HALLIWELL'S FILM & VIDEO GUIDE 2001

Also edited by John Walker

HALLIWELL'S WHO'S WHO IN THE MOVIES

HALLIWELL'S FILM & VIDEO GUIDE 2001

LESLIE HALLIWELL

16th EDITION
Revised and Updated

Edited by
JOHN WALKER

HarperResource
An Imprint of HarperCollinsPublishers

This book is published in Great Britain by
HarperCollins*Publishers* under the title
Halliwell's Film and Video Guide 2001 (16th edition)

HarperCollins books may be purchased for educational,
business, or sales promotional use. For information,
please write: Special Markets Department, HarperCollins
Publishers Inc., 10 East 53rd Street, New York, NY 10022.

First HarperResource Edition published 2000.

ISBN 0-06-095798-0

Contents

Introduction

It has been a great year for films, including, as it does, Sam Mendes' brilliant debut *American Beauty*, scripted by Alan Ball, on the sterility and the pleasures of suburban living, Ridley Scott reinvigorating a moribund genre with his *Gladiator*, Mike Leigh breathing new life into period drama with *Topsy-Turvy*, and Spike Jonze and screenwriter Charlie Kaufman's witty exploration of identity, the wholly original *Being John Malkovich*.

There were also searing dramas such as *Boys Don't Cry*, David Lynch's delightful road movie *The Straight Story*, Michael Mann's exposé of corporate politics *The Insider* and such foreign pleasures as Pedro Almodovar's *All About My Mother*, Tom Tykwer's *Run Lola Run* and Hirokazu Kore-Eda's *After Life*.

Yet, at the beginning of a new millennium (as Stanley Kubrick knew, it arrived in 2001), these may be the last gasp of 20th-century cinema. For movies are changing with the times, and there is a perceptible shift happening in the way films are made, seen and enjoyed. Inevitably, this is the result of the switch to digital methods of reproduction and distribution.

At the expensive end of film making, we can witness the re-creation of ancient Rome in *Gladiator*, or the incredible ballet of bullets and people in *The Matrix*. At the cheap end, the masses can now afford to make movies with digital cameras and computerized editing systems. Many wannabe directors will have been inspired by *The Blair Witch Project*, a cheaply made movie with an unknown cast that, cleverly marketed at low cost on the Internet, outperformed at the box office heavily-promoted Hollywood blockbusters featuring $20m stars.

Already, Danish directors such as Lars von Trier and Thomas Vinterberg have demonstrated the change and charge that can be got from dramas filmed with hand-held cameras using available light. The Iranian director Abbas Kiarostami has made films on minimal budgets based on real-life incidents, in which people have played themselves. (Imagine *Erin Brokovich* with Erin Brokovich rather than Julia Roberts in the lead.)

The success of web cameras on the Internet shows there is an apparently insatiable demand to glimpse the lives of other people. Films, too, are being made specifically to be shown on the World Wide Web. For the first time since the early days of film, the means to create movies is available to the many.

Hollywood has reacted so far by releasing films of interminable length and throwing millions of dollars at spectacular special digital effects. But that is an approach that will soon lose its novelty value. Once you can conjure up anything digitally, then the extraordinary soon becomes ordinary. The quality of imagination, the visionary collaboration of writers, artists and actors, will be what matters.

Hollywood, of course, will absorb the lessons, and many of the talents, that the digital revolution throws up. But for every George Lucas filming the next episode of *Star Wars* at vast cost with digital cameras, there will be a Michael Almereyda (who not so long ago was making movies with a Fisher-Price toy Pixel camera) using video to film *Hamlet* on a minimal budget, or a Mike Figgis, experimenting with split screens and simultaneous stories in a way that would have been impossibly expensive in the past.

Neither Figgis's or Almereyda's newest films will be found here, as they have yet to reach the UK. But some 400 new films have been added to this edition. For reasons of space, these do not include films made specifically for television, which still fall into the category of the missable. For the first time, too, some entries from earlier editions have been dropped. Unfortunately, this was inevitable, since the *Guide* cannot get any bigger. The movies eliminated from this edition are listed in an appendix.

The *Guide* in its entirety, together with its companion volume, *Halliwell's Who's Who in the Movies*, will, however, be accessible on the Internet through Coppernob, a new and exciting site on the World Wide Web, that will, among many other matters of interest, provide extensive coverage of films. See you there!

I am grateful to the many readers who have taken the time to write to me, both with encouragement and complaints. I also owe thanks to Val Hudson and Monica Chakraverty and the technical wizards Graham Bell and Alan Trewartha at HarperCollins, and to my agents Rivers Scott and Gloria Ferris; my love goes to my wife Barbara, whose sense and sensitivity makes the hard work worthwhile.

John Walker (E-mail film@coppernob.net)

Explanatory Notes

Alphabetical Order

Unlike some books which take the complete title into account, as though there were no gaps between words, we have always persevered with the old-fashioned word-at-a-time arrangement. Thus, all titles starting with *In*, including *In Which We Serve*, are used up before one goes on to titles beginning *Incredible*, *Inspector*, *Intolerance*. Hyphenated or apostrophized words are counted as one word. Compressions such as *Dr* and *St* are treated as though they had been spelled out, as *Doctor* and *Saint*. *Mac* and *Mc* are regarded as interchangeable under *Mac*. Titles consisting of initials, such as *C. C. and Company* or *D.O.A.* are dealt with at the beginning of each alphabetical section, except where they have become acronyms (i.e. pronounceable as one word, e.g. AWOL). In all cases the complete title is given as billed, though the definite and indefinite articles are not counted in the alphabetical arrangement where they occur as the first word of a title. The spelling of the country of origin is used, e.g. *My Favorite Blonde* and not *My Favourite Blonde*.

Individual Entries

All entries follow the same format and the notes are set out below in the order in which they will be encountered.

Publicity tags These were used in the promotion of the film and, in the manner of trailers, precede the entry.

Ratings These range from none to four stars. Four stars indicate a film outstanding in many ways, a milestone in cinema history, remarkable for acting, direction, writing, photography or some other aspect of technique. Three stars indicate a very high standard of professional excellence or great historical interest. Or, if you like, three strong reasons for admiring it. Two stars indicate a good level of competence and a generally entertaining film. One star indicates a film not very satisfactory as a whole; it could be a failed giant or a second feature with a few interesting ideas among the dross. No stars at all indicates a totally routine production or worse; such films may be watchable but are at least equally missable.

Country of origin This is the first item on the second line.

Year of release This comes after the country of origin and is intended to indicate the year when the film was first shown, which is not necessarily the year that it was made. Dating is sometimes an onerous task, and the result debatable.

Running time This is given in minutes, signified by 'm'. So far as possible, this is the original release time. Very many films are cut as they appear in different countries, sometimes by twenty minutes or more. An engineering function of British television results in an imperceptible speeding-up of projection and a consequent loss of one minute in every twenty-five. A hundred-minute film, therefore, will run only ninety-six minutes on the box.

Colour This is indicated by 'bw' for black and white films and 'colour' for the others. The colour process used, such as Technicolor, is given when known.

Other notable points These are given at the end of the second line, indicating the use of a special process, such as Panavision.

Production credit This is the central credit on the third line. To the left comes the name of the distributor, which is followed by the production company if different. To the right comes the name or names of the actual producer – in brackets, unless he has a stake in the production, in which case he follows an oblique. These days, many films tend to have more producers of one kind or another than actors. The credit here refers to the person bearing the title of producer rather than to the executive producer, associate producer, production executive and so on.

Family viewing 👨‍👦 indicates that the film is suitable for family viewing, i.e. by parents together with young film-goers aged from four to fourteen.

Video ▣ indicates that the film has been released on VHS video-cassette for the British PAL system. ▣ indicates that the film has been released on VHS video-cassette for the British PAL system in wide-screen format. ✿ indicates that the film has been released on VHS video-cassette in a computer-colourized version. ▤ indicates that the film has been released in the American NTSC format (which is not compatible with the British PAL system). ✇ indicates that the film is available on laser disc in either American NTSC format or British PAL format. ⊚ indicates that the film is available on Video CD. ∩ indicates that the film's soundtrack music has been released on compact disc. Video and record releases come and go with great rapidity these days; all that it is possible to indicate is whether a title has been available at some time. If a film or soundtrack has been available in the past, then it is very likely to become available again in the future. If you are desperate to acquire a particular film or soundtrack album, then it would be worthwhile checking film magazines for advertisements from companies that specialize in tracking down deleted titles. ⊚ indicates DVD (Digital Video Disc) releases in Region 1 and ⊚ indicates DVD releases in Region 2.

Alternative title This is given on a separate line, usually with a note of the country in which it was used. If no such distinction exists, the formula aka (also known as) is used. Alternative titles are also listed individually, cross-referenced to the main entry for the film to which they belong.

Synopsis This is a brief description of the film's plot.

Assessment Again, this is brief and to the point.

Writer credit (*w*) This appears first since the script precedes direction and is therefore, at least sometimes, more important than the director credit. The author of the screenplay is given; if this derives from a novel, play, musical, or story, this is given next, together with the original author.

Director credit (*d*) This follows next. If the director is also the writer, then there will be a combined *wd* credit.

Photography credit (*ph*) This indicates the cinematographer or lighting cameraman, otherwise known as the director of photography, rather than the actual camera operator.

Music credit (*m*) This means the composer of the background music score. Sometimes there is only a music director (*md*) who orchestrates library or classical music. When noteworthy songs are performed in a film, or are specially written for it, those responsible are indicated by a credit for music and lyrics (*m/ly*) or simply *songs*.

Other credits These include art director (*ad*), choreographer (*ch*), costume designer (*costume*), film editor (*ed*), production designer (*pd*) and special effects (*sp*). They are given when they seem important and when they can be found. In some cases it has not been possible to track down all the credits one would wish.

Cast ☆ A list of the principal actors is given, roughly in order of importance.

Italics These denote a contribution of a particularly high standard.

Critical comments Brief quotes from well-known professional critics are appended to many entries, sometimes because they wittily confirm the assessments and sometimes because they provide alternative opinions. The absence of a quote casts no reflection whatever on the film, only on the difficulty of finding an opinion worth quoting.

Additional notes Any points of interest about the film are given after the symbol †. The symbol ♫ indicates notable songs which appear in the film.

Academy Awards Awards 🏆 and nominations 𝟙 are listed for all principal categories, including best picture, acting, direction, photography, music score and songs, and some minor ones, such as sound and make-up, when they seem of interest. British Academy of Film and Television Arts awards follow the symbol ♕.

A Bout de Souffle ****
France 1960 90m bw
SNC (Georges de Beauregard)
aka: *Breathless*
A young car thief kills a policeman and goes on the run with his American girlfriend.
Casual, influential, New Wave reminiscence of both Quai des Brumes and innumerable American gangster thrillers. (The film is dedicated to Monogram.) One of the first and most influential films of the French New Wave.
w Jean-Luc Godard *story* François Truffaut
d Jean-Luc Godard *ph* Raoul Coutard *m* Martial Solal *ed* Cécile Decugis
☆ *Jean-Paul Belmondo, Jean Seberg, Daniel Boulanger, Jean-Pierre Melville, Jean-Luc Godard*
'A film all dressed up for rebellion but with no real tangible territory on which to stand and fight.' – *Peter John Dyer*
† See also *Breathless, American remake.*

A Double Tour
France/Italy 1959 110m Eastmancolor
Paris/Panitalia (Robert and Raymond Hakim)
aka: *Web of Passion*
A wealthy wine grower has trouble with his wife, his children, his best friend, and his mistress across the way, who is murdered.
Talented but irritating mixture of Hitchcock and Les Parents Terribles; rather an undergraduatish romp.
w Paul Gégauff *novel* La Clé de la Rue Saint-Nicolas *d* Claude Chabrol *ph* Henri Decaë *m* Paul Misraki
☆ Jacques Dacqmine, Madeleine Robinson, Jean-Paul Belmondo, Bernadette Lafont, Antonella Lualdi, André Jocelyn

A la Folie: see *Six Days, Six Nights*

A la Place du Coeur *
France 1998 112m colour
Artificial Eye/Agat/Diaphana/La Seot/France2/Canal+ (Gilles Sandoz, Michel Saint-Jean, Robert Guédiguian)
In Marseille, a pregnant 16-year-old white girl struggles to defend the black father of her expected child, who is accused of raping a Bosnian refugee.
An often clumsy French version of Baldwin's angry novel, which was set in Harlem; the change in locale has not affected the racial tension at the heart of the drama.
w Jean-Louis Milesi, Robert Guédiguian *novel* If Beale Street Could Talk *by* James Baldwin *d* Robert Guédiguian *ph* Bernard Cavalié *ad* Michel Vandestien *ed* Bernard Sasia
☆ Ariane Ascaride, Christine Brücher, Jean-Pierre Darroussin, Gérard Meylan, Alexandre Ogou, Laure Raoust, Véronique Ballme, Pierre Banderet
'A highly individual and personal piece of work. It's one that deserves a place in everyone's heart.' – *James Mottram, Film Review*

A Nos Amours: see *To Our Loves*

A Nous Deux **
France/Canada 1979 109m Eastmancolor
Films 13/Cinévidéo (Claude Lelouch, Denis Heroux, Joseph Beaubien)
aka: *An Adventure for Two*
aka: *The Two of Us*
A thief escapes from prison and goes on the run, becoming involved along the way with a man-hating prostitute who is also wanted by the police.
Clever, witty thriller, full of little visual surprises, and one that plays games with an audience's expectations.
wd Claude Lelouch *ph* Bernard Zitzermann *m* Francis Lai *m* Jean-Louis Poveda *ed* Sophie Bhaud, Hugues Darmois

☆ Catherine Deneuve, Jacques Dutronc, Jacques Villeret, Paul Préboist, Bernard Lecoq, Gilberte Geniat, Monique Melinand, Jacques Godin, Daniel Auteuil

A Nous la Liberté ****
France 1931 95m bw
Tobis
US title: *Freedom for Us*
A factory owner is blackmailed about his past, and helped by an old prison friend, with whom he finally takes to the road.
Operetta-style satirical comedy with leftish attitudes and several famous sequences later borrowed by Chaplin for Modern Times. In terms of sheer film flair, a revelation, though the plot has its tedious turns.
wd René Clair *ph* Georges Périnal *m* Georges Auric *pd* Lazare Meerson
☆ Raymond Cordy, Henri Marchand, Rolla France, Paul Olivier
'Different from the usual run ... easily understandable even to those who do not know French.' – *Variety*
'He demonstrates that sound pictures can be as fluid as silents were, and the picture is rightly considered a classic.' – *Pauline Kael, 1970s*
'I was close to the extreme left ... I wanted to attack the Machine, which led men into starvation instead of adding to their happiness.' – *René Clair*

A Propos de Nice *
France 1930 30m bw
A satirical documentary on the millionaire's paradise of the French Riviera.
Cheaply made and rather naïve-looking after sixty years, this amusingly belligerent lampoon still has its striking moments.
wd Jean Vigo *ph* Boris Kaufman

A Toute Vitesse
France 1996 85m colour
Dangerous to Know/Magouric/Téléma/France2/Rhône-Alpes (Laurent Bénégui)
A young French writer befriends a homosexual Algerian in order to obtain material for his next novel.
An effective drama of racial, sexual and class prejudice, though it has nothing new to say about them.
wd Gaël Morel *ph* Jeanne Lapoirie *ad* Frédérique Hurpeau *ed* Catherine Schwartz
☆ élodie Bouchez, Pascal Cerve, Stéphane Rideau, Meziane Bardadi, Romain Auger, Salim Kechiouche, Mohammed Dib
'Gives the impression of being less than the sum of its parts.' – *Sight and Sound*

Aan *
India 1952 190m Technicolor
All India Film Corporation/Mehboob Productions
aka: *Savage Princess*
A usurping young prince and his sister are tamed by an athletic peasant and his girlfriend.
One of the few examples to reach the West of Indian costume melodrama with music, spectacle and swashbuckling. Distinctly intriguing, if overpowering.
w Chaudary, Ali Raza *d* Mehboob *ph* Faredoon A. Irani *m* Naushad Dilip
☆ Kumar, Nimmi, Premnath, Nadira
'Disarmingly enthusiastic ... exotic and yet charmingly naïve.' – *MFB*

De Aanslag: see *The Assault*

Aaron Slick from Punkin Crick *
US 1952 95m Technicolor
Paramount (William Perlberg, George Seaton)
GB title: *Marshmallow Moon*
A small-town girl is tricked into selling her farm and moving to the city, but eventually marries the simple farmer who rescues her.
Homespun entertainment based on a staple success of the American provincial theatre, with pleasant songs added.
wd Claude Binyon *play* Walter Benjamin Hare *ph* Charles B. Lang Jnr *m/ly* Jay Livingston, Ray Evans *ch* Charles O'Curran
☆ Alan Young, Dinah Shore, Robert Merrill, Adele Jergens, Minerva Urecal

Abandon Ship: see *Seven Waves Away*

Abbot and Costello in Society: see *In Society*

'They're too wild for one world!'
Abbott and Costello Go to Mars
US 1953 76m bw
U-I (Howard Christie)
Two incompetents accidentally launch a space ship and land first in Louisiana, then on Venus.
Dismal knockabout, badly made.
w John Grant, D. D. Beauchamp *d* Charles Lamont *ph* Clifford Stine *m* Joseph Gershenson
☆ Bud Abbott, Lou Costello, Mari Blanchard, Robert Paige, Martha Hyer

Abbott and Costello in Hollywood *
US 1945 85m bw
MGM (Martin Gosch)
Two agents have hectic adventures in a film studio.
Tolerable star romp on one of their biggest budgets, climaxing in a roller coaster ride.
w Nat Perrin, Lou Breslow *d* S. Sylvan Simon *ph* Charles Schoenbaum *m* George Bassman
☆ Bud Abbott, Lou Costello, Frances Rafferty, Warner Anderson, Robert Z. Leonard

Abbott and Costello in the Foreign Legion
US 1950 80m bw
U-I (Robert Arthur)
Incompetent legionnaires become heroes to the fury of their sergeant.
Dull star vehicle on ramshackle sets, with no memorable routines.
w John Grant, Leonard Stern, Martin Ragaway *d* Charles Lamont *ph* George Robinson *m* Joseph Gershenson
☆ Bud Abbott, Lou Costello, Patricia Medina, Walter Slezak, Douglass Dumbrille

Abbott and Costello in the Navy: see *In the Navy*

Abbott and Costello Lost in Alaska
US 1952 76m bw
U-I (Howard Christie)
Two San Francisco firemen take a melancholy prospector back to Alaska to find a gold mine.
Sub-standard comedy vehicle with poor production.
w Martin Ragaway, Leonard Stern *d* Jean Yarbrough *ph* George Robinson *m* Joseph Gershenson
☆ Bud Abbott, Lou Costello, *Tom Ewell*, Mitzi Green, Bruce Cabot

Abbott and Costello Meet Captain Kidd *
US 1952 70m Supercinecolor
Warner/Woodley (Alex Gottlieb)
Two servants have a treasure map, and a fearsome pirate wants it.
Crude knockabout: the stars are way below their best, and a famous actor is embarrassed.
w Howard Dimsdale, John Grant *d* Charles Lamont *ph* Stanley Cortez *m* Raoul Kraushaar
☆ Bud Abbott, Lou Costello, Charles Laughton, Hillary Brooke, Leif Erickson

Abbott and Costello Meet Dr Jekyll and Mr Hyde *
US 1953 77m bw
U-I (Howard Christie)
In Victorian London, two rookie policemen catch a monster.
Quite a lively spoof with some well-paced comedy sequences.
w John Grant, Lee Loeb *d* Charles Lamont *ph* George Robinson *m* Hans Salter
☆ Bud Abbott, Lou Costello, Boris Karloff, Reginald Denny, Craig Stevens, Helen Westcott, John Dierkes
'Gracious Boris Karloff is superior to his surroundings.' – *MFB* (Though it is doubtful whether he ever got behind the Hyde make-up.)
† In Britain, the film was given an 'X' certificate, though it later played on children's television.

'Jeepers! the creepers are after somebody – and guess who! More howls than you can shake a shiver at!!!'
Abbott and Costello Meet Frankenstein **
US 1948 83m bw
U-I (Robert Arthur)
GB title: *Abbott and Costello Meet the Ghosts*
Two railway porters deliver crates containing the Frankenstein monster, Dracula, and the Wolf Man.
Fairly lively spoof which put an end to Universal's monsters for a while. Good typical sequences for the stars, a few thrills, and some good lines. Dracula to Costello, lovingly: 'What we need is young blood ... and brains...'
w Robert Lees, Frederic I. Rinaldo, John Grant *d* Charles Barton *ph* Charles van Enger *m* Frank Skinner
☆ Bud Abbott, Lou Costello, Bela Lugosi, Lon Chaney Jnr, Glenn Strange, Lenore Aubert, Jane Randolph
WOLF MAN: 'You don't understand. Every night when the moon is full, I turn into a wolf.'
COSTELLO: 'You and twenty million other guys!'
† Probably the Abbott and Costello film which survives best.

Abbott and Costello Meet the Ghosts:
see *Abbott and Costello Meet Frankenstein*

Abbott and Costello Meet the Invisible Man *
US 1951 82m bw
U-I (Howard Christie)
A boxer accused of murder makes himself invisible while two detectives clear him.
Quite a bright comedy with good trick effects.
w Robert Lees, Frederic I. Rinaldo, John Grant *d* Charles Lamont *ph* George Robinson *m* Hans Salter
☆ Bud Abbott, Lou Costello, Arthur Franz, Nancy Guild, Adele Jergens, Sheldon Leonard

'When every face wore a custard pie, and vamps broke hearts with a winking eye!'

Abbott and Costello Meet the Keystone Kops *
US 1954 79m bw
U-I (Howard Christie)

In pioneer film days, two incompetents are sold a dud studio by a con man, but succeed as stunt men.
Flabby comedy which never seems to get going until the chase finale; notable chiefly for a guest appearance by Mack Sennett.
w John Grant d Charles Lamont ph Reggie Lanning m Joseph Gershenson
☆ Bud Abbott, Lou Costello, Lynn Bari, Fred Clark, Frank Wilcox, Maxie Rosenbloom

'More ghoulish glee than when they met Frankenstein!'

Abbott and Costello Meet the Killer, Boris Karloff *
US 1948 84m bw
U-I (Robert Arthur)

Two bellboys help to solve mysterious murders in a remote hotel.
This clumsily titled comedy really does not work until the last sequence in a cavern. Boris Karloff is not the killer and appears very little.
w Hugh Wedlock Jnr, Howard Snyder, John Grant d Charles Barton ph Charles van Enger md Milton Schwarzwald
☆ Bud Abbott, Lou Costello, Boris Karloff, Gar Moore, Lenore Aubert, Alan Mowbray

'It has been said that a man's best friend is his mummy...'

Abbott and Costello Meet the Mummy *
US 1955 77m bw
U-I (Howard Christie)

A missing medallion leads to a lost tomb and a living mummy.
The comedians show their age in this one, but there is some typical if predictable humour and a thrill or two.
w John Grant d Charles Lamont ph George Robinson m Hans Salter
☆ Bud Abbott, Lou Costello, Kurt Katch, Marie Windsor, Michael Ansara, Dan Seymour
COSTELLO: 'How stupid can you get?'
ABBOTT: 'How stupid do you want me to be?'

The Abdication
GB 1974 102m Technicolor
Warner (Robert Fryer, James Cresson)
17th-century Queen Christina of Sweden journeys to Rome to embrace the Catholic church and falls in love with a cardinal.
Sombre historical fantasia, more irritating than interesting.
w Ruth Wolff play Ruth Wolff d Anthony Harvey ph Geoffrey Unsworth m Nino Rota
☆ Liv Ullmann, Peter Finch, Cyril Cusack, Paul Rogers, Graham Crowden, Michael Dunn, Lewis Fiander, Harold Goldblatt
'Dainty debauchery and titillating tease straight from twenties women's pulp magazines.' – Variety
'Embalmed in such reverence for its own cultural elevation that it loses all contact with the audience.' – Pauline Kael

The Abductors *
US 1957 80m bw Regalscope
TCF/Regal (Ray Wander)
Around 1870, criminals steal Lincoln's body as ransom to effect a convict's release.
Interesting minor melodrama, but not sufficiently well made.
w Ray Wander d Andrew V. McLaglen ph Joseph LaShelle m Paul Glass
☆ Victor McLaglen, Gavin Muir, George Macready

Abdul the Damned *
GB 1935 111m bw
BIP/Capitol (Max Schach)
In 1900 Turkey, an opera gives herself to a villainous sultan to protect her fiancé.
Thoroughgoing hokum, well produced, which pleased some people in its day.
w Ashley Dukes, Warren Chetham Strode, Robert Burford d Karl Grune ph Otto Kanturek

☆ Fritz Kortner, Adrienne Ames, Nils Asther, John Stuart, Esme Percy, Walter Rilla, Patric Knowles, Eric Portman

Abdulla's Harem: see Abdulla the Great

Abe Lincoln in Illinois **
US 1940 110m bw
RKO (Max Gordon)

GB title: Spirit of the People
Episodes in the political and domestic life of Abraham Lincoln.
Pleasant, muted, careful film based on a Broadway success: generally informative and interesting.
w Grover Jones play Robert E. Sherwood d John Cromwell ph James Wong Howe m Roy Webb
☆ Raymond Massey, Ruth Gordon, Gene Lockhart, Mary Howard, Dorothy Tree, Minor Watson, Howard da Silva
'If you want attitudes, a five gallon hat, famous incidents, and One Nation Indivisible, they're all here. As a picture and as a whole, it just doesn't stick.' – Otis Ferguson
♫ Raymond Massey, James Wong Howe

Abel **
Netherlands 1985 96m colour
First Floor Features (Laurens Geels, Dick Maas, Rob Swaab)
A 31-year-old mother's boy, thrown out of home, moves in with his father's mistress.
Witty, neatly plotted black farce of family life.
wd Alex Van Warmerdam ph Marc Felperlaan ad Harry Ammerlaan ed Hans Van Dongen
☆ Alex Van Warmerdam, Henri Garcin, Olga Zuiderhoek, Annet Malherbe, Loes Luca

Abgeschminkt!: see Making Up

Abie's Irish Rose
US 1946 96m bw
UA/Bing Crosby Productions (Edward A. Sutherland)
Flat filming of the twenties Broadway play about Irish girl marrying Jewish boy, leading to a clash of families.
w Anne Nichols play Anne Nichols d A. Edward Sutherland ph William Mellor m John Scott Trotter
☆ Joanne Dru, Richard Norris, Michael Chekhov, Eric Blore, Art Baker
† There had been a silent version in 1928, and the plot was borrowed, to say the least, for the 1972 TV series Bridget Loves Bernie.

Abilene Town *
US 1946 89m bw
UA (Jules Levey)

An upright marshal routs crooked cattlemen.
Vigorous, enjoyable Western programmer.
w Harold Shumate d Edwin L. Marin
☆ Randolph Scott, Ann Dvorak, Rhonda Fleming, Edgar Buchanan, Lloyd Bridges

'Love means never having to say you're ugly!'

The Abominable Dr Phibes *
GB 1971 94m Movielab
AIP (Louis M. Heyward, Ron Dunas)

A disfigured musical genius devises a series of horrible murders, based on the ten curses of Pharaoh, for the surgeons who failed to save his wife.
Brisk but uninspired treatment of a promising theme, with more unintended nastiness than intended laughs. Some good moments and interesting low-budget thirties sets.
w James Whiton, William Goldstein d Robert Fuest ph Norman Warwick m Basil Kirchen, Jack Nathan pd Brian Eatwell
☆ Vincent Price, Joseph Cotten, Hugh Griffith, Terry-Thomas, Peter Jeffrey, Virginia North, Aubrey Woods
'The sets are awful, the plot ludicrous and the dialogue inane – what more could a horror freak desire?' – Motion Picture Guide
† Sequel: Dr Phibes Rises Again (1973).

'See it with someone brave!'

The Abominable Snowman *
GB 1957 91m bw RegalScope
Warner/Hammer/Clarion (Aubrey Baring)

US title: The Abominable Snowman of the Himalayas
Himalayan explorers are attacked one by one by the Yeti and their own fear.
A thin horror film with intelligent scripting: more philosophizing and characterization than suspense. The briefly glimpsed Yeti are disappointing creations.
w Nigel Kneale TV play Nigel Kneale d Val Guest ph Arthur Grant m Humphrey Searle md John Hollingsworth pd Bernard Robinson ed Bill Lenny
☆ Peter Cushing, Forrest Tucker, Maureen Connell, Richard Wattis, Robert Brown, Arnold Marle

About Face
US 1952 96m Technicolor
Warner (William Jacobs)
Moronic remake of Brother Rat (qv), shorn of all wit, pace and style.
w Peter Milne d Roy del Ruth ph Bert Glennon m/ly Charles Tobias, Peter de Rose
☆ Eddie Bracken, Gordon MacRae, Dick Wesson, Virginia Gibson, Phyllis Kirk, Joel Grey

About Last Night
US 1986 113m MGM Color
Tri-Star (Jason Brett, Stuart Oken)

The ups and downs of an unmarried relationship.
Smart, slick, up-to-the-minute account of human coupling and uncoupling in the eighties ... but no plot.
w Tim Kazurinsky, Denise DeClue play Sexual Perversity in Chicago by David Mamet d Edward Zwick ph Andrew Dintenfass m Miles Goodman pd Ida Random
☆ Rob Lowe, Demi Moore, Jim Belushi, Elizabeth Perkins, George DiCenzo
'Savvy enough to recognize points of conflict but not daring enough to look beneath the surface.' – Variety

About Mrs Leslie *
US 1954 104m bw
Paramount (Hal B. Wallis)
An ageing nightclub singer has a platonic affair with a mysterious wealthy man, who leaves her enough money to buy a boarding house.
Odd, likeable romantic drama tailored for an unusual star; but its plot is too thin and its direction too drab for real success.
w Ketti Frings, Hal Kanter novel Vina Delmar d Daniel Mann ph Ernest Laszlo m Victor Young
☆ Shirley Booth, Robert Ryan, Alex Nicol, Marjie Millar, Eilene Janssen
'This quiet and curious film has an unexpectedly gentle, civilized flavour.' – Gavin Lambert
'It's all sunny disposition and sweet sadness for Miss Booth.' – Judith Crist
'One is reminded alternately of Chekhov and of Back Street.' – Sight and Sound

'The love story behind the billion dollar secret!'

Above and Beyond *
US 1952 122m bw
MGM (Melvin Frank, Norman Panama)

The training of Colonel Paul Tibbets, who dropped the first atomic bomb on Japan.
Overstretched flagwaver with laborious domestic interludes. Of little real interest then or now.
w Melvin Frank, Norman Panama story Beirne Lay Jnr d Melvin Frank, Norman Panama ph Ray June m Hugo Friedhofer
☆ Robert Taylor, Eleanor Parker, James Whitmore, Larry Keating, Larry Gates
♫ Beirne Lay Jnr, Hugo Friedhofer

Above Suspicion *
US 1943 91m bw
MGM (Victor Saville)

Just before World War II, an Oxford professor on a continental honeymoon is asked to track down a missing agent.
Patchy, studio-bound spy comedy-drama with a couple of good sequences. Notable also for Mr MacMurray's impersonation of a professor who hails a Nazi as 'Hiya, dope!'

w Keith Winter, Melville Baker, Patricia Coleman novel Helen MacInnes d Richard Thorpe ph Robert Planck m Bronislau Kaper
☆ Fred MacMurray, Joan Crawford, Conrad Veidt, Basil Rathbone, Reginald Owen, Felix Bressart, Richard Ainley
'Will need more than strong support for passable biz.' – Variety

Above the Law
US 1988 99m Technicolor
Warner (Steven Seagal, Andrew Davis)

aka: Nico
A cop, who is also a martial arts expert, uncovers dirty work in the CIA.
Woodenly acted, violent action movie with an unusual anti-establishment slant.
w Steven Pressfield, Ronald Shusett, Andrew Davis story Andrew Davis, Steven Seagal d Andrew Davis ph Robert Steadman m David M. Frank pd Maher Ahmad ed Michael Brown sp Art Brewer, Lee Solis
☆ Steven Seagal, Pam Grier, Henry Silva, Daniel Faraldo, Sharon Stone, Nicholas Kusenko

'The hardest part of winning is choosing sides.'

Above the Rim
US 1994 93m DeLuxe
First Independent/New Line (Jeff Pollack, Ben Medina)

A troubled, talented basketball player, who refuses to play for his high school team, becomes involved with a drug dealer and his brother, a former star player now working as a school security guard.
An attempt to combine the usual sports movie plot, with victory being snatched at the last minute, with the street credibility of the usual drug movie, with death for the bad guys and redemption for the good in the last reel; two sets of clichés do not make a classic.
w Barry Michael Cooper, Jeff Pollack, Ben Medina d Jeff Pollack ph Tom Priestley Jnr m Marcus Miller pd Ina Mayhew ed Michael Ripps, James Mitchell
☆ Duane Martin, Tupac Shakur, Leon, David Bailey, Tonya Pinkins, Marlon Wayans, Bernie Mac
'A fine cast and the movie's general energy can't overcome that mix of clichés and technical flaws, which should conspire to prevent any high flying at the box-office.' – Brian Lowry, Variety

'A story of impudent gallantry!'

Above Us the Waves *
GB 1955 99m bw
Rank/London Independent Producers (William Macquitty)

In World War II, midget submarines attack a German battleship in a Norwegian fjord.
Archetypal stiff-upper-lip war drama with disappointing action sequences and jumbled continuity.
w Robin Estridge d Ralph Thomas ph Ernest Steward m Arthur Benjamin
☆ John Mills, John Gregson, Donald Sinden, James Robertson Justice, Michael Medwin, Lee Patterson, Lyndon Brook
'It tells a heroic story without any flowery effects at all.' – Manchester Guardian

'The wonder film of the century, about the most romantic figure who ever lived!'

Abraham Lincoln **
US 1930 97m bw
UA/Art Cinema Corporation/D. W. Griffith

An account of Lincoln's entry into politics and his years of power.
Rather boring even at the time, this straightforward biopic has the virtues of sincerity and comparative fidelity to the facts.
w Stephen Vincent Benet, Gerrit Lloyd d D. W. Griffith ph Karl Struss m Hugo Riesenfeld pd William Cameron Menzies
☆ Walter Huston, Una Merkel, Edgar Dearing, Russell Simpson, Henry B. Walthall
'A startlingly superlative accomplishment, one rejuvenating a greatest Griffith ... one smooth roll of literally pulsating passion, pathos, laughter ... it should be his greatest contribution to the exhibitor.' – Variety
'It brings to us – with a curious finality of disappointment, a sentimental sense of the closing of a chapter – the impression of a

---

♙♙ film suitable for family viewing
▥ VHS video-cassette for the British PAL system
▥ VHS video-cassette for the British PAL system in wide screen-format
✿ Video cassette in a computer-colourised version
▬ American NTSC video-cassette
Ⓛ Laser disc

director who has nowhere made a valid contact with the condition of the screen today.' – C. A. Lejeune

'A treasure trove of magnificent moments.' – *MFB*, 1973

'Dull, episodic, overlong … it is difficult to understand why contemporary critics were so impressed.' – *Anthony Slide, 70s*

† There was a silent biopic in 1924 starring George A. Billings, but it lacked cinematic interest. Written by Frances Marion and directed by Phil Rosen, for Rocket/Lincoln/AFN.

Abraham Valley

Portugal/France/Switzerland 1993 189m colour
Artificial Eye/Mandragoa/Gemini/Light Night (Paulo Branco)

📺

original title: *Vale Abraao*

A lame and glamorous woman with romantic inclinations is frustrated both by her marriage and her affairs.

A deft variation of Flaubert's Madame Bovary, in which the husband encourages his wife's infidelity without making her any more contented, but one that lacks heart.

wd Manoel de Oliveira *novel* Augustina Bessa-Luis *ph* Mário Barroso *ad* Maria José Branco *ed* Manoel de Oliveira, Valérie Loiseleux
☆ Leonor Silveira, Cecile Sanz de Alba, Luis Miguel Cintra, Rui de Carvalho, Luis Lima Barreto, Mário Barroso

Abre Los Ojos: see Open Your Eyes

'Two roaring Romeos who thought even the dames were on lend lease!'

Abroad with Two Yanks *

US 1944 80m bw
Edward Small

▦

Adventures around the Pacific with two woman-chasing sailors.

This simple-minded farce with its punny title was a great success in its day, and still generates a laugh or two.

w Charles Rogers, Wilkie Mahoney, Ted Sills d Allan Dwan ph Charles Lawton m Lud Gluskin
☆ Dennis O'Keefe, William Bendix, Helen Walker, John Abbott, John Loder

Abschied von Gestern *

West Germany 1966 90m bw
Kairos Film/Independent/Alexander Kluge
aka: *Yesterday Girl*

A Jewish girl escapes from East to West Germany but is disillusioned and gives herself up.

Witty and remarkably light-hearted satirical comedy which can be fully understood only by those living in Germany in the sixties.

wd Alexander Kluge ph Edgar Reitz, Thomas Mauch ed Beata Mainka
☆ Alexandra Kluge, Günther Mack, Hans Korte, Eva Marie Meinecke

Absence of Malice *

US 1981 116m DeLuxe
Columbia/Mirage (Sydney Pollack)

📺 ▦ 📀 🎧

When a longshoremen's union leader disappears, a lady journalist throws an unfair spotlight on an innocent suspect.

Well-meaning but overwritten attack on journalistic abuses, notable for some unsuitable leading performances.

w Kurt Luedtke d Sydney Pollack ph Owen Roizman m Dave Grusin pd Terence Marsh
☆ Paul Newman, Sally Field, Bob Balaban, Melinda Dillon, Luther Adler, Barry Primus
'Pollack seems to be carving out a new niche for himself as an updater of Hollywood's most tried and true methods of sugaring a message.' – *Richard Combs, MFB*
'A thoroughly craftsmanlike movie that never quite delivers on the commercial or the artistic front.' – *Guardian*
'The story is perfunctory and disappointing in a movie that promises but does not deliver.' – *Motion Picture Guide*
ਊ screenplay; Paul Newman; Melinda Dillon

Absent without Leave

New Zealand 1993 96m Eastmancolor
Meridian/NZFC/Avalon/NFU (Robin Laing)

In New Zealand in 1942, a soldier, who is about to be sent overseas, goes absent so that he can take home to her parents his young wife, who has had a miscarriage.

Amiable, meandering domestic drama of no particular interest.

w James Edwards, Graeme Tetley d John Laing ph Allen Guilford m Don McGlashan, David Long, Mark Austin pd Rick Kofoed ed Paul Sutorius
☆ Craig McLachlan, Katrina Hobbs, Judie Douglass, Tony Barry, Ken Blackburn, Tony Burton

'It's all about a wacky prof who invents an anti-gravity goo that flew!'

The Absent-Minded Professor *

👫 US 1961 97m bw
Walt Disney (Bill Walsh)

A lighter-than-air substance called flubber enables its inventor to drive his Model-T through the sky and catch some spies.

Foolishly engaging fantasy comedy with goodish trick effects.

w Bill Walsh d Robert Stevenson ph Edward Colman m George Bruns sp Robert A. Mattey, Peter Ellenshaw, Eustace Lycett
☆ Fred MacMurray, Tommy Kirk, Keenan Wynn, Nancy Olson, Leon Ames, Ed Wynn, Edward Andrews
† Sequel: *Son of Flubber* (1963) (qv).
†† Remake: *Flubber* (1997) (qv).
ਊ Edward Colman

Absinthe: see Madame X (1929)

'Welcome to the world of your dreams!'

Absolute Beginners

GB 1986 107m Super Techniscope
Virgin/Goldcrest/Palace (Stephen Woolley, Chris Brown)

📺 ▦ 📀 🎧

Teen life and pop fashion in 1958 London.

Deafening, mindless, musical, multi-screen pot-pourri of teen culture which sadly needs narrative links not to mention better music and firmer control.

w Richard Burridge, Christopher Wicking, Don MacPherson *novel* Colin MacInnes d Julien Temple ph Oliver Stapleton m *David Bowie, Ray Davies, et al.* pd John Beard
☆ Eddie O'Connell, Patsy Kensit, David Bowie, Ray Davies, James Fox, Lionel Blair, Steven Berkoff, Mandy Rice Davies
'All that noise, all that energy, so little governing thought.' – *Time Out*

Absolute Power *

US 1997 120m Technicolor Panavision
Columbia/Castle Rock/Malpaso (Clint Eastwood, Karen Spiegel)

📺 ▦ 📀 ◎ 🎧

A thief attempts to prove that the US President was an accomplice in the murder of a woman.

Old-fashioned, lacklustre thriller with an implausible plot, though it does occasionally crank up the suspense.

w William Goldman *novel* David Baldacci d Clint Eastwood ph Jack N. Green m Lennie Niehaus pd Henry Bumstead ed Joel Cox
☆ Clint Eastwood, Gene Hackman, Ed Harris, Laura Linney, Judy Davis, Scott Glenn, Dennis Haysbert, E. G. Marshall, Melora Hardin
'Glum and depersonalized, as if Eastwood couldn't muster the energy to guide us through this maze of improbable twists.' – *Owen Gleiberman, Entertainment Weekly*

Absolute Quiet *

US 1936 71m bw
MGM (John Considine Jnr)

A planeload of strangers is forced down on a financier's ranch.

Interestingly-cast programmer, efficiently directed.

w Harry Clork d George B. Seitz
☆ Lionel Atwill, Louis Hayward, Raymond Walburn, Stuart Erwin, Wallace Ford, J. Carrol Naish

Absolution *

GB 1978 95m Technicolor
Bulldog (Danny O'Donovan, Elliott Kastner)

📺 ▦

TV title: *Murder by Confession*

A schoolmaster priest at a Roman Catholic boarding school is taunted by a malicious pupil into committing murder.

Interesting and suspenseful, though finally too complicated compromise between a thriller of the Sleuth type and a downbeat character study.

w Anthony Shaffer d Anthony Page ph John Coquillon m Stanley Myers
☆ Richard Burton, Dominic Guard, Dai Bradley, Billy Connolly, Andrew Keir
'A dire slice of clever-clever narrative trickery.' – *Paul Taylor, MFB*
'You can't make real bricks from this kind of straw, since a potentially interesting study of character and environment is gradually weakened by the constraints of a second-rate murder mystery.' – *Guardian*

Abwärts: see Out of Order

'A place on earth more awesome than anywhere in space.'

The Abyss

US 1989 140m DeLuxe
Fox (Gale Anne Hurd)

📺 📺 ▦ 📀 🎧

Attempting to rescue a nuclear submarine, divers working on underwater drilling encounter aliens.

Despite some clever special effects, a tedious, overlong fantasy that is more excited by machinery than people.

wd James Cameron ph Mikael Salomon m Alan Silvestri pd Leslie Dilley ed Joel Goodman sp Laura Buff, John Bruno, ILM, Dennis Muren
☆ Ed Harris, Mary Elizabeth Mastrantonio, Michael Biehn, Leo Burmester, Todd Graff, John Bedford Lloyd, J. C. Quinn, Kimberly Scott
'For the most part, as exciting an undersea drama as one could imagine.' – *MFB*
† *The Abyss Special Edition* released on video and Laserdisc contained an extra 27m cut from the original cinema release.
🏆 visual effects
ਊ cinematography; art direction

Accattone *

Italy 1961 120m bw
Cino del Duca/Arco (Alfredo Bini)

📺 📺 ▦ 🎧

A Roman pimp and thief is beset by troubles, and is finally killed escaping from the police.

Sordid and rough-edged but vividly realistic melodrama.

wd Pier Paolo Pasolini ph Tonino delli Colli md Carlo Rustichelli ad Bernardo Bertolucci
☆ Franco Citti, Franca Pasut, Silvana Corsini, Paola Giudi, Roberto Scaringella, Adele Cambria
'Discontinuous, lackadaisical, sometimes improbable, almost always superficial.' – *John Simon*

Accent on Love

US 1941 61m bw
TCF

A real estate executive walks out to become spokesman for his former underprivileged tenants.

Thin Capraesque romantic comedy.

w John Larkin *story* Dalton Trumbo d Ray McCarey
☆ George Montgomery, Osa Massen, J. Carrol Naish, Cobina Wright Jnr, Stanley Clements, Thurston Hall, Minerva Urecal

Accent on Youth *

US 1935 77m bw
Paramount (Douglas Maclean)

A secretary falls in love with her middle-aged playwright employer.

Reasonably sparkling comedy from a popular play, later remade as Mr Music and But Not for Me.

w Herbert Fields, Claude Binyon *play* Samson Raphaelson d Wesley Ruggles ph Leon Shamroy
☆ Herbert Marshall, Sylvia Sidney, Philip Reed, Astrid Allwyn, Holmes Herbert
'Well adapted, presented and produced for box office satisfaction.' – *Variety*

Accident **

GB 1967 105m Eastmancolor
London Independent Producers (Joseph Losey, Norman Priggen)

📺 ▦

An Oxford undergraduate is killed in a car crash; his tutor looks back over the tangle of personal relationships that contributed to his death.

Ascetic drama in which the audience is too often left to observe at length and draw its own conclusions; good characterizations nevertheless.

w Harold Pinter *novel* Nicholas Mosley d Joseph Losey ph Gerry Fisher m John Dankworth
☆ Dirk Bogarde, Stanley Baker, Jacqueline Sassard, Vivien Merchant, Michael York
'The whole thing is such a teapot tempest, and it is so assiduously underplayed that it is neither strong drama nor stinging satire. It is just a sad little story of a wistful don.' – *Bosley Crowther*
'Everything is calm, unruffled, lacquered in a veneer of civilization, yet underneath it all, one gradually begins to realize, the characters are tearing each other emotionally to shreds.' – *MFB*
'Uneven, unsatisfying, but with virtuoso passages of calculated meanness.' – *New Yorker, 1977*

Accidental Hero: see Hero

The Accidental Tourist ***

US 1988 121m Technicolor
Warner (Lawrence Kasdan, Charles Okun, Michael Grillo)

📺 ▦ 📀 🎧

Left by his wife, an uptight travel writer falls in love with an exuberant dog-trainer.

A liberating domestic drama, notable for some excellent acting.

w Frank Galati, Lawrence Kasdan *novel* Anne Tyler d Lawrence Kasdan ph John Bailey m John Williams pd Bo Welch ed Carol Littleton
☆ William Hurt, Kathleen Turner, Geena Davis, Amy Wright, Bill Pullman, Robert Gorman, David Ogden Stiers, Ed Begley Jnr
🏆 Geena Davis
ਊ picture; adapted screenplay; John Williams

Accidents Will Happen

US 1938 62m bw
Warner (Bryan Foy)

An insurance claims adjuster takes to crime.

Slack little programmer.

w George Bricker, Anthony Coldeway d William Clemens
☆ Ronald Reagan, Dick Purcell, Gloria Blondell, Addison Richards, Hugh O'Connell

Acción Mutante

Spain 1993 94m Fujicolour Cinemascope
Feature Film/El Deseo/CIBY 2000 (Agustin Almodóvar, Pedro Almodóvar)

📺

In 2012, a disfigured man leads a group of disabled in a terrorist war against the healthy and perfectly formed for his own advantage.

Bizarre horror that can be taken as a black or sick joke, depending on your attitude to a movie with such characters as a half-dead, half-alive Siamese twin. Whatever, after a brisk beginning, it soon palls and even appals, with its emphasis on the gruesome.

w Jorge Guerricaechevarria, Alex de la Iglesia d Alex de la Iglesia ph Carles Gusi m Juan Carlos Cuello ad José Luis Arrizabalaga ed Pablo Blanco sp Oliver Gleyze, Yves Domenjoud, Jean-Bapiste Bonetto, Bernard-André le Boetti
☆ Antonio Resines, Frédérique Feder, Alex Angulo, Juan Viades, Karra Elejalde, Saturnino Garcia, Fernando Guillén, Jaime Blanch
'Officially a promising first film, this feels more like a disappointing second one.' – *Empire*

L'Accompagnatrice: see The Accompanist

The Accompanist

France 1992 111m colour
Gala/Film Par Film/De la Boissière Orly/Sedif France/3 Cinema (Jean-Louis Livi)

📺

original title: *L'Accompagnatrice*

In occupied Paris of the early 1940s, a young star-struck woman becomes the accompanist to a fashionable French singer and her rich husband, a reluctant collaborator with the Germans.

The wartime setting is presumably intended to give resonance to this otherwise trite, but charming, tale of

self-sacrifice; instead it makes the soul-searching of the central characters seem a luxury and an irrelevance.
w Claude Miller, Luc Béraud *novel* Nina Berberova d Claude Miller ph Yves Angelo m Alain Jomy pd Jean-Pierre Kohut Svelko ed Albert Jurgenson
☆ Ronald Bohringer, Elena Safonova, Romane Bohringer, Bernard Verley, Samuel Labarthe, Nelly Borgeaud, Julien Rassam, Jean-Pierre Kohut Svelko
'Dramatically, the movie doesn't cover much ground ... all he ends up with is the thin old story of a supporting artist who lives by proxy.' – *Michael Sragow, New Yorker*
'The film's uniform visual and narrative dullness does act as a pretty effective anaesthetic. And it also fits a certain, rather unpleasant way of looking at French history in which these stories and images that we've seen a thousand times take on a mythical quality.' – *Martin Bright, Sight and Sound*

According to Mrs Hoyle
US   1951   60m   bw
Monogram
A retired schoolteacher lives in a hotel run by criminals, and becomes involved.
Uninspired sentimental comedy providing a rare star part for a well-liked character actress.
w W. Scott Darling, Barney Gerard d Jean Yarbrough
☆ Spring Byington, Anthony Caruso, Brett King, Tanis Chandler

Account Rendered
GB   1957   60m   bw
Rank/Major Productions (John Temple-Smith)
A detective inspector tracks down the killer of a banker's flirtatious wife.
Indifferent thriller lacking any distinguishing features.
w Barbara S. Harper *novel* Pamela Barrington d Peter Graham Scott ph Walter J. Harvey ad Norman Arnold ed Tom Simpson
☆ Honor Blackman, Griffith Jones, Ursula Howells, Ewen Solon, Robert Raikes, John Van Eyssen

'The standout suspense triumph of the year!'
The Accused *
US   1948   101m   bw
Paramount (Hal B. Wallis)
aka: *Strange Deception*
In self-defence a lady professor kills a student who has sexually attacked her.
Dullish suspenser with the outcome never in doubt, though the production values are beyond reproach.
w Ketti Frings d William Dieterle ph Milton Krasner m Victor Young
☆ Loretta Young, Robert Cummings, Wendell Corey, Sam Jaffe, Douglas Dick

The Accused *
US   1988   110m   Technicolor
UIP/Paramount (Stanley R. Jaffe, Sherry Lansing)
▣▣   ▤   ◉∿
A provocatively-dressed woman is raped after performing a sexy dance at a seedy bar.
Unconvincing problem picture that fails to explore the issues it raises.
w Tom Topor d Jonathan Kaplan ph Ralf Bode m Brad Fiedel pd Richard Kent Wilcox ed Jerry Greenberg, O. Nicholas Brown
☆ Kelly McGillis, Jodie Foster, Bernie Coulson, Ann Hearn, Steve Antin, Tom O'Brien
'Another box-office winner which once again negotiates a fine line between social concern, feminism and exploitation.' – *MFB*
♟ Jodie Foster

Accused of Murder
US   1956   76m   Trucolor   Naturama
Republic
When a crooked lawyer is murdered, his mistress is suspected.
Flat little mystery with unappetizing characters.
w Bob Williams, W. R. Burnett *novel* Vanity Row by W. R. Burnett d Joe Kane
☆ Vera Ralston, David Brian, Sidney Blackmer, Virginia Grey, Warren Stevens, Lee Van Cleef

Ace in the Hole ***
US   1951   111m   bw
Paramount (Billy Wilder)
aka: *The Big Carnival*
In order to prolong the sensation and boost newspaper sales, a self-seeking journalist delays the rescue of a man trapped in a cave.
An incisive, compelling melodrama taking a sour look at the American scene; one of its director's masterworks.
w Billy Wilder, Lesser Samuels, Walter Newman d Billy Wilder ph Charles B. Lang Jnr m Hugo Friedhofer
☆ Kirk Douglas, Jan Sterling, Porter Hall, Bob Arthur, Richard Benedict, Ray Teal, Frank Cady
   LORRAINE TO TATUM: 'I've met some hard-boiled eggs, but you – you're twenty minutes!'
   LORRAINE: 'I don't go to church. Kneeling bags my nylons.'
   TATUM TO EDITOR: 'I've done a lot of lying in my time. I've lied to men who wear belts. I've lied to men who wear suspenders. But I'd never be so stupid as to lie to a man who wears both belt and suspenders.'
   TATUM, DYING, TO EDITOR: 'How'd you like to make a thousand dollars a day, Mr Boot? I'm a thousand-dollar-a-day newspaperman. You can have me for nothing.'
'Few of the opportunities for irony, cruelty and horror are missed.' – *Gavin Lambert*
'Style and purpose achieve for the most part a fusion even more remarkable than in *Sunset Boulevard*.' – *Penelope Houston*
'As stimulating as black coffee.' – *Richard Mallett, Punch*
'Americans expected a cocktail and felt I was giving them a shot of vinegar instead.' – *Billy Wilder*
'Some people have tried to claim some sort of satirical brilliance for it, but it's really rather nasty, in a sociologically pushy way.' – *New Yorker, 1980*
'A brilliant arrangement of cause and effect ... unique as a mirror of the morbid psychology of crowds ... revolting but incontrovertibly true.' – *New York Times*
† Locations were at Gallup, New Mexico.
§ script

Ace of Aces *
US   1933   76m   bw
RKO
On the outbreak of World War I an American sculptor is branded a coward when he does not immediately enlist; but he disappears and turns up in France a hero, though with a sour taste in his mouth.
Melodrama of disillusion, dated in many respects but interesting to compare with The Dawn Patrol *and* The Last Flight.
w John Monk Saunders, H. W. Hanemann *story* Bird of Prey by John Monk Saunders d J. Walter Ruben ph Henry Cronjager m Max Steiner
☆ Richard Dix, Elizabeth Allan, Theodore Newton, Ralph Bellamy, Joseph Sawyer, Frank Conroy, William Cagney
'It's the fine photography and crashes that provide the thrills.' – *Variety*

'He's the best there is! (Actually, he's the only one there is.)'
Ace Ventura, Pet Detective
♙♙   US   1994   93m   colour
Warner/Morgan Creek (James G. Robinson)
▣▣   ▤   ◉∿   ◉   ⌂
A private eye who recovers missing pets is hired to recover the Miami Dolphins' dolphin mascot.
Featuring a relentlessly mugging comedian who makes Jerry Lewis seem as restrained as Buster Keaton, this is an extraordinarily inept comedy, with feeble jokes parodying other movies, feebler slapstick and much homophobia and misogyny; it also provides Sean Young with the most demeaning role of her career.
w Jack Bernstein, Tom Shadyac, Jim Carrey d Tom Shadyac ph Julio Macat m Ira Newborn pd William Elliott ed Don Zimmerman
☆ Jim Carrey, Courteney Cox, Sean Young, Dan Marino, Noble Willingham, Troy Evans, Udo Kier, Tone Loc
'Doesn't display the comic pedigree needed for the rubber-faced-and-limbed comedian to collar breakthrough dollars. That said, dumb good

times still wield a strong lure for the Saturday night date crowd.' – *Variety*
† The film was an unexpected hit in America, earning more than $65m at the box-office and raising Jim Carrey's price per picture from $350,000 to a reported $7m.

Ace Ventura: When Nature Calls
US   1995   92m   Technicolor
Warner/Morgan Creek (James G. Robinson)
▣▣   ▤   ◉∿   ◉   ⌂
A pet detective goes to Africa to find a sacred white bat, a creature he dislikes.
Carrey extends his range of lavatorial humour to include spit and vomit, and an exit from the anus of a mechanical rhinoceros. The bad-taste episodic narrative, resembling a very old version of King Solomon's Mines, has no other function than to give him plenty of scope for his unrestrained mugging.
wd Steve Oedekerk ph Donald E. Thorin m Robert Folk pd Stephen J. Lineweaver ed Malcolm Campbell
☆ Jim Carrey, Ian McNeice, Simon Callow, Maynard Eziashi, Bob Gunton, Sophie Okonedo, Tommy Davidson, Adewalé, Andrew Steel, Bruce Spence
'As fresh, brash and outrageous as the original' – *Variety*
† Director Tom DeCerchio left after shooting began, to be replaced by writer Steve Oedekerk. The film took $37.8m on its opening weekend in the United States, the highest figure so far for a comedy, and went on to gross more than $104m at the US box-office and another $37m elsewhere during 1995.

Aces High *
GB   1976   114m   Technicolor
EMI/S. Benjamin Fisz/Jacques Roitfeld
▣▣
In the air force during World War I, young pilots are needlessly sacrificed.
Spirited if rather unnecessary remake of Journey's End *transposed to the air war, which makes it almost identical to* The Dawn Patrol.
w Howard Barker d Jack Gold ph Gerry Fisher, Peter Allwork m Richard Hartley
☆ Malcolm McDowell, Christopher Plummer, Simon Ward, Peter Firth, John Gielgud, Trevor Howard, Richard Johnson, Ray Milland

'Their best and final mission.'
Aces: Iron Eagle III
US   1992   98m   CFI color
New Line/7 Arts (Ron Samuels)
▤   ⌂
Veteran fighter pilots battle against South American drug barons.
Energetic but mindless action, with a little slapstick thrown in, and featuring muscle-woman Rachel McLish.
w Kevin Elders d John Glen ph Alec Mills m Harry Manfredini pd Robb Wilson King ed Bernard Gribble sp John Richardson
☆ Louis Gossett Jnr, Rachel McLish, Paul Freeman, Horst Buchholz, Christopher Cazenove, Sonny Chiba, Fred Dalton Thompson, Mitchell Ryan

Acid House
GB   1998   118m   colour
Film Four/Picture Palace North/Umbrella/Channel 4 (David Muir, Alex Usborne)
▣▣   ▤   ◉
Three stories about life in Scotland: 'The Granton Star Cause', in which God turns a failure into a fly; 'The Soft Touch', in which a man takes back his unfaithful wife; 'The Acid House', in which a drug-taking youth switches personalities with a baby.
Unsubtle portmanteau movie, in which anarchic wit struggles against a browbeating style and loses; the overall effect is dispiriting.
w Irvine Welsh *stories* Irvine Welsh d Paul McGuigan ph Alasdair Walker m Primal Scream, Nick Cave et al. pd Richard Bridgland, Mike Gunn ed Andrew Hulme
☆ 'The Granton Star Cause': Stephen McCole, Maurice Roeves, Garry Sweeney, Jenny McCrindle, Irvine Welsh, 'A Soft Touch': Kevin McKidd, Michelle Gomez, Tam Dean Burn, Gary McCormack, 'The Acid House': Ewen Bremner, Martin Clunes, Jemma Redgrave, Arlene Cockburn, Jane Stabler
'The acting throughout is broad, the direction has a sledgehammer coarseness, and the lack of

compassion, though this cannot be intentional, seems absolute.' – *Philip French, Observer*

Across 110th Street ***
US   1972   102m   DeLuxe
UA/Film Guarantors (Fouad Said, Ralph Serpe)
▤   ⌂
Police and the Mafia go after three blacks disguised as cops who rob a Harlem numbers bank and kill its operators.
Tough, clever thriller, set within a well-observed society of violence and deprivation.
w Luther Davis *novel* Wally Ferris d Barry Shear ph Jack Priestley m J. J. Johnson ad Perry Watkins ed Bryan Brandt
☆ Anthony Quinn, Yaphet Kotto, Anthony Franciosa, Paul Benjamin, Ed Barnard, Richard Ward, Antonio Fargas
† The film was cut to 99m on its British release.

'Once A Master Of Millions ... Now A Fugitive In Flight!'
Across the Bridge *
GB   1957   103m   bw
Rank/IPF (John Stafford)
▤
A fugitive financier kills his pursuer, finds he was a murderer, and tries to hide out across the Mexican border.
This star tour de force is unconvincing in detail and rather unattractive to watch (British films never could cope with American settings), but the early sequences have suspense.
w Guy Elmes, Denis Freeman *novel* Graham Greene d Ken Annakin ph Reg Wyer m James Bernard
☆ Rod Steiger, David Knight, Marla Landi, Noel Willman, Bernard Lee

Across the Pacific ***
US   1942   99m   bw
Warner (Hal B. Wallis)
▤   ◉∿
Just before Pearl Harbor, an army officer is cashiered by arrangement in order to contact pro-Japanese sympathizers.
Hasty, easy-going and very enjoyable hokum, partly ship-set and successfully reteaming three stars of The Maltese Falcon.
w Richard Macaulay *serial* Aloha Means Goodbye by Robert Carson d John Huston ph Arthur Edeson m Adolph Deutsch
☆ Humphrey Bogart, Mary Astor, Sydney Greenstreet, Sen Yung, Monte Blue, Richard Loo, Chester Gan, Kam Tong
'A spy picture which tingles with fearful uncertainties and glints with the sheen of blue steel.' – *Bosley Crowther*
† Huston was called up before the film was completed, and allegedly reshaped the script before leaving in order to put the hero in an impossible situation. Direction was eventually completed by Vincent Sherman.
†† Monte Blue, who has a tiny last-reel part as the heroine's drunken father, starred in a 1926 silent film with the same title but a totally different plot. He played an army officer fighting Philippine guerrillas. Darryl F. Zanuck wrote the script, and Roy del Ruth directed, for Warner.

Across the Tracks
US   1991   100m   CFI color
Desert Productions (Dale Rosenbloom)
▣▣   ▤   ◉∿
Two athletic brothers of differing temperaments become rivals.
A well-intentioned movie about teenage problems that may appeal to adolescents but not to adults.
wd Sandy Tung ph Michael Delahoussaye m Joel Goldsmith pd Thomas Meleck ed Farrel Levy
☆ Rick Schroder, Brad Pitt, Carrie Snodgress, David Anthony Marshall, Thomas Mikal Ford, John Linton

Across the Wide Missouri *
US   1951   77m   Technicolor
MGM (Robert Sisk)
In the 1820s, a trapper marries an Indian girl and lives with her people.
Promising credits produce an unsatisfactory Western: despite honest efforts, the elements do not jell into a convincing whole.
w Talbot Jennings d William Wellman ph William C. Mellor m David Raksin

---

☆ Clark Gable, Ricardo Montalban, John Hodiak, Adolphe Menjou, Maria Elena Marques, J. Carrol Naish, Jack Holt, Alan Napier, Howard Keel

Act of Love *
US 1954 104m bw
UA/Benagoss (Anatole Litvak)
In Paris in 1944, an American with the liberation army falls in love with a French girl, who commits suicide when he is posted and cannot make their rendezvous.
Cheerless romantic drama, rather thin and unmemorable despite the efforts of all concerned.
w Irwin Shaw *novel* The Girl on the Via Flaminia by Alfred Hayes d Anatole Litvak ph Armand Thirard m Michael Emer, Joe Hajos pd Alexander Trauner
☆ Kirk Douglas, Dany Robin, Barbara Laage, Robert Stauss, Gabrielle Dorziat, Gregoire Aslan, Fernand Ledoux, Serge Reggiani, Brigitte Bardot
† Made in France, an early Hollywood foreign location film.

Act of Murder **
GB 1964 62m bw
Merton Park (Jack Greenwood)
A couple arrange a holiday by swapping houses with strangers, and a complex plot ensues.
Slick, superior example of the Edgar Wallace second feature series.
w Lewis Davidson d Alan Bridges ph James Wilson m Bernard Ebbinghouse
☆ John Carson, Anthony Bate, Justine Lord, Duncan Lewis, Dandy Nichols
'This uncommonly intelligent little thriller is just the sort of film which is likely to arouse critical sneers for reaching too high on a low budget.' – Tom Milne

An Act of Murder *
US 1948 90m bw
U-I (Jerry Bresler)
aka: *Live Today for Tomorrow*
A judge insists on being tried for the mercy killing of his incurably ill wife.
Earnest social drama which despite excellent acting can only reach an inconclusive ending.
w Michael Blankfort, Robert Thoeren *novel* The Mills of God by Ernst Lothar d Michael Gordon ph Hal Mohr m Daniele Amfitheatrof
☆ Fredric March, Florence Eldridge, Edmond O'Brien, Geraldine Brooks

Act of Violence **
US 1948 82m bw
MGM (William Wright)
After the war, an ex-GI tracks down a prison camp informer.
Moody, glossy melodrama with tension well sustained, though the sentimental ending is a cop-out.
w Robert L. Richards *story* Collier Young d Fred Zinnemann ph Robert Surtees m Bronislau Kaper
☆ Van Heflin, Robert Ryan, Janet Leigh, Mary Astor
'Strong characterization, fine direction and good photography combine to put this film high among its kind.' – MFB
'An effortless narrative control and a real power to maintain tension.' – Richard Winnington

Act One *
US 1963 110m bw
Warner (Dore Schary)
Poor Brooklyn boy Moss Hart rises to Broadway eminence via his writing partnership with George S. Kaufman.
Incredibly stilted film version of an excellent autobiography, notable only for fragments of acting and the fact that a film so totally uncommercial was made at all.
wd Dore Schary ph Arthur J. Ornitz m Skitch Henderson
☆ George Hamilton, Jason Robards Jnr, Jack Klugman, Sam Levene, George Segal, Ruth Ford, Eli Wallach
'From the moment young Hart takes pencil in hand, we have nowhere to go except to that happy ending; and despite all the painstaking detail, we don't believe a word of it.' – Judith Crist

Action for Slander *
GB 1937 83m bw
London Films/Saville (Victor Saville)
A bankrupt officer, accused of cheating at cards, defends his honour with a writ.
Lively melodrama of the old school.
w Ian Dalrymple, Miles Malleson *novel* Mary Borden d Tim Whelan ph Harry Stradling md Muir Mathieson
☆ Clive Brook, Ann Todd, Margaretta Scott, Arthur Margetson, Ronald Squire, Athole Stewart, Percy Marmont, Frank Cellier, Morton Selten
'Hollywood in its most lavish spurt of extravagance never went to such pains to assemble a cast … general run of patrons however will chafe under the lack of physical movement.' – Variety

Action in the North Atlantic *
US 1943 127m bw
Warner (Jerry Wald)
An American convoy bound for Russia comes under U-boat attack.
Efficient propaganda potboiler; studio bound, but still works as a war actioner.
w John Howard Lawson *story* Guy Gilpatric d Lloyd Bacon ph Ted McCord m Adolph Deutsch
☆ Humphrey Bogart, Raymond Massey, Alan Hale, Julie Bishop, Ruth Gordon, Sam Levene, Dane Clark
'The production has interludes of tremendous power. What is lacking is dramatic cohesion.' – Howard Barnes
'Directly in line of descent from The Perils of Pauline.' – Time
'The American equivalent of our war documentaries … tough, exciting, with no concession to flim flam.' – New Statesman
'I cannot think I have ever seen such realistic battles, or lived so intimately with the characters who comprise the crew.' – Evening Standard
⌗ Guy Gilpatric

Action Jackson
US 1988 96m Metrocolor
Guild/Lorimar (Joel Silver)
A maverick cop is framed for a murder while investigating the killings of union officials.
Violent action movie, with spectacular deaths and car chases, a ludicrous plot and a hissable villain.
w Robert Reneau d Craig R. Baxley ph Matthew F. Leonetti m Herbie Hancock, Michael Kamen ad Virginia Randolph ed Mark Helfrich
☆ Carl Weathers, Craig T. Nelson, Vanity, Sharon Stone, Thomas F. Wilson, Bill Duke, Robert Davi

Action of the Tiger
GB 1957 93m Technicolor Cinemascope
MGM/Claridge (Kenneth Harper)
An adventurer helps a French girl to rescue her brother from political imprisonment in Albania.
Dull and poorly constructed action melodrama.
w Robert Carson *novel* James Wellard d Terence Young ph Desmond Dickinson m Humphrey Searle
☆ Van Johnson, Martine Carol, Herbert Lom, Gustavo Rojo, Anthony Dawson, Helen Haye, Sean Connery

Actors and Sin *
US 1952 91m bw
UA/Sid Kuller (Ben Hecht)
Two short stories. When an unsuccessful actress commits suicide, her father makes it look like murder so that for once she shall get attention. The authoress of a romantic script bought by Hollywood is discovered to be a horrid little 9-year-old.
Interesting but incompetent compendium which descends almost to the home movie level and leaves the actors struggling.
wd Ben Hecht ph Lee Garmes m George Antheil
☆ Edward G. Robinson, Marsha Hunt, Dan O'Herlihy, Rudolph Anders, Eddie Albert, Alan Reed, Jenny Hecht
'A depressing double bill.' – Lindsay Anderson

An Actor's Revenge **
Japan 1963 113m Daieicolor Daieiscope
Daiei (Masaichi Nagata)
original title: *Yukinojo Henge*
In the early 19th century, a touring actor comes upon the rich merchant who had ruined his parents, and his revenge involves several deaths.
Complex, fascinating period melodrama, both rich and strange, with strong echoes of Jacobean melodrama.
w Daisuke Ito, Teinosuke Kinugasa, Natto Wada *novel* Otokichi Mikami d Kon Ichikawa ph Setsuo Kobayashi m Yasushi Akutagawa
☆ Kazuo Hasegawa, Fujiko Yamamoto, Ayako Wakao, Ganjiro Nakamura

The Actress *
US 1928 90m bw silent
MGM
GB title: *Trelawny of the 'Wells'*
A young Victorian actress marries a rich admirer.
Pleasing, well-cast version of a celebrated play.
w Albert Lewin, Richard Schayer *play* Sir Arthur Wing Pinero d Sidney Franklin ph William Daniels
☆ Norma Shearer, Ralph Forbes, O. P. Heggie, Owen Moore, Roy D'Arcy
'A thoughtful, rounded and provocative entertainment.' – New York Times
† Opening attraction at London's Empire Theatre, Leicester Square.

The Actress
US 1953 91m bw
MGM (Lawrence Weingarten)
Ruth Jones becomes an actress against the wishes of her stubborn seafaring father.
Episodes from Ruth Gordon's early life, based on her Broadway play Years Ago, make a pleasant though scarcely engrossing film: it is all a shade too discreet and wanly winning, and the few key events take place offscreen.
w Ruth Gordon d George Cukor ph Harold Rosson m Bronislau Kaper ad Cedric Gibbons, Arthur Lonergan
☆ Jean Simmons, Spencer Tracy, Teresa Wright, Anthony Perkins, Ian Wolfe, Mary Wickes

Actresses
Spain 1996 88m colour
Downtown/Els Films de la Rambla (Ventura Pons)
original title: *Actrius*
Before auditioning for the role of a legendary actress, a drama student interviews three of her former pupils.
This leisurely examination of the influence of past events on present lives reveals its theatrical origins by its static style; it also provides little opportunity for its cast to revel in the pleasures of acting.
w Ventura Pons, J. M. Benet I Jornet *play* E.R. by J. M. Benet I Jornet d Ventura Pons ph Tomás Pladevall m Carles Cases pd Rosa Ros ed Pere Abadal
☆ Nuria Espert, Rosa Maria Sardà, Anna Lizaran, Mercè Pons
'I can't think of anyone this film could possibly interest. It has the dramatic momentum of a slug.' – James Christopher, The Times

Acts of Love: see Carried Away

Ad Ogni Costo: see Grand Slam

Ada *
US 1961 109m Metrocolor Cinemascope
MGM/Avon/Chalmar (Lawrence Weingarten)
A political candidate marries a call girl who becomes his strong right arm and weathers a threat to reveal her past.
Indecisive romantic drama which pulls too many punches but has interesting background detail.
w Arthur Sheekman, William Driskill *novel* Ada Dallas by Wirt Williams d Daniel Mann ph Joseph Ruttenberg m Bronislau Kaper
☆ Susan Hayward, Dean Martin, Wilfrid Hyde-White, Ralph Meeker, Martin Balsam
'A bonanza for connoisseurs of perfectly awful movies.' – Judith Crist
'Its characterizations are sketchy, its political setting routine and symbolic.' – New York Herald Tribune

Adalen 31 **
Sweden 1969 115m Technicolor Techniscope
Svensk Filmindustri
A prolonged strike at a small-town paper mill ends in tragedy when the troops move in.
Effective period piece which emphasizes the idyllic qualities of the backgrounds rather than the foreground terrors.
wd Bo Widerberg ph Jorgen Persson
☆ Peter Schildt, Kerstin Tidelius, Roland Hedlund, Stefan Feierbach, Anita Bjork
⌗ foreign film

Adam *
GB 1991 7m colour
Aardman Animations (Christopher Moll)
A solitary figure living on a small world becomes excited when his creator decides to make him a companion.
Amusing cartoon of the beginning of the sex wars.
wd Peter Lord ph David Sproxton m Stuart Gordon ed Nigel Bell
⌗ animated film

Adam and Eva *
US 1923 83m bw silent
Paramount/Cosmopolitan
An extravagant girl reforms when her father goes bust.
Moral comedy with a happy ending: a hit of its day.
w Luther Reed *play* Guy Bolton and George Middleton d Robert G. Vignola
☆ Marion Davies, T. Roy Barnes, Tom Lewis, William Norris, Percy Ames

Adam and Evelyne
GB 1949 92m bw
Rank/Two Cities (Harold French)
A society playboy adopts his dead friend's daughter, and falls in love with her.
Undernourished romantic drama, a mild variation on Daddy Longlegs.
w Noel Langley, Lesley Storm, George Barraud, Nicholas Phipps d Harold French ph Guy Green m Mischa Spoliansky
☆ Stewart Granger, Jean Simmons, Helen Cherry, Edwin Styles, Beatrice Varley, Wilfrid Hyde-White

Adam at 6 A.M. *
US 1970 100m colour
National General (Robert Christiansen, Rick Rosenberg)
A disillusioned Californian university professor returns to Missouri and takes a labouring job.
Interesting and unconventional drama of a liberal kind.
w Stephen Karpf, Elinor Karpf d Robert Scheerer ph Charles Rosher ad Dale Hennessey ed Jack McSweeney
☆ Michael Douglas, Lee Purcell, Joe Don Baker, Grayson Hall, Charles Aidman, Louise Latham, Meg Foster

Adam Had Four Sons *
US 1941 81m bw
Columbia (Robert Sherwood)
A widower's family is cared for by a governess.
Modest magazine fiction which established Ingrid Bergman as an American star.
w Michael Blankfort, William Hurlbut *novel* Legacy by Charles Bonner d Gregory Ratoff ph Peverell Marley m W. Franke Harling
☆ Warner Baxter, Ingrid Bergman, Susan Hayward, Richard Denning, Fay Wray

Adam's Rib *
US 1922 86m bw silent
Paramount (Cecil B. de Mille)
By offering herself in her stead, an American girl tries to prevent her mother's adultery with a European ex-monarch.
One of its director's 'sin in high life' melodramas, which packed 'em in at the time, this has nothing but decoration to offer to a modern audience.
w Jeanie MacPherson d Cecil B. de Mille
☆ Milton Sills, Elliott Dexter, Theodore Kosloff, Anna Q. Nilsson, Pauline Garon, Julia Faye

---

Adam's Rib **

US   1949   101m   bw
MGM (Lawrence Weingarten)

Husband and wife lawyers are on opposite sides of
an attempted murder case.
*A superior star vehicle which also managed to introduce
four promising personalities; slangily written and
smartly directed, but perhaps a shade less funny than it
once seemed.*
w *Ruth Gordon, Garson Kanin* d *George Cukor*
ph *George J. Folsey* m *Miklos Rozsa*
☆ *Spencer Tracy, Katharine Hepburn, David Wayne,
Tom Ewell, Judy Holliday, Jean Hagen, Hope
Emerson, Clarence Kolb*
  'Hepburn and Tracy are again presented as the
  ideal US Mr and Mrs of upper-middle income.
  This time, as well as being wittily urbane, both
  are lawyers.' – *Time*
  'It isn't solid food but it certainly is meaty and
  juicy and comically nourishing.' – *Bosley
  Crowther*
† A 1972 TV series of the same title provided a
boring imitation, with Ken Howard and Blythe
Danner.
&. Ruth Gordon and Garson Kanin

Adamson of Africa: see *The Killers of
Kilimanjaro*

'Creepy. Kooky. Spooky. Ooky.'
The Addams Family *

👫   US   1991   99m   DeLuxe
Columbia TriStar/Paramount/Orion (Scott Rudin)

An impostor turns up at the Addams family
mansion, claiming to be a long-lost elder brother.
*Owing more to the TV series of the 1960s than to the
macabre wit of the original New Yorker cartoons, an
ill-conceived, coarse-grained comedy that nevertheless
was a success at the box-office.*
w *Caroline Thompson, Larry Wilson characters
created by* Charles Addams d *Barry Sonnenfeld*
ph *Owen Roizman* m *Marc Shaiman* pd *Richard
MacDonald* ed *Dede Allen, Jim Miller* sp visual
effects supervisor Alan Munro, Chuck Comisky
☆ *Anjelica Huston, Raul Julia, Christopher Lloyd,
Dan Hedaya, Elizabeth Wilson, Judith Malina,
Carel Struycken, Dana Ivey, Paul Benedict,
Christopher Hart*
  'Plays like a collection of sitcom one-liners
  augmented by feature-film special effects – a
  combination that is stretched well beyond its
  limits.' – *Variety*
  'Misguided graveyard slapstick.' – *New Yorker*

'Motherhood just got a little stranger.'
Addams Family Values *

👫   US   1993   94m   colour
UIP/Paramount (Scott Rudin)

The Addams children try to kill the new baby, but
he is damage-proof; while their parents hire a
nanny who is also a serial killer.
*This is less a movie and more a sequence of gags set in
an elongated sit-com, of which few are inspired and
most too ordinary to amuse, but it has its moments.*
w *Paul Rudnick* d *Barry Sonnenfeld* ph *Donald
Peterman* m *Marc Shaiman* pd *Ken Adam*
ed *Arthur Schmidt, Jim Miller*
☆ *Anjelica Huston, Raul Julia, Christopher Lloyd,
Joan Cusack, Christina Ricci, Carol Kane, Jimmy
Workman, Carel Struycken, David Krumholtz,
Christopher Hart*
  'It's the kind of wicked delicious comedy one can
  savor without adding the proviso of guilty
  pleasure.' – *Variety*
  'The film does not know when to stop, has little
  idea of how to begin, and moves forward by a
  process of "Quick, who's got the next gimmick"
  jolts and nudges.' – *Nigel Andrews, Financial
  Times*
  'The storyline is almost too slim to recall and the
  cast simply earn their bread and butter doing
  revue turns.' – *Derek Malcolm, Guardian*
&. Ken Adam

Addicted to Love *

US   1997   100m   Technicolor
Warner/Outlaw/Miramax (Jeffrey Silver, Bobby
Newmyer)

When his girlfriend leaves him for a French
restaurateur, an astronomer joins with the man's
jilted fiancée to break up their romance.
*A romantic comedy with a cutting edge, as people
behave badly to one another in the name of fidelity.*
w *Robert Gordon* d *Griffin Dunne* ph *Andrew
Dunn* m *Rachel Portman* pd *Robin Standefer*
ed *Elizabeth Kling*
☆ *Meg Ryan, Matthew Broderick, Kelly Preston,
Tcheky Karyo, Maureen Stapleton, Nesbitt
Blaisdell, Remak Ramsay, Dominick Dunne*
  'This odd juxtaposition of light drama and
  outrageous antics is apt to confuse more than
  charm audience.' – *Leonard Klady, Variety*

The Addiction

US   1995   82m   bw
Guild/Fast Films (Denis Hann, Fernando Sulichin)

A philosophy student turns vampire and is turned
on by the writings of Nietzsche.
*Ferrara bites off more than he can chew in this horror
movie, using images of massacres and concentration
camp victims to emphasize his depiction of power-
crazed bloodlust let loose on society; but his fiction
shrivels in the light of these actual horrors.*
w *Nicholas St John* d *Abel Ferrara* ph *Ken
Kelsch* m *Joe Delia* pd *Charlie Lagola* ed *Mayin
Lo*
☆ *Lili Taylor, Christoper Walken, Annabella
Sciorra, Edie Falco, Paul Calderon, Fredro Star,
Kathryn Erbe, Michael Imperioli*
  'Dramatically surprising, stylishly made in black-
  and-white and very well acted.' – *Variety*
  'Offensively pretentious.' – *Sunday Times*

The Adding Machine *

GB   1968   99m   Technicolor
Universal/Associated London (Jerome Epstein)

Downtrodden clerk Mr Zero rebels against society
by murdering his boss. Tried and executed, he
spends thirty years in heaven before being
'laundered' and sent back to start again as another
nonentity.
*Elmer Rice's satirical fantasy of the twenties is here
robbed of its expressionist staging and presented
naturalistically, a fatal error from which the film never
for one moment recovers.*
wd *Jerome Epstein* ph *Walter Lassally* m *Mike
Leander, Lambert Williamson*
☆ *Phyllis Diller, Milo O'Shea, Billie Whitelaw,
Sydney Chaplin, Julian Glover, Raymond Huntley,
Phil Brown, Libby Morris*

Addio, Fratello Crudele: see *'Tis Pity She's a
Whore*

Address Unknown **

US   1944   72m   bw
Columbia (William Cameron Menzies)

A German-American becomes a Nazi and is
incriminated by false letters from his one-time
friend.
*Reasonably engrossing, cheaply-made adaptation of a
slim little thriller which was widely read during World
War II.*
w *Kressman Taylor, Herbert Dalmas
novel* Kressman Taylor d *William Cameron
Menzies* m *Rudolph Maté* m *Ernst Toch*
ad *Lionel Banks, Walter Holscher*
☆ *Paul Lukas, Carl Esmond, Peter Van Eyck, Mady
Christians, Emory Parnell*
&. Ernst Toch; art direction

Adieu Philippine *

France/Italy   1962   106m   bw
Unitec/Alpha/Rome-Paris (Georges de Beauregard)

A young TV cameraman is torn between two girls.
*Flimsy but attractive romantic comedy, slightly marred
by New Wave improvisation with consequent rough
edges.*
w *Michèle O'Glor, Jacques Rozier* d *Jacques
Rozier* ph *René Mathelin* m *various*
☆ *Jean-Claude Aimini, Yveline Céry, Stefania
Sabatini, Vittorio Caprioli*

Adios, Sabata: see *The Bounty Hunters*

Adj Kiraly Katonat: see *The Princess*

'Sex ... Power ... Obsession.'
The Adjuster *

Canada   1991   102m   colour
Metro/Ego Film Arts/Téléfilm Canada/Ontario Film
Development Corp. (Atom Egoyan)

An insurance loss adjuster becomes involved in the
sexual activities of his clients.
*Offbeat movie that takes an oblique approach to the
relationship between cinema and voyeurism.*
wd *Atom Egoyan* ph *Paul Sarossy* m *Mychael
Danna* d *Linda Del Rosario, Richard Paris*
ed *Susan Shipton*
☆ *Elias Koteas, Arsinée Khanjian, Maury
Chaykin, Gabrielle Rose, Jennifer Dale, David
Hemblen, Rose Sarkisyan, Armen Kokorian*
  'Utterly compelling, a visual treat and, above all,
  a fiercely intelligent piece of work.' – *Empire*

The Admirable Crichton *

GB   1957   93m   Technicolor   Vistavision
Columbia/Modern Screenplays (Ian Dalrymple)
US title: *Paradise Lagoon*

Lord Loam and his family are shipwrecked on a
desert island, where his manservant proves the
undisputed leader.
*Few laughs are to be had from this blunt, sentimental
version of a famous play, but the photography and
decor are excellent.*
w *Vernon Harris play* J. M. Barrie d *Lewis
Gilbert* ph *Wilkie Cooper* m *Douglas Gamley,
Richard Addinsell* ad *William Kellner*
cos *Bernard Nevill devices* Emmett
☆ *Kenneth More, Cecil Parker, Sally Ann Howes,
Diane Cilento, Martita Hunt, Jack Watling, Peter
Graves, Gerald Harper*
  'Barrie's play now seems more remote than
  Gammer Gurton.' – *David Robinson*

The Admiral Was a Lady

US   1950   87m   bw
Roxbury (Albert S. Rogell, Jack M. Warner)

Four ex-airmen and an ex-Wac try to live on their
wits.
*Unappealing comedy which gives the impression that it
has tried to find a new style, and failed.*
w *Sidney Salkow, John O'Dea* d *Albert S. Rogell*
ph *Stanley Cortez*
☆ *Edmond O'Brien, Wanda Hendrix, Rudy
Vallee, Johnny Sands, Steve Brodie, Richard
Erdman, Hillary Brooke, Richard Lane*

The Adolescent

France/West Germany   1979   93m   colour
Janus (Phillipe Dussart)
original title: *L'Adolescente*

In France in 1939, a 12-year-old girl is infatuated
with a young Jewish doctor.
*A solidly acted but otherwise uninspired account of the
stirrings of adolescent angst.*
w *Henriette Jelinek, Jeanne Moreau* d *Jeanne
Moreau* ph *Pierre Gautard* m *Philippe Sarde*
ed *Albert Jurgenson*
☆ *Simone Signoret, Laetitia Chauveau, Edith
Clever, Jacques Weber, Francis Huster*

Adolf Hitler – My Part in His Downfall *

GB   1972   102m   Technicolor
UA/Norcon (Gregory Smith, Norman Cohen)

Episodes in the life of a conscript at the beginning
of World War II.
*Lumbering anarchic comedy based on Spike Milligan's
own sidesplitting memoirs; an enfeebled British
M*A*S*H.*
w *Johnny Byrne* d *Norman Cohen* ph *Terry
Maher* m *Wilfred Burns*
☆ *Jim Dale, Spike Milligan, Arthur Lowe, Bill
Maynard, Windsor Davies, Pat Coombs, Tony
Selby, Geoffrey Hughes*
  'A convincing period shabbiness and sleaziness
  which are endearing when they're not being
  overstated.' – *MFB*

Adorable *

US   1933   85m   bw
Fox

A Ruritanian princess falls in love with a naval
officer.
Charming, lightweight romance of the old school.
w *George Marion Jnr, Jane Storm story* Paul
Frank, Billy Wilder d *William Dieterle* ph *John
Seitz* m/ly *Werner Richard Heymann, George
Marion, Richard Whiting*

☆ *Janet Gaynor, Henri Garat, C. Aubrey Smith,
Herbert Mundin, Blanche Friderici, Hans von
Twardowski*
† The film was remade from German-French
originals under a title which translated as *Her
Majesty Commands.* The German version starred
Kaethe von Nagy and Willy Fritsch, the French
Lillian Harvey and Henri Garat.

Adorable Creatures

France   1952   105m   bw
Sirius/Jacques Roitfeld

A Paris fashion executive recalls his love affairs.
*A collection of four short sex comedies which did well
on the heels of La Ronde.*
w *Charles Spaak, Jacques Companeez*
d *Christian-Jaque* ph *Christian Matras*
m *Georges Van Parys*
☆ *Daniel Gélin, Danielle Darrieux, Edwige
Feuillère, Antonella Lualdi, Martine Carol,
Marilyn Buferd*

Adorable Julia

Austria/France   1962   97m   bw
Wiener Mundus/Etoile

GB title: *The Seduction of Julia*

A middle-aged actress takes on a lover.
*Moderately pleasing sex comedy, rather more heavily
directed than Maugham would have liked.*
w *Johanna Sibelius, Eberhard Keindorff
novel Theatre by* Somerset Maugham d *Alfred
Weidenmann*
☆ *Lilli Palmer, Charles Boyer, Jean Sorel, Jeanne
Valerie*

Adorable Lies **

Cuba   1991   100m   colour
ICAIC (Evelio Delgado)
original title: *Adorables Mentiras*

A married, unsuccessful scriptwriter pretends to be
a film director in his efforts to seduce a woman he
fancies, who turns out to be a frustrated actress
married to a corrupt government official.
*A deft and witty farce of false identities that makes fun
of marriage, desire and ideologically correct cinema.
Not surprisingly, it ran into censorship problems in
Cuba and was hardly seen there.*
w *Senel Paz* d *Gerardo Chijona* ph *Julio Valdes*
m *Edesio Alejandro, Gerardo Garcia* pd *Onelio
Larralde* ed *Jorge Abello*
☆ *Isabel Santos, Luis Alberto Garcia, Mirtha
Ibarra, Thais Valdes, Carlos Cruz, Silvia Planas,
Santiago Alvarez*
  'Combines comedy and melodrama with uneven
  results. At times it seems to be a tongue-in-
  cheek soap opera, but in other scenes its tone
  becomes too dark. While there are some funny
  moments, this Cuban sudser goes on too long
  and eventually grows tiring.' – *Variety*

Adorables Mentiras: see *Adorable Lies*

Adrenalin: Fear the Rush

US   1996   77m   colour
Columbia TriStar/Largo/Toga (Tom Karnowski, Gary
Schmoeller)

In Boston in 2007, two cops try to track down a
mad killer, who has escaped from a quarantine
camp and is infected with a plague that
depopulated Europe.
*Daft and strikingly unoriginal action movie, which
leaves its characters and its audience in the dark for
much of the time.*
wd *Albert Pyun* ph *George Mooradian* m *Tony
Riparetti* pd *Nenad Pecur* ed *Ken Morrisey*
sp *John McLeod; Kevin Marks*
☆ *Christophe Lambert, Natasha Henstridge,
Norbert Weisser, Elizabeth Barondes, Craig Davis,
Xavier Declie, Nicholas Guest, Andrew Divoff*
† Despite being set in Boston, the film was shot in
Bratislava, which accounts for the police cars being
marked *Policia*.

Adua e le Compagne

Italy   1960   150m   bw
Zebra Film
GB title: *Hungry for Love*

When brothels in Italy are officially closed, four of
the old girls open a restaurant.
*Immensely overlong comedy drama whose rewards
come entirely from the actors.*

---

w Ruggero Maccari, Ettore Scola, Antonio Pietrangeli, Tullio Pinelli d Antonio Pietrangeli ☆ Simone Signoret, Marcello Mastroianni, Sandra Milo, Emmanuele Riva, Gina Rovere

'The script becomes increasingly episodic, and clichés abound.' – MFB

Advance to the Rear *
US 1964 97m bw Panavision
MGM/Ted Richmond
GB title: Company of Cowards?
After the Civil War, a troop of misfits is sent west out of harm's way, but manages to capture a rebel spy and save a gold shipment.
Semi-satirical Western action comedy with a farcical climax; quite sharply made.
w Samuel A. Peeples, William Bowers story Jack Schaefer d George Marshall ph Milton Krasner m Randy Sparks
☆ Glenn Ford, Melvyn Douglas, Stella Stevens, Jim Backus, Joan Blondell, Andrew Prine, Alan Hale, James Griffith, Preston Foster

'Gable's back and Garson's got him!'
Adventure *
US 1945 126m bw
MGM (Sam Zimbalist)
A roughneck sailor marries a librarian, but only settles down to love her when their child is born.
Uniquely embarrassing (and fascinating) mishmash of pretentious dialogue and cardboard characters.
w Frederick Hazlitt Brennan, Vincent Lawrence novel Clyde Brion Davis d Victor Fleming ph Joseph Ruttenberg m Herbert Stothart
☆ Clark Gable, Greer Garson, Thomas Mitchell, Joan Blondell, John Qualen, Richard Haydn
'MGM proudly announce Adventure as the meeting of a red-blooded man with a blue-blooded woman. Its impact on the bloodstream of your critic was a chilling one. Fifty years of the cinema, he thought, and this is where we've landed.' – Richard Winnington

Adventure for Two: see The Demi-Paradise

An Adventure for Two: see A Nous Deux

Adventure in Baltimore
US 1949 89m bw
RKO (Richard H. Berger)
GB title: Bachelor Bait
In 1905, a young society girl becomes a suffragette.
Inconsequential period comedy which did nothing for its young star's fading career.
w Lionel Houser story Christopher Isherwood, Lesser Samuels d Richard Wallace ph Robert de Grasse m Frederick Hollander
☆ Shirley Temple, Robert Young, John Agar, Albert Sharpe, Josephine Hutchinson, Johnny Sands, John Miljan, Norma Varden

Adventure in Manhattan
US 1936 73m bw
Columbia
GB title: Manhattan Madness
An actress helps an ace reporter to foil a bank robbery by a master criminal.
Flat romantic mystery comedy which wastes a good cast.
w Sidney Buchman, Harry Sauber, Jack Kirkland d Edward Ludwig ph Henry Freulich
☆ Jean Arthur, Joel McCrea, Thomas Mitchell, Reginald Owen, Herman Bing

Adventure Island
US 1947 67m Cinecolor
Paramount
Seafarers chance on an uncharted island, ruled by a deadly fanatic.
Hokum rehash of Stevenson's Ebb Tide, with Paul Kelly as the madman.
w Maxwell Shane d Peter Stewart (Sam Newfield)
☆ Paul Kelly, Rory Calhoun, Rhonda Fleming

The Adventure of Sherlock Holmes' Smarter Brother
GB 1975 91m DeLuxe
TCF/Jouer (Richard A. Roth)
More by good luck than good management, Sherlock's younger brother solves one of his cases.

Infuriating parody with little sense of the original and a hit-or-miss style all of its own. Amusing moments fail to atone for the general waste of opportunity.
wd Gene Wilder ph Gerry Fisher m John Morris pd Terry Marsh
☆ Gene Wilder, Marty Feldman, Madeline Kahn, Leo McKern, Dom DeLuise, Roy Kinnear, John Le Mesurier, Douglas Wilmer, Thorley Walters
'Like a compilation of the kind of numbers actors like to do at parties.' – Howard Kissel
'He has bitten off more than he can chew or I can swallow.' – John Simon
'A few stray chuckles but nothing more.' – Sight and Sound
'There's no mystery, and since you can't have a parody of a mystery without a mystery, there's no comic suspense.' – New Yorker, 1980

The Adventurer ***
US 1917 21m bw silent
Mutual
An escaped convict rescues two wealthy women from drowning and is invited to their home.
Hilarious early Chaplin knockabout, with his physical gags at their most streamlined.
wd Charles Chaplin ph William C. Foster, Rollie Totheroh
☆ Charles Chaplin, Edna Purviance, Eric Campbell, Henry Bergman

The Adventurers
GB 1950 86m bw
Rank/Mayflower (Maxwell Setton, Aubrey Baring)
US title: The Great Adventure
aka: Fortune in Diamonds
In 1902, two Boers and a cashiered English officer set out to recover stolen diamonds.
Lethargic South African Western in the wake of Treasure of the Sierra Madre; clumsy and unconvincing, with cardboard characters.
w Robert Westerby d David MacDonald ph Oswald Morris m Cedric Thorpe Davie
☆ Dennis Price, Jack Hawkins, Siobhan McKenna, Peter Hammond, Bernard Lee, Grégoire Aslan

The Adventurers *
US 1970 170m Technicolor Panavision
Paramount/Avco Embassy/Adventurers Film (Lewis Gilbert)
A sensualist brought up amid Europe's luxuries returns to his Central American homeland to take vengeance on the brutal security chief who raped and murdered his mother.
Sprawling, sexy, bloodstained extravaganza from a Harold Robbins novel. Expensive to look at and riddled with sensation, but that's about all.
w Michael Hastings, Lewis Gilbert d Lewis Gilbert ph Claude Renoir m Antonio Carlos Jobim pd Tony Masters
☆ Bekim Fehmiu, Alan Badel, Candice Bergen, Ernest Borgnine, Olivia de Havilland, Rossano Brazzi, Charles Aznavour, Sydney Tafler, Fernando Rey, Leigh Taylor-Young, Thommy Berggren, John Ireland
'A three-hour slog through every imaginable cliché of writing and direction … in addition to an abundance of flaccid sex and violence, it offers drugs, sadism, orchids, fireworks, orgies, lesbianism, a miscarriage, a private torture chamber, and the hell of several fashion shows with loud pop music accompaniment. This might well be described as the film with everything; trouble is, it is difficult to imagine anybody wanting any of it.' – MFB
'Lovers of rotten movies and close-up violence can revel in it.' – Judith Crist

Adventures in Babysitting: see Night On the Town

'Ladies...if you can't do-it-yourself call a plumber!'
Adventures of a Plumber's Mate
GB 1978 88m Eastmancolor
Salon (Stanley Long)
A plumber with debts is chased by crooks and by lustful women.
Tired sexploitation farce with little narrative, merely a succession of episodes in which women lose their clothes.
w Stephen D. Frances, Aubrey Cash d Stanley Long ph Peter Sinclair m Christopher Neil ad Carlotta Barrow ed Jo Gannon

☆ Christopher Neil, Arthur Mullard, Stephen Lewis, Nina West, Anna Quayle, Prudence Drage, Elaine Paige, William Rushton
'A glum essay in blue-nosed British farce.' – Tim Pulleine, MFB

Adventures of a Taxi Driver
GB 1975 89m Eastmancolor
Alpha/Salon (Peter Long, Stanley Long)
A taxi driver finds that his sex life is both busy and confusing.
Lamentable British comedy, in which a cast of reliable performers are allowed to embarrass themselves and their audience.
w Suzanne Mercer d Stanley Long ph Peter Sinclair ed Jo Gannon
☆ Barry Evans, Judy Geeson, Adrienne Posta, Diana Dors, Liz Fraser, Ian Lavender, Stephen Lewis, Robert Lindsay, Henry McGee, Brian Wilde
'A crass, lobotomised production, with no discernible style, humour or purpose.' – MFB

Adventures of a Young Man: see Hemingway's Adventures of a Young Man

The Adventures of Arsène Lupin *
France/Italy 1956 103m Eastmancolor
Chavane-SNE-Gaumont/Lambor-Costellazione (Robert Sussfeld)
In 1912, the famous jewel thief conducts several successful robberies and outwits the Kaiser.
The most stylish Lupin film, though not based on the original stories.
w Jacques Becker, Albert Simonin, based on the character created by Maurice Leblanc d Jacques Becker ph André Mondellini
☆ Robert Lamoureux, Liselotte Pulver, Otto Hasse, Henri Rollan

Adventures of Baron Munchausen **
GB/West Germany 1989 126m Eastmancolor
Prominent Features/Laura Film/Columbia-Tri Star (Thomas Schühly)
A German soldier tells tall stories of his escapades.
Ambitious, extravagant fantasy in which some of the parts are better than the whole.
w Charles McKeown, Terry Gilliam story Rudolph Erich Raspe d Terry Gilliam ph Giuseppe Rotunno m Michael Kamen pd Dante Ferretti ed Peter Hollywood sp Richard Conway
☆ John Neville, Eric Idle, Sarah Polley, Oliver Reed, Charles McKeown, Winston Dennis, Jack Purvis, Valentina Cortese, Jonathan Pryce, Bill Paterson, Peter Jeffrey, Uma Thurman
'Munchausen's inability to get into gear rather defeats what would seem the point of the picture: whereas the source is adroit at slipping between fantasy and reality, Gilliam's fiction can't even handle a flashback.' – MFB
⚆ art direction; costume design; makeup
Ⓥ Dante Ferretti

The Adventures of Baron Munchausen: see Münchausen (1943)

The Adventures of Barry Mackenzie *
Australia 1972 114m Eastmancolor
Columbia/Longford (Philip Adams)
A sex-hungry Australian gets into all kinds of trouble on a visit to the Old Country.
Occasionally funny, defiantly crude and tasteless, but poorly produced comedy-misadventure from the Private Eye comic strip. Australian slang combines with bad sound recording to make much of the film unintelligible.
w Barry Humphries, Bruce Beresford d Bruce Beresford ph Don McAlpine m Peter Best
☆ Barry Crocker, Barry Humphries, Peter Cook, Spike Milligan, Dennis Price, Avice Landone, Dick Bentley, Joan Bakewell, William Rushton
'A wildly uneven concoction of antipodean bad taste, probably only fully appreciated by Earls Court exiles.' – Sight and Sound
† Sequel 1974: Barry Mackenzie Holds His Own

The Adventures of Buckaroo Banzai Across the Eighth Dimension *
US 1984 102m colour
Sherwood (Neil Canton/W. D. Richter)
A Renaissance man – physicist, surgeon and rock star – crashes into the eighth dimension and releases evil aliens.
Genial spoof of science fiction and other movie genres.
w Earl MacRauch, W. D. Richter ph Fred J. Koenekamp m Michael Boddicker pd J. M. Riva ed Richard Marks, George Bowers
☆ Peter Weller, John Lithgow, Ellen Barkin, Jeff Goldblum, Christopher Lloyd

The Adventures of Bullwhip Griffin *
♟♟ US 1965 110m Technicolor
Walt Disney (Bill Anderson)
In the 1849 California Gold Rush, two aristocrats and their butler head west.
Rather splendid spoof Western with careful attention to detail and comedy pointing, well above the average Disney standard.
w Lowell S. Hawley novel By the Great Horn Spoon by Sid Fleischman d James Neilson ph Edward Colman m George Bruns titles Ward Kimball
☆ Roddy McDowall, Suzanne Pleshette, Bryan Russell, Karl Malden, Harry Guardino, Richard Haydn, Mike Mazurki, Hermione Baddeley, Cecil Kellaway

The Adventures of Captain Fabian
US 1951 100m bw
Republic/Silver (William Marshall)
A sea captain returns to New Orleans to revenge himself on the family which had defrauded his father.
Stilted, old-fashioned Monte Cristoish melodrama with some curiosity value but little verve in the playing or production. An awful warning to independent producers.
w Errol Flynn novel Fabulous Ann Medlock by Robert Shannon d William Marshall ph Marcel Grignon m René Cloerec
☆ Errol Flynn, Micheline Presle, Agnes Moorehead, Vincent Price, Victor Francen, Jim Gerald
† Made in France.

The Adventures of Captain Marvel *
US 1941 bw serial: 12 eps
Republic
When a scientific expedition goes to Siam, the assistant radio operator is endowed by the mysterious Shazam with the power to transform himself into Captain Marvel, and to defeat the evil Scorpion.
Modest classic serial, good for more than a few laughs.
d William Witney, John English
☆ Tom Tyler, Frank Coghlan Jnr, William Benedict, Louise Currie

Adventures of Casanova
US 1948 83m bw
Eagle-Lion
Casanova returns to Sicily and helps overthrow the tyrannical rule of the King of Naples.
Robin Hood transplanted, with a few amorous asides; but this is a totally stilted production which fails to entertain.
w Crane Wilbur, Walter Bullock, Ken de Wolf d Roberto Gavaldon
☆ Arturo de Cordova, Lucille Bremer, Turhan Bey

The Adventures of Don Juan **
US 1949 110m Technicolor
Warner (Jerry Wald)
GB title: The New Adventures of Don Juan
A reformed 17th-century rake saves his queen from the machinations of her first minister.
Expensive, slightly uneasy, but generally very entertaining swashbuckler with elements of self-spoofery. Flynn's last big-budget extravaganza.
w George Oppenheimer, Harry Kurnitz d Vincent Sherman ph Elwood Bredell m Max Steiner ad Edward Carrere
☆ Errol Flynn, Viveca Lindfors, Romney Brent, Robert Douglas, Alan Hale, Ann Rutherford, Robert Warwick, Jerry Austin, Douglas Kennedy, Una O'Connor, Aubrey Mather, Raymond Burr
'A lavish film on a truly magnificent scale.' – The Times
⚆ art direction

ⒹDigital Video Disc Region 2   ⒹDigital Video Disc Region 1   ⌁Soundtrack released on compact disc   ☆Cast in approximate order of importance   †Points of interest   ♫Notable songs   ▲Academy Award   ⚆Academy Award nomination   ⓋBAFTA

Adventures of Ford Fairlane
US 1990 104m DeLuxe Panavision
TCF (Joel Silver, Steve Perry)
🎞 🎦 ⚬ 🎧

A conceited rock 'n' roll detective solves the murder of a Los Angeles disc jockey.
Drearily vulgar comedy, featuring one of the more obnoxious stand-up comedians of the 90s and about as entertaining as stepping in something nasty in the street. It was a flop at the box-office, resulting in Fox's decision not to release Clay's concert film Dice Rules (qv).
w Daniel Waters, James Cappe, David Arnott based on characters created by Rex Weiner
d Renny Harlin ph Oliver Wood m Yello
pd John Vallone ed Michael Tronick
☆ Andrew Dice Clay, Wayne Newton, Priscilla Presley, Morris Day, Lauren Holly, Maddie Corman, Robert Englund, Ed O'Neill
'Surprisingly funny and expectedly rude.' – *Variety*
'What can you say about a movie whose comic highlight is the hanging of a koala bear?' – *Empire*

The Adventures of Gallant Bess
US 1948 71m Cinecolor
Eagle Lion
🎦

The master of a trained rodeo horse becomes a range wanderer.
Easy-going animal interest saga with a pleasant ending.
w Matthew Rapf d Lew Landers
☆ Cameron Mitchell, Audrey Long, Fuzzy Knight, James Millican, Ed Gargan

The Adventures of Gerard *
GB 1970 91m DeLuxe Panavision
UA/Sir Nigel Films (Henry Lester, Gene Gutowski)
A hussar of Napoleon becomes involved in a double spy game but comes out trumps and wins a fair lady.
A lighthearted historical spoof of military pomp, with plenty of attractive elements which unfortunately fail to jell into a satisfying film.
w H. A. L. Craig and others stories Arthur Conan Doyle d Jerzy Skolimowski ph Witold Sobocinski
m Riz Ortolani
☆ Peter McEnery, Claudia Cardinale, Eli Wallach, Jack Hawkins, Mark Burns, Norman Rossington, John Neville
'Enormously graceful and witty ... picks its way with amazing delicacy through the reefs of facetiousness.' – *Tom Milne*

The Adventures of Hajji Baba *
👥 US 1954 93m DeLuxe Cinemascope
Allied Artists/Walter Wanger
In ancient Arabia, a barber helps and falls in love with an escaping princess.
A reasonably dashing sword and sandal romp which no one takes very seriously.
w Richard Collins d Don Weis ph Harold Lipstein m Dimitri Tiomkin pd Gene Allen
☆ John Derek, Elaine Stewart, Thomas Gomez, Amanda Blake, Paul Picerni, Rosemarie Bowe

The Adventures of Huck Finn
👥 US 1993 108m Technicolor
Buena Vista/Walt Disney/Mighty Miss/Steve White
(Laurence Mark)
🎞 🎦 ⚬ 🖥 📀 🎧

Huck Finn, escaping from his brutal father, goes on the run with Jim, an escaped slave, and takes to the river.
Bland and fussy remake of the familiar story, one that ignores the vigour of the original in favour of cuteness.
wd Stephen Sommers novel The Adventures of Huckleberry Finn by Mark Twain ph Janusz Kaminski m Bill Conti pd Richard Sherman
ed Bob Ducsay
☆ Elijah Wood, Courtney B. Vance, Robbie Coltrane, Jason Robards, Ron Perlman, Dana Ivey, James Gammon, Anne Heche, Paxton Whitehead
'Wholesome family entertainment with a worthy anti-slavery message.' – *Empire*

The Adventures of Huckleberry Finn: see *Huckleberry Finn (1960)*

The Adventures of Ichabod and Mr Toad: see *Ichabod and Mr Toad*

The Adventures of Marco Polo *
US 1938 100m bw
Samuel Goldwyn
🎦

The medieval Italian explorer discovers China, fireworks, and a beautiful maiden.
One gets the impression that this began as a standard adventure and that during production it switched to comedy; whatever the cause, lively and amusing scenes fail to add up to more than a thinly scripted pantomime.
w Robert E. Sherwood d Archie Mayo
ph Rudolph Maté m Hugo Friedhofer md Alfred Newman ad Richard Day
☆ Gary Cooper, Sigrid Gurie, Basil Rathbone, Ernest Truex, Binnie Barnes, Alan Hale, George Barbier
'In spite of its elaborate settings and the presence of Gary Cooper, it never quite lives up to its promises.' – *New York Sun*
'Goldwyn's most ambitious endeavour ... deserves and will get enthusiastic exhibitor plugging. Sherwood's more concerned with entertainment than with history.' – *Variety*
† Release prints were in sepiatone.

The Adventures of Mark Twain **
US 1944 130m bw
Warner (Jesse L. Lasky)
The life of America's foremost humorous writer, from a Mississippi riverboat to his becoming an honorary fellow of Oxford University.
Conventional biopic, quite watchable and with unusual side turnings, but eventually lacking the zest of the subject.
w Harold M. Sherman, Alan le May, Harry Chandler d Irving Rapper ph Sol Polito m Max Steiner ad John J. Hughes
☆ Fredric March, Alexis Smith, Donald Crisp, Alan Hale, C. Aubrey Smith, John Carradine, William Henry, Robert Barrat, Walter Hampden
'It's not that it's much worse than most cinematized biographies, because it does have its good moments. It's just that once more biographical inaccuracy is rampant, and once more the best dramatic possibilities have been overlooked, so it's hard to think of anything new, in the line of protest, to say.' – *David Lardner, New Yorker*
🎵 Max Steiner; John J. Hughes

The Adventures of Martin Eden
US 1942 87m bw
Columbia (B. P. Schulberg)
An American seaman fights a brutal captain and wins better conditions for his comrades.
Routine actioner based on what are virtually the author's memoirs.
w W. L. River story Jack London d Sidney Salkow
☆ Glenn Ford, Evelyn Keyes, Claire Trevor, Stuart Erwin, Dickie Moore

Adventures of Milo and Otis (dubbed) *
👥 Japan 1986 75m Eastmancolor
Panavision
Virgin/Fuji (Hisashi Hieda)
🎞 🎦 ⚬

original title: *Koneko Monogatari*
A puppy leaves a farm to search for his friend, a kitten, who has floated downriver in a box.
Innocuous adventure, using real animals, that may appeal to the very young.
w Mark Saltzman story Masanori Hata
d Masanori Hata ph Hideo Fuji, Shinji Tomita
m Michael Boddicker ad Takeharu Sakahuchi
ed Chizuko Osada
☆ Dudley Moore
'Youngsters and pet lovers will adore this film. Grown-ups with a less positive attitude to the animal kingdom are well advised to stay away.' – *Empire*
† The film was the second most popular ever made in Japan.

The Adventures of Pinocchio *
👥 GB/US/France/Germany 1996 96m
DeLuxe
New Line/Savoy/Pangaea/Twin Continental (Raju Patel, Jeffrey M. Sneller)
🎞 🎦 🎧

The adventures of a wooden puppet who comes to life after he has been made by a lonely wood-carver.
A live-action account, with an animatronic puppet, of a story most familiar from Disney's version; it does not match up to the animated feature, but manages a certain charm.
w Sherry Mills, Steve Barron, Tom Benedek, Barry Berman novel Carlo Collodi d Steve Barron
ph Juan Ruiz-Anchia m Rachel Portman
pd Allan Cameron ed Sean Barton sp Jim Henson's Creature Shop
☆ Martin Landau, Jonathan Taylor Thomas, Geneviève Bujold, Udo Kier, Bebe Neuwirth, Rob Schneider, Griff Rhys Jones, Dawn French, John Sessions
'Well-crafted and gently charming.' – *Variety*

'Finally, a comedy that will change the way you think, the way you feel and, most importantly, the way you dress.'
The Adventures of Priscilla Queen of the Desert **
Australia 1994 103m colour Arriscope
Rank/Polygram/AFFC/Latent Image/Specific Films (Al Clark, Michael Hamlyn)
🎞 🎦 ⚬ 📀 🎧

Two transvestites and a transsexual drive a bus from Sydney to Alice Springs for a cabaret engagement at a hotel run by a former wife of one of them.
A bright and brittle road movie, gaudy and fun and refusing to take seriously even the occasional glimpse of genuine emotion.
wd Stephan Elliott ph Brian J. Breheny m Guy Gross pd Owen Paterson ed Sue Blainey
☆ Terence Stamp, Hugo Weaving, Guy Pearce, Bill Hunter, Sarah Chadwick, Mark Holmes, Julia Cortez
'A cheerfully vulgar and bitchy, but essentially warmhearted, road movie with a difference.' – *David Stratton, Variety*
'A slick, shrewdly ingratiating entertainment that jumps from highlight to highlight and lives on sparkle.' – *David Denby, New York*
† Al Clark's book *The Lavender Bus* (1999) tells the story of the production of the film.
👔 costume design (Lizzy Gardiner, Tim Chappell)

The Adventures of Quentin Durward:
see *Quentin Durward*

'Only the rainbow can duplicate its brilliance!'
The Adventures of Robin Hood ****
👥 US 1938 102m Technicolor
Warner (Hal B. Wallis)
🎞 🎦 ⚬ 🎧

Rebel outlaw Robin Hood outwits Guy of Gisbourne and the Sheriff of Nottingham, and saves the throne for the absent King Richard.
A splendid adventure story, rousingly operatic in treatment, with dashing action highlights, fine comedy balance, and incisive acting all round. Historically notable for its use of early three-colour Technicolor; also for convincingly recreating Britain in California.
w Seton I. Miller, Norman Reilly Raine d William Keighley, Michael Curtiz ph Tony Gaudio, Sol Polito, W. Howard Greene m Erich Wolfgang Korngold ad Carl Jules Weyl ed Ralph Dawson
☆ Errol Flynn, Basil Rathbone, Claude Rains, Olivia de Havilland, Alan Hale, Patric Knowles, Eugene Pallette, Ian Hunter, Melville Cooper, Una O'Connor, Herbert Mundin, Montagu Love, Howard Hill
PRINCE JOHN: 'Any objections to the new tax, from our Saxon friends?'
ROBIN TO GISBOURNE DURING DUEL: 'Did I upset your plans?'
GISBOURNE: 'You've come to Nottingham once too often!'
ROBIN: 'When this is over, my friend, there'll be no need for me to come again!'
PRINCE JOHN: 'Ho, varlets, bring Sir Robin food! Such insolence must support a healthy appetite!'
ROBIN: 'It's injustice I hate, not the Normans!'
'Magnificent, unsurpassable ... the film is lavish, brilliantly photographed, and has a great Korngold score.' – *NFT, 1974*
'Mostly the picture is full of movement, some of it dashing in fine romantic costume style, some of it just sprightly. The excitement comes from fast action – galloping steeds, men swinging Tarzan-like from the trees, hurling tables and chairs, rapid running swordplay, the sudden whiz of Robin's arrows coming from nowhere to startle his enemies – more than from any fear that Robin might be worsted. Somehow the whole thing has the air of being a costume party, a jolly and rather athletic one, with a lot of well-bred Englishmen playing at being in the greenwood.' – *James Shelley Hamilton, National Board of Review*
† At the time of its release this was Warner's most expensive film, costing more than two million dollars. Chico, California, stood in for Sherwood Forest; the archery contest was shot at Busch Gardens, Pasadena. Curtiz took over direction when it was felt that the action lacked impact.
🎵 Erich Wolfgang Korngold; Carl Jules Weyl; Ralph Dawson
👕 picture

The Adventures of Robinson Crusoe ***
Mexico 1953 89m Pathécolor
Tepeyac (Oscar Dancigers, Henry F. Ehrlich)
A 17th-century mariner is shipwrecked on an uninhabited tropical island.
Fascinating version of a famous story, with only one character on screen until the belated arrival of Friday and the escape to civilization. Subtle and compelling, with only the colour unsatisfactory.
w Luis Buñuel, Phillip Roll novel Daniel Defoe
d Luis Buñuel ph Alex Phillips m Anthony Collins
☆ Dan O'Herlihy, Jaime Fernandez
'A film of which the purity, the tense poetic style, evokes a kind of wonder.' – *Gavin Lambert*
'Free of that deadly solicitude which usually kills off classics.' – *New Yorker, 1977*
🎵 Dan O'Herlihy

The Adventures of Sadie: see *Our Girl Friday*

The Adventures of Sherlock Holmes **
US 1939 83m bw
TCF (Gene Markey)
🎞 🎦 ⚬

GB title: *Sherlock Holmes*
Moriarty sends Holmes on a false trail while he plots to steal the Crown jewels.
An engaging piece of pseudo-Victoriana: all elements smooth save an unconvincing plot.
w Edwin Blum, William Drake d Alfred Werker
ph Leon Shamroy m Cyril Mockridge
☆ Basil Rathbone, Nigel Bruce, George Zucco, Ida Lupino, Alan Marshal, Terry Kilburn, E. E. Clive, Henry Stephenson, Mary Gordon
'The "elementary my dear Watson" type of dialogue is soft-pedalled for more modern phrases or understandable patter.' – *Variety*
'Told with more movie art per foot than seven reels of anything the intellectual men have been finding good this whole year or more.' – *Otis Ferguson*
† This was the second and last of Rathbone's costume outings as Holmes, and the one in which he sang a comic song in disguise.

The Adventures of Tartu *
GB 1943 103m bw
MGM (Irving Asher)
US title: *Tartu*
During World War II, a British spy goes to Czechoslovakia to dismantle a poison gas factory.
Halting and artificial comedy-thriller, saved only by a graceful star performance.
w Howard Emmett Rogers, John Lee Mahin, Miles Malleson d Harold S. Bucquet ph John J. Cox
m Hubert Bath md Louis Levy
☆ Robert Donat, Valerie Hobson, Walter Rilla, Glynis Johns, Martin Miller
'You are seeing all it has, and bald spots as well, first time around, whereas with a good Hitchcock or even a good Carol Reed, the pleasures visible at a first seeing stand up, or intensify, at a third or a fifth.' – *James Agee*

Adventures of the Wilderness Family
👥 US 1975 101m colour
Pacific International
🎦

An urban family runs into trouble when it takes to the wilds.
Naïve little four-wall family movie in which the pretty scenery (Utah and the Canadian Rockies) and the animals compensate for the dramatic inadequacies.
wd Stewart Raffill
☆ Robert Logan, Susan Damante Shaw
† *Further Adventures of the Wilderness Family* appeared in 1977.

The Adventures of Tom Sawyer ***
👫 ▦ US 1938 91m Technicolor
David O. Selznick (William H. Wright)
▦ ▩ ◉
Small-town Mississippi boy tracks down a
murderer, Injun Joe.
*Set-bound but excellent version of the children's classic
by Mark Twain.*
w John Weaver d Norman Taurog ph James
Wong Howe, Wilfrid Cline m Max Steiner
ad Lyle Wheeler
☆ Tommy Kelly, May Robson, Walter Brennan,
Victor Jory, Victor Kilian, Jackie Moran, Ann
Gillis, Donald Meek, Margaret Hamilton, Marcia
Mae Jones
'The familiar characters emerge in all their old
amiability, the atmosphere is there and so is the
excitement.' – MFB
'Should make Mark Twain circulate in his grave
like a trout in a creel.' – Otis Ferguson
'Another Selznick International box office
clean-up ... that there exists a broad audience
for films whose essential appeal is to the family
trade has always been true. Snow White touched
a source of almost unlimited audience draw: Tom
Sawyer follows to the same customers.' – Variety
⚑ Lyle Wheeler

The Adventuress: see I See a Dark Stranger

Advice to the Lovelorn *
US 1933 62m bw
TCF/Darryl F. Zanuck
A reporter is demoted to the lonelyhearts column
and becomes absorbed in it.
Springy vehicle for Lee Tracy.
w Leonard Praskins novel Miss Lonelyhearts by
Nathanael West d Alfred Werker
☆ Lee Tracy, Sally Blane, Sterling Holloway,
Isabel Jewell, Jean Adair
† Compare the Paul Muni vehicle Hi Nellie. It was
remade in 1958 as Lonelyhearts (qv).

'Are the men and women of Washington really like
this?'
Advise and Consent **
US 1962 139m bw Panavision
Columbia/Alpha-Alpina/Otto Preminger
▦ ▩ ◉ ✡
The President's choice of an unpopular secretary of
state leads to divisions in the Senate and the
blackmail and suicide of a senator.
*Absorbing political melodrama from a novel which
aimed to lift the lid off Washington. Many character
actors make their mark, but the harsh-contrast
photography seems misjudged.*
w Wendell Mayes novel Allen Drury d Otto
Preminger ph Sam Leavitt m Jerry Fielding
titles Saul Bass
☆ Don Murray, Charles Laughton, Henry Fonda,
Walter Pidgeon, Lew Ayres, Edward Andrews,
Burgess Meredith, Gene Tierney, Franchot Tone,
George Grizzard, Paul Ford, Peter Lawford, Inga
Swenson, Will Geer
'The result is supremely ambivalent, a battle
between fascinatingly real props and procedures
and melodramatically unreal characters and
situations.' – Peter John Dyer
'The parade of people helps to take one's mind
off the overwrought melodrama.' – New Yorker,
1980

Aelita *
USSR 1924 70m bw silent
Mezhrabpom
Two Russian rocket pioneers land on Mars and
start a revolution against the planet's queen.
*Notable early space fiction, with footage of twenties
Moscow as well as interesting set designs.*
w Fedor Ozep, Alexei Faiko novel Alexei Tolstoy
d Yakov Protazanov ph Yuri Zhelabuzhsky
pd Sergei Kozlovsky
☆ Yulia Solntseva, Nikolai Batalov, Igor Ilinsky

Aerial Gunner
US 1943 78m bw
Paramount (William H. Pine, William G. Thomas)
A US air force pilot in hospital thinks back to his
training and his young brother's problems.
*A watered-down Wings (with process footage to
match) which also starred Arlen.*
w Maxwell Shane d William H. Pine
☆ Richard Arlen, Chester Morris, Jimmy Lydon,
Lita Ward, Dick Purcell

Aerograd **
USSR 1935 81m bw
Mosfilm/Ukrainfilm
aka: Frontier
Guards keep Japanese spies out of Siberia, where
an airport is being built.
An action film with style and pretensions.
wd Alexander Dovzhenko ph Edouard Tissé,
Mikhail Gindin m Dmitri Kabalevsky
☆ Semyon Shagaida, Stepan Shkurat, Sergei
Stolyarov

Affair at the Villa Fiorita: see The Battle of
the Villa Fiorita

Affair in Monte Carlo: see Twenty-Four Hours
of a Woman's Life

Affair in Trinidad *
US 1952 98m bw
Columbia/Beckworth (Vincent Sherman)
▦ ◉
A nightclub singer whose husband is killed by
gangsters works undercover for the police and routs
the gang with the help of her husband's brother.
*A tired tropical melodrama intended to follow up the
success of Gilda, but without the verve. Some routine
pleasures, though.*
w Oscar Saul, James Gunn d Vincent Sherman
ph Joseph Walker m Morris Stoloff, George
Duning
☆ Rita Hayworth, Glenn Ford, Alexander
Scourby, Torin Thatcher, Valerie Bettis, Steve
Geray, Karel Stepanek, George Voskovec
'Improbable, foolish, but glossy.' – Penelope
Houston

An Affair to Remember **
US 1957 114m Eastmancolor
Cinemascope
TCF (Jerry Wald)
▦ ▩ ◉ ◉ ◉
An ex-nightclub singer falls in love with a wealthy
bachelor on a transatlantic liner, but an accident
prevents her from attending their subsequent
rendezvous.
*Remake of Love Affair, a surprisingly successful
mixture of smart lines, sentiment and tears, all applied
with style and assurance.*
w Delmer Daves, Leo McCarey d Leo McCarey
ph Milton Krasner m Hugo Friedhofer
☆ Cary Grant, Deborah Kerr, Cathleen Nesbitt,
Richard Denning, Neva Patterson
'A lush slice of Hollywood romanticism.' – MFB
'90 masterly minutes of entrancing light comedy
and 25 beastly minutes of beastly, melodramatic,
pseudo-tragic guff.' – Paul Dehn
⚑ Milton Krasner; Hugo Friedhofer; title song
(mHarry Warren, ly Harold Adamson, Leo
McCarey)

Affair with a Stranger *
US 1953 87m bw
RKO (Robert Sparks)
Five friends reminisce about a marriage which
seems about to break up.
*This would-be-smart comedy has a good idea
unsatisfactorily worked out, and could have used a
more sparkling cast.*
w Richard Flournoy d Roy Rowland ph Harry J.
Wild m Roy Webb
☆ Jean Simmons, Victor Mature, Mary Jo Tarola,
Monica Lewis, Jane Darwell, Nicholas Joy, Wally
Vernon, Dabbs Greer

L'Affaire est dans le Sac *
France 1932 47m bw
Pathé/Nathan
aka: It's in the Bag
Two would-be kidnappers end up (a) married to
and (b) employed by their intended victims.
Semi-professional nonsense comedy with political jokes.
w Jacques Prévert d Pierre Prévert ph A.
Giboury, Eli Lotar m Maurice Jaubert
☆ J.-P. Le Chanois, Jacques Brunius, Etienne
Decroux, Lucien Raimbourg, Julien Carette, Lora
Hays

Affairs of a Rogue: see The First Gentleman

The Affairs of Anatol *
US 1921 95m bw silent
Famous Players-Lasky/de Mille-Paramount
A socialite interrupts his honeymoon to go looking
for romance.
*Dated but historically very interesting sophisticated
farce from a time when Hollywood was aping Viennese
naughtiness.*
w Jeanie MacPherson, Beulah Marie Dix, Lorna
Moon, Elmer Harris from Granville Barker's
paraphrase of the play Anatol by Arthur Schnitzler
d Cecil B. de Mille ph Alvin Wyckoff, Karl Struss
ed Anne Bauchens
☆ Wallace Reid, Gloria Swanson, Bebe Daniels,
Elliott Dexter, Monte Blue, Wanda Hawley,
Theodore Roberts
'Should be enormously popular, especially with
those who think Schnitzler is a cheese.' – Robert
E. Sherwood
'The man who doesn't sell out for every
performance of a double run should turn his
show shop into a Quaker meeting house.' –
Motion Picture Herald

The Affairs of Annabel *
US 1938 69m bw
RKO (Lee Marcus, Lou Lusty)
▦ ◉
A crackpot Hollywood press agent sends his star to
jail as a publicity stunt.
*An amusing frenetic comedy of its time, successful
enough to warrant a sequel, Annabel Takes a Tour,
in the same year.*
w Bert Granet, Paul Yawitz d Ben Stoloff
ph Russell Metty m Roy Webb
☆ Lucille Ball, Jack Oakie, Ruth Donnelly,
Bradley Page, Fritz Feld, Thurston Hall, Elisabeth
Risdon, Granville Bates, James Burke

The Affairs of Cellini *
US 1934 90m bw
Twentieth Century (Darryl F. Zanuck)
The complex amours of a 16th-century Florentine
rake.
*Lively period bedroom farce somewhat hampered by
censorship.*
w Bess Meredyth play The Firebrand by Edwin
Justus Mayer d Gregory La Cava ph Charles
Rosher m Alfred Newman ad Richard Day
☆ Fredric March, Constance Bennett, Frank
Morgan, Fay Wray, Vince Barnett, Louis Calhern,
Jessie Ralph
'Gay and entertaining though whipped up
synthetically like circus ice cream.' – Variety
⚑ Charles Rosher; Frank Morgan; Richard Day

The Affairs of Dobie Gillis
US 1953 74m bw
MGM (Arthur M. Loew Jnr)
Adventures of an indolent and accident-prone
university student.
*Scatty comedy with good talent and musical numbers
encased in a tatty production.*
w Max Shulman d Don Weis ph William Mellor
md Jeff Alexander
☆ Bobby Van, Debbie Reynolds, Hans Conried,
Barbara Ruick, Bob Fosse

Affairs of Sally: see The Fuller Brush Girl

'She's so romantic she drives four men frantic!'
The Affairs of Susan **
US 1945 110m bw
Paramount (Hal B. Wallis)
Four men in Susan's life see her differently.
*Occasionally witty comedy designed as a champagne
vehicle for its star. It seemed quite good at the time.*
w Richard Flournoy story Laszlo Gorog, T.
Monroe d William A. Seiter ph David Abel
m Frederick Hollander
☆ Joan Fontaine, George Brent, Walter Abel, Don
Defore, Dennis O'Keefe
'The cast enters into the irresponsibilities with
gusto.' – MFB
'A bright thing, a bit too long.' – Richard Mallett,
Punch
⚑ Laszlo Gorog, T. Monroe

Affectionately Yours
US 1941 88m bw
Warner (Mark Hellinger)
A foreign correspondent hurries home when he
hears that his wife plans to divorce him.
Thin lightweight comedy, unsuitably cast.

w Edward Kaufman d Lloyd Bacon ph Tony
Gaudio m Heinz Roemheld
☆ Merle Oberon, Dennis Morgan, Rita Hayworth,
George Tobias, Ralph Bellamy, James Gleason,
Hattie McDaniel

Affliction **
US 1997 113m DeLuxe
Largo (Linda Reisman)
▦ ◉
In a small snowbound town, the local sheriff finally
breaks under life's many humiliations.
*A stolid drama of a cycle of childhood abuse spanning
the generations; the excellent performances seem
somehow stranded by the austere directorial approach.*
wd Paul Schrader novel Russell Banks ph Paul
Sarossy m Michael Brook pd Anne Pritchard
ed Jay Rabinowitz
☆ Nick Nolte, Sissy Spacek, James Coburn, Willem
Dafoe, Mary Beth Hurt, Jim True, Marian Seldes,
Homes Osborne, Brigid Tierney, Sean McCann,
Wayne Robson
'This is a powerhouse picture which comes to
grips with some horrific home truths.' – Kim
Newman, Empire
🏆 James Coburn
⚑ Nick Nolte

Afraid of the Dark *
GB/France 1992 91m colour
Rank/Sovereign/Telescope/Les Films Ariane/Cine Cinq
(Simon Bosanquet)
▦ ▩ ◉
A near-sighted 11-year-old boy with a blind
mother worries about the identity of the slasher
who is attacking blind women.
*A thriller that turns out to be not what it seems, but the
twist is ultimately an uninteresting one, though the film
does work up a degree of terror.*
wd Mark Peploe ph Bruno de Keyzer m Richard
Hartley pd Caroline Ames ed Scott Thomas
☆ James Fox, Fanny Ardant, Paul McGann, Clare
Holman, Ben Keyworth
'A rather stiff and self-conscious film, not
without its pretensions, but also informed by
considerable intelligence.' – Derek Malcolm,
Guardian

Africa Screams
US 1949 79m bw
UA (Edward Nassour)
▦ ◉
Two dumbbells go on safari with a treasure map.
Lower-case comedy.
w Earl Baldwin d Charles Barton ph Charles
Van Enger
☆ Bud Abbott, Lou Costello, Hillary Brooke, Max
Baer, Shemp Howard

Africa Texas Style *
👫 GB 1967 109m Eastmancolor
Paramount/Vantors (Andrew Marton)
A Kenyan settler hires two Texas cowboys to help
in his scheme of wild game ranching.
*Excellent location sequences are dragged down by a
very boring script, but it's a good family film
nevertheless.*
w Andy White d Andrew Marton ph Paul
Beeson m Malcolm Arnold
☆ John Mills, Hugh O'Brian, Nigel Green, Tom
Nardini, Adrienne Corri, Ronald Howard
† Forerunner of TV series, Cowboy in Africa.

African Fury: see Cry the Beloved Country

'They never dreamed of being in each other's arms,
yet the mystic spell of the jungle swept them to
primitive, hungry embrace! The greatest adventure a
man ever had ... with a woman!'
The African Queen ***
GB 1951 103m Technicolor
IFD/Romulus-Horizon (Sam Spiegel)
▦ ▩ ◉
In 1915, a gin-drinking river trader and a prim
missionary make odd companions for a boat trip
down a dangerous river, culminating in an attack
on a German gunboat.
*Despite some unfortunate studio sets mixed in with real
African footage achieved through great hardship by all
concerned, this is one of those surprising films that
really work, a splendidly successful mixture of comedy,
character and adventure.*
w James Agee novel C. S. Forester d John Huston
ph Jack Cardiff m Allan Gray

☆ *Humphrey Bogart*, Katharine Hepburn, Robert Morley, Peter Bull, Theodore Bikel
ROSE: 'I never dreamed that any experience could be so stimulating!'
'Entertaining but not entirely plausible or original.' – *Robert Hatch*
'The movie is not great art but it is great fun, essentially one long, exciting, old-fashioned movie chase.' – *Time*
'A Technicolor Cook's Tour of jungle wonders, enriched by performances unmatched by anything Hepburn or Bogart have yet contributed to the screen.' – *Cue*
† Peter Viertel's book, *White Hunter Black Heart*, filmed by Clint Eastwood, is basically about Huston during the making of this film. In 1987 Katharine Hepburn wrote a book about her experiences, entitled *The Making Of The African Queen, or How I went to Africa with Bogart, Bacall and Huston and almost lost my mind.*
♟ Humphrey Bogart
♟ James Agee; John Huston; Katharine Hepburn

Afrodite Dea Dell'Amore: see *Aphrodite, Goddess of Love*

'Seduced Beyond The Limits Of Deception. Betrayed Beyond The Limits Of Desire.'

After Dark, My Sweet
US   1990   111m   colour
Virgin/Avenue (Ric Kidney, Bob Redlin)
◙◙ ◙◙. ◯
A disturbed young drifter becomes involved with an alcoholic widow and a former policeman in a plan to kidnap a child.
Wildly melodramatic thriller with dull performances.
w Bob Redlin *novel* Jim Thompson d James Foley *m* Mark Plummer *m* Maurice Jarre ad Kenneth A. Hardy *ed* Howard Smith
☆ Jason Patric, Rachel Ward, Bruce Dern, George Dickerson, James Cotton

After Eight Hours: see *Society Doctor*

'When it's after midnight in New York City, you don't have to look for love, laughter and trouble. They'll all find you!'

After Hours **
US   1985   97m   DuArt
Warner/Geffen/Double Play (Amy Robinson, Griffin Dunne, Robert F. Colesberry)
◙◙ ▬ ◙◙.
Through a chapter of accidents, a mild-mannered computer programmer has a bad time in the night streets of New York.
An unsettling kind of black comedy with moments of malaise: nobody denies its touches of brilliance, but few people want to see it again.
w Joseph Minion d *Martin Scorsese* ph Michael Ballhaus *m* Howard Shore *pd* Jeffrey Townsend ed Thelma Schoonmaker
☆ Griffin Dunne, Rosanna Arquette, Verna Bloom, Thomas Chong, Teri Garr, Cheech Marin, Linda Fiorentino, John Heard
'The cinema of paranoia and persecution reaches an apogee … would have been pretty funny if it didn't play like a confirmation of everyone's worst fears about contemporary urban life.' – *Variety*
'A film so original, so particular, that one is uncertain from moment to moment exactly how to respond to it. Interesting.' – *Roger Ebert*

'What Is The One Memory You Would Take With You?'

After Life ****
Japan   1998   118m   colour
ICA/TV Man Union/Engine (Shiho Sato, Masayuki Akieda)
aka: *Wonderful Life*
original title: *Wandafuru Raifu*
After they die, people are processed by bureaucrats who allow them to take one memory of their life, in the form of a film re-creation, into eternity.
Simple, straightforward drama, mixing actual memories with imagined ones, that manages to touch deep emotions; it is both witty and moving in its depiction of the newly dead and the stranded officials who attempt to deal both with their lives and those fleeting moments that gave them meaning.
wd Hirokazu Kore-Eda ph Yamazaki Hiroshi m Yasuhiro Kasamatsu ad Toshihiro Isomi, Hideo Gunji ed Hirokazu Kore-Eda

☆ Arata, Erika Oda, Susumu Terajima, Tsuyoshi Naito, Kyoko Kagawa, Kei Tani, Takashi Naito, Sadao Abe
'A profound meditation on life's meaning and value and the relationship of movies, memories and dreams.' – *Stephen Holden, New York Times*

After Midnight: see *Captain Carey USA* (1950)

After Midnight
US   1989   90m   colour
MGM/High Bar (Richard Arlook, Peter Greene, Ken and Jim Wheat)
◙◙ ▬
A lecturer on the psychology of fear invites his students to scare each other by telling frightening stories.
Portmanteau horror that relies on violent shocks for its effect.
wd Ken and Jim Wheat ph Phedon Papamichael m Marc Donahue pd Paul Chadwick ed Phillip Linson, Quinnie Martin Jnr
☆ Judie Aronson, Marg Helgenberger, Marc McClure, Ed Monaghan, Alan Rosenberg, Monique Salcido, Tracy Wells, Jillian McWhirter

After Midnight
Ireland   1990   100m   colour
Lazer/Channel 4/Dublin Cinema Group (Maxine Julius)
An alcoholic nightwatchman in a Dublin hotel redeems himself with the help of a new assistant.
Despite the valiant efforts of Jaffrey, a broad farce that fails to amuse and sticks instead to clichéd characters and situations.
wd Shanis Grewal ph Jack Conroy m Mickey Gallagher pd Brien Vahey ed Carl Thomson
☆ Saeed Jaffrey, Hayley Mills, Ian Dury, Dhirendra, Vladek Sheybal

After Office Hours *
US   1935   75m   bw
MGM (Bernard H. Hyman)
A newspaperman and his socialite reporter solve a murder mystery.
Crisply-written, fast-moving comedy melodrama; good stuff of its time and type.
w Herman J. Mankiewicz d Robert Z. Leonard ph Charles Rosher
☆ *Clark Gable*, Constance Bennett, Stuart Erwin, Billie Burke, Harvey Stephens, Katherine Alexander, Henry Travers, Henry Armetta
'One of the best balanced pix of the season; it has practically everything.' – *Film Daily*
'Mildly satisfactory entertainment … story deficiencies are surprising … Gable and Bennett will have to carry this one.' – *Variety*

After the Ball *
GB   1957   89m   Eastmancolor
IFD/Beaconsfield (Peter Rogers)
The life and loves of music-hall singer Vesta Tilley, who married into the nobility.
Adequate if uninspired biopic with entertaining detail and songs.
w Hubert Gregg d Compton Bennett ph Jack Asher md Muir Mathieson ad Norman Arnold
☆ Pat Kirkwood, Laurence Harvey, Clive Morton, Jerry Verno, June Clyde

After the Fox *
US/Italy   1966   103m   Technicolor
Panavision
UA/Nancy/CCM (John Bryan)
▬
The Fox escapes from jail to execute a gold bullion caper and save his young sister from the streets.
Unlikeable and unfunny farce which sets its star among excitable Italians and hopes for the best, adding a few wild stabs at satire on movie-making styles. Mature agreeably sends up his old image.
w Neil Simon, Cesare Zavattini d Vittorio de Sica m Leonida Barboni m Burt Bacharach
☆ Peter Sellers, Victor Mature, Britt Ekland, Lidia Brazzi, Paolo Stoppa, Akim Tamiroff, Martin Balsam
'Never even begins to get off the ground.' – *MFB*

After the Rehearsal **
Sweden   1984   72m   colour
Svenskfilmindustri/SV2
▬
After a rehearsal for Strindberg's *Dream Play*, the director sits and remembers the circumstances surrounding an earlier production.
Typical but satisfyingly unpretentious Bergman piece of the second rank.
wd Ingmar Bergman
☆ Erland Josephson, Ingrid Thulin, Lena Olin
'What we are left with is the very strong sense of an artist who has sacrificed many lives for the sake of his art, and now wonders if perhaps one of those lives was his own.' – *Roger Ebert*

After the Thin Man **
US   1936   113m   bw
MGM (Hunt Stromberg)
▬ ◙◙.
Nick and Nora Charles, not forgetting Asta, solve another murder.
Overlong but well-carpentered sequel to The Thin Man, developing the thesis that a married couple, even if they are detectives and drink too much, can be interesting and lovable.
w Frances Goodrich, Albert Hackett d W. S. Van Dyke II ph Oliver T. Marsh m Herbert Stothart, Edward Ward
☆ William Powell, Myrna Loy, James Stewart, Elissa Landi, Joseph Calleia, Jessie Ralph, Alan Marshal, Sam Levene
'It is evident that it was almost impossible to make a better mystery comedy than *The Thin Man*. Early speed would have helped, but … few films this season have contained more risibles.' – *Variety*
♟ Frances Goodrich; Albert Hackett

After Tomorrow
US   1932   70m   bw
Fox
Family troubles and small salaries prevent a young couple from getting married.
Rather curious drama which was sold on the fact that it retained the sex discussion from its stage original.
w Sonya Levien play John Golden, Hugh Stange d Frank Borzage
☆ Charles Farrell, Marian Nixon, Minna Gombell, Josephine Hull, William Collier Snr, William Pawley
'In several sequences it pioneers for the picture business. That financial success is doubtful is rather unfortunate.' – *Variety*

After Tonight
US   1933   71m   bw
RKO
GB title: *Sealed Lips*
During World War I a Russian lady spy falls for an Austrian officer.
Tediously talky romantic vehicle which barely gets started before it bogs down.
w Jane Murfin d George Archainbaud
☆ Constance Bennett, Gilbert Roland, Edward Ellis, Mischa Auer

Afterglow *
US   1997   113m   DeLuxe
Entertainment/Moonstone/Sandcastle 5/Elysian Dreams (Robert Altman)
◙◙ ▬
A middle-aged handyman, who is married to a washed-up 'B'-movie actress, begins an affair with a wealthy young woman; in retaliation, his wife spends a weekend with the woman's husband.
Glossy romantic drama that takes a great deal of time to say very little about relationships; the performances don't help.
wd Alan Rudolph ph Toyomichi Kurita m Mark Isham pd François Séguin ed Suzy Elmiger
☆ Julie Christie, Nick Nolte, Lara Flynn Boyle, Jonny Lee Miller
'Serious and comic, frivolous and substantial, giddy and lyrical all at once.' – *Emanuel Levy, Variety*
♟ Julie Christie

Agaguk: see *Shadow of the Wolf*

Against a Crooked Sky
US   1975   89m   colour
Doty/Dayton
Two Westerners set out to find the sister of one of them, who has been kidnapped by Indians.
Very ordinary variation on The Searchers, which in itself was a bit tedious at times.
w Douglas G. Stewart, Eleanor Lamb d Earl Bellamy
☆ Richard Boone, Stewart Petersen, Geoffrey Land, Jewel Blanch, Henry Wilcoxon

Against All Flags *
US   1952   83m   Technicolor
U-I (Howard Christie)
▬
A daring British seaman routs Spanish ships at the request of the king.
Standard pirate yarn, almost Flynn's last swashbuckler; production below par.
w Aeneas Mackenzie, Joseph Hoffman d George Sherman ph Russell Metty m Hans Salter
☆ Errol Flynn, Maureen O'Hara, Anthony Quinn, Mildred Natwick
† Remade as *The King's Pirate* (qv)
†† Though Flynn did most of his own stunts for this picture, he balked at the one involving sliding down through a sail on a rapier blade, which was originated by Douglas Fairbanks in *The Black Pirate*; it was performed by a stunt double.

Against All Odds
US   1984   121m   Metrocolor
Columbia/Delphi (Jerry Bick)
◙◙ ▬ ◙◙. ◯
An unemployed football player is hired by a bookmaker to find his missing wife.
Complex and lugubrious remake of Out of the Past (qv), which long outstays its welcome.
w Eric Hughes d Taylor Hackford ph Donald Thorin, E. Pershing Flynn m Michel Colombier, Larry Carlton ad Richard James Lawrence
☆ Jeff Bridges, Rachel Ward, James Woods, Richard Widmark, Jane Greer (from the original cast), Alex Karras, Dorian Harewood, Swoosie Kurtz
'It has so many convoluted double crosses that each time you are told what really went on behind the scene you just witnessed, you care less.' – *Time Out*
'A tedious concatenation of narrative twists.' – *MFB*
'The best thing to do is accept the plot, then disregard it, and pay attention to the scenes of passion.' – *Roger Ebert*
♟ title song (Phil Collins)

Against the Wind *
GB   1947   96m   bw
Ealing (Sidney Cole)
◙◙
In London during World War II, men and women are trained as saboteurs, and one of them is a traitor.
Thoughtful, well-made spy thriller with good performances; but a bit dour.
w T. E. B. Clarke, Michael Pertwee d Charles Crichton ph Lionel Banes m Leslie Bridgewater
☆ Simone Signoret, Robert Beatty, Jack Warner, Gordon Jackson, Paul Dupuis, Gisele Preville, John Slater, Peter Illing, James Robertson Justice

Agantuk **
India/France   1991   120m   colour
Artificial Eye/National Film Development Corporation of India/Erato/DD/Soprofilms/Canal (Satyajit Ray)
◙◙ ▬
aka: *The Stranger*
A Calcutta family suspect that a long-lost uncle who comes to stay may be an impostor.
A charming and humorous examination of cultural differences and ingrained prejudices.
wd Satyajit Ray ph Barun Raha m Satyajit Ray ed Dulal Dutt
☆ Dipankar De, Mamata Shankar, Bikram Bhattacharya, Utpal Dutt, Dhritiman Chatterjee, Rabi Ghosh, Subrata Chatterjee
'A wise, witty and benevolent work, a worthy sign-off from a great film-maker.' – *Philip Kemp, Sight and Sound*
'Mitra, in Utpal Dutt's performance, combines, as Ray himself did, a powerful intellect and an unsentimental insight into human behaviour with a generosity of spirit and genuine humility.' – *Philip French, Observer*
† It was Ray's last film.

♟♟ film suitable for family viewing   　◙◙ VHS video-cassette for the British PAL system   　◙◙ VHS video-cassette for the British PAL system in wide screen-format   　✿ Video cassette in a computer-colourised version   　▬ American NTSC video-cassette   　◙◙. Laser disc

Agatha *

GB 1979 105m Technicolor
Warner/First Artists/Sweetwall/Casablanca (Jarvis Astaire, Gavrik Losey)

🖭 ▦ ⊕↝

In 1926, Agatha Christie disappears after marital difficulties and tries to commit suicide in a Harrogate hotel under a pseudonym.
Lushly recreated but still imaginary and unconvincing solution to a real-life disappearance, complete with romantic encounter with an American newspaperman.
w Kathleen Tynan, Arthur Hopcraft d Michael Apted ph Vittorio Storaro m Johnny Mandel pd Shirley Russell
☆ Vanessa Redgrave, Dustin Hoffman, Timothy Dalton, Helen Morse, Timothy West, Tony Britton, Alan Badel
'With its shadowy characters, paucity of plot, and an abundance of stylistic red herrings, one doubts whether *Agatha* would have met Mrs Christie's own requirements for a thriller, though she may well have enjoyed its sumptuous recreation of hotel interiors in the 1920s.' – *Geoff Brown, MFB*
'It has a general air of knowingness, but seems to be missing the scenes which would explain why it was made.' – *New Yorker*

L'Age d'Or **

France 1930 63m bw
Vicomte de Noailles
A collection of strange events satirizing religion and the social order.
Deliberately shocking and possibly quite meaningless, this wily surrealist film is chiefly interesting now for its flashforwards to Buñuel's later work.
w Luis Buñuel, Salvador Dali d Luis Buñuel ph Albert Dubergen m Georges van Parys ed Luis Buñuel
☆ Gaston Modot, Lya Lys, Max Ernst, Pierre Prévert, Jacques Brunius
'In some way the juxtaposition of images causes in almost every spectator a train of reactions of unprecedented violence.' – *Basil Wright, 1972*
'The story is also a sequence of moral and surrealist aesthetic. The sexual instinct and the sense of death form its substance.' – *Luis Buñuel*
'It retains its outrageous anarchic vitality, as though unwilling to admit its age.' – *Observer 1980*

The Age for Love

US 1931 81m bw
UA/Howard Hughes
A wife does not want children; her husband leaves her and marries a woman who does.
Shapeless and would-be shocking, this forgotten film was written off as soon as it was made.
w Robert E. Sherwood, Frank Lloyd, Ernest Pascal novel Ernest Pascal d Frank Lloyd m Alfred Newman
☆ Billie Dove, Adrian Morris, Charles Starrett, Lois Wilson, Edward Everett Horton, Mary Duncan
'Everybody makes mistakes, and this is one by Howard Hughes.' – *Variety*

Age of Consent *

Australia 1969 103m Technicolor
Columbia/Nautilus (James Mason, Michael Powell)

🖭 ▦

An artist seduces the granddaughter of a drunken harridan with whom he shares a Barrier Reef island.
Mildly likeable but self-conscious and overlong South Pacific idyll.
w Peter Yeldham novel Norman Lindsay d Michael Powell ph Hannes Staudinger m Stanley Myers
☆ James Mason, Helen Mirren, Jack MacGowran, Neva Carr-Glyn, Frank Thring

Age of Innocence

US 1934 71m bw
RKO
In the 1870s, a young attorney's career is threatened when he falls in love with a divorcee.
Dated romantic drama, rather thinly performed and presented.
w Sarah Y. Mason, Victor Heerman novel Edith Wharton d Philip Moeller
☆ Irene Dunne, John Boles, Lionel Atwill, Laura Hope Crews, Helen Westley, Julie Haydon

'It will take smart selling to protect it at the box office, especially away from the social registers of the land.' – *Variety*

Age of Innocence

Canada/GB 1977 101m Eastmancolor
Judson/Willoughby (Henning Jacobsen)
After World War I, an English teacher in Canada develops pacifist views which stir up local resentment and lead to violence.
Rather uninteresting melodrama which never really comes to the boil despite care all round.
w Ratch Wallace d Alan Bridges ph Brian West m Lucio Agostini
☆ David Warner, Honor Blackman, Trudy Young, Cec Linder, Tim Henry, Lois Maxwell, Robert Hawkins

The Age of Innocence **

US 1993 138m Technicolor Super 35mm
Columbia (Barbara de Fina)

🖭 ▦ ⊕↝ ♫

In New York in the 1870s, a wealthy and conventional lawyer falls in love with his wife's cousin, a woman of dubious reputation.
A deft study of a repressed society with some effective set-pieces, let down by an insufficiently dramatized narrative; the emotional weight of the film is carried not by the actors, but by the voice-over, which severely limits its impact.
w Jay Cocks, Martin Scorsese novel Edith Wharton d Martin Scorsese ph Michael Ballhaus m Elmer Bernstein pd Dante Ferretti ed Thelma Schoonmaker
☆ Daniel Day-Lewis, Michelle Pfeiffer, Winona Ryder, Richard E. Grant, Alec McCowen, Geraldine Chaplin, Mary Beth Hurt, Stuart Wilson, Miriam Margolyes, Sian Phillips, Michael Gough, Alexis Smith, Jonathan Pryce, Robert Sean Leonard
'Scorsese has met most of the challenges inherent in tackling such a formidable period piece, but the material remains cloaked by the very propriety, stiff manners and emotional starchiness the picture delineates in such copious detail.' – *Variety*
'The great virtue of the film is that it takes the past seriously and sets about the task of bringing it to life detail by detail, without false immediacy.' – *Adam Mars-Jones*
'For those whose idea of bliss is watching handsome people in a well-told story of love and denial, this is ecstasy from scene one.' – *Angie Errigo, Empire*
⅋ Winona Ryder; Jay Cocks, Martin Scorsese; Elmer Bernstein; Dante Ferretti; costume design (Gabriella Pescucci)
🎭 Miriam Margolyes

Agency

Canada 1981 94m colour
Farley

▦

An advertising agency gets into political hands which send out messages through special TV packs.
Faded melodrama which did nothing for anyone involved in it.
w Noel Hynd novel Paul Gottlieb d George Kaczender
☆ Robert Mitchum, Lee Majors, Valerie Perrine, Saul Rubinek, Alexandra Stewart

Agent 8*: see **Hot Enough for June**

Agent for Harm

US 1966 84m colour
Universal (Joseph F. Robertson)
A Washington agency prevents the Russians from abducting a scientist.
Spy spoof somewhat below the level of the TV UNCLE films.
w Blair Robertson d Gerd Oswald
☆ Wendell Corey, Mark Richman, Martin Kosleck, Carl Esmond, Barbara Bouchet

The Agitator *

GB 1944 98m bw
British National (Louis H. Jackson)
An embittered mechanic becomes a loud-mouthed union spokesman, but fate eventually takes him into management.
Fairly absorbing, modest narrative of the flaws of socialism.
w Edward Dryhurst novel Peter Pettinger by William Riley d John Harlow ph James Wilson

☆ William Hartnell, Mary Morris, John Laurie, Moore Marriott, George Carney, Edward Rigby, Elliot Mason, Frederick Leister, Cathleen Nesbitt, Moira Lister

'When Agnes Brown's husband died she discovered something amazing... Herself.'

Agnes Browne

Ireland 1999 92m Technicolor
UIP/October/Hell's Kitchen

🎧

In Dublin in the mid 60s, a widow with seven children struggles to stay solvent.
Maudlin domestic drama of a plucky, warm-hearted woman battling against the odds that leaves no cliché of Irish life at all unfilmed or unspoken.
w John Goldsmith, Brendan O'Carroll novel The Mammy by Brendan O'Carroll d Anjelica Huston ph Anthony B. Richmond m Paddy Moloney pd David Brockhurst ed Eva Gardos
☆ Anjelica Huston, Marion O'Dwyer, Ray Winstone, Arno Chevrier, Gerard McSorley, Niall O'Shea, Ciaran Owens, Roxana Williams, Carl Power, Mark Power, Tom Jones
'Huston is no stranger to the comic tics of Dublin life, so frankly she should be lynched for directing a theme park ride as appalling as this.' – *James Christopher, Times*
'Hopelessly silly and sentimental.' – *Edward Porter, Sunday Times*

Agnes of God *

US 1985 98m Metrocolor
Columbia/Delphi IV (Patrick Palmer, Norman Jewison)

🖭 ▦ ⊕↝ 🎧

A young nun is accused of giving birth and then killing her baby.
Heavy hysterical weather with no clear solution, but a field day for three actresses.
w John Pielmeier play John Pielmeier d Norman Jewison ph Sven Nykvist m Georges Delerue pd Ken Adam ed Antony Gibbs
☆ Jane Fonda, Anne Bancroft, Meg Tilly
'Predictably, religion and reason play to something like a draw.' – *Variety*
⅋ Anne Bancroft; Meg Tilly (supporting actress); music

Agonia: see **Agony**

Agony **

USSR 1975 148m colour/bw
Mosfilm/Second Film Group

▦

original title: *Agonia*
aka: *Rasputin*
As discontent at the rule of the Tsar increases, and revolution looms in Russia, the monk Rasputin becomes the power behind the throne.
A gripping account of the downfall of the Romanovs and the extraordinary life and death of Rasputin, mixing drama and contemporary newsreels; at times it comes near to being a history lesson, but it fascinates for all that. Nine years in the making, it was banned for ten years by the Soviet authorities.
w Semyon Lungin, Ilya Nusinov d Elem Klimov ph Leonid Kalashnikov m Alfred Schittke md Eri Klas
☆ Alexei Petrenko, Anatoly Romashin, Velta Linne, Alisa Freindlikh
† The film also exists in a version that runs for 107m.

The Agony and the Ecstasy *

US 1965 140m DeLuxe Todd-AO
TCF/International Classics Inc (Carol Reed)

🖭 ▦ ⊕↝ 🎧

Pope Julius II persuades Michelangelo to leave his sculptures and paint the ceiling of the Sistine Chapel.
Dully reverent comic strip approach to art and history; generally heavy going, but good looking.
w Philip Dunne novel Irving Stone d Carol Reed ph Leon Shamroy m Alex North pd John DeCuir
☆ Charlton Heston, Rex Harrison, Diane Cilento, Harry Andrews, Alberto Lupo, Adolfo Celi
JULIUS: 'You dare to dicker with your pontiff?'
'The vulgarity of the whole concept has none of the joyfully enthusiastic philistinism of a de Mille; rather its tone is a dry, almost cynical, condescension.' – *Brenda Davies*
'All agony, no ecstasy.' – *Judith Crist*

'Not a strong and soaring drama but an illustrated lecture of a slow artist at work.' – *Bosley Crowther*
'Heston hits the ceiling.' – *New York Times*
† The film is said to have cost 12 million dollars and earned 4.
†† Michelangelo was apparently both a dwarf and a homosexual. He is played by Charlton Heston.
⅋ Leon Shamroy; Alex North

Aguirre, Wrath of God ****

West Germany 1972 95m colour
Hessicher Rundfunk/Werner Herzog

🖭 ▦ ⊕↝ 🎧

In 1560, one of Pizarro's lieutenants takes a party of forty down river by raft, and succumbs to megalomania.
Absorbing conquistador melodrama, vividly assembled and impossible to forget.
wd Werner Herzog ph Thomas Mauch m Popol Vuh
☆ Klaus Kinski, Ruy Guerra, Helena Rojo, Cecilia Rivera
'It ingeniously combines Herzog's gift for deep irony, his strong social awareness, and his worthy ambition to fashion a whole new visual perspective on the world around us via mystical, evocative, yet oddly direct imagery. It is a brilliant cinematic achievement.' – *David Skerritt, Christian Science Monitor*

Ah! Les Belles Bacchantes: see **Femmes de Paris**

'The play that startled the nation!'

Ah, Wilderness **

US 1935 101m bw
MGM (Hunt Stromberg)

Problems of a small-town family at the turn of the century.
Well-acted, affectionately remembered version of a play later musicalized as Summer Holiday. The commercial success of this film led to the Hardy family series.
w Albert Hackett, Frances Goodrich play Eugene O'Neill d Clarence Brown ph Clyde de Vinna m Herbert Stothart
☆ Wallace Beery, Lionel Barrymore, Eric Linden, Spring Byington, Mickey Rooney, Aline MacMahon, Charley Grapewin, Cecilia Parker, Frank Albertson, Bonita Granville
'A job of picture making, in craftsmanship and feeling, that is wonderful to see.' – *Otis Ferguson*
'That it is a fine artistic effort will not be denied anywhere, but for the public at large it will need all the boosting it can get.' – *Variety*

A-Haunting We Will Go *

US 1942 68m bw
TCF (Sol M. Wurtzel)

🖭

Gangsters dupe Laurel and Hardy into escorting a coffin, which is accidentally switched with one used in a magic act.
Nothing whatever to do with haunting: a poor comedy with no typical material for the stars, but interesting as a record of the touring show of Dante the Magician.
w Lou Breslow d Alfred Werker ph Glen MacWilliams m Emil Newman
☆ Stan Laurel, Oliver Hardy, Dante, Sheila Ryan, John Shelton, Elisha Cook Jnr
'The comedians' lack of enthusiasm for their material is rather evident.' – *William K. Everson, 1967*

Ahfei Zhenjuang: see **Days of Being Wild**

Ai No Borei *

Japan/France 1978 105m Eastmancolor
Argos/Oshima (Anatole Dauman)

🖭 ▦ ⊕↝

aka: *Empire of Passion*
aka: *Phantom Love; In the Realm of Passion*
In the 1890s, an adulterous wife and her young lover kill her husband and are haunted by his ghost.
A drama of lust, love and guilt set in a small, close-knit community; its formal quality distances the audience from the action so that it remains for the most part uninvolving.
wd Nagisa Oshima story Itoko Nakamura ph Yoshio Miyajima m Toru Takemitsu ad Josho Toda ed Keiichi Uraoka

---

☆ Tatsuya Fuji, Kazuko Yoshiyuki, Takahiro Tamura, Takuzo Kawatani, Akiko Koyama, Taiji Tonoyama

† Oshima won the award for best director at the Cannes Film Festival in 1978 with this film, a companion piece to *Ai No Corrida* (qv).

Ai No Corrida **

France/Japan 1976 105m Eastmancolor
Argos/Oshima/Shibata (Anatole Dauman)
French title: *L'Empire des Sens*
aka: *Empire of the Passions; Empire of the Senses*
A sexually complicated servant girl has an intense affair with the master of the house, and finally murders and mutilates him.
Strong but stylish stuff, a kind of Japanese Last Tango in Paris. Those who like this kind of thing will like it a lot.
wd Nagisa Oshima ph Hideo Ito m Minoru Miki
☆ Tatsuya Fuji, Eiko Matsuda, Aoi Nakajima, Meika Seri
'By the final sequence, we are all implicated in the continuing social system which makes such love impossible. It is not Sade, but the censor in all of us who ultimately wields the knife.' – *Jan Dawson, MFB*
† The film was not given a certificate by the BBFC or a cinema release in Britain until 1991, although it had been shown in cinema clubs.

Aida

Italy 1953 95m Ferrania colour
Oscar Film (Ferrucio de Martino, Federico Teti)
A young Egyptian army officer loves the captive princess of the Ethiopians.
Stuffy, over-dressed, pantomimish version of the opera, with some pretension to cinematic vitality.
w various opera Verdi d Clemente Fracassi
ph Piero Portalupi ad Flavio Mogherini
☆ Sophia Loren (sung by Renata Tebaldi), Lois Maxwell, Luciano della Marra

Aimez-Vous les Femmes?: see Do You Like Women?

Ain't Misbehavin' *

US 1955 81m Technicolor
U-I (Samuel Marx)
A young millionaire marries a cabaret girl, who determines to improve her mind and manners.
Lively American version of Pygmalion, with musical numbers and some bright lines.
w Edward Buzzell, Philip Rapp, Devery Freeman
d Edward Buzzell m Wilfrid Cline m Joseph Gershenson ch Kenny Williams, Lee Scott
☆ Rory Calhoun, *Piper Laurie, Reginald Gardiner*, Jack Carson, Barbara Britton, Mamie Van Doren

Air America

US 1990 118m DeLuxe
Guild/Indieprod/Carolco (Daniel Melnick)
▣ ▤ ◎ ◎ ◯
CIA pilots indulge in illicit activities in Laos.
Frenetic mix of action and comedy – and unsuccessful at both.
w Jim Eskow, Richard Rush book Christopher Robbins d Roger Spottiswoode ph Roger Deakins
m Charles Gross pd Allan Cameron ed John Bloom, Lois Freeman-Fox
☆ Mel Gibson, Robert Downey Jnr, Nancy Travis, Ken Jenkins, David Marshall Grant, Lane Smith, Art La Fleur, Ned Eisenberg, Marshall Bell

Air Bud

👫 US 1997 97m Technicolor
Buena Vista/Walt Disney/Keystone (Robert Vince, William Vince)
▣ ▤ ◎ ◎ ◯
A lonely young boy befriends a basketball-playing dog.
An enjoyable piece of whimsy that should appeal to the young.
w Paul Tamasy, Aaron Mendelsohn character created by Kevin DiCicco d Charles Martin Smith
ph Mike Southon m Brahm Wenger pd Elizabeth Wilcox ed Alison Grace
☆ Michael Jeter, Kevin Zegers, Wendy Makkena, Bill Cobbs, Eric Christmas, Brendan Fletcher, Norman Browning, Buddy
'An old-fashioned heart-tugger in the tradition of *Old Yeller*.' – *Variety*
† Buddy, the golden retriever, was found to be suffering from cancer and had a leg amputated soon

after filming finished; he died at the age of 10 in 1998.

'For one typical family, this Friday is to be like no other.'

Un Air de Famille **

France 1996 119m colour Panavision
Metro/Tartan/Téléma/Canal/France2 (Charles Gassot)
▣ ◯
aka: *Family Resemblances*
A special family gathering in a café is marked by rifts and reconciliations.
A familiar setting – a celebratory occasion at which family members settle old scores and open fresh wounds – is made fresh by excellent acting and sparkling dialogue.
w Agnès Jaoui, Jean-Pierre Bacri, Cédric Klapisch play Agnès Jaoui, Jean-Pierre Bacri d Cédric Klapisch ph Benoît Delhomme pd François Emmanuelli ed Francine Sandberg
☆ Jean-Pierre Bacri, Jean-Pierre Darroussin, Catherine Frot, Agnès Jaoui, Claire Maurier, Wladimir Yordanoff
'A barbed but finally affectionate group portrait, all the more entertaining if your French is good enough to keep up with the argy-bargy.' – *Alexander Walker, London Evening Standard*

Air Force *

US 1943 124m bw
Warner (Hal B. Wallis)
▣ ◯
A Flying Fortress and its crew see action in Manila, Pearl Harbor and the Coral Sea.
Propaganda piece concentrating on the characters of the crew members, with action set-pieces largely provided by newsreel; but skilled direction still conveys plenty of punch.
w Dudley Nichols d Howard Hawks ph James Wong Howe, Elmer Dyer, Charles Marshall
m Franz Waxman ed George Amy
☆ John Garfield, Gig Young, Arthur Kennedy, Charles Drake, John Ridgely, Harry Carey, George Tobias, Stanley Ridges, Moroni Olsen, Edward Brophy
'Maybe the story is high-flown, maybe it overdraws a recorded fact a bit. We'd hate to think it couldn't happen – or didn't – because it leaves you feeling awfully good.' – *Bosley Crowther*
'The film is one crisis after another, and the director stages the air battles handsomely, but for the rest it helps if you're interested in the factors involved in getting a bomber somewhere and back.' – *Pauline Kael, 70s*
⚙ George Amy
⚙ Dudley Nichols; James Wong Howe, Elmer Dyer, Charles Marshall

'Five miles up, The President of the United States is waging war on terrorism. Face to face.'
'Harrison Ford *is* the President.'

Air Force One

US 1997 124m Technicolor 'Scope
Columbia/Beacon/Radiant (Armyan Bernstein, Wolfgang Petersen, Gail Katz, Jon Shestack)
▣ ▤ ◎ ◎ ◯
The US President shows he is a man of action when, with the aid of a US agent, Russians hijack the presidential jet and hold his wife and daughter hostage.
Silly, implausible jingoistic thriller of surprising banality.
w Andrew W. Marlowe d Wolfgang Petersen
ph Michael Ballhaus m Jerry Goldsmith
pd William Sandell ed Richard Francis-Bruce
☆ Harrison Ford, Gary Oldman, Glenn Close, Wendy Crewson, Paul Guilfoyle, William H. Macy, Liesel Matthews, Dean Stockwell, Jürgen Prochnow
'Think of it as *Fly Hard* and you'll be in the right ballpark.' – *Jay Carr, Boston Globe*
'So preposterous that it begins to seem like a science-fiction artefact in its own right, the product of a parallel-universe 1990s which somehow bypassed the decades since the 1950s, in every area except technology ... utterly unreal in terms of story and character.' – *Adam Mars-Jones, Independent*
† The director rejected Randy Newman's original score for the film
†† The film grossed $172m at the US box-office and another $126m around the world.
⚙ Richard Francis-Bruce; sound

Air Mail *

US 1932 84m bw
Universal
Brash young pilot effects a daring rescue and gets the mail through.
Moderate actioner of its time.
w Dale Van Every, Frank Wead d John Ford
☆ Pat O'Brien, Ralph Bellamy, Russell Hopton, Gloria Stuart, Lillian Bond, Slim Summerville
'Far short of a smash ... it has no sock name, it is weak on the romantic side and the story material is directed at men.' – *Variety*
† There was also a good silent version in 1925, with Warner Baxter and Douglas Fairbanks Jnr, written by James Shelley Hamilton and directed by Irvin Willat; both had remarkable similarities to *Only Angels Have Wings* (1938).

Air Raid Wardens

👫 US 1943 67m bw
MGM (B. F. Zeidman)
▣
Rejected by the armed services, two incompetent air raid wardens accidentally round up Nazi spies.
Well below par star comedy: their incomparable dignity has disappeared.
w Jack Jevne, Martin Rackin, Charles Rogers, Harry Crane d Edward Sedgwick ph Walter Lundin m Nathaniel Shilkret
☆ Stan Laurel, Oliver Hardy, Edgar Kennedy, Jacqueline White, Stephen McNally, Nella Walker, Donald Meek

The Air Up There *

👫 US 1994 108m Technicolor
Buena Vista/Hollywood/Interscope/Polygram (Ted Field, Rosalie Swedling, Robert W. Cort)
▣ ▤ ◎ ◎ ◯
An American basketball coach has to train an African team to win a game in order to settle a tribal dispute, recruit a new star and save his job.
Amiable drama of a man discovering that sport is not all that matters in life.
w Max Apple d Paul M. Glaser ph Dick Pope
m David Newman pd Roger Hall ed Michael E. Polakow
☆ Kevin Bacon, Charles Gitonga Maina, Yolanda Vasquez, Winston Ntshona, Mabutho 'Kid' Sithole, Sean McCann, Dennis Patrick, Nigel Miguel, Ilo Mitumbo
'Mildly entertaining ... isn't quite as stale as the numerous clichés it launches.' – *Brian Lowry, Variety*

Airborne

👫 US 1993 90m Technicolor
Warner/Icon (Bruce Davey, Stephen McEveety)
An unhappy surfer, forced to move to Cincinnati, becomes a skateboard champion.
A movie aimed at young 'teens, who may not mind the way it sticks to tried and test formulae, but who will appreciate its spectacular rollerblade sequences.
w Bill Apablasa, Stephen McEveety d Rob Bowman ph Daryn Okada m Stewart Copeland
pd John Myhre ed Harry B. Miller III
☆ Shane McDermott, Seth Green, Brittney Powell, Chris Conrad, Edie McClurg, Patrick O'Brien, Jack Black

Airborne

Canada 1997 90m DeLuxe
Le Monde/C3 (John Gillespie)
An elite team of agents attempt to recover a deadly virus stolen from a germ warfare laboratory.
Risible thriller with moments of meaningless slow-motion; despite the permanent scowl, designer stubble and scars, Guttenberg makes an unconvincing action hero.
w Tony Johnston, Julian Grant d Julian Grant
ph Russell Goozee m Christophe Beck pd Oleg Savytskyiy ed Paul Day
☆ Steve Guttenberg, Kim Coates, Torri Higginson, Colm Feore, Sean Bean, Philip Akin, David Fraser

Airheads

US 1994 92m DeLuxe
TCF/Island World (Robert Simonds, Mark Burg)
▣ ▤ ◎ ◯
An unsuccessful rock band hold up a radio station and demand that their demo tape is played on the air.

A dim comedy of dimmer characters which simply keeps repeating its single joke.
w Rich Wilkes d Michael Lehmann ph John Schwartzman m Carter Burwell pd David Nichols ed Stephen Semel
☆ Brendan Fraser, Steve Buscemi, Chris Farley, Adam Sandler, Michael McKean, Judd Nelson, Ernie Hudson, Amy Locane, David Arquette, Joe Mantegna
'An anarchic screwball comedy for the Beavis and Butthead generation.' – *Nigel Robinson, Film Review*
'Unspeakable.' – *Observer*

Airplane **

US 1980 88m Metrocolor
Paramount/Howard W. Koch (Jon Davison)
▣ ▤ ◎
A former pilot gets his nerve back when called upon to land a passenger plane because the crew all have food poisoning.
Arthur Hailey's play Flight into Danger and the film Zero Hour which was made from it get the zany parody treatment in this popular movie which is often funny but sometimes merely crude. It rang the box-office bell more loudly than most expensive epics of its year.
wd Jim Abrahams, David and Jerry Zucker
ph Joseph Biroc m Elmer Bernstein pd Ward Preston
☆ Robert Stack, Lloyd Bridges, Robert Hays, Julie Hagerty, Peter Graves, Leslie Nielsen, Lorna Patterson, Ethel Merman, Kareem Abdul-Jabbar
'Parody may be the lowest form of humour, but few comedies in ages have rocked the laugh meter this hard.' – *Variety*
'It keeps going, like a dervish with skids on.' – *Derek Malcolm, Guardian*
'Proof that the cinema is alive and well and bursting with ingenuity.' – *David Hughes, Sunday Times*
'It's compiled like a jokebook and has the kind of pacing that goes with a laugh track.' – *Pauline Kael*
'All pretty juvenile really, though the relentless pace and sheer poor taste make up for a lack of originality.' – *Time Out, 1984*
'Practically a satirical anthology of movie clichés ... it compensates for its lack of original comic invention by its utter willingness to steal, beg, borrow and rewrite from anywhere.' – *Roger Ebert*

'Just when you thought it safe to go back into the departure lounge'

Airplane II: The Sequel

US 1982 85m Metrocolor
Paramount (Howard W. Koch)
▣ ▤ ◎
A space shuttle gets into trouble but is rescued in the nick of time.
Palsied sequel to a funny film, with some of the same cast and some of the same jokes.
wd Ken Finkleman ph Joe Biroc m Elmer Bernstein pd William Sandell ed Dennis Virkler
☆ Robert Hays, Julie Hagerty, Lloyd Bridges, Peter Graves, William Shatner, Chad Everett, Steven Stucker, Sonny Bono, Raymond Burr, Chuck Connors, Rip Torn, John Dehner, Kent McCord, John Vernon
'All the pleasure lies in the humour's weakness.' – *Observer*

Airport ***

US 1970 136m Technicolor Todd-AO
Universal/Ross Hunter (Jacque Mapes)
▣ ▤ ◎ ◎ ◯
Events of one snowy night at a midwestern international airport, culminating in airborne melodrama when a mad bomber is killed and the damaged plane has to be talked down.
Glossy, undeniably entertaining, all-star version of a popular novel, with cardboard characters skilfully deployed in Hollywood's very best style.
wd George Seaton novel Arthur Hailey
ph Ernest Laszlo m Alfred Newman ed Stuart Gilmore
☆ Burt Lancaster, Dean Martin, Jean Seberg, *Helen Hayes*, Van Heflin, Jacqueline Bisset, George Kennedy, Maureen Stapleton, Barry Nelson, Dana Wynter, Lloyd Nolan, Barbara Hale, Gary Collins, Jessie Royce Landis
'The best film of 1944.' – *Judith Crist*

'For sheer contentment there is nothing to beat the sight of constant catastrophe happening to others.' – *Alexander Walker*

'A *Grand Hotel* in the sky ... every few years or so some more show-biz types would crowd onto a plane that would threaten to crash, collide with another, meet with terrorists, or otherwise be subjected to the perils of Pauline.' – *Les Keyser, Hollywood in the Seventies*

† The film cost 10 million dollars and earned 45.

👤 Helen Hayes

Ⓐ best picture; George Seaton (as writer); Ernest Laszlo; Alfred Newman; Maureen Stapleton; editing; costumes (Edith Head)

'Something hit us ... the crew is dead ... help us, please, please help us!'

Airport 1975

US   1974   105m   Technicolor   Panavision
Universal (Jennings Lang, William Frye)
▦ ◎ 🎧

A private aircraft collides with a jet plane and kills or immobilizes its crew, so a stewardess has to manoeuvre the jumbo to safety.

Inept airborne suspenser loaded with stars who do nothing and marred by continuity lapses and boring dialogue.

w Don Ingalls d Jack Smight ph Philip Lathrop m Jim Cacavas

☆ Charlton Heston, *Karen Black*, George Kennedy, Helen Reddy, Efrem Zimbalist Jnr, Susan Clark, Myrna Loy, Gloria Swanson, Linda Blair, Dana Andrews, Roy Thinnes, Sid Caesar, Ed Nelson, Nancy Olson, Martha Scott

'Aimed squarely for the yahoo trade.' – *Variety*
'Processed schlock. One can have a fairly good time laughing at it, but it doesn't sit too well as a joke, because the people on the screen are being humiliated.' – *Pauline Kael, New Yorker*
'Good exciting corny escapism, and the kind of movie you would not want to watch as an inflight film.' – *Roger Ebert*

Airport '77

US   1977   114m   Technicolor   Panavision
Universal (William Frye)
▦ ▦ ◎

A private airliner loaded with guests and art treasures hits an oil rig and settles underwater on a sandbank.

Hysteria, rescue, and guest stars with nothing to do; the mixture as before.

w Michael Scheff, David Spector story H. A. L. Craig, Charles Kuenstle d Jerry Jameson ph Philip Lathrop m John Cacavas pd George C. Webb

☆ Jack Lemmon, James Stewart, Brenda Vaccaro, Joseph Cotten, Olivia de Havilland, Lee Grant, Darren McGavin, Christopher Lee, Robert Foxworth, Robert Hooks, Monte Markham, Kathleen Quinlan, James Booth, George Kennedy

'Neither as riveting as it should be, nor as much fun as its absurd plotline would suggest.' – *Verina Glaessner, MFB*

† See also: *The Concorde – Airport '79.*

Airport '80: The Concorde: see The Concorde: Airport '79

Akahige: see Redbeard

Akasen Chitai: see Street of Shame

Ake and His World *

Sweden   1984   103m   colour
Sandrew/Svenska Film Institute/Scentext
original title: *Ake Och Hans Värld*

In the 1930s the six-year-old son of a Swedish country doctor observes the lives and deaths of his father's patients.

Charming, episodic, gently nostalgic account of childhood.

wd Allan Edwall ph Jörgen Persson m Thomas Lindahl ad Anna Asp ed Lars Hagström

☆ Martin Lindstrom, Loa Falkman, Gunnel Fred, Katja Blomquist, Ulla Sjöblom, Susanne Ernrup, Björn Gustafson, Allan Edwall

Akenfield *

GB   1974   98m   Techniscope
Angle Films/LWT (Peter Hall, Rex Pyke)

Semi-dramatized film version of a book which documented a Suffolk village by interviewing its older inhabitants.

An interesting venture ruined by imprecision, misty photography, lack of narrative drive or any compensating detail, and the appalling error of using a cheap wide screen process.

w Ronald Blythe book Ronald Blythe d Peter Hall ph Ivan Strasberg m Michael Tippett ad Ian Whittaker, Roger Christian

☆ Garrow Shand, Peggy Cole, Barbara Tilney, Lyn Brooks, Ida Page, Ted Dedman, Peter Tuddenham

'One of the best films – certainly the most unusual – made in England and about England.' – *Alexander Walker*
'A parochial drama-documentary, commercially dubious but otherwise an impressive achievement.' – *Variety*
'About the impact of the leading players, the beauty of the Edwardian scenes and the triumphantly enhancing use of music, there need be no reservations at all.' – *Michael Ratcliffe*

Akira (dubbed) **

Japan   1987   124m   colour
ICA/Akira Committee (Ryohei Suzuki, Shunzo Kato)
▦ ▦ ◎

In a future neo-Tokyo, filled with revolutionaries, terrorists and warring government factions, a young biker becomes the subject of experiments to create a super-being.

Brilliantly animated film, based on a comic-book, that eschews cartoon violence for the more realistic style of action movies. The narrative, which begins as fantasy and shifts into mysticism, is less enthralling.

w Katsuhiro Otomo, Izo Hashimoto comic Katsuhiro Otomo d Katsuhiro Otomo ph Katsuji Misawa m Shoji Yamashiro ad Toshiharu Mizutani ed Takeshi Seyama

'Probably the first animated feature with a genuinely novelistic density of incident and character.' – *Tony Rayns, MFB*

Akira Kurosawa's Dreams *

US   1990   119m   colour
Warner/Akira Kurosawa USA (Hisao Kurosawa, Mike Y. Inoue)
▦ ▦ ◎

Eight dream sequences, concerning animals, ghosts, spirits and nuclear destruction, the most successful of which involves entering the paintings of Van Gogh.

A lesser work of a master: visually fascinating, though too often trite in content.

wd Akira Kurosawa ph Takao Saito, Masaharu Ueda m Shinichiro Ikebe ad Yoshiro Muraki, Akira Sakuragi ed Tome Minami

☆ Mitsuko Baisho, Toshihiko Nakano, Mitsunori Isaki, Mie Suzuki, Akira Terao, Mieko Harada, Yoshitaka Zushi, Martin Scorsese, Chosuke Ikariya, Chishu Ryu

'His is not to shock us into surrendering to his visions but to seduce our consent to them. And this he does in one of the most lucid dreamworks ever placed on film.' – *Richard Schickel, Time*

'Fearlessly Told! Authentic! True!'
'He built a vicious crime syndicate of illegal liquor, vice and gambling that we are still fighting today!'

Al Capone **

US   1959   105m   bw
Allied Artists (John H. Burrows, Leonard J. Ackerman)
▦ ▦

An account of Chicago's most famous gangster, up to his arrest for income tax evasion.

Only slightly overplayed, semi-documentary retelling of a larger-than-life true story. Steiger gives a clever impersonation on the border of caricature.

w Malvin Wald, Henry Greenberg d Richard Wilson ph Lucien Ballard m David Raksin

☆ Rod Steiger, Fay Spain, Murvyn Vye, Nehemiah Persoff, Martin Balsam, James Gregory, Joe de Santis

'The most remarkable thing about it is its truth.' – *Daily Telegraph*
'This powerful production may turn out to be the definitive gangster film of all time.' – *Film Daily*

'Imagine if you had three wishes, three hopes, three dreams and they all could come true.'

Aladdin ****

🎬 US   1992   90m   Technicolor
Buena Vista/Walt Disney (John Musker, Ron Clements)
▦ ▦ ◎ 🎧

An urchin with a magic lamp falls in love with a runaway princess.

Another brilliant return to classic form from Disney, notable for its quick-change genie to match the exuberance of Robin Williams' characterization, and some innovative computer animation.

wd John Musker, Ron Clements, Ted Elliott, Terry Rossio m Alan Menken m/ly Alan Menken, Howard Ashman, Tim Rice pd R. S. Vander Wende ed H. Lee Peterson

☆ Featuring the voices of Scott Weinger, Brad Kane (Aladdin's singing), Robin Williams, Linda Larkin, Lea Salonga (Jasmine's singing), Jonathan Freeman, Frank Welker, Gilbert Gottfried, Douglas Seale

'Floridly beautiful, shamelessly derivative and infused with an irreverent, sophisticated comic flair.' – *Variety*
'A rollicking, bodaciously choreographed fantasy right out of Busby Berkeley.' – *Washington Post*

† It was followed by two sequels released direct to video: *Return of Jafar*, edited from an animated TV series, and *Aladdin and the King of Thieves*.

👤 Alan Menken (score); song: 'Whole New World' (mAlan Menken, lyTim Rice)

Ⓐ song: 'Friends like Me' (mAlan Menken, lyHoward Ashman); sound; sound effects editing

Alakazam the Great *

🎬 Japan   1960   88m   Eastmancolor
Toei (Hiroshi Okawa)
▦

original title: *Saiyu-ki*

The arrogant monkey king of the animals is sent by his human master on a pilgrimage; he defeats evil King Gruesome and returns a hero.

Smartly animated, Disney-inspired cartoon based on the same legend as Monkey, translated by Arthur Waley.

w Osamu Tezuka, Keinosuke Uekusa d Taiji Yabushita

'The Mission That Became A Fortress ... The Fortress That Became A Shrine...'

The Alamo *

US   1960   193m   Technicolor   Todd-AO
UA/Batjac/John Wayne
▦ ▦ ▦ ◎ 🎧

In 1836 a small southern fort becomes the centre of Texas' fight for independence, but it is suddenly annihilated by a Mexican raid, and all its defenders killed.

Sprawling historical epic with many irrelevant episodes and distracting changes of mood.

w James Edward Grant d John Wayne ph William H. Clothier m Dimitri Tiomkin ed Stuart Gilmore

☆ John Wayne, Richard Widmark, Laurence Harvey, Richard Boone, Frankie Avalon, Patrick Wayne, Linda Cristal, Chill Wills, Joseph Calleia

CROCKETT: 'Republic. I like the sound of the word. It means people can live free, talk free, go or come, buy or sell, be drunk or sober, however they choose. Some words give you a feeling. Republic is one of those words that makes me tight in the throat – the same tightness a man gets when his baby takes his first step or his first baby shaves and makes his first sound like a man. Some words can give you a feeling that makes your heart warm. Republic is one of those words.'

'Its sole redeeming feature lies in one of those crushing climaxes of total massacre which Hollywood can still pull off thunderingly well.' – *Peter John Dyer*

Ⓐ picture; William H. Clothier; Dimitri Tiomkin; Chill Wills; song 'The Green Leaves of Summer' (mDimitri Tiomkin, ly Paul Francis Webster); editing

Alamo Bay

US   1985   98m   Metrocolor
Tri-Star/Delphi III (Louis and Vincent Malle)
▦ ▦ ◎ 🎧

Fisherfolk in Galveston Bay resent the intrusion of refugee Vietnamese.

Unsympathetic, slow-paced melodrama which ends up seeming pointless despite a Ku Klux Klan confrontation.

w Alice Arlen d Louis Malle ph Curtis Clark m Ry Cooder pd Trevor Williams ed James Bruce

☆ Amy Madigan, Ed Harris, Donald Moffat, Rudy Young, Ho Nguyen

'A failed piece of social consciousness.' – *Variety*

An Alan Smithee Film: Burn, Hollywood, Burn!

US   1997   86m   colour
Buena Vista/Hollywood/Cinergi (Ben Myron)
▦ ▦ ◎

After he loses control of his blockbuster film, a director steals the negative; those involved in its making explain what went wrong.

A lamentable, heavy-handed, ham-fisted attempt at a satire on Hollywood, in which all the jokes misfire.

w Joe Eszterhas d Alan Smithee (Arthur Hiller) ph Reynaldo Villalobos m Gary G-Wiz, Chuck D pd David L. Snyder ed Jim Langlois

☆ Ryan O'Neal, Coolio Leon, Chuck D, Richard Jeni, Eric Idle, Leslie Stefanson, Sandra Bernhard, Cheri Lunghi, Harvey Weinstein, Gavin Polone, MC Lite, Marcello Thedford, Nicole Nagel, Stephen Tobolowsky

'It becomes obvious well before the end that there wasn't really a movie here after all, at least not one that will be terribly edifying for general audiences.' – *Todd McCarthy, Variety*

† Those appearing as themselves include: Sylvester Stallone, Whoopi Goldberg, Jackie Chan, Billy Bob Thornton, Joe Eszterhas, Robert Evans and Shane Black

†† Alan Smithee is the pseudonym used by a director when he wants his name removed from the film's credits. In this instance Arthur Hiller, who asked for his name to be removed after a dispute with Joe Eszterhas

††† It was voted the worst film of 1998 in the Golden Raspberry Awards.

The Alarmist

US   1997   91m   FotoKem
Columbia TriStar/Life During Wartme (Dan Stone, Lisa Zimble)

A security system salesman suspects his boss of murdering one of his clients in order to increase sales.

Dim social comedy with misjudged performances and a sense of increasing desperation about its narrative twists.

wd Evan Dunsky play Life During Wartime by Keith Reddin ph Alex Nepomniaschy m Christopher Beck pd Amy B. Ancona ed Norman Buckley

☆ David Arquette, Stanley Tucci, Mary McCormack, Kate Capshaw, Tricia Vessey, Ryan Reynolds, Hoke Howell, Ruth Miller, Michael Learned, Lewis Arquette, Richmond Arquette

'A cinematic experience not unlike being savaged by a sheep.' – *Kieron Corless, Sight and Sound*

Alaska

🎬 US   1995   109m   Technicolor
Columbia/Castle Rock (Carol Fuchs, Andy Burg)
▦ ▦ ◎

Two children go in search of their father after he crashes his plane in Alaska.

Uninspired adventure movie, demonstrating that children and animals (a bear cub this time around) are not infallible scene-stealers.

w Andy Burg, Scott Myers d Fraser Heston ph Tony Westman m Reg Powell pd Douglas Higgins ed Rob Kobrin

☆ Thora Birch, Vincent Kartheiser, Dirk Benedict, Charlton Heston, Duncan Fraser, Gordon Tootoosis

Alaska Highway

US   1943   66m   bw
Paramount/Pine-Thomas

Engineer brothers blaze a trail for the Army Engineer Corps, and fall for the same girl.

Routine sock-it-to-me adventure romance with process photography.

w Maxwell Shane, Lewis R. Foster d Frank McDonald

☆ Richard Arlen, Jean Parker, Ralph Sanford, Bill Henry

Alaska Seas

US   1953   78m   bw
Paramount (Mel Epstein)

Alaska fishermen oppose the crooked owner of the local cannery.

Insipid remake of Spawn of the North (qv).

w Geoffrey Homes, Walter Doniger d Jerry Hopper ph William C. Mellor md Irvin Talbot

☆ Robert Ryan, Gene Barry, Jan Sterling, Brian Keith, Richard Shannon

---

Ⓓ Digital Video Disc Region 2   Ⓡ Digital Video Disc Region 1   🎧 Soundtrack released on compact disc   ☆ Cast in approximate order of importance   † Points of interest   🎵 Notable songs   👤 Academy Award   Ⓐ Academy Award nomination   Ⓑ BAFTA

The Alaskan *

US 1924 80m bw

Famous Players/Paramount

An Alaskan defies robber barons intent on corrupting the new state.

Tough, effective and straightforward action drama, one of its star's best roles.

w Willis Goldbeck *novel* James Oliver Curwood d Herbert Brenon

☆ *Thomas Meighan*, Estelle Taylor, John Sainpolis, Anna May Wong

L'Albatross (dubbed)

France 1971 90m Eastmancolor

Antony Balch/Balzac/Profilm/Belstar (Jean-Pierre Mocky, Jacques Dorfmann, Frédérick Dorfmann)

GB title: Love Hat

After escaping from prison, a man accused of murder goes on the run, taking as hostage the daughter of a left-wing politician.

Complex romantic and political thriller, with an atmosphere ruined by its insensitive dubbing.

w Jean-Pierre Mocky, Claude Veillot, Raphael Delpard d Jean-Pierre Mocky *ph* Marcel Weiss m Léo Ferré *ad* Jacques Flamand, Jacques Dor ed Marguerite Renoir

☆ Jean-Pierre Mocky, Marion Game, André Le Gall, Paul Muller, Francis Terzian

Albert RN **

GB 1953 88m bw

Dial (Daniel M. Angel)

US title: Break to Freedom

Prisoners of war construct a lifelike dummy to cover the absence of escaping prisoners.

Competent, entertaining version of a successful play: an archetypal POW comedy drama.

w Guy Morgan, Vernon Harris *play* Guy Morgan, Edward Sammis d Lewis Gilbert *ph* Jack Asher m Malcolm Arnold

☆ Jack Warner, Anthony Steel, Robert Beatty, William Sylvester, Anton Diffring, Eddie Byrne, Guy Middleton, Paul Carpenter, Frederick Valk

Albino Alligator *

US 1996 97m colour 'Scope

Miramax/UGC DA/Motion Picture Corp (Brad Krevoy, Steve Stabler)

Three incompetent robbers take refuge in a basement bar, which is surrounded by armed police.

An efficient, claustrophobic suspense movie of a familiar kind.

w Christian Forte d Kevin Spacey *ph* Mark Plummer m Michael Brook *pd* Nelson Coates ed Jay Cassidy

☆ Matt Dillon, Faye Dunaway, Gary Sinise, William Fichtner, Viggo Mortensen, John Spencer, Skeet Ulrich, M. Emmet Walsh, Joe Mantegna

'Pro cast and muscular lensing aren't quite enough to overcome a script that isn't nearly as ingenious as it would like to seem.' *Lisa Nesselson, Variety*

Albuquerque

US 1947 89m Cinecolor

Pine-Thomas/Paramount

GB title: Silver City

The nephew of a town tyrant steps in to save an independent wagon line.

Formula Western with adequate action.

w Gene Lewis and Clarence Upson Young *novel* Luke Short d Ray Enright

☆ Randolph Scott, Barbara Britton, George 'Gabby' Hayes, George Cleveland, Lon Chaney Jnr, Russell Hayden

Alcatraz Island

US 1937 64m bw

Warner/Cosmopolitan

The federal government decides to build a top-security prison on a rock in San Francisco Bay.

Cheap routine treatment of what might have been an interesting subject.

w Crane Wilbur d William McGann

☆ Ann Sheridan, Mary Maguire, Dick Purcell, Addison Richards, *George E. Stone*, Doris Lloyd, John Litel

'Should about complete the Warner file on prisons.' – *Variety*

The Alchemist

US 1981 84m DeLuxe

Video Form/Ideal Films (Lawrence Applebaum)

A beautiful woman cures a man of his century-old curse.

Low-budget amalgam of horror movie clichés, inexpertly combined.

w Alan J. Adler d Charles Band *ph* Andrew W. Friend m Richard H. Band *pd* Dale A. Pelton ad Pam Warner ed Ted Nicolaou

☆ Robert Ginty, Lucinda Dooling, John Sanderford, Viola Kate Stimpson, Robert Glaudini

Alex *

New Zealand/Australia 1992 92m colour

Isambard/Total/NZFC/NZOA/AFFC (Tom Parkinson, Phil Gerlach)

A 15-year-old New Zealand swimmer overcomes personal and professional difficulties to win a place in the 1960 Olympic Games.

Pleasant, sentimental account of a strong-willed girl succeeding against the odds.

w Ken Katran *book* Tessa Duder d Megan Simpson *ph* Donald Duncan m Todd Hunter, Johanna Pigott *pd* Kim Sinclair ed Tony Kavanagh

☆ Chris Haywood, Lauren Jackson, Josh Picker, Catherine Godbold, Elizabeth Hawthorn

Alex and the Gypsy

US 1976 99m DeLuxe

TCF (Richard Shepherd)

A cynical California bailbondsman involved in illicit activities chooses romantic freedom with a gypsy girl.

Incoherent hardbitten romance with an unconvincing set of characters.

w Lawrence B. Marcus *novel The Bailbondsman* by Stanley Elkin d John Korty *ph* Bill Butler m Henry Mancini

☆ Jack Lemmon, Geneviève Bujold, James Woods, Gino Ardito, Robert Emhardt

'Even if it were well done (which it is not) it would be banal, predictable and cloying.' – *Frank Rich*

'Off the beaten track, but that's just about the only thing you can give it points for.' – *Pauline Kael*

Alex in Wonderland

US 1970 109m colour

MGM (Larry Tucker)

A Hollywood director finds life tedious.

So did the small paying audiences who saw this pale imitation of Fellini. (Some wags called it One and a Half.)

w Paul Mazursky, Larry Tucker d Paul Mazursky *ph* Laszlo Kovacs m Tom O'Horgan *pd* Pato Guzman ed Stuart H. Pappe

☆ Donald Sutherland, Jeanne Moreau, Ellen Burstyn, Federico Fellini

'The Fellini elements are laid onto the film and don't quite sink in – but the human story does work, remarkably well.' – *Roger Ebert*

Alexander Hamilton *

US 1931 73m bw

Warner

The life of America's 18th-century financier.

Star biopic, highly satisfying in its day.

w Julien Josephson, Maude Howell, George Arliss d John G. Adolfi *ph* James Van Trees

☆ George Arliss, Doris Kenyon, Montagu Love, Dudley Digges, Lionel Belmore, Ralf Harolde, Alan Mowbray

Alexander Nevsky ****

USSR 1938 112m bw

Mosfilm

In 1242, Prince Alexander Nevsky defeats the invading Teutonic Knights in a battle on the ice of Lake Peipus.

A splendid historical pageant which shows the director at his most inventively pictorial and climaxes in a superb battle sequence using music instead of natural sound.

w Pyotr Pavlenko, Sergei Eisenstein d *Sergei Eisenstein* *ph* Edouard Tissé m Prokofiev ad I. Shpinel, N. Soloviov, K. Yeliseyev

☆ Nikolai Cherkassov, Nikolai Okhlopkov, Andrei Abrikosov, Dmitri Orlov

'The picture will meet with good results wherever its political sentiments find established adherents. Otherwise it's almost nil for general appeal.' – *Variety*

'Superb sequences of cinematic opera that pass from pastoral to lamentation and end in a triumphal cantata.' – *Georges Sadoul*

'The colossus who conquered the world! The most colossal motion picture of all time!'

Alexander the Great *

US 1956 135m Technicolor Cinemascope

UA/Robert Rossen

The life and early death at 33 of the Macedonian warrior who conquered the entire known world.

Dour impassive epic which despite good intelligent stretches makes one long for Hollywood's usual more ruthless view of history.

wd Robert Rossen *ph* Robert Krasker m Mario Nascimbene *ad* Andrei Andreiev

☆ Richard Burton, Fredric March, Danielle Darrieux, Claire Bloom, Barry Jones, Harry Andrews, Peter Cushing, Stanley Baker, Michael Hordern, Niall MacGinnis

'Not a scene is held for a second longer than it is worth; greatness is pictured in constant dissolve.' – *Alexander Walker*

'Rossen has aimed for greatness and lost honourably.' – *Andrew Sarris*

Alexander's Ragtime Band ***

US 1938 106m bw

TCF (Darryl F. Zanuck, Harry Joe Brown)

Between 1911 and 1939, two songwriters vie for the affections of a rising musical comedy star.

Archetypal chronicle musical with 26 songs: well-paced, smartly made, and bursting with talent.

w Kathryn Scola, Lamar Trotti, Richard Sherman d Henry King *ph* Peverell Marley m/ly Irving Berlin *md* Alfred Newman *ad* Bernard Herzbrun, Boris Leven ed Barbara McLean

☆ Tyrone Power, Alice Faye, Don Ameche, Ethel Merman, Jack Haley, Jean Hersholt, Helen Westley, John Carradine, Paul Hurst, Wally Vernon, Ruth Terry, Eddie Collins, Douglas Fowley, Chick Chandler

'A grand filmusical which stirs and thrills, finding response in the American heart to memories of the exciting, sentimental and patriotic moments of the past quarter of a century.' – *Variety*

♫ 'Alexander's Ragtime Band'; 'Everybody's Doin' It'; 'When the Midnight Choo-Choo Leaves for Alabam'; 'Oh, How I Hate to Get Up in the Morning'; 'Say It with Music'; 'A Pretty Girl Is Like a Melody'; 'Blue Skies'; 'What'll I Do'; 'Easter Parade'; 'Heat Wave'.

♟ Alfred Newman

♟ picture; Irving Berlin (for original story); Irving Berlin (for song, 'Now It Can Be Told'); art direction; editing

Alf, Bill and Fred *

GB 1964 8m Eastmancolor

Biographic 4 (Bob Godfrey)

A man, a duck and a dog enjoy bouncing together.

Bittersweet cartoon fable which pleases much more than its synopsis might suggest.

w Stan Hayward d Bob Godfrey

† Animation by Bob Godfrey.

The Alf Garnett Saga

GB 1972 90m colour

Columbia/Associated London Films (Ned Sherrin, Terry Glinwood)

Bigoted Alf is exasperated by his council flat, his son-in-law, and the possibility that his daughter is pregnant by a black man.

Second inflation of the TV series, Till Death Us Do Part, even cruder and less funny than the first; listlessly written and developed.

w Johnny Speight d Bob Kellett *ph* Nic Knowland m Georgie Fame

☆ Warren Mitchell, Dandy Nichols, Adrienne Posta, Paul Angelis, John Le Mesurier, Joan Sims, John Bird, Roy Kinnear

'One long, repetitive and unfunny diatribe.' – *MFB*

Alfie **

GB 1966 114m Techniscope

Paramount/Sheldrake (Lewis Gilbert)

A Cockney Lothario is proud of his amorous conquests, but near-tragedy finally makes him more mature.

Garish sex comedy, an immense box-office success because of its frankness and an immaculate performance from its star.

w Bill Naughton *play* Bill Naughton d Lewis Gilbert *ph* Otto Heller m Sonny Rollins

☆ *Michael Caine*, Vivien Merchant, Shirley Anne Field, Millicent Martin, Jane Asher, Julia Foster, Shelley Winters, Eleanor Bron, Denholm Elliott

'A film exceptionally well made; never boring; composed of remarkable performances, scenes sharply observed and music neatly attuned.' – *Dilys Powell*

'Paramount thought it was a good bet because it was going to be made for 500,000 dollars, normally the sort of money spent on executives' cigar bills.' – *Lewis Gilbert*

♟ picture; Bill Naughton; Michael Caine; Vivien Merchant; title song (m Burt Bacharach, ly Hal David)

♟ Vivien Merchant

Alfie Darling

GB 1975 102m Technicolor

EMI/Signal (Dugald Rankin)

Further repetitive amorous exploits of the Cockney Lothario, now a continental truck driver.

Soft porn adventures quite unworthy of the writer-director, and tedious to sit through; the touch of tragedy at the end only makes matters worse.

wd Ken Hughes *ph* Ousama Rawi m Alan Price

☆ Alan Price, Jill Townsend, Paul Copley, Joan Collins, Sheila White, Annie Ross, Hannah Gordon, Rula Lenska

Alfred the Great *

GB 1969 122m Metrocolor Panavision

MGM/Bernard Smith

In AD 871 Alfred takes over kingship from his weak elder brother.

A 'realistic' youth-oriented view of history: blood and four-letter words alternate with cliché to make a dispiriting, disunified whole, though the background detail is interesting and the battle scenes vivid.

w Ken Taylor, James R. Webb d Clive Donner *ph* Alex Thomson m Ray Leppard *pd* Michael Stringer

☆ David Hemmings, Michael York, Prunella Ransome, Colin Blakely, Julian Glover, Ian McKellen, Alan Dobie

Alfredo Alfredo

Italy/France 1971 110m Technicolor

CIC/RPA/Rizzoli/Francoriz (Pietro Germi)

A bank clerk, determined to divorce his sexually insatiable wife, recalls his courtship and their difficult marriage.

A laboured and inane comedy of marital misunderstanding; it's possible that you need to be Italian to find it at all interesting.

w Leo Benvenuti, Piero de Bernardi, Tullio Pinelli, Pietro Germi d Pietro Germi *ph* Aiace Parolin m Carlo Rustichelli *ad* Carlo Egidi ed Sergio Montanari

☆ Dustin Hoffman, Stefania Sandrelli, Carla Gravina, Clara Colosimo, Daniele Patella

'It simply limps on and on and on to no point or purpose.' – *Tom Milne, MFB*

† The version released in Britain ran for 98m.

Alf's Button

GB 1930 96m bw/colour

Gaumont

A soldier has a button, which, when rubbed, summons an all-powerful genie.

Not the first version (there was one in 1920 with Leslie Henson) but the first in sound of a lively knockabout comedy. It even had a colour sequence.

w L'Estrange Fawcett *play* W. A. Darlington d W. P. Kellino *ph* Percy Strong, William Shenton *ad* A. L. Mazzei

☆ Jimmy Nervo, Teddy Knox, Tubby Edlin, Alf Goddard, Nora Swinburne, Polly Ward, Anton Dolin

---

Alf's Button Afloat **
GB   1938   89m   bw
Gainsborough (Edward Black)

Six itinerants encounter a genie, whose granting of their wishes brings riches and embarrassment.
Archetypal music hall farce descending at moments into surrealism (the lovers are eaten by a bear). It starred the six original members of the Crazy Gang, and all concerned are on top form.
w *Marriott Edgar, Val Guest, Ralph Smart* novel *Alf's Button by W. A. Darlington* d *Marcel Varnel* ph *Arthur Crabtree* md *Louis Levy* ad *Vetchinsky* ed *R. E. Dearing, Alfred Roome*
☆ *Bud Flanagan, Chesney Allen, Jimmy Nervo, Teddy Knox, Charles Naughton, Jimmy Gold, Alastair Sim, Wally Patch, Peter Gawthorne*

Algiers **
US   1938   95m   bw
Walter Wanger
▤

A romantic Casbah thief makes the mistake of falling in love.
Seminal Hollywood romantic drama based closely on a French original, Pepe le Moko; laughed at for years because of the alleged line 'Come with me to the Casbah' (which is never actually said), it holds up remarkably well in its fashion.
w *John Howard Lawson, James M. Cain* d *John Cromwell* ph *James Wong Howe* m *Vincent Scotto, Mohammed Igorbouchen*
☆ *Charles Boyer, Hedy Lamarr, Sigrid Gurie, Gene Lockhart, Joseph Calleia, Alan Hale, Johnny Downs*
'A quality of sustained suspense and excitement … there is nothing makeshift about the production.' – *Variety*
'Few films this season, or any other, have sustained their mood more brilliantly.' – *New York Times*
'The general tone is that of the decent artistry we must demand and enjoy in pictures, which should someday be as respectable as books, only more near and vivid.' – *Otis Ferguson*
'This version is pure Hollywood, sacrificing everything to glamour, and the heavy make-up and studio lighting make it seem so artificial one can get giggly.' – *New Yorker, 1977*
† Remake: *Casbah* (qv).
♫ *James Wong Howe; Charles Boyer; Gene Lockhart*

'Wild nights of sheer delights! Burning days of bold adventure! When beauty was the booty and the prize of all was love!'
Ali Baba and the Forty Thieves *
🎠 US   1944   87m   Technicolor
Universal (Paul Malvern)
▤   ⊚

A deposed prince pretending to be a bandit regains his rightful throne.
Absurd but likeable wartime pantomime without much humour: a typical big-budget production of its studio and period.
w *Edmund L. Hartmann* d *Arthur Lubin* ph *George Robinson* m *Edward Ward*
☆ *Jon Hall, Maria Montez, Scotty Beckett, Turhan Bey, Frank Puglia, Andy Devine, Kurt Katch*
† Remake: *Sword of Ali Baba*, which over twenty years later used much of the same footage.

Ali Baba and the Forty Thieves *
🎠 France   1954   90m   Eastmancolor
Films du Cyclope

Ali Baba is sent to buy a new wife for his master, and accidentally finds a thieves' treasure cave…
Sporadically amusing but finally disappointing version of the Arabian Nights story; it looks hasty.
w *Jacques Becker, Marc Maurette, Maurice Griffe* d *Jacques Becker* ph *Robert Le Fèbvre* m *Paul Misraki*
☆ *Fernandel, Samia Gamal, Dieter Borsche, Henri Vilbert*

Ali Baba and the Seven Saracens (dubbed)
Italy   1965   82m   Eastmancolor   Totalscope
AVIS (Aldo Occhipinti)

Ali Baba competes with seven other champions to become ruler of all the desert tribes and overthrow a tyrant.
Risible, camp extravaganza, not helped by its tacky settings and stolid dialogue.

w *Benito Ilforte, Sergio Tocci, Emimmo Salvi* d *Emimmo Salvi* ph *Mario Parapetti* m *Italo Fischetti* ad *Peppino Ranieri* ed *Enzo Alfonsi*
☆ *Gordon Mitchell, Dan Harrison, Bella Cortez, Mike Moore, Nat Koster, Carrol Brown, Lilly Zander*

Ali Baba Goes to Town *
US   1937   81m   bw
TCF (Lawrence Schwab)

A hobo falls off a train into a film set and thinks he is back in the Arabian Nights.
Rather flat star vehicle with a few compensations.
w *Harry Tugend, Jack Yellen* d *David Butler* ph *Ernest Palmer* m *Louis Silvers* m/ly *Mack Gordon, Harry Revel* ch *Sammy Lee*
☆ *Eddie Cantor, Tony Martin, Roland Young, John Carradine, June Lang*
'An elaborately produced filmusical which satirizes the New Deal policies, politicians and politics.' – *Variety*
♫ *Sammy Lee*

Alias Bulldog Drummond: see Bulldog Jack

Alias Jesse James *
US   1959   92m   DeLuxe
Hope Enterprises (Jack Hope)

An incompetent insurance salesman sells a policy to Jesse James and has to protect his client until he can get it back.
Ho-hum star comedy saved by a climax in which Hope is protected by every cowboy star in Hollywood.
w *William Bowers, D. D. Beauchamp* d *Norman Z. McLeod* ph *Lionel Lindon* m *Joseph J. Lilley*
☆ *Bob Hope, Rhonda Fleming, Wendell Corey, Jim Davis, Will Wright*

Alias Jimmy Valentine
US   1928   75m   bw
MGM

Crook comedy drama previously made in 1920.
This version is notable only as the first MGM sound film.
w *Sarah Y. Mason, A. P. Younger* d *Jack Conway*
☆ *William Haines, Karl Dane, Lionel Barrymore*

Alias 'La Gringa' *
Peru/Spain   1991   100m   colour
Perfo/TV Española/Channel 4 (Andres Malatesta, Emilio Salomon)

A criminal returns to jail to rescue the university professor who, in the middle of a riot by terrorists, saved his life.
Harsh exposé of prison life, inspired by a true story, and providing a little insight into Peruvian life and politics.
w *Alberto Durant, José Watanabé, José María Salcedo* d *Alberto Durant* ph *Mario García Joya* m *Pochi Marambio* pd *Matanabé* ed *Gianfranco Annichini*
☆ *Germano Gonzales, Elsa Oliveros, Orlando Sacha, Juan Manuel Ochoa, Enrique Victoria, Gonzalo de Miguel*
'Basically action for undemanding Latino auds, but on its own terms it's efficiently and briskly handled.' – *Variety*

Alias Mary Dow
US   1935   65m   bw
Universal

A millionaire persuades a chorus girl to pose as his long-lost kidnapped daughter, to satisfy his wife.
Obvious audience-pleaser of its time.
w *Gladys Unger, Rose Franken, Arthur Caesar* d *Kurt Neumann*
☆ *Ray Milland, Sally Eilers, Henry O'Neill, Katherine Alexander*
'Not a bad picture … small towns should like it best.' – *Variety*

'No man ever held more terrible power over women than this tall dark handsome stranger from nowhere! The shock-filled story of a man whose love was more dangerous than a loaded gun!'
Alias Nick Beal ***
US   1949   93m   bw
Paramount (Endre Bohem)
GB title: *The Contact Man*

A politician is nearly corrupted by a mysterious stranger offering wealth and power.
Highly satisfactory modern version of Faust, done in gangster terms but not eschewing a supernatural explanation. Acting, photography and direction all in the right key.

w *Jonathan Latimer* story *Mindret Lord* d *John Farrow* ph *Lionel Lindon* m *Franz Waxman*
☆ *Ray Milland, Thomas Mitchell, Audrey Totter, George Macready, Fred Clark*

Alias the Deacon
US   1940   74m   bw
Ben Pivar/Universal

A sentimental cardsharp is mistaken by smalltown folk for their new deacon.
Modest rural comedy from a well-worn play.
w *Nat Perrin, Charles Grayson* play *John B. Hymer, Leroy Clemens* d *Christy Cabanne*
☆ *Bob Burns, Mischa Auer, Peggy Moran, Dennis O'Keefe, Edward Brophy, Thurston Hall, Jack Carson*
† Remake of *Half a Sinner* (qv).

Alias the Doctor
US   1932   70m   bw
First National/Warner

A natural man of the soil tries to follow his mother's wish that he should become a doctor.
Dated drama of family sentiment.
w *Benjamin McGill, Houston Branch* play *Emric Foldes* d *Lloyd Bacon*
☆ *Richard Barthelmess, Laura la Plante, Marian Marsh, Norman Foster, Oscar Apfel*
'It misses big league rating, but will satisfy on the average programme.' – *Variety*

Alibi *
US   1929   90m   bw
Roland West
▤

An ex-convict marries a policeman's daughter and uses her in his plan for the perfect murder.
Early talkie drama, mostly risible now but with interesting fragments of technique and imagination.
w *Roland West, C. Gardner Sullivan* play *Nightstick by Elaine Sterne Carrington, John Wray, J. C. Nugent* d *Roland West* ph *Ray June* m *Hugo Riesenfeld* ad *William Cameron Menzies*
☆ *Chester Morris, Eleanor Griffith, Regis Toomey, Mae Busch, Harry Stubbs*
♫ *picture; Chester Morris; William Cameron Menzies*

Alibi
GB   1931   75m   bw
Twickenham

Hercule Poirot proves that an apparent suicide was murder.
Tame adaptation, without the narrative gimmick of Agatha Christie's The Murder of Roger Ackroyd.
w *H. Fowler Mear* d *Leslie Hiscott*
☆ *Austin Trevor, Franklin Dyall, Elizabeth Allan, J. H. Roberts, Mary Jerrold*

Alibi *
GB   1942   82m   bw
Corona (Josef Somlo)

A nightclub mindreader forces the lady owner to give him a murder alibi.
Interesting but disappointing minor suspenser copied from a sharper French original.
w *uncredited* novel *Marcel Achard* d *Brian Desmond Hurst* ph *Otto Heller* m *Jack Beaver*
☆ *Margaret Lockwood, Hugh Sinclair, James Mason, Raymond Lovell, Enid Stamp-Taylor, Hartley Power, Jane Carr, Rodney Ackland, Edana Romney, Elizabeth Welch, Olga Lindo, Muriel George*
† The French film, *L'Alibi*, was made in 1939 by B-N Films. The girl was Jany Holt, with Erich von Stroheim as the villain and Louis Jouvet as the inspector. Pierre Chenal directed.

Alibi Ike *
US   1935   73m   bw
Warner (Edward Chodorov)

A baseball pitcher gets involved in all kinds of trouble.
Above average star comedy vehicle.
w *William Wister Haines* story *Ring Lardner* d *Ray Enright* ph *Arthur Todd* md *Leo F. Forbstein*
☆ *Joe E. Brown, Olivia de Havilland, Ruth Donnelly, Roscoe Karns, William Frawley*

Alice ***
🎠 GB/Switzerland/West Germany   1988   85m
Eastmancolor
Condor-Hessisches/SRG/Film Four (Peter-Christian Fueter)
▤   ⊚
original title: *Neco z Alenky*

A young girl follows a rabbit through a broken glass case into Wonderland.
A free, sometimes disturbing interpretation with surrealist overtones, of Lewis Carroll's masterpiece by a great animator that, with its mix of live actors and animation, comes closer than any other to conjuring the curious atmosphere of the original.
wd *Jan Svankmajer* novel *Alice in Wonderland by Lewis Carroll* ph *Svatoluk Maly* ad *Eva Svankmerova, Jiri Blaha* ed *Marie Drvotova*
☆ *Kristyna Kohoutova*
'A film for children of a certain kind, for the quiet solitary ones who spend hours in conversation with their dolls; who invest the smallest cast-off objects with secret significance.' – *Terrence Rafferty, New Yorker*

Alice *
US   1990   106m   DuArt
Orion/Jack Rollins, Charles H. Joffe
▤   ⊚

A bored housewife indulges in a fantasy life.
Moderately amusing comedy of a search for individuality.
wd *Woody Allen* ph *Carlo di Palma* pd *Santo Loquasto* ad *Speed Hopkins*
☆ *Mia Farrow, Joe Mantegna, Alec Baldwin, Blythe Danner, Judy Davis, William Hurt, Keye Luke, Bernadette Peters, Cybill Shepherd, Gwen Verdon*
'A likable little pic that will please his fans.' – *Variety*
♫ *original screenplay*

Alice Adams **
US   1935   99m   bw
RKO (Pandro S. Berman)
▤   ⊚

A social-climbing small-town girl falls in love.
Dated but interesting star vehicle with good production values.
w *Dorothy Yost, Mortimer Offner, Jane Murfin* novel *Booth Tarkington* d *George Stevens* ph *Robert de Grasse* m *Max Steiner, Roy Webb*
☆ *Katharine Hepburn, Fred MacMurray, Evelyn Venable, Frank Albertson, Fred Stone, Ann Shoemaker, Charles Grapewin, Grady Sutton, Hedda Hopper*
'Sturdy cinematic substance, virtually audience proof.' – *Variety*
'A nice middle-class film, as trivial as a schoolgirl's diary, and just about as pathetically true.' – *C. A. Lejeune*
'What was in 1922 a biting and observant novel emerges in 1935 as a bitingly satiric portrait of an era.' – *Time*
♫ *picture; Katharine Hepburn*

Alice au Pays de Merveilles: see Alice in Wonderland (1951)

'A picture for anyone who has ever dreamed of a second chance'
Alice Doesn't Live Here Any More ***
US   1974   112m   Technicolor
Warner (David Susskind, Audrey Maas)
▤   ⊚

A widow sets off with her young son for Monterey and a singing career.
Realistically squalid and foul-mouthed but endearing look at a slice of America today, with firm handling and excellent performances in a surprisingly old-fashioned theme.
w *Robert Getchell* d *Martin Scorsese* ph *Kent L. Wakeford* m *various* md *Richard La Salle* pd *Toby Carr Rafelson*
☆ *Ellen Burstyn, Alfred Lutter, Kris Kristofferson, Billy Green Bush, Diane Ladd, Lelia Goldoni, Jodie Foster*
'What Scorsese has done is to rescue an American cliché from the bland, flat but much more portentous naturalism of such as Harry and Tonto and restore it to an emotional and intellectual complexity through his particular brand of baroque realism.' – *Richard Combs*
'Full of funny malice and breakneck vitality.' – *New Yorker*

'A tough weepie, redeemed by its picturesque locations and its eye for social detail.' – *Michael Billington, Illustrated London News*
† The film inspired the TV sitcom *Alice* (1976–85).
👤 Ellen Burstyn
🏆 Robert Getchell; Diane Ladd
🎬 picture; Robert Getchell; Ellen Burstyn; Diane Ladd

Alice in the Cities

West Germany   1974   110m   bw
Filmverlag der Autoren
📼 📼
original title: *Alice in den Städten*
A German journalist in America reluctantly escorts a small girl back to Germany.
Interesting but overlong collection of modern metaphors, occasionally reminiscent of Paper Moon.
w Wim Wenders ph Robby Müller, Martin Schäfer m Irmin Schmid, Can ed Peter Przygodda
☆ Rüdiger Vogler, Yella Röttlander, Lisa Kreuzer, Edda Köchel

Alice in Wonderland **

👪👪   US   1933   75m   bw
Paramount (Louis D. Lighton)
Intriguing but disappointing version of the nonsense classic, keeping to the Tenniel drawings by dressing an all-star cast in masks, thereby rendering them ineffective.
w Joseph L. Mankiewicz, William Cameron Menzies *novel* Lewis Carroll d Norman Z. McLeod ph Henry Sharp, Bert Glennon m Dimitri Tiomkin
☆ Charlotte Henry, W. C. Fields, Cary Grant, Gary Cooper, Edward Everett Horton, Edna May Oliver, Jack Oakie, Leon Errol, Charles Ruggles, May Robson, Louise Fazenda, Ned Sparks, Alison Skipworth
'Nothing grows out of anything else in this phantasmagoria. It's like reading a whole volume of separate four-line gags.' – *Variety*
'Lavishly produced, with great care given to costumes and settings and make-up, but the spirit is missing.' – *New Yorker, 1977*
† Ida Lupino was brought from the UK for the title role, but not used.

Alice in Wonderland *

👪👪   US   1951   75m   Technicolor
Walt Disney
📼 🖥 📼 @~ 🎧
Fully animated cartoon version which has good moments but modernizes and Americanizes the familiar characters.
w various d Clyde Geronimi, Hamilton Luske, Wilfred Jackson m Oliver Wallace *supervisor* Ben Sharpsteen
☆ Featuring the voices of Kathryn Beaumont, Ed Wynn, Richard Haydn, Sterling Holloway, Jerry Colonna, Verna Felton, Bill Thompson
🎵 Oliver Wallace

Alice in Wonderland *

USA/France/Great Britain   1951   83m
Anscocolor
UGC/Rank/Lou Bunin
aka: *Alice au Pays de Merveilles*
Often interesting if sometimes crude version with Bunin's puppets, filmed in Nice; the simultaneous Disney cartoon version effectively kept it off the world's screens.
☆ Carol Marsh, Stephen Murray, Pamela Brown, Felix Aylmer

Alice, Sweet Alice: see *Communion (1978)*

Alice's Adventures in Wonderland *

👪👪   GB   1972   101m   Eastmancolor   Todd-AO
TCF/Josef Shaftel (Derek Horne)
📼
Live-action version which starts amiably enough but soon becomes flat and uninventive, with a star cast all at sea and tedium replacing the wit of the original.
wd William Sterling ph Geoffrey Unsworth m John Barry pd Michael Stringer
☆ Fiona Fullerton, Michael Crawford, Robert Helpmann, Dudley Moore, Spike Milligan, Peter Sellers, Dennis Price, Flora Robson, Rodney Bewes, Peter Bull, Michael Hordern, Ralph Richardson
🎬 Geoffrey Unsworth

Alice's Restaurant *

US   1969   110m   DeLuxe
UA/Florin (Harold Leventhal)
📼 📼
Folk singer Arlo Guthrie, on the verge of being drafted, gets some varied experience of life among the drop-outs of Montana, Massachusetts and New York.
Typical of the freakish, anti-Vietnam, do-as-you-please movies which splurged from Hollywood in the wake of Easy Rider, this has the minor benefits of good production values and a few jokes.
w Venable Herndon, Arthur Penn d Arthur Penn ph Michael Nebbia m/songs Arlo Guthrie
☆ Arlo Guthrie, Pat Quinn, James Broderick, Michael McClanathan, Geoff Outlaw
'A subtle, funny, tender and original movie that may not perhaps increase Arthur Penn's present high standing but will certainly do nothing to diminish it.' – *Philip French, Sight and Sound*
🎵 Arthur Penn

'In space, no one can hear you scream!'
Alien ****

GB   1979   117m   Eastmancolor   Panavision
TCF/Brandywine (Walter Hill, Gordon Carroll, David Giler)
📼 📼 🖥 @~ ⊙ ⊙ 🎧
Astronauts returning to Earth visit an apparently dead planet and are infected by a violent being which has unexpected behaviour patterns and eliminates them one by one.
Deliberately scarifying and highly commercial shocker. On its own terms, a classic of suspense – and art direction.
w Dan O'Bannon d Ridley Scott ph Derek Vanlint, Denys Ayling m Jerry Goldsmith *chief designer* H. R. Giger
☆ Tom Skerritt, Sigourney Weaver, John Hurt, Veronica Cartwright, Harry Dean Stanton, Ian Holm, Yaphet Kotto
'A sort of inverse relationship to *The Thing* invites unfavourable comparisons.' – *Sight and Sound*
'Empty bag of tricks whose production values and expensive trickery cannot disguise imaginative poverty.' – *Time Out*
'It was not, as its co-author admitted, a think piece. The message he intended was simple: Don't close your eyes or it will get ya.' – *Les Keyser, Hollywood in the Seventies*
† It was followed by three sequels, *Aliens*, *Alien3* and *Alien Resurrection*.
👤 visual effects (H. R. Giger, Carlo Rambaldi and others)
🎬 production design (Michael Seymour)

Alien Nation

US   1988   94m   DeLuxe
Fox (Gale Anne Hurd, Richard Kobritz)
📼 📼 @~
A detective, one of a despised minority of aliens stranded on Earth, is partnered with a bigoted human cop to solve a murder.
What begins as an interestingly oblique look at the problems of racism soon turns into a lacklustre action movie.
w Rockne S. O'Bannon d Graham Baker ph Adam Greenberg m Curt Sobel pd Jack T. Collis
☆ James Caan, Mandy Patinkin, Terence Stamp

Alien Resurrection *

US   1997   108m   DeLuxe   Panavision
TCF/Brandywine (Bill Badalato, Gordon Carroll, David Giler, Walter Hill)
📼 📼 🖥 ⊙ ⊙ 🎧
Two hundred years after being impregnated with an alien queen and killing herself to save the world, Ripley is cloned as part of an experiment to bring the creatures back to life.
Stylish, occasionally impressive movie that all too soon settles into familiar routine.
w Joss Whedon d Jean-Pierre Jeunet ph Darius Khondji m John Frizzell pd Nigel Phelps ed Herve Schneid
☆ Sigourney Weaver, Winona Ryder, Ron Perlman, Dominique Pinon, Michael Wincott, Dan Hedaya, Gary Dourdan, Kim Flowers, J. E. Freeman, Brad Dourif
'It's a shame that this effort – though far more coherent, entertaining and exciting than Alien3 – should be the first film in the series to be

almost anonymous.' – *Kim Newman, Sight and Sound*
† Sigourney Weaver was reportedly paid $11m for her role. The film cost $80m and took around $48m at the US box-office and more than $75m elsewhere.

'The Bitch Is Back.'
Alien3

US   1992   115m   Rank Colour   Panavision
TCF/Brandywine (Gordon Carroll, David Giler, Walter Hill)
📼 📼 🖥 @~ ⊙ ⊙ 🎧
Ripley crash-lands on a mining planet inhabited by convicts and discovers that she has brought an alien with her.
Grim, grey sequel that struggles, and fails, to add something new to the now familiar story.
w David Giler, Walter Hill, Larry Ferguson *story* Vincent Ward d David Fincher ph Alex Thomson m Elliot Goldenthal pd Norman Reynolds ed Terry Rawlings sp George Gibbs, Richard Edlund
☆ Sigourney Weaver, Charles S. Dutton, Charles Dance, Paul McGann, Brian Glover, Ralph Brown, Danny Webb, Christopher John Fields, Lance Henriksen
'A muddled effort offering little more than visual splendor to recommend it.' – *Variety*
'In space, no one can hear you snore.' – *Andy Klein, Los Angeles Reader*
🎵 visual effects

The Alienator

US   1989   92m   colour
Amazing/American Independent/Majestic (Jeffrey C. Hogue)
📼 🖥 @~
An alien outlaw escapes to Earth, pursued by an indestructible android.
Any resemblance to Predator and The Terminator is presumably deliberate, and merely points up the general ineptitude on display.
w Paul Garson d Fred Olen Ray ph Gary Graver m Chuck Cirino ad Lindah Lauderbaugh ed Chris Roth
☆ Jan-Michael Vincent, John Phillip Law, Ross Hagen, Dyana Ortelli, Dawn Wildsmith, P. J. Soles, Jesse Dabson

Aliens *

US   1986   137m   DeLuxe
TCF/Brandywine (Gale Anne Hurd)
📼 📼 🖥 @~ ⊙ ⊙ 🎧
The sole survivor of the space team in *Alien* goes back with another team to the mystery planet, and finds more monsters.
Frightening but mechanical sequel with none of the half-assed poetry of the original.
w James Cameron, Walter Hill, David Giler d James Cameron ph Adrian Biddle m James Horner pd Peter Lamont ed Ray Lovejoy
☆ Sigourney Weaver, Carrie Henn, Michael Biehn, Paul Reiser
'Audiences will be riveted to their seats with drooling dread in anticipation of the next horrifying attack.' – *Variety*
'I'm giving the movie a high rating for its skill and professionalism, and because it does the job it says it will do. I am also advising you not to eat before you see it.' – *Roger Ebert*
† A special edition was released on video running for 154m.
👤 special visual effects (Robert Skotak, Stan Winston, John Richardson, Suzanne Benson)
🎵 music; production design; Ray Lovejoy; Sigourney Weaver

Alive

US   1992   127m   Technicolor
UIP/Paramount (Robert Watts, Kathleen Kennedy)
📼 📼 🖥 @~ 🎧
Members of a South American rugby team whose plane crash-lands on an inaccessible mountain-top are forced to eat their dead in order to survive.
Efficient re-telling of a true story, but one that adds little to the sum of human knowledge or happiness.
w John Patrick Shanley *book* Piers Paul Read d Frank Marshall ph Peter James m James Newton Howard pd Norman Reynolds ed Michael Kahn, William Goldenberg
☆ Ethan Hawke, Vincent Spano, Josh Hamilton, Bruce Ramsay, John Haymes Newton, David Kriegel, Kevin Breznahan, Sam Behrens

'Neither the exploitative gross-out teens might be looking for nor quite the rousing adventure it needs to be.' – *Kim Newman, Sight and Sound*
† In 1976 the story was filmed in Mexico by director Rene Cardona as *Survive!* (qv).

Alive and Kicking: see *Indian Summer (1993)*

Alive and Kicking *

GB   1958   94m   bw
ABP (Victor Skutezky)
Three old ladies escape from a home to an Irish island.
Agreeable minor comedy, a showcase for its elderly but vigorous stars.
w Denis Cannan d Cyril Frankel ph Gilbert Taylor m Philip Green
☆ Sybil Thorndike, Kathleen Harrison, Estelle Winwood, Stanley Holloway, Joyce Carey, Eric Pohlmann, Colin Gordon

Alive and Kicking *

GB   1996   99m   Rank Colour
Film Four/Channel 4 (Martin Pope)
An HIV-positive ballet dancer, in a dance troupe whose numbers are dwindling because of AIDS, has problems at work and at home, in his relationship with an older man.
A sometimes witty and engaging movie about loss and love, though its feel-good ending is unconvincing.
w Martin Sherman d Nancy Meckler ph Chris Seager m Peter Salem pd Cecelia Brereton ed Rodney Holland
☆ Jason Flemyng, Anthony Sher, Dorothy Tutin, Anthony Higgins, Bill Nighy, Philip Voss, Diane Parish, Aiden Waters, Natalie Roles
'Both watchable and moving, even if it falls into the by now well-worn category of gay suffering.' – *Derek Malcolm, Guardian*

'The most provocative picture of the year!'
All About Eve ***

US   1950   138m   bw
TCF (Darryl F. Zanuck)
📼 📼 @~
An ageing Broadway star suffers from the hidden menace of a self-effacing but secretly ruthless and ambitious young actress.
A basically unconvincing story with thin characters is transformed into a screenplay scintillating with savage wit and a couple of waspish performances into a movie experience to treasure.
wd Joseph L. Mankiewicz ph Milton Krasner m Alfred Newman ad Lyle Wheeler, George Davis ed Barbara McLean
☆ Bette Davis, George Sanders, Anne Baxter, Celeste Holm, Thelma Ritter, Gary Merrill, Hugh Marlowe, Gregory Ratoff, Marilyn Monroe, Barbara Bates, Walter Hampden
MARGO: 'Fasten your seat belts, it's going to be a bumpy night!'
ADDISON: 'That I should want you at all suddenly strikes me as the height of improbability … you're an improbable person, Eve, but so am I. We have that in common. Also a contempt for humanity, an inability to love or be loved, insatiable ambition – and talent. We deserve each other.'
BIRDIE: 'The bed looks like a dead animal act.'
ADDISON: 'That's all television is, dear – just auditions.'
BIRDIE: 'What a story! Everything but the bloodhounds snappin' at her rear end!'
ADDISON: 'I have lived in the theatre as a Trappist monk lives in his faith. In it I toil not, neither do I spin. I am a critic and a commentator. I am essential to the theatre – as ants to a picnic, as the boll weevil to a cotton field.'
'The wittiest, the most devastating, the most adult and literate motion picture ever made that had anything to do with the New York Stage.' – *Leo Mishkin*
'The dialogue and atmosphere are so peculiarly remote from real life that they have sometimes been mistaken for art.' – *Pauline Kael, 1968*
'Plenty of surface cynicism, but no detachment, no edge and no satire. Boiled down it is a plush backstage drama.' – *Richard Winnington*
'Long, but continuously, wonderfully entertaining in a way I had almost forgotten was possible for films.' – *Richard Mallett, Punch*
'Someone remarked of this witty, exaggerated, cruel and yet wildly funny film that the secret of its success was the extreme bad taste shown throughout by all concerned (though I hope

they didn't mean to include Milton Krasner's tactful camerawork in this.' – *Basil Wright, 1972*
'The picture seemed long – though it was not by today's standards of length – and the crispness of the dialogue was not matched by equally crisp editing.' – *Hollis Alpert, 1962*
† The idea for the film came from a short story, 'The Wisdom of Eve', by Mary Orr.
👤 picture; Joseph L. Mankiewicz (as writer); Joseph L. Mankiewicz (as director); George Sanders
🏆 Milton Krasner; Alfred Newman; Bette Davis; Anne Baxter; Celeste Holm; Thelma Ritter; art direction; editing
🏆 picture

'Ever get the feeling you're being watched?'
All About My Mother ***
Spain/France 1999 101m
Pathé/El Deseo/France2/Via Digital (Agustin Almodovar)
▣ ▤ ◎ ♫
original title: *Todo Sobre Mi Madre*
After the death of her teenage son, an actress and single mother goes in search of the boy's father, a transsexual prostitute.
Drawing on the themes of All About Eve and A Streetcar Named Desire, this is an engrossing melodrama of love and death, the difference between real and imagined emotions, the kindness of strangers and the waywardness of life.
wd Pedro Almodovar ph Affonso Beato m Alberto Iglesias ad Antxon Gomez ed Jose Salcedo
☆ *Cecilia Roth, Eloy Azorin, Marisa Paredes, Penelope Cruz, Candela Pena, Antonia San Juan, Rosa Maria Sarda, Toni Canto*
'Weaves a silky web of emotional truths wrapped up in a shimmering cascade of glossy photography, glamorous close-ups and glorious acting from the cream of Spanish cinema.' – *Alan Jones, Film Review*
👤 foreign film
🏆 Pedro Almodovar (as director); foreign film

All Ashore
US 1952 80m Technicolor
Columbia (Jonie Taps)
Three sailors on shore leave work their passage to Catalina.
Very lightweight musical, no rival for On the Town.
w Blake Edwards, Richard Quine d Richard Quine ph Charles Lawton Jnr m Morris Stoloff, George Duning ly Robert Wells
☆ Mickey Rooney, Dick Haymes, Ray McDonald, Peggy Ryan, Barbara Bates, Jody Lawrance

All at Sea: see *Barnacle Bill*

All Coppers Are...
GB 1972 87m colour
Rank/Peter Rogers (George H. Brown)
A crook and a cop both fancy the same girl.
Pointlessly titled lowlife melodrama with no style whatever; any episode of Z Cars would be vastly preferable.
w Allan Prior d Sidney Hayers
☆ Nicky Henson, Martin Potter, Julia Foster, Ian Hendry

All Creatures Great and Small *
🎬 GB 1974 92m Eastmancolor
EMI/Venedon (David Susskind, Duane Bogie)
▣
The pre-war Yorkshire life of a country vet.
Simple-minded popular entertainment of a long-forgotten kind, oddly sponsored by American TV in the shape of Readers' Digest and the Hallmark Hall of Fame.
w Hugh Whitemore novel James Herriot d Claude Whatham ph Peter Suschitzky m Wilfred Josephs
☆ Anthony Hopkins, Simon Ward, Lisa Harrow, Freddie Jones, Brian Stirner, T. P. McKenna, Brenda Bruce, John Collin
† 1976 sequel: *It Shouldn't Happen to a Vet.*

All Dogs Go to Heaven
🎬 Eire 1989 85m colour
Rank/Sullivan Bluth/Goldcrest/Don Bluth, Gary Goldman, John Pomeroy
▣ ▤ ◎ ♫
A dead dog returns to Earth to seek revenge on the vicious gangster dog who had him killed.

Skilful animation goes to waste in a confused and confusing narrative.
w David N. Weiss d Dan Kuenster, Gary Goldman m Ralph Burns m/ly Charles Strouse, T. J. Kuenster, Al Kasha/Joel Hirschhorn/Michael Lloyd pd Don Bluth, Larry Leker
☆ Featuring the voices of Burt Reynolds, Vic Tayback, Judith Barsi, Dom DeLuise, Loni Anderson, Melba Moore, Charles Nelson Reilly

All Dogs Go to Heaven 2
🎬 US 1996 82m colour
MGM (Paul Sabella, Jonathan Dern, Kelly Ward, Mark Young)
▤
Two dogs are despatched from heaven to rescue Gabriel's trumpet.
Tame sequel, slow-moving, unexciting and unlikely to set any tails wagging.
w Arne Olsen, Kelly Ward, Mark Young d Paul Sabella, Larry Leker m Mark Watters m/ly Barry Mann, Cynthia Weil ad Deane Taylor ed Tony Garber
☆ Featuring the voices of: Ernest Borgnine, Sheena Easton, Bebe Neuwirth, Charlie Sheen, George Hearn, Dom DeLuise, Wallace Shawn, Adam Wylie
'Won't be bow-wowing them at the box-office.' – *Variety*

All Fall Down *
US 1962 111m bw Panavision
MGM (John Houseman)
▤
A young man reveres his ne'er-do-well elder brother but determines to shoot him when he causes a girl's death.
Another gallery of middle American failures, competently portrayed by a writer and actors very practised at this sort of thing.
w William Inge novel James Leo Herlihy d John Frankenheimer ph Lionel Lindon m Alex North
☆ Warren Beatty, Brandon de Wilde, Angela Lansbury, Karl Malden, Eva Marie Saint
'That strange area of nostalgic Americana where the familiar is the Freudian grotesque.' – *New Yorker, 1982*

All for Mary *
GB 1955 82m Eastmancolor
Rank/Paul Soskin
Two rivals for the hand of the pretty daughter of a Swiss hotelier are struck down by chicken pox and cared for by the old nanny of one of them.
Simple-minded farce in which two grown men quail like children before a forceful old lady; on the strength of the latter characterization and a few funny lines the original play was a considerable West End success.
w Peter Blackmore, Paul Soskin play Harold Brooke, Kay Bannerman d Wendy Toye ph Reg Wyer m Robert Farnon
☆ Kathleen Harrison, Nigel Patrick, David Tomlinson, Jill Day, David Hurst, Leo McKern

All Good Citizens: see *All My Good Countrymen*

All Hands on Deck
US 1961 98m DeLuxe Cinemascope
TCF (Oscar Brodney)
Romantic and farcical adventures of sailors on leave.
Tired musical comedy romp with a second team cast.
w Jay Sommars novel Donald R. Morris d Norman Taurog ph Leo Tover m Cyril Mockridge m/ly Jay Livingston, Ray Evans
☆ Pat Boone, Buddy Hackett, Dennis O'Keefe, Barbara Eden, Warren Berlinger, Gale Gordon, Joe E. Ross

All I Desire
US 1953 79m bw
U-I (Ross Hunter)
A woman who had deserted her husband and family for a life on the stage returns for her daughter's graduation and is reconciled.
Resilient star melodrama with all stops out.
w James Gunn, Robert Blees d Douglas Sirk ph Carl Guthrie md Joseph Gershenson
☆ Barbara Stanwyck, Richard Carlson, Lyle Bettger, Maureen O'Sullivan, Richard Long, Lori Nelson

'How Far Would You Go To Make A Wish Come True?'
All I Want For Christmas
US 1991 92m Technicolor
Paramount (Marykay Powell)
▣ ▤ ◎. ◎
The Christmas wish of two children is that their divorced parents should get together again.
Dim comedy that even the season of good-will cannot make palatable.
w Thom Eberhardt, Richard Kramer d Robert Lieberman ph Robbie Greenberg m Bruce Broughton pd Herman Zimmerman ed Richard Berger, Dean Goodhill
☆ Ethan Randall, Thora Birch, Harley Jane Kozak, Jamey Sheridan, Lillian Brooks, Lauren Bacall

All In
GB 1936 71m bw
Gainsborough
A young man whose rich aunt opposes gambling finds himself the owner of a wrestling arena as well as a racing stable.
w Leslie Arliss, Val Guest play *Tattenham Corner* by Bernard Merivale, Brandon Fleming d Marcel Varnel
☆ Ralph Lynn, Gina Malo, Jack Barty, Claude Dampier, Sydney Fairbrother, Garry Marsh

All in a Night's Work
US 1961 94m Technicolor
Paramount/Hal B. Wallis-Joseph Hazen
▣ ▤
A publishing heir falls for a girl he suspects of having been his uncle's mistress.
Unpolished and not very amusing comedy which falters after an intriguing start.
w Edmund Beloin, Maurice Richlin, Sidney Sheldon d Joseph Anthony ph Joseph LaShelle m André Previn
☆ Shirley MacLaine, Dean Martin, Charles Ruggles, Cliff Robertson, Norma Crane, Gale Gordon, Jerome Cowan, Jack Weston
'Tame and aimless sex-and-big-business comedy.' – *MFB*

All Men Are Enemies
US 1934 78m bw
Rocket/Fox
Sweethearts parted by the war are reunited at last, despite another woman.
Tedious romantic drama which failed to make a Hollywood star of its British lead.
w Samuel Hoffenstein, Lenore Coffee novel Richard Aldington d George Fitzmaurice
☆ Hugh Williams, Helen Twelvetrees, Mona Barrie, Herbert Mundin, Henry Stephenson, Walter Byron, Una O'Connor, Halliwell Hobbes

'She Longed To Be Remembered ... By A Man Who Wanted To Forget'
All Men Are Mortal
GB/Netherlands/France 1995 90m colour
Warner/Nova/Sigma/Rio (Rudolph Wichmann, Matthias Van Heijningen)
▣
A successful actress ambitious for immortality begins an affair with a 700-year-old prince who cannot die.
A depressingly dull fantasy, with a cast that appears understandably unhappy and lost amid the trappings of existentialist Paris.
w Olwen Wymark, Ate de Jong, Stephen Gaydos novel Simone de Beauvoir d Ate de Jong ph Bruno de Keyzer m Michael Gibbs, Simon Fisher Turner pd Ben van Os ed Nicolas Gaster
☆ Stephen Rea, Irène Jacob, Marianne Sägebrecht, Colin Salmon, Derek de Lint, John Nettles, Maggie O'Neill, Chiara Mastroianni
'It has, and unerringly combines, all the ingredients for disaster.' – *Sheila Johnston, Independent*

All Mine To Give *
US 1956 102m Technicolor RKOscope
RKO (Sam Wiesenthal)
GB title: *The Day They Gave Babies Away*
In 1856, a pioneer couple in Wisconsin train their children to carry on the family after their own deaths.
Weird sentimental sob story, even odder under its English title. Surprisingly, some of it works quite well.

w Dale and Katherine Eunson (apparently about their own ancestors) d Allen Reisner ph William Skall m Max Steiner
☆ Glynis Johns, Cameron Mitchell, Patty McCormack, Rex Thompson, Ernest Truex, Hope Emerson, Alan Hale
'A strong mood of folksy western reminiscence.' – *MFB*

All My Good Countrymen **
Czechoslovakia 1968 126m colour
Filmove Studio Barrandov (Jaroslav Jilovec)
original title: *Všichni Dobří Rodáci*
aka: *All Good Citizens*
Life and death among seven friends following the turmoil following the Second World War and the rise of the Communist party.
Lyrical and moving account of political expediency and corruption and the human sacrifice it entails. Awarded the best director prize at the Cannes Film Festival in 1969, it was then banned by the Czech government and its director went into exile.
wd Vojtěch Jasný ph Jaroslav Kučera m Svatoplick Havelka ed Oldřich Mach
☆ Vlastimil Brodský, Radoslav Brzobohatý, Vladimir Mensik, Waldemar Matuška, Drahomira Hofmanová, Pavel Pavlovský

All My Sons *
US 1948 94m bw
U-I (Chester Erskine)
A young man establishes that his father sold defective airplanes during the war.
Heady family melodrama from a taut and topical stage play. The film is well-meaning but artificial and unconvincing.
w Chester Erskine play Arthur Miller d Irving Reis ph Russell Metty m Leith Stevens
☆ Edward G. Robinson, Burt Lancaster, Mady Christians, Howard Duff

All Neat in Black Stockings
GB 1969 99m Eastmancolor
Anglo Amalgamated/Miton (Leon Clore)
Sex adventures of an amorous window cleaner.
Modish comedy drama with surface entertainment of a sort, but no depth.
w Jane Gaskell, Hugh Whitemore d Christopher Morahan ph Larry Pizer m Robert Cornford
☆ Victor Henry, Susan George, Jack Shepherd, Anna Cropper, Clare Kelly, Terence de Marney

All Night *
US 1918 57m bw silent
Bluebird Films
A bright young entrepreneur throws a dinner for would-be investors.
Theatrical farce, with most characters pretending to be what they're not, this must have worked better on the stage but by all accounts did pretty well on film.
w Fred Myton d Paul Powell
☆ Rudolph Valentino, Carmel Myers, Charles Dorian, Mary Warren

All Night Long *
GB 1961 95m bw
Rank/Bob Roberts (Michael Relph, Basil Dearden)
Because of rumour set about by a jealous rival, a jazz trumpeter at an all-night party tries to strangle his wife.
Cheeky updating of Othello with jazz accompaniment, played a shade too grimly by an excellent cast. An interesting misfire. The soundtrack features jazz musicians Dave Brubeck, Tubby Hayes and John Dankworth.
w Nel King, Peter Achilles d Basil Dearden ph Ted Scaife m Philip Green
☆ Patrick McGoohan, Richard Attenborough, Keith Michell, Betsy Blair, Marti Stevens, Paul Harris, Bernard Braden

All Night Long
US 1981 87m Technicolor
Universal (Leonard Goldberg, Jerry Weintraub)
▣
The wife of the night manager of a supermarket has a hyperactive sex life.
Curiously misjudged and outdated farce which offers very few laughs.
w W. D. Richter d Jean-Claude Tramont ph Philip Lathrop m Ira Newborn, Richard Hazard pd Peter Jamison
☆ Barbra Streisand, Gene Hackman, Diane Ladd, Dennis Quaid, Kevin Dobson, William Daniels, Ann Doran

---

'Neither screenplay nor direction seem very clear what they're trying to say, and large chunks of it make no sense at all.' – *Daily Mail*

'There are two kinds of women, but only one kind of love!'

All of Me
US   1934   70m   bw
Paramount (Louis Lighton)
An engineering professor on his way to Boulder Dam finds his life affected by the problems of a criminal.
Confused and uninteresting romantic melodrama with a good cast all at sea.
w Sidney Buchman, Thomas Mitchell *play Chrysalis* by Rose Porter *d* James Flood *ph* Victor Milner *m/ly* Ralph Rainger, Leo Robin
☆ Fredric March, Miriam Hopkins, George Raft, Helen Mack, Nella Walker, William Collier Jnr, Gilbert Emery, Blanche Friderici, Edgar Kennedy
'The most startling glorification of criminals that even the movies have ever dared.' – *New York Sun*
'The gags aren't thought out visually in terms of the L.A. locations, and the film has the bland ugliness of sitcoms.' – *Pauline Kael, New Yorker*

All of Me
US   1984   91m   Technicolor
Thorn-EMI/Kings Road/Universal (Stephen Friedman)
A guru accidentally transfers a woman's soul after death into her lawyer's body.
Curiously vulgar sitcom with a familiar team trying and failing to go one better on The Man With Two Brains.
w Phil Alden Robinson *novel Me Two* by Ed Davis *d* Carl Reiner *ph* Richard H. Kline *m* Patrick Williams *pd* Edward Carfagno *ed* Bud Molin
☆ Steve Martin, Lily Tomlin, Victoria Tennant, Madolyn Smith, Dana Elcar

All Over Me
US   1997   90m   colour
Medusa/Slam/Baldini (Dolly Hall)
Two teenage girls begin to explore their sexuality and their emergence into an adult world of confusion and violence.
A drab little adolescent drama, one of those movies that keeps nudging its audience in the ribs to emphasize its own sensitivity.
w Sylvia Sichel *d* Alex Sichel *ph* Joe DeSalvo *m* Miki Navazio *pd* Amy Beth Silver *ed* Sabine Hoffman
☆ Alison Folland, Tara Subkoff, Cole Hauser, Wilson Cruz, Ann Dowd
'This gritty drama is so rich in ideas that it goes beyond being a coming-out or even a lesbian-themed story ... a gem. It is rare for an American film to portray with such delicacy, subtlety and candor the complex processes of coming of age.' – *Emanuel Levy, Variety*

All Over the Town *
GB   1949   88m   bw
Rank/Wessex (Ian Dalrymple)
Two reporters revivify a West of England local newspaper, and expose local corruption.
Fresh, agreeable romantic comedy on sub-Ealing lines.
w Derek Twist and others *d* Derek Twist *ph* C. Pennington-Richards *m* Temple Abady
☆ Norman Wooland, Sarah Churchill, Fabia Drake, Cyril Cusack, James Hayter

All Over Town
US   1937   62m   bw
Republic
A pair of vaudevillians with a trained seal save a theatre on the skids.
Routine knockabout comedy.
w Jack Townley, Jerome Chodorov *d* James Horne
☆ Ole Olsen, Chic Johnson, Mary Howard, Harry Stockwell, Chic Johnson, Mary Howard, Harry Stockwell, James Finlayson, Franklin Pangborn

All Quiet on the Western Front ****
US   1930   130m   bw
Universal (Carl Laemmle Jnr)
In 1914, a group of German teenagers volunteer for action on the Western Front, but they become disillusioned, and none of them survives.

A landmark of American cinema and Universal's biggest and most serious undertaking until the sixties, this highly emotive war film with its occasional outbursts of bravura direction fixed in millions of minds the popular image of what it was like in the trenches, even more so than Journey's End which had shown the Allied viewpoint. Despite dated moments, it retains its overall power and remains a great pacifist work. Milestone's direction is reminiscent of Eisenstein and Lang.
w Lewis Milestone, Maxwell Anderson, Del Andrews, George Abbott *novel* Erich Maria Remarque *d* Lewis Milestone *ph* Arthur Edeson *m* David Broekman
☆ Lew Ayres, Louis Wolheim, Slim Summerville, John Wray, Raymond Griffith, Russell Gleason, Ben Alexander, Beryl Mercer
TJADEN: 'Me and the Kaiser, we are both fighting. The only difference is, the Kaiser isn't here.'
KATCZINSKY: 'At the next war let all the Kaisers, Presidents and Generals and diplomats go into a big field and fight it out first among themselves. That will satisfy us and keep us at home.'
PAUL: 'We live in the trenches out there. We fight. We try not to be killed, but sometimes we are. That's all.'
'A magnificent cinematic equivalent of the book ... to Mr. Milestone goes the credit of effecting the similitude in united and dynamic picture terms. The sound and image mediums blend as one, as a form of artistic expression that only the motion screen can give.' – *National Board of Review*
'Nothing passed up for the niceties; nothing glossed over for the women. Here exhibited is war as it is, butchery. The League of Nations could make no better investment than to buy up the master-print, reproduce it in every language to be shown to every nation every year until the word war is taken out of the dictionaries.' – *Variety*
'A trenchant and imaginative audible picture ... most of the time the audience was held to silence by its realistic scenes.' – *New York Times*
† ZaSu Pitts originally played the role of Mrs Baumer in the film. When preview audiences, used to seeing her in comedies, were confused by her performance, her scenes were reshot with Beryl Mercer in the part.
picture; Lewis Milestone (as director)
& Lewis Milestone, Maxwell Anderson, Del Andrews, George Abbott; Arthur Edeson

'Together again ... surpassing their performances in "Magnificent Obsession"'

All that Heaven Allows
US   1955   89m   Technicolor
U-I (Ross Hunter)
A sad widow falls in love with the gardener at her winter home, and marries him despite local prejudice.
Standard tearjerker in the tradition of Magnificent Obsession, reuniting the same stars, producer and director in the same rich musical and photographic sauce.
w Peg Fenwick *d* Douglas Sirk *ph* Russell Metty *m* Frank Skinner
☆ Jane Wyman, Rock Hudson, Agnes Moorehead, Conrad Nagel, Virginia Grey, Charles Drake
'As laboriously predictable as it is fatuously unreal.' – *MFB*

All That Jazz ***
US   1979   123m   Technicolor
COL/TCF (Robert Alan Aurthur, Daniel Melnick)
A stage musical director pushes himself too hard, and dies of a surfeit of wine, women and work.
Self-indulgent, semi-autobiographical tragi-comic extravaganza complete with heart operations and a recurring angel of death. Flashes of brilliant talent make it a must for Fosse fans.
w Robert Alan Aurthur, Bob Fosse *d* Bob Fosse *ph* Giuseppe Rotunno *m* Ralph Burns *pd* Philip Rosenberg, Tony Walton *ed* Alan Heim
☆ Roy Scheider, Jessica Lange, Ann Reinking, Leland Palmer, Ben Vereen, Cliff Gorman
'Egomaniacal, wonderfully choreographed, often compelling ... more an art item than a broad commercial prospect.' – *Variety*
'An improbable mixture of crass gags, song 'n' dance routines and open heart surgery. Not for the squeamish.' – *Time Out*
'By the end I felt I'd learned more about Fosse than I actually cared to know.' – *Daily Mail*

'High cholesterol hokum. Enjoyable, but probably not good for you.' – *Pauline Kael, New Yorker*
art direction; editing; musical adaptation; costume design (Albert Wolsky)
& picture; Bob Fosse; Roy Scheider; Giuseppe Rotunno; script
cinematography; editing; sound

All that Money Can Buy ****
US   1941   106m   bw
RKO/William Dieterle (Charles L. Glett)
aka: *The Devil and Daniel Webster*
aka: *Daniel and the Devil; Here Is a Man*
A hard-pressed farmer gives in to the Devil's tempting, but is saved from the pit by a famous lawyer's pleading at his 'trial'.
A brilliant Germanic Faust set in 19th-century New Hampshire and using historical figures, alienation effects, comedy asides and the whole cinematic box of tricks which Hollywood had just learned again through Citizen Kane. A magic act in more ways than one.
w Dan Totheroh *story The Devil and Daniel Webster* by Stephen Vincent Benet *d* William Dieterle *ph* Joseph August *m* Bernard Herrmann *ad* Van Nest Polglase *sp* Vernon L. Walker
☆ Walter Huston, James Craig, Anne Shirley, Simone Simon, Edward Arnold, Jane Darwell, Gene Lockhart, John Qualen, H. B. Warner
MR SCRATCH: 'A soul. A soul is nothing. Can you see it, smell it, touch it? No. Think of it – this soul – your soul – a nothing, against seven whole years of good luck! You will have money and all that money can buy.'
'Some of those in the movie industry who saw it restively called it a dog; but some of them cried it was another catapult hurling the cinema up to its glorious destiny.' – *Cecilia Ager*
Bernard Herrmann
& Walter Huston

All the Brothers Were Valiant *
US   1953   94m   Technicolor
MGM (Pandro S. Berman)
Rivalry between brothers on a whaling schooner.
Remake of a silent melodrama with predictable vengefulness and formula heroism, capably but unmemorably portrayed.
w Harry Brown *novel* Ben Ames Williams *d* Richard Thorpe *ph* George Folsey *m* Miklos Rozsa
☆ Stewart Granger, Robert Taylor, Ann Blyth, Betta St John, Keenan Wynn, James Whitmore, Kurt Kasznar, Lewis Stone
& George Folsey

All the Fine Young Cannibals
US   1960   122m   Metrocolor   Cinemascope
MGM/Avon (Pandro S. Berman)
The son of a country clergyman loves the daughter of another clergyman; they both find the realities of life in New York a horrid shock.
The glum joys of sex and dope in the big city are revealed in this boring rather than daring farrago which is not even unintentionally funny.
w Robert Thom *novel The Bixby Girls* by Rosamond Marshall *d* Michael Anderson *ph* William H. Daniels *m* Jeff Alexander
☆ Robert Wagner, Natalie Wood, Pearl Bailey, Susan Kohner, George Hamilton, Jack Mullaney, Onslow Stevens, Anne Seymour

All the King's Horses
US   1935   87m   bw
Paramount
A Hollywood star revisiting his native Langenstein turns out to be a double of the king, and finds himself romancing the queen.
Operetta-style entertainment grafted onto the plot of The Prisoner of Zenda; *by no means unacceptable even now.*
w Frank Tuttle, Frederick Stephani *play* Lawrence Clark, Max Giersberg *d* Frank Tuttle *ch* LeRoy Prinz
☆ Carl Brisson, Mary Ellis, Edward Everett Horton, Eugene Pallette, Katherine de Mille
& LeRoy Prinz

'He thought he had the world by the tail – till it exploded in his face, with a bullet attached!'

All the King's Men ***
US   1949   109m   bw
Columbia (Robert Rossen)
An honest man from a small town is elected mayor and then governor, but power corrupts him absolutely and he ruins his own life and those of his friends before being assassinated.
Archetypal American political melodrama based on the life of southern senator Huey Long. The background is well sketched in and there are excellent performances, but the overall narrative is rather flabby.
w Robert Rossen *novel* Robert Penn Warren *d* Robert Rossen *ph* Burnett Guffey *m* Louis Gruenberg *ad* Sturges Carne *ed* Robert Parrish, Al Clark
☆ Broderick Crawford, John Ireland, Mercedes McCambridge, Joanne Dru, John Derek, Anne Seymour, Shepperd Strudwick
'More conspicuous for scope and worthiness of intention than for inspiration.' – *Gavin Lambert*
'The film is like one of those lifeless digests, designed for people who cannot spare the time to read whole books. Perhaps that accounts for its popularity.' – *Lindsay Anderson*
'A superb pictorialism which perpetually crackles and explodes.' – *Bosley Crowther*
'Realism comes from within as well as without and the core of meaning that might have made this film a step forward from Boomerang does not exist amid all the courageous camera-work.' – *Richard Winnington*
'Broderick Crawford's Willie Stark might just make you feel better about the President you've got ... By no means a great film, but it moves along.' – *Pauline Kael, New Yorker*
picture; Broderick Crawford; Mercedes McCambridge
& Robert Rossen (as writer); Robert Rossen (as director); John Ireland; editing

'Of all God's creatures...man is the cruellest.'

All The Little Animals
GB   1998   111m   Technicolor   'Scope
Entertainment/Recorded Pictures/British Screen, J&M/IofMFC/BBC (Jeremy Thomas)
A brain-damaged adolescent, running away from his unhappy home, is befriended by an eccentric old man who protects wild animals from harm.
An unsatisfactory fable of the superiority of the natural world, yoked to a melodramatic tale of a usurping, wicked stepfather.
w Eski Thomas *novel* Walker Hamilton *d* Jeremy Thomas *ph* Mike Molloy *m* Richard Hartley *pd* Andrew Sanders *ed* John Victor Smith
☆ John Hurt, Christian Bale, Daniel Benzali, James Faulkner, John O'Toole
'Modest in ambition and accomplishment.' – *Variety*

All the Marbles...
US   1981   113m   Metrocolor
MGM/Aldrich Company (William Aldrich)
GB title: *The California Dolls*
Problems of a women's wrestling team in the midwest.
Tasteless and tedious exploitation comedy with just a few flashes of the director's old flair.
w Mel Frohman *d* Robert Aldrich *ph* Joseph Biroc *m* Frank de Vol *pd* Carl Anderson *ed* Irving C. Rosenblum, Richard Lane
☆ Peter Falk, Vicki Frederick, Laurene Landon, Burt Young, Tracy Reed

'The most devastating detective story of the century!'

All the President's Men ****
US   1976   138m   Technicolor
Warner/Wildwood (Robert Redford, Walter Coblenz)
A reconstruction of the discovery of the White House link with the Watergate affair by two young reporters from the *Washington Post*.
An absorbing drama from the headlines which despite its many excellences would have been better with a more audible dialogue track, less murky photography and a clearer introduction of the characters concerned. The acting however is a treat.
w William Goldman *book* Carl Bernstein, Bob Woodward *d* Alan J. Pakula *ph* Gordon Willis *m* David Shire *pd* George Jenkins

☆ *Robert Redford, Dustin Hoffman*, Jason Robards Jnr, Martin Balsam, Hal Holbrook, Jack Warden, Jane Alexander, Meredith Baxter

'It works as a detective thriller (even though everyone knows the ending), as a credible (if occasionally romanticized) primer on the prosaic fundamentals of big league investigative journalism, and best of all, as a chilling tone poem that conveys the texture of the terror in our nation's capital during that long night when an aspiring fascist regime held our democracy under siege.' – *Frank Rich, New York Post*

🏅 William Goldman; Jason Robards Jnr

👤 picture; Alan J. Pakula; Jane Alexander

All the Right Moves

US 1983 91m colour
Fox (Stephen Deutsch)

An ambitious high school football star is helped to get an athletics scholarship.
Rather dislikeable melodrama with specifically American atmosphere.
w Michael Kane d Michael Chapman ph Jan de Bont m David Campbell ad Mary Ann Biddle ed David Garfield
☆ Tom Cruise, Craig T. Nelson, Lea Thompson, Charles Cioffi, Christopher Penn

All the Right Noises *

GB 1969 91m Eastmancolor
(TCF) Trigon (Anthony Hope)
The electrician of a touring company has an affair with a 15-year-old actress, but finally returns to his wife.
Sharp, sensible treatment of a cliché situation, as watchable as a superior television play.
wd Gerry O'Hara ph Gerry Fisher m John Cameron
☆ Tom Bell, Judy Carne, Olivia Hussey, John Standing
'Built on a solid framework of disciplined direction and animated performances.' – *MFB*

All the Vermeers in New York

US 1990 87m TVC Color
Complex Corporation (Henry S. Rosenthal)
A Wall Street trader begins a relationship with a French woman he meets at the Metropolitan Museum of Art.
A desultory, minimalist film that proceeds in a haphazard fashion, picking up and then dropping the threads of the story.
wd Jon Jost ph Jon Jost m Jon A. English ed Jon Jost
☆ Emmanuelle Chaulet, Stephen Lack, Grace Phillips, Laurel Kiefer, Gordon Joseph Weiss, Katherine Bean, Gracie Mansion, Roger Ruffin

'Love is not a thing that grows only in the dark!'
All the Way Home **

US 1963 107m bw
Paramount/Talent Associates (David Susskind)
In 1916 Tennessee, the beloved father of a family is killed in a car crash, and after the trauma wears off, mother helps the children to rebuild their lives.
Tactful, charming though finally depressing slice of small town period Americana, with generally eloquent performances.
w Philip Reisman Jnr play Tad Mosel novel A Death in the Family by James Agee d Alex Segal ph Boris Kaufman m Bernard Green
☆ Robert Preston, Jean Simmons, Aline MacMahon, Pat Hingle, Michael Kearney
'A heart-wrenching blend of nostalgia and sorrow.' – *Judith Crist*
'Terribly earnest, pictorial, and well intentioned. And a terrible mistake.' – *Pauline Kael, New Yorker*

All the Way Up *

GB 1970 97m Technicolor
Granada/EMI (Philip Mackie)
Social-climbing Dad makes his way by treachery and blackmail, but gets his come-uppance when his son takes after him.
Crudely farcical adaptation of a thoughtful comedy of its time; the treatment works in fits and starts but leaves one in no mood for the talkative finale.
w Philip Mackie play Semi Detached by David Turner d James MacTaggart ph Dick Bush m Howard Blake

☆ Warren Mitchell, Pat Heywood, Elaine Taylor, Kenneth Cranham, Vanessa Howard, Richard Briers, Adrienne Posta, Bill Fraser

All the Young Men

US 1960 87m bw
Columbia (Hall Bartlett/Jaguar)

A marine patrol in Korea is commanded by a black man, and racial tensions take precedence over fighting the enemy.
Simple-minded, parsimoniously-budgeted war melodrama.
wd Hall Bartlett ph Daniel Fapp m George Duning
☆ Alan Ladd, Sidney Poitier, Ingemar Johansson, Glenn Corbett, James Darren, Mort Sahl
'Strenuously engaged in exploiting the entertainment values of nostalgia, fear, suspense, hatred and sex.' – *MFB*

All the Youthful Days: see The Boys from Fengkuei

All These Women: see Now About All These Women…

All This and Glamour Too: see Vogues of 1938

All This and Heaven Too **

US 1940 143m bw
Warner (Jack L. Warner, Hal B. Wallis)

A 19th-century French nobleman falls in love with his governess and murders his wife.
Romantic, melodramatic soap opera from a mammoth best seller; well made for those who can stomach it, with excellent acting and production values.
w Casey Robinson novel Rachel Field d Anatole Litvak ph Ernest Haller m Max Steiner
☆ Charles Boyer, Bette Davis, Barbara O'Neil, Virginia Weidler, Jeffrey Lynn, Helen Westley, Henry Daniell, Harry Davenport, Walter Hampden, George Coulouris, Janet Beecher, Montagu Love
'Deserves extended runs and upped admissions … completely shorn of spectacle, but replete with finely drawn characters in absorbingly dramatic situations.' – *Variety*
'Litvak had it all on paper: he planned every move. There is not the spontaneity or flexibility.' – *Bette Davis*
👤 picture; Ernest Haller; Barbara O'Neil

All This and Money Too: see Love is a Ball

All This and World War Two *

US 1977 88m bw/DeLuxe
Fox/Lou Reizner Productions
Wartime newsreels are interwoven with pop songs and clips from feature films.
A messy mélange with obvious items of interest, but totally confusing and uninformative for the young historian.
d Susan Winslow
'Desperately straining to make any kind of sense, it is reduced to making parallels that are either glib or facetious.' – *MFB*

'Killer Bogart takes the Gestapo for a ride!'
All Through the Night *

US 1942 107m bw
Warner (Jerry Wald)

Gangsters help to track down fifth columnists in World War II New York.
Highly entertaining muddle of several styles which somehow works well and allows several favourites to do their thing.
w Leonard Spigelgass, Edwin Gilbert d Vincent Sherman ph Sid Hickox m Adolph Deutsch
☆ Humphrey Bogart, Conrad Veidt, Peter Lorre, Karen Verne, Judith Anderson, Jane Darwell, Frank McHugh, Jackie Gleason, William Demarest, Phil Silvers
'Exciting slaphappy stuff.' – *Kine Weekly*
'The thrills and the jokes have both been sharpened to a pin point.' – *New Statesman*

The All-American

US 1932 73m bw
Universal
GB title: *Sport of a Nation*
A college football star finds his fame of little use to him in the outside world.
Lively drama of its day, but with little permanent interest.
w Frank Wead, Ferdinand Reyher, Richard Schayer, Dale Van Every d Russell Mack
☆ Richard Arlen, Andy Devine, Gloria Stuart, James Gleason, Preston Foster
'A pleaser for all audiences, having more than the football stuff to recommend it.' – *Variety*

The All-American

US 1952 83m bw
U-I (Aaron Rosenberg)
GB title: *The Winning Way*
When his parents are killed on the way to a match, a college football hero rejects sport for the groves of *academe.*
Very modest formula drama.
w D. D. Beauchamp d Jesse Hibbs ph Maury Gertsman m Joseph Gershenson
☆ Tony Curtis, Mamie Van Doren, Lori Nelson, Gregg Palmer, Richard Long, Paul Cavanagh

The All-American Boy

US 1973 118m colour Panavision
Warner
A young boxer has got to the top too fast, and is depressed by the future.
Uninteresting character study.
wd Charles Eastman
☆ Jon Voight, Carol Androsky, Anne Archer

Allan Quatermain and the Lost City of Gold

US 1987 99m colour JDC
Cannon (Menahem Golan, Yoram Globus)
A mysterious old gold piece sends Quatermain looking for his brother, missing in Africa after seeking a lost white race.
Abysmal follow-up to 1985's ghastly King Solomon's Mines.
w Gene Quintano d Gary Nelson ph Alex Phillips, Frederick Elmes m Michael Linn pd Trevor Williams, Leslie Dilley ed Alain Jakubowicz
☆ Richard Chamberlain, Sharon Stone, James Earl Jones, Henry Silva, Robert Donner
'The embarrassing screenplay jettisons Haggard's enduring fantasy and myth-making in favour of a back-of-the-envelope plotline and anachronistic jokes about Cleveland.' – *Daily Variety*

Allegheny Uprising

US 1939 98m bw
RKO (P. J. Wolfson)
GB title: *The First Rebel*
A young frontiersman smashes liquor traffic with the Indians.
Modestly efficient Western with an impressive cast.
w P. J. Wolfson story Neil Swanson d William A. Seiter ph Nicholas Musuraca
☆ John Wayne, Claire Trevor, Brian Donlevy, George Sanders, Wilfrid Lawson, Robert Barrat, Moroni Olsen, Eddie Quillan, Chill Wills
'Long on horsemanship and action, short on romance and suspense.' – *Variety*

Allegro Ma Troppo *

France 1963 16m Eastmancolor
Films Je Vois Tout
One night in Paris viewed through accelerated motion.
An amusing if not original conceit, smartly executed.
m François de Roubaix ed Robert Enrico w/d/ph Paul de Roubaix

Allegro Non Troppo *

Italy 1977 74m colour/bw
Essential/Bruno Bozzetto
A mix of live action and animation to create a modernistic version of *Fantasia*, e.g. Ravel's 'Bolero' is danced by a Coca-Cola bottle.
w Bruno Bozzetto, Guido Manuli, Maurizio Nichetti d Bruno Bozzetto ph Mario Masini m Debussy, Dvorak, Ravel, Sibelius, Vivaldi, Stravinsky md Herbert von Karajan, Hans Stadlmair, Lorin Maazel

☆ Maurizio Nichetti, Nestor Garay, Maurizio Micheli, Maria Luisa Giovanni

Alley of Nightmares: see She Freak

Alligator *

US 1980 91m DeLuxe
Group 1/Alligator Associates (Brandon Chase)

A pet baby alligator is flushed down the toilet and later, grown to enormous size, goes on the rampage.
Jaws-type monster movie made tolerable by occasional flashes of humour but not otherwise remarkable.
w John Sayles d Lewis Teague ph Joseph Mangine m Craig Hundley sp Richard O. Helmer
☆ Robert Forster, Robin Ryker, Michael Gazzo, Dean Jagger, Jack Carter, Henry Silva
'Hair raising, funny, shrewdly scripted and politically telling.' – *Margaret Hinxman, Daily Mail*

Alligator Eyes *

US 1990 101m DuArt
Castle Hill/Laughing Man (John Feldman, Ken Schwenker)

Three friends from New York, driving off on holiday, pick up a beautiful hitchhiker, not realizing that she is blind and has her own sinister agenda.
Intriguing and suspenseful road movie for the most part, though its resolution disappoints.
wd John Feldman ph Todd Crockett m Sheila Silver ed Cynthia Rogers
☆ Annabelle Larsen, Roger Kabler, Mary McLain, Allen McCullough, John Mackay
'As a road movie, this one's unusually well-written, directed and acted.' – *Variety*

Alligator II: The Mutation

US 1991 90m DeLuxe Panavision
Golden Hawk (Brandon Chase)

After an unscrupulous property developer dumps toxic waste in the city sewers, a monstrous man-eating alligator emerges to terrorize the town.
Uninvolving sequel that follows a familiar and predictable pattern and lacks the wit and pace of the original.
w Curt Allen d Jon Hess ph Joseph Mangine m Jack Tillar pd George Costello ed Marshall Harvey, Chris Ellis
☆ Joseph Bologna, Dee Wallace Stone, Richard Lynch, Woody Brown, Holly Gagnier, Bill Dailey, Steve Railsback, Brock Peters

An Alligator Named Daisy

GB 1955 88m Technicolor Vistavision
Rank (Raymond Stross)
A young songwriter finds himself saddled with a pet alligator.
The ultimate in silly animal comedies, this does score a few laughs.
w Jack Davies novel Charles Terrot d J. Lee-Thompson ph Reg Wyer m Stanley Black
☆ Donald Sinden, Diana Dors, Jean Carson, James Robertson Justice, Stanley Holloway, Roland Culver, Margaret Rutherford, Avice Landone, Richard Wattis, Frankie Howerd, Jimmy Edwards, Gilbert Harding
'Apart from a fairly Kafkaesque scene in which Daisy is discovered in an upright piano, the situation is treated with little wit or comic invention.' – *MFB*

'Nerve-Shattering Terror'
'Her Honeymoon Turned Into A Nightmare Of Horror!'
The Alligator People

US 1959 73m bw Cinemascope
TCF (Jerry Wald)
A doctor uses a revolutionary serum which unfortunately turns patients into the alligators from which it was derived.
Moderately inventive 'B' chiller.
w Orville H. Hampton d Roy del Ruth ph Karl Struss m Irving Gertz
☆ George Macready, Frieda Inescort, Beverly Garland, Bruce Bennett, Lon Chaney Jnr

The Allnighter

US 1987 94m CFI color
Universal/Aurora (Tamar Simon Hoffs)

Three girls party during their final days at college.
Unbelievably crass teen pic that is enough to put an entire generation off higher education – or sex, for that matter.
w M. I. Kessler, Tamar Simon Hoffs d Tamar Simon Hoffs ph Joseph Urbanczyk m Charles Bernstein pd Cynthia Sowder ed Dan M. Rich
☆ Susanna Hoffs, Dedee Pfeiffer, Joan Cusack, Michael Ontkean, Pam Grier, James Anthony Shanta, John Terlesky

All's Fair...

US 1989 90m colour
Midwood (John Gordon)

Working for a firm run on macho-military lines, the female executives challenge their bosses to a weekend war game.
Coarse, loud, dispiriting one-joke comedy, in which shouting and over-acting substitute for humour.
w Randee Russell, John Finnegan, Tom Rondinella, William Pace d Rocky Lang ph Peter Lyons Collister m Bill Meyers pd Cynthia Charette ed Maryann Brandon
☆ Sally Kellerman, George Segal, Jane Kaczmarek, Jennifer Edwards, John Kapelos, Lou Ferrigno, Robert Carradine

Almonds and Raisins *

GB 1983 90m bw
Willowgold/Brook Productions and the National Center for Jewish Film
The story of the Yiddish cinema in thirties New York.
Interesting documentary compilation majoring in the work of Edgar G. Ulmer.
w Wolf Mankowitz d Russ Karel

Almost: see Wendy Cracked a Walnut

Almost a Bride: see A Kiss for Corliss

Almost an Angel

US 1990 95m DeLuxe
UIP/Paramount (John Cornell)

A petty crook returns to Earth as a good angel.
Trite comedy with little substance and fewer laughs.
w Paul Hogan d John Cornell ph Russell Boyd m Maurice Jarre pd Henry Bumstead ad Bernie Cutler ed David Stiven
☆ Paul Hogan, Elias Koteas, Linda Kozlowski, Doreen Lang, Robert Sutton, Travis Venable, Douglas Seale, Ruth Warshawsky

Almost Angels

US 1962 93m colour
Buena Vista

A boy joins the Vienna Boys' Choir.
The singing outweighs the story in this overlong but often pleasing filler.
w Vernon Harris story R. A. Stemmle d Steven Previn
☆ Vincent Winter, Peter Weck, Sean Scully, Hans Holt

Almost Married

US 1932 50m bw
TCF

An insane Bolshevik breaks out of hospital when he hears of his wife's bigamous marriage.
Oddly-titled melodrama with flashes of interest, previously filmed by MGM in 1919.
w Wallace Smith novel Devil's Triangle by Andrew Soutar d William Cameron Menzies
☆ Violet Heming, Ralph Bellamy, Alexander Kirkland, Alan Dinehart

An Almost Perfect Affair *

US 1979 93m DeLuxe
Paramount/Terry Carr

A young film producer at the Cannes Festival falls for the wife of an Italian impresario.
Lively detail lifts many scenes of this eccentric romance, but the routine plot is a downer.
w Walter Bernstein, Don Petersen d Michael Ritchie ph Henri Decae m Georges Delerue
☆ Keith Carradine, Monica Vitti, Raf Vallone, Christian de Sica

Almost Summer

US 1978 88m colour
Universal (Rob Cohen)

High-school students hold an election for their new president.
Mercifully short farcical comedy, aimed at a teenage audience.
w Judith Berg, Sandra Berg, Martin Davidson, Marc Reid Rubel d Martin Davidson ph Stevan Larner m Ron Altbach, Charles Lloyd ad William F. Hiney ed Lynzee Klingman
☆ John Friedrich, Bruno Kirby, Lee Purcell, Didi Conn, Thomas Carter, Tim Matheson, Patronia Paley

Almost You

US 1984 96m DuArt
TCF/Wescom (Mark Lipson)

After his wife dislocates her hip, her wealthy and bored husband is attracted to the live-in nurse he hires to look after her.
A tedious romantic comedy that overstates the obvious.
w Mark Horowitz story Adam Brooks d Adam Brooks ph Alexander Gruszynski m Jonathan Elias ad Nora Chavoosian ed Mark Burns
☆ Brooke Adams, Griffin Dunne, Karen Young, Marty Watt, Laura Dean, Josh Mostel, Christine Estabrook, Spalding Gray

Aloha Bobby and Rose

US 1975 89m Metrocolor
Warner/Cine Artists International (Fouad Said)

A Los Angeles motor mechanic becomes unwittingly involved in crime and finds himself fleeing for the Mexican border with a girlfriend.
Warmed-over retread of They Live By Night, not badly done but of no abiding interest.
wd Floyd Mutrux ph William A. Fraker
☆ Paul Le Mat, Dianne Hull, Tim McIntire, Leigh French, Noble Willingham, Robert Carradine
'As accurate a picture of Southern California as I've yet seen.' – Guardian

Aloha Summer

US 1988 97m CFI color
Hanauma Bay (Mike Greco)

An American teenager holidaying in Hawaii learns about racial prejudice, sex and violence.
Typical teen picture, directed with a heavy hand.
w Mike Greco d Tommy Lee Wallace ph Steven Poster m Jesse Frederick, Bennet Salvay ad Donald Harris ed James Coblentz, Jack Hofstra, Jay Cassidy
☆ Chris Makepeace, Yuji Okumoto, Don Michael Paul, Tia Carrere, Sho Kosugi, Lorie Griffin

'Pagan love – in an exotic, exciting tropic paradise!'

Aloma of the South Seas

US 1941 77m Technicolor
Paramount (Monta Bell)

A young Polynesian chieftain returns to quell trouble on his island after being educated in the US.
Hoary goings-on in gory colour, a remake of a silent epic devised to display the star's sarong and the backlot's expensive volcano.
w Frank Butler, Seena Owen, Lillie Hayward d Alfred Santell ph Karl Struss, Wilfrid M. Cline, William Snyder m Victor Young sp Gordon Jennings
☆ Dorothy Lamour, Jon Hall, Lynne Overman, Philip Reed, Katherine de Mille, Fritz Leiber, Dona Drake, Esther Dale
'The mountain has the privilege of belching when it is dissatisfied, which is something no well-bred critic should do.' – C. A. Lejeune
† A silent version in 1926 had starred Gilda Gray. Directed by Maurice Tourneur, it adhered more closely to the original play (by John B. Hymer and Leroy Clemens).
♫ Karl Struss, Wilfrid M. Cline, William Snyder

Alone in the Dark

US 1982 93m Cineffects
New Line/Masada

Maximum-security prisoners in a mental hospital are liberated by a power failure.
Pretentious but incompetent horror flick of the Halloween school with a plot partly borrowed from Spellbound.
wd Jack Sholder

☆ Jack Palance, Donald Pleasence, Martin Landau, Dwight Schultz, Deborah Hedwall

Alone on the Pacific **

Japan 1963 104m Eastmancolor
Cinemascope
Ishihara-Nikkatsu (Akira Nakai)
original title: Taiheiyo Hitoribochi

A young man crosses from Osaka to San Francisco in a small yacht.
Fascinating Robinson-Crusoe-like exercise, with flashbacks to life on dry land.
w Natto Wada, based on the experiences of Kenichi Horie d Kon Ichikawa ph Yoshihiro Yamazaki m Yasushi Akatagawa, Tohru Takemitsu
☆ Yujiro Ishihara, Masayuki Mori, Kinuyo Tanaka, Ruriko Asaoko
'Wonderfully comic moments emerge, but they never overshadow the film's sheer pictorial value.' – Brenda Davies, MFB

Along Came Jones *

US 1945 90m bw
UA/Cinema Artists Corporation (Gary Cooper)

Two cowboys are mistaken for killers.
Very mild Western comedy melodrama, with the star at his most self-effacing and production only mediocre.
w Nunnally Johnson novel Alan le May d Stuart Heisler ph Milton Krasner m Charles Maxwell, Arthur Lange, Hugo Friedhofer
☆ Gary Cooper, Loretta Young, William Demarest, Dan Duryea, Russell Simpson

Along Came Sally: see Aunt Sally

Along the Great Divide

US 1950 88m bw
Warner (Anthony Veiller)

A marshal prevents an old man from being hanged for murder, and eventually discovers the real culprit.
Adequate, modest Western with an unusual detective element.
w Walter Doniger, Lewis Meltzer d Raoul Walsh ph Sid Hickox m David Buttolph
☆ Kirk Douglas, Virginia Mayo, Walter Brennan, John Agar, Ray Teal

Along the Rio Grande

US 1941 64m bw
RKO (Bert Gilroy)

A cowboy and his two friends claim to be bank robbers to bring to justice a cattle rustler and outlaw.
Cheerful but unexceptional Western.
w Arthur V. Jones, Morton Grant story Stuart Anthony d Edward Killy ph Frank Redman m Paul Sawtell ad Van Nest Polglase ed Frederic Knudtson
☆ Tim Holt, Ray Whitley, Betty Jane Rhodes, Emmett Lynn, Robert Fiske, Hal Taliaferro

Alphabet City

US 1984 85m colour
Atlantic (Andrew Braunsberg)

A New York drug dealer decides it is time to go straight, providing he can pay his debts and stay alive.
Introspective, atmospheric low-life drama that is short on action.
w Amos Poe, Gregory Heller d Amos Poe ph Oliver Wood m Nile Rogers ad Stephen Lineweaver ed Grahame Weinbren
☆ Vincent Spano, Michael Winslow, Kate Vernon, Jami Gertz, Zohra Lampert, Raymond Serra, Kenny Marino

The Alphabet Murders

GB 1965 90m bw
MGM (Ben Arbeid)

Hercule Poirot solves a series of murders by an apparent lunatic choosing his victims in alphabetical order.
Ruination of a classic whodunnit novel, misguided both in its attempt to mix slapstick with detection and in its terrible central performance.
w David Pursall, Jack Seddon novel The ABC Murders by Agatha Christie d Frank Tashlin ph Desmond Dickinson m Ron Goodwin

☆ Tony Randall, Robert Morley, Anita Ekberg, Maurice Denham, Guy Rolfe, James Villiers, Clive Morton

Alphaville *

France/Italy 1965 98m bw
Chaumiane/Filmstudio (André Michelin)

A special agent travels across space to find out what happened to his predecessor, and finds himself in a loveless society.
A rather chill futuristic fantasy on the lines of 1984 but with an outer space background and a hero borrowed from Peter Cheyney. Interesting but not endearing.
wd Jean-Luc Godard ph Raoul Coutard m Paul Misraki
☆ Eddie Constantine, Anna Karina, Akim Tamiroff, Howard Vernon, Laszlo Szabo
'One surrenders to an experience which is the more disturbing for being so near the recognisable normal.' – Dilys Powell

Alpine Fire **

Switzerland 1985 117m colour
Electric/SRG/WDR/Rex/Bernard Lang
original title: Höhenfeuer

A sister and her deaf-mute brother, isolated on an Alpine farm, embark on an incestuous relationship.
Unsensational and austere, it creates an atmosphere all its own.
wd Fredi M. Murer novel Fredi M. Murer ph Pio Corradi m Mario Beretta ed Helena Gerber
☆ Thomas Nock, Johanna Lier, Dorothea Moritz, Rolf Illig, Tilli Breidenbach, Joerg Odermatt

älskande Par: see Loving Couples

Altered States *

US 1980 102m Technicolor
Warner/Howard Gottfried, Daniel Melnick

A psychophysiologist uses a sensory deprivation tank to hallucinate himself back into primitive states of human evolution, in which guise he emerges to kill...
Amusing elaboration of Jekyll and Hyde, not to mention the Karloff mad doctor second features of the forties. All very po-faced now, and certainly impeccably done.
w Sidney Aaron (Paddy Chayefsky) novel Paddy Chayefsky d Ken Russell ph Jordan Cronenweth m John Corigliano pd Richard McDonald
☆ William Hurt, Blair Brown, Bob Balaban, Charles Haid
'Russell clomps from one scene to the next, the psychedelic visions come at you like choppy slide shows, and the picture has a dismal, tired, humanistic ending.' – Pauline Kael, New Yorker
'A feast for special effects lovers and drugged philosophy majors only.' – Roger Ebert
♪ John Corigliano

'A herd of cattle against a herd of cannon!'

Alvarez Kelly

US 1966 116m Technicolor Panavision
Columbia/Ray David (Sol C. Siegel)

The owner of a herd of 2500 cattle finds himself between two sides in the American Civil War.
Unusual if rather tepid Western which balances historical interest against social conscience and throws in a variety of other elements.
w Franklin Coen d Edward Dmytryk ph Joseph MacDonald m John Green
☆ William Holden, Richard Widmark, Janice Rule, Patrick O'Neal, Victoria Shaw, Roger C. Carmel, Richard Rust
'One of the soppiest and sloppiest of Civil War cow-operas to have come our way in years.' – Judith Crist

Alvin Purple

Australia 1973 97m colour
Hexagon (Tim Burstall)

A young man who finds himself irresistible to women finally lands a job ... as gardener in a convent.
Dismal sex farce which nevertheless helped to start the present world-wide popularity of Australian cinema. It took over a million dollars at the Australian box-office.
w Alan Hopgood d Tim Burstall
☆ Graeme Blundell, Abigail, Lynette Curran, Christine Amor, Dina Mann
† A sequel Alvin Rides Again (qv) followed.

Alvin Rides Again

Australia 1974 89m colour
Hexagon (Tim Burstall)
Alvin continues to be irresistible to women.
Dire sequel to dim comedy, but one that failed to find an appreciative audience.
w Alan Hopgood d David Bilcock, Robin Copping
☆ Graeme Blundell, Alan Finney, Frank Thring, Chantal Contouri, Abigail

Always *

US 1989 123m DeLuxe
UIP/Amblin/Steven Spielberg, Frank Marshall, Kathleen Kennedy
▣ ▣ ◉ ⊙ ⌒
A dead pilot returns as a ghost to aid a romance between another flyer and his girl-friend.
Sentimental remake of the 1944 movie A Guy Named Joe (qv).
w Jerry Belson, Diane Thomas d Steven Spielberg ph Mikael Salomon m John Williams pd James Bissell ed Michael Kahn
☆ Richard Dreyfuss, Holly Hunter, Brad Johnson, John Goodman, Audrey Hepburn, Roberts Blossom, Keith David, Ed Van Nuys

Always Goodbye

US 1931 62m bw
Fox
A much-jilted girl finally believes she has met Mr Right.
Fairly pointless romantic comedy which must have pleased some people in the early days of talkies.
w Kate MacLaurin d William Cameron Menzies, Kenneth MacKenna
☆ Elissa Landi, Lewis Stone, Paul Cavanagh, John Garrick, Frederick Kerr

Always Goodbye

US 1938 75m bw
TCF (Raymond Griffith)
An unwed mother gives up her baby and later wants it back.
Tired sentimental warhorse, a remake of Gallant Lady (qv).
w Kathryn Scola, Edith Skouras d Sidney Lanfield ph Robert Planck md Louis Silvers
☆ Barbara Stanwyck, Herbert Marshall, Ian Hunter, Cesar Romero, Lynn Bari, Binnie Barnes
'A fair summer attraction ... should do satisfactorily on the strength of its cast.' – *Variety*

Always in My Heart *

US 1942 92m bw
Warner (Walter McEwen, William Jacobs)
A convict returns home to find his daughter a stranger and his wife about to marry again.
Well acted sentimental drama.
w Adele Commandini play Fly Away Home by Dorothy Bennett, Irving White d Jo Graham ph Sid Hickox m Heinz Roemheld
☆ Walter Huston, Kay Francis, Gloria Warren, Frankie Thomas, Sidney Blackmer, Una O'Connor
♫ title song (mErnest Lecuona, ly Kim Gannon)

Always Leave Them Laughing *

US 1949 116m bw
Warner (Jerry Wald)
A vaudeville comedian craves the spotlight at the expense of his private life.
Raucous backstage vehicle, crammed with sentimental and melodramatic cliché but affording tantalizing glimpses of the stage acts of its two stars.
w Jack Rose, Mel Shavelson d Roy del Ruth ph Ernest Haller md Ray Heindorf ly Sammy Cahn
☆ Milton Berle, Bert Lahr, Virginia Mayo, Ruth Roman, Alan Hale, Jerome Cowan

Always Together *

US 1947 78m bw
Warner
Dying millionaire bequeaths his all to a working girl, then recovers and tries to retrieve it.
Oddball comedy about a girl who has film fantasies, killed by dull title.
w Henry and Phoebe Ephron, I. A. L. Diamond d Frederick de Cordova
☆ Joyce Reynolds, Robert Hutton, Cecil Kellaway, Ernest Truex, Errol Flynn (cameo), Humphrey Bogart (cameo)

Ama

GB 1991 100m colour
Artificial Eye/Efiri Tete (Kwesi Owusu, Kwate Nee-Owoo)
A young girl, who learns by means of a computer disk that she is an ancestral messenger of the Asante, is warned that disaster will overtake her brother and father unless they change their plans.
Confused story, overloaded with fantasy, of Africans living unhappily in London.
w Kwesi Owusu d Kwesi Owusu, Kwate Nee-Owoo ph Jonathan Collinson, Roy Cornwall m Kwesi Owusu, Vico Mensah ad Ruhi Chaudry, Nigel Ashby, Keith Khan ed Justin Hrish
☆ Thomas Baptiste, Anima Misa, Roger Griffiths, Nii Oma Hunter, Joy Elias Rilwan, Georgina Ackerman
'The film's nostalgia for the past, like all forms of sentimentality, implies an unwillingness to engage in reality.' – *Sight and Sound*

'The Man ... The Music ... The Madness ... The Murder ... The Motion Picture ... Everything you've heard is true.'

Amadeus ***

US 1984 160m Technicolor Panavision
Saul Zaentz
▣ ▣ ▣ ◉ ⊙ ⊙ ⌒
Dying in 1823, the jealous composer Salieri claims to have murdered Mozart.
A musical legend performed with success and economy on stage now becomes an exciting baroque film, like an opera in high-pitched dialogue. Great to look at, and only the American accents jar the ear.
w Peter Shaffer play Peter Shaffer d Milos Forman ph Miroslav Ondricek md Neville Marriner pd Patrizia Van Brandenstein ed Nena Danevic, Michael Chandler
☆ F. Murray Abraham, Tom Hulce, Elizabeth Berridge, Simon Callow, Roy Dotrice, Christine Ebersole
♟ picture; direction; F. Murray Abraham; adapted screenplay; make-up
♟ Tom Hulce; photography; editing; art direction
▽ Miroslav Ondricek

Amantes: see Lovers

Amanti d'Oltretomba: see Night of the Doomed

Les Amants **

France 1958 88m bw Dyaliscope
Nouvelles Editions (Louis Malle)
▣ ▣
aka: The Lovers
A rich provincial wife has a secret life in Paris, but finds real satisfaction in an affair with a young man.
A passionate romance which had some censorship difficulties at the time, this rather gloomy film never quite whirls one away as it should, and it doesn't have the eye for detail of Brief Encounter.
w Louis Malle, Louise de Vilmorin novel Point de Lendemain by Dominique Vivant d Louis Malle ph Henri Decae m Brahms ad Jacques Saulnier, Bernard Evein ed Léonide Azar
☆ Jeanne Moreau, Alain Cuny, Jean-Marc Bory, Judith Magre

Les Amants de Montparnasse: see The Lovers of Montparnasse

Les Amants de Vérone *

France 1948 110m bw
CICC (Raymond Borderie)
aka: The Lovers of Verona
In modern Venice a film is being made of Romeo and Juliet, and the stand-ins for the stars feel they are re-enacting the old story.
A superbly stylish if rather empty piece, the dazzling detail being much more interesting than the main story.
w André Cayatte, Jacques Prévert d André Cayatte ph Henri Alekan m Joseph Kosma ad Moulaert
☆ Pierre Brasseur, Serge Reggiani, Anouk Aimée, Louis Salou, Marcel Dalio
'Visually exciting, immaculately made.' – *Penelope Houston*

Les Amants du Pont-Neuf

France 1991 125m colour
Artificial Eye/Christian Fechner
▣
aka: Lovers on the Pont-Neuf
An artist, who fears she is going blind, takes to the streets and ends up on the Pont-Neuf, inhabited by an old tramp and a young fire-eating drop-out, with whom she has an affair.
An anti-romantic love story: grim, grey and ultimately boring with its uninteresting characters upstaged by the locations.
wd Leos Carax ph Jean-Yves Escoffier m Benjamin Britten, Johann Strauss and others ad Michael Vandestien ed Nelly Quettier
☆ Juliette Binoche, Denis Lavant, Klaus-Michael Gruber
'Neo-Godardian new wave: lazy in script, crazy in characterisation, wilfully disjunctive but undeniably powerful in performance and visual panache.' – *Ian Johnstone, Sunday Times*
'One of the most visually exhilarating and surprising films of recent years, a true "cinema of attractions" with music, colour, dazzling camerawork, melodramatic coincidences and tour de force performances.' – *Ginette Vincendeau, Sight and Sound*
'One has to admire the audacity, even if the result could be considered mere flim-flam.' – *Derek Malcolm, Guardian*
† The film, originally budgeted at 32 million francs (£3.2 million), became one of the most expensive of French films; its cost soared to between 100–160 million francs (£10–16 million) owing to building an elaborate set recreating the Pont-Neuf and its environs.

Les Amants du Tage: see The Lovers of Lisbon

Amarcord **

Italy/France 1973 123m Technicolor
FC Produzione/PECF (Franco Cristaldi)
▣ ⊙ ⌒
Memories of a small Italian town during the fascist period.
A bizarre, intriguing mixture of fact, fantasy and obscurity, generally pleasing to watch though hardly satisfying. The title means 'I remember'.
w Federico Fellini, Tonino Guerra d Federico Fellini ph Giuseppe Rotunno m Nino Rota ad Danilo Donati
☆ Pupella Maggio, Magali Noel, Armando Brancia, Ciccio Ingrassia
'A rich surface texture and a sense of exuberant melancholia.' – *Michael Billington, Illustrated London News*
'Peaks of invention separated by raucous valleys of low comedy.' – *Sight and Sound*
'Some idea of attitudes within the film business may be conveyed by the fact that this witty, tender, humane, marvellously photographed picture has been booked into a cinema with 132 seats.' – *Benny Green, Punch*
'Hitchcock once said that he wanted to play his audiences like a piano. Fellini requires the entire orchestra.' – *Roger Ebert*
♟ foreign film
♟ script; direction

Amateur **

US/France 1994 105m colour
UGC/Zenith/True Fiction (Ted Hope, Hal Hartley)
▣ ▣ ⌒
A former nun turned pornographer helps an amnesiac crook discover who he really is, a search that involves sex, violence and death.
Enjoyably downbeat thriller that prefers philosophical asides to shoot-outs, though it manages to encompass both.
wd Hal Hartley ph Michael Spiller m Ned Rifle, Jeffrey Taylor pd Steve Rosenzweig ed Steven Hamilton
☆ Isabelle Huppert, Martin Donovan, Elina Lowensohn, Damian Young, Pamela Stewart, David Simmonds, Chuck Montgomery
'He's an acquired taste, but the new film has a warmth, humour and humanity that might please even hostile palates.' – *Sheila Johnston, Independent*

The Amateur

US 1981 111m Technicolor
TCF/Joel B. Michaels, Garth B. Drabinsky
▣ ▣ ⌒
A computer expert goes into action on his own account when his girlfriend is killed in the Munich consulate and the CIA takes no reprisals.
Ho-hum espionage adventure which has its moments but barely got released.
w Robert Littell, Diana Maddox novel Robert Littell d Charles Jarrott ph John Coquillon m Ken Wannberg
☆ John Savage, Christopher Plummer, Marthe Keller, Arthur Hill, Ed Lauter
'Ill constructed and largely implausible, with occasional atmospheric touches.' – *Guardian*

Amateur Daddy

US 1932 71m bw
Fox
A promise to a dying friend leaves a construction engineer with four orphans to look after.
Sentimental drama of the Daddy Longlegs school, with backwoods atmosphere which makes it seem even more dated than it is.
w William Conselman, Doris Malloy and Frank Dolan novel Scotch Valley by Mildred Cram d John Blystone
☆ Warner Baxter, Marian Nixon, Rita LaRoy, William Pawley, David Landau
'Strikes a strong human interest note ... more than often very agreeable entertainment.' – *Variety*

The Amateur Gentleman *

GB 1936 102m bw
Criterion (Marcel Hellman, Douglas Fairbanks Jnr)
A Regency innkeeper's son poses as a travelling pugilist in order to clear his father's name of theft.
Dated but rather fascinating period adventure, quite a lively production of its time.
w Clemence Dane, Edward Knoblock, Sergei Nolbandov novel Jeffrey Farnol d Thornton Freeland ph Gunther Krampf m Richard Addinsell
☆ Douglas Fairbanks Jnr, Elissa Landi, Gordon Harker, Basil Sydney, Hugh Williams, Irene Browne, Margaret Lockwood, Coral Browne, Frank Pettingell, Athole Stewart, Esmé Percy

Amator: see Camera Buff

Amazing Adventure: see The Amazing Quest of Ernest Bliss

The Amazing Captain Nemo

↟↟ US 1978 103m colour
Warner
Underwater explosions in 1978 release Captain Nemo and his submarine from a hundred years of suspended animation; he continues his search for the lost continent of Atlantis while helping US naval intelligence agents deal with a mad scientist.
Moderate adventure story that may keep the young quiet for a time, though it lacks any big thrills.
w Norman Katkov, Preston Wood, Robert C. Dennis, William Keys, Mann Rubin, Robert Bloch, Larry Alexander d Alex March ph Lamar Boren m Richard LaSalle ad Eugene Lourie, Duane Alt ed Bill Brame
☆ José Ferrer, Burgess Meredith, Tom Hallick, Burr Debenning, Lynda Day George, Mel Ferrer, Richard Angarola, Horst Buchholz

'Growing! growing! growing! When will it stop?'

The Amazing Colossal Man *

US 1957 80m bw
AIP/Malibu (Bert I. Gordon)
GB title: The Terror Strikes
A plutonium explosion causes an army colonel to grow at the rate of ten feet a day.
Modest, quite well written sci-fi let down by shaky trick work.
w Bert I. Gordon, Mark Hanna d Bert I. Gordon ph Joe Biroc m Albert Glasser
☆ Glenn Langan, Cathy Downs, William Hudson, James Seay
† Sequel: War of the Colossal Beast (qv).

The Amazing Dobermans

👫 US 1977 96m colour
Golden (David Chudnow)

▤

A con man with five trained dogs helps a treasury agent get the better of a gangster.
So-so doggedly doggy comedy.
w Michael Kraike, William Goldstein, Richard Chapman d Byron Chudnow ph Gregory Sandor m Alan Silvestri ed James Potter
☆ Fred Astaire, James Franciscus, Barbara Eden, Jack Carter, Billy Barty, Parley Baer

The Amazing Dr Clitterhouse **

US 1938 87m bw
Warner (Robert Lord)

A criminologist researcher joins a gangster's mob and becomes addicted to crime.
Amusing, suspenseful, well acted comedy-melodrama.
w John Huston, John Wexley play Barre Lyndon d Anatole Litvak ph Tony Gaudio m Max Steiner
☆ *Edward G. Robinson*, Humphrey Bogart, Claire Trevor, Allen Jenkins, Gale Page, Donald Crisp, Maxie Rosenbloom
'An unquestionable winner ... the picture inculcates a bit of the sherlocking theme and modified romance.' – *Variety*
'The story is ingenious, but Anatole Litvak and his producing-acting crew have so thoroughly kept the larky mood of it while setting up the necessary mood of interest and suspense that it is hard to see where conception leaves off and the shaping of it into motion begins.' – *Otis Ferguson*

The Amazing Dr X

US 1948 78m bw
Eagle-Lion (Ben Stoloff)
GB title: *The Spiritualist*
A widow seeks comfort from a fraudulent medium.
An interesting subject for a thriller is muffed by naïve handling.
w Muriel Roy Bolton, Ian McLellan Hunter story Crane Wilbur d Bernard Vorhaus ph John Alton m Alexander Laszlo
☆ Lynn Bari, Richard Carlson, Turhan Bey, Cathy O'Donnell

Amazing Grace and Chuck

US 1987 115m colour
Tri-Star/Rastar (David Field)
▤ ◕~ ⬢
GB title: *Silent Voice*
On both sides of the Iron Curtain, a weird selection of public personalities stand up in favour of the elimination of nuclear weapons.
Expensive but inept propaganda apparently motivated by Ted Turner.
w David Field d Mike Newell ph Robert Elswit m Elmer Bernstein pd Dena Roth ed Peter Hollywood
☆ Jamie Lee Curtis, Alex English, Gregory Peck, William L. Petersen, Joshua Zuehike
'As amazingly bad as it is audacious.' – *Daily Variety*

The Amazing Mr Beecham: see The Chiltern Hundreds

The Amazing Mr Blunden **

👫 GB 1972 99m Eastmancolor
Hemdale/Hemisphere (Barry Levinson)
▤

In 1918, a widow and her two children meet a kindly gentleman who offers them work in his old mansion. Here they meet two ghost children, discover that he is a ghost too, and travel a hundred years back in time to right a wicked wrong.
Involved ghost story for intellectual children, made generally palatable by oodles of period charm and good acting.
wd Lionel Jeffries story The Ghosts by Antonia Barker m Gerry Fisher m Elmer Bernstein pd Wilfrid Shingleton
☆ Laurence Naismith, Diana Dors, James Villiers, David Lodge, Lynne Frederick, Dorothy Alison, Rosalyn Lander, Marc Granger
'Easy period charm ... fills every crevice.' – *Clyde Jeavons*

The Amazing Mr Forrest: see The Gang's All Here (1939)

The Amazing Mr Williams *

US 1939 86m bw
Columbia (Everett Riskin)
About-to-be-marrieds investigate a murder.
Brisk comedy-thriller on Thin Man lines.
w Dwight Taylor, Sy Bartlett, Richard Maibaum d Alexander Hall ph Arthur Todd md Morris Stoloff
☆ Melvyn Douglas, Joan Blondell, Ruth Donnelly, Clarence Kolb, Ed Brophy, Donald MacBride, Don Beddoe

The Amazing Mrs Holliday

US 1943 98m bw
Universal (Bruce Manning, Frank Shaw)
Torpedoed in mid-Pacific, a missionary's daughter arrives in San Francisco with eight Chinese orphans.
Unusual sentimental vehicle for its star; of no particular interest or merit in itself, but with the usual interludes for song.
w Frank Ryan, John Jacoby d Bruce Manning ph Elwood Bredell m Hans Salter, Frank Skinner md Charles Previn
☆ Deanna Durbin, Edmond O'Brien, Frieda Inescort, Barry Fitzgerald, Arthur Treacher, Harry Davenport, Grant Mitchell
'Timely drama with human interest angles.' – *Variety*
♫ Hans Salter, Frank Skinner

The Amazing Panda Adventure

👫 US 1995 84m Technicolor Panavision
Warner (Lee Rich, John Wilcox, Gary Foster, Dylan Sellers)
▦ ▤ ◕~ ⌂
An American boy and a Chinese girl help save a baby panda and its nature reserve in China.
Inoffensively bland family entertainment that may appeal to those who still take a teddy bear to bed with them.
w Jeff Rothberg, Laurice Elehwany story John Wilcox, Steven Allredge d Christopher Cain ph Jack N. Green m William Ross pd John Willett ed Jack Hofstra sp panda effects: Rick Baker
☆ Stephen Lang, Ryan Slater, Yi Ding, Huang Fei
'Harmless family fare might be deemed politically correct for its concern for endangered species, but whitewashing of Chinese regime will strike adults aware of current events as somewhat bizarre.' – *Variety*

The Amazing Quest of Ernest Bliss

GB 1936 63m bw
UA/Garrett-Klement (Alfred Zeisler)
▦
aka: *The Amazing Adventure*
aka: *Romance and Riches*
A millionaire bets that he can rise to the top from his job as a chauffeur without using his wealth.
Mild comedy that depends on Cary Grant's charm to carry it through.
w John L. Balderston novel E. Phillips Oppenheim d Alfred Zeisler ph Otto Heller ad David Rawnsley ed Merrill White
☆ Cary Grant, Mary Brian, Henry Kendall, Leon M. Lion, Ralph Richardson

Amazon Women on the Moon

US 1987 85m colour
Universal (Robert K. Weiss)
▦ ▤ ⬢ ⬢
A parody of a 1950s low-budget science fiction movie is interrupted by a series of supposedly comic sketches.
While the parody is precise and amusing, the surrounding material, which occupies the majority of the film, is weak and silly.
w Michael Barrie, Jim Mulholland d Joe Dante, Carl Gottlieb, Peter Horton, John Landis, Robert K. Weiss ph Daniel Pearl ed Bert Lovitt, Marshall Harvey, Malcolm Campbell
☆ Rosanna Arquette, Ralph Bellamy, Carrie Fisher, Griffin Dunne, Steve Guttenberg, Michelle Pfeiffer

The Ambassador

US 1984 95m TVC Color
Cannon/Northbrook (Isaac Kol)
▤
An American ambassador to Israel gets in the line of fire with the Arabs; meanwhile his wife is having an affair with a man who is secretly a leader of the PLO.
Aged stars go gloomily through some tasteless paces in this politically unwise pseudo-thriller.
w Max Jack novel 52 Pick Up by Elmore Leonard d J. Lee Thompson ph Avi Karpik, Ofer Yanov, Rami Siman Tov m Dov Seltzer
☆ Robert Mitchum, Ellen Burstyn, Rock Hudson, Fabio Testi, Donald Pleasence
'Not wild enough to be funny.' – *Sight and Sound*
† Not much more than a year later, the original novel was filmed under its own title in its original setting (qv).

Ambassador Bill

US 1931 68m bw
Fox

An Oklahoma cattle man is appointed US ambassador to a foreign country ruled by a regency.
Poorly tailored star vehicle.
w Guy Bolton story Vincent Sheean d Sam Taylor
☆ Will Rogers, Marguerite Churchill, Greta Nissen, Gustav von Seyffertitz, Ray Milland
'Wilting yarn, illogical hoke.' – *Variety*

The Ambassador's Daughter *

US 1956 102m Technicolor Cinemascope
UA/Norman Krasna

An American senator in Paris decides that the presence of US forces in Paris constitutes a moral danger. The ambassador's daughter decides to investigate.
Thin comedy of the old-fashioned type: smart lines and intimate playing not helped by the vast screen.
wd Norman Krasna ph Miche Kelber m Jacques Metehen
☆ Olivia de Havilland, John Forsythe, Edward Arnold, Adolphe Menjou, Myrna Loy, Francis Lederer, Tommy Noonan, Minor Watson
'An experienced cast approach the story's frivolities with poise and style.' – *MFB*

The Ambulance

US 1990 95m DeLuxe Panavision
Epic/Sarlui/Diamant (Moctesuma Esparza, Robert Katz)
▦ ▤ ◕~
Aided by an old reporter, a photographer investigates the disappearance of people from the streets of New York.
Absurd thriller, with rather better acting than it deserves.
wd Larry Cohen ph Jacques Haitkin m Jay Chattaway pd Lester Cohen ed Arnold Lebowitz, Claudia Finkle
☆ Eric Roberts, James Earl Jones, Megan Gallagher, Richard Bright, Janine Turner, Eric Braeden, Red Buttons
'A seamless thriller with top-notch thrills.' – *Empire*

Ambush *

US 1938 62m bw
Paramount
A girl proves her brother innocent and brings gangsters to book.
Brisk second feature with an unexpected writing credit.
w S. J. and Laura Perelman d Kurt Neumann
☆ Gladys Swarthout, Lloyd Nolan, Ernest Truex
'Hard hitting, fast moving and at all times plausible.' – *Variety*

Ambush *

US 1949 89m bw
MGM (Armand Deutsch)
An army scout leads a posse to capture an Indian chief who is holding a white woman hostage.
Good, clean, robust Western, well produced and acted.
w Marguerite Roberts d Sam Wood ph Harold Lipstein m Rudolph Kopp
☆ Robert Taylor, John Hodiak, Arlene Dahl, Don Taylor, Jean Hagen, Leon Ames

'One man against the west!'
Ambush at Tomahawk Gap

US 1953 73m Technicolor
Columbia (Wallace MacDonald)
▤
Four ex-convicts seek hidden loot in a ghost town.
Standard co-feature Western with rather more violence than usual for its date.

w David Lang d Fred F. Sears ph Henry Freulich m Ross Di Maggio
☆ John Hodiak, John Derek, David Brian, Maria Elena Marques, Ray Teal, John Qualen

Ambush Bay

US 1966 109m DeLuxe
UA/Aubrey Schenck
In 1944, nine Marines try to escape from a Japanese-held island.
Routine, lengthy, sub-standard heroics for action addicts.
w Marve Feinberg, Ib Melchior d Ron Winston ph Emanuel Rojas m Richard La Salle
☆ Hugh O'Brian, Mickey Rooney, James Mitchum, Tisa Chang, Harry Lauter

The Ambushers

US 1967 102m Technicolor
Columbia/Meadway/Claude (Irving Allen)
▦ ◕~
An experimental flying disc disappears on a test run, and the trail leads Matt Helm to the Mexican jungle.
The third Matt Helm adventure had such a stupid script that all concerned decided to send it up, unfortunately with too obvious a tendency to smirk at their own bravado.
w Herbert Baker d Henry Levin ph Burnett Guffey, Edward Colman m Hugo Montenegro
☆ Dean Martin, Senta Berger, Janice Rule, Kurt Kasznar, James Gregory, Albert Salmi
'Plot, jokes and gadgets all well below par.' – *MFB*

'Love of tender girlhood! Passionate deeds of heroes! A rushing, leaping drama of charm and excitement!'
America *

US 1924 122m bw silent
(UA)
⬢
Various characters experience the Revolutionary War.
The Birth of a Nation, one war back. Much of interest, but nothing new; Griffith was basically repeating himself.
w John Pell d D. W. Griffith ph Billy Bitzer, Hendrik Sartow, Marcel le Picard, Hal Sintzenich
☆ Neil Hamilton, Carol Dempster, Lionel Barrymore, Erville Alderson
'Here is the romance of one hundred million people, told in heartthrobs!' – *D. W. Griffith*
† As the English were the villains, the film was banned in Britain, but later released under the title *Love and Sacrifice*.

America, America *

US 1963 177m bw
Warner/Athena Enterprises (Elia Kazan)
▦ ◕~
GB title: *The Anatolian Smile*
In 1896 Turkey, a young Greek dreams of emigrating to America, and finally does so.
A massive piece of self-indulgence by a one-man band, fascinating for his family circle but so poorly constructed as to be of very limited interest elsewhere.
wd Elia Kazan ph Haskell Wexler m Manos Hadjidakis
☆ Stathis Giallelis, Frank Wolff, Harry Davis, Elena Karam, Estelle Hemsley, Lou Antonio
'Kazan has failed to film the adventure implicit in his material, and a potentially exciting story has gone to waste.' – *MFB*
'If he sinks his teeth in a scene or a sequence that he enjoys, the audience can just sit around and be damned.' – *Stanley Kauffmann*
'Every episode, almost every shot, has its own beginning, middle and end, and the numberless playlets are cemented together into a strip which after the first two hours threatens to stretch grimly into eternity.' – *Robert Hatch, The Nation*
♫ picture; Elia Kazan (as writer); Elia Kazan (as director)

'...look closer'
American Beauty ****

US 1999 122m Technicolor Panavision
DreamWorks (Bruce Cohen, Dan Jinks)
▦ ▤ ◕~
A dying suburban husband and father reviews his life and the events that led to his murder.
A terrific, biting comedy of a man dealing, in an adolescent way, with a midlife crisis and the aridities of the life he and those around him are living; it manages

---

not only to expose the inanities of a conformist society, but also to suggest an alternative, in the small pleasures that existence affords. There is not a false note in either the acting or the direction.

w Alan Ball & Sam Mendes ph Conrad L. Hall m Thomas Newman pd Naomi Shohan ed Tariq Anwar, Christopher Greenbury

☆ Kevin Spacey, Annette Bening, Thora Birch, Wes Bentley, Mena Suvari, Peter Gallagher, Allison Janney, Scott Bakula, Sam Robards, Chris Cooper
'A film of incredible flair and formal, compositional brilliance.' – *Peter Bradshaw, Guardian*
'An acerbic, darkly comic critique of how social conventions can lead people into false, sterile and emotionally stunted lives.' – *Todd McCarthy, Variety*
'The picture is a con. Can't educated liberals see that it sucks up to them at every plot turn?' – *Pauline Kael*

🏆 picture; Kevin Spacey; Sam Mendes; Alan Ball; Conrad L. Hall
🏆 Annette Bening; Thomas Newman; Tariq Anwar, Christopher Greenbury
🏆 picture; Annette Bening; Kevin Spacey; Conrad L. Hall; Tariq Anwar, Christopher Greenbury; Thomas Newman

The American Beauty: see *La Belle Américaine*

American Blue Note *
US 1989 97m Technicolor
Vested Interests/Fakebook (Ralph Toporoff)
📼 🇺🇸 🔊
aka: *Fakebook*
In the 1960s the leader of a jazz quintet struggles to find an audience for his music.
Gentle, well-observed off-beat film with a sense of humour.
w Gilbert Girion d Ralph Toporoff ph Joey Forsyte m Larry Schanker pd Charles Lagola ed Jack Haigis
☆ Peter MacNicol, Carl Capotorto, Tim Guinee, Bill Christopher-Myers, Jonathan Walker, Charlotte D'Amboise, Trini Alvarado

American Boyfriends
Canada 1989 90m Alpha Cine
Alliance/First Choice/Backseat (Steve Denure)
🇺🇸
Three Canadian girls go across the border to attend a wedding and see California.
Dull sequel to My American Cousin, in which aimless talk and movement substitute for character and action.
wd Sandy Wilson ph Brenton Spencer m Terry Frewer pd Philip Schmidt ed Lara Mazur
☆ Margaret Langrick, John Wildman, Jason Blicker, Lisa Repo-Martell, Michele Bardeaux, Delia Brett

American Buffalo **
US, GB 1996 88m colour
Film Four/Capitol/Samuel Goldwyn/Channel 4/Punch (Gregory Mosher)
📼 🇺🇸 🔊 🔊
A junkshop owner discusses robbing the home of a coin collector with his teenage helper and a petty thief.
A conversation piece that shows its theatrical origins, but survives the transition to the screen thanks to Mamet's demotic dialogue and the expert performances it receives.
w David Mamet play David Mamet d Michael Corrente ph Richard Crudo m Thomas Newman pd Daniel Talpers ed Kate Sanford
☆ Dustin Hoffman, Dennis Franz, Sean Nelson

An American Dream
US 1966 103m Technicolor
Warner (William Conrad)
GB title: *See You in Hell, Darling*
A TV commentator is goaded into murdering his wife, becomes involved with gangsters and, tortured by guilt, allows them to kill him for shielding the girlfriend of one of them.
Ludicrously heavy-handed version of a semi-surrealist book which presumably had something to say about modern America, at least in its author's mind. Nothing comes through but relentless boredom at watching sordid and unlikely events, and sympathy for those involved. Eleanor Parker's one-scene role of screaming bitchery has to be seen to be believed.
w Mann Rubin novel Norman Mailer d Robert Gist ph Sam Leavitt m Johnny Mandel

☆ Stuart Whitman, Janet Leigh, Eleanor Parker, J. D. Cannon, Lloyd Nolan, Barry Sullivan, Murray Hamilton
'An idiotic melodrama laced with the salacious syndromes and little-boy nastiness that are the hall-mark of today's "mature film".' – *Judith Crist*
🎵 song, 'A Time for Love' (mJohnny Mandel, ly Paul Francis Webster)

American Dreamer
US 1984 105m Technicolor
Warner/Rank/CBS (Doug Chapin)
📼
An Ohio housewife writes a novel, wins a trip to Paris, and finds her romantic dreams coming true.
A kind of lower-case reprise of Romancing the Stone, this modest comedy works only in fits and starts.
w Jim Kouf, David Greenwalt story Ann Biderman d Rick Rosenthal ph Giuseppe Rotunno m Lewis Furey pd Brian Eatwell ed Anne Goursaud
☆ JoBeth Williams, Tom Conti, Giancarlo Giannini, Coral Browne, James Staley
'A pleasant throwback to earlier forms of Hollywood farce.' – *Variety*

'The nation-blazing epic of America's westward march!'
American Empire
US 1942 82m bw
Harry Sherman/UA
🇺🇸
GB title: *My Son Alone*
Brothers fall out over management of their Texas ranch.
Reasonable but forgettable semi-Western.
w Ben Grauman Kohn, Gladys Atwater, Robert Bren d William McGann
☆ Richard Dix, Preston Foster, Frances Gifford, Leo Carrillo

American Flyers
US 1985 114m Technicolor
Warner/Gareth Wigan, Paula Weinstein
📼 🇺🇸
Two brothers compete in a gruelling bicycle race.
Ambitious but ineffective drama with too much effort to explore personal dramas instead of getting on with the action.
w Steve Tesich d John Badham ph Don Peterman m Lee Ritenour, Greg Mathieson pd Lawrence G. Paull ed Frank Morriss
☆ Kevin Costner, David Grant, Rae Dawn Chong, Alexandra Paull, Janice Rule
'Overblown production just pumps hot air in too many directions and comes up limp.' – *Variety*

The American Friend *
West Germany 1977 127m colour
Road Movies/WDR/Wim Wenders
📼 🇺🇸
original title: *Der amerikanische Freund*
A Hamburg picture-framer thinks he is dying and is persuaded to become a Mafia hitman.
Strange melodrama which got the ear of the cognoscenti.
w Wim Wenders, Fritz Müller-Scherz novel *Ripley's Game* by Patricia Highsmith d Wim Wenders ph Robby Müller m Jürgen Knieper
☆ Dennis Hopper, Bruno Ganz, Lisa Kreuzer, Gerard Blain, Nicholas Ray, Samuel Fuller

American Friends *
GB 1991 95m Eastmancolor
Virgin/British Screen/Millennium/Mayday/Prominent Features (Patrick Cassavetti, Steve Abbott)
📼 🇺🇸 🔊
In Victorian England, a middle-aged Oxford academic, who is about to be elected president of his college, a post for a bachelor, falls in love with an American woman.
Gentle, quirky tale of romantic and academic intrigue that yields small pleasures.
w Michael Palin, Tristram Powell d Tristram Powell ph Philip Bonham-Carter m Georges Delerue pd Andrew McAlpine ed Dennis McTaggart
☆ Michael Palin, Trini Alvarado, Connie Booth, Bryan Pringle, Fred Pearson, Alfred Molina, Susan Denaker, Robert Eddison
'Not really the stuff of the big screen, but rather a perfectly acceptable, reasonably touching TV drama.' – *Empire*

'He's the highest paid lover in Beverly Hills!'
American Gigolo
US 1980 117m Metrocolor
Paramount/Pierre Associates (Freddie Fields)
A male prostitute finds that a client won't clear him when he is falsely charged with murder.
Thoroughly unattractive wallow on the seamy side of Los Angeles, with none of Midnight Cowboy's compassion.
wd Paul Schrader ph John Bailey m Giorgio Moroder
☆ Richard Gere, Lauren Hutton, Hector Elizondo, Nina Van Pallandt
'A hot subject, cool style and overly contrived plotting don't all mesh.' – *Variety*
'A perverse film devoted to perversity, typical of Schrader's apparently sadistic intent to pillory his audience with every kind of degenerate act he can manufacture.' – *Motion Picture Guide*
† Christopher Reeve allegedly refused one million dollars to play the lead. John Travolta also turned down the role.

American Gothic
GB/Canada 1988 90m colour
Manor Ground/Vidmark (John Quested/Christopher Harrop)
🇺🇸 🔊
A murderous family, living in an old house on an otherwise deserted island, invites some stranded travellers to stay.
Ludicrous, hammily acted horror.
w Burt Wetanson, Michael Vines d John Hough ph Harvey Harrison m Alan Parker pd David Hiscox ed John Victor Smith sp Allen Benjamin
☆ Rod Steiger, Yvonne de Carlo, Sarah Torgov, Michael J. Pollard, Fiona Hutchinson, William Hootkins

'Where were you in '62?'
American Graffiti ***
US 1973 110m Techniscope
Universal/Lucasfilm/Coppola Company (Francis Ford Coppola, Gary Kurtz)
📼 🇺🇸 🔊
In 1962 California, four young men about to leave for college gather for a night's girl-chasing and police-baiting.
Nostalgic comedy recalling many sights and sounds of the previous generation and carefully crystallizing a particular time and place. Successful in itself, it led to many imitations.
wd George Lucas ph Ron Eveslage, Jan D'Alquen m popular songs
☆ Richard Dreyfuss, Ronny Howard, Paul le Mat, Charlie Martin Smith, Cindy Williams, Candy Clark, Mackenzie Phillips
† The film cost 750,000 dollars, and grossed 55 million.
🏆 picture; George Lucas (as writer); George Lucas (as director); Candy Clark

An American Guerilla in the Philippines
US 1950 104m colour
TCF (Lamar Trotti)
aka: *I Shall Return*
A stranded American naval officer forms a guerrilla band to fight the Japanese after the fall of the Philippines.
Muddled war story with a weak script; both its director and star disliked making the movie, and it shows.
w Lamar Trotti novel Ira Wolfert d Fritz Lang ph Harry Jackson m Cyril J. Mockridge md Lionel Newman ad Lyle Wheeler ed Robert Simpson
☆ Tyrone Power, Micheline Presle, Tom Ewell, Bob Patten, Tommy Cook, Juan Torena, Jack Elam, Carleton Young

'Jack Kelson is going straight. And his son's breaking the law to help him.'
American Heart *
US 1992 114m colour
Entertainment/Avenue/World Films (Rosilyn Heller, Jeff Bridges)
📼 🇺🇸 🔊
Out on parole, a former prisoner tries to go straight and also look after his teenage son.
An interesting attempt to deal with the lower reaches of American life in a realistic manner, but one that is only partly successful.
w Peter Silverman story Martin Bell, Mary Ellen Mark, Peter Silverman d Martin Bell ph James R.

Bagdonas m James Newton Howard pd Joel Schiller ed Nancy Baker
☆ Jeff Bridges, Edward Furlong, Lucinda Jenney, Don Harvey, Tracey Tyla Kapisky, John Boylan
'Has plenty of passion and commitment but is rather too straightforward and disappointingly resolved to qualify as a total success.' – *Variety*
'The film tries now and then to be upbeat in the familiar American manner but doesn't press it and is rarely sentimental. Bell goes for the jugular when he can.' – *Derek Malcolm, Guardian*

American History X *
US 1998 118m DeLuxe
Entertainment/New Line (John Morrissey)
📼 🇺🇸 🔊 🔊 🔊 🔊
The leader of a neo-Nazi gang undergoes a reform in prison.
Tense melodrama of racism that looks a great deal better than it sounds; along the way, though, it invests its skinhead thugs with a kind of glamour.
w David McKenna d Tony Kaye ph Tony Kaye m Anne Dudley pd Jon Gary Steele ed Jerry Greenberg, Alan Heim
☆ Edward Norton, Edward Furlong, Fairuza Balk, Stacy Keach, Elliott Gould, Avery Brooks, Beverly D'Angelo, Paul Le Mat
'Norton's performance lets the film retain its primal power. But it doesn't redeem the overall concern such a film must cause us. You don't construct an anti-Nazi polemic that gratifies an audience's taste for brutality, nor end it so nihilistically that resistance to fascism seems futile.' – *Alexander Walker, London Evening Standard*
† Tony Kaye disowned the released version of his film. At the Berlin Film Festival in 1999, he issued a statement which said, in part: 'My vision of the film never made it to the screen. Edward Norton was permitted by the producers to edit and alter the film, which he did by increasing his role while decreasing the integrity of the film. The producers denied me the opportunity to present a black voice to provide depth and balance to the film. They denied me the opportunity to let a thousand voices be heard, if need be, so that a person watching the film might make an intelligent and informed decision about the compelling questions of our time.' Norton later commented, 'Let's not make any mistake: Tony Kaye is a victim of his own spiritual and creative immaturity.'
🏆 Edward Norton

American Hot Wax
US 1978 91m Metrocolor
Paramount (Art Linson)
The early days of rock and roll as seen by a prominent disc jockey of the time.
Mildly entertaining ragbag of semi-historical facts and authentic music, strictly for the youth market.
w John Kaye, Art Linson d Floyd Mutrux ph William A. Fraker md Kenny Vance
☆ Tim McIntire, Fran Drescher, Jay Leno, Laraine Newman, Chuck Berry, Jerry Lee Lewis, Screamin' Jay Hawkins

An American in Paris ****
US 1951 113m Technicolor
MGM (Arthur Freed)
📼 🇺🇸 🔊 🔊
A carefree young artist scorns a rich woman's patronage and wins the love of a gamine.
Altogether delightful musical holiday, one of the highspots of the Hollywood genre, with infectious enthusiasm and an unexpected sense of the Paris that was.
w Alan Jay Lerner d Vincente Minnelli ph Al Gilks, John Alton m George Gershwin ch Gene Kelly ad Cedric Gibbons, Preston Ames ed Adrienne Fazan ly Ira Gershwin
☆ Gene Kelly, Oscar Levant, Nina Foch, Leslie Caron, Georges Guetary
'Too fancy and overblown, but the principal performers are in fine form and the Gershwin music keeps everything good-spirited.' – *New Yorker, 1977*
† Chevalier was originally paged for the Georges Guetary role, but turned it down because he lost the girl. The production cost $2,723,903, of which $542,000 went on the final ballet.
🎵 'I Got Rhythm'; 'Embraceable You'; 'By Strauss'; 'Swonderful'; 'Tra La La'; 'Our Love Is Here to Stay'; 'Stairway to Paradise'; 'Concerto in F' (instrumental); 'An American in Paris' (ballet)

♟ picture; Alan Jay Lerner; Al Gilks, John Alton; musical arrangement (Saul Chaplin, Johnny Green); art direction; costumes (Walter Plunkett, Irene Sharaff)
⚅ Vincente Minnelli; editing

American Madness **
US 1932 80m bw
Columbia
📼 🇺🇸

When a bank failure threatens, hundreds of small savers increase their deposits to save the situation.
Vivid, overstressed topical melodrama with crowd scenes typical of its director's later output.
w Robert Riskin d Frank Capra ph Joseph Walker
☆ Walter Huston, Pat O'Brien, Kay Johnson, Constance Cummings, Gavin Gordon, Berton Churchill

'It's a money picture. That goes both ways. It's about money and banks and spells dough for the box office. It's timely, topical, human, dramatic, punchy and good entertainment at one and the same time.' – *Variety*
'The sequence of the mounting panic and the storming of the bank are effectively staged, but the resolution is the usual Capra/Riskin populist hokum.' – *New Yorker, 1977*

American Me **
US 1992 125m DeLuxe
Y.O.Y. (Sean Daniel, Robert M. Young, Edward James Olmos)
📼 🇺🇸 💿 📀 🎧

A young Hispanic hoodlum serves an 18-year jail sentence and tries to make sense of his life on his release.
Grim, forceful and engrossing depiction of a savage world, inside and outside prison, where violence, crime and drugs are the shaping influences.
w Floyd Mutrux, Desmond Nakano d Edward James Olmos ph Reynaldo Villalobos m Dennis Lambert, Claude Gaudette pd Joe Aubel ed Arthur R. Coburn, Richard Candib
☆ *Edward James Olmos*, William Forsythe, Pepe Serna, Danny de La Paz, Evelina Fernandez, Cary-Hiroyuki Tagawa, Daniel Villareal, Sal Lopez

'Represents a massive downer by any conventional audience standards, and also runs the risk of attracting the type of crowd that will groove on the violence and ignore the message.' – *Variety*
'True tragedy; there are moments of Shakespearean power as well as graphic violence.' – *John Anderson, Newsday*

American Ninja
US 1986 95m TVC Color
Cannon/Menahem Golan/Yoram Globus
📼 🇺🇸 💿 🎧

GB title: *American Warrior*
Two GIs use extreme violence to thwart gun-runners and other enemies in the Philippines.
Flaccid martial arts movie.
w Paul de Mielche story Avi Kleinberger, Gideon Amir d Sam Firstenberg ph Hanania Baer m Michael Linn pd Adrian H. Gorton ed Andrew Horvitch
☆ Michael Dudikoff, Steve James, Judie Aronson, Guich Koock

American Ninja 2: The Confrontation
US 1987 100m TVC Color
Cannon/Menahem Golan/Yoram Globus
📼 🇺🇸 💿 📀 🎧

Two US Army Rangers are sent to a small Caribbean island to investigate a mystery of disappearing marines.
Non-stop action, leavened with a touch of humour.
w Gary Conway, James Booth d Sam Firstenberg ph George S. Clinton pd Holger Gross ed Michael J. Duthie
☆ Michael Dudikoff, Steve James, Larry Poindexter, Gary Conway, Jeff Weston

American Ninja 3: Blood Hunt
US 1989 93m Rank Colour
Cannon/Breton (Harry Alan Towers)
📼 🇺🇸 💿 🎧

The toughest man in the world takes his revenge after he is infected with a deadly disease by the men who murdered his father.
Dreary action movie, full of ineptly-staged fights.

wd Cedric Sundstrom story Gary Conway ph George Bartels m George S. Clinton pd Ruth Strimling ed Michael J. Duthie
☆ David Bradley, Steve James, Marjoe Gortner, Michele Chan, Yehuda Efroni, Calvin Jung

American Ninja 4: The Annihilation
US 1991 95m colour
Cannon (Christopher Pearce)
📼 🇺🇸 💿

A teacher reverts to his martial arts training to rescue friends taken prisoner by an evil sheikh.
Dim and unexciting sequel, with little sign of life or interest from the participants.
w David Geeves d Cedric Sundstrom ph Joseph Wein m Nicolas Tenbroek pd Ruth Strimling ed Claudio Yrtuc
☆ Michael Dudikoff, David Bradley, James Booth, Dwayne Alexandre, Robin Stille, Ken Gampu

'Low-budget, no-talent programmer … Even the genre's most devoted fans will be disappointed by the lack of imagination and energy in the fight scenes.' – *Variety*

'There is no escape from destiny.'
American Perfekt
US 1997 99m Foto-Kem
Blue Dolphin/Nu Image (Irvin Kershner)
🇺🇸

A serial killer, who leads his life according to the throw of a coin, gets his come-uppance.
The unexpected never happens in this predictable movie of women in peril from a madman; it's best to take a chance and avoid it.
wd Paul Chart ph William Wages m Simon Boswell pd Katherine Vallin ed Michael Russo
☆ Fairuza Balk, Robert Forster, Amanda Plummer, Paul Sorvino, David Thewlis, Geoffrey Lewis, Chris Sarandon, Joanna Gleason

'Within the arthousey road movie formula, it seems, sometimes there is no escape from predictability.' – *Tom Doyle, Empire*

'Have you had that loving filling?'
'There's something about your first piece.'
American Pie *
US 1999 96m DeLuxe
Universal (Warren Zide, Craig Perry, Chris Moore, Chris Weitz)
📼 🇺🇸 💿 🎧

Four high school youths are determined to lose their virginity before they graduate.
The 90s equivalent of Porky's, a gross comedy of crude jokes about adolescent sexuality; its success was due to the fact that it went further than its predecessors.
w Adam Herz d Paul Weitz ph Richard Crudo m David Lawrence pd Paul Peters ed Priscilla Nedd-Friendly
☆ Jason Biggs, Shannon Elizabeth, Alyson Hannigan, Chris Klein, Natasha Lyonne, Thomas Ian Nicholas, Tara Reid, Seann W. Scott, Mena Suvari, Eddie Kaye Thomas, Eugene Levy

'Crude in more ways than one, this cheesy homage to a level of horniness Austin Powers could only imagine will be a dream movie for many a teenage boy.' – *Todd McCarthy*
'Marks a major shift in contemporary teen culture by making the girls as hip to sex as the boys.' – *Owen Gleiberman, Entertainment Weekly*
'The movie industry is dominated by 12-year-olds. I mean, I'm not trying to sound snobbish, but *American Pie*? Sticking your dick in a pie? That's a movie? Come on.' – *Spike Lee*
† It grossed around $102m at the US box office.

The American President *
US 1995 113m Technicolor Panavision
Columbia/Castle Rock/Wildwood (Rob Reiner)
📼 🇺🇸 💿 📀 🎧

A US president who lacks a wife decides to date an attractive lobbyist, with the result that his popularity with his party and the public begins to slide.
This is a clever idea for a romantic comedy, as the most important man in America tries to behave like the boy next door, but it is one that is soon reduced to blandness by a refusal to take risks: playing safe may be good political practice but it does not make for more general hilarity.
w Aaron Sorkin d Rob Reiner ph John Seale m Marc Shaiman pd Lilly Kilvert ed Robert Leighton
☆ Michael Douglas, Annette Bening, Martin Sheen, Michael J. Fox, David Paymer, Samantha Mathis, Richard Dreyfuss

'Genial middlebrow fare that coasts a long way on the charm of its two stars.' – *Todd McCarthy, Variety*
'Its success will be a sign that movie-goers have scaled down their expectations for romantic comedy.' – *Terrence Rafferty, New Yorker*
† Robert Redford was to have starred, but was replaced after a disagreement with Reiner.
⚅ Marc Shaiman

'Killer looks.'
'No introductions necessary.'
American Psycho **
US/Canada 2000 101m DeLuxe Panavision
Entertainment/Lions gate/MUSE (Edward R. Pressman, Chris Hanley, Christian Halsey Solomon)
A successful, promiscuous Wall Street broker fantasises about becoming a serial killer.
A deft, elegant portrait of a self-obsessed, fashionable, design-conscious man descending into psychosis as a result of his obsessions.
w Mary Harron, Guinevere Turner novel Bret Easton Ellis d Mary Harron ph Andrzej Sekula m John Cale pd Gideon Ponte ed Andrew Marcus
☆ Christian Bale, Willem Dafoe, Jared Leto, Reese Witherspoon, Samantha Mathis, Chloe Sevigny, Justin Theroux, Josh Lucas, Guinevere Turner, Matt Ross, Bill Sage, Cara Seymour

'A stylish, disquieting, unexpectedly witty piece of cinema.' – *Peter Bradshaw, Guardian*
'The idea that a culture of rapacious consumerism breeds killers like Bateman is just too facile to take seriously. This is a satire with no roots in reality.' – *Cosmo Landesman, Sunday Times*
† Christian Bale bowed out of the film when Leonardo DiCaprio announced his interest in playing Bateman, and a new director was also sought. Bale and Harron returned when DiCaprio changed his mind.

An American Romance *
US 1944 151m Technicolor
MGM (King Vidor)
The life of a European immigrant who becomes a master of industry.
Mind-boggling pageant of the American dream, coldly presented and totally humourless. Its saving grace is its smooth physical presentation.
w Herbert Dalmas, William Ludwig d King Vidor ph Harold Rosson m Louis Gruenberg
☆ Brian Donlevy, Ann Richards, John Qualen, Walter Abel, Stephen McNally

'A thousand chances to inform, excite or even interest have been flung away.' – *Richard Winnington*
'The whole aim of it is to boost The American Way.' – *Richard Mallett, Punch*

American Samurai
US 1992 87m colour
Cannon/Global (Allan Greenblatt)
📼 🇺🇸

An American journalist investigating a murder using a samurai sword is forced to enter a fight to the death.
Mundane action film, offering little that cannot be found in a dozen similar movies of equal banality.
w John Corcoran d Sam Firstenberg ph David Gurfinkel m Robbie Patton pd Kuly Sander ed Sebastian Serrell-Watts, Shlomo Chazan
☆ David Bradley, Mark Dacascos, Valarie Trapp, Rex Ryon, Melissa Hellman, John Fujioka

'Cheap and trite, this is yet another hymn to the ability of a handsome white guy to beat up ethnic opponents.' – *Empire*

The American Success Company *
US 1980 94m colour
Columbia (Edgar J. Scherick and Daniel H. Blatt)
The inexperienced son of a credit card tycoon becomes a tough guy.
Tilts at the American myth: not a notable success.
w William Richert, Larry Cohen d William Richert
☆ Jeff Bridges, Belinda Bauer, Ned Beatty, Steven Keats, Bianca Jagger

An American Tail *
👪 US 1986 80m DeLuxe
Universal/Steven Spielberg (Don Bluth, John Pomeroy, Gary Goldman)
📼 🇺🇸 💿 🎧

Russian mice encounter all kinds of trouble when in the 1880s they emigrate to the United States.
Expensive cartoon feature with old-fashioned full animation but not much in the way of narrative interest or indeed humour.
w Judy Freudberg, Tony Geiss d Don Bluth (also designer)
☆ voices: Cathianne Blore, Christopher Plummer, Dom DeLuise, Madeline Kahn

'Every character and every situation have been presented a thousand times before … anyone over the age of 12 will likely experience more boredom than pleasure.' – *Variety*
⚅ song, 'Somewhere Out There' (James Horner, Barry Mann, Cynthia Weil)

'Look Out Pardeners, There's A New Mouse In Town!'
An American Tail: Fievel Goes West **
👪 US 1991 75m colour
UIP/Universal/Amblin (Steven Spielberg, Robert Watts)
📼 🇺🇸 💿 🎧

A confidence trickster of a cat persuades a family of mice to move to the West.
Enjoyable and high-spirited animated film that borrows plot and attitudes from classic Westerns.
w Flint Dille story Charles Swenson d Phil Nibbelink, Simon Wells m James Horner
☆ Featuring the voices of Phillip Glasser, James Stewart, Erica Yohn, Cathy Cavadini, Nehemiah Persoff, Dom DeLuise, Amy Irving, John Cleese, Jon Lovitz

'Drama that happens around you every day – when the wild life of impetuous youth burns away age-old barriers!'
An American Tragedy **
US 1931 95m bw
Paramount
An ambitious young man murders his pregnant fiancée when he has a chance to marry a rich girl.
Dated but solidly satisfying adaptation of a weighty novel, more compelling than the 1951 remake A Place in the Sun.
wd Josef von Sternberg novel Theodore Dreiser ph Lee Garmes ad Hans Dreier
☆ Phillips Holmes, Sylvia Sidney, Frances Dee, Irving Pichel, Frederick Burton, Claire McDowell

'It unreels as an ordinary programme effort with an unhappy ending … as Sternberg has seen fit to present it the celluloid structure is slow, heavy and not always interesting drama. Its box office success is very doubtful.' – *Variety*
'It is the first time, I believe, that the subjects of sex, birth control and murder have been put into a picture with sense, taste and reality.' – *Pare Lorentz*
'An aimless, lugubrious mess. The fireworks may dazzle to schoolboys of criticism, but they will add no permanent color to the motion picture.' – *Harry Alan Potamkin*

American Warrior: see *American Ninja*

An American Werewolf in London ***
GB 1981 97m Technicolor
Polygram/Lycanthrope (Peter Guber, Jon Peters)
📼 🇺🇸 💿 🎧

Two American tourists are bitten by a werewolf.
Curious but oddly endearing mixture of horror film and spoof, of comedy and shock, with everything grist to its mill including tourist Britain and the wedding of Prince Charles. The special effects are notable, and signalled new developments in this field.
wd John Landis ph Robert Paynter m Elmer Bernstein sp Effects Associates, Rick Baker
☆ David Naughton, Jenny Agutter, Griffin Dunne, John Woodvine

'The gear changes of tone and pace make for a very jerkily driven vehicle.' – *Sunday Times*
'Seems curiously unfinished, as though Landis spent all his energy on spectacular set-pieces and then didn't want to bother with things like transitions, character development, or an ending.' – *Roger Ebert*

👪 film suitable for family viewing
📼 VHS video-cassette for the British PAL system
🇺🇸 VHS video-cassette for the British PAL system in wide screen-format
💿 Video cassette in a computer-colourised version
🟥 American NTSC video-cassette
📀 Laser disc

'Things Are Going to Get A Little Hairy.'
An American Werewolf in Paris *
US/GB/France/Luxembourg 1997 98m colour
Entertainment/Stonewood/Hollywood/Cometstone/J
&M (Richard Claus)

An American tourist in Paris is seduced and bitten
by a female werewolf.
*A sequel to An American Werewolf in London
which often resembles a remake of the original, though
it lacks that film's engaging mix of horror and black
humour.*
w Tim Burns, Tom Stern, Anthony Waller *based
on characters created by* John Landis d Anthony
Waller ph Egon Werdin m Wilbert Hirsch
pd Matthias Kammermeier ed Peter R. Adam
sp Santa Barbara Studios; Peter Lloyd; Magicon &
Crawley Creatures
☆ Tom Everett Scott, Julie Delpy, Vince Vieluf,
Phil Buckman, Julie Bowen, Pierre Cosso, Tom
Novémbre, Thierry Lhermitte
'Not funny enough, not scary enough, and
deeply in need of a silver bullet.' – *Darren
Bignell, Empire*

American Yakuza
US/Japan 1993 91m Foto-Kem
Overseas Filmgroup/First Look/Ozla/Neo (Michael
Leahy, Aki Komine)

An FBI agent infiltrates Japanese gangsters trying
to muscle in on the Mafia.
*Slick, moderately engaging action film that makes all
the expected and customary moves of the genre.*
w Max Strom, John Allen Nelson *story* Taka
Ichise d Frank Cappello ph Richard Clabaugh
m David C. Williams pd Shay Austin ed Sonny
Baskin
☆ Viggo Mortensen, Ryo Ishibashi, Michael
Nouri, Franklyn Ajaye, Cristina Lawson, Yuji
Okumoto, Robert Forster
'A stylish action-thriller directed with flair.' –
Sight and Sound

American Yakuza 2: Back to Back
US/Japan 1996 87m Foto-Kem
Overseas Filmgroup/Ozla/Neo (W. K. Border, Aki
Komine)

In Los Angeles, a bad-tempered ex-detective with
family problems is forced to help a Japanese
gangster wage war on the Mafia and a corrupt cop.
*Slick, violent, tongue-in-cheek, over-the-top action
movie that takes delight in the excesses of the genre.*
w Roger Nygard, Lloyd Keith d Roger Nygard
ph Mark W. Gray m Walter Werzowa
pd Anthony Stabley ed Roger Nygard
☆ Michael Rooker, Ryo Ishibashi, Danielle Harris,
John Laughlin, Koh Takasugi, Tim Thomerson,
Stephen Furst, Vincent Schiavella, Frank
D'Amico, Bobcat Goldthwait
'A stylishly packaged combo of black humour,
violence and well-staged action.' – *Film Review*

The Americanization of Emily *
US 1964 115m bw
MGM/Filmways (John Calley)

World War II: just before the Normandy landings,
a war widow driver falls for an American
commander who is a self-confessed coward.
*Bizarre comedy full of eccentric characters, an uneasy
choice for its female star but otherwise successful in
patches in its random distillation of black comedy, sex
and the tumbling of old-fashioned virtues.*
w Paddy Chayefsky *novel* William Bradford Huie
d Arthur Hiller ph Philip Lathrop, Chris Challis
m Johnny Mandel
☆ Julie Andrews, James Garner, *Melvyn Douglas*,
James Coburn, Liz Fraser, Joyce Grenfell, Edward
Binns, Keenan Wynn, William Windom
'Out of it all there comes the definite feeling
that Hitler's war is incidental to Paddy
Chayevsky's war of ideas … no plot synopsis
could begin to suggest how much the characters
talk.' – *MFB*
↯ Philip Lathrop

The Americano
US 1916 60m bw silent
Triangle (D. W. Griffith)

A young American engineer becomes involved in
a revolution in Patagonia.
*Early star adventure vehicle, an immense popular
success; the last film Fairbanks made for Griffith.*

w Anita Loos, John Emerson *novel* Blaze
Derringer by Eugene P. Lyle Jnr d John Emerson
ph Victor Fleming
☆ *Douglas Fairbanks*, Alma Rubens, Spottiswoode
Aitken, Lillian Langdon

The Americano
US 1955 85m Technicolor
RKO (Robert Stillman)

A Westerner takes three prize bulls to Brazil, but
finds the buyer has been murdered.
*A Western with a twist, but otherwise extremely dull,
with poor pace, colour and use of settings.*
w Guy Trosper d William Castle ph William
Snyder m Roy Webb
☆ Glenn Ford, Frank Lovejoy, Abbe Lane, Cesar
Romero, Ursula Thiess

L'Amérique des autres: see Someone Else's
America

L'Ami de Mon Amie: see My Girlfriend's
Boyfriend

L'Ami Retrouvé: see Reunion

Un Ami Viendra ce Soir
France 1946 111m bw
CGC (R. Artus)

During World War II a French patriot uses a
lunatic asylum as a resistance headquarters.
Rather glum wartime melodrama, lacking in tension.
w Jacques Companeez, Raymond Bernard
d Raymond Bernard ph Robert Le Fèbvre
m Arthur Honegger
☆ Michel Simon, Louis Salou, Saturnin Fabre,
Paul Bernard, Madeleine Sologne, Marcel André

Le Amiche *
Italy 1955 90m bw
Trionfalcine (Giovanni Addessi)
aka: *The Girl Friends*
The interaction of five girls living together in
Turin.
*Highbrow lending library stuff, quite watchable but
equally forgettable.*
w Suso Cecchi d'Amico, Alba de Cespedes
story Tra Donne Sole by Cesare Pavese
d Michelangelo Antonioni ph Gianni di Venanzo
m Giovanni Fusco
☆ Eleonora Rossi Drago, Valentina Cortese,
Yvonne Furneaux, Gabriele Ferzetti, Franco
Fabrizi, Madeleine Fischer

La Amiga
Argentina/West Germany 1988 108m colour
Journal/Alma/Jorge Estrada Mora (Jorge Estrada,
Klaus Volkenberg)
aka: *The Girlfriend*
Stages in the life of two women in Buenos Aires:
one a Jewish actress, the other a mother who
becomes politically involved after her son is taken
away by security officers and never seen alive
again.
*Involved and somewhat sentimental drama of survival
in a hostile world.*
w Jeanine Meerapfel, Alcides Chiesa d Jeanine
Meerapfel ph Axel Block pd Jorge Marchegiano,
Rainer Schaper ed Juliane Lorenz
☆ Liv Ullmann, Cipe Lincovsky, Federico Luppi,
Victor Laplace, Harry Baer, Lito Cruz, Greger
Hansen, Nicolas Frei

Amistad **
US 1997 152m Technicolor 'Scope
DreamWorks/HBO (Steven Spielberg, Debbie Allen,
Colin Wilson)

African slaves who escape their chains and kill the
crew of a slave ship are tried in America for
murder, while the ship's owners, the salvagers and
the Spanish Queen claim them as their property.
*Earnest and dogged, well meaning but too often
dramatically inert, this tells a true story from a white
viewpoint, in which the slaves remain exotic accessories
to the real conflict, which takes place in courtrooms.*
w David Franzoni d Steven Spielberg ph Janusz
Kaminski m John Williams pd Rick Carter
ed Michael Kahn
☆ Matthew McConaughey, Anthony Hopkins,
Morgan Freeman, Nigel Hawthorne, Djimoun
Hounsou, David Paymer, Pete Postlethwaite,
Stellan Skarsgård, Anna Paquin, Tomas Milian,
Austin Pendleton

'Artistically solid, if not always dramatically
exciting.' – *Variety*
♫ Anthony Hopkins; Janusz Kaminski; John
Williams; Ruth E. Carter (costumes)

Amityville 3: The Demon: see Amityville 3-D

Amityville 3-D
US 1984 93m colour ArriVision 3-D
EMI/Universal/Dino de Laurentiis/Orion (Stephen F.
Kesten)

aka: *Amityville 3: The Demon*
A sceptical journalist moves into the haunted
house but is jolted out of his complacency.
*Ragbag of supernatural incident with neither cohesion
nor plausibility, but good 3-D.*
w William Wales d Richard Fleischer ph Fred
Schuler m Howard Blake ad Giorgio Postiglione,
Justin Scoppa ed Frank J. Urioste
☆ Tony Roberts, Tess Harper, Robert Joy, Candy
Clark, John Beal, Leora Dana
'An assortment of unrelated happenings
precedes the final appearance of a crude bug-
eyed monster.' – *MFB*

Amityville Dollhouse
US 1996 93m colour
Promark/Spectacor/Zeta (Zane W. Levitt, Mark Yellen,
Steve White)

A family move into a new home, which includes a
dollhouse that carries the curse of the Amityville
horror.
*A dull horror movie that begins by locating horrors at
the heart of normal family life, but soon abandons this
promising approach for the usual predictable shocks.*
w Joshua Michael Stern m Steve White ph Tom
Callaway m Ray Colcord pd Jerry Fleming
ed Kert VanderMeulen
☆ Robin Thomas, Starr Andreeff, Clayton
Murray, Lenore Kasdorf, Allen Cutler, Rachel
Duncan, Franc Ross, Lisa Robin Kelly, Jarrett
Lennon

The Amityville Horror
US 1979 118m Movielab
AIP/Cinema 77 (Ronald Saland, Elliot Geisinger)

Newlyweds move into a house where a murder was
committed, and experience strange manifestations
which drive them away.
*Sub-Exorcist goings on, a shameless exaggeration of
some of the alleged facts retailed in the best-selling
book. A shocker for the uncritical.*
w Sandor Stern *book* Jay Anson d Stuart
Rosenberg ph Fred J. Koenekamp m Lalo
Schifrin
☆ James Brolin, Margot Kidder, Rod Steiger, Don
Stroud, Murray Hamilton
♫ Lalo Schifrin

Amityville II: The Possession
US 1982 104m DeLuxe
Dino de Laurentiis/Orion (Ira N. Smith, Stephen R.
Greenwald)

The sequel turns out to be a prequel, dealing with
the events that led to the house at Amityville
becoming haunted.
*Everything but the kitchen sink is thrown into this
ghoulish brew, and most of it is red; but the script is
hopeless from the start.*
w Tommy Lee Wallace *book* Murder in Amityville
by Hans Holzer d Damiano Damiani ph Franco
Di Giacomo m Lalo Schifrin pd Pierluigi Basile
ed Sam O'Steen
☆ Burt Young, Rutanya Alda, James Olson, Jack
Magner, Andrew Prine
'There probably isn't a more unsympathetic
bunch on screen this year. They're sure to make
audiences root for the house.' – *Variety*

Amnesia *
Chile 1994 90m Eastmancolor
Arca/Cine Chile/Fondart

After a civil war, a soldier and a survivor of a
prison camp take revenge on a brutal sergeant.
*A tense and gripping drama concerned with individual
responsibility which also touches on the theme of
national amnesia about atrocities committed on behalf
of the state.*
w Gustavo Frias, Gonzalo Justiniano d Gonzalo
Justiniano ph Hans Burmann m José Miguel

Tobar, Miguel Miranda ad Carlos Garrido
ed Danielle Fillios
☆ Julio Jung, Pedro Vicuña, Nelson Villagra, José
Secall, Marcela Osorio, Carla Cristi
'An offbeat, sometimes nightmarish black
comedy.' – *Variety*

Amok: see Schizo

'Some heights can only be reached by the heart.'
Among Giants *
GB 1998 96m colour
Kudos/British Screen/Capitol/Arts Council/YMPA/BBC

An Australian backpacker becomes the only
female member of a group of climbers who earn
their living painting electricity pylons.
*A working-class romantic tragi-comedy that does not
scale the heights.*
w Simon Beaufoy d Sam Miller ph Witold Stok
m Tim Atack pd Luana Hanson ed Paul Green,
Elen Pierce Lewis
☆ Pete Postlethwaite, Rachel Griffiths, James
Thornton, Rob Jarvis, Andy Serkis, Lennie James,
Alan Williams, Emma Cunniffe
'This small-scale, bittersweet film has many fine
qualities, but it lacks the crucial dramatic spark
that would have made it truly memorable.' –
Stephen Farber, Movieline

Among the Living *
US 1941 68m bw
Paramount (Sol C. Siegel)
In a small town live twin brothers, one of whom is
a murderer.
Offbeat suspenser with effective performances.
w Lester Cole, Garrett Fort d Stuart Heisler
ph Theodor Sparkuhl
☆ Albert Dekker, Susan Hayward, Frances Farmer,
Harry Carey, Gordon Jones
'Head and shoulders above all the filler shows
ground out by Hollywood to perpetuate the
double feature system.' – *Howard Barnes, New
York Herald Tribune*

'Born With Everything They Had To Have More.'
Amongst Friends
US 1993 87m Technicolor
Rank/Last Outlaw/Island World (Matthew Blumberg)

Three boyhood friends from the wealthy middle
class fall out when they try to become gangsters.
*Heavily influenced by Martin Scorsese's Mean
Streets, this lacks any sense of observable reality,
relying instead on fast talking and undistinguished songs
to carry the action, which disintegrates into violence to
compensate for its lack of anything better to show.*
wd Rob Weiss ph Michael Bonvillain m Mick
Jones pd Terrence Foster ed Leo Trombetta
☆ Steve Parlavecchio, Joseph Lindsey, Patrick
McGaw, Mira Sorvino, Chris Santos, Brett
Lambson, Michael Artura, Frank Medrano, Louis
Lombardi
'A truly numbskulled use of violence.' – *Nigel
Andrews, Financial Times*
'The whole structure is a mess and there's a
strong sense of been-here-before about the
project.' – *Derek Malcolm, Guardian*

El Amor Brujo: see A Love Bewitched

L'Amore *
Italy 1948 79m bw
Tevere Film (Roberto Rossellini)
Two short films. *The Human Voice*: a woman talks
on the phone to the man who has forsaken her.
The Miracle: a peasant woman is seduced and is
convinced she will give birth to a new Messiah.
*A tour de force by an actress to be reckoned with; but
hardly compulsive as cinema.*
w Tullio Pinelli, Roberto Rossellini, Federico
Fellini *play* Jean Cocteau d Roberto Rossellini
ph Robert Juillard, Aldo Tonti m Renzo
Rossellini
☆ Anna Magnani, Federico Fellini
† *The Miracle* was separately released in some
countries.

'She searched for the truth but found only lies...'
L'Amore Molesto *
Italy 1995 103m Technicolor
Arrow/Kucky Red/Teatri Uniti (Angelo Curti, Andrea Occhipinti, Kermit Smith)
⬛
aka: *Wounded Love*
A middle-aged comic-book artist investigates her mother's mysterious death.
Complex thriller, structured around flashbacks that may, or may not, be accurate memories of the past; it does not entirely reward the effort required to understand its somewhat sleazy subject matter.
wd Mario Martone *novel* Elena Ferrante *ph* Luca Bigazzi *ad* Giancarlo Muselli *ed* Jacopo Quadri
☆ Anna Bonaiuto, Angela Luce, Gianni Cajafa, Peppe Lanzetta, Licia Maglietta, Anna Calato, Italo Celero
'A moody rather than an event-filled thriller which holds the viewer with its eccentric charm and quite nasty after-taste.' – *Marianne Gray, Film Review*

'The rollicking story of a ribald century that should have been ashamed of itself!'
The Amorous Adventures of Moll Flanders
GB 1965 125m Technicolor Panavision
Paramount/Winchester (Marcel Hellman)
⬛
An ambitious servant girl loses her virtue to a succession of rich gentlemen but finally settles for a highwayman.
The aim was to make a female Tom Jones, but this bawdy romp never achieves the freewheeling fluency of that surprise success, and a vacuous central performance makes the constant couplings more boring than exciting.
w Denis Cannan, Roland Kibbee *novel* Daniel Defoe d Terence Young *ph* Ted Moore m John Addison *pd* Syd Cain
☆ Kim Novak, Richard Johnson, George Sanders, Lilli Palmer, Angela Lansbury, Leo McKern, Vittorio de Sica, Cecil Parker, Daniel Massey
'Further from Defoe than *Tom Jones* was from Fielding, but with much the same combination of crude table manners and clean sets to stand in for period flavour.' – *MFB*

The Amorous Milkman
GB 1975 94m colour
Variety/Lanka (Derren Nesbitt)
A young milkman becomes engaged to two women at the same time.
Trivial and heavy-handed comedy, in which the hero is the victim of rapacious women; intended to titillate, it fails miserably.
wd Derren Nesbitt *novel* Derren Nesbitt *ph* Jim Allen m Roger Webb *ad* Tony Curtis *ed* Russell Lloyd
☆ Julie Ege, Diana Dors, Brendan Price, Donna Reading, Nancie Wait, Alan Lake, Bill Fraser, Fred Emney, Patrick Holt, Roy Kinnear, Ray Barrett, Anthony Sharp, Megs Jenkins, Arnold Ridley, Sam Kydd
'All in all, this is British graffiti at its worst.' – *MFB*

The Amorous Prawn *
GB 1962 89m bw
BL/Covent Garden (Leslie Gilliat)
US title: *The Playgirl and the War Minister (an attempt to cash in on the Profumo case)*
A hard-up general's wife invites American paying guests to their official highland home.
This film version of a stage success seems very mild, but the cast is eager to please: the result is a frantic high-class farce.
w Anthony Kimmins, Nicholas Phipps *play* Anthony Kimmins d Anthony Kimmins *ph* Wilkie Cooper m John Barry
☆ Joan Greenwood, Ian Carmichael, Cecil Parker, Dennis Price, Robert Beatty, Finlay Currie, Liz Fraser, Derek Nimmo

Amos & Andrew
US 1993 94m Technicolor
Columbia/Castle Rock/New Line (Gary Goetzman)
⬛ ⬛ ⚬ ⬛ ⚬
A black writer moves into an exclusive neighbourhood and finds himself taken for a burglar, befriended by a petty crook and involved in a shoot-out with police.
A crass farce of mistaken identity, a would-be satire of racial attitudes that neither illumines nor entertains.

wd E. Max Frye *ph* Walt Lloyd m Richard Gibbs *pd* Patricia Norris *ed* Jane Kurson
☆ Nicolas Cage, Samuel L. Jackson, Dabney Coleman, Michael Lerner, Margaret Colin, Brad Dourif, Giancarlo Esposito, Bob Balaban
'Raises the question: "How did this film ever get made?" Few audience members will sit through its entirety to ponder the issue.' – *Lawrence Cohn, Variety*

L'Amour à Mort *
France 1984 90m colour
Dussart/Ariane/A2 (Philippe Dussart)
An archaeologist and his mistress come to the conclusion that their love will reach its fullest expression in death.
Chilly symbolic drama, a continuation of the same team's preoccupations with the meaning of life which were previously explored (via the same four actors) in Mon Oncle d'Amérique *and* La Vie est un Roman. *Interesting but not especially rewarding.*
w Jean Gruault d Alain Resnais *ph* Sacha Vierny m Hans Werner Henze
☆ Sabine Azema, Fanny Ardant, Pierre Arditi, André Dussolier

Un Amour de Pluie: see *Loving in the Rain*

Un Amour de Swann: see *Swann in Love*

L'Amour, L'Après-midi *
France 1972 97m colour
Les Films du Losange/Barbet Schroeder (Pierre Cottrell)
⬛
US title: *Chloë in the Afternoon*
aka: *Love in the Afternoon*
A married man's flirtation with an old flame leads him to a greater appreciation of his wife.
The last of Rohmer's six moral tales and the least interesting.
wd Eric Rohmer *ph* Nestor Almendros m Arié Dzierlatka *ad* Nicole Rachline *ed* Cécile Decugis, Martine Kalfon
☆ Bernard Verley, Zouzou, Françoise Verley, Daniel Ceccaldi, Malvina Penne, Babette Ferrier
'The director shows life going on realistically enough. But the elegance with which he presents it, the wit – and the film doesn't merely sound witty, it looks witty – remove it from the tedium of the realistic.' – *Dilys Powell*

Les Amours de la Reine Elisabeth: see *Queen Elizabeth*

Amsterdam Affair
GB 1968 91m Eastmancolor
LIP/Trio/Group W (Gerry Willoughby)
Inspector Van der Valk investigates when a writer is accused of murdering his mistress.
Tolerable roman policier.
w Edmund Ward *novel* Love in Amsterdam by Nicolas Freeling d Gerry O'Hara *ph* Gerry Fisher m Patrick John Scott
☆ Wolfgang Kieling, William Marlowe, Catherina von Schell

The Amsterdam Kill
Hong Kong 1977 93m Technicolor
Panasonic
Golden Harvest/Fantastic Films/Raymond Chow
⬛ ⬛
An American ex-Drug Enforcement Agency officer tries to protect an old friend caught in the Hong Kong drug wars.
Roughly made and uninventive thriller in which the Hong Kong film makers fail to consolidate the international ground they gained with kung fu films.
w Robert Clouse, Gregory Teifer d Robert Clouse *ph* Alan Hume m Hal Schaffer
☆ Robert Mitchum, Bradford Dillman, Richard Egan, Leslie Nielsen, Keye Luke

'Be glad you're afraid. It means you're still alive'
Amsterdamned *
Netherlands 1988 113m colour
Vestron/First Floor Features (Laurens Geels, Dick Maas)
⬛ ⬛ ⚬
A cop is assigned to discover the murderer of a prostitute found floating in a canal.
Deft action picture that makes the most of its waterfront setting.
wd Dick Maas *ph* Marc Felperlaan m Dick Maas *pd* Dick Schillemans *ed* Hans Van Dongen

☆ Huub Stapel, Monique Van de Ven, Serge-Henri Valcke, Tanneke Hartsuiker, Wim Zomer, Hidde Maas

Amy
👪 US 1981 100m Technicolor
Walt Disney
⬛
A spinster is taught a little about life and love.
Unmemorable family comedy drama.
w Noreen Stone d Vincent McEveety
☆ Jenny Agutter, Barry Newman, Kathleen Nolan, Chris Robinson, Margaret O'Brien, Nanette Fabray

'In the heart of an outcast He found his destiny. In the passion of an outsider She found her home.'
Amy Foster
GB/US/France 1997 113m Technicolor
Panavision
Columbia TriStar (Polly Tapson, Charles Steel, Beeban Kidron)
⬛ ⬛ ⚬ ⚬ ⚬
US title: *Swept from the Sea*
In Cornwall, a shipwrecked Russian marries a local servant girl, but the course of true love is far from smooth.
A period story of love blossoming in an inward-looking and isolated community, this good-looking movie is curiously short of felt emotion; it may look more at home on video or TV.
w Tim Willocks *story* Joseph Conrad d Beeban Kidron *ph* Dick Pope m John Barry *pd* Simon Holland *ed* Alex Mackie, Andrew Mondshein
☆ Vincent Perez, Rachel Weisz, Ian McKellen, Joss Ackland, Kathy Bates, Tom Bell, Zoë Wanamaker, Tony Haygarth
'Almost exemplary of present Hollywood practice in that prodigious amounts of touch, care and technical skill have succeeded in turning Conrad's hard nugget of a yarn into a piece of sumptuous mush.' – *Peter Matthews, Sight and Sound*

'When you can't breathe, you can't scream.'
'It will take your breath away.'
Anaconda
US 1997 89m colour Panavision
Columbia/CL Cinema Line (Verna Harrah, Leonard Rabinowitz, Carole Little)
⬛ ⬛ ⚬ ⚬ ⚬
An anthropologist goes looking for a tribe of Indians in the rainforest and finds a gigantic killer snake instead.
A bungled rip-off of Jaws, *with Voight, who seems to relish his role as an expert snake-hunter, providing what sounds like a parody of Brando at his most excessive; otherwise the action is decidedly tame.*
w Hans Bauer, Jim Cash, Jack Epps Jnr & Luis Llosa *ph* Bill Butler m Randy Edelman *pd* Kirk M. Petruccelli *ed* Michael R. Miller *sp* Walt Conti, John Nelson
☆ Jennifer Lopez, Ice Cube, Jon Voight, Eric Stoltz, Jonathan Hyde, Owen Wilson, Kari Wuhrer, Vincent Castellanos, Danny Trejo
'The big, bad anaconda never really develops any personality – menacing or otherwise – and remains nothing more than a jack-in-the-box gimmick.' – *Joe Leydon, Variety*
† Like *Congo* the year before, it was a bad adventure film that found an audience, grossing $66m in the US, and another $70m elsewhere.

'You try telling him his 50 minutes are up.'
Analyze This **
US 1999 103m Technicolor
Warner/Village Roadshow/NPV/Baltimore/Spring Creek/Face/Tribeca (Paula Weinstein, Jane Rosenthal)
⬛ ⬛
An ageing Mafia gangster consults a psychiatrist about his anxiety attacks.
A witty comedy that lets De Niro play to good effect against his more familiar Mafia roles and which also has fun at the excesses of psychobabble.
w Peter Tolan, Kenneth Lonergan d Harold Ramis *st* Stuart Dryburgh m Howard Shore *pd* Wynn Thomas *ed* Christopher Tellefsen
☆ Robert De Niro, Billy Crystal, Lisa Kudrow, Joe Viterelli, Chazz Palminteri, Bill Macy, Leo Rossi, Kyle Sabihy, Rebecca Schull, Molly Shannon, Max Casella, Pat Cooper
'Has a funny title, an even funnier premise and inspired odd-couple casting that's enough to prompt laughter just on the basis of its two-shots

in the ad campaign. Think of it as an offer you can't refuse.' – *Janet Maslin, New Yorker*

'The most amazing conspiracy the world has ever known, and love as it never happened to a man and woman before!'
Anastasia **
GB 1956 105m Eastmancolor
Cinemascope
TCF (Buddy Adler)
⬛ ⚬ ⚬
In 1928 Paris, a group of exiled White Russians claim to have found the living daughter of the Tsar, presumed executed in 1918; but the claimant is a fake schooled by a general, with whom she falls in love.
Slick, highly theatrical entertainment for the upper classes; it dazzles and satisfies without throwing any light on history. The film marked Bergman's Hollywood comeback after some years in Europe under a cloud for her 'immoral' behaviour
w Arthur Laurents *play* Marcelle Maurette, Guy Bolton d Anatole Litvak *ph* Jack Hildyard m Alfred Newman *ad* Andrei Andreiev, Bill Andrews
☆ Ingrid Bergman, Yul Brynner, Helen Hayes, Martita Hunt, Akim Tamiroff, Felix Aylmer, Ivan Desny
'Little weight but considerable and urbane charm.' – *John Cutts*
Ⓐ Ingrid Bergman
Å Alfred Newman

'Discover the Adventure Behind the Greatest Mystery of Our Time.'
Anastasia
👪 US 1997 94m Technicolor
Cinemascope
TCF (Don Bluth, Gary Goldman)
A young girl travels from Russia to Paris, claiming to be the long-lost Anastasia, the daughter of Tsar Nicholas.
An extraordinarily misguided attempt to make a Disney-styled animated feature from events that do not fit the formula: the villains here are a dead Rasputin and his pet bat.
w Susan Gautheir, Bruce Graham, Bob Tzudiker, Noni White *play* Marcelle Maurette, adapted by Guy Bolton *screenplay* Arthur Laurents, *adapted by* Eric Tuchman d Don Bluth, Gary Goldman m David Newman *m/ly* Lynn Ahrens, Stephen Flaherty *ed* Fiona Trayler
☆ Featuring the voices of: Meg Ryan, John Cusack, Kelsey Grammer, Christopher Lloyd, Hank Azaria, Bernadette Peters, Kirsten Dunst; singers: Liz Callaway, Lacey Chabert, Jim Cummings, Jonathan Dokuchitz
'An ambitious, serious but not particularly stimulating musical feature that unconvincingly attempts to graft warm and cuddly family fare onto turbulent aspects of modern history and mythology.' – *Todd McCarthy, Variety*
Å Stephen Flaherty, Lynn Ahrens, David Newman; song 'Journey to the Past' (m Stephen Flaherty, *ly* Lynn Ahrens)

Anatahan
Japan 1953 92m bw
Daiwa (K. Takimura)
aka: *The Saga of Anatahan*
During World War II, Japanese seamen are shipwrecked on the same deserted island as a man and a woman; the latter causes jealousy and murder.
Downright peculiar studio-set melodrama, based on true events and its creator through interpreters, with results far from happy.
m A. Ifukube *wd/ph* Josef von Sternberg
☆ Akemi Negishi, T. Sugunuma, K. Onoe, T. Bandoh
'The main impression is of tedium relieved by moments of far from intentional humour.' – *Penelope Houston*

The Anatolian Smile: see *America, America*

'Last year's number one best seller. This year's (we hope) number one motion picture!'
Anatomy of a Murder **
US 1959 161m bw
Columbia/Carlyle/Otto Preminger
⬛ ⬛ ⚬ ⚬
A small-town lawyer successfully defends an army officer accused of murdering a bartender who had assaulted his wife.

Overlong and over-faithful version of a highly detailed courtroom bestseller. The plot is necessarily equivocal, the characterizations overblown, but the trial commands some interest, and the use of 'daring' words in evidence caused controversy at the time. It was Scott's first notable role, as the prosecutor.

w Wendell Mayes novel Robert Traver d Otto Preminger ph Sam Leavitt m Duke Ellington pd Boris Leven ed Louis R. Loeffler

☆ James Stewart, Ben Gazzara, Lee Remick, Eve Arden, Arthur O'Connell, George C. Scott, Kathryn Grant, Orson Bean, Murray Hamilton

† The trial judge was played by Joseph N. Welch, a real-life judge who had gained fame in 1954 by representing the army against Senator McCarthy.

�ჰ picture; Wendell Mayes; Sam Leavitt; James Stewart; Arthur O'Connell; George C. Scott; editing

Anchoress
GB/Belgium 1993 108m bw
BFI/Corsan (Paul Breuls, Ben Gibson)
📺 ⊚

In 14th-century England, a young woman obsessed by the Virgin Mary is walled up in a small cell in the village church and then decides she wants to leave.

Grimly downbeat account of medieval life, hovering on the edge of parody and lacking narrative drive.

w Judith Stanley-Smith, Catherine Vandeleene d Chris Newby ph Michel Baudour m Niek Kortekaas ed Brand Thumin

☆ Natalie Morse, Eugene Bervoets, Toyah Wilcox, Peter Postlethwaite, Christopher Eccleston, Michael Pas, Brenda Bertin

'Evocatively designed period pic creates a long ago world yet remains relevant on such issues as what recourse women have in a man's world and how faith grounded in nature fares against that dictated by the clergy.' – Variety

Anchors Aweigh **
👫 US 1945 139m Technicolor
MGM (Joe Pasternak)
📺 ▦ ⊚ ∩

Two sailors on leave in Los Angeles get involved with a small boy who wants to join the navy.

Rather droopy musical most notable as a forerunner of On the Town, though on much more conventional lines. Amiable performances, and a brilliant dance with a cartoon mouse, save the day.

w Isobel Lennart d George Sidney ph Robert Planck, Charles Boyle m George Stoll m/ly Jule Styne, Sammy Cahn pd Cedric Gibbons

☆ Frank Sinatra, Gene Kelly, Kathryn Grayson, Jose Iturbi, Sharon McManus, Carlos Ramirez, Dean Stockwell, Pamela Britton

♫ 'We Hate to Leave'; 'What Makes the Sun Set?'; 'The Charm of You'; 'I Begged Her'; 'I Fall in Love Too Easily'; 'The Worry Song'

🎖 George Stoll

ჰ picture; Robert Planck; Gene Kelly; song 'I Fall in Love Too Easily' (mJule Styne, ly Sammy Cahn)

And Baby Makes Three
US 1950 83m bw
Columbia (Robert Lord)
A wife divorces her compromised husband before discovering that she is pregnant.

Thin marital comedy with minor compensations.

w Lou Breslow, Joseph Hoffman d Henry Levin ph Burnett Guffey m George Duning

☆ Robert Young, Barbara Hale, Billie Burke, Robert Hutton, Janis Carter, Nicholas Joy, Lloyd Corrigan

'It has everything but a story that hangs together.' – New York Herald Tribune

'And God created woman. But the Devil created Brigitte Bardot'

And God Created Woman
France 1957 90m Eastmancolor
Cinemascope
Iēna-Hodu/UCIL/Cocinor (Raoul Lévy)
📺 ▦ ⊚ ∩

original title: Et Dieu Créa la Femme
aka: And Woman ... Was Created

An 18-year-old finds herself fatally attracted towards men.

Rather a feeble excuse for its star to strip on the St Tropez beach, but one that made her an international star.

w Roger Vadim, Raoul Lévy d Roger Vadim ph Armand Thirard m Paul Misraki ad Jean André

☆ Brigitte Bardot, Curt Jurgens, Jean-Louis Trintignant, Christian Marquand, Georges Poujouly, Jane Marken, Paul Faivre

'An open violation of conventional morality.' – Catholic Legion of Decency

'I'm prepared to bet an overcoat to a bikini that this film will make its star Miss Sex of the Universe.' – Sketch

'One of the most genuine, youthful and original works produced in France since 1945.' – Louis Marcorelles, Sight and Sound

† Vadim made a second film with this title (US 1987), see below.

And God Created Woman
US 1987 100m DeLuxe
Crow/Vestron (George P. Braunstein/Ron Hamady)

A woman marries so that she can get parole from prison and pursue her ambition to become a rock star.

Silly raucous remake that has nothing in common with Vadim's original but the title. This time the stripping is done by Rebecca de Mornay.

w R. J. Stewart d Roger Vadim ph Stephen M. Katz m Tom Chase, Steve Rucker pd Victor Kempster ed Suzanne Pettit

☆ Rebecca de Mornay, Vincent Spano, Frank Langella, Donovan Leitch

And Hope to Die
US/Fr/Canada 1972 104m bw
Serge Silberman/TCF
▦

original title: La Course du lièvre à travers les champs

A fugitive Frenchman in Canada runs foul of criminals and gypsies and causes several deaths.

Muddled melodrama of the worst 'international' kind.

w Sebastien Japrisot d René Clément

☆ Jean-Louis Trintignant, Robert Ryan, Aldo Ray, Tisa Farrow, Lea Massari

And Justice for All
US 1979 119m Metrocolor
Columbia/Malton (Joe Wizan)
📺 ▦ ⊚

An American lawyer gets into all kinds of trouble, including the defence of a judge on a rape charge.

Not so much a satire as a series of random pot-shots at the legal system, sometimes funny but cumulatively stultifying.

w Valerie Curtin, Barry Levinson d Norman Jewison ph Frank Holgate m Dave Grusin

☆ Al Pacino, Jack Warden, John Forsythe, Lee Strasberg, Christine Lahti, Sam Levene, Jeffrey Taybor

'Most incriminating is its own hysterical imprecision and sentimental pleading.' – Sight and Sound

ჰ Al Pacino; screenplay

And Life Goes On... **
Iran 1992 108m colour
ICA/I.I.D.C.Y.A. (Ali Reza Zarrin)
📺

original title: Zendegi Va Digar Hich...

A film director and his son visit part of Iran hit by an earthquake to discover if a boy who starred in his recent film is still alive.

An austere road movie composed of small episodes, in which, despite their tragedies, the survivors continue with the mundane matter of getting through the day.

wd Abbas Kiarostami ph Homayun Payvar m Vivaldi ed Abbas Kiarostami

☆ Ferhed Kherdamend, Buba Bayour

...and millions will die!
Australia 1973 96m Eastmancolor
Allied Artists/Apa (Mende Brown)

A scientist tracks down a hidden store of nerve gas, secreted by a Nazi war criminal, that threatens the population of Hong Kong.

Muddled thriller with irrelevant and undeveloped subplots; it lacks suspense, probably because the bad guys are killed off early in the film.

w Michael Fisher d Leslie H. Martinson ph Paul Onorato m Laurie Lewis ed Richard Hindley

☆ Richard Basehart, Susan Strasberg, Leslie Nielsen, Peter Sumner, Joseph Furst, Alwyn Kurts, Tony Wager

And Now for Something Completely Different **
👫 GB 1971 88m colour
Columbia/Kettledrum/Python (Patricia Casey)
📺 ▦ ⊚

Monty Python's Flying Circus perform again a selection of sketches from the BBC television series.

The first Monty Python film, intended to introduce the team's humour to an American audience. It lacks any overall coherence, but many of the individual sketches are a joy.

w Graham Chapman, John Cleese, Terry Gilliam, Eric Idle, Terry Jones, Michael Palin d Ian MacNaughton ph David Muir ad Colin Grimes ed Thom Noble

☆ Graham Chapman, John Cleese, Terry Gilliam, Eric Idle, Terry Jones, Michael Palin, Carol Cleveland

'Very funny.' – MFB

And Now Miguel *
US 1965 95m Technicolor
Universal/Robert B. Radnitz

A 10-year-old Mexican boy proves himself worthy to work on the mountain with the sheep.

A children's film typical of its producer: good to look at, documentarily convincing, but too slight and too slow.

w Ted Sherdeman, Jane Klove novel Joseph Krumgold d James B. Clark ph Clifford Stine m Phillip Lambro

☆ Pat Cardi, Guy Stockwell, Clu Gulager, Michael Ansara, Joe de Santis

And Now My Love **
France/Italy 1974 121m Technicolor
Avco Embassy/Films 13/Rizzoli (Pierre Pardon)

original title: Toute une Vie

The love stories of three generations, from 1900 to 1974: a son is born to the wife of a soldier who dies in the First World War; he marries a woman who dies in childbirth; their daughter finds happiness with a film director.

An enjoyably romantic, if somewhat bland, panorama of the 20th century, taking in on the way most of the major events, seen as a background to individual relationships; the passage of time is paralleled by the development of cinema, the story beginning with grainy black and white photography and moving through the silent period to colour.

w Claude Lelouch, Pierre Uytterhoeven d Claude Lelouch ph Jean Collomb m Francis Lai ad François de Lamothe ed George Klotz

☆ Marthe Keller, André Dussolier, Charles Denner, Carla Gravina, Charles Gerard, Gilbert Bécaud, Alain Basnir, Daniel Boulanger

'No amount of technical wizardry can fully disguise the naivety of Lelouch's basic concept.' – Geoff Brown, MFB

† The version released in France ran for 150m and included a sequence set in the future.

ჰ screenplay

And Now The Screaming Starts
GB 1973 91m colour
Amicus (Max J. Rosenberg, Milton Subotsky)
📺 ▦

A new bride in a country house is haunted by hallucinations of the past.

Grisly ghost story which overplays its hand and outstays its welcome.

w Roger Marshall novel Fengriffen by David Case d Roy Ward Baker ph Denys Coop m Douglas Gamley

☆ Peter Cushing, Stephanie Beacham, Herbert Lom, Patrick Magee, Ian Ogilvy, Geoffrey Whitehead, Guy Rolfe, Rosalie Crutchley

'Who are you that a man can't make love to you?'

And Now Tomorrow *
US 1944 86m bw
Paramount (Fred Kohlmar)

A rich girl goes deaf, loses her fiancé, but wins the poor doctor who cares for her.

Bestselling slush turned into a routine star romance. It was Ladd's first film in confirmed top-star status after a meteoric rise interrupted by war service.

w Frank Partos, Raymond Chandler (!) novel Rachel Field d Irving Pichel ph Daniel L. Fapp m Victor Young

☆ Loretta Young, Alan Ladd, Susan Hayward, Beulah Bondi, Cecil Kellaway, Barry Sullivan

'A vernal sign of the boys getting back to one of their favourite legends after the wintry days of war.' – Richard Winnington

And One Was Beautiful
US 1940 68m bw
MGM (Frederick Stephani)

A girl sets a trap for a playboy, who falls for her sister.

Cinderella-style second feature, quite unremarkable.

w Harry Clork story Alice Duer Miller d Robert Sinclair

☆ Robert Cummings, Laraine Day, Jean Muir, Billie Burke, Esther Dale

And So They Were Married
US 1935 74m bw
Columbia (B. P. Schulberg)

A widow and a widower try to get married despite the ill-feeling of their children.

Predictable romantic farce.

w Doris Anderson, Joseph Anthony d Elliott Nugent ph Henry Freulich m Howard Jackson

☆ Melvyn Douglas, Mary Astor, Edith Fellows, Jackie Moran, Donald Meek, Dorothy Stickney

And Soon the Darkness *
GB 1970 99m colour
Associated British (Albert Fennell, Brian Clemens)

Of two young nurses on a cycling holiday in France, one is murdered by a local sex maniac and the other almost shares her fate.

Slow, overstretched, often risible suspenser on vanishing lady lines; long on red herrings and short on humour, but with some pretension to style. The action all takes place along a mile or two of sunlit country road.

w Brian Clemens, Terry Nation d Robert Fuest ph Ian Wilson m Laurie Johnson

☆ Pamela Franklin, Michele Dotrice, Sandor Eles, John Nettleton

And Sudden Death
US 1936 60m bw
Paramount

A young man denies a hit and run charge but confesses on his death bed.

Preachy melodrama with little entertainment value.

w Joseph Moncure March d Charles Barton

☆ Randolph Scott, Tom Brown, Frances Drake, Billy Lee, Fuzzy Knight, Porter Hall

'There's nothing but trouble in Paradise when the bandleader tries to make love to a whole sister act – simultaneously!'

And the Angels Sing *
US 1943 95m bw
Paramount (E. D. Leshin)

Four singing sisters have hectic adventures with a bandleader.

Mildly disarming romantic comedy with music, more firmly set in a recognizable social milieu than the usual fan product from this studio.

w Melvin Frank, Norman Panama, Claude Binyon d George Marshall ph Karl Struss m Victor Young m/ly Johnny Burke, Jimmy Van Heusen

☆ Dorothy Lamour, Diana Lynn, Betty Hutton, Mimi Chandler, Fred MacMurray, Raymond Walburn, Eddie Foy Jnr, Fred Albertson, Mikhail Rasumny

'Slapstick sophistication in a sub-Sturges manner.' – MFB

'Cruel, soggily professional, over-elaborate, and inclined towards snobbish whimsy.' – James Agee

And the Band Played On *
US 1993 141m colour
ITC/Odyssey/HBO (Midge Sanford, Sarah Pillsbury)
📺 ▦ ⊚ ∩

Doctors investigating a disease affecting homosexual men in America discover that it is sexually transmitted and first name it GRID (Gay Related Immune Deficiency) and then, when it is discovered that the virus is no respecter of sexuality, call it AIDS.

A confusing dramatization of Shilts's angry book on the first years of AIDS and the inactivity of the government and other organizations in dealing with it; it leaves one little wiser, though sadder, than before.

w Arnold Schulman book Randy Shilts d Roger Spottiswoode ph Paul Elliott, Paul Ryan m Carter Burwell pd Victoria Paul ed Lois Freeman-Fox

☆ Matthew Modine, Alan Alda, Richard Gere, Patrick Bauchau, Nathalie Baye, Christian Clemenson, Phil Collins, Bud Cort, Alex Courtney, David Dukes, David Clennon, Anjelica Huston, Steve Martin, Ian McKellen, Lily Tomlin

---

'Spottiswoode's engrossing, powerful work still accomplishes its mission: Shilts' book, with all its shock, sorrow and anger, has been transferred decisively to the screen.' – *Variety*

'The result is sometimes both informative and moving but also in places a little dull and unfocused, as if those who made the film were too conscientious to leave anything out and too scared to make a proper fiction out of history.' – *Derek Malcolm, Guardian*

† The film, made for American television, was given a cinema release in Britain. The book was originally optioned in 1989 but twice plans to film it fell through. This version had a troubled production, with two directors quitting and Spottiswoode leaving during the post-production process, and it was criticized by Shilts himself shortly before his death in February 1994.

And the Same To You

GB   1960   70m   bw
Monarch

A clergyman's nephew decides to become a boxer.
Uninventive and unfunny comedy.
w John Paddy Carstairs, John Junkin *play* A. P. Dearsley *d* George Pollock
☆ Brian Rix, Leo Franklyn, William Hartnell, Vera Day, Tommy Cooper, Dick Bentley, Sid James

And the Ship Sails On *

Italy/France   1983   132m   Technicolor
Panavision
RAI/Vides/Gaumont (Franco Cristaldi)
⊞ ▤ ⌕

original title: *E la Nave Va*
From Naples in 1914 a luxurious liner sets forth to scatter the ashes of an opera singer.
Less a Ship of Fools than a theatre of the absurd, with familiar Fellini caricatures going through their paces against studio sets. Fascination alternates with boredom.
w Federico Fellini, Tonino Guerra *d* Federico Fellini *m* Giuseppe Rotunno *m* Gianfranco Plenizio *ad* Dante Ferretti *ed* Ruggero Mastroianni
☆ Freddie Jones, Barbara Jefford, Victor Poletti, Peter Cellier, Elisa Mainardi, Norma West
'A genial movie, although a bit discontinuous.' – *Alberto Moravia*
'A vessel that is chock-full of his best gags, visual fun and love of cinema as artful technique.' – *Variety*
'Too much a work of the pure imagination with the result that the audience is cast adrift on a styrofoam sea without a lifeline to any kind of recognizable reality.' – *Andrew Sarris, Village Voice*

And Then There Were None ****

US   1945   97m   bw
Popular Pictures/Harry M. Popkin (René Clair)
⊞ ▤

GB title: *Ten Little Niggers*
Ten people are invited to a house party on a lonely island, and murdered one by one.
A classic mystery novel is here adapted and directed with the utmost care to provide playful black comedy, stylish puzzlement, and some splendid acting cameos.
w Dudley Nichols *novel* Agatha Christie (aka: Ten Little Niggers) *d* René Clair *ph* Lucien Andriot *m* Mario Castelnuovo-Tedesco
☆ Walter Huston, Barry Fitzgerald, Louis Hayward, June Duprez, Roland Young, Richard Haydn, C. Aubrey Smith, Judith Anderson, Queenie Leonard, Mischa Auer
MISS BRENT: 'Very stupid to kill the only servant in the house. Now we don't even know where to find the marmalade.'
JUDGE QUINCANNON: 'Mr Owen could only come to the island in one way. It's perfectly clear. Mr Owen is one of us.'
ROGERS: 'Never in my life have I been accused of any crime, sir – and if that's what you think of me, I shan't serve any dinner.'
'Rich in the elements which have made mystery melodramas popular, yet not in the precise form of any previously made.' – *Hollywood Reporter*
'The efforts at sprightly, stylish comedy don't gain much momentum.' – *Pauline Kael, New Yorker, 70s*

And Then There Were None

GB   1974   98m   Technicolor
EMI/Filibuster (Harry Alan Towers)
US title: *Ten Little Indians*
Ten people are lured to an isolated Persian hotel and murdered one by one.
Listless remake, often so inept you could scream.
w Peter Welbeck (Harry Alan Towers) *d* Peter Collinson *ph* Fernando Arribas *m* Bruno Nicolai
☆ Oliver Reed, Richard Attenborough, Elke Sommer, Herbert Lom, Gert Frobe, Stéphane Audran, Charles Aznavour, Adolfo Celi, Alberto de Mendoza, Maria Rohm

And There Was Jazz *

Poland   1981   90m   bw
Zespoly Filmowe (Andrzej Soltysik)
aka: *Byl Jazz*
In Poland of the 1950s, a group of students playing classic jazz become a symbol of opposition in a conformist society.
Like its subject matter, a small but engaging gesture of revolt. It was banned by the Polish authorities.
wd Feliks Falk *ph* Witold Sobocinski *m* Jerzy Matula *ad* Teresa Smus-Barska *ed* Miroslawa Garlicka
☆ Bozena Adamkowna, Michal Bajor, Andrzej Grabarczyk, Kazimierz Wysota, Jerzy Gudejko, Adrzej Chichlowski, Jacek Strzemzalski, Jacek Sass-Uhrynowski

And Woman ... Was Created: see *And God Created Woman*

And You Thought Your Parents Were Weird

👫 US   1991   92m   CFI color
Trimark/Panorama/Just Betzer
⊞ ▤

Two young inventors create a robot which is then possessed by the spirit and voice of their dead father.
Dull, sickly family comedy, which also exhibits some dubious attitudes to deception and death.
wd Tony Cookson *ph* Paul Elliot *m* Randy Miller *pd* Alexandra Kicenik *ed* Michael Ornstein
☆ Marcia Strassman, Joshua Miller, Edan Gross, John Quade, Sam Behrens, Alan Thicke (voice), Susan Gibney, A. J. Langer
'Cookson lays on the sentiment with a spatula towards the end. Still, story has plenty of heart, cast is enjoyable and Cookson has an instinct for the material that makes this humble outing uncalculated and even a bit soulful.' – *Variety*
† The film was released direct to video in Britain.

The Anderson Tapes *

US   1971   98m   Technicolor   Panavision
Columbia/Robert M. Weitman
⊞ ▤ ⌕

An ex-con forms a gang to rob a building, not knowing that police and others, for various purposes, are making tape recordings of his conversations.
Superficially slick and fashionable crime thriller, marred by unnecessarily flashy direction, a failure to explain enough about the tapes, and a climax which oddly mixes bloodshed and farce.
w Frank R. Pierson *novel* Lawrence Sanders *d* Sidney Lumet *ph* Arthur J. Ornitz *m* Quincy Jones
☆ Sean Connery, Martin Balsam, Dyan Cannon, Alan King, Ralph Meeker

'Out of the sea and into your heart.'

Andre *

👫 US   1994   94m   Eastmancolor
Rank/Kushner-Locke (Annette Handley, Adam Shapiro)
⊞ ▤ ⌕ ⊚

A seven-year-old girl befriends a baby seal and protects it from the locals who regard it as a pest.
A film, based on a true story, to delight most children and which for the most part successfully skirts sentimentality; it gains immeasurably from the exuberant personality of its animal star.
w Dana Baratta *novel* A Seal Called Andre by Harry Goodridge, Lew Dietz *d* George Miller *ph* Thomas Burstyn *m* Bruce Rowland *pd* William Elliot *ed* Harry Hitner, Patrick Kennedy
☆ Keith Carradine, Tina Majorino, Chelsea Field, Aidan Pendleton, Shane Meier, Keith Szarabajka, Joshua Jackson, Tory

'For people who like to see animals put through their paces in the world's Marinelands without getting wet their own feet wet.' – *Alexander Walker, London Evening Standard*
'Call me heartless, but somehow I can't warm to a hero who resembles a giant garden slug in a false moustache.' – *Jonathan Romney, Guardian*
† Andre is played not by a seal but by a sea lion.

Andrei Rublev ****

USSR   1966   181m   bw/colour   Cinemascope
Mosfilm
⊞ ▤ ⊚ ⌕

Imaginary episodes from the life of a 15th-century icon painter.
A superb recreation of medieval life dramatizes the eternal problem of the artist, whether to take part in the life around him or merely comment on it.
w Andrei Mikhalkov-Konchalovsky, Andrei Tarkovsky *d* Andrei Tarkovsky *ph* Vadim Yusov *m* Vyacheslav Tcherniaiev
☆ Anatoly Solonitsin, Ivan Lapikov, Nikolai Grinko, Nikolai Sergeyev
'The one indisputable Russian masterpiece of the last decade.' – *Nigel Andrews, MFB, 1973*
'With the exception of the great Eisenstein, I can't think of any film which has conveyed a feeling of the remote past with such utter conviction ... a durable and unmistakable masterpiece.' – *Michael Billington, Illustrated London News*

Androcles and the Lion **

US   1952   96m   bw
RKO (Gabriel Pascal)

A slave takes a thorn from the paw of a lion which later, in the arena, refuses to eat him.
Shavian drollery, with interpolated discussions on faith, is scarcely ideal cinema material, but gusto in the performances keeps it going despite stolid direction.
w Chester Erskine *play* Bernard Shaw *d* Chester Erskine *ph* Harry Stradling *m* Frederick Hollander *ad* Harry Horner
☆ Alan Young, Jean Simmons, Robert Newton, Victor Mature, Maurice Evans, Reginald Gardiner, Elsa Lanchester, Alan Mowbray, Gene Lockhart
† Production had previously begun with Harpo Marx as Androcles and Rex Harrison as Caesar.

Android *

US   1982   80m   DeLuxe
New World/Android (Mary Ann Fisher)
⊞ ▤

In 2036, a police transport vehicle is hijacked in space, and the scientists on board, some of them androids, react in unexpected ways.
Cheaply made, but a bobby dazzler for science fiction addicts.
w James Reigle, Don Opper *d* Aaron Lipstadt *ph* Tim Suhrstedt *m* Don Preston
☆ Klaus Kinski, Brie Howard, Norbert Weisser, Crofton Hardester, Kendra Kirchner, Don Opper
'The best first feature since *Dark Star*.' – *Tom Milne, MFB*

The Andromeda Strain **

US   1970   131m   Technicolor   Panavision
Universal/Robert Wise
⊞ ▤ ⌕ ⊚

Scientists work frantically to neutralize an infected village, knowing that the least infection will cause their laboratory to self-destruct.
Solemn and over-detailed but generally suspenseful thriller, with a sense of allegory about man's inhumanity to man.
w Nelson Gidding *novel* Michael Crichton *d* Robert Wise *ph* Richard H. Kline *m* Gil Melle *ad* Boris Leven
☆ Arthur Hill, David Wayne, James Olson, Kate Reid, Paula Kelly

Andy Hardy Comes Home *

👫 US   1958   81m   bw
MGM (Red Doff)
Fortyish Andy returns to Carvel, his home town, to negotiate a land deal.
Rather dismal sequel to the celebrated series of Hardy family comedies which were enormously popular in the early forties – a thirteen-year gap is too long, and although most of the family is reunited the old Judge is sadly missed.
w Edward Everett Hutshing, Robert Morris Donley *d* Howard W. Koch *ph* William W. Spencer, Harold E. Wellman *m* Van Alexander

☆ Mickey Rooney, Fay Holden, Cecilia Parker, Patricia Breslin, Sara Haden, Jerry Colonna
† See also under *Hardy Family*.

Andy Warhol's Bad

US   1976   109m   Technicolor
EMI/Andy Warhol (Jeff Tornberg)
▤ ⌕

A housewife, who runs an assassination bureau using young female killers, employs a man – with fatal results.
A tedious, sloppily made horror movie.
w Pat Hackett, George Abagnalo *d* Jed Johnson *ph* Alan Metzger *m* Mike Bloomfield *ad* Eugene Rudolf *ed* David McKenna
☆ Carroll Baker, Perry King, Charles Oas-Heim, Cyrinda Fox, Matthew Anton, Cathy Roskam, Susan Tyrrell, Brigid Polk, Lawrence Tierney
† The film was cut to 104m on its British release.

Andy Warhol's Dracula: see *Dracula*

Andy Warhol's Flesh: see *Flesh*

Andy Warhol's Heat: see *Heat*

Andy Warhol's Lonesome Cowboys: see *Lonesome Cowboys*

Andy Warhol's Trash: see *Trash*

'I want love – and I'm going to get it!'

Angel *

US   1937   98m   bw
Paramount (Ernst Lubitsch)
▤ ⌕

The wife of an English diplomat finds herself neglected and almost has an affair with his old friend.
A curious romantic comedy in many ways typical of its time, yet with very few laughs, showing none of its director's usual cinematic sense, and compromised by the censor's refusal to let a spade be called a spade. Underplaying, and a sense that we watch a way of life about to be swept away, just about save it.
w Samson Raphaelson *play* Melchior Lengyel *d* Ernst Lubitsch *ph* Charles Lang *m* Frederick Hollander
☆ Marlene Dietrich, Herbert Marshall, Melvyn Douglas, Edward Everett Horton, Laura Hope Crews, Ernest Cossart
MARIA: 'What's the matter, darling? Is it France?'
SIR FREDERICK: 'No, no. Jugoslavia.'
MARIA: 'Oh, I see.'
'It isn't Hollywood dish that copies foreign recipes. It's a good picture and in the keys, especially for the carriage trade, it can't miss.' – *Variety*
'Very sophisticated, very subtle, very chic, vastly polished and entertaining.' – *Literary Digest*
'The production is performed with studied deliberation.' – *New York Times*
'This movie isn't essentially different from the best of Lubitsch, but it's attenuated. It's the sort of cultivated triangular love affair in which each of the three has a turn at the piano.' – *Pauline Kael, 70s*

Angel *

Eire   1982   92m   Technicolor
Motion Picture Company of Ireland/Irish Film Board/Channel 4 (John Boorman)
⊞ ▤

US title: *Danny Boy*
Against a background of the Irish troubles, a saxophonist is drawn into a maze of violence when he attempts to avenge the murder of a mute girl.
Glumly Irish thriller with metaphysical overtones as well as references to the state of Ireland. Keen narrative style is dissipated by overkill.
wd Neil Jordan *ph* Chris Menges *m* Verdi
☆ Stephen Rea, Veronica Quilligan, Alan Devlin, Peter Caffrey
'The film's style might be called flamboyant or baroque – or damned as pretentious – but it's a genuine style, a way of speaking. No one else speaks quite this way.' – *Michael Wilmington, Los Angeles Times*

👫 film suitable for family viewing   ⊞ VHS video-cassette for the British PAL system   ▤ VHS video-cassette for the British PAL system in wide screen-format   ⌕ Video cassette in a computer-colourised version   ▤ American NTSC video-cassette   ⌕ Laser disc

'Honor student by day – hooker by night!'
'You're young, attractive and healthy – and swimming in a toilet bowl!'

Angel
US 1983 93m CFI color
New World/Adam's Apple/Angel (Sandy Howard)

A 15-year-old student doubles as a Hollywood hooker and takes on a psychopathic killer.
Yucky melodrama with no holds barred, not even moments of humour.
w Robert Vincent O'Neil, Joseph M. Cala
d Robert Vincent O'Neil ph Andrew Davis
m Craig Safan
☆ Cliff Gorman, Donna Wilkes, Rory Calhoun, Susan Tyrrell, Dick Shawn, John Diehl, Elaine Giftos
'A tasteless blend of realism and farce.' – *Sunday Times*
† A sequel appeared in 1985 under the title *Avenging Angel*. Betsy Russell was the girl, now hunting down her mentor.

Angel and the Badman *
US 1946 100m bw
Republic (John Wayne)

The love of a Quaker girl converts a wounded gunslinger to an honourable life.
Thoughtful Western with good background detail and a fair measure of action.
wd James Edward Grant ph Archie Stout
m Richard Hageman pd Ernst Fegte
☆ John Wayne, Gail Russell, Harry Carey, Bruce Cabot, Irene Rich, Tom Powers
'Unpretentious, sweet-tempered and quite likeable.' – *James Agee*

Angel, Angel, Down We Go
US 1969 93m colour
AIP (Jerome F. Katzman)
Decadence in Hollywood: rock and rollers invade the lives of a rich family.
Unpleasant blather with a star well past her prime.
wd Robert Thom
☆ Jennifer Jones, Jordan Christopher, Roddy McDowall, Lou Rawls, Holly Near, Charles Aidman

An Angel at My Table **
New Zealand/Australia 1990 160m colour
Hibiscus Films/N.Z. Film Commission/TV New Zealand/ABC (Bridget Ikin)

A shy and introverted writer is wrongly diagnosed as a schizophrenic.
The biography of a notable poet, edited from a three-hour television miniseries.
w Laura Jones book Janet Frame's autobiographies
d Jane Campion ph Stuart Dryburgh m Don McGlashan pd Grant Major ed Veronica Haussler
☆ Kerry Fox, Alexia Keogh, Karen Fergusson, Iris Churn, K. J. Wilson, Melina Bernecker, Glynis Angell, Sarah Smuts-Kennedy, Colin McColl
'A potentially magical and harrowing film is imbued with gentle humor and great compassion, which makes every character (even the unappealing ones) come vividly to life.' – *Variety*

Angel Baby *
US 1960 97m bw
Madera (Thomas F. Woods)

A mute girl is cured by an evangelist, and renounces her sins.
Strident, vigorous low-budget melodrama.
w Oris Borstem, Samuel Roeca, Paul Mason novel Jenny Angel by Elsie Oaks Barbour d Paul Wendkos ph Haskell Wexler, Jack Marta m Wayne Shanklin
☆ Salome Jens, George Hamilton, Joan Blondell, Mercedes McCambridge, Henry Jones, Burt Reynolds

'In Love. In Deep. In Danger.'
Angel Baby *
Australia 1995 103m colour
AFFC/Stamen/Meridian (Timothy White, Jonathan Shteinman)

After they meet at a clinic, two psychiatric patients fall in love and decide to set up home together.

A grim and harrowing tale of a doomed love, a relationship between damaged people in a world that fails to understand them; its tragic protagonists lack depth, and are characterized mainly by their sickness.
wd Michael Rymer ph Ellery Ryan m John Clifford White, Gavin Friday, Maurice Seezer pd Chris Kennedy ed Danny Cooper
☆ John Lynch, Jacqueline McKenzie, Colin Friels, Deborra-Lee Furness, Robyn Nevin, David Argue, Jane Menelaus
'Should click with young auds who'll connect with the radiant but deeply troubled lovers.' – *Variety*

Angel Dust *
France 1987 95m colour
UGC/President Films/Top No 1/FR3/Films de La Saga/La Sofica (Jacques-Eric Strauss)

aka: *Poussière d'Ange*
A detective, whose life begins to fall to pieces after his wife leaves him, becomes involved with a young girl and a series of strange murders.
Acerbic thriller about the corrupting influence of sexual desire.
w Edouard Niermans, Jacques Audiard, Alain le Henry d Edouard Niermans ph Bernard Lutic m Leon Senza, Vincent-Marie Bouvot pd Dominique Maleret ed Yves Deschamps, Jacques Witta
☆ Bernard Giraudeau, Fanny Bastien, Fanny Cottencon, Michel Aumont, Jean-Pierre Sentier, Gérard Blain, Luc Lavandier

El Angel Exterminador: see *The Exterminating Angel*

Angel Face *
US 1952 91m bw
RKO (Otto Preminger)
A demented girl murders her father and stepmother, involving her chauffeur, whom she finally kills, and commits suicide.
Outrageous melodrama, so absurd as to be almost endearing.
w Frank Nugent, Oscar Millard d Otto Preminger ph Harry Stradling m Dimitri Tiomkin
☆ Jean Simmons, Robert Mitchum, Herbert Marshall, Barbara O'Neil, Leon Ames, Mona Freeman, Kenneth Tobey, Raymond Greenleaf
'The one lyrical nightmare in the cinema.' – *Ian Cameron*

An Angel from Texas *
US 1940 69m bw
Warner (Robert Fellows)
Misadventures of a country boy in New York.
Modest revamping of a much filmed farce, also made as The Tenderfoot (1928) and Dance Charlie Dance (1937).
w Fred Niblo Jnr, Bertram Millhauser play *The Butter and Egg Man* by George F. Kaufman d Ray Enright ph Arthur L. Todd m Howard Jackson
☆ Eddie Albert, Rosemary Lane, Wayne Morris, Ronald Reagan, Milburn Stone

Angel Heart *
US 1987 113m Technicolor
Tri-Star/Kassar-Vajna/Carolco/Winkast-Union (Alan Marshall, Elliott Kastner)

In 1955, a New York private eye descends into Hell.
He does, literally, in pursuit of a missing person who's opted out of a pact with the devil. Thoroughly unpleasant in detail, this wallow in the private eye cult constantly takes the eye with its pictorial qualities, even at its most nauseating.
wd Alan Parker novel *Falling Angel* by William Hjortsberg ph Michael Seresin m Trevor Jones pd Brian Morris
☆ Mickey Rourke, Robert De Niro, Lisa Bonet, Charlotte Rampling, Stocker Fontelieu, Brownie McGhee
'Faustian theme, heavy bloodletting and pervasive grimness may represent barriers too great for general audiences to surmount.' – *Daily Variety*

Angel in Exile *
US 1948 90m bw
Republic
An ex-con heads for an abandoned Arizona mine to recover stolen gold.
Modest, effective Western about a baddie who reforms.

w Charles Larson d Allan Dwan, Philip Ford ph Reggie Lanning m Nathan Scott
☆ John Carroll, Adele Mara, Thomas Gomez

Angel in My Pocket
US 1969 105m Technicolor
Universal (Ed Montagne)
A minister and his family arrive in a small town.
Simplistic comedy-drama with nothing to distinguish it from a dozen others in similar vein.
w Jim Fritzell, Everett Greenbaum d Alan Rafkin
☆ Andy Griffith, Jerry Van Dyke, Kay Medford, Edgar Buchanan, Margaret Hamilton, Gary Collins, Lee Meriwether, Henry Jones

The Angel Levine *
US 1970 105m DeLuxe
UA/Belafonte Enterprises (Chiz Schultz)
An elderly Jewish tailor complains to God of his bad luck; a black angel appears and seems to help him for a while.
Muddled and seemingly pointless parable with occasional felicities.
w Bill Gunn, Ronald Ribman story Bernard Malamud d Jan Kadar ph Richard Kratina m Zdenek Linka pd George Jenkins
☆ Zero Mostel, Harry Belafonte, Ida Kaminska, Milo O'Shea, Eli Wallach, Anne Jackson, Gloria Foster
'A prolonged variation on the theme that faith can produce miracles, but only if there is enough of it.' – *John Gillett*

The Angel of Broadway *
US 1927 82m bw silent
DeMille/Pathé
A night-club entertainer haunts Salvation Army missions in search of material, but ultimately joins the cause.
Fairly impressive propaganda piece of its time.
w Lenore J. Coffee d Lois Weber
☆ Leatrice Joy, Victor Varconi, May Robson, Alice Lake

Angel on My Shoulder **
US 1946 101m bw
UA/Charles R. Rogers

The devil promises leniency to a dead gangster if he will return to Earth and take over the body of a judge who is stamping out evil.
Crude but lively fantasy on the tail-end of the Here Comes Mr Jordan cycle, and by the same author.
w Harry Segall, Roland Kibbee d Archie Mayo ph James Van Trees m Dimitri Tiomkin
☆ Paul Muni, Claude Rains, Anne Baxter, Erskine Sanford, Hardie Albright
'The story is so imitative that it's hard to feel any more towards it than a mildly nostalgic regard.' – *Bosley Crowther*
'Witty, caustic and exciting.' – *Motion Picture Guide*

Angel on the Amazon
US 1948 86m bw
Republic (John H. Auer)
GB title: *Drums Along the Amazon*
An elderly white lady resident of the Amazon jungle looks only 25 after being scared by a panther…
Ludicrous melodrama which the actors take seriously.
w Lawrence Kimble d John H. Auer ph Reggie Lanning m Nathan Scott
☆ George Brent, Constance Bennett, Vera Hruba Ralston, Brian Aherne, Fortunio Bonanova, Alfonso Bedoya, Gus Schilling

Angel Sharks *
France 1997 93m colour 'Scope
Blue Light/Les Films de la Suane/Studio Image 2/La Sept/Lelia (Philippe Rousselet)
original title: *Marie Baie des Anges*
In a coastal area where teenage gangs roam, two outsiders come together for a brief moment of happiness.
Episodic low-life drama of petty crimes and promiscuity among doomed youth, directed with a sometimes haphazard energy.
wd Manuel Pradal ph Christopher Pollock m Carlo Crivelli pd Javier Po, Véronique Mellery ed Valerie Deseine
☆ Nicolas Welbers, Amira Casar, Swan Carpio, Jamie Harris, Frédéric Malgras, Vahina Giocante, Andrew Clover

'The plot simply isn't coherent or interesting enough to stop boredom setting in about halfway through and winds up really testing the outer regions of patience.' – *Jessica Mellor, Empire*

Angel Square *
Canada 1990 106m colour
Rendez-Vous/Wheeler-Hendren/Western International/Arvi Liimatainen

During Christmas in the late 1940s, a dreamy youth solves the mystery of who attacked the father of his Jewish friend.
Genial account of boyhood fantasies, complete with excursions into cartoon-like parodies of comic-strip adventures.
w James Defelice, Anne Wheeler novel Brian Doyle d Anne Wheeler ph Tobias Schliessler m George Blondheim pd John Blackie ed Peter Svab, Lenka Svab
☆ Ned Beatty, Jeremy Radick, Guillaume Lemay Thivierge, Marie Stefane Gaudry, Sarah Meyette, Nicola Cavendish, Brian Dooley, Michel Barrette

Angel Street: see *Gaslight* (1939)

The Angel Who Pawned Her Harp *
GB 1954 76m bw
Group Three (Sidney Cole)
A real angel arrives on a goodwill visit to seamy Islington, and manages to right a few wrongs.
Simple-minded whimsy, spottily effective, with good performances.
w Charles Terrot, Sidney Cole d Alan Bromly ph Arthur Grant m Antony Hopkins
☆ Diane Cilento, Felix Aylmer, Robert Eddison, Jerry Desmonde, Sheila Sweet, Alfie Bass

The Angel with the Trumpet
GB 1949 98m bw
British Lion/London Films (Karl Hartl)
An Austrian lady has an affair with a crown prince but marries for security and dies in defiance of the Nazis.
Curious European cavalcade, dully directed to keep the budget down and accommodate long stretches of an Austrian original. An eccentricity.
w Karl Hartl, Franz Tassie novel Ernst Lothar d Anthony Bushell ph Robert Krasker m Willy Schmidt-Gentner
☆ Eileen Herlie, Basil Sydney, Norman Wooland, Anthony Bushell, Maria Schell, John Justin, Oskar Werner, Andrew Cruickshank

The Angel Wore Red
US 1960 105m bw
MGM/Titanus/Spectator (Gottfredo Lombardo)
The love story of a priest and a prostitute in the Spanish Civil War.
Turgid farrago, unsatisfactory both romantically and politically.
wd Nunnally Johnson ph Giuseppe Rotunno m Bronislau Kaper
☆ Ava Gardner, Dirk Bogarde, Joseph Cotten, Vittorio de Sica, Aldo Fabrizi, Finlay Currie
'The stars show no apparent surprise that a film so empty of reward should take itself so seriously.' – *Peter John Dyer*

Angela
US 1955 81m bw
TCF/Patricia/Telecinema (Steven Pallos)
A former American racing driver working as a salesman in Italy finds himself involved in murder when he falls in love with a secretary.
Moody, unoriginal thriller in the film noir tradition, given a slight twist by being set in Rome.
w Jonathan Rix, Eduardo Anton story Steve Carruthers d Dennis O'Keefe ph Leonida Barboni m Mario Nascimbene ad Alfredo Montori ed Giancarlo Cappelli
☆ Dennis O'Keefe, Mara Lane, Rossano Brazzi, Arnoldo Foa, Galeazzo Benti, Nino Crisman, Enzo Fiermonte, John Fostini, Aldo Pini, Maria Teresa Paliani

Angela's Ashes **
US 1999 145m Technicolor
Universal/Paramount/Dirty Hands (Scott Rudin/David Brown/Alan Parker)

An Irish writer remembers his miserable Catholic childhood in Limerick, before he left to live in the United States.

Based on a best-selling memoir, this puts a Hollywood gloss on the rain-soaked poverty it depicts which, coupled with miscasting of the leading role, mutes its impact; it sputters only sporadically to life.
w Laura Jones, Alan Parker book Frank McCourt d Alan Parker ph Michael Seresin m John Williams pd Geoffrey Kirkland ed Gerry Hambling
☆ Emily Watson, Robert Carlyle, Joe Breen, Ciaran Owens, Michael Legge, Ronnie Masterson, Pauline McLynn, Liam Carney, Eanna Macliam, Andrew Bennett (narrator)
'This is the kind of film about hardship in which nobody has indoor plumbing, but everyone has clean hair.' – Janet Maslin, New York Times
'The resilience of McCourt is admirable, but the film doesn't manage to enlist one's sympathies for his hard lot so much as eventually sow the suspicion that he's working it off on us.' – Alexander Walker, London Evening Standard
& John Williams

The Angelic Conversation

GB   1985   80m   colour
BFI/Derek Jarman (James Mackay)
🖭
Readings from Shakespeare's sonnets by Judi Dench are accompanied by a film of young men striking Christ-like poses or caressing each other. Moody, grainy photography, much of it in jerky slow-motion, fails to illuminate the text.
d Derek Jarman ph Derek Jarman m Coil ed Cerith Wyn Evans, Peter Cartwright
☆ Paul Reynolds, Philip Williamson

Angelina *

Italy   1947   98m   bw
Lux-Ora (Paulo Frasca)
An impoverished housewife becomes the spokeswoman for her community on flooding, housing and other slum problems.
Reasonably rewarding star vehicle in the neo-realist tradition, this time angled for comedy.
w Suso Cecchi d'Amico, Piero Tellini, Luigi Zampa d Luigi Zampa ph Mario Craveri m Enzio Masetti
☆ Anna Magnani, Nando Bruno, Gianni Glori, Franco Zeffirelli
'At once kindly and fierce, witty and humorous, sad and richly gay. It warms your heart and breaks it, and has you laughing almost continuously.' – Fred Majdalany
'Behind the bubble and the chatter, the shouting and the running, the crowd and corteges that the Italians have always adored in their cinema, there is a genuine spring of fun that can only rise from a hopeful attitude towards God, and the right sort of optimism about one's neighbour.' – C. A. Lejeune

Angélique

France/West Germany/Italy   1964   116m
Eastmancolor   Dyaliscope
Francos/CICC/Gloria/Fona Roma (Francis Cosne)
🎧
original title: Angélique Marquise des Anges
Adventures of a nobleman's daughter at the court of Louis XIV.
Watchable swashbuckling nonsense, a kind of French Forever Amber. Several sequels were made.
w Claude Brûlé, Bernard Borderie, Francis Cosne novel Serge and Anne Golon d Bernard Borderie ph Henri Pérsin m Michel Magne
☆ Michèle Mercier, Robert Hossein, Giuliano Gemma, Jean Rochefort, François Maistre, Jacques Toja

Angelo My Love

US   1982   116m   colour
Lorton
🖭 ⚙
Adventures of an eight-year-old gypsy boy in Manhattan.
Angelo is a precocious little rogue, but two hours is a long haul for this kind of ethnic medley.
wd Robert Duvall
☆ Angelo Evans, Michael Evans, Ruthie Evans, Steve Tsigonoff
'Duvall has done wonders with his actors and then robbed them of their glory by mishandling the tempo of the piece.' – Sunday Times

Angelos

Greece   1982   119m   colour
Cannon/Greek Film Centre (Yorgos Katakouzinos)
A youth falls in love with a sailor and becomes a transvestite prostitute.
Doom-ridden tale unlikely to interest an audience of any sexual orientation.
wd Yorgos Katakouzinos ph Tasos Alexakis m Stamatis Spanoudakis ed Aristide Karydis-Maniatis
☆ Michalis Maniatis, Dionisis Xanthos, Katerina Chelmi, Maria Alkaiou

Angels: see Angels in the Outfield (1994)

'An elegant seduction. An erotic deception. A stunning revelation.'

Angels & Insects *

GB/US   1995   117m   Technicolor
Film Four/Samuel Goldwyn/Playhouse (Joyce Herlihy, Belinda Haas)
🖭 🖭 🎧
A naturalist from a working-class background, who goes to work for an aristocrat, is attracted by his patron's eldest daughter and marries her, with unexpected results.
A dry, austere and sometimes stilted period drama, emphasizing the resemblance between the human and the insect world that obsesses the hero, though the final revelation seems more anagrammatic than anything else.
w Belinda Haas, Philip Haas novel Morpho Eugenia by A. S. Byatt d Philip Haas ph Bernard Zitzerman m Alexander Balanescu pd Jennifer Kernke ed Belinda Haas
☆ Mark Rylance, Kristin Scott-Thomas, Patsy Kensit, Jeremy Kemp, Douglas Henshall, Annette Badland, Chris Larkin, Anna Massey, Saskia Wickham
'It's not the usual period piece, but its literary origins are too evident and the passion for insect metaphors soon begins to pall.' – Tom Shone, Sunday Times
& Paul Brown (costumes)

Angels and the Pirates: see Angels in the Outfield (1952)

Angel's Dance

US   1999   102m   FotoKem
Promark/Videal (David Bixler)
🖭 🖭 🎧
A hitman and his apprentice are stalked by the woman they tried to use for target practice.
Tacky thriller, given to cheap sentimentality and risible situations.
wd David L. Corley ph Michael G. Wojciechowski m Tim Truman pd Patti Podesta ed Sean Albertson
☆ James Belushi, Sheryl Lee, Kyle Chandler, Frank John Hughes, Ned Bellamy, Mark Carlton, Mac Davis, Jon Polito

Angels Hard as They Come

US   1971   90m   Metrocolor
New Realm/New World (Jonathan Demme)
🖭
Three bikers run into trouble in a ghost town inhabited by hippies but controlled by another gang of bikers.
Ponderous action movie, with a plot that seems to have been wrenched from some spaghetti Western, in which violence is seen as a force for good.
w Jonathan Demme, Joe Viola d Joe Viola ph Steve Katz m Richard Hieronymous, Carp ad Jack Fisk ed Joe Ravetz
☆ Scott Glenn, Charles Dierkop, Gilda Texter, James Iglehart, Garry Littlejohn, Gary Busey, Janet Wood, Don Carerra, Brendan Kelly, Larry Tucker
'The film's strivings for social and political significance are effectively smothered by the obligatory overlay of sex and violence.' – John Raisbeck, MFB
† The film was cut to 82m on its British release.

Angel's Holiday

US   1937   74m   bw
John Stone/TCF
The niece of a newspaper editor rounds up a gang of racketeers.
Smart comedy vehicle for Shirley Temple's only rival.
w Frank Fenton, Lynn Root d James Tinling
☆ Jane Withers, Robert Kent, Joan Davis, Sally Blane, Harold Huber, Frank Jenks, John Qualen, Lon Chaney Jnr

Angels in the Outfield

👪 US   1952   99m   bw
MGM (Clarence Brown)
GB title: Angels and the Pirates
The profane and bad-tempered manager of an unsuccessful baseball team gets help from an angel.
Unamusing, saccharine whimsy which does not deserve its excellent production values.
w Dorothy Kingsley, George Wells d Clarence Brown ph Paul C. Vogel m Daniele Amfitheatrof
☆ Paul Douglas, Janet Leigh, Keenan Wynn, Lewis Stone, Donna Corcoran, Spring Byington, Bruce Bennett

'Ya Gotta Believe! It Could Happen.'

Angels in the Outfield

US   1994   102m   Technicolor
Buena Vista/Walt Disney/Caravan (Irby Smith, Joe Roth, Roger Birnbaum)
GB title: Angels
A boy enlists the aid of angels so that a baseball team can be transformed from losers to winners, enabling him to be reunited with his father.
A remake that has made many alterations to the original story and added fancy special effects so that the angels are now visible; it is also far sweeter and no more successful as entertainment.
w Dorothy Kingsley, George Wells, Holly Goldberg Sloan d William Dear ph Matthew F. Leonetti m Randy Edelman pd Dennis Washington ed Bruce Green sp Giedra Rackauskas
☆ Danny Glover, Tony Danza, Brenda Fricker, Christopher Lloyd, Ben Johnson, Taylor Negron, Jay O. Sanders, Milton Davis Jnr
'Serves up its corn so unabashedly it's hard to take offence at its sappiness.' – Variety

Angels One Five *

GB   1952   98m   bw
Templar (John W. Gossage)
🖭
A slice of life in an RAF fighter station during the Battle of Britain.
Underplayed semi-documentary drama with stiff upper lips all round and the emphasis on characterization rather than action. A huge commercial success in Britain.
w Derek Twist d George More O'Ferrall ph Christopher Challis, Stanley Grant (air scenes) m John Wooldridge
☆ Jack Hawkins, John Gregson, Michael Denison, Andrew Osborn, Cyril Raymond, Humphrey Lestocq, Dulcie Gray, Veronica Hurst

Angels Over Broadway

US   1940   80m   bw
Columbia/Ben Hecht
🖭 🖭 🖭
During one rainy New York night, three of life's failures have one last stab at success.
Would-be poetic, moralizing melodrama very typical of its author; interesting but not a success.
w Ben Hecht d Ben Hecht, Lee Garmes ph Lee Garmes m George Antheil
☆ Douglas Fairbanks Jnr, Rita Hayworth, Thomas Mitchell, John Qualen, George Watts, Ralph Theodore
'There's a genial, original spirit to it.' – New Yorker, 1978
'It has excitement, fast talk, some knowable people, cynicism and sentiment.' – Otis Ferguson
† Sample dialogue: 'This town's a giant dice game … come on, seven!'
& Ben Hecht (as writer)

The Angels Wash Their Faces *

US   1939   86m   bw
Warner (Max Siegel)
original title: The Battle of City Hall
A bad boy joins the Dead End Kids, but they all reform in the end.
Routine programmer, hastily concocted after the success of Angels with Dirty Faces.
w Michael Fessier, Niven Busch, Robert Buckner d Ray Enright ph Arthur Todd m Adolph Deutsch
☆ Ann Sheridan, Ronald Reagan, the Dead End Kids, Bonita Granville, Frankie Thomas, Henry O'Neill, Berton Churchill, Eduardo Ciannelli
'Ray Enright's terrific meller pace makes it the sort of fare the average audience will eat up … he has an eye for the spectacular, including a

thrilling fire sequence and a dramatic courtroom scene.' – Variety

Angels with Dirty Faces ****

US   1938   97m   bw
Warner (Sam Bischoff)
A Brooklyn gangster is admired by slum boys, but for their sake pretends to be a coward when he goes to the electric chair.
A shrewd, slick entertainment package and a seminal movie for all kinds of reasons. It combined gangster action with fashionable social conscience; it confirmed the Dead End Kids as stars; it provided archetypal roles for its three leading players and catapulted the female lead into stardom. It also showed the Warner style of film-making, all cheap sets and shadows, at its most effective.
w John Wexley, Warren Duff story Rowland Brown d Michael Curtiz ph Sol Polito m Max Steiner
☆ James Cagney, Pat O'Brien, Humphrey Bogart, The Dead End Kids, Ann Sheridan, George Bancroft, Edward Pawley
'Should do fair business, but the picture itself is no bonfire.' – Variety
'A rousing, bloody, brutal melodrama.' – New York Mirror
& Rowland Brown; Michael Curtiz; James Cagney

Les Anges du Péché *

France   1943   73m   bw
Synops/Robert Paul
A novice nun has trouble with the mother superior because of her obsessive interest in a rebellious delinquent girl, and dies before taking her vows.
Interesting study of an enclosed society, notable as its director's first film.
w R. P. Bruckberger, Jean Giraudoux, Robert Bresson d Robert Bresson ph Philippe Agostini m Jean-Jacques Grunenwald
☆ Renée Faure, Jany Holt, Sylvie, Mila Parély, Marie-Hélène Dasté

Angi Vera ***

Hungary   1978   93m   Eastmancolor
Mafilm/Objektiv
🖭
English title: The Education of Vera
In the late 40s, an idealistic 18-year-old girl becomes a dedicated Communist Party worker and learns that betrayal is part of the system.
A deft and moving examination of the totalitarian mind-set, expressed in human terms; at the time, it was a courageous film to make.
w Pál Gábor story Endre Vészi ph Lajos Koltai m György Selmeczi ed Éva Karmentö
☆ Veronika Papp, Erzsi Pásztor, Eva Szabó, Tamás Dunai, László Horváth

'Angie wants to stay single, have a baby, and fall in love. But she's willing to negotiate.'

Angie *

US   1994   108m   Technicolor
Buena Vista/Hollywood Pictures/Caravan/Morra-Brezner-Steinberg-Tenenbaum (Larry Brezner, Patrick McCormick)
🖭 🖭 ⚙ 🎧
A Brooklyn girl grows up and decides that life should have more to offer than her pregnancy by a plumber she's known since her schooldays.
Drama of a woman searching for some meaning to her life, enjoyable mainly for the performances of Geena Davis and Stephen Rea as her casual lover; it falls away towards the end to a neat and sentimental resolution that falsifies what has gone before.
w Todd Graff novel Angie, I Says by Avra Wing d Martha Coolidge m Johnny E. Jensen m Jerry Goldsmith pd Mel Bourne ed Steven Cohen
☆ Geena Davis, James Gandolfini, Aida Turturro, Stephen Rea, Philip Bosco, Jenny O'Hara, Michael Rispoli
'One of the year's dampest celluloid squibs.' – James Keen, Film Review
† The role of Angie was originally written for Madonna.

Anglagård: see House of Angels

Angora Love **

👪 US   1929   20m   bw   silent
Hal Roach
🖭
Laurel and Hardy keep a goat in their lodgings.

Lively comedy, even funnier when remade two years later as Laughing Gravy.
w Leo McCarey and H. M. Walker d Lewis R. Foster
☆ Laurel and Hardy, Edgar Kennedy, Charlie Hall

The Angry Dragon
Hong Kong 1974 80m Eastmancolor Scope
Mark Associates/Oriental Film (Mah Jam Sheng)
A police inspector defeats a local gangster with the aid of martial arts students.
The usual high-kicking kung-fu mayhem, with an uninteresting narrative and unattractive leads.
wd Chiang Hung
☆ Cheng Lei, Christine Hui, Lee Wan Chung
'Possibly the least prepossessing of all independent Hong Kong features.' – Tony Rayns, MFB

Angry Harvest: see Bittere Ernte

The Angry Hills
GB 1959 105m bw
MGM/Raymond Stross
In 1940, an American war correspondent is helped by Greek freedom fighters.
Laboured war melodrama with pretentious dialogue but little characterization.
w A. I. Bezzerides novel Leon Uris d Robert Aldrich ph Stephen Dade m Richard Rodney Bennett ad Ken Adam
☆ Robert Mitchum, Gia Scala, Elisabeth Mueller, Stanley Baker, Donald Wolfit, Kieron Moore, Theodore Bikel, Sebastian Cabot, Peter Illing, Marius Goring, Leslie Phillips

The Angry Red Planet *
US 1959 83m colour Cinemagic
Sino (Sid Pink, Norman Maurer)
Four astronauts who land on Mars fight for their lives against a variety of monsters and giant Martians.
Enjoyably quaint science fiction, filmed in a process that gives a pink tinge to the action.
w Ib Melchior, Sid Pink d Ib Melchior ph Stanley Cortez ad Herman Townsley, Michael Sternlight, Art Wasson
☆ Gerald Mohr, Nora Hayden, Les Tremayne, Jack Kruschen

The Angry Silence **
GB 1960 94m bw
British Lion/Beaver (Richard Attenborough, Bryan Forbes)
A worker who refuses to join an unofficial strike is 'sent to Coventry' by his mates; the matter hits national headlines, and the communists use it to their own advantage.
Irresistibly reminding one of a po-faced I'm All Right Jack, this remains a fresh and urgent film which unfortunately lost excitement in its domestic scenes.
w Bryan Forbes story Michael Craig, Richard Gregson d Guy Green ph Arthur Ibbetson m Malcolm Arnold
☆ Richard Attenborough, Michael Craig, Pier Angeli, Bernard Lee, Alfred Burke, Laurence Naismith, Geoffrey Keen
'Vastly entertaining as well as thought-provoking. Matter and manner are for once wholly in harmony.' – Daily Mail
'A film made by people who care about the screen and care about what they are saying on it.' – Dilys Powell
⅋ Bryan Forbes, Richard Gregson, Michael Craig
Ⓥ Bryan Forbes

Die Angst des Tormanns beim Elfmeter: see The Goalkeeper's Fear of the Penalty Kick

Angus *
🎟 US 1995 90m colour
Entertainment/Atlas/BBC/Syalis/Tele München/Quality/Turner (Dawn Steel, Charles Roven)
An overweight teenager, who is mocked at school, finds the courage to fight back.
Pleasant, old-fashioned, though unexceptional comedy of an outsider who insists on being part of a community.
w Jill Gordon story Chris Crutcher d Patrick Read Johnson ph Alexander Grusynski m David Russo pd Larry Miller ed Janice Hampton

☆ Kathy Bates, George C. Scott, Charlie Talbert, Ariana Richards, James Van Der Beek, Chris Owen, Lawrence Pressman, Rita Moreno
'Fat kids deserve a better deal from this movie that merely manages to re-establish American college students as the most obnoxiously cruel species since the Hitler Youth went out of fashion. Angus gets his moment of triumph, but it's the sour taste of juvenile hostility that lasts a lot longer.' – Tom Hutchinson, Film Review

Animal Behavior
US 1989 89m DeLuxe
Millimeter (Kjehl Rasmussen)
A university music teacher is attracted to an animal behavourist, who is teaching a chimpanzee sign language, but finds it difficult to communicate her own feelings.
A would-be romantic comedy that is ambitious in its scope, trying to cram in several plot strands while examining the odd behaviour of humans, but fatally flawed in its execution, and with an unhappily mannered performance from Karen Allen.
w Susan Rice d H. Anne Riley ph David Spellvin m Cliff Eidelman pd Jeannine Oppewall ed Joseph Weintraub
☆ Karen Allen, Armand Assante, Holly Hunter, Josh Mostel, Richard Libertini, Alexa Kenin, Jon Matthews, Nan Martin
† H. Anne Riley is a name that hides the real identity of director Jenny Bowen, who began making the film in 1984, and its producer, who completed it much later; after that, it sat on the shelf before being released in the US, and was not seen in Britain until 1997, when the new TV station Channel 5 inflicted it upon its viewers.

Animal Crackers ***
🎟 US 1930 98m bw
Paramount
Thieves covet a valuable oil painting unveiled at a swank party.
An excuse for the Marx Brothers, and a lively one in patches, though sedate and stagebound in treatment. The boys are all in top form, and many of the dialogue exchanges are classics.
w Morrie Ryskind musical play Morrie Ryskind, George S. Kaufman d Victor Heerman ph George Folsey m/ly Bert Kalmar, Harry Ruby
☆ Groucho, Chico, Harpo, Zeppo, Margaret Dumont, Lillian Roth, Louis Sorin, Robert Greig, Hal Thompson
GROUCHO: 'You're the most beautiful woman I've ever seen, which doesn't say much for you.'
GROUCHO: 'One morning I shot an elephant in my pajamas. How he got into my pajamas I'll never know.'
GUESTS: 'Hooray for Captain Spaulding, the African explorer!'
GROUCHO: 'Did someone call me schnorrer?'
GUESTS: 'Hooray, hooray, hooray!'
ZEPPO: 'He went into the jungle, where all the monkeys throw nuts.'
GROUCHO: 'If I stay here, I'll go nuts.'
GUESTS: 'Hooray, hooray, hooray!'
He put all his reliance
In courage and defiance
And risked his life for science.'
GROUCHO: 'Hey, hey!'
MRS RITTENHOUSE: 'He is the only white man who covered every acre…'
GROUCHO: 'I think I'll try and make her…'
GUESTS: 'Hooray, hooray, hooray!'
'A hit on the screen before it opened, and in the money plenty.' – Variety

Animal Farm **
🎟 GB 1955 75m Technicolor
Louis de Rochemont/Halas and Batchelor
Oppressed by the cruelty and inefficiency of their master, the animals take over a farm but find fresh tyrants among themselves.
George Orwell's political fable – 'all animals are equal but some animals are more equal than others' – is faithfully followed in this ambitious but rather disappointingly flat cartoon version.
m Matyas Seiber w/p/d John Halas, Joy Batchelor
☆ Featuring voices: Maurice Denham
'A melodramatic fantasy that is mordant, tender and quixotic, shot with ironic humour.' – New York Times

The Animal Kingdom *
US 1932 95m bw
RKO (David O. Selznick)
GB title: The Woman in His House
An intellectual publisher tries to justify keeping both a wife and a mistress.
Smart comedy-drama from a Broadway success, later bowdlerized as One More Tomorrow (qv).
w Horace Jackson play Philip Barry d Edward H. Griffith ph Lucien Andriot m Max Steiner
☆ Leslie Howard, Ann Harding, Myrna Loy, Neil Hamilton, William Gargan, Henry Stephenson, Ilka Chase
'A wise and engaging picture addressed to the upper levels of fandom.' – Variety

'Two billion years in the making!'
The Animal World *
US 1956 80m Technicolor
Warner/Windsor (Irwin Allen)
The evolution of animals from their primitive beginnings.
Ambitious documentary with a popular science approach; very variable, with poorish model work.
wd Irwin Allen ph Harold Wellman m Paul Sawtell sp Willis O'Brien, Ray Harryhausen

The Animals
US 1970 86m Technicolor Techniscope
MGM-EMI/XYZ (Richard Bakalyan)
aka: Five Savage Men
A schoolteacher, raped by a sadistic killer and his gang, takes her revenge with the aid of an Indian who saves her life.
Notably grim and violent Western, made with no sense of style or period and overweighted by the heavy irony of its climax.
w Richard Bakalyan d Ron Joy ph Keith Smith m Rupert Holmes ed Pier Laskey
☆ Henry Silva, Keenan Wynn, Michele Carey, John Anderson, Joseph Turkel, Pepper Martin, Bobby Hall, Peter Hellmann
'As with other forms of pornography, the possibilities of originality within the pornography of violence are distinctly finite.' – James D. White, MFB

The Animals Film *
GB/US 1981 136m colour/bw
Slick Pix
A hard-hitting documentary recording human ill-treatment of animals, with obvious hints that humans themselves will be next. Narrated by Julie Christie.
Not for the squeamish.
wd Victor Schonfeld

Animalympics
🎟 US 1979 80m Technicolor
Lisburger (Steven Lisburger, Donald Kushner)
Wild animals from around the world compete in athletic events.
A lively, though inconsequential, animated spoof of the Olympics, with a US bias; its hyperactive style, though, seems tame alongside the hysteria of TV coverage of the actual event.
w Michael Fremer, Steven Lisburger story Steven Lisburger, Roger Allers, John Norton d Steven Lisburger, Bill Kroyer m Graham Gouldman ad Roger Allers, John Norton, Peter Mueller ed Matt Cope
☆ Featuring the voices of: Gilda Radner, Billy Crystal, Harry Shearer, Michael Fremer

Animated Genesis *
GB 1952 22m Technicolor (blown up from 16mm)
Korda/British Lion
Greed and the machine enslave mankind.
Ambitious and decorative cartoon conceived and drawn by Joan and Peter Foldes, from whom little was subsequently heard.
m Thomas Henderson

Ann Vickers *
US 1933 72m bw
RKO (Pandro S. Berman)
A feminist social worker is taught a thing or two by life and settles down with a corrupt judge.
Reasonably effective version of a popular though heavy-going novel of the time.

w Jane Murfin novel Sinclair Lewis d John Cromwell ph David Abel, Edward Cronjager m Max Steiner
☆ Irene Dunne, Walter Huston, Conrad Nagel, Bruce Cabot, Edna May Oliver, Mitchell Lewis, Murray Kinnell
'Her sufferings are bearable and her ultimate happiness is assured, so this is vicarious enjoyment for any woman. Lovely romance, moderate penance, final respectability. All of which suggests that Ann Vickers should do moderately good biz.' – Variety

Anna
Italy 1951 100m bw
Lux (Ponti/de Laurentiis)
A novice nun recalls her former life and almost gives up her vocation.
Soupy woman's picture of no particular merit.
w Giuseppe Berto, Dino Risi, Ivo Perilli, Franco Brusati, Rodolfo Sonego d Alberto Lattuada ph Otello Martelli m Nino Rota
☆ Silvana Mangano, Raf Vallone, Vittorio Gassman, Gaby Morlay, Jacques Dumesnil

Anna
US 1987 100m TVC Color
Magnus (Zanne Devine, Yurek Bogayevicz)
A Czech-born actress in the New York fringe theatre is betrayed by a young female admirer.
Echoes of All About Eve seem less important than the political asides, and the whole thing is a bit of a muddle.
w Agnieszka Holland d Yurek Bogayevicz ph Bobby Bukowski m Greg Hawkes
☆ Sally Kirkland, Robert Fields, Paulina Porizkova
⅋ Sally Kirkland

Anna and the King *
🎟 US 1999 148m DeLuxe Panavision
TCF (Lawrence Bender, Ed Albert)
In the 1860s an Englishwoman becomes tutor to the children of the embattled King of Siam.
A lavish production, often gorgeous to look at, is laced with sentimentality and a simple approach to history; Foster adds a little frosty femininity to the role of Anna, which chills the romantic interludes.
w Steve Meerson, Peter Krikes diaries Anna Leonowens d Andy Tennant ph Caleb Deschanel m George Fenton pd Luciana Arrighi cos Jenny Beavan
☆ Jodie Foster, Chow Yun-Fat, Bai Ling, Tom Felton, Syed Alwi, Randall Duk Kim, Lim Kay Siu, Melissa Campbell, Deanna Yusoff
'A schmaltzy, ultra-elaborate, overly long production, all too consciously conceived as an old-fashioned family entertainment.' – Emanuel Levy, Variety
'Picturesque but stodgy…unfolds like an exotic historical diorama with dramatic vignettes thrown in for spice.' – Stephen Holden, New York Times
⅋ Luciana Arrighi; Jenny Beavan

Anna and the King of Siam **
US 1946 128m bw
TCF (Louis D. Lighton)
In 1862 an English governess arrives in Bangkok to teach the 67 children of the king.
Unusual and lavish drama, tastefully handled and generally absorbing despite miscasting and several slow passages.
w Talbot Jennings, Sally Benson book Margaret Landon d John Cromwell ph Arthur Miller m Bernard Herrmann ad Lyle Wheeler, William Darling
☆ Irene Dunne, Rex Harrison, Linda Darnell, Gale Sondergaard, Lee J. Cobb, Mikhail Rasumny
'A film that never touches the imagination, a film that leaves the mind uninformed and the memory unburdened.' – Richard Winnington
'It's pitifully unauthentic, and not a very good movie either, but the story itself holds considerable interest.' – Pauline Kael, 70s
🏆 Arthur Miller
⅋ Talbot Jennings, Sally Benson; Bernard Herrmann; Gale Sondergaard

---

'Garbo talks!'

Anna Christie **
US 1930 86m bw
MGM
▣ ▣
A waterfront prostitute falls in love with a young seaman.
Primitive sound version of an earthy theatrical warhorse: it has a niche in history as the film in which Garbo first talked.
w Frances Marion *play* Eugene O'Neill
d Clarence Brown *ph* William Daniels
☆ *Greta Garbo*, Charles Bickford, *Marie Dressler*, James T. Mack, Lee Phelps
'Great artistically and tremendous commercially ... in all respects a wow picture.' – *Variety*
'A very talkie, uncinematic affair, more old-fashioned than the silent movies. If it were not so well acted it would be pretty tiresome.' – *National Board of Review*
† A 1923 silent version starred Blanche Sweet and was directed by John Wray.
⚷ Clarence Brown; William Daniels; Greta Garbo

Anna Karenina: see *Leo Tolstoy's Anna Karenina (1997)*

Anna Karenina **
US 1935 95m bw
MGM (David O. Selznick)
▣ ▣
The wife of a Russian aristocrat falls for a dashing cavalry officer.
Well-staged but finally exasperating romantic tragedy, sparked by good performances and production.
w Clemence Dane, Salka Viertel *novel* Leo Tolstoy d Clarence Brown *ph* William Daniels m Herbert Stothart
☆ *Greta Garbo*, Fredric March, *Basil Rathbone*, Freddie Bartholomew, Maureen O'Sullivan, May Robson, Reginald Owen, Reginald Denny
'Cinch b.o. anywhere. In the foreign markets it should come close to establishing modern-day highs.' – *Variety*
'A dignified and effective drama which becomes significant because of that tragic, lonely and glamorous blend which is the Garbo personality.' – *André Sennwald*
'It reaches no great heights of tragedy or drama but rather moves forward relentlessly and a little coldly.' – *The Times*
† Previously filmed as a 1928 silent called *Love*, with Garbo and John Gilbert.

Anna Karenina *
GB 1948 139m bw
London Films (Alexander Korda)
▣ ▣ ⌕
Tiresomely overlong but very handsomely staged remake marred by central miscasting.
w Jean Anouilh, Guy Morgan, Julien Duvivier d Julien Duvivier *ph* Henri Alekan m Constant Lambert *ad* André Andrejew *ed* Russell Lloyd
☆ Vivien Leigh, Kieron Moore, *Ralph Richardson*, Marie Lohr, Sally Ann Howes, Niall MacGinnis, Michael Gough, Helen Haye, Mary Kerridge
'Vivien Leigh is lashed about by the tremendous role of Anna like a pussy cat with a tigress by the tail. She is not helped by a script which insists on sentimentally ennobling one of fiction's most vehemently average women.' – *James Agee*

Anna Lucasta *
US 1949 86m bw
Columbia/Security (Philip Yordan)
The bad girl of a farming family comes home to marry, but her past catches up with her.
Polish immigrant melodrama, a touring company staple, adequately transferred to the screen.
w Philip Yordan, Arthur Laurents *play* Philip Yordan d Irving Rapper *ph* Sol Polito m David Diamond
☆ Paulette Goddard, Oscar Homolka, Broderick Crawford, William Bishop, Gale Page, Mary Wickes

Anna Lucasta *
US 1958 97m bw
(UA) Longridge Enterprises (Sidney Harmon)
Black version of the long-running play; performances standard.
w Philip Yordan d Arnold Laven *ph* Lucien Ballard m Elmer Bernstein
☆ Eartha Kitt, Frederick O'Neal, Sammy Davis Jnr, Henry Scott, Rex Ingram, James Edwards

Anna of Brooklyn
Italy/France/US 1958 106m colour
Technirama
Circeo Cinematografica/France Cinema/RKO (Milko Skofic)
An attractive widow returns from New York to her native Italian village in search of a husband.
Footling romantic drama which wastes its cast and budget.
w Ettore Margadonna, Dino Risi d Reginald Denham, Carlo Lasticati *ph* Giuseppe Rotunno m Alessandro Cicognini, Vittorio de Sica
☆ Gina Lollobrigida, Dale Robertson, Vittorio de Sica, Amedeo Nazzari, Peppino de Filippo, Gabriella Palotta

Annabel Takes a Tour
US 1939 69m bw
RKO
▣
A star on a publicity tour balks at the stunts she is expected to perform.
Thinnish sequel to The Affairs of Annabel (qv).
w Bert Granet and Olive Cooper d Lew Landers
☆ Lucille Ball, Jack Oakie, Ruth Donnelly, Bradley Page, Ralph Forbes

Annabelle Partagée
France 1990 80m colour
Gala/ça Films (Sophie Delochée, Anne Fieschl)
▣
A student dancer ditches her middle-aged boyfriend for someone younger.
Dull film, in which little happens and nothing of any consequence.
wd Francesca Comencini *ph* Michel Abramowicz m Les Valentins, Etienne Daho *ad* Valérie Grall *ed* Yves Deschamps
☆ Delphine Zingg, François Marthouret, Jean-Claude Adelin
'A French film about l'amour in which l'ennui takes over early on.' – *Nigel Andrews, Financial Times*
'The one notable moment of Francesca Comencini's mildly feminist debut is an erect penis, slightly out of focus and looking rather like a toadstool, seen in the foreground of the opening shot. This might be a small milestone, so to speak, in popular French cinema.' – *Philip French, Observer*

Annabelle's Affairs
US 1931 74m bw
Fox
▣
When her husband disappears, a young bride becomes head cook at his rival's home. Then the husband turns up.
Standard farce which worked pretty well in its day.
w Leon Gordon *play* Good Gracious Annabelle by Clare Kummer d Alfred Werker
☆ Jeanette MacDonald, Victor McLaglen, Roland Young, Sam Hardy, William Collier Snr

An Annapolis Story
US 1955 81m colour
Allied Artists/Walter Mirisch
▣
GB title: *The Blue and the Gold*
Two cadets at the naval academy love the same girl.
Artless recruiting poster heroics.
w Dan Ullman d Don Siegel *ph* Sam Leavitt m Marlin Skiles
☆ Diana Lynn, John Derek, Kevin McCarthy, Pat Dooley, L. Q. Jones
'Seldom have so many scrubbed, wholesome-looking young people thronged any picture.' – *New York Times*

Anne and Muriel ***
France 1971 108m Eastmancolor
Gala/Les Films du Carrosse/Cinetel (Marcel Berbert)
▣
original title: *Les Deux Anglaises et le Continent*
A French writer falls in love with two English sisters.
Elegant variation on the eternal triangle.
w François Truffaut, Jean Gruault *novel* Henri-Pierre Roche d François Truffaut *ph* Nestor Almendros m Georges Delerue *ad* Michel de Broin *ed* Yann Dedet
☆ Jean-Pierre Léaud, Kika Markham, Stacey Tendeter, Sylvia Marriott, Marie Mansart, Philippe Léotard, Irene Tunc

Anne of Green Gables *
👫 US 1934 79m bw
RKO (Kenneth MacGowan)
An orphan girl goes to the country to live with her aunt.
Standard version of the classic for young girls. Anne Shirley had been known as Dawn O'Day and legally adopted the name of her character in this, her first starring role.
w Sam Mintz *novel* L. M. Montgomery d George Nicholls Jnr *ph* Lucien Andriot m Max Steiner
☆ Anne Shirley, Tom Brown, O. P. Heggie, Helen Westley, Sara Haden, Charley Grapewin
'Made up and monotonous – tragedy having its breakfast in bed.' – *Otis Ferguson*
† *Anne of Windy Poplars* (qv), with the same stars and production team, followed in 1940.

Anne of the Indies *
US 1951 87m Technicolor
TCF (George Jessel)
Lady pirate Anne Bonney, the terror of the Caribbean, is at odds with her former master Blackbeard.
Routine swashbuckler, generally well handled.
w Philip Dunne, Arthur Caesar d Jacques Tourneur *ph* Harry Jackson m Franz Waxman
☆ Jean Peters, Louis Jourdan, Debra Paget, Herbert Marshall, Thomas Gomez, James Robertson Justice, Sean McClory, Francis Pierlot

Anne of the Thousand Days *
GB 1969 146m Technicolor Panavision
Universal/Hal B. Wallis
▣ ▣
Henry VIII divorces his wife to marry Anne Boleyn, but soon finds evidence of adultery.
A somewhat unlikely view of history, rather boringly presented on a woman's magazine level, but with occasional good moments from a cast of British notables.
w John Hale, Bridget Boland *play* Maxwell Anderson d Charles Jarrott *ph* Arthur Ibbetson m Georges Delerue *pd* Maurice Carter *cos* Margaret Furse
☆ *Richard Burton, Geneviève Bujold, John Colicos*, Irene Papas, Anthony Quayle, Michael Hordern, Katharine Blake, Peter Jeffrey, William Squire, Esmond Knight, Nora Swinburne
'The costumes, beautiful in themselves, have that unconvincing air of having come straight off the rack at Nathan's.' – *Brenda Davies*
'A decent dullness is, alas, the keynote.' – *Michael Billington, Illustrated London News*
'The quintessential work of art for people who haven't the foggiest notion of what art is.' – *John Simon*
'Intelligent from line to line, but the emotions supplied seem hypocritical, and the conception lacks authority ... Burton's performance is colourless. It's as though he *remembered* how to act but couldn't work up much enthusiasm or involvement.' – *Pauline Kael*
⚹ Margaret Furse
⚷ picture; John Hale, Bridget Boland; Arthur Ibbetson; Georges Delerue; Richard Burton; Geneviève Bujold; Anthony Quayle

Anne of Windy Poplars
👫 US 1940 88m bw
RKO (Cliff Reid)
The newly appointed vice-principal of a small-town school charms her way out of a neighbourhood feud.
Pleasant family drama in a minor key, but all very forgettable.
w Michael Kanin, Jerry Cady *novel* L. M. Montgomery d Jack Hively *md* Roy Webb *ad* Van Nest Polglase *ed* George Hively
☆ Anne Shirley, James Ellison, Henry Travers, Patric Knowles, Slim Summerville, Elizabeth Patterson, Louise Campbell, Joan Carroll
† It was a sequel to *Anne of Green Gables* (qv).

Anne Trister
Canada 1986 100m colour
Vision 4 (Roger Frappier, Claude Bonin)
After the death of her father, a young Jewish artist leaves her boyfriend and moves from her Swiss home to Quebec to make sense of her life; there she falls in love with a woman friend.
Sombre, slow-paced study of a woman seeking her true identity; there is a great deal of heart-searching but not much action.
w Marcel Beaulieu, Léa Pool d Léa Pool *ph* Pierre Mignot m René Dupéré *ad* Vianney Gauthier *ed* Michel Arcand
☆ Albane Guilhe, Louise Marleau, Hugues Quester, Lucie Laurier, Nuvit Ozdogru, Guy Thauvette, Kim Yaroshevskaya

L'Année Dernière à Marienbad: see *Last Year at Marienbad*

Annie
👫 US 1982 128m Metrocolor
Panavision
Columbia/Ray Stark (Joe Layton)
▣ ▣ ⌕
In 1933 an orphan waif charms a munitions millionaire and is adopted by him.
Misguided opening-out of a charming stage musical based on the comic strip which is basically a reversal of Oliver Twist. Some of the best numbers have been discarded, the dancing is ponderous, the acting distinctly uneasy, and the choice of director stupefying. None of it works at all.
w Carol Sobieski, from the stage play *book* Thomas Meehan *comic strip* Harold Gray d John Huston *ph* Richard Moore m Ralph Burns *pd* Dale Hennesy *ly* Martin Charnin
☆ Albert Finney, Carol Burnett, Aileen Quinn, Ann Reinking, Bernadette Peters, Tim Curry, Geoffrey Holder, Edward Herrmann
'Whatever indefinable charm the stage show had is completely lost in this lumbering and largely uninteresting and uninvolving exercise, where the obvious waste reaches almost Pentagonian proportions.' – *Variety*
'The whole thing has the air of a vast, hollow Christmas tree bauble intended not so much for children as for the infantile-minded middle-aged.' – *Sunday Times*
'This is the film I want on my tombstone.' – *Ray Stark*
'Funeral services may be held starting this week at a theatre near you.' – *Time*
† The cost of *Annie*, starting with $9,000,000 for the rights, rose to $42,000,000. It was not recovered.
⚷ art direction; original song score

Annie Get Your Gun *
US 1950 107m Technicolor
MGM (Arthur Freed)
♬
A young female hillbilly joins Frank Butler's sharpshooting act, and is sophisticated by her love for him.
Gaudy, stagey, generally uninspired screen version of the famous musical show based remotely on a historical character of post-wild-west days. There is a lack of dancing, the direction is stodgy, and in general flair the production falls disappointingly below MGM's usual standard.
w Sidney Sheldon *musical play* Herbert and Dorothy Fields d George Sidney *ph* Charles Rosher *m/ly* Irving Berlin *md* Adolph Deutsch, Roger Edens *ch* Robert Alton *ad* Cedric Gibbons, Paul Groesse
☆ Betty Hutton, Howard Keel, Edward Arnold, J. Carrol Naish, Louis Calhern
† The real Annie Oakley was born Phoebe Ann Oakley Mozie in 1860, and died in 1926. The role was to have been played by Judy Garland, who was fired after displays of temperament; also considered were Doris Day, Judy Canova and Betty Garrett.
†† Louis Calhern replaced Frank Morgan, who died during production.
♫ 'Colonel Buffalo Bill'; 'Doing What Comes Naturally'; 'The Girl That I Marry'; 'You Can't Get a Man with a Gun'; 'There's No Business Like Show Business'; 'My Defenses Are Down'; 'I'm an Indian Too'; 'I Got the Sun in the Morning'; 'Anything You Can Do'; 'They Say It's Wonderful'
⚹ music direction
⚷ Charles Rosher

Annie Hall ****
US 1977 93m DeLuxe
UA/Jack Rollins-Charles H. Joffe (Fred T. Gallo)
▣ ▣ ⌕ ⌕
Sub-title: *A Nervous Romance*
Against the neuroses of New York and Los Angeles, a Jewish comedian has an affair with a midwestern girl.

Semi-serious collage of jokes and bits of technique, some of the former very funny and some of the latter very successful. For no very good reason it hit the box-office spot and turned its creator, of whom it is very typical, from a minority performer to a superstar.
w Woody Allen, Marshall Brickman d Woody Allen ph Gordon Willis m various
☆ Woody Allen, Diane Keaton, Tony Roberts, Carol Kane, Paul Simon, Shelley Duvall
ALLEN: 'Hey, don't knock masturbation. It's sex with someone I love.'

'The film's priceless vignettes about the difficulties in chitchatting with strangers, the awkward moments in family visits, and the frequent breakdowns in communication and failures in intimacy, its reminiscences about the palpable horrors of growing up in Brooklyn, and its comic encounters with lobsters in the kitchen or spiders in the bathroom, all seem like snapshots from Allen and Keaton's own romance.' – Les Keyser, Hollywood in the Seventies
† The narrative supposedly mirrors the real-life affair of the stars, who separated before the film came out. (Diane Keaton's family name is Hall.)
♟ picture; script; direction; Diane Keaton
♟ Woody Allen (as actor)
♟ picture; script; Woody Allen (as director); Diane Keaton

Annie Oakley *
US 1935 90m bw
RKO (Cliff Reid)
▣
The historical story, more or less, of the lady later immortalized in Annie Get Your Gun.
Lively semi-Western with good dialogue but gluey plot development.
w Joel Sayre, John Twist d George Stevens ph J. Roy Hunt md Alberto Colombo ad Van Nest Polglase
☆ Barbara Stanwyck, Preston Foster, Melvyn Douglas, Moroni Olsen, Pert Kelton, Andy Clyde, Chief Thunderbird
'A swell idea that doesn't quite come through.' – Variety

Annie's Coming Out *
Australia 1984 93m Eastmancolor
Film Australia (Don Murray)
A physically handicapped child, wrongly characterized as mentally retarded also, is brought out by a devoted teacher.
Fictionalized version of a true story: predictably well intentioned, shocking, and consistently watchable.
w John Patterson, Chris Borthwick book Rosemary Crossley d Gil Brealey ph Mick Van Borneman m Simon Walker
☆ Angela Punch-McGregor, Drew Forsythe, Tina Arhondis, Liddy Clark, Monica Maughan

The Annihilators
US 1985 84m colour
New World (Allan C. Pedersen, Tom Chapman)
▣▣ ▣
Vietnam veterans are hired as small-town vigilantes.
Violent action film of no visible merit.
w Brian Russell d Charles E. Sellier Jnr ph Henning Schellerup m Bob Summers ad Simon Gittins ed Dan Gross
☆ Christopher Stone, Andy Wood, Lawrence Hilton-Jacobs, Gerrit Graham, Dennis Redfield, Paul Koslo

The Anniversary *
GB 1968 95m Technicolor
Warner/Hammer (Jimmy Sangster)
A malevolent one-eyed widow will stop at nothing to prevent her grown sons from leaving the family orbit, and they meet each year to mourn the death of the husband she really hated.
Agreeable but over-talkative black comedy with a splendid role for its star and some good scattered moments, marred by a general lack of style.
w Jimmy Sangster play Bill MacIlwraithA d Roy Ward Baker ph Harry Waxman m Philip Martell ad Reece Pemberton ed James Needs, Peter Weatherley
☆ Bette Davis, Jack Hedley, James Cossins, Sheila Hancock, Elaine Taylor, Christian Roberts, Timothy Bateson
'It all reminds one of a love scene in a funeral parlour.' – Variety

'Magisterially grotesque in elegantly tailored eye-patch and exotic gown, she snaps out her bitchy insults with all 57 varieties of relish.' – MFB
† Alvin Rakoff was replaced as director during filming.

Ano Natsu, Ichiban Shizukana Umi: see A Scene at the Sea

El Anonimo
Spain 1990 87m Eastmancolor
Sagutxo (Alfonso Arandia)
Four students try to recover an incriminating letter addressed to one of their professors.
Amiable, lackadaisical comedy.
w Alfonso Arandia, Jose Antonio Gomez d Alfonso Arandia ph Gonzalo F. Berridi m Mikel Erentxum ed Juan I. Sanmateo
☆ Miguel Molina, Jorge de Juan, Martxelo Rudio, Carlos Zabala, Nacho Martinez, Rosa Maria Sarda, Alejandra Greppi

The Anonymous Letter: see El Anonimo

Another 48 Hrs
US 1990 95m Technicolor
Paramount/Eddie Murphy Productions (Lawrence Gordon, Robert D. Wachs)
▣▣ ▣ ▣ ▣ ▣
A cop enters into a partnership with a criminal to catch a drug dealer.
A virtual remake of 48 Hours (qv), but lacking in energy or interest.
w John Fasano, Jeb Stuart, Larry Gross story Fred Braughton d Walter Hill ph Matthew F. Leonetti m James Horner pd Joseph C. Nemec III ad Gary Wissner ed Freeman Davies, Carmel Davies, Donn Aron
☆ Eddie Murphy, Nick Nolte, Brion James, Kevin Tighe, Ed O'Ross, David Anthony Marshall, Andrew Divoff, Bernie Casey, Brent Jennings, Ted Markland, Tisha Campbell
'Disappoints in its failure, after eight years, to introduce even the faintest wrinkle of something new.' – Variety

'Convention outraged ... a class abandoned ... a country betrayed!'
Another Country *
GB 1984 90m colour
TCF/Virgin/Goldcrest (Alan Marshall)
▣▣ ▣ ▣
A homosexual defector to Russia reflects on the public school pressures which influenced him.
Upper-crust militarism, arrogance, sadism and homosexuality rolled up in a package which pleased the West End theatre crowds but seems faintly absurd on film. Not much of a recruiting poster for Eton.
w Julian Mitchell play Julian Mitchell d Marek Kanievska ph Peter Biziou m Michael Storey pd Brian Morris
☆ Rupert Everett, Colin Firth, Michael Jenn, Robert Addie, Anna Massey, Rupert Wainwright, Betsy Brantley
'Inevitably it went down well at the Cannes Film Festival, where movies critical of their own country's shortcomings are always favoured.' – Margaret Hinxman, Daily Mail

Another Dawn
US 1937 73m bw
Warner (Harry Joe Brown)
In a British army post in Africa, a wife is torn between duty and romance.
Absurdly sudsy melodrama, a potboiler for stars between more important assignments.
w Laird Doyle d William Dieterle ph Tony Gaudio m Erich Wolfgang Korngold
☆ Errol Flynn, Kay Francis, Ian Hunter, Frieda Inescort, Herbert Mundin
† In every Warner film where a cinema canopy was shown, the title advertised was Another Dawn, so its use here as an actual title is presumably a piece of cynicism.

Another Day in Paradise **
US 1998 100m CFI
Metrodome/Chinese Bookie (Stephen Chin, Larry Clark, James Woods)
▣ ▣
In the 1970s, a middle-aged drug dealer and his girlfriend career across Oklahoma with a young junkie and his girlfriend.
Hectic road movie, set in sleazy motels and featuring various varieties of low-life, given an extra jolt by the

nervy authenticity of the performances of Woods and Griffith.
w Christopher Landon, Stephen Chin book Eddie Little d Larry Clark ph Eric Edwards pd Aaron Osborne ed Luis Colina
☆ James Woods, Melanie Griffith, Vincent Kartheiser, Natasha Gregson Wagner, James Otis, Peter Sarsgaard, Paul Hipp, Brent Briscoe, Branden Williams, Kim Flowers
'This imperfect but compelling outlaw drama may be too raw and unflinching to make a wide splash, but should find an audience ready to respond to its gritty aesthetic.' – David Rooney, Variety
† Lou Diamond Phillips appears uncredited as Jewels.

Another Face
US 1935 72m bw
RKO
GB title: It Happened in Hollywood
A gangster has his face lifted and becomes a film star.
Rather heavy comedy with some good laughs.
w Garrett Graham, John Twist, Ray Mayer, Thomas Dugan d Christy Cabanne
☆ Brian Donlevy, Wallace Ford, Phyllis Brooks, Erik Rhodes, Molly Lamont, Alan Hale

Another Fine Mess **
US 1930 30m bw
Hal Roach
On the run from a cop, Stan and Ollie masquerade as master and maid.
Elaborate star comedy with spoken introduction instead of titles; very satisfying but not quite vintage.
w H. M. Walker, from a sketch by Stan Laurel's father d James Parrott
☆ Laurel and Hardy, James Finlayson, Thelma Todd, Charles Gerrard

Another Girl, Another Planet
US 1992 56m bw Pixelvision
ICA/Michael Almereyda, Robin O'Hara, Bob Gosse
▣▣
A man attempts to seduce women passing through his apartment by showing them old cartoon films, while his married neighbour looks on or discusses the meaning of life.
Depression as an art form: a minimalist film shot with a toy camera that renders everything slightly out of focus and provides at best a murky image of shadows and fog, turning human life into a grey smear on the wall.
wd Michael Almereyda ph Jim Denault ed David Leonard
☆ Nic Ratner, Barry Sherman, Mary Ward, Lisa Perisot, Maggie Rush
'An elegantly-crafted chamber piece that effortlessly belies its no-budget origins.' – Steve Bode, London Film Festival
'We're so often up to the director's pretensions in angst that despair starts to creep almost palpably off the screen and into the auditorium. Joyful it ain't.' – Tom Hutchinson, Film Review
† The film was shot using a Fisher-Price PXL 2000 child's camcorder, made of moulded plastic, with a fixed lens, and recording on standard audio cassettes. The images it produces fade rapidly and are composed of easily visible pixels, like an over-enlarged computer image. The camera, which was made as a toy for Christmas 1987 and discontinued soon after, has become a favourite of a group of experimental film-makers because of its technical limitations.

Another Language
US 1933 75m bw
MGM (Walter Wanger)
A young wife does not fit in with her husband's snobby family and falls in love with his nephew.
Flat treatment of a dated play.
w Herman J. Mankiewicz, Gertrude Purcell, Donald Ogden Stewart play Rose Franken d Edward H. Griffith ph Ray June
☆ Helen Hayes, Robert Montgomery, John Beal, Louise Closser Hale, Henry Travers, Margaret Hamilton
'A very good picture that will get more than average box office attention ... everything is handled with intellect and due restraint.' – Variety

Another Man, Another Chance
France/US 1977 132m Eastmancolor
UA/Films 13/Ariane (Alexandre Mnouchkine, George Dancigers)
▣
French title: Un Autre Homme, une Autre Chance
aka: Another Man, Another Woman
A Yank vet and a French widow meet and fall in love in the old west.
Pretty, overlong, rather enervating romance with an unusual and not entirely convincing setting.
wd Claude Lelouch ph Jacques Lefrançois m Francis Lai
☆ James Caan, Geneviève Bujold, Francis Huster, Susan Tyrrell

Another Man's Poison *
GB 1951 89m bw
Douglas Fairbanks Jnr/Daniel M. Angel
A lady novelist poisons her husband and lover, then unwittingly takes a fatal dose herself.
Hysterical vehicle for a fading Hollywood star reduced to repeating her tantrums in an English studio on a low budget; she should have stayed home, as should her director.
w Val Guest play Deadlock by Leslie Sands d Irving Rapper ph Robert Krasker m John Greenwood
☆ Bette Davis, Anthony Steel, Gary Merrill, Emlyn Williams, Barbara Murray, Reginald Beckwith, Edna Morris
'Barnstormers as rich and improbable as this are rare ... the general atmosphere takes one back to 1935.' – Gavin Lambert
'Like reading Ethel M. Dell by flashes of lightning.' – Frank Hauser
'The melodramatic gamut has seldom experienced such a workout.' – Hollywood Reporter

Another Part of the Forest *
US 1948 108m bw
U-I (Jerry Bresler)
In the post-Civil War years, Marcus Hubbard leads his family to worldly success by cheating and the misuse of power: he lives to regret it, as the children learn their lessons all too well.
This backwards sequel to The Little Foxes (qv), showing how the characters of that play got to be their nasty selves, is quite absorbingly acted but stagily presented, with plenty of care but no style.
w Vladimir Pozner play Lillian Hellman d Michael Gordon ph Hal Mohr m Daniele Amfitheatrof
☆ Fredric March, Florence Eldridge, Ann Blyth, Dan Duryea, Edmond O'Brien, John Dall
'The Hubbards are the greatest collection of ghouls since The Old Dark House.' – Pauline Kael, 70s

Another Shore *
GB 1948 77m bw
Ealing (Ivor Montagu)
A young Irishman dreams of life in the South Seas but gives up his fancies for love.
Curiously whimsical, artificial and unconvincing comedy drama from a famous studio, but not without its moments of interest.
w Walter Meade novel Kenneth Reddin d Charles Crichton ph Douglas Slocombe m Georges Auric
☆ Robert Beatty, Stanley Holloway, Moira Lister, Michael Medwin, Dermot Kelly, Wilfrid Brambell, Irene Worth

'The Perfect Family Has Just Moved Into The Neighbourhood.'
Another Stakeout
US 1993 108m Technicolor Scope
Buena Vista/Touchstone (Jim Kouf, Cathleen Summers, Lynn Bigelow)
▣▣ ▣ ▣
Two cops and a lawyer pretend to be a family when they stake out a house for the witness to a murder.
Slight and ineffectual flop that substitutes poor gags for thrills.
w Jim Kouf d John Badham ph Roy H. Wagner m Arthur B. Rubinstein pd Lawrence G. Paull ed Frank Morris, Kevin Stitt
☆ Richard Dreyfuss, Emilio Estevez, Rosie O'Donnell, Dennis Farina, Marcia Strassman, Cathy Moriarty, Madeleine Stowe, John Rubinstein, Miguel Ferrer
'The "another" ... is a declaration by the makers of Stakeout, a successful 1987 comedy-thriller,

that this follow-up is a reprise rather than a sequel, and an indication that they suspect the targeted audience might have trouble reading roman numerals.' – *Philip French, Observer*

'It's one of those sequels that, though reasonably entertaining, go in one eye and out the other.' – *Derek Malcolm, Guardian*

'It's a blessed event!'
Another Thin Man
US 1939 102m bw
MGM (Hunt Stromberg)
▣ ◑
Nick Charles solves a murder on a Long Island weekend.
Overwritten and distinctly tedious star sequel to The Thin Man and After the Thin Man (qv). The title refers (erroneously) to Nick and Nora's baby.
w Frances Goodrich, Albert Hackett d W. S. Van Dyke II ph Oliver T. Marsh, William Daniels m Edward Ward
☆ William Powell, Myrna Loy, Otto Kruger, C. Aubrey Smith, Virginia Grey, Nat Pendleton, Tom Neal, Ruth Hussey, Sheldon Leonard
'The screenplay tosses shootings and skulduggery and repartee at us before we're ready, and then Nick Charles takes an unconscionable amount of time sorting things out.' – *Pauline Kael, 70s*

Another Time, Another Place
GB 1958 98m bw Vistavision
Paramount/Kaydor (Lewis Allen, Smedley Aston)
▣ ▤ ◑
During World War II an American newspaperwoman has an affair with a British war correspondent; when he is killed in action, she consoles his widow.
Drippy romance, unsympathetically played and artificially set in a Cornish village.
w Stanley Mann novel Lenore Coffee d Lewis Allen ph Jack Hildyard m Douglas Gamley
☆ Lana Turner, Barry Sullivan, Glynis Johns, Sean Connery, Sidney James

Another Time, Another Place **
GB 1983 102m Eastmancolor
Cinegate/Umbrella/Rediffusion/Channel 4/Scottish Arts Council (Simon Perry)
▣
In the late 40s, a Scottish farmer's wife falls in love with an Italian prisoner-of-war working on her husband's isolated farm.
The puritan north meets the sensual south in an emotional encounter, in which overheated passions contrast with a bleak landscape.
wd Michael Radford novel Jessie Kesson ph Roger Deakins m John McLeod ad Hayden Pearce ed Tom Priestley
☆ Phyllis Logan, Giovanni Mauriello, Denise Coffey, Gian Luca Favilla, Tom Watson, Gregor Fisher, Paul Young, Claudio Rosini
'More than adequately fills the big screen with bold imagery and emotions.' – *Film Yearbook*
† The film was made for television, but was given a cinema release.
▨ Phyllis Logan

Another Way **
Hungary 1982 109m colour
Mafilm/Dialog Filmstudio
▣
original title: *Egymásra Nézve*
In 1958, a married journalist recalls her love affair with an uncompromising lesbian colleague which led to attempted murder, death and misery.
A passionate, timely and excellently acted examination of the state of the nation through the individual experience of those seeking freedom from repression.
w Károly Makk, Erzsébet Galgóczi novel Erzsébet Galgóczi d Károly Makk ph Tamás Andor m László Dés, János Másik ed György Sivó
☆ Jadwiga Jankowska, Grazyna Szapolowska, Jozef Kroner, Adám Szirtes, Judit Pogány, Gábor Reviczky
† Jadwiga Jankowska won the best actress award at the Cannes Film Festival in 1982 for her performance.

Another Woman *
US 1988 84m colour
Rank/Orion/Jack Rollins, Charles H. Joffe (Robert Greenhut)
▣ ▤ ◑
An unemotional academic discovers her inner self.
Woody Allen at his most gloomy and introspective.

wd Woody Allen ph Sven Nykvist pd Santo Loquasto ed Susan E. Morse
☆ Gena Rowlands, Mia Farrow, Ian Holm, Blythe Danner, Gene Hackman, Betty Buckley, Martha Plimpton, John Houseman
'Not only Allen's most wholly personal movie since Stardust Memories but arguably the most substantial achievement of his career.' – *Tim Pulleine, MFB*

Ansiktet: see *The Face*

Antefatto: see *A Bay of Blood*

Anthony Adverse *
US 1936 141m bw
Warner (Henry Blanke)
◎
Adventures of an ambitious young man in early 19th-century America.
A rousing spectacle of its day, from a bestselling novel, this award-winning movie quickly dated and now seems very thin and shadowy despite the interesting talents involved.
w Sheridan Gibney novel Hervey Allen d Mervyn Le Roy m Tony Gaudio m Erich Wolfgang Korngold ad Anton Grot ed Ralph Dawson
☆ Fredric March, Olivia de Havilland, Gale Sondergaard, Edmund Gwenn, Claude Rains, Anita Louise, Louis Hayward, Steffi Duna, Donald Woods, Akim Tamiroff, Ralph Morgan, Henry O'Neill
'A bulky, rambling and indecisive photoplay which has not merely taken liberties with the letter of the original but with its spirit.' – *Frank S. Nugent, New York Times*
'In the dramatizing there is shown no relish or conviction, only a retentive memory for all the old clothes of show business.' – *Otis Ferguson*
'A lavish gold-leaf from Hervey Allen's book, an earnest cinema endeavour, taxing alike its studio's purse and artistry.' – *Douglas Gilbert, New York World Telegraph*
'The show is fairly glutted with plot and counter-plot and is apt to make one feel that one is witnessing a serial run off continuously at a single performance.' – *Howard Barnes, New York Herald Tribune*
'It goes on too long, otherwise it might have been the funniest film since The Crusades.' – *Graham Greene*
♟ Tony Gaudio; Erich Wolfgang Korngold; Gale Sondergaard; Ralph Dawson
♟ picture; Anton Grot

Anti-Extortion Woman

Antoine et Antoinette *
France 1947 87m bw
SNEG/Gaumont
A young married couple find they have won a lottery but lost the ticket.
A bubbly soufflé, most expertly served but leaving one still a little hungry; not quite in the Clair class.
w Françoise Giroud, M. Griffe, Jacques Becker d Jacques Becker ph Pierre Montazel m Jean-Jacques Grunenwald
☆ Roger Pigaut, Clair Maffei

Antonia's Line ***
Netherlands/Belgium/GB 1995 102m
Fujicolour
Guild/Antonia's Line/Bergen/Prime Time/Bard/NPS (Hans de Weers)
▣ ▤ ◎
On her deathbed, an elderly woman recalls the events of her life and of those she gave a home to over a period of 40 years.
A celebration of domestic and feminine virtues, a vivid, sprawling account that mixes fantasy and reality to heighten the story of love and survival.
wd Marleen Gorris ph Willy Stassen m Ilona Sekacz ad Harry Ammerlaan ed Michiel Reichwein, Wim Louwrier
☆ Willeke van Ammelrooy, Els Dottemans, Jan Decleir, Mil Seghers, Marina de Graaf, Jan Steen, Veerle van Overloop, Dora van der Groen
'A delightful, enjoyable and generous film.' – *Film Review*
♟ foreign film

Antonio (dubbed)
Chile 1973 82m colour
Saga/Claudio Guzmán
A poor village potter, given an expensive car by an indulgent American millionaire, drives to Santiago so that he can return the gift.
A confused and innocuous little fable about the corruption of urban life, aimed at a family audience.
w Mervin Walkenstein, Claudio Guzmán d Claudio Guzmán ph Andres Martorell m Ralph Ferraro pd Pato Guzmán
☆ Trini Lopez, Larry Hagman, Naomi Guerrero, Mervin Walkenstein

Antonio das Mortes **
Brazil 1969 95m Eastmancolor
Connoisseur/Produções Cinematograficas
Mapa/Glauber Rocha (Claude-Antoine Mapa, Glauber Rocha)
original title: *O Dragao da Maldade contra o Santo Guerreiro*
A mercenary, hired by a rich landowner to kill an outlaw and his poor followers, realizes that he is supporting the wrong side.
Vivid, exotic South American Western with political overtones, a sequel of sorts to Black God, White Devil (qv).
wd Glauber Rocha ph Alfonso Beato m Marlos Nobre, Walter Queiroz, Sergio Ricardo ad Glauber Rocha ed Eduardo Escorel
☆ Mauricio Do Valle, Odete Lara, Hugo Carvana, Othon Bastos, Joffre Soares, Lorival Pariz
'Rocha's magnificent film is in fact firmly tied to the present-day political and social reality of his underdeveloped homeland.' – *Konstantin Bazarov, MFB*

Antony and Cleopatra *
GB/Spain/Switzerland 1972 170m
Technicolor Todd-AO 35
Transac/Izaro/Folio Films (Peter Snell)
▣ ▤ ◎
Well-meaning, well-mounted, but quite uninspired rendering.
wd Charlton Heston play William Shakespeare ph Rafael Pacheco m John Scott pd Maurice Pelling
☆ Charlton Heston, Hildegarde Neil, Eric Porter, John Castle, Fernando Rey, Freddie Jones, Peter Arne, Roger Delgado
† Olivier and Orson Welles were both sought for the lead.

'See the world from a whole new perspective.'
Antz **
US 1998 83m Technicolor
DreamWorks/PDI (Brad Lewis, Aron Warner, Patty Wooton)
A worker ant, who falls in love with a princess ant, prevents a coup by her soldier-ant fiancé.
Enjoyable computer-animated feature with a verbal wit that may well appeal more to adults than children; the narrative follows a familiar outline, but the animation itself is brilliantly done.
w Todd Alcott, Chris Weitz, Paul Weitz d Eric Darnell, Tim Johnson m Harry Gregson-Williams, John Powell pd John Bell ed Stan Webb
☆ Featuring the voices of: Woody Allen, Dan Aykroyd, Anne Bancroft, Jane Curtin, Danny Glover, Gene Hackman, Jennifer Lopez, John Mahoney, Paul Mazursky, Sylvester Stallone, Sharon Stone, Christopher Walken
'Winds up overplotted in bizarrely grandiose ways. Must every child-friendly adventure film boil down to a struggle for world domination? And did this one really need to invoke genocide in its final reel?' – *Janet Maslin, New York Times*

'Life Is A Contact Sport. Play. Or Be Played.'
Any Given Sunday *
US 1999 162m Technicolor Panavision
Warner/Ixtlan/The Donners' Co (Lauren Shuler Donner, Clayton Townsend, Dan Halsted)
◎
A veteran coach and a commercially-minded owner of a football team clash over attitudes and tactics, while the players undergo crises of their own.
Stone has said the film was intended as a homage to Robert Aldrich, and it has as its subject the same aggressive, amoral masculinity and bonding of the two movies, The Dirty Dozen and The Longest Yard, that inspired it: the problem for many non-US

audiences will be trying to summon up some interest in American football.
w John Logan, Oliver Stone, Daniel Pyne d Oliver Stone ph Salvatore Totino m Robbie Robertson, Paul Kelly, Richard Horowitz pd Victor Kempster ed Tom Nordberg, Keith Salmon, Stuart Waks, Stuart Levy
☆ Al Pacino, Cameron Diaz, Dennis Quaid, James Woods, Jamie Foxx, LL Cool J, Dr Ollie Powers, Jim Brown, Charlton Heston, Ann-Margret, Aaron Eckhart, John C. McGinley, Lauren Holly
'A rambunctious, hyperkinetic, testosterone-and-adrenaline-drenched look at that American obsession known as professional football.' – *Todd Mccarthy, Variety*
'Delivers a credible, action-charged vision of the frenzied world of professional sports as a metaphor for the volatility of American culture.' – *Stephen Holden, New York Times*
† Oliver Stone cut 12 minutes from the film for its European version.

Any Number Can Play *
US 1949 103m bw
MGM (Arthur Freed)
A gambling casino owner has health problems, is reconciled with his son and retires from the game.
Rather boring drama redeemed by slightly offbeat dialogue and excellent star acting, albeit in routine roles.
w Richard Brooks novel E. H. Heth d Mervyn Le Roy ph Harold Rosson m Lennie Hayton
☆ Clark Gable, Alexis Smith, Mary Astor, Wendell Corey, Audrey Totter, Lewis Stone, Frank Morgan, Marjorie Rambeau, Barry Sullivan

Any Old Port *
▧ US 1932 20m bw
Hal Roach
▤
Stan and Ollie are sailors on leave, and Ollie enters Stan for a boxing match.
Minor star comedy with good moments but a weak finish.
w H. M. Walker d James W. Horne
☆ Stan Laurel, Oliver Hardy, Walter Long

Any Wednesday *
US 1966 109m Technicolor
Warner (Julius J. Epstein)

GB title: *Bachelor Girl Apartment*
A millionaire businessman spends every Wednesday with his mistress, but complications arise when his young associate is accidentally sent to use the company flat.
Overlong screen version of a thinly scripted Broadway ... which seems gradually overtake laughs.
Rosemary Murphy is a breath of fresh air as the deceived wife who doesn't mind.
w Julius J. Epstein play Muriel Resnik d Robert Ellis Miller ph Harold Lipstein m George Duning
☆ Jane Fonda, Dean Jones, Jason Robards Jnr, Rosemary Murphy, Ann Prentiss, King Moody

Any Which Way You Can
US 1980 116m DeLuxe
Malpaso/Warner (Fritz Manes)
The hero of *Every Which Way But Loose* (qv) becomes involved in further brawls and car crashes, with the help of his friendly orang-utan.
A sequel designed entirely for the box-office, its tone set by the scene in which the villains on motorcycles are covered in tar.
w Stanford Sherman d Buddy Van Horn ph David Worth md Steve Dorf pd William J. Creber ed Ferris Webster, Ron Spang
☆ Clint Eastwood, Ruth Gordon, Sondra Locke, Geoffrey Lewis, William Smith, Harry Guardino
'This kind of thing is clearly beyond or beneath criticism.' – *Variety*
'Where the previous comedy set up a zany situation, this one ploughs it into the ground.' – *Daily Mail*

Anybody's Woman
US 1930 80m bw
Paramount
A drunken lawyer marries a chorus girl and regrets it, but she reforms him.
Tedious matrimonial drama.
w Zoe Akins, Doris Anderson, Gouverneur Morris d Dorothy Arzner

---

☆ Ruth Chatterton, Clive Brook, Paul Lukas, Huntley Gordon, Virginia Hammond

'It can't lose through that title and the stars.' – Variety

Anything Can Happen *

US 1952 93m bw
Paramount/William Perlberg, George Seaton

Adventures of a Russian immigrant family in New York.

A standard Hollywood product based on a sentimental best-seller.

w George Seaton, George Oppenheimer book George and Helen Papashvily d George Seaton ph Daniel L. Fapp m Victor Young
☆ José Ferrer, Kim Hunter, Kurt Kasznar, Alex Danaroff, Oscar Beregi

'Exploits to the hilt the somewhat limited possibilities of quaintness and whimsicality with a broken accent.' – *Penelope Houston*

Anything Goes **

US 1936 92m bw
Paramount (Benjamin Glazer)
TV title: *Tops is the Limit*

Romantic adventures on board a transatlantic liner.

Amiably batty musical comedy, zestfully directed and blithely performed.

w Guy Bolton, P. G. Wodehouse, Howard Lindsay, Russel Crouse, from their Broadway show d Lewis Milestone ph Karl Struss m/ly Cole Porter md Victor Young ad Hans Dreier
☆ Bing Crosby, Ethel Merman, Charles Ruggles, Grace Bradley, Ida Lupino, Chill Wills, the Avalon Boys, Arthur Treacher
† Only three of Cole Porter's songs were retained from the Broadway show: 'Anything Goes', 'You're the Top' and 'I Get a Kick out of You'. Others by various hands include 'Moonburn', 'Sailor Beware', 'My Heart and I', 'Am I Awake?', 'Hopelessly in Love'.

Anything Goes *

US 1956 106m Technicolor Vistavision
Paramount (Robert Emmett Dolan)

The male stars of a musical comedy each sign a girl to play the female lead; resulting complications are ironed out during a transatlantic voyage.

Below-par reworking of the 1936 film in which technical gloss and dull sets virtually reduce the characters to puppets. A few good moments transcend the general lack of imagination.

w Sidney Sheldon, from show as credited in 1936 version d Robert Lewis ph John F. Warren m/ly Cole Porter md Joseph J. Lilley ch Nick Castle, Roland Petit ad Hal Pereira, Joseph M. Johnson
☆ Bing Crosby, Donald O'Connor, Zizi Jeanmaire, Mitzi Gaynor, Phil Harris, Kurt Kasznar

'The story of a mother who knows best... and a daughter who knows better.'

Anywhere But Here

US 1999 114m DeLuxe 'Scope
TCF/Fox 2000 (Laurence Mark)

A mother and her 14 year-old daughter find it hard to cope with one another when they move from Wisconsin to Los Angeles.

A domestic drama skewed in favour of the younger of two women, who is presented as more mature than her childlike mother, possibly in the hope of appealing to a highschool audience; adults may find it harder going.

w Alvin Sargent novel Mona Simpson d Wayne Wang ph Roger Deakins m Danny Elfman pd Donald Graham Burt ed Nicholas C. Smith
☆ Susan Sarandon, Natalie Portman, Eileen Ryan, Ray Baker, John Diehl, Shawn Hatosy, Bonnie Bedelia, Caroline Aaron, Hart Bochner

'A sumptuously crafted but extremely old-fashioned comedy-drama, made in the manner of Hollywood weepies of yesteryear.' – *Emanuel Levy, Variety*

† Contemporary with the movie was *Tumbleweeds* (qv),on a very similar mother-daughter conflict.

Anzio

Italy 1968 117m Technicolor Panavision
Columbia/Dino de Laurentiis (Marcel Bebert)

GB title: *The Battle for Anzio*

A war correspondent joins American and British troops preparing for the 1944 landing in Italy.

Threadbare war film which wastes an all-star American cast.

w H. A. L. Craig book Wynford Vaughan Thomas d Edward Dmytryk ph Giuseppe Rotunno m Riz Ortolani
☆ Robert Mitchum, Peter Falk, Arthur Kennedy, Robert Ryan, Earl Holliman, Mark Damon, Reni Santoni, Anthony Steel, Patrick Magee

'It must be a long time since a script managed to pack in so many crassly portentous statements about why men fight wars.' – MFB

Apache *

US 1954 91m Technicolor
UA/Hecht-Lancaster (Harold Hecht)

After the surrender of Geronimo, one Apache leader is unconquered; after creating much havoc, he settles for domesticity, and the white men let him go unharmed.

Sober Western in the wake of Broken Arrow (qv), with a predictably sympathetic star performance and a surprising happy ending. More decency than excitement along the way.

w James R. Webb novel Bronco Apache by Paul I. Wellman d Robert Aldrich ph Ernest Laszlo m David Raksin
☆ Burt Lancaster, Jean Peters, John McIntire, Charles Bronson, John Dehner, Paul Guilfoyle, Walter Sande, Monte Blue

'The picture was seriously compromised. You make a picture about one thing, the inevitability of Massai's death. His courage is measured against the inevitable. The whole previous two hours becomes reduced if at the end he can just walk away.' – *Robert Aldrich*

Apache Drums

US 1951 75m Technicolor
U-I (Val Lewton)

A gambler helps a town under Indian attack.

Standard co-feature Western, perfectly adequate but showing no sign of its producer's former tastes and skills.

w David Chandler d Hugo Fregonese ph Charles Boyle m Hans Salter
☆ Stephen McNally, Willard Parker, Coleen Gray, Arthur Shields, James Griffith

Apache Rifles

US 1964 92m DeLuxe
Admiral Pictures/TCF

In 1879 Arizona, an Indian-hating officer falls for a half-caste.

Tolerable mid-budget Western.

w Charles B. Smith d William H. Witney
☆ Audie Murphy, Michael Dante, Linda Lawson, L. Q. Jones

Apache Trail

US 1942 66m bw
MGM (Sam Marx)

A highwayman's brother guards the stagecoach mail box.

Routine Western support, quite watchable.

w Maurice Geraghty story Ernest Haycox d Richard Thorpe
☆ Lloyd Nolan, Donna Reed, William Lundigan, Ann Ayars, Connie Gilchrist, Chill Wills, Miles Mander, Gloria Holden

Apache Uprising

US 1965 90m Techniscope
Paramount/A. C. Lyles

Assorted passengers in a stagecoach survive an Indian attack at a way station.

It sounds like a remake, and almost is, but the handling is lively enough and the producer's usual cast of nostalgic stars is in evidence.

w Harry Sanford, Max Lamb d R. G. Springsteen ph W. Wallace Kelley m Jimmie Haskell
☆ Rory Calhoun, Corinne Calvet, John Russell, Lon Chaney Jnr, Gene Evans, DeForest Kelley, Arthur Hunnicutt, Richard Arlen, Johnny Mack Brown, Jean Parker

Apache War Smoke

US 1952 67m bw
MGM

An Indian killer is among those sheltering in a desert outpost before an Apache raid.

Talkative but tense lower-berth Western.

w Jerry Davis story Ernest Haycox d Harold Kress

☆ Gilbert Roland, Robert Horton, Glenda Farrell, Barbara Ruick, Henry Morgan

Apache Woman

US 1955 82m Pathecolor
AIP/Golden State (Roger Corman)

A government agent discovers that a series of killings blamed on Apaches are caused by a gang led by a half-breed.

Routine Western, to which Corman added a subplot about racial prejudice, which may have improved its liberal credentials but does little for it as a movie.

w Lou Rusoff d Roger Corman ph Floyd Crosby m Ronald Stein ed Ronald Sinclair
☆ Lloyd Bridges, Joan Taylor, Lance Fuller, Morgan Jones, Paul Birch, Lou Place, Paul Dubov, Dick Miller, Chester Conklin
† The film was shot in under two weeks at a cost of around $80,000. Dick Miller played both a cowboy and an Apache in the film.

Aparajito ****

India 1956 113m bw
Epic Films Private Ltd (Satyajit Ray)

aka: *The Unvanquished*

After his father's death, a poor country boy is helped by his mother to study for the university.

A detailed and moving study of two characters who are universally familiar despite an unusual background.

wd Satyajit Ray ph Subrata Mitra m Ravi Shankar
☆ Pinaki Sen Gupta, Karuna Banerjee, Kanu Banerjee
† This was the sequel to *Pather Panchali*, and was itself followed by *The World of Apu* (qv).

'Movie-wise, there has never been anything like it – laugh-wise, love-wise, or otherwise-wise!'

The Apartment **

US 1960 125m bw Panavision
UA/Mirisch (Billy Wilder)

A lonely, ambitious clerk rents out his apartment to philandering executives and finds that one of them is after his own girl.

Overlong and patchy but agreeably mordant and cynical comedy with a sparkling view of city office life and some deftly handled individual sequences.

w Billy Wilder, I. A. L. Diamond d Billy Wilder ph Joseph LaShelle m Adolph Deutsch ad Alexander Trauner ed Daniel Mandell
☆ Jack Lemmon, Shirley MacLaine, Fred MacMurray, Ray Walston, Jack Kruschen, Joan Shawlee, Edie Adams, David Lewis

BAXTER'S OPENING NARRATION: 'On November 1st, 1959, the population of New York City was 8,042,753. If you laid all these people end to end, figuring an average height of five feet six and a half inches, they would reach from Times Square to the outskirts of Karachi, Pakistan. I know facts like this because I work for an insurance company – Consolidated Life of New York. We are one of the top five companies in the country. Last year we wrote nine point three billion dollars worth of policies. Our home office has 31,259 employees, which is more than the entire population of Natchez, Mississippi, or Gallup, New Mexico. I work on the 19th floor – Ordinary Policy department – Premium Accounting division – Section W – desk number 861.'

BAXTER: 'Miss Kubelik, one doesn't get to be a second administrative assistant around here unless he's a pretty good judge of character, and as far as I'm concerned you're tops. I mean, decency-wise and otherwise-wise.'

BAXTER: 'You know, I used to live like Robinson Crusoe – shipwrecked among eight million people. Then one day I saw a footprint in the sand and there you were. It's a wonderful thing, dinner for two.'

MISS KUBELIK (LAST LINE OF FILM): 'Shut up and deal.'

'Without either style or taste, shifting gears between pathos and slapstick without any transition.' – *Dwight MacDonald*

'Billy Wilder directed this acrid story as if it were a comedy, which is a cheat, considering that it involves pimping and a suicide attempt and many shades of craven ethics.' – *New Yorker*, 1980

🏆 picture; Billy Wilder, I. A. L. Diamond (as writers); Billy Wilder (as director)

♫ Joseph LaShelle; Jack Lemmon; Shirley MacLaine; Jack Kruschen; art direction; editing
🎬 picture; Jack Lemmon; Shirley MacLaine

Apartment for Peggy *

US 1948 98m Technicolor
TCF (William Perlberg)

A retired professor finds a new lease of life through caring for the homeless family of an ex-GI.

Sentimental comedy with serious undertones (the professor twice attempts suicide). Signs of enterprise are smothered by regulation charm.

wd George Seaton story Faith Baldwin ph Harry Jackson m David Raksin
☆ Edmund Gwenn, Jeanne Crain, William Holden, Gene Lockhart, Henri Letondal, Charles Lane, Houseley Stevenson

'A first rate experience for observers with comprehending minds.' – *Bosley Crowther, New York Times*

The Apartment on the 13th Floor: see *Cannibal Man*

Apartment Zero

UK 1988 125m colour
Mainline/The Summit Company (Martin Donovan, David Koepp)

In Buenos Aires, a repressed crypto-Englishman takes as a lodger a mysterious American.

Unpleasant psychological thriller about unlovely people.

w Martin Donovan, David Koepp d Martin Donovan ph Miguel Rodriguez m Elia Cmiral pd Miguel Angel Lumaldo ed Conrad M. Gonzalez
☆ Colin Firth, Hart Bochner, Dora Bryan, Liz Smith, Cipe Lincovsky

The Ape

US 1940 61m bw
Monogram (Scott R. Dunlap)

Dr Adrian seeks to cure polio by means of a serum which can only be obtained from the spinal fluid of a human being. He kills an escaped ape and dresses in its skin to seek victims.

Silly and rather boring addition to the mad doctor cycle.

w Curt Siodmak, Richard Carroll play Adam Shirk d William Nigh ph Harry Neumann m Edward Kay
☆ Boris Karloff, Maris Wrixon, Gertrude Hoffman, Henry Hall

Ape and Super Ape

Netherlands/USA 1972 103m Technicolor
Unicorn (Bert Haanstra Films)

original title: *Bij de Beesten Af*

An alleged documentary comparing human and animal behaviour seems regrettably to turn into a series of episodes depicting animal savagery in close-up.

wd Bert Haanstra ph Anton Van Munster ed Bert Haanstra

'It lacks even associational interest for the wild-life enthusiast, and is best written off as an inconclusive, unoriginal and often repellent exercise unworthy of its maker.' – *John Baxter, MFB*
🎬 documentary

The Ape Man

US 1943 64m bw
Monogram (Sam Katzman, Jack Dietz)

GB title: *Lock Your Doors*

A scientist injects himself with spinal fluid which turns him into an ape creature.

Cheap rubbish shot in a couple of corners and offering no thrill whatever.

w Barney A. Sarecky story They Creep in the Dark by Karl Brown d William Beaudine ph Mack Stengler m Edward Kay
☆ Bela Lugosi, Wallace Ford, Louise Currie, Minerva Urecal

'Bela Lugosi, rigged out in a shaggy beard and formal morning attire, ambling like an ape and sharing a cage with a gorilla, scares nobody. It's strictly a dual support.' – *Variety*
† A supposed sequel the following year, *Return of the Ape Man*, had in fact no plot connection. In this Lugosi thawed out a neanderthal man, inserted

John Carradine's brain, and the composite turned into George Zucco!

APEX
US 1994 103m Foto-Kem
Republic/Green Communications (Talaat Captan)
📺 ▦ ◎~

A time-traveller, sent back a hundred years to 1973 to find a malfunctioning robot, catches a virus that alters the future, turning it into a disease-ridden epoch, alive with killer robots.
Enjoyable low-budget variation on a familiar science-fiction theme of man versus machines, which borrows from bigger-budget successes such as The Terminator, among others. The title is an acronym for Advanced Prototype Extermination Unit.
w Phillip J. Roth, Ronald Schmidt d Phillip J. Roth ph Mark W. Gray m Jim Goodwin ed Daniel Lawrence sp Ultra Matrix; make-up: Altered Anatomy FX
☆ Richard Keats, Mitchell Cox, Lisa Russell, Marcus Aurelius, Adam Lawson, Brian Richard Peck
'Made with more imagination than skill, and more resourcefulness than polish, pic makes the absolute most of an obviously limited budget.' – *Variety*

Der Apfel ist ab **
West Germany 1949 105m bw
Camera Film/Helmut Beck-Herzog
Translated title: The Apple Fell
Adam and Eve have marital problems in Paradise, and consult a psychiatrist.
Lively sophisticated fantasy, perhaps a bit arch for general consumption, but almost as interesting in post-war Nazi Germany as Caligari was in 1919.
w Kurd E. Heyne, Helmut Kautner, Bobby Todd, from their musical comedy d Helmut Kautner ph Igor Oberberg m Bernhard Eichhorn
☆ Bobby Todd, Bettina Moissi, Joana Maria Gorvin
'Hollywood should look over this Kautner. He has a Lubitsch touch that runs all over this picture.' – *Variety*

Aphrodite, Goddess of Love
Italy 1958 90m Ferrania colour
Schermi (Adriano Merkel)
original title: *Afrodite Dea Dell'Amore*
aka: *Slave Women of Corinth*
The governor of Corinth has to cope with the Emperor Nero, his infatuation with a prostitute, plague, Christians and revolting people.
Better-than-average example of its genre, mixing power politics and romance to some effect.
w Ugo Moretti, Mario Bonnard, Sergio Leone, Mario Di Nardo d Mario Bonnard ph Tino Santoni m Giovanni Fusco pd Saverio D'Eugenio ed Nella Nannuzzi
☆ Isabelle Corey, Antonio de Teffe, Irene Tunc, Ivo Garrani, Giulio Donnini, Carlo Tamberlani

Apocalypse Now **
US 1979 153m Technicolor Technovision
Omni Zoetrope (Francis Coppola)
📺 📺 ▦ ◎~ 🎧

A Vietnam captain is instructed to eliminate a colonel who has retired to the hills and is fighting his own war.
Pretentious war movie, made even more hollow-sounding by the incomprehensible performance of Brando as the mad martinet. Some vivid scenes along the way, and some interesting parallels with Conrad's Heart of Darkness, but these hardly atone for the director's delusion that prodigal expenditure of time and money will result in great art. (The movie took so long to complete that it was dubbed Apocalypse Later.)
w John Milius, Francis Coppola d Francis Coppola ph Vittorio Storaro m Carmine Coppola, Francis Coppola pd Dean Tavoularis ed Richard Marks, Walter Murch, Gerald B. Greenberg, Lisa Fruchtman
☆ Martin Sheen, Robert Duvall, Frederic Forrest, Marlon Brando, Sam Bottoms, Dennis Hopper
'The characters are living through Vietnam as pulp adventure fantasy, as movie, as stoned humour.' – *New Yorker*
'Emotionally obtuse and intellectually empty.' – *Time*
† Coppola admitted the following at the Cannes Film Festival: 'It's more of an experience than a movie. At the beginning there's a story. Along the river the story becomes less important and the experience more important.'

🎥 Vittorio Storaro; sound (Walter Murch, Mark Berger, Richard Beggs, Nat Boxer)
⚜ picture; John Milius, Franics Coppola (script); Francis Coppola (as director); Robert Duvall; art direction; editing
📹 Francis Coppola; Robert Duvall

'Houston, we have a problem.'
Apollo 13 **
US 1995 140m colour
Imagine (Brian Grazer)
📺 📺 📺 ◎~ ⊘ ⊘ 🎧

In 1970 NASA Mission Control works feverishly to bring back three astronauts alive when there is an explosion aboard the Apollo 13 spacecraft to the moon.
A gripping documentary-style recreation of an averted tragedy, excellently done but one that is an uncritical celebration of the American way and which makes no attempt to put the mission into a wider historical context; it settles for simple patriotism.
w William Broyles Jnr, Al Reinert book Lost Moon by Jim Lovell, Jeffrey Kluger d Ron Howard ph Dean Cundey m James Horner pd Michael Corenblith ed Mike Hill, Dan Hanley
☆ Tom Hanks, Bill Paxton, Kevin Bacon, Ed Harris, Gary Sinise, Kathleen Quinlan, Mary Kate Schellhardt, Emily Ann Lloyd
'Makes all the right moves, but lacks inspiration.' – *Sight and Sound*
'Plays boringly safe ... The drama proceeds in a narrow line that leaves no room for poetry, surprise or true excitement.' – *Geoff Brown, The Times*
† The film took more than $331m at the box-office worldwide.
🎬 Mike Hill, Dan Hanley; sound effects
⚜ picture; Ed Harris; Kathleen Quinlan; James Horner; Michael Corenblith; William Broyles Jnr, Al Reinert; visual effects

The Apostle **
US 1997 134m CFI color
Universal/October/Butchers Run (Rob Carliner)
📺 📺 ▦ ◎~

After he loses his church and beats his wife's lover unconscious with a baseball bat, a middle-aged preacher leaves Texas and goes to a small Louisiana town, where he starts a new church.
Engrossing portrait of a man driven by the need to communicate his religion, though it is not always easy to empathize with a preacher whose approach is wholly emotional, and never rational.
wd Robert Duvall ph Barry Markowitz m David Mansfield pd Linda Burton ed Stephen Mack
☆ Robert Duvall, Farrah Fawcett, Todd Allen, John Beasley, June Carter Cash, Walton Goggins, Billy Joe Shaver, Billy Bob Thornton, Miranda Richardson
'A triumph on every level but one: its excessive running time.' – *Emanuel Levy, Variety*
† Robert Duvall put up $5m of his own money to make the film.
⚜ Robert Duvall

The Appaloosa *
US 1966 99m Techniscope
Universal (Alan Miller)
📺 ▦ ◎~

GB title: *Southwest to Sonora*
A cowboy's plan to start a stud farm with his magnificent horse is interrupted by badmen who think he has molested their girl.
Mannered, slow Western set on the Mexican border, with star and director apparently striving to upstage each other.
w James Bridges, Roland Kibbee novel Robert MacLeod d Sidney J. Furie ph Russell Metty m Frank Skinner
☆ Marlon Brando, Anjanette Comer, John Saxon, Rafael Campos, Frank Silvera
'Seems intent less on telling a story than in carving out the incidental details.' – *MFB*
'The camerawork concentrates on beady eyes, sweaty foreheads, spurred boots and anonymous midriffs being studied through a variety of frames, ranging from tequila bottles to cook fires to grillwork to fingers to feet.' – *Judith Crist*
'A dog of a movie about a horse.' – *Pauline Kael*

L'Appartement **
France/Spain/Italy 1996 102m colour
Artificial Eye/Ima/UGC/La Sept/M6/Mate/Cecchi Gori (Georges Benayoun)

In Paris, a young executive neglects his job because of his involvement with three women – his fiancée, a former lover he tracks down, and an actress he saves from suicide – who also lead complex lives.
Intriguing, complex tragi-comedy of tangled love affairs, in which the audience is led on a quest as baffling and rewarding as that of its protagonist; it acknowledges its debt to Shakespeare's A Midsummer Night's Dream.
wd Gilles Mimouni ph Thierry Arbogast m Peter Chase ad Philippe Chiffre ed Caroline Biggerstaff, Françoise Bonnot
☆ Romane Bohringer, Vincent Cassel, Jean-Philippe Ecoffey, Monica Bellucci, Sandrine Kiberlain, Olivier Granier
'The kind of movie that you'll want to actively consume rather than passively watch ... thoroughly engaging cinema.' – *Helen Van Kruyssen, Film Review*
† foreign film

L'Appât: see The Bait

'Is Kitty a mother?'
Applause **
US 1929 78m bw
Paramount (Jesse L. Lasky, Walter Wanger)
▦

A vaudeville star gradually loses the love of her daughter.
Absorbing treatment of a has-been tearjerking theme, full of cinematic touches and with unusual use of New York locations.
w Garrett Fort novel Beth Brown d Rouben Mamoulian ph George Folsey
☆ Helen Morgan, Joan Peers, Henry Wadsworth, Fuller Mellish Jnr
'An oasis of filmic sophistication in a desert of stage-bound early talkies.' – *William Everson, 1966*
'A cohesive, well integrated series of pictures. Its intensity, its sharp projection of tragedy, emerge from the eye of the camera; an omniscient, omnipresent eye that slides easily over the links of the story and emphasizes only the true and the relevant.' – *Thornton Delehanty, The Arts*

The Apple **
Iran/France 1997 85m colour
Artificial Eye/MK2
original title: *Sib*
Two 12-year-old twin girls, who have been kept locked away in their home by their unemployed father and blind mother, experience the outside world for the first time.
An extraordinary film, based on an actual event, with the cast playing themselves; it occupies an unusual space between documentary and drama, but is in no way exploitative.
w Mohsen Makhmalbaf d Samirah Makhmalbaf ph Ebrahim Ghafouri ed Mohsen Makhmalbaf
☆ Massoumeh Naderi, Za Naderi, Ghorban Ali-Naderi, Azizeh Mohamadi, Zahra Sagharisaz, Amir Hossein Khosrojerdi
'A remarkable achievement, proving poignant, funny and very human.' – *James Mottram, Film Review*

The Apple Dumpling Gang
👫 US 1974 100m Technicolor
Walt Disney (Bill Anderson)
📺 ▦ ◎~

Three orphan children strike gold in 1878 California.
Better-than-average Disney romp.
w Don Tait novel Jack M. Bickham d Norman Tokar ph Frank Phillips m Buddy Baker
☆ Bill Bixby, Susan Clark, David Wayne, Don Knotts, Tim Conway, Slim Pickens, Harry Morgan, John McGiver, Marie Windsor, Iris Adrian

The Apple Dumpling Gang Rides Again
👫 US 1979 88m Technicolor
Walt Disney (Ron Miller)
▦

Two incompetent bank robbers trying to go straight find themselves in trouble with a sheriff, the cavalry, Indians and a rival gang.

Limp, slow-paced comedy Western that is a dull sequel to an ordinary original.
w Don Tait d Vincent McEveety ph Frank Phillips m Buddy Baker ad John B. Mansbridge, Frank T. Smith ed Gordon D. Brenner
☆ Tim Conway, Don Knotts, Tim Matheson, Kenneth Mars, Elyssa Davalos, Jack Elam, Robert Pine, Harry Morgan, Ruth Buzzi

The Apple Fell: see Der Apfel ist ab

Appleseed (dubbed)
Japan 1991 71m colour
Manga/Gainax/AIC/Centre Studio/Tohokushinsha/Bandai/Movie (Taro Maki, Atsushi Sugita, Masaki Sawanobori, Tohru Miura)
📺

Power struggles in Olympus, a haven built after World War III, between humans, terrorist outlaws, cyborgs and biodroids, half-human, half-robot creatures developed to protect the city, who wish to control it as well.
Poorly animated science-fiction thriller with a predictable narrative, dubbed with too many expletives. The stories on which the film is based were highly regarded in Japan, so something must have been lost in their translation to the screen.
wd Kazuyoshi Katayama stories Appleseed by Masamune Shirow m Norimasa Yamanaka ad Hiroaki Ogura
☆ Featuring the voices of Larissa Murray, Bill Roberts, David Reynolds, Lorelei King, Vincent Marzello, Julia Brahms

The Appointment *
US 1969 100m colour
MGM (Martin Poll)
A businessman suspects his wife of spare time prostitution.
Unusual sophisticated fable, dressed to kill but rather stretched out for its substance. Shades of El and The Chinese Room.
w James Salter d Sidney Lumet m John Barry, Don Walker
☆ Omar Sharif, Anouk Aimée, Lotte Lenya

Appointment for Love *
US 1941 89m bw
Universal (Bruce Manning)
A doctor and a playwright agree to marry 'without love'.
A familiar theme quite amusingly explored by a practised cast.
w Bruce Manning, Felix Jackson d William A. Seiter ph Joseph Valentine m Frank Skinner, Charles Previn
☆ Charles Boyer, Margaret Sullavan, Eugene Pallette, Rita Johnson, Gus Schilling, Reginald Denny, Ruth Terry

Appointment in Berlin
US 1943 77m bw
Columbia (Sam Bischoff)
An RAF wing commander expresses unpopular views and is recruited by the Nazis as a 'voice of truth' broadcaster.
World War II potboiler.
w Horace McCoy, Michael Hogan d Alfred E. Green ph Franz Planer m Werner Heymann
☆ George Sanders, Marguerite Chapman, Gale Sondergaard, Onslow Stevens, Alan Napier, H. P. Sanders (the star's father)

Appointment in Honduras
US 1953 79m Technicolor
RKO/Benedict Bogeaus
▦

Three assorted types and four criminals escape through the jungle from a revolution.
Predictable adventure drama sabotaged by poor colour.
w Karen de Wolf d Jacques Tourneur ph Joseph Biroc m Louis Forbes
☆ Glenn Ford, Ann Sheridan, Zachary Scott, Rodolfo Acosta, Jack Elam

Appointment in London *
GB 1952 96m bw
Mayflower (Aubrey Baring, Maxwell Setton)
📺

The exploits of a squadron of Bomber Command during one month in 1943.
Dullish war film with standard credits.
w John Wooldridge, Robert Westerby d Philip Leacock ph Stephen Dade m John Wooldridge

☆ Dirk Bogarde, Ian Hunter, Dinah Sheridan, Bill Kerr, Bryan Forbes, William Sylvester, Charles Victor

Appointment with a Shadow

US 1957 72m bw Cinemascope
Universal-International
GB title: The Big Story

An alcoholic reporter redeems himself by capturing a criminal single-handed.

Maudlin melodrama which takes itself too seriously.

w Alec Coppel, Norman Jolley d Richard Carlson

☆ George Nader, Joanna Moore, Brian Keith, Virginia Field

Appointment with Crime

GB 1945 97m bw
British National

Ex-convict revenges himself on the former friends who shopped him.

Stodgy melodrama which seemed about to make a big star of William Hartnell.

wd John Harlow

☆ William Hartnell, Robert Beatty, Joyce Howard, Raymond Lovell, Herbert Lom

Appointment with Danger *

US 1949 89m bw
Paramount (Robert Fellows)

A nun becomes the government's chief witness in identifying the murderers of a US postal inspector.

Routine but entertaining star thick ear.

w Richard Breen, Warren Duff d Lewis Allen ph John Seitz m Victor Young

☆ Alan Ladd, Phyllis Calvert, Paul Stewart, Jan Sterling, Jack Webb, Henry Morgan

Appointment with Death

GB 1988 108m colour
Cannon (Michael Winner)

Another starry Hercule Poirot tale, this time in 30s Palestine.

w Anthony Shaffer, Peter Buckman, Michael Winner *novel* Agatha Christie d Michael Winner ph David Gurfinkel m Pino Donaggio pd John Blezard

☆ Peter Ustinov, Lauren Bacall, Carrie Fisher, John Gielgud, Piper Laurie

'They came home with the milk!'

Appointment with Venus **

GB 1951 89m bw
GFD/British Film Makers (Betty E. Box)
US title: Island Rescue

During World War II, a pedigree cow is rescued from the German-occupied Channel Islands.

Curious but generally agreeable mixture of comedy and war adventure, pleasantly shot on Sark.

w Nicholas Phipps *novel* Jerrard Tickell d Ralph Thomas ph Ernest Steward m Benjamin Frankel

☆ David Niven, Glynis Johns, George Coulouris, Barry Jones, Kenneth More, Noel Purcell, Bernard Lee, Jeremy Spenser

Apprentice to Murder

Norway 1988 94m colour
New World (Howard K. Grossman)

In Pennsylvania in the 1920s, a teenaged boy comes under the influence of a faith healer who is cursed by the devil.

Odd little thriller that relies too heavily on special effects to hold an audience's attention.

w Allan Scott, Wesley Moore d R. L. Thomas ph Kelvin Pike m Charles Gross pd Gregory Bolton ed Patrick McMahon sp Derek Meddings, Mark Meddings, Roy Spencer

☆ Donald Sutherland, Chad Lowe, Mia Sara, Knut Husebo, Rutanya Alda, Eddie Jones, Mark Burton, Adrian Sparks

The Apprenticeship of Duddy Kravitz *

Canada 1974 121m Bellevue-Pathé
Panavision
Duddy Kravitz Syndicate (Gerald Schneider)

An ambitious young Jew finds that it is best to be liked.

Amusing adventures of an anti-hero; good scenes but rather patchy technique.

w Mordecai Richler *novel* Mordecai Richler d Ted Kotcheff ph Miklos Lente m Stanley Myers

☆ Richard Dreyfuss, Micheline Lanctot, Jack Warden, Randy Quaid, Denholm Elliott, Joseph Wiseman

 Å Mordecai Richler

Les Apprentis *

France 1995 98m colour
Gala/Péléas/Glem (Philippe Martin)

A would-be photographer makes and loses a friend when he moves into a flat with an older writer.

Desultory but amusing comedy of an odd couple who share no more than a desire for love and an inability to find employment.

w Pierre Salvadori, Philippe Harel, Marc Syrigas, Nicolas Cuche, Franck Bauchard d Pierre Salvadori ph Gilles Henry m Philippe Eidel ad François Emmanuelli ed Hélène Viard

☆ François Cluzet, Guillaume Depardieu, Judith Henry, Claire Laroche, Philippe Girard, Barnard Yerles, Marie Trintignant

'Feels as if it was written from day to day and heavily dependent on how its stars were feeling when they got up. Might have been better to stay in bed.' – *Alexander Walker*

Après l'Amour *

France 1992 105m colour
Mayfair/Alexandre/TF1/Prodeve (Jean-Bernard Fetoux)

Love and desire among the thirty-somethings of Parisian glitterati.

A complex story of sexual relationships over a period of a year, enjoyable enough if you can keep track of all the shifting couplings, but not particularly insightful.

w Diane Kurys, Antoine Lacomblez d Diane Kurys ph Fabio Conversi m Yves Simon, Serge Parathoner, Jannick Top ad Tony Egry ed Hervé Schneid

☆ Isabelle Huppert, Bernard Giraudeau, Hippolyte Girardot, Lio, Yvan Attal, Judith Reval, Ingrid Held, Laure Killing, Mehdi Ioossen, Florian Billon

'It copes with agony, bluster, lies and voyeurism in a cynically relaxed spirit that places it firmly in the French "relationship movie" genre; though with the difference, outdated as it may seem anywhere except France, that it is a woman through whose eyes we look.' – *Amanda Lipman, Sight and Sound*

'He has a wife. She has a husband. With so much in common they just have to fall in love.'

The April Fools *

US 1969 95m Technicolor Panavision
Cinema Center/Jalem (Gordon Carroll)

An unhappy New York husband elopes to Paris with an unhappy wife.

Whimsical romantic comedy which rather strains its resources without giving full value for money in romance, humour or simple charm. Good moments, though.

w Hal Dresner d Stuart Rosenberg ph Michel Hugo m Marvin Hamlisch pd Richard Sylbert

☆ Jack Lemmon, Catherine Deneuve, Myrna Loy, Charles Boyer, Peter Lawford, Jack Weston, Harvey Korman, Sally Kellerman

'Painfully modish, from the opening party in an apartment filled with fashionable objets d'art to the final mad dash to the airport in an expensive sports car.' – *MFB*

April Fool's Day

US 1986 88m Metrocolor Panavision
Paramount/Hometown (Frank Mancuso Jnr)

College friends go to spend a weekend in an isolated house with a wealthy practical joker, who has a taste for murderous pranks.

A teenage slasher movie with an original twist, but one that does not alter the usual tedium of the genre.

w Danilo Bach d Fred Walton ph Charles Minsky m Charles Bernstein ad Stewart Campbell ed Bruce Green

☆ Jay Baker, Deborah Foreman, Deborah Goodrich, Ken Olandt, Griffin O'Neal, Leah King Pinsent, Clayton Rohner

April in Paris *

US 1952 100m Technicolor
Warner (William Jacobs)

A chorus girl is mistakenly invited to a US Arts Festival in Paris, and bewitches the bureaucrat in charge.

Poorly produced star musical with a thin plot and a few redeeming wisps of wit.

w Jack Rose, Melville Shavelson d David Butler ph Wilfrid Cline m/ly Sammy Cahn, Vernon Duke, E. Y. Harburg md Ray Heindorf ch Le Roy Prinz

☆ Doris Day, *Ray Bolger*, Claude Dauphin, Eve Miller, George Givot

April Love

US 1957 99m Eastmancolor Cinemascope
TCF (David Weisbart)

For stealing a car, a teenager is sent on probation to his uncle's stud farm, where circumstances seem once again to put him in trouble with the law.

Easygoing star vehicle with little to recommend it to adults.

w Winston Miller *novel* George Agnew Chamberlain d Henry Levin ph Wilfrid Cline m/ly Sammy Fain, Paul Francis Webster

☆ Pat Boone, Shirley Jones, Dolores Michaels, Arthur O'Connell, Jeanette Nolan

† A remake of *Home in Indiana* (qv).

Å title song (m Sammy Fain, ly Paul Francis Webster)

April One

Canada 1993 85m colour
Astral/April One (Julia Sereny)

In Ottawa, a diplomat becomes protective towards the confused ex-convict who takes her hostage.

Based on a true story, a suspenseless thriller that leaves its audience no wiser than before, or any more understanding of the motives of those involved.

wd Murray Battle ph Mark Irwin m Jonathan Goldsmith ad Ian Brock ed Roger Mattiussi

☆ Stephen Shellen, Djanet Sears, David Strathairn, Wayne Robson, Gordon Clapp, Pierre Curzi, Martin Julien

April Romance: see Blossom Time

April Showers *

US 1948 94m bw
Warner (William Jacobs)

In a family vaudeville act, Dad takes to drink.

Hoary musical melodrama enlivened by occasional acts.

w Peter Milne *musical adaptation* Max Steiner d James V. Kern ph Carl Guthrie md Ray Heindorf *songs* various

☆ Jack Carson, Robert Alda, Ann Sothern, Robert Ellis, S. Z. Sakall

Aprile *

Italy/France 1998 78m Technicolor
Metro Tartan/Sacher/BAC (Angelo Barbagallo, Nanni Moretti)

A film director begins and abandons a musical, starts a political documentary, wishes he were making a musical and is distracted by the birth of his son and the sense that time is running out.

Moretti managed to transform his life into art with his charming Dear Diary (qv). This time around his autobiographical concerns are so personal that the result is too inward-looking to fully engage the interest of others.

wd Nanni Moretti ph Giuseppe Lanci ad Marta Maffucci ed Angelo Nicolin

☆ Nanni Moretti, Silvio Orlando, Silvia Nono, Pietro Moretti, Agata Apicella Moretti, Nuria Schoenberg, Angelo Barbagallo, Silvia Bonucci, Quentin de Fouchecour, Renato De Maria, Daniele Luchetti, Andrea Molaioli, Nicola Piepoli, Corrado Stajano

'The film is a delight to watch (even more so if you know anything about Italy). It is also a cinematic masterpiece.' – *Chris Wagstaff, Sight and Sound*

Apt Pupil **

US/France 1997 111m Technicolor
Panavision
Columbia TriStar/Phoenix/Bad Hat Harry/Canal+ (Jane Hamsher, Don Murphy, Bryan Singer)

In California, a schoolboy threatens a former Nazi with disclosure unless he tells him about the Holocaust.

An effective drama about the corruption caused by contact with evil, though it descends into horror-movie clichés towards the end.

w Brandon Boyce *novella* Stephen King d Bryan Singer ph Newton Thomas Sigel m John Ottman pd Richard Hoover ed John Ottman

☆ Ian McKellen, Brad Renfro, Bruce Davison, Elias Koteas, Joe Morton, Jan Triska, Michael Byrne, Heather McComb, David Schwimmer

'Has more than enough chilling dramatic scenes to rivet the attention but suffers from some hokey contrivances and underlying insufficiencies of motivation.' – *Todd McCarthy, Variety*

'I didn't like my character. He didn't seem very deep. He just seemed a representative of evil.' – *Ian McKellen*

Aquila Nera: see Black Eagle

The Arab: see The Barbarian

Arabella

US/Italy 1969 91m Technicolor
Cram Film/Universal

A female confidence trickster needs the money to pay her grandmother's back taxes.

Floppy, tedious comedy adventure with an international cast all at sea.

w Adriano Barocco d Mauro Bolognini

☆ Virna Lisi, James Fox, Terry-Thomas, Margaret Rutherford

Arabesque **

US 1966 118m Technicolor Panavision
Universal (Stanley Donen)

An Oxford professor is asked by Middle Eastern oil magnates to decipher a hieroglyphic, and finds afterwards that he is marked for assassination.

The ultimate in sixties spy kaleidoscopes, in which the working out of the plot matters much less than the stars, the jokes and the lavish backgrounds. Fast moving, amusing and utterly forgettable.

w Julian Mitchell, Stanley Price, Pierre Marton *novel The Cipher* by Gordon Cotler d Stanley Donen ph Christopher Challis m Henry Mancini ad Reece Pemberton

☆ Gregory Peck, Sophia Loren, *Alan Badel*, Kieron Moore, Carl Duering

'Nothing could look more "with it", or somehow matter less.' – *MFB*

'A strikingly visual chase and intrigue yarn.' – *Robert Windeler*

'All rather too flashy for comfort.' – *Sight and Sound*

† Pierre Marton was a pen name for Peter Stone.

Ü Christopher Challis

Arabian Adventure

GB 1979 98m colour
Badger Films/John Dark

The dictator of Jadur promises his daughter's hand in marriage if a young prince will seek and find a magic rose.

Artless juggling of elements from The Thief of Baghdad, including magic carpets, monsters and a bottle djinn.

w Brian Hayles d Kevin Connor ph Alan Hume m Ken Thorne pd Elliot Scott

☆ Christopher Lee, Oliver Tobias, Mickey Rooney, Milo O'Shea, Elizabeth Welch, Peter Cushing, Capucine

'Resolutely well mounted, but somehow lacking that necessary fillip of Hollywood vulgarity or exuberance.' – *John Pym, MFB*

Arabian Nights

US 1942 86m Technicolor
Universal (Walter Wanger)

The Caliph of Baghdad is deposed by his half-brother but wins back his throne with the help of a dancer and an acrobat.

Well presented oriental adventure which has nothing to do with its source material but entertained multitudes in search of relief from total war and was followed by several vaguely similar slices of hokum with the same stars.

w Michael Hogan d John Rawlins ph Milton Krasner, William V. Skall, W. Howard Greene m Frank Skinner ad Alexander Golitzen, Jack Otterson

☆ Jon Hall, Maria Montez, Sabu, Leif Erickson, Thomas Gomez, Turhan Bey, John Qualen, Billy Gilbert, Shemp Howard

⅋ Milton Krasner, William V. Skall, W. Howard Greene; Frank Skinner; art direction

'Eight legs. Two fangs. And an attitude.'

Arachnophobia **

US   1990   109m   DeLuxe
Hollywood Pictures/Amblin/Tangled Web (Kathleen Kennedy, Richard Vane)
⬚⬚ ▇ ℚ ✿ ❍ ◠

A doctor moves with his family from the town to the country to find himself confronting local hostility and a plague of killer spiders.
Executive producer Steven Spielberg's influence is evident in this effectively scary movie set in a small town threatened by a menace it doesn't understand.

w Don Jacoby, Wesley Strick story Don Jacoby, Al Williams d Frank Marshall ph Mikael Salomon m Trevor Jones pd James Bissell ad Christopher Burian-Mohr ed Michael Kahn sp Chris Walas (creatures effects)

☆ Jeff Daniels, Harley Jane Kozak, John Goodman, Julian Sands, Stuart Pankin, Brian McNamara, Mark L. Taylor, Henry Jones

'Not since Jaws has a film come along to make audiences jump in their seats so regularly and enjoyably.' – Variety

Aranyer Din Ratri: see Days and Nights in the Forest

The Arc

US   1991   95m   colour
Cinema Parallel/Film Four (J. K. Eareckson)
A welder, who loses his job, his house, his friends and his wife, decides to take the first bus out of Baltimore.
An episodic, eccentric, low-budget road movie of occasional sharp humour, but more often given over to windy philosophizing.

wd Rob Tregenza ph Rob Tregenza pd Dolores Deluxe

☆ Jason Adams, Kathryn Kelley, Catherine Fogarty, Jennifer Mendenhall

'The story of an outcast and a killer!'

Arch of Triumph *

US   1948   120m   bw
Enterprise (David Lewis)
⬚⬚ ▇

In postwar Paris, an embittered refugee seeks his former Nazi tormentor and has a tragic romance with a would-be suicide.
Doleful, set-bound melodrama knee-deep in misery and artificial melodramatics. An expensive, ambitious failure, both commercially and artistically, but an interesting one.

w Lewis Milestone, Harry Brown novel Erich Maria Remarque d Lewis Milestone ph Russell Metty m Leonard Gruenberg md Morris Stoloff

☆ Ingrid Bergman, Charles Boyer, Charles Laughton, Louis Calhern

'Cutting Arch of Triumph improved it considerably. It was terrible for four hours, but now it is only terrible for two hours.' – Charles Boyer

† The film cost 5 million dollars and grossed 1.5 million. The story was remade for TV in 1984.

La Ardilla Roja: see The Red Squirrel

Are Husbands Necessary?

US   1942   79m   bw   Paramount
A bickering couple decide to adopt a baby.
Mild marital comedy in a familiar mould.

w Tess Slesinger, Frank Davis story Mr and Mrs Cugat by Isabel Scott Rorick d Norman Taurog ph Charles Lang m Robert Emmett Dolan

☆ Ray Milland, Betty Field, Patricia Morison, Eugene Pallette, Charles Dingle, Cecil Kellaway, Leif Erickson, Richard Haydn, Elisabeth Risdon

'A chaos of farcical situations, conceived without gusto and played without conviction.' – Richard Mallett, Punch

Are These Our Children?

US   1931   75m   bw
RKO
A teenager gets into bad company and ends up facing the electric chair.
Shapeless and uncompelling moralistic farrago of no entertainment value.

w Howard Estabrook d Wesley Ruggles

☆ Eric Linden, Rochelle Hudson, Arline Judge, Ben Alexander, Robert Quirk, Beryl Mercer

Are These Our Parents?

US   1944   74m   bw
Monogram (Jeffrey Bernerd)
GB title: They Are Guilty
Parents neglect their children, who become suspects in a murder case.
Cheap yellow press sensationalism without much production expertise to back it up.

w Michel Jacoby, Hilary Lynn d William Nigh

☆ Helen Vinson, Lyle Talbot, Ivan Lebedeff, Addison Richards

'Juvenile delinquency yarn is a dualer, twenty years too late; must rely on exploitation for biz.' – Variety

Are We All Murderers?: see Nous Sommes Tous les Assassins

Are You a Mason?

GB   1934   70m   bw
Twickenham
A stockbroker has been pretending to be a Masonic grand master so that he can get out nights.
Fairly simple-minded farce which could have done with slicker production.

w H. Fowler Mear play Leo Dietrichstein, Emmanuel Lederer d Henry Edwards

☆ Sonnie Hale, Robertson Hare, Davy Burnaby, Gwyneth Lloyd, Bertha Belmore

Are You Being Served?

GB   1977   95m   Technicolor
EMI (Andrew Mitchell)
⬚⬚

The staff of the clothing section of a department store go on holiday to the Costa Plonka.
Feeble enlargement of an old-fashioned but very popular TV series relying heavily on sexual badinage and ancient jokes.

w Jeremy Lloyd, David Croft d Bob Kellett ph Jack Atcheler m various

☆ John Inman, Frank Thornton, Mollie Sugden, Trevor Bannister, Wendy Richard, Arthur Brough, Nicholas Smith, Arthur English, Harold Bennett, Glyn Houston

'A withering selection of patent British puns.' – John Pym, MFB

Are You Listening?

US   1932   73m   bw
MGM
A radio continuity announcer accidentally kills his wife.
Curious disjointed melodrama, the sidelights on the new radio business being its main interest.

w Dwight Taylor story J. P. McEvoy d Harry Beaumont

☆ William Haines, Karen Morley, Madge Evans, Anita Page, Neil Hamilton, Wallace Ford, Jean Hersholt

Are You With It? *

US   1948   90m   bw
Universal-International (Robert Arthur)
An insurance executive with doubts joins a fun fair and has a whale of a time.
Pleasantly lively low-budget musical.

w Oscar Brodney musical comedy Sam Perrin, George Balzer d Jack Hively ph Maury Gertsman m/ly Sidney Miller, Inez James md Walter Scharf

☆ Donald O'Connor, Olga San Juan, Martha Stewart, Lew Parker

Arena

US   1953   83m   Anscocolor   3-D
MGM (Arthur M. Loew Jnr)
A rodeo rider regains his wife and his sense when his best friend is killed.
Routine actioner, distinguished by 3-D camerawork.

w Harold Jack Bloom d Richard Fleischer ph Paul C. Vogel m Rudolph G. Kopp

☆ Gig Young, Jean Hagen, Polly Bergen, Henry Morgan, Barbara Lawrence, Robert Horton, Lee Van Cleef

The Arena

US   1973   83m   Technicolor   Techniscope
EMI/New World (Mark Damon)
▇
aka: Naked Warriors
Female slaves, who have been forced to fight one another as gladiators, rebel against their small-town owner.
Standard exploitation picture, ringing a slight change on the genre's usual women's prison dramas but employing many of the same clichés.

w John William Corrington, Joyce Hooper Corrington d Steve Carver ph Aristide Massacessi m Francesco de Masi ad Mimmo Scavia ed Joe Dante, Piera Bruni

☆ Pam Grier, Margaret Markov, Lucretia Love, Paul Muller, Daniel Vargas, Marie Louise, Mary Count

Aren't Men Beasts! *

GB   1937   66m   bw
BIP (Walter Mycroft)
A dentist poses as his aunt to stop a plot to prevent his son's marriage.
Archetypal British star farce.

w Marjorie Deans, William Freshman play Vernon Sylvaine d Graham Cutts ph Roy Kellino

☆ Robertson Hare, Alfred Drayton, June Clyde, Billy Milton, Judy Kelly

L'Argent *

Switzerland/France   1983   84m   colour
EOS/Marion's Films/FR3 (Jean-Marc Henchoz)
⬚⬚ ▇

A tragic chain of events is started when a forged note is passed in a photographer's shop.
A bleak Bressonian study of conscience, fate and atonement.

wd Robert Bresson story The False Note by Leo Tolstoy ph Emmanuel Machuel, Pasqualino de Santis m Bach

☆ Christian Patey, Sylvie Van Den Elsen, Michel Briguet, Caroline Lang

L'Argent de Poche: see Small Change

Argentine Nights

US   1940   75m   bw
Universal
The Ritz Brothers and the Andrews Sisters head for Argentina to avoid their creditors.
Fair low-budget musical.

w Arthur Horman, Ray Golden, Sid Kuller d Albert S. Rogell

☆ The Ritz Brothers, the Andrews Sisters, Constance Moore, George Reeves, Peggy Moran, Anne Nagel

Aria

GB/US   1988   98m   colour
Virgin Vision/Warner (Don Boyd)
▇ ℚ ◠

A man wanders through Italian streets and buildings, a journey interrupted as operatic arias are combined with glossy visuals.
Ten directors, given freedom to illustrate the music in any manner they wanted, display a paucity of imagination.

w Nicolas Roeg, Charles Sturridge, Jean-Luc Godard, Julien Temple, Bruce Beresford, Robert Altman, Franc Roddam, Ken Russell, Derek Jarman, Bill Bryden, Don Boyd d Nicolas Roeg, Charles Sturridge, Jean-Luc Godard, Julien Temple, Bruce Beresford, Robert Altman, Franc Roddam, Ken Russell, Derek Jarman, Bill Bryden ph Harvey Harrison, Gale Tattersall, Carolyn Champetier, Oliver Stapleton, Dante Spinotti, Pierre Mignot, Frederick Elmes, Gabriel Beristain, Mike Southon, Christopher Hughes m Verdi, Lully, Korngold, Rameau, Wagner, Puccini, Charpentier, Leoncavallo md Ralph Mace pd Diana Johnstone, Andrew McAlpine, Stephen Altman, Piers Plowden, Scott Bushnell, John Hay, Matthew Jacobs, Paul Dufficey, Christopher Hobbs ed Marie Therese Boiche, Mike Cragg, Tony Lawson, Matthew Longfellow, Neil Abrahamson, Jennifer Auge, Rich Elgood, Michael Bradsell, Peter Cartwright, Angus Cook

☆ Theresa Russell, Nicola Swain, Jack Kyle, Marion Peters, Valerie Allain, Buck Henry, Anita Morris, Beverly D'Angelo, Elizabeth Hurley, Peter Birch, Bertrand Bonvoison, Julie Hagerty, Bridget Fonda, James Mathers, Linzi Drew and also Andreas Wisniewski, Tilda Swinton, Spencer Leigh, John Hurt, Sophie Ward

Ariane

Germany   1931   78m   bw
Nerofilm
An innocent young girl falls for a man of the world and makes him think she is a cocotte.
Sophisticated comedy later remade as Love in the Afternoon (qv); this version is interesting chiefly for its presentation of a new star.

w Paul Czinner, Carl Mayer novel Claude Anet d Paul Czinner

☆ Elisabeth Bergner, Rudolf Forster, Annemarie Steinsieck, Hertha Guthmar

Ariel *

Finland   1988   72m   colour
Electric/Villealfa (Aki Kaurismäki)
⬚⬚ ▇

A redundant miner is forced by circumstances to take to a life of crime.
Episodic movie with not much sense of reality.

wd Aki Kaurismäki ph Timo Salminen pd Risto Karhula ed Raija Talvio

☆ Turo Pajala, Susanna Haavisto, Matti Pellonpää, Eetu Hilkamo, Erkki Pajala, Matti Jaaranen, Hannu Viholainen

'It's a documentation of the destruction of Finland.' – Aki Kaurismäki

'Here's the gay, glorious story of a war correspondent and a war ace … a romance that could happen only in 1940!'

Arise My Love ***

US   1940   113m   bw
Paramount (Arthur Hornblow Jnr)
American reporters in Europe and in love survive the Spanish Civil War, a wrathful editor in Paris and the sinking of the Athenia.
Unique sophisticated entertainment gleaned from the century's grimmest headlines, ending with a plea against American isolationism. A significant and stylish comedy melodrama.

w Charles Brackett, Billy Wilder d Mitchell Leisen ph Charles Lang m Victor Young ad Hans Dreier, Robert Usher

☆ Claudette Colbert, Ray Milland, Walter Abel, Dennis O'Keefe, George Zucco, Dick Purcell, Frank Puglia, Esther Dale

WALTER ABEL (MR PHILLIPS): "I'm not happy. I'm not happy at all…"

'Against the background of European fisticuffs, Paramount brings forth a film of absorbing romantic interest, proving that love will find a way through the hazards of air raids, torpedo attacks and enemy invasions.' – Variety

† Joel McCrea was originally cast for the Milland role.

♟ original story (Benjamin Glazer, John S. Toldy)

⅋ Charles Lang; Victor Young; art direction

The Aristocats **

👪👪 US   1970   78m   Technicolor
Walt Disney (Wolfgang Reitherman, Winston Hibler)
⬚⬚ ▇ ℚ ◠

Two cats are deliberately lost by a butler who fears they will inherit his mistress's wealth; but a variety of animal friends restore them to their rightful place.
Cartoon feature, a moderate example of the studio's work after Disney's death, with rather too few felicitous moments.

w Larry Clemmons and others d Wolfgang Reitherman

☆ Featuring the voices of Phil Harris, Eva Gabor, Sterling Holloway, Scatman Crothers, Paul Winchell, Hermione Baddeley, Roddy Maude-Roxby

Arizona

US   1940   125m   bw
Columbia (Wesley Ruggles)
▇

A Tucson wildcat meets her match in a travelling Missourian who helps her outwit villains who are sabotaging her wagon trains.
Loosely built, deliberately paced Western which for all its pretensions makes very little impact.

w Claude Binyon d Wesley Ruggles ph Joseph Walker, Harry Hollenberger, Fayte Brown m Victor Young ad Lionel Banks, Robert Peterson
☆ Jean Arthur, William Holden, Warren William, Porter Hall, Paul Harvey, George Chandler, Byron Foulger, Regis Toomey, Edgar Buchanan
'Lacks the sweep and dramatic impulse that would have made it a great picture.' – *Variety*
♫ Victor Young; art direction

Arizona Bushwhackers

US 1968 86m Techniscope
Paramount (A. C. Lyles)
▣ ◎.
A Confederate prisoner is given a chance as a Western sheriff.
Stolid Western, notable only, as is usual with this producer, for its gallery of ageing but still reliable familiar faces.
w Steve Fisher d Lesley Selander ph Lester Shorr m Jimmie Haskell
☆ Howard Keel, Yvonne de Carlo, Brian Donlevy, John Ireland, Marilyn Maxwell, Scott Brady, Barton MacLane, James Craig

Arizona Dream **

US/France 1991 142m colour
Electric/Constellation/UGC/Hachette (Claudie Ossard, Yves Marmion)
▣ ◎.
A young New York fish counter visits his uncle in Arizona and falls in love with an older woman.
A quirky fantasy, sometimes engaging, sometimes maddening in its deliberate oddness, but always original and often surprising.
w David Atkins d Emir Kusturica ph Vilko Filac m Goran Bregovic pd Miljen Kljakovic ed Andrija Zafranovic
☆ Johnny Depp, Faye Dunaway, Jerry Lewis, Lili Taylor, Paulina Porizkova, Vincent Gallo, Candyce Mason
'A marathon, self-indulgent, often profoundly tedious sprawl which you go with, part of the time at least, for its sudden flashes of visionary splendour.' – *Sheila Johnston, Independent*
† The film was cut to 119m for its British and US releases. Kusturica walked off the film at one point following a dispute with his producers, and only returned when he was allowed to continue without interference.

The Arizona Kid

US 1930 84m bw
Fox
A wanted bandit finds a secret gold mine in Utah.
Disappointing semi-sequel to In Old Arizona (qv): *same star, much less talent to back him up.*
w Ralph Block d Alfred Santell
☆ Warner Baxter, Mona Maris, Carole Lombard, Theodore von Eltz

Arizona Raiders

US 1965 88m Techniscope
Admiral/Columbia
▣
Two of Quantrell's Raiders are offered a pardon if they will round up renegades.
Stereotyped Western, poorly processed.
w Alex Gottlieb, Mary and Willard Willingham d William Witney
☆ Audie Murphy, Michael Dante, Ben Cooper, Buster Crabbe, Gloria Talbott

Arizona to Broadway

US 1933 66m bw
Fox
A small-town girl in the big city is changed by a con man.
Fast-moving support which has its moments.
w William Conselman, Henry Johnson d James Tinling
☆ James Dunn, Joan Bennett, Herbert Mundin, Sammy Cohen, Theodore von Eltz, J. Carrol Naish, Walter Catlett

The Arizonian

US 1935 72m bw
RKO
Lawless Silver City gets a reform marshal.
Adequate first-feature Western, but not a spectacular.
w Dudley Nichols d Charles Vidor
☆ Richard Dix, Margot Grahame, Preston Foster, Louis Calhern
'Through the names it can slip into the keys where westerns rarely treat, and where,

therefore, horse operas are regarded as refreshing novelties.' – *Variety*

The Arkansas Traveller

US 1938 85m bw
Paramount
A small-town widow is helped to keep her newspaper going by a stranger who happens to be passing through.
Archetypal mid-American fantasy.
w Viola Brothers Shore, George Sessions Perry story Jack Cunningham d Alfred Santell
☆ Bob Burns, Fay Bainter, Jean Parker, Irvin S. Cobb
'It will get over nicely in the key spots, but its biggest b.o. will be in the nabes and smaller communities.' – *Variety*

'How Well Do You Know Your Neighbour?'
Arlington Road **

US 1999 DeLuxe Panavision
Sony/Screen Gems/Lakeshore Entertainment (Peter Samuelson, Tom Gorai, Marc Samuelson)
▣ ◎. ▣
A history professor suspects that his suburban neighbour is a terrorist.
Clever psychological thriller, in which the paranoia is justified.
w Ehren Kruger d Mark Pellington ph Bobby Bukowski m Angelo Badalamenti pd Therese Deprez ed Conrad Buff
☆ Jeff Bridges, Tim Robbins, Joan Cusack, Hope Davis, Robert Gossett, Mason Gamble, Spencer Treat Clark, Stanley Anderson
'An intelligent, insidiously plotted Hitchcockian thriller directed in souped-up, modern expressionistic style.' – *Todd McCarthy, Variety*

Armageddon

Canada/Netherlands 1997 93m colour
Nu Image (Brian Irving)
▣
In an authoritarian Russia of the future, a former CIA agent, murdered in Moscow by his partner-in-crime, is brought back to life to take revenge on his killer.
Turgid and violent action movie that offers no surprises, due to its reliance on the usual clichés of the genre; it is, however, sillier than most of its kind.
w Tibor Takacs, Brian Irving d Tibor Takacs ph Zoltan David m Guy Zerafa pd Istvan Ocztos ed Neil Grieve
☆ Rutger Hauer, Mark Dacascos, Yvonne Scio, Patrick Dreihauss, Randall William Cook
'Eye-catching production values, some nicely atmospheric lighting and a winning line in throwaway humour buoy up this classy action fodder.' – *Sight and Sound*

Armageddon

US 1998 150m Technicolor Panavision
Buena Vista/Touchstone/Valhalla (Jerry Bruckheimer, Gale Anne Hurd, Michael Bay)
▣ ◎. ▣ ◎. ▣
A maverick gang of oil-drillers go into space to put a nuclear bomb on an asteroid that threatens to destroy the Earth.
Loud and brainless action movie that was among the top box-office successes of 1998.
w Jonathan Hensleigh, J. J. Abrams, Robert Roy Pool, Tony Gilroy, Shane Salerno d Michael Bay ph Jon Schwartzman m Trevor Rabin pd Michael White ed Mark Goldblatt, Chris Lebenzon, Glen Scantlebury sp Pat McClung, Richard Hoover; Dream Quest Images
☆ Bruce Willis, Billy Bob Thornton, Liv Tyler, Ben Affleck, Will Patton, Peter Stormare, Keith David, Steve Buscemi, Owen Wilson, William Fichtner, Jessica Steen, Jason Isaacs, Grace Zabriskie, Udo Kier, Michael Clarke Duncan and also Charlton Heston (narrator)
'Effects-obsessed and dramatically be-numbed.' – *Variety*
† The film cost $150m and took more than $464m at the box-office worldwide. It was preceded by *Deep Impact* (qv), a film with an identical theme.
♫ song 'I Don't Want to Miss a Thing (m/ly Diane Warren); sound; sound effects editing; visual effects

Armed and Dangerous

US 1985 85m DeLuxe
Columbia (Brian Grazer, James Keach)
▣ ◎.
An ex-cop and a former lawyer uncover criminal activities at a private security company.

Comedy in which most of the humour depends on high-speed car crashes.
w Harold Ramis, Peter Torokvei story Brian Grazer, Harold Ramis, James Keach d Mark L. Lester ph Fred Schuler pd David L.Snyder ed Michael Hill, Daniel Hanley, Gregory Prange
☆ John Candy, Eugene Levy, Robert Loggia, Kenneth McMillan, Meg Ryan, Brion James, Jonathan Banks, Don Stroud, Larry Hankin
'In a way, this is a highly immoral film. It is made for the very young and will undoubtedly give them the idea that they can drive as recklessly and the like without doing anyone serious damage. Not a pint of blood is spilled. Victims climb unscathed out of cars that have been reduced to so much abstract sculpture. This is bad propaganda, but, like so much that is immoral, it is highly entertaining.' – *Quentin Crisp*

Armed Response

US 1986 85m United Color
Cinetel (Paul Hertzberg)
▣ ◎.
A private eye retrieves a jade antique for a Japanese gangster.
Violent low budgeter with allusions for film buffs.
w T. L. Lankford d Fred Olen Ray
☆ David Carradine, Lee Van Cleef, Mako, Lois Hamilton, Ross Hagen

L'Armée Des Ombres: see *The Army in the Shadows*

Armored Attack: see *North Star*

Armored Car Robbery *

US 1950 67m bw
RKO (Herman Schlom)
▣
A police lieutenant leads the recovery of half a million dollars stolen by gangsters.
Good competent second feature with Los Angeles locations and detailed observation of police methods.
w Earl Felton, Gerald Drayson Adams d Richard Fleischer ph Guy Roe m Constantin Bakaleinikoff
☆ Charles McGraw, Adele Jergens, William Talman, Douglas Fowley, Steve Brodie

Armored Command

US 1961 105m bw
Allied Artists (Ron W. Alcorn)
▣
During the Battle of the Bulge, a ravishing Nazi spy is infiltrated into an American army outpost.
Incredible Mata Hari melodrama posing as a war film, nicely shot in bleak snowscapes. Not exactly rewarding, but unusual.
w Ron W. Alcorn d Byron Haskin ph Ernest Haller m Bert Grund
☆ Howard Keel, Tina Louise, Burt Reynolds, Earl Holliman, Warner Anderson, Carleton Young, Marty Ingels

The Armour of God

Hong Kong 1987 90m colour
Golden Harvest (L. K. C. Ho, Chua Lam)
▣
original title: *Long Xiong Hu Di*
A martial arts expert goes in search of a valuable suit of armour.
Standard kung-fu adventure.
w Edward Tang story Barry Wong d Jackie Chan ph Bob Thompson m Michael Rai ad William Cheung ed Cheung Yiu Chung
☆ Jackie Chan, Alan Tam, Rosamund Kwan, Lola Forner

Armour of God II: see *Operation Condor*

Arms and the Girl: see *Red Salute*

Arms and the Man

GB 1932 85m bw
BIP/Wardour
A soldier who finds discretion the better part of valour hides in a girl's bedroom.
Faithful but uninspired version of Bernard Shaw's play.
wd Cecil Lewis play George Bernard Shaw ad John Mead ed Walter Stokvis
☆ Barry Jones, Anne Grey, Angela Baddeley

Arms and the Woman: see *Mr Winkle Goes to War*

Army Girl

US 1938 90m bw
Republic
GB title: *The Last of the Cavalry*
Old loyalties flare at an army post when tanks replace cavalry troops.
Modest flagwaver which got by at the time.
w Barry Trivers, Sam Ornitz d George Nicholls Jnr ph Ernest Miller, Harry Wild m Victor Young
☆ Madge Evans, Preston Foster, James Gleason, H. B. Warner, Ruth Donnelly, Neil Hamilton, Billy Gilbert, Heather Angel, Ralph Morgan
'Thoroughly entertaining … suitable as single in smaller spots, or action half of double bill in keys.' – *Variety*
♫ Ernest Miller, Harry Wild; Victor Young

The Army in the Shadows ***

France/Italy 1969 143m colour
Films Corona/Fono Roma (Jacques Dorfman)
original title: *L'Armée Des Ombres*
A group of Resistance fighters in Lyon try to discover the traitors in their midst.
Moving, harrowing and, in its depiction of a bungled execution, horrific account of the French Resistance at work, notable for the excellence of the direction and acting.
wd Jean-Pierre Melville novel Joseph Kessel ph Pierre L'homme m Eric de Marsan ad Théobald Meurisse ed Françoise Bonnot
☆ Lino Ventura, Simone Signoret, Jean-Pierre Cassel, Paul Meurisse, Claude Mann, Paul Crauchet, Christian Barbier

Army of Darkness

US 1992 109m DeLuxe
Guild/Renaissance/Introvision (Robert Tapert)
▣ ◎. ◎. ▣ ◎.
aka: *Evil Dead III*
aka: *Army of Darkness: The Medieval Dead*
Thrust back in time to medieval England, a supermarket assistant searches for a spell to return him to his own time and instead causes the dead to rise from their graves.
Comic horror of uncertain tone, which occasionally raises a smile, but is much influenced for the worse by the work of the Three Stooges.
w Sam Raimi, Ivan Raimi d Sam Raimi ph Bill Pope m Joseph LoDuca pd Tony Tremblay ed Bob Murawski, R. O. C. Sandstorm
☆ Bruce Campbell, Embeth Davidtz, Marcus Gilbert, Ian Abercrombie, Richard Grove, Michael Earl Reid, Bridget Fonda
'Preoccupied with repetitive and clumsy battle scenes and mild, bloodless effects, *Army of Darkness* falls off the knife-edge between humour and horror.' – *Kim Newman*
'Neither fantastic nor funny enough, despite its plethora of special effects and artful jokiness, to pass muster as anything much.' – *Derek Malcolm, Guardian*
† It was the third film in Raimi's sequence, following *The Evil Dead* and *The Evil Dead II* (qqv).

Arnold

US 1973 95m DeLuxe
Avco/Fenady (Charles A. Pratt, Andrew Fenady)
▣
Via cassette recordings, a dead man toys with his would-be heirs, and several are murdered.
Unpleasant and very laboured black comedy on the lines of And Then There Were None *and a hundred others, all better than this.*
w Jameson Brewer, John Fenton Murray d George Fenady ph William Jurgenson m George Duning
☆ Stella Stevens, Roddy McDowall, Elsa Lanchester, Shani Wallis, Farley Granger, Victor Buono, John McGiver, Bernard Fox, Patric Knowles
† Apparently made back to back with *Terror in the Wax Museum* (qv), which has very similar credits.

Around the World

US 1943 81m bw
RKO (Allan Dwan)
▣
Kay Kyser's band goes on a world tour to entertain troops overseas.
Typical wartime patriotic musical, now of sociological interest.
w Ralph Spence d Allan Dwan ph Russell Metty m George Duning m/ly Jimmy McHugh, Harold Adamson md Constantin Bakaleinikoff
☆ Kay Kyser, Ish Kabibble, Ginny Simms, Joan Davis, Mischa Auer

'It's a wonderful world, if you'll only take the time to go around it!'

Around the World in Eighty Days ***

US   1956   178m   Technicolor   Todd-AO
UA (Michael Todd)

A Victorian gentleman and his valet win a bet that they can go round the world in eighty days.
Amiable large-scale pageant resolving itself into a number of sketches, which could have been much sharper, separated by wide screen spectacle. What was breathtaking at the time seems generally slow and blunted in retrospect, but the fascination of recognizing 44 cameo stars remains. The film is less an exercise in traditional skills than a tribute to its producer's energy.
w James Poe, John Farrow, S. J. Perelman
novel Jules Verne d Michael Anderson, Kevin McClory ph Lionel Lindon m Victor Young ad James W. Sullivan, Ken Adams ed Gene Ruggiero, Paul Weatherwax titles Saul Bass
☆ *David Niven, Cantinflas, Robert Newton, Shirley MacLaine, Charles Boyer, Joe E. Brown, Martine Carol, John Carradine, Charles Coburn, Ronald Colman, Melville Cooper, Noël Coward, Finlay Currie, Reginald Denny, Andy Devine and also Marlene Dietrich, Luis Dominguin, Fernandel, John Gielgud, Hermione Gingold, Jose Greco, Cedric Hardwicke, Trevor Howard, Glynis Johns, Buster Keaton, Evelyn Keyes, Beatrice Lillie, Peter Lorre, Edmund Lowe, A. E. Matthews, Mike Mazurki, Tim McCoy, Victor McLaglen, John Mills, Alan Mowbray, Robert Morley, Jack Oakie, George Raft, Gilbert Roland, Cesar Romero, Frank Sinatra, Red Skelton, Ronald Squire, Basil Sidney, Harcourt Williams, Ed Murrow*
'Michael Todd's "show", shorn of the ballyhoo and to critics not mollified by parties and sweetmeats, is a film like any other, only twice as long as most … the shots of trains and boats seem endless.' – *David Robinson*
🏆 picture; James Poe, John Farrow, S. J. Perelman; Lionel Lindon; Victor Young
🏅 Michael Anderson; art direction; editing

Around the World in Eighty Minutes

US   1931   80m   bw
United Artists
An account of Douglas Fairbanks's travels, mainly in the Far East.
Awfully padded travelogue which seems to have been a bore even at the time, despite a few magic-carpet tricks.
w Robert E. Sherwood d Douglas Fairbanks, Victor Fleming
'Fairbanks enlivens much of the drab footage with his acrobatics.' – *Variety*

Around the World under the Sea

US   1966   110m   Metrocolor   Panavision
MGM/Ivan Tors (Andrew Marton)
An ultra-modern underwater craft travels around the seabed fixing sensors to give early warning of volcanoes.
Earnest, dullish, elementary sci-fi with cardboard characters providing routine five men-one woman skirmishes.
w Arthur Weiss, Art Arthur d Andrew Marton, Ricou Browning ph Clifford Poland, Lamar Boren m Harry Sukman
☆ Lloyd Bridges, Shirley Eaton, Brian Kelly, David McCallum, Keenan Wynn, Marshall Thompson, Gary Merrill

Arouse and Beware: see The Man from Dakota

The Arrangement **

US   1969   127m   Technicolor   Panavision
Warner/Athena (Elia Kazan)

A wealthy advertising man fails in a suicide attempt and spends his convalescence reflecting on his unsatisfactory emotional life.
A lush, all-American melodrama, rich in technique but peopled by characters who have nothing to say; the film makes no discernible point except as a well-acted tirade against the compromises of modern urban living.
wd Elia Kazan novel Elia Kazan ph Robert Surtees m David Amram pd Malcolm C. Bert
☆ Kirk Douglas, Faye Dunaway, Deborah Kerr, Richard Boone, Hume Cronyn
'The sort of collage that won't fit together, no matter where you stand.' – *PS*
'As dead as a flower arrangement in an undertaker's parlour … all possible cinematic

cleverness – usually yesterday's – are dragged out in an endless parade, to illustrate a senseless and banal story that reels from platitude to platitude.' – *John Simon*

Arrest Bulldog Drummond: see Bulldog Drummond

The Arrival *

US   1996   115m   Technicolor
Entertainment/Live/Steelwork (Thomas G. Smith, James Steel)

An astronomer realizes that aliens are among us.
Conspiratorial science fiction exhibiting some interesting ideas and managing to incorporate them into a sometimes suspenseful story.
wd David Twohy ph Hiro Narita m Arthur Kempel pd Michael Novotny ed Martin Hunter sp Pacific Data Images
☆ Charlie Sheen, Ron Silver, Lindsay Crouse, Teri Polo, Richard Schiff, Leon Rippy, Tony T. Johnson
'Confusing and incoherent, implausible even by SF standards.' – *Sight and Sound*

Arrivederci Baby: see Drop Dead Darling

Arrow in the Dust

US   1954   80m   Technicolor
Allied Artists (Hayes Goetz)
An army deserter assumes the identity of a cavalry captain to help defend a wagon-train from marauding Indians.
Effective minor Western, gaining from its redemptive, reluctant hero, forced to act against his own best interests.
w Don Martin novel L.L. Foreman d Lesley Selander ph Ellis W. Carter m Marlin Skiles ad David Milton ed William Austin
☆ Sterling Hayden, Coleen Gray, Keith Larsen, Tom Tully, Jimmy Wakely, Tudor Owen, Lee Van Cleef, John Pickard, Carleton Young

Arrowhead

US   1953   105m   Technicolor   3D
Paramount (Nat Holt)

Enmity between an army scout and an Indian chief is resolved by single combat.
Standard Western, good-looking but rather lifeless.
wd Charles Marquis Warren novel W. R. Burnett ph Ray Rennahan m Paul Sawtell
☆ Charlton Heston, Jack Palance, Katy Jurado, Brian Keith, Milburn Stone

Arrowsmith *

US   1931   108m   bw
Samuel Goldwyn

The self-sacrificing career of a doctor.
Emotionally satisfactory, dramatically slow and unsurprising variation on a theme which has since been treated far too often.
w Sidney Howard novel Sinclair Lewis d John Ford ph Ray June m Alfred Newman ad Richard Day
☆ Ronald Colman, Helen Hayes, Richard Bennett, Myrna Loy, Charlotte Henry, Beulah Bondi, A. E. Anson
'Pictures would do better to stay clear of these elaborately biographical novels with their wealth of actionless detail … That portion of the citizenry which read the Sinclair Lewis novel will probably be in sympathy with the film, those who didn't will not be prone to deem this macabre tale entertainment.' – *Variety*
† The negative was later cut to about 89m for reissue, and this version, virtually eliminating Myrna Loy, is the only one now available.
🏅 best picture; Sidney Howard; Ray June; Richard Day

Arsenal **

USSR   1929   99m (16 fps)   bw   silent
VUFKU
The 1914 war is made worse by strikes at home.
Patchy propagandist drama with brilliant sequences.
wd Alexander Dovzhenko ph Danylo Demutsky
☆ S. Svashenko, A. Buchma, M. Nademsky
'A romantic and lyrical masterpiece.' – *Georges Sadoul*

The Arsenal Stadium Mystery

GB   1939   85m   bw
G&S/GFD

A footballer is poisoned during a match.
Brisk little mystery, with an amiable star performance.
w Thorold Dickinson, Donald Bull novel Leonard Gribble d Thorold Dickinson
☆ Leslie Banks, Greta Gynt, Esmond Knight, Brian Worth
'This picture is as good to watch as either of the Thin Man films, and Dickinson gives us wit instead of facetiousness – wit of cutting and wit of angle.' – *Graham Greene*

Arsène Lupin **

US   1932   75m   bw
MGM
The Parisian gentleman thief accomplishes some daring robberies and is almost caught stealing the Mona Lisa.
Amusing crook comedy with a few flat passages but much sparkle in between, and a lively finale.
w Carey Wilson, Lenore Coffee, Bayard Veiller play Maurice Le Blanc, Francis de Croisset d Jack Conway ph Oliver Marsh ad Cedric Gibbons ed Hugh Wynn
☆ John Barrymore, Lionel Barrymore, Karen Morley, Tully Marshall, John Miljan
'First screen appearance of John and Lionel together and their acting of this old standard detective story ensures its box office in spite of the absence of other qualities that make for notable screen successes … At least it addresses itself to a higher class of fans than the lurid type of dime novel subject.' – *Variety*

Arsène Lupin Returns

US   1938   81m   bw
MGM (John W. Considine Jnr)
The reformed jewel thief helps an American detective to track down a French criminal.
Smooth but disappointingly scripted sequel which never quite rises to a climax despite sympathetic casting.
w James Kevin McGuinness, Howard Emmett Rogers, George Harmon Coxe d George Fitzmaurice ph George Folsey m Franz Waxman
☆ Melvyn Douglas, Warren William, Virginia Bruce, John Halliday, Nat Pendleton, Monty Woolley, George Zucco, E. E. Clive
'A first-class mystery jewel theft combo … for the top side of the marquee pairing, missing A classification quite a little, but still being okay.' – *Variety*

Arsenic and Old Lace ***

US   1944   118m   bw
Warner (Frank Capra)

Two dear, well-meaning old ladies invite lonely old men to their Brooklyn home, poison them with elderberry wine, and have their mad brother, who believes the corpses are yellow fever victims, bury them in the cellar. A homicidal nephew then turns up with bodies of his own.
A model for stage play adaptations, this famous black farce provided a frenzy of hilarious activity, and its flippant attitude to death was better received in wartime than would have been the case earlier or later. The director coaxed some perfect if overstated performances from his star cast, and added his own flair for perpetuating a hubbub.
w Julius J. and Philip G. Epstein, with help from Howard Lindsay, Russel Crouse play Joseph Kesselring d Frank Capra ph Sol Polito m Max Steiner
☆ Cary Grant, Josephine Hull, Jean Adair, Priscilla Lane, Raymond Massey, John Alexander, Peter Lorre, James Gleason, Jack Carson, Edward Everett Horton, Grant Mitchell
MORTIMER: 'Insanity runs in my family. It practically gallops.'
MARTHA: 'One of our gentlemen found time to say "How delicious!" before he died…'
† Made in 1992 but not released immediately.

The Art of Dying

US   1991   93m   Foto-Kem
PM (Richard Pepin, Joseph Merhi)

A maverick cop tracks down a pornographer who films and kills his victims from the movies.

Slow, unpleasant homophobic thriller about a cut-rate Dirty Harry; the emphasis is on atmosphere and the hero's uninteresting love-life rather than on action.
w Joseph Merhi d Wings Hauser ph Richard Pepin m John Gonzalez pd Greg Martin ed Geraint Bell, Paul Volk
☆ Wings Hauser, Kathleen Kinmont, Michael J. Pollard, Gary Werntz, Mitch Hara, Sarah Douglas, Sydney Lassick

The Art of Love

US   1965   99m   Technicolor
Universal/Cherokee/Ross Hunter
To stimulate interest in his work, a penniless artist fakes suicide, subsequently becoming so famous that he finds it difficult to reappear.
A pleasant black comedy idea is buried under lush production, dull direction and a host of unattractive Parisian sets.
w Carl Reiner d Norman Jewison ph Russell Metty m Cy Coleman
☆ James Garner, Dick Van Dyke, Angie Dickinson, Elke Sommer, Ethel Merman, Pierre Olaf

The Art of Love (dubbed)

France/Italy   1983   87m   colour
ZT/Distribuzione/Nija/Oitra Impex/Man International (Ugo Tucci)

In Rome, Ovid lectures on the subject of love, while some of his pupils practise his teachings.
Soft-core eroticism with a little twist at the end, done with slightly more style than usual.
wd Walerian Borowczyk m Luis Bacalov ed Walerian Borowczyk
☆ Marina Pierro, Massimo Girotti, Laura Betti, Milena Vukotic, Philippe Lemaire, Michele Placido

'I race cars, I play tennis, I fondle women, but I have weekends off and I am my own boss!'

Arthur *

US   1981   97m   Technicolor
Warner/Orion (Robert Greenhut)

A rich New York layabout is forced to moderate his life style in order to qualify for his inheritance.
An unattractive excuse for the star to do his drunk act. In effect his thunder was stolen by Gielgud as the valet who is not above a few choice four-letter words; but over the whole enterprise hung a pall of desperation. It is a sign of its times that it made a lot of money.
wd Steve Gordon ph Fred Schuler m Burt Bacharach pd Stephen Hendrikson
☆ Dudley Moore, John Gielgud, Liza Minnelli, Geraldine Fitzgerald, Jill Eikenberry, Stephen Elliott
'It comes as no surprise to find the funniest sequences packed into the first half-hour.' – *Martyn Auty, MFB*
'Gielgud may be the most poised and confident funnyman you'll ever see.' – *New Yorker*
'Arthur may be the surprise hit of 1981, but to me he's a pain in the neck.' – *Margaret Hinxnan, Daily Mail*
🏆 John Gielgud (supporting actor); song 'Best That You Can Do' (Burt Bacharach, Carole Bayer Sager, Christopher Cross, Peter Allen)
🏅 screenplay; Dudley Moore

Arthur 2: On the Rocks

US   1988   113m   colour
Warner (Robert Shapiro)

Arthur's fortune is threatened by his former fiancée's father, bent on revenge, while his wife wants to adopt a baby.
Moore and friends are much less funny the second time around, and much more sentimental; it's just a sloppy would-be comedy.
w Andy Breckman d Bud Yorkin ph Stephen H. Burum m Burt Bacharach mad Michael Kahn
☆ Dudley Moore, Liza Minnelli, Geraldine Fitzgerald, Paul Benedict, John Gielgud
'Still manages to be an amusing romp.' – *Variety*

'When the heroes are forgotten. When the stakes are life and death. There's one stand you've got to take. There's one rule you've got to break.'

Article 99

US 1992 100m DeLuxe

Orion/Gruskoff/Levy (Michael Gruskoff, Michael I. Levy)

Doctors and surgeons at a Veterans' Administration hospital ignore red tape in order to treat their patients.

A frenetic movie with more than a touch of hysteria in its treatment of an emotive subject.

w Ron Cutler d Howard Deutch ph Richard Bowen m Danny Elfman pd Virginia L. Randolph ed Richard Halsey

☆ Ray Liotta, Kiefer Sutherland, Forest Whitaker, Lea Thompson, John Mahoney, John C. McGinley, Keith David, Kathy Baker, Eli Wallach

'Is ultimately more successful in awakening the viewer to a desperate situation than in providing a good time.' – *Variety*

An Artist with Ladies: see *Coiffeur pour Dames*

Artistes at the Top of the Big Top: Disorientated **

West Germany 1968 103m bw/colour

Kairos Film

The daughter of a dead trapezist dreams of creating the ideal circus with a moral for mankind but step by step gives up her ambition.

A melancholy satire, told in fragmented fashion with some brilliant tricks and memorable sequences.

wd Alexander Kluge ph Gunther Hörmann, Thomas Mauch

☆ Hannelore Hoger, Siegfried Graue, Alfred Edel, Bernd Höltz

'Those who interpret it simply as an allegory of German politics or of the present crisis in film-making narrow it unnecessarily.' – *Jan Dawson, MFB*

Artists and Models *

US 1937 97m bw

Paramount (Lewis E. Gensler)

An advertising man has to find the right girl as symbol for a silverware company.

Fairly stylish comedy musical with many elements typical of its studio.

w Walter de Leon, Francis Martin d Raoul Walsh ph Victor Milner m Victor Young songs various

☆ Jack Benny, Ida Lupino, Richard Arlen, Gail Patrick, Ben Blue, Judy Canova, Martha Raye, Donald Meek, Hedda Hopper, André Kostelanetz and his Orchestra, Louis Armstrong and his Orchestra

'Should be a box-office bonanza for exhibitors. It holds enough variety, comedy, colour, spectacle, flash, dash and novelty for a couple of pictures.' – *Variety*

♫ song 'Whispers in the Dark' (m Frederick Hollander, ly Leo Robin)

Artists and Models *

US 1955 109m Technicolor Vistavision

Paramount/Hal B. Wallis

A goonish young man receives telepathic top secret information in his nightmares, which are used by his artist friend in comic strips; foreign agents and the CIA get interested.

A good zany idea is worked into an overlong dyspeptic comedy which neither the stars nor frantic treatment can hope to save.

w Frank Tashlin, Don McGuire d Frank Tashlin ph Daniel Fapp m Walter Scharf

☆ Dean Martin, Jerry Lewis, Shirley MacLaine, Dorothy Malone, Eddie Mayehoff, Eva Gabor, Anita Ekberg, George 'Foghorn' Winslow, Jack Elam

'It's an ooh-la-lalapalooza!'

Artists and Models Abroad *

US 1938 90m bw Paramount (Arthur Hornblow Jnr)

GB title: *Stranded in Paris*

Stranded in Paris, a troupe of girls and their manager are helped by a Texas oil millionaire.

Generally agreeable comedy musical with emphasis on fashion.

w Howard Lindsay, Russel Crouse, Ken Englund d Mitchell Leisen ph Ted Tetzlaff md Boris Morros ad Hans Dreier, Ernst Fegte songs various

☆ Jack Benny, Joan Bennett, Mary Boland, Charley Grapewin, Joyce Compton, the Yacht Club Boys, Fritz Feld, G. P. Huntley, Monty Woolley

'Straight farce comedy. The models are in a fashion show and the artists are missing entirely.' – *Variety*

The Aryan *

US 1916 75m bw silent

Triangle (Thomas Ince)

A gold prospector is cheated by a woman and becomes an outlaw.

Striking early star Western.

w C. Gardner Sullivan d William S. Hart, Clifford Smith ph Joseph August, Clyde de Vinna

☆ William S. Hart, Bessie Love, Louise Glaum, Herschel Mayall

'A comedy from the heart that goes for the throat.'

As Good as It Gets ***

US 1997 138m Technicolor

Columbia TriStar/Gracie (James L. Brooks, Bridget Johnson, Kristi Zea)

A misanthropic writer suffering from a compulsive-obsessive disorder learns to love again when he reluctantly involves himself in the lives of a neighbour and a waitress.

A sour-toned comedy about damaged people that, for all its occasional glibness and the ease with which its problems are solved, somehow works; it convinces as long as the movie lasts.

w Mark Andrus, James L. Brooks d James L. Brooks ph John Bailey m Hans Zimmer pd Bill Brzeski ed Richard Marks

☆ Jack Nicholson, Helen Hunt, Greg Kinnear, Cuba Gooding Jnr, Skeet Ulrich, Shirley Knight, Yeardley Smith, Lupe Ontiveros

'A sporadically funny romantic comedy with all the dramatic plausibility and tonal consistency of a TV variety show.' – *Todd McCarthy, Variety*

🏆 Jack Nicholson; Helen Hunt

🏅 Best picture; Greg Kinnear; Mark Andrus, James L. Brooks; Richard Marks; Hans Zimmer

As Husbands Go

US 1934 65m bw

Fox/Jesse Lasky

Lover and husband become friends, making infidelity impossible.

Minor smart-set comedy from a then popular play.

w Sam Behrman, Sonya Levien play Rachel Crothers d Hamilton McFadden

☆ Warner Baxter, Helen Vinson, Warner Oland, G. P. Huntley Jnr, Catherine Doucet

'Pleasant entertainment all the way, but a lack of action will bore children and annoy that not inconsiderable body of Americans who violently resent too much suavity of speech and manner.' – *Variety*

As Long as They're Happy *

GB 1955 91m Eastmancolor

Rank/Regroup (Raymond Stross)

The suburban home of a London stockbroker is invaded by an American sob singer.

Frantic farce expanded from a stage satire of the Johnnie Ray cult; a patchy but sometimes funny star vehicle.

w Alan Melville play Vernon Sylvaine d J. Lee-Thompson ph Gilbert Taylor m Stanley Black

☆ Jack Buchanan, Brenda de Banzie, Diana Dors, Jean Carson, Janette Scott, Susan Stephen, Jerry Wayne, Hugh McDermott

As Long as You're Near Me

West Germany 1954 94m colour

Warner/NDF

original title: *Solange Du da bist*

A film director almost ruins a small-part actress's life by insisting on making her a star.

Reasonably absorbing drama chiefly remarkable for being a great hit in the US when dubbed.

w Jochen Huth d Harold Braun

☆ O. W. Fischer, Hardy Kruger, Maria Schell

As Tears Go By **

Hong Kong 1988 94m colour

In-Gear (Rover Tang)

original title: *Mongkok Kamun*

An aggressive debt collector, living on the edge, finds himself drawn back by his loyalties into a world of urban gangsters when he tries to escape to a quieter life with his country cousin.

Tough thriller, in which the violent fight scenes have a disturbing reality; the direction occasionally strains after effect in an otherwise tense movie of thugs who come to believe in their own publicity.

wd Wong Kar-Wai ad William Cheung

☆ Andy Lau, Maggie Cheung, Jacky Cheung

'A superbly gritty debut, let down by Wong's tendency to go for the big scene – complete with MTV-style music – every five minutes.' – *Sight and Sound*

As the Earth Turns

US 1934 73m bw

Warner

The problems of three farming families in Maine.

Reliable rustic soap opera, pretty well presented.

w Ernest Pascal book Gladys Hasty Carroll d Alfred E. Green

☆ Jean Muir, Donald Woods, Emily Lowry, William Janney, David Landau, Dorothy Peterson

'What it may lack in box office, it makes up in entertainment … the sort of story that commands attention and favour.' – *Variety*

As Time Goes By

Australia 1987 94m colour

Valhalla/Monroe Stahr (Chris Kiely)

A man travels into the outback to keep a rendezvous made by his mother 25 years earlier, and finds an interplanetary traveller waiting for him.

Oddball comedy that runs out of steam at the halfway mark, though it tries hard; the alien, who talks in dialogue culled from old movies, may interest film buffs (and the credits include, along with Best Boy, Worst Boy).

wd Barry Peak ph John Ogden m Peter Sullivan pd Paddy Reardon ed Ralph Strasser

☆ Bruno Lawrence, Nique Needles, Ray Barrett, Marcelle Schmitz, Mitchell Faircloth, Max Gillies

'You don't need us to tell you not to miss this film. You couldn't be kept away!'

As You Desire Me *

US 1931 71m bw

MGM (George Fitzmaurice)

The amnesiac mistress of a novelist rediscovers her real husband and falls in love with him again.

Interesting star vehicle with good cast and production.

w Gene Markey play Luigi Pirandello d George Fitzmaurice ph William Daniels

☆ Greta Garbo, Melvyn Douglas, Erich von Stroheim, Owen Moore, Hedda Hopper, Rafaela Ottiano

'Pretty subtle for the generality of fans. It was more of a courageous gesture towards production ideals than good business judgement that dictated its choice for filming in the first place.' – *Variety*

As You Like It *

GB 1936 96m bw

TCF/Inter-Allied (Joseph M. Schenck, Paul Czinner)

The fortunes of an exiled king take a turn in the Forest of Arden.

Stylized, rather effete but often amusing version of Shakespeare's pastoral comedy.

w J. M. Barrie, Robert Cullen play William Shakespeare d Paul Czinner ph Harold Rosson m William Walton

☆ Elisabeth Bergner, Laurence Olivier, Sophie Stewart, Leon Quartermaine, Henry Ainley, Richard Ainley, Felix Aylmer, Mackenzie Ward, Aubrey Mather, John Laurie, Peter Bull

'Rather too respectably lighthearted, but by no means a contemptible production.' – *New Yorker, 1978*

'There are far too many dull middle-length shots from a fixed camera, so that we might just as well be seated in the circle above the deep wide stage at Drury Lane.' – *Graham Greene*

As You Like It

GB 1992 117m colour

Squirrel/Sands Films (Richard Goodwin)

Banished from City of London splendour to a grimy slum where locals live in cardboard boxes, Orlando falls in love with the banished and disguised Rosalind.

Modern-dress version of the play, with the Forest of Arden becoming an urban wasteland inhabited by the homeless. It sounds as ugly as it looks, with some wretched speaking of the verse.

play William Shakespeare d Christine Edzard ph Robin Vidgeon m Michel Sanvoisin ed Christine Edzard

☆ James Fox, Emma Croft, Cyril Cusack, Griff Rhys Jones, Andrew Tiernan, Miriam Margolyes, Don Henderson, Celia Bannerman, Murray Melvin

'We feel like victims of a mobile theatre experiment, moving our camp stools from one daft venue to the next as we follow a bunch of under-rehearsed actors belting it out into the void.' – *Nigel Andrews, Financial Times*

'In this misguided and also perversely endearing version, Christine Edzard ultimately proves the Bard's resilience, but she proves it the hard way.' – *Adam Mars-Jones, Independent*

'Edzard restores to filmed Shakespeare the means and immediacy of cinema, daring to present, as the theatre has been doing since the nineteenth century, Shakespearean text in a modern context.' – *Ilona Halberstadt, Sight and Sound*

As Young as You Feel *

US 1951 77m bw

TCF (Lamar Trotti)

An elderly employee, forced to retire, impersonates the company president, saves the firm from bankruptcy, and proves his continued worth.

Good-natured comedy, ably presented.

w Lamar Trotti story Paddy Chayefsky d Harmon Jones ph Joe MacDonald m Cyril Mockridge

☆ Monty Woolley, Constance Bennett, Thelma Ritter, David Wayne, Jean Peters, Marilyn Monroe, Allyn Joslyn, Albert Dekker

Ascendancy *

GB 1982 85m colour

British Film Institute Production Board (Penny Clark, Ian Elsey)

In 1920 Belfast a shipyard owner's daughter, shocked by the death of her brother in the war, cannot come to terms with the sectarian slaughter around her.

Unilluminatingly argumentative character study which fails to make its purpose very clear despite a stunning central performance.

w Edward Bennett, Nigel Gearing d Edward Bennett ph Clive Tickner m Ronnie Leahy

☆ Julie Covington, Ian Charleson, John Phillips, Susan Engel, Philip Locke

Ascenseur pour l'Echafaud: see *Lift to the Scaffold*

Ash Wednesday

US 1973 99m Technicolor

Sagittarius (Dominick Dunne)

An ageing American beauty rejuvenates herself via plastic surgery, leads a vivid sex life, and leaves her stolid husband.

The bloodthirsty operation scenes are revolting, yet this joyless saga seems meant as a celebration of the wonders of cosmetic surgery and Sex for the Aged. Hypnotic but hardly rewarding.

w Jean Claude Tramont d Larry Peerce ph Ennio Guarnieri m Maurice Jarre

☆ Elizabeth Taylor, Henry Fonda, Helmut Berger, Keith Baxter, Maurice Teynac

'Endless shots of Elizabeth Taylor expensively attired against the plush background of Cortina.' – *Michael Billington, Illustrated London News*

'A long-drawn-out ghoulish commercial for cosmetic surgery – made apparently for people who can't think of anything to do with their lives but go backwards.' – *Pauline Kael*

Ashanti

Switzerland 1979 117m Technicolor
Panavision
Columbia/Beverly (Luciano Sacripanti)
🔲 ▤

In West Africa, the wife of a member of the World Health Organization is seized by slave traders.
Absurd and rather unattractively brutal adventure story, decked out with appearances by guest stars.
w Stephen Geller *novel* Ebano *by* Alberto Vasquez-Figueroa d Richard Fleischer ph Aldo Tonti m Michael Melvoin
☆ Michael Caine, Omar Sharif, Peter Ustinov, Rex Harrison, Kabir Bedi, William Holden, Zia Mohyeddin, Beverly Johnson

Ashes and Diamonds ****

Poland 1958 104m bw
Film Polski
🔲 ▤

original title: Popiol y Diament
A Polish partisan is confused by the apparent need to continue killing after the war is over.
A chilling account of the intellectual contradictions to which war leads, and a moving and sensitive film in its own right.
wd Andrzej Wajda *novel* Jerzy Andrzejewski ph Jerzy Wojcik
☆ Zbigniew Cybulski, Ewa Krzyzanowska, Adam Pawlikowski

Ashik Kerib **

USSR 1988 78m colour
Georgia Film Studio
▤

aka: The Lovelorn Minstrel
A poor minstrel goes to seek his fortune so that he can marry the daughter of a rich Turkish merchant.
Richly coloured, episodic fable, told in the artful and artless manner of silent cinema.
w Giya Badridze *story* Mikhail Lermontov d Sergei Paradjanov, David Abashidze ph Albert Yavuryan m Zhavanshir Kuliev pd G. Meskhishvili, Shota Gogolashvili, Nikolai Zandukeli, K. Davidov
☆ Yuri Mgoyan, Veronique Matonidze, Levan Natroshvili, Solico Chaureli
'The film chronicles a spiritual journey in profane, worldly terms, and it is the earthy vulgarity of the detail that gives the spirituality its edge.' – Tony Rayns, MFB

Ask a Policeman **

GB 1938 82m bw
Gainsborough (Edward Black)
In a small coastal village, incompetent policemen accidentally expose smugglers who are scaring the locals with a headless horseman legend.
One of the best comedies of an incomparable team, with smart dialogue, good situations and a measure of suspense.
w Marriott Edgar, Val Guest, J. O. C. Orton d Marcel Varnel ph Derek Williams md Louis Levy
☆ Will Hay, Moore Marriott, Graham Moffatt, Glennis Lorimer, Peter Gawthorne, Herbert Lomas, Charles Oliver
'A good laugh getter and safe second feature on any programme.' – Variety

Ask Any Girl *

US 1959 98m Metrocolor Cinemascope
MGM/Euterpe (Joe Pasternak)
A husband-hunting receptionist in New York catches the eye of a wealthy playboy but finally settles for his elder brother.
Predictable Cinderella story with a lively but forgettable script and actors going through familiar paces.
w George Wells *novel* Winifred Wolfe d Charles Walters ph Robert Bronner m Jeff Alexander
☆ David Niven, Shirley MacLaine, Gig Young, Rod Taylor, Jim Backus, Claire Kelly
'Like a comic strip transposed to the glossy pages of Vogue.' – MFB
🎬 Shirley MacLaine

Asking for Trouble *

GB 1941 81m bw
British National
A bookie poses as a big game hunter.
The last opportunity to see a great music hall comic on film, his style admittedly bowdlerized.
w Oswald Mitchell, Con West d Oswald Mitchell

☆ Max Miller, Carole Lynne, Wilfrid Hyde-White, Mark Lester

Aspern *

Portugal 1981 96m colour
VO/Oxala (Paulo Branco)
The French biographer of a deceased poet goes to Venice to get unpublished papers from his aged mistress.
This very well-known story (see also The Lost Moment *and various theatrical versions) is styled with exceeding solemnity in this well-acted but boring version.*
w Michael Graham *story* Henry James d Eduardo de Grigorio ph Acacio de Almeida m mainly from Mozart
☆ Alida Valli, Jean Sorel, Bulle Ogier, Ana Marta

Asphalt *

Germany 1929 101m bw
UFA
A young policeman accidentally kills his rival for a worthless girl.
Heavily expressionist melodrama, overlong but good to watch.
w Rolf Vanloo, Fred Majo, Hans Szekely d Joe May ph Günther Rittau
☆ Gustav Fröhlich, Betty Amann, Else Heller, Albert Steinruck, Hans Albers
'So well produced that it is good entertainment in spite of itself.' – Variety

The Asphalt Jungle ***

US 1950 112m bw
MGM (Arthur Hornblow Jnr)
🔲 ▤
An elderly crook comes out of prison and assembles a gang for one last robbery.
Probably the very first film to show a 'caper' from the criminals' viewpoint (a genre which has since been done to death several times over), this is a clever character study rather than a thriller, extremely well executed and indeed generally irreproachable yet somehow not a film likely to appear on many top ten lists; perhaps the writer-director stands too far back from everybody, or perhaps he just needed Humphrey Bogart.
w Ben Maddow, John Huston *novel* W. R. Burnett d John Huston ph Harold Rosson m Miklos Rozsa
☆ Sterling Hayden, Louis Calhern, Sam Jaffe, Jean Hagen, James Whitmore, John McIntire, Marc Lawrence, Marilyn Monroe, Barry Kelley
RIEDENSCHNEIDER: 'Crime is a left-handed form of human endeavour.'
'Where this film excels is in the fluency of its narration, the sharpness of its observation of character and the excitement of its human groupings.' – Dilys Powell
'That Asphalt Pavement thing is full of nasty, ugly people doing nasty things. I wouldn't walk across the room to see a thing like that.' – Louis B. Mayer (who was head of the studio which made it)
† Apart from imitations, the film has been directly remade as The Badlanders, Cairo *and* A Cool Breeze (qqv).
🅰 Ben Maddow, John Huston (writers); John Huston (as director); Harold Rosson; Sam Jaffe

The Asphyx

GB 1972 99m Eastmancolor Todd-AO 35
Glendale (John Brittany)
🔲 ▤
A Victorian aims to become immortal by separating the spirit of death from his body.
Interminable hocus pocus with a plethora of talk, seldom exciting but watchable because of its remarkable cast and other credits.
w Brian Comport d Peter Newbrook ph Freddie Young m Bill McGuffie sp Ted Samuels
☆ Robert Stephens, Robert Powell, Jane Lapotaire

The Assam Garden

GB 1985 90m colour
Contemporary/Moving Picture Company (Nigel Stafford-Clark)
A widow returns from Assam to the English house where many years previously her husband had created a garden full of eastern plants, and where events now help her to free herself of the past.
Muted and somewhat ineffective treatment of a familiar television theme. Not unpleasant to watch despite obvious economies, but instantly forgettable.

w Elisabeth Bond d Mary McMurray ph Bryan Loftus m Richard Harvey
☆ Deborah Kerr, Madhur Jaffrey, Alec McCowen, Zia Mohyeddin, Iain Cuthbertson

Assassin: see Point of No Return (1993)

Assassin

GB 1973 83m Technicolor
Pemini (David M. Jackson)
MI5 arranges the liquidation of an Air Ministry spy.
Old hat espionage melodrama, top heavy with artiness which makes it look like an endless TV commercial.
w Michael Sloan d Peter Crane ph Brian Jonson m Zack Lawrence
☆ Ian Hendry, Edward Judd, Frank Windsor, Ray Brooks, John Hart Dyke

The Assassin: see Gunfighters (1947)

The Assassin: see Venetian Bird

1952

The Assassin **

Italy/France 1961 105m bw
Titanus-Vides-SGC (Franco Cristaldi)
A prosperous antique dealer is accused of murder and his unsavoury past is revealed; but when he is freed, he prides himself on his new personality.
A careful, detailed and wholly enjoyable character study, somewhere between comedy and drama.
w Elio Petri and others d Elio Petri ph Carlo di Palma m Piero Piccioni
☆ Marcello Mastroianni, Salvo Randone, Micheline Presle, Andrea Checci

Assassin for Hire *

GB 1951 67m bw
Merton Park (Julian Wintle/Anglo Amalgamated)
A professional killer is trapped into admitting a murder he didn't do.
Taut little suspenser, quite watchable.
w Rex Rienits d Michael McCarthy
☆ Sydney Tafler, Ronald Howard, John Hewer, Martin Benson

L'Assassin habite au 21 **

France 1947 83m bw
Mage/Liote
aka: The Murderer Lives at 21
A police detective assumes the guise of a clergyman to investigate mass killings which seem to centre on a boarding house.
Agreeable, straight-faced but tongue-in-cheek comedy thriller which was probably even funnier in French.
wd Henri-Georges Clouzot *novel* S. A. Steerman ph Armand Thirard
☆ Pierre Fresnay, Suzy Delair, Pierre Larquey, Noel Roquevert

Assassin of the Tsar (dubbed)

Russia/GB 1991 104m Eastmancolor
Blue Dolphin/Mosfilm/Spectator/Courier (Christopher Gawor, Erik Vaisberg, Anthony Sloman)
🔲
Russian title: Tsareubiitsa
A doctor decides on a dangerous plan to cure a patient in a Russian psychiatric ward who believes he is both the killer of Tsar Alexander II in 1881 and one of the murderers of Tsar Nicholas and his family in 1918.
An odd movie that is unsuccessful in its attempt to frame the demise of the Russian royal family within a modern-day story; the result is confusing and unconvincing.
w Aleksandr Borodianski, Karen Shakhnazarov d Karen Shakhnazarov ph Nikolai Nemoliaev m John Altman, Vladislav Shut ad Liudmila Kusakova ed Lidiia Miliotti
☆ Malcolm McDowell, Oleg Yankovsky, Armen Dzhigarkhanyan, Iurii Sherstnev, Angela Ptashuk, Viktor Seferov
'Both a compelling modern pyschodrama and a powerful recreation of one of the pivotal events of modern history, addressing Russian history and the current turbulent state of the country in an effective and compelling manner.' – Kim Newman, Empire
'Unsatisfactory psychology and unsatisfactory historiography.' – Sight and Sound

Assassination

US 1986 88m TVC Color
Cannon (Pancho Kohner)
🔲 ▤ ◎
A White House secret service man finds himself on the run with the first lady.
Mildly diverting but over-mysterious chase movie, less violent than the Bronson norm.
w Richard Sale d Peter Hunt
☆ Charles Bronson, Jill Ireland, Stephen Elliott, Jan Gan Boyd, Randy Brooks, Michael Ansara

The Assassination Bureau *

GB 1968 110m Technicolor
Paramount/Heathfield (Michael Relph)
▤
In 1906 a lady journalist breaks up an international gang of professional killers by falling in love with their leader.
Black comedy period pastiche which resolves itself into a series of sketches leading up to a spectacular zeppelin climax. Plenty going on, but the level of wit is not high.
w Michael Relph, Wolf Mankowitz d Basil Dearden ph Geoffrey Unsworth m Ron Grainer
☆ Oliver Reed, Diana Rigg, Telly Savalas, Curt Jurgens, Philippe Noiret, Warren Mitchell, Clive Revill, Beryl Reid, Kenneth Griffith

The Assassination of the Duc de Guise *

France 1908 15m bw silent
Film d'Art
Henry III arranges the killing of the Duc de Guise when he comes to court.
Influential early story film.
w Henri Lavedan d Charles le Bargy m Saint-Saëns
☆ Charles le Bargy, Albert Lambert, Gabrielle Lavinne

'For one moment, they hold history in their hands. With one terrible blow, they make it'
The Assassination of Trotsky

Italy/GB/France 1972 103m Technicolor
Dino de Laurentiis/Josef Shaftel/Cinetel (Norman Priggen, Joseph Losey)
▤ ◎ 🎧
In 1940, Trotsky is hiding out in Mexico; a Stalinist infiltrates his presence and kills him with an ice pick.
Glum historical reconstruction with much fictitious padding; basically undramatic.
w Nicholas Mosley, Masolino d'Amico d Joseph Losey ph Pasquale de Santis m Egisto Macchi
☆ Richard Burton, Alain Delon, Romy Schneider, Valentina Cortese, Jean Desailly
'Not for anyone who knows, or cares, anything about Leon Trotsky.' – New Yorker, 1977

Assassino ... è al telefono: see The Killer Is on the Phone

Assassins

US 1995 132m Technicolor
Warner/Silver Pictures (Richard Donner, Joel Silver, Bruce Evans, Raynold Gideon, Andrew Lazar, Jim Van Wyck)
🔲 ▤ ◎ 🎦 🎦
A top hitman, who has decided that it is time to quit, is menaced by a younger rival.
Even by the standards of some other of Stallone's movies, this is relentlessly silly stuff about extremely nasty characters; you may keep watching just to discover what illogicality happens next, in which case the ending will not disappoint you.
w Andy Wachowski, Larry Wachowski, Brian Helgeland d Richard Donner ph Vilmos Zsigmond m Mark Mancina pd Tom Sanders ed Richard Marks
☆ Sylvester Stallone, Antonio Banderas, Julianne Moore, Anatoly Davydow, Muse Watson, Stephen Kahan
'Has a few suspenseful confrontations, but to get to them you have to wade through countless scenes of monosyllabic brooding, all shot in the kind of elegantly sterile beige and slate tones that suggest someone's half-baked idea of a "minimalist" thriller.' – Entertainment Weekly

Les Assassins du Dimanche

France 1956 94m bw Cinepanoramic
EDIC
aka: Every Second Counts
Dozens of people help to track down a holiday car which has been driven away from a garage in a dangerous condition.

Watchable but artificial suspenser.
w Alex Joffe, Gabriel Arout d Alex Joffe ph Jean Bourgoin
☆ Barbara Laage, Jean-Marc Thibault, Dominique Wilms, Paul Frankeur

Assault
GB 1970 91m Eastmancolor
Rank/Peter Rogers (George H. Brown)
An art mistress helps police to solve a case of multiple rape in an English village.
Old-fashioned police mystery with new-fangled shock treatment. Routine excitements.
w John Kruse *novel* Kendal Young d Sidney Hayers ph Ken Hodges m Eric Rogers
☆ Frank Finlay, Suzy Kendall, James Laurenson, Lesley-Anne Down, Freddie Jones, Tony Beckley, Anthony Ainley, Dilys Hamlett
  'All right for that wet afternoon.' – *Michael Billington, Illustrated London News*

The Assault ***
Netherlands 1986 148m colour
Cannon (Fons Rademakers)
⬚ ▤
original title: *De Aanslag*
An adult is forced to recall the traumatic events of his childhood, when he saw his family murdered by the Nazis.
Part gripping thriller, part indictment of those who would forget the past, and wholly watchable.
w Gerard Soeteman *novel* Harry Mulisch d Fons Rademakers ph Their Van Der Sande m Jurriaan Andriessen ed Kees Linthorst
☆ Derek de Lint, Marc Van Uchelen, Monique Van de Ven, John Kraaykamp, Huub Van Der Lubbe, Elly Weller, Ina Van Der Molen
🏆 best foreign film

Assault on a Queen
US 1966 106m Technicolor Panavision
Paramount/Seven Arts/Sinatra Enterprises (William Goetz)
▤
Crooks dredge up a submarine and use it to hi-jack the *Queen Mary.*
Strained caper film which remains uncertain whether to play for drama or thrills, and achieves neither. Special effects unconvincing.
w Rod Serling *novel* Jack Finney d Jack Donohue ph William Daniels m Duke Ellington
☆ Frank Sinatra, Virna Lisi, Tony Franciosa, Alf Kjellin, Errol John, Richard Conte, Murray Matheson, Reginald Denny
  'Just about as enthralling as plastic boats in the bath.' – *MFB*

Assault on Precinct 13 ***
US 1976 91m Metrocolor Panavision
CKK (Joseph Kaufman)
⬚ ▤ ⊚ ○
Gang members on a vendetta attack a police station.
Violent but basically efficient and old-fashioned programmer which shows that not all the expertise of the forties in this then-familiar field has been lost.
ph Douglas Knapp wd/m John Carpenter
☆ Austin Stoker, Darwin Joston, Laurie Zimmer, Martin West
  'One of the most effective exploitation movies of the last ten years … Carpenter scrupulously avoids any overt socio-political pretensions, playing instead for laughs and suspense in perfectly balanced proportions.' – *Time Out*

The Assignment
Canada/US 1997 115m colour
Columbia TriStar/Triumph/Allegro (Tom Berry, Franco Battista)
⬚ ▤ ⊚ ○
An American naval officer, who is the double of Carlos 'The Jackal' Sanchez, is persuaded by the CIA to impersonate the terrorist.
Tepid spy thriller, which seems more like propaganda than entertainment; despite its use of fact, it never suggests a convincing reality.
w Dan Gordon, Sabi H. Shabtai d Christian Duguay ph David Franco m Normand Corbeil pd Michael Joy ed Yves Langlois
☆ Aidan Quinn, Donald Sutherland, Ben Kingsley, Claudia Ferri, Celine Bonnier, Vlasta Vrana, Liliana Komorowska
  'Visually proceedings veer between made-for-television stodge and inexpert gimmickry.' – *Danny Leigh, Sight and Sound*

Assignment in Brittany
US 1943 96m bw
MGM (J. Walter Ruben)
A Free French soldier stays in occupied France to fight the Nazis.
Routine propagandist actioner, totally unbelievable.
w Anthony Veiller, William Wright, Howard Emmett Rogers *novel* Helen MacInnes d Jack Conway ph Charles Rosher m Lennie Hayton
☆ Jean Pierre Aumont, Signe Hasso, Susan Peters, Reginald Owen, Richard Whorf, Margaret Wycherly, John Emery, Miles Mander, George Coulouris

  'Any moment the world might blow up in their double faces!'
Assignment K
GB 1968 97m Techniscope
Columbia/Mazurka (Ben Arbeid, Maurice Foster)
The European head of a toy firm is also head of a special spy unit.
Dreary espionage thriller, instantly forgettable, and only watchable at odd moments while it's on.
w Val Guest, Bill Strutton, Maurice Foster *novel* Hartley Howard d Val Guest ph Ken Hodges m Basil Kirchin
☆ Stephen Boyd, Michael Redgrave, Camilla Sparv, Leo McKern, Jeremy Kemp

Assignment Paris
US 1952 85m bw
Columbia (Sam Marx, Jerry Bresler)
A reporter on the Paris staff of the *New York Herald-Tribune* goes to Yugoslavia, is arrested as a spy, and has to be exchanged.
Dim cold war melodrama with occasional entertaining moments.
w William Bowers *novel* Trial by Terror by Paul Gallico d Robert Parrish ph Burnett Guffey, Ray Cory m George Duning
☆ George Sanders, Dana Andrews, Sandro Giglio, Marta Toren, Audrey Totter, Herbert Berghof

Assignment Redhead
GB 1956 79m bw
Butcher's (W. G. Chalmers)
A gang of Continental crooks searches for forged Nazi banknotes in London.
Convoluted but uninteresting thriller, lacking in suspense.
wd Maclean Rogers *novel* Lindsay Hardy ph Ernest Palmer md Wilfred Burns ad John Stoll ed Peter Mayhew
☆ Richard Denning, Carole Mathews, Ronald Adam, Danny Green, Brian Worth, Jan Holden, Elwyn Brook-Jones, Ronald Leigh-Hunt

Assignment to Kill
US 1967 99m Technicolor Panavision
Warner Seven Arts (William Conrad)
A New York insurance company hires a private eye to investigate a dubious European financier.
Routine international intrigue with muddled plot and unusual cast. A nice production wasted.
wd Sheldon Reynolds ph Harold Lipstein m William Lava
☆ Patrick O'Neal, John Gielgud, Peter Van Eyck, Joan Hackett, Herbert Lom, Eric Portman, Oscar Homolka, Leon Greene

The Assisi Underground
Italy/US 1985 178m colour
Cannon (Menahem Golan, Yoram Globus)
▤ ○
During World War II, Assisi monasteries hide Jewish refugees.
Expansive but generally abysmal war adventure which was released in various forms, including a television miniseries. No amount of re-editing can disguise an empty script and incompetent direction.
wd Alexander Ramati *novel* Alexander Ramati ph Giuseppe Rotunno m Dov Seltzer pd Luciano Spadoni
☆ Ben Cross, James Mason, Irene Papas, Maximilian Schell, Simon Ward, Giancarlo Giannini
  'There is simply not enough story to fill three hours, so the scenery upstages the actors.' – *Variety*

The Associate
US 1996 113m Technicolor
Polygram/Interscope (Frédérick Golchan, Patrick Markey, Adam Leipzig)
⬚ ▤ ⊚ ○
Faced with the problems of succeeding in a man's world, a female financial analyst invents a male partner, and then discovers she needs to impersonate him.
Perhaps it was time for a male impersonation, after an overdose of other drag acts in mainstream films, but this vehicle is too ramshackle and lacking in humour to make the effort seem worthwhile.
w Nick Thiel *novel* El socio by Jenaro Prieto d Donald Petrie ph Alex Nepomniaschy m Christopher Tyng pd Andrew Jackness ed Bonnie Koehler *film* L'Associé
☆ Whoopi Goldberg, Dianne Wiest, Tim Daly, Bebe Neuwirth, Eli Wallach, Austin Pendleton, Lainie Kazan, George Martin, Kenny Kerr
  'Shallow cut-and-paste Hollywood formula.' – *Sight and Sound*

Asterix & Obelix Take on Caesar
(dubbed) *
 👫 France/Germany/Italy 1999 110m colour Super 35
Pathé/Katharina/Renn/TF1/Bavaria/Melampo (Claude Berri)
original title: *Astérix & Obélix contre Caesar*
In Gaul, a small village, where the men are made strong by their druid's magic potion, holds out against Julius Caesar's invading army.
Lavish live-action version of the much-loved comic books, well-cast but suffering in the English-language version from the dubbing, which loses much of the humour.
w Claude Zidi, Gérard Lauzier (English version: Terry Jones) *characters created by* Albert Uderzo, René Goscinny d Claude Zidi ph Tony Pierce-Roberts pd Jean Rabasse ed Nicole Saunier, Hervé de Luze
☆ Christian Clavier, Gérard Depardieu, Roberto Benigni, Michel Galabru, Claude Piéplu, Daniel Prévost, Pierre Palmade, Laetitia Casta, Arielle Dombasle, Sim, Marianne Sagebrecht, Gottfried John, Jean-Pierre Castaldi, Jean-Jacques Devaux, Jean-Roger Milo
  'Trades in suitably lively slapstick but perhaps without ever doing the cool Gaul total justice.' – *William Thomas, Empire*
† One of the most expensive films ever made in France, it was also a smash hit at the French box-office.

Asterix and the Big Fight
 👫 France/West Germany 1989 81m Eastmancolor
Palace/Gaumont/Extrafilm (Nicolas Pesques)
⬚
original title: *Le Coup de Menhir*
Asterix attempts to restore the village soothsayer's memory in order to make a potion to defeat the invading Romans.
Dull adaptation of a far wittier comic-book original.
w George Roubicek *novel* Asterix and the Big Fight by Rene Goscinny and Alberto Uderzo d Philippe Grimond ph Craig Simpson m Michel Colombier pd Nicolas Pesques ed Jean Goudier
☆ Featuring the voices of Bill Oddie, Bernard Bresslaw, Ron Moody, Sheila Hancock, Peter Hawkins, Brian Blessed, Michael Elphick, Andrew Sachs, Tim Brooke-Taylor, Douglas Blackwell

Asterix Conquers America
 👫 Germany 1994 85m colour
TCF/Extrafilm (Jürgen Wohlrabe)
⬚
Asterix and friends end up accidentally in America, where they spend some time with an Indian tribe before returning home to fight the Romans once more.
Uninventive animated cartoon, making mild and inoffensive fun of national characteristics.
w Thomas Platt, Rhett Rooster, Robin Lyons, Andrew Offiler d Gerhard Hahn m Harold Faltermayer ed Ulrich Steinvorth
☆ Featuring the voices of John Rye, Craig Charles, Howard Lewis, Henry McGee, Geoffrey Bayldon, Christopher Biggins
  'Pretty weary stuff, suitable only for avid fans.' – *Guardian*

Asterix in Britain
 👫 Denmark/France 1986 74m Eastmancolor
Gaumont Dargaud (Yannik Piel)
⬚
Asterix and friends go to Britain to help the locals repel the Roman invasion.
Amiable animated version of the comic-book characters, poking good-natured fun at national stereotypes.
w Pierre Tchernia *comic* Goscinny and Uderzo d Pino Van Lamsweerde m Vladimir Cosma
☆ Featuring the voices of Jack Beaver, Bill Kearns, Graham Bushnell, Herbert Baskind, Ed Marcus

The Asthenic Syndrome ***
Russia 1989 153m bw/Fujicolor
Odessa Film Studio
original title: *Asteniceskij Sindrom*
A bleak tale of a woman who cannot come to terms with her bereavement turns out to be a film within the film; the real story is of modern-day Moscow and events centring around a narcoleptic teacher.
The film opens with a chorus of three old ladies chanting, 'In my childhood and youth I thought that if everybody read Leo Tolstoy carefully they would understand absolutely everything and would become very kind and wise.' What follows in this witty, episodic, structurally bold, harshly ironic account is the obverse: a society of uncaring and hostile people who will not wake up to their condition.
w Kira Muratova, Sergei Popov, Alexander Tschernych d Kira Muratova ph Vladimir Pankov ed Vladimir Olinik
☆ Olga Antonova, Sergei Popov, Galina Zakhrudayeva
† The film was banned on its release, and was only seen in Russia after it won the Special Jury Prize at the Berlin Film Festival in 1990.

The Astonished Heart *
GB 1949 89m bw
Gainsborough/Sydney Box (Anthony Darnborough)
A psychiatrist is permitted by his wife to fall in love with another woman but finds the situation intolerable and kills himself.
The star, looking like a Chinese mandarin, reached his nadir in this unwise screen adaptation, inelegantly directed, of one of his slightest short plays about boring and effete people. It sank without trace.
w Noël Coward *play* Noël Coward d Terence Fisher, Anthony Darnborough ph Jack Asher m Noël Coward
☆ Noël Coward, Margaret Leighton, Celia Johnson, Graham Payn, Joyce Carey, Ralph Michael, Michael Hordern

The Astounding She-Monster
US 1957 59m bw
Hollywood International (Ronnie Ashcroft)
▤
GB title: *Mysterious Invader*
In a remote spot, some crooks and a scientist combat a female space visitor with remarkable powers.
An early sub-Corman pot-boiler with only its camp qualities to recommend it.
w Frank Hall d Ronnie Ashcroft
☆ Robert Clarke, Kenne Duncan, Marilyn Harvey

  'Imagine the face of terror is the one you love.'
The Astronaut's Wife
US 1999 109m DeLuxe
Entertainment/New Line/Mad Chance (Andrew Lazar)
▤ ⊚ ○
An astronaut's wife comes to believe that, while in space, her husband was taken over by an alien entity; then she becomes pregnant.
A sort of science-fiction variation on Rosemary's Baby, but much less effective and interesting.
wd Rand Ravich ph Allen Daviau pd Jan Roelfs ed Steve Mirkovich, Tim Alverson
☆ Johnny Depp, Charlize Theron, Joe Morton, Clea DuVall, Donna Murphy, Samantha Eggar, Gary Grubbs, Blair Brown, Tom Noonan
  'The abiding atmosphere is one of tedium and unreality.' – *James Christopher, Times*

Asya's Happiness **
USSR 1967 94m bw
Artificial Eye/Mosfilm (M. Zarzhitskaya)
original title: *Istoria Asi Klyachinoi, kotoraya lyubila, da nie vshla zamuzh*

The film's epigraph is 'The story of a woman who loved but did not marry', but it is more a loving account of a rural community at work and play.

A candid portrait of Soviet life, using amateur actors, that was banned for more than 20 years for reasons only the Russians will understand.

w Yuri Klepikov d Andrei Mikhalkov-Konchalovsky ph Georgy Rerberg pd Mikhail Romadin ed L. Pokrovskoi

☆ Iya Savvina, Lyubov Sokolova, Alexander Surin, Gennady Yegorychev, Ivan Petrov

'A major film in its own right, a worthy addition to that great agrarian cinema of Vidor and Ford.' – Ian Christie, MFB

'You have nothing to lose but your mind!'
Asylum *
GB 1972 88m Eastmancolor
Amicus (Max J. Rosenberg, Milton Subotsky)
aka: *House of Crazies*

A doctor applies for a job at an asylum, hears weird stories from four patients, and finds himself in the middle of a weirder one.

Lively horror compilation with echoes of Caligari and Dead of Night. Gruesomeness sometimes overdone.

w Robert Bloch d Roy Ward Baker ph Denys Coop m Douglas Gamley

☆ Patrick Magee, Robert Powell, Geoffrey Baylдon, Barbara Parkins, Sylvia Syms, Richard Todd, Peter Cushing, Barry Morse, Britt Ekland, Charlotte Rampling, James Villiers, Megs Jenkins, Herbert Lom

At Close Range
US 1986 111m CFI color Panavision
Orion/Hemdale (Elliott Lewitt, Don Guest)

In Pennsylvania, a gang of young robbers is picked off one by one by the father of one of them, who feels they know too much about his own criminal activities.

Relentlessly brutal, dispiriting and quite pointless melodrama, even with the saving grace of a factual basis.

w Nicholas Kazan d James Foley ph Juan Ruiz-Anchia m Patrick Leonard

☆ Sean Penn, Christopher Walken, Mary Stuart Masterson, Christopher Penn, Millie Perkins, Eileen Ryan, Candy Clark

'A very tough picture … runs the risk of being an audience turnoff.' – Variety

At Dawn We Die: see *Tomorrow We Live*

'Seeing is believing.'
At First Sight
US 1999 128m DeLuxe Panavision
MGM (Irwin Winkler, Rob Cowan)

A blind masseur is encouraged by his girlfriend to have an operation that may restore his sight.

A sentimental romantic drama that should be neither seen nor heard.

w Steve Levitt story *To See and Not See* by Oliver Sacks d Irwin Winkler ph John Seale m Mark Isham pd Jane Musky ed Julie Monroe

☆ Val Kilmer, Mira Sorvino, Kelly McGillis, Steven Weber, Bruce Davison, Nathan Lane, Ken Howard

'Fluffy, oversweet and not particularly nourishing.' – Lael Loewenstein, Variety

'The film itself could have done with an eye-test, since it apparently can't see its story except in soft-focus.' – Alexander Walker, London Evening Standard

At Gunpoint
US 1955 80m Technicolor Cinemascope
Allied Artists
GB title: *Gunpoint*

A Western storekeeper accidentally kills a bank robber, whose brothers seek revenge; will the townsfolk come to his aid?

Fair Western on the lines of High Noon.

w Dan Ullman d Alfred Werker

☆ Fred MacMurray, Dorothy Malone, Walter Brennan, John Qualen, Skip Homeier

'A new kind of musical!'
At Long Last Love
US 1975 114m Technicolor
TCF/Copa de Oro (Peter Bogdanovich)

The 1935 romance of a New York millionaire and a musical star.

An attempt to recapture the simple pleasures of an Astaire-Rogers musical; unfortunately true professionalism is lacking and the wrong kind of talent is used. The result is awful to contemplate.

wd Peter Bogdanovich ph Laszlo Kovacs m Cole Porter pd Gene Allen

☆ Burt Reynolds, Cybill Shepherd, Eileen Brennan, Madeline Kahn, Duilio del Prete, John Hillerman, Mildred Natwick

'He works hard at reducing all his sets and costumes to variations of black against silver or white on white, and uncovers in his most oft-repeated visual motif – the elegant mirrors before which his cast seem at all times to be posed – the perfect metaphor for this endlessly narcissistic, thoroughly calcified enterprise.' – Richard Combs

'It just lies there, and it dies there.' – Variety

'Studios bury more films than the public or the critics. Fox gave up on At Long Last Love instantly. A six million dollar film was written off while it was doing well because their lawyers told them they could make more money that way.' – Peter Bogdanovich

'It is justly included on most lists of the ten worst films ever made.' – Les Keyser, Hollywood in the Seventies

'Stillborn … a relentlessly vapid pastiche.' – Pauline Kael

At Play in the Fields of the Lord *
US 1991 186m Technicolor
Entertainment/Saul Zaentz

American mercenaries become embroiled in a battle for the land and souls of an Indian tribe in the Amazon.

Over-long and over-earnest treatment of a fashionable theme, though it does have its moments.

w Jean-Claude Carrière, Hector Babenco novel Peter Mathiessen d Hector Babenco ph Lauro Escorel m Zbigniew Preisner pd Clovis Bueno ed William Anderson, Aremn Minasian, Louise Innes

☆ Tom Berenger, John Lithgow, Daryl Hannah, Aidan Quinn, Tom Waits, Kathy Bates, Stenio Garcia, Nelson Xavier

'The Amazonian tragedy is surely not best served by three hours of tedium.' – Empire

At Sword's Point *
US 1952 81m Technicolor
RKO (Jerrold T. Brandt)
GB title: *Sons of the Musketeers*

The sons of the three musketeers rally around their ageing queen to prevent her daughter's marriage to a villain.

Adequate swashbuckler with plenty of pace and a sound cast.

w Walter Ferris, Joseph Hoffman d Lewis Allen ph Ray Rennahan m Roy Webb

☆ Cornel Wilde, Maureen O'Hara, Gladys Cooper, Robert Douglas, Dan O'Herlihy, Alan Hale Jnr, Blanche Yurka, Nancy Gates

At the Circus **
US 1939 87m bw
MGM (Mervyn Le Roy)
aka: *The Marx Brothers at the Circus*

A shyster lawyer and two incompetents save a circus from bankruptcy.

This film began the decline of the Marx Brothers; in it nothing is ill done but nothing is very fresh either apart from the rousing finale which shows just what professionalism meant in the old Hollywood. Highlights include Groucho singing about Lydia the tattooed lady, his seduction of Mrs Dukesbury, and the big society party.

w Irving Brecher d Edward Buzzell ph Leonard M. Smith m Franz Waxman m/ly Harold Arlen, E. Y. Harburg

☆ Groucho, Chico, Harpo, Margaret Dumont, Florence Rice, Kenny Baker, Eve Arden, Nat Pendleton, Fritz Feld

GROUCHO: 'I don't know what I'm doing here when I could be at home in bed with a hot toddy. That's a drink.'

'Rousing physical comedy and staccato gag dialogue … geared for fine b.o. and general audience appeal.' – Variety

'We must regretfully accept the fact that, thanks to the Metro millions, the Marx Brothers are finally imprisoned in the Hollywood world.' – Graham Greene

♫ 'Lydia', 'Two Blind Loves', 'Step up and Take a Bow'

At the Earth's Core
GB 1976 90m Technicolor
Amicus (John Dark)

Scientists testing a geological excavator are carried by it to the centre of the Earth, and find a prehistoric land inhabited by feuding tribes.

Mainly feeble science fiction for kids, with occasional amusing moments.

w Milton Subotsky novel Edgar Rice Burroughs d Kevin Connor ph Alan Hume m Mike Vickers pd Maurice Carter sp Ian Wingrove

☆ Doug McClure, Peter Cushing, Caroline Munro, Cy Grant, Godfrey James, Keith Barron

'Papier mâché people-eaters, idiotic situations, and a frequent sense of confusion as to what is going on.' – David Stewart, Christian Science Monitor

At the Stroke of Nine
GB 1957 72m bw
Tower/Grand National

A mad concert pianist plots to murder a young girl reporter.

Absurd and rather endearing melodrama of the very old school.

w Tony O'Grady, Harry Booth, Jon Pennington, Michael Deeley d Lance Comfort

☆ Stephen Murray, Patricia Dainton, Patrick Barr, Dermot Walsh

At the Villa Rose
This murder mystery by A. E. W. Mason has had three British filmings: in 1920 with Teddy Arundell as Inspector Hanaud; in 1930 with Austin Trevor; in 1939 with Keneth Kent. All were adequate to their time. The story concerns a medium framed for the murder of a rich widow.

At War with the Army
US 1951 93m bw
Paramount/Fred K. Finklehoffe

A couple of song and dance men have trouble as army recruits.

American service farce, based on a play and confined largely to one set; rather untypical of Martin and Lewis, yet oddly enough the film which sealed their success.

w Fred Finklehoffe play James Allardice d Hal Walker ph Stuart Thompson m Joseph Lilley

☆ Dean Martin, Jerry Lewis, Mike Kellin, Polly Bergen, Jimmie Dundee

L'Atalante *
France 1934 89m bw
J. L. Nounez-Gaumont

A barge captain takes his new wife down river.

One of those classics which no longer provide the authentic thrill; its lack of incident and plot leads quickly to boredom.

w Jean Guinée, Jean Vigo, Albert Riera d Jean Vigo ph Boris Kaufman, Louis Berger m Maurice Jaubert

☆ Jean Dasté, Dita Parlo, Michel Simon, Giles Margaritis

'The singular talent – for once I think I may say genius – of the film lies in its translation into visual images of the mysterious and terrible and piteous undertones of even the simplest human life.' – Dilys Powell

¡Atame!: see *Tie Me Up! Tie Me Down!*

El Ataque de los Muertos sin Ojo: see *The Return of the Evil Dead*

Athena
US 1954 96m Eastmancolor
MGM (Joe Pasternak)

A young lawyer falls in love with the eldest of seven sisters brought up to high standards of moral conduct and physical fitness.

Promising but unfulfilling light musical which smothers a good idea in routine treatment.

w William Ludwig, Leonard Spigelgass d Richard Thorpe ph Robert Planck m/ly Hugh Martin, Ralph Blane md George Stoll

☆ Edmund Purdom, Jane Powell, Debbie Reynolds, Louis Calhern, Evelyn Varden, Vic Damone, Linda Christian, Ray Collins

'The Leviathan of Talkies'
'A thunderbolt of drama impossible to describe'
Atlantic
GB 1929 90m bw
BIP

A passenger liner sinks in mid-Atlantic.

Veiled retelling of the Titanic story, here in a clumsy Anglo-German version with extremely primitive sound and a plethora of pregnant silences.

w Victor Kendall play *The Berg* by Ernest Raymond d E. A. Dupont

☆ Franklin Dyall, Madeleine Carroll, Monty Banks, John Stuart, John Longden, Ellaline Terriss

'If you want to be mentally shipwrecked or lost at sea, see *Atlantic* … It's something unnecessary to see; something no one wants to see; something horrible to even think of.

'…It will draw to and drive away from the box office. Draw to because it holds horror, thrills and suspense; drive away through children not being permitted to see it and the suggested gruesomeness too strong for many, not only women.

'…A faint try at comedy with a valet was like a ghoul in a cemetery … but Franklin Dyall excelled as an aged invalid with John Longden as a ship's officer, making a splendid appearance.' – Variety

Atlantic Adventure *
US 1935 68m bw
Columbia

A reporter captures a murderer on an ocean liner.

Lively double-biller, better than average in all departments.

w John T. Neville, Nat Dorfman story Diana Bourbon d Albert Rogell ph John Stumar ed Ted Kent

☆ Nancy Carroll, Lloyd Nolan, Harry Langdon, Arthur Hohl, Robert Middlemass, John Wray, E. E. Clive

'Only lack of cast names keeps this in dual pix classification.' – Variety

Atlantic City *
US 1944 87m bw
Republic (Albert J. Cohen)
aka: *Atlantic City, U.S.A.*

Before World War I, a young showman aims to make Atlantic City the entertainment centre of the world.

Simple-minded romantic musical, quite pacy and effectively staged for a Republic product.

w Doris Gilbert, Frank Gill Jnr, George Carleton Brown d Ray McCarey ph John Alton m/ly various

☆ Constance Moore, Brad Taylor, Jerry Colonna, Charley Grapewin

Atlantic City ***
Canada/France 1981 105m colour
Cine-Neighbour/Selta Films (Denis Heroux)

Small-time crooks congregate round Atlantic City's new casinos.

Elegiac character drama which often achieves the mood it seeks but on the whole remains too understated for its own good.

w John Guare d Louis Malle ph Richard Ciupka m Michel Legrand pd Anne Pritchard

☆ Burt Lancaster, Susan Sarandon, Kate Reid, Michel Piccoli, Hollis McLaren

📖 best picture; John Guare; Burt Lancaster; Susan Sarandon; Louis Malle

🎬 best direction; Burt Lancaster

Atlantic Episode: see *Catch As Catch Can*

Atlantic Ferry *
GB 1941 108m bw
Warner (Max Milder)
US title: *Sons of the Sea*

In 1837 Liverpool, two brothers build the first steamship to cross the Atlantic.

Ponderous historical romance with points of interest.

👪 film suitable for family viewing   ▣ VHS video-cassette for the British PAL system   ▣ VHS video-cassette for the British PAL system in wide screen-format   ☻ Video cassette in a computer-colourised version   ▤ American NTSC video-cassette   ⌕ Laser disc w Gordon Wellesley, Edward Dryhurst, Emeric Pressburger d Walter Forde ph Basil Emmott m Jack Beaver

☆ Michael Redgrave, Valerie Hobson, Griffith Jones, Margaretta Scott, Hartley Power, Bessie Love, Milton Rosmer

'Probably the finest collection of model shots in captivity.' – C. A. Lejeune

L'Atlantide *

France 1921 125m bw silent
Thalman

Two explorers find the lost continent of Atlantis and fall in love with its queen.

Highly commercial adventure fantasy of its day; it cost two million francs and ran in Paris for a year. Some scenes still sustain, and the desert scenes are impressive.

Other versions include:

1932 *Queen of Atlantis*, Germany, d G. W. Pabst, with Brigitte Helm

1948 *Siren of Atlantis*, US, d Gregg Tallas, with Maria Montez

1961 *L'Atlantide*, France/Italy, d Edgar G. Ulmer
wd Jacques Feyder *novel* Pierre Benoît
ph Georges Specht, Victor Morin

☆ Jean Angelo, Stacia Napierkowska, Georges Melchior

Atlantis **

⋔⋔ France 1991 75m colour
Warner/Gaumont/Cecchi Gori

An episodic documentary, with musical accompaniment, on life under the sea.

A fascinating attempt at what its director defined as an 'underwater opera', full of quirky detail and showing various species that may soon die out.

d Luc Besson ph Christian Petron m Eric Serra ed Luc Besson

Atlantis, the Lost Continent

⋔⋔ US 1961 91m Metrocolor
MGM/Galaxy/George Pal

A Greek fisherman is imprisoned when he returns a maiden he has rescued to her island home of Atlantis, but escapes just before volcanic eruption overtakes the doomed nation.

Penny-pinching fantasy spectacle with very little entertainment value.

w Daniel Mainwaring *play* Sir Gerald Hargreaves
d George Pal ph Harold E. Wellman m Russell Garcia

☆ Anthony Hall, Joyce Taylor, John Dall, Edward Platt, Frank de Kova, Jay Novello

Atoll K: see Robinson Crusoeland

Atolladero

Spain 1995 99m colour Panavision
FDG/Canal+ (Arturo Duque)
🔲

In 2048 in Texas, where despots rule over desert regions, an epileptic cop tries to escape from the small community in which he lives.

Curious pulp science fiction which mixes comic-book characters with the style of a slightly surreal spaghetti Western; most of the action takes place off-screen.

wd Oscar Aibar ph Carles Gusi m Javier Navarrete ad Llorenç Miquel ed Anastasi Rinos, Xavier Cabrera

☆ Pere Ponce, Joaquin Hinojosa, Iggy Pop, Félix Rotaeta, Carlos Lucas, Pep Molina, Oriol Tramvia, Ion Gabella, Xevi Collelmir

'Strong on atmosphere and character, but let down by flimsy plotting.' – *Sight and Souns*

The Atomic City *

US 1952 85m bw
Paramount (Joseph Sistrom)

The young son of a leading atomic scientist is kidnapped but his father and the FBI rescue him.
Routine but well-paced thriller with a documentary background of research at Los Alamos.

w Sydney Boehm d Jerry Hopper ph Charles B. Lang Jnr m Leith Stevens

☆ Gene Barry, Lydia Clarke, Lee Aaker, Nancy Gates, Milburn Stone

🎵 Sydney Boehm

The Atomic Kid

US 1954 86m bw
Republic/Mickey Rooney (Maurice Duke)
🔲

After an atomic blast, a prospector accidentally left in the area proves immune to uranium, and after various adventures rounds up some communist spies.

Inane romp which raises a few laughs.

w Benedict Freeman, John Fenton Murray *story* Blake Edwards d Leslie H. Martinson
ph John L. Russell Jnr m Van Alexander

☆ Mickey Rooney, Robert Strauss, Elaine Davis, Bill Goodwin, Whit Bissell

Atomic Submarine

US 1959 72m bw
Allied Artists (Alex Gordon)
📀 🔲

The crew of an atomic submarine save the world from an alien invasion under the North Pole.
Engaging nonsense of the period.

w Orville H. Hampton d Spencer Gordon Bennet ph Gilbert Warrenton m Alexander Laszlo ad Dan Haller, Dan Ament ed William Austin

☆ Arthur Franz, Dick Foran, Brett Halsey, Tom Conway, Paul Dubov, Bob Steele, Victor Varconi, Selmer Jackson

The Atonement of Gösta Berling **

Sweden 1924 200m bw silent
Svensk Filmindustri
🔲

original title: *Gösta Berlings Saga*

A pastor is defrocked for drinking, becomes a tutor, and has various love affairs.

Lumpy but often engrossing picturization of a famous novel, veering mostly into melodrama but finding its way to a happy ending.

w Mauritz Stiller, Ragnar Hylten-Cavallius *novel* Selma Lagerlof d Mauritz Stiller ph Julius Jaenzon

☆ Lars Hanson, Gerda Lundeqvist, Ellen Cederstrom, Mona Martensson, Jenny Hasselqvist, Otto Elg-Lundberg, Greta Garbo

'Stiller was a master at unifying visual beauty and emotional effect; the complicated narrative is blurry, but there are sequences as lovely and expressive as any on film.' – *New Yorker, 1980*

† It was her small role in this film which led directly to Greta Garbo's American stardom.

Attack **

US 1956 104m bw
UA/Associates and Aldrich
📀

In 1944 Belgium, an American infantry command is led by a coward.

High-pitched, slick, violent and very effective war melodrama, even though by the end we seem to be in the company of raving lunatics rather than soldiers.

w James Poe *play* Fragile Fox by Norman Brooks d Robert Aldrich ph Joseph Biroc m Frank de Vol

☆ Jack Palance, Eddie Albert, Lee Marvin, Buddy Ebsen, Robert Strauss, Richard Jaeckel, William Smithers, Peter Van Eyck

'The film does not so much tackle a subject as hammer it down.' – *Penelope Houston*

Attack Force Z

Australia 1981 110m colour
John McCallum/Central Motion Picture Corp (Lee Robinson)
📀 🔲

A secret commando group attempts to rescue survivors of a plane crash in Japanese-held territory during the Second World War.

Downbeat adventure, which was intended as a tribute to Australasian special operations, but conveys instead the waste of humanity that war entails.

w Roger Marshall d Tim Burstall ph Lin Hun-Chung m Eric Jupp ed David Stiven

☆ John Phillip Law, Mel Gibson, Sam Neill, Chris Haywood, John Waters, Koo Chuan-Hsiung, Sylvia Chang, O Ti

Attack of the 50 Ft. Woman

US 1993 90m colour
Entertainment/HBO/Bartleby (Debra Hill)
📀 🔲

After an encounter with a UFO a woman grows to enormous size and deals with her philandering husband.

A feminist remake that adds nothing of interest to the original, merely seeming a story yanked out of its time.

w Joseph Dougherty d Christopher Guest ph Russell Carpenter m Nicholas Pike pd Joseph T. Garrity ed Harry Keramidas sp Fantasy II Film Effects

☆ Daryl Hannah, Daniel Baldwin, William Windom, Frances Fisher, Paul Benedict, O'Neal Compton, Cristi Conaway

† Made for cable TV, the film had a brief cinema showing in Britain.

The Attack of the 50-Foot Woman

US 1958 72m bw
Allied Artists (Bernard Woolner)
🔲 📀

A neurotic woman is lured inside a space ship, becomes radio-active, and grows to alarming proportions.

Hilarious tailpiece to the fifties monster cycle, a dismal movie worth remembering only for its title.

w Mark Hanna d Nathan Hertz (Nathan Juran) ph Jacques Marquette m Ronald Stein ed Edward Mann

☆ Allison Hayes, William Hudson, Roy Gordon

'From the depths of the sea ... A Tidal Wave of Terror!'

Attack of the Crab Monsters

US 1956 62m bw
Allied Artists (Roger Corman)
🔲

25-foot mutant crabs cause landslides on a Pacific island.

Bottom-of-the-barrel monster mayhem from this tongue-in-cheek producer; now a cult.

w Charles B. Griffith d Roger Corman ph Floyd Crosby m Ronald Stein ed Charles Gross Jnr

☆ Richard Garland, Pamela Duncan, Russell Johnson

Attack of the Giant Leeches

US 1959 62m bw
Corman/AIP

aka: *Demons of the Swamp*

A bar owner forces his wife and her lover into a swamp to be eaten by monsters.

The bottom of the Corman/AIP barrel, good only for a few unintentional laughs.

w Leo Gordon d Bernard Kowalski ph John M. Nickolaus Jnr

☆ Ken Clark, Michael Emmet, Yvette Vickers, Bruno Ve Sota

Attack of the Killer Tomatoes

US 1978 87m colour
Four Square/NAI
📀 🔲 📀

Vegetables go berserk in the big city.

Apparently a cult film made deliberately as such, which is a contradiction in terms. Nothing for the ordinary audience, anyway.

w Costa Dillon, Steve Peace, John de Bello d John de Bello

☆ David Miller, George Wilson, Sharon Taylor, Jack Riley

'Though the idea sounds funny, actually sitting through nearly 90 minutes of it is enough to make anyone long for Attack of the Fifty Foot Woman.' – *Motion Picture Guide*

Attack of the Puppet People

US 1957 79m bw
Alta Vista (Bert I. Gordon)
GB title: *Six Inches Tall*

A doll-maker has also learned to shrink people.
Inferior entry in the Dr Cyclops mould; mildly amusing moments are sandwiched between chunks of tedium.

w George Worthing Yates d Bert I. Gordon

☆ John Hoyt, John Agar, June Kenny

Attack on the Iron Coast

GB 1967 90m DeLuxe
UA/Mirisch (John Champion)

In World War II, a Canadian commando unit destroys a German installation on the French coast.

Stagey low-budgeter with modest action sequences.

w Herman Hoffman d Paul Wendkos ph Paul Beeson m Gerard Schurmann

☆ Lloyd Bridges, Andrew Keir, Mark Eden, Sue Lloyd

Attila the Hun

Italy/France 1954 79m Technicolor
Lux Ponti de Laurentiis/LCCF (Georgio Andriani)

original title: *Attilo Flagello di Dio*

The barbarian chief attacks the forces of the Emperor Valentinian and marches on Rome.
Predictably violent adventures after de Mille; a bit slow to start.

w Ennio de Concini, Primo Zeglio d Pietro Francisci ph Aldo Tonti m Enzo Masetti

☆ Anthony Quinn, Sophia Loren, Henri Vidal, Irene Papas, Ettore Manni, Claude Laydu

Attilo Flagello di Dio: see Attila the Hun

Attorney for the Defense

US 1932 70m bw
Columbia

A prosecutor's wiles result in an innocent man being executed, so he turns crusader and takes on defence cases.

Punchy if unconvincing courtroom melodrama which would certainly satisfy at the time.

w Jo Swerling, J. K. McGuinness d Irving Cummings

☆ Edmund Lowe, Evelyn Brent, Constance Cummings, Donald Dillaway, Dorothy Peterson, Dwight Frye, Nat Pendleton, Clarence Muse

Au delà des Grilles

Italy/France 1949 90m bw
Italia Produzione/Francinex (Alfredo Guarini)
Italian title: *La mura de Malapaga*
aka: *Beyond the Gates; The Walls of Malapaga*

A murderer on the run in Genoa falls in love with a waitress and loses his chance of escape.

Quai des Brumes reworked against an Italian neo-realist setting; dramatic values less interesting now than historical ones.

w Jean Aurenche, Pierre Bost, Cesare Zavattini, Suso Cecchi d'Amico d René Clément ph Louis Page m Roman Vlad

☆ Jean Gabin, Isa Miranda, Vera Talchi, Andrea Checci

🏆 best foreign film

Au Hasard, Balthazar: see Balthazar

Au Pair Girls

GB 1972 86m Eastmancolor
LMG/Kenneth Shipman (Guido Coen)
📀

The adventures of four au pair girls in London.
Dire comedy in the depressing cycle of British sexploitation films of the 70s, one that wasted some excellent talents.

w Val Guest, David Adnopoz *story* David Grant d Val Guest ph John Wilcox m Roger Webb ad Roy Smith ed John Colville

☆ Gabrielle Drake, Astrid Frank, Nancie Wait, Me Me Lay, Richard O'Sullivan, John Le Mesurier, Geoffrey Bayldon, Rosalie Crutchley, Ferdy Mayne, John Standing, Johnny Briggs

'Val Guest hits rock bottom with this humourless attempt at a sex comedy.' – *Derek Elley, MFB*

Au Revoir Les Enfants ****

France 1988 107m Eastmancolor
Nouvelles éditions de Films/MK2/Stella Films (Louis Malle)
📀 🔲 📀 🎧

During the German occupation of France, a boy at a Catholic school inadvertently betrays his Jewish schoolfriend to the Nazis.

A coolly-understated, intensely personal, semi-autobiographical movie much admired by the French and winner of the Golden Lion at the Venice Film Festival.

wd Louis Malle ph Renato Berta ad Willy Holt ed Emmanuelle Castro

☆ Gaspard Manesse, Raphaël Fejtö, Francine Racette, Stanislas Carre de Malberg, Philippe Morier-Genoud, François Berleand

'Malle has said of Au Revoir, "I reinvented the past in the pursuit of a haunting and timeless truth." Maybe that's why I felt as if I were watching a faded French classic, something I dimly recalled.' – *Pauline Kael, New Yorker*

🏆 best foreign film; Louis Malle (as writer)

🎖 Louis Malle (as director)

Au Royaume des Cieux
France   1949   108m   bw
Regina (Julien Duvivier)
aka: *Woman Hunt*
An 18-year-old girl suffers at a reform school.
Shoddy melodrama, more sensational than Hollywood ever dared to be.
wd Julien Duvivier *ph* Victor Armenise
☆ Suzanne Cloutier, Serge Reggiani, Monique Mélinand, Suzy Prim, Jean Davy, Juliette Greco
   'A depressing exhibit from a director who once had a serious reputation.' – *Gavin Lambert*

L'Auberge Rouge: see *The Red Inn*

Auch Zwerge Haben Klein Angefangen:
see *Even Dwarfs Started Small*

Audrey Rose *
US   1977   113m   DeLuxe   Panavision
United Artists (Joe Wizan, Frank de Felitta)
⬛ ▦
A man believes that a 12-year-old girl is the reincarnation of his dead daughter.
Rather painful and not very persuasive spiritualist thriller in the wake of The Exorcist; only moments of dramaturgy survive.
w Frank de Felitta *novel* Frank de Felitta
d Robert Wise *ph* Victor J. Kemper *m* Michael Small *pd* Harry Horner
☆ Anthony Hopkins, Marsha Mason, John Beck, Susan Swift, Norman Lloyd, John Hillerman, Robert Walden

'You can live a whole lifetime in a single weekend...'
August *
GB   1995   94m   colour
Film Four/Majestic/Newcomm/Granada (June Wyndham Davies, Pippa Cross)
⬛ ▦ ❧ ∩
A visit by the head of the family and his much younger wife to the estate managed by his brother-in-law precipitates a crisis which leads its members to examine the disappointments of their lives.
An elegant, civilized version, though lacking in urgency, of Chekhov's play, which translates well to the Wales of the 1890s, with a narrative that gives some sense of life outside the stifled family at its centre.
w Julian Mitchell *play Uncle Vanya* by Anton Chekhov *d* Anthony Hopkins *ph* Robin Vidgeon *m* Anthony Hopkins *pd* Eileen Diss *ed* Edward Mansell
☆ Anthony Hopkins, Leslie Phillips, Kate Burton, Gawn Grainger, Hugh Lloyd, Rhoda Lewis, Menna Trussler, Rhian Morgan
   'It is very much an actor's piece. Lines are delivered rather than spoken, and the cast frequently freezes into a tableau, everyone staring rigidly into the distance.' – *George Perry*

Aunt Clara *
GB   1954   84m   bw
London Films (Colin Lesslie, Anthony Kimmins)
A pious old person inherits from a reprobate uncle five greyhounds, a pub and a brothel.
Extremely mild star vehicle with a gallery of comedy character cameos.
w Kenneth Horne *novel* Noel Streatfeild
d Anthony Kimmins *ph* C. Pennington-Richards
m Benjamin Frankel
☆ Margaret Rutherford, Ronald Shiner, A. E. Matthews, Fay Compton, Nigel Stock, Jill Bennett, Reginald Beckwith, Raymond Huntley

Aunt Julia and The Scriptwriter: see *Tune In Tomorrow*

Aunt Sally
GB   1933   84m   bw
Gainsborough (Michael Balcon)
US title: *Along Came Sally*
A fake French star saves a night-club owner from gangsters.
Predictable star vehicle.
w Austin Melford, Guy Bolton, A. R. Rawlinson
d Tim Whelan *ph* Charles Van Enger
ad Vetchinsky
☆ Cicely Courtneidge, Sam Hardy, Billy Milton, Phyllis Clare, Hartley Power

Auntie Mame *
US   1958   144m   Technirama
Warner (Morton da Costa)
▦ ❧
An orphan boy is adopted by his volatile extravagant aunt, whose giddy escapades fill his memory of the twenties and thirties.
A rather unsatisfactory star revue from a book and play later turned into a musical, Mame (qv). *A few splendid moments, otherwise rather dull and irritating.*
w Betty Comden, Adolph Green *play* Jerome Lawrence, Robert E. Lee *novel* Patrick Dennis
d Morton da Costa *ph* Harry Stradling
m Bronislau Kaper *ad* Malcolm Bert *ed* William Ziegler
☆ Rosalind Russell, Forrest Tucker, Coral Browne, Fred Clark, Roger Smith, Patric Knowles, Peggy Cass, Lee Patrick, Joanna Barnes
⚖ best picture; Harry Stradling; Rosalind Russell; Peggy Cass; art direction; editing

The Aurora Encounter
♙♙   US   1985   90m   colour
New World (Jim McCullough)
▦
In the 1890s, an alien visits a small Texas town in a flying saucer.
Unexciting, soft-centred family fare, featuring Elam in his later incarnation as an avuncular buffoon.
w Jim McCullough Jnr *d* Jim McCullough
ph Joseph Wilcots *m* Ron F. Dilulio *pd* Drew E. Hunter *ed* Sheri Galloway
☆ Jack Elam, Peter Brown, Carol Bagdasarian, Dottie West, Mickey Hays, Spanky McFarland

Aus Einem Deutschen Leben: see *Death Is My Trade*

Une Aussi Longue Absence *
France/Italy   1961   96m   bw
Procinex/Lyre/Galatea (Jacques Nahum)
aka: *The Long Absence*
A widow who owns a Paris café meets an amnesiac tramp who may be her long-lost husband.
Romantic character study which just about comes off thanks to good acting.
w Marguerite Duras, Gérald Jarlot *d* Henri Colpi
ph Marcel Weiss *m* Georges Delerue
☆ Alida Valli, Georges Wilson, Jacques Harden

Austerlitz
France/Italy/Liechtenstein/Yugoslavia   1959
166m   Eastmancolor   Dyaliscope
CFPI/SCLF/Galatea/Michael Arthur/Dubrava
(Alexander and Michael Salkind)
aka: *The Battle of Austerlitz*
Napoleon defeats the Austro-Russian army.
Elaborate pageant with a hopelessly cluttered narrative line arranged to take in a roster of guest stars who merely distract from the central theme.
wd Abel Gance *ph* Henri Alekan, Robert Juillard
m Jean Ledrut
☆ Pierre Mondy, Jean Mercure, Jack Palance, Orson Welles, Michel Simon, Jean-Louis Trintignant, Martine Carol, Leslie Caron, Claudia Cardinale, Rossano Brazzi, Ettore Manni, Jean Marais, Vittorio de Sica
   'Strictly for connoisseurs of Gance's brand of hyperbolic history.' – *Peter John Dyer, MFB*

'"Shall we shag now, or shall we shag later?" – Austin Powers'
Austin Powers: International Man of Mystery *
US   1997   89m   CFI color   Panavision
Guild/New Line/Capella/KC Medien/Eric's Boy
(Suzanne Todd, Demi Moore, Jennifer Todd, Mike Myers)
⬛ ▦ ◉ ⊘ ⊘ ∩
A cryogenically frozen spy from the 60s is thawed out to deal with a master criminal who threatens the peace of the world.
Very late in the day comes a spoof of James Bond and films of swinging London that manages to be engaging, mainly by contrasting the fashions of yesterday with those of today.
w Mike Myers *d* Jay Roach *ph* Peter Deming
m George S. Clinton *pd* Cynthia Charette
ed Debra Neil-Fisher
☆ Mike Myers, Elizabeth Hurley, Michael York, Mimi Rogers, Robert Wagner, Seth Green, Fabiana Udenio, Charles Napier

'For noise, enthusiasm and silliness, Austin Powers is a bit of a gas.' – *Richard Williams, Guardian*
† The film cost $17m and took $54m at the US box-office.
⚖ make-up (Michele Burke, Mike Smithson)

'First he fought for the Crown. Now he's fighting for the Family Jewels.'
Austin Powers: The Spy Who Shagged Me *
US   1999   95m   DeLuxe
New Line/Eric's Boy/Moving Pictures/Team Todd
(Suzanne Todd, Jennifer Todd, Demi Moore, Eric McLeod, John Lyons, Mike Myers)
⬛ ▦ ◉ ⊘ ⊘ ∩
A secret agent goes back in time to recover his lost mojo.
The mixture is much as before, though with a greater preponderance of fart jokes, and a few engagingly silly moments. This time around, audiences who had stayed away from the first Powers film flocked to see this one.
w Mike Myers, Michael McCullers *d* Jay Roach
ph Ueli Steiger *m* George S. Clinton *pd* Rusty Smith *ed* Jon Poll, Debra Neil-Fisher
☆ Mike Myers, Heather Graham, Michael York, Robert Wagner, Rob Lowe, Seth Green, Mindy Sterling, Verne J. Troyer, Elizabeth Hurley, Kristen Johnston, Gia Carides
   'Tickles the funny bone ably enough for 95 minutes, yet feels like a quickie where it ultimately counts most: in the writing.' – *Dennis Harvey, Variety*
† The film also includes cameos by Burt Bacharach, Elvis Costello, Woody Harrelson, Charles Napier, Willie Nelson, Tim Robbins, and Jerry Springer.
†† It was the fourth most successful movie of 1999, grossing more than $250m at the box-office.

Australia
France/Belgium/Switzerland   1989   124m
colour
Christian Bourgois/AO/Les Films de La
Dreve/CAB/RTBF/Cine 5 (Marie Pascale Osterrieth)
A Belgium wool merchant, returning home from Australia to sort out a family problem, falls in love with a married woman.
Superior soap opera.
w Jean Gruault, Jacques Audiard, Jean-Jacques Andrien *d* Jean-Jacques Andrien *ph* Yorgos Arvanitis *m* Nicola Piovani *pd* Herbert Westbrook *ed* Ludo Troch
☆ Jeremy Irons, Fanny Ardant, Tcheky Karyo, Agnes Soral, Danielle Lyttleton, Helene Surgere

Austria 1700: see *Mark of the Devil*

Author, Author! *
US   1982   109m   TVC Color
TCF (Irwin Winkler)
⬛ ▦
A Broadway playwright has worries about his wife's fidelity.
Like a sixties update of All About Eve, *this thin but sometimes witty sex-behind-the-footlights comedy had nothing to offer the general audience of the eighties, and one can only speculate as to why it was made. The acting does help, but it's a long haul.*
w Israel Horovitz *d* Arthur Hiller *ph* Victor J. Kemper *m* Dave Grusin *pd* Gene Rudolf
ed William Reynolds
☆ Al Pacino, Dyan Cannon, Tuesday Weld, Bob Dishy, Bob Elliott
   'In trying to dig a little deeper than the average Neil Simon comedy, it only prepares its own grave.' – *Observer*

Autobiography of a Princess *
GB   1975   59m   colour
Contemporary/Merchant-Ivory (Ismail Merchant)
⬛ ▦
In London, the exiled daughter of a maharajah and her father's former English secretary watch ancient home movies and swap barbed reminiscences about India in the days of Empire.
A gently bitter look back in regret and disappointment, as two elderly people reinterpret the past to suit their own concerns.
w Ruth Prawer Jhabvala *d* James Ivory
ph Walter Lassally *m* Vic Flick *ad* Jaquemine Charrot-Lodwidge *ed* Humphrey Dixon
☆ James Mason, Madhur Jaffrey, Keith Varnier, Diane Fletcher, Timothy Bateson, Johnny Stuart, Nazrul Rahman
   'Undoubtedly Ivory's best film to date.' – *MFB*

Autobus *
France   1991   98m   colour
Artificial Eye/Les Productions Lazennec/FR3/SGGC/La Générale d'Images/Canal (Alain Rocca)
⬛ ∩
French title: *Aux yeux du monde*
A frustrated and unemployed youth hijacks a bus full of schoolchildren so that he can go to visit his girlfriend.
An unexpected and uplifting exploration of a familiar theme which manages to avoid all the conventional routes.
wd Eric Rochant *ph* Pierre Novion *m* Gérard Torikian *pd* Pascale Fenouillet *ed* Catherine Quesemand
☆ Yvan Attal, Kristin Scott-Thomas, Marc Berman, Charlotte Gainsbourg, Renan Mazeas
   'Slight and well-meaning, and less incisive than it could be. But it is also more appealing than its rather whimsical premise would suggest.' – *Verina Glaessner, Sight and Sound*

Automania 2000 *
GB   1963   10m   Eastmancolor
Halas and Batchelor
New cars have the ability to reproduce themselves: city dwellers of the future consequently live in stationary vehicles piled on top of each other.
Amusing cartoon fantasy, neatly executed.
w Joy Batchelor *d* John Halas

Un Autre Homme, une Autre Chance: see *Another Man, Another Chance*

An Autumn Afternoon *
Japan   1962   113m   Agfa-Shochikucolor
Shochiku
▦
original title: *Samma no Aji*
A widower, horrified by the thought of his daughter becoming an old maid by looking after him, is encouraged by his friends to find her a husband.
Ozu's last film, in which form matters as much as content, is an elegiac account of the disintegration of family life and the prospect of lonely old age.
w Kogo Noda, Yasujiro Ozu *d* Yasujiro Ozu
ph Yuharu Atsuta *m* Kojun Saito *ad* Tatsuo Hamada *ed* Yoshiyasu Hamamura
☆ Shima Iwashita, Chishu Ryu, Keiji Sada, Mariko Okada, Shinichiro Mikami, Teruo Yoshida, Noriko Maki, Nobuo Nakamura, Eijiro Tono

Autumn Crocus
GB   1934   86m   bw
ATP
A British schoolmistress on holiday falls for her Tyrolean innkeeper.
Difficult now to conceive the popularity in its day of this novelettish romance, which seems frozen in amber.
wd Basil Dean *play* C. L. Anthony
☆ Ivor Novello, Fay Compton, Jack Hawkins, Diana Beaumont, Muriel Aked, George Zucco

'In the dark, when I feel his heart pounding against mine – is it love? or frenzy? or terror?'
Autumn Leaves *
US   1956   108m   bw
Columbia/William Goetz
A middle-aged spinster marries a young man who turns out to be a pathological liar and tries to murder her.
Skilfully tailored star vehicle for female audiences.
w Jack Jevne, Lewis Meltzer, Robert Blees
d Robert Aldrich *ph* Charles Lang *m* Hans Salter
☆ Joan Crawford, Cliff Robertson, Lorne Greene, Vera Miles, Ruth Donnelly, Shepperd Strudwick

Autumn Moon *
Hong Kong/Japan   1992   108m   colour
ICA/Trix (Clara Law/Fong Ling Ching)
⬛
original title: *Qiuyue*
A Japanese youth in Hong Kong forms a friendship with a young girl, soon to emigrate to Canada to be with her family, and her grandmother who has to remain behind.
Charming, understated exploration of uprooted lives and uncertain futures.
w Fong Ling Ching *d* Clara Law *ph* Tony Cheung *m* Lau Lee Tat *ad* Timmy Yip *ed* Fong Ling Ching

---

♙♙ film suitable for family viewing   ▦ VHS video-cassette for the British PAL system   ▦ VHS video-cassette for the British PAL system in wide screen-format   ⟳ Video cassette in a computer-colourised version   ⬛ American NTSC video-cassette   ❧ Laser disc

☆ Masatoshi Nagase, Li Pui Wei, Maki Kiuchi, Choi Siu Wan, Suen Ching Hung, Sung Lap Yeung
'A way of life is seen to be tragically on the wane. Clara Law's fascinating movie catches its dying glow with engrossing sensitivity.' – Tom Hutchinson, Film Review

Autumn Sonata *
Sweden/West Germany/GB   1978   97m   colour
ITC/Personafilm (Ingmar Bergman)
📀 📼

When her lover dies, a concert pianist visits the daughter she has not seen for many years.
Typically Bergmanesque, understated conversation piece with no obvious happy ending for anybody.
wd Ingmar Bergman *ph* Sven Nykvist *m* Chopin, Handel, Bach
☆ Ingrid Bergman, Liv Ullmann, Halvar Bjork
'Professional gloom.' – Time
'It fills these middle-class rooms with the deep music of conflict and reconciliation that must strike home to any audiences in any culture or society.' – Jack Kroll, Newsweek
🎗 script; Ingrid Bergman

An Autumn Tale: see *Conte D'Automne*

Aux yeux du monde: see *Autobus*

'Six million tons of icy terror!'
Avalanche
US   1978   91m   Metrocolor
New World (Roger Corman)
📀 📼

Snow threatens holidaymakers at a ski lodge.
A disaster movie which, while quite competent in most ways, is no better than TV movies of this kind, especially as it resorts for its climaxes to scratched old stock film.
w Claude Pola, Corey Allen *d* Corey Allen *ph* Pierre-William Glenn *m* William Kraft
☆ Rock Hudson, Mia Farrow, Robert Forster, Jeanette Nolan, Rick Moses, Steve Franken, Barry Primus

Avalanche Express
Eire   1979   88m   DeLuxe   Panavision
TCF/Lorimar (Mark Robson)
📀 📼

Spies of all nations converge on a train from Milan to Rotterdam.
Fitfully amusing hodgepodge which had to be finished off in a hurry following the death of its star and director in mid-production.
w Abraham Polonsky *novel* Colin Forbes *d* Mark Robson *ph* Jack Cardiff *m* Allyn Ferguson
☆ Robert Shaw, Lee Marvin, Linda Evans, Maximilian Schell, Mike Connors, Joe Namath, Horst Buchholz
'The most impressive work of montage to emerge from a big-budget adventure movie.' – Richard Combs, MFB
'Pell-mell direction and editing perform a precarious, oddly suspenseful balancing act.' – Sight and Sound

Les Avaleuses: see *Female Vampire*

Avalon *
US   1990   128m   Technicolor
Columbia TriStar/Baltimore Pictures (Mark Johnson, Barry Levinson)
📀 📼 📀 🎧

The lives and good times over half-a-century of an immigrant family in Baltimore.
Sprawling, episodic and too stolid for its ambitions, but with enjoyable moments from the ensemble cast.
wd Barry Levinson *ph* Allen Daviau *m* Randy Newman *man* Reynolds *ed* Stu Linder
☆ Armin Mueller-Stahl, Elizabeth Perkins, Joan Plowright, Kevin Pollak, Aidan Quinn, Leo Fuchs, Eve Gordon, Lou Jacobi
'A lifeless experience devoid of a central conflict or purpose … The film is mostly a celebration of the mundane, and, while watching grandma and grandpa bicker at the dinner table may spur a fond glimmer of recognition, it's a wispy premise on which to hang this sort of lavish undertaking.' – Variety
'This movie is an elegy to a mythical past. That's probably why people escape from the theatre sniffling.' – Pauline Kael, New Yorker
🎗 Barry Levinson (as writer); Allen Daviau; Randy Newman; costume design (Gloria Gresham)

'When someone knocks at your door and says "Permesso?", be careful before you say…'
Avanti! *
US   1972   144m   DeLuxe
UA/Mirisch/Phalanx/Jalem (Billy Wilder)
📀

A young American goes to Ischia to collect the body of his father who has died on holiday. He finds that the fatal accident had also killed his father's mistress, and amid overwhelming bureaucratic problems proceeds to fall in love with her daughter.
Absurdly overlong black comedy, with compensations in the shape of a generally witty script and some fine breakneck sequences of culminating confusion.
w Billy Wilder, I. A. L. Diamond *play* Samuel Taylor *d* Billy Wilder *ph* Luigi Kuveiller *m* Carlo Rustichelli
☆ Jack Lemmon, Juliet Mills, Clive Revill, Edward Andrews, Gianfranco Barra
'A movie flatter than a pizza.' – Donald J. Mayerson, Cue

Avanti-Popolo
Israel   1986   88m   colour
TTG/Kastel Communications (Rafi Bukaee)
In the final hours of the Six Day War between Israel and Egypt in 1967, two Egyptian conscripts flee towards the safety of the Suez Canal.
Drama on the futility of war that lacks the performances to compensate for its snail-like pace, or the style to accommodate its mix of comedy and death.
wd Rafi Bukaee *ph* Yoav Kosh *m* Uri Ofir *ad* Ariel Glazer *ed* Zohar Sela
☆ Salim Daw, Suheil Haddad, Dani Roth, Dani Segev, Tuvya Gelber

The Avenger: see *Texas Addio*

The Avengers: see *The Day Will Dawn (1942)*

'She's Peel. He's Steed. Their world is a dangerous place. And they love it.'
'Saving The World In Style.'
'Two Amazing Secret Agents. One Diabolical Madman. Conditions Are Dark. The Forecast Is Deadly. Tea, Anyone?'
The Avengers
US   1998   89m   Technicolor
Warner (Jerry Weintraub)
📀 📼 📀 🎧 ⊙

A secret agent foils a mad meteorologist's plans to hold the world to ransom by controlling its weather.
A complete dud, a direly boring thriller: miscast, mishandled and miserable. Nothing about it works, from its over-insistent score and over-elaborate plot to its unsophisticated attempt at urbanity.
w Don Macpherson *d* Jeremy Chechik *ph* Roger Pratt *m* Joel McNeely *pd* Stuart Craig *ed* Mick Audsley
☆ Ralph Fiennes, Uma Thurman, Sean Connery, Patrick MacNee, Jim Broadbent, Fiona Shaw, Eddie Izzard, Eileen Atkins, John Wood, Carmen Ejogo, Keeley Hawes
'About as inviting as a cement soufflé.' – Philip French, Observer
'An abomination. As the awful movie version of the brilliant TV classic of the Swinging '60s, it is worse than anyone ever imagined it might be.' – Bruce Kirland, Toronto Sun
'I heard actual cries of "Ugh!" on the way out of the door.' – New York Times
† The film, which cost some $60m, opened simultaneously in the UK and the US without being given a press show or a première. Of the 32 leading British and American critics who reviewed the film, only one liked it
†† The Avengers was one of the most successful British TV series, starring Patrick MacNee as the bowler-hatted secret agent John Steed; his various female sidekicks included Diana Rigg as Emma Peel. It ran from 1961 to 1969.

'May God Have Mercy On His Enemies!'
The Avenging Boxer (dubbed)
Hong Kong   1973   90m   colour
Alpha Motion Picture Co. (Jimmy Shaw)
US title: *Fearless Young Boxer*
A son learns kung fu so that he can avenge his father's death at the hands of a hired killer.
Standard martial-arts mayhem consisting of acrobatic fights interspersed with broad comedy, although it does manage a spectacular finale.

wd Jimmy Shaw *m* Chang Fang Gi *ad* David Wong *ed* W. C. Leung
☆ Peter Chang, Ca Sa Fa, Lee Lo Ling, Lee Kwun, Chan Wai Lau, Lung Fee

The Avenging Conscience *
US   1914   58m   bw   silent
Mutual
An elaboration of Poe's *The Tell Tale Heart* in which Griffith first shows his ability to control a feature-length movie, with many cinematic devices.
wd D. W. Griffith *ph* Billy Bitzer
☆ Henry B. Walthall, Blanche Sweet, Spottiswoode Aitken, Mae Marsh

The Avenging Hand
GB   1936   64m   bw
Motion Pictures (John Stafford)
A Chicago gangster holidaying in London turns detective to track down a murderer.
Tepid thriller built around Beery's brash and breezy performance.
w Reginald Long *d* Frank Richardson *ph* James Wilson *md* Jack Beaver *ad* MacDonald Sutherland *ed* Sidney Cole
☆ Noah Beery, Kathleen Kelly, Louis Borell, Charles Oliver, Reginald Long, Penelope Parkes, Tarver Penna, Joan Kemp-Welch

L'Avenir d'Emilie: see *The Future of Emily*

Les Aventures de Rabbi Jacob
France/Italy   1973   94m   Eastmancolor
Fox-Rank/Films Pomereu/Horse Film (Bernard Javal)
GB title: *The Mad Adventures of 'Rabbi' Jacob*
A French businessman with anti-Semitic views is forced by an Arab agitator on the run to impersonate a rabbi presiding at a Bar Mitzvah in Paris.
Broad comedy that raises a few laughs at the expense of xenophobia.
w Gérard Oury, Daniele Thompson, Josy Eisenberg *d* Gérard Oury *ph* Henri Decae *m* Vladimir Cosma *ad* Théo Meurisse *ed* Albert Jurgenson
☆ Louis de Funès, Suzy Delair, Marcel Dalio, Claude Giraud, Claude Piéplu, Renzo Montagnani
'Much loved in France, this comedy of errors has not travelled well and turns up in Britain looking painfully unfunny.' – David McGillivray

L'Aveu: see *The Confession*

The Aviator
US   1930   73m   bw
Warner
A timid clerk lends his name to a technical book on aviation, and finds himself having to back up the pretence by flying.
Predictable star comedy.
play James Montgomery *d* Roy del Ruth
☆ Edward Everett Horton, Patsy Ruth Miller, Johnny Arthur, Lee Moran
'Peg this as a good one.' – Variety

The Aviator
US   1985   96m   Metrocolor
MGM-UA/Mace Neufeld
In 1928, a spoiled rich girl is cared for by a sullen pilot when they crashland in the Sierras.
Drawn-out, actionless adventure concerning unattractive characters; it has been seen before in at least two TV movies.
w Marc Norman *novel* Ernest Gann *d* George Miller *ph* David Connell *m* Dominic Frontiere *pd* Brenton Swift *ed* Duane Hartzell
☆ Christopher Reeve, Rosanna Arquette, Jack Warden, Sam Wanamaker, Scott Wilson, Tyne Daly
'Doesn't fly.' – Variety

The Aviator's Wife *
France   1980   106m   Eastmancolor (blown up from 16mm)
Les Films du Losange (Margaret Menegoz)
📀
original title: *La Femme de L'Aviateur*
Anne and François are having an affair, but each has other entanglements.
Meticulously arranged conversations in this director's best style, but this time not seeming to amount to very much.
wd Eric Rohmer *ph* Bernard Lutic *m* Jean-Louis Valero

☆ Philippe Marlaud, Marie Rivière, Anne-Laure Maeury, Mathieu Carrière
'Does the aviator Christian's wife exist? It really does not matter: she is a formal device in a play of formalist devices.' – Jill Forbes, MFB

De Avonden: see *Evenings*

L'Avventura *
Italy/France   1960   145m   bw
Cino del Duca/PCE/Lyre (Amato Pennasilico)
🎧
Young people on a yachting holiday go ashore on a volcanic island. One of them disappears; this affects the lives of the others, but she is never found.
Aimless, overlong parable with lots of vague significance; rather less entertaining than the later Picnic at Hanging Rock (qv), it made its director a hero of the highbrows.
w Michelangelo Antonioni, Elio Bartolini, Tonino Guerra *d* Michelangelo Antonioni *ph* Aldo Scavarda *m* Giovanni Fusco
☆ Monica Vitti, Lea Massari, Gabriele Ferzetti, Dominique Blanchar, James Addams, Lelio Luttazi
'A film of complete maturity, sincerity and creative intuition.' – Peter John Dyer, MFB

The Awakening
GB   1980   105m   Technicolor
EMI/Orion (Robert Solo)
📀 📼 📀
An obsessed archaeologist believes that the spirit of a long-dead Egyptian queen has entered into the soul of his daughter.
Unpersuasive and humourless mumbo jumbo from the same intractably complex novel that provided the basis for Blood from the Mummy's Tomb (qv).
w Allan Scott, Chris Bryant, Clive Exton *novel* Jewel of the Seven Stars by Bram Stoker *d* Mike Newell *ph* Jack Cardiff *m* Claude Bolling *pd* Michael Stringer
☆ Charlton Heston, Susannah York, Jill Townsend, Stephanie Zimbalist, Patrick Drury, Bruce Myers
'An almost total waste of the talents involved.' – Sunday Times
'It is difficult to imagine a film more likely to put you to sleep.' – Guardian

Awakenings *
US   1990   121m   Technicolor   Panavision
Columbia TriStar (Walter F. Parkes, Lawrence Lasker)
📀 📼 📀 🎧
A young doctor discovers a treatment that temporarily revives sufferers from encephalitis who have been in a state of suspended animation for 30 years or more.
Over-sentimentalized treatment of a fascinating subject, too insistent on leaving its audience feeling good.
w Steven Zaillian *book* Oliver Sacks *d* Penny Marshall *ph* Miroslav Ondricek *m* Randy Newman *pd* Anton Furst *ed* Jerry Greenberg, Battle Davis
☆ Robert De Niro, Robin Williams, Julie Kavner, Ruth Nelson, John Heard, Penelope Ann Miller, Alice Drummond, Judith Malina, Barton Heyman, Max von Sydow
'The movie douses everything fiery. Everything is shaped for you to root for the resurrections, and then nothing much happens … the humanism is so pallid that the awakened patients don't seem very different from the way they were in their comatose states.' – Pauline Kael, New Yorker
🎗 best picture; Robert De Niro; Steven Zaillian

Away All Boats
US   1956   114m   Technicolor   Vistavision
U-I (Howard Christie)
📼 ⊙
Adventures of a small transport boat during the Pacific War.
Competent drum-beating war heroics with expensive action sequences.
w Ted Sherdeman *novel* Kenneth M. Dodson *d* Joseph Pevney *ph* William Daniels, Clifford Stine *m* Frank Skinner
☆ Jeff Chandler, George Nader, Julie Adams, Lex Barker, Keith Andes, Richard Boone, Frank Faylen

The Awful Dr Orloff

Spain   1962   88m   bw
Hispamer (Serge Newman, Leo Lax)
▣▣ ▆

original title: *Gritos en la Noche*
A mad doctor tries to restore his disfigured
daughter to beauty by kidnapping and skinning
young women.
*Sleazy ill-made horror, notable only for being the first
of a sequence of films featuring the awful doctor.*
wd Jesús Franco novel David Kuhne
ph Godofredo Pacheco
☆ Howard Vernon, Conrado Sanmartin, Perla
Cristal, Diana Lorys, Ricardo Valle
  'An utterly dreadful movie.' – *The Dark Side*

The Awful Truth ***

US   1937   90m   bw
Columbia (Leo McCarey)
▣▣ ▆ ◎~

A divorcing couple endure various adventures
which lead to reconciliation.
*Classic crazy comedy of the thirties, marked by a
mixture of sophistication and farce and an irreverent
approach to plot.*
w Vina Delmar play Arthur Richman d Leo
McCarey ph Joseph Walker md Morris Stoloff
ed Al Clark
☆ Irene Dunne, Cary Grant, Ralph Bellamy,
Alexander D'Arcy, Cecil Cunningham, Molly
Lamont, Esther Dale, Joyce Compton
  IRENE DUNNE: 'You've come back and caught me

in the truth, and there's nothing less logical than
the truth.'
  CARY GRANT: 'In the spring a young man's fancy
lightly turns to what he's been thinking about all
winter.'
  'Fast, smart comedy that will please everywhere
and do strong general biz.' – *Variety*
  'The funniest picture of the season.' – *Otis
Ferguson*
  'Among the ingredients the raising powder is the
important thing and out of the oven comes a
frothy bit of stuff that leaves no taste in the
mouth and is easy on the stomach.' – *Marion
Fraser, World Film News*
  'Delightfully effective entertainment.' – *Time
Out, 1985*
† Remade 1953 as *Let's Do It Again* (qv).
🏆 Leo McCarey
🏅 best picture; script; Irene Dunne; Ralph
Bellamy; Al Clark

'In A World Of Make Believe Stella Is About To
Discover The Difference Between True Love ... And
Real Life.'
An Awfully Big Adventure *

GB   1994   112m   Metrocolor
TCF/Portman/British Screen/BBC/Wolfhound (Hilary
Heath, Philip Hinchcliffe)
▣▣ ▆ ◎~ ∩

In 1947, a gullible 15-year-old girl joins a rundown
Liverpool repertory theatre, where she falls in love
with its manipulative director and begins an affair

with its flamboyant leading actor.
*Good on atmospherics and the detail of backstage
bitchery and theatrical ambition, but flawed in its wider
ambitions of a girl growing to maturity in circumstances
of betrayal, this is a broken-backed melodrama: the
first half belongs to Grant's ambiguous director, the
second to Rickman's reckless leading man, but the
innocent girl at its centre is not a strong enough
character to hold it together as a satisfying whole.*
w Charles Wood novel Beryl Bainbridge d Mike
Newell ph Dick Pope m Richard Hartley
pd Mark Geraghty ed Jon Gregory
☆ Georgina Cates, Hugh Grant, Alan Rickman,
Peter Firth, Alun Armstrong, Prunella Scales, Rita
Tushingham, Edward Petherbridge, Nicola Pagett,
Alan Cox, Carol Drinkwater, Clive Merrison,
Gerard McSorley
  'The unsympathetic characters and oblique
storytelling make large demands on the
audience, limiting the film's appeal essentially to
art-house aficionados.' – *Colin Brown, Screen
International*

AWOL

US   1990   108m   colour
Guild/Wrong Bet Productions/Imperial Entertainment
(Ash R. Shah, Eric Karson)
▆ ◎~ ∩
US title: *Lionheart*
aka: *The Wrong Bet*
A deserter from the Foreign Legion becomes a
bare-knuckle fighter in America.

*Musclebound action movie, sentimental when it is not
violent.*
wd Sheldon Lettich, Jean-Claude Van Damme
ph Robert C. New m John Scott pd Gregory
Pickrell ed Mark Conte
☆ Jean-Claude Van Damme, Harrison Page,
Deborah Rennard, Lisa Pelikan, Ashley Johnson,
Brian Thompson

Ay, Carmela! **

Spain/Italy   1990   103m   colour
Iberoamericana/Ellepi/Television Espanola (Andres
Vicente Gomez)
▣▣ ▆ ◎~ ∩

During the Spanish Civil War a trio of vaudeville
performers entertaining the Republican troops are
taken prisoner by the Nationalist army.
*Very watchable but flawed political film with a bungled
ending.*
w Rafael Azcona, Carlos Saura play José Sanchis
Sinistierra d Carlos Saura ph José Luis Alcaine
m Alejandro Masso ad Rafael Palmero ed Pablo
G. Del Amo
☆ Carmen Maura, Andres Pajares, Gabino Diego,
Maurizio de Razza, José Sancho, Mario de Candia

B

B.F.'s Daughter *
US   1948   106m   bw
MGM (Edwin A. Knopf)
GB title: *Polly Fulton*
The wife of a penniless lecturer secures her husband's rise to fame without his knowing that she is the daughter of a millionaire.
Solid upper-class romantic drama with a touch of Peg's Paper.
w Luther Davis *novel* John P. Marquand
d Robert Z. Leonard *ph* Joseph Ruttenberg
m Bronislau Kaper
☆ Barbara Stanwyck, Van Heflin, Charles Coburn, Richard Hart, Keenan Wynn, Margaret Lindsay, Spring Byington, Marshall Thompson

B.S. I Love You
US   1971   98m   DeLuxe
Motion Pictures International/Fox (A. M. Broidy)
A director of TV commercials is beset by passionate women.
Tiresomely trendy sex comedy with a visual style that never lets up.
wd Steven Hilliard Stern *ph* David Dans
m Jimmy Dale, Mark Shekter
☆ Peter Kastner, Joanna Cameron, Louise Sorel, Gary Burghoff, Joanna Barnes, Richard B. Shull
† The initials in the title are short for bullshit.

Ba Mua: see *Three Seasons*

Ba Wang Bie Ji: see *Farewell My Concubine*

Baara
Mali   1979   93m   colour
Souleymanne Cissé Productions
A factory owner orders the killing of his manager for calling a meeting of workers to improve their conditions.
A slice of African industrial life, contrasting the lives of the rich and corrupt with the poor and exploited.
wd Souleymane Cissé *ph* Etienne Carton de Grammont *m* Lamine Konté
☆ Balla Moussa Keita, Baba Niaré, Bubakar Keita, Umu Diarra, Ismaila Sarr, Umir Kone

Bab El Hadid: see *Cairo Station*

Bab el-Oued City *
Algeria/France   1994   93m   colour
Les Matins/Flash Back/La Sept/ZDF/Thelma (Tahar Harhoura)
A carefree young baker finds himself driven from his home and the woman he loves by a gang of Moslem fundamentalists.
Well-made, low-key and topical drama of the current political unrest in Algiers, with a wider theme of bigotry and intolerance; its general appeal, though, is likely to be limited.
wd Merzak Allouache *ph* Jean-Jacques Mréjen
m Rachid Bahri *ed* Marie Colonna
☆ Nadia Kaci, Mohamed Ourdache, Hassan Abdou, Mabrouk Ait Amara, Messaoud Hattou, Mourad Khen, Djamila, Nadia Samir, Simone Vignote, Michel Such
  'To date the most lucid depiction on film of the rise of Islamic fundamentalism in Algeria and its perils. It's essential viewing for anyone interested in getting insight into the people's reaction to this broad political change.' – *Deborah Young, Variety*
† The film won the International Critics' Prize at the 1994 Cannes Film Festival.

Babar: The Movie
♙♙   Canada/France   1989   76m   colour
Winstone/Nelvana/Ellipse (Patrick Loubert, Michael Hirsch, Clive A. Smith)
King Babar tells his children of his adventures as a young elephant.

Lacklustre story, with simple animation.
w Peter Sauder, J. D. Smith, John de Klein, Raymond Jaffelice, Alan Bunce *story* Peter Sauder, Patrick Loubert, Michael Hirsch *based on characters created by* Jean de Brunhoff, Laurent de Brunhoff *d* Alan Bunce *m* Milan Kymlicka
m/ly Maribeth Solomon *pd* Ted Bastien *ad* Clive Powsey, Carol Bradbury *ed* Evan Landis
☆ Featuring the voices of Gordon Pinsent, Elizabeth Hanna, Lisa Yamanaka, Marsha Moreau, Bobby Beckon, Amos Crawley, Gavin Magrath, Sarah Polley

Babbitt *
US   1934   74m   bw
Warner (Sam Bischoff)
Problems of a middle-aged man in a small American town.
A minor attempt to film a major novel: quite tolerable but lacking density.
w Mary McCall Jnr *novel* Sinclair Lewis
d William Keighley *ph* Arthur Todd
☆ Guy Kibbee, Aline MacMahon, Claire Dodd, Maxine Doyle, Minor Watson, Minna Gombell, Alan Hale, Berton Churchill, Russell Hicks, Nan Grey
  'Smooth, pleasant but trite.' – *Variety*
† Previously filmed in 1924 with Willard Louis.

Babe ***
♙♙   Australia   1995   94m   colour
Universal/Kennedy Miller (George Miller, Doug Mitchell, Bill Miller)
An orphaned piglet is adopted by a sheepdog and decides that he wants to grow up and follow in his mother's pawprints.
Delightful, witty, clever and almost irresistible children's film with a wide appeal; the mid-Atlantic voices given the animals take a little getting used to, but otherwise it's a pleasure all the way.
w George Miller, Chris Noonan *novel* The Sheep-Pig by Dick King-Smith *d* Chris Noonan
ph Andrew Lesnie *m* Nigel Westlake *pd* Roger Ford *ed* Marcus D'Arcy, Jay Friedkin
☆ James Cromwell, Magda Szubanski, Roscoe Lee Browne and also the voices of Christine Cavanaugh, Miriam Margolyes, Danny Mann, Hugo Weaving
  'A dazzling family entertainment with enormous charm and utilizing breathtaking technical innovation.' – *Leonard Klady, Variety*
♙ visual effects
☐ best picture; Chris Noonan; George Miller, Chris Noonan (screenplay adaptation); James Cromwell; Marcus D'Arcy, Jay Friedkin; Roger Ford

The Babe
US   1992   115m   DeLuxe
Universal (John Fusco)
Biopic of the life of the baseball player Babe Ruth.
An undistinguished film with little appeal outside America, although Goodman brings some individuality to his portrayal of the flawed hero.
w John Fusco *d* Arthur Hiller *ph* Haskell Wexler
m Elmer Bernstein *pd* James D. Vance *ed* Robert C. Jones
☆ John Goodman, Kelly McGillis, Trini Alvarado, Bruce Boxleitner, James Cromwell, Peter Donat, Bernard Kates, Michael McGrady
  'The thinly dramatised, overly episodic Babe Ruth biopic resembles a telepic that has lost its way to the big screen.' – *Variety*

'In the heart of the city, a pig with heart.'
Babe: Pig in the City *
Australia   1998   97m   Atlab
Universal (George Miller, Doug Mitchell, Bill Miller)
A hero for winning the sheepdog trials, a pig visits the city and rescues a motley collection of animals impounded by the authorities.
A muddled sequel that lacks the charm of the original; its approach to humour is laborious and overelaborate.
w George Miller, Judy Morris, Mark Lamprell *characters created by* Dick King-Smith *d* George Miller *ph* Andrew Lesnie *m* Nigel Westlake
pd Roger Ford *ed* Jay Friedkin, Margaret Sixel
sp Rhythm & Hues, Mill Film, Animal Logic Film, Neal Scanlan Studio
☆ Magda Szubanski, James Cromwell, Mary Stein, Mickey Rooney, Julie Godfrey and also the voices of: E. G. Daily, Danny Mann, Glenne Headly, Steven Wright, James Cosmo, Roscoe Lee Browne
  'There is plenty of fun in this cinematic menagerie, consummate screen magic and a series of well-intentioned messages that sidestep the cloying and saccharine.' – *Leonard Klady, Variety*
† The film cost around $100m to make and market. Its failure at the box-office led to the departure of several top executives from Universal.
♫ song 'That'll Do' (*m/ly* Randy Newman)

The Babe Ruth Story
US   1948   107m   bw
Allied Artists (Roy del Ruth)
The biography of a baseball player who was thought of as something of a saint.
Dim, sentimental and faintly mystical biopic, throughout which the star presents his familiar image.
w Bob Considine, George Callahan *d* Roy del Ruth *ph* Philip Tannura, James Van Trees
m Edward Ward
☆ William Bendix, Claire Trevor, Charles Bickford

Babes in Arms **
♙♙   US   1939   96m   bw
MGM (Arthur Freed)
The teenage sons and daughters of retired vaudevillians put on a big show.
Simple-minded backstage musical which marked the first enormously successful teaming of its two young stars.
w Jack McGowan, Kay Van Riper *Broadway show* Rodgers and Hart *ph* Ray June *m* Roger Edens, George Stoll *m/ly* Rodgers and Hart and others *d/ch* Busby Berkeley
☆ Judy Garland, Mickey Rooney, Charles Winninger, Douglas Macphail, Leni Lynn, June Preisser
  'A topflight filmusical entertainment. It will click mightily in the key deluxers, and roll up hefty profits for exhibits in the subsequent runs and smaller situations.' – *Variety*
♫ 'Where or When'; 'Babes in Arms'; 'I Cried for You'; 'God's Country'; 'Good Morning'; 'You Are My Lucky Star'
☐ Roger Edens, George Stoll; Mickey Rooney

Babes in Baghdad
US   1952   77m   Exotic Color
UA (Danziger Brothers)
Harem ladies go on strike.
Embarrassing attempt at satire by stars who are over the hill and not helped by abysmal technique.
w Felix E. Feist, Joe Anson *d* Edgar G. Ulmer
☆ Paulette Goddard, Gypsy Rose Lee, Richard Ney, John Boles, Sebastian Cabot

Babes in Toyland **
♙♙   US   1934   77m   bw
Hal Roach
aka: *Wooden Soldiers*
aka: *March of the Wooden Soldiers; Laurel and Hardy in Toyland*
Santa Claus's incompetent assistants accidentally make some giant wooden soldiers, which come in useful when a villain tries to take over Toyland.
Comedy operetta in which the stars have pleasant but not outstanding material; the style and decor are however sufficient to preserve the film as an eccentric minor classic.
w Nick Grinde, Frank Butler *original book* Glen MacDonough *d* Gus Meins, Charles Rogers
ph Art Lloyd, Francis Corby *m* Victor Herbert
☆ Stan Laurel, Oliver Hardy, Charlotte Henry, Henry Brandon, Felix Knight, Florence Roberts, Johnny Downs, Marie Wilson
  'It is amusing enough to entertain older persons who remember when they were young.' – *Variety*

Babes in Toyland
♙♙   US   1961   105m   Technicolor
Walt Disney
The wicked Barnaby is foiled in his plans to get rid of Tom Piper so that he can marry Mary Contrary.
A misfiring remake, all charm and no talent apart from some excellent special effects at the climax. Bolger is miscast as the villain, and Sheldon and Calvin imitate Laurel and Hardy.
w Ward Kimball, Joe Rinaldi, Lowell S. Hawley *operetta* Victor Young, Glenn McDonough *d* Jack Donohue *ph* Edward Colman *m/ly* Victor Young; George Bruns, Mel Leven *md* George Bruns
ch Tommy Mahoney *ad* Carroll Clark, Marvin Aubrey Davis *ed* Robert Stafford *sp* Eustace Lycett, Robert A. Mattey, Bill Justice, Xavier Atencio, Yale Gracey
☆ Ray Bolger, Tommy Sands, Annette Funicello, Tommy Kirk, Gene Sheldon, Henry Calvin, Ed Wynn, Kevin Corcoran, Mary McCarty
♫ I Can't Do the Sum, Just a Toy, Floretta, Castle in Spain, We Won't Be Happy Till We Get It, Lemonade, Just a Whisper Away, March of the Toys, Toyland, The Workshop Song, Slowly He Sank into the Sea.
☐ George Bruns

Babes on Broadway **
US   1941   118m   bw
MGM (Arthur Freed)
A sequel to *Babes in Arms*, in which the kids get to Broadway and share some disillusion.
Inflated and less effective than the original, but with good numbers.
w Fred Finklehoffe, Elaine Ryan *ph* Lester White *m/ly* Burton Lane, Ralph Freed *d/ch* Busby Berkeley
☆ Judy Garland, Mickey Rooney, Virginia Weidler, Ray Macdonald, Richard Quine, Fay Bainter
  'Enough energy and enthusiasm to make older people wish they were young, and young people glad that they are.' – *MFB*
† The Virginia Weidler role was originally intended for Shirley Temple, but TCF wouldn't loan her.
☐ song 'How About You' (*m* Burton Lane, *ly* Ralph Freed)

Babette Goes to War
France   1959   103m   Eastmancolor
Cinemascope
Iéna (Raoul Lévy)
original title: *Babette S'en Va-t-en Guerre*
In 1940 a French refugee girl is sent by British intelligence from London to Paris as bait in a plot

---

to kidnap a German general and delay the Nazi invasion of England.
Witless war farce which goes on for ever.
w Raoul Lévy, Gérard Oury d Christian-Jaque ph Armand Thirard m Gilbert Bécaud
☆ Brigitte Bardot, Jacques Charrier, Hannes Messemer, Yves Vincent, Ronald Howard, Francis Blanche
'A kind of *Private's Progress* without comedians.' – MFB

Babette S'en Va-t-en Guerre: see *Babette Goes to War*

Babette's Feast **
Denmark 1987 103m Eastmancolor
Panorama/Nordisk/Danish Film Institute
🔲 ■ ◎ ⌒ ⏚
A French refugee in 19th-century Norway wins 10,000 francs in a lottery and spends it all on preparing a sumptuous banquet for her Lutheran employers and their friends.
Ironic and elegant fable juxtaposing bacchanalian extravagance with narrow piety.
wd Gabriel Axel story Isak Dinesen ph Henning Kristiansen m Per Norgard ad Sven Wichman
☆ Stéphane Audran, Jean-Philippe Lafont, Jarl Kulle, Bibi Andersson, Bodil Kjer, Birgitte Federspiel
🏆 best foreign film
🎬 best foreign film

'Torture ... Terror ... It's A Nightmare You'll Never Forget!'
The Baby
US 1973 102m colour
Quintet (Milton Polsky, Abe Polsky)
■ ◎
A social worker becomes obsessed by one of her charges: a mentally retarded man who behaves like a one-year-old in a household dominated by his mad mother and two disturbed sisters.
Unpleasant low-budget shocker, with over-the-top performances and general grotesqueness.
w Abe Polsky d Ted Post ph Michael Margulies m Gerald Fried ad Michael Devine ed Dick Wormell, Bob Crawford Snr
☆ Anjanette Comer, Ruth Roman, Marianna Hill, Suzanne Zenor, Tod Andrews, Michael Pataki, Beatrice Manley Blau, David Manzy
'Ultimately, it seems a long walk round a very small sick joke.' – *Tom Milne, MFB*

The Baby and the Battleship
GB 1956 96m Eastmancolor
British Lion/Jay Lewis
■
Two sailors hide an Italian baby on their battleship.
Simple-minded lower decks farce, with lots of confusion and cooing over the baby, but not much to laugh at.
w Jay Lewis, Gilbert Hackforth-Jones, Bryan Forbes d Jay Lewis ph Harry Waxman m James Stevens
☆ John Mills, Richard Attenborough, André Morell, Bryan Forbes, Michael Howard, Lisa Gastoni, Ernest Clark, Lionel Jeffries, Thorley Walters
'In this British film the predicament is made splendidly funny.' – *Dilys Powell*

Baby Be Good: see *Brother Rat and a Baby*

Baby Blue Marine *
US 1976 90m Metrocolor
Columbia/Spelling-Goldberg (Robert LaVigne)
In 1943, a failed marine returns home and pretends to be a war hero.
Careful small-town drama with good period feel but not much dramatic punch: Hail the Conquering Hero *(qv) did it better.*
w Stanford Whitmore d John Hancock ph Laszlo Kovacs m Fred Karlin
☆ Jan-Michael Vincent, Glynnis O'Connor, Katherine Helmond, Dana Elcar, Bert Remsen, Richard Gere
'A rickety structure of strange events.' – *New York Post*

Baby Boom
US 1987 110m colour
UIP/MGM
🔲 ■ ◎ ⌒
The life of a busy executive changes when she acquires a small baby.

Moderately enjoyable comedy, though it lacks any particular distinction.
w Nancy Meyers, Charles Shyer d Charles Shyer ph William A. Fraker m Bill Conti pd Jeffrey Howard ed Lynzee Klingman
☆ Diane Keaton, Harold Ramis, Sam Wanamaker, Sam Shepard, James Spader, Pat Hingle, Britt Leach
'If there were justice in the world of entertainment, *Baby Boom* would be unwatchable. But Diane Keaton gives a smashing, glamorous performance that rides over many of the inanities.' – *Pauline Kael, New Yorker*

'19 years old and married ... but not really!'
Baby Doll **
US 1956 116m bw
Warner/Elia Kazan
🔲 ■
In the deep South, the child wife of a broken-down cotton miller is seduced by her husband's revenge-seeking rival.
An incisive, cleverly-worked-out study of moral and physical decay; whether it was worth doing is another question, for it's a film difficult to remember with affection.
w Tennessee Williams play 27 Wagonloads of Cotton by Tennessee Williams d Elia Kazan ph Boris Kaufman m Kenyon Hopkins ad Richard Sylbert
☆ Karl Malden, Eli Wallach, Carroll Baker, Mildred Dunnock, Lonny Chapman
'Just possibly the dirtiest American-made motion picture that has ever been legally exhibited, with Priapean detail that might well have embarrassed Boccaccio.' – *Time*
'He views southern pretensions with sardonic humor, and builds an essentially minor story into a magnificently humorous study of the grotesque and the decadent.' – *Hollis Albert*
'A droll and engrossing carnal comedy.' – *Pauline Kael, 1968*
'A film in which everything works: narration, casting, tempo, rhythm, dramatic tension.' – *Basil Wright, 1972*
† Another publicity tag read: 'Condemned by Cardinal Spellman!'
§ script: Boris Kaufman; Carroll Baker; Mildred Dunnock
🎬 Eli Wallach (best newcomer)

'She climbed the ladder of success – wrong by wrong!'
Baby Face **
US 1933 70m bw
Warner (Ray Griffith)
■ ◎
Amorous adventures of an ambitious working girl.
Sharp melodrama very typical of its time, with fast pace and good performances.
w Gene Markey, Kathryn Scola story Mark Canfield (Darryl F. Zanuck) d Alfred E. Green ph James Van Trees ad Anton Grot
☆ Barbara Stanwyck, George Brent, Donald Cook, Margaret Lindsay, Arthur Hohl, John Wayne, Henry Kolker, Douglass Dumbrille
'Blue and nothing else. It possesses no merit for general or popular appeal, is liable to offend the family trade and can't count on any juve attendance.
'...This is reputed to be a remake on the first print, which was considered too hot. Anything hotter than this for public showing would call for an asbestos audience blanket.' – *Variety*

Baby Face Harrington
US 1935 63m bw
MGM
A timid man is mistakenly identified as a public enemy, and chased by both cops and rival gangsters.
Thin but appealing comedy.
w Nunnally Johnson, Edwin Knopf d Raoul Walsh
☆ Charles Butterworth, Una Merkel, Nat Pendleton, Eugene Pallette, Donald Meek
'Weak satire, grievously overacted.' – *Variety*

Baby Face Morgan
US 1942 60m bw
Jack Schwartz/PRC
The son of a racketeer is made a figurehead by his father's old mob.

Curious comedy of non-violent crime; also non-entertaining.
w Edward Dein, Jack Rubin, Oscar Brodney d Arthur Dreifuss
☆ Richard Cromwell, Mary Carlisle, Robert Armstrong, Chick Chandler, Warren Hymer, Vince Barnett

'Don't see it unless your nerves are bullet proof!'
Baby Face Nelson *
US 1957 85m bw
UA/Fryman-ZS (Al Zimbalist)
Fragmentary account of the life of a thirties public enemy, with the star over the top and the technicians doing what they can on an obviously low budget.
w Irving Shulman, Daniel Mainwaring d Don Siegel ph Hal Mohr m Van Alexander
☆ Mickey Rooney, Cedric Hardwicke, Carolyn Jones, Chris Dark, Ted de Corsia, Leo Gordon, John Hoyt, Anthony Caruso, Jack Elam

Baby It's You *
US 1982 104m colour
Paramount/Double Play (Griffin Dunne, Amy Robinson)
■ ◎
In the sixties, a well-heeled high school girl is wooed and won by a greasy street sheikh with ambitions.
Curious sweet-and-sour romance with a determination to be modern; agreeable in parts but basically empty, and rather undermined by a torrent of rock music on the sound track.
wd John Sayles story Amy Robinson ph Michael Ballhaus md Joel Dorn pd Jeffrey Townsend
☆ Rosanna Arquette, Vincent Spano, Joanna Merlin, Jack Davidson, Nick Ferrari, Leora Dana

Baby Love
GB 1968 93m Eastmancolor
Avco/Avton/Michael Klinger (Guido Coen)
An orphaned nymphet causes trouble among the men in her foster home.
Ludicrous sexploiter which embarrasses a good cast and descends into bathos.
w Alastair Reid, Guido Coen, Michael Klinger novel Tina Chad Christian d Alastair Reid ph Desmond Dickinson m Max Harris
☆ Linda Hayden, Ann Lynn, Keith Barron, Derek Lamden, Diana Dors, Patience Collier, Dick Emery

The Baby Maker
US 1970 109m Technicolor
Robert Wise/National General (Richard Goldstone)
■
A freewheeling girl agrees to have a baby for a childless couple.
Stretched-out fable for our time which refrains from pointing a moral and is generally tastefully done but nevertheless outstays its welcome.
wd James Bridges m Fred Karlin, Tylwyth Kymry
☆ Barbara Hershey, Collin Wilcox-Horne, Sam Groom, Scott Glenn, Jeannie Berlin
§ Fred Karlin, Tylwyth Kymry

The Baby of Macon **
GB/Netherlands/France/Germany 1993 122m colour
Allarts/UGC/La Sept/Cine Electra II/Channel 4/Filmstiftung/Canal (Kees Kasander)
🔲 ⏚
In the 1650s, encouraged by a naïve and sadistic prince, a play about a miraculous child, exploited by his sister and the church, becomes all too real, and rape, death and dismemberment follow.
A puzzling and audacious work, visually sumptuous and frequently confusing in its mix of artifice and actuality, but original and intriguing as it explores the themes of art and its influence, the translation of experience into consumerism, alienation and voyeurism. Audiences are likely to love or hate the film, though at Cannes and elsewhere it mostly met with a hostile reception.
wd Peter Greenaway ph Sacha Vierny m Henry Purcell, Matthew Locke and others pd Jan Roelfs, Ben van Os ed Chris Wyatt
☆ Julia Ormond, Ralph Fiennes, Philip Stone, Jonathan Lacey, Don Henderson, Celia Gregory, Jeff Nuttall, Kathryn Hunter, Gabrielle Reidy, Jessica Stevenson, Frank Egerton
'An uneven film which, for all its formal excellence, is a major let-down.' – *Geoffrey Macnab, Sight and Sound*
'All fluff and no filling.' – *Variety*

Baby on Board
Canada 1992 90m colour
Rose & Ruby/WEN/Sandy Howard/ABC/Prism (Damian Lee)
🔲 ■ ◎
A taxi driver's life becomes complicated after he finds in his cab the small daughter of a Mafia widow, who is on the run for accidentally shooting the hitman who mistakenly killed her husband.
A comedy that tries too hard to be amusing to be amusing.
w Damian Lee story Doug Moore d Francis A. Schaeffer ph Curtis Petersen m Ronald J. Weiss ed Douglas Caron, Allan Mestel
☆ Judge Reinhold, Carol Kane, Geza Kovacs, Alex & Holly Stapley, Conrad Bergschneider, Lou Pitoscias, Errol Slue

Baby – Secret of the Lost Legend
🎦 US 1985 95m Technicolor
Supertechnirama
Touchstone (Jonathan T. Taplin)
■ ◎
Palaeontologists in the African jungle discover a family of living dinosaurs.
Technically and dramatically less than effective, this latter-day King Kong *demonstrates yet again the Disney company's difficulties in hitting the right note for the modern family audience.*
w Clifford and Ellen Green d B. W. L. Norton ph John Alcott m Jerry Goldsmith sp Philip Meador, Peter Anderson
☆ William Katt, Sean Young, Patrick McGoohan, Julian Fellowes

Baby Take a Bow *
🎦 US 1934 76m bw
Fox
An ex-convict is accused of theft, but his small daughter unmasks the real culprit.
Shirley Temple's first star vehicle was a solid enough commercial property to take her right to the top.
w Philip Klein, E. E. Paramore Jnr d Harry Lachman
☆ Shirley Temple, James Dunn, Claire Trevor, Alan Dinehart
'A pretty obvious and silly melodrama, but it has Shirley Temple, so it can go down in the books as a neat and sure b.o. hit.' – *Variety*

'The more he gets into trouble, the more he gets under her skin!'
Baby, the Rain Must Fall
US 1964 100m bw
Columbia/Pakula-Mulligan (Alan Pakula)
■ ◎
A parolee rejoins his wife and daughter in a Southern town, but his outbursts of violence separate them again.
Hard work by all concerned scarcely produces absorbing interest in this filmed play of the Tennessee Williams school.
w Horton Foote play The Travelling Lady by Horton Foote d Robert Mulligan ph Ernest Laszlo m Elmer Bernstein
☆ Steve McQueen, Lee Remick, Don Murray, Paul Fix, Josephine Hutchinson, Ruth White, Charles Watts

The Baby Vanishes: see *Broadway Limited*

'When The Big City Called He Had To Answer.'
'Born To Go Wild!'
Baby's Day Out
🎦 US 1994 98m DeLuxe
TCF (John Hughes, Richard Vane)
🔲 ■
A baby escapes from his kidnappers and leads them a chase across the city, using methods taken from his favourite book.
The Home Alone *formula, of cute kid, dim crooks and violent slapstick topped with sentimentality, fails to raise a laugh this time around.*
w John Hughes d Patrick Read Johnson ph Thomas Ackerman m Bruce Broughton pd Doug Kraner ed David Rawlins
☆ Joe Mantegna, Lara Flynn Boyle, Joe Pantoliano, Brian Haley, Cynthia Nixon, Fred Dalton Thompson, John Neville, Matthew Glave, Eddie Bracken
'A tired retread of past comic formulas played a pitch higher, a rhythm faster. It tries too hard to please and fails miserably.' – *Leonard Klady, Variety*

The Bacchantes

Italy/France 1961 96m colour
Cino Del Duca/Vic Film/Lyre Film (Gian Paolo Bigazzi)
original title: *Le Baccanti*
Dionysius takes his revenge after King Pentheus bans his worship in his home city of Thebes.
Enjoyably silly mythological romp, with bacchantes looking as if they had stepped out of the pages of pin-up magazines.
w Giorgio Stegani, Giorgio Ferroni *play The Bacchae* by Euripides d Giorgio Ferroni ph Pier Ludovico Pavoni m Mario Nascimbene ch Herbert Ross ad Arrigo Equini
☆ Taina Elg, Pierre Brice, Alberto Lupo, Alessandro Panaro, Raf Mattioli, Akim Tamiroff

The Bachelor

US 1999 101m DeLuxe Panavision
Entertainment/New Line/George Street
🖭 ◉
A bachelor, who must marry on his 30th birthday in order to inherit $100m, is pursued by hundreds of prospective brides.
A re-make of Buster Keaton's Seven Chances (qv), but one singularly lacking in humour, romance and charm.
w Chris O'Donnell *play Seven Chances* by Roi Copper Megrue *screenplay* Clyde Bruckman, Jean Havez, Joseph Mitchell d Gary Sinyor ph Simon Archer m David A. Hughes, JohnMurphy pd Craig Stearns ed Robert Reitano cos Terry Dresbach
☆ Chris O'Donnell, Renee Zellweger, Hal Holbrook, James Cromwell, Artie Lange, Edward Asner, Marley Shelton, Sarah Silverman, Stacy Edwards, Rebecca Cross, Jennifer Esposito, Katharine Towne, Peter Ustinov, Mariah Carey, Brooke Shields
  'Crude, frantic yuppie farce.' – *New York Times*

The Bachelor and the Bobbysoxer ***

US 1947 95m bw
RKO (Dore Schary)
🖭 ◎
GB title: *Bachelor Knight*
A lady judge allows her impressionable young sister to get over her crush on an errant playboy by forcing them together.
Simple but unexpectedly delightful vehicle for top comedy talents, entirely pleasant and with several memorable moments.
w Sidney Sheldon d Irving Reis ph Robert de Grasse, Nicholas Musuraca m Leigh Harline
☆ Cary Grant, Myrna Loy, Shirley Temple, *Ray Collins*, Rudy Vallee, *Harry Davenport*, Johnny Sands, Don Beddoe
  'Sure-fire stuff guaranteed to do no conceivable harm ... the audience laughed so loud I missed some of the lines.' – *Shirley O'Hara, New Republic*
🏆 Sidney Sheldon

Bachelor Apartment

US 1931 77m bw
RKO (William Le Baron)
🖭
A virtuous working girl in New York falls for a rich woman-chasing bachelor.
Mildly agreeable early talking romantic comedy.
w J. Walter Ruben, John Howard Lawson d Lowell Sherman ph Leo Tover
☆ Irene Dunne, Lowell Sherman, Mae Murray, Norman Kerry, Claudia Dell, Ivan Lebedeff
  'It oversteps the reasonable limits of sophisticated art ... thus the film is doubtful for small towns.' – *Variety*

Bachelor Bait: see *Adventure in Baltimore*

Bachelor Father

US 1931 90m bw
MGM (B. P. Fineman)
A much-married elderly man visits his grown children.
Unremarkable star comedy of its day.
w Laurence E. Johnson *play* Edward Childs Carpenter d Robert Z. Leonard ph Oliver T. Marsh
☆ Marion Davies, C. Aubrey Smith, Ray Milland, Ralph Forbes, Halliwell Hobbes, Guinn Williams, David Torrence
  'Where they have used the old hoke they have masked it with commendable skill.' – *Variety*

Bachelor Flat

US 1961 91m DeLuxe Cinemascope
TCF/Jack Cummings
An English professor at an American university is unrelentingly pursued by girls.
Flat one-joke comedy which simply hasn't the style to sustain itself.
w Frank Tashlin, Budd Grossman *play* Budd Grossman d Frank Tashlin ph Daniel L. Fapp m Johnny Williams
☆ Terry-Thomas, Richard Beymer, Tuesday Weld, Celeste Holm, Francesca Bellini, Howard McNear

Bachelor Girl Apartment: see *Any Wednesday*

Bachelor Girls: see *The Bachelor's Daughters*

Bachelor in Paradise

US 1961 109m Metrocolor Cinemascope
MGM/Ted Richmond
A famous writer of advice to the lovelorn settles incognito in a well-heeled Californian community to observe its social habits.
Mildly amusing satire is too frequently interrupted by unsuitable romantic interludes in this rather ill-considered star comedy.
w Valentine Davies, Hal Kanter d Jack Arnold ph Joseph Ruttenberg m Henry Mancini
☆ Bob Hope, Lana Turner, Janis Paige, Don Porter, Paula Prentiss, Jim Hutton, Virginia Grey, Reta Shaw, John McGiver, Agnes Moorehead
🎵 title song (m Henry Mancini, ly Mack David)

Bachelor Knight: see *The Bachelor and the Bobbysoxer*

'Just ten tiny fingers and ten tiny toes ... Trouble? Scandal? Gosh, nobody knows!'

Bachelor Mother ***

US 1939 82m bw
RKO (B. G. de Sylva)
🖭 🖭 ◎
A shopgirl finds an abandoned baby and is thought to be its mother; the department store owner's son is then thought to be the father.
Blithely-scripted comedy which stands the test of time and provided several excellent roles.
w Norman Krasna *story* Felix Jackson d Garson Kanin ph Robert de Grasse m Roy Webb
☆ Ginger Rogers, David Niven, Charles Coburn, Frank Albertson, E. E. Clive, Ernest Truex
  'Carries some rather spicy lines aimed at the adult trade, but broad enough in implication to catch the fancy of general audiences ... a surprise laugh hit that will do biz generally and overcome hot weather box office lethargy.' – *Variety*
  'An excellent comedy, beautifully done.' – *Richard Mallett, Punch*
  'This is the way farce should be handled, with just enough conviction to season its extravagances.' – *New York Times*
† Remade as *Bundle of Joy* (qv).
🏅 Felix Jackson

Bachelor of Hearts

GB 1958 94m Technicolor
Rank/Independent Artists (Vivian A. Cox)
Adventures of a German student at Cambridge University.
Sometimes agreeable, sometimes annoying, especially when romance gets in the way of the possibilities for fun.
w Leslie Bricusse, Frederic Raphael d Wolf Rilla ph Geoffrey Unsworth m Hubert Clifford
☆ Hardy Kruger, Sylvia Syms, Ronald Lewis, Eric Barker, Newton Blick

Bachelor Party

US 1984 105m DeLuxe
Fox/Aspect Ratio/Twin Continental (Ron Moler, Bob Israel)
🖭 🖭 ◎
A bachelor party is beset by a series of disasters.
Crude, exploitative farce full of physical mess and tending to get most of its humour from the destruction of order and some teetering on the brink of pornography.
w Neal Israel, Pat Proft *story* Bob Israel d Neal Israel ph Hal Trussell m Robert Folk ad Kevin Conlin, Martin Price ed Tom Walls
☆ Tom Hanks, Tawny Kitaen, Adrian Zmed, George Grizzard, Barbara Stuart, Robert Prescott

The Bachelor Party ***

US 1957 93m bw
UA/Norma (Harold Hecht)
New York book-keepers throw a wedding eve party for one of their fellows, but drink only brings to the fore their own private despairs.
Though the last half-hour lets it down, most of this is a brilliantly observed social study of New York life at its less attractive, and the acting matches the incisiveness of the script.
w Paddy Chayefsky *TV play* Paddy Chayefsky d Delbert Mann ph Joseph LaShelle m Alex North
☆ Don Murray, E. G. Marshall, *Jack Warden*, Philip Abbott, Larry Blyden, Patricia Smith, Carolyn Jones
🏅 Carolyn Jones

Bachelor's Affairs

US 1931 64m bw
Fox
A middle-aged bachelor thinks he needs a young wife, but can't keep up with the one he gets.
Strained star comedy of no surviving interest.
w Barry Conners, Philip Klein *play* Precious by James Forbes d Alfred Werker
☆ Adolphe Menjou, Minna Gombell, Arthur Pierson, Joan Marsh, Alan Dinehart
  'Neither farce nor a social problem development, it misses throughout.' – *Variety*

The Bachelor's Daughters *

US 1946 90m bw
UA/Andrew Stone
GB title: *Bachelor Girls*
Four shopgirls and a floorwalker rent a Long Island house and pass themselves off as a wealthy family in order to lure suitable husbands for the girls.
Mildly amusing comedy with good performances.
wd Andrew Stone ph Theodor Sparkuhl m Heinz Roemheld
☆ Adolphe Menjou, Gail Russell, Claire Trevor, Billie Burke

Back Door to Heaven

US 1939 81m bw
Odessco/Paramount (William K. Howard)
🖭
A boy born on the wrong side of the tracks is prevented from going straight, and, having escaped execution for murder, is bumped off by gangsters.
Heavy-going indictment of society; too glum to work, it seems to have finished off the career of its talented director.
w John Bright, Robert Tasker *story* William K. Howard d William K. Howard
☆ Wallace Ford, Aline MacMahon, Stuart Erwin, Jimmy Lydon, William Harrigan, Bert Frohman
  'Artistic drama, too heavy and slow-tempoed for general b.o.' – *Variety*
† William K. Howard also appears as the prosecuting attorney.

'Lost Together ... Locked Together In The Jungle.'
'As the Jivaro drums grew louder, love changed to fear, selfishness to tenderness, passion to pity.'

Back from Eternity

US 1956 97m bw
RKO (John Farrow)
🖭 ◎
An airliner is forced to crashland in headhunter country, and when repairs are made only five of the eight survivors can be carried.
Remake by the same producer-director of his own 1939 'B', Five Came Back (qv), this time to considerably less effect despite superior production.
w Jonathan Latimer d John Farrow ph William Mellor m Franz Waxman
☆ Robert Ryan, Anita Ekberg, Rod Steiger, Phyllis Kirk, Gene Barry, Keith Andes, Beulah Bondi, Fred Clark, Cameron Prud'homme, Jesse White

Back from the Dead

US 1957 78m bw Regalscope
TCF/Regal (Robert Stabler)
A girl on honeymoon becomes possessed by the spirit of her husband's first wife.
Blithe Spirit played for real but getting just as many laughs, unintentional this time.
w Catherine Turney *novel The Other One* by Catherine Turney d Charles Marquis Warren ph Ernest Haller m Raoul Kraushaar

☆ Peggie Castle, Arthur Franz, Marsha Hunt, Don Haggerty

Back in Circulation

US 1937 80m bw
Warner
Girl news reporter wins her editor's attention by solving a murder.
Sub-Front Page melodrama, of no intrinsic interest.
w Warren Duff d Ray Enright
☆ Pat O'Brien, Joan Blondell, Margaret Lindsay
  'The newspaper boys, the goofy photographers and the hysterical city are on the murder trail, relentlessly pursuing the accused, telling coroners, district attorneys and defence counsel how to conduct their business.' – *Variety*

Back in the USSR

US 1991 87m DeLuxe
Warner/Largo/JVC/Mosfilm (Lindsay Smith, Ilmar Taska)
🖭
In Moscow, an American tourist becomes involved in murder and the theft of a priceless icon from a country church.
Involved and unconvincing thriller with enough twists and turns in the narrative to confuse anyone patient enough to watch it until the end.
w Lindsay Smith d Deran Sarafian ph Yuri Neyman m Les Hooper pd Vladimir Philippov ed Ian Crafford
☆ Frank Whaley, Roman Polanski, Natalya Negoda, Dey Young, Andrew Divoff, Brian Blessed, Ravil Issyanov
  'The plot is contrived and lacklustre and the performances, with a few exceptions, profoundly lacking in presence. The only laughs are unintentional, and the thrills negligible.' – *James Keen, Film Review*

Back of Beyond

Australia 1995 85m colour
Imagine/AFFC/Back of Beyond/Peter Szabo/Tourist/John Sexton
A diamond thief and his girlfriend are stranded in the desert, near a derelict garage, where a mechanic mourns the death of his sister.
An odd little ghost story about loss and love, lacking in much substance.
w Paul Leadon, A. M. Brooksbank, Richard J. Sawyer *original treatment* Michael Robertson d Michael Robertson ph Stephen Dobson m Mark Moffatt, Wayne Goodwin pd Ross Major ed Timothy Wellburn
☆ Paul Mercurio, Colin Friels, John Polson, Dee Smart, Bob Mazza

Back Roads

US 1981 95m DeLuxe Panavision
CBS Theatrical/Meta Films (Ronald Shedlo)
🖭
A hooker and an ex-boxer hitch-hike to California.
Tiresomely with-it update of It Happened One Night (qv); the humour and romance of the original are preferable to this dollop of bad language, boring people and bed-hopping.
w Gary DeVore d Martin Ritt ph John A. Alonzo m Henry Mancini
☆ Sally Field, Tommy Lee Jones, David Keith, Miriam Colon, Michael Gazzo
  'Decidedly sticky, and instantly forgettable.' – *Guardian*

Back Room Boy *

GB 1942 82m bw
GFD/Gainsborough (Edward Black)
🖭
A timid meteorologist is sent to an Orkney lighthouse and unmasks a bunch of spies.
Fairly spirited star comedy of interest as a shameless rip-off of The Ghost Train (qv) and Oh Mr Porter (qv), whose plotlines are milked but not improved: note also that Askey took over Will Hay's discarded stooges.
w Val Guest, Marriott Edgar d Herbert Mason ph Jack Cox
☆ Arthur Askey, Moore Marriott, Graham Moffatt, Googie Withers, Vera Frances, John Salew

Back Street *

US 1932 93m bw
Universal (Carl Laemmle Jnr)
A married man has a sweet-tempered mistress who effaces herself for twenty years.

Popular version of a sudsy bestselling novel.
w Gladys Lehman, Lynn Starling *novel Fannie Hurst* d John M. Stahl *ph* Karl Freund
☆ Irene Dunne, John Boles, June Clyde, George Meeker, ZaSu Pitts, Doris Lloyd
  'Swell romance, a little tear-jerking, and a woman's picture – which means a money production.' – *Variety*

Back Street *
US   1941   89m   bw
Universal (Bruce Manning)
Competent remake.
w Bruce Manning, Felix Jackson d Robert Stevenson *ph* William Daniels *m* Frank Skinner
☆ Margaret Sullavan, Charles Boyer, Richard Carlson, Frank McHugh, Tim Holt, Frank Jenks, Esther Dale, Samuel S. Hinds
♫ Frank Skinner

Back Street *
US   1961   107m   Technicolor
U-I/Ross Hunter/Carrollton
▦
Glossy remake typical of its producer: unfortunately it fails to work because the heroine suffers too luxuriously.
w Eleanore Griffin, William Ludwig d David Miller *ph* Stanley Cortez *m* Frank Skinner
☆ Susan Hayward, John Gavin, Vera Miles, Virginia Grey, Charles Drake, Reginald Gardiner
  'Though there is a lot to be said for this new version's thesis that one can be just as lonely in a series of apartments and lovers' nests apparently never less than a hundred yards wide, the illusion is quickly shattered the moment one gets the impression that the lovers prefer to keep much the same distance during their moments of passion.' – *Peter John Dyer*
  'Ross Hunter has updated this old faithful and given it a contemporary lack of significance.' – *Hollis Alpert, Saturday Review*
  'The bathrooms look like the lobby of the Beverly Hilton … the fallen woman falls, not into the pit of shame, but into the lap of luxury.' – *Time*

Back to Bataan
US   1945   97m   bw
RKO (Robert Fellows)
▦ ▦ ▦
When Bataan is cut off, a Marine colonel organizes guerrilla resistance.
Modestly made and rather dislikeable flagwaver.
w Ben Barzman, Richard Landau d Edward Dmytryk *ph* Nicholas Musuraca *m* Roy Webb
☆ John Wayne, Anthony Quinn, Beulah Bondi, Fely Franquelli, Leonard Strong, Richard Loo, Philip Ahn, Lawrence Tierney, Paul Fix

Back to God's Country
US   1953   78m   Technicolor
U-I (Howard Christie)
A sea captain battles the Canadian winter and a villain who wants his wife and his cargo of furs.
Old-fashioned adventure story, moderately well presented.
w Tom Reed *novel* James Oliver Curwood d Joseph Pevney *ph* Maury Gertsman *m* Frank Skinner
☆ Rock Hudson, Steve Cochran, Marcia Henderson, Hugh O'Brian

Back to School
US   1986   94m   DeLuxe
Orion/Paper Clip (Chuck Russell)
▦ ▦ ▦ ▦
A millionaire enrols in university as a freshman so as to teach his son the ropes.
Crass and ineptly made comedy vehicle for a star with distinct limitations.
w Steven Kampmann, Harold Ramis, Will Porter, Peter Torokvei d Alan Metter *ph* Thomas E. Ackerman *m* Danny Elfman *pd* David Snyder *ed* David Rawlins
☆ Rodney Dangerfield, Sally Kellerman, Burt Young, Keith Gordon, Paxton Whitehead

Back to the Beach
US   1987   92m   colour
Paramount (Frank Mancuso Jnr)
▦ ▦ ▦
Former teenage surfers return to the beach in middle age and help kids with problems.
Not so bad as it sounds, but for cultists only.

w Peter Krikes, Steve Meerson, Christopher Thompson d Lyndall Hobbs *ph* Bruce Surtees *m* Steve Dorff *pd* Michael Helmy *ed* David Finfer
☆ Annette Funicello, Frankie Avalon, Connie Stevens, Lori Loughlin, Tommy Hinkley, Bob Denver, Jerry Mathers, Pee-wee Herman, Don Adams
  'A wonderfully campy trip down pop culture's trash-filled memory lane.' – *Daily Variety*

Back to the Future ***
🏃 US   1985   116m   Technicolor
Universal/Steven Spielberg (Bob Gale, Neil Canton)
▦ ▦ ▦ ▦
With the help of a not-so-crazy scientist, a teenager goes back thirty years to make a man out of his dimwit father.
Lighthearted Twilight Zone fantasy which certainly pleased the international multitudes.
w Robert Zemeckis, Bob Gale d Robert Zemeckis *ph* Dean Cundey *m* Alan Silvestri *pd* Lawrence G. Paull *ed* Arthur Schmidt, Harry Keramidas
☆ Michael J. Fox, Christopher Lloyd, Crispin Glover, Lea Thompson, Claudia Wells
  'Accelerates with wit, ideas, and infectious, wide-eyed wonder.' – *Variety*
♫ original screenplay; song ('The Power of Love'); sound

Back to the Future II
🏃 US   1989   108m   DeLuxe
UIP/Amblin Entertainment (Bob Gale, Neil Canton)
▦ ▦ ▦ ▦ ▦
A scientist and his young friend discover, on their return from a trip to the future, that the present has been altered for the worse.
Extraordinarily raucous, confusingly plotted, poorly performed (rarely have actors aged so unconvincingly) sequel that amounts to little more than a trailer for the third part of the series.
w Bob Gale *story* Bob Gale, Robert Zemeckis d Robert Zemeckis *ph* Dean Cundey *m* Alan Silvestri *pd* Rick Carter *ad* Margie Stone McShirley *ed* Arthur Schimdt, Harry Keramidas
☆ Michael J. Fox, Christopher Lloyd, Lea Thompson, Thomas F. Wilson, Harry Waters Jnr, Charles Fleischer, Joe Flaherty

  'They've saved the best trip to the last. But this time they may have gone too far.'

Back to the Future III **
🏃 US   1990   118m   DeLuxe
UIP/Amblin (Bob Gale, Neil Canton)
▦ ▦ ▦ ▦
A teenager travels back in time to rescue his friend, a scientist stranded in the Wild West.
Good-natured fun at the expense of classic Western movies.
w Bob Gale *story* Robert Zemeckis d Robert Zemeckis *ph* Dean Cundey *m* Alan Silvestri *pd* Rick Carter *ed* Arthur Schmidt, Harry Keramidas
☆ Michael J. Fox, Christopher Lloyd, Mary Steenburgen, Thomas F. Wilson, Lea Thompson, Elisabeth Shue, Matt Clark, Richard Dysart, James Tolkan
  'Has a joyousness seldom seen on the screen these days, a sense of exuberance in the breaking of boundaries of time, space and genre.' – *Variety*

Backbeat *
GB   1993   100m   Eastmancolor Panavision
Rank/Polygram/Scala/Channel 4 Films/Royal Dwyer, Stephen Woolley)
▦ ▦ ▦ ▦
Stuart Sutcliffe, a promising young painter, plays with the Beatles in Hamburg, where he falls for a German photographer and decides his future is with art not rock.
A deft and enjoyable movie about the birth of the 60s and the Beatles, concentrating on the tragically short life of Sutcliffe, who died of a brain tumour in 1962.
w Iain Softley, Michael Thomas, Stephen Ward d Iain Softley *ph* Ian Wilson *m* Don Was *pd* Joseph Bennett *ed* Martin Walsh
☆ Sheryl Lee, Stephen Dorff, Ian Hart, Gary Bakewell, Chris O'Neill, Scot Williams, Kai Wiesinger, Jennifer Ehle
  'Shrewd rather than clever, lively rather than memorable and possessed of just enough wit and heart to convince that it is essentially more than a nostalgia-stirring package.' – *Derek Malcolm, Guardian*

'Has quite a bit going for it in the way of cultural and musical history but lacks a crucial, heightened artistic quality and point of view that would have given it real distinction.' – *Variety*
🎞 music

Backdraft *
US   1991   136m   DeLuxe
UIP/Trilogy/Imagine (Richard B. Lewis, Pen Densham, John Watson)
▦ ▦ ▦ ▦ ▦ ▦
Two brothers track down an arsonist and expose corruption in the fire department.
Overheated, muddled melodrama saved from tedium by its fiery special effects.
w Gregory Widen d Ron Howard *ph* Mikael Salomon *m* Hans Zimmer *pd* Albert Brenner *ed* Daniel Hanley, Michael Hill *sp* Visual effects: Industrial Light and Magic. Pyrotechnics: Allen Hall
☆ Kurt Russell, William Baldwin, Robert De Niro, Donald Sutherland, Jennifer Jason Leigh, Scott Glenn, Rebecca DeMornay, Jason Gedrick, J. T. Walsh
  'Visually, pic is often exhilarating, but it's shapeless and dragged down by corny, melodramatic characters and situations.' – *Variety*

Backfire
US   1949   90m   bw
Warner (Anthony Veiller)
A war veteran solves the murder of which his best friend is accused.
Confusing murder mystery of a very familiar kind, adequately made but with no particular style. Flashbacks don't help.
w Larry Marcus, Ivan Goff, Ben Roberts d Vincent Sherman *ph* Carl Guthrie *m* Ray Heindorf *ad* Anton Grot
☆ Gordon MacRae, Virginia Mayo, Edmond O'Brien, Dane Clark, Viveca Lindfors, Ed Begley

Backfire
US   1987   91m   colour
Virgin/ITC (Danton Rissner)
▦ ▦
A Vietnam veteran with nightmares seems to be in the middle of a murder plot.
Too-murky thriller which takes an awful long time to come clean.
w Larry Brand, Rebecca Reynolds d Gilbert Cates *ph* Tak Fujimoto *m* David Shire *pd* Daniel Lomino *ed* Melvin Shapiro
☆ Karen Allen, Keith Carradine, Jeff Fahey, Bernie Casey, Dean Paul Martin

Background *
GB   1953   82m   bw
Group Three (Herbert Mason)
US title: Edge of Divorce
Two people decide on divorce, but thoughts of their children bring them together again.
Low-budget, stiff-upper-lip marriage guidance tract, well acted but more well-intentioned than memorable.
w Warren Chetham Strode, Don Sharp *play* Warren Chetham Strode d Daniel Birt *ph* Arthur Grant
☆ Valerie Hobson, Philip Friend, Norman Wooland, Janette Scott, Mandy Miller, Jeremy Spenser, Richard Wattis

Background to Danger
US   1943   80m   bw
Warner (Jerry Wald)
▦
An adventurer thwarts Nazi intrigue in Turkey.
Flat, studio-bound wartime potboiler with a good cast all at sea.
w W. R. Burnett *novel Uncommon Danger* by Eric Ambler d Raoul Walsh *ph* Tony Gaudio *m* Frederick Hollander
☆ George Raft, Brenda Marshall, Sydney Greenstreet, Peter Lorre, Osa Massen, Turhan Bey, Kurt Katch
  'You could use this film for one kind of measurement of the unconquerable difference between a good job by Hitchcock and a good job of the Hitchcock type.' – *James Agee*
  'There's nothing for the cast to do other than concentrate on the display of melodramatics.' – *Variety*

Backlash *
US   1956   84m   Technicolor
U-I (Aaron Rosenberg)
A gunman seeks the father he has never met, who turns out to be a villain who sold his partners for gold to attacking Indians.
Rather unusual suspense Western, very watchable for its mystery elements.
w Borden Chase d John Sturges *ph* Irving Glassberg *m* Herman Stein
☆ Richard Widmark, Donna Reed, John McIntire, William Campbell, Barton MacLane

Backlash
Australia   1986   110m   colour
Mermaid Beach/Multifilms (Bill Bennett)
▦
An antagonistic pair of cops – one male, one female – are stranded in the outback with an Aborigine woman accused of the castration and murder of her employer.
Glum melodrama: its heart may be in the right place, but its mind is elsewhere.
wd Bill Bennett *ph* Tony Wilson *m* Michael Atkinson, Michael Spicer *ed* Denise Hunter
☆ David Argue, Gia Carides, Lydia Miller, Brian Syron

Backsliding
Australia/GB   1991   88m   colour
Film4/Itel/AFFC/Charles and Simon Target (Sue Wild)
An incompetent engineer is stranded in the outback with a born-again Christian, who has a violent past and believes that he is being tempted by the devil.
Creepy little psychological drama, but one that lacks much in the way of suspense or character development.
w Simon Target, Ross Wilson d Simon Target *ph* Tom Cowan *m* Nigel Westlake *pd* Ross Major *ed* Nicolas Holmes
☆ Tim Roth, Jim Holt, Odile Le Clezio, Ross McGregor, Michelle Fillery, Patrick Duggan, Jim Morlock, Adrian Shirley

Backstreet Dreams
US   1990   104m   DeLuxe
Trimark (Jason O'Malley, Lance H. Robbins)
▦ ▦
A petty gangster decides to go straight to care for his autistic son.
Lurid melodrama, alternately mawkish and violent, but never bearing any resemblance to an observable reality.
w Jason O'Malley d Rupert Hitzig *ph* Stephen M. Katz *m* Bill Conti *ed* Robert Gordon
☆ Jason O'Malley, Brooke Shields, Sherilyn Fenn, Tony Fields, Nick Cassavetes, Ray Mancini, Burt Young, Anthony Franciosa, Joe Pantoliano
  'A vanity production unsuccessfully mixing exploitation film clichés with fake uplift of a tv disease-of-the-week pic.' – *Variety*

The Bacon Grabbers *
US   1929   20m   bw   silent
Hal Roach
Bailiffs fail to recover a radio on which the instalments are overdue.
Modestly pleasing star comedy on the lines of Big Business (qv).
w Leo McCarey, H. M. Walker d Lewis R. Foster
☆ Stan Laurel, Oliver Hardy, Edgar Kennedy, Jean Harlow, Charlie Hall

'The story of a blonde who wanted to go places, and a brute who got her there – the hard way!'
The Bad and the Beautiful **
US   1952   118m   bw
MGM (John Houseman)
▦ ▦
A director, a star, a screenwriter and an executive recall their experiences at the hands of a go-getting Hollywood producer.
Very much a Hollywood 'in' picture, this rather obvious flashback melodrama offers good acting chances and a couple of intriguing situations; never quite finding the style it seeks, it offers good bitchy entertainment along the way, and there are references back to it in Two Weeks in Another Town (qv), made ten years later.
w Charles Schnee d Vincente Minnelli *ph* Robert Surtees *m* David Raksin *ad* Cedric Gibbons, Edward Carfagno
☆ Kirk Douglas, Lana Turner, Walter Pidgeon, Dick Powell, Barry Sullivan, Gloria Grahame,

Gilbert Roland, Leo G. Carroll, Vanessa Brown, Paul Stewart

'For all the cleverness of the apparatus, it lacks a central point of focus.' – *Penelope Houston*
'Clever, sharply observed little scenes reflect the Hollywood surface: the egotistic babble at a party, the affectations of European directors, the sneak preview, the trying on of suits for catmen in a B picture.' – *MFB*
'It is a crowded and colourful picture, but it is choppy, episodic and vague. There does not emerge a clear picture of exactly how movies are made.' – *Bosley Crowther*
† The relationship between Jonathan Shields and Georgia Lorrison is modelled on that between producer David Selznick and actress Jennifer Jones.
🏆 Charles Schnee; Robert Surtees; art direction; Gloria Grahame
🏵 Kirk Douglas

Bad Bascomb *
US   1946   110m   bw
MGM (Orville Dull)
A sentimental bank robber becomes the hero of a group of travelling Mormons.
Pleasing though overlong star Western, with good production values.
w William Lipman, Grant Garrett d S. Sylvan Simon ph Charles Schoenbaum m David Snell
☆ *Wallace Beery*, Margaret O'Brien, Marjorie Main, J. Carrol Naish, Russell Simpson, Sara Haden

'The Mother, The Planner And The Gobshite.'
Bad Behaviour
GB   1993   104m   colour
First Independent/Channel 4/British Screen/Parallax (Sarah Curtis)
📀 📀 📺
An Irish couple living in North London with their two young sons muddle through life, not helped by the attentions of a neighbour, an unscrupulous landlord and his slapdash friends in the building trade.
A small-scale improvised comedy that concerns itself with the details of everyday existence to the detriment of drama; it may be realistic, but it is often uninteresting, despite the best efforts of its cast.
d Les Blair ph Witold Stok m John Altman pd Jim Grant ed Martin Walsh
☆ Stephen Rea, Sinead Cusack, Philip Jackson, Clare Higgins, Phil Daniels, Saira Todd, Mary Jo Randle

'A delightful comedy of manners ... The pic is character, not knockabout, comedy, but this is a group of mild eccentrics you want to follow to the end.' – *Variety*

Bad Blood *
New Zealand/GB   1981   105m   colour
Southern (Andrew Brown)
📺
A paranoid farmer kills seven people and goes on the run.
Based on a true story, a grim, tense thriller that maintains its excitement.
w Andrew Brown book Manhunt: The Story of Stanley Graham by Howard Willis d Mike Newell ph Gary Hansen m Richard Hartley ad Kai Hawkins ed Peter Hollywood
☆ Jack Thompson, Carol Burns, Dennis Lill, Donna Akersten, Martyn Sanderson, Marshall Napier

Bad Blood: see The Night Is Young (1986)

Bad Boy Bubby **
Australia/Italy   1993   114m   colour
Entertainment/Fandango/Bubby (Domenico Procacci, Giorgio Draskovic, Rolf de Heer)
📀 📺
A retarded 35-year-old, who has never been allowed out of his home, murders his parents and experiences the wider world.
An odd and disturbing black comedy of a man who replays everything said and done to him; many may find it repugnant, but it offers a skewed and satirical perspective on everyday life and communication.
wd Rolf de Heer ph Ian Jones m Graham Tardiff pd Mark Abbott ed Suresh Ayyar
☆ Nicholas Hope, Claire Benito, Ralph Cotterill, Sid Brisbane, Norman Kaye, Carmel Johnson, Bridget Walters

'Provocative, stylistically daring and inventive.' – *Variety*

† Apart from its director of photography, the film used 30 other cinematographers, one for each location. The film won awards for best director, best actor, best original screenplay and best editing at the 1994 Australian Film Institute awards.

Bad Boys
US   1983   123m   Astrocolor
EMI/Robert Solo
📺 📀
Delinquents get out of control in a Juvenile Correctional Facility.
Ugly but yawnworthy saga of up-to-date Dead End Kids.
w Richard di Lello d Rick Rosenthal ph Bruce Surtees, Don Thorin m Bill Conti
☆ Sean Penn, Reni Santoni, Jim Moody, Eric Gurry, Esai Morales, Ally Sheedy

'It has been made in a brutal, realistic neo-Warners style ... Even when episodes are powerful, they're banal.' – *New Yorker*

'Watcha Gonna Do?'
Bad Boys *
US   1995   118m   Technicolor
Columbia (Don Simpson, Jerry Bruckheimer)
📀 📀 📺 📀 📀 📀 🎧
Two Miami cops go after the gang that stole a fortune in heroin from their station-house.
High-octane entertainment in which smart dialogue alternates with frenetic action and large-scale destruction.
w Michael Barrie, Jim Mulholland, Doug Richardson story George Gallo d Michael Bay ph Howard Atherton m Mark Mancina pd John Vallone ed Christian Wagner
☆ Martin Lawrence, Will Smith, Téa Leoni, Tcheky Karyo, Theresa Randle, Marg Helgenberger, Joe Pantoliano

'Ultra-slick combination of expensive action, rude attitude, sassy humor, trendy locations, fast cars, heavy soundtrack and decorous violence.' – *Variety*
'A wholly unambitious reworking of a stock formula.' – *Sheila Johnston, Independent*

Bad Company ***
US   1972   92m   Technicolor
Paramount (Stanley R. Jaffe)
📺
During the Civil War, two youths on the run team up and become outlaws.
A successful attempt to recreate the feeling of past time, by the writers of another criminal myth, Bonnie and Clyde.
w David Newman, Robert Benton d Robert Benton ph Gordon Willis m Harvey Schmidt
☆ Jeff Bridges, Barry Brown, Jim Davis, David Huddleston, John Savage

Bad Company
Canada   1994   108m   Technicolor
Buena Vista/Touchstone (Amedeo Ursini, Jeffrey Chernov)
📺
A former CIA agent becomes involved in industrial espionage and murder.
Lacklustre thriller about uninteresting characters being unpleasant to one another; it lives up to its title.
w Ross Thomas d Damian Harris ph Jack N. Green m Carter Burwell pd Andrew McAlpine ed Stuart Pappe
☆ Ellen Barkin, Laurence Fishburne, Frank Langella, Michael Beach, Gia Carides, David Ogden Stiers, Spalding Gray

'With its uninvolving story, listless delivery and the unsympathetic characters ... would-be suspenser fails even on the erotic level.' – *Godfrey Cheshire, Variety*
† It was released direct to video in Britain.

Bad Day at Black Rock ****
US   1955   81m   Eastmancolor   Cinemascope
MGM (Dore Schary)
📺 📺 📀
A one-armed stranger gets off the train at a sleepy desert hamlet and is greeted with hostility by the townsfolk, who have something to hide.
Seminal suspense thriller – the guilty town motif became a cliché – with a terse script and professional presentation. The moments of violence, long awaited, are electrifying.

w Millard Kaufman story Bad Time at Hondo by Howard Briskin d John Sturges ph William C. Mellor m André Previn
☆ Spencer Tracy, Robert Ryan, Dean Jagger, Walter Brennan, Ernest Borgnine, Lee Marvin, Anne Francis, John Ericson, Russell Collins

'A very superior example of motion picture craftsmanship.' – *Pauline Kael*
'The movie takes place within twenty-four hours. It has a dramatic unity, an economy of word and action, that is admirable in an age of flabby Hollywood epics that maunder on forever.' – *William K. Zinsser, New York Herald Tribune*
'The skill of some sequences, the mood and symbiosis between man and nature makes this film sometimes superior to High Noon.' – *G. N. Fenin*
🏵 Millard Kaufman; John Sturges; Spencer Tracy

Bad Dreams
US   1988   84m   DeLuxe
TCF (Gale Anne Hurd)
📺 📀
After 13 years in a coma, a woman who survived a mass suicide discovers that the murderous spirit of her cult leader is still active.
Unsuccessful horror movie, too imitative of others of the genre and too feeble in its own right to be effective.
w Andrew Fleming, Steven E. de Souza d Andrew Fleming ph Alexander Gruszynski m Jay Michael Ferguson pd Ivo Crisante ed Jeff Freeman
☆ Jennifer Rubin, Bruce Abbott, Richard Lynch, Harris Yulin, Dean Cameron, Susan Barnes

Bad for Each Other
US   1954   83m   bw
Columbia (William Fadiman)
A doctor back from the army scorns his home town for high society, but a mine disaster reverses his decision.
Misleadingly titled cliché drama, patterned after The Citadel (qv). Actors ill at ease, handling competent but routine.
w Irving Wallace, Horace McCoy novel Horace McCoy d Irving Rapper ph Franz Planer md Mischa Bakaleinikoff
☆ Charlton Heston, Lizabeth Scott, Dianne Foster, Mildred Dunnock, Arthur Franz, Ray Collins, Marjorie Rambeau

Bad Girl *
US   1931   90m   bw
Fox
Two New York youngsters have to get married and find life bewildering.
Typical Borzage sentiment which was well received at the time.
w Edwin Burke novel Vina Delmar d Frank Borzage ph Chester Lyons
☆ Sally Eilers, James Dunn, Minna Gombell, William Pawley, Frank Darien
🏆 Frank Borzage; Edwin Burke
🏵 best picture

'It was a dangerous time to be a woman. And a good time to have friends.'
Bad Girls
US   1994   99m   DeLuxe
TCF (Albert S. Ruddy, André E. Morgan, Charles Finch)
📀 📺 📀 🎧
Four prostitutes flee town after a killing and head for the wide open spaces to become outlaws.
Comic and unconvincing Western romp, impossible to take seriously and too silly to be amusing.
w Ken Friedman, Yolande Finch story Albert S. Ruddy, Charles Finch, Gray Frederickson d Jonathan Kaplan ph Ralf Bode m Jerry Goldsmith pd Guy Barnes ed Jane Kurson
☆ Madeleine Stowe, Mary Stuart Masterson, Andie MacDowell, Drew Barrymore, James Russo, Robert Loggia, Dermot Mulroney

'Drinks from an empty trough of wit and style.' – *Variety*
† Tamra Davis was the original director, but left soon after shooting began.

Bad Influence *
US   1990   99m   DeLuxe
Entertainment/Epic/Sarlui/Diamant (Steve Tisch)
📀 📺
A mysterious stranger manipulates the life of a disgruntled office worker.

Thriller requiring a more-than-usual suspension of disbelief.
w David Koepp d Curtis Hanson ph Robert Elswit m Trevor Jones ed Bonnie Koehler
☆ Rob Lowe, James Spader, Lisa Zane, Christian Clemenson, Kathleen Wilhoite, Tony Maggio, Marcia Cross

'A reasonably taut, suspenseful thriller that provides its share of twists before straying into silliness during its final third.' – *Variety*

Bad Jim
US   1990   90m   Rank Colour
21st Century (Joseph Wouk)
A cowboy buys Billy the Kid's horse and turns bank robber, riding across the country with his gang, doing a few good turns.
Amiable, unmemorable Western that goes through familiar routines without much enthusiasm.
wd Clyde Ware ph David Golia m Jaime Sheriff pd Michael E. Forrell ed Glenn Garland
☆ James Brolin, Richard Roundtree, John Clark Gable, Harry Carey Jnr, Rory Calhoun, Pepe Serna, Ty Hardin

Bad Lieutenant
US   1992   96m   colour
Guild/Pressman (Edward R. Pressman, Mary Kane)
A corrupt cop goes from bad to worse.
A lurid and exploitative melange of drugs, sex, masturbation, rape and religiosity, hardly justified by the suggestion of redemption tacked on to its end. What does save it, even if it doesn't justify it, is the force of Harvey Keitel's performance.
w Zoe Lund, Abel Ferrara d Abel Ferrara ph Ken Kelsch m Joe Delia pd Charles Logola ed Anthony Redman
☆ Harvey Keitel, Frankie Thorn, Zoe Lund, Anthony Ruggiero, Eddie Daniels, Bianca Bakija

'Film's frank treatment of drug addiction, obsessive sexuality and loss of religious faith spells instant controversy.' – *Variety*
'Not exactly comfortable viewing, of course, but this is disturbing, raw filmmaking and award-winning acting.' – *Kim Newman, Empire*

Bad Little Angel
US   1939   72m   bw
MGM
A sad little girl flees an orphanage and brightens up several lives in a small town.
Pollyanna-type period drama, definitely for small-town audiences but well enough done.
w Dorothy Yost novel Looking after Sandy by Margaret Turnbull d William Thiele
☆ Virginia Weidler, Gene Reynolds, Guy Kibbee, Ian Hunter, Elizabeth Patterson, Reginald Owen, Henry Hull, Lois Wilson

'Homespunner for the nabes.' – *Variety*

The Bad Lord Byron *
GB   1949   85m   bw
Triton (Aubrey Baring)
Byron lies dying, and imagines his life and loves under review in a heavenly court.
Thought risible at the time, this historical romance in flashback now seems no worse and even a little more stylish than most, though the script suffers from too many cooks.
w Terence Young, Anthony Thorne, Peter Quennell, Laurence Kitchin, Paul Holt d David MacDonald ph Stephen Dade m Cedric Thorpe Davie
☆ Dennis Price, Mai Zetterling, Linden Travers, Joan Greenwood, Sonia Holm, Raymond Lovell, Leslie Dwyer
† The end of the British costume cycle which began with The Man in Grey (qv).

The Bad Man
US   1940   70m   sepia
MGM (J. Walter Ruben)
GB title: Two Gun Cupid
A Mexican outlaw helps a former friend and unites two lovers.
Forgettable Western comedy drama with a sterling cast.
w Wells Root play Porter Emerson Browne d Richard Thorpe ph Clyde de Vinna m Franz Waxman
☆ Wallace Beery, Lionel Barrymore, Laraine Day, Ronald Reagan, Henry Travers

---

Bad Man of Brimstone

US   1937   89m   bw
MGM
An old bandit discovers his long-lost son and sees the light.
Hilariously predictable but enjoyable star vehicle, quite palatable when it isn't too lachrymose.
w Richard Maibaum, Cyril Hume d J. Walter Ruben
☆ Wallace Beery, Virginia Bruce, Noah Beery, Dennis O'Keefe, Lewis Stone, Guy Kibbee, Joseph Calleia

Bad Man of Wyoming: see *Wyoming* (1940)

Bad Man's River

Spain/Italy/France   1972   90m   Eastmancolor
Franscope
Zurbano/Apollo/Roitfeld (Bernard Gordon)
Four outlaws accept the job of blowing up a government arsenal in Mexico.
Lurid Western with comedy leanings and a somewhat eccentric cast.
w Philip Yordan, Eugenio Martin d Eugenio Martin ph Alexander Ulloa m Waldo de Los Rios
☆ Lee Van Cleef, James Mason, Gina Lollobrigida, Simon Andreu, Diana Lorys
  'When shooting a western in Spain one should not say to oneself, "Never mind, no one is going to see it," because that will be just the film which the Rank Organization will choose to release in England.' – *James Mason*

Bad Medicine

US   1985   96m   DeLuxe
TCF/Lantana (Alex Winitsky, Arlene Sellers)
A student goes to medical school in Mexico.
Condescending farce which the Mexicans certainly won't like. Nothing much in it for general audiences either.
wd Harvey Miller novel Steven Horowitz ph Kelvin Pike m Lalo Schifrin pd Les Dilley
☆ Steve Guttenberg, Alan Arkin, Julie Hagerty, Bill Macy
  'With the tone shifting constantly from realistic to slapstick, the film has no center and just sprawls on.' – *Variety*

Bad Men of Missouri

US   1941   72m   bw
Warner
The Younger brothers become outlaws when they fight the influence of carpetbaggers.
Whitewashing of a family of Western criminals; good double-bill entertainment.
w Charles Grayson d Ray Enright
☆ Dennis Morgan, Arthur Kennedy, Wayne Morris, Jane Wyman, Victor Jory, Walter Catlett

Bad Moon

US   1996   79m   colour
Warner/Morgan Creek (James G. Robinson)
An American photojournalist turns werewolf after being attacked by a creature in Nepal.
Dull horror movie that sticks to familiar clichés, lacking any sense of conviction.
wd Eric Red novel Thor by Wayne Smith ph Jan Kiesser m Daniel Licht pd Richard Paris, Linda Del Rosario ed C. Timothy O'Meara sp make-up fx: Steve Johnson
☆ Mariel Hemingway, Michael Paré, Mason Gamble, Primo
  'Too silly to be suspenseful, yet not quite awful enough – or unintentionally funny enough – to qualify as camp.' – *Variety*

The Bad News Bears

US   1976   103m   Movielab
Paramount (Stanley Jaffe)
An ex-baseball professional coaches a team of tough kids.
Rough-tongued, sentimental star comedy.
w Bill Lancaster d Michael Ritchie ph John A. Alonzo m Jerry Fielding (after Bizet)
☆ Walter Matthau, Tatum O'Neal, Vic Morrow, Joyce Van Patten

The Bad News Bears Go to Japan

US   1978   91m   Movielab
Paramount (Michael Ritchie)
Yet another unnecessary sequel with a self-explanatory title.
w Bill Lancaster d John Berry ph Gene Polito m Paul Chihara
☆ Tony Curtis, Jackie Earle Haley, Tomisaburo Wayakama, George Wyner

The Bad News Bears in Breaking Training

US   1977   100m   Movielab
Paramount/Leonard Goldberg (Fred T. Gallo)
The Bears are invited to play in the Houston Astrodome but have trouble finding a coach.
Dimwitted and alarmingly sentimental sequel to a raucously vulgar oncer which should have been left alone.
w Paul Brickman d Michael Pressman ph Fred J. Koenekamp m Craig Safan from Tchaikovsky's 1812 Overture ed John W. Wheeler
☆ William Devane, Clifton James, Jackie Earle Haley, Jimmy Baio, Chris Barnes

The Bad One

US   1930   70m   bw
UA/Art Cinema Corporation
A prostitute falls for a client and saves him from prison.
Artificial to the point of risibility, this incredible melodrama demeans all concerned with it.
w Carey Wilson, Howard E. Rogers, John Farrow d George Fitzmaurice
☆ Dolores del Rio, Edmund Lowe, Don Alvarado, Blanche Friderici

The Bad Seed *

US   1956   129m   bw
Warner (Mervyn Le Roy)
A sweet-looking 8-year-old girl is a liar and a murderess; her mother finds out and attempts to kill her and commit suicide.
A real curiosity from an unexpected stage hit: absurd melodrama treated with astonishing high literary style and some censor-induced levity; at the end, after the little villainess has been struck by lightning, a curtain call shows her being soundly spanked. Nancy Kelly rather uneasily recreates her stage role as the mother.
w John Lee Mahin play Maxwell Anderson novel William March d Mervyn Le Roy ph Harold Rosson m Alex North
☆ Nancy Kelly, Patty McCormack, Henry Jones, Eileen Heckart, Evelyn Varden, William Hopper, Paul Fix, Jesse White
  Harold Rosson; Nancy Kelly; Patty McCormack; Eileen Heckart

Bad Sister: see *The White Unicorn* (1947)

Bad Sister

US   1931   71m   bw
Universal (Carl Laemmle Jnr)
A small-town coquette falls for a city slicker, and her quiet sister gets her steady boyfriend.
A teenage potboiler of its day, remarkable only for its cast.
w Raymond L. Schrock, Tom Reed story The Flirt by Booth Tarkington d Hobart Henley ph Karl Freund
☆ Conrad Nagel, Sidney Fox, Bette Davis, Humphrey Bogart, ZaSu Pitts, Slim Summerville, Emma Dunn, Bert Roach

The Bad Sleep Well **

Japan   1960   151m   bw
Toho (Tomoyuki Tanaka, Akira Kurosawa)
original title: *Warui Yatsu Yoku Nemuru*
As part of his plan for revenge, a man marries the daughter of the businessman responsible for his father's death.
Moody thriller, in the style of American gangster movies of the 40s, but with an ending that Hollywood would have rejected as too downbeat.
w Akira Kurosawa, Hideo Oguni, Eijiro Kusaka, Ryuzo Kikushina, Shinobu Hashimoto novel Ed McBain d Akira Kurosawa ph Yazuru Aizawa m Sasuru Sato
☆ Toshiro Mifune, Masayuki Mori, Kyoko Kagawa, Tatsuya Mihashi, Takashi Shimura, Akira Nishimura, Takeshi Kato

Bad Taste

New Zealand   1987   92m   colour
Blue Dolphin/Wing Nut Films/Peter Jackson
Alien fast-food restaurateurs add humans to their menu.
A deliberately gross low-budget movie, mixing gore and comedy, that gained a cult following among those with strong stomachs. Chacun à son goût.
w Peter Jackson, Tony Hiles, Ken Hammon m Michelle Scullion ed Peter Jackson, Jamie Selkirk sp Peter Jackson d/ph Peter Jackson
☆ Terry Potter, Pete O'Herne, Craig Smith, Mike Minett, Peter Jackson, Doug Wren
  'Some kind of triumph in its horror-comic verve.' – *MFB*

Bad Timing

GB   1980   123m   colour   Technovision
Rank/Recorded Picture Company (Jeremy Thomas)
In Vienna, an American divorcee has a strange and unhappy affair with a psychoanalyst.
Weird and unsympathetic sex melodrama, presented with the disconnected style expected from this director as a series of flashbacks from the heroine's near-deathbed.
w Yale Udoff d Nicolas Roeg ph Anthony Richmond m Richard Hartley
☆ Art Garfunkel, Theresa Russell, Harvey Keitel, Denholm Elliott, Daniel Massey
  'An enervating experience. Technically flashy, and teeming with degenerate chic, the downbeat tale is unrelieved by its tacked-on thriller ending, and deals purely in despair.' – *Variety*

Badge 373

US   1973   116m   Technicolor
Paramount (Howard W. Koch)
A police detective is enraged by the murder of his partner and his own suspension after the death of a suspect.
'Realistic' (i.e. violent and foul-mouthed) cop thriller in the wake of The French Connection, tolerable only for action highlights.
w Pete Hamill, from the exploits of Eddie Egan d Howard W. Koch ph Arthur J. Ornitz m J. J. Johnson
☆ Robert Duvall, Verna Bloom, Henry Darrow, Eddie Egan, Felipe Luciano, Tina Christiana, Marina Durell
  'A deeply divided and scarcely reassuring addition to the movies' composite portrait of the American police force.' – *John Gillett*
  'Nasty, violent and humourless.' – *Sight and Sound*
  'A movie well worth protesting about.' – *Michael Billington, Illustrated London News*

The Badge of Marshal Brennan

US   1957   75m   bw
Allied Artists
A man on the run takes on the identity of a dying marshal, and cleans up a corrupt town.
Satisfying lower-case Western.
w Thomas G. Hubbard d Albert C. Gannaway
☆ Jim Davis, Arleen Whelan, Louis Jean Heydt, Lee Van Cleef

Badkonake Sefid: see *The White Balloon*

The Badlanders *

US   1958   83m   Metrocolor   Cinemascope
MGM/Arcola (Aaron Rosenberg)
Crooked Westerners plan to rob a goldmine.
Rather sloppy Western remake of The Asphalt Jungle (qv).
w Richard Collins d Delmer Daves ph John Seitz
☆ Alan Ladd, Ernest Borgnine, Katy Jurado, Claire Kelly, Kent Smith, *Nehemiah Persoff*, Robert Emhardt

Badlands ****

US   1973   94m   CFI color
Warner/Pressman/Williams/Badlands (Terrence Malick)
A teenage girl and a young garbage collector wander across America leaving a trail of murder behind them.

A violent folk tale for moderns; very well put together, it quickly became a cult film. It has proved to be a seminal film in its depiction of aimless anger as a means of attempting to connect with the world.
wd Terrence Malick ph Brian Probyn, Tak Fujimoto, Stevan Larner m George Tipton
☆ Martin Sheen, Sissy Spacek, Warren Oates, Ramon Bieri
  'One of the finest literate examples of narrated cinema since the early days of Welles and Polonsky.' – *Jonathan Rosenbaum*
  'So preconceived that there's nothing left to respond to.' – *New Yorker*

Badman's Country

US   1958   72m   bw
Warner
Pat Garrett, Wyatt Earp, Buffalo Bill Cody and Bat Masterson have a showdown with Butch Cassidy.
Wildly unhistorical Western.
w Orville H. Hampton d Fred F. Sears
☆ George Montgomery, Buster Crabbe, Malcolm Atterbury, Gregory Walcott, Neville Brand

'The west's worst killers strike again!'

Badman's Territory

US   1946   97m   bw
RKO
The brutality of the Texas state police forces a sheriff to seek help from outlaws.
Unconvincing Western with good moments.
w Jack Natteford, Luci Ward d Tim Whelan
☆ Randolph Scott, Steve Brodie, Gabby Hayes, Ann Richards

Bagdad Café ***

West Germany   1988   91m   Eastmancolor
Mainline/Pelemele/Pro-Ject (Percy and Eleonore Adlon)
aka: *Out of Rosenheim*
A middle-aged Bavarian woman, left stranded in the Mojave desert by her husband, transforms a seedy motel she stumbles across.
High-spirited comedy, full of gentle wit and charm.
w Percy and Eleonore Adlon, Christopher Doherty d Percy Adlon ph Bernd Heinl m Bob Telson ad Bernt Amadeus Capra ed Norbert Herzner
☆ *Marianne Sägebrecht*, Jack Palance, C. C. H. Pounder, Christine Kaufmann, Monica Calhoun, Darron Flagg
† The success of the film resulted in an American TV series starring Whoopi Goldberg.
  song 'Calling You' (m/l)Bob Telson)

Baghdad

US   1949   81m   Technicolor
U-I (Robert Arthur)
A chieftain's daughter seeks revenge for her father's death.
Thinly-conceived Arabian Nights modernization, unsure whether to take itself seriously.
w Robert Hardy Andrews d Charles Lamont ph Russell Metty m Frank Skinner, Jack Brooks
☆ Maureen O'Hara, Vincent Price, Paul Christian, John Sutton, Jeff Corey, Frank Puglia
  'Silly, but not in the least muddle-headed. The producers are fully aware that all the customers want to see of Baghdad is Maureen O'Hara, with a touch of leopard-skin at the throat to warm up a generous décolletage.' – *C. A. Lejeune*

'The two most gorgeous humans you've ever beheld – caressed by soft tropic winds – tossed by the tides of love!'

Bahama Passage

US   1941   82m   Technicolor
Paramount (Edward H. Griffith)
A sophisticated girl is determined to live on a salt-mining island in the West Indies.
Forgettable tropical romance in very pleasing early colour.
w Virginia Van Upp novel Nelson Hayes d Edward H. Griffith ph Leo Tover m David Buttolph
☆ Madeleine Carroll, Sterling Hayden, Flora Robson, Leo G. Carroll, Cecil Kellaway, Dorothy Dandridge

La Baie des Anges **
France 1962 85m bw
Sud-Pacifique (Paul-Edmond Decharme)
GB title: Bay of Angels
A bank clerk who has had unexpected winnings at the Nice Casino falls in love with a compulsive gambler.
Good-looking romantic drama utilizing many of the cinema's most dazzling resources.
wd Jacques Demy ph Jean Rabier m Michel Legrand
☆ Jeanne Moreau, Claude Mann, Paul Guers, Henri Nassiet
'Immense lightness, speed and gaiety … stunning visual texture.' – Tom Milne, MFB
'It's like a French attempt to purify, to get to the essence of, a Warner's movie of the 30s.' – Pauline Kael

Baisers Volés: see Stolen Kisses

Bait
US 1954 79m bw
Columbia (Hugo Haas)
Gold prospectors fall out over a mine and a woman.
Antediluvian melodrama typical of this director, made more risible than usual by Cedric Hardwicke's introduction in the shape of Satan.
w Samuel W. Taylor d Hugo Haas ph Edward P. Fitzgerald m Vaclav Divina
☆ Hugo Haas, Cleo Moore, John Agar, Emmett Lynn

'They are young. They want results. She is…'
The Bait *
France 1995 117m colour
Artificial Eye/Mayfair/Hachette/Little Bear/France 2/M6 (René Cleitman, Frederic Bourboulon)
◉◉
original title: L'Appât
Two layabouts use an 18-year-old shop assistant to flirt with wealthy men and gain access to their apartments so that they can be robbed.
Grim little parable of the acquisitive society, but one that offers little in the way of fresh insights.
w Colo Tavernier O'Hagan, Bertrand Tavernier book Morgan Sportès d Bertrand Tavernier ph Alain Choquart m Philippe Haim ad Emile Ghico ed Luce Grunenwaldt
☆ Marie Gillain, Olivier Sitruk, Bruno Putzulu, Richard Berry, Philippe Duclos, Marie Ravel
'It simply trundles out shock horror with very little interpretation.' – Derek Malcolm, Guardian
† It was winner of the Golden Bear award for best film at the 1995 Berlin Film Festival.

The Baited Trap: see The Trap

Baker's Hawk *
US 1976 96m colour
Doty-Dayton
▦
A reclusive Westerner becomes the victim of hoodlum vigilantes and is helped by a boy and his father.
Refreshingly simple-minded Western for the family audience.
w Dan Greer, Hal Harrison Jnr novel Jack Bickham d Lyman D. Dayton
☆ Clint Walker, Burl Ives, Diane Baker, Lee H. Montgomery, Alan Young

The Baker's Wife: see La Femme du Boulanger

Bakushu: see Early Summer

Le Bal **
France/Italy/Algeria 1982 112m Fujicolour
S.A./A2/Massfil/Oncic (Giorgio Silvagni)
Scenes from the history of a small Paris ballroom between 1936 and 1983.
Striking if overlong attempt at a totally speechless drama, with handling very nearly good enough to meet the challenge, though the result will not be to everyone's taste, and one's reaction in any case will depend very much on mood.
w Jean-Claude Penchenat, Ruggero Maccari, Furio Scarpelli, Ettore Scola, from an idea by the first-named and the stage production by the Théâtre du Campagnol d Ettore Scola ph Ricardo Aranovich m Vladimir Cosma
☆ Jean-Claude Penchenat, Chantal Capron, Etienne Guichard

Balalaika *
US 1939 102m bw
MGM (Lawrence Weingarten)
Russian exiles gather in Paris.
Mildly pleasing star musical.
w Jacques Deval, Leon Gordon play Eric Maschwitz d Reinhold Schunzel ph Joseph Ruttenberg, Karl Freund m Herbert Stothart
☆ Nelson Eddy, Ilona Massey, Charles Ruggles, Frank Morgan, C. Aubrey Smith, Lionel Atwill, Walter Woolf King, Joyce Compton
'A sumptuously produced operetta in the opulent MGM tradition.' – Variety
† Only the title song was retained from the original score
♫ 'At the Balalaika'; 'Tanya'; 'Ride, Cossack, Ride'; 'Shadows on the Sand'; 'Tale of the Tailors'; 'Beneath the Winter's Snows'; 'In a Heart as Brave as Your Own'; 'Soldiers of the Czar'; 'How Many Miles to Go'; 'The Magic of Your Love'; 'My Heart Is a Gypsy'

La Balance ***
France 1982 102m colour
Les Films Ariane/Films A2 (Georges Dancigers, Alexandre Mnouchkine)
◉◉
A pimp and his girlfriend are pressured by the police into becoming informers.
Tough thriller in which the only difference between the cops and the crooks is that the police are the more violent. A box-office success in France, where it was voted the best film of the year.
w M. Fabiani, Bob Swaim d Bob Swaim ph Bernard Zitzermann m Roland Bocquet pd Eric Moulard ed Françoise Javet
☆ Nathalie Baye, Philipe Léotard, Richard Berry, Maurice Ronet

Balboa
US 1983 91m DeLuxe
Entertainment/Production Associates (James Polakof)
◉◉ ▦
Plans by a crooked Californian entrepreneur to set up a casino are opposed by the daughter of the man he ruined.
A glossy and confused soap opera of plot and counter-plot, cut from from a TV mini-series that, understandably, was never broadcast.
w James Polakof, Gail Willumsen, Nicki Lewis d James Polakof ph Christopher Lynch m Richard Hieronymus pd Charles D. Tomlinson ed Millie Paul
☆ Tony Curtis, Carol Lynley, Chuck Connors, Sonny Bono, Steve Kanaly, Jennifer Chase, Martine Beswick

The Balcony *
US 1963 86m bw
Walter Reade/Sterling/Allen Hodgdon/City Film (Joseph Strick, Ben Maddow)
▦ ◎
In a war-torn world, a brothel continues to attract customers of every variety.
Low-budget adaptation of a rather confused allegorical play: vivid moments hardly atone for reels of surrealist groping.
w Ben Maddow play Jean Genet d Joseph Strick ph George Folsey m Igor Stravinsky
☆ Shelley Winters, Peter Falk, Lee Grant, Peter Brocco, Kent Smith, Ruby Dee, Jeff Corey, Leonard Nimoy
'Relentlessly funny, shaggy, shocking.' – The Times
'Unfit for exhibition to man, woman or child.' – People
🎞 George Folsey

Ball of Fire *
US 1941 111m bw
Samuel Goldwyn
▦ ◎
working title: The Professor and the Burlesque Queen
Seven professors compiling a dictionary give shelter to a stripteaser on the run from gangsters.
Rather overstretched but fitfully amusing romp inspired by Snow White and the Seven Dwarfs.
w Charles Brackett, Billy Wilder d Howard Hawks ph Gregg Toland m Alfred Newman
☆ Barbara Stanwyck, Gary Cooper, Oscar Homolka, Henry Travers, S. Z. Sakall, Tully Marshall, Leonid Kinskey, Richard Haydn, Aubrey Mather, Allen Jenkins, Dana Andrews, Dan Duryea

'It's played as if it were terribly bright, but it's rather shrill and tiresome.' – New Yorker, 1982
† Ginger Rogers was first choice for the Stanwyck role.
🎞 original story (Thomas Monroe, Billy Wilder); Alfred Newman; Barbara Stanwyck

Ballad in Blue
GB 1964 88m bw
(Warner) Alexander and Miguel Salkind (Herman Blaser)
▤
US title: Blues for Lovers
A famous pianist becomes friendly with a blind boy and helps reconcile his parents.
Curious sentimental drama with the star playing himself; competent but hardly rousing.
w Burton Wohl d Paul Henreid ph Ron Taylor m Ray Charles, Stanley Black
☆ Ray Charles, Mary Peach, Dawn Addams, Tom Bell, Piers Bishop, Betty McDowall

Ballad of a Soldier **
USSR 1959 89m bw
Mosfilm
▤ ◎
original title: Ballada o Soldate
A soldier is granted four days' home leave before returning to be killed at the front.
Lyrical tear-jerker most notable for its impeccably photographed detail of Russian domestic and everyday life.
w Valentin Yoshov, Grigori Chukrai d Grigori Chukrai ph Vladimir Nikolayev, Era Saveleva m Mikhail Ziv
☆ Vladimir Ivashev, Sharma Prokhorenko, Antonina Maximova
'In an epoch when the entertainment in most entertainment films is little more than offensive, its persuasive charm is particularly welcome.' – MFB
🎞 Valentin Yoshov, Grigori Chukrai
🏆 best picture

The Ballad of Berlin: see Berliner Ballade

The Ballad of Cable Hogue *
US 1970 121m Technicolor
Warner/Phil Feldman (Sam Peckinpah)
◉◉ ▤ ◎ ∩
A gold prospector takes a lengthy and ineffectual revenge on men who robbed him, and dies trying to be a hero.
Curious peripatetic Western with the director in uncharacteristically experimental and comparatively non-violent mood. All concerned seem to be enjoying themselves, but the fun is not always communicated.
w John Crawford, Edmund Penney d Sam Peckinpah ph Lucien Ballard m Jerry Goldsmith
☆ Jason Robards, David Warner, Strother Martin, Slim Pickens, L. Q. Jones, Peter Whitney, R. G. Armstrong, Gene Evans, Stella Stevens
'A curiously compelling film. Like a child's playhouse, we come to love it not for its perfect symmetry but for the open way it expressed the feelings of its creator.' – Richard Schickel

The Ballad of Joe Hill **
Sweden 1971 115m Eastmancolor
Bo Widerberg Film (Waldemar Bergendahl)
aka: Joe Hill
In 1902, a Swedish immigrant in New York becomes a revolutionary and is executed for the murder of a grocer.
Romantic propaganda which incidentally gives a delightfully detailed outsider's view of period America.
wd Bo Widerberg ph Peter Davidson, Jorgen Persson m Stefan Grossman ad Ulf Axen
☆ Thommy Berggren, Anja Schmidt, Evert Anderson, Cathy Smith

The Ballad of Josie *
US 1967 102m Techniscope
Universal (Marty Melcher)
Cleared of the manslaughter of her husband, a Western widow renovates a derelict ranch and sets up as a sheep farmer.
Tediously whimsical, unsuitably cast women's lib comedy with so few laughs that it may require to be taken seriously.
w Harold Swanton d Andrew V. McLaglen ph Milton Krasner m Frank de Vol
☆ Doris Day, Peter Graves, George Kennedy, William Talman, Andy Devine, Audrey Christie

'In 1866, A Woman Had Two Choices … She Could Be A Wife Or She Could Be A Whore. Josephine Monaghan Made The Boldest Choice Of All. She Chose To Be A Man.'
The Ballad of Little Jo *
US 1993 121m Technicolor Panavision
Rank/Fine Line/Polygram/Joco (Fred Berner, Brenda Goodman)
◉◉ ▤ ◎ ∩
A New York woman disguises herself as a man and becomes a cowboy and rancher.
Based on a true story, this becomes a feminist tract about the impossibility of being free and female in the West, which may also be true but here makes for a dull movie.
wd Maggie Greenwald ph Declan Quinn m David Mansfield pd Mark Friedberg ed Keith Reamer
☆ Suzy Amis, Bo Hopkins, Ian McKellen, David Chung, Carrie Snodgress, Rene Auberjonois, Heather Graham, Sam Robards, Tom Bower
'This well-intentioned, revisionist frontier saga is too solemn and dramatically unexciting to generate wild appeal beyond a core of female viewers and ardent followers of indie pics.' – Variety
'It has a nice feeling for the smallness of man and his or her tenuous presence on the Western landscape.' – Philip French, Observer

The Ballad of Narayama *
Japan 1983 130m colour
Cannon/Toei
original title: Narayama Bushi-Ko
An old woman prepares to die in a community where the elderly are exposed on a mountainside when they reach the age of 70.
Often ponderous, though gripping, remake of Keisuke Kinoshita's more restrained movie, made in 1958. It won the prize for the best film at the Cannes Film Festival in 1983.
wd Shohei Imamura novel Narayama Bushi-Ko by Shichiro Fukazawa ph Masao Tochizawa m Shinichiro Ikebe pd Toshio Inagaki ed Hajime Okayasu
☆ Ken Ogata, Sumiko Sakamoto, Tonpei Hidari, Takejo Aki, Shoichi Ozawa, Mitsuaki Fukamizu
'One of the most intense portraits of personal fulfilment in all cinema.' – Tony Rayns, MFB

The Ballad of Tam-Lin: see Tam-Lin

The Ballad of the Sad Café
US/GB 1990 101m Technicolor
Hobo/Merchant Ivory (Ismail Merchant)
◉◉ ▤ ◎ ∩
On his release from prison, a rejected husband takes his revenge on his wife, a small-town store-owner.
A Southern Gothic fairy-tale transferred poorly to the screen.
w Michael Hirst play Edward Albee novel Carson McCullers d Simon Callow ph Walter Lassally m Richard Robbins pd Bruno Santini ed Andrew Marcus
☆ Vanessa Redgrave, Keith Carradine, Cork Hubbert, Rod Steiger, Austin Pendleton, Beth Dixon, Lanny Flaherty, Mert Hatfield, Earl Hindman, Anne Pitoniak
'A film of quite exceptional gracelessness.' – Tom Milne, Sight and Sound
'Difficult to respond to and probably will not engage mainstream audiences.' – Variety

Ballada o Soldate: see Ballad of a Soldier

Ballet Mécanique *
France 1924 10m bw silent
Fernand Léger, Dudley Murphy
Famous experimental short in which everyday images form abstract patterns.
A key to all subsequent surrealist experiments in the cinema.
wd Fernand Léger, Dudley Murphy m Georges Antheil

Balthazar *
France/Sweden 1966 95m bw
Parc/Ardos/Athos/Svenska Filminstitutet (Philippe Dussart)
◉◉
original title: Au Hasard, Balthazar
The life of a talented donkey, born in the Swiss alps and eventually killed during a smuggling escapade.

Something between Black Beauty *and a Christian parable, this quiet, episodic film is counted by some as its director's best work.*
wd *Robert Bresson* ph *Ghislain Cloquet* m *Jean Wiener (and Schubert)* ad *Pierre Charbonnier* ed *Raymond Lamy*
☆ Anne Wiazemsky, François Lafarge, Walter Green

Baltic Deputy *
USSR 1937 100m bw Lenfilm
An old professor is finally reconciled to the 1917 revolution.
Propagandist biography (of scientist K. A. Timiriazev) with interesting scenes and a strong central performance.
w *the directors and others* d *Alexander Zharki, Josef Heifits* ph *M. Kaplan* m *M. Timofeyev*
☆ Nikolai Cherkassov, M. Damasheva, A. Melnikov

The Baltimore Bullet
US 1980 103m Eastmancolor
Avco Embassy/Filmfair (John F. Brescia)
▥ ▤
Adventures of a pair of pool sharks.
Flabby comedy attempting a lighthearted version of The Hustler *(qv). The rewards are meagre.*
w *John F. Brescia, Robert Vincent O'Neill* d *Robert Ellis Miller* ph *James A. Crabe* m *Johnny Mandel*
☆ James Coburn, Omar Sharif, Bruce Boxleitner, Ronee Blakley, Calvin Lockhart
'It manages to be stupidly macho and hopelessly incompetent at one and the same time.' – *Guardian*

Balto
👫 US/GB 1995 77m DeLuxe
Universal/Amblin (Steve Hickner)
▥ ▤ ◷ ◯
A woman explains to her granddaughter how a statue in New York's Central Park commemorates Balto, a half-wolf, half-dog which led a sled team that brought antitoxins to the town of Nome, Alaska, during an epidemic of diphtheria in 1925.
Bland family entertainment that begins as live action and then becomes a rather dull animated film that attempts to make some point about miscegenation.
w *Cliff Ruby, Elana Lesser, David Steven Cohen, Roger S. H. Schulman* d *Simon Wells* ph *Jan Richter-Friis* m *James Horner* pd *Hans Bacher* ed *Nick Fletcher, Sim Evan-Jones*
☆ Miriam Margolyes, Lola Bates-Campbell and also the voices of: Kevin Bacon, Bob Hoskins, Bridget Fonda, Jim Cummings, Phil Collins, Donald Sinden
'Grossly sentimentalised as the triumph of an unwanted mongrel, but it won't do much harm to small children.' – *Derek Malcolm, Guardian*
† Balto and the other dogs in his sled team starred in a silent movie, *Balto's Race to Nome*, before becoming sideshow attractions, from which they were rescued and moved to Cleveland Zoo, where Balto lived until his death at the age of 11 in 1933.

La Bamba: see *Bamba*

Bambi ****
👫 US 1942 72m Technicolor
Walt Disney
▥ ▤ ◷ ◯
The story of a forest deer, from the book by Felix Salten.
Anthropomorphic cartoon feature, one of Disney's most memorable and brilliant achievements, with a great comic character in Thumper *the rabbit and a climactic forest fire sequence which is genuinely thrilling. A triumph of the animator's art.*
m *Frank Churchill, Edward Plumb* supervisor *David Hand*
☆ Featuring the voices of Peter Behn, Paula Winslow
'The ultimate stag movie.' – *anon*
'The film, charming and touching as it can be, belongs more to the Disney of whimsy and sentiment than it does to the creative artist; and those who remember the Schubert in *Fantasia* will know what I mean when I say that a good deal of this tale of a forest deer is in Disney's Ave Maria manner.' – *Dilys Powell*
'Sheer enchantment.' – *C. A. Lejeune*
♫ Frank Churchill, Edward Plumb; song 'Love Is a Song' (m Frank Churchill, ly Larry Morey)

The Bamboo Blonde
US 1946 68m bw
Herman Schlom/RKO
A night-club singer falls for a B29 pilot who christens her – and his plane – The Bamboo Blonde.
Mediocre filler with the star ill at ease except when singing.
w *Olive Cooper, Lawrence Kimble, Wayne Williams* d *Anthony Mann*
☆ Frances Langford, Ralph Edwards, Russell Wade, Iris Adrian, Jane Greer

The Bamboo Prison
US 1955 80m bw
Columbia
An American prisoner-of-war in Korea poses as a collaborator in order to get secret information.
Forlorn war drama which makes little impact.
w *Edwin Blum, Jack de Witt* d *Lewis Seiler*
☆ Robert Francis, Brian Keith, E. G. Marshall, Dianne Foster, Jerome Courtland

Banana Ridge
GB 1941 87m bw
ABPC
A business man's old flame presents him with an alleged son.
Stagey farce salvaged by star performances.
w *Walter C. Mycroft, Lesley Storm, Ben Travers* play *Ben Travers* d *Walter C. Mycroft*
☆ Robertson Hare, Alfred Drayton, Isabel Jeans, Nova Pilbeam, Adele Dixon, Stewart Rome

Bananas *
US 1971 81m DeLuxe
UA/Rollins and Joffe (Jack Grossberg)
▥ ▤ ◷
A meek and mild product tester for a New York corporation accidentally becomes a South American rebel hero.
Disjointed anarchic comedy with a few good jokes typical of their author.
w *Woody Allen, Mickey Rose* d *Woody Allen* ph *Andrew M. Costikyan* m *Marvin Hamlisch*
☆ Woody Allen, Louise Lasser, Carlos Montalban, Jacobo Morales
'Full of hilarious comic ideas and lines, supplied by Allen and his collaborator; then Allen, the director and actor, murders them.' – *Stanley Kauffmann*
† Asked why his film was called *Bananas*, Allen replied: 'Because there are no bananas in it.'

The Bananas Boat: see *What Changed Charley Farthing?*

'You're no blue blood any more, honey. The master bought you ... and now he's waitin'!'
Band of Angels
US 1957 127m Warnercolor
Warner (no producer credited)
◯
In 1865, a Kentucky girl learns that her mother was black and is sold as a slave, but quickly becomes her owner's mistress.
Long-winded romantic adventure, rather lamely scripted and developed. The star's presence reinforces the impression of sitting through the ghost of Gone with the Wind.
w *John Twist, Ivan Goff, Ben Roberts* novel *Robert Penn Warren* d *Raoul Walsh* ph *Lucien Ballard* m *Max Steiner*
☆ Clark Gable, Yvonne de Carlo, Sidney Poitier, Efrem Zimbalist Jnr, Patric Knowles, Rex Reason, Torin Thatcher, Andrea King
'Too absurd to be dislikeable.' – *MFB*

The Band Plays On
US 1934 87m bw
MGM
Four street kids are saved by football and eventually become national stars.
Ho-hum sentimental melodrama with plot trouble.
w *Bernard Schubert, Ralph Spence, Harvey Gates* d *Russell Mack*
☆ Robert Young, Stuart Erwin, Leo Carrillo, Betty Furness, Ted Healy, Preston Foster, Russell Hardie, William Tannen
'Slow, long, and weak on cast names.' – *Variety*

Band Waggon *
GB 1939 85m bw
GFD/Gainsborough (Edward Black)
Comedians running a pirate TV station in a ghostly castle round up a gang of spies.
Film version of a long-running radio comedy series; quite a serviceable record of a phenomenon.
w *Marriott Edgar, Val Guest* d *Marcel Varnel* ph *Henry Harris*
☆ Arthur Askey, Richard Murdoch, Jack Hylton and his band, Pat Kirkwood, Moore Marriott, Peter Gawthorne, Wally Patch, Donald Calthrop

The Band Wagon ****
US 1953 112m Technicolor
MGM (Arthur Freed)
▥ ▤ ◷ ◯
A has-been Hollywood dancer joins forces with a temperamental stage producer to put on a Broadway musical.
Simple but sophisticated musical with the bare minimum of plot, told mostly in jokes, and the maximum of music and song. Numbers include those listed below, as well as a spoof Mickey Spillane ballet finale. Level of technical accomplishment very high.
w *Adolph Green, Betty Comden* d *Vincente Minnelli* ph *Harry Jackson* m *Adolph Deutsch* m/ly *Howard Dietz, Arthur Schwartz* ad *Cedric Gibbons, Preston Ames*
☆ Fred Astaire, Jack Buchanan, Oscar Levant, Cyd Charisse, Nanette Fabray
'The best musical of the month, the year, the decade, or for all I know of all time.' – *Archer Winsten*
† The Jack Buchanan character, Jeffrey Cordova, was first offered to Clifton Webb. It was loosely based on José Ferrer, who in the early fifties produced four Broadway shows all running at the same time, and acted in a fifth.
♫ 'A Shine on Your Shoes', 'By Myself', 'That's Entertainment', 'Dancing in the Dark', 'Triplets', 'New Sun in the Sky', 'I Guess I'll Have to Change My Plan', 'Louisiana Hayride', 'I Love Louisa', 'Girl Hunt' ballet.
⌕ Adolph Green, Betty Comden; Adolph Deutsch

Bande à Part
France 1964 95m bw
Anouchka/Orsay (Philippe Dussart)
aka: *The Outsiders*
Aimless young people plan a robbery which ends in murder.
Despite the plot, the emphasis is on fragments of lyricism, and the film is not among its director's greatest successes.
wd *Jean-Luc Godard* novel *Fool's Gold* by Dolores Hitchens ph *Raoul Coutard* m *Michel Legrand*
☆ Anna Karina, Claude Brasseur, Sami Frey, Louisa Colpeyn
'In a sense, the whole film is a metaphor illustrating this glancing collision, when fantasy and reality merge but one may still remain unsure which is which.' – *Tom Milne, MFB*

Bandido
US 1956 92m DeLuxe Cinemascope
UA/Robert L. Jacks
Mexico 1916: an American adventurer helps a rebel leader to defeat a gun runner.
Standard action fare, rather slackly handled.
w *Earl Felton* d *Richard Fleischer* ph *Ernest Laszlo* m *Max Steiner*
☆ Robert Mitchum, Gilbert Roland, Zachary Scott, Ursula Thiess

The Bandit *
Brazil 1953 119m bw
Companhia Cinematographica (Cid Leite da Silva)
original title: *O'Cangaceiro*
The leader of a gang of outlaws comes to grief after falling out with his second in command over a woman.
One of the few Brazilian films to achieve international popularity, mainly because of its memorable theme tune. The film itself looks attractive but becomes a bit of a bore.
wd *Lima Barreto* ph *Chick Fowle* m *Gabriel Migliori*
☆ Alberto Ruschel, Milton Ribeiro, Marisa Prado

The Bandit of Sherwood Forest *
👫 US 1946 87m Technicolor
Columbia (Leonard S. Picker, Clifford Sanforth)
Robin Hood frustrates the Regent who plans to usurp the throne from the boy king.
A lively romp through Sherwood Forest with a capable cast.
w *Wilfrid H. Pettitt, Melvin Levy* novel *Son of Robin Hood* by Paul A. Castleton d *George Sherman, Henry Levin* ph *Tony Gaudio, William Snyder, George Meehan* m *Hugo Friedhofer*
☆ Cornel Wilde, Anita Louise, Edgar Buchanan, Jill Esmond, Henry Daniell, George Macready, Russell Hicks, John Abbott, Lloyd Corrigan

The Bandit of Zhobe
GB 1959 81m Technicolor Cinemascope
Warwick/Columbia
An Indian chieftain kidnaps a British major's daughter in retaliation for the death of his wife.
Tinpot action melodrama in the wake of the rather better Zarak *(qv).*
wd *John Gilling*
☆ Victor Mature, Anthony Newley, Anne Aubrey, Norman Wooland

Bandit Queen *
GB/India 1994 120m colour
Mainline/Kaleidoscope/Channel 4 (Sundeep Singh Bedi)
▥ ▤ ◷ ◯
Phoolan Devi, an illiterate, low-caste, much-abused woman, becomes a feared leader of outlaws and takes her revenge on her tormentors before surrendering to the authorities.
An Indian movie made for the West, often stirring and always interesting but raising more questions than it answers in its treatment of its real-life heroine, who is alternately presented as a victim and a victimizer.
w *Mala Sen, Ranjit Kapoor* d *Shekar Kapur* ph *Ashok Mehta* m *Nusrat Fateh Ali Khan* pd *Eve Mavrakis* ed *Renu Saluja*
☆ Seema Biswas, Nirmal Pandey, Manoj Bajpai, Rajesh Vivek, Raghuvir Yadav, Saurabh Shukla, Govind Namdeo
'This makes a welcome breather from all the usual air-brushed Raj epics and dotty Bollywood excesses, presenting an India which is dirty, unglamorous but still so mysterious.' – *Steve Beard, Empire*
'Essentially *Bandit Queen* just transforms Phoolan Devi from being India's best-known bandit into history's most famous victim of rape.' – *Arundhati Roy, Independent*
† The film's Indian release was delayed after Phoolan Devi sued Channel 4 and the makers of the film for invasion of her privacy by depicting her rape and for prejudicing her forthcoming trial by implicating her in a mass murder that she denies.

The Bandit Queen
US 1950 69m bw
Lippert (William Berke)
▤
The daughter of murdered Spaniards in California takes revenge against violent settlers from the east.
Predictable Western adventure on a low budget.
w *Victor West and Budd Lesser* d *William Berke*
☆ Barbara Britton, Willard Parker, Barton MacLane, Philip Reed, Victor Kilian, Thurston Hall

Bandit Ranger
US 1942 60m bw
RKO (Bert Gilroy)
A rancher, attempting to expose a phoney Texas Ranger and a gang of cattle-rustlers, finds himself framed for murder.
Second-feature Western with a better than average narrative, though otherwise it's the usual mix of action, romance, a song or two, and a little comedy.
w *Bennett R. Cohen, Morton Grant* d *Lesley Selander* ph *Nicholas Musuraca* m *Paul Sawtell* m/ly *Fred Rose, Ray Whitley* ad *Albert S. D'Agostino, Walter E. Keller* ed *Les Millbrook*
☆ Tim Holt, Cliff Edwards, Joan Barclay, Kenneth Harlan, Glenn Strange, Leroy Mason

Banditi a Orgosolo: see *Bandits of Orgosolo*

Bandits of Corsica *
US 1951 83m bw
Global/UA
GB title: *The Return of the Corsican Brothers*
Mario and his gypsy twin get together to unseat a tyrant.
Rather muffled actioner with adequate highlights.
w Richard Schayer d Ray Nazarro
☆ Richard Greene, Paula Raymond, Raymond Burr, Dona Drake, Raymond Greenleaf, Lee Van Cleef
† See also: *The Corsican Brothers.*

Bandits of Orgosolo
Italy 1961 98m bw
Vittorio de Seta/Titanus
A Sardinian shepherd shelters some bandits and becomes one of them.
Rather slow character adventure which achieved some international reputation on its first release.
w Vittorio de Seta, Vera Gherarducci
m Valentino Bucci d/ph Vittorio de Seta
☆ Michele Cossu, Peppeddu Cuccu, and amateur cast

Bandolero! *
US 1968 108m DeLuxe Panavision
Fox (Robert L. Jacks)
In Texas, fugitive outlaw brothers run into trouble with their Mexican counterparts.
Dour and downbeat but well-staged Western with emphasis on hanging and rape; an unusual mixture but smoothly assembled.
w James Lee Barrett d Andrew V. McLaglen ph William H. Clothier m Jerry Goldsmith
☆ James Stewart, Dean Martin, Raquel Welch, George Kennedy, Will Geer, Andrew Prine

Bang: see *The Big Bang Theory* (1995)

Bang *
US 1996 110m colour
Polygram/Eagle Eye (Daniel M. Berger, Ladd Vance)
Thrown out of her apartment for non-payment of rent and humiliated by everyone she meets, a Los Angeles actress steals a cop's uniform, motorbike and gun after he propositions her for sex, and discovers how empowering her appearance becomes.
Energetic, low-budget, independent movie that shows signs of haste in its making, but also of a quirky and individual talent.
wd Ash ph David Gasperik pd Daniel M. Berger ed Ash, Daniel M. Berger
☆ Darling Narita, Peter Greene, Michael Newland, David Allan Graff, Stanley Herman, Noble James, Art Cruz, Luis Guizar
† The film was made at a cost of $20,000.

Bang the Drum Slowly
US 1973 96m Movielab
Paramount (Maurice and Lois Rosenfield)
A baseball star finds that he is dying of leukemia.
Cliché-ridden tearjerker in the modern style.
w Mark Harris *novel* Mark Harris d John Hancock ph Richard Shore m Stephen Lawrence
☆ Michael Moriarty, Robert De Niro, Vincent Gardenia, Phil Foster
ደ Vincent Gardenia

Bang, You're Dead
GB 1954 88m bw
British Lion/Wellington (Lance Comfort)
US title: *Game of Danger*
A small boy accidentally shoots a local villain, and another man is arrested.
Singularly pointless and unattractive melodrama, a long way behind The Window and The Yellow Balloon (qqv).
w Guy Elmes, Ernest Borneman d Lance Comfort ph Brendan J. Stafford m Eric Spear
☆ Jack Warner, Derek Farr, Veronica Hurst, Gordon Harker, Michael Medwin, Anthony Richmond, Philip Saville

Banjo on my Knee **
US 1936 95m bw
TCF (Nunnally Johnson)
In a Mississippi riverboat shanty town, a wedding night is interrupted when the groom is arrested during a brawl.

Unusual, easy-going comedy in which the stars sing and dance as well as fool around.
w Nunnally Johnson *novel* Harry Hamilton d John Cromwell ph Ernest Palmer m Arthur Lange m/ly Jimmy McHugh, Harold Adamson
☆ Barbara Stanwyck, Joel McCrea, Buddy Ebsen, Walter Brennan, Helen Westley, Walter Catlett, Tony Martin, Katherine de Mille
'Too complicated for any better than moderate reception.' – *Variety*

The Bank Breaker: see *Kaleidoscope*

The Bank Detective: see *The Bank Dick*

The Bank Dick ***
US 1940 73m bw
Universal
🖭 📺
GB title: *The Bank Detective*
In Lompoc, California, a ne'er-do-well accidentally stops a hold-up, is made a bank detective, acquires deeds to a worthless mine and interferes in the production of a film.
Imperfect, but probably the best Fields vehicle there is: the jokes sometimes end in mid-air, but there are delicious moments and very little padding. The character names are sometimes funnier than the script: they include Egbert Sousè (accent grave over the 'e'), J. Pinkerton Snoopington, Ogg Oggilbie and Filthy McNasty.
w Mahatma Kane Jeeves (W. C. Fields) d Eddie Cline ph Milton Krasner md Charles Previn
☆ W. C. Fields, Franklin Pangborn, Una Merkel, Shemp Howard, Jack Norton, Grady Sutton, Cora Witherspoon
'One of the great classics of American comedy.' – *Robert Lewis Taylor*
'When the man is funny he is terrific ... but the story is makeshift, the other characters are stock types, the only pace discernible is the distance between drinks or the rhythm of the fleeting seconds it takes Fields to size up trouble coming and duck the hell out.' – *Otis Ferguson*
'Individualistic display of broad comedy ... adequate program supporter.' – *Variety*
† Fields's writing nom-de-plume was allegedly borrowed from noble characters in old English plays he squirmed through as a youth. They kept saying: 'M'hat, m'cane, Jeeves.'

Bank Holiday *
GB 1938 86m bw
GFD/Gainsborough (Edward Black)
US title: *Three on a Weekend*
The lives of various people intertwine during a day out in Brighton.
Simple but effective slice-of-life comedy-drama, establishing several actors and a director. Still quite refreshing.
w Hans Wilhelm, Rodney Ackland, Roger Burford d Carol Reed ph Arthur Crabtree md Louis Levy ad Vetchinsky ed R. E. Dearing, Alfred Roome
☆ Margaret Lockwood, Hugh Williams, John Lodge, Kathleen Harrison, Wally Patch, Rene Ray, Linden Travers, Garry Marsh, Wilfrid Lawson
'Ranges from pathos to farce with a nice avoidance of overstatement.' – *Daily Telegraph*

Bank Robber
US 1993 91m Foto-Kem
IRS/Initial (Lisa Cazés)
🖭 📺
A bank robber hides in a seedy hotel where every guest recognizes him and demands a share of the loot in return for keeping quiet about it.
Vacuous comedy that lacks jokes and tries to compensate by putting the emphasis on sex.
wd Nick Mead ph Andrzej Sekula m Stewart Copeland
☆ Patrick Dempsey, Lisa Bonet, Judge Reinhold, Forest Whitaker, Olivia D'Abo, Mariska Hargitay, Michael Jeter
'File under misfire.' – *Film Review*

The Bank Shot *
US 1974 83m DeLuxe
UA/Hal Landers, Bobby Roberts
🖭
Using house-moving equipment, an escaped convict steals a whole bank.
Extended chase comedy with scenes of gleeful destruction. Acceptable for those in the mood, but a shade overdone.

w Wendell Mayes *novel* Donald E. Westlake d Gower Champion ph Harry Stradling Jnr m John Morris
☆ George C. Scott, Joanna Cassidy, Sorrell Booke, G. Wood, Clifton James

Bannerline *
US 1951 87m bw
MGM (Henry Berman)
To comfort a dying old man, a young reporter prints a fake newspaper showing the indictment of the old man's gangster enemy. By an odd chain of events, the story becomes true.
Worthy but rather dull MGM 'B', typical of the regime of Dore Schary, boasting a pleasing small-town atmosphere and a remarkable cast of old actors.
w Charles Schnee *story* Samson Raphaelson d Don Weis ph Harold Lipstein m Rudolph Kopp
☆ Lionel Barrymore, Keefe Brasselle, Sally Forrest, Lewis Stone, Elisabeth Risdon, J. Carrol Naish, Spring Byington, Larry Keating

Banning
US 1967 102m Techniscope
Universal (Dick Berg)
A golf pro has sporting and amorous adventures at a country club.
Tedious, complexly plotted melodrama of life among the idle rich; handling generally laboured. A showcase for the studio's young contract talent.
w James Lee d Ron Winston ph Loyal Griggs m Quincy Jones
☆ Robert Wagner, Anjanette Comer, Jill St John, Guy Stockwell, James Farentino, Susan Clark, Howard St John, Mike Kellin, Sean Garrison, Gene Hackman
♫ song 'The Eyes of Love' (mQuincy Jones, ly Bob Russell)

BAPS
US 1997 92m DeLuxe
Entertainment/New Line/Island (Mark Burg, Loretta Jones)
🖭 📺
A waitress is offered a small fortune to impersonate the lost granddaughter of a dying millionaire's old love.
Exceptionally dreary and raucous comedy, feebly plotted.
w Troy Beyer d Robert Townsend ph Bill Dill m Stanley Clarke pd Keith Brian Burns ed Patrick Kennedy
☆ Halle Berry, Martin Landau, Ian Richardson, Natalie Desselle, Troy Beyer, Luigi Amodeo, Jonathan Fried
'Words cannot convey the multi-hued frightfulness of this film.' – *Derek Malcolm, Guardian*
† The title is an acronym for Black American Princesses.

'Finally ... a romantic comedy without men.'
Bar Girls *
US 1994 94m Foto-Kem
Lavender Hill Mob (Lauren Hoffman, Marita Giovanni)
🖭
A lesbian begins a relationship with a married actress whom she picks up at her local bar.
A slick, somewhat theatrical low-budget movie that isn't likely to have much appeal outside its target audience; its emphasis on courtship rituals among its youngish lesbians has an earnestness that precludes both romance and wit.
w Lauren Hoffman *play* Lauren Hoffman d Marita Giovanni ph Michael Ferris m Lenny Meyers ad Darryl Fong, Keith Brunsmann ed Carter De Haven
☆ Nancy Allison Wolfe, Liza D'Agostino, Camila Griggs, Lisa Parker, Justine Slater, Paula Sorge, Michael Harris

The Bar Sinister *
US 1955 87m Eastmancolor Cinemascope
MGM (Henry Berman)
🖭
GB title: *It's a Dog's Life*
The rise in lifestyle of a Bowery bull terrier, as told by himself.
Tolerable whimsy, in MGM's best family manner; ten years earlier it might have been a hit.
w John Michael Hayes *story* Richard Harding Davis d Herman Hoffman ph Paul Vogel m Elmer Bernstein

☆ Edmund Gwenn, Jeff Richards, Jarma Lewis, Dean Jagger

Barabbas *
Italy/US 1962 144m Technirama
Columbia/Dino de Laurentiis
🖭 🖥 📺
Pardoned instead of Christ, Barabbas is sentenced to the silver mines, turns Christian, and becomes a gladiator.
Overblown epic which starts with a genuine eclipse of the sun and has nowhere to go but down. The cast sparks a few moments, but it is generally a gaudy display of carnage.
w Christopher Fry, Nigel Balchin, Diego Fabbri, Ivo Perilli *novel* Pär Lagerkvist d Richard Fleischer ph Aldo Tonti m Mario Nascimbene ad Mario Chiari
☆ Anthony Quinn, Silvana Mangano, Vittorio Gassman, Ernest Borgnine, Jack Palance, Arthur Kennedy, Norman Wooland, Valentina Cortese, Harry Andrews, Katy Jurado, Michael Gwynn
'Unacceptable in its pain-preoccupation and its religiosity.' – *Peter John Dyer*
† The eclipse of the sun at the beginning is a real one, photographed at Nice.

'A world beyond words.'
Baraka *
US 1992 97m colour 70mm
Mayfair/Magidson (Mark Magidson)
🖭 🖥 📺 ⊚ 📺
Scenes of nature are followed by those of religious celebrations around the world, of human life and work, of death in war and funeral rituals.
A film made by the cinematographer of Koyaanisqatsi (qv), and similar in style, though less coherent in its selection of images, stunning though they often are.
w Ron Fricke, Mark Magidson, Bob Green d Ron Fricke ph Ron Fricke m Michael Stearns ed Ron Fricke, Mark Magidson, David E. Aubrey, Alton Walpole
'Comes over as an animated National Geographic.' – *Sight and Sound*
'Perhaps one needs to see it on a psychedelic substance to discern a pattern or coherent structure.' – *Empire*

'In A World Gone To Hell Even Angels Carry Guns.'
Barb Wire *
US 1996 99m Technicolor
Polygram/Propaganda/Dark Horse (Mike Richardson, Todd Moyer, Brad Wyman)
🖭 🖥 📺
In 2017, while civil war rages in the States, a club-owner and bounty hunter, who favours tight black leather and high heels, goes in search of some contact lenses that can save the world.
A film that renders criticism superfluous: a comic-book adventure that seems even more cartoon-like than the original.
w Chuck Pfarrer, Ilene Chaiken d David Hogan ph Rick Bota m Michel Colombier pd Jean-Philippe Carp ed Peter Schink
☆ Pamela Anderson Lee, Temuera Morrison, Victoria Rowell, Jack Noseworthy, Xander Berkeley, Udo Kier, Steve Railsback, Clint Howard
'Resembles *Mad Max* with brassieres and deserves to be mocked.' – *Guardian*
'A slow, dim-witted, second-rate rock video that is devoid of energy, excitement or imagination.' – *Sunday Times*

'See her do her thing!'
Barbarella *
France/Italy 1967 98m Technicolor Panavision
Marianne/Dino de Laurentiis
🖭 🖥 📺
A beautiful young 40th-century astronaut prevents the positronic ray from getting into the wrong hands.
Campy and slightly sick adventures with angels and other space people, from a highly censorable comic strip; some ingenious gadgetry and design, but not much of interest in the foreground.
w Terry Southern *book* Jean-Claude Forest d Roger Vadim ph Claude Renoir m Bob Crewe, Charles Fox pd Mario Garbuglia
☆ Jane Fonda, John Phillip Law, Anita Pallenberg, Milo O'Shea, David Hemmings, Marcel Marceau, Ugo Tognazzi, Claude Dauphin
'A leading science fiction authority has claimed that if Lewis Carroll were alive today he would

inevitably have written not *Alice's Adventures in Wonderland* but *Lolita*. He might perhaps equally well have written *Barbarella*.' – *Jack Ibberson*
'A flaccid, jaded appeal to our baser appetites, always liberally doused with essence of cop-out, resulting in elucubrated, anaemic pornography.' – *John Simon*

The Barbarian

US   1933   82m   bw
MGM
GB title: *A Night in Cairo*
An American lady travelling in the Middle East falls for a local potentate.
Shades of The Sheik *(qv). Actually this version was first filmed in 1915 by Edgar Selwyn from his own play, then again in 1924. Any version would seem fairly hysterical now.*
w Anita Loos, Elmer Harris *play* Edgar Selwyn d Sam Wood *ph* Harold Rosson
☆ Ramon Novarro, Myrna Loy, Reginald Denny, C. Aubrey Smith, Louise Closser Hale, Edward Arnold
'An abrupt switch to melodrama at the halfway mark makes this a maudlin, doubtful desert melodrama.' – *Variety*

The Barbarian and the Geisha *

US   1958   105m   Eastmancolor
Cinemascope
TCF (Eugene Frenke)
📺 🇺🇸 📼 💿
In 1856 the first US diplomat to visit Japan meets local opposition but is helped by a geisha.
Episodic semi-historical romance which scarcely suits the talents of those involved.
w Charles Grayson d John Huston *ph* Charles G. Clarke m Hugo Friedhofer
☆ John Wayne, Eiko Ando, Sam Jaffe, So Yamamura
'It is saddening to think that the director of *The Asphalt Jungle* has gained professional freedom and international celebrity to become, at 51, yet another taskmaster who goes out in the midday sun.' – *Arlene Croce*

Barbarian Queen

US   1985   82m   colour
Concorde/Rodeo (Frank Isaac, Alex Sessa)
📺 🇺🇸
When their men are kidnapped, women warriors go on the warpath.
One of the reasons that the fad for films of the sword and sorcery genre was so short-lived – muscle-bound men and scantily clad women of minimal acting ability are not enough to attract an audience.
d Hector Olivera *ph* Rudy Donovan m Chris Young, Jamie Horner *pd* Julia Bertram *ed* Sylvia Roberts, Leslie Rosenthal *sp* Willy Smith, Arny Alfieri
☆ Lana Clarkson, Katt Shea, Frank Eugarino, Dawn Dunlap, Susana Traverso, Victor Bo, Arman Chapman, Andrea Barbizon
† A sequel of even less interest, *Barbarian Queen 2*, directed by Joe Finley, followed in 1988.

The Barbarians

US/Italy   1987   88m   colour
Cannon (John Thompson)
📺 🇺🇸 💿 🎧
In a primitive world, twin musclemen take on warring tribes and wizards to rescue their queen.
Dim-witted sword and sorcery movie that never rises above the risible.
w James R. Silke d Ruggero Deodato *ph* Lorenzo Battaglia m Pino Donaggio *pd* Giuseppe Mangano *ed* Eugene Alabiso
☆ David Paul, Peter Paul, Richard Lynch, Eva La Rue, Virginia Bryant, Sheeba Alahani, Michael Berryman, Nanni Bernini

Barbarosa *

US   1981   90m   Eastmancolor
ITC/Wittliff-Nelson-Busey (Paul N. Lazarus III)
🇺🇸 💿
An outlaw's legend grows along with his enemies.
Undercast but interestingly directed Western, with more than enough elegiac qualities mixed with some nods to the old enjoyable style.
w William D. Wittliff d Fred Schepisi *ph* Ian Baker m Bruce Smeaton
☆ Willie Nelson, Gary Busey, Isela Vega, Gilbert Roland, George Voskovec
'The most spirited and satisfying new western epic in several years.' – *New Yorker*
'More than its share of artistic merit.' – *Variety*

Barbary Coast **

US   1935   91m   bw
Samuel Goldwyn
📺 🇺🇸
During San Francisco's gold rush days a ruthless club owner builds a lonely girl into a star attraction but cannot win her love.
Juicy melodrama tailored for its stars, but with excellent background detail, sets and lighting.
w Ben Hecht, Charles MacArthur d Howard Hawks *ph* Ray June m Alfred Newman
☆ Edward G. Robinson, Miriam Hopkins, Joel McCrea, Walter Brennan, Frank Craven, Brian Donlevy, Donald Meek
'More than a year ago Sam Goldwyn picked Barbary Coast as a title and called in Hecht and MacArthur to write a story to fit. Result is a picture that has all it takes to get along in thoroughbred company.' – *Variety*
† David Niven made his first screen appearance as an extra.
🎞 Ray June

Barbary Coast Gent

US   1944   87m   bw
MGM (Orville Dull)
A bandit from the Californian goldfields tries to go straight in San Francisco.
Star comedy drama, somewhat below par despite attractive settings and good production.
w William Lipman, Grant Garrett, Harry Ruskin d Roy del Ruth *ph* Charles Salerno Jnr m David Snell
☆ Wallace Beery, Binnie Barnes, Frances Rafferty, Chill Wills, Ray Collins, John Carradine, Noah Beery, Morris Ankrum, Henry O'Neill, Donald Meek, Paul Hurst, Louise Beavers

Barbed Wire *

US   1927   85m   bw   silent
Paramount
A French girl falls for a German prisoner of war.
Almost forgotten war film which seems at least worthy of comparison with All Quiet on the Western Front *(qv), which was made three years later.*
w Jules Furthman and Rowland V. Lee *novel* The Woman of Knockaloe *by* Hall Caine d Rowland V. Lee *ph* Bert Glennon
☆ Pola Negri, Clive Brook, Einar Hanson, Claude Gillingwater, Gustav von Seyffertitz

'Americans. Anti-Americans. In love.'
Barcelona *

US   1994   101m   Technicolor
Rank/Castle Rock//Westerly (Whit Stillman)
📺 🇺🇸 💿 🎧
In the mid-1980s, two American cousins find that life and love in Spain are fraught with problems.
A leisurely exploration of cultural and racial differences that is intermittently interesting but not always convincing; it consists of a great deal of talk about not very much.
wd Whit Stillman *ph* John Thomas m Mark Suozzo *pd* José Mareia Botines *ed* Christopher Tellefsen
☆ Taylor Nichols, Chris Eigeman, Tushka Bergen, Mira Sorvino, Hellena Schmied, Pep Munne, Nuria Badia, Francis Creighton
'Although the picture begins promisingly, its charm peters out fast. Every scene seems to make the same not very interesting point: that Americans get a bum rap from foreigners.' – *Terrence Rafferty, New Yorker*
'The city of Barcelona looks beautiful, but everything in the movie is negligent, underdeveloped, unfelt.' – *David Denby, New York*

Bardelys the Magnificent

US   1926   88m   bw   silent
MGM
A 16th-century French adventurer finally wins his fair lady.
Laboured swashbuckler.
w Dorothy Farnum *novel* Rafael Sabatini d King Vidor
☆ John Gilbert, Eleanor Boardman, George K. Arthur

The Bare Breasted Countess: see *Female Vampire*

Barefaced Flatfoot ***

US   1952   7m   Technicolor
UPA (Stephen Bosustow)
Mr Magoo battles shortsightedly to save his nephew from the underworld.
Archetypal Magoo cartoon. ('Didn't we meet in Heidelberg?' he murmurs to the dummy he is duelling with his umbrella.) The title is a spoof on a contemporary Columbia movie, The Barefoot Mailman (qv).
pd John Hubley

'The world's most beautiful animal!'
The Barefoot Contessa *

US   1954   128m   Technicolor
UA/Figaro (Forrest E. Johnston)
📺 🇺🇸
A glamorous barefoot dancer in a Spanish cabaret is turned into a Hollywood star, but her sexual frustrations lead to a tragic end.
A fascinating farrago of addled philosophy and lame wisecracks, very typical of a writer-director here not at his best, decorated by a splendid gallery of actors and some attractive settings.
wd Joseph L. Mankiewicz *ph* Jack Cardiff m Mario Nascimbene
☆ Humphrey Bogart, Ava Gardner, Edmond O'Brien, Marius Goring, Valentina Cortesa, Rossano Brazzi, Elizabeth Sellars, Warren Stevens, Franco Interlenghi, Mari Aldon
HARRY: 'Life, every now and then, behaves as though it had seen too many bad movies, when everything fits too well – the beginning, the middle, the end – from fade-in to fade-out.'
'This example of the Higher Lunacy must vie with *Johnny Guitar* for the silliest film of the year.' – *Gavin Lambert*
'A trash masterpiece: a Cinderella story in which the prince turns out to be impotent.' – *Pauline Kael, 1968*
🏆 Edmond O'Brien
🎞 Joseph L. Mankiewicz (as writer)

The Barefoot Executive *

👪 US   1970   96m   Technicolor
Walt Disney (Bill Anderson)
A TV network discovers that its most infallible average viewer is a chimpanzee.
Quite a beguiling little farcical comedy with mild doses of satire.
w Joseph L. McEveety d Robert Butler *ph* Charles F. Wheeler m Robert F. Brunner
☆ Kurt Russell, Harry Morgan, Joe Flynn, Wally Cox, Heather North, Alan Hewitt, Hayden Rorke

'Break the rules! Make love! Fall over laughing!'
Barefoot in the Park **

US   1967   105m   Technicolor
Paramount/Hal B. Wallis
📺 🇺🇸 💿
A pair of New York newlyweds rent a cold water flat at the top of a liftless building, and manage to marry the bride's mother to an eccentric neighbour.
Breezy but overlong adaptation of a stage play which succeeded through audience response to its one-liners, which on the screen sometimes fall flat. The people are nice, though.
w Neil Simon *play* Neil Simon d Gene Saks *ph* Joseph LaShelle m Neal Hefti
☆ Robert Redford, Jane Fonda, Mildred Natwick, Charles Boyer, Herb Edelman, Mabel Albertson, Fritz Feld
ETHEL: 'Make him feel important. If you do that, you'll have a happy and wonderful marriage – like two out of every ten couples.'
ETHEL: 'I feel like we've died and gone to heaven – only we had to climb up.'
🎞 Mildred Natwick

The Barefoot Mailman

US   1951   82m   Supercinecolor
Columbia (Robert Cohn)
In 19th-century Florida, the mailman is joined by a confidence trickster who later has a change of heart.
Inept comedy adventure which never really gets started.
w James Gunn, Francis Swann *novel* Theodore Pratt d Earl McEvoy *ph* Ellis W. Carter m George Duning
☆ Robert Cummings, Jerome Courtland, Terry Moore, John Russell, Will Geer, Arthur Shields, Trevor Bardette

† This is the title parodied by the Mr Magoo cartoon *Barefaced Flatfoot (qv)*.

Barfly *

US   1987   99m   TVC Color
Cannon/Barbet Schroeder, Fred Roos, Tom Luddy
📺 🇺🇸 💿
A self-styled poet of the bottle lords it over a Los Angeles bar.
Unrelieved serio-comic wallow in the underside of American life. For connoisseurs and idiots as well as star fans.
w Charles Bukowski d Barbet Schroeder *ph* Robby Muller m none *pd* Bob Ziembicki
☆ Mickey Rourke, Faye Dunaway, Alice Krige, Jack Nance

The Bargee *

GB   1964   106m   Techniscope
AB/Galton-Simpson (W. A. Whitaker)
📺
A canal barge Casanova is trapped into marriage.
The long-awaited comedy which was supposed to make a film star out of TV's Young Steptoe turned out to be rough and vulgar but not very funny.
w Ray Galton, Alan Simpson d Duncan Wood *ph* Harry Waxman m Frank Cordell
☆ Harry H. Corbett, Ronnie Barker, Hugh Griffith, Eric Sykes, Julia Foster, Miriam Karlin, Eric Barker, Derek Nimmo, Norman Bird, Richard Briers

Baritone **

Poland   1984   96m   colour
PRF Zespoly Filmowe/Zespol Perspektywa (Barbara Pec-Slesicka)
original title: *Baryton*
In the early 1930s a famous Polish opera singer returns home after 25 years, only to lose his voice before a celebratory concert.
Zestful satiric portrayal of egomania and doublecross, set against the rise of Nazism.
w Feliks Falk d Janusz Zaorski *ph* Witold Adamek m Jerzy Satanowski *ad* Allan Starski *ed* Halina Pruga-Ketling
☆ Zbigniew Zapasiewicz, Piotr Fronczewski, Janusz Błyczyński, Marcin Troński, Malgorzata Pieczyńska, Zofia Saretok

The Barkleys of Broadway *

US   1949   109m   Technicolor
MGM (Arthur Freed)
📺 🇺🇸 💿 🎧
A quarrelling couple of musical comedy stars split up, and she becomes a serious actress.
A rather flat and unattractive reunion for a famous pair, with a witless script, poorish numbers and very little style. The compensations are minor.
w Adolph Green, Betty Comden d Charles Walters *ph* Harry Stradling m/ly Harry Warren, Ira Gershwin *md* Lennie Hayton
☆ Fred Astaire, Ginger Rogers, Oscar Levant, Jacques François, Billie Burke
† Ginger Rogers was in fact second choice; Judy Garland was cast but withdrew through illness.
🎞 Harry Stradling

Barnabo of the Mountains

France/Italy/Switzerland   1994   124m   colour
Artificial Eye/Nautilus/Number One/Flach/RAI-1 (Tommaso Dazzi, Gabriella Lazzoni)
original title: *Barnabo della Montagne*
In the early 20s, a mountain ranger with pacifist tendencies is sacked for failing to shoot at some murderous poachers and, after much wandering, returns to the mountains.
More a celebration of the Dolomites than an exploration of character, this is a film where little happens, very slowly; its mainly amateur cast are required only to register rock-like characteristics and to blend with the magnificence of the landscape.
w Angelo Pasquini, Mario Brenta, Francesco Alberti, Enrico Soci *novel* Dino Buzzati d Mario Brenta *ph* Vincenzo Marano m Stefano Caprioli *ad* Giorgio Bertolini *ed* Roberto Missiroli
☆ Marco Pauletti, Alessandra Milan, Marco Tonin, Duilo Fontana, Carlo Caserotti, Antonio Vecellio, Angelo Chiesura
'This sort of art movie is easy to mock. And hardly for the likes of those who enjoy the familiar narrative drive and special effects driven melodramas that cram the cinemas.' – *Derek Malcolm, Guardian*

'Like watching three coats of paint dry.' – *Independent*

Barnaby and Me

Australia 1977 90m colour
ABC/Force Ten/Transatlantic (Matthew N. Herman)

A koala recalls how an American con man disrupted the lives of an Australian family.
Affable but silly family comedy that relies too heavily on the skills of Caesar to provide some amusement and features a koala with a heavy American accent.
w James Henderson d Norman Panama ph Peter Hendry m Brian May ad George Liddle ed Tim Wellburn
☆ Sid Caesar, Juliet Mills, Sally Boyden, Hugh Keays-Byrne, Rangi Nicholls, James Condon, Kenneth Laird, Bruce Spence, Daws Butler (voice)

Barnacle Bill

US 1941 90m bw
MGM (Milton Bren)
A fishing boat skipper gets romantic in the hope of financing his enterprises.
Adequate waterfront comedy on Min and Bill lines, consolidating a popular star teaming.
w Jack Jevne, Hugo Butler d Richard Thorpe ph Clyde de Vinna m Bronislau Kaper
☆ Wallace Beery, Marjorie Main, Leo Carrillo, Virginia Weidler, Donald Meek, Barton MacLane, Connie Gilchrist, Sara Haden
♫ 'They Can't Take That Away from Me', 'Shoes with Wings On', 'My One and Only Highland Fling', 'Swing Trot', 'Manhattan Downbeat', 'You'd Be So Hard to Replace', 'A Weekend in the Country', 'Sabre Dance'

Barnacle Bill *

GB 1957 87m bw
Ealing (Michael Balcon)
US title: *All at Sea*
The last of a long line of sailors suffers from seasickness, and takes command of a decaying Victorian pier at an English seaside resort.
Quite an amusing comedy which had the misfortune to come at the tag-end of the Ealing classics and so seemed too mild and predictable. Perhaps it was a little staid.
w T. E. B. Clarke d Charles Frend ph Douglas Slocombe m John Addison
☆ Alec Guinness, Irene Browne, Percy Herbert, Harold Goodwin, Maurice Denham, George Rose, Lionel Jeffries, Victor Maddern

Barney's Great Adventure

US 1998 75m DeLuxe
Polygram/Lyrick (Sheryl Leach, Dennis DeShazer)

With the aid of a toy that turns into a lifesize dinosaur, two children hunt for a special egg.
A tacky film for children about an irrepressibly cheerful purple dinosaur, whose appeal is less than universal.
w Stephen White d Steve Gomer ph Sandi Sissel ch Debra Brown pd Vincent Jefferds ed Richard Halsey sp Cinemotion Pictures
☆ George Hearn, Shirley Douglas, Trevor Morgan, Kyla Pratt, Diana Rice, David Joyner, Bob West

'No film could have a higher must-see rating among the 2-to-5-year-old target audience.' – *Variety*

Barocco *

France 1976 105m Eastmancolor
La Boétie/Sara (André Génovès, Alain Sarde)

A woman manipulates the killer of her boyfriend, murdered for his part in a political scandal, into becoming the double of the dead man.
A stylized, stylish thriller that hovers on the edge of parody, it is enjoyable to watch, even though its narrative is sometimes difficult to follow.
w André Téchiné, Marilyn Goldin d André Téchiné ph Bruno Nuytten m Philippe Sarde ad Ferdinando Scarfiotti ed Claudine Merlin
☆ Isabelle Adjani, Gérard Depardieu, Marie-France Pisier, Hélène Surgère, Jean-François Stevenin, Julien Guiomar, Claude Brasseur, Jean-Claude Brialy

Baron Blood (dubbed)

Italy/West Germany 1972 92m Technicolor
Leone International/Cinevision (Alfred Leone)

original title: *Gli Orrori del Castello di Norimberga*
aka: *Chamber of Tortures; The Thirst of Baron Blood; The Torture Chamber of Baron Blood*
In Austria, an American student brings back to life his sadistic 300-year-old ancestor, who resumes his old pastime of torturing the locals.
Dull, unimaginative and lurid horror; in which the director's penchant for pointless zooms detracts from his attempts at atmosphere; an occasional chase sequence reveals what might have been, if those involved had been more committed or if its stars had bothered to act.
w Vincent Fotre, William A. Bairn d Mario Bava ph Antonio Rinaldi m Stelvio Cipriani ad Enzo Bulgarelli ed Carlo Reali sp Franco Tocci
☆ Joseph Cotten, Elke Sommer, Massimo Girotti, Rada Rassimov, Antonio Cantafora, Humi Raho, Alan Collins, Dieter Tressler

Le Baron Fantôme *

France 1943 100m bw
Consortium de Productions de Films (Robert Florat)
GB title: *The Phantom Baron*
In the early 19th century, the disappearance of a nobleman causes problems for his heirs.
Macabre fairy tale with effective scenes which seem to relate to Cocteau's later fantasies; the film as a whole is less effective.
wd Serge de Poligny ph Roger Hubert m Louis Beydts narrator Jean Cocteau
☆ Jany Holt, Odette Joyeux, Alain Cuny, Gabrielle Dorziat

Baron Münchhausen *

Czechoslovakia 1962 81m Agfacolor
Ceskoslovensky Film

original title: *Baron Prasil*
An astronaut finds on the moon the famous liar Baron Münchhausen, who takes him back to Earth and a variety of exaggerated adventures.
Amusing variation on the old stories, using live action against deliberately artificial backgrounds.
wd Karel Zeman novel Gottfried Burger (illustrations by Gustave Doré) ph Jiri Tarantik m Zdenek Liska
☆ Milos Kopecky, Rudolf Jelinek, Jana Becjchova

The Baron of Arizona

US 1950 85m bw
Lippert (Carl Hittleman)

In the 19th century a clerk tries to claim the whole of Arizona by false land grants.
Initially appealing but basically rather feeble tall tale, ineffectively worked out and decidedly undernourished as a production.
wd Samuel Fuller ph James Wong Howe m Paul Dunlap
☆ Vincent Price, Ellen Drew, Beulah Bondi, Vladimir Sokoloff, Reed Hadley, Robert Barrat

Baron Prasil: see Baron Münchhausen

The Baroness and the Butler

US 1938 75m bw
TCF (Raymond Griffith)
The Hungarian prime minister's butler is loved by a princess.
Thin mittel-European romantic star whimsy.
w Sam Hellman, Lamar Trotti, Kathryn Scola play *The Lady Has a Heart* by Ladislaus Bus-Fekete d Walter Lang ph Arthur Miller md Louis Silvers
☆ William Powell, Annabella, Henry Stephenson, Nigel Bruce, Helen Westley, Joseph Schildkraut, J. Edward Bromberg, Lynn Bari

Barquero!

US 1970 114m DeLuxe
Aubrey Schenck (Hal Klein)
A Western ferryman is taken prisoner by bandits but turns the tables.
Long, violent, rather uninteresting Western in the Spanish manner.
w George Schenck, William Marks d Gordon Douglas ph Jerry Finnerman m Dominic Frontiere
☆ Lee Van Cleef, Forrest Tucker, Warren Oates, Kerwin Mathews, Mariette Hartley, Brad Weston, John Davis Chandler

'When poets love, heaven and earth fall back to watch!'

The Barretts of Wimpole Street **

US 1934 109m bw
MGM (Irving Thalberg)

TV title: *Forbidden Alliance*
Invalid Elizabeth Barrett plans to marry poet Robert Browning, against her tyrannical father's wishes.
Claustrophobic but well-acted adaptation of a stage play which has become more forceful than history. Stilted now, but still better than the remake.
w Ernst Vajda, Claudine West, Donald Ogden Stewart play Rudolf Besier d Sidney Franklin ph William Daniels m Herbert Stothart
☆ Norma Shearer, Fredric March, Charles Laughton, Maureen O'Sullivan, Katherine Alexander, Una O'Connor, Ralph Forbes, Ian Wolfe
  'Box office for all its celluloid lethargy ... truly an actor's picture, with long speeches and verbose philosophical observations.' – *Variety*
  ஃ best picture; Norma Shearer

The Barretts of Wimpole Street

GB 1956 105m Metrocolor Cinemascope
MGM (Sam Zimbalist)
Dreadful, miscast remake of the above, with emphasis on the Freudian father-daughter relationship.
An unattractive and boring film.
w John Dighton d Sidney Franklin ph Frederick A. Young m Bronislau Kaper
☆ Jennifer Jones, Bill Travers, John Gielgud, Virginia McKenna
  'That rarity – a remake of an established Hollywood classic that is exceptionally fine in every respect.' – *New York Times*

Barricade

US 1939 71m bw
TCF (Edward Kaufman)
A newsman and a girl with a past fight Mongolian bandits in North China.
A bagful of clichés which does not quite add up to entertainment.
w Granville Walker d Gregory Ratoff ph Karl Freund m David Buttolph
☆ Warner Baxter, Alice Faye, Charles Winninger, Arthur Treacher, Keye Luke, Willie Fung, Doris Lloyd
  'Inadequate and confusing ... it was launched as an A, but winds up as a B that will have to groove generally in the supporting spots.' – *Variety*

Barricade

US 1949 75m Technicolor
Warner (Saul Elkins)
A tough mine-owner who runs a camp miles from civilization meets his come-uppance when three strangers are forced to accept his hospitality.
Rough Western only notable as an (almost) scene-for-scene steal from The Sea Wolf (qv): a text-book adaptation.
w William Sackheim d Peter Godfrey ph Carl Guthrie m William Lava
☆ Raymond Massey, Dane Clark, Ruth Roman, Robert Douglas, Morgan Farley

The Barrier

US 1926 79m bw silent
MGM
A brutal sea captain tries to prevent his protégé's marriage.
Brooding melodrama climaxing in an Alaskan storm. It was Barrymore's first film for the studio where he spent the rest of his career.
w Rex Beach d George Hill
☆ Lionel Barrymore, Henry B. Walthall, Marceline Day, Norman Kerry

The Barrier

US 1937 90m bw
Paramount/Harry Sherman
A gold rush prospector kidnaps a child and brings her up in the belief that she is a half-breed.
Lyceum-like melodrama against spectacular natural settings; somehow not of interest.
w Bernard Schubert, Mordaunt Shairp, Harrison Jacobs novel Rex Beach d Lesley Selander
☆ Leo Carrillo, Jean Parker, Robert Barrat, James Ellison, Otto Kruger, Andy Clyde, Addison Richards, Sara Haden

Barry Lyndon **

GB 1975 187m Eastmancolor
Warner/Hawk/Peregrine (Stanley Kubrick)

Adventures of an 18th-century Irish gentleman of fortune.
A curiously cold-hearted enterprise, like an art gallery in which the backgrounds are sketched in loving detail and the human figures totally neglected; there is much to enjoy, but script and acting are variable to say the least, and the point of it all is obscure, as it certainly does not tell a rattling good story.
wd Stanley Kubrick novel W. M. Thackeray ph John Alcott md Leonard Rosenman pd Ken Adam
☆ Ryan O'Neal, Marisa Berenson, Patrick Magee, Hardy Kruger, Steven Berkoff, Gay Hamilton, Marie Kean, Murray Melvin, André Morell, Leonard Rossiter, Philip Stone, Michael Hordern
  'The motion picture equivalent of one of these very large, very expensive, very elegant and very dull books that exist solely to be seen on coffee tables.' – *Charles Champlin*
  'Watching the movie is like looking at illustrations for a work that has not been supplied.' – *John Simon*
  'All art and no matter: a series of still pictures which will please the retina while denying our hunger for drama. And far from re-creating another century, it more accurately embalms it.' – *Michael Billington, Illustrated London News*
  ⚱ John Alcott; Leonard Rosenman; Ken Adam; costumes (Britt Soderlund, Milena Canonero)
  ஃ best picture; Stanley Kubrick (as writer); Stanley Kubrick (as director)
  Ⓣ Stanley Kubrick (as director); John Alcott

Barry McKenzie Holds His Own

Australia 1974 98m Eastmancolor
Panavision
EMI/Reg Grundy (Bruce Beresford)

The twin nephews of Edna Everage, an Australian housewife, go to her rescue when she is mistaken for the Queen and kidnapped by Transylvanians.
Coarse slapstick comedy of a deliberately tasteless kind.
w Barry Humphries, Bruce Beresford d Bruce Beresford ph Don McAlpine m Peter Best pd John Stoddart ed William Anderson
☆ Barry Crocker, Barry Humphries, Donald Pleasence, Dick Bentley, Ed Devereaux, Tommy Trinder, Frank Windsor, Deryck Guyler, Arthur English, Roy Kinnear, John Le Mesurier

Bartleby *

GB 1970 79m Eastmancolor
Pantheon (Rodney Carr-Smith)

A young clerk gradually refuses to take part in life.
A non-action film from an independent source, praiseworthy but overlong and fairly lacking in any kind of appeal except to literary connoisseurs.
w Anthony Friedmann, Rodney Carr-Smith story Herman Melville d Anthony Friedmann ph Ian Wilson m Roger Webb
☆ Paul Scofield, John McEnery, Thorley Walters, Colin Jeavons

'There's Only One Thing Stranger Than What's Going On Inside His Head. What's Going On Outside.'
'Between Heaven and Hell there's always Hollywood.'

Barton Fink ***

US 1991 116m colour
Rank/Circle (Ethan Coen)

In the 1940s an intellectual left-wing playwright goes to work in Hollywood, where he is told to write a wrestling picture for Wallace Beery.
What begins as a satire on the film industry, with a central character owing much to Clifford Odets, turns halfway through into something darker and more disturbing, a dizzying trip inside two disturbed minds.
w Ethan and Joel Coen d Joel Coen m Carter Burwell pd Dennis Gassner ed Roderick Jaynes
☆ John Turturro, John Goodman, Judy Davis, Michael Lerner, John Mahoney, Tony Shalhoub, Jon Polito, Steve Buscemi
  'Scene after scene is filled with a ferocious strength and humour.' – *Variety*
  † The film took an unprecedented three prizes at the 1991 Cannes Film Festival: Palme d'Or for best film, best actor (John Turturro) and best director.
  ஃ Michael Lerner; Dennis Gassner

Baryton: see *Baritone*

Bas Ya Bahar: see *La Mer Cruelle*

BASEketball

US   1998   103m   DeLuxe
Universal (David Zucker, Robert LoCash, Gil Netter)

Two basketball players invent a new variation on the game, in which teams can insult one another and try to unsettle opposing players.
Broad comedy which sends up the clichés of sports movies without managing to be particularly amusing.
w David Zucker, Robert LoCash, Lewis Friedman, Jeff Wright *d* David Zucker *ph* Steve Mason *m* James Ira Newborn *pd* Steven Jordan *ed* Jeffrey Reiner
☆ Trey Parker, Matt Stone, Yasmine Bleeth, Jenny McCarthy, Robert Vaughn, Ernest Borgnine, Dian Bachar
'The broad, bawdy antics onscreen will be a slam-dunk at the box office.' – *Leonard Klady, Variety*

Les Bas-fonds *

France   1936   92m   bw
Albatros (Alexander Kamenka)
aka: *The Lower Depths*
A clash of temperaments flares up between derelicts in a dosshouse.
Uneven transposition of a famous work, with patches of good acting.
w Jean Renoir, Charles Spaak and others *play* Maxim Gorky *d* Jean Renoir *ph* Jean Bachelet *m* Jean Wiener
☆ Jean Gabin, Louis Jouvet, Vladimir Sokoloff, Robert Le Vigan, Suzy Prim

'Flesh seduces. Passion kills.'
Basic Instinct *

US   1991   128m   Technicolor   Panavision
Guild/Carolco/Canal (Alan Marshall)

A violent, suspended detective falls in love with the chief suspect in a murder investigation, a bisexual millionairess whose latest novel contains a detailed description of a similar killing.
Overheated, overlong melodramatic thriller with an implausible plot that requires its audience to accept that Michael Douglas is irresistibly attractive to bisexual women. But the skill and pace of the direction makes one regret that they were not exercised on better material.
w Joe Esterhas *d* Paul Verhoeven *ph* Jan de Bont *m* Jerry Goldsmith *pd* Terence Marsh *ed* Frank J. Urioste *sp* Rob Bottin
☆ Michael Douglas, Sharon Stone, George Dzundza, Jeanne Tripplehorn, Denis Arndt, Leilani Sarelle, Dorothy Malone
'Saddled with extremely unattractive characters, vile dialogue and sex that appeals only to your baser instincts.' – *Jami Bernard, New York Post*
'The film falls down simply because its three-million-dollar script is just a gimmick, an unfeeling house of cards which falls apart when the loopholes and logical flaws that sustain the ambiguous resolution come to light.' – *Kim Newman, Sight and Sound*
'An outrageous film, a great big rubbishy sort of popcorn Saturday night movie with bags of sex and violence, blokes being blokes and ice-cool blondes being just that, and even a couple of quite stupendous car chases thrown in just for old times' sake.' – *Empire*
⬧ Jerry Goldsmith; editing

Basil, The Great Mouse Detective: see *The Great Mouse Detective*

'The Tenant In Room Seven Is Very Small, Very Twisted And Very Mad.'
Basket Case

US   1982   93m   TVC Color
Alpha (Edgar Ievins)

Siamese twins, one a tiny, deformed creature, take revenge on the doctors who separated them.
Grisly, jokey, low-budget horror that gained a cult following.
wd Frank Henenlotter *ph* Bruce Torbet *m* Gus Russo *ad* Frederick Loren *ed* Frank Henenlotter
☆ Kevin Van Hentenryck, Terri Susan Smith, Beverly Bonner, Robert Vogel, Diana Browne, Lloyd Pace

Basket Case 2

US   1990   90m   TVC Color
Medusa/Shapiro, Glickenhaus Entertainment/Ievins-Henenlotter (Edgar Ievins)

Twins, one of them a deformed creature in a basket, take refuge in a community of freaks.
Tediously grotesque comedy.
wd Frank Henenlotter *ph* Robert M. Baldwin *m* Joe Renzetti *pd* Michael P. Moran *ad* Daniel Ouellette *ed* Kevin Tent
☆ Kevin Van Hentenryck, Judy Grafe, Annie Ross, Heather Rattray, Chad Brown, Beverly Bonner, Leonard Jackson, Alexandra Auder
'Henenlotter seems unsure whether to play his outré offerings for laughs, shocks or sympathy, and this remains an uncertain (and somewhat unnecessary) sequel to a sure-footed original.' – *MFB*

'It's Time To Build A Bigger Basket!'
Basket Case 3: The Progeny

US   1992   90m   TVC Color
Shapiro, Glickenhaus (Edgar Ievins)

A deformed twin becomes a father of monsters, but has to battle to protect them from the forces of law and order.
The mixture much as before, only of interest to fans of cheap horror.
w Frank Henenlotter, Robert Martin *d* Frank Henenlotter *ph* Bob Paone *m* Joe Renzetti *pd* William Barclay *ed* Greg Sheldon *sp* creature effects: Gabe Bartalos, David Kindlon
☆ Annie Ross, Kevin Van Hentenryck, Dan Biggers, Gil Roper, Tina Louise Hilbert, James O'Doherty
'The flick's fast pace, perverse tone, clever dialog and suitably grotesque cartoon-styled gore make it a legit treat for frightcoms.' – *New York Daily News*
'Henenlotter's mix of wild over-acting, cartoon color scheme and heavy-handed message regarding tolerance is tough to take for the uninitiated.' – *Variety*

'The true story of the death of innocence and the birth of an artist...'
The Basketball Diaries *

US   1995   102m   Technicolor
New Line/Island (Liz Heller)

A rebellious teenager at a Catholic school becomes a heroin addict, prostitute and thief.
The precocious Carroll's diaries might have once caused a minor sensation, but their attitudinizing romanticism has palled, and there is little of value to be found in the lower depths as depicted here, in a bio-pic that gives little indication of a specific time or place for its action.
w Bryan Goluboff *book* Jim Carroll *d* Scott Kalvert *ph* David Phillips *m* Graeme Revell *pd* Christopher Nowak *ed* Dana Congdon
☆ Leonardo DiCaprio, Bruno Kirby, Lorraine Bracco, Ernie Hudson, Patrick McGaw, James Madio, Mark Wahlberg, Michael Rapaport
'It has lost its uniquely disturbing quality by being relocated by director Scott Kalvert in present-day New York, where the incidents are now simply a string of junkie clichés.' – *Alexander Walker*
† DiCaprio took over the leading role after River Phoenix died of a drug overdose.

Basquiat *

US   1996   106m   DuArt
Guild/Eleventh Street/Miramax (Jon Kilik, Randy Ostrow, Sigurjon Sighvatsson)

A graffiti artist gains a mainstream reputation, but succumbs to drug addiction.
Biopic of Jean-Michel Basquiat, who died in 1988 at the age of 27; it has its moments, yet the story is told in a cautious manner, and displays little insight into his extraordinary career and the environment which nurtured and, possibly, destroyed him.
wd Julian Schnabel *story* Lech Majewski, John Bowe *ph* Ron Fortunato *m* John Cale *pd* Dan Leigh *ed* Michael Berenbaum
☆ Jeffrey Wright, David Bowie, Dennis Hopper, Gary Oldman, Claire Forlani, Michael Wincott, Parker Posey, Elina Löwensohn, Willem Dafoe, Tatum O'Neal, Benicio Del Toro, Christopher Walken, Courtney Love, Paul Bartel
'Decently modest, though decidedly unexciting.' – *Variety*

† Basquiat's estate refused permission for his paintings to be used in the film. Those shown were painted by Schnabel.

'When it flies, someone dies!'
The Bat

US   1959   78m   bw
AA/Liberty (C. J. Tevlin)

A lady mystery writer rents a spooky old house and finds herself and her guests at the mercy of a maniac in search of hidden loot.
Poor remake of a standard twenties stage thriller; everyone chews the scenery.
wd Crane Wilbur *play* Mary Roberts Rinehart *ph* Joseph Biroc *m* Louis Forbes
☆ Vincent Price, Agnes Moorehead, Gavin Gordon, John Sutton, Lenita Lane, Darla Hood

Bat 21 **

US   1988   105m   DeLuxe
Tri-Star/Vision/Eagle (David Fisher, Gary A. Neill, Michael Balson)

In Vietnam an American pilot attempts to rescue a 53-year-old Air Force missile intelligence expert when he is shot down behind enemy lines.
Effective and suspenseful drama of the muddle and moral expediencies of war, based on a true story.
w William C. Anderson, George Gordon *book* William C. Anderson *d* Peter Markle *ph* Mark Irwin *m* Christopher Young *pd* Vincent Cresciman *ed* Stephen E. Rivkin
☆ Gene Hackman, Danny Glover, Jerry Reed, David Marshall Grant, Clayton Rohner, Erich Anderson, Joe Dorsey

'Greatest all talking thriller!'
The Bat Whispers **

US   1930   82m   bw
UA (Roland West)

Classic early sound version of *The Bat* (qv) by the director of the 1926 silent version.
Excellent use of camera, sets, and unusual models.
wd Roland West *ph* Ray June, Robert Planck
☆ Chester Morris, Una Merkel, Chance Ward, Grayce Hampton, Maude Eburne, Spencer Charters, Gustav von Seyffertitz
† Originally released in a 'wide screen' process.

'The story America will never forget!'
Bataan *

US   1943   114m   bw
MGM (Irving Starr)

Thirteen soldiers holding a bridge against the Japanese die one by one.
Uncredited remake of The Lost Patrol (qv) transposed to the Pacific war, with stereotyped characters and much flagwaving. Very dated, but a big box-office film of its time, despite its studio jungles.
w Robert D. Andrews *d* Tay Garnett *ph* Sidney Wagner *m* Bronislau Kaper
☆ Robert Taylor, George Murphy, Thomas Mitchell, Lloyd Nolan, Lee Bowman, Robert Walker, Desi Arnaz, Barry Nelson, Philip Terry
'Naïve, coarse-grained, primitive, honest, accomplished and true.' – *James Agee*
'One of the most convincing attempts I have ever seen to show a bit of hell on the screen.' – *Observer*

La Bataille du Rail **

France   1945   87m   bw
CGCF

Reconstructions of heroic resistance work by the French railwaymen during World War II.
Reasonably compulsive documentary fiction which was plainly more inspiring at the time than it seems now.
wd René Clément *ph* Henri Alekan *m* Yves Baudrier
☆ Salina, Daurand, Lozach, Tony Laurent
'There is no lingering, no declaiming, no attempt to hide a certain volatile small boy's enjoyment of sabotage (an aspect of resistance never before touched upon), there is a natural unescapable dramatic tension and speed and perfect unostentatious playing by everybody.' – *Richard Winnington*

Bathing Beauty

US   1944   101m   Technicolor
MGM (Jack Cummings)

A songwriter plans to retire and settle down, but his publisher schemes to set his fiancée against him.
Witless, artificial aqua-musical, with plenty of unpersuasive high jinks but no real style despite a capable cast.
w Dorothy Kingsley, Allen Boretz, Frank Waldman *d* George Sidney *ph* Harry Stradling *m* Johnny Green *ch* John Murray Anderson
☆ Esther Williams, Red Skelton, Basil Rathbone, Keenan Wynn, Ethel Smith, Xavier Cugat, Bill Goodwin
'I could not resist the wish that MGM had topped its aquatic climax – a huge pool full of girls, fountains and spouts of flame – by suddenly draining the tank and ending the show with the entire company writhing like goldfish on a rug.' – *James Agee*
♫ 'Faculty Row'; 'Tico Tico'; 'Echo of a Serenade'; 'I Cried for You'; 'Bim Bam Boom'; 'By the Waters of Minnetonka'; 'I've Got a Problem'; 'I'll Take the High Note'

Batman

US   1943   bw   serial: 15 eps
Columbia

With the help of the Boy Wonder, the Caped Crusader battles an enemy underground ring led by Dr Daka.
Reasonably spirited romp marred by the usual tinpot sets.
d Lambert Hillyer
☆ Lewis Wilson, Douglas Croft, J. Carrol Naish, William Austin
† *Batman and Robin* (15 eps) followed in 1948, directed by Spencer Bennet. The leads were played by Robert Lowery and John Duncan: they combated The Wizard with the help of Lyle Talbot as the police commissioner.

Batman *

US   1966   105m   DeLuxe
TCF/Greenlawn/National Periodical Publications (William Dozier)

The cloaked avenger saves an important executive from the clutches of four of the world's most notorious criminals.
Glossy feature version of the old and new serials about the comic strip hero who scurries around in his Batmobile making sure that justice is done. The scriptwriter's invention unfortunately flags halfway, so that despite a fairly sharp production the result is more childish than camp.
w Lorenzo Semple Jnr *d* Leslie Martinson *ph* Howard Schwartz *m* Nelson Riddle
☆ Adam West, Burt Ward, Cesar Romero, Frank Gorshin, Burgess Meredith, Lee Meriwether, Alan Napier, Neil Hamilton

Batman **

US   1989   126m   Technicolor
Warner (Jon Peters, Peter Guber)

A young boy who witnesses his parents' murder grows up to become Batman, a masked and emotionally disturbed vigilante who battles against an arch-criminal known as The Joker.
The campness of earlier versions of the comic-book hero gives way to a gloomier psychological interpretation that loses much of the fun of the original, while the brilliant production design, of a grim, grey Metropolis, overshadows all. Narrative is reduced to a succession of set-pieces.
w Sam Hamm, Warren Skaaren *d* Tim Burton *ph* Roger Pratt *m* Danny Elfman *m/ly* Prince, John L. Nelson *pd* Anton Furst *ed* Ray Lovejoy *sp* John Evans
☆ Michael Keaton, Jack Nicholson, Kim Basinger, Robert Wuhl, Pat Hingle, Billy Dee Williams, Michael Gough, Jack Palance, Jerry Hall
'A moderately entertaining fantasy, with good design, some strong performances and a desperate need of a script doctor.' – *Adam Mars-Jones, Independent*
⬧ best art direction

Batman & Robin

US   1997   130m   Technicolor
Warner (Peter Macgregor-Scott)

Batman thwarts the ambitions of Mr Freeze, a deformed scientist who has to acquire diamonds to survive.

The dullest of the series so far, gaudy but empty of emotional or narrative interest, and the action soon palls.

w Akiva Goldsman d Joel Schumacher ph Stephen Goldblatt m Elliot Goldenthal pd Barbara Ling ed Dennis Virkler sp John Dykstra

☆ George Clooney, Arnold Schwarzenegger, Chris O'Donnell, Uma Thurman, Alicia Silverstone, Michael Gough, Pat Hingle, John Glover, Elle Macpherson, Vivica A. Fox

'A film which tries hard but seldom manages to be anything more than moderately entertaining.' – *Derek Malcolm, Guardian*

† The film grossed some $107m in the US and another $126m elsewhere.

Batman Forever *

US   1995   121m   Technicolor
Warner (Tim Burton, Peter MacGregor-Scott)

With the aid of Robin, Batman battles against criminals Two Face and The Riddler while resisting the temptations of a female psychologist.

A high-camp sequel, with the tone set by the redesigned, ever-more fetishistic Batman costume, the arrival of Robin, and the unrestrained antics of The Riddler; it's fun for much of the time.

w Lee Batchler, Janet Scott Batchler, Akiva Goldsman d Joel Schumacher ph Stephen Goldblatt m Elliot Goldenthal pd Barbara Ling ed Dennis Virkler

☆ Val Kilmer, Tommy Lee Jones, Jim Carrey, Chris O'Donnell, Nicole Kidman, Michael Gough, Pat Hingle, Drew Barrymore, Rene Auberjonois

'It doesn't have much on its mind except emptying yours for two hours.' – *Tom Shone, Sunday Times*

† The film took more than $333m at the box-office worldwide.

⚬ Stephen Goldblatt; sound; sound effect editing

Batman Returns **

US   1992   126m   Technicolor
Warner (Denise Di Novi, Tim Burton)

Batman does battle with Catwoman and The Penguin.

More comic-strip story-telling, done as a succession of set pieces, with the towering design of the city and its sewers overshadowing the performances.

w Daniel Waters story Daniel Waters, Sam Hamm d Tim Burton ph Stefan Czapsky m Danny Elfman pd Bo Welch ed Chris Lebenzon, Bob Badami

☆ Michael Keaton, Danny DeVito, Michelle Pfeiffer, Christopher Walken, Michael Gough, Michael Murphy, Cristi Conaway, Pat Hingle

'Resembles nothing so much as a blacker, spikier but less focused version of a Disney animation feature made flesh.' – *Derek Malcolm, Guardian*

'A blend of playful novelty and reassuring familiarity – a difficult mixture to get right.' – *New Yorker*

⚬ Visual effects; make-up

La Battaglia di Algeri: see The Battle of Algiers

La Battaglia di El Alamein: see The Battle of El Alamein

La Battaglia di Maratona: see The Giant of Marathon

I Battellieri del Volga: see Prisoner of the Volga

Battement de Coeur **

France   1940   100m   bw
Ciné Alliance/Osso

A poor Parisienne joins a school for pickpockets but falls for the ambassador she robs.

Amusing romance later remade in the US as Heartbeat *(qv).*

w Jean Villeme, Max Colpet, Michel Duran d Henri Decoin

☆ Danielle Darrieux, André Luguet, Claude Dauphin, Julien Carette, Saturnin Fabre

'Dauphin fails to rate in hero roles … he lacks personality, is short of stature, and dresses like a bank clerk.' – *Variety*

Batteries Not Included

US   1987   106m   DeLuxe
UIP/Universal (Ronald L. Schwary)

A Manhattan neighbourhood where everyone has problems is helped out by miniature flying saucers with angelic intentions.

Frank Capra would have done it much better.

w Matthew Robbins, Brad Bird, Brent Maddock, S. S. Wilson story Mick Garris d Matthew Robbins ph John McPherson m James Horner pd Ted Haworth ed Cynthia Scheider

☆ Hume Cronyn, Jessica Tandy, Frank McRae, Elizabeth Pena, Michael Carmine

The Battle *

France   1934   85m   bw
Lionofilm (Leon Garganoff)

English language version aka: *Thunder in the East, Hara Kiri*

A Japanese aristocrat urges his wife to befriend an English naval attaché and steal secrets from him; she does, and falls in love.

Stagey but discreet melodrama of the old school, quite well made and acted.

w Nicolas Farkas, Bernard Zimmer, Robert Stevenson novel Claude Farrère d Nicolas Farkas ph Roger Hubert

☆ Charles Boyer, Merle Oberon, John Loder, Betty Stockfeld, Miles Mander

The Battle at Bloody Beach

US   1961   80m   bw   Cinemascope
TCF/API (Richard Maibaum)

GB title: *Battle on the Beach*

Guerrillas fight Japs in the Philippines.

Tedious war melodrama with interludes for an eternal triangle.

w Richard Maibaum, Willard Willingham d Herbert Coleman ph Kenneth Peach m Henry Vars

☆ Audie Murphy, Gary Crosby, Dolores Michaels, Alejandro Rey

Battle Beneath the Earth *

GB   1967   92m   Technicolor
MGM/Reynolds/Vetter (Charles Reynolds)

US title: *Battle Beneath the Sea*

Enemy agents burrow under the US by means of a giant laser.

Agreeable schoolboy science fiction with fair special effects.

w L. Z. Hargreaves d Montgomery Tully ph Kenneth Talbot m Ken Jones sp Tom Howard

☆ Kerwin Mathews, Viviane Ventura, Robert Ayres, Peter Arne, Martin Benson

Battle Beneath the Sea: see Battle Beneath the Earth

Battle Beyond the Stars *

US   1980   104m   Metrocolor
New World/Roger Corman (Ed Carlin)

A small planet hires help to repel invaders.

Impertinent and sometimes amusing space fiction rip-off of Seven Samurai *(qv), with plenty of in-jokes and quite pleasant special effects.*

w John Sayles d Jimmy T. Murakami ph Daniel Lacambre m James Horner ad Jim Cameron, Charles Breen

☆ Richard Thomas, Robert Vaughn, John Saxon, George Peppard, Sam Jaffe, Morgan Woodward, Darlanne Fluegel, Sybil Danning

Battle Circus

US   1952   90m   bw
MGM (Pandro S. Berman)

A patriotic nurse and a disillusioned major fall in love at a mobile army hospital in Korea.

A flat, studio-bound potboiler with miscast stars, bound to provoke hilarity now as a serious version of M*A*S*H.

wd Richard Brooks ph John Alton m Lennie Hayton

☆ Humphrey Bogart, June Allyson, Keenan Wynn, Robert Keith, William Campbell

'It is disappointing that Brooks, whose early work … suggested considerable promise, should have descended to such a glib, uninteresting piece of film-making.' – *MFB*

'The men who fought … The women who waited. And the stolen moments they shared.'

Battle Cry

US   1955   148m   Warnercolor   Cinemascope
Warner (producer not credited)

During World War II, marines endure tough training before combat in Saipan; their sex lives come a close second to the war.

Interminable cheapie epic with both eyes on the box-office: the cast salvages an odd moment or two, but violence of all kinds is the key to the entertainment.

w Leon Uris novel Leon Uris d Raoul Walsh ph Sid Hickox m Max Steiner

☆ Van Heflin, Aldo Ray, Mona Freeman, Dorothy Malone, Raymond Massey, Nancy Olson, James Whitmore, Tab Hunter, Anne Francis, William Campbell

⚬ Max Steiner

The Battle Cry of Peace *

US   1915   120m   bw   silent
Blackton/VIT

Lost film in which New York was invaded by forces of apparently German origin.

It caused great political unrest and was followed by Thomas Ince's Civilization *which took the pacifist point of view.*

w J. Stuart Blackton book Defenceless America by Hudson Maxim d Wilfred North

☆ Charles Richman, L. Rogers Lytton, Charles Kent, James Morrison

The Battle for Anzio: see Anzio

Battle for Music *

GB   1943   87m   bw
Strand Films (Donald Taylor)

The story of the wartime ups and downs of the London Philharmonic Orchestra.

Not many films feature a classical orchestra, and this simple tribute, a mediocre production at best, has considerable historical interest.

w St John L. Clowes d Donald Taylor

☆ Hay Petrie, Joss Ambler, Eileen Carson, Jack Hylton, J. B. Priestley, Eileen Joyce, Moiseiwitch, Sir Adrian Boult, Sir Malcolm Sargent

Battle for Russia ***

US   1943   80m   bw
US Army Signal Corps (Anatole Litvak)

Fifth of Frank Capra's Why We Fight documentaries, and like the others a brilliant compilation of carefully selected footage.

m Dimitri Tiomkin commentary Anthony Veiller

Battle for the Planet of the Apes

US   1973   86m   DeLuxe   Panavision
TCF/APJAC (Frank Capra Jnr)

Following a nuclear war, apes are the only surviving leaders of society, but begin to fight among themselves.

Fifth and last in an increasingly confusing chronology, this is at least more thoughtful than violent.

w John William Corrington, Joyce Hooper Corrington d J. Lee-Thompson ph Richard H. Kline m Leonard Rosenman make-up John Chambers

☆ Roddy McDowall, Claude Akins, John Huston, Natalie Trundy, Severn Darden, Lew Ayres, Paul Williams

† See Planet of the Apes.

Battle Hell: see Yangtse Incident

Battle Hymn

US   1957   108m   Technicolor   Cinemascope
U-I (Ross Hunter)

An American preacher with a guilt complex volunteers to help the South Koreans and after many adventures founds an orphanage.

Earnest, somnolent biopic of one Dean Hess; its mixture of drama, comedy, religion and war heroics is indigestible despite professional handling.

w Charles Grayson, Vincent B. Evans d Douglas Sirk ph Russell Metty m Frank Skinner

☆ Rock Hudson, Anna Kashfi, Dan Duryea, Don Defore, Martha Hyer, Jock Mahoney, James Edwards, Carl Benton Reid

'The film seems to infer that heroic self-sacrifice, a little homely Eastern philosophy and a capacity for combining battle experience with an awareness of spiritual values are enough to overcome all emergencies.' – *John Gillett*

'The Revolt That Stirred The World!'

The Battle of Algiers ****

Algeria/Italy   1965   135m   bw
Casbah/Igor (Antonio Musi, Yacef Saadi)

original title: *La Battaglia di Algeri*

In 1954 Algiers, an ex-convict joins the terrorists in rebellion against the French government.

Politically oriented reconstruction of a bitter period of French colonial history, made better propaganda by its wealth of effective detail.

w Franco Solinas d Gillo Pontecorvo ph Marcello Gatti m Ennio Morricone, Gillo Pontecorvo

☆ Brahim Haggiag, Jean Martin, Yacef Saadi, Tommaso Neri

'An astonishing piece of work in directorial technique processing to achieve not merely a newsreel tempo but a grainy realism unmatched by the average news film and all too rarely approached by even the better ventures into cinema verité. What is equally noteworthy is Pontecorvo's objectivity in showing both the exhilaration and the heart-break of a fight for liberation, with neither the oppressed nor the oppressor able to survive at ease with his conscience.' – *Judith Crist*

⚬ best foreign film; Franco Solinas; Gillo Pontecorvo (as director)

The Battle of Austerlitz: see Austerlitz

Battle of Britain ***

US   1943   52m   bw

Fourth of the Why We Fight series. (See Battle for Russia.)

'It will emerge as one of the vital documents depicting a people's courage when the torch of freedom flickered at its lowest.' – *Variety*

Battle of Britain *

GB   1969   131m   Technicolor   Panavision
UA/Spitfire (Harry Saltzman, Ben Fisz)

Summer 1940: England defends itself against aerial onslaught.

Plodding attempt to cover an historic event from too many angles and with too many guest stars, all indistinguishable from each other when masked in the cockpit during the repetitive and interminable dogfight sequences. On the ground, things are even duller.

w James Kennaway, Wilfred Greatorex d Guy Hamilton ph Frederick A. Young m William Walton, Ron Goodwin

☆ Laurence Olivier, Robert Shaw, Michael Caine, Christopher Plummer, Kenneth More, Susannah York, Trevor Howard, Ralph Richardson, Patrick Wymark, Curt Jurgens, Michael Redgrave, Nigel Patrick, Robert Flemyng, Edward Fox

† The film lost ten million dollars worldwide.

Battle of Broadway

US   1938   84m   bw
TCF

Two American legionnaires at a New York convention try to break up the infatuation of their boss's son with a showgirl.

Amiably rowdy Flagg-and-Quirt imitation.

w Lou Breslow, John Patrick d George Marshall

☆ Victor McLaglen, Brian Donlevy, Gypsy Rose Lee, Raymond Walburn, Lynn Bari, Jane Darwell, Hattie McDaniel

'Flagg and Quirt shenanigans … rowdy, good-natured fun.' – *Variety*

The Battle of City Hall: see The Angels Wash Their Faces

The Battle of El Alamein

Italy/France   1968   105m   Eastmancolor
Cromoscope
Zenith Cinematografica/Les Films Corona (Mino Loy, Luciano Martino)

■

original title: *La Battaglia di El Alamein*
aka: *Desert Tanks*
In June 1942 Italian troops, who have been ordered to beat their German allies to Alexandria, run into British resistance.
The North African campaign as seen from an Italian viewpoint: the Italian troops are gallant and courageous, the British foolish and treacherous, and the Germans coldly inhumane and equally treacherous.
w Ernesto Gastaldi, Remigio Del Grosso d Calvin Jackson Padget (Giorgio Ferroni) ph Sergio D'Offizi m Carlo Rustichelli ed Eugenio Alabiso
☆ Frederick Stafford, George Hilton, Michael Rennie, Robert Hossein, Marco Guglielmi, Ettore Manni, Gérard Herter, Ira Furstenberg, Enrico Maria Salerno
　'An ingenious attempt to whitewash Italy's military record in the last war and to justify her alliance with Germany as part of that lovable Mediterranean characteristic of being "too trusting".' – *Jan Dawson, MFB*

The Battle of Gallipoli: see *Tell England*

The Battle of Midway: see *Midway*

The Battle of Neretva

Yugoslavia/US/Italy/W. Germany   1969   106m
colour   Cinemascope
Jadran-Bosna
■   ∩
In 1943, Yugoslav partisans resist German and Italian invaders.
War spectacular with international cast; despite brilliant handling of the climaxes it didn't travel.
w Ugo Pirro and others d Veljko Bulajic
☆ Yul Brynner, Curt Jurgens, Sylva Koscina, Orson Welles, Hardy Kruger, Franco Nero
⚅ best foreign film

The Battle of Paris

US   1929   71m   bw   Paramount
A lady music seller teams up with a pickpocket and falls for an American artist.
Primitive sound musical notable chiefly for its cast.
w Gene Markey d Robert Florey ph Bill Steiner m/ly Cole Porter
☆ Gertrude Lawrence, Charles Ruggles, Walter Petrie, Arthur Treacher, Gladys du Bois

Battle of Powder River: see *Tomahawk*

The Battle of Rogue River

US   1954   71m   Technicolor
Columbia
A disciplinarian major at a Western fort discovers that his friend is fanning hatred between Indians and whites, for personal reasons.
Tatty Western with little action, and that very lame.
w Douglas Heyes d William Castle
☆ George Montgomery, Richard Denning, Martha Hyer, John Crawford

Battle of the Bulge **

US   1965   167m   Technicolor   Ultra
Panavision
Warner/United States Pictures (Sidney Harmon, Milton Sperling, Philip Yordan)
■   ⚘   ∩
In December 1944, the Allies take longer than expected to win a land battle in the Ardennes because of a crack Nazi Panzer commander.
Bloody and unbowed war spectacle, quite literate and handsome but deafeningly noisy and with emphasis on strategy rather than character.
w Philip Yordan, Milton Sperling, John Melson d Ken Annakin ph Jack Hildyard m Benjamin Frankel
☆ Henry Fonda, Robert Shaw, Robert Ryan, Telly Savalas, Dana Andrews, George Montgomery, Ty Hardin, Pier Angeli, Barbara Werle, Charles Bronson, James MacArthur, Werner Peters

The Battle of the Century **

US   1927   20m   bw   silent
Hal Roach
⚅
The manager of an unsuccessful boxer accidentally starts a marathon pie fight.

The first reel is lost, but the pie sequence is what matters, being one of the most celebrated pieces of slapstick in cinema history.
w Hal Roach, H. M. Walker d Clyde Bruckman
☆ Stan Laurel, Oliver Hardy, Eugene Pallette

Battle of the Coral Sea

US   1959   85m   bw
Columbia (Charles H. Schneer)
⚅
During World War II a submarine commander, sent to photograph the Japanese fleet, is captured but escapes.
Routine, unconvincing war heroics.
w Dan Ullman, Stephen Kandel d Paul Wendkos
☆ Cliff Robertson, Gia Scala, Patricia Cutts

The Battle of the River Plate *

GB   1956   119m   Technicolor   Vistavision
Rank/Powell and Pressburger
⚅⚅   ⚅
US title: *Pursuit of the Graf Spee*
Semi-documentary account of the 1939 trapping of the German pocket battleship *Graf Spee* in Montevideo Harbour, and of her subsequent scuttling.
A sympathetic view of a German hero, Commander Langsdorff (not unexpected from these producers), is the most notable feature of this disappointingly patchy and studio-bound war epic, with too many actors in ill-defined bit parts, too undisciplined a storyline, and too confusing scenes of battle.
wd Michael Powell, Emeric Pressburger
ph Christopher Challis m Brian Easdale
☆ John Gregson, Anthony Quayle, Peter Finch, Bernard Lee, Ian Hunter, Jack Gwillim, Lionel Murton, Anthony Bushell, Peter Illing
　'It is difficult to understand how English film-makers can have done thus badly with material so apt to their gifts.' – *Stanley Kauffmann*

The Battle of the Sexes

US   1914   60m   bw   silent
Mutual/Reliance-Majestic
A wealthy middle-aged man is taken in by a fortune-hunting couple.
A commercial potboiler, made on the cheap but enormously successful.
wd D. W. Griffith play *The Single Standard* by Daniel Carson Goodman ph G. W. Bitzer
☆ Lillian Gish, Owen Moore, Mary Alden, Fay Tincher, Robert Harron
† In 1928 Griffith remade the property with Phyllis Haver, Jean Hersholt, Belle Bennett, Sally O'Neil and Don Alvarado.

The Battle of the Sexes *

GB   1960   83m   bw
Prometheus (Monja Danischewsky)
⚅⚅   ⚅
A lady efficiency expert upsets the even tenor of life at an Edinburgh tweed manufactory, and the chief accountant plans to eliminate her.
Sub-Ealing black comedy which tends to misfire despite effort all round.
w Monja Danischewsky story *The Catbird Seat* by James Thurber d Charles Crichton ph Freddie Francis m Stanley Black
☆ Peter Sellers, Constance Cummings, Robert Morley, Jameson Clark, Moultrie Kelsall, Alex Mackenzie, Roddy McMillan, Ernest Thesiger

The Battle of the V1

GB   1958   109m   bw
Criterion (George Maynard)
US titles: *Unseen Heroes*
aka: *Missiles from Hell*
Polish patriots sabotage the German rocket installation at Peenemünde.
Effective though schoolboyish war adventure shot on a low budget: story development reasonably brisk though predictable.
w Jack Hanley, Eryk Wlodek book Bernard Newman d Vernon Sewell ph Basil Emmott m Robert Sharples
☆ Michael Rennie, Patricia Medina, Milly Vitale, David Knight, Esmond Knight, Christopher Lee

The Battle of the Villa Fiorita

GB   1964   111m   Technicolor   Panavision
Warner (Delmer Daves)
US title: *Affair at the Villa Fiorita*
Two children aim to break up their mother's romance with an Italian concert pianist.

Quite lively, old-fashioned romantic comedy-drama largely set in a splendid Mediterranean villa; happy ending never in doubt.
wd Delmer Daves novel Rumer Godden
ph Oswald Morris m Mischa Spoliansky
☆ Maureen O'Hara, Rossano Brazzi, Richard Todd, Phyllis Calvert, Olivia Hussey, Martin Stephens, Elizabeth Dear

Battle on the Beach: see *The Battle at Bloody Beach*

Battle Stations

US   1956   81m   bw
Columbia
Life on an aircraft carrier as seen by the padre.
Cliché-strewn, mini-budgeted war thriller.
w Crane Wilbur d Lewis Seiler
☆ John Lund, William Bendix, Keefe Brasselle, Richard Boone

Battle Stripe: see *The Men*

Battle Taxi

US   1954   82m   bw
UA (Ivan Tors)
A newcomer to the helicopter rescue service in Korea resents his non-combatant status, but becomes a hero.
The story takes second place to one damned rescue after another in this lively but overlong second feature.
w Malvin Wald d Herbert L. Strock
☆ Sterling Hayden, Arthur Franz, Marshall Thompson

'The guts! The girls! The glory! of a lot of wonderful guys!'

Battleground *

US   1949   118m   bw
MGM (Dore Schary)
■   ⚘
How a group of American soldiers in 1944 endured the Battle of the Bulge.
Enormously successful at the box-office, this studio-bound production now seems stilted and unpersuasive, despite some good writing and direction.
w Robert Pirosh d William Wellman ph Paul C. Vogel m Lennie Hayton ed John Dunning
☆ Van Johnson, John Hodiak, Ricardo Montalban, George Murphy, Marshall Thompson, Jerome Courtland, Don Taylor, Bruce Cowling, James Whitmore, Douglas Fowley, Guy Anderson, Richard Jaeckel, Leon Ames
　'Engrossingly well done.' – *Richard Mallett, Punch*
⚅ Robert Pirosh; Paul C. Vogel
⚅ best picture; William Wellman; James Whitmore; editing

Battles of Chief Pontiac

US   1953   75m   bw
Jack Broder
In the mid-18th century, peace talks with the Detroit Indians are sabotaged.
Slightly unusual but undistinguished slice of Western history.
w Jack de Witt d Felix E. Feist
☆ Lon Chaney Jnr, Lex Barker, Helen Westcott, Berry Kroeger, Roy Roberts

The Battleship Potemkin ****

USSR   1925   75m   bw   silent; sound version
65m
Goskino
⚅⚅   ⚘   ⊘
original title: *Bronenosets Potemkin*
A partly fictitious account of the mutiny at Odessa, an episode in the 1905 revolution. (The film was made as part of the 20th anniversary celebrations.)
A textbook cinema classic, and masterpiece of creative editing, especially in the famous Odessa Steps sequence in which innocent civilians are mown down in the bloodshed; the happenings of a minute are drawn into five by frenzied cross-cutting. The film contains 1,300 separate shots, and was judged the best film ever made in 1948 and 1958 by a panel of international judges.
wd Sergei Eisenstein ph Edouard Tissé, V. Popov
☆ A. Antonov, Grigori Alexandrov, Vladimir Barsky, Levshin

Battlestar Galactica

↟↟   US   1979   125m   colour
Universal (John Dykstra)
■   ⚘   ∩
A spaceship crew battles its way back towards Earth.

Cobbled together from episodes of an unsuccessful TV series, the movie resembles a space version of another TV series, Bonanza, and borrows heavily from Star Wars to little effect.
w Glen A. Larson d Richard A. Colla ph Ben Coleman m Stu Phillips, John E. Chilberg II ed Robert L. Kimble, Leon Ortiz-Gil, Larry Strong sp Apogee
☆ Richard Hatch, Dirk Benedict, Lorne Greene, Ray Milland, Lew Ayres, Jane Seymour, Wilfrid Hyde-White, John Colicos, Patrick Macnee

Battletruck

New Zealand   1981   94m   colour
Battletruck Films (Lloyd Phillips, Rob Whitehouse)
■
aka: *Warlords of the 21st Century*
In the future, when civilization has been reduced to a few isolated communities, a lone hero on a motorbike battles a ruthless gang leader and his armoured truck.
A latter-day Western, full of gratuitous sadism, and no more than a pale shadow of Mad Max (qv).
w Irving Austin, Harley Cokliss, John Beech d Harley Cokliss ph Chris Menges m Kevin Peek pd Gary Hansen ed Michael Horton
☆ Michael Beck, Annie McEnroe, James Wainwright, Bruno Lawrence, John Bach, John Ratzenberger, Randolph Powell

Battling Bellhop: see *Kid Galahad* (1937)

Battling Butler *

US   1926   68m   bw   silent
MGM (Joseph M. Schenck)
■   ⚘
A young millionaire pretends to be a boxer in order to win a sweetheart.
Middling star comedy.
w Al Boasberg, Charles Smith, Paul Gerard Smith, Lex Neal d Buster Keaton ph J. Devereux Jennings, Bert Haines
☆ Buster Keaton, Sally O'Neil

The Bawdy Adventures of Tom Jones

GB   1976   94m   Technicolor
Universal/Robert Sadoff

See *Tom Jones*, of which this is a musical version. *Not quite as bad as one would expect, but not up to the original.*
w Jeremy Lloyd play Don McPherson d Cliff Owen ph Douglas Slocombe m Ron Grainer m/ly Paul Holden
☆ Nicky Henson, Trevor Howard, Terry-Thomas, Arthur Lowe, Georgia Brown, Joan Collins, William Mervyn, Murray Melvin, Geraldine McEwan, Michael Bates, James Hayter, Isabel Dean, Gladys Henson
　'A cheap, crude, sexed-up rehash with only three actual musical numbers … more boring than bawdy.' – *Kevin Thomas, Los Angeles Times*

Baxter *

GB   1972   100m   Technicolor
EMI/Performing Arts (Arthur Lewis)
An American son of divorced parents comes to London with his mother, meets tragedy in the shape of a friend's death, and responds to treatment for a speech defect.
Slight, appealing case history of a maladjusted 12-year-old; a rather unnecessarily uncommercial slice of life with no easy solution offered.
w Reginald Rose d Lionel Jeffries ph Geoffrey Unsworth m Michael J. Lewis ad Anthony Pratt ed Teddy Darvas
☆ Patricia Neal, Scott Jacoby, Britt Ekland, Jean-Pierre Cassel, Lynn Carlin, Paul Eddington, Sally Thomsett, Paul Maxwell

The Bay Boy

Canada/France   1984   101m   colour
Rank/Hachette Fox/Antenne 2/A2/CTV/HBO/Orion (John Kemeny, Denis Héroux)
■   ⚘
In 1937 Nova Scotia, a 16-year-old boy is distracted by real-life problems from his supposed vocation as a priest.
Doleful, weatherbeaten slice of autobiography which remains of interest only to those who know the country and the people.
wd Daniel Petrie ph Claude Agostini m Claude Bolling pd Wolf Kroeger ed Susan Shanks
☆ Liv Ullmann, Kiefer Sutherland, Peter Donat, Alan Scarfe, Chris Wiggins

Bay of Angels: see *La Baie des Anges*

'The first motion picture to require a face-to-face warning. May be the last shock film you will ever want to see!'

A Bay of Blood (dubbed)

Italy 1971 90m colour
Nuovo Linea (Giuseppe Zaccariello)

🖳 🖦

original title: *Ecologia del Delitto*
aka: *Antefatto; Bloodbath Bay of Blood; Carnage; Last House on the Left Part II; Twitch of the Death Nerve*

In a struggle to gain control of a beautiful bay ripe for development, thirteen people are murdered.
There's not much narrative in this movie, which is more an exercise in thinking up inventive ways for people to die, with each victim killed by a different means. It is original, in that there are multiple killers at work, as each murderer becomes a victim in turn, and it is done with some style and a heavy irony.
w Mario Bava, Joseph McLee (Giuseppe Zaccariello), Filippo Ottoni *story* Dardano Sacchetti, Franco Barberi *d* Mario Bava *ph* Mario Bava *m* Stelvio Cipriani *ad* Sergio Canevari *ed* Carlo Realy
☆ Claudine Auger, Luigi Pistilli, Claudio Volonte, Anna M. Rosati, Chris Avram, Leopoldo Trieste, Laura Betti, Brigitte Skay, Isa Miranda
† The British video release runs for 81m. When it was first shown in America, as a gimmick ticket-holders had to pass through a 'final warning station' before being allowed to see the film.

Be Big *
👥 US 1931 20m bw
Hal Roach

🖳 🖦

Ollie feigns illness to avoid a trip with his wife, but Stan's help proves disastrous.
Comedy warm-up for Sons of the Desert (qv); Ollie spends most of the second reel trying to rid himself of a tight boot.
w H. M. Walker *d* James Parrott
☆ Stan Laurel, Oliver Hardy, Anita Garvin, Isabelle Keith

'Somewhere on this planet it must exist.'

The Beach *
US 2000 120m Technicolor 'Scope
TCF/Figment (Andrew Macdonald)
🎧

An American backpacker discovers that the rumour is true of a hippy community living by a perfect beach on a remote Thailand island.
Fitfully engaging tale of an expulsion from paradise, hampered by being too obviously fitted around the requirements of its star.
w John Hodge *novel* Alex Garland *d* Danny Boyle *ph* Darius Khondji *m* Angelo Badalamenti *pd* Andrew McAlpine *ed* Masahiro Hirakubo
☆ Leonardo DiCaprio, Tilda Swinton, Virginie Ledoyen, Guillaume Canet, Paterson Joseph, Robert Carlyle, Peter Youngblood Hills, Jerry Swindall, Lars Arentz Hansen
'Not a terrible movie. just an insubstantial one. All of Mr DiCaprio's charisma and the director's savvy are used to divert us from the fact that there's not much going on.' – *Elvis Mitchell, New York Times*

Beach Blanket Bingo
US 1965 98m Pathécolor Panavision
Orion/AIP (James H. Nicholson, Samuel Z. Arkoff)

🖳 🖦

Teenage surfers become involved with a publicity man organizing a series of stunts to make a star of a new singer.
It has sea, surf, sand, slapstick, sky-diving, a mermaid and a little cynicism, making fun of youth-oriented pop while at the same time celebrating it; possibly the best of its imperturbably bland genre.
w William Asher, Leo Townsend *d* William Asher *ph* Floyd Crosby *m* Les Baxter *ch* Jack Baker *ad* Howard Campbell *ed* Fred Feitshans, Eve Newman
☆ Frankie Avalon, Annette Funicello, Deborah Walley, Harvey Lembeck, John Ashley, Jody McCrea, Donna Loren, Marta Kristen, Linda Evans, Timothy Carey, Paul Lynde, Don Rickles, Buster Keaton, Earl Wilson
† The fifth in AIP's beach movies, it was followed by *How to Stuff a Wild Bikini* (qv).

The Beach Girls and the Monster
US 1966 70m bw
Edward Janis/Films

An oceanographer finds something very strange emerging from the waters of Waikiki Beach.
Elementary horror flick which fails to scare and is only notable for the re-emergence of its star.
w Joan Gardner *d* Jon Hall
☆ Jon Hall, Sue Casey, Walker Edmiston, Arnold Lessing

Beach House
US 1982 76m TVC Color
New Line/Galaxy Industries (Marino Amoruso)

🖳

Teenagers congregate in Ocean City to indulge in banal dialogue, stupid pranks, dull sex and duller rock.
Garish, jejune, indifferently acted and directed attempt at a comedy that even the youth of its participants cannot excuse.
d John Gallagher *ph* Peter Stein *m* C. P. Roth *m/ly* Adam Roth *ed* Victor Kanefsky, John Bloomgarden
☆ Ileana Seidel, Richard Duggan, Kathy McNeil, John Cosola, Marino Amoruso, Spence Waugh, Paul Anderson, Adam Roth

The Beach of Lost Children
Mali 1991 88m colour
Paris Plage/Herakles (Mohamed Abderrahman Tazi)
aka: *La Plage des Enfants Perdus*

A father hides away his simple-minded daughter when he discovers that she is pregnant by a local taxi driver.
Leaden and curiously inert treatment of a dramatic story.
wd Jillali Ferhati *ph* Gilberto Azevedo, Jacques Besse *m* Djamel Allam *ad* Abdelkrim Akkelach *ed* Natalie Perrey
☆ Souad Ferhati, Mohamed Timod, Fatima Loukili, Larbi El Yacoubi, Nezha Zakaria, Mohamed Larbi Khazzan, Safia Ziani

Beach Party *
US 1963 104m Pathécolor Panavision
AIP/Alta Vista (James H. Nicholson, Lou Rusoff)

🖳

An anthropologist sets up house on a California beach to study the mating habits of young people but becomes personally involved when one of them falls for him.
Vaguely satirical pop musical with relaxed performances; quite tolerable in itself, it started an excruciating trend.
w Lou Rusoff *d* William Asher *ph* Kay Norton *m* Les Baxter *ad* Daniel Haller *ed* Homer Powell
☆ Bob Cummings, Dorothy Malone, Annette Funicello, Frankie Avalon, Vincent Price, Harvey Lembeck, Morey Amsterdam, Jody McCrea

Beach Red *
US 1967 105m Technicolor
UA/Theodora (Cornel Wilde)

🖳 🖦

In 1943, American assault craft take a Japanese-held Pacific island.
Brutal, pacifist war film, simply and clearly portrayed but not exactly entertaining.
w Clint Johnston, Donald A. Peters, Jefferson Pascal *d* Cornel Wilde *ph* Cecil R. Cooney *m* Antonio Buenaventura
☆ Cornel Wilde, Rip Torn, Burr de Benning, Jean Wallace

The Beachcomber: see *Vessel of Wrath* (1938)

The Beachcomber *
GB 1954 90m Technicolor
GFD/London Independent (William MacQuitty)

🖳

An alcoholic ne'er-do-well in the Dutch East Indies reforms after an unexpected adventure with a lady missionary.
Styleless remake of Vessel of Wrath (qv); the acting just about holds the interest, but all other contributions are flat.
w Sydney Box *story* Somerset Maugham *d* Muriel Box *ph* Reg Wyer *m* Francis Chagrin
☆ Robert Newton, Glynis Johns, Donald Sinden, Paul Rogers, Donald Pleasence, Walter Crisham, Michael Hordern, Ronald Lewis

Beaches *
US 1988 123m Metrocolor
Warner/Touchstone/An All Girl Production (Bonnie Bruckheimer-Martell, Bette Midler, Margaret Jennings South)

🖳 🖦 🎧

A singer visits her dying friend, a lawyer, and recalls their long and volatile friendship.
In another age, this sentimental feminist weepie would have been classified as a woman's picture, though Midler's singing gives it a wider appeal.
w Mary Agnes Donoghue *novel* Iris Rainer Dart *d* Garry Marshall *ph* Dante Spinotti *m* Georges Delerue *pd* Albert Brenner *ad* Garrett Lewis *ed* Richard Halsey
☆ Bette Midler, Barbara Hershey, John Heard, Spalding Gray, Lainie Kazan, James Read, Grace Johnston, Mayim Bialik, Marcie Leeds
⚉ best art direction

The Beads of One Rosary *
Poland 1979 116m colour
Cinegate/PRF-Zespol Filmowy
original title: *Paciorki Jednego Różańca*

A retired miner and his wife defy attempts by property developers to demolish their cottage.
There is something of the charm of an Ealing comedy in this tale of a little man standing up to bureaucratic pressures.
wd Kazimierz Kutz *ph* Wieslaw Zdort *m* Wojciech Kilar *ad* Andrzej Plocki, Miroslaw Krelik *ed* Jozef Bartczak
☆ Augustyn Halotta, Marta Straszna, Ewa Wiśniewska, Franciszek Pieczka

'The Ultimate Disaster Movie'

Bean *
👥 GB 1997 90m colour
Polygram/Working Title/Tiger Aspect (Tim Bevan, Eric Fellner, Peter Bennett-Jones)

🖳 🖦 🖳. 📀 🎧

An accident-prone attendant at London's Royal National Gallery accompanies *Whistler's Mother* to America.
Slapstick farce of embarrassment, based on a highly successful television series; it features one of the least likeable and most mean-spirited of comic creations.
w Richard Curtis, Robin Driscoll, Rowan Atkinson *d* Mel Smith *ph* Francis Kenny *m* Howard Goodall *pd* Peter Larkin *ed* Chris Blunden
☆ Rowan Atkinson, Peter MacNicol, Pamela Reed, Harris Yulin, Burt Reynolds, John Mills, Richard Gant, Tricia Vessey, Andrew Lawrence, Peter Egan, Peter Capaldi
'Not only consistently entertaining, but frequently laugh-out-loud funny.' – *Caroline Westbrook, Empire*
'The ultimate movie disaster.' – *Mike Higgins, Independent*
† The film cost £17m and grossed around $45m in the US, and another $172m elsewhere.

The Bear **
👥 France 1989 98m Eastmancolor Panavision
Tri-Star/Renn/Price Entertainment (Claude Berri)

🖳 🖦 🖳. 📀 🎧

An orphaned bear cub tries to cope with life in the wild.
Charming film, told from the bear's point of view, with natural sounds substituting for dialogue.
w Gérard Brach *novel* *The Grizzly King* by James Oliver Curwood *d* Jean-Jacques Annaud *ph* Philippe Rousselot *m* Philippe Sarde *pd* Toni Ludi *ed* Noelle Boisson
☆ Bart, Youk, Jack Wallace, Tcheky Karyo, André Lacombe
⚉ best film editing

Bear Country: see *The Living Desert*

'Below freezing and beyond fear ... will anyone survive its terror?'

Bear Island
GB/Canada 1979 118m colour Panavision
Columbia/Bear Island/Selkirk (Peter Snell)

🖳 🖦

Meteorological experts on an Arctic island are menaced by neo-Nazis.
Highly implausible adventure yarn, indifferently presented.
w David Butler, Don Sharp *novel* Alistair MacLean *d* Don Sharp *ph* Alan Hume *m* Robert Farnon
☆ Vanessa Redgrave, Donald Sutherland, Richard Widmark, Christopher Lee, Barbara Parkins, Lloyd Bridges

The Bears and I
👥 US 1974 89m Technicolor
Walt Disney (Winston Hibler)

🖳

An army veteran goes to live near an Indian settlement and adopts three bear cubs, later becoming a Park Ranger.
Simple, pleasing outdoor family film.
w John Whedon *novel* Robert Franklin Leslie *d* Bernard McEveety *ph* Ted D. Landon *m* Buddy Baker
☆ Patrick Wayne, Chief Dan George, Andrew Duggan, Michael Ansara

The Beast
US 1988 109m colour
Columbia/A&M (John Fiedler)

aka: *The Beast of War*

In 1981 in Afghanistan a Russian soldier turns rebel after he is left to die by his brutal comrades, who are trying to reach safety with their tank while being attacked by Afghan guerrillas.
Dull, violent, unilluminating war movie, conducted on a pitch of hysteria.
w William Mastrosimone *play* *Nanawatai* by William Mastrosimone *d* Kevin Reynolds *ph* Douglas Milsome *m* Mark Isham *ad* Richard James
☆ George Dzundza, Jason Patric, Steven Bauer, Stephen Baldwin, Don Harvey, Erick Avari, Kabir Bedi
'This superior war movie effortlessly fuses the moral complexity of scriptwriter William Mastrosimone's original stage play with the visual spectacle and narrative drive of a full-blown cinema feature.' – *Time Out*

'A Thrill-Story Beyond All Imagining!'
'King of Prehistoric Sea Giants ... Raging Up From The Bottom of Time!'

The Beast from Twenty Thousand Fathoms
US 1953 80m bw
Warner (Hal Chester, Jack Dietz)

🖳 🖳.

Heat generated by an atomic bomb test in the Arctic thaws out a prehistoric rhedosaurus which travels down the American coast to cause havoc in New York until cornered and destroyed on Coney Island.
Flat-footed addition to the monster cycle, with an interminable wait for the beast's appearance and inferior trick work when he goes on the rampage.
w Lou Morheim, Fred Freiberger *d* Eugène Lourié *ph* Jack Russell *m* David Buttolph *sp* Ray Harryhausen
☆ Paul Christian, Paula Raymond, Cecil Kellaway, Kenneth Tobey, Donald Woods, Lee Van Cleef

The Beast in the Cellar
GB 1970 87m Eastmancolor
Tigon-Leander (Tony Tenser, Graham Harris)

A rampaging killer in the Lancashire woods turns out to be the deranged ex-soldier brother of two elderly spinsters who have kept him locked up for thirty years.
Idiotically boring farrago, totally lacking in suspense and wasting good talent.
wd James Kelly *ph* Harry Waxman, Desmond Dickinson *m* Tony Macaulay
☆ Flora Robson, Beryl Reid, Tessa Wyatt, John Hamill, T. P. McKenna

The Beast Must Die: see *Que la Bête Meure* (1969)

The Beast Must Die *
GB 1974 93m Technicolor
BL/Amicus (Milton Subotsky)

🖳 🖦

aka: *Black Werewolf*

A millionaire big game hunter holds a weekend party to track down a werewolf, but his guest list rapidly gets smaller...

A savage variation on Ten Little Indians *(qv), not badly done, with such gimmicks as a 'guess who' break near the end.*

w Michael Winder *story* James Blish *d* Paul Annett *ph* Jack Hildyard *m* Douglas Gamley
☆ Calvin Lockhart, Peter Cushing, Charles Gray, Anton Diffring, Marlene Clark, Ciaran Madden, Michael Gambon

The Beast of Hollow Mountain

US/Mexico   1956   78m   DeLuxe
Cinemascope/Regiscope
UA/Peliculas Rodriguez (William and Edward Nassour)

An American rancher in Mexico has to deal with a jealous rival and a rampaging tyrannosaurus rex.
Uneasy mix of routine cowboy movie and substandard science fiction.

w Robert Hill, Jack DeWitt *story* Willis O'Brien *d* Edward Nassour, Ismael Rodriguez *ph* Jorge Stahl Jnr *m* Raul Lavista *ed* Holbrook Todd, Maury Wright
☆ Guy Madison, Patricia Medina, Carlos Rivas, Edward Noriega, Julio Villareal, Mario Navorro
'It should rack up handsome returns for its producers and provide moppet audiences particularly with edge-of-the-seat entertainment during its fantasy sequences.' – *Variety*
† The Regiscope system promised 'animation in depth', but its stop motion effects with fuzzy back projection are comic rather than horrific. The central notion of this first science-fiction Western turned up again in *Valley of Gwangi* (qv).

Beast of Morocco: see The Hand of Night

Beast of the City

US   1932   80m   bw
MGM

A police captain is determined to get a ruthless racketeer by fair means or foul.
Curiously dour little crime melodrama with a high death rate; the cast does not quite save it.

w John Lee Mahin *story* W. R. Burnett *d* Charles Brabin *ph* Barney McGill
☆ Walter Huston, Jean Harlow, Wallace Ford, Jean Hersholt, Dorothy Peterson, Tully Marshall, John Miljan
'A gang story for rural and home circle consumption, preaching the gospel of civic righteousness and the glory of steadfast purpose. Aiming at domestic patronage, they even make Miss Harlow keep her skirts down.' – *Variety*
'Endowed with vitality and realism.' – *New York Times*

The Beast of War: see The Beast

The Beast with a Million Eyes

US   1955   84m   bw
San Matteo/AIP

A malicious space creature lands in the desert but is defeated by human love.
Semi-professional would-be horror story, on a level with the German horrors of the period

w Tom Filer *d* David Karmansky
☆ Paul Birch, Lorna Thayer, Dick Sargent

The Beast with Five Fingers *

US   1946   88m   bw
Warner (William Jacobs)

A famous pianist dies and his severed hand returns to commit murder.
Slow-moving, Italian-set horror thriller which wastes an excellent original; a superb central performance and clever trick effects can hardly redeem the stodgy script or the ending which reveals the hauntings as a hallucination.

w Curt Siodmak *story* W. F. Harvey *d* Robert Florey *ph* Wesley Anderson *m* Max Steiner
☆ Peter Lorre, Andrea King, Robert Alda, J. Carrol Naish, Victor Francen, Charles Dingle

Beastcops

Hong Kong   1998   108m   colour
Media Asia/People's Production (F.K. Ma, John Chong)

original title: Yeshou Xingling
Two mismatched cops become involved with girls and gangsters when the Triad boss leaves town.
Violent thriller with some bloody fight scenes and a lot of desultory action as the two cops become buddies.

w Chan Hing-kai, Gordon Chan *d* Gordon Chan *ph* Tony Cheung *m* T2 *ad* Alfred Yau *ed* Chan Ki-hop
☆ Michael Fitzgerald Wong, Anthony Wong, Kathy Chau, Roy Cheung, Sam Lee
'High on testosterone, but short on lyricism or humour.' – *Sight and Sound*
† It was voted Best Film at the Hong Kong Film Awards in 1999.

The Beastmaster

US   1982   118m   colour
EMI/Ecta/Leisure Investments (Paul Pepperman, Sylvio Tabet)

A royal child, stolen at birth by a witch, is rescued by a peasant who brings him up skilled in the martial arts.
Comic strip sword and sorcery: fairly high budget but very low intelligence.

w Don Coscarelli, Paul Pepperman *d* Don Coscarelli *ph* John Alcott *m* Lee Holdridge *pd* Conrad E. Angone *ed* Roy Watts
☆ Marc Singer, Tanya Roberts, Rip Torn, John Amos, Rod Loomis

Beastmaster 2: Through the Portals of Time

US   1991   107m   CFI color
Republic/Films 21 (Sylvio Tabet)

A mythical warrior and his animal friends are transported through time to present-day Los Angeles to battle against his evil brother.
More comic-strip sword and sorcery: very low budget, even lower intelligence.

w R. J. Robertson, Jim Wynorski, Sylvio Tabet, Ken Hauser, Doug Miles *novel* The Beastmaster *by* André Norton *d* Sylvio Tabet *ph* Ronn Schmid *m* Robert Folk *pd* Allen Jones *ed* Adam Bernardi
☆ Marc Singer, Kari Wuhrer, Wings Hauser, Sarah Douglas, Charles Young

The Beat Generation

US   1959   95m   bw   Cinemascope
Albert Zugsmith

aka: This Rebel Age

A vicious rapist joins the beatniks.
Bankrupt exploitation melodrama, not easy to sit through.

w Richard Matheson, Lewis Meltzer *d* Charles Haas *ph* Walter H. Castle *m* Albert Glasser
☆ Ray Danton, Steve Cochran, Fay Spain, Mamie Van Doren, Jackie Coogan, Louis Armstrong, Maggie Hayes, Jim Mitchum, Irish McCalla, Maxie Rosenbloom
'An enervating mixture of slapstick, religiosity, psychological hokum and grubby sensationalism.' – *MFB*

'Beat' Girl

GB   1960   85m   bw
Renown

US title: Wild for Kicks
An architect's teenage daughter goes to the dogs.
Risible exposé-style melodrama.

w Dail Ambler *d* Edmond T. Gréville *ph* Walter Lassally *m* John Barry
☆ David Farrar, Noelle Adam, Christopher Lee, Gillian Hills, Adam Faith, Peter McEnery, Nigel Green

Beat Street

US   1984   106m   DeLuxe Movielab
Orion (David V. Picker, Harry Belafonte)

An aspiring DJ from South Bronx has trouble getting into showbiz.
For teenagers only; a rehash of Saturday Night Fever *(qv) applied to the new fad of break-dancing.*

w Andy Davis, David Gilbert, Paul Golding *d* Stan Lathan *ph* Tom Priestley *m* Harry Belafonte *pd* Patrizia von Brandenstein *ed* Dov Hoenig
☆ Rae Dawn Chong, Guy Davis, Jon Chardiet, Leon W. Grant, Saundra Santiago

'Adventure at its boldest! Bogart at his best!'
Beat the Devil *

GB   1953   100m   bw
Romulus/Santana (Jack Clayton)

In a small Mediterranean port, and subsequently on a boat bound for the African coast, oddly assorted travellers plan to acquire land known to contain uranium deposits. Unsatisfactory, over-talkative and inconsequential burlesque of the director's own *The Maltese Falcon* and *Across the Pacific* (qv).
Good fun was obviously had by the cast, but audiences were mostly baffled by the in-jokes, the extra-strange characters, and the lack of attention to pace, suspense and plot development.

w Truman Capote, John Huston *novel* James Helvick *d* John Huston *ph* Oswald Morris *m* Franco Mannino
☆ Humphrey Bogart, *Jennifer Jones*, Gina Lollobrigida, *Edward Underdown*, Peter Lorre, Robert Morley, *Ivor Barnard*, Bernard Lee, Marco Tulli
GWENDOLEN: 'Harry, we must beware of these men. They're desperate characters. Not one of them looked at my legs.'
DANNREUTHER: 'Trouble with England, it's all pomp and no circumstance. You're very wise to get out of it, escape while you can.'
O'HARA: 'Time! Time! What is time? The Swiss manufacture it. The French hoard it. Italians want it. Americans say it is money. Hindus say it does not exist. Do you know what I say? I say time is a crook.'
'A potential treat emerged as a wet firecracker … the incidents remain on a naggingly arch and lagging verbal keel.' – *New York Times*
'Each of its cinematic clichés appears to be placed in the very faintest of mocking quotation marks.' – *Time*
'Only the phonies liked it. It's a mess!' – *Humphrey Bogart*
'The formula of *Beat the Devil* is that everyone is slightly absurd.' – *John Huston*
† James Helvick was the pseudonym of Claud Cockburn.

Beau Brummell *

US   1924   104m   bw   silent
Warner

A Regency dandy becomes the right-hand man of the Prince of Wales, but falters through his own arrogance.
Elegant period romance which marked the beginning of its star's great movie decade.

w Dorothy Farnum *d* Harry Beaumont
☆ John Barrymore, Mary Astor, Carmel Myers, Willard Louis

Beau Brummell *

GB   1954   111m   Eastmancolor
MGM (Sam Zimbalist)

A Regency dandy enjoys a close relationship with the Prince of Wales, and when this is eventually withdrawn he dies in penury.
Stodgy historical romance with entertaining patches; the main story is too graceful and conventional to be believed.

w Karl Tunberg *play* Clyde Fitch *d* Curtis Bernhardt *ph* Oswald Morris *m* Richard Addinsell *ad* Alfred Junge
☆ Stewart Granger, Elizabeth Taylor, *Peter Ustinov*, Robert Morley, James Donald, James Hayter, Rosemary Harris, Paul Rogers, Noel Willman, Peter Bull, Peter Dyneley

Beau Chumps: see Beau Hunks

'Hard lives, quick deaths, undying love!'
Beau Geste **

US   1926   120m   bw (colour sequences)   silent
Paramount (Herbert Brenon)

Three English brothers join the Foreign Legion, suffer under a brutal sergeant, and die fighting the Arabs.
Although outmoded even when first filmed, this tale of derring-do and self sacrifice usually works, and in this case it gave its star a fresh image. One of the best remembered silents of the twenties.

w Paul Schofield *novel* P. C. Wren *d* Herbert Brenon *ph* Roy Hunt *ad* Julian Boone Fleming

☆ Ronald Colman, Neil Hamilton, Ralph Forbes, Alice Joyce, Mary Brian, *Noah Beery*, William Powell, Victor McLaglen
† Remade 1939 and 1966; sequel, *Beau Ideal*, 1931.

'Three against the world! Brothers and soldiers all!'
Beau Geste **

US   1939   120m   bw
Paramount (William Wellman)

Spirited remake, with the famous flashback opening of the desert fort defended by corpses.
Style and acting generally satisfactory.

w Robert Carson *d* William Wellman *ph* Theodor Sparkuhl, Archie Stout *m* Alfred Newman *ad* Hans Dreier, Robert Odell
☆ Gary Cooper, Ray Milland, Robert Preston, *Brian Donlevy*, *J. Carrol Naish*, Susan Hayward, Heather Thatcher, James Stephenson, Donald O'Connor, G. P. Huntley Jnr, Albert Dekker, Broderick Crawford
FOREWORD: 'The love of a man for a woman waxes and wanes like the moon, but the love of brother for brother is steadfast as the stars and endures like the word of the prophet…' Arabian proverb
MARKOFF: "Keep shooting, you scum! You'll get a chance yet to die with your boots on!"
'Its melodrama is sometimes grim but never harrowing, its pace is close to hectic and its suspense is constant.' – *Herbert Cohn, Brooklyn Daily Eagle*
'A morbid picture, but I doubt whether any morality council will take action, the whole story being so wrapped up in the school colours – in comradeship and loyalty and breeding, and the pure girl left behind; morbid because the brutality has no relation whatever to the real world; it is uncriticized daydreaming.' – *Graham Greene*
'A handsome treatment of a well-loved adventure tale.' – *New York Daily Mirror*
'Will do nominal biz, but lacks punch for smash proportions.' – *Variety*
† Shot in Buttercup Valley, west of Yuma
†† The nasty sergeant, originally Lejeune, became Markoff to avoid offending the French.
⌘ Brian Donlevy; Hans Dreier, Robert Odell

Beau Geste

US   1966   105m   Techniscope
Universal (Walter Seltzer)

The central desert section of the story is here augmented, with violence stressed, and Beau allowed to survive at the end.
A cheap leery melodrama is what results from the jettisoning of all the romantic portions of the original. Savalas is rampant as the sadistic sergeant.

wd Douglas Heyes *ph* Bud Thackery *m* Hans Salter
☆ Telly Savalas, Guy Stockwell, Doug McClure, Leslie Nielsen, Leo Gordon, Michael Constantine

Beau Hunks **

US   1931   40m   bw
Hal Roach

GB title: Beau Chumps
A fool and his friend join the Foreign Legion to forget.
Patchy but amiable star comedy with memorable high spots. In-joke: the woman the whole legion wants to forget is Jean Harlow.

w H. M. Walker *d* James W. Horne
☆ Stan Laurel, Oliver Hardy, Charles Middleton

Beau Ideal

US   1931   75m   bw
RKO (William Le Baron)

John Geste and a new legionnaire friend become involved in a religious war started by a rascally emir.
Lame sequel to Beau Geste *(qv), fettered by primitive dialogue.*

w Paul Schofield *novel* P. C. Wren *d* Herbert Brenon *ph* J. Roy Hunt *m* Max Steiner
☆ Lester Vail, Ralph Forbes, Don Alvarado, Loretta Young, Irene Rich
'Ordinary programme picture with slight romance. Doubtful draw for women.' – *Variety*

'He took New York for its wildest joy ride!'

Beau James *
US 1957 107m Technicolor Vistavision
Paramount/Hope Enterprises (Jack Rose)

The vaguely crooked career of Jimmy Walker, mayor of New York in the twenties.

Romanticized biopic with few funny moments: Hope cannot cope with the drama, and the result is a creaking vehicle apart from a well-recreated twenties atmosphere and excellent production values.

w Jack Rose, Melville Shavelson book Gene Fowler d Melville Shavelson ph John F. Warren m Joseph J. Lilley

☆ Bob Hope, Paul Douglas, Vera Miles, Alexis Smith, Darren McGavin, Joe Mantell, Walter Catlett

Le Beau Mariage *
France 1981 97m colour
Les Films du Losange/Les Films du Carrosse (Margaret Menegoz)
▭

GB title: *A Good Marriage*

An art student abandons her many affairs and announces her intention of getting married, but her intended proves reluctant ...

Quietly amusing conversation piece in the style expected of this director; an after-dinner entertainment for the Sunday Times set.

wd Eric Rohmer ph Bernard Lutic m Ronan Girre, Simon des Innocents

☆ Beatrice Ronand, André Dussollier, Feodor Atkine, Arielle Dombasle

Le Beau Serge *
France 1958 97m bw
AYJM (Jean Cotet)

A student returns to his home town and tries to redeem his old friend who has become a drunkard.

Enjoyable character drama with well observed village backgrounds. Credited with being the spearhead of the 'new wave'.

wd Claude Chabrol ph Henri Decaë m Emile Delpierre

☆ Gérard Blain, Jean-Claude Brialy, Michèle Meritz, Bernadette Lafont

Beaumarchais *
France 1996 100m colour
Artificial Eye/Téléma/Canal+/France 2/France 3 (Charles Gossot)
▭

original title: *Beaumarchais l'Insolent*

The playwright Beaumarchais overcomes imprisonment and adversity to support revolution in America and France.

Enjoyable and episodic period romp, stronger on decor than narrative.

w Edouard Molinaro, Jean-Claude Brisville play Sacha Guitry d Edouard Molinaro ph Michaël Epp m Jean-Claude Petit ad Jean-Marc Kerdelhue, Jamie Leonard ed Véronique Parnet

☆ Fabrice Luchini, Manuel Blanc, Sandrine Kiberlain, Michael Serrault, Jacques Weber, Michel Piccoli, Jean-Claude Brialy, Murray Head, Jean Yanne, Claire Nebout

'This gorgeous film is witty, intelligent and consistently thought-provoking.' – *Marianne Gray, Film Review*

Beau-Père *
France 1981 120m colour
Antenne 2/Sara
▭

aka: *Stepfather*

After the death of her mother, an adolescent girl decides to seduce her stepfather.

A drama of innocence and experience that is played mainly for comedy, though there is also an underlying tenderness.

wd Bertrand Blier novel Bertrand Blier ph Sacha Vierny m Philippe Sarde ad Theobald Meurisse ed Claudine Merlin

☆ Patrick Dewaere, Ariel Besse, Maurice Ronet, Nicole Garcia, Nathalie Baye, Maurice Risch, Genevieve, Macha Meril

La Beauté du Diable **
Italy/France 1949 96m bw
AYJM

The Faust story with the protagonists agreeing to change places.

Dazzling plot twists and cinematic virtuosity make this a richly enjoyable fantasy, though perhaps not among Clair's greatest works.

w René Clair, Armand Salacrou d René Clair ph Michel Kelber m Roman Vlad ad Léon Barsacq

☆ Michel Simon, Gérard Philipe, Raymond Cordy, Nicole Besnard, Gaston Modot, Paolo Stoppa

The Beautician and the Beast *
US 1997 105m DeLuxe
Paramount/Koch/High School Sweethearts (Howard W. Koch Jnr, Todd Graff)
▭

An ambitious beautician, mistakenly hired as a tutor to the children of an eastern European dictator, falls for her boss.

An attempt at a romantic frivolity, relying on a clash between New York Jewish humour and communist rigidity for its humour; its appeal is likely to be limited to New Yorkers.

w Todd Graff d Ken Kwapis ph Peter Lyons Collister m Cliff Eidelman pd Rusty Smith ed Jon Poll

☆ Fran Drescher, Timothy Dalton, Ian McNeice, Patrick Malahide, Lisa Jakub, Michael Lerner, Phyllis Newman

'The cinematic equivalent of a cheesy, multi-accented and self-consciously naïve college production.' – *Emanuel Levy, Variety*

'She's got the biggest six-shooters in the west!'

The Beautiful Blonde from Bashful Bend *
US 1949 77m Technicolor
TCF (Preston Sturges)
▭

A temperamental saloon entertainer accidentally shoots the sheriff and takes refuge as a schoolmistress.

A dishevelled Western farce unworthy of its creator, but with the advantage of appearances by many of his usual repertory of players.

wd Preston Sturges ph Harry Jackson m Cyril Mockridge

☆ Betty Grable, Cesar Romero, El Brendel, Hugh Herbert, Rudy Vallee, Olga San Juan, Sterling Holloway, Porter Hall, Esther Howard, Margaret Hamilton

'It erects a fabric of roaring slapstick on a conventional western foundation, and from time to time it succeeds in being very funny.' – *Richard Mallett, Punch*

'Somehow the ramshackle air of Bashful Bend itself seems to have permeated the whole film.' – *MFB*

Beautiful but Broke *
US 1944 74m bw
Columbia (Irving Briskin)

An agent and a girls' band get romantically marooned on the way to a date in Cleveland.

Haphazard comedy with music; just an occasional smile amid the tedium.

w Monte Brice, Manny Seff story Arthur Housman d Charles Barton

☆ Joan Davis, Jane Frazee, John Hubbard, Judy Clark, Bob Haymes, Danny Mummert, Byron Foulger

'Commonplace B entry.' – *Variety*

Beautiful but Dangerous (1952): see *She Couldn't Say No*

Beautiful but Dangerous (dubbed)
Italy/France 1955 115m Eastmancolor
GESI/SEDIF (Maleno Malenotti)

original title: *La Piu Bella Donna del Mondo*

An orphaned Italian singer falls in love with a Russian prince.

A lively piece of kitsch, which at one moment has Lollobrigida imitating Botticelli's Venus as part of a music-hall act.

w Cesare Cavagna, Liana Ferri, Luciano Martino, Mario Monicelli, Piero Pierotti, Franco Solinas, Giovanna Soria d Robert Z. Leonard ph Mario Bava m Renzo Rossellini ch Margherita Wallman ad Alberto Boccianti ed Eraldo da Roma

☆ Gina Lollobrigida, Vittorio Gassman, Robert Alda, Anne Vernon, Tamara Lees, Gino Sinimberghi, Enzo Biliotti, Peter Trent, Mario del Monaco

The Beautiful Cheat: see *What a Woman*

Beautiful Dreamers
Canada 1990 105m colour
Blue Dolphin/Starway/National Film Board of Canada (Michael MacLear, Martin Walters, Sally Bochner)
▭ ▭

The poet Walt Whitman forms a friendship with the liberal superintendent of a Canadian mental asylum.

Hokum, disguised as a life-enhancing drama.

wd John Kent Harrison ph François Protat m Lawrence Shragge pd Seamus Flannery ed Ron Wisman

☆ Colm Feore, Rip Torn, Wendel Meldrum, Sheila McCarthy, Colin Fox, David Gardner, Barbara Gordon, Marsha Moreau, Albert Schultz

The Beautiful End of This World
West Germany 1983 95m colour
Pentagramma (Rainer Erler)

Sent to Australia to establish a pesticide factory, a German chemical engineer is persuaded that the project would be an ecological disaster.

Dull, if well-meaning, demonstrating that, in movies, good intentions are never enough.

wd Rainer Erler ph Wolfgang Grasshoff m Eugen Thomass ad Chris Harrison, Michael Pilz ed Ulrike Pahl

☆ Robert Atzorn, Claire Oberman, Judy Winter, Gotz George

'Good times never seemed so good.'

Beautiful Girls *
US 1996 107m DeLuxe
Buena Vista/Miramax (Cary Woods)
▭ ▭ ▭

Returning home from New York for a high-school reunion, a bar-room pianist meets his old friends, now in dead-end jobs, to talk about their problems with women.

A single-minded ensemble piece, in which sex is relentlessly discussed; its cast is rather young for the prevalent repining for the recent past.

w Scott Rosenberg d Ted Demme ph Adam Kimmel m David A. Stewart pd Dan Davis ed Jeffrey Wolf

☆ Matt Dillon, Noah Emmerich, Tim Hutton, Natalie Portman, Annabeth Gish, Lauren Holly, Rosie O'Donnell, Max Perlich, Mira Sorvino, Uma Thurman, Martha Plimpton

'A great title in search of a movie to live up to, this startlingly uneventful compendium of thick-headed boy-talk and female tolerance squanders a fine cast on incredibly ordinary characters and situations.' – *Todd McCarthy, Variety*

Beautiful People **
GB 1999 109m colour
Warner/Channel Four/Tall Stories (Ben Woolford)
▭

In London, in 1993, Serbian and Croatian refugees from Bosnia attempt to carry on their dispute, which widens to involve locals.

An often contrived and ramshackle drama-cum-romantic comedy, but one that is also lively and convincing in its depiction of the confusions of life (not for nothing is a new baby, conceived as the result of a rape, called Chaos); its upbeat ending is tempered by its final image of a clenched fist.

wd Jasmin Dizdar ph Barry Ackroyd m Garry Bell pd Jon Henson ed Justin Krish

☆ Charlotte Coleman, Charles Kay, Rosalind Ayres, Roger Sloman, Heather Tobias, Danny Nussbaum, Siobhan Redmond, Gilbert Martin, Steve Sweeney, Linda Bassett, Nicholas Farrell, Edin Dzandzanovic

'Derives a dramatic charge from dark and intractable issues, only to suggest that warm-hearted comedy is their solvent.' – *Peter Bradshaw, Guardian*

'There's basically nothing going on here beyond pantomime of the lamest kind.' – *Derek Elley, Variety*

The Beautiful Rebel: see *Janice Meredith*

Beautiful Stranger
GB 1954 89m bw
Marksman (Maxwell Setton, John R. Sloan)
▭

US title: *Twist of Fate*

On the Riviera, an actress discovers that her fiancé is a criminal.

Tawdry star melodrama of virtually no interest.

w Robert Westerby, Carl Nystrom d David Miller ph Robert Day, Ted Scaife m Malcolm Arnold

☆ Ginger Rogers, Jacques Bergerac, Herbert Lom, Stanley Baker, Margaret Rawlings, Eddie Byrne, Coral Browne

Beautiful Thing *
GB 1995 91m colour
Film Four/World (Tony Garnett, Bill Shapter)
▭ ▭

Two teenage schoolboys on a South London housing estate fall in love with each other.

A reticent, feelgood summer romance, to the music of the Mamas and the Papas; it deals more in nostalgic fantasy than reality, despite its gritty, urban setting.

w Jonathan Harvey play Jonathan Harvey d Hettie Macdonald ph Chris Seager m John Altman pd Mark Stevenson ed Don Fairservice

☆ Linda Henry, Glen Berry, Scott Neal, Ben Daniels, Tameka Empson

'If *Beautiful Thing* was any more desperate to be liked, it would be following the audience home, wagging its tail and wanting to be thrown choc drops.' – *Adam Mars-Jones, Independent*

Beauty!: see *Beauty for Sale*

Beauty and the Beast: see *La Belle et la Bête* (1946)

'The most beautiful love story ever told.'

Beauty and the Beast **
♔♔ US 1991 85m Technicolor
Buena Vista/Walt Disney/Silver Screen Partners IV (Don Hahn)
▭ ▭ ▭ ▭ ▭ ▭

A prince, turned into a beast by enchantment, is rescued by the love of a beautiful girl.

A return to top form by Disney, with excellent animation and a singable score. The picture has been credited with starting a new Hollywood fashion for animated musicals.

w Linda Woolverton d Gary Trousdale, Kirk Wise m/ly Alan Menken, Howard Ashman ad Brian McEntee ed John Carnochan

☆ Featuring the voices of Paige O'Hara, Robby Benson, Jerry Orbach, Angela Lansbury, Richard White, David Ogden Stiers, Jesse Corti, Rex Everhart, Bradley Michael Pierce, Jo Anne Worley, Kimmy Robertson

'A lovely film that ranks with the best of Disney's animated classics.' – *Variety*

'It's got storytelling vigour and clarity, bright eclectic animation, and a frisky musical wit.' – *New Yorker*

♪ Alan Menken; song 'Beauty and the Beast' (mAlan Menken, ly Howard Ashman)
♫ film; song 'Belle'; song 'Be Our Guest'; sound

Beauty and the Boss
US 1932 75m bw
Warner

A girl down on her luck becomes secretary to an amorous banker and eventually becomes his wife.

Artless Cinderella story in an uneasy Viennese setting.

w Joseph Jackson play The Church Mouse by Ladislas Fodor, Paul Frank d Roy del Ruth

☆ Warren William, Marian Marsh, Charles Butterworth, Frederick Kerr, Lillian Bond

'Elementary stuff for the B houses, titularly phrased for flap appeal.' – *Variety*

Beauty for Sale
US 1933 85m bw
MGM

aka: *Beauty!*

An innocent girl snares a rich man while working in a beauty parlour.

Well-mounted romantic comedy-drama with most of the elements the 1933 public wanted.

w Zelda Sears, Eve Greene novel Beauty by Faith Baldwin d Richard Boleslawski

☆ Madge Evans, Alice Brady, Una Merkel, Otto Kruger, May Robson, Phillips Holmes, Eddie Nugent, Hedda Hopper

'Pulp magazine fiction made for subway-riding stenographers ... romantic hoke skilfully dressed up.' – *Variety*

Beauty for the Asking
US 1939 68m bw
RKO
▭

Jealousies flourish among the women in a cosmetics showroom.

Average supporting drama for female audiences.

---

w Doris Anderson, Paul Jarrico d Glenn Tryon
☆ Lucille Ball, Frieda Inescort, Patric Knowles, Donald Woods, Inez Courtney

The Beauty Jungle *

GB   1964   114m   Eastmancolor
Cinemascope
Rank/Val Guest
US title: *Contest Girl*

A typist enters a beauty contest and step by step becomes Miss Globe; but her descent is equally rapid.

Wicked show biz and the road to ruin in one glossy package, predictable, but not badly done; always something going on, and performed with gusto.

w Robert Muller, Val Guest d Val Guest
ph Arthur Grant m Laurie Johnson
☆ Janette Scott, Ian Hendry, Ronald Fraser, Edmund Purdom, Kay Walsh, Norman Bird, Janina Faye, Tommy Trinder, Francis Matthews

Beavis and Butthead Do America *

US   1996   80m   DeLuxe
Paramount/Geffen/MTV (Abby Terkuhle)
📼 🎦 🎧

Two simple- and dirty-minded teenagers travel from Las Vegas to Washington for the wrong reasons.

Crudely, if effectively, animated lowbrow comedy, most likely to be enjoyed by those familiar with the dim-witted duo's appearances on MTV.

w Mike Judge, Joe Stillman d Mike Judge
m John Frizell ed Terry Kelley, Gunter Glinka, Neil Lawrence
☆ Featuring the voices of: Mike Judge, Cloris Leachman, Robert Stack, David Spade, Eric Bogosian, Richard Linklater, Bruce Willis (uncredited), Demi Moore (uncredited)
  'Has some genuinely amusing moments of dumb and dumber silliness. But it arrives too late in the day to fully exploit the popularity of the once-trendy MTV series.' – Joe Leydon, Variety

Because of Him *

US   1945   88m   bw
Universal (Felix Jackson)

A waitress pesters a Broadway author and actor for a leading role in their new show.

Moderately sprightly star vehicle with bonuses in the leading men; handling disappointingly routine.

w Edmund Beloin d Richard Wallace ph Hal Mohr m Miklos Rozsa
☆ Deanna Durbin, Charles Laughton, Franchot Tone, Helen Broderick, Stanley Ridges, Donald Meek

'Even in the first wild joy of his arms, she realized that she would be ... an unfit mother!'

Because of You

US   1952   95m   bw
U-I (Albert J. Cohen)

A female ex-convict marries on parole but does not tell her husband of her past. Her old associates involve her innocently in another crime, and her husband divorces her; but years later she gets him and their child back.

Soap opera of the stickiest kind, made quite tolerable by good production.

w Ketti Frings d Joseph Pevney ph Russell Metty m Frank Skinner
☆ Loretta Young, Jeff Chandler, Alex Nicol, Frances Dee, Lynne Roberts, Alexander Scourby, Mae Clarke
  'Shows the most whole-hearted devotion to woman's magazine conventions.' – MFB

'Whoever you are, you're in this picture! Because this tells of youth's challenge to grown-ups who can't understand!'

Because They're Young

US   1960   98m   bw
Columbia/Drexel (Jerry Bresler)

A high school teacher helps one of his tougher pupils not to slip into crime.

Routine sentimental melodrama, slightly redeemed by directorial expertise.

w James Gunn novel Harrison High by John Farris d Paul Wendkos ph Wilfrid Cline m Johnny Williams
☆ Dick Clark, Michael Callan, Tuesday Weld, Victoria Shaw, Warren Berlinger, Doug McClure

Because You're Mine

US   1952   103m   Technicolor
MGM (Joe Pasternak)
📺

An opera singer becomes a GI and wins the sergeant's sister.

Lumberingly inept star vehicle, giving the impression of nothing at all happening between the songs.

w Leonard Spigelgass, Karl Tunberg d Alexander Hall ph Joseph Ruttenberg md Johnny Green
☆ Mario Lanza, Doretta Morrow, James Whitmore, Dean Miller, Paula Corday, Jeff Donnell, Spring Byington
  'On a dull day in Manchester it will bring colour to the greyness of life.' – Sunday Express
♫ title song (mNicholas Brodszky, ly Sammy Cahn)

'The screen explodes with rage and passion and greatness!'

Becket **

GB   1964   149m   Technicolor   Panavision
Paramount/Hal B. Wallis
📺 🔵

Henry II leans on his boisterous Saxon friend Thomas à Becket, but when the latter is made first chancellor and then archbishop a rift between them widens and ends in Becket's assassination by Henry's over-eager knights.

Jean Anouilh's bitter stage comedy is filmed literally and soberly as a rather anaemic epic, so that the point is lost and the edge blunted. The paucity of physical action causes good scenes to alternate with long stretches of tedium.

w Edward Anhalt d Peter Glenville ph Geoffrey Unsworth m Laurence Rosenthal pd John Bryan
☆ Richard Burton, Peter O'Toole, Donald Wolfit, John Gielgud, Martita Hunt, Pamela Brown, Sian Phillips, Paolo Stoppa
  'Handsome, respectable and boring.' – John Simon
  'The power of the film is in the close-up, the concentration on the two protagonists. And what is so fascinating is that Burton and O'Toole provide no ultimate answers for each other or for us.' – Judith Crist
🏆 Edward Anhalt
♫ best picture; Peter Glenville; Geoffrey Unsworth; Laurence Rosenthal; Richard Burton; Peter O'Toole; John Gielgud
🎖 John Bryan; Geoffrey Unsworth

Becky Sharp **

US   1935   83m   Technicolor
RKO (Kenneth MacGowan)
📺

An ambitious girl makes her way into Regency society.

Chiefly notable as the first feature in three-colour Technicolor, this rather theatrical piece has its civilized enjoyments and the director made a few predictable cinematic experiments; the overall effect, however, is patchy.

w Francis Edward Faragoh play Landon Mitchell novel Vanity Fair by W. M. Thackeray d Rouben Mamoulian ph Ray Rennahan m Roy Webb pd Robert Edmond Jones
☆ Miriam Hopkins, Cedric Hardwicke, Frances Dee, Billie Burke, Alison Skipworth, Nigel Bruce, Alan Mowbray, Colin Tapley, G. P. Huntley Jnr
  'Beautiful cinematographically but weak on story. No cinch, and should be sold on colour angle.' – Variety
  'As pleasing to the eye as a fresh fruit sundae, but not much more.' – Otis Ferguson
  'If colour is to be of permanent importance a way must be found to use it realistically, not only as a beautiful decoration. It must be made to contribute to our sense of truth. The machine gun, the cheap striped tie, the battered Buick and the shabby bar will need a subtler colour sense than the Duchess of Richmond's ball, the girls of Miss Pinkerton's Academy, the Marquess of Steyne's dinner for two. Can Technicolor reproduce with the necessary accuracy the suit that has been worn too long, the oily hat?' – Graham Greene
♫ Miriam Hopkins

Bed and Board **

France/Italy   1970   97m   Eastmancolor
Columbia/Les Films du Carrosse/Valoria/Fida Cinematografica (Marcel Berbert)
📼

original title: *Domicile Conjugal*

Antoine Doinel, the hero of three previous films, becomes a husband, father, writer and adulterer.

The fourth, and least rewarding, of the series of five films, although it has some amusing moments.

w François Truffaut, Claude de Givray, Bernard Revon d François Truffaut ph Nestor Almendros m Antoine Duhamel ad Jean Mandaroux ed Agnes Guillemot
☆ Jean-Pierre Léaud, Claude Jade, Hiroko Berghauer, Daniel Ceccaldi, Claire Duhamel, Barbara Laage

'It's nice to have a man around the house.'

Bed and Breakfast

US   1992   98m   DuArt
Hemdale (Jack Schwartzman)
📼 📺 🔵 🎧

A widow running a seaside boarding house falls for an affable con man.

Mundane romantic drama that trundles along on familiar lines.

w Cindy Myers d Robert Ellis Miller ph Peter Sova m David Shire pd Suzanne Cavedon ed John F. Burnett
☆ Roger Moore, Talia Shire, Colleen Dewhurst, Nina Siemaszko, Ford Rainey, Stephen Root, Jamie Walters, Cameron Arnett
  'Pic is so predictable and sentimental that it will be quickly forgotten at the box office.' – Variety
† The film was released direct to video in Britain.

Bed of Roses

US   1995   88m   DeLuxe
Entertainment (Allan Mindel, Denise Shaw)
📼 📺 🔵 🎦 🎧

A florist, whose wife died in childbirth, falls for a lonely workaholic banker who had an abusive stepfather.

An attempt to update the type of romantic movie made in the 40s by adding a dash of dysfunction and a little New Age back-to-nature dressing; the result is as remote from reality as ever and poor escapism as well.

wd Michael Goldenberg ph Adam Kimmel m Michael Convertino pd Stephen McCabe ed Jane Kurson
☆ Christian Slater, Mary Stuart Masterson, Pamela Segall, Josh Brolin, Ally Walker, Debra Monk
  'One of those acutely sensitive American movies about love and loss that manage to be, despite their sincerity, incredibly dull.' – Derek Malcolm, Guardian

The Bed Sitting Room *

GB   1969   91m   DeLuxe
UA/Oscar Lewenstein (Richard Lester)

Surrealist romance, after a nuclear war, motley survivors in the waste lands turn into bed sitting rooms, cupboards and parakeets.

Arrogantly obscure fantasy, a commercial flop which kept its director in the wilderness for four years. Fans of Monty Python may salvage a joke or two.

w John Antrobus play John Antrobus, Spike Milligan d Richard Lester ph David Watkin m Ken Thorne pd Assheton Gorton
☆ Ralph Richardson, Rita Tushingham, Michael Hordern, Arthur Lowe, Mona Washbourne, Peter Cook, Dudley Moore, Spike Milligan, Harry Secombe, Marty Feldman, Jimmy Edwards

Bedazzled *

GB   1967   96m   DeLuxe   Panavision
TCF/Stanley Donen
📼 📺 🔵

A short order cook is saved from suicide by Mr Spiggott, who offers him seven wishes in exchange for his soul.

A camped-up version of Faust which resolves itself into a series of threadbare sketches for the stars. All rather desperate apart from the leaping nuns.

w Peter Cook d Stanley Donen ph Austin Dempster m Dudley Moore
☆ Peter Cook, Dudley Moore, Michael Bates, Raquel Welch, Eleanor Bron

Bedelia

GB   1946   90m   bw
John Corfield (Isadore Goldsmith)

A psychotic woman is discovered to have poisoned three husbands.

Dreary upper-class British murder drama, totally devoid of style or suspense but a big star hit of the time.

w Vera Caspary, Moie Charles, Herbert Victor, Roy Ridley, Isadore Goldsmith novel Vera Caspary d Lance Comfort ph F. A. Young
☆ Margaret Lockwood, Ian Hunter, Barry K. Barnes, Anne Crawford, Jill Esmond, Ellen Pollock

Bedevilled

US   1955   86m   Eastmancolor   Cinemascope
MGM (Henry Berman)

In Paris, a novice priest befriends a girl on the run from gangsters. She turns out to be a murderess and is shot by her victim's brother.

Absurd high-flown bosh, unsuitably cinemascoped in ugly colour, and surprisingly badly handled by old professionals.

w Jo Eisinger d Mitchell Leisen ph Frederick A. Young m William Alwyn
☆ Anne Baxter, Steve Forrest, Simone Renant, Victor Francen, Maurice Teynac, Joseph Tomelty
  'This mixture of melodrama and religion provides a most unedifying entertainment.' – MFB

The Bedford Incident ***

GB   1965   102m   bw
Columbia/Bedford Productions (James B. Harris)
📺

A ruthlessly efficient US destroyer captain in the Arctic chases a Russian submarine and accidentally fires an atomic weapon.

Gripping mixture of themes from Dr Strangelove and The Caine Mutiny (qqv), very tense and forceful, with excellent acting. It was Poitier's first role with no reference to his colour.

w James Poe novel Mark Rascovich d James B. Harris ph Gilbert Taylor m Gerard Schurmann
☆ Richard Widmark, Sidney Poitier, James MacArthur, Eric Portman, Wally Cox, Martin Balsam, Phil Brown, Michael Kane, Gary Cockrell, Donald Sutherland
  'Strong on virtues of a rather negative kind.' – Penelope Houston

Bedknobs and Broomsticks

👪 US   1971   117m   Technicolor
Walt Disney (Bill Walsh)
📼 🇺🇸 🔵

In 1940 three evacuee children and a kindly witch ride on a magic bedstead and defeat the invasion of England.

Extraordinarily dishevelled and incompetent Disney follow-up to Mary Poppins (qv), a very muddled narrative with few high points and evidence of much cutting. Redeemed occasionally by camera trickery.

w Bill Walsh, Don DaGradi d Robert Stevenson ph Frank Phillips m/ly Richard M. Sherman, Robert B. Sherman sp Eustace Lycett, Alan Maley, Danny Lee
☆ Angela Lansbury, David Tomlinson, Roy Snart, Cindy O'Callaghan, Sam Jaffe, Roddy McDowall, Bruce Forsyth, Tessie O'Shea, Reginald Owen
🏅 special visual effects (Alan Maley, Eustace Lycett, Danny Lee)
♫ Richard M. Sherman, Robert B. Sherman; song 'The Age of Not Believing' by the Shermans

Bedlam **

US   1946   80m   bw
RKO (Val Lewton)
📺 🔵

In 18th-century London, a sane girl is confined by the malevolent asylum master.

Interesting but rather flatly handled addition to the Val Lewton gallery of horrors, perhaps too carefully and discreetly done for pace or suspense.

w Mark Robson, Carlos Keith d Mark Robson ph Nicholas Musuraca m Roy Webb
☆ Boris Karloff, Anna Lee, Billy House, Richard Fraser, Glenn Vernon
† Carlos Keith was Val Lewton's pseudonym
†† Bedlam was never granted a certificate in Britain.

The Bedroom
Japan 1992 63m colour
Kokuei (Daisuke Asakura)
📺

A woman becomes unable to distinguish between fantasy and reality after her sister dies in a club where men act out their fantasies on drugged women.
Odd, unpleasant, voyeuristic, poorly subtitled Japanese erotica, given a modish treatment; its images of inert, passive women are most likely to appeal to necrophiliacs.
w Yumeno Shiro d Sato Hisayasu ph Masashi Inayashi ed Shoji Sakai
☆ Ito Kiyomi, Asano Mamori, Nakamura Kyoko, Sagawa Issei
'Inventively shot in a sub-David Lynch sort of way, but pretty repugnant all the same.' – *Sight and Sound*

Bedroom Eyes
Canada 1984 90m Medallion
Alliance/RSL (Robert Lantos, Stephen J. Roth)
📺 ◎~

A stockbroker, who is a peeping Tom by night, is accused of murder when the woman he spies on is killed.
Dull and risible psychological thriller, which uses sex as a substitute for narrative interest and excitement.
w Michael Alan Eddy d William Fruet ph Miklos Lente m John Tucker pd Lindsey Goddard ed Tony Lower
☆ Kenneth Gilman, Dayle Haddon, Christine Cattell, Lawrence K. Philips, Jayne Catling, Barbara Law

The Bedroom Window
US 1986 115m colour JDC Widescreen
De Laurentiis (Robert Towne, Martha Schumacher)
📺 ◎~

From her boyfriend's apartment window, an adulterous wife witnesses an assault, and sends her boyfriend to the police in her place.
Sub-Hitchcock thriller, almost as creaky as it sounds.
wd Curtis Hanson ph Gil Taylor m Michael Shrieve, Patrick Gleeson ed Scott Conrad
☆ Steve Guttenberg, Elizabeth McGovern, Isabelle Huppert, Paul Shenar, Frederick Coffin, Wallace Shawn
'Less than riveting entertainment.' – *Daily Variety*

'Re-Model Your Love Life.'
Bedrooms & Hallways
GB/France/Germany 1998 96m Rank Colour
Alliance/ARP/Pandora/BBC (Ceci Dempsey, Dorothy Berwin)
📺

A group of friends enjoy varied sexual relationships with one another.
A slight comedy of bisexuality and serial partners.
w Robert Farrar d Rose Troche ph Ashley Rowe m Alfredo D. Troche, Ian MacPherson pd Richard Bridgland ed Christopher Blunden
☆ Kevin McKidd, Hugo Weaving, James Purefoy, Tom Hollander, Christopher Fulford, Julie Graham, Con O'Neill, Paul Higgins, Jennifer Ehle, Simon Callow, Harriet Walter
'Watching B&H is a bit like sitting in a lukewarm bath, waiting for someone to turn the hot water back on. The longer you wait, the colder it gets.' – *Charlotte O'Sullivan, Independent*

Bedside Manner
US 1945 79m bw
UA (Andrew Stone)
📺

A lady doctor falls for a war worker.
Flat and contrived comedy which just about manages to keep going.
w Frederick Jackson, Malcolm Stuart Boylan story Robert Carson d Andrew Stone
☆ Ruth Hussey, John Carroll, Charles Ruggles, Ann Rutherford, Claudia Drake, Grant Mitchell, Frank Jenks

Bedtime for Bonzo
US 1951 83m bw
U-I (Michel Kraike)

To prove that environment determines character, a chimpanzee is brought up as a human baby.
Very moderate fun and games which proved successful enough for a sequel, Bonzo Goes to College.

w Val Burton, Lou Breslow d Frederick de Cordova ph Carl Guthrie m Frank Skinner
☆ Ronald Reagan, Diana Lynn, Walter Slezak, Lucille Barkley, Herbert Heyes

Bedtime Story *
US 1942 85m bw
Columbia (B. P. Schulberg)

A playwright's wife wants to retire instead of acting in his next play.
Pleasantly sparkling comedy with good performances.
w Horace Jackson, Grant Garrett, Richard Flournoy d Alexander Hall ph Joseph Walker m Werner Heymann
☆ *Fredric March, Loretta Young*, Robert Benchley, Allyn Joslyn, Eve Arden, Helen Westley, Joyce Compton, Tim Ryan

Bedtime Story *
US 1964 99m Eastmancolor
U-I/Lankershim/Pennebaker (Stanley Shapiro)

Two Riviera confidence tricksters outwit each other.
A fairly lively script is defeated by dull handling, but performances and backgrounds are attractive.
w Stanley Shapiro, Paul Henning d Ralph Levy ph Clifford Stine m Hans Salter
☆ David Niven, Marlon Brando, Shirley Jones, Dody Goodman, Aram Stephan, Marie Windsor
'The most vulgar and embarrassing film of the year.' – *Daily Express*
† It was remade as *Dirty Rotten Scoundrels* (qv).

A Bedtime Story *
US 1933 89m bw
Paramount (Emanuel Cohen)

A breezy Frenchman has to interrupt his romances to look after an abandoned baby.
Mild star vehicle in which the agreeable comedy is largely supplanted by sentimental cooing.
w Benjamin Glazer novel Bellamy the Magnificent by Roy Horniman d Norman Taurog ph Charles Lang m/ly Ralph Rainger, Leo Robin
☆ Maurice Chevalier, Helen Twelvetrees, Baby LeRoy, Edward Everett Horton, Adrienne Ames

A Bee in the Rain
Portugal 1968 74m bw
Media (Fernando Matos Silva)
original title: *Uma Abelha na Chuva*

A farmer's unhappy marriage to an aristocratic wife brings tragedy in its wake.
Slow-moving, doom-laden tale of marital discord, not helped by the self-consciously arty direction, with freeze frames and lingering, inconsequential close-ups.
wd Fernando Lopes novel Carlos de Oliveira ph Manuel Costa e Silva m Manuel Jorge Veloso ed Fernando Lopes
☆ Laura Soveral, João Guedes, Zita Duarte, Ruy Furtado, Carlos Ferreiro, Adriano Reys

The Beekeeper **
Greece/France 1986 122m colour
Greek Film Centre/ERTI/MK2/Theodoros Angelopoulos
🎧
original title: *O Melissokomos*

A retired schoolmaster, visiting the sites of beehives around Greece, picks up a teenage hitchhiker, an act which is to drive him to desperation.
Melancholy but moving film, with a finely judged performance from Mastroianni.
w Theodoros Angelopoulos, Dimitris Nollas d Theodoros Angelopoulos ph Giorgos Arvantis m Helen Karaindrou ad Mikes Karapiperis ed Takis Yannopoulos
☆ *Marcello Mastroianni*, Nadia Mourouzi, Serge Reggiani, Jenny Roussea, Dinos Iliopoulos, Vassia Panagopolou, Dimitris Poulikakos

Beer
US 1985 82m DeLuxe
Orion (Robert Chartoff)
📺
original title: *The Selling of America*

A lady executive on Madison Avenue promotes a brand of beer by promoting three honest Joes from the street and turning them into macho media figures.
Another shred of proof that satire is what closes Saturday night. A few smiles, but no release.

w Allan Weisbecker d Patrick Kelly ph Bill Butler m Bill Conti pd Bill Brodie ed Alan Heim
☆ Loretta Swit, Rip Torn, Kenneth Mars, David Alan Grier, William Russ, Dick Shawn

Bees in Paradise
GB 1943 75m bw
Gainsborough

Four airmen find themselves on a South Sea island ruled by women who kill their spouses after the honeymoon.
Saucy farce, too talkative to be very interesting even in the dark days of war.
w Val Guest, Marriott Edgar d Val Guest
☆ Arthur Askey, Peter Graves, Max Bacon, Anne Shelton, Jean Kent

'The head of the family is the one with the tail.'
Beethoven
🕊 US 1992 87m DeLuxe
UIP/Universal (Joe Medjuck, Michael C. Gross)
📺 🎬 ◎~ ◉ 🎧

A St Bernard dog causes havoc in a family household to the delight of the children and the annoyance of their father.
Predictable comedy of the dreariest kind.
w Edmond Dantes, Amy Holden Jones d Brian Levant ph Victor J. Kemper m Randy Edelman pd Alex Tavoularis ed Sheldon Kahn, William D. Gordean
☆ Charles Grodin, Bonnie Hunt, Dean Jones, Oliver Platt, Stanley Tucci, David Duchovny, Patricia Heaton, Laurel Cronin, O-Lan Jones
'Could be called harmless if it wasn't so badly made and blandly characterised.' – *Derek Malcolm, Guardian*
'Laugh? We wait like locked-in dogs whose noses are pressed to the window for the first sign of life or human interest coming up the driveway. Wit we have already despaired of in reel one.' – *Nigel Andrews, Financial Times*

Beethoven's 2nd
🕊 US 1993 89m DeLuxe
Universal (Michael C. Gross, Joe Medjuck)
📺 🎬 ◎~ ◉ 🎧

Beethoven becomes the father of pups, which are promptly kidnapped.
A sentimental sequel that will be enjoyed by fans of large, slobbering dogs and obvious jokes.
w Len Blum d Rod Daniel ph Bill Butler m Randy Edelman pd Lawrence Miller ed Sheldon Kahn, William D. Gordean
☆ Charles Grodin, Bonnie Hunt, Nicholle Tom, Christopher Castile, Sarah Rose Karr, Debi Mazar, Chris Penn, Ashley Hamilton, Maury Chaykin
'Universal unleashes what should be a big, slobbering hit with this reasonably entertaining sequel, certainly a more pleasing tale than the one that sired it.' – *Variety*
'It's so insubstantial that it flies from the mind's eye almost as soon as the lights go up.' – *Derek Malcolm, Guardian*
'All the wit and spontaneity of a suet pudding.' – *Sight and Sound*
🎵 song 'The Day I Fall In Love' (m/ly Carole Bayer Sager, James Ingram, Cliff Magness)

Beetlejuice *
US 1988 92m Technicolor
Warner Bros/Geffen (Michael Bender)
📺 🎬 ◎~ ◉

The newly dead at a New England barn try to scare off objectionable new buyers.
Mainly unpleasant and seldom funny fantasy.
w Michael McDowell, Warren Skaaren d Tim Burton ph Thomas Ackerman m Danny Elfman pd Bo Welch
☆ Alec Baldwin, Geena Davis, Michael Keaton, Catherine O'Hara, Glenn Shadix

'A murder. A suspect. A shadow of a doubt.'
Before and After
US 1996 108m Technicolor
Buena Vista/Hollywood/Caravan (Barbet Schroeder, Susan Hoffman)
📺 🎬 ◎~ 🎧

When their teenage son is accused of murdering his girlfriend, his parents take differing attitudes on how best to deal with the situation.
Indifferent and windy drama that avoids any proper conflict or confrontation of the issues; it doesn't even hold the interest of its participants.

w Ted Tally novel Rosellen Brown d Barbet Schroeder ph Luciano Tovoli m Howard Shore pd Stuart Wurtzel ed Lee Percy
☆ Meryl Streep, Liam Neeson, Edward Furlong, Alfred Molina, Julia Weldon, Daniel von Bargen, John Heard
'A wan, flat little anecdote, implausible to a preposterous degree.' – *Alexander Walker*

Before Dawn *
US 1933 60m bw
RKO

Three murders take place in a mysterious mansion.
Lively comedy-thriller which won't bore anybody: good in its class.
w Garrett Fort, Marion Dix, Ralph Block story Edgar Wallace d Irving Pichel m Max Steiner
☆ Warner Oland, Stuart Erwin, Dorothy Wilson, Dudley Digges, Oscar Apfel

Before Hindsight **
GB 1977 78m Eastmancolor
Elizabeth Taylor-Mead

Interviews and clips show how inadequately cinema newsreels covered world events in the 1930s.
Hard tack for entertainment seekers, but a clear exposition of a proven case of importance to film-makers and politicians.
w Elizabeth Taylor-Mead d Jonathan Lewis
'Certainly not the kind of picture people will pay money to see.' – *Variety*

'Beware! When Karloff Stops The Clock ... Your Hour Has Come!'
Before I Hang *
US 1940 71m bw
Columbia (Wallace MacDonald)
📺 ◎~

A research scientist experiments with a new serum which turns him into a murderer.
Archetypal Karloff mad doctor flick, Jekyll and Hyde model: still quite tolerable.
w Robert D. Andrews d Nick Grinde ph Benjamin Kline md Morris Stoloff
☆ Boris Karloff, Evelyn Keyes, Bruce Bennett, Pedro de Cordoba, Edward Van Sloan, Don Beddoe
'Karloff is so good he makes you believe this nonsense.' – *The Dark Side*

Before Sunrise *
US 1995 101m Technicolor
Rank/Castle Rock/Detour/Filmhaus (Anne Walker-McBay)
📺 🎬 ◎~ ◉

A young American meets a French woman on a train and persuades her to spend the night talking and walking around Vienna.
A conversation piece that has a certain inconsequential charm but cannot sustain itself for the length of the film; the talk is simply not interesting enough.
w Richard Linklater, Kim Krizan d Richard Linklater ph Lee Daniel pd Florian Reichmann ed Sandra Adair
☆ Ethan Hawke, Julie Delpy
'This two character talkfest wins points for daring to be a love story – how defiantly unhip is that? – and is presumably meant as sensitivity training for 20-year-olds. But in reaching for winsome charm, the film falls flat. This meeting of bright minds often plays like desperate showing off.' – *Richard Corliss, Time*
'While pic remains sympathetic and appealing, the endless dialogue and repetitive settings become wearing through the couple's one long night together, and the artifice of the premise may contribute to the difficulty the film has in coming to romantic life.' – *Todd McCarthy, Variety*

Before the Nickelodeon **
US 1982 60m bw/colour
Film for Thought

The life, times and films of the pioneer Edwin S. Porter.
Valuable documentary on a little-known figure, with films ranging from 1896 to 1907.
w Warren D. Leight, Charles Musser d Charles Musser

Before the Night: see *One Night Stand* (1995)

Before the Rain ***

GB/France/Macedonia   1994   113m
Eastmancolor
Electric/Aim/Noe/Vardar (Judy Counihan, Cedomir
Kolar, Sam Taylor, Cat Villiers)

original title: *Pred Dozdot*

An expatriate Macedonian photographer leaves his
pregnant English lover in London and returns to
his homeland, caught in the conflict that has
destroyed Yugoslavia, to witness the effects of the
civil war on the village where he grew up.
Three separate stories intertwine in a gripping drama,
although the connections between them, and the way
each leads forward and back to the other, is not evident
until the final moments; the construction mirrors the
circle of violence the film depicts, with its characters
mired in unthinking hate.
wd Milcho Manchevski ph Manuel Teran
m Anastasia pd Sharon Lamofsky, David Munns
ed Nicolas Gaster
☆ Katrin Cartlidge, Rade Serbedzija, Gregoire
Colin, Labina Mitevska, Jay Villiers, Silvija
Stojanovska, Phyllida Law
'Dense with threat and tense with the possibility
of its release.' – *Tom Shone, Sunday Times*
⅄ best foreign film

Before the Revolution *

Italy   1964   115m   bw
Cineriz/Iride

original title: *Prima della Rivoluzione*
The suicide of a friend leads a middle-class youth
living in Parma to consider his own life and
attitudes before opting for safe conformity.
A talented but confused debate on politics, which upset
Catholic authorities at the time, but leaves an audience
only a little wiser.
wd Bernardo Bertolucci m Gino Paoli, Ennio
Morricone md Aldo Scavarda ad Romano
Pampaloni ed Roberto Perpignani
☆ Francesco Barilli, Adriana Asti, Alain
Midgette, Morando Morandini
'He captures what has rarely been seen on the
screen – the extravagance and poetry of youthful
ardour.' – *Pauline Kael, New Yorker*

Before Winter Comes *

GB   1968   107m   Technicolor
Columbia/Windward (Robert Emmett Ginna)
Austria 1945: a British major in charge of displaced
persons is helped and hindered by a cheerful
Yugoslav refugee who turns out to be a Russian
deserter.
Likeable, well-produced drama hampered by a plot
which becomes unnecessarily schematic, coincidental
and downbeat in its attempts to tug at the heartstrings.
w Andrew Sinclair novel *The Interpreter* by
Frederick L. Keefe d J. Lee-Thompson ph Gilbert
Taylor m Ron Grainer
☆ David Niven, Topol, Ori Levi, Anna Karina,
John Hurt, Anthony Quayle
'One of those films with a message on every page
of its script.' – *MFB*

Beg, Borrow or Steal

US   1937   70m   bw
MGM
An American expatriate lives by his wits in Paris.
Flabby comedy which misses on all cylinders.
w Leonard Lee, Harry Ruskin, Marion Parsonnet
d William Thiele
☆ Frank Morgan, Florence Rice, John Beal, Janet
Beecher, Herman Bing, Erik Rhodes, E. E. Clive,
Reginald Denny, George Givot
'Nothing quite so incredible as this story has
been tossed to the double bills since the major
studios started competing among themselves to
turn out low-grade entertainment for the filler-in
spots.' – *Variety*

Beggars in Ermine

US   1934   70m   bw
Monogram
A steelworker who loses his legs and his livelihood
organizes beggars into a wealthy union.
Curious semi-fantasy, probably worth a mark for
trying.
w Tristam Tupper novel Esther Lynd Daly d Phil
Rosen
☆ Lionel Atwill, Henry B. Walthall, Betty
Furness, Jameson Thomas, Astrid Allwyn

Beggars of Life *

US   1928   80m   bw   part-talkie
Paramount
Adventures of a hobo.
Curious melodramatic farrago notable chiefly for
technical advances but far from boring to watch for its
own sake.
w Benjamin Glazer, Jim Tully d William
Wellman
☆ Richard Arlen, Wallace Beery, Louise Brooks,
Edgar Blue Washington, H. A. Morgan, Roscoe
Karns

The Beggar's Opera *

GB   1952   94m   Technicolor
British Lion/Imperadio (Herbert Wilcox, Laurence
Olivier)

A highwayman in Newgate jail devises an opera
based on his own exploits.
Exuberant potted version of the 1728 low opera,
generally likeable but lacking a strong coherent
approach and marred by violent colour and raggedly
theatrical presentation. It nearly but not quite comes
off.
w Denis Cannan, Christopher Fry opera John
Gay d Peter Brook ad Guy Green ad George
Wakhevitch, William C. Andrews musical
arrangement and additions Arthur Bliss
☆ Laurence Olivier, Stanley Holloway, Dorothy
Tutin, Daphne Anderson, Mary Clare, George
Devine, Athene Seyler, Hugh Griffith, Margot
Grahame, Sandra Dorne, Laurence Naismith
'The failure is equalled only by the ambition.' –
Gavin Lambert

'New Thrills! New Shocks! New Terror!'
The Beginning of the End

US   1957   73m   bw
ABPT/Republic (Bert I. Gordon)

Radiation breeds giant grasshoppers which are only
stopped when they can't withstand the waters of
Lake Michigan.
Bottom-of-the-sci-fi-barrel rubbish, very boring to
watch.
w Fred Freiberger, Lester Corn d Bert I. Gordon
☆ Peggie Castle, Peter Graves, Morris Ankrum,
James Seay, Richard Benedict, Pierre Watkin

The Beginning or the End

US   1947   112m   bw
MGM (Samuel Marx)
During World War II American scientists continue
to perfect the atom bomb despite their own
misgivings, and one dies in an explosion.
Semi-documentary marred by sentimental personal
asides and of very little continuing interest.
w Robert Considine d Norman Taurog ph Ray
June m Daniele Amfitheatrof
☆ Brian Donlevy, Robert Walker, Tom Drake,
Beverly Tyler, Hume Cronyn, Audrey Totter,
Godfrey Tearle
'The documentary value is so offset by sickly
sentiment that it is practically just another love
story.' – *W. A. Wilcox, Sunday Dispatch*

Begone Dull Care ****

Canada   1953   9m   colour
National Film Board (Norman McLaren)
Abstract images drawn directly onto the film are
accompanied by three pieces of jazz performed by
the Oscar Peterson Trio.
The central movement is a little too slow, but the first
piece is witty and the climax is an irresistible frenzy of
sound and image. Undeniably a classic short, and
probably McLaren's best.
conceived and made by Norman McLaren

'One man ... seven women ... in a strange house!'
The Beguiled *

US   1971   109m   Technicolor
Universal/Malpaso (Don Siegel)

A wounded Unionist soldier hides out in a
Confederate ladies' school; the teachers fend for
him until he causes trouble among the sexually
frustrated women, who eventually kill him.
Eccentric melodrama which does not really work
despite its credentials and patient work all round.
w John B. Sherry, Grimes Grice novel Thomas
Cullinan d Don Siegel ph Bruce Surtees m Lalo
Schifrin pd Ted Haworth

☆ Clint Eastwood, Geraldine Page, Elizabeth
Hartman, Jo Ann Harris, Darleen Carr, Mae
Mercer
'A must for sadists and woman-haters.' – *Judith*
Crist

Behave Yourself *

US   1951   81m   bw
RKO (Jerry Wald, Norman Krasna)

A young married couple and their dog get mixed
up in a chain of murders.
Zany black comedy in the wake of A Slight Case of
Murder and The Thin Man (qqv). The humour is
spread too thin for success.
wd George Beck ph James Wong Howe m Leigh
Harline
☆ Farley Granger, Shelley Winters, William
Demarest, Francis L. Sullivan, Margalo Gillmore,
Lon Chaney, Hans Conried, Elisha Cook Jnr

Behemoth the Sea Monster: see The Giant
Behemoth

Behind Convent Walls (dubbed)

Italy   1977   95m   Telecolor
Trust International (Giuseppe Vezzani)

original title: *Interno d'un Convento*
US title: *Sex Life in a Convent; aka: Within a Cloister*
A mother superior finds that her sisters are more
interested in carnal knowledge than religious faith.
A staple of soft-core porn – nuns behaving badly – is
given a little visual distinction in an otherwise dull and
predictable offering.
wd Walerian Borowczyk stories Promenades
Romanes by Stendhal ph Luciano Tovolli
m Sergio Montori ad Luciano Spadoni
☆ Ligia Branice, Howard Ross, Marina Pierro,
Gabriella Giaccobe, Rodolfo Dal Pra', Loredana
Martinez, Mario Maranzana

Behind Prison Gates

US   1939   63m   bw
Columbia
A secret agent follows bank robbers into prison.
Standard undercover crime support.
w Arthur T. Horman, Leslie T. White d Charles
Barton
☆ Brian Donlevy, Jacqueline Wells, Joseph
Crehan, Paul Fix

Behind Prison Walls

US   1943   64m   bw
PRC (Arthur Ripley)
GB title: *Youth Takes a Hand*
Too-honest son gets his tycoon father sent to
prison, but ends up there himself.
Curious moral comedy drama which can't work on a
low budget.
w Van Norcross, W. A. Ulman Jnr d Steve Sekely
☆ Alan Baxter, Tully Marshall, Gertrude Michael,
Edwin Maxwell, Matt Willis

Behind That Curtain

US   1929   91m   bw
Fox

Murder follows when a ne'er-do-well aspires to
marry an heiress.
Nominally the third Charlie Chan film, but Chan,
played by E. L. Park, is whittled down to a tiny role.
As it stands, a clumsy effort, but could be worth
remaking.
w Sonya Levien, Clarke Silvernail novel Earl
Derr Biggers d Irving Cummings
☆ Warner Baxter, Lois Moran, Gilbert Emery,
Claude King, Philip Strange, Boris Karloff

Behind the Door: see The Man with Nine Lives

Behind the Eight Ball

US   1942   60m   bw
Universal
GB title: *Off the Beaten Track*
Actors are mistaken for spies.
Very patchy but commendably brief star comedy.
w Stanley Roberts, Mel Ronson d Edward F.
Cline
☆ The Ritz Brothers, Carol Bruce, Dick Foran,
William Demarest

Behind the High Wall

US   1956   85m   bw
U-I (Stanley Rubin)
A prison warder, taken as hostage by escaping
convicts, steals some of the money they have
taken.
Glum melodrama, capably presented.
w Harold Jack Bloom d Abner Biberman
ph Maury Gertsman m Joseph Gershenson
☆ Tom Tully, Sylvia Sidney, John Gavin, Betty
Lynn, John Larch, Barney Phillips, Don Beddoe

Behind the Iron Mask: see The Fifth
Musketeer

'Who is the murdering monster?'
Behind the Mask

US   1932   68m   bw
Columbia
A crazy doctor operates fatally on those who know
too much.
Semi-horror mystery using two members of the
Frankenstein cast.
w Jo Swerling d John Francis Dillon
☆ Jack Holt, Constance Cummings, Edward Van
Sloan, Boris Karloff
'Exploited as another horror picture, this doesn't
horrify sufficiently to class with preceding baby-
scarers. But its virtues are a not-so-bad Secret
Service story, well-acted by a cast of veterans.' –
Variety

Behind the Mask *

GB   1958   99m   Eastmancolor
BL/GW Films (Sergei Nolbandov, Josef Somlo)
Political infighting causes tension on the board of a
local hospital.
Oddly titled social drama with interesting detail but not
much tension or conclusion.
w John Hunter novel *The Pack* by John Rowan
Wilson d Brian Desmond Hurst ph Robert
Krasker m Geoffrey Wright
☆ Michael Redgrave, Tony Britton, Carl Mohner,
Niall MacGinnis, Vanessa Redgrave, Ian Bannen,
Brenda Bruce, Lionel Jeffries, Miles Malleson, John
Welsh, Ann Firbank

Behind the Rising Sun *

US   1943   88m   bw
RKO

An American-educated Japanese goes home in the
thirties, comes under the influence of war-mongers,
and causes his father to commit hara-kiri.
Outrageous wartime flagwaver designed to vilify 'Uncle
Tojo's dogs', from the writer and director of the similar
Hitler's Children (qv).
w Emmet Lavery novel James R. Young d Edward
Dmytryk ph Russell Metty m Roy Webb
☆ J. Carrol Naish, Tom Neal, Margo, Robert
Ryan, Gloria Holden, Don Douglas, Adeline de
Walt Reynolds

Behold a Pale Horse *

US   1964   121m   bw
Columbia/Highland/Brentwood (Fred Zinnemann,
Alexander Trauner)

A Spanish guerrilla goes into exile at the end of
the Civil War. Twenty years later he is persuaded
to return and kill a brutal police chief.
An action film which unfortunately insists on saying
something significant about morality, destiny and
death. Impeccably made, but somehow not very
interesting apart from the action sequences.
w J. P. Miller novel *Killing a Mouse on Sunday* by
Emeric Pressburger d Fred Zinnemann ph Jean
Badal m Maurice Jarre ad Alexander Trauner
☆ Gregory Peck, Omar Sharif, Anthony Quinn,
Raymond Pellegrin, Paolo Stoppa, Mildred
Dunnock, Daniela Rocca, Christian Marquand
'A fine example of a high class failure.' – *Judith*
Crist

'Her savage heart pounded with revenge when her
love went unwanted!'
Behold My Wife

US   1934   79m   bw
Paramount (B. P. Schulberg)
A wealthy young man brings back and marries a
New Mexico Indian girl to show up his snobbish
family.
Dated melodrama, of interest solely for its racial theme.

👫 film suitable for
family viewing
📼 VHS video-cassette for
the British PAL system
📼 VHS video-cassette for the British
PAL system in wide screen-format
💾 Video cassette in a computer-
colourised version
📺 American NTSC video-cassette
💿 Laser disc

w William R. Lipman, Oliver LaFarge novel *The Translation of a Savage* by Sir Gilbert Parker d Mitchell Leisen ph Leon Shamroy
☆ Sylvia Sidney, Gene Raymond, Juliette Compton, Laura Hope Crews, H. B. Warner, Monroe Owsley, Ann Sheridan
'Frank melodrama of the hokiest sort.' – *Variety*

Beijing Bastards *

China/Hong Kong 1993 95m colour
Beijing Bastards (Cui Jian, Zhang Yuan, Shu Qi, Du Kefeng)

original title: *Beijing Zazhong*

Groups of friends with artistic aspirations drink, fight, talk, drink, play music and complain about their aimless lives.
A disjointed look at the disaffected young, in which the slight narrative is disrupted by rock performances; interesting mainly for its portrait of a shiftless generation not usually seen on film.
w Zhang Yuan, Tang Danian, Cui Jian d Zhang Yuan ph Zhang Jian m Cui Jian, Dou Wei, Ha Yong ad Liu Xiaodong ed Feng Shuangyuan
☆ Cui Jian, Li Wei, Wu Gang, Bian Tianshuo, Tang Danian, Bian Wing
'The first film to tackle the anger and frustration of today's youth in China … communicates a strong sense of squalor and brutishness, a depressing lack of purpose and lack of contact between people. All told, pic is quite a downer.' – *Deborah Young, Variety*
† The film was banned by the Chinese authorities, who also tried to prevent it being shown at the Locarno Festival in 1993.

Beijing Zazhong: see *Beijing Bastards*

'Suddenly one Summer…'
Being at Home with Claude

Canada 1993 85m colour/bw
Out on a Limb/Les Productions du Cerf (Louise Gendron)

A young hustler explains to a policeman why he murdered his lover, a shy intellectual.
This small-scale play transferred to the screen retains its theatrical air, being all talk and no action; the talk, though, and the interaction between the two protagonists retain one's interest for the most part.
wd Jean Beaudin play René-Daniel Dubois ph Thomas Vamos m Richard Grégoire ed André Corriveau
☆ Roy Dupuis, Jacques Godin, Jean-François Pichette, Gaston Lepage
'It's hard not to respect something so extreme in its stylisation, emotional intensity and naked romanticism, but it's also hard to cosy up to a film which combines such posiness with hidebound theatre conventions. Beautifully crafted but entirely resistible.' – *Kim Newman, Empire*

'From the dawn of time man has struggled for just four things. Food. Safety. Someone to Love. And a pair of shoes that fit.'
Being Human *

US/GB 1994 122m Technicolor
Warner/Enigma/Fujisankei/BSB/NatWest Ventures (Robert F. Colesberry, David Puttnam)

In five historical eras, from the Bronze Age to modern-day America, a father fails to provide for his family and ends alone and in near-despair.
Bleak variations on the theme of man's inability to make sense of the world, of people inventing stories to comfort themselves in impossible situations. There are moments of wry amusement, but despite its originality, it has too little variation in pace, and the episodes are too inconclusive to provide much satisfaction.
wd Bill Forsyth ph Michael Coulter m Michael Gibbs pd Norman Garwood ed Michael Ellis
☆ Robin Williams, John Turturro, Anna Galiena, Vincent D'Onofrio, Hector Elizondo, Lorraine Bracco, Lindsay Crouse, Jonathan Hyde, Bill Nighy, Theresa Russell
'An affecting piece that follows its own path against the odds, and certainly does not need any excuses made for it.' – *Jonathan Romney, Guardian*
'This still-born series of little fables is so flat and ill-conceived that it could convince the uninitiated that neither Robin Williams nor the highly idiosyncratic Scottish writer/director Bill Forsyth had any talent.' – *Todd McCarthy, Variety*

† After being left on the shelf for a year, the film, which cost $20m to make, flopped at the US box-office, taking $2m, and was released direct to video in Britain.

Being John Malkovich ***

US/GB 1999 112m colour
Universal/Gramercy/Propaganda/Single Cell (Michael Stipe, Sandy Stern, Steve Golin, Vincent Landay)

Having discovered a portal that allows him to spend time inside the brain of John Malkovich, an unhappily married, unsuccessful puppeteer decides to exploit the situation.
A witty, highly original comedy that manages to be both surreal and ordinary in its depiction of the world and the everyday oddballs that inhabit it, though it does disappear up its own inventiveness towards the end.
w Charlie Kaufman d Spike Jonze ph Lance Acord m Carter Burwell pd K. K. Barrett ed Eric Zumbrunnen
☆ John Cusack, Cameron Diaz, Catherine Keener, Orson Bean, Mary Kay Place, John Malkovich, Charlie Sheen
'Touches on questions of love, identity, sex, gender and penetration with a playful perverseness few other semi-mainstream productions would ever dare to dabble in. Devilishly inventive and so far out there it's almost off the scale.' – *David Rooney, Variety*
'Manages any number of resourceful riffs on the cult of success without losing its own sweetness.' – *Adam Mars-Jones, Times*
† Sean Penn, Brad Pitt and Christopher Bing appear uncredited as themselves.
⅙ Catherine Keener; Spike Jonze; Charlie Kaufman
☝ Charlie Kaufman

'Getting there is half the fun; being there is all of it!'
Being There **

US 1979 130m Metrocolor
Lorimar/North Star/CIP (Andrew Braunsberg)

An illiterate gardener is taken for a homespun philosopher and becomes a national celebrity.
Overlong serio-comic parable hinging on a somewhat dubious star performance. Chance made it a popular urban success, but few who saw it were enthused.
w Jerzy Kosinski novel Jerzy Kosinski d Hal Ashby ph Caleb Deschanel m John Mandel pd Michael Haller
☆ Peter Sellers, Shirley MacLaine, Melvyn Douglas, Jack Warden, Richard Dysart, Richard Basehart
'It pulls off its long shot and is a confoundingly provocative movie.' – *Roger Ebert*
⚹ Melvyn Douglas
⅙ Peter Sellers
☝ screenplay

Beiqing Chengshi *

Taiwan 1989 160m colour
Artificial Eye/3-H/Era International (Qui Fusheng)

aka: *A City of Sadness*

During the 1940s, from the end of the Japanese occupation of Taiwan to the communist takeover of the Chinese mainland, a family, headed by a local gangster, undergoes domestic upheavals.
Winner of the Golden Lion at the Venice Film Festival in 1989, it nevertheless remains fairly impenetrable to Western audiences not familiar with the political intricacies of the period.
w Wu Nianzhen, Zhu Tianwen d Hou Hsiao-Hsien ph Chen Huai'en m Tachikawa Naoki, Zhang Hongyi pd Liu Zhihua, Lin Chongwen ed Liao Qingsong
☆ Li Tianlu, Chen Songyong, Gao Jie, Tony Leung, Wu Yifang, Xin Shufen, Chen Shufang, Ke Suyun, Lin Liqing, He Aiyun
'Its balance between the personal and the political is spectacular and exemplary, as if a brilliant miniaturist had miraculously filled a huge canvas.' – *Tony Rayns, MFB*

Bela Lugosi Meets a Brooklyn Gorilla

US 1952 74m bw
Jack Broder

GB title: *The Monster Meets the Gorilla*

A tropical island scientist turns one half of a stranded comedy team into a gorilla.
Stupid farce which never rises to the occasion.
w Tim Ryan d William Beaudine

☆ Bela Lugosi, Duke Mitchell, Sammy Petrillo, Ray 'Crash' Corrigan, Muriel Landers
'Neighbourhood and small-town audiences will get some laughs.' – *Box Office*

Believe in Me

US 1971 90m colour
MGM (Irwin Winkler, Robert Chartoff)

Two young marrieds take to drugs.
Tedious and unenlightening modern drama which seems to think it's saying something new.
w Israel Horovitz d Stuart Hagmann ph Dick Kratina, Richard C. Brooks m Fred Karlin
☆ Michael Sarrazin, Jacqueline Bisset, Jon Cypher, Allen Garfield

The Believers *

US 1987 114m DeLuxe
Orion/John Schlesinger, Michael Childers, Beverly Camhe

New York's occult underworld is permeated by a sinister Catholic ritual.
Most of the time it's hard to say what's going on in this intensely melodramatic thriller, but there are the odd rewards along the way. Not too many, actually.
w Mark Frost book *The Religion* by Nicholas Conde d John Schlesinger ph Robby Müller m J. Peter Robinson pd Simon Holland ed Peter Honess
☆ Martin Sheen, Helen Shaver, Harley Cross, Robert Loggia, Elizabeth Wilson, Harris Yulin
'If nothing else, Schlesinger knows how to produce a film where pain and horror are beautiful to watch.' – *Daily Variety*

'A bewitching comedy about an enchanting subject!'
Bell, Book and Candle *

US 1958 103m Technicolor
Columbia/Phoenix (Julian Blaustein)

A publisher slowly becomes aware that his new girlfriend is a witch.
A gossamer stage comedy has been fatally flattened in translation; most of the actors are miscast, and sentiment soaks the script. But it remains a civilized entertainment.
w Daniel Taradash play John Van Druten d Richard Quine ph James Wong Howe m George Duning ad Cary Odell
☆ James Stewart, Kim Novak, Jack Lemmon, Ernie Kovacs, Hermione Gingold, Elsa Lanchester, Janice Rule
'Rarely has so much cinematic talent been expended so successfully on so little.' – *Films in Review*
⅙ art direction

Bell Bottom George

GB 1943 97m bw
Columbia

A medically exempt waiter dons uniform and catches a ring of spies.
Formula star comedy, too long and too familiar.
w Peter Fraser, Edward Dryhurst d Marcel Varnel
☆ George Formby, Anne Firth, Reginald Purdell, Peter Murray Hill

A Bell for Adano *

US 1945 104m bw
TCF (Louis D. Lighton, Lamar Trotti)

An American major takes over an Italian town and wins affection by replacing the local bell.
Slight end-of-war mood piece, still quite pleasant but without the undercurrents of feeling it had at the time.
w Lamar Trotti, Norman Reilly Raine novel John Hersey d Henry King ph Joseph LaShelle m Alfred Newman
☆ John Hodiak, Gene Tierney, William Bendix, Glenn Langan, Richard Conte, Stanley Prager, Henry Morgan

The Bell Jar

US 1979 107m colour
Peerce-Goldston/Avco

A teenage girl becomes mentally ill when her father dies.
Numbingly tedious case history without much apparent point.
w Marjorie Kellogg novel Sylvia Plath d Larry Peerce
☆ Marilyn Hassett, Julie Harris, Anne Jackson, Barbara Barrie

Belladonna

GB 1934 91m bw
Twickenham (Julius Hagen)

A selfish woman tries to poison her husband for love of an Egyptian.
Intriguingly-cast version of a story that was later filmed in Hollywood as Temptation *(qv).*
w H. Fowler Mear play J. B. Fagan novel Robert Hichens d Robert Milton ph Sydney Blythe, William Luff ad James Carter
☆ Mary Ellis, Conrad Veidt, Cedric Hardwicke, John Stuart, Michael Shepley

Il Bell'Antonio *

Italy/France 1960 105m bw
Cina del Duca-Arco/Lyre Cinématographique (Alfredo Bini)

GB title: *Handsome Antonio*

A youngish man returns to his native town with the reputation of a lady-killer, but when married turns out to be impotent.
Amusing but finally exhausting Sicilian comedy with all the expected exaggeration of speech and gesture.
w Pier Paolo Pasolini, Gino Visentini novel Vitaliano Brancati d Piero Piccioni
☆ Marcello Mastroianni, Claudia Cardinale, Pierre Brasseur, Rina Morelli, Tomas Milian

The Bellboy *

US 1960 72m bw
Paramount/Jerry Lewis Productions (Jerry Lewis)

An incompetent bellboy causes havoc in a Miami hotel.
Plotless essence of a comedian who divides opinion and will never be better than variable. This ragbag of old gags at least prevents his usual sentimental excesses, and is mercifully short.
wd Jerry Lewis ph Haskell Boggs m Walter Scharf
☆ Jerry Lewis, Alex Gerry, Bob Clayton, Herkie Styles, Milton Berle

La Belle Américaine *

France 1961 101m bw (colour finale)
CCFC/Film d'Art/Panorama/Corflor (Henri Diamant-Berger, Arthur Lesser)

GB and US titles: *What a Chassis*
aka: *The American Beauty*

A Parisian factory worker gets into all kinds of trouble when he buys an American supercar for a ridiculously low price.
Some brilliant gags are separated by long dull spots of unnecessary storytelling.
w Robert Dhéry, Pierre Tchernia, Alfred Adam d Robert Dhéry ph Ghislain Cloquet m Gérard Calvi
☆ Robert Dhéry, Louis de Funes, Colette Brosset, Alfred Adam, Bernard Lavalette, Annie Ducaux

Belle de Jour ****

France/Italy 1967 100m Eastmancolor
Paris Film/Five Film (Robert and Raymond Hakim)

A surgeon's wife finds herself drawn to afternoon work in a brothel.
Fascinating Buñuel mixture of fact and fantasy, impeccably woven into a rich fabric.
w Luis Buñuel, Jean-Claude Carrière novel Joseph Kessel d Luis Buñuel ph Sacha Vierny m none ad Robert Clavel ed Louisette Hautecoeur, Walter Spohr
☆ Catherine Deneuve, Jean Sorel, Michel Piccoli, Genevieve Page, Pierre Clémenti
'Oppressively powerful. Like being buried alive in Sarah Bernhardt's dressing room.' – *Wilfred Sheed*
'The rhythm of the writing, the color changes, acting tempos, camera angles, the whole editing – all this is perfect. There is not one extraneous shot, not one that is missing. Disparate elements are embraced in a self-possessed, lucidly enchanting flow.' – *John Simon*

Belle Epoque *

Spain 1992 109m Eastmancolor
Cinemascope
Mayfair/Lola/Animatografo/French Production/Fernando Trueba

In Spain in the early 30s, a deserter from the army hides in the house of a widower with four attractive daughters, who teach him the pleasures of life.

A leisurely, enjoyable film of the past, as seen through rose-coloured spectacles; it is inoffensive and amusing without being particularly memorable.

w Rafael Azcona *story* Rafael Azcona, José Luis Garcia Sanchez, Fernando Trueba d Fernando Trueba *ph* José Luis Alcaine *m* Antoine Duhamel *ad* Juan Botella *ed* Carmen Frias

☆ Fernando Fernán Gómez, Jorge Sanz, Maribel Verdú, Ariadna Gil, Miriam Diaz-Aroca, Penélope Cruz, Gabino Diego, Michel Galabru

'The tone is merry as well as erotic, but generally takes the easy way out, suggesting there is more than one country in Europe that sees the benefit of making warmly pleasurable period films that will attract nostalgic audiences.' – *Derek Malcolm, Guardian*

�ⵣ best foreign film

La Belle Equipe *

France 1936 74m bw
Ciné Arts

Five unemployed Parisians win the lottery and open a restaurant, but things do not go smoothly.
Interesting but rather lumpy star drama which finally descends into melodrama; alternative tragic and happy endings were originally offered.

w Charles Spaak, Julien Duvivier d Julien Duvivier *ph* Jules Kruger, Marc Fessard *m* Maurice Yvain

☆ Jean Gabin, Charles Vanel, Viviane Romance, Raymond Aimos, Robert Lynen, Raymond Cordy, Raphael Medina

La Belle et la Bête **

France 1946 96m bw
Discina (André Paulvé)

aka: *Beauty and the Beast*
Beauty gives herself to the Beast who has kidnapped her father; through love the monster turns into a handsome prince.
Slightly heavy-handed though usually stunning-looking adaptation of the fairy tale.

wd Jean Cocteau *story* Madame LePrince de Beaumont *ph* Henri Alekan *m* Georges Auric *ad* Christian Bérard *ed* Claude Ibéria

☆ Jean Marais, Josette Day, Mila Parély, Marcel André, Nane Germon, Michel Auclair

'Perhaps the most sumptuously elegant of all filmed fairy tales.' – *New Yorker, 1980*
'Absolute magic: diamond cold and lunar bright.' – *CBS*
'A sensuously fascinating film, a fanciful poem in movement given full articulation on the screen.' – *Bosley Crowther, New York Times*

Une Belle Fille Comme Moi

France 1972 98m colour
Columbia/Les Films du Carrosse (Marcel Berbert, Claude Ganz)

US title: *Such a Gorgeous Kid Like Me*
A gullible sociologist hears the confession of a promiscuous murderess.
Moderately interesting black comedy.

w Jean-Loup Dabadie, François Truffaut *novel* Henry Farrell d François Truffaut *ph* Pierre-William Glenn *m* Georges Delerue *ad* Jean-Pierre Kohut *ed* Yann Dedet, Martine Barraque

☆ Bernadette Lafont, Claude Brasseur, Charles Denner, Guy Marchand, André Dussollier, Anne Kreis, Philippe Léotard

La Belle Noiseuse ***

France 1991 240m colour
Artificial Eye/Pierre Grise

The beautiful young mistress of a friend inspires a famous artist to finish a painting, for which his wife modelled, that he put aside ten years before.
A gripping and penetrating movie on the themes of obsession, art and love, although it offers little in the way of conventional narrative.

w Pascal Bonitzer, Christine Laurent, Jacques Rivette *story* Le Chef d'Oeuvre Inconnu (The Unknown Masterpiece) by Honoré de Balzac d Jacques Rivette *ph* William Lubtchansky *m* Stravinsky *ad* Emmanuel de Chauvigny *ed* Nicole Lubtchansky

☆ Michel Piccoli, Jane Birkin, Emmanuelle Béart, Marianne Denicourt, David Bursztein, Gilles Arbona

'Perhaps the most meticulous and seductive depiction in movies of the hard work of making art.' – *Richard Corliss, Time*

† Artist Bernard Dufour, whose hand is the only part of him to be seen, did the painting
†† *La Belle Noiseuse: Divertimento,* a two-hour version of the film using different takes, was produced for French TV and also given a cinema and video release.

The Belle of New York *

US 1952 82m Technicolor
MGM (Arthur Freed)

An 1890s playboy falls for a Salvation Army girl.
A rather dreary version of the old musical, with undistinguished additions.

w Robert O'Brien, Irving Elinson *play* Hugh Morton d Charles Walters *ph* Robert Planck *m/ly* Johnny Mercer, Harry Warren *md* Adolph Deutsch *ad* Jack Martin Smith

☆ Fred Astaire, Vera-Ellen, Marjorie Main, Keenan Wynn, Alice Pearce, Clinton Sundberg, Gale Robbins

† Vera-Ellen's singing was dubbed by Anita Ellis
♫ 'When I'm Out with the Belle of New York'; 'Oops'; 'Baby Doll'; 'Naughty but Nice'; 'Seeing's Believing'; 'Thank You Mr Currier, Thank You Mr Ives'; 'I Love to Beat a Big Bass Drum'; 'I Wanna Be a Dancing Man'; 'Let a Little Love Come In'

Belle of the Nineties *

US 1934 75m bw
Paramount (William Le Baron)

A saloon entertainer loves two men, one of whom is a crook.
Much-laundered star vehicle which despite superior production seems a pale shadow of the star's better pieces.

w Mae West d Leo McCarey *ph* Karl Struss *m/ly* Arthur Johnston, Sam Coslow

☆ Mae West, Roger Pryor, John Miljan, John Mack Brown, Katherine de Mille, Duke Ellington and his Orchestra

'It's been sufficiently denatured from within, yet not completely emasculated.' – *Variety*

Belle of the Yukon *

US 1945 84m Technicolor
International

A troupe of saloon entertainers in the Yukon become involved with a bank robbery.
Threads of plot support comedy, dancing and songs in this but reasonably fresh musical imitation of The Spoilers (qv).

w James Edward Grant d William A. Seiter *ph* Ray Rennahan *md* Arthur Lange

☆ Gypsy Rose Lee, Randolph Scott, Dinah Shore, Charles Winninger, Bob Burns

ⵣ Arthur Lange; song 'Sleigh Ride in July' *(m*Jimmy Van Heusen, *ly* Johnny Burke)

Belle Starr

US 1941 87m Technicolor
TCF (Kenneth MacGowan)

Absurdly laundered version of the life of the west's most notorious female outlaw, with the star laughably miscast.

w Lamar Trotti d Irving Cummings *ph* Ernest Palmer, Ray Rennahan *m* Alfred Newman

☆ Gene Tierney, Randolph Scott, Dana Andrews, Shepperd Strudwick, Elizabeth Patterson, Chill Wills, Louise Beavers

Les Belles de Nuit **

France/Italy 1952 89m bw
Franco London/Rizzoli

A discontented music teacher dreams of beautiful women through the ages.
Charming but very slight dream fantasy with many of the master's touches. (He claims to have intended a comic Intolerance.)

wd René Clair *ph* Armand Thirard, Robert Juilliard, Louise Née *m* Georges Van Parys *ad* Léon Barsacq

☆ Gérard Philipe, Gina Lollobrigida, Martine Carol, Magali Vendeuil, Paolo Stoppa, Raymond Bussières, Raymond Cordy

The Belles of St Trinian's *

GB 1954 91m bw
BL/London Films/Launder and Gilliat

At an unruly and bankrupt school for girls, more time is spent backing horses than studying subjects,

and the headmistress's bookmaker brother has a scheme or two of his own.
Fairly successful film version of Ronald Searle's awful schoolgirl cartoons, the emphasis shifted to a grotesque older generation with the star in drag. An enormous commercial success, but the three sequels, Blue Murder at St Trinian's, The Pure Hell of St Trinian's, The Great St Trinian's Train Robbery (qqv) went from bad to awful.

w Frank Launder, Sidney Gilliat, Val Valentine d Frank Launder *ph* Stan Pavey *m* Malcolm Arnold

☆ Alastair Sim, George Cole, Joyce Grenfell, Hermione Baddeley, Betty Ann Davies, Renée Houston, Beryl Reid, Irene Handl, Mary Merrall, Joan Sims, Sidney James

'Not so much a film as an entertainment on celluloid, a huge charade, a rich pile of idiotic and splendidly senseless images.' – *David Robinson*

Belles on Their Toes

US 1952 89m Technicolor
TCF (Samuel G. Engel)

Further adventures in the growing up of the twelve Gilbreth children.
Flat sequel to Cheaper by the Dozen (qv) with sentimentality instead of Clifton Webb. Period atmosphere attractive.

w Phoebe and Henry Ephron *book* Frank B. Gilbreth Jnr and Ernestine Gilbreth Carey d Henry Levin *ph* Arthur E. Arling *m* Cyril Mockridge

☆ Myrna Loy, Jeanne Crain, Debra Paget, Jeffrey Hunter, Edward Arnold, Hoagy Carmichael, Barbara Bates, Robert Arthur

Bellissima *

Italy 1951 100m bw
Bellissima Films (Salvo d'Angelo)

A mother struggles to get a part in a film for her 7-year-old daughter.
Highly detailed, very noisy star vehicle with neo-realist working-class backgrounds. Exhausting.

w Suso Cecchi d'Amico, Francesco Rosi, Luchino Visconti, Cesare Zavattini d Luchino Visconti *ph* Piero Portalupi *m* Franco Mannino

☆ Anna Magnani, Walter Chiari, Tina Apicella, Gastone Renzelli, Alessandro Blasetti

Bellman and True *

GB 1987 122m Technicolor
Handmade/Euston (Michael Wearing, Christopher Neame)

A young burglar in a heist is protected by an older crook's computer skills.
Good crime drama with television derivation.

w Desmond Lowder, Richard Loncraine, Michael Wearing *novel* Desmond Lowder d Richard Loncraine *ph* Ken Westbury *m* Colin Towns *pd* Jon Bunker *ed* Paul Green

☆ Bernard Hill, Derek Newark, Kieran O'Brien, Richard Hope, Frances Tomelty

The Bells

GB 1931 75m bw
PDC/BSFP (Sergei Nolbandov)

An Alsatian burgomaster is forced by conscience to confess to the killing of a Jew.
Only sound version of a famous melodrama first played on stage by Henry Irving in 1871.

w C. H. Dand *play* Le Juif Polonais by Erckmann and Chatrian d Oscar M. Werndorff, Harcourt Templeman (in three language versions) *ph* Gunther Krampf, Eric Cross *m* Gustav Holst *ad* Oscar Werndorff *ed* Lars Moen, Michael Hankinson

☆ Donald Calthrop, Jane Welsh, Edward Sinclair

† In a 1926 silent version Lionel Barrymore played the murderer and Boris Karloff the mesmerist.

Bells Are Ringing *

US 1960 126m Metrocolor Cinemascope
MGM (Arthur Freed)

A telephone answering service operator becomes passionately involved in the lives of her clients.
Dull, rather ugly and boring transcription of a Broadway musical, with all talents below par, not enough dancing and too much plot.

w Betty Comden, Adolph Green *play* Betty Comden, Adolph Green d Vincente Minnelli *ph* Milton Krasner *m* Jule Styne *md* André

Previn *ch* Charles O'Curran *ad* George W. Davis, Preston Ames *ly* Betty Comden, Adolph Green

☆ Judy Holliday, Dean Martin, Fred Clark, Eddie Foy Jnr, Jean Stapleton, Ruth Storey, Frank Gorshin

ⵣ André Previn

The Bells Go Down *

GB 1943 89m bw
Ealing (S. C. Balcon)

The exploits of a London firefighting unit during World War II.
Tragi-comedy with lively scenes, a good record of the historical background of the blitz.

w Roger Macdougall, Stephen Black d Basil Dearden *ph* Ernest Palmer *m* Roy Douglas

☆ Tommy Trinder, James Mason, Mervyn Johns, Philippa Hyatt, Finlay Currie, Philip Friend, Meriel Forbes, Beatrice Varley, Billy Hartnell

Bells of St Angelo

US 1947 78m Trucolor
Republic (Edward J. White)

In between songs, Roy Rogers foils smugglers who are taking silver across the Mexican border.
A tougher movie than usual for Rogers, but still a curious mixture of comedy, songs, fist-fights and death.

w Sloan Nibley *story* Paul Gangelin d William Witney *ph* Jack Marta *md* Morton Scott *ad* Gano Chittenden *ed* Les Orlebeck

☆ Roy Rogers, Dale Evans, Andy Devine, Bob Nolan and the Sons of the Pioneers

'Your heart will be wearing a smile!'

The Bells of St Mary's **

US 1945 126m bw
RKO/Rainbow (Leo McCarey)

At a big city Catholic school, Father O'Malley and Sister Benedict indulge in friendly rivalry, and succeed in extending the school through the gift of a building.
Sentimental and very commercial sequel to Going My Way (qv), with the stars at their peak and the handling as cosy and well-paced as might be expected.

w Dudley Nichols d Leo McCarey *ph* George Barnes *m* Robert Emmett Dolan *ed* Harry Marker

☆ Bing Crosby, Ingrid Bergman, Henry Travers, William Gargan, Ruth Donnelly, Rhys Williams, Una O'Connor, Eva Novak

'The picture is full of shrewd and pleasant flashes. It is also fascinating to watch as a talented, desperate effort to repeat the unrepeatable. But on the whole it is an unhappy film.' – *James Agée*

ⵣ best picture; Leo McCarey; Robert Emmett Dolan; Bing Crosby; Ingrid Bergman; song 'Aren't You Glad You're You' *(m*Jimmy Van Heusen,*ly* Johnny Burke); Harry Marker

Belly

US 1998 96m DeLuxe
Alliance/Artisan/Big Dog (Ron Rotholz, Hype Williams, Robert Salerno, Larry Meistrich)

Two successful young black gangsters face an uncertain future.
A first feature from a director of music-videos, which has flash and style but little characterisation; you could say it suffers from substance abuse: there's not enough of it beneath the slick surface and raucous hiphop soundtrack.

w Hype Williams, Anthony Bodden, Nas d Hype Williams *ph* Malik Sayeed *m* Stephen Cullo *pd* Regan Jackson *ed* David Leonard

☆ Nas, DMX, Taral Hicks, Tionne 'T-Boz' Watkins, Method Man, Hassan Johnson, Power, Louie Rankin, Tyrin Turner, Minister Benjamin F. Muhammed

'Shackled to a threadbare plot and guided by primary school philosophy, unfortunately Belly fails in every department.' – *Ben Falk, Empire*

The Belly of an Architect

GB/Italy 1987 118m Technicolor
Recorded Releasing/Mondial/Tangram/Film Four International/British Screen (Colin Callender, Walter Donohue)

An American architect in Rome discovers he is terminally ill, is deserted by his wife, and commits suicide.

Ravishing evocation of 18th-century Roman architecture is no compensation for the multi-layered psychological complexity.
wd Peter Greenaway ph Sacha Vierny m Wim Mertens ad Luciana Vedovelli ed John Wilson
☆ Brian Dennehy, Chloe Webb, Lambert Wilson

Beloved
US 1933 80m bw
Universal (Bennie F. Zeidman)
A composer ages from 10 to 90 while trying to place his symphony; he dies happy.
Curious fictional biopic with plenty of incident but no plot.
w Paul Gangelin, George O'Neil d Victor Schertzinger
☆ John Boles, Gloria Stuart, Albert Conti, Dorothy Peterson, Morgan Farley
'Too hopelessly muddled in conception to reach the important money class.' – *Variety*

Beloved *
US 1998 172m Technicolor
Buena Vista/Touchstone/Harpo/Clinica Estetico (Edward Saxon, Jonathan Demme, Gary Goetzman, Oprah Winfrey, Kate Forte)
📀 ▦ ◎ 🎧
In Ohio in the 1870s, a former slave gives a home to a strange young woman, who seems to be the ghost of her dead daughter.
Meticulous version of a novel dealing with the effects and aftermath of slavery; it is, though, both too earnest and too long to be entirely satisfactory.
w Akosua Busia, Richard LaGravenese, Adam Brooks novel Toni Morrison d Jonathan Demme ph Tak Fujimoto m Rachel Portman pd Kristi Zea ed Carol Littleton, Andy Keir
☆ Oprah Winfrey, Danny Glover, Thandie Newton, Kimberly Elise, Beah Richards, Lisa Gay Hamilton, Albert Hall, Irma P. Hall, Carol Jean Lewis, Kessia Kordelle, Jason Robards
'They should have called it Belaboured.' – *Tom Shone, Sunday Times*
⚘ Colleen Atwood (costumes)

The Beloved
US/Greece 1972 94m Technicolor
Filmex Curtwel/Pageant (Patrick Curtis, Yorgo (George) Pan Cosmatos)
▦
aka: *Sin*
aka: *Restless*
Returning from London to his Greek island home, a man begins an affair with the wife of a friend and connives in his death.
Glossy, folksy, and very dull domestic drama, as unconvincing as you would expect from a production that casts Raquel Welch in the role of a Greek peasant.
wd Yorgo (George) Pan Cosmatos ph Mercello Gatti m Yannis Markopoulos pd John Corbidge ed Terry Williams
☆ Raquel Welch, Richard Johnson, Jack Hawkins, Flora Robson, Renato Romano, Frank Wolff

The Beloved Bachelor
US 1931 72m bw
Paramount
A man falls in love with his adopted daughter.
Innocuous tearjerker made with some style.
w Sidney Buchman, Raymond Griffith, Agnes Brand Leahy, Edward H. Peple d Lloyd Corrigan
☆ Paul Lukas, Dorothy Jordan, Betty Van Allen, Charles Ruggles, Vivienne Osborne
'A particularly femme appealing yarn with apt dialogue and natural continuity.' – *Variety*

'There she sat ... Tense ... Silent ... Watching!'
Beloved Enemy *
US 1936 90m bw
Samuel Goldwyn (George Haight)
During the 1921 Irish rebellion, the fiancée of a British army officer falls in love with the leading revolutionary.
Dreamy-eyed romance with little relevance to the real situation; not badly done of its kind.
w John Balderston, Rose Franken, William Brown Meloney, David Hart d H. C. Potter ph Gregg Toland m Alfred Newman
☆ Brian Aherne, Merle Oberon, David Niven, Karen Morley, Jerome Cowan, Henry Stephenson, Donald Crisp
'One of the most incredible screen yarns which has been shown in many a day ... If when the film is shown in Dublin a tidal wave engulfs

Hollywood, it will be caused by the Emerald Isle turning somersaults.' – *Variety*

Beloved Infidel *
US 1959 123m DeLuxe Cinemascope
TCF/Company of Artists (Jerry Wald)
▦
Sheilah Graham, a British chorus girl turned Hollywood columnist, lives with Scott Fitzgerald but fails to cure him of alcoholism.
A bitter and even sordid true story becomes a slice of Hollywood romance, with stars unsuitably cast. On all levels it falls between two stools, satisfying nobody.
w Sy Bartlett book Sheilah Graham, Gerold Frank d Henry King ph Leon Shamroy m Franz Waxman
☆ Gregory Peck, Deborah Kerr, Eddie Albert, Philip Ober, Herbert Rudley, Karin Booth, Ken Scott
'Catastrophically misguided.' – *Penelope Houston*

The Beloved Rogue *
US 1927 99m bw silent
Art Cinema Corporation
▦ ◎
15th-century poet and thief François Villon becomes a friend of the king, but is banished when he falls for a lady of the court.
Stylish star vehicle remade as If I Were King (qv).
w Paul Bern d Alan Crosland pd William Cameron Menzies
☆ John Barrymore, Conrad Veidt, Marceline Day, Mack Swain, Slim Summerville

'He kissed many but loved one!'
The Beloved Vagabond *
GB 1936 78m bw
ABFD/Ludovico Toeplitz
At the turn of the century, a jilted French artist becomes a vagabond and falls in love with an orphan girl.
Mildly amusing bi-lingual production from a bestselling picaresque novel; production quite lively.
w Wells Root, Arthur Wimperis, Hugh Mills, Walter Creighton novel W. J. Locke d Curtis Bernhardt ph Franz Planer m Darius Milhaud md Leslie Bridgewater ad Andrei Andreiev ed Doug Myers
☆ Maurice Chevalier, Margaret Lockwood, Betty Stockfeld, Desmond Tester, Austin Trevor, Peter Haddon, Cathleen Nesbitt
'A weak sister, mostly for the duals.' – *Variety*

Below Zero **
👥 US 1930 20m bw
Hal Roach
Street musicians treat a policeman to lunch on the contents of a found wallet which turns out to be his.
Slow-paced but likeable star comedy from their best period.
w H. M. Walker d James Parrott
☆ Laurel and Hardy, Frank Holliday, Tiny Sandford

The Belstone Fox *
👥 GB 1973 103m Eastmancolor Todd-AO 35
Rank/Independent Artists (Sally Shuter)
📀
A fox and a hound grow up together but the fox leads to tragedy for its masters.
Good animal and countryside photography barely compensate for a fragmentary story with unpleasant moments or for a muddled attitude towards humans and animals; one is not clear what audience the result is supposed to appeal to.
wd James Hill novel The Ballad of the Belstone Fox by David Rook ph John Wilcox, James Allen m Laurie Johnson
☆ Eric Porter, Rachel Roberts, Jeremy Kemp, Bill Travers, Dennis Waterman

Beltenebros
Spain 1991 114m Eastmancolor
Panavision
Metro/Iberoamerican/Floradora (Andrés Vicente Gómez)
📀
aka: *Prince of Shadows*
In the early 1960s, a Spanish political exile is sent to kill a traitor to the anti-fascist cause.
Good-looking but dull and disastrously miscast drama of betrayal.

w Pilar Miró, Mario Camus, Juan Antonio Porto novel Beltenebros by Antonio Muñoz Molina d Pilar Miró ph Javier Aguirresarobe m José Nieto pd Fernando Saénz, Luis Vallés, Ewa Braun ed José Luis Matesanz
☆ Terence Stamp, Patsy Kensit, José Luis Gómez, John McEnery, Geraldine James, Simón Andreu, Aleksander Bardini, Bernice Stegers

Ben
US 1972 92m DeLuxe
Cinerama/Bing Crosby (Mort Briskin)
▦
A sickly boy inherits an army of trained rats.
Boring reprise of Willard (qv) in which the audience knows only too well what to expect. Production and development quite routine.
w Gilbert A. Ralston d Phil Karlson ph Russell Metty m Walter Scharf
☆ Lee Harcourt Montgomery, Arthur O'Connell, Rosemary Murphy, Meredith Baxter, Kaz Garas, Paul Carr, Kenneth Tobey, Joseph Campanella
♫ title song (m Walter Scharf, ly Don Black)

Benchley
The one-reel shorts in which Robert Benchley, sitting behind a desk, delivered nonsensical lectures on aspects of modern life were very popular with better-class audiences, and launched Benchley onto his movie career as a light actor. Here is a list of them:
1928 The Treasurer's Report, The Sex Life of the Polyp, The Spellbinder
1929 Lesson Number One (2 reels), Furnace Trouble (2 reels), Stewed, Fried and Boiled (2 reels)
1933 Your Technocracy and Mine (2 reels)
1935 How to Break 90 at Croquet, How to Sleep
1936 How to Behave, How to Train a Dog, How to Vote, How to Be a Detective
1937 The Romance of Digestion, How to Start the Day, A Night at the Movies
1938 How to Figure Income Tax, Music Made Simple, An Evening Alone, How to Raise a Baby, The Courtship of the Newt, How to Read, How to Watch Football, Opening Day, Mental Poise, How to Sublet
1939 An Hour for Lunch, Dark Magic, Home Early, How to Eat, The Day of Rest, See Your Doctor
1940 That Inferior Feeling, Home Movies, The Trouble with Husbands
1941 Waiting for Baby, Crime Control, The Forgotten Man, How to Take a Vacation
1942 Nothing but Nerves, The Witness, Keeping in Shape, The Man's Angle
1943 My Tomato, No News Is Good News
1944 Important Business, Why, Daddy?
1945 Boogie Woogie (2 reels), I'm a Civilian Here Myself
† In the late seventies a feature compilation was made under the title *Those Marvellous Benchley Shorts*.

Bend of the River *
US 1952 91m Technicolor
U-I (Aaron Rosenberg)
📀 ▦ ◎
GB title: *Where the River Bends*
1880 wagon trains arrive in Oregon, and the pioneers have trouble with the local bad man.
Good standard Western with pace and period feeling but not much plot sense.
w Borden Chase novel Bend of the Snake by William Gulick d Anthony Mann ph Irving Glassberg m Hans Salter ad Bernard Herzbrun, Nathan Juran ed Russell Schoengarth
☆ James Stewart, Arthur Kennedy, Rock Hudson, Julia Adams, Lori Nelson, Jay C. Flippen, Henry Morgan, Royal Dano, Stepin Fetchit

Beneath the Planet of the Apes *
US 1969 94m DeLuxe Panavision
TCF/APJAC (Mort Abrahams)
📀 ▦ ◎
Astronauts on the ape planet discover that it is really Earth and that subterranean human mutants are nursing a live atom bomb.
Violence replaces the thoughtfulness of the original, but this is not at all a bad sequel as sequels go.
w Paul Dehn, Mort Abrahams d Ted Post ph Milton Krasner m Leonard Rosenman
☆ James Franciscus, Charlton Heston, Linda Harrison, Kim Hunter, Maurice Evans, Paul

Richards, Victor Buono, Jeff Corey, James Gregory, Thomas Gomez
† See *Planet of the Apes*.

Beneath the Twelve Mile Reef
US 1953 102m Technicolor Cinemascope
TCF (Robert Bassler)
▦ ◎ 🎧
Jealousy, tragedy and romance among the Florida sponge fishers.
Fox's early Cinemascope production involved much underwater shooting, a trick octopus, and predictable plot devices.
w A. I. Bezzerides, d Robert D. Webb ph Edward Cronjager m Bernard Herrmann
☆ Robert Wagner, Terry Moore, Gilbert Roland, Peter Graves, J. Carrol Naish, Richard Boone, Angela Clarke, Jay Novello
'The dead weight of a melodramatic script overtaxes the gallant attempts at conviction.' – *MFB*
⚘ Edward Cronjager

Benefit of the Doubt
US/Germany 1993 91m DeLuxe
Warner/Benefit/Cine Vox/Monument (Michael Spielberg, Brad M. Gilbert)
📀 ▦
Out on parole after more than 20 years in prison for the murder of his wife, a man goes to live near his daughter, persuading her that he is innocent of the crime.
A dull thriller that warms over familar plot devices to little purpose.
w Jeffrey Polman, Christopher Keyser story Michael Lieber d Jonathan Heap ph Johnny E. Jensen m Hummie Mann pd Marina Kieser ed Sharyn L. Ross
☆ Donald Sutherland, Amy Irving, Rider Strong, Christopher McDonald, Graham Greene, Theodore Bikel, Gisela Kovach, Ferdinand Mayne
'The result is pretty silly and demeaning.' – *Derek Malcolm, Guardian*

Bengal Brigade
US 1954 87m Technicolor
U-I (Ted Richmond)
GB title: *Bengal Rifles*
In 19th-century India, an officer is cashiered through false evidence, and becomes an undercover man with the wicked local rajah.
Routine Hollywood heroics with a few unintended laughs.
w Richard Alan Simmons novel Bengal Tiger by Hall Hunter d Laslo Benedek ph Maury Gertsman m Hans Salter
☆ Rock Hudson, Arlene Dahl, Dan O'Herlihy, Ursula Thiess, Torin Thatcher, Michael Ansara, Arnold Moss

Bengal Rifles: see Bengal Brigade

Bengazi
US 1955 79m bw Superscope
RKO/Panamint (Sam Wiesenthal, Eugene Tevlin)
Various unsavoury characters set out into the African desert to look for gold hidden by the Nazis.
Poor potboiler on predictable lines.
w Endre Bohem, Louis Vittes d John Brahm ph Joseph Biroc m Roy Webb
☆ Richard Conte, Victor McLaglen, Richard Carlson, Mala Powers, Richard Erdman, Gonzales Gonzales, Hillary Brooke

'The great decade (1915–25) of the progress of motion picture art reaches its summit! A cast of 125,000!'
'The inspired love of the prince of Hur for the gentle lovely Esther!'
Ben-Hur ***
US 1925 170m bw (colour sequence) silent
MGM
📀 ▦ ◎
In the time of Christ, a Jew suffers mightily under the Romans.
The American silent screen's biggest epic; the sea battle and the chariot race are its most famous sequences.
w Bess Meredyth, Carey Wilson novel Lew Wallace d Fred Niblo ph Karl Struss, Clyde de Vinna, and others ad Horace Jackson, Ferdinand Pinney Earle
☆ Ramon Novarro, Francis X. Bushman, Carmel Myers, May McAvoy, Betty Bronson

---

'Masterpiece of study and patience, a photodrama filled with artistry.' – *New York Times*

† To begin with, the film was directed by Charles Brabin and starred George Walsh. Both were replaced after Louis Mayer saw the first rushes. Previously filmed in 1907.

Ben-Hur **

US   1959   217m   Technicolor   Camera 65
MGM (Sam Zimbalist)

Solid, expensive, surprisingly unimaginative remake; generally less sprightly than the silent version.

w Karl Tunberg d William Wyler, Andrew Marton ph Robert L. Surtees m Miklos Rozsa ad William A. Horning, Edward Carfagno ed Ralph E. Winters, John D. Dunning

☆ Charlton Heston, Haya Harareet, Jack Hawkins, Stephen Boyd, Hugh Griffith, Martha Scott, Sam Jaffe, Cathy O'Donnell, Finlay Currie, Frank Thring, Terence Longdon, André Morell, George Relph

'Watching it is like waiting at a railroad crossing while an interminable freight train lumbers by, sometimes stopping altogether.' – *Dwight MacDonald*
'A Griffith can make a hundred into a crowd while a Wyler can reduce a thousand to a confused cocktail party.' – *Ibid.*
'The most tasteful and visually exciting film spectacle yet produced by an American company.' – *Albert Johnson, Film Quarterly*
'Spectacular without being a spectacle … not only is it not simple-minded, it is downright literate.' – *Saturday Review*
'A major motion picture phenomenon.' – *Films in Review*

† The production cost four million dollars, twice the maximum at the time. Rock Hudson, Marlon Brando and Burt Lancaster were all sought in vain for the lead before Heston was selected
†† This version was subtitled 'A Tale of the Christ'.
⚹ best picture; William Wyler; Robert L. Surtees; Miklos Rozsa; Charlton Heston; Hugh Griffith; art direction; editing; special effects (Arnold Gillespie, Robert MacDonald, Milo Lory)
⚹ Karl Tunberg
⚹ best picture

Benjamin, or The Diary of an Innocent Young Man

France   1966   104m   Eastmancolor
Paramount/Parc/Marianne (Mag Bodard)
In the 18th century, a 17-year-old orphan is taken in hand by his wealthy aunt and initiated into the mysteries of sex.
Imitation Tom Jones (qv), quite good to look at but rather boring.
w Nina Companeez d Michel Déville ph Ghislain Cloquet
☆ Pierre Clémenti, Michèle Morgan, Catherine Deneuve, Michel Piccoli, Francine Bergé, Anna Gaël, Odile Versois
'Heavy with Gallic naughtiness rather than airy charm … a plethora of colourful costumes, foliage and fireworks.' – *MFB*
'A marathon tease … an unending series of interrupted coitions … a gorgeously wrapped and beribboned Christmas package containing an empty box.' – *John Simon*

Benji *

US   1974   86m   CFI color
Mulberry Square (Joe Camp)

A stray mongrel dog saves two kidnapped children.
Family film par excellence which rang the box-office bell in a big way in the US. Its modest merits are rather beside the point.
wd Joe Camp ph Don Reddy m Euel Box
☆ Peter Breck, Edgar Buchanan, Terry Carter, Christopher Connelly
† A sequel, *For the Love of Benji* (qv), followed in 1977. In 1980 came the offbeat *Oh Heavenly Dog* (qv). Then in 1987 the same team presented a quirky movie of a different kind: *Benji the Hunted* (qv).
⚹ song 'I Feel Love' (m Euel Box, ly Betty Box)

Benji the Hunted

US   1987   88m   CFI color
Mulberry Square/Embark/Buena Vista (Ben Vaughn)

A mongrel dog is shipwrecked and fosters a pack of cougar cubs.
Freaky fable about a dog with a high IQ; but the training is remarkable.
wd Joe Camp ph Don Reddy m Euel Box, Betty Box sp Bryan L. Renfro, Frank and Juanita Inn (Benji's trainers)
☆ Benji, Frank Inn, Red Steagall

'Benny's breaking up his sister Joon's romance. Isn't that what big brothers are for?'
'A romance on the brink of reality.'

Benny and Joon

US   1993   99m   DeLuxe
MGM (Susan Arnold, Donna Roth)

A mentally disturbed painter falls for a fey mime, to the displeasure of her uptight brother.
A romantic comedy about mental illness, by turns whimsical and sentimental and never less than saccharine.
w Barry Berman, Leslie McNeil d Jeremiah Chechik ph John Schwartzman m Rachel Portman pd Neil Spisak ed Carol Littleton
☆ Johnny Depp, Mary Stuart Masterson, Aidan Quinn, Julianne Moore, Oliver Platt, C. C. H. Pounder, Dan Hedaya, Joe Grifasi
'Embarrassingly, relentlessly cute.' – *Observer*

The Benny Goodman Story *

US   1955   117m   Technicolor
U-I (Aaron Rosenberg)

A clarinettist from the Jewish section of Chicago becomes internationally famous.
Sentimental biopic of a familiar figure which comes to life when the sound track is given its head (and the real Goodman's clarinet).
wd Valentine Davies ph William Daniels md Joseph Gershenson
☆ Steve Allen, Donna Reed, Berta Gersten, Herbert Anderson, Robert F. Simon, Sammy Davis Snr, Harry James, Martha Tilton, Gene Krupa
'The customary fictional liberties appear to have been taken.' – *MFB*

Benny's Video *

Austria/Switzerland   1992   105m   colour
ICA/Wega/Bernard Lang
A bored, middle-class, video-obsessed teenager picks up a girl at a video-rental store, takes her home and kills her on camera.
A low-budget movie of alienation that creates unease and questions the role of video violence in society.
wd Michael Haneke ph Christian Berger pd Christoph Kanter ed Marie Homolkova
☆ Arno Frisch, Angela Winkler, Ulrich Mühe, Ingrid Stassner
'Neatly states its case against the anesthetizing properties of too much violent imagery too soon. Urban terror story plays like an icy thriller, but the message runs deeper, lending an intellectual edge.' – *Variety*
† The director has said that the film is a statement 'about the American sensational cinema and its power to rob viewers of their ability to form their own opinions'.

Bent

GB/US/Japan   1996   116m   colour
Film Four/NDF/Ask Kodansha/Channel 4/Nippon (Michael Solinger, Dixie Linder)
A homosexual man, sent to a German concentration camp, forms an intense relationship with another prisoner.
A briefly controversial play of the 70s, in which love flourished under appalling conditions, transfers to the screen and just lies there.
w Martin Sherman play Martin Sherman d Sean Mathias ph Yorgos Arvanitis m Philip Glass pd Stephen Brimson Lewis ed Isabel Lorente
☆ Lothaire Bluteau, Clive Owen, Brian Webber, Ian McKellen, Mick Jagger, Nikolaj Waldau, Jude Law, Sian Bentish
'Makes all the right motions on screen. But it's hard to feel for its argument the way that people did in a theatre.' – *Alexander Walker, London Evening Standard*

Benvenuta *

Belgium   1983   106m   Eastmancolor
Artificial Eye/La Nouvelle Imageries/UGC/Europe 1/FR3/Opera Film (Jean-Claude Batz)
A screenwriter meets a reclusive novelist to write a treatment of her once-famous semi-autobiographical book.
Constantly shifting between fiction and reality, between appearance and fantasy, it soon wears out its welcome.
wd André Delvaux novel La Confession Anonyme by Suzanne Lilar ph Charlie Van Damme m Frédérick Devreese ad Claude Pignot ed Jean Goudier
☆ Fanny Ardant, Vittorio Gassman, Françoise Fabian, Mathieu Carrière, Claire Wauthion, Philippe Geluck

Bequest to the Nation *

GB   1973   116m   Technicolor
Universal/Hal B. Wallis
US title: *The Nelson Affair*
The story of Nelson's long affair with the tempestuous Lady Hamilton.
Undistinguished historical drama from a thin play which despite hard work all round makes very ordinary screen entertainment. Glenda Jackson's performance is way over the top.
w Terence Rattigan play Terence Rattigan d James Cellan Jones ph Gerry Fisher m Michel Legrand pd Carmen Dillon
☆ Peter Finch, Glenda Jackson, Michael Jayston, Anthony Quayle, Margaret Leighton, Dominic Guard, Nigel Stock, Roland Culver
'As empty as an out-of-town matinee.' – *MFB*

Berkeley Square **

US   1933   87m   bw
Fox (Jesse L. Lasky)
A London house reincarnates its owner as his 18th-century ancestor.
Romantic fantasy on a time lapse theme, the first of many and perhaps the most stylish and self-assured.
w Sonya Levien, John Balderston play John Balderston d Frank Lloyd ph Ernest Palmer m Louis de Francesco ad William Darling
☆ Leslie Howard, Heather Angel, Valerie Taylor, Irene Browne, Beryl Mercer, Colin Keith-Johnston, Alan Mowbray
'Too far above the heads of ordinary theatergoers and too British in tempo and execution to break any box office records.' – *Variety*
† Remade as *The House in the Square* (qv).
⚹ Leslie Howard

Berlin Correspondent

US   1942   70m   bw
TCF (Bryan Foy)
In pre-war Germany an American reporter is kidnapped by the Nazis and replaced by a double…
Preposterous melodrama, so silly as to be often quite funny.
w Steve Fisher, Jack Andrews d Eugene Forde ph Virgil Miller md Emil Newman
☆ Dana Andrews, Virginia Gilmore, Mona Maris, Martin Kosleck, Sig Rumann, Kurt Katch, Torben Meyer

Berlin, die Symphonie einer Grosstadt:
see *Berlin, Symphony of a Great City*

Berlin Express *

US   1948   87m   bw
RKO (Bert Granet)
Police of four nations guard a German VIP on a crack train to Berlin.
Rather muddled suspenser with attempts at political moralizing; the cast provides some good moments.
w Harold Medford story Curt Siodmak d Jacques Tourneur ph Lucien Ballard m Frederick Hollander
☆ Merle Oberon, Robert Ryan, Charles Korvin, Paul Lukas, Robert Coote

Berlin, Symphony of a Great City ***

Germany   1927   70m   bw   silent
Fox-Europa
original title: *Berlin, die Symphonie einer Grosstadt*
An impression of the life of a city from dawn to midnight, expressed by cinematic montages, angles, sequences, etc, and set to music.
A leader in the field of 'impressionistic' documentaries which are now so familiar (Rien que les Heures did a

similar job for Paris at around the same time), this still has moments of poetry which have seldom been equalled.
w Walter Ruttman, Karl Freund, Carl Mayer d Walter Ruttman ph Reimar Kuntze, Robert Baberske, Laszlo Schäffer m Edmund Meisel ed Walter Ruttman

Berliner Ballade *

Germany   1948   77m   bw
Comedia Film (Alf Teichs)
aka: *The Ballad of Berlin*
Otto Nobody, an unwilling soldier, returns home to find himself at the mercy of bureaucrats and black marketeers.
Melancholy satire presented as a series of sketches, almost a forerunner of That Was the Week That Was.
w Gunter Neumann d Robert Stemmle ph Georg Krause m/ly Gunter Neumann, Werner Eisbrenner
☆ Gert Fröbe, Anton Zeithammer, Tatjana Sais, O. E. Hasse
'Very much the film of a defeated people.' – *Penelope Houston*

Bermuda Affair

GB   1956   77m   bw
Bermuda Studio Productions
The pilot of a West Indian airline falls for his partner's wife but dies in an air accident.
Tedious and unconvincing marital drama with back-projected local colour.
w Robert J. Shaw, Edward Sutherland d Edward Sutherland
☆ Kim Hunter, Gary Merrill, Ron Randell, Zena Marshall

The Bermuda Mystery

US   1944   65m   bw
TCF
Friends who have invested in a joint insurance policy are murdered one by one.
Competent lower-berth murder mystery.
w W. Scott Darling story John Larkin d Ben Stoloff
☆ Preston Foster, Ann Rutherford, Charles Butterworth, Helene Reynolds, Richard Lane

Bernadette

France   1988   105m   colour
Cannon/Films de L'Etoile D'Or/Bernadette Association International (Jacques Quintard)
A peasant girl sees visions of the Virgin Mary at Lourdes and invokes the hostility of the authorities.
Ponderously reverent treatment of a saintly girl, providing no more than moments of piety.
w Jean Delannoy, Robert Arnaut d Jean Delannoy ph Jean-Bertrand Penzer m Francis Lai ad Alain Paroutaud ed Annick Charvein
☆ Sydney Penney, Jean-Marc Bory, Michèle Simonnet, Roland Lesaffre, Bernard Dhéran, François Dalout, Stephan Garcin

Bernardine *

US   1957   95m   Eastmancolor   Cinemascope
TCF (Samuel G. Engel)
A college student forced to swot for exams asks a friend's elder brother to look after his girl.
Henry Aldrich-style high school comedy, showing the lighter side of Rebel without a Cause (qv). Notable for the clean-living hero played by a clean-living singing star, and the reappearance of Janet Gaynor for the only time since 1939, in a routine mother role.
w Theodore Reeves play Mary Chase d Henry Levin ph Paul Vogel m Lionel Newman
☆ Pat Boone, Richard Sargent, Terry Moore, Janet Gaynor, Walter Abel, Dean Jagger, Natalie Schafer, James Drury

Berry Gordy's The Last Dragon: see *The Last Dragon*

Berserk!

GB   1967   96m   Technicolor
Columbia (Herman Cohen)

A lady circus owner revels in the publicity brought about by a series of murders.
Grisly and unattractive thriller with an ageing star in a series of unsuitably abbreviated costumes; the script is beyond redemption.

w Herman Cohen, Aben Kandel *d* Jim O'Connolly *ph* Desmond Dickinson *m* Patrick John Scott

☆ Joan Crawford, Diana Dors, Ty Hardin, Judy Geeson, Michael Gough, Robert Hardy, Geoffrey Keen, Sydney Tafler, Philip Madoc

Bert Rigby, You're a Fool

USA   1989   94m   Metrocolor
Warner/Lorimar/A Clear Production (George Shapiro)

A former miner becomes a mostly unsuccessful song-and-dance man in Hollywood.
Dim comedy, intended as a showcase for the slight charm of Robert Lindsay.
wd Carl Reiner *ph* Jan de Bont *m* Ralph Burns *pd* Terence Marsh *ad* Dianne Wager, Michael Seirton *ed* Bud Molin, Stephen Myers
☆ Robert Lindsay, Anne Bancroft, Corbin Bernsen, Robbie Coltrane, Cathryn Bradshaw, Jackie Gayle, Bruno Kirby, Liz Smith, Lila Kaye
'Mixes sentimentality with vulgarity with reckless abandon.' – *John Pym, MFB*

Berth Marks

↟↟   US   1929   20m   bw   silent
Hal Roach

Stan and Ollie, on a train, have to share an upper berth.
Overstretched single-situation comedy, one of the team's poorest.
w Leo McCarey, H. M. Walker *d* Lewis R. Foster
☆ Stan Laurel, Oliver Hardy

Die Berührte: see *No Mercy No Future*

Besieged

Italy   1998   94m   Technicolor
Fiction/Navert/Mediaset (Massimo Cortesi)
In Rome, a British pianist falls in love with his African maid and agrees to help her husband, who is being held as a political prisoner.
Turgid drama of obsessive love that fails to engage emotionally or intellectually.
w Clare Peploe, Bernardo Bertolucci *story* James Lasdun *d* Bernardo Bertolucci *ph* Fabio Cianchetti *m* Alessio Vlad *pd* Gianni Silvestri *ed* Jacopo Quadri
☆ Thandie Newton, David Thewlis, Claudio Santamaria
'A dull, simple-minded, almost deliberately clumsy affair.' – *Philip French, Observer*

The Bespoke Overcoat **

GB   1956   33m   bw
Romulus (Jack Clayton)
A clerk in a clothing warehouse is refused a coat and asks a tailor friend to make him one. But he dies of cold and his ghost persuades the tailor to steal the coat he deserved.
The story seems stiff, but the production has a rich Dickensian feel and may be the best short drama filmed in Britain.
w Wolf Mankowitz *story* Gogol *d* Jack Clayton *ph* Wolfgang Suschitzky *m* Georges Auric
☆ Alfie Bass, David Kossoff
'A triumph of talent, small means and originality.' – *New Statesman*
🏆 best short

Best Boy ***

US   1979   111m   colour   16mm
Ira Wohl

A documentary, shot by his cousin, of the problems of a mentally retarded 53-year-old man whose elderly parents are ailing.
A film with many moving elements, though they would have been even sharper at half the length.
wd Ira Wohl
🏆 best documentary

Best Defense

US   1984   94m   Movielab
Paramount (Gloria Katz)

A US tank goes hopelessly out of control in Kuwait; intercut with this are some of the problems which confronted its designer two years earlier.
Weird, unappetizing and disjointed farce, composed mainly of irrelevancies.
w Gloria Katz, Willard Huyck *novel* Easy and Hard Ways Out by Robert Grossbach *d* Willard

Huyck *ph* Don Peterman *m* Patrick Williams *pd* Peter Jamison
☆ Dudley Moore, Eddie Murphy, Kate Capshaw, George Dzundza, Helen Shaver
'As bereft of charm and spontaneity as it is overburdened with tedious gesticulation.' – *Tim Pulleine, MFB*
'About as funny as getting hi-jacked by a group of kamikaze terrorists.' – *Derek Malcolm, Guardian*
'How did I get involved? The door opened, and four men came in carrying a cheque.' – *Eddie Murphy*

Best Foot Forward

US   1943   94m   Technicolor
MGM (Arthur Freed)

A glamorous publicity-seeking film star accepts an invitation to a military college ball.
Old-fashioned formula musical based on a lightweight Broadway success.
w Irving Brecher, Fred Finklehoffe *play* John Cecil Holmes *d* Edward Buzzell *ph* Leonard Smith *m/ly* Hugh Martin, Ralph Blane *md* Lennie Hayton *ch* Charles Walters
☆ Lucille Ball, William Gaxton, Virginia Weidler, Harry James and his Orchestra, June Allyson, Gloria de Haven
† Lucille Ball's singing was dubbed by Martha Mears.

Best Friends *

US   1982   116m   Technicolor
Warner/Joe Wizan/Norman Jewison

Two writers who have enjoyed a peaceful professional relationship find problems when they get married and visit their respective families.
Rather a heavy comedy which seems to have no real point; this gets by on enjoyable sequences and star performances.
w Valerie Curtin, Barry Levinson *d* Norman Jewison *ph* Jordan Cronenweth *m* Michel Legrand *ad* Joe Russo *ed* Don Zimmerman
☆ Burt Reynolds, Goldie Hawn, Jessica Tandy, Barnard Hughes, Audra Lindley, Keenan Wynn
'A print-out of a script conference at which everyone collapsed at everyone else's contributory sally.' – *Sunday Times*
🎵 song 'How Do You Keep the Music Playing?' (Michel Legrand, Alan and Marilyn Bergman)

The Best House in London *

GB   1968   96m   Eastmancolor
MGM/Bridge/Carlo Ponti (Philip Breen, Kurt Unger)
A Victorian publicity agent tries to organize a government-sponsored brothel.
Cheerful slam-bang historical send-up with as many dull thuds of banality as pleasant witticisms.
w Denis Norden *d* Philip Saville *ph* Alex Thomson *m* Mischa Spoliansky *pd* Wilfrid Shingleton
☆ David Hemmings, George Sanders, Joanna Pettet, Warren Mitchell, Dany Robin, William Rushton

The Best Intentions ***

Sweden   1992   181m   colour
Artificial Eye/STV1/ZDF/Channel 4/RAIDU/La Sept/DR/YLE 2/NRK/RUV (Lars Bjälkeskog)

original title: Den Goda Viljan
In Sweden in the early 1900s, a priest overcomes parental objections to marry a nurse, but their union is a troubled one.
A sharply observed, fascinating semi-biographical account by a son of the early years of his parents' marriage, ending just before his birth.
w Ingmar Bergman *d* Bille August *ph* Jörgen Persson *m* Stefan Nilsson *ad* Anna Asp *ed* Janus Billeskov Jansen
☆ Samuel Fröler, Pernilla August, Max von Sydow, Ghita Norby, Lennart Hjulström, Mona Malm, Lena Endre, Keve Hjelm
'The picture is uniformly well acted, has a wonderful feeling for the distinct Scandinavian seasons, and re-creates social occasions with an acute moral edge.' – *Philip French, Observer*
'Ingmar Bergman may have officially retired from film direction, but his genius marches on.' – *Geoff Brown, The Times*
† At the 1992 Cannes Film Festival, the film won the Palme D'Or for best film and Pernilla August the award for best actress.

Best Laid Plans *

US   1999   93m   Technicolor
TCF/Fox 2000/Dogstar (Alan Greenspan, Betsy Beers, Chris Moore, Sean Bailey)

Robberies go wrong for a man trying to raise money to escape his dreary life and pay off a local hoodlum.
Quirky thriller that begins well but ends with a whimper, never exploring the increasingly unlikely motivations needed to keep the narrative moving.
w Ted Griffin *d* Mike Barker *ph* Ben Seresin *m* Craig Armstrong *pd* Sophie Becher *ed* Sloane Klevin
☆ Alessandro Nivola, Reese Witherspoon, Josh Brolin, Rocky Carroll, Michael G. Hagerty, Terence Howard, Jimmy Marsh, Gene Wolande
'Fundamentally, it's a small pleasure rather than a fully-blown triumph.' – *Peter Bradshaw, Guardian*

The Best Little Whorehouse in Texas

US   1982   114m   Technicolor   Panavision
Universal/RKO (Thomas L. Miller, Edward K. Milkis, Robert L. Boyett)

A long-established Texas whorehouse becomes the object of a clean-up campaign.
Flat and feeble screen version of a limp and tuneless musical which astonishingly was a Broadway hit, perhaps because people thought it was naughty. Onscreen the acting is too easy-going and the script too coy for anybody to have a good time.
w Larry L. King, Peter Masterson *play* Larry L. King, Peter Masterson *d* Colin Higgins *ph* William A. Fraker *m* Patrick Williams *m/ly* Carol Hall *pd* Robert F. Boyle
☆ Burt Reynolds, Dolly Parton, Charles Durning, Dom DeLuise, Jim Nabors, Robert Mandan, Lois Nettleton, Noah Beery Jnr
'Rancid, self-deceiving, hypocritical stuff.' – *Observer*
'A sanitized, coyly predictable piece of brothel creeping, set to musak by a poorly programmed computer.' – *Guardian*
'Almost everything about it is misjudged.' – *Daily Mail*
'High on jollity, low on country and western, and very uncertainly directed.' – *Sight and Sound*
'Never gets beyond the concept stage.' – *Roger Ebert*
🏆 Charles Durning

The Best Man ***

US   1964   104m   bw
UA/Stuart Millar, Lawrence Turman

Two contenders for a presidential nomination seek the support of the dying ex-president.
Brilliant political melodrama, ingeniously adapted on a low budget from an incisive play, with splendid dramatic scenes, memorable performances and good convention detail.
w Gore Vidal *play* Gore Vidal *d* Franklin Schaffner *ph* Haskell Wexler *m* Mort Lindsey
☆ Henry Fonda, Cliff Robertson, Lee Tracy, Margaret Leighton, Edie Adams, Kevin McCarthy, Shelley Berman, Ann Sothern, Gene Raymond, Mahalia Jackson
'A fine opportunity to watch pros at work in a hard-hitting and cogent drama that seems to become more topical and have more relevance with each showing.' – *Judith Crist*
'Some of the wittiest lines since *Strangelove* … the acting fairly crackled with authenticity.' – *Isabel Quigly*
'You are left gasping at its sheer professionalism.' – *Evening News*
🏆 Lee Tracy

The Best Man Wins

US   1934   75m   bw
Columbia

A harbour cop finds himself tracking down the friend who had saved his life.
Predictable tough-guy programmer.
w Ethel Hill, Bruce Manning *d* Erle C. Kenton
☆ Edmund Lowe, Jack Holt, Bela Lugosi, Florence Rice, Forrester Harvey

Best Men *

US/GB   1997   89m   DeLuxe   Panavision
Film Four/Orion/Rank (Brad Krevoy, Steve Stabler, Brad Jenkel, Deborah Ridpath)

When a bank robbery on the way to a wedding goes wrong, five friends are trapped with their hostage inside a bank, surrounded by the police and FBI.
Talky confessional thriller, in which everyone blames society for their particular failings; despite its sometimes desperate contrivances, it has a slight charm.
w Art Edler Brown, Tracy Fraim *d* Tamra Davis *ph* James Glennon *m* Mark Mothersbaugh *pd* Tony Corbett *ed* Paul Trejo
☆ Dean Cain, Andy Dick, Sean Patrick Flanery, Mitchell Whitfield, Luke Wilson, Fred Ward, Raymond J. Barry, Drew Barrymore, Brad Dourif
'It's the sheer *joie de vivre* and good timing that enables this tragi-comedy about a group of misfits to succeed.' – *Nina Caplan, Sight and Sound*

The Best of Enemies

US/Italy   1961   104m   colour   Technirama
Columbia/Dino de Laurentiis
During the Abyssinian campaign of 1941, an Italian and a British officer learn mutual respect.
Mild satirical comedy drama with a few points to make about war; the elements blend rather obviously and dispiritingly.
w Jack Pulman *d* Guy Hamilton *ph* Giuseppe Rotunno *m* Nino Rota
☆ David Niven, Alberto Sordi, Michael Wilding, Amedeo Nazzari, Harry Andrews, David Opatoshu, Kenneth Fortescue, Duncan Macrae

The Best of Everything *

US   1959   121m   DeLuxe   Cinemascope
TCF (Jerry Wald)
Personal problems of a New York publisher's female staff.
Slick novelette on the lines of a naughty Peg's Paper; pure Hollywood gossamer.
w Edith Sommer, Mann Rubin *novel* Rona Jaffe *d* Jean Negulesco *ph* William C. Mellor *m* Alfred Newman
☆ Hope Lange, Stephen Boyd, Joan Crawford, Louis Jourdan, Suzy Parker, Martha Hyer, Diane Baker, Brian Aherne, Robert Evans, Brett Halsey, Donald Harron
'A cautionary tale sensationally told.' – *Alexander Walker*
🎵 title song (*m* Alfred Newman, *ly* Sammy Cahn)

Best of the Badmen *

US   1951   84m   Technicolor
RKO (Herman Schlom)
At the end of the Civil War Jeff Clanton organizes the break-up of Quantrell's Raiders, but is himself arrested on a trumped-up charge and needs the Raiders' help.
Standard Western notable for a good cast and for bringing in a remarkable number of historical outlaws, doing rather unhistorical things.
w Robert Hardy Andrews, John Twist *d* William D. Russell *ph* Edward Cronjager *m* Paul Sawtell
☆ Robert Ryan, Claire Trevor, Jack Buetel, Robert Preston, Walter Brennan, Bruce Cabot, John Archer, Lawrence Tierney

'Apart, They're Tough. Together, They're Awesome.'

Best of the Best

US   1989   97m   CFI color
Entertainment/Best of the Best/Kuys (Phillip Rhee, Peter E. Strauss)

An American Taekwondo team prepares to compete against the Korean champions.
Plodding, sentimental and over-familiar variation on The Karate Kid and Rocky (qqv).
w Paul Levine *story* Phillip Rhee, Paul Levine *d* Bob Radler *ph* Doug Ryna *pd* Kim Rees *ed* William Hoy
☆ Eric Roberts, James Earl Jones, Sally Kirkland, John P. Ryan, John Dye, David Agresta, Tom Everett, Louise Fletcher, Simon Rhee

---

Best of the Best II

US   1992   100m   DeLuxe
Entertainment/Picture Securities (Peter E. Strauss, Phillip Rhee)

Members of the US karate team avenge a friend's death at the hands of a ruthless champion who wants them killed.

The stock plot of virtually every martial arts movie is wheeled out yet again, together with the obligatory violence and the chest-thumping moral that might is right; it is no more convincing this time around.

w Max Strom, John Allen Nelson   d Robert Radler   ph Fred Tammes   m David Michael Frank   pd Gary Frutkoff   ed Bert Lovitt

☆ Eric Roberts, Phillip Rhee, Edan Gross, Ralph Moeller, Christopher Penn, Sonny Landham, Wayne Newton, Meg Foster

'Film looks and plays like a drive-in picture of 20 years ago, only less fun.' – *Variety*

The Best of Times

US   1985   104m   Technicolor
Universal/Kings Road (Gordon Carroll)

A small-town loser determines to have one more shot at the big time.

Curious, almost plotless comedy drama with nothing to draw the punters.

w Ron Shelton   d Roger Spottiswoode
ph Charles F. Wheeler   m Arthur B. Rubinstein   ad Anthony Brockliss   ed Garth Craven

☆ Robin Williams, Kurt Russell, Pamela Reed, Holly Palance, Donald Moffat, M. Emmet Walsh

'Required magic is in too short supply and box office returns should be also.' – *Variety*

The Best Pair of Legs in the Business *

GB   1972   97m   Technicolor
Sunny (Andrew Mitchell, Johnny Goodman)

An ageing comedian, reduced to working at a caravan holiday camp, is forced to face up to his own inadequacies and his wife's adultery.

A sad story of a seedy, miserable comic that provides Varney with an opportunity to display some acting skill, but which overstays its welcome.

w Kevin Laffan   d Christopher Hodson   ph Jimmy Allen   m Harry Robinson   ad Robert Jones   ed Richard Best

☆ Reg Varney, Diana Coupland, Lee Montague, Jean Harvey, Johnny Briggs, Geoffrey Chater, Michael Hadley, Clare Kelly, Jane Seymour

Best Revenge

Canada   1983   94m   colour
John Watson, Pen Densham (Michael M. Lebowitz)

Two American friends become involved in a drug deal in Morocco that goes wrong.

A dull thriller that never commands attention, thanks to an ill-constructed script and uninspired direction.

w David Rothberg, Rick Rosenthal, Logan N. Danforth   d John Trent   ph John Coquillon   m Keith Emerson   pd William Beeton   ed James Symons

☆ John Heard, Levon Helm, Alberta Watson, Stephen McHattie, Moses Znaimer, John Rhys-Davies, Benjamin Gordon

Best Seller *

US   1987   110m   CFI color
Orion/Hemdale (Carter de Haven)

A former hit-man helps an ex-cop write a book based on an old unsolved case.

Tortuous but generally lively and interesting melodrama which at least tries to be different.

w Larry Cohen   d John Flynn   ph Fred Murphy   m Jay Ferguson   pd Gene Rudolf   ed David Rosenbloom

☆ James Woods, Brian Dennehy, Victoria Tennant, Allison Balson, Paul Shenar, George Coe

Best Shot: see *Hoosiers*

The Best Things in Life Are Free *

US   1956   103m   Eastmancolor
Cinemascope
TCF (Henry Ephron)

From Broadway to Hollywood in the twenties, the story of songwriting team de Sylva, Brown and Henderson.

Gangsters, movie studios and the writing of 'Sonny Boy' for Al Jolson all figure in this amiable musical

which spends more time on jokes than romance; the numbers are disappointing despite good tunes.

w William Bowers, Phoebe Ephron   d Michael Curtiz   m Leon Shamroy   md Lionel Newman

☆ Ernest Borgnine, Gordon MacRae, Dan Dailey, Sheree North, Jacques d'Amboise, Norman Brooks, Murvyn Vye

& Lionel Newman

'Three wonderful loves in the best picture of the year!'

The Best Years of Our Lives ****

US   1946   182m   bw
Samuel Goldwyn

Three men come home from war to a small middle-American community, and find it variously difficult to pick up where they left off.

The situations and even some of the characters now seem a little obvious, but this was a superb example of high-quality film-making in the forties, with smiles and tears cunningly spaced, and a film which said what was needed on a vital subject.

w Robert Sherwood   novel Glory for Me by Mackinlay Kantor   d William Wyler   ph Gregg Toland   m Hugo Friedhofer   ed Daniel Mandell

☆ Fredric March, Myrna Loy, Teresa Wright, Dana Andrews, Virginia Mayo, Cathy O'Donnell, Hoagy Carmichael, Harold Russell, Gladys George, Roman Bohnen, Ray Collins

'One of the best pictures of our lives!' – *Variety*
'The result is a work of provocative and moving insistence and beauty.' – *Howard Barnes*
'One recognizes everything and in the end this recognition is all the excitement, for what is on the screen becomes finally as accustomed and undramatic as the shabby decor of the theatre itself.' – *Robert Warshow, The Immediate Experience*
'One of the very few American studio-made movies in years that seem to me profoundly pleasing, moving and encouraging.' – *James Agee*
'Easily the best film from Hollywood on the warrior's return.' – *Sunday Graphic*

† In 1977 came a TV remake *Returning Home* but it did not lead to the expected series.

†† Harold Russell was a handless veteran, with no training as an actor, whose only film this was until *Inside Moves* in 1980.

⬥ best picture; Robert Sherwood; William Wyler; Hugo Friedhofer; Fredric March; Harold Russell; Daniel Mandell

⬦ best picture

La Bête Humaine **

France   1938   99m   bw
Paris Films (Robert Hakim)

aka: *The Human Beast*
aka: *Judas Was a Woman*

A psychopathic train driver falls for a married woman, plans with her to kill her husband, but finally strangles her instead.

Curious melodrama with strong visual sequences, flawed by its ambivalent attitude to its hero-villain.

wd Jean Renoir   novel Emile Zola   ph Curt Courant   m Joseph Kosma

☆ Jean Gabin, Simone Simon, Julien Carette, Fernand Ledoux, Jean Renoir

'French production at its best.' – *Variety*
'Marvellous atmosphere and a fine cast, but the material turns oppressive.' – *New Yorker, 1978*
'What is most deft is the way Renoir works the depot and the man's job into every scene – conversations on platforms, in washrooms and canteens, views from the station master's window over the steaming metal waste: the short sharp lust worked out in a wooden platelayer's shed among shunted trucks under the steaming rain.' – *Graham Greene*

† Remade in Hollywood as *Human Desire* (qv).

Betrayal *

GB   1982   95m   colour
Horizon/Sam Spiegel (Eric Rattray)

The story of a publisher, his wife and her lover is told in scenes that go backwards in time.

Sharply acted stuff very typical of its author, for audiences with wideawake minds; but more theatrical than cinematic.

w Harold Pinter   play Harold Pinter   d David Jones   ph Mike Fash   m Dominic Muldowney

☆ Jeremy Irons, Ben Kingsley, Patricia Hodge, Avril Elgar

'Occasionally I pined for a little zest – perhaps a nude lesbian chariot race on ice.' – *Quentin Crisp*

& screenplay adaptation

Betrayal from the East

US   1945   83m   bw
RKO (Herman Schlom)

Japanese out to sabotage the Panama Canal are thwarted by a carnival showman.

Extravagant but penny-pinching flagwaver.

w Kenneth Gamet, Aubrey Wisberg   novel Alan Hynd   d William Berke   ph Russell Metty   m Roy Webb

☆ Lee Tracy, Nancy Kelly, Richard Loo, Abner Biberman, Regis Toomey, Philip Ahn, Addison Richards, Sen Yung, Drew Pearson

Betrayed: see *When Strangers Marry* (1944)

Betrayed

US   1954   108m   Eastmancolor
MGM (Gottfried Reinhardt)

In 1943 a Dutch intelligence officer works with a resistance leader who turns out to be a traitor.

Slow-moving, studio-set romantic melodrama of the old school; not very lively.

w Ronald Millar, George Froeschel   d Gottfried Reinhardt   ph Frederick A. Young   m Walter Goehr

☆ Clark Gable, Victor Mature, Lana Turner, Louis Calhern, O. E. Hasse, Wilfrid Hyde-White, Ian Carmichael, Niall MacGinnis, Nora Swinburne

Betrayed *

US   1988   128m   Alpha/Astro
MGM/UA/Irwin Winkler (Joe Eszterhas)

Following the murder of a radio talk show hostess, a couple on the run find themselves in a web of political intrigue.

Heavygoing piece with Something to Say, but not much to watch.

w Joe Eszterhas   d Costa-Gavras   ph Patrick Blossier   m Bill Conti   pd Patrizia von Brandenstein

☆ Debra Winger, Tom Berenger, John Heard, Betsy Blair, John Mahoney

Betrogen bis zum Jüngsten Tag: see *Duped Till Doomsday*

'The Harold Robbins people: what you dream, they do!'

The Betsy

US   1977   125m   Technicolor
Allied Artists/Harold Robbins International (Robert R. Weston)

Jockeying for power in the boardroom and the family life of an aged car manufacturer.

Rather tame and obvious melodrama enlivened by its star performance.

w William Bast, Walter Bernstein   novel Harold Robbins   d Daniel Petrie   ph Mario Tosi   m John Barry

☆ Laurence Olivier, Robert Duvall, Tommy Lee Jones, Katharine Ross, Jane Alexander, Lesley-Anne Down, Joseph Wiseman, Edward Herrmann

'Almost compulsively dreadful.' – *Derek Malcolm, Guardian*

Betsy's Wedding *

US   1990   94m   Technicolor
Warner/Touchstone/Silver Screen Partners IV (Martin Bregman, Louis A. Stroller)

A father gives his daughter a no-expense-spared wedding.

Intermittently amusing comedy of domestic mishaps.

wd Alan Alda   ph Kelvin Pike   m Bruce Broughton   pd John Jay Moore   ed Michael Polakow

☆ Alan Alda, Joey Bishop, Madeline Kahn, Anthony LaPaglia, Catherine O'Hara, Joe Pesci, Molly Ringwald, Ally Sheedy, Burt Young

'Surges ahead with tart one-liners, absurd spectacle, and ebullient side turns.' – *MFB*

Better Late Than Never

US   1983   87m   colour
Warner (Jack Haley Jnr, David Niven Jnr)

From two possibilities, an heiress selects her true grandfather. (Her grandmother wasn't sure.)

Would-be risqué comedy which fails to spark despite the talents involved.

wd Bryan Forbes   m Henry Mancini

☆ David Niven, Art Carney, Maggie Smith, Kimberley Partridge, Catherine Hicks, Lionel Jeffries

'As predictable as a rumbling stomach after a bowl of chilli.' – *Motion Picture Guide*

Better Off Dead

US   1985   98m   Technicolor
Warner/A&M (Michael Jaffe)

When his fickle girlfriend leaves him, a lonely teenager becomes despondent, but the sun shines when another girl shows interest.

Plotless, almost legless comedy drama with no direction whatever.

wd Savage Steve Holland   ph Isidore Mankovsky   m Rupert Hine   pd Herman Zimmerman

☆ John Cusack, David Ogden Stiers, Kim Darby, Demian Slade, Scooter Stevens, Diane Franklin

'Kids deserve better than this.' – *Variety*

The Better 'Ole

US   1926   97m   bw   silent
Warner

A British sergeant in Flanders proves that his major is actually a German spy.

Comedy-drama based on the cartoons of Old Bill by Bruce Bairnsfather. (The title comes from one in which Old Bill, in the trenches, is saying to a disgruntled soldier: 'If yer knows of a better 'ole, go to it.'). Criticism is irrelevant now, but the piece has historical interest.

w Charles Reisner, Darryl F. Zanuck   d Charles Reisner   ph Ed Du Par, Walter Robinson

☆ Syd Chaplin, Doris Hill, Harold Goodwin, Edgar Kennedy

A Better Tomorrow *

Hong Kong   1987   95m   colour
Atlas/Cinema City/Film Workshop (Tsui Hark)

original title: *Yingxiong Bense*

Two gangsters fall on hard times when they attempt to go straight, and the younger brother of one, a naïve but ambitious cop, finds that he cannot get promotion because of their relationship.

Sentimental tale of male bonding and sibling relationships, intercut with action set-pieces and culminating in a violent dockside shoot-out.

w Chan Hing Kai, Leung Suk Wah   d John Woo   ph Wong Wing Hang

☆ Chow Yun-Fat, Ti Lung, Leslie Cheung, Emily Chu

† The film was released on video in a dubbed and a wide-screen subtitled version.

A Better Tomorrow II

Hong Kong   1987   100m   colour
Golden Princess/Cinema City (Tsui Hark)

Two brothers, one a cop and the other a convicted criminal, go undercover as rivals to expose a counterfeiting racket, while an American-based restaurateur seeks revenge on local protection racketeers and the gangsters who drove his friend mad.

An unconvincing and, for those who have not seen the original film, confusing action melodrama, particularly in its New York scenes, partly redeemed by the final half-hour of balletic violence. The subtitling uses somewhat erratic English.

wd John Woo (action director: Ching Siu Tung)   story Tsui Hark   ph Wong Wing Hang   m Joseph Koo   ad Andy Lee

☆ Chow Yun-Fat, Leslie Cheung, Dean Shek, Ti Lung, Emily Chu, Kwan San, Kent Tsang, Regina Kent

'The mesmerising shoot-out at the conclusion makes up for any shortcomings in the plot.' – *Sight and Sound*

'The Making of a Killer.'

A Better Tomorrow III *
Hong Kong 1989 107m colour
Golden Princess/Film Workshop (Tsui Hark)
🎬 📼 📀 🎧

In the confusion of the fall of Saigon, a Hong Kong mechanic takes revenge against the crime boss who was responsible for the death of his uncle and falls in love with the boss's gun-toting mistress.
A prequel to John Woo's original film, alternating violence and romance and with an over-the-top melodramatic finale combining both, done with a certain panache.
d Tsui Hark
☆ Chow Yun-Fat, Tony Leung, Anita Mui, Saburo Tokito

Betty Blue *
France 1986 120m Fujicolour
Gaumont/Constellation/Cargofilms (Claudie Ossard)
🎬 📼 📀 🎧

original title: *37.2 au matin*
A waitress indulges her animal attraction for an odd job man but discovers him to be a literary genius.
What virtues this film has are more in style than content, but most people will find it over the top anyway.
wd Jean-Jacques Beineix novel Philippe Dijan ph Jean-François Robin m Gabriel Yared ed Monique Prim
☆ Béatrice Dalle, Jean-Hugues Anglade, Consuelo de Haviland

Between Heaven and Hell *
US 1956 94m Eastmancolor Cinemascope
TCF (David Weisbart)
📼

After Pearl Harbor a young Southern landowner is called up and finds himself on active service with mixed racial types.
Vaguely anti-war, pro-understanding action thriller which ends up going through predictable heroics in a professional but not too sympathetic manner.
w Harry Brown novel *The Day the Century Ended* by Francis Gwaltney d Richard Fleischer ph Leo Tover m Hugo Friedhofer
☆ Robert Wagner, Buddy Ebsen, Broderick Crawford, Brad Dexter, Mark Damon, Robert Keith, Ken Clark, Skip Homeier, Harvey Lembeck
♫ Hugo Friedhofer

Between Midnight and Dawn
US 1950 89m bw
Columbia (Hunt Stromberg)

Radio policemen track down a racketeer.
Competent, undistinguished programmer.
w Eugene Ling d Gordon Douglas ph George E. Diskant m George Duning
☆ Mark Stevens, Edmond O'Brien, Gale Storm, Donald Buka, Gale Robbins, Roland Winters

Between the Lines *
US 1977 101m TVC Color
Essential/Midwest Film Productions (Raphael Silver)
🎬 📼

Workers on a Boston underground newspaper are worried by rumours of an impending sale.
Sharply observed but slackly structured slice of provincial life.
w Fred Barron d Joan Micklin Silver ph K. V. Sickle pd Stuart Wurtzel ed John Carter
☆ John Heard, Lindsay Crouse, Jeff Goldblum, Jill Eikenberry, Bruno Kirby, Stephen Collins, Michael J. Pollard

Between Two Women
US 1937 88m bw
MGM

Romance between doctor and nurse is interrupted by his alcoholic husband and his infatuation with a patient.
Incident-packed men-in-white melodrama.
w Carey Wilson story Erich von Stroheim d George B. Seitz
☆ Franchot Tone, Maureen O'Sullivan, Virginia Bruce, Edward Norris, Cliff Edwards, Janet Beecher
'Class B that almost grew up. Eternal triangle in a hospital; okay dualler for nabes.' – *Variety*
† Title later changed to *Surrounded by Women* to avoid confusion with a *Dr Kildare* episode.

Between Two Worlds *
US 1944 112m bw
Warner (Mark Hellinger)

A number of air-raid victims, and two lovers who have committed suicide, find themselves on a luxury ship en route to the next world.
Nice-looking but slow and turgid remake of Outward Bound (qv), largely sunk in its own misery but redeemed by two performances.
w Daniel Fuchs play Sutton Vane d Edward A. Blatt ph Carl Guthrie m Erich Wolfgang Korngold
☆ John Garfield, Edmund Gwenn, Eleanor Parker, Paul Henreid, Sydney Greenstreet, Sara Allgood, George Tobias, Faye Emerson, George Coulouris, Dennis King, Isobel Elsom
'For ferry service from a world so saturated with death, the ship seems strangely empty – a fact that was not obtrusive in a day when death was not intrusive.' – *James Agee*

Between Us Girls
US 1942 89m bw
Universal (Henry Koster, Phil Karlson)

A mother and daughter are both involved in romances which tend to cross.
Mild comedy, a disappointing bid for stardom for a disappointing young star.
w Myles Connolly, True Boardman play *Le Fruit Vert* by Regis Gignoux, Jacques Thery d Henry Koster pd Joseph Valentine m Frank Skinner
☆ Diana Barrymore, Kay Francis, Robert Cummings, John Boles, Scotty Beckett, Ethel Griffies

The Beverly Hillbillies
👫 US 1993 93m DeLuxe
TCF (Ian Bryce, Penelope Spheeris)
🎬 📼 📀 🎧

A hillbilly family strikes oil and moves to live in a Beverly Hills mansion.
Based on the mouldering television sit-com, this is a wearisome concoction of old jokes about country folk trying to cope with city ways; its unsophisticated appeal is limited.
w Lawrence Konner, Mark Rosenthal, Jim Fisher, Jim Staahl d Penelope Spheeris ph Robert Brinkmann m Lalo Schifrin pd Peter Jamison ed Ross Albert
☆ Diedrich Bader, Dabney Coleman, Erika Eleniak, Cloris Leachman, Rob Schneider, Lea Thompson, Lily Tomlin, Jim Varney, Buddy Ebsen, Zsa Zsa Gabor, Dolly Parton
'Just as corny and stupid as the long-running series, pic version has been cleverly cast and shrewdly skewed to appeal jointly to original fans of the show and younger viewers only vaguely familiar with it.' – *Variety*
† The TV series ran from 1962 to 1971 and starred Buddy Ebsen in Jim Varney's role as Jed Clampett, Irene Ryan in Cloris Leachman's role as Granny, Donna Douglas in Erika Eleniak's role as the nubile Elly May, and Max Baer Jnr in Diedrich Bader's role of the dim Jethro. Created by Paul Henning, in its early years it was the most popular programme on American television, with a weekly audience of around 60 million.

Beverly Hills Brats
US 1989 91m Technicolor
Taurus (Terry Moore, Jerry Rivers)
🎬 📼 📀

The teenage son of wealthy, preoccupied parents decides to arrange his own kidnapping in order to remind them of his existence.
Tedious and unsubtle comedy, ploddingly directed and shrilly acted.
w Linda Silverthorn story Terry Moore, Jerry Rivers d Dimitri Sotirakis ph Harry Mathias m Barry Goldberg pd George Costello ed Jerry Frizell
☆ Burt Young, Martin Sheen, Terry Moore, Peter Billingsley, Natalie Schafer, Ramon Sheen, Cathy Podewell

Beverly Hills Cop **
US 1984 105m Technicolor
Paramount/Don Simpson/Jerry Bruckheimer
🎬 📼 📀 🎧

A Detroit cop races to Los Angeles to track down the killers of his best friend.
Filled with foul language and frenetic action, this rough-edged action comedy became one of the top box-office grossers of its year. So much for its year.
w Daniel Petrie Jnr d Martin Brest ph Bruce Surtees m Harold Faltermeyer pd Angelo Graham ed Billy Weber, Arthur O. Coburn
☆ Eddie Murphy, Judge Reinhold, Lisa Eilbacher, John Ashton, Ronny Cox, Steven Berkoff
'The film's only function is to provide Murphy with the opportunity to work a dozen or so variations on his familiar and oddly endearing routine.' – *Time*
† The role was originally tailored for Sylvester Stallone.
♫ original screenplay

'Axel Foley Is Back. Back Where He Doesn't Belong.'

Beverly Hills Cop 2
US 1987 102m Technicolor Panavision
UIP/Paramount/Don Simpson-Jerry Bruckheimer/Eddie Murphy
🎬 📼 📀 🎧

A cop returns to Beverly Hills to solve a series of crimes.
Further helpings from the same bowl. In no respect is the second film an improvement on the first.
w Larry Ferguson, Warren Skaaren, David Giler, Dennis Klein story Eddie Murphy, Robert D. Wachs d Tony Scott ph Jeffrey L. Kimball m Harold Faltermeyer pd Ken Davis ed Billy Weber, Chris Lebenzon, Michael Tronick
☆ Eddie Murphy, Judge Reinhold, Jurgen Prochnow, Ronny Cox, Allen Garfield, Brigitte Nielsen, Dean Stockwell, Paul Guilfoyle
'A noisy, numbing, unimaginative, heartless remake … all has gone sour and cold.' – *Daily Variety*

'In For The Ride Of His Life.'

Beverly Hills Cop 3
US 1994 104m DeLuxe
UIP/Paramount
🎬 📼 📀 🎧

A cop discovers that the head of security at a Los Angeles theme park is a murderer and counterfeiter.
The law of diminishing returns features yet again in this violent, noisy and predictable thriller that trades on past success but offers nothing for the future.
w Steven E. de Souza d John Landis ph Mac Ahlberg m Nile Rodgers pd Michael Seymour ed Dale Beldin
☆ Eddie Murphy, Judge Reinhold, Hector Elizondo, Timothy Carhart, Stephen McHattie, Theresa Randle, John Saxon, Alan Young, Bronson Pinchot
'A soulless, faceless, worthless dud.' – *Kim Newman, Empire*
♫ song 'Shakedown' (m Harold Faltermeyer; Keith Forsey; ly Harold Faltermeyer; Keith Forsey; Bob Seger)

'Kung Fool!'

Beverly Hills Ninja
US 1997 88m Foto-Kem
TriStar/Motion Picture Corp (Brad Krevoy, Steve Stabler, Brad Jenkel)
🎬 📼 📀

A woman wanting a martial arts expert to track down her missing boyfriend gets an overweight incompetent instead.
Dim-witted, ponderously performed slapstick featuring a comedian of very limited appeal.
w Mark Feldberg, Mitch Klebenoff d Dennis Dugan ph Arthur Albert m George S. Clinton pd Ninkey Dalton ed Jeff Gourson
☆ Chris Farley, Nicolette Sheridan, Robin Shou, Nathaniel Parker, Chris Rock, Soon-Tek Oh
'By no means a black belt in comedy or action choreography. Still, you have to give it high marks for tenacity and the ability to get the job done.' – *Leonard Klady, Variety*

Beware My Lovely
US 1952 77m bw
RKO/Filmmakers (Collier Young)
📼 📀

A handyman employed by a widow turns out to be a mental defective who imprisons and threatens to rape and murder her.
Dismal suspenser with a lot of screaming and running around but very little flair.
w Mel Dinelli play *The Man* by Mel Dinelli d Harry Horner ph George E. Diskant m Leith Stevens
☆ Ida Lupino, Robert Ryan, Taylor Holmes, Barbara Whiting

'Inept characterization and ludicrously repetitive situations will surely rank this among the silliest films of the year.' – *MFB*

Beware of Children: see *No Kidding*

Beware of Pity *
GB 1946 106m bw
Two Cities (W. P. Lipscomb)

An officer courts a crippled girl out of pity. She finds out and kills herself.
Ambitious but rather artificial and dreary drama, a shade too pleased with its own literariness; performances straitjacketed by production.
w W. P. Lipscomb, Elizabeth Baron, Marguerite Steen novel Stefan Zweig d Maurice Elvey ph Derick Williams
☆ Lilli Palmer, Albert Lieven, Cedric Hardwicke, Gladys Cooper, Linden Travers, Ernest Thesiger, Emrys Jones

Beware Spooks!
US 1939 65m bw
Columbia (Robert Sparks)

A nervous policeman routs crooks operating from a fairground.
Standard star comedy with some funny moments.
w Richard Flournoy, Albert Duffy, Brian Marlow d Edward Sedgwick
☆ Joe E. Brown, Mary Carlisle, Clarence Kolb, Marc Lawrence, Don Beddoe

Beware! The Blob
US 1971 88m DeLuxe
Jack H. Harris
🎬 📼

GB title: *Son of Blob*
A mysterious jelly from outer space consumes most of the population of a small town.
Spoofy sequel to one of the original space monster movies of the fifties. It's all too laboured to raise a thrill or a smile.
w Jack Woods, Anthony Harris d Larry Hagman ph Al Hamm m Mort Garson sp Tim Baar
☆ Robert Walker, Gwynne Gilford, Godfrey Cambridge, Richard Webb, Shelley Berman, Carol Lynley, Burgess Meredith, Gerrit Graham, Larry Hagman

Der Bewegte Man: see *The Most Desired Man*

Bewitched
US 1945 65m bw
MGM (Jerry Bresler)

A girl with twin personalities has her murderous element exorcized by a spiritualist.
Hilarious nonsense, ancestor of the Eve and Lizzie schizos of the fifties.
wd Arch Oboler story *Alter Ego* by Arch Oboler ph Charles Salerno Jnr m Bronislau Kaper
☆ Phyllis Thaxter, Edmund Gwenn, Addison Richards, Kathleen Lockhart
'Oboler manages the first persuasive imitations of stream of consciousness I know of in a movie. Much more often, he bores to desperation with the vulgarity and mere violence of his effects.' – *James Agee*

Beyond a Reasonable Doubt *
US 1956 80m bw
RKO (Bert Friedlob)
🎬 📼

A novelist is persuaded by a crusading newspaper proprietor to fake circumstantial evidence incriminating himself in a murder, thus proving the uselessness of such evidence.
Ingenious but rather cheerless and mechanical thriller. The actors extract what they can from a script intent on sleight of hand, but the distinguished director is at his most flatulent.
w Douglas Morrow d Fritz Lang ph William Snyder m Herschel Burke Gilbert
☆ Dana Andrews, Joan Fontaine, Sidney Blackmer, Philip Bourneuf, Shepperd Strudwick, Arthur Franz, Edward Binns

Beyond Bedlam
GB 1994 89m Technicolor
Feature Film/Metrodome (Paul Brooks)
🎬 📼

A detective's murder investigations lead him to a psychiatrist experimenting with mind-altering drugs on a serial killer.
Convoluted and unengrossing thriller, lacking any credibility and relying on most of the stereotypes of this

---

kind of fiction: aggressive cop, insane killer, glamorous psychiatrist.
w Rob Walker, Vadim Jean *novel* Harry Adam Knight d Vadim Jean *ph* Gavin Finney m David A. Hughes, John Murphy *pd* James Helps *ed* Liz Webber
☆ Craig Fairbrass, Elizabeth Hurley, Keith Allen, Anita Dobson, Craig Kelly, Jesse Birdsall, Georgina Hale
'A profound failure.' – *Sight and Sound*
'More than a bit of a mess, combining fantasy and reality in such a way that it is difficult to decide which is which.' – *Derek Malcolm, Guardian*

'An adventure which cowards quit early and weaklings never finish at all!'
Beyond Glory
US 1948 82m bw
Paramount (Robert Fellows)
The honour of a West Point cadet is vindicated.
Proficient but dramatically turgid vehicle for an absurdly over-age star.
w Jonathan Latimer, Charles Marquis Warren, William Wister Haines d John Farrow *ph* John F. Seitz m Victor Young
☆ Alan Ladd, Donna Reed, George Coulouris, George Macready, Audie Murphy

Beyond Mombasa
GB 1955 90m Technicolor
Columbia/Hemisphere (Adrian Worker)
In East Africa, an American avenges his brother's death at the hands of the Mau Mau (here called the Leopard Men and revealed to be run by a mad English missionary).
Tasteless and rather humdrum jungle adventure using real-life problems purely as a backdrop.
w Richard English, Gene Levitt *novel* Mark of the Leopard by James Eastwood d George Marshall *ph* Frederick A. Young m Humphrey Searle *ed* Ernest Walter
☆ Cornel Wilde, Donna Reed, Leo Genn, Ron Randell, Christopher Lee

'Truth has a witness...'
Beyond Rangoon **
US 1995 97m Technicolor Panavision
Columbia/Castle Rock (Barry Spikings, Eric Pleskow)
🎞 📼 ⊕~ 🎧
aka: Rangoon
In 1988, an American doctor visits Burma and becomes aware of the country's political situation, with a repressive dictatorship crushing any moves towards democracy.
An earnest and slightly uneasy attempt to combine a narrative of an innocent in peril with a polemic exposing an unlovely regime: it works better on the level of a suspense drama than as a political one.
w Alex Lasker, Bill Rubenstein d John Boorman *ph* John Seale m Hans Zimmer *pd* Anthony Pratt *ed* Ron Davis
☆ Patricia Arquette, Frances McDormand, Spalding Gray, U Aung Ko, Victor Slezak, Adelle Lutz
'A remarkably well-judged attempt to educate an audience's consciousness without altogether abandoning the function of entertainment.' – *Adam Mars-Jones*
'At the heart of *Beyond Rangoon* is an embarrassing contradiction. The heroine is presumably there to be the audience's representative. But since the focus is entirely on her naïveté, her struggle, her growth, the film effectively reduces the Burmese quagmire to a vacation from hell.' – *Entertainment Weekly*

Beyond Reasonable Doubt *
New Zealand 1980 127m colour
Endeavour/Fay, Richwhite/Brierley/Bob Jones/BRD (John Barnett)
In 1970, a police inspector frames a farmer for the murder of a couple from a neighbouring farm.
Based on a true story, this intriguing and disturbing exposé, of official corruption and suppression of evidence is given a somewhat stolid treatment.
w David Yallop *book* David Yallop d John Laing *ph* Alun Bollinger m Dave Fraser
☆ David Hemmings, John Hargreaves, Tony Barry, Martyn Sanderson, Grant Tilly, Diana Rowan, Ian Watkin, Terence Cooper, Bruno Lawrence

'The queen of the tropics finds a new jungle man!'
Beyond the Blue Horizon *
US 1942 76m Technicolor
Paramount (Monta Bell)
An orphan white girl grows up on a tropical island with a chimpanzee and a swimming tiger; when rescued and her story doubted, she leads an expedition back to prove it.
The most tongue-in-cheek of the Lamour jungle extravaganzas, with plenty of simple fun.
w Frank Butler d Alfred Santell *ph* Charles Boyle m Victor Young
☆ Dorothy Lamour, Richard Denning, Jack Haley, Patricia Morison, Walter Abel, Helen Gilbert, Elizabeth Patterson

Beyond the Clouds **
France/Italy/Germany 1995 109m
Eastmancolor
Artificial Eye/Sunshine/Cine B/France 3/Cecchi Gori/Road Movies (Stéphane Tchal Gadjieff, Arlette Danys, Philippe Carcassonne)
A film director imagines or remembers four stories involving partings between a man and a woman.
A slight but enjoyable postscript to Antonioni's career, with pared-down anecdotes of the disabling power of love.
w Wim Wenders, Michelangelo Antonioni, Tonino Guerra *stories* Quel Bowling sul Tevere by Michelangelo Antonioni d Michelangelo Antonioni, Wim Wenders *ph* Alfio Contini, Robby Müller m Lucio Dalla, Laurent Petitgang, Van Morrison, U2 *ad* Thierry Flamand *ed* Claudio di Mauro, Michelangelo Antonioni, Peter Przygodda, Luciano Segura
☆ Sophie Marceau, Vincent Perez, Irène Jacob, Marcello Mastroianni, Fanny Ardant, John Malkovich, Kim Rossi Stuart, Chiara Caselli, Jean Reno, Peter Weller, Jeanne Moreau, Ines Sastre
'Might be the most intimate, personal film Michelangelo Antonioni has ever made, but it may also be his least significant.' – *Deborah Young, Variety*

Beyond the Curtain
GB 1960 88m bw
Rank/Welbeck (John Martin)
A flying officer rescues a stewardess whose plane has been forced down in East Germany.
Inept, penny-pinching cold war melodrama in which very little happens.
w John Cresswell, Compton Bennett *novel* Thunder Above by Charles F. Blair d Compton Bennett *ph* Eric Cross m Kenneth Pakeman
☆ Richard Greene, Eva Bartok, Marius Goring, Lucie Mannheim, Andree Melly, George Mikell, John Welsh

Beyond the Door: see *Devil within Her*

'A twelve o'clock girl in a nine o'clock town!'
'Nobody's as good as Bette when she's bad!'
Beyond the Forest
US 1949 96m bw
Warner (Henry Blanke)
🎞
The discontented wife of a small-town doctor has an affair with a wealthy Chicagoan, murders a witness, attempts suicide, and dies of fever.
The star caricatures herself in this overblown melodrama which marked the unhappy end of her association with the studio. The rest of the cast suffer more dumbly from the script's unintentional hilarities.
w Lenore Coffee *novel* Stuart Engstrand d King Vidor *ph* Robert Burks m Max Steiner
☆ Bette Davis, Joseph Cotten, David Brian, Minor Watson, Dona Drake, Regis Toomey
ROSA: 'What a dump!'
ROSA: 'If I don't get out of here, I'll just die!'
Living here is like waiting for the funeral to begin.'
'This peerless piece of camp.' – *New Yorker, 1978*
'Miss Davis makes a regrettably melodramatic mess of what is undoubtedly one of the most unfortunate stories she has ever tackled.' – *Newsweek*
🎵 Max Steiner

Beyond the Gates: see *Au delà des Grilles*

Beyond the Limit: see *The Honorary Consul*

Beyond the Poseidon Adventure
US 1979 114m Technicolor Panavision
Warner/Irwin Allen
🎞
When rescuers reach the topsy-turvy passenger liner, one of them is intent on plunder.
Dreary alternative ending to The Poseidon Adventure (qv), with cardboard character studies, cut-price action, and tenth-rate technicalities.
w Nelson Gidding d Irwin Allen *ph* Joseph Biroc m Jerry Fielding *pd* Preston Ames
☆ Michael Caine, Telly Savalas, Karl Malden, Sally Field, Peter Boyle, Jack Warden, Shirley Knight, Shirley Jones, Slim Pickens

Beyond the River: see *The Bottom of the Bottle*

Beyond the Rockies
US 1932 55m bw
RKO
🎞
A singing deputy marshal disguises himself as an outlaw to bring to justice a female cattle baron.
Primitive early Western of no intrinsic interest.
w Oliver Drake *story* John P. McCarthy d Fred Allen *ph* Ted McCord *ad* Carroll Clark *ed* William Clemens
☆ Tom Keene, Rochelle Hudson, Marie Wells, Julian Rivero, Ernie Adams, Hank Bell, William Welsh, Tom London, Ted Adams

Beyond the Stars
US 1989 94m TVC Color
Five Star Entertainment (Joseph Perez)
🎞 📼 ⊕~
aka: Personal Choice
A mixed-up adolescent, determined to walk on the moon, strikes up a friendship with a former astronaut who has become a reclusive alcoholic after a strange incident on his last mission.
Meandering and sentimental account of a youth's coming of age, overweighted with messages about the environment.
wd David Saperstein *ph* John Bartley m Geoff Levin, Chris Many *pd* John J. Moore *ed* Frank Irvine, Stanley Warnow, Judith Blume
☆ Martin Sheen, Christian Slater, Robert Foxworth, Sharon Stone, Olivia d'Abo, F. Murray Abraham

'Trapped! ... in the incredible cosmic world that moves 100 years beyond time!'
'Adam and Eve of the year 2024! Only they could repopulate the world!'
Beyond the Time Barrier
US 1959 75m bw
AIP/Pacific International/Miller-Consolidated (Robert Clarke)
🎞
A test pilot crosses the fifth dimension and finds himself in 2024 when civilization has gone underground to avoid nuclear contamination.
Crude science fiction, roughly on the level of Flash Gordon but less entertaining.
w Arthur C. Pierce d Edgar G. Ulmer *ph* Meredith Nicholson m Darrell Calker
☆ Robert Clarke, Darlene Tompkins, Arianne Arden, Vladimir Sokoloff, Stephen Bekassy

Beyond the Universe
US 1978 90m colour/bw
Gold Key
A hundred years after a nuclear holocaust, a scientist trying to save a dying Earth uncovers a plot to exterminate all the sick and elderly.
Earnest, deadly dull ecological fable. Fortunately the entire cast is sucked into a black hole; unfortunately, they survive.
w uncredited d Robert Emenegger *pd* José Luis Mignone *ad* Michael Scheffe *ed* Brian Varaday
☆ David Ladd, Jacqueline Ray, Christopher Cary, John Dewey-Carter, Frank A. Miller, Stephanie Faulkner, Henry Darrow

Beyond the Valley of the Dolls
US 1970 109m DeLuxe Panavision
TCF (Russ Meyer)
🎞 📼 ⊕~
Three girls in Hollywood enjoy the wilder reaches of show biz high life.
The skinflick director's first film for a major studio, with positively no connection with Valley of the Dolls, is not explicitly pornographic but pussyfoots around with as many general excesses as can be crammed into

two hours. If taken as high camp it provides a laugh or two, but is chiefly notable as marking a major studio's deepest dip into muddy waters.
w Roger Ebert d Russ Meyer *ph* Fred J. Koenekamp m Stu Phillips, William Loose
☆ Dolly Read, Cynthia Myers, Marcia McBroom, John La Zar, Michael Blodgett, Edy Williams
'If one can resist walking out, the last half hour is quite manic.' – *MFB*
'A film whose total, idiotic, monstrous badness raises it to the pitch of near-irresistible entertainment.' – *Alexander Walker*
'Awful, stupid and preposterous ... also weirdly funny and a real curio, rather like a Grandma Moses illustration for a work by the Marquis de Sade.' – *John Simon*

Beyond Therapy
US 1986 93m colour
Entertainment/Sandcastle 5/New World (Steven M. Haft)
Psychiatrists become personally involved in the hang-ups of young New Yorkers.
Unfunny film version of a play which may have had something.
w Robert Altman, Christopher Durang *play* Christopher Durang d Robert Altman *ph* Pierre Mignot m Gabriel Yared *pd* Stephen Altman *ed* Jennifer Agué
☆ Glenda Jackson, Tom Conti, Julie Hagerty, Jeff Goldblum, Christopher Guest, Genevieve Page

Beyond This Place *
GB 1959 90m bw
Renown/Georgefield (Maxwell Setton, John R. Sloan)
US title: *Web of Evidence*
An American visiting London finds his supposedly dead father in prison serving a life sentence for murder; he delves into history and finds the real culprit.
Spiritless murder mystery with less serious intent than the original novel; tolerable entertainment.
w Kenneth Taylor *novel* A. J. Cronin d Jack Cardiff *ph* Wilkie Cooper m Douglas Gamley *ad* Ken Adam
☆ Van Johnson, Vera Miles, Bernard Lee, Emlyn Williams, Jean Kent, Moultrie Kelsall, Leo McKern, Ralph Truman

Beyond Tomorrow
US 1940 84m bw
RKO
🎞
Two elderly ghosts return at Christmas to help young lovers.
An amiably modest example of the kind they don't do any more.
w Adele Commandini *story* Mildred Cram d Edward Sutherland
☆ Richard Carlson, Jean Parker, C. Aubrey Smith, Charles Winninger

Bez Konca: see *No End*

Bez Svidetelei: see *A Private Conversation*

Bezhin Lug: see *Bezhin Meadow*

Bezhin Meadow **
USSR 1937 31m bw
Mosfilm
🎞
original title: *Bezhin Lug*
Fragments from an incomplete Eisenstein film are held together by freeze frames.
Even this collection of bits and pieces shows the power of the master.
w Alexander Rozhdestvenski *story* Ivan Turgenev d Sergei Eisenstein *ph* Edouard Tissé
☆ Vitya Kartashov, Boris Zakhava, Igor Pavlenko
† The film was reconstructed in 1966.

Bezness **
Tunis/France 1992 100m colour
CTF/Flach/TMP/Canal (Ahmed Baha Eddine Attia, Jean-François Lepetit)
A young Tunisian offering sexual and other services to tourists is torn between Islamic and Western ways of life and confused by his own double standards.
Absorbing account of cultural conflict, of exploitation and corruption told through the interlocking lives of a gigolo, the girl he wishes to marry, and a French photographer.

---

wd Nouri Bouzid *ph* Alain Levent *m* Anouar Braham *ad* Khaled Joulak *ed* Kahena Attia
☆ Abdel Kechiche, Jacques Penot, Ghalia Lacroix, Ahmed Ragoubi

'A Day To Set Yourself Free!'
Bhaji on the Beach *
GB 1993 101m colour
First Independent/Umbi/Channel 4 (Nadine Marsh-Edwards)
▦ ▤ ଼

A group of Asian women living in Birmingham go on a day trip to the seaside at Blackpool.
An enjoyable slice of life, covering not only racism and culture clashes, but the generational differences between the young and the old women as well as problems of gender.
w Meera Syal *d* Gurinda Chadha *ph* John Kenway *m* Craig Pruess, John Altman, Kuljit Bhamra *pd* Derek Brown *ed* Oral Norrie Otley
☆ Kim Vithana, Jimmi Harkishin, Sarita Khajuria, Mo Sesay, Lalita Ahmed, Shaheen Khan, Zohra Segal, Amer Chadha-Patel, Nisha Nayar
'As a look at the Afro-Asian community in Britain, it's everything one could ask for: funny and serious at the same time, good-tempered but not afraid of giving offence.' – *Alexander Walker*

Bhowani Junction *
GB 1956 110m Eastmancolor
Cinemascope
MGM (Pandro S. Berman)
▤ ⊛

Adventures of an Anglo-Indian girl during the last years of British India.
Disappointingly anaemic semi-epic from a gutsy novel, variably handled by all concerned.
w Sonya Levien, Ivan Moffat *novel* John Masters *d* George Cukor *ph* Frederick A. Young *m* Miklos Rozsa
☆ Ava Gardner, Stewart Granger, *Francis Matthews*, Bill Travers, Abraham Sofaer, Marne Maitland, Peter Illing, Freda Jackson, Edward Chapman
'An unwieldy, flatly-conceived charade.' – MFB
'One may believe with Henry Ford that history is bunk; if so, be assured that the labour pains of India are not half as much bunk as the romance of Victoria Jones, daughter of a Hindu lady, and a Welsh engine driver.' – *Alexander Walker*

Bian Zhou Bian Chang: see Life on a String

The Bible *
US/Italy 1966 174m DeLuxe Dimension 150 (70mm)
TCF/Dino de Laurentiis (Luigi Luraschi)
▤ ⊛ ଼

Through the Old Testament from Adam to Isaac.
A portentous creation with whispered commentary gives way to a dull misty Eden with decorous nudes, a sprightly Noah's Ark, a spectacular Babel, a brooding Sodom and a turgid Abraham. The pace is killingly slow and the script has little religious sense, but the pictures are often pretty.
w Christopher Fry and others *d* John Huston *ph* Giuseppe Rotunno *m* Toshiro Mayuzumi *ad* Mario Chiari
☆ Michael Parks, Ulla Bergryd, Richard Harris, *John Huston*, Stephen Boyd, George C. Scott, Ava Gardner, Peter O'Toole
'An Old Testament spectacular like any other.' – *David Robinson*
'At a time when religion needs all the help it can get, John Huston may have set its cause back a couple of thousand years.' – *Rex Reed*
⅄ Toshiro Mayuzumi

'One robot's 200 year journey to become an ordinary man.'
Bicentennial Man
US 1999 140m Technicolor
Buena Vista/Columbia/Touchstone/1492/Radiant (Wolfgang Petersen, Gail Katz, Neal Miller, Laurence Mark, Chris Columbus, Mark Radcliffe, Michael Barnathan)
▤ ଼

A domestic android gradually achieves his ambition to become fully human
This is a movie that covers a span of 200 years in which nothing very interesting happens, although the time does provide scope for one of Williams's more simpering performances.
w Nicholas Kazan *story* Isaac Asimov *novel* The Positronic Man by Isaac Asimov, Robert Silverberg

d Chris Columbus *ph* Phil Meheux *m* James Horner *pd* Norman Reynolds *ed* Neil Travis
☆ Robin Williams, Sam Neill, Wendy Crewson, Embeth Davidtz, Oliver Platt, Hallie Kate Eisenberg, Stephen Root, Lynne Thigpen, Bradley Whitford, Kiersten Warren
'Perhaps, one day, there will be robot film reviewers. And if they beg not to be sent to Robin Williams movies, we'll know they are developing human feelings.' – *Edward Porter, Sunday Times*
'An ambitious tale handled in a dawdling, sentimental way.' – *Todd McCarthy. Variety*
⅄ make-up (Greg Cannon)

Les Biches **
France/Italy 1968 99m Eastmancolor
La Boétie/Alexandra (André Génovès)
▦

aka: *The Does*
Two lesbians form an uneasy *ménage à trois* with a young architect, who loves both of them.
Fascinating and well-detailed character study with more depth than at first appears.
w Paul Gégauff, Claude Chabrol *d* Claude Chabrol *ph* Jean Rabier *m* Pierre Jansen
☆ Stéphane Audran, Jacqueline Sassard, Jean-Louis Trintignant
'You can almost see tubes attached to the heels of all the characters, through which the meaning has been sucked out of them and Chabrol pumped in.' – *John Simon*

Bicycle Thieves ***
Italy 1948 90m bw
PDS-ENIC (Umberto Scarparelli)

original title: *Ladri di Biciclette*
US title: *Bicycle Thief*
An Italian workman, long unemployed, is robbed of the bicycle he needs for his new job, and he and his small son search Rome for it.
The epitome of Italian neo-realism, the slight human drama is developed so that it has all the force of King Lear, and both the acting and the backgrounds are vividly compelling.
w Cesare Zavattini *d* Vittorio de Sica *ph* Carlo Montuori *m* Alessandro Cicognini
☆ Lamberto Maggiorani, Enzo Staiola
'A film of rare humanity and significance.' – *Gavin Lambert*
'A memorable work of art with the true flavour of reality. To see it is an experience worth having.' – *Richard Mallett, Punch*
'My idea is to de-romanticize the cinema.' – *Vittorio de Sica*
⅄ best foreign film
⅄ Cesare Zavattini
☗ best picture

Big **
↟↟ US 1988 102m DuArt/DeLuxe
TCF (James L. Brooks, Robert Greenhut)
▦ ▤ ⊛ ଼

A 13-year-old boy has his wish to grow 'big' granted by a carnival wishing machine.
Magic fun, better done than it has been since Turnabout (qv) in 1940.
w Gary Ross, Anne Spielberg *d* Penny Marshall *ph* Barry Sonnenfeld *m* Howard Shore *pd* Santo Loquasto
☆ Tom Hanks, Elizabeth Perkins, John Heard, Jared Rushton, Robert Loggia, David Moscow
⅄ Tom Hanks; best original screenplay

The Big and the Bad (dubbed)
Italy/France/Spain 1971 84m Technicolor
MGM-EMI/Sancrosiap-Terzafilm/Jaques Roitfeld/Atlantida (Alfonso Sansone, Enrico Chroscicki)
original title: *Si Può Fare ... Amigo*
A gunfighter hunts for the man who seduced his sister so that he can force him to marry her before he kills him.
Comic, slapstick spaghetti Western, with heavy-handed jokes.
w Rafael Azcona *story* Ernesto Gastaldi *d* Maurizio Lucidi *ad* Aldo Tonti *m* Luis Enriquez Bacalov *ad* Eduardo Torre della Fuentes *ed* Renzo Lucidi
☆ Jack Palance, Bud Spencer (Carlo Pedersoli), Francisco Rabal, Renato Cestiè, Dany Saval

'Men, money and moonshine ... when it comes to vice, Mama knows best!'
Big Bad Mama
US 1974 85m Metrocolor
Santa Cruz (Roger Corman)
▤

In 1932 Texas, a desirable widow becomes a bank robber.
Fast moving, violent nonsense, like a caricature of Bonnie and Clyde (qv), which was itself a caricature.
w William Norton, Frances Doel *d* Steve Carver *ph* Bruce Logan *m* David Grisman
☆ Angie Dickinson, William Shatner, Tom Skerritt, Susan Sennett, Robbie Lee

Big Bad Mama II
US 1987 85m colour
Concorde (Roger Corman)
▦ ▤

A mother and her daughters rob banks as a revenge for her husband's death.
A sequel that is more like a re-run of the original movie, and it is less interesting and stylish the second time around.
w R. J. Robertson, Jim Wynorski *d* Jim Wynorski *ad* Billie Breenbaum
☆ Angie Dickinson, Robert Culp, Danielle Brisebois, Julie McCullough, Jeff Yagher, Bruce Glover, Ebbe Roe Smith, Charles Cyphers

The Big Bang *
US 1989 81m colour
Kanter/Toback (Joseph H. Kanter)

A documentary in which people, from a nun to a gangster, a restaurant owner to a basketball player, are asked about the meaning of life.
Engaging conversational piece, cutting quickly from one person to another, that holds one's interest.
d James Toback *ad* Nicole C. Nicola *ed* Stephanie Kempf, Keith Robinson
☆ Emma Astner, Missy Boyd, Max Brockman, Darryl Dawkins, Eugene Fodor, Polly Frost, Veronica Geng, Julius Hemphill, Fred Hess, Elaine Kaufman, Sheila Kennedy, Anne Marie Keyes, Charles Lassiter, Marcia Oakley, Jack Richardson and also Don Simpson, Tony Sirico, José Torres, Barbara Traub

The Big Bang Theory *
US 1995 100m colour
Polygram/Renegade/Eagle Eye/Asylum (Daniel M. Bergers, Ladd Vance)
▦ ▤

GB title: *Bang*
In Los Angeles, a young woman discovers the power a uniform and a gun give her when she takes them from a cop who tried to sexually assault her.
Offbeat, episodic, independent movie that deals sympathetically with the dispossessed, and treats with disdain those that abuse their authority.
wd Ash *ph* Dave Gasperik *pd* Daniel M. Berger *ed* Ash, Daniel M. Berger
☆ Darling Narita, Peter Greene, Everlast, Michael Arturo, James Sharpe, Luis Guizar
'A powerful sleeper, convincing, provocative and exciting – an adventure in "guerrilla filmmaking" that uses an unexpected story device to hold up a mirror to a big US city.' – *Roger Ebert, Chicago Sun-Times*

The Big Bankroll: see King of the Roaring Twenties

The Big Blockade *
GB 1941 73m bw
Ealing (Alberto Cavalcanti)
▦

A semi-documentary showing the importance of blockading Germany in winning the war.
A curious all-star propaganda revue with some sketches more effective than others. It was Will Hay's only serious role.
w Charles Frend, Angus Macphail *d* Charles Frend *m* Wilkie Cooper *m* Richard Addinsell
☆ Leslie Banks, Michael Redgrave, John Mills, Will Hay, Frank Cellier, Robert Morley, Alfred Drayton, Michael Rennie, Marius Goring, Bernard Miles
'Topical subject matter, graphic descriptive work, pungent commentary, thrilling spectacle, clever characterisation.' – *Kine Weekly*

The Big Blue
US 1988 119m Eastmancolor
Cinemascope
TCF (Patrice Ledoux)
▦ ▤ ▤ ⊛ ଼

Two competitive deep-sea divers combine to rescue a dolphin.
Bizarre, over-long fantasy, much of it filmed murkily underwater.
w Luc Besson, Robert Garland, Marilyn Goldin, Jacques Mayol, Marc Perrier *d* Luc Besson *ph* Carlo Varini, Luc Besson, Christian Petron *m* Eric Serra, Bill Conti *pd* Dan Weil *ed* Olivier Mauffroy
☆ Rosanna Arquette, Jean-Marc Barr, Jean Reno
'The director's future as a significant cinematic navigator looks, on this evidence, rather less than watertight.' – *Philip Strick, MFB*
† The film was cut by nine minutes for its US release. It was released on video in two versions, one running for the same length of time as the cinema release, and the other, a special edition, running for 168m.

The Big Boodle
US 1957 83m bw
UA/Monteflor (Lewis F. Blumberg)
GB title: *Night in Havana*
A croupier in a Havana gambling casino is suspected of knowing where counterfeited plates are hidden...
An undistinguished chase film with the star very tired and a long way from home.
w Jo Eisinger *novel* Robert Sylvester *d* Richard Wilson *ph* Lee Garmes *m* Raul Lavista
☆ Errol Flynn, Pedro Armendariz, Gia Scala, Rossana Rory

The Big Boss (dubbed) **
Hong Kong 1971 98m Eastmancolor
Dyaliscope
Cathay/Golden Harvest (Raymond Chow)
▦

aka: *Fists of Fury*
A worker in an ice factory takes revenge on a gang of heroin smugglers led by his crooked and murderous boss.
Possibly Bruce Lee's best film; certainly it is the one that shows his skills to best advantage.
wd Lo Wei *ph* Chen Ching Cheh *m* Wang Fu Ling *ed* Fan Chia Kun
☆ Bruce Lee, Maria Yi Yi, James Tien, Nora Miao

The Big Bounce
US 1969 102m Technicolor Panavision
Warner/Greenway (William Dozier)
An ex-GI with a criminal record gets into sexual and criminal trouble while working at a Californian motel.
Unattractive melodrama with no discernible point, certainly not to entertain.
w Robert Dozier *novel* Elmore Leonard *d* Alex March *ph* Howard R. Schwartz *m* Michael Curb
☆ Ryan O'Neal, Leigh Taylor Young, Van Heflin, James Daly, Robert Webber, Lee Grant

Big Boy
US 1930 68m bw
Warner
⊛
A jockey wins a big race.
Star musical from a Broadway original; routine except that Jolson plays in blackface, then comes on as himself for the finale.
w William K. Wells, Perry Vekroff *d* Alan Crosland
☆ Al Jolson, Louise Closser Hale, Noah Beery
'Comedy entertaining in hoke way, but production inferior to previous Jolson pictures.' – *Variety*

The Big Brawl
US 1980 95m Technicolor Panavision
Warner Brothers/Golden Harvest (Raymond Chow)
▤

The son of a Chinese restaurateur in Chicago outwits gangsters.
Silly but quite entertaining chopsocky melodrama laced with comedy.
wd Robert Clouse *ph* Robert Jessup *m* Lalo Schifrin
☆ Jackie Chan, José Ferrer, Kristine de Bell, Mako, David Sheiner

---

The Big Broadcast **
US   1932   78m   bw
Paramount
A failing radio station is saved by an all-star show.
Revue-style show with a minimum of plot, valuable as archive material covering many stars of the time.
w George Marion Jnr *novel* Wild Waves by William Ford Manley d Frank Tuttle ph George Folsey
☆ Bing Crosby, Kate Smith, George Burns, Gracie Allen, Stuart Erwin, Leila Hyams, Cab Calloway, the Mills Brothers, the Boswell Sisters
'Flock of radio names ensures b.o. interest, especially in hinterland.' – *Variety*
♫ 'Please'; 'Here Lies Love'; 'Hot Toddy'; 'Where the Blue of the Night Meets the Gold of the Day'; 'Tiger Rag'; 'Crazy People'; 'It Was So Beautiful'; 'Kicking the Gong Around'

'A musical meteor of songs, comedy and romance!'
The Big Broadcast of 1936 *
US   1935   97m   bw
Paramount (Ben Glazer)
The 'radio lover' of a small radio station is kidnapped by a man-hungry countess.
Zany comedy with interpolated variety acts and a totally Marxian climax.
w Walter de Leon, Francis Martin, Ralph Spence d Norman Taurog ph Leo Tover ch LeRoy Prinz
☆ Jack Oakie, George Burns, Gracie Allen, Henry Wadsworth, Wendy Barrie, Lyda Roberti, C. Henry Gordon, Benny Baker, Bing Crosby, Ethel Merman, Richard Tauber, Amos 'n Andy, Mary Boland, Charles Ruggles, Virginia Weidler and also Guy Standing, Gail Patrick, Bill Robinson, the Nicholas Brothers, the Vienna Boys Choir, Akim Tamiroff
'Names are in and out as fast and as often as a firefly's tail light.' – *Variety*
'It hasn't much story, but the lack won't bother.' – *Variety*
♫ 'Miss Brown to You'; 'Through the Doorway of Dreams'; 'Double Trouble'; 'Why Dream?'; 'Amargura'; 'I Wished on the Moon'; 'Crooner's Lullaby'; 'Why Stars Come Out at Night'
♫ LeRoy Prinz

The Big Broadcast of 1937 **
US   1936   100m   bw
Paramount (Lewis Gensler)
A radio station manager has trouble with his sponsors.
More recorded acts separated by a measure of plot.
w Erwin Gelsey, Arthur Kober, Barry Travers, Walter de Leon, Francis Martin d Mitchell Leisen ph Theodor Sparkuhl *songs* various
☆ Jack Benny, George Burns, Gracie Allen, Bob Burns, Martha Raye, Shirley Ross, Ray Milland, Benny Fields, Benny Goodman and his Orchestra, Leopold Stokowski and the Philadelphia Orchestra, Eleanore Whitney, Larry Adler, Louis da Pron
'It isn't a comedy and it isn't a musical, but it has a lot of laughs, the best in several types of music, and I don't know where in the world you will see anything like it.' – *Otis Ferguson*

The Big Broadcast of 1938 **
US   1937   90m   bw
Paramount (Harlan Thompson)
A steamship owner engaged in a transatlantic race is hampered by his practical joking twin brother.
Glamorous, empty-headed all-star nonsense with the expected bevy of interpolated acts.
w Walter de Leon, Francis Martin, Ken Englund, Frederick Hazlitt Brennan d Mitchell Leisen ph Harry Fischbeck m/ly Ralph Rainger, Leo Robin
☆ W. C. Fields, Bob Hope, Martha Raye, Dorothy Lamour, Shirley Ross, Lynne Overman, Ben Blue, Leif Erickson, Kirsten Flagstad, Tito Guizar, Shep Fields and his Rippling Rhythm Orchestra
'Pictorially original and alluring, with the rejuvenated W. C. Fields at his inimitable best.' – *Variety*
♫ 'Thanks for the Memory'; 'Don't Tell a Secret to a Rose'; 'You Took the Words Right Out of My Heart'; 'Mama That Moon Is Here Again'; 'This Little Ripple Has Rhythm'; 'The Waltz Lives On'; 'Zuni Zuni'; 'Sawing a Woman in Half'
♫ song 'Thanks for the Memory' (mRalph Rainger, lyLeo Robin)

Big Brown Eyes
US   1936   76m   bw
Paramount (Walter Wanger)
A private detective and his wisecracking girlfriend catch a jewel thief.
Minor league Thin Man stuff, quite acceptably done.
w Raoul Walsh, Bert Hanlon d Raoul Walsh ph George Clemens m Gerard Carbonara md Morris Stoloff
☆ Cary Grant, Joan Bennett, Walter Pidgeon, Lloyd Nolan, Alan Baxter, Marjorie Gateson, Isabel Jewell, Douglas Fowley
'A fast, well-directed and quite unsentimental gangster film, pleasantly free from emotion – for emotion on the screen is nearly always false emotion.' – *Graham Greene*

'A comedy for the kid in all of us.'
Big Bully
US   1996   93m   colour
Warner/Morgan Creek (Lee Rich, Gary Foster)
▭▭
A former schoolboy bully reverts to his old ways when, 25 years later, his victim returns to their old school as a teacher.
Raucous slapstick comedy of minimal interest.
w Mark Steven Johnson d Steve Miner ph Daryn Okada m David Newman pd Ian Thomas ed Marshall Harvey
☆ Rick Moranis, Tom Arnold, Julianne Phillips, Carol Kane, Jeffrey Tambor, Curtis Armstrong, Faith Prince, Tony Pierce, Don Knotts
'This moronic, half-arsed and desperately obvious comedy has about the same level of entertainment as toothache.' – *Empire*

The Big Bus
US   1976   88m   Movielab   Panavision
Paramount (Fred Freeman, Lawrence J. Cohen)
▭▭
Misadventures of a giant atomic-powered bus on its first cross-country trip.
Rather feeble spoof on disaster pictures, with some good moments.
w Fred Freeman, Lawrence J. Cohen d James Frawley ph Harry Stradling Jnr m David Shire pd Joel Schiller
☆ Joseph Bologna, Stockard Channing, John Beck, René Auberjonois, Ned Beatty, Bob Dishy, José Ferrer, Ruth Gordon, Harold Gould, Larry Hagman, Sally Kellerman, Richard Mulligan, Lynn Redgrave
'It's all fast, bright, surface stuff, almost obsessively intent on never letting a laugh get away, misfiring, backfiring, skidding and crashing gears gaily all the way, often quite as thrilling, if not always as ludicrous, as some of the films it mocks.' – *Alan Brien, Sunday Times*
'It has been produced with such consummate bad taste, schlock acting and feeble attempts at verbal and visual humour that whatever laughs are engendered are at it rather than with it.' – *Dave Pomeroy, Film Information*

Big Business ****
↟↟   US   1929   20m   bw   silent
Hal Roach
▭▭
Stan and Ollie fail to sell a Christmas tree to a belligerent householder.
Classic silent comedy consisting largely of a brilliant tit-for-tat routine of reciprocal destruction, to which scripting, acting and editing equally combine.
w Leo McCarey, H. M. Walker d James W. Horne ed Richard Currier
☆ Stan Laurel, Oliver Hardy, James Finlayson

Big Business
US   1988   97m   Metrocolor
Buena Vista/Touchstone/Silver Screen Partners III
(Steve Tisch, Michael Peyser)
▭▭   ▭▭
Big business complexities are made more so by the fact that the principals are discovered to have been exchanged at birth.
Loud-shouting farce which just about gets by on star value.
w Dori Pierson, Marc Rubel d Jim Abrahams ph Dean Cundey m Lee Holdridge
☆ Bette Midler, Lily Tomlin, Fred Ward, Edward Herrmann

The Big Cage
US   1933   71m   bw
Universal
A lion tamer is worshipped by an orphan boy.
Pretty awful programme filler capitalizing on the animal act from the Ringling Brothers circus.
w Edward Anthony, Ferdinand Reyher d Kurt Neumann
☆ Clyde Beatty, Andy Devine, Mickey Rooney, Anita Page, Vince Barnett, Wallace Ford, Raymond Hatton

The Big Carnival: see Ace in the Hole

The Big Cat
US   1949   75m   Technicolor
Eagle-Lion
Feuding mountain families combine to track a marauding lion.
Standard outdoor melodrama, almost a straight version of Track of the Cat *(qv).*
w Morton Grant, Dorothy Yost d Phil Karlson
☆ Peggy Ann Garner, Lon McCallister, Preston Foster, Forrest Tucker, Skip Homeier, Sara Haden

'How much love, sex, fun and friendship can a person take?'
'In a cold world, you need your friends to keep you warm!'
The Big Chill **
US   1983   105m   Metrocolor
Columbia/Carson Productions (Michael Shamberg)
▭▭   ▭▭   ⌨   ✇   ☊
University contemporaries try to comfort each other after the death of a friend.
Wry satirical comedy which seems to be nostalgic for the sixties, but is funny anyway.
w Lawrence Kasdan, Barbara Benedek d Lawrence Kasdan ph John Bailey m various pd Ida Random ed Carol Littleton
☆ Tom Berenger, Glenn Close, Jeff Goldblum, William Hurt, Kevin Kline, Mary Kay Place, Meg Tilly, JoBeth Williams, Don Galloway
'The final impression left is of a collage of small relishable moments.' – *Kim Newman, MFB*
'An entertainment in which humour and sentiment are finely balanced and profundities are artfully skirted.' – *Sight and Sound*
'A splendid technical exercise … but there's no pay-off and it doesn't lead anywhere.' – *Roger Ebert*
♫ best picture; Glenn Close; screenplay

The Big Circus *
US   1959   109m   Technicolor   Cinemascope
AA (Irwin Allen)
▭▭   ▭▭
A bankrupt circus owner tries to get his show back on the road despite the murderous schemes of his ex-partners.
Fast-paced melodrama which makes little sense but generally provides the expected thrills.
w Irwin Allen, Charles Bennett, Irving Wallace d Joseph Newman ph Winton C. Hoch m Paul Sawtell, Bert Shefter
☆ Victor Mature, Red Buttons, Rhonda Fleming, Kathryn Grant, Vincent Price, Peter Lorre, Gilbert Roland, David Nelson, Adele Mara, Steve Allen

Big City
US   1948   103m   bw
MGM (Joe Pasternak)
In New York's East Side, a little girl is the adopted daughter of three bachelors, but trouble looms when they all get ideas of romance.
Latter-day star vehicle for which the young star is really too old and all else is excessively sentimental and sprawling.
w Whitfield Cook, Anne Chapin d Norman Taurog ph Robert Surtees
☆ Margaret O'Brien, Robert Preston, Danny Thomas, George Murphy, Karin Booth, Jackie Butch Jenkins, Betty Garrett, Lotte Lehmann, Edward Arnold
† Margaret O'Brien's singing was dubbed by Marni Nixon.

The Big City
US   1927   80m   bw   silent
MGM
A cabaret owner has a jewel robbery gang as a sideline.
Minor star melodrama.
w Waldemar Young, Tod Browning d Tod Browning
☆ Lon Chaney, Betty Compson, James Murray, Marceline Day

The Big City *
US   1937   80m   bw
MGM (Norman Krasna)
An honest cab driver and his wife hold out against corruption.
Sentimental realism of the type expected of its director. Smooth and syrupy.
w Dore Schary, Hugo Butler d Frank Borzage ph Joseph Ruttenberg m William Axt
☆ Spencer Tracy, Luise Rainer, Charley Grapewin, Janet Beecher, Irving Bacon, William Demarest, Eddie Quillan
'Domesticity and tenderness are heavily laid on: people in this film are *too* happy before disaster: no one is as happy as all that, no one so little prepared for what life is bound to do sooner or later.' – *Graham Greene*

The Big City **
India   1963   131m   bw
R. D. Bansal
original title: Mahanagar
A poverty-stricken Calcutta bank accountant sends his wife out to work; then the bank crashes, and she becomes the sole breadwinner.
Immensely detailed, overlong, but mainly fascinating account of modern urban India and its attitudes.
wd Satyajit Ray *novel* Narendra Nath Mitra ph Subrata Mitra m Satyajit Ray
☆ Madhabi Mukherjee, Anil Chatterjee, Haren Chatterjee, Haradhan Banerjee

Big City Blues
US   1932   65m   bw
Warner
A country boy gets into trouble on his first trip to New York.
Predictable comedy drama which seems to have no point other than the obvious one.
w Ward Morehouse, Lillie Hayward d Mervyn Le Roy
☆ Joan Blondell, Eric Linden, Inez Courtney, Evalyn Knapp, Guy Kibbee, Walter Catlett, Humphrey Bogart, Ned Sparks

'The strangest and most savage manhunt in history!'
The Big Clock *
US   1947   95m   bw
Paramount (John Farrow)
▭▭
A publishing magnate murders his mistress and assigns one of his editors to solve the crime.
Slick but rather empty thriller with judicious use of adequate talent.
w Jonathan Latimer *novel* Kenneth Fearing d John Farrow ph John Seitz m Victor Young
☆ Charles Laughton, Ray Milland, Maureen O'Sullivan, Rita Johnson, Elsa Lanchester
† Remade as *No Way Out* (1987) (qv).

The Big Combo *
US   1955   80m   bw
Allied Artists/Security-Theodora (Sidney Harmon)
▭▭   ▭▭
The police crush a crime syndicate.
An otherwise uninspired thriller memorable for starting the new violence, with some ugly scenes of torture which suffered at the time from the censor.
w Philip Yordan d Joseph H. Lewis ph John Alton m David Raksin
☆ Cornel Wilde, Richard Conte, Jean Wallace, Brian Donlevy, Robert Middleton, Lee Van Cleef, Ted de Corsia, Helen Walker, John Hoyt

The Big Country ***
US   1958   165m   Technicolor   Technirama
UA/Anthony/Worldwide (William Wyler, Gregory Peck)
▭▭   ▭▭   ☊
The Terrills and the Hannesseys feud over water rights, and peace is brought about only with the deaths of the family heads.
Big-scale Western with a few pretensions to say something about the Cold War. All very fluent, star-laden and easy to watch.

---

w James R. Webb, Sy Bartlett, Robert Wilder
novel Donald Hamilton d William Wyler ph Franz
Planer m Jerome Moross
☆ Gregory Peck, Jean Simmons, Charlton Heston,
Carroll Baker, Burl Ives, Charles Bickford, Alfonso
Bedoya, Chuck Connors
'Has, in fact, most of the elements one asks for in
the Western. Especially it has a feeling of size
and space … Yet something, I think, is missing:
the romantic heart.' – Dilys Powell
♪ Burl Ives
♫ Jerome Moross

'Once you adopt a kid, you've got to keep him.'
Big Daddy
US 1999 93m Technicolor
Columbia/Out of the Blue (Sid Ganis, Jack
Giarraputo)
A thirties-something playboy adopts a five-year-old
in the hope of impressing his girlfriend.
Sandler's familiar persona of a dim but charming
manchild wears ever thinner here, in a heavy-handed,
predictable and sentimental comedy.
w Steve Franks, Tim Herlihy, Adam Sandler
d Dennis Dugan ph Theo Van de Sande
m Teddy Castellucci pd Perry Andelin Blake
ed Jeff Gourson
☆ Adam Sandler, Joey Lauren Adams, Jon
Stewart, Cole Sprouse, Dylan Sprouse, Josh
Mostel, Leslie Mann, Allen Covert, Rob
Schneider, Kristy Swanson, Joe Bologna, Steve
Buscemi
'Easily the laziest, most slapdash and altogether
crummiest picture Sandler's done to date.' – New
York Post
'Sandler's goofy, infantile act, profoundly
unattractive when juxtaposed with an actual
infant, is about as amusing as a broken collar-
bone.' – Peter Bradshaw, Guardian
† The film was among the box-office successes of
the year, grossing more than $163m in the USA.

Big Deal at Dodge City: see A Big Hand for
the Little Lady

Big Deal on Madonna Street: see Persons
Unknown

The Big Doll House
US 1971 93m colour
MGM/New World (Jane Schaffer)
Tough new revolutionary inmates plan an escape
from a woman's prison run by a sadistic wardress.
Dull, cheap exploitation movie, concentrating on
nudity and violence; it is indifferently acted, and
perfunctorily written and directed.
w Don Spencer, Jack Hill ph Fred Conde
m Hall Daniels pd Ben Otico ed Cliff Fenneman
☆ Judy Brown, Roberta Collins, Pam Grier,
Brooke Mills, Pat Woodell, Sid Haig, Christiane
Schmidtmer

The Big Easy *
US 1986 108m DeLuxe
Kings Road (Stephen Friedman)
A New Orleans homicide detective is persuaded by
a lady investigator from the DA's office to look into
irregularities in the department.
Sassy, easy-going melodrama with comedy asides.
w Dan Petrie Jnr d Jim McBride ph Affonso
Beato m Brad Fiedel pd Jeannine Claudia
Oppewall
☆ Dennis Quaid, Ellen Barkin, Ned Beatty, John
Goodman, Ebbe Roe Smith
'The cooks did the best they could with
ingredients that tasted good but were a little
tough to chew.' – Daily Variety

Big Executive
US 1933 70m bw
Paramount
A go-getting market operator finds himself
competing with the grandfather of the girl he
loves.
Ho-hum melodrama with no compelling angles.
w Laurence Stallings story Alice Duer Miller
d Erle C. Kenton
☆ Ricardo Cortez, Richard Bennett, Elizabeth
Young, Sharon Lynn, Dorothy Peterson, Barton
MacLane
'It will be anything but big at the box office.' –
Variety

Big Fella *
GB 1937 73m bw
British Lion/Fortune (H. Fraser Passmore)
In Marseilles, a black man returns a lost child to
his English parents.
Pleasant light vehicle with the star in typical easy form.
w Fenn Sherie, Ingram d'Abbes novel Banjo by
Claude McKay d J. Elder Wills ph Cyril Bristow
m Eric Ansell
☆ Paul Robeson, Elizabeth Welch, Roy Emerton,
Marcelle Rogez
'A very unpretentious vehicle.' – Variety

The Big Fisherman
US 1959 166m Technicolor Panavision
Centurion (Rowland V. Lee)
An Arab princess meets disciple Simon Peter, who
dissuades her from her plan to assassinate her
stepfather Herod.
Well-meaning but leaden adaptation of a bestselling
novel which followed on from The Robe (qv). Too
reverent by half, and in many respects surprisingly
incompetent.
w Howard Estabrook, Rowland V. Lee
novel Lloyd C. Douglas d Frank Borzage ph Lee
Garmes m Albert Hay Malotte pd John DeCuir
☆ Howard Keel, Alexander Scourby, Susan
Kohner, John Saxon, Martha Hyer, Herbert Lom,
Ray Stricklyn, Beulah Bondi
'Its overall flatness of conception and execution
is a stiff price to pay for the lack of spectacular
sensationalism characterizing its fellow-epics.' –
MFB
'The picture is three hours long, and, except for
those who can be dazzled by big gatherings of
props, horses and camels, it is hard to find three
minutes of entertainment in it.' – Hollywood
Reporter
♫ Lee Garmes; John DeCuir

The Big Fix
US 1978 108m Technicolor
Universal (Carl Borack, Richard Dreyfuss)
An industrial investigator fancies himself as a
private eye and gets involved in a political
corruption case.
Hard to follow and harder still to care about, this rather
sloppy, with-it movie is a little too pleased with itself
from the word go.
w Roger L. Simon novel Roger L. Simon
d Jeremy Paul Kagan ph Frank Stanley m Bill
Conti pd Robert F. Boyle
☆ Richard Dreyfuss, Susan Anspach, Bonnie
Bedelia, John Lithgow
'The strength of this film lies in the cool,
meandering discretion with which its central
theme is fleshed out: regret for lost illusions as
the protest generation of the sixties finds its
arteries hardening.' – Tom Milne, MFB

The Big Gamble *
US 1960 100m DeLuxe Cinemascope
TCF/Darryl F. Zanuck
Three people drive an ailing truck to a remote
African township where they hope to start a
haulage business.
Curious comedy-drama-adventure which starts off with
family matters in Dublin and gradually develops into
a lighter-hearted Wages of Fear (qv). It has its
moments.
w Irwin Shaw d Richard Fleischer, Elmo Williams
ph William Mellor, Henri Persin m Maurice Jarre
☆ Stephen Boyd, Juliette Greco, David Wayne,
Gregory Ratoff, Sybil Thorndike, Fernand Ledoux

Big Girls Don't Cry ... They Get Even
US 1992 104m CFI color
Rank/New Line/Perlman/MG Entertainment (Laurie
Perlman, Gerald T. Olson)
GB title: Stepkids
A 13-year-old girl runs away from home, unhappy
at the lack of attention she is getting from her
mother and her new family, and from her father
who has started another family of his own.
Sentimental domestic drama that is no more than a
soap opera screened large.
w Frank Mugavero story Mark Goddard, Melissa
Goddard d Joan Micklin Silver ph Theo Van de
Sande m Patrick Williams pd Victoria Paul
ed Janice Hampton

☆ Griffin Dunne, Dan Futterman, Patricia
Kalember, Jenny Lewis, Ben Savage, Adrienne
Shelly, David Strathairn, Trenton Teigen, Margaret
Whitton, Hillary Wolf
'Promises much, delivers little.' – Kim Newman,
Empire

The Big Gundown
Italy/Spain 1966 105m Techniscope
PEA/PC (Alberto Grimaldi)
Italian title: La Resa dei Conti
A Texas lawman is hired to catch a Mexican
outlaw, who repeatedly escapes and finally proves
his innocence.
Violent but moderately enjoyable spaghetti Western.
w Sergio Donati, Sergio Sollima d Sergio Sollima
ph Carlo Carlini m Ennio Morricone
☆ Lee Van Cleef, Tomas Milian, Walter Barnes,
Luisa Rivelli

'All the action you can take … all the adventure you
can wish for!'
A Big Hand for the Little Lady **
US 1966 96m Technicolor
Warner/Eden (Fielder Cook)
GB title: Big Deal at Dodge City (though the action
clearly takes place in Laredo)
Five rich poker players are outwitted by a family of
confidence tricksters.
Diverting but thinly stretched acting-piece from a much
shorter TV original; still, suspense builds nicely until
the disappointingly handled revelation.
w Sidney Carroll TV play Sidney Carroll
d Fielder Cook ph Lee Garmes m David Raksin
☆ Henry Fonda, Joanne Woodward, Jason Robards,
Paul Ford, Kevin McCarthy, Charles Bickford,
Robert Middleton, Burgess Meredith, John Qualen

The Big Hangover
US 1950 82m bw
MGM (Norman Krasna)
A lawyer struggling to mingle with the mighty
finds he is allergic to strong drink.
Woefully unfunny comedy with virtually no plot.
wd Norman Krasna ph George Folsey m Adolph
Deutsch
☆ Van Johnson, Elizabeth Taylor, Percy Waram,
Fay Holden, Leon Ames, Edgar Buchanan,
Rosemary de Camp, Gene Lockhart, Selena Royle

The Big Heart: see Miracle on 34th Street

Big Hearted Herbert
US 1934 60m bw
Warner
A prosperous plumber becomes more concerned
with money than with his family's happiness.
Pleasing moral comedy, well cast.
w Lillie Hayward, Ben Markson play Sophie Kerr,
Anna Steese Richardson d William Keighley
☆ Guy Kibbee, Aline MacMahon, Patricia Ellis,
Philip Reed, George Chandler
† 1940 brought a remake under the title Father Is a
Prince, with Grant Mitchell.

'A hard cop and a soft dame!'
The Big Heat **
US 1953 90m bw
Columbia (Robert Arthur)
A police detective's wife is killed by a bomb meant
for himself; he quits his job to track down the
gangsters responsible.
Considered at the time to reach a new low in violence
(boiling coffee in the face), this dour little thriller also
struck a new note of realism in crime films and
produced one of Glenn Ford's most typical
performances.
w Sydney Boehm novel William P. McGivern
d Fritz Lang ph Charles Lang m Arthur Morton
md Mischa Bakaleinikoff
☆ Glenn Ford, Gloria Grahame, Alexander
Scourby, Jocelyn Brando, Lee Marvin, Jeanette
Nolan, Peter Whitney
'The main impression is of violence employed
arbitrarily, mechanically and in the long run
pointlessly.' – Penelope Houston

'Executed with style.'
The Big Hit *
US 1998 91m DeLuxe
TriStar/Amen Ra Films/Zide-Perry/Lion Rock (Warren
Zide, Wesley Snipes)
A hitman who begins to fall for the girl he has
kidnapped is betrayed by his confederate in the
crime.
All the hallmarks of Hong Kong action films, with their
gun-battles and intricately choreographed mayhem, are
here translated to an American setting, with the
addition of wisecracking gangsters and sick jokes.
w Ben Ramsey d Che-Kirk Wong ph Danny
Nowak m Graeme Revell pd Taavo Soodor
ed Robin Russell, Pietro Scalia
☆ Mark Wahlberg, Lou Diamond Phillips,
Christina Applegate, Avery Brooks, Bokeem
Woodbine, China Chow, Antonio Sabato Jnr,
Lainie Kazan, Elliott Gould, Sab Shimono
'A fleet piece of sock-'em entertainment, its
kinetic force plows through myriad plot holes
and inconsistencies with game abandon.' –
Leonard Klady, Variety

The Big House **
US 1930 88m bw
MGM (Irving Thalberg)
Tensions in prison lead to an attempted breakout
and a massacre.
Archetypal prison melodrama and a significant advance
in form for early talkies.
w Frances Marion d George Hill ph Harold
Wenstrom
☆ Chester Morris, Wallace Beery, Robert
Montgomery, Lewis Stone, Leila Hyams, George F.
Marion, J. C. Nugent, Karl Dane
'Not a two-dollar talker, but virile, realistic
melodrama, a cinch for any week-stand and
hold-overable generally.' – Variety
'We all gave our roles the best that was in us,
and the virility and truthfulness of the picture
were more satisfying than anything I've ever
done.' – Chester Morris, 1953
† The role played by Wallace Beery had been
intended for Lon Chaney, who died during
preparation.
♪ Frances Marion
♫ best picture; Wallace Beery

Big House USA
US 1954 82m bw
UA/Bel Air (Aubrey Schenck)
Convicts stage a break-out to get at hidden loot.
Though less explicit in its violence than many later
films, this is a singularly unpleasant melodrama with
not one attractive character.
w John C. Higgins d Howard W. Koch
ph Gordon Avil m Paul Dunlap
☆ Broderick Crawford, Ralph Meeker, Lon
Chaney, Charles Bronson, William Talman, Reed
Hadley

Big Jack
US 1949 85m bw
MGM (Gottfried Reinhardt)
Adventures of a couple of amiable scoundrels in
1890 Virginia.
The elements don't jell in this outdoor comedy-drama,
which was its star's last film.
w Gene Fowler, Marvin Borowsky, Otto Van Eyss
d Richard Thorpe ph Robert Surtees m Herbert
Stothart
☆ Wallace Beery, Marjorie Main, Richard Conte,
Edward Arnold, Vanessa Brown, Clinton
Sundberg, Charles Dingle, Clem Bevans

Big Jake *
US 1971 110m Technicolor Panavision
Batjac/Cinema Center (Michael A. Wayne)
An elderly Texas cattleman swings into action
when his grandson is kidnapped.
Satisfactory example of the star's later vehicles, with
efficient production and familiar cast and brawling.
w Harry Julian Fink, R. M. Fink d George
Sherman ph William Clothier m Elmer
Bernstein
☆ John Wayne, Richard Boone, Maureen O'Hara,
Patrick Wayne, Chris Mitchum, Bobby Vinton,
Bruce Cabot, Glenn Corbett, Harry Carey Jnr,
John Agar
'Another genial celebration of Big John's ability
to carry a film practically single-handed.' – MFB

Big Jim McLain
US 1952 90m bw
Wayne/Fellows (Robert Fellows)
🎞 ⊘~

A special agent for the House of UnAmerican Activities Committee routs communists in Hawaii.
Curious and rather offensive star vehicle in which the right-wing political shading interferes seriously with the entertainment value.
w James Edward Grant d Edward Ludwig
ph Archie Stout m Paul Dunlap md Emil Newman
☆ John Wayne, Nancy Olson, James Arness, Alan Napier, Veda Ann Borg, Hans Conried, Gayne Whitman

'Brings to the screen all the unattractively hysterical mentality of the witch hunt.' – *Penelope Houston*

The Big Job
GB 1965 88m bw
Allied Artists/Adder (Peter Rogers)
🎞

After 15 years in prison, a gang of inept bank robbers discover that the hollow tree in which they hid their loot now stands in the yard of a new police station.
Broad slapstick comedy, involving many of the Carry On team, that has some occasional amusing moments, though the best joke, when the gang make their getaway in a hearse, comes at the beginning.
w Talbot Rothwell story John Antrobus
d Gerald Thomas ph Alan Hume m Eric Rogers
ad Bert Davey ed Rod Keys
☆ Sidney James, Sylvia Syms, Dick Emery, Lance Percival, Joan Sims, Jim Dale, Edina Ronay, Deryck Guyler, Reginald Beckwith, Wanda Ventham

'The Hottest Hunk Of Film Hollywood Ever Shot!'
The Big Knife *
US 1955 111m bw
UA/Aldrich and Associates
🎞 ⊘~

A depressed Hollywood star who wants better things for himself is blackmailed into signing a new contract.
Overheated argument between Art and Mammon, with rather disagreeable people shouting at each other, for too long a time. Limited interest is provided by the acting.
w James Poe play Clifford Odets d Robert Aldrich ph Ernest Laszlo m Frank de Vol
☆ Jack Palance, Ida Lupino, Rod Steiger, Everett Sloane, Jean Hagen, Shelley Winters, Wendell Corey, Ilka Chase, Wesley Addy

'... it is with great relish and unbridled zest paced too fast and pitched too high, immorality is attacked with almost obscene relish, the knife turns into a buzz saw.' – *Pauline Kael, 1968*

The Big Land
US 1957 92m Warnercolor
Warner/Jaguar (George C. Bertholon)
GB title: *Stampeded*
Cattlemen encourage the building of a rail link for Texas.
Undistinguished star Western.
w David Dortort, Martin Rackin novel *Buffalo Grass* by Frank Gruber d Gordon Douglas
ph John F. Seitz m David Buttolph
☆ Alan Ladd, Virginia Mayo, Edmond O'Brien, Anthony Caruso, Julie Bishop, John Qualen

'Hackneyed, humdrum western.' – *Howard Thompson*

Big Leaguer
US 1953 73m bw
MGM (Matthew Rapf)
An ageing baseball player is given the job of running a youth training camp.
Even the synopsis is boring. A routine job from the doldrums of the star's career.
w Herbert Baker d Robert Aldrich ph William Mellor md Alberto Colombo
☆ Edward G. Robinson, Vera-Ellen, Jeff Richards, William Campbell, Richard Jaeckel

'The film treats its subject with an almost hushed reverence and its appeal is restricted almost entirely to baseball enthusiasts.' – *MFB*

'Her Life Was In Their Hands. Now Her Toe Is In The Mail.'
The Big Lebowski **
US 1998 127m Technicolor
Polygram/Working Title (Ethan Coen)
🖥 🎞 ⊘~ ⊙ ⊙ 🎧

A middle-aged nobody is attacked having been mistaken for his namesake, a millionaire whose wife, an actress in pornographic films, has apparently been kidnapped.
A meandering thriller that provides a great deal of incidental pleasures on a journey to nowhere in particular.
w Joel and Ethan Coen d Joel Coen ph Roger Deakins m Carter Burwell pd Rick Heinrichs ed Roderick Jaynes, Tricia Cooke
☆ Jeff Bridges, John Goodman, Julianne Moore, Steve Buscemi, Peter Stormare, David Huddleston, Sam Elliott, John Turturro, David Thewlis, Ben Gazzara

'A pseudo-mystery thriller with a keen eye and ear for societal mores and modern figures of speech, nonetheless adds up to considerably less than the sum of its often scintillating parts, simply because the film does not seem to be about anything other than its own cleverness.' – *Todd McCarthy, Variety*

'A shaggy dog story out for a constitutional.' – *Alexander Walker, London Evening Standard*

The Big Lift *
US 1950 119m bw
TCF (William Perlberg)
🎞

When the Russians blockade Berlin, British and American airmen get supplies there via a massive airlift; two men on one plane hold opposite views of the matter, and both have chastening experiences.
Rather heavy-going fiction based on fact, with earnest performances and good production.
wd George Seaton ph Charles G. Clarke m Alfred Newman
☆ Montgomery Clift, Paul Douglas, Cornell Borchers, O. E. Hasse, Bruni Lobel

'There are some acute touches ... just enough to make the slick evasions of the rest all the more regrettable.' – *Gavin Lambert*

The Big Man
GB 1990 116m colour
Palace/Miramax/BSB/British STV Film Enterprises (Stephen Woolley)
🖥 ⊘~
US title: *Crossing the Line*
An unemployed miner becomes a bare-knuckle fighter.
What begins as social realism, at its most powerful in a brutal fight sequence, ends as a mess of sentimental claptrap with a lot of labour politics.
w Don MacPherson novel William McIlvanney
d David Leland ph Ian Wilson m Ennio Morricone pd Carol Amies ed George Akers
☆ Liam Neeson, Joanne Whalley-Kilmer, Billy Connolly, Ian Bannen, Maurice Roeves, Kenny Ireland, John Beattie, Amanda Walker

'Rarely plausible, frequently risible, occasionally embarrassing, this morally confused melodrama falls with a dull thud between social realism and mythic fable.' – *Philip French, Observer*

The Big Money
GB 1956 86m Technicolor Vistavision
Rank (Joseph Janni)
A family of petty crooks is ashamed of its eldest son, who is an incompetent thief.
A would-be high-spirited lark in which none of the jokes comes off, and a note of forced artificiality hangs over the whole production.
w John Baines d John Paddy Carstairs ph Jack Cox m Van Phillips
☆ Ian Carmichael, Belinda Lee, Kathleen Harrison, Robert Helpmann, James Hayter, George Coulouris, Jill Ireland, Renée Houston, Leslie Phillips

The Big Mouth
US 1967 107m Pathecolor
Columbia (Jerry Lewis)
🎞
A meek bank auditor finds he is the double of a dying gangster and is put on the trail of stolen diamonds.
The comedian at his worst, most repetitive and long drawn out.
w Jerry Lewis, Bill Richmond d Jerry Lewis
ph W. Wallace Kelley, Ernest Laszlo m Harry Betts
☆ Jerry Lewis, Harold J. Stone, Susan Bay, Buddy Lester, Del Moore

'Comedy with Taste.'
Big Night **
US 1996 108m DeLuxe
Rysher/Timpano (Jonathan Filley)
🖥 🎞 ⊘~
In New Jersey in the late 50s, two brothers, who run an authentic but failing Italian restaurant, prepare a feast in the belief that entertainer Louis Prima will be coming for a meal.
Charming small-scale comedy of brotherly rivalry and love, immaculately done.
w Stanley Tucci, Joseph Tropiano d Stanley Tucci, Campbell Scott ph Ken Kelsch m Gary DeMichele pd Andrew Jackness ed Suzy Elmiger
☆ Minnie Driver, Ian Holm, Isabella Rossellini, Tony Shalhoub, Stanley Tucci, Caroline Aaron, Marc Anthony, Allison Janney

'A smartly made, delightfully acted period piece whose sensibility neatly straddles art films and the mainstream.' – *Todd McCarthy, Variety*

The Big Night
US 1951 75m bw
UA/Philip A. Waxman
A 17-year-old youth goes on the rampage in the underworld to avenge the beating up of his father by gangsters.
Hysterical melodrama presenting a rather false and dismal view of the world. Amazingly typical of its director's later output.
w Stanley Ellin, Joseph Losey novel *Dreadful Summit* by Stanley Ellin d Joseph Losey ph Hal Mohr m Lyn Murray
☆ John Barrymore Jnr, Preston Foster, Howard St John, Philip Bourneuf, Howland Chamberlin, Emile Meyer, Dorothy Comingore, Joan Lorring

'We are in that familiar underworld of the American cinema: dark streets gleaming with rain, sleazy apartments, garish night clubs, with Negro singers, drunks who spout philosophy, discontented blondes and fierce pock-marked thugs.' – *Gavin Lambert*

The Big Noise
US 1944 74m bw
TCF (Sol M. Wurtzel)
Two incompetent detectives accidentally round up a spy gang.
Very thin star vehicle consisting largely of poorly staged and warmed up versions of a few old routines.
w Scott Darling d Mal St Clair ph Joe MacDonald m Cyril Mockridge
☆ Stan Laurel, Oliver Hardy, Doris Merrick, Arthur Space, Veda Ann Borg

The Big Operator
US 1959 91m bw Cinemascope
MGM/Albert Zugsmith-Fryman (Red Doff)
The racketeer head of a labour union goes berserk when the government has him investigated.
Unpleasant gangster exploitation melodrama from the bottom of the barrel.
w Robert Smith, Allen Rivkin d Charles Haas
ph Walter H. Castle m Van Alexander
☆ Mickey Rooney, Steve Cochran, Mamie Van Doren, Mel Tormé, Ray Danton, Jim Backus, Jackie Coogan, Ray Anthony, Charles Chaplin Jnr

'The epic of the American doughboy!'
The Big Parade ***
US 1925 115m silent
MGM
🖥 🎞 ⊘~
A young American enlists in 1917, learns the realities of war, is wounded but survives.
Enormously successful commercially, this 'anti-war' film survives best as a thrilling spectacle and a well-considered piece of film-making.
w Laurence Stallings, Harry Behn d King Vidor
ph John Arnold m William Axt, David Mendoza
☆ John Gilbert, Renee Adoree, Hobart Bosworth, Karl Dane, George K. Arthur

'The human comedy emerges from a terrifying tragedy.' – *King Vidor*

'A cinegraphically visualized result of a cinegraphically imagined thing ... something conceived in terms of a medium and expressed by that medium as only that medium could properly express it.' – *National Board of Review*

'The extraordinary impression of the rush of lorries, the queer terror of the woods ... it was amazing how much fear could be felt in the mere continuous pace of movement.' – *Bryher, Close Up*
† The biggest grossing silent film of all.

The Big Parade **
China 1986 103m colour Scope
ICA/Guangxi Film Studio (Chen Liguo)
original title: *Da Yuebing*
Four hundred volunteers from the Airborne Division of the People's Liberation Army train for the National Day Parade in Beijing's Tiananmen Square.
Well-made film that concentrates on the relationship between individuals and the institution they serve. Changes to the movie were forced on the director by the People's Army, including the final scenes of the parade itself.
w Gao Lili d Chen Kaige ph Zhang Yimou
m Qu Xiasong, Zhao Jiping ad He Qun ed Zhou Xinxia
☆ Wang Xueqi, Sun Chun, Lu Lei, Wu Ruofu, Guan Qiang, Kang Hua

The Big Parade of Comedy **
US 1964 90m bw
MGM (Robert Youngson)
aka: *MGM's Big Parade of Comedy*
A compilation by Robert Youngson, including material as diverse as *Ninotchka*, Laurel and Hardy and the Marx Brothers.
One is grateful for the excerpts but the assembly of them is somewhat graceless.

The Big Picture **
US 1988 101m DeLuxe
Hobo/Columbia (Michael Varhol)
🖥 🎞 ⊘~
A student film maker goes to Hollywood.
Amusing satire of the movie business.
w Michael Varhol, Christopher Guest, Michael McKean d Christopher Guest ph Jeff Jur
m David Nichtern pd Joseph T. Garrity
ad Patrick Tagliaferro ed Martin Nicholson
☆ Kevin Bacon, Emily Longstreth, J. T. Walsh, Jennifer Jason Leigh, Martin Short, Michael McKean, Kim Miyori, Teri Hatcher

The Big Pond *
US 1930 79m bw
Paramount (Monta Bell)
The son of an important French family acts as a tourist guide in Venice.
Reasonably lively, semi-satirical early musical with pleasant touches but a faint air of the jejune.
w Robert Presnell, Garrett Fort, Preston Sturges
play George Middleton, A. E. Thomas d Hobart Henley ph George Folsey m arranged by John Green songs various
☆ Maurice Chevalier, Claudette Colbert, George Barbier, Nat Pendleton, Marion Ballou

'An amiable and ingratiating comedy that will give the Chevalier momentum another good shove.' – *Variety*
♫ Maurice Chevalier

The Big Punch
US 1948 80m bw
Warner
A boxer refuses to throw a fight and is framed for murder.
Routine time-passer with a second team before and behind the camera.
w Bernard Girard d Sherry Shourds
☆ Gordon MacRae, Wayne Morris, Lois Maxwell, Mary Stewart

Big Red
👪 US 1962 89m Technicolor
Walt Disney (Winston Hibler)
🎞
An orphan boy protects a dog which later saves him from a mountain lion.
Simple boy-and-dog yarn with impressive Canadian settings.
w Louis Pelletier d Norman Tokar ph Edward Colman m Oliver Wallace
☆ Walter Pidgeon, Gilles Payant, Emile Genest

The Big Red One **
US 1980 111m colour
UA/Lorimar (Gene Corman)

Five foot-soldiers survive action in several theatres of war between 1940 and 1945.
Symbolic action drama, very well made but finally lacking a cumulative impact.
w/d *Samuel Fuller* ph *Adam Greenberg* m *Dana Kaproff*
☆ Lee Marvin, Mark Hamill, Robert Carradine, Bobby DiCicco, Kelly Ward, Stéphane Audran, Serge Marquand
  'A picture of palpable raw power which manages both intense intimacy and great scope at the same time.' – *Variety*
  'Like all Fuller movies, about an inch from cliché all the way.' – *Guardian*

The Big Shakedown *
US 1934 64m bw
Warner (Sam Bischoff)
A racketeer finds a new gimmick: cut-price medicine.
Action programmer with emphasis on the young couple forced into helping the racket.
w *Niven Busch, Rian James* d *John Francis Dillon* ph *Sid Hickox*
☆ Bette Davis, Ricardo Cortez, Charles Farrell, Glenda Farrell, Allen Jenkins, Henry O'Neill, Samuel S. Hinds
  'A routine assortment of gang-film impedimenta.' – *New York Times*

The Big Shave **
US 1967 6m colour 16mm
Contemporary/McGraw-Hill

To the soundtrack accompaniment of Bunny Berigan's 'I Can't Get Started', a man shaves in a white bathroom, imperturbably cutting himself almost with every stroke until his face runs with blood.
A short, gruesome, macabre joke, intended by Scorsese as an angry comment on the process of self-mutilation that was the war in Vietnam.
w/d *Martin Scorsese* ph *Ares Demertzis*
☆ Peter Bernuth
† The film carries the credit 'Whiteness Herman Melville' as well as the line 'Viet '67'. It was released on video with three other shorts under the title *Scorsese x 4*.

The Big Shot *
US 1942 82m bw
Warner (Walter MacEwen)
An ill-fated criminal has trouble with women and his former companions.
Dullish star vehicle.
w *Bertram Millhauser, Abem Finkel, Daniel Fuchs* d *Lewis Seiler* ph *Sid Hickox* m *Adolph Deutsch*
☆ Humphrey Bogart, Irene Manning, Richard Travis, Donald Crisp, Stanley Ridges, Henry Hull, Susan Peters, Howard da Silva

The Big Show
US 1961 113m DeLuxe Cinemascope
TCF/API (Ted Sherdeman)
A circus proprietor dominates his sons; after his death they fight for supremacy.
Another remake of House of Strangers, which was also remodelled as Broken Lance (qqv). Not too bad as circus melodramas go.
w *Ted Sherdeman* d *James B. Clark* ph *Otto Heller* m *Paul Sawtell, Bert Shefter*
☆ Esther Williams, Cliff Robertson, Nehemiah Persoff, Robert Vaughn, Carol Christensen, Margia Dean, David Nelson

The Big Silence
France/Italy 1969 115m Eastmancolor
Adelphia/Corona
original title: *Il Grande Silencio*
A mute gunfighter comes to a small lawless town to kill a ruthless bounty hunter.
Brutal Western in which the bad guys win, but one with a genuine feeling for the genre and the snowbound landscape.
w/d *Sergio Corbucci* ph *Silvano Ippoliti* m *Ennio Morricone*
☆ Jean-Louis Trintignant, Klaus Kinski, Vonetta McGee

The Big Sky *
US 1952 122m bw
RKO/Winchester (Howard Hawks)

In 1830 two Kentucky mountain men join an exploration up the Missouri and become preoccupied with Indian trouble.
A large-scale adventure, loaded with talent, which becomes oddly tedious.
w *Dudley Nichols* novel *A. B. Guthrie Jnr* d *Howard Hawks* ph *Russell Harlan* m *Dimitri Tiomkin*
☆ Kirk Douglas, Arthur Hunnicutt, Elizabeth Threatt, Dewey Martin, Buddy Baer, Steve Geray, Jim Davis
  'It has the timeless, relentless quality of the long American historical novel.' – *Penelope Houston*
  ♫ Russell Harlan; Arthur Hunnicutt

The Big Sleep ***
US 1946 114m bw
Warner (Howard Hawks)

Private eye Philip Marlowe is hired to protect General Sternwood's wild young daughter from her own indiscretions, and finds several murders later that he has fallen in love with her elder sister.
Inextricably complicated, moody thriller from a novel whose author claimed that even he did not know 'who done it'. The film is nevertheless vastly enjoyable along the way for its slangy script, star performances and outbursts of violence, suspense and sheer fun.
w *William Faulkner, Leigh Brackett, Jules Furthman* novel *Raymond Chandler* d *Howard Hawks* ph *Sid Hickox* m *Max Steiner*
☆ Humphrey Bogart, Lauren Bacall, John Ridgely, Martha Vickers, Dorothy Malone, Regis Toomey, Charles Waldron, Charles D. Brown, Elisha Cook Jnr, Louis Jean Heydt, Bob Steele, Peggy Knudsen, Sonia Darrin
  MARLOWE: 'My, my, my. Such a lot of guns around town and so few brains.'
  GENERAL: 'You may smoke, too. I can still enjoy the smell of it. Nice thing when a man is too indulge his vices by proxy.'
  VIVIAN: 'So you're a private detective. I didn't know they existed, except in books – or else they were greasy little men snooping around hotel corridors. My, you're a mess, aren't you?'
  MARLOWE: 'I don't mind if you don't like my manners. I don't like 'em myself. They're pretty bad. I grieve over 'em on long winter evenings.'
  GENERAL: 'If I seem a bit sinister as a parent, Mr Marlowe, it's because my hold on life is too slight to include any Victorian hypocrisy. I need hardly add that any man who has lived as I have and indulges for the first time in parenthood at the age of 55 deserves all he gets.'
  MARLOWE: 'Speaking of horses … you've got a touch of class, but I don't know how far you can go.'
  VIVIAN: 'A lot depends on who's in the saddle. Go ahead Marlowe. I like the way you work. In case you don't know it, you're doing all right.'
  'A sullen atmosphere of sex saturates the film, which is so fast and complicated you can hardly catch it.' – *Richard Winnington*
  'A violent, smoky cocktail shaken together from most of the printable misdemeanours and some that aren't.' – *James Agee*
  'Harder, faster, tougher, funnier and more laconic than any thriller since.' – *NFT, 1974*
  'Wit, excitement and glamour in generous doses.' – *Francis Wyndham*

'Some days business is good – and some days it's murder!'
The Big Sleep
GB 1977 99m DeLuxe
Winkast (Elliott Kastner, Michael Winner)

An American private eye is hired by a crippled General to protect his uncontrolled younger daughter.
Straight remake of the 1946 film, curiously and ineffectively set in London.
w/d *Michael Winner* ph *Robert Paynter* m *Jerry Fielding*
☆ Robert Mitchum, Sarah Miles, Richard Boone, Candy Clark, Edward Fox, Joan Collins, John Mills, James Stewart, Oliver Reed, Harry Andrews, Richard Todd, James Donald, Colin Blakely

'The 1946 film takes on even more stature in light of this. For a Winner film, however, it's quite good.' – *Variety*

The Big Stampede
US 1932 54m bw
Warner

A deputy sheriff cleans up Arizona, gets the girl and defeats a cattle rustler.
Pleasant undemanding Western with Wayne working on his taciturn screen presence while remaking Ken Maynard's silent oaters, in this instance, Land beyond the Law.
w *Kurt Kempler* story *Marion Jackson* d *Tenny Wright* ph *Ted McCord* ed *Frank Ware*
☆ John Wayne, Noah Beery, Mae Madison, Berton Churchill, Paul Hurst, Sherwood Bailey, Luis Alberni, Lafe McKee, Paul Hurst

The Big Steal **
US 1949 72m bw
RKO (Jack J. Gross)

An army officer is framed for the theft of a payroll, and sets off across Mexico in hectic pursuit of the real culprit.
Unexpectedly enjoyable comedy melodrama with a plethora of twists and a pace that never lets up. Routine Hollywood at a level seldom achieved, and short enough to leave one asking for more.
w *Gerald Drayson Adams, Geoffrey Homes* story *The Road to Carmichael's* by *Richard Wormser* d *Don Siegel* ph *Harry J. Wild* m *Leigh Harline*
☆ Robert Mitchum, Jane Greer, William Bendix, Ramon Novarro, Patric Knowles, Don Alvarado, John Qualen
  'Vigour and excellent craftsmanship.' – *Gavin Lambert*

'He Wants The Key To Her Heart. They Want The Key To His Car.'
The Big Steal *
Australia 1990 100m colour
Hobo/Cascade/Film Victoria/Australia Film Finance Corp. (David Parker, Nadia Tass)

An 18-year-old boy plots revenge against the car salesman who sold him a faulty Jaguar with which he had hoped to impress his new girl-friend.
Mildly amusing comedy of the eccentricity underlying suburban life.
w *David Parker, Max Dunn* d *Nadia Tass* ph *David Parker* m *Philip Judd* pd *Paddy Reardon* ed *Peter Carrodus*
☆ Ben Mendelsohn, Claudia Karvan, Steve Bisley, Marshall Napier, Damon Herriman, Angelo D'Angelo, Tim Robertson, Maggie King
  'Has a low-key charm that's appealing, and a couple of riotously funny scenes.' – *Variety*

The Big Store *
US 1941 83m bw
MGM (Louis K. Sidney)

An eccentric private eye saves a department store from the hands of crooks.
Reckoned to be the Marx Brothers' weakest MGM vehicle, but it has its moments, especially the first reel and the bedding department scene, also Groucho's rendering of 'Sing While You Sell'.
w *Sid Kuller, Hal Fimberg, Ray Golden* d *Charles Reisner* ph *Charles Lawton* m *George Stoll*
☆ Groucho, Chico, Harpo, Margaret Dumont, Douglass Dumbrille, Tony Martin, Virginia Grey, Virginia O'Brien, Henry Armetta

The Big Story: see *Appointment with a Shadow* (1957)

The Big Story *
GB 1995 2m bw
Screwball Films

A reporter demands to be given a big story to cover.
Witty compendium of newspaper movie clichés, in which all the animated characters resemble Kirk Douglas.
w/d *Tim Watts, David Stoten* ph *Tristan Oliver*
☆ Featuring voices: Frank Gorshin
  ♫ animated short

The Big Street *
US 1942 88m bw
RKO (Damon Runyon)
A Broadway night-club waiter falls in love with a crippled singer who selfishly accepts his help without loving him in return.
Unusual but mawkish material from an author who never really suited the screen; a mixture of laughs, tears and sentimentality, with a comic gangster background.
w *Leonard Spigelgass* story *Little Pinks* by *Damon Runyon* d *Irving Reis* ph *Russell Metty* m *Roy Webb*
☆ Henry Fonda, Lucille Ball, Eugene Pallette, Virginia Weidler, Agnes Moorehead, Barton MacLane, Ozzie Nelson and his Orchestra, Sam Levene, Ray Collins, Marion Martin

'Five Couples. With One Big Idea.'
The Big Swap
GB 1997 122m colour
Film Four/Mayfair/Moonlit (Niall Johnson)

Five couples who are old friends decide to swap partners for a night, and find their lives are changed.
An earnest, low-budget movie about relationships; but the group of thirtysomethings involved are an unsympathetic bunch, and the concentration on their behaviour in bed becomes claustrophobic.
w/d *Niall Johnson* ph *Gordon Hickie* m *Jason Flinter, Craig Johnson* pd *Craig Johnson* ed *David Thrasher*
☆ Mark Adams, Sorcha Brooks, Mark Caven, Alison Egan, Richard Cherry, Julie-Ann Gillitt, Antony Edridge, Clarke Hayes, Thierry Harcourt, Jackie Sawiris, Kevin Howarth
  'In attempting to deliver a slight, soft-porn comedy for the upwardly mobile, Johnson gives all he's got in the first hour.' – *Jessica Mellor, Empire*

'He Saw. He Combed. He Conquered.'
The Big Tease *
US 1999 86m DeLuxe
Warner/Crawford P/I Should Coco (Philip Rose)
A Glaswegian hairdresser goes to Los Angeles in the expectation of competing in the World Freestyle Hairdressing Championship.
A fitfully amusing comedy, done in documentary style but lacking bite, and relying on Ferguson's performance to maintain any comic momentum.
w *Sacha Gervasi, Craig Ferguson* d *Kevin Allen* ph *Seamus McGarvey* m *Mark Thomas* pd *Joseph Hodges* ed *Chris Peppe*
☆ Craig Ferguson, Frances Fisher, Chris Langham, Mary McCormack, Donal Logue, Larry Miller, David Rasche, Kevin Allen, Charles Napier, Isabella Aitken
  'A silly, often funny and finally engaging mocku-comedy that's the This Is Spinal Tap of the Hollywood crimping scene.' – *Derek Elley, Variety*
  'It overstays its limited welcome by nearly an hour, freewheeling uphill to an embarrassing climax.' – *Philip French, Observer*

Big Time Operators: see *The Smallest Show on Earth*

Big Town
US 1947 59m bw
Paramount/Pine-Thomas
Adventures of the crusading editor of a city newspaper.
Anaemic support which surprisingly started a series.
w *Geoffrey Homes* from radio scripts d *William Thomas*
☆ Philip Reed, Hillary Brooke, Robert Lowery, Byron Barr, Veda Ann Borg

The Big Town
US 1987 110m colour
Rank/Columbia (Martin Ransohoff, Don Carmody)
A crapshooter on a winning streak goes to the big city to make good.
Ineffectual drama of a youth learning about life from his elders, chiefly women.
w *Robert Roy Pool* novel *The Arm* by *Clark Howard* d *Ben Bolt* ph *Ralf D. Bode* m *Michael Melvoin* pd *Bill Kenney* ed *Stuart Pappe*

☆ Matt Dillon, Diane Lane, Tommy Lee Jones, Bruce Dern, Tom Skerritt, Lee Grant, David Marshall Grant, Don Francks

Big Town Girl *

US   1937   66m   bw
TCF (Milton H. Feld)
A night-club singer adopts a disguise to elude her escaped convict husband.
Satisfactory supporting comedy-melodrama.
w Lou Breslow, John Patrick, Robert Ellis, Helen Logan d Alfred Werker
☆ Claire Trevor, Donald Woods, Alan Dinehart, Alan Baxter, Murray Alper, Spencer Charters
'First-class dualler which should please everywhere.' – *Variety*

The Big Trail *

US   1930   125m   bw
Fox
A wagon train struggles along the Oregon trail.
Simple-minded early talkie Western spectacular with a new young star who took another nine years to make it big. Originally shown on a giant 70mm gauge and intended for big screens.
w Jack Peabody, Marie Boyle, Florence Postal d Raoul Walsh ph Lucien Andriot, Arthur Edeson
☆ John Wayne, Marguerite Churchill, El Brendel, Tully Marshall, Tyrone Power Snr, David Rollins, Ward Bond, Helen Parrish
'Failing to own a kick or a punch, other than scenically, and with no outstanding cast names, it remains only a western of the pioneering sort, so thoroughly made familiar by those pioneering epics preceding it.' – *Variety*
'Printed upon the new wide film and projected upon the vastly large Grandeur screen, the landscapes, wagon trains, vistas and camp scenes achieve an incredibly greater sweep [than *The Covered Wagon*]. *The Big Trail* is often stagey, melodramatic, ranty.' – *Theatre Magazine*

The Big Trees **

US   1952   89m   Technicolor
Warner (Louis F. Edelman)
An unscrupulous lumberman tries to exploit California's giant redwood forests but is won over by the local Quakers who hold the trees in awe.
Pleasing, old-fashioned outdoor drama with a plot which allows the star much opportunity for derring-do.
w John Twist, James R. Webb d Felix Feist ph Bert Glennon m Heinz Roemheld
☆ Kirk Douglas, Eve Miller, Patrice Wymore, Edgar Buchanan, John Archer, Alan Hale Jnr
† A remake of *Valley of the Giants* (qv).

Big Trouble

US   1984   93m   Metrocolor
Columbia/Delphi III (Michael Lobell)
Two incompetent con men try to swindle an insurance company.
Witless comic farrago apparently designed to cash in on the success of The In-Laws (qqv) by utilizing the plot of Double Indemnity (qqv). Not a goer.
w Warren Bogle (Andrew Bergman) d John Cassavetes ph Bill Butler m Bill Conti
☆ Peter Falk, Alan Arkin, Beverly D'Angelo, Charles Durning, Paul Dooley, Robert Stack, Valerie Curtin

Big Trouble in Little China

US   1986   99m   DeLuxe   Panavision
TCF/Paul Monash, Keith Barish (Larry J. Franco)
A philosophizing truck driver in San Francisco finds himself combating an ancient, evil Chinese magician.
Misfiring attempt to equal the nonsense of the Indiana Jones sagas; occasional effective action moments don't stop the whole from being tiresome.
w W. D. Richter, Gary Goldman, David Z. Weinstein d John Carpenter ph Dean Cundey m John Carpenter pd John J. Lloyd
☆ Kurt Russell, Kim Cattrall, Dennis Dun, James Hong, Victor Wong, Kate Burton
'Glitzy sets, vacuous characters, limping fantasy.' – *Sight and Sound*

Big Wednesday *

US   1978   119m   Metrocolor   Panavision
Warner/A-Team (Alex Rose, Tamara Asseyev)
Three California surfing friends of the early sixties get back together after the Vietnam war.
It isn't clear whether the intent is to extol or deride the mystical camaraderie of surfing, but for those who can stand rumbustious beach behaviour this curious movie may have at least as much to say as The Deer Hunter (qv).
w John Milius, Dennis Aaberg d John Milius ph Bruce Surtees m Basil Poledouris surfing photography Greg MacGillivray
☆ Jan-Michael Vincent, William Katt, Gary Busey, Darrell Fetty

The Big Wheel

US   1949   92m   bw
UA/Popkin/Stiefel/Dempsey (Samuel H. Stiefel)
The son of a racing driver is determined to follow in father's footsteps.
Grubby star actioner.
w Robert Smith d Edward Ludwig ph Ernest Laszlo m Nat W. Finston
☆ Mickey Rooney, Spring Byington, Thomas Mitchell, Mary Hatcher, Allen Jenkins

Big Zapper

GB   1973   90m   Technicolor   Techniscope
Miracle/Lindsay Shonteff
aka: The Sex Life of a Female Private Eye
A tough female detective with a masochistic boyfriend, Rock Hard, is hired to discover the fate of a brother and sister, who have been murdered by a pimp.
Dreary and sniggering would-be erotic thriller, concerned solely and ineptly with sex and violence.
w Hugh Brody d Lindsay Shonteff ph John C. Taylor m Colin Pearson ad Spencer Reeve
☆ Linda Marlowe, Richard Monette, Gary Hope, Sean Hewitt, Michael O'Malley
'A paltry and nasty sexual fantasy which looks as though it has been dreamed up for the entertainment of impotent sadists.' – *Sylvia Miller, MFB*

'Wanted by two women!'
The Bigamist *

US   1953   80m   bw
Filmmakers (Collier Young)
A travelling salesman has two wives.
Minor melodrama which took its subject seriously but failed to make absorbing drama of it. Very much a family affair, starring the producer's present and past wives, the latter also directing.
w Collier Young d Ida Lupino ph George Diskant m Leith Stevens
☆ Edmond O'Brien, Joan Fontaine, Ida Lupino, Edmund Gwenn, Jane Darwell
'The film seems to have summoned all its energy to shout defiantly that bigamous marriages exist and, finding no one to defy, retires deflated.' – *MFB*

The Bigamist *

Italy/France   1956   97m   bw
Royal/Filmel/Alba
An innocent young salesman is accused of bigamy and dragged into court.
Noisy comedy of mistaken identity; some laughs, but the talents are not at their best.
w Sergio Amidei, Age Scarpelli, Francesco Rosi, Elio Talarico d Luciano Emmer ph Mario Montuori m Alessandro Cicognini
☆ Marcello Mastroianni, Vittorio de Sica, Franca Valeri, Giovanna Ralli

Bigfoot and the Hendersons: see *Harry and the Hendersons*

Bigger than Life *

US   1956   95m   Eastmancolor   Cinemascope
TCF/James Mason
A small-town schoolteacher is prescribed cortisone for arthritis; it gradually turns him into a bullying megalomaniac full of grandiose schemes.
Exaggerated and sensationalized but still not very dramatic expansion of a genuine case history. A curious choice for all concerned.
w Cyril Hume, Richard Maibaum d Nicholas Ray ph Joe MacDonald m David Raksin

☆ James Mason, Barbara Rush, Walter Matthau, Robert Simon, Roland Winters

'This is the world's sexiest robbery!'
The Biggest Bundle of Them All

US   1967   110m   Metrocolor   Panavision
MGM/Shaftel-Stewart
A retired gangster is kidnapped by other gangsters and shows them how to steal five million dollars worth of platinum.
Very moderately amusing international comedy caper.
w Josef Shaftel, Sy Salkowitz d Ken Annakin ph Piero Portalupi m Riz Ortolani
☆ Raquel Welch, Robert Wagner, Vittorio de Sica, Edward G. Robinson, Godfrey Cambridge, Davy Kaye
'It begins like one of these really bad movies that are unintentionally funny. Then it becomes clear that it intends to be funny, and it isn't.' – *Renata Adler*

Biggles

GB   1986   92m   Technicolor
UIP/Compact Yellowbill/Tambarle (Kent Walwin, Pom Oliver)
US title: Biggles: Adventures in Time
A young New York businessman is transported back in time to 1917, and his help solicited by a daredevil airman.
The bookends set a spoofy tone, but most of the movie is the same old teenage gunge.
w John Groves, Kent Walwin, characters created by Captain W. E. Johns d John Hough ph Ernest Vincze m Stanislas pd Terry Pritchard
☆ Neil Dickson, Alex Hyde-White, Peter Cushing, Fiona Hutchison, Marcus Gilbert, William Hootkins
'If you're in the right undemanding mood it's just daft enough to be enjoyable.' – *The Dark Side*

Bij de Beesten Af: see *Ape and Super Ape*

Les Bijoutiers du Clair de Lune: see *Heaven Fell That Night*

Bike Boy *

US   1967   96m   Eastmancolor
Vaughan/Factory Films (Andy Warhol)
A motorcyclist from the West Coast visiting New York has encounters with various women, one of whom seduces him.
Leisurely and occasionally witty exploration of low life, enlivened by the casually commanding presence of Viva.
w Andy Warhol and cast d Andy Warhol ph Paul Morrissey
☆ Joe Spencer, Viva, Brigid Polk, Ingrid Superstar, Ed Hood
'A strikingly pure exposition of Warhol's belief that the actor is the most important element in a film, and that the film-maker's job is simply to situate the actor to his best advantage.' – *Tony Rayns, MFB*

Bikini Beach

US   1964   100m   Pathécolor
American International
A California beach is disputed by surfers, motor bikers, and a businessman who wants to build a retirement community.
Mindless youth nonsense with flashes of satire.
w William Asher, Leo Townsend, Robert Diller d William Asher
☆ Frankie Avalon, Annette Funicello, Martha Hyer, Don Rickles, Harvey Lembeck, Keenan Wynn, John Ashley, Boris Karloff (cameo)

Bill and Coo

US   1947   61m   colour
Republic
Trials and tribulations of the inhabitants of Chirpendale are enacted entirely by birds, mostly wearing hats and neckties.
An eccentricity which won its creator, Ken Murray, a special Academy Award.
'By conservative estimate, the goddamnedest thing ever seen.' – *James Agee*

'Once ... they made history. Now ... they are history.'
Bill & Ted's Bogus Journey

US   1991   93m   DeLuxe
Columbia TriStar/Orion/Nelson Entertainment (Scott Kroopf)
Killed by robots designed to resemble them, two inept college boys trick Death, enlist the help of God and become heavy-metal heroes.
A sequel that, like the original, has attracted a cult following, though the joke, depending on the slang spoken by its dim heroes, remains a thin one.
w Ed Solomon, Chris Matheson d Pete Hewitt ph Oliver Wood m David Newman ed David Finfer
☆ Alex Winter, Keanu Reeves, Jeff Miller, David Carrera, George Carlin, Joss Ackland, William Sadler
'A sequel that contrives another elaborate but non-excellent adventure.' – *Variety*

Bill and Ted's Excellent Adventure

US   1988   89m   Technicolor   Panavision
Castle Premier/Interscope Communications/Soisson-Murphey Productions/De Laurentiis Film Partners (Scott Kroopf, Michael S. Murphey, Joel Soisson)
In order to improve their essays, two high-school students, with the aid of a time machine, abduct famous historical figures and take them to modern-day America.
Mild comedy depending for its effect on an understanding of teenage Californian mores.
w Chris Matheson, Ed Solomon d Stephen Herek ph Timothy Suhrstedt m David Newman pd Roy Forge Smith, Lynda Paradise ad Gordon White, Pierluigi Basile ed Larry Bock, Patrick Rand
☆ Keanu Reeves, Alex Winter, Robert V. Barron, Terry Camilleri, Clifford David, Al Leong, Rod Loomis, Dan Shor, Tony Steedman, Jane Wiedlin

A Bill of Divorcement **

US   1932   76m   bw
RKO/David O. Selznick
A middle-aged man, released from a mental institution, comes home and meets his strong-willed daughter.
Pattern play which became a celebrated star vehicle; now very dated but the performances survive. It was Hepburn's first film.
w Howard Estabrook, Harry Wagstaff Gribble play Clemence Dane d George Cukor ph Sid Hickox m Max Steiner, W. Franke Harling
☆ John Barrymore, Katharine Hepburn, Billie Burke, David Manners, Paul Cavanagh, Henry Stephenson, Elizabeth Patterson
'A money picture for all classes of houses ... the most potent tear jerker in many a moon.' – *Variety*
'A very good picture, tender, emotional and intensely gripping.' – *Picturegoer*

A Bill of Divorcement *

US   1940   69m   bw
RKO
GB title: Never To Love
Virtually a scene-for-scene remake of the above.
Again the acting holds the material together.
w Dalton Trumbo d John Farrow ph Nicholas Musuraca m Roy Webb
☆ Adolphe Menjou, Maureen O'Hara, Patric Knowles, Herbert Marshall, C. Aubrey Smith, Dame May Whitty

Billie

US   1965   87m   Technicolor   Techniscope
UA/Peter Lawford (Don Weis)
A teenage tomboy runs into trouble because she is better at sport than her boyfriends.
Routine American college/domestic comedy with a young star and good comedy support.
w Ronald Alexander play Time Out for Ginger by Ronald Alexander d Don Weis ph John Russell m Dominic Frontière
☆ Patty Duke, Jim Backus, Jane Greer, Warren Berlinger, Billy de Wolfe, Charles Lane, Dick Sargent, Richard Deacon

---

Billion Dollar Brain

GB 1967 111m Technicolor Panavision
UA/Lowndes (Harry Saltzman)

Ex-secret agent Harry Palmer agrees to take a mysterious canister to Finland and becomes involved in an American megalomaniac's bid to take over the world.

Incomprehensible spy story smothered in the kind of top dressing now expected from this director, but which almost killed his career at the time. Occasional pictorial pleasures, but the total kaleidoscopic effect is enough to drive most audiences to the exit.

w John McGrath *novel* Len Deighton d Ken Russell ph Billy Williams m Richard Rodney Bennett pd Syd Cain

☆ Michael Caine, Oscar Homolka, Françoise Dorléac, Karl Malden, Ed Begley

Billion Dollar Scandal

US 1932 81m bw
Paramount

Ex-convicts are involved by a millionaire in a shady oil deal.

Competent but complex and talky melodrama 'from the headlines'.

w Gene Towne, Graham Baker d Harry Joe Brown

☆ Robert Armstrong, Constance Cummings, Frank Morgan, Olga Baclanova, James Gleason, Irving Pichel

A Billion for Boris

US 1990 89m TVC Color
Comworld Pictures (Sandy Russell Gartin, Ned Kandel)

An adolescent boy, who has problems with his mother, tries to get rich quick after he discovers that his old TV set shows the next day's programmes.

Predictable, soft-centred, slow-moving, lacklustre comedy.

w Sandy Russell Gartin *novel* Mary Rodgers d Alex Grasshoff ph Peter Stein m Robert Christianson pd Dan Leigh ed Sheila Bakerman

☆ Scott Tiler, Mary Tanner, Seth Green, Tim Kazurinsky, Lee Grant

Billy Bathgate

US 1991 106m DuArt
Warner/Touchstone (Arlene Donovan, Robert F. Colesbury)

A teenager becomes an assistant to gangster Dutch Schultz.

Curiously uninvolving and tepid thriller, with a lacklustre central performance.

w Tom Stoppard *novel* E. L. Doctorow d Robert Benton m Nestor Almendros m Mark Isham pd Patrizia von Brandenstein ed Alan Heim, Robert Reitano

☆ Dustin Hoffman, Nicole Kidman, Loren Dean, Bruce Willis, Steven Hill, Steve Buscemi, Billy Jaye

'This refined, intelligent drama about thugs appeals considerably to the head but has little impact in the gut, which is not exactly how it should be with gangster films.' – *Variety*
'A film of minor virtues and major faults.' – *Sight and Sound*
'It has a grace and gravity rare just now in American films.' – *Richard Corliss, Time*

Billy Budd *

GB 1962 125m bw Cinemascope
Anglo-Allied (A. Ronald Lubin, Peter Ustinov)

In 1797 the sadistic master at arms of a British warship terrorizes the crew and is killed by young Billy Budd, who must hang for his unpremeditated crime.

Handsomely photographed but obtusely scripted and variously acted attempt at the impossible, an allegory of good and evil more suited to opera or the printed page than film: in any case, a hopelessly and defiantly uncommercial enterprise. Some actors bore, others chew the scenery.

w Peter Ustinov, Robert Rossen *novel* Herman Melville d Peter Ustinov ph Robert Krasker m Antony Hopkins

☆ Peter Ustinov, Robert Ryan, Terence Stamp, Melvyn Douglas, Paul Rogers, John Neville, Ronald Lewis, David McCallum, Lee Montague, John Meillon, Thomas Heathcote, Niall MacGinnis, Cyril Luckham

'A beautiful, terrifying and heartbreaking film.' – *Time*
§ Terence Stamp

Billy Galvin *

US 1986 94m colour
American Playhouse/Vestron (Sue Jett, Tony Mark)

Frictions develop between father and son in blue collar Boston.

Old-fashioned family drama, quite rewarding for old-fashioned audiences.

wd John Gray ph Eugene Shlugleit pd Shay Austin ed Lou Kleinman

☆ Karl Malden, Lenny von Dohlen, Joyce Van Patten, Toni Kalem, Paul Guilfoyle

Billy Jack *

US 1971 113m Technicolor
Warner/National Student Film Corporation (Mary Rose Solti)

A half-breed Vietnam veteran roams the Arizona desert protecting wild mustangs and a runaway teenager.

A trendy radical drama, virtually a one-man show which had an enormous success in the US and led to a sequel, The Trial of Billy Jack.

w Tom Laughlin, Delores Taylor d Tom Laughlin (T. C. Frank) ph Fred Koenekamp, John Stephens m Mundell Lowe

☆ Tom Laughlin, Delores Taylor, Bert Freed, Clark Howat, Julie Webb, Ken Tobey, Victor Izay

'A plea for the alternative society with a format of the crudest melodrama.' – *MFB*

Billy Liar ***

GB 1963 98m bw Cinemascope
Vic Films (Joe Janni)

In a drab North Country town, an undertaker's clerk lives in a world of fantasy.

Flawed only by its unsuitable Cinemascope ratio, this is a brilliant urban comedy of its time, seminal in acting, theme, direction and permissiveness.

w Keith Waterhouse, Willis Hall *play* Keith Waterhouse, Willis Hall *novel* Keith Waterhouse inspired by Thurber's Walter Mitty d John Schlesinger ph Denys Coop m Richard Rodney Bennett

☆ Tom Courtenay, Julie Christie, Wilfred Pickles, Mona Washbourne, Ethel Griffies, Finlay Currie, Rodney Bewes, Leonard Rossiter

'John Schlesinger's direction, I am delighted to say, is rich in wit.' – *Dilys Powell*
† It was later turned into a TV series and a successful stage musical, making Billy a universal figure of the period.

Billy Madison

US 1995 90m DeLuxe
Universal (Robert Simonds)

A rich slacker vows to work his way through a different grade of school every two weeks to prove himself to his father so that he can inherit the family business.

Dim and coarse-toned comedy that does not travel well, featuring a performer of slight appeal outside the US, and material that might have sufficed for a funny five minutes.

w Tim Herlihy, Adam Sandler d Tamra Davis ph Victor Hammer m Randy Edelman pd Perry Blake ed Jeffrey Wolf

☆ Adam Sandler, Darren McGavin, Bridgette Wilson, Bradley Whitford, Josh Mostel, Norm MacDonald

'As derivative a compound as the dross left over from a particularly noxious junior school chemistry experiment.' – *Leslie Felperin, Sight and Sound*
† Steve Buscemi appears uncredited.

Billy Rose's Diamond Horseshoe: see *Diamond Horseshoe*

Billy Rose's Jumbo: see *Jumbo*

Billy the Kid *

US 1930 90m bw
MGM

A young Western outlaw is relentlessly pursued by Sheriff Pat Garrett.

Mildly interesting early talkie Western with the usual romanticized view of Billy. Originally made and shown in 70mm.

w Wanda Tuchock, Laurence Stallings, Charles MacArthur d King Vidor ph Gordon Avil

☆ Johnny Mack Brown, Wallace Beery, Kay Johnson, Karl Dane, Roscoe Ates

'Should stand up for slightly better than average business where shown on Realife. Otherwise just an ordinary western.' – *Variety*

Billy the Kid *

US 1941 95m Technicolor
MGM (Irving Asher)

Remake of the above, equally false and rather less well acted, but a striking outdoor colour film of its period.

w Gene Fowler d David Miller ph Leonard Smith, William V. Skall m David Snell

☆ Robert Taylor, Brian Donlevy, Ian Hunter, Mary Howard, Gene Lockhart, Henry O'Neill, Frank Puglia, Cy Kendall, Ethel Griffies
§ Leonard Smith, William V. Skall

Billy the Kid and the Green Baize Vampire

GB 1985 93m colour
ITC/Zenith (Simon Mallin)

A hustling young snooker player takes on a formidable opponent.

Predictable sporting melodrama with curious supernatural overtones; not a coherent whole.

w Trevor Preston d Alan Clarke ph Clive Tickner m George Fenton pd Jamie Leonard

☆ Phil Daniels, Alun Armstrong, Bruce Payne, Louise Gold, Eve Ferret

'Weird, not to say downright perverse.' – *Sight and Sound*

Billy the Kid vs Dracula

US 1965 89m Pathécolor
Avco Embassy/Circle/Embassy (Carroll Case)

Billy the Kid rescues his fiancée from the clutches of Dracula.

Comic treatment of horror and Westerns, with Billy as a clean-cut hero, that may appeal to fans of bad movies.

w Carl K. Hittleman d William Beaudine ph Lothrop Worth m Raoul Kraushaar ad Paul Sylos, Harry Reif ed Roy Livingston

☆ Chuck Courtney, John Carradine, Melinda Plowman, Virginia Christine, Walter Janovitz, Olive Carey, Harry Carey Jnr

'Great fun, pleasingly economical, and by no means an unworthy conclusion to Beaudine's career' – *David McGillivray, MFB*

Billy Two Hats

US 1973 99m Technicolor
UA/Algonquin (Norman Jewison, Patrick Palmer, Mitchell Lifton)

aka: *The Lady and the Outlaw*

The friendship of an old Scottish outlaw and a young half-breed is broken only by the old man's death.

Curiously miscast Western shot in Israel; it makes no discernible point and is not very entertaining.

w Alan Sharp d Ted Kotcheff ph Brian West m John Scott

☆ Gregory Peck, Desi Arnaz Jnr, Jack Warden, Sian Barbara Allen, David Huddleston

Billy's Hollywood Kiss

'Lights... Camera... Attraction!'

US 1998 92m colour Panavision
Revolutionary Eye LLC (David Moseley)

A gay photographer desires his male model, who claims to be heterosexual.

Trivial romantic comedy, so insubstantial as to hardly register at all.

wd Tommy O'Haver ph Mark Mervis m Alan Ari Lazar ch Michele Spears, Joseph McKee pd Franco-Giacomo Carbone ed Jeff Betancourt

☆ Sean P. Hayes, Brad Rowe, Richard Ganoung, Meredith Scott Lynn, Matthew Ashford, Armando Valdes-Kennedy, Paul Bartel, Carmine D. Giovinazzo, Holly Woodlawn, Christopher Bradley

'I felt like I'd seen it many, many times before.' – *Peter Bradshaw, Guardian*

Biloxi Blues *

US 1988 106m colour Panavision
Universal/Rastar (Ray Stark)

Standard, quite pleasing version of a Broadway comedy about a conscript called up in 1945 when World War Two was ending.

w Neil Simon *play* Neil Simon d Mike Nichols ph Bill Butler m Georges Delerue pd Paul Sylbert ed Sam O'Steen

☆ Matthew Broderick, Christopher Walken, Matt Mulhern, Corey Parker

Bingo

US 1991 90m Technicolor
Tri-Star (Thomas Baer)

A runaway circus dog follows across country the boy who befriended him, when his family moves home.

Dully dogged comedy in which the animals behave like humans; it may amuse small children given to anthropomorphism, but I doubt it.

w Jim Strain d Matthew Robbins ph John McPherson m Richard Gibbs pd Mark Freeborn ed Maryann Brandon

☆ Cindy Williams, David Rasche, Robert J. Steinmiller Jnr, David French, Kurt Fuller, Joe Guzaldo, Glenn Shadix

The Bingo Long Traveling All-Stars and Motor Kings

US 1976 111m Technicolor
Universal (Rob Cohen)

Adventures of a black baseball team in the 1940s.

High-spirited japes and exhibitions of athleticism which dramatically do not add up to very much.

w Hal Barwood, Matthew Robbins *novel* William Brashler d John Badham ph Bill Butler m William Goldstein

☆ Billy Dee Williams, James Earl Jones, Richard Pryor, Rico Dawson

'Modest pleasures and dull stretches co-exist in equal abundance.' – *Frank Rich, New York Times*

Bio-Dome

US 1996 95m colour
MGM/Motion Picture Corp/Weasel/3 Arts (Brad Krevoy, Steve Stabler, Brad Jenkel)

Two dim students are inadvertently trapped for a year in a sealed dome where scientists are carrying out environmental experiments.

Yet another in the 90s cycle of dumb comedies involving stupid heroes and their bodily functions; this, though, may be the dumbest so far.

w Kip Koenig, Scott Marcano *story* Adam Leff, Mitchell Peck, Jason Blumenthal d Jason Bloom ph Phedon Papamichael m Andrew Gross pd Michael Johnston ed Christopher Greenbury

☆ Pauly Shore, Stephen Baldwin, William Atherton, Joey Lauren Adams, Teresa Hill, Henry Gibson, Kevin West, Kylie Minogue

'Definitely a dome of doom, the "Bio" pic is likely to leapfrog the endangered list for deserved extinction.' – *Leonard Klady, Variety*

Biography (of a Bachelor Girl) *

US 1935 84m bw
MGM (Irving Thalberg)

The biography of a sophisticated lady portrait painter reveals surprising details of her love life.

Leaden, bowdlerized screen version of a sparkling Broadway play, fragments of which do however survive. It isn't helped by the miscasting of Ann Harding.

w Anita Loos *play* S. N. Behrman d Edward H. Griffith ph James Wong Howe m Herbert Stothart

☆ Ann Harding, Robert Montgomery, Edward Everett Horton, Edward Arnold, Una Merkel, Charles Richman, Donald Meek

'Smart entertainment for top houses. Possibly too smart for the other end.' – *Variety*

Birch Interval

US 1976 105m colour
Gamma III (Robert B. Radnitz)

A twelve-year-old girl goes to live with her Amish relations in the country.

Simple-minded moral tale which needed some old-fashioned style to bring it off.

---

w Joanna Crawford *novel* Joanna Crawford
d Delbert Mann
☆ Eddie Albert, Rip Torn, Susan McClung, Ann Wedgeworth, Bill Lucking

Bird *
US 1988 161m Technicolor
Warner/Malpaso (Clint Eastwood)

The life of Charlie Parker.
Long, downbeat, heavygoing treatment of America's greatest black alto saxophonist; but not a popular choice.
w Joel Oliansky *d* Clint Eastwood *ph* Jack N. Green *m* Lennie Niehaus
☆ Forest Whitaker, Diane Venora, Michael Zelniker

Bird of Paradise
US 1932 80m bw
RKO (David O. Selznick)

An adventurer on a South Sea island marries a native girl and causes trouble.
Never-never romance which remains stilted despite care obviously taken.
w Wells Root *d* King Vidor *ph* Clyde de Vinna *m* Max Steiner
☆ Joel McCrea, John Halliday, Dolores del Rio, Skeets Gallagher
'The old tropical romance nicely done. OK for the main stem stands.' – *Variety*

Bird of Paradise
US 1951 100m Technicolor
TCF (Harmon Jones)

Opulent remake of the above; the trappings make it even more absurd, and the ritual sacrifice of the heroine seems misplaced in what is otherwise a pantomime.
wd Delmer Daves *ph* Winton Hoch *m* Daniele Amfitheatrof
☆ Louis Jourdan, Jeff Chandler, Debra Paget, Maurice Schwartz, Everett Sloane, Jack Elam
'The Kahuna is a naively grotesque figure, with a Central European accent and carrying what appears to be an outsize radish: he personifies the film's dubious approach to Polynesian myth and culture.' – *Gavin Lambert*

Bird of Prey
US/Bulgaria 1995 101m Foto-Kem
BMS/Sneak Preview/First Private Bank (Boyan Milushev, Jonathan Debin)

A policeman's son takes revenge on an American drug and arms dealer who murdered his father, beginning with the seduction of the man's daughter.
The Bulgarian setting is the only novelty in an otherwise unremarkable movie, full of the usual confrontations, gun battles and explosions of the genre.
w Boyan Milushev, James J. Mellon, Tracy Hall Adams, Lynette Prucha *d* Temistocles Lopez *ph* David Knaus *m* Brian Clifton *pd* Robert Harbour *ed* Ila von Hasperg, Tracy Hall Adams
☆ Jennifer Tilly, Boyan Milushev, Richard Chamberlain, Lesley Ann Warren, Lenny von Dohlen
'A conventional thriller that hasn't quite got the extra punch needed to elevate it above video fare.' – *Variety*

Bird on a Wire
US 1990 111m DeLuxe
UIP/Universal/Badham-Cohen-Interscope Communications (Ron Cohen)

A lawyer and her former lover run from their would-be assassins.
Chase comedy, too frenetic to be funny.
w David Seltzer, Louis Venosta, Eric Lerner *d* John Badham *ph* Robert Primes *m* Hans Zimmer *pd* Philip Harrison *ad* Richard Hudolin *ed* Frank Morriss, Dallas Puett
☆ Mel Gibson, Goldie Hawn, David Carradine, Bill Duke, Joan Severance, Stephen Tobolowsky, Harry Caesar, Jeff Corey
'One of those star vehicles from deepest Hollywood for which there seems no adequate reason other than to pay someone's mortgage.' – *Derek Malcolm, Guardian*

The Bird with the Crystal Plumage
Italy 1969 98m colour
Salvatore Argento

GB title: The Gallery Murders
A supposed murderer is vindicated when his alleged next victim turns out to be a psychopath.
Tolerable shocker which was popular in dubbed version.
wd Dario Argento
☆ Suzy Kendall, Tony Musante

'What could possibly come between a match made in heaven? The parents. Dinner. And a nightclub called..'

The Birdcage *
US 1996 119m Technicolor Panavision
United Artists (Mike Nichols)

The son of a homosexual club-owner persuades his father to act the heterosexual at a dinner with his future in-laws, a right-wing senator and his wife, but his father's lover, a drag artiste, insists on appearing as his mother.
An American version of a 20-year-old French farce; it has some funny moments, but, despite the best efforts of all concerned, seems resolutely old-fashioned and adds nothing to the original; the jokes at the expense of effeminacy begin to wear after a while.
w Elaine May *script La Cage aux Folles* by Francis Veber, Edouard Molinaro, Marcello Danon, Jean Poiret *d* Mike Nichols *ph* Emmanuel Lubezki *m* Jonathan Tunick, Steven Goldstein *pd* Bo Welch *ed* Arthur Schmidt
☆ Robin Williams, Nathan Lane, Gene Hackman, Dianne Wiest, Christine Baranski, Hank Azaria, Dan Futterman, Calista Flockhart
'This is a copy of an old success which doesn't bother much about reality, and ends more like a pantomime than a proper dramatic entity.' – *Derek Malcolm, Guardian*
'Performed with matchless aplomb and made with a plush professionalism, pic serves up pure pleasure from beginning to end.' – *Todd McCarthy, Variety*
† The film is a remake of the French hit *La Cage aux Folles* (qv). It was a hit, taking more than $110m at the US box-office.
⅄ Bo Welch

Birdman of Alcatraz *
US 1962 148m bw
UA/Hecht-Lancaster (Stuart Millar, Guy Trosper)

An imprisoned murderer makes a name for himself as an ornithologist.
Overlong and rather weary biopic of Robert Stroud, who spent nearly sixty years in prison and became a cause célèbre. One cannot deny many effective moments, notably of direction, but it's a long haul.
w Guy Trosper *book* Thomas E. Gaddis *d* John Frankenheimer *ph* Burnett Guffey *m* Elmer Bernstein
☆ Burt Lancaster, Karl Malden, Thelma Ritter, Edmond O'Brien, Betty Field, Neville Brand, Hugh Marlowe, Telly Savalas, James Westerfield
⅄ Burnett Guffey; Burt Lancaster; Thelma Ritter; Telly Savalas
⅄ Burt Lancaster

'Suspense and shock beyond anything you have ever seen or imagined!'

The Birds ***
US 1963 119m Technicolor
Universal/Alfred Hitchcock

In a Californian coastal area, flocks of birds unaccountably make deadly attacks on human beings.
A curiously absorbing work which begins as light comedy and ends as apocalyptic allegory, this piece of Hitchcockery has no visible point except to tease the audience and provide plenty of opportunity for shock, offbeat humour and special effects (which despite the drumbeating are not quite as good as might be expected). The actors are pawns in the master's hand.
w Evan Hunter *story* Daphne du Maurier *d* Alfred Hitchcock *ph* Robert Burks *sp* Lawrence A. Hampton *sound consultant* Bernard Herrmann
☆ Rod Taylor, Tippi Hedren, Jessica Tandy, Suzanne Pleshette, Ethel Griffies
'Enough to make you kick the next pigeon you come across.' – *Judith Crist*

'The dialogue is stupid, the characters insufficiently developed to rank as clichés, the story incohesive.' – *Stanley Kauffmann*
'We must sit through half an hour of pachydermous flirtation between Rod and Tippi before the seagull attacks, and another fifteen minutes of tedium … before the birds attack again. If one adds later interrelations between mother, girlfriend and a particularly repulsive child actress, about two-thirds of the film is devoted to extraneous matters. Poe would have been appalled.' – *Dwight MacDonald*

The Birds and the Bees: see *Three Daring Daughters* (1948)

The Birds and the Bees
US 1956 94m Technicolor Vistavision
Paramount (Paul Jones)

On a transatlantic voyage a wealthy simpleton is fleeced by a card sharp and his daughter; but the latter falls in love with her victim.
Competent but uninspired reworking of The Lady Eve (qv) as a vehicle for a rather charmless comic. Lacking Preston Sturges at the helm, the mixture of slapstick and sentiment fails to jell.
w Sidney Sheldon after Preston Sturges *d* Norman Taurog *ph* Daniel Fapp *m* Walter Scharf
☆ George Gobel, David Niven, Mitzi Gaynor, Fred Clark, Reginald Gardiner, Harry Bellaver, Hans Conried

'Beneath her icy composure lay a deep desire to love!'

Birds Come to Die in Peru
France 1968 98m Technicolor Franscope
Universal France (Jacques Natteau)

On a Peruvian beach a tormented nymphomaniac makes love to several men and attempts suicide, but is rescued by her true love.
Elaborate high-flown bosh, quite fun to watch.
wd Romain Gary *ph* Christian Matras *m* Kenton Coe
☆ Jean Seberg, Maurice Ronet, Danielle Darrieux, Pierre Brasseur

Birds Do It
US 1966 88m colour
Columbia (Ivan Tors, Stanley Colbert)

A janitor at an atomic plant is accidentally ionized and finds he can fly, which enables him to catch a spy or two.
Childish stunt comedy.
w Arnie Kogen *d* Andrew Marton *ph* Howard Winner *m* Samuel Maltovsky
☆ Soupy Sales, Tab Hunter, Arthur O'Connell, Edward Andrews, Doris Dowling, Beverly Adams, Louis Quinn

Birds of a Feather: see *La Cage aux Folles*

The Birds, the Bees and the Italians
Italy/France 1965 98m colour
Dear Film/Films du Siècle (Robert Haggiag, Pietro Germi)

original title: Signore e Signori
Stories of adultery in an Italian provincial town.
Mainly tedious sex comedy full of gesticulating actors.
w Furio Scarpelli, Luciano Vincenzoni, Pietro Germi *d* Pietro Germi *ph* Aiace Parolin *m* Carlo Rustichelli
☆ Gastone Moschin, Virna Lisi, Alberto Lionello, Gigi Ballista, Beba Loncar, Franco Fabrizi

The Birdwatcher *
Estonia 1987 84m colour
Palinfilm

A young man studying seagulls on a remote island nature reserve has a stormy relationship with a grouchy middle-aged widow.
Enjoyable account of a clash of temperaments – town against country, idealism versus pragmatism, masculine and feminine – with an unexpectedly harsh ending.
w Marina Sheptunova *d* Arvo Ikho *ph* Tatyana Loginova *m* Lepo Sumera
☆ Svetlana Tormakhova, Eric Ruus

Birdy
US 1984 120m Metrocolor
Tri-Star (Alan Marshall)

A psychologically disturbed war veteran thinks he can fly like a bird.

A case history which somewhat lacks plot advancement. Too self-indulgent even to earn marks for trying.
w Sandy Kroopf, Jack Behr *novel* William Wharton *d* Alan Parker *m* Peter Gabriel *pd* Geoffrey Kirkland
☆ Matthew Modine, Nicolas Cage, John Harkins, Sandy Baron
'Likely will fall short of taking full flight at the box office.' – *Variety*

Birth of a Legend *
US 1966 26m bw
Mary Pickford Corporation

Sprightly compilation of clips from the films of Mary Pickford and Douglas Fairbanks; the treatment is cursory but sympathetic.
wd Matty Kemp

'The dawn of a new art!'

The Birth of a Nation ****
US 1915 185m bw silent
Epoch (D. W. Griffith, Harry E. Aitken)

Northern and Southern families are caught up in the Civil War.
The cinema's first and still most famous epic, many sequences of which retain their mastery despite negro villains, Ku Klux Klan heroes, and white actors in blackface. Originally shown as The Clansman; a shorter version with orchestral track was released in 1931.
w D. W. Griffith, Frank E. Woods *novel The Klansman* by Thomas Dixon Jnr *d* D. W. Griffith *ph* G. W. Bitzer
☆ Henry B. Walthall, Mae Marsh, Miriam Cooper, Lillian Gish, Robert Harron, Wallace Reid, Donald Crisp, Joseph Henabery, Raoul Walsh, Eugene Pallette, Walter Long
'A film version of some of the melodramatic and inflammatory material contained in *The Clansman* … a great deal might be said concerning the sorry service rendered by its plucking at old wounds. But of the film as a film, it may be reported simply that it is an impressive new illustration of the scope of the motion picture camera.' – *New York Times*
'Griffith was, in his prime, a nineteenth-century humanist working in a twentieth-century medium. And, speaking for myself, I should welcome today some infusion of that unashamed humane sentiment into the smart machine-made films I see every week.' – *Dilys Powell, 1945*
† The soundtrack album features a recording of the score written by Joseph Carl Breil to accompany the film in 1915.

The Birth of the Blues *
US 1941 85m bw
Paramount (B. G. de Sylva, Monta Bell)

Trials and tribulations of a jazz band in New Orleans.
Thin fiction on which is strung a multitude of jazz-influenced musical entertainment. Not bad, even now.
w Harry Tugend, Walter de Leon *d* Victor Schertzinger *ph* William C. Mellor *md* Robert Emmett Dolan
☆ Bing Crosby, Mary Martin, Brian Donlevy, Jack Teagarden, Eddie 'Rochester' Anderson, Carolyn Lee
♫ 'The Birth of the Blues'; 'By the Light of the Silvery Moon'; 'Wait 'til the Sun Shines, Nellie'; 'My Melancholy Baby'; 'The Waiter and the Porter and the Upstairs Maid'; 'St Louis Blues'.
⅄ Robert Emmett Dolan

The Birthday Party *
GB 1968 126m Technicolor
Palomar (Max Rosenberg, Milton Subotsky)

The down-at-heel lodger in a seaside boarding house is menaced by two mysterious strangers, who eventually take him away.
Overlong but otherwise satisfactory film record of an entertaining if infuriating play, first of the black absurdities which proliferated in the sixties to general disadvantage, presenting structure without plot and intelligence without meaning.
w Harold Pinter *play* Harold Pinter *d* William Friedkin *ph* Denys Coop *m* none *pd* Edward Marshall
☆ Sydney Tafler, Patrick Magee, Robert Shaw, Dandy Nichols, Moultrie Kelsall

---

The Birthday Present *
GB   1957   100m   bw
BL/Jack Whittingham
A toy salesman's life is changed when he is charged with smuggling a watch through the customs.
Downcast, prolonged and rather uninteresting domestic drama; attention is held by generally good acting.
w Jack Whittingham d Pat Jackson ph Ted Scaife m Clifton Parker
☆ Tony Britton, Sylvia Syms, Jack Watling, Walter Fitzgerald, Geoffrey Keen, Howard Marion Crawford, John Welsh

Biruma no Tategoto: see *The Burmese Harp*

Bis ans Ende der Welt: see *Until the End of the World*

The Biscuit Eater
GB title, 1940 version: *God Gave Him a Dog*
Two versions exist of this story by James Street about a white and a black boy who turn a stray into a crack hunting dog. The first was by Stuart Heisler for Paramount in 1940; it starred Billy Lee and made quite a box-office impact. The second was by Vincent McEveety for Disney in 1972, with Johnny Whittaker; despite the presence of Earl Holliman and Lew Ayres it made no impact at all.

The Bishop Misbehaves *
US   1935   87m   bw
MGM
GB title: *The Bishop's Misadventures*
A bishop gets on the wrong side of the law when he helps a young girl to see justice done.
Amusing trifle with strong cast.
w Leon Gordon, George Auerbach play Frederick Jackson d E. A. Dupont
☆ Edmund Gwenn, Maureen O'Sullivan, Lucile Watson, Reginald Owen, Robert Greig, Dudley Digges, Melville Cooper, Lillian Bond
'Reaches a grade above the average programmer, but points mainly to sophisticated patronage.' – *Variety*

The Bishop Murder Case
US   1930   91m   bw
MGM
Philo Vance unmasks a killer who sends warning notes in rhyme.
Mildly interesting early talkie detection which moves at too stately a pace.
w Lenore Coffee novel S. S. Van Dine d Nick Grinde, David Burton
☆ Basil Rathbone, Leila Hyams, Alec B. Francis, Roland Young, George Marion

The Bishop's Misadventures: see *The Bishop Misbehaves*

The Bishop's Wife **
US   1947   108m   bw
Samuel Goldwyn
◉ ▦ @. ⊘
An angel is sent down to mend the ways of a bishop whose absorption with cathedral buildings has put him out of touch with his wife and parishioners.
Whimsical, stolid and protracted light comedy saved by its actors and its old-fashioned Hollywood style.
w Robert E. Sherwood, Leonardo Bercovici novel Robert Nathan d Henry Koster ph Gregg Toland m Hugo Friedhofer ed Monica Collingwood
☆ Cary Grant, Loretta Young, David Niven, Monty Woolley, James Gleason, Gladys Cooper, Elsa Lanchester, Sara Haden, Regis Toomey
'It is the Protestant comeback to the deadly successful RC propaganda of *Going My Way* and *The Bells of St Mary's*. It surpasses in tastelessness, equals in whimsy and in technique falls well below those crooning parables. It is really quite a monstrous film.' – *Richard Winnington, News Chronicle*
'When a film undertakes to bring audiences a spiritual message, we wonder whether the director doesn't owe it to us to clothe such messages in less muddled characterizations and to dispense with caricature.' – *Scholastic Magazine*
'A sophisticated *Christmas Carol.*' – *Philip Hartung*
'As cheerful an invasion of the realm of conscience as we have seen.' – *New York Times*

† Director William A. Seiter was replaced when the film was half complete; this caused nearly one million dollars to be wasted.
🛡 best picture; Henry Koster; Hugo Friedhofer; editing

A Bit of Scarlet *
GB   1996   75m   colour
BFI/Channel 4/Maya Vision (Rebecca Dobbs)
Documentary on the way homosexuality has been treated or ignored by the British cinema, with clips to illustrate various rules of representation.
Irritating approach to an interesting subject, cutting from one unidentified film clip to another in a specious but ultimately unconvincing manner.
d Andrea Weiss m John Eacott ed Andrea Weiss
☆ Ian McKellen

The Bit Player: see *Salut l'Artiste*

The Bitch
GB   1979   94m   colour
Brent Walker (John Quested)
A woman of much influence in London's underworld has a temporary liaison with a young gangster wanted by the Mafia.
Intolerable sexed-up sequel to The Stud *(qv), hard on both eyes and ears.*
wd Gerry O'Hara story Jackie Collins ph Denis Lewiston m Biddu ad Malcolm Middleton ed Ed Joseph
☆ Joan Collins, Kenneth Haigh, Michael Coby, Ian Hendry, Carolyn Seymour, Sue Lloyd, Mark Burns
'Appropriately enough for a film whose sole rationale seems to be its chic consumerist decoration (and of course its disco soundtrack), *The Bitch* ruthlessly pares away any other elements of interest.' – *Richard Combs, MFB*

The Bitch
France   1984   100m   colour
Sara Films/FR3 (Alain Sarde)
French title: *La Garce*
After serving a six-year sentence for rape, a former cop finds work as a private detective and finds himself investigating the girl he assaulted.
Routine thriller of double-crossed lovers.
w Pierre Fabre, Laurent Heynemann, Christine Pascal, A. M. Delocque Fourcaud d Christine Pascal ph Raoul Coutard m Philippe Sarde ed Jacques Comets
☆ Isabelle Huppert, Richard Berry, Vittorio Mezzogiorno, Jean Benguigui, Jean-Claude Legay, Jean-Pierre Moulin, Clement Harrari

Bite the Bullet
US   1975   131m   Metrocolor   Panavision
Columbia/Persky-Bright/Vista (Richard Brooks)
▦ @.
Several cowboys compete in a 700-mile endurance horse race.
Episodic adventure story with too much muddled chat and a very thin connecting story line; good to look at, though.
wd Richard Brooks ph Harry Stradling Jnr m Alex North
☆ Gene Hackman, Candice Bergen, James Coburn, Ben Johnson, Ian Bannen, Jan-Michael Vincent, Paul Stewart
🛡 Alex North

Bits and Pieces
Italy   1995   109m   Technicolor
Electric/Fandango/Colorado (Domenico Procacci, Maurizio Totti)
original title: *Il cielo è sempre più blu*
As a jogger takes his exercise, events involving theft, desire, deception and death happen in Rome.
An episodic account of a day in the life of an urban jungle, full of casual betrayals, curious happenings and cruelty; but there is a sense of randomness about the events, which fail to come together to form a bigger picture.
w Daniele Cesarano, Paolo Marchesini d Antonella Grimaldi ph Alessandro Pesci m Enzo Favata, Jana Project ad Giada Calabria ed Angelo Nicolini
☆ Asia Argento, Luca Barbareschi, Margherita Buy, Roberto Citran, Enrico Lo Verso, Ivano Marescotti, Dario Argento

'I want something good to happen to me before I die!'
Bitter Harvest
GB   1963   96m   Eastmancolor
Rank/Independent Artists (Albert Fennell)
An innocent Welsh girl comes to London, is deflowered, and sets off in search of wealth and luxury at any price.
Naïve 60s version of the road to ruin, quite well done if you like that kind of thing.
w Ted Willis d Peter Graham Scott ph Ernest Steward m Laurie Johnson
☆ Janet Munro, John Stride, Anne Cunningham, Alan Badel, Thora Hird, Vanda Godsell, Terence Alexander

'Some lovers never know when to stop...'
Bitter Moon
GB/France   1992   139m   colour
Columbia Tristar/Les Films Alain Sarde/Canal/R.P. Productions/Timothy Burrill Productions (Roman Polanski)
◉ ▦ @. ⌕
original title: *Lunes de Fiel*
On board a liner an English couple are drawn into the sadistic sexual fantasies of a crippled American writer and his French wife.
Incoherent melodrama of the corruption of innocence; but we've all been here too many times before for this treatment to carry any appeal.
w Roman Polanski, Gérard Brach, John Brownjohn novel Pascal Bruckner d Roman Polanski ph Tonino Delli Colli m Vangelis pd Willy Holt, Gérard Viard ed Hervé de Luze
☆ Peter Coyote, Emmanuelle Seigner, Hugh Grant, Kristin Scott-Thomas, Victor Banerjee, Sophie Patel, Stockard Channing
'A slick psycho-drama ... the work of a perverse, exhausted talent narrated by a perverse, exhausted, talentless writer to trap a dim-witted listener.' – *Philip French, Observer*

Bitter Rice *
Italy   1949   108m   bw
Lux Films
▦
original title: *Riso Amaro*
In the rice fields of the Po valley, a thief on the run meets a girl who tries to steal his loot.
Well-made exploitation melodrama which made a star of the well-endowed Mangano but is not otherwise more memorable than its innumerable American counterparts.
w Carlo Lizzani, Carlo Musso, Gianni Puccini, Corrado Alvaro, Ivo Perilli, Giuseppe de Santis d Giuseppe de Santis ph Otello Martelli m Goffredo Petrassi
☆ Silvana Mangano, Raf Vallone, Doris Dowling, Vittorio Gassman
† Its scene of peasant women in the mud of the paddy fields is said to have inspired one of William de Kooning's best-known paintings, *Excavation* (1950).
🛡 original story

Bitter Springs *
GB   1950   89m   bw
Ealing (Leslie Norman)
A pioneer family in Australia buys a patch of ground but has trouble with aborigines.
Thinnest of the Ealing attempts to make movies down under, suffering from a lack of pace and sharpness as well as obvious studio settings.
w Monja Danischewsky, W. P. Lipscomb d Ralph Smart m George Heath m Vaughan Williams
☆ Chips Rafferty, Tommy Trinder, Gordon Jackson, Jean Blue, Charles Tingwell

Bitter Sweet
GB   1933   93m   bw
UA/British and Dominion (Herbert Wilcox)
▦
In 1875 Vienna, a violinist marries a girl dancer and is later killed by a gambler.
Rather feeble filming of Noël Coward's operetta: it pleased a lot of people at the time.
w Lydia Hayward, Herbert Wilcox, Monckton Hoffe d Herbert Wilcox ph Freddie Young m Noël Coward md Lew Stone ad L. P. Williams
☆ Anna Neagle, Fernand Gravet, Ivy St Helier, Miles Mander, Esmé Percy, Hugh Williams, Pat Paterson, Kay Hammond

Bitter Sweet
US   1940   94m   Technicolor
MGM (Victor Saville)
▦
Remake of the above, retailored for unsuitable leads and with the story and music unattractively rearranged.
w Lesser Samuels d W. S. Van Dyke II ph Oliver T. Marsh, Allen Davey m Noël Coward ad Cedric Gibbons, John S. Detlie
☆ Jeanette Macdonald, Nelson Eddy, George Sanders, Felix Bressart, Ian Hunter, Fay Holden, Sig Rumann, Herman Bing, Curt Bois
'It's now chiefly eye-and-ear entertainment, with the original sentimental charm and romance missing.' – *Variety*
🛡 Oliver T. Marsh, Allen Davey; art direction

The Bitter Tea of General Yen **
US   1932   89m   bw
Columbia (Walter Wanger)
◉◉
An American lady missionary in Shanghai is captured by a Chinese warlord and falls in love with him.
Arty miscegenation story which bids fair to become a cult film and certainly has a number of interesting sequences.
w Edward Paramore story Grace Zaring Stone d Frank Capra ph Joseph Walker m W. Franke Harling
☆ Barbara Stanwyck, Nils Asther, Toshia Mori, Walter Connolly, Gavin Gordon, Lucien Littlefield
'It is doubtful whether this picture can make the grade without support ... photographic advantages cannot overcome the queer story.' – *Variety*
† The film chosen to open Radio City Music Hall.

The Bitter Tears of Petra von Kant
West Germany   1972   124m   colour
Tango/Rainer Werner Fassbinder, Michael Fengler
▦
original title: *Die bitteren Tränen der Petra von Kant*
Lesbian jealousies in the fashion world.
Interesting but exhausting hothouse confection, no more likeable than the Hollywood kind for being more intelligent about its perversions.
wd Rainer Werner Fassbinder ph Michael Ballhaus m The Platters and others ed Thea Eymèsz
☆ Margit Carstensen, Irm Hermann, Hanna Schygulla, Eva Mattes
'Dazzling in the brittle brilliance of its execution, the precision of its structure and movement, the total hermetic self-containment of the little world it creates.' – *David Robinson, The Times*

Bitter Victory
US/France   1957   100m   bw   Cinemascope
Columbia/Transcontinental/Robert Laffont
Two officers sent on a document raid in Libya during World War II become poor soldiers because one suspects the other of an affair with his wife.
Glum desert melodrama, turgidly scripted and boringly made.
w René Hardy, Nicholas Ray, Gavin Lambert novel Bitter Victory by René Hardy d Nicholas Ray ph Michel Kelber m Maurice Le Roux
☆ Richard Burton, Curt Jurgens, Ruth Roman, Raymond Pellegrin, Anthony Bushell, Andrew Crawford, Nigel Green, Christopher Lee

Bittere Ernte **
West Germany   1985   102m   colour
Filmkunst (Artur Brauner)
GB title: *Angry Harvest*
An inhibited farmer shelters a Jewish woman from the authorities, with tragic results.
Intermittently moving, though heavy going at times.
w Paul Hengge, Agnieszka Holland d Agnieszka Holland ph Josef Ort-Snep m Jorg Strass Burger ed Barbara Kunze
☆ Armin Muller-Stahl, Elisabeth Trissenaar, Kathe Jaenicke, Hans Beerhenke, Isla Haller, Margit Carstensen
🛡 best foreign film

Bittersweet Love
US   1976   92m   colour
Zappala-Slott
Newlyweds discover that they both had the same father.

Old-fashioned family shocker which needed a lot more zip if it was going to shock anybody.
w Adrian Morrall, D. A. Kellogg d David Miller
☆ Lana Turner, Robert Alda, Celeste Holm, Robert Lansing, Scott Hylands, Denise DeMirjian
'Performances and settings are all very high class. I mean, when you have all that money and those great surroundings you can still suffer, but you do have multiple choices.' – *Archer Winsten, New York Post*

Bizarre, Bizarre: see Drôle de Drame

The Black Abbot

GB 1934 56m bw
Ambassador/Real Art (Julius Hagen)
Crooks take advantage of a legend of a ghost to kidnap a wealthy man.
Dire upper-class thriller with stilted acting and excruciating comic relief supplied by the servants.
w Terence Egan *novel The Grange Mystery* by Philip Godfrey d George A. Cooper ph Ernest Palmer ad James A. Carter ed Lister Laurance
☆ John Stuart, Judy Kelly, Richard Cooper, Edgar Norfolk, Ben Welden

Black and White in Colour *

France/Switzerland/Ivory Coast 1976 100m Eastmancolor
Reggane/SFP/Artco/Société Ivorienne de Production (Arthur Cohn, Jacques Perrin, Giorgio Silvagni)
⬛ @~
original title: *La Victoire en Chantant*
In French West Africa in 1915, easy-going colonials learn of the outbreak of war and prepare to attack a neighbouring German garrison.
Curious mixture of Ealing-style comedy and mordant satire; interesting without being wholly engaging.
w Georges Conchon, Jean-Jacques Annaud d Jean-Jacques Annaud ph Claude Agostini, Eduardo Serra, Nanamoudou Magassouda m Pierre Bachelet, Mat Camison
☆ Jean Carmet, Jacques Dufilho, Catherine Rouvel, Jacques Spiesser, Dora Doll
🏆 best foreign film

Black Angel *

US 1946 80m bw
U-I (Roy William Neill, Tom McKnight)
A drunk sets out to find the murderer of his wife, and finds it was himself.
Stylish but empty version of a tired theme, interesting for performances and atmosphere.
w Roy Chanslor *novel* William Irish d Roy William Neill ph Paul Ivano m Frank Skinner
☆ Dan Duryea, Peter Lorre, Broderick Crawford, June Vincent, Wallace Ford, Hobart Cavanaugh, Constance Dowling

The Black Arrow

US 1948 76m bw
Columbia
⬛
GB title: *The Black Arrow Strikes*
During the Wars of the Roses, an English knight seeks the murderer of his father.
Pennypinching swashbuckler which contrives to entertain despite total disregard of probability.
w Richard Schayer, David P. Sheppard, Thomas Seller *novel* R. L. Stevenson d Gordon Douglas ph Charles Lawton Jnr
☆ Louis Hayward, Janet Blair, George Macready, Edgar Buchanan, Paul Cavanagh

The Black Arrow Strikes: see The Black Arrow

Black Bart

US 1948 80m Technicolor
U-I (Leonard Goldstein)
GB title: *Black Bart, Highwayman*
Lola Montez, on an American tour, falls for an American bandit.
Acceptable Western programmer with historical trimmings and some evidence of tongue-in-cheek attitudes.
w Luci Ward, Jack Natteford, William Bowers d George Sherman ph Irving Glassberg m Frank Skinner
☆ Yvonne de Carlo, Dan Duryea, Jeffrey Lynn, Percy Kilbride, Lloyd Gough, Frank Lovejoy, John McIntire, Don Beddoe

Black Bart, Highwayman: see Black Bart

Black Beauty

🏠🏠 US 1946 74m bw
TCF (Edward L. Alperson)
⬛
In Victorian England, a girl searches for her lost colt.
Stilted children's film with little relation to the book.
w Lillie Hayward, Agnes Christine Johnston *novel* Anna Sewell d Max Nosseck ph J. Roy Hunt m Dimitri Tiomkin
☆ Mona Freeman, Richard Denning, Evelyn Ankers, J. M. Kerrigan, Terry Kilburn

Black Beauty *

🏠🏠 GB 1971 106m colour
Tigon/Chilton (Tony Tenser)
⬛ @~
A luckless horse passes from hand to hand but is finally restored to its original young master and has a happy retirement.
Pleasant, episodic animal story which stays pretty close to the book. A shade yawn-inducing for adults, but fine for children.
w Wolf Mankowitz *novel* Anna Sewell d James Hill ph Chris Menges m Lionel Bart, John Cameron
☆ Mark Lester, Walter Slezak, Peter Lee Lawrence, Patrick Mower, John Nettleton, Maria Rohm

Black Beauty

🏠🏠 GB/US 1994 88m Technicolor
Warner (Robert Shapiro, Peter MacGregor-Scott)
⬛ ⬛ @~ ◎ ♩
An old horse put out to pasture tells the story of his life, from pampered pet and heroic coach-horse to broken-down cart-horse.
Sadly inert version of the classic tale, narrated by the horse itself, a device that robs the story of any dramatic quality, since the events tend to be described before they are shown, and which also plays down any human interest.
wd Caroline Thompson *novel* Anna Sewell ph Alex Thomson m Danny Elfman pd John Box ed Claire Simpson
☆ Alan Cumming, Sean Bean, David Thewlis, Jim Carter, Peter Davison, Eleanor Bron, Alun Armstrong, John McEnery, Peter Cook
'Certainly beautiful in both the equine and cinematic senses, but its penchant for lengthy montages could leave its young viewers squirming in their seats.' – *Denis Seguin, Screen International*

The Black Bird

US 1975 98m colour
Columbia/Rastar (Michael Levee, Lou Lombardo)
⬛
Sam Spade's son finds himself beset by crooks still after the Maltese falcon.
Dismal, witless, boring parody of a classic crime film, with none of the humour of the original.
wd David Giler ph Philip Lathrop m Jerry Fielding
☆ George Segal, Stéphane Audran, Lee Patrick Elisha Cook Jnr, Lionel Stander, John Abbott, Signe Hasso, Felix Silla
'A dumb comedy with an insecure tone and some good ideas mixed up with some terrible ones.' – *Variety*
'It doesn't work because it has nothing to say.' – *Michael Billington, Illustrated London News*

The Black Book *

US 1949 88m bw
Eagle-Lion
GB title: *Reign of Terror*
A member of a secret organization which plans to replace Robespierre with a moderate goes undercover with the French Revolutionaries.
Moderate period melodrama with an attractive though artificial look.
w Philip Yordan, Aeneas Mackenzie d Anthony Mann ph John Alton m Sol Kaplan
☆ Robert Cummings, Arlene Dahl, Richard Basehart, Richard Hart, Arnold Moss

Black Caesar

US 1973 87m DeLuxe
Gala/Larco (Larry Cohen)
⬛ ⬛ @~
GB title: *The Godfather of Harlem*
A black hoodlum takes over Mafia territory to become a Harlem big-shot.

Slapdash movie that attempts to update the style of Warner's 30s gangster movies.
wd Larry Cohen ph Fenton Hamilton, James Signorelli m James Brown pd Larry Lurin ed George Folsey Jnr
☆ Fred Williamson, D'Urville Martin, Julius W. Harris, Gloria Hendry, Art Lund, Val Avery, Minnie Gentry
'A welcome attempt to move black films off the beaten track.' – *David McGillivray, MFB*
† The film was cut to 84m on its British release. It was followed by a sequel, *Hell up in Harlem.*

The Black Camel

US 1931 67m bw
Fox
Charlie Chan solves the murder of a film starlet in Honolulu.
Second in the Oland series (see under Charlie Chan), not easy to see these days.
w Barry Conners, Philip Klein d Hamilton McFadden
☆ Warner Oland, Dorothy Revier, Bela Lugosi, Sally Eilers, Victor Varconi, Robert Young

Black Candles (dubbed)

Spain 1981 82m colour
Films Around The World
⬛
original title: *Los Ritos Sexuales del Diablo*
A woman investigates the sudden death of her brother and discovers that he was a victim of black magic.
Cheaply made soft-core porn that combines devil worship, blasphemy, lesbianism, interminable scenes of love-making and tedium.
wd Joseph Braunstein (José Ramón Larraz) ph Alan Clarke m Cam ad John Hanford ed Harold Wallmann
☆ Martha Belton, Vanesa Ashley, Jeffrey Healey, Betty Webster, Christopher Bright, John McGrat
'No-one in that film could act. So what do you do with them? You put them in bed and have them jump on each other.' – *José Ramón Larraz*

The Black Cannon Incident *

China 1985 99m colour
ICA/Xi'an Film Studio (Wu Tiangming, Manfred Durniok)
An engineer and interpreter involved in a project with the Germans is replaced by an incompetent after Party members suspect him of spying.
A satire on bureaucratic bungling, one of the few to have emerged from China.
w Li Wei *story Langman de Heipao* by Zhang Xianliang d Huang Jianxin ph Wang Xinsheng, Feng Wei m Zhu Shirui ad Liu Yichuan ed Chen Dali
☆ Liu Zifeng, Gerhard Olschewski, Gao Ming, Wang Yi, Yang Yazhou, Ge Hui

The Black Castle

US 1952 80m bw
Universal-International (William Alland)
⬛
An 18th-century knight avenges the deaths of two friends who have attended a hunting party at the castle of a sadistic Viennese count.
A variation on The Most Dangerous Game (qv), and not a good one: the pace is far too plodding and the atmosphere unpleasant.
w Jerry Sackheim d Nathan Juran ph Irving Glassberg m Hans Salter md Joseph Gershenson
☆ Richard Greene, Stephen McNally, Boris Karloff, Lon Chaney Jnr, Paula Corday, John Hoyt, Michael Pate

Black Cat: see Kuroneko (1968)

'It's tremonstrous! The absolute apex of the super-shivery!'

The Black Cat *

US 1934 65m bw
Universal (Carl Laemmle Jnr)
⬛ ⬛ @~
GB title: *House of Doom*
A revengeful doctor seeks out the Austrian architect and devil-worshipper who betrayed his country in World War I.
Absurd and dense farrago set in a modernistic but crumbling castle which is eventually blown to bits just as its owner is skinned alive. Mostly rather dull despite the extraordinary plot, but the thing has moments of style, a delightful cod devil worship sequence (especially for audiences with a rudimentary knowledge of Latin)

and nothing at all to do with the title or Edgar Allan Poe.
w Peter Ruric d Edgar G. Ulmer ph John Mescall md Heinz Roemheld ad Charles D. Hall
☆ Boris Karloff, Bela Lugosi, David Manners, Jacqueline Wells, Egon Brecher
'On the counts of story, novelty, thrills and distinction, the picture is sub-normal.' – *Variety*
'A truly bizarre concoction of mayhem, necrophilia, sadism and satanism.' – *Clive Hirschhorn, 1980s*

The Black Cat *

US 1941 70m bw
Universal (Burt Kelly)
Murder follows the summoning of the family to the spooky house of a cat-loving recluse.
Disappointing mystery which squanders a splendid cast on a script full of non-sequiturs and makes heavy weather of its light relief.
w Robert Lees, Fred Rinaldo, Eric Taylor, Robert Neville d Albert S. Rogell ph Stanley Cortez
☆ Basil Rathbone, Gladys Cooper, Broderick Crawford, Hugh Herbert, Gale Sondergaard, Anne Gwynne, Alan Ladd, Cecilia Loftus, Bela Lugosi
HUGH HERBERT (READING INSCRIPTION): 'That house is doubly blest, Which to our feline friends gives rest.'
BRODERICK CRAWFORD (NOT IMPRESSED): 'Her hats are full of bats, For spending all her dough on cats.'

The Black Cat (dubbed)

Italy 1981 91m Technicolor Technovision
Selenia (Giulio Sbarigia)
⬛
original title: *Il Gatto Nero*
A black cat and its owner, an eccentric medium, are locked in a battle of wills, one that results in many deaths in an English village.
A ghoulish and moderately stylish modern-day variation on Poe's story; hampered by its low budget, it is nevertheless an effective little shocker.
w Biagio Proietti, Lucio Fulci *story* Edgar Allan Poe d Lucio Fulci ph Sergio Salvati m Pino Donaggio pd Francesco Calabrese ed Vincenzo Tomassi
☆ Patrick Magee, Mimsy Farmer, David Warbeck, Al Cliver, Dagmar Lassander, Bruno Corazzari, Geoffrey Copleston, Daniela Dorio
'Aims for a more psychological approach, even if it is for the most part bogged down by Fulci's usual muddled style.' – *Shivers*

Black Cat, White Cat *

France/Germany/Yugoslavia 1998 129m colour
October/Ciby 2000/Pandora/Komuna (Karl Baumgartner)
⬛ ⬛
When a robbery goes wrong, a Yugoslavian crook can only extricate himself by agreeing to marry his son to the unattractive daughter of a scheming gypsy godfather.
Sprawling, exuberant, messy comedy that finally outstays its welcome.
w Gordan Mihic, Emir Kusturica d Emir Kusturica ph Thierry Arbogast, Michel Amathieu m D. Nele Karajilic, Vajislav Aralica, Dejo Sparavalo pd Milenko Jeremic ed Svetolik Mica Zajc
☆ Bajram Severdzan, Florijan Ajdini, Salija Ibraimova, Branka Katic, Srdan Todorovic, Zabit Memedov, Sabri Sulejman, Jasar Destani, Ljubica Adzovic
'A colorful, frenetic mixture of slapstick and folklore that stands a good chance of delighting arthouse audiences the world over.' – *David Stratton, Variety*

The Black Cauldron *

🏠🏠 US 1985 80m Technicolor
Walt Disney Productions (Joe Hale)
♩
A medieval hero combats magic swords, wicked witches and skeletal tyrants.
Assured but somehow quite forgettable Disney cartoon feature.
w David Jonas, Vance Gerry, Ted Berman, Richard Rich, Al Wilson, Roy Morita, Peter Young, Art Stevens, Joe Hale, *from The Chronicles of Prydain by Lloyd Alexander* d Ted Berman, Richard Rich m Elmer Bernstein *key animator* Walt Stanchfield

☆ Featuring the voices of Freddie Jones, Nigel Hawthorne, John Hurt, John Huston, John Byner, Arthur Malet
† Production allegedly took ten years and cost 25 million dollars.

'If this doesn't make your skin crawl ... it's on too tight!'
Black Christmas
Canada 1974 97m Technicolor
EMI/Film Funding/Vision IV (Robert Clark)
📀
aka: Silent Night, Evil Night
Girls in a college sorority house are attacked by a lurking psychopath.
Moderate suspense chiller.
w Roy Moore d Bob Clark
☆ Olivia Hussey, Keir Dullea, Margot Kidder, Andrea Martin, John Saxon, Marian Waldman, Art Hindle

Black Diamond Rush
US 1993 100m colour
Black Diamond (Kurt Miller, Peter Speek)
A documentary on the pleasures of skiing.
A celebration of skiers as exemplars of personal freedom, filmed to a rock soundtrack; it is likely to appeal only to the initiated.
w Warren Miller d Kurt Miller, Peter Speek ph Don Brolin m Middleman ed Paul Burack, Kim Schneider
☆ Warren Miller

Black Dog
US 1998 88m DeLuxe
Universal/Mutual/Prelude (Raffaella de Laurentiis, Peter Saphier, Mark W. Koch)
📀
An ex-convict, tricked into driving a truck that contains guns from Georgia to New Jersey, is harassed by hijackers.
Predictable action fare, done with energy but no originality.
w William Mickelberry, Dan Vining d Kevin Hooks ph Buzz Feitshans IV m George S. Clinton pd Victoria Paul ed Debra Neil Fisher, Sabrina Plisco Morris
☆ Patrick Swayze, Meat Loaf, Randy Travis, Gabriel Casseus, Brian Vincent, Brenda Strong, Stephen Tobolowsky, Charles S. Dutton
'Overly familiar but fitfully exciting.' – Variety

Black Eagle
US 1988 93m colour
Rotecon/Magus (Shimon Arama)
📀
Americans hire a top agent to foil a Russian attempt to recover a US plane fitted with top-secret equipment that crashed into the Mediterranean.
An action picture full of meaningless and irrelevant action; it seems to have been made in the belief that innumerable gun and fist fights will compensate for the lack of characterization and engrossing narrative, and also to disguise the fact that few of its leading characters speak comprehensible English.
w A. E. Peters, Michael Gonzales story Shimon Arama d Eric Karson ph George Koblasa m Terry Plumeri ed Michael Kelly
☆ Sho Kosugi, Jean-Claude Van Damme, Doran Clark, Bruce French, Vladimir Skomarovsky, Kane Kosugi, Shane Kosugi

Black Eyes
GB 1939 72m bw
Associated British (Walter Mycroft)
A Moscow head waiter has raised his daughter to believe he's a big wheel in the business world.
Well-made comedy drama from a French original, Les Yeux Noirs.
w Dudley Leslie d Herbert Brenon ph Gunther Krampf m Walford Hyden, Bela Bizoni ad Ian White
☆ Otto Kruger, Mary Maguire, Walter Rilla, John Wood

Black Eyes **
Italy 1987 117m colour
Excelsior/RAI (Silvia D'Amico Bendico)
📀
original title: Oci Ciornie
GB title: Dark Eyes
At the turn of the century, an aged Italian recounts his lapses.

Highly amusing star vehicle based on stories by Chekhov.
w Nikita Mikhalkov, Alexander Adabachian, Suso Cecchi d'Amico d Nikita Mikhalkov ph Franco di Giacomo m Francis Lai pd Mario Garbuglia, Alexander Adabachian
☆ Marcello Mastroianni, Silvana Mangano, Marthe Keller, Elena Sofonova
'The film effortlessly swings from farce to tenderness, love to betrayal, exuberance to poignancy without missing a beat.' – Daily Variety
♗ Marcello Mastroianni

Black Flowers
Argentina/Mexico 1993 106m colour
Aleph/IMDC/Channel 4
original title: Un Muro de Silencio
aka: A Wall of Silence
A British film director, visiting Buenos Aires in 1990 to make a feature about the repressive regime of the mid-70s, discovers that many Argentinians prefer to forget their recent past.
Confusing drama, switching back and forth in time and between a film within a film and the actual lives of its protagonists; the result is sometimes interesting, but never gripping.
w Lita Stantic, Graciela Maglie, Gabriela Massuh d Lita Stantic ph Félix Monti m Néstor Marconi ad Margarita Jusid ed Juan Carlos Macias
☆ Vanessa Redgrave, Ofelia Medina, Lautaro Murúa, Lorenzo Quinteros, Soledad Villamil, André Melançon, Alberto Segado, Julio Chávez
'Pic's awkward structure, slow pacing and unexciting direction result in a moderately absorbing drama that will appeal mainly to viewers interested in political cinema.' – Emanuel Levy, Variety

Black Flowers for the Bride: see Something for Everyone

Black Fox
US 1962 89m bw
Jack Le Vien
Slick documentary on the rise of Hitler, using the expected newsreels reinforced but too artfully by references to art and to the medieval folk tale of Reynard the Fox.
wd Louis Clyde Stoumen
☆ Marlene Dietrich
🏆 best documentary

Black Friday *
US 1940 70m bw
Universal (Burt Kelly)
🎧
After an accident, a college professor is given a gangster's brain, and the surgeon encourages him to believe that he is the gangster so as to find hidden loot.
Plot-packed melodrama which fails to provide the chills suggested by the cast, but passes the time agreeably enough.
w Curt Siodmak, Eric Taylor d Arthur Lubin ph Woody Bredell m Hans Salter
☆ Boris Karloff, Bela Lugosi, Stanley Ridges, Anne Nagel, Anne Gwynne, Virginia Brissac, Paul Fix
† Lugosi was originally cast as the professor, but proved wrong for the part; Stanley Ridges replaced him and walked off with the movie.

Black Fury *
US 1934 95m bw
Warner (Robert Lord)
📀
A coal miner comes up against union problems, unsafe conditions and corruption.
Typical Warner social drama, good for its time but now very obvious.
w Abem Finkel, Carl Erickson play Bohunk by Harry R. Irving d Michael Curtiz ph Byron Haskin md Leo Forbstein
☆ Paul Muni, Karen Morley, William Gargan, Barton MacLane, John Qualen, J. Carrol Naish, Vince Barnett, Tully Marshall, Henry O'Neill
'Basic box office, packed with promotional potentialities.' – Variety
'The most powerful strike picture that has yet been made, and I am aware of the better-known Soviet jobs in the field.' – Otis Ferguson

The Black Glove: see Face the Music

Black God, White Devil **
Brazil 1964 110m bw
New Cinema/Luiz Augusto Mendes/Copacabana (Glauber Rocha)
original title: Deus e o Diabo na Terra do Sol
A peasant follows the teachings of a fanatical prophet who preaches a gospel of suffering and death and becomes an outlaw.
Grim and violent tale of striving humanity at the mercy of a desolate landscape which established the reputation of its director as a new and disquieting voice in international cinema.
wd Glauber Rocha ph Waldemar Lima m Villa-Lobos ad Glauber Rocha ed L. Ririra
☆ Yona Magalhaes, Geraldo Del Rey, Othon Bastos, Mauricio Do Valle, Lidio Silva
'One is left wondering what a film so locked in its own oppressive landscape can really communicate to a European audience – other than the seduction of alien violence and alien despair.' – Penelope Houston, Sight and Sound
† The hired killer Antonio das Mortes became the eponymous hero of a film Rocha made in 1969 (qv).

Black Gold
US 1947 90m Cinecolor
Allied Artists
📀
An Indian couple on the reservation adopt a Chinese boy who becomes a famous jockey.
Tears all round in this enterprising if rather muddled B picture with a social conscience.
w Agnes Christine Johnston story Caryl Coleman d Phil Karlson
☆ Anthony Quinn, Katherine de Mille, Elyse Knox, Kane Richmond, Ducky Louie, Raymond Hatton, Thurston Hall, Alan Bridge

Black Gold
US 1963 98m bw
Warner
Novice wildcatter makes it rich in Oklahoma despite villains on every side.
Absolutely predictable actioner which unspools like a remake even if it isn't.
w Bob and Wanda Duncan d Leslie H. Martinson
☆ Philip Carey, Diane McBain, Claude Akins, Iron Eyes Cody, James Best

Black Gunn
US 1972 95m Eastmancolor
Columbia-Warner/Champion (John Heyman, Norman Priggen)
📀
With the aid of a group of black militants, an LA club owner takes revenge on gangsters who killed his brother.
Mundane action film, with nothing to distinguish it from a hundred others.
w Franklin Coen, Robert Shearer d Robert Hartford-Davis ph Richard H. Kline m Tony Osborne ad Jack DeShields ed Pat Somerset
☆ Jim Brown, Martin Landau, Brenda Sykes, Luciana Paluzzi, Vida Blue, Stephen McNally, Keefe Brasselle

Black Hand *
US 1949 92m bw
MGM (William H. Wright)
📀
In New York at the turn of the century, an Italian boy avenges his father's death at the hands of the Mafia.
Neatly produced, studio-set melodrama, unusual in subject but very stereotyped and artificial in treatment.
w Luther Davis d Richard Thorpe ph Paul C. Vogel m Alberto Colombo
☆ Gene Kelly, J. Carrol Naish, Teresa Celli, Marc Lawrence, Frank Puglia, Barry Kelley

'A journey that begins where everything ends!'
The Black Hole *
👥 US 1979 98m Technicolor
Technovision
Walt Disney (Ron Miller)
📀
A research team in space is welcomed aboard a mysterious survey ship poised on the edge of a black hole.
The special effects are superb, though achieved through a general gloom which is barely acceptable. But the story is an ill-worked-out remake of Twenty Thousand Leagues under the Sea (qv), the

characterization is ridiculously inept, and the final disclosure that black holes are doorways to hell sends one home rather bemused.
w Jeb Rosebrook, Gerry Day d Gary Nelson ph Frank Phillips m John Barry pd Peter Ellenshaw
☆ Maximilian Schell, Robert Forster, Anthony Perkins, Joseph Bottoms, Yvette Mimieux, Ernest Borgnine
'As pastiche, it sounds promising; as drama, encumbered with references to Cicero and Goethe, it is merely tedious.' – John Halford, MFB
'Rated PG, but the only danger to children is that it may make them think that outer space is not much fun any more.' – New Yorker
♗ Frank Phillips

Black Horse Canyon
US 1954 81m Technicolor
Universal-International
Two cowpunchers help a lady rancher to capture and train a wild black stallion.
Slight but agreeable outdoor programmer.
w Geoffrey Homes d Jesse Hibbs
☆ Joel McCrea, Mari Blanchard, Race Gentry, Murvyn Vye, Irving Bacon

Black Ice: see A Passion for Murder

Black Jack
👥 GB 1979 110m colour
Enterprise/Kestrel (Tony Garnett)
In 1750 Yorkshire, a rascally French sailor recovers from a hanging and has adventures on the road with a young apprentice.
The purpose of this costume adventure, from these creators, is obscure, but the execution of it is muddled and amateurish.
w none credited novel Leon Garfield d Ken Loach ph Chris Menges m Bob Pegg ad Martin Johnson ed Bill Shapter
☆ Jean Franval, Stephen Hirst, Louise Cooper
'Ploddingly unpersuasive. Not only narrative clarity but simple credibility is lacking.' – Tim Pulleine, MFB

Black Joy *
GB 1977 109m Eastmancolor
Winkast/West One (Elliott Kastner, Martin Campbell)
A Guyanan immigrant in Brixton is tricked by a Jamaican good-for-nothing but later goes into partnership with him and learns to stand up for his rights.
Vivid but eventually wearying ethnic comedy-melodrama.
w Anthony Simmons, Jamal Ali play Dark Days and Light Nights by Jamal Ali d Anthony Simmons ph Philip Meheux md Lou Reizner from reggae songs
☆ Norman Beaton, Trevor Thomas, Floella Benjamin, Dawn Hope
'I wanted to show the reality of life in an immigrant area, angry and frustrated like so many parts of Britain – but full of hope and humour.' – Anthony Simmons

The Black Knight
GB 1954 85m Technicolor
Warwick (Irving Allen, Albert R. Broccoli)
A humble swordmaker reveals a traitor to King Arthur.
Hilarious travesty of English historical legend, meant seriously for Anglo-American consumption. Shades of Zorro, Babes in the Wood and 1066 and All That.
w Alec Coppel d Tay Garnett ph John Wilcox m John Addison
☆ Alan Ladd, Peter Cushing, Patricia Medina, Harry Andrews, André Morell, Anthony Bushell, Patrick Troughton, Laurence Naismith, John Laurie, Ronald Adam, Elton Hayes
'Alan Ladd galahads with wild west gentillesse in this Technicolored rampage through British history.' – MFB

'Unmasking America's brotherhood of butchery!'
Black Legion **
US 1937 83m bw
Warner (Robert Lord)
A factory worker becomes involved with the Ku Klux Klan.
Social melodrama typical of its studio, and good of its kind.
w Robert Lord, Abem Finkel, William Wister Haines d Archie Mayo ph George Barnes

☆ Humphrey Bogart, Erin O'Brien Moore, Dick Foran, Ann Sheridan, Robert Barrat, John Litel, Charles Halton

'Powerful story of the horror spread by the hooded order; Surefire man's picture.' – *Variety*
'An honest job of film work, and one of the most direct social pieces released from Hollywood.' – *Otis Ferguson*
§ Robert Lord (original story)

Black Limelight *
GB 1938 70m bw
ABPC (Walter C. Mycroft)
The wife of a man convicted of killing his mistress proves that a 'moon murderer' did it.
Naïve but effective little chiller.
w Dudley Leslie, Walter Summers *play* Gordon Sherry d Paul Stein ph Claude Friese-Greene ad Cedric Dawe
☆ Raymond Massey, Joan Marion, Walter Hudd, Henry Oscar, Coral Browne

Black Lucia: see *The Premonition*

'The biggest picture in ten years! The greatest cavalcade of intrigue, spectacle, adventure and excitement you'll ever see on the screen'

Black Magic *
US 1949 105m bw
Edward Small (Gregory Ratoff)
Cagliostro the magician becomes involved in a plot to supply a double for Marie Antoinette.
Deliriously complicated historical romp which unfortunately suffers from a stolid script and production which kill all the flights of fancy.
w Charles Bennett d Gregory Ratoff ph Ubaldo Arata, Anchise Brizzi m Paul Sawtell
☆ Orson Welles, Nancy Guild, Akim Tamiroff, Valentina Cortese, Margot Grahame, Charles Goldner, Frank Latimore, Stephen Bekassy

'At times a grotesque, and at others a melancholy spectacle; including one scene of humiliating burlesque at the expense of physical disability that is as vile as anything I have witnessed in a cinema. But on the whole, absurdity predominates, and one must grin if one is to bear it. Whether Mr Welles deliberately enhanced the joke by adding bad acting to bad material is between him and his own soul.' – C. A. Lejeune

Black Mama, White Mama
US 1972 85m Movielab
New Realm/Four Associates (Eddie Romero, John Ashley)
aka: *Hot, Hard and Mean*
In Latin America, a black prostitute and a white guerrilla leader escape from a women's prison chained together.
Cheap and uninteresting exploitation movie, much in the manner of The Hot Box (qv), from the same writers.
w H. R. Christian *story* Jonathan Demme, Joseph Viola d Eddie Romero ph Justo Paulino m Harry Betts ad berto Formoso ed Asagni V. Pastor
☆ Pam Grier, Margaret Markov, Sid Haig, Lynn Borden, Zaldy Zshornack, Laurie Burton

'Despite Eddie Romero's years of experience in filming in the Philippines, the location possibilities are consistently thrown away; and no one has made any attempt to integrate the crude sexploitation sequences.' – *Tony Rayns, MFB*

The Black Marble
US 1980 113m DeLuxe
Avco/Frank Capra Jnr
A drunken cop redeems himself when teamed with a policewoman who is less cynical about the work.
Curious cop show with emphasis on child murders and dog torturing. An unhappy film with a garbled message.
w Joseph Wambaugh *novel* Joseph Wambaugh d Harold Becker ph Owen Roizman m Maurice Jarre
☆ Robert Foxworth, Paula Prentiss, Harry Dean Stanton, Barbara Babcock, John Hancock

Black Market Babies
US 1946 71m bw
Monogram (Jeffrey Bernerd)
An ex-medico runs a baby farm for illegitimate offspring.
Routine exploitationer with no surprises.
w George Morris, George W. Sayre d William Beaudine
☆ Ralph Morgan, Kane Richmond, Teala Loring, George Meeker
'Should bring fair returns on double bills.' – *Variety*

Black Moon Rising
US 1985 100m CFI color
Thorn EMI/New World (Joel B. Michaels, Douglas Curtiss)
An adventurer in the pay of the US government hides much-wanted evidence in the back of a super-high-powered car.
Absurd, almost impenetrable action shenanigans with more than enough violent action.
w John Carpenter, Desmond Nakano, William Gray d Harley Cokliss ph Misha Suslov m Lalo Schifrin pd Bryan Ryman ed Todd Ramsay
☆ Tommy Lee Jones, Linda Hamilton, Robert Vaughn, Richard Jaeckel, Keenan Wynn

Black Narcissus ***
GB 1947 100m Technicolor
GFD/The Archers (Michael Powell, Emeric Pressburger)
Anglo-Catholic nuns in the Himalayas have trouble with climate, morale, and one of their number who goes mad with sexual frustration.
An unlikely theme produces one of the cinema's most beautiful films, a visual and emotional stunner despite some narrative uncertainty.
wd Michael Powell, Emeric Pressburger *novel* Rumer Godden ph Jack Cardiff m Brian Easdale
☆ Deborah Kerr, David Farrar, Sabu, Jean Simmons, Kathleen Byron, Flora Robson, Esmond Knight, Jenny Laird, May Hallatt, Judith Furse
§ Jack Cardiff

Black on White *
Finland 1967 95m Eastmancolor
Jorn Donner/FJ Film
original title: *Mustaa Valkoisella*
A successful young executive falls in love with a girl hitch-hiker, but when his wife leaves him the girl is no longer interested.
Showy romantic melodrama which tries to make rather too much of a slender theme.
wd Jorn Donner ph Esko Nevaleinen m George Riedel
☆ Jorn Donner, Kristina Halkola, Liisamaija Laaksonen

The Black Orchid *
US 1958 95m bw Vistavision
Paramount (Carlo Ponti, Marcello Girosi)
A widower incurs hostility from his daughter when he plans to marry a gangster's widow.
Rather solemn New York/Italian romantic melodrama, with much gesticulation all round.
w Joseph Stefano d Martin Ritt ph Robert Burks m Alessandro Cicognini
☆ Sophia Loren, Anthony Quinn, Ina Balin, Jimmy Baird, Mark Richman

Black Orpheus *
France/Italy/Brazil 1958 106m Eastmancolor Cinemascope
Dispatfilm/Gemma/Tupan (Sacha Gordine)
original title: *Orfeu Negro*
Against a background of the Rio carnival, a black tram driver accidentally kills his girlfriend, and kills himself to be with her.
Rather irritating and noisy attempt to update a legend, without showing very much reason for doing so.
w Vinitius de Moraes d Marcel Camus ph Jean Bourgoin m Luis Bonfa, Antonio Carlos Jobim
☆ Breno Mello, Marpessa Dawn, Ademar da Silva, Lourdes de Oliviera
§ best foreign film

The Black Parachute
US 1944 65m bw
Jack Fier/Columbia
An American soldier parachutes into a mythical European kingdom to free its king from the Nazis.
Thick-ear propaganda fare; it has its moments.
w Clarence Upson Young d Lew Landers
☆ Larry Parks, John Carradine, Osa Massen, Jeanne Bates, Jonathan Hale

Black Patch
US 1957 84m bw
Warner/Montgomery
A marshal is wrongly suspected of murder.
Dour, dark Western, occasionally worth looking at.
wd Allen H. Miner
☆ George Montgomery, Diane Brewster, Tom Pittman, Leo Gordon

The Black Pirate ***
US 1926 76m Technicolor silent
Douglas Fairbanks
A shipwrecked mariner swears revenge on the pirates who blew up his father's ship.
Cheerful swashbuckler with the star in top form.
w Douglas Fairbanks, Jack Cunningham d Albert Parker ph Henry Sharp ad Oscar Borg, Dwight Franklin
☆ Douglas Fairbanks, Billie Dove, Donald Crisp, Sam de Grasse

Black Rain *
Japan 1988 123m bw
Artificial Eye/Imamura Productions/Hayashibara/Tohokushinsha (Hisa Iino)
original title: *Kuroi Ame*
Caught in the destruction of Hiroshima, a Japanese family copes with the onset of radiation sickness in the ensuing years.
Intermittently moving, despite its uncertainties of tone.
w Toshiro Ishido, Shohei Imamura *novel* Masuji Ibuse d Shohei Imamura ph Takashi Kawamata m Toru Takemitsu ad Hiasao Inagaki ed Hajime Okayasu
☆ Yoshiko Tanaka, Kazuo Kitamura, Etsuko Ichihara, Shoichi Ozawa, Norihei Miki
'When Imamura conjures a string of imagery out of next to nothing, he achieves results as disquieting and resonant as anything he has ever done.' – *Tony Rayns, MFB*

Black Rain *
US 1989 125m Technicolor
UIP/Paramount/Stanley R. Jaffe, Sherry Lansing
A rebellious and corrupt New York cop tracks down an escaped killer in Tokyo.
Effective thriller, though many may find unappetising its theme of redemption through revenge and violence.
w Craig Bolotin, Warren Lewis d Ridley Scott ph Jan de Bont m Hans Zimmer pd Norris Spencer ad John J. Moore, Herman F. Zimmerman, Kazuo Takenaka ed Tom Rolf
☆ Michael Douglas, Andy Garcia, Ken Takakura, Kate Capshaw, Yusaku Matsuda, Shigeru Koyama, John Spencer

Black Rainbow
GB 1989 103m colour
Palace/Goldcrest (John Quested, Geoffrey Helman)
A medium foretells the violent death of members of her audience, including her father.
Unconvincing story of the supernatural.
wd Mike Hodges ph Gerry Fisher m John Scott pd Voytek ad Patty Klawonn ed Malcolm Cooke
☆ Rosanna Arquette, Jason Robards, Tom Hulce, Mark Joy, Ron Rosenthal, John Bennes, Linda Pierce

The Black Rider
GB 1954 66m bw
Butcher's/Balblair (A. R. Rawlinson)
A journalist investigating the legend of a haunted castle exposes a gang of foreign saboteurs.
Plodding thriller that begins promisingly, but soon settles for genteel tedium.
w A. R. Rawlinson d Wolf Rilla ph Geoffrey Faithfull m Wilfred Burns ad John Stoll ed John Trumper
☆ Jimmy Hanley, Rona Anderson, Leslie Dwyer, Lionel Jeffries, Beatrice Varley, Michael Golden,

Valerie Hanson, Vincent Ball, Edwin Richfield, Kenneth Connor, Robert Rietty

Black Robe ***
Canada/Australia 1991 100m Eastmancolor
Samuel Goldwyn/Alliance/Samson/Telefilm Canada (Robert Lantos, Stephane Reichel, Sue Milliken)
In the 17th century, a Jesuit priest travels through Quebec to convert the Indians.
Tough-minded, compassionate, excellently acted account of inadvertent tragedy.
w Brian Moore *novel* Brian Moore d Bruce Beresford ph Peter James m Georges Delerue pd Herbert Pinter ed Tim Wellburn
☆ Lothaire Bluteau, Aden Young, Sandrine Holt, August Schellenberg, Tantoo Cardinal, Frank Wilson
'A magnificently staged combination of top talents delivering a gripping and tragic story.' – *Variety*
'An adventure story in the truest sense: the filmmakers lead us into unknown territory, and keep pushing us farther and farther on, until, by the end, we find ourselves deep in the wilderness of the seventeenth-century consciousness.' – *Terrence Rafferty, New Yorker*

The Black Room *
US 1935 70m bw
Columbia
A nobleman's power is claimed by his evil twin brother.
Rather splendid old barnstormer with touches of horror, a neatly produced star vehicle.
w Henry Myers, from the writings of Arthur Strawn d Roy William Neill ph Al Siegler
☆ Boris Karloff, Marian Marsh, Katherine de Mille, Thurston Hall
'Eerie affair, dull and destined for negative results. Its best qualities are scenic investiture and photography, which do not excite dollars to elope from people's pokes.' – *Variety*
'Mrs Radcliffe would not have been ashamed of this wild and exciting film, of the bones in the oubliette, the scene at the altar when the dog leaps and the paralysed arm comes to life in self-defence, of the Count's wild drive back to the castle, the rearing horses, the rocketing coach, the strange valley of rocks with its leaning cross and neglected Christ, the graveyard with its owls and ivy.' – *Graham Greene*

The Black Rose *
GB 1950 120m Technicolor
TCF (Louis D. Lighton)
A 13th-century English scholar journeys to the land of the Mongols, and after many adventures returns to a knighthood for his scientific discoveries.
Portentous and slow-moving adventure with good things along the way.
w Talbot Jennings *novel* Thomas B. Costain d Henry Hathaway ph Jack Cardiff m Richard Addinsell ad Paul Sheriff
☆ Tyrone Power, Orson Welles, Cecile Aubry, Jack Hawkins, Finlay Currie, Henry Oscar, Michael Rennie

'This is the night of the nightmare ... when a headless corpse rides the cold night wind, when a woman's soul inhabits the body of a buzzing fly.'

Black Sabbath
Italy 1963 99m Pathécolor
American International
Three supernatural stories introduced by Boris Karloff. *The Drop of Water* (Jacqueline Pierreux); *The Telephone* (Michele Mercier); *The Wurdelak* (Boris Karloff, Mark Damon).
Tolerable horror portmanteau.
stories Anton Chekhov, Howard Snyder, Leo Tolstoy d Mario Bava

'The management reserves the right to put up the lights any time the audience becomes too emotionally disturbed. We urge you not to panic or bolt from your seats.'

The Black Scorpion
US 1957 88m bw
Warner (Frank Melford, Jack Dietz)
Volcanic explosions uncover a nest of prehistoric giant scorpions near a Mexican village.

Apart from a genuinely terrifying sequence in the scorpion's lair, this is a poor monster movie in which excessively dark photography seems intended to cover up very variable trick work.
w David Duncan, Robert Blees d Edward Ludwig ph Lionel Lindon m Paul Sawtell sp Willis O'Brien
☆ Richard Denning, Mara Corday, Carlos Rivas, Mario Navarro

Black Shack Alley: see *Rue Cases Nègres*

Black Shampoo
US 1975 83m Movielab
Transit/World Amusement (Alvin L. Fast)

A hairdresser fights back when a rival sends thugs to wreck his salon.
Presumably intended as an attempt to cash in on the success of Shampoo (qv), it develops instead into a dull gangster movie; or maybe it was always a dull gangster movie, and was given a catch-penny title.
w Alvin L. Fast, Greydon Clark d Greydon Clark ph Dean Cundey, Michael J. Mileham m Gerald Lee ed Earl Watson Jnr
☆ John Daniels, Tanya Boyd, Joe Ortiz, Skip Lowe, Gary Allen, Bruce Kerley, Jack Mehoff
'Script and performances are strictly make-and-mend; the direction, which contrives several flashily irrelevant optical effects, and finally sacrifices all for a blood bath involving a fashionable chain-saw, is audacious.' – David McGillivray, MFB

Black Sheep
US 1935 70m bw
Fox
A high-class gambler finds his forgotten son on a transatlantic liner.
Mouldy compromise of sophistication and soul-searching.
wd Allan Dwan
☆ Edmund Lowe, Claire Trevor, Tom Brown, Eugene Pallette, Herbert Mundin, Adrienne Ames
'It doesn't rate as a solo performer.' – Variety

Black Sheep
US 1996 87m DeLuxe
Paramount (Lorne Michaels)

A politician's aide is detailed to see that the candidate's accident-prone brother stays out of trouble.
Crass and coarse comedy, relying for laughs on uninspired slapstick.
w Fred Wolf d Penelope Spheeris ph Daryn Okada m William Ross pd Peter Jamison ed Ross Albert
☆ Chris Farley, David Spade, Tim Matheson, Christine Ebersole, Gary Busey, Grant Heslov, Timothy Carhart
'Not only is the film sickeningly unfunny, it is crassly sentimental and predictable as well.' – James Cameron-Wilson, Film Review

The Black Sheep of Whitehall *
GB 1941 80m bw
Ealing (S. C. Balcon)
An incompetent teacher is mistaken for an economics expert and saves the real expert from spies who run a nursing home.
Pretty good wartime star comedy, with a succession of briskly timed gags.
w Angus Macphail, John Dighton d Basil Dearden, Will Hay ph Gunther Krampf
☆ Will Hay, John Mills, Basil Sydney, Frank Cellier, Felix Aylmer

The Black Shield of Falworth *
US 1954 99m Technicolor Cinemascope
U-I (Robert Arthur, Melville Tucker)
The son of a disgraced knight prevents an attempt against the throne of King Henry IV.
An amiable romp which alternates between comic strip dialogue and a surprisingly convincing sense of medieval custom. The training scenes are as sharp as the romantic asides are pallid.
w Oscar Brodney novel Men of Iron by Howard Pyle d Rudolph Maté ph Irving Glassberg m Herman Stein, Hans Salter ed Ted J. Knight
☆ Tony Curtis, Janet Leigh, David Farrar, Barbara Rush, Herbert Marshall, Rhys Williams, Dan O'Herlihy, Torin Thatcher, Ian Keith

'A straightforward piece of hokum with no pretensions, and spoken in a variety of accents that only Hollywood could muster.' – John Gillett

'A horror horde of monster mutants walk the earth!'
The Black Sleep
US 1956 81m bw
UA/Bel Air (Howard W. Koch)

A Victorian brain surgeon experiments on human beings and produces freaks who eventually turn on him.
Gruesome and humourless horror film notable only for its gallery of wasted talent.
w John C. Higgins d Reginald Le Borg ph Gordon Avil m Les Baxter
☆ Basil Rathbone, Bela Lugosi, Lon Chaney Jnr, John Carradine, Akim Tamiroff, Tor Johnson, Herbert Rudley, Patricia Blake

The Black Stallion *
US 1980 117m Technicolor
UA/Omni Zoetrope (Fred Ross, Tom Sternberg)

After a 1946 shipwreck, a boy and a stallion are cast up on the African shore; many years later, he rides the horse to victory at Santa Anita.
1980 seems a bit late for boy-and-horse pictures, but this one is so beautifully directed and photographed, if drastically overlong, that most adults thought their children should see it.
w Melissa Mathison, Jeanne Rosenberg, William D. Witliff novel Walter Farley d Carroll Ballard ph Caleb Deschanel m Carmine Coppola
☆ Kelly Reno, Mickey Rooney, Teri Garr, Clarence Muse, Hoyt Axton
'A perfect gem – the beautiful craftsmanship alone makes it a joy to behold.' – Variety
⚧ Mickey Rooney

The Black Stallion Returns
US 1983 93m Technicolor
MGM-UA/Coppola/Zoetrope (Tom Sternberg)

Rather desperate sequel in which a teenager loses his horse in Morocco and gets him back after various daredevil adventures.
Tame, predictable and boring.
w Richard Kletter, Jerome Kass novel Walter Farley d Robert Dalva ph Carlo DiPalma m Georges Delerue ad Aurelio Crugnolo ed Paul Hirsch
☆ Kelly Reno, Ferdy Mayne, Woody Strode, Vincent Spano, Allen Goorwitz
'Well-intentioned, but overall it doesn't look like a winner.' – Variety

Black Sunday: see *Mask of Satan*

'The undead demons of hell terrorize the world!'
Black Sunday *
Italy 1960 83m bw
Galatra/Jolly

aka: Mask of the Demon
A beautiful witch is put to death in an iron maiden but rises from the dead to wreak vengeance.
Stylish horror comic which started the Italian cult for such things.
wd Mario Bava story Gogol
☆ Barbara Steele, John Richardson, Ivo Garrani

Black Sunday *
US 1977 143m Movielab Panavision
Paramount (Robert Evans)

The Black September movement threatens a football game to be held in Miami's Superbowl.
Spectacular, heavily detailed, but somehow unexciting disaster melodrama.
w Ernest Lehman, Kenneth Ross, Ivan Moffat novel Thomas Harris d John Frankenheimer ph John A. Alonzo m John Williams
☆ Robert Shaw, Marthe Keller, Bruce Dern, Fritz Weaver, Steven Keats, Bekim Fehmiu, Michael V. Gazzo, William Daniels, Walter Gotell
'There's only one real motivation for this movie, and that's the desire to make money. Why else would anyone make an ostensibly anti-terrorist film that in actuality could end up promoting terrorism?' – Frank Rich, New York Post

The Black Swan ***
US 1942 85m Technicolor
TCF (Robert Bassler)
Morgan the pirate is made governor of Jamaica and enlists the help of his old friends to rid the Caribbean of buccaneers.
Rousing adventure story with comic asides: just what action hokum always aimed to be, with a spirited gallery of heroes and villains and an entertaining narrative taken at a spanking pace.
w Ben Hecht, Seton I. Miller novel Rafael Sabatini d Henry King ph Leon Shamroy m Alfred Newman
☆ Tyrone Power, Maureen O'Hara, Laird Cregar, Thomas Mitchell, George Sanders, Anthony Quinn, George Zucco, Edward Ashley
'Performed by actors as though to the hokum born.' – Time
'Battles between sailing ships, realistic sword fights, assaults, abductions, tortures and love making.' – CEA Report
♠ Leon Shamroy
⚧ Alfred Newman

The Black Tent
GB 1956 93m Technicolor Vistavision
Rank/William MacQuitty

During a Libyan battle a wounded army captain is cared for by Arabs and marries the sheikh's daughter. Ten years later, after his death, his son elects to live with the tribe.
Pleasantly shot but otherwise dull, formless and interminable romantic drama, all very stiff upper lip.
w Robin Maugham, Bryan Forbes d Brian Desmond Hurst ph Desmond Dickinson m William Alwyn
☆ Anthony Steel, Donald Sinden, André Morell, Anna Maria Sandri, Ralph Truman, Donald Pleasence, Anthony Bushell, Michael Craig

'What was the deadly power that desired and devoured the women of Fordyke?'
The Black Torment *
GB 1964 85m Eastmancolor
Compton-Tekli (Robert Hartford-Davis)
The second wife of an 18th-century baronet investigates the hauntings which have followed the apparent suicide of his first.
Agreeably unpretentious period ghost story (with a rational explanation). Not exactly good, but better than one might expect.
w Donald and Derek Ford d Robert Hartford-Davis ph Peter Newbrook m Robert Richards
☆ John Turner, Heather Sears, Ann Lynn, Joseph Tomelty, Peter Arne, Raymond Huntley

Black Tuesday *
US 1954 80m bw
UA/Leonard Goldstein (Robert Goldstein)
A killer escapes from Death Row and hides out with hostages in a disused warehouse.
Starkly melodramatic gangster vehicle with the star up to his oldest tricks. Good tension, but generally rather unpleasant.
w Sydney Boehm d Hugo Fregonese ph Stanley Cortez m Paul Dunlap
☆ Edward G. Robinson, Jean Parker, Peter Graves, Milburn Stone, Warren Stevens, Jack Kelly, James Bell

'An electrifying drama about a predatory female! All the suspense your system can take!'
Black Widow *
US 1954 95m DeLuxe Cinemascope
TCF (Nunnally Johnson)
A Broadway producer is suspected of the murder of an ambitious young girl.
Reasonably classy whodunnit with glamorous settings and an able cast, but a little lacking in wit and pace.
wd Nunnally Johnson novel Fatal Woman by Patrick Quentin ph Charles G. Clarke m Leigh Harline
☆ Ginger Rogers, Van Heflin, George Raft, Gene Tierney, Peggy Ann Garner, Reginald Gardiner, Virginia Leith, Otto Kruger, Hilda Simms, Cathleen Nesbitt

Black Widow *
US 1987 103m colour
TCF/Laurence Mark (Harold Schneider)

A lady cop tracks down a lady murderer in Hawaii.

Watchable but overlong cop show with nothing very surprising about it once the plot is clear: TV movies have done just as well.
w Ronald Bass d Bob Rafelson ph Conrad Hall m Michael Small pd Gene Callahan
☆ Debra Winger, Theresa Russell, Sami Frey, Dennis Hopper, Nicol Williamson, Lois Smith
'A moderately interesting tale of one woman's obsession for another's glamorous and criminal lifestyle.' – Daily Variety

The Black Widow
GB 1951 62m bw
Exclusive/Hammer (Anthony Hinds)
A man succeeds in killing his would-be murderer; his wife schemes to bury the body as her real husband so that she can marry again.
A whole lot less interesting than it sounds, acting and direction being alike laborious.
w Alan MacKinnon serial Return from Darkness by Lester Powell d Vernon Sewell ph Walter Harvey ed James Needs
☆ Christine Norden, Robert Ayres, Anthony Forwood, John Longden

The Black Windmill *
GB 1974 106m Technicolor Panavision
Universal/Zanuck-Brown (Don Siegel)

A secret service agent has to fight a lone battle when his young son is kidnapped by spies.
Unconvincing variant on The Man Who Knew Too Much (qv), with an unwieldy and incoherent plot and more borrowings from Hitchcock than you can count. It ends up as fair predictable fun despite its jaded air.
w Leigh Vance novel Seven Days to a Killing by Clive Egleton d Don Siegel ph Ousama Rawi m Roy Budd
☆ Michael Caine, Janet Suzman, Joseph O'Conor, Donald Pleasence, Delphine Seyrig, John Vernon, Joss Ackland
'A flaccid spy thriller, vaguely reminiscent of Hitchcock and Foreign Correspondent, with direction as blank as the expression on Michael Caine's face throughout.' – Sight and Sound

'Fang And Claw Killers Stalk The City Streets!'
Black Zoo
US 1962 88m Eastmancolor Panavision
Allied Artists/Herman Cohen
The owner of a private Los Angeles zoo trains his animals to kill his enemies.
Stultifyingly inept and uninteresting horror film.
w Herman Cohen d Robert Gordon ph Floyd Crosby m Paul Dunlap
☆ Michael Gough, Jeanne Cooper, Rod Lauren, Virginia Grey, Jerome Cowan, Elisha Cook Jnr, Marianna Hill

Blackbeard the Pirate *
US 1952 99m Technicolor
RKO (Edmund Grainger)

In the 17th century, reformed pirate Sir Henry Morgan is commissioned to rid the Caribbean of the rascally Blackbeard.
A farrago of action clichés with the star giving his eye-rolling all. The romantic element is dreary and the whole a shade bloodthirsty for family fare.
w Alan le May d Raoul Walsh ph William E. Snyder m Victor Young
☆ Robert Newton, Linda Darnell, Keith Andes, William Bendix, Torin Thatcher, Irene Ryan, Alan Mowbray, Richard Egan

Blackbeard's Ghost
US 1967 107m Technicolor
Walt Disney (Bill Walsh)

The famous pirate returns as a ghost to help the old ladies who own a hotel he loved.
Ponderous and lengthy comedy, partially salvaged by performances.
w Bill Walsh, Don Da Gradi d Robert Stevenson ph Edward Colman m Robert F. Brunner
☆ Peter Ustinov, Dean Jones, Suzanne Pleshette, Elsa Lanchester, Richard Deacon

The Blackbird
US 1925 70m bw silent
MGM
A Limehouse thief pretends to be a cripple, and after committing a murder finds that he is.
Standard star vehicle with recollections of several others.
wd Tod Browning

☆ Lon Chaney, Renee Adoree, Owen Moore, Doris Lloyd

'I'm a teacher. My pupils are the kind you don't turn your back on, even in class!'

The Blackboard Jungle *
US   1955   101m   bw
MGM (Pandro S. Berman)
⬛ ▦ ⍟

In a slum school, a teacher finally gains the respect of his class of young hooligans.
Seminal fifties melodrama more notable for its introduction of 'Rock Around the Clock' behind the credits than for any intrinsic interest.
wd Richard Brooks novel Evan Hunter
ph Russell Harlan m Bill Haley and the Comets
ad Cedric Gibbons, Randall Duell ed Ferris Webster
☆ Glenn Ford, Anne Francis, Louis Calhern, Margaret Hayes, John Hoyt, Richard Kiley, Emile Meyer, Warner Anderson, Basil Ruysdael, *Sidney Poitier*, Vic Morrow, Rafael Campos
    'It could just as well have been the first good film of this kind. Actually, it will be remembered chiefly for its timely production and release.' – G. N. Fenin, *Film Culture*
& Richard Brooks (as writer); Russell Harlan; art direction; editing

Blackjack: see Captain Blackjack

Blackjack Ketchum, Desperado
US   1956   76m   bw
Columbia (Sam Katzman)
A former gunslinger turns sheriff and defeats the local badman.
Standard lower-case Western with predictable excitements.
w Luci Ward, Jack Natteford novel Louis L'Amour d Earl Bellamy
☆ Howard Duff, Victor Jory, Maggie Mahoney, Angela Stevens

Blackmail ***
GB   1929   78m   bw
BIP (John Maxwell)
⬛ ▦ ⍟

A Scotland Yard inspector finds that his girl is involved in a murder; he conceals the fact and is blackmailed.
Hitchcock's first talkie is now a very hesitant entertainment but fully bears the director's stamp and will reward patient audiences in several excitingly staged sequences.
w Alfred Hitchcock, Benn W. Levy, Charles Bennett play Charles Bennett d Alfred Hitchcock ph Jack Cox m Campbell and Connelly, arranged Hubert Bath, Henry Stafford md John Reynders ad Wilfred and Norman Arnold ed Emile de Ruelle
☆ Anny Ondra, Sara Allgood, John Longden, Charles Paton, Donald Calthrop, Cyril Ritchard
    'Hitchcock's ending was to have been ironic, the detective seeing the cell door shut on the arrested girl, going home and then being asked if he was going out with his girlfriend that evening. His answer: "Not tonight." This was unacceptable commercially and a happy ending was substituted.' – George Perry

Blackmail
US   1939   81m   bw
MGM (John Considine Jnr)
A man is released from prison after serving a sentence for a crime he did not commit. Immediately a blackmailer pounces…
Co-feature drama for a star marking time; not bad in its way.
w David Hertz, William Ludwig d H. C. Potter ph Clyde de Vinna m David Snell, Edward Ward
☆ Edward G. Robinson, Ruth Hussey, Gene Lockhart, Guinn Williams, Esther Dale
    'The family circuit will accept it as sufficient entertainment for a suspenseful evening.' – *Variety*

Blackmailed
GB   1950   85m   bw
GFD/Harold Huth
Several victims of a blackmailer are involved in his murder.
Interestingly plotted and well cast melodrama which suffers from a flat script and production.

w Hugh Mills, Roger Vadim novel Mrs Christopher by Elizabeth Myers d Marc Allégret ph George Stretton m John Wooldridge
☆ Dirk Bogarde, Mai Zetterling, Fay Compton, Robert Flemyng, Michael Gough, James Robertson Justice, Joan Rice, Wilfrid Hyde-White, Harold Huth

Blackout: see Contraband (1940)

Blackout
GB   1950   73m   bw
Tempean/Eros
A man supposedly killed in an air crash turns out to be the head of a counterfeiting ring.
Fairly entertaining British support of its time.
w John Gilling d Robert S. Baker, Monty Berman
☆ Dinah Sheridan, Maxwell Reed, Patric Doonan, Eric Pohlmann

'Sex+Drugs+Alcohol+'
The Blackout
US   1997   94m   Technicolor
Feature/Films Number One/CIPA/MDP (Edward R. Pressman, Clayton Townsend)
⬛ ▦

A self-destructive Hollywood star hastens along the primrose path before deciding to clean up his act.
Drearily self-indulgent stuff, in which the only pleasure is the cruel one of watching its actors slowly drown in its pretensions.
w Marla Hanson, Chris Zois, Abel Ferrara d Abel Ferrara ph Ken Kelsch m Joe Delia pd Richard Hoover ed Anthony Redman
☆ Matthew Modine, Claudia Schiffer, Dennis Hopper, Béatrice Dalle, Sarah Lassez
    'It's doubtful that even Ferrara's hard-core fans will like this sleazy, borderline exploitation movie that is burdened by psychological and therapeutic concerns.' – *Emanuel Levy, Variety*
    'Imbecilic piffle.' – *Empire*

Blackwell's Island
US   1939   71m   bw
Warner (Bryan Foy)
A reporter goes to jail to get the goods on a smart gangster.
Forgettable exposé of the lighter kind.
w Crane Wilbur d William McGann ph Sid Hickox
☆ John Garfield, Rosemary Lane, Dick Purcell, Victor Jory, Stanley Fields
    'An exploitation natural … a portrayal of incredible events taken from real life.' – *Variety*

Blacula
US   1972   93m   Movielab
AIP (Joseph T. Naar)
▦ ⍟

In 1815 in Transylvania, an African prince falls victim to Dracula. A hundred and fifty years later, his body is shipped to Los Angeles and accidentally revivified.
Jaded semi-spoof notable chiefly as the first black horror film. The star's performance is as stately as could be wished in the circumstances.
w Joan Torres, Raymond Koenig d William Crain ph John Stevens m Gene Page
☆ William Marshall, Vonetta McGee, Denise Nicholas, Gordon Pinsent, Charles Macaulay

'The power of an immortal. The soul of a human. The heart of a hero.'
Blade *
US   1998   121m   colour   'Scope
New Line/Amen Ra/Imaginary Forces (Peter Frankfurt, Wesley Snipes, Robert Engleman)
⬛ ▦ ⍟ ⍟ ⍟ ⍟

A half-human, half-vampire hero battles to prevent vampires from ruling the world.
Comic-book hokum done with some style and a great deal of noisy action; its nonsense is taken more seriously than it deserves.
w David S. Goyer characters created by Marv Wolfman, Gene Colan d Stephen Norrington ph Theo Van de Sande m Mark Isham pd Kirk M. Petruccelli ed Paul Rubell sp make-up fx: Greg Cannom
☆ Wesley Snipes, Stephen Dorff, Kris Kristofferson, N'Bushe Wright, Donal Logue, Udo Kier, Arly Jover, Traci Lords, Kevin Patrick Walls, Tim Guinee, Sanaa Lathan, Eric Edwards
    'Though slick and diverting in some aspects, increasingly silly pic has trouble meshing

disparate elements – horror, superhero fantasy, straight-up action – into a workable whole.' – *Dennis Harvey, Variety*

'A chilling, bold, mesmerizing, futuristic detective thriller.'
Blade Runner **
US   1982   117m   Technicolor   Panavision
Warner/Ladd/Blade Runner Partnership (Michael Deeley, Ridley Scott)
⬛ ▦ ⍟ ⍟ ⍟

Los Angeles, AD 2019; a licensed-to-kill policeman tracks down and destroys a group of intelligent robots who have hijacked a space shuttle and returned to Earth.
Gloomy futuristic thriller, looking like a firework display seen through thick fog, and for all the tiring tricks and expense adding up to little more than an updated Philip Marlowe case.
w Hampton Fancher, David Peoples novel Do Androids Dream of Electric Sheep? by Philip K. Dick d Ridley Scott ph Jordan Cronenweth m Vangelis pd Lawrence G. Paull
☆ Harrison Ford, Rutger Hauer, Sean Young, Edward James Olmos, M. Emmet Walsh, Daryl Hannah
    'The sets are indeed impressive, but they are no compensation for a narrative so lame that it seems in need of a wheelchair.' – *Tom Milne, MFB*
    'A richly detailed and visually overwhelming trip to 2019 which sticks with you like a recurrent nightmare.' – *Sunday Times*
    'A massive assault on the senses which seems to have been launched from a madhouse equipped with all computerized mod cons.' – *Daily Mail*
    'Glitteringly and atmospherically designed; but ultimately mechanics win out over philosophizing.' – *Sight and Sound*
† Ridley Scott's original cut of the film, which dispenses for the most part with the voice-over narration and has a different ending, was shown to general critical approval in 1991 and also released on video and DVD.
& art direction; visual effects (Douglas Trumbull, Richard Yuricich, David Dryer)
⍟ Jordan Cronenweth; Lawrence G. Paull

The Blair Witch Project ***
US   1998   81m   bw/colour
Pathé/Haxan (Gregg Hale, Robin Cowie)
⬛ ▦

Three students set out to film a documentary about a local legend of a witch; they are never heard of again, but the footage they shot is found a year later.
A extraordinary box-office success, this looks and sounds like the amateur movie it's meant to be, yet somehow, with its horrors never quite seen, scared audiences the world over, so well-faked was its feeling of reality.
wd Daniel Myrick, Eduardo Sanchez ed Daniel Myrick, Eduardo Sanchez
☆ Heather Donahue, Michael Williams, Joshua Leonard, Bob Griffith, Jim King, Sandra Sanchez, Ed Swanson, Patricia Decou
    'An intensely imaginative piece of conceptual filmmaking that also delivers the goods as a dread-drenched horror movie.' – *Todd McCarthy, Variety*
    'The sort of film that gets its best effects by creeping up on you unawares and whispering scary things in the dark.' – *Kim Newman, Empire*
† The film's three actors were shown how to use a video and a 16mm camera and then sent out into the woods for eight days, with the directors leaving messages for them at pre-established points. Within these limits, the film was improvised, with the cast not knowing what would happen next.
†† The original film was made at a cost of $25,000, though more was spent later on improving its quality. It took more than $140.5m at the US box-office, making it probably the most profitable film so far released.

'She's the hottest thing on the beach. She's also his best friend's daughter!'
Blame It on Rio
US   1983   100m   Metrocolor
Sherwood (Stanley Donen)
⬛ ▦ ⍟

A businessman is enlisted by his best friend to find his daughter's seducer, who is in fact himself.

Totally joyless and witless comedy with a South American background which is supposedly presumed to take away the bad taste.
w Charlie Peters, Larry Gelbart, from Claude Berri's 1977 film Un Moment d'Egarement d Stanley Donen ph Reynaldo Villalobos md Ken Wannberg
☆ Michael Caine, Joseph Bologna, Valerie Harper, Michelle Johnson, Demi Moore

'Murder, mistresses, madness and mayhem … It's all part of the service.'
Blame It on the Bellboy
GB   1992   78m   Technicolor
Warner/Bellboy/Hollywood Pictures (Jennifer Howarth)
⬛ ▦ ⍟

At a hotel in Venice, a bellboy confuses the identities of a hitman, a timid estate agent and a mayor who has arranged a romantic assignation.
Tired and tepid farce, given the performances it deserves.
wd Mark Herman ph Andrew Dunn md Guy Dagel pd Gemma Jackson ed Mike Ellis
☆ Dudley Moore, Bryan Brown, Richard Griffiths, Andreas Katsulas, Patsy Kensit, Alison Steadman, Penelope Wilton, Bronson Pinchot, Lindsay Anderson
    'A lightweight ensemble comedy that should check out fast from most hospices. Ingenious plotting is let down by weak dialog and stop-go direction that largely squanders the talent involved.' – *Variety*

Blame It on the Night
US   1984   85m   Technicolor
Tri-Star (Gene Taft)
▦

A rock star tries to make friends with the 13-year-old son he's only just met.
Resolutely uninteresting pattern play which slouches its way to a predictable ending.
w Len Jenkin d Gene Taft ph Alex Phillips m Ted Whitfield pd Ted Haworth ed Tony Lombardo
☆ Nick Mancuso, Byron Thames, Leslie Ackerman, Dick Bakalyan

Blanche *
France   1971   92m   Eastmancolor
Telepresse/Abel et Charton (Dominique Duvergé, Philippe d'Argila)
⬛

In 13th-century France, a baron's beautiful young wife excites dark passions in her stepson and in the king.
An adult fairy tale full of symbols for those who seek them; but its main virtue is its highly decorative pictorialism.
wd Walerian Borowczyk novel Mazepa by Juliusz Słowacki ph Guy Durban m 13th-century music
☆ Ligia Branice, Michel Simon, Lawrence Trimble, Jacques Perrin
    'Live-action Jeux des Anges, a brilliant, terrifying ballad of imprisonment.' – *Philip Strick, MFB*

Blanche Fury
GB   1948   95m   Technicolor
GFD/Cineguild (Anthony Havelock-Allan)
⬛

A governess marries a wealthy heir, then with a steward connives at his murder.
Chilly Victorian melodrama without much interest outside the decor: the actors have unplayable roles and the handling is very flat.
w Audrey Erskine Lindop, Hugh Mills, Cecil McGivern novel Joseph Shearing d Marc Allégret ph Guy Green, Geoffrey Unsworth m Clifton Parker
☆ Valerie Hobson, Stewart Granger, Walter Fitzgerald, Michael Gough, Maurice Denham, Sybilla Binder
    'This is all about murder, mayhem and seduction among the Furys in 1860. Our interest in them is not enhanced by the necessity of watching Miss Hobson pose against fulsome backgrounds for long stretches, though she is very beautifully coloured and they are very beautifully decorated.' – *Richard Winnington*

'He knew what to do with a million dollars.'
'Every kid's dream … every parent's nightmare!'

Blank Check

US   1994   93m   Technicolor
Buena Vista/Walt Disney (Craig Baumgarten, Gary Adelson)

GB title: Blank Cheque

An 11-year-old boy is mistakenly given a blank cheque by a crook and cashes it for one million dollars.

A greed-is-good movie for young teens.

w Blake Snyder, Colby Carr d Rupert Wainwright ph Bill Pope m Nicholas Pike pd Nelson Coates ed Hubert C. de La Bouillerie, Jill Savitt

☆ Brian Bonsall, Karen Duffy, Miguel Ferrer, James Rebhorn, Tone Loc, Rick Ducommun, Jayne Atkinson, Debbie Allen, Michael Lerner
  'Charmless tripe.' – Film Review

Blank Man

US   1994   92m   Technicolor
Columbia/Wife'N'Kids (Eric L. Gold, C. O. Erickson)

An inventor, worried by the amount of crime in his neighbourhood, makes himself a cloak out of his grandmother's housecoat and becomes a masked avenger of evil.

Rough slapstick parody of Superman and Batman (qqv) that manages high spirits but not much actual humour; its likely audience is the young.

w Damon Wayans, J. F. Lawton d Mike Binder ph Tom Sigel m Miles Goodman pd James Spencer ed Adam Weiss

☆ Damon Wayans, David Alan Grier, Robin Givens, Christopher Lawford, Lynne Thigpen, Jon Polito, Jason Alexander
  'Young viewers will rejoice at a comic-book fable that celebrates a self-appointed neighborhood crime fighter in the "Superman" mold. Adults, however, may find the film too goofy, too loud and vastly uneven in humor and execution.' – Emanuel Levy, Variety

Blast from the Past *

US   1999   111m   colour   'Scope
New Line/Midnight Sun (Renny Harlin, Hugh Wilson)

A family emerges from a nuclear fallout shelter after 35 years.

Amiable comedy of a culture clash, with Fraser perfecting his standard role as an innocent exposed to experience.

w Bill Kelly, Hugh Wilson d Hugh Wilson ph Jose Luis Alcaine m Steve Dorff pd Robert Ziembicki ed Don Brochu

☆ Brendan Fraser, Alicia Silverstone, Christopher Walken, Sissy Spacek, Dave Foley, Joey Slotnick, Dale Raoul
  'Expends scant imagination or style on a fun premise that seems an open invitation to both.' – Dennis Harvey, Variety

Blast Off: see Jules Verne's Rocket to the Moon

Blaze *

US   1989   117m   DuArt
Warner/Touchstone/Silver Screen Partners IV/A&M (Gil Friesen, Dale Pollock)

Earl Long, the governor of Louisiana, enjoys an affair with a stripper.

Warmed-over political scandal from the 1950s.

w Ron Shelton book Blaze Starr by Blaze Starr, Huey Perry d Ron Shelton ph Haskell Wexler m Bennie Wallace pd Armin Ganz ad Edward Richardson ed Robert Leighton, Adam Weiss

☆ Paul Newman, Lolita Davidovich, Jerry Hardin, Gailard Sartain, Jeffrey DeMunn, Garland Bunting
  'The combination of sex and political intrigue would probably be enough to make Blaze a winner, but Shelton's characteristically quirky perspective and surreal ear for dialogue propels the film into a higher league.' – MFB
☆ best cinematography

'She kept her love for one – by sharing it with all!'

Blaze of Noon

US   1947   91m   bw
Paramount (John Farrow)

Three stunt-flyer brothers in the 20s leave their circus to start a commercial airline.

Predictable romantic drama with little flying: tragic pretensions, routine performances.

w Frank Wead, Arthur Sheekman d John Farrow ph William C. Mellor m Adolph Deutsch

☆ William Holden, Anne Baxter, Sonny Tufts, Sterling Hayden, William Bendix, Howard da Silva
  'So long as it sticks to stunt flying and mild comedy it is pleasant enough, but the last half, during which the obsessed brothers come one by one to grief and the little woman waits it out, gets pretty monotonous.' – James Agee

The Blazing Forest

US   1952   90m   Technicolor
Paramount/Pine–Thomas (William H. Pine, William C. Thomas)

A lady landowner has trouble with her rival timber bosses.

Fair period programmer.

w Lewis R. Foster, Winston Miller d Edward Ludwig ph Lionel Lindon m Lucien Cailliet

☆ John Payne, Agnes Moorehead, William Demarest, Richard Arlen, Susan Morrow, Roscoe Ates, Lynne Roberts

Blazing Magnum

Canada   1976   99m   colour   Panavision
Security Investment Trust Inc

A tough cop solves his sister's murder.

Tired rehash of the Dirty Harry formula, with plenty of violent action.

w Vincent Mann, Frank Clark d Martin Herbert

☆ Stuart Whitman, John Saxon, Martin Landau, Tisa Farrow, Gayle Hunnicutt, Carole Laure
  'The stunts are well-managed and staged; the script, performances and direction make it unlikely that any viewer will care who survives them.' – Scott Meek, MFB

Blazing Saddles *

US   1974   93m   Technicolor   Panavision
Warner/Crossbow (Michael Herzberg)

A black railroad worker and an alcoholic ex-gunfighter foil a crooked attorney and his henchmen.

Wild Western parody in which the action eventually shifts to the Warner backlot, after which the actors repair to Grauman's Chinese Theater to find out what happened at the end of the story. At least as many misses as hits, and all aimed squarely at film buffs.

w Norman Steinberg, Mel Brooks, Andrew Bergman, Richard Pryor, Alan Unger d Mel Brooks ph Joseph Biroc m John Morris

☆ Cleavon Little, Gene Wilder, Slim Pickens, Harvey Korman, Madeline Kahn, Mel Brooks, Burton Gilliam, Alex Karras
  'One suspects that the film's gradual disintegration derives not from the makers' inability to end it, so much as from their inability to stop laughing at their own jokes.' – Jan Dawson
  'A surfeit of chaos and a scarcity of comedy.' – Judith Crist
  '"I just about got everything out of me," said Brooks, "all my furor, my frenzy, my insanity, my love of life and hatred of death." Audiences flocked to this insane affirmation of dancing girls, Hollywood production numbers, stomach gas around the campfire, and gallows humor. Brooks had found the perfect vehicle for the age.' – Les Keyser, Hollywood in the Seventies
♫ Madeline Kahn; title song (m John Morris, ly Mel Brooks)

Bleak Moments *

GB   1971   110m   Eastmancolor
Autumn/Memorial/BFI (Leslie Blair)

Scenes from drab lives in a south London suburb.

Clearly not likely to appeal to the entertainment-seeking masses, and undeniably overlong, this small movie nevertheless has plenty of telling and even amusing detail about life as most of us recognize it.

wd Mike Leigh ph Bahram Manoochehri songs Mike Bradwell

☆ Anne Raitt, Sarah Stephenson, Eric Allan, Mike Bradwell
  'A prolonged poem to inhibitions, speechlessness, and social unease.' – John Coleman, New Statesman

Die Blechtrommel: see The Tin Drum

Die Bleierne Zeit: see The German Sisters

Bless the Beasts and Children *

US   1971   110m   colour
Columbia/Stanley Kramer

Six boys on an adventure holiday try to free a herd of buffalo earmarked for destruction.

Rather obviously pointed melodrama, well enough done but not very interesting.

w Mac Benoff novel Glendon Swarthout d Stanley Kramer

☆ Bill Mumy, Barry Robins, Miles Chapin, Jesse White, Ken Swofford
♫ title song (m/ly Barry de Vorzon, Perry Botkin Jnr)

Bless This House

GB   1972   89m   Eastmancolor
Rank/Peter Rogers

A suburbanite's multifarious frustrations culminate in preparations for his son's wedding.

This tedious spin-off from a TV sitcom virtually abandons plot in favour of an endless series of slapstick gags which could have been better presented.

w Dave Freeman d Gerald Thomas

☆ Sid James, Diana Coupland, Terry Scott, June Whitfield, Peter Butterworth, Sally Geeson, Robin Askwith, Bill Maynard

Blessed Event **

US   1932   84m   bw
Warner (Ray Griffith)

A gossip columnist gets himself into hot water.

Amusing vehicle for a fast-talking star, and quite an interesting historical document.

w Howard Green play Manuel Seff, Forest Wilson d Roy del Ruth ph Sol Polito

☆ Lee Tracy, Ned Sparks, Mary Brian, Dick Powell, Ruth Donnelly, Frank McHugh, Allen Jenkins
  'A potential clean-up … a sustained hour and a half or so of smart entertainment.' – Variety
  'Quick and pacy and very likeable.' – Pauline Kael, 70s
† A historically interesting note was small-part actress Emma Dunn's use of the expression 'Well I'll be damned', which was technically forbidden at the time.

Blighty *

GB   1926   93m   bw   silent
Gainsborough–Piccadilly (Michael Balcon, Carlyle Blackwell)

A chauffeur becomes an officer and after the war finds himself looking after the master's family.

Fairly unwatchable in a normal sense, but of historical interest as one of the key British films of the twenties to make a comment about the war.

w Elliot Stannard, Charles McEvoy, Ivor Montagu d Adrian Brunel

☆ Jameson Thomas, Ellaline Terriss, Lilian Hall Davis, Godfrey Winn, Wally Patch, Seymour Hicks
  'It was, quietly, an anti-war picture rather than a pro-war picture.' – Adrian Brunel

Blind Adventure

US   1933   65m   bw
RKO

An American in London gets mixed up with blackmailers and kidnappers.

Light-hearted but ill-explained second feature.

w Ruth Rose d Ernest B. Schoedsack m Max Steiner

☆ Robert Armstrong, Helen Mack, Roland Young, Ralph Bellamy, John Miljan, Laura Hope Crews, Henry Stephenson, Phyllis Barry
  'Has some fine things but won't mean much more than a programmer in the split spots.' – Variety
† The film seems to have been undertaken as a diversion by the makers of King Kong (qv).

Blind Alley **

US   1939   68m   bw
Columbia

An escaped killer takes refuge in the home of a psychiatrist, who explores his subconscious and tames him.

Unusual lowercase thriller with effective dream sequences; it was much imitated.

w Michael Blankfort, Albert Duffy play James Warwick d Charles Vidor ph Lucien Ballard m Morris Stoloff

☆ Chester Morris, Ralph Bellamy, Ann Dvorak, Melville Cooper, Rose Stradner, Marc Lawrence
  'Psychoanalysis of a criminal provides a new twist to what would otherwise be another crime picture of general trend.' – Variety
  'As un-Hollywood as anything that has come from France this year.' – New York Daily News
  'Survive a sticky ten minutes and you have a thriller of quite unusual merit.' – Graham Greene
† Remake: The Dark Past (qv).

Blind Alley

US   1984   91m   colour
Hemdale (Paul Kurta)

aka: Perfect Strangers

A three-year-old witnesses a murder, and the hitman responsible begins a relationship with the boy's mother.

Lacklustre thriller, lacking in any tension or suspense.

wd Larry Cohen ph Paul Glickman m Dwight Dixon ed Armond Lebowitz

☆ Anne Carlisle, Brad Rijn, John Woehrle, Matthew Stockley, Stephen Lack
  'Abandon everything – even sex – to watch it … its real power lies not in what we are shown but in what we fear may happen. Interest never flags from the grim beginning of this tale to its appalling climax.' – Quentin Crisp

A Blind Bargain *

US   1922   60m   bw   silent
Goldwyn

A demented scientist creates an ape monster.

Interesting star vehicle, a precursor of many hokum thrillers.

w J. G. Hawks novel The Octave of Claudius by Barry Pain d Wallace Worsley

☆ Lon Chaney, Jacqueline Logan, Raymond McKee, Virginia True Boardman

Blind Date

US   1934   71m   bw
Columbia

A working girl jilts a man because he is not the marrying kind, then regrets it.

Tedious homespun drama.

w Ethel Hill d Roy William Neill

☆ Ann Sothern, Neil Hamilton, Paul Kelly, Mickey Rooney, Jane Darwell, Spencer Charters
  'Vida Hurst is credited with the basic story, but a lot of others used it before her. Used to be a favourite with Corinne Griffith.' – Variety

Blind Date *

GB   1959   95m   bw
Rank/Sydney Box/Independent Artists (David Deutsch)

US title: Chance Meeting

A young Dutch painter in London discovers his mistress's body and finds himself in a web of deceit.

Tolerable, comparatively sophisticated murder puzzle; rather glum looking, but the plot holds the interest.

w Ben Barzman, Millard Lampell novel Leigh Howard d Joseph Losey ph Christopher Challis m Richard Rodney Bennett

☆ Hardy Kruger, Stanley Baker, Micheline Presle, Robert Flemyng, Gordon Jackson, John Van Eyssen

Blind Date *

US   1987   93m   Metrocolor
Tri-Star/Blake Edwards (Tony Adams)

A company executive needs a date for a company function, and takes a remote relative who turns out to be an easy drunk.

One-note gag movie which spurs some laughs but wears out its welcome.

w Dale Launer d Blake Edwards ph Harry Stradling Jnr m Henry Mancini

☆ Kim Basinger, Bruce Willis, John Larroquette, William Daniels, Phil Hartman, Alice Hirson
  'In short, hokey and hip – which in this case is a foolproof formula.' – Daily Variety

The Blind Dead: see Tombs of the Blind Dead

Blind Fury

US   1989   86m   Technicolor
Columbia TriStar (Daniel Grodnik, Tim Matheson)

A blind martial arts expert takes on a drug dealer and his gang.

Violent American variation on a Japanese samurai series of the 1960s featuring Zatoichi the blind swordsman, which gains nothing from being transferred from the 1800s to present-day Los Angeles.
w Charles Robert Carner *screenplay* Ryozo Kasahara d Phillip Noyce ph Don Burgess m J. Peter Robinson pd Peter Murton ad John Myhre ed David Simmons
☆ Rutger Hauer, Terrance O'Quinn, Brandon Call, Noble Willingham, Lisa Blount, Nick Cassavetes, Rick Overton, Randall 'Tex' Cobb

The Blind Goddess
GB   1947   88m   bw
Gainsborough (Betty Box)
The private secretary to a public figure finds that his idol has feet of clay, and suffers in court for his discovery.
Courtroom drama from an old-fashioned stage play: surefire for addicts, but routine as a film.
w Muriel and Sydney Box *play* Patrick Hastings d Harold French ph Ray Elton
☆ Eric Portman, Anne Crawford, Hugh Williams, Michael Denison, Nora Swinburne, Claire Bloom, Raymond Lovell, Frank Cellier

Blind Husbands **
US   1919   90m   bw   silent
Universal (Erich von Stroheim)
An Austrian officer, on holiday in the Alps, seduces the wife of a rich American.
Stroheim's first comedy of sexual manners, now of mainly archival interest.
wd Erich von Stroheim ph Ben Reynolds ad Erich von Stroheim
☆ Erich von Stroheim, Sam de Grasse, Gibson Gowland, Francella Billington

Blind Man's Bluff: see *Cauldron of Blood* (1968)

Blind Man's Buff
GB   1936   72m   bw
Present Day/Fox British
A doctor jealous of his wife does not reveal the fact that he has been cured of blindness.
Yawnworthy melodrama.
w Cecil Maiden *play* Smoked Glasses by William Foster, B. Scott-Elder d Albert Parker ph Roy Kellino
☆ Basil Sydney, James Mason, Enid Stamp-Taylor, Barbara Greene, Iris Ashley

'No Witness, No Evidence, No Way Out.'
Blind Side
US   1993   CFI color
HBO (Jay Roewe)
Returning from Mexico, a couple run over a cop and leave his apparently dead body by the roadside; later, a stranger who claims to have witnessed the accident turns up to blackmail them.
A non-too-serious variation on the familiar theme of the psychopath who comes to call, with over the top performances and a parody of a spaghetti Western to add a little novelty.
w Stewart Lindh, Solomon Weingarten, John Carlen d Geoff Murphy ph Paul Elliott m Brian May pd Nina Ruscio ed Rick Shaine
☆ Rutger Hauer, Rebecca DeMornay, Ron Silver, Jonathan Banks, Mariska Hargitay, Tamara Clatterbuck
'A cracking thriller combining an ingenious script, effective direction and good acting.' – *Sight and Sound*

Blind Terror
GB   1971   89m   colour
Columbia/Filmways/Genesis (Leslie Linder)
US title: *See No Evil*
A blind girl is the sole, hunted survivor of a maniac's rampage on a lonely estate.
Shocks, screams and starts fill a cliché-ridden but still effective script which is faithfully turned into a competent but routine heart-stopper.
w Brian Clemens d Richard Fleischer ph Gerry Fisher m Elmer Bernstein
☆ Mia Farrow, Robin Bailey, Dorothy Alison, Diane Grayson, Norman Eshley, Brian Rawlinson
'For those who like to watch folks pull the wings off flies.' – *Judith Crist*

Blind Vision
US   1990   92m   DeLuxe
Saban/Vertigo (Jonathon Braun)
A repressed, mother-dominated amateur photographer is suspected of murdering the boyfriend of a woman on whom he spies obsessively from his flat opposite.
Dreary, fourth-rate, risible thriller, not helped by being told mainly from the viewpoint of its unsympathetic protagonist, a voyeuristic nerd.
w Shuki Levy, Winston Richard d Shuki Levy ph Frank Byers m Shuki Levy, Hiram Titus ad Jayne Asman ed Jon Braun, Shuki Levy
☆ Lenny von Dohlen, Deborah Shelton, Stoney Jackson, Robert Vaughn, Ned Beatty, Louise Fletcher

Blindfold **
US   1965   102m   Technicolor   Panavision
Universal (Marvin Schwartz)
A society psychiatrist is enlisted by the CIA to make regular blindfold journeys to a secret destination where he treats a neurotic physicist. Discovering that his contacts are really enemy agents, he tracks down the destination by sound and guesswork, and routs the villains.
Lively spy spoof with rather too much knockabout between the Hitchcockian suspense sequences; it has indeed the air of a script which Hitchcock rejected, but provides reliable entertainment.
w Philip Dunne, W. H. Menger *novel* Lucille Fletcher d Philip Dunne ph Joseph MacDonald m Lalo Schifrin
☆ Rock Hudson, Claudia Cardinale, Jack Warden, Guy Stockwell, Brad Dexter

Blindman (dubbed)
US/Italy   1971   96m   Technicolor   Techniscope
Fox-Rank/ABKCO/Primex (Tony Anthony, Saul Swimmer)
A blind man goes in search of 50 mail-order brides who have been stolen by a bandit and his gang.
Comic spaghetti Western in which the only point of interest, apart from its bizarre hero, lies in seeing a former Beatle in the role of a Mexican outlaw.
w Tony Anthony, Piero Anchisi, Vincenzo Cerami *story* Tony Anthony d Ferdinando Baldi ph Riccardo Pallottino m Stelvio Cipriani ad Gastone Garsetti ed Reberto Perpignani
☆ Tony Anthony, Ringo Starr, Agneta Eckemyr, Lloyd Batista, Magda Konopka, Raf Baldassare
'Indistinguishable from the ruck in its crude direction, garbled plot, obsessive violence, variable technical achievements, and pot-pourri cast and acting styles.' – *Tom Milne, MFB*
† The original version of the film ran for 105m.

'Illusion. Deception. Murder.'
'In the blink of an eye things are not what they seem.'
Blink
US   1994   106m   DeLuxe
Guild/New Line (David Blocker)
A cop investigating a murder is attracted by the only witness, a formerly blind woman who has just regained her sight but is not sure of what she sees.
Dumb woman-in-peril thriller that relies on cliché to see it through to its unexciting end.
w Dana Stevens d Michael Apted ph Dante Spinotti m Brad Fiedel pd Dan Bishop ed Rick Shaine
☆ Madeleine Stowe, Aidan Quinn, Laurie Metcalf, Peter Friedman, James Remar, Bruce A. Young, Paul Dillon, Matt Roth
'So numbingly banal and predictable it might as well have been called *Wink*, of which you need 40 to get through it.' – *Leslie Felperin Sharman, Sight and Sound*

Bliss *
Australia   1985   111m   colour
Entertainment (Anthony Buckley)
After a heart attack, an advertising executive realizes the rottenness of his wife and children and seeks happiness elsewhere.
Energetic black comedy, intermittently entertaining, that won awards in its home country.
w Ray Lawrence, Peter Carey *novel* Peter Carey d Ray Lawrence ph Paul Murphy m Peter Best ad Owen Paterson ed Wayne Leclos

☆ Barry Otto, Lynette Curran, Helen Jones, Miles Buchanan, Gia Carides, Tim Robertson, Jeff Truman, Bryan Marshall

'Love is only the beginning.'
Bliss
US   1997   103m   colour
Triumph (Allyn Stewart)
A newly married wife seeks the advice of a therapist, who has sexual relationships with his patients.
Bizarre and risible would-be erotic drama that frequently resembles an instructional video for the unenlightened.
wd Lance Young ph Michael Molloy m Jan A. P. Kaczmarek pd John Willett, David Lloyd Fischer ed Allan Lee
☆ Craig Sheffer, Sheryl Lee, Terence Stamp, Casey Siemaszko, Spalding Gray, Leigh Taylor Young, Lois Chiles
'Tone of the film is too smug, the earnestness of its lesson creating the off-putting impression of the recently converted trying to preach newly acquired wisdom to the masses.' – *Todd McCarthy, Variety*

The Bliss of Mrs Blossom
GB   1968   93m   Technicolor
Paramount (Josef Shaftel)
The wife of a bra manufacturer keeps her lover in the attic.
Silly, wild-eyed sex comedy decorated with the flashy tinsel of swinging London's dying fall.
w Alec Coppel, Denis Norden d Joe McGrath ph Geoffrey Unsworth m Riz Ortolani pd Assheton Gorton
☆ Richard Attenborough, Shirley MacLaine, James Booth, Freddie Jones, William Rushton, Bob Monkhouse, Patricia Routledge

Blithe Spirit ***
GB   1945   96m   Technicolor
Two Cities/Cineguild (Anthony Havelock-Allan)
A cynical novelist's second marriage is disturbed when the playful ghost of his first wife materializes during a séance.
Direction and acting carefully preserve a comedy which on its first West End appearance in 1941 achieved instant classic status. The repartee scarcely dates, and altogether this is a most polished job of film-making.
w Noël Coward *play* Noël Coward *scenario* David Lean, Anthony Havelock-Allan, Ronald Neame d David Lean ph Ronald Neame m Richard Addinsell
☆ Rex Harrison, Kay Hammond, Constance Cummings, Margaret Rutherford, Hugh Wakefield, Joyce Carey, Jacqueline Clark
'Ninety minutes of concentrated, cultivated fun.' – *C. A. Lejeune*
† After seeing this, Noël Coward reputedly told Rex Harrison: 'After me you're the best light comedian in the world.'

Blitz on Britain *
GB   1960   71m   bw
Anglo-Continental/British Lion
A very acceptable record of the Battle of Britain as it affected the home front, narrated by Alistair Cooke.
w Patrick Brawn d/ed Harry Booth

'Indescribable ... Indestructible! Nothing Can Stop It!'
The Blob
US   1958   83m   DeLuxe
Tonylyn/Jack H. Harris
A small town combats a slimy space invader.
Padded hokum for drive-ins, with a few effective moments.
w Theodore Simonson, Kate Phillips d Irvin S. Yeaworth Jnr ph Thomas Spalding m Ralph Carmichael
☆ Steve McQueen, Aneta Corseaut, Olin Howlin, Earl Rowe
'Classic teen horror which really sums up the spirit of 50s drive-in movies.' – *The Dark Side*
† Sequel 1971: *Beware! The Blob* (aka *Son of Blob*).

The Blob
US   1988   92m   Technicolor
Tri-Star (Jack H. Harris/Elliott Kastner)
Fifties sci-fi horror dressed up for the 80s.
w Chuck Russell, Frank Darabont d Chuck Russell ph Mark Irwin m Michael Hoenig pd Craig Stearns ed Terry Stokes, Tod Feuerman
☆ Shawnee Smith, Kevin Dillon, Donovan Leitch, Jeffrey de Munn, Candy Clark, Joe Seneca
'A great B-movie with an A-pic budget.' – *Variety*

Block Busters
US   1944   60m   bw
Monogram/Banner (Sam Katzman, Jack Dietz)
The East Side Kids are upset when a rich French boy moves into the neighbourhood.
Lacklustre programmer, although jazz fans may enjoy a rare, if brief, glimpse of the great clarinettist Jimmy Noone in action.
w Houston Branch d Wallace Fox ph Marcel LePicard md Edward Kay ad David Milton ed Carl Pierson
☆ Leo Gorcey, Huntz Hall, Gabriel Dell, Billy Benedict, Frederick Pressel, Noah Beery, Harry Langdon, Bernard Gorcey

Blockade *
US   1938   84m   bw
Walter Wanger
During the Spanish Civil War, a peace-loving young farmer has to take up arms to defend his land.
Much touted as Hollywood's first serious contribution to international affairs, this dogged drama was in fact so bland that audiences had difficulty ascertaining which side it was on, especially as neither Franco nor the Fascists were mentioned. As a romantic action drama, however, it passed muster.
w John Howard Lawson d William Dieterle ph Rudolf Maté m Werner Janssen
☆ Henry Fonda, Madeleine Carroll, Leo Carrillo, John Halliday, Vladimir Sokoloff, Robert Warwick, Reginald Denny
'It misses any claim to greatness because it pulls its punches ... and it's going to be tough to sell.' – *Variety*
'The film has a curious unreality considering the grim reality behind it.' – *Frank S. Nugent*
'There is achieved a deadly numb level of shameless hokum out of which anything true or decent rises only for a second to confound itself.' – *Otis Ferguson*
† Original publicity carried this disclaimer: NOTE: Care has been taken to prevent any costume of the production from being accurately that of either side in the Spanish Civil War. The story does not attempt to favour any cause in the present conflict.
♫ John Howard Lawson; Werner Janssen

Blockheads ***
US   1938   60m   bw
Hal Roach/Stan Laurel
Twenty years after World War I, Stan is still guarding a trench because nobody told him to stop. Ollie takes him home to meet the wife, with disastrous consequences.
The last first-class Laurel and Hardy comedy is shapeless but hilarious, a fragmented reworking of earlier ideas, all of which work beautifully. Gags include encounters with a tip-up truck and an automatic garage, and a brilliantly worked out sequence up and down several flights of stairs.
w James Parrott, Harry Langdon, Felix Adler, Charles Rogers, Arnold Belgard d John G. Blystone ph Art Lloyd m Marvin Hatley
☆ Stan Laurel, Oliver Hardy, Billy Gilbert, Patricia Ellis, Minna Gombell, James Finlayson
'Hodge-podge of old-fashioned slapstick and hoke.' – *Variety*
♫ Marvin Hatley

Den Blodiga Tiden: see *Mein Kampf*

Blonde Bombshell: see *Bombshell*

Blonde Crazy *

US   1931   74m   bw

Warner

▤   ©⌐

GB title: Larceny Lane

A bellhop and a chambermaid set out to fleece all-comers.

Smart con man comedy with the star in excellent form.

w Kubec Glasmon, John Bright   d Roy del Ruth   ph Sid Hickox

☆ James Cagney, Joan Blondell, Ray Milland, Louis Calhern, Guy Kibbee, Polly Walters, Charles Lane, Maude Eburne

'Naughty cracks galore, and one says "Nuts". But he doesn't push a grapefruit in the girlfriend's face, though they expect it any time.' – Variety

'A chipper, hard-boiled, amusing essay in petty thieving.' – Time

Blonde Fever

US   1944   69m   bw

MGM

A middle-aged husband falls for a blonde waitress.

Very ho-hum comedy on familiar lines.

w Patricia Coleman play Ferenc Molnar   d Richard Whorf

☆ Philip Dorn, Mary Astor, Gloria Grahame, Felix Bressart, Marshall Thompson, Curt Bois

Blonde Fist

GB   1991   102m   colour

Blue Dolphin/Film Four (Christopher Figg, Joseph D'Morais)

The fighting daughter of a bare-knuckle boxer goes in search of her father and of a new life.

Brain-damaged knockabout comedy.

wd Frank Clarke   ph Bruce McGowan   m Alan Gill   pd Colin Pocock   ed Brian Peachey

☆ Margi Clarke, Carroll Baker, Ken Hutchinson, Sharon Power, Angela Clarke, Lewis Bester

The Blonde from Peking

US/France   1968   80m   colour

Paramount

The CIA thinks that a girl with amnesia may know Chinese nuclear secrets.

Witless international spy stuff, neither funny nor thrilling.

w Nicolas Gessner and Marc Behm story James Hadley Chase   d Nicolas Gessner

☆ Mireille Darc, Claudio Brook, Edward G. Robinson, Pascale Roberts

A Blonde in Love: see Loves of a Blonde

Blonde Sinner: see Yield to the Night

'What could she do but flee from love? She loved two men at once!'

Blonde Venus *

US   1932   97m   bw

Paramount

▤   ◉   ©⌐

A German café singer marries an English research chemist, but their marriage doesn't run smoothly.

Rather dreary, fragmented star vehicle with good moments, notably the star's opening appearance as a gorilla.

w Jules Furthman, S. K. Lauren   d Josef von Sternberg   ph Bert Glennon   m Oscar Potoker

☆ Marlene Dietrich, Herbert Marshall, Cary Grant, Dickie Moore

'Weak story, inept direction and generally sluggish total count heavily against it … it'll require plenty of bally.' – Variety

'The story has all the dramatic integrity of a sashweight murderer's tabloid autobiography.' – Pare Lorentz

'There is more pleasure for the eye in Blonde Venus than in a hundred of its fellows. But what does beauty ornament? The story of a wife who becomes a kept woman for the sake of her husband, and a prostitute for the sake of her child.' – Forsyth Hardy, Cinema Quarterly

Blondes for Danger

GB   1938   68m   bw

British Lion/Herbert Wilcox

A Cockney taxi driver takes an unwanted fare and becomes involved in a deep dark plot.

Modest but effective star vehicle.

w Gerald Elliott novel Red for Danger by Evadne Price   d Jack Raymond

☆ Gordon Harker, Enid Stamp-Taylor, Ivan Brandt

Blondie *

US   1938   68m   bw

Columbia

▤

Misadventures of a harassed suburban family man.

Dagwood Bumstead and his wife Blondie were Mr and Mrs Small Town America throughout the thirties and forties, and received their perfect screen incarnations in this unambitious but quite watchable series, which provided familiar and often quite observant fun. Other episodes were as follows:

1939 Blondie Meets the Boss, Blondie Takes a Vacation, Blondie Brings Up Baby

1940 Blondie on a Budget, Blondie Has Servant Trouble, Blondie Plays Cupid

1941 Blondie Goes Latin, Blondie in Society

1942 Blondie Goes to College, Blondie's Blessed Event, Blondie for Victory

1943 It's a Great Life, Footlight Glamour

1945 Leave It to Blondie

1946 Blondie Knows Best, Life with Blondie, Blondie's Lucky Day

1947 Blondie's Big Moment, Blondie's Holiday, Blondie in the Dough, Blondie's Anniversary

1948 Blondie's Reward

1949 Blondie's Secret, Blondie's Big Deal, Blondie Hits the Jackpot

1950 Blondie's Hero, Beware of Blondie

w Richard Flournoy comic strip Chic Young   d Frank R. Strayer   ph Henry Freulich

☆ Arthur Lake, Penny Singleton, Larry Simms, Daisy the Dog, Jonathan Hale, Gene Lockhart, Ann Doran, Irving Bacon

'Light fare, but universal in appeal … could be clicko series.' – Variety

† TV series were started in the fifties and sixties, but both failed.

Blondie Johnson

US   1933   67m   bw

Warner

The career of a female larcenist who eventually takes her medicine.

Competent programmer very typical of its studio and year.

w Earl Baldwin   d Ray Enright

☆ Joan Blondell, Chester Morris, Allen Jenkins, Claire Dodd

'After she departs for the pen, she lets the public in on the fact that crime doesn't pay. Neither will the picture.' – Variety

Blondie of the Follies *

US   1932   97m   bw

MGM (Marion Davies)

Two New York showgirls graduate from tenements to luxury.

Adequate comedy-melodrama with an interesting cast and good dialogue.

w Frances Marion, Anita Loos   d Edmund Goulding   ph George Barnes   m William Axt

☆ Marion Davies, Jimmy Durante, Robert Montgomery, Billie Dove, James Gleason, ZaSu Pitts, Sidney Toler, Douglass Dumbrille

'Not bad, but not very good, with chances that it will just get by. Length and slow pace the drawbacks … It isn't padded out, it's just flatfooted.' – Variety

'An unjustly forgotten film.' – New Yorker, 1979

Blood Alley

US   1955   115m   Warnercolor   Cinemascope

Warner/Batjac (no producer credited)

◉   ♫

An American sailor is helped by local people to escape from a Chinese jail; he then escorts them to Hong Kong.

Rudimentary anti-Red heroics with expensive spectacle punctuating a tacky script.

w A. S. Fleischman novel A. S. Fleischman   d William Wellman   ph William H. Clothier   m Roy Webb   pd Alfred Ybarra

☆ John Wayne, Lauren Bacall, Paul Fix, Joy Kim, Berry Kroeger, Mike Mazurki, Anita Ekberg

'Becomes A Terror House Of Blood!!'

'Guaranteed! The 8 Greatest Shocks Ever Filmed!'

Blood and Black Lace

Italy   1964   90m   Eastmancolor

Emmepi

▤

original title: Sei Donne per l'Assassino

Six women are nastily murdered in a fashion house.

Vaguely necrophiliac but trendy suspense-horror flick in the wake of Psycho (qv).

w Marcello Fondato, Giuseppe Barilla, Mario Bava   d Mario Bava

☆ Cameron Mitchell, Thomas Reiner, Mary Arden

'The wooden nature of the script and performances makes it hard to get into the complicated narrative. Don't bother. Just settle back and enjoy the sex and violence.' – The Dark Side

Blood and Roses

France/Italy   1960   87m   colour   Technirama

Eger/Documento (Raymond Eger)

▤

original title: Et Mourir de Plaisir

Carmilla takes on the vampiric personality of her ancestress Millarca, whom she closely resembles.

A rather half-hearted attempt to make an elegant horror story; boring rather than charming or frightening.

w Claude Brûlé, Claude Martin, Roger Vadim   d Roger Vadim   ph Claude Renoir   m Jean Prodromidès

☆ Mel Ferrer, Elsa Martinelli, Annette Vadim, Marc Allégret

Blood and Sand *

US   1922   80m   bw   silent

Paramount

▤   ©⌐

A matador falls under the spell of an aristocratic woman.

Elegant star vehicle which established his image.

w June Mathis novel Vicente Blasco Ibanez   d Fred Niblo

☆ Rudolph Valentino, Nita Naldi, Lila Lee, Walter Long

'Love flamed in the shadow of death!'

Blood and Sand *

US   1941   123m   Technicolor

TCF (Darryl F. Zanuck, Robert T. Kane)

◉◉   ⌂

A matador's life goes wrong when he is torn between the love of his wife and the attractions of a vamp.

Rather boring version, fine to look at but dramatically deadly.

w Jo Swerling novel Vicente Blasco Ibanez   d Rouben Mamoulian   ph Ernest Palmer, Ray Rennahan   m Alfred Newman   ad Richard Day, Joseph C. Wright

☆ Tyrone Power, Rita Hayworth, Linda Darnell, Nazimova, Anthony Quinn, J. Carrol Naish, John Carradine, Lynn Bari, Laird Cregar, Monty Banks

† Carole Landis turned down the role that made a star of Rita Hayworth because she refused to change her hair colour from blonde to red.

🏆 Ernest Palmer, Ray Rennahan

👤 Richard Day, Joseph C. Wright

'There is no honor amongst thieves.'

Blood & Wine *

US   1996   98m   DeLuxe

TCF/Blood & Wine/Marmont/Recorded Picture/Majestic (Jeremy Thomas)

▤   ⌂

A wine merchant steals a valuable necklace, but loses it to his wife and stepson.

A grim and violent thriller with some effective performances; but its portrait of a greedy and dysfunctional family leaves little lasting impression.

w Nick Villiers, Alison Cross   d Bob Rafelson   ph Newton Thomas Sigel   m Michel Lorenc   pd David Sylbert   ed Steven Cohen

☆ Jack Nicholson, Michael Caine, Stephen Dorff, Jennifer Lopez, Judy Davis, Harold Perrineau Jnr

'The film doesn't seem very significant. Everyone's good, but it's less than the sum of its watchable parts.' – Derek Malcolm, Guardian

Blood Beach

US   1980   90m   colour

Miracle/Empress (Steven Nalevansky)

▤

A monster, lurking beneath the sand of a beach, swallows passers-by.

Dull, lethargic, low-budget variation on Jaws (qv); not only could they not afford much of a monster, they also skimped on the script and actors.

w Jeffrey Bloom story Jeffrey Bloom, Steven Nalevansky   d Jeffrey Bloom   ph Steve Poster   m Gil Mellé   ad William Sandell   ed Gary Griffen

☆ David Huffman, Marianna Hill, John Saxon, Otis Young, Stefan Gierasch, Burt Young

'It's so slow and boring, just like a bad television movie.' – The Dark Side

Blood Beast from Outer Space: see The Night Caller

The Blood Beast Terror

GB   1967   88m   Eastmancolor

Tigon (Arnold L. Miller)

A Victorian entomologist creates human beings who can change themselves into monster death's-head moths.

Unpersuasive and totally idiotic cheapjack horror fare.

w Peter Bryan   d Vernon Sewell   ph Stanley A. Long   m Paul Ferris

☆ Robert Flemyng, Peter Cushing, Wanda Ventham, Vanessa Howard, David Griffin, John Paul, Kevin Stoney, Roy Hudd

The Blood Demon

West Germany   1967   76m   colour

New Realm/Constantin (Wolfgang Kuehnlenz)

▤

original title: Die Schlangengrube und das Pendel

aka: The Torture Chamber of Dr Sadism

An aristocrat dismembered after killing 12 virgins returns from the dead to kill a 13th and achieve immortality.

An extremely free adaptation of Poe, given over to narrative incoherence and startling images.

w Manfred R. Koehler story The Pit and the Pendulum by Edgar Allan Poe   d Harald Reinl   ph Ernst W. Kalinke

☆ Christopher Lee, Lex Barker, Karin Dor, Carl Lange, Vladimir Medar, Christiane Rucker, Dieter Eppler

Blood Feud

Italy   1979   112m   Technospes

ITC/Liberty Films (Harry Columbo)

▤

aka: Revenge

In Sicily, as the fascists come to power, a rich socialist lawyer and a small-time crook court the same vengeful woman.

Unsatisfactory, melodramatic mix of romance and politics.

wd Lina Wertmuller   ph Tonino Delli Colli   m Dangio-Nando de Luca   ad Enrico Job   ed Franco Fraticelli

☆ Sophia Loren, Marcello Mastroianni, Giancarlo Giannini, Mario Scarpetta

Blood for Dracula: see Dracula (1974)

Blood from the Mummy's Tomb *

GB   1971   94m   Technicolor

MGM-EMI/Hammer (Howard Brandy)

Twenty years after a female mummy is brought back to England, members of the expedition are killed one by one, and their leader's daughter is possessed by the spirit of the dead princess.

Interesting but over-complicated and hard-to-enjoy attempt to maintain the mummy saga without an actual marauding mummy. Intelligently handled but sadly lacking in a sense of humour.

w Christopher Wicking novel Jewel of the Seven Stars by Bram Stoker   d Seth Holt, Michael Carreras   ph Arthur Grant   m Tristram Cary   ad Scott MacGregor   ed Peter Weatherley

☆ Andrew Keir, Valerie Leon, James Villiers, Hugh Burden, George Coulouris, Mark Edwards, Rosalie Crutchley, Aubrey Morris, David Markham

'Makes the genre seem like new.' – Tony Rayns

† Seth Holt died while the shooting was still incomplete, and Michael Carreras took over for the last few days.

'Two Cats...One Car...And A World Of Hurt'

Blood Guts Bullets & Octane *
US   1997   86m   colour
Downtown/Short Fuse/Next Wave (Dan Leis, Leon Corcos, Patrick Lynn)

Two car dealers, given money to look after a Pontiac Le Mans, decide to steal the car instead, not knowing that the FBI believe it contains drugs and was used by a serial killer.
A low-budget movie, made with enough verve and energy to overcome its familiar, low-life narrative.
wd Joe Carnahan ph John Alexander Jimenez m Mark Priolo, Martin Birke ad Eric Lutes ed Joe Carnahan
☆ Joe Carnahan, Dan Leis, Ken Rudulph, Dan Harlan, Hugh McChord, Kurt Johnson, Mark S. Allen, Kellee Benedic

Blood In, Blood Out **
US   1992   180m   Technicolor
Buena Vista/Hollywood Pictures/Touchstone Pacific Partners I (Taylor Hackford, Jerry Gershwin)

A decade in the life of three Chicanos, two half-brothers and their half-white cousin, caught up in gang warfare on the streets and in prison.
Tough, violent, gripping drama of oppression and redemption in the East Los Angeles barrio, depicting an aspect of America not often seen on-screen; its length is justified not only by its narrative drive but by the fleshing out of individual lives caught in a destructive system.
w Jimmy Santiago Baca, Jeremy Iacone, Floyd Mutrux story Ross Thomas d Taylor Hackford ph Gabriel Beristain m Bill Conti pd Bruno Rubeo ed Fredric Steinkamp, Karl F. Steinkamp
☆ Jesse Borrego, Benjamin Bratt, Enrique Castillo, Damian Chapa, Delroy Lindo, Tom Wilson, Karmin Murcelo, Ving Rhames, Jenny Gago
'Triumphs over cliché to sustain its vast length and space. The key to this success lies in its epic size, a mood and a scale more akin to a mini-series than grandiose cinema.' – *Olly Blackburn, Sight and Sound*
'Seems compelled to say something profound but too often stands on a soapbox to do it.' – *Variety*

Blood Is My Heritage: see *Blood of Dracula*

Blood Money: see *Requiem for a Heavyweight (1962)*

Blood Money *
US   1933   66m   bw
Fox/Darryl F. Zanuck
The decline of a bail-bond racketeer.
Smartly made melodrama with good work all round.
wd Rowland Brown
☆ George Bancroft, Judith Anderson, Chick Chandler, Frances Dee, Blossom Seeley

Blood Oath
Australia   1990   108m   Eastmancolor
Rank/Sovereign/Village Roadshow/Siege (Graham Burke, Greg Coote, John Tarnoff)

In 1946, an Australian Army captain prosecutes the Japanese commandant of a camp where the bodies of more than 300 prisoners were discovered in a mass grave.
A routine courtroom drama of no particular interest, despite its factual basis.
w Denis Whitburn, Brian A. Williams d Stephen Wallace ph Russell Boyd m David McHugh ad Virginia Bieneman ed Nicholas Beauman, Bernard Hides
☆ Bryan Brown, George Takei, Terry O'Quinn, John Bach, Toshi Shioya, John Clarke, Deborah Unger, Jason Donovan
'Reduces the moral complexities of war to the simplest *Boy's Own* level.' – *Sight and Sound*

The Blood of a Poet **
France   1931   58m   bw
Vicomte de Noailles

original title: *Le Sang d'un Poète*
Aspects of a poet's vision, taking place while a chimney is falling down.
An indescribable film full of striking imagery which may, or may not, be meaningful. Its author claims that it is not surrealist, but that label for most people will do as well as any other.

wd Jean Cocteau ph Georges Périnal m Georges Auric ad Jean Gabriel d'Aubonne
☆ Lee Miller, Enrique Rivero, Pauline Carton, Feral Benga, Jean Desbordes, Barbette, Odette Talazac
'It must be placed among the classic masterpieces of the seventh art.' – *Revue du Cinéma*

'In her eyes Desire! In her veins the blood of a ... Monster!'

Blood of Dracula
US   1957   68m   bw
Anglo Amalgamated/Carmel/AIP (Herman Cohen)

GB title: *Blood Is My Heritage*
aka: *Blood of the Demon*
A feminist high-school chemistry teacher hypnotizes an unhappy student into becoming a vampire to prove that men control, and will destroy, the world.
Risible mix of horror and teenage rebellion movies that does not miss a cliché of either genre.
w Ralph Thornton d Herbert L. Strock ph Monroe Askins m Paul Dunlap ad Leslie Thomas ed Robert Moore sp Philip Scheer
☆ Sandra Harrison, Louise Lewis, Gail Ganley, Jerry Blaine, Heather Ames, Malcolm Atterbury, Mary Adams
† With a change in gender for the leading characters and a different monster, the script was recycled by Thornton as *I Was a Teenage Werewolf* (qv).

Blood of the Demon: see *Blood of Dracula*

Blood of the Dragon
Japan   1974   88m   Eastmancolor
Eural/Toei-Kyoto Eiga/Titan (Norimichi Matsudaira)

original title: *Satsujinken 2*
Double-crossed by his employers, who front for the Mafia, an assassin goes on the rampage.
Convoluted martial arts mayhem that makes little narrative sense; but then all that matters is its fights.
w Hajime Takaiwa, Shigehiro Ozawa story Koji Yakada d Sonny Chiba, Gerald Yamada, Doris Nakajima, Tony Cetera, Tatsuro Endo, Masashi Ishibashi m Tony Tsushima ad Tokumichi Igawa ed Kozo Horiike
☆ Sonny Chiba, Yoko Ichiji, Masafumi Suzuki, Kaoru Nakajima, Naoki Shima, Masashi Ishibashi

Blood of the Undead: see *Schizo*

Blood of the Vampire
GB   1958   85m   Eastmancolor
Baker-Berman/Artistes Alliance

A doctor, raised from the dead, takes over an asylum and experiments on the inmates.
Heavy-handed, crudely made horror comic.
w Jimmy Sangster d Henry Cass ph Monty Berman m Stanley Black ad John Elphick ed Douglas Myers
☆ Donald Wolfit, Barbara Shelley, Vincent Ball, Victor Maddern, Andrew Faulds, John Le Mesurier, Bernard Bresslaw

Blood on His Lips: see *The Hideous Sun Demon*

Blood on My Hands: see *Kiss the Blood Off My Hands*

Blood on Satan's Claw
GB   1970   93m   Eastmancolor
Tigon-Chilton (Tony Tenser, Malcolm B. Heyworth, Peter L. Andrews)

aka: *Satan's Skin*
A devil's claw wreaks havoc among children in a 17th-century English village.
Moderately frightening, rather silly but at least original period horror comic.
w Robert Wynne-Simmons d Piers Haggard ph Dick Bush m Marc Wilkinson
☆ Patrick Wymark, Linda Hayden, Barry Andrews, Avice Landon, Simon Williams, Tamara Ustinov, Anthony Ainley

Blood on the Arrow
US   1964   91m   DeLuxe
Leon Fromkess/Allied Artists
An outlaw is the only survivor of an Indian raid, and later becomes a hero when the Indians attack again.
Unremarkable Western, with every turn of plot to order.
w Robert E. Kent d Sidney Salkow
☆ Dale Robertson, Martha Hyer, Wendell Corey, Paul Mantee, Ted de Corsia

Blood on the Moon *
US   1948   88m   bw
RKO (Sid Rogell, Theron Warth)

A homesteader finds that his best friend is the villainous leader of a group of cattlemen.
Good-looking but rather pedestrian Western, generally well handled.
w Lillie Hayward novel *Gunman's Choice* by Luke Short d Robert Wise ph Nicholas Musuraca m Roy Webb
☆ Robert Mitchum, Barbara Bel Geddes, Robert Preston, Walter Brennan

Blood on the Streets: see *Borsalino & Co*

Blood on the Sun *
US   1945   94m   bw
Cagney Productions (William Cagney)

In the twenties, the American editor of a Tokyo newspaper reveals a Japanese militarist plan for world conquest.
Satisfactory star actioner with good production and exciting highlights.
w Lester Cole d Frank Lloyd ph Theodor Sparkuhl m Miklos Rozsa ad Wiard Ihnen
☆ James Cagney, Sylvia Sidney, Wallace Ford, Rosemary de Camp, Robert Armstrong, John Emery, Leonard Strong, Frank Puglia
'It ought to be fine for those who enjoy a good ninety-minute massacre.' – *New Yorker*
'Tough, hard-hitting and explosive, with just enough rudimentary suspense.' – *Bosley Crowther*
'Pure unadulterated melodrama has a safe niche in cinematic offerings, but this folderol is more pretentious than persuasive.' – *Howard Barnes*
🎭 Wiard Ihnen

Blood Relatives
Canada/France   1977   100m   colour
Panavision
Classic/Cinevideo/Filmel (Denis Heroux, Eugene Lepecier)

aka: *Les Liens du Sang*
A 15-year-old girl accuses her brother of murdering their 17-year-old cousin.
Dull psychological thriller, with stock characters and showing none of the flair that Chabrol has exhibited when examining the French middle classes under pressure.
w Claude Chabrol, Sydney Banks novel Ed McBain d Claude Chabrol ph Jean Rabier m Howard Blake pd Anne Pritchard ed Yves Langlois
☆ Donald Sutherland, Stéphane Audran, Micheline Lanctot, Aude Landry, Lisa Langlois, Laurent Malet, Donald Pleasence, David Hemmings

Blood Simple *
US   1983   99m   DuArt
Palace/River Road (Ethan Coen)

A saloon owner hires a hit man to kill his unfaithful wife and her lover, but the plot rebounds on him.
Yet another variation on The Postman Always Rings Twice (qv), and one with strong moments.
w Joel and Ethan Coen d Joel Coen ph Barry Sonnenfeld m Carter Burwell pd Jane Musky ed Roderick Jaynes, Don Wiegmann, Peggy Connolly
☆ John Getz, Frances McDormand, Dan Hedaya, M. Emmet Walsh

Blood Sisters: see *Sisters*

The Blood Virgin: see *Symptoms*

Blood Wedding **
Spain   1981   72m   Eastmancolor
Artificial Eye/Emiliano Piedra

Dancers of the Antonio Gades company first prepare for, and then rehearse in a bare room, their flamenco-ballet treatment of Lorca's play of passion, jealousy and death.
An exhilarating treatment of both Lorca and the dancers, moving from a documentary style to one more involved in the commitment, energy and techniques on display.
play Federico Garcí Lorca d Carlos Saura ph Teo Escamilla m Emilion de Diego ch Antonio Gades ad Rafael Lammero ed Pablo del Amo
☆ Antonio Gades, Cristina Hoyos, Juan Antonio, Pilar Cardenas, Carmen Villena, Marisol, Pepe Blanco, El Guito, Lario Diaz
'A feast for dance lovers.' – *Sight and Sound*

Bloodbath at the House of Death
GB   1983   92m   colour
EMI/Wildwood (Ray Cameron)
Scientists investigate a haunted house.
Spoof tailored to the requirements of a zany television comedian who never knows when enough is enough. Too much gore and far too much smut.
w Ray Cameron, Barry Cryer d Ray Cameron ph Brian West, Dusty Miller m Mike Moran, Mark London
☆ Kenny Everett, Pamela Stephenson, Vincent Price, Gareth Hunt, Don Warrington, John Fortune, Sheila Steafel, Graham Stark
'Presumably intended as high camp; looks like low-grade *Carry On*.' – *Martyn Auty, MFB*

Bloodbath Bay of Death: see *A Bay of Blood*

Bloodbrothers
US   1978   116m   Technicolor
Warner/Stephen Friedman/Kings Road

The disintegration through failure and inadequacy of a noisy Italian-American family.
The kind of self-indulgence that has one seeking the exit before it's half over.
w Walter Newman novel Richard Price d Robert Mulligan ph Robert Surtees m Elmer Bernstein pd Gene Callahan
☆ Paul Sorvino, Tony Lo Bianco, Richard Gere, Lelia Goldoni
'The director is trying for something crude, powerful, volatile ... but it goes terribly wrong. People laugh with hysterical heartiness, or say things like: "Life can hurt. It's made me feel close to all those doing the hurting dance."' – *Pauline Kael, New Yorker*
🎭 Walter Newman

Bloodfist
US   1989   85m   colour
Concorde (Roger Corman)

A kick-boxer seeks to avenge his brother's death.
Unexciting and turgid action movie.
w Robert King d Terence H. Winkless ph Ricardo Jacques Gale m Sasha Matson ed Karen Horn
☆ Don 'The Dragon' Wilson, Joe Marie Avellana, Michael Shaner, Riley Bowman, Rob Kamen, Billy Blanks, Kris Aguilar

Bloodfist II
US   1990   88m   colour
Concorde (Roger Corman)

A kick-boxer attempts to infiltrate an island fortress.
A cheap re-run of Enter the Dragon (qv) with a far less charismatic hero.
w Catherine Cyran d Andy Blumenthal ph Bruce Dorfman m Nigel Holton ed Karen Joseph
☆ Don 'The Dragon' Wilson, Rina Reyes, Joe Marie Avellana, Robert Marius, Maurice Smith, Tim Baker, James Warring

Bloodfist III
US   1992   88m   Foto-Kem
Concorde (Roger Corman)

A wrongly imprisoned kick-boxer goes to the aid of a friend attacked by fellow convicts.

Fast action movie, with some fierce fights, which should satisfy fans of the genre.
w Allison Burnett, Charles Mattera d Oley Sassone ph Rick Bota m Nigel Holton pd James Shumaker ed Eric L. Beason
☆ Don 'The Dragon' Wilson, Richard Roundtree, Gregory McKinney, Rick Dean, Richard Paul, Charles Boswell, John Cardone

Bloodhounds of Broadway *
US 1952 90m Technicolor
TCF (George Jessel)
With the help of a gangster, an orphan girl and her pet bloodhounds make a big hit in cabaret.
Absurd but sporadically amusing gangster burlesque, typical of its author. Lively production values.
w Sy Gomberg story Damon Runyon d Harmon Jones ph Edward Cronjager m David Raksin md Lionel Newman
☆ Mitzi Gaynor, Scott Brady, Mitzi Green, Marguerite Chapman, Michael O'Shea, Wally Vernon, George E. Stone

Bloodhounds of Broadway
US 1989 90m DeLuxe
Columbia (Howard Brookner)
Interwoven stories of the escapades of gangsters, guys and dolls on New Year's Eve, 1928.
Bland and forgettable and lacking the particular flavour of the original tales.
wd Howard Brookner short stories Damon Runyon ph Elliot Davis m Jonathan Sheffer pd Linda Conway-Parsole ed Camilla Toniolo
☆ Josef Sommer, Madonna, Tony Azito, Jennifer Grey, Tony Longo, Rutger Hauer, Matt Dillon, Julie Hagerty, Randy Quaid, William Burroughs

Bloodline
US 1979 117m Movielab
Paramount/Geria (David V. Picker, Sidney Beckerman)
A pharmaceutical tycoon is murdered and his daughter seems likely to be the next victim.
Involved all-star suspense shocker which seems constantly about to be better than it ever is.
w Laird Koenig novel Sidney Sheldon d Terence Young ph Freddie Young m Ennio Morricone pd Ted Haworth
☆ Audrey Hepburn, Ben Gazzara, James Mason, Claudia Mori, Omar Sharif, Irene Papas, Maurice Ronet, Romy Schneider, Beatrice Straight, Gert Frobe, Michelle Phillips
'Unutterably chic, inexpressibly absurd, and saved from being painfully tedious only by a personable cast doing their damnedest.' – Tom Milne, MFB

Bloodsport
US 1988 92m TVC Color
Cannon (Mark DiSalle)
An American commando goes to Hong Kong to take part in the Kumite, a clandestine martial arts competition.
Despite being based on the true story of Frank Dux (who supervised the fight sequences), the movie emerges as pulp fiction that will be of interest only to martial arts enthusiasts, who may not wonder why an American should speak with a heavy Belgian accent.
w Sheldon Lettich, Christopher Crosby, Mel Friedman d Newt Arnold ph David Worth m Paul Hertzog pd David Searl ed Carl Kress
☆ Jean-Claude Van Damme, Donald Gibb, Leah Ayres, Norman Burton, Forest Whitaker, Roy Chiao, Philip Chan, Pierre Rafini, Bolo Yeung

The Bloodstained Shadow (dubbed)
Italy 1978 107m Technospes
PAC (Teodoro Agrimi)
original title: Solamente Nero
The visit of an overworked university lecturer to his brother, a priest, coincides with a series of murders.
Dull and slow-moving thriller, with an explanation of the crimes that makes very little sense, although a similar and equally unlikely plot turns up in Dario Argento's Creepers (qv).
w Antonio, Marisa Andalo, Domenico Malan d Antonio Bido ph Mario Vulpiani m Stelvio Cipriani ad Carlo Leva ed Amedeo Giomini

☆ Lino Capolicchio, Stefania Casini, Craig Hill, Massimo Serato, Juliette Mayniel, Laura Nucci, Attilio Duse

Bloodstream
US 1993 90m CFI color
HBO Showcase (John Bard Manulis)
In the near, grim future, a woman falls in love with the leader of a resistance movement against government policy, in which people suffering from an AIDS-like disease are imprisoned while order is maintained by gangs of young vigilantes.
Moderately effective science-fiction drama of an era when individual liberty is subordinated to the interests of the state, though making only a perfunctory attempt to explore the concept in any depth.
wd Stephen Tolkin play Beirut by Alan Bowne ph Tom Sigel m Michel Colombier pd Leslie Pope ed Brunilda Torres
☆ Cuba Gooding Jnr, Moira Kelly, Omar Epps, Martha Plimpton, Alice Drummond, David Eigenberg, Jon Seda, Nick Chinlund
'Maintains a delicate balance between fantasy and reality, enveloping its political message in an easy-to-swallow dramatic capsule … a real find.' – Sight and Sound
† The film was made for cable TV.

Bloodsuckers: see Incense of the Damned

Bloodsucking Freaks
US 1977 93m colour Ghoulovision
Troma (Alan Margolin)
aka: The Incredible Torture Show
Nasty things happen during a Grand Guignol-style stage show given over to sadism and the white slave trade.
Extraordinarily unpleasant farrago, in which one of the pleasanter moments has someone's brain being sucked out with a straw. According to Troma's Lloyd Kaufman, it is 'only for the demented'; but it won't do them any good.
wd Joel M. Reed ph Gerry Toll m Michael Sahl ed Victor Kanevsky
☆ Seamus O'Brien, Niles McMaster, Luis de Jesus, Viju Krim, Alan Dellay

The Bloody Bushido Blade: see The Bushido Blade

'The family that stays together slays together!'
Bloody Mama *
US 1969 90m Movielab
AIP (Roger Corman)
In the thirties, outlaw Kate Barker and her four sons conduct a reign of terror until what's left of the gang is riddled with machine gun bullets.
Violent gangster story with a star on the rampage; the attempt to philosophize is more than the facts will bear, but the production moves smartly enough.
w Robert Thom d Roger Corman ph John Alonzo m Don Randi
☆ Shelley Winters, Pat Hingle, Don Stroud, Diane Varsi, Bruce Dern, Clint Kimbrough, Robert De Niro, Robert Walden, Alex Nicol

Bloomfield
GB 1969 95m Technicolor
World Film Services/Limbridge (John Heyman, Wolf Mankowitz)
US title: The Hero
A 10-year-old Israeli boy hitchhikes to Jaffa to see his football idol play his last game.
Sentimental whimsy, unattractively interpreted.
w Wolf Mankowitz d Richard Harris ph Otto Heller m Johnny Harris
☆ Richard Harris, Romy Schneider, Kim Burfield, Maurice Kaufmann, Yossi Yadin

Blossom Time
GB 1934 90m bw
BIP (Walter Mycroft)
US title: April Romance
In old Vienna, a composer stands by while the girl he loves weds a dragoon.
Stilted musical romance redeemed by its star's singing presence.
w John Drinkwater, Walter Burford, Paul Perez, G. H. Clutsam story Franz Schulz d Paul Stein ph Otto Kanturek, Bryan Langley m Schubert

md Idris Lewis ad David Rawnsley, Clarence Elder ed Leslie Norman
☆ Richard Tauber, Jane Baxter, Carl Esmond, Athene Seyler

Blossoms in the Dust **
US 1941 99m Technicolor
MGM (Irving Asher)
A woman who loses her husband and child founds a state orphanage.
Archetypal tearjerker of the forties, a glossy 'woman's picture' which distorts the facts into a star vehicle. Excellent colour helped to make it an enormous success.
w Anita Loos, based on the life of Edna Gladney d Mervyn Le Roy ph Karl Freund, W. Howard Greene m Herbert Stothart ad Cedric Gibbons, Urie McCleary
☆ Greer Garson, Walter Pidgeon, Felix Bressart, Marsha Hunt, Fay Holden, Samuel S. Hinds
🏆 art direction
🏆 best picture; Karl Freund, W. Howard Greene; Greer Garson

'Heading for the laff round-up!'
Blossoms on Broadway
US 1937 88m bw
Paramount (B. P. Schulberg)
A girl who owns a Death Valley gold mine comes to New York and is hounded by confidence men.
Tolerably fast-moving comedy.
w Theodore Reeves d Richard Wallace
☆ Edward Arnold, Shirley Ross, John Trent, Weber and Fields, Frank Craven, Rufe Davis, William Frawley
'Won't do much b.o. blossoming. Good songs, but story stumbles badly.' – Variety

Blotto *
US 1930 20m bw
Hal Roach
Ollie helps Stan escape his wife for a night on the town, but the lady takes revenge.
Palatable star comedy with a strained second half following a splendidly typical opening.
w Leo McCarey, H. M. Walker d James Parrott
☆ Stan Laurel, Oliver Hardy, Anita Garvin

'Murder has a sound all of its own!'
Blow Out
US 1981 108m Technicolor Panavision
Filmways/Cinema 77/Geria (George Litto)
A sound effects man accidentally captures on film what turns out to be a murder.
Showily unpleasant thriller concocted of equal parts of The Conversation, Blow Up, and Kennedy at Chappaquiddick; the work of a copycat talent operating below par.
wd Brian de Palma ph Vilmos Zsigmond m Pino Donaggio pd Paul Sylbert
☆ John Travolta, Nancy Allen, John Lithgow, Dennis Franz, John McMartin, John Aquino
'The camera is better deployed than the script.' – Guardian

Blow to the Heart
Italy 1982 105m colour
Other Cinema/RAI/Antea Cinematografica (Enzo Porcelli)
original title: Colpire Al Cuore
A conformist son suspects his radical father of terrorist sympathies.
Moderately gripping, though it suffers from indecision over whether its subject matter is politics or family relationships.
w Gianni Amelio, Vincenzo Cerami d Gianni Amelio ph Tonino Nardi m Franco Piersanti ad Marco Dentici ed Anna Napoli
☆ Jean-Louis Trintignant, Laura Morante, Fausto Rossi, Sonia Gessner, Vanni Corbellini

Blowing Wild *
US 1953 88m bw
Warner/United States (Milton Sperling)
A Mexican oil driller becomes involved with the psychotic wife of an old friend; the triangle leads to murder and retribution.
Pot-boiling star vehicle with adequate melodramatic interest, full of reminiscences of other movies, with a wicked lady to end them all.

w Philip Yordan d Hugo Fregonese ph Sid Hickox m Dimitri Tiomkin
☆ Gary Cooper, Barbara Stanwyck, Anthony Quinn, Ruth Roman, Ward Bond

'Trusting Someone Can Be Deadly.'
Blown Away
Canada 1992 92m colour
Norstar (Peter R. Simpson)
A young resort worker becomes involved with the spoilt, self-destructive 17-year-old daughter of his violent boss.
Tawdry tale of thwarted teenage sex that is both trivial and tedious, shot in the style of an unimaginative promotional video for a pop song.
w Robert Cooper d Brenton Spencer ph Perci Young m Paul J. Zaza ad Ian Brock ed Bill Towgood
☆ Corey Haim, Corey Feldman, Nicole Eggert, Gary Farmer, Kathleen Robertson, Jean LeClerc
'Daft "erotic" thriller.' – Sight and Sound

'5-4-3-2-1-Time's Up.'
Blown Away
US 1994 121m DeLuxe Panavision
MGM/Trilogy (John Watson, Richard Lewis, Pen Densham)
A Boston bomb disposal expert hunts down an escaped Irish bomber who knows his guilty secret and is killing his friends.
An action movie with more holes in its plot than there are in some of its mad bomber's victims; the cast give the impression that they were anxious to be somewhere else, but it is enjoyable enough in a mindless way, as long as you do not expect it to make any sense.
w Joe Batteer, John Rice d Stephen Hopkins ph Peter Levy m Alan Silvestri pd John Graysmark ed Timothy Wellburn
☆ Jeff Bridges, Tommy Lee Jones, Lloyd Bridges, Forest Whitaker, Suzy Amis
'Diehard action seekers may be drawn into its technical bag of tricks, but those in search of a gripping, emotional genre pic will be disappointed.' – Leonard Klady, Variety

Blow-Out **
France/Italy 1973 133m Eastmancolor Panavision
Gala/Mara/Les Films 66/Capitolina (Jean-Pierre Rassam)
original title: La Grande Bouffe
A master chef, a television personality, a pilot and a judge get together for a prolonged orgy of gourmandizing and sex that ends with their deaths.
Grotesque celebration of, or satire on, the consumer society in which amusement gradually turns to disgust.
w Marco Ferreri, Rafael Azcona, Francis Blanche d Marco Ferreri ph Mario Vulpiani m Philippe Sarde ad Michel de Broin ed Claudine Merlin, Gina Pignier
☆ Marcello Mastroianni, Ugo Tognazzi, Michel Piccoli, Philippe Noiret, Andréa Ferreol, Solange Florence, Blondeau Giorgetti, Michele Alexandre, Monique Chaumette
'The film is never negligible thanks to Ferreri's consistently inventive use of detail; and whatever else, it stands as an overdue riposte to the contemporary cinema's ubiquitous hymns to male camaraderie.' – Tony Rayns, MFB

Blow-Up **
GB 1966 110m Eastmancolor
MGM/Carlo Ponti
A London fashion photographer thinks he sees a murder, but the evidence disappears.
Not a mystery but a fashionable think-in on the difference (if any) between fantasy and reality.
Agreeable to look at for those who can stifle their irritation at the non-plot and non-characters; a huge audience was lured by flashes of nudity and the trendy 'swinging London' setting.
wd Michelangelo Antonioni ph Carlo di Palma m Herbert Hancock ad Asshelton Gorton
☆ David Hemmings, Sarah Miles, Vanessa Redgrave
'A beautiful and startling film, startling because if the credits didn't say it was coauthored and directed by Michelangelo Antonioni you'd never believe it on the basis of the movie itself, and beautiful because in his first made-in-England English-language film the Italian director proves

himself a master of the use of color, both literally and figuratively.' – *Judith Crist*
§ Michelangelo Antonioni (as writer and director)

Blue

US 1968 113m Technicolor Panavision
Paramount/Kettledrum (Judd Bernard, Irwin Winkler)
▣ ◕

The white adopted son of a Mexican bandit prevents his cohorts from raping a white girl, and falls in love with her.
Pretentious, self-conscious, literary Western without much zest.
w Meade Roberts, Ronald M. Cohen d Silvio Narizzano ph Stanley Cortez m Manos Hadjidakis
☆ Terence Stamp, Joanna Pettet, Karl Malden, Ricardo Montalban
'I don't know which is worse – bad cowboy movies or bad arty cowboy movies. *Blue* is both.' – *Rex Reed*

Blue **

GB 1993 76m Technicolor
Basilisk/Uplink (James Mackay, Takashi Asai)
▣ ▤ ◕ ◠

A meditation on AIDS and the colour blue; the screen is suffused with a blue light as the director muses on the death of friends and his own illness and deteriorating sight.
Jarman's valediction to the cinema is more a radio play than a film, but is nevertheless a superior piece of radio.
wd Derek Jarman m Simon Fisher Turner
☆ Featuring the voices of John Quentin, Derek Jarman, Nigel Terry, Tilda Swinton
'Given the choice between art and socially oriented moviemaking, he has opted for art.' – *Robert Horton, Film Comment*
† *Blue* was given a simultaneous first broadcast on British television and stereo radio. Jarman himself said of it, 'I think it's quite nice to have that visual silence in the cinema.'

The Blue and the Gold: see *An Annapolis Story*

The Blue Angel ****

Germany 1930 98m bw
UFA (Erich Pommer)
▣ ◕

A fuddy-duddy professor is infatuated with a tawdry night-club singer. She marries him but is soon bored and contemptuous; humiliated, he leaves her and dies in his old classroom.
A masterwork of late twenties German grotesquerie, and after a slowish beginning an emotional powerhouse, set in a dark nightmare world which could be created only in the studio. Shot also in English, it was highly popular and influential in Britain and America. It instantly catapulted Dietrich to international stardom.
w Robert Liebmann, Karl Zuckmayer, Karl Vollmoeller *novel Professor Unrath* by Heinrich Mann d Josef von Sternberg ph Günther Rittau, Hans Schneeberger m Frederick Hollander (inc 'Falling in Love Again', 'They Call Me Wicked Lola') ad Otto Hunte, Emil Hasler
☆ Emil Jannings, Marlene Dietrich, Kurt Gerron, Hans Albers
'It will undoubtedly do splendidly in the whole of Europe and should also appeal strongly in the States ... only fault is a certain ponderousness of tempo which tends to tire.' – *Variety*
'At the time I thought the film was awful and vulgar and I was shocked by the whole thing. Remember, I was a well brought up German girl.' – *Marlene Dietrich*

The Blue Angel

US 1959 107m DeLuxe Cinemascope
TCF (Jack Cummings)
Ill-advised attempt at a 'realistic', updated remake of the above; the result is a total travesty, with the actors aware that stylized melodrama is turning before their eyes into unintentional farce.
w Nigel Balchin d Edward Dmytryk ph Leon Shamroy m Hugo Friedhofer
☆ Curt Jurgens, May Britt, Theodore Bikel, John Banner
'It totally lacks the stifling atmosphere of sordid and oppressive sexuality which is essential to give conviction to the German sadism of the story.' – *Brenda Davies*

The Blue Bird ***

⚣ US 1940 98m Technicolor (bw prologue)
TCF (Gene Markey)
▤

In a Grimm's Fairy Tale setting, the two children of a poor woodcutter seek the bluebird of happiness in the past, the future and the Land of Luxury, but eventually discover it in their own back yard.
An imaginative and often chilling script clarifies Maurice Maeterlinck's fairy play, and the art direction is outstanding, but the children are necessarily unsympathetic and the expensive production paled beside the success of the more upbeat Wizard of Oz (qv), which was released almost simultaneously. Slashed for re-release, the only existing prints now open with confusing abruptness and no scene-setting before the adventures begin.
w Ernest Pascal d Walter Lang ph Arthur Miller, Ray Rennahan m Alfred Newman ad Richard Day, Wiard B. Ihnen
☆ Shirley Temple, Johnny Russell, Gale Sondergaard, Eddie Collins, Nigel Bruce, Jessie Ralph, Spring Byington, Sybil Jason, Helen Ericson, Russell Hicks, Al Shean, Cecilia Loftus
'One of the most deliciously lovely productions to be brought to the screen.' – *MFB*
§ Arthur Miller, Ray Rennahan

The Blue Bird

⚣ US/USSR 1976 83m Technicolor Panavision
TCF/Edward Lewis/Lenfilm
Abortive remake of the above, widely touted as the first Russian–American co-production, but sabotaged by a flabby script, unsuitable casting and unresolved production problems.
w Hugh Whitemore, Alfred Hayes d George Cukor ph Freddie Young, Ionas Gritzus m Irwin Kostal, Andrei Petrov
☆ Elizabeth Taylor, Ava Gardner, Cicely Tyson, Jane Fonda, Harry Andrews, Will Geer, Mona Washbourne, George Cole
'It works so hard at making history that it forgets to make sense.' – *David Sterritt, Christian Science Monitor*
'If you have any naughty children you want to punish, take them to *The Blue Bird* and make them sit all the way through it.' – *William Wolf, Cue*
'It turns a work for adults that children can enjoy into a charade for children that must sicken adults.' – *John Simon, New Yorker*
'Senile and interminable.' – *Stephen Farber, New West*
'Lavishly done; limited box office.' – *Variety*

Blue Black Permanent

GB 1992 86m colour
BFI/Channel 4/Viz Permanent (Barbara Grigor)
An Edinburgh photographer remembers her childhood in the Orkneys and returns there with her lover to sort out the problems that plague her.
A shifting and complex narrative explores feminine identity across two generations.
wd Margaret Tait ph Alex Scott m John Gray pd Andrew Semple ed John MacDonnell
☆ Celia Imrie, Jack Shepherd, Gerda Stevenson, James Fleet, Sean Scanlan, Hilary Maclean, Walter Leask, Sheena Mar
'Tait's achievement is to suggest the processes that lie behind our ways of seeing, our declarations, and to find a style that enacts, or at least simulates, those very processes.' – *Robert Yates, Sight and Sound*

Blue Blood

GB 1973 86m Technicolor
Mallard-Impact Quadrant (Kent Walwin, John Trent)
A German governess arrives at an English stately home and finds the malevolent butler plotting to show his supremacy over his effete master.
An extremely unattractive, would-be satirical melodrama which plays like a Grand Guignol version of The Servant (qv).
wd Andrew Sinclair *novel The Carry-Cot* by Alexander Thynne ph Harry Waxman m Brian Gascoigne
☆ Oliver Reed, Derek Jacobi, Fiona Lewis, Anna Gael, Meg Wynn Owen

Blue Canadian Rockies

US 1952 60m bw
Columbia/Gene Autry (Armand Schaefer)
▤

A ranch foreman goes to Canada to stop the boss's daughter from marrying the wrong man.
Uninteresting Western with a flimsy plot and minimal action, interrupted by some indifferent songs.
w Gerald Geraghty d George Archainbaud ph William Bradford md Mischa Bakaleinikoff ad George Brooks ed James Sweeney
☆ Gene Autry, Champion, Pat Buttram, Gail Davis, Carolina Cotton, Ross Ford, Tom London, Mauritz Hugo, Cass County Boys

Blue Chips *

US 1994 108m Technicolor
Paramount (Michele Rappaport)
▣ ▤ ◠

A college basketball coach, in trouble with a losing streak, condones bribery to get the talent he needs for his team.
A loud and frenetic melodrama of endemic corruption with an appeal likely to be limited to fans of the sport.
w Ron Shelton d William Friedkin ph Tom Priestley Jnr m Nile Rodgers, Jeff Beck, Jed Leiber pd James Bissell ed Robert K. Lambert, David Rosenbloom
☆ Nick Nolte, Mary McDonnell, J. T. Walsh, Ed O'Neill, Alfre Woodard, Bob Cousy, Shaquille O'Neal, Matt Nover, Louis Gossett Jnr, Robert Wuhl, Anfernee 'Penny' Hardaway
'A riveting, intelligent work.' – *Independent*
'A deafness-inducing but otherwise ho-hum would-be exposé of shady recruiting practices by college basketball programs.' – *Todd McCarthy, Variety*

Blue City

US 1986 83m Technicolor
Paramount (William Hayward, Walter Hill)
▣ ▤ ◕

A drifter returns home to discover that his father has been murdered and his step-mother is living with the probable killer.
Dull, predictable and unpleasantly amoral thriller in which the hero's investigative methods into the killing consist of beating up most people he meets while waging a criminal war against his enemies.
w Lukas Heller, Walter Hill *novel* Ross MacDonald d Michelle Manning ph Steven Poster m Ry Cooder ad Richard Lawrence ed Ross Albert
☆ Judd Nelson, Ally Sheedy, David Caruso, Paul Winfield, Scott Wilson, Anita Morris, Julie Carmen, Luis Contreras

Blue Collar ***

US 1978 114m Technicolor
Universal/TAT (Don Guest)
▣ ▤ ◕ ◠

Three car factory workers try to improve their lot by unionization and robbery.
Salty, rough, downbeat but impressively realistic modern drama, a belated American equivalent of Saturday Night and Sunday Morning (qv).
w Paul Schrader, Leonard Schrader d Paul Schrader ph Bobby Byrne m Jack Nitzsche
☆ Richard Pryor, Harvey Keitel, Yaphet Kotto, Ed Begley Jnr, Harry Bellaver
'This is Schrader's first directing job and the best elements in the script fit his ability like a role tailored for an actor. His work is easy and quick, imaginative but not ostentatious.' – *Stanley Kauffmann*

'Tamed by a brunette – framed by a blonde – blamed by the cops!'

The Blue Dahlia **

US 1946 99m bw
Paramount (John Houseman)
A returning war veteran finds his faithless wife murdered and himself suspected.
Hailed on its first release as sharper than average, this mystery suspenser is now only moderately compelling despite the screenplay credit; direction and editing lack urgency and the acting lacks bounce.
w Raymond Chandler d George Marshall ph Lionel Lindon m Victor Young
☆ Alan Ladd, Veronica Lake, William Bendix, Howard da Silva, Doris Dowling, Tom Powers, Hugh Beaumont, Howard Freeman, Will Wright
'It threatens to turn into something, but it never does.' – *New Yorker, 1978*

'The picture is as neatly stylized and synchronized, and as uninterested in moral excitement, as a good ballet; it knows its own weight and size perfectly and carries them gracefully and without self-importance; it is, barring occasional victories and noble accidents, about as good a movie as can be expected from the big factories.' – *James Agee*
§ Raymond Chandler

Blue Denim *

US 1959 89m bw Cinemascope
TCF (Charles Brackett)
GB title: *Blue Jeans*
Teenagers confronted with the prospect of illegitimate parenthood consult an abortionist, but all ends with wedding bells.
First of its rather dreary kind but better than most, this only slightly mawkish domestic drama has its heart in the right place and steers surprisingly towards a nick-of-time chase climax.
w Edith Sommer, Philip Dunne *play* James Leo Herlihy, William Noble d Philip Dunne ph Leo Tover m Bernard Herrmann
☆ Carol Lynley, Brandon de Wilde, Macdonald Carey, Marsha Hunt, Nina Shipman, Warren Berlinger

Blue Fire Lady

⚣ Australia 1978 95m Eastmancolor
AIFC (Anthony Ginnane)
A young girl defies her father's opposition to work with horses.
A soft-centred romance between a girl and a horse which follows the usual pattern – girl meets horse, girl loses horse, girl gets horse – and which will appeal to other horse-lovers.
w Bob Maumill d Ross Dimsey
☆ Cathryn Harrison, Mark Holden, Peter Cummins, Marion Edward, Lloyd Cunnington, Syd Conabere, Philip Barnard-Brown, Gary Waddell

The Blue Gardenia

US 1953 90m bw
Warner/Gloria/Blue Gardenia (Alex Gottlieb)
⌖
A girl gets drunk and wakes up in a strange apartment with a dead man by her side.
Totally undistinguished mystery which leaves egg on the actors' faces.
w Charles Hoffman d Fritz Lang ph Nicholas Musuraca m Raoul Kraushaar
☆ Anne Baxter, Richard Conte, Ann Sothern, Raymond Burr, Jeff Donnell, Richard Erdman, Nat King Cole

Blue Hawaii

US 1961 101m Technicolor Panavision
Hal B. Wallis
▣ ▤ ◕ ⌖ ◠
A GI comes home to Honolulu and becomes a beachcomber.
Lifeless star vehicle shot on glamorous locations.
w Hal Kanter d Norman Taurog ph Charles Lang Jnr m Joseph J. Lilley
☆ Elvis Presley, Joan Blackman, Nancy Walters, Roland Winters, Angela Lansbury, John Archer, Howard McNear

Blue Heat

US 1990 106m colour
Rank/Orion/Davis (John A. Davis)
▣ ▤ ◕
US title: *The Last of the Finest*
An ex-cop goes after the drugs and arms dealer who caused his resignation from the force.
Standard cops 'n' robbers mayhem.
w Jere Cunningham, Thomas Lee Wright, George Armitage d John MacKenzie ph Juan Ruiz-Anchia m Jack Nitzsche, Michael Hoenig pd Lawrence G. Paull ed Graham Walker, Gregory Mark Gerlich, Albert Coleman, Karen Dale Greene
☆ Brian Dennehy, Joe Pantoliano, Jeff Fahey, Bill Paxton, Michael C. Gwynne

'If Harry's past ever catches up with him, he won't live long enough to regret it.'

Blue Ice

US 1992 105m colour
Guild/M&M (Martin Bregman, Michael Caine)
▣ ▤ ◕
A jazz-club owner, a former secret agent, is asked by his mistress to find an old boyfriend and becomes embroiled in murder and arms smuggling.

⚣ film suitable for family viewing   ▣ VHS video-cassette for the British PAL system   ▩ VHS video-cassette for the British PAL system in wide screen-format   ⌖ Video cassette in a computer-colourised version   ▤ American NTSC video-cassette   ◕ Laser disc

Dreary thriller, lacking in surprise and suspense, with a cast that gives the impression that its attention is understandably elsewhere.

w Ron Hutchinson *novel* Ted Allbeury d Russell Mulcahy ph Denis Crossan m Michael Kamen pd Grant Hicks ed Seth Flaum

☆ Michael Caine, Sean Young, Ian Holm, Bobby Short, Alun Armstrong, Sam Kelly, Jack Shepherd, Philip Davis, Patricia Hayes, Alan MacNaughton, Bob Hoskins

'Belongs to that familiar genre, the bad British thriller, with Michael Caine playing a version of Harry Palmer depoliticised for the Nineties and Sean Young giving the non-performance of her career.' – *Sheila Johnston, Independent*

'A resolutely old-fashioned thriller which, in its quaint view of London (all Tower Bridge and Soho dives), seems like an inflated 50s quota quickie.' – *Kim Newman, Sight and Sound*

The Blue Iguana
US 1988 88m CFI color
TCF/Polgram/Propaganda (Sigurjon Sighvatsson, Steven Colin)

An incompetent and down-at-heel bounty hunter is forced by inland revenue agents to undertake a suicidal mission in Mexico.

A comic take on the clichés of tough-guy thrillers that suffers from overstatement, with jokes being repeated three or four times in case you missed the point first time around.

wd John Lafia ph Rodolfo Sanchez m Ethan James pd Cynthia Sowder ed Scott Chestnut

☆ Dylan McDermott, Jessica Harper, James Russo, Tovah Feldshuh, Dean Stockwell, Pamela Gidley, Yano Anaya, Flea

---

'Just Over The Bridge, Around The Corner From Reality Is A Place That's Out Of This World. Welcome To Planet Brooklyn.'

Blue in the Face
US 1995 89m DuArt
Miramax (Greg Johnson, Peter Newman, Diana Phillips)

Customers drop in to a Brooklyn cigar store, presided over by an affable manager, while residents talk about life in the locality.

A semi-improvised film that grew out of rehearsals for Smoke *(qv), its more structured companion piece; it may well be rewarding for those who enjoyed that film, but is otherwise of limited interest.*

wd Wayne Wang, Paul Auster ph Adam Holender m John Lurie pd Kalina Ivanov ed Christopher Tellefsen

☆ Harvey Keitel, Lou Reed, Roseanne, Michael J. Fox, Jim Jarmusch, Lily Tomlin, Mel Gorham, Jared Harris, Giancarlo Esposito, Victor Argo, Madonna, Keith David, Mira Sorvino

'The pointlessness would be vastly more appealing if Wang and Auster didn't make such a point of it.' – *Terrence Rafferty, New Yorker*

Blue Jean Cop
US 1988 105m colour
Universal/Shapiro-Glickenhaus Entertainment (J. Boyce Harman Jnr)

US title: *Shakedown*

A lawyer defending a drug dealer uncovers corruption in the police force.

Over-the-top car chases and gun battles mar what might have been a good action thriller.

wd James Glickenhaus ph John Lindley m Jonathan Ellis pd Charles Bennett ed Paul Fried

☆ Peter Weller, Sam Elliott, Patricia Charbonneau, Antonio Fargas, William Prince, Blanche Baker

Blue Jeans: see Blue Denim

'On the waves, he's the king. On land, he's in trouble.'
'One Life. Use It.'

Blue Juice *
GB 1995 98m colour
Film Four/Pandora/Skreba (Peter Salmi, Simon Relph)

Surfers gather in Cornwall for one last fling before they succumb to life's responsibilities.

Pleasing small-scale movie of people searching for something to commit to, and finding, for the most part, only stormy weather.

w Carl Prechezer, Peter Salmi d Carl Prechezer ph Richard Greatrex m Simon Davison pd Mark Tildesley ed Michael Ellis

☆ Sean Pertwee, Catherine Zeta Jones, Steven Mackintosh, Ewan McGregor, Peter Gunn, Heathcote Williams, Keith Allen, Jenny Agutter

'Absolutely charming, unabashedly offbeat.' – *Variety*

The Blue Kite **
China/Japan 1993 138m colour
Longwick/Beijing Film Studio

original title: *Lan Fengzheng*

A boy recalls his mother's three marriages and the troubles that beset his family life during the 1950s and 60s, a time of political upheaval during China's Great Leap Forward and the Cultural Revolution inspired by the Red Guards.

A gripping, though often depressing, domestic drama seen against the ideological upheavals that made a hero of one period a villain of the next; there is warmth and humour in the telling, but the story is one of personal tragedy.

w Xiao Mao d Tian Zhuangzhuang ph Hou Yong m Yoshihide Otomo ad Zhang Xiande ed Qian Lengleng

☆ Zhang Wenyao, Chen Xiaoman, Lu Piping, Pu Quanxin, Li Xuejian, Guo Baochang, Zhong Ping, Chu Qhuangzhong, Song Xiaoying, Zhang Hong

'Major surprise of the movie is that, despite a story and multi-character cast that looks more fitted to a mini-series, it works on a simple emotional level as a feature film. Characters emerge as real people rather than political stereotypes.' – *Variety*

'Vividly and touchingly conveys the insecurity, fear and confusion of the family.' – *Sheila Johnston, Independent*

† The film had a troubled production with interference from Chinese officials, who forbade a print to leave the country for post-production work. The film was finished from the director's script and notes after a print was smuggled out of the country. In a statement made at the 1993 Cannes Film Festival the director said, 'The stories in the film are real, and they are related with total sincerity. What worries me is that it is precisely a fear of reality that has led to the ban on such stories being told.' It has not been shown in China, and in April 1994 Tian Zhuangzhuang was one of seven film directors banned from making films in mainland China.

The Blue Lagoon *
GB 1949 103m Technicolor
GFD/Individual (Frank Launder, Sidney Gilliat)

A shipwrecked boy and girl grow up on a desert island, ward off smugglers, have a baby, and eventually sail away in search of civilization.

Rather lifeless, though pretty, treatment of a famous novel: the story never becomes vivid despite splendid Fijian locations.

w Frank Launder, John Baines, Michael Hogan *novel* H. de Vere Stacpoole d Frank Launder ph Geoffrey Unsworth m Clifton Parker

☆ Jean Simmons, Donald Houston, Noel Purcell, Cyril Cusack, James Hayter

The Blue Lagoon
US 1980 102m Colorfilm
Columbia/Randal Kleiser

Remake of the above with poor narrative balance and a great deal of nudity and adolescent frankness about sex.

Adolescents are probably its only audience.

w Douglas Day Stewart d Randal Kleiser ph Nestor Almendros m Basil Poledouris

☆ Brooke Shields, Christopher Atkins, Leo McKern, William Daniels

'At best a damp dream, a Sunday school fairy tale which makes the story of Adam and Eve seem like hard porn, as hygienically sanitized as a Hilton Hotel lavatory seat.' – *Sunday Times*

'A total fraud from beginning to end.' – *Guardian*

'The film has an inevitable, built-in prurience. All we have to look forward to is: when are these two going to discover fornication?' – *Pauline Kael, New Yorker*

'This movie made me itch.' – *Roger Ebert*

♫ Nestor Almendros

The Blue Lamp ***
GB 1949 84m bw
Ealing (Michael Relph)

A young man joins London's police force. The elderly copper who trains him is killed in a shootout, but the killer is apprehended.

Seminal British police film which spawned not only a long line of semi-documentary imitations but also the twenty-year TV series Dixon of Dock Green *for which the shot PC was happily revived. As an entertainment, pacy but dated; more important, it burnished the image of the British copper for generations.*

w T. E. B. Clarke d Basil Dearden ph Gordon Dines md Ernest Irving

☆ Jack Warner, Jimmy Hanley, Dirk Bogarde, Meredith Edwards, Robert Flemyng, Bernard Lee, Patric Doonan, Peggy Evans, Gladys Henson, Dora Bryan

'The mixture of coyness, patronage and naive theatricality which has vitiated British films for the last ten years.' – *Gavin Lambert*

'A soundly made crime thriller which would not be creating much of a stir if it were American.' – *Richard Mallett, Punch*

'It is not only foreigners who find the English policeman wonderful, and, in composing this tribute to him, the Ealing Studios are giving conscious expression to a general sentiment.' – *The Times Film Correspondent*

🏆 best British picture

The Blue Light *
Germany 1932 68m bw
H. R. Sokal/Leni Riefenstahl

In the early 19th century, a painter defies a local legend to climb a Dolomite mountain.

Romantic fairy tale with a story more suited to a ballet. It still takes the eye, and is recognizable as the work of its director.

wd Leni Riefenstahl ph Hans Schneeberger, Henry Jaworsky m Giuseppe Becce

☆ Leni Riefenstahl, Matthias Wieman, Max Holsboer

† This version was put together in 1950 after the original negative had been lost; among other things, a flashback frame was removed.

'There was no quiet on the western front for the heroes and cowards who flew to their rendezvous with hell!'

The Blue Max *
US 1966 156m DeLuxe Cinemascope
TCF (Christian Ferry)

In Germany after World War I an ambitious and skilful pilot causes the death of his comrades and steals the wife of his High Command superior, who eventually finds a means of revenge.

For once, an action spectacular not too badly let down by its connecting threads of plot, apart from some hilarious and unnecessary bedroom scenes in which the female star's bath towel seems to become conveniently adhesive.

w David Pursall, Jack Seddon, Gerald Hanley *novel* Jack Hunter d John Guillermin ph Douglas Slocombe m Jerry Goldsmith pd Wilfred Shingleton

☆ George Peppard, James Mason, Ursula Andress, Jeremy Kemp, Karl Michael Vogler, Anton Diffring, Derren Nesbitt

'Addicts of flying movies swear by this one, but for others, the monoplanes and biplanes can't smash or burn fast enough.' – *Pauline Kael*

🏆 Wilfred Shingleton

Blue Murder at St Trinians *
GB 1957 86m bw
British Lion/John Marvel (Launder and Gilliat)

The awful schoolgirls win a UNESCO prize trip which takes them to Rome where they become involved with a jewel thief.

Possibly the best of this series, which isn't saying much. See The Belles of St Trinians.

w Frank Launder, Val Valentine, Sidney Gilliat d Frank Launder m Gerald Gibbs m Malcolm Arnold

☆ Terry-Thomas, George Cole, Joyce Grenfell, Alastair Sim, Judith Furse, Sabrina, Lionel Jeffries, Lloyd Lamble, Thorley Walters, Kenneth Griffith, Eric Barker, Richard Wattis

Blue Parrot
GB 1953 69m bw
ACT (Stanley Haynes)

An American detective helps Scotland Yard solve a murder mystery.

Uninteresting thriller, no more than a programme-filler.

w Allan MacKinnon *story* Percy Hoskins d John Harlow ph Bob Navarro ad Don Russell ed Robert Hill

☆ Dermot Walsh, Jacqueline Hill, Ballard Berkeley, June Ashley, Victor Lucas, John Le Mesurier, Arthur Rigby, Ferdy Mayne, Richard Pearson, Edwin Richfield

The Blue Peter
GB 1955 93m Eastmancolor
British Lion/Beaconsfield (Herbert Mason)

US title: *Navy Heroes*

A confused war hero becomes a trainer at an Outward Bound school for boys.

Pleasant but uninspired open air adventure for young people.

w Don Sharp, John Pudney d Wolf Rilla ph Arthur Grant m Antony Hopkins

☆ Kieron Moore, Greta Gynt, Sarah Lawson, Mervyn Johns, Ram Gopal, Edwin Richfield, Harry Fowler, John Charlesworth

---

'It's the nearest thing to heaven!'

Blue Skies *
US 1946 104m Technicolor
Paramount (Sol C. Siegel)

A dancing star and a night-club owner fight for years over the same girl.

Thin musical with splendid Irving Berlin tunes and lively individual numbers, including Astaire dancing 'Puttin' on the Ritz'.

w Arthur Sheekman d Stuart Heisler ph Charles Lang Jnr, William Snyder md Robert Emmett Dolan ad Hans Dreier, Hal Pereira ed LeRoy Stone

☆ Fred Astaire, Bing Crosby, Joan Caulfield, Billy de Wolfe, Olga San Juan, Robert Benchley, Frank Faylen, Victoria Horne, Jack Norton

♫ A Couple of Song and Dance Men; Getting Nowhere; I'll Dance Rings Around You; It's A Lovely Day for a Walk; Puttin' on the Ritz; Heat Wave; How Deep is the Ocean?; A Pretty Girl is Like a Melody; All By Myself; Blue Skies; I've Got My Captain Working For Me Now; Russian Lullaby; White Christmas

🏆 Robert Emmett Dolan; song 'You Keep Coming Back Like a Song' (m/ly Irving Berlin)

'In a world of secrets, love is the most powerful weapon.'

Blue Sky **
US 1994 101m DeLuxe
Orion (Robert H. Solo)

In the early 60s, an army scientist involved in dubious nuclear experiments has problems with his work and his marriage.

An old-fashioned melodrama that gains from some good performances, though its resolution is unconvincing.

w Rama Laurie Stagner, Arlene Sarner, Jerry Leichtling d Tony Richardson ph Steve Yaconelli m Jack Nitzsche pd Timian Alsaker ed Robert K. Lambert

☆ Jessica Lange, Tommy Lee Jones, Powers Boothe, Carrie Snodgress, Amy Locane, Chris O'Donnell, Mitchell Ryan, Annie Ross

† Made in 1991.

🏆 Jessica Lange

Blue Steel
US 1934 54m bw
Lone Star (Paul Malvern)

A sheriff goes undercover to expose a gang of crooks attempting to swindle a town out of its riches.

Lacklustre Western enlivened by a few stunts.

wd Robert N. Bradbury ph Archie Stout ed Carl Pierson

☆ John Wayne, Eleanor Hunt, George Hayes, Edward Peil, Yakima Canutt, George Cleveland

---

'For a rookie cop, there's one thing more dangerous than uncovering a killer's fantasy. Becoming it.'

Blue Steel

US　1990　102m　Technicolor
Vestron/Lightning Pictures/Precision Films/Mack-Taylor Productions (Edward R. Pressman, Oliver Stone)

📼 📼 ▬ ℚ.

A new cop, hunting a serial killer, falls for the chief suspect.
Lurid and ludicrous melodrama.
w Kathryn Bigelow, Eric Red　d Kathryn Bigelow
ph Amir Mokri　m Brad Fiedel　pd Tony Corbett
ed Hal Levinsohn
☆ Jamie Lee Curtis, Ron Silver, Clancy Brown, Elizabeth Pena, Louise Fletcher, Philip Bosco

'He's A Cop That's Not. Believe That!'

Blue Streak

US　1999　95m　DeLuxe
Columbia/Global (Toby Jaffe, Neal H. Moritz)

▬ ◎ ◎ 🎧

After serving his prison sentence, a jewel thief discovers that his hiding place for his loot is now a police station.
A corny excuse for a comedy is given occasional life by the vigorous performance of its star, but even he cannot salvage such hand-me-down material.
w Michael Berry, John Blumenthal, Steve Carpenter　d Les Mayfield　ph David Eggby
m Edward Shearmur　pd Bill Brzeski　ed Michael Tronick
☆ Martin Lawrence, Luke Wilson, Peter Greene, Dave Chappelle, William Forsythe, Nicole Ari Parker, Graham Beckel, Robert Miranda, Olek Krupa, Saverio Guerra
'Though unevenly devised as an homage to the whole range of '70s crime pics from blaxploitation to buddie cop comedies, modest production plays closer to a made-for-TV project than anything worthy of the big screen.' – Robert Koehler, Variety

Blue Thunder *

US　1983　110m　Technicolor　Panavision
Columbia/Rastar/Gordon Carroll

📼 📼 ▬ ℚ. ◎ 🎧

A policeman in Los Angeles' Astro Division is haunted by memories of Vietnam and goes berserk when using his new ultra-sophisticated helicopter to wage war against crime.
Slick but hollow thriller most remarkable for its helicopter stunting between city skyscrapers. Otherwise, it is too often fashionably inaudible and almost invisible.
w Dan O'Bannon, Don Jakoby　d John Badham
ph John A. Alonzo　m Arthur B. Rubinstein
ed Frank Morriss, Edward Abroms　aerial photography Frank Holgate
☆ Roy Scheider, Warren Oates, Candy Clark, Daniel Stern, Malcolm McDowell
† A watered-down TV version was quickly assembled, but its comic-strip dialogue grounded it after 13 episodes.
🎞 film editing

Blue Tiger

US　1994　87m　colour
NEO/Ozla (Michael Leahy, Aki Komine)

📼

After her young son is accidentally shot by a Japanese gangster, his mother searches for his killer, a man with a distinctive tattoo of a blue tiger.
On its own undemanding level, an enjoyable and well-made thriller.
w Joel Soisson　d Norberto Barba　ph Christopher Walling　md Larry Scharf　ed Caroline Ross
☆ Virginia Madsen, Harry Dean Stanton, Toru Nakamura, Ryo Ishibashi, Dean Hallo, Sal Lopez, Lewis Arquette, Henry Mortensen
'Handsome photography, slick direction and a fun script make this a top quality B-movie.' – Sight and Sound

The Blue Veil *

US　1951　114m　bw
RKO/Wald-Krasna (Raymond Hakim)
The vocational career of a children's nurse who descends into poverty but is rescued by one of her own charges, now grown up.
Sober American remake of a French tearjerker (Le Voile bleu) with the star suffering nobly but being upstaged by the cameo players.
w Norman Corwin, from the original by François Campaux　d Curtis Bernhardt　ph Franz Planer
m Franz Waxman
☆ Jane Wyman, Charles Laughton, Richard Carlson, Joan Blondell, Agnes Moorehead, Don Taylor, Audrey Totter, Everett Sloane, Cyril Cusack, Natalie Wood, Warner Anderson
🎞 Jane Wyman; Joan Blondell

Blue Velvet **

US　1986　120m　colour
De Laurentiis (Richard Roth)

📼 📼 📼 ℚ. ◎ ◎ ◎ 🎧

Murder, mutilation and sexual perversion in Middle America..
Bizarrely stylish exercise by the director of The Elephant Man (qv), popular at the box-office.
wd David Lynch　ph Frederick Elmes　m Angelo Badalamenti　pd Patricia Norris
☆ Kyle MacLachlan, Isabella Rossellini, Dennis Hopper, Laura Dern, Hope Lange, Dean Stockwell
'Horrifying in ways that genre horror movies never are … Lynch's nightmare has a sort of irregular, homemade quality, as if it had been cooked up with familiar but not entirely wholesome ingredients – a fresh apple pie with a couple of worms poking through the crust.' – Terrence Rafferty, Nation
🎞 David Lynch

Blue Water, White Death *

US　1971　99m　Techniscope
Blue Water Films/Cinema Center
A skilful and quite frightening documentary about the habits of the Great White Shark, with a lead-up showing events on the expedition which set out in search of it.
wd Peter Gimbel　ph James Lipscomb

Bluebeard: see Landru (1962)

Bluebeard *

US　1944　73m　bw
PRC

▬ ◎

A strangler of young girls is at large in Paris.
Poverty Row chiller with effective moments; possibly the most interesting film ever to come from PRC (which isn't saying very much).
w Pierre Gendron　d Edgar G. Ulmer　ph Jockey Feindel
☆ John Carradine, Jean Parker, Ludwig Stossel, Nils Asther, Iris Adrian

Bluebeard

France/Italy/Germany　1972　124m　Technicolor
Barnabé/Gloria/Geiselgasteig (Alexander Salkind)

▬

The lady-killer in this case is an Austrian aristocrat who has been driven to desperation and murder by a long line of mistresses whose bodies he keeps frozen in his cellar.
Would-be macabre comedy which becomes totally off-putting by its emphasis on close-up death agonies.
w Ennio de Concini, Edward Dmytryk, Maria Pia Fusco　d Edward Dmytryk　ph Gabor Pogany
m Ennio Morricone
☆ Richard Burton, Raquel Welch, Joey Heatherton, Virna Lisi, Nathalie Delon, Marilu Tolo
'Somewhere between (and a long way behind) Kind Hearts and Coronets and The Abominable Dr Phibes.' – Clyde Jeavons, MFB

Bluebeard's Eighth Wife *

US　1938　85m　bw
Paramount (Ernst Lubitsch)
The daughter of an impoverished French aristocrat marries for money a millionaire who has had seven previous wives, and determines to teach him a lesson.
Very thin sophisticated comedy with unsympathetic characters and little wit after the first scene; a disappointment from the talent involved.
w Charles Brackett, Billy Wilder　play Alfred Savoir　d Ernst Lubitsch　ph Leo Tover　m Werner Heymann, Frederick Hollander
☆ Claudette Colbert, Gary Cooper, David Niven, Edward Everett Horton, Elizabeth Patterson, Herman Bing, Warren Hymer, Franklin Pangborn
'Light and sometimes bright, but it gets a bit tiresome.' – Variety
'In these days it is bad enough to have to admire millionaires in any circumstances; but a

millionaire with a harem complex simply can't help starting the bristles on the back of a sensitive neck.' – New York Times
† A previous version, released by Paramount in 1923 and directed by Sam Wood, starred Gloria Swanson and Huntley Gordon.

Bluebeard's Seven Wives *

US　1926　94m　bw　silent
First National
A bank teller becomes a film star and is transformed, notably by seven imaginary marriages.
Amusing spoof on the film industry that was.
w Blanche Merrill, Paul Scofield　d Alfred Santell
☆ Ben Lyon, Lois Wilson, Blanche Sweet, Dorothy Sebastian, Sam Hardy

Bluebeard's Ten Honeymoons

GB　1960　93m　bw
Anglo-Allied (Roy Parkinson)
Another version of the story of Landru, alternating wildly between fantasy, farce and melodrama.
Not a success in any of its moods.
w Myles Wilder　d W. Lee Wilder　ph Stephen Dade　m Albert Elms
☆ George Sanders, Corinne Calvet, Patricia Roc, Ingrid Hafner, Jean Kent, Greta Gynt, Maxine Audley, Selma Vaz Diaz, George Coulouris
'The undefying narrative is developed along the most obvious lines imaginable.' – MFB

Blueberry Hill

US　1988　93m　colour
MGM/Mediacom/Prism/MVA-1/Tricoast (Mark Michaels)

▬

In an isolated logging community, a mother tries to conceal from her daughter the truth about her dead father.
Unoriginal domestic drama of young rebellion, set in the 50s, which provides the excuse for its soundtrack of rock 'n' roll hits.
w Lonon Smith　d Strathford Hamilton　ph David Lewis　m Ira Ingber　pd John Sperry Wade
ed Marcy Hamilton
☆ Carrie Snodgress, Margaret Avery, Jennifer Rubin, Matt Lattanzi, Tommy Swerdlow

The Bluebird: see The Blue Bird

A Blueprint for Murder *

US　1953　77m　bw
TCF (Michael Abel)
After the death of his brother and niece, a man proves that his sister-in-law is a murderess.
Unpleasant but efficient murder story with enough twists to keep one watching.
wd Andrew Stone　ph Leo Tover　m David Raksin
md Lionel Newman
☆ Jean Peters, Joseph Cotten, Gary Merrill, Catherine McLeod, Jack Kruschen

Blueprint for Robbery *

US　1960　87m　bw
Paramount (Bryan Foy)
Crooks plan and execute a robbery, agreeing not to touch the proceeds for two and a half years. But some get tired of waiting...
Minor but effective crime melodrama in semi-documentary vein.
w Irwin Winehouse, A. Sanford Wolf　d Jerry Hopper　ph Loyal Griggs　m Van Cleave
☆ J. Pat O'Malley, Robert Gist, Romo Vincent, Marion Ross, Tom Duggan
'A not uninteresting entry in the screen log-book on crime.' – MFB

The Blues Brothers *

US　1980　133m　Technicolor
Universal (Robert K. Weiss)

📼 📼 ▬ ◎ 🎧

A massive car chase develops when two brothers collect money for their old orphanage without too much regard for law and order.
Fashionable chase comedy with so many stunts that its cost ran up to 33,000,000 dollars. The public stayed away, though it has gained a cult following since.
w Dan Aykroyd, John Landis　d John Landis
ph Stephen M. Katz　md Ira Newborn　pd John Lloyd
☆ John Belushi, Dan Aykroyd, Kathleen Freeman, James Brown, Henry Gibson, Cab Calloway, Carrie Fisher
'It meanders expensively like some pedigreed shaggy dog through 70s/80s American cinema

and 50s/60s American rock, cocking its leg happily at every popular landmark on the way.' – Paul Taylor, MFB
'There's not a soupçon of wit or ingenuity in this brainless exercise in overspending.' – Daily Mail
'There's even room, in the midst of the carnage and mayhem, for a surprising amount of grace, humor and whimsy.' – Roger Ebert

Blues Brothers 2000

US　1998　123m　DeLuxe
Universal (John Landis, Dan Aykroyd, Leslie Belzberg)

📼 ▬ ℚ. ◎ 🎧

Chased by cops, gangsters and militia, an ex-jailbird and singer tries to reassemble his old band.
Virtually a remake of The Blues Brothers; even those who enjoyed its conspicuous destruction and ersatz rhythm and blues the first time around may find this more is worse.
w Dan Aykroyd, John Landis　d John Landis
ph David Herrington　m Paul Shaffer　pd Bill Brodie　ed Dale Beldin
☆ Dan Aykroyd, John Goodman, Joe Morton, J. Evan Bonifant, Nia Peeples, Frank Oz, Steve Lawrence, Aretha Franklin, James Brown, B. B. King
'A warmed-up corpse of a movie, having neither the courage to do anything new or the wit to make a joke out of its own unoriginality.' – Adam Smith, Empire

Blues for Lovers: see Ballad in Blue

Blues in the Night *

US　1941　88m　bw
Warner (Henry Blanke)
Career and romantic problems for the members of a travelling jazz band.
Atmospheric little melodrama with good score and smart dialogue.
w Robert Rossen　play Hot Nocturne by Edwin Gilbert　d Anatole Litvak　ph Ernest Haller
m/ly Harold Arlen, Johnny Mercer
☆ Priscilla Lane, Richard Whorf, Lloyd Nolan, Betty Field, Jack Carson, Elia Kazan, Wallace Ford, Billy Halop, Peter Whitney
🎞 title song (mHarold Arlen, lyJohnny Mercer)

Blume in Love *

US　1973　116m　Technicolor
Warner (Paul Mazursky)

▬

A divorced American lawyer in Venice reminisces about his love life.
Shapeless but enjoyable 'serious comedy' with star and director in good form.
wd Paul Mazursky　ph Bruce Surtees　m various
☆ George Segal, Susan Anspach, Kris Kristofferson, Marsha Mason, Shelley Winters

BMX Bandits

🏃 Australia　1984　90m　colour
Panavision
Rank/BMX/Nilsen (Tom Broadbridge, Paul Davies)
Bike enthusiasts become unpopular when they cause havoc in the streets, but become heroes when they capture bank robbers.
Lively action piece with unacceptable behaviour followed by reformation and an old-fashioned moral for early teenagers.
w Patrick Edgeworth　story Russell Hagg　d Brian Trenchard-Smith　ph John Seale　m Colin Stead, Frank Strangio　pd Ross Major　ed Alan Lake
☆ David Argue, John Ley, Nicole Kidman, Bryan Marshall, Angelo d'Angelo

Boardwalk

US　1979　100m　Eastmancolor
ITC/Stratford (Gerald T. Herrod)
An old couple in Coney Island are affected by escalating violence.
Well-meaning but somewhat absurd moral tale for our times, in which the harassed septuagenarian finally chokes the young punk leader to death.
w Stephen Verona, Leigh Chapman　d Stephen Verona　ph Billy Williams　m various
☆ Ruth Gordon, Lee Strasberg, Janet Leigh, Joe Silver, Eddie Barth
'One would probably have to reach as far back as The Birth of a Nation to find a more direct incitement to racial hatred.' – Richard Combs, MFB

The Boat **

West Germany 1981 149m Fujicolour
Columbia/Bavaria Atelier/Radiant Film (Gunter Röhrbach)

original and US title: *Das Boot*

Adventures of a German U-boat during World War II.

Well-crafted but totally unsurprising saga of heroism and self-sacrifice; a decent view of war from the German side, designed to impress world markets. It did so only moderately.

wd Wolfgang Petersen ph Jost Vacano m Klaus Doldinger ad Rolf Zehetbauer

☆ Jürgen Prochnow, Herbert Grönemeyer, Klaus Wennemann, Hubertus Bengsch, Martin Semmelrogge

† A director's cut, running for 209m, was released in 1997.

⚱ direction; screenplay (adaptation); cinematography; editing; sound; sound editing

The Boatmen: see *Prisoner of the Volga*

The Boatniks *

🧍🧍 US 1970 100m Technicolor
Walt Disney (Ron Miller)

An accident-prone coastguard officer creates havoc at a yachting marina but is acclaimed a hero after catching three jewel thieves.

Simple fresh-air farce for the family, pleasantly set but flatly directed.

w Arthur Julian d Norman Tokar ph William Snyder m Robert F. Brunner

☆ Phil Silvers, Robert Morse, Stefanie Powers, Norman Fell, Mickey Shaughnessy, Wally Cox, Don Ameche, Joey Forman

Bob & Carol & Ted & Alice **

US 1969 105m Technicolor
Columbia/M. J. Frankovich (Larry Tucker)

Two California couples, influenced by a group therapy session advocating natural spontaneous behaviour, decide to admit their extra-marital affairs and narrowly avoid a wife-swapping party.

Fashionable comedy without the courage of its convictions: it starts and finishes very bashfully, but there are bright scenes in the middle. An attempt to extend it into a TV series was a failure.

w Paul Mazursky, Larry Tucker d Paul Mazursky ph Charles E. Lang m Quincy Jones

☆ Natalie Wood, Robert Culp, Elliott Gould, Dyan Cannon, Horst Ebersberg

'An old-fashioned romantic comedy disguised as a blue picture.' – *Arthur Schlesinger Jnr*

⚱ Paul Mazursky, Larry Tucker; Charles E. Lang; Elliott Gould; Dyan Cannon

The Bob Mathias Story

US 1954 80m bw
Allied Artists

GB title: *The Flaming Torch*

The biography of an American athlete who won the Decathlon in the 1952 Olympics.

Predictable low-budgeter of no abiding interest.

w Richard Collins d Francis D. Lyon

☆ Bob Mathias, Ward Bond, Melba Mathias, Ann Doran, Howard Petrie

Bob Roberts **

US 1992 104m Technicolor
Rank/Polygram/Working Title/Live Entertainment (Forrest Murray)

An American folk singer and right-wing politician makes a record that goes to the top of the hit parade and wins a seat in the Senate.

Clever satire on politics, done as a documentary film, that has the message that it is appearance and the manipulation of the media that counts, not reality.

wd Tim Robbins ph Jean Lépine m David Robbins pd Richard Hoover ed Lisa Churgin

☆ Tim Robbins, Giancarlo Esposito, Alan Rickman, Ray Wise, Brian Murray, Gore Vidal, Rebecca Jenkins, Harry J. Lennix, Susan Sarandon, John Cusack, Bob Balaban

'Both a stimulating social satire and a depressing commentary on the devolution of the US political system.' – *Variety*

Bob, Son of Battle

US 1947 110m Technicolor
TCF (Robert Bassler)

aka: *Thunder in the Valley*

A surly old shepherd discovers that his sheepdog, which he loves above his son, is a killer.

Soft-centred family drama that relies overmuch on Gwenn's roguish charm and sudden redemption.

w Jerome Cady novel Alfred Ollivant d Louis King ph Charles Clarke m Cyril Mockridge

☆ Edmund Gwenn, Lon McCallister, Peggy Ann Garner, Reginald Owen, Charles Irwin, Dave Thursby, John Rogers, Leyland Hodgson

Bobbikins

GB 1959 90m bw Cinemascope
TCF (Oscar Brodney, Bob McNaught)

A downtrodden variety artist finds that his baby can not only talk but also give him tips on the stock exchange.

Not at all a good idea, and feebly executed.

w Oscar Brodney d Robert Day ph Geoffrey Faithfull m Philip Green

☆ Max Bygraves, Shirley Jones, Billie Whitelaw, Barbara Shelley, Colin Gordon, Charles Tingwell, Lionel Jeffries, Rupert Davies

'He had to meet her – to find himself!'

Bobby Deerfield

US 1977 123m Metrocolor Panavision
Warner/First Artists (Sydney Pollack)

A depressive motor racing driver falls for a girl with an incurable illness.

A kind of understated Love Story (qv) for intellectuals; nicely made, but nothing that anybody will be wildly concerned about.

w Alvin Sargent novel Heaven Has No Favourites by Erich Maria Remarque d Sydney Pollack ph Henri Decaë m Dave Grusin pd Stephen Grimes

☆ Al Pacino, Marthe Keller, Anny Duperey, Walter McGinn, Romolo Valli, Jaime Sanchez

The Bobo

US 1967 105m Technicolor
Warner/Gina (Elliott Kastner, Jerry Gershwin) (David R. Schwartz)

An unsuccessful and timid bullfighter is offered a contract if within three days he can seduce the local belle.

Stylized, silly and boring comedy from an obviously dated play; Chaplinesque pathos was not this star's strong suit.

w David R. Schwartz play David R. Schwartz novel Olimpia by Burt Cole d Robert Parrish ph Gerry Turpin m Francis Lai

☆ Peter Sellers, Britt Ekland, Rossano Brazzi, Adolfo Celi, Hattie Jacques, Ferdy Mayne, Kenneth Griffith, John Wells

Bob's Birthday **

GB 1993 11m colour
Snowden Fine Animation/Channel 4/NFBC (Alison Snowden, David Fine)

A dentist is unhappy about celebrating his 40th birthday, while his wife prepares a surprise party for him.

Witty animated cartoon about middle-aged angst and embarrassment.

wd Alison Snowden, David Fine m Patrick Godfrey

☆ Featuring the voices of: Andy Hamilton, Harry Enfield, Alison Snowden

🧍 animated short

La Boca del Lobo **

Peru/Spain 1988 116m Agfacolor
New People's Cinema/Twinray/Inca Films/Tornasol Films (Gerardo Herrero, Francisco J. Lombardi)

English title: *The Lion's Den*

A tough and embittered lieutenant orders his troops to massacre villagers sympathetic to the Communists.

Gripping investigation of the morality of war, based on a true incident.

w Augusto Cabada, Giovanni Pollarolo, Gerardo Herrero d Francisco J. Lombardi ph Jose Luis Lopez Linares m Bernardo Bonezzi pd Marta Mendez ed Juan San Mateo

☆ Gustavo Bueno, Tono Vega, Joe Tejada, Gilberto Torres, Antero Sanchez, Aristoteles Picho, Fernando Vasquez, Luis Saavedra, Bertha Pagaza

Boccaccio '70 *

Italy/France 1962 210m Eastmancolor
TCF/CCC/Cineriz/Francinex/Gray Films (Antonio Cervi, Carlo Ponti)

Four modern stories which Boccaccio might have written (on an off day).

Overlong portmanteau with inevitable bright moments but many more longueurs. The fourth episode was dropped when the film was released in the States and elsewhere.

The Temptation of Dr Antonio

w Federico Fellini, Tullio Pinelli, Ennio Flaiano d Federico Fellini ph Otello Martelli; with Anita Ekberg

The Job

w Suso Cecchi d'Amico, Luchino Visconti d Luchino Visconti ph Giuseppe Rotunno; with Romy Schneider, Tomas Milian

The Raffle

w Cesare Zavattini d Vittorio de Sica ph Otello Martelli; with Sophia Loren

Renzo and Luciana

d Mario Monicelli

Boda Secreta: see *Secret Wedding*

Bodies, Rest and Motion

US 1993 94m DeLuxe
Electric/Fine Line/August (Allan Mindel, Denise Shaw, Eric Stoltz)

A couple split up: he goes in search of his parents with a stolen television set, she begins a casual affair with a decorator.

An aimless movie about feckless people, the sort of film you'd continue watching on television if the remote control was not to hand.

w Roger Hedden d Michael Steinberg ph Bernd Heinl m Michael Convertino pd Stephen McCabe ed Jay Cassidy

☆ Phoebe Cates, Bridget Fonda, Tim Roth, Eric Stoltz, Alicia Witt, Sandra Lafferty, Peter Fonda

'Uncompelling but moderately engaging throughout.' – *Variety*

'Billed as a comedy, it's mighty short on laughs.' – *Sheila Johnston, Independent*

Body and Soul

US 1931 82m bw
Fox

In the 1914–1918 war, a flyer falls for the wife of his dead buddy.

Tedious and often risible romantic melodrama.

w Jules Furthman play Squadrons by A. E. Thomas d Alfred Santell

☆ Charles Farrell, Elissa Landi, Humphrey Bogart, Myrna Loy, Donald Dillaway

'Kidding is almost bound to creep in.' – *Variety*

Body and Soul *

US 1947 104m bw
Enterprise (Bob Roberts)

A young boxer fights his way unscrupulously to the top.

Melodramatic but absorbing study of prizefighting's seamy side. (Is there any other?) Inventively studio-bound and almost impressionist in treatment.

w Abraham Polonsky d Robert Rossen ph James Wong Howe m Hugo Friedhofer md Rudolph Polk ed Francis Lyon, Robert Parrish

☆ John Garfield, Lilli Palmer, Hazel Brooks, Anne Revere, William Conrad, Joseph Pevney, Canada Lee

'Here are the gin and tinsel, squalor and sables of the depression era, less daring than when first revealed in *Dead End* or *Golden Boy* but more valid and mature because shown without sentiment or blur.' – *National Board of Review*

🧍 Francis Lyon, Robert Parrish

⚱ Abraham Polonsky; John Garfield

Body and Soul

US 1981 122m colour
Cannon/Golan-Globus (Cliff Roquemore)

An amateur boxer turns professional to earn money for medical treatment for his kid sister.

Blood in the ring, sentimentality on the sidelines. Despite the credit, this repellent movie has virtually no connection with the previous 'version'.

The Body Disappears

US 1941 72m bw
Warner (Ben Stoloff)

A professor invents an invisibility formula.

Uninspired comedy switch on a familiar theme.

w Scott Darling, Erna Lazarus d D. Ross Lederman ph Allen G. Seigler m Howard Jackson

☆ Edward Everett Horton, Jeffrey Lynn, Jane Wyman, Herbert Anderson, Marguerite Chapman, Craig Stevens, David Bruce, Willie Best

w Leon Isaac Kennedy screenplay Abraham Polonsky d George Bowers ph James Forrest m Webster Lewis

☆ Leon Isaac Kennedy, Jayne Kennedy, Muhammad Ali, Michael Gazzo, Perry Lang, Kim Hamilton, Peter Lawford

Body Count

GB/US 1997 84m DeLuxe
Polygram/Island/Main Line (Mark Burg, Doug McHenry, George Jackson)

Four quarrelling art thieves, on the run from cops, pick up a double-crossing woman along the way.

Slick but uninvolving thriller, with an unhelpful style in flashbacks.

w Theodore Witcher d Robert Patton-Spruill ph Charles Mills m Curt Sobel pd Tim Eckel ed Richard Nord

☆ David Caruso, Linda Fiorentino, John Leguizamo, Ving Rhames, Donnie Wahlberg, Forest Whitaker

Body Double

US 1984 114m Metrocolor
Columbia/Delphi II (Brian de Palma)

An out-of-work actor finds himself drawn into a nightmare when he spies on a lady stripteaser across the street.

Semi-porno melodrama with many echoes of Hitchcock overlaid with fashionable extremes of violence.

w Robert J. Avrech, Brian de Palma d Brian de Palma ph Stephen H. Burum m Pino Donaggio pd Ida Random ed Jerry Greenberg, Bill Pankow

☆ Craig Wasson, Gregg Henry, Melanie Griffith

'De Palma lets all his obsessions hang out.' – *Variety*

'She taught him everything he knew – about passion and murder!'

Body Heat **

US 1981 113m Technicolor
Warner/Ladd (Fred T. Gallo)

A Florida lawyer becomes involved with a married woman and they plot to kill her businessman husband.

Oversexed and superfluous, not to mention uncredited, revamp of Double Indemnity (qv). Some evidence of flair does not relieve that 'I have been here before' feeling.

wd Lawrence Kasdan ph Richard H. Kline m John Barry pd Bill Kenney ed Carol Littleton

☆ William Hurt, Kathleen Turner, Richard Crenna, Ted Danson

'Film noir, if it is to be successfully reworked, needs to be approached with a sense of analysis, rather than simple excess.' – *Steve Jenkins, MFB*

Body Melt

Australia 1993 84m colour
Dumb Films/Australian Film Commission/Film Victoria (Rod Bishop, Daniel Scharf)

A mad scientist invents a vitamin supplement that has an appalling side-effect: it causes people to explode or disintegrate.

A gruesomely visceral horror with stomach-turning effects; beneath all the gore there are signs of a certain wit and intelligence at work.

w Philip Brophy, Rod Bishop d Philip Brophy ph Ray Argall m Philip Brophy pd Maria Kozic ed Bill Murphy sp Bob McCarron

☆ Gerard Kennedy, Andrew Daddo, Ian Smith, Vince Gil, Regina Gaigalas, Maurie Annese, Nick Polites, William McInnes

'A schlocky, tongue-in-cheek gore pic … cheerfully sick humor.' – *Variety*

† The film's credits include the unusual lines: 'Testicles Philip Brophy, Buttocks Maria Kozic'.

Body of Evidence

US   1992   99m   DeLuxe
UIP/Dino de Laurentiis
⊞ ▤ ▦ ℚ ♫

A woman, who is accused of killing the elderly man who left her a fortune in his will, begins an affair with her defence counsel.
Almost silly enough to be enjoyable, in its calculated mix of kinky sex and courtroom scenes, but finally it is just too silly for words.
w Brad Mirman d Uli Edel ph Doug Milsome m Graeme Revell pd Victoria Paul ed Thom Noble
☆ Madonna, Willem Dafoe, Joe Mantegna, Anne Archer, Julianne Moore, Jurgen Prochnow, Frank Langella, Stan Shaw
    'This showcase for the singer-thesp as femme fatale is titillating enough to lure an initially curious public and follow up as a good video title, but its theatrical endurance would seem closer to that of her victim than to Madonna's.' – *Variety*

Body Parts

US   1991   88m   Technicolor   Panavision
Paramount (Frank Mancuso Jnr)
⊞ ▤ ▦ ℚ

A psychiatrist, injured in a car crash, is one of several patients to have body parts transplanted from a homicidal maniac, with predictable results.
Dull horror movie that tries to revive an old, familiar plot by injecting plenty of gore.
w Eric Red, Norman Snider novel *Choice Cuts* by Boileau-Narcejac story Patricia Herskovic, Joyce Taylor d Eric Red ph Theo Van de Sande m Loek Dikker pd Bill Brodie ed Anthony Redman
☆ Jeff Fahey, Lindsay Duncan, Zakes Mokae, Kim Delaney, Peter Murnik, Paul Benvictor, Brad Dourif

'There are movies that define every decade... One night will change eight lives forever.'
Body Shots

US   1999   106m   DeLuxe   Panavision
Entertainment/New Line (Jennifer Keohane, Harry Colomby)
▤ ♫

The sexual misadventures of four young men and women in Los Angeles.
A drama of casual coupling, centred around the accusation of rape from one participant; what begins as comedy ends as a more earnest investigation of varying sexual attitudes, but it never strikes the right note in either part.
w David McKenna d Michael Cristofer ph Rodrigo García m Mark Isham pd David J Bomba ed Eric Sears
☆ Sean Patrick Flanery, Jerry O'Connell, Amanda Peet, Tara Reid, Ron Livingston, Emily Procter, Brad Rowe, Sybil Temchen
    'Essentially an exercise in adult TV framed for widescreen. The project exudes a lush look entombed in a self-important manner that's culturally tone-deaf.' – *Robert Koehler, Variety*

Body Slam

US   1987   89m   CFI color
Musifilm/Hemdale (Shel Lytton, Mike Curb)
▤

A promoter on the skids accidentally creates the rock 'n' wrestling craze.
Easy-going comedy which would have benefited from more confident production.
w Shel Lytton, Steve Burkow d Hal Needham ph Mike Shea m Michael Lloyd, John D'Andrea ad Pamela Warner ed Randy Thornton
☆ Dirk Benedict, Tanya Roberts, Roddy Piper, Lou Albano, Charles Nelson Reilly, Billy Barty, Barry Gordon, John Astin

'Shriek And Shudder.'
'Graves Raided! Coffins Robbed! Corpses Carved! Midnight Murder! Body Blackmail! Stalking Ghouls! Mad Thrills Of Terror And Macabre Mystery!'
The Body Snatcher ***

US   1945   77m   bw
RKO (Val Lewton)
⊞ ▤ ℚ

In 19th-century Edinburgh a doctor obtains 'specimens' from grave-robbers, and murder results when supplies run short.

A familiar theme very imaginatively handled, and well acted, though the beginning is slow. The best of the Lewton thrillers.
w Philip MacDonald, Carlos Keith (Val Lewton) story R. L. Stevenson d Robert Wise ph Robert de Grasse m Roy Webb
☆ Henry Daniell, Boris Karloff, Bela Lugosi, Edith Atwater, Russell Wade
    'A humane sincerity and a devotion to good cinema ... However, most of the picture is more literary than lively.' – *Time*

'Imagine ... You're Gone And Someone Else Is Living Inside Your Body.'
Body Snatchers **

US   1993   90m   Technicolor
Warner (Robert H. Solo)
⊞ ▤

Aliens replicate and replace the inhabitants of military camps.
An effective and suspenseful retelling of the classic of conformity and paranoia, given a modern gloss with its teenage heroine and its concerns about toxic waste and environmental damage.
w Stuart Gordon, Dennis Paoli, Nicholas St John novel Jack Finney story Raymond Cistheri, Larry Cohen d Abel Ferrara ph Bojan Bazelli m Joe Delia pd Peter Jamison ed Anthony Redman
☆ Gabrielle Anwar, Terry Kinney, Billy Wirth, Meg Tilly, Christine Elise, R. Lee Ermey, G. Elvis Phillips, Reilly Murphy, Kathleen Doyle, Forest Whitaker
    'A tremendously exciting thriller that compares favourably with Don Siegel's classic.' – *Variety*
    'A gem which seduces the eye, captures the imagination and makes the adrenalin race.' – *Sight and Sound*
† The film was released direct to video in Britain. Jack Finney's novel was filmed in 1956 by Don Siegel and remade in 1978 by Philip Kaufman under the title *Invasion of the Body Snatchers* (qqv), the later version also being produced by Robert H. Solo.

Body Stealers

GB   1969   91m   colour
Tigon (Tony Tenser)
US title: *Thin Air*
A NATO general calls for an investigation when parachutists training for space disappear in mid-air.
Conventional low-budget science fiction, predictable from the first moment to the last.
w Mike St Clair, Peter Marcus d Gerry Levy ph Johnny Coquillon m Reg Tilsey ad Wilfred Arnold ed Howard Lanning
☆ George Sanders, Maurice Evans, Patrick Allen, Hilary Dwyer, Lorna Wilde, Neil Connery, Robert Flemyng, Allan Cuthbertson

The Bodyguard: see Yojimbo (1961)

'Never let her out of your sight. Never let your guard down. Never fall in love.'
The Bodyguard

US   1992   129m   Technicolor
Warner/Tig/Kasdan Pictures (Lawrence Kasdan, Jim Wilson, Kevin Costner)
⊞ ▤ ℚ ⊛ ⊚ ♫

A former CIA agent is hired as a bodyguard by a singer who has received threats on her life.
Predictable mix of song, romance and action that found surprising favour at the box-office.
w Lawrence Kasdan d Mick Jackson ph Andrew Dunn m Alan Silvestri pd Jeffrey Beecroft ed Richard A. Harris
☆ Kevin Costner, Whitney Houston, Gary Kemp, Bill Cobbs, Ralph Waite, Tomas Arana, Michele Lamar Richards, Mike Starr
    'A jumbled mess with a few enjoyable moments but little continuity or flow.' – *Variety*
    'The film is highly professional and perfectly watchable. But there's nothing memorable in it at all.' – *Derek Malcolm, Guardian*
♫ Song: 'I Have Nothing' (mJud Friedmann, lyAllan Rich); song: 'Run to You'

'The big comedy of nineteen sexty-sex!'
Boeing-Boeing

US   1965   102m   Technicolor
Paramount/Hal B. Wallis
▤ ℚ

By successfully juggling with plane schedules, a Paris journalist manages to live with three air hostesses at the same time.

Frenetic, paper-thin sex comedy from a one-joke play; film style generally undistinguished. It was Jerry Lewis's first 'straight' role.
w Edward Anhalt play Marc Camoletti d John Rich ph Lucien Ballard m Neal Hefti
☆ Tony Curtis, Jerry Lewis, Dany Saval, Christiane Schmidtmer, Suzanna Leigh, Thelma Ritter
    'A sort of jet-age French farce.' – *Judith Crist*

The Bofors Gun *

GB   1968   105m   Technicolor
Rank/Everglades (Robert A. Goldston, Otto Plaschkes)
In 1954 Germany a British army unit runs into trouble when a violent and unstable Irish private picks on a weakly National Service corporal.
Keen, fascinating, but often crude and eventually rather silly expansion of a TV play chiefly notable for the excellent acting opportunities provided by its unattractive but recognizable characters.
w John McGrath play *Events While Guarding the Bofors Gun* by John McGrath d Jack Gold ph Alan Hume m Carl Davis
☆ Nicol Williamson, John Thaw, David Warner, Ian Holm
ⓣ Ian Holm

Bogus

US   1996   110m   DeLuxe   Panavision
Warner/Regency/Yorktown/New Regency (Arnon Milchan, Norman Jewison, Jeff Rothberg)
⊞ ▤ ℚ

An orphan who goes to live with his child-hating aunt invents an imaginary friend.
Slight and sentimental fantasy that depends too much on the slender charms of its stars, who are at their most smug.
w Alvin Sargent story Jeff Rothberg, Francis X. McCarthy d Norman Jewison ph David Watkin m Marc Shaiman pd Ken Adam ed Stephen Rivkin
☆ Whoopi Goldberg, Gérard Depardieu, Haley Joel Osment, Nancy Travis, Denis Mercier, Ute Lemper, Sheryl Lee Ralph
    'Sweetly sentimental and anachronistically whimsical.' – *Variety*

La Bohème *

France/Italy   1988   107m   Eastmancolor
Electric Pictures/Erato Films/La Sept/SFPC/Generale d'Images, Travelling Productions/Video-Schermo (Jean-Claude Borlat)
Uncinematic treatment of Puccini's opera, though well enough sung.
w Giuseppe Giacosa, Luigi Illica novel *Scènes de la vie de Bohème* by Henri Murger d Luigi Comencini ph Armando Nannuzzi m Giacomo Puccini md James Conlon ad Paolo Comencini ed Sergio Buzi, Reine Wekstein
☆ Barbara Hendricks, Luca Canonici, Jose Carreras (voice only), Angela Maria Blasi, Gino Quilico

The Bohemian Girl *

↟↟ US   1936   74m   bw
Hal Roach
⊞ ▤ ℚ ✿

Gypsies kidnap a nobleman's daughter and bring her up as their own.
One of several operettas reworked for Laurel and Hardy, this is an inoffensive entertainment which devotes too little care to their need for slowly built-up gag structure; their sequences tend to fizzle out and the singing is a bore.
operetta Michael W. Balfe d James Horne, Charles Rogers ph Art Lloyd, Francis Corby md Nathaniel Shilkret ed Bert Jordan, Louis McManus
☆ Stan Laurel, Oliver Hardy, Mae Busch, Antonio Moreno, Jacqueline Wells, Darla Hood, Zeffie Tilbury, James Finlayson, Thelma Todd
† There was in 1922 a British silent version with a splendid cast including Ivor Novello, Gladys Cooper, C. Aubrey Smith, Ellen Terry and Constance Collier.

Il Boia di Venezia: see Executioner of Venice

'Welcome to the New American Dream'
Boiler Room *

US   2000   120m   DeLuxe
Entertainment/New Line (Suzanne Todd, Jennifer Todd)
A college drop-out joins a brokerage firm that makes its money by selling dubious stocks to gullible clients.
A study in high pressure salesmanship that updates Wall Street and Glengarry Glenn Ross without quite matching the verve or guilty fascination of either.
wd Ben Younger ph Enrique Chediak m The Angel pd Anne Stuhler ed Chris Peppe
☆ Giovanni Ribisi, Vin Diesel, Nia Long, Nicky Katt, Scott Caan, Ron Rifkin, Jamie Kennedy, Taylor Nichols, Tom Everett Scott, Ben Affleck
    'Portrays the testosterone-flavoured soup of the trading floor superbly.' – *James White, Total Film*
    'Seductive and disturbing...a dynamic piece of film-making.' – *James Cameron-Wilson, Film Review*

Boiling Point *

Japan   1990   96m   colour
ICA/Bandai/Shochiku/Fuji (Hisao Nabeshima, Takio Yoshida, Masayuki Mori)
⊞ ▤
original title: *3-4x Jugatsu*
An ineffectual garage worker discovers that passivity gets you nowhere when he becomes embroiled in a violent vendetta after punching a bullying local gangster.
An offbeat mix of deadpan comedy and deader-pan thriller with a disjointed narrative style, enlivened by quirky directorial touches and a visual wit.
wd Takeshi Kitano ph Katsumi Yanagishima ad Osumu Sasaki ed Toshio Taniguchi
☆ 'Beat' Takeshi (Takeshi Kitano), Masahiko Ono, Yuriko Ishida, Takahito Iguchi, Minoru Iizuka, Hisashi Igawa, Bengal, Katsuo Tokashiki
    'Formally inventive, profligate with visual and dramatic ideas, and always giving the sense that it has more creative horsepower under its bonnet than it needs to use, this film is a delight.' – *Tony Rayns, Sight and Sound*
    'As an absurdist gangster melodrama it has enough insight in its brutality to make Scorsese look to his Oriental laurels.' – *Tom Hutchinson, Film Review*

Boiling Point *

US/France   1993   92m   Technicolor
Guild/Warner/Hexagon (Marc Frydman, Leonardo de la Fuente)
⊞ ▤ ℚ

Two men have a week to solve their problems: a Treasury agent, obsessed with avenging the murder of his partner, and the [...] responsible for the killing.
Although promoted as an action film, this is more an engaging character study that hovers on the edge of cliché but manages to maintain its balance.
wd James B. Harris novel *Money Men* by Gerald Petievich ph King Baggot m Cory Lerois, John D'Andrea pd Ron Foreman ed Jerry Brady
☆ Wesley Snipes, Dennis Weaver, Lolita Davidovich, Viggo Mortensen, Dan Hedaya, Seymour Cassel, Jonathan Banks, Christine Elise, Tony Lo Bianco, Valerie Perrine
    'Low-key and bland in the extreme, it's strictly for film buffs.' – *Variety*
    'Hardly substantial, but it's also consistently entertaining.' – *Sight and Sound*

The Bold and the Brave

US   1956   87m   bw   Superscope
RKO/Hal E. Chester
An assortment of American types come together in the Italian campaign of 1944.
Routine war heroics chiefly remembered (if at all) for a crap game sequence.
w Robert Lewin d Lewis Foster ph Sam Leavitt m Herschel Burke Gilbert
☆ Wendell Corey, Mickey Rooney, Nicole Maurey, Don Taylor
§ Robert Lewin; Mickey Rooney

'He rose to fame on a ladder of dancing ladies!'
Bolero *

US   1934   85m   bw   Paramount
A New York dancer neglects his personal life to become king of the European night-club circuit.
Lively romantic drama which performed remarkably at the box-office and led to a kind of sequel, Rumba (qv).

↟↟ film suitable for family viewing   ⊞ VHS video-cassette for the British PAL system   ⊞ VHS video-cassette for the British PAL system in wide screen-format   ✿ Video cassette in a computer-colourised version   ▤ American NTSC video-cassette   ℚ Laser disc

Sally Rand performs the fan dance, for which she was famous.
w Carey Wilson, Kubec Glasmon, Ruth Ridenour, Horace Jackson d Wesley Ruggles ph Leo Tover
☆ George Raft, *Carole Lombard*, Sally Rand, Frances Drake, William Frawley, Ray Milland, Gertrude Michael

'A studio conference product: lots of surefire elements. On screen it's a little enervating … depends on Raft's popularity with the women.' – *Variety*

Bolero

US 1984 104m colour
Cannon/City (Bo Derek)
▦ ⊚↝

In 1926, a wealthy romantic girl travels the world in search of a man worthy of the sacrifice of her virginity.
Ludicrous sexual charade with unpleasant overtones resulting from the fact that the star's husband wrote and photographed this embarrassing piece of near-pornography.
wd John Derek ph John Derek m Peter Bernstein pd Alan Roderick-Jones
☆ Bo Derek, George Kennedy, Andrea Occhipinti, Greg Bensen, Ana Obregon

'The only ecstatic moment a filmgoer might derive will be at the discovery that it's over.' – *Philip Strick, MFB*

Bomba the Jungle Boy

↟↟ US 1949 71m bw or sepia
Monogram (Walter Mirisch)
Photographers in Africa meet a junior Tarzan who rescues their girlfriend.
Cut-rate hokum starring the lad who had played Johnny Weissmuller's 'son' in earlier Tarzan movies; it led to several tedious sequels.
Sequels were as follows:
1948 Bomba on Panther Island (76m, with Allene Roberts)
1949 Bomba and the Lost Volcano (76m, with Donald Woods), Bomba and the Hidden City (71m, with Paul Guilfoyle)
1950 Bomba and the Elephant Stampede (71m, with Myron Healey)
1951 Bomba and the African Treasure (70m, with Lyle Talbot), Bomba and the Jungle Girl (70m, with Karen Sharpe), Bomba and the Lion Hunters (75m, with Morris Ankrum)
1953 Safari Drums (71m, with Douglas Kennedy)
1954 The Golden Idol (71m, with Paul Guilfoyle), Killer Leopard (70m, with Beverly Garland)
1955 Lord of the Jungle (69m, with Wayne Morris)
w Jack de Witt, from the comic strip by Roy Rockwell d Ford Beebe ph William Sickner m Edward Kay
☆ Johnny Sheffield, Peggy Ann Garner, Onslow Stevens, Charles Irwin

Bombardier

US 1943 99m bw
RKO (Robert Fellows)
▦
Cadet bombardiers learn the realities of war on raids over Japan.
Totally routine recruiting poster heroics.
w John Twist d Richard Wallace ph Nicholas Musuraca m Roy Webb
☆ Pat O'Brien, Randolph Scott, Anne Shirley, Eddie Albert, Walter Reed, Robert Ryan, Barton MacLane

Bombay Clipper

US 1941 54m bw
Universal
On a clipper bound for Bombay, a reporter becomes involved in mystery and romance.
Capsule actioner with stock studio talent.
w Roy Chanslor, Stanley Rubin d John Rawlins
☆ William Gargan, Irene Hervey, Maria Montez, Charles Lang, Turhan Bey, Lloyd Corrigan, Mary Gordon

Bombay Mail

US 1933 66m bw
Universal
On a train between Calcutta and Bombay a Scotland Yard detective solves the murder of the Governor of Bengal.
Very tolerable mystery filler.
w Tom Reed, L. G. Blochman d Edwin L. Marin
☆ Edmund Lowe, Shirley Grey, Onslow Stevens, Ralph Forbes, Hedda Hopper

'It mixes a colourful set of characters and maintains a moderately absorbing pace.' – *Variety*

Bombay Talkie *

India 1970 105m Eastmancolor
Merchant-Ivory (Ismail Merchant)
▦
A sophisticated American woman comes to Bombay and falls for two men involved in film-making.
Interesting but unsatisfactory romantic drama, rather pointlessly set against film studio backgrounds.
w Ruth Prawer Jhabvala, James Ivory d James Ivory ph Subrata Mitra m Shankar Jaikishan
☆ Jennifer Kendal, Shashi Kapoor, Zia Mohyeddin

Bombers B-52

US 1957 106m Warnercolor Cinemascope
Warner (Richard Whorf)
GB title: *No Sleep till Dawn*
A USAF sergeant considers applying for a discharge so that he can earn more money in civilian life.
Glossy domestic melodrama punctuated by aircraft shots.
w Irving Wallace d Gordon Douglas ph William Clothier m Leonard Rosenman
☆ Karl Malden, Marsha Hunt, Natalie Wood, Efrem Zimbalist Jnr, Don Kelly

'No one questions the basic assumption – that the good life consists of servicing bigger and better bombers.' – *MFB*

Bomber's Moon

US 1943 70m bw
TCF
An American pilot crashlands into Germany and makes for the coast.
Modestly budgeted war adventure with conventional thrills.
w Kenneth Gamet d 'Charles Fuhr' (Edward Ludwig and Harold Schuster)
☆ George Montgomery, Annabella, Kent Taylor, Walter Kingsford, Martin Kosleck

Bombshell ***

US 1933 91m bw
MGM (Hunt Stromberg)
▦
GB title and aka: *Blonde Bombshell*
A glamorous film star yearns for a new image.
Crackpot farce which even by today's standards moves at a fair clip and enabled the star to give her best comedy performance.
w Jules Furthman, John Lee Mahin play Caroline Francke, Mack Crane d Victor Fleming ph Chester Lyons, Hal Rosson
☆ Jean Harlow, Lee Tracy, Frank Morgan, Franchot Tone, Pat O'Brien, Ivan Lebedeff, Una Merkel, Ted Healy, Isabel Jewell, C. Aubrey Smith, Louise Beavers, Leonard Carey, Mary Forbes

'Bound to click and the best legitimate comedy in a long time.' – *Variety*

Bombsight Stolen: see *Cottage to Let*

Bon Voyage *

US 1962 133m Technicolor
Walt Disney (Bill Walsh, Ron Miller)
An American family spends a holiday in Paris.
Simple-minded, overlong comedy of mishaps, with Daddy finally trapped in the sewer. Smoothly done of its kind.
w Bill Walsh novel Marrijane and Joseph Hayes d James Neilson ph William Snyder m Paul Smith
☆ Fred MacMurray, Jane Wyman, Michael Callan, Deborah Walley, Jessie Royce Landis, Tommy Kirk, Ivan Desny

Bonaventure: see *Thunder on the Hill*

Bond Street

GB 1948 107m bw
ABP/World Screenplays (Anatole de Grunwald)
Four stories, each concerning an item of an expensive wedding trousseau.
Mild and laboured short story compendium.
w Anatole de Grunwald d Gordon Parry ph Otto Heller m Benjamin Frankel

☆ Roland Young, Jean Kent, Paula Valenska, Kathleen Harrison, Derek Farr, *Kenneth Griffith*, Hazel Court, Ronald Howard

'Even a glimpse of actual Bond Street makes little contact with reality.' – *MFB*

'Two cops on the trail of a serial killer. They must see as one…They must act as one… They must think as one… Before another victim falls.'

The Bone Collector

US 1999 118m DeLuxe Super 35
Universal/Columbia (Martin Bregman, Louis A. Stroller, Michael Bregman)
▦ ⊚ ⌒
A paralysed former detective and forensic expert works with an inexperienced female cop to catch a serial killer.
A wearying, downbeat thriller of a familiar kind, dragged down by a script that makes little narrative sense and leaves too many questions unanswered.
w Jeremy Iacone novel Jeffery Deaver d Phillip Noyce ph Dean Semler m Craig Armstrong pd Nigel Phelps ed William Hoy
☆ Denzel Washington, Angelina Jolie, Queen Latifah, Michael Rooker, Mike McGlone, Leland Orser, Luis Guzman, John Benjamin Hickey

'One of the year's most gruesome movies… ingenious but preposterous.' – *Stephen Holden, New York Times*

Bone Daddy

Canada 1998 87m DeLuxe
Kushner-Locke (Lewis B. Chesler, Jean Desormeaux)
▦▦
After a former medical examiner writes a bestselling novel based on unsolved serial murders that happened seven years earlier, the killings begin again.
Gruesome and predictable thriller of no particular interest.
w Tom Szollosi d Mario Azzopardi ph Danny Nowak m Christophe Beck pd Jeff Ginn ed Dean Balser
☆ Rutger Hauer, Barbara Williams, R. H. Thomson, Joseph Kell, Robin Gammell, Blu Mankuma, Mimi Kuzyk

'Take one Wall Street tycoon, his Fifth Avenue mistress, a reporter hungry for fame, and make the wrong turn in The Bronx … then sit back and watch the sparks fly'

The Bonfire of the Vanities

US 1990 125m Technicolor
Warner (Brian de Palma)
▦▦ ⊚ ⌒
The successful life of a New York bond dealer crumbles when he is arrested for injuring a black youth in a street accident.
Strained attempt at social satire, miscast and missing all its targets.
w Michael Cristofer novel Tom Wolfe d Brian de Palma ph Vilmos Zsigmond m Dave Grusin pd Richard Sylbert ad Peter Lansdown Smith ed David Ray, Bill Pankow
☆ Tom Hanks, Bruce Willis, Melanie Griffith, Kim Cattrall, Saul Rubinek, Morgan Freeman, F. Murray Abraham, John Hancock, Kevin Dunn, Clifton James

'A misfire of inanities.' – *Variety*
† Julie Salamon's book *The Devil's Candy: The Bonfire of the Vanities Goes to Hollywood* follows the production from its inception to its release.

Le Bonheur *

France 1965 79m Eastmancolor
Parc/Mag Bodard
A young carpenter is happy with his wife and family, happier still when he finds a mistress, whom he marries when his wife is found drowned.
Slight, good looking, ambivalent little fable which finally expires in a surfeit of style.
wd Agnès Varda ph Jean Rabier, Claude Beausoleil m Mozart
☆ Jean-Claude Drouot, Claire Drouot, Marie-France Boyer

Le Bonheur Est dans le Pré *

France 1995 106m colour
Guild/Téléma/Canal+/Champ Poirier/France 2/France 3 (Charles Gassot)
▦▦
An unhappy factory owner leaves home to start a new life with a Spanish woman whose missing husband he resembles.

Undemanding comedy of sexual mishap, lacking the bite of its director's earlier movies.
w Florence Quentin d Etienne Chatiliez ph Philippe Welt m Pascal Andreaccchio ad Stéphane Makedonshy ed Ann Lafarge
☆ Michel Serrault, Eddy Mitchell, Sabine Azéma, Carmen Maura, François Morel, Guillaine Londez, Virginie Darmon, Eric Cantona

'A feel-good movie first and foremost, in which only the occasional force-fed duck or woman clipped round the ear is likely to dissent from the bucolic chorus of bliss.' – *Keith Reader, Sight and Sound*

Bonjour Tristesse *

GB 1957 93m Technicolor Cinemascope
Columbia/Wheel Films (Otto Preminger)
▦
A teenage girl becomes involved with her sophisticated father's amours and causes the death of his would-be mistress.
The novel's rather repellent characters are here played like royal personages against a background of Riviera opulence. The result is very odd but often entertaining, especially when it slips into self-parody.
w Arthur Laurents novel Françoise Sagan d Otto Preminger ph Georges Périnal m Georges Auric pd Roger Furse
☆ David Niven, Deborah Kerr, Jean Seberg, Mylene Demongeot, Geoffrey Horne, Juliette Greco, Martita Hunt, Walter Chiari, Jean Kent, Roland Culver

'An elegant, ice-cold charade of emotions.' – *Judith Crist*
'Sagan not so much translated as traduced – opened out, smartened up, the sickness overlaid with Riviera suntan.' – *Alexander Walker*
'Long, untidy, muddled and mushy.' – *Financial Times*
† Shot in monochrome for Paris, colour for the Riviera.

La Bonne Année: see *Happy New Year*

Bonne Chance

France 1935 75m bw
Sacha Guitry
An artist who wins a lottery takes on holiday with him, on a purely platonic basis, the girl who gave him half her ticket.
Modest star comedy which pleased at the time.
wd Sacha Guitry
☆ Sacha Guitry, Jacqueline Delubac, Robert Darthez

La Bonne Soupe

France/Italy 1963 97m bw
Belstar/Du Siècle/Dear Film (André Hakim)
A high-class prostitute tells her life story.
A saucy frolic complete with three-in-a-bed and rapidly closing doors; quite enjoyable of its kind.
wd Robert Thomas play Félicien Marceau ph Roger Hubert m Raymond le Sénéchal
☆ Annie Girardot, Marie Bell, Gérard Blain, Bernard Blier, Jean-Claude Brialy, Claude Dauphin, Sacha Distel, Daniel Gélin, Blanchette Brunoy, Jane Marken, Raymond Péllégrin, Franchot Tone

Les Bonnes Femmes **

France 1960 102m bw
Paris/Panitalia (Robert and Raymond Hakim)
⌒
aka: *The Girls*
Four shop assistants dream of getting away from the boredom and mediocrity of their lives.
Tough and compassionate study of women trapped in a second-rate world, from which death offers the only real escape.
w Paul Gégauff, Claude Chabrol d Claude Chabrol ph Henri Decaë m Paul Misraki, Pierre Jansen ed Jacques Gaillard
☆ Bernadette Lafont, Clotilde Joano, Stéphane Audran, Lucile Saint-Simon, Pierre Bertin, Jean-Louis Maury, Claude Berri, Mario David

'Uneven and, in parts, somewhat tedious and tawdry, yet it has more tenderness and is more emotionally compelling than much of Chabrol's more refined work.' – *Pauline Kael*

'They're young ... they're in love ... and they kill people!'
Bonnie and Clyde ****
US   1967   111m   Technicolor
Warner/Seven Arts/Tatira/Hiller (Warren Beatty)

In the early thirties, a car thief and the daughter of his intended victim team up to become America's most feared and ruthless bank robbers.
Technically brilliant evocation of sleepy mid-America at the time of the public enemies, using every kind of cinematic trick including fake snapshots, farcical interludes, dreamy soft-focus and a jazzy score. For all kinds of reasons a very influential film which even made extreme violence quite fashionable (and very bloody it is).
w David Newman, Robert Benton d Arthur Penn ph Burnett Guffey m Charles Strouse, using 'Foggy Mountain Breakdown' by Flatt and Scruggs
☆ Warren Beatty, Faye Dunaway, Gene Hackman, Estelle Parsons, Michael J. Pollard, Dub Taylor, Denver Pyle, Gene Wilder
  'It is a long time since we have seen an American film so perfectly judged.' – MFB
  '...all to the rickety twang of a banjo and a saturation in time and place.' – Judith Crist
  'The formula is hayseed comedy bursting sporadically into pyrotechnic bloodshed and laced with sentimental pop-Freudianism.' – John Simon
  'A film from which we shall date reputations and innovations in the American cinema.' – Alexander Walker
  'It works as comedy, as tragedy, as entertainment, as a meditation on the place of guns and violence in American society.' – Roger Ebert
  ⬥ Burnett Guffey; Estelle Parsons
  ⬥ best picture; David Newman, Robert Benton; Arthur Penn; Warren Beatty; Faye Dunaway; Gene Hackman; Michael J. Pollard
  ⬥ Faye Dunaway

The Bonnie Parker Story
US   1958   80m   bw
James H. Nicholson, Sam Arkoff
A waitress joins up with a cheap crook in a series of bank raids.
Tinpot 'B' gangster film chiefly notable for comparison with the later Bonnie and Clyde (qv). All it really has is a certain exuberance in the action sequences.
w Stan Shpetner d William Witney ph Jack Marta m Ronald Stein
☆ Dorothy Provine, Jack Hogan, Richard Bakalyan, Joseph Turkel

Bonnie Prince Charlie
GB   1948   140m   Technicolor
British Lion/London Films (Edward Black)

The hope of the Stuarts returns from exile but is eventually forced to flee again.
Good highland photography combines with appalling studio sets, an initially confused narrative, a draggy script and uneasy performances to produce an ill-fated attempt at a British historical epic. Alexander Korda, who masterminded it, sulked in public at the critical roasting, but on this occasion the critics were right.
w Clemence Dane d Anthony Kimmins ph Robert Krasker m Ian Whyte
☆ David Niven, Margaret Leighton, Jack Hawkins, Judy Campbell, Morland Graham, Finlay Currie, John Laurie
  'I have a sense of wonder about this film, beside which The Swordsman seems like a dazzling work of veracity and art. It is that London Films, having surveyed the finished thing, should not have quietly scrapped it.' – Richard Winnington
  'The picture is not lacking in moments of unconscious levity, what with David Niven rallying his hardy Highlanders to his standard in a voice hardly large enough to summon a waiter.' – New Yorker
  'Time has made it the film industry's biggest joke. But the joke turns a little sour when one reflects how extravagance, recklessness and sheer bungling administration during the fat and prosperous years left the British film industry so poor and vulnerable when the hard times came along.' – Gerald Garret, 1975

Bonnie Scotland *
US   1935   80m   bw
MGM/Hal Roach

Two Americans journey to Scotland to collect a non-existent inheritance, then follow their friend in the army and wind up in India.
Generally disappointing star comedy which still contains excellent sequences when it is not vainly trying to preserve interest in a boring plot. An obvious parody on Lives of a Bengal Lancer (qv), released earlier that year; Scotland has almost nothing to do with it.
w Frank Butler, Jeff Moffitt d James Horne ph Art Lloyd, Walter Lundin ed Bert Jordan
☆ Stan Laurel, Oliver Hardy, James Finlayson, Daphne Pollard, William Janney, June Lang
  'Packed with Laurel and Hardy hokum and good for plenty of laughs' – Boxoffice

Bonnie's Kids
US   1972   105m   Eastmancolor
Variety/Tommy J. Productions (Charles Stroud)

After killing their lecherous stepfather, two young women take to a life of sex and crime.
Cut-rate exploitation picture, celebrating amorality, that attempts to cash in on the success of Bonnie and Clyde (qv).
wd Arthur Marks ph Robert Charles Wilson m Carson Whitsett ed Richard Greer
☆ Tiffany Bolling, Robin Mattson, Leo Gordon, Steve Sandor, Scott Brady, Leonore Stevens, Alex Rocco, Timothy Brown

'You'll be tickled to death over this gay chiller diller!'
The Boogie Man Will Get You
US   1944   66m   bw
Columbia (Colbert Clark)
Bodies accumulate when mad doctors get to work creating supermen in a small village.
Desperately unfunny spoof notable only for the fact that it was attempted with these players and at that time.
w Edwin Blum d Lew Landers ph Henry Freulich md Morris Stoloff
☆ Boris Karloff, Peter Lorre, Maxie Rosenbloom, Jeff Donnell, Larry Parks, Maude Eburne, Don Beddoe

'The life of a dreamer, the days of a business and the nights in between.'
Boogie Nights **
US   1997   156m   DeLuxe   Panavision
Entertainment/New Line/Ghoulardi/Lawrence Gordon (Lloyd Levin, Paul Thomas Anderson, John Lyons, Joanne Sellar)

The rise and fall of a well-endowed youth who becomes a star of pornographic movies in the 70s.
An entertaining and sometimes savage account of the last moments of hard-core films, just before the industry switched to video; witty and satiric for much of the time, it is spoilt by its use of gratuitous violence to overcome its narrative flaws.
wd Paul Thomas Anderson ph Robert Elswit m Toby Emmerich pd Bob Ziembicki ed Dylan Tichenor
☆ Mark Wahlberg, Burt Reynolds, Julianne Moore, John C. Reilly, Don Cheadle, Heather Graham, Luis Guzman, Philip Seymour Hoffman, William H. Macy, Alfred Molina
  'Darkly comic, vastly entertaining and utterly original.' – Variety
  ⬥ Burt Reynolds; Julianne Moore; Paul Thomas Anderson (as writer)

The Book of Life
US/France   1998   63m   colour
La Sept Arte/Haut et Court/True Fiction (Thierry Cagianut, Matthew Myers)
On the last day of 1999, Jesus arrives in New York, reluctant to carry out his mission to bring the world to an end.
Disjointed, aimless movie in which the jerky, blurred handheld camera-work is a distraction, though the loquacious script is no aid to enjoyment, either.
wd Hal Hartley m Jim Denault ad Andy Biscontini ed Steve Hamilton
☆ Martin Donovan, Anna Köhler, Martin Pfeffercorn, Olga Alexandrova, Michael Ornstein, Paul Albe, Don Creech, Joseph McKenna, Abby Royle, P.J. Harvey

Book of Love *
US   1990   87m   CFI color
Entertainment/New Line

A successful writer remembers when he was 16 and was too shy to ask the girl he loved to go to the prom.
Pleasantly done, nostalgic rites-of-passage movie. It travels over familiar ground, but with a light tread.
w William Kotzwinkle novel Jack in the Box by William Kotzwinkle d Robert Shaye ph Peter Deming m Stanley Clarke pd C. J. Strawn ed Terry Stokes
☆ Chris Young, Keith Coogan, Aeryk Egan, Josie Bissett, Tricia Leigh Fisher, Danny Nucci, John Cameron Mitchell, Beau Dremann

Book of Numbers *
US   1973   80m   colour
Brut (Raymond St Jacques)

Black waiters set up a numbers racket in a small Arkansas town during the Depression, to the annoyance of white gangsters.
Enjoyable blaxploitation movie, energetic and driven by a genuine anger, perception and humour – the high spot is a courtroom scene – which overcomes many of its low-budget inadequacies.
w Larry Spiegel novel Robert Deane Pharr d Raymond St Jacques ph Gayne Rescher m Al Schackman, Sonny Terry, Brownie McGhee ad Robert D. Shepherd, Edward Burbridge ed Irving G. Rosenblum
☆ Raymond St Jacques, Philip M. Thomas, Freda Payne, Hope Clarke, D'Urville Martin, Gilbert Green

'She outlived six rich men!'
Boom!
GB   1968   113m   Technicolor   Panavision
Universal/World Film Services/Moon Lake Productions (John Heyman, Norman Priggen)
On the volcanic Mediterranean island which she owns, a dying millionairess plans to take as her last lover a wandering poet who is the angel of death.
Pretentious, boring nonsense, showing that when talent goes awry it certainly goes boom.
w Tennessee Williams play The Milk Train Doesn't Stop Here Any More by Tennessee Williams d Joseph Losey ph Douglas Slocombe m John Barry
☆ Elizabeth Taylor, Richard Burton, Noël Coward, Michael Dunn, Joanna Shimkus
  'It's a beautiful picture, the best ever made of one of my plays.' – Tennessee Williams
  'A pointless, pompous nightmare.' – Paul D. Zimmermann, Newsweek
  'An ordeal in tedium.' – Hollywood Reporter
  'Outright junk.' – Saturday Review
  'The title could not be more apt: it is precisely the sound of a bomb exploding.' – Richard Schickel, Life
  'Boom! isn't doing little business; it's doing no business at all.' – Universal executive

Boom in the Moon (dubbed)
Mexico   1946   90m   bw
Alsa (Alexander Salkind)

original title: El Moderno Barba Azul
A shipwrecked sailor is mistaken for a mass murderer and sent on the first expedition to the moon.
Embarrassingly bad, feebly scripted and cheaply made comedy in which Keaton displays none of his skill or invention, but sleepwalks through his role.
w Victor Trivas, Jaime Salvador d Jaime Salvador m George Tzipine
☆ Buster Keaton, Angel Garasa, Virginia Seret, Luis Bareiro, Fernando Sotto
† The film was never released in American cinemas and was hardly seen outside Mexico until its video release; it surfaces occasionally on television in a version that runs for 70m.

Boom Town **
US   1940   120m   bw
MGM (Sam Zimbalist)

Two friendly oil drillers strike it rich.
Enjoyable four-star, big-studio product of its time: world-wide entertainment of assured success, with a proven mix of romance, action, drama and comedy.

w John Lee Mahin story James Edward Grant d Jack Conway ph Harold Rosson m Franz Waxman ad Cedric Gibbons
☆ Clark Gable, Spencer Tracy, Claudette Colbert, Hedy Lamarr, Frank Morgan, Lionel Atwill, Chill Wills
  'Western high jinks, a wee child, and courtroom speeches about individual enterprise constitute the various come-ons in a scrambled and inept picture.' – New York Herald Tribune
  'More colourful action in the oil fields and less agitation indoors might have made it a great picture.' – Bosley Crowther
  ⬥ Harold Rosson

Boomerang ***
US   1947   88m   bw
TCF (Louis de Rochemont)
In a New England town, a clergyman is shot dead on the street. The DA prevents an innocent man from being convicted, but cannot track down the guilty party.
Incisive real life thriller: based on a true case, it was shot in an innovative documentary style which was much copied, and justice is not seen to be done, though the murderer is known to the audience. A milestone movie of its kind.
w Richard Murphy d Elia Kazan ph Norbert Brodine m David Buttolph
☆ Dana Andrews, Jane Wyatt, Lee J. Cobb, Cara Williams, Arthur Kennedy, Sam Levene, Taylor Holmes, Robert Keith, Ed Begley
  'A study of integrity, beautifully developed by Dana Andrews against a background of political corruption and chicanery that is doubly shocking because of its documentary understatement.' – Richard Winnington
  'For the first time in many a moon we are treated to a picture that gives a good example of a typical small American city – the people, their way of living, their mode of government, the petty politics practised, the power of the press.' – Frank Ward, National Board of Review
  ⬥ Richard Murphy

'A Player Who's About To Be Played.'
Boomerang
US   1992   117m   Technicolor
UIP/Paramount (Brian Grazer, Warrington Hudlin)

An executive in a cosmetics firm has an unsuccessful affair with his boss before finding true love.
Dim comedy that substitutes gloss for wit and deprives its star of everything except uncritical adulation.
w Barry W. Blaustein, David Sheffield d Reginald Hudlin ph Woody Omens m Marcus Miller pd Jane Musky ed Earl Watson, John Carter, Michael Jablow
☆ Eddie Murphy, Robin Givens, Halle Berry, David Alan Grier, Martin Lawrence, Grace Jones, Geoffrey Holder, Eartha Kitt, Melvin Van Peebles
  'This Eddie Murphy vehicle tries hard to be positive. It's a pity that the movie isn't any good.' – Michael Sragow, New Yorker
  'An ill-fitting comedy vehicle that's desperately in need of a reality check.' – Variety

The Boost *
US   1988   95m   colour
Hemdale/Becker-Blatt-Ponicsan (Daniel H. Blatt)

A fast-talking salesman and his wife are ruined by their addiction to cocaine.
Cautionary tale of an acquisitive society, coolly told.
w Darryl Ponicsan novel Ludes by Benjamin Stein d Harold Becker ph Howard Atherton m Stanley Myers ad Ken Hardy ed Maury Winetrobe
☆ James Woods, Sean Young, John Kapelos, Steven Hill, Kelle Kerr, John Rothman, Amanda Blake, Grace Zabriskie

Das Boot: see The Boat

Boots! Boots!
GB   1934   80m   bw
Blakeley/John E. Blakeley
A simple hotel employee turns entertainer with the scullery maid.
Formby's first film, based on a stage show, and filmed cheaply and with little imagination: the camera remains static as if the proceedings are being viewed from the stalls. It retains some slight interest as an example of popular entertainment of the period.

w Jack Cottrill, George Formby d Bert Tracey ph James S. Hodgson md Harry Hudson ad Thomas Fleetwood

☆ George Formby, Beryl Formby, Arthur Kingsley, Tonie Forde, Lillian Keyes, Donald Reid, Constance Fletcher, Wallace Boscoe, Betty Driver

Boots Hill (dubbed) *
Italy 1969 106m Technicolor Techniscope
San Marco/Crono
original title: *La Collina degli Stivali*

A man wounded and hunted by a gang of killers takes refuge with a travelling circus.

Lively spaghetti Western that threatens to be more original than most, with its chase narrative concerned with greed and exploitation, but which finally settles, with the arrival of Bud Spencer at the halfway mark, for broad comedy, gunfights and pub brawls.

wd Giuseppe Colizzi ph Marcello Masciocchi m Carlo Rustichelli ad Gastone Carsetti ed Tatiana Morigi Casini

☆ Terence Hill (Mario Girotti), Woody Strode, Bud Spencer (Carlo Pedersoli), Victor Buono, Lionel Stander, Edward Ciannelli, Luca Montefiori, Glauca Onorato

Boots Malone
US 1952 103m bw
Columbia (Milton Holmes)
▦

A would-be jockey tags along with a down-at-heel agent who gets him work and finally persuades him not to throw a crooked race.

Dullish racetrack melodrama bogged down by repetitive and unsympathetic plot twists.

w Milton Holmes d William Dieterle ph Charles Lawton Jnr m Elmer Bernstein

☆ William Holden, Johnny Stewart, Stanley Clements, Basil Ruysdael, Carl Benton Reid, Ed Begley, Henry Morgan

'Some guys will do anything for a little something.'
Booty Call
US 1997 79m DeLuxe
Columbia (John Morrissey)
▦ ▤ ◎ ◎

Two couples decide to indulge in intercourse providing the men equip themselves with condoms.

A prolonged, comic commercial for safe sex that detumesces quickly.

w Takashi Bufford d Jeff Pollack ph Ron Orieux m Robert Folk pd Sandra Kybartas ed Christopher Greenbury

☆ Jamie Foxx, Tommy Davidson, Vivica A. Fox, Tamala Jones, Scott LaRose, Gedde Watanabe

'An oddly effective comic mix of the politically correct and outré stereotyping.' – *Variety*

† Art Malik appears uncredited.

Bopha! *
US 1993 121m DeLuxe
Paramount/Arsenio Hall/Taubman
▦

In South Africa in 1980, a black policeman, living in a turbulent township, finds himself torn between supporting his repressive white boss or approving the actions of his outspoken son, who believes in revolution.

A sincere, well-acted movie about apartheid and its consequences, but over-simplistic and too conventional in its approach.

w Brian Bird, John Wierick play Percy Mtwa d Morgan Freeman ph David Watkin m James Horner pd Michael Philips ed Neil Travis

☆ Danny Glover, Malcolm McDowell, Rosie Mangena, Marius Weyers, Maynard Eziashi, Malick Bowens, Michael Chinyamurindi, Christopher John Hall

'A handsomely crafted, potently played drama that brings the issue of apartheid down to a visceral human dimension.' – Leonard Klady, *Variety*

The Border
US 1982 108m Technicolor Panavision
Universal/RKO (Neil Hartley)
▦ ▤ ◎

A Los Angeles cop joins the border patrol in El Paso and becomes involved in the squalor, violence and double-dealing.

A rather solemn elaboration on a well-worn theme, with nothing very memorable except its excesses.

w Deric Washburn, Walon Green, David Freeman d Tony Richardson ph Ric Waite m Ry Cooder pd Toby Rafelson ed Robert K. Lambert

☆ Jack Nicholson, Harvey Keitel, Valerie Perrine, Warren Oates, Elpidia Carrillo

Border Incident
US 1949 93m bw
MGM (Nicholas Nayfack)

Police stop the illegal immigration of labourers from Mexico.

Routine semi-documentary cops and robbers, well enough made.

w John C. Higgins d Anthony Mann ph John Alton m André Previn

☆ Ricardo Montalban, George Murphy, Howard da Silva, James Mitchell, Alfonso Bedoya

Border Radio
US 1987 84m bw
Coyote/Marcus de Leon
▤

A punk rock musician goes on the run to Mexico after stealing money from a promoter who failed to pay him.

Probably a learning experience for those involved: the jerky narrative (one title reads '2 or 6 months later'), abrupt editing, deliberately inconsequential, improvised dialogue and amateurish acting suggest that its participants were determined to make a film but were uncertain of precisely how to do it.

wd Allison Anders, Dean Lent, Kurt Voss ph Dean Lent m Dave Alvin

☆ Chris D., Luana Anders, Chris Shearer, John Doe, Dave Alvin, Iris Berry, Devon Anders, Texacala Jones

† The credits include: 'Many curses on: Those Who Tried To Thwart Us'.

Border Shootout
US 1990 110m colour
Turner/Phoenix
▤

A naïve rancher becomes the sheriff of a town in thrall to the crooked son of its largest landowner.

Inept Western, in which the various strands of the narrative never quite come together; the acting is variable – from acceptable to bad – and the direction clumsy. Despite his star billing, Ford, whose mind seems to be on other things, plays a secondary role.

wd C. T. McIntyre novel *The Law at Randado* by Elmore Leonard ph Dennis Dalzell m Coley Music Group pd Craig B. Stein ed Grant Johnson

☆ Glenn Ford, Charlene Tilton, Jeff Kaake, Michael Horse, Russell Todd, Cody Glenn, Sergio Calderon, Michael Ansara

Borderline
US 1980 97m colour
ITC (Martin Starger)

A Mexican border patrolman chases illegal immigrants and the big time crooks making money out of them.

Routine, quite effective action programmer.

w Steve Kline, Jerrold Freedman d Jerrold Freedman ph Tak Fujimoto m Gil Melle

☆ Charles Bronson, Bruno Kirby, Karmin Murcelo, Michael Lerner, Ed Harris

Borderlines: see *The Caretakers*

Bordertown *
US 1934 80m bw
Warner (Robert Lord)

In a North Mexican town, a shabby lawyer becomes infatuated with the neurotic wife of a businessman.

Satisfying melodrama whose plot climax was later borrowed from They Drive by Night (qv).

w Laird Doyle, Wallace Smith novel Carroll Graham d Archie Mayo ph Tony Gaudio md Leo Forbstein

☆ Paul Muni, Bette Davis, Margaret Lindsay, Eugene Pallette, Robert Barrat, Henry O'Neill, Hobart Cavanaugh

'A strictly box office film, well written and paced.' – *Variety*

† *Blowing Wild* (qv) was also a partial uncredited remake.

Bordertown Cafe
Canada 1991 95m colour
Cinexus/Flat City/NFBC (Norma Bailey)

A woman running a small-town café has problems with her mother, son and truck-driving former husband.

Fraught and talkative soap opera of regrets and disappointments.

w Kelly Rebar d Norma Bailey ph Ian Elkin m Ben Mink pd John Blackie ed Lara Mazur

☆ Susan Hogan, Janet Wright, Gordon Michael Woolvett, Sean McCann, Nicholas Campbell

Born Again
US 1978 110m Technicolor
Robert L. Munger/Frank Capra Jnr
▤

Charles Colson, sent to prison after Watergate, becomes a devout Christian.

Part evangelism, part reconstruction through rose-tinted spectacles; not particularly entertaining or instructive as either.

w Walter Block d Irving Rapper ph Harry Stradling Jnr m Les Baxter

☆ Dean Jones, Anne Francis, Jay Robinson, Dana Andrews, Raymond St Jacques, George Brent, Harry Spillman

Born for Glory: see *Brown on Resolution*

Born for Trouble: see *Murder in the Big House*

Born Free **
👫👫 GB 1966 95m Technicolor
Panavision
Columbia/Open Road (Carl Foreman)/High Road/Atlas (Sam Jaffe, Paul Radin)
▤ ▦ ◎ ◎

A Kenyan game warden and his wife rear three lion cubs, one of which eventually presents them with a family.

Irresistible animal shots salvage this rather flabbily put together version of a bestselling book. An enormous commercial success, it was followed by the even thinner Living Free (qv), by a TV series, and by several semi-professional documentaries.

w Gerald L. C. Copley book Joy Adamson d James Hill ph Kenneth Talbot m John Barry

☆ Virginia McKenna, Bill Travers, Geoffrey Keen

🏆 John Barry; title song (mJohn Barry, lyDon Black)

Born in East L.A.
US 1987 87m colour
Universal (Peter Macgregor-Scott)
▤ ▦ ◎ ◎

An American Mexican is mistaken for an illegal immigrant and deported to Tijuana.

Mercifully short brain-dead comedy.

wd Cheech Marin ph Alex Phillips m Lee Holdridge ed Don Brochu

☆ Cheech Marin, Daniel Stern, Paul Rodriguez, Jan Michael Vincent, Kamala Lopez, Tony Plana

Born Losers
US 1967 112m colour
AIP (Delores Taylor)
▤

California teeny-boppers claim to have been gang-raped by wandering motorcyclists.

Teenage shocker, only notable for its credits, and for being the first Billy Jack film.

wd Tom Laughlin ph Gregory Sandor m Mike Curb

☆ Tom Laughlin, Jane Russell, Elizabeth James, Jeremy Slate, William Wellman Jnr

'It's so pokey and crudely obvious that it seems almost guileless – helplessly inept.' – *Pauline Kael*

'A true story of innocence lost and courage found'
Born on the Fourth of July **
US 1989 144m DeLuxe Panavision
UIP/Ixtlan (A Kitman Ho, Oliver Stone)
▤ ▦ ◎ ◎ 🎧

A crippled Vietnam veteran joins the anti-war movement.

Rousing drama, based on fact.

w Oliver Stone, Ron Kovic book Ron Kovic d Oliver Stone ph Robert Richardson m John Williams pd Bruno Rubeo ad Victor Kempster, Richard L. Johnson ed David Brenner

☆ Tom Cruise, Bryan Larkin, Raymond J. Barry, Caroline Kava, Josh Evans, Seth Allan, Jamie Talisman, Sean Stone, Anne Bobby, Jenna von Oy

🏆 Oliver Stone; best film editing

🏅 Tom Cruise; John Williams; best picture; best adapted screenplay; best cinematography

Born Reckless
US 1930 73m bw
Fox

Doings of an Italian gangster bootlegger.

A generally poorly regarded early work of its director.

w Donald Henderson Clarke novel *Louis Beretti* by Donald Henderson Clarke d John Ford

☆ Edmund Lowe, Catherine Dale Owen, Lee Tracy, Marguerite Churchill, Warren Hymer, Frank Albertson

'A singularly full and sprawling scenario … Fox originally intended the yarn for Paul Muni. It's possible the script got kicked around the lot and came out as beef stew.' – *Variety*

Born Reckless
US 1937 60m bw
TCF

Big-town taxi drivers start a war among themselves.

Second-feature actioner, well enough done.

w John Patrick, Helen Logan, Robert Ellis d Malcolm St Clair

☆ Brian Donlevy, Rochelle Hudson, Barton MacLane, Robert Kent, Harry Carey, Pauline Moore, Chick Chandler

'Houses in the knuckle districts will give it its best play.' – *Variety*

Born to Be Bad
US 1934 70m bw
Twentieth Century (William Goetz, Raymond Griffith)

A girl schemes to seduce the man who has adopted her illegitimate son.

Batty mother-love melodrama.

w Ralph Graves d Lowell Sherman ph Barney McGill m Alfred Newman

☆ Loretta Young, Cary Grant, Jackie Kelk, Henry Travers, Russell Hopton, Andrew Tombes, Harry Green

Born to Be Bad
US 1950 70m bw
RKO (Robert Sparks)
▤

An ambitious girl marries a millionaire but continues her affair with a novelist; finally both men discover her true character.

Tentative bad girl novelette, just about passable.

w Edith Sommer novel *All Kneeling* by Anne Parrish d Nicholas Ray ph Nicholas Musuraca m Frederick Hollander

☆ Joan Fontaine, Robert Ryan, Zachary Scott, Joan Leslie, Mel Ferrer

'Trash story too much for cast and director to live down.' – *Variety*

Born to Be Wild
👫👫 US 1995 100m Technicolor
Warner/Fuji/Outlaw (Robert Newmyer, Jeffrey Silver)
▤ ▦ ◎

A teenage delinquent makes a friend of a gorilla in a research laboratory who can communicate by sign language; when she is reclaimed by her unpleasant owner, he runs off with her.

Pleasant, undemanding entertainment; when attention flags, you can try to decide whether or not the ape is real or a large, electronically controlled puppet.

w John Bunzel, Paul Young d John Gray ph Donald M. Morgan m Mark Snow pd Roy Forge Smith ed Maryann Brandon

☆ Wil Horneff, Helen Shaver, Peter Boyle, Jean Marie Barnwell, John McGinley, Marvin J. McIntyre

'Contains all the requisite charms and values of a feel-good, politically correct child-animal story.' – *Variety*

Born to Dance *
US 1936 108m bw
MGM (Jack Cummings)
▤ ◎

A sailor meets a girl in New York.

Well remembered musical with good numbers but a rather lame tone.

w Jack McGowan, Sid Silvers, B. G. de Sylva d Roy del Ruth ph Ray June m/ly Cole Porter md Alfred Newman ch Dave Gould ad Cedric Gibbons ed Blanche Sewell

☆ Eleanor Powell, James Stewart, Virginia Bruce, Una Merkel, Sid Silvers, Frances Langford,

Raymond Walburn, *Reginald Gardiner*, Buddy Ebsen

'Corking entertainment … Cast is youthful, sight stuff is lavish, the specialities are meritorious, and as for songs, the picture is positively filthy with them.' – *Variety*
'The plot is a half-hearted reprise of *42nd Street* … this time Eleanor Powell is the understudy who replaces the star … and by the time she finishes the finale, you're overpowered and feel you should cheer.' – *Pauline Kael, 70s*
♫ 'I've Got You Under My Skin'; 'Easy to Love'; 'Rap Tap on Wood'; 'Swinging the Jinx Away'; 'Rolling Home'; 'Hey Babe Hey'; 'Love Me Love My Pekinese'
♫ song 'I've Got You Under My Skin'; Dave Gould

Born to Kill: see *Cockfighter (1974)*

Born to Kill *
US   1947   92m   bw
RKO
▤
GB title: *Lady of Deceit*
A psychotic involves his new wife in his criminal pursuits.
Unusual, heavy-going, well acted melodrama.
w Eve Greene, Richard Macaulay *novel* James Gunn d Robert Wise ph Robert de Grasse m Paul Sawtell
☆ Lawrence Tierney, Claire Trevor, Walter Slezak, Phillip Terry, Elisha Cook Jnr

Born to Love
US   1931   84m   bw
RKO
During World War I a nurse bears the child of an army pilot who is reported missing; but he turns up after she has married an English milord.
A useful compendium of thirties romantic clichés, quite attractively packaged.
w Ernest Pascal d Paul Stein ph John Mescall
☆ Constance Bennett, Joel McCrea, Paul Cavanagh, Frederick Kerr, Anthony Bushell, Louise Closser Hale, Edmund Breon, Mary Forbes

Born to Ride
US   1991   88m   Technicolor
Warner/Inconvent (Fred Weintraub, Sandra Weintraub)
▤
In 1939, a biker is hired by the army to teach the cavalry to switch from horses to motorbikes and rescue an American scientist from fascist kidnappers.
A curious attempt to combine the style of a 60s biker movie with a period war film; it very quickly runs out of gas.
w Michael Pardridge, Janice Hickey d Graham Baker ph Frank Gell m Shirley Walker
pd Francis I. Pezza ed Alan Balsam
☆ John Stamos, John Stockwell, Teri Polo, Sandy McPeak, Kriss Kamm, Keith Cooke

Born to Run
👪 US   1977   90m   Technicolor
Walt Disney (Jerome Courtland)
📼 ▤
In Australia at the turn of the century, a boy and his colt win a race to save the family farm.
Pleasant if unmemorable film that will appeal to young horse-lovers.
w Ed Jurist *novel* Walter D. Edmonds d Don Chaffey ph Geoff Burton m Ron Goodwin
ad David Copping ed Peter Boita
☆ Tom Farley, Robert Bettles, Andrew McFarlane, Mary Ward, Julieanne Newbould, John Meillon

Born to Sing
👪 US   1941   82m   bw
Frederick Stephani/MGM
Kids put together a patriotic show.
Curiously undernourished family musical in the wake of Babes in Arms (qv): lots of talent but no star.
w Franz Spencer, Harry Clork d Edward Ludwig
☆ Virginia Weidler, Douglas McPhail, Leo Gorcey, Ray McDonald, Rags Ragland, Sheldon Leonard, Margaret Dumont, Larry Nunn, Henry O'Neill

'A perfectly swell motion picture!'
Born Yesterday **
US   1950   103m   bw
Columbia (S. Sylvan Simon)
📼 ▤ ⊚
The ignorant ex-chorus girl mistress of a scrap iron tycoon takes English lessons, falls for her tutor, and politically outmanoeuvres her bewildered lover.
Pleasant film version of a cast-iron box-office play, subtle and intelligent in all departments yet with a regrettable tendency to wave the flag.
w Albert Mannheimer *play* Garson Kanin d George Cukor ph Joseph Walker m Frederick Hollander
☆ Judy Holliday, Broderick Crawford, William Holden, Howard St John
† The original choices for the Judy Holliday role were Rita Hayworth and Jean Parker (who had played it on tour).
🏆 Judy Holliday
♫ best picture; Albert Mannheimer; George Cukor

Born Yesterday
US   1993   100m   Technicolor
Warner/Hollywood/Touchwood Pacific Partners I (D. Constantine Conte)
📼 ▤ ⊚
A journalist turns a millionaire's seemingly dumb chorus-girl mistress into a bright and intelligent woman, falling in love with her in the process.
A remake that does nothing but point up the superiority of the original and, in particular, Judy Holliday's priceless gift for comedy; the jokes are mistimed here and the romance is hardly in evidence.
w Douglas McGrath *play* Garson Kanin d Luis Mandoki ph Lajos Koltai m George Fenton
pd Lawrence G. Paull ed Lesley Walker
☆ Melanie Griffith, John Goodman, Don Johnson, Edward Herrmann, Max Perlich, Benjamin C. Bradlee, Sally Quinn, William Frankfather, Fred Dalton Thompson
'This version has great casting, canny scripting and only fair direction, but still jollies along nicely.' – *Kim Newman, Empire*

The Borrower
US   1989   88m   colour
Cannon/Vision (R. P. Sekon, Steven A. Jones)
📼 ▤
An alien murderer is 'genetically devolved' and marooned on Earth; but his head keeps exploding so he replaces it by ripping off fresh human ones.
Hysterical gore-filled horror – so ineptly made that the body of the alien also changes whenever he gains a new head (since he is played by a different actor each time).
w Mason Nage, Richard Fire d John McNaughton ph Julio Macat, Robert New m Robert McNaughton, Ken Hale, Steven A. Jones pd Robert Henderson ed Elena Maganini
☆ Rae Dawn Chong, Don Gordon, Antonio Fargas, Tom Towles

'Small Is Awesome.'
The Borrowers **
👪 GB   1997   83m   Technicolor
Polygram/Working Title (Tim Bevan, Eric Fellner, Rachel Talalay)
📼 ▤ ⊚ ⊚ ⌐
The future of a family of tiny people, who live under the floorboards of a house, is threatened by an unscrupulous lawyer.
Clever, if hectic and noisy, children's film; it doesn't have the quiet humour of the original books, but nevertheless creates an odd, fanciful world that mixes English and American influences.
w Gavin Scott, John Camps *novels* Mary Norton d Peter Hewitt ph John Fenner, Trevor Brooker m Harry Gregson-Williams pd Gemma Jackson ed David Freeman, Annie Kocur
☆ John Goodman, Jim Broadbent, Mark Williams, Hugh Laurie, Bradley Pierce, Flora Newbigin, Tom Felton, Raymond Pickard, Celia Imrie
'A top-notch family film that welds English quaintness and eccentricity with high-tech effects.' – *Derek Elley, Variety*
'It blends old with new, irony with sincerity, and plain with fancy in such a way as to give post-modernism a good name and to entertain an audience of all ages.' – *Richard Williams, Guardian*

Borsalino *
France/Italy   1970   126m   Eastmancolor
Adel-Marianne-Mars (Alain Delon)
⌐
In the thirties two Marseilles gangsters become firm friends and join forces.
Semi-spoof, but with 'real' blood, and period atmosphere laid on thick. The stars just about keep it ticking over.
w Jean-Claude Carrière, Claude Sautet, Jacques Deray, Jean Cau d Jacques Deray ph Jean-Jacques Tarbès m Claude Bolling
☆ Jean-Paul Belmondo, Alain Delon, Michel Bouquet, Catherine Rouvel, Corinne Marchand
'Rather like a Hollywood musical where someone has forgotten to insert the production numbers.' – *MFB*

Borsalino & Co (dubbed)
France/Italy/West Germany   1974   91m   Eastmancolor
Adel/Comacico/Medusa/TIT (Maurice Jacquin, Alain Delon)
⌐
aka: *Blood on the Streets*
A fascist gangleader runs into trouble when he tries to take over Marseilles.
A violent thriller, a sequel to Borsalino but lacking wit and substance. It was among the top ten box-office successes of the year in France.
w Pascal Jardin d Jacques Deray ph Jean-Jacques Tarbès m Claude Bolling ad François de Lamothe ed Henri Lanoë
☆ Alain Delon, Catherine Rouvel, Riccardo Cucciolla, Daniel Ivernel

Bosambo: see *Sanders of the River*

The Boss *
US   1956   89m   bw
UA/Frank N. Seltzer
▤
After World War I, a ne'er-do-well becomes a corrupt small town political boss.
Low budgeted, complexly plotted, occasionally quite powerful and efficient crime melodrama.
w Ben L. Parry d Byron Haskin ph Hal Mohr m Albert Glasser
☆ John Payne, William Bishop, Gloria McGhee, Doe Avedon, Joe Flynn

Le Bossu **
France/Italy   1997   128m   colour   Panavision
Aliceleo/TFI/CGG Tiger/Gemini
aka: *On Guard!*
In the early 18th century, a swordsman rescues a baby girl from a murderous nobleman, and promises revenge.
Enjoyable period romp, a romantic swashbuckler performed with great panache.
w Jean Cosmos, Jerome Tonnerre, Philippe de Broca *novel* Paul Feval d Philippe de Broca ph Jean-François Robin m Philippe Sarde ad Bernard Vezat ed Henri Lanoë
☆ Daniel Auteuil, Fabrice Luchini, Vincent Perez, Marie Gillain, Yann Collette, Jean-François Stevenin, Didier Pain, Philippe Noiret
'Has an energy and a thrill that restore the swashbuckler to its rightful place in screen society.' – *Gaby Wood, Guardian*
† Paul Feval's novel has been filmed in France at least six times since 1914; notably starring Jean Marais in 1959.

Boston Blackie
An American second feature series made by Columbia between 1941 and 1949. There had been silent films about the character, a reformed crook and con man who has to solve crimes because he is suspected by the law.
Cheap but sometimes vigorous productions, they had a loyal following and starred Chester Morris with George E. Stone as his assistant The Runt.
The titles were:
1941 Meet Boston Blackie, Confessions of Boston Blackie
1942 Alias Boston Blackie, Boston Blackie Goes to Hollywood
1943 After Midnight with Boston Blackie
1944 One Mysterious Night
1945 Boston Blackie Booked on Suspicion, Boston Blackie's Rendezvous
1946 A Close Call for Boston Blackie, The Phantom Thief

1947 Boston Blackie and the Law
1948 Trapped By Boston Blackie
1949 Boston Blackie's Chinese Venture
† A television series starring Kent Taylor followed in 1951.

'Going mad … going places … going straight … going nowhere...'
Boston Kickout *
GB   1996   105m   colour
First Independent/Boston/Aramanth/Trijbits Worrell (Paul Hills, Danny Cannon)
📼 ▤ ⊚ ⌐
A teenager manages to free himself from the delinquency and despair that motivate his unemployed friends.
Disaffection in the concrete wilderness of Stevenage makes for less than revelatory viewing, despite energetic performances from its talented cast.
w Paul Hills, Diane Whitley, Roberto Troni d Paul Hills ph Roger Bonnici m Robert Hartshorne pd Simon Elliott ed Melanie Adams
☆ John Simm, Emer McCourt, Marc Warren, Andrew Lincoln, Richard Hanson, Nathan Valente, Derek Martin, Vincent Phillips
'One of the best recent British films.' – *Danny Boyle*

The Boston Strangler **
US   1968   118m   DeLuxe   Panavision
TCF (Robert Fryer)
📼 ▤
A semi-factual account of the sex maniac who terrified Boston in the mid-sixties.
Ambitious policier rendered less effective by pretentious writing and flashy treatment, including multi-image sequences; the investigation is more interesting than the psychoanalysis.
w Edward Anhalt *book* Gerold Frank d Richard Fleischer ph Richard Kline m Lionel Newman
☆ Henry Fonda, Tony Curtis, George Kennedy, Mike Kellin, Hurd Hatfield, Murray Hamilton, Sally Kellerman, Jeff Corey, George Voskovec

The Bostonians
GB   1984   122m   colour
Merchant Ivory/WGBH/Rediffusion/Almi (Ismail Merchant)
▤ ⊚ ⊚
In 1876 Boston, the cause of female emancipation wrecks Verena Tarrant's relationship with the determined Basil Ransome.
Another sluggish literary adaptation from the heavily meaningful Merchant Ivory team: the material, one feels, would have worked better as a TV bestseller.
w Ruth Prawer Jhabvala *novel* Henry James d James Ivory ph Walter Lassally m Richard Robbins pd Leo Austin
☆ Christopher Reeve, Vanessa Redgrave, Madeleine Potter, Jessica Tandy, Nancy Marchand, Linda Hunt, Wesley Addy
'Although it's not so limp as some of their other collaborations, they don't dramatize the material, and Ivory doesn't shape the performances.' – *Pauline Kael, New Yorker*
♫ Vanessa Redgrave

Botany Bay
US   1952   94m   Technicolor
Paramount (Joseph Sistrom)
▤
On a convict ship in 1787 an American student unjustly accused of robbery clashes with the brutal captain for the favours of the only woman aboard.
Cramped and brutal action melodrama, a let-down considering the talent involved.
w Jonathan Latimer *novel* Charles Nordhoff, James Hall d John Farrow ph John Seitz m Franz Waxman
☆ James Mason, Alan Ladd, Patricia Medina, Cedric Hardwicke, Murray Matheson, Jonathan Harris

Both Ends of the Candle: see *The Helen Morgan Story*

Both Sides of the Law: see *Street Corner*

Bottle Rocket *
US   1996   95m   Technicolor
Columbia/Gracie/Boyle-Taylor (Polly Platt, Cynthia Hargrave)
📼 ▤ ⊚
Three young incompetents decide to embark on a life of crime.

Enjoyable and witty small-scale independent film that manages some original variations on a familiar theme.
w Owen C. Wilson, Wes Anderson d Wes Anderson ph Robert Yeoman m Mark Mothersbaugh pd David Wasco ed David Moritz
☆ Luke Wilson, Owen C. Wilson, Robert Musgrave, Andrew Wilson, Lumi Cavazos, James Caan, Teddy Wilson, Jim Ponds
'Full of surprising warmth and charm, unexpected plot turns and droll characters that bounce off each other in refreshing ways.' – *David Rooney, Variety*

The Bottom of the Bottle
US 1956 86m Eastmancolor Cinemascope
TCF (Buddy Adler)
GB title: *Beyond the River*
A wealthy attorney is visited by his drunken brother, on the run from the police and needing help to escape into Mexico.
Dreary drama in muddy colour, a clearly misguided enterprise.
w Sydney Boehm novel Georges Simenon d Henry Hathaway ph Lee Garmes m Leigh Harline
☆ Joseph Cotten, Van Johnson, Ruth Roman, Jack Carson

'For those who like to laugh and sing when tears get in their eyes!'

Bottoms Up
US 1934 85m bw
Fox (B. G. de Sylva)
A slick promoter in Hollywood disguises his pals as British nobility and gets them lucrative jobs.
Mild musical with a rather interesting cast.
w B. G. de Sylva, David Butler, Sid Silvers d David Butler ph Arthur Miller md Constantin Bakaleinikoff
☆ Spencer Tracy, Pat Paterson, John Boles, Harry Green, Herbert Mundin, Sid Silvers, Thelma Todd, Robert Emmett O'Connor
'In the best 1934 filmusical manner and contributes handily toward the perpetuation of the cycle.' – *Variety*

Bottoms Up
GB 1959 89m bw
ABPC (Mario Zampi)
A seedy schoolmaster passes off his bookie's son as an eastern prince.
Rambling film version of a successful TV series Whacko!, *written by Frank Muir and Denis Norden.*
w Michael Pertwee d Mario Zampi ph Gilbert Taylor m Stanley Black ad Ivan King ed Richard Best
☆ Jimmy Edwards, Arthur Howard, Martita Hunt, Sydney Tafler, Raymond Huntley, Reginald Beckwith, Vanda Hudson, Richard Briers

Le Boucher ***
France/Italy 1969 94m Eastmancolor
La Boétie/Euro International (André Génovès)
aka: *The Butcher*
Murders in a small French town are traced to the inoffensive-seeming young butcher who is courting the local schoolmistress.
Curious, mainly charming film which can't make up its mind whether to be an eccentric character study or a Hitchcock thriller, but has its moments as each.
wd Claude Chabrol ph Jean Rabier m Pierre Jansen
☆ Stéphane Audran, Jean Yanne, Antonio Passalia, Mario Beccaria
'A thriller, but a superlative example of the genre.' – *Times*

Boudu Sauvé des Eaux ***
France 1932 87m bw
Michel Simon/Jean Gehret
aka: *Boudu Saved from Drowning*
A scruffy tramp is not grateful for being rescued from suicide, and plagues the family who invite him to stay.
A minor classic of black comedy, interesting equally for its characterizations, its acting, and its film technique.
wd Jean Renoir play René Fauchois ph Marcel Lucien m from Raphael and Johann Strauss
☆ Michel Simon, Charles Granval, Marcelle Hainia, Séverine Lerczinska, Jean Dasté, Jacques Becker
'A beautifully rhythmed film that makes one nostalgic for the period when it was made.' – *New Yorker, 1977*

† Remade 1985, more or less, as *Down and Out in Beverly Hills* (qv).

Boudu Saved from Drowning: see *Boudu Sauvé des Eaux*

Bought
US 1931 70m bw
Warner
An ambitious working girl rebels against her slum existence and seeks a rich man.
Typical star vehicle of its time, with a predictable and unlikely change of heart for a finale.
w Charles Kenyon, Raymond Griffith novel *Jackdaw's Strut* by Harriet Henry d Archie Mayo ph Ray June
☆ Constance Bennett, Ben Lyon, Richard Bennett, Dorothy Peterson, Ray Milland, Doris Lloyd, Maude Eburne
'It's an entertainment in itself to be seated among women auditors during a Constance Bennett picture. They love that girl and she mustn't be worsted by men.' – *Variety*

Boulder Dam
US 1936 70m bw
Sam Bischoff/Warner
A mechanic accidentally kills a man and seeks anonymity among the crews building Boulder Dam.
Routine melo with an unusual setting.
w Sy Bartlett, Ralph Block d Frank McDonald
☆ Ross Alexander, Patricia Ellis, Lyle Talbot, Eddie Acuff, Henry O'Neill

Boulevard
US 1994 96m colour
Norstar (Peter Simpson, Ray Sager)
An abused wife becomes a prostitute and is victimized by a ruthless pimp.
Brutal thriller of little merit which makes the most of its frequent bouts of violence.
w Rae Dawn Chong d Penelope Buitenhuis ph David Frazee m Ian Thomas pd Jasna Stefanovic ed Bernadette Kelly
☆ Rae Dawn Chong, Lou Diamond Phillips, Lance Henriksen, Kari Wuhrer, Joel Bissonnette
'Suggests the importance of female camaraderie, but ultimately the violence against women is so excessive and exploitational that it's shocking to realise pic was written and directed by women.' – *Emanuel Levy, Variety*

Boulevard Nights
US 1979 102m colour
Warner (Bill Benenson)
Two Mexican-American brothers become involved with a street gang.
Well-meaning but uninvolving account of life lived at an inescapably violent level.
w Desmond Nakano d Michael Pressman ph John Bailey m Lalo Schifrin pd Jackson DeGovia ed Richard Halsey
☆ Richard Yniguez, Danny de La Paz, Marta Du Bois, James Victor, Betty Carvalho
'Earnest, uninspired.' – *Pauline Kael*

'A Trust So Deep It Cuts Both Ways.'
'Stealing's a lot like sex. You've got two people who want the same thing.'

Bound **
US 1996 108m DeLuxe
Guild/Dino de Laurentiis/Summit/Newmarket (Andrew Lazar, Stuart Boros)
In Chicago, a lesbian thief falls for a gangster's mistress, and the pair decide to make a new life with the Mob's millions.
A lesbian twist on a familiar film noir narrative, delivered with a campily violent knowingness and much twirling of the camera.
wd Andy Wachowski, Larry Wachowski ph Bill Pope m Don Davis pd Eve Cauley ed Zach Staenberg
☆ Jennifer Tilly, Gina Gershon, Joe Pantoliano, John P. Ryan, Christopher Meloni, Richard C. Sarafian, Barry Kivel
'Who needs good taste when you can have this much fun? It's a blast.' – *Neil Norman, London Evening Standard*

Bound and Gagged – A Love Story
US 1992 94m colour
Metro Tartan/Cinescope (Dennis J. Mahoney)
A woman, married to a violent husband, is abducted by her female lover and her friend, a suicidal, unhappily married man who has lost the ability to speak.
A doggedly well-meaning movie about abusive and dependent behaviour that is also virtually unwatchable.
wd Daniel B. Appleby ph Dean Lent m William Murphy pd Dane Pizzuti Krogman ed Kaye Davis
☆ Ginger Lynn Allen, Karen Black, Chris Denton, Elizabeth Saltarrelli, Mary Ella Ross, Chris Mulkey
'This is not a good film. In fact, it is a pretty bad one – unevenly acted, scripted without much real wit and directed with the kind of careless abandon that sometimes passes for imagination when one's had too much of Hollywood's professional vacuity.' – *Derek Malcolm, Guardian*
'Resolutely unengaging, almost repugnant. It is muddily photographed and poorly scripted.' – *Caren Myers, Sight and Sound*
† The film has been described by its director, who is noted for his documentaries on similar subject-matter, as a labour of love, taking two and a half years to make.

Bound for Glory *
US 1976 148m DeLuxe Panavision
UA/Robert F. Blumhofe, Harold Leventhal
In 1936 Woody Guthrie leaves the Texas dust bowl for California, and after various hardships his musical talent is recognized.
Care and occasional beauty in the photography do not obscure memories of The Grapes of Wrath *(qv), which told much the same story more dramatically and succinctly, and with less earnestness and self-pity.*
w Robert Getchell autobiography Woody Guthrie d Hal Ashby ph Haskell Wexler m Leonard Rosenman pd Michael Haller songs Woody Guthrie
☆ David Carradine, Ronny Cox, Melinda Dillon, Gail Strickland, John Lehne
'The movie spends two-and-a-half hours and seven million dollars gazing wistfully at a little man and a big country, and it ends up prettily embalming them both.' – *Janet Maslin, Newsweek*
🏆 Haskell Wexler; Leonard Rosenman
🅰 best picture; Robert Getchell

Boundaries of the Heart *
Australia 1988 100m colour
IFM/Tra La La/FGH (Patrick Juillet)
In a dying desert town, where only 49 people remain, two unexpected visitors disrupt the life of a hotel owner and his unhappy daughter.
Intense, claustrophobic, domestic drama, of disappointments in life and love.
w Peter Yeldham d Lex Marinos ph David Sanderson, Geoff Simpson m Sharon Calcraft pd Melody Cooper ed Philip Howe
☆ Wendy Hughes, John Hargreaves, Norman Kaye, Max Cullen, Julie Nihill, Michael Siberry, John Clayton

The Bounty *
GB 1984 133m Technicolor Panavision
Dino de Laurentiis (Bernard Williams)
William Bligh is summoned before a court martial to explain the events leading to the famous mutiny.
Rather independent version of the twice-told movie tale, and the least compelling of all. Despite the emphasis on character, only occasionally interesting.
w Robert Bolt book *Captain Bligh and Mr Christian* by Anthony Hough d Roger Donaldson ph Arthur Ibbetson m Vangelis pd John Graysmark
☆ Anthony Hopkins, Mel Gibson, Laurence Olivier, Edward Fox, Daniel Day-Lewis, Bernard Hill, Liam Neeson
'A long voyage to nowhere.' – *Nick Roddick, MFB*
'This misshapen movie doesn't work as an epic – it doesn't have the scope or the emotional surge.' – *Pauline Kael, New Yorker*
'A great adventure, a lush romance, and a good movie.' – *Roger Ebert*

The Bounty Hunter
US 1954 79m WarnerColor
Warner (Samuel Bischoff)
Three respectable citizens are unmasked as masterminds behind a series of train robberies.
Predictable but enjoyable star action fare.
w Winston Miller d André de Toth ph Edwin DuPar m David Buttolph
☆ Randolph Scott, Dolores Dorn, Marie Windsor, Ernest Borgnine

The Bounty Hunters (dubbed) *
Italy 1970 106m Technicolor Techniscope
UA/PEA (Alberto Grimaldi)
original title: *Indio Black, Sai che ti Dico: Sei un Gran Figlio di...*
aka: *Adios, Sabata*
In Mexico in the 1860s, a time of revolution, a bounty hunter leads an expedition to steal a shipment of Austrian gold.
Dubbing turned the central character from Indio Black into Sabata, a role played by Lee Van Cleef in a successful movie made by the same director a year earlier; this time around, the result was more conventional and less enjoyable.
w Renato Izzo, Gianfranco Parolini d Frank Kramer (Gianfranco Parolini) ph Sandro Mancori m Bruno Nicolai ad Pierluigi Basile ed Gianfranco Parolini, Salvatore Avantario
☆ Yul Brynner, Dean Reed, Pedro Sanchez (Ignazio Spalla), Gerard Herter, Sal Borgese, Franco Fantasia, Gianni Rizzo
'Since the characterisations are quite lively and the message agreeably cynical ... it is a pity that so much of the action is clogged up by that old stand-by of the Italian Western – extras falling off roofs in graceful death-falls.' – *Tom Milne, MFB*
† *Return of Sabata*, a sequel to the original *Sabata* (qqv), appeared in 1972.

The Bowery ***
US 1933 92m bw
Twentieth Century (Darryl F. Zanuck) (Raymond Griffith, William Goetz)
In 1890s New York, two boisterous rivals settle their differences after one has jumped off the Brooklyn Bridge for a bet.
Roistering saga of cross and double cross on the seamy side, splendidly vigorous in acting and treatment.
w Howard Estabrook, James Gleason novel Michael L. Simmons, Bessie Roth Solomon d Raoul Walsh ph Barney McGill m Alfred Newman ad Richard Day
☆ Wallace Beery, George Raft, Pert Kelton, Jackie Cooper, Fay Wray, Herman Bing
'It delivers as entertainment. It should draw by itself, while the cast will be a considerable help.' – *Variety*
'A model of skilful reconstruction and ingenious research.' – *Times*
'Fairly reeking with authentic, rowdy, hurdy-gurdy atmosphere ... a grand evening of fun for everybody.' – *Photoplay*
† *The Bowery* was the first production of Twentieth Century
†† Gable was sought for the Raft role, but proved unavailable.

Bowery at Midnight
US 1942 61m bw
Monogram
A criminal by night doubles as a mission proprietor by day.
Star horror cheapie with echoes of Lugosi's previous Dark Eyes of London *(qv).*
w Gerald Schnitzer d Wallace Fox
☆ Bela Lugosi, John Archer, Wanda McKay, Tom Neal, Dave O'Brien, Vince Barnett

The Bowery Boys
A cheap and cheerful series of American second features, immensely popular between 1946 and 1958, these adventures of a group of ageing Brooklyn layabouts had their origin in the 1937 film *Dead End*, from which the Dead End Kids graduated to other features at Warner: *Crime School, They Made Me a Criminal, Angels with Dirty Faces, Angels Wash their Faces* (qqv), etc. A couple of the 'boys' then defected to Universal and made *Little Tough Guy* (qv) and a series of half a dozen subsequent pictures; while in 1940 Monogram took a couple more and built up another group called

the East Side Kids. In 1946 a formal merger of talent at Monogram consolidated the remaining members into the Bowery Boys. The members were Leo Gorcey, Huntz Hall, Bobby Jordan, Gabriel Dell (all from the Dead End Kids), Bernard Gorcey, David Gorcey, Billy Benedict, and Bennie Bartlett. The films are:

1946 In Fast Company, Bowery Bombshell, Live Wires, Spook Busters, Mr Hex
1947 Bowery Buckaroos, Hard Boiled Mahoney, News Hounds, Angels' Alley
1948 Jinx Money, Smuggler's Cove, Trouble Makers
1949 Angels in Disguise, Fighting Fools, Hold That Baby, Master Minds
1950 Blonde Dynamite, Blues Busters, Lucky Losers, Triple Trouble
1951 Bowery Battalion, Crazy over Horses, Ghost Chasers, Let's Go Navy
1952 Feudin' Fools, Here Come the Marines, Hold That Line, No Holds Barred
'1953 Clipped Wings, Jalopy, Loose in London, Private Eyes
1954 The Bowery Boys Meet the Monsters, Jungle Gents, Paris Playboys
1955 Bowery to Bagdad, High Society, Jail Busters, Spy Chasers
1956 Dig That Uranium, Crashing Las Vegas, Fighting Trouble, Hot Shots
1957 Spook Chasers, Hold That Hypnotist, Looking for Danger
1958 Up in Smoke, In the Money

Bowery to Broadway

US 1944 94m bw
Universal (John Grant)
In the 1890s, a Bowery songstress makes it to the big time.
Simple-minded musical in which the drama has no drive and the guest stars are given inferior material.
w Joseph Lytton, Arthur T. Horman d Charles Lamont ph Charles Van Enger md Edward Ward
☆ Maria Montez, Turhan Bey, Susanna Foster, Jack Oakie, Donald Cook, Louise Allbritton, Andy Devine, Rosemary de Camp, Ann Blyth, Donald O'Connor, Peggy Ryan, Frank McHugh, Leo Carrillo, Evelyn Ankers, Mantan Moreland
♫ 'The Love Waltz'; 'There'll Always Be a Moon'; 'My Song of Romance'; 'Montevideo'; 'Coney Island Waltz' (plus standards)

'They're going to lie, cheat and steal—but in a nice way.'
Bowfinger *
US 1998 97m DeLuxe
Universal/Imagine (Brian Grazer)
An unsuccessful producer decides to use a superstar in his new film without the actor being aware of what's happening.
Mildly amusing comedy of Hollywood wheeling and dealing, with a few good jokes but rather more poor ones.
w Steve Martin d Frank Oz ph Ueli Steiger m David Newman pd Jackson DeGovia ed Richard Pearson
☆ Steve Martin, Eddie Murphy, Heather Graham, Christine Baranski, Jamie Kennedy, Adam Alexi-Malle, Kohl Sudduth, Barry Newman, Robert Downey Jnr, Terence Stamp
'A splendidly funny piece of work.' – *Empire*

'Some people have a hard time unwinding.'
Box of Moonlight *
US 1996 112m Technicolor
First Independent/Lakeshore/Largo/JVC/Lemon Sky (Marcus Viscidi, Thomas A. Bliss)
A boring construction foreman gives a lift to a young drop-out, who teaches him to relax and enjoy life moment by moment.
A somewhat unconvincing paean to spontaneity, as opposed to the mundane realities of life, but given a little boost by Turturro's performance as an uptight family man; it is less an example of carpe diem, though, and more caveat emptor.
wd Tom DiCillo ph Paul Ryan m Jim Farmer pd Thérèse DePrez ed Camilla Toniolo
☆ John Turturro, Sam Rockwell, Catherine Keener, Lisa Blount, Annie Corley, Rica Martens, Ray Aranha, Alexander Goodwin, Dermot Mulroney

Boxcar Bertha *
US 1972 88m DeLuxe
AIP (Roger Corman)
In early thirties Arkansas, an unhappy girl falls in with gangsters and train robbers.
Competent imitation of Bonnie and Clyde (qv).
w Joyce H. and John W. Corrington d Martin Scorsese ph John Stephens m Gib Guilbeau, Thad Maxwell
☆ Barbara Hershey, David Carradine, Barry Primus, Bernie Casey, John Carradine

'Love is always worth fighting for.'
The Boxer **
GB/Ireland/US 1997 113m Technicolor
Universal/Hell's Kitchen (Jim Sheridan, Arthur Lappin)
A former IRA prisoner takes up his old profession of boxing and opens a gym for young hopefuls with the aid of an alcoholic trainer.
A tough and gritty drama about controlled violence as redemption. The fight sequences have an authentic, sweaty feel about them; the rest is too schematic in its condemnation of bigotry to convince.
w Jim Sheridan, Terry George d Jim Sheridan ph Chris Menges m Gavin Friday, Maurice Seezer pd Brian Morris ed Gerry Hambling
☆ Daniel Day-Lewis, Emily Watson, Brian Cox, Ken Stott, Gerard McSorley, Eleanor Methven, Ciaran Fitzgerald, Kenneth Cranham
'An involving but rather prosaic report from the Belfast front with a melancholy undertow of romantic yearning.' – *Todd McCarthy, Variety*
† Daniel Day-Lewis spent several years in preparation for his role, and was trained by former world champion boxer, and Irish hero, Barry McGuigan.

'A Deep Dark Obsession That Bares A Woman's Body And A Man's Soul.'
Boxing Helena
US 1993 105m Technicolor Panavision
Entertainment/Main Line (Carl Mazzocone)
A surgeon seemingly takes advantage of an accident to amputate the legs and arms of the woman who rejected his love.
A tedious, neurotic tale that would have benefited from hefty cuts; it is unable to sustain interest in either its minimal plot or its unsympathetic characters.
wd Jennifer Chambers Lynch story Philippe Caland ph Frank Byers m Graeme Revell ad Paul Huggins ed David Finfer
☆ Julian Sands, Sherilyn Fenn, Bill Paxton, Art Garfunkel, Betsy Clark, Kurtwood Smith
'Not only is the script unbelievably bad – packed with clumsy, forced and often banal dialogue – but some of the acting has to be seen to be believed.' – *Amanda Lipman, Sight and Sound*
'Just might have passed muster as a 15-minute film school gag. With performances as inept as the script, the self-parody cannot be passed off as intentional.' – *David Robinson, The Times*
'Simply cannot be taken seriously, in a large part because it takes itself so seriously that we can only respond to it with gales of derisive crowing.' – *Michael Atkinson, Movieline*
† The film was most memorable for what happened off-screen, when Kim Basinger was sued for changing her mind over her agreement to star in it, and ordered to pay some $8 million in damages. In a settlement reached in 1995, she agreed to pay around $3 million.

A Boy a Girl and a Bike
GB 1949 92m bw
Gainsborough (Ralph Keene)
Romantic jealousies arise between members of a Yorkshire cycling club.
Mild comedy drama with the advantage of fresh air locations.
w Ted Willis d Ralph Smart ph Ray Elton m Kenneth Pakeman
☆ John McCallum, Honor Blackman, Patrick Holt, Diana Dors, Leslie Dwyer, Thora Hird, Anthony Newley, Megs Jenkins, Maurice Denham

'A rather kinky tale of survival.'
A Boy and His Dog *
US 1975 89m colour
LG Jaf (Alvy Moore)
While searching for food in an apocalyptic future, a young man and his more intelligent telepathic dog find an apparently Utopian community that needs masculine input.
Quirky science fiction, not to be taken too seriously, and managing a surprise ending.
wd L. Q. Jones story Harlan Ellison ph John Arthur Morrill m Tim McIntire pd Ray Boyle ed Scott Conrad
☆ Don Johnson, Susanne Benton, Jason Robards, Ron Feinberg, Tim McIntire, Charles McGraw

The Boy and the Bridge
GB 1959 91m bw
Xanadu (Kevin McClory)
A boy who believes he has committed a murder hides in the ramparts of Tower Bridge.
This tiny fable adds up to very weak entertainment, despite inventive photography, because it has virtually no plot development.
w Geoffrey Orme, Kevin McClory, Desmond O'Donovan d Kevin McClory ph Ted Scaife m Malcolm Arnold
☆ Ian MacLaine, Liam Redmond, James Hayter, Norman MacOwan, Geoffrey Keen, Jack MacGowran, Royal Dano, Rita Webb

The Boy and the Pirates
↟↟ US 1960 84m Eastmancolor
Perceptovision
United Artists
A small boy finds an old bottle on the seashore, wishes he could live in pirate days, and hey presto.
Modest juvenile fantasy on the lines of The Wizard of Oz (qv) but without the talent.
w Lillie Hayward, Jerry Sackheim d Bert I. Gordon
☆ Charles Herbert, Susan Gordon, Murvyn Vye, Paul Guilfoyle

A Boy Called Hate
US 1995 98m CFI colour
Pacific/J&M
A young biker rescues a girl from rape by shooting her assailant, and is soon being sought by the police for murder.
Trashy story of two young killers on the run, featuring a great deal of moody teenage posturing, in a sub-James Dean manner, and lacking any moral or wider social dimension.
wd Mitch Marcus ph Paul Holahan m Pray for Rain
☆ Scott Caan, Missy Crider, Elliott Gould, Adam Beach, James Caan

The Boy Cried Murder
GB/West Germany/Yugoslavia 1965 86m Eastmancolor
CCC/Carlos/Avala
A small boy has such a vivid imagination that nobody except the criminal believes him when he says he has witnessed a murder.
Flat and unnecessary remake of The Window (which was later done again as Eye Witness) (qqv).
w Robin Estridge story Cornell Woolrich d George Breakston
☆ Frazer MacIntosh, Veronica Hurst, Phil Brown, Tim Barrett

'No more bubble bath, she screamed!'
Boy, Did I Get a Wrong Number
US 1966 99m DeLuxe
UA/Edward Small (George Beck)
Trying to phone his wife, an estate agent gets involved with a runaway actress.
Lifeless and generally resistible star comedy, the first of several hard and unfunny vehicles for an ageing Bob Hope seeming to hark back to the least attractive aspects of burlesque rather than the sympathetic wisecracking which suits him best.
w Burt Styler, Albert E. Lewin, George Kennett d George Marshall ph Lionel Lindon m Richard Lasalle ly By Dunham
☆ Bob Hope, Elke Sommer, Phyllis Diller, Marjorie Lord, Cesare Danova, Benny Baker

The Boy Friend *
GB 1971 125m Metrocolor Panavision
MGM/Russflix (Ken Russell)
On a wet Wednesday afternoon in Portsmouth in the late twenties, a tatty company with backstage problems puts on an empty-headed musical.
Russell the mastermind effectively destroys Sandy Wilson's charming period pastiche, sending up all the numbers (via badly staged dream sequences on the wrong shape screen) in a Busby Berkeley manner which had not yet been invented. Moments do work, but a non-star doesn't help, and the whole thing is an artistic disaster of some significance both to Russell's career and to the cinema of the early seventies.
wd Ken Russell musical play Sandy Wilson ph David Watkin md Ian Whittaker, Peter Greenwell, Peter Maxwell Davies pd Tony Walton
☆ Twiggy, Christopher Gable, Max Adrian, Tommy Tune, Barbara Windsor, Moyra Fraser, Bryan Pringle, Vladek Sheybal, Antonia Ellis, Glenda Jackson
'The glittering, joyless numbers keep coming at you: you never get any relief from Russell's supposed virtuosity.' – *New Yorker, 1977*
'The acting was too broad, the gags too laboured and the pacing too slow.' – *Ken Russell*
⅃ Ian Whittaker, Peter Greenwell, Peter Maxwell Davies

The Boy from Barnardo's: see Lord Jeff

The Boy from Mercury *
GB/France 1996 87m colour
Blue Dolphin/Mercurian/Blue Dahlia/Blue Rose/Jo Manuel (Marina Hughes)
In Ireland in the late 50s, a young boy fantasizes that he is from the planet Mercury and has been sent to investigate the Earth.
Nostalgic, gently humorous account of childhood, in which small events assume large proportions.
wd Martin Duffy ph Seamus Deasy m Stephen McKeon pd Tom Conroy ed John Victor Smith
☆ Rita Tushingham, Tom Courtenay, Hugh O'Conor, James Hickey, Ian McElhinney, Joanne Gerard

The Boy from Oklahoma *
US 1953 88m Warnercolor
Warner (David Weisbart)
A genial plainsman studying law becomes sheriff of a small town and uncovers its mayor as a killer.
Modest, pleasing Western with the star imitating his father.
w Frank Davis, Winston Miller d Michael Curtiz ph Robert Burks m Max Steiner
☆ Will Rogers Jnr, Nancy Olson, Lon Chaney Jnr, Anthony Caruso, Wallace Ford, Clem Bevans, Merv Griffin

The Boy in Blue
Canada 1986 97m DeLuxe
TCF/ICC/Denis Heroux/John Kemeny
In the 1870s, a young ne'er-do-well Canadian oarsman becomes a world champion.
The true story of Ned Hanlan, straightforwardly and unremarkably told.
w Douglas Bowie idea John Trent d Charles Jarrott ph Pierre Mignot m Roger Webb pd William Beeton ed Rit Wallis
☆ Nicolas Cage, Christopher Plummer, Cynthia Dale, David Naughton, Sean Sullivan, Melody Anderson

Boy Meets Girl: see A Lover and His Lass (1975)

Boy Meets Girl *
US 1938 86m bw
Warner (George Abbott)
Two crazy Hollywood scenario writers make a star of an infant yet unborn.
Freewheeling film version of a hilarious play: fine crazy comedy and excellent Hollywood satire.
w Bella and Sam Spewack (play) Bella and Sam Spewack d Lloyd Bacon ph Sol Polito m Leo Forbstein
☆ James Cagney, Pat O'Brien, Marie Wilson, Ralph Bellamy, Frank McHugh, Dick Foran, Bruce Lester, Ronald Reagan, James Stephenson
'Satisfactory, but not socko.' – *Variety*

↟↟ film suitable for family viewing   ▣▣ VHS video-cassette for the British PAL system   ▤ VHS video-cassette for the British PAL system in wide screen format   ⌗ Video cassette in a computer-colourised version   ▬ American NTSC video-cassette   ◎ Laser disc

'It bounces from one hilarious absurdity to another with all the resilience of a rubber ball.' – *MFB*

Boy Meets Girl *
France 1984 100m bw
Other Cinema/Abilene (Patricia Moraz)
📺

An aimless youth ends his romance with one girl and starts a new one with another.
A low-budget movie, made by its writer-director at the age of 22, of interest mainly for its photography of Paris by night.
wd Leos Carax ph Jean-Yves Escoffier m Jacques Pinault ad Serge Marzolff, Jean Bauer ed Nelly Meunier, Francine Sandberg
☆ Denis Lavant, Mireille Périer, Carroll Brooks, Elie Poicard, Anna Baldaccini

Boy of the Streets
US 1937 75m bw
Monogram
A city youngster falls in with racketeers.
Ho-hum Dead End melodrama.
w Scott Darling, Gilson Brown d William Nigh
☆ Jackie Cooper, Maureen O'Connor, Kathleen Burke, Marjorie Main, Robert Emmett O'Connor
'Will do biz for independents ... easily Monogram's most ambitious production effort to date.' – *Variety*

Boy on a Dolphin *
US 1957 111m Eastmancolor
Cinemascope
TCF (Samuel G. Engel)
📺 ▦ 🎧

A Greek girl diver discovers a sunken artifact of great value and the news spreads to an American archaeologist and an unscrupulous collector.
Likeable, sunswept Mediterranean adventure romance marred by the miscasting of the male lead.
w Ivan Moffat, Dwight Taylor novel David Divine d Jean Negulesco ph Milton Krasner m Hugo Friedhofer md Lionel Newman
☆ Alan Ladd, Sophia Loren, Clifton Webb, Laurence Naismith, Alexis Minotis, Jorge Mistral
♫ Hugo Friedhofer

Boy Slaves
US 1938 70m bw
RKO
A boy leaves home and ends up in a forced labour camp.
Topical preachment drama which kicked up a bit of dust at the time.
w Albert Bein, Ben Orkow d P. J. Wolfson
☆ Anne Shirley, Roger Daniel, James McCallion, Alan Baxter.
'Devoid of essential entertainment factors for general theatre showings.' – *Variety*

A Boy Ten Feet Tall: see *Sammy Going South*

Boy Trouble
US 1939 75m bw
Paramount
A small-towner finds his life upset when his wife adopts two orphans.
Sentimental comedy which caused a few tears to trickle.
w Laura and S. J. Perelman story Lloyd Corrigan, Monte Brice d George Archainbaud
☆ Charles Ruggles, Mary Boland, Donald O'Connor, Joyce Matthews, Billy Lee, Andrew Tombes
'Good old hokum with an emotional wallop ... Exhibitors can use more pictures of this type.' – *Variety*

The Boy Who Could Fly
👫 US 1986 114m DeLuxe Panavision
TCF/Lorimar (Gary Adelson)
📺 ▦ 🎦

After the death of their father, two children move with their mother to a new home and make friends with the boy next door, who believes that he can fly.
A family drama, about the problems of coping with loss, that moves into fantasy without altogether losing its slight charm and effectiveness.
wd Nick Castle ph Steven Poster, Adam Holender m Bruce Broughton pd Jim Bissell ed Patrick Kennedy

☆ Lucy Deakins, Jay Underwood, Bonnie Bedelia, Fred Savage, Colleen Dewhurst, Fred Gwynne, Mindy Cohen, Janet MacLachlan, Jason Priestley

'Those who don't believe – are dead!'
The Boy Who Cried Werewolf
US 1973 93m Technicolor
Universal
On a camping trip, a boy and his father are attacked by a werewolf, and later on Dad starts acting mighty strange...
Disappointingly straight rewrite of the old hokum.
w Bob Homel d Nathan Juran
☆ Kerwin Mathews, Elaine Devry, Scott Sealey

The Boy Who Had Everything
Australia 1985 94m colour
Multi Films/Alfred Roads (Richard Mason, Julia Overton)
In 1965, as Australian troops are about to be sent to Vietnam a university freshman submits to initiation rites but renounces his mother and his future.
Angry, rather muddled character study which seems to be drawn from life but doesn't know what moral to point.
wd Stephen Wallace ph Geoff Burton m Ralph Schneider
☆ Jason Connery, Diane Cilento, Laura Williams, Lewis Fitz-Gerald

The Boy Who Stole a Million
👫 GB 1960 81m bw
British Lion/Fanfare/George H. Brown
A young page in a Spanish bank 'borrows' some money to help his father but finds Dad, police and crooks all after him.
Half-hearted attempt at a British Bicycle Thieves (qv), oddly set in Spain and never quite managing to convince or interest us.
w John Eldridge, Charles Crichton story Neils West Larsen, Antonio de Leon d Charles Crichton ph Douglas Slocombe m Tristram Cary ad Maurice Carter ed Peter Bezencenet
☆ Maurice Reyna, Virgilio Teixeira, Harold Kasket, George Coulouris, Edwin Richfield, Curt Christian, Bill Nagy, Marianne Benet, Cyril Shaps, Warren Mitchell

The Boy with Green Hair
US 1948 82m Technicolor
RKO (Stephen Ames)
▦ 🎦

When he hears that his parents were killed in an air raid, a boy's hair turns green; other war orphans encourage him to parade himself publicly as an image of the horror and futility of war.
Muddled, pretentious and unpersuasive fantasy, typical of this producer's do-goodery. One of those oddities which make Hollywood endearing, but not very entertaining apart from Pat O'Brien's garrulous grandpa.
w Ben Barzman, Alfred Lewis Levitt story Betsy Beaton d Joseph Losey ph George Barnes m Leigh Harline
☆ Dean Stockwell, Pat O'Brien, Robert Ryan, Barbara Hale

The Boyars' Plot: see *Ivan the Terrible*

Boys
US 1996 89m Technicolor
Polygram/Interscope (Peter Frankfurt, Paul Feldsher, Erica Huggins)
📺 ▦ 🎧

A frustrated high-school student discovers a mysterious young woman, who is unconscious after a fall from her horse, and takes her back to his room.
Thin and vapid tale of a mixed-up teenager, almost totally lacking in either content or interest; clumsily structured, it fails to reach a satisfactory or acceptable conclusion.
wd Stacy Cochran story Twenty Minutes by James Salter ph Robert Elswit m Stewart Copeland pd Dan Bishop ed Camilla Toniolo
☆ Winona Ryder, Lukas Haas, John C. Reilly, James LeGros, Skeet Ulrich, Spencer Vrooman, Charlie Hofheimer, Bill Sage, Jessica Harper
'Never advances beyond banality, and the cop-out ending is both glib and unreal.' – *George Perry, Sunday Times*

The Boys
GB 1962 123m bw Cinemascope
Gala/Columbia (Sidney J. Furie)
Four boys are on trial for killing a garage attendant.
Elaborate courtroom drama with flashbacks, stars for counsel, a tricksy director, and about forty minutes too much footage.
w Stuart Douglass d Sidney J. Furie ph Gerald Gibbs m The Shadows
☆ Richard Todd, Robert Morley, Felix Aylmer, Dudley Sutton, Ronald Lacey, Tony Garnett, Jess Conrad, Wilfrid Brambell, Allan Cuthbertson, Colin Gordon

The Boys *
Australia 1998 84m Movielab
Globe/Arenafilm/AFC (Robert Connolly, John Maynard)
◉

Released from prison, a violent man returns home to disrupt family life.
Chilling portrait of a manipulative and aggressive psychopath; by the end we are no wiser, though more appalled, than we were at the beginning.
w Stephen Sewell play Gordon Graham d Rowan Woods ph Tristan Milani m The Necks pd Luigi Pittorino ed Nick Meyers
☆ David Wenham, Toni Collette, Lynette Curran, John Polson, Anthony Hayes, Jeanette Cronin, Anna Lise, Pete Smith

'A True Story About Finding The Courage To Be Yourself.'
Boys Don't Cry ***
US 1999 118m DeLuxe
TCF/Killer Films (Jeffrey Sharp, John Hart, Eva Kolodner, Christine Vachon)
▦ ◉

In Nebraska in the early 90s, a girl decides to live as a boy.
Abrasive, jolting drama of shock and outrage, more disturbing than the grisliest horror movie because, based on fact, it exposes a desperation at the heart of America.
w Kimberly Peirce, Andy Bienen d Kimberly Peirce m Jim Denault m Nathan Larson pd Michael Shaw ed Lee Percy, Tracy Granger
☆ Hilary Swank, Chloe Sevigny, Peter Sarsgaard, Brendan Sexton III, Alison Folland, Alicia Goranson, Matt McGrath, Rob Campbell, Jeannetta Arnette
'Audacious, accomplished pic should play well with open minded viewers seeking edgy, mature fare.' – *Emanuel Levy, Variety*
'A delicately conceived, fearless movie.' – *David Denby, New Yorker*
'Scorches the screen like a prairie fire.' – *J. Hoberman, Village Voice*
🏆 Hilary Swank
♟ Chloe Sevigny

'94 men must die to keep alive a dream – or a nightmare!'
The Boys from Brazil *
US/GB 1978 124m DeLuxe
ITC/Producer Circle (Martin Richards, Stanley O'Toole)
📺 ▦ 🎦 🎧

A renegade Nazi in hiding has a sinister plot to reconquer the world.
Suspense fantasy firmly based on a gripping book; excellent performances, but a shade too long.
w Heywood Gould novel Ira Levin d Franklin Schaffner ph Henri Decaë m Jerry Goldsmith pd Gil Parrando
☆ Gregory Peck, Laurence Olivier, James Mason, Lilli Palmer, Uta Hagen, Steve Guttenberg, Denholm Elliott, Rosemary Harris, John Dehner, John Rubinstein, Anne Meara, David Hurst, Michael Gough
♟ Jerry Goldsmith; Laurence Olivier

The Boys from Fengkuei **
Taiwan 1983 104m colour
Evergreen
original title: *Feng-Kuei-Lai-Te Jen*
aka: *All the Youthful Days*
In search of excitement, three youths move to the city from the fishing village where they were born.
Absorbingly detailed drama of the young coming to terms with the pleasures and problems of adult life.
w Chu T'ien-wen d Hou Hsiao-hsien ph Ch'en K'un'hou
☆ Niu Cheng-tse, Lin Xiuling, To Tsung-hua, Chang Shih

The Boys from Syracuse *
US 1940 74m bw
Universal (Jules Levey)
The Comedy of Errors with modern wisecracks, and a few songs.
Predictable well-drilled confusion arises from master and slave having identical twins, but the general tone is a bit flat for an adaptation from a hilarious Broadway success. Still, the songs are lively and the chariot race finale shows spirit.
w Leonard Spigelgass, Charles Grayson, Paul Gerard Smith play George Abbott, William Shakespeare d A. Edward Sutherland songs Joseph Valentine m Frank Skinner m/ly Richard Rodgers, Lorenz Hart md Charles Previn ad Jack Otterson
☆ Allan Jones, Joe Penner, Charles Butterworth, Rosemary Lane, Irene Hervey, Martha Raye, Alan Mowbray
† The writing credit on screen ends: 'After a play by William Shakespeare ... long, long after!
♫ 'Who Are You?'; 'This Can't be Love'; 'Falling in Love with Love'; 'The Greeks Have No Word for It'; 'Sing for Your Supper'; 'He and She'
♟ John Otterson

The Boys in Blue
GB 1983 91m colour
Elstree/Rank
Village policemen catch art thieves.
Horribly incompetent remake of Ask a Policeman (qv), with a totally untalented star team.
wd Val Guest
☆ Tommy Cannon, Bobby Ball, Suzanne Danielle, Roy Kinnear, Eric Sykes, Jack Douglas, Edward Judd, Jon Pertwee, Arthur English
'The perfect antidote to sweeping claims about the British renaissance.' – *Geoff Brown, MFB*

Boys in Brown
GB 1949 84m bw
Gainsborough (Anthony Darnborough)
Life in a Borstal institution.
The stars make elderly boys, but Jack Warner is a cuddly governor. Boring and unpersuasive non-documentary fiction in Britain's most tiresome style.
wd Montgomery Tully play Reginald Beckwith ph Gordon Lang, Cyril Bristow m Doreen Carwithen
☆ Jack Warner, Dirk Bogarde, Michael Medwin, Jimmy Hanley, Richard Attenborough, Alfie Bass, Barbara Murray, Thora Hird
† Made by the Independent Frame method, which blended real backgrounds with studio sets.

The Boys in Company C
Hong Kong 1977 125m Technicolor
Panavision
Golden Harvest (Andre Morgan)
▦ 🎦

Five marines find their lives changed by the Vietnam war.
Crude action melodrama.
w Rick Natkin, Sidney J. Furie d Sidney J. Furie ph Godfrey Godar m Jaime Mendoza-Nava
☆ Stan Shaw, Andrew Stevens, James Canning, Michael Lembeck, Craig Wasson, James Whitmore Jnr
'Laden with barrack room dialogue and played at the enlisted man's level.' – *Variety*
'An exploitation war movie, like dirty TV.' – *New Yorker*

The Boys in the Band *
US 1970 120m Technicolor
Cinema Center/Leo (Mart Crowley, Kenneth Utt)
📺 ▦ 🎦

Tempers fray and true selves are revealed when a heterosexual is accidentally invited to a homosexual party.
Careful but claustrophobic filming of a Broadway play, which at the screen's closer quarters becomes overpowering well before the end.
w Mart Crowley play Mart Crowley d William Friedkin ph Arthur J. Ornitz m none
☆ Leonard Frey, Kenneth Nelson, Cliff Gorman, Frederick Combs, Reuben Greene, Robert La Tourneaux, Laurence Luckinbill, Keith Prentice, Peter White
'They crack jokes while their hearts are breaking.' – *New Yorker*

Boys' Night Out

US 1962 115m Metrocolor Cinemascope
MGM/Filmways (Martin Ransohoff)
Three married men and their bachelor friend share a flat and a 'mistress'.
Would-be saucy comedy in which nothing sexy ever happens and the helpless players are as witless as the script.
w Ira Wallach d Michael Gordon ph Arthur E. Arling m Frank de Vol
☆ James Garner, Kim Novak, Tony Randall, Howard Duff, Howard Morris, Oscar Homolka, Janet Blair, Patti Page, Jessie Royce Landis

Boys on the Side

US 1995 117m Technicolor
Warner/Canal/Regency/Alcor (Arnon Milchan, Steven Reuther, Herbert Ross)
Three women – a lesbian musician, a heterosexual with AIDS and the pregnant, confused girlfriend of a drug dealer – go on the road together.
Manipulative twaddle, mired in sentimentality and remote from reality, a modern version of a woman's picture, all female bonding and buddies together, and extremely old-fashioned under its slick, hip surface.
w Don Roos d Herbert Ross ph Donald E. Thorin m David Newman pd Ken Adam ed Michael R. Miller
☆ Whoopi Goldberg, Mary Louise Parker, Drew Barrymore, Matthew McConaughey, James Remar, Billy Wirth, Anita Gillette
'Lush, weepy, topically correct, emotional button pusher – a chick flick for women who sing "We Are Family" too much.' – *Lisa Schwarzbaum, Entertainment Weekly*

'More laughs than Laurel and Hardy! More thrills than *Test Pilot*! More tears than *Captains Courageous*!'

Boys Town *

US 1938 93m bw
MGM (John W. Considine Jnr)
The story of Father Flanagan and his school for juvenile delinquents.
Well-made, highly successful, but sentimental crowd pleaser.
w John Meehan, Dore Schary story Eleanore Griffin, Dore Schary d Norman Taurog ph Sidney Wagner m Edward Ward
☆ Spencer Tracy, Mickey Rooney, Henry Hull, Gene Reynolds, Sidney Miller, Frankie Thomas, Bobs Watson, Tommy Noonan
'A production that should build goodwill for the whole industry.' – *Variety*
🏆 Eleanore Griffin, Dore Schary; Spencer Tracy
🏆 best picture; John Meehan, Dore Schary; Norman Taurog

Boys Will Be Boys **

GB 1935 75m bw
Gaumont/Gainsborough (Michael Balcon)
An incompetent headmaster thwarts a jewel robber.
The first recognizable Will Hay vehicle, based in part on J. B. Morton's Narkover sketches.
w Will Hay, Robert Edmunds d William Beaudine ph Charles Van Enger m Louis Levy
☆ Will Hay, Gordon Harker, Jimmy Hanley, Davy Burnaby, Norma Varden, Claude Dampier, Charles Farrell, Percy Walsh
'It is hard to see how his distinctive sketch writing could have found a satisfactory screen equivalent. Nevertheless, a good augury of the films to come.' – *Ray Seaton and Roy Martin, 1978*

'Increase The Peace.'

Boyz N The Hood **

US 1991 112m DeLuxe
Columbia TriStar (Steve Nicolaides)
Young blacks try to survive in the hostile urban world of Los Angeles gangs.
Episodic in form and over-schematic in its depiction of social difficulties, particularly those caused by absentee fathers, but it holds one's interest throughout.
wd John Singleton ph Charles Mills m Stanley Clarke ad Bruce Bellamy ed Bruce Cannon
☆ Ice Cube, Cuba Gooding Jnr, Morris Chestnut, Larry Fishburne, Nia Long, Tyra Ferrell

'An absorbing, smartly made dramatic encyclopedia of problems and ethics in the black community, 1991.' – *Variety*
'Conveys a vivid sense of the dangers, both physical and emotional, of day-to-day existence in this ravaged urban environment.' – *New Yorker*
🎭 John Singleton (as director); John Singleton (screenplay)

The Brady Bunch Movie *

US 1995 88m DeLuxe
Paramount (Sherwood Schwartz, Lloyd Schwartz, David Kirkpatrick)
In a troubled modern-day Los Angeles, the Brady family behave as if they were still living in the mid-70s, displaying sweetness and good behaviour on every possible occasion.
Pleasantly amusing comedy that exploits the gap between the fantasy of family relationships and the reality, though it will mean most to viewers of the original TV sitcom.
w Laurice Elehwany, Rick Copp, Bonnie Turner, Terry Turner d Betty Thomas ph Mac Ahlberg m Guy Moon pd Steven Jordan ed Peter Teschner
☆ Shelley Long, Gary Cole, Michael McKean, Jean Smart, Henriette Mantel, Christopher Daniel Barnes, Christine Taylor, Jennifer Elise Cox, Jesse Lee, Olivia Hack, RuPaul
'It's a very good-humoured, unspiteful movie, and mounted with great energy. Everyone acts in that manic, twitchy, over-emphatic manner of bad US sitcoms, while Betty Thomas directs with speed and wit.' – *Sheila Johnston, Independent*
'This is not a very good film, being less well-written than it might have been and directed as if we are all as moronic as the people in the movie.' – *Derek Malcolm, Guardian*
† *The Brady Bunch*, created by Sherwood Schwartz, was a clean-cut television sitcom that ran from 1969 to 1974 and was followed by an animated version, *The Brady Kids* (1972–74). The family returned for *The Brady Bunch Hour* in 1977 and *The Bradys* in 1990 and also made several TV movies. None of TV's Brady Bunch appeared in the film.

The Brain: see Vengeance (1962)

The Brain

France/US 1969 115m colour
Paramount (Alain Poire)
original title: *Le Cerveau*
A British colonel leads an international crew in an attempt to rob NATO.
Exhausting and generally misfiring international crook comedy.
w Gérard Oury, Marcel Julian, Daniele Thompson d Gérard Oury ph Vladimir Ivanov, Armand Thirard m Georges Delerue
☆ David Niven, Jean-Paul Belmondo, Bourvil, Eli Wallach, Silvia Monti

Brain Damage

US 1988 90m colour
Palace/Frank Henenlotter (Edgar Levins)
A man is provided with hallucinatory pleasures in return for helping a brain-eating parasite.
Low-budget nastiness intended to amuse rather than shock.
wd Frank Henenlotter ph Bruce Torbet m Gus Russo, Clutch Reiser ad Ivy Rosovsky ed James Y. Kwei, Frank Henenlotter
☆ Rick Herbst, Jennifer Lowry, Gordon Macdonald, Theo Barnes, Lucille Saint-Peter, Vicki Darnell

Brain Donors

US 1992 79m colour
Paramount/Zucker (Gil Netter, James D. Brubaker)
A trio of idiots attempt to part a widow from her wealth by running a ballet company for her.
A misfiring farce and a leaden attempt to revive the Marx Brothers' style of comedy. Inspired by A Night at the Opera, it doesn't even approach the low level of Love Happy (qqv).
w Pat Proft d Dennis Dugan ph David M. Walsh m Ira Newborn pd William J. Cassidy ed Malcolm Campbell

☆ John Turturro, Bob Nelson, Mel Smith, Nancy Marchand, John Savident, George de La Pena
'Sounds like a horror film and for those expecting a comedy, it is.' – *Variety*

'Crawling, Slimy Things Terror-Bent On Destroying The World!'

The Brain Eaters

US 1958 60m bw
AIP/Corinthian (Edwin Nelson)
Parasites from the Earth's core isolate a small town and begin to take over its citizens.
Low-budget imitation of Invasion of The Body Snatchers (qv), but with little evidence of intelligence in its making.
w Gordon Urquhart d Bruno Ve Sota ph Larry Raimond m Tom Jonson ad Burt Shonberg ed Carlo Lodato
☆ Edwin Nelson, Alan Frost, Jack Hill, Joanna Lee, Jody Fair, David Hughes, Leonard Nimoy
† Leonard Nimoy is credited as Nemoy and plays a bearded ancient.

'Science-fiction's most astounding story!'

The Brain from Planet Arous

US 1957 70m bw
Howco International (Jacques Marquette)
A criminal alien, consisting of a disembodied brain, takes possession of the body of a nuclear scientist.
Laughably inept science fiction that leaves few clichés unspoken.
w Ray Buffum d Nathan Hertz (Nathan Juran) ph Jacques Marquette m Walter Greene ed Irving Schoenberg
☆ John Agar, Joyce Meadows, Robert Fuller, Thomas B. Henry, Henry Travis
'It's not actually as hilariously awful as you might think, but bad movie buffs will still get a kick out of it.' – *The Dark Side*

The Brain Machine *

GB 1954 83m bw
Alec Snowden/Merton Park
Through an electroencephalograph, a hospital psychiatrist recognizes a patient as a dangerous psychopath.
Very tolerable crime thriller with a fresh angle.
wd Ken Hughes
☆ Elizabeth Allan, Patrick Barr, Maxwell Reed, Russell Napier, Vanda Godsell, Gibb McLaughlin

Brain Waves

US 1982 80m colour
CinAmerica Pictures (Ulli Lommel)
A brain-dead accident victim is brought back to life through the electronic transfer of the brain patterns of a murder victim, with disastrous results.
Ponderous and sentimental fantasy, a high-tech variation on Frankenstein.
wd Ulli Lommel ph Jon Kranhouse m Robert O. Ragland ed Richard Brummer
☆ Tony Curtis, Keir Dullea, Suzanne Love, Vera Miles, Percy Rodrigues, Paul Willson

'A romantic comedy about a boy, a girl and their power tools.'

Braindead

New Zealand 1992 104m colour
Polygram/Wingnut Films (Jim Booth)
US title: *Dead Alive*
A bite from a rat monkey turns a woman into a zombie; soon her cellar is full of other zombies.
Grossly gory horror, played for sick laughs, with a climactic massacre of the zombies by lawnmower that must rank as one of the bloodiest twenty minutes on film. It is difficult to understand why the British censors are happy to let us watch such jejune and tiresome stuff uncut while refusing a video release for such films as Straw Dogs and Reservoir Dogs (qqv).
w Stephen Sinclair, Frances Walsh, Peter Jackson d Peter Jackson ph Murray Milne pd Kenneth Leonard-Jones ad Jamie Selkirk
☆ Timothy Balme, Diana Penalver, Elizabeth Moody, Ian Watkin, Brenda Kendal, Stuart Devenie, Jed Brophy
'Soon jettisons characterisations and story development in favour of an orgy of tasteless effects.' – *Kim Newman*

'It's impossible to imagine anyone out-grossing the New Zealander's effort, or wanting to.' – *Sight and Sound*

Brainscan

US 1994 95m colour
Guild/Coral (Michael Roy)
A youth finds that the deaths in a computer game he is playing are happening in the real world.
A tasteless dose of teenage fantasy, just another failed attempt to bridge the gap between cinema and computer games.
w Andrew Kevin Walker story Brian Owens d John Flynn ph François Protat pd Paola Ridolfi ed Jay Cassidy visual effects and character design René Daalder
☆ Edward Furlong, Frank Langella, T. Ryder Smith, Amy Hargreaves, Jamie Marsh, Victor Ertmanis, David Hemblen
'May be too tame for the creature-feature fans and slasher devotees who will be drawn by its ad campaign.' – *Variety*

Brainstorm

US 1965 110m bw Panavision
Warner/Kodima (William Conrad)
A passer-by saves a married woman from suicide, has an affair with her, and conspires to murder her husband. This accomplished, she leaves him and he goes insane.
Overlong thriller which starts off agreeably in the Double Indemnity vein; but goes slow and solemn around the half way mark.
w Mann Rubin d William Conrad ph Sam Leavitt m George Duning
☆ Jeffrey Hunter, Anne Francis, Dana Andrews, Viveca Lindfors, Stacy Harris
'A sub-B potboiler for those who find comic books too intellectual.' – *Judith Crist*

'Open the doors to your mind…'

Brainstorm

US 1983 106m Metrocolor Super Panavision
MGM/UA/JF (Douglas Trumbull)
A technological device records emotions so faithfully as to make other people feel them through each of the five senses. The enemy is discovered to be using it for brainwashing purposes; but it has recorded the experience of death…
Scientific mumbo jumbo which went far too far as an attack on the audience's senses, and was jinxed by the death of its star during production.
w Robert Stitzel, Philip Frank Messina, Bruce Joel Rubin d Douglas Trumbull ph Richard Yuricich m James Horner pd John Vallone
☆ Natalie Wood, Christopher Walken, Louise Fletcher, Cliff Robertson, Jordan Christopher, Alan Fudge
'A monstrous bore, with uninteresting characters buried beneath a mass of even less interesting technology.' – *Tom Milne, MFB*

Brainwashed

France/Italy 1972 Eastmancolor
Lira/Fox Europa/Pegaso (Roland Girard, Jean Bolvary)
original title: *Le Droit d'Aimer*
aka: *The Right to Love*
After a two-year wait, a woman visits her lover, a political prisoner held on a grim island jail, and discovers that their relationship has changed.
A glum fable of requited love.
w Jean-Claude Carrière, Françoise Xenakis, Jean Bolvary, Eric Le Hung novel Elle Lui Dirait dans l'Ile by Françoise Xenakis d Eric Le Hung ph Henri Decaë m Philippe Sarde ed Jacqueline Thiédot
☆ Omar Sharif, Florinda Bolkan, Pierre Michael, Gilles Ségal

Bram Stoker's Count Dracula

Spain/Italy/West Germany/Liechtenstein 1970 98m Eastmancolor Panavision
Hemdale/Fénix/Corona/Filmar/Towers of London (Harry Alan Towers)
original title: *El Conde Dracula*
aka: *Count Dracula, Dracula 71*
An English solicitor, Jonathan Harker, tracks Dracula to his castle after the Count kills his wife's friend, and destroys him by burning his coffin.
A feeble effort, in which a good cast is wasted by directorial incompetence. It was claimed, wrongly, that it was the first film to stick closely to the original story.

---

w Peter Welbeck (Harry Alan Towers), Carlo Fadda, Milo C. Cuccia, Dietmar Behnke novel *Dracula* by Bram Stoker d Jess (Jesús) Franco ph Manuel Merino m Bruno Nicolai sp Sergio Pagoni

☆ Christopher Lee, Herbert Lom, Klaus Kinski, Frederick Williams, Maria Rohm, Soledad Miranda, Jack Taylor

'Disappointingly unimaginative in treatment … the evidently low budget reveals day-for-day shots for what they are, also permitting a cardboard rock clearly to be seen bouncing off a horse's head before "crushing" a peasant.' – *John Raisbeck, MFB*

'Love Never Dies.'

Bram Stoker's Dracula

US 1992 128m Technicolor
Columbia TriStar/American Zoetrope/Osiris (Francis Ford Coppola, Fred Fuchs, Charles Mulvehill)

⊙ ▦ ◎ ⊚ ⊘ ⌒

In the 1480s Dracula curses God and becomes a vampire after his wife, thinking that he has died in battle, commits suicide; 400 or so years later in London he falls in love with a woman who seems to be her reincarnation.

A lush, over-dressed Gothic romance that plays down the menace and dread of the original, with performances that range from the inadequate to the over-ripe.

w James V. Hart d Francis Ford Coppola ph Michael Ballhaus m Wojciech Kilar pd Thomas Sanders ed Nicholas C. Smith, Glen Scantlebury, Anne Goursaud sp Roman Coppola

☆ Gary Oldman, Winona Ryder, Anthony Hopkins, Keanu Reeves

'Remains in essentials a fairly comprehensive and often vulgar mess … The whole somehow seems to sum up what people want from cinema nowadays: style hinting at content but gradually drowning it out with pyrotechnics.' – *Derek Malcolm, Guardian*

'You emerge from the vampire's feast hungry and disappointed.' – *Geoff Brown, The Times*

'Everybody knows that Dracula has a heart; Coppola knows that it is more than an organ to drive a stake into. To the director, the count is a restless spirit who has been condemned for too many years to interment in cruddy movies. This luscious film restores the creature's nobility and gives him peace.' – *Richard Corliss, Time*

♟ Eiko Ishioka (costumes); make-up; sound effects editing

♟ Thomas Sanders

Bram Stoker's Legend of the Mummy

US 1997 93m colour
Goldbar/Unapix (Harel Goldstein, Bill Barnett)

▦ ▦

aka: *Bram Stoker's The Mummy*

An archaeologist summons to life the preserved body of an ancient queen of Egypt.

A horror movie shocking only in its cheapness and incompetence: it has several scenes of people fighting off an invisible assailant, no doubt to save the cost of providing a mobile mummy, who is otherwise impersonated by a set of false teeth and some bandages.

wd Jeffrey Obrow novel *The Jewel of Seven Stars* by Bram Stoker ph Antonio Soriano m Rick Cox pd Ken Larson ed Gary Meyers

☆ Louis Gossett Jnr, Amy Locane, Eric Lutes, Mark Lindsay-Chapman, Richard Karn, Lloyd Bochner, Victoria Tennant, Aubrey Morris

The Bramble Bush

US 1960 105m Technicolor
Warner/United States (Milton Sperling)

A doctor returns to his home town and finds himself involved in old tragedies including the mercy killing of his friend.

Sordid small-town melodrama in the Peyton Place vein, with adequate production values but dispiriting treatment.

w Milton Sperling, Philip Yordan novel Charles Mergendahl d Daniel Petrie ph Lucien Ballard m Leonard Rosenman

☆ Richard Burton, Barbara Rush, Jack Carson, Angie Dickinson, James Dunn, Tom Drake, Henry Jones, Frank Conroy, Carl Benton Reid, William Hansen

The Branches of the Tree **

India 1990 120m colour
Erato/DD/Soproffilms

When their famous father is taken ill, his three successful sons and their wives and children return home to visit him.

A rigorous examination of family relationships and values.

wd Satyajit Ray ph Sandip Ray m Satyajit Ray

☆ Ajit Banerjee, Soumitra Chatterjee, Maradan Banerjee, Lily Charraborty, Deepankar De, Mamata Shankar, Ranjit Malik

'An honest, thoughtful, compassionate film.' – *Philip French, Observer*

Branded

US 1950 104m Technicolor
Paramount (Mel Epstein)

▦ ◎

A gunman poses as a rancher's lost heir, but redeems himself by finding the real one.

Competent, brisk Western.

w Sydney Boehm, Cyril Hume d Rudolph Maté ph Charles Lang Jnr m Roy Webb

☆ Alan Ladd, Charles Bickford, Mona Freeman, Robert Keith, Joseph Calleia, Peter Hansen, Selena Royle, Tom Tully

Branded to Kill **

Japan 1967 91m colour Nikkatsu-scope
Nikkatsu (Iwai Kaneo)

▦ ⊘

original title: *Koroshi No Rakuin*

The number three hitman in Tokyo, whose fetish is smelling boiled rice, finds himself the target of the top killer.

A strange but enjoyable thriller, with its quirky originality, odd angles and odder hero as well as some effective suspense.

w Guryu Hachiro d Suzuki Seijun ph Nagatsuka Kazue m Yamamoto Naozumi ad Kawahara Sukezo ed Tanji Mutsuo

☆ Shishido Jo, Ogawa Mariko, Mari Annu, Nanbara Koji, Tamagawa Isao, Minami Hiroshi

'His film-making remains a wonderful subversion of commercial genres, wildly over-the-top, stylistically imaginative and totally watchable for its sheer (possibly ironic) audacity.' – *Derek Malcolm, Guardian*

'One of Suzuki's greatest, and it stands as his last word to date on the yakuza genre.' – *Tony Rayne*

† The film caused Suzuki's sacking from the Nikkatsu studios, when he became a scapegoat for a change in policy.

Brandy for the Parson *

GB 1951 79m bw
Group Three (Alfred Shaughnessy)

A couple on a yachting holiday find themselves unwittingly smuggling brandy into Britain.

Pleasant little sub-Ealing comedy with agreeable locations but not much drive.

w John Dighton, Walter Meade story Geoffrey Household d John Eldridge ph Martin Curtis m John Addison

☆ James Donald, Kenneth More, Jean Lodge, Frederick Piper, Charles Hawtrey, Michael Trubshawe, Alfie Bass, Reginald Beckwith

'Detective-Lieutenant Brannigan is in London … God Save the Queen!'

Brannigan *

GB 1975 111m DeLuxe Panavision
UA/Wellborn (Jules Levy, Arthur Gardner)

▦ ⊘

A Chicago policeman is sent to London to pick up a gangster.

Cheerful crime pastiche and tour of London, quite an agreeable entertainment despite its obviously over-age star.

w Christopher Trumbo, Michael Butler, William P. McGivern, William Norton d Douglas Hickox ph Gerry Fisher m Dominic Frontière

☆ John Wayne, Richard Attenborough, Judy Geeson, Mel Ferrer, John Vernon, Daniel Pilon, John Stride, James Booth, Barry Dennen

The Brasher Doubloon *

US 1946 72m bw
TCF

GB title: *The High Window*

Philip Marlowe investigates the theft of a rare coin and finds himself involved in a series of murders.

The poorest of the Chandler adaptations, previously filmed as Time to Kill, still contains good moments, though the star is lightweight and the production low-budget.

w Dorothy Bennett novel *The High Window* by Raymond Chandler d John Brahm ph Lloyd Ahern m David Buttolph

☆ George Montgomery, Nancy Guild, Florence Bates, Conrad Janis, Fritz Kortner

The Brass Bottle

↟↟ US 1964 89m Eastmancolor
U-I/Scarus (Robert Arthur)

A young architect finds an old brass bottle which contains a troublesome genie.

Simple-minded farce with little invention and poor trickwork.

w Oscar Brodney novel F. Anstey d Harry Keller ph Clifford Stine m Bernard Green sp Roswell Hoffman

☆ Tony Randall, Burl Ives, Barbara Eden, Edward Andrews, Ann Doran

The Brass Legend

US 1956 79m bw
UA (Herman Cohen/Bob Goldstein)

A sheriff finds himself in trouble when he tries to protect his fiancée's young brother.

Stolid programmer of the High Noon school, but without the flair.

w Don Martin d Gerd Oswald

☆ Hugh O'Brian, Nancy Gates, Raymond Burr, Reba Tassell

The Brass Monkey

GB 1948 84m bw
Diadem/Alliance/UA (N. A. Bronsten)

aka: *Lucky Mascot*

A radio singer thwarts the theft of a Buddhist idol.

Flat thriller based round a radio 'discovery' programme.

w Alec Coppel, Thornton Freeland d Thornton Freeland m Basil Emmott

☆ Carole Landis, Carroll Levis, Herbert Lom, Avril Angers, Ernest Thesiger

Brass Target

US 1978 111m Metrocolor
MGM (Berle Adams)

▦ ◎

The alleged story behind the death of General Patton, who according to these sources was eliminated because he had discovered a bullion robbery attempt.

Good-looking but interminably complex and talkative, with nothing much for its star cast to do.

w Alvin Boretz novel *The Algonquin Project* by Frederick Nolan d John Hough ph Tony Imi m Laurence Rosenthal

☆ Sophia Loren, George Kennedy, Max von Sydow, John Cassavetes, Patrick McGoohan, Robert Vaughn, Bruce Davison, Edward Herrmann, Ed Bishop

Brassed Off *

GB 1996 107m Rank Colour
Film Four/Miramax/Prominent Features (Steve Abbott)

▦ ▦ ▦ ⊚ ⌒

A mining community, facing the closure of its pit, struggles to keep its brass band going so that it may play in a national competition.

Sentimental comedy mixed with political preaching, saved from bathos by some good character acting.

wd Mark Herman m Andy Collins m Trevor Jones pd Don Taylor ed Michael Ellis

☆ Pete Postlethwaite, Tara Fitzgerald, Ewan McGregor, Jim Carter, Stephen Tompkinson, Ken Colley, Stephen Moore, Peter Gunn, Mary Healey, Melanie Hill

'Full to the brim with lazy effects, grabbing at a sentimentality it hasn't earned and a seriousness of tone for which it hasn't put in an inch of work.' – *Tom Shone, Sunday Times*

Brats *

↟↟ US 1930 20m bw
Hal Roach

Stan and Ollie have trouble baby-sitting their own mischievous kids.

Fairly ambitious star comedy with trick sets and photography enabling Laurel and Hardy to play their own sons. About half the gags come off.

w Leo McCarey, H. M. Walker, Hal Roach d James Parrott ph George Stevens ed Richard Currier

☆ Stan Laurel, Oliver Hardy

The Bravados *

US 1958 98m Eastmancolor Cinemascope
TCF (Herbert B. Swope)

A widower chases four killers who, he believes, raped and murdered his wife.

Dour Western with a downbeat ending; production good, but entertainment uneasy.

w Philip Yordan novel Frank O'Rourke d Henry King ph Leon Shamroy m Hugo Friedhofer md Emil Newman

☆ Gregory Peck, Stephen Boyd, Joan Collins, Albert Salmi, Henry Silva, George Voskovec, Barry Coe, Lee Van Cleef

The Brave and the Beautiful: see The Magnificent Matador

The Brave Bulls

US 1951 108m bw
Columbia (Robert Rossen)

A Mexican matador regains his courage but loses his girl in a car crash.

Muddled narrative with dollops of bull-fighting mystique; a rather miserable movie despite effort all round.

w John Bright novel Tom Lea d Robert Rossen ph James Wong Howe, Floyd Crosby

☆ Mel Ferrer, Miroslava, Anthony Quinn, Eugene Iglesias

The Brave Don't Cry *

GB 1952 90m bw
Group Three (John Baxter)

Over a hundred men are rescued in a Scottish mine disaster.

Semi-documentary based on a real incident well done on a small budget, but hardly memorable.

w Montagu Slater d Philip Leacock ph Arthur Grant m none

☆ John Gregson, Meg Buchanan, John Rae, Fulton Mackay, Andrew Keir, Russell Waters, Jameson Clark, Jean Anderson, Eric Woodburn

The Brave Little Toaster

↟↟ US 1987 90m DeLuxe
Castle Premier/Hyperion/Kushner-Locke/Wang Film/Global Communications (Donald Kushner, Thomas L. Wilhite)

▦ ◎

Domestic appliances go in search of their owner.

Odd fantasy of pots and pans with no more than adequate animation.

w Jerry Rees, Joe Ranft novel Thomas M. Disch d Jerry Rees m David Newman

☆ Featuring the voices of Jon Lovitz, Tim Stack, Timothy E. Day, Thurl Ravenscroft, Deanna Oliver, Phil Hartman, Joe Ranft

The Brave One *

↟↟ US 1956 100m Technicolor
Cinemascope
King Brothers

▦ ◎

A small boy saves the life of his pet bull when it is sent into the ring.

Mildly beguiling minor drama for those who adore small boys and bulls.

w Harry Franklin, Merrill G. White story Robert Rich d Irving Rapper ph Jack Cardiff m Victor Young ed Merrill G. White

☆ Michel Ray, Rodolfo Hoyos, Elsa Cardenas, Joi Lansing, Carlos Navarro

♟ Robert Rich. (There was much confusion when the mysterious Rich turned out to be Dalton Trumbo, who was blacklisted at the time.)

♟ editing

'His passion captivated a woman. His courage inspired a country. His heart defied a king.'

Braveheart ***

US 1995 177m DeLuxe
TCF/Icon/Ladd (Mel Gibson, Alan Ladd Jnr, Bruce Davey)

▦ ▦ ▦ ◎ ⌒

William Wallace leads a Scottish rebellion against the claims of the English king, Edward I.

A stirring nationalistic epic, acted and directed with great verve; some of the history may be suspect, but the film creates a sense of myth with its sweep and passion.

---

w Randall Wallace d Mel Gibson ph John Toll m James Horner pd Tom Sanders ed Steven Rosenblum

☆ Mel Gibson, Sophie Marceau, Patrick McGoohan, Catherine McCormack, Brendan Gleeson, James Cosmo, Alun Armstrong, Angus Macfadyen, Ian Bannen

'At last: a costume drama that wears its costumes with pride, a period drama that has the courage of its convictions.' – Tom Shone, Sunday Times

† The film took $168.5m at the box-office worldwide, according to Variety's figures.

🎬 best film; Mel Gibson (as director); John Toll; makeup; sound effects editing

🎬 Randall Wallace; James Horner; Steven Rosenblum; costume design (Charles Knode); sound

Brazil

US 1944 91m bw
Republic (Robert North)

A lady novelist goes to Brazil for material; a local composer poses as her guide in order to pay her back for her previous remarks about his country.
Acceptable lower case musical with pleasant tunes and humour.

w Frank Gill Jnr, Laura Kerr d Joseph Santley ph Jack Marta m Walter Scharf songs Bob Russell and others

☆ Virginia Bruce, Tito Guizar, Edward Everett Horton, Roy Rogers

🎬 song 'Rio de Janeiro' (m Ary Barrosa, ly Ned Washington); Walter Scharf

Brazil *

GB 1985 142m colour
Embassy (Arnon Milchan)
🖭 🖭 ◎ ◎ 🎧

A comically pessimistic view of the future, seen through the eyes of a dutiful civil servant who is eventually crushed by the system.
An expensive, wild, overlong, hit-or-miss Orwellian satire: enough good jabs to please the intelligentsia, but a turnoff for patrons at the local Odeon.

w Terry Gilliam, Tom Stoppard, Charles McKeown d Terry Gilliam ph Roger Pratt m Michael Kamen pd Norman Garwood ed Julian Doyle

☆ Jonathan Pryce, Robert De Niro, Michael Palin, Kim Greist, Katherine Helmond, Ian Holm, Ian Richardson, Peter Vaughan, Bob Hoskins

'It will not be everybody's cup of poisoned tea.' – Variety

'Exuberantly violent, cruelly funny and sometimes sickeningly scatological ... the whole is wrapped up in a melancholy wistfulness.' – Sight and Sound

🎬 original screenplay, art direction
🎬 production design

Breach of Promise

GB 1941 79m bw
British Mercury/MGM
US title: Adventure in Blackmail

A girl chases the man she wants by filing a breach of promise suit against him.
Dated but lively comedy with agreeable playing.

w Roland Pertwee d Harold Huth, Roland Pertwee

☆ Clive Brook, Judy Campbell, C. V. France, Marguerite Allan, Percy Walsh

Bread and Chocolate *

Italy 1973 112m Eastmancolor
Verona Cinematografica (Maurizio Lodo-Fe)

An Italian waiter in Switzerland is accused of murder and indecent exposure.
Amusing and often pathetic account of an inveterate loser, its flavour impossible to define.

w Franco Brusati, Iaia Fiastri, Nino Manfredi d Franco Brusati ph Luciano Tovoli md Daniele Patrucchi

☆ Nino Manfredi, Anna Karina, Johnny Dorelli, Paolo Turco

Bread, Love and Dreams *

Italy 1953 90m bw
Titanus (Marcello Girosi)

The new sergeant of police in a small rural village comes looking for a wife.
Pleasant rather than exciting rural comedy which spun off a number of vaguely related sequels (Bread, Love and Jealousy, etc).

---

w Luigi Comencini story Ettore Margadonna d Luigi Comencini ph Arturo Gallea m Alessandro Cicognini

☆ Vittorio de Sica, Gina Lollobrigida, Marisa Merlini, Roberto Risso

🎬 Ettore Margadonna

The Break

GB 1962 76m bw
Mancunian (Tom Blakeley)

Guests arrive at a remote Dartmoor farmhouse hotel, where a violent escaped criminal is being hidden by its owner, a smuggler.
Dull thriller which, with its Cold Comfort Farm-like setting, hovers unwittingly on the edge of parody, but, even so, offers little of interest.

w Pip and Jane Baker d Lance Comfort ph Basil Emmott m Brian Fahey ad George Provis ed Peter Pitt

☆ Tony Britton, William Lucas, Eddie Byrne, Robert Urquhart, Sonia Dresdel, Edwin Richfield, Gene Anderson, Christina Gregg

Break in the Circle

GB 1955 91m Eastmancolor (bw in US)
Exclusive/Hammer (Michael Carreras)
🖭

The owner of a cabin cruiser is hired to smuggle a scientist out of Germany.
Routine action yarn of cross and double-cross, tolerably staged.

wd Val Guest novel Philip Lorraine ph Walter Harvey m Doreen Carwithen ad J. Elder Wills ed Bill Lenny

☆ Forrest Tucker, Eva Bartok, Marius Goring, Eric Pohlmann, Guy Middleton, Arnold Marlé

Break of Hearts

US 1935 80m bw
RKO (Pandro S. Berman)
🖭 ◎

A girl composer falls in love with a distinguished conductor who becomes a dipsomaniac.
Well acted soap opera, not really worthy of its stars.

w Sarah Y. Mason, Victor Heerman, Anthony Veiller d Philip Moeller ph Robert de Grasse m Max Steiner

☆ Katharine Hepburn, Charles Boyer, Jean Hersholt, John Beal, Sam Hardy

'A stale turnip story that relies entirely upon characterization to hide the basic dullness.' – Variety

'In spite of some capable acting, it lacks a certain compelling warmth. The audience's heart never breaks.' – Eileen Creelman, New York Sun

Break the News *

GB 1938 78m bw
GFD/Jack Buchanan

A dancer arranges his partner's 'death' for publicity reasons but is sent to jail when the partner disappears.
Thin but lively comedy with a remarkable couple of song and dance men. Negative apparently lost.

w Geoffrey Kerr novel La Mort en Fuite by Loic de Gouriadec d René Clair ph Phil Tannura m Theo Mackeben m/ly Cole Porter md Van Phillips ad Lazare Meerson ed Francis Lyon, Fred Wilson

☆ Jack Buchanan, Maurice Chevalier, June Knight, Marta Labarr, Garry Marsh, Felix Aylmer, Robb Wilton

† Various remakes include The Art of Love (qv).

Break to Freedom: see Albert RN

Breakdance: see Breakin'

Breakdance 2: Electric Boogaloo: see Breakin' 2: Electric Boogaloo

Breakdown **

US 1997 93m DeLuxe Super 35
TCF/Dino de Laurentiis/Spelling
🖭 🖭 ◎ ◎

After his car breaks down, a man finds that his wife has disappeared and that a gang of roughnecks want to steal all his money.
Slick, unpretentious action thriller that effectively exploits urban fears of wide-open spaces.

w Jonathan Mostow, Sam Montgomery d Jonathan Mostow d Doug Milsome m Basil Poledouris pd Victoria Paul ed Derek Brechin, Kevin Stitt

---

☆ Kurt Russell, J. T. Walsh, Kathleen Quinlan, M. C. Gainey, Jack Noseworthy, Rex Linn, Ritch Brinkley, Moira Harris

'A tremendously tense thriller that expertly keeps tightening the screws throughout its taut running time.' – Variety

'A rough-hewn thriller, enjoyable in its simplicity and occasional silliness.' – Edward Porter, Sunday Times

Breaker Morant ***

Australia 1980 107m Eastmancolor Panavision
South Australian Film Corporation (Matthew Carroll)
🖭 🖭 ◎ ◎

During the Boer War three Australian officers are courtmartialled for murdering prisoners.
Careful, moving military drama which gives a more sympathetic view of the facts than history does.

w Jonathan Hardy, Bruce Beresford, David Stevens play Kenneth Ross d Bruce Beresford ph Donald McAlpine md Phil Cuneen

☆ Edward Woodward, Jack Thompson, John Waters, Charles Tingwell, Terence Donovan, Vincent Ball

'It is impossible to suppress a feeling that the spirit of Stanley Kramer is abroad on the veldt.' – Tim Pulleine, MFB

🎬 screenplay

Breakfast at Tiffany's *

US 1961 115m Technicolor
Paramount (Martin Jurow, Richard Shepherd)
🖭 🖭 ◎ ◎ 🎧

A young New York writer has as neighbour the volatile Holly Golightly, a slightly crazy call girl with an exotic social and emotional life.
Impossibly cleaned up and asexual version of a light novel which tried to be the American I Am a Camera (qv). Wild parties, amusing scenes and good cameos, but the pace is slow, the atmosphere is unconvincingly clean and luxurious, and the sentimentality kills it.

w George Axelrod novel Truman Capote d Blake Edwards ph Franz Planer m Henry Mancini

☆ Audrey Hepburn, George Peppard, Patricia Neal, Buddy Ebsen, Martin Balsam, John McGiver, Mickey Rooney

🎬 Henry Mancini; song 'Moon River' (mHenry Mancini, lyJohnny Mercer)

🎬 George Axelrod; Audrey Hepburn

The Breakfast Club

US 1985 97m Technicolor
A&M/Universal (Ned Tanen, John Hughes)
🖭 🖭 ◎ ◎ 🎧

Five rebellious students at Shermer High blame their parents for their misfortunes.
Abysmal apologia for loutish teenage behaviour.

wd John Hughes ph Thomas Del Ruth, George Bouillet m Keith Forsey ed Dede Allen

☆ Emilio Estevez, Judd Nelson, Molly Ringwald, Anthony Michael Hall, Ally Sheedy

Breakfast for Two *

US 1937 65m bw
RKO (Edward Kaufman)

A Texas heiress turns a playboy into a businessman.
Star crazy comedy with some wildly funny scenes.

w Charles Kaufman, Paul Yawitz, Viola Brothers Shore d Alfred Santell ph J. Roy Hunt

☆ Barbara Stanwyck, Herbert Marshall, Donald Meek, Glenda Farrell, Eric Blore, Etienne Girardot

'Heaps of laughs in a breezily-paced farce.' – Variety

Breakfast in Hollywood

US 1945 90m bw
Golden Pictures/United Artists
🖭

GB title: The Mad Hatter

A day in the life of a radio breakfast show host.
Topical programme filler, more interesting historically than entertaining.

w Earl W. Baldwin d Harold Schuster

☆ Tom Breneman, Bonita Granville, Beulah Bondi, Eddie Ryan, Raymond Walburn, Billie Burke, ZaSu Pitts, Spike Jones and his City Slickers, Andy Russell, Hedda Hopper

---

Breakheart Pass *

US 1975 94m DeLuxe
UA/Elliott Kastner (Jerry Gershwin)
🖭 ◎

Various mysterious passengers on an 1873 train across the frozen west to Fort Humboldt turn out to have smuggling and murder in mind.
Botched murder mystery on wheels: there are some exciting scenes, but the plot makes little sense and the 'action finale' is muddled.

w Alistair MacLean novel Alistair MacLean d Tom Gries ph Lucien Ballard m Jerry Goldsmith

☆ Charles Bronson, Ben Johnson, Richard Crenna, Jill Ireland, Charles Durning, Archie Moore, Ed Lauter

Breakin'

US 1984 87m Metrocolor
MGM-UA/Cannon (Allen DeBevoise, David Zito)
🖭 ◎ 🎧

GB title: Breakdance

Youngsters promote a new form of dancing.
Minor exploitation item, the form little improved on Rock around the Clock (qv) thirty years earlier.

w Charles Parker, Allen DeBevoise, Gerald Scaife d Joel Silberg ph Hanania Baer m Gary Remal, Michael Boyd pd Ivo Cristante ed Mark Helfrich

☆ Lucinda Dickey, Adolfo 'Shabba-Doo' Quinones, Michael 'Boogaloo-Shrimp' Chambers, Ben Lokey, Phineas Newborn III, Tracey 'Ice T' Marrow

Breakin' 2: Electric Boogaloo

US 1984 94m TVC Color
Cannon
🖭 ◎ 🎧

GB title: Breakdance 2: Electric Boogaloo

Youngsters raise 200,000 dollars to save their local community centre; a dance show does it.
Hurried sequel of no interest apart from the briefly popular musical gyrations.

w Jan Ventura, Julie Reichert d Sam Firstenberg

☆ Lucinda Dickey, Adolfo Quinones, Michael Chambers, Susie Bono

Breaking Away *

US 1979 101m DeLuxe
TCF (Peter Yates)
🖭 ◎

An imaginative teenager has trouble adjusting to adult life after high school.
Andy Hardy would have felt at home in this fragmented comedy of the American hinterland; 1979 audiences found it a welcome relief from the stronger brews to which they had become accustomed.

w Steve Tesich d Peter Yates ph Matthew F. Leonetti m Patrick Williams md Lionel Newman

☆ Dennis Christopher, Dennis Quaid, Daniel Stern, Jackie Earle Haley, Barbara Barrie, Paul Dooley

'Affection for the middle classes, the landscapes of Indiana, and bicycle racing.' – New Yorker

'It is not devoid of pleasures ... but it fatally lacks a clear purpose and identity.' – Geoff Brown, MFB

'Here's a sunny, goofy, intelligent little film about coming of age in Bloomington, Indiana.' – Roger Ebert

† An unsuccessful TV series followed in 1980.

🎬 Steve Tesich

🎬 best picture; Peter Yates; Patrick Williams; Barbara Barrie

🎬 Dennis Christopher

'The experience is shattering!'
Breaking Glass

GB 1980 104m Technicolor Panavision
GTO/Film and General (Dodi Fayed)
🖭 🎧

Vicissitudes of a pop band and of its singer who can't stand the pace.
Garish, freakish musical with unattractive characters strung along an oft-told tale. Some commendable vigour in the presentation, but it won't appeal to anybody over 21.

wd Brian Gibson ph Stephen Goldblatt md Tony Visconti

☆ Hazel O'Connor, Phil Daniels, Jon Finch, Jonathan Pryce

Breaking In *

US   1989   94m   colour

Castle Premier/Breaking In Productions/Sam Goldwyn Company (Harry Gittes)

A veteran safe-breaker teaches a teenager the tricks of the trade.

Mildly rewarding comedy of crooked manners.

w John Sayles d Bill Forsyth ph Michael Coulter pd Adrienne Atkinson, John Willett ed Michael Ellis

☆ Burt Reynolds, Casey Siemaszko, Sheila Kelley, Lorraine Toussaint, Albert Salmi, Harry Carey, Maury Chaykin

'Less a barrel of laughs than elliptically funny in its observation of the unconscious discrepancy between word and deed.' – *Tom Milne, MFB*

The Breaking of Bumbo

GB   1970   90m   colour

Associated British (Jeffrey Selznick)

A misfit of a Guards officer goes to pieces thanks to his own, and his fellow officers', shortcomings.

A misfiring comedy which, like its hero, falls flat on its face.

wd Andrew Sinclair novel Andrew Sinclair

☆ Richard Warwick, Joanna Lumley, Natasha Pyne, Jeremy Child, John Bird, Donald Pickering

† The film was never given a general release and was shown briefly in one London cinema, although it is occasionally seen on television.

'Innocence and fury don't mix – they explode!'

Breaking Point

Canada   1976   92m   colour   Panavision

TCF/Astral Belle Vue (Harold Greenberg, Harold Pariser)

An innocent witness against the Mafia takes off against them vigilante style when his partner is murdered and his own life threatened.

Comic strip thuggery with performances to match; plenty of excitement for toughies.

w Roger E. Swaybill, Stanley Mann d Bob Clark ph Marc Champion m David McLey

☆ Bo Svenson, Robert Culp, John Colicos, Belinda J. Montgomery, Stephen Young

'There's nothing more deadly than a gentle man pushed too far!'

The Breaking Point *

US   1950   97m   bw

Warner (Jerry Wald)

A charterboat owner becomes involved with crooks but turns them in when they have killed his friend.

Adequate if slightly humdrum attempt by Warner to atone for what they had done to a Hemingway novel, the infidelity of To Have and Have Not *and the unauthorized variation of* Key Largo *(qqv). (See also:* The Gun Runners.*)*

w Ranald MacDougall novel To Have and Have Not by Ernest Hemingway d Michael Curtiz ph Ted McCord m (uncredited) William Lava, Max Steiner

☆ John Garfield, Patricia Neal, Phyllis Thaxter, Juano Hernandez, Wallace Ford, Edmon Ryan, William Campbell

'All the character, color, and cynicism of Mr Hemingway's lean and hungry tale are wrapped up in this realistic picture.' – *New York Times*

The Breaking Point

GB   1961   59m   bw

Butcher's (Peter Lambert)

A high-living, bankrupt executive of a firm printing banknotes is persuaded to take part in a currency swindle.

Drab, poverty-stricken melodrama with no sparkle or style.

w Peter Lambert novel Laurence Meynell d Lance Comfort ph Basil Emmott m Albert Elms ad John Earl ed Peter Pitt

☆ Peter Reynolds, Dermot Walsh, Joanna Dunham, Lisa Gastoni, Jack Allen, Brian Cobby, Arnold Diamond

Breaking the Ice

US   1938   80m   bw

RKO/Sol Lesser

A Pennsylvania Dutch boy runs away to the city so that his mother can afford her own farm.

Slim star musical which had its pleasing moments.

w Mary McCall Jnr, Manuel Seff, Bernard Schubert d Edward F. Cline ph Jack MacKenzie m Victor Young

☆ Bobby Breen, Charles Ruggles, Dolores Costello, Robert Barrat, Dorothy Peterson, John King, Billy Gilbert, Margaret Hamilton

'Moderately engrossing, combination folk drama and musical.' – *Variety*

⅄ Victor Young

Breaking the Sound Barrier: see *The Sound Barrier*

'Love is a mighty power.'

Breaking the Waves ****

Denmark/Sweden/France/Netherlands   1996   159m   colour

Guild/Zentropa/Trust/Liberator/Argus/Northern Lights (Vibeke Windeløv, Peter Aalbaek Jensen)

In a remote part of Scotland, a young woman humiliates herself in the hope of saving the life of her husband, paralysed in an accident on an oil rig.

A remarkable and striking film, though in some ways a dislikeable one. It has a raw, emotional power rarely encountered on film, owing to its soulful and guileless central performance and the restlessly casual, close-up camerawork; but its theme, an apparent celebration of self-sacrifice through sexual degradation, is often unlovely and hard to take.

w Lars von Trier, Peter Asmussen d Lars von Trier ph Robby Müller m Joachim Holbek ad Karl Juliusson ed Anders Refn

☆ Emily Watson, Stellan Skarsgård, Katrin Cartlidge, Jean-Marc Barr, Udo Kier, Adrian Rawlins, Jonathan Hackett, Sandra Voe

'An astonishing film, so well thought-out and passionately executed that it's only afterwards, if then, that audiences will wonder exactly what they have been persuaded to think and feel.' – *Adam Mars-Jones, Independent*

'Acted with a conviction you rarely find, it's one of those movies that affects you in such a profound way. Believe me, this one's a life-altering experience.' – *Alan Jones, Film Review*

† The film won the Grand Jury Prize at the Cannes Film Festival in 1996.

⅄ Emily Watson

Breaking Up

US   1996   90m   colour

Warner/Regency (Robert Greenwald, George Moffly)

A married couple recount their on-and-off relationship.

A small-scale film in which two people bicker and make up without seeming of any interest to anyone else.

w Michael Cristofer d Robert Greenwald ph Mauro Fiore m Mark Mothersbaugh pd Terence Foster ed Suzanne Hines

☆ Russell Crowe, Salma Hayek, Abraham Alvarez

'An exercise in tedium that has you looking at your watch wondering why time is passing so slowly.' – *George Perry, Sunday Times*

'The sort of picture that can sap your will to live.' – *Ryan Gilbey, Independent*

Breakout: see *Danger Within* (1958)

Breakout

US   1975   96m   colour   Panavision

Columbia/Persky-Bright (Robert Chartoff, Irwin Winkler)

A professional rescuer gets an innocent man out of a Mexican jail.

Rough and ready adventure thriller which starts slowly and confusingly but later works up a fair head of steam.

w Howard B. Kreitsek, Frank Kowalski novel Ten Second Jailbreak by Howard B. Kreitsek, Frank Kowalski d Tom Gries ph Lucien Ballard m Jerry Goldsmith

☆ Charles Bronson, Robert Duvall, John Huston, Jill Ireland, Randy Quaid, Sheree North

Breakthrough: see *Sergeant Steiner* (1978)

Breakthrough

US   1950   91m   bw

Warner (Bryan Foy)

Adventures of a US army unit in Normandy after D-Day.

Routine low-budgeter which improves after a slow start.

w Bernard Girard, Ted Sherdeman, Joseph I. Breen Jnr d Lewis Seiler ph Edwin DuPar m William Lava

☆ David Brian, John Agar, Frank Lovejoy, William Campbell, Paul Picerni, Greg McClure, Edward Norris, Matt Willis, Dick Wesson

The Breakup: see *La Rupture*

Breath of Scandal: see *His Glorious Night* (1929)

A Breath of Scandal

US   1960   98m   Technicolor

Paramount/Titanus/Ponti-Girosi (Carlo Ponti, Marcello Girosi)

A spirited Ruritanian princess falls for an American industrialist.

Exceedingly flat-footed and boring international co-production of an old Molnar play; if anyone concerned had bright ideas, they don't show.

w Walter Bernstein play Olimpia by Ferenc Molnar d Michael Curtiz, Mario Russo ph Mario Montuori m Alessandro Cicognini

☆ Sophia Loren, Maurice Chevalier, John Gavin, Isabel Jeans, Angela Lansbury, Roberto Risso, Friedrich Ledebur, Tullio Carminati, Milly Vitale

† A remake of *His Glorious Night* (qv), filmed by MGM in 1929.

Breathless: see *A Bout de Souffle* (1959)

Breathless

US   1983   101m   DeLuxe

Miko/Breathless Associates/Greenberg Brothers (Martin Erlichman)

A street-smart hustler steals a car in Las Vegas and heads for the coast.

Fashionable amalgam of sex and violence, borrowed from A Bout de Souffle *(qv) but far too long after the event.*

w L. M. Kit Carson, Jim McBride d Jim McBride ph Richard H. Kline m Jack Nitzche pd Richard Sylbert

☆ Richard Gere, Valerie Kaprisky, William Tepper, John P. Ryan, Art Metrano

'Not much more than an ego trip for a bankable star.' – *Daily Mail*

A Breed Apart

US   1984   101m   colour   Panavision

Hemdale/Sagittarius (John Daly, Derek Gibson)

A rich collector hires a mountaineer to rob the almost inaccessible nest of a rare bald eagle, guarded by a militant conservationist.

Ecological propaganda given the sugar coating of a sentimental love story with a little action thrown in.

w Paul Wheeler d Philippe Mora m Geoffrey Stephenson m Maurice Gibb pd William Barclay ed Christopher Lebenzon

☆ Rutger Hauer, Powers Boothe, Kathleen Turner, Brion James, Donald Pleasence

Breezy

US   1973   107m   Technicolor

Universal/Malpaso (Robert Daley)

A divorced 50-year-old real estate agent is rejuvenated by an affair with a young girl hippy.

An abrasive veneer covers the most stereotyped of January/May love stories. Technically an attractive piece of work.

w Jo Heims d Clint Eastwood ph Frank Stanley m Michel Legrand

☆ William Holden, Kay Lenz, Roger C. Carmel, Marj Dusay, Joan Hotchkis

Brewster McCloud

US   1970   105m   Metrocolor   Panavision

MGM/Adler-Phillips/Lion's Gate (Lou Adler)

A man hides out under the roof of the Houston Astrodrome, prepares to learn to fly with man-made wings, and refuses all offers of help; when he launches himself, he falls to his death.

Anarchic, allegorical fantasy, a delight no doubt for connoisseurs of way-out humour. Everyone else, forget it.

w Doran William Cannon d Robert Altman ph Lamar Boren, Jordan Cronenweth m Gene Page

☆ Bud Cort, Sally Kellerman, Michael Murphy, William Windom, Shelley Duvall, René Auberjonois, Stacy Keach, John Schuck, Margaret Hamilton

'Amorphous and rather silly ... the idea seems to be left over from a Victorian fable, but the style is like a Road Runner cartoon.' – *New Yorker, 1974*

Brewster's Millions *

GB   1935   84m   bw

British and Dominion (Herbert Wilcox)

If he can spend a million pounds within two months, a playboy will inherit many millions more.

Artless but lively version of a famous comedy which provided a good role for its star.

w Arthur Wimperis, Paul Gangelin, Douglas Furber, Clifford Grey, Donovan Pedelty, Wolfgang Wilhelm play George Barr McCutcheon, Winchell Smith novel George Barr McCutcheon d Thornton Freeland ph Henry Harris, Barney McGill m Ray Noble ad L. P. Williams ed Merrill White

☆ Jack Buchanan, Lili Damita, Nancy O'Neil, Amy Veness, Sydney Fairbrother, Fred Emney, Sebastian Shaw

'As near 100% film entertainment as can be expected.' – *Variety*

† There had been silent versions in 1916 (with Edward Abeles) and 1921 (with Roscoe Arbuckle).

Brewster's Millions *

US   1945   79m   bw

Edward Small

Competent American remake of the above.

w Sig Herzig, Charles Rogers d Allan Dwan ph Charles Lawton Jnr m Hugo Friedhofer

☆ Dennis O'Keefe, Eddie 'Rochester' Anderson, Helen Walker, Gail Patrick, Mischa Auer, June Havoc, Joe Sawyer, Nana Bryant, John Litel, Thurston Hall, Byron Foulger

† Remade as *Three on a Spree* (GB 1961).

⅄ Lou Forbes (music scoring)

Brewster's Millions

↑↑   US   1985   97m   Technicolor

Universal (Lawrence Gordon, Joel Silver)

A baseball player learns that in order to inherit 30 million dollars he must spend one million a day for 30 days.

Frantically noisy remake of an old chestnut.

w Herschel Weingrod, Timothy Harris d Walter Hill m Ric Waite m Ry Cooder pd John Vallone ed Freeman Davis, Michael Ripps

☆ Richard Pryor, John Candy, Lonette McKee, Stephen Collins, Jerry Orbach, Pat Hingle, Tovah Feldshuh

The Bribe *

US   1949   98m   bw

MGM (Pandro S. Berman)

A US agent tracks down a group of criminals in Central America.

Steamy melodrama with pretensions but only moderate entertainment value despite high gloss. The rogues' gallery, however, is impressive.

w Marguerite Roberts d Robert Z. Leonard ph Joseph Ruttenberg m Miklos Rozsa

☆ Robert Taylor, Ava Gardner, Charles Laughton, Vincent Price, John Hodiak

The Bridal Path *

GB   1959   95m   Technicolor

Vale (Sidney Gilliat, Frank Launder)

A stalwart Hebridean islander journeys to the mainland in search of a wife.

Mild, episodic, very pleasant open-air comedy set amid splendid locations.

w Frank Launder, Geoffrey Willans novel Nigel Tranter d Frank Launder ph Arthur Ibbetson m Cedric Thorpe Davie

☆ Bill Travers, Fiona Clyne, George Cole, Duncan Macrae, Gordon Jackson, Dilys Laye, Bernadette O'Farrell

Bridal Suite

US   1939   70m   bw

MGM

A playboy seldom turns up for his own weddings, but his new intended takes him and his mother in hand.

Frothy comedy with dependable cast.

---

w Samuel Hoffenstein d William Thiele

☆ Robert Young, Annabella, Walter Connolly, Billie Burke, Reginald Owen, Arthur Treacher

'Dull and uninteresting, with static direction, commonplace story and situations, and inability to catch audience attention except for brief moments.' – *Variety*

† First known as *Maiden Voyage*.

'A woman born of electricity ... a man driven by passion!'

The Bride

US   1985   118m   Rank Colour

Columbia/Victor Drai

Frankenstein creates a bride for his monster, but she falls for him instead, and the monster goes off with a garrulous dwarf.

Insane romantic-feminist remake of The Bride of Frankenstein (qv), extremely dull and aimless after an arresting start.

w Lloyd Fonvielle d Franc Roddam ph Stephen H. Burum m Maurice Jarre pd Michael Seymour ed Michael Ellis

☆ Sting, Jennifer Beals, Clancy Brown, David Rappaport, Geraldine Page, Anthony Higgins, Quentin Crisp

'A misbegotten exercise.' – *Sight and Sound*

The Bride Came C.O.D. *

US   1941   92m   bw

Warner (Hal B. Wallis)

A charter pilot agrees to kidnap a temperamental heiress, but is stuck with her when they crashland in the desert.

Feeble comedy with a script totally unworthy of its stars. The mass of talent does however provide a smile or two towards the end.

w Julius J. and Philip G. Epstein d William Keighley ph Ernest Haller m Max Steiner

☆ Bette Davis, James Cagney, Harry Davenport, Stuart Erwin, Eugene Pallette, Jack Carson, George Tobias, William Frawley, Edward Brophy, Chick Chandler

'Neither the funniest comedy ever made, nor the shortest distance between two points, but for the most part a serviceable romp.' – *Theodore Strauss*

'Both of them mug good-naturedly, and it's pleasantly fast.' – *New Yorker, 1977*

The Bride Comes Home *

US   1935   82m   bw

Paramount (Wesley Ruggles)

A penniless socialite helps a wealthy man and his roughneck bodyguard in a magazine venture.

Slight but freshly handled romantic comedy, still worth a look.

w Elizabeth Sanxay Holding, Claude Binyon d Wesley Ruggles ph Leo Tover

☆ Claudette Colbert, Robert Young, Fred MacMurray, William Collier Snr, Donald Meek, Edgar Kennedy, Richard Carle, Jimmy Conlin

'Another galloping lithograph off the boy-and-girl-always-fighting woodblock.' – *Variety*

Bride for Sale

US   1949   87m   bw

RKO (Jack H. Skirball)

A practical-minded businesswoman has two admirers.

Skittish romantic comedy for ageing stars.

w Bruce Manning, Islin Auster d William D. Russell ph Joseph Valentine m Frederick Hollander

☆ Claudette Colbert, George Brent, Robert Young, Max Baer, Gus Schilling, Charles Arnt, Thurston Hall

The Bride Goes Wild

US   1948   98m   bw

MGM (William H. Wright)

As his lady illustrator finds out, a writer of children's books is not quite the sober uncle she expected, especially when he has to pretend to adopt an unruly orphan.

Scatty comedy with farcical interludes, quite pleasantly played but lacking style.

w Albert Beich d Norman Taurog ph Ray June m Rudolf Kopp

☆ June Allyson, Van Johnson, Jackie 'Butch' Jenkins, Hume Cronyn, Richard Derr

The Bride Is Much Too Beautiful (dubbed)

France   1956   90m   bw

Leo Lax/Production Générale/Pathé-Cinéma (Fred Surin)

original title: *La Mariée Est Trop Belle*

A village girl becomes a top magazine model and falls for her editor.

Routine film, made just before Bardot's stardom, which even she admitted to finding silly.

w Philippe Agostini, Juliette Saint-Giniez novel Odette Joyeux d Pierre Gaspard-Huit ph Louis Page m Norbert Glanzberg pd Pierre Duquesne, Marc Frederix, Jean d'Eaubonne ed Louisette Hautcoeur

☆ Louis Jourdan, Brigitte Bardot, Micheline Presle, Marcel Amont, Marcelle Arnold, Roger Dumas, Jean-François Calvé

'The Honeymoon's Gonna Be Killer.'

Bride of Chucky *

US   1998   89m   DeLuxe

Universal (David Kirschner, David Gilroy)

The girlfriend of a dead serial killer resurrects his spirit in the body of a doll; she then becomes a living doll herself.

Horror movie done with some panache, and a nod or two in the direction of The Bride of Frankenstein.

w Don Mancini d Ronnie Yu ph Peter Pau m Graeme Revell pd Alicia Keywan ed David Wu, Randolph K. Bricker sp puppet fx: Kevin Yagher

☆ Jennifer Tilly, Katherine Heigl, Nick Stabile, John Ritter, Alexis Arquette, Gordon Michael Woolvett, Lawrence Dane, Michael Johnson, James Gallanders, Janet Kidder, Kathy Najimy, Brad Dourif

'Emerges with recharged batteries and a mordantly funny edge that's attuned to the dawning millennium. A relatively straightforward genre piece, it has flair and a dash of wit.' – *Leonard Klady, Variety*

† The film was a sequel to the *Child's Play* series (qv).

'The monster demands a mate!'

The Bride of Frankenstein ****

US   1935   90m   bw

Universal (Carl Laemmle Jnr)

Baron Frankenstein is blackmailed by Dr Praetorius into reviving his monster and building a mate for it.

Frankenstein was startlingly good in a primitive way; this sequel is the screen's sophisticated masterpiece of black comedy, with all the talents working deftly to one end. Every scene has its own delights, and they are woven together into a superb if wilful cinematic narrative which, of its gentle mocking kind, has never been surpassed.

w John L. Balderston, William Hurlbut d James Whale ph John Mescall m Franz Waxman

☆ Boris Karloff, Colin Clive, Ernest Thesiger, Valerie Hobson, E. E. Clive, Dwight Frye, O. P. Heggie, Una O'Connor, Elsa Lanchester, Gavin Gordon, Douglas Walton

FRANKENSTEIN: 'I've been cursed for delving into the mysteries of life!'

'It is perhaps because Whale was by now master of the horror film that this production is the best of them all.' – *John Baxter, 1968*

'An extraordinary film, with sharp humour, macabre extravagance, and a narrative that proceeds at a fast, efficient pace.' – *Gavin Lambert, 1948*

'A great deal of art has gone into it, but it is the kind of art that gives the healthy feeling of men with their sleeves rolled up and working, worrying only about how to put the thing over in the best manner of the medium – no time for nonsense and attitudes and long hair.' – *Otis Ferguson*

† The regular release version runs 75m, having dropped part of the Mary Shelley prologue and a sequence in which the monster becomes unsympathetic by murdering the burgomaster.

†† The title was originally to have been *The Return of Frankenstein*.

Bride of the Gorilla

US   1951   65m   bw

Jack Broder Productions

The manager of a rubber plantation is poisoned by a native woman and turns into a gorilla.

Incredibly inane two-bit shocker, a strong contender for any list of the worst films of all time.

wd Curt Siodmak

☆ Barbara Payton, Lon Chaney Jnr, Raymond Burr, Tom Conway, Paul Cavanagh

---

'The screen's master of the weird ... In his newest and most daring shocker!'

Bride of the Monster

US   1953   69m   bw

Rolling M (Edward D. Wood)

Dr Vornoff has an atomic machine which will convert people into beings of superhuman strength; it is turned on himself, but a giant octopus, also with superoctopus strength, gets him.

A perfectly terrible movie, on a par with this director's other works.

w Edward D. Wood Jnr, Alex Gordon d Edward D. Wood Jnr

☆ Bela Lugosi, Tor Johnson, Tony McCoy, Loretta King, Harvey Dunne

Bride of the Re-Animator: see Re-Animator 2

Bride of the Regiment

US   1930   79m   Technicolor

First National

GB title: *Lady of the Rose*

In northern Italy a band of aristocrats rises against the invading Austrians.

Early talkie operetta, well received at the time. No colour material survives.

w Ray Harris operetta *The Lady in Ermine* by Rudolph Schanzer, Ernest Wellsch d John Francis Dillon ph Dev Jennings, Charles Schoenbaum m/ly Al Bryan, Ed Ward ch Jack Haskell

☆ Vivienne Segal, Allan Prior, Walter Pidgeon, Louise Fazenda, Ford Sterling, Myrna Loy, Lupino Lane

'Entertaining all the way, deserves returns above the average.' – *Variety*

Bride of Vengeance *

US   1948   91m   bw

Paramount (Richard Maibaum)

The story of the Borgias (whitewashing Lucretia) and the Duke of Ferrara.

Superb looking but appallingly acted and rather stodgily directed piece of historical melodrama. Totally studio-bound, but one of these days it could find a sympathetic audience.

w Cyril Hume, Michael Hogan d Mitchell Leisen ph Daniel L. Fapp m Hugo Friedhofer ad Hans Dreier, Roland Anderson, Albert Nozaki

☆ Paulette Goddard, John Lund, Macdonald Carey, Albert Dekker, Raymond Burr

'A dud ... it just couldn't be that bad by accident.' – *Los Angeles Times*

The Bride Walks Out

US   1936   81m   bw

RKO (Edward Small)

A successful mannequin tries to manage on her engineer husband's lowly salary.

Thin, pleasant marital comedy with no surprises.

w P. J. Wolfson, Philip G. Epstein d Leigh Jason ph J. Roy Hunt m Roy Webb

☆ Barbara Stanwyck, Gene Raymond, Robert Young, Ned Sparks, Helen Broderick, Willie Best, Robert Warwick, Billy Gilbert, Hattie McDaniel, Irving Bacon

The Bride Wasn't Willing: see Frontier Gal

The Bride Wore Black *

France/Italy   1968   107m   Eastmancolor

UA/Films du Carrosse/Artistes Associés/Dino de Laurentiis (Marcel Bébert)

original title: *La Mariée était en Noir*

A melancholy lady traces and kills the five men responsible for her fiancé's death.

Uncertain and not very entertaining attempt to turn a Hitchcock situation into a character study.

w François Truffaut, Jean-Louis Richard novel William Irish d François Truffaut ph Raoul Coutard m Bernard Herrmann ad Pierre Guffroy ed Claudine Bouché

☆ Jeanne Moreau, Jean-Claude Brialy, Michel Bouquet, Charles Denner, Claude Rich, Michel Lonsdale

'Truffaut has called the film a love story; others have taken it as a tribute to his master, a Hitchcockian thriller. In fact it is neither; it is a piece of junk.' – *John Simon*

The Bride Wore Boots

US   1946   86m   bw

Paramount (Seton I. Miller)

A woman who loves horses is married to a man who does not.

Flimsy, silly, but mainly quite tolerable light comedy sustained by its stars.

w Dwight Mitchell Wiley d Irving Pichel ph Stuart Thompson m Frederick Hollander

☆ Barbara Stanwyck, Robert Cummings, Diana Lynn, Patric Knowles, Peggy Wood, Robert Benchley, Willie Best, Natalie Wood

The Bride Wore Red *

US   1937   103m   bw

MGM (Joseph L. Mankiewicz)

A whimsical count arranges for a chorus girl to spend two weeks at an aristocratic Tyrol resort, where she is pursued by two rich men.

Cinderella retold in fancy dress; a typically unreal but quite entertaining star confection of its day.

w Tess Slesinger, Bradbury Foote play *The Girl from Trieste* by Ferenc Molnar d Dorothy Arzner ph George Folsey m Franz Waxman

☆ Joan Crawford, Robert Young, Franchot Tone, Billie Burke, Reginald Owen, George Zucco, Lynne Carver, Mary Philips, Paul Porcasi

'Marquee values will have to bolster this one.' – *Variety*

'In the privacy of a girls' school he sought his prey – turning innocent beauty into a thing of unspeakable horror!'

The Brides of Dracula **

GB   1960   85m   Technicolor

U-I/Hammer/Hotspur (Anthony Hinds)

Baron Meinster, a disciple of Dracula, is locked up by his mother; but a servant lets him out and he goes on the rampage in a girls' school.

The best of the Hammer Draculas, with plenty of inventive action, some classy acting and a good sense of place and period.

w Jimmy Sangster, Peter Bryan, Edward Percy d Terence Fisher ph Jack Asher m Malcolm Williamson ed James Needs, Alfred Cox

☆ David Peel, Peter Cushing, Freda Jackson, Martita Hunt, Yvonne Monlaur, Andrée Melly, Mona Washbourne, Henry Oscar, Miles Malleson

The Brides of Fu Manchu *

GB   1966   94m   Eastmancolor

Anglo Amalgamated

The yellow peril kidnaps twelve young women in order to blackmail their influential boyfriends.

Very adequate sequel to The Face of Fu Manchu (qv for details of series), after which Fu Manchu went rapidly downhill.

w Harry Alan Towers (Peter Welbeck) d Don Sharp

☆ Christopher Lee, Douglas Wilmer, Howard Marion Crawford, Marie Versini, Tsai Chin, Rupert Davies

The Bridge *

West Germany   1959   106m   bw

Fono/Jochen Severin (Hermann Schwerin)

In 1945, only a handful of 16-year-old schoolboys is left to defend the bridge of a small German town.

Painful but memorable war vignette, almost an updating of All Quiet on the Western Front (qv).

w Michael Mansfield, Karl-Wilhelm Vivier novel Manfred Gregor d Bernhard Wicki ph Gerd von Bonen m Hans-Martin Majewski

☆ Volker Bohnet, Fritz Wepper, Michael Hinz, Frank Glaubrecht, Karl Michael Balzer, Gunther Hoffman

⅄ foreign film

The Bridge
GB 1991 99m Fujicolour
Moonlight/British Screen/Film Four (Lyn Goleby)
🔲 ◑

A young artist and a bored wife, who is on holiday with her young daughters, fall in love.
Genteel period drama, lacking in any dramatic impetus.
w Adrian Hodges d Sydney MacCartney
ph David Tattersall m Richard G. Mitchell
pd Terry Pritchard ed Michael Ellis
☆ Saskia Reeves, David O'Hara, Joss Ackland, Anthony Higgins, Rosemary Harris, Geraldine James
'Beautiful but inert … firmly belongs to the Laura Ashley school of genteel British cinema.' – *Variety*
'Frozen with timidity. This British costume drama sits on the screen like little Miss Muffet, spinning the trite tale of a summer's dalliance.' – *Geoff Brown, The Times*

The Bridge at Remagen *
US 1968 116m DeLuxe Panavision
UA/Wolper (David L. Wolper)
🔲 ◎ ⊘

February 1945: Germans and Americans fight over a Rhine bridge.
Disenchanted, violent war film in which incessant bang-bang, adroitly staged, is all that matters.
w Richard Yates, William Roberts d John Guillermin ph Stanley Cortez m Elmer Bernstein
☆ George Segal, Robert Vaughn, Ben Gazzara, Bradford Dillman, E. G. Marshall, Peter Van Eyck
'Viable viewing if explosions and clichés are your shtick and exciting if you're not sure who won that war.' – *Judith Crist*

The Bridge of San Luis Rey *
US 1944 85m bw
UA/Benedict Bogeaus
🔲 ◎ ⊘

Five people die when a Peruvian rope bridge collapses; the film investigates why they were each on the bridge at the time.
An intriguing novel is turned into tedious film drama, with actors, director, scenarist and production designer all making heavy weather.
w Howard Estabrook novel Thornton Wilder
d Rowland V. Lee ph John Boyle m Dimitri Tiomkin
☆ Lynn Bari, Francis Lederer, Nazimova, Louis Calhern, Akim Tamiroff, Blanche Yurka, Donald Woods
'As a remake for present-day audiences, up to their ears in war news, this picture will be a welcome divertissement.' – *Variety*
† A silent version, with a few minutes of hasty talk, was made in 1929 by Charles Brabin for MGM, from a script by Alice Duer Miller, Ruth Cummings and Marian Ainslee. The cast included Lili Damita, Ernest Torrence, Don Alvarado, Raquel Torres, and Henry B. Walthall.
♫ Dimitri Tiomkin

'It spans a whole new world of entertainment!'
The Bridge on the River Kwai ****
GB 1957 161m Technicolor Cinemascope
Columbia/Sam Spiegel
🔲 🔳 ◎ ☊

British POWs in Burma are employed by the Japs to build a bridge; meanwhile British agents seek to destroy it.
Ironic adventure epic with many fine moments but too many centres of interest and an unforgivably confusing climax. It is distinguished by Guinness's portrait of the English CO who is heroic in his initial stand against the Japs but finally cannot bear to see his bridge blown up: and the physical detail of the production is beyond criticism.
w Carl Foreman novel Pierre Boulle d David Lean ph Jack Hildyard m Malcolm Arnold ed Peter Taylor
☆ Alec Guinness, William Holden, Jack Hawkins, Sessue Hayakawa, James Donald, Geoffrey Horne, Andre Morell, Percy Herbert
'It may rank as the most rousing adventure film inspired by the last World War.' – *Alton Cook, New York World Telegram*
† Cary Grant was originally sought for the William Holden role
†† The script was actually written by Michael Wilson, who was blacklisted by the anti-communists.

👤 best picture; best adaptation (now credited to Carl Foreman, Michael Wilson and Pierre Boulle); David Lean; Jack Hildyard; Malcolm Arnold; Alec Guinness; editing
♫ Sessue Hayakawa
🎬 best picture; best British picture; Alec Guinness; best screenplay

Bridge to the Sun *
France/US 1961 112m bw
MGM/Cité Films (Jacques Bar)

Just before Pearl Harbor, an American girl marries a Japanese diplomat and goes to live in Tokyo.
Romantic drama which oddly sides with the Japanese and shows America in a poor light. Interesting if not very compelling, with some unfamiliar views of Japan.
w Charles Kaufman autobiography Gwendolen Terasaki d Etienne Périer ph Marcel Weiss, Seiichi Kizuka, Bill Kelly m Georges Auric
☆ Carroll Baker, James Shigeta, James Yagi, Tetsuro Tamba
'In yet another burst of national flagellation, Hollywood turns on itself and unthinking Americans for being so beastly about the wartime Japanese.' – *MFB*

A Bridge Too Far **
US/GB 1977 175m Technicolor Panavision
UA/Joseph E. Levine (John Palmer)
🔲 ◎ ⊘ ☊

The story of the Allied defeat at Arnhem in 1944.
Like all large-scale military films, this one fails to make its tactics clear, and its sober intent conflicts with its roster of guest stars. For all that, there are impressive moments of acting and production.
w William Goldman book Cornelius Ryan
d Richard Attenborough (and Sidney Hayers)
ph Geoffrey Unsworth, Harry Waxman, Robin Browne m John Addison pd Terence Marsh
☆ Dirk Bogarde, James Caan, Michael Caine, Sean Connery, Edward Fox, Elliott Gould, Gene Hackman, Anthony Hopkins, Hardy Kruger, Laurence Olivier, Ryan O'Neal, Robert Redford, Maximilian Schell, Liv Ullmann, Arthur Hill and also Wolfgang Preiss
'A film too long.' – *Anon*
'So wearily, expensively predictable that by the end the viewer will in all likelihood be too enervated to notice Attenborough's prosaic moral epilogue.' – *John Pym, MFB*
🎬 Geoffrey Unsworth; Edward Fox; John Addison

The Bridges at Toko-Ri *
US 1954 104m Technicolor
Paramount/Perlberg-Seaton
🔲 ◎

The comradeship and death of two jet pilots during the Korean War.
Ambitiously staged action thriller with points to make about war, death and politics: a well-worn American formula pitched very hard.
w Valentine Davies novel James A. Michener
d Mark Robson ph Loyal Griggs m Lyn Murray
ed Alma Macrorie
☆ William Holden, Mickey Rooney, Grace Kelly, Fredric March, Robert Strauss, Charles McGraw, Earl Holliman, Willis Bouchey
'A taut, thrilling, top flight documentary drama of men, war, ships and planes.' – *Cue*
♫ editing

The Bridges of Madison County **
US 1995 135m Technicolor
Warner/Amblin/Malpaso (Clint Eastwood, Kathleen Kennedy)
🔲 🔳 ◎ ⊘ ☊

An Italian-born farmer's wife in Iowa has a passionate four-day affair with a photographer.
Eastwood's restraint, both as actor and director, adds a little rigour to a swooningly sentimental best-seller, and Meryl Streep surprisingly finds some truth in her character; but for all their efforts, it is a thin thing.
w Richard LaGravenese d Clint Eastwood
ph Jack N. Green m Lennie Niehaus
pd Jeannine Oppewall ed Joel Cox
☆ Clint Eastwood, Meryl Streep, Annie Corley, Victor Slezak, Jim Haynie
'A handsomely crafted, beautifully acted adult love story.' – *Variety*
'Dull, dull, dull.' – *Pauline Kael*
† The film took more than $172m at the box-office worldwide.
♫ Meryl Streep

Brief Encounter ****
GB 1945 86m bw
Eagle-Lion/Cineguild (Anthony Havelock-Allan, Ronald Neame)
🔲 🔳 ◎

A suburban housewife on her weekly shopping visits develops a love affair with a local doctor; but he gets a job abroad and they agree not to see each other again.
An outstanding example of good middle-class cinema turned by sheer professional craft into a masterpiece; even those bored by the theme must be riveted by the treatment, especially the use of a dismal railway station and its trains.
w Noël Coward, David Lean, Ronald Neame, Anthony Havelock-Allan play Still Life by Noël Coward d David Lean ph Robert Krasker
m Rachmaninov md Muir Mathieson ad L. P. Williams ed Jack Harris
☆ Celia Johnson, Trevor Howard, Stanley Holloway, Joyce Carey, Cyril Raymond
'Both a pleasure to watch as a well-controlled piece of work, and deeply touching.' – *James Agee*
'Polished as is this film, its strength does not lie in movie technique, of which there is plenty, so much as in the tight realism of its detail.' – *Richard Winnington*
'A celebrated, craftsmanlike tearjerker, and incredibly neat. There's not a breath of air in it.' – *Pauline Kael, 70s*
† A TV film version was made in 1975 by ITC, starring Richard Burton and Sophia Loren and directed by Alan Bridges. It was an unqualified disaster.
♫ script; David Lean; Celia Johnson

A Brief History of Time **
GB/US 1992 84m Technicolor
(David Hickman)
🔲

A documentary on the theories of Stephen Hawking concerning the origins and likely fate of the universe.
A more accessible but less complex approach to Hawking's views than his bestselling, if seldom finished, book. It includes interviews with Hawking himself.
wd Errol Morris book Stephen Hawking ph John Bailey m Philip Glass pd Ted Bafaloukos
ed Brad Fuller

Brigadoon *
US 1954 108m Anscocolor Cinemascope
MGM (Arthur Freed)
🔲 🔳 ◎ ☊

Two Americans in Scotland find a ghost village which awakens only once every hundred years.
Likeable but disappointing adaptation of a Lost Horizonish Broadway musical, marred by artificial sets and jaded direction.
w Alan Jay Lerner play Alan Jay Lerner
d Vincente Minnelli ph Joseph Ruttenberg
m/ly Frederick Loewe, Alan Jay Lerner
md Johnny Green ad Cedric Gibbons, Preston Ames
☆ Gene Kelly, Cyd Charisse, Van Johnson, Jimmy Thompson, Elaine Stewart, Barry Jones, Eddie Quillan
'The whimsical dream world it creates holds no compelling attractions.' – *Penelope Houston*
† Cyd Charisse's singing was dubbed by Carole Richards.
♫ art direction

The Brigand *
US 1952 93m Technicolor
Columbia

A Moroccan adventurer looks like the king and is reprieved from execution if he will impersonate the latter and root out his enemies.
Cheeky revamp of The Prisoner of Zenda (qv), quite acceptably done.
w Jesse Lasky Jnr d Phil Karlson ph W. Howard Greene m Mario Castelnuovo-Tedesco
☆ Anthony Dexter, Jody Lawrance, Gale Robbins, Anthony Quinn, Carl Benton Reid, Ron Randell

The Brigand of Kandahar
GB 1965 81m Technicolor Scope
EMI/Hammer (Anthony Nelson-Keys)

A cashiered Bengal Lancer officer throws in his lot with a troublesome bandit.
Feeble frontier adventure with nothing ringing true.

wd John Gilling ph Reg Wyer m Don Banks
pd Bernard Robinson ed James Needs
☆ Oliver Reed, Ronald Lewis, Duncan Lamont, Yvonne Romain, Catherine Woodville, Glyn Houston

Brigham Young *
US 1940 112m bw
TCF (Kenneth MacGowan)

The story of the Mormon trek to Utah.
Ambitious but rather dull interpretation of history, seen as a Western with romantic fictional trimmings.
w Lamar Trotti story Louis Bromfield d Henry Hathaway ph Arthur Miller m Alfred Newman
☆ Dean Jagger, Tyrone Power, Linda Darnell, Brian Donlevy, Jane Darwell, John Carradine, Mary Astor, Vincent Price, Moroni Olsen
'A big picture in every respect.' – *Variety*
'One of the year's outstanding films.' – *Newsweek*
† The production had a 133-day schedule, and cost 2,700,000 dollars.

Bright Eyes *
👣 US 1934 84m bw
Fox (Sol M. Wurtzell)

An orphan finds herself torn between foster-parents.
The first of Shirley Temple's genuine star vehicles has a liveliness and cheerfulness hard to find today. As a production, however, it is decidedly economical.
w William Conselman d David Butler ph Arthur Miller m Samuel Kaylin
☆ Shirley Temple, James Dunn, Lois Wilson, Jane Withers, Judith Allen
'It seems a cinch to please generally, the family and sentimental strata particularly.' – *Variety*

Bright Leaf
US 1950 110m bw
Warner (Henry Blanke)

A 19th-century tobacco farmer builds a cigarette empire.
Quite agreeable but disjointed fictional biopic, more about love than tobacco.
w Ranald MacDougall novel Robert Wilder
d Michael Curtiz ph Karl Freund m Victor Young
☆ Gary Cooper, Lauren Bacall, Patricia Neal, Jack Carson, Donald Crisp, Gladys George, Elizabeth Patterson, Jeff Corey, Taylor Holmes

Bright Lights *
US 1935 86m bw
Warner
GB title: *Funny Face*
A vaudevillian lets success go to his head.
The plot served for a score or more of thirties musicals, but this had Busby Berkeley routines and an unusual star role for Joe E. Brown.
w Bert Kalmar, Harry Ruby d Busby Berkeley
☆ Joe E. Brown, Ann Dvorak, Patricia Ellis, William Gargan
'Practically an 86-minute monologue, with the star doing everything but taking tickets.' – *Variety*
† The same title covered a 1925 MGM silent with Charles Ray as a country boy in love with a Broadway star, also a 1930 Warner film with Frank Fay.

Bright Lights, Big City
US 1988 107m colour
UIP/United Artists (Mark Rosenberg, Sydney Pollack)
🔲 🔳 ◎ ☊

A cocaine-snorting magazine researcher goes to pieces in New York.
Some good performances compensate for the unsympathetic central character of a lightweight drama.
w Jay McInerney novel Jay McInerney d James Bridges ph Gordon Willis m Donald Fagen
pd Santo Loquasto ed John Bloom
☆ Michael J. Fox, Kiefer Sutherland, Phoebe Cates, Frances Sternhagen, Dianne Wiest, Swoosie Kurtz, John Houseman, Jason Robards, Tracy Pollan
'The banality comes down on you like drizzle.' – *Pauline Kael, New Yorker*

Bright Road *
US 1953 69m bw
MGM (Sol Baer Fielding)

In an all-black school, a problem child finds himself when he helps to rid the school of a swarm of bees.
Slight but attractive second feature, unostentatiously set in a black community.

w Emmet Lavery d Gerald Mayer ph Alfred Gilks m David Rose

☆ Dorothy Dandridge, Harry Belafonte, Robert Horton, Philip Hepburn, Barbara Ann Sanders

Bright Victory *
US 1951 97m bw
Universal (Robert Buckner)
GB title: Lights Out
A blinded soldier adjusts to civilian life.
Well-meaning if rather slow and sticky, this drama is more sentimental than realistic but has good performances.
w Robert Buckner novel Baynard Kendrick d Mark Robson ph William Daniels m Frank Skinner
☆ Arthur Kennedy, Peggy Dow, Julie Adams, James Edwards, Will Geer, Minor Watson, Jim Backus
& Arthur Kennedy

A Brighter Summer Day ***
Taiwan 1991 237m colour
ICA/Yang and His Gang (Yu Welyan)
original title: *Guling Jie Shaonian Sha Ren Shijan*
In the early 1960s, a 14-year-old boy falls in love with the girlfriend of a young gang leader.
A long but engrossing film, set against troubled times and the fear of Communist China, which provides a detailed examination of the society of the time.
w Edward Yang, Yan Hongya, Yang Shunqing, Lai Mingtang d Edward Yang ph Zhang Hulgong, Li Longyu pd Yu Welyan, Edward Yang ed Chen Bowen
☆ Lisa Yang, Zhang Zhen, Zhang Guozhu, Elaine Jin, Wang Juan, Zhang Han
'One of the major feats of non-American cinema of its time ... Gathers an extraordinary momentum, showing that you really can delineate the lives of ordinary people in an extraordinary way without either flashiness or pretension.' – Derek Malcolm, Guardian
† The film also exists in a version that is 50m shorter. The longer version is the director's preferred cut.

Brightness: see Yeelen

Brighton Beach Memoirs *
US 1986 108m colour
Universal/Rastar (David Chasman)
In 1937 Brooklyn, a lower-middle-class Jewish family has assorted crises.
Standard picturization of a Neil Simon play, somewhat flattened out in the process but with funny moments.
w Neil Simon play Neil Simon d Gene Saks ph John Bailey m Michael Small
☆ Blythe Danner, Bob Dishy, Brian Drillinger, Stacey Glick, Judith Ivey, Lisa Waltz
'Simon instinctively makes things easy and palatable, and there's a penalty: it's the retrograde, pepless snooziness of the picture. You come out feeling half dead.' – New Yorker

Brighton Rock ***
GB 1947 92m bw
Associated British/Charter Films (Roy Boulting)
US title: Young Scarface
The teenage leader of a racetrack gang uses a waitress as alibi to cover a murder, and marries her. He later decides to be rid of her, but fate takes a hand in his murder plot.
A properly 'seedy' version of Graham Greene's 'entertainment', very flashily done for the most part but with a trick ending which allows the heroine to keep her illusions.
w Graham Greene, Terence Rattigan novel Graham Greene d John Boulting ph Harry Waxman m Hans May
☆ Richard Attenborough, Hermione Baddeley, Harcourt Williams, William Hartnell, Alan Wheatley, Carol Marsh, Nigel Stock
'The film is slower, much less compelling, and, if you get me, less cinematic than the book, as a child's guide to which I hereby offer it.' – Richard Winnington
'It proceeds with the efficiency, the precision and the anxiety to please of a circular saw.' – Dilys Powell

The Brighton Strangler
US 1945 67m bw
RKO (Herman Schlom)
An actor takes over in real life the part he is playing – of a murderer.
This hoary plot had seen better days even in 1945, and was not helped by an establishing shot which put Parliament on the wrong side of the Thames.
w Arnold Phillips, Max Nosseck d Max Nosseck ph J. Roy Hunt m Leigh Harline
☆ John Loder, June Duprez, Miles Mander

Brimstone
US 1949 90m Trucolor
Republic
A US Marshal tracks down Public Outlaw Number One.
High-spirited Western co-feature.
w Thames Williamson d Joseph Kane
☆ Rod Cameron, Walter Brennan, Adrian Booth, Forrest Tucker, Jack Holt, Jim Davis, James Brown, Guinn Williams

Brimstone and Treacle *
GB 1982 87m colour
Namara/Alan E. Salke/Herbert Solow
A strange young man has a sinister effect on the family of a middle-aged writer of doggerel, whose crippled daughter he finally rapes.
Similar in mood to Pennies from Heaven (qv), this is basically a television play very typical of its author. (Some years ago it was taped and then banned by the BBC.) In substance no more than a reversal of The Passing of the Third Floor Back (qv), its points of interest are mainly technical.
w Dennis Potter play Dennis Potter d Richard Loncraine ph Peter Hannan m Sting pd Milly Burns
☆ Sting, Denholm Elliott, Joan Plowright, Suzanna Hamilton, Benjamin Whitrow, Dudley Sutton

Bring 'Em Back Alive
US 1932 65m bw
RKO/Van Beuren
A documentary showing how an animal hunter scoured Malayan jungles for specimens to stock the world's zoos.
Very dated now, but quite an attraction in its day. The title was used again in 1982 for a TV series in which Bruce Boxleitner played Buck; the emphasis now, however, was on serial-like intrigue.
d Clyde Elliott
☆ Frank Buck
'Will get money but needs alert exploitation.' – Variety

'It's got guts!'
Bring Me the Head of Alfredo Garcia
US 1974 112m DeLuxe
UA/Optimus/Churubusco (Martin Baum)
A wealthy Mexican offers a million dollars for the head of a man who seduced his daughter, and claimants find that grave robbing is involved.
Gruesome, sickly action melodrama with revolting detail; the nadir of a director obsessed by violence.
w Gordon Dawson, Sam Peckinpah d Sam Peckinpah ph Alex Phillips Jnr m Jerry Fielding
☆ Warren Oates, Gig Young, Isela Vega, Robert Webber, Helmut Dantine, Emilio Fernandez, Kris Kristofferson
'Few movies are as tedious. Bring me the head of the studio that released this one.' – Gene Shalit
'The only kind of analysis it really invites is psychoanalysis.' – Wall Street Journal
'Peckinpah clearly doesn't lack talent – what he lacks is brains.' – John Simon

Bring Me the Head of Mavis Davis
GB 1997 99m Technicolor
Feature/Goldcrest/BBC/Mission (Stephen Colegrave, Joanne Reay)
A record producer hires a hitman when he suddenly realizes that his star singer would be worth more to him dead than alive.
Some slick performances fail to save this would-be black comedy from being unpleasant and unamusing.

w Craig Strachan idea Joanne Reay d John Henderson m Clive Tickner m Christopher Tyng pd Michael Carlin ed Paul Endacott
☆ Rik Mayall, Jane Horrocks, Danny Aiello, Ronald Pickup, Philip Martin-Brown, Jaclyn Mendoza, Ross Boatman, Paul Shearer
'A TV-style effort decapitated by a lame script and often clumsy direction.' – Derek Elley, Variety

Bring On the Girls
US 1945 92m Technicolor
Paramount (Fred Kohlmar)
A millionaire joins the navy in the hope that a girl will love him for himself.
A good example of the gaily-coloured but witless drivel which occasionally came out of the big studios towards the end of the war.
w Karl Tunberg, Darrell Ware d Sidney Lanfield ph Karl Struss md Robert Emmett Dolan
☆ Veronica Lake, Eddie Bracken, Sonny Tufts, Marjorie Reynolds, Grant Mitchell, Alan Mowbray, Porter Hall

Bring Your Smile Along
US 1955 83m Technicolor
Columbia
A lady schoolteacher goes to New York to write songs.
Amiable musical filler with rather flat jokes.
wd Blake Edwards
☆ Frankie Laine, Keefe Brasselle, Constance Towers, Lucy Marlow

Bringing Out the Dead ***
US 1999 120m DeLuxe Panavision
Buena Vista/Paramount/Touchstone (Scott Rudin, Barbara De Fina)
In New York City, an overworked ambulance driver careers towards a breakdown over the unremitting horrors of his night shift.
Scorsese revisits familiar territory for him and his audience: hellish streets inhabited by low-life predators and victims; but his perspective has shifted from his customary petty gangsters and psychopaths to the good guys, however unbalanced they may seem. Despair is here tempered with humanity.
w Paul Schrader novel Joe Connelly d Martin Scorsese ph Robert Richardson m Elmer Bernstein pd Dante Ferretti ed Thelma Schoonmaker sp Industrial Light & Magic
☆ Nicolas Cage, Patricia Arquette, John Goodman, Ving Rhames, Tom Sizemore, Marc Anthony, Mary Beth Hurt, Cliff Curtis, Nestor Serrano, Aida Turturro
'An intense, volatile movie full of sorrow and wild, mordant humor.' – Janet Maslin, New York Times
'This is a work of bad imitation from an immature talent who thinks he's Martin Scorsese.' – Cosmo Landesman, Sunday Times

Bringing Up Baby ***
US 1938 102m bw
RKO (Howard Hawks)
A zany girl causes a zoology professor to lose a dinosaur bone and a pet leopard in the same evening.
Outstanding crazy comedy which barely pauses for romance and ends up with the whole splendid cast in jail.
w Dudley Nichols, Hagar Wilde d Howard Hawks ph Russell Metty m Roy Webb
☆ Katharine Hepburn, Cary Grant, May Robson, Charles Ruggles, Walter Catlett, Fritz Feld, Jonathan Hale, Barry Fitzgerald
'Harum-scarum farce comedy ... definite box-office.' – Variety
'I am happy to report that it is funny from the word go, that it has no other meaning to recommend it ... and that I wouldn't swap it for practically any three things of the current season.' – Otis Ferguson
'It may be the American movies' closest equivalent to Restoration comedy.' – Pauline Kael
'Crazy comedies continue to become crazier, and there will soon be few actors and actresses left who have no straw in their hair.' – Basil Wright
† The dog George was played by Asta from The Thin Man movies.

Bringing Up Father
US 1928 70m bw silent
MGM
Mild domestic comedy about a henpecked husband, from the famous comic strip.
It marked the successful comeback of Marie Dressler (as the maid).
w Frances Marion d Jack Conway
☆ J. Farrell MacDonald, Marie Dressler, Polly Moran, Gertrude Olmsted, Grant Withers
† Two or three second features about Jiggs and Maggie, featuring Renie Riano and Joe Yule, appeared in the late forties.

Brink of Hell: see Toward the Unknown

Brink of Life: see So Close to Life

The Brinks Job
US 1978 103m Technicolor
Universal/Dino de Laurentiis (Ralph Serpe)
In 1944, amateur criminals bring off a raid on the vaults of a Boston security company.
Farcical variation of a much-told true tale. Despite much mugging by the stars and a frantic narrative style, it does not come off.
w Walon Green book Big Stick-Up at Brinks by Noel Behn d William Friedkin ph Norman Leigh m Richard Rodney Bennett pd Dean Tavoularis
☆ Peter Falk, Warren Oates, Peter Boyle, Allen Goorwitz, Gena Rowlands, Paul Sorvino, Sheldon Leonard

Britannia Hospital
GB 1982 116m colour
EMI/Film and General/NFFC (Davina Belling, Clive Parsons)
Problems besetting a British hospital celebrating its 500th anniversary include strikes, demonstrators, and a mad doctor who transplants heads.
Looking as crummy as a Carry On at the end of its tether, this intended lampoon of the state of the nation never warms up and can only fire off stale jokes in all directions while repelling the eye with its Frankenstein scenes.
w David Sherwin d Lindsay Anderson ph Mike Fash m Alan Price pd Norris Spencer
☆ Malcolm McDowell, Leonard Rossiter, Graham Crowden, Fulton Mackay, Vivian Pickles, Joan Plowright, Peter Jeffrey, Robin Askwith, Dandy Nichols, Valentine Dyall, Roland Culver, Alan Bates, Arthur Lowe, Marsha Hunt
'It has all the intensity, along with the flailing incoherence, of a soapbox jeremiah.' – Richard Combs, MFB
'Having once created a general shambles, the film is at a loss to clean it up.' – Margaret Hinxman, Daily Mail
'Inexplicably muddled and inconclusive.' – Guardian
'It mentholates the tubes and oxygenates the brain.' – Sunday Telegraph

Britannia Mews
GB 1948 91m bw
TCF (William Perlberg)
US title: The Forbidden Street
In Victorian times, the widow of a puppetmaster eventually marries his lookalike who rebuilds their puppet theatre.
Curious and uncertain comedy drama set among yesterday's high society, with poorly played leads but an interesting supporting cast and technical assurance.
w Ring Lardner Jnr novel Margery Sharp d Jean Negulesco ph Georges Périnal m Malcolm Arnold ad Andrei Andreiev
☆ Dana Andrews, Maureen O'Hara, Sybil Thorndike, Wilfrid Hyde-White, Fay Compton, A. E. Matthews

British Agent *
US 1934 75m bw
Warner (Henry Blanke)
In 1910 Russia, a Britisher falls in love with a lady spy.
Sluggish and dated romantic melodrama, notable only for Howard's performance and some directional felicities.
w Laird Doyle novel H. Bruce Lockhart d Michael Curtiz ph Ernest Haller ad Anton Grot

---

☆ *Leslie Howard*, Kay Francis, William Gargan, *Irving Pichel*, Philip Reed, Walter Byron, J. Carrol Naish, Halliwell Hobbes

'One of those rare cases of a film both artistically and cinematically good entertainment … an exciting story well told, excellent acting, draw names and production value.' – *Variety*

British Intelligence *
US   1940   63m   bw
Warner (Bryan Foy)
📼 ⊘
GB title: *Enemy Agent*
During World War I a German lady spy becomes a guest in the house of a British war official, the butler of which is the leader of a German spy ring.
Second feature remake of Three Faces East *(qv); still quite an entertaining melodrama.*
w Lee Katz *play* Anthony Paul Kelly d Terry Morse ph Sid Hickox m Heinz Roemheld
☆ Boris Karloff, Margaret Lindsay, Maris Wrixon, Bruce Lester, Leonard Mudie, Holmes Herbert

Broadcast News *
US   1987   31m   DeLuxe
UKFD/Fox/Gracie Films (James L. Brooks)
📼 📀 ⌂
An ambitious TV news reader with personality but little talent gets to the top.
Mildly satirical look at the world of television journalism that slips into romantic comedy.
wd James L. Brooks ph Michael Ballhaus m Bill Conti pd Charles Rosen ed Richard Marks
☆ William Hurt, Albert Brooks, *Holly Hunter*, Robert Prosky, Lois Chiles, Joan Cusack, Jack Nicholson (uncredited cameo)
⚹ best picture; William Hurt; Holly Hunter; Albert Brooks; best original screenplay; best cinematography; best film editing

Broadminded *
US   1931   65m   bw
First National
A bashful swain leaves town after a misunderstanding and becomes involved in an intercontinental chase.
Modest star vehicle with some hilarious moments.
w Bert Kalmar, Harry Ruby d Mervyn Le Roy
☆ *Joe E. Brown*, Ona Munson, William Collier Jnr, Marjorie White, Holmes Herbert, Bela Lugosi
'Best he has ever done … any audience will enjoy it.' – *Variety*

Broadway
US   1942   90m   bw
Universal (Bruce Manning)
George Raft recalls his days as a hoofer in a New York speakeasy, and in particular a murder involving gangsters and chorus girls.
Minor crime melodrama which after interminable scene-setting paints an effective picture of the twenties but has too slack a grip on narrative.
w Felix Jackson, John Bright *play* Philip Dunning, George Abbott d William A. Seiter ph George Barnes md Charles Previn
☆ George Raft, Pat O'Brien, S. Z. Sakall, Janet Blair, Broderick Crawford, Marjorie Rambeau

Broadway Bad
US   1933   59m   bw
Fox
A scheming chorus girl makes a rich marriage.
Paper-thin melodrama, one of a hundred on similar lines.
w Arthur Kober, Maude Fulton d Sidney Lanfield
☆ Joan Blondell, Ginger Rogers, Ricardo Cortez, Adrienne Ames, Spencer Charters, Donald Crisp

Broadway Bill **
US   1934   104m   bw
Columbia (Frank Capra)
📼 📀 ⌂
GB title: *Strictly Confidential*
A cheerful horse trainer finds he has a winner.
Easygoing romantic comedy with the energetic Capra style in fairly full bloom.
w Robert Riskin *story* Mark Hellinger d *Frank Capra* ph Joseph Walker
☆ Warner Baxter, Myrna Loy, Walter Connolly, Helen Vinson, Douglass Dumbrille, Raymond Walburn, Lynne Overman, Clarence Muse, Margaret Hamilton, Paul Harvey, Claude Gillingwater, Charles Lane, Ward Bond

'The effect of capable direction is discernible in every foot.' – *Variety*
'It will be a long day before we see so little made into so much: it is gay and charming and will make you happy, and I am sorry to say I do not know recommendations much higher.' – *Otis Ferguson*
† Remade as *Riding High* (qv).

Broadway Bound *
US   1991   94m   colour
Blue Dolphin/ABC Productions (Terry Nelson)
📼 📀
In the 40s, two brothers struggle to become writers and move away from home, where their father and mother quarrel and their grandfather grumbles.
An autobiographical slice of life, delivered with a gently effective humour.
w Neil Simon *play* Neil Simon d Paul Bogart ph Isidore Mankofsky m David Shire pd Ben Edwards ed Andy Zall
☆ Anne Bancroft, Hume Cronyn, Corey Parker, Jonathan Silverman, Jerry Orbach, Michele Lee
'Certain to delight those with a taste for the theatrical.' – *Empire*

Broadway Danny Rose *
US   1984   84m   DeLuxe
Orion (Robert Greenhut)
📼 📀 ⌂ ⌂
An artists' agent and former comic falls foul of the Mafia while promoting a client.
Generally appealing comedy-melodrama with rather less self-examination than has latterly been typical of its star.
wd Woody Allen ph Gordon Willis md Dick Hyman pd Mel Bourne ed Susan E. Morse
☆ Woody Allen, Mia Farrow, Nick Apollo Forte, Craig Vandenburgh, Herb Reynolds
⚹ direction, original screenplay
Ⓣ original screenplay

Broadway Gondolier
US   1935   98m   bw
Warner
A taxi driver wants to become a radio singer.
Rather tedious musical with second-rate elements.
w Warren Duff, Sig Herzig d Lloyd Bacon m/ly Al Dubin, Harry Warren
☆ Dick Powell, Adolphe Menjou, Joan Blondell, Louise Fazenda, the Mills Brothers, Judy Canova, Ted Fiorito and his band
'Loose on story and even lethargic, it holds enough for gate values.' – *Variety*

Broadway Hostess
US   1935   69m   bw
Warner
A small-town girl becomes a night-club singer.
Modest musical which failed to create a new star.
w George Bricker d Frank McDonald ch Bobby Connolly
☆ Wini Shaw, Genevieve Tobin, Lyle Talbot, Allen Jenkins, Phil Regan, Marie Wilson, Spring Byington
'Adequate for family audience consumption.' – *Variety*
⚹ Bobby Connolly

Broadway Limited *
US   1941   75m   bw
Hal Roach
📼
GB title: *The Baby Vanishes*
On an express train, a Hollywood publicity stunt backfires.
Wild farce which is not very funny as a whole but has entertaining comic performances.
w Rian James d Gordon Douglas ph Henry Sharp m Charles Previn
☆ Victor McLaglen, Patsy Kelly, *Leonid Kinskey*, Marjorie Woodworth, Dennis O'Keefe, ZaSu Pitts, George E. Stone

'The pulsating drama of Broadway's bared heart speaks and sings with a voice to stir your soul!'
'The new wonder of the screen!'
Broadway Melody *
US   1929   110m   bw (Technicolor scenes)
MGM (Lawrence Weingarten)
📼 ⌂
Chorus girls try to make it big on Broadway.
The screen's very first musical, exceedingly primitive by the standards of even a year later, but rather endearing and with a splendid score.

w James Gleason, Norman Houston, Edmund Goulding d Harry Beaumont ph John Arnold m/ly Nacio Herb Brown, Arthur Freed ad Cedric Gibbons
☆ Charles King, Anita Page, Bessie Love, Jed Prouty, Kenneth Thomson, Mary Doran, Eddie Kane
'A basic story with some sense to it, action, excellent direction, laughs, a tear, a couple of great performances and plenty of sex.' – *Variety*
† The plot resurfaced in *Two Girls On Broadway* (qv), made by MGM in 1940.
⚹ best picture
⚹ Harry Beaumont, Bessie Love

'You have waited seven years for this!'
Broadway Melody of 1936 **
US   1935   103m   bw
MGM (John W. Considine Jnr)
📼 ⌂
A Broadway producer is at loggerheads with a columnist.
Fairly lively musical with lavish numbers.
w Jack McGowan, Sid Silvers, Harry Conn *story* Moss Hart d Roy del Ruth ph Charles Rosher m/ly Nacio Herb Brown, Arthur Freed md Alfred Newman ch Dave Gould ed Blanche Sewell
☆ Jack Benny, Robert Taylor, Una Merkel, *Eleanor Powell*, June Knight, Vilma and Buddy Ebsen, Nick Long Jnr
'Smash musical with strong dancing and comedy framework.' – *Variety*
♫ 'You Are My Lucky Star'; 'I've Gotta Feelin' You're Foolin''; 'Broadway Rhythm'; 'On a Sunday Afternoon'; 'Sing Before Breakfast'; 'All I Do Is Dream Of You'
⚹ Dave Gould
⚹ best picture; Moss Hart

'So Big It Tops Them All. So New It's A Year Ahead!'
Broadway Melody of 1938 *
US   1937   110m   bw
MGM (Jack Cummings)
📼 ⌂ ⌂
Backstage problems threaten the opening of a musical show.
Lavish but fairly forgettable musical with top talent.
w Jack McGowan, Sid Silvers d Roy del Ruth ph William Daniels m/ly Nacio Herb Brown, Arthur Freed md George Stoll ed Blanche Sewell
☆ Eleanor Powell, George Murphy, *Sophie Tucker*, Judy Garland, Robert Taylor, Buddy Ebsen, Sid Silvers, Billy Gilbert, Raymond Walburn
'Explosion in the cash drawers … will do smash business everywhere.' – *Variety*
♫ 'Some of These Days'; 'Your Broadway and My Broadway'; 'Yours and Mine'; 'I'm Feelin'' Like a Million'; 'Dear Mr Gable'

Broadway Melody of 1940 *
US   1939   102m   bw
MGM (Jack Cummings)
📼 ⌂
A dance team gets to the top.
Splendidly produced but thinly plotted extravaganza with good numbers.
w Leon Gordon, George Oppenheimer *story* Jack McGowan, Dore Schary d Norman Taurog ph Oliver T. Marsh, Joseph Ruttenberg m/ly Cole Porter md Alfred Newman ad Cedric Gibbons ed Blanche Sewell
☆ *Fred Astaire, Eleanor Powell*, George Murphy, Douglas Macphail, Florence Rice, Frank Morgan, Ian Hunter
♫ 'I Concentrate on You'; 'Begin the Beguine'; 'Between You and Me'

Broadway Musketeers
US   1938   62m   bw
Warner (Bryan Foy)
Three girls from the same orphanage meet again in New York.
Uninspired remake of Three on a Match *(qv).*
w Don Ryan, Ken Gamet d John Farrow
☆ Ann Sheridan, Marie Wilson, Margaret Lindsay, John Litel, Dick Purcell
'A programmer of average distinction … ought to get by satisfactorily.' – *Variety*

Broadway Rhythm *
US   1943   113m   Technicolor
MGM (Jack Cummings)
📼
Originally intended as *Broadway Melody of 1944*, this putting-on-a-show extravaganza had only the numbers to commend it.
w Dorothy Kingsley, Harry Clork *operetta* Very Warm for May *by Jerome Kern and Oscar Hammerstein* d Roy del Ruth ph Leonard Smith m/ly various md John Green
☆ George Murphy, Ginny Simms, Charles Winninger, Gloria de Haven, Lena Horne, Nancy Walker, Hazel Scott, Eddie Anderson, Ben Blue, Tommy Dorsey and his Orchestra
'It contains perhaps three minutes of good acrobatic dancing and lasts nearly two hours.' – *James Agee*

Broadway Serenade
US   1939   114m   bw
MGM (Robert Z. Leonard)
📼
GB title: *Serenade*
Career problems split the marriage of a songwriter and his singing wife.
Lavish but rather dull romantic drama with music.
w Charles Lederer, Lew Lipton, John T. Foote, Hans Kraly d Robert Z. Leonard ph Oliver T. Marsh md Herbert Stothart
☆ Jeanette Macdonald, Lew Ayres, Frank Morgan, Ian Hunter, Rita Johnson, Virginia Grey, William Gargan, Katherine Alexander
'With all its lavishness, it impresses as only mild box office material.' – *Variety*
♫ 'No Time to Argue'; 'Time Changes Everything but Love'; 'For Every Lonely Heart'; 'Broadway Serenade'; 'High Flyin''; 'One Look at You'

Broadway Singer: see *Torch Singer*

Broadway thru a Keyhole *
US   1933   90m   bw
UA/Twentieth Century (William Goetz, Raymond Griffith)
A tough New York gangster falls for a singer in his night-club.
Reputed acid observation of the New York scene distinguishes this low-budget gangster drama.
w Gene Towne, Graham Baker *story* Walter Winchell d Lowell Sherman ph Barney McGill m/ly Mack Gordon, Harry Revel
☆ Constance Cummings, Russ Columbo, Paul Kelly, *Blossom Seeley*, Gregory Ratoff, *Texas Guinan*, Hobart Cavanaugh, C. Henry Gordon
'Not a big picture, but good entertainment.' – *Variety*
† The film was based on Ruby Keeler's relationships with gangster Johnny Costello and Al Jolson.

Broadway to Hollywood
US   1933   90m   bw
MGM
GB title: *Ring Up the Curtain*
A vaudeville family makes it in movies.
Cliché-strewn rags-to-riches saga with songs; good moments.
wd Willard Mack
☆ Frank Morgan, Alice Brady, Jackie Cooper, Madge Evans, Jimmy Durante, Nelson Eddy, May Robson, Una Merkel, Mickey Rooney
'A saga of the theatre that will please.' – *Variety*
† Some material was salvaged from an abandoned MGM musical of 1929, *The March of Time*.

'For just a little while, it was all so perfect.'
'How far would you go to protect a friend?'
Brokedown Palace *
US   1999   100m   DeLuxe   Panavision
TCF/Fox 2000 (Adam Fields)
📼 📀 ⊘ ⌂
Two teenage girls are jailed in Thailand after being tricked into carrying heroin through customs.
Mundane drama with nothing to lift it out of the ordinary.
w David Arata, Adam Fields d Jonathan Kaplan ph Newton Thomas Sigel m David Newman pd James Newport ed Curtiss Clayton
☆ Claire Danes, Kate Beckinsale, Bill Pullman, Jacqueline Kim, Lou Diamond Phillips, Daniel Lapaine, Tom Amandes, Aimee Graham, John Doe, Kay Tong Lim

---

'Utterly indistinguishable from the heap of Third World prison movies involving gullible Westerners.' – *James Christoper, Times*

Broken Arrow *
US   1950   92m   Technicolor
TCF (Julian Blaustein)
📼 ▦

A US army scout brings about peace between white man and Apache.
Solemn Western which at the time was acclaimed for giving the Indian's point of view (something which had scarcely happened since silent days). As entertainment it was not exciting, but it set Jeff Chandler off on a career playing Cochise with variations, and a TV series of the same name surfaced in 1956.
w Michael Blankfort *novel Blood Brother* by Elliott Arnold d Delmer Daves ph Ernest Palmer m Hugo Friedhofer md Alfred Newman
☆ James Stewart, Jeff Chandler, Debra Paget, Basil Ruysdael, Will Geer, Arthur Hunnicutt, Jay Silverheels
'It has probably done more to soften racial hostilities than most movies designed to instruct, indict and inspire.' – *Pauline Kael*
& Michael Blankfort; Ernest Palmer; Jeff Chandler

'Prepare To Go Ballistic!'
Broken Arrow
US   1996   86m   DeLuxe   Panavision
TCF/WCG (Mark Gordon, Bill Badalato, Terence Chang)
📼 ▦ ◷ ⊚ 🎧

A pilot chases a rival who has stolen a Stealth bomber containing live nuclear bombs.
An object lesson in how to make violence aesthetically interesting, but it is a pity the director cannot do the same with the plot or the characters; the narrative is implausible and the people little more than automatons equipped with a couple of vaguely human characteristics.
w Graham Yost d John Woo ph Peter Levy m Hans Zimmer pd Holger Gross ed John Wright, Steve Mirkovich, Joe Hutshing
☆ John Travolta, Christian Slater, Samantha Mathis, Delroy Lindo, Bob Gunton, Frank Whaley, Howie Long, Vondie Curtis-Hall, Jack Thompson
'Highly proficient and almost totally empty.' – *Derek Malcolm, Guardian*
'For explosion nerds only.' – *Tom Shone, Sunday Times*

Broken Blossoms **
US   1919   105m   bw   silent
UA/D. W. Griffith
📼 ▦ ◷ ⊚

In slummy Limehouse, a young Chinaman loves the daughter of a brute, who kills her; the Chinaman then kills him and commits suicide.
Victorian-style melodrama presented by Griffith with all the stops out; sometimes striking, but very dated even on its first appearance.
wd D. W. Griffith *story Limehouse Nights (The Chink and the Child)* by Thomas Burke ph G. W. Bitzer, Hendrik Sartov, Karl Brown
☆ Lillian Gish, Donald Crisp, Richard Barthelmess
'This is a Limehouse which neither Mr Burke nor anybody else who knows his East End of London will be able to recognize … but *Broken Blossoms* is a genuine attempt to bring real tragedy onto the screen as opposed to machine-made drama, and for that Mr Griffith deserves the thanks of all who are convinced of the potentialities of the film.' – *The Times*
'I know of no other picture in which so much screen beauty is obtained … attributable to the Whistlerian fogs and shadows, with that dock in Limehouse recurring like some pedal point.' – *James Agate, 1928*
† The film was made for $88,000, but Adolph Zukor regarded it as uncommercial and sold it to United Artists for $250,000. It went on to make a profit of $700,000. Leslie Henson appeared in a parody, *Broken Bottles*, in 1920.

Broken Blossoms *
GB   1936   84m   bw
Twickenham (Julius Hagen)
A remake originally intended to be directed by Griffith.
Quite stylish, and in some ways more interesting than its predecessor.
w Emlyn Williams d John Brahm ph Curt Courant

☆ Dolly Haas, Arthur Margetson, Emlyn Williams, Donald Calthrop, Ernest Sefton, Kathleen Harrison, Basil Radford
'There isn't much reason for this one.' – *Variety*

'The language of love, honour and betrayal.'
Broken English **
New Zealand   1996   92m   colour
First Independent/Communicado/Village Roadshow (Robin Scholes)
In New Zealand, a young Croatian woman, eager to escape her domineering father, falls in love with the Maori chef at the Chinese restaurant where she works.
Tough, compelling account of immigrant life, and of love, of fears of the future on the part of those locked in their past, of culture clashes and misunderstandings.
w Gregor Nicholas, Johanna Pigott, Jim Salter d Gregor Nicholas ph John Toon m Murray Grindlay, Murray McNabb pd Michael Kane ed David Coulson
☆ Rade Serbedzija, Aleksandra Vujcic, Julian Arahanga, Marton Csokas, Madeline McNamara, Zhoa Jing, Yang Li, Temuera Morrison
'Well-intentioned but overly harrowing viewing which will leave its audience craving a shot of escapism.' – *Rob Driscoll, Empire*

The Broken Horseshoe
GB   1953   79m   bw
Butchers/Nettlefold (Ernest G. Roy)
A doctor becomes implicated in the murder of a patient when he falls for a mysterious woman.
A thriller with an over-reliance on plot to maintain an audience's interest, which it soon dissipates with its implausibility.
w A. R. Rawlinson *TV serial* Francis Durbridge d Martyn C. Webster ph Gerald Gibbs m Wilfred Burns ad Bernard Robinson ed Joseph Sterling
☆ Robert Beatty, Elizabeth Sellars, Peter Coke, Hugh Kelly, Vida Hope, Janet Butler, Ferdy Mayne, George Benson, Roger Delgado

Broken Journey
GB   1948   89m   bw
Gainsborough (Sydney Box)
A plane crashes in the Alps, and the survivors take different attitudes to their situation.
Unpersuasive and stagey melodrama which wastes some good talent.
w Robert Westerby d Ken Annakin ph Jack Cox m John Greenwood
☆ Phyllis Calvert, James Donald, Margot Grahame, Francis L. Sullivan, Raymond Huntley, Derek Bond, Guy Rolfe, David Tomlinson

Broken Lance *
US   1954   96m   DeLuxe   Cinemascope
TCF (Sol C. Siegel)
📼 ▦ ◷

An autocratic cattle baron causes dissension among his sons.
Western remake of House of Strangers (qv), quite well done.
w Richard Murphy *story* Philip Yordan d Edward Dmytryk ph Joe MacDonald m Leigh Harline
☆ Spencer Tracy, Richard Widmark, Robert Wagner, Jean Peters, Katy Jurado, Earl Holliman, Hugh O'Brian, Eduard Franz, E. G. Marshall
🏆 Philip Yordan
& Katy Jurado

Broken Lullaby *
US   1931   77m   bw   Paramount
GB and original title: *The Man I Killed*
A young Frenchman goes to Germany to seek out the family of the man he killed in the war, and is accepted by them as a friend.
This most untypical Lubitsch film now seems very dated but was deeply felt at the time and has plenty of cinematic grip.
w Ernest Vajda, Samson Raphaelson *play L'Homme que J'ai Tué* by Maurice Rostand d Ernst Lubitsch ph Victor Milner m W. Franke Harling ad Hans Dreier
☆ Lionel Barrymore, Phillips Holmes, Nancy Carroll, Tom Douglas, ZaSu Pitts, Lucien Littlefield, Louise Carter, Emma Dunn
'Well made, but heavy themes and actionless … hardly attuned to film patronage as a whole.' – *Variety*
'The best talking picture that has yet been seen and heard.' – *Robert E. Sherwood*

'I cannot remember a film so beautifully made, so completely fine in its execution.' – *John Grierson*
'Lubitsch can't entirely escape his own talent, and the film is beautifully crafted, but he mistook drab, sentimental hokum for ironic, poetic tragedy.' – *Pauline Kael, 70s*

Broken Mirrors
Holland   1984   116m   Eastmancolor
Sigma (Matthijs van Heijningen)
Brothel girls consider the worthlessness of their lives.
Would-be symbolic melodrama with feminist overtones. Hard to take from beginning to end.
wd Marleen Gorris ph Frans Bromet m Lodewijk de Boer
☆ Lineke Rijxman, Henriette Tol, Edda Barends, Coby Stunnenberg

Broken Noses *
US   1987   77m   bw/colour
Mainline/Kira Films (Emie Ameniya)
Documentary of a young boxer training younger boys.
Ambivalent account of a violent sport, chicly photographed.
d Bruce Weber ph Julio Macat md Cherry Vanilla ed Phyllis Famiglietti, Howie Weisbrot
☆ Andy Minsker, The Mount Scott Boxing Club
'This is not so much a sporting profile as a poetic essay on American masculinity using boxing as a metaphor for the transformations involved in acquiring male identity.' – *MFB*

Broken Vessels **
US   1998   92m   DeLuxe
Feature/Unapix/Zeitgeist (Roxana Zal, Scott Ziehl)
⊚

In Los Angeles, a newcomer to an ambulance service lives on the edge, under the influence of the veteran paramedic with whom he is teamed.
An engaging, low-budget, drug-fuelled movie with a dark sense of humour, a tragic projectory and a disregard for propriety.
w David Baer, John McMahon, Scott Ziehl d Scott Ziehl ph Antonio Calvache m Bill Laswell, Martin Blasick, Brent David Fraser pd Rodrigo Castillo ed David Moritz, Chris Figler
☆ Todd Field, Jason London, Roxana Zal, Susan Traylor, James Hong, Patrick Cranshaw, Brent David Fraser, Stephanie Feury, David Nelson, William Smith, David Baer
'Is powered by a contagious headlong energy and is often outrageously funny.' – *Philip Kemp, Sight and Sound*

The Broken Wing
US   1932   71m   bw   Paramount
A Mexican girl jilts a bandit for an American pilot.
Hokey romantic melodrama.
w Grover Jones, William Slavens McNutt *play* Paul Dickey, Charles Goddard d Lloyd Corrigan ph Henry Sharp
☆ Lupe Velez, Leo Carrillo, Melvyn Douglas, George Barbier, Willard Robertson
'Too much of a monologue to get far as a talker. Entire first half is just a stage-setter for what follows, and what follows isn't important.' – *Variety*

Bronco Billy **
US   1980   116m   DeLuxe   Panavision
Warner/Second Street (Neal Dobrofsky, Dennis Hackin)
📼 ▦ ◷

A New Jersey shoe salesman takes over a rundown wild west show.
Enjoyable, sentimental, satirical comedy which unaccountably let down its star's box-office record.
w Dennis Hackin d Clint Eastwood ph David Worth md Snuff Garrett, Steve Dorff ad Eugene Lourie
☆ Clint Eastwood, Sondra Locke, Geoffrey Lewis, Scatman Crothers, Bill McKinney, Sam Bottoms
'Eastwood seems to have most enjoyed toying with some distinctly old-fashioned materials: a runaway heiress, a murder plot that isn't, some consequent punning on points of identity, and the most mischievously brittle set of greedy Eastern sophisticates since Frank Capra.' – *Richard Combs, MFB*

Bronco Buster
US   1952   80m   Technicolor
U-I (Ted Richmond)
A champion rodeo rider meets a challenge from a younger man.
Totally routine programmer.
w Horace McCoy, Lillie Hayward d Budd Boetticher
☆ John Lund, Scott Brady, Joyce Holden, Chill Wills, Don Haggerty

Bronenosets Potemkin: see The Battleship Potemkin

A Bronx Tale *
US   1993   121m   Technicolor
Rank/Price/Tribeca (Jane Rosenthal, Jon Kilik, Robert De Niro)
📼 ▦ ◷ ⊚ 🎧

In the 1960s, in the Italian neighbourhood of the Bronx, a boy grows up, torn between affection for his father, a bus driver, and admiration for the local gang boss, and caught in the growing struggle for control between blacks and whites.
An enjoyable stroll through familiar territory, which at least shows the ordinary life of the time, even if it, too, is seduced by the glamour of the gangsters.
w Chazz Palminteri *play* Chazz Palminteri d Robert De Niro ph Reynaldo Villalobos m Butch Barbella pd Wynn Thomas ed David Ray, R. Q. Lovett
☆ Robert De Niro, Chazz Palminteri, Lillo Brancato, Francis Capra, Taral Hicks, Katherine Narducci, Clem Caserta, Joe Pesci, Alfred Sauchelli Jnr
'A wonderfully vivid snapshot of a colorful place and time, as well as a very satisfactory directorial debut.' – *Variety*

The Brood
Canada   1979   91m   colour
Mutual/Elgin (Claude Heroux)
▦ ◷

The rage of a mentally disturbed woman produces homicidal 'babies'.
Idiotic and repellent shocker.
wd David Cronenberg ph Mark Irwin m Howard Shore ad Carol Spier ed Alan Collins
☆ Oliver Reed, Samantha Eggar, Art Hindle, Cindy Hinds
'In Cronenberg's hands, horror is no longer a disreputable bastard genre but a new avenue of expression, glistening with possibility … Horror is his native language. He dreams in it.' – *Stephen Schiff*

A Brooklyn State of Mind
Canada   1997   87m   colour
Norstar/Storm (Peter R. Simpson)
A gangster discovers the truth about the killing of his father 20 years earlier, and decides to avenge his death.
Mundane gangster drama, containing nothing that has not been better done before.
w Frank Rainone, Frederick Stroppel d Frank Rainone ph Ken Kelsch m Paul J. Zaza pd William Barclay ed Nick Rotundo
☆ Danny Aiello, Vincent Spano, Maria Grazia Cucinotta, Abe Vigoda, Tony Danza, Morgana King
'Dramatically functional but has little to add to the well-trodden genre.' – *Variety*

Broth of a Boy
Eire   1958   77m   bw
Emmet Dalton (Alec Snowden)
TV covers the village festivities celebrating an old poacher's 110th birthday.
Mildly amusing regional comedy.
w Patrick Kirwan, Blanaid Irvine *play The Big Birthday* by Hugh Leonard d George Pollock ph Walter J. Harvey m Stanley Black
☆ Barry Fitzgerald, June Thorburn, Tony Wright, Harry Brogan, Eddie Golden, Marie Kean, Godfrey Quigley, Dermot Kelly

Brother Can You Spare a Dime?
GB   1975   109m   bw
VPS/Goodtimes
▦

A 'documentary' picture of America in the thirties, attempted by an apparently random collage of newsreel and feature film extracts, sometimes difficult to tell one from the other.

Sometimes entertaining but mainly unpardonable.
wd Philippe Mora

The Brother from Another Planet

US 1984 108m Movielab
A-Train Films

An alien lands in Harlem and is protected by locals from the horrors he finds there.
Moderately amusing combination of science fiction, farce and satire, which outstays its welcome by at least half an hour.
wd John Sayles
☆ Joe Morton, Tom Wright, Caroline Aaron, Randy Sue Carter

Brother John *

US 1970 94m Eastmancolor
Columbia/E and R (Joel Glickman)

A mysterious black man comes to town for a family funeral and is suspected by the townsfolk of various sinister motives, but when they imprison him he is freed by a sympathizer.
The humans are all mean-minded, the saintly visitor is either Christ or an emissary from another planet. Either way, we have been here before, but although this little fantasy has nothing clear to say it is quite enjoyable on the surface.
w Ernest Kinoy d James Goldstone ph Gerald Perry Finnerman m Quincy Jones
☆ Sidney Poitier, Bradford Dillman, Will Geer, Beverly Todd, Ramon Bieri, Warren J. Kemmerling, Paul Winfield, Lincoln Kilpatrick
'It starts out as an engaging mystery with sociological overtones but ends up as a muddle-headed doomsday parable.' – *Judith Crist, 1977*

Brother Orchid *

US 1940 91m bw
Warner (Hal B. Wallis)

A gangster, 'taken for a ride' by his former friends, escapes and becomes a monk.
Rather uneasy blend of comedy, drama and religion, with some good scenes.
w Earl Baldwin story Richard Connell d Lloyd Bacon ph Tony Gaudio m Heinz Roemheld
☆ Edward G. Robinson, Humphrey Bogart, Donald Crisp, Ann Sothern, Ralph Bellamy, Allen Jenkins, Cecil Kellaway

Brother Rat *

US 1938 89m bw
Warner (Robert Lord)
Fun and games with the cadets at a military academy.
Brisk but dated farce from a highly successful Broadway original; remade as About Face (qv).
w Richard Macaulay, Jerry Wald play Fred Finklehoffe, John Monks Jnr d William Keighley ph Ernest Haller
☆ Wayne Morris, Eddie Albert, Ronald Reagan, Priscilla Lane, Jane Bryan, Jane Wyman, Johnnie Davis, Henry O'Neill
'Exhibs who dig into exploitation fields will hit paydirt.' – *Variety*

Brother Rat and a Baby

US 1939 87m bw
Warner (Robert Lord)
GB title: *Baby Be Good*
Scatty follow-up to the above, with the cadets graduating.
w Jerry Wald, Richard Macaulay d Ray Enright ph Charles Rosher m Heinz Roemheld
☆ Wayne Morris, Eddie Albert, Ronald Reagan, Priscilla Lane, Jane Wyman, Jane Bryan, Arthur Treacher, Moroni Olsen

Brother Sun, Sister Moon

GB/Italy 1972 122m Technicolor
Panavision
Paramount/Vic Films/Euro International (Luciano Perugia)

The life of Francis of Assisi.
Good-looking but relentlessly boring view of a medieval saint as a kind of early flower person.
w Suso Cecchi d'Amico, Kenneth Ross, Lina Wertmuller, Franco Zeffirelli d Franco Zeffirelli ph Ennio Guarnieri m Donovan, Riz Ortolani pd Lorenzo Mongiardino ed Reginald Mills, John Ruston

☆ Graham Faulkner, Judi Bowker, Alec Guinness, Leigh Lawson, Kenneth Cranham, Lee Montague, Valentina Cortese, Michael Feast, Nicholas Willatt, John Sharp
'If I were Pope, I would burn it.' – *Stanley Kauffmann*

The Brotherhood *

US 1968 96m Technicolor
Paramount/Brotherhood Company (Kirk Douglas)

A Mafia executive welcomes his younger brother into the syndicate, but is finally executed by him.
Dour melodrama with tragic pretensions: well made but rather tedious and violent.
w Lewis John Carlino d Martin Ritt ph Boris Kaufman m Lalo Schifrin
☆ Kirk Douglas, Alex Cord, Luther Adler, Irene Papas, Susan Strasberg, Murray Hamilton, Eduardo Ciannelli

The Brotherhood of Satan *

US 1970 93m Techniscope
Columbia/LQJAF/Four Star Excelsior (L. Q. Jones, Alvy Moore)

A village is isolated by an outbreak of diabolism.
Fresh and intriguing minor horror film with imaginative touches.
w William Welch d Bernard McEveety ph John Arthur Morril m Jaime Mendoza-Nava
☆ Strother Martin, L. Q. Jones, Charles Bateman, Ahna Capri, Charles Robinson, Alvy Moore, Geri Reischl

Brotherly Love: see Country Dance

The Brothers **

GB 1947 98m bw
Triton (Sydney Box)
An orphan girl comes to a Skye fishing family at the turn of the century, and causes superstition, sexual jealousy and tragedy.
Wildly melodramatic but good-looking open-air melodrama, a surprising and striking British film of its time. Macrae gives a splendidly malevolent performance.
w Muriel and Sydney Box novel L. A. G. Strong d David Macdonald ph Stephen Dade m Cedric Thorpe Davie
☆ Patricia Roc, Maxwell Reed, Duncan Macrae, Will Fyffe, Andrew Crawford, Finlay Currie
'Heavy breathing, heavier dialect, and any number of queer folk customs ... the island and its actual inhabitants are all right; the rest is Mary Webb with hair on her chest.' – *James Agee*

Brothers in Arms (dubbed)

France 1989 125m Eastmancolor
Alexandre/SGGC/FR3 (Alexandre Arcady)
In Paris, a Jewish cop and an Algerian-born undercover agent form an uneasy partnership to combat Islamic fundamentalists who are planning a terrorist campaign using drugs and violence.
Tough and topical, though otherwise unremarkable, thriller.
w Daniel Saint-Hamont, Alexandre Arcady, Pierre Aknine d Alexandre Arcady ph Robert Alazraki m Jean-Jacques Goldman, Roland Romanelli pd Gerard Daoudal, Tony Egry ed Joële Van Effenterre, Anne-Marie Leduc
☆ Richard Berry, Patrick Bruel, Bruno Cremer, Claude Brasseur, Marthe Villalonga, Saïd Amadis, Corinne Dacla, Amidou

Brothers in Law *

GB 1957 97m bw
British Lion/The Boultings (John Boulting)

A young barrister has comic misdemeanours in and out of court.
The lighter side of the law, from a bestseller by a judge; mechanically amusing and not in the same street as its predecessor Private's Progress *(qv), though it seemed hilarious at the time.*
w Roy Boulting, Frank Harvey, Jeffrey Dell novel Henry Cecil d Roy Boulting ph Max Greene m Benjamin Frankel
☆ Ian Carmichael, Terry-Thomas, Richard Attenborough, Miles Malleson, Eric Barker, Irene Handl, John Le Mesurier, Olive Sloane, Kynaston Reeves
FOREWORD: IF ALL THE CHARACTERS IN THIS FILM WERE NOT FICTITIOUS – IT WOULD BE ALARMING!

CLERK: 'You start with a blue robing bag, sir. Then if you do good work for counsel, he'll give you a red one. If at the end of seven years you haven't been given a red bag – use a suitcase.'
☑ Eric Barker (best newcomer)

'A story of survival and belonging.'

Brothers in Trouble *

GB 1996 103m colour
BFI/BBC/Renegade/Kinowelt/Mikado (Robert Buckler)

In the 60s, a Pakistani arrives in Britain as an illegal immigrant and eventually prospers, despite the fear in which he at first lives with other immigrants.
Revealing look at English life from an unusual viewpoint.
w Robert Buckler novel Return Journey by Abdullah Hussein d Udayan Prasad ph Alan Almond m Stephen Warbeck pd Chris Townsend ed Barrie Vince
☆ Om Puri, Pavan Malhotra, Angeline Ball, Ahsen Bhatti, Bhasker, Pravesh Kumar, Badi Uzzaman
'A touching, optimistic fable about friendship and survival.' – *Empire*

The Brothers Karamazov *

US 1958 146m Metrocolor
MGM/Avon (Pandro S. Berman)

In 19th-century Russia, the father of three sons is murdered and the wrong brother is found guilty.
Decent but decidedly unenthralling Hollywood compression of a classic, faithful to the letter but not the spirit of the book, and with few memorable moments or performances.
w Richard Brooks novel Fyodor Dostoyevsky d Richard Brooks ph John Alton m Bronislau Kaper ad William A. Horning, Paul Groesse
☆ Yul Brynner, Maria Schell, Richard Basehart, Claire Bloom, Lee J. Cobb, Albert Salmi, William Shatner, Judith Evelyn
'A picture full of ferocity and passion, with streaks of genius in the lighting, mounting and music.' – *News of the World*
† In 1968 came Ivan Pyryev's massive 220m Russian version, little seen in the west.
♫ Lee J. Cobb

'Jack is Trying to Save His Marriage. Patrick is in a Hopeless Relationship. But Their Biggest Problem is Barry's Brotherly Advice.'
'Sometimes the Best Friends Are the Ones You've Known Your Whole Life.'

The Brothers McMullen **

US 1995 118m DuArt
TCF/Marlboro Road Gang/Videography/Good Machine (Edward Burns, Dick Fisher)

Three Irish-American brothers are having trouble with their relationships.
A character-driven, low-budget film that is observant in its examination of the dynamics of interaction between the brothers and the women in their lives; for most of the time, it steers clear of mawkishness.
wd Edward Burns ph Dick Fisher m Seamus Egan ed Dick Fisher
☆ Jack Mulcahy, Mike McGlone, Edward Burns, Connie Britton, Maxine Bahns, Elizabeth P. McKay, Shari Albert, Jennifer Jostyn
'Straightforward and disarming in its utter disregard for trendiness and current fashion.' – *Todd McCarthy, Variety*

The Brothers Rico

US 1957 91m bw
Columbia/William Goetz (Lewis J. Rachmil)
An accountant fails to retrieve his brothers from a life of crime.
Moderate gangster fare with good credentials but more talk than action.
w Lewis Meltzer, Ben Perry novel Georges Simenon d Phil Karlson ph Burnett Guffey m George Duning
☆ Richard Conte, James Darren, Dianne Foster, Kathryn Grant, Larry Gates, Lamont Johnson, Harry Bellaver

Brown of Harvard

US 1926 70m bw silent
MGM
Two college students, one academic and one sporty, love the same girl.

Best-known version of a 1909 play first filmed in 1917: archetypal campus drama.
w Donald Ogden Stewart, A. P. Younger play Rida Johnson Young d Jack Conway
☆ William Haines, Jack Pickford, Mary Brian

Brown on Resolution *

GB 1935 80m bw
Gaumont (Michael Balcon)

Later retitled: *Forever England*
US title: *Born for Glory*
In the 1914 war in the Mediterranean, a seaman holds a German warship at bay with a rifle.
Uneasy amalgam of adventure heroics and character study, interesting for its effort.
w Michael Hogan, Gerard Fairlie, J. O. C. Orton novel C. S. Forester d Walter Forde ph Bernard Knowles
☆ John Mills, Betty Balfour, Barry Mackay, Jimmy Hanley, Howard Marion Crawford, H. G. Stoker
'A milestone in British pictures ... an attractive and interesting feature anywhere.' – *Variety*

The Browning Version *

GB 1951 90m bw
GFD/Javelin (Teddy Baird)

Retiring through ill health, a classics master finds that he is hated by his unfaithful wife, his headmaster and his pupils. An unexpected act of kindness gives him courage to face the future.
A rather thin extension of a one-act play, capped by a thank-you speech which is wildly out of character. Dialogue and settings are smooth, but the actors are not really happy with their roles.
w Terence Rattigan play Terence Rattigan d Anthony Asquith ph Desmond Dickinson ad Carmen Dillon ed John D. Guthridge
☆ Michael Redgrave, Jean Kent, Nigel Patrick, Wilfrid Hyde-White, Bill Travers, Ronald Howard
'If the sustained anguish of the role does not allow Redgrave a great deal of room to move around in, it does give him a chance to show what he can do in tight quarters, and that, it turns out, is considerable.' – *Pauline Kael, 70s*

The Browning Version *

GB 1994 97m colour
UPI/Percy Main (Ridley Scott, Mimi Polk)

As he retires, a repressed and disliked schoolteacher, treated badly by his headmaster and adulterous wife, comes to terms with himself.
A remake of no particular distinction or point, cut adrift from its original period setting and losing in credibility because of it.
w Ronald Harwood play Terence Rattigan d Mike Figgis ph Jean-François Robin m Mark Isham pd John Beard ed Hervé Schneid
☆ Albert Finney, Greta Scacchi, Matthew Modine, Julian Sands, Michael Gambon, Ben Silverstone, James Sturgess, Joe Beattie, Mark Bolton, Heathcote Williams
'Strong and affecting – perhaps because neither the director nor the star has worked with this sort of material before.' – *Terrence Rafferty, New Yorker*
'One can't help returning to the question of why the film was made if neither director, scriptwriter nor star had anything new to add to the innumerable Browning Versions that have gone before it.' – *Geoffrey McNab, Sight and Sound*
'The play is done all the time but who under the age of 30 knows it? Doing it in period would have no bearing on younger audiences and I wanted to attract them.' – *Mike Figgis*

Brown's Requiem *

US 1998 104m DeLuxe
J&T/Savvy Lad (Tim Youd, David Scott Rubin)

In Los Angeles, an alcoholic ex-cop turned private eye runs into trouble when he is hired to investigate a young girl's relationship with an elderly, wealthy crook.
A thriller stuck in a sub-Chandler mode, with a world-weary hero in a situation he doesn't comprehend; the clichés are neatly shuffled, but overfamiliarity leads to ennui before the end.
wd Jason Freeland novel James Ellroy ph Seo Mutarevic m Cynthia Millar pd Marc Rizzo ed Toby Yates
☆ Michael Rooker, Tobin Bell, Selma Blair, Jack Conley, Kevin Corrigan, Brad Dourif, Harold

Gould, Brion James, Barry Newman, Valerie
Perrine, William Sasso

Brubaker *

US   1980   130m   DeLuxe
TCF (Ron Silverman)
😎 ▦ ◕

A new governor fails to make much headway with
his reform plan at Wakefield Prison Farm.
*Fairly brutal but unsurprising prison drama which takes
itself somewhat too seriously.*
w W. D. Richter d Stuart Rosenberg ph Bruno
Nuytten m Lalo Schifrin
☆ Robert Redford, Yaphet Kotto, Jane Alexander,
Murray Hamilton, David Keith, Morgan Freeman
  'It's hard to imagine a broad audience wanting to
  share the two hours of agony.' – *Variety*
Ω screenplay

The Brute *

Mexico   1952   83m   bw
International Cinematografica
▦

original title: El Bruto
Victimized slum tenants call for help to a slow-
witted giant, who kills the landlord and falls in
love with his daughter.
*Eccentric melodrama which doesn't quite seem to make
its point.*
wd Luis Buñuel ph Augustin Jiminez m Raul
Lavista
☆ Pedro Armendariz, Katy Jurado, Rosita Arenas,
Andres Soler

The Brute

GB   1975   90m   Technicolor
Rank/Trigon (John Quested)
A model is married to a man who beats her and
threatens to take away her son if she complains.
*Glumly fashionable domestic drama that is more
interested in displaying violence than explaining it.*
wd Gerry O'Hara ph Dennis Lewiston
m Kenneth V. Jones ad Terence Pritchard
ed Gerry Hambling
☆ Sarah Douglas, Julian Glover, Bruce Robinson,
Jenny Twigge, Suzanne Stone, Peter Bull,
Charlotte Cornwell
  'A glossy piece of pornography pretentiously
  packaged and sold under the guise of a social
  document.' – *MFB*

Brute Force **

US   1947   96m   bw
U-I (Mark Hellinger)
Six violent convicts revolt against a sadistic
warden and try to escape.
*Vivid and rather repellent prison melodrama leading up
to an explosive climax; its savagery seemed at the time
to break fresh ground.*
w Richard Brooks d Jules Dassin ph William
Daniels m Miklos Rozsa
☆ Burt Lancaster, Charles Bickford, Hume
Cronyn, Ella Raines, Yvonne de Carlo

The Brute Man

US   1946   60m   bw
Universal
▦ ◕

A disfigured paranoic is helped by a blind pianist
and kills again to help her.
Schlock horror programmer.
w George Bricker, M. Coates Webster d Jean
Yarbrough
☆ Rondo Hatton, Tom Neal, Jane Adams
† Universal were so ashamed of it that they farmed
it out to PRC

El Bruto: see *The Brute*

The Brylcreem Boys

GB   1996   105m   Rank Colour
Rough Magic (Alan Latham, Bernie Stampfer, Terence
Ryan, Paul Madigan)
😎 ◕

During the Second World War, English and
German prisoners of war share the same camp in
Ireland.
*Apparently based on a real-life situation, this stumbles
from romantic comedy to drama with no sense of
direction or style.*
w Terence Ryan, Jamie Brown, Susan Morrall
d Terence Ryan ph Gerry Lively m Richard
Hartley pd Steve Hardie ed Emma E. Hickox

☆ Bill Campbell, William McNamara, Angus
MacFadyen, Gabriel Byrne, Jean Butler, John
Gordon Sinclair, Oliver Tobias
  'A toe-curlingly terrible film.' – *Peter Bradshaw,
  Guardian*
  'It gets on the list of the 10 worst films about the
  war.' – *Philip French, Observer*

The Bubble *

US   1966   112m   Eastmancolor   Spacevision
(aka Stereovision 3D)
Arch Oboler
▦

aka: Fantastic Invasion of Planet Earth
Three people find themselves trapped in a small
town that is surrounded by an invisible bubble of
energy.
*Originally made in 3D, the film was a good
advertisement for that process but not, with its
indifferent acting and talky, slow-moving narrative, for
any other reason.*
wd Midwestern Magic-Vuers (Arch Oboler)
ph Charles F. Wheeler m Paul Sawtell, Bert
Shefter ad Marvin Chomsky ed Igo Kanter
☆ Michael Cole, Deborah Walley, Johnny
Desmond, Virginia Gregg, Chester Jones
† The film was cut to 94m and re-released in 1972
as *Fantastic Invasion of Planet Earth*, though no
invasion occurs during the film. It has been
released on video in its 3D version.

The Buccaneer *

US   1938   125m   bw
Paramount (Cecil B. de Mille)
During the 1812 war, pirate Jean Lafitte helps
general Andrew Jackson to repel the British.
*Sprightly adventure romance with generally good
production and acting.*
w Jeanie Macpherson, Edwin Justus Mayer, Harold
Lamb, C. Gardner Sullivan d Cecil B. de Mille
ph Victor Milner m Georges Antheil md Boris
Morros
☆ Fredric March, Franciska Gaal, Akim Tamiroff,
Margot Grahame, Walter Brennan, Ian Keith,
Spring Byington, Douglass Dumbrille, Robert
Barrat, Hugh Sothern, Beulah Bondi, Anthony
Quinn, Montagu Love
  'A cinch for big box-office returns around the
  world.' – *Variety*
  'From de Mille's skilled craftsmanship have come
  other pictures quite as ambitious, none more
  adroitly fabricated, skilfully adjusted to the norm
  of appeal to the world audience that such
  imposing and costly productions must
  command.' – *Terry Ramsaye*
Ω Victor Milner

The Buccaneer

US   1958   121m   Technicolor   Vistavision
Paramount/Cecil B. de Mille (Henry Wilcoxon)
▦ ◕

Slow, slack and stolid remake of the 1938 film,
with practically no excitement or interest and very
obvious studio sets.
w Jesse L. Lasky Jnr, Bernice Mosk, from the
earlier screenplay d Anthony Quinn ph Loyal
Griggs m Elmer Bernstein
☆ Yul Brynner, Claire Bloom, Charles Boyer,
Inger Stevens, Henry Hull, Charlton Heston, E. G.
Marshall, Douglass Dumbrille, Lorne Greene, Ted
de Corsia, Robert F. Simon

Buccaneer's Girl

US   1949   77m   Technicolor
Universal-International
A New Orleans entertainer helps to free a pirate
who was her friend.
Cheerful action programmer.
w Harold Shumate, Joseph Hoffman d Frederick
de Cordova
☆ Yvonne de Carlo, Philip Friend, Robert
Douglas, Elsa Lanchester

Buchanan Rides Alone

US   1958   78m   colour
Columbia (Harry Joe Brown)
A wandering Texan helps a young Mexican
accused of murder.
Very moderate star Western.
w Charles Lang novel *The Name is Buchanan* by
Jonas Ward d Budd Boetticher ph Lucien Ballard
☆ Randolph Scott, Craig Stevens, Barry Kelley,
Peter Whitney

Die Büchse der Pandora: see *Pandora's Box*

Buck and the Preacher

US   1971   103m   colour
Columbia/E and R/Belafonte (Joel Glickman)
Nightriders chasing escaped slaves are outwitted by
a wagon train guide and a con man.
*Lively, easygoing Western with a largely black cast,
and a message of militancy sugar-coated by Hollywood
hokum.*
w Ernest Kinoy d Sidney Poitier ph Alex
Phillips m Benny Carter
☆ Sidney Poitier, Harry Belafonte, Ruby Dee,
Cameron Mitchell, Denny Miller, Nita Talbot,
John Kelly

Buck Benny Rides Again *

US   1940   82m   bw
Paramount (Mark Sandrich)
A radio comedian goes west but finds he's no
cowboy.
*Moderate filming of episodes and characters from the
star's weekly radio show.*
w William Morrow, Edmund Beloin d Mark
Sandrich
☆ Jack Benny, Ellen Drew, Eddie Anderson, Andy
Devine, Phil Harris, Dennis Day
  'Swell mass entertainment.' – *Variety*

Buck Privates *

👪 US   1941   84m   bw
Universal (Alex Gottlieb)
▦ ◕

GB title: Rookies
Two incompetents accidentally enlist in the army.
*Abbott and Costello's first starring vehicle is a tired
bundle of army jokes and old routines separated by plot
and romance, but it sent the comedians right to the top,
where they stayed for ten years.*
w Arthur T. Horman d Arthur Lubin ph Milton
Krasner md Charles Previn
☆ Bud Abbott, Lou Costello, Lee Bowman, Alan
Curtis, Jane Frazee, The Andrews Sisters, Nat
Pendleton, Samuel S. Hinds, Shemp Howard
Ω Charles Previn; song 'The Boogie Woogie Bugle
Boy of Company B' (mHugh Prince, lyDon Raye)

Buck Privates Come Home

👪 US   1946   77m   bw
U-I (Robert Arthur)
▦ ◕

GB title: Rookies Come Home
Incompetent war veterans are demobilized and find
civilian life tough.
Thin star comedy with a good final chase.
w John Grant, Frederic I. Rinaldo, Robert Lees
d Charles T. Barton ph Charles Van Enger
☆ Bud Abbott, Lou Costello, Beverly Simmons,
Tom Brown, Nat Pendleton

Buck Rogers *

US   1939   bw   serial: 12 eps
Universal
After crashing in the Arctic and being preserved
by gas for five hundred years, Buck discovers that
the world has been conquered by gangsters led by
Killer Kane.
*Acceptable science fiction hokum with moments of
ingenuity.*
d Ford Beebe, Saul Goodkind
☆ Buster Crabbe, Constance Moore, Jackie
Moran, Jack Mulhall, Anthony Warde

Buck Rogers in the 25th Century

👪 US   1979   89m   colour
Universal (Richard Coffey)
Launched 500 years into the future, an astronaut
helps save civilization.
*Dull and bland version of comic strip heroics, originally
made for television, which lacks even the low-budget
charm of the 30s serial.*
w Glen A. Larson, Leslie Stevens d Daniel Haller
ph Frank Beascoechea m Stu Phillips ad Paul
Peters ed John J. Dumas
☆ Gil Gerard, Pamela Hensley, Erin Gray, Henry
Silva, Tim O'Connor, Joseph Wiseman, Duke
Butler, Felix Silla, Mel Blanc

  'You'll be sick – from laughing!'

A Bucket of Blood

US   1959   65m   bw
Alta Vista (Roger Corman)
😎 ◕

A waiter becomes a renowned sculptor when he
hits on the idea of moulding clay round corpses.
*Heavy-handed spoof with a few choice if bloody
moments.*
w Charles B. Griffith d Roger Corman ph Jack
Marquette m Fred Katz ad Daniel Haller
ed Anthony Carras
☆ Dick Miller, Barboura Morris, Antony Carbone,
Ed Nelson

Buckskin

US   1968   97m   Pathécolor
Paramount/A. C. Lyles
▦ ◕

In the frontier town of Gloryhole a gambler is
routed by the new marshal.
*Routine old-fashioned Western with this producer's
predictable gallery of weatherbeaten familiar faces.*
w Michael Fisher d Michael Moore ph W.
Wallace Kelley m Jimmie Haskell
☆ Barry Sullivan, Joan Caulfield, Lon Chaney Jnr,
John Russell, Richard Arlen, Barbara Hale, Bill
Williams, Barton MacLane

Buckskin Frontier

US   1943   75m   bw
United Artists/George Sherman
GB title: The Iron Road
In the 1860s, cattle empires are born as the railroad
stretches west.
Ambitious mini-Western; a bit stodgy.
w Norman Houston novel *Buckskin Empire* by
Harry Sinclair Drago d Lesley Selander
☆ Richard Dix, Jane Wyatt, Lee J. Cobb, Albert
Dekker, Victor Jory

Budbringeren: see *Junk Mail*

Buddies

Australia   1983   95m   colour   Panavision
J. D. Productions/John Dingwall
Two sapphire miners outwit an attempt by an
unscrupulous rival to grab their claim.
*Comic celebration of what an Australian premier once
described as 'mateship'.*
w John Dingwall d Arch Nicholson ph David
Eggby m Chris Neal pd Philip Warner ad Ron
Highfield ed Martyn Down
☆ Colin Friels, Harold Hopkins, Kris McQuade,
Norman Kaye, Dennis Miller, Bruce Spence

Buddy

👪 US   1997   84m   Technicolor
Columbia/Jim Henson/American Zoetrope (Steve
Nicolaides, Fred Fuchs)
😎 ◕

In the 20s, a wealthy Brooklyn woman saves a baby
gorilla and raises him as a member of her animal-
filled household.
*One of those movies where you cannot quite imagine
why it was made, though it has a slight, cutesy
animal appeal.*
wd Caroline Thompson book *Animals are My
Hobby* by Gertrude Davies Linz ph Steve Mason
m Elmer Bernstein pd David Nichols, Daniel
Lomino ed Jonathan Shaw sp Jim Henson's
Creature Shop
☆ René Russo, Robbie Coltrane, Alan Cumming,
Irma P. Hall, Peter Elliott, Paul Reubens
  'I watched this movie with steadily mounting
  incredulity. I was trying to find the category for
  it, and there isn't one … It could be a study in
  undiagnosed mental illness, if it weren't shot on
  perky 1930s sets, scored with upbeat music and
  played by the actors like a *Thin Man* movie with
  Nick and Nora on Prozac.' – *Roger Ebert, Chicago
  Sun-Times*

Buddy Buddy

US   1981   96m   Metrocolor   Panavision
MGM (Jay Weston)
😎

A hit man on a job is hampered by a woebegone
fellow intent on committing suicide.
*Painful remake of the French L'Emmerdeur (A Pain
in the A …) (qv). Lugubriously funny at times, but
generally much less attractive than the original.*
w Billy Wilder, I. A. L. Diamond play *Francis
Veber* d Billy Wilder ph Harry Stradling Jnr
m Lalo Schifrin pd Daniel A. Lomino

👪 film suitable for   😎 VHS video-cassette for   ◨ VHS video-cassette for the British   ⟳ Video cassette in a computer-   ▦ American NTSC video-cassette   ◕ Laser disc
family viewing   the British PAL system   PAL system in wide screen-format   colourised version

☆ Walter Matthau, Jack Lemmon, Paula Prentiss, Klaus Kinski, Dana Elcar

'The saddest episode in Wilder's career.' – *Richard Combs, MFB*

The Buddy Holly Story

🏃 US 1978 113m colour
Columbia/Innovisions/ECA (Fred Bauer)

The life of a fifties rock-and-roller who died young in an accident.

Solidly carpentered showbiz biopic for the youth market.

w Robert Gittler d Steve Rash ph Stevan Larner md Joe Renzetti

☆ Gary Busey, Don Stroud, Charles Martin Smith, William Jordan, Maria Richwine

'A B movie leavened by grade-A talent.' – *Les Keyser, Hollywood in the Seventies*

🏆 Joe Renzetti
🏅 Gary Busey

Buddy's Song

🏃 GB 1990 106m Eastmancolor
Castle Premier/Buddy/Bill Curbishley, Roy Baird, Roger Daltrey

A rock 'n' roll father becomes manager of his son's more modern band, with mixed results.

Dreary attempt at a generation gap musical, unlikely to appeal to any age-group.

w Nigel Hinton *novel* Nigel Hinton d Claude Whatham ph John Hooper m Roger Daltrey pd Grant Hicks ed John Grover

☆ Roger Daltrey, Chesney Hawkes, Sharon Duce, Michael Elphick, Douglas Hodge, Paul McKenzie

'Breezy, anodyne fare better suited to the tube.' – *Variety*

'In Havana, music isn't a pastime ...it's a way of life.'

Buena Vista Social Club ***

Germany 1998 105m colour
Film Four/Road Movies/Kintop/Arte/ICAIC (Ulrich Felsberg, Deepak Nayar)

A documentary on a forgotten generation of now elderly Cuban musicians, brought back into the limelight by guitarist Ry Cooder for a best-selling record album.

Charming account of some exceptional musicians enjoying a late flowering; their enjoyment of life and the style of music they developed is evident, with the energetic, 90-year-old Compay Segundo slyly stealing the show with his reminiscences and vocals.

d Wim Wenders ph Joerg Widmer, Robby Mueller, Lisa Renzler ed Brian Johnson

☆ Ry Cooder, Compay Segundo, Ruben Gonzalez, Ibrahim Ferrer, Eliades Ochoa, Omara Portuondo, Manuel 'Guajiro' Mirabal, Orlando 'Cachaito' Lopez, Barbarito Torres, Manuel 'Puntillita' Licea, Raul Planes, Felix Valoy, Maceo Rodriguez, Richard Eques, Joaquim Cooder

'A film of ineffable sweetness and glorious music, which puts the shallow, affectless popular culture of our prosperous west to shame.' – *Peter Bradshaw, Guardian*

🏅 documentary

Buffalo '66 *

US 1998 112m colour
Lions Gate/Cinepix/Muse (Chris Hanley)

In order to impress his parents, who believe him to have been on government work, a newly released convict kidnaps a dancer and persuades her to pretend to be his wife.

An oddity: this has the look and style of a gritty low-life drama about one of life's unloveliest losers, but the content is closer to absurdist drama with its close-up study of a comically dysfunctional family.

w Vincent Gallo, Alison Bagnall d Vincent Gallo ph Lance Acord m Vincent Gallo pd Gideon Ponte ed Curtiss Clayton

☆ Vincent Gallo, Christina Ricci, Anjelica Huston, Ben Gazzara, Kevin Corrigan, Mickey Rourke, Rosanna Arquette, Jan-Michael Vincent

'A small but almost perfectly formed film.' – *Guardian*

'A sustained and dolorous hymn to male self-pity.' – *Sunday Times*

Buffalo Bill *

US 1944 89m Technicolor
TCF (Harry Sherman)

A moderately fictitious account of the life of William Cody, from buffalo hunter to wild west showman.

Easygoing entertainment which turns from Western excitements to domestic drama. Generally watchable.

w Aeneas Mackenzie, Clements Ripley, Cecile Kramer d William Wellman ph Leon Shamroy m David Buttolph

☆ Joel McCrea, Maureen O'Hara, Linda Darnell, Thomas Mitchell, Edgar Buchanan, Anthony Quinn, Moroni Olsen

Buffalo Bill and the Indians, or Sitting Bull's History Lesson

US 1976 118m colour Panavision
EMI/Dino de Laurentiis (Robert Altman)

During winter camp for his wild west show, Buffalo Bill Cody and his friends discuss life and his own myth.

Anti-action, alienation-effect talk piece which has some points of interest for sophisticates but is likely to set Western addicts asking for their money back.

w Alan Rudolph, Robert Altman *play* Indians by Arthur Kopit d Robert Altman ph Paul Lohmann m Richard Baskin

☆ Paul Newman, Burt Lancaster, Joel Grey, Kevin McCarthy, Geraldine Chaplin, Harvey Keitel, John Considine, Denver Pyle

'The western is an enormously resilient form, but never has that resilience been tested quite so much as in this movie ... it isn't really a movie, it's a happening.' – *Arthur Knight*

'Whereas Kopit's play offered a hallucinatory mosaic, Altman's script has the one-dimensional clarity of a cartoon.' – *Michael Billington, Illustrated London News*

'That American history is the creation of flamboyant lies and showmanship strikes us at first as an amusing trifle and then quickly becomes an epigram shaggy-dogging its way across two hours of eccentric Altmanship.' – *Will Aitken, Take One*

Buffalo Bill – Hero of the Far West

France/Italy/West Germany 1964 90m
Technicolor Techniscope
Gloria/Corona/Cinematografica

Buffalo Bill thwarts a gang of gun-runners selling rifles to renegade Indians.

Standard Western, slavishly imitating its Hollywood models.

w Nino Stresa, Luciano Martino d J. W. Fordson (Mario Costa) ph Jack Dalmas

☆ Gordon Scott, Jan Hendricks, Mirko Ellis, Mario Brega, Roldano Lupi, Hans von Borsody, Peter Lull

Buffet Froid **

France 1979 93m Eastmancolor
Sara Films/Antenna 2 (Alain Sarde)

US title: *Cold Cuts*

A police inspector joins up with two new acquaintances: they discover that they all like killing people.

Satirical black comedy which goes on a little too long for its own good; invention gives way to glumness.

wd Bertrand Blier ph Jean Penzer m classical extracts

☆ Gérard Depardieu, Bernard Blier, Jean Carmet, Geneviève Page

Buffy the Vampire Slayer

US 1992 94m DeLuxe
TCF/Sandollar/Kuzui (Kaz Kazui, Howard Rosenman)

A Californian bimbo learns that her destiny is to be a killer of vampires.

Curiously ineffectual teen comedy.

w Joss Whedon d Fran Rubel Kuzui ph James Hayman m Carter Burwell pd Lawrence Miller ed Camilla Toniolo, Jill Savitt, Richard Candib

☆ Kristy Swanson, Donald Sutherland, Paul Reubens, Rutger Hauer, Luke Perry, Michele Abrams, Hilary Swank, Paris Vaughan, David Arquette, Natasha Gregson Wagner

'A bloodless comic resurrection of the undead that goes serious just when it should get wild and woolly.' – *Variety*

'To enjoy this moronic rubbish, you need to put your IQ into total unconsciousness.' – *Alexander Walker, Evening Standard*

† The film was the basis of a successful TV series in 1997, created by Joss Whedon and starring Sarah Michelle Gellar.

The Bug

US 1975 101m Movielab
Paramount/William Castle

Large rocklike insects appear after an earthquake and set fire to themselves and their victims.

Absurd, overlong and rather nasty horror film with no visible redeeming features.

w William Castle, Thomas Page *novel* The Hephaestus Plague by Thomas Page d Jeannot Szwarc ph Michel Hugo, Ken Middleham m Charles Fox

☆ Bradford Dillman, Joanna Miles, Richard Gilliland, Jamie Smith Jackson, Alan Fudge, Patty McCormack

'The finer scientific points are to say the least elusive.' – *David Robinson*

The Bugle Sounds

US 1941 101m bw
MGM (J. Walter Ruben)

An old cavalry sergeant, discharged for insubordination, rounds up fifth columnists and is reinstated.

Ho-hum star vehicle on familiar lines but at undue length.

w Cyril Hume d S. Sylvan Simon ph Clyde de Vinna m Lennie Hayton

☆ Wallace Beery, Marjorie Main, Lewis Stone, George Bancroft, William Lundigan, Henry O'Neill, Donna Reed, Chill Wills, Roman Bohnen, Jerome Cowan, Tom Dugan, Guinn Williams, Jonathan Hale

Bugles in the Afternoon

US 1952 85m Technicolor
Warner/Cagney Productions (William Cagney)

In the US army at the time of Custer's last stand, a young officer is victimized by a jealous rival.

Modest, adequate Western with nice scenery but no surprises.

w Geoffrey Homes, Harry Brown *novel* Ernest Haycox d Roy Rowland ph Wilfrid Cline m Dimitri Tiomkin

☆ Ray Milland, Hugh Marlowe, Helena Carter, Forrest Tucker, Barton MacLane, George Reeves, James Millican, Gertrude Michael

A Bug's Life **

US 1998 96m Technicolor Cinemascope
Buena Vista/Walt Disney/Pixar (Darla K. Anderson, Kevin Reher)

A worker ant enlists the help of some circus bugs in defeating a threatening gang of grasshoppers.

Enjoyable computer-animated feature, though pleasure in its technical qualities – the play of light and shade – outweighs its narrative virtues and its lack of outstanding characterization.

w Andrew Stanton, Donald McEnery, Bob Shaw, John Lasseter, Joe Ranft d John Lasseter ph Sharon Calahan m Randy Newman pd William Cone ed Lee Unkrich

☆ Featuring the voices of: Dave Foley, Kevin Spacey, Julia Louis-Dreyfus, Hayden Panettiere, Phyllis Diller, Richard Kind, David Hyde Pierce, Joe Ranft, Denis Leary, Jonathan Harris, Madeline Kahn, Bonnie Hunt, Michael McShane, John Ratzenberger, Roddy McDowall

'Makes jaunty, imaginative use of both extraordinary technology and bold storytelling possibilities within the insect world.' – *Janet Maslin, New York Times*

'A pale imitation of Disney's best.' – *Derek Malcolm, Guardian*

† *Antz* (qv) is another computer-animated film on a similar theme.

🏅 Randy Newman

Bugsy **

US 1991 135m Technicolor
Columbia TriStar/Mulholland/Baltimore (Mark Johnson, Barry Levinson, Warren Beatty)

A starstruck gangster goes to Las Vegas and transforms the place into a gambler's paradise.

Romanticized account of the life and violent death of Bugsy Siegel, done with charm and style.

w James Toback d Barry Levinson ph Allen Daviau m Ennio Morricone pd Dennis Gassner ed Stu Linder

☆ Warren Beatty, Annette Bening, Harvey Keitel, Ben Kingsley, Elliott Gould, Joe Mantegna, Bebe Neuwirth, Wendy Phillips, Richard Sarafian, Bill Graham

'Elegantly made, wickedly perverse and very smart.' – *Richard Schickel, Time*

'An absorbing narrative flow and a parade of colourful underworld characters vie for screen time with an unsatisfactory central romance.' – *Variety*

🏆 Dennis Gassner; costume (Albert Wolsky)
🎬 film; Barry Levinson; Warren Beatty; Harvey Keitel; Ben Kingsley; James Toback; Allen Daviau; Ennio Morricone

Bugsy Malone **

🏃 GB 1976 93m Eastmancolor
Rank/Bugsy Malone Productions (David Puttnam, Allan Marshall)

New York 1929: gangster Fat Sam fights it out with Dandy Dan, and the best man wins the girl.

Extremely curious musical gangster spoof with all the parts played by children and the guns shooting ice cream. Very professionally done, but one wonders to whom it is supposed to appeal.

wd Alan Parker ph Michael Seresin, Peter Biziou pd Geoffrey Kirkland m/songs Paul Williams

☆ Scott Baio, Jodie Foster, Florrie Dugger, John Cassisi

'If for nothing else, you would have to admire it for the sheer doggedness of its eccentricity.' – *David Robinson, The Times*

'All the pizazz in the world couldn't lift it above the level of empty camp.' – *Frank Rich, New York Post*

'I only wish the British could make adult movies as intelligent as this one.' – *Michael Billington, Illustrated London News*

'In an uncanny way the movie works as a gangster movie and we remember that the old Bogart and Cagney classics had a childlike innocence too. The world was simpler then. Now it's so complicated maybe only a kid can understand the Bogart role.' – *Roger Ebert*

🏅 Paul Williams
🎬 Alan Parker (script); Geoffrey Kirkland; Jodie Foster

Build My Gallows High: see Out of the Past

Bull Durham *

US 1988 108m colour
Rank/Orion/Mount Company (Thom Mount, Mark Burg)

An English teacher prevaricates between choosing a rookie or an experienced baseball player as her latest lover.

Odd-ball movie, more in love with the game than its characters.

wd Ron Shelton ph Bobby Byrne m Michael Convertino pd Armin Ganz ad David Lubin ed Robert Leighton, Adam Weiss

☆ Kevin Costner, Susan Sarandon, Tim Robbins, Trey Wilson, Robert Wuhl, William O'Leary, David Neidorf, Danny Gans

🏅 best original screenplay

The Bulldog Breed

🏃 GB 1960 97m bw
Rank (Hugh Stewart)

A grocer joins the navy.

Elementary raw recruit comedy with many familiar ruses.

w Jack Davies, Henry Blyth, Norman Wisdom d Robert Asher

☆ Norman Wisdom, Edward Chapman, Ian Hunter, David Lodge, Robert Urquhart, Eddie Byrne, Peter Jones

'A farce which ought never to have put to sea.' – *MFB*

Bulldog Drummond *

US 1929 90m bw
Samuel Goldwyn

After advertising for adventure, ex-war hero Drummond is approached by an American girl

whose uncle is being held prisoner in a fake nursing home by villainous Carl Petersen.
This is the closest the screen ever came to the original Drummond character, debonair yet taking personal and unnecessary vengeance on the chief villain. A fairly primitive talkie with little movement, yet consistently interesting.
w Sidney Howard *play Sapper* by H. C. McNeile d F. Richard Jones *ph* George Barnes, Gregg Toland *ad William Cameron Menzies*
☆ Ronald Colman, Joan Bennett, Claud Allister, Lilyan Tashman, Montagu Love, Lawrence Grant
⚸ Ronald Colman; William Cameron Menzies

Bulldog Drummond at Bay
GB   1937   78m   bw
BIP/ABPC (Walter Mycroft)
📼
Foreign spies use a peace club as a front, but are routed by Drummond the adventurer.
A very poor entry in this occasional series: production, directing and acting are as bad as the dialogue.
w Patrick Kirwan, James Parrish *novel Sapper* by H. C. McNeile d Norman Lee *ph* Walter Harvey *ad* John Mead *ed* J. Corbett
☆ John Lodge, Dorothy Mackaill, Victor Jory, Claud Allister, Richard Bird

Bulldog Drummond Strikes Back *
US   1934   83m   bw
UA/Twentieth Century (Darryl F. Zanuck)
Drummond gets married, but delays his honeymoon to investigate a mysterious London house with a disappearing body.
Slow-starting, then intriguing light mystery which becomes repetitive and silly. Performances and production enjoyable.
The full complement of Drummond films is as follows:
1922 Bulldog Drummond (GB, silent with Carlyle Blackwell)
1925 The Third Round (GB, silent with Jack Buchanan)
1929 Bulldog Drummond (US, see above)
1930 Temple Tower (US, lost Fox film with Kenneth MacKenna)
1934 The Return of Bulldog Drummond (GB, perhaps the most Fascist of the series, with Ralph Richardson)
1934 Bulldog Jack (GB, amiable spoof with Jack Hulbert and Richardson as the Moriarty-like villain; finale in an Underground tunnel)
1934 Bulldog Drummond Strikes Back (US, see above)
1936 Bulldog Drummond at Bay (GB, see above)
1937 Bulldog Drummond Escapes (US, start of minor series with Ray Milland, later replaced by John Howard, and Guy Standing as Colonel Neilson)
1937 Bulldog Drummond Comes Back (US, John Howard takes over from Milland, John Barrymore from Standing)
1938 Bulldog Drummond's Revenge (US, Howard and Barrymore)
1938 Bulldog Drummond's Peril (US, ditto)
1938 Bulldog Drummond in Africa (US, Howard and H. B. Warner)
1938 Arrest Bulldog Drummond (US, ditto)
1939 Bulldog Drummond's Secret Police (US, ditto)
1939 Bulldog Drummond's Bride (US, ditto)
1939 Bulldog Sees It Through (GB, imitation with Jack Buchanan)
1947 Bulldog Drummond at Bay (US, second feature with Ron Randell)
1947 Bulldog Drummond Strikes Back (US, see above)
1948 The Challenge (US, with Tom Conway)
1948 Thirteen Lead Soldiers (US, ditto)
1951 Calling Bulldog Drummond (GB, with Walter Pidgeon)
1967 Deadlier than the Male (GB, Richard Johnson as a Bond-like Drummond)
1970 Some Girls Do (GB, Johnson again in a feeble sequel)
w Nunnally Johnson d Roy del Ruth *ph* Peverell Marley *m* Alfred Newman
☆ Ronald Colman, Loretta Young, C. Aubrey Smith, Charles Butterworth, Warner Oland, Mischa Auer, Una Merkel
'Zippy, snappy comedy melodrama with a swashbuckling flavour. Packed with what it takes.' – *Variety*

Bulldog Jack *
GB   1934   72m   bw
Gaumont (Michael Balcon)
📼
US title: Alias Bulldog Drummond
A playboy poses as Bulldog Drummond when the real man is injured, and manages to foil the thieves and save the girl.
After a slowish start, this comedy thriller works up into a fine frenzy with exciting scenes on the London Underground and in the British Museum.
w Gerard Fairlie, J. O. C. Orton, Sidney Gilliat, Jack Hulbert *novel Sapper* d Walter Forde *ph* Mutz Greenbaum (Max Greene) *md* Louis Levy *ad* Alfred Junge *ed* Otto Ludwig
☆ Jack Hulbert, Ralph Richardson, Claude Hulbert, Fay Wray, Athole Fleming, Paul Graetz
'There is … a mad train ride towards the terminus and destruction, as good as anything in screen melodrama.' – *Peter John Dyer, 1965*
'A sense of showmanship that is rewarded in a full quota of thrills and laughs.' – *Kine Weekly*

Bullet
US   1995   90m   CFI color
Village Roadshow-Clipsal/Red Ruby (John Flock)
📼 ⌨
A self-destructive drug addict gets out of prison and returns to his old thieving and violent ways in Brooklyn.
Brutal and uninteresing drama of street life, with a subtext of bad feeling between Jews and blacks; the movie provides Rourke with an opportunity to punch people and walls and wear several silly hats.
w Bruce Rubenstein, Sir Eddie Cook d Julien Temple *ph* Crescenzo G. P. Notarile *pd* Christopher Nowak *ed* Niven Howie
☆ Mickey Rourke, Tupac Shakur, Ted Levine, Adrien Brody, John Enos III, Suzanne Shepherd, Jerry Grayson
'The sundry ultra-violent confrontations play like an action-movie parody.' – *Sight and Sound*

Bullet for a Badman
US   1964   80m   Technicolor
Universal-International
An ex-Texas Ranger escapes from prison to prove his innocence of murder.
Lively Western programmer.
w Mary and Willard Willingham d R. G. Springsteen
☆ Audie Murphy, Darren McGavin, Ruta Lee, Skip Homeier, George Tobias

A Bullet for Joey
US   1955   85m   bw
UA/Sam Bischoff, David Diamond
A Canadian policeman prevents the murder of an atomic scientist.
Listless low-budgeter with familiar stars below par.
w Geoffrey Homes, A. I. Bezzerides d Lewis Allen *ph* Harry Neumann *m* Harry Sukman
☆ Edward G. Robinson, George Raft, Audrey Totter, George Dolenz, Peter Hanson, Peter Van Eyck

A Bullet for the General (dubbed) *
Italy   1966   126m   colour   Scope
MCM (Bianco Manini)
📼 ⌨
original title: El Chucho, Quién Sabe?
An American mercenary joins a gang of bandits in order to assassinate a Mexican revolutionary leader.
Slow-paced, interesting spaghetti Western concerned with matters of life and death and the making of moral choices.
w Salvatore Laurani, Franco Solinas d Damiano Damiani *m* Tony Secchi *m* Luis Bacalov *md* Ennio Morricone *ad* Sergio Canevari *ed* Renato Cinquini
☆ Gian-Maria Volonté, Klaus Kinski, Martine Beswick, Lou Castel, Jaime Fernandez
† The film exists in several versions, ranging in length from 77 to 135 minutes, with the shorter concentrating on its moments of violence.

Bullet in the Head
Hong Kong   1990   100m   colour
Milestone/John Woo
📼 ⌨
Three young tough Chinese gangsters continue their criminal activities in Saigon during the Vietnamese war.

Blood-soaked adventure with an individual, frenetic style.
w John Woo, Patrick Leung, Janet Chun d John Woo *ph* Ardy Lam, Wilson Chan, Somchai Kittikun, Wong Wing-Hang *m* James Wong, Romeo Diaz *ad* James Leung *ed* John Woo
☆ Tony Leung, Jacky Cheung, Waise Lee, Simon Yam, Yolinda Yan
'Graphically violent, vile and thoroughly disturbing depiction of war.' – *Variety*

A Bullet Is Waiting
US   1954   82m   Technicolor
Columbia/Welsch (Howard Welsch)
📼
A plane accident brings a policeman and his prisoner to a lonely farm, where a girl and her father bring a fresh twist to the situation.
Disappointing melodrama full of pretentious moralizing and fey characterization.
w Thames Williamson, Casey Robinson d John Farrow *ph* Franz Planer *m* Dimitri Tiomkin
☆ Jean Simmons, Rory Calhoun, Stephen McNally, Brian Aherne

Bullet Scars
US   1942   59m   bw
Warner
A doctor is kidnapped to patch up a bullet-scarred gunman.
Just another second feature.
w Robert E. Kent d D. Ross Lederman
☆ Regis Toomey, Adele Longmire, Howard da Silva, John Ridgely

Bullet to Beijing
GB/Canada/Russia   1995   122m   colour
Quebec 3099-3081/Lenfilm/Harry Palmer (Alexander Goloutva, John Dunning, André Link)
📼 ⌨
Retired on a reduced pension, a British secret agent is hired by a mysterious Russian to recover a deadly biological weapon that has gone missing.
Caine returns to the role of Harry Palmer, the unconventional agent he first played in the 60s, but the reunion is not a happy one; the problem is the dull script that defeats everyone.
w Peter Welbeck (Harry Alan Towers) *novel* Len Deighton d George Mihalka *ph* Peter Benison, Terence Cole *m* Rick Wakeman *pd* Yuri Pashigorie *ed* François Gill
☆ Michael Caine, Jason Connery, Mia Sara, Michael Gambon, Michael Sarrazin, Lev Prygunov, Anatoly Davidov, Sue Lloyd, Burt Kwouk, Patrick Allen

Bulletproof
US   1987   94m   colour
Virgin/Bulletproof Productions (Paul Hertzberg, N. C. Lundell)
📼 ⌨ 🎧
A Los Angeles cop undertakes a dangerous mission against terrorists in Mexico.
Absurd action picture.
w T. L. Lankford, Steve Carver d Steve Carver *ph* Francis Grumman *m* Tom Chase, Steve Rucker *pd* Adrian H. Gorton *ed* Jeff Freeman
☆ Gary Busey, Darlanne Fluegel, Henry Silva, Thalmus Rasulala, L. Q. Jones, Rene Enriquez, Mills Watson, James Andronica

Bulletproof
US   1996   85m   DeLuxe
Universal (Robert Simonds)
📼 ⌨ 🎧
A car thief discovers that his partner is actually an undercover cop.
Frenetic action movie that tries no new variations on the plot of an ill-assorted, bickering couple trying to straighten out a confused situation with as much shooting and noise as possible.
w Joe Gayton, Lewis Colick d Ernest Dickerson *ph* Steven Bernstein *m* Elmer Bernstein *ad* Perry Andelin Blake, William F. Matthews *ed* George Folsey Jnr
☆ Damon Wayans, Adam Sandler, James Caan, Jeep Swenson, James Farentino, Kristen Wilson, Bill Nunn
'Industrial-strength action comedy.' – *Time*

'Murder was his game, until she changed the rules.'
Bulletproof Heart
US   1994   98m   colour
First Independent/Keystone/Worldvision (Robert Vince, William Vince)
📼
GB title: Killer
A burned-out hitman is hired to kill a woman who wants to die, but also wants to talk about it, after first seducing him.
A killer who needs a psychiatrist meets a woman whose shrink has a drinking problem. The result is a great deal of psycho-babble in a thriller with pretensions above its genre; the action is divided into chapters, for no perceptible reason.
w Gordon Melbourne *story* Mark Malone d Mark Malone *ph* Tobias Schliessler *m* Graeme Coleman *pd* Lynne Stopkewich *ed* Robin Russell
☆ Anthony LaPaglia, Mimi Rogers, Matt Craven, Peter Boyle, Monika Schnarre, Joseph Maher
'What the film lacks is suspense and a pinch of human credibility. It would have made a good short, though.' – *Film Review*

Bullets for O'Hara
US   1941   50m   bw
Warner
A gangster's wife helps an FBI man to trap her husband.
Fast-moving filler with action scenes lifted from its original, Public Enemy's Wife (qv).
w Raymond L. Schrock d William K. Howard
☆ Roger Pryor, Anthony Quinn, Joan Perry, Maris Wrixon, Dick Purcell

'Every real citizen should see it!'
Bullets or Ballots *
US   1936   81m   bw
Warner (Lou Edelman)
📼 📼 🎧
A city cop goes undercover to break the mob.
Vivid routine gangster thriller, not quite of the top flight, but nearly.
w Seton I. Miller d William Keighley *ph* Hal Mohr *m* Heinz Roemheld
☆ Edward G. Robinson, Joan Blondell, Humphrey Bogart, Barton MacLane, Frank McHugh, Dick Purcell, George E. Stone
'A good gangster film of the second class … all the old chivalrous situations of *Chums* and the *Boy's Own Paper* are agreeably translated into sub-machine gun terms.' – *Graham Greene*

Bullets over Broadway **
US   1994   99m   colour
Buena Vista/Magnolia/Sweetland (Robert Greenhut)
📼 📼 ⌨ ⌨ 🎧
In 1920s New York, a writer agrees to hire an untalented actress so that her lover, a gangster, will back his new play; but her bodyguard has other ideas when he realizes she is ruining the production.
Witty and entertaining backstage comedy on the theme of artistic integrity, performed and directed in a sprightly manner.
w Woody Allen, Douglas McGrath d Woody Allen *ph* Carlo Di Palma *pd* Santo Loquasto *ed* Susan E. Morse
☆ John Cusack, Jack Warden, Chazz Palminteri, Joe Viterelli, Jennifer Tilly, Rob Reiner, Mary-Louise Parker, Dianne Wiest, Harvey Fierstein, Jim Broadbent, Tracey Ullman
'Allen bathes his fable in a seductive, rosy light, grants everyone in the wonderful ensemble cast a comic high point, and gives us a film that combines impeccable craftsmanship and a basic exuberance that's been missing from his work for years.' – *Richard Schickel, Time*
'What's fatally missing from the movie is any love for the way of life being mocked. There's too much contempt – contempt joined strangely with self-exculpation.' – *New York*
🏆 Dianne Wiest
⚸ Woody Allen (as director); Woody Allen, Douglas McGrath (screenplay); Chazz Palminteri; art direction; costume design

The Bullfighter and the Lady
US   1951   87m   bw
Republic/John Wayne (Budd Boetticher)
📼 ⌨
A young American in Mexico is fascinated by bullfighting but during training accidentally causes the death of a great matador.

👫 film suitable for family viewing   📼 VHS video-cassette for the British PAL system   📼 VHS video-cassette for the British PAL system in wide screen-format   ⌨ Video cassette in a computer-colourised version   ▦ American NTSC video-cassette   🎧 Laser disc

Predictable, rather boring plot given routine treatment: for aficionados only.
w James Edward Grant d Budd Boetticher
ph Jack Draper m Victor Young
☆ Robert Stack, Gilbert Roland, Joy Page, Katy Jurado, Virginia Grey, John Hubbard
⅋ original story (Budd Boetticher, Ray Nazarro)

The Bullfighters *
US 1945 60m bw
TCF (William Girard)
😊 😊
Two detectives in Mexico find that one of them resembles a famous matador.
Laurel and Hardy's last American feature is poor enough as a whole, but at least has a few sequences in their earlier style.
w Scott Darling d Mal St Clair ph Norbert Brodine m David Buttolph ad Lyle Wheeler, Chester Gore ed Stanley Rabjohn
☆ Stan Laurel, Oliver Hardy, Richard Lane, Margo Woode, Carol Andrews

Bullitt **
US 1968 113m Technicolor
Warner/Solar (Philip D'Antoni)
😊 😊 😊 😊 😊 😊 😊
A San Francisco police detective conceals the death of an underground witness in his charge, and goes after the killers himself.
Routine cop thriller with undoubted charisma, distinguished by a splendid car chase which takes one's mind off the tedious plot. Technical credits first class.
w Harry Kleiner, Alan R. Trustman novel Mute Witness by Robert L. Pike d Peter Yates ph William A. Fraker m Lalo Schifrin ed Frank P. Keller
☆ Steve McQueen, Jacqueline Bisset, Robert Vaughn, Don Gordon, Robert Duvall, Simon Oakland
  'It has energy, drive, impact, and above all, style.' – Hollis Alpert
🏆 Frank P. Keller

Bullseye!
US 1990 92m colour
Castle Premier/21st Century (Michael Winner)
😊 😊 😊
Two con-men impersonate crooked nuclear scientists.
Tedious comedy with few laughs.
w Leslie Bricusse, Laurence Marks, Maurice Gran story Leslie Bricusse, Michael Winner, Nick Mead d Michael Winner ph Alan Jones pd John Blezard ad Alan Cassie ed Arnold Crust
☆ Michael Caine, Roger Moore, Sally Kirkland, Deborah Barrymore, Lee Patterson, Mark Burns, Derren Nesbitt
  'Wallowing in its excremental humour, Bullseye! is content to reinforce the crudest of racial and sexual stereotypes.' – MFB

Bullshot
GB 1983 88m Technicolor
HandMade (Ian La Frenais)
😊
In the twenties, Bullshot Crummond is pitted against his arch enemy Count Otto von Bruno.
Very flat-footed spoof which belies the talents involved.
w Ron House, Diz White, Alan Shearman d Dick Clement ph Alex Thomson m John Du Prez pd Norman Garwood
☆ Alan Shearman, Diz White, Ron House, Frances Tomelty, Michael Aldridge, Ron Pember, Mel Smith, Billy Connolly, Geoffrey Bayldon, Bryan Pringle
  'Unrelievedly ghastly … even canned laughter would be hard pressed to raise a titter.' – Gilbert Adair, MFB
  'Behind every mannered line you can hear technicians laughing the fun to death on the studio floor.' – Sunday Times

Bulworth *
US 1998 107m Technicolor
TCF (Warren Beatty, Pieter Jan Brugge)
😊 😊 😊
Having arranged his assassination in order to provide wealth for his family, a Democratic senator decides to tell the unvarnished truth during his election campaign.
A satire on the corporate control of political parties that, however accurate, lacks bite; Beatty's embrace of urban black culture, as his senator breaks into rap, seems self-indulgent rather than revolutionary.
w Warren Beatty, Jeremy Pikser d Warren Beatty ph Vittorio Storaro m Ennio Morricone pd Dean Tavoularis ed Robert C. Jones, Billy Weber
☆ Warren Beatty, Halle Berry, Don Cheadle, Oliver Platt, Paul Sorvino, Jack Warden, Isaiah Washington, Joshua Malina, Christine Baranski, Richard Sarafian, Amiri Baraka, Sean Astin, Laurie Metcalf, Wendell Pierce
  'One of the best films to emerge from a Hollywood studio in the 90s.' – Richard Kelly, Sight and Sound
⅋ Warren Beatty, Jeremy Pikser (script)

Bun Ngo Tsong Tinngai: see Wild Search

Bundle of Joy
US 1956 98m Technicolor RKOscope
RKO/Edmund Grainger
😊
A shopgirl finds an abandoned baby and everyone thinks it is hers.
Tame musical remake of Bachelor Mother (qv); some laughs, but poor numbers.
w Norman Krasna, Arthur Sheekman, Robert Carson d Norman Taurog ph William Snyder m Josef Myrow
☆ Debbie Reynolds, Eddie Fisher, Adolphe Menjou, Melville Cooper, Tommy Noonan, Nita Talbot, Una Merkel, Robert H. Harris
  'As bad as I was, the picture was worse.' – Eddie Fisher

Bunker Bean
US 1936 67m bw
RKO
aka: His Majesty Bunker Bean
A meek office clerk rises to power after a personality course.
Old-fashioned comedy previously filmed in 1917 and 1924.
w Edmund North, James Gow and Dorothy Yost novel Harry Leon Wilson d William Hamilton, Edward Killy
☆ Owen Davis Jnr, Lucille Ball, Berton Churchill, Louise Latimer, Jessie Ralph, Hedda Hopper

Bunny Lake Is Missing **
GB 1965 107m bw Panavision
Columbia/Wheel (Otto Preminger)
The 4-year-old illegitimate daughter of an American girl in London disappears, and no one can be found to admit that she ever existed.
A nightmarish gimmick story, with more gimmicks superimposed along the way to say nothing of a Psychoish ending; some of the decoration works and makes even the unconvincing story compelling, while the cast alone is worth the price of admission.
w John and Penelope Mortimer novel Evelyn Piper d Otto Preminger ph Denys Coop m Paul Glass pd Don Ashton titles Saul Bass
☆ Laurence Olivier, Carol Lynley, Keir Dullea, Noël Coward, Martita Hunt, Finlay Currie, Clive Revill, Anna Massey, Lucie Mannheim
  'It has the enjoyable hallmarks of really high calibre professionalism.' – Penelope Houston

Bunny O'Hare
US 1971 92m Movielab
AIP (Gerd Oswald, Norman T. Herman)
A middle-aged widow and an ex-con plumber become bank robbers, dressed as hippies and escaping on a motor cycle.
Unappealing, ill-thought-out comedy with pretensions to satire, an unhappy venture for both stars.
w Stanley Z. Cherry, Coslough Johnson d Gerd Oswald ph Loyal Griggs, John Stephens m Billy Strange
☆ Bette Davis, Ernest Borgnine, Jack Cassidy, Joan Delaney, Jay Robinson, John Astin

Buona Sera Mrs Campbell *
US 1968 113m Technicolor
UA/Connaught (Melvin Frank)
😊 😊
Wartime USAF comrades reassemble twenty years later in an Italian village, and three find that they have been paying paternity money to the same local glamour girl.
Agreeably cast, pleasantly set and photographed, quite funny in parts, this comedy of middle age unfortunately outstays its welcome and lets its invention peter out.
w Melvin Frank, Denis Norden, Sheldon Keller d Melvin Frank ph Gabor Pogany m Riz Ortolani

☆ Gina Lollobrigida, Telly Savalas, Phil Silvers, Peter Lawford, Lee Grant, Marian Moses, Shelley Winters

Il Buono, il Brutto, il Cattivo: see The Good, the Bad and the Ugly

The 'burbs **
US 1988 102m DeLuxe
UIP/Imagine (Michael Finnell, Larry Brezner)
😊 😊 😊 😊
Neighbours decide that there is something sinister about a new family on the block.
One-joke black comedy that has its moments.
w Dana Olsen d Joe Dante ph Robert Stevens m Jerry Goldsmith pd James Spencer ed Marshall Harvey
☆ Tom Hanks, Bruce Dern, Carrie Fisher, Rick Ducommun, Corey Feldman, Wendy Schaal, Henry Gibson, Brother Theodore, Courtney Gains, Gale Gordon
  'For the most part, this is one of the most extraordinary major studio films of the late 80s.' – Kim Newman, MFB

Bureau of Missing Persons *
US 1933 73m bw
Warner
😊
Police chief helps a girl find her husband, who turns out to have been murdered.
Fast-moving potboiler typical of its studio.
w Robert Presnell story Missing Men by John H. Ayers, Carol Bird d Roy del Ruth
☆ Pat O'Brien, Bette Davis, Lewis Stone, Glenda Farrell, Allen Jenkins, Hugh Herbert
  'Pretty fair entertainment. Nothing socko, but it will please.' – Variety

Burglar
US 1987 102m Technicolor
Warner/Nelvana (Kevin McCormick, Michael Hirsch)
😊 😊 😊 😊
An ex-con turns tec to avoid arrest as a cat burglar.
Strained comedy which is too goofy to sustain its mystery elements.
w Joseph Loeb III, Matthew Weisman, Hugh Wilson books Lawrence Block d Hugh Wilson ph William A. Fraker m Sylvester Levay
☆ Whoopi Goldberg, Bob Goldthwait, G. W. Bailey, Lesley Ann Warren, James Handy, Anne de Salvo

The Burglar *
US 1957 80m bw
Columbia (Louis W. Kellerman)
A burglar is shadowed by a policeman who is also after the loot.
Slightly pretentious but watchable low-budgeter.
w David Goodis novel David Goodis ph Don Malkames m Sol Kaplan d/ed Paul Wendkos
☆ Dan Duryea, Jayne Mansfield, Martha Vickers, Peter Capell

The Burglar
Russia 1987 89m colour
First Film Group/Lenfilm
original title: Vzlomshchik
A youth steals a synthesiser in order to prevent his elder brother, a rock musician, from committing the crime.
Teenage alienation among Soviet punk rockers.
w Valeri Priyomkhov d Valery Ogorodnikov ph Valery Mironov m Viktor Kisin ad Irakli Kvirikadze
☆ Oleg Elykomov, Konstantin Kirchev, Yuri Tsapnik, Svetlana Gaitan, Polina Petrenko, Mikhail Parfonov, Pyotr Semak, Oleg Garkusha, Valdimir Dyatlov

The Burglars
France/Italy 1971 120m Eastmancolor
Panavision
Columbia/Vides (Henri Verneuil)
original title: La Casse
A determined policeman chases three burglars and their girl accomplice.
Expensive, camped-up version of The Burglar, with plenty going on, most of it borrowed from other films.
w Vahe Katcha, Henri Verneuil novel The Burglar by David Goodis d Henri Verneuil ph Claude Renoir m Ennio Morricone

☆ Omar Sharif, Jean-Paul Belmondo, Dyan Cannon, Robert Hossein, Nicole Calfan, Renato Salvatori
  'Electronic equipment, wild action, exotic locales and bland villainy.' – Tom Milne, MFB

Buried Alive
US 1991 91m colour
21st Century/Breton (Harry Alan Towers)
😊 😊
A psychiatrist, made mad by his father's experiments, turns a former asylum into a school for disturbed girls.
Dim and gory exploitation movie that borrows ideas from several of Poe's stories but has little notion of what to do with them.
w Jake Clesi, Stuart Lee story Edgar Allan Poe d Gérard Kikoine ph Gérard Loubeau m Frederic Targorn pd Leonardo Coen Calgi ed Gilbert Kikoine
☆ Robert Vaughn, Donald Pleasence, Karen Witter, John Carradine, Nia Long, Ginger Lynn Allen, Bill Butler
† It was John Carradine's last film.

Burke and Hare
GB 1971 91m DeLuxe
UA/Kenneth Shipman/Armitage (Guido Coen)
The story of anatomist Dr Knox and his body snatchers, retold with emphasis on the local brothel.
Depressing in its childish attempts to be gruesome and perverted.
w Ernie Bradford d Vernon Sewell ph Desmond Dickinson m Roger Webb
☆ Harry Andrews, Derren Nesbitt, Glynn Edwards, Yootha Joyce, Dee Sjendery, Alan Tucker

Burke and Wills *
Australia 1985 140m Eastmancolor
Panavision
Hoyts Edgley (Graeme Clifford, John Sexton)
😊 😊
An account of the 1860 expedition across Australia.
Downbeat epic with interesting highlights; but the length is against it.
w Michael Thomas d Graeme Clifford ph Russell Boyd m Peter Sculthorpe pd Ross Major
☆ Jack Thompson, Nigel Havers, Greta Scacchi, Matthew Fargher
† A parody film, Wills and Burke, appeared simultaneously.

Burma Convoy
US 1941 72m bw
Universal
A trucking convoy on the Burma Road is terrorized by enemy smugglers.
Adequately two-fisted second feature.
w Stanley Rubin, Roy Chanslor d Noel M. Smith
☆ Charles Bickford, Evelyn Ankers, Cecil Kellaway, Frank Albertson, Keye Luke, Turhan Bey, Willie Fung

The Burmese Harp ***
Japan 1956 116m bw
Nikkatsu (Masayuki Takagi)
😊 😊
original title: Biruma no tategoto
A shell-shocked Japanese soldier stays in the Burmese jungle to bury the unknown dead.
Deeply impressive and horrifying war film with an epic, folk-tale quality, emphasized by superbly controlled direction.
w Natto Wada novel Michio Takeyama d Kon Ichikawa ph Minoru Yokoyama m Akira Ifukube
☆ Shoji Yasui, Rentaro Mikuni, Tatsuya Mihashi
⅋ best foreign film

Burn!: see Queimada!

Burn 'Em Up O'Connor
US 1938 70m bw
MGM
The life and loves of a speedway ace.
Modestly effective second from the time when the studios were trying to make a star of Dennis O'Keefe.
w Milton Merlin, Byron Morgan novel Salute to the Gods by Sir Malcolm Campbell d Edward Sedgwick
☆ Dennis O'Keefe, Harry Carey, Cecilia Parker, Nat Pendleton, Charley Grapewin

---

'Will fill better half of duals for good b.o.' –
Variety

Burn, Witch, Burn: see *Night of the Eagle*

'Don't look he'll see you. Don't breathe he'll hear
you. Don't move you're dead.'

The Burning
US 1981 91m colour
HandMade/Miramax (Harvey Weinstein)
■

An incinerated caretaker takes his revenge on
teenagers at a summer camp.
*Dire, totally predictable, uninventive low-budget
horror.*
w Peter Lawrence, Bob Weinstein *story* Harvey
Weinstein, Tony Maylam, Brad Grey d Tony
Maylam ph Harvey Harrison m Rick Wakeman
ad Peter Politanoff ed Jack Sholder
☆ Brian Matthews, Leah Ayres, Brian Backer,
Larry Joshua, Jason Alexander, Ned Eisenberg,
Holly Hunter

Burning an Illusion
GB 1981 111m Eastmancolor
BFI (Vivien Pottersman)
A black secretary in London, reluctantly intrigued
by the activities of her political boyfriend, becomes
a political militant.
*Most people would sigh at the thought of sitting through
this decently made but rather earnest document which
preaches only to the converted.*
wd Menelik Shabazz ph Roy Cornwall
songs various
☆ Cassie McFarlane, Victor Romero, Beverley
Martin, Angela Wynter

The Burning Cross
US 1947 79m bw
Screen Guild
A frustrated war veteran succumbs temporarily to
the wiles of the Ku Klux Klan.
*Cheap semi-documentary with a clear exploitation
purpose.*
w Aubrey Wisberg d Walter Colmes
☆ Hank Daniels, Virginia Patton, Raymond Bond

The Burning Hills
US 1956 92m Warnercolor Cinemascope
Warner (Richard Whorf)
A young rancher gets even with a cattle baron who
had his brother killed.
Reasonable but unexciting star vehicle.
w Irving Wallace *novel* Louis L'Amour d Stuart
Heisler
☆ Natalie Wood, Tab Hunter, Skip Homeier,
Eduard Franz, Earl Holliman

The Burning Question: see *Reefer Madness*

Burning Rubber
West Germany 1980 84m colour
Ocean Films/Safe Productions (Stefan Abendroth,
Barrie Saint Clair)
A car mechanic becomes a drag-racer with the aid
of a rich girlfriend.
*An attempt to combine the appeals of pop music and
motor-racing, to the detriment of both.*
w Dale Cutts, Bill Flynn d Norman Cohen
ph Keith Jones m Bay City Rollers ed Wayne
Lines
☆ Olivia Pascal, Alan Longmuir, Sascha Hehn,
Stuart 'Woody' Wood, Derek Longmuir, Duncan
Faure

Burning Secret *
UK/US 1988 105m colour
Vestron/NFH/CLG Films (Norma Heyman, Eberhard
Junkersdoft, Carol Lynn Greene)
■■ ■ ℚ~ ⌂
An asthmatic boy on the edge of adolescence
interferes in a holiday romance between his
mother and a stranger.
*Constantly promising more than it delivers, though
with some interesting stops on an unsatisfying journey.*
wd Andrew Birkin *story Brennendes Geheimnis* by
Stefan Zweig ph Ernest Day m Hans Zimmer
pd Bernd Lepel ed Paul Green
☆ Faye Dunaway, David Eberts, Klaus Maria
Brandauer, Ian Richardson
'Stately, elegant, and stiflingly old-fashioned,
producing many exquisite coils of smoke but
nothing resembling a real fire.' – *Philip Strick,
MFB*

Burnt by the Sun ***
Russia/France 1994 134m colour
Studio Trite/Camera One (Nikita Mikhalkov, Michel
Seydoux)
■■ ■ ℚ~ ⌂
original title: Utomlennye Solntsem
In rural Russia in the Stalinist mid-30s, an ageing
military hero of the Revolution is betrayed by a
former acquaintance, his wife's old boyfriend, who
is a turncoat White Russian now working for the
secret police.
*Complex and tragic, at times almost Chekhovian,
evocation of an ambiguous time, of unthinking
brutality darkening a summer landscape.*
w Nikita Mikhalkov, Rustam Ibragimbekov
d Nikita Mikhalkov ph Vilen Kaliuta m Eduard
Artemiev ad Aleksandr Samuelekin, Vladimir
Aronin ed Enzo Meniconi, Joëlle Hache
☆ Nikita Mikhalkov, Oleg Menchikov, Ingeborga
Dapkunaité, Nadya Mikhalkov, Viacheslav
Tikhonov, Svetlana Kriuchkova, Vladimir Ilyin
'The acting is excellent and the direction
sympathetic to it, so that the whole glimmers in
the mind's eye in a totally different way to
anything the American cinema seems capable of
at the moment.' – *Derek Malcolm, Guardian*
'Surely the most charming movie about the
horrors of totalitarianism ever made.' – *Tom
Shone, Sunday Times*
† The film shared the Grand Prix at the Cannes
Film Festival in 1995. It is dedicated to 'everyone
who was burnt by the sun of Revolution'.
♟ best foreign film

Burnt Offerings
US 1976 115m DeLuxe
UA/PEA-Dan Curtis (Robert Singer)
■
An evil house restores itself by feeding on its
tenants.
*An agreeably macabre idea for a five-page story is
dragged out to interminable length, and seizes the
attention only by a few shock moments. The title is
mysteriously irrelevant.*
w William F. Nolan, Dan Curtis *novel* Robert
Marasco d Dan Curtis ph Jacques Marquette
m Robert Colbert pd Eugene Lourie
☆ Oliver Reed, Karen Black, Bette Davis, Lee
Montgomery, Burgess Meredith, Eileen Heckart,
Dub Taylor
'Before the ludicrous dénouement, the movie
merely piles on one special effect after another –
none of them too special – and stalls for time.' –
Janet Maslin, Newsweek

Bury Me Dead *
US 1947 78m bw
Charles F. Reisner/Eagle Lion
A girl reappears on the day of her 'funeral', and
determines to discover who is being buried in her
name.
*Complex mystery which might have been worthy of a
Grade A production.*
w Karen de Wolf, Dwight V. Babcock *story* Irene
Winston d Bernard Vorhaus
☆ Cathy O'Donnell, June Lockhart, Hugh
Beaumont, Mark Daniels, Greg McClure

Bus Riley's Back in Town *
US 1965 93m Eastmancolor
U-I (Elliott Kastner)
An ex-sailor wants to settle back into small-town
life but finds that his girlfriend has married.
*Watchable, middling, routine small-town drama in the
style of Picnic (qv).*
w Walter Gage (William Inge) d Harvey Hart
ph Russell Metty m Richard Markowitz
☆ Michael Parks, Ann-Margret, Jocelyn Brando,
Janet Margolin, Kim Darby, Brad Dexter, Larry
Storch, Crahan Denton, Mimsy Farmer, David
Carradine

Bus Stop **
US 1956 96m Eastmancolor Cinemascope
TCF (Buddy Adler)
■■ ■
TV title: The Wrong Kind of Girl
In a rodeo town, a simple-thinking cowboy meets a
café singer and asks her to marry him.
*Sex comedy-drama, a modest entertainment in familiar
American vein, very well done but rather over-inflated
by its star.*

w George Axelrod *play* William Inge d Joshua
Logan ph Milton Krasner m Alfred Newman,
Cyril Mockridge
☆ Marilyn Monroe, Don Murray, Betty Field,
Arthur O'Connell, Eileen Heckart, Robert Bray,
Hope Lange, Hans Conried, Casey Adams
'The film demands of its principal performers a
purely physical display of their bodies viewed as
sexual machinery.' – *David Robinson*
♟ Don Murray

Bush Christmas
↟↟ GB 1947 77m bw
ABFD/Children's Entertainment Films (Ralph Smart)
Australian children on holiday help catch horse
thieves.
*Rather stolid family feature which got a reputation it
hardly deserved.*
wd Ralph Smart
☆ Chips Rafferty, John Fernside, Stan Tolshurst,
Pat Penny, Thelma Grigg, John McCallum

The Bushido Blade
GB/US 1978 92m colour
Trident/Rankin-Bass (Arthur Rankin Jnr)
■
aka: The Bloody Bushido Blade
Yokohama 1854; a US-Japanese treaty is in
jeopardy because the Shogun's gift of a ceremonial
sword has been stolen.
*Unappealing hybrid with much beheading and other
random action, but little sense.*
w William Overgard d Tom Kotani ph Shoji
Uedo m Maury Laws
☆ Richard Boone, Frank Converse, Laura Gemser,
Toshiro Mifune, Sonny Chiba, James Earl Jones,
Mako

Bushwhacked
US 1995 90m DeLuxe
TCF (Charles B. Wessler, Paul Schiff)
■■ ■
Framed for murder, a dim-witted van driver heads
for the mountains to prove his innocence and is
forced to impersonate a Ranger Scout leader who is
taking a troop on an overnight jaunt.
*Crude, brash, loud would-be comedy, with a manic
central performance; its intended audience of children
is likely to find it as unamusing as any adults
unfortunate enough to watch it.*
w John Jordan, Danny Byers, Tommy Swerdlow,
Michael Goldberg d Greg Beeman ph Theo Van
de Sande m Bill Conti pd Mark W. Mansbridge,
Sandy Veneziano ed Ross Albert
☆ Daniel Stern, Jon Polito, Brad Sullivan, Ann
Dowd, Anthony Heald, Tom Wood, Blake Bashoff,
Corey Carrier, Michael Galeota

A Business Affair
GB/France/Germany/Spain 1993 102m colour
Entertainment/Film and General/Osby/Connexion
(Clive Parsons, Davina Belling, Xavier Larere)
An author with writer's block is annoyed by his
wife's success as a novelist and her decision to
leave him for his agent.
*Slick, forgettable romantic nonsense, through which its
talented cast dispiritedly flounders.*
w William Stadiem, Lucy Flannery *novel Tears
before Bedtime, Weep No More* by Barbara Skelton
d Charlotte Brandstorm ph Willy Kurant
m Didier Vasseur pd Sophie Becher ed Laurence
Méry-Clark
☆ Christopher Walken, Jonathan Pryce, Carole
Bouquet, Sheila Hancock, Anna Manahan, Tom
Wilkinson
'A whimsical love-triangle saga with the
production values of a mineral water
commercial.' – *Geoffrey Macnab, Sight and Sound*

Business and Pleasure
US 1931 76m bw
Fox
A down-to-earth husband is tempted by a *femme
fatale.*
Mild star comedy for his regular fans.
w Gene Towne, William Conselman *novel The
Plutocrat* by Booth Tarkington d David Butler
☆ Will Rogers, Jetta Goudal, Joel McCrea,
Dorothy Peterson, Jed Prouty
'West of Albany, perhaps, it will see some good
business.' – *Variety*

Business As Usual
GB 1987 90m colour
Cannon (Sara Geater)
■
The manageress of a shop, sacked for objecting to
her boss's sexual harassment of his staff, fights back.
Agit-prop drama with some forceful performances.
wd Lezli-An Barrett ph Ernie Vincze
ad Hildegarde Betchler ed Henry Richardson
☆ Glenda Jackson, John Thaw, Cathy Tyson, Mark
McGann, Buki Armstrong, Stephen McGann,
Philip Foster, Natalie Duffy, James Hazeldine, Mel
Martin

Busman's Honeymoon *
GB 1940 99m bw
MGM (Harold Huth)
US title: Haunted Honeymoon
Lord Peter Wimsey finds a murder to be solved in
his honeymoon cottage.
*Pleasant, slightly flat film version of a favourite old-
fashioned detective novel.*
w Monckton Hoffe, Angus MacPhail, Harold
Goldman *novel* Dorothy L. Sayers d Arthur
Woods ph F. A. Young m Louis Levy ad Alfred
Junge ed Al Barnes
☆ Robert Montgomery, Constance Cummings, Leslie
Banks, Seymour Hicks, Robert Newton, Googie
Withers, Frank Pettingell, Joan Kemp-Welch

Busses Roar
US 1942 61m bw
Warner
A saboteur fixes a bomb to explode on a bus as it
passes through an oilfield.
Passable time-filler.
w Anthony Coldeway, George Bilson d D. Ross
Lederman
☆ Richard Travis, Eleanor Parker, Julie Bishop,
Charles Drake

Buster
GB 1988 102m colour
Vestron/The Movie Group (Norma Heyman)
■■ ■ ℚ~ ⌂
True story of Great Train Robber, actually a small-
time thief, on the run.
*Uneasy combination of romantic comedy and chase
thriller.*
w Colin Schindler d David Green ph Tony Imi
m Anne Dudley pd Simon Holland ed Lesley
Walker
☆ Phil Collins, Julie Walters, Larry Lamb,
Stephanie Lawrence, Martin Jarvis, Sheila
Hancock, Anthony Quayle
♟ best song 'Two Hearts' (*mflp Lamont Dozier,
Phil Collins*)

Buster and Billie
US 1973 99m CFI color
Black Creek Billie/Columbia
■
A sensitive high school senior elects to marry the
school's derided 'easy lay', with tragic results.
*Unattractive reminiscences of rural Georgia with a
rather desperate appeal to oversexed teenagers.*
w Ron Turbeville d Daniel Petrie ph Mario Tosi
☆ Jan-Michael Vincent, Pamela Sue Martin, Joan
Goodfellow, Clifton James

Buster Keaton: A Hard Act to Follow ***
GB 1987 156m colour/bw
Thames TV (Kevin Brownlow, David Gill)
■■
A three-part investigation of the art and life of
Keaton, including many clips from his films as well
as interviews with him and those who worked with
him.
*An exemplary and fascinating documentary on one of
the greatest of cinematic clowns.*
w Kevin Brownlow, David Gill m Carl Davis
☆ Lindsay Anderson

The Buster Keaton Story *
US 1957 91m bw Vistavision
Paramount (Sidney Sheldon, Robert Smith)
A biopic of the great silent comedian, with the
emphasis on his years of downfall through drink.
*An interesting recreation of Hollywood in the twenties
and thirties is the main asset of this otherwise dismal
tribute to a man whose greatness the star is unable to
suggest apart from a few acrobatic moments.*
w Robert Smith, Sidney Sheldon d Sidney
Sheldon ph Loyal Griggs m Victor Young

☆ Donald O'Connor, Rhonda Fleming, Ann Blyth, Peter Lorre, Larry Keating, Richard Anderson, Dave Willock

Bustin' Loose

US 1981 94m Technicolor
Universal/Richard Pryor (William Greaves)

🖭 ⌖

A thief on parole learns to look after a school for maladjusted children en route to a mountain retreat.
A fairly nauseous compendium of pratfalls and sentiment, not too bad while it keeps on the move.
w Roger L. Simon d Oz Scott ph Dennis Dalzell m Mark Davis, Roberta Flack
☆ Richard Pryor, Cicely Tyson, Angel Ramirez, Jimmy Hughes
'The sort of forties-style warm experience I could well do without.' – *Derek Malcolm, Guardian*

Busting

US 1973 92m DeLuxe
UA/Chartoff-Winkler (Henry Gellis)

🖭

Two Los Angeles vice squad officers fight corruption inside and outside the force.
Violent, exhausting, but totally routine police caper of the seventies.
wd Peter Hyams ph Earl Rath m Billy Goldenberg
☆ Elliott Gould, Robert Blake, Allen Garfield, Antonio Fargas
'The farcical version of *Serpico*.' – *Michael Billington, Illustrated London News*

Busy Bodies **

👫 US 1933 20m bw
MGM/Hal Roach

🖭

Stan and Ollie are involved in various disasters in a sawmill.
Though not among their most sympathetic comedies, this is a sustained and brilliantly contrived slapstick sequence.
w Anon (and Stan Laurel) d Lloyd French ph Art Lloyd ed Bert Jordan
☆ Laurel and Hardy, Tiny Sandford, Charlie Hall

The Busy Body

US 1966 102m Technicolor Techniscope
Paramount/William Castle
A gangster is buried in a suit with a million dollar lining which various people are out to get.
Unfunny black comedy; laboured handling makes it a joke in poor taste.
w Ben Starr novel Donald E. Westlake d William Castle ph Hal Stine m Vic Mizzy
☆ Robert Ryan, Sid Caesar, Arlene Golonka, Anne Baxter, Kay Medford, Charles McGraw

But Not for Me

US 1959 105m bw
Paramount (William Perlberg, George Seaton)

🖭

An ageing, washed-up Broadway producer is loved by his young drama student secretary.
Rather heavy-going remake of Accent on Youth (qv), efficiently performed but lacking the original gaiety.
w John Michael Hayes d Walter Lang ph Robert Burks m Leith Stevens
☆ Clark Gable, Carroll Baker, Lilli Palmer, Lee J. Cobb, Barry Coe, Thomas Gomez

But the Flesh Is Weak

US 1932 82m bw
MGM
A widower and his son both decide to marry wealthy widows.
Amusing high society comedy from Ivor Novello's The Truth Game.
w Ivor Novello d Jack Conway
☆ Robert Montgomery, C. Aubrey Smith, Heather Thatcher, Edward Everett Horton, Nils Asther

Butch and Sundance: The Early Days *

US 1979 112m DeLuxe
TCF (Gabriel Katzka, Stephen Bach)

🖭

Early episodes in the careers of the famous outlaws, culminating in a train robbery.
'Prequel' to a more celebrated but not a fresher or more lyrical Western.

w Allan Burns d Richard Lester ph Laszlo Kovacs m Patrick Williams pd Brian Eatwell
☆ Tom Berenger, William Katt, Jeff Corey, John Schuck, Michael C. Gwynne, Brian Dennehy, Peter Weller

'Not that it matters, but most of it is true!'
Butch Cassidy and the Sundance Kid ****

US 1969 110m DeLuxe Panavision
TCF/Campanile (John Foreman)

🖭 🖭 ⌖ ♫ ⌒

A hundred years ago, two Western train robbers keep one step ahead of the law until finally tracked down to Bolivia.
Humorous, cheerful, poetic, cinematic account of two semi-legendary outlaws, winningly acted and directed. One of the decade's great commercial successes, not least because of the song 'Raindrops Keep Fallin' on My Head'.
w William Goldman d George Roy Hill ph Conrad Hall m Burt Bacharach
☆ Paul Newman, Robert Redford, Katharine Ross, Strother Martin, Henry Jones, Jeff Corey, Cloris Leachman, Ted Cassidy, Kenneth Mars
'A mere exercise in smart-alecky device-mongering, chock-full of out of place and out of period one-upmanship, a battle of wits at a freshman smoker.' – *John Simon*
'The film does wonderful things with mood and atmosphere. The touches are fleeting, but they are there.' – *Hollis Alpert, Saturday Review*
🏆 William Goldman; Conrad Hall; Burt Bacharach; song 'Raindrops Keep Fallin' on My Head' (m Burt Bacharach, ly Hal David)
⚖ best picture; George Roy Hill
🏵 best picture; George Roy Hill; Conrad Hall; Burt Bacharach; William Goldman; Robert Redford; Katharine Ross

The Butcher: see Le Boucher

Butcher Boy ***

Ireland/US 1997 110m Technicolor
Warner/Geffen (Redmond Morris, Stephen Woolley)

🖭 ⌒

In the early 60s, an Irish boy with an alcoholic father and suicidal mother grows up to be a murderer.
Sustained by a superb performance in the title role, this is a bleak, dark drama of alienation and despair, shot through with a gallows humour.
w Neil Jordan, Patrick McCabe novel Patrick McCabe d Neil Jordan ph Adrian Biddle m Elliot Goldenthal pd Anthony Pratt ed Tony Lawson
☆ Stephen Rea, Fiona Shaw, Eamonn Owens, Alan Boyle, Brendan Gleeson, Milo O'Shea, Ian Hart, Sinead O'Connor, Patrick McCabe
'A heart-wrenching black comedy.' – *Paddy Barrett, Screen International*
'Grips like *The 400 Blows* crossed with *A Clockwork Orange*.' – *Alexander Walker*

'It's not about meat, it's about magic.'
The Butcher's Wife

US 1991 105m Technicolor
Blue Dolphin/Paramount (Wallis Nicita, Lauren Lloyd)

🖭 🖭 ⌖

A clairvoyant marries a butcher and tells customers of her premonitions concerning them.
Whimsical romantic comedy that sank without a trace.
w Ezra Litwak, Marjorie Schwartz d Terry Hughes ph Frank Tidy m Michael Gore pd Charles Rosen ed Donn Cambern
☆ Demi Moore, Jeff Daniels, George Dzundza, Mary Steenburgen, Frances McDormand, Margaret Colin, Max Perlich, Miriam Margolyes
'The jokes and folksy apopthegms are the sort that fill out the pages of *Reader's Digest*, the over-acting is the kind of thing good performers resort to in long-running Broadway plays.' – *Philip French, Observer*

The Butler's Dilemma

GB 1943 83m bw
British National/Shaftesbury (Elizabeth Hiscott)
A jewel thief has to pose as his fiancée's butler.
Predictable comedy of pretence and mistaken identity; a tolerable co-feature of its day.
w Michael Barringer d Leslie Hiscott ph James Wilson m John Blore
☆ Richard Hearne, Francis L. Sullivan, Judy Kelly, Hermione Gingold, Henry Kendall, Wally Patch

Butley *

US/GB 1973 130m Eastmancolor
American Express/Ely Landau/Cinevision

🖭

Personal problems assail an English lecturer at a university college.
Adequate but not outstanding transcription (for the American Film Theater) of a successful and percipient play.
w Simon Gray play Simon Gray d Harold Pinter ph Gerry Fisher m none ad Carmen Dillon
☆ Alan Bates, Jessica Tandy, Richard O'Callaghan, Susan Engel, Michael Byrne

The Butter and Egg Man

This pleasant George S. Kaufman comedy about a cowboy in New York was filmed as a silent in 1928, with Jack Mulhall; in 1932 as *The Tenderfoot* (qv) with Joe E. Brown; in 1937 as *Dance Charlie Dance* with Stuart Erwin; and in 1940 as *An Angel from Texas* (qv) with Eddie Albert.

The Buttercup Chain *

GB 1970 95m Technicolor Panavision
Columbia (Leslie Gilliat, John Whitney, Philip Waddilove)
A hothouse sex quartet changes partners with bewildering rapidity against a background of European splendour.
Chi-chi romance with a fashionably disillusioned and tragic ending. As watchable as the best TV commercials, but totally empty.
w Peter Draper novel Janice Elliott d Robert Ellis Miller ph Douglas Slocombe m Richard Rodney Bennett
☆ Hywel Bennett, Leigh Taylor-Young, Jane Asher, Sven-Bertil Taube, Clive Revill, Roy Dotrice
'British bathos about the unhappy overprivileged.' – *Variety*

'The most desirable woman in town, and the easiest to find!'
Butterfield Eight

US 1960 108m Metrocolor Cinemascope
MGM/Afton/Linebrook (Pandro S. Berman)

🖭 🖭 ⌖

A society call girl has a complex love life.
This coy sex drama seemed mildly daring in 1960, but has since been well outclassed in that field and certainly has nothing else going for it except good production values.
w Charles Schnee, John Michael Hayes novel John O'Hara d Daniel Mann ph Joseph Ruttenberg, Charles Harten m Bronislau Kaper
☆ Elizabeth Taylor, Laurence Harvey, Eddie Fisher, Dina Merrill, Mildred Dunnock, Betty Field, Jeffrey Lynn, Kay Medford, Susan Oliver
'The mixture resolutely refuses to come to the boil.' – *John Gillett*
🏆 Elizabeth Taylor
⚖ Joseph Ruttenberg, Charles Harten

Butterflies Are Free

US 1972 109m Eastmancolor
Columbia/M. J. Frankovich

🖭

An aspiring actress falls for a blind neighbour but is handicapped by his possessive mother.
Three-character comedy-drama from a slight, sentimental but successful Broadway play.
w Leonard Gershe play Leonard Gershe d Milton Katselas ph Charles B. Lang m Bob Alcivar
☆ Goldie Hawn, Edward Albert, Eileen Heckart
🏆 Eileen Heckart
⚖ Charles B. Lang

Butterfly

US 1981 108m Metrocolor
Par Par (Matt Cimber)

🖭 🖭 ⌖ ⌒

A 17-year-old sexpot reappears in her father's life, commits incest with him, and sets in train a grotesque series of plot developments.
Risible concatenation of murders, repentances, illegitimate sex and various kinds of lust, all revolving round butterfly marks and set in 1937 backwoods Arizona. Tobacco Road it ain't, though.
w John Goff, Matt Cimber novel The Butterfly by James M. Cain d Matt Cimber ph Eddy Van Der Enden m Ennio Morricone

☆ Stacy Keach, Pia Zadora, Orson Welles, Lois Nettleton, Edward Albert, Stuart Whitman, Ed MacMahon, June Lockhart, James Franciscus

The Butterfly Effect

Spain/France/GB 1995 109m colour
Blue Dolphin/Fernando Colomo/Mainstream/Portman/Oceandeep (Beatriz de la Gindara)
The tangled love life of a student and his family in London brings down the Spanish government.
Chaos theory, in which minor happenings can have major effects, is meant to underpin this camp comedy; those who watch it may be put off international co-productions for life.
w Joaquin Oristrell, Fernando Colomo d Fernando Colomo ph Jean-François Robin m Ketama ad John Roberts ed Miguel Angel Santamaria
☆ Maria Barranco, Coque Malla, Rosa Maria Sarda, James Fleet, Peter Sullivan, Cécile Pallas, John Faal
'A delightful comedy of manners. Its cross-cultural observations on Spanish and British cultural mores are perceptively written.' – *José Arroyo, Sight and Sound*
'This one's entire cast should be garrotted. You thought there couldn't be a worse director in Spain than the punk cartoonist Almodovar. Wrong: his name is Fernando Colomo.' – *Alexander Walker, London Evening Standard*

Butterfly Kiss *

GB 1995 88m colour/bw
Electric/Dan/British Screen (Julie Baines)

🖭

An assistant at a motorway services shop takes in a suicidal young wanderer and the couple begin a lesbian affair; they travel the roads together, killing those they meet.
A grim and downbeat tale of obsessive love and despair, displaying an undeniable, though depressing, talent.
w Frank Cottrell Boyce d Michael Winterbottom ph Seamus McGarvey m John Harle ad Rupert Miles ed Trevor Waite
☆ Amanda Plummer, Saskia Reeves, Kathy Jamieson, Des McAleer, Freda Dowie, Lisa Jane Riley, Ricky Tomlinson
'The film's quiet sense of style, its sensibly short length, expert editing and sure touch … proclaim an exceptional new director for the cinema.' – *Derek Malcolm, Guardian*
'Resembles nothing so much as a trawl through dirt-cheap, one dimensional thrilleramics. A film unlikely to do much for either the serial killer genre or motorway services tourist trade.' – *Clark Collis, Empire*

The Butterfly Murders ***

Hong Kong 1979 colour
Ng See Yuen (Ng See Kin)
A wandering scholar, at a time of warring factions, solves the mystery of an aristocratic family apparently plagued by killer butterflies.
A visually splendid martial arts fantasy with elaborately choreographed fight sequences, done with immense melodramatic style.
w Lam Fan d Tsui Hark ph Fun Chin Yu
☆ Lau Siu Ming, Wong Shee Tong, Michelle, Chan Chi Chi, Cheong Kwok Chu, Kuo Hung, Wong Cheong, Kiu Fung

Buy & Cell

US 1989 95m colour
Empire/Altar (Frank Yablans)

🖭 🖭 ⌖

Framed for embezzlement, a stockbroker runs a successful investment company from inside prison.
Dire comedy on the theme that greed makes brothers of us all; every scene goes on too long and unsubtle performances are encouraged.
w Ken Krauss, Merrin Holt story Leonard Montana, Louis Peraino d Robert Boris ph Daniele Nannuzzi m Mark Shreeve pd Giovanni Natalucci ed Bert Glatstein
☆ Robert Carradine, Michael Winslow, Ben Vereen, Malcolm McDowell, Randall 'Tex' Cobb, Imogene Coca, Fred Travalena, Roddy Piper, Lise Cutter, Tony Plana, Michael Goodwin

---

Buy Me That Town *

US   1941   70m   bw
Paramount (Sol C. Siegel)
Gangsters take over a small town and pull the community out of bankruptcy.
Unusual comedy-drama, quite well done for a second feature.
w Gordon Kahn d Eugene Forde ph Theodor Sparkuhl
☆ Lloyd Nolan, Albert Dekker, Constance Moore, Sheldon Leonard, Vera Vague, Edward Brophy, Horace MacMahon, Warren Hymer

Bwana Devil

US   1952   79m   Anscocolor   3D
(UA)
At the turn of the century, two man-eating lions threaten an African railroad.
Inept actioner notable only as the first film in 3-D ('Natural Vision'), advertised with the famous slogan 'A lion in your lap'.
wd Arch Oboler ph Joseph Biroc m Gordon Jenkins
☆ Robert Stack, Barbara Britton, Nigel Bruce, Ramsay Hill

By Candlelight *

US   1933   70m   bw
Universal (Carl Laemmle Jnr)
On a transcontinental train a woman meets a butler and takes him for a prince; he does not disillusion her.
Moderately pleasing romantic comedy of the old school.
w Hans Kraly, F. Hugh Herbert, Karen de Wolf, Ruth Cummings play Siegfried Geyer d James Whale
☆ Elissa Landi, *Paul Lukas*, Nils Asther
'A nice little class picture that should make money all round.' – *Variety*
'A dazzling display of romantic confidence trickery which takes on Lubitsch in his own territory.' – *Tom Milne, 1978*

By Hook or by Crook: see I Dood It

By Love Possessed *

US   1961   116m   DeLuxe   Panavision
UA/Mirisch/Seven Arts (Walter Mirisch)
A Massachusetts lawyer reflects on the outlandish sexual mores of himself, his family and friends.
Peyton Place moved up in the social scale; a reasonably absorbing melodrama but hardly memorable.
w John Dennis novel James Gould Cozzens d John Sturges ph Russell Metty m Elmer Bernstein
☆ Lana Turner, Efrem Zimbalist Jnr, Jason Robards Jnr, Barbara Bel Geddes, George Hamilton, Susan Kohner, Thomas Mitchell, Yvonne Craig, Everett Sloane
'A talky succession of soap opera situations.' – *Robert Windeler*

'The most warm-hearted musical under the sun!'

By the Light of the Silvery Moon *

US   1953   101m   Technicolor
Warner (William Jacobs)
In a small American town in 1918, the Winfield family has several problems arising from the return of daughter Marjorie's soldier boyfriend.
A sequel to On Moonlight Bay (qv), presenting further situations from the Penrod stories retailored for Doris Day. Inoffensive, well-made, old-fashioned entertainment with nostalgic songs and an archetypal family.
w Robert O'Brien, Irving Elinson stories Booth Tarkington d David Butler ph Wilfrid M. Cline m Max Steiner
☆ Doris Day, Gordon MacRae, *Leon Ames, Rosemary de Camp, Mary Wickes*
♟ William Goldman

By Your Leave

US   1934   81m   bw
RKO
A restless husband tries to be a Don Juan.
Very mild domestic comedy.
w Allan Scott play Gladys Hurlbut, Emma B. C. Wells d Lloyd Corrigan
☆ Frank Morgan, Genevieve Tobin, Neil Hamilton, Marian Nixon, Glenn Anders, Gene Lockhart, Margaret Hamilton, Betty Grable, Charles Ray
'Once the customers are in they'll get some laughs, but they're not going to be easy to entice.' – *Variety*

Bye Bye Birdie

US   1963   112m   Eastmancolor   Panavision
Columbia/Fred Kohlmar/George Sidney
▤ ◎ ♫
Havoc suffuses the last TV show of a pop star before he goes into the army.
Noisy, frenetic musical, hard to follow and even harder to like, with all the satire of the stage original subtracted. For young audiences who enjoy incoherence.
w Irving Brecher musical Michael Stewart d George Sidney ph Joseph Biroc m/ly Charles Strouse, Lee Adams md Johnny Green
☆ Janet Leigh, Dick Van Dyke, Maureen Stapleton, Ann-Margret, Bobby Rydell, Jesse Pearson, Ed Sullivan, Paul Lynde, Robert Paige
♟ Johnny Green

Bye Bye Blues

Canada   1989   117m   colour
Artificial Eye/True Blue Films/Allarcom/Telefilm Canada/CFCN TV/CITV (Anne Wheeler, Arvi Liimatainen, Jerry Krepakevich)
▤ ♫
A mother with two young children awaits the return of her soldier husband.
Uninteresting throwback to women's movies of the 1940s.
wd Anne Wheeler ph Vic Sarin m George Blondheim pd John Blackie ad Scott Dobbie, Jayoo Patwarchan, Chinu Patwarchan ed Christopher Tate
☆ Michael Ontkean, Rebecca Jenkins, Luke Reilly, Stuart Margolin, Wayne Robson, Robyn Stevan
'A film which, without exactly bowling one over, will probably remain in the memory longer than most.' – *Derek Malcolm, Guardian*

Bye Bye Braverman *

US   1968   92m   Technicolor
Warner/Sidney Lumet
New Yorkers get drunk and disillusioned on their way home from the funeral of a friend.
Witty, downbeat Jewish comedy which does not quite come off and would in any case be caviare to the general.
w Herbert Sargent novel To an Early Grave by Wallace Markfield d Sidney Lumet ph Boris Kaufman m Peter Matz
☆ George Segal, Jack Warden, Joseph Wiseman, Sorrell Booke, Jessica Walter, Phyllis Newman, Zohra Lampert, Alan King, Godfrey Cambridge
'You don't have to be Jewish to love it, but it helps a lot to be a New Yorker.' – *Robert Hatch, The Nation*

Bye Bye Love

US   1995   106m   DeLuxe
TCF/UBU (Gary David Goldberg, Brad Hall, Sam Weisman)
▣ ▤
Three divorced fathers spend the weekend with their kids in various ways.
Bland and innocuous comedy in favour of family values and McDonald's hamburgers, though not necessarily in that order.
w Gary David Goldberg, Brad Hall d Sam Weisman ph Kenneth Zunder m J. A. C. Redford pd Linda DeScenna ed Roger Bondelli
☆ Matthew Modine, Randy Quaid, Paul Reiser, Janeane Garofalo, Rob Reiner, Amy Brenneman, Eliza Dushku, Ed Flanders, Maria Pitillo, Lindsay Crouse
'Funny and poignant, with the good-natured effort and its affable cast elevating a sometimes schematic story.' – *Leonard Klady, Variety*

Bye Bye Monkey

Italy/France   1977   114m   Eastmancolor
18 Dicembre/Prospectacle/Action Film (Giorgio Nocella, Maurice Bernart)
▣ ◎
original title: *Ciao Maschio*
A Frenchman, dividing his time between a wax museum and a theatre group run by women, finds a chimpanzee and adopts it as his son.
Desultory drama of misfits drifting through New York that is never sharp or observant enough to be either amusing or interesting; and the deaths at the end do not make it tragic.
w Marco Ferreri, Gérard Brach, Rafael Azcona d Marco Ferreri ph Luciano Tovoli m Philippe Sarde ad Dante Ferretti ed Ruggero Mastroianni
☆ Gérard Depardieu, James Coco, Marcello Mastroianni, Geraldine Fitzgerald, Gail Lawrence, Stefania Casini, Francesca de Sapio, Mimsy Farmer

C.C. and Company
US   1971   84m   colour
Allan Carr-Roger Smith/Avco Embassy
Adventures of a motorcycle gang.
Bottom of the barrel programme-filler.
w Roger Smith d Seymour Robbie
☆ Joe Namath, Ann-Margret, William Smith, Jennifer Billingsley, Don Chastain

C.H.O.M.P.S.: see *Chomps*

C Man
US   1949   75m   bw
Film Classics
Customs agents track down a murderer.
Lively little independent co-feature of its day.
w Berne Giler d Joseph Lerner
☆ Dean Jagger, John Carradine, Lotte Elwen, Harry Landers

Ca Commence Aujourd'hui: see *It All Starts Today*

Ça Peut Pas être L'Hiver, On N'a Même Pas Eu été: see *It Can't Be Winter, We Haven't Had Summer Yet*

'A divinely decadent experience!'
Cabaret ****
US   1972   123m   Technicolor
ABC Pictures/Allied Artists (Cy Feuer)
In the early thirties, Berlin is a hot-bed of vice and anti-semitism. In the Kit Kat Klub, singer Sally Bowles shares her English lover with a homosexual German baron, and her Jewish friend Natasha has troubles of her own.
This version of Isherwood's Berlin stories regrettably follows the plot line of the play I Am a Camera rather than the Broadway musical on which it is allegedly based, and it lacks the incisive remarks of the MC, but the very smart direction creates a near-masterpiece of its own, and most of the songs are intact.
w Jay Presson Allen novel Goodbye to Berlin by Christopher Isherwood ph Geoffrey Unsworth m/ly John Kander, Fred Ebb md Ralph Burns pd Rolf Zehetbauer d/ch Bob Fosse
☆ Liza Minnelli, Joel Grey, Michael York, Helmut Griem, Fritz Wepper, Marisa Berenson
'A stylish, sophisticated entertainment for grown-up people.' – John Russell Taylor
'Film journals will feast for years on shots from this picture; as it rolled along, I saw page after illustrated page from a not-too-distant book called The Cinema of Bob Fosse.' – Stanley Kauffmann
🏆 Bob Fosse (as director); Geoffrey Unsworth; Ralph Burns; Liza Minnelli; Joel Grey
⚬ best picture; Jay Presson Allen
🏆 best picture; Rolf Zehetbauer; Geoffrey Unsworth; Bob Fosse; Liza Minnelli; Joel Grey

Cabeza de Vaca *
Mexico/Spain   1990   111m   Eastmancolor
Iguana Productions (Rafael Cruz, Jorge Sánchez, Julio Solórzano Foppa, Bertha Navarro)
In the 1520s, the leader of a group of Spanish conquistadores, shipwrecked off the coast of Florida, survives ambush, torture and privation by learning to live with the natives.
An ambitious, overlong, often mystic and sometimes violent epic, taken from a contemporary account, which is on the side of the native Americans.
w Guillermo Sheridan, Nicolás Echevarria book Naufragios by Alvar Nunez Cabeza de Vaca d Nicolás Echevarria ph Guillermo Navarro m Mario Lavista ad José Luis Aguilar Gil ed Rafael Castanedo
☆ Juan Diego, Daniel Gimenez Cacho, Roberto Sosa, Carlos Castañón, Roberto Villarreal, Roberto Cobo, José Flores

'It's a demanding pic for audiences, but they will be well rewarded with a film that's exotic, mysterious, bizarre (shades of Alexandro Jodorowsky) and dramatic.' – Variety

Cabin Boy
US   1994   80m   Foto-Kem
Hollywood (Tim Burton, Denise di Novi)
A rich and snobbish youth boards the wrong boat and finds himself in rough and fantastic company.
Coarse and unattractive comedy that veers into a spoof of Sinbad's adventures with some ill-chosen fantasy.
wd Adam Resnick ph Steve Yaconelli m Steve Bartek pd Steven Legler ed Jon Poll
☆ Chris Elliott, Richard Brinkley, James Gammon, Brian Doyle-Murray, Brion James, Russ Tamblyn, Ricki Lake
'Obnoxious, snide and pointless, this ill-fated spoof carries the bonus of being as crude and gamy as the hold of an old fishing barge.' – Brian Lowry, Variety
† Made in 1992.

The Cabin in the Cotton *
US   1932   79m   bw
Warner (Hal B. Wallis)
A sharecropper is almost ruined by a Southern belle.
Dated melodrama with interesting style and performances.
w Paul Green novel Harry Harrison Kroll d Michael Curtiz ph Barney McGill
☆ Richard Barthelmess, Dorothy Jordan, Bette Davis, David Landau, Tully Marshall, Henry B. Walthall, Hardie Albright
'Not well done … less than a moderate grosser all round.' – Variety
† The film in which Bette Davis drawled: 'Ah'd love to kiss yuh, but Ah just washed mah hair.'

'Broadway's big, fun-jammed music show is on the screen at last – crowded with stars and songs and spectacle in the famed MGM manner!'
Cabin in the Sky **
US   1943   99m   bw
MGM (Arthur Freed)
An idle, gambling husband is reformed by a dream of his own death, with God and Satan battling for his soul.
Consistently interesting, often lively, but generally rather stilted all-black musical which must have seemed a whole lot fresher on the stage. Still, a good try.
w Joseph Schrank musical play Lynn Root d Vincente Minnelli ph Sidney Wagner m/ly Harold Arlen, E. Y. Harburg, Vernon Duke, John Latouche, Ted Fetter md George Stoll ad Cedric Gibbons, Leonid Vasian
☆ Eddie 'Rochester' Anderson, Ethel Waters, Lena Horne, Louis Armstrong, Rex Ingram, Kenneth Spencer, John W. Sublett ('Bubbles'), Ford L. Washington ('Buck'), Mantan Moreland, Willie Best
'Whatever its box office fate, a worthwhile picture for Metro to have made, if only as a step toward Hollywood recognition of the place of the colored man in American life.' – Variety
🎵 'Li'l Black Sheep'; 'Ain't It De Truth'; 'Life's Full Of Consequence'; 'Honey in the Honeycomb'; 'Taking a Chance on Love'; 'Going Up'; 'I Got A Song'; 'Shine'
⚬ song 'Happiness Is Just a Thing Called Joe' (mHarold Arlen, lyE. Y. Harburg)

'No one permitted out or in during the last thirteen nerve-shattering minutes!'
The Cabinet of Caligari
US   1962   105m   bw   Cinemascope
TCF/Lippert (Roger Kay)
A young woman whose car breaks down near a country house is held prisoner by the sinister Caligari. Eventually it transpires that the mystery is all in her imagination: he is a psychiatrist and she an old lady whose sexual fantasies he has been curing.
Interminably talkative and frequently (unintentionally) funny trick film with the odd moment of effective suspense. The original ending, which cast some doubt on who was mad and who sane, is no longer available. The actors do not entirely escape absurdity.
w Robert Bloch d Roger Kay ph John Russell m Gerald Fried
☆ Glynis Johns, Dan O'Herlihy, Constance Ford, Dick Davalos, Lawrence Dobkin
'It is impossible to be grateful for the film on any of its levels.' – MFB
'The most complete essay in the décor of delirium.' – New Yorker, 1979
† The fact that the story is told through the eyes of a mad person is the only link with the 1919 classic.

'See the sleepwalker, floating down the street, ripped from some nightmare! A street of misshapen houses with brooding windows, streaked by dagger strokes of light and darkened by blots of shadow! You will immediately feel the terror in the movements of that floating grotesque!'
The Cabinet of Dr Caligari ****
Germany   1919   90m   bw   silent
Decla-Bioscop (Erich Pommer)
A fairground showman uses a somnambulist for purposes of murder and is finally revealed to be the director of a lunatic asylum; but the whole story is only the dream of a madman.
Faded now, but a film of immense influence on the dramatic art of cinema, with its odd angles, stylized sets and hypnotic acting, not to mention the sting in the tail of its story (added by the producer).
w Carl Mayer, Hans Janowitz d Robert Wiene ph Willy Hameister ad Hermann Warm, Walter Röhrig, Walter Reiman
☆ Werner Krauss, Conrad Veidt, Lil Dagover, Friedrich Feher, Hans von Twardowski
'The first hundred shocks are the hardest.' – New York Evening Post, 1924
† The film cost 18,000 dollars to make.

Cabiria ***
Italy/France   1957   110m   bw
Dino De Laurentiis/Les Films Marceau
original title: Le Notti di Cabiria
aka: Nights of Cabiria
A Roman prostitute has dreams of romance and respectability.
A bitter Cinderella story which was later turned into the Broadway musical Sweet Charity. Much of interest, but the leading lady is too Chaplinesque.
w Federico Fellini, Ennio Flaiano, Tullio Pinelli d Federico Fellini ph Aldo Tonti m Nino Rota
☆ Giulietta Masina, François Périer, Amedeo Nazzari, Franca Marzi, Dorian Gray
'Any nobility in the original conception slowly suffocates in an atmosphere of subjective indulgence bordering dangerously on self-pity.' – Peter John Dyer
'Stylistically the whole film with its dejected setting and its riotously fluent movement is brilliant. And the acting is superb.' – Dilys Powell
🏆 best foreign film

'Are You Ready To Get Wired?'
The Cable Guy
US   1996   96m   Technicolor
Columbia (Andrew Licht, Jeffrey A. Mueller, Judd Apatow)
A yuppie businessman is at first befriended and then terrorized by a cable TV installation man.
Carrey's frenetic mugging here sits oddly with the naturalistic style of the rest of the cast; some satire at the expense of a television-fixated generation is no doubt intended, but is too heavy-handed to be effective.
w Lou Holtz Jnr d Ben Stiller ph Robert Brinkman m John Ottman pd Sharon Seymour ed Steven Weisberg
☆ Jim Carrey, Matthew Broderick, Leslie Mann, George Segal, Diane Baker, Jack Black, Ben Stiller, Janeane Garofalo, Eric Roberts, Charles Napier
'This fuzzy-focus outing is hopelessly disconnected and ultimately unsatisfying.' – Variety
† Carrey was paid $20m for his role, which had originally been intended for Chris Farley. The movie took around $60m at the US box-office and another $42m worldwide.

Caboblanco
US   1981   87m   colour   Panavision
Avco/Martin V. Smith
A café proprietor in the Caribbean dodges various groups of criminals.
Witless spoof of Casablanca which seems to have been cobbled together from a half-finished negative.
w Mort Fine, Milton Gelman d J. Lee Thompson ph Alex Phillips Jnr m Jerry Goldsmith
☆ Charles Bronson, Jason Robards Jnr, Dominique Sanda, Fernando Rey, Simon MacCorkindale, Camilla Sparv, Denny Miller, Gilbert Roland

Caccia Tragica *
Italy   1947   89m   bw
Lux/ANPI
aka: The Tragic Pursuit
A bandit is hunted through the Po valley but finally allowed to escape.
Minor peripatetic melodrama, well-handled and exciting but uncertain in mood.
w Giuseppe de Santis, Michelangelo Antonioni, Cesare Zavattini, Carlo Lizzani, Umberto Barbaro d Giuseppe de Santis ph Otello Martelli m Giuseppe Rosati
☆ Massimo Girotti, Andrea Checchi, Vivi Gioi

Cactus *
Australia   1986   96m   colour
Dofine/Film Victoria/AFC (Jane Ballantyne, Paul Cox)
A Frenchwoman, whose eyesight begins to deteriorate after a car crash, falls in love with a blind man.
Austere and sensitive drama about a woman finding herself, but too underplayed to be entirely effective.
w Paul Cox, Bob Ellis, Norman Kaye, Morris Lurie d Paul Cox ph Yuri Sokol pd Asher Bilu ed Tim Lewis
☆ Isabelle Huppert, Robert Menzies, Norman Kaye, Monica Maughan, Banduk Marika, Sheila Florance

Cactus Flower *
US   1969   103m   Technicolor
Columbia/M. J. Frankovich
To deceive his mistress, a dentist employs his starchy secretary to pose as his wife, and falls for her when she loosens up.
Amusing sophisticated comedy, generally well handled.
w I. A. L. Diamond play Abe Burrows, French original by Pierre Barillet, Jean Pierre Gredy

d Gene Saks *ph* Charles E. Lang *m* Quincy Jones *pd* Robert Clatworthy

☆ Ingrid Bergman, Walter Matthau, Goldie Hawn, Jack Weston, Rick Lenz, Vito Scotti, Irene Hervey

🎭 Goldie Hawn

Cactus in the Snow: see *You Can't Have Everything*

Cactus Jack: see *The Villain*

Cadaveri Eccellenti: see *Illustrious Corpses*

Caddie *
Australia   1976   106m   Eastmancolor
Roadshow/Anthony Buckley
🎥
A deceived wife takes off with her two children and becomes a barmaid.
Desultory account of aimless low life to which Caddie brings a spark of sunshine. Watchable but forgettable.
w Joan Long, from the autobiography by 'Caddie' *d* Donald Crombie *ph* Peter James *m* Peter Flynn
☆ Helen Morse, Takis Emmanuel, Kirrily Nolan, Jacki Weaver, Jack Thompson

The Caddy *
US   1953   95m   bw
Paramount (Paul Jones)
🎥
A music hall comedy act recall how they got together.
Less a feature than a series of short sketches, this ragbag has its choice moments, but they are few.
w Edmund Hartmann, Danny Arnold *d* Norman Taurog *ph* Daniel L. Fapp *m* Joseph L. Lilley
☆ Dean Martin, Jerry Lewis, Donna Reed, Barbara Bates, Joseph Calleia, Fred Clark, Clinton Sundberg, Marshall Thompson
🎵 song 'That's Amore' (*m*Harry Warren, *ly*Jack Brooks)

Caddyshack
US   1980   98m   Technicolor
Warner/Orion (Douglas Kenney)
🎥 🎥 🎥 🎧
Misadventures at a golf club.
A relentlessly crude and lumbering series of farcical incidents which mainly fail to raise laughs.
w Brian Doyle-Murray, Harold Ramis, Douglas Kenney *d* Harold Ramis *ph* Stevan Larner *m* Johnny Mandel *pd* Stan Jolley *ed* William Carruth
☆ Chevy Chase, Rodney Dangerfield, Ted Knight, Michael O'Keefe
'There are jests about vomiting and nose-picking, while the most elaborate gag sequence involves a chocolate bar falling into a swimming pool and being mistaken for a turd … a sustained exercise in tiresomeness.' – *Tim Pulleine, MFB*

Caddyshack II
US   1988   99m   colour
Warner (Neil Canton, Jon Peters, Peter Guber)
🎥 🎥 🎥
A self-made millionaire is persuaded by his upwardly mobile daughter to apply for membership of an exclusive golf club.
Dim sequel that reprises the central situation of the original without even managing its crude humour; this one is just crude.
w Harold Ramis, Peter Torokvei *d* Allan Arkush *ph* Harry Stradling Jnr *m* Ira Newborn *pd* Bill Matthews *ed* Bernard Gribble
☆ Jackie Mason, Robert Stack, Dina Merrill, Dyan Cannon, Jonathan Silverman, Randy Quaid, Chevy Chase, Dan Aykroyd

Cadillac Man
US   1990   97m   colour
Rank/Orion (Charles Roven, Roger Donaldson)
🎥 🎥 🎥
A car salesman is held hostage by a jealous husband.
Frenetic farce that is rarely funny.
w Ken Friedman *d* Roger Donaldson *ph* David Gribble *m* J. Peter Robinson *pd* Gene Rudolf *ed* Richard Francis-Bruce
☆ Robin Williams, Tim Robbins, Pamela Reed, Fran Drescher, Zack Norman, Annabella Sciorra, Lori Petty, Paul Guilfoyle, Bill Nelson, Eddie Jones
'A rarity among recent films – a comedy that is in touch with a recognizable reality.' – *Richard Schickel, Time*

'Days of magnificent adventure … nights of maddest revelry … a temptation in Technicolor!'
Caesar and Cleopatra **
GB   1945   135m   Technicolor
Rank/Gabriel Pascal
🎥
An elaborate screen treatment of Bernard Shaw's comedy about Caesar's years in Alexandria.
Britain's most expensive film is an absurd extravaganza for which the producer actually took sand to Egypt to get the right colour. It has compensations however in the sets, the colour, the performances and the witty lines, though all its virtues are theatrical rather than cinematic and the play is certainly not a major work.
w Bernard Shaw *d* Gabriel Pascal *ph* F. A. Young, Robert Krasker, Jack Hildyard, Jack Cardiff *m* Georges Auric *decor/costumes* Oliver Messel *sets* John Bryan
☆ Claude Rains, Vivien Leigh, Cecil Parker, Stewart Granger, Flora Robson, Francis L. Sullivan, Raymond Lovell, Anthony Harvey, Anthony Eustrel, Basil Sydney, Ernest Thesiger, Stanley Holloway, Leo Genn, Jean Simmons, Esmé Percy and also Michael Rennie
'It cost over a million and a quarter pounds, took two and a half years to make, and well and truly bored one spectator for two and a quarter hours.' – *Richard Winnington*
'It is so wonderful as to make my other films look naive.' – *Bernard Shaw*
'When Rains played a small part he sometimes gave the impression that he was carrying the movie, but here his impish grin and his equanimity aren't enough.' – *Pauline Kael, 70s*
🎵 John Bryan

Café Colette
GB   1936   73m   bw
Garrick (W. Devenport Hackney)
US title: *Danger in Paris*
A diplomat in charge of a secret formula falls for a Russian princess.
Old-hat spy melodrama, quite neatly staged.
w Eric Maschwitz, Val Gielgud, Walford Hyden *d* Paul L. Stein *ph* Ronald Neame *m* George Posford, Walford Hyden
☆ Paul Cavanagh, Greta Nissen, Sally Gray, Bruce Seton, Donald Calthrop, Dino Galvani

Café Metropole
US   1937   83m   bw
TCF (Nunnally Johnson)
An heiress in Paris romances a Russian nobleman who is actually a penniless American.
Lighter-than-air romance which passed the time at the time.
w Jacques Duval *d* Edward H. Griffith *ph* Lucien Andriot *md* Louis Silvers
☆ Loretta Young, Adolphe Menjou, Tyrone Power, Charles Winninger, Gregory Ratoff, Christian Rub, Helen Westley
'It's smart, sophisticated (not too much so), has the proper romantic ingredients, and will pull 'em in almost anywhere.' – *Variety*
'Here is a very amusing script, admirable acting … all thrown away by inferior direction. The camera is planked down four-square before the characters like a plain, honest, inexpressibly dull guest at a light and loony party.' – *Graham Greene*

Café of Seven Sinners: see *Seven Sinners*

'The Gay, Giddy Goings-On Inside The Most Glamorous Social Circle In The World…'
Café Society
US   1939   84m   bw
Paramount
A publicity-seeking socialite impulsively marries a reporter who has annoyed her, but instead of making a fool of him she falls in love.
Faded light comedy which was never outstanding.
w Virginia Van Upp *d* Edward H. Griffith *ph* Ted Tetzlaff
☆ Madeleine Carroll, Fred MacMurray, Shirley Ross, Claude Gillingwater
'Good cast will carry it nicely into okay if not wow business.' – *Variety*

La Cage aux Folles *
France/Italy   1978   91m   Eastmancolor
UA/PAA/Da Ma (Marcello Danon)
🎥 🎥 🎥 🎧
aka: *Birds of a Feather*
A homosexual night-club owner is persuaded by his straight son to behave properly in front of his girlfriend's parents, but chaos comes on the night of the party.
Internationally popular near-the-knuckle farce with excellent moments and some longueurs.
w Francis Veber, Edouard Molinaro, Marcello Danon, Jean Poiret *play* Jean Poiret *d* Edouard Molinaro *ph* Armando Nannuzzi *m* Ennio Morricone
☆ Ugo Tognazzi, Michel Serrault, Michel Galabru, Claire Maurier, Remi Laurent
🎵 Edouard Molinaro (as director); script

La Cage aux Folles II
France/Italy   1980   99m   Technicolor
UA/PAA/Da Ma (Marcello Danon)
🎥 🎥
An ageing homosexual tells his partner he is too old to be an effective female impersonator. Trying to prove the opposite, the partner becomes involved in a spy search for hidden microfilm.
Rather dimwitted sequel to a comedy which though deliberately 'naughty' showed some restraint; here, all is noise and excess.
w Jean Poiret, Francis Veber, Marcello Danon *d* Edouard Molinaro *ph* Armando Nannuzzi *m* Ennio Morricone
☆ Ugo Tognazzi, Michel Serrault, Marcel Bozzuffi, Paola Borboni
'The juxtaposition of campy histrionics with the dreariest kind of espionage comedy offers quickly diminishing returns.' – *Gilbert Adair, MFB*

La Cage aux Folles III
France/Italy   1985   87m   Eastmancolor
Da Ma/Columbia (Marcello Danon)
🎥 🎥
In order to inherit a fortune, Albin must marry and produce an heir.
Yawnworthy attempt to milk more gags out of a formula which exhausted itself with number one.
w Philippe Nicaud, Christine Carere, Marcello Danon, Jacques Audiard, Michel Audiard, Georges Lautner, Gerald Lamballe *d* Georges Lautner *ph* Luciano Tavoli *m* Ennio Morricone *pd* Mario Garbuglia *ed* Michelle David, Elisabeth Guido, Lidia Pascolini
☆ Ugo Tognazzi, Michel Serrault, Michel Galabru, Antonella Interlenghi
'Lots of cooks but not much broth.' – *Variety*

La Cage aux Rossignols *
France   1947   88m   bw
Gaumont
GB title: *A Cage of Nightingales*
A reform school teacher fires difficult pupils with new hope.
Low-key star vehicle with moderately pleasing results.
w Noel-Noel, René Wheeler *d* Jean Dreville
☆ Noel-Noel, Micheline Francey, Georges Biscot, René Blancard
🎵 Georges Chaperot, René Wheeler (original story)

Cage of Doom: see *Terror from the Year 5000*

Cage of Gold *
GB   1950   83m   bw
Ealing (Michael Relph)
A girl's philandering ex-husband comes back into her life and is murdered.
Mild mystery melodrama in which the puzzle comes too late.
w Jack Whittingham *d* Basil Dearden *ph* Douglas Slocombe *m* Georges Auric
☆ Jean Simmons, David Farrar, James Donald, Madeleine Lebeau, Maria Mauban, Herbert Lom, Bernard Lee, Gladys Henson, Harcourt Williams, Grégoire Aslan

A Cage of Nightingales: see *La Cage aux Rossignols*

'Will she come out woman or wildcat?'
Caged *
US   1949   96m   bw
Warner (Jerry Wald)
After being involved in a robbery a 19-year-old girl is sent to prison, and finds the staff more terrifying than the inmates.
Slick, superficial, hysterically harrowing women-in-prison melodrama; predictably overblown but also effective and powerful.
w Virginia Kellogg, Bernard Schoenfeld *d* John Cromwell *ph* Carl Guthrie *m* Max Steiner
☆ Eleanor Parker, Agnes Moorehead, Ellen Corby, Hope Emerson, Betty Garde, Jan Sterling, Lee Patrick, Olive Deering, Jane Darwell, Gertrude Michael, Joan Miller
† Remade in 1962 as *House of Women*, directed by Walter Doniger, with Shirley Knight.
🎵 Virginia Kellogg, Bernard Schoenfeld; Eleanor Parker; Hope Emerson

Caged Heat *
US   1974   83m   DeLuxe
Target/Artists Entertainment Complex/Renegade Women (Samuel Gelfman)
🎥
A new convict is horrified by the way a crippled governess runs a women's prison.
Quirky, individual, anti-authoritarian take on the standard ingredients of an exploitation picture set among female prisoners.
wd Jonathan Demme *ph* Tak Fujimoto *m* John Cale *ad* Eric Thierman *ed* Johanna Demetrakis, Carolyn Hicks
☆ Juanita Brown, Roberta Collina, Erica Gavin, Ella Reid, Lynda Gold, Warren Miller, Barbara Steele, Toby Carr
'A distinctly exceptional exploitation movie.' – *Tony Rayns, MFB*
† The British release was cut to 79m.

Caged Virgins: see *Requiem for a Vampire*

'Break the law and he's the last man you'll want to see. And the last man you ever will!'
Cahill, US Marshal
US   1973   103m   Technicolor   Panavision
Warner/Batjac (Michael A. Wayne)
🎥 🎥 🎥
A stalwart Western marshal finds that his own young sons are involved in a robbery he is investigating.
Satisfactory but sentimental John Wayne vehicle with the star too often yielding place to the rather boring young folk.
w Harry Julian Fink, Rita M. Fink *d* Andrew V. McLaglen *ph* Joseph Biroc *m* Elmer Bernstein
☆ John Wayne, George Kennedy, Gary Grimes, Neville Brand, Clay O'Brien, Marie Windsor, Royal Dano, Denver Pyle, Jackie Coogan

La Caida: see *The Fall*

'It's unlike any musical you've ever seen before – Timed to the Tantalizing Tempo of Today!'
Cain and Mabel *
US   1936   90m   bw
Warner (Sam Bischoff)
Tribulations of a prizefighter in love with a chowgirl
Generously produced but weakly written comedy drama with rather unexpected musical numbers; not a successful whole, but interesting.
w Laird Doyle, H. C. Witwer *d* Lloyd Bacon *ph* George Barnes *m/ly* Harry Warren, Al Dubin *ch* Bobby Connolly
☆ Clark Gable, Marion Davies, Allen Jenkins, Roscoe Karns, Walter Catlett, Hobart Cavanaugh, Pert Kelton, Ruth Donnelly, E. E. Clive
🎵 Bobby Connolly

'As big as the ocean!'
The Caine Mutiny **
US   1954   125m   Technicolor
Columbia/Stanley Kramer
🎥 🎥 🎥 🎥 🎥
Jealousies and frustrations among the officers of a peacetime destroyer come to a head when the neurotic captain panics during a typhoon and is relieved of his post. At the resulting trial the officers learn about themselves.
Decent if lamely paced version of a bestseller which also made a successful play; the film skates too lightly over the characterizations and even skimps the courtroom scene, but there are effective scenes and performances.

---

w Stanley Roberts *novel* Herman Wouk
d Edward Dmytryk *ph* Franz Planer *m* Max
Steiner *ed* William A. Lyon, Henry Batista
☆ *Humphrey Bogart*, José Ferrer, Van Johnson,
Fred MacMurray, Robert Francis, May Wynn, Tom
Tully, E. G. Marshall, Lee Marvin, Claude Akins

QUEEG: 'There are four ways of doing things on
board my ship. The right way, the wrong way, the
navy way, and my way. If they do things my way,
we'll get along.'

QUEEG: 'Ah, but the strawberries! That's where I
had them. They laughed and made jokes, but I
proved beyond the shadow of a doubt, and with
geometric logic, that a duplicate key to the
wardroom icebox did exist. And I'd have produced
that key if they hadn't pulled the *Caine* out of
action. I know now they were out to protect some
fellow officer.'

KEEFER: 'There is no escape from the *Caine*, save
death. We're all doing penance, sentenced to an
outcast ship, manned by outcasts, and named after
the greatest outcast of them all.'
↧ best picture; Stanley Roberts; Max Steiner;
Humphrey Bogart; Tom Tully; editing

Cairo *
US 1942 100m bw
MGM (Joseph L. Mankiewicz)
An American war reporter in Egypt meets a screen
star and thinks she is a spy.
*Mildly pleasing light comedy-drama with self-spoofing
elements.*
w John McClain *d* W. S. Van Dyke II *ph* Ray
June *md* Herbert Stothart
☆ Jeanette MacDonald, Robert Young, Ethel
Waters, Reginald Owen, Lionel Atwill, Mona
Barrie, Eduardo Ciannelli, Dennis Hoey, Dooley
Wilson
'Confusing if not amusing.' – *Variety*

Cairo
GB 1963 91m bw
MGM (Ronald Kinnoch)
▥
Crooks plan to steal Tutankhamun's jewels from
the Cairo Museum.
Spiritless remake of The Asphalt Jungle (qv).
w Joanne Court *d* Wolf Rilla *ph* Desmond
Dickinson *m* Kenneth V. Jones
☆ George Sanders, Richard Johnson, Faten
Hamama, John Meillon, Eric Pohlmann, Walter
Rilla

Cairo Road
GB 1950 95m bw
ABP (Aubrey Baring)
An Egyptian police chief lays traps for drug
smugglers.
*Oddly cast, reasonably lively but routine police
adventure in an unfamiliar setting.*
w Robert Westerby *d* David MacDonald
ph Oswald Morris *m* Robert Gill
☆ Eric Portman, Laurence Harvey, Maria
Mauban, Karel Stepanek, Harold Lang, Camelia,
Grégoire Aslan, Oscar Quitak

Cairo Station
Egypt 1958 95m bw
Gabriel Talhami
original title: *Bab El Hadid*
A crippled newspaper seller goes mad through
thwarted love.
Popular melodrama, acted with verve.
d Youssef Chahine *ph* Alvise *m* Fouad El Zahiry
ad Gabriel Karraze *ed* Kamal Abul Ela
☆ Farid Chawki, Hind Rostom, Youssef Chahine,
Safia Sarwat, Assaad Kellam, Sherine

Cal *
GB 1984 102m colour
Warner/Goldcrest/Enigma (Stuart Craig, David
Puttnam)
▥ ▤ ◠
A young Catholic in Ulster falls for the widow of
the policeman in whose murder he has been an
accomplice.
*More clichés about the troubles: the film belies its
publicity as 'a love story which happens to take place in
Northern Ireland'. But it has style.*
w Bernard MacLaverty *novel* Bernard MacLaverty
d Pat O'Connor *ph* Jerzy Zielinski *m* Mark
Knopfler *pd* Stuart Craig
☆ Helen Mirren, John Lynch, Donal McCann,
John Kavanagh, Ray McAnally

Calabuch *
Spain/Italy 1956 93m bw
Aguila/Constellaxione (José Luis Jerez)
An atomic scientist settles delightedly in a
peaceful Spanish village, but sacrifices his own
privacy when he invents a sky rocket.
*Semi-satirical Ealing-type comedy which starts
engagingly but runs out of steam.*
w Leonardo Martin, Ennio Flaiano, Florentino
Soria, Luis Berlanga *d* Luis Berlanga *ph* Francisco
Sempere *m* Francesco Lavagnino
☆ *Edmund Gwenn*, Valentina Cortese, Franco
Fabrizi

Calamity Jane **
↟↟ US 1953 101m Technicolor
Warner (William Jacobs)
▥ ▤ ◠
Calamity helps a saloon owner friend find a star
attraction, and wins the heart of Wild Bill Hickok.
*Agreeable, cleaned-up, studio-set Western musical
patterned after Annie Get Your Gun, but a much
friendlier film, helped by an excellent score.*
w James O'Hanlon *d* David Butler *ph* Wilfrid
Cline *m/ly* Sammy Fain, Paul Francis Webster
md Ray Heindorf *ch* Jack Donohue
☆ *Doris Day, Howard Keel*, Allyn McLerie, Phil
Carey, Dick Wesson, Paul Harvey
♩ song 'Secret Love'
↧ Ray Heindorf

Calamity Jane and Sam Bass
US 1949 85m Technicolor
Universal-International
Sam Bass murders the man who poisoned his horse,
becomes an outlaw, and tangles with Jane
Carraway.
Routine Western programmer from this stable.
w Maurice Geraghty, Melvin Levy *d* George
Sherman
☆ Yvonne de Carlo, Howard Duff, Dorothy Hart,
Willard Parker, Houseley Stevenson, Ann Doran,
Norman Lloyd

Calculated Risk
GB 1963 72m bw
Bryanston/William McLeod
A convict comes out of prison to plan a bank
robbery.
*Moderate second-feature thriller, competently done but
unexciting and unoriginal.*
w Edwin Richfield *d* Norman Harrison
ph William McLeod *m* George Martin *ad* John
St John Earl *ed* John Trumper
☆ William Lucas, John Rutland, Dilys Watling,
Shay Gorman, Terence Cooper, David Brierley,
Warren Mitchell

Calcutta
US 1946 83m bw
Paramount (Seton I. Miller)
Two flyers seek the murderer of their friend in the
hotels and bazaars of Calcutta.
*Studio-bound action potboiler, simple-minded but quite
good fun.*
w Seton I. Miller *d* John Farrow *ph* John F. Seitz
m Victor Young
☆ Alan Ladd, Gail Russell, William Bendix, June
Duprez, Lowell Gilmore

Calendar
Canada/Germany 1993 75m colour
ZDF/Ego Film Arts
▤
A Canadian photographer of Armenian descent
recalls how his wife left him for his guide while
they were on assignment to photograph Armenian
churches for a calendar.
*A meditation on what it means to be Armenian and on
photography and its limitations. It is so personal to its
maker as to be somewhat impenetrable to anyone else;
at the least, it requires tolerance from the viewer.*
wd Atom Egoyan *ph* Norayr Kasper *m* Duduk
ed Atom Egoyan
☆ Arsinée Khanjian, Ashot Adamian, Atom
Egoyan
'The photographer has been freed from his
assimilation assignment, but at what cost? Given
the self-referential and revisionist subtext of the
film, this open-ended question evokes a sense of
genuine anticipatory excitement for Egoyan's
next venture.' – *Farrah Anwar, Sight and Sound*

Calendar Girl
US 1993 90m colour
Columbia/Parkway (Debbie Robins, Gary Marsh)
▥ ▤ ◠
Three 60s students go to Los Angeles in the hope
of meeting Marilyn Monroe.
*Uninteresting drama of teenage wish-fufilment that
may please fans of its star but few others.*
w Paul W. Shapiro *d* John Whitesell *ph* Tom
Priestley *m* Hans Zimmer *pd* Bill Groom
ed Wendy Greene Bricmont
☆ Jason Priestley, Gabriel Olds, Jerry O'Connell,
Joe Pantoliano, Steve Railsback, Kurt Fuller,
Stephen Tobolowsky, Chubby Checker
'A dull, sanctimonious morality tale about the
meaning of friendship and manhood.' – *Variety*

'No town would have her! No man could tame her!'

California
US 1946 97m Technicolor
Paramount (Seton I. Miller)
An army deserter joins the 1848 California gold
rush.
*Standard glamorized star Western; not bad if you
accept the conventions.*
w Frank Butler, Theodore Strauss *d* John Farrow
ph Ray Rennahan *m* Victor Young
☆ Ray Milland, Barbara Stanwyck, Barry
Fitzgerald, Albert Dekker, George Coulouris,
Anthony Quinn
'It quickly loses its stirrups and ends up caught
by the chaps in a bed of cactus.' – *Newsweek*

California Conquest
US 1952 79m Technicolor
Columbia (Sam Katzman)
Spanish Californians band together against
Russian would-be invaders.
*Tedious and unsympathetic historical Western on a 'B'
budget.*
w Robert E. Kent *d* Lew Landers
☆ Cornel Wilde, Teresa Wright, Alfonso Bedoya,
Lisa Ferraday, Ivan Lebedeff, John Dehner

The California Dolls: see *All the Marbles*

California Holiday: see *Spinout*

California Man: see *Encino Man*

California Split *
US 1974 109m Metrocolor Panavision
Columbia/Persky-Bright/Reno (Robert Altman, Joseph
Walsh)
Two cheerful gamblers get drunk, laid, cheated and
happy.
*Sporadically entertaining character comedy sunk in a
sea of chatter.*
w Joseph Walsh *d* Robert Altman *ph* Paul
Lohmann *m* Phyllis Shotwell
☆ Elliott Gould, George Segal, Gwen Welles,
Ann Prentiss, Joseph Walsh
'The film seems to be being improvised ... we
catch at events and personalities by the ends of
threads.' – *New Yorker*
† An end title reads: FOR BARBARA,
1933–1973. This was Barbara Ruick, who played
the barmaid and died on location.

California Straight Ahead *
US 1937 57m bw
Universal (Trem Carr)
A nationwide race is held between a special train
and a convoy of high-powered trucks.
*Unusual and quite lively second feature shot on
location.*
w Scott Darling *story* Herman Boxer *d* Arthur
Lubin *ph* Harry Neumann *m* Charles Previn
☆ John Wayne, Louise Latimer, Robert McWade,
Tully Marshall
'Everything happens as the audience expects and
wishes, so in its field it will do okay.' – *Variety*

California Suite *
US 1978 103m colour
Columbia/Ray Stark
▥ ▤ ◠
Misadventures of four groups of guests at the
Beverly Hills Hotel.
*Two hits, two misses; closer intercutting might have
helped. No doubt that Maggie Smith and Michael
Caine come off best, with bitcheries about the
Academy Awards.*
w Neil Simon *play* Neil Simon *d* Herbert Ross
ph David M. Walsh *m* Claude Bolling *pd* Albert
Brenner
☆ Michael Caine, Maggie Smith, Walter
Matthau, Elaine May, Alan Alda, Jane Fonda,
Richard Pryor, Bill Cosby
'By turns silly and thoughtful, tedious and
charming, broad and delicate.' – *Frank Rich*
♙ Maggie Smith
↧ Neil Simon; art direction

'What would you have done if you had been given
absolute power of life and death over everyone else
in the whole wide world?'

Caligula
Italy/US 1979 150m Eastmancolor
GTO/Felix/Penthouse Films (Bob Guccione, Franco
Rossellini)
▥ ▤ ◠ ⏀
The violent life and times of a decadent Roman
emperor.
*What would have been a dull and worthless pseudo-
epic has been perked up by violence and hardcore sex.
The result is a vile curiosity of interest chiefly to sado-
masochists.*
w Bob Guccione *screenplay* Gore Vidal *d* Tinto
Brass, Giancarlo Lui, Bob Guccione *ph* Danilo
Donati *m* Paul Clemente *ed* Nino Bragli
☆ Malcolm McDowell, John Gielgud, Peter
O'Toole, Helen Mirren, Teresa Ann Savoy, John
Steiner
'An anthology of sexual aberrations in which
incest is the only face-saving relationship ... far
more Gore than Vidal.' – *Variety*
'It just keeps rolling along at inordinate length,
suggesting de Mille grinding slowly to a frequent
stoppage for a display of bums, breasts and pubic
hair.' – *Time Out*

Call a Messenger
US 1939 65m bw
Universal
Working as telegraph messengers, the Little Tough
Guys prevent a hold-up.
*Second-feature offshoot of the Dead End Kids, some of
whom had now departed to become the East Side Kids
(who later blossomed forth as the Bowery Boys).*
w Arthur T. Horman *d* Arthur Lubin
☆ Billy Halop, Huntz Hall, Billy Benedict, David
Gorcey, Robert Armstrong, Mary Carlisle, Anne
Nagel, Victor Jory, El Brendel, Larry 'Buster'
Crabbe
'A rowdy, gripping production patterned as
heavy bolstering in dual set-ups.' – *Variety*

Call Harry Crown: see *99 and 44/100 Per Cent
Dead*

Call Her Savage *
US 1932 88m bw
Paramount (Sam E. Rork)
Trials and tribulations of a half-breed Indian girl
who marries a cad and later takes to the streets.
*Rough and ready melodrama for female audiences; the
penultimate appearance of a star who did not take to
talkies.*
w Edwin Burke *novel* Tiffany Thayer *d* John
Francis Dillon *ph* Lee Garmes
☆ Clara Bow, Gilbert Roland, Monroe Owsley,
Thelma Todd, Estelle Taylor
'The return of Clara Bow in a madcap role
makes a natural ... the result is bound to be
money.' – *Variety*

Call Him Mr Shatter: see *Shatter*

Call Him Savage
France/Italy 1975 103m colour
Lira/Produzioni Artistiche Internazionali (Raymond
Danon)
aka: *Lovers Like Us*
A French *parfumier*, trying to escape from his
business, meets a woman on the run from her
Venezuelan fiancé.
Dim attempt at a romantic comedy.
w Jean-Paul Rappeneau, Elizabeth Rappeneau,
Jean-Loup Dabadie *d* Jean-Paul Rappeneau
ph Pierre Lhomme *m* Michel Legrand *ed* Marie-
Joseph Yoyotte
☆ Yves Montand, Catherine Deneuve, Tony
Roberts, Luigi Vannucchi, Dana Wynter

Call It a Day *
US 1937 89m bw
Warner (Henry Blanke)
An upper-class British family has problems during a single day.
Surprising, and not very effective, Hollywood treatment of a very British comedy.
w Casey Robinson *play* Dodie Smith d Archie Mayo *ph* Ernest Haller
☆ Olivia de Havilland, Ian Hunter, Anita Louise, Alice Brady, Roland Young, Frieda Inescort, Bonita Granville, Peggy Wood, Walter Woolf King, Una O'Connor, Beryl Mercer
'A fine cast rowing a very thin boat ... charm, many a giggle but nary a sock laugh.' – *Variety*

Call It Murder: see *Midnight*

Call Me Bwana *
GB 1962 93m Eastmancolor
Rank/Eon (Harry Saltzman, Albert R. Broccoli)
A fake African explorer is sent to the jungle to recover a space capsule.
Moderate star farce with occasional bright moments.
w Nate Monaster, Johanna Harwood d Gordon Douglas *ph* Ted Moore m Monty Norman
☆ Bob Hope, Anita Ekberg, Edie Adams, Lionel Jeffries, Percy Herbert, Paul Carpenter, Orlando Martins

Call Me Genius: see *The Rebel*

Call Me Madam ***
US 1953 114m Technicolor
TCF (Sol C. Siegel)
A Washington hostess is appointed Ambassador to Lichtenberg and marries the foreign minister.
Studio-bound but thoroughly lively transcription of Irving Berlin's last big success, with most of the performers at their peak and some topical gags which may now be mystifying.
w Arthur Sheekman *play* Howard Lindsay, Russel Crouse d Walter Lang *m* Leon Shamroy *m/ly* Irving Berlin *md* Alfred Newman *ch* Robert Alton
☆ Ethel Merman, Donald O'Connor, George Sanders, Vera-Ellen, Billy de Wolfe, Helmut Dantine, Walter Slezak, Steve Geray, Ludwig Stossel
'Good-tempered, warm, generous and about as quiet as a massed brass band festival.' – *Dilys Powell*
† Vera-Ellen's singing was dubbed by Carole Richards
♫ 'The Hostess with the Mostes"; 'Can You Use Any Money Today?'; 'Marrying for Love'; 'It's a Lovely Day Today'; 'That International Rag'; 'The Ocarina'; 'What Chance Have I with Love?'; 'The Best Thing for You'; 'Something to Dance About'; 'You're Just in Love'.
♦ Alfred Newman

Call Me Mister
US 1951 95m Technicolor
TCF (Fred Kohlmar)
A husband and wife dance team entertain the troops in Japan and after the war.
Passable musical of a very predictable kind.
w Albert E. Lewin, Burt Styler *book* Arnold Auerbach, Arnold B. Horwitt d Lloyd Bacon *ph* Arthur E. Arling m Harold Rome *m/ly* various *ch* Busby Berkeley
☆ Betty Grable, Dan Dailey, Danny Thomas, Dale Robertson, Richard Boone

Call Northside 777 **
US 1948 111m bw
TCF (Otto Lang)
A Chicago reporter helps a washerwoman prove her son not guilty of murdering a policeman.
Overlong semi-documentary crime thriller based on a real case. Acting and detail excellent, but the sharp edge of Boomerang is missing.
w Jerome Cady, Jay Dratler d Henry Hathaway *ph* Joe MacDonald m Alfred Newman
☆ James Stewart, Lee J. Cobb, Helen Walker, Kasia Orzazewski, Betty Garde, Richard Conte
'A most satisfying thriller, generously streaked with class.' – *Daily Mail*
'Absorbing, exciting, realistic.' – *Star*

Call of the Wild *
♠♠ US 1935 81m bw
Twentieth Century (Darryl F. Zanuck)
A young widow falls in love with a wild Yukon prospector.
Inaccurate but pleasing adaptation of an adventure novel with dog interest.
w Gene Fowler, Leonard Praskins *novel* Jack London d William Wellman *ph* Charles Rosher m Alfred Newman
☆ Clark Gable, Loretta Young, Jack Oakie, Reginald Owen, Frank Conroy
'The lion-hearted dog emerges as a stooge for a rather conventional pair of human lovebirds ... looks like box office.' – *Variety*

Call of the Wild
♠♠ GB/W. Germany/Spain/Italy/France 1972 105m Eastmancolor
Massfilms/CCC/Izaro/Oceania/UPF (Harry Alan Towers)
■■
During the Klondike gold rush, a stolen dog becomes a miner's best friend before joining the wolf-pack.
Closer to the book than the previous version, but curiously scrappy and unsatisfactory.
w Harry Alan Towers, Wyn Wells, Peter Yeldham d Ken Annakin *ph* John Cabrera, Dudley Lovell m Carlo Rustichelli
☆ Charlton Heston, Michèle Mercier, Raimund Harmstorf, George Eastman

Call Out the Marines *
US 1942 67m bw
RKO
■■
Two adventurers re-enlist in the Marines and foil a spy plot.
The last of many action comedies featuring the original Flagg and Quirt from What Price Glory?
wd Frank Ryan, William Hamilton
☆ Victor McLaglen, Edmund Lowe, Binnie Barnes, Paul Kelly, Franklin Pangborn

Call the Cops!: see *Find the Lady*

Callan *
GB 1974 106m Eastmancolor
EMI/Magnum (Derek Horne)
■■
aka: The Neutralizer
A former secret agent is seconded to a government section devoted to the elimination of undesirables.
Expanded rewrite of the first episode of a long-running TV series, quite fresh and vivid in the circumstances, especially as it comes at the tail end of ten years of similar bouts of blood and thunder.
w James Mitchell *novel* A Magnum for Schneider by James Mitchell d Don Sharp *ph* Ernest Steward m Wilfred Josephs
☆ Edward Woodward, Eric Porter, Carl Mohner, Catherine Schell, Peter Egan, Russell Hunter, Kenneth Griffith

Callaway Went Thataway *
US 1951 81m bw
MGM (Melvin Frank, Norman Panama)
GB title: *The Star Said No*
The old movies of a Hollywood cowboy become popular on TV, but the star has become a hopeless drunk and an actor is hired to pose as him for public appearances.
Reasonably engaging comedy using charm rather than acid.
wd Melvin Frank, Norman Panama *ph* Ray June m Marlin Skiles
☆ Dorothy McGuire, Fred MacMurray, Howard Keel, Jesse White, Natalie Schafer

Calle Mayor *
Spain/France 1956 95m bw
Play Art Iberia/Cesareo Gonzales
aka: Grande Rue
In a small Spanish town, a young stud pretends for a bet to be in love with a plain spinster.
Interesting but rather unattractive and certainly unconvincing little comedy-drama, rather too obviously styled for its American star after her success in Marty.
wd Juan Antonio Bardem *ph* Michel Kelber m Joseph Kosma
☆ Betsy Blair, Yves Massard, René Blancard, Lila Kedrova

Calling Bulldog Drummond
GB 1951 80m bw
MGM (Hayes Goetz)
Drummond goes undercover to catch a gang of thieves.
Minor-league quota quickie addition to the exploits of a long-running character (see Bulldog Drummond).
w Howard Emmett Rogers, Gerard Fairlie, Arthur Wimperis d Victor Saville *ph* F. A. Young m Rudolph Kopp
☆ Walter Pidgeon, Margaret Leighton, Robert Beatty, David Tomlinson, Peggy Evans, Charles Victor, Bernard Lee, James Hayter

'Terror strikes as a madman rules!'
Calling Doctor Death
US 1943 63m bw
Universal
A doctor's wife is murdered; her lover is arrested; but did the doctor himself do it?
Probably not, as the tendency of the tinpot Inner Sanctum series, of which this was the first, was to make its star look anguished for six reels and then show him to be as innocent as the film was (mercifully) short.
w Edward Dein d Reginald Le Borg
☆ Lon Chaney, Patricia Morison, Fay Helm, David Bruce, Ramsay Ames, J. Carrol Naish

Calling Dr Gillespie *
US 1942 84m bw
MGM
A deranged ex-patient breaks into Blair Hospital for the purpose of killing Dr Gillespie.
The point at which cranky old wheelchair-bound Dr Gillespie took over the Kildare series, its star (Lew Ayres) having effectually abdicated from acting by declaring himself a conscientious objector. Production values up to par.
w Kubec Glasmon, Willis Goldbeck, Harry Ruskin d Harold S. Bucquet
☆ Lionel Barrymore, Philip Dorn, Phil Brown, Donna Reed, Nat Pendleton, Mary Nash, Alma Kruger, Walter Kingsford
† See *Dr Kildare* for titles in series.

Calling Dr Kildare *
US 1939 86m bw
MGM
Kildare becomes innocently involved in murder and needs Dr Gillespie's help.
The second in the Kildare series had the confidence that comes of box-office approval.
w Harry Ruskin, Willis Goldbeck d Harold S. Bucquet
☆ Lew Ayres, Lionel Barrymore, Lana Turner, Nat Pendleton, Samuel S. Hinds, Laraine Day, Alma Kruger

Calling Philo Vance *
US 1939 62m bw
Warner
A manufacturer is murdered and foreign agents are discovered among his servants.
Essentially a remake of The Kennel Murder Case; inferior as a whole, but with an excellent new Vance.
w Tom Reed d William Clemens
☆ James Stephenson, Margot Stevenson, Henry O'Neill, Ed Brophy, Ralph Forbes, Martin Kosleck

Calm Yourself
US 1935 70m bw
MGM
An advertising man helps solve a kidnapping.
Spoofy comedy-drama which simply doesn't work.
w Edward Hope, Arthur Kober d George B. Seitz
☆ Robert Young, Madge Evans, Betty Furness, Nat Pendleton, Hardie Albright, Ralph Morgan
'Strictly for the not too particular nabe clientele.' – *Variety*

Caluga o Menta
Chile 1991 90m colour
Arca/TVE/Filmocentro (Patricia Navarrete)
aka: Candy or Mint
In Santiago, a gang of disaffected youngsters turn to crime and drug-running to relieve the everyday monotony of their lives.
A downbeat study of no-hopers, filmed with a partly non-professional cast, which is mainly of sociological interest.
w Gonzalo Justiniano, Gustavo Frias, Jose Andres Peña d Gonzalo Justiniano *ph* Gaston Roca m Jaime de Aguirre *ed* Claudio Martinez

☆ Mauricio Vega, Patricia Rivadeneira, Aldo Parodi, Myriam Palacios

Camelot **
♠♠ US 1967 181m Technicolor
Panavision 70
Warner (Jack L. Warner)
■■ ■■ ⚙ ⚙ 🎧
King Arthur marries Guinevere, loses her to Lancelot, and is forced into war.
A film version of a long-running Broadway show with many excellent moments. Unfortunately the director cannot make up his mind whether to go for style or realism, and has chosen actors who cannot sing. The result is cluttered and overlong, with no real sense of period or sustained imagination, but the photography and the music linger in the mind.
w Alan Jay Lerner *novel* The Once And Future King by T. H. White d Joshua Logan *ph* Richard H. Kline *m/ly* Frederick Loewe, Alan Jay Lerner *md* Ken Darby, Alfred Newman *ad* Edward Carrere *pd/costumes* John Truscott
☆ Richard Harris, Vanessa Redgrave, David Hemmings, Lionel Jeffries, Laurence Naismith, Franco Nero
'One wonders whether the fashion for musicals in which only the chorus can actually sing may be reaching its final stage.' – *MFB*
'Three hours of unrelieved glossiness, meticulous inanity, desperate and charmless striving for charm.' – *John Simon*
'The sets and costumes and people seem to be sitting there on the screen, waiting for the unifying magic that never happens.' – *New Yorker, 1977*
† Franco Nero's singing was dubbed by Gene Merlina
♫ 'The Merry Month of May'; 'Camelot'; 'If Ever I Would Leave You'; 'Take Me to the Fair'; 'C'est Moi'
♦ art direction; costumes; music direction
♢ cinematography

The Camels are Coming
GB 1934 80m bw
Gainsborough (Michael Balcon)
An officer in the camel corps catches Egyptian drug smugglers.
Light, bouncy star vehicle.
w Jack Hulbert, Guy Bolton, W. P. Lipscomb d Tim Whelan *ph* Glen MacWilliams, Bernard Knowles m Ray Noble, Max Kester, Noel Gay *md* Louis Levy *ad* Oscar Werndorff *ed* Frederick Y. Smith
☆ Jack Hulbert, Anna Lee, Hartley Power, Harold Huth, Allan Jeayes

Camera Buff *
Poland 1979 112m colour
Cinegate/Zespoly Filmowe/Film Polski
original title: *Amator*
A factory worker finds himself in conflict with his bosses when he becomes obsessed with making films at work.
Lively political allegory.
wd Krzysztof Kieslowski *ph* Jacek Petrycki m Krzysztof Knittel *ad* Rafal Waltenberger *ed* Halina Nawrocka
☆ Jerzy Stuhr, Malgorzata Zabkowska, Ewa Pokas, Stefan Czyzewski, Jerzy Nowak, Tadeusz Bradecki, Krzysztof Zanussi

The Cameraman ***
US 1928 78m bw silent
MGM (Lawrence Weingarten)
■■ ⚙
In order to woo a film star, a street photographer becomes a newsreel cameraman.
Highly regarded chapter of farcical errors, among the star's top features.
w Clyde Bruckman, Lex Lipton, Richard Schayer d Edward Sedgwick *ph* Elgin Lessley, Reggie Manning
☆ Buster Keaton, Marceline Day, Harry Gribbon, Harold Goodwin
† The film was remade in 1948 for Red Skelton as *Watch the Birdie*, with Keaton supervising the gags but sadly getting no credit.

The Cameraman's Revenge **
Russia   1912   11m   bw/tinted
Ladislaw Starewicz
📺

Two beetles, a brother and a sister, try to conceal their marriages from one another so that they may inherit the family fortune of a pot of beer.
An early and still impressive example of stop-motion animation.
wd Ladislaw Starewicz m Roger White
† The film has been released on video with the feature-length *The Tale of the Fox* (qv) and four other shorts under the title *Ladislaw Starewicz: Selected Films.*

Cameron's Closet
US   1987   87m   colour
Medusa/Smart Egg (Luigi Cingolani)
📺 ▦ 🎧

Subjected by his father to experiments in psychokinesis, a boy summons up a demon.
Ineffectual horror, with a boring monster.
w Gary Brandner novel Gary Brandner d Armand Mastroianni ph Russell Carpenter m Harry Manfredini pd Michael Bingham ed Frank de Palma
☆ Cotter Smith, Mel Harris, Scott Curtis, Chuck McCann, Leigh McCloskey, Kim Lankford
'The contents of this particular closet are decidedly shop-worn and second-hand.' – MFB

Camila **
Argentina/Spain   1984   97m   colour
GEA Cinematografica/Impala (Lila Stanic)
In Argentina in the 1840s the strong-willed daughter of an upper-class family scandalizes Church and government by eloping with a priest.
A powerful drama that manages to say much about present-day repression despite its period setting.
w Maria Luisa Bemberg, Beda Docampo Feijoo, Juan Bautista Stagnaro d Maria Luisa Bemberg ph Fernando Arribas m Luis Maria Serra ad Miguel Rodriguez ed Luis Cesar D'Angiolillo
☆ Susu Pecoraro, Imanol Arias, Hector Alterio, Carlos Muñoz, Hector Pelligrini, Juan Levrado, Cecilio Madanes, Mona Maris, Elena Tasisto

Camilla
GB/Canada   1994   95m   Colour
Entertainment/Shaftesbury/Skreba (Christina Jennings, Simon Relph)
📺 ▦

An unhappily married woman, a frustrated musician, abandons her husband and goes on the road with an elderly former concert violinist, anxious to get away from her son.
Jessica Tandy, in her last role, provides the watchable moments in an otherwise undernourished and meandering movie that covers a lot of ground without getting anywhere very interesting.
w Paul Quarrington story Ali Jennings d Deepa Mehta ph Guy Dufeau m Daniel Lanois pd Sandra Kybartas ed Barry Farrell
☆ Jessica Tandy, Bridget Fonda, Elias Koteas, Maury Chaykin, Hume Cronyn, Graham Greene
'Endless drollery and treacle, with amiable eccentrics lurking at every pit-stop.' – Jonathan Romney, Guardian

'You who are so young – where can you have learned all you know about women like me?'
'Their lips meet for the first time … a superb thrill seared in your memory forever!'

Camille **
US   1937   108m   bw
MGM (Irving Thalberg, Bernard Hyman)
▦ 🎧

A dying courtesan falls for an innocent young man who loves her, and dies in his arms.
This old warhorse is an unsuitable vehicle for Garbo but magically she carries it off, and the production is elegant and pleasing.
w Frances Marion, James Hilton, Zoe Akins novel Alexandre Dumas d George Cukor ph William Daniels m Herbert Stothart
☆ Greta Garbo, Robert Taylor, Lionel Barrymore, Henry Daniell, Elizabeth Allan, Lenore Ulric, Laura Hope Crews, Rex O'Malley, Jessie Ralph, E. E. Clive
'Pretty close to the top mark in showmanship, direction, photography and box office names.' – Variety
'The slow, solemn production is luxuriant in its vulgarity: it achieves that glamor which MGM

traditionally mistook for style.' – Pauline Kael, 1968
'The surprise is to find a story that should by rights be old hat coming to such insistent life on the screen.' – Otis Ferguson
'It steadily builds up an impression of being a spectacle of manners and fashions, a socially true background for its characters to move against.' – National Board of Review
'This is not death as mortals know it. This is but the conclusion of a romantic ritual.' – Bosley Crowther
† A 1927 silent version starred Norma Talmadge with Gilbert Roland.
🏆 Greta Garbo

Camille Claudel **
France   1988   174m   colour   Panavision
Cannon/Films Christian Fechner/Lilith Films/Gaumont/A2 TV France/Films A2/DD Productions (Bernard Artigues)
📺 ▦ 🎧

A talented sculptress becomes Rodin's pupil and mistress with tragic results.
Overlong, and lacking a visual flair to match its subject, but nevertheless engrossing for the most part.
w Bruno Nuytten, Marilyn Goldin book Reine-Marie Paris d Bruno Nuytten ph Pierre Lhomme m Gabriel Yared ad Bernard Vezat ed Joëlle Hache, Jeanne Kef
☆ Isabelle Adjani, Gérard Depardieu, Laurent Grevill, Alain Cuny, Philippe Clevenot, Katrine Boorman, Danielle Lebrun, Maxime Leroux
'As a cultural coffee-table artefact, it has everything.' – Tom Milne, MFB
🏆 Isabelle Adjani; best foreign film

El Camino del Sur: see Journey to the South

Il Cammino della Speranza *
Italy   1950   105m   bw
Lux (Luigi Rovere)
aka: The Road to Hope
Unemployed Sicilian miners travel to France in search of work.
Episodic location melodrama with a social conscience, a kind of Italian Grapes of Wrath. Very watchable, but not moving.
w Federico Fellini, Tullio Pinelli d Pietro Germi ph Leonido Barboni m Carlo Rustichelli
☆ Raf Vallone, Elena Varzi, Saro Urzi, Franco Navarra

Camorra: the Naples Connection
Italy   1985   106m   colour
Cannon/Italian International (Menahem Golan, Yoram Globus)
original title: Un complicato intrigo di donne, vicoli e delitto
Mothers take revenge on the drug dealers who have killed their children.
Highly charged, full of sound and fury and signifying very little.
w Lina Wertmuller, Elvio Porta d Lina Wertmuller ph Giuseppe Lanci m Tony Esposito ad Enrico Job ed Luigi Zita
☆ Angela Molina, Francisco Rabal, Harvey Keitel, Daniel Ezralow

Camp de Thiaroye **
Senegal/Algeria/Tunisia   1988   152m   colour
Metro/SNPC/ENAPROC/SATPEC (Mamadou Mbengue)
African soldiers, returning home after fighting in the Second World War, are massacred in a dispute over pay.
Powerful indictment of colonialism.
wd Ousmane Sembène, Thierno Faty Sow ph Ismail Lakhdar Hamina m Ismaila Lo ad El hadj Abdoulaye Diouf ed Kahena Attia-Riveill
☆ Ibrahima Sane, Sigiri Bakara, Hamed Camara, Ismaila Cissé, Ababacar Sy Cissé

Camp Nowhere
👨‍👧 US   1994   96m   Technicolor
Buena Vista/Hollywood (Michael Peyser)
📺 ▦

A group of disaffected kids decide to create their own summer camp to escape from their parents' expectations.
Moderate comedy that pretends to be rebellious before settling for an affirmation of family values.
w Andrew Kurtzman, Eliot Wald d Jonathan Prince ph Sandi Sissel m David Lawrence pd Rusty Smith ed Jon Poll, David Street

☆ Christopher Lloyd, Wendy Makkena, M. Emmet Walsh, Jonathan Jackson, Andrew Keegan, Melody Kay, Ray Baker, Kate Mulgrew, Burgess Meredith
'Interesting premise needed more than the so-so treatment delivered here.' – Variety

The Camp on Blood Island
GB   1958   81m   bw   MegaScope
Columbia/Hammer (Anthony Hinds)
The sadistic commandant of a Japanese POW camp swears to kill all the inmates. Japan surrenders, and a great effort is made to prevent the news from reaching him.
Dubious melodrama parading sadism and brutality as entertainment.
w Jon Manchip White, Val Guest d Val Guest ph Jack Asher m Gerard Schurmann ad John Stoll ed James Needs, Bill Lenny
☆ André Morell, Carl Mohner, Edward Underdown, Michael Goodliffe, Ronald Radd, Walter Fitzgerald, Phil Brown, Barbara Shelley, Michael Gwynn, Richard Wordsworth, Marne Maitland, Mary Merrall

Campbell's Kingdom *
GB   1957   102m   Eastmancolor
Rank (Betty E. Box)
A young man who thinks he is dying arrives in the Canadian Rockies to take over his father's oil valley, but a scheming contractor opposes him.
Competent and entertaining romantic thick ear.
w Robin Estridge novel Hammond Innes d Ralph Thomas ph Ernest Steward m Clifton Parker
☆ Dirk Bogarde, Michael Craig, Stanley Baker, Barbara Murray, Athene Seyler, Mary Merrall, James Robertson Justice
'Yet another large budget British film doggedly maintaining a B-picture standard' – John Osborne, London Evening Standard

Campfire Tales
US   1996   83m   Foto-Kem/bw
Vault/Kunert/Manes (Eric Manes, Lori Miller, Larry Weinberg)
📺 ▦

After crashing their car on a remote road at night, four teenagers shelter in a ruined church and tell each other horror stories.
A compendium of three stories, each favouring a slow build-up to moments of shock and content, for the most part to retread over-familiar ways.
w Martin Kunert, Eric Manes, Matt Cooper d David Semel, Martin Kunert, Matt Cooper ph John Peters m Andrew Rose pd Shay Austin ed Luis Colina, Steve Nevius, Richard H. Fields
☆ Jay R. Ferguson, Christine Taylor, Christopher Kennedy Masterson, Kim Murphy, Ron Livingston, Jennifer MacDonald, Hawthorne James, Alex McKenna, Devon Odessa, Jonathan Fuller
'A superior horror compendium.' – Sight and Sound

Can Can
US   1960   131m   DeLuxe   Todd-AO
TCF/Suffolk-Cummings (Jack Cummings)
▦ 🎧 🎵

A Parisian night-club dancer in the 90s is sued for performing the Can Can.
Flat film of a dull musical, with just a few plums in the pudding.
w Dorothy Kingsley, Charles Lederer play Abe Burrows d Walter Lang ph William Daniels m/ly Cole Porter md Nelson Riddle ch Hermes Pan
☆ Frank Sinatra, Shirley MacLaine, Maurice Chevalier, Louis Jourdan, Juliet Prowse, Marcel Dalio, Leon Belasco
🏆 Nelson Riddle

Can Hieronymus Merkin Ever Forget Mercy Humppe and Find True Happiness?
GB   1969   117m   Technicolor
Universal/Taralex (Anthony Newley)
A performer on a beach assembles a huge pile of personal bric-à-brac and reminisces about his life in the style of a variety show.
Obscure and pointless personal fantasy, financed at great expense by a major film company as a rather seedy monument to Anthony Newley's totally uninteresting sex life, and to the talent which he

obviously thinks he possesses. The few mildly amusing moments are not provided by him.
w Herman Raucher, Anthony Newley d Anthony Newley ph Otto Heller m Anthony Newley
☆ Anthony Newley, Joan Collins, George Jessel, Milton Berle, Bruce Forsyth, Stubby Kaye, Patricia Hayes, Victor Spinetti
'If I'd been Anthony Newley I would have opened it in Siberia during Christmas week and called it a day.' – Rex Reed
'The kindest thing for all concerned would be that every available copy should be quietly and decently buried.' – Michael Billington, Illustrated London News

Can She Bake a Cherry Pie?
US   1983   90m   DuArt
Jagfilm/International Rainbow
▦

An abandoned wife has an experimental affair with a hypochondriac divorcé.
What the writer-director calls 'a bitter-sweet comedy about loneliness and love' has more to say to him than to an audience; but there are wryly amusing moments.
wd Henry Jaglom ph Robert Fiore
☆ Karen Black, Michael Emil, Michael Margotta, Frances Fisher

Can This Be Dixie?
US   1936   68m   bw
TCF (Sol M. Wurtzel)
In the old South, a medicine showman and his daughter help a bankrupt Kentucky colonel.
Agreeable supporting material, with elements of satire, spoof and musical comedy.
w Lamar Trotti d George Marshall
☆ Jane Withers, Slim Summerville, Claude Gillingwater, Helen Wood, Thomas Beck, Sara Haden, Donald Cook, Hattie McDaniel
'Plenty of ingredients were thrown into the soup … it will hold its own in the duals.' – Variety

Can You Keep It Up For A Week?
GB   1974   94m   Technicolor
Pyramid (Elton Hawke)
A woman tells her accident-prone lover that she will marry him only if he can hold down a job for seven days.
Little more than a succession of archly delivered double entendres, it enjoyed a surprising success at the time of its original release, though now it is merely indicative of the banality of the British film industry of the period.
w Robin Gough d Jim Atkinson ph Ricky Briggs m Dave Quincy md Harry South ad Jacquemine Charrott-Lodwige ed David Docker
☆ Jeremy Bulloch, Neil Hallett, Sue Longhurst, Jill Damas, Richard O'Sullivan, Jenny Cox, Joy Harrington, Valerie Leon
'Dreary sexual encounters, rudimentary direction and 94 minutes of witless Old English puns.' – David McGillivray
† The producer's name was a pseudonym for Hazel Adair, best known as co-creator of the TV soap opera Crossroads, and TV wrestling commentator Kent Walton.

Canadian Bacon
US   1995   90m   DeLuxe/bw
Polygram/Propaganda/Maverick (Michael Moore, David Brown, Ron Rotholz, Steve Golin)
📺 ▦

The American President, needing to boost his popularity by belligerence, decides that Canada is a threat to the free world.
A one-joke movie that will mean little outside North America, and not a great deal more inside it.
wd Michael Moore ph Haskell Wexler m Elmer Bernstein, Peter Bernstein pd Carol Spier ed Wendy Stanzler, Michael Berenbaum
☆ Alan Alda, John Candy, Rhea Perlman, Kevin Pollak, Rip Torn, Bill Nunn, Kevin J. O'Connor, G. D. Spradlin, Carlton Watson, James Belushi, Dan Aykroyd
'An amusing outing for a sophisticate crowd. More hip and flip than broadly humorous, pic is too much of an in-joke to translate to the mainstream.' – Variety

'The blazing saga of untamed men and a savage wilderness!'

Canadian Pacific

US   1949   95m   Cinecolor

TCF (Nat Holt)

A surveyor discovers the vital pass through the Rockies, and chooses between a lady doctor and a wilful half-breed.

Fairly unhistorical Western; watchable, though.

w Jack de Witt, Kenneth Gamet   d Edwin L. Marin

☆ Randolph Scott, Jane Wyatt, Nancy Olson, J. Carrol Naish, John Victor, Robert Barrat

The Canadians

GB/Canada   1961   85m   DeLuxe

Cinemascope

TCF (Herman E. Webber)

After Custer's defeat at Little Big Horn, 6,000 Sioux flee north and are victimized by villainous Canadians; but the Mounties come to the rescue.

Dreary, stumbling semi-Western which set back Canadian production by a year or two. The blame seems to be equally shared by all concerned.

wd Burt Kennedy   ph Arthur Ibbetson   m none

☆ Robert Ryan, John Dehner, Torin Thatcher, Burt Metcalfe, Teresa Stratas, Michael Pate, John Sutton

Cancel My Reservation

US   1972   99m   Technicolor

Naho Enterprises

A TV talk show host retreats to his ranch and finds himself mixed up with murder.

Bob Hope's last film, though it reverted to farce and his bumbling coward persona, proved a sorry affair with egg on the face of everybody concerned.

w Arthur Marx, Robert Fisher *novel* The Broken Gun by Louis L'Amour   d Paul Bogart

☆ Bob Hope, Eva Marie Saint, Ralph Bellamy, Forrest Tucker, Anne Archer, Keenan Wynn, Doodles Weaver

The Candidate ***

US   1972   110m   Technicolor

Warner/Redford-Ritchie (Walter Coblenz)

A young Californian lawyer is persuaded to run for senator; in succeeding, he alienates his wife and obscures his real opinions.

Put together in a slightly scrappy but finally persuasive style, this joins a select band of rousing, doubting American political films.

w Jeremy Larner   d Michael Ritchie   ph Victor J. Kemper   m John Rubinstein

☆ Robert Redford, Peter Boyle, *Don Porter*, Allen Garfield, Karen Carlson, Quinn Redeker, Morgan Upton, *Melvyn Douglas*

'Decent entertainment … it is never boring, but it is never enlarging, informationally or emotionally or thematically.' – *Stanley Kauffmann*

🏆 Jeremy Larner

Candide

France   1960   90m   bw

CLM/SN Pathé (Clément Duhour)

Ever optimistic, a 20th-century Candide tours Nazi prison camps, communist countries and various South American revolutions.

Scrappily-made satire which soon overstays its welcome.

wd Norbert Carbonneaux *novel* Voltaire   ph Robert Le Fèbvre   m Hubert Rostaing

☆ Jean-Pierre Cassel, Daliah Lavi, Pierre Brasseur, Nadia Gray, Michel Simon, Louis de Funès

Candlelight in Algeria

GB   1943   85m   bw

British Aviation

Spies seek whereabouts of Allied rendezvous.

Elementary spy thriller using modest talents.

w Katherine Strueby, Brock Williams   d George King

☆ Carla Lehmann, James Mason, Walter Rilla, Raymond Lovell, Enid Stamp Taylor

Candles at Nine

GB   1944   86m   bw

British National

A young heiress in her benefactor's old mansion is menaced by her housekeeper.

Elementary Cat and the Canary reprise; cast understandably uneasy.

w John Harlow, Basil Mason *novel* Anthony Gilbert   d John Harlow

☆ Jessie Matthews, John Stuart, Beatrix Lehmann, Winifred Shotter, Reginald Purdell

Candleshoe

👪   GB   1977   101m   Technicolor

Walt Disney Productions (Hugh Attwooll)

An attempt to pass off a fake heiress to an English stately home is prevented by the resourceful butler.

Slackly handled comedy adventure full of easy targets and predictable incidents.

w David Swift, Rosemary Anne Sisson *novel* Christmas at Candleshoe by Michael Innes   d Norman Tokar   ph Paul Beeson   m Ron Goodwin

☆ David Niven, Helen Hayes, Jodie Foster, Leo McKern, Veronica Quilligan, Ian Sharrock, Vivian Pickles

'It might have been conceived by a computer called upon to produce the definitive pastiche of a Disney film of the 1970s.' – *Financial Times*

Candy

US/France/Italy   1968   124m   Technicolor

Selmur/Dear/Corona (Robert Haggiag)

An innocent girl defends herself from a fate worse than death in a variety of international situations.

Witless and charmless perversion of a sex satire in which the point (if any) was that the nymphet gladly surrendered herself to all the gentlemen for their own good. A star cast flounders helplessly in a morass of bad taste, bad film-making, and boredom.

w Buck Henry *novel* Terry Southern   d Christian Marquand   ph Giuseppe Rotunno   m Dave Grusin

☆ Ewa Aulin, Richard Burton, Marlon Brando, James Coburn, Walter Matthau, Charles Aznavour, John Huston, Elsa Martinelli, Ringo Starr, John Astin

'Hippy psychedelics are laid on with the self-destroying effect of an overdose of garlic.' – *MFB*

'As an emetic, liquor is dandy, but Candy is quicker.' – *John Simon*

The Candy Man

US   1968   98m   Eastmancolor

Sagittarius

A British drug pusher in Mexico City plots the kidnap of an American film star's child.

Abysmal independent thriller with a star at the end of his tether.

wd Herbert J. Leder

☆ George Sanders, Leslie Parrish, Gina Roman, Manolo Fabregas

Candy Mountain *

Switzerland/France/Canada   1987   92m   Eastmancolor

Oasis/Xanadu/Films Plant Chant/Films Vision 4 (Ruth Waldburger)

An enterprising musician goes in search of a reclusive guitar-maker.

An occasionally engaging road movie, accompanied by many songs, of an innocent being taken for a ride, literally and metaphorically.

w Rudy Wurlitzer   d Robert Frank, Rudy Wurlitzer   ph Pio Corradi   m Dr John, David Johansen, Leon Redbone and others   ed Jennifer Auge

☆ Kevin J. O'Connor, Harris Yulin, Tom Waits, Bulle Ogier, Roberts Blossom, Leon Redbone, Dr John, Rita McNeil, Joe Strummer, Laurie Metcalf

Candy or Mint: see Caluga o Menta

Candyman *

US   1992   93m   DeLuxe

Columbia TriStar/Polygram/Propaganda (Steve Golin, Sigurjon Sighvatsson, Alan Poul)

An anthropology student becomes convinced of the reality of a mythical hook-handed serial killer, the son of a murdered slave.

Effective horror that manages not only to be scary but also delivers a parable on contemporary attitudes to race and sex.

wd Bernard Rose *story* The Forbidden by Clive Barker   ph Anthony B. Richmond   m Philip Glass   pd Jane Ann Stewart   ed Dan Rae   sp Image Animation

☆ Virginia Madsen, Tony Todd, Xander Berkeley, Kasi Lemmons, Vanessa Williams, DeJuan Guy, Michael Culkin, Stanley DeSantis, Gilbert Lewis

'An upper-register horror item that delivers the requisite shocks and gore but doesn't cheat or cop out.' – *Variety*

Candyman: Farewell to the Flesh

US   1995   94m   DeLuxe

Polygram/Propaganda (Sigurjon Sighvatsson, Gregg D. Fienberg)

A teacher discovers that the Candyman has been conjured into life once again, after her brother is accused of murdering an expert on the legend.

At its second outing, the urban myth of a hook-handed victim of injustice has deteriorated into just another slasher movie.

w Rand Ravich, Mark Kruger *story* Clive Barker   d Bill Condon   ph Tobias Schliessler   m Philip Glass   pd Barry Robison   ed Virginia Katz

☆ Tony Todd, Kelly Rowan, Timothy Carhart, Veronica Cartwright, William O'Leary, Fay Hauser, Bill Nunn, Joshua Gibran Mayweather

'Still delivers a requisite number of shocks to satisfy the core cult that propelled the original to hitdom.' – *Variety*

'Eleven dead bodies. One dead cat. No breasts. Hand hacked off. One bar-room brawl, with head through mirror. Multiple hooks through the breast, with spurtin' goo. Multiple killer-bee attacks, with facial goo … Four stars. Joe Bob says check it out.' – *Joe Bob Briggs*

Cannery Row

US   1982   120m   Metrocolor

MGM/Michael Philips

Incidents in the life of a 1940s marine biologist who lives on the waterfront with bums and floozies.

Badly out of its time, this curious attempt at sentimental realism was long in the works but emerged as a bloodless, stultifying entertainment.

wd David S. Ward *novel* John Steinbeck   ph Sven Nykvist   m Jack Nitzsche   pd Richard MacDonald   ed David Bretherton

☆ Nick Nolte, Debra Winger, Audra Lindley, Frank McRae, M. Emmet Walsh, John Huston

'Another MGM item in which the entertainment values are difficult to locate.' – *Variety*

† Raquel Welch, originally cast for the Winger role, was fired in mid-production.

Cannibal Girls

Canada   1972   84m   Eastmancolor

Target/Scary Pictures (Daniel Goldberg)

A couple whose car breaks down check into a motel in a small town where the inhabitants are cannibals.

Standard undistinguished and improvised horror fare, influenced by George Romero's Night of the Living Dead and itself an influence on The Texas Chainsaw Massacre. The film is not helped by the gimmick of a buzzer that sounds just before shock scenes and a bell that signals when the horror is over.

w Robert Sandler   d Ivan Reitman   ph Robert Saad   m Doug Riley   ed Daniel Goldberg   sp Richard Whyte, Michael Lotosky

☆ Eugene Levy, Andrea Martin, Ronald Ulrich, Randall Carpenter, Bonnie Neilson, Mira Pawluk

'Aggravatingly hammy and corny.' – *MFB*

Cannibal Man (dubbed)

Spain   1972   120m   colour

Atlas (Joe Truchado)

original title: La Semana del Asesino

aka: The Apartment on the 13th Floor; Week of the Killer

A slaughterhouse worker embarks on a killing spree to cover up his murder of a taxi driver during an argument over the fare.

An unconvincing psychological thriller. Cannibalism plays no part in the story other than, indirectly, when human remains are fed with other meat into a machine for making soup.

w Eloy de la Iglesia, Anthony Fos, Robert H. Oliver   d Eloy de la Iglesia   ph Raul Artigot   m Fernando G. Morcillo   ed Joe Louis Martinez   sp Baquero

☆ Vincent Parra, Emma Cohen, Eusebio Poncela, Vicky Lagos, Lola Herrera

† The English video release was cut to 92m.

Cannibal! The Musical

US   1996   105m   colour

Troma/Avenging Conscience/Cannibal (Ian Hardin, Alexandra Kelly, Jason McHugh, Trey Parker, Matthew Stone)

In the 1880s, an imprisoned goldminer tells a female reporter how he was accused of cannibalism in Colorado.

Claiming to be a restoration of a 1954 film with violent scenes 'edited out for your viewing pleasure', this deliberately amateurish movie begins and ends with an excess of gore played for comedy; in between there are moments of the ghoulish humour better known from Stone and Parker's TV series South Park.

wd Trey Parker   ph Matthew Bonifacio, Chris Graves   m Trey Parker, Rich Sanders   m/ly Trey Parker   pd David Hedge   ed Ian Hardin

☆ Juan Schwartz, Ian Hardin, Matt Stone, Jon Hegel, Jason McHugh, Dian Bachar, Toddy Walters, Robert Muratore, Stan Brakhage

The Cannibals

Italy   1969   87m   Technicolor   Techniscope

Cinegate/Doria/San Marco (Enzo Doria, Bino Cicogna)

original title: I Cannibali

In Milan, where a harsh military ruler brutally puts down a revolution, a woman searches for the dead body of her brother so that she can bury him.

An unsuccessful updating of Sophocles, with the emphasis on sensationalism rather than tragedy.

w Italo Moscati, Liliana Cavani, Fabrizio Onofri *play* Antigone by Sophocles   d Liliana Cavani   ph Giulio Albonico   m Ennio Morricone   ad Ezio Frigerio   ed Nino Baragli

☆ Britt Ekland, Pierre Clémenti, Tomas Milian, Francesco Leonetti, Delia Boccardo

Cannon for Cordoba

US   1970   104m   DeLuxe   Panavision

UA/Mirisch (Stephen Kandel, Vincent Fennelly)

In 1912, the Mexican bandit Cordoba is outgunned and outwitted by a US army captain.

Fast-moving but rather uninteresting action adventure.

w Stephen Kandel   d Paul Wendkos   ph Antonio Macasoli   m Elmer Bernstein

☆ George Peppard, Raf Vallone, Giovanna Ralli, Pete Duel, Don Gordon, Nico Minardos, John Russell

'A free-wheeling, stunt-studded, dented and demented story of a road racer without rules.'

Cannonball

US/Hong Kong   1976   93m   Metrocolor

Harbor/Shaw Brothers (Samuel W. Gelfman)

GB title: Carquake

Aggressive drivers compete in the Trans-American Grand Prix.

The plot is a thin excuse for multiple pile-ups and other road disasters. Moments amuse, but the violence quickly palls.

w Paul Bartel, Donald C. Simpson   d Paul Bartel   ph Tak Fujimoto   m David A. Axelrod

☆ David Carradine, Bill McKinney, Veronica Hamel, Gerrit Graham, Judy Canova

Cannonball Fever: see Speed Zone

The Cannonball Run

👪   US   1980   95m   Technicolor

Golden Harvest (Albert S. Ruddy)

The adventures of ill-assorted contestants in the illegal Cannonball coast-to-coast race.

Well-known stars are all at sea in this comedy/disaster extravaganza, which seems to have begun as a joke rather than a script.

w Brock Yates   d Hal Needham   ph Michael Butler   md Al Capps

☆ Burt Reynolds, Roger Moore, Farrah Fawcett, Dom DeLuise, Dean Martin, Sammy Davis Jnr, Adrienne Barbeau, Jack Elam, Bert Convy, Jamie Farr, Peter Fonda, Molly Picon, Bianca Jagger

'Lacking any recognizable plot or characterization, or indeed incidental invention, it merely offers a parade of inept whimsy and lame intra-mural reference.' – *Tim Pulleine*, MFB

'Moviegoers who relish the screech of tyres taking a fast turn on a narrow bend should have a whale of a time.' – *Daily Mail*

Cannonball Run II
US 1983 108m Technicolor
Golden Harvest/Warner (Albert S. Ruddy)

An Arab sheik puts up a million-dollar prize for the Cannonball Run.
Dispirited rehash of number one, with poor technique and non-performances by stars who should have known better than to get involved.
w Hal Needham, Albert S. Ruddy, Harvey Miller d Hal Needham ph Nick McLean m Al Capps ad Thomas E. Azzari ed William Gordean, Carl Kress
☆ Burt Reynolds, Dom DeLuise, Sammy Davis Jnr, Dean Martin, Jamie Farr, Telly Savalas, Shirley MacLaine, Frank Sinatra, Susan Anton, Catherine Bach, Richard Kiel, Tim Conway, Sid Caesar, Don Knotts, Ricardo Montalban and also Jim Nabors, Henry Silva

Canon City *
US 1948 82m bw
Eagle Lion/Bryan Foy (Robert T. Kane)
Convicts break out of the Colorado State Prison.
Minor semi-documentary melodrama, quite effectively presented.
wd Crane Wilbur ph John Alton
☆ Scott Brady, Jeff Corey, Whit Bissell, Stanley Clements, DeForest Kelley

Can't Buy Me Love
US 1987 94m colour
Warner/Touchstone (Thom Mount)

A wimp hires a popular cheerleader to be his girlfriend for a month to improve his social standing.
Predictable comedy aimed at a teenage audience, and they are welcome to it.
w Michael Swerdlick d James Foley ph Peter Lyons Collister m Robert Folk pd Donald Light-Harris ed Jeff Gourson
☆ Patrick Dempsey, Amanda Peterson, Courtney Gains, Seth Green, Tina Caspary, Devin Devasquez, Darcy de Moss, Eric Bruskotter

Can't Hardly Wait
US 1998 98m Technicolor
Columbia/Tall Trees

At a wild party to celebrate graduation from high school, a shy youth approaches the girl he loves, who has just broken up with her boyfriend.
Noisy lowbrow comedy of American school life, unlikely to interest anyone who's not an adolescent of limited horizons.
wd Harry Elfont, Deborah Kaplan ph Lloyd Ahern m David Kitay, Matthew Sweet pd Marcia Hinds-Johnson ed Michael Jablow
☆ Jennifer Love Hewitt, Ethan Embry, Charlie Korsmo, Lauren Ambrose, Seth Green, Peter Facinelli, Adam Hann-Byrd
'A mediocre attempt to recapture the exuberance and candid portraiture of such high school movie classics as *American Graffiti*.' – *Emanuel Levy, Variety*

Can't Help Singing *
US 1944 90m Technicolor
Universal (Frank Ross)
A Washington heiress chases her army lieutenant lover across the Wild West to California.
Lively star musical which could have used a little more wit in its lighthearted script.
w Lewis Foster, Frank Ryan d Frank Ryan ph Woody Bredell, W. Howard Greene m/ly Jerome Kern, E. Y. Harburg md Jerome Kern, Hans Salter
☆ Deanna Durbin, David Bruce, Robert Paige, Akim Tamiroff, Leonid Kinskey, Ray Collins, Thomas Gomez
'This could have been a beautiful and gay picture, but it is made without much feeling for beauty or gaiety.' – *James Agee*
'She can carry a simple part charmingly; she looks very well; her manners are impeccable; and she can sing a role just short of grand opera better than any actress on the screen.' – *Observer*
♫ 'Elbow Room'; 'Any Moment Now'; 'Californ-i-ay'; 'Swing Your Sweetheart round the Fire'; 'Finale Ultimo'
♪ Jerome Kern, Hans Salter; song 'More and More'

Can't Stop the Music
US 1980 124m Metrocolor
Panavision
EMI/Allan Carr

A Greenwich Village pop group hits the bigtime.
Curiously old-fashioned youth musical, unwisely touted as something special, which it isn't.
w Bronte Woodward, Allan Carr d Nancy Walker ph Bill Butler m Jacques Morali
☆ The Village People, Valerie Perrine, Paul Sand, Bruce Jenner, Tammy Grimes, June Havoc, Barbara Rush, Jack Weston
'The hype disaster of the 80s, a grisly rehash of the let's-start-a-group-of-our-own plot, peopled with butch gay stereotypes of both sexes pretending to be straight. The pervasive tackiness is unrelieved.' – *Time Out*
'Desperately knowing about the eighties but fixed remorselessly in a time warp of fifties hokum.' – *Guardian*
'All noise, lights, slogans, movement and dazzle, like a 124m commercial devoted to selling you a product you can't use.' – *Sunday Times*
'One doesn't watch it, one is attacked by it.' – *New England Entertainment Digest*
'Considering the low level of wit, perhaps the Village People should consider renaming themselves the Village Idiots.' – *Los Angeles Magazine*
'This shamefully tacky musical extravaganza fails on every aesthetic level.' – *Los Angeles Herald Examiner*
'A forced marriage between the worst of sitcom plotting and the highest of high camp production numbers.' – *New West*

Cantata de Chile *
Cuba 1976 119m colour
ICAIC (Orlando de La Huerta, Camilo Vives)
Revolutionary history of Cuba, told from a Marxist viewpoint.
An ambitious, epic mix of realism, symbolic action, songs and poems, intermixed with scenes of appalling violence, and filmed with exuberance and panache. But two hours in the company of excessively noble peasants is too much.
wd Humberto Solas ph Jorge Herrera m Leo Brouwer pd Fedora Robles ed Nelson L. Rodriguez
☆ Nelson Villagra, Shenda Roman, Eric Heresmann

A Canterbury Tale **
GB 1944 124m bw
Rank/Archers (Michael Powell, Emeric Pressburger)

A batty magistrate is unmasked by a land girl, an army sergeant and a GI.
Curious would-be propaganda piece with Old England bathed in a roseate wartime glow, but the plot seems to have little to do with Chaucer. Indeed, quite what Powell and Pressburger thought they were up to is hard to fathom, but the detail is interesting.
wd Michael Powell, Emeric Pressburger ph Erwin Hillier
☆ Eric Portman, Sheila Sim, John Sweet, Dennis Price, Esmond Knight, Charles Hawtrey, Hay Petrie, George Merritt, Edward Rigby
'To most people the intentions of the filmmakers remained highly mysterious; nor did this picture commend itself to the authorities, who showed some reluctance to encourage its export to our allies.' – *Basil Wright, 1972*

The Canterbury Tales
Italy/France 1971 109m Technicolor
UA/PEA/PAA (Alberto Grimaldi)

Medieval pilgrims amuse each other by telling stories on the way to Canterbury.
A sweaty selection of the tales in their more prurient aspects, with relentless emphasis on excrement and sex perversions.
wd Pier Paolo Pasolini, after Chaucer ph Tonino Delli Colli m Ennio Morricone
☆ Pier Paolo Pasolini, Hugh Griffith, Laura Betti, Tom Baker, Ninetto Davoli, Franco Citti
'Caricature Chaucer, with pilgrims losing the way to Canterbury amid a forest of male genitalia.' – *Sight and Sound*
'The vivid depiction of taboo subjects emerges less as an affirmation of the Chaucerian belief that all human activity lies within the artist's

scope, than as a bludgeoning over-emphasis on physical appetite as man's primal motive for action.' – *Nigel Andrews, MFB*

The Canterville Ghost *
US 1944 95m bw
MGM (Arthur Field)

The young girl heiress of an English castle introduces GIs to the resident ghost.
Leaden comedy a long way after Oscar Wilde, sunk by slow script and direction, but partly salvaged by the respective roguishness and infant charm of its stars.
w Edwin Blum d Jules Dassin ph Robert Planck m George Bassman
☆ Charles Laughton, Margaret O'Brien, Robert Young, William Gargan, Rags Ragland, Peter Lawford, Una O'Connor, Mike Mazurki
† In the mid 1970s, a television version starring David Niven was made by HTV. Another TV version followed in 1996, starring Patrick Stewart and Neve Campbell.

Canyon Pass: see *Raton Pass*

Canyon Passage *
US 1946 99m Technicolor
Universal (Walter Wanger)
In the 1850s along the pioneering tracks the west's first towns were being built…
Simple, scrappy but generally pleasing film which gives a vivid picture of pioneering life while minimizing its hardships.
w Ernest Pascal, William Fosche d Jacques Tourneur ph Edward Cronjager m Frank Skinner
☆ Dana Andrews, Patricia Roc, Hoagy Carmichael, Brian Donlevy, Susan Hayward, Ward Bond, Andy Devine, Lloyd Bridges
'Miles of beautiful scenery, lavishly punctuated with rough-and-tumble episodes, moments of tender romance and a smattering of folk customs.' – *New York Times*
♪ song 'Ole Buttermilk Sky' (m/ly Hoagy Carmichael, Jack Brooks)

Cape Fear *
US 1961 106m bw
U-I/Melville-Talbot (Sy Bartlett)

An ex-convict blames a lawyer for his sentence and threatens to rape the lawyer's wife.
Unpleasant and drawn out suspenser with characters of cardboard and situations from stock.
w James R. Webb novel *The Executioners* by John D. MacDonald d J. Lee-Thompson ph Sam Leavitt m Bernard Herrmann
☆ Gregory Peck, Robert Mitchum, Polly Bergen, Martin Balsam, Lori Martin, Jack Kruschen, Telly Savalas

'There is nothing in the dark that isn't there in the light. Except fear.'
Cape Fear **
US 1991 128m Technicolor Panavision
Universal/Amblin/Cappa/Tribeca (Barbara de Fina)

A psychopathic ex-convict returns to threaten the family of the lawyer who unsuccessfully defended him on a charge of rape.
A remake superior to the original, a grimly effective thriller, filled with a sense of brooding menace.
w Wesley Strick novel *The Executioners* by John D. MacDonald screenplay James R. Webb d Martin Scorsese ph Freddie Francis m Bernard Herrmann md Elmer Bernstein pd Henry Bumstead ed Thelma Schoonmaker
☆ Robert DeNiro, Nick Nolte, Jessica Lange, Juliette Lewis, Joe Don Baker, Robert Mitchum, Gregory Peck, Martin Balsam, Illeana Douglas
'A highly potent thriller that will strike fear into the hearts of a sizable public.' – *Variety*
'The film begins as it goes on; undeviatingly and unrelievedly brutal. This said, I must admit I mistrust myself for admiring it so much. For more than two hours it puts one's moral conscience under assault, not just one's nerves.' – *Alexander Walker, London Evening Standard*
'A picture whose sole aim is to give its audience huge, bowel-loosening shocks; the veneer of moral seriousness and psychological complexity that Scorsese brings to the enterprise feels like an attempt to convince himself that he's not doing what he's doing … This is Scorsese's worst picture – an ugly, incoherent piece of work.' – *New Yorker*

'Have our lives truly become so hollow that this kind of unapologetic bludgeoning of our sensibilities passes for jolly weekend entertainment?' – *Kenneth Turan, Los Angeles Times*
'I'm glad I saw the film. I found it as gripping and offensive as Scorsese intended. But, apart from de Niro's transcendent performance, I'm not sure I'd want to see it again.' – *Ian Johnstone, Sunday Times*
† Gregory Peck, Robert Mitchum and Martin Balsam all featured in the 1962 version, as did Bernard Herrmann's score.
♟ Robert DeNiro, Juliette Lewis

The Caper of the Golden Bulls *
US 1966 104m Pathécolor
Embassy (Clarence Greene)

GB title: *Carnival of Thieves*
Ex-air-aces rob banks in order to pay for the restoration of a French cathedral they had to bomb; to avoid incrimination they are blackmailed into doing one last job in Pamplona.
Ingeniously plotted, flatly executed suspenser set in Pamplona during the bull run.
w Ed Waters, William Moessinger novel William P. McGivern d Russel Rouse ph Hal Stine m Vic Mizzy
☆ Stephen Boyd, Giovanna Ralli, Yvette Mimieux, Walter Slezak, Vito Scotti

Capetown Affair
US/SA 1967 100m DeLuxe
TCF/Killarney (Robert D. Webb)

A pickpocket on a South African bus steals a purse containing secret microfilm.
Flatulent remake of Pickup on South Street with nothing but the unfamiliar locale to recommend it.
w Harold Medford, Samuel Fuller d Robert D. Webb ph David Millin m Bob Adams
☆ James Brolin, Jacqueline Bisset, Claire Trevor, Bob Courtney, Jon Whiteley

'The man who made the twenties roar! Now, after 45 years, his true story can be told!'
Capone
US 1975 101m DeLuxe
TCF/Santa Fe (Roger Corman)
Exploitation version of the Capone story, with the emphasis on unpleasant violence.
w Howard Browne d Steve Carver ph Vilis Lapenieks m David Grisman
☆ Ben Gazzara, Sylvester Stallone, Susan Blakely, Harry Guardino, John Cassavetes, John Davis Chandler, Peter Maloney, Royal Dano
† See also: *Al Capone*.

Le Caporal Epinglé: see *The Vanishing Corporal*

Caprice *
US 1967 98m DeLuxe Cinemascope
TCF/Aaron Rosenberg, Marty Melcher

A career girl investigating the death of her boss discovers that a cosmetics empire is the front for international drug smuggling.
Incoherent kaleidoscope which switches from farce to suspense and Bond-style action, scattering in-jokes along the way. Bits of it however are funny, and it looks good.
w Jay Jayson, Frank Tashlin d Frank Tashlin ph Leon Shamroy (who also appears) m Frank de Vol
☆ Doris Day, Richard Harris, Edward Mulhare, Ray Walston, Jack Kruschen, Lilia Skala, Irene Tsu, Michael Romanoff, Michael J. Pollard

Capricious Summer *
Czechoslovakia 1968 75m Eastmancolor
Ceskoslovensky Film (Jan Libora)
The beautiful assistant of a wandering tightrope walker sets up sexual tensions when they stop at a sleepy riverside town.
Amusing little period comedy in a period setting.
wd Jiri Menzel m Jaromir Sofr m Jiri Sust
☆ Rudolf Hrusinsky, Vlastimil Brodsky, Frantisek Rehak, Jana Drchalova, Jiri Menzel

Capricorn One

US   1978   128m   CFI color   Panavision
Associated General/Lew Grade (Paul N. Lazarus III)
📼 💿 ⊙ ⌕

A reporter discovers that the first manned space flight to Mars was a hoax.
Smartly packaged topical adventure thriller rather marred by its all star cast.
wd Peter Hyams ph Bill Butler m Jerry Goldsmith pd Albert Brenner
☆ Elliott Gould, James Brolin, Brenda Vaccaro, Sam Waterston, O. J. Simpson, Hal Holbrook, Telly Savalas, Karen Black, David Huddleston
'After weighing in with some Watergate/Bernstein pretensions, the makers then opt for boring, Bondish derring-do.' – *Sight and Sound*

Captain America

US   1989   97m   Eastmancolor
Castle/21st Century/Marvel/Jadran Film (Menahem Golan)
📼

Frozen in the ice for decades, Captain America is freed to battle against an arch-criminal The Red Skull.
Comic-book nonsense, half-heartedly presented.
w Stephen Tolkin d Albert Pyun ph Philip Alan Waters m Barry Goldberg ed David Reale
☆ Matt Salinger, Ronny Cox, Ned Beatty, Darren McGavin, Michael Nouri, Melinda Dillon, Francesca Neri, Bill Mumy, Kim Gillingham
'It comprises reams of tedious exposition interlarded with out-dated heroics.' – *MFB*

Captain Apache

US/Spain   1971   94m   Technicolor   'Scope
Benmar (Milton Sperling, Philip Yordan, Irving Lerner)
📼

An Indian serving with US army intelligence tracks down a gun runner.
An old formula tarted up with the new violence. Very ho-hum.
w Philip Yordan, Milton Sperling novel S. E. Whitman d Alexander Singer ph John Cabrera m Dolores Claman
☆ Lee Van Cleef, Carroll Baker, Stuart Whitman, Percy Herbert, Tony Vogel

Captain Applejack

US   1931   70m   bw
Warner

A timid man turns the tables on crooks who plan to find treasure beneath his ancestral home.
Early talkie version of a well-worn play previously filmed in 1923.
w Maude Fulton novel Ambrose Applejohn's Adventure by Walter Hackett d Hobart Henley
☆ John Halliday, Kay Strozzi, Arthur Edmund Carewe, Mary Brian, Louise Closser Hale

Captain Bill

GB   1935   81m   bw
Leslie Fuller (Joe Rock)

A bargee saves a schoolmistress from trouble with crooks.
By reputation the best of its star's modest comedies, which have not yet been rediscovered.
w Val Valentine, Syd Courtenay and George Harris d Ralph Ceder
☆ Leslie Fuller, Georgie Harris, Judy Kelly, Hal Gordon, O. B. Clarence

Captain Blackjack

US/France   1952   90m   bw
Alsa/Jungla (Julien Duvivier)
aka: *Blackjack*

A Riviera socialite pretends to be an undercover agent but is really a smuggler; she is unmasked by a doctor who is really a detective.
Trashy hodgepodge with a remarkable cast of ageing stars.
w Julien Duvivier, Charles Spaak, Michael Pertwee story Robert Gaillard d Julien Duvivier ph André Thomas m Joseph Kosma
☆ George Sanders, Agnes Moorehead, Herbert Marshall, Patricia Roc, Marcel Dalio, Howard Vernon, Dennis Wyndham
† The film was meant to take eight weeks to shoot; instead, it took seven months, which is why Sanders, who ate too much out of boredom, is thin in some scenes and fat in others. The stars were to be paid out of the film's receipts and, as a result, earned no money from the picture.

'A million dollars worth of adventure! To do justice in words to its fascination is impossible!'
'His sword carved his name across the continents – and his glory across the seas!'

Captain Blood **

👨‍👩‍👧 US   1935   119m   bw
Warner (Harry Joe Brown)
📼 💿 ⊙

A young British surgeon, wrongly condemned by Judge Jeffreys for helping rebels, escapes and becomes a Caribbean pirate.
Modestly produced but quite exhilarating pirate adventure notable for making a star of Errol Flynn. Direction makes the most of very limited production values.
w Casey Robinson novel Rafael Sabatini d Michael Curtiz ph Hal Mohr m Erich Wolfgang Korngold ad Anton Grot
☆ Errol Flynn, Olivia de Havilland, Basil Rathbone, Lionel Atwill, Guy Kibbee, Ross Alexander, Henry Stephenson, Forrester Harvey, Hobart Cavanaugh, Donald Meek
'A lavish, swashbuckling saga of the Spanish Main … it can't fail at the wickets.' – *Variety*
'Here is a fine spirited mix-up with clothes and wigs which sometimes hark back to the sixteenth century and sometimes forward to the period of Wolfe … one is quite prepared for the culminating moment when the Union Jack breaks proudly, anachronistically forth at Peter Blood's masthead.' – *Graham Greene*
'Magnificently photographed, lavishly produced, and directed with consummate skill.' – *Picturegoer*
⚜ best picture

Captain Blood, Fugitive: see Captain Pirate

Captain Boycott *

GB   1947   93m   bw
GFD/Individual (Frank Launder, Sidney Gilliat)

In 1880, poor Irish farmers rebel against their tyrannical English landlords.
Modest historical drama in which a splendid cast is rather subdued.
w Wolfgang Wilhelm, Frank Launder, Paul Vincent Carroll, Patrick Campbell novel Philip Rooney d Frank Launder ph Wilkie Cooper m William Alwyn ad Ted Carrick
☆ Stewart Granger, Kathleen Ryan, Alastair Sim, Robert Donat (cameo), Cecil Parker, Mervyn Johns, Noel Purcell, Niall MacGinnis
'It is said that no actor can survive playing opposite a child or a dog. Let me add here that it is just as lethal playing with the Abbey Players. Apart from being able to act you off the stage, they can also drink you under the table.' – *Sidney Gilliat, 1982*

Captain Carey USA

US   1950   83m   bw
Paramount (Richard Maibaum)
GB title: *After Midnight*

After the war, a military officer returns to an Italian village to expose the informer who betrayed his comrades.
Muddled and rather boring melodrama with a labyrinthine plot which seems to have stultified all concerned. It did produce a hit song, 'Mona Lisa'.
w Robert Thoeren novel Dishonoured by Martha Albrand d Mitchell Leisen ph John F. Seitz m Hugo Friedhofer
☆ Alan Ladd, Francis Lederer, Wanda Hendrix, Joseph Calleia, Celia Lovsky, Angela Clarke, Jane Nigh, Frank Puglia, Luis Alberni
🎵 song 'Mona Lisa' (m/ly Ray Evans, Jay Livingston)

Captain Caution

👨‍👩‍👧 US   1940   84m   bw
Hal Roach

In 1812, a girl takes over her dead father's ship and fights the British.
Lively though unconvincing adventure with emphasis on comedy.
w Grover Jones novel Kenneth Roberts d Richard Wallace ph Norbert Brodine m Phil Ohman
☆ Victor Mature, Louise Platt, Bruce Cabot, Leo Carrillo, Robert Barrat, Vivienne Osborne, Alan Ladd

---

Captain China

US   1949   97m   bw
Paramount/Pine-Thomas (William H. Pine, William C. Thomas)

A wandering seafarer seeks the mate who betrayed him.
Action melodrama with a second team look; all rather listless.
w Lewis R. Foster, Gwen Bagni d Lewis R. Foster ph John Alton m Lucien Cailliet
☆ John Payne, Gail Russell, Jeffrey Lynn, Lon Chaney Jnr, Michael O'Shea, Ellen Corby

Captain Clegg *

GB   1962   82m   Technicolor
Universal/Hammer (John Temple-Smith)
US title: *Night Creatures*

The vicar of an 18th-century village in Romney Marsh is really a retired pirate, now doing a little smuggling on the side.
Mild remake of Dr Syn with a few moments of violence added; watchable for those who like totally predictable plot development.
w John Elder (Anthony Hinds) d Peter Graham Scott ph Arthur Grant m Don Banks ad Bernard Robinson, Don Mingaye ed James Needs, Eric Boyd-Perkins
☆ Peter Cushing, Patrick Allen, Michael Ripper, Oliver Reed, Derek Francis, Milton Reid, Martin Benson, David Lodge, Yvonne Romain

Captain Eddie

US   1945   107m   bw
TCF/Eureka

Eddie Rickenbacker, adrift on a life raft after a plane crash in the Pacific, thinks back on his adventurous life in aviation.
Flat and surprisingly poorly made biopic with little to hold the attention.
w John Tucker Battle d Lloyd Bacon ph Joe MacDonald m Cyril Mockridge
☆ Fred MacMurray, Lynn Bari, Thomas Mitchell, Lloyd Nolan, Charles Bickford

Captain from Castile

US   1947   140m   Technicolor
TCF (Lamar Trotti)
📼 🎧

A young 15th-century Spaniard hopes for fame and fortune in the New World.
Rather empty and boring adventure epic from a bestseller; high production values produce moments of interest.
w Lamar Trotti novel Samuel Shellabarger d Henry King ph Charles Clarke, Arthur E. Arling m Alfred Newman ad Richard Day, James Basevi
☆ Tyrone Power, Jean Peters, Lee J. Cobb, Cesar Romero, John Sutton, Antonio Moreno, Thomas Gomez, Alan Mowbray, Barbara Lawrence, George Zucco, Roy Roberts, Marc Lawrence
'The first few reels have flow and a kind of boy's-book splendour; the rest is locomotor ataxia.' – *James Agee*
⚜ Alfred Newman

Captain Fury *

US   1939   91m   bw
Hal Roach

In 19th-century Australia, an adventurer fights the evil head of a penal colony.
Shades of Zorro and Robin Hood in a brawling, comic actioner typical of this producer.
w Grover Jones, Jack Jevne, William de Mille d Hal Roach ph Norbert Brodine m Marvin Hatley ad Charles D. Hall
☆ Brian Aherne, Victor McLaglen, Paul Lukas, June Lang, John Carradine
'Action, fast riding, gunplay, surprise attacks, some broad comedy and a few dashes of romance … will do pretty good biz in the keys, but will hit a more profitable stride in the subsequents.' – *Variety*
⚜ Charles D. Hall

The Captain Hates the Sea *

US   1934   92m   bw
Columbia

Crime and comedy on an ocean voyage.
Zany, rather endearing comedy which gave the star his last role.
w Wallace Smith d Lewis Milestone ph Joseph August
☆ John Gilbert, Victor McLaglen, Walter Connolly, Alison Skipworth, Wynne Gibson,

---

Helen Vinson, Leon Errol, Walter Catlett, Donald Meek, Arthur Treacher, Akim Tamiroff
'A fine cast, excellent comedy relief and expert direction.' – *Variety*
'The best neglected picture in two years.' – *Otis Ferguson, 1936*

Captain Horatio Hornblower RN

GB   1951   117m   Technicolor
Warner (Raoul Walsh)
📼 💿

Events from the adventure novels about a 19th-century sailor who outwits the Spaniards and the French and marries his admiral's widow.
Sprawling, plotless sea saga with the cast ill at ease in highly unconvincing sets: no air seems to blow across the decks of the Lydia.
w Ivan Goff, Ben Roberts, Aeneas Mackenzie novels C. S. Forester d Raoul Walsh ph Guy Green m Robert Farnon ad Tom Morahan
☆ Gregory Peck, Virginia Mayo, Robert Beatty, James Robertson Justice, Terence Morgan, Moultrie Kelsall, Richard Hearne, Denis O'Dea
'No point makes a strong enough impression to suggest a main line of criticism.' – *Richard Mallett, Punch*

The Captain Is a Lady *

US   1940   63m   bw
MGM

A sea captain is forced by ill-fortune to send his wife to an old ladies' home, but he dresses as a woman to be with her.
Absurd-sounding comedy not without a certain lunatic charm.
w Harry Clork play Rachel Crothers d Robert Sinclair
☆ Charles Coburn, Billie Burke, Beulah Bondi, Dan Dailey, Virginia Grey, Helen Broderick, Helen Westley

Captain Jack

👨‍👩‍👧 GB   1998   100m   colour
Feature Film/Captain Jack (John Goldschmidt)
📼

A sailor sets out on an unseaworthy vessel with an amateur crew to commemorate the 200th anniversary of a voyage from Whitby to the Arctic.
Ramshackle drama, based on a real incident, that unsuccessfully attempts to revive the style of Ealing comedies.
w Jack Rosenthal article Nick Davies d Robert Young ph John McGlashan m Richard Harvey pd Simon Holland ed Edward Mansell
☆ Bob Hoskins, Sadie Frost, Gemma Jones, Anna Massey, Peter McDonald, David Troughton, Maureen Lipman, Patrick Malahide, Michelle Dotrice
'The result is ham-fisted and more than a little irritating.' – *Empire*

Captain January *

👨‍👩‍👧 US   1936   74m   bw
TCF (Darryl F. Zanuck)
📼

A little girl is rescued from a shipwreck by a lighthouse keeper.
Standard Shirley Temple vehicle with pleasing dialogue and numbers.
w Sam Hellman, Gladys Lehman, Harry Tugend novel Laura E. Richards d David Butler ph John F. Seitz m Louis Silvers m/ly Lew Pollack, Sidney Mitchell, Jack Yellen
☆ Shirley Temple, Guy Kibbee, Buddy Ebsen, Slim Summerville, June Lang, Sara Haden, Jane Darwell
'Sentimental, a little depraved, with an appeal interestingly decadent.' – *Graham Greene*

Captain Kidd

US   1945   90m   bw
Benedict Bogeaus

A pirate tricks King William III into giving him royal orders, but enemies he believes dead return to see him hanged.
Rather poorly produced vehicle for a star who however rants and raves to some effect.
w Norman Reilly Raine d Rowland V. Lee ph Archie Stout m Werner Janssen
☆ Charles Laughton, Randolph Scott, Barbara Britton, Reginald Owen, John Carradine, Gilbert Roland, Sheldon Leonard
⚜ Werner Janssen

Captain Kidd and the Slave Girl

US 1954 82m CFI color
Reliance/UA

A scheming earl reprieves Captain Kidd so that he can steal his treasure.
Cut-price swashbuckler with more vigour than some.
w Aubrey Wisberg, Jack Pollexfen d Lew Landers
☆ Anthony Dexter, Eva Gabor, Alan Hale Jnr, James Seay

Captain Kronos, Vampire Hunter *

GB 1973 91m colour
Hammer (Albert Fennell, Brian Clemens)
🎞️

The title explains almost all; in this case he tackles an old vampire crone who becomes young when she sucks blood.
Lively horror yarn with amusing asides.
wd Brian Clemens ph Ian Wilson m Laurie Johnson pd Robert Jones ed James Needs
☆ Horst Janson, John Carson, Shane Briant, Caroline Munro, John Cater, Wanda Ventham

Captain Lightfoot

US 1955 92m Technicolor Cinemascope
U-I (Ross Hunter)

Adventures of a 19th-century Irish rebel.
Dullish adventure story with the star ill at ease.
w W. R. Burnett, Oscar Brodney d Douglas Sirk
ph Irving Glassberg m Hans Salter
☆ Rock Hudson, Barbara Rush, Jeff Morrow, Kathleen Ryan, Finlay Currie, Denis O'Dea, Geoffrey Toone

Captain Moonlight: see D'Ye Ken John Peel?

Captain Nemo and the Underwater City

🎬 GB 1969 106m Metrocolor
Panavision
MGM/Omnia (Steven Pallos, Bertram Ostrer)

Six survivors from an Atlantic shipwreck are picked up by a mysterious submarine and have adventures in a spectacular underwater city.
Further adventures of Jules Verne's engaging Victorian character from Twenty Thousand Leagues under the Sea. Here however the general production values are stolid rather than solid, and the script makes heavy weather.
w Pip Baker, Jane Baker, A. Wright Campbell
d James Hill ph Alan Hume, Egil Woxholt
m Walter Stott ad Bill Andrews
☆ Robert Ryan, Chuck Connors, Bill Fraser, Kenneth Connor, Nanette Newman, John Turner, Luciana Paluzzi, Allan Cuthbertson

Captain Newman MD *

US 1963 126m Eastmancolor
Universal-Brentwood-Reynard (Robert Arthur)
🎞️

At an army air base during World War II, a psychiatrist has varied success with his patients.
A decidedly curious comedy drama on the fringe of bad taste; it should have turned out better than it does, but will entertain those who like hospital heroics drenched in bitter-sweet sentimentality.
w Richard L. Breen, Phoebe and Henry Ephron
novel Leo Rosten d David Miller ph Russell Metty m Joseph Gershenson
☆ Gregory Peck, Tony Curtis, Angie Dickinson, Eddie Albert, Bobby Darin, James Gregory, Jane Withers, Bethel Leslie, Robert Duvall, Larry Storch, Robert F. Simon, Dick Sargent
⚜ script; Bobby Darin

Captain of the Guard

US 1930 83m bw
Carl Laemmle/Universal

During the French Revolution, a guards captain changes sides.
Unexciting historical melodrama which failed to make the intended impression.
w Arthur Ripley story Houston Branch d Paul Fejos, John S. Robertson m Charles Wakefield Cadman
☆ John Boles, Laura La Plante, Lionel Belmore, Sam de Grasse, James Marcus, Otis Harlan
'Universal's most pretentious release of the season … liberal expenditure shows on the screen.' – Variety

---

'Passions run hot and blood runs cold!'

Captain Pirate

US 1952 85m Technicolor
Columbia (Harry Joe Brown)
GB title: Captain Blood, Fugitive

A reformed pirate, accused of sacking Cartagena, returns to piracy to discover the perpetrators.
Lively buccaneering programmer with an adequate budget and plenty of high spirits.
w Robert Libbott, Frank Burt, John Meredyth Lucas novel Captain Blood Returns by Rafael Sabatini d Ralph Murphy ph Charles Lawton Jnr
m George Duning
☆ Louis Hayward, Patricia Medina, John Sutton, George Givot, Rex Evans, Ted de Corsia, Charles Irwin

---

'The only thing Martin wanted was a nice, quiet family vacation. Instead, he got … Captain Ron.'

Captain Ron

US 1992 100m Technicolor
Touchstone/Touchwood Pacific Partners I (David Permut, Paige Simpson)
📺 🎞️ 🔊

An American family inherits an ancient yacht in the Caribbean and hire a dubious one-eyed captain to help them sail it back to the States.
Tedious and indifferently acted comedy, in which the jokes consist of people either falling over or falling into the water.
w John Dwyer, Thom Eberhardt d Thom Eberhardt ph Daryn Okada m Nicholas Pike
pd William F. Matthews ed Tina Hirsch
☆ Kurt Russell, Martin Short, Mary Kay Place, Benjamin Salisbury, Meadow Sisto, Paul Anka
'Inoffensive but unexciting.' – Variety
† The film was released direct to video in Britain.

Captain Scarlett

US 1952 75m Technicolor
UA/Craftsman (Howard Dimsdale)

After the Napoleonic wars, southern France is in need of a protector against the villainous Duke of Corlaine. Captain Scarlett rides into action…
Robin Hood in all but name, an old tale retold without much flair.
w Howard Dimsdale d Thomas Carr ph Charles Carbajal m Elias Breeskin
☆ Richard Greene, Leonora Amar, Nedrick Young, Eduardo Noriega

Captain Sinbad *

🎬 US/Germany 1963 88m Eastmancolor
Wonderscope
King Brothers
🎞️

Sinbad returns to Baristan and by means of magic deposes a sultan.
Rather splendid adventure fantasy with a European flavour, good trick effects and full-blooded performances.
w Samuel B. West, Harry Relis d Byron Haskin
ph Gunther Senftleben, Eugen Shuftan m Michel Michelet ad Werner and Isabell Schlicting
sp Tom Howard
☆ Guy Williams, Pedro Armendariz, Heidi Bruhl, Abraham Sofaer

Captain Tugboat Annie

US 1945 70m bw
Republic

Annie wants to adopt a small boy but by clerical error gets a young man instead.
A silly story which prevented this reworking of the old Dressler-Beery vehicle from becoming a series.
w George Callahan d Phil Rosen
☆ Jane Darwell, Edgar Kennedy, Charles Gordon

Captains Courageous **

🎬 US 1937 116m bw
MGM (Louis D. Lighton)
📺 🎞️ 🔊

A spoiled rich boy falls off a cruise liner and lives for a while among fisherfolk who teach him how to live.
Semi-classic Hollywood family film which is not all that enjoyable while it's on but is certainly a good example of the prestige picture of the thirties. (It also happened to be good box-office.)
w John Lee Mahin, Marc Connelly, Dale Van Every novel Rudyard Kipling d Victor Fleming
ph Harold Rosson m Franz Waxman ed Elmo Veron
☆ Spencer Tracy, Lionel Barrymore, Freddie Bartholomew, Mickey Rooney, Melvyn Douglas,

---

Charley Grapewin, Christian Rub, John Carradine, Walter Kingsford, Leo G. Carroll, Charles Trowbridge
'Will not have to go begging for patronage … one of the best pictures of the sea ever made.' – Variety
'Another of those grand jobs of movie-making we have come to expect from Hollywood's most profligate studio.' – Frank S. Nugent, New York Times
† 1977 brought a TV movie remake, as did 1995, both inferior to the movie.
♟ Spencer Tracy
⚜ best picture; script; editing

Captains of the Clouds

US 1942 113m Technicolor
Warner (Hal B. Wallis, William Cagney)

A flippant Canadian Air Force pilot proves his worth under fire.
Recruiting poster heroics, reasonably well done but lacking the vital spark.
w Arthur T. Horman, Richard Macaulay, Norman Reilly Raine d Michael Curtiz ph Sol Polito, Wilfrid M. Cline m Max Steiner ad Ted Smith
☆ James Cagney, Dennis Morgan, Brenda Marshall, George Tobias, Alan Hale, Reginald Gardiner, Reginald Denny, Paul Cavanagh, Clem Bevans, J. M. Kerrigan
'Pure tribute to the unchanging forcefulness of James Cagney.' – New York Post
⚜ Sol Polito, Wilfrid M. Cline; Ted Smith

The Captain's Paradise *

GB 1953 89m bw
BL/London (Anthony Kimmins)
📺 🎞️ 🔊

The captain of a steamer plying between Gibraltar and Tangier has a wife in each port, one to suit each of his personalities.
Over-dry comedy in which the idea is much funnier than the script. One is left with the memory of a pleasant star performance.
w Alec Coppel, Nicholas Phipps d Anthony Kimmins ph Ted Scaife m Malcolm Arnold
☆ Alec Guinness, Celia Johnson, Yvonne de Carlo, Charles Goldner, Miles Malleson, Bill Fraser, Nicholas Phipps, Ferdy Mayne, George Benson
⚜ original story (Alec Coppel)

The Captain's Table *

GB 1958 89m Eastmancolor
Rank (Joseph Janni)
🎞️

A cargo skipper is given command of a luxury liner and has to watch his manners.
Lively adaptation of a frivolous book of obvious jokes, most of which come up quite funny amid the luxurious surroundings.
w John Whiting, Bryan Forbes, Nicholas Phipps novel Richard Gordon d Jack Lee ph Christopher Challis m Frank Cordell
☆ John Gregson, Peggy Cummins, Donald Sinden, Reginald Beckwith, Nadia Gray, Richard Wattis, Maurice Denham, Nicholas Phipps, Joan Sims, Miles Malleson

The Captive City **

US 1951 91m bw
UA/Aspen (Theron Warth)

Small-town corruption imposed by the Mafia is revealed by a crusading editor who defies threats to his wife and family and tells all to the Kefauver Commission.
Excellent documentary melodrama made in a style then original, also notable for use of the Hoge deep focus lens.
w Karl Lamb, Alvin Josephy Jnr d Robert Wise
ph Lee Garmes m Jerome Moross
☆ John Forsythe, Joan Camden, Harold J. Kennedy, Marjorie Crossland, Victor Sutherland, Ray Teal, Martin Milner, Hal K. Dawson

The Captive City

Italy 1963 110m bw
Paramount
Italian title: La Città Prigionera

Rebels keep an assorted group of people captive in an Athens hotel.
Dim would-be thriller which rambles on far too long.
w Guy Elmes, Eric Bercovici, Marc Brandel
novel John Appleby d Joseph Anthony
☆ David Niven, Lea Massari, Ben Gazzara, Daniela Rocca, Martin Balsam, Michael Craig, Percy Herbert

---

La Captive du Desert

France 1990 101m colour
Artificial Eye/La Sept/Roger Diamantis/St-André-des-Arts/Jean-Bernard Fetoux/SGGC/Jean-Luc Larguier/Titane (Pascale Dauman, Jean-Luc Ormires)

A Frenchwoman is held captive in the desert by nomadic tribesmen.
A minimalist movie, based on a true story, with little dialogue or action but a great deal of sand.
wd Raymond Depardon ph Raymond Depardon
m Jean-Jacques Lemtre ed Roger Ikhief, Camille Cotte, Pascale Charolais
☆ Sandrine Bonnaire, Dobi Kor, Fadi Taha, Dobi Wachink, Badei Barka
'Half the audience with whom I watched the film left before the end while the other half remained, fascinated by the vividness of the photography and the highly personal nature of the film. It is one of those in which nothing, and everything, happens.' – Derek Malcolm, Guardian

The Captive Heart **

GB 1946 108m bw
Ealing (Michael Relph)
📺

Stories of life among British officers in a German POW camp, especially of a Czech who has stolen the papers of a dead Britisher.
Archetypal POW drama lacing an almost poetic treatment with humour and melodrama.
w Angus MacPhail, Guy Morgan story Patrick Kirwan d Basil Dearden ph Douglas Slocombe
m Alan Rawsthorne ad Michael Relph
☆ Michael Redgrave, Jack Warner, Basil Radford, Mervyn Johns, Jimmy Hanley, Gordon Jackson, Ralph Michael, Derek Bond, Karel Stepanek, Guy Middleton, Jack Lambert, Gladys Henson, Rachel Kempson, Meriel Forbes
'A warm, emotional, intensely human document, entitled to rate among the best twenty films of the last ten years.' – News of the World

Captive Hearts: see Fire with Fire (1986)

Captive Hearts

US 1987 97m Metrocolor
MGM/Kurissama (John A. Kuri)
🎞️

Rescued from instant execution and put to work by the headman of a remote village after being shot down over Japan in 1944, an American soldier falls in love with a local woman
Simple-minded romance that lacks dramatic impetus or interest.
w Patrick N. Morita, John A. Kuri story The Hawk by Sargon Tamimi d Paul Almond
ph Thomas Vamos m Osamu Kitajima
pd François de Lucy, Steve Sardanis ed Yurij Luhovy
☆ Noriyuki (Pat) Morita, Chris Makepeace, Michael Sarrazin, Mari Sato, Seth Sakai, Denis Akiyama

---

'A human form with animal instincts!'

Captive Wild Woman

US 1943 60m bw
Universal

A doctor finds a way of developing the glands of an ape and turning it into a beautiful girl.
Lamebrain horror item which amazingly spawned two sequels, Jungle Woman (1944) and Jungle Captive (1945).
w Griffin Jay, Henry Sucher d Edward Dmytryk
☆ Evelyn Ankers, Acquanetta, John Carradine, Martha Vickers, Milburn Stone

Captives

GB 1994 100m Rank Colour
Entertainment/BBC/Distant Horizon (David M. Thompson)
📺 🎞️

A female dentist is blackmailed after she begins an affair with a convicted murderer.
An oddly unconvincing melodrama, in which the contrivances of the plot prevent the development of character.
w Frank Deasy d Angela Pope ph Remi Adefarasin m Colin Towns pd Stuart Walker
ed Dave King
☆ Julia Ormond, Tim Roth, Richard Hawley, Jeff Nuttall, Kenneth Cope, Keith Allen, Bill Moody, Peter Capaldi
'A botched job, with many an unfilled plot cavity.' – Guardian

---

The Capture

US   1950   91m   bw
RKO/Showtime (Niven Busch)

On the run from the police, a former oil company field boss explains to a priest how he, by accident, came to be a fugitive.

Run-of-the-mill melodrama, all talk and no action.

w Niven Busch d John Sturges ph Edward Cronjager m Daniele Amfitheatrof pd William E. Flannery

☆ Lew Ayres, Teresa Wright, Victor Jory, Jacqueline White, Victor Hunt, Edwin Rand, Duncan Renaldo

Captured

US   1933   72m   bw
Warner

A prisoner-of-war discovers that his best friend was his wife's lover.

Turgid and heavy-going early variation on a theme which would become very familiar indeed; the stars couldn't save it.

w Edward Chodorov novel Sir Philip Gibbs d Roy Del Ruth

☆ Leslie Howard, Paul Lukas, Douglas Fairbanks Jnr, Margaret Lindsay, J. Carrol Naish, Arthur Hohl

'Too many obviously adverse ingredients, chiefly story, to chalk this one up as a winner … at best its earnings shape up as spotty.' – *Variety*

'Is it a phantom, a demon, or the devil himself?'

The Car

US   1977   98m   Technicolor   Panavision
Universal (Marvin Birdt, Elliot Silverstein)

A small south-western town is terrorized by a driverless car which may be a creation of the devil.

Silly suspense with a draggy midsection.

w Dennis Shryack, Michael Butler, Lane Slate d Elliot Silverstein ph Gerald Hirschfeld m Leonard Rosenman

☆ James Brolin, Kathleen Lloyd, John Marley, John Rubinstein, R.G. Armstrong

Car 99

US   1935   70m   bw
Paramount

A novice state trooper redeems early failure by capturing bank robbers.

Competent routine programmer which helped to establish its star.

w Karl Detzer, C. Gardner Sullivan d Charles Barton

☆ Fred MacMurray, Ann Sheridan, Sir Guy Standing

'Heaps of excitement and comedy make a swell hour of entertainment for the nabe element.' – *Variety*

Car of Dreams

GB   1935   72m   bw
Gaumont-British (Michael Balcon)

A rich man's son buys a car for one of his father's factory girls.

Silly comedy with sillier music, remade from a German original.

w Austin Melford d Austin Melford, Graham Cutts ph Mutz Greenbaum m Mischa Spoliansky ad Alfred Junge

☆ John Mills, Grete Mosheim, Mark Lester, Robertson Hare, Norah Howard

Car Trouble

GB   1986   93m   colour
Thorn EMI/GTO/Goldfarb (Howard Malin, Gregory J. DeSantis)

A woman having an affair with a car salesman finds herself sexually locked to him in her husband's new vehicle.

This weird premise for a comedy rings up remarkably few laughs.

w James Whaley, A. J. Tipping d David Green ph Michael Garfath

☆ Julie Walters, Ian Charleson, Stratford Johns, Vincenzo Ricotta

Car Wash

US   1976   96m   Technicolor
Universal

Various eccentrics congregate around the Dee Luxe Car Wash.

Zany ethnic (black) comedy with little rhyme or reason in its development but a certain vigour in some of its sketches. A subsequent TV series didn't last.

w Joel Schumacher d Michael Schultz

☆ Franklyn Ajaye, Sully Boyar, Richard Pryor, Ivan Dixon, Antonio Fargas, Tracy Reed

'Its specialty is yanking laughs by having blacks do dirtier versions of the standard pranks that naughty kids used to do in comedies.' – *Pauline Kael*

Caravaggio *

GB   1986   89m   Technicolor
BFI/Channel 4/Nicholas Ward-Jackson (Sarah Radclyffe)

An imaginary biopic of the Italian painter who died in 1610, with emphasis on homosexual models, a variety of scandals, and jokey anachronisms.

A classic for the gay crowd; something of a mystery for everyone else.

wd Derek Jarman ph Gabriel Beristain m Simon Fisher Turner pd Christopher Hobbs

☆ Nigel Terry, Sean Bean, Garry Cooper, Spencer Leigh

'It rises above its financial restrictions to prove that less can be a lot more.' – *Variety*

Caravan

US   1934   101m   bw
Fox

A countess marries a gypsy.

Odd romantic drama with music: too whimsical to succeed.

w Samson Raphaelson d Erik Charell ph Ernest Palmer, Theodor Sparkuhl m/ly Werner R. Heymann, Gus Kahn

☆ Loretta Young, Charles Boyer, Jean Parker, Phillips Holmes, Louise Fazenda, Eugene Pallette, C. Aubrey Smith, Charley Grapewin, Noah Beery, Dudley Digges

'Big, beautiful and boring … peasants come popping out of nowhere, in pairs, tens, hundreds, thousands, and burst into song.' – *Variety*

Caravan

GB   1946   122m   bw
Gainsborough (Harold Huth)

A young man on a mission in Spain is left for dead by emissaries of his rival in love; he is nursed back to health by a gypsy girl who falls in love with him.

Artificial, romantic, high-flown period tosh without the courage of its lack of convictions. At the time, an exhibitor's dream.

w Roland Pertwee novel Lady Eleanor Smith d Arthur Crabtree ph Stephen Dade

☆ Stewart Granger, Jean Kent, Anne Crawford, Robert Helpmann, Dennis Price, Gerard Heinz, Enid Stamp-Taylor, David Horne, John Salew

Caravan to Vaccares

GB/France   1974   98m   Eastmancolor Panavision
Crowndale (Geoffrey Reeve)

An American drifter on the Riviera is employed to escort a mysterious Hungarian to New York.

Lumpy Alistair MacLean action thriller, all a bit déjà vu.

w Paul Wheeler d Geoffrey Reeve ph Frederic Tammes m Stanley Myers

☆ David Birney, Charlotte Rampling, Michel Lonsdale, Marcel Bozzuffi, Michael Bryant

'An undernourished plot advanced only by a series of venerable clichés.' – *MFB*

'The biggest load of schoolboy hokum since Boy's Own Paper ceased circulation.' – *Michael Billington, Illustrated London News*

Caravans

US/Iran   1978   123m   Technicolor Panavision
Ibex/FIDCI (Elmo Williams)

In the Middle East in 1948, a junior diplomat is sent to bring back the daughter of a US politician, who has married an Arab, left him, and joined a Bedouin caravan.

Curiously halting succession of pretty pictures and not much plot; what there is tends to take second place to philosophy and eastern promise.

w Nancy Voyles Crawford, Thomas A. MacMahon, Lorraine Williams novel James Michener d James Fargo ph Douglas Slocombe m Mike Batt

☆ Anthony Quinn, Michael Sarrazin, Jennifer O'Neill, Christopher Lee, Joseph Cotten, Barry Sullivan, Jeremy Kemp

'A tiresome exercise in anti-climax.' – *Tim Pulleine, MFB*

† The film cost 14 million dollars and is said to have been financed by the Shah of Iran.

Carbine Williams

US   1952   93m   bw
MGM (Armand Deutsch)

An imprisoned bootlegger perfects a new gun and is pardoned.

Flat fictionalization of a true story, with the star miscast.

w Art Cohn d Richard Thorpe ph William Mellor m Conrad Salinger

☆ James Stewart, Jean Hagen, Wendell Corey, Carl Benton Reid, Paul Stewart, Otto Hulett, James Arness

Carbon Copy

US   1981   91m   Metrocolor
Hemdale/RKO (Stanley Shapiro, Carter de Haven)

An executive is shocked when his long-lost son turns out to be black.

Stale comedy. The producers clearly think the basic idea worth ramming home a score of times; the characterization is thin and the production undernourished.

w Stanley Shapiro d Michael Schultz ph Fred J. Koenekamp m Bill Conti

☆ George Segal, Susan Saint James, Jack Warden, Dick Martin, Denzel Washington, Paul Winfield

'It makes *Guess Who's Coming to Dinner?* look like a tract for the nineties.' – *Derek Malcolm, Guardian*

'He's the cheekiest man in town!'

The Card **

GB   1952   91m   bw
Rank/British Film Makers (John Bryan)

US title: *The Promoter*

A bright young clerk from the potteries finds many ingenious ways of improving his bank account and his place in society.

Pleasing period comedy with the star in a made-to-measure role and excellent production values.

w Eric Ambler novel Arnold Bennett d Ronald Neame ph Oswald Morris m William Alwyn ad T. Hopwell Ash

☆ Alec Guinness, Glynis Johns, Petula Clark, Valerie Hobson, Edward Chapman, Veronica Turleigh, Gibb McLaughlin, Frank Pettingell

Card of Fate: see *Le Grand Jeu*

Cardboard Cavalier *

GB   1949   96m   bw
Rank/Two Cities (Walter Forde)

In Cromwellian England, a jovial commission a barrow boy to carry a secret letter. Helped by Nell Gwynn, he succeeds after encounters with a castle ghost and custard pies.

A pantomime crossed with an Aldwych farce in a period setting. It failed at the time but now seems a brave try, with nice judgment all round.

w Noel Langley d Walter Forde ph Jack Hildyard m Lambert Williamson

☆ Sid Field, Margaret Lockwood, Mary Clare, Jerry Desmonde, Claude Hulbert, Irene Handl, Brian Worth, Edmund Willard

Cardiac Arrest

US   1980   80m   DeLuxe
Film Ventures (Richard Helzberg)

A murderer in San Francisco cuts out the hearts of his victims.

Trivial slasher movie.

☆ Gerry Goodrow, Mike Chan, Max Gail, Susan O'Connell, Ray Reinhardt

Cardigan's Last Case: see *State's Attorney*

The Cardinal *

US   1963   175m   Technicolor   Panavision 70
Gamma/Otto Preminger

A 1917 ordinand becomes a Boston curate, a fighter of the Ku Klux Klan, a Rome diplomat, and finally gets a cardinal's hat.

Heavy-going documentary melodrama with many interesting sequences marred by lack of cohesion, too much grabbing at world problems, and over-sensational personal asides.

w Robert Dozier novel Henry Morton Robinson d Otto Preminger ph Leon Shamroy m Jerome Moross pd Lyle Wheeler titles Saul Bass

☆ Tom Tryon, Carol Lynley, Dorothy Gish, Maggie MacNamara, Cecil Kellaway, John Saxon, John Huston, Robert Morse, Burgess Meredith, Jill Haworth, Raf Vallone, Tullio Carminati, Ossie Davis, Chill Wills, Arthur Hunnicutt and also Murray Hamilton, Patrick O'Neal, Romy Schneider

'Very probably the last word in glossy dishonesty posturing as serious art.' – *John Simon*

'Mere and sheer wide screen Technicolor movie.' – *Stanley Kauffmann*

& Otto Preminger; Leon Shamroy; John Huston

'To thwart a king's passion, he gambled the fate of a nation!'

Cardinal Richelieu *

US   1935   83m   bw
Twentieth Century (Darryl F. Zanuck)

Fictionalized biography of the unscrupulous cardinal who was the grey eminence behind Louis XIII.

One of George Arliss's better star vehicles, with not much conviction but excellent production values.

w Maude Howell, Cameron Rogers, W. P. Lipscomb d Rowland V. Lee ph Peverell Marley m Alfred Newman

☆ George Arliss, Maureen O'Sullivan, Edward Arnold, Cesar Romero

'In selecting the churchly cardinal of Bulwer-Lytton rather than the cavalier-cardinal beloved of Dumas, they have lost romance and dash but gained compensating dignity … a fine technical production.' – *Variety*

† Nunnally Johnson, who wrote the original script, asked for his name to be removed from the credits because he objected to the way Arliss rewrote his lines.

The Care Bears' Adventure In Wonderland!

Canada   1987   75m   colour
Fox/Nelvana Productions (Michael Hirsch, Patrick Loubert, Clive A. Smith)

The Care Bears go through the looking glass with Alice.

Undemanding and uninteresting whimsy for the under-sixes.

w Susi Snooks, John DeKlein story Peter Sauder d Raymond Jafelice m Trish Cullen, John Sebastian

☆ Featuring the voices of Colin Fox, Bob Dermer, Eva Almos, Dan Hennessy, Jim Henshaw

The Care Bears Movie

US   1985   75m   colour
Nelvana (Michael Hirsch, Patrick Loubert, Clive Smith)

Magical bears combat an evil spirit who aims to make everybody miserable.

Cartoon feature, sluggishly animated and narrated, with appeal to nobody over five years old. Produced as a back-up to a range of toys.

w Peter Sauder d Arna Selznick m John Sebastian

☆ Featuring the voices of Mickey Rooney, Georgia Engel, Harry Dean Stanton

Care of the Spitfire Grill: see *The Spitfire Grill*

Career

US   1939   80m   bw
RKO (Robert Sisk)

A respected small-town storekeeper has old scores to settle against the local banker.

Modest, pleasing, rather faded 'B' picture.

w Dalton Trumbo, Bert Granet novel Phil Stong d Leigh Jason ph Frank Redman

☆ Edward Ellis, Samuel S. Hinds, Anne Shirley, Janet Beecher, Leon Errol, Raymond Hatton, Hobart Cavanaugh

'Small-town story will sell better outside major playdates.' – *Variety*

† The film featured the winners of the Gateway to Hollywood talent contest, John Archer and Alice Eden.

Career *

US 1959 105m bw

Paramount/Hal B. Wallis (Paul Nathan)

🖵

An actor from the midwest finally gets his chance in New York.

A location melodrama with the feel of a documentary, well played but slow and rather indeterminate.

w James Lee *play* James Lee d Joseph Anthony ph Joseph LaShelle m Franz Waxman

☆ Anthony Franciosa, Dean Martin, Shirley MacLaine, Carolyn Jones, Joan Blackman, Robert Middleton, Frank McHugh, Donna Douglas

ℒ Joseph LaShelle

Career Girls *

GB 1997 87m Metrocolor

Film Four/Thin Man/Matrix (Simon Channing-Williams)

🖵 🖵

Two flatmates who studied at the North London Polytechnic meet again 10 years later to recall their past times together.

With a cast twitching away like contestants at a St Vitus's dance marathon, this is an intensely caricatured, unenlightening account of student life and its aftermath.

wd Mike Leigh ph Dick Pope m Marianne Jean-Baptiste, Tony Remy pd Eve Stewart ed Robin Sales

☆ Katrin Cartlidge, Lynda Steadman, Kate Byers, Mark Benton, Andy Serkis, Joe Tucker, Margot Stanley, Michael Hay

'A masterly observation of the foibles of the human condition, rendered with an incisive bite and delivered with a boisterous wit.' – *Christopher Hemblade, Empire*

'Manages to be bleak, lightweight and histrionic at the same time. Even Leigh aficionados might balk at such relentless toothlessness.' – *John Diamond, New Statesman*

Career Opportunities

US 1991 85m DeLuxe

Universal/Hughes Entertainment (John Hughes, A. Hunt Lowry)

🖵 🖵 ⊙ ⊚ ∩

A young nightwatchman outwits thieves trying to rob a department store.

Tired teen comedy that runs out of jokes long before the end.

w John Hughes d Bryan Gordon ph Don McAlpine m Thomas Newman pd Paul Sylbert ed Glenn Farr, Peck Prior

☆ Frank Whaley, Jennifer Connelly, Dermot Mulroney, Kieran Mulroney, John M. Jackson, Jenny O'Hara, Noble Willingham, Barry Corbin, John Candy (uncredited)

'Plenty of absorbing characters, smart, snappy dialog and delightful stretches of comic foolery.' – *Variety*

Career Woman

US 1936 75m bw

TCF

A shyster lawyer helps a girl student to win a murder case.

Passable programme material which didn't bore.

w Lamar Trotti *story* Gene Fowler d Lewis Seiler

☆ Michael Whalen, Claire Trevor, Isabel Jewell, Eric Linden, Virginia Field, Gene Lockhart, Ed Brophy, El Brendel

'Teeters between farce and stark realism ... not exactly for the family trade.' – *Variety*

Carefree *

US 1938 85m bw

RKO (Pandro S. Berman)

🖵 🖵

A humourless lawyer sends his undecided girlfriend to an alienist, with whom she falls in love.

Slight, frothy comedy musical; quite palatable, but it signalled the end of the Astaire-Rogers series.

w Allan Scott, Ernest Pagano d Mark Sandrich ph Robert de Grasse m/ly Irving Berlin md Victor Baravalle ch Hermes Pan ad Van Nest Polglase

☆ Fred Astaire, Ginger Rogers, Ralph Bellamy, Luella Gear, Clarence Kolb, Jack Carson, Franklin Pangborn, Walter Kingsford, Hattie McDaniel

'Perhaps their poorest musical ... a disappointing story and the stars alone may save it.' – *Variety*

♫ 'I Used to Be Colour Blind'; 'The Yam'; 'The Night Is Filled with Music'

ℒ Victor Baravalle; Van Nest Polglase; song 'Change Partners'

Careful

Canada 1992 100m colour

ICA/Greg and Tracy Film Ministry (Greg Klymkiw, Tracy Traeger)

Sex and death engulf two families living in constant danger of being killed by Alpine avalanches.

A deliberately over-the-top melodramatic concoction, a heady stew of rape, incest, requited and unrequited love, a deformed child kept hidden in an attic and ghosts bringing warnings of doom. It's a low-budget camp extravaganza that can amuse, but can as easily infuriate by its knowing air.

w George Toles, Guy Maddin d Guy Maddin ph Guy Maddin m John McCulloch pd Guy Maddin ed Guy Maddin

☆ Kyle McCulloch, Gosia Dobrowolska, Sarah Neville, Brent Neale, Paul Cox, Victor Cowie, Jackie Burroughs

'In a film which can afford real animals but not real mountains, a couple of goats running up a slope – swathed in dry ice, shot in purple or blue monochrome and captioned to tell us the altitude – stand in for the Alps.' – *Claire Monk, Sight and Sound*

Careful, Soft Shoulder *

US 1942 69m bw

TCF (Walter Morosco)

A Washington socialite becomes a spy for both sides.

Modest, slightly unusual second feature which over the years has gathered for itself more reputation than it really deserves.

wd Oliver H. P. Garrett ph Charles Clarke m Leigh Harline, Emil Newman

☆ Virginia Bruce, James Ellison, Aubrey Mather, Sheila Ryan, Ralph Byrd

Careless Lady

US 1932 76m bw

Fox

A young girl from the country pretends to be a married society woman and finds herself with a husband she doesn't want.

It was the scriptwriter who was careless: the story doesn't make much sense.

w Guy Bolton *story* Reita Lambert d Kenneth MacKenna

☆ Joan Bennett, John Boles, Minna Gombell, Weldon Heyburn, Raul Roulien, Fortunio Bonanova, Josephine Hull

'Reaching house averages will be beyond expectations regardless of campaign.' – *Variety*

The Caretaker *

GB 1964 105m bw

Caretaker Films (Michael Birkett)

US title: *The Guest*

Two brothers invite a revolting tramp to share their attic.

Rather doleful filming of the fashionable play with its non-plot, irregular conceits and interesting interplay of character. It remains a theatrical experience.

w Harold Pinter d Clive Donner ph Nicolas Roeg m Ron Grainer

☆ Alan Bates, Robert Shaw, Donald Pleasence

'Now the screen tells what makes a woman – and what breaks her!'

The Caretakers *

US 1963 97m bw

UA/Hall Bartlett

GB title: *Borderlines*

The interrelationship of several cases in a state mental hospital.

Rather hysterical melodrama, lacking in the stature required for its subject, but sometimes perversely entertaining.

w Henry F. Greenberg *novel* Daniel Telfer d Hall Bartlett ph Lucien Ballard m Elmer Bernstein

☆ Polly Bergen, Robert Stack, Joan Crawford, Diane McBain, Janis Paige, Van Williams, Robert Vaughn, Herbert Marshall, Constance Ford

ℒ Lucien Ballard

The Carey Treatment *

US 1972 101m Metrocolor Panavision

MGM (William Belasco)

A Boston pathologist investigating the death of an abortion victim becomes the potential murder victim of a father turned killer.

Pretentious thriller with a tendency to make moral points among the bloodshed; vigorously but variably made.

w James P. Bonner (Irving Ravetch, Harriet Frank Jnr, John D. F. Black) *novel* A Case of Need by Jeffrey Hudson (Michael Crichton) d Blake Edwards ph Frank Stanley m Roy Budd

☆ James Coburn, Jennifer O'Neill, Skye Aubrey, Pat Hingle, Dan O'Herlihy, Elizabeth Allen, Alex Dreier, Regis Toomey

Cargo of Innocents: see *Stand By for Action*

Cargo to Capetown

US 1950 84m bw

Columbia

A merchant ship captain shanghais his friend on a long voyage.

Routine, competently staged thick ear.

w Lionel Houser d Earl McEvoy

☆ Broderick Crawford, John Ireland, Ellen Drew, Edgar Buchanan, Ted de Corsia

Caribbean

US 1952 94m Technicolor

Paramount/Pine-Thomas (William H. Pine, William C. Thomas)

GB title: *Caribbean Gold*

An 18th-century pirate captures the nephew of his old enemy.

Adequate but not very exciting swashbuckler with fair production values.

w Frank L. Moss, Edward Ludwig d Edward Ludwig ph Lionel Lindon m Lucien Cailliet

☆ John Payne, Arlene Dahl, Cedric Hardwicke, Francis L. Sullivan, Dennis Hoey

Caribbean Gold: see *Caribbean*

The Caribbean Mystery

US 1945 65m bw

William Girard/TCF

A retired cop investigates the disappearance of several geologists on an oil company payroll.

Modest mystery, previously filmed as Murder in Trinidad.

w W. Scott Darling *novel* John W. Vandercook d Robert Webb

☆ James Dunn, Sheila Ryan, Edward Ryan, Jackie Paley, Reed Hadley

The Cariboo Trail *

US 1950 80m Cinecolor

TCF (Nat Holt)

🖵 ⊙

A cattle rancher from Montana takes his cows along when he goes prospecting for gold in British Columbia.

In its brief length, it manages to cram just about every standard Western ingredient – cowboys and Indians, fist and gun fights, cows and gold, a wicked town boss and a glamorous saloon owner – without displaying any originality; its underlying theme, the appropriation of Indian lands, no longer seems as heroic as it once did.

w Frank Gruber *story* John Rhodes Sturdy d Edwin L. Marin ph Fred Jackman m Paul Sawtell ad Arthur Lonergan ed Philip Martin

☆ Randolph Scott, George 'Gabby' Hayes, Bill Williams, Victor Jory, Karin Booth, Dale Robertson

'A dream called freedom. A nightmare called Nicaragua.'

Carla's Song *

GB/Germany/Spain 1996 125m Metrocolor

Polygram/Channel 4/GFF/Parallax/Road Movies/Tornasol (Sally Hibbin)

🖵 🖵

In the mid-80s, a Glaswegian bus driver falls in love with a Nicaraguan woman and returns with her to her homeland in search of her missing boyfriend.

A political and personal drama played out against the civil war in Nicaragua, it too often lapses into confused agitprop to convince an audience of its relevance or point.

w Paul Laverty d Ken Loach ph Barry Ackroyd m George Fenton pd Martin Johnson ed Jonathan Morris

☆ Robert Carlyle, Oyanka Cabezas, Scott Glenn, Salvador Espinoza, Louise Goodall, Richard Loza, Gary Lewis

'What the film clearly intends is a lest-we-forget drama, and this is an angry film, understandably so. But, strangely, the angrier it gets, the less effective it becomes.' – *Derek Malcolm*

Carlito's Way *

US 1993 145m DeLuxe

Universal (Martin Bregman, Willi Baer, Michael A. Bregman)

🖵 🖵 🖵 ⊙ ⊚ ∩

A drug dealer finds it tough when he tries to go straight.

A good, if unoriginal, gangster movie with some action sequences that add a little distinction; it would benefit, though, from being shorter.

w David Koepp *novels* Carlito's Way, After Hours by Edwin Torres d Brian de Palma ph Stephen H. Burum m Patrick Doyle pd Richard Sylbert ed Bill Pankow, Kristina Boden

☆ Al Pacino, Sean Penn, Penelope Ann Miller, John Leguizamo, Ingrid Rogers, Luis Guzman, John Rebhorn, Viggo Mortensen

'Handsomely made, expertly directed and colorfully acted, it should satisfy action buffs and slightly more sophisticated audiences.' – *Variety*

'An old-style gangster movie with some neat contemporary knobs on.' – *Derek Malcolm*

Carlton-Browne of the FO

GB 1958 88m bw

British Lion/Charter Films (John Boulting)

🖵

US title: *Man in a Cocked Hat*

When valuable mineral deposits are found in a small British colony, the diplomat sent to cement good relations does quite the reverse.

Hit-or-miss farcical comedy several rungs below the Ealing style, with all concerned in poor form.

wd Jeffrey Dell, Roy Boulting ph Max Greene m John Addison

☆ Terry-Thomas, Peter Sellers, Ian Bannen, Thorley Walters, Raymond Huntley, John Le Mesurier, Luciana Paluzzi, Miles Malleson, Kynaston Reeves, Marie Lohr

Carmen *

Spain 1983 101m Eastmancolor

Emiliano Piedra Productions/Television Española (Emiliano Piedra)

🖵 ⊙

A rehearsal for the ballet Carmen finds dancers playing out in reality the parts of the drama.

Enjoyable but exhausting melodrama with elements of The Red Shoes; meticulous choreography and direction are its chief assets.

w Carlos Saura, Antonio Gades *novel* Prosper Mérimée d Carlos Saura ph Teo Escamilla m Paco de Lucia ad Felix Murcia ed Pedro del Rey

☆ Antonio Gades, Laura del Sol, Paco de Lucia, Cristina Hoyos

'Extremely enjoyable, but lacks the edge that would make it in any way compelling.' – *Jill Forbes, MFB*

ℒ best foreign film

Ⴆ best foreign film

Carmen *

Italy/France 1984 152m Eastmancolor Panavision

Opera/Gaumont (Patrice Ledoux)

🖵 🖵 ⊙ ∩

A luxuriantly filmed version of Bizet's opera, generally received with critical rapture.

d Francesco Rosi ph Pasqualino De Santis pd Enrico Job

☆ Julia Migenes-Johnson, Placido Domingo, Ruggero Raimondi

† Silent versions stretch back to 1915 – that one starred Geraldine Farrar the opera singer (in a silent movie, by producer Cecil B. de Mille's whim).

Carmen Jones *

US 1954 105m DeLuxe Cinemascope

TCF (Otto Preminger)

A factory girl marries a soldier, and is strangled by him for infidelity.

Black American updating of Bizet's opera, not really satisfactory but given full marks for trying, though the main singing is dubbed and the effect remains doggedly theatrical.

w Harry Kleiner d Otto Preminger ph Sam Leavitt md Herschel Burke Gilbert ly Oscar Hammerstein II titles Saul Bass

☆ *Dorothy Dandridge, Harry Belafonte, Pearl Bailey, Olga James, Joe Adams, Roy Glenn, Nick Stewart, Diahann Carroll, Brock Peters*

'All one regrets is that the director has been unable to impose a unifying style on this promising material.' – *Gavin Lambert*

† Joe Adams's vocals were dubbed by Marvin Hayes, Harry Belafonte's by LeVerne Hutcherson, Diahann Carroll's by Bernice Peterson, and Dorothy Dandridge's by Marilyn Horne.

♫ Herschel Burke Gilbert; Dorothy Dandridge

Carmin Profond: see *Deep Crimson*

Carnage: see *A Bay of Blood*

Carnal Knowledge *

US   1971   97m   Technicolor   Panavision
Avco Embassy/Icarus (Mike Nichols)

⊞ ▤ ◖.

A college student embarks on an enthusiastic and varied sex life but by middle age is bored and empty.

Hampered by an unsuitable wide screen, this pretentious but fragmented comedy drama is embarrassingly conscious of its own daring in subject and language, and good performances are weighed down by an unsubtle script and tricksy direction.

w Jules Feiffer d Mike Nichols ph Giuseppe Rotunno m various songs pd Richard Sylbert

☆ Jack Nicholson, Arthur Garfunkel, Candice Bergen, Ann-Margret, Rita Moreno

♫ Ann-Margret

Carne Tremula: see *Live Flesh*

Carnegie Hall

US   1947   134m   bw
Federal Films (Boris Morros, William Le Baron)

The story of New York's music centre, based on a fiction about a cleaner who finally becomes a concert organizer when her son is a famous pianist.

Slim and risible excuse for a classical concert, featuring among others Bruno Walter, Leopold Stokowski, Artur Rubinstein, Jascha Heifetz, Lily Pons, Rise Stevens, Ezio Pinza, Jan Peerce, Harry James, Vaughn Monroe and the New York Philharmonic Symphony Orchestra.

w Karl Kamb d Edgar G. Ulmer ph William Miller

☆ Marsha Hunt, William Prince, Frank McHugh, Martha O'Driscoll

'The thickest and sourest mess of musical multigatawny I have yet had to sit down to.' – *James Agee*

Un Carnet de Bal **

France   1937   135m   bw
Lévy/Strauss/Sigma
aka: *Life Dances On*

A rich widow seeks her partners at a ball she remembers from her youth, finding that they are all failures and the ball a village hop.

Considering its fame, this is a lumpy porridge of a picture, good in parts but often slow, pretentious and banal. Its gallery of actors is, however, unique.

w Jean Sarment, Pierre Wolff, Bernard Zimmer, Henri Jeanson, Julien Duvivier d Julien Duvivier ph Michel Kelber, Philippe Agostini m Maurice Jaubert

☆ Marie Bell, Françoise Rosay, *Louis Jouvet, Raimu, Harry Baur, Fernandel, Pierre Blanchar*

'Recent winner of the Mussolini Cup is loaded with top names, but it is not the film of the year ... it tries to take in too much and takes too long to put across.' – *Variety*

† The film's international success took Duvivier to Hollywood, where he half-remade it as *Lydia* and went on to other multi-story films such as *Tales of Manhattan* and *Flesh and Fantasy*.

Les Carnets de Major Thompson: see *The Diary of Major Thompson*

Carnival

US   1934   77m   bw
Columbia

A widowed puppeteer takes custody of his child, which is sought by the maternal grandfather, and seeks anonymity in a circus.

Curious sentimental melodrama with the stars shown in an unusual light.

w Robert Riskin d Walter Lang

☆ Lee Tracy, Jimmy Durante, Sally Eilers, Dickie Walters, Thomas Jackson, Florence Rice, Lucille Ball

'This should hold its own, though it probably will not climb to big grosses.' – *Variety*

Carnival

GB   1946   93m   bw
Rank/Two Cities (John Sutro, William Sassoon)

In the 1890s, a ballet dancer marries a dour Cornish farmer, who shoots her when her erstwhile lover comes after her.

Flimsy screen version of a solidly old-fashioned romantic drama.

w Eric Maschwitz novel Compton Mackenzie d Stanley Haynes ph Guy Green

☆ Sally Gray, Michael Wilding, Bernard Miles, Cathleen Nesbitt, Stanley Holloway, Jean Kent, Nancy Price, Hazel Court, Brenda Bruce, Catherine Lacey

† The story was previously filmed in 1931, as *Dance Pretty Lady*, with Ann Casson and Carl Harbord. The 1931 film *Carnival*, with Matheson Lang, is based on a story identical to *Men Are Not Gods* and *A Double Life*: an actor becomes obsessed with the part of Othello and strangles his wife.

Carnival in Costa Rica

US   1947   97m   Technicolor
TCF (William A. Bacher)

A young Costa Rican, engaged to an American singer, returns home to find that his parents expect him to marry his childhood sweetheart.

Decidedly rundown musical in which incessant carnival largely supplants the wispy plot.

w John Larkin, Samuel Hoffenstein, Elizabeth Reinhardt d Gregory Ratoff ph Harry Jackson m/ly Harry Ruby, Ernesto Lecuona ch Leonid Massine

☆ Dick Haymes, Vera-Ellen, Celeste Holm, J. Carrol Naish, Cesar Romero

Carnival in Flanders: see *La Kermesse Héroïque*

Carnival of Souls

US   1962   80m   bw
Herts-Lion (Herk Harvey)

⊞ ▤ ◖.

After an accident, a lady ghost emerges to become the new church organist.

Absurd but occasionally compelling independently made horror film which would have been better in half-hour form.

w John Clifford d Herk Harvey ph Maurice Prather m Gene Moore ed Dan Palmquist, Bill de Jarnette

☆ Candace Hilligoss, Herk Harvey, Francis Feist, Sidney Berger

'Has the power to detach you from your surroundings and put you in the middle of its own distinctive nowhere.' – *Terrence Rafferty, New Yorker*

† Made in Kansas, allegedly for less than 100,000 dollars.

Carnival of Terror: see *The Funhouse*

Carnival of Thieves: see *The Caper of the Golden Bulls*

Carnival Story

US/Germany   1954   95m   Technicolor
The King Brothers

▤

A starving girl becomes a trapezist at a German circus and stirs up jealousy among her partners.

Bleak reworking of The Three Maxims (qv), reworked again with more expertise in Trapeze (qv); this version is a cheap and unattractive co-production.

w Kurt Neumann, Hans Jacoby d Kurt Neumann ph Ernest Haller m Willy Schmidt-Gentner

☆ Anne Baxter, Steve Cochran, Lyle Bettger, George Nader, Jay C. Flippen

'63 million years ago they ruled the Earth. They're back, and it's no theme park!'

Carnosaur

US   1993   83m   Foto-Kem
New Horizons (Mike Elliott)

⊞ ▤ ◖. ◎

A scientist breeds giant meat-eating mutant chickens in an attempt to recreate dinosaurs and replace humans by a kinder species.

Cheap attempt to cash in on the Jurassic Park craze from Roger Corman's outfit, recast as a conventional, gory, monster-on-the-loose, mad-scientist horror pic: nasty, brutish and, fortunately, short.

wd Adam Simon novel Harry Adam Knight (John Brosnan) ph Keith Holland m Nigel Holton pd Aaron Osborne ed Richard Genter sp John Buechler, Magical Media Industries, Alan Lasky

☆ Diane Ladd, Raphael Sbarge, Jennifer Runyon, Harrison Page, Ned Bellamy, Clint Howard

'This breezy outing is a not-very-filling popcorn treat. Predictably plotted with bargain-basement effects, it's a serviceable programmer.' – *Variety*

Carny

US   1980   105m   Technicolor
Lorimar/Jonathan Taplin (Robbie Robertson)

▤

Three wacky characters join a travelling carnival.

Sordid, sexy melodrama which seems to be doing a Jules and Jim with no holds barred. Not badly made, but full of people one would cross the road to avoid.

w Thomas Baum story Phoebe Kaylor, Robert Kaylor, Robbie Robertson d Robert Kaylor ph Harry Stradling Jnr m Alex North

☆ Gary Busey, Jodie Foster, Robbie Robertson, Kenneth McMillan, Meg Foster, Elisha Cook Jnr, Fred Ward

'Too dark and turbulent a vision to be palatable to a large public.' – *Variety*

Caro Diario: see *Dear Diary*

Carolina

US   1934   85m   bw
Fox (Darryl F. Zanuck)
GB title: *House of Connelly*

A Yankee farmer's daughter falls in love with a Southern plantation owner.

Mildly pleasing period piece.

w Reginald Berkeley play *The House of Connelly* by Paul Green d Henry King ph Hal Mohr m Louis de Francesco

☆ Janet Gaynor, Lionel Barrymore, Robert Young, Henrietta Crosman, Mona Barrie, Richard Cromwell, Stepin Fetchit

'An arresting saga of a proud old southern family that starts out threateningly strong but peters to the point where it misses being another *State Fair*.' – *Variety*

Caroline Chérie

France   1951   115m   bw
SNEG/Cinéphonie

Adventures of an attractive and willing young French girl in the days of the revolution.

A cheerful French imitation of Forever Amber; witless and not very entertaining despite good period sense and a certain amount of self-mockery.

w Jean Anouilh novel Cécil Saint-Laurent d Richard Pottier ph Maurice Barry m Georges Auric

☆ Martine Carol, Jacques Dacqmine, Marie Déa, Paul Bernard, Pierre Cressoy

† After several sequels, a colour remake appeared in 1967.

Carousel *

US   1956   128m   Eastmancolor
Cinemascope 55
TCF (Henry Ephron)

⊞ ▤ ◖. ◎ ◖

A ne'er-do-well dies while committing a holdup. Fifteen years later he returns from heaven to set his family's affairs in order.

Based on a fantasy play with an honourable history, this super-wide-screen version of an effective stage musical is hollow and boring, a humourless whimsy in which even the songs seem an intrusion.

w Phoebe and Henry Ephron, from the musical based on Ferenc Molnar's play Liliom d Henry King ph Charles G. Clarke m/ly Rodgers and Hammerstein ch Rod Alexander, Agnes de Mille

☆ Gordon MacRae, Shirley Jones, Cameron Mitchell, Gene Lockhart, Barbara Ruick, Robert Rounseville

'This is adult entertainment!'

The Carpetbaggers **

US   1964   150m   Technicolor   Panavision
Paramount/Embassy (Joseph E. Levine)

▤

A young playboy inherits an aircraft business, becomes a megalomaniac tycoon, and moves to Hollywood in his search for power.

Enjoyable pulp fiction clearly suggested by the career of Howard Hughes. Lashings of old-fashioned melodrama, quite well pointed by all concerned.

w John Michael Hayes novel Harold Robbins d Edward Dmytryk ph Joseph MacDonald m Elmer Bernstein ad Hal Pereira, Walter Tyler

☆ George Peppard, Carroll Baker, Alan Ladd, Martin Balsam, Bob Cummings, Martha Hyer, Elizabeth Ashley, Lew Ayres, Ralph Taeger, Archie Moore, Leif Erickson, Audrey Totter

'One of those elaborate conjuring tricks in which yards and yards of coloured ribbon are spread all over the stage merely to prove that the conjuror has nothing up his sleeve.' – *Tom Milne*

† It was Ladd's last film.

'A dad in a hurry. A man on the run. And five kids with an attitude.'

Carpool

US   1996   119m   Technicolor
Warner/Regency (Arnon Milchan, Michael Nathanson)

⊞ ▤ ◖.

A harassed businessman, together with a car load of children is taken hostage by an incompetent armed robber.

Dumb, ramshackle comedy, of infantile adults and precocious children, that is a pain to sit through.

w Don Rhymer d Arthur Hiller m David M. Walsh m John Debney pd James D. Vance ed William Reynolds, L. James Langlois

☆ Tom Arnold, David Paymer, Rhea Perlman, Kim Coates, Obba Babatundé, Rachel Leigh Cook, Micah Gardener, Jordan Blake Warkol, Rod Steiger

† Tom Arnold was awarded a Golden Raspberry as worst actor of the year for his performance.

Carquake: see *Cannonball*

Carrefour *

France   1938   75m   bw
BUP Tuscherer

A French manufacturer, wounded during the war, finds himself the centre of blackmail plots.

Intriguing melodrama which was later rather flatly remade in Hollywood as Crossroads.

w Hans Kafka d Kurt Bernhardt

☆ Charles Vanel, Jules Berry, Suzy Prim, Tania Fedor

'One of the best French films of the late season, and worthy of American attention.' – *Variety*

Carrie **

US   1952   122m   bw
Paramount (William Wyler)

▤ ◖.

In the early 1900s a country girl comes to Chicago, loses her innocence and goes on the stage, meanwhile reducing a wealthy restaurant manager to penury through love for her.

A famous satirical novel is softened into an unwieldy narrative with scarcely enough dramatic power to sustain interest despite splendid production values. Heavy pre-release cuts remain obvious, and the general effect is depressing; but it is very good to look at.

w Ruth and Augustus Goetz novel Sister Carrie by Theodore Dreiser d William Wyler ph Victor Milner m David Raksin ad Hal Pereira, Roland Anderson

☆ Laurence Olivier, Jennifer Jones, Miriam Hopkins, Eddie Albert, Basil Ruysdael, Ray Teal, Barry Kelley, Mary Murphy

'Olivier is so impassioned and so painfully touching that everything else in the movie, including the girl whose story it's meant to be, fades into insignificance.' – *Variety*

'They shot the later episodes for the strongest dramatic effect only, despite the fact that the story had stopped following a melodramatic line and become a sociological study ... each additional episode exploits the audience's hope that things will be brought to a satisfactory conclusion, but they never are.' – *Films in Review*

♫ art direction

Carrie *

US 1976 98m MGM-DeLuxe
UA/Red Bank (Paul Monash)

A repressed teenager with remarkable mental powers takes a macabre revenge on classmates who taunt and persecute her.
Stylish but unattractive shocker which works its way up to a fine climax of gore and frenzy, and takes care to provide a final frisson just when the audience thinks it can safely go home.
w Lawrence D. Cohen *novel* Stephen King d Brian de Palma *ph* Mario Tosi *m* Pino Donaggio
☆ Sissy Spacek, Piper Laurie, Amy Irving, William Katt, John Travolta
'Combining Gothic horror, offhand misogyny and an air of studied triviality, *Carrie* is de Palma's most enjoyable movie in a long while, and also his silliest.' – *Janet Maslin, Newsweek*
'The horror is effective only once, and the attempts at humour are never very successful and come almost when one is inclined to be moved by somebody's plight, so that the non-jokes yield authentic bad taste.' – *John Simon, New York*
⚲ Sissy Spacek; Piper Laurie

'No man is safe from temptation...'

Carried Away *

US 1995 108m Alpha Cine
First Independent/Cinetel (Lisa Hansen, Paul Hertzberg)

GB title: *Acts of Love*
In a small Texan town, a middle-aged schoolteacher is seduced by a teenaged schoolgirl.
Slow-paced story of restricted lives, carrying some convincing emotion owing to Hopper's performance as a downtrodden man discovering a renewed enthusiasm for life.
w Ed Jones *novel Farmer* by Jim Harrison d Bruno Barreto *ph* Declan Quinn *m* Bruce Broughton *pd* Peter Paul Raubertas *ed* Bruce Cannon
☆ Dennis Hopper, Amy Irving, Amy Locane, Julie Harris, Gary Busey, Hal Holbrook, Christopher Pettiet
'The film wins out through refreshing performances and a vibrant irresistible charm.' – *Empire*

The Carriers Are Waiting: see *Les Convoyeurs Attendent*

'A Love Story So Unusual It Has To Be True'

Carrington *

GB/France 1995 120m Technicolor
Polygram/Freeway/Shedlo/Dora (Ronald Shedlo, John McGrath)

A woman artist falls in love with the writer Lytton Strachey, a homosexual, and he with her.
The tangled love-life of the Bloomsbury group is exhibited in one of its more curious relationships, for the couple's love survived Carrington's marriage and she ended her life following Strachey's death; despite the film's title, it is Strachey who dominates the film, partly owing to a miscast and querulous Emma Thompson, but also because Carrington remains a cipher throughout, seen only in relationship to the men in her life.
wd Christopher Hampton *book Lytton Strachey* by Michael Holroyd *ph* Denis Lenoir *m* Michael Nyman *pd* Caroline Amies *ed* George Akers
☆ Emma Thompson, Jonathan Pryce, Steven Waddington, Samuel West, Rufus Sewell, Penelope Wilton, Janet McTeer, Peter Blythe
'Prettily dressed, but cinematically stilted, and makes its characters' anguish and chatter seem ultimately of little consequence.' – *Geoff Brown, The Times*
'Emerges as an unsentimental salute to unselfish love and friendship.' – *Stephen Farber, Movieline*
'What the film wants to pass off as a dangerous liaison looks more like the ultimate in safe sex.' – *Entertainment Weekly*
† The film won the Special Jury Prize and Jonathan Pryce the Best Actor award at the 1995 Cannes Film Festival. It was originally to have been directed by Herbert Ross, and then by Mike Newell. Hampton wrote his original script in the mid-70s.

Carrington VC *

GB 1954 106m bw
British Lion/Romulus (Teddy Baird)

US title: *Court Martial*
An army major is courtmartialled for embezzling mess funds.
Good courtroom drama with a few plot surprises, convincing characters, and very serviceable acting and direction.
w John Hunter *play* Dorothy and Campbell Christie d Anthony Asquith *ph* Desmond Dickinson
☆ David Niven, Margaret Leighton, Noelle Middleton, Laurence Naismith, Clive Morton, Mark Dignam, Allan Cuthbertson, Victor Maddern, John Glyn-Jones, Raymond Francis, Newton Blick, John Chandos

Le Carrosse d'Or: see *The Golden Coach*

Carry Me Back

New Zealand 1982 90m colour
Kiwi Films/New Zealand Film Commission (Graeme Cowley)

Two sons attempt to smuggle their father's corpse from the city to their farm in order to benefit from his will.
Blackish comedy of mishaps and misfits that occasionally amuses.
w Derek Morton, Keith Aberdein, John Reid *story* Joy Cowley d John Reid *ph* Graeme Cowley *m* Tim Bridgewater, James Hall *ad* Jim Barr *ed* Simon Reece, Michael Horton
☆ Grant Tilley, Kelly Johnson, Dorothy McKegg, Derek Hardwick, Joanne Mildenhall

Carry On Abroad *

♈ GB 1972 88m Eastmancolor
Fox-Rank/Peter Rogers

A couple who go on a package holiday to Spain find that their hotel is still being built and there is a staff of no more than three.
Every opportunity for bathroom jokes is relished in what is otherwise an average effort.
w Talbot Rothwell d Gerald Thomas *ph* Alan Hume *m* Eric Rogers *ad* Lionel Couch *ed* Alfred Roome
☆ Sidney James, Kenneth Williams, Charles Hawtrey, Joan Sims, Bernard Bresslaw, Barbara Windsor, Kenneth Connor, Peter Butterworth, Jimmy Logan, June Whitfield, Hattie Jacques
'Travelling well-trodden paths of slapstick, *double entendre* and nudging innuendo.' – *Nigel Andrews*

Carry On Admiral

GB 1957 83m bw Spectascope
George Minter

aka: *The Ship Was Loaded*
In a drunken moment, an MP changes clothes with a naval officer and is forced to adopt his friend's identity aboard ship.
Bland and undemanding farce, taken at a too-leisurely pace.
wd Val Guest *play Off the Record* by Ian Hay, Stephen King-Hall *ph* Arthur Grant *m* Philip Green
☆ David Tomlinson, Peggy Cummins, Ronald Shiner, Brian Reece, A. E. Matthews, Joan Sims, Ronald Adam, Alfie Bass
† The film has no connection with the long-running *Carry On* series.

Carry On Again Doctor

♈ GB 1969 89m Eastmancolor
Rank/Adder (Peter Rogers)

A doctor, exiled to a tropical island, returns to Britain with a special slimming cure.
A slight air of desperation hangs over the often-used setting of a hospital, and most of the jokes remain in intensive care.
w Talbot Rothwell d Gerald Thomas *ph* Ernest Steward *m* Eric Rogers *pd* Jack Blezard *ed* Alfred Roome
☆ Sidney James, Kenneth Williams, Jim Dale, Charles Hawtrey, Joan Sims, Barbara Windsor, Hattie Jacques, Patsy Rowlands, Peter Butterworth, Pat Coombs
'Perhaps the team go that much further than ever before. Their fans will be delighted; those

who aren't won't care.' – *Richard Davis, Films and Filming*

Carry On at Your Convenience

♈ GB 1971 90m Eastmancolor
Rank/Peter Rogers

A union leader at the firm of W. A. Boggs, makers of fine toiletware, keeps ordering the workers to come out on strike.
No toilet joke is left unplumbed here, and the result is dire.
w Talbot Rothwell d Gerald Thomas *ph* Ernest Steward *m* Eric Rogers *ed* Alfred Roome
☆ Sidney James, Kenneth Williams, Charles Hawtrey, Joan Sims, Bernard Bresslaw, Hattie Jacques, Kenneth Cope, Patsy Rowlands, Jacki Piper, Richard O'Callaghan
'One of the least funny of this staggeringly successful series.' – *Eric Braun*
'Even more scrappily assembled than usual and, with the exception of a fairly amusing parody of sex education films, the level of humour, though noticeably cleaner than of late, is still rock bottom.' – *David McGillivray*

Carry On Behind **

♈ GB 1975 90m Eastmancolor
Fox-Rank/Peter Rogers

Archaeologists arrive to search for Roman remains at a caravan site full of holiday-makers.
One of the best of the series and certainly the last watchable film the team produced.
w Dave Freeman d Gerald Thomas *ph* Ernest Steward *m* Eric Rogers *ed* Alfred Roome
☆ Elke Sommer, Kenneth Williams, Joan Sims, Bernard Bresslaw, Kenneth Connor, Peter Butterworth, Jack Douglas, Windsor Davies, Liz Fraser, Patsy Rowlands
'Emerges as the most consistently funny *Carry On* in many years ... a strong vein of comedy is mined from the simple situation of campsite overcrowding, with some of the best sight gags involving a lugubrious Irish wolf-hound and a foul-mouthed mynah bird.' – *Verina Glaessner, MFB*

Carry On Cabby *

♈ GB 1963 91m bw
Anglo Amalgamated/Peter Rogers

The neglected wife of the owner of a taxi firm sets up a rival firm with women drivers.
A deft farcical battle of the sexes.
w Talbot Rothwell d Gerald Thomas *ph* Alan Hume *m* Eric Rogers *ed* Archie Ludski
☆ Sidney James, Charles Hawtrey, Kenneth Connor, Hattie Jacques, Esma Cannon, Liz Fraser, Bill Owen, Milo O'Shea, Jim Dale
'The golden formula of the *Carry On* series is back with a bang.' – *Variety*

Carry On Camping *

GB 1969 88m Eastmancolor
Rank/Peter Rogers

Two men take their girlfriends on holiday to a nudist camp in the hope that it will make them less inhibited.
A partly successful attempt to provide the characters with fewer sexual repressions than usual.
w Talbot Rothwell d Gerald Thomas *ph* Ernest Steward *m* Eric Rogers *ad* Lionel Couch *ed* Alfred Roome
☆ Sidney James, Kenneth Williams, Joan Sims, Charles Hawtrey, Terry Scott, Barbara Windsor
'Suffers somewhat in comparison to some of its predecessors in that it lacks a storyline, however slim.' – *Variety*

Carry On Cleo *

♈ GB 1964 92m Eastmancolor
Anglo Amalgamated/Peter Rogers

Ancient Britons are captured by the Romans while Mark Antony carries on with Cleopatra.
Sporadically amusing parody of the Elizabeth Taylor epic, though it should have been much funnier.
w Talbot Rothwell d Gerald Thomas *ph* Alan Hume *m* Eric Rogers *ad* Bert Davey *ed* Archie Ludski
☆ Sidney James, Kenneth Williams, Charles Hawtrey, Joan Sims, Kenneth Connor, Jim Dale,

Amanda Barrie, E. V. H. Emmett, Sheila Hancock, Jon Pertwee
'Gags, both verbal and visual, suffer from repetition.' – *Variety*
† As a result of a court case for breach of copyright brought by Twentieth Century-Fox, the film's poster, which parodied the advertising for *Cleopatra*, had to be withdrawn.

'Up your anchor for a well crewed voyage!!'

Carry On Columbus

♈ GB 1992 91m colour
Island World/Comedy House/Peter Rogers (John Goldstone)

Columbus's voyage to find a route to the East is sabotaged by spies in the pay of the Sultan of Turkey.
Ill-starred attempt, with a succession of single entendres and some inept performances, to revive a tired old formula.
w Dave Freeman d Gerald Thomas *ph* Alan Hume *m* John Du Prez *pd* Harry Pottle *ed* Chris Blunden
☆ Jim Dale, Bernard Cribbins, Maureen Lipman, Peter Richardson, Rik Mayall, Alexei Sayle, Charles Fleischer, Larry Miller, Leslie Phillips, Julian Clary, Sara Crowe, Rebecca Lacey, Nigel Planer, June Whitfield, Richard Wilson
'Painfully unfunny, lacking imagination and energy.' – *Philip French, Observer*

Carry On Constable *

♈ GB 1960 86m bw
Anglo Amalgamated/Peter Rogers

Four new and inept constables report for duty at their local police station.
In part a parody of the popular TV series Dixon of Dock Green and moderately amusing despite the absence of a plot.
w Norman Hudis *story* Brock Williams d Gerald Thomas *ph* Ted Scaife *m* Bruce Montgomery *ad* Carmen Dillon *ed* John
☆ Sidney James, Kenneth Williams, Charles Hawtrey, Joan Sims, Kenneth Connor, Eric Barker, Leslie Phillips, Hattie Jacques, Shirley Eaton, Cyril Chamberlain, Irene Handl, Esma Cannon, Freddie Mills
'Simply an anthology of police gags and situations.' – *Variety*

'How The West Was Lost!!'

Carry On Cowboy **

♈ GB 1965 95m Eastmancolor
Anglo Amalgamated/Peter Rogers

A sanitary engineer is given the task of cleaning up a town being terrorized by outlaws.
Amusing parody of High Noon and other classic Westerns.
w Talbot Rothwell d Gerald Thomas *ph* Alan Hume *m* Eric Rogers *ad* Bert Davey *ed* Rod Keys
☆ Sidney James, Kenneth Williams, Charles Hawtrey, Joan Sims, Jim Dale, Percy Herbert, Angela Douglas, Bernard Bresslaw, Peter Butterworth, Jon Pertwee
'Less a string of irrelevant situations than usual, giving the team more opportunity for comedy thesping.' – *Variety*

Carry On Cruising

♈ GB 1962 89m Eastmancolor
Anglo Amalgamated/Peter Rogers

The captain of a cruise liner finds his peace of mind threatened by new crew members and tourists.
Weak comedy that doesn't seem to know where it's going.
w Norman Hudis *story* Eric Barker d Gerald Thomas *ph* Alan Hume *m* Bruce Montgomery, Douglas Gamley *ad* Carmen Dillon *ed* John Shirley
☆ Sidney James, Kenneth Williams, Kenneth Connor, Liz Fraser, Dilys Laye, Esma Cannon, Lance Percival, Ronnie Stevens, Cyril Chamberlain, Anton Rodgers
'Direction by Gerald Thomas is boisterously effective.' – *Variety*

Carry On Dick

👫 GB 1974 91m Eastmancolor
Rank/Peter Rogers
📼

Bow Street Runners ask a village clergyman to help them catch the highwayman Dick Turpin, better known as Big Dick.
Inspiration flags in a comedy where both cast and director seem hardly interested in what they were doing, probably because they had been doing it for too long.
w Talbot Rothwell *story* Lawrie Wyman, George Evans d Gerald Thomas *ph* Ernest Steward m Eric Rogers ed Alfred Roome
☆ Sidney James, Kenneth Williams, Kenneth Connor, Barbara Windsor, Hattie Jacques, Bernard Bresslaw, Joan Sims, Peter Butterworth, Jack Douglas, Patsy Rowlands, Bill Maynard
'These tireless upholders of the "saucy" postcard tradition soldier on with their perennial rib-poking, elbow-nudging, albeit scarcely jaw-breaking esprit ... Maybe their continuing appeal is beyond criticism – or according to taste, beneath it.' – *Nigel Gearing, MFB*
'The script is utterly banal. It is incredible that human minds can put such muck on to paper.' – *Kenneth Williams*

Carry On Doctor *

👫 GB 1968 94m Eastmancolor
Rank/Peter Rogers
📼 ▇

Hospital patients revolt against a tyrannical matron when their favourite doctor is sacked.
Occasionally amusing farce.
w Talbot Rothwell d Gerald Thomas *ph* Alan Hume m Eric Rogers ed Alfred Roome
☆ Frankie Howerd, Sidney James, Kenneth Williams, Jim Dale, Charles Hawtrey, Joan Sims, Barbara Windsor, Hattie Jacques, Anita Harris, Bernard Bresslaw, Peter Butterworth
'Usual unabashed mixture of double-meanings, down-to-earth vulgarity, blue jokes.' – *Variety*

Carry On – Don't Lose Your Head

👫 GB 1966 90m Eastmancolor
Rank/Peter Rogers
📼

aka: *Don't Lose Your Head*
A foppish Briton, the Black Fingernail, rescues French aristocrats from the guillotine during the French Revolution.
A limp parody of The Scarlet Pimpernel causes no more than a few chuckles.
w Talbot Rothwell d Gerald Thomas *ph* Alan Hume m Eric Rogers ed Rod Keys
☆ Sidney James, Kenneth Williams, Jim Dale, Charles Hawtrey, Joan Sims, Peter Butterworth, Dany Robin, Peter Gilmore
'A crazy debauch of duelling, doublecrossing and disaster. The troupers jump through their well-known hoops with agility.' – *Variety*

Carry On Emmannuelle

GB 1978 88m Technicolor
Hemdale/Peter Rogers
📼

The wife of an impotent French ambassador to England seduces every man she meets.
A doomed attempt to update the formula for more sexually permissive times that resulted in the worst of the series, and the last for fourteen years, until it was revived in 1992.
w Lance Peters d Gerald Thomas *ph* Alan Hume m Eric Rogers ad Jack Shampan ed Peter Boita
☆ Suzanne Danielle, Kenneth Williams, Kenneth Connor, Jack Douglas, Joan Sims, Peter Butterworth, Larry Dann, Beryl Reid, Eric Barker
'This one is rude, certainly, but the relentless phallic innuendo is as labored as makers' determination to show nothing to worry the censor. Leaden comic timing...' – *Variety*
'It's rather like watching endearing elderly relatives disgracing themselves at a party.' – *Andy Medhurst, Sight and Sound*

Carry On England

GB 1976 89m colour
Rank/Peter Rogers
📼

In 1940 the men and women who form an experimental anti-aircraft battery prefer to make love rather than war, to the annoyance of their new commanding officer.
One of the weakest of the series and a sign that the series was running out of energy, unable to find suitable replacements for its usual team and handicapped more than usual by a weak script.
w Jack Seddon, David Pursall d Gerald Thomas *ph* Ernest Steward m Max Harris ad Lionel Couch ed Richard Marden
☆ Kenneth Connor, Windsor Davies, Patrick Mower, Judy Geeson, Jack Douglas, Diane Langton, Melvyn Hayes, Joan Sims, Peter Jones, Peter Butterworth, David Lodge
'Suffers from a particularly unfortunate hangup. It's not funny.' – *Variety*
'The laboured puns and overacting are as tiresome as ever.' – *MFB*

Carry On – Follow That Camel

👫 GB 1966 90m Eastmancolor
Rank/Peter Rogers
📼

aka: *Follow That Camel*
An English gentleman, accused of behaving badly at cricket, joins the Foreign Legion to regain his honour.
An ill-match between American and English styles of vaudeville and music-hall humour results in a direly unamusing movie.
w Talbot Rothwell d Gerald Thomas *ph* Alan Hume m Eric Rogers ed Alfred Roome
☆ Phil Silvers, Kenneth Williams, Jim Dale, Charles Hawtrey, Joan Sims, Peter Butterworth, Anita Harris, Bernard Bresslaw, Angela Douglas, Peter Gilmore
'It all works with considerable bounce, with elements of parody of Beau Geste-style movies for those alert to them. All the regular comics are on first-rate form.' – *Variety*

Carry On Girls

GB 1973 88m Eastmancolor
Fox-Rank/Peter Rogers
📼

The organizer of a seaside beauty contest annoys the local members of the Women's Liberation movement.
Below average romp.
w Talbot Rothwell d Gerald Thomas *ph* Alan Hume m Eric Rogers ed Alfred Roome
☆ Sidney James, Kenneth Connor, Joan Sims, Barbara Windsor, Bernard Bresslaw, Peter Butterworth, June Whitfield, Jack Douglas, Patsy Rowlands, Jimmy Logan, Joan Hickson, David Lodge
'Herculean efforts on the part of the entire cast do eventually pull off (in the context, I must insist this is not meant as a *double entendre*) some fairly effective slapstick.' – *Eric Braun*
'Thriving as ever on the sexual repression of its audience, Talbot Rothwell's windy, radio-style script ... turns out the routine quota of puns on such words as bang, boob, bed, bust, bristol and bash, and makes such weary labour of it that every joke can be heard creaking into place long before the arrival of the punch-line.' – *Gareth Jones, MFB*

'A Great Guy With His Chopper!'
Carry On Henry **

👫 GB 1971 89m Eastmancolor
Rank/Adder (Peter Rogers)
📼 ▇

US title: *Carry On Henry VIII*
King Henry tries to get rid of his wife when he discovers she smells of garlic.
A coarsely successful parody of Anne of the Thousand Days and other period films.
w Talbot Rothwell d Gerald Thomas *ph* Alan Hume m Eric Rogers ed Alfred Roome
☆ Sidney James, Kenneth Williams, Charles Hawtrey, Joan Sims, Terry Scott, Barbara Windsor, Kenneth Connor, Peter Butterworth, Peter Gilmore, Patsy Rowlands
'They have managed to come up with a bit of a winner ... there is a delicious send up of that most boring and perennial line of cinematic yawns, the historical romance.' – *Peter Buckley*
'The cast is the familiar stock company at full force; the script is from Talbot Rothwell at his most characteristic; and the film is at any rate better looking than most of its shoe-string predecessors.' – *John Pidgeon, MFB*
'I read the script of *Carry On Henry* and I think it's abysmal.' – *Kenneth Williams, 1970*
'We saw the TV and it was *Carry On Henry* ... amazing how well this was made! Everyone in it was competent and the sheer *look* of the thing was very professional.' – *Kenneth Williams, 1979*

'ITV showed *Carry On Henry*. Oh dear! It was so bad in places ... truly chronic dialogue ... dreadful acting. Sid James had never been quite as bad as this. A collection of such rubbish you're amazed it could ever have been stuck together. Only an audience of illiterates could ever have found this tripe amusing.' – *Kenneth Williams, 1988*

Carry On Jack

👫 GB 1964 91m Eastmancolor
Anglo Amalgamated/Peter Rogers
📼

US title: *Carry On Venus*
A midshipman finds himself at the mercy of a bullying captain and they are both put overboard after a mutiny.
Salty but unamusing parody of Mutiny on The Bounty and other sea-faring sagas.
w Talbot Rothwell d Gerald Thomas *ph* Alan Hume m Eric Rogers ad Jack Shampan ed Archie Ludski
☆ Bernard Cribbins, Kenneth Williams, Charles Hawtrey, Juliet Mills, Donald Houston, Percy Herbert, Peter Gilmore, Jim Dale, Anton Rodgers, Cecil Parker, Patrick Cargill
'Gerald Thomas steers his cast through a maze of mixups and misadventures.' – *Variety*

Carry On Loving

GB 1970 88m Eastmancolor
Rank/Adder (Peter Rogers)
📼

Assorted misfits try their luck at a computer dating agency.
Limp comedy for which the regulars show little enthusiasm.
w Talbot Rothwell d Gerald Thomas *ph* Ernest Steward m Eric Rogers ad Lionel Couch ed Alfred Roome
☆ Sidney James, Kenneth Williams, Charles Hawtrey, Joan Sims, Terry Scott, Hattie Jacques, Richard O'Callaghan, Bernard Bresslaw, Jacki Piper, Imogen Hassall, Patsy Rowlands, Bill Maynard
'Full of tired jokes, obvious situations and ludicrous performances, we have all been here at least three times before, but the crew have a way of working over the old material.' – *Peter Buckley, Films and Filming*
'Scrapings from the bottom of Talbot Rothwell's barrel of well-worn double entendre, delivered with mechanical efficiency by an equally well-worn cast.' – *MFB*

Carry On Matron *

👫 GB 1972 87m Eastmancolor
Rank/Peter Rogers
📼

A con man persuades his son to dress as a nurse in order to infiltrate a maternity hospital to steal contraceptive pills.
Intermittently amusing comedy.
w Talbot Rothwell d Gerald Thomas *ph* Ernest Steward m Eric Rogers ad Lionel Couch ed Alfred Roome
☆ Sidney James, Kenneth Williams, Charles Hawtrey, Joan Sims, Hattie Jacques, Bernard Bresslaw, Terry Scott, Kenneth Cope, Barbara Windsor, Kenneth Connor, Jacki Piper, Patsy Rowlands, Jack Douglas
'A largely successful if slightly patchy addition to the series; its comic highlight involves Sid James, required to assume a medical alias, introducing himself as "Dr Zhivago".' – *Kenneth Thompson, MFB*

Carry On Nurse **

👫 GB 1959 86m bw
Anglo Amalgamated/Peter Rogers
📼 ▇

Male patients in a hospital rebel against the dictatorial matron.
The first true Carry On, done when the whole notion was still fresh and the cast responded with glee to its crudities.
w Norman Hudis *story* Patrick Cargill, Jack Searle d Gerald Thomas *ph* Reg Wyer m Bruce Montgomery ad Alex Vetchinsky ed John Shirley
☆ Shirley Eaton, Kenneth Williams, Charles Hawtrey, Hattie Jacques, Joan Sims, Kenneth Connor, Terence Longdon, Bill Owen, Leslie Phillips, Wilfrid Hyde-White, Irene Handl
'The yocks come thick and fast.' – *Variety*

'A seaside postcard come to life, a shameless procession of vulgarities. Utterly irresistible.' – *Andy Medhurst, Sight and Sound*
† The film topped the box-office in Britain and was surprisingly successful in the US where it ran for two-and-a-half years.

Carry On Regardless

👫 GB 1961 90m bw
Anglo Amalgamated/Peter Rogers
📼

A group of incompetent unemployed join an odd-job agency.
Less a film than a series of sketches, which are very variable in quality.
w Norman Hudis d Gerald Thomas *ph* Alan Hume m Bruce Montgomery ed John Shirley
☆ Sidney James, Kenneth Williams, Charles Hawtrey, Joan Sims, Kenneth Connor, Bill Owen, Liz Fraser, Terence Longdon, Esma Cannon, Hattie Jacques, Fenella Fielding
'Ingenuity of scriptwriter Norman Hudis is sometimes a bit strained, but he has come up with some sound comedy situations.' – *Variety*

Carry On Screaming *

👫 GB 1966 97m Eastmancolor
Anglo Amalgamated/Peter Rogers
📼

Police investigate a mad doctor and his sister, who are turning young women into mannequins.
A send-up of Hammer horrors that manages to emulate the garishness of the originals.
w Talbot Rothwell d Gerald Thomas *ph* Alan Hume m Eric Rogers ed Rod Keys
☆ Harry H. Corbett, Kenneth Williams, Jim Dale, Charles Hawtrey, Fenella Fielding, Joan Sims, Angela Douglas, Bernard Bresslaw, Peter Butterworth, Jon Pertwee
'Puts the skids under horror pix. Snag is that most horror films themselves teeter on the edge of parody and it is rather tough trying to burlesque a parody.' – *Variety*

Carry On Sergeant

👫 GB 1958 83m bw
Anglo Amalgamated/Insignia (Peter Rogers)
📼

An army training sergeant accepts a bet that his last platoon of raw recruits will win the Star Squad award.
Shabby farce with humdrum script and slack direction, saved by energetic performances.
w Norman Hudis *play* The Bull Boys by R. F. Delderfield d Gerald Thomas *ph* Peter Hennessy m Bruce Montgomery
☆ Bob Monkhouse, William Hartnell, Kenneth Williams, Charles Hawtrey, Shirley Eaton, Eric Barker, Dora Bryan, Bill Owen, Kenneth Connor

'They're At It Again – O.O.O.H!'
Carry On Spying

👫 GB 1964 87m bw
Anglo Amalgamated/Peter Rogers
📼

British spies are sent to recapture a secret formula stolen by the Society for the Total Extinction of Non-Conforming Humans, otherwise known as Stench.
A feeble parody of the Bond films.
w Talbot Rothwell, Sid Colin d Gerald Thomas *ph* Alan Hume m Eric Rogers ed Archie Ludski
☆ Kenneth Williams, Bernard Cribbins, Charles Hawtrey, Barbara Windsor, Eric Pohlmann, Eric Barker, Dilys Laye, Jim Dale, Richard Wattis
'A dazzling return to form, milking every last drop from the ripe targets of espionage in general and Bond in particular.' – *Andy Medhurst, Sight and Sound*

Carry On Teacher *

👫 GB 1959 86m bw
Anglo Amalgamated/Peter Rogers
📼

Pupils at a school sabotage the headmaster's attempts to get another job because they don't want to lose him.
Amiable comedy that is less frenetic than many in the series, and all the better for it.
w Norman Hudis d Gerald Thomas *ph* Reginald Wyer m Bruce Montgomery ed John Shirley
☆ Ted Ray, Kenneth Williams, Charles Hawtrey, Leslie Phillips, Joan Sims, Kenneth Connor, Hattie Jacques, Rosalind Knight, Cyril Chamberlain
'The laughs come readily.' – *Variety*

👫 film suitable for family viewing   📼 VHS video-cassette for the British PAL system   📼 VHS video-cassette for the British PAL system in wide screen-format   ♻ Video cassette in a computer-colourised version   ▇ American NTSC video-cassette   💿 Laser disc

Carry On up the Jungle

👫 GB 1970 89m Eastmancolor
Rank/Peter Rogers
📀

An ornithologist journeys to Africa in search of the rare Oozulum bird.

A tired parody of Tarzan and jungle films; the jokes get lost in the undergrowth.

w Talbot Rothwell d Gerald Thomas ph Ernest Steward m Eric Rogers ad Alex Vetchinsky ed Alfred Roome
☆ Frankie Howerd, Sidney James, Charles Hawtrey, Joan Sims, Terry Scott, Kenneth Connor, Bernard Bresslaw, Jacki Piper
'The film is an assured success.' – *Films and Filming*

Carry On up the Khyber ***

👫 GB 1968 88m Eastmancolor
Rank/Adder (Peter Rogers)
📀

A Scots regiment, the Third Foot and Mouth, fails to defend British interests in India.

The best of the series, a wonderfully vulgar and ripe low comedy on an imperial theme.

w Talbot Rothwell d Gerald Thomas ph Alan Hume m Eric Rogers ad Alex Vetchinsky ed Alfred Roome
☆ Sidney James, Kenneth Williams, Charles Hawtrey, Joan Sims, Roy Castle, Bernard Bresslaw, Peter Butterworth, Terry Scott, Angela Douglas, Cardew Robinson, Julian Holloway, Peter Gilmore
'Continues to rely primarily on low-comedy visual and verbal gag situations for its yocks.' – *Variety*
† The movie was filmed in Wales.

Carry On Venus: see *Carry On Jack*

The Cars that Ate Paris *

Australia 1974 88m Eastmancolor
Panavision
Saltpan/AFDC/Royce Smeal (Jim and Howard McElroy)
📀 📺

Car travellers become victims of a small town whose youthful inhabitants live on the pickings of engineered road accidents.

Another small town with a guilty secret, in this case more suitable to a half-hour than a feature, but with rewarding attention to detail.

wd Peter Weir ph John McLean m Bruce Smeaton
☆ Terry Camilleri, John Meillon, Melissa Jaffa, Kevin Miles

Carson City *

US 1952 87m Warnercolor
Warner (David Weisbart)

A stagecoach service suffers from bandit raids, so a local banker finances a railroad.

Agreeably conventional Western with plenty of reliable plot and a satisfactory outcome for the goodies.

w Sloan Nibley, Winston Miller d André de Toth ph John Boyle m David Buttolph
☆ Randolph Scott, Raymond Massey, Lucille Norman, Richard Webb, James Millican, Larry Keating, George Cleveland

Cartouche

Italy/US 1954 85m bw
Venturini/RKO (John Nasht)

A French prince clears himself of a murder charge and brings the villain to book.

Flat costume drama.

w Louis Stevens, Tullio Pinelli d Steve Sekely, Gianni Vernuccio ph Massimo Dallamano m Bruce Montgomery
☆ Richard Basehart, Patricia Roc, Massimo Serato, Akim Tamiroff

Cartouche **

France/Italy 1961 114m Eastmancolor
Dyaliscope
Ariane/Filmsonor/Vides (Georges Danciger)
📀 📺

aka: *Swords of Blood*

An 18th-century cooper's son becomes a quick-witted and gallant thief.

Slightly bitter fairy tale based on a French legend, vigorously encompassing tragedy, farce, violence and high-flown adventure.

w Daniel Boulanger, Philippe de Broca d Philippe de Broca ph Christian Matras m Georges Delerue

☆ Jean-Paul Belmondo, Claudia Cardinale, Odile Versois, Marcel Dalio, Philippe Lemaire, Jean Rochefort
'A tour de force of virtuosity.' – *Peter John Dyer, MFB*

Carve Her Name with Pride *

GB 1958 119m bw
Rank/Keyboard (Daniel M. Angel)
📀

In 1940, the young British widow of a French officer is enlisted as a spy, and after various adventures dies before a German firing squad.

Slightly muddled if ultimately moving biopic in which initial light comedy gives way to romance, documentary, character study, blazing war action and finally tragedy. Generally well made.

w Vernon Harris, Lewis Gilbert book R. J. Minney d Lewis Gilbert ph John Wilcox m William Alwyn
☆ Virginia McKenna, Paul Scofield, Jack Warner, Sydney Tafler, Denise Grey, Alain Saury, Maurice Ronet, Nicole Stéphane, Noel Willman, Bill Owen, William Mervyn, Anne Leon
'What is missing is the deeply charged passion which would have gone beyond the quietly decent statement intermittently achieved.' – *John Gillett*

La Casa del Angel: see *The House of the Angel*

'As big and timely a picture as ever you've seen! You can tell by the cast it's important! gripping! big!'

Casablanca ****

US 1942 102m bw
Warner (Hal B. Wallis)
📀 📺 📀 📀 🎧 ⚙

Rick's Café in Casablanca is a centre for war refugees awaiting visas for America. Rick abandons his cynicism to help an old love escape the Nazis with her underground leader husband.

Cinema par excellence: a studio-bound Hollywood melodrama which after various chances just fell together impeccably into one of the outstanding entertainment experiences of cinema history, with romance, intrigue, excitement, suspense and humour cunningly deployed by master technicians and a perfect cast.

w Julius J. Epstein, Philip G. Epstein, Howard Koch play Everybody Comes to Rick's by Murray Burnett, Joan Alison d Michael Curtiz ph Arthur Edeson m Max Steiner ed Owen Marks
☆ Humphrey Bogart, Ingrid Bergman, Paul Henreid, Claude Rains, Sydney Greenstreet, Peter Lorre, S. Z. Sakall, Conrad Veidt, Dooley Wilson, Marcel Dalio, Joy Page, John Qualen, Ludwig Stossel, Leonid Kinskey, Helmut Dantine and also Ilka Gruning

RICK: 'I stick out my neck for nobody. I'm the only cause I'm interested in.'
LOUIS: 'How extravagant you are, throwing away women like that. Someday they may be scarce.'
RICK: 'Ilse, I'm no good at being noble, but it doesn't take much to see that the problems of three little people don't amount to a hill of beans in this crazy world. Someday you'll understand that. Not now. Here's looking at you, kid.'
RICK: 'I came to Casablanca for the waters.'
LOUIS: 'What waters? We're in the desert.'
RICK: 'I was misinformed.'
RICK: 'Louis, I think this is the beginning of a beautiful friendship.'
'A picture which makes the spine tingle and the heart take a leap ... they have so combined sentiment, humour and pathos with taut melodrama and bristling intrigue that the result is a highly entertaining and even inspiring film.' – *New York Times*
'Its humour is what really saves it, being a mixture of Central European irony of attack and racy Broadway-Hollywood Boulevard cynicism.' – *Herman G. Weinberg*
'The happiest of happy accidents, and the most decisive exception to the auteur theory.' – *Andrew Sarris, 1968*
'A film which seems to have been frozen in time ... the sum of its many marvellous parts far exceeds the whole.' – *NFT, 1974*
'It's far from a great film, but it has an appealingly schlocky romanticism, and you're never really pressed to take its melodramatic twists and turns seriously.' – *Pauline Kael, 70s*
† Originally named for the leads were Ronald Reagan, Ann Sheridan and Dennis Morgan

🎵 'As Time Goes By', 'Knock on Wood'
🏆 best picture; Julius J. and Philip G. Epstein, Howard Koch; Michael Curtiz
🏆 Arthur Edeson; Max Steiner; Humphrey Bogart; Claude Rains; Owen Marks

Casanova

Italy 1976 163m Technicolor Scope
TCF/PEA (Alberto Grimaldi)
📺 🎧

aka: *Fellini's Casanova*

Episodes from the life of the 18th-century libertine, in the course of which he seduces, among others, a nun, a mechanical doll, and a hunchbacked nymphomaniac.

A curiously rarefied spectacle which seldom comes to anything like life and despite its vast expense seems more likely to provoke yawns than lust.

w Federico Fellini, Bernardino Zapponi d Federico Fellini ph Giuseppe Rotunno m Nino Rota pd Danilo Donati, Federico Fellini
☆ Donald Sutherland, Tina Aumont, Cicely Browne, Carmen Scarpitta
'It may well be the most ponderous specimen of imaginative vacuity ever devised.' – *John Simon, New York*
🏆 script
🏆 Danilo Donati

Casanova Brown

US 1944 99m bw
International/Christie (Nunnally Johnson)

Just as his divorce comes through, a man discovers that his wife is pregnant.

Very mild star comedy which tiptoes round its subject.

w Nunnally Johnson play Bachelor Father by Floyd Dell, Thomas Mitchell d Sam Wood ph John F. Seitz m Arthur Lange ad Perry Ferguson
☆ Gary Cooper, Teresa Wright, Frank Morgan, Anita Louise, Patricia Collinge, Edmund Breon, Jill Esmond, Isobel Elsom, Mary Treen, Halliwell Hobbes
'There is so much clowning with so little subject that one is exposed to the impression that anything went for a laugh.' – *Bosley Crowther, New York Times*
† A remake of Little Accident (qv).
🏆 Arthur Lange; Perry Ferguson

Casanova in Burlesque

US 1944 74m bw
Republic

A professor has a secret summer life as a burlesque performer.

Unusual, amiable comedy.

w Frank Gill d Leslie Goodwins
☆ Joe E. Brown, June Havoc

Casanova's Big Night

US 1954 86m Technicolor
Paramount (Paul Jones)
📀 📺 📀

In old Italy, the great lover is fleeing from his creditors and changes places with a tailor's apprentice.

The last of Bob Hope's big-budget, big-studio burlesques is a lumbering vehicle which wastes its star cast and mistimes its laughs. Joan Fontaine is an unhappy comedy foil.

w Hal Kanter, Edmund Hartmann d Norman Z. McLeod ph Lionel Lindon m Lyn Murray
☆ Bob Hope, Joan Fontaine, Basil Rathbone, Vincent Price, Audrey Dalton, Hugh Marlowe, John Carradine, Primo Carnera, Arnold Moss, Lon Chaney Jnr

Casbah

US 1948 94m bw
Universal (Erik Charell)

Remake of *Algiers* (qv) with songs added.

Not too bad in the circumstances, but a wholly artificial exercise, and another version was really not needed. The sets seem overlit and claustrophobic.

w Ladislaus Bus-Fekete, Arnold Manoff novel Detective Ashelbe musical Erik Charell d John Berry ph Irving Glassberg m/ly Harold Arlen, Leo Robin
☆ Tony Martin, Yvonne de Carlo, Marta Toren, Peter Lorre, Hugo Haas
🏆 song 'For Every Man There's a Woman'

The Case against Brooklyn

US 1958 81m bw
Charles H. Schneer/Columbia

An undercover cop smashes a gambling syndicate.

Competent second feature treatment of a story we have heard somewhere before.

w Raymond T. Marcus d Paul Wendkos
☆ Darren McGavin, Maggie Hayes, Warren Stevens, Emile Meyer, Nestor Paiva

'Is she an unfit mother?'

The Case against Mrs Ames

US 1936 85m bw
Paramount (Walter Wanger)

The prosecutor in a murder case is convinced of the defendant's innocence.

Tired rehash of a familiar theme.

w Gene Towne, Graham Baker d William A. Seiter ph Lucien Andriot md Boris Morros
☆ Madeleine Carroll, George Brent, Arthur Treacher, Alan Baxter, Beulah Bondi, Alan Mowbray, Esther Dale, Ed Brophy

A Case for P.C. 49

GB 1950 80m bw
Hammer

A police constable solves a millionaire's murder.

Incompetent and virtually unwatchable transcription of a juvenile TV series.

w Alan Stranks, Vernon Harris from their series d Francis Searle
☆ Brian Reece, Joy Shelton, Christine Norden, Leslie Bradley, Gordon McLeod

The Case of Charles Peace

GB 1949 88m bw
John Argyle

The story of a burglar and murderer of the 1870s whose career caught the public fancy.

Antediluvian and largely fictitious treatment of a Victorian cause célèbre.

w Doris Davison, Norman Lee d Norman Lee
☆ Michael Martin Harvey, Chili Bouchier, Valentine Dyall, Bruce Belfrage, Ronald Adam

The Case of Mrs Pembroke: see *Two Against the World*

The Case of the Black Cat

US 1936 66m bw
Warner

An old man is murdered after changing his will: Perry Mason investigates.

One of the better tales of the lawyer sleuth.

w F. Hugh Herbert d William McGann
☆ Ricardo Cortez, Harry Davenport, June Travis, Jane Bryan

The Case of the Curious Bride

US 1935 80m bw
Warner

Perry Mason helps a woman who is being blackmailed by her 'dead' husband.

Smoothish mystery.

w Tom Reed story Erle Stanley Gardner d Michael Curtiz
☆ Warren William, Margaret Lindsay, Donald Woods, Claire Dodd, Allen Jenkins, Errol Flynn

The Case of the Frightened Lady

GB 1940 81m bw
Pennant

A dowager knows that her son is mad and tries to prevent him from strangling his cousin.

Quite a lively suspenser of its time.

w Edward Dryhurst novel Edgar Wallace d George King
☆ Marius Goring, Penelope Dudley Ward, Helen Haye, Patrick Barr, Felix Aylmer
† A previous version was released in 1932 as *The Frightened Lady* (qv).

The Case of the Howling Dog

US 1934 75m bw
Warner

Two men claim the same woman as their wife.

Adequate Perry Mason mystery.

w Ben Markson story Erle Stanley Gardner d Alan Crosland
☆ Warren William, Mary Astor, Allen Jenkins, Grant Mitchell, Helen Trenholme, Dorothy Tree

---

The Case of the Lucky Legs
US   1935   77m   bw
Warner

Perry Mason chases a beauty contest promoter who skips town with the winnings.
Fair lighthearted mystery, with a somewhat dissipated sleuth.
w Ben Markson, Brown Holmes *story* Erle Stanley Gardner *d* Archie Mayo
☆ Warren William, Genevieve Tobin, Allen Jenkins, Patricia Ellis, Lyle Talbot, Barton MacLane
   'An admirable film.' – *Graham Greene*

The Case of the Missing Blonde: see *Lady in the Morgue*

The Case of the Stuttering Bishop
US   1937   70m   bw
Warner

Perry Mason investigates an heiress who may be an impostor.
Thin mystery with another different star in the lead.
w Don Ryan, Kenneth Gamet *story* Erle Stanley Gardner *d* William Clemens
☆ Donald Woods, Ann Dvorak, Anne Nagel, Linda Perry

The Case of the Velvet Claws
US   1936   63m   bw
Warner

Perry Mason's honeymoon is postponed when he finds himself on a murder charge.
Moderate light-hearted mystery, but they should have awarded prizes to anyone who could explain the title.
w Tom Reed *story* Erle Stanley Gardner *d* William Clemens
☆ Warren William, Claire Dodd, Wini Shaw, Gordon Elliott, Addison Richards

Casey's Shadow
US   1978   116m   Metrocolor   Panavision
Columbia/Ray Stark (Michael Levee)

A Cajun family in New Mexico breeds a champion horse which wins the annual race.
Shades of Maryland: an old-fashioned movie of the kind which absolutely nobody should want to revive, at least not so ineptly or at such length.
w Carol Sobieski *story* Ruidoso by John McPhee *d* Martin Ritt *ph* John A. Alonzo *m* Patrick Williams
☆ Walter Matthau, Alexis Smith, Robert Webber, Murray Hamilton, Andrew A. Rubin, Stephan Burns, Michael Hershewe

C.A.S.H.: see *W.H.I.F.F.S.*

Cash
GB   1933   73m   bw
Paramount/London Films (Alexander Korda)

US title: *For Love Or Money*
aka: *If I Were Rich*
A bank clerk embezzles money.
Quota quickie that never rises above the totally mundane.
w Arthur Wimperis *story* Anthony Gibbs, Dorothy Greenhill *d* Zoltan Korda *ph* Robert Martin *ed* Stephen Harrison
☆ Edmund Gwenn, Wendy Barrie, Robert Donat, Morris Harvey, Lawrence Grossmith

Cash and Carry: see *Ringside Maisie*

Cash McCall
US   1960   102m   Technicolor
Warner (Henry Blanke)

A Napoleon of the stock market gets into trouble for the first time when love interferes with business.
Slightly unusual comedy drama, quite sharply made and played, but not adding up to much.
w Lenore Coffee, Marion Hargrove *novel* Cameron Hawley *d* Joseph Pevney *ph* George Folsey *m* Max Steiner
☆ James Garner, Natalie Wood, Nina Foch, Dean Jagger, E. G. Marshall, Henry Jones, Otto Kruger, Roland Winters

Cash on Demand *
GB   1963   86m   bw
Columbia/Woodpecker/Hammer (Michael Carreras)
A fussy bank manager outwits a classy robber.

Quietly effective suspenser with an admirable middle-aged cast and no love interest.
w Lewis Greifer, David T. Chantler *TV play* Jacques Gillies *d* Quentin Lawrence *ph* Arthur Grant *m* Wilfred Josephs
☆ Peter Cushing, André Morell, Richard Vernon, Norman Bird, Edith Sharpe

Casino ***
US   1995   178m   Technicolor
Universal/Syalis/Legende/De Fina/Cappa (Barbara de Fina)

A gambler who is put in charge of a Las Vegas casino by the Mafia runs into trouble when he tries to run the business honestly and falls in love with a call-girl.
Deft, involving and intriguing depiction of the inescapable corruption of the spirit, in a city built on greed. It begins in a leisurely, documentary style before focusing on individuals as flawed as the system they operate and as expendable as the chips they bet.
w Nicholas Pileggi, Martin Scorsese *book* Nicholas Pileggi *d* Martin Scorsese *ph* Robert Richardson *pd* Dante Ferretti *ed* Thelma Schoonmaker
☆ Robert DeNiro, Sharon Stone, Joe Pesci, James Woods, Don Rickles, Alan King, Kevin Pollak, L. Q. Jones, Dick Smothers
   'I simply can't see any urgent reason for *Casino* to exist. Scorsese has always been a master of camera movement, but here the camera is just going through the motions.' – *Tom Shone, Sunday Times*
   'It doesn't seem too much to ask, in exchange for three hours of our lives, to be offered an emotion less tainted than watching nasty people fall foul of one another.' – *Adam Mars-Jones, Independent*
   'A must-see for cinema-savvy audiences.' – *Variety*
   ⚷ Sharon Stone

Casino de Paree: see *Go Into Your Dance*

The Casino Murder Case
US   1935   85m   bw
MGM

Philo Vance solves a murder in a family of neurotics.
Rather heavy-going detection.
w Florence Ryerson, Edgar Allan Woolf *story* S. A. Van Dine *d* Edwin Marin
☆ Paul Lukas, Rosalind Russell, Eric Blore, Donald Cook, Louise Fazenda, Ted Healy, Isabel Jewell, Leo G. Carroll

Casino Royale
GB   1967   130m   Technicolor   Panavision
Columbia/Famous Artists (Charles K. Feldman, Jerry Bresler)

The heads of the allied spy forces call Sir James Bond out of retirement to fight the power of SMERSH.
Woeful all-star kaleidoscope, a way-out spoof which generates far fewer laughs than the original. One of the most shameless wastes of time and talent in screen history.
w Wolf Mankowitz, John Law, Michael Sayers *novel* Ian Fleming *d* John Huston, Ken Hughes, Val Guest, Robert Parrish, Joe McGrath, Richard Talmadge *ph* Jack Hildyard *m* Burt Bacharach *pd* Michael Stringer
☆ David Niven, Deborah Kerr, Orson Welles, Peter Sellers, Ursula Andress, Woody Allen, William Holden, Charles Boyer, John Huston, Joanna Pettet, Daliah Lavi, Kurt Kasznar, Jacqueline Bisset, Derek Nimmo, George Raft and also Ronnie Corbett, Peter O'Toole, Jean-Paul Belmondo, Geoffrey Bayldon, Duncan Macrae
   'One of those wild wacky extravaganzas in which the audience is expected to have a great time because everybody making the film did. It seldom works out that way, and certainly doesn't here.' – *John Russell Taylor*
   'The dialogue is witless and unhampered by taste, and the interminable finale is a collection of clichés in a brawl involving the cavalry, parachuted Indians, split-second appearances by George Raft and Jean-Paul Belmondo, every variety of mayhem, and Woody Allen burping radiation as a walking atom bomb.' – *Judith Crist*
   'The worst film I ever enjoyed.' – *Donald Zec*
   ⚷ song 'The Look of Love' (mBurt Bacharach, lyHal David)

'No Such Things As Ghosts?'
Casper
US   1995   100m   DeLuxe
UIP/Amblin/Harvey (Colin Wilson)

A greedy woman searches for treasure in a haunted house, with the aid of an expert in ghosts and his teenage daughter.
An unpleasant attempt to revive a comic-book character, both sickly with sentiment and tasteless in its attitudes to life and death; the special effects are spectacular, though.
w Sherri Stoner, Deanna Oliver *story* Casper the Friendly Ghost by Joseph Oriolo, Seymour Rait *d* Brad Silberling *ph* Dean Cundey *m* James Horner *pd* Leslie Dilley *ed* Michael Kahn *sp* Michael Lantieri
☆ Christina Ricci, Bill Pullman, Cathy Moriarty, Eric Idle and also the voices of Malachi Pearson, Joe Nipote, Joe Alaskey, Brad Garrett
   'Attempts, with a host of clever special effects, to be both wise and innocent as well as funny and scary. But it is outrageously sentimental; half of the fun of the piece is buried in buttery popcorn covering.' – *Derek Malcolm, Guardian*
   'Purest ectoplasmic slush.' – *Sunday Times*
   † The film took more than $277m at the box-office worldwide
   †† In 1997 came a prequel, *Casper, a Spirited Beginning*, which was released direct to video and aimed at a young audience.

Casque d'Or ***
France   1952   96m   bw
Speva/Paris (Robert Hakim)
aka: *Golden Marie*

1898. In the Paris slums, an Apache finds passionate love but is executed for murder.
A tragic romance which on its first release seemed bathed in a golden glow and is certainly an impeccable piece of film-making.
w Jacques Becker, Jacques Companeez *d* Jacques Becker *ph* Robert Le Fèbvre *m* Georges Van Parys
☆ Simone Signoret, Serge Reggiani, Claude Dauphin, Raymond Bussières, Gaston Modot
   'Takes its place alongside *Le Jour Se Lève* among the masterpieces of the French cinema.' – *Karel Reisz*
   'A screen alive with sensuousness and luminous figures.' – *Dilys Powell*
   ⚷ Simone Signoret

Cass Timberlane *
US   1947   119m   bw
MGM (Arthur Hornblow Jnr)

A judge marries a working-class girl, who is unsettled at first but finally comes to realize her good fortune.
Solid drama with an understanding star performance and good production values.
w Donald Ogden Stewart *novel* Sinclair Lewis *d* George Sidney *ph* Robert Planck *m* Roy Webb
☆ Spencer Tracy, Lana Turner, Zachary Scott, Tom Drake, Mary Astor, Albert Dekker, Selena Royle, Josephine Hutchinson, Margaret Lindsay

Cassandra
Australia   1987   93m   colour
Parallel (Trevor Lucas)

A young woman's nightmares of murder begin to turn into reality.
Spooky little chiller with a certain amount of suspense but not much substance.
w Colin Eggleston, John Ruane, Chris Fitchett *d* Colin Eggleston *ph* Garry Wapshott *m* Trevor Lucas, Ian Mason *pd* Stewart Burnside *ed* Josephine Cook
☆ Shane Briant, Briony Behets, Kit Taylor, Lee James, Susan Barling, Tim Burns, Tessa Humphries

The Cassandra Crossing
GB/Italy/West Germany   1976   129m
Technicolor   Panavision
AGF/CCC/International Cine (Lew Grade, Carlo Ponti)

A terrorist carrying a deadly plague virus boards a transcontinental train.
Disaster spectacular with a number of fashionable interests but no observable filmmaking technique.
w Tom Mankiewicz, Robert Katz, George Pan Cosmatos *d* George Pan Cosmatos *ph* Ennio Guarnieri *m* Jerry Goldsmith *pd* Aurelio Crugnola

☆ Sophia Loren, Richard Harris, Ava Gardner, Burt Lancaster, Martin Sheen, Ingrid Thulin, Lee Strasberg, John Phillip Law, Lionel Stander, Ann Turkel, O. J. Simpson, Alida Valli

La Casse: see *The Burglars*

Cast a Dark Shadow *
GB   1955   82m   bw
Frobisher/Daniel M. Angel (Herbert Mason)

A wife-murderer marries an ex-barmaid and tries again.
Unambitious but enjoyable melodrama, well acted though with directorial opportunities missed.
w John Cresswell *play* Murder Mistaken by Janet Green *d* Lewis Gilbert *ph* Jack Asher *m* Antony Hopkins
☆ Dirk Bogarde, Margaret Lockwood, Kay Walsh, Kathleen Harrison, Robert Flemyng, Mona Washbourne, Walter Hudd

'Outnumbered – unarmed – unprepared – they hurled back their answer in flesh and flame!'
Cast a Giant Shadow *
US   1966   141m   DeLuxe   Panavision
UA/Mirisch/Llenroc/Batjac (Melville Shavelson)

An American military lawyer and ex-colonel goes to Israel in 1947 to help in the fight against the Arabs.
Spectacular war biopic with all concerned in good form but lacking the clarity and narrative control of a real smash.
w Melville Shavelson, from Ted Berkman's biography of Col. David Marcus *d* Melville Shavelson *ph* Aldo Tonti *m* Elmer Bernstein *pd* Michael Stringer
☆ Kirk Douglas, Angie Dickinson, Senta Berger, Luther Adler, Stathis Giallelis, Chaim Topol, John Wayne, Frank Sinatra, Yul Brynner, James Donald, Gordon Jackson, Michael Hordern, Gary Merrill, Allan Cuthbertson, Jeremy Kemp

Cast a Long Shadow
US   1959   82m   bw
Mirisch/UA

A hard-drinking drifter thinks he may be the illegitimate son of a dead cattle baron.
Would-be psychological Western with not enough going for it.
w Martin M. Goldsmith, John McGreevey *novel* Wayne D. Overholser *d* Thomas Carr
☆ Audie Murphy, John Dehner, Terry Moore, James Best, Denver Pyle

Cast Iron: see *The Virtuous Sin*

Castaway
GB   1986   118m   Fujicolour
Cannon/United British Artists (Rick McCallum)

A bored London girl answers an ad placed by a man who wants a wife to take to a tropical island for a year; but he expects sex and she doesn't.
Extended absurdity uncharacteristic of its director.
w Allan Scott *book* Lucy Irvine *d* Nicolas Roeg *ph* Harvey Harrison *m* Stanley Myers *pd* Andrew Sanders *ed* Tony Lawson
☆ Oliver Reed, Amanda Donohoe, Georgina Hale
   'Prospects are good for those interested in beautiful scenery and naked bodies.' – *Daily Variety*

The Castaway Cowboy *
US   1974   91m   Technicolor
Walt Disney (Ron Miller, Winston Hibler)

In 1850, a Shanghaied sailor on Hawaii helps a lady potato farmer to turn her land into a cattle ranch.
Unexciting and unexceptional family fare.
w Don Tait *d* Vincent McEveety *ph* Andrew Jackson *m* Robert F. Brunner
☆ James Garner, Vera Miles, Robert Culp, Eric Shea, Elizabeth Smith

---

🏃 film suitable for family viewing   📼 VHS video-cassette for the British PAL system   📼 VHS video-cassette for the British PAL system in wide screen-format   ♻ Video cassette in a computer-colourised version   ▤ American NTSC video-cassette   ◷ Laser disc

The Castle
West Germany 1969 93m colour
Maximilian Schell/Alfa/Glarus/Rudolf Noelte

A surveyor is summoned to a remote castle but prevented by the villagers from getting there.
Attempt, partly successful, to film an unfinished Kafka obscurity. Marks all round for trying.
wd Rudolf Noelte
☆ Maximilian Schell, Cordula Trantow, Trudik Daniel, Franz Misar

The Castle *
Australia 1997 85m Cinevex
UIP/Village Roadshow/Working Dog/Frontline TV (Debra Choate)
A dim-witted family, living happily at the edge of an airport, fights the government's plan to extend the runways by demolishing its home.
Low-budget comedy of victory for the little man, enjoyable in its ramshackle way.
w Rob Sitch, Santo Cilauro, Tom Gleisner, Jane Kennedy d Rob Sitch ph Miriana Marusic m Craig Harnath pd Carrie Kennedy ed Wayne Hyett
☆ Michael Caton, Anne Tenney, Sophie Lee, Anthony Simcoe, Stephen Curry, Wayne Hope, Eric Bana, Tiriel Mora, Charles (Bud) Tingwell, Robyn Nevin, Costas Kilias
'Inanity elevated to a jubilantly funny and optimistic fable, beautifully acted with unflagging sincerity.' – *Angie Erigo, Empire*

Castle Freak
US/Italy 1994 95m colour
Full Moon (Maurizio Maggi)
An American family inherit an Italian castle with a grisly secret.
Ineffectual horror that fails to generate much suspense.
w Dennis Paoli d Stuart Gordon ph Mario Vulpiani m Richard Band ad Frank Vanorio ed Bert Glastein
☆ Jeffrey Combs, Barbara Crampton, Jonathan Fuller, Jessica Dollarhide, Massimo Sarchielli, Elizabeth Kaza, Luca Zingaretti, Helen Stirling

Castle in the Air
GB 1952 90m bw
Hallmark/ABP
A nobleman fails to turn his castle into a hotel but hopes to sell it to the Coal Board.
Topical comedy which sparkled rather more on the stage.
w Alan Melville, Edward Dryhurst play Alan Melville d Henry Cass
☆ David Tomlinson, Helen Cherry, Margaret Rutherford, Barbara Kelly, A. E. Matthews, Pat Dainton, Brian Oulton, Ewan Roberts

Castle in the Desert *
US 1942 62m bw
TCF
Murders take place at the remote castle of an eccentric millionaire.
One of the sharpest Charlie Chan mysteries, with a lively plot and some good lines.
w John Larkin d Harry Lachman
☆ Sidney Toler, Arleen Whelan, Richard Derr, Douglass Dumbrille, Henry Daniell, Steve Geray, Sen Yung, Ethel Griffies, Milton Parsons

'A one-eyed major and his oddball heroes fight a twentieth-century war in a tenth-century castle!'
Castle Keep *
US 1969 107m Technicolor Panavision
Columbia/Filmways (Martin Ransohoff, John Calley)
During World War II seven battle-weary American soldiers occupy a 10th-century castle filled with art treasures, then die defending it. Or are they dead all the time?
The film version of this fantastic novel never seems quite sure, and the uncertainty finally deadens it despite careful work all round.
w Daniel Taradash, David Rayfiel novel William Eastlake d Sydney Pollack ph Henri Decaë m Michel Legrand
☆ Burt Lancaster, Peter Falk, Jean Pierre Aumont, Patrick O'Neal, Al Freeman Jnr, Scott Wilson, Tony Bill, Bruce Dern, Astrid Heeren

Castle of Evil
US 1966 81m Eastmancolor
NTA
A disfigured industrialist summons six people to a remote Caribbean island for the reading of his will.
Tedious variation on Ten Little Niggers and The Cat and the Canary, with horror asides and the lowest of budgets.
w Charles A. Wallace d Francis D. Lyon
☆ Virginia Mayo, Scott Brady, David Brian, Lisa Gaye, Hugh Marlowe

Castle of Fu Manchu
West Germany/Spain/Italy/GB 1968 92m Eastmancolor
Terra Filmkunst/Balcazar/Italian International/Towers of London
The yellow peril wrecks an ocean-going liner by turning water into ice, and keeps the inventor a prisoner.
Extraordinarily tatty entry in a series which started off well. (See Fu Manchu for list.)
w Harry Alan Towers d Jesus Franco ph Manuel Merino m Carlo Camilleri
☆ Christopher Lee, Richard Greene, Howard Marion Crawford, Gunther Stoll, Maria Perschy

Castle of the Doomed: see Kiss Me Monster

Castle on the Hudson *
US 1940 77m bw
Warner (Sam Bischoff)
GB title: Years without Days
A hardened criminal is not helped by his years in prison.
Adequate, gloomy remake of Twenty Thousand Years in Sing Sing.
w Seton I. Miller, Brown Holmes, Courteney Terrett d Anatole Litvak ph Arthur Edeson m Adolph Deutsch
☆ John Garfield, Pat O'Brien, Ann Sheridan, Burgess Meredith, Jerome Cowan, Henry O'Neill, Guinn Williams, John Litel

Casual Sex?
US 1988 97m colour
Universal/Jascat (Ilona Herzberg, Sheldon Kahn)
Two women, one promiscuous, the other prim, who are both scared of being single, find true love at a health resort.
Based on a stage musical and transferred to the screen without songs, it is an inconsequential jejune look at sexual relationships, full of direct-to-camera monologues that are at best coy and often embarrassing.
w Wendy Goldman, Judy Toll play book and lyrics Wendy Goldman, Judy Toll, music Alan Axelrod d Genevieve Robert ph Rolf Kestermann m Van Dyke Parks pd Randy Ser ed Sheldon Kahn, Donn Cambern
☆ Lea Thompson, Victoria Jackson, Stephen Shellen, Jerry Levine, Mary Gross, Peter Dvorsky, Andrew Dice Clay

Casualties of War *
US 1989 113m DeLuxe Panavision
Columbia TriStar (Art Linson)
In Vietnam, a soldier is horrified when others kidnap and rape a village girl.
Simple minded, melodramatic account of a true incident.
w David Rabe book Daniel Lang d Brian de Palma m Stephen H. Burum m Ennio Morricone pd Wolf Kroeger ed Bill Pankow
☆ Michael J. Fox, Sean Penn, Don Harvey, John C. Reilly, John Leguizamo, Thuy Thu Le, Erik King, Jack Gwaltney
'This new film is the kind that makes you feel protective. When you leave the theatre, you'll probably find that you're not ready to talk about it. You may also find it hard to talk lightly about anything.' – *Pauline Kael*

The Cat *
France 1973 88m colour
Raymond Danon
After twenty-five years of marriage an embittered trapeze star and her husband simply don't talk to each other.
Absorbing drama for two characters, brilliantly acted, but with a somewhat unsatisfactory conclusion.

w Pascal Jardin d Pierre Granier-Deferre
☆ Jean Gabin, Simone Signoret

Cat and Mouse *
GB 1958 79m bw
Eros/Anvil (Paul Rotha)
The daughter of a man executed for murder is threatened by criminals seeking hidden loot.
Interesting rather than exciting second feature thriller directed by a documentary maker.
wd Paul Rotha novel Michael Halliday ph Wolfgang Suschitzky
☆ Lee Patterson, Ann Sears, Hilton Edwards, Victor Maddern, George Rose, Roddy McMillan

The Cat and the Canary ***
US 1927 84m bw silent
Universal
Greedy relatives assemble in an old house to hear an eccentric's will, and a young girl's sanity is threatened.
Archetypal spooky house comedy horror, here given an immensely stylish production which influenced Hollywood through the thirties and was spoofed in The Old Dark House.
w Alfred Cohn, Robert F. Hill play John Willard d Paul Leni ph Gilbert Warrenton ad Charles D. Hall
☆ Creighton Hale, Laura La Plante, Forrest Stanley, Tully Marshall, Flora Finch, Gertrude Astor, Arthur Carewe

The Cat and the Canary ***
US 1939 72m bw
Paramount (Arthur Hornblow Jnr)
A superbly staged remake, briskly paced, perfectly cast and lusciously photographed.
The comedy-thriller par excellence, with Bob Hope fresh and sympathetic in his first big star part.
w Walter de Leon, Lynn Starling d Elliott Nugent ph Charles Lang m Dr Ernst Toch ad Hans Dreier, Robert Usher ed Archie Marshek
☆ Bob Hope, Paulette Goddard, Gale Sondergaard, Douglass Montgomery, John Beal, George Zucco, Nydia Westman, Elizabeth Patterson, John Wray
CICILY: 'Do you believe people come back from the dead?'
WALLY: 'You mean like Republicans?'
CICILY: 'Don't these big empty houses scare you?'
WALLY: 'Not me, I was in vaudeville.'
WALLY: 'I get goose pimples. Even my goose pimples have goose pimples.'
'The objective is carried out briskly and to our complete satisfaction.' – *New York Times*
'A top programmer for upper-bracket bookings in the keys, and will hit a consistent stride down the line in the subsequents.' – *Variety*
'Beautifully shot, intelligently constructed.' – *Peter John Dyer, 1966*

The Cat and the Canary
GB 1979 98m Technicolor
Gala/Grenadier (Richard Gordon)
An overpoweringly cast but half-heartedly scripted remake of the above, which after a spirited beginning bores more than it thrills.
wd Radley Metzger ph Alex Thomson m Steven Cagan
☆ Honor Blackman, Michael Callan, Edward Fox, Wendy Hiller, Beatrix Lehmann, Olivia Hussey, Daniel Massey, Carol Lynley, Peter McEnery, Wilfrid Hyde-White
'So mechanically are characters shunted through the indistinguishable rooms and corridors that one is surprised not to see the parquet marked off in neat little squares, as on a Cluedo board.' – *Gilbert Adair, MFB*

The Cat and the Fiddle
US 1933 90m bw (colour sequence)
MGM (William K. Howard)
In a taxi in Brussels, a leading lady of Broadway musicals meets a European composer.
Very lightweight musical comedy.
w Sam and Bella Spewack stageshow Jerome Kern, Otto Harbach d William K. Howard ph Harold Rosson, Charles Clarke md Herbert Stothart ad Alexander Toluboff ed Frank Hull
☆ Jeanette MacDonald, Ramon Novarro, Charles Butterworth, Frank Morgan, Jean Hersholt, Vivienne Segal, Henry Armetta

'The only thing remaining of merit is the music.' – *Variety*

Cat Ballou **
US 1965 96m Technicolor
Columbia (Harold Hecht)
Young Catherine Ballou hires a drunken gunfighter to protect her father from a vicious gunman, but despite her efforts he is shot, so she turns outlaw.
Sometimes lively, sometimes somnolent Western spoof which considering the talent involved should have been funnier than it is. The linking ballad helps.
w Walter Newman, Frank R. Pierson novel Roy Chanslor d Elliot Silverstein ph Jack Marta m Frank de Vol
☆ Jane Fonda, Lee Marvin, Michael Callan, Dwayne Hickman, Nat King Cole, Stubby Kaye, Tom Nardini, John Marley, Reginald Denny
'Uneven, lumpy, coy and obvious.' – *Pauline Kael*
'The ultimate American spoof of the American Western, done with a judicious restraint and sly satire and, above all, a consistency all too rarely found in Hollywood.' – *Judith Crist*
🏆 Lee Marvin
🏅 Walter Newman, Frank R. Pierson; Frank de Vol; song 'The Ballad of Cat Ballou' (mJerry Livingston, lyMack David)
🎬 Lee Marvin

Cat Chaser
US 1988 98m Technicolor
Whiskers Productions (Peter A. Davis, William Panzer)
A motel owner becomes involved with an old girlfriend, who is now married to an exiled Dominican thug who keeps a fortune in banknotes in a secret hiding place.
Another botched attempt to find the cinematic equivalent to Leonard's tense, witty novels, not helped by an obtrusive voice-over.
w James Borelli, Elmore Leonard novel Elmore Leonard d Abel Ferrara ph Anthony B. Richmond m Chick Corea pd Dan Leigh ed Anthony Redman
☆ Peter Weller, Kelly McGillis, Charles Durning, Frederic Forrest, Tomas Milian, Juan Fernandez, Phil Leeds, Kelly Jo Minter, Tony Bolano

The Cat Creeps *
US 1930 71m bw
Universal
A sound remake of the 1927 Cat and the Canary.
Not too bad on its own account.
w Gladys Lehman, William Hurlbut d Rupert Julian
☆ Helen Twelvetrees, Raymond Hackett, Neil Hamilton, Jean Hersholt, Montagu Love, Blanche Friderici, Elizabeth Patterson, Theodore von Eltz, Lilyan Tashman, Lawrence Grant

The Cat Creeps
US 1946 58m bw
Universal
A reporter and photographer solve a murder and uncover missing millions.
Terrible programme filler, nothing to do with The Cat and the Canary.
w Edward Dein, Jerry Warner d Erle C. Kenton
☆ Noah Beery Jnr, Lois Collier, Paul Kelly, Douglass Dumbrille, Rose Hobart, Jonathan Hale

The Cat from Outer Space
🎞 US 1978 103m Technicolor
Walt Disney Productions (Ron Miller)
A superintelligent extraterrestrial cat is forced to land on Earth for running repairs.
Fairly modest studio offering which pleased its intended market but could have been sharper.
w Ted Key d Norman Tokar ph Charles F. Wheeler m Lalo Schifrin sp Eustace Lycett, Art Cruickshank, Danny Dee
☆ Ken Berry, Roddy McDowall, Sandy Duncan, Harry Morgan, McLean Stevenson, Jesse White, Alan Young, Hans Conried

Cat o' Nine Tails
Italy/France/Germany 1971 112m Technicolor Techniscope
Spettacoli/Mondial/Terra/Labrador (Salvatore Argento)
A blind reporter overhears an industrial espionage plot that turns into murder.
Smart surface mechanics camouflage poor storytelling.

---

wd Dario Argento *story* Dario Argento, Luigi Collo, Dardano Sacchetti *ph* Enrico Menczer *m* Ennio Morricone *ad* Carlo Leva *ed* Franco Fraticelli

☆ Karl Malden, James Franciscus, Catherine Spaak

'The sort of thriller where professional expertise amd a certain visual elegance struggle to give "tone" and "style" to blandly undistinguished material.' – *Richard Combs, MFB*

Cat on a Hot Tin Roof **
US   1958   108m   Metrocolor
MGM/Avon (Lawrence Weingarten)

A rich plantation owner, dying of cancer, finds his two sons unsatisfactory: one is a conniver, the other a neurotic who refuses to sleep with his wife.

Slightly bowdlerized version of Tennessee Williams's most straightforward melodrama, watchable for the acting but still basically a theatrical experience.

w Richard Brooks, James Poe *play* Tennessee Williams *d* Richard Brooks *ph* William Daniels *m* uncredited

☆ *Paul Newman*, Burl Ives, Elizabeth Taylor, Jack Carson, Judith Anderson, Madeleine Sherwood, Larry Gates

BIG DADDY: 'Truth is pain and sweat and paying bills and making love to a woman that you don't love any more. Truth is dreams that don't come true and nobody prints your name in the paper until you die.'

MAGGIE: 'Win what? What is the victory of a cat on a hot tin roof?'

BRICK: 'Just staying on it, I guess.'

🏆 best picture; Richard Brooks, James Poe; Richard Brooks (as director); William Daniels; Paul Newman; Elizabeth Taylor

'Kiss me and I'll claw you to death!'
Cat People **
US   1942   73m   bw
RKO (Val Lewton)

A beautiful Yugoslavian girl believes she can turn into a panther; before she is found mysteriously dead, several of her acquaintances are attacked by such a beast.

The first of Lewton's famous horror series for RKO is a slow starter but has some notable suspense sequences. It was also the first monster film to refrain from showing its monster.

w De Witt Bodeen *d* Jacques Tourneur *ph* Nicholas Musuraca *m* Roy Webb

☆ Simone Simon, Kent Smith, Tom Conway, Jane Randolph, Jack Holt

'(Lewton) revolutionized scare movies with suggestion, imaginative sound effects and camera angles, leaving everything to the fear-filled imagination.' – *Pauline Kael, 1968*

† *Curse of the Cat People* (qv) was a very unrelated sequel.

Cat People
US   1982   118m   Technicolor
Universal (Charles Fries)

A kinky version of the 1942 horrorpic. The feline lady now has an incestuous relationship with her brother, only changes after sex, and then must kill to become human again. (It is therefore safe to mate only with relatives.)

One presumes that among the eroticism and bloodlust a statement is being made, but it is never evident.

w Alan Ormsby *d* Paul Schrader *ph* John Bailey *m* Giorgio Moroder *ed* Jacqueline Cambas *sp* Tom Burman, Albert Whitlock *visual consultant* Ferdinando Scarfiotti

☆ Nastassja Kinski, Malcolm McDowell, John Heard, Annette O'Toole, Ruby Dee, Ed Begley Jnr

'The final impression is of a phantasmagoric indulgence in sound and vision by a filmmaker who fears sex and is excited by violence.' – *Sunday Times*

'The hobgoblins of an actual horror movie aren't easily translatable into the demons that haunt a Schrader hero on his way to a religious transcendence that is also a renunciation.' – *Richard Combs, MFB*

The Cat that Hated People **
US   1948   7m   Technicolor
MGM

A weary Manhattan cat rockets to the moon but finds it even noisier and is glad to come home.

Violent but dazzlingly inventive cartoon from this madcap director; a little classic of its kind.

w Heck Allen *d* Tex Avery

'See: The Lost City Of Love-Starved Cat-Women!'
Cat Women of the Moon
US   1953   63m   bw   3D
Three Dimensional Pictures

aka: *Rocket to the Moon*

Five American astronauts find the moon inhabited solely by ravenous cat women.

One of the top claimants to film history's booby prize, along with such other space fiction entrants as Fire Maidens from Outer Space, Plan 9 from Outer Space and Santa Claus Conquers the Martians. It has more than a chance.

w Roy Hamilton *d* Arthur Hilton

☆ Sonny Tufts, Victor Jory, Marie Windsor, William Phipps, Douglas Fowley

'The special effects look like they came free with a cornflakes packet.' – *The Dark Side*

Catacombs
GB   1964   90m   bw
Parroch/McCallum

A rich woman is murdered by her husband and her male secretary.

Involved melodrama with rather too many twists.

w Dan Mainwaring *d* Gordon Hessler

☆ Gary Merrill, Neil McCallum, Georgina Cookson, Jane Merrow, Rachel Thomas, Jack Train

Catch 22 *
US   1970   122m   Technicolor   Panavision
Paramount/Filmways (John Calley, Martin Ransohoff)

At a US Air Force base in the Mediterranean during World War II, one by one the officers are distressingly killed; a survivor paddles towards neutral Sweden.

Intensely black comedy, more so than M*A*S*H and less funny, effectively mordant in places but too grisly and missing several tricks.

w Buck Henry *novel* Joseph Heller *d* Mike Nichols *ph* David Watkin *m* none *pd* Richard Sylbert

☆ Alan Arkin, Martin Balsam, Richard Benjamin, Art Garfunkel, Jack Gilford, Buck Henry, Bob Newhart, Anthony Perkins, Paula Prentiss, Jon Voight, Martin Sheen, Orson Welles

'There are startling effects and good revue touches here and there, but the picture keeps going on and on, as if it were determined to impress us.' – *New Yorker, 1977*

'As hot and heavy as the original was cool and light.' – *Richard Schickel*

'It goes on so long that it cancels itself out, even out of people's memories; it was long awaited and then forgotten almost instantly.' – *Pauline Kael*

'Dr Strangelove out of Alice in Wonderland.' – *Daily Mail*

Catch As Catch Can
GB   1937   71m   bw
Fox British

aka: *Atlantic Episode*

Crooks after a valuable diamond converge on a transatlantic liner.

Modest comedy-thriller.

w Richard Llewellyn *d* Roy Kellino

☆ James Mason, Viki Dobson, Eddie Pola, Finlay Currie

Catch Me a Spy
GB   1971   94m   Technicolor
Rank/Ludgate/Capitol/Films de la Pleiade (Steven Pallos)

A British agent smuggling Russian manuscripts into England falls for the wife of a Russian spy and finally gets his money as well.

Complex, patchy comedy thriller with dispirited action scenes in Bucharest and Scotland. Technical credits rather dim.

w Dick Clement, Ian La Frenais *novel* George Marton, Tibor Meray *d* Dick Clement *ph* Christopher Challis *m* Claude Bolling *ad* Carmen Dillon *ed* John Bloom

☆ Kirk Douglas, Trevor Howard, Tom Courtenay, Marlene Jobert, Patrick Mower, Bernadette Lafont, Bernard Blier

Catch Me If You Can
US   1989   105m   Foto-Kem
Medusa/Management Company Entertainment Group/Sterling Entertainment (Jonathan D. Krane)

A high-school student becomes a champion drag-racer to prevent his school from closing through lack of funds.

A drive-in movie for undemanding adolescents.

wd Stephen Sommers *m* Tangerine Dream *ad* Stuart Blatt *ed* Bob Ducsay

☆ Matt Lattanzi, Loryn Locklin, Grant Heslov, Billy Morrissette, M. Emmet Walsh

Catch My Soul
US   1973   95m   DeLuxe
Fox-Rank/Metromedia (Richard Rosenbloom, Jack Good)

A black evangelist, led astray by a member of his congregation possessed by a demon, becomes jealous of his wife and murders her.

A rock and country musical version of Othello, in which the tragic original is trivialized to the point of boredom.

w Jack Good *musical play* Jack Good from Shakespeare's Othello *d* Patrick McGoohan *ph* Conrad Hall *m* Paul Glass *m/ly* Tony Joe White, Jack Good *md* Delaney Bramlett *pd* Tex Reed *ed* Sid Levin

☆ Richie Havens, Lance LeGault, Season Hubley, Tony Joe White, Susan Tyrrell

'A sort of comic strip travesty of the play.' – *Tom Milne, MFB*

Catch Us If You Can
GB   1965   91m   bw
Anglo Amalgamated/Bruton (David Deutsch)

US title: *Having a Wild Weekend*

Freelance stuntmen have various adventures in the west of England.

The first film of a pretentious director is a bright but wearisomely high-spirited imitation of A Hard Day's Night.

w Peter Nichols *d* John Boorman *ph* Manny Wynn *m* Dave Clark

☆ The Dave Clark Five, Barbara Ferris, David Lodge, Robin Bailey, Yootha Joyce

'An uneven script, rather uncertainly making its point about disillusionment and capitulation to the sham; but – like Mr Boorman's direction – at its best well worth your attention.' – *Dilys Powell*

Catchfire
US   1989   99m   CFI color
Vestron/Precision Films/Mack-Taylor Productions (Dick Clark, Dan Paulson)

A female artist who witnessed a Mafia killing falls in love with the man sent to murder her.

Unbelievable, though occasionally enjoyable, thriller.

w Rachel Kronstadt Mann, Ann Louise Bardach *d* Alan Smithee (Dennis Hopper) *ph* Ed Lachman *m* Curt Sobel *pd* Ron Foreman *ed* David Rawlins

☆ Dennis Hopper, Jodie Foster, Dean Stockwell, Vincent Price, John Turturro, Joe Pesci, Fred Ward, Julie Adams, G. Anthony Sirico

The Catered Affair *
US   1956   93m   bw
MGM (Sam Zimbalist)

GB title: *Wedding Breakfast*

When the daughter of a New York taxi driver gets married, her mother insists on a bigger function than they can afford.

Rather heavy-going comedy with amusing dialogue, from the period when Hollywood was seizing on TV plays like Marty and Twelve Angry Men.

w Gore Vidal *TV play* Paddy Chayefsky *d* Richard Brooks *ph* John Alton *m* André Previn

☆ Bette Davis, Ernest Borgnine, Debbie Reynolds, Barry Fitzgerald, Rod Taylor, Robert Simon, Madge Kennedy, Dorothy Stickney

Catherine the Great *
GB   1934   93m   bw
London Films/Alexander Korda

aka: *The Rise of Catherine the Great*

How Catherine married the mad prince and slowly conquered the Russian court.

Dated but well acted and written account, sober by comparison with The Scarlet Empress which came out at the same time.

w Lajos Biro, Arthur Wimperis, Marjorie Deans *play* The Czarina by Melchior Lengyel, Lajos Biro *d* Paul Czinner *ph* Georges Périnal, Robert Lapresle *m* Ernest Toch *md* Muir Mathieson *ad* Vincent Korda *ed* Harold Young

☆ Elisabeth Bergner, Douglas Fairbanks Jnr, Flora Robson, Gerald du Maurier, Irene Vanbrugh, Griffith Jones, Joan Gardner, Diana Napier

'It rates no raves but is a good piece of merchandise.' – *Variety*

† The style is typified by a speech given to Grand Duke Peter: 'If she wasn't on the throne she'd be on the street.'

Catholic Boys: see *Heaven Help Us*

Cathy Tippel: see *Keetje Tippel*

Catlow *
GB   1971   101m   Metrocolor
MGM/Euan Lloyd

A likeable outlaw tries to avoid problems while recovering his hidden gold.

Light-hearted, cheerfully cast, fast-moving, Spanish-located Western.

w Scot Finch, J. J. Griffith *novel* Louis L'Amour *d* Sam Wanamaker *ph* Ted Scaife *m* Roy Budd

☆ Yul Brynner, Leonard Nimoy, Richard Crenna, Daliah Lavi, Jo Ann Pflug, Jeff Corey, Bessie Love, David Ladd

Catman of Paris
US   1946   63m   bw
Republic (Marek M. Libkov)

An amnesia victim may be the mad killer who prowls the boulevards.

Poverty Row thriller with a few sharp moments.

w Sherman Lowe *d* Lesley Selander

☆ Carl Esmond, Lenore Aubert, Adele Mara, Douglass Dumbrille, Gerald Mohr, Fritz Feld

'Settings have solid mahogany look but the script has only a literate veneer.' – *Variety*

Cat's Eye
US   1985   93m   Technicolor
Famous Films/Dino de Laurentiis (Martha J. Schumacher)

Three semi-horror stories linked by a cat.

This omnibus is weak in every department.

w Stephen King *d* Lewis Teague *ph* Jack Cardiff *m* Alan Silvestri *pd* Giorgio Postiglione

☆ Drew Barrymore, James Woods, Alan King, Kenneth McMillan, Robert Hays, Candy Clark, James Naughton

'It creeps in on foggy feet.' – *Variety*

The Cat's Paw *
US   1936   101m   bw
Harold Lloyd

The son of a Chinese missionary returns home and finds himself in the middle of a Tong war.

Very moderate star comedy from the time when he was considering himself a character comedian rather than a slapstick ace.

w Harold Lloyd, Sam Taylor *story* Clarence Budington Kelland *d* Sam Taylor

☆ Harold Lloyd, George Barbier, Una Merkel, Nat Pendleton, Grant Mitchell, Vince Barnett

'The picture gets its laughs all right, but it approaches them at a crawl.' – *Variety*

Cattle Annie and Little Britches
🏕 US   1980   98m   CFI color
Hemdale/UATC (Rupert Hitzig, Alan King)

In 1893, two girls head west in search of adventure.

Rather winsome family Western, with too little real action and too much romping about.

w Robert Ward, David Eyre *novel* Robert Ward *d* Lamont Johnson *ph* Larry Pizer *m* Sanh Berti, Tom Slocum

☆ Burt Lancaster, John Savage, Rod Steiger, Diane Lane, Amanda Plummer, Scott Glenn, Steven Ford

'Its storyline meanders and it never clinches any central conflict. But it has qualities of feeling that grab-'em movies can't approach.' – *Peter Rainer, Los Angeles Herald Examiner*

Cattle Drive

US 1951 78m Technicolor
Universal-International (Aaron Rosenberg)
The spoiled teenage son of a magnate finds humanity and friendship with a cowhand during a cattle drive.
Captains Courageous out west, not badly done.
w Jack Natteford, Lillie Hayward d Kurt Neumann
☆ Joel McCrea, Dean Stockwell, Chill Wills, Leon Ames, Bob Steele

Cattle Empire

US 1958 82m DeLuxe Cinemascope
TCF (Robert Stabler)
A trail boss out of prison gets a new assignment and signs up helpers who had previously made life difficult for him.
Fair general Western, entirely dependent on its star.
w Endre Bohem, Eric Norden d Charles Marquis Warren ph Brydon Baker m Paul Sawtell, Bert Shefter
☆ Joel McCrea, Gloria Talbott, Don Haggerty, Phyllis Coates, Paul Brinegar

Cattle King

US 1963 90m Metrocolor
MGM/Missouri (Nat Holt)
GB title: *Guns of Wyoming*
A big rancher opposes a cattle trail and starts a range war.
Moderately expert but very familiar star Western.
w Thomas Thompson d Tay Garnett ph William E. Snyder m Paul Sawtell
☆ Robert Taylor, Joan Caulfield, Robert Middleton, Robert Loggia, Larry Gates, Malcolm Atterbury

Cattle Queen of Montana

US 1954 88m Technicolor
RKO/Benedict Bogeaus
A tough woman inherits her father's rangeland and resists cattle rustlers.
A Western which runs in predictable grooves, and could have done with more vigour.
w Robert Blees, Howard Estabrook story Robert Blackburn d Allan Dwan ph John Alton md Louis Forbes
☆ Barbara Stanwyck, Ronald Reagan, Gene Evans, Lance Fuller, Anthony Caruso, Jack Elam

Cattle Town

US 1952 71m bw
Warner
After the Civil War, returning ranch owners find their land appropriated by squatters.
Reach-me-down Western programmer.
w Tom Blackburn d Noel Smith
☆ Dennis Morgan, Amanda Blake, Rita Moreno, Ray Teal, Philip Carey

Caught!

US 1931 71m bw
Paramount
A US cavalry officer discovers that Calamity Jane is his mother.
Curious mother-love Western.
w Agnes Brand Leahy, Keene Thompson, Sam and Bella Spewack d Edward Sloman
☆ Richard Arlen, Louise Dresser, Frances Dee

Caught *

US 1948 88m bw
Enterprise (Wolfgang Reinhardt)
The ill-treated wife of a vicious millionaire leaves him for a doctor, but finds she is to have the millionaire's baby.
Pretentious film noir, rather typical of its time, with much talent squandered on a very boring plot.
w Arthur Laurents novel *Wild Calendar* by Libbie Block d Max Ophuls ph Lee Garmes m Frederick Hollander ed Robert Parrish
☆ James Mason, Robert Ryan, Barbara Bel Geddes, Natalie Schafer, Curt Bois
'Ophuls had suffered at Hughes' hands ... had wasted time on worthless projects ... and had been referred to as "the oaf". Laurents built the script on stories which Ophuls told him about Hughes, and on the accounts given by one of Hughes' girls.' – *Pauline Kael*

Caught

US 1995 109m DuArt
Cinehaus/DuArt/Circle Films (Richard Brick, Irwin Young)
Tensions within a Hispanic family explode after an Irish drifter moves in.
A thriller that works a few variations on a familiar theme, but lacks the style to capture and maintain an audience's interest.
w Edward Pomerantz novel *Into It* by Edward Pomerantz d Robert M. Young ph Michael Barrow m Chris Botti pd Hilary Rosenfeld ed Norman Buckley
☆ Edward James Olmos, Maria Conchita Alonso, Arie Verveen, Steven Schub, Bitty Schram, Shawn Elliott

Caught in the Act

GB 1996 97m colour
Midsummer (Christopher Milburn)
Smitten by a theatrical agent, a young woman persuades her two equally unmusical friends to form a singing group to perform on his talent show.
Feeble comedy that never rises above sitcom predictability.
w Caroline Hill, Mark Greenstreet d Mark Greenstreet ph David Evans m Simon May pd James Hendy ed Nick Arthurs
☆ Sara Crowe, Annette Badland, Nadia Sawalha, Paul Shelley, Leslie Phillips, Guy Henry, Tim McMullan, Gerard Kelly, Nickolas Grace, Gaye Brown

Caught in the Draft **

US 1941 82m bw
Paramount (B. G. de Sylva)
A nervous film star cannot avoid being drafted into the army.
Sprightly comedy from the star's best period, with gags and supporting cast well up to form.
w Harry Tugend d David Butler ph Karl Struss m Victor Young
☆ Bob Hope, Lynne Overman, Dorothy Lamour, Clarence Kolb, Eddie Bracken, Paul Hurst, Irving Bacon

Caught Plastered

US 1931 68m bw
RKO
In helping an old lady save her drug store, two hams get mixed up with bootleggers.
Tedious star farce.
w Ralph Spence, Douglas MacLean d William Seiter
☆ Bert Wheeler, Robert Woolsey, Dorothy Lee, Lucy Beaumont, Jason Robards
'Best for combo and three-dayers.' – *Variety*

Caught Short

US 1930 75m bw
Cosmopolitan/MGM
Feuding boarding house landladies play the stock market – and win.
Lumbering comedy which marked the first big success for the team of Dressler and Moran.
w Willard Mack, Robert Hopkins d Charles Reisner
☆ Marie Dressler, Polly Moran, Charles Morton, Anita Page
'A gold mine ... the apex of the career of this pair of sublimated film-makers ... a box office smash for all classes anywhere.' – *Variety*
† A credit reads: Story suggested by Eddie Cantor's gag book.

Caught Up *

US 1998 97m DeLuxe
Heller Highwater/Live/Mediaworks
A former convict forms a relationship with a duplicitous woman when a hitman opens fire on them both.
Enjoyable, slickly directed modern excursion into film noir, set among the black community of South Central Los Angeles.
wd Darin Scott ph Thomas Callaway m Marc Bonilla pd Terrence Foster ed Charles Bornstein
☆ Cynda Williams, Bokeem Woodbine, Joseph Lindsey, Clifton Powell, Basil Wallace, Tony Todd, LL Cool J, Snoop Doggy Dog, Jeffrey Combs
'An engrossing, skillful yarn that takes its protag on a twisted path of murder, deceit, treachery and passion.' – *Leonard Klady, Variety*

Cauldron of Blood

Spain/US 1968 97m Eastmancolor
Tigon/Hispamer/Robert D. Weinbach
aka: *Blind Man's Bluff*
A sculptor, blinded in a car crash, is unaware that his wife has turned killer to keep him supplied with the skeletons he uses in his work.
Dreary horror movie that is interesting only for the presence of Karloff, and even he seems to wish himself elsewhere.
w John Melson, Edward Mann, José Luis Bayonas d Edward Mann (Santos Alcocer) ph Francisco Sempere m Ray Ellis ad Gil Parrondo ed J. Antonio Rojo sp Thierre Pathé
☆ Boris Karloff, Viveca Lindfors, Jean-Pierre Aumont, Jacqui Speed
'Its heavy Freudian symbolism becomes almost laughable in conjunction with the wooden dialogue and ludicrous situations.' – *David Pirie, MFB*
† The film was cut to 87m for its British release.

Cause for Alarm *

US 1951 74m bw
MGM (Tom Lewis)
A housewife tries frantically to retrieve a posted letter containing manufactured evidence which may put her on a murder charge.
Minor-league suspenser, watchable but disappointingly handled.
w Mel Dinelli, Tom Lewis d Tay Garnett ph Joe Ruttenberg m André Previn
☆ Loretta Young, Barry Sullivan, Bruce Cowling, Margalo Gillmore, Irving Bacon

'A love that suffered and rose triumphant above the crushing events of this modern age! The march of time measured by a mother's heart!'

Cavalcade **

US 1933 109m bw
Fox (Winfield Sheehan)
The story of an upper-class English family between the Boer War and World War I.
Rather static version of the famous stage spectacular, very similar in setting and style to TV's later Upstairs Downstairs. *Good performances, flat handling.*
w Reginald Berkeley play Noël Coward d Frank Lloyd m Ernest Palmer m Louis de Francesco ad William Darling war scenes William Cameron Menzies
☆ Clive Brook, Diana Wynyard, Ursula Jeans, Herbert Mundin, Una O'Connor, Irene Browne, Merle Tottenham, Beryl Mercer, Frank Lawton, Billy Bevan
'Dignified and beautiful spectacle that will demand respect.' – *Variety*
'If there is anything that moves the ordinary American to uncontrollable tears, it is the plight – the constant plight – of dear old England ... a superlative newsreel, forcibly strengthened by factual scenes, good music, and wonderful photography.' – *Pare Lorentz*
'Greater even than *Birth of a Nation*!' – *Louella Parsons*
'An orgy of British self-congratulation.' – *Pauline Kael, 70s*
🏆 best picture; Frank Lloyd; William Darling
⧣ Diana Wynyard

The Cave Dwellers: see *One Million BC*

The Cave Man

US 1926 78m silent
Warner
A bored socialite cuts a high denomination note in half, throws one half away, and offers riches to the first man to find it.
Typical twenties comedy which seemed very modern at the time.
w Darryl F. Zanuck d Lewis Milestone
☆ Marie Prevost, Matt Moore, Phyllis Haver, Myrna Loy

Cave of Outlaws

US 1951 76m Technicolor
Universal-International
After surviving a long prison term, a bandit returns to the caves where his partners hid their booty.
Modest Western with scenes shot in the Carlsbad Caverns.
w Elizabeth Wilson d William Castle

☆ Macdonald Carey, Alexis Smith, Edgar Buchanan, Victor Jory, Hugh O'Brian, Houseley Stevenson

Caveman

US 1981 91m Technicolor
UA (Lawrence Turman, David Foster)
Adventures of a prehistoric man.
Witless farrago of puns and farts on a lower level than Mel Brooks, if such a thing were possible.
w Rudy de Luca, Carl Gottlieb d Carl Gottlieb ph Alan Hume m Lalo Schifrin pd Philip M. Jefferies ed Gene Fowler
☆ Ringo Starr, Dennis Quaid, Jack Gilford, Barbara Bach, Avery Schreiber
'Too gross and leery for children and not nearly sprightly or sly enough for adults.' – *Daily Mail*
'Worth about half an hour of anybody's time. Unfortunately it runs 97 minutes.' – *Guardian*

El Cazador de la Muerte: see *Deathstalker*

CB4

US 1993 88m DeLuxe
Universal (Nelson George)
Clean-living middle-class youths form a gangsta rap group called Cell Block 4 and pretend to be tough.
Brief appearances from Ice T, Ice Cube, Flavour Flav and others add a little authenticity to a slight but amusing satire at the expense of the macho posturing of rappers. It will be most enjoyed by those attuned to the phenomenon of hip hop.
w Chris Rock, Nelson George, Robert LoCash d Tamra Davis ph Karl Walter Lindenlaub m John Barnes pd Nelson Coates ed Earl Watson
☆ Chris Rock, Allen Payne, Deezer D, Phil Hartman, Arthur Evans, Theresa Randle, Willard E. Pugh, Richard Gant, Charlie Murphy, Chris Elliott
'Lively is the word for its better parts. Terminally disorganised would be the best one for the rest.' – *Derek Malcolm, Guardian*
'The satire is feeble, the pastiche documentary botched. Stereotypes are peeled away to reveal stereotypes beneath.' – *Philip French, Observer*

Cease Fire

US 1985 97m Continental Color
Double Helix/Cineworld (William Grefe)
Ex-Vietnam vets in Miami have trouble getting work and forgetting the past.
Honest but predictable drama from behind the headlines.
w George Fernandez play *Vietnam Trilogy* by George Fernandez d David Nutter ph Henning Schellerup m Gary Fry ad Alan Avchen ed Julio Chaves
☆ Don Johnson, Lisa Blount, Robert F. Lyons, Richard Chaves, Rick Richards

Ceiling Zero *

US 1935 95m bw
Warner/Cosmopolitan (Harry Joe Brown)
Amorous and airborne adventures of an irresponsible but brilliant civil airlines pilot.
Splendid star vehicle which turns maudlin in the last reel but until then provides crackling entertainment.
w Frank 'Spig' Wead play Frank Wead d Howard Hawks ph Arthur Edeson
☆ James Cagney, Pat O'Brien, June Travis, Stuart Erwin, Henry Wadsworth, Isabel Jewell, Barton MacLane
'An entertainment wallop of extraordinary power.' – *Variety*
'The best of all airplane pictures.' – *Otis Ferguson, 1939*
'Directed at a breakneck pace which emphasizes its lean fibre and its concentration on the essentials of its theme.' – *Andrew Sarris, 1963*
† Remade in 1939 as *International Squadron*.

Cela s'appelle l'Aurore *

France/Italy 1955 108m bw
Marceau/Laetitia
A Corsican company doctor falls for a young widow while his wife is on holiday, and events lead to tragedy.
Efficient melodrama, given an extra dimension by its auteur.

---

w Luis Buñuel, Jean Ferry novel Emmanuel
Robles d Luis Buñuel ph Robert Le Fèbvre
m Joseph Kosma
☆ Georges Marchal, Lucia Bose, Gianni Esposito,
Julien Bertheau, Henri Nassiet

The Celebration: see *Festen*

'A new comedy about people who will do anything
to get famous ... or stay famous.'

Celebrity *
US   1998   113m   bw
Buena Vista/Sweetland (Jean Doumanian)
📼 ⬛ 🎧
After a marital break-up, a promiscuous journalist
and his insecure former wife look for love.
*With the neurotic centre of energy being occupied by
both Branagh and Davis, Allen's on-screen presence is
much missed here, while on the other side of the camera
he recycles his usual attitudes to relationships without
much apparent enthusiasm but with the occasional good
joke.*
wd Woody Allen ph Sven Nykvist pd Santo
Loquasto ed Susan E. Morse
☆ Hank Azaria, Kenneth Branagh, Judy Davis,
Leonardo DiCaprio, Melanie Griffith, Famke
Janssen, Michael Lerner, Joe Mantegna, Bebe
Neuwirth, Winona Ryder, Charlize Theron
'Annoyingly mannered in performance as well as
tiresomely familiar in the way it trots out its
angst-ridden urban characters' problems.' – *Todd
McCarthy, Variety*

Céleste
West Germany   1981   106m   Eastmancolor
Artificial Eye/Pelemele/Bayerische Rundfunk
(Eleonore Adlon)
⬛
Proust's housekeeper recalls their life together.
*Stifling, slow-moving account, likely to interest only
admirers of the author.*
wd Percy Adlon book Monsieur Proust by Céleste
Albaret ph Jürgen Martin, Horst Becker, Helmo
Sahliger, Hermann Ramelow m Cesar Franck
ad Hans Gailling ed Clara Fabry
☆ *Eva Mattes,* Jürgen Arndt, Norbert
Wartha, Wolf Euba, Joseph Manoth, Leo
Bardischewski

Celia
GB   1949   67m   bw
Exclusive/Hammer (Anthony Hinds)
An impecunious actress becomes a temporary
private eye investigating the case of a rich aunt
who marries a man young enough to be her son
and refuses to meet her relatives.
*Mildly amusing, cheaply made comedy thriller, based
on a BBC radio serial by Mason.*
w A. R. Rawlinson, Edward J. Mason, Francis
Searle, Roy Plomley d Francis Searle ph Cedric
Williams md Frank Spencer, Rupert Grayson
ad Denis Wreford ed R. C. Cox
☆ Hy Hazell, Bruce Lester, John Bailey, Joan
Hickson, Elsie Wagstaff

Celia *
Australia   1988   103m   colour
BCB/Seon (Timothy White, Gordon Glenn)
📼
Grieving over the death of her grandmother
and caught up in political and sexual acrimony
that she doesn't understand, a nine-year
old girl retreats into a fantasy world of childish
violence.
*Unconvincing tale of a child's development, warped by
the red-baiting, rabbit-hating suburban Australian
society of the 1950s.*
wd Ann Turner ph Geoffrey Simpson m Chris
Neal pd Peta Lawson ed Ken Sallows
☆ Rebecca Smart, Nicholas Eadie, Victoria
Longley, Mary-Anne Fahey

Celine and Julie Go Boating *
France   1974   192m   Eastmancolor
Les Films du Losange (Barbet Schroeder)
📼
Two girls change the outcome of a drama played
daily in a haunted house.
*Odd, dreamlike, absurdly long and semi-
improvisational mood piece, with reverberations from
Alice in Wonderland and Orphée. Not an
unpleasant experience, but sometimes a tiresome one.*
w Eduardo de Gregorio, Juliet Berto, Dominique
Labourier, Bulle Ogier, Marie-France Pisier, Jacques
Rivette, partly suggested by two stories by Henry

James d Jacques Rivette ph Jacques Renard
m Jean-Marie Senia
☆ Juliet Berto, Dominique Labourier, Bulle Ogier,
Marie-France Pisier, Barbet Schroeder
'Rivette uncannily combines slapstick, suspense
and tears in his most watchable assault on the
narrative form.' – *Jan Dawson*
† Shot in 16mm.

Cell 2455 Death Row
US   1955   77m   bw
Columbia (Wallace MacDonald)
A convicted murderer staves off execution with
appeal after appeal.
*Cheap run-off of the case of Caryl Chessman, who
was executed ten years after his trial for rape and
murder. Retold in a 1977 TV movie, Kill Me If You
Can.*
w Jack de Witt book Caryl Chessman d Fred F.
Sears ph Fred Jackman Jnr md Mischa
Bakaleinikoff
☆ William Campbell, Kathryn Grant, Harvey
Stephens, Marian Carr, Vince Edwards

The Celluloid Closet **
US   1995   101m   colour
Electric/Reflective/Telling Pictures/HBO/Channel 4/ZD
(Rob Epstein, Jeffrey Friedman)
⬛ 🔍
A documentary, illustrated with interviews and
excerpts from films, about the way homosexuals
have been presented in Hollywood movies.
*An interesting and provocative examination of
Hollywood attitudes towards sexuality, though it never
quite gets to grips with how far movies reflect and
influence the attitudes of a wider society.*
w Rob Epstein, Jeffrey Friedman, Sharon Wood,
Armistead Maupin book Vito Russo d Rob
Epstein, Jeffrey Friedman m Nancy Schreiber
m Carter Burwell ad Scott Chambliss ed Jeffrey
Friedman, Arnold Glassman
☆ Tony Curtis, Armistead Maupin, Susie Bright,
Whoopi Goldberg, Quentin Crisp, Harvey
Fierstein, Arthur Laurents, Gore Vidal, Farley
Granger, Paul Rudnick, Shirley MacLaine, Tom
Hanks, John Schlesinger, Lily Tomlin
'Fascinating, insightful, often funny.' – *George
Perry*

Celtic Pride
US   1996   91m   Technicolor
Buena Vista/Hollywood/Caravan (Roger Birnbaum)
📼 ⬛ 🔍
Two basketball fans kidnap the star player from a
rival team so that their own team can win an
important game.
*A comedy of working-class passion for sporting heroes
which does not travel well.*
w Judd Apatow d Tom De Cerchio ph Oliver
Wood m Basil Poledouris pd Stephen Marsh
ed Hubert de la Bouillerie
☆ Damon Wayans, Daniel Stern, Dan Aykroyd,
Gail O'Grady, Adam Hendershott, Paul Guilfoyle
'An uneven but largely likeable basketball-
themed comedy.' – *Variety*

Celui Qui Doit Mourir: see *He Who Must Die*

'Love Knows No Limits.'
The Cement Garden *
GB/Germany/France   1993   105m   colour
Metro Tartan/Constantin/Torii/Sylvia
Montalti/Laurentic (Bee Gilbert, Ene Vanaveski)
📼
After their parents die, a teenage boy and girl,
while trying to look after their younger brothers
and sisters, begin an incestuous affair.
*A cool, distanced and unsettling account of adolescent
angst and sexuality, notable for some excellent acting.*
wd Andrew Birkin novel Ian McEwan
ph Stephen Blackman m Edward Shearmur
pd Bernd Lepel ed Toby Tremlett
☆ *Andrew Robertson, Charlotte Gainsbourg,* Alice
Coulthard, Ned Birkin, Sinead Cusack, Hanns
Zischler, Jochen Horst, Gareth Brown, William
Hootkins
'Neither a black comedy nor a horror story, but a
delicate and beautifully filmed and performed
account of the innocence and confusions of
youth, within an adult world, unlikely to be
mature enough to comprehend it.' – *Derek
Malcolm, Guardian*
† Birkin won the award for best director at the
Berlin Film Festival.

Cemetery Man *
France/Italy   1994   100m   Eastmancolor
Technovision
KG/Canal+/Audifilm/Urania (Tilde Corsi, Gianni
Romoli, Michele Soavi)
📼 ⬛ 🎧
original title: *Dellamorte Dellamore*
The watchman at a cemetery where the dead rise
from their graves after seven days begins an affair
with a beautiful young widow when she visits her
newly buried husband.
*A horror film that is more original than most, as it
veers between elegance and sudden goriness, eroticism
and necrophilia, camp humour and sudden shock,
coarseness and mysticism. It is not, however, for the
squeamish.*
w Gianni Romoli novel Tiziano Sclavi
d Michele Soavi ph Mauro Marchetti m Manuel
de Sica pd Antonello Geleng ed Franco Fraticelli
sp Sergio Stivaletti
☆ Rupert Everett, François Hadji-Lazaro, Anna
Falci, Mickey Knox, Fabiana Formica, Clive Riche,
Katja Anton, Stefano Masciarelli
'A hip, offbeat horror item floating on a bed of
dark philosophy.' – *Variety*

Centennial Summer **
🚸 US   1946   102m   Technicolor
TCF (Otto Preminger)
A Philadelphia family responds to the Great
Exposition of 1876.
*Pleasing family comedy with music, the kind of
harmless competence Hollywood used to throw off with
ease but can no longer manage.*
w Michael Kanin novel Albert E. Idell d Otto
Preminger ph Ernest Palmer m Alfred Newman
m/ly Jerome Kern, Oscar Hammerstein II, E. Y.
Harburg, Leo Robin
☆ Jeanne Crain, Cornel Wilde, Linda Darnell,
William Eythe, Walter Brennan, *Constance
Bennett, Dorothy Gish*
† Jeanne Crain's songs were dubbed by Louanne
Hogan.
♫ Alfred Newman; song 'All Through the Day'
(mJerome Kern, lyOscar Hammerstein II)

Central Airport
US   1933   75m   bw
Warner
After the war the only job an ace pilot can get is as
'chauffeur' to a lady parachutist.
*Rather stiff romantic drama with aeronautics thrown
in.*
w Rian James, James Seymour story Hawk's Mate
by Jack Moffitt d William A. Wellman ph Sid
Hickox md Leo F. Forbstein ad Jack Okey
ed James Morley
☆ Richard Barthelmess, Sally Eilers, Tom Brown,
Glenda Farrell, Harold Huber
'The aerial excitement should bring sufficient
response to bring it over to the right side of the
box office.' – *Variety*

Central Do Brasil: see *Central Station*

Central Park
US   1932   57m   bw
Warner
Stories of life in New York's park.
Nifty portmanteau which moves fast and does not bore.
w Ward Morehouse, Earl Baldwin d John Adolfi
☆ Joan Blondell, Guy Kibbee, Wallace Ford,
Henry B. Walthall, Patricia Ellis, Spencer Charters

Central Station ***
Brazil/France   1998   110m   colour   'Scope
MACT/Videofilms/Riofilme/Canal+ (Arthur Cohn,
Martine de Clermont-Tonnerre)
📼 ⬛
original title: *Central Do Brasil*
A cynical elderly former schoolteacher
accompanies a young boy across Brazil in search of
his father.
*A delight – a charming, but tough, study in loss and
redemption, wise, witty and compassionate without
losing touch with the harsher realities of life.*
w João Emanuel Carneiro, Marcos Bernstein
idea Walter Salles d Walter Salles ph Walter
Carvalho m Antonio Pinto, Jaques Morelembaum
pd Cassio Amarante, Carla Caffe ed Isabelle
Rathery, Felipe Lacerda
☆ *Fernanda Montenegro,* Marilia Pera, Vinicius de
Oliveira, Soia Lira, Othon Bastos, Otavio Augusto,

Stela Freitas, Matheus Nachtergaele, Caio
Junquaria
'A melancholy Brazilian road movie shot
through with gently stressed cultural
commentary.' – *Todd McCarthy, Variety*
'Shrewd, tough and big-hearted.' – *David Denby,
New Yorker*
♀ foreign-language film; Fernanda Montenegro
🎬 foreign-language film

Century *
GB   1994   112m   colour
Electric/BBC/Beambright (Therese Pickard)
📼 🎧
At the end of the 19th century, a Jewish doctor
goes to work at a research institute where the
doctor in charge is sterilizing poor women to
prevent them breeding.
*An interesting drama of the beginning of the 20th
century, but one that often seems too diagrammatic in
its concerns to be convincing.*
wd Stephen Poliakoff ph Witold Stok
m Michael Gibbs pd Michael Pickwoad
ed Michael Parkinson
☆ Charles Dance, Clive Owen, Miranda
Richardson, Robert Stephens, Joan Hickson, Lena
Headey, Neil Stuke, Liza Walker
'Deserves to be celebrated for its effortless
integration of contemporary issues –
immigration, genetic engineering in the broadest
sense of that phrase – with a convincing
historical story.' – *Adam Mars-Jones, Independent*
'While rarely less than intelligent and
provocative, Century is frequently implausible –
dramatically, psychologically and historically.' –
Philip French, Observer

Le Cercle Rouge: see *The Red Circle*

La Cérémonie **
France/Germany   1995   112m   colour
Gala/MK2/France3/Prokino/Olga/ZDF (Marin Karmitz)
📼
aka: *A Judgement in Stone*
Two women, an illiterate new housekeeper to a
wealthy couple and the local postmistress, form a
close friendship and begin to resent those in
authority over them.
*A deft psychological thriller, sympathetic towards its
apparently servile rebels, and enjoying the way that its
middle-class characters get their come-uppance.*
w Claude Chabrol, Caroline Eliacheff novel A
Judgement in Stone by Ruth Rendell d Claude
Chabrol ph Bernard Zitzermann m Matthieu
Chabrol ad Daniel Mercier ed Monique Fardoulis
☆ Sandrine Bonnaire, Isabelle Huppert, Jean-
Pierre Cassel, Jacqueline Bisset, Virginie Ledoyen,
Jean-François Perrier
'Deliriously nasty.' – *Sunday Times*

The Ceremony
US/Spain   1963   107m   bw
UA/Magla (Laurence Harvey)
In a Tangier jail, a bank robber awaits the firing
squad, but he and his brother have an escape plan.
*Murky and pretentious melodrama with aspirations to
high style and symbolism. A bore.*
w Ben Barzman novel Frederic Grendel
d Laurence Harvey ph Oswald Morris m Gerard
Schurmann
☆ Laurence Harvey, Sarah Miles, Robert Walker,
John Ireland, Ross Martin, Lee Patterson, Jack
MacGowran, Murray Melvin, Fernando Rey

A Certain Smile *
US   1958   105m   Eastmancolor
Cinemascope
TCF (Henry Ephron)
A girl student falls in love with her philandering
uncle.
*Another sordid novella by Françoise Sagan (see
Bonjour Tristesse), transformed by Hollywood into a
glowing romantic saga of life among the Riviera rich.
On this level, very competent.*
w Frances Goodrich, Albert Hackett d Jean
Negulesco ph Milton Krasner m Alfred Newman
ad Lyle R. Wheeler, John DeCuir
☆ Christine Carere, Rossano Brazzi, Joan
Fontaine, Bradford Dillman, Eduard Franz, Kathryn
Givney, Steve Geray
♫ title song (mSammy Fain, lyPaul Francis
Webster); art direction

Cervantes

Spain/Italy/France 1968 119m Eastmancolor
Supertotalvision
Prisma/Protor/Procinex (Alexander Salkind)
US title: *The Young Rebel*
Cervantes, an assistant papal envoy, helps persuade
Philip of Spain to join the Holy League, then turns
soldier and has various adventures.
Rather boring spectacular with conventional set-pieces.
w Enrique Llovet, Enrico Bomba *novel* Bruno
Frank d Vincent Sherman ph Edmond Richard
m Jean Ledrut
☆ Horst Buchholz, Gina Lollobrigida, Louis
Jourdan, José Ferrer, Fernando Rey, Francisco
Rabal

César: see Marius (1931)

César ***

France 1936 117m bw
La Société des Films Marcel Pagnol
A son sets out to find his real father, who returns
home after 20 years of unhappy exile.
*The triumphant climax of Pagnol's trilogy, marked with
the same wit, warmth and humanity as the previous
episodes.*
wd Marcel Pagnol ph Willy m Vincent Scotto
ed Suzanne de Troeye, Jeanette Ginestet
☆ *Raimu*, Orane Demazis, Pierre Fresnay, Fernand
Charpin, André Fouché, Alida Rouffe, Robert
Vattier, Auguste Mouriès, Milly Mathis, Maupi,
Edouard Delmont, Paul Dulac
† This was the third film in Pagnol's Marseilles
trilogy, following *Marius* and *Fanny* (qqv).

César and Rosalie *

France/Italy/West Germany 1972 105m
Eastmancolor
Fildebroc/UPS/Mega Paramount/Orion (Michèle de
Broca)
A divorcee living with a rich merchant becomes
attracted to a young artist. Unexpectedly, the two
become friends…
Wryly amusing comedy for adults.
w Jean-Loup Dabadie, Claude Sautet d Claude
Sautet ph Jean Boffety m Philippe Sarde
☆ *Yves Montand*, Romy Schneider, Sami Frey,
Umberto Orsini

C'est arrivé près de chez vous: see Man Bites Dog

C'est la Vie *

France 1990 96m colour
Electric/Contemporary/Alexandre/SGGC/A2/CNC
(Alexandre Arcady)
original title: *La Baule-les pins*
During a summer holiday, two sisters are onlookers
at the end of their parents' marriage as their
mother begins a romance with a younger man.
*A slight domestic tale, but filmed with some charm and
humour.*
w Diane Kurys, Alain Le Henry d Diane Kurys
ph Giuseppe Lanci m Philippe Sarde ad Tony
Egry ed Raymonde Guyot
☆ Nathalie Baye, Richard Berry, Zabou, Jean-
Pierre Bacri, Vincent Lindon, Valéria Bruni-
Tedeschi, Didier Benureau, Julie Bataille, Candice
Lefranc

Chacun cherche son chat: see When the Cat's Away

Chad Hanna *

US 1940 86m Technicolor
TCF (Darryl F. Zanuck, Nunnally Johnson)
Life in a New York state circus in the 1840s.
*Mild romantic drama from a bestseller; local colour
excellent, dramatic interest thin.*
w Nunnally Johnson *novel* Red Wheels Rolling by
Walter D. Edmonds d Henry King ph Ernest
Palmer m David Buttolph
☆ Henry Fonda, Dorothy Lamour, Linda Darnell,
Guy Kibbee, Jane Darwell, John Carradine, Ted
North, Roscoe Ates

The Chain *

GB 1984 100m Eastmancolor
Quintet/County Bank/Channel 4 (Victor Glynn)
Seven groups of people, corresponding to the seven
deadly sins, are involved in a house-moving chain.
*Rather tedious and predictable 'all star' comedy with
effective moments but no narrative command.*

w Jack Rosenthal d Jack Gold ph Wolfgang
Suschitzky m Stanley Myers
☆ Denis Lawson, Maurice Denham, Nigel
Hawthorne, Billie Whitelaw, Judy Parfitt, Leo
McKern, Warren Mitchell, Gary Waldhorn, Anna
Massey

Chain Lightning

US 1950 94m bw
Warner (Anthony Veiller)
After World War II a bomber pilot learns how to
control the new jets.
Absolutely routine romance and heroics.
w Liam O'Brien, Vincent Evans d Stuart Heisler
ph Ernest Haller m David Buttolph
☆ Humphrey Bogart, Eleanor Parker, Raymond
Massey, Richard Whorf, James Brown, Roy
Roberts, Morris Ankrum

Chain of Desire

US 1992 107m Technicolor
Distant Horizon/Anant Singh (Brian Cox)
Sexual permutations link a group of 14 people.
*A bisexual updating of La Ronde for the AIDS
generation, among people given over to the kinkier
forms of sex; for all that its treatment tends to the
unsophisticated and lacks any sense of irony.*
wd Temistocles Lopez ph Nancy Schreiber
m Nathan Birnbaum pd Scott Chambliss
ed Suzanne Fenn
☆ Linda Fiorentino, Elias Koteas, Tim Guinee,
Grace Zabriskie, Assumpta Serna, Patrick
Bauchau, Seymour Cassel, Malcolm McDowell
'An uneven but alluringly sexy melodrama that
gets better as it goes along.' – *Variety*
'Avoid.' – *Empire*

Chain Reaction

US 1996 106m colour Panavision
TCF/Zanuck Co./Chicago Pacific (Arne L. Schmidt,
Andrew Davis)
After discovering how to make limitless energy
from water, scientists go on the run from secret
agents who plan to kill them.
*In the tradition of recent action movies, the narrative is
paranoid and impenetrable, and the action is
spectacular; but it's a chase movie that leads nowhere
interesting.*
w Josh Friedman, J. F. Lawton, Michael Bortman
d Andrew Davis ph Frank Tidy m Jerry
Goldsmith pd Maher Ahmad ed Donald Brochu,
Dov Hoenig, Arthur Schmidt sp Digital Domain
☆ Keanu Reeves, Morgan Freeman, Rachel Weisz,
Fred Ward, Brian Cox, Kevin Dunn, Joanna
Cassidy, Chelcie Ross
'One attends this sort of claptrap for the delights
of overscaled technological barbarism; and
indeed the exploding megatonnage in the
opening and closing sequences is shot and edited
to knock you out of your seat.' – *Peter Matthews,
Sight and Sound*

The Chain Reaction

Australia 1980 90m colour
Palm Beach (David Elfick)
aka: *Nuclear Run*
A scientist dying from a fatal dose of radiation in
an accident at a nuclear plant attempts to warn the
public of the danger they face from contaminated
water.
*Paranoid thriller that tries too hard to conjure up a
sinister atmosphere of multinational conspiracies; with
its mute assassin, amnesiac scientist and interminable
car chases, it swiftly becomes absurd.*
wd Ian Barry ph Russell Boyd m Andrew
Thomas Wilson ad Graham Walker ed Tim
Wellburn
☆ Steve Bisley, Arna-Maria Winchester, Ross
Thompson, Ralph Cotterill, Hugh Keays-Byrne,
Lorna Lesley, Richard Moir
† George Miller, director of *Mad Max*, was
responsible for second-unit direction.

Chaindance

Canada 1991 110m colour
R&R/Telefilm Canada/BC (Richard Davis)
An armed robber in a tough prison learns the error
of his ways after being involved in a rehabilitation
programme, working in a home for the
handicapped.

*Often brutal drama that, in trying to avoid
sentimentality, ascends into heated melodrama and
loses credibility.*
w Alan Aylward, Michael Ironside d Allan A.
Goldstein ph Tobias Schliessler m Graeme
Coleman pd Phil Schmidt ed Allan Lee
☆ Michael Ironside, Rae Dawn Chong, Brad
Dourif, Bruce Glover, Ken Pogue, Sheila Moore,
Leslie Carlson

'When she's in his arms, it's the grandest thrill the
screen can give!'

Chained *

US 1934 77m bw
MGM (Hunt Stromberg)
A devoted wife has a shipboard romance with
another man.
Moderate star romantic drama.
w John Lee Mahin d Clarence Brown ph George
Folsey m Herbert Stothart
☆ Joan Crawford, Clark Gable, Otto Kruger,
Stuart Erwin, Una O'Connor, Akim Tamiroff
'Simple in story and unoriginal in idea, its
weight is in words rather than action and
dramatic potency.' – *Variety*

Chained for Life

US 1950 70m bw
Classic films
One of two girl Siamese twins is accused of murder.
*Real life freak show starring the English Hilton twins
(1908–64) who were joined at the hip. Hard to watch
because of the subject but otherwise a routine lower-
case effort.*
w Nat Tanchuck d Harry L. Fraser
☆ Violet and Daisy Hilton, Allen Jenkins

Chained to Yesterday: see Limbo

The Chairman: see The Most Dangerous Man in the World

Chairman of the Board

US 1998 95m colour Panavision
Trimark/101st Street (Peter M. Lenkov, Rupert
Harvey)
A mad inventor helps an old man and inherits a
multimillion-dollar corporation, causing
annoyance to the man's heirs and associates.
*Broad comedy by a gadget-obsessed stand-up
comedian, whose appeal does not travel well.*
w Al Septien, Turi Meyer, Alex Zamm d Alex
Zamm ph David Lewis m Chris Hajian
pd Aaron Osborne ed Jim Hill
☆ Carrot Top, Courtney Thorne-Smith, Larry
Miller, Raquel Welch, Mystro Clark, Jack Plotnick,
Jack Warden, M. Emmet Walsh
'Peppered with the comic's signature gag
inventions and enough fart jokes to keep your
average 11-year-old in hysterics.' – *Glenn Lovell,
Variety*

A Chairy Tale **

Canada 1957 10m bw
National Film Board of Canada
A young man finds that a kitchen chair is
unwilling for him to sit on it, but they arrive at a
compromise.
*The simplest and most effective of fantasies is told at
somewhat excessive length but remains among its
director's more memorable creations.*
wd Norman McLaren
☆ Claude Jutra

The Chalk Garden *

GB 1964 106m Technicolor
U-I/Quota Rentals (Ross Hunter)
The governess in a melancholy household has an
effect on the lives of her aged employer and the
young granddaughter.
*Sub-Chekhovian drama in a house by the sea, flattened
by routine handling into something much less
interesting than it was on the stage.*
w John Michael Hayes *novel* Enid Bagnold
d Ronald Neame ph Arthur Ibbetson
m Malcolm Arnold
☆ Edith Evans, Deborah Kerr, Hayley Mills, John
Mills, Felix Aylmer, Elizabeth Sellars, Lally Bowers,
Toke Townley
'Crashing symbolism, cracker-motto
sententiousness.' – *MFB*
⚖ Edith Evans

The Challenge

US 1948 69m bw
Reliance (TCF)
Bulldog Drummond solves the mystery of a yacht
which is stolen after its owner is murdered.
Modest addition to a long-running series.
w Frank Gruber, Irving Elman d Jean Yarbrough
☆ Tom Conway, June Vincent, Richard Stapley

The Challenge

GB 1960 89m bw
John Temple-Smith/Alexandra
US title: *It Takes a Thief*
In search of buried loot, a lady gangster kidnaps a
convict's son.
Murky and unsympathetic melodrama.
wd John Gilling
☆ Jayne Mansfield, Anthony Quayle, Carl
Mohner, Barbara Mullen, Peter Reynolds, Dermot
Walsh

The Challenge

US 1982 112m Eastmancolor
CBS Theatrical Film Group (Lyle Poncher, Robert L.
Rosen, Ron Beckman)
An American boxer in Japan becomes involved in
a feud between two brothers.
*Belated martial arts saga with a good deal of head-
lopping and plenty of pretensions but no apparent
message to spike its dismal entertainment values.*
w Richard Maxwell, John Sayles d John
Frankenheimer ph Kozo Okazaki m Jerry
Goldsmith pd Yoshiyuki Ishida ed Jack Wheeler
☆ Scott Glenn, Toshiro Mifune, Donna Kei Benz,
Atsuo Nakamura, Calvin Young, Clyde Kusatsu
'Ridiculous, demeaning stuff.' – *Guardian*

A Challenge for Robin Hood *

GB 1967 96m Technicolor
Hammer (Clifford Parkes)
A retelling of the original Robin Hood legend.
Unassuming, lively, predictable adventure hokum.
w Peter Bryan d C. Pennington-Richards
ph Arthur Grant m Gary Hughes
☆ Barrie Ingham, James Hayter, Leon Greene,
John Arnatt, Peter Blythe, Gay Hamilton, William
Squire

Challenge to Lassie *

US 1949 76m Technicolor
MGM (Robert Sisk)
In Edinburgh in the 1860s, a sheepdog keeps vigil
over the grave of its dead master.
*Well-made sentimental tale, though it's possible that its
winsome charm may no longer find a receptive
audience.*
w William Ludwig *novel* Greyfriars Bobby by
Eleanor Atkinson d Richard Thorpe ph Charles
Schoenbaum m André Previn ad Cedric
Gibbons, Eddie Imazu ed George White
☆ Edmund Gwenn, Donald Crisp, Geraldine
Brooks, Reginald Owen, Alan Webb, Ross Ford,
Henry Stephenson, Alan Napier, Sara Allgood,
Lassie
† Eleanor Atkinson's novel, originally about a
Skye terrier, was also filmed in 1961 as *Greyfriars
Bobby* (qv).

The Chamber *

US 1996 110m DeLuxe Panavision
Universal/Imagine/Brian Grazer/Davis Entertainment
(John Davis, Brian Grazer, Ron Howard)
A young lawyer, whose father killed himself, tries
to prevent his grandfather, convicted of a racist
atrocity, from being executed.
*Unconvincing and rather plodding drama, though
Hackman's performance almost manages to keep one's
interest alive.*
w William Goldman, Chris Reese *novel* John
Grisham d James Foley ph Ian Baker m Carter
Burwell pd David Brisbin ed Mark Warner
☆ Chris O'Donnell, *Gene Hackman*, Faye
Dunaway, Robert Prosky, Lela Rochon, Raymond
Barry, Bo Jackson, David Marshall Grant, Nicholas
Pryor, Harve Presnell
'An intelligently proficient thriller that works
more effectively as a family drama than a legal
thriller.' – *Emanuel Levy, Variety*
† Grisham was paid $3.7m for his story outline,
before writing the novel. The film cost around
$45m and took $14.5m at the US box-office.

Chamber of Horrors: see *The Door with Seven Locks* (1940)

'The unspeakable vengeance of the crazed Baltimore strangler!'
Chamber of Horrors
US 1966 99m Warnercolor
Warner (Hy Averback)
A maniacal murderer is finally trapped by two amateur criminologists who run a wax museum in Baltimore.
Zany horror thriller originally meant for TV; it turned out a shade too harrowing. Advertised as 'the picture with the Fear Flasher and the Horror Horn', shock gimmicks which proved much more startling than the crude events they heralded.
w Stephen Kandel d Hy Averback ph Richard Kline m William Lava
☆ Patrick O'Neal, Cesare Danova, Wilfrid Hyde-White, Laura Devon, Patrice Wymore, Suzy Parker, Jeanette Nolan, Tony Curtis

Chamber of Tortures: see *Baron Blood*

'Don't fail to get a ringside seat!'
'The knockout picture of the year!'
The Champ *
US 1931 87m bw
MGM (Harry Rapf)
A young boy has faith in a washed-up prizefighter.
Maudlin drama, highly commercial in its day and a box-office tonic for its two stars. Remade as The Clown (qv).
w Leonard Praskins, Frances Marion d King Vidor ph Gordon Avil
☆ Wallace Beery, Jackie Cooper, Irene Rich, Roscoe Ates, Edward Brophy
'This picture will hit 'em all, large or small, and that means lots of money.' – *Variety*
♦ original story (Frances Marion); Wallace Beery
♦ best picture; King Vidor

The Champ *
US 1979 122m Metrocolor
MGM (Dyson Lovell)
A remake of the above, with Florida racetrack asides.
A lush version, so little updated in mood that its tearfulness seems to have strayed from another age.
w Walter Newman d Franco Zeffirelli ph Fred J. Koenekamp m Dave Grusin pd Herman A. Blumenthal
☆ Jon Voight, Faye Dunaway, Ricky Schroder, Jack Warden, Arthur Hill, Strother Martin, Joan Blondell, Elisha Cook
♦ Dave Grusin

Champagne
GB 1928 90m bw silent
BIP (John Maxwell)
A millionaire pretends to be bankrupt so that his daughter won't marry.
Tedious comedy drama with very few of the master's touches.
w Eliot Stannard, Walter C. Mycroft, Alfred Hitchcock d Alfred Hitchcock ph Jack Cox
☆ Betty Balfour, Jean Bradin, Gordon Harker, Theodore von Alten
'Dreadful.' – *Alfred Hitchcock*

Champagne Charlie
US 1936 60m bw
TCF (Edward T. Lowe)
A gambler double-crosses the gangsters who financed him to seduce and marry an heiress.
Efficient, fast-moving 'B'-movie thriller.
w Allen Rivkin d James Tinling dr Daniel B. Clark md Samuel Kaylin ad Duncan Cramer, Lewis Creber ed Nick de Maggio
☆ Paul Cavanagh, Helen Wood, Thomas Beck, Minna Gombell, Herbert Mundin, Noel Madison

Champagne Charlie *
GB 1944 107m bw
Ealing (John Croydon)
The life of Victorian music hall singer George Leybourne and his rivalry with the Great Vance.
Careful period reconstruction and good songs and acting are somehow nullified by unsympathetic handling and photography.

w Austin Melford, Angus Macphail, John Dighton d Alberto Cavalcanti ph Wilkie Cooper md Ernest Irving ad Michael Relph
☆ Tommy Trinder, Stanley Holloway, Betty Warren, Austin Trevor, Jean Kent, Guy Middleton, Frederick Piper, Harry Fowler, James Robertson Justice
'Cavalcanti's taste for the bizarre and the vigour of the performances make it something more than a museum piece.' – *Time Out, 1984*

Champagne for Caesar *
US 1950 99m bw
Cardinal (George Moskov)
A self-confessed genius with a grudge against a soap company determines to win astronomical sums on its weekly radio quiz.
Agreeable, mildly satirical star comedy which tends to peter out halfway.
w Hans Jacoby, Fred Brady d Richard Whorf ph Paul Ivano m Dimitri Tiomkin
☆ Ronald Colman, Vincent Price, Celeste Holm, Barbara Britton, Art Linkletter

Champagne for Everybody: see *Here Come the Girls*

The Champagne Murders
France 1967 107m Techniscope
Universal (France) (Jacques Natteau)
original title: *Le Scandale*
A disturbed champagne millionaire thinks he may be a murderer.
Complex but uninvolving mystery story in which the director's eye seems to be more on satire than on narrative.
w Claude Brûlé, Derek Prouse, Paul Gégauff d Claude Chabrol ph Jean Rabier m Pierre Jansen
☆ Anthony Perkins, Maurice Ronet, Stéphane Audran, Yvonne Furneaux, Suzanne Lloyd

'As gay and sparkling as a champagne cocktail!'
Champagne Waltz
US 1937 90m bw
Paramount (Harlan Thompson)
A press agent takes a swing band to Vienna.
Rather tedious romantic comedy with music.
w Don Hartman, Frank Butler story Billy Wilder, H. S. Kraft d Edward Sutherland ph William Mellor ed Paul Weatherwax
☆ Fred MacMurray, Gladys Swarthout, Jack Oakie
'On the slow side, but should do fairly.' – *Variety*

'This is the only sport in the world where two guys get paid for doing something they'd be arrested for if they got drunk and did it for nothing.'
Champion **
US 1949 99m bw
Stanley Kramer
An ambitious prizefighter alienates his friends and family, and dies of injuries received in the ring.
Interesting exposé of the fight racket, presented in good cinematic style and acted with great bravura.
w Carl Foreman story Ring Lardner d Mark Robson ph Franz Planer m Dimitri Tiomkin ed Harry Gerstad
☆ Kirk Douglas, Arthur Kennedy, Marilyn Maxwell, Paul Stewart, Ruth Roman, Lola Albright, Luis Van Rooten
♦ Harry Gerstad
♦ Carl Foreman; Franz Planer; Dimitri Tiomkin; Kirk Douglas; Arthur Kennedy

Champions: see *The Mighty Ducks* (1992)

Champions *
GB 1983 115m colour
Embassy/Archerwest/Ladbroke/United British Artists (Peter Shaw, Eva Monley)
A leading jockey develops cancer and his horse receives a leg injury, but both survive to win the Grand National.
Gruelling factual story which could have done with a little more drama, not to mention a more sympathetic hero.
w Evan Jones book Bob Champion, Jonathan Powell d John Irvin ph Ronnie Taylor m Carl Davis
☆ John Hurt, Edward Woodward, Ben Johnson, Jan Francis, Peter Barkworth, Ann Bell, Judy Parfitt

'It ignores any inner aspect, the better to concentrate on tearjerking externals.' – *Tom Milne, MFB*
'Told as an indecent tearjerker, directed with the discretion of a rampaging steamroller.' – *Sight and Sound*

Chan Is Missing *
US 1981 80m bw
Wayne Wang Productions/Wayne Wang
In San Francisco, two Chinese-American cab drivers search for a friend who has disappeared with $4,000 of their money.
Rambling but engaging in its different perspective on America.
w Isaac Cronin, Wayne Wang, Terrel Seltzer d Wayne Wang ph Michael Chin m Robert Kikuchi-Yngojo
☆ Wood Moy, Marc Hayashi, Lauren Chew, Peter Wang, George Woo

Chance Meeting: see *The Young Lovers* (1954)

Chance Meeting: see *Blind Date* (1959)

Chance of a Lifetime *
GB 1950 93m bw
Pilgrim Pictures (Bernard Miles)
The owner of a small engineering works, impatient with the unionism of his men, gives them a chance to run the factory themselves.
Quiet comedy-drama on sub-Ealing lines; always interesting, it never quite catches fire despite a reliable cast.
w Walter Greenwood, Bernard Miles d Bernard Miles ph Eric Cross
☆ Bernard Miles, Basil Radford, Niall MacGinnis, Geoffrey Keen, Julien Mitchell, Josephine Wilson, Kenneth More, Hattie Jacques
'The film's triumph lies in the integrity with which it draws its picture of factory life and it is flawlessly acted.' – *The Times*
'It held me from beginning to end. I found it amusing, exciting and at times moving enough to raise some embarrassing and surreptitious tears.' – *Milton Shulman*
'British workmen are shown for the first time as characters, not comic caricatures. They are authentic, breezy and warm, sympathetically played by comparatively fresh actors.' – *Richard Winnington*
† The major circuits in Britain refused to give a showing to this independent movie, which was made at a cost of 150,000, on the grounds that it wasn't entertaining. They were forced to do so after its director appealed to the Film Selection Committee.

Chance or Coincidence *
France/Canada 1998 121m colour
Panavision
Films13/TF1/SDA/UGC/Neuilly/FCC (Claude Lelouch)
original title: *Hasards ou Coincidences*
A man becomes infatuated with a ballerina he sees on some stolen video-tapes.
A melodramatic narrative, of loss and grief, betrayal and unexpected love, all hinging on unlikely accidents, is offset by some luxuriant scene-setting: the result is a feast for the eyes, but not the mind.
wd Claude Lelouch ph Pierre-William Glenn m Francis Lai, Claude Bolling ch Richard Wherlock ed Hélène du Luze
☆ Alessandra Martines, Pierre Arditi, Marc Hollonge, Laurent Hilaire, Véronique Moreau, Patrick Labbé, Geoffrey Holder, Luigi Bonino
'Full of staggering images as well as entrancing techniques to constantly engage the audience.' – *Alan Jones, Film Review*

Chances *
US 1931 72m bw
Warner
In wartime London, two soldiers on leave fall for the same girl.
Unexpectedly sensitive and pleasing romance, generally well handled.
w Waldemar Young novel Hamilton Gibbs d Allan Dwan
☆ Douglas Fairbanks Jnr, Anthony Bushell, Rose Hobart
'Enough contributing sidelights to keep the emphasis away from the combat … should be pleasant b.o.' – *Variety*

Chances Are *
US 1989 108m Metrocolor
Tri-Star (Mike Lobell)
A widow realizes that her daughter's boyfriend is the reincarnation of her dead husband.
Excessively contrived romantic comedy; we have all been here before and there is nothing noteworthy about this particular variation on a familiar theme.
w Perry Howze, Randy Howze d Emile Ardolino ph William A. Fraker m Maurice Jarre pd Dennis Washington ed Harry Keramidas
☆ Cybill Shepherd, Robert Downey Jnr, Ryan O'Neal, Mary Stewart Masterson, Christopher McDonald, Josef Sommer, Joe Grifasi, Henderson Forsythe
♪ song 'Chances Are' (m/l Tom Snow, Dean Pitchford)

Chandler
US 1971 88m Metrocolor Panavision
MGM
An ex-private eye becomes a security guard and an alcoholic but even worse befalls when he agrees to keep an eye on a government witness.
Downbeat, generally unamusing and little seen piece of thick ear which harks back unsuccessfully to the forties.
w John Sacret Young d Paul Magwood
☆ Warren Oates, Leslie Caron, Alex Dreier, Mitchell Ryan, Gordon Pinsent, Charles McGraw, Richard Loo, Walter Burke, Gloria Grahame, Royal Dano, Scatman Crothers

Chandu the Magician *
US 1932 74m bw
Fox
A spiritualist battles against a madman with a death ray which could destroy the world.
Rather dim serial-like thriller, with interesting talent not at its best.
w Philip Klein, Barry Conners d Marcel Varnel, William Cameron Menzies ph James Wong Howe m Louis de Francesco
☆ Edmund Lowe, Bela Lugosi, Irene Ware, Herbert Mundin, Henry B. Walthall
† Sequels (whittled down from serials) include *The Return of Chandu* and *Chandu and the Magic Isle*.

Chanel Solitaire
France/GB 1981 124m colour
Gardenia/Todrest (Larry G. Spangler)
Fashion designer Coco Chanel thinks back on her long career.
Moderately elegant but frigid autobiopic with very little entertainment value.
w Julian More novel Claude Dulay d George Kaczender ph Ricardo Aronovich m Jean Musy
☆ Marie-France Pisier, Timothy Dalton, Rutger Hauer, Karen Black, Brigitte Fossey
'The producer says the film is devoted to providing what every woman wants – men, money, jewellery, castles, caviare, champagne and love, love, love. I never realized they could be so boring.' – *Sunday Times*

Chang **
US 1927 71m bw silent
Paramount
The life of a rice-grower in Thailand.
Influential but now rather boring documentary with animal interest.
wd/ph/ed Merian C. Cooper, Ernest B. Schoedsack
'I can remember no more terrible adventure in the kinema than the moment in the middle of Chang when suddenly the curtains divide, and the screen seems to swell and tremble and burst its bounds, and the great herd of elephants comes trampling out of the picture and bears down upon us in a multitude of tossing trunks and angry feet.' – *C. A. Lejeune*
♦ Unique and Artistic Picture

Change of Habit
US 1969 97m colour
Universal
A young doctor working in a ghetto has his opinions changed by three nuns.
A notably unsuccessful attempt by a star to change his image.
w James Lee, S. S. Schweitzer, Eric Bercovici d William Graham ph Russell Metty m Billy

Goldenberg *ad* Alexander Golitzen *ed* Douglas Stewart

☆ Elvis Presley, Mary Tyler Moore, Barbara McNair, Ed Asner, Leora Dana, Jane Elliot, Robert Emhardt

Change of Heart: see *Hit Parade of 1943 (1943)*

Change of Heart
US   1934   74m   bw
Fox
Four young Californian students make good in New York.
Minor fairy tale which marked the last of twelve teamings for Gaynor and Farrell.
w Sonya Levien, James Gleason, Samuel Hoffenstein *novel* Kathleen Norris *d* John G. Blystone *ph* Hal Mohr *m* Louis de Francesco
☆ Janet Gaynor, Charles Farrell, Ginger Rogers, James Dunn, Beryl Mercer, Gustav von Seyffertitz, Shirley Temple
'They are on the back of a nag that never quite gets started … most of the time it causes that tired feeling.' – *Variety*

Change of Heart
US   1937   65m   bw
TCF (Sol M. Wurtzel)
A bored man and wife go their separate ways but are eventually reconciled.
Bright little comedy on a tired old theme.
w Frances Hyland, Albert Ray *d* James Tinling
☆ Michael Whalen, Gloria Stuart, Lyle Talbot, Jane Darwell
'More originality, freshness of treatment and solid entertainment than in half the more expensive efforts from the Hollywood studios.' – *Variety*

Change of Mind
US   1969   98m   Eastmancolor
Sagittarius (Seeleg Lester, Richard Wesson)
The life of a liberal white DA can only be 'saved' by transplanting his brain into the body of a dead black man.
Fantasy melodrama with a social conscience, about a half-and-half which is acceptable to neither whites nor blacks. Very obvious and rather boring.
w Seeleg Lester, Richard Wesson *d* Robert Stevens *ph* Arthur J. Ornitz *m* Duke Ellington
☆ Raymond St Jacques, Susan Oliver, Janet McLachlan, Leslie Nielsen

A Change of Seasons
US   1980   102m   DeLuxe
TCF/Martin Ransohoff/Film Finance Group Ltd
▦
A college professor takes a mistress and his wife retaliates.
Zestless and unhumorous rehash of Who's Afraid of Virginia Woolf? and Bob and Carol and Ted and Alice. Not a new thought anywhere.
w Erich Segal, Ronni Kern, Fred Segal *d* Richard Lang *ph* Philip Lathrop *m* Henry Mancini *pd* Bill Kenney
☆ Shirley MacLaine, Anthony Hopkins, Bo Derek, Michael Brandon, Mary Beth Hurt, Ed Winter
'A tired rehash of themes that might have been provocative a decade ago … it would take a Lubitsch to do justice to the incredibly tangled relationships.' – *Variety*
'The situation soon melts into a gooey mess, like a Mars bar left too long in a trouser pocket.' – *Sunday Times*

The Changeling
Canada   1979   107m   colour   Panavision
Chessman Palk Productions (Joel B. Michaels, Garth H. Drabinsky)
▦   ⊙
A widowed academic takes on an old house haunted by the spirit of a murdered child.
Tedious and not very brief, this uninspired ghost story comes very late in the horror stakes and contains very little to make one care about its outcome.
w William Gray, Diana Maddox *d* Peter Medak *ph* John Coquillon *m* Rick Wilkins
☆ George C. Scott, Melvyn Douglas, Trish Van Devere, John Colicos, Jean Marsh, Barry Morse
'None of its most eerily untoward occurrences proceed from any spectral intervention, but from the worst abuses of Peter Medak's infuriatingly fidgety camera.' – *Gilbert Adair, MFB*

Changing Habits
US   1997   95m   colour
Teagarden/Initial (Abra Edelman, James Dodson)
▦   ⊙   ⊙
An unhappy, shoplifting artist is given a room at a convent, where she secretly paints a mural in an abandoned chapel.
A film about a woman's journey in search of her identity; only the very patient would wish to accompany her.
w Scott Davis Jones *d* Lynn Roth *ph* Michael Mayers *m* David McHugh *pd* Dena Roth, Gail Bennett *ed* Susan Godfrey, Clayton Halsey
☆ Moira Kelly, Christopher Lloyd, Dylan Walsh, Shelley Duvall, Bob Gunton, Marissa Ribisif, Anne Hanley, Frances Bay, Eileen Brennan, Teri Garr
'Never locates the charm and depth it hopes for, thanks largely to an unappealingly conceived protagonist.' – *Dennis Harvey, Variety*

Channel Crossing *
GB   1933   70m   bw
Gaumont (Angus MacPhail, Ian Dalrymple)
Various characters converge on a ferry boat to France.
Somewhat stilted potboiler with interesting cast.
w W. P. Lipscomb, Cyril Campion *d* Milton Rosmer *ph* Phil Tannura *ad* Alfred Junge *ed* Dan Birt
☆ Matheson Lang, Max Miller, Constance Cummings, Edmund Gwenn, Anthony Bushell, Dorothy Dickson, Nigel Bruce

The Chant of Jimmie Blacksmith ****
Australia   1978   122m   Eastmancolor   Panavision
Film House (Fred Schepisi)
In 1900, a half-caste mingles with high-class whites, goes berserk, and slaughters several of them with an axe.
A powerful film on the tragedy of an outcast at home in no society, torn between the world he has lost and the one he cannot gain. The violence is shocking, as it is meant to be. It is one of the great achievements of Australian cinema.
wd Fred Schepisi *novel* Thomas Keneally *ph* Ian Baker *m* Bruce Smeaton *pd* Wendy Dickson *ed* Brian Cavanagh
☆ Tommy Lewis, Ray Barrett, Jack Thompson, Freddy Reynolds
'One of the greatest pieces of political film making I know, because it doesn't impose rhetorical nobility on its characters or twist their lives into social statement.' – *Stephen Schiff*
'This is a large scale film – a visually, impassioned epic.' – *Pauline Kael*
'A big film intended for a big audience. On its own terms, it is a powerful indictment of the insidious, pervasive canker of white racism.' – *David Wilson, Sight and Sound*

Chapayev *
USSR   1934   94m   bw
Lenfilm
▦
Exploits of a Red Army commander during the 1919 battles.
Moderately striking propaganda piece.
wd Sergei and Georgy Vasiliev *ph* Alexander Sigayev *m* Gavril Popov
☆ Boris Babochkin, B. Blinov, Leonid Kmit
'Easily the best film turned out in Russia since sound.' – *Variety*

Un Chapeau de Paille d'Italie: see *An Italian Straw Hat*

'He made the whole world laugh and cry. He will again.'
'Everyone has a wild side. Even a legend.'

Chaplin **
GB   1992   145m   Technicolor
Guild/Lambeth/Carolco/Studio Canal (Richard Attenborough, Mario Kassar)
▦   ▦   ⊙   ⊙
In old age, Charlie Chaplin tells the story of his life to a biographer – from his early childhood to his Hollywood triumphs, his exile from America and his honorary Oscar in 1972.
Somewhat stolid biopic that tries to cram in too much of a long life, but which has a fascinating story to tell and often tells it well; it might have been better had it been longer.
w William Boyd, Bryan Forbes, William Goldman *book* My Autobiography by Charles Chaplin; Chaplin – His Life and Art by David Robinson *story* Diana Hawkins *d* Richard Attenborough *ph* Sven Nykvist *m* John Barry *pd* Stuart Craig *ed* Anne V. Coates
☆ Robert Downey Jnr, Dan Aykroyd, Geraldine Chaplin, Kevin Dunn, Anthony Hopkins, Milla Jovovich, Kevin Kline, Diane Lane, Penelope Ann Miller, Paul Rhys, John Thaw, Marisa Tomei, Nancy Travis, James Woods
'Old-fashioned bio-pic does an inadequate job of getting beneath the skin of one of the most famous Englishmen of the century.' – *Iain Johnstone, Sunday Times*
⧓ Robert Downey Jnr; Stuart Craig; John Barry
⦿ Robert Downey Jnr

The Chapman Report
US   1962   125m   Technicolor
Warner/Darryl F. Zanuck (Richard D. Zanuck)
Dr Chapman conducts a study of female sex behaviour in an American suburb.
Influenced by the Kinsey report, this melodramatic compendium takes itself far too seriously, and the director's smooth style is barely in evidence.
w Wyatt Cooper, Don M. Mankiewicz *novel* Irving Wallace *d* George Cukor *ph* Harold Lipstein *m* Leonard Rosenman
☆ Shelley Winters, Claire Bloom, Glynis Johns, Efrem Zimbalist Jnr, Jane Fonda, Ray Danton, Ty Hardin, Andrew Duggan, John Dehner, Henry Daniell, Corey Allen, Harold J. Stone
'We had a preview which went very well, and then it was sent over to Mr Zanuck, who did what I thought was a most horrendous job of cutting it up.' – *George Cukor*

Chapter Two
US   1979   127m   Metrocolor
Columbia/Rastar (Margaret Booth)
▦   ⊙
A widowed novelist reluctantly embarks on an affair with a divorcee.
Simon in sad mood means that the wisecracks are still there but the pauses between them are longer. The thin but heavy-going plot finally militates against enthusiasm.
w Neil Simon *d* Robert Moore *m* David M. Walsh, Richard Kratina *m* Marvin Hamlisch *pd* Gene Callahan
☆ James Caan, Marsha Mason, Joseph Bologna, Valerie Harper, Alan Fudge
'The regular Neil Simon Broadway takeaway for people who watch movies with their ears. Over two hours of theatrical smart talk and unfailing wit-under-pressure as Simon-surrogate Caan and the real Mrs Simon swap marital repartee in front of a reverent camera.' – *Time Out*
'All the couple have to do is swap wisecracks and nurse their rather pretty emotional bruises.' – *Observer*
'More than two hours of discussions, arguments, debates, reconciliations and accusations that quickly become tedious.' – *Roger Ebert*
⧓ Marsha Mason

Character **
Netherlands   1997   125m   colour
Gala/Almerica/NPS Made (Laurens Geels)
original title: Karakter
A grasping bailiff persecutes his illegitimate son, an unsuccessful businessman.
Powerful, downbeat, Oedipal drama of obsession in a period setting.
w Mike van Diem, Laurens Geels, Ruud van Megen *novel* Karakter by F. Bordewijk *d* Mike van Diem *ph* Rogier Stoffers *m* Het Paleis van Boem *pd* Jelier & Schaaf *ed* Jessica de Koning
☆ Jan Decleir, Fedja van Huêt, Betty Schuurman, Tamar van den Dop, Victor Löw, Hans Kesting
'Turgid, interminable … strong on atmosphere but surprisingly weak on variation in tone.' – *James Cameron-Wilson, Film Review*
⚑ foreign film

Charade
US   1952   83m   bw
Portland (James Mason)
Three stories conceived and produced by the stars.
Everything about this triptych is on the dull side, and Mason himself later regretted embarking on it.
w James and Pamela Mason *d* Roy Kellino
☆ James Mason, Pamela Mason, Scott Forbes, Paul Cavanagh, Bruce Lester
† Roy Kellino was Pamela Mason's first husband.

Charade **
US   1963   113m   Technicolor
Universal/Stanley Donen
▦   ▦   ⊙   ⊙
A Parisienne finds her husband murdered. Four strange men are after her, and she is helped by a handsome stranger … but is he hero, spy or murderer?
Smoothly satisfying sub-Hitchcock nonsense, effective both as black romantic comedy and macabre farce.
w Peter Stone *d* Stanley Donen *ph* Charles Lang Jnr *m* Henry Mancini
☆ Cary Grant, Audrey Hepburn, Walter Matthau, James Coburn, George Kennedy, Ned Glass, Jacques Marin
'One hesitates to be uncharitable to a film like Charade, which seeks only to provide a little innocent merriment and make a pot of money … Of itself, it is a stylish and amusing melodrama, but in the context of the bloodlust that seems unloosed in our land it is as sinister as the villains who stalk Miss Hepburn through the cobbled streets of Paris.' – *Arthur Knight*
† Cary Grant conceals his age of sixty by taking a shower fully clothed.
♫ song 'Charade' (*m*Henry Mancini, *ly*Johnny Mercer)
⦿ Audrey Hepburn

The Charge at Feather River *
US   1953   96m   Warnercolor
Warner (David Weisbart)
An army platoon composed of men from the guardhouse tries to rescue two women kidnapped by Indians.
Formula Western distinguished by 3-D photography, probably the best to be achieved in the brief life of the medium. Warnerphonic sound was less successfully added; the sum total would be trying for nervous people.
w James R. Webb *d* Gordon Douglas *ph* Peverell Marley *m* Max Steiner
☆ Guy Madison, Frank Lovejoy, Vera Miles, Helen Westcott, Dick Wesson, Onslow Stevens, Steve Brodie
'From the start we are involved in a whirl of frenzied activity: a cavalry charge, knife throwing, sabre practice, flaming arrows – not a trick missed.' – *MFB*

The Charge Is Murder: see *Twilight of Honor*

Charge of the Lancers
US   1953   74m   Technicolor
Columbia (Sam Katzman)
During the Crimean War, the Russians capture an English major who knows the details of a new cannon.
Action cheapie which seems to be largely shot in the producer's back garden but provides a laugh or two.
w Robert E. Kent *d* William Castle
☆ Paulette Goddard, Jean-Pierre Aumont, Richard Stapley, Karin Booth, Lester Matthews

'The reckless lancers sweep on and on – so that a woman's heart might not be broken! You're not fighting a single legion – you're fighting the entire British army, Surat Khan!'

The Charge of the Light Brigade ***
US   1936   115m   bw
Warner (Hal B. Wallis, Sam Bischoff)
▦   ⊙   ⊙
An army officer deliberately starts the Balaclava charge to even an old score with Surat Khan, who's on the other side.
Though allegedly 'based on the poem by Alfred Lord Tennyson', this is no more than a travesty of history, most of it taking place in India. As pure entertainment however it is a most superior slice of Hollywood hokum and the film which set the seal on Errol Flynn's superstardom.
w Michel Jacoby, Rowland Leigh *d* Michael Curtiz *ph* Sol Polito, Fred Jackman *m* Max Steiner
☆ Errol Flynn, Olivia de Havilland, Patric Knowles, Donald Crisp, C. Aubrey Smith, David Niven, Henry Stephenson, Nigel Bruce, C. Henry Gordon, Spring Byington, E. E. Clive, Lumsden Hare, Robert Barrat, J. Carrol Naish
'When the noble six hundred, lances level and stirrups touching, pace, canter and, finally, charge down the mile-long valley, with the enemy guns tearing great holes in their ranks, you are a dead stock if your pulses don't thunder and your heart quicken perceptibly. This scene

---

may be villainous history, but it is magnificent cinema, timed, shot, and cut with brilliance. It only cramps the patriotic effect a trifle that the Union Jack, nine times out of ten in the picture, is shown resolutely flying upside down.' – C. A. Lejeune

♫ Max Steiner

The Charge of the Light Brigade *

GB   1968   141m   DeLuxe   Panavision
UA/Woodfall (Neil Hartley)
▣

An historical fantasia with comic, sociological and cartoon embellishments.
This version for the swinging sixties has a few splendid moments but apes Tom Jones all too obviously and leaves audiences with an even dimmer view of history than they started with.
w Charles Wood d Tony Richardson ph David Watkin, Peter Suschitzky m John Addison ad Edward Marshall animation Richard Williams
☆ Trevor Howard, John Gielgud, David Hemmings, Vanessa Redgrave, Jill Bennett, Harry Andrews, Peter Bowles, Mark Burns
'Considering the lucid book on which it is largely based, it is almost as inexcusably muddled as the British commanders at Balaclava.' – John Simon
'The point of the film is to recreate mid-Victorian England in spirit and detail.' – Stanley Kauffmann
'Notions for at least three interesting films are on view … what seems signally lacking is a guiding hand, an overriding purpose.' – John Coleman
'This epic has so little feeling for the courage that went with the idiocies of the past that it diminishes itself along with its targets.' – Pauline Kael

Charing Cross Road

GB   1935   72m   bw
British Lion (Herbert Smith)
Struggling boy and girl singers try to move into high society.
Dated and artificial filler.
w Con West, Clifford Grey play Gladys and Clay Keys d Albert de Courville ph Phil Tannura m Percival Mackey, Arthur Young ad Norman Arnold
☆ John Mills, June Clyde, Derek Oldham, Jean Colin, Judy Kelly

'Two men chasing dreams of glory!'
Chariots of Fire ***

♠♠   GB   1981   121m   colour
TCF/Allied Stars/Enigma (David Puttnam)
▣ ☺ ⊘ ◎
In the 1924 Paris Olympics, a Jew and a Scotsman run for Britain.
A film of subtle qualities, rather like those of a BBC classic serial. Probably not quite worth the adulation it received, but full of pleasant romantic touches and sharp glimpses of the wider issues involved.
w Colin Welland d Hugh Hudson ph David Watkin m Vangelis
☆ Ben Cross, Ian Charleson, Nigel Havers, Nicholas Farrell, Daniel Gerroll, Cheryl Campbell, Alice Krige, John Gielgud, Lindsay Anderson, Nigel Davenport, Ian Holm, Patrick Magee
'The whole contradictory bundle is unexpectedly watchable.' – Jo Imeson, MFB
'A piece of technological lyricism held together by the glue of simple-minded heroic sentiment.' – Pauline Kael
'A hymn to the human spirit as if scored by Barry Manilow.' – Richard Corliss, Film Comment
♟ best picture; Colin Welland; Vangelis; costume design (Milera Canonero)
♫ Hugh Hudson; editing (Terry Rawlings); Ian Holm (supporting actor)
▼ best picture; costume design; Ian Holm

Charles and Lucie *

France   1979   97m   colour
Avon/Cythere Films/Films de La Chouette/Antenne 2 (Claude Makovski)
original title: Charles et Lucie
An antique dealer and a singer, both down on their luck, are the victims of a confidence trick.
An enjoyable divertissement.
w Jean Chapot d Nelly Kaplan ph Gilbert Sandoz m Pierre Perret ed Nelly Kaplan, Jean Chapot

☆ Daniel Ceccaldi, Ginette Garcin, Jean-Marie Proslier, Samson Fainsilber, Georges Claisse, Guy Grosso

Charley and the Angel *

♠♠   US   1974   93m   Technicolor
Walt Disney (Bill Anderson)
▣
A small-town sporting goods storekeeper in the thirties escapes death three times and finds an impatient angel waiting for him.
Mild sentimental whimsy on the lines of On Borrowed Time, but with a happy ending and attractive period trappings.
w Roswell Rogers novel The Golden Evenings of Summer by Will Stanton d Vincent McEveety ph Charles F. Wheeler m Buddy Baker ad John B. Mansbridge ed Ray de Leuw, Bob Bring
☆ Fred MacMurray, Cloris Leachman, Harry Morgan, Kurt Russell, Kathleen Cody, Edward Andrews, Barbara Nichols

Charley Moon *

GB   1956   92m   Eastmancolor
Colin Lesslie, Aubrey Baring
A music hall comic becomes swollen-headed but returns to his home village and marries his childhood sweetheart.
Faltering musical lacking the gusto of its background, but providing a generally believable impression of life on the halls.
novel Reginald Arkell d Guy Hamilton ph Jack Hildyard m Francis Chagrin w/songs Leslie Bricusse
☆ Max Bygraves, Dennis Price, Michael Medwin, Florence Desmond, Shirley Eaton, Patricia Driscoll, Reginald Beckwith

'When he runs out of dumb luck he always has genius to fall back on!'
Charley Varrick ***

US   1973   111m   Technicolor   Panavision
Universal (Don Siegel)
▣
A bank robber discovers he has stolen Mafia money, and devises a clever scheme to get himself off the hook.
Sharp, smart, well-observed but implausible thriller, astringently handled and agreeably set in Californian backlands. Accomplished, forgettable entertainment.
w Howard Rodman, Dean Riesner novel The Looters by John Reese d Don Siegel ph Michael Butler m Lalo Schifrin
☆ Walter Matthau, Joe Don Baker, Felicia Farr, Andy Robinson, John Vernon, Sheree North, Norman Fell
'It proves there is nothing wrong with an auteur director that a good script can't cure.' – Stanley Kauffmann
'The narrative line is clean and direct, the characterizations economical and functional, and the triumph of intelligence gloriously satisfying.' – Andrew Sarris
▼ Walter Matthau

Charley's American Aunt: see Charley's Aunt

Charley's Aunt **

US   1941   81m   bw
TCF (William Perlberg)
GB title: Charley's American Aunt
For complicated reasons, an Oxford undergraduate has to impersonate his friend's rich aunt from Brazil (where the nuts come from).
Very adequate version of the Victorian farce, with all concerned in excellent form.
w George Seaton play Brandon Thomas d Archie Mayo ph Peverell Marley m Alfred Newman ad Richard Day, Nathan Juran
☆ Jack Benny, Kay Francis, James Ellison, Anne Baxter, Laird Cregar, Edmund Gwenn, Reginald Owen, Richard Haydn, Arleen Whelan, Ernest Cossart
† See also: Where's Charley?

Charley's Big-Hearted Aunt

GB   1940   76m   bw
Gainsborough (Edward Black)
Rather disappointing British version of the famous farce, dully assembled and rather unsuitably cast.
w Marriott Edgar, Val Guest d Walter Forde ph Jack Cox

☆ Arthur Askey, Phyllis Calvert, Moore Marriott, Graham Moffatt, Richard Murdoch, Jeanne de Casalis, J. H. Roberts, Felix Aylmer, Wally Patch

Charlie Bubbles ***

GB   1968   91m   Technicolor
Universal/ Memorial (Michael Medwin, George Pitcher)
A successful novelist loathes the pointlessness of the good life and tries unsuccessfully to return to his northern working class background.
A little arid and slow in its early stages, and with a rather lame end (our hero escapes by air balloon), this is nevertheless a fascinating, fragmentary character study with a host of wry comedy touches and nimbly sketched characters; in its unassuming way it indicts many of the symbols people lived by in the sixties.
w Shelagh Delaney d Albert Finney ph Peter Suschitzky m Mischa Donat
☆ Albert Finney, Billie Whitelaw, Liza Minnelli, Colin Blakely, Timothy Garland, Diana Coupland, Alan Lake, Yootha Joyce, Joe Gladwin
'A modest thing, but like all good work in minor keys it has a way of haunting the memory.' – Richard Schickel
'The supreme deadweight is Liza Minnelli, whose screen debut proves easily the most inauspicious since Turhan Bey's.' – John Simon
▼ Billie Whitelaw

Charlie Chan

The Oriental detective created by Earl Derr Biggers began his film career as a minor character (played by George Kuwa) in a 1926 serial called HOUSE WITHOUT A KEY. In 1928 Kamiyama Sojin had a bigger role in THE CHINESE PARROT, but in 1929 E. L. Park did almost nothing in BEHIND THAT CURTAIN. In 1931 however began the fully-fledged Chan movies, which entertained a generation. Chan, based on a real-life Chinese detective named Chang Apana, became a citizen of Honolulu and was developed as a polite family man, aided by his impulsive number one or number two son (out of a family of fourteen), in solving murder puzzles. He had a treasury of aphorisms (a whole book of which has been published), and his technique was to gather all the suspects into one room before unmasking one as the murderer. The films built to a peak around 1936–9, but tailed off disastrously in the mid-forties. They were never noted for production values, but many retain interest for their scripts, their puzzles, and their casts of budding stars, as well as the central character. This is a complete list:
For Fox (later Twentieth Century Fox), with Warner Oland as Chan:
1931 Charlie Chan Carries On*, The Black Camel
1932 Charlie Chan's Chance
1933 Charlie Chan's Greatest Case
1934 Charlie Chan's Courage, Charlie Chan in London
1935 Charlie Chan in Paris*, Charlie Chan in Egypt, Charlie Chan in Shanghai
1936 Charlie Chan's Secret*, Charlie Chan at the Circus*, Charlie Chan at the Race Track, Charlie Chan at the Opera**
1937 Charlie Chan at the Olympics, Charlie Chan on Broadway*, Charlie Chan at Monte Carlo
For Twentieth Century Fox, with Sidney Toler:
1938 Charlie Chan in Honolulu
1939 Charlie Chan in Reno, Charlie Chan on Treasure Island**, City of Darkness
1940 Charlie Chan in Panama, Charlie Chan's Murder Cruise, Charlie Chan at the Wax Museum*, Murder over New York
1941 Dead Men Tell, Charlie Chan in Rio, Castle in the Desert*
For Monogram, with Sidney Toler:
1944 Charlie Chan in the Secret Service, The Chinese Cat, Black Magic
1945 The Scarlet Clue, The Jade Mask, Shanghai Cobra, Red Dragon
1946 Shadows over Chinatown, Dangerous Money
1947 The Trap
For Monogram, with Roland Winters:
1947 The Chinese Ring
1948 Docks of New Orleans, Shanghai Chest, The Golden Eye, The Feathered Serpent
1949 Sky Dragon
† In the late fifties J. Carrol Naish appeared in a half-hour TV series as Chan, but the episodes were dull. In 1971 Universal tried to revive the character in a 96-minute pilot film Happiness is a

Warm Clue, but Ross Martin was woefully miscast. See also below.

Charlie Chan and the Curse of the Dragon Queen

US   1980   95m   CFI color
UA/American Cinema/Jerry Sherlock
The villainous Dragon Queen puts a curse on Chan and his descendants, and works it out some years later in San Francisco.
The targets in this spoof are somewhat elementary (the sinister housekeeper is Mrs Danvers, the wheelchair-bound butler Gillespie) and almost all the jokes fall flat on their faces.
w Stan Burns, David Axelrod d Clive Donner ph Paul Lohmann m Patrick Williams
☆ Peter Ustinov, Angie Dickinson, Richard Hatch, Brian Keith, Roddy McDowall, Rachel Roberts, Johnny Sekka, Michelle Pfeiffer

Charlie McCarthy, Detective

US   1939   65m   bw
Universal
Ventriloquist Edgar Bergen helps to solve a murder.
Slightly tiresome mystery comedy with no real place for the wisecracking dummy.
w Edward Eliscu d Frank Tuttle
☆ Edgar Bergen, Robert Cummings, Constance Moore, John Sutton, Louis Calhern, Edgar Kennedy, Samuel S. Hinds, Warren Hymer, Harold Huber
'Looks like a corner-cutter … will have to struggle as top half of the duallers.' – Variety

Charlie the Lonesome Cougar *

♠♠   US   1967   75m   colour
Disney
⊚
The growing-up of a cougar.
Amiable true-life adventure.
w Jack Speirs d Winston Hibler

Charlotte

France/Italy/West Germany   1974   103m   Eastmancolor
New Realm/Claude Capra/Sedimo/Gerico/TIT (Roger Vadim)
original title: La Jeune Fille Assassinée
An author investigates the unsolved murder of a former lover, a police chief's promiscuous daughter, at the invitation of a rich German who claims to have killed her.
A glossy, essentially trivial mix of sex and murder.
wd Roger Vadim ph William Glenn m Mike Oldfield ed Victoria Mercanton
☆ Sirpa Lane, Michel Duchaussoy, Mathieu Carrière, Roger Vadim, Alexandre Astruc
† The film was cut to 99m on its British release.

Charlotte's Web

♠♠   US   1972   96m   Technicolor
Sagittarius/Hanna-Barbera
▣   ☺   ⊘
Farmyard animals who sense their fate are stimulated and encouraged by a resourceful spider.
Interesting but overlong and rather plodding version of a stylish book for children; the animation has no style at all.
w Earl Hamner Jnr novel E. B. White d Charles A. Nichols, Iwao Takamoto m/ly Richard and Robert Sherman md Irwin Kostal
☆ Featuring the voices of Debbie Reynolds, Henry Gibson, Paul Lynde, Martha Scott, Agnes Moorehead

Charly *

US   1968   106m   Techniscope
Selmur/Robertson Associates (Ralph Nelson)
▣   ☺   ⊘
New methods of surgery cure a mentally retarded young man, who becomes a genius, but the effects wear off.
Smooth, unconvincing, rather pointless fantasy which ultimately leaves a bad taste in the mouth.
w Stirling Silliphant novel Flowers for Algernon by Daniel Keyes d Ralph Nelson ph Arthur J. Ornitz m Ravi Shankar
☆ Cliff Robertson, Claire Bloom, Leon Janney, Lilia Skala
'The most distressing thing about Charly is not its ticklish subject, nor yet its clumsily modish surface, but its insistent, persistent sentimentality.' – Tom Milne
♟ Cliff Robertson

Charmant Garçons: see *Too Many Lovers*

Le Charme Discret de la Bourgeoisie: see *The Discreet Charm of the Bourgeoisie*

Charming Sinners
US 1929 66m bw
Paramount
A society wife schemes to regain the attention of her wayward husband.
Early talkie version of Somerset Maugham's The Constant Wife; of historical interest only.
w Doris Anderson d Robert Milton
☆ Ruth Chatterton, Clive Brook, William Powell, Mary Nolan, Florence Eldridge

Charro
US 1969 98m Technicolor Panavision
National General (Charles Marquis Warren)
▦
A reformed outlaw is framed for the theft of a cannon.
Dismal Western with a singing star playing straight. A bad experience.
wd Charles Marquis Warren ph Ellsworth Fredricks m Hugo Montenegro
☆ Elvis Presley, Ina Balin, Barbara Werle, Lynn Kellogg, Victor French, Solomon Sturges

Chartroose Caboose
US 1960 76m Eastmancolor Panavision
Red-Bill/U-I
A runaway couple take refuge with a retired train conductor in his converted rolling stock home.
Old-fashioned to the point of seeming half-witted, this comedy has little to offer but geniality.
w Rod Peterson d William Reynolds
☆ Molly Bee, Ben Cooper, Edgar Buchanan, O. Z. Whitehead, Slim Pickens

Charulata *
India 1964 117m bw
RDP (R. D. Bansal)
aka: *The Lonely Wife*
In Calcutta in the 1880s, the neglected wife of a wealthy newspaper editor turns to her husband's cousin for the love she craves.
A sombre story of repressed passion and domestic tragedy, but told at a too leisurely pace so that the tensions slacken and thin.
wd Satyajit Ray *novella* Nastanirh by Rabindranath Tagore ph Subrata Mitra m Satyajit Ray ad Bansi Chandragupta ed Dulal Dutta
☆ Soumitra Chatterjee, Madhabi Mukherjee, Sailen Mukherjee, Syamal Ghosal, Gitali Roy, Bholanath Koyal, Suku Mukherjee, Dilip Bose
'Ray's most nearly flawless film … a flowing opulent tale that seems to be lit from the inside like a velvet-lined carriage with a lantern in it rocked by a hot monsoon wind.' – *Penelope Gilliat, New Yorker*
'Unutterably boring.' – *John Simon*
† Ray had to take care in photographing Madhabi Mukherjee in order to conceal the fact that her lower teeth were in poor condition and stained black.

The Chase *
US 1947 84m bw
Nero Pictures (Seymour Nebenzal)
A shell-shocked ex-serviceman foils a criminal and falls for his wife.
Weird Cuban-set film noir with a strange cast and stranger atmosphere. A genuine bomb, but worth a look for its pretensions, its cast, and its trick ending.
w Philip Yordan *novel* The Black Path of Fear by Cornell Woolrich d Arthur Ripley ph Franz Planer m Michel Michelet
☆ Robert Cummings, Michèle Morgan, Peter Lorre, Steve Cochran, Lloyd Corrigan, Jack Holt

The Chase *
US 1966 135m Technicolor Panavision
Columbia/Sam Spiegel
▤ @ᵥ 🎧
When a convict escapes and heads for his small Texas home town, almost all the inhabitants are affected in one way or another.
Expensive but shoddy essay in sex and violence, with Brando as a masochistic sheriff lording it over Peyton-Place-in-all-but-name. Literate moments do not atone for the general pretentiousness, and we have all been here once too often.

w Lillian Hellman *novel* Horton Foote d Arthur Penn ph Joseph LaShelle m John Barry pd Richard Day
☆ Marlon Brando, Jane Fonda, Robert Redford, Angie Dickinson, Janice Rule, James Fox, Robert Duvall, E. G. Marshall, Miriam Hopkins, Henry Hull
'The worst thing that has happened to movies since Lassie played a war veteran with amnesia.' – *Rex Reed*
'Considering all the talent connected with it, it is hard to imagine how The Chase went so haywire.' – *Philip T. Hartung*

'Life can be Hell loving in the fast lane…'
'A high-speed romance.'
The Chase
US 1994 88m colour
TCF/Hercules (Brad Wyman, Cassian Elwes)
▦ ▤ @ᵥ 🎧
An escaped prisoner kidnaps a glamorous heiress and heads for Mexico in her car chased by police and journalists.
This is a hectic, jokey journey to nowhere in particular, with nothing to engage the eye or mind along the way.
wd Adam Rifkin ph Alan Jones m Richard Gibbs pd Sherman Williams ed Peter Schink
☆ Charlie Sheen, Kristy Swanson, Henry Rollins, Josh Mostel, Ray Wise, Wayne Grace, Rocky Carroll, Miles Dougal
'A romantic road movie of acute banality. A film which relies more heavily on its music score and its stars to carry it through. I doubt if either will be enough.' – *Derek Malcolm, Guardian*

Chase a Crooked Shadow **
GB 1957 87m bw
ABP/Associated Dragon Films (Douglas Fairbanks Jnr)
An heiress finds her home invaded by a stranger posing as her dead brother.
Tricksy, lightly controlled suspense melodrama with a perfectly fair surprise ending. Handling equivocal but competent.
w David D. Osborn, Charles Sinclair d Michael Anderson ph Erwin Hillier m Matyas Seiber
☆ Richard Todd, Anne Baxter, Faith Brook, Herbert Lom, Alexander Knox, Alan Tilvern
'It'll lead the wisest guessers up the garden and give them the surprise of their life!' – *Kine Weekly*
† The plot was borrowed from an episode in *The Whistler* TV series, and later reversed for a 1975 TV film, *One of my Wives is Missing*.

The Chaser
US 1938 73m bw
MGM
An ambulance-chasing lawyer falls for the girl whose intent is to show him up.
Tolerable second feature.
w Everett Freeman, Bella and Sam Spewack, Harry Ruskin d Edwin L. Marin
☆ Dennis O'Keefe, Ann Morriss, Lewis Stone, Nat Pendleton, Henry O'Neill, John Qualen

'It was supposed to be a routine prison transfer. But this was no ordinary prisoner.'
Chasers
US 1994 101m Technicolor
Warner/Morgan Creek (James G. Robinson)
▦ ▤ @ᵥ 🎧
A glamorous woman uses her sex-appeal to outwit the two men who are escorting her to a naval prison.
Uninteresting comedy, with thinly realized characters, contrived situations, and only the occasional eccentric moment from its minor characters to give it any life.
w Joe Batteer, John Rice d Dennis Hopper ph Ueli Steiger m Dwight Yoakam, Peter Anderson pd Robert Pearson ed Christian A. Wagner
☆ Tom Berenger, William McNamara, Erika Eleniak, Crispin Glover, Dean Stockwell, Gary Busey, Seymour Cassel, Frederic Forrest, Matthew Glave, Marilu Henner, Dennis Hopper
'Mangy, dimwitted gender switch on *The Last Detail*.' – *Variety*

'Sex Is Easy. Love Is Hard.'
Chasing Amy **
US 1997 111m Technicolor
Metrodome/Miramax/View Askew (Scott Mosier)
▦ ▤
A comic-book artist is attracted to a lesbian with wide sexual experience.

Enjoyable, often witty low-budget movie about the complexities of love and friendship.
wd Kevin Smith ph David Klein m David Pirner pd Robert 'Ratface' Holtzman ed Kevin Sith, Scott Mosier
☆ Ben Affleck, Joey Lauren Adams, Jason Lee, Dwight Ewell, Jason Mewes, Kevin Smith
'Fundamentally amusing and appealing.' – *Variety*
† The film was made for $250,000
†† The credits include the dedication: 'To the critics who hated our last flick – all is forgiven.'

Chasing Dreams
US 1982 105m CFI color
Nascent (Therese Conte, David G. Brown)
▤
A shy youth with family problems and a handicapped brother discovers that he has a gift for playing baseball.
Sentimental family drama that is unlikely to stir any interest outside its home country.
w David G. Brown d Sean Roche ph Connie Holt m Gregory Conte pd Bobbi Peterson Himber ed Jerry Weldon, Robert Sinise
☆ David G. Brown, John Fife, Jim Shane, Matthew Clark, Lisa Kingston, Kevin Costner

Chasing Rainbows
US 1929 100m bw (colour sequence)
MGM
True love finds a way while a big musical is rehearsing.
Naïve attempt to repeat the success of Broadway Melody.
w Bess Meredyth d Charles Riesner
☆ Bessie Love, Charles King, Marie Dressler, Polly Moran, Jack Benny
'Numerous exploitable names and a snappy set of tunes.' – *Variety*
🎵 'Happy Days Are Here Again'; 'Everybody Tap'; 'Lucky Me, Loveable You'; 'Poor but Honest'; 'Dynamic Personality'; 'Love Ain't Nothing but the Blues'; 'Gotta Feeling for You'

Chasing the Deer
GB 1994 97m colour
Feature Film/Cromwell/La Mancha (Bob Carruthers)
🎧
A father and son find themselves, by force of circumstances, on opposite sides at the Battle of Culloden in 1746, when Bonnie Prince Charlie's Jacobite forces were defeated by the Duke of Cumberland.
Rather like the rebellion it celebrates, a gallant failure; it looks good but sadly lacks inspiration.
w Jerome Vincent, Bob Carruthers, Steve Gillham d Graham Holloway ph Alan M. Trow m John Wetton ed Patrick Moore
☆ Brian Blessed, Iain Cuthbertson, Fish, Matthew Zajax, Sandy Welch, Brian Donald, Peter Gordon, Lynn Ferguson
'You do need scale and a certain directorial flair. It's the lack of that which makes this properly sincere film into what is essentially a bit of a plod.' – *Derek Malcolm, Guardian*
† The producers raised much of the film's budget of £460,000 by offering roles as extras to those who invested in it.

Chasing Yesterday
US 1935 78m bw
RKO
An elderly archaeologist seeks to renew his lost youth through the daughter of the woman he once loved but lost.
Slow and old-fashioned melodrama.
w Francis E. Faragoh *novel* The Crime of Sylvestre Bonnard by Anatole France d George Nicholls Jnr
☆ O. P. Heggie, Anne Shirley, Elizabeth Patterson, Helen Westley, John Qualen, Etienne Girardot
'Prospects not bright.' – *Variety*

The Chastity Belt
Italy 1967 110m Eastmancolor
Warner/Julia (Francesco Mazzei)
aka: *On My Way to the Crusades I Met a Girl Who…*
A 12th-century knight is called to the Crusades just as he is consummating his marriage, and when he locks his wife in a chastity belt she follows him.
Abysmal international romp which looks nice but is killed stone dead by writing, dubbing and direction.
w Luigi Magni, Larry Gelbart d Pasquale Festa Campanile ph Carlo di Palma m Riz Ortolani

☆ Tony Curtis, Monica Vitti, Hugh Griffith, John Richardson, Nino Castelnuovo

Chastnaya Zhizn: see *Private Life*

Le Château de Ma Mère *
France 1990 98m Eastmancolor
Gaumont/Gueville/TF1 (Marc Goldstaub, Guy Azzi)
▦ ▤ @ᵥ
aka: *My Mother's Castle*
A novelist and film-maker remembers his childhood holidays spent among the hills of Provence.
Slow-paced, soft-centred account of a blissful past; nostalgia is laid on with a trowel.
w Jérôme Tonnerre, Yves Robert *autobiography* Marcel Pagnol d Yves Robert m Robert Alazraki m Vladimir Cosma ad Jacques Dugied ed Pierre Gillette
☆ Philippe Caubère, Nathalie Roussel, Didier Pain, Thérèse Liotard, Julien Ciamaca, Victorien Delamare, Joris Molinas, Julie Timmerman, Jean Carmet, Jean Rochefort, Georges Wilson, Jean-Pierre Darras
† A sequel to *La Gloire de Mon Papa* (qv).

Chato's Land
GB 1971 100m Technicolor
UA/Scimitar (Michael Winner)
▤
An Apache half-breed kills a man in self-defence, subsequently eluding and destroying the sheriff's posse.
Exhaustingly violent Western in which the audience is spared no gory detail; efficiently put together for those who like this kind of fracas.
w Gerald Wilson m Michael Winner ph Robert Paynter m Jerry Fielding
☆ Charles Bronson, Jack Palance, Richard Basehart, James Whitmore, Simon Oakland, Richard Jordan, Ralph Waite, Victor French, Lee Patterson

Chattahoochee
US 1989 97m TVC Color
Hemdale (Aaron and Faye Schwab)
▦ ▤ @ᵥ
In the mid-1950s a veteran of the Korean War suffers a breakdown and is sent to a decaying, violent mental hospital.
Downbeat and depressing.
w James Hicks d Mick Jackson ph Andrew Dunn m John Keane pd Joseph T. Garrity ed Don Fairservice
☆ Gary Oldman, Dennis Hopper, Frances McDormand, Pamela Reed, Ned Beatty, M. Emmet Walsh

Chatterbox
US 1935 68m bw
RKO
A country maiden aspires to the stage.
Mildly likeable comedy for family audiences.
w Sam Mintz *play* David Carb d George Nicholls Jnr
☆ Anne Shirley, Phillips Holmes, Edward Ellis, Erik Rhodes, Margaret Hamilton, Granville Bates
'Discounting the nice job all around, the picture isn't there.' – *Variety*

Chatterbox
US 1943 77m bw
Republic (Albert J. Cohen)
A radio cowboy gets a film contract but can't stand horses.
Flat star comedy which borrows some well-worn situations but handles them badly.
w George Carleton Brown, Frank Gill Jnr d Joseph Santley ph Ernest Miller md Walter Scharf
☆ Joe E. Brown, Judy Canova, Rosemary Lane, John Hubbard, Chester Clute

Che?: see *What?*

'With a dream of justice, he created a nightmare of violence!'
Che!
US 1969 94m DeLuxe Panavision
TCF (Sy Bartlett)
▤
Fidel Castro is helped in his subversion of Batista's Cuban regime by an Argentinian doctor named Che Guevara.

⊚ Digital Video Disc Region 2   ⊚ Digital Video Disc Region 1   🎧 Soundtrack released on compact disc   ☆ Cast in approximate order of importance   † Points of interest   🎵 Notable songs   🏆 Academy Award   🏆 Academy Award nomination   🏆 BAFTA

Fictionalized biography, and a dull one, of a man who became a myth.
w Michael Wilson, Sy Bartlett d Richard Fleischer ph Charles Wheeler m Lalo Schifrin
☆ Omar Sharif, Jack Palance, Cesare Danova, Robert Loggia, Woody Strode, Barbara Luna
'It goes at the pace of a drugged ox, and hasn't an ounce of political or historical sense in its nut.' – *New Yorker*

The Cheap Detective
US 1978 92m Metrocolor Panavision
Columbia/Ray Stark
▦ ▤ ☙

Forties private eye Lou Peckinpaugh is involved in a complex case with echoes of *Casablanca*, *The Big Sleep*, *The Maltese Falcon* and *Farewell My Lovely*.
Lame spoof which might have seemed funnier on a small screen in black and white; as it is, the strain is evident and desperate.
w Neil Simon d Robert Moore ph John A. Alonzo m Patrick Williams
☆ Peter Falk, John Houseman, Nicol Williamson, Louise Fletcher, Fernando Lamas, Madeline Kahn, Dom DeLuise, Paul Williams, Marsha Mason, Ann-Margret, Eileen Brennan, Stockard Channing, Sid Caesar, Scatman Crothers, Phil Silvers and also Abe Vigoda, Vic Tayback
'Frankly they did this sort of thing just as well, and a lot more quickly, on *The Carol Burnett Show*.' – *Richard Shickel, Time*
'There is about enough talent around for a twenty-minute sketch at the Edinburgh fringe.' – *Derek Malcolm, Guardian*
† The film was a follow-up to the not much more effective but at least more controlled *Murder by Death*.

Cheaper by the Dozen **
👫 US 1950 86m Technicolor
TCF (Lamar Trotti)
Efficiency expert Frank Gilbreth and his wife Lillian have twelve children, a fact which requires mathematical conduct of all their lives.
Amusing family comedy set in the twenties, unconvincing in detail though based on a book by two of the children. A great commercial success and a Hollywood myth-maker. Sequel: Belles on their Toes (qv).
w Lamar Trotti book Frank B. Gilbreth Jnr, Ernestine Gilbreth Carey d Walter Lang ph Leon Shamroy m Cyril Mockridge md Lionel Newman ad Lyle Wheeler, Leland Fuller
☆ Clifton Webb, Myrna Loy, Jeanne Crain, Edgar Buchanan, Barbara Bates, Betty Lynn, Mildred Natwick, Sara Allgood

The Cheat *
US 1915 95m bw silent
Famous Players Lasky/Paramount
A society lady borrows from a rich Japanese, and he brands her when she refuses to become his mistress.
Hoary melodrama which caused a sensation in its day.
w Hector Turnbull d Cecil B. de Mille ph Alvin Wyckoff
☆ Fanny Ward, Jack Dean, Sessue Hayakawa, James Neill
† Remade in 1923 by George Fitzmaurice, in 1931 by George Abbott, and in 1937 (in France, as *Forfaiture*) by Marcel L'Herbier.

The Cheaters *
US 1945 86m bw
Republic
A selfish and ostentatious family is reformed by the ministrations of a down-and-out actor.
Fairly engaging variation on The Passing of the Third Floor Back, with sweetness and light brought into people's lives by a fireside recital of A Christmas Carol.
w Frances Hyland d Joseph Kane ph Reggie Lanning m Walter Scharf
☆ Joseph Schildkraut, Billie Burke, Eugene Pallette, Ona Munson, Raymond Walburn

Cheating Cheaters
US 1934 67m bw
Universal
Two groups of jewel thieves clash when posing as society swells.
Tolerable programmer from an old stage hit.
w Gladys Unger, Allen Rivkin play Max Marcin d Richard Thorpe

☆ Fay Wray, Cesar Romero, Minna Gombell, Hugh O'Connell, Henry Armetta, Francis L. Sullivan, Ann Shoemaker
'Rather creaky entertainment, but it will about get by.' – *Variety*

Check and Double Check
US 1930 71m bw
RKO
▤ ☙
Comic adventures of a couple of black handymen.
Feeble comedy notable only for the film appearance of radio's immensely popular Amos 'n' Andy, played by white actors in blackface.
w Bert Kalmar, Harry Ruby, J. Walter Ruben d Melville Brown ph William Marshall m Max Steiner
☆ Freeman F. Gosden, Charles V. Correll, Sue Carol, Charles Morton, Irene Rich, Ralf Harolde, Duke Ellington and his Orchestra
'The best picture for children ever put on the screen … as a freak talking picture it's in the money immediately.' – *Variety*

The Checkered Coat
US 1948 66m bw
TCF (Sam Baerwitz)
A psychopathic killer is captured during one of his cataleptic seizures.
Fairly routine programme filler which manages to keep the attention.
w John C. Higgins d Edward L. Cahn
☆ Tom Conway, Hurd Hatfield, Noreen Nash, James Seay

Checkers
👫 US 1937 79m bw
TCF
The niece of a ne'er-do-well horse owner brings him success.
One of the most successful vehicles of Shirley Temple's arch rival.
w Lynn Root, Frank Fenton, Karen de Wolf play Rida Johnson Young d H. Bruce Humberstone
☆ Jane Withers, Stuart Erwin, Una Merkel, Marvin Stephens, Andrew Tombes, Minor Watson
'Will delight the moppet's following … due for heavy dual booking.' – *Variety*

Checking Out
GB 1988 95m Technicolor
Virgin/Handmade (Ben Myron)
▦ ▤ ☙
A successful advertising man becomes a hypochondriac after the sudden death of a friend.
Mildly amusing comedy.
w Joe Eszterhas d David Leland ph Ian Wilson m Carter Burwell pd Barbara Ling ed Lee Percy
☆ Jeff Daniels, Melanie Mayron, Michael Tucker, Kathleen York, Ann Magnuson, Allan Harvey, Jo Harvey Allen, Ian Wolfe

Checkpoint *
GB 1956 84m Eastmancolor
Rank (Betty Box)
A tycoon sends an industrial spy to Italy in search of new motor racing car designs.
Acceptable hokum, cleanly assembled, with motor race highlights.
w Robin Estridge d Ralph Thomas ph Ernest Steward m Bruce Montgomery
☆ Anthony Steel, Stanley Baker, James Robertson Justice, Odile Versois, Maurice Denham, Michael Medwin, Lee Patterson

Cheech and Chong: Still Smokin'
US 1983 92m colour
Paramount/Cheech & Chong's Comedy Film Festival Number One Inc (Peter MacGregor-Scott)
Two slobbish comedians attend a Burt Reynolds-Dolly Parton film festival in Amsterdam.
Dreary, plotless exercise in futility that reaches its nadir in excerpts from the duo's concert performance.
w Thomas Chong, Cheech Marin d Thomas Chong ph Harvey Harrison m George A. Clinton ad Ruud Van Dijk ed David Ramirez, James Coblenz
☆ Cheech Marin, Thomas Chong, Hans Man In't Veld, Carol Van Herwijnen, Shireen Strocker, Susan Hahn

Cheech and Chong's Next Movie
US 1980 95m Technicolor
Howard Brown/Universal
▦ ▤ ☙
GB title: *High Encounters of the Ultimate Kind*
Two dopers have various rude adventures.
Totally repulsive comedy which gives a bad name to self-indulgence.
w Cheech Marin, Thomas Chong d Thomas Chong
☆ Cheech Marin, Thomas Chong, Evelyn Guerrero, Betty Kennedy, Sy Kramer

Cheech and Chong's The Corsican Brothers
US 1984 90m colour
Orion (Peter MacGregor-Scott)
▤ ☙
Twin brothers run amuck during the French Revolution.
Coarse and unfunny parody of a swashbuckling adventure.
w Cheech Marin, Thomas Chong d Thomas Chong ph Harvey Harrison m GEO ad Daniel Budin ed Tom Avildsen
☆ Cheech Marin, Thomas Chong, Roy Dotrice, Shelby Fiddis, Rikki Marin, Edie McClurg, Rae Dawn Chong, Robbi Chong

Cheer Boys Cheer
GB 1939 84m bw
ATP (Michael Balcon)
Brewery owners hate each other but their children fall in love.
A highly predictable plot provides some incidental pleasures in this modest precursor of the Ealing comedies.
w Roger MacDougall, Allan MacKinnon story Ian Dalrymple, Donald Bull d Walter Forde ph Ronald Neame, Gordon Dines md Ernest Irving ad Wilfred Shingleton ed Ray Pitt
☆ Nova Pilbeam, Edmund Gwenn, Jimmy O'Dea, Moore Marriott, Graham Moffatt, C. V. France, Alexander Knox

Cheer Up!
GB 1936 72m bw
Associated British/Stanley Lupino
An unemployed actor is mistaken for a millionaire by an out-of-work actress.
Jolly though undistinguished musical, hampered by its low humour and lower budget.
w Michael Barringer story Stanley Lupino d Leo Mittler ph Curt Courant m/ly Billy Mayerl, Val Guest, Noel Gay, Frank Eyton, Stanley Lupino, Desmond Carter md Percy Mackey ad J. Elder Wills ed Sam Simmonds, Ronald Deeming
☆ Stanley Lupino, Sally Gray, Roddy Hughes, Wyn Weaver, Marjorie Chard, Ernest Sefton, Gerald Barry, Kenneth Kove, Doris Rogers, Arthur Rigby

Cheers for Miss Bishop *
US 1941 94m bw
UA (Richard A. Rowland)
▤
The life of a schoolmistress in a small mid-western town.
Acceptable sentimental hokum, quite pleasantly done.
w Adelaide Heilbron novel Bess Streeter Aldrich d Tay Garnett ph Hal Mohr m Edward Ward
☆ Martha Scott, William Gargan, Edmund Gwenn, Sterling Holloway, Sidney Blackmer, Mary Anderson, Dorothy Peterson
♪ Edward Ward

Cheetah
👫 US 1984 84m Metrocolor
Buena Vista/Walt Disney (Robert Halmi)
▦ ▤ ☙
Two American teenagers, who spend six months in Africa with their parents, rescue and rear a cheetah cub.
Bland and innocuous entertainment aimed at children, but too tame to hold their interest for long.
w Erik Tarloff, John Cotter, Griff du Rhone book The Cheetahs by Alan Caillou d Jeff Blyth ph Tom Burstyn m Bruce Rowland pd Jane Cavedon ed Eric Albertson
☆ Keith Coogan, Lucy Deakins, Timothy Landfield, Breon Gorman, Collin Mothupi

Chelovek sKinoapparatom: see *The Man with the Movie Camera*

The Chelsea Girls **
US 1966 255m bw/colour
Andy Warhol
Episodic look at life in a series of hotel rooms, consisting of unedited conversations between spaced-out individuals – the Pope of Greenwich Village hearing confessions and losing his temper, a drug dealer talking to a customer as she injects them both, a woman being reduced to tears by aggressive questioning, a mother chastising her son, a dancer stripping as he talks about his desires, and so on.
Shown on a double screen, with two different rooms visible at a time, but only one conversation audible, this was the film which, more than any other, brought the underground to public attention. It has worn less well than some of Morrissey and Warhol's other work but survives as a monument of sorts, exactly capturing the sights and sounds of a particular era despite its technical shortcomings.
d Paul Morrissey ph Andy Warhol m The Velvet Underground
☆ Marie Mencken, Mary Woronov, Gerard Malanga, International Velvet, Ingrid Superstar, Ondine, Mario Montez, Eric Emerson, Nico, Brigid Polk
'An epic movie-novel.' – *Jonas Mekas*
'Warhol's people are more real than real because the camera encourages their exhibitionism. They are all "performing" because their lives are one long performance and their party is never over.' – *Andrew Sarris, Village Voice*
'It has come time to wag a warning finger at Andy Warhol and his underground friends and tell them politely but firmly that they are pushing a reckless thing too far.' – *Bosley Crowther, New York Times*
'A three and a half hour cesspool of vulgarity and talentless confusion which is about as interesting as the inside of a toilet bowl.' – *Rex Reed*
† The film, which cost less than $3,000 to make, took more than $300,000 in its first six months.

Chère Inconnue: see *I Sent a Letter To My Love*

'America's favourite two-gun star battles for love and glory!'
Cherokee Strip
US 1940 86m bw
Harry Sherman/Paramount
A marshal brings law and order to a frontier town.
Competent Western programmer.
w Norman Houston, Bernard McConville d Lesley Selander
☆ Richard Dix, Florence Rice, William Henry, Victor Jory, Andy Clyde

Cherry 2000
US 1988 93m DeLuxe
Orion (Edward R. Pressman, Caldecot Chubb)
▦ ▤ ☙
In the year 2017 after his robotic sex-toy breaks down, a man discovers human romance when he hires a female mercenary to obtain the spare part he needs to repair it from a heavily guarded desert warehouse.
Post-apocalyptic fantasy of a familiar kind, silly but enjoyable if you are in a tolerant enough mood to accept Melanie Griffith as the female equivalent of Mad Max.
w Michael Almereyda story Lloyd Fonvielle d Steve de Jarnatt ph Jacques Haitkin m Basil Poledouris pd John J. Moore ed Edward Abroms, Duwayne Dunham
☆ Melanie Griffith, David Andrews, Ben Johnson, Brion James, Tim Thomerson, Harry Carey Jnr, Pamela Gidley
† The film was made in 1985.

Cherry, Harry and Raquel!
US 1969 71m colour
Panamint/Eve (Russ Meyer)
A crooked sheriff gets his come-uppance.
Little more than a series of violent or sexual incidents, which only have a vague connection with each other; as with Meyer's other films, there's time to contemplate why his characters are always so angry with each other.
w Tom Wolfe, Russ Meyer d Russ Meyer ph Russ Meyer m William Loose ed Russ Meyer, Richard S. Brummer
☆ Larissa Ely, Linda Ashton, Charles Napier, Bert Santos, Franklin H. Bolger, Astrid Lillimor, John Milo

The Cherry Picker

GB 1972 92m Eastmancolor
Fox-Rank/Elsinore (Peter Curran, Derek Kavanagh)

The rich, hippy son of an American tycoon loses his appetite for the sybaritic life.

Typical British product of its time; a failed attempt to mix sex and satire; what we get instead is a cheap-looking movie with a confused narrative and an uncertain tone.

wd Peter Curran *novel* Pick Up Sticks *by* Mickey Phillips *ph* Billy Jordan *m* Bill McGuffie *pd* Frank White *ed* Jack Knight

☆ Lulu, Bob Sherman, Wilfrid Hyde-White, Spike Milligan, Patrick Cargill, Robert Hutton, Priscilla Morgan, Jack Hulbert, Terry-Thomas

'The film dithers over an inadequately scripted and crudely shot narrative that might be charitably described as "rambling" or "picaresque".' – *MFB*

Chess Fever *

USSR 1925 20m bw silent
Mezhrabpom-Russ

A chess fanatic is so absorbed that he misses his wedding.

Spirited visual comedy which still raises the intended laughs.

w Nikolai Shpikovsky d Nikolai Shpikovsky, Vsevolod Pudovkin

☆ Vladimir Fogel, Anna Zemtsova

The Chess Players *

India 1977 129m Eastmancolor
Devki Chitra (Suresh Jindal)

original title: *Shatranj Ke Khilari*

In 1856 Lucknow, two noblemen are more interested in playing chess than in their state's imminent annexation by the British.

Patchy but frequently charming historical piece with more specifically Indian elements than are usual from its director.

wd Satyajit Ray *story* Prem Chand *m* Satyajit Ray *ad* Bansi Chandragupta *ed* Dulal Dutta

☆ Sanjeev Kumar, Saeed Jaffrey, Richard Attenborough, Amjad Khan

Le Cheval d'Orgueil: see The Proud Ones

Cheyenne

US 1947 100m bw
Warner

later retitled: *The Wyoming Kid*

A gambler turns lawman, catches a robber and marries his wife.

Rather sluggish Western which later inspired a long-running TV series.

w Alan Le May, Thames Williamson d Raoul Walsh

☆ Dennis Morgan, Bruce Bennett, Jane Wyman, Arthur Kennedy, Janis Paige, Alan Hale

Cheyenne Autumn *

US 1964 170m Technicolor Panavision 70
Warner/Ford-Smith (Bernard Smith)

In the 1860s, Cheyenne Indians are moved to a new reservation 1500 miles away; wanting aid, they begin a trek back home, and various battles follow.

Dispirited, shapeless John Ford Western with little of the master's touch; good to look at, however, with effective cameos, notably an irrelevant and out-of-key comic one featuring James Stewart as Wyatt Earp.

w James R. Webb *novel* Mari Sandoz d John Ford *ph* William H. Clothier *m* Alex North *ad* Richard Day *ed* Otho Lovering

☆ Richard Widmark, Carroll Baker, Karl Malden, Dolores del Rio, Sal Mineo, Edward G. Robinson, James Stewart, Ricardo Montalban, Gilbert Roland, Arthur Kennedy, Patrick Wayne, Elizabeth Allen, Victor Jory, John Carradine, Mike Mazurki and also John Qualen, George O'Brien

'Although one would like to praise the film for its high-minded aims, it is hard to forget how ponderous and disjointed it is.' – *Moira Walsh*

'The acting is bad, the dialogue trite and predictable, the pace funereal, the structure fragmented and the climaxes puny.' – *Stanley Kauffmann*

୫ William H. Clothier

The Cheyenne Social Club *

US 1970 102m Technicolor Panavision
National General (James Lee Barrett, Gene Kelly)

Two itinerant cowboys inherit a high-class brothel.

Disappointing star comedy Western with pleasing moments and a lively climactic shootout. Perhaps the girls are just a shade too winsome.

w James Lee Barrett *d* Gene Kelly *ph* William H. Clothier *m* Walter Scharf

☆ James Stewart, Henry Fonda, Shirley Jones, Sue Ane Langdon, Robert Middleton, Arch Johnson

'Co-starring Shirley Jones and Rigor Mortis, who enters early and stays through the very last scene.' – *Rex Reed*

Chi L'ha Vista Morire?: see Who Saw Her Die?

Chi sei?: see Devil within Her

Chicago Calling *

US 1951 75m bw
UA/Arrowhead/Joseph Justman (Peter Berneis)

A drunk cannot pay his phone bill and is waiting for a vital call about his daughter's involvement in a car crash.

Moderate, location-shot minor melodrama with a few good ideas.

w John Reinhardt, Peter Berneis d John Reinhardt *ph* Robert de Grasse *m* Heinz Roemheld

☆ Dan Duryea, Mary Anderson, Gordon Gebert, Ross Elliott

Chicago, Chicago: see Gaily, Gaily

Chicago Confidential

US 1957 74m bw
Peerless/UA

A gambling syndicate takes over a labour union and frames its incorruptible president for murder.

Very routine gangster potboiler.

w Raymond T. Marcus d Sidney Salkow

☆ Brian Keith, Beverly Garland, Dick Foran, Elisha Cook Jnr

Chicago Deadline

US 1949 87m bw
Paramount (Robert Fellows)

A reporter researches the life of a lonely girl who died of tuberculosis.

Flat star vehicle consisting mainly of overplayed cameos.

w Warren Duff, Tiffany Thayer d Lewis Allen *ph* John F. Seitz *m* Victor Young

☆ Alan Ladd, Donna Reed, June Havoc, Berry Kroeger, Arthur Kennedy, Gavin Muir, Shepperd Strudwick

† Remade as the TV pilot of *The Name of the Game*.

'Where desire has no limits ... Fantasies become dangerous realities!'

Chicago Joe and the Showgirl

GB 1989 103m colour
Palace/New Line/Polygram/Working Title/BSB (Tim Bevan)

During the Second World War, an American deserter and his English girlfriend, a stripper, enhance their affair by committing a series of crimes.

Based on actual events, but a movie that rarely seems more than a laboured fantasy and one that the public ignored.

w David Yallop d Bernard Rose *ph* Mike Southon *m* Hans Zimmer, Shirley Walker *pd* Gemma Jackson *ed* Dan Rae

☆ Kiefer Sutherland, Emily Lloyd, Patsy Kensit

Chicago Masquerade: see Little Egypt

Chicago Syndicate

US 1955 86m bw
Clover/Columbia

A young accountant breaks up an outwardly respectable crime syndicate.

Formula racket-busting melodrama.

w Joseph Hoffman d Fred F. Sears

☆ Dennis O'Keefe, Abbe Lane, Paul Stewart, Xavier Cugat, Alison Hayes

The Chicken Chronicles

US 1977 94m CFI color
Chicken Enterprises/Avco Embassy

Problems of a teenager in an American small town.

Extremely boring comedy drama, obsessed with sex and lacking background detail.

w Paul Diamond d Francis Simon

☆ Phil Silvers, Ed Lauter, Steve Guttenberg, Meredith Baer, Lisa Reeves

Chicken Every Sunday *

US 1949 94m bw
TCF

The Hefferans have run a boarding house for twenty years, but dad's wild schemes run away with any possible profit.

Archetypal, folksy, American small-town chronicle, reasonably well made, for an audience that later watched The Waltons.

w George Seaton, Valentine Davies d George Seaton *ph* Harry Jackson *m* Alfred Newman

☆ Dan Dailey, Celeste Holm, Colleen Townsend, Alan Young, Natalie Wood

The Chicken Wagon Family

US 1939 81m bw
TCF

Louisiana backwoods make a trip to New York.

Feeble country cousin comedy.

w Viola Brothers Shore d Herbert I. Leeds

☆ Jane Withers, Leo Carrillo, Marjorie Weaver, Spring Byington, Kane Richmond, Hobart Cavanaugh

'Nabes and second runs will write best ledger marks.' – *Variety*

Chickens Come Home *

US 1931 30m bw
Hal Roach

Stan helps his boss Ollie to evade the attentions of an old flame.

Rather heavy and untypical, but mainly very enjoyable star comedy, a remake of Love 'Em and Weep in which all three leading players had appeared four years earlier in different roles.

w H. M. Walker *story* Hal Roach d James W. Horne *ph* Art Lloyd, Jack Stevens *ed* Richard Currier

☆ Stan Laurel, Oliver Hardy, James Finlayson, Mae Busch, Thelma Todd

The Chief

US 1933 80m bw
MGM

GB title: *My Old Man's a Fireman*

A fireman's son becomes a Bowery candidate for alderman.

Feeble comedy with the star ill at ease.

w Arthur Caesar, A. E. Hopkins d Charles F. Riesner

☆ Ed Wynn, Dorothy Mackaill, Charles 'Chic' Sale, William Boyd, George Givot, C. Henry Gordon

'With the radio draw angle discarded it is weak entertainment.' – *Variety*

Chief Crazy Horse

US 1954 86m Technicolor Cinemascope
U-I (William Alland)

GB title: *Valley of Fury*

The tribal problems of the Indian chief who defeated Custer at Little Big Horn.

Competent pro-Indian Western.

w Franklin Coen, Gerald Drayson Adams d George Sherman *ph* Harold Lipstein *m* Frank Skinner

☆ Victor Mature, Suzan Ball, John Lund, Ray Danton, Keith Larsen, Paul Guilfoyle, David Janssen

Un Chien Andalou *

France 1928 17m bw silent
Luis Buñuel

Famous surrealist short which includes dead donkeys on pianos and starts with a woman's eyeball being cut by a razor blade.

It had meaning for its makers, but very few other people saw anything in it but sensationalism.

w Luis Buñuel, Salvador Dali d Luis Buñuel *ph* Albert Dubergen *ed* Luis Buñuel

☆ Simone Mareuil, Pierre Batcheff, Jaime Miravilles, Salvador Dali, Luis Buñuel

La Chienne *

France 1931 85m bw
Braunberger-Richebé

A bank clerk falls for a prostitute and later kills her; her pimp is executed for the crime and the bank clerk becomes a tramp.

Heavy-going, old-fashioned melodrama with some interesting detail.

wd Jean Renoir *novel* Georges de la Fouchardière *ph* Theodor Sparkuhl, Roger Hubert

☆ Michel Simon, Janie Marèze, Georges Flament, Jean Gehret

'If the English translation of the title is unfit to print, the film's dialogue cannot be translated into English. Okay for sophisticated audiences that look for a taste of spice in a ritzy spot.' – *Variety*

† Remade as *Scarlet Street* (qv).

La Chiesa: see The Church

Child in the House

GB 1956 88m bw
Eros/Golden Era (Ben Fisz)

When her mother is ill and her father in hiding from the police, a 12-year-old girl goes to stay with her fussy uncle and aunt.

Modest family drama of the novelette type in which adult problems are put right by the wisdom of a child.

wd C. Raker Endfield *novel* Janet McNeill *ph* Otto Heller *m* Mario Nascimbene *ad* Ken Adam

☆ Eric Portman, Phyllis Calvert, Stanley Baker, Mandy Miller, Dora Bryan, Joan Hickson, Victor Maddern, Percy Herbert

A Child Is Born

US 1939 79m bw
Warner (Sam Bischoff)

A slice of life in the maternity ward.

Adequately dramatic sequence of cameos, with mothers-to-be including a gangster's moll: a remake of Life Begins (qv).

w Robert Rossen *play* Mary M. Axelson d Lloyd Bacon *ph* Charles Rosher *m* Heinz Roemheld

☆ Geraldine Fitzgerald, Jeffrey Lynn, Gladys George, Gale Page, Spring Byington, Henry O'Neill, John Litel, Gloria Holden, Eve Arden, Nanette Fabares, Hobart Cavanaugh, Johnny Downs, Johnnie Davis

A Child Is Waiting **

US 1963 104m bw
UA/Stanley Kramer

A mixed-up spinster joins the staff of a school for mentally handicapped children.

Worthy semi-documentary marred by having a normal boy play the central character (albeit very well). A little over-dramatized but cogent and unsentimental.

w Abby Mann d John Cassavetes *ph* Joseph LaShelle *m* Ernest Gold

☆ Burt Lancaster, Judy Garland, Bruce Ritchey, Steven Hill, Gena Rowlands, Paul Stewart, Lawrence Tierney

The Childhood of Maxim Gorky ***

USSR bw
Soyuzdetfilm

Orphan Gorky is raised by his grandparents, and becomes a ship's cook and a painter before going on to university.

This simple and direct story is told in three beautifully detailed if rather overlong films: 'The Childhood of Maxim Gorky' (1938, 101m), 'Out in the World' (1939, 98m), 'My Universities' (1940, 104m).

w Mark Donskoi, I. Grudzev d Mark Donskoi *ph* Pyotr Yermolov *m* Lev Schwartz *ad* I. Stepanov

☆ Alexei Lyarsky, Y. Valbert, M. Troyanovski, Valeria Massalitinova

'This is for grown-up minds. It is episodic and sprawling, the photography is by no means good – quite inferior to the polished camera work of the average Hollywood product – but it touches the mind and heart as no film within years has done.' – *Richard Winnington*

The Children *
GB/West Germany   1990   115m   colour
Isolde/Arbo Film & Maran/Channel 4 (Andrew Montgomery)
📼
Returning from Brazil to marry a rich widow, an engineer finds his plans disrupted when he becomes guardian to the boisterous children of an old friend.
A leisurely account of thwarted love, held together by Kingsley's strong central performance of repressed emotion.
w Timberlake Wertenbaker *novel* Edith Wharton d Tony Palmer *ph* Nic Knowland *m* Benjamin Britten, Samuel Barber, Vaughan Williams, Evelyn Glennie *pd* Chris Bradley, Paul Templeman
☆ Ben Kingsley, Kim Novak, Siri Neal, Geraldine Chaplin, Joe Don Baker, Britt Ekland, Karen Black, Donald Sinden, Robert Stephens, Rupert Graves, Rosemary Leach

Children of a Lesser God *
US   1986   110m   Film Lab Color
Paramount (Burt Sugarman, Patrick Palmer)
📼 ▦ ☋ 🎧
A deaf woman falls in love with her speech therapist.
Sluggish adaptation of a play which meant more on the stage.
w Hesper Anderson, Mark Medoff *play* Mark Medoff d Randa Haines *ph* John Seale m Michael Convertino *pd* Gene Callahan ed Lisa Fruchtman
☆ William Hurt, Marlee Matlin, Piper Laurie, Philip Bosco
🏆 Marlee Matlin
🏆 best picture; William Hurt; Piper Laurie; screenplay

Children of Chance
GB/Italy   1949   99m   bw
British Lion/Ortus/Lux (John Sutro, Ludovico Toeplitz)
At the end of the Second World War, a woman on the island of Ischia discovers that her savings, which she sent to her village priest for safe-keeping, have been spent on opening a home for the illegitimate children of Allied soldiers.
A slow-moving, sentimental drama which, although based on a true story and filmed on location, lacks authenticity owing to the restrained performances of its impeccably English cast.
w Piero Tellini, Michael Medwin d Luigi Zampa *ph* Carlo Montuori *m* Nino Rota
☆ Patricia Medina, Manning Whiley, Yvonne Mitchell, Barbara Everest, Eliot Makeham, George Woodbridge, Frank Tickle, Eric Pohlmann

Children of Hiroshima **
Japan   1952   97m   bw
Kendai Eiga Lyokai/Gekidan Mingei
A young teacher returns to Hiroshima seven years after the bomb.
Restrained yet harrowing social documentary in fiction form, with the most effective use of flashbacks to show the horror of the bomb and its aftermath.
wd Kaneto Shindo *novel* Arata Osada *ph* Takeo Itoh *m* Akira Ifukube
☆ Nobuko Otowa, Chikako Hosbawa, Niwa Saito

Children of Paradise: see *Les Enfants du Paradis*

The Children of Sanchez
US/Mexico   1978   126m   colour
Hall Bartlett
📼
A macho Mexican and one of his daughters have ideas above the semi-slum in which they live.
The star is still looking for another Zorba the Greek, but this isn't it. Glum, glum, glum.
w Cesare Zavattini, Hall Bartlett *novel* Oscar Lewis d Hall Bartlett *ph* Gabriel Figueroa m Chuck Mangione
☆ Anthony Quinn, Dolores del Rio, Lupita Ferrer, Katy Jurado, Stathis Giallelis

Children of the Corn
US   1984   92m   CFI color
New World/Angeles/Cinema Group (Donald P. Borchers, Terence Kirby)
📼 ▦ ☋
A doctor and his girlfriend run down a child, discover that his throat has been cut, and find

themselves in a community of murderous adolescents.
Nightmarish modern fantasy with style but very little to like.
w George Goldsmith *story* Stephen King d Fritz Kiersch *ph* Raoul Lomas *m* Jonathan Elias
☆ Peter Horton, Linda Hamilton, R. G. Armstrong, John Franklin
'The aim seems to be to reassure rather than to disturb.' – Robert Murphy, MFB

Children of the Corn II: The Final Sacrifice
US   1992   Foto-Kem
Fifth Avenue Entertainment (Scott A. Stone, David G. Stanley)
📼 ▦ ☋ 🎧
Teenagers who have killed all the adults in a small town in the Bible Belt are moved to another small town, where they proceed to do the same.
Inept sequel, so predictable as to be almost unwatchable.
w A. L. Katz, Gilbert Adler *story* Children of the Corn by Stephen King d David F. Price *ph* Levie Isaacks *m* Daniel Licht *pd* Greg Melton ed Barry Zetlin *sp* Bob Keen
☆ Terence Knox, Paul Scherrer, Ryan Bollman, Christie Clark, Rosalind Allen, Ned Romero
'More effective on a shock and shriek level than the original but not a major contribution to anything.' – Empire
† Children of the Corn III; Urban Harvest, Children of the Corn IV; The Gathering, and Children of the Corn V: Fields of Terror followed, providing ever-diminishing returns.

'So young, so innocent, so deadly – they came to conquer the world!'
Children of the Damned *
GB   1964   90m   bw
MGM (Ben Arbeid)
📼 ☋
Six super-intelligent children of various nations are brought to London by UNESCO, and turn out to be invaders from another planet.
Moderate sequel to Village of the Damned, well made but with no new twists.
w John Briley d Anton M. Leader *ph* David Boulton *m* Ron Goodwin *ad* Elliot Scott ed Ernest Walter
☆ Ian Hendry, Alan Badel, Barbara Ferris, Alfred Burke, Sheila Allen, Ralph Michael, Martin Miller, Harold Goldblatt

Children Shouldn't Play with Dead Things
US   1972   87m   colour
Geneni (Bob Clark, Gary Goch)
📼 🎧
A group of film-makers travel to an isolated island cemetery, where they try to raise the dead as a joke, and find they have created zombie cannibals.
A low-budget horror that begins slowly and then quickens to a gory finale, though those who have seen Night of the Living Dead may experience a feeling of déjà vu.
w Benjamin Clark (Bob Clark), Alan Ormsby d Benjamin Clark (Bob Clark) *ph* Jack McGowan
☆ Alan Ormsby, Anya Ormsby, Valerie Manches, Jane Daly, Jeff Gillen, Paul Cronin, Bruce Solomon, Seth Sklarey

The Children's Hour *
US   1962   108m   bw
UA/Mirisch (William Wyler)
📼 ☋
GB title: *The Loudest Whisper*
A spoilt schoolgirl spreads a rumour that her schoolmistresses are lesbians.
Frank sixties version of a play originally filmed in a much bowdlerized version as These Three. Unfortunately frankness in this case leads to dullness, as nothing is done with the theme once it is stated, and the treatment is heavy-handed.
w Lillian Hellman *play* Lillian Hellman d William Wyler *ph* Franz Planer *m* Alex North
☆ Audrey Hepburn, Shirley MacLaine, James Garner, Miriam Hopkins, Fay Bainter, Karen Balkin
'All very exquisite, and dead as mutton.' – Tom Milne
🏆 Franz Planer; Fay Bainter

Child's Play *
GB   1952   68m   bw
British Lion/Group 3 (Herbert Mason)
Village children find a way to create atomic energy and use the power to set up a flourishing popcorn business.
A lively children's feature that has now acquired a quaint charm in its attitude to nuclear energy.
w Peter Blackmore *story* Don Sharp, Margaret Thomson d Margaret Thomson *ph* Denny Densham *m* Anthony Hopkins *ad* Michael Stringer ed John Legard
☆ Mona Washbourne, Peter Martyn, Dorothy Alison, John Sharp, Peter Sallis, Christopher Beeny, Wendy Westcott
'A child's chief glories are its energy and its noise; and this picture very properly bombinates with both.' – Paul Dehn

Child's Play *
US   1972   100m   colour   Movielab
Paramount (David Merrick)
In a Catholic boarding school for boys, an unpopular master is hounded and discredited by another whose motives may be diabolic.
Enjoyable overblown melodrama with hints of many nasty goings on, rather spoiled by too much talk and too little local colour.
w Leon Prochnik *play* Robert Marasco d Sidney Lumet *ph* Gerald Hirschfeld *m* Michael Small
☆ James Mason, Robert Preston, Beau Bridges, Ronald Weyand

Child's Play
US   1988   87m   Astrocolor
UIP/United Artists (David Kirschner)
📼 ▦ ☋ 🎧
The personality of a serial killer is transferred to a young boy's doll.
Unexciting horror, too predictable to be frightening.
w Don Mancini, John Lafia, Tom Holland d Tom Holland *ph* Bill Butler *m* Joe Renzetti *pd* Daniel A. Lomino ed Edward Warschilka, Roy E. Peterson
☆ Catherine Hicks, Chris Sarandon, Alex Vincent, Brad Dourif, Dinah Manoff, Tommy Swerdlow

Child's Play 2
US   1990   85m   DeLuxe
Universal (David Kirschner)
📼 ▦ ☋ 🎧
A doll possessed by the spirit of a mass murderer attempts to kill a small boy.
Tiresome and unpleasant.
w Don Mancini d John Lafia *ph* Stefan Czapsky m Graeme Revell *pd* Ivo Cristante *ad* Donald Maskovich ed Edward Warschilka
☆ Alex Vincent, Jenny Agutter, Gerrit Graham, Christine Elise, Brad Dourif, Grace Zabriskie
'Another case of rehashing the few novel elements of the original to the point of utter numbness.' – Variety

Child's Play 3
US   1991   89m   DeLuxe
Universal/David Kirschner (Robert Latham Brown)
📼 ▦ ☋
A killer doll infiltrates a military school in order to kill the students.
Mindless and unpleasant sequel, ever straining for effect.
w Don Mancini d Jack Bender *ph* John A. Leonetti *m* Cory Lerios, John D'Andrea pd Richard Sawyer ed Edward Warschilka
☆ Justin Whalin, Perrey Reeves, Jeremy Sylvers, Travis Fine, Dean Jacobson, Brad Dourif, Andrew Robinson
† It was followed in 1998 by a sequel, Bride of Chucky (qv).

Chilly Scenes of Winter: see *Head Over Heels (1980)*

The Chiltern Hundreds *
GB   1949   84m   bw
Rank/Two Cities (George H. Brown)
US title: *The Amazing Mr Beecham*
An aged earl is bewildered when his son fails to be elected to parliament as a socialist but his butler gets in as a Tory.
Satisfactory filming of an amusing stage comedy, with the aged A. E. Matthews repeating his delightful if irrelevant act as the dotty earl.

w William Douglas Home, Patrick Kirwan play William Douglas Home d John Paddy Carstairs *ph* Jack Hildyard *m* Benjamin Frankel
☆ A. E. Matthews, Cecil Parker, David Tomlinson, Marjorie Fielding, Joyce Carey

Chimes at Midnight **
Spain/Switz   1966   119m   bw
Internacional Films Española/Alpine (Alessandro Tasca)
▦ 🎧
aka: *Falstaff*
Prince Hal becomes King Henry V and rejects his old friend Falstaff.
Clumsy adaptation of Shakespeare with brilliant flashes and the usual Welles vices of hasty production, poor synchronization and recording, etc. One wonders why, if he wanted to make a telescoped version of the plays, he did not spare the time and patience to make it better.
wd Orson Welles *ph* Edmond Richard *m* Angelo Francesco Lavagnino *pd* Gustavo Quintano ed Fritz Mueller
☆ Orson Welles, Keith Baxter, John Gielgud, Margaret Rutherford, Jeanne Moreau, Norman Rodway, Alan Webb, Marina Vlady, Tony Beckley, Fernando Rey, Michael Aldridge
'One of Orson Welles' best and least-seen movies … The film is a near-masterpiece.' – New Yorker
'Ridiculous is the word for the whole enterprise – not funny and certainly not moving.' – John Simon
'A testament to the enduring genius of Orson Welles as screenwriter, director and actor … does justice to Shakespeare, to cinema and to his own great talents.' – Judith Crist

The Chimp *
👪 US   1932   30m   bw
Hal Roach
📼
Stan and Ollie try to get lodgings without revealing that their friend is a chimp, their share of a bankrupt circus.
The circus scenes are better than the rather tired farce which follows, especially as it is so similar to Laughing Gravy.
w H. M. Walker d James Parrott *ph* Walter Lundin ed Richard Currier
☆ Stan Laurel, Oliver Hardy, James Finlayson, Billy Gilbert, Tiny Sandford

'Alan Ladd and twenty girls – trapped by the rapacious Japs!'
China
US   1943   79m   bw
Paramount (Richard Blumenthal)
An oil salesman joins a Chinese guerrilla force and sacrifices himself.
Solemnly hilarious propaganda piece tailored to its star, showing the immense superiority of one lone American to the entire Japanese army.
w Frank Butler *novel* The Fourth Brother by Reginald Forbes d John Farrow *ph* Leo Tover m Victor Young
☆ Alan Ladd, Loretta Young, William Bendix, Philip Ahn, Iris Wong, Sen Yung, Richard Loo, Tala Birell

China 9, Liberty 37 *
Spain/Italy   1978   109m   Technicolor   Technovision
Lorimar/Compagnia Europe Cinematografica/Aspa (Gianni Bozzacchi, Valerio de Paolis, Monte Hellman)
▦ 🎧
aka: *Gunfire*
Hired to shoot a retired killer, a gunfighter runs off with his wife instead and is pursued by the irate husband and his brothers.
Intriguing spaghetti Western, slow-paced, with a brooding atmosphere and some sharp dialogue.
w Jerry Harvey, Douglas Venturelli d Monte Hellman *ph* Giuseppe Rotunno *m* Pino Donaggio *ad* Luciano Spadoni ed Cesare D'Amico
☆ Warren Oates, Fabio Testi, Jenny Agutter, Sam Peckinpah, Isabel Mestres, Gianrico Tondivelli, Franco Interlenghi, Carlos Bravo
† The title refers to a signpost which a travelling hangman passes at the beginning of the film. He takes the road to China.

China Caravan: see *A Yank on the Burma Road*

China Clipper *

US 1936 89m bw
Warner (Sam Bischoff)

An aviator neglects his wife while building up a trans-Pacific civil aviation link.

Solid entertainment feature of its day, with adequate production and performance.

w Frank 'Spig' Wead d Ray Enright ph Arthur Edeson m Bernhard Kaun, W. Franke Harling
☆ Pat O'Brien, Beverly Roberts, Ross Alexander, Humphrey Bogart, Marie Wilson, Henry B. Walthall, Joseph Crehan, Addison Richards

China Corsair

US 1951 76m bw
Columbia

An American ship's engineer is stranded on an island off the China coast.

Routine escapist hokum.

w Harold A. Greene d Ray Nazarro
☆ Jon Hall, Lisa Ferraday, Ron Randell, Douglas Kennedy, Ernest Borgnine

China Cry

US 1991 107m CFI color
TBN/Parakletos (Don LeRoy Parker)

During Mao's revolution, a young middle-class woman, who is condemned to a labour camp for aiding her husband's escape from China, survives hardship to join him in Hong Kong.

An interesting story of a spoilt child maturing through the experience of war and injustice, but so flatly told that it makes little emotional impact.

wd James F. Collier book Nora Lam, Irene Burke ph David Worth m Al Kasha, Joel Hirschhorn pd Norman Baron ed Duane Hartzell
☆ Julia Nickson-Soul, Russell Wong, James Shigeta, France Nuyen, Philip Tan, Elizabeth Sung

China Doll

US 1958 99m bw
Romina/Batjac (Frank Borzage)

In 1943 an American air force officer accidentally buys the services of a young Chinese housekeeper. He marries her but they are both killed in action; years later their daughter is welcomed to America by members of his old air crew.

Incurably sentimental and icky romantic drama in the style of the director's silent films; something of a curiosity for historians.

w Kitty Buhler d Frank Borzage ph William H. Clothier m Henry Vars
☆ Victor Mature, Li Li Hua, Bob Mathias, Ward Bond, Stuart Whitman

'An American dynamiter love-locked in war-locked China!'

China Gate

US 1957 90m bw Cinemascope
TCF (Samuel Fuller)

A Eurasian girl guides her American husband to a communist arms dump.

Anti-Red thick ear, slick but undistinguished.

wd Samuel Fuller ph Joseph Biroc m Victor Young, Max Steiner
☆ Gene Barry, Angie Dickinson, Nat King Cole, Paul Dubov, Lee Van Cleef, George Givot

China Girl

US 1943 95m bw
TCF (Ben Hecht)

A newsreel cameraman in China falls in love with a Eurasian schoolteacher.

Routine adventure romance with splodges of love and self-sacrifice.

w Ben Hecht d Henry Hathaway ph Lee Garmes m Hugo Friedhofer
☆ Gene Tierney, George Montgomery, Lynn Bari, Victor McLaglen, Alan Baxter, Sig Rumann, Myron McCormick, Philip Ahn

China Girl

US 1987 90m colour
Vestron (Michael Nozik)

In New York an Italian youth with Mafia connections falls in love with a Chinese girl from a family involved with the Triads.

Romeo and Juliet updated to Little Italy and Chinatown and used as an occasion for blood-letting and much gang violence.

w Nicholas St John d Abel Ferrara ph Bojan Bazelli m Joe Delia ed Anthony Redman
☆ James Russo, Richard Panebianco, Sari Chang, David Caruso, Russell Wong, Joey Chin, Judith Malina, James Hong

'A masterfully directed, uncompromising drama and romance.' – Variety

'Even die-hard fans of New York urban violence movies will find this tough going.' – Stefan Jaworzyn, Shock Xpress

China Moon *

US 1994 99m DeLuxe
Orion (Barrie M. Osborne)

A seductive woman, married to an adulterous wife-beating banker, persuades a detective to forget about law and order.

Accomplished but sometimes predictable foray into film noir, an agreeable time-waster.

w Roy Carlson d John Bailey ph Willy Kurant m George Fenton pd Conrad Angone ed Carol Littleton, Jill Savitt
☆ Ed Harris, Madeleine Stowe, Charles Dance, Pruitt Taylor Vince, Patricia Healy, Benicio del Toro

'Avoids slick montage and the cheap thrills of shock cuts and instead aims for the eyes – and heart.' – Emanuel Levy, Variety

† The film was made in 1992.

China, My Sorrow: see Niu-Peng

China O'Brien

US 1988 90m Image Transform colour
Golden Harvest/Fred Weintraub

A former cop replaces her murdered father as sheriff of a small town.

The usual martial arts mayhem with the novelty of a high-kicking female hero.

wd Robert Clouse story Sandra Weintraub ph Kent Wakeford m David Wheatley, Paul Antonelli ed Mark Harrah
☆ Cynthia Rothrock, Richard Norton, Keith Cooke, Patrick Adamson, David Blackwell

China O'Brien II

US 1989 86m colour
Imperial/Golden Harvest (Fred Weintraub)

A female sheriff is threatened by an escaped drug pusher.

Routine high-kicking martial arts, with the usual rudimentary acting.

w James Hennessy, Craig Clyde story Sandra Weintraub d Kent Wakeford m David Wheatley, Paul F. Antonelli ed Mark Harrah
☆ Cynthia Rothrock, Richard Norton, Keith Cooke, Frank Magner, Harlow Marks, Tiffany Soter

'A haphazard affair, generating little interest.' – Variety

China Seas **

US 1935 89m bw
MGM (Albert Lewin)

Luxury cruise passengers find themselves involved with piracy.

Omnibus shipboard melodrama, tersely scripted and featuring a splendid cast all somewhere near their best; slightly dated but very entertaining.

w Jules Furthman, James Kevin McGuinness novel Crosbie Garstin d Tay Garnett ph Ray June m Herbert Stothart
☆ Clark Gable, Jean Harlow, Wallace Beery, Rosalind Russell, Lewis Stone, C. Aubrey Smith, Dudley Digges, Robert Benchley

'It will do double-barrelled duty, drawing business and providing ace entertainment.' – Variety

'The hell with art this time. I'm going to produce a picture that will make money.' – Irving Thalberg

China Sky

US 1945 78m bw
RKO (Maurice Geraghty)

Two American doctors live with Chinese guerrillas; the jealousy of the wife of one of them causes problems.

Routine adventure romance with generally unconvincing production and performance.

w Brenda Weisberg, Joseph Hoffman novel Pearl Buck d Ray Enright ph Nicholas Musuraca m Roy Webb
☆ Randolph Scott, Ellen Drew, Ruth Warrick, Anthony Quinn, Carol Thurston, Richard Loo, Philip Ahn

The China Syndrome ***

US 1979 122m Metrocolor
Columbia/IPC (Michael Douglas)

The controller of a nuclear power plant discovers an operational flaw which could lead to disaster, but the unscrupulous authorities want to cover it up.

Topical thriller-with-a-moral, absorbingly done in the old style but perhaps in the end a shade too hysterical and self-congratulatory.

w Mike Gray, T. A. Cook, James Bridges d James Bridges m James Crabe m various pd George Jenkins ed David Rawlins
☆ Jane Fonda, Jack Lemmon, Michael Douglas, Scott Brady, Peter Donat, James Hampton

'The performances are so good, and the screen so bombarded with both action and informative images … that it's only with considerable hindsight that one recovers sufficient breath to reproach the script with the occasional glib symmetry.' – Jan Dawson, MFB

♬ Jack Lemmon, Jane Fonda; script
ᴛ Jack Lemmon; Jane Fonda

China Venture

US 1953 83m bw
Columbia (Anson Bond)

In 1945, American marines are sent into the Chinese jungle to recover a Japanese admiral held captive there.

Topical thick ear, played and presented without conviction.

w George Worthing Yates, Richard Collins d Don Siegel
☆ Edmond O'Brien, Barry Sullivan, Jocelyn Brando, Richard Loo

Chinatown ****

US 1974 131m Technicolor Panavision
Paramount/Long Road (Robert Evans)

In 1937, a Los Angeles private eye takes on a simple case and burrows into it until it leads to murder and a public scandal.

Teasing, complex mystery that uses the conventions of detective stories to explore civic and personal corruption, in the style of Raymond Chandler, but adding a more modern perspective. It is eminently watchable, with effective individual scenes and performances and photography which is lovingly composed though tending to suggest period by use of an orange filter.

w Robert Towne d Roman Polanski ph John A. Alonso m Jerry Goldsmith pd Richard Sylbert
☆ Jack Nicholson, Faye Dunaway, John Huston, Perry Lopez, John Hillerman, Roman Polanski, Darrell Zwerling, Diane Ladd

'You are swept along as helpless as any of the corpses so unaccountably drowned in empty lake-beds.' – Dilys Powell

'The success of Chinatown – with its beautifully structured script and draggy, overdeliberate direction – represents something dialectically new: nostalgia (for the thirties) openly turned to rot, and the celebration of rot.' – Pauline Kael

♬ Robert Towne
♬ best picture; Roman Polanski; John A. Alonso; Jerry Goldsmith; Jack Nicholson; Faye Dunaway
ᴛ Roman Polanski; Robert Towne; Jack Nicholson

Chinatown at Midnight

US 1949 67m bw
Columbia

Police seek a killer in Chinatown.

Efficient lower-case police thriller.

w Robert Libott, Frank Burt d Seymour Friedman
☆ Hurd Hatfield, Jean Willes, Tom Powers, Ray Walker

Chinese Box

US/France/Japan 1997 109m colour
Canal+/NDF/WW (Lydia Dean Pilcher, Jean-Louis Piel)

As the British prepare to hand over Hong Kong to the Chinese, a dying English journalist tries to

make his own farewells through his relationship with two contrasting women.

Tepid topical drama that uses TV newscasts to provide an urgency that is otherwise lacking.

w Jean-Claude Carriere, Larry Gross d Wayne Wang ph Vilko Filac m Graeme Revell pd Chris Wong ed Christopher Tellefsen
☆ Jeremy Irons, Gong Li, Maggie Cheung, Ruben Blades, Michael Hui

'This tale of impossible cross-cultural love is rendered dreary by lukewarm chemistry between stars Jeremy Irons and Gong Li, and a script that provides no character depth.' – David Rooney, Variety

Chinese Boxes

GB 1984 87m colour
Palace/Road Movies (Chris Sievernich)

An American in Berlin discovers a dead 15-year-old girl in his apartment.

A thriller that resembles a jigsaw with some of the pieces missing. It is told in such an elliptical fashion as to leave the viewer not only confused but indifferent.

w L. M. Kit Carson, Christopher Petit d Christopher Petit ph Peter Harvey m Günter Fischer ad Edgar Hinz, Klaus Beiger ed Fred Srp
☆ Will Patton, Gottfried John, Adelheid Arndt, Robbie Coltrane, Beate Jensen, L. M. Kit Carson, Chris Sievernich, Christopher Petit

The Chinese Bungalow

GB 1939 72m bw
George King
US title: Chinese Den

A Chinese merchant plots to kill the lover of his English wife.

Stolid version of an old melodrama which can hardly fail; previously filmed in 1926 with Matheson Lang and Genevieve Townsend (directed by Sinclair Hill) and in 1930 with Matheson Lang and Anna Neagle (directed by J. B. Williams).

w A. R. Rawlinson, George Wellesley play Matheson Lang, Marian Osmond d George King ph Hone Glendinning
☆ Paul Lukas, Jane Baxter, Robert Douglas, Kay Walsh, Jerry Verno

The Chinese Connection: see Fist of Fury

Chinese Den: see The Chinese Bungalow

A Chinese Feast

Hong Kong 1995 107m colour
Mandarin/Film Workshop

original title: Gamyuk Muntong

An inept chef seeks the help of a one-time master, now a derelict, to enter a contest to cook the Qing and Han Imperial Feast, an elaborate banquet of more than 100 dishes.

Broad slapstick comedy that is unlikely to be to Western tastes, any more than the main dishes prepared for the banquet: bear's paw, elephant's trunk and monkey's brains with shark's fin.

w Tsui Hark, Ng Man-fai, Tseng Tsung-tai d Tsui Hark ph Peter Pau m Lowell Lo pd, William Chang ed Mak Tsi-sin
☆ Leslie Cheung, Anita Yuen, Kenny Bee, Ni Shu-chun, Lo Ka-ying, Zhao Wenzhuo, Hung Yan-yan

'A comic kung-food movie about dueling chefs that's funny, skillful and a heart-warmer to boot.' – Derek Elley, Variety

† Subtitles on the video are so small as to be almost unreadable, and even when they can be read they are frequently incomprehensible ('Make sure dismoral to the fish, not me').

A Chinese Ghost Story

Hong Kong 1988 98m colour
Film Workshop (Tsui Hark)

original title: Qiannu Youhun

A wandering tax collector falls in love with a ghost condemned to lure men to their death.

Fast-moving mix of horror, romance and martial arts; its narrative, involving reincarnation and a soul-sucking tree demon with a killer tongue, confuses as much as it entertains.

story Pu Songling d Ching Siu-tung ph Poon Hang-Seng m Romeo Diaz pd Xi Zhongwen ed David Wu
☆ Leslie Cheung, Joey Wong, Wu Ma, David Lam

A Chinese Ghost Story II

Hong Kong   1990   104m   colour
Golden Princess (Tsui Hark)
⊚

original title: *Qiannu Youhun – Renjian Dao*
A wandering scholar falls for the reincarnation of
his ghostly lover and rescues her father from evil
spirits.
*With its half-comic, half-horrific demon creeping up
behind the hero, magic spells, broad humour and evil
golden Buddha, this, in Western terms, resembles a
lavish pantomime; on that level, it is moderately
enjoyable.*
d Ching Siu-tung   ph Wong Ngok-Tai
☆ Leslie Cheung, Joey Wong, Jackie Cheung,
Michelle Reis, Waise Lee, Wu Ma, Ku Feng

Chinese Roulette *

West Germany/France   1976   86m
Eastmancolor
Albatros/Losange (Rainer Werner Fassbinder)
📼   ▦   ⚟

Various related people, mainly adulterous, meet in
a country château and play a truth game which
ends in violence.
*Interestingly enigmatic character melodrama
reminiscent of Bergman at his prime, but concerning
people who barely seem to matter.*
wd Rainer Werner Fassbinder   ph Michael Ballhaus
m Peer Raben
☆ Margit Carstensen, Andrea Schober, Ulli
Lommel, Anna Karina, Macha Meril
 'Locked into their private hell ... this vicious
 octet form their own coherent and compelling
 universe.' – Jan Dawson, MFB

Chino

US/Italy   1973   98m   colour
Dino de Laurentiis
▦   ⚟

A runaway boy helps a half-breed run a ranch in
New Mexico.
Undistinguished Western.
w Clair Huffaker novel Lee Hoffman d John
Sturges
☆ Charles Bronson, Jill Ireland, Vincent Van
Patten

La Chinoise ***

France   1967   95m   Eastmancolor
Fair Enterprises/Productions de la
Guéville/Parc/Simar/Anouchka/Athos
In 1967, five Parisian Maoist revolutionaries
debate the best ways of achieving the end of the
capitalist system, from closing the universities to
acting Brecht, and decide that terrorism is the way
forward.
*With hindsight, a prophetic movie of the student politics
that shook Paris a year later, which is still a troubling
and wittily intriguing film in its search for new means of
cinematic expression.*
wd Jean-Luc Godard   ph Raoul Coutard   m Karl-
Heinz Stockhausen   ed Agnès Guillemot,
Delphine Desfons
☆ Anne Wiazemsky, Jean-Pierre Léaud, Michel
Sémeniako, Lex de Brujin, Juliet Berto, Omar
Diop, Francis Jeanson
 'The movie is like a speed-freak's anticipatory
 vision of the political horrors to come; it's
 amazing.' – Pauline Kael
 'A piece of mitigated trash ... Godard, his
 material, his pretentiousness and undisciplined
 garrulity, are boring when not exasperating.' –
 John Simon

Chip off the Old Block

US   1944   76m   bw
Universal (Bernard W. Burton)
The son of a seafaring family gets into expected
romantic trouble.
*Lightweight comedy-musical which performed
adequately at the time.*
w Eugene Conrad, Leo Townsend   d Charles
Lamont
☆ Donald O'Connor, Peggy Ryan, Ann Blyth,
Patric Knowles, Helen Broderick, Helen Vinson,
Arthur Treacher, J. Edward Bromberg, Ernest Truex
 'Effervescing juvenile comedy-drama for wide
 audience appeal.' – Variety

Chisum *

US   1970   110m   Technicolor   Panavision
Warner/Batjac (Michael Wayne, Andrew J. Fenady)
📼   ▦

A corrupt businessman plots against the head of a
vast cattle empire, who is saved by the
intervention of numerous friends including Pat
Garrett and Billy the Kid.
*Desultory, overlong, friendly Western in the Ford
manner. Easy to watch and easier to forget.*
w Andrew J. Fenady   d Andrew V. McLaglen
ph William H. Clothier   m Dominic Frontière
☆ John Wayne, Forrest Tucker, Christopher
George, Ben Johnson, Glenn Corbett, Bruce
Cabot, Andrew Prine, Patric Knowles, Richard
Jaeckel, Lynda Day George, John Agar, Ray Teal,
Glenn Langan, Alan Baxter, Abraham Sofaer
 'A curious mixture of styles and myths.' – John
 Gillett

Chitty Chitty Bang Bang

👫   GB   1968   145m   Technicolor   Super
Panavision 70
UA/Warfield/DFI (Albert R. Broccoli)
📼   ▦   ⚟

An unsuccessful inventor rescues a derelict car and
gives it magical properties, then helps the children
who own it to overthrow the government of a
country which hates children.
*A bumpy ride. Sentiment, slapstick, whimsy and mild
scares do not combine but are given equal shares of the
limelight, while poor trickwork prevents the audience
from being transported.*
w Roald Dahl, Ken Hughes   d Ken Hughes
ph Christopher Challis   m Irwin Kostal   m/ly The
Sherman Brothers   ad Rowland Emmett
☆ Dick Van Dyke, Sally Ann Howes, Lionel
Jeffries, Robert Helpmann, Gert Frobe, Benny Hill,
James Robertson Justice
⚟ title song

Chloë in the Afternoon: see L'Amour, L'Après-midi

Le Choc: see The Shock

Chocolat **

France/Germany/Cameroon   1988   105m
colour
Electric/Cinemanuel/MK2/Cerio/Wim Wenders
Produktion/TF1/SEPT/Caroline/FODIC (Alain
Belmondo, Gerard Crosnier)
📼   ▦   ⚟

A French woman recalls her colonial childhood in
French West Africa and her relationship with the
family servant.
*Cool, distanced, semi-autobiographical account of
racism and its effects.*
w Claire Denis, Jean-Pol Fargeau   d Claire Denis
ph Robert Alazraki   m Abdullah Ibrahim
pd Thierry Flamand   ed Claudine Merlin
☆ Isaach de Bankole, Giula Boschi, François
Cluzet, Jean-Claude Adelin
 'Undoubtedly over-generous, fictionalised and
 nostalgic, but it is also well paced, well observed
 and shot through with a dry sense of humour.' –
 Jill Forbes, MFB

The Chocolate Soldier *

US   1941   102m   bw
MGM (Victor Saville)
▦

Married opera singers fall out backstage.
*Talky musical remake of The Guardsman: nearly
comes off but not quite.*
w Keith Winter, Leonard Lee   d Roy del Ruth
ph Karl Freund   m Herbert Stothart, Bronislau
Kaper   m/ly Oscar Straus
☆ Nelson Eddy, Rise Stevens, Nigel Bruce,
Florence Bates, Nydia Westman
⚟ Karl Freund; Herbert Stothart, Bronislau Kaper

The Choice

Burkina Faso   1987   88m   colour
Les Films de L'Avenir
original title: *Yam Daabo*
The pleasures and tribulations of African village
life.
*Rudimentary and episodic first feature, lacking the
resonance of the director's later films such as Yaaba
and Tilai (qv).*
wd Idrissa Ouedraogo   ph Jean Monsigny, Sekou
Ouedraogo, Issaka Thiombiano   m Francis Bebey
ed Arnaud Blin

☆ Aoua Guiraud, Moussa Bologo, Ousmana
Sawadogo, Fatima Ouedraogo

Choice of Arms *

France   1981   130m   Fujicolour
Sara/Parafrance/Antenne 2/RMC (Daniel Deschamps)
original title: *Le Choix des Armes*
A successful, retired gangster is drawn back into a
world of violence when, after a jail break, a
seriously wounded friend seeks refuge at his stud
farm together with a young, violent, reckless
hoodlum.
*Interesting but too-leisurely account of people unable to
escape their past.*
w Michel Grisolia, Alain Corneau   d Alain
Corneau   ph Pierre William Glenn   m Philippe
Sarde   ad Jean-Pierre Kohut Svelko   ed Thierry
Derocles
☆ Yves Montand, Gérard Depardieu, Catherine
Deneuve, Michel Galabru, Gérard Lanvin, Jean-
Claude Dauphin, Jean Rougerie, Christian
Marquand, Richard Anconina

Choice of Weapons: see Trial by Combat

The Choirboys

US   1978   119m   Technicolor
Lorimar/Airone (Lee Rich, Merv Adelson)
▦

Members of a police department are if anything
more delinquent, vicious and mentally retarded
than their quarries.
*A vulgar and repellent anti-establishment display,
apparently intended as black comedy. Just the thing to
put an end to the art of the movie once and for all.*
w Christopher Knopf   novel Joseph Wambaugh
d Robert Aldrich   ph Joseph Biroc   m Frank de
Vol
☆ Charles Durning, Lou Gossett Jnr, Perry King,
Stephen Macht, Tim McIntire, Clyde Kusatsu,
Randy Quaid, Don Stroud, Robert Webber, Blair
Brown

Le Choix des Armes: see Choice of Arms

Chomps

👫   US   1979   89m   Movielab
American International (Joseph Barbera)
▦

A young inventor is successful with a robot dog
(Canine Home Protection System).
Rather feeble family-oriented comedy.
w Dick Robbins, Duane Poole   story Joseph
Barbera   d Don Chaffey   ph Charles F. Wheeler
m Hoyt Curtin   pd Ted Shell   ed Warner
Leighton, Dick Darling
☆ Wesley Eure, Jim Backus, Valerie Bertinelli,
Chuck McCann, Regis Toomey, Red Buttons,
Hermione Baddeley

Choose Me

US   1984   106m   Movielab
Island Alive/Tartan (Carolyn Pfeiffer, David Blocker)
📼   ▦   ⚟

Two lonely people in LA become a couple.
*Even for those not irritated by the director's style and
interests, this is an entertainment which goes around in
circles and gets nowhere, except Las Vegas.*
wd Alan Rudolph   ph Jan Kiesser   m Luther
Vandross   pd Steve Legler   ed Mia Goldman
☆ Geneviève Bujold, Keith Carradine, Lesley
Ann Warren, Patrick Bachau, Rae Dawn Chong
 'An L.A. flower, a neon orchid – hip,
 outrageous, beautiful. It's a romance – music at
 its heart and farce around its edges – for those
 afraid to be in love.' – Sheila Benson, Los Angeles
 Times

Choose Your Partner: see Two Girls on Broadway

A Chorus Line

US   1985   111m   Technicolor   Panavision
Embassy/Polygram (Cy Feuer, Ernest Martin)
📼   ▦   ⚟

A Broadway musical chorus is selected.
*Overpraised musical drama which took nine years to
reach the screen because nobody could figure out how
to 'open it up' despite Universal's payment of 5.5
million dollars for the rights. The present team has not
solved the problem.*
w Arnold Schulman   play Nicholas Dante, James
Kirkwood   d Richard Attenborough   ph Ronnie

Taylor   m/ly Marvin Hamlisch, Edward Kleban
pd Patrizia von Brandenstein   ed John Bloom
☆ Michael Douglas, Terrence Mann, Alyson
Reed, Cameron English, Vicki Frederick
 'Static and confined, rarely venturing beyond
 the immediate.' – Variety
 'He makes his camera fly like a bird around the
 near-deserted theatre.' – Shaun Usher, Daily Mail
⚟ editing; song 'Surprise, Surprise' (mMarvin
Hamlisch, lyEdward Kleban)

A Chorus of Disapproval *

GB   1988   99m   colour
Hobo/Curzon/Palisades Entertainment (André Blay,
Elliott Kastner)
📼   ▦   ⚟

A new tenor joins an amateur choir to find the
sopranos lusting after him.
*Ponderous direction almost ruins a witty comedy of
suburban life.*
w Michael Winner, Alan Ayckbourn play Alan
Ayckbourn   d Michael Winner   ph Alan Jones
pd John Du Prez   ed Arnold Crust
☆ Anthony Hopkins, Jeremy Irons, Richard
Briers, Gareth Hunt, Patsy Kensit, Alexandra Pigg,
Prunella Scales, Jenny Seagrove, Peter Lee-Wilson,
Barbara Ferris, Lionel Jeffries, Sylvia Sims, David
King

The Chosen: see Holocaust 2000 (1977)

The Chosen

US   1981   108m   Movielab
The Chosen Film Company (Edie and Ely Landau)

In New York in the early forties, a family feud
between Zionist and Hassidic Jews interferes with a
friendship between two boys.
*A sentimental minority piece which does what it has to
do quite effectively.*
w Edwin Gordon   novel Chaim Potok   d Jeremy
Paul Kagan   ph Arthur Ornitz   m Elmer Bernstein
pd Stuart Wurtzel
☆ Maximilian Schell, Rod Steiger, Robby Benson,
Barry Miller, Hildy Brooks, Kaethe Fine

Chosen Survivors

US   1974   98m   colour
Alpine/Metromedia (Charles Fries)
Ten people with special skills are chosen to test
human reaction to thermo-nuclear war, but find
themselves at the mercy of vampire bats.
*Another misfit group united by disaster; more shocks
than suspense, and not much characterization, but for
adventure/horror addicts it will pass the time.*
w H. B. Cross, Joe Reb Moffly   d Sutton Roley
ph Gabriel Torres   m Fred Karlin
☆ Jackie Cooper, Alex Cord, Richard Jaeckel,
Diana Muldaur, Lincoln Kilpatrick, Bradford
Dillman, Pedro Armendariz Jnr, Gwen Mitchell,
Barbara Babcock, Christina Moreno

Les Choses de la Vie

France/Italy   1969   89m   Eastmancolor
Lira/Fida (Raymond Danon)
📼   🎧
aka: *These Things Happen*
aka: *The Things of Life*
An architect has his wife and mistress neatly
balanced when an accident upsets his scheme of
things.
*Nicely observed tragi-comedy in the best French
manner; since it starts with the car crash, a mini-
Bridge of San Luis Rey.*
w Paul Guimard, Claude Sautet, Jean-Loup
Dabadie   novel Paul Guimard   d Claude Sautet
ph Jean Boffety   m Philippe Sarde
☆ Michel Piccoli, Romy Schneider, Lea Massari,
Gérard Lartigau, Jean Bouise

Christ Stopped at Eboli ***

Italy/France   1979   155m   Technospes   Vides
Cinematografica/RAI/Action Film/Gaumont (Franco
Cristaldi, Nicola Carraro)
V, V*
In 1935 an Italian doctor is exiled because of his
political views to a remote southern part of the
country.
*An attractively faithful account of a book which was
part personal statement, part symbolism, part political
opinion and part local colour. Non-Italians will be
unable to extract the full flavour.*
w Francesco Rosi, Tonino Guerra, Raffaele La
Capria   book Carlo Levi   d Francesco Rosi
ph Pasqualino de Santis   m Piero Piccioni

👫 film suitable for family viewing   📼 VHS video-cassette for the British PAL system   📼 VHS video-cassette for the British PAL system in wide screen-format   ⚟ Video cassette in a computer-colourised version   ▦ American NTSC video-cassette   ⚟ Laser disc

☆ Gian Maria Volonte, Alain Cuny, Paolo Bonacelli, Lea Massari, Irene Papas, François Simon
ⓥ best foreign film

The Christian Licorice Store
US 1971 90m colour
National General
A Hollywood tennis player succumbs to corrupting influences.
Odd item with interesting credits but not much flesh on the bones.
w Floyd Mutrux d James Frawley
☆ Beau Bridges, Maud Adams, Gilbert Roland, Alan Arbus, Monte Hellman

Christiane F *
West Germany 1981 131m colour
Maran Film/Popular Film/Hans H. Kaden/TCF (Bernd Eichinger, Hans Weth)
A teenage girl becomes a drug addict.
Slick melodrama hoked up from 'true' confessions with excellent background detail.
w Herman Weigel d Ulrich Edel ph Justus Pankau, Jürgen Jürges m David Bowie ed Jane Seitz
☆ Natja Brunckhorst, Thomas Haustein, Jens Kuphal

Christina: see Virgin among the Living Dead

'How do you kill something that can't possibly be alive?'
Christine
US 1983 110m Technicolor Panavision
Columbia/Delphi (Richard Kobritz)
A diabolical car maims and kills its owner's girlfriends.
Thin and gruesomely extended horror flick which never begins to be convincing. For teenagers only.
w Bill Phillips novel Stephen King d John Carpenter ph Donald M. Morgan m John Carpenter pd Daniel Lomino
☆ Keith Gordon, John Stockwell, Alexandra Paul, Robert Prosky, Harry Dean Stanton, Christine Belford

A Christmas Carol *
US 1938 69m bw
MGM (Joseph L. Mankiewicz)
Scrooge the miser is reformed when four ghosts visit him on Christmas Eve.
Standard Dickensian frolic, quite well mounted.
w Hugo Butler d Edwin L. Marin ph Sidney Wagner m Franz Waxman
☆ Reginald Owen, Gene Lockhart, Kathleen Lockhart, Terry Kilburn, Leo G. Carroll, Lynne Carver
'Top production, inspired direction, superb acting.' – Variety
† See also Scrooge.

Christmas Eve *
US 1947 92m bw
Benedict Bogeaus
aka: Sinners' Holiday
An old lady needs the help of her three adopted sons to prevent herself from being swindled.
Basically three short stories sealed by a Christmas Eve reunion, this is old-fashioned sentimental stuff, but it works on its level and the cast is interesting.
w Laurence Stallings d Edwin L. Marin ph Gordon Avil m Heinz Roemheld
☆ Ann Harding, George Raft, Randolph Scott, George Brent, Joan Blondell, Virginia Field, Reginald Denny

Christmas Holiday
US 1944 93m bw
Universal (Felix Jackson)
A young girl marries a murderer, and later, as a shady songstress in a night-club, is forced to help him escape.
A weird change of pace for Deanna Durbin, whose forte had been sweetness and light, this relentlessly grim and boring melodrama was also a travesty of the novel on which it was based.
w Herman J. Mankiewicz novel Somerset Maugham d Robert Siodmak ph Elwood Bredell m Hans Salter
☆ Deanna Durbin, Gene Kelly, Dean Harens, Gladys George, Richard Whorf, Gale Sondergaard

'A jolly title for a Deanna Durbin film, but it's the only jolly thing about it. Miss Durbin is an accomplished singer; so they cut her songs to two and make them blues numbers. She has a naturally modest and ingenuous manner, so they cast her as a hostess in a seedy night club.' – C. A. Lejeune
♫ Hans Salter

Christmas in Connecticut *
US 1945 101m bw
Warner (William Jacobs)
GB title: Indiscretion
The spinster writer of a successful column about love and marriage has to conjure up a family for herself in the cause of publicity.
Predictable but fairly brisk comedy with excellent talent well deployed.
w Lionel Houser, Adele Commandini d Peter Godfrey ph Carl Guthrie m Frederick Hollander
☆ Barbara Stanwyck, Dennis Morgan, Sydney Greenstreet, Reginald Gardiner, S. Z. Sakall, Robert Shayne, Una O'Connor, Frank Jenks
† Arnold Schwarzenegger directed a remake for cable television in 1992 starring Dyan Cannon, Kris Kristofferson and Tony Curtis.

'If you can't sleep at night, it isn't the coffee – it's the bunk!'
Christmas in July **
US 1940 67m bw
Paramount
A young clerk and his girl win first prize in a big competition.
Slightly unsatisfactory as a whole, this Preston Sturges comedy has echoes of Clair and a dully predictable plot line, but is kept alive by inventive touches and a gallery of splendid character comedians.
wd Preston Sturges ph Victor Milner m Sigmund Krumgold
☆ Dick Powell, Ellen Drew, Ernest Truex, Al Bridge, Raymond Walburn, William Demarest
'The perfect restorative for battered humors and jangled nerves.' – Bosley Crowther
'Agreeable enough, but it lacks the full-fledged Sturges lunacy.' – New Yorker, 1977

Christmas Present *
Italy 1986 101m Telecolor Technovision
Duea/DMV/RAI Uno (Antonio Avati)
original title: Regalo di Natale
Four old friends, each needing money, get together on Christmas Eve to play poker in the hope of fleecing a rich industrialist.
Enjoyably sour little drama of masculine pride, obsession and betrayal.
wd Pupi Avati ph Pasquale Rachini m Riz Ortolani pd Giuseppe Pirrotta ed Amedeo Salfa
☆ Diego Abatantuono, Gianni Cavina, Alessandro Haber, Carlo delle Piane, George Eastman, Kristina Sevieri

A Christmas Story *
👫 US 1983 93m colour
MGM/UA (René Dupont, Bob Clark)
In an Indiana suburb during the 1940s, a schoolboy hopes to get a rifle for Christmas.
Curious, almost plotless family comedy of the old school, with the difference that some grotesquerie and tastelessness is added. On the whole, however, an amusing entertainment for adults who don't mind their mood of sentimental nostalgia being tilted at by the director of Porky's.
w Jean Shepherd, Leigh Brown, Bob Clark novel In God We Trust, All Others Pay Cash by Jean Shepherd d Bob Clark ph Reginald H. Morris m Carl Zittrer, Paul Zaza pd Gavin Mitchell ed Stan Cole
☆ Peter Billingsley, Melinda Dillon, Darren McGavin, Ian Petrella

The Christmas Tree
France/Italy 1969 110m Eastmancolor
Corona/Jupiter (Robert Dorfmann)
The small son of a millionaire widower is fatally infected by radioactivity.
Painfully sentimental and overdrawn weepie, the most lachrymose film of the sixties.
wd Terence Young novel Michel Bataille ph Henri Alekan m Georges Auric

☆ William Holden, Virna Lisi, Brook Fuller, Bourvil
'Depending on your taste threshold, there may not be a dry eye – nor a full stomach – in the house.' – Judith Crist

Christopher Bean *
US 1933 80m bw
MGM
aka: Her Sweetheart
A dying artist appoints his housekeeper as his executor.
Solid family entertainment very typical of its studio.
w Laurence Johnson, Sylvia Thalberg play The Late Christopher Bean by Sidney Howard d Sam Wood
☆ Marie Dressler, Lionel Barrymore, Beulah Bondi, Helen Mack, George Coulouris, H. B. Warner, Jean Hersholt
† It was Marie Dressler's final film.

Christopher Columbus
US 1949 104m Technicolor
Rank/Gainsborough/Sydney Box (Betty E. Box)
Columbus seeks and receives the patronage of the Spanish court for his voyage to the west.
An extraordinarily tediously paced historical account of basically undramatic events; interesting without being stimulating.
w Muriel and Sydney Box, Cyril Roberts d David MacDonald ph Stephen Dade m Arthur Bliss
☆ Fredric March, Florence Eldridge, Francis L. Sullivan, Linden Travers
'Even ten-year-olds will find it about as thrilling as an afternoon spent looking at Christmas cards.' – Time

Christopher Columbus: The Discovery
US 1992 121m Technicolor Panavision
Rank/Peel Enterprises (Alexander Salkind, Ilya Salkind)
Backed by Spain, Columbus sets sail to discover the New World on a disastrous voyage, but returns in triumph to be created Viceroy of the Indies.
Risible pageant with some notably poor performances and little to maintain one's interest.
w John Briley, Cary Bates, Mario Puzo d John Glen ph Alec Mills, Arthur Wooster m Cliff Eidelman pd Gil Parrondo ed Matthew Glen
☆ Marlon Brando, Tom Selleck, George Corraface, Rachel Ward, Robert Davi, Catherine Zeta Jones, Oliver Cotton, Benicio Del Toro, Mathieu Carrière, Nigel Terry
'Dead meat. It's the sort of film that makes you worry not about its characters but about the actors playing them … The basic trouble is that the whole film is devised in cliché terms.' – Derek Malcolm, Guardian

'She gave herself to the great God speed, and tried to run away from the fires within her!'
'The personal story of a million daughters!'
Christopher Strong *
US 1933 72m bw
RKO (Pandro S. Berman)
A daring lady aviator has an affair with a married businessman and commits suicide when she finds herself pregnant.
A curious and unsatisfactory yarn for Hepburn's second film; well enough made, it died at the box-office.
w Zoe Akins novel Gilbert Frankau d Dorothy Arzner ph Bert Glennon m Max Steiner
☆ Katharine Hepburn, Colin Clive, Billie Burke, Helen Chandler, Ralph Forbes, Irene Browne, Jack La Rue
'Draggy society play with circusy aeroplane stunt incidentals … interest in the star will outweigh other elements.' – Variety

Chronicle of a Death Foretold **
Italy/France 1987 110m Eastmancolor Panavision
Virgin/Italmedia/Soprafilms/Ariane/FR3/RAI (Frances von Buren, Yves Gasset)
original title: Cronica di una Morte Annunciata
After 27 years a doctor returns to his home-town to discover the truth about the death of his best friend.

Despite its stately rhythm, a powerful examination of the codes of masculine honour and female virtue.
w Francesco Rosi, Tonino Guerra novel Gabriel García Marquez d Francesco Rosi ph Pasqualino de Santis m Piero Piccioni pd Andrea Crisanti ed Ruggero Mastroianni
☆ Rupert Everett, Ornella Muti, Gian Maria Volonte, Irene Papas, Lucia Bose, Anthony Delon, Alain Cuny

Chronique d'un été *
France 1961 90m bw
Argos
Parisians talk about their lives.
Curious but rather stimulating acted documentary, with two interviewers pontificating; saved by shrewd editing to keep interest at its maximum.
wd Jean Rouch, Edgar Morin ph various

Chu Chin Chow *
GB 1934 102m bw
Gaumont British/Gainsborough (Michael Balcon)
In old Arabia, a slave girl foils a robber posing as a dead mandarin.
Second screen version (the first was silent) of the old Arabian Nights stage musical. A curiosity.
w Edward Knoblock, L. DuGarde Peach, Sidney Gilliat play Oscar Asche, Frederick Norton d Walter Forde ph Max Greene m/ly Frederick Norton md Louis Levy ch Anton Dolin ad Ernö Metzner ed Derek Twist
☆ George Robey, Fritz Kortner, Anna May Wong, John Garrick, Pearl Argyle, Malcolm MacEachern, Dennis Hoey, Francis L. Sullivan, Sydney Fairbrother
'A colourful, extravagant costume film that makes its bid for attention purely on an extravaganza platform, and makes the grade.' – Variety
'Gaumont British have broken away for the first time from their careful refinement, and produced something that has guts as well as grace.' – C. A. Lejeune

Chu Chu and the Philly Flash
US 1981 100m colour
TCF (Jay Weston)
A one-woman band performer and a drunken ex-baseball player lay claim to the same lost briefcase.
Weird comedy which doesn't come off except at odd moments.
w Barbara Dana d David Lowell Rich
☆ Carol Burnett, Alan Arkin, Jack Warden, Danny Aiello, Adam Arkin, Ruth Buzzi

Chubasco
US 1967 100m Technicolor Panavision
Warner Seven Arts (William Conrad)
A wild beach boy takes a job on a tuna fishing boat.
Old-fashioned boy-makes-good melodrama à la Captains Courageous. Excellent action sequences at sea.
wd Allen H. Miner ph Louis Jennings, Paul Ivano m William Lava
☆ Chris Jones, Richard Egan, Susan Strasberg, Ann Sothern, Simon Oakland, Preston Foster, Audrey Totter, Peter Whitney

Chuka
US 1967 105m Technicolor
Paramount/Rod Taylor
A wandering gunfighter defends the inhabitants of a fort against Indian attack.
Ill-assorted characters under stress is the theme of this rather pedestrian and slightly pretentious Western.
w Richard Jessup d Gordon Douglas ph Harold Stine m Leith Stevens
☆ Rod Taylor, Ernest Borgnine, John Mills, Luciana Paluzzi, James Whitmore, Louis Hayward, Angela Dorian

A Chump at Oxford **
👫 US 1940 63m bw
Hal Roach
Two street cleaners foil a bank hold-up and are presented with an Oxford education.
Patchy but endearing Laurel and Hardy romp, starting with an irrelevant two reels about their playing butler and maid, but later including Stan's burlesque impersonation of Lord Paddington.

---

w Charles Rogers, Harry Langdon, Felix Adler d Alfred Goulding ph Art Lloyd m Marvin Hatley ed Bert Jordan

☆ Stan Laurel, Oliver Hardy, James Finlayson, Forrester Harvey, Wilfred Lucas, Peter Cushing

'Ranks with their best pictures – which, to one heretic, are more agreeable than Chaplin's. Their clowning is purer; they aren't out to better an unbetterable world; they've never wanted to play Hamlet.' – Graham Greene

Chung On Tsou: see Crime Story

Chunghing Samlam: see Chungking Express

Chungking Express **
Hong Kong 1994 103m colour
ICA/Jet Tone (Chan Yi-Kan)
▣▣ ▤
original title: Chunghing Samlam

A film in two parts: in the first, a lonesome policeman, whose girlfriend has left him, becomes involved with a female drug dealer; in the second, another solitary cop is loved from afar by a woman working in a fast-food restaurant.

A mood of nostalgia-tinged melancholia pervades this enjoyable movie of young, urban workers caught in a web of disappointment and desire, but still hopelessly optimistic.

wd Wong Kar-Wai ph Christopher Doyle, Lau Wai-Keung m Frankie Chan, Roel A. Garcia ad William Chang ed William Chang, Hai Kit-Wai, Kwong Chi-Leung

☆ Brigitte Lin, Takeshi Kineshiro, Tony Leung, Faye Wong, Valerie Chow, 'Piggy' Chan

'A curious mix of maudlin male romanticism … and impish absurdity.' – Sheila Johnston, Independent

'Not only the zingiest visit to Heartbreak Hotel in many years but also one of the first films of the 90s to feel genuinely fresh and original.' – Tony Rayns, Sight and Sound

'It Will Make You Squirm.'
The Church (dubbed)
Italy 1991 98m colour
ADC/Cecchi Gori/Tiger/Reteitalia (Dario Argento)
▣▣ ▤
aka: La Chiesa

A group of worshippers are trapped in a cathedral where the new librarian has been possessed by the spirits of devil worshippers, massacred in medieval times and buried beneath the building.

Stylishly gruesome horror with a confused narrative, much influenced by the work of its producer and co-writer Dario Argento and likely to appeal to admirers of his work.

w Dario Argento, Franco Ferrini, Michele Soavi d Michele Soavi ph Renato Tafuri m Keith Emerson, The Goblins ad Antonello Geleng ed Franco Fraticelli

☆ Hugh Quarshie, Tomas Arana, Feodor Chaliapin, Barbara Cupisti, Antonella Vitale, Giovanni Lombardo Radice, Asia Argento

'Inventively gory deaths, lavish surreal set-pieces and lashings of religious hokum make this a treat which yields greater rewards on subsequent viewings.' – Sight and Sound

'Visually it's great, but don't bother trying to strain your brain figuring out the plot.' – Dark Side

Ciao Maschio: see Bye Bye Monkey

Cible émouvante: see Wild Target

'A story about how far we must travel to find the place where we belong.'
The Cider House Rules **
US 1999 131m DeLuxe 'Scope
Miramax/FilmColony (Richard N. Gladstein)
◌

A young man leaves the orphanage where he feels safe and needed to discover his destiny.

A leisurely drama, of a boy growing to manhood, that has an intensely nostalgic feel to it, so that even unpleasant moments have a warm glow to them; this is life seen through rose-coloured memories, given some touch of reality by its quality of acting

w John Irving novel John Irving d Lasse Hallstrom ph Oliver Stapleton m Rachel Portman pd David Gropman ed Lisa Zeno Churgin

☆ Tobey Maguire, Charlize Theron, Delroy Lindo, Paul Rudd, Michael Caine, Jane Alexander, Kathy Baker, Erykah Badu, Kieran Culkin, Kate Nelligan

'A touching, old-fashioned charmer that ultimately satisfies.' – David Rooney, Variety

'Beautifully enacted literary cinema.' – Angie Errigo, Empire

🏆 Michael Caine; John Irving
🏆 picture; Lasse Hallstrom; Lisa Zeno Churgin; Rachel Portman; David Gropman

Il cielo è sempre più blu: see Bits and Pieces

'Earth-shaking in its grandeur! A titanic canvas sprung to life!'
Cimarron *
US 1930 130m bw
RKO (Louis Sarecky)
▤

The life of an Oklahoma homesteader from 1890 to 1915.

Sprawling Western family saga; a big early talkie, it dates badly.

w Howard Estabrook novel Edna Ferber d Wesley Ruggles ph Edward Cronjager m Max Steiner ad Max Ree

☆ Richard Dix, Irene Dunne, Estelle Taylor, Nance O'Neil, William Collier Jnr, Roscoe Ates, George E. Stone, Stanley Fields, Edna May Oliver

'An elegant example of super film-making … big money feature for all classes.' – Variety

🏆 best picture; Howard Estabrook
🏆 Wesley Ruggles; Edward Cronjager; Richard Dix; Irene Dunne; Max Ree

Cimarron *
US 1960 147m Metrocolor Cinemascope
MGM (Edmund Grainger)

Flabby, relentlessly boring remake of the above.

w Arnold Schulman d Anthony Mann ph Robert L. Surtees m Franz Waxman ad George W. Davis, Addison Hehr

☆ Glenn Ford, Maria Schell, Anne Baxter, Lili Darvas, Russ Tamblyn, Henry Morgan, David Opatoshu, Charles McGraw, Aline MacMahon, Edgar Buchanan, Arthur O'Connell, Mercedes McCambridge, Vic Morrow, Robert Keith, Mary Wickes and also Royal Dano, Vladimir Sokoloff

🏆 art direction

The Cincinnati Kid **
US 1965 113m Metrocolor
MGM/Filmways (Martin Ransohoff, John Calley)
▣▣ ▤ ◌

In New Orleans in the late thirties, stud poker experts compete for supremacy.

This is to poker what The Hustler was to pool, a fascinating suspense study of experts at work; as before, the romantic asides let down the effectiveness of the others.

w Ring Lardner Jnr, Terry Southern novel Richard Jessup d Norman Jewison ph Philip Lathrop m Lalo Schifrin

☆ Steve McQueen, Edward G. Robinson, Karl Malden, Ann-Margret, Tuesday Weld, Joan Blondell, Rip Torn, Jack Weston, Cab Calloway, Jeff Corey

'I took out all the primaries. There are no reds, greens, whites or blues in the film outside of the red cards and the cockfight.' – Norman Jewison

Cinderella **
🏃 US 1950 75m Technicolor
Walt Disney
▣▣ ▤ ◌ ◌

The Perrault fairy tale embroidered with animal characters.

A feature cartoon rather short on inspiration, though with all Disney's solid virtues. The mice are lively and the villainous cat the best character.

d Wilfred Jackson, Hamilton Luske, Clyde Geronimi m Oliver Wallace, Paul J. Smith supervisor Ben Sharpsteen

☆ Featuring the voices of Ilene Woods, William Phipps, Eleanor Audley, Rhoda Williams, Lucille Bliss, Verna Felton

🏆 Oliver Wallace, Paul J. Smith; song 'Bibbidy Bobbidy Boo' (m/ly Mack David, Al Hoffman, Jerry Livingston)

Cinderella Jones
US 1946 89m bw
Warner (Alex Gottlieb)

To collect an inheritance, a girl must marry a brainy man.

Witless comedy for the easily pleased.

w Charles Hoffman story Philip Wylie d Busby Berkeley ph Sol Polito m Frederick Hollander

☆ Joan Leslie, Robert Alda, S. Z. Sakall, Edward Everett Horton, Julie Bishop, William Prince, Charles Dingle, Ruth Donnelly, Elisha Cook Jnr, Hobart Cavanaugh, Chester Clute

'A movie for every woman who thinks she can never fall in love again!'
Cinderella Liberty
US 1974 117m DeLuxe Panavision
TCF/Sanford (Mark Rydell)
▣▣

A sailor on shore leave picks up a prostitute and falls in love with her.

Assertively 'modern' yet glutinously sentimental love story in squalid settings. It presumably has an audience.

w Darryl Ponicsan novel Darryl Ponicsan d Mark Rydell ph Vilmos Zsigmond m John Williams

☆ James Caan, Marsha Mason, Eli Wallach, Kirk Calloway, Allyn Ann McLerie

'A sordid, messy affair which wants to jerk tears but just doesn't have the knack.' – New Yorker

🏆 John Williams; Marsha Mason; song 'You're So Nice To Be Around' (mJohn Williams, lyPaul Williams)

Cinderfella
US 1960 91m Technicolor
Paramount/Jerry Lewis
▣▣ ▤

Luxury pantomime featuring a male Cinderella.

Annoyingly lavish and empty star vehicle with precious little to laugh at: Lewis's own jokes are strung out to snapping point and no one else gets a look in.

wd Frank Tashlin ph Haskell Boggs m Walter Scharf

☆ Jerry Lewis, Ed Wynn, Judith Anderson, Anna Maria Alberghetti, Henry Silva, Robert Hutton, Count Basie

'A drought of comic inspiration, followed by a flood of mawkish whimsy, gradually reducing one's early misgivings to a degree which finally verges on revulsion.' – Peter John Dyer

Cinema Paradiso ****
Italy/France 1989 122m colour
Palace/Films Ariana/RAI TRE/Forum/Franco Cristaldi
▣▣ ▣▣ ▤ ◌ ◌ ◌
original title: Nuovo Cinema Paradiso

A film director remembers his early life and his boyhood friendship with the projectionist at his local cinema.

Nostalgic in its celebration of the cinema, beautifully detailed in its enjoyment of the rituals of small-town life wish, underneath it all, a toughness in its depiction of a child's growth to maturity.

wd Giuseppe Tornatore ph Blasco Giurato m Ennio Morricone, Andrea Morricone pd Andrea Crisanti ed Mario Morra

☆ Antonelli Attli, Enzo Cannavale, Isa Danieli, Leo Gullotta, Marco Leonardi, Pupella Maggio, Agnese Nano, Leopoldo Trieste, Salvatore Cascio, Jacques Perrin, Philippe Noiret

† A director's cut lasting 175m was released in 1994.

🏆 best foreign film
🏆 best foreign film; original screenplay; Philippe Noiret; Salvatore Cascio; Ennio and Andrea Morricone

Cinque Bambole per la Luna d'Agosto:
see Five Dolls for an August Moon

Le Cinquième Elément: see The Fifth Element

La Ciociara: see Two Women

The Circle
US

Somerset Maugham's brittle play contrasting noble breeding with vulgar riches was filmed by Frank Borzage as a Hollywood silent, in 1925 for MGM, with Eleanor Boardman, Creighton Hale and Alec B. Francis. In 1930 the same studio made it as a talkie under the title Strictly Unconventional, with Catherine Dale Owen, Tyrrell Davis and Lewis

Stone; directed by David Burton. Neither version really worked.

The Circle: see The Vicious Circle (1957)

Circle of Danger *
GB 1950 89m bw
Coronado/David Rose (Joan Harrison)

An American in England investigates the strange death some years earlier of his brother during a commando raid.

Individual scenes are well milked for suspense and dramatic emphasis, but the plot line has virtually no mystery and absolutely no danger. It all seems mildly reminiscent of several Hitchcock films.

w Philip MacDonald d Jacques Tourneur ph Oswald Morris m Robert Farnon

☆ Ray Milland, Patricia Roc, Marius Goring, Hugh Sinclair, Naunton Wayne, Marjorie Fielding, Edward Rigby, Colin Gordon, Dora Bryan

Circle of Deceit *
West Germany/France 1981 109m
Eastmancolor
Bioskop/Artemis/Hessischer Rundfunk/Argos (Eberhard Junkersdorf)
original title: Die Fälschung

A German journalist has a crisis of conscience while covering the war in Beirut.

Fashionable self-scrutiny based on a published 'faction'. As a film, quite engrossing and occasionally hair-raising.

w Volker Schlöndorff, Jean-Claude Carrière, Margarethe von Trotta, Kai Hermann novel Nicolas Born d Volker Schlöndorff ph Igor Luther m Maurice Jarre

☆ Bruno Ganz, Hanna Schygulla, Jerzy Skolimowski, Gila von Weitershausen

'Rarely can a fiction film about war have had such a vividly authentic background, with real corpses and real destruction lending a bleak chill never captured by staged reconstructions.' – Tom Milne, MFB

Circle of Deception
GB 1960 100m bw Cinemascope
TCF (T. H. Morahan)

An officer is parachuted into Germany with the intention that he should crack under interrogation and reveal false information.

Depressing World War II tall tale, with suspense sacrificed by flashback structure.

w Nigel Balchin, Robert Musel novel Alec Waugh d Jack Lee ph Gordon Dines m Clifton Parker

☆ Bradford Dillman, Harry Andrews, Suzy Parker, Robert Stephens, John Welsh, Paul Rogers, Duncan Lamont, Michael Ripper

Circle of Friends *
Ireland/US 1995 96m colour
Rank/Price/Lantana (Arlene Sellers, Alex Winitsky, Frank Price)
▣▣ ▤ ◌ ◌

Three young women from an Irish village go to Dublin University, where one falls in love with a handsome, rugby-playing medical student.

Pleasant, sugar-coated account of growing up, set in the 50s and much concerned with Catholic notions of sin; it is all neatly and glossily done, and the acting carries more conviction than might be expected from its conventional story.

w Andrew Davies novel Maeve Binchy d Pat O'Connor ph Ken MacMillan m Michael Kamen pd Jim Clay ed Jim Jympson

☆ Chris O'Donnell, Minnie Driver, Geraldine O'Rawe, Alan Cumming, Colin Firth, Ciaran Hinds, Saffron Burrows, Tony Doyle

'Sentimental, old-fashioned fare.' – Variety

Circle of Two
Canada 1980 105m colour
Film Consortium of Canada (Henk Van der Kolk)

A 60-year-old artist falls for a teenage student.

Dreary and uninteresting star drama which never really gets going.

w Thomas Hedley novel A Lesson in Love by Marie Terese Baird d Jules Dassin ph Lazlo George m Paul Hoffert

☆ Richard Burton, Tatum O'Neal, Nuala FitzGerald, Kate Reid, Robin Gammell, Patricia Collins

---

Circonstances Atténuantes *

France 1939 85m bw

CCFC

A retired magistrate becomes innocently involved with a gang of crooks.

Nimble farce, most skilfully acted.

w Jean-Pierre Feydeau *novel* Marcel Arnac d Jean Boyer

☆ Michel Simon, Arletty, Suzanne Dantes, Arnoux, Mila Parely

Circuitry Man

US 1990 93m Foto-Kem

IRS Media (Steven Reich, John Schouweiler)

■ ⌂

In subterranean Los Angeles in the near future, a woman and an android go on the run with a suitcase containing contraband computer chips.

Drear science-fiction flick that sticks close to standard thriller conventions; it takes place in no convincing reality, or fantasy for that matter. The cast content themselves with attitudinizing, which is understandable considering the clichés they have been hired to enunciate.

w Steven Lovy, Robert Lovy d Steven Lovy ph Jamie Thompson m Deborah Holland pd Robert Lovy ed Jonas Thaler

☆ Jim Metzler, Dana Wheeler-Nicholson, Barbara Alyn Woods, Lu Leonard, Andy Goldberg, Vernon Wells, Dennis Christopher, Paul Willson

† A sequel, *Plughead Rewired: Circuitry Man II*, followed in 1994, directed by Steven and Robert Lovy.

The Circus *

♔♔ US 1928 72m bw silent

(UA)

■ ■ ⌂ ◉

A tramp on the run from the police takes refuge in a circus and falls for an equestrienne.

Pathos often descends to bathos in this self-constructed star vehicle which has far too few laughs.

wd *Charles Chaplin* ph Rollie Totheroh, Jack Wilson, Mark Marlott

☆ Charles Chaplin, Merna Kennedy, Allan Garcia, Harry Crocker

♟ Special Award to Chaplin for acting, writing, directing and producing the film

Circus Boys *

Japan 1989 106m bw

ICA/Eizo Tanteisha/CBS Sony (Mituhisa Hida, Yoichi Sakurai)

■

original title: *Ni ju-seiki Shonen Dokuhon*

A boy grows up to become a circus clown before leaving to work as an itinerant pedlar and falling in love with a gangster's concubine.

Strange and wayward film with a powerful poetic quality.

wd Kaizo Hayashi ph Yuichi Nagata ad Takeo Kimura, Hidemitsu Yamazaki ed Osamu Tanaka

☆ Hiroshi Mikami, Moe Kamura, Xia Jian, Michiru Akiyoshi, Yuki Asayama, Sanshi Katsura, Haruko Wanibuchi

'It isn't very often you see a film that understands so well that the cinema should be a place with some magic in it as well as simple story-telling ability.' – *Derek Malcolm, Guardian*

Circus of Fear

GB 1966 83m Eastmancolor

Circus Films (Harry Alan Towers)

aka: *Psycho-Circus*

A circus performer is the mastermind behind a daring daylight robbery on Tower Bridge.

Efficient B-movie thriller with a few traces of wit and a better cast than might have been expected.

w Peter Welbeck (Harry Alan Towers) d John Moxey ph Ernest Steward m Johnny Douglas ad Frank White ed John Trumper

☆ Christopher Lee, Leo Genn, Maurice Kaufmann, Anthony Newlands, Heinz Drache, Klaus Kinski, Eddi Arent, Margaret Lee, Suzy Kendall, Cecil Parker, Victor Maddern

'One man's lust turns men into beasts, strips women of their souls!'

Circus of Horrors

GB 1960 91m Eastmancolor

Anglo Amalgamated/Lynx/Independent Artists (Norman Priggen)

■ ⌂

A plastic surgeon staffs a semi-derelict circus with criminals whose faces he has altered, and murders any who try to flee.

Stark horror comic; quite professionally made, but content-wise a crude concoction of sex and sadism.

w George Baxt d Sidney Hayers ph Douglas Slocombe m Franz Reizenstein, Muir Mathieson

☆ Anton Diffring, Erika Remberg, Yvonne Monlaur, Donald Pleasence, Jane Hylton, Kenneth Griffith, Conrad Phillips, Jack Gwillim

The Circus Queen Murder *

US 1933 63m bw

Columbia

Thatcher Colt solves murders in a travelling circus.

Reasonably slick second feature of its period.

w Jo Swerling *novel* Anthony Abbot d Roy William Neill

☆ Adolphe Menjou, Greta Nissen, Ruthelma Stevens, Dwight Frye, Donald Cook

Circus World

US 1964 138m Technicolor Super Technirama 70

Bronston/Midway (Samuel Bronston)

■ ⌂

GB title: *The Magnificent Showman*

An American circus owner tours Europe in search of his alcoholic ex-wife who left him when her lover fell to death from the trapeze.

Lethargic big-screen epic which exhausts its spectacle in the first hour and then settles down to a dreary will-daughter-guess-who-the-strange-lady-is plot, without even the plus of an exciting finale.

w Ben Hecht, Julian Halevy, James Edward Grant *story* Philip Yordan, Nicholas Ray d Henry Hathaway ph Jack Hildyard m Dimitri Tiomkin pd John DeCuir ed Dorothy Spencer

☆ John Wayne, *Rita Hayworth*, Claudia Cardinale, John Smith, Lloyd Nolan, Richard Conte, Wanda Rotha, Kay Walsh

'To sit through this film is something like holding an elephant on your lap for two hours and fifteen minutes.' – *Time*

The Cisco Kid

The Cisco Kid, a ruthless Mexican bandit originally created by O. Henry in a short story, was turned by Hollywood into a dashing wild Western Robin Hood in twenty-three sound features (following a few silent ones) and a long-running TV series. In most of them he was accompanied by his fat side-kick Pancho.

For Fox:

1929 In Old Arizona (Warner Baxter)

1931 The Cisco Kid (Baxter)

For Twentieth Century Fox:

1939 The Return of the Cisco Kid (Baxter), The Cisco Kid and the Lady (Cesar Romero: who played the role in all the remaining TCF movies).

1940 Viva Cisco Kid, Lucky Cisco Kid, The Gay Caballero

1941 Romance of the Rio Grande, Ride On, Vaquero

For Monogram:

1945 The Cisco Kid Returns (Duncan Renaldo), The Cisco Kid in Old New Mexico (Renaldo), South of the Rio Grande (Renaldo)

1946 The Gay Cavalier (Gilbert Roland), South of Monterey (Roland), Beauty and the Bandit (Roland)

1947 Riding the California Trail (Roland), Robin Hood of Monterey (Roland), King of the Bandits (Roland)

For United Artists (all with Renaldo):

1949 The Valiant Hombre, The Gay Amigo, The Daring Caballero, Satan's Cradle

1950 The Girl from San Lorenzo

† The 50s TV series starred Renaldo with Leo Carrillo.

Cisco Kid and The Lady

US 1939 73m bw

TCF (John Stone)

The Cisco Kid accidentally acquires, and sensibly disposes of, a baby and a gold mine.

Lively 'B' feature, full of action, humour and narrative twists.

w Frances Hyland *story* Stanley Rauh *character created by* William Sydney Porter (O. Henry) d Herbert I. Leeds ph Barney McGill md Samuel Kaylin ad Richard Day, Chester Gore ed Nick de Maggio

☆ Cesar Romero, Marjorie Weaver, Chris-Pin Martin, George Montgomery, Robert Barrat, Virginia Field, Harry Green, Ward Bond

Cisco Pike

US 1971 94m Eastmancolor

Columbia/Acrobat (Gerald Ayres)

A former pop group leader and drug pusher is blackmailed by a cop into selling marijuana.

Low-key, would-be realistic study of a section of life in 70s LA. Flashy, boring and almost plotless.

wd Bill L. Norton ph Vilis Lapenieks m Sonny Terry, Sir Douglas Quintet, Lee Montgomery, Kris Kristofferson pd Rosanna White ed Robert C. Jones

☆ Kris Kristofferson, Gene Hackman, Karen Black, Harry Dean Stanton, Viva, Roscoe Lee Browne

'A moody, melancholy little film whose strength lies in its evocation of the rootless, aimless, irresponsible life-style of the pop/drug culture.' – *Brenda Davies*

The Citadel: see *El Kalaa*

'Secrets of a doctor as told by a doctor!'

The Citadel **

GB 1938 113m bw

MGM (Victor Saville)

■

A young doctor has a hard time in the mining villages but is later swayed by the easy rewards of a Mayfair practice.

Solidly produced adaptation of a bestseller; the more recent deluge of doctors on television make it appear rather elementary, but many scenes work in a classical way. One of the first fruits of MGM's British studios which were closed by World War II.

w Elizabeth Hill, Ian Dalrymple, Emlyn Williams, Frank Wead *novel* A. J. Cronin d King Vidor ph Harry Stradling m Louis Levy ad Lazare Meerson, Alfred Junge ed Charles Frend

☆ *Robert Donat*, Rosalind Russell, Ralph Richardson, Emlyn Williams, Penelope Dudley Ward, Francis L. Sullivan, Rex Harrison

'General audience limited … strong for the Anglo market.' – *Variety*

'I think any doctor will agree that here is a medical picture with no Men in White hokum, no hysterical, incredible melodrama, but with an honest story, honestly told. And that's a rare picture.' – *Pare Lorentz*

'We are grateful that a worthy idea has been handled with intelligence and imagination, that Vidor has shown respect both for his talent and for the sensibilities of the audience.' – *Robert Stebbins*

'Numerous passages shine brilliantly with those deft touches that first brought Vidor to prominence.' – *Variety*

'The pace of Hollywood, the honest characterization of England's best.' – *New York Times*

† The parts played by Russell and Richardson were originally intended for Elizabeth Allan and Spencer Tracy.

♟ best picture; script; King Vidor; Robert Donat

Citizen Kane ****

US 1941 119m bw

RKO (Orson Welles)

■ ■ ⌂ ◉ ◉ ⌂

A newspaper tycoon dies, and a magazine reporter interviews his friends in an effort to discover the meaning of his last words.

A brilliant piece of Hollywood cinema using all the resources of the studio; despite lapses of characterization and gaps in the narrative, almost every shot and every line is utterly absorbing both as entertainment and as craft. See The Citizen Kane Book by Pauline Kael, and innumerable other writings.

w Herman J. Mankiewicz, Orson Welles d Orson Welles ph Gregg Toland m Bernard Herrmann ad Van Nest Polglase ed Robert Wise sp Vernon L. Walker

☆ *Orson Welles, Joseph Cotten, Dorothy Comingore, Everett Sloane, Ray Collins, Paul Stewart, Ruth Warrick, Erskine Sanford, Agnes Moorehead, Harry*

Shannon, George Coulouris, William Alland, Fortunio Bonanova

NEWSREEL: 'Then, last week, as it must to all men, death came to Charles Foster Kane.'

BERNSTEIN: 'Old age … it's the only disease you don't look forward to being cured of.'

THOMPSON: 'Mr Kane was a man who got everything he wanted, and then lost it. Maybe Rosebud was something he couldn't get, or something he lost. Anyway, I don't think it would have explained everything. I don't think any word can explain a man's life. No, I guess Rosebud is just a piece in a jigsaw puzzle … a missing piece.'

SUSAN: 'Forty-nine acres of nothing but scenery and statues. I'm lonesome.'

KANE: 'You're right, Mr Thatcher, I did lose a million dollars last year. I expect to lose a million dollars this year. I expect to lose a million dollars next year. You know, Mr Thatcher, at the rate of a million dollars a year, I'll have to close this place – in sixty years.'

KANE: 'I run a couple of newspapers. What do you do?'

BERNSTEIN: 'One day back in 1896 I was crossing over to Jersey on the ferry, and as we pulled out, there was another ferry pulling in, and on it there was a girl waiting to get off. A white dress she had on. She was carrying a white parasol. I only saw her for one second. She didn't see me at all, but I'll bet a month hasn't gone by since that I haven't thought of that girl.'

'On seeing it for the first time, one got a conviction that if the cinema could do that, it could do anything.' – *Penelope Houston*

'What may distinguish *Citizen Kane* most of all is its extracting the mythic from under the humdrum surface of the American experience.' – *John Simon, 1968*

'Probably the most exciting film that has come out of Hollywood for twenty-five years. I am not sure it isn't the most exciting film that has ever come out of anywhere.' – *C. A. Lejeune*

'At any rate Orson Welles has landed in the movies, with a splash and a loud yell.' – *James Shelley Hamilton*

'More fun than any great movie I can think of.' – *Pauline Kael, 1968*

'It is a fascinating picture, but because of its congestion of technical stunts, it fails to move us.' – *Egon Larsen*

'A quite good film which tries to run the psychological essay in harness with the detective thriller, and doesn't quite succeed.' – *James Agate*

♟ Herman J. Mankiewicz, Orson Welles (script)

♟ best picture; Orson Welles (as director); Gregg Toland; Bernard Herrmann; Orson Welles (as actor); art direction; Robert Wise

Citizens' Band: see *FM*

Citizens Band: see *Handle with Care (1977)*

La Città delle Donne: see *City of Women*

La Città Si Difende

Italy 1951 90m bw

Cines (Carlo Civallero)

A gang is recruited to rob a football stadium.

Moderate forerunner of The Good Die Young, The Killing, and a hundred other caper films.

w Federico Fellini, Tullio Pinelli, Luigi Comencini d Pietro Germi ph Carlo Montuori m Carlo Rustichelli

☆ Fausto Tozzi, Gina Lollobrigida, Patrizia Manca, Enzo Maggio

'As anonymous as the average B picture.' – *Gavin Lambert*

The City *

US 1939 32m bw

American Institute of Planners

A historical, social and psychoanalytical study of urban living.

Slightly guarded but convention-breaking documentary which though of its time still fascinates mildly by its style.

w Henwar Rodakiewicz *book* The Culture of Cities by Lewis Mumford d Ralph Steiner, Willard Van Dyke ph Ralph Steiner, Willard Van Dyke

City across the River

US 1949 91m bw

U-I (Howard Christie)

Brooklyn delinquents get involved in murder.

Semi-documentary throwback to the Dead End Kids, with location shooting influenced by The Naked City. Dull.

w Maxwell Shane, Dennis Cooper *novel* The Amboy Dukes *by* Irving Shulman d Maxwell Shane *ph* Maury Gertsman *m* Walter Scharf

☆ Stephen McNally, Barbara Whiting, Peter Fernandez, Al Ramsen, Joshua Shelley, Anthony Curtis

City after Midnight: see *That Woman Opposite*

The City and the Dogs ★★
Peru 1985 135m colour
Inca Films (Francisco J. Lombardi)
original title: La Ciudad Y Los Perros
With the aid of an incorruptible officer, a cadet tries to expose the organized brutality at a military academy.
A passionate allegory of military dictatorship.
w José Watanabe *novel* Mario Vargas Llosa d Francisco J. Lombardi *ph* Pili Flores Guerra *m* Enrique Iturriaga *ad* Lloyd Moore *ed* Gianfranco Annichini, Augusto Tamayo San Roman

☆ Pablo Serra, Gustavo Bueno, Luis Alvarez, Jan Manuel Ochva, Eduardo Adrianzen

City beneath the Sea
👪 US 1953 87m Technicolor
U-I (Albert J. Cohen)
Deep sea divers fall out over a sunken treasure.
Adequate double-biller with little to stir the interest.
w Jack Harvey, Ramon Romero d Budd Boetticher *ph* Charles P. Boyle *md* Joseph Gershenson

☆ Robert Ryan, Anthony Quinn, Mala Powers, Suzan Ball, George Mathews, Karel Stepanek, Lalo Rios

City beneath the Sea
US 1970 98m DeLuxe
Warner/Kent/Motion Pictures International (Irwin Allen)
GB theatrical release title: One Hour to Doomsday
An undersea city is threatened by an errant planetoid.
Futuristic adventure from a familiar stable; it will satisfy followers of Voyage to the Bottom of the Sea. *Originally made for TV.*
w John Meredyth Lucas d Irwin Allen *ph* Kenneth Peach *m* Richard La Salle *ad* Rodger E. Maus, Stan Jolley

☆ Stuart Whitman, Robert Wagner, Rosemary Forsyth, Robert Colbert, Burr de Benning, Richard Basehart, Joseph Cotten, James Darren, Sugar Ray Robinson, Paul Stewart

City for Conquest ★★
US 1940 106m bw
Warner (Anatole Litvak)
🖳 🔍
An East Side truck driver becomes a boxer but is blinded in a fight; meanwhile his composer brother gives up pop music for symphonies.
Phony but oddly persuasive melodrama set in a studio in New York and heavily influenced by the pretensions of the Group theatre.
w John Wexley *novel* Aben Kandel d Anatole Litvak *m* Sol Polito, James Wong Howe *m* Max Steiner

☆ James Cagney, Ann Sheridan, Frank Craven, Donald Crisp, *Arthur Kennedy*, Frank McHugh, George Tobias, Anthony Quinn, Jerome Cowan, Lee Patrick, Blanche Yurka, Thurston Hall

'Sometimes we wonder whether it wasn't really the Warner brothers who got New York from the Indians, so diligent and devoted have they been in feeling the great city's pulse, picturing its myriad facets and recording with deep compassion the passing life of its seething population.' – Bosley Crowther

City Girl
US 1930 77m bw
Fox
A city girl finds rural life has its own drama.
Rural drama distinguished by directorial touches.
w Berthold Viertel, Marion Orth *play* The Mud Turtle *by* Elliott Lester d F. W. Murnau *ph* Ernest Palmer *m* Arthur Kay

☆ Charles Farrell, Mary Duncan, David Torrence, Edith Yorke, Dawn O'Day (Anne Shirley)

City Girl
US 1937 60m bw
TCF
A slightly dumb waitress becomes a gangster's moll.
Fast-moving B picture which undoubtedly gave satisfaction.
w Frances Hyland, Robin Harris, Lester Ziffren d Alfred Werker

☆ Phyllis Brooks, Ricardo Cortez, Robert Wilcox, Douglas Fowley, Chick Chandler, Esther Muir

'It Started With A Shootout On A Rainswept Street And Ended In A Scandal That Shattered New York.'

City Hall ★★
US 1996 111m Technicolor
Rank/Castle Rock (Edward R. Pressman, Ken Lipper, Charles Mulvehill, Harold Becker)
🖳 🖳 🔍
Investigation of a triple shooting in Brooklyn, involving a cop and a gangster, reveals high-level corruption among city officials.
An involving political thriller that is less interested in the guilt of its participants and more concerned with examining the compromises and short-cuts that are necessary to run a big city, and the dangers they involve.
w Ken Lipper, Paul Schrader, Nicholas Pileggi, Bo Goldman d Harold Becker *ph* Michael Seresin *m* Jerry Goldsmith *pd* Jane Musky *ed* Robert C. Jones, David Bretherton

☆ Al Pacino, John Cusack, Bridget Fonda, Danny Aiello, Martin Landau, David Paymer, Tony Franciosa, Lindsay Duncan

'A film that aims to tell the dark truth about a modern metropolis yet doesn't stint on fun.' – Variety

'If the message is ho-hum, so is the plot of this talky, convoluted, predictable tale. Despite the best efforts of an impressive cast, this wan thriller has virtually no thrills at all.' – Stephen Farber, Movieline

† Frank Pierson worked uncredited on the screenplay. Ken Lipper was deputy mayor of New York under Ed Koch.

City Heat
US 1984 97m Technicolor
Warner/Malpaso/Deliverance (Fritz Manes)
🖳 🖳 🔍
In the early thirties, a private eye's partner is bumped off, and he teams against the baddies with an old cop friend.
A tedious teaming for two tired stars who seem to imagine that all they have to do is show up.
w Sam O. Brown (Blake Edwards), Joseph C. Stinson d Richard Benjamin *ph* Nick McLean *m* Lennie Niehaus *pd* Edward Carfagno

☆ Clint Eastwood, Burt Reynolds, Jane Alexander, Madeline Kahn, Rip Torn, Irene Cara, Richard Roundtree, Tony Lo Bianco

'It evaporates from the mind instantly upon its conclusion.' – Variety

The City Is Dark: see *Crime Wave*

The City Jungle: see *The Young Philadelphians*

City Lights ★★★
👪 US 1931 87m bw silent (with music and effects)
UA/Charles Chaplin
🖳 🖳 🔍 🔍
A tramp befriends a millionaire and falls in love with a blind girl.
Sentimental comedy with several delightful sequences in Chaplin's best manner.
ph Rollie Totheroh *md* Alfred Newman *wd/m* Charles Chaplin

☆ Charles Chaplin, Virginia Cherrill, Florence Lee, Harry Myers

'Chaplin has another good picture, but it gives indications of being short-winded, and may tire fast after a bombastic initial seven days … he has sacrificed speed to pathos, and plenty of it.' – Variety

'Even while laughing, one is aware of a faint and uneasy feeling that Chaplin has been pondering with more than a bit of solemnity on conventional story values, and it has led him further than ever into the realms of what is often called pathetic.' – National Board of Review

'She Didn't Believe In Angels Until She Fell In Love With One.'

City of Angels
US/Germany 1998 117m Technicolor Panavision
Warner/Regency/Atlas (Charles Roven, Dawn Steel)
🖳 🖳 🔍 🔍
An angel, who watches over Los Angeles, decides to become human after he falls in love with a heart surgeon.
Slick romantic comedy with ambitions beyond its reach; it settles, finally, for heavy sentimentality.
w Dana Stevens d Brad Silberling *ph* John Seale *m* Gabriel Yared *pd* Lilly Kilvert *ed* Lynzee Klingman *sp* Sony Picture Imageworks *film* Wings of Desire *by* Wim Wenders

☆ Nicolas Cage, Meg Ryan, Andre Braugher, Dennis Franz, Colm Feore, Robin Bartlett, Joanna Merlin, Sarah Dampf

'The film is glossy and soft, and has none of the intelligence or bitter humour of Wenders' film.' – Gaby Wood, Guardian

City of Bad Men ★
US 1953 82m Technicolor
TCF (Leonard Goldstein)
In Carson City during the Corbett/Fitzsimmons boxing match, outlaws plan to rob the arena of its receipts.
Slightly unusual Western suspenser with generally accomplished handling.
w George W. George, George Slavin d Harmon Jones *ph* Charles G. Clarke *md* Lionel Newman

☆ Dale Robertson, Jeanne Crain, Richard Boone, Lloyd Bridges, Carl Betz, Carole Mathews, Whitfield Connor

City of Chance ★
US 1939 57m bw
Sol M. Wurtzel/TCF
A girl reporter crusades against gangster gamblers.
Smart little second feature with no time to be boring.
w John Larkin, Barry Trivers d Ricardo Cortez

☆ Lynn Bari, C. Aubrey Smith, Donald Woods, Amanda Duff, June Gale, Richard Lane

'A half crazed man in a terror crazed town!'

City of Fear
US 1958 81m bw
Columbia/Orbit (Leon Chooluck)
🔍
A convict escapes with a canister of radioactive cobalt, which he believes to be heroin. After terrifying the city, he finally dies of exposure to it.
Rough-edged but occasionally gripping minor thriller from an independent company.
w Steven Ritch, Robert Dillon d Irving Lerner *ph* Lucien Ballard *m* Jerry Goldsmith

☆ Vince Edwards, John Archer, Patricia Blair, Steven Ritch, Lyle Talbot

City of Gold ★★
Canada 1957 23m bw
National Film Board of Canada
The story of Dawson City, capital of the Klondike in 1897–8, is told by an accumulation of details from still photographs.
A film with much to answer for, being the first documentary exclusively using the rostrum camera, a technique later adopted extensively by television. The subject matter is fascinating.
w and narrated by Pierre Berton *d/ph* Colin Low, Wolf Koenig

City of Hope ★★★
US 1991 130m DuArt Panavision
Mainline/Esperanza
🖳 🖳 🔍 🔍
Corruption and crime in Hudson City, New Jersey touches the lives of locals, from building contractors and petty thieves to the mayor.
Complex and engrossing, with a narrative style that brings to busy life a whole community.
wd John Sayles *ph* Robert Richardson *m* Mason Daring *pd* Dan Bishop, Dianna Freas *ed* John Sayles

☆ Vincent Spano, Joe Morton, Tony Lo Bianco, Barbara Williams, Stephen Mendillo, Chris Cooper, Charlie Yanko, Jace Alexander, Todd Graff, Scott Tiler, John Sayles, Frankie Faison, Gloria Foster, Tom Wright

'A major film, suggesting that Sayles might become as significant a film-maker for the 90s as Altman was for the 70s.' – Kim Newman, Sight and Sound

'Epic, masterly, urgent, adult and unforgettable. Put simply – which is grossly unfair to its complexity – it is Bonfire of the Vanities without the vanities.' – Alexander Walker, London Evening Standard

'It plays as if it were still on the drawing board.' – Michael Sragow, New Yorker

'Wanting a man dead can be reason enough to live.'

City of Industry ★
US 1996 97m DeLuxe
Largo (Evzen Kolar, Ken Solarz)
🖳 🖳 🔍 🔍
The surviving member of a gang of jewel robbers hunts down the person who double-crossed his friends and escaped with the loot.
Forceful, violent revenge thriller; the narrative is predictable, but the action is directed in an appropriately hard-hitting style, and Keitel – 'I'm my own police' – brings an angry intensity to his role as the implacable and indestructible avenger.
w Ken Solarz d John Irvin *ph* Thomas Burstyn *m* Stephen Endelman *pd* Michael Novotny *ed* Mark Conte

☆ Harvey Keitel, Stephen Dorff, Timothy Hutton, Famke Janssen, Wade Dominguez, Michael Jai White, Elliott Gould (uncredited)

'In its detached way, the film seems to be trying to get at the quintessence of revenge movies, free of all superfluity.' – Rob White, Sight and Sound

'He was a man who couldn't care less … until he met a man who couldn't care more.'

City of Joy ★
GB/France 1992 135m Eastmancolor
Warner/Lightmotive/Pricel (Jake Eberts, Roland Joffé)
🖳 🖳 🔍 🔍
In Calcutta an American doctor becomes involved in a clinic for the poor and helps them in their struggle against local gangsters.
Well-meaning movie that tends to talk about, rather than dramatize, its theme of the need for commitment.
w Mark Medoff *book* Dominic LaPierre d Roland Joffé *ph* Peter Biziou *m* Ennio Morricone *pd* Roy Walker *ed* Gerry Hambling

☆ Patrick Swayze, Pauline Collins, Om Puri, Shabana Azmi, Art Malik, Ayesha Dharker, Santu Chowdhury, Imran Badsah Khan

'Joffé's noble attempt to portray the tenacity and strength of the human spirit under the most trying conditions comes off as curiously ineffectual due to predictable plotting and character evolution.' – Variety

'Hopelessly fraudulent, with an uplifting finale that could make a strong man heave.' – Stephen Farber, Movieline

City of Lost Children ★
France 1995 111m colour Technovision
Entertainment/Lumiere/Canal Plus/France 3 (Claudie Ossard)
🖳 🖳 🔍 🔍
original title: La Cité des Enfants Perdus
A circus strongman goes in search of his adopted child, kidnapped, like many others, by a madman who lives in mid-ocean and hopes to steal the children's dreams to make up for the loss of his own.
A bizarre, hyperactive fantasy that yields many incidental pleasures, although coherence is not among them.
w Gilles Adrien, Jean-Pierre Jeunet, Marc Caro d Jean-Pierre Jeunet, Marc Caro *ph* Darius Khondji *m* Angelo Badalamenti *ad* Marc Caro *ed* Hervé Schneid

☆ Ron Perlman, Daniel Emilfork, Judith Vittet, Dominique Pinon, Jean-Claude Dreyfus, Genevieve Brunet, Odile Mallet, Ticky Holgado, Jean-Louis Trintignant

'The film's obscure plot, its vast assemblage of weird characters and its refusal to centre any of them securely in the emotions make for a peculiarly imperfect general effect.' – Derek Malcolm, Guardian

A City of Sadness: see *Beiqing Chengshi*

City of Silent Men
US 1942 64m bw
PRC (Dixon R. Harwin)
Two ex-convicts finally get work but are hounded by a newspaper publisher.
Decent second feature, a cut above the average for its source.

w Joseph Hoffman, Robert E. Kent d William Nigh

☆ Frank Albertson, June Lang, Jan Wiley, Richard Clarke

City of the Dead *
GB 1960 78m bw
Vulcan (Donald Taylor)
US title: Horror Hotel

In Massachusetts, a woman burned as a witch 250 years ago is still 'alive', running a local hotel and luring unwary strangers into becoming sacrificial victims.

A deadly first half gives way to splendid cinematic terror when the scene shifts to the village by night, all dry ice and limpid fog, and the heroine becomes a human sacrifice. A superior horror comic.

w George Baxt story Milton Subotsky d John Moxey ph Desmond Dickinson m Douglas Gamley, Ken Jones ad John Blezard

☆ Patricia Jessel, Betta St John, Christopher Lee, Dennis Lotis, Valentine Dyall, Venetia Stevenson, Norman MacOwan, Fred Johnson

'From The Bowels Of The Dead They Came To Collect The Living...'

City of the Living Dead (dubbed)
Italy 1980 93m colour
Dania/Medusa/National Cinematografia (Giovanni Masini)

original title: *Paura nella Città dei Morti Viventi*
aka: *Gates of Hell; Twilight of The Dead; The Fear*

In the Massachusetts town of Dunwich a priest hangs himself and opens a gateway to hell, through which stagger the living dead.

A slow-moving horror with little narrative and a great deal of gore. It was supposedly inspired by H. P. Lovecraft, although it bears little resemblance to his stories.

w Lucio Fulci, Dardano Sacchetti d Lucio Fulci ph Sergio Salvati m Fabio Frizzi pd Massimo Antonello Geleng ed Vincenzo Tomassi

☆ Christopher George, Katriona MacColl, Carlo de Mejo, Antonella Interlenghi, Giovanni Lombardo Radice, Daniela Doria, Janet Agren
'The ending is somewhat incomprehensible and acting and dialogue as usual leave a good deal to be desired. However, one doesn't really look to the "fantastique" for that kind of thing.' – *Julian Petley, Films and Filming*

† The film was cut to 92m on its British cinema release in 1982 and to 86m for its video release, removing the goriest episodes, including a youth having an electric drill pushed through his head, and making the narrative, like a few of its characters, somewhat disjointed.

City of Women *
Italy-France 1980 140m Eastmancolor
Opera Film-Gaumont (Renzo Rossellini)

original title: *La Città delle Donne*

A businessman finds himself trapped and threatened by women *en masse.*

Often leaden but sometimes spectacular fantasy in which the director spews out his views of the war between men and women. Fascinating in patches, but generally indigestible.

w Federico Fellini, Bernardino Zapponi d Federico Fellini ph Giuseppe Rotunno m Luis Bacalov

☆ Marcello Mastroianni, Anna Prucnal, Bernice Stegers, Ettore Manni, Donatella Damiani
'Another visual tour de force in an elaborate dream framework; narrative thin, overlong, and finally overweight.' – *Variety*

City on Fire
Canada/US 1979 106m colour
Rank/Astral Bellevue/Pathé/Sandy Howard/Harold Greenberg (Claude Héroux)

A slum fire threatens an entire city.
Shoddy disaster movie which does its cast no favour.
w Jack Hill, David P. Lewis, Celine La Frenière d Alvin Rakoff ph René Verzier m William and Matthew Macauley pd William McCrow ed Jean-Pol Passer, Jacques Clairoux sp Cliff Wenger, Carol Lynn

☆ Barry Newman, Susan Clark, Shelley Winters, Henry Fonda, Leslie Nielsen, James Franciscus, Ava Gardner

City on Fire *
Hong Kong 1987 101m colour
Cinema City (Ringo Lam)

An undercover cop reluctantly replaces a murdered colleague and infiltrates a ruthless gang planning a big jewel robbery.

Brutal action thriller that was one of the inspirations for Quentin Tarantino's Reservoir Dogs, though it concerns loyalty and rivalry between an elderly inspector and a brash new cop as much as dissension between gangsters.

w Tommy Sham story Ringo Lam d Ringo Lam ph Andrew Lau m Teddy Robin, Kwan ad Luk Tze Fung ed Wong Ming Lam

☆ Chow Yun-Fat, Sun Yeuh, Lee Sau Yin, Carrie Ng, Roy Cheung, Danny

'Three urban hombres heading west, seeking adventure, craving excitement ... and longing for room service.'

City Slickers ***
US 1991 114m CFI color
First Independent/Castle Rock/Nelson/Face (Irby Smith)

Three friends, all facing midlife crises, decide to spend their vacation on a cattle drive.

A witty and engaging comedy for the most part, with some affectionate parodies of moments from classic Westerns.

w Lowell Ganz, Babaloo Mandel d Ron Underwood ph Dean Semler m Marc Shaiman, Hummie Mann ed Lawrence G. Paull ed O. Nicholas Brown

☆ Billy Crystal, Daniel Stern, Bruno Kirby, Patricia Wettig, Helen Slater, Jack Palance, Josh Mostel, David Paymer, Noble Willingham
'A deft blend of wry humour and warmth (albeit with a little too much thirty-something-esque angst for its own good).' – *Variety*

⚭ Jack Palance

City Slickers II: The Legend of Curly's Gold
US 1994 116m Technicolor Panavision
Columbia TriStar/Face/Castle Rock (Billy Crystal)

Three city friends head west in search of treasure buried by a dead cowboy, helped and hindered by his twin brother.

Disappointing sequel that settles for tired comedy routines and slack jokes about old movies.

w Billy Crystal, Lowell Ganz, Babaloo Mandel d Paul Weiland ph Adrian Biddle, Craig Haagensen m Marc Shaiman pd Stephen J. Lineweaver ed William Anderson, Armen Minasian

☆ Billy Crystal, Daniel Stern, Jon Lovitz, Jack Palance, Patricia Wettig, Bill McKinney, Pruitt Taylor Vince, Beth Grant, Noble Willingham
'A sure-shootin' entertainment that shouldn't have much trouble rounding up an audience for the high jinks on the range.' – *Variety*
'A charmless, redundant sequel that replaces greed for character development and skimps on the laughs. Dull, dull, dull.' – *Movie Collector*

'Love and courage pitted against a ruthless hate!'

City Streets **
US 1931 86m bw
Paramount (Rouben Mamoulian)

A gangster's daughter is sent to jail for a murder she did not commit, and on release narrowly escapes being 'taken for a ride'.

Tense, dated gangland melodrama of primary interest because of its director's very cinematic treatment.

w Max Marcin, Oliver H. P. Garrett, Dashiell Hammett story Ladies of the Mob by Ernest Booth d Rouben Mamoulian ph Lee Garmes

☆ Sylvia Sidney, Gary Cooper, Paul Lukas, Guy Kibbee, William (Stage) Boyd, Stanley Fields, Wynne Gibson
'So many brilliant touches that anyone who sees it will have to predict for Mamoulian a brilliant career.' – *Film Spectator*
'Too much attempt to artify hurts though the sophisticated treatment and elegant settings will help.' – *Variety*
'A love story in a gangster setting which got carried away into so much fancy expressionism and symbolism that it seems stylized out of all relationship to the actual world.' – *Pauline Kael, 70s*

City that Never Sleeps
US 1953 90m bw
Republic (John H. Auer)

The work of the Chicago police force during one night.

Adequate minor semi-documentary police yarn.

w Steve Fisher d John H. Auer ph John I. Russell m R. Dale Butts

☆ Gig Young, Mala Powers, William Talman, Edward Arnold, Chill Wills, Paula Raymond, Marie Windsor

'They dared the most romantic journey that has ever challenged the imagination!'

City under the Sea
GB 1965 84m Eastmancolor
Colorscope
Bruton/AIP (Daniel Haller)

US title: *War Gods of the Deep*

An American heiress in Cornwall meets Victorian smugglers who have lived a hundred years under the sea in Lyonesse.

Childlike, unpersuasive nonsense which wastes some good talent.

w Charles Bennett, Louis M. Heyward d Jacques Tourneur ph Stephen Dade m Stanley Black

☆ Vincent Price, David Tomlinson, Susan Hart, Tab Hunter, Henry Oscar, John Le Mesurier

City War
Hong Kong 1988 93m colour
Cinema City (Catherine Lau)

A drug dealer who gets out of jail after serving a 10-year sentence vows to kill the bad-tempered cop who put him away.

Violent, efficient thriller that also charts changes in the local landscape, with cops playing by the rules, or suffering the consequences, and gangsters going legitimate.

w Tung Lo, Leung Wai Ting, Chung Kai-Cheong d Sun Chung ph Li Hsin Yeh m Michael Lai ad Jason Mok, Eric Lam ed Wong Ming Lam

☆ Chow Yun-Fat, Ti Lung, Tien Niu, Chui Siu Kwung, Mary Hon, Michael Chow, Teresa Carpio

City without Men
US 1943 75m bw
Columbia

A boarding house near a prison is filled with women awaiting the parole of their menfolk.

Stereotyped programmer.

w W. L. River, George Sklar, Donald Davis d Sidney Salkow

☆ Linda Darnell, Michael Duane, Sara Allgood, Edgar Buchanan, Glenda Farrell, Leslie Brooks, Margaret Hamilton, Sheldon Leonard

A City's Child
Australia 1971 80m Eastmancolor
Pleasant Pastures/Brian Kavanagh

A reclusive woman, who becomes obsessed with dolls after her mother's death, takes as a lover a young man who may not exist.

A daft excursion into experimental cinema which fails to hold the attention.

w Don Battye story Brian Kavanagh d Brian Kavanagh ph Bruce McNaughton m Peter Pinne ad Trevor Ling ed Brian Kavanagh

☆ Monica Maughan, Sean Scully, Moira Carleton, Vivean Gray, Marguerite Lofthouse

The City's Edge
Australia 1985 86m colour
Eastcaps (Pom Oliver, Errol Sullivan)

A troubled man takes a room in a Bondi boarding house and finds others worse off than himself.

Dreary mini-dramas, somewhat arbitrarily linked and without a shred of hope in sight for anybody.

w Robert J. Merritt, Ken Quinnell novel W. A. Harbinson d Ken Quinnell

☆ Hugo Weaving, Tommy Lewis, Shirley Cameron, Mark Lee, Ralph Cotterill

La Ciudad Y Los Perros: see The City And The Dogs

A Civil Action **
US 1998 112m DeLuxe
Buena Vista/Paramount/Touchstone (Scott Rudin, Robert Redford, Rachel Pfeffer)

A successful lawyer runs into difficulties when he sets out to prove that the dumping of toxic waste by a chemical company has caused the death of several children.

Engrossing, muted drama, taken from a true story, that is as much concerned with the cost of the awakening of an individual's social conscience as the case itself.

wd Steven Zaillian book Jonathan Harr ph Conrad L. Hall m Danny Elfman pd David Gropman ed Wayne Wahrman

☆ John Travolta, Robert Duvall, Tony Shalhoub, William H. Macy, Zeljko Ivanbeck, Bruce Norris, John Lithgow, Kathleen Quinlan, Peter Jacobson, Sydney Pollack
'A solid and intelligent legal thriller that may be too complex in its issues, and too low-key and unexciting in its style, for today's market demands.' – *Emanuel Levy, Variety*

⚭ Robert Duvall; Conrad L. Hall

Civilization ***
US 1916 68m bw silent
Triangle

A mythical country starts war, but one of the principals has a vision of Christ on the battlefields and the king is persuaded to sign a peace treaty.

Surprisingly impressive parable showing this early director at his best; intended as a pacifist tract in the middle of World War I.

w C. Gardner Sullivan d Thomas Ince ph Irvin Willat

☆ Enid Markey, Howard Hickman, J. Barney Sherry

Claire Dolan *
France/US 1998 95m DuArt
ICA/MK2/Serene (Ann Ruark)

An introverted Irish prostitute in New York tries to start a new life.

A claustrophobic film about repressed emotions; its lack of overt passion and its restrained approach will deter many, but there are rewards for those who persevere with its enigmatic style.

wd Lodge Kerrigan ph Teodoro Maniaci m Ahrin Mishan, Simon Fisher Turner pd Sharon Lomofsky ed Kristina Boden

☆ Katrin Cartlidge, Vincent D'Onofrio, Colm Meaney, John Doman, Maryanne Plunkett, Miranda Stuart-Rhyne, Kate Skinner, David Little, Lola Pashalinski, Jim Frangione, Ed Hodson
'Of possible appeal only to the most intellectual critics and viewers, some of whom will be very taken with the film's cinematic discipline, this will fall in the watching-paint-dry category even for specialized audiences.' – *Todd McCarthy, Variety*

Claire of the Moon
US 1992 107m Foto-Kem
Demi-Monde (Pamela S. Kuri)

At a women writers' retreat, an untidy, promiscuous heterosexual novelist finds herself sharing an apartment with an introverted lesbian sexual behaviourist.

Humourless, slow-moving romance, given over to psycho-babble and caricature.

wd Nicole Conn ph Randolph Sellars m Michael Allen Harrison ed Michael Solinger

☆ Trisha Todd, Karen Trumbo, Faith McDevitt, Caren Graham, Sheila Dickinson
'A talky drama that plays like a lesbian version of The Odd Couple.' – *Variety*

Claire's Knee ***
France 1970 106m Eastmancolor
Gala/Les Films du Losange (Pierre Cottrell)

original title: *Genou de Claire*

A 35-year-old diplomat who is about to be married confides to a female friend that he is attracted to a 16-year-old girl and her 17-year-old half-sister.

Witty and perceptive conversation piece, probably the best of Rohmer's explorations of the ambiguities of love and desire.

wd Eric Rohmer ph Nestor Almendros ed Cécile Decugis

◎ Digital Video Disc Region 2 | ◉ Digital Video Disc Region 1 | ♫ Soundtrack released on compact disc | ☆ Cast in approximate order of importance | † Points of interest | ♫ Notable songs | ⚭ Academy Award | ⚭ Academy Award nomination | ♔ BAFTA

☆ Jean-Claude Brialy, Aurora Cornu, Béatrice Romand, Laurence de Monaghan, Michèle Montel, Gérard Falconetti, Fabrice Luchini
'Rohmer's quiet, complacent movie-novel game is pleasing.' – *Pauline Kael, New Yorker*

'Hexed By The Evil Eye. Ruled By A Female Svengali.'
The Clairvoyant *
GB   1934   80m   bw
Gainsborough (Michael Balcon)
🖿

A fraudulent mindreader predicts a disaster which comes true.
Effective minor suspenser on predictable but enjoyable lines.
w Charles Bennett, Bryan Edgar Wallace, Robert Edmunds *novel* Ernst Lothar d Maurice Elvey ph Glen MacWilliams ad Alfred Junge
☆ Claude Rains, Fay Wray, Jane Baxter, Mary Clare, Athole Stewart, Ben Field, Felix Aylmer, Donald Calthrop

Clambake
US   1967   98m   Technicolor   Techniscope
UA/Rhodes (Laven-Gardner-Levy)
🖿🖿 🖿

The son of an oil millionaire sets out to see life.
Painless, forgettable star vehicle.
w Arthur Browne Jnr d Arthur H. Nadel ph William Margulies m Jeff Alexander
☆ Elvis Presley, Shelley Fabares, Bill Bixby, James Gregory, Will Hutchins, Gary Merrill

Clan of the Cave Bear
US   1985   98m   Technicolor   Technovision
Warner/PSO/Guber-Peters/Jozak-Decade/Jonesfilm
(Gerald I. Isenberg)
🖿 🖚 🖿 🎧

In Neanderthal days, a blonde outcast girl is adopted by a swarthy tribe who think her ugly.
Comic-strip prehistory: better revive One Million BC or even the 1912 Griffith epic Man's Genesis.
w John Sayles *novel* Jean M. Auel d Michael Chapman ph Jan de Bont m Alan Silvestri pd Anthony Masters
☆ Daryl Hannah, Pamela Reed, James Remar, Thomas G. Waites
𝔔 make-up (Michael G. Westmore, Michele Burke)

Clancy Street Boys
US   1943   66m   bw
Pathé/Monogram/Banner (Sam Katzman, Jack Dietz)
Muggs has to produce five brothers and a sister when a rich relation comes to call.
Ponderous comic outing for the East Side Kids, though it comes briefly to life when Huntz Hall pretends to be a girl.
w Harvey Gates d William Beaudine ph Mack Stengler md Edward Kay ad Dave Milton ed Carl Pierson
☆ Leo Gorcey, Huntz Hall, Bobby Jordan, Noah Beery, Lita Ward, Bennie Bartlett, Rick Vallin, Billy Benedict

Clarence the Cross-Eyed Lion
👭 US   1965   98m   Metrocolor
MGM (Leonard Kaufman)
🖿

Adventures of animal farmers in Africa.
Amiable theatrical 'pilot' for the Daktari TV series.
w Alan Caillou, Marshall Thompson, Art Arthur d Andrew Marton ph Lamar Boren
☆ Marshall Thompson, Betsy Drake, Richard Haydn, Cheryl Miller

'Livin' in my house! Lovin' another man! Is that what you call honest? That's just givin' it a nice name!'
Clash by Night *
US   1952   105m   bw
RKO (Harriet Parsons) (A Wald-Krasna Production)
🖿 🖿 🖚

In a northern fishing village, jealousy and near-tragedy are occasioned by the return home of a hardened girl from the big city.
Absurdly overblown melodrama of the Anna Christie school, burdened with significance and doggedly acted by a remarkable cast.
w Alfred Hayes *play* Clifford Odets d Fritz Lang ph Nicholas Musuraca m Roy Webb
☆ Barbara Stanwyck, Paul Douglas, Robert Ryan, Marilyn Monroe, J. Carrol Naish, Keith Andes
'When Stanwyck snarls into a pub and belts down a straight shot, we think we're watching a

remake of *Anna Christie*; when she is shyly and ineptly courted by Douglas we think it's a remake of *Min and Bill*; a sub-plot involving Monroe and Andes plays like *Gidget Faces an Identity Crisis*.' – *Kit Parker catalogue*

Clash of the Titans
👭   GB   1981   118m   Metrocolor   Dynarama
MGM/Charles H. Schneer, Ray Harryhausen
🖿🖿 🖿 🖚

Perseus sets out to win Andromeda despite the impossible obstacles set for him by Thetis, which include a number of mythical monsters.
Star-packed but feebly imagined mythological spectacular, further hampered by gloomy photography which is presumably required to offset the jerkiness of the monsters. A very few moments provide the right kind of elation.
w Beverley Cross d Desmond Davis ph Ted Moore m Laurence Rosenthal pd Frank White sp Ray Harryhausen
☆ Laurence Olivier, Claire Bloom, Maggie Smith, Ursula Andress, Jack Gwillim, Harry Hamlin, Judi Bowker, Burgess Meredith, Siân Phillips, Flora Robson, Freda Jackson, Donald Houston
'There's a real possibility some audiences will be turned to stone before Medusa even appears.' – *Geoff Brown, MFB*
'Unspeakable dialogue, muddy photography and a motley, lacklustre cast.' – *Sight and Sound*

'The good news is, Jonathan's having his first affair. The bad news is, she's his roommate's mother!'
Class
US   1983   98m   Astrocolor
Orion/Martin Ransohoff
🖿🖿 🖿 🖚

A shy student has an affair with an older woman who turns out to be his best friend's mother.
Ghastly travesty of The Graduate which aspires to every kind of sophistication it can think of but ends nowhere.
w Jim Kouf, David Greenwalt d Lewis John Carlino ph Ric Waite m Elmer Bernstein ad Jack Poplin
☆ Jacqueline Bisset, Cliff Robertson, Rob Lowe, Andrew McCarthy, Stuart Margolin, John Cusack
'It is not often that one comes across a film of such muddled aspirations and widely divergent achievements.' – *Nick Roddick, MFB*

Class Act
US   1992   98m   Technicolor
Warner/Wizan Black/Gordy de Passe (Todd Black, Maynell Thomas)
🖿🖿 🖿 🖚 🎧

Two high-school students – one an intellectual, the other a delinquent – swop identities.
Dim-witted teen comedy.
w John Semper, Cynthia Friedlob *story* Michael Swerdlick, Wayne Rice, Richard Brenne d Randall Miller ph Francis Kenny m Vassal Benford ph David L. Snyder ed John F. Burnett
☆ Christopher Reid, Christopher Martin, Karyn Parsons, Alysia Rogers, Meshach Taylor, Doug E. Doug, Lamont Johnson

'Nothing Personal. It's Just Father vs Daughter In The Fight Of Their Lives.'
Class Action
US   1990   109m   colour
TCF/Interscope (Ted Field, Scott Kroopf, Robert W. Cort)
🖿🖿 🖿 🖚 🎧

A father and a daughter, both lawyers, find themselves on opposing sides in the courtroom.
Moderately engrossing, though predictable, drama.
w Carolyn Shelby, Christopher Ames, Samantha Shad d Michael Apted ph Conrad L. Hall m James Horner pd Todd Hallowell ed Ian Crafford
☆ Gene Hackman, Mary Elizabeth Mastrantonio, Colin Friels, Joanna Merlin, Larry Fishburne, Donald Moffat, Jan Rubes, Matt Clark
'A remarkably well-made and well-mannered film.' – *Sight and Sound*
'Pic's parameters may be worn, but Apted's keen focus on its emotional core helps it transcend the everyday.' – *Variety*

Class of 1999
US   1989   93m   colour
Original Pictures (Mark L. Lester)
🖿🖿 🖿

Three android teachers, hired to bring discipline to a lawless high school, go haywire.
A sort of robot Blackboard Jungle, aimed at teenage audiences in love with violence.
w C. Courtney Joyner *story* Mark L. Lester d Mark L. Lester ph Mark Irwin m Michael Hoenig pd Steven Legler ed Scott Conrad
☆ Bradley Gregg, Traci Lin, John P. Ryan, Pam Grier, Patrick Kilpatrick, Joshua Miller, Stacy Keach, Malcolm McDowell

Class of '44
US   1973   95m   Technicolor   Panavision
Warner (Paul Bogart)

Sex problems of college students during World War II.
Thin sequel to Summer of '42, nostalgic to Americans over forty but not much of a trip for anyone else.
w Herman Raucher d Paul Bogart ph Andrew Laszlo m David Shire
☆ Gary Grimes, Jerry Houser, Oliver Conant, William Atherton, Sam Bottoms, Deborah Winters

Class of 84
Canada   1981   98m   colour
Columbia/Guerrilla (Arthur Kent)
🖿 🖚

A new teacher finds his students involved in drug and vice rackets.
The Blackboard Jungle goes several steps further, to general indifference.
w Mark Lester, John Saxton, Tom Holland d Mark Lester ph Albert Dunk m Lalo Schifrin ad no credit
☆ Perry King, Merrie Lynn Ross, Timothy Van Patten, Roddy McDowall

The Class of Miss McMichael
GB   1978   90m   colour
Brut/Kettledrum (Judd Bernard)
🖿

A dedicated schoolmistress has no chance against her slum surroundings.
The Blackboard Jungle lives on, very boringly.
w Judd Bernard *novel* Sandy Hutson d Silvio Narizzano ph Alex Thomson m Stanley Myers
☆ Glenda Jackson, Oliver Reed, John Standing, Michael Murphy, Rosalind Cash
'Poorly mannered, simple minded, badly disciplined … gives social science a bad name.' – *Variety*

Class of Nuke 'Em High
US   1986   92m   colour
Troma/TNT (Lloyd Kaufman, Michael Hertz)
🖿🖿 🖿 🖚 🖚

After nuclear waste contaminates the water supply, students who don't turn nasty are terrorized by a monster.
Cheap, over-the-top horror movie that makes fun of its lack of pretension.
w Richard W. Haines, Mark Rudnitsky, Lloyd Kaufman, Stuart Strutin d Richard W. Haines, Lloyd Kaufman ph Michael Mayers m Michael Lattanzi, Biohazard ad Art Skopinsky, Arthur Lorenz ed Richard Haines
☆ Janelle Brady, Gilbert Brenton, Robert Prichard, R. L. Ryan, James Nugent Vernon, Brad Dunker, Gary Schneider
† It was followed by two sequels, *Class of Nuke 'Em High 2: Subhumanoid Meltdown*, and *Class of Nuke 'Em High 3: The Good, the Bad and the Subhumanoid*.

Claudelle Inglish
US   1961   99m   bw
Warner (Leonard Freeman)
GB title: *Young and Eager*

A poor farmer's daughter scorns a wealthy man for a succession of young studs.
Would-be sensational novelette from the author of Tobacco Road; it does not begin to be interesting.
w Leonard Freeman *novel* Erskine Caldwell d Gordon Douglas ph Ralph Woolsey m Howard Jackson
☆ Diane McBain, Arthur Kennedy, Constance Ford, Chad Everett, Claude Akins, Will Hutchins, Robert Colbert, Ford Rainey, James Bell

Claudia **
US   1943   92m   bw
TCF (William Perlberg)

A middle-class husband helps his child-wife to mature.
Typical of the best of Hollywood's 'woman's pictures' of the period, this is a pleasant domestic comedy-drama featuring recognizably human characters in an agreeable setting.
w Morrie Ryskind *novel and play* Rose Franken d Edmund Goulding ph Leon Shamroy m Alfred Newman
☆ Dorothy McGuire, Robert Young, Ina Claire, Reginald Gardiner, Olga Baclanova, Jean Howard, Elsa Janssen
'It won't leave a dry eye in the house.' – *Variety*
† Cary Grant was sought for the Robert Young part.

Claudia and David *
US   1946   78m   bw
TCF (William Perlberg)
Claudia and her husband survive assorted crises including their son's illness and David's involvement in a car crash.
Patchwork sequel to Claudia, quite pleasant but obviously contrived quickly from scraps.
w Rose Franken, William Brown Meloney d Walter Lang ph Joseph LaShelle m Cyril Mockridge
☆ Dorothy McGuire, Robert Young, Mary Astor, John Sutton, Gail Patrick, Florence Bates

Claudine
US   1974   92m   DeLuxe
Fox-Rank/Third World Cinema/Joyce Selznick, Tina Pine (Hannah Weinstein)

A garbage collector falls for a poor woman with six kids.
Sugar-coated account, with romantic overtones, of life at the bottom in New York.
w Tina and Lester Pine d John Berry ph Gayne Rescher m Curtis Mayfield pd Ted Haworth ed Luis San Andres
☆ Diahann Carroll, James Earl Jones, Lawrence Hilton-Jacobs, Tamu, David Kruger, Yvette Curtis, Eric Jones
'Substitute white actors for the black cast, tone down the fashionably outspoken situations a little, and it would be just like one of those perennial Disney movies about happy families and the difficulty of living and loving in this problematic world.' – *Tom Milne, MFB*
𝔔 Diahann Carroll

Claws
US   1977   100m   colour
Alaska Pictures (Chuck D. Keen)
🖿

A grizzly bear, wounded by hunters, turns maneater and begins to kill the inhabitants of a small Alaskan town.
Cheap and unimaginative Jaws rip-off, displaying no creativity whatsoever, though the landscape is impressive.
w Chuck D. Keen, Brian Russell d Richard Bansbach, Robert E. Pierson ph Chuck D. Keen m Gene Kauer, Douglas Lackey ed Richard Bansbach
☆ Jason Evers, Leon Ames, Anthony Caruso, Carla Layton, Glenn Sipes, Buck Young, Myron Healey

The Clay Pigeon **
US   1949   63m   bw
RKO (Herman Schlom)
🖿

An amnesiac sailor finds himself courtmartialled for treason, but discovers the real culprit.
Tidily efficient second feature thriller; good enjoyable stuff of its kind.
w Carl Foreman d Richard Fleischer ph Robert de Grasse m Paul Sawtell
☆ Bill Williams, Barbara Hale, Richard Quine, Richard Loo, Frank Fenton

'Lester Long Never Forgets A Friend.'
Clay Pigeons
US   1998   104m   colour
Gramercy/Scott Free (Ridley Scott, Chris Zarpas)
🖿 🖚 🖚

An affable, adulterous but guileless gas station attendant is suspected of being a serial killer.

👭 film suitable for family viewing   🖿🖿 VHS video-cassette for the British PAL system   🖿 VHS video-cassette for the British PAL system in wide screen-format   🖚 Video cassette in a computer-colourised version   🖿 American NTSC video-cassette   🖚 Laser disc

A blackish comedy of escalating disaster that rarely strikes the requisite heartless tone; a little more wit might have helped.
w Matt Healy d David Dobkin ph Eric Edwards m John Lurie pd Clark Hunter ed Stan Salfas
☆ Vince Vaughn, Joaquin Phoenix, Janeane Garofalo, Georgina Cates, Scott Wilson, Phil Morris, Vince Vieluf, Nikki Arlyn
'Pic's air of jaunty (albeit somewhat flat) humor, plus its lack of genuine tension or character empathy, renders the serial-sadist aspect slightly distasteful, even irresponsible.' – Dennis Harvey, Variety

Clean and Sober **
US 1988 124m Technicolor
Warner/Imagine Entertainment (Tony Ganz, Deborah Blum)

An embezzler hides out in a rehabilitation clinic, refusing to admit to himself that he is an alcoholic and cocaine addict.
Unrelenting and powerful drama.
w Tod Carroll d Glenn Gordon Caron ph Jan Kiesser m Gabriel Yared pd Joel Schiller ed Richard Chew
☆ Michael Keaton, Kathy Baker, Morgan Freeman, Tate Donovan, Henry Judd Baker, Claudia Christian, M. Emmet Walsh, Luca Bercovici
'I only wish there were some honest way of describing this movie that would make everyone go and see it.' – Philip French, Observer

Clean, Shaven **
US 1993 77m DuArt
ICA/DSM III (Lodge Kerrigan)

A schizophrenic man goes looking for his daughter in Canada while being chased by a detective who believes he murdered a young girl.
A brilliant, but downbeat and difficult to watch, evocation of a shattered mind, full of pain and aggression and shot in a dislocated style.
wd Lodge Kerrigan ph Teodoro Maniaci m Hahn Rowe pd Tania Ferrier ed Jay Rabinowitz
☆ Peter Greene, Robert Albert, Megan Owen, Molly Castelloe, Jennifer MacDonald, Alice Levitt
'An almost unbearably intense, exceedingly concentrated study of schizophrenia by a clearly talented new filmmaker. Using a fragmented narrative and some avant-garde techniques, pic is so unsettling that many viewers won't be able to tolerate it.' – Todd McCarthy, Variety
† The film was made over a period of two years.

Clean Slate: see Coup de Torchon (1981)

Clean Slate
US 1994 107m DeLuxe
MGM (Richard D. Zanuck, Lili Fini Zanuck)

A private detective forgets everything whenever he falls asleep.
A shaggy dog comedy in which all the laughs are stolen by a one-eyed Jack Russell terrier; it is a pity he couldn't have been persuaded to write the script.
w Robert King d Mick Jackson ph Andrew Dunn m Alan Silvestri pd Norman Reynolds ed Priscilla Nedd-Friendly
☆ Dana Carvey, Valeria Golino, James Earl Jones, Kevin Pollak, Michael Gambon, Michael Murphy
'This convoluted comedy feels like a pale follow-up to Groundhog Day.' – Variety

'Truth needs a soldier.'
Clear and Present Danger *
US 1994 141m DeLuxe Panavision
Paramount (Mace Neufeld, Robert Rehme)

A leading CIA agent investigating the Colombian drug trade discovers that its corruption reaches the highest level of American government.
Fast-moving thriller of betrayal and the abuse of power, simple-minded but effective entertainment.
w Donald Stewart, Steven Zaillian, John Milius novel Tom Clancy d Phillip Noyce ph Donald McAlpine m James Horner pd Terence Marsh ed Neil Travis
☆ Harrison Ford, Willem Dafoe, Anne Archer, Henry Czerny, Joaquim de Almeida, Harris Yulin, Donald Moffat, Miguel Sandoval, James Earl Jones
'Long, uneven and sometimes downright tedious.' – Screen International
'The filmmakers haven't simply tamed the rogue elephant of Clancy's narrative; they've turned it

into something that moves as gracefully and powerfully as a gazelle.' – Terrence Rafferty, New Yorker
♫ sound; sound effects editing

Clearcut
Canada 1991 98m colour
Northern Arts/Cinexus (Stephen J. Roth, Ian McDougal)

After losing a court battle to save Native American lands from a logging company, an idealistic lawyer witnesses the kidnapping of the sawmill's manager by an enigmatic Native American who believes in primitive vengeance.
A flawed film that abandons thoughtfulness in favour of brutal action; it is almost worth watching for Greene's performance as a nightmare figure beyond the reach of reason.
w Rob Forsyth novel A Dream Like Mine by M. T. Kelly d Richard Bugajski ph François Protat m Shane Harvey pd Perri Gorrara ed Michael Rea
☆ Ron Lea, Graham Greene, Michael Hogan, Rebecca Jenkins, Floyd Red Crow Westerman
'Despite its surface blandness, and though it wobbles precariously on the brink of oversimplification, it's as radical in its message as any picture you're likely to see.' – Hal Hinson, Washington Post

Cleo from 5 to 7 *
France/Italy 1961 90m bw/colour
Rome/Paris (Bruno Drigo)

original title: Cleo de 5 à 7
A girl waiting for the result of a medical examination wanders around Paris thinking she has cancer.
Impressively handled character sketch with gratifying attention to detail.
wd Agnès Varda ph Jean Rabier m Michel Legrand
☆ Corinne Marchand, Antoine Bourseiller, Dorothée Blanck, Michel Legrand

'The love affair that shook the world!'
Cleopatra **
US 1934 101m bw
Paramount/Cecil B. de Mille

After Julius Caesar's death, Cleopatra turns her attention to Mark Antony.
More of the vices than the virtues of its producer are notable in this fustian epic, which is almost but not quite unwatchable because of its stolid pace and miscasting. Some of the action montages and the barge scene, however, are superb cinema.
w Waldemar Young, Vincent Lawrence d Cecil B. de Mille ph Victor Milner m Rudolph Kopp ed Anne Bauchens
☆ Claudette Colbert, Henry Wilcoxon, Warren William, Gertrude Michael, Joseph Schildkraut, Ian Keith, C. Aubrey Smith, Leonard Mudie, Irving Pichel, Arthur Hohl, Ian MacLaren
'He has certainly made the most sumptuous of Roman circuses out of Roman history ... a constant succession of banquets, dancers, triumphs, and a fleet set on fire.' – The Times
'Gorgeous optically but mentally weak ... a handpicked audience was polite but not over-enthusiastic.' – Variety
'A great cinematic achievement, a spectacle of breathtaking brilliance.' – Daily Express
'It is remarkable how Cecil B. de Mille can photograph so much on such a vast scale and still say nothing ... it reeks of so much pseudo-artistry, vulgarity, philistinism, sadism, that it can only be compared with the lowest form of contemporary culture: Hitlerism. This is the type of "culture" that will be fed to the audience of Fascist America.' – Irving Lerner, 1968
🏆 Victor Milner
♫ best picture; Anne Bauchens

'The motion picture the world has been waiting for!'
Cleopatra
US 1963 243m DeLuxe Todd-AO
TCF (Walter Wanger)

The unsurprising story is told at inordinate length and dullness in this all-starred epic, one of the most heralded, and mismanaged, in film history. (Its story is best told in the producer's My Life with Cleopatra.)

The most expensive film ever made, for various reasons which do not appear on the screen.
w Joseph L. Mankiewicz, Ranald MacDougall, Sidney Buchman, and others d Joseph L. Mankiewicz (and others) ph Leon Shamroy m Alex North ad John DeCuir, Jack Martin Smith, and others
☆ Elizabeth Taylor, Richard Burton, Rex Harrison, Pamela Brown, George Cole, Hume Cronyn, Cesare Danova, Kenneth Haigh, Andrew Keir, Martin Landau, Roddy McDowall, Robert Stephens, Francesca Annis, Martin Benson, Herbert Berghof and also Grégoire Aslan, Richard O'Sullivan
'Whatever was interesting about it clearly ended up somewhere else: on the cutting room floor, in various hotel rooms, in the newspaper columns ... it lacks not only the intelligent spectacle of Lawrence of Arabia but the spectacular unintelligence of a Cecil B. de Mille product...' – John Simon
'The small screen does more than justice to this monumental mouse.' – Judith Crist
'I only came to see the asp.' – Charles Addams
'Surely the most bizarre piece of entertainment ever to be perpetrated.' – Elizabeth Taylor
† Archivists are attempting to restore a six-hour 'director's cut' of the film. After its opening, it was also shown in versions running for 227m and 192m.
🏆 Leon Shamroy; John DeCuir and others; costumes (Irene Sharaff, Vittorio Nino Novarese, Renie); special visual effects (Emil Kosa Jnr)
♫ best picture; Alex North; Rex Harrison

Cleopatra Jones
US 1973 89m Technicolor Panavision
Warner

A black female CIA agent eliminates a ring of dope peddlers.
Grotesque comic strip fantasy with a high mortality rate.
w Max Julien, Sheldon Keller d Jack Starrett
☆ Tamara Dobson, Shelley Winters, Bernie Casey, Brenda Sykes
'It hampers the cause of racial entente more effectively than any work since Uncle Tom's Cabin.' – John Baxter, MFB

Cleopatra Jones and the Casino of Gold
US/Hong Kong 1975 96m Technicolor Panavision
Warner/Shaw Bros (William Tennant, Run Run Shaw)

A tough female government agent goes to Hong Kong to smash a drugs ring.
Feeble sequel lacking the brashness of the original, but equally tasteless.
w William Tennant d Chuck Bail ph Alan Hume m Dominic Frontiere ad Johnson Tsao ed Willy Kemplen
☆ Tamara Dobson, Stella Stevens, Tanny, Norman Fell, Albert Popwell
'The film is cut together quite incoherently, and Chuck Bail's barely competent direction seizes up completely when called upon now and then for some large-scale action set-piece.' – Verina Glaessner, MFB

Clerks **
US 1994 103m bw
Artificial Eye/View Askew (Kevin Smith, Scott Mosier)

An unhappy clerk is forced to work in a grocery store on his day off, which turns out to be full of mishaps and laconic conversations with his friend, who runs the low-class neighbourhood video shop.
Witty, episodic, foul-mouthed account of the slacker generation doing what it does best: nothing in particular; it is often inventive, making the most of its low-budget restrictions, if too determinedly quirky.
wd Kevin Smith ph David Klein m Scott Angley ed Scott Mosier, Kevin Smith
☆ Brian O'Halloran, Jeff Anderson, Marilyn Ghigliotti, Lisa Spoonauer, Jason Mewes, Kevin Smith
'A randy, irreverent, slice-of-life no-budgeter that's played for laughs and gets them.' – Todd McCarthy, Variety
† The film was shot on 16mm for $27,000.

'A district attorney out for a conviction. A new lawyer out of her league. A young boy who knew too much.'
The Client *
US 1994 121m Technicolor
Warner/Regency/Alcor (Arnon Milchan, Steven Reuther)

A female lawyer is hired to protect an 11-year-old boy, being chased by the Mafia and hounded by the FBI because he knows where the body of a murder victim is buried.
Slick and enjoyable thriller that lacks subtlety but maintains a high level of tension.
w Akiva Goldsman, Robert Getchell novel John Grisham d Joel Schumacher ph Tony Pierce-Roberts m Howard Shore pd Bruno Rubeo ed Robert Brown
☆ Susan Sarandon, Tommy Lee Jones, Mary-Louise Parker, Anthony LaPaglia, J. T. Walsh, Anthony Edwards, Brad Renfro, Will Patton, Ossie Davis
'Safe-as-houses entertainment, directed with no particular finesse, but it's refreshingly straightforward and unpretentious.' – Terrence Rafferty, New Yorker
♫ Susan Sarandon
🇬🇧 Susan Sarandon

'Hang on.'
Cliffhanger *
US 1993 112m Technicolor
Carolco/Canal/Pioneer/RCS Video (Alan Marshall, Renny Harlin)

A mountain rescue expert turns the tables on violent gangsters who crash in the Rocky Mountains with suitcases stuffed with money.
Enjoyably silly action adventure, with some spectacular, edgy stunts, although it never touches reality at any point and has one of the more ludicrous lip-smacking villains this side of melodrama.
w Michael France, Sylvester Stallone story Michael France based on a premise by John Long d Renny Harlin ph Alex Thomson m Trevor Jones pd John Vallone ed Frank J. Urioste sp Neil Krepela, John Richardson, John Bruno, Pamela Easley
☆ Sylvester Stallone, John Lithgow, Michael Rooker, Janine Turner, Rex Linn, Caroline Goodall, Leon, Craig Fairbrass, Gregory Scott Cummins, Paul Winfield, Ralph Waite
'Harlin displays perfect pitch, not just with the individual scenes of jaw-dropping stunt work, but in the way these episodes flow into each other with varying degrees of intensity.' – Henry Sheehan, Sight and Sound
'A two-hour roller-coaster ride that never stops from first minute to last. A high-octane action suspenser with thrilling vertiginous footage unlike anything seen before in a feature.' – Variety
♫ sound; sound effects editing; visual effects

A Climate for Killing
US 1991 103m Foto-Kem
Propaganda

aka: A Row of Crows
A new cop who goes by the book finds himself at odds with an old-style sheriff and in love with his daughter as they investigate the murder of a woman who apparently died 16 years earlier.
Competent but unexciting murder mystery.
wd J. S. Cardone ph Michael Cardone m Robert Folk
☆ John Beck, Steven Bauer, Mia Sara, Katharine Ross, John Diehl, Dedee Pfeiffer, Phil Brock, Tony Frank

'The screen's classic of suspense!'
The Climax *
US 1944 86m Technicolor
Universal (George Waggner)

A young opera singer is hypnotized by a mad doctor, who has kept his murdered mistress embalmed for ten years.
Gothic romantic melodrama invented to capitalize on the success – and the sets – of Phantom of the Opera. Curiously endearing, with a good eye-rolling part for Karloff.
w Curt Siodmak, Lynn Starling play Edward Cochran d George Waggner ph Hal Mohr, W. Howard Greene m Edward Ward ad John B. Goodman, Alexander Golitzen

☆ Boris Karloff, Susanna Foster, Gale Sondergaard, Turhan Bey, Thomas Gomez, Scotty Beckett

'All quite unalarming, which is a bit of a handicap.' – *New Yorker, 1978*

& art direction

Climbing High *
GB   1938   78m   bw
Gaumont (Michael Balcon)

A rich man pretends to be a male model in order to win a girl.

Light-hearted romantic musical with interesting credits.

w Stephen Clarkson *story* Lesser Samuels, Marian Dix *d* Carol Reed *ph* Mutz Greenbaum (Max Greene) *ad* Alfred Junge *ed* Michael Gordon

☆ Jessie Matthews, Michael Redgrave, Noel Madison, Alastair Sim, Margaret Vyner, Mary Clare, Francis L. Sullivan

The Clinging Vine *
US   1926   71m   bw   silent
Cecil B. de Mille

The president's secretary is the real driving force of a paint company, but finds that love is more important than business.

Interesting silent predecessor of many career girl comedies of the thirties and forties.

w Jeannie Macpherson *d* Paul Sloane

☆ Leatrice Joy, Tom Moore, Toby Claude, Robert Edeson

'People are going to **** whether you like it or not – and this place is here to see that they enjoy it!'

The Clinic *
Australia   1982   92m   colour
Film House/Generation Films (Bob Weis, Robert le Tet)
▤

One day in the life of a clinic for venereal diseases.

Slightly dishevelled comedy-drama which will be generally remembered as a very naughty carry-on.

w Greg Millen *d* David Stevens

☆ Chris Haywood, Simon Burke, Gerda Nicolson, Rona McLeod, Suzanne Roylance

'Six words from a woman changed the map of Asia!'

Clive of India *
US   1934   90m   bw
Twentieth Century (Darryl F. Zanuck, William Goetz, Raymond Griffith)

The life of the 18th-century empire builder, with special emphasis on his marriage.

A very tame and now faded epic, with more romance than adventure. The production relies more on stars than technique, but it works.

w W. P. Lipscomb, R. J. Minney *play* W. P. Lipscomb, R. J. Minney *d* Richard Boleslawski *ph* Peverell Marley *m* Alfred Newman

☆ Ronald Colman, Loretta Young, Colin Clive, Francis Lister, Montagu Love, Robert Greig, Leo G. Carroll, C. Aubrey Smith, Mischa Auer

'It may be spoken of as another of the best British pictures made in Hollywood ... Should be strong b.o.' – *Variety*

'Patriotic pageantry, undistorted by facts.' – *J. R. Parish*

& art direction

'The moment he fell in love was his moment of greatest danger!'

Cloak and Dagger *
US   1946   106m   bw
United States Pictures (Milton Sperling)
▦▦   ▤   ⌕

A physics professor joins the secret service and is parachuted into Germany to interview a kidnapped scientist.

Supposedly authoritative espionage adventure which turned out dull and humourless; plot routine, direction absent-minded.

w Albert Maltz, Ring Lardner Jnr *d* Fritz Lang *ph* Sol Polito *m* Max Steiner

☆ Gary Cooper, Lilli Palmer, Robert Alda, Vladimir Sokoloff, J. Edward Bromberg, Ludwig Stossel, Helene Thimig, Marc Lawrence

'Just a B plot dressed up in A trimmings.' – *Newsweek*

Clochemerle
France   1948   93m   bw
Cinéma Productions (Ralph Baum)

The progressive mayor of a French village erects a gentlemen's convenience in the main street and shocks the local reactionaries.

Most of the book's political satire was ironed out in this cheap and opportunist production which got a few easy laughs but failed to sustain itself.

w Gabriel Chevalier *novel* Gabriel Chevalier *d* Pierre Chénal *ph* Robert Le Fèbvre *m* Henri Sauguet

☆ Brochard, Maximilienne, Simone Michels, Jane Marken, Paul Demange, Felix Oudart, Saturnin Fabre

The Clock **
US   1945   90m   bw
MGM (Arthur Freed)
▤   ⌕
GB title: *Under the Clock*

A girl meets a soldier at New York's Grand Central Station and marries him during his 24-hour leave.

Everyone now seems far too nice in this winsome romance full of comedy cameos and convincing New York locations, but if you can relive the wartime mood it still works as a corrective to the Betty Grable glamour pieces.

w Robert Nathan, Joseph Schrank *story* Paul and Pauline Gallico *d* Vincente Minnelli *ph* George Folsey *m* George Bassman

☆ Judy Garland, Robert Walker, James Gleason, Lucille Gleason, Keenan Wynn, Marshall Thompson, Chester Clute

'Sweetly charming, if maybe too irresistible ... fortunately the director fills the edges with comic characters.' – *New Yorker, 1978*

'The emotion may have been honest, but the method was too rich for my eyes, and the writing as used on the screen too weak for my mind.' – *Stephen Longstreet*

'Strictly a romance ... safely told, disappointing and angering in the thought of the great film it might have been.' – *James Agee*

'Amazingly, it was all shot in the studio, using street sets and back projection; even the old Penn Station, where so much of the action takes place, is a set.' – *Pauline Kael, 70s*

Clockers **
US   1995   128m   DeLuxe
UIP/Universal/40 Acres and a Mule (Martin Scorsese, Spike Lee, Jon Kilik)
▦▦   ▤   ◈   ⌕

After a drug pusher is shot, a Brooklyn detective suspects that the man who confesses to the crime is doing so to protect his younger brother who is a clocker, a small-time crack dealer working on the streets.

A harsh report from the urban front line, where drugs cause blacks to kill blacks and even those who reject that culture find themselves unable to escape it; it is a powerful and despairing film, but often tends to be more didactic than dramatic.

w Richard Price, Spike Lee *novel* Richard Price *d* Spike Lee *ph* Malik Hassan Sayeed *m* Terence Blanchard *pd* Andrew McAlpine *ed* Sam Pollard

☆ Harvey Keitel, John Turturro, Delroy Lindo, Mekhi Phifer, Isaiah Washington, Keith David, Pee Wee Love, Regina Taylor, Sticky Fingaz

'A kaleidoscopic vision of a community mired in betrayal, psychosis, and murder. The images are like something out of a nightmare newsreel, raw and grainy and pulsatingly alive.' – *Owen Gleiberman, Entertainment Weekly*

'Confirms Lee's position as the cinema's great surgeon-general, alternately taking the pulse of America and probing its open wounds. But it is still, in many ways, a bad film – so full of holes you can see right through it.' – *Tom Shone, Sunday Times*

† Originally, the film was to have been directed by Martin Scorsese. But he decided to make *Casino* instead, and Lee took over as director, rewriting the script to change its emphasis: in Price's novel, the protagonist was the Brooklyn detective played by Harvey Keitel.

Clockwise *
GB   1986   97m   Technicolor
EMI/Moment (Michael Codron)

A headmaster on his way to a conference is delayed by circumstance.

What was intended as an escalating climax of comic chaos falls away as the script runs out of steam, but the nation's need for comedy ensured box-office success.

w Michael Frayn *d* Christopher Morahan *ph* John Coquillon *m* George Fenton *pd* Roger Murray-Leach *ed* Peter Boyle

☆ John Cleese, Alison Steadman, Penelope Wilton, Stephen Moore, Joan Hickson, Charon Maiden

'Whichever way you point him, as soon as you let Conrad go ... He's off and over the edge.'

Clockwork Mice
GB   1995   99m   colour
Feature Film/Metrodome
▦▦

An idealistic young teacher attempts to encourage a young boy in cross-country running when he goes to work in a special school.

Confused and episodic drama that veers abruptly from actuality to fantasy before climaxing with an unconvincing finale and unlikely romance; quite what the point of it all is, is impossible to know.

w Rod Woodruff *d* Vadim Jean *ph* Gordon Hickie *m* John Murphy, David Hughes *pd* David Munns *ed* Liz Webber

☆ Ian Hart, Ruaidhri Conroy, Catherine Russell, Art Malik, John Alderton, Claire Skinner, James Bolam, Nigel Planer, Lilly Edwards, Frankie Bruno

'If you can keep your cynicism in check, this is that rarest of breeds, a stirring British movie with a mind of its own.' – *Empire*

'Being the adventures of a young man whose principal interests are rape, ultra-violence, and Beethoven!'

A Clockwork Orange *
GB   1971   136m   colour
Warner/Polaris (Bernard Williams)
▦▦   ◈   ⌕

In a future Britain of desolation and violence, a young gangster guilty of rape and murder obtains a release from prison after being experimentally brainwashed: he finds society more violent than it was in his time.

A repulsive film in which intellectuals have found acres of social and political meaning; the average judgement is likely to remain that it is pretentious and nasty rubbish for sick minds who do not mind jazzed-up images and incoherent sound.

wd Stanley Kubrick *novel* Anthony Burgess *ph* John Alcott *m* Walter Carlos *pd* John Barry

☆ Malcolm McDowell, Michael Bates, Adrienne Corri, Patrick Magee, Warren Clarke

'Very early there are hints of triteness and insecurity, and before half an hour is over it begins to slip into tedium ... Inexplicably the script leaves out Burgess' reference to the title.' – *Stanley Kauffmann*

'It might be the work of a strict and exacting German professor who set out to make a porno violent sci-fi comedy.' – *New Yorker, 1980*

'Kubrick handles his medium with a confidence almost insolent. For the rest – the flashes of farce, the variations on distance and distortion and dream-imagery – he has given us the most audacious of horror-films. And the most inhuman.' – *Dilys Powell*

& best picture; Stanley Kubrick (as writer and director)

'We are not alone...'

Close Encounters of the Third Kind *
US   1977   135m   Metrocolor   Panavision
Columbia/EMI (Julia and Michael Phillips)
▦▦   ▥   ▤   ◈   ⌕

A series of UFOs takes Indiana by surprise, and a workman is led by intuition and detection to the landing site which has been concealed from the public.

There's a lot of padding in this slender fantasy, which has less plot and much less suspense than It Came from Outer Space which was made on a tiny budget in 1955; but the technical effects are masterly though their exposure is over-prolonged, and the benevolent mysticism filled a current requirement of popular taste, accounting for the enormous box-office success of a basically flawed film. Much of the dialogue is inaudible.

wd Steven Spielberg *ph* Vilmos Zsigmond *m* John Williams *pd* Joe Alves *ed* Michael Kahn *sp* Douglas Trumbull

☆ Richard Dreyfuss, François Truffaut, Teri Garr, Melinda Dillon, Cary Guffey

'It somehow combines Disney and 1950s SF and junk food into the most persuasive (if arrested) version of the American dream yet.' – *Time Out*

'It has visionary magic and a childlike comic spirit, along with a love of surprises and a skeptical, let's-try-it-on spirit.' – *New Yorker*

† The cost of this film was estimated at 20,000,000 dollars

†† In 1980 a 'special edition' was released with some success: this pared down the idiotic middle section and extended the final scenes of the space ship, including some new interiors

††† This film used the largest set in film history: the inside of an old dirigible hangar. Of the special edition, Derek Malcolm in the *Guardian* wrote: 'One is inclined to feel that with all the money at his disposal, Spielberg might have got it right the first time.'

⚲ Vilmos Zsigmond

& direction; John Williams; Melinda Dillon; visual effects (Douglas Trumbull and others)

▽ Joe Alves

Close My Eyes
GB   1991   108m   colour
Artificial Eye/Beambright/Film Four (Thérèse Pickard)

A long-separated brother and sister meet and fall in love.

Hysterical and dull, peopled by fashionable but inert characters given to boring introspection.

wd Stephen Poliakoff *ph* Witold Stok *m* Michael Gibbs *pd* Luciana Arrighi *ed* Michael Parkinson

☆ Alan Rickman, Saskia Reeves, Clive Owen, Karl Johnson, Lesley Sharp, Kate Gartside, Karen Knight, Niall Buggy

'Should have a solid career ahead of it and is a major plus for all concerned.' – *Variety*

'Drags itself across the screen. After much huffing and puffing, the script refuses to become the sum of its many, many scholarly observations about life, love, the universe. The lack of feeling is fatal.' – *John Lyttle, Independent*

A Close Shave **
GB   1995   30m   colour
BBC/Aardman Animations (Carla Shelley, Michael Rose)
▦▦   ▤

Wallace and Gromit defeat a sheep-rustling operation; in the process Wallace experiences the pangs of requited love and Gromit is accused of murder.

Enjoyable slapstick comedy of misapplied ingenuity, with nostalgic overtones, close in spirit to the British 'little man' comedies of the 50s with a few nods to more modern movies, such as The Terminator, along the way.

w Bob Baker, Nick Park *d* Nick Park *ph* David Alex Riddett *m* Julian Nott *ad* Phil Lewis *ed* Helen Garrard

☆ Featuring the voices of: Peter Sallis, Anne Reid

⚲ best animated short

Close to Eden: see *Urga* (1991)

Close to Eden
US   1992   111m   colour
Rank/Propaganda/Sandollar/Isis (Steve Golin, Sigurjon Sighvatsson, Howard Rosenman)
▦▦   ▤   ⌕
aka: *A Stranger Among Us*

A female cop infiltrates the Hasidic community in New York to track down a murderer.

An odd and unconvincing thriller, ignoring the narrative for much of the time as it becomes almost a promotional film on behalf of the Hasidim.

w Robert J. Avrech *d* Sidney Lumet *ph* Andrzej Bartkowiak *m* Jerry Bock *pd* Philip Rosenberg *ed* Andrew Mondshein

☆ Melanie Griffith, Eric Thal, John Pankow, Tracy Pollan, Lee Richardson, Mia Sara, Jamey Sheridan, Jake Weber

'With its Fiddler on the Roof score and some sneakily hypocritical espousing of deeply conservative religious values, this is little more than a 111-minute love letter to Sidney Lumet's rabbi.' – *Kim Newman, Empire*

🏠 film suitable for family viewing   ▦▦ VHS video-cassette for the British PAL system   ▥ VHS video-cassette for the British PAL system in wide screen-format   ✿ Video cassette in a computer-colourised version   ▤ American NTSC video-cassette   ⌕ Laser disc

Close to My Heart
US 1951 90m bw
Warner (William Jacobs)
An adopted baby is discovered to have a murderer for a father; but environment is proved to be more important than heredity.
Routine sentimental drama.
wd William Keighley story *A Baby for Midge* by James R. Webb ph Robert Burks m Max Steiner
☆ Ray Milland, Gene Tierney, Fay Bainter, Howard St John, Mary Beth Hughes

Closely Observed Trains **
Czechoslovakia 1966 92m bw
Ceskoslovensky Film (Zdenek Oves)
During World War II, an apprentice railway guard at a country station falls in love and becomes a saboteur.
Warm, amusingly detailed comedy with a disconcerting downbeat ending.
wd Jiri Menzel novel Bohumil Hrabal ph Jaromir Sofr m Jiri Pavlik
☆ Vaclav Neckar, Jitka Bendova, Vladimir Valenta, Josef Somr
'Like Forman, Menzel seems incapable of being unkind to anybody.' – Tom Milne
'The director has made extraordinarily effective use of the solitude which the characters share.' – Dilys Powell
🏆 best foreign film

Closet Land *
US 1991 89m DeLuxe
Universal/Imagine (Janet Meyers)
A children's writer is arrested, interrogated and tortured by a government official on a charge of subverting the young.
Intense psychological drama of a battle of wills, but lacking the required emotional impact through being set in no recognizable society; the acting almost carries it, but its heavy-handed symbolism sinks it before the end.
wd Radha Bharadwaj ph Bill Pope m Richard Einhorn pd Eiko Ishioka ed Lisa Churgin
☆ Madeleine Stowe, Alan Rickman
'Not an experience many filmgoers will want to put down money for.' – Variety
† Philip Glass was credited with 'creative musical supervision'.

Close-Up **
Iran 1989 93m colour
BFI/IIDCYA (Hassan Agha-Karimi)
original title: *Namayeh Nazdik*
A young man is tried for fraud after he persuades a family that he is the director Mohsen Makhmalbaf, and borrows money from them.
An oddity, and a fascinating one: a true story of a fantasist, part re-enacted, part actual, as the trial itself was filmed at the request of the accused.
wd Abbas Kiarostami ph Ali Reza Zarrin-Dast ed Abbas Kiarostami
☆ Hossain Sabzian, Mohsen Makhmalbaf, Abolfazi Ahankhah, Mehrdad Ahankhah, Manoochehr Ahankhah, Hossein Farazmand, Abbas Kiarostami

The Cloud Capped Star **
India 1960 127m bw
BFI/Chitrakalpa (Ritwik Ghatak)
original title: *Meghe Dhaka Tara*
In Calcutta, the daughter of a refugee family struggling to survive sacrifices herself for the sake of her heedless parents and siblings.
A powerful and enraged account of suffering and waste, of exile and disappointment.
wd Ritwik Ghatak story Shaktipada Rajguru ph Dinen Gupta m Jyotirindra Moitra ad Ravi Chattopadhyay ed Ramesh Joshi
☆ Supriya Choudhury, Anil Chatterjee, Bijon Bhattacharya, Guita De, Gita Ghatak, Dwiju Bhawal, Niranjan Roy
'An underrated modern masterpiece.' – Film Review

Cloud Dancer
US 1977 108m colour
Melvin Simon
Episodes in the life of a stunt flyer.
Technically proficient, loosely assembled amble through the problems of a man with an obsession for danger; not a great crowd-puller.

w William Goodhart d Barry Brown
☆ David Carradine, Jennifer O'Neill, Joseph Bottoms, Albert Salmi, Salome Jens, Colleen Camp

Cloudburst
GB 1951 92m bw
Exclusive/Hammer (Anthony Hinds)
A vengeful code expert goes after the criminals who ran down his wife in making a getaway.
Watchable potboiler.
w Leo Marks, Francis Searle d Francis Searle ph Walter Harvey m Frank Spencer
☆ Robert Preston, Elizabeth Sellars, Colin Tapley, Sheila Burrell, Harold Lang
† The US version ran for 83m.

The Clouded Yellow *
GB 1950 96m bw
Sydney Box/Carillon (Betty Box)
A sacked secret service agent gets work tending a butterfly collection and finds that this involves him in a murder plot.
Implausible but quite engaging thriller in the Hitchcock style, involving a chase across the Lake District.
w Janet Green, Eric Ambler d Ralph Thomas ph Geoffrey Unsworth
☆ Trevor Howard, Jean Simmons, Barry Jones, Sonia Dresdel, Maxwell Reed, Kenneth More, André Morell

Clouds Over Europe: see *Q Planes*

The Clown
US 1952 91m bw
MGM (William H. Wright)
A drunken clown, once a great star, is idolized by his son who believes in a comeback.
Maudlin reworking of The Champ (qv), with not a surprise in the plot and a star way over the top.
w Martin Rackin d Robert Z. Leonard ph Paul C. Vogel m David Rose
☆ Red Skelton, Jane Greer, Tim Considine, Loring Smith, Philip Ober

A Clown Must Laugh: see *Pagliacci*

The Club **
Australia 1980 90m colour Panavision
South Australia Film Corp/New South Wales Film Corp (Matt Carroll)
aka: *Players*
The arrival of an expensive, university-educated player precipitates a crisis among management and players at a football club.
Incisive, excellently acted drama of boardroom manoeuvres and conflicting loyalties.
w David Williamson play David Williamson d Bruce Beresford ph Don McAlpine pd David Copping ed William Anderson
☆ Jack Thompson, Harold Hopkins, Graham Kennedy, John Howard, Frank Wilson, Alan Cassell

Club Extinction: see *Dr M*

Club Havana
US 1946 62m bw
PRC
Several stories come to a head in a night-club.
Slight musical multi-drama with moments of interest.
w Raymond L. Schrock, Fred Jackson d Edgar G. Ulmer
☆ Tom Neal, Margaret Lindsay, Don Douglas, Isabelita, Ernest Truex, Renie Riano, Paul Cavanagh, Marc Lawrence

Club Paradise
US 1986 104m Technicolor
Warner (Michael Shamberg)
A Chicago fireman retires to a Caribbean island to manage a rundown club.
Dismal waste of talent.
w Harold Ramis, Brian Doyle-Murray story Ed Roboto, Tom Leopold, Chris Miller, David Standish d Harold Ramis ph Peter Hannan m David Mansfield, Van Dyke Parks pd John Graysmark ed Marion Rothman
☆ Robin Williams, Peter O'Toole, Rick Moranis, Jimmy Cliff, Twiggy, Adolph Caesar, Eugene Levy, Joanna Cassidy

'Like one of those giddy, casual farces that Paramount turned out in the thirties … Those pictures often got terrible reviews but kept audiences giggling cheerfully.' – Pauline Kael, New Yorker

Clubbed to Death
France/Portugal/Netherlands 1997 88m colour
Artificial Eye/Madar/La Sept/Grupo de Estudos/Meteor (Odile Gervais)
A young, middle-class woman is thrilled to discover rave culture and a drug-taking, impotent Arab boxer in the Parisian suburbs.
A slim narrative with little worthwhile dialogue, on which is hung the pounding music and pill-popping antics of the rave scene; for addicts only.
w Yolande Zauberman, Noémie Lvovsky d Yolande Zauberman ph Denis Lenoir m various pd Olivier Radot ed François Gédigier
☆ Elodie Bouchez, Roschdy Zem, Béatrice Dalle, Richard Courcet, Alex Descas
'Nothing other than a pretentious attempt to portray meaning to a culture that most of us couldn't care less about.' – Helen Van Kruyssen, Film Review

Clue
US 1985 87m Metrocolor
Paramount/Guber-Peters/Debra Hill/Polygram
A murder game becomes reality.
A rather arch attempt to film an internationally popular board game; those not in on the joke may tend to restlessness.
wd Jonathan Lynn ph Victor J. Kemper m John Morris pd John Lloyd
☆ Eileen Brennan, Tim Curry, Madeline Kahn, Christopher Lloyd, Michael McKean, Lesley Ann Warren
'Enough wit, neuroses and motive to intrigue even the most inept whodunnit solver.' – Variety
† Three alternative solutions were originally provided.

Clueless **
US 1995 97m DeLuxe
Paramount (Robert Lawrence, Scott Rudin)
A Beverly Hills teenager, the daughter of a successful lawyer, worries about losing her position as the most popular girl in the school and winning the boy she wants.
A surprisingly successful comedy about a girl who loves to shop, an activity that satisfies when all else fails. The dialogue is witty, the performances are smart and the tone is one of affectionate amusement touched with a little irony; the result is greatly enjoyable.
wd Amy Heckerling ph Bill Pope m David Kitay pd Steve Jordan ed Debra Chiate
☆ Alicia Silverstone, Stacey Dash, Brittany Murphy, Paul Rudd, Dan Hedaya, Donald Faison, Elisa Donovan, Wallace Shawn
'A highly satisfactory piece of work.' – Adam Mars-Jones, Independent
'The plot, a blend of Heathers and Sandra Dee, makes you feel as if you're biting into a tamale filled with Marshmallow Fluff.' – Entertainment Weekly
† The film is loosely based on Jane Austen's Emma.

Cluny Brown **
US 1946 100m bw
TCF (Ernst Lubitsch)
A plumber's niece goes into service and falls for a Czech refugee guest.
Romantic comedy in a never-never pre-war England; it does no more than poke casual fun at upper-class conventions, but the smooth direction and some excellent character comedy keep it well afloat.
w Samuel Hoffenstein, Elizabeth Reinhardt novel Margery Sharp d Ernst Lubitsch ph Joseph LaShelle m Cyril Mockridge, Emil Newman
☆ Jennifer Jones, Charles Boyer, Richard Haydn, Una O'Connor, Peter Lawford, Helen Walker, Reginald Gardiner, Reginald Owen, C. Aubrey Smith, Sara Allgood, Ernest Cossart, Florence Bates, Billy Bevan
'A lovely, easygoing comedy, full of small surprising touches.' – Pauline Kael, 70s

The Clutching Hand *
US 1936 bw serial: 15 eps
Stage and Screen
A scientist with a formula for synthetic gold is kidnapped, and rescue attempts are hampered by a sinister shadowy figure.
Archetypal spooky house serial.
d Albert Herman
☆ Jack Mulhall, Marion Shilling, Yakima Canutt, Reed Howes, William Farnum

Coal Miner's Daughter ***
US 1980 124m Technicolor
Universal (Bob Larson)
The wife of a Kentucky hillbilly becomes a pop star.
'With-it' version of the old show business story: gradual success, stardom, nervous breakdown, reconciliation. Based on the life of Loretta Lynn, but mainly notable for its depiction of backwoods Kentucky.
w Tom Rickman d Michael Apted ph Ralf D. Bode md Owen Bradley pd John W. Corso
☆ Sissy Spacek, Tommy Lee Jones, Levon Helm, Jennifer Beasley, Phyllis Boyens
🏆 Sissy Spacek
🏆 best picture; Tom Rickman; Ralf D. Bode; editing (Arthur Schmidt); art direction (John W. Corso, John M. Dwyer)

Coast to Coast
US 1980 94m Movielab
Paramount (Terry Carr)
A Los Angeles wife flees her husband and hitches a lift from a truck driver with problems.
Comedy for easy watching: pleasant characters are given very little of interest to do.
w Stanley Weiser d Joseph Sargent ph Joel King m Charles Bernstein
☆ Dyan Cannon, Robert Blake, Quinn Redeker, Michael Lerner, Bill Lucking, Maxine Stuart

Coastal Command **
GB 1942 69m bw
Crown Film Unit (Ian Dalrymple)
The RAF's Coastal Command at work, protecting a homeward-bound convoy of 42 merchant ships threatened by U-boats and a German raider.
Gripping documentary, full of exciting action, that has acquired additional historical worth with the passing of the years; it is also notable for Vaughan Williams's evocative score.
d J. B. Holmes ph Jonah Jones, F. Gamage m Ralph Vaughan Williams md Muir Mathieson ed Michael Gordon
'The whole piece is full of action, and yet it is somehow possible to watch it with imperturbability. A little more perturbation, and some humour, too, perhaps might not have hurt this picture.' – C. A. Lejeune

Cobb
US 1994 128m Technicolor
Warner/Regency/Alcor (David Lester)
A sports writer working on the official biography of Ty Cobb, the legendary American baseball player, discovers that the sporting hero is a thoroughly unpleasant person.
A revisionist biopic, with a larger-than-life performance in the title role; it is only likely to appeal to a dedicated sports fan.
wd Ron Shelton book Cobb: A Biography by Al Stump ph Russell Boyd m Elliot Goldenthal pd Armin Ganz, Scott Ritenour ed Paul Seydor, Kimberly Ray
☆ Tommy Lee Jones, Robert Wuhl, Lolita Davidovich, Stephen Mendillo, Lou Myers, J. Kenneth Campbell, William Utay, Rhoda Griffis
'It's neither character study nor historic drama. It's ambitious but oblique and unfocused, and only the most generous of viewers will forgive its numerous lapses and vagaries.' – Leonard Klady, Variety

Cobra
US 1925 85m bw silent
Ritz-Carlton
An impoverished Italian nobleman collects women as a hobby.
The star's first independent production won no plaudits and was thought to be a mistake conceived by his wife

Natacha Rambova, who appeared in a dance act with him.
w Anthony Coldeway d Joseph Henabery
☆ Rudolph Valentino, Nita Naldi, Casson Ferguson, Gertrude Olmstead, Hector V. Sarno

Cobra

US 1986 87m Technicolor
Warner/Cannon (James D. Brubaker)
📺 ▦ ◎ ⌑ ⌒

A tough LA cop tracks down a serial killer.
Relentless but unsurprising carbon of Dirty Harry, a bit too tough for its own good.
w Sylvester Stallone *novel Fair Game* by Paula Gosling d George Pan Cosmatos ph Ric Waite m Sylvester Levay pd Bill Kenney ed Don Zimmerman, James Symons
☆ Sylvester Stallone, Brigitte Nielsen, Reni Santoni, Andrew Robinson
† 2,131 prints were made for the launch
†† It was remade in 1995 as *Fair Game* (qv), starring Cindy Crawford.

Cobra Verde

West Germany 1988 111m colour
Palace/Concorde/Werner Herzog Film Production/ZDF/Ghana Film Industry Corp (Luigi Stipetic)
📺 ⌒

A Brazilian peasant-turned-bandit goes to West Africa to revive the slave trade.
Disjointed, episodic and uninteresting.
w Werner Herzog *novel The Viceroy of Ouidah* by Bruce Chatwin d Werner Herzog ph Viktor Ruzicka m Popol Vuh pd Ulrich Bergfelder ed Maximiliane Mainka
☆ Klaus Kinski, King Ampaw, Jose Lewgoy, Salvatore Basile

Cobra Woman

US 1944 71m Technicolor
U-I (George Waggner)

A South Seas girl is abducted by snake worshippers ruled by her evil twin.
A monument of undiluted hokum with some amusing sets and performances but not enough self-mockery in the script.
w Richard Brooks, Gene Lewis d Robert Siodmak ph George Robinson, W. Howard Greene m Edward Ward
☆ Maria Montez, Jon Hall, Sabu, Lon Chaney Jnr, Mary Nash, Edgar Barrier, Lois Collier, Samuel S. Hinds, Moroni Olsen
'Among the exotic treats: a rumbling volcano, a pet chimp, ominous gong sounds, forest glade love scenes, human sacrifices, handmaidens in high-heeled pumps, Tollea's imperious writhing during a demonic dance, and the good Nadja's plea for the symbol of the power that is rightly hers: "Gif me the cobra jool."' – *Pauline Kael, 70s*

The Cobweb

US 1955 124m Eastmancolor
Cinemascope
MGM (John Houseman)
◎

Tensions among the staff of a private mental clinic reach a new high over the purchase of curtains.
The patients seem saner than the doctors in this strained and verbose character drama which despite its cast and big studio look never begins to engage the interest.
w John Paxton *novel* William Gibson d Vincente Minnelli ph George Folsey m Leonard Rosenman
☆ Richard Widmark, Lauren Bacall, Charles Boyer, *Lillian Gish*, Gloria Grahame, John Kerr, Susan Strasberg, *Oscar Levant*, Paul Rettig, Paul Stewart, Adèle Jergens
'An overwrought and elaborately artificial exercise, made scarcely more plausible by reliance on the basic jargon of psychiatry.' – *Penelope Houston*
'By the mid-50s, nobody was surprised that the new variant on *Grand Hotel* was an expensive, exclusive loony bin.' – *Pauline Kael, 70s*

The Coca-Cola Kid

Australia 1985 94m Eastmancolor
Palace/Cinema Enterprises/Film Gallery/Columbia (David Roe)
📺 ▦ ◎

A Coca-Cola rep is sent to Australia to combat a remote land baron who brews and distributes his own brand.

Flaccid drama with an eventually mystifying superabundance of style.
w Frank Moorhouse d Dusan Makavejev ph Dean Semler m William Motzing pd Graham (Grace) Walker ed John Scott
☆ Eric Roberts, Greta Scacchi, Bill Kerr, Max Gillies, Kris McQuade

Cockeyed Cavaliers

US 1934 72m bw
RKO
▦

Two idiots have various adventures in medieval England.
Fairly tolerable slapstick from a team which never seemed quite at its best.
w Edward Kaufman, Ben Holmes d Mark Sandrich
☆ Bert Wheeler, Robert Woolsey, Thelma Todd, Noah Beery, Dorothy Lee, Franklin Pangborn, Robert Greig
'With a fair quota of laughs, it eclipses their previous releases.' – *Variety*

The Cockeyed Cowboys of Calico County

US 1969 99m Technicolor
Universal
A Western blacksmith stops working when his mail order bride doesn't arrive.
Styleless American rehash of La Femme du Boulanger, with all concerned trying too hard.
w Ranald MacDougall d Tony Leader
☆ Dan Blocker, Nanette Fabray, Mickey Rooney

The Cockeyed Miracle

US 1946 92m bw
MGM
GB title: *Mr Griggs Returns*
Family ghosts return to sort out domestic chaos.
Moderate 'Topper'-style comedy with amiable cast.
w Karen de Wolf *play* George Seaton d S. Sylvan Simon
☆ Frank Morgan, Cecil Kellaway, Gladys Cooper, Audrey Totter, Marshall Thompson, Leon Ames

The Cockeyed World *

US 1929 115m bw
Fox
Further adventures of Sergeants Flagg and Quirt, the boisterous heroes of *What Price Glory.*
Lively early talkie; the adventure comedy remains interesting, though the technique is badly faded.
w William K. Wells, Laurence Stallings, Maxwell Anderson, Wilson Mizner, Tom Barry d Raoul Walsh ph Arthur Edeson
☆ Victor McLaglen, Edmund Lowe, Lili Damita, Lelia Karnelly, El Brendel, Bob Burns, Stuart Erwin

Cockfighter

US 1974 92m Metrocolor
Rio Pinto/New World/Artists Entertainment Complex (Roger Corman)
▦
aka: *Born to Kill*
A professional cockfighter ends a run of bad luck but loses his girl.
Not badly made but rather seedy film about appalling people.
w Charles Willeford *novel* Charles Willeford d Monte Hellman ph Nestor Almendros m Michael Franks
☆ Warren Oates, Richard B. Shull, Harry Dean Stanton, Ed Begley Jnr, Laurie Bird, Troy Donahue

Cockleshell Heroes

GB 1955 97m Technicolor Cinemascope
Columbia/Warwick (Phil C. Samuel)
📺
During World War II, ten marines are trained to travel by canoe into Bordeaux harbour and attach limpet mines to German ships.
Absolutely predictable semi-documentary war heroics, with barrack-room humour turning eventually into tragedy. The familiar elements, including a display of stiff upper lips, ensured box-office success.
w Bryan Forbes, Richard Maibaum d José Ferrer ph John Wilcox, Ted Moore m John Addison
☆ José Ferrer, Trevor Howard, Dora Bryan, Victor Maddern, Anthony Newley, Peter Arne, David Lodge, Walter Fitzgerald, Beatrice Campbell

Cocktail

US 1988 103m Metrocolor
Warner/Touchstone/Silver Screen Partners III/Interscope Communications (Ted Field, Robert W. Cort)
📺 ▦ ◎ ⌒

A young man becomes a bartender in the belief he will meet rich and beautiful women.
Glossy nonsense.
w Heywood Gould *novel* Heywood Gould d Roger Donaldson ph Dean Semler m Peter Robinson ad Dan Davis ed Neil Travis, Barbara Dunning
☆ Tom Cruise, Bryan Brown, Elisabeth Shue, Lisa Banes, Laurence Luckinbill, Kelly Lynch, Gina Gershon, Ron Dean

Cocoanut Grove

US 1938 85m bw
Paramount (George Arthur)
A band is fired from an excursion boat but makes it big in a Los Angeles night-club.
Vacuous comedy musical with a watchable number or two.
w Sy Bartlett, Olive Cooper d Alfred Santell ph Leo Tover m/ly various
☆ Fred MacMurray, Harriet Hilliard, The Yacht Club Boys, Ben Blue, Eve Arden, Billy Lee, Rufe Davis
'No mind-wearier as to plot, it shapes up as nice summer film fare.' – *Variety*

The Cocoanuts **

US 1929 96m bw
Paramount (Walter Wanger, James R. Cowan)
▦ ◎ ◉

A chiselling hotel manager tries to get in on the Florida land boom.
Considering its age and the dismal prints which remain, this is a remarkably lively if primitive first film by the Marxes, with some good routines among the excess footage.
w George S. Kaufman, Morrie Ryskind d Robert Florey, Joseph Santley ph George Folsey m/ly Irving Berlin
☆ The Four Marx Brothers, Margaret Dumont, Oscar Shaw, Mary Eaton, Kay Francis, Basil Ruysdael
'The camerawork showed all the mobility of a concrete fire hydrant caught in a winter freeze.' – *Paul D. Zimmermann*

Cocoon **

US 1985 117m DeLuxe
TCF/Zanuck-Brown (Lili Zanuck)
📺 ▦ ▦ ⌒

Aliens from another galaxy leave pods in the pool of a Florida retirement home, whose bathers are rejuvenated.
Unusual, amusing and sentimentally effective movie of the kind which gets hearty word-of-mouth recommendation.
w Tom Benedek *novel* David Saperstein d Ron Howard ph Don Peterman m James Horner pd Jack T. Collis ed Daniel Hanley, Michael J. Hill
☆ Don Ameche, Wilford Brimley, Hume Cronyn, Brian Dennehy, Jack Gilford, Steve Guttenberg, Maureen Stapleton, Jessica Tandy, Gwen Verdon
'A mesmerizing tale that's a certified audience pleaser.' – *Variety*
🏆 best supporting actor, Don Ameche

Cocoon: The Return

US 1988 116m DeLuxe
Fox/Richard D. Zanuck, David Brown, Lili Fini Zanuck
📺 ▦ ◎ ⌒

After a visit to another planet, three rejuvenated elderly couples return to Earth to rescue alien pods.
Lacklustre sequel, a concept in search of a script.
w Stephen McPherson *story* Stephen McPherson, Elizabeth Bradley d Daniel Petrie ph Tak Fujimoto m James Horner pd Lawrence Paull ed Mark Warner
☆ Don Ameche, Wilford Brimley, Courteney Cox, Hume Cronyn, Jack Gilford, Steve Guttenberg, Barret Oliver, Maureen Stapleton, Elaine Stritch, Jessica Tandy, Gwen Verdon, Tahnee Welch
'Extraordinarily scrappy.' – *MFB*

Code Name: Emerald

US 1985 93m Metrocolor
NBC/MGM-UA
▦ ◎

A double agent is sent to Paris in 1944 to make sure that a captured American officer doesn't talk about the D-Day plans.
Plodding, old hat war melodrama with no specific virtues.
w Ronald Bass *novel The Emerald Illusion* by Ronald Bass d Jonathan Sanger ph Freddie Francis
☆ Ed Harris, Max von Sydow, Horst Buchholz, Helmut Berger, Graham Crowden

Code Name: Trixie: see *The Crazies*

Code Name: Zebra

US 1985 96m Foto-Kem
Pac-West (Joseph Lucchese)
▦

On his release from prison, a gangster takes his revenge against a gang of ex-Vietnam War veterans who put him inside.
Cheap and nasty exploitation film that rehashes in a ham-fisted manner all the usual shoot-outs, car crashes and casual violence; if it has any originality, it is that the good guys are even more unpleasant than the bad.
w Robert Leon d Joe Tornatore ph Bill Dickson, Tom Denove m Louis Febre, Peter Rotter ed Ed Hansen
☆ Jim Mitchum, Mike Lane, Timmy Brown, Joe Dante, Chuck Morrell, Deana Jurgens, Lindsey Crosby, Frank Sinatra Jnr

Code of Scotland Yard: see *The Shop at Sly Corner*

Code of Silence

US 1985 101m Astrocolor
Rank/Orion (Raymond Wagner)
📺 ▦

A Chicago cop raids a drug den and sets off a gang war.
Routine tough stuff which just about avoids self-parody.
w Michael Butler, Dennis Shryack, Mike Gray d Andy Davis ph Frank Tidy m David Frank pd Maher Ahmed ed Peter Parasheles, Christopher Holmes
☆ Chuck Norris, Henry Silva, Bert Remsen, Molly Hagan

Code of the Secret Service

US 1939 58m bw
Warner
Agents track a gang who stole treasury banknote plates.
Serial-like adventures, one of several from the same stable, all featuring the future president of the US.
w Lee Katz, Dean Franklin d Noel Smith
☆ Ronald Reagan, Eddie Foy Jnr, Rosella Towne, Moroni Olsen, Edgar Edwards
'Filler fodder; a wild actioner for lower dual bookings.' – *Variety*

Code Two

US 1953 69m bw
MGM
Three young men join the police academy.
Predictable second biller.
w Marcel Klauber d Fred M. Wilcox
☆ Ralph Meeker, Sally Forrest, Keenan Wynn, James Craig, Robert Horton, Elaine Stewart, Jeff Richards

Codename Wild Geese

Italy 1984 101m colour
Entertainment/Ascot/Gico Cinematografica (Erwin C. Dietrich)
📺

Mercenaries are sent to destroy heavily guarded opium depots in Thailand.
Brisk but undistinguished action movie, with a large cast of expendable Orientals.
w Michael Lester d Anthony M. Dawson (Antonio Margheriti) ph Peter Baumgartner m Jan Nemec
☆ Lewis Collins, Lee Van Cleef, Ernest Borgnine, Klaus Kinski, Manfred Lehmann, Mimsy Farmer, Thomas Dannenberg, Wolfgang Pampel, Harmut Neugebauer

---

Un Coeur en Hiver *

France 1991 104m colour
Artificial Eye/Film Par
Film/Cinea/Orly/Sedif/Paravision/DA Films/FR 3 (Jean-Louis Livi, Philippe Carcassonne)

aka: A Heart in Winter

A young violinist, about to leave the home of her female manager to live with a violin maker, falls in love with his friend and partner.
A familiar story, impeccably acted but failing to touch the emotions, possibly because of its distanced direction and the rigid, symphonic structure which restricts its humanity.
w Claude Sautet, Jacques Fieschi, Jérôme Tonnerre d Claude Sautet ph Yves Angelo m Philippe Sarde ad Christian Marti ed Jacqueline Thiedot
☆ Daniel Auteuil, Emmanuelle Béart, André Dussollier, Elisabeth Bourgine, Brigitte Catillon, Maurice Garrel
'Extremely subtle and intensely enjoyable, impressive pic deserves international art house attention.' – *Variety*

Coffy

US 1973 91m Movielab
Focus/AIP (Robert A. Papazian)

A nurse pretends to be a drug addict in order to exact revenge on those responsible for destroying the life of her 11-year-old sister.
Lively, violent blaxploitation movie, in which Grier moves like an avenging angel through a corrupt society.
wd Jack Hill ph Paul Lohmann m Roy Ayers ad Perry Ferguson ed Charles McClelland
☆ Pam Grier, Booker Bradshaw, Robert DoQui, William Elliott, Allan Arbus, Sid Haig, Barry Cahill
'What distinguishes this superficially rough and routine effort from the run of the black sexploitation mill is its all-embracing grimness. Its moral blackness, in fact.' – *Verina Glaessner, MFB*

Cohen and Tate

US 1988 86m DeLuxe
Guild/Nelson Films (Antony Rufus Isaacs, Jeff Young)

Two hit men kidnap a boy who witnessed a gangland murder.
A thriller lacking suspense.
wd Eric Red ph Victor J. Kemper pd David M. Haber ed Edward Abroms
☆ Roy Scheider, Adam Baldwin, Harley Cross, Cooper Huckabee, Suzanne Savoy, Marco Perella, Tom Campitelli, Andrew R. Gill

The Cohens and the Kellys

Seven comedies were made, all for Universal, about the friendly rivalry of Jewish and Irish neighbours. They were:
1926 The Cohens and Kellys
1928 The Cohens and Kellys in Paris
1929 The Cohens and Kellys in Atlantic City
1930 The Cohens and Kellys in Scotland
1931 The Cohens and Kellys in Africa
1932 The Cohens and Kellys in Hollywood
1933 The Cohens and Kellys in Trouble
George Sidney played Cohen in all of the series and Charlie Murray played Kelly in five films. He was replaced by J. Farrell MacDonald in *Paris* and by Mack Swain in *Atlantic City*.

Coiffeur pour Dames

France 1952 87m bw
Hoche (Jean Boyer)
GB title: *An Artist with Ladies*
A Provençal sheep shearer becomes a fashionable ladies' hairdresser with a Champs-élysées salon, and finds that his clients are all susceptible to his charms.
Obvious star comedy with a fair measure of laughs; more in fact than the much later Shampoo.
w Serge Véber, Jean Boyer play P. Armont, M. Gerbidon d Jean Boyer ph Charles Suin m Paul Misraki
☆ Fernandel, Blanchette Crunoy, Renée Devillers, Arlette Poirier

Cold around the Heart

US 1997 96m colour
TCF/Illusion/Baumgarten-Prophet/Kushner Locke (Dan Halsted, Craig Baumgarten, Adam J. Merims)

aka: Cold Heart

A jewel thief is double-crossed by his girlfriend and framed for the murders she has committed.
Tough thriller set among crooks to whom duplicity is as natural as breathing, and who like to discuss their attitudes to one another at length.
wd John Ridley ph Malik Hassan Sayeed m Mason Daring pd Kara Lindstrom, Missy Okum ed Eric L. Beason
☆ David Caruso, Kelly Lynch, Stacey Dash, Chris Noth, John Spencer, Pruitt Taylor Vince, Richard Kind
'A derivative but fitfully effective modern *film noir*.' – *Sight and Sound*

Cold Blood (dubbed)

West Germany 1975 76m colour
City/Televox

A teacher becomes involved with a pilot who is on the run after stealing a million dollars from gangsters.
Run-of-the-mill thriller, with an ending that attempts to be clever but is merely botched.
w Günter Vaessen d Ralf Gregan ph Michael Ballhaus m Rolg Bauer pd Herbert Kluver ed Christel Orthmann
☆ Rutger Hauer, Vera Tschechowa, Horst Frank, Walter Richter, Günther Stoll

Cold Comfort

Canada 1989 88m colour
Norstar/Telefilm (Lana Frank, Ray Sager)
A snowbound motorist is kidnapped by an unbalanced truck driver as a birthday present for his 18-year-old daughter.
Claustrophobic thriller that lacks suspense.
w Richard Beattie, Elliot L. Sims play James Garrard d Vic Sarin ph Vic Sarin m Jeff Dana ad Jo-Ann Chorney ed Nick Rotundo
☆ Maury Chaykin, Margaret Langrick, Paul Gross

Cold Comfort Farm *

GB 1995 95m colour
BBC/Thames TV (Alison Gilby)

A London cousin brings changes to the family who inhabit a decaying farm, ruled by an ageing matriarch who once saw something nasty in the woodshed.
Enjoyable comedy that doesn't quite capture the flavour of the original satire or the high and rural romanticism of Mary Webb's novels.
w Malcolm Bradbury novel Stella Gibbons d John Schlesinger ph Chris Seager m Robert Lockhart pd Malcolm Thornton ed Mark Day
☆ Eileen Atkins, Kate Beckinsale, Sheila Burrell, Stephen Fry, Freddie Jones, Joanna Lumley, Ian McKellen, Miriam Margolyes, Rufus Sewell
'A deliciously eccentric, fabulously acted comedy of manners.' – *Variety*
† Shown on television in Britain, it was given a cinema release in the US.

Cold Cuts: see Buffet Froid

Cold Dog Soup

US 1989 88m Technicolor
Palace/HandMade/Aspen (Richard G. Abramson, William E. McEuen)

Given a dead dog to bury by his new girlfriend, a man attempts to sell it to a furrier and a Chinese restaurateur.
Dismal attempt at a black comedy.
w Thomas Pope book Stephen Dobyns d Alan Metter ph Frederick Elmes m Michael Kamen, Mark Snow pd David L. Snyder ed Kaja Fehr
☆ Randy Quaid, Frank Whaley, Christine Harnos, Sheree North, Nancy Kwan
'Miserably unwatchable.' – *MFB*

Cold Eyes of Fear

Italy/Spain 1971 95m colour
Cinemar/Atlantida (José Frade)

A lawyer and a prostitute are held hostage by two convicts, one of whom is intent on killing the lawyer's uncle, a judge who wrongly condemned him to prison.

Low-budget thriller in which a battle of wits holds the attention for a time.
w Leo Anchoriz, Tito Carpi, Enzo G. Castellari d Enzo G. Castellari ph Antonio Ballesteros m Ennio Morricone pd Roman Calatayud ed Vincenzo Tomassi
☆ Giovanna Ralli, Frank Wolff, Fernando Rey, Julian Mateos, Gianni Garko, Karin Schubert, Leon Lenoir, Franco Marletta

Cold Feet *

US 1989 94m colour
Virgin/Avenue Pictures (Cassian Elwes)

Three petty crooks fall out after smuggling emeralds into America inside a horse.
Amusingly ramshackle semi-Western.
w Thomas McGuane, Jim Harrison d Robert Dornhelm ph Brian Duggan m Tom Bahler pd Bernt Capra
☆ Keith Carradine, Sally Kirkland, Tom Waits, Bill Pullman, Rip Torn, Kathleen York, Macon McCalman

Cold Fever *

US/Denmark/Germany/Iceland 1995 86m colour
Theatrical Experience/Icicle/IFC/Film Fonds/Sunrise/Pandora/Zentropa/Alta (Jim Stark)
A Japanese man travels by bus, car and horse to a remote part of Iceland to hold a memorial service for his parents, who died there.
A quirky road movie where different cultures don't so much clash as collide head-on.
w Jim Stark, Fridrik Thor Fridriksson d Fridrik Thor Fridriksson ph Ari Kristinsson m Hilmar Orn Hilmarsson pd Arni Poll Johansson ed Steingrimur Karlsson
☆ Masatshi Nagase, Lili Taylor, Fisher Stevens, Gisli Halldorsson, Laura Hughes, Seijun Suzuki, Katrin Olafsdottir
'Drive-by surrealism with ice on top.' – *Tom Shone, Sunday Times*

Cold Front

Canada 1989 96m colour
Beacon Group (Ed Richardson, Sean Allan)

An American and a Canadian cop become entangled in dirty deals made by the KGB and the CIA when they investigate a killing.
Cheap, nasty and stupidly violent thriller with no redeeming qualities.
w Sean Allan, Stefan Arngrim d Paul Bnarbic (Allan Goldstein) ph Thomas Burstyn m Braun Farnon, Craig Zurba pd Sarina Rotstein-Cheikes ed Martin Hunter
☆ Martin Sheen, Michael Ontkean, Kim Coates, Beverly D'Angelo, Jan Rubes, Yvan Ponton, Miguel Fernandes

Cold Heart: see Cold around the Heart

Cold Heaven

US 1992 105m colour
(Allan Scott, Jonathan Crane)

An adulterous wife, a lapsed Catholic, has a vision of the Virgin Mary while on holiday in Mexico after she believes that her husband has been killed in a boating accident.
A flawed attempt to transfer to the screen a novel dealing with thought and feelings rather than action; it holds the attention without satisfying.
w Allan Scott novel Brian Moore d Nicolas Roeg ph Francis Kenny m Stanley Myers pd Steve Legler ed Tony Lawson
☆ Theresa Russell, Mark Harmon, James Russo, Talia Shire, Will Patton, Richard Bradford, Seymour Cassel
'Confused and confusing, dazzling and disturbing, fascinating and frustrating.' – *Film Review*

The Cold Light of Day

Netherlands 1995 96m colour
Polygram/Meteor/Capitol (Chris Brouwer, Haig Balian)

In Eastern Europe, an obsessional former police inspector determines to track down the killer of young children, after his chief, facing re-election, forces a drug addict to confess to the crimes.
Melodramatic and implausible drama, with occasional moments of suspense.

w Doug Magee story Es geschah am hellichten Tag by Friedrich Dürrenmatt d Rudolf Van Den Berg ph Igor Luther m Stefan Truyman, Yves Elegeert ad Zdenek Fleming ed Kant Pan
☆ Richard E. Grant, Lynsey Baxter, Simon Cadell, James Laurenson, Heathcote Williams, Thom Hoffman, Gerard Thoolen, Perdita Weeks
'This ludicrous thriller lacks atmosphere, while the cast's English accents are idiotically at odds with the locale.' – *Sight and Sound*

The Cold Summer of '53 **

USSR 1987 100m colour
Mosfilm
In the period after Stalin's death when criminals were freed, an exile in a remote part of Siberia is roused from his apathy to defend a small community when it is terrorized by a gang of thugs.
A tense and gripping, though slow-paced, thriller that can also be seen as a sharp comment on the changing politics of its time.
w Edgar Dubrovsky d Alexander Proshkin ph Boris Brozhovsky m V. Martynov pd Valery Filippov
☆ Valeri Priyomykhov, Anatoli Papanov, Victor Stepanov, Nina Usatova, Zoya Buryak, Yuri Kuznetsov, Vladimir Kashpur
† It was the second-highest grossing movie in the USSR in 1988.

Cold Sweat

Italy/France 1970 94m colour
Corona/Fair (Robert Dorfmann)

aka: The Man With Two Shadows
An American living peaceably on the Riviera is forced into drug smuggling.
Reliable tough stuff for those who like that sort of thing.
w Shimon Wincelberg, Albert Simonin novel Ride the Nightmare by Richard Matheson d Terence Young ph Jean Rabier m Michel Magne
☆ Charles Bronson, James Mason, Liv Ullmann, Jill Ireland, Jean Topart

Cold Turkey *

US 1970 102m DeLuxe
UA/Tandem/DFI (Norman Lear)

A tobacco company offers 25 million dollars to any town which can give up smoking for thirty days.
Rather wild and strained but sporadically amusing satirical comedy, aggressively littered with unpleasant detail.
w Norman Lear novel I'm Giving Them Up for Good by Margaret and Neil Rau d Norman Lear ph Charles F. Wheeler m Randy Newman
☆ Dick Van Dyke, Pippa Scott, Tom Poston, Edward Everett Horton, Bob Newhart, Vincent Gardenia, Jean Stapleton
'An eager desire to debunk and shock at the same time.' – *David McGillivray*

Cold Water: see L'Eau Froide

A Cold Wind in August *

US 1960 77m bw
UA/Troy Films (Robert L. Ross, Philip Hazleton)
An ageing stripper seduces a 17-year-old janitor but the affair ends when he sees her do her act.
Roughly-made, well-acted sex drama which at the time seemed mildly shocking but can only survive for its central acting performance.
w Burton Wohl novel Burton Wohl d Alexander Singer ph Floyd Crosby m Gerald Fried
☆ Lola Albright, Scott Marlowe, Joe de Santis, Herschel Bernardi

The Colditz Story **

GB 1954 97m bw
British Lion/Ivan Foxwell

Adventures of British POWs in the German maximum security prison in Saxony's Colditz Castle during World War II.
Probably the most convincing of the British accounts of POW life, with a careful balance of tragedy and comedy against a background of humdrum, boring daily existence. A TV series followed in 1972.
w Guy Hamilton, Ivan Foxwell book P. R. Reid d Guy Hamilton ph Gordon Dines m Francis Chagrin
☆ John Mills, Eric Portman, Christopher Rhodes, Lionel Jeffries, Bryan Forbes, Ian Carmichael,

Richard Wattis, Frederick Valk, Anton Diffring, Eugene Deckers, Theodore Bikel
'It has all the realism, dignity and courage of the men it commemorates.' – *News of the World*

'You won't dare open your mouth, but you'll be screaming for her to escape!'

The Collector *
US 1965 119m Technicolor
Columbia (Jud Kinberg, John Kohn)
🎬 🔲 ⊛ 🎧
An inhibited young butterfly specialist kidnaps a girl to add to his collection.
Talkative and unrewarding suspenser with pretensions, sluggishly handled and not very interestingly acted.
w Stanley Mann, John Kohn *novel* John Fowles d William Wyler *ph* Robert L. Surtees, Robert Krasker *m* Maurice Jarre
☆ Terence Stamp, Samantha Eggar, Mona Washbourne
⅄ Stanley Mann, John Kohn; William Wyler; Samantha Eggar

Colleen *
US 1936 89m bw
Warner (Robert Lord)
Boy meets Irish girl in New York.
Typical light musical of the period with standard studio talent.
w Peter Milne, F. Hugh Herbert, Sig Herzig d Alfred E. Green *ph* Byron Haskin, Sol Polito *m/ly* Harry Warren, Al Dubin *ch* Bobby Connolly *gown* Orry-Kelly
☆ Dick Powell, Ruby Keeler, Jack Oakie, Joan Blondell, Hugh Herbert, Louise Fazenda, Paul Draper, Marie Wilson, Luis Alberni, Hobart Cavanaugh, Berton Churchill

'You'll graduate with a perpetual smile!'

College *
🎬🎬 US 1927 65m bw silent
Buster Keaton Productions (Joseph M. Schenck)
🔲 ⊛
A brainy high school student becomes a college football star.
Disappointing comedy from this great stone-faced clown: the plums are there, but few and far between.
w Carl Harbaugh, Bryan Foy d James W. Horne *ph* J. Devereux Jennings, Bert Haines
☆ Buster Keaton, Ann Cornwall, Harold Goodwin, Snitz Edwards, Florence Turner

College Coach
US 1933 75m bw
Warner
A tough football coach finds that his best star is a timid chemistry student.
Unremarkable studio programmer despite a strong cast.
w Niven Busch, Manuel Seff d William A. Wellman
☆ Dick Powell, Pat O'Brien, Ann Dvorak, Arthur Byron, Lyle Talbot, Hugh Herbert, Guinn Williams, Donald Meek
'Hasn't enough punch for real sock grosses.' – *Variety*

College Confidential
US 1960 91m bw
Universal (Albert Zugsmith)
A professor surveys the sexual habits of his students.
Tinpot exposé of a highly dubious kind.
w Irving Shulman d Albert Zugsmith
☆ Steve Allen, Jayne Meadows, Mamie Van Doren, Rocky Marciano, Mickey Shaughnessy, Herbert Marshall, Conway Twitty

College Holiday
US 1936 87m bw
Paramount (Harlan Thompson)
Bright young specimens are invited to spend a summer with a lady hotelier interested in eugenics.
Boisterous fun and games which may have seemed funny at the time.
w J. P. McEvoy, Harlan Ware, Jay Gorney, Henry Myers d Frank Tuttle *ph* Theodor Sparkuhl *m/ly* various
☆ Jack Benny, George Burns, Gracie Allen, Mary Boland, Martha Raye, Etienne Girardot, Marsha Hunt, Leif Erickson, Eleanore Whitney, Johnny Downs, Olympe Bradna, Ben Blue, Jed Prouty
'For a picture that permits the cast to run around practically on the loose, it gets along remarkably well.' – *Variety*

College Humor
US 1933 84m bw
Paramount
A freshman discovers that football and necking are at least as important as studies.
Easy-going comedy-musical which helped to establish its star.
w Claude Binyon, Frank Butler *story* Dean Fales d Wesley Ruggles *ph* Leo Tover *m/ly* Arthur Johnston, Sam Coslow
☆ Bing Crosby, Jack Oakie, George Burns, Gracie Allen, Richard Arlen, Mary Carlisle
'A light frothy musical that doesn't give the customers much of a mental workout.' – *Variety*

College Rhythm
US 1934 75m bw
Paramount
A college football team fights to help an old-fashioned department store to modernize itself.
Of its time, a pleasant 'youth' movie, but with nothing for posterity.
w Walter de Leon, John McDermott, Francis Martin, George Marion Jnr d Norman Taurog *m/ly* Mack Gordon, Harry Revel
☆ Jack Oakie, Joe Penner, Mary Brian, Lanny Ross, Helen Mack, Lyda Roberti, George Barbier, Franklin Pangborn, Dean Jagger
'Entertaining semi-musical with bright box-office possibilities.' – *Variety*
🎵 'Stay as Sweet as You Are'; 'Goo Goo'; 'Let's Give Three Cheers for Love'; 'Take a Number from One to Ten'

College Scandal
US 1935 75m bw
Paramount
A killer attacks three male students.
After College Humor and College Rhythm, this amounts to College Murder. With stars, it could have been memorable.
w Frank Partos, Charles Brackett, Marguerite Roberts d Elliott Nugent
☆ Arline Judge, Kent Taylor, Wendy Barrie, Mary Nash, William Stack, William Frawley, Benny Baker, Johnny Downs
'Worthwhile summer fare for high-grade dual houses.' – *Variety*

College Swing
US 1938 86m bw
Paramount (Lewis Gensler)
GB title: *Swing, Teacher, Swing*
A dumb girl must graduate if a college is to inherit a fortune.
Mild comedy more notable for its cast than its script.
w Walter de Leon, Francis Martin d Raoul Walsh *ph* Victor Milner *m/ly* various
☆ George Burns, Gracie Allen, Martha Raye, Bob Hope, Edward Everett Horton, Florence George, Ben Blue, Betty Grable, Jackie Coogan, John Payne, Cecil Cunningham, Robert Cummings
'A medley of vaude specialties, bits and numbers strung together in not too happy a manner.' – *Variety*

La Collina degli Stivali: see Boots Hill

Colonel Blimp: see The Life and Death of Colonel Blimp

'Back from the dead … To reclaim his life and the woman he loved.'

Le Colonel Chabert *
France 1994 111m colour Panavision
Guild/Film Par
Film/DD/Paravision/Sidonie/Orly/Sedif/TF1 (Jean Louis-Livi)
🔲 🎧
Ten years after his supposed death in battle, an army officer returns to France to reclaim his identity, his fortune and his wife, now married to an ambitious politician.
Impressive moments, particularly the opening scenes of the aftermath of battle, do not quite compensate for the often stilted approach to a period drama of loss and betrayal.
w Jean Cosmos, Yves Angelo *novel* Honoré de Balzac d Yves Angelo *ph* Bernard Lutic m Beethoven, Mozart, Schubert *ad* Bernard Vezat *ed* Thierry Derocles
☆ Gérard Depardieu, Fanny Ardant, Fabrice Luchini, André Dussollier, Daniel Prévost, Claude Rich, Romane Bohringer, Maxime Leroux
'Predictable and uninspiring.' – *Sight and Sound*

Colonel Effingham's Raid
US 1946 70m bw
TCF (Lamar Trotti)
🔲
GB title: *Man of the Hour*
A retired Southern colonel tries to straighten out a corrupt Georgia town.
Competent, unsurprising programmer.
w Kathryn Scola *novel* Berry Fleming d Irving Pichel *ph* Edward Cronjager m Cyril Mockridge
☆ Charles Coburn, Joan Bennett, William Eythe, Allyn Joslyn, Elizabeth Patterson, Donald Meek, Frank Craven, Thurston Hall, Cora Witherspoon, Emory Parnell, Henry Armetta, Roy Roberts, Charles Trowbridge

Colonel Redl **
Hungary/West Germany/Austria 1984 149m Eastmancolor
Mafilm/Mokep/Manfred Durniok/ZDF/ORF
🔲 🎧
original title: *Oberst Redl*
The career of a railwayman's son who in the early years of the century rises high in the military but is condemned by his own insecurities and forced to commit suicide as a spy.
Whether or not one cares for the ironic parable (also treated by John Osborne in his play A Patriot for Me) this is a handsome film full of brilliant visuals.
w Istvan Szabo, Peter Dobai d Istvan Szabo *ph* Lajos Koltai m Zdenko Tamassy
☆ Klaus Maria Brandauer, Hans-Christian Blech, Armin Müller-Stahl, Gudrun Landgrebe, Jan Niklas
⅄ best picture
🎬 best foreign film

The Color of Money **
US 1986 119m DuArt
Touchstone (Irving Axelrod, Barbara de Fina)
🔲 🔲 ⊛ 🎧
Twenty-five years later, the hero of *The Hustler* teaches a young man his skills.
Slackly told but consistently enjoyable adventures of Fast Eddie Felson in his older age.
w Richard Price, based on characters created by Walter Tevis d Martin Scorsese *ph* Michael Ballhaus m Robbie Robertson
☆ Paul Newman, Tom Cruise, Mary Elizabeth Mastrantonio, Helen Shaver, Bill Cobbs, John Turturro
'Fast and absorbing and often thrillingly well made, but there's something impure about it: it's a streamlined, best-sellerish replay of Scorsese's work in the 1970s.' – *Terrence Rafferty, Nation*
👤 Paul Newman
⅄ Michael Balhaus; Boris Leven (art direction); Kevin J. O'Hara (sound); Mary Elizabeth Mastrantonio; Richard Price

Color of Night
US 1994 123m colour
Guild/Cinergi/Hollywood Pictures (David Matalon, Buzz Feitshans)
🔲 🔲 ⊛ 🎧
A traumatized psychiatrist takes over a group of patients that includes the person who murdered his colleague.
A ludicrous thriller that reaches depths of absurdity rarely seen on screen, particularly in its risibly overblown finale. Willis acts in Die Hard mode while the rest of the cast twitch uncontrollably around him.
w Matthew Chapman, Billy Ray d Richard Rush *ph* Dietrich Lohmann m Dominic Frontiere *pd* James L. Schoppe *ed* Jack Hofstra
☆ Bruce Willis, Jane March, Ruben Blades, Lesley Ann Warren, Scott Bakula, Brad Dourif, Lance Henriksen, Shirley Knight
'A sure bet for many Worst of the Year lists, this wholly terrible movie is far more enjoyable and astonishing than many halfway good ones.' – *Kim Newman, Sight and Sound*
'It's hard not to regard this as another woeful addition to the ever-growing canon of Willis stinkers.' – *Empire*
'This trashy, over the top, often funny feature has sex, nudity, gore, Vertigo scenes and lots of nutty patients.' – *Psychotronic Video*
† The version shown in cinemas was recut by the production company. The director's cut, lasting six minutes longer, was released on video.

The Color Purple **
US 1985 152m DeLuxe
Warner/Amblin (Steven Spielberg, Kathleen Kennedy, Frank Marshall, Quincy Jones)
🔲 🔲 ⊛ 🎬 🎧
The growth of a Southern black family during the first half of the century.
Well-intentioned and gracious but not always dramatically cohesive generation saga from a director trying to prove he has depth.
w Menno Meyjes *novel* Alice Walker d Steven Spielberg *ph* Allen Daviau m Quincy Jones *pd* J. Michael Riva *ed* Michael Kahn
☆ Whoopi Goldberg, Danny Glover, Margaret Avery, Oprah Winfrey, Willard Pugh, Adolph Caesar
⅄ best picture; Whoopi Goldberg; Margaret Avery (supporting actress); Oprah Winfrey (supporting actress); adapted screenplay; photography; music; editing; costumes (Aggie Guerard Rodgers); song 'Miss Celie's Blues' (mQuincy Jones, Rod Tempeston, lyLionel Richie)

Colorado Territory *
US 1949 93m bw
Warner (Anthony Veiller)
An outlaw escapes from prison planning one last robbery but is shot in the attempt.
Moderate Western remake of High Sierra.
w John Twist, Edmund H. North d Raoul Walsh *ph* Sid Hickox m David Buttolph
☆ Joel McCrea, Virginia Mayo, Dorothy Malone, Henry Hull, John Archer, James Mitchell, Morris Ankrum, Basil Ruysdael, Frank Puglia

Colors *
US 1988 120m Metrocolor
Rank/Orion (Robert H. Solo)
🔲 🔲 ⊛ 🎧
A veteran cop and his young and cocky partner try to keep the peace between rival Los Angeles street gangs.
A documentary-style look at street violence and its relationship to poverty and drugs. It works well for the first half-hour, but soon loses coherence as a narrative and goes on too long before the effective climax.
w Michael Schiffer d Dennis Hopper *ph* Haskell Wexler m Herbie Hancock *pd* Ron Foreman *ed* Robert Estrin
☆ Sean Penn, Robert Duvall, Maria Conchita Alonso, Randy Brooks, Grand Bush, Don Cheadle, Damon Wayans
'A solidly crafted depiction of some current big-city horrors.' – *Variety*

The Colossus of Rhodes
Italy 1961 129m Technicolor
SuperTotalScope
MGM (Michele Scaglione)
In 300 BC, a huge statue doubles as a fortress to prevent the Phoenicians from invading.
Good-looking spectacle with the usual muddled script.
w Sergio Leone and seven others d Sergio Leone *ph* Emilio Foriscot, Antonio Lopez Ballesteros m Angelo Francesco Lavagnino
☆ Rory Calhoun, Lea Massari, Georges Marchal

Colossus, the Forbin Project: see The Forbin Project

Colour Me Dead
Australia 1970 97m colour
Goldsworthy (Eddie Davis)
🔲
An accountant discovers that he has been given a slow-acting poison.
Poor remake of the 1949 semi-classic D.O.A.: no reason to see it.
w Russel Rouse, Clarence Greene *d/p* Eddie Davis
☆ Tom Tryon, Carolyn Jones, Rick Jason, Patricia Connolly

The Colour of Pomegranates ***
USSR 1969 73m colour
Armenfilm
🔲 🔲
original title: *Tsvet Granata*
Biopic of the 18th-century Armenian poet Sayat Nova, as he rises from a child working as a wool dyer to courtier and monk, told in the manner of his poems.
Extraordinary lyrical film, full of richly coloured emblematic images, like a succession of animated icons.

wd Sergei Paradjanov *ph* Suren Shakhbazian *m* Tieran Mansurian *ad* Stepan Andranikan ☆ Sofiko Chiaureli, M. Alekian, V. Glastian, G. Gegechkori, O. Minasian

Colpire Al Cuore: see Blow to the Heart

Colt 45
US　1950　74m　Technicolor
Warner (Saul Elkins)
US TV title: *Thundercloud*
A new kind of gun, intended to bring law and order to the west, gets into the wrong hands.
Routine, watchable Western which achieved a surprising popularity.
w Thomas Blackburn *d* Edwin L. Marin *ph* Wilfred M. Cline *m* William Lava
☆ Randolph Scott, Zachary Scott, Ruth Roman, Lloyd Bridges, Chief Thundercloud
'Has all the artistry of a picture-strip.' – C. A. Lejeune

Coma *
US　1978　113m　Metrocolor
MGM (Martin Erlichman)
📀 📼 ☊ ♫
A lady doctor suspects that patients are being put deliberately into coma so that their organs can be sold, and finds herself in deadly peril.
Hitchcockian suspense thriller with nobody but the audience believing the heroine; the fact that there are more dead than living characters makes it slightly too ghoulish at times.
wd Michael Crichton *novel* Robin Cook *ph* Victor J. Kemper, Gerald Hirschfeld *m* Jerry Goldsmith *pd* Albert Brenner
☆ Geneviève Bujold, Michael Douglas, Richard Widmark, Elizabeth Ashley, Rip Torn, Lois Chiles, Hari Rhodes, Tom Selleck
'A stupid, silly mad-scientist thriller, with a plucky Girl-Surgeon out to solve the mysteries of some strange deaths.' – Stanley Kauffmann

Comanche
US　1955　87m　DeLuxe　Cinemascope
UA (Carl Krueger)
♫
In 1875 New Mexico, a renegade Indian prevents peace between white and red man.
Cheerful action Western, satisfying to the easily pleased.
w Carl Krueger *d* George Sherman *m* Herschel Burke Gilbert
☆ Dana Andrews, Kent Smith, Nestor Paiva, Henry Brandon, John Litel, Lowell Gilmore, Mike Mazurki

Comanche Station
US　1960　74m　Technicolor　Cinemascope
Columbia (Budd Boetticher)
📀
A man seeks his wife, taken prisoner by Indians.
Below-par star Western, indifferently plotted.
w Burt Kennedy *d* Budd Boetticher *ph* Charles Lawton Jnr *md* Mischa Bakaleinikoff
☆ Randolph Scott, Nancy Gates, Claude Akins, Skip Homeier

Comanche Territory
US　1950　76m　Technicolor
Universal (Leonard Goldstein)
Jim Bowie prevents an Indian war by stopping settlers taking over the silver mines on Comanche land.
Routine Western, given more handsome treatment than it deserves.
w Oscar Brodney, Lewis Meltzer *d* George Sherman *ph* Maury Gertsman *m* Frank Skinner *ad* Bernard Herzbrun, Richard H. Riedel *ed* Frank Gross
☆ Maureen O'Hara, Macdonald Carey, Will Geer, Charles Drake, Pedro de Cordoba, Ian MacDonald, Edmond Cobb, Glenn Strange

The Comancheros **
US　1961　107m　DeLuxe　Cinemascope
TCF (George Sherman)
♫
A Texas Ranger and his gambler prisoner join forces to clean up renegade gunmen operating from a remote armed compound.
Easy-going, cheerfully violent Western with lively roughhouse sequences.
w James Edward Grant, Clair Huffaker *d* Michael Curtiz *ph* William H. Clothier *m* Elmer Bernstein
☆ John Wayne, Stuart Whitman, Nehemiah Persoff, Lee Marvin, Ina Balin, Bruce Cabot

Come and Get It *
US　1936　99m　bw
Samuel Goldwyn (Merritt Hulburd)
📼 📀
The life and loves of a lumber tycoon in 19th-century Wisconsin.
Disappointingly conventional, mainly studio-bound action drama using top talent of the period.
w Jules Furthman, Jane Murfin *novel* Edna Ferber *d* Howard Hawks, William Wyler *ph* Gregg Toland, Rudolph Maté *m* Alfred Newman *ed* Edward Curtiss
☆ Edward Arnold, Joel McCrea, Frances Farmer, Walter Brennan, Andrea Leeds
🏆 Walter Brennan
🏵 Edward Curtiss

Come Back Charleston Blue *
US　1972　101m　Technicolor
Warner/Formosa (Samuel Goldwyn Jnr)
Harlem detectives Coffin Ed Johnson and Gravedigger Jones investigate the case of a long-dead gangster who seems to be still taking vengeance.
Occasionally funny but disturbingly violent crime kaleidoscope with a black ambience, more sophisticated and therefore more generally acceptable than its predecessor Cotton Comes to Harlem (qv).
w Bontche Schweig, Peggy Elliott *novel* The Heat's On by Chester Himes *d* Mark Warren *ph* Dick Kratina *m* Donny Hathaway
☆ Godfrey Cambridge, Raymond St Jacques, Peter de Anda, Jonelle Allen, Percy Rodrigues, Minnie Gentry

'That girl in their house spelled trouble!'
Come Back Little Sheba *
US　1952　99m　bw
Paramount (Hal B. Wallis)
📼 📀
An ex-alcoholic is let down not only by his slovenly wife but by the young girl he idolizes.
Stagey but theatrically effective transcription of a popular domestic drama, with one outstanding performance.
w Ketti Frings *play* William Inge *d* Daniel Mann *ph* James Wong Howe *m* Franz Waxman *ed* Warren Low
☆ Shirley Booth, Burt Lancaster, Terry Moore, Richard Jaeckel
🏆 Shirley Booth
🏵 Terry Moore; editing

Come Back Peter: see Some Like It Sexy

Come Back to Me: see Doll Face

Come Back to the Five and Dime, Jimmy Dean, Jimmy Dean
US　1983　110m　DuArt
Sandcastle 5/Mark Goodman/Viacom
📼 📀 ☊
Misfits meet to celebrate the twentieth anniversary of the death of James Dean.
Filmed play which descends from cynicism through gloom to hysteria and is never very revealing.
w Ed Graczyk *play* Ed Graczyk *d* Robert Altman *ph* Pierre Mignot *m* various
☆ Sandy Dennis, Karen Black, Cher, Sudie Bond, Kathy Bates
'It may seem perverse to describe as Altman's masterpiece so self-contained and "alien" a work, with an existence pre-dating his own involvement and a thrusting (if perverse) biological life that owes nothing to the audience's willingness to participate. But the irony depends solely on which side of Altman's own two-way world one stands.' – Richard Combs, MFB

Come Blow Your Horn *
US　1963　112m　Technicolor　Panavision
Paramount/Lear and Yorkin
📼
A country boy in New York is envious of his older brother's sophisticated life.
Amusing characters and funny lines permeate this stolid transcription of an early Neil Simon success; the big screen is not the place for them.
w Norman Lear *play* Neil Simon *d* Bud Yorkin *ph* William Daniels *m* Nelson Riddle
☆ Frank Sinatra, Tony Bill, Lee J. Cobb, Molly Picon, Jill St John, Barbara Rush, Dan Blocker

Come Clean **
🎭 US　1931　20m　bw
Hal Roach
Two much-married men go out for ice-cream and bring back a woman of the streets they have saved from suicide.
Splendid star comedy with the famous characterizations fully rounded.
w H. M. Walker *d* James W. Horne *ph* Art Lloyd *ed* Richard Currier
☆ Stan Laurel, Oliver Hardy, Mae Busch, Charlie Hall, Gertrude Astor, Linda Loredo
† Remade in 1942 as *Brooklyn Orchid*, with William Bendix and Joe Sawyer.

Come Fill the Cup *
US　1951　113m　bw
Warner (Henry Blanke)
An alcoholic newspaperman cures himself, then his boss's alcoholic son who is involved with gangsters.
Unlikely but solidly entertaining melodrama, powerfully cast.
w Ivan Goff, Ben Roberts *novel* Harlan Ware *d* Gordon Douglas *ph* Robert Burks *m* Ray Heindorf
☆ James Cagney, Gig Young, Raymond Massey, Phyllis Thaxter, James Gleason, Selena Royle, Larry Keating
🏵 Gig Young

Come Fly with Me
US　1962　109m　Metrocolor　Panavision
MGM/Anatole de Grunwald
The romantic adventures of three air hostesses.
Good-looking girls and airplanes but little else make thin entertainment.
w William Roberts *d* Henry Levin *ph* Oswald Morris *m* Lyn Murray
☆ Hugh O'Brian, Dolores Hart, Karl Malden, Pamela Tiffin, Lois Nettleton, Karl Boehm

Come Live with Me *
US　1941　86m　bw
MGM (Clarence Brown)
In order to stay in America, a girl refugee from Vienna arranges a strictly platonic marriage with a struggling author.
Hypnotically predictable comedy, quite well presented and performed.
w Patterson McNutt, Virginia Van Upp *d* Clarence Brown *ph* George Folsey *m* Herbert Stothart
☆ James Stewart, Hedy Lamarr, Ian Hunter, Verree Teasdale, Donald Meek, Barton MacLane, Adeline de Walt Reynolds

Come Next Spring *
US　1955　92m　Trucolor　Republic
A drunkard returns to his Arkansas farm family and wins the respect of them and the community.
D. W. Griffith-type pastoral melodrama which surprisingly works pretty well and leaves one with the intended warm glow.
w Montgomery Pittman *d* R. G. Springsteen *ph* Jack Marta *m* Max Steiner
☆ Ann Sheridan, Steve Cochran, Walter Brennan, Sherry Jackson, Richard Eyer, Edgar Buchanan, Sonny Tufts, Mae Clarke
'An unpretentious film with a good deal of charm.' – MFB

The Come On
US　1956　83m　bw　Superscope
AA (Lindley Parsons)
Husband and wife confidence tricksters get homicidal when she falls in love.
In trade parlance, strictly a lower berth item; but with points of mild interest.
w Warren Douglas *novel* Whitman Chambers *d* Russell Birdwell *ph* Ernest Haller *m* Paul Dunlap
☆ Anne Baxter, Sterling Hayden, John Hoyt, Jesse White, Paul Picerni

Come on George *
GB　1939　88m　bw
ATP/Ealing (Jack Kitchin)
📼
A stableboy calms a nervous racehorse and rides him to victory.
Standard comedy vehicle, well mounted, with the star at his box-office peak.
w Anthony Kimmins, Leslie Arliss, Val Valentine *d* Anthony Kimmins *ph* Ronald Neame, Gordon Dines *m* Ernest Irving *ad* Wilfred Shingleton *ed* Ray Pitt
☆ George Formby, Pat Kirkwood, Joss Ambler, Meriel Forbes, Cyril Raymond, George Carney, Ronald Shiner

Come Out Fighting
US　1945　62m　bw
Monogram/Pathé/Banner (Sam Katzman, Jack Dietz)
The East Side Kids reform the naïve, ballet-dancing son of the police commissioner by saving him from crooked gamblers.
Dull programmer, with rough-and-ready direction and performances and lacking the series' usual boisterous humour.
w Earle Snell *d* William Beaudine *ph* Ira Morgan *md* Edward Kay *ad* David Milton *ed* William Austin
☆ Leo Gorcey, Huntz Hall, Billy Benedict, Gabriel Dell, June Carlson, Amelita Ward, Johnny Duncan

Come Out of the Pantry
GB　1935　73m　bw
British and Dominions (Herbert Wilcox)
An English milord is forced by circumstance to take a job as his boss's footman.
Pleasing if obvious comedy, later remodelled as Spring in Park Lane.
w Austin Parker, Douglas Furber *story* Alice Duer Miller *d* Jack Raymond *ph* Freddie Young, Henry Harris *ad* L. P. Williams *ed* Frederick Wilson
☆ Jack Buchanan, Fay Wray, James Carew, Ronald Squire, Olive Blakeney, Fred Emney

Come See the Paradise *
US　1990　133m　DeLuxe
Fox (Robert F. Colesberry)
📼 📀 ☊ ♫
After Pearl Harbor, a Japanese-American woman, married to an Irish-American soldier, is interned with her family.
A fascinating subject, of racism and culture clash, is submerged by a concentration on an ordinary romance.
wd Alan Parker *m* Michael Seresin *m* Randy Edelman *pd* Geoffrey Kirkland *ed* Gerry Hambling
☆ Dennis Quaid, Tamlyn Tomita, Sab Shimono, Shizuko Hoshi, Stan Egi, Ronald Yamamoto, Akemi Nishino, Naomi Nakano, Brady Tsurutani, Elizabeth Gilliam

Come September
US　1961　112m　Technicolor　CinemaScope
Universal/7 Pictures Corporation/Raoul Walsh Enterprises (Robert Arthur)
A wealthy American discovers that his Italian villa is being used as a hotel by his once-a-year mistress, who is about to marry.
Clumsy sex farce with lush trimmings and generation gap asides; effort more noticeable than achievement.
w Stanley Shapiro, Maurice Richlin *d* Robert Mulligan *ph* William Daniels *m* Hans J. Salter
☆ Rock Hudson, Gina Lollobrigida, Sandra Dee, Bobby Darin, Walter Slezak, Brenda de Banzie, Joel Grey, Rossana Rory, Ronald Howard

Come to the Stable *
US　1949　94m　bw
TCF (Samuel G. Engel)
Two French nuns arrive in New England to build a local hospital, and melt the hearts of the local grumps.
This old-time charmer simply brims with sweetness and light and is produced with high-class studio efficiency.
w Oscar Millard, Sally Benson *story* Clare Boothe Luce *d* Henry Koster *ph* Joseph LaShelle *m* Cyril Mockridge *md* Lionel Newman *ad* Lyle Wheeler, Joseph C. Wright
☆ Loretta Young, Celeste Holm, Hugh Marlowe, Elsa Lanchester, Thomas Gomez, Dorothy Patrick, Basil Ruysdael, Dooley Wilson, Regis Toomey, Henri Letondal

---

⚨ Clare Boothe Luce; Joseph LaShelle; Loretta Young; Celeste Holm; Elsa Lanchester; song 'Through a Long and Sleepless Night' (mAlfred Newman, lyMack Gordon); art direction

'Millions loved him, could someone hate him enough to kill and kill again?'

The Comeback
GB   1978   100m   colour
Enterprise (Peter Walker)
📺

aka: The Day the Screaming Stopped

An American singer in London deals with the murder of his wife – and with her ghost.
Dim mixture of mystery and horror, not at all persuasive.
w Murray Smith d Peter Walker m Stanley Myers
☆ Jack Jones, Sheila Keith, Pamela Stephenson, David Doyle, Bill Owen, Richard Johnson

The Comedians *
US/Bermuda/France   1967   160m   Metrocolor
Panavision
MGM/Maximilian/Trianon (Peter Glenville)
📺

A variety of English-speaking eccentrics are caught up in the violent events of Haiti under Papa Doc Duvalier.
Clumsy and heavy-going compression of a too-topical novel, with most of the plot left in at the expense of character. Neither entertaining nor instructive, but bits of acting please.
w Graham Greene novel Graham Greene
d Peter Glenville ph Henri Decaë m Laurence Rosenthal
☆ Richard Burton, Elizabeth Taylor, Alec Guinness, Peter Ustinov, Lillian Gish, Paul Ford, Roscoe Lee Browne, James Earl Jones, Raymond St Jacques, Cicely Tyson
'So thick and fast do the clichés come that one feels the script can only have been salvaged from some New Statesman competition.' – Tom Milne
'It's pleasant to spend two hours again in Greeneland, still well-stocked with bilious minor crucifixions, furtive fornication, cynical politics, and reluctant hope.' – Stanley Kauffmann

The Comedy Man *
GB   1964   92m   bw
British Lion-Gray-Consort (Jon Pennington)
📺

A middle-aged actor on the skids desperately rounds up his contacts and becomes the star of a TV commercial.
Determinedly depressing satirical melodrama with engaging moments; comedy emphasis would have better suited the talents.
w Peter Yeldham novel Douglas Hayes d Alvin Rakoff ph Ken Hodges m Bill McGuffie
☆ Kenneth More, Cecil Parker, Dennis Price, Billie Whitelaw, Norman Rossington, Angela Douglas, Edmund Purdom, Frank Finlay, Alan Dobie
'Humour and intelligent irony.' – Sunday Express
'A merciless and accurate picture of the brave band of actors who live from hand to mouth and commute between the Salisbury Arms pub and the Poland Street Labour exchange.' – Evening News

The Comedy of Terrors *
US   1963   88m   Pathécolor   Panavision
Alta Vista/AIP (Anthony Carras, Richard Matheson)
📺   💿

Two impecunious funeral directors decide to speed up the demise of their prospective clients.
Disappointingly slackly-handled and rather tiresome macabre frolic, notable for a few splendid moments and an imperishable cast.
w Richard Matheson d Jacques Tourneur
ph Floyd Crosby m Les Baxter
☆ Vincent Price, Peter Lorre, Boris Karloff, Basil Rathbone, Joe E. Brown, Joyce Jameson

Comes a Horseman
US   1978   118m   Technicolor   Panavision
UA/Chartoff-Winkler (Robert Caan)
📺   💿

In the forties, Montana ranchers have a hard time holding onto their land against the pressures of progress and a villainous cattle baron.

Portentous and wholly unexciting modern Western, not helped by a loftily unexplained title and show-off photography.
w Dennis Lynton Clark d Alan J. Pakula
ph Gordon Willis m Michael Small pd George Jenkins
☆ Jane Fonda, Jason Robards Jnr, James Caan, George Grizzard, Richard Farnsworth, Jim Davis
'It's a film of few words (and about a quarter of them mangled by the sound recording). The melodrama is smothered under sullen, overcast skies. How can you get involved in the conflict between the good guys and the bad guys if you can't even see them?' – Pauline Kael
⚨ Richard Farnsworth

Comet over Broadway
US   1938   65m   bw
Warner

An actress, having been involved in a murder, is torn between burning ambition and mother love.
Arrant melodrama which overtaxes its star.
w Mark Hellinger, Robert Buckner story Faith Baldwin d Busby Berkeley
☆ Kay Francis, Ian Hunter, John Litel, Donald Crisp, Minna Gombell, Sybil Jason, Melville Cooper
'A backstage yarn that goes overboard on assorted heartbreaks.' – Variety

Comfort and Joy *
GB   1984   106m   colour
Lake/EMI/STV (Davina Belling, Clive Parsons)
📺   📺

A Scottish radio disc jockey becomes involved in a war between two ice-cream firms.
Heavy comedy, short of laughs and sympathy; a distinct descent from Local Hero, which was a comedown after Gregory's Girl.
wd Bill Forsyth ph Chris Menges m Mark Knopfler
☆ Bill Paterson, Eleanor David, C. P. Grogan, Alex Norton

The Comfort of Strangers
Italy/GB   1990   104m   Technicolor
Rank/Erre/Sovereign/Reteitalia (Angelo Rizzoli)
📺   📺   🎧

original title: Cortesie per gli ospiti
On holiday in Venice, a conventional husband and wife become involved with a sadomasochistic couple.
Bleak and icy tale that will induce a shiver, although the mannered performances aren't an attraction.
w Harold Pinter novel Ian McEwan d Paul Schrader ph Dante Spinotti m Angelo Badalamenti pd Gianni Quaranta ed Bill Pankow
☆ Christopher Walken, Rupert Everett, Natasha Richardson, Helen Mirren, Manfredi Aliquo

The Comic *
US   1969   95m   Technicolor
Columbia (Carl Reiner)
📺   💿

The success, downfall and old age of a silent film comedian in Hollywood.
Remarkably bright and cinematic tragicomedy obviously based on Buster Keaton, with a Citizen Kane-type framework. Not a commercial success, but a must for professionals.
w Carl Reiner, Aaron Rubin d Carl Reiner
ph W. Wallace Kelley m Jack Elliott
☆ Dick Van Dyke, Mickey Rooney, Cornel Wilde, Carl Reiner, Michele Lee, Pert Kelton
'Offers a variety of delights.' – Judith Crist
'A furious editorial about a business that treats its veterans like over-exposed celluloid.' – Variety

Comic Book Confidential **
US/Canada   1989   90m   bw/colour
Sphinx/Don Haig/Martin Harbury/Charles Lippincott (Ron Mann)
📺   💿

A documentary on the evolution of the comic book in North America, from its beginnings in the 30s, with interviews with leading exponents.
Graphic montage of comic books and the controversies and cults they have started, concentrating in particular on the 50s, when they were condemned as corrupters of the young, followed by a period of self-censorship and the return of the Superheroes in the 60s; it is accompanied by a well-chosen soundtrack of the more eccentric songs of each era.

d Ron Mann ph Robert Fresco, Joan Churchill
ad Gerlinde Scharinger ed Robert Kennedy, Ron Mann
☆ Lynda Barry, Charles Burns, Sue Coe, Robert Crumb, Will Eisner, Al Feldstein, Shary Flenniken, William M. Gaines, Bill Griffith, Jaime Hernandez, Jack Kirby, Harvey Kurtzman, Stan Lee, Paul Mavrides, Frank Miller and also Victor Moscoso, Françoise Mouly, Dan O'Neill, Harvey Pekar, Gilbert Shelton, Spain, Art Spiegelman

Comic Strip Hero: see Jeu de Massacre

Comin' at Ya!
US   1981   101m   Technicolor
Dimensionscope 3-D
GTO Films (Marshall Lupo, Stan Torchia)

An ex-outlaw goes in search of three outlaws who kidnapped his wife-to-be.
Determined three-dimensional attack on the sensibilities, with nothing to interest in story or acting.
w Wolf Lowenthal, Lloyd Battista, Gene Quintano story Tony Petitto d Ferdinando Baldi
ph Fernando Arribas m Carlo Savina ad Luciano Spadoni ed Franco Fraticelli
☆ Tony Anthony, Gene Quintano, Victoria Abril, Ricardo Palacios

Comin' thro' the Rye
GB   1923   85m   bw   silent
Hepworth Picture Plays

In Victorian England, lovers meet periodically in a rye field, but events move against them.
Statuesque romantic drama whose reputation may be largely due to its accidental survival. (There was a previous version from the same producer in 1916, with the same leading actress.)
w Blanche McIntosh novel Helen Mathers
d Cecil M. Hepworth ph Geoffrey Faithfull
☆ Alma Taylor, Shayle Gardner, Eileen Dennes, Ralph Forbes, Francis Lister
'My best and most important film.' – Cecil M. Hepworth
'Hepworth's directorial style reaches its material in simplicity.' – Geoff Brown, MFB, 1976

'A man who believed in war! A man who believed in nothing! And a woman who believed in both of them!'

Coming Home *
US   1978   128m   DeLuxe
UA/Jerome Hellman
📺   💿   🎧

An embittered Vietnam veteran falls for the wife of a serving soldier.
Self-pitying romantic wallow which must mean more to American audiences than to others. Goodish acting.
w Waldo Salt, Robert C. Jones story Nancy Dowd d Hal Ashby ph Haskell Wexler m various
pd Mike Haller ed Don Zimmerman
☆ Jane Fonda, Jon Voight, Bruce Dern, Robert Carradine, Penelope Milford
'Just one more story about a wife who gets entangled with another man while her husband is away. Everything in the script that is contemporary is mere updating of that perennial story.' – Stanley Kauffmann
🏆 Jon Voight; Jane Fonda; best screenplay
⚨ best picture; Hal Ashby; Bruce Dern; Penelope Milford; editing

Coming to America
US   1988   116m   Technicolor
UIP/Paramount (George Folsey Jnr, Robert D. Wachs)
📺   💿   🎧

A wealthy African prince poses as a poor student in New York so he can find a bride who will love him for himself.
Tired comedy that fails to exploit Murphy's strengths, despite his popping up heavily disguised in several minor roles.
w David Sheffield, Barry W. Blaustein story Eddie Murphy d John Landis ph Woody Omens
m Nile Rodgers ed Malcolm Campbell, George Folsey Jnr sp make-up: Rick Baker
☆ Eddie Murphy, Arsenio Hall, John Amos, James Earl Jones, Shari Headley, Madge Sinclair
'A true test for loyal fans.' – Variety

Coming Up Roses *
GB   1986   93m   Eastmancolor
Red Rooster/S4C
Welsh Title: Rhosyn a Rhith
When the local cinema closes down the local community takes it over for mushroom-growing.
Charming curiosity in Welsh with English subtitles, reminiscent of Ealing in its heyday.
w Ruth Carter d Stephen Bayley ph Dick Pope
m Michael Story pd Hildegard Bechtler
☆ Dafydd Hywel, Iola Gregory, Olive Michael, Mari Emlyn

A Coming-Out Party: see Very Important Person

The Command
US   1954   94m   Warnercolor   Cinemascope
Warner (David Weisbart)
A cavalry troop escorts a wagon train through Indian country.
Competent but unsurprising 'second team' Western.
w Russell Hughes novel James Warner Bellah
d David Butler ph Wilfrid M. Cline m Dimitri Tiomkin
☆ Guy Madison, Joan Weldon, James Whitmore, Carl Benton Reid, Harvey Lembeck, Ray Teal, Bob Nichols

'Heroes, cowards, fighters, braggarts, liars ... and what goes on in their hearts!'

Command Decision *
US   1949   111m   bw
MGM (Sidney Franklin)
📺   💿

War among the back-room boys; a general, his staff and his peers debate the aerial bombardment of Germany.
Plainly reproduced version of a determinedly serious play, with a remarkable cast partly at sea.
w William R. Laidlaw, George Froeschel
play William Wister Haines d Sam Wood
ph Harold Rosson m Miklos Rozsa
☆ Clark Gable, Walter Pidgeon, Van Johnson, Brian Donlevy, John Hodiak, Charles Bickford, Edward Arnold, Marshall Thompson, Richard Quine, Cameron Mitchell, Clinton Sundberg, Ray Collins, Warner Anderson, John McIntire, Moroni Olsen

Command Performance
GB   1937   84m   bw
Grosvenor (Harcourt Templeman)
Fearing a breakdown through overwork a singer takes to the open road and falls in love with a gypsy.
Innocuous musical, which is mainly a vehicle for Tracy to sing sentimental ballads and attempt an operatic aria.
w Stafford Dickens, George Pearson, Michael Hankinson story Sinclair Hill d Sinclair Hill
ph Cyril Bristow m/ly Tolchard Evans, Stanley Damerell, Irwin Dash md Louis Levy ad C. Wilfred Arnold ed Michael Hankinson
☆ The Street Singer (Arthur Tracy), Lilli Palmer, Mark Daly, Finlay Currie, Jack Milford, Stafford Hilliard

'He's getting even ... by breaking all the rules.'

Commandments
US   1997   86m   DeLuxe
Gramercy/Northern Lights (Michael Chinich, Daniel Goldberg, Joe Medjuck)
📺   💿   🎧

Having lost everything that makes his life worthwhile, a doctor decides to break every one of the Ten Commandments.
A blackish comedy with an uncertain tone and an often squeamish approach to its subject matter.
wd Daniel Taplitz ph Slavomir Idziak m Joseph Vitarelli pd Robin Standefer ed Michael Jablow
☆ Aidan Quinn, Courteney Cox, Anthony LaPaglia, Louis Zorich, Pamela Gray, Pat McNamara, Tom Aldredge
'Too glib and too oblique to break out of niche interest.' – Variety

Commando
US   1985   88m   DeLuxe
TCF (Joel Silver)
📺   💿

Unlikely mates are thrown together in pursuit of a deadly Latin dictator.

🏃 film suitable for family viewing   📺 VHS video-cassette for the British PAL system   📺 VHS video-cassette for the British PAL system in wide screen-format   💠 Video cassette in a computer-colourised version   ▦ American NTSC video-cassette   💿 Laser disc

Hard action nonsense with the saving grace of humour.
w Steven de Souza d Mark L. Lester m James Horner pd John Vallone ed Mark Goldblatt, John F. Link, Glenn Farr
☆ Arnold Schwarzenegger, Rae Dawn Chong, Dan Hedaya, Vernon Wells, David Patrick Kelly
'Palatable actioner, inoffensively silly.' – *Variety*

The Commandos Strike at Dawn *
US 1942 98m bw
Columbia (Lester Cowan)

Norwegian commandos outwit the Nazis with the help of the British navy.
Standard war adventure shot on Vancouver Island.
w Irwin Shaw story C. S. Forester d John Farrow ph William C. Mellor m Louis Gruenberg
☆ Paul Muni, Anna Lee, Lillian Gish, Cedric Hardwicke, Robert Coote, Ray Collins, Rosemary de Camp, Richard Derr, Alexander Knox, Rod Cameron
♫ Louis Gruenberg

La Commare Secca: see *The Grim Reaper*

The Commissar: see *Komissar*

'They Had Absolutely Nothing. But They Were Willing To Risk It All.'

The Commitments **
US 1991 118m Technicolor
TCF/Beacon/First Film/Dirty Hands (Roger Randall-Cutler, Lynda Myles)
⊙ ⊚ ⌒ ♫

Dublin youths, believing that the Irish are the blacks of Europe, form a soul band.
Lively and energetic account of backstage traumas, troubles and triumphs.
w Dick Clement, Ian La Frenais, Marc Abraham novel Roddy Doyle d Alan Parker ph Gale Tattersall pd Brian Morris ed Gerry Hambling
☆ Robert Arkins, Michael Aherne, Angeline Ball, Maria Doyle, Dave Finnegan, Bronagh Gallagher, Félim Gormley, Glen Hansard, Dick Massey, Johnny Murphy, Kenneth McCluskey, Andrew Strong
'Isn't likely to overwhelm at the box-office, any more than a band like this one devoted to covering classics would get much mileage in the music industry. Still, the pic is so fresh, well-executed and original that, properly handled, it should enjoy a long if modest run and inspire much hardcore devotion among music fans.' – *Variety*
'A hilariously funny, richly humane, consistently truthful story … the movie pulsates with vitality, high spirits and the exhilarating feeling of people growing as they work together to transcend the seeming hopelessness of their surroundings.' – *Philip French, Observer*
♫ editing
♛ best picture; adapted screenplay; Alan Parker

Common Clay
US 1930 68m bw
Fox

A speakeasy hostess becomes a maid in a wealthy household and falls in love with her betters.
Archetypal soap opera which caused a mild sensation and sent its star into half a dozen imitations.
w Jules Furthman novel Cleves Kincaid d Victor Fleming ph Glen MacWilliams
☆ Constance Bennett, Lew Ayres, Tully Marshall, Matty Kemp, Purnell Pratt, Beryl Mercer
'Emotional play of 1916 bearing the marks of that artificial school … heavy for fan diet.' – *Variety*

The Common Touch *
GB 1941 104m bw
British National (John Baxter)

A rich young man poses as a tramp to save a dosshouse from destruction.
Naïve drama with a social conscience, remade from the 1932 talkie Dosshouse. A brave try.
w Barbara K. Emery, Geoffrey Orme novel Herbert Ayres d John Baxter ph James Wilson
☆ Geoffrey Hibbert, Greta Gynt, Joyce Howard, Harry Welchman, Edward Rigby, George Carney, Bransby Williams, Wally Patch, Eliot Makeham, Bernard Miles, Bill Fraser, John Longden

Common-Law Cabin
US 1967 70m colour
Eve (Russ and Eve Mayer)

A group of tourists are stranded on an isolated pleasure beach on the Colorado River.
A typical Meyer product, which mixes sex and a little violence in a confused narrative of inadequate men, and willing women.
w John Moran d Russ Meyer ph Wady C. Medawar, Jack Lucas ed Russ Meyer
☆ Jack Moran, Babette Bardot, Adele Rein, Franklin Bolger, Alaina Capri, John Furlong, Ken Swofford, Andrew Hagara

Communion
US 1977 108m colour
Allied Artists (Richard K. Rosenberg)
⊙ ⊚
aka: *Alice, Sweet Alice*
aka: *Holy Terror*

A young girl is suspected of killing several of her relatives.
Moderate low-budget thriller, mainly of interest for the brief appearances of Brooke Shields, in her first film, and of Roth as a pathologist.
w Rosemary Ritvo, Alfred Sole d Alfred Sole ph John Friberg, Chuck Hall m Stephen Lawrence pd John Lawless ed Edward Salier
☆ Paula Sheppard, Brooke Shields, Linda Miller, Jane Lowry, Alphonso DeNoble, Rudolph Willrich, Lillian Roth
'One of the most complex and satisfying American films in years.' – *Colin Pahlow, MFB*
'Strictly formulaic.' – *Sight and Sound*

'On December 25 1985 Whitley Strieber had a dream. Weeks later he discovered his family had the same dream. Months later he made the most shocking discovery of his life. Now, you will discover it.'

Communion
US 1990 101m DeLuxe
Vestron/Pheasantry Films/Allied Vision/The Picture Property Co. (Philippe Mora, Whitley Strieber, Dan Allingham)
⊙ ⊚ ⊚ ⌒

A writer recalls his meeting with extra-terrestrials and resolves to write a book about it.
Supposedly based on fact, the film has the style of an ill-conceived fantasy more rewarding to its author than to any audience.
w Whitley Strieber book Whitley Strieber d Philippe Mora ph Louis Irving m Eric Clapton pd Linda Pearl ed Lee Smith
☆ Christopher Walken, Lindsay Crouse, Joel Carlson, Frances Sternhagen, Andreas Katsulas, Terri Hanauer, Basil Hoffman

Como agua para chocolate: see *Like Water for Chocolate*

Compañeros *
Italy/Spain/West Germany 1970 118m
Technicolor Techniscope
TCF/Tritone/Atlantida/Terra
⊚
aka: *Vamos a Matar, Compañeros!*

A Swedish mercenary and a Mexican free a revolutionary being held by the Americans in order to get their hands on a fortune.
A baroque spaghetti Western, what with Nero as a straw-hatted Swede and Palance as a wooden-handed gunman, whose real hand was eaten by his pet hawk; underneath the extravagant action is buried a message about the exploitation of the poor.
w Sergio Corbucci, Dino Maiuri, Massimo de Rita, Fritz Ebert d Sergio Corbucci ph Alejandro Ulloa m Ennio Morricone ad Adolfo Cofiño ed Eugenio Alabiso
☆ Franco Nero, Tomas Milian, Jack Palance, Fernando Rey, Iris Berben, Karin Schubert, Francisco Bodalo
'Nasty, brutish and not particularly short.' – *Tom Milne, MFB*
'Tremendously entertaining.' – *Sight and Sound*
† It was a sequel to *The Mercenary* (qv).

Company Business
US 1991 98m Technicolor
MGM (Steven-Charles Jaffe)
⊙ ⊚ ⊚ ⌒

An ageing agent is recalled by the CIA to make a covert spy swap with the KGB, only to discover it is a set-up, and he and his prisoner are to be killed.
Paranoid thriller that begins well but soon degenerates into a great deal of chasing around to little effect.

wd Nicholas Meyer ph Gerry Fisher m Michael Kamen pd Ken Adam ed Ronald Roose
☆ Gene Hackman, Mikhail Baryshnikov, Kurtwood Smith, Terry O'Quinn, Daniel von Bargen, Oleg Rudnick, Geraldine Danon
'This comedic thriller, which asks what spies do after the cold war, doesn't figure to have much company or do much business.' – *Variety*

Company Limited **
India 1971 112m bw
Chitranjali (Bharat Shamsher Rana)
original title: *Seemabaddha*

A sales manager uses underhand methods to gain promotion.
Long-winded drama of Calcutta life among westernized young executives where ambition stifles morality.
wd Satyajit Ray novel *Seemabaddha* by Shankar ph Soumendu Roy m Satyajit Ray ad Ashoke Bose ed Dulal Dutta
☆ Sharmila Tagore, Barun Chanda, Parumita Chowdhury

Company of Cowards: see *Advance to the Rear*

The Company of Strangers **
Canada 1990 101m colour
Electric/Contemporary/National Film Board of Canada (David Wilson)
⊙ ⊚
aka: *Strangers In Good Company*

Seven old women are forced to camp out for several days in a derelict farmhouse after their bus breaks down.
A small gem of a movie, using a cast of non-actors to great effect.
w Gloria Demers, Cynthia Scott, David Wilson, Sally Bochner, Cynthia Scott ph David de Volpi m Marie Bernard ed David Wilson
☆ Alice Diabo, Constance Garneau, Winifred Holden, Cissy Meddings, Mary Meigs, Catherine Roche, Michelle Sweeney, Beth Webber
'In its quiet way this truthful, affecting, unsentimental movie tells us as much as any film I know about the female experience in this century.' – *Philip French, Observer*

The Company of Wolves **
GB 1984 95m colour
ITC/Palace (Chris Brown, Stephen Woolley)
⊙ ⊚ ⊚ ⌒

A young girl dreams of wolves and werewolves.
Fragmentary adult fantasy which had an unexpected box-office success, chiefly because of its sexual allusiveness, its clever make-up and its pictorial qualities.
w Angela Carter, Neil Jordan stories Angela Carter d Neil Jordan ph Bryan Loftus m George Fenton pd Anton Furst special effects Christopher Tucker
☆ Angela Lansbury, David Warner, Graham Crowden, Brian Glover, Sarah Patterson, Micha Bergese, Stephen Rea
'A horror film as literate as it is visionary, it's great fun – and that's not a cheap thrill.' – *J. Hoberman, Village Voice*

The Company She Keeps
US 1950 83m bw
RKO (John Houseman)

A self-sacrificing parole officer allows a parolee to steal her fiancé.
Considering the credits, a dismally novelettish drama of almost no interest.
w Ketti Frings d John Cromwell ph Nicholas Musuraca m Leigh Harline
☆ Lizabeth Scott, Jane Greer, Dennis O'Keefe, Fay Baker, John Hoyt, James Bell, Don Beddoe, Bert Freed
'Of the two dozen films I have produced this is the only one of which I am totally ashamed – it is silly and bad – absurd soap opera.' – *John Houseman*

Compartiment Tueurs: see *The Sleeping Car Murders*

The Competition *
US 1980 129m Metrocolor
Columbia/Rastar/William Sackheim
⊚ ⌒

An ageing piano prodigy has one last shot at fame in a San Francisco piano competition.

Slightly curious, old-fashioned but heavy-handed romance which aims to do for the piano what The Turning Point did for ballet. It doesn't sustain its length but at least the milieu is interesting.
wd Joel Oliansky ph Richard H. Kline pd Dale Hennesy ed David Blewitt m/md Lalo Schifrin
☆ Richard Dreyfuss, Lee Remick, Amy Irving, Sam Wanamaker, Joseph Cali
♫ film editing; best song 'People Alone' (m Lalo Schifrin, ly Wilbur Jennings)

Un Complicato Intrigo di Donne, Vicoli e Delitto: see *Camorra: The Naples Connection*

Compromising Positions
US 1985 98m colour
Paramount (Frank Perry)
⊚ ⌒

The murder of a philandering dentist has repercussions among his various mistresses.
Combination sex comedy and whodunnit which never seems to hit the right groove.
w Susan Isaacs novel Susan Isaacs d Frank Perry ph Barry Sonnenfeld m Brad Fiedel pd Peter Larkin ed Peter Frank
☆ Susan Sarandon, Raul Julia, Edward Herrmann, Judith Ivey, Mary Beth Hurt, Joe Mantegna

Compulsion *
US 1959 103m bw Cinemascope
TCF/Darryl F. Zanuck Productions (Richard F. Zanuck)

In the twenties, two Chicago students kidnap and murder a young boy for kicks.
Rather dogged but earnest fictionalization of the Leopold-Loeb case with solid performances and production.
w Richard Murphy novel Meyer Levin d Richard Fleischer ph William C. Mellor m Lionel Newman ed William Reynolds
☆ Dean Stockwell, Bradford Dillman, Orson Welles, Diane Varsi, E. G. Marshall, Martin Milner, Richard Anderson, Robert Simon
† Welles's cameo court appearance as a lawyer is based on Clarence Darrow.

The Computer Wore Tennis Shoes
↟↟ US 1970 90m Technicolor
Disney
⊚

While mending a computer a college student gets an electric shock and becomes omniscient.
Ho-hum Disney comedy, eager to please but instantly forgotten.
w Joseph L. McEveety d Robert Butler
☆ Kurt Russell, Cesar Romero, Joe Flynn, William Schallert, Alan Hewitt

Comrade X *
US 1940 89m bw
MGM (Gottfried Reinhardt)

An American correspondent in Russia is blackmailed into smuggling a girl out of the country.
Lame satirical comedy in the wake of Ninotchka; a few good moments, but generally heavy-handed.
w Ben Hecht, Charles Lederer story Walter Reisch d King Vidor ph Joseph L. Ruttenberg m Bronislau Kaper
☆ Clark Gable, Hedy Lamarr, Felix Bressart, Oscar Homolka, Eve Arden, Sig Rumann
'Broadest comedic strokes and not-too-subtle satire … a smacko entry for topflight biz.' – *Variety*
♫ Walter Reisch

Comrades ***
GB 1987 180m colour
Curzon/Skreba/National Film Finance (Simon Relph)

In the 1830s six Dorset farm labourers who form a union to campaign against low wages are tried and transported to Australia as criminals.
Subtitled 'a lanternist's account', and based on the true story of the Tolpuddle Martyrs, it is a flawed masterpiece: too long and too preachy, yet its qualities outweigh these defects.
wd Bill Douglas ph Gale Tattersall m Hans Werner Henze, David Graham pd Michael Pickwoad ed Mick Audsley
☆ Robin Soans, William Gammara, Stephen Bateman, Philip Davis, Jeremy Flynn, Keith Allen, Alex Norton, Michael Clark, Arthur Dignam, James Fox, John Hargreaves, Michael Hordern, Freddie Jones, Vanessa Redgrave, Robert Stephens and also Murray Melvin, Barbara Windsor, Imelda Staunton

Comradeship: see *Kameradschaft (1931)*

Comradeship *
GB   1919   67m   bw   silent
Stoll
Two friends endure varying fortunes during World War I.
An early British 'A' feature which was highly popular in its day.
w Jeffrey Bernerd d Maurice Elvey
☆ Lily Elsie, Gerald Ames, Guy Newall, Peggy Carlisle

La Comtesse aux Seins Nu: see *Female Vampire*

La Comtesse Noire: see *Female Vampire*

'Buckle up ... and hang on.'
Con Air *
US   1997   115m   Technicolor   Panavision
Buena Vista/Touchstone (Jerry Bruckheimer)
▦ ▤ ⊘ ◎ ◠
A tough parolee decides to support law and order when a violent criminal hijacks a convict transport plane.
Uproarious but enjoyable nonsense, marked by much gunfire, loud explosions, over-the-top acting and, when it can be heard, some witty dialogue.
w Scott Rosenberg d Simon West ph David Tattersall m Mark Mancina, Trevor Rabin ad Edward T. McAvoy ed Chris Lebenzon, Steve Mirkovich, Glen Scantlebury
☆ Nicolas Cage, John Cusack, John Malkovich, Steve Buscemi, Ving Rhames, Colm Meaney, Mykelti Williamson, Rachel Ticotin, Monica Potter, Dave Chappelle, M. C. Gainey
  'For a bit of dumb fun, the fun goes out of *Con Air* pretty quickly.' – *Sunday Times*
† The film was among the most commercially successful of the year, grossing some $101m in the US, and another $122m elsewhere.
♫ song 'How Do I Live' (*m/ly* Dianne Warren); sound

'Thief. Warrior. Gladiator. King.'
Conan the Barbarian
US   1981   129m   Technicolor   Todd-AO
Dino de Laurentiis/Edward R. Pressman (Buzz Feitshans, Raffaella de Laurentiis)
▦ ▤ ⊘ ◎ ◠
In the Dark Ages, a young stalwart seeks out the barbarian tribe which murdered his parents.
Intolerably doomladen, slow-moving and mainly unintelligible rubbish which failed to put a lift into the long-announced sword-and-sorcery cycle.
w John Milius, Oliver Stone, from a character created by Robert E. Howard d John Milius ph Duke Callaghan m Basil Poledouris pd Ron Cobb ed C. Timothy O'Meara
☆ Arnold Schwarzenegger, James Earl Jones, Max von Sydow, Sandahl Bergman, Ben Davidson, Mako, Gerry Lopez
  'A ragbag of half-witted kitsch, where even locations resemble a set, actors look like extras, violence like a stunt and life a bad dream.' – *Sunday Times*
  'An indigestible blend of anti-liberal braggadocio, post-60s mysticism and echt-60s blockbusting.' – *Sight and Sound*

Conan the Destroyer
US   1984   101m   Technicolor   Scope
Dino de Laurentiis
▦ ▤ ⊘ ◎ ◠
An evil queen offers to bring Conan's last love back to life, if he will undertake a magical quest for her.
More heavy-handed and unpleasant nonsense, with a slightly better pace than before.
w Stanley Mann d Richard Fleischer ph Jack Cardiff
☆ Arnold Schwarzenegger, Grace Jones, Wilt Chamberlain, Mako, Tracey Walter, Sarah Douglas

Concealment: see *The Secret Bride*

Concerto: see *I've Always Loved You*

The Concierge: see *For Love or Money*

The Concorde: Airport '79
US   1979   113m   Technicolor
Universal (Jennings Lang)
▤
GB title: *Airport '80: The Concorde*
Various disasters befall the Concorde on its way from Washington to Paris.
Stultified final (one presumes) effort in the Airport series; it could hardly be funnier if it were intended as a comedy, but somehow it entertains.
w Eric Roth d David Lowell Rich ph Philip Lathrop m Lalo Schifrin
☆ Alain Delon, Susan Blakely, Robert Wagner, Sylvia Kristel, George Kennedy, Eddie Albert, Bibi Andersson, John Davidson, Martha Raye, Cicely Tyson, Mercedes McCambridge
  'Larger-than-life characters are thrown together on a storyboard and must fend for themselves against attacks, chases and assorted escapades ... this would be soporific even as a transatlantic inflight movie.' – *Martyn Auty, MFB*

The Concrete Jungle: see *The Criminal*

El Conde Dracula: see *Bram Stoker's Count Dracula*

'A kiss that cannot be forgotten!'
Condemned *
US   1929   86m   bw
Samuel Goldwyn
aka: *Condemned to Devil's Island*
A bank robber is sent to Devil's Island and falls in love with the wife of the brutal warden.
Slow-moving but pictorially attractive melodrama with old-style performances.
w Sidney Howard novel *Condemned to Devil's Island* by Blair Niles d Wesley Ruggles ph George Barnes, Gregg Toland pd William Cameron Menzies
☆ Ronald Colman, Ann Harding, Louis Wolheim, Dudley Digges, William Elmer
  'A piece of nonsense from which it would appear that French convicts on Devil's Island live a life consisting entirely of hot-towel shaves and flirtations with the governor's wife.' – *James Agate*
♫ Ronald Colman

The Condemned of Altona *
Italy/France   1962   113m   bw
(TCF) Titanus/SGC (Carlo Ponti)
The head of a German shipping empire discovers he has only a few months to live and tries to bring his family to order.
Strident intellectual melodrama whose credits tell all. Watchable for the acting, but very glum.
w Abby Mann, Cesare Zavattini play Jean-Paul Sartre d Vittorio de Sica ph Roberto Gerardi m Dmitri Shostakovich
☆ Fredric March, Sophia Loren, Robert Wagner, Maximilian Schell, Françoise Prévost, Alfredo Franchi
  'This film is such a hopeless mess that it is difficult to know where to begin criticizing it.' – *Tom Milne*

Condemned to Death *
GB   1932   75m   bw
Twickenham (Julius Hagen)
A condemned killer hypnotizes a judge into murdering those who turned him in.
Irresistible nonsense of the old school, with spirited direction and a good cast.
w Bernard Merivale, Harry Fowler Mear, Brock Williams play Jack O'Lantern by George Goodchild, James Dawson d Walter Forde ph Sidney Blythe, William Luff
☆ Arthur Wontner, Gillian Lind, Edmund Gwenn, Gordon Harker, Jane Welsh, Cyril Raymond
  'A weak daily changer with double-headed programming its merited rating.' – *Variety*
  'It would be difficult to find a dull moment.' – *The Bioscope*

Condemned to Devil's Island: see *Condemned*

Condemned to Life: see *Life for Ruth*

Condorman
↟↟   US   1981   90m   Technicolor
Panavision
Walt Disney (Jan Williams)
▤
The author of a 'superman' comic tries to act like his hero in real life.
Very mildly amusing spy spoof with inadequate special effects.
w Marc Sturdivant, Glen Caron, Mickey Rose novel *The Game of X* by Robert Sheckley d Charles Jarrott ph Charles F. Wheeler m Henry Mancini pd Albert Witherick sp Art Cruickshank
☆ Michael Crawford, Oliver Reed, Barbara Carrera, James Hampton, Jean-Pierre Kalfon

Conduct Unbecoming
GB   1975   107m   Technicolor
British Lion/Crown (Michael Deeley, Barry Spikings)
▦ ▤
In an officers' mess in India in the 1890s, a cadet is accused of assault on a lady but the real culprit is a paranoic who has taken to pigsticking in quite the wrong way.
Disappointingly flatly-handled and quite unatmospheric picturization of an absorbing West End melodrama. The cast is largely wasted, but stretches of dialogue maintain their interest.
w Robert Enders play Barry England d Michael Anderson ph Bob Huke m Stanley Myers
☆ Michael York, Stacy Keach, Trevor Howard, Christopher Plummer, Richard Attenborough, Susannah York, James Faulkner, James Donald

The Conductor *
Poland   1979   102m   Orwocolor
PRF/X Films of Poland
original title: *Dyrygent*
A Polish girl violinist finds her life affected when an elderly international conductor returns to her town.
Initially interesting but finally tedious and muddled allegory, further handicapped by stilted post-synching of the English version.
w Andrzej Kijowski d Andrzej Wajda ph Slawomir Idziak m from Beethoven
☆ John Gielgud, Krystyna Janda, Andrzej Seweryn

Cone of Silence *
GB   1960   92m   bw
British Lion/Bryanston (Aubrey Baring)
US title: *Trouble in the Sky*
A seasoned pilot is condemned for an error which caused a crash and later dies in similar circumstances. A flying examiner discovers scientific reasons for exonerating him.
Tolerable suspense drama let down by thin dialogue and confused characterization.
w Robert Westerby novel *David Beaty* d Charles Frend ph Arthur Grant m Gerard Schurmann
☆ Michael Craig, Bernard Lee, Peter Cushing, George Sanders, Elizabeth Seal, André Morell, Gordon Jackson, Delphi Lawrence, Noel Willman, Charles Tingwell

'Young ones! Parental units! We summon you!'
Coneheads
US   1993   88m   DeLuxe
Paramount (Lorne Michaels)
▦ ▤ ⊘ ◠
An illegal pointy-headed alien crash-lands in the United States.
Dim one-joke comedy at the expense of suburbia.
w Tom Davis, Dan Aykroyd, Bonnie Turner, Terry Turner d Steve Barron m David Newman pd Gregg Fonseca ed Paul Trejo
☆ Dan Aykroyd, Jane Curtin, Michael McKean, Laraine Newman, Jason Alexander, Lisa Jane Persky, Chris Farley, David Spade, Michelle Burke
  'A sweet, funny, anarchic pastiche that should find broad-based popularity.' – *Variety*
  'Quite extraordinarily bad ... worth renting only if you take a perverse pleasure in watching a very large amount of someone else's money going down the drain.' – *Jonathan Ross, Empire*
† The film was released direct to video in Britain.

Coney Island *
US   1943   96m   Technicolor
TCF (William Perlberg)
Two fairground showmen vie for the affections of a songstress.

Brassy, simple-minded, entertaining musical. Very typical of its time; later remade as Wabash Avenue (qv).
w George Seaton d Walter Lang ph Ernest Palmer m Alfred Newman m/ly Leo Robin, Ralph Rainger ch Hermes Pan ad Richard Day, Joseph C. Wright
☆ Betty Grable, George Montgomery, Cesar Romero, Charles Winninger, Phil Silvers, Matt Briggs, Paul Hurst, Frank Orth, Andrew Tombes, Alec Craig, Hal K. Dawson
♫ Alfred Newman

Confession
US   1937   90m   bw
Warner (Henry Blanke)
An errant mother shoots her former lover to protect her daughter.
Stilted romantic melodrama copied scene for scene from a 1936 German film Mazurka.
w Julius J. Epstein, Margaret Le Vino original screenplay Hans Rameau d Joe May ph Sid Hickox m Peter Kreuder md Leo F. Forbstein ad Anton Grot
☆ Kay Francis, Ian Hunter, Basil Rathbone, Jane Bryan, Donald Crisp, Dorothy Peterson, Laura Hope Crews, Robert Barrat
  'Distinctly in the upper bracket and made to order for important first runs.' – *Variety*

Confession
GB   1955   90m   bw
Anglo Guild
US title: *The Deadliest Sin*
A murderer stalks the priest who knows his guilt through the confessional but may not reveal it.
So-so reworking of the theme that daunted Hitchcock in I Confess; some pleasant touches are nullified by slow pacing.
wd Ken Hughes
☆ Sydney Chaplin, Audrey Dalton, John Welsh, John Bentley, Peter Hammond

The Confession: see *Quick Let's Get Married (1965)*

The Confession *
France/Italy   1970   160m   Eastmancolor
Films Corona/Films Pomereu/Selena Cinematografica (Robert Dorfmann)
original title: *L'Aveu*
In Prague in 1951, a minister is secretly imprisoned and interrogated, and finally confesses under duress to anti-communist activities.
Brutally long but frequently impressive anti-Soviet tract, extremely well acted but less exciting than Z. Based on a true account.
w Jorge Semprun book *Lise and Artur London* d Costa-Gavras ph Raoul Coutard m not credited
☆ Yves Montand, Simone Signoret, Gabriele Ferzetti, Michel Vitold

Le Confessional **
Canada/GB/France   1995   101m   colour/bw
Artificial Eye/Téléfilm
Canada/Cinémaginaire/Enigma/Cinéa (Denise Robert, David Puttnam, Philippe Carcassonne)
▦ ▤
Returning home to Quebec for his father's funeral, an artist helps his adopted brother, now a homosexual prostitute, search for his real father, who they suspect may have been a priest.
Stylish, intelligent mystery story, full of echoes of Hitchcock, and moving between 1989 and 1952, where the tragedy that engulfs them had its roots. Set against Hitchcock's filming of I Confess, it is told in a cool, distancing manner that is emotionally uninvolving; it is to be admired more than enjoyed.
wd Robert Lepage ph Alain Dostie m Sacha Puttnam ad François Laplante ed émmanuelle Castro
☆ Lothaire Bluteau, Patrick Goyette, Kristin Scott-Thomas, Jean-Louis Millette, Richard Fréchette, François Papineau, Marie Gignac, Ron Burrage
  'A few moments of daftness aside, this is a superbly watchable and seamlessly structured film.' – *Nigel Robinson, Film Review*

Confessions from a Holiday Camp

GB 1977 88m colour
Columbia/Swiftdown (Greg Smith)

An entertainments officer at a holiday camp attempts to deal with the disciplinarian in charge while seducing every woman he meets.

Heavy-handed slapstick comedy intended to titillate, in the style of a lower-budget Carry On, with single entendres and no laughs.

w Christopher Wood *novel* Timothy Lea (Christopher Wood) d Norman Cohen ph Ken Hodges m Ed Welch ad Harry Pottle ed Geoffrey Foot

☆ Robin Askwith, Anthony Booth, Doris Hare, Bill Maynard, Sheila White, Colin Crompton, Liz Fraser, Linda Hayden, John Junkin, Lance Percival

'Strained and patronising low comedy.' – *MFB*

Confessions of a Counterspy: see *Man on a String*

Confessions of a Driving Instructor

GB 1976 90m colour
Columbia-Warner/Swiftdown (Greg Smith)
🔲

A newly qualified driving instructor seduces his female pupils and all the other women he meets.

A tired farce that cannot even rise to the level of the Carry On series' double entendres.

w Christopher Wood *novel* Timothy Lea d Norman Cohen ph Ken Hodges m Ed Welch ad Albert Witherick ed Geoffrey Foot

☆ Robin Askwith, Anthony Booth, Sheila White, Doris Hare, Bill Maynard, Windsor Davies, Liz Fraser, Irene Handl, Lynda Bellingham, Avril Angers

'A fifth-rate potboiler of proven commercial value.' – *John Pym, MFB*

Confessions of a Nazi Spy ***

US 1939 110m bw
Warner (Robert Lord)

How G-men ferreted out Nazis in the United States.

Topical exposé with all concerned in top form; a semi-documentary very typical of Warner product throughout the thirties and forties, from G-Men to Mission to Moscow and I Was a Communist for the FBI: well made, punchy, and smartly edited, with a loud moral at the end.

w Milton Krims, John Wexley, from materials gathered by former FBI agent Leon G. Turrou d Anatole Litvak ph Sol Polito m Max Steiner

☆ Edward G. Robinson, Paul Lukas, George Sanders, Francis Lederer, Henry O'Neill, Lya Lys, James Stephenson, Sig Rumann, Dorothy Tree, Joe Sawyer

'Its social implications are far more important than the immediate question of how much money the release makes for Warner Brothers.' – *Variety*

'The Warner brothers have declared war on Germany with this one … with this precedent there is no way any producer could argue against dramatizing any social or political theme on the grounds that he's afraid of domestic or foreign censorship. Everybody duck.' – *Pare Lorentz*

'Has a remarkable resemblance to a full-length *Crime Does Not Pay*.' – *David Wolff*

'One of the most sensational movie jobs on record, workmanlike in every respect and sprang across the headlines.' – *Otis Ferguson*

Confessions of a Pop Performer

GB 1975 91m colour
Columbia-Warner/Swiftdown
🔲

A window cleaner joins a rock group and enjoys the groupies.

A broad and unsubtle slapstick comedy.

w Christopher Wood *novel* Confessions from the Pop Scene by Timothy Lea d Norman Cohen ph Alan Hume m Bugatti Musker pd Robert Jones ed Geoffrey Foot

☆ Robin Askwith, Anthony Booth, Sheila White, Doris Hare, Bill Maynard, Bob Todd, Jill Gascoine, Peter Jones, Diane Langton, Ian Lavender

'Creaky gags, overly familiar slapstick routines, sniggering innuendo, grimly facetious mugging and a nervously regular injection of titillating sequences on the lines of the average German sex comedy.' – *Verina Glaessner, MFB*

Confessions of a Sex Maniac

GB 1974 81m Eastmancolor
Oppidan/Rothernorth (Alan Birkinshaw)

aka: Design for Lust

aka: The Man Who Couldn't Get Enough

An architect searches for the perfect breast so that he can use it as the design for a new building.

Tired farce, intended to titillate, but more likely to act as a soporific.

w Alan Paz d Alan Birkinshaw ph Arthur Lavis m Derek Warne, John Shakespeare ad Tessa Davis ed David White

☆ Roger Lloyd Pack, Vicki Hodge, Derek Royle, Stephanie Marrian, Louise Rush, Candy Baker

'A perilously weak plot premise is just about kept alive by the two appealing lead performances, before being smothered by a platitudinous ton of groping and grappling.' – *Richard Combs*

Confessions of a Window Cleaner

GB 1974 90m Eastmancolor
Columbia-Warner/Swiftdown (Greg Smith)
🔲

A window cleaner discovers many amorous housewives on his round.

A broad, but not bawdy, comedy for the sexually repressed. Despite its low level, it did well enough at the box-office to spawn several sequels.

w Christopher Wood, Val Guest d Val Guest ph Norman Warwick m Sam Sklair pd Robert Jones ed Bill Lenny

☆ Robin Askwith, Anthony Booth, Sheila White, Dandy Nichols, Bill Maynard, Linda Hayden, John Le Mesurier, Joan Hickson, Richard Wattis, Katya Wyeth, Sam Kydd

'The humour is of the sniggering, innuendo-squeezing variety and is aimed with unnerving mediocrity at a particular kind of embarrassed – and distinctly British – audience reaction.' – *Gareth Jones, MFB*

† The lead role was turned down by Nicky Henson, Dennis Waterman and Richard Beckinsale.

'Take One Daring Step Beyond The Threshold Of Your Own Imagination!'

Confessions of an Opium Eater

US 1962 85m bw
Albert Zugsmith
🔲

GB title: *Evils of Chinatown*

In San Francisco in the 1890s, a seaman falls into the clutches of a tong.

The hero is called de Quincey, but that is the only association with the famous book of the same title. This absurd melodrama is just about bad enough to be funny, but not very.

w Robert Hill d Albert Zugsmith ph Joseph Biroc m Albert Glasser ad Eugene Lourié

☆ Vincent Price, Linda Ho, Richard Loo, Philip Ahn, June Kim

'Has to be seen to be believed … starved girls captive in cages, secret panels, sliding doors, sewer escape routes, opium dens and nightmares…' – *MFB*

Confidential

US 1935 70m bw
Equity/Mascot (Bernard Smith)

An FBI agent goes undercover to expose the seemingly respectable businessman who ruthlessly controls the nation's gambling rackets.

Slick, tightly constructed 'B'-movie thriller with a few touches of class.

w Wellyn Totman, Olive Cooper *story* John Rathmell, Scott Darling d Edward L. Cahn ph Ernest Miller, Jack Marta ed Joseph H. Lewis, Ray Curtiss

☆ Donald Cook, Evalyn Knapp, Warren Hymer, J. Carrol Naish, Herbert Rawlinson, Theodore von Eltz

Confidential

Canada 1987 88m colour
Brightstar (Anthony Kramreither)
🔲

A reporter goes missing on an assignment to track down a woman who killed her father with an axe years before.

Undistinguished, claustrophobic thriller, a low-budget pastiche of hard-boiled pulp fiction, tightly shot to try to hide the paucity of its sets.

wd Bruce Pittman ph John Herzog m Bruce Ley ed Bruce Pittman

☆ August Schellenberg, Chapelle Jaffe, Neil Munro, Tom Butler, Anthony Parr, Linda Goranson, Doris Petrie, Michael Fletcher

Confidential Agent **

US 1945 122m bw
Warner (Robert Buckner)

An emissary of Franco's Spain comes to England in the late thirties to make a munitions deal, and falls in love with the tycoon's daughter.

Heavy-going simplification of Graham Greene's lowering novel, with cast and (especially) set designers all at sea but nevertheless providing striking moments.

w Robert Buckner d Herman Shumlin ph James Wong Howe m Franz Waxman

☆ Charles Boyer, Lauren Bacall, Katina Paxinou, Peter Lorre, Victor Francen, George Coulouris, Wanda Hendrix, George Zucco, Miles Mander

'In some ways an exciting and good picture, the best attempt yet, though still inadequate, to make the best of a Greene novel.' – *James Agee*

Confidential Report

Spain 1955 99m bw
Sevilla Studios (Louis Dolivet, Orson Welles)
🔲 🔲 ◎~

aka: Mr Arkadin

A wealthy and powerful financier employs a young American to seek out figures from his own past, who are soon found dead…

Silly melodrama which might have been suspenseful if done by Hitchcock, or even by Welles at his peak; as it is, weak writing and sloppy production remove most of the interest and reveal it as a very obvious bag of tricks.

wd Orson Welles *novel* Mr Arkadin by Orson Welles ph Jean Bourgoin m Paul Misraki pd Orson Welles ed Renzo Lucidi

☆ Orson Welles, Michael Redgrave, Katina Paxinou, Akim Tamiroff, Mischa Auer, Patricia Medina, Jack Watling, Peter Van Eyck, Paola Mori, Robert Arden, Grégoire Aslan, Suzanne Flon

'Tilted camera angles, heavy atmospheric shots, overlapping dialogue – all the trademarks are here, sometimes over-used to an almost hysterical degree, but they have little significance … (the film) springs not from life but from the earlier cinematic world of Welles himself and from the kind of thriller written about thirty years ago by E. Philips Oppenheim.' – *Gavin Lambert*

'The quality of the soundtrack is quite disastrous, but there is a certain grandeur about the carelessness of the film's construction which makes one forget everything except the immediacy of the moment.' – *Basil Wright, 1972*

Confidentially Connie

US 1953 71m bw
MGM

A Texas rancher starts a price war when he strikes a deal with a local butcher so that the rancher's impecunious son can get half-price meat for his family.

Modest comedy which adequately filled the lower half of a bill.

w Max Shulman *story* Max Shulman, Herman Wouk d Edward Buzzell

☆ Louis Calhern, Janet Leigh, Van Johnson, Walter Slezak, Gene Lockhart, Hayden Rorke

Confirm or Deny *

US 1941 78m bw
TCF (Len Hammond)

An American reporter falls for a wireless operator in wartime London.

Artificial but watchable minor romantic melodrama.

w Jo Swerling, Henry Wales, Samuel Fuller d Archie Mayo ph Leon Shamroy

☆ Don Ameche, Joan Bennett, Roddy McDowall, Arthur Shields, Raymond Walburn, John Loder

† Fritz Lang directed some scenes.

Conflict *

US 1945 86m bw
Warner (William Jacobs)
🔲 🔲

A man murders his wife and is apparently haunted by her; but the odd happenings have been arranged by a suspicious psychiatrist.

Leaden and artificial melodrama with both stars miscast; a few effective moments.

w Arthur T. Horman, Dwight Taylor d Curtis Bernhardt ph Merritt Gerstad m Frederick Hollander

☆ Humphrey Bogart, Sydney Greenstreet, Alexis Smith, Rose Hobart, Charles Drake, Grant Mitchell

† The film was completed in August 1943.

Conflict of Wings *

GB 1953 84m Eastmancolor
Group Three (Herbert Mason)

US title: *Fuss over Feathers*

East Anglian villagers fight to save a bird sanctuary from being taken over by the RAF as a rocket range.

Sub-Ealing comedy-drama with a highly predictable outcome; generally pleasant but without much bite.

w Don Sharp, John Pudney d John Eldridge ph Arthur Grant m Philip Green

☆ John Gregson, Muriel Pavlow, Kieron Moore, Niall MacGinnis, Sheila Sweet, Harry Fowler, Barbara Hicks, Charles Lloyd Pack

The Conformist ***

Italy/France/West Germany 1969 108m Technicolor
Mars/Marianne/Maran (Giovanni Bertolucci)
🔲 🔲 ◎~

original title: *Il Conformista*

In 1938 an inhibited young man tries to conform to the prevailing mood of Fascism, but gets out of his depth when he turns informer.

Psychologically confusing but brilliantly realized recreation of an age.

wd Bernardo Bertolucci *novel* Alberto Moravia ph Vittorio Storaro m Georges Delerue

☆ Jean-Louis Trintignant, Stefania Sandrelli, Gastone Moschin, Enzo Tarascio, Dominique Sanda, Pierre Clementi

'It's a triumph of feeling and of style – lyrical, flowing, velvety style, so operatic that you come away with sequences in your head like arias.' – *New Yorker*

🎭 Bernardo Bertolucci (as writer)

Il Conformista: see *The Conformist*

'Where you are the endangered species.'

Congo

US 1995 108m DeLuxe
UIP/Paramount (Kathleen Kennedy, Sam Mercer)
🔲 🔲 ◎~

A talking gorilla, a primatologist, a woman in search of rare blue diamonds, a mysterious Romanian and a great black hunter combine on an expedition to Africa where they find King Solomon's mines guarded by killer apes.

Heady nonsense, a throwback to those old movies based on Victorian adventure stories; it is hokum of a sort rarely seen since the days of Nyoka the Jungle Girl.

w John Patrick Shanley *novel* Michael Crichton d Frank Marshall ph Allen Daviau m Jerry Goldsmith pd J. Michael Riva ed Anne V. Coates sp Industrial Light and Magic; Stan Winston Studio

☆ Dylan Walsh, Laura Linney, Ernie Hudson, Tim Curry, Joe Don Baker, Grant Heslov

'A shamelessly inane confection.' – *Sight and Sound*

† The film took more than $151m worldwide at the box-office, $81m in the US.

Congo Crossing

US 1956 85m Technicolor
U-I (Howard Christie)

Assorted fugitives from justice gather at Congotanga, which has no extradition laws.

The poor man's Casablanca, quite good looking but dully written and presented.

w Richard Alan Simmons d Joseph Pevney ph Russell Metty m Joseph Gershenson

☆ George Nader, Virginia Mayo, Peter Lorre, Michael Pate, Rex Ingram

Congorilla *

US 1932 74m bw
Fox

A record of two years spent in the Belgian Congo by Mr and Mrs Martin Johnson.

Excellent exploration documentary of its time.

wd The Johnsons

'Replete with thrills, adventure and laughs, making withal for an excellent entertainment.' – *Variety*

◎ Digital Video Disc Region 2   ◎ Digital Video Disc Region 1   🎧 Soundtrack released on compact disc   ☆ Cast in approximate order of importance   † Points of interest   🎵 Notable songs   🏆 Academy Award   🎭 Academy Award nomination   🏆 BAFTA

Congress Dances *

Germany 1931 92m bw
UFA (Erich Pommer)
original title: Der Kongress Tanzt
At the Congress of Vienna, Metternich attempts to decoy the Tsar with a countess; but the Tsar has a double.
Lubitsch-like treatment of sexual dalliance in high places; no doubt a stunner in its time, but rather faded now.
w Norbert Falk, Robert Liebmann d Erik Charell ph Carl Hoffmann m Werner Heymann ad Robert Herlth, Walter Röhrig
☆ Conrad Veidt, Willy Fritsch, Lilian Harvey, Lil Dagover, Henry Garat, Gib McLaughlin
'A revue more than a story … grace, taste and a light hand.' – Variety

A Connecticut Yankee *

US 1931 96m bw
Fox
A man dreams himself back to the court of King Arthur, and teaches the Middle Ages a thing or two about modern living.
First sound version of Mark Twain's classic fantasy, also filmed in 1921 and 1949. Creaky now, but amiable.
w William Conselman d David Butler ph Ernest Palmer
☆ Will Rogers, Maureen O'Sullivan, Myrna Loy, Frank Albertson, William Farnum
'Good deluxe comedy … should draw substantial grosses.' – Variety

'Its laughter will ring through the centuries!'

A Connecticut Yankee in King Arthur's Court *

US 1949 106m Technicolor
Paramount (Robert Fellows)
GB title: A Yankee in King Arthur's Court
Gossamer musical version of the above with the emphasis on song and knockabout.
Palatable, with the 'Busy Doin' Nothin' sequence the most memorable.
w Edmund Beloin d Tay Garnett ph Ray Rennahan m/ly Johnny Burke, Jimmy Van Heusen md Victor Young
☆ Bing Crosby, Rhonda Fleming, William Bendix, Cedric Hardwicke, Murvyn Vye
'The tacky pageantry is more suited to the opening of a West Coast supermarket than to an English court in the 6th century.' – Pauline Kael, 70s

Connecting Rooms

GB 1969 103m Technicolor
Telstar/Franklin Gollings (Harry Field)
In a seedy Bayswater boarding house, a dismissed schoolmaster befriends a failed cellist whose protégé is a sponging songwriter.
Aggressively dismal melodrama which would be hilarious if it were not so sadly slow and naïve.
wd Franklin Gollings play The Cellist by Marion Hart ph John Wilcox m John Shakespeare
☆ Bette Davis, Michael Redgrave, Alexis Kanner, Kay Walsh, Gabrielle Drake, Leo Genn, Olga Georges-Picot, Richard Wyler, Brian Wilde

The Connection

US 1961 110m bw
Shirley Clarke/Lewis Allen
Junkies hang around waiting for a fix and are filmed by a documentary unit.
Unattractive low-budgeter with occasional impressive moments.
w Jack Gelber play Jack Gelber d Shirley Clarke ph Arthur J. Ornitz m Freddie Redd ad Richard Sylbert
☆ Warren Finnerty, Jerome Raphael, Jim Anderson, Carl Lee, Roscoe Browne

The Conquering Horde

US 1931 73m bw
Paramount
In Texas after the Civil War, resistance to railroads hampers the movement of cattle.
Stronaish Western of its period, but of no continuing interest.
w Grover Jones, William Slavens McNutt d Edward Sloman

☆ Richard Arlen, Fay Wray, Claude Gillingwater, Ian MacLaren
'Good story, plenty of love interest, action and comedy … will do above average.' – Variety

'Spectacular as its barbaric passions and savage conquests!'

The Conqueror

US 1955 112m Technicolor Cinemascope
Howard Hughes (Dick Powell)
A romance of the early life of Genghis Khan, who captures and is enamoured by the daughter of an enemy.
Solemn pantomime with a measure of bloodthirsty action and dancing girls, has featuring too many dull spots between, especially as the star is the most unlikely of eastern warriors and the production values careful but not too steady.
w Oscar Millard d Dick Powell ph Joseph LaShelle, Leo Tover, Harry J. Wild m Victor Young
☆ John Wayne, Susan Hayward, Pedro Armendariz, Agnes Moorehead, Thomas Gomez, John Hoyt, William Conrad, Ted de Corsia, Lee Van Cleef
GENGHIS KHAN: 'This tartar woman is for me, and my blood says, take her!'
'Simply an oriental western.' – New York Times
'History has not been well served and nor has the popcorn public.' – Richard Hatch, Nation
'It's all that its makers wanted it to be.' – Manchester Guardian
'John Wayne as Genghis Khan – history's most improbable piece of casting unless Mickey Rooney were to play Jesus in King of Kings.' – Jack Smith, L.A. Times
† The location was Utah's Escalante Desert, and three local mountains were renamed Mount Wayne, Mount Hughes and Mount Powell. The desert had been used for atom bomb tests, and twenty-five years after the production, questions were asked when several members of the cast died of cancer
†† Wayne asked for his role. 'The way the screenplay reads, this is a cowboy picture, and that's how I am going to play Genghis Khan. I see him as a gunfighter.'

The Conqueror Worm: see Witchfinder General

The Conquerors

US 1932 88m bw
RKO (David O. Selznick)
TV title: Pioneer Builders
Nebraska settlers in the 1870s set the seeds of a banking empire.
Routine family epic with the star playing himself and his own grandson.
w Robert Lord story Howard Estabrook d William Wellman ph Edward Cronjager m Max Steiner
☆ Richard Dix, Ann Harding, Edna May Oliver, Guy Kibbee, Donald Cook, Julie Haydon, Jed Prouty
'As good as a depression story can be, which isn't much box office.' – Variety

Conquest **

US 1937 115m bw
MGM (Bernard Hyman)
GB title: Marie Walewska
The life of Napoleon's most enduring mistress.
Measured, dignified, and often rather dull historical fiction, lightened by excellent performances and production.
w Samuel Hoffenstein, Salka Viertel, S. N. Behrman, from a Polish play dramatized by Helen Jerome d Clarence Brown ph Karl Freund m Herbert Stothart ad Cedric Gibbons
☆ Greta Garbo, Charles Boyer, Reginald Owen, Alan Marshal, Henry Stephenson, Dame May Whitty, Leif Erickson
'For special first-run openings – and then the clean up.' – Variety
'Ornate, unexpectedly tasteful, carefully detailed – and lifeless.' – Pauline Kael, 70s
§ Charles Boyer; Cedric Gibbons

Conquest of Cochise

US 1953 78m Technicolor
Columbia (Sam Katzman)
An army major is sent to make peace with Cochise, the Apache.
Feeble Western cheapie.
w Arthur Lewis, De Vallon Scott d William Castle
☆ Robert Stack, John Hodiak, Joy Page

The Conquest of Everest *

GB 1953 73m Technicolor
British Lion/Group 3/Countryman Films
Documentary on the successful 11th attempt on Everest, the expedition led by Colonel John Hunt.
A documentary with some fascinating footage of early expeditions, and of the detailed planning of the expedition, opening in a burst of patriotism as success followed the coronation of Queen Elizabeth II.
w Louis MacNeice d uncredited ph Thomas Stobart, George Lowe, Captain J. B. L. Noel m Arthur Benjamin md Muir Mathieson ed Adrian de Potier
☆ Meredith Edwards

'See how it will happen – in your lifetime!'

Conquest of Space

US 1954 80m Technicolor
Paramount (George Pal)
In 1980, the Americans have built a space station in the atmosphere, and plan a voyage to the moon but are sent to Mars instead.
So history catches up with science fiction. This sober prophecy looks good but very little happens and the result is as dull as it is bright and shiny.
w James O'Hanlon book Chesley Bonestell, Willy Ley d Byron Haskin ph Lionel Lindon m Van Cleeve ad Hal Pereira, James McMillan Johnson sp John P. Fulton, Irmin Roberts, Paul Lerpae, Ivyl Burks, Jan Domella
☆ Eric Fleming, Walter Brooke, Mickey Shaughnessy, William Hopper, Ross Martin

Conquest of the Air

GB 1940 71m bw
London Films/Alexander Korda
A history of man's discovery of the power of flight.
Curious schoolbook documentary, of historical interest.
w Hugh Gray, Peter Bezencenet d Zoltan Korda and others
☆ Laurence Olivier, Franklin Dyall, Henry Victor, Hay Petrie, John Turnbull
† Work began on the film in 1935, when it was planned as part of a series on land, sea and air transport through the ages. It was completed in 1937 but not released for another three years.

Conquest of the Planet of the Apes

US 1972 85m DeLuxe Todd-AO 35
TCF/APJAC (Arthur P. Jacobs)
In the 1990s, apes used as slaves revolt against their human masters.
Ragged science fiction in a series that was going rapidly downhill.
w Paul Dehn d J. Lee Thompson ph Bruce Surtees m Tom Scott ad Philip Jefferies ed Marjorie Fowler, Allan Jaggs
☆ Roddy McDowall, Don Murray, Ricardo Montalban, Natalie Trundy, Hari Rhodes, Severn Darden
'In spite of some crude allegorical pretensions, it can't really be considered seriously as more than another excuse for APJAC to get maximum wear out of an expensive set of costumes. Even on that score, the film falls down rather badly.' – Clyde Jeavons, MFB
† The film was fourth in the series that began with The Planet of the Apes, and continued with Beneath the Planet of the Apes and Escape from the Planet of the Apes. It was followed by Battle for the Planet of the Apes (qqv).

Conquest of the South Pole

GB 1989 95m colour
Jam Jar Films/Channel 4 (Gareth Wardell)
Five unemployed Glaswegian youths recreate Amundsen's expedition to Antarctica in a decaying urban landscape.
Awkward transfer to the screen of an impressionistic play.
w Gareth Wardell play Manfred Karge d Gillies Mackinnon ph Sean Van Hales m Guy

Woolfenden ad Andy Harris ed Stephen Singleton
☆ Stefan Rimkus, Ewen Bremner, Leonard O'Malley, Laura Girling, Gordon Cameron, Alastair Galbraith, John Michie, Julie-Kate Olivier

Conrack *

US 1974 106m DeLuxe Panavision
TCF (Martin Ritt, Irving Ravetch)
A young white teacher is assigned to an all-black school in South Carolina, and after some difficulty makes friends with children and parents.
Nostalgically mellow happy-film, lit by bright smiles all around.
w Irving Ravetch, Harriet Frank Jnr novel The Water Is Wide by Pat Conroy d Martin Ritt ph John Alonzo m John Williams
☆ Jon Voight, Paul Winfield, Hume Cronyn, Madge Sinclair, Tina Andrews
'For all its craftsman-like virtues, it seems a conscious turning aside from the complexities of modern cinema to the simpler alternatives of yesteryear. Indeed, with underprivileged white children instead of black and Greer Garson substituting for Jon Voight, the film might have been made all of thirty years ago.' – John Raisbeck

'Thou Shalt Not Covet Thy Neighbor's Wife.'

Consenting Adults

US 1992 99m Technicolor
Buena Vista/Hollywood Pictures (Alan J. Pakula, David Permut)
A money-obsessed financial adviser accuses his friend of murdering his wife after a night in which they swopped partners.
A thriller that owes much to Hitchcock but is unable to maintain either interest or suspense.
w Matthew Chapman d Alan J. Pakula ph Stephen Goldblatt m Michael Small pd Carol Spier ed Sam O'Steen
☆ Kevin Kline, Mary Elizabeth Mastrantonio, Kevin Spacey, Rebecca Miller, E. G. Marshall, Forest Whitaker
'Initially seems a little brainier than its brethren but soon gives way to the same cavernous lapses in logic and formula ending.' – Variety
'Nobody can do anything much to enliven this ponderous telling of a barely credible story and the result is curiously flat and unholding.' – Derek Malcolm, Guardian

Consider Your Verdict

GB 1938 40m bw
Charter (John Boulting)
A juror proves an accused man not guilty by falsely confessing to the crime himself.
Fairly smart little entry into the feature film scene for the Boulting Brothers, from a popular radio play of the time.
w Francis Miller play Laurence Housman d Roy Boulting ph D. P. Cooper
☆ Marius Goring, Manning Whiley, Olive Sloane, Hay Petrie, George Carney

Consolation Marriage

US 1931 62m bw
RKO
A wife keeps a stiff upper lip when her husband strays.
Ho-hum domestic drama with attempts at comedy relief.
w Humphrey Pearson d Paul Sloane
☆ Irene Dunne, Pat O'Brien, John Halliday, Matt Moore, Myrna Loy
'Fair entertainment; will satisfy with good stage support.' – Variety

'What conflict in the heart of a nun would make her break her vows?'

Conspiracy of Hearts *

GB 1960 113m bw
Rank (Betty E. Box)
During World War II, Italian nuns smuggle Jewish children across the border from a nearby prison camp.
Highly commercial combination of exploitable sentimental elements: Germans, Jews, nuns, children, war, suspense. Remarkably, it gets by without causing nausea.
w Robert Presnell Jnr d Ralph Thomas ph Ernest Steward m Angelo Lavagnino

---

☆ Lilli Palmer, Sylvia Syms, Yvonne Mitchell, Albert Lieven, Ronald Lewis, Peter Arne, Nora Swinburne, Michael Goodliffe, Megs Jenkins, David Kossoff, Jenny Laird, George Coulouris, Phyllis Neilson-Terry

'What You Know Could Kill You...'

Conspiracy Theory
US 1997 135m Technicolor Panavision
Warner (Joel Silver, Richard Donner)
🖭 ◉ ◉ ◉ ◉

A Manhattan taxi driver's obsessions, with government conspiracies and a beautiful lawyer, put his life in danger.
Ridiculously paranoid thriller that degenerates into an overlong chase movie.
w Brian Helgeland d Richard Donner ph John Schwartzman m Carter Burwell pd Paul Sylbert ed Frank J. Urioste, Kevin Stitt
☆ Mel Gibson, Julia Roberts, Patrick Stewart, Cylk Cozart, Stephen Kahan, Terry Alexander
'Sporadically amusing but listless thriller that wears its humorous, romantic and political components like mismatched articles of clothing.' – *Todd McCarthy, Variety*

Conspirator
GB 1949 87m bw
MGM (Arthur Hornblow Jnr)
A guards officer, unknown to his young wife, is a communist spy.
Singularly awful romantic melodrama which never convinces or entertains for a moment.
w Sally Benson, Gerard Fairlie *novel* Humphrey Slater d Victor Saville ph F. A. Young m John Wooldridge
☆ Robert Taylor, Elizabeth Taylor, Harold Warrender, Robert Flemyng, Marie Ney

The Conspirators *
US 1944 101m bw
Warner (Jack Chertok)
A Dutch underground leader escapes to Lisbon and clears up international intrigue.
Interestingly cast but often listless wartime melodrama, a doomed attempt to reprise Casablanca without Humphrey Bogart.
w Vladimir Pozner, Leo Rosten *novel* City of Shadows by Frederick Prokosch d Jean Negulesco ph Arthur Edeson m Max Steiner
☆ Hedy Lamarr, Paul Henreid, Sydney Greenstreet, Peter Lorre, Victor Francen, Carol Thurston, Vladimir Sokoloff, Joseph Calleia, Edward Ciannelli, Steve Geray, Kurt Katch, George Macready
SYDNEY GREENSTREET (AS QUINTANILLA): 'This may seem to you melodramatic, but indulge me, please, I like melodrama.'
'As exciting as baseball and almost as gentlemanly as cricket.' – *New Statesman*
'I enjoyed it as much as any Warner melodrama since *Casablanca*.' – *Observer*

Conspirators of Pleasure **
Czech Republic/Switzerland/GB 1996 75m colour
ICA/Athanor/Pierre Assouline/Delfilm/Keith Griffiths/Koninck (Jaromir Kallista)
◉

original title: Spiklenci slasti
In Prague, various people indulge in solitary acts of love which have unexpected consequences.
Surreal film on the way perversity interacts with normal life, odd and intriguing in its own perverse way.
wd Jan Svankmajer ph Miloslav Spála md Norbert Baxter pd Jan Svankmajer ed Marie Zemanová
☆ Petr Meissel, Gabriela Wilhelmová, Barbora Hrzánová, Anna Wetlinská
'A Freudian shaggy-dog story that is as hilarious, idiosyncratic and terrifying as the most unspeakable sexual fantasy you've ever entertained. Yes, that good.' – *Independent*

Constans: see *The Constant Factor*

The Constant Factor *
Poland 1980 91m Eastmancolor
Cinegate/PRF/Zespol Filmowy
original title: Constans
A precise idealist refuses to adjust to the petty corruptions of life.
Cool dissection of human fallibility.

wd Krzysztof Zanussi ph Slawomir Idziak m Wojciech Kilar ad Tadeusz Wybult, Maciej Putowski ed Urszula Sliwinska, Ewa Smal
☆ Tadeusz Bradecki, Zofia Mrozowska, Malgorzata Zajaczkowska, Cezary Morawski, Witold Pyrkosz

The Constant Husband *
GB 1955 88m Technicolor
British Lion/London Films (Frank Launder, Sidney Gilliat)
An amnesiac discovers that he is a multiple bigamist, still wanted by each of his five wives.
Flimsy comedy which never really gets going despite an attractive cast.
w Sidney Gilliat, Val Valentine d Sidney Gilliat ph Ted Scaife m Malcolm Arnold
☆ Rex Harrison, Kay Kendall, Margaret Leighton, Cecil Parker, Nicole Maurey, George Cole, Raymond Huntley, Michael Hordern, Eric Pohlmann, Robert Coote

The Constant Nymph *
GB 1933 98m bw
Gaumont (Michael Balcon)
In the Tyrol, a composer leaves his rich wife for a schoolgirl suffering from a heart condition.
Archetypal romantic drama from Margaret Kennedy's book, first filmed in 1928 by the same producer (and then directed by Adrian Brunel, starring Ivor Novello and Mabel Poulton). A standard production of its time, which seems to have vanished with the literary copyright.
w Margaret Kennedy, Basil Dean, from their play based on her novel d Basil Dean ph Max Greene m John Greenwood
☆ Brian Aherne, Victoria Hopper, Leonora Corbett, Lyn Harding, Mary Clare, Jane Baxter
'Beautifully done artistic success from England, of doubtful box office for America.' – *Variety*
'One can say that it has a beginning, a middle and an end, but it lacks something vital.' – *E. V. Lucas, Punch*

The Constant Nymph *
US 1943 112m bw
Warner (Henry Blanke)
Artificially well-produced, overlong Hollywood version of the above.
w Kathryn Scola d Edmund Goulding ph Tony Gaudio m Erich Wolfgang Korngold
☆ Charles Boyer, Joan Fontaine, Alexis Smith, Brenda Marshall, Charles Coburn, Dame May Whitty, Peter Lorre, Joyce Reynolds, Jean Muir, Edward Ciannelli, Montagu Love, André Charlot
⅋ Joan Fontaine

Consuming Passions
GB/US 1988 100m colour
Samuel Goldwyn/Euston Films (William Cartlidge)
🖭 ▤ ◎
By adding a new ingredient to chocolate – human flesh – a young man rises to the top of his profession.
Dire attempt to revive the tradition of Ealing comedy.
w Paul D. Zimmerman, Andrew Davies *play* Secrets by Michael Palin, Terry Jones d Giles Foster ph Roger Pratt m Richard Hartley pd Peter Lamont ed John Grover
☆ Vanessa Redgrave, Freddie Jones, Jonathan Pryce, Tyler Butterworth, Sammi Davis, Thora Hird, Prunella Scales

'A message from deep space. Who will be the first to go? A journey to the heart of the universe.'

Contact *
US 1997 150m Technicolor Panavision
Warner/South Side Amusement
🖭 ▤ ◎ ◉ ◉ ◖
An astronomer picks up a signal from intelligent life on another planet.
After a brilliant beginning, an awe-inspiring journey through space, the film soon settles for sentimentality and psychobabble, being less interested in the consequences of the possibilities of alien contact than in self-help and exploring one's inner being.
w James V. Hart, Michael Goldenberg *novel* Carl Sagan d Robert Zemeckis ph Don Burgess m Alan Silvestri pd Ed Verreaux ed Arthur Schmidt
☆ Jodie Foster, Matthew McConaughey, James Woods, John Hurt, Tom Skerritt, Angela Bassett
'A serious and sober piece of speculative fiction, designed to play off of apprehensions about the forthcoming millennium in a positive and uplifting manner.' – *Variety*
⅋ sound

The Contact Man: see *Alias Nick Beal*

Conte D'Automne **
France 1998 112m colour
Artificial Eye/Films du Losange/La Sept (Margaret Ménégoz)
🖭
aka: An Autumn Tale
Friends of a lonely widow, who works as a wine grower in the Rhone valley, conspire to find her a new man.
Gently perceptive, witty drama, given a physical and spiritual autumnal setting, and one that is rooted in the realities of everyday life.
wd Eric Rohmer ph Diane Baratier m Claude Marti, Gérard Pansanel, Pierre Peyras, Antonello Salis ed Mary Stephen
☆ Marie Riviere, Béatrice Romand, Alain Libolt, Didier Sandre, Alexia Portal, Stéphane Darmon, Aurélia Alcais, Mathieu Davette, Yves Alcais
'Like Woody Allen, Rohmer may be remaking the same film again and again, but this time it's a great one.' – *Ian Freer, Empire*

Conte de Printemps **
France 1990 110m colour
Roissy Films/Films du Losange (Margaret Ménégoz)
🖭 ▤ ◎
aka: A Spring Tale
A teenage daughter, whose parents are separated, attempts to persuade her father to change girlfriends.
Witty, sophisticated comedy of manners.
wd Eric Rohmer ph Luc Pages m Beethoven, Schumann ed Lisa Garcia
☆ Anne Teyssedre, Hugues Quester, Florence Durrell, Eloise Bennett, Sophie Robin

Conte d'été *
France 1996 114m colour
Artificial Eye/Films du Losange/La Sept (Françoise Etchegaray)
aka: A Summer's Tale
A young musician on holiday toys with the affections of three women.
Slight and inconsequential tale of an indecisive protagonist drifting through life, given a certain charm by the performances.
wd Eric Rohmer ph Diane Baratier m Philippe Eidel, Sébastien Erms ed Mary Stephen
☆ Melvil Poupaud, Amanda Langlet, Gwenaëlle Simon, Aurélia Nolin, Aimé Lefèvre, Alain Guellaff
'Fans of French cinema should delight in its playful and leisurely insights into the teenage condition.' – *James Cameron-Wilson, Film Review*

Conte d'hiver **
France 1992 114m bw
Artificial Eye/Films du Losange (Margaret Ménégoz)
🖭
aka: A Winter's Tale
A French hairdresser, waiting in hope for the man who fathered her child to return to her, has unsatisfactory relationships with two other men.
An enjoyable variation on the themes of Shakespeare's play, complete with happy ending and as little concerned with reality.
wd Eric Rohmer ph Luc Pages, Maurice Giraud m Sebastian Erms ed Mary Stephen
☆ Charlotte Very, Frederic Van Den Driessche, Michel Voletti, Hervé Furic, Ava Loraschi, Christiane Desbois, Rosette, Jean-Luc Revol
'Fittingly, Rohmer's winter story has an affirmative inner glow.' – *Philip Strick, Sight and Sound*

Contempt **
France/Italy 1963 103m Technicolor
Rome-Paris/Concordia/CCC (Carlo Ponti, Joseph E. Levine)
🖭 ▤ ◎
original title: Le Mépris
In Rome, a screenwriter has troubles with his wife as he tries to set up a film of *The Odyssey* with a philistine American producer.
A clever and engrossing account of a marital crisis and of film-making; in both, none of the principals are able to communicate with the other.
wd Jean-Luc Godard *novel* A Ghost at Noon by Alberto Moravia ph Raoul Coutard m Georges Delerue ed Agnès Guillemot, Lila Lakshmanan
☆ Brigitte Bardot, Michel Piccoli, Jack Palance, Fritz Lang, Giorgia Moll, Jean-Luc Godard

'Portentous without having anything to say, improvisatory without imagination, full of esoteric references without relevance and in-group allusions without interest. Its puppets behave with meaningless meanness if not with sheer meaninglessness.' – *John Simon*
'We are still subjected to the banalities of film "in" jokes, the fake spontaneity that is supposed to cover up the plotless pointlessness of his work and the meandering literalism of his camera.' – *Judith Crist*
† The disdain for producers shown in the film was mirrored by real events: Godard had his name removed from the Italian version owing to cuts imposed by the producers and other changes, which included redubbing to remove the different languages spoken by the participants, and a new musical score by Piero Piccioni.

Contest Girl: see *The Beauty Jungle*

Continental Divide
US 1981 103m Technicolor
Universal/Amblin (Bob Larson)
▤ ◎
A national columnist finds himself banished to the wilds with a lady ornithologist studying the bald eagle.
Old-fashioned comedy, a cross between Bringing Up Baby and Woman of the Year. Not actually bad, but somewhat lacking in personality.
w Lawrence Kasdan d Michael Apted ph John Bailey m Michael Small
☆ John Belushi, Blair Brown, Allen Goorwitz, Carlin Glynn

Continuavamo a Chiamarlo Trinity: see *Trinity Is Still My Name*

Contraband **
GB 1940 92m bw
British National (John Corfield)
▤
US title: Blackout
A Danish merchant captain and a girl in wartime London expose a gang of spies using a cinema as headquarters.
Enjoyable lightweight comedy melodrama on Hitchcock lines, reuniting the unlikely star team from The Spy in Black.
w Emeric Pressburger, Michael Powell, Brock Williams d Michael Powell ph F. A. Young
☆ Conrad Veidt, Valerie Hobson, Esmond Knight, Hay Petrie, Raymond Lovell, Harold Warrender, Charles Victor, Manning Whiley
'A light romantic comedy with bondage overtones.' – *Ken Russell*

Contraband Spain
GB 1955 82m Eastmancolor
Diadem/ABP
An American agent in Barcelona investigates the death there of a compatriot involved in drug smuggling.
Pretty awful formula thick ear with bland stars and a boring look.
wd Lawrence Huntington
☆ Richard Greene, Anouk Aimée, Michael Denison, John Warwick

The Contract **
Poland 1980 111m colour
Cinegate/PRF/Zespol Filmowy
original title: Kontrakt
Despite the reluctance of a couple to marry, the groom's father celebrates with a lavish reception.
Comic and satirical look at Polish high life.
wd Krzysztof Zanussi ph Slawomir Idziak m Wojciech Kilar ad Tadeusz Wybult ed Urszula Sliwinska, Ewa Smal
☆ Maja Komorowska, Tadeusz Lomnicki, Magda Jaroszowna, Krzysztof Kilberger, Leslie Caron

Convention City *
US 1933 78m bw
Warner (Henry Blanke)
Extra-marital fun and games at a Chicago convention.
Amusing and rather risqué comedy which helped to bring down on Hollywood the wrath of the Legion of Decency.
w Robert Lord d Archie Mayo ph William Reese
☆ Joan Blondell, Guy Kibbee, Adolphe Menjou, Dick Powell, Mary Astor, Frank McHugh, Ruth Donnelly, Hugh Herbert, Hobart Cavanaugh

---

'Not a dull foot … probably the fastest complex comedy of the year and a certain money picture.' – *Variety*

The Conversation ***
US 1974 113m Technicolor
Paramount/Francis Ford Coppola
A bugging device expert lives only for his work, but finally develops a conscience.
Absorbing but extremely difficult to follow in detail, this personal, timely (in view of Watergate), Kafkaesque suspense story centres almost entirely on director and leading actor, who have a field day.
wd Francis Ford Coppola ph Bill Butler m David Shire
☆ Gene Hackman, John Cazale, Allen Garfield, Frederic Forrest
'A private, hallucinatory study in technical expertise and lonely guilt.' – *Sight and Sound*
'A terrifying depiction of a ransacked spirit.' – *New Yorker, 1977*
'Alert, truthful, unarty and absolutely essential viewing.' – *Michael Billington, Illustrated London News*
& best picture; Francis Ford Coppola (as writer)

Conversation Piece
Italy/France 1974 121m Technicolor Todd-AO 35
Rusconi/Gaumont (Giovanni Bertolucci)
original title: *Gruppo di Famiglia in un Interno*
When a reclusive professor is persuaded to let his top floor to a young couple he is brought face to face with his latent homosexuality and his approaching death.
Death in Venice revisited, but with much less style and even more obscurity.
w Luchino Visconti, Suso Cecchi d'Amico, Enrico Medioli d Luchino Visconti ph Pasqualino de Santis m Franco Mannino
☆ Burt Lancaster, Helmut Berger, Claudia Marsani, Silvana Mangano

Convict 99 *
GB 1938 91m bw
Gainsborough (Edward Black)
A seedy schoolmaster accidentally becomes a prison governor and lets the convicts run the place.
Patchily funny if overlong and in some ways rather serious Will Hay comedy, not quite typical of him.
w Marriott Edgar, Val Guest, Ralph Smart, Jack Davies d Marcel Varnel ph Arthur Crabtree md Louis Levy ad Vetchinsky ed R. E. Dearing
☆ Will Hay, Graham Moffatt, Moore Marriott, Googie Withers, Garry Marsh, Peter Gawthorne, Basil Radford, Kathleen Harrison

Convicted *
US 1950 91m bw
Columbia (Jerry Bresler)
When a prison informer is killed, one convict knows who did it.
Routine, over-plotted, strongly cast prison melodrama.
w William Bowers, Fred Niblo Jnr, Seton I. Miller play Martin Flavin d Henry Levin ph Burnett Guffey m George Duning
☆ Glenn Ford, Broderick Crawford, Millard Mitchell, Dorothy Malone, Frank Faylen, Carl Benton Reid, Will Geer

Convicts Four *
US 1962 106m bw
Allied Artists-Lubin-Kaufman (A. Ronald Lubin)
original and GB title: *Reprieve*
A convict reprieved from the electric chair spends eighteen years in prison, becomes a painter, and is rehabilitated.
Odd and unsatisfactory mixture of documentary, melodrama, sentimentality and character study, with stars unexpectedly popping in for cameo appearances. Something worthier was obviously intended.
wd Millard Kaufman autobiography John Resko ph Joseph Biroc m Leonard Rosenman
☆ Ben Gazzara, Vincent Price, Rod Steiger, Broderick Crawford, Stuart Whitman, Ray Walston, Jack Kruschen, Sammy Davis Jnr

Convoy *
GB 1940 90m bw
Ealing (Sergei Nolbandov)
A German pocket battleship menaces a British convoy, and a merchant ship sacrifices itself to prevent disaster.
Fluent British war film of the early days, the only substantial work of a much vaunted director who was subsequently killed.
w Pen Tennyson, Patrick Kirwan d Pen Tennyson ph Gunther Krampf, Roy Kellino m Ernest Irving
☆ Clive Brook, John Clements, Edward Chapman, Judy Campbell, Penelope Dudley Ward, Edward Rigby, Allan Jeayes, Albert Lieven

Convoy *
US 1978 110m DeLuxe Panavision
UA/EMI (Robert M. Sherman)
A folk hero truck driver survives several crashes and his policeman nemesis.
A virtually plotless anthology of wanton destruction. Too noisy to sleep through.
w B. W. L. Norton, based on the song by C. W. McCall d Sam Peckinpah ph Harry Stradling Jnr m Chip Davis
☆ Kris Kristofferson, Ali MacGraw, Ernest Borgnine, Burt Young, Madge Sinclair
'There's a whole lot of nothing going on here … strictly a summer popcorn picture for the nondiscriminating.' – *Variety*
'Roughly as much fun as a ride on the New Jersey turnpike with the window open. It not only numbs the brain but pollutes the senses.' – *Richard Schickel, Time*

Les Convoyeurs Attendent **
France/Belgium/Switzerland 1999 94m bw
Entertainment/K-Star/K2/RTBF/CAB/SSR (Dominique Janne)
aka: *The Carriers Are Waiting*
Desperate to win a car in a competition, a moped-riding newspaper photographer forces his teenage son to attempt the world record for opening and closing a door for 24 hours.
Quirky, dark-tinged comedy of a dysfunctional father that still somehow manages to celebrate the pleasures of family life.
w Emmanuelle Bada, Benoit Mariage, Jean-Luc Seigle d Benoit Mariage ph Philippe Guilbert m Stéphane Huguenin, Yves Sanna ad Chris Cornil ed Philippe Bourgueil
☆ Benoit Poelvoorde, Morgane Simon, Bouli Lanners, Dominique Baeyens, Philippe Grand'Henry, Jean-Francois Devigne, Lisa LaCroix, Philippe Nahon, Edith Lemerdy, Patrick Audin
'As moving and as thought-provoking a film as you would hope to see, offering a unique and insightful sideways glance at the world we live in.' – *James Mottram, Film Review*

Coogan's Bluff **
US 1968 94m Technicolor
Universal (Don Siegel)
An Arizona sheriff takes an escaped killer back to New York, and when the man escapes uses Western methods to recapture him.
Violent, well-done police story which inspired the TV series McCloud.
w Herman Miller, Dean Riesner, Howard Rodman d Don Siegel ph Bud Thackery m Lalo Schifrin
☆ Clint Eastwood, Lee J. Cobb, Susan Clark, Don Stroud, Tisha Sterling, Betty Field, Tom Tully

The Cook, the Thief, His Wife & Her Lover **
GB/France 1989 124m colour
Cinemascope
Palace/Allarts Cook/Erato Films (Kees Kasander)
A coarse gangster holds court in a fashionable restaurant while his wife conducts a passionate affair in the kitchens with a fellow diner.
Elegant, stylized, painterly and extremely brutal variation on a Jacobean revenge tragedy, though some have seen it as a political satire on our materialistic times.
wd Peter Greenaway ph Sacha Vierny m Michael Nyman pd Ben Van Os, Jan Roelfs ed John Wilson
☆ Richard Bohringer, Michael Gambon, Helen Mirren, Alan Howard, Tim Roth, Ciaran Hinds,

Gary Olsen, Ewan Stewart, Roger Ashton Griffiths, Ron Cook, Liz Smith
'Watching this picture is like being trapped in a nightmare art-history seminar: we sit there, cowed and miserable, as the teacher spews high-toned abstractions and dares us, smirkingly, to raise a common-sense objection – we know we'll be ridiculed if we do.' – *Terrence Rafferty, New Yorker*

Cookie
US 1989 93m DuArt
Warner/Lorimar (Laurence Mark)
A gangster's daughter shows that she has her father's dubious skills.
Lame drama of family relationships in gangland setting.
w Nora Ephron, Alice Arlen d Susan Seidelman ph Oliver Stapleton m Thomas Newman pd Michael Haller ad Bill Groom ed Andrew Mondshein
☆ Peter Falk, Dianne Wiest, Emily Lloyd, Michael V. Gazzo, Brenda Vaccaro, Adrian Pasdar, Lionel Stander, Jerry Lewis, Bob Gunton, Ben Rayson, Ricki Lake
'Cookie has the feel of a worn-out vehicle grinding to a halt.' – *Pam Cook, MFB*

'Where there's a will, there's a way.'
Cookie's Fortune **
US 1999 159m DeLuxe
Alliance/October/Sandcastle 5/Elysian Dreams (Robert Altman, Etchie Stroh)
Fearing scandal in a small Southern town, a woman attempts to cover up the suicide of her wealthy aunt, which leads to a black oddjob man being accused of murder.
Enjoyable, leisurely, ramshackle social comedy that gives its characters room to blossom and reveal their humanity.
w Anne Rapp d Robert Altman ph Toyomichi Kurita m David A. Stewart pd Stephen Altman ed Abraham Lim
☆ Glenn Close, Julianne Moore, Liv Tyler, Chris O'Donnell, Charles S. Dutton, Patricia Neal, Ned Beatty, Courtney B. Vance, Donald Moffat, Lyle Lovett, Danny Darst, Ruby Wilson
'May or not be Robert Altman's best film in years, but it is certainly his most pleasurable.' – *Todd McCarthy, Variety*

'Seven savage punks on a binge of violence.'
The Cool and the Crazy
US 1958 78m bw
AIP/Imperial Productions (E. C. Rhoden Jnr)
A rebellious high-school student causes havoc after he persuades his fellow students to smoke marijuana.
Typical teen drive-in drama of its time, never less than hysterical and acted by a cast who look as if they've left puberty far behind.
w Richard C. Sarafian d William Witney ph Harry Birch m Raoul Kraushaar ed Helene Turner
☆ Scott Marlowe, Gigi Perreau, Dick Bakalyan, Dick Jones

Cool as Ice
US 1991 93m DeLuxe
Universal/Alive (Carolyn Pfieffer, Lionel Wigram)
A new biker in town helps save the parents of the girl he fancies when they are threatened by gangsters.
A failed attempt to make a film star out of a white rapper.
w David Stenn d David Kellogg ph Janusz Kaminski m Stanley Clarke pd Nina Ruscio ed Debra Goldfield, Caroline Biggerstaff
☆ Vanilla Ice, Kristin Minter, Michael Gross, Sydney Lassick, Dody Goodman, Naomi Campbell, Candy Clark
'Universal's hopes of springing another Elvis Presley on the screen are, at best, laughable.' – *Variety*

Cool Breeze
US 1972 102m Metrocolor
MGM/Penelope (Gene Corman)
A miscellaneous gang of crooks is rounded up to commit a robbery, which ultimately fails.
Third, all-black remake of The Asphalt Jungle (the others being The Badlanders and Cairo). Fashionable

violence against a Los Angeles backdrop, but not at all memorable.
wd Barry Pollack ph Andy Davis m Solomon Burke
☆ Thalmus Rasulala, Judy Pace, Jim Watkins, Raymond St Jacques, Lincoln Kilpatrick

'What we've got here is a failure to communicate.'
Cool Hand Luke **
US 1967 126m Technicolor Panavision
Warner/Jalem (Gordon Carroll)
Sentenced to two years' hard labour with the chain gang, a convict becomes a legend of invulnerability but is eventually shot during an escape.
Allegedly a Christ-allegory, this well-made and good-looking film is only partially successful as an entertainment; slow stretches of soul-searching alternate with brutality, and not much acting is possible.
w Donn Pearce, Frank R. Pierson novel Donn Pearce d Stuart Rosenberg ph Conrad Hall m Lalo Schifrin
☆ Paul Newman, George Kennedy, Jo Van Fleet, J. D. Cannon, Lou Antonio, Robert Drivas, Strother Martin, Clifton James
'May be the best American film of 1967.' – *John Simon*
♟ George Kennedy
& Donn Pearce, Frank R. Pierson; Lalo Schifrin; Paul Newman

Cool Mikado
GB 1963 81m colour
UA/Gilbert and Sullivan Operas (Harold Baim)
In Japan, the son of an American judge is kidnapped when he falls in love with a girl engaged to a gangster.
An updated and unsuccessful version of the Gilbert and Sullivan operetta, one that allows little scope for its cast of comedians.
w Michael Winner, Maurice Browning, Lew Schwartz operetta The Mikado by W. S. Gilbert and Arthur Sullivan d Michael Winner m Denys Ayling, Martin Curtis md John Barry pd Derek Barrington ed Frank Galvin
☆ Frankie Howerd, Stubby Kaye, Tommy Cooper, Dennis Price, Mike Winters, Bernie Winters, Lionel Blair, Tsai Chin, Kevin Scott, Glen Mason, Peter Murray, Dermot Walsh, The John Barry Seven

The Cool Ones
US 1967 96m Technicolor Panavision
Warner (William Conrad)
Former pop singer makes a comeback.
Zazzy showbiz saga with ear-splitting track, quite professionally assembled.
w Joyce Geller d Gene Nelson ph Floyd Crosby m Ernie Freeman
☆ Roddy McDowall, Debbie Watson, Robert Coote, Phil Harris, Nita Talbot

Cool Runnings *
♚♚ US 1993 97m Technicolor
Buena Vista/Walt Disney (Dawn Steel)
A Jamaican athlete who fails to qualify for the Olympics decides to compete by forming a bobsled team with the aid of a white coach living on the island.
Based on the true story of the Jamaican bobsled team in the 1988 Olympics, an amiable, good-natured comedy of some charm.
w Lynn Siefert, Tommy Swerdlow, Michael Goldberg story Lynn Siefert, Michael Ritchie d Jon Turteltaub ph Phedon Papamichael m Hans Zimmer pd Stephen Marsh ed Bruce Green
☆ John Candy, Leon, Doug E. Doug, Malik Yoba, Rawle D. Lewis, Raymond Barry, Larry Gilman, Peter Outerbridge, Paul Coeur
'The offbeat, fact-based saga is enlivened by the perfect balance of humor, emotion and insight.' – *Variety*

Cool World
US 1992 102m Technicolor
Blue Dolphin/Paramount (Frank Mancuso Jnr)
A cartoonist and his creations flit in and out of the real world and the Cool World of his imagination.
Dreary attempt to marry live action and cartoon characters, with a plot obsessed by the possibility of sex

---

between the two, which seems nothing to get excited about.

w Michael Grais, Mark Victor d Ralph Bakshi ph John A. Alonzo m Mark Isham, John Dixon pd Michael Corenblith ed Steve Mirkovich, Annamaria Szanto

☆ Kim Basinger, Gabriel Byrne, Brad Pitt, Michele Abrams, Deirdre O'Connell, Janni Brenn-Lowen

'A combination funhouse ride/acid trip that will prove an ordeal for most visitors in the form of trial by animation. Visually dazzling but utterly soulless.' – *Variety*

Cooley High
US 1975 107m Movielab
Brent Walker/AIP (Steve Krantz)
▦ ⌖

The adventures of high-school students in Chicago of the mid-60s.
A lively first feature, full of energy but lacking in focus.
w Eric Monte d Michael Schultz ph Paul von Brack m Freddie Perren ad William B. Fosser ed Christopher Holmes

☆ Glynn Turman, Lawrence-Hilton Jacobs, Garrett Morris, Cynthia Davis, Corin Rogers, Maurice Leon Havis

'The promising debut of a very talented director, intermittently doing what he can with an uneven and somewhat routine script.' – *Jonathan Rosenbaum, MFB*

† The film was the basis of a US TV sitcom, *What's Happening* (1976–79).

The Co-Optimists *
GB 1929 83m bw
New Era (Edwin Greenwood)

A revue by a popular pierrot troupe of the time.
Famous as Britain's first musical, this is a dated but valuable record of a stage performance of the kind long vanished.
w Melville Gideon, Laddie Cliff d Edwin Greenwood, Laddie Cliff ph Basil Emmott, Sydney Blythe

☆ Davy Burnaby, Stanley Holloway, Laddie Cliff, Phyllis Monkman, Melville Gideon, Gilbert Childs, Betty Chester, Elsa MacFarlane, Peggy Petronella, Harry S. Pepper

Cop
US 1987 110m colour
Entertainment/Atlantic (James B. Harris)
▦ ⌖

A cop tracks down a serial killer to the detriment of his marriage and his relationship with his colleagues.
Tough, violent but not particularly memorable thriller.
wd James B. Harris novel *Blood on the Moon* by James Ellroy ph Steve Dubin m Michel Colombier pd Gene Rudolf ed Anthony Spano

☆ James Woods, Lesley Ann Warren, Charles Durning, Charles Haid, Raymond J. Barry, Randi Brooks, Steven Lambert, Christopher Wynne, Jan McGill

Le Cop *
France 1985 107m Eastmancolor
Panavision
Cannon/Films 7/Editions 23

A corrupt veteran cop is teamed with an incorruptible recruit.
Enjoyably comic exposé, much admired by the French.
w Claude Zidi story Simon Michael d Claude Zidi ph Jean-Jacques Tarbes m Francis Lai ad Françoise de Leu ed Nicole Saunier

☆ Philippe Noiret, Thierry Lhermitte, Regine, Grace de Capitani, Claude Brosset, Albert Simono

Le Cop 2
France 1989 108m Eastmancolor
Gala/Films 7/Orly/Sedif/TF1 (Pierre Gauchet)
▦

original title: *Ripoux contre ripoux*
Two corrupt policemen, suspended from duty, turn the tables on the crooks and cops who try to put them out of the force.
Weak sequel, with a complicated but uninteresting plot and nowhere to go for its central characters.
w Simon Michael, Claude Zidi, Didier Kaminka d Claude Zidi ph Jean-Jacques Tarbes m Francis Lai ad Françoise Deleu ed Nicole Saunier

☆ Philippe Noiret, Thierry Lhermitte, Guy Marchand, Line Renaud, Grace de Capitani, Michel Aumont, Jean-Pierre Castaldi, Jean-Claude Brialy

Cop and a Half
⫟ US 1993 97m DeLuxe
Universal/Imagine (Paul Maslansky)
▦ ▦ ⌖

An eight-year-old boy, witness to a murder, gets to be a cop for a day.
Ghastly, sentimental comedy aimed at the lowest common demonitor.
w Arne Olsen d Henry Winkler ph Bill Butler m Alan Silvestri pd Maria Caso ed Daniel Hanley, Roger Tweten, C. Timothy O'Meara

☆ Burt Reynolds, Norman D. Golden II, Ruby Dee, Holland Taylor, Ray Sharkey, Sammy Hernandez, Frank Sivero

'Unashamedly caters to children's crudest fantasies and leaves the rest of the world at a loss. There are few adult pleasures to be had.' – *Sight and Sound*

Cop au Vin *
France 1984 110m Eastmancolor
Panavision
Virgin/MK2/Marin Karmitz

original title: *Poulet au Vinaigre*
An unorthodox police inspector investigates two deaths in a small provincial town.
Glossy thriller exposing the pettiness of the bourgeoisie.
w Dominique Roulet, Claude Chabrol novel *Un Mort En Trop* by Dominique Roulet d Claude Chabrol ph Jean Rabier m Matthieu Chabrol ad Françoise Benoît-Fresco ed Monique Fardoulis

☆ Jean Poiret, Stéphane Audran, Michel Bouquet, Jean Topart, Lucas Blevaux, Pauline Lafont, Caroline Cellier, Josephine Chaplin

'No One Is Above The Law.'

Cop Land **
US 1997 105m DeLuxe
Buena Vista/Woods Entertainment (Cary Woods, Cathy Konrad, Ezra Swerdlow)
▦ ▦ ⌖ ⊚ ⌂

A sheriff in a small New Jersey town that is home to many policemen investigates the deaths of two youths at the hands of a cop.
A thriller interesting mainly for Stallone's attempt to get away from his usual macho roles by playing an overweight, deaf sheriff, though it is never less than enjoyable.
wd James Mangold ph Eric Edwards m Howard Shore pd Lester Cohen ed Craig McKay

☆ Sylvester Stallone, Harvey Keitel, Ray Liotta, Robert de Niro, Peter Berg, Janeane Garofalo, Robert Patrick, Michael Rapaport, Annabella Sciorra, Noah Emmerich, Cathy Moriarty

'Has the feel of a classic frontier Western in which the amiable sheriff is forced to wake up to the dastardly doings of the community's most prominent citizens.' – *Todd McCarthy, Variety*

Copacabana
US 1947 91m bw
UA/Sam Coslow
▦ ⌖

A quick-thinking agent forms two acts out of one client, which makes things awkward when both are needed at once.
Thinly produced comedy with both stars doing what is expected of them in surroundings less glamorous than those to which they were previously accustomed.
w Allen Boretz, Howard Harris story Laslo Vadnay d Alfred E. Green ph Bert Glennon m Edward Ward

☆ Groucho Marx, Carmen Miranda, Steve Cochran, Gloria Jean, Andy Russell

Copper Canyon
US 1949 84m Technicolor
Paramount
▦ ⌖

After the Civil War, Southern veterans trying to rebuild their homes are helped by a gunslinger.
Shiny unpersuasive Western with stars ill at ease.
w Jonathan Latimer d John Farrow

☆ Ray Milland, Hedy Lamarr, Macdonald Carey, Mona Freeman, Harry Carey Jnr

Cops ***
⫟ US 1922 20m bw silent
First National/Comique Film (Joseph M. Schenck)
▦

An innocent disrupts a parade and is pursued by a horde of policemen.
The perfect Keaton short, a careful assembly of perfectly timed gags.
wd Buster Keaton ph Elgin Lessley

☆ Buster Keaton, Virginia Fox

Cops and Robbers *
US 1973 89m DeLuxe
UA/EK Corp (Elliott Kastner)
▦

Two New York cops turn crook and pull off a job for the Mafia.
Trendily anti-establishment comedy, quite snappy and smart when you can follow it.
w Donald E. Westlake d Aram Avakian ph David L. Quaid m Michel Legrand

☆ Cliff Gorman, Joe Bologna, Dick Ward, Shepperd Strudwick, Ellen Holly, John P. Ryan

Cops and Robbersons
US 1994 93m Technicolor
TriStar/Channel (Ned Tanen, Nancy Graham Tanen, Ronald L. Schwary)
▦ ▦ ⌖

Two cops move in with a suburban family to keep watch on a forger who lives next door.
Tame, formulaic comedy that pulls its punches in its depiction of the conventionalities of middle-class life, although Palance, as a cop who eats his food with a cigarette stuck in the corner of his mouth, provides moments of pleasure.
w Bernie Somers d Michael Ritchie ph Gerry Fisher m William Ross pd Stephen J. Lineweaver ed Stephen A. Rotter, William S. Scharf

☆ Chevy Chase, Jack Palance, Dianne Wiest, Robert Davi, David Barry Gray, Jason James Richter, Fay Masterson, Miko Hughes

'Best suited to a juvenile crowd who will thrive on the obvious nature of the proceedings.' – *Variety*

Copycat *
US 1995 123m Technicolor
Warner/New Regency/Monarchy (Arnon Milchan, Mark Tarlov)
▦ ▦ ⌖ ⊚ ⊚ ⌂

A female detective and an agoraphobic psychologist team up to track down a serial killer who copies the style of murders carried out by other serial killers
A well-acted thriller on over-familiar themes; the performances do not compensate for its sense of staleness.
w Ann Biderman, David Madsen d Jon Amiel ph Laszlo Kovacs m Christopher Young pd Jim Clay ed Alan Heim, Jim Clark

☆ Sigourney Weaver, Holly Hunter, Dermot Mulroney, William McNamara, Harry Connick Jnr, J. E. Freeman, Will Patton, John Rothman

'An upscale suspenser by virtue of its classy cast, its extremely bright characters and the chillingly intellectual approach of the murderer, this shrewdly devised pulse-pounder may actually be too refined to click in a big way with mass audiences.' – *Todd McCarthy, Variety*

'This all-too-aptly titled film suggests it is time to find another dead horse to flog.' – *Kim Newman, Empire*

Coquette
US 1929 75m bw
Mary Pickford
▦

A Southern belle has a flirtatious nature.
Disappointing talkie start for a first lady of the silents; she did not recover from it, despite her Oscar.
w John Grey, Allen McNeil, Sam Taylor play George Abbott, Anne Preston d Sam Taylor

☆ Mary Pickford, Johnny Mack Brown, Matt Moore, William Janney

🎔 Mary Pickford

Le Corbeau **
France 1943 92m bw
L'Atelier Français
US title: *The Raven*
Poison pen letters disturb a small provincial town.
Impressively characterized whodunnit with the usual French qualities of detail and discretion. Remade in Hollywood to less effect as The Thirteenth Letter (qv).
w Louis Chavance d Henri-Georges Clouzot ph Nicholas Hayer m Tony Aubain

☆ Pierre Fresnay, Pierre Larquey, Ginette Leclerc, Hélène Manson

'By no means as malign or as brilliant as it's cracked up to be, but a sour, clever, amusing job.' – *James Agee*

Coriolanus – Hero without a Country
(dubbed)
Italy/France 1965 100m Eastmancolor
Euroscope
Dorica/Explorer/CFFP (Diego Alchimede)
original title: *Coriolano, Eroe senza Patria*
aka: *Thunder of Battle*
In a Rome riven by class conflict, its greatest general, Coriolanus, is exiled by the popular leaders.
Above-average Italian historical epic.
w Remigio Del Grosso d Giorgio Ferroni ph Augusto Tiezzi m Carlo Rustichelli ad Arrigo Equini ed Antonietta Zita

☆ Gordon Scott, Alberto Lupo, Lilla Brignone, Philippe Hersent, Rosalba Neri

The Corn Is Green *
⫟ US 1945 118m bw
Warner (Jack Chertok)
▦

In 1895 Miss Moffat starts a village school for Welsh miners, and after some tribulations sees one of them off to Oxford.
A very theatrical production with unconvincing sets and mannered acting, but the original play has its felicities.
w Casey Robinson, Frank Cavett play Emlyn Williams d Irving Rapper ph Sol Polito m Max Steiner ad Carl Jules Weyl

☆ Bette Davis, John Dall, Nigel Bruce, Joan Lorring, Rhys Williams, Rosalind Ivan, Mildred Dunnock, Arthur Shields

'It's very apparent that Hollywood isn't Wales … but the film lingers in the memory anyway.' – *New Yorker, 1978*

† Remade as a TV movie in 1978, with Katharine Hepburn.

⅄ John Dall; Joan Lorring

Cornered *
US 1945 102m bw
RKO
▦ ⌖

After demobilization, a French-Canadian pilot tracks down the collaborationist responsible for the death of his wife.
Well-made but humourless revenge thriller.
w John Paxton story John Wexley d Edward Dmytryk ph Harry J. Wild m Roy Webb

☆ Dick Powell, Micheline Cheirel, Walter Slezak, Morris Carnovsky

Coronado
US 1935 77m bw
Paramount
Marital misunderstandings abound at a swanky beach hotel.
Thinly plotted but star-spotted comedy musical, notable now for the talent.
w Don Hartman, Frank Butler d Norman McLeod

☆ Jack Haley, Leon Errol, Eddy Duchin and his Orchestra, Johnny Downs, Betty Burgess, Andy Devine, Alice White, Jameson Thomas

Coroner Creek
US 1948 89m Cinecolor
Columbia (Harry Joe Brown)
▦

A Western crusader tracks down the man behind a stagecoach raid.
Solid action Western between the A and B categories.
w Kenneth Gamet novel Luke Short d Ray Enright

☆ Randolph Scott, Marguerite Chapman, George Macready, Sally Eilers, Edgar Buchanan, Barbara Reed, Wallace Ford, Forrest Tucker, Douglas Fowley

Corps Profond *
France 1963 21m Technicolor
Delpire
A tour inside the human body by courtesy of micro-photography.
Spellbinding and educative documentary of a new kind, and just the right length; the later British imitation, The Body, outstayed its welcome.
wd Igor Barrière, Etienne Lalou

The Corpse Came COD
US 1947 87m bw
Columbia (Sam Bischoff)
Rival reporters try to solve the mystery of a wandering body.

⊚ Digital Video Disc Region 2   ▦ Digital Video Disc Region 1   ⌂ Soundtrack released on compact disc   ☆ Cast in approximate order of importance   † Points of interest   ♫ Notable songs   🎔 Academy Award   ⅄ Academy Award nomination   ⍟ BAFTA

Routine crime comedy with too few smart lines.
w George Bricker, Dwight Babcock *novel* Jimmy Starr d Henry Levin *ph* Lucien Andriot
m George Duning
☆ George Brent, Joan Blondell, Adele Jergens, Jim Bannon, Leslie Brooks, Grant Mitchell, Una O'Connor

'Horror to make your hair stand on end!'
The Corpse Vanishes
US   1942   70m   bw
Monogram (Sam Katzman)
▤ ◉
A botanist kidnaps young brides for their body fluids, in the hope of reviving his dead wife.
An especially dreary example of Poverty Row horror.
w Harvey Gates d Wallace Fox
☆ Bela Lugosi, Frank Moran, Minerva Urecal, Luana Walters

Corregidor
US   1943   74m   bw
PRC/Dixon R. Harwin-Edward Finney
▤
Doctors on Corregidor sort out an eternal triangle while US forces fight the Japs.
Feeble wartime quickie, inept in almost every respect.
w Doris Malloy, Edgar G. Ulmer d William Nigh
☆ Elissa Landi, Otto Kruger, Donald Woods, Frank Jenks, Rick Vallin, Ian Keith

Corridor of Mirrors
GB   1948   105m   bw
Cartier-Romney-Apollo (Rudolph Cartier)
An eccentric art collector believes that he and his mistress are reincarnations of 400-year-old lovers in a painting; but they are separated by murder.
Pretentious melodrama of no urgent narrative interest, with all concerned sadly at sea.
w Rudolph Cartier, Edana Romney *novel* Chris Massie d Terence Young *ph* André Thomas
m Georges Auric
☆ Eric Portman, Edana Romney, Barbara Mullen, Hugh Sinclair
'It has aimed at Art. It is, in fact, Effect. Some members of the cast wander in and out of the scenes as if they are not quite sure what has happened to them. Their confusion is not beyond comprehension.' – *MFB*

Corridors of Blood *
GB   1958   86m   bw
Producers' Associates (John Croydon)
▤ ▦
original title: *Doctor from Seven Dials*
Seeking to discover anaesthetics, a Victorian doctor falls a prey to resurrection men.
Unpleasant but well-mounted semi-horror backed by strong cast and art direction.
w Jean Scott Rogers d Robert Day *ph* Geoffrey Faithfull m Buxton Orr *ad* Anthony Masters
☆ Boris Karloff, Christopher Lee, Finlay Currie, Frank Pettingell, Betta St John, Francis Matthews, Adrienne Corri, Marian Spencer
† Not released until 1964.

'An enchanting comedy comedy.'
Corrina, Corrina
👫 US   1994   114m   colour
Guild/New Line (Paula Mazur, Steve Tisch, Jessie Nelson)
▦ ▤ ◎ 🎧
In the late 1950s, a new housekeeper forms a motherly relationship with a nine-year-old girl, struck dumb by the death of her mother, and also becomes close to the girl's father.
A sentimental movie movie, which seems to have been mainly designed to sell its soundtrack album of the songs of the period.
wd Jessie Nelson *ph* Bruce Surtees m Rick Cox
pd Jeannine Claudia Oppewall *ed* Lee Percy
☆ Ray Liotta, Whoopi Goldberg, Tina Majorino, Wendy Crewson, Larry Miller, Jenifer Lewis, Erica Yohn, Joan Cusack, Don Ameche
'Hopelessly pedantic – chock full of lessons about grief, racism, and, so help us, God.' – *Michael Sragow, New Yorker*
'Like *The Sound of Music* remade as an AT & T commercial.' – *Entertainment Weekly*

The Corrupt Ones: see *The Peking Medallion*

Corruption
GB   1967   91m   Technicolor
Columbia/Titan (Peter Newbrook)
A surgeon kills for pituitary gland fluid to restore his fiancée's beauty.
Highly derivative shocker with no inspiration of its own except an accumulation of gory detail.
w Donald and Derek Ford d Robert Hartford Davis *ph* Peter Newbrook m Bill McGuffie
☆ Peter Cushing, Sue Lloyd, Noel Trevarthen, Kate O'Mara, David Lodge

'You can't play by the rules when there aren't any.'
The Corruptor *
US   1999   110m   DeLuxe   Panavision
New Line/Illusion (Dan Halsted)
🎧
A young New York cop whose beat is Chinatown discovers that his new Asian-American partner has links to the Triads.
Tough, street-smart thriller on familiar themes of integrity and betrayal, given a fresh twist by its setting and its subject-matter of illegal immigration.
w Robert Pucci d James Foley *ph* Juan Ruiz-Anchia m Carter Burwell *pd* David Brisbin
ed Howard E. Smith
☆ Chow Yun-Fat, Mark Wahlberg, Ric Young, Paul Ben-Victor, Jon Kit Lee, Andrew Pang, Brian Cox, Elizabeth Lindsey, Byron Mann, Kim Chan, Bill Macdonald, Susie Trinh, Tovah Feldshuh
'The movie may be a conventional story of police corruption, temptation and conflicting loyalties, but it never loses its smarts.' – *Stephen Holden, New York Times*

Corsa dell'Innocente: see *Flight of the Innocent*

Corsair *
US   1931   75m   bw
Roland West
A college football hero turns hi-jacker.
Modest gangster saga with signs of style smothered by the script.
w Josephine Lovett *novel* Walon Green
d Roland West
☆ Chester Morris, Alison Loyd, William Austin, Frank McHugh, Ned Sparks
'A bit out-dated … will take a lot of nursing to reach average grosses.' – *Variety*
† Alison Loyd was a name momentarily adopted by Thelma Todd.

The Corsican Brothers *
US   1941   111m   bw
UA/Edward Small
▤
Siamese twins are separated but remain spiritually tied through various adventures.
Adequately exciting picturization of the Dumas swashbuckler.
w George Bruce, Howard Estabrook d Gregory Ratoff *ph* Harry Stradling m Dimitri Tiomkin
☆ Douglas Fairbanks Jnr, Akim Tamiroff, Ruth Warrick, J. Carrol Naish, H. B. Warner, Henry Wilcoxon
† In 1953 came an undistinguished sequel, *Bandits of Corsica* (GB: *The Return of the Corsican Brothers*), with Richard Greene, Paula Raymond, Raymond Burr and Dona Drake. Written by Richard Schayer; directed by Ray Nazarro; for Global/UA. A comic version, *Cheech and Chong's Corsican Brothers* (qv), was released in 1984.
♫ Dimitri Tiomkin

Cortesie per gli ospiti: see *The Comfort of Strangers*

Corvette K 225 *
US   1943   97m   bw
Universal (Howard Hawks)
GB title: *The Nelson Touch*
A Canadian corvette commander encounters submarines and bombers in mid-Atlantic.
Good war film of its period, marred by romantic interest.
w Lt John Sturdy d Richard Rosson *ph* Tony Gaudio m David Buttolph
☆ Randolph Scott, James Brown, Ella Raines, Barry Fitzgerald, Andy Devine, Richard Lane
♫ Tony Gaudio

Corvette Summer
US   1979   104m   Metrocolor
MGM/Plotto (Hal Barwood)
▤
GB title: *The Hot One*
A Los Angeles student spends the summer looking for his stolen customized car, and has various adventures around Las Vegas.
There are a few choice moments in this disconnected comedy drama, but the appeal is almost entirely to moonstruck teenagers.
w Hal Barwood, Matthew Robbins d Matthew Robbins *ph* Frank Stanley m Craig Safan
☆ Mark Hamill, Annie Potts, Eugene Roche, Kim Milford, Richard McKenzie

Cosh Boy
GB   1952   75m   bw
Romulus (Daniel M. Angel)
US title: *The Slasher*
A young thug resists all attempts to reform him.
A competent social drama of its time; it has not worn well, though it remains of interest for what it reveals about the attitudes of the period.
w Lewis Gilbert, Vernon Harris *play* Master Crook by Bruce Walker d Lewis Gilbert *ph* Jack Asher m Lambert Williamson *ad* Bernard Robinson
ed Charles Hasse
☆ James Kenney, Joan Collins, Hermione Baddeley, Hermione Gingold, Betty Ann Davies, Robert Ayres, Nancy Roberts, Laurence Naismith, Ian Whittaker
'There is something about this film which goes beyond the sordid nature of the subject and leaves a peculiarly distasteful impression. Whether by design or accident, there is a feeling about the piece that this sort of behaviour is not a deadly public menace, but a half-humorous escapade of youth.' – *C. A. Lejeune*
† The film, which was an early recipient of a British 'X' certificate, opens with an on-screen message: 'By itself, the "Cosh" is the cowardly implement of a contemporary evil; in association with "Boy", it marks a post-war tragedy – the juvenile delinquent. "Cosh Boy" portrays starkly the development of a young criminal, an enemy of society at sixteen. Our Judges and Magistrates, and the Police, whose stern duty it is to resolve the problem, agree that its origins lie mainly in the lack of parental control and early discipline. The problem exists – and we cannot escape it by closing our eyes. This film is presented in the hope that it will contribute towards stamping out this social evil.'

The Cosmic Man
US   1958   72m   bw
Futura (Robert A. Terry)
▦
An alien is met with hostility when he visits Earth preaching peace.
Typical low-budget sci-fi movie of its time that offers nothing out of the ordinary.
w Arthur C. Pierce m Herbert Greene *ph* John F. Warren m Paul Sawtell, Bert Shefter *ed* Helene Turner
☆ Bruce Bennett, John Carradine, Angela Greene, Paul Langton, Scotty Morrow, Lyn Osborn, Walter Maslow

Cosmic Monsters: see *Strange World of Planet X*

Costa Brava *
Spain   1994   92m   colour
DTK/Marta Balletbò-Coll
A female engineer falls in love with a lesbian writer.
Slight, pleasant romantic comedy set in Barcelona and with its Spanish cast speaking English.
w Marta Balletbò-Coll, Ana Simón Cerezo, Steven Winchell, Marel Malaret, Desi del Valle d Marta Balletbò-Coll *ph* Teo López Garcia m Emili Remolins Casas, Xavier Martorell, Miquel Amor *pd* Gloria Marti-Palanques *ed* Ignacio Pérez de Olaguer Córdoba
☆ Desi del Valle, Marta Balletbò-Coll, Montserrat Gausachs, Josep Maria Brugués, Ramon Mari, Sergi Schaaff
'A lesbian fairy tale with the lightest of touches, a fragile but charming confection.' – *Sight and Sound*

Cottage on Dartmoor
GB   1929   75m   bw
BIP (Bruce Woolfe)
US title: *Escaped from Dartmoor*
A farmer's wife shelters her ex-lover when he breaks jail.
Crude early talkie notable only as an immature work of its director.
wd Anthony Asquith *story* Herbert Price *ph* Stanley Rodwell *md* William Hodgson *ad* Ian Campbell-Gray
☆ Norah Baring, Uno Hemming, Hans Schlettow, Judd Green

Cottage to Let *
GB   1941   90m   bw
Gainsborough (Edward Black)
▦ ▤
US title: *Bombsight Stolen*
Evacuated to Scotland, a Cockney helps prevent spies from kidnapping his inventor foster-father.
Stagey but often amusing comedy-thriller which after a shaky start becomes agreeably Hitchcockian.
w Anatole de Grunwald, J. O. C. Orton *play* Geoffrey Kerr d Anthony Asquith *ph* Jack Cox *md* Louis Levy
☆ Leslie Banks, *Alastair Sim*, John Mills, Jeanne de Casalis, George Cole, Carla Lehmann, Michael Wilding, Frank Cellier, Wally Patch, Muriel Aked, Muriel George, Catherine Lacey, Hay Petrie

'Where crime lords rub elbows with the rich and famous!'
The Cotton Club
US   1984   127m   Technicolor   Panavision
Zoetrope (Robert Evans)
▦ ▤ ◎ 🎧
The story of Harlem's famous night-club and the gangsters who frequented it.
A lumpy vehicle, eventually costing fifty million dollars, for some of the talents who made The Godfather *ten years earlier. Despite a few effective moments, a prime example of the careless extravagance which all but killed the film business.*
w William Kennedy, Francis Coppola d Francis Coppola *ph* Stephen Goldblatt m John Barry
pd Richard Sylbert *ed* Barry Malkin, Robert Lovett
☆ Richard Gere, Gregory Hines, Diane Lane, Lonette McKee, Bob Hoskins, James Remar, Nicolas Cage, Allen Garfield, Fred Gwynne, Gwen Verdon
'The narrative is a mess, and keeps interrupting the heartstopping hoofing.' – *Time Out*
♫ editing, art direction

Cotton Comes to Harlem
US   1970   97m   DeLuxe
Formosa/UA
▤
Two black detectives try to beat the police to a bale of cotton containing a fortune in stolen dollars.
Rickety vehicle for two amiable black characters presented rather more surely in Come Back Charleston Blue *(qv).*
w Arnold Perl, Ossie Davis, Chester Himes *novel* Chester Himes d Ossie Davis
☆ Godfrey Cambridge, Raymond St Jacques, Calvin Lockhart, Judy Pace, Redd Foxx

Cotton Mary *
GB   1999   123m   Technicolor
UIP/Merchant Ivory (Nayeem Hafizka, Richard Hawley)
An Anglo-Indian nurse in a white household in India in the 1950s imagines that she can supplant her mistress.
An effective drama of colonialism and racial identity, fought out within a family that is losing its cohesion.
w Alexandra Viets *play* Alexandra Viets d Ismail Merchant *ph* Pierre Lhomme m Richard Robbins *pd* Alison Riva *ed* John David Allen
☆ Greta Scacchi, Madhur Jaffrey, James Wilby, Sarah Badel, Riju Bajaj, Gerson Da Cunha, Joanna David, Neena Gupta, Sakina Jaffrey, Gemma Jones, Firdausi Jussawalla
'An enjoyable, sturdy little film that is uniformly well-acted and beautifully shot.' – *Clayton Hickman, Film Review*

👫 film suitable for family viewing   ▦ VHS video-cassette for the British PAL system   ▤ VHS video-cassette for the British PAL system in wide screen-format   ↻ Video cassette in a computer-colourised version   ▤ American NTSC video-cassette   ◎ Laser disc

Cotton Queen

GB 1937 bw

British Independent Exhibitors/Joe Rock

Two fiercely competitive Manchester mill-owners agree, after many misunderstandings, to co-operate.

Drear provincial comedy, in which a talented cast is given no opportunity to shine.

w Syd Courtenay, Barry Peak, Scott Pembroke, Louis Golding d Bernard Vorhaus ph Eric Cross md Cyril Ray ad George Provis ed Sam Simmonds, Dr Max Brenner

☆ Will Fyffe, Stanley Holloway, Mary Lawson, Jimmy Hanley, Helen Haye, Marcelle Rogez, Syd Courtenay

The Couch Trip *

US 1988 98m colour

Rank/Orion (Lawrence Gordon)

A mental patient escapes to Los Angeles where he becomes a success as a radio doctor.

Sporadically amusing comedy that mocks obvious targets.

w Steven Kampmann, Will Port, Sean Stein novel Ken Kolb d Michael Ritchie ph Donald E. Thorin m Michel Colombier pd Jimmy Bly ed Richard A. Harris

☆ Dan Aykroyd, Walter Matthau, Charles Grodin, Donna Dixon, Richard Romanus, Mary Gross, David Clennon

Council of the Gods *

Germany 1950 106m bw

DEFA (Adolf Fischer)

A research chemist working for a big chemical company denounces them after the war when he finds they have been producing poison gas for the concentration camps.

Self-flagellatory expiation of war crimes encased in an absorbing drama.

w Friedrich Wolff, Philipp Gebb d Kurt Maetzig ph Friedl Behn-Grund m Hanns Eisler, Erwin Lehn

☆ Paul Bildt, Agnes Windeck, Yvonne Merin, Fritz Tillman

Counsel for Crime

US 1937 61m bw

Columbia

A crooked lawyer fixes alibis for his clients before they commit a crime, until he finds his own son on the other side of one of his cases.

Adequate programmer.

w Fred Niblo Jnr, Grace Neville, Lee Loeb, Harold Buchman d John Brahm

☆ Otto Kruger, Douglass Montgomery, Jacqueline Wells, Thurston Hall, Nana Bryant

'Won't disappoint those who get caught with it on a dual.' – *Variety*

Counsellor at Law *

US 1933 78m bw

Universal (Henry Henigson)

Life in the New York office of a successful Jewish lawyer.

Practised film-making from a Broadway hit.

w Elmer Rice play Elmer Rice d William Wyler ph Norbert Brodine

☆ John Barrymore, Bebe Daniels, Melvyn Douglas, Doris Kenyon, Onslow Stevens, Isabel Jewell, Thelma Todd, Mayo Methot

'Good drama, well produced and with strong b.o. potentialities.' – *Variety*

† Paul Muni was the first choice for the lead, but refused to play a Jewish role.

Counsel's Opinion

GB 1933 76m bw

London Films (Alexander Korda)

A widow wins a barrister by pretending to be a flighty socialite.

Semi-sophisticated comedy; this rather thin quickie version was done over four years later and became The Divorce of Lady X (qv).

w Dorothy Greenhill, Arthur Wimperis play Gilbert Wakefield d Allan Dwan ph Bernard Browne ad Holmes Paul ed Harold Young

☆ Henry Kendall, Binnie Barnes, Cyril Maude, Lawrence Grossmith

'There is perhaps more naivety than usual about this comedy of a divorce counsel who imagines himself mixed up in his own case. The director is an American, Allan Dwan, who must either

have come or gone away with odd ideas of British humour.' – *Observer*

Count A Lonely Cadence: see *Stockade*

Count Dracula: see *Bram Stoker's Count Dracula*

Count Five and Die *

GB 1957 92m bw Cinemascope

TCF/Zonic (Ernest Gartside)

British intelligence seeks to give the Nazis false information about the 1944 invasion, but conviction grows that a double agent is among them.

Terse, downbeat war suspenser, gripping in parts but quite forgettable.

w Jack Seddon, David Pursall d Victor Vicas ph Arthur Grant m John Wooldridge

☆ Nigel Patrick, Jeffrey Hunter, Anne-Marie Duringer, David Kossoff

The Count of Monte Cristo ***

♔♔ US 1934 114m bw

Reliance (Edward Small)

After spending years in prison, Edmond Dantes escapes and avenges himself on those who framed him.

Classic swashbuckler, extremely well done with due attention to dialogue as well as action; a model of its kind and period.

w Philip Dunne, Dan Totheroh, Rowland V. Lee novel Alexandre Dumas d Rowland V. Lee ph Peverell Marley m Alfred Newman

☆ Robert Donat, Elissa Landi, Louis Calhern, Sidney Blackmer, Raymond Walburn, O. P. Heggie, William Farnum

'A near-perfect blend of thrilling action and grand dialogue.' – *Variety*

The Count of the Old Town

Sweden 1935 75m bw

Svensk Filmindustri/AB Fribergs Filmbyra

original title: *Munkbrogreven*

A mysterious stranger moves into a hotel frequented by some elderly work-shy drinkers, and begins a romance with the maid.

A broad and episodic comedy of clever crooks and dim cops, dominant women and henpecked men, with enough absurd impetus to its set-pieces to still raise a smile or two.

w Gösta Stevens play Greven Av Gamla Sta'n by Siegfried and Arthur Fischer d Edvin Adolphson ph Åke Dahlquist m Eric Bengtson ed Rolf Husberg

☆ Waldemar Dalquist, Julia Caesar, Sigurd Wallén, Tollie Zellman, Edvin Adolphson, Ingrid Bergman, Eric Abrahamson, Weyler Hildebrand

† It was Ingrid Bergman's first film.

Count the Hours

US 1953 74m bw

RKO (Benedict Bogeaus)

GB title: *Every Minute Counts*

A man's wife and lawyer fight to save him from the gallows.

Stiff and unconvincing suspenser.

w Doane R. Hoag, Karen DeWolf d Don Siegel ph John Alton m Louis Forbes

☆ Teresa Wright, Macdonald Carey, Dolores Moran, Adele Mara, Edgar Barrier, John Craven, Jack Elam

Count Three and Pray

US 1955 92m Technicolor Cinemascope

Columbia/Copa (Ted Richmond)

After the Civil War a roistering Southerner comes home to rebuild his town and become its parson.

Moderate semi-Western, fresh and pleasing but not memorable.

w Herb Meadow d George Sherman ph Burnett Guffey m George Duning

☆ Van Heflin, Joanne Woodward, Phil Carey, Raymond Burr, Allison Hayes, Myron Healey, Nancy Kulp, James Griffiths

'Don't dare come alone!'

Count Yorga Vampire

US 1970 90m Movielab

Erica/AIP (Michael Macready)

aka: *The Loves of Count Iorga, Vampire*

Inquisitive Los Angeles teenagers are vampirized by a suave foreign visitor.

A semi-professional film that looks it but amid the longueurs provides one or two nasty frissons.

wd Bob Kelljan ph Arch Archambault m William Marx

☆ Robert Quarry, Roger Perry, Michael Murphy, Michael Macready, Donna Anders, Judith Lang

† The Return of Count Yorga followed a year later.

Count Your Blessings

US 1959 102m Metrocolor Cinemascope

MGM (Karl Tunberg)

An English girl marries an aristocratic Frenchman, but the war and other considerations make them virtual strangers until their son is nine years old, when it becomes clear that daddy is a philanderer.

Slight upper-crust comedy, basically rather tedious but kept buoyant by Chevalier as commentator.

w Karl Tunberg novel The Blessing by Nancy Mitford d Jean Negulesco ph Milton Krasner, George Folsey m Franz Waxman

☆ Deborah Kerr, Maurice Chevalier, Rossano Brazzi, Martin Stephens, Tom Helmore, Ronald Squire, Patricia Medina, Mona Washbourne

'Negulesco's aspirations to elegance are now familiar ... this is far too absurd an example of Hollywood's infatuation with Old Europe to arouse much interest.' – *MFB*

Countdown *

US 1967 101m Technicolor Panavision

Warner (William Conrad)

Russian and American spaceships race for the moon.

Earnest, simply-plotted science-fiction in which technology is the centre of interest.

w Loring Mandel d Robert Altman ph William W. Spencer m Leonard Rosenman ad Jack Poplin

☆ James Caan, Robert Duvall, Barbara Baxley, Joanna Moore, Charles Aidman, Steve Ihnat

Counterattack

US 1945 89m bw

Columbia

GB title: *One against Seven*

Resistance fighters go behind enemy lines for purposes of sabotage.

Standard World War II actioner, the star appearing above his surroundings.

w John Howard Lawson play Janet and Philip Stevenson d Zoltan Korda ph James Wong Howe m Louis Gruenberg

☆ Paul Muni, Marguerite Chapman, Larry Parks, George Macready, Roman Bohnen

Counterblast

GB 1948 99m bw

British National

An escaped Nazi poses as a British scientist in a research laboratory.

Overlong espionage thick ear with some compensations.

w Jack Whittingham story Guy Morgan d Paul Stein

☆ Robert Beatty, Mervyn Johns, Nova Pilbeam, Margaretta Scott, Marie Lohr, Karel Stepanek, Alan Wheatley

The Counterfeit Traitor *

US 1962 140m Technicolor

Paramount/Perlberg-Seaton

An oil importer, a naturalized Swede born in America, is blackmailed by the Allies into becoming a spy.

Heavy-going espionage drama which divides its time between action and moralizing. Excellent production does not quite make it exciting.

wd George Seaton book Alexander Klein ph Jean Bourgoin m Alfred Newman

☆ William Holden, Lilli Palmer, Hugh Griffith, Werner Peters, Eva Dahlbeck

'The picture is too long, it is also incessantly exciting, occasionally witty ... and in its expression of organized sadism comparatively subtle.' – *Time*

The Counterfeiters

US 1948 73m bw

TVF/Reliance (Maurice H. Conn)

A Scotland Yard detective and a US Treasury agent team up to track down a gang of forgers who are flooding Europe with fake twenty-dollar bills and five-pound notes.

Undemanding and undistinguished time-filler with a reliance on stereotype – the Englishman cop smokes a

pipe, the American cigarettes – and with Chaney doing the dim hulk routine that he perfected in Of Mice and Men.

w Fred Myton, Barbara Worth story Maurice H. Conn d Peter Stewart (Sam Newfield) ph James S. Brown m Irving Gertz ad Frank Dexter ed Martin G. Cohn

☆ John Sutton, Doris Merrick, Hugh Beaumont, Lon Chaney, George O'Hanlon, Douglas Blackley, Herbert Rawlinson

Counterpoint *

US 1967 107m Technicolor Techniscope

Universal (Dick Berg)

In 1944, an American symphony orchestra is captured by the Germans and threatened with execution.

Bizarre war suspenser, quite unconvincing but with effectively suspenseful moments and an old-fashioned portrayal of the Nazis as sadistic music-loving Huns.

w James Lee, Joel Oliansky novel The General by Alan Sillitoe d Ralph Nelson ph Russell Metty m Bronislau Kaper

☆ Charlton Heston, Maximilian Schell, Anton Diffring, Kathryn Hays, Leslie Nielsen

Countess Dracula

GB 1971 93m Eastmancolor

Rank/Hammer (Alexander Paal)

A Hungarian noblewoman restores her youth by bathing in the blood of young virgins.

Risibly sub-Freudian addition to a grotesque Hammer gallery of monsters, indistinguishable from the others once it gets going.

w Jeremy Paul story Alexander Paal, Peter Sasdy, Gabriel Ronay d Peter Sasdy ph Ken Talbot m Harry Robinson ad Philip Harrison ed Henry Richardson

☆ Ingrid Pitt, Nigel Green, Sandor Eles, Maurice Denham, Patience Collier, Peter Jeffrey, Lesley-Anne Down

'At its best the film employs the kind of romantic imagery one associates with Keats; and if it doesn't quite live up to that comparison, it is at least a worthy companion to Corman's Bloody Mama.' – *David Pirie, MFB*

† Ingrid Pitt's performance was dubbed because the director found her accent caused problems in some key scenes.

A Countess from Hong Kong

GB 1967 120m Technicolor

Universal (Jerome Epstein)

An American millionaire diplomat is followed from Hong Kong by his Russian émigrée girlfriend, and complications mount when his wife boards the ship at Hawaii.

Flatulent comedy with neither the sparkle of champagne nor even the fizz of lemonade: Chaplin's writing, direction and music are alike soporific, and commiserations are due to the cast.

ph Arthur Ibbetson pd Don Ashton wd/m Charles Chaplin

☆ Marlon Brando, Sophia Loren, Patrick Cargill, Margaret Rutherford, Charles Chaplin, Sydney Chaplin, Oliver Johnston, John Paul

'An unfunny, mindless mess.' – *Robert Windeler*

'So old-fashioned and dull that one can hardly believe it was made now.' – *Philip T. Hartung*

Countess of Monte Cristo

US 1948 76m bw

Universal International/Westwood

Two Norwegian barmaids visit a smart resort, pretending to be a countess and her maidservant.

Lacklustre musical comedy that brought Henie's US career to an end.

w William Bowers story Walter Reisch d Frederick De Cordova ph Edward Cronjager m Walter Scharf m/ly Saul Chaplin, Jack Brooks ch Louis Da Pron ad Bernard Herzbrun, Emrich Nicholson ed Edward Curtiss

☆ Sonja Henie, Michael Kirby, Olga San Juan, Dorothy Hart, Arthur Treacher, Hugh French, Ransom Sherman, Freddie Trenkler

† The film was a musical remake of a 1934 movie of the same name.

♫ Friendly Polka, Count Your Blessings, Who Believes in Santa Claus?

The Countess of Monte Cristo

US   1933   74m   bw
Universal
A bit player in a musical convinces her friends she is a countess.
Mild comedy.
w Karen de Wolf, Gene Lewis d Karl Freund
☆ Fay Wray, Paul Lukas, Patsy Kelly, Reginald Owen
† It was remade in 1948 as an even milder vehicle for Sonja Henie.

Country *

US   1984   109m   Technicolor   Panavision
Touchstone/Far West/Pangaea (William D. Wittliff, Jessica Lange)
▣ ▣ ◗
Iowa farmers, on the breadline after a tornado, face foreclosure.
Deeply felt modern variation on The Grapes of Wrath, *not particularly dramatic for those who have not felt the pressure.*
w William D. Wittliff d Richard Pearce
ph David M. Walsh m Charles Gross pd Ron Hobbs ed Bill Yahraus
☆ Jessica Lange, Sam Shepard, Wilford Brimley, Matt Clark, Therese Graham
♧ Jessica Lange

Country Dance

GB   1969   112m   Metrocolor
MGM/Keep-Windward (Robert Emmett Ginna)
aka: *Brotherly Love*
An eccentric baronet's incestuous love for his sister finally breaks up her marriage.
Rambling melodrama with O'Toole going mad in squire's tweeds; tediously fashionable but too pallid for general success, it was barely released.
w James Kennaway novel Household Ghosts by James Kennaway d J. Lee-Thompson ph Ted Moore m John Addison
☆ Peter O'Toole, Susannah York, Michael Craig, Harry Andrews, Cyril Cusack, Judy Cornwell, Brian Blessed

The Country Doctor *

US   1936   94m   bw
TCF (Darryl F. Zanuck)
A rural physician becomes famous when quintuplets are born to one of his patients.
Fictionalization of the birth of the Dionne Quintuplets; pleasantly nostalgic even sixty years after its raison d'être.
w Sonya Levien d Henry King ph John F. Seitz, Daniel B. Clark
☆ Jean Hersholt, the Dionne Quins, Dorothy Peterson, June Lang, Slim Summerville, Michael Whalen, Robert Barrat
'Admirably genuine: the camera – rare occasion in the cinema – doesn't lie, and Mr Jean Hersholt gives one of the most sympathetic performances I have seen this year.' – *Graham Greene*
† Sequels: *Reunion* (1936), *Five of a Kind* (1938).

Country Gentlemen

US   1936   66m   bw
Republic
A couple of con men help a widow who runs a small-town hotel.
Strained comedy in which the gag men misguidedly try to play straight.
w Milton Raison, Jack Harvey, Jo Graham
d Ralph Staub
☆ Ole Olsen, Chic Johnson, Joyce Compton, Lila Lee, Pierre Watkin
'Missing is the rapidfire buffoonery with which they have been identified in vaudeville.' – *Variety*

'How far should a woman go to redeem the man she loves?'

The Country Girl *

US   1954   104m   bw
Paramount (William Perlberg)
⌂
The wife of an alcoholic singer blossoms when he is stimulated into a comeback.
Theatrically effective but highly unconvincing, this rather glum stage success made a cold film, miscast with an eye on the box-office.
w Stanley Roberts play Clifford Odets d George Seaton ph John F. Warren m Victor Young m/ly Ira Gershwin, Harold Arlen ad Hal Pereira, Roland Anderson

☆ Bing Crosby, Grace Kelly, William Holden, Anthony Ross, Gene Reynolds
'The dramatic development is not really interesting enough to sustain a film of the intensity for which it strives.' – *Karel Reisz*
'Rather inexplicably, this sado-masochist morass was one of the biggest box office hits of its year.' – *Pauline Kael, 70s*
♦ Grace Kelly
♧ best picture; John F. Warren; Bing Crosby; George Seaton; Stanley Roberts; art direction

Country Life **

Australia   1994   117m   colour
Metro Tartan/AFFC/Robin Dalton
▣ ◗
Just after the end of the First World War, a snobbish, failed literary critic returns from London with his young wife to the Australian sheep farm run by his brother-in-law.
Gentle, well-observed comedy of unfulfilled lives and broken dreams.
wd Michael Blakemore play Uncle Vanya by Anton Chekhov ph Stephen Windon m Peter Best pd Laurence Eastwood ed Nicholas Beauman
☆ Greta Scacchi, Sam Neill, John Hargreaves, Kerry Fox, Michael Blakemore, Googie Withers, Patricia Kennedy, Ron Blanchard, Maurie Fields
'A very funny film with a rippling undercurrent of imminent melancholy. It does more than entertain, with an observant view of humanity's pardonable frailties.' – *Alexander Walker, London Evening Standard*

The County Chairman

US   1934   85m   bw
Fox
A small-town attorney competes with his prospective son-in-law for the post of public prosecutor.
Small-town period comedy drama, not among its star's best.
w Sam Hellman, Gladys Lehman novel George Ade d John Blystone
☆ Will Rogers, Evelyn Venable, Kent Taylor, Louise Dresser, Mickey Rooney, Stepin Fetchit, Berton Churchill

County Hospital **

♦♦   US   1932   20m   bw
Hal Roach
▣ ✿
Ollie is in hospital; Stan brings him some hardboiled eggs and some nuts, and nearly wrecks the place.
Archetypal star comedy with brilliant character and slapstick sequences, let down by a badly processed car ride home.
w H. M. Walker d James Parrott ph Art Lloyd ed Bert Jordan, Richard Currier
☆ Stan Laurel, Oliver Hardy, Billy Gilbert, William Austin, May Wallace

Coup de Foudre *

France   1983   111m   colour   Cinemascope
Gala/Partners Productions/Alexandre Films/Hachette Première/A2/SFPC (Ariel Zeitoun)
▣ ▣
US title: *Entre Nous*
Two women leave their husbands to live and work together.
Charm predominates in this nostalgic piece, based on the life of the director's mother.
w Olivier Cohen, Diane Kurys book Diane Kurys d Diane Kurys ph Bernard Lutic m Luis Bacalov pd Jacques Bufnoir ed Joele Van Effenterre
☆ Miou-Miou, Isabelle Huppert, Guy Marchand, Jean-Pierre Bacri, Robin Renucci, Patrick Bauchau, Jacques Alric
♧ best foreign film

Coup de Torchon *

France   1981   128m   colour
Les Films de la Tour/Les Films A2/Little Bear (Adolphe Viezzi)
GB title: *Clean Slate*
In French West Africa in 1938, an apparently easy-going police officer is inspired to commit a series of murders.
Well-made, heavy-going study of mania.

w Jean Aurenche, Bertrand Tavernier novel POP. 1280 by Jim Thompson d Bertrand Tavernier ph Pierre William Glenn m Philippe Sarde
☆ Philippe Noiret, Isabelle Huppert, Jean-Pierre Marielle, Stéphane Audran, Eddy Mitchell
♧ best foreign film

'A movie for everyone who's ever struggled to love a brother … Or strangle one.'

Coupe de Ville **

US   1990   97m   DeLuxe
Warner/Morgan Creek (Larry Brezner, Paul Schiff)
▣ ▣ ◗ ◗
In the early 1960s, a father asks his three sons to drive a 1950s Cadillac Coupe de Ville from Michigan to Miami for their mother's birthday.
Engaging and amusing low-key road movie centring on family relationships.
w Mike Binder d Joe Roth ph Reynaldo Villalobos m James Newton Howard pd Angelo Graham ed Paul Hirsch
☆ Patrick Dempsey, Arye Gross, Daniel Stern, Annabeth Gish, Rita Taggart, Joseph Bologna, Alan Arkin
'A road movie with a difference, this one has heart and quality.' – *Shaun Usher, Daily Mail*
'For the most part a very shrewd, well-made and well-acted film.' – *Derek Malcolm, Guardian*

Courage: see *Raw Courage (1985)*

Courage

US   1930   65m   bw
Warner
▣
A widow has a large family of which the one sweet-natured son is left a fortune by the old lady next door.
Glutinous mother-love saga from a popular play.
w Walter Anthony d Archie Mayo
☆ Belle Bennett, Marian Nixon, Rex Bell, Leon Janney, Blanche Friderici
'Should be certain in neighbourhood houses. For abroad, a perfect picture for a glimpse of a real American boy of breeding and the sort of mother who lives in every nation.' – *Variety*

Courage Fuyons *

France   1979   98m   Eastmancolor
Gaumont/Gueville (Yves Robert)
A middle-aged man embarks on a series of surprising romantic adventures.
A mainly enjoyable exercise in wish-fulfilment, sharply written and acted.
w Jean-Loup Dabadie, Yves Robert d Yves Robert ph Yves Lafaye m Vladimir Cosma
☆ Jean Rochefort, Catherine Deneuve, Robert Webber, Philippe Leroy-Beaulieu

Courage Mountain

♦♦   US   1989   98m   CFI color
Entertainment/Epic/Stone Group (Stephen Ujlaki)
▣ ▣
A Swiss schoolgirl, stranded in Italy with some friends, makes her way back home.
A new adventure, told in an old-fashioned way, of that one-time children's favourite Heidi.
w Weaver Webb story Fred Brogger, Mark Brogger d Christopher Leitch ph Jacques Steyn m Sylvester Levay pd Robb Wilson King ed Martin Walsh
☆ Juliette Caton, Charlie Sheen, Leslie Caron, Yorgo Voyagis, Laura Betti, Jan Rubes, Joanna Clarke

Courage Under Fire *

US   1996   115m   DeLuxe
TCF/Fox 2000/Davis Entertainment (Joseph M. Singer, David T. Friendly)
▣ ▣ ◗ ◗ ◗
A colonel investigates the suitability of awarding a posthumous Medal of Honor to a female helicopter pilot killed in the Gulf War.
A film that begins as a complex investigation into behaviour in wartime but ends as a straightforward flag-waving exercise.
w Patrick Sheane Duncan d Edward Zwick ph Roger Deakins m James Horner pd John Graysmark ed Steven Rosenblum
☆ Denzel Washington, Meg Ryan, Lou Diamond Phillips, Michael Moriarty, Matt Damon, Bronson Pinchot, Scott Glenn, Sean Astin
'An intelligent well-crafted film that pays few concessions to Hollywood melodrama.' – *James Cameron-Wilson, Film Review*

The Courageous Mr Penn: see *Penn of Pennsylvania*

The Courier

Ireland   1987   85m
Palace/City Vision (Hilary McLoughlin)
◗
A motorcycle messenger becomes an unknowing carrier of drugs.
Violent, low-budget thriller with no redeeming qualities.
w Frank Deasy d Joe Lee, Frank Deasy ph Gabriel Beristain m Declan MacManus pd David Wilson ed Derek Trigg, Annette D'Alton
☆ Gabriel Byrne, Ian Bannen, Cait O'Riordan, Padraig O'Loingsigh, Patrick Bergin, Andrew Connolly

Cours du Soir

France   1967   25m   colour
Telecip/Specta (Bernard Maurice)
▣
An evening-class lecturer demonstrates the various ways people smoke, walk and play sport.
Tati goes through some of his familiar routines, but the setting is not a sympathetic one and he looks tired and unenthusiastic about what he is doing.
w Jacques Tati d Nicolas Rybowski ph Jean Badal m Léo Petit ed Nicole Cauduchon
☆ Jacques Tati

The Court Jester ***

♦♦   US   1955   101m   Technicolor
Vistavision
Paramount/Dena (Melvin Frank, Norman Panama)
▣ ▣ ◗ ◗
Opposition to a tyrannical king is provided by the Fox, but it is one of the rebel's meekest men who, posing as a jester, defeats the usurper.
One of the star's most delightful vehicles, this medieval romp has good tunes and lively action, not to mention an exceptional cast and the memorable 'chalice from the palace' routine.
wd Norman Panama, Melvin Frank ph Ray June m/ly Sylvia Fine, Sammy Cahn ad Hal Pereira, Roland Anderson
☆ Danny Kaye, Glynis Johns, Basil Rathbone, Cecil Parker, Mildred Natwick, Angela Lansbury, Edward Ashley, Robert Middleton, Michael Pate, Alan Napier

Court Martial: see *Carrington VC*

The Court Martial of Billy Mitchell *

US   1955   100m   Warnercolor   Cinemascope
United States Pictures (Milton Sperling)
▣ ▣ ◗
GB title: *One Man Mutiny*
In the early twenties, an American general of the Army Air Service is court-martialled for accusing the war department of criminal negligence.
Adequate recreation of a historical incident, with a cast of excellent actors converging for a courtroom scene of some effectiveness.
w Milton Sperling, Emmet Lavery d Otto Preminger ph Sam Leavitt m Dimitri Tiomkin
☆ Gary Cooper, Rod Steiger, Ralph Bellamy, Charles Bickford, Elizabeth Montgomery, Fred Clark, Darren McGavin, James Daly
♧ Milton Sperling, Emmet Lavery

The Courtney Affair: see *The Courtneys of Curzon Street*

The Courtneys of Curzon Street *

GB   1947   120m   bw
Imperadio (Herbert Wilcox)
▣
US title: *The Courtney Affair*
In Victorian times, a baronet's son marries a lady's maid … and many years later, their grandson marries a factory worker.
Unbelievable upstairs-downstairs romantic drama spanning three generations; all to be taken with a gigantic pinch of salt, but a huge success when released.
w Nicholas Phipps novel Florence Tranter d Herbert Wilcox ph Max Greene m Anthony Collins ad William C. Andrews ed Flora Newton, Vera Campbell
☆ Anna Neagle, Michael Wilding, Gladys Young, Coral Browne, Michael Medwin, Daphne Slater, Jack Watling, Helen Cherry, Bernard Lee
'The dignity of Curzon Street is Hollywoodized, and it is rare in 1945 that people in their sixties

look as though they have one foot in the grave.'
– MFB
'If my livelihood depended on booking the right
film into the average cinema, this is one I would
not dare to miss.' – *Observer*

The Courtship of Eddie's Father *
US 1962 117m Metrocolor Panavision
MGM/Joe Pasternak
▇
The small son of a widower tries to interest Dad in
another woman.
*Fairly icky American-style sentimental comedy with
most of the stops pulled out; way over-length and too
self-indulgently solemn in the last part, but with
professional touches.*
w John Gay *novel* Muriel Toby d Vincente
Minnelli ph Milton Krasner m George Stoll
☆ Glenn Ford, Ronny Howard, Shirley Jones,
Stella Stevens, Dina Merrill
† A TV series starring Bill Bixby followed in 1971.

'Who Knew Deception, Treachery And Revenge
Could Be This Much Fun…'
'A Delicious Tale Of Revenge.'
Cousin Bette *
US 1998 107m colour Panavision
Fox Searchlight (Sarah Radclyffe)
▣ ▇ ◉ ⌂
A hard-up seamstress plots revenge against her
wealthy cousins.
*Slight but enjoyable version of a more complex novel, a
period romp with a hissable villainess.*
w Lynn Siefert, Susan Tarr *novel* Honoré de
Balzac d Des McAnuff ph Andrzej Sekula
m Simon Boswell pd Jane Gibson ed Hugo
Luczyc-Wyhowksi ed Tariq Anwar, Barry
Alexander Brown
☆ Jessica Lange, Elisabeth Shue, Bob Hoskins,
Hugh Laurie, Kelly Macdonald, Aden Young,
Geraldine Chaplin, Toby Stephens, John Sessions
'As a frothy confection it can't be faulted.' –
Ryan Gilbey, Independent

Cousin Bobby *
US 1992 69m colour
Electric/Tesauro
▇
A documentary on the life and work of the Rev.
Robert Castle, an outspoken Episcopalian priest
working in Harlem, made by his film director
cousin.
*Well-made and interesting account of a dedicated priest
that cuts from the public life to the private man.*
d Jonathan Demme ed Ernest Dickerson, Craig
Haagensen, Tony Jannelli, Jacek Laskus, Declan
Quinn m Anton Sanko ed David Greenwald
'A low-key, occasionally touching documentary
… essentially a home movie, but one with broad
appeal.' – *Variety*

Cousin, Cousine ***
France 1975 95m Eastmancolor
Pomereu/Gaumont (Bertrand Javal)
▣ ▇ ◉ ⌂
Various furtive love affairs centre on a family
wedding.
*Sprightly satirical comedy full of pleasing touches,
mostly jibes at French bourgeois standards.*
wd Jean-Charles Tacchella ph Georges Lendi
m Gerard Anfosso
☆ Marie-France Pisier, Marie-Christine Barrault,
Victor Lanoux, Guy Marchand, Ginette Garcin
'One of those rare delights you want to see again
and again just to share the sheer joy of living,
zest for love, genuine affection, all-too-human
absurdity, and pure happiness of all those
delicious people on screen.' – *Judith Crist,
Saturday Review*
⌀ best foreign film; script; Marie-Christine
Barrault

Cousins
US 1989 113m Technicolor
UIP/Paramount (William Allyn)
▣ ▇ ◉ ⌂
Two couples, who meet at a relative's wedding,
swop partners.
*An adaptation of the French film Cousin, Cousine
without the exuberant charm of the original.*
w Stephen Metcalfe d Joel Schumacher ph Ralf
Bode m Angelo Badalamenti pd Mark S.
Freeborn ed Robert Brown

☆ Ted Danson, Isabella Rossellini, Sean Young,
William Petersen, Lloyd Bridges, Norma Aleandro,
Keith Coogan, Gina DeAngelis, George Coe
'Combines satire, near-farce, and incipient
fantasy with great dexterity.' – *Tim Pulleine, MFB*

Les Cousins *
France 1959 110m bw
AJYM (Claude Chabrol)
⌂
A law student stays with his sophisticated cousin in
Paris, and his life is altered.
*The country cousin fable filled with undramatic detail
and given a rather perverse ending without any
apparent point.*
wd Claude Chabrol ph Henri Decaë m Paul
Misraki ad Jacques Saulnier, Bernard Evein
ed Jacques Gaillard
☆ Jean-Claude Brialy, Gérard Blain, Juliette
Mayniel, Claude Cerval

A Covenant with Death
US 1966 97m Technicolor
Warner (William Conrad)
A half-Mexican judge in a border town convicts a
man who accidentally kills the hangman just as the
real murderer confesses.
*Dreary moral melodrama with accents, nicely
photographed but cold, remote and drawn out.*
w Larry Marcus, Saul Levitt *novel* Stephen
Becker d Lamont Johnson ph Robert Burks
m Leonard Rosenman
☆ George Maharis, Katy Jurado, Earl Holliman,
Sidney Blackmer, Laura Devon, Gene Hackman

'Too thrilling for words, so they set it to music!'
Cover Girl **
US 1944 107m Technicolor
Columbia (Arthur Schwartz)
▣ ▇ ◉
The road to success for magazine cover models.
*Wartime glamour musical with a stronger reputation
than it really deserves apart from Kelly's solos; it does
however manage a certain joie de vivre which should
not be despised.*
w Virginia Van Upp d Charles Vidor
ph Rudolph Maté m/ly Jerome Kern, Ira
Gershwin md Morris Stoloff, Carmen Dragon
ad Lionel Banks, Cary Odell
☆ Rita Hayworth, Gene Kelly, Phil Silvers, Lee
Bowman, Jinx Falkenburg, Otto Kruger, Eve
Arden, Ed Brophy
'Kelly and Silvers are better than Kelly and
Hayworth, though she does look sumptuous, and
her big smile could be the emblem of the period.'
– *New Yorker, 1977*
'Much of it is not as fresh as it may seem; but its
second-handedness and its occasional failures
cannot obliterate the pleasure of seeing the work
of a production company which obviously
knows, cares about and enjoys what it is doing.'
– *James Agee*
† Rita Hayworth's singing was dubbed by Martha
Mears.
♟ Morris Stoloff, Carmen Dragon
⌀ Rudolph Maté; song 'Long Ago and Far Away';
art direction

Cover Girl Killer
GB 1960 61m bw
Butcher's/Parroch (Jack Parsons)
A short-sighted man in a badly fitting wig begins
to murder girls who pose on the covers of a pin-up
magazine.
Competent, if uninspired, minor programmer.
wd Terry Bishop ph Gerald Gibbs m William
Davies ad Andrew Campbell ed John Trumper
☆ Harry H. Corbett, Felicity Young, Spencer
Teakle, Victor Brooks, Bernadette Milnes,
Christina Gregg, Tony Doonan, Charles Lloyd
Pack, Dermot Kelly

Cover Up
US 1948 82m bw
Strand/UA
An insurance investigator finds senior officials
conspiring to obscure the facts of a small-town
murder.
*Modest mystery, initially intriguing but finally
unsatisfying.*
w Jerome Odlum, Jonathan Ritz d Alfred E.
Green
☆ Dennis O'Keefe, William Bendix, Barbara
Britton, Art Smith

The Covered Wagon *
US 1923 103m bw silent
Paramount/Famous Players-Lasky
▇ ◉
Pioneer settlers travel west by wagon train.
*A classic Western which now seems painfully
undernourished in terms of plot and character but still
retains moments of epic sweep.*
w Jack Cunningham *novel* Emerson Hough
d James Cruze ph Karl Brown
☆ Ernest Torrence, Tully Marshall, J. Warren
Kerrigan, Lois Wilson, Alan Hale
'There wasn't a false whisker in the film.' – *James
Cruze*
'Forthright, impressive and vigorous, it brought a
breath of fresh air into the jazz-ridden film
world.' – *Lewis Jacobs*

The Cow and I
France 1959 119m bw
Cyclope/Omnia (Walter Rupp)
original title: *La Vache et le Prisonnier*
A French soldier escapes from a prison camp and
takes a farm cow as cover.
*Curiously overlong war adventure which hovers
uncertainly between comedy and suspense.*
w Henri Verneuil, Henri Jeanson, Jean Manse
d Henri Verneuil ph Roger Hubert m Paul
Durand
☆ Fernandel, René Havard, Albert Remy, Bernard
Musson

'Authentic Greatness!'
Cowboy *
US 1958 92m Technicolor
Columbia/Phoenix (Julian Blaustein)
Frank Harris becomes a cattle herder for love of a
lady but is quickly disillusioned with the outdoor
life.
*Fashioned from a lively autobiography, this has
interesting moments but is never as fascinating as one
would expect.*
w Edmund H. North *book* On the Trail by Frank
Harris d Delmer Daves ph Charles Lawton Jnr
m George Duning ed William A. Lyon, Al Clark
☆ Jack Lemmon, Glenn Ford, Brian Donlevy,
Anna Kashfi, Dick York, Richard Jaeckel, King
Donovan
'Describes with an engaging mixture of
saddlesore truth and reach-for-leather fiction
what a cowboy's life was like in the Old West.' –
Time
⌀ editing

The Cowboy and the Girl: see A Lady Takes a
Chance

The Cowboy and the Lady
US 1938 91m bw
Samuel Goldwyn
▣ ▇ ◉
The daughter of a presidential candidate becomes
infatuated with a rodeo cowboy.
*Insubstantial and witless romantic comedy which
suffered many sea changes from script to screen.*
w Leo McCarey, S. N. Behrman, Sonya Levien
d H. C. Potter ph Gregg Toland m Alfred
Newman
☆ Gary Cooper, Merle Oberon, Patsy Kelly,
Walter Brennan, Fuzzy Knight, Henry Kolker,
Harry Davenport
'By and large only mildly diverting … the
interest and promise of the early reels is not
sustained in the latter half.' – *Variety*
'Just a lot of chestnuts pulled out of other
people's dead fires.' – *Otis Ferguson*
⌀ Alfred Newman; title song (mLionel Newman,
lyArthur Quenzer)

Cowboy from Brooklyn
US 1938 80m bw
Warner
A supposed cowboy crooner is taken out west and
proves to be terrified of animals.
Genial but witless spoof of a trend of the times.
w Earl Baldwin *play* Howdy Stranger by Robert
Sloane, Louis Pelletier Jnr d Lloyd Bacon
☆ Pat O'Brien, Dick Powell, Priscilla Lane, Dick
Foran, Ann Sheridan, Ronald Reagan, Johnnie
Davis, James Stephenson
† Remade as *Two Guys from Texas*.

'How the East was won.'
The Cowboy Way
US 1994 105m DeLuxe
Universal/Imagine/Brian Grazer
▣ ▇ ◉
Two rodeo stars go to New York in search of a
kidnapped daughter of a Cuban friend.
*Smug and unlikeable lead performances sink this
comedy from the start, though it would have sunk
anyway, whoever had played the roles.*
w Joe Gayton, William Wittliff d Gregg
Champion ph Dean Semler m David Newman
ed Michael Tronick
☆ Woody Harrelson, Kiefer Sutherland, Ernie
Hudson, Dylan McDermott, Cara Buono, Marg
Helgenberger, Tomas Milian
'The action sequences are lacklustre and the
bickering and bonding between the likeable
leads is drearily predictable.' – *Film Review*

The Cowboys *
US 1972 128m Technicolor Panavision 70
Sanford/Warner (Mark Rydell)
▣ ▇ ◉ ◎
Deserted by his ranch hands, a cattle drover on a
long trail enlists the help of eleven schoolboys,
who later avenge his death.
*Ambling, climactically violent, extremely unlikely
Western with good scenes along the way.*
w Irving Ravetch, Harriet Frank Jnr
novel William Dale Jennings d Mark Rydell
ph Robert Surtees m John Williams
☆ John Wayne, Roscoe Lee Browne, Bruce Dern,
Colleen Dewhurst, Slim Pickens, Sarah
Cunningham, A. Martinez, Robert Carradine,
Alfred Barker Jnr, Nicolas Beauvy, Steve Benedict,
Norman Howell Jnr, Stephen Hudis, Sean Kelly,
Clay O'Brien and also Sam O'Brien, Mike Pyeatt
† A TV series followed in 1974 but was shortlived.

Coyote (dubbed)
Canada 1993 99m colour
Alliance/Stock International/Molecule/Canal+
(Richard Sadler, Henry Lange)
A student film-maker falls in love with a free-
thinking woman.
*Turgid 'teen romance, visually and dramatically
undistinguished, and unconvincing in its moments of
joy and misery.*
w Michel Michaud, Richard Sadler, Richard
Ciupka, Louise Anne Bouchard *novel* Michel
Michaud d Richard Ciupka ph Steve Danyluk
m Reinhardt Wagner ad Jean-Baptiste Tard
ed Jean-Guy Monpetit
☆ Mitsou, Patrick Labbé, Thierry Magnier,
Claude Legault, François Massicotte, Jean-Claude
Dreyfus

Crack in the Mirror
US 1960 97m bw Cinemascope
TCF/Darryl F. Zanuck
A young lawyer and his ageing mentor are at
opposite sides of a murder case.
*Pointless Paris-set melodrama in which for no obvious
reason each of the three stars plays two roles.
Relentlessly boring.*
w Mark Canfield (Darryl F. Zanuck) d Richard
Fleischer ph William C. Mellor m Maurice Jarre
☆ Orson Welles, Bradford Dillman, Juliette
Greco, William Lucas, Alexander Knox, Catherine
Lacey

Crack in the Mirror
US 1988 94m colour
Blue Dolphin/Jubran Group (Fred Berner, Jubran
Jubran)
▣ ▇
A drug-dealer, on the run from a rival gangster,
asks a friend to look after his business.
*Convoluted tale of killers and addicts, full of heavy-
handed anti-drugs polemic.*
w Robert Madero d Robby Benson ph Neil
Smith m Nile Rodgers ed Alan Miller, Craig
McKay
☆ Robby Benson, Tawny Kitaen, Danny Aiello,
Kevin Gray, Cliff Bemis, Tony Gillan, Paul
Herman, Tony Sirico, Mark Ornstein

'Thank God it's only a motion picture!'
Crack in the World
US 1965 96m Technicolor
Paramount/Security (Philip Yordan, Bernard Glasser,
Lester A. Sansom)
A dying scientist fires a missile into the Earth's
centre, and nearly blows the planet apart.

⊚ Digital Video Disc Region 2 ◉ Digital Video Disc Region 1 ⌂ Soundtrack released on compact disc ☆ Cast in approximate order of importance † Points of interest ♫ Notable songs ♟ Academy Award ⌀ Academy Award nomination ▽ BAFTA

Jaded science-fiction melodrama, overburdened with initial chat but waking up when the special effects take over.

w Jon Manchip White, Julian Halevy d Andrew Marton ph Manuel Berenguer m John Douglas ad Eugene Lourié sp John Douglas

☆ Dana Andrews, Janette Scott, Kieron Moore, Alexander Knox, Peter Damon, Gary Lasdun

Crack Up *
US 1946 93m bw
RKO
▤ ☏

A museum curator with an eye for forgery is discredited by crooks who make him appear drunk or half-crazed when he recounts a set of strange events which have happened to him…

The intriguing mystery of the opening reels, when solved, is replaced by rather dull detection, but this remains a thriller with a difference, generally well presented.

w John Paxton d Irving Reis ph Robert de Grasse m Leigh Harline

☆ Pat O'Brien, Claire Trevor, Herbert Marshall, Ray Collins

Cracked Nuts
US 1931 65m bw
RKO

Two Americans get mixed up in a revolution in a mythical country.

Padded farce vehicle for a comedy team.

w Al Boasberg, Ralph Spence d Edward Cline

☆ Bert Wheeler, Robert Woolsey, Ben Turpin, Edna May Oliver, Dorothy Lee

'As a two-reeler it would be fair entertainment.' – *Variety*

Crackerjack *
GB 1938 79m bw
Gainsborough (Edward Black)
US title: *The Man with a Hundred Faces*

A gentleman thief poses as butler at a stately home.

Fairly smart sardonic star vehicle.

w A. R. Rawlinson, Michael Pertwee, Basil Mason novel W. B. Ferguson d Albert de Courville ph J. J. Cox

☆ Tom Walls, Lilli Palmer, Noel Madison, Leon M. Lion, Edmund Breon, Charles Heslop

'Carelessly made but fairly engrossing.' – *Variety*

Crackers
US 1984 92m Technicolor
Universal/Edward Lewis
▤ ☏

Incompetent crooks run a pawnshop.

Insufficiently rethought, San Francisco set, updating of Monicelli's 1956 comedy Big Deal on Madonna Street (I Soliti Ignoti). No longer at all funny.

w Jeffrey Fiskin d Louis Malle ph Laszlo Kovacs m Paul Chihara pd John L. Lloyd

☆ Donald Sutherland, Jack Warden, Sean Penn, Wallace Shawn, Larry Riley, Trinidad Silva, Charlaine Woodard, Irwin Corey

'One can sense that it would all sound much funnier in Italian.' – *Variety*

The Cracksman
GB 1963 112m Technicolor Cinemascope
ABPC
▦

A master locksmith becomes the unwitting dupe of a gang of safecrackers.

The most elaborate vehicle devised for this diminutive star; despite bright moments, conventional mounting and over-generous length finally defeat it.

w Lew Schwartz, Charlie Drake d Peter Graham Scott

☆ Charlie Drake, George Sanders, Dennis Price, Nyree Dawn Porter, Eddie Byrne, Finlay Currie, Percy Herbert

Cradle Song *
US 1933 78m bw
Paramount (E. Lloyd Sheldon)

A nun adopts a foundling.

Stately transcription of a once-fashionable play, too concerned with its own artistic background and handicapped by a star who didn't travel well, except to those partial to Jewish nuns.

w Marc Connelly play G. M. Martinez Sierra d Mitchell Leisen ph Charles Lang m W. Franke Harling

☆ Dorothea Wieck, Evelyn Venable, Sir Guy Standing, Louise Dresser, Kent Taylor, Gertrude Michael, Nydia Westman, Eleanor Wesselhoeft

'It moves slowly, laboriously … as a commercial entry decidedly dubious.' – *Variety*

The Cradle Will Rock **
US 1999 135m Technicolor
Buena Vista/Touchstone/Havoc (Jon Kilik, Lydia Dean Pilcher, Tim Robbins)
▤ ◎

When, in New York in 1936, the authorities prevent the opening of Marc Blitzstein's musical play *The Cradle Will Rock*, the cast march to another theatre and, forbidden to act on stage, play it from the auditorium.

A true story, and a fascinating and important one, is given a rousing treatment, providing a panoramic view of the artistic ferment of the time, when passions ran high, and art and politics could be united in a common cause.

wd Tim Robbins ph Jean Yves Escoffier m David Robbins m/ly Marc Blitzstein pd Richard Hoover ed Geraldine Peron cos Ruth Myers

☆ Hank Azaria, Ruben Blades, Joan Cusack, John Cusack, Cary Elwes, Philip Baker Hall, Cherry Jones, Angus Macfadyen, Bill Murray, Vanessa Redgrave, Susan Sarandon, Jamey Sheridan, John Turturro, Emily Watson, Bob Balaban and also Barnard Hughes, Barbara Sukowa, John Carpenter, Gretchen Mol, Harris Yulin

'What Robbins also achieves here is an astonishingly moving tribute to the power of theatre…but you have to actually be *interested* in the subject matter to appreciate it.' – *Lorien Haynes, Film Review*

'Exorcise Your Rites.'

The Craft
US 1996 100m Technicolor
Columbia (Douglas Wick)
▦ ☐ ◎ ◎ ◎ ◖

A new girl at school joins forces with three others who practise witchcraft.

Tiresome and unoriginal teenage horror, notably lacking in any imaginative use of the powers its protagonists summon up.

w Peter Filardi, Andrew Fleming d Andrew Fleming ph Alexander Gruszynski m Graeme Revell pd Marek Dobrowolski ed Jeff Freeman

☆ Robin Tunney, Fairuza Balk, Neve Campbell, Rachel True, Skeet Ulrich, Christine Taylor, Breckin Meyer, Nathaniel Marston, Cliff de Young, Helen Shaver, Assumpta Serna

'Full of gorgeous young actresses – high school girls have rarely been given such an appealing lustre – but it also has great visuals, sure drama and applied intelligence; a rare combination in horror movies.' – *Chris Savage King, Sight and Sound*

Craig's Wife *
US 1936 77m bw
Columbia
▤

A middle class wife lets her house take precedence over her husband.

Capable picturization of a Broadway success, later remade as Harriet Craig (qv).

w Mary McCall Jnr, George Kelly play George Kelly d Dorothy Arzner ph Lucien Ballard md Morris Stoloff

☆ Rosalind Russell, John Boles, Billie Burke, Jane Darwell, Dorothy Wilson, Alma Kruger, Thomas Mitchell, Elizabeth Risdon, Raymond Walburn

Crainquebille *
France 1922 70m bw silent
Trarieux Films

A street trader is unjustly accused and imprisoned, afterwards finding happiness as a tramp.

Somewhere between Chaplin and Kafka, this fable was long admired for its style.

wd Jacques Feyder story Anatole France ph Léonce Burel

☆ Maurice de Féraudy, Françoise Rosay, Felix Oudart

† Remade 1933 by Jacques de Baroncelli with Maurice Tramel; 1954 by Ralph Habib with Yves Deniaud.

The Cranes Are Flying **
USSR 1957 94m bw
Mosfilm
▤ ☏

original title: *Letyat Zhuravli*

When her lover goes to war, a girl refuses to believe later reports of his death even though she has suffered much, including marriage to a bully, in the interim.

Sleek, moving love story with most of the Hollywood production virtues plus an attention to detail and a realism which are wholly Russian.

w Victor Rosov d Mikhail Kalatozov ph Sergei Urusevski

☆ Tatiana Samoilova, Alexei Batalov, Vasili Merkuriev

Crash!
US 1977 85m DeLuxe Panavision
Group One/Charles Band

A crippled husband sets out to murder his wife, but she is protected by a good-luck charm with magic powers.

Ineffably silly occult thriller, consisting mainly of unspectacular car crashes which are all reprised towards the end of the film to ensure total tedium.

w Marc Marais d Charles Band ph Andrew Davis, Bill Williams m Andrew Belling ad Patrick McFadden ed Harry Keramidas

☆ José Ferrer, Sue Lyon, John Ericson, Leslie Parrish, John Carradine, Jerome Guardino, Reggie Nalder

Crash **
Canada 1996 98m DeLuxe
Columbia TriStar/Alliance (David Cronenberg)
▦ ☐ ◎ ◎ ◖

After being injured in a car crash, a man and a woman are initiated into a group that is sexually aroused by such occurrences.

A compelling, not very likeable movie that gives new meaning to auto-eroticism, in an account of technological fetishism that is stylishly made and seriously intended.

wd David Cronenberg novel J. G. Ballard ph Peter Suschitzky m Howard Shore pd Carol Spier ed Ronald Sanders

☆ James Spader, Holly Hunter, Elias Koteas, Deborah Unger, Rosanna Arquette, Peter MacNeill

'A forbiddingly frigid piece of esoteric erotica.' – *Todd McCarthy, Variety*

† After much controversy, the film was passed uncut in Britain; the British Board of Film Classification consulted a forensic psychologist, an audience of the disabled and a QC, who concluded that 'rather than sympathising or identifying with the attitudes or tastes of the characters in this film, the average viewer would in the end be repelled by them, and would reject the values and sexual proclivities displayed.' The *Daily Mail* condemned the BBFC's decision, commenting, 'All the psychobabble in the world cannot refute the simple fact: The film is sick. It should not be shown.'

The Crash
US 1932 59m bw
Warner

An unfaithful wife finds her life changed by the stock market crash.

Dim high-society goings-on make a poor star vehicle.

w Earl Baldwin novel Children of Pleasure by Larry Barratto d William Dieterle

☆ Ruth Chatterton, George Brent, Paul Cavanagh, Henry Kolker, Barbara Leonard

'A weak sister … nothing happens to pique interest or capture sympathy or even provoke hostility.' – *Variety*

Crash Dive *
US 1943 105m Technicolor
TCF (Milton Sperling)

A submarine lieutenant and his commander love the same girl.

Well-staged war thrills in the final reels are prefaced by a long romantic comedy build-up, which probably seemed good propaganda at the time.

w Jo Swerling story W. R. Burnett d Archie Mayo ph Leon Shamroy m David Buttolph md Emil Newman sp Fred Sersen

☆ Tyrone Power, Anne Baxter, Dana Andrews, James Gleason, Dame May Whitty, Henry Morgan, Frank Conroy, Minor Watson

'One of those films which have no more sense of reality about this war than a popular song.' – *Bosley Crowther*

The Crash of Silence: see *Mandy*

Crashing Hollywood *
US 1937 60m bw
RKO

A studio screenwriter selects a criminal as collaborator, and gets into all kinds of trouble.

Lively melodramatic star vehicle with a reasonably vivid background.

w Paul Yawitz, Gladys Atwater play Paul Dickey, Mann Page d Lew Landers

☆ Lee Tracy, Joan Woodbury, Paul Guilfoyle, Lee Patrick, Richard Lane, Jack Carson, Tom Kennedy

'Completely satisfactory programme picture.' – *Variety*

Crashout
US 1955 83m bw
Hal E. Chester/Standard
▤

Six convicts escape from prison, but most of them die en route.

Watchable melodrama, fairly savage for its day.

w Hal E. Chester, Lewis R. Foster d Lewis R. Foster

☆ William Bendix, Arthur Kennedy, Luther Adler, William Talman, Gene Evans, Marshall Thompson, Beverly Michaels

The Crawling Eye: see *The Trollenberg Terror*

Craze
GB 1973 95m Technicolor
EMI/Harbour (Herman Cohen)
▤

An African idol accidentally causes a death which brings money to its owner, who kills again and again in the hope of more loot.

Crude shocker from the bottom of even this producer's barrel, notable for the star cast which was surprisingly roped in.

w Aben Kandel, Herman Cohen novel Infernal Idol by Henry Seymour d Freddie Francis ph John Wilcox m John Scott

☆ Jack Palance, Diana Dors, Julie Ege, Edith Evans, Hugh Griffith, Trevor Howard, Michael Jayston, Suzy Kendall, Martin Potter, Percy Herbert, Kathleen Byron

The Crazies *
US 1973 102m colour
Pittsburgh Films/Cambist/Lee Hessel (A. C. Croft)
▣

aka: *Code Name: Trixie*

The army seals off a small town when its inhabitants become mad and violent following the crash of a plane carrying a deadly virus; but the locals object to martial law.

Fast-moving, low-budget horror movie that also attempts to be a satire on rigid, military attitudes; it does achieve a certain frisson by its driving relentlessness and copious killing.

wd George A. Romero story Paul McCollough ph S. William Hinzman m Bruce Roberts ed George A. Romero sp Regis Survinski, Tony Pantanello

☆ Lane Carroll, W. G. McMillan, Harold Wayne Jones, Lloyd Hollar, Lynn Lowry, Richard Liberty, Richard France, Harry Spillman

'Average paranoia movie … Romero is better at maintaining a high body count than being profound.' – *Sight and Sound*

Crazy Desires of a Murderer
Italy 1977 95m Eastmancolor Vistavision
GI.BA.SI. (Salvatore Siciliano)
▣

original title: *I Vizi Morbosi di una Governante*

A limping inspector investigates murders at a castle inhabited by a senile baron whose mad son is incarcerated in the cellars, his promiscuous daughter, her decadent friends, an alcoholic doctor, and criminal servants.

An unpalatable mix of old-fashioned detective mystery, melodrama, gruesome horror and irrelevant couplings; the solution to the mystery leaves much unexplained.

w Ambrogio Molteni d Peter Rush (Filippo Ratti) ph Gino Santini m Piero Piccioni ad Gino Tonni ed Sergio Muzzi

☆ Corrado Gaipa, Roberto Zattin, Isabelle Marchal, Anie Edel, Gaetano Russo, Beppe

---

Colombo, Sergio Orsi, Claudio Peticchio, Patrizia Gori
† The British video release runs for 85m.

Crazy House: see *The House in Nightmare Park (1973)*

Crazy House
US 1943 80m bw
Universal (Erle C. Kenton)
Olsen and Johnson go to Hollywood to make a film.
Lame sequel to Hellzapoppin; after an explosively well edited first reel of panic in the studio, it degenerates into a slew of below-par variety turns.
w Robert Lees, Frederic I. Rinaldo d Edward Cline ph Charles Van Enger md George Hale, Milt Rosen
☆ Ole Olsen, Chic Johnson, Martha O'Driscoll, Patric Knowles, Percy Kilbride, Cass Daley, Thomas Gomez, Edgar Kennedy
† Sherlock Holmes fans may or may not wish to record a two-line comic bit by Basil Rathbone and Nigel Bruce in character.

Crazy Joe
US/Italy 1973 99m Technicolor
Bright-Persky/De Laurentiis
The rise and fall of a Mafia hood in New York.
Noisy, violent, reasonably proficient gangster movie which seems to have some pretensions to play against stereotype.
w Lewis John Carlino d Carlo Lizzani
☆ Peter Boyle, Paula Prentiss, Fred Williamson, Charles Cioffi, Rip Torn, Luther Adler, Eli Wallach, Henry Winkler

Crazy Love *
Belgium 1987 87m Eastmancolor
Mainline/Multimedia (Erwin Provoost, Alain Keytsman)
US title: *Love Is a Dog from Hell*
A frustrated boy, full of romantic longings, grows up to be a necrophiliac.
Episodic and squalid story of a journey from innocence to drug-addicted desperation, told with style.
w Marc Didden, Dominique Deruddere story The Copulating Mermaid of Venice, California and other works by Charles Bukowski d Dominique Deruddere ph Willy Stassen m Raymond Van Het Groenewoud pd Hubert Pouille, Erik Van Belleghem ed Ludo Troch, Guido Henderickx
☆ Josse de Pauw, Geert Hunaerts, Michael Pas, Gene Bervoets, Amid Chakir, François Beukelaers, Florence Beliard, Carmela Locantore
'A movie for people with a perverse sense of humor or a persistent sexual acne – a low-keyed sexual reverie.' – *Pauline Kael, New Yorker*

Crazy Mama *
US 1975 80m colour
New World (Julie Corman)
In 1958 Arkansas, mother and daughter set off on a series of robberies and kidnaps which end in violence.
Exploitation crime movie with no apparent basis in fact; as such, occasionally exciting for those who can tolerate this kind of thing.
w Robert Thom d Jonathan Demme ph Bruce Logan m Snotty Scotty and the Hankies
☆ Cloris Leachman, Ann Sothern, Stuart Whitman, Jim Backus, Linda Purl, Brian Englund

Crazy Moon
Canada 1987 90m colour
Miramax/Tom Berry, Stefan Wodoslawsky
A rich, clever, miserable and inhibited youth falls for a tough-minded, deaf shop assistant.
While the couple may have enjoyed a moment's happiness, it is doubtful whether an audience will; a dull drama of teenage traumas, acted and directed without much conviction.
w Tom Berry, Stefan Wodoslawsky d Allan Eastman ph Savas Kalogeras m Lou Forestieri ad Guy Lalande ed Franco Battista
☆ Kiefer Sutherland, Vanessa Vaughan, Peter Spence, Sean McCann, Bronwen Mantel, Eve Napier, Ken Pogue

Crazy People
US 1990 92m Technicolor
UIP/Paramount (Thomas Barad)
An ad-man runs his business from a rest home for mental patients.
Unsatisfactory would-be satire.
w Mitch Markowitz d Tony Bill ph Victor J. Kemper m Cliff Eidelman ad Steven Schwartz ed Mia Goldman
☆ Dudley Moore, Daryl Hannah, Paul Reiser, J. T. Walsh, Bill Smitrovich, Alan North, David Paymer
'Damp, indulgent squib of a film.' – *Geoff Brown, MFB*
† Markowitz began as director, with John Malkovich in the leading role. When Markowitz was replaced, Malkovich left, to be replaced by Dudley Moore.

The Crazy Ray: see *Paris Qui Dort*

Crazy Streets: see *Forever Lulu*

Crazy to Kill: see *Dr Gillespie's Criminal Case*

The Crazy World of Julius Vrooder
US 1974 98m colour
TCF
A Vietnam veteran withdraws from the world.
Well-meaning but tiresome problem pic which gets nowhere.
w Daryl Henry d Arthur Hiller
☆ Timothy Bottoms, Barbara Seagull, Lawrence Pressman, Albert Salmi

The Crazy World of Laurel and Hardy *
US 1964 83m bw
Hal Roach/Jay Ward
A compilation of Laurel and Hardy extracts from their classic period.
Although the material is in itself excellent and some of the build-up sequences well done, the clips are all too short to achieve maximum impact, and virtually none is identified.
w Bill Scott m Jerry Fielding narrator Garry Moore

Creator
US 1985 107m Technicolor
Entertainment/Universal/Kings Road (Stephen Friedman)
A research scientist tries to clone his dead wife.
Sentimental and eccentric comedy of little interest.
w Jeremy Leven novel Jeremy Leven d Ivan Passer ph Robbie Greenberg m Sylvester Levay ad Josan F. Russo ed Richard Chew
☆ Peter O'Toole, Mariel Hemingway, Vincent Spano, Virginia Madsen, David Ogden Stiers, John Dehner

Creature Comforts **
GB 1989 5m colour
Aardman Animations/Channel 4 (Sara Mullock)
Animals discuss the pleasures and disadvantages of living in a zoo.
A clever and witty marrying of stop-motion animation with vox-pop interviews; it was successful enough to spawn a series of similar TV commercials and product merchandising.
d Nick Park ed William Ennals
👤 animated short

'Not since the beginning of time has the world beheld terror like this!'
The Creature from the Black Lagoon
US 1954 79m bw 3-D
U-I (William Alland)
Up the Amazon, scientists encounter a fearful fanged creature who is half man, half fish.
Unpersuasive and unsuspenseful horror hokum from the bottom drawer of imagination: it did, however, coin enough pennies to generate two even worse sequels, Revenge of the Creature (1955) and The Creature Walks Among Us (1956). And the underwater photography is super.
w Harry Essex, Arthur Ross d Jack Arnold ph William E. Snyder m Herman Stein, Hans Salter md Joseph Gershenson
☆ Richard Carlson, Julie Adams, Richard Denning, Antonio Moreno, Nestor Paiva, Ricou Browning

The Creature with the Atom Brain
US 1955 80m bw
Columbia (Sam Katzman)
A scientist creates super-strong robot men, who go on the rampage.
Comic strip style chiller, not too bad to sit through.
w Curt Siodmak d Edward L. Cahn
☆ Richard Denning, Angela Stevens, Gregory Gaye, Tristram Coffin

Creatures the World Forgot
GB 1971 95m Technicolor
Columbia/Hammer (Michael Carreras)
Quarrels break out between rival tribes of Stone Age men.
Feeble follow-up to One Million Years BC and When Dinosaurs Ruled the Earth: someone forgot to order any monsters.
w Michael Carreras d Don Chaffey ph Vincent Cox m Mario Nascimbene pd John Stoll ed Chris Barnes
☆ Julie Ege, Brian O'Shaughnessy, Robert John, Marcia Fox, Rosalie Crutchley

The Creeper
US 1948 63m bw
TCF
Scientists disagree over a serum which changes humans into cats.
Nonsense horror item with stalwart cast.
w Maurice Tombragel d Jean Yarbrough
☆ Ralph Morgan, Eduardo Ciannelli, Onslow Stevens, June Vincent, Richard Lane

Creepers
Italy 1984 110m Eastmancolor
Palace/Dacfilm (Dario Argento)
aka: *Phenomena*
In Switzerland, a sleep-walking schoolgirl with the ability to communicate with insects is helped by a wheelchair-bound entomologist and his chimpanzee to track down a serial killer who murders girls and keeps their bodies.
Daft and gruesome horror that lacks style and sense; it has a plethora of murderers, it is never fully explained who did what to whom, its intention is to disgust rather than shock, and its heavy-metal soundtrack is a frequent distraction.
w Dario Argento, Franco Ferrini d Dario Argento ph Romano Albani m Goblin, Bill Wyman, Iron Maiden, Motorhead, Andy Sex Gang and others pd Maurizio Garrone, Nello Giorgetti, Luciano Spadoni, Umberto Turco ed Franco Fraticelli
☆ Jennifer Connelly, Daria Nicolodi, Dalila di Lazzaro, Donald Pleasence, Patrick Bauchau, Fiore Argento, Federica Mastroianni, Fiorenza Tessari, Michele Soavi
'The saddest aspect of this farrago is the way that, even in this toned-down version, Argento goes for sickness after the manner of Lucio Fulci.' – *Kim Newman, MFB*
'Argento is the rock Toscanini of the hack-em-up.' – *David Edelstein, Village Voice*
† The version released in Britain runs for 83m. It was Argento's first English-language film.

The Creeping Flesh *
GB 1972 91m Eastmancolor
Tigon/World Film Services (Michael Redbourn)
A Victorian scientist discovers that water causes the recomposing of tissue on the skeleton of a Neanderthal man.
Absurd but persuasive horror film, quite well done in all departments.
w Peter Spenceley, Jonathan Rumbold d Freddie Francis ph Norman Warwick m Paul Ferris
☆ Peter Cushing, Christopher Lee, Lorna Heilbron, George Benson, Kenneth J. Warren, Duncan Lamont, Michael Ripper
'The theme of the different attempts to locate and hence control evil is interestingly and sensitively worked out.' – *Robin Wood, MFB*

The Creeping Unknown: see *The Quatermass Experiment*

'The most fun you'll ever have being scared!'
Creepshow
US 1982 120m colour
United Film Distribution/Laurel Show (Richard P. Rubenstein)
A boy reads five gruesome stories from a horror comic.
Supposedly funny but mainly rather nasty recreation of a famous 'comic' style; far too extended for its own good.
w Stephen King d George A. Romero ph Michael Gornick m John Harrison pd Tom Savini
☆ Carrie Nye, Viveca Lindfors, Stephen King, Leslie Nielsen, Hal Holbrook, Adrienne Barbeau, E. G. Marshall
'Robert Bloch and Freddie Francis did it all so much better in Torture Garden.' – *Tom Milne, MFB*

Creepshow 2
US 1987 89m colour
Laurel/New World (David Ball)
Cheapjack sequel, of no interest whatsoever.
w George A. Romero stories Stephen King d Michael Gornick ph Dick Hart, Tom Hurwitz m Les Reed ed Peter Weatherly
☆ Lois Chiles, George Kennedy, Dorothy Lamour, Tom Savini, Page Hannah

'The night the loving ended and the killing began!'
Crescendo *
GB 1970 95m Technicolor
Warner/Hammer (Michael Carreras)
A girl researcher goes to stay with the widow of a famous composer, and finds herself in mortal danger…
Lunatic Hammer horror with the courage of its shameless borrowings from Taste of Fear, Fanatic, Nightmare, Maniac and all the films about mad twin brothers, to which this chaotic brew adds dollops of sex and heroin addiction.
w Jimmy Sangster, Alfred Shaughnessy d Alan Gibson ph Paul Beeson m Malcolm Williamson ad Scott MacGregor ed Chris Barnes
☆ Stefanie Powers, James Olson, Margaretta Scott, Jane Lapotaire, Joss Ackland

Crest of the Wave: see *Seagulls over Sorrento*

Le Cri de Hibou *
France/Italy 1987 102m colour
Italfrance Films/TF1 (Gerard Croce)
aka: *The Cry of the Owl*
As his divorce to his vindictive wife becomes absolute, a depressed commercial artist introduces himself to a young woman on whose apparently happy life he has been spying; before long, he finds himself accused of murder and the target of a killer.
An intriguing, downbeat psychological thriller, a study of a man who seems to carry death with him, and of jealousy, revenge and love, observed with a dispassionate eye.
w Odile Barski, Claude Chabrol novel Patricia Highsmith d Claude Chabrol ph Jean Rabier m Matthieu Chabrol md Michel Ganot ed Monique Fardoulis
☆ Christophe Malavoy, Mathilda May, Jacques Penot, Jean-Pierre Kalfon, Virginie Thevenet
'For the most part shows Chabrol at his best.' – *Sight and Sound*

Le Cri du Coeur *
France 1994 86m colour
Les Films de la Plaine/De L'Avenir/CEC Rhône-Alpes (Bernard Granger)
An 11-year-old boy, who travels with his mother from his African village to join his father in Paris, is haunted by visions of a hyena roaming the city streets.
Interesting drama of assimilation into a foreign land and culture, as seen through the eyes of a child, but lacking in dramatic impetus.
w Idrissa Ouédraogo, Robert Gardner, Jacques Akchoti, Olivier Douyère d Idrissa Ouédraogo ph Jean Monsigny, Jean-Paul Meurisse m Henri Texler ad Olivier Paultre, Alain Poirot ed Luc Barnier
☆ Richard Bohringer, Said Diarra, Félicité Wouassi, Alex Descas, Clémentine Célarié, Jean-Yves Gautier

---

'Well-made, dignified … though pic's main audience will be viewers interested in African cinema.' – *Variety*

Cria!: see *Raise Ravens*

Cria Cuervos: see *Raise Ravens*

Cries and Whispers ****
Sweden   1972   91m   Eastmancolor
Cinematograph (Ingmar Bergman)
🎞
original title: *Viskningar och Rop*
A young woman dying of cancer in her family home is tended by her two sisters.
Quiet, chilling, classical chapter of doom which variously reminds one of Chekhov, Tolstoy and Dostoievsky but is also essential Bergman. Tough but important viewing, it lingers afterwards in the mind like a picture vividly painted in shades of red.
wd Ingmar Bergman ph Sven Nykvist m Chopin and Bach
☆ Harriet Andersson, Kari Sylwan, Ingrid Thulin, Liv Ullmann
  'Harrowing, spare and perceptive, but lacking the humour that helps to put life and death into perspective.' – *Michael Billington, Illustrated London News*
🏃 Sven Nykvist
& best picture; Ingmar Bergman (as writer); Ingmar Bergman (as director)

Crime and Punishment *
US   1935   88m   bw
Columbia
A student kills a pawnbroker and is tortured by remorse.
Heavy-going rendering of Dostoievsky with some pictorial interest.
w S. K. Lauren, Joseph Anthony d Josef von Sternberg ph Lucien Ballard m Arthur Honegger md Louis Silvers
☆ Peter Lorre, Edward Arnold, Tala Birell, Marian Marsh, Elizabeth Risdon, Mrs Patrick Campbell
  'Will have to be sold, but should average fair takings.' – *Variety*

Crime and Punishment *
France   1935   110m   bw
Incisive, well-acted French version.
w Marcel Aymé d Pierre Chenal m Arthur Honegger
☆ Pierre Blanchar, Harry Baur, Marcelle Geniat, Madeleine Ozeray
  'There's a real picture in this Dostoievsky book, and the French have proved it.' – *Variety*

Crime and Punishment USA
US   1958   96m   bw
Allied Artists/Sanders Associates (Terry Sanders)
A student murders an old pawnbroker and is driven mad by guilt.
Pointless updating of Dostoievsky by two young film-makers who seemed for years to be on the brink of a masterpiece but never actually produced it. Some points of interest, but the low budget is cramping.
w Walter Newman d Denis Sanders ph Floyd Crosby m Herschel Burke Gilbert
☆ George Hamilton, Frank Silvera, Mary Murphy, John Harding, Marian Seldes
  'There is about it a strange quality of aimlessness which nullifies much of its effect.' – *MFB*

Crime by Night *
US   1944   72m   bw
Warner (William Jacobs)
A private detective reluctantly solves a small-town murder, and finds a spy.
Second feature which was thought at the time to have established a new pair of married detectives in the tradition of The Thin Man. However, one poor sequel, Find the Blackmailer, put paid to the idea.
w Richard Weil, Joel Malone novel Forty Whacks by Geoffrey Homes d William Clemens ph Henry Sharpe
☆ Jerome Cowan, Jane Wyman, Faye Emerson, Charles Lang, Eleanor Parker, Cy Kendall, Creighton Hale

Crime Doctor
US   1934   75m   bw
RKO
A criminologist uses his special knowledge to wreak vengeance on his wife's lover.

Smart co-feature which doubtless pleased a good many audiences.
w Jane Murfin story Israel Zangwill d John Robertson
☆ Otto Kruger, Karen Morley, Nils Asther, Judith Wood, William Frawley, Donald Crisp
  'Good in every department, with mounting suspense.' – *Variety*

Crime Doctor *
US   1943   66m   bw
Columbia
An amnesiac becomes a successful psychiatrist, then discovers that he was once a wanted gangster.
Time-passing second feature from a popular radio series. Ten Crime Doctor films were made between 1943 and 1949, all starring Warner Baxter, all except the first being locked room mysteries which seldom played fair with the audience.
The sequels:
1943 Crime Doctor's Strangest Case
1944 Shadows in the Night, Crime Doctor's Courage
1945 Crime Doctor's Warning
1946 Crime Doctor's Manhunt, Just before Dawn
1947 The Millerson Case
1948 Crime Doctor's Gamble
1949 Crime Doctor's Diary
w Graham Baker, Louise Lantz d Michael Gordon m Louis Silvers
☆ Warner Baxter, Margaret Lindsay, John Litel, Ray Collins, Harold Huber, Leon Ames, Don Costello

Crime Does Not Pay
A celebrated series of two-reel shorts made by MGM between 1935 and 1947.
In a hard-driving, tensely commentated manner more reminiscent of Warner filmmaking, they gave ample scope to trainee actors and directors in allegedly truthful re-enactments of contemporary crimes, often introduced by the state governor or police commissioner. The titles were as follows:
The titles were as follows:
1935 Buried Loot, d George B. Seitz; with Robert Taylor, Robert Livingston
1935 Racket, d George B. Seitz
1935 Desert Death, d George B. Seitz; with Raymond Hatton, Harvey Stephens
1935 A Thrill for Thelma, d Edward Cahn; with Irene Hervey, Robert Warwick
1935 Hit and Run Driver, d Edward Cahn; with Morgan Wallace, Jonathan Hale
1935 Perfect Set-up, d Edward Cahn
1936 Foolproof, d Edward Cahn; with Niles Welch, Alonzo Price
1936 The Public Pays, d Errol Taggart; with Paul Stanton, Cy Kendall
1936 Torture Money, d Harold S. Bucquet
1937 It May Happen to You, d Harold S. Bucquet
1937 Soak the Poor, d Harold S. Bucquet
1937 Give Till it Hurts, d Felix Feist; with Janet Beecher, Howard Hickman
1937 Behind the Criminal, d Harold S. Bucquet; with Edward Emerson, Walter Kingsford
1938 What Price Safety, d Harold S. Bucquet; with John Wray, George Houston
1938 Miracle Money, d Leslie Fenton; with John Miljan, Claire DuBrey
1938 Come Across, d Harold S. Bucquet; with Bernard Nedell, Donald Douglas
1938 A Criminal is Born, d Leslie Fenton; with George Breakston, David Durand
1938 They're Always Caught, d Harold S. Bucquet; with Stanley Ridges, John Eldredge
1938 Think it Over, d Jacques Tourneur; with Lester Matthews, Dwight Frye
1938 The Wrong Way Out, d Gustav Machaty; with Linda Terry, Kenneth Howell
1939 Money to Loan, d Joe Newman; with Alan Dinehart, Paul Guilfoyle
1939 While America Sleeps, d Fred Zinnemann; with Dick Purcell, Roland Varno
1939 Help Wanted, d Fred Zinnemann; with Tom Neal, Jo Ann Sayers
1939 Think First, d Roy Rowland; with Laraine Day, Marc Lawrence, Sara Haden
1939 Drunk Driving, d David Miller; with Dick Purcell, Jo Ann Sayers
1940 Pound Foolish, d Felix Feist; with Neil Hamilton, Lynne Carver
1940 Know Your Money, d Joe Newman; with Dennis Moore, Noel Madison
1940 Jackpot, d Roy Rowland; with Tom Neal, Ann Morriss

1940 Women in Hiding, d Joe Newman; with Marsha Hunt, C. Henry Gordon
1940 Buyer Beware, d Joe Newman; with Charles Arnt
1940 Soak the Old, d Sammy Lee; with Ralph Morgan, Kenneth Christy
1940 You the People, d Roy Rowland; with C. Henry Gordon, Paul Everton
1941 Respect the Law, d Joe Newman.
1941 Forbidden Passage, d Fred Zinnemann; with Harry Woods
1941 Coffins on Wheels, dJoe Newman; with Cy Kendall, Darryl Hickman
1941 Sucker List, d Roy Rowland; with Lynne Carver, John Archer
1942 For the Common Defense, d Allen Kenward; with Van Johnson, Douglas Fowley
1942 Keep 'em Sailing, d Basil Wrangell; with Jim Davis, Lou Smith
1943 Plan for Destruction, d Edward Cahn; with Lewis Stone
1944 Patrolling the Ether, d Paul Burnford
1944 Easy Life, dWalter Hart; with Bernard Thomas, Steve Geray
1944 Dark Shadows, d Paul Burnford; with Arthur Space, Henry O'Neill
1945 Fall Guy, d Paul Burnford; with Leon Ames
1945 The Last Instalment, d Walter Hart; with Cameron Mitchell, Walter Sande
1945 Phantoms Inc., d Harold Young; with Frank Reicher, Ann Shoemaker
1945 A Gun in His Hand, d Joseph Losey; with Anthony Caruso, Richard Gaines
1945 Purity Squad, d Harold Kress; with Byron Foulger, Dick Elliott
1947 Luckiest Guy in the World, d Joe Newman; with Barry Nelson, Eloise Hardt

Crime in the Streets *
US   1956   91m   bw
Allied Artists (Vincent M. Fennelly)
🎞
Rival knife gangs bring havoc to tenement dwellers.
Lively semi-documentary low-life melodrama; routine subject, excellent credits.
w Reginald Rose TV play Reginald Rose d Don Siegel ph Sam Leavitt m Franz Waxman
☆ John Cassavetes, James Whitmore, Sal Mineo, Mark Rydell

The Crime of Dr Crespi
US   1935   64m   bw
Republic
🎞
A surgeon induces suspended animation in a hated rival, and has him buried.
Crude and tasteless variation on Poe's 'The Premature Burial'.
w Lewis Graham, Edward Olmstead d John H. Auer
☆ Erich von Stroheim, Dwight Frye, Paul Guilfoyle, Harriet Russell
  'As a baby scarer it's a weak entry.' – *Variety*

The Crime of Dr Forbes
US   1936   75m   bw
TCF
A gravely injured scientist asks to be put out of his misery, and a colleague is accused of murder.
Competently handled minor item, more a mystery story than a consideration of euthanasia.
w Frances Hyland, Saul Elkins d George Marshall
☆ Robert Kent, J. Edward Bromberg, Gloria Stuart, Henry Armetta, Sara Haden, Alan Dinehart

The Crime of Monsieur Lange **
France   1936   85m   bw
Obéron (André Halley des Fontaines)
🎞
When the hated boss of a publishing house is believed killed, the workers turn it into a successful co-operative. When he reappears, he is killed.
The political elements of this fable now seem unimportant, but it still shows its original charm and cinematic skill.
w Jacques Prévert d Jean Renoir ph Jean Bachelet m Jean Wiener
☆ René Lefèbvre, Jules Berry, Florelle, Sylvia Bataille, Henri Guisol

Crime of Passion
US   1956   86m   bw
UA/Bob Goldstein (Herman Cohen)
An executive's wife sleeps her way to the top, but when the boss does not come through with promotion she shoots him.
Old-fashioned star melodrama on a low budget.
w Jo Eisinger d Gerd Oswald ph Joseph LaShelle m Paul Dunlap
☆ Barbara Stanwyck, Sterling Hayden, Raymond Burr, Fay Wray, Royal Dano, Virginia Grey

Crime of the Century
US   1933   74m   bw
Paramount (B. P. Schulberg)
A doctor commits a robbery by hypnotism, but is himself assaulted and the money disappears.
Smart exploitation mystery with an intermission for the audience to check the clues, and a revelation that the police investigator is the guilty man.
w Florence Ryerson, Brian Marlow play The Grootman Case by Walter Maria Espe d William Beaudine
☆ Jean Hersholt, Robert Elliott, Wynne Gibson, Stuart Erwin, Frances Dee, David Landau
  'Can be built up into a better than average below the de luxe theatres.' – *Variety*

The Crime of the Century: see *Walk East on Beacon* (1952)

Crime over London
GB   1936   84m   bw
UA/Criterion (Marcel Hellman, Douglas Fairbanks Jnr)
A department store becomes a hide-out for gangsters.
Stolid attempt at a British gangster picture; doesn't come off.
w Norman Alexander, Harold French novel House of a Thousand Windows by Louis de Wohl d Alfred Zeisler ph Victor Armenise, Claude Friese-Greene ad Edward Carrick ed Conrad von Molo
☆ Margot Grahame, Paul Cavanagh, Joseph Cawthorn, Basil Sydney, Rene Ray

Crime School *
US   1938   86m   bw
Warner (Bryan Foy)
Problems of the warden of a reform school.
Predictable vehicle for the Dead End Kids; watchable at the time.
w Crane Wilbur, Vincent Sherman d Lewis Seiler ph Arthur Todd m Max Steiner
☆ Humphrey Bogart, Gale Page, Billy Halop, Huntz Hall, Leo Gorcey, Bobby Jordan, Gabriel Dell, Bernard Punsley, Paul Porcasi, Al Bridge
  'A rough entertainment, sometimes brutal … should do well where audiences like 'em tough.' – *Variety*

Crime Story *
Hong Kong   1993   100m   colour
Golden Harvest (Leonard K. C. Ho)
📼
original title: *Chung On Tsou*
A cop hunts down the ruthless kidnappers who have grabbed the millionaire he was assigned to guard.
There is less action and more acting than usual from its star in a tough and tense thriller, which builds to a satisfactory climax.
w Cheun Tin-nam, Chan Man-keung, Cheung Lai-ling d Kirk Wong ph Leu Wai-keung m James Wong ad Tony Au, Lui Cho-hung, Luk Tsi-leung ed Peter Cheung
☆ Jackie Chang, Kent Cheng, K'o Shou-liang, Ng Wing-mei, Poon Ling-ling
  'Action set pieces and firepower are both high caliber, with a simmering tension that holds the whole together.' – *Variety*

Crime Wave
US   1954   74m   bw
Warner
GB title: *The City Is Dark*
An ex-con is prevented from going straight.
Basically humdrum programmer with lively detail.
w Crane Wilbur d André de Toth
☆ Sterling Hayden, Gene Nelson, Phyllis Kirk, Ted de Corsia, Charles Bronson

---

'He had tired of her – and for that he was sorry! He was tied to her – and for that he hated her!'

Crime without Passion **

US   1934   82m   bw
Paramount (Ben Hecht, Charles MacArthur)

A lawyer is driven to commit murder.

Effective melodrama notable for then-new techniques which were blended into the mainstream of movie-making, and for the first appearance in Hollywood of a smart new writer-producer-director team.

wd *Ben Hecht, Charles MacArthur story Caballero of the Law by Ben Hecht, Charles MacArthur ph Lee Garmes m Oscar Levant sp Slavko Vorkapich*

☆ Claude Rains, Margo, Whitney Bourne, Stanley Ridges

'It turns a lot of established motion picture conventions topsy-turvy ... shouldn't have much trouble at the box office, and inside the theatre it is safe.' – *Variety*

'The whole venture seems to take a long stride forward for the movies.' – *Otis Ferguson*

'A flamboyant, undisciplined, but compulsively fascinating film classic.' – *Peter John Dyer, 1966*

Crimes and Misdemeanors ***

US   1989   104m   DeLuxe
Rank/Orion (Robert Greenhut)

Brothers-in-law deal with marital crises.

Two interlinked stories, one comic, the other tragic, form a winning combination.

wd *Woody Allen ph Sven Nykvist md Joe Malin pd Santo Loquasto ed Susan E. Morse*

☆ Caroline Aaron, Alan Alda, Woody Allen, Claire Bloom, Mia Farrow, Joanna Gleason, Anjelica Huston, Martin Landau, Jenny Nichols, Jerry Orbach

⅋ best director; best original screenplay; Martin Landau

Crimes at the Dark House

GB   1939   69m   bw
Pennant (George King)

A Victorian landowner kills his wife and conceals the fact by using a lunatic as her double.

Cheeky adaptation of a classic to make one of the star's most lip-smacking barnstormers.

w *Edward Dryhurst, Frederick Hayward, H. F. Maltby novel The Woman in White by Wilkie Collins d George King ph Hone Glendinning*

☆ Tod Slaughter, Hilary Eaves, Sylvia Marriott, Hay Petrie, David Horne

Crimes of Passion

US   1984   104m   colour
New World (Barry Sandler)

A prostitute tells her story at a group therapy session.

Predictably from this director, a hysterically overheated stew of sex and murder; one to walk away from.

w *Barry Sandler d Ken Russell ph Dick Bush m Rick Wakeman*

☆ Kathleen Turner, Anthony Perkins, John Laughlin, Annie Potts

'Film walks an uneasy line at times between comedy and drama, but is entertaining in the manner of a great B picture all about sex.' – *Variety*

'One of the silliest movies in a long time.' – *Roger Ebert*

The Crimes of Stephen Hawke

GB   1936   69m   bw
MGM (George King)

A 19th-century moneylender is exposed as the mysterious murderer who had terrorized London.

Amusing barnstormer.

w *H. F. Maltby story Jack Celestin d George King ph Ronald Neame*

☆ Tod Slaughter, Eric Portman, Marjorie Taylor, Gerald Barry

Crimes of the Heart *

US   1986   105m   Technicolor
De Laurentiis/Freddie Fields-Burt Sugarman

Three sisters try to reconcile themselves with their family past.

Somewhat overwrought but generally compelling Southern comedy-drama.

w *Beth Henley play Beth Henley d Bruce Beresford ph Dante Spinotti m Georges Delerue pd Ken Adam*

☆ Diane Keaton, Jessica Lange, Sissy Spacek, Sam Shepard, Tess Harper, David Carpenter, Hurd Hatfield

⅋ Sissy Spacek, Tess Harper; Beth Henley

'To be seen is to exist.'

Crimetime *

GB/US/Germany   1996   118m   colour
First Independent/Focus/Channel 4/Pandora/Trimark (David Pupkewitz)

An actor begins to identify with a serial killer after he plays the murderer on a television show recreating the crimes as they occur.

A thriller that promises more than it finally delivers, raising intriguing questions about TV and identity which it then ignores.

w *Brendan Somers d George Sluizer ph Jules van den Steenhoven m David A. Stewart pd Bernd Lepel ed Fabienne Rawley*

☆ Stephen Baldwin, Pete Postlethwaite, Sadie Frost, Geraldine Chaplin, Karen Black, James Faulkner, Philip Davis, Marianne Faithfull

'Not helped by a succession of unappealing performances, nor the faintly surreal atmosphere, the mishmash of styles, accents and performances, or a host of dramatic short cuts that do no favours for credibility.' – *Anwar Brett, Film Review*

Crimewave

US   1986   83m   Technicolor
Embassy/Pressman/Renaissance (Robert Tapert)

Two psychopaths are hired by a timid security man to murder his double-crossing partner.

Broad black farcical horror that is very noisy, but never funny.

w *Ethan Coen, Joel Coen, Sam Raimi d Sam Raimi ph Robert Primes m Arlon Ober ad Gary Papierski ed Michael Kelly, Kathie Weaver*

☆ Louise Lasser, Paul L. Smith, Brion James, Sheree J. Wilson, Edward R. Pressman, Bruce Campbell, Reed Birney

'A fiasco.' – *Bruce Campbell*

The Criminal *

GB   1960   97m   bw
Merton Park (Jack Greenwood)

US title: The Concrete Jungle

Sent to jail for a racecourse snatch, a gangster comes out fifteen years later to regain the loot and is followed by other criminals who kill him.

Relentlessly grim saga of prison life, with a few sensational trimmings.

w *Alun Owen, Jimmy Sangster d Joseph Losey ph Robert Krasker m Johnny Dankworth*

☆ Stanley Baker, Sam Wanamaker, Margit Saad, Patrick Magee, Noel Willman, Grégoire Aslan, Jill Bennett, Kenneth J. Warren, Nigel Green, Patrick Wymark, Murray Melvin

'A savage, almost expressionistic picture of English underworld life.' – *NFT, 1973*

The Criminal Code *

US   1930   97m   bw
Columbia (Harry Cohn)

A young man kills in self-defence, is railroaded into jail and becomes involved in another murder.

Impressive melodrama with good performances and sharp handling.

w *Seton I. Miller, Fred Niblo Jnr play Martin Flavin d Howard Hawks ph James Wong Howe, Ted Tetzlaff*

☆ Walter Huston, Phillips Holmes, Constance Cummings, Mary Doran, De Witt Jennings, John Sheehan, Boris Karloff

† Remade as *Penitentiary* (1938) with Walter Connolly and *Convicted* (1950) with Broderick Crawford.

⅋ Seton I. Miller, Fred Niblo Jnr

Criminal Court

US   1946   63m   bw
RKO

A lawyer is blackmailed by a crooked club owner.

Stock crime and lawcourt yarn, rather stodgily put together but with interesting moments.

w *Lawrence Kimble d Robert Wise*

☆ Tom Conway, Martha O'Driscoll, Robert Armstrong, Addison Richards

'Whoever fights monsters should see to it that in the process he does not become a monster.' Nietzsch'

Criminal Law

US   1989   118m   colour   Panavision
Hemdale/Northwood (Robert MacClean, Hilary Heath)

A successful lawyer decides that his client is a murderer.

Hysterical thriller that never convinces on any level.

w *Mark Kasdan d Martin Campbell ph Philip Meheux m Jerry Goldsmith ed Chris Wimble*

☆ Gary Oldman, Kevin Bacon, Karen Young, Joe Don Baker, Tess Harper, Ron Lea, Karen Woolridge, Terence Labrosse, Jennie Walker

'It dares to elaborate on its unbelievable central relationship between a driven yuppie lawyer and a charming old-money psychopath with hokey devices more redolent of some 40s old-dark-house movie than of a supposedly "serious" modern thriller.' – *Kim Newman, MFB*

Criminal Lawyer

US   1937   72m   bw
RKO

A smart lawyer who has devoted his career to getting criminals off the hook has a change of heart when appointed district attorney.

Standard programmer with a first-rate star performance.

w *G. V. Atwater, Thomas Lennon story Louis Stevenson d Christy Cabanne*

☆ Lee Tracy, Margot Grahame, Eduardo Ciannelli, Erik Rhodes

'Strong fronter for a dual, but can go solo where Tracy's name will draw.' – *Variety*

The Criminal Life of Archibaldo de la Cruz *

Mexico   1955   91m   bw
Alianza Cinematografica (Roberto Figueroa)

original title: Ensayo de un Crimen

A fantasist determines to kill all women who cross his path, but fate intervenes.

Cheaply made macabre joke, one of its director's throwaway oddities: not too smooth, but often amusing.

w *Luis Buñuel, E. Ugarte d Luis Buñuel ph Augusto Jimenez md Jorge Perez*

☆ Ernesto Alonso, Ariadna Welter, Miroslava Stern, Rita Macedo

'Buñuel has not only given a frightful reality to melodramatic obsessions; he has created, in place of the grimaces, by now laughable, of the conventional madman of the screen, a whole repertory of erotic and deathly gestures which chill the flesh.' – *Dilys Powell*

The Crimson Blade: see *The Scarlet Blade*

The Crimson Canary

US   1945   64m   bw
Universal (Bob Faber)

A jazz band vocalist is murdered.

Routine murder mystery with appearances by Coleman Hawkins, Oscar Pettiford and Josh White.

w *Henry Blankfort, Peggy Phillips d John Hoffman*

☆ Noah Beery Jnr, Lois Collier, Danny Morton, John Litel, Steve Geray

The Crimson Circle

GB   1936   76m   bw
Wainwright/Richard Wainwright

Scotland Yard rounds up a blackmail gang.

Lively Edgar Wallace adaptation.

w *Howard Irving Young story Edgar Wallace d Reginald Denham ph Phil Tannura*

☆ Hugh Wakefield, Alfred Drayton, Noah Beery, June Duprez, Niall MacGinnis

'Considerably superior to pictures of its kind coming out of the tight little isle.' – *Variety*

† An earlier version in 1929 (part-talkie) with Stewart Rome was directed by Fred Zelnick for British Talking Pictures.

The Crimson Cult: see *Curse of the Crimson Altar*

The Crimson Curtain *

France   1952   43m   bw
Argos

original title: Le Rideau Cramoisi

An officer billeted with a bourgeois family is visited at night by the beautiful daughter, who finally dies in his arms.

A curious polished fragment with narration replacing spoken dialogue. For those in the mood, it works.

wd *Alexandre Astruc story Barbey d'Aurevilly ph Eugene Schufftan m Jean-Jacques Grunenwald*

☆ Jean-Claude Pascal, Anouk Aimée, Madeleine Garcia, Jim Gerald

'In its limited time, with the greatest economy of means, it evokes an authentic sense of the past, as well as telling a story movingly and dramatically.' – *Richard Roud*

The Crimson Kimono *

US   1959   82m   bw
Columbia/Globe (Samuel Fuller)

Detectives seeking the murderer of a stripper in Los Angeles' Little Tokyo both fall in love with a witness.

Self-conscious local colour, though quite freshly observed and well photographed, finally overwhelms an ordinary little murder mystery.

wd *Samuel Fuller ph Sam Leavitt m Harry Sukman*

☆ Glenn Corbett, James Shigeta, Victoria Shaw, Anna Lee, Paul Dubov

'Ask me no questions: believe only what you see!'

The Crimson Pirate *

↟↟ GB   1952   104m   Technicolor
Warner/Norma (Harold Hecht)

An 18th-century pirate and an eccentric inventor lead an island's people in rebellion against a tyrant.

One suspects that this started off as a straight adventure and was turned halfway through production into a spoof; at any rate, the effect is patchy but with spirited highlights, and the star's acrobatic training is put to good use.

w *Roland Kibbee d Robert Siodmak ph Otto Heller m William Alwyn*

☆ Burt Lancaster, Nick Cravat, Eva Bartok, Torin Thatcher, James Hayter, Margot Grahame, Noel Purcell, Frank Pettingell

Crimson Romance

US   1934   70m   bw
Mascot

Two Americans join the German Air Force and one is killed fighting Americans.

Very curious action drama which does not make its actual sympathies very clear.

w *Al Martin, Sherman Lowe d David Howard*

☆ Ben Lyon, James Bush, Erich von Stroheim, Sari Maritza, Bodil Rosing, Herman Bing

'By indie standards a pretentious production ... but not very promising for localities where resentment is rife.' – *Variety*

Crimson Tide **

US   1995   116m   Technicolor   Panavision
Buena Vista/Hollywood (Don Simpson, Jerry Bruckheimer)

The veteran captain of a US submarine and his Harvard-educated executive officer clash over what action should be taken after Russian rebels seize a nuclear missile base and they are under attack.

A thriller that grips and entertains despite its predictability and the familiarity of its doomsday scenario.

w *Michael Schiffer d Tony Scott ph Dariusz Wolsky m Hans Zimmer pd Michael White ed Chris Lebenzon*

☆ Denzel Washington, Gene Hackman, George Dzundza, Viggo Mortensen, James Gandolfini, Matt Craven, Rick Schroder, Jason Robards (uncredited)

'The Caine Mutiny on steroids.' – *Tom Shone, Sunday Times*

'A boy's movie all the way, with enough expensive military hardware and tough-guy power plays to appeal to teenagers of all ages.' – *Todd McCarthy, Variety*

† Quentin Tarantino, Robert Towne and Steve Zaillian worked uncredited on the script.

⅋ Chris Lebenzon; sound; sound effects editing

◎ Digital Video Disc Region 2   ◎ Digital Video Disc Region 1   ♫ Soundtrack released on compact disc   ☆ Cast in approximate order of importance   † Points of interest   ♫ Notable songs   ▲ Academy Award   ⅋ Academy Award nomination   ♔ BAFTA

Crin Blanc **
France   1953   47m   bw
Albert Lamorisse
aka: *Wild Stallion*
A small boy befriends and rides a wild horse in the Camargue.
A favourite short film of great beauty, but a shade overlong for its content.
wd Albert Lamorisse ph Edmond Séchan
m Maurice Le Roux
☆ Alain Emery, Pascal Lamorisse

'For every man who struck gold – a hundred tried to take it away from him!'
Cripple Creek
US   1952   78m   colour
Columbia (Edward Small)
A federal agent uncovers smugglers during a gold rush.
Adequate co-feature Western in murky colour.
w Richard Schayer d Ray Nazarro
☆ George Montgomery, Karin Booth, Jerome Courtland, William Bishop, Richard Egan, Don Porter

La Crise *
France   1992   95m   colour
Electric/TFI/Leader/Raidue/Canal/Alain Sarde
A man loses his wife and his job on the same day and cannot find anyone, apart from a drunk, to sympathize with his predicament.
An amusing, if slightly mechanical comedy, of a workaholic discovering that life has more to offer than work.
wd Coline Serreau ph Robert Alazraki m Sonia Wieder-Atherton pd Guy-Claude François
ed Catherine Renault
☆ Vincent Lindon, Patrick Timsit, Annik Alane, Valerie Alane, Gilles Privat, Nanou Garcia, Christian Benedetti, Didier Flamand
   'Amiable, crowd-pleasing entertainment with more than its fair share of good jokes.' – *Sight and Sound*

Crisis *
US   1950   96m   bw
MGM (Arthur Freed)
A brain surgeon is forced to operate secretly on a South American dictator, and his wife is kidnapped by revolutionaries.
Dour intellectual suspense piece, in key with the genteel enlightenment of the Dore Schary regime at MGM. Well made but cold.
wd Richard Brooks story George Tabori ph Ray June m Miklos Rozsa
☆ Cary Grant, José Ferrer, Signe Hasso, Paula Raymond, Ramon Navarro, Antonio Moreno, Leon Ames, Gilbert Roland
   'Original, arresting and considered ... so far the most striking example of Dore Schary's policy of encouraging the development of new talents.' – *Gavin Lambert*
   'A bold piece of movie adventuring.' – *L.A. Mirror*

Criss Cross *
US   1948   87m   bw
U-I (Michel Kraike)
An armoured car guard and his double-crossing ex-wife get mixed up with vicious gangsters.
Sordid film noir with a poor plot but suspenseful sequences.
w Daniel Fuchs novel Don Tracy d Robert Siodmak ph Franz Planer m Miklos Rozsa
☆ Burt Lancaster, Yvonne de Carlo, Dan Duryea, Stephen McNally, Richard Long, Tom Pedi, Alan Napier
   'Siodmak's talent for brooding violence and the sombre urban setting gives the film a relentlessly mounting tension.' – *Peter John Dyer*

CrissCross
US   1992   100m   colour
MGM/Hawn-Sylbert (Anthea Sylbert)
A 12-year-old boy turns to crime to help his mother who works as a waitress and a stripper in order to support them.
Slow-moving domestic drama that fails to sustain one's interest.

w Scott Sommer novel Scott Sommer d Chris Menges ph Ivan Strasburg m Trevor Jones
pd Crispian Sallis ed Tony Lawson
☆ Goldie Hawn, Arliss Howard, James Gammon, David Arnott, Keith Carradine, J. C. Quinn, Steve Buscemi

'At Memorial Hospital no one ever dies ... until their insurance runs out.'
Critical Care
US   1997   105m   DeLuxe
Live Entertainment/Mediaworks (Steven S. Schwartz, Sidney Lumet)
An ambitious young hospital doctor is drawn into a battle between two sisters over the fate of their comatose father and his money.
Ailing satire on the medical profession, a heavy-handed melodrama with occasional pleasures.
w Steven S. Schwartz book Richard Dooling
d Sidney Lumet ph David Watkin m Michael Convertino pd Philip Rosenberg ed Tom Swartwout
☆ James Spader, Kyra Sedgwick, Helen Mirren, Margo Martindale, Jeffrey Wright, Wallace Shawn, Anne Bancroft, Albert Brooks, Philip Bosco, Edward Herrmann, Colm Feore
   'A sadly anemic and uncharacteristically unenergetic addition to Sidney Lumet's career.' – *Todd McCarthy, Variety*

Critical Condition
US   1986   100m   Technicolor
Paramount (Ted Field, Robert Cort)
Pretending to be mad in order to escape the Mafia, our hero is instead mistaken for a doctor.
Zany, hepped-up comedy which fails on all counts.
w Denis and John Hamill d Michael Apted
ph Ralf D. Bode m Alan Silvestri pd John Lloyd ed Robert K. Lambert
☆ Richard Pryor, Rachel Ticotin, Ruben Blades, Joe Mantegna, Bob Dishy
   'Fans will find little to cheer about.' – *Daily Variety*

Critic's Choice
US   1963   100m   Technicolor   Panavision
Warner/Frank P. Rosenberg
A ruthless Broadway critic is forced by his scruples to write a bad review of his wife's play.
Unsuitable vehicle for stars who have shorn a good comedy of wit and strive vainly for sentiment, wisecracks and pratfalls.
w Jack Sher play Ira Levin d Don Weis
ph Charles Lang m George Duning
☆ Bob Hope, Lucille Ball, Marilyn Maxwell, Rip Torn, Jessie Royce Landis, John Dehner, Jim Backus, Marie Windsor
   'For instant stultification.' – *Judith Crist*

Critters
US   1986   86m   DeLuxe
Sho Films/Smart Egg/New Line (Rupert Harvey)
Hair-ball-like creatures arrive from an asteroid and devastate Kansas.
Childish horror spoof which makes Gremlins look like War and Peace.
w Stephen Herek, Domonic Muir d Stephen Herek ph Tim Suhrstedt, Chris Tufty m David Newman pd Gregg Fonseca ed Larry Bock
☆ Dee Wallace Stone, M. Emmet Walsh, Billy Green Bush, Scott Grimes
   'Irritatingly insipid and lightweight.' – *Variety*

Critters 2
US   1988   86m   colour
Palace/New Line/Sho films (Barry Opper)
original title: *Critters 2: The Main Course*
Killer aliens terrorise a town.
Even judged by the standards of the original, a dull and boring movie.
w D. T. Twohy, Mick Garris d Mick Garris ph Russell Carpenter m Nicholas Pike pd Philip Dean Foreman ed Charles Bornstein
☆ Terrence Mann, Don Opper, Cynthia Garris, Scott Grimes, Al Stevenson, Tom Hodges, Douglas Rowe, Liane Curtis
   'A soft-centred remake of its amiable but unremarkable original.' – *MFB*

Critters 3
US   1992   86m   colour
Newline/OH Films (Barry Opper, Rupert Harvey)
Furry man-eating aliens invade an apartment block in Los Angeles.
A mixture of gore and comedy that borrows from Die Hard.
w David J. Schow story Barry Opper, Rupert Harvey d Kristine Peterson ph Tom Callaway m David C. Williams pd Philip Dean Foreman ed Terry Stokes
☆ Aimee Brooks, John Calvin, Katherine Cortez, Leonardo DiCaprio, Geoffrey Blake, Don Opper, Diana Bellamy, Terrence Mann

Critters 4
US   1992   90m   colour
New Line/OH Films (Barry Opper, Rupert Harvey)
A space salvage crew is trapped on a space station between the last surviving Krites and ruthless killers who want the creatures for biological warfare.
Almost a standard low-budget space parody of Alien, with a couple of jokes and the Critters reduced to occasional roll-on, roll-off roles.
w Joseph Lyle, David J. Schow story Barry Opper, Rupert Harvey d Rupert Harvey ph Tom Callaway m Peter Manning Robinson pd Philip Dean Foreman ed Terry Stokes
☆ Don Opper, Paul Whitthorne, Angela Bassett, Anders Hove, Eric DaRe, Brad Dourif

'Crocodile' Dundee *
Australia   1986   102m   Kodak Color
Panavision
Paramount/Hoyts/Rimfire (John Cornell)
An outback hero goes to Manhattan and puts New Yorkers in their place.
Easygoing comedy with no real style, which astounded the industry by becoming one of America's most popular films in 1986.
w Paul Hogan, Ken Shadie d Peter Faiman
ph Russell Boyd m Peter Best
☆ Paul Hogan, Linda Koslowski, John Meillon, Mark Blum
   'Romancing the Stone combined with Tarzan's New York Adventure.' – *Sight and Sound*
   'A movie doggedly designed to make you feel good.' – *Vincent Canby, New York Times*
   ♗ best original screenplay

'Crocodile' Dundee II
Australia   1988   111m   DuArt   Panavision
Paramount/Rimfire (John Cornell, Jane Scott)
Hunted in New York by drug dealers seeking the return of an incriminating photograph, 'Crocodile' Dundee returns to the Australian bush where his superior skills can outwit them.
Ineffectual sequel that offers nothing new for its central character to do and merely recycles episodes from the first hit.
w Paul Hogan, Brett Hogan d John Cornell
ph Russell Boyd m Peter Best pd Lawrence Eastwood ed David Stiven
☆ Paul Hogan, Linda Kozlowski, John Meillon, Ernie Dingo, Steve Rackman, Charles Dutton, Juan Fernandez, Hechter Ubarry
   'A wasted opportunity if ever there was one.' – *MFB*

Cromwell *
GB   1970   141m   Technicolor   Panavision
Columbia/Irving Allen (Andrew Donally)
An account of the rise of Cromwell to power, the execution of Charles 1, and the Civil War.
Disappointingly dull schoolbook history, with good production values but glum handling.
wd Ken Hughes ph Geoffrey Unsworth m Frank Cordell pd John Stoll
☆ Richard Harris, Alec Guinness, Robert Morley, Dorothy Tutin, Frank Finlay, Timothy Dalton, Patrick Wymark, Patrick Magee, Nigel Stock, Charles Gray, Michael Jayston, Anna Cropper, Michael Goodliffe
   'It tries to combine serious intentions with the widest kind of popular appeal and falls unhappily between the two. It will offend the purists and bore the kiddies.' – *Brenda Davies*
   'Shakespeare spoiled us for this sort of thing. We wait for great speeches and witty remarks, for

rage and poetry, and we get dedicated stodginess.' – *Pauline Kael*
🎩 costumes (Nino Novarese)
♗ Frank Cordell

Cronica di una Morte Annunciata: see *Chronicle of a Death Foretold*

Cronos **
Mexico   1992   92m   Foto-Kem
October Films/Iguana/Ventana (Arthur H. Gorson)
An antique dealer finds a 400-year-old clockwork device containing a blood-sucking insect that confers immortality upon its user; but a rich, ruthless, dying industrialist is determined to obtain it for himself.
Deft, imaginative, original and gruesome variation on the vampire myth, stylishly directed and conjuring an atmosphere of genuine horror.
wd Guillermo del Toro ph Guillermo Navarro pd Tolita Figueroa ed Raul Davalos
☆ Federico Luppi, Ron Perlman, Claudio Brook, Margarita Isabel, Tamara Shanath
   'With spot-on pulp dialogue, simple, poetic imagery and gothic sound-effects, this is nothing short of a near-masterpiece.' – *Steve Beard, Empire*
   'Audaciously reinvents the vampire legend in order to deliver a completely satisfying film that is both entertaining and intelligent in a manner that few contemporary horror films are.' – *Michael Lucas, Guardian*

The Crook: see *Le Voyou*

The Crooked Billet
GB   1929   82m   bw
Gainsborough (Michael Balcon)
Spies and detectives converge on an old inn where documents are hidden.
Fairly unwatchable now, this once-entertaining melodrama was shot as a silent and had sound clumsily added.
w Angus Macphail play Dion Titherage
d Adrian Brunel ph Claude McDonnell
md Louis Levy ed Ian Dalrymple
☆ Carlyle Blackwell, Madeleine Carroll, Miles Mander, Gordon Harker
   'The subject never appealed to me – it was a conventional crook melodrama – and I had raging toothache during most of the shooting.' – *Adrian Brunel*

The Crooked Road
GB/Yugoslavia   1964   92m   bw
Agro/Triglav
An American journalist plans to expose as a crook the dictator of a small Balkan state, but finds himself framed for murder.
Lugubrious and too-talkative melodrama of political intrigue.
w J. Garrison, Don Chaffey novel The Big Story by Morris West d Don Chaffey
☆ Robert Ryan, Stewart Granger, Marius Goring, Nadia Gray, Catherine Woodville, George Coulouris

The Crooked Way
US   1949   87m   bw
Benedict Bogeaus
An amnesiac ex-veteran finds that he was once a minor gangster.
Predictable thick ear with film noir aspirations.
w Richard Landau play No Blade Too Sharp by Robert Monroe d Robert Florey ph John Alton
☆ John Payne, Sonny Tufts, Ellen Drew, Rhys Williams

The Crooked Web
US   1955   77m   bw
Columbia (Sam Katzman)
A restaurant owner is lured into a scheme to recover buried Nazi gold from Germany, but finds it is a means of arresting him on an old murder charge.
Ingenious but somehow uninteresting puzzle melodrama.
w Lou Breslow d Nathan Juran
☆ Frank Lovejoy, Richard Denning, Mari Blanchard

'A sweet concoction of 70's soul and fun, fun, fun!'
Crooklyn *
US 1994 114m colour
Electric Triangle/40 Acres and a Mule/Child Hoods
(Spike Lee)

▣ ▦ ◷ ◉ ◎

In Harlem during the 1970s, an out-of-work jazz musician and his wife, a teacher, struggle to bring up their five unruly children.
A semi-autobiographical film, which may explain why it is as undisciplined as the family at its centre, as if the director were too close to his material to control it; much of the action is seen through the eyes of a 10-year-old girl, including a long sequence, shown in squeezed images, in which she is sent away to relatives; it has moments of vitality in which all the elements cohere.
w Joie Susannah Lee, Cinqué Lee, Spike Lee
d Spike Lee ph Arthur Jafa m Terence Blanchard
pd Wynn Thomas ed Barry Alexander Brown
☆ Alfre Woodard, Delroy Lindo, Spike Lee, Zelda Harris, Carlton Williams, Sharif Rashed
'The juke-box principle of film-making was never applied so enthusiastically, with practically every scene anchored by a song. But it's all too tempting to shut your eyes and pretend you're listening to The Best Soul Album Ever, since the film's dramatic content is so confused.' – *Jonathan Romney, Guardian*

Crooks and Coronets
GB 1969 106m Technicolor
Warner Seven Arts/Herman Cohen

▦

US title: *Sophie's Place*
American gangsters plan to rob a stately home but are taken over by the dowager in charge.
Overlong and mainly flatulent comedy, with a good climax involving a vintage plane.
wd Jim O'Connolly ph Desmond Dickinson
m Patrick John Scott
☆ Telly Savalas, Edith Evans, Warren Oates, Nicky Henson, Cesar Romero, Harry H. Corbett

Crooks Anonymous *
GB 1962 87m bw
Anglo Amalgamated (Nat Cohen)
A pretty thief joins an organization for reforming criminals, but is tempted again … and so are they.
Amusingly devised and plotted minor comedy with an exceptional cast.
w Jack Davies, Henry Blyth d Ken Annakin
ph Ernest Steward m Muir Mathieson, Henry Martin
☆ Leslie Phillips, Stanley Baxter, Wilfrid Hyde-White, Julie Christie, James Robertson Justice, Robertson Hare, Charles Lloyd Pack

Crooks in Cloisters
👥 GB 1963 97m Technicolor Scope
ABPC
Forgers pose as monks but are reformed by the country life.
Busy comedy full of familiar faces; perhaps a small cut above the Carry Ons.
w Mike Watts d Jeremy Summers
☆ Ronald Fraser, Barbara Windsor, Grégoire Aslan, Bernard Cribbins, Davy Kaye, Wilfrid Brambell

Crooks in Clover: see *Penthouse*

Crooks' Tour *
GB 1940 84m bw
British National (John Corfield)
English tourists are mistaken for spies by Nazis in Baghdad.
Amusing vehicle for two comic actors who excelled at portraying the English abroad.
w John Watt, Max Kester radio serial Sidney Gilliat, Frank Launder d John Baxter ph James Wilson m Kennedy Russell
☆ Basil Radford, Naunton Wayne, Greta Gynt, Abraham Sofaer, Gordon McLeod
'Their bland imperturability in the face of extraordinary circumstances provides no little fun.' – *Picture Show*

Crooner
US 1932 64m bw
Warner
A radio singer who is more than something of a prig gets his come-uppance.
Would-be satire with more bore than bite.

w Charles Kenyon story Rian James d Lloyd Bacon
☆ David Manners, Ann Dvorak, Ken Murray, William Janney, Eddie Nugent, J. Carrol Naish
'A general slap at that ether pest who for a time held popular sway … but there is no sympathy for anybody in the cast.' – *Variety*

The Cross and the Switchblade
US 1970 106m colour
Fox/Dick Ross Associates

▦

A minister sets out to rid his New York streets of delinquents.
Arrant but alas unconvincing do-goodery.
w Don Murray, James Bonnet d Don Murray
☆ Pat Boone, Erik Estrada, Jackie Giroux, Jo-Ann Robinson

Cross Country
Canada 1983 104m colour
Filmline/Yellowbill
The boyfriend of a murdered girl finds himself being driven west at gunpoint by a mad nymphomaniac and her protector.
No-holds-barred 'adult' thriller whose excesses become risible.
w Logan N. Danforth (John Hunter) d Paul Lynch
☆ Richard Beymer, Nina Axelrod, Michael Ironside, Brent Carver

'The true story about the woman who wrote *The Yearling'*
Cross Creek *
US 1983 122m Technicolor
EMI/Radnitz/Ritt (Robert B. Radnitz)

▦

In 1928 Marjorie Kinnan Rawlings leaves her journalist husband and goes to live in the Florida backwoods, where she hopes to write a Gothic romance.
Elongated study of writer's block (though the subject did eventually write The Yearling). Altogether too typical of its producer and director – and too slow – to hold much surprise or interest.
w Dalene Young memoirs Marjorie Kinnan Rawlings d Martin Ritt ph John A. Alonzo
m Leonard Rosenman pd Walter Scott Herndon
☆ Mary Steenburgen, Rip Torn, Peter Coyote, Dana Hill, Ike Eisenmann, Alfre Woodard
'The landscapes are attractive, but much too lushly filmed with lyrical inserts in which the wonders of the bayou are contemplated. Good performances fail to mask the fact that the characters are stereotypes from start to finish.' – *Tom Milne, MFB*
'Everything is lighted to look holy, and when the score isn't shimmering and burnishing, nature is twittering.' – *New Yorker*
⌂ Rip Torn, Alfre Woodard, Leonard Rosenman

Cross My Heart *
US 1945 83m bw
Paramount (Harry Tugend)
A romantic girl confesses to murder, is acquitted, and finds the real murderer.
Modest remake of True Confession (qv), with frenetic pace but not much style.
w Claude Binyon, Harry Tugend, Charles Schnee d John Berry ph Charles Lang Jnr m Robert Emmett Dolan
☆ Betty Hutton, Sonny Tufts, Michael Chekhov, Rhys Williams, Ruth Donnelly, Al Bridge, Howard Freeman, Iris Adrian

Cross My Heart
US 1987 90m DeLuxe
Universal (Lawrence Kasdan)

▦

As they begin to fall in love, a man and a woman are unable to be honest with each other on a date that first goes disastrously wrong and then miraculously right.
Slight romantic comedy that needed the injection of a little more pace and variation to hold an audience's attention; it has a certain charm, though.
w Armyan Bernstein, Gail Parent d Armyan Bernstein ph Thomas del Ruth m Bruce Broughton pd Lawrence G. Paull ed Mia Goldman
☆ Martin Short, Annette O'Toole, Paul Reiser, Joanna Kerns

Cross My Heart *
Canada 1990 105m colour
Belbo (Ludi Boeken, Jacques Fansten)

▣ ▦

original title: *La Fracture du Myocarde*
Frightened of being sent to an orphanage, a 12-year-old boy tries to conceal the death of his mother.
Enjoyable comedy that stretches credulity at times but at least presents believable children living in a recognizable world.
wd Jacques Fansten ph Jean-Claude Saillier m Jean Marie Senia pd Gilbert Gagneux
☆ Sylvain Copans, Nicolas Parodi, Cecilia Rouaud, Lucie Blossier, Delphine Gouttman
'Delightfully offbeat first feature … Few will remain unmoved.' – *Variety*

Cross of Iron *
GB/West Germany 1977 133m Technicolor
EMI-Rapid Film/Terra Filmkunst (Wolf. C. Hartwig)

▣ ▦ ◉

Militarily and emotionally at the end of its tether, a German battalion is decimated while fighting the Russians in 1943.
Painful to follow, occasionally beautiful to watch, this quite horrid film offers too much opportunity for its director to wallow in unpleasant physical details, and its main plot of bitter rivalry offers no relief.
w Julius J. Epstein, Herbert Asmodi novel *The Willing Flesh* by Willi Heinrich d Sam Peckinpah ph John Coquillon m Ernest Gold
☆ James Coburn, James Mason, Maximilian Schell, David Warner, Klaus Löwitsch, Senta Berger
'Morally dubious but technically brilliant.' – *Michael Billington, Illustrated London News*

The Cross of Lorraine *
US 1944 91m bw
MGM (Edwin Knopf)
In a German camp for French prisoners, an escape leads to a rising by local villagers.
Standard war propaganda piece, made with enthusiasm on unconvincing sets.
w Michael Kanin, Ring Lardner Jnr, Alexander Esway, Robert Andrews d Tay Garnett ph Sidney Wagner m Bronislau Kaper
☆ Gene Kelly, Jean-Pierre Aumont, Cedric Hardwicke, Peter Lorre, Joseph Calleia, Richard Whorf, Hume Cronyn
'Half a football team worked on the story, yet except for a foolish coda it is one of the most edged, well-characterized, and naturally cinematic scripts of the year.' – *James Agee*

Cross Shot
Italy 1976 95m colour
P.A.C. (Teodoro Agrimi)
A quick-tempered police inspector, a sensational journalist and a gangster attempt to track down a young cop-killer.
Portentous, studiedly slow thriller with nothing to recommend it, not even Lee J. Cobb (in a minor role, despite his star billing) as a blind Mafioso.
w Lucio de Caro, Piero Poggio, Maurizio Mengoni, Dardano Sacchetti, Ted Rusoff story Lucio de Caro d Stelvo Massi ph Mario Vulpiani m Piero Pintucci pd Carlo Leva ed Mauro Bonanni
☆ John Saxon, Lee J. Cobb, Renzo Palmer, Rosanna Fratello, Antonella Lualdi, Lino Capolicchio

Crossed Swords: see *The Prince and the Pauper* (1977)

Crossed Swords
Italy/USA 1954 83m Pathécolor
Viva Films (J. Barrett Mahon, Vittorio Vassarotti)
original title: *Il Maestro di Don Giovanni*
The son of an Italian duke prevents an uprising.
A thin swashbuckler showing the perils of early co-production.
wd Milton Krims ph Jack Cardiff
☆ Errol Flynn, Gina Lollobrigida, Cesare Danova, Nadia Gray, Paola Mori

'Sensational? No, it's dynamite!'
Crossfire ****
US 1947 86m bw
RKO (Adrian Scott)

▦ ◷

A Jew is murdered in a New York hotel, and three soldiers are suspected.

Tense, talky thriller shot entirely at night with pretty full expressionist use of camera technique; notable for style, acting, experimentation, and for being the first Hollywood film to hit out at racial bigotry.
w John Paxton novel *The Brick Foxhole* by Richard Brooks d Edward Dmytryk ph J. Roy Hunt m Roy Webb
☆ Robert Young, Robert Mitchum, Robert Ryan, Gloria Grahame, Paul Kelly, Sam Levene, Jacqueline White, Steve Brodie
'Another murder story that holds its own with any on the basis of suspense and speed.' – *Richard Winnington*
⌂ best picture; John Paxton; Edward Dmytryk; Robert Ryan; Gloria Grahame

The Crossing
Australia 1990 92m colour
Beyond (Sue Seeary)

▦ ▦

A young man returns home from the city, hoping to marry the girl he left behind, and disrupts a small community.
Heavy-handed domestic melodrama that looks like an imitation of American films of teenage rebellion and unsatisfactory parent–child relationships.
w Ranald Allan d George Ogilvie ph Jeff Darling m Martin Armiger pd Igor Nay ed Henry Dangar
☆ Russell Crowe, Robert Mammone, Danielle Spencer, Emily Lumbers, Rodney Bell, Ben Oxenbould, Myles Collins

Crossing Delancey *
US 1988 97m DuArt
Warner (Michael Nozik)

▣ ▦ ◷

A bookshop manager vacillates between an author and a pickle manufacturer as a suitable lover.
Small but enjoyable celebration of the simple life.
w Susan Sandler play Susan Sandler d Joan Micklin Silver ph Theo Van de Sande m Paul Chihara, The Roches pd Dan Leigh ed Rick Shaine
☆ Amy Irving, Peter Riegert, Reizl Bozyk, Jeroen Krabbe, Sylvia Miles, George Martin, John Bedford Lloyd

The Crossing Guard *
US 1995 114m DeLuxe
Buena Vista/Miramax (Sean Penn, David S. Hamburger)

▣ ▦ ◷

An alcoholic jeweller plans to kill the man, just released from prison, who killed his daughter in a drunk-driving accident six years previously.
Grim, over-emphatic, slow-moving drama of loss and guilt, but one that elicts some good performances from the principals.
wd Sean Penn ph Vilmos Zsigmond m Jack Nitzsche, Joseph Vitarelli pd Michael Haller ed Jay Cassidy
☆ Jack Nicholson, David Morse, Anjelica Huston, Robin Wright, Piper Laurie, Richard Bradford, Robbie Robertson, John Savage
'A tough guy's weepie … It's a trademark of the tough guy's weepie, incidentally, that it takes emotion seriously, but only among people who fight against it, i.e. men. Women get paradoxically short shrift, because they're meant to be good at that stuff.' – *Adam Mars-Jones, Independent*

The Crossing of the Rhine *
France/Italy/West Germany 1960 125m bw
Franco-London-Gibe-Jonia-UFA (Ralph Baum)
original title: *Le Passage du Rhin*
Two French soldiers escape from the Germans in 1940 and after various adventures meet up again in Paris in 1945.
Two crowded plots and not a great deal of point emerge from this watchable war film full of conventional set-pieces.
w André Cayatte, Armand Jammot d André Cayatte ph Roger Fellous m Louiguy
☆ Charles Aznavour, Nicole Courcel, Georges Rivière, Cordula Trantow

Crossing the Line: see *The Big Man*

Crossplot
GB 1969 97m Eastmancolor
UA/Tribune (Robert S. Baker)
An advertising executive gets involved in a spy ring.

Old-fashioned, London-set amalgam of secret codes, disappearing bodies, helicopter attacks, and a finale frustrating the assassination of a statesman in Hyde Park.

w Leigh Vance d Alvin Rakoff ph Brendan J. Stafford m Stanley Black

☆ Roger Moore, Martha Hyer, Alexis Kanner, Francis Matthews, Bernard Lee

Crossroads **

Japan   1928   80m   bw   silent
Shochiku
original title: *Jujiro*

A woman kills her seducer. Her brother thinks he has killed a man and takes refuge with her, only to die of shock when he sees the man alive.

The only widely distributed Japanese silent film, this curious piece is fragmentarily told and will remind many of Rashomon with its mixture of flashbacks and dreams.

wd Teinosuke Kinugasa ph Kohei Sugiyama

☆ J. Bandoha, A. Tschihaya, Yujiko Ogawa, I. Sohma

Crossroads *

US   1942   84m   bw
MGM (Edwin Knopf)

A French diplomat who once lost his memory is blackmailed by crooks who claim he was once a criminal.

Smooth mystery melodrama adapted from the French film Carrefour.

w Guy Trosper story Howard Emmett Rogers, John Kafka d Jack Conway ph Joseph Ruttenberg m Bronislau Kaper

☆ William Powell, Hedy Lamarr, Basil Rathbone, Claire Trevor, Margaret Wycherly, Felix Bressart, Sig Rumann

'Well directed and acted with polish, delightful romantic moments breaking up the general atmosphere of excitement and suspense.' – *Picturegoer*

Crossroads

US   1986   96m   Technicolor
Delphi IV/Columbia (Mark Carliner)
▄▄ ◎～

Urged by a young musician, an old blues singer travels the South in search of his legendary companion's lost music.

Rather specialized and unsatisfactory road pic which loses its way well before the end.

w John Fusco d Walter Hill ph John Bailey m Ry Cooder ad Albert Heschong ed Freeman Davies

☆ Ralph Macchio, Joe Seneca, Jami Gertz, Joe Morton

'You can tell what's wrong with *Crossroads* when you try to describe it to friends. Half-way through the plot description, their eyes glaze over.' – *People*

Crosswinds

US   1951   93m   Technicolor
Paramount/Pine/Thomas

Treasure-hunting boatmen fall out in New Guinea.

Adequate outdoor thick ear; good value for money as the lower half of a double bill.

wd Lewis R. Foster

☆ John Payne, Rhonda Fleming, Forrest Tucker, Robert Lowery, Alan Mowbray, John Abbott

Crossworlds

US   1996   91m   colour
Trimark (Rupert Harvey, Lloyd Segan)
▄▄ ▄▄ ◎～

A youth is hunted by beings from another dimension, who want the crystal left to him by his father, which unlocks the boundaries between worlds.

Low-budget, brainless science-fiction; it displays a paucity of imagination, as well as a paunchy Hauer, looking uncomfortable in the role of an action hero.

w Raman Rao, Krishna Rao d Krishna Rao ph Christopher Walling m Christopher Beck pd Aaron Osborne ed Anita Brandt-Burgoyne

☆ Rutger Hauer, Josh Charles, Stuart Wilson, Andrea Roth, Perry Anzilotti, Richard McGregor, Jack Black

'He hates cheats.'

Croupier

GB/Ireland/France/Germany   1997   94m   colour
BFI/Little Bird/Tatfilm/Compagnie des Phares & Balises/La Sept/Channel4 (Jonathan Cavendish)

A would-be novelist and former croupier returns to working in a casino where he avoids the temptation to be dishonest.

Cool, impersonal thriller that keeps its distance from the events it shows, becoming a somewhat arid account of a man trapped in a world he understands but dislikes.

w Paul Mayersberg d Mike Hodges ph Mike Garfath m Simon Fisher Turner pd Jon Bunker ed Les Healey

☆ Clive Owen, Kate Hardie, Alex Kingston, Gina McKee, Nicholas Ball, Nick Reding, Alexander Morton

'Lurches from stylish tension and dry comedy to toe-curling awkwardness with perplexing regularity.' – *Tom Doyle, Empire*

'One of the niftiest noir character studies to have come along in a long time.' – *Andrew Sarris, New York Observer*

'Believe In Angels.'
'Darker than the bat.'

The Crow *

US   1994   101m   DeLuxe
Entertainment/Jeff Most/Edward R. Pressman
▄▄ ▄▄ ◎ ◎ ◎～

Accompanied by a crow, a rock guitarist returns from the dead to kill those responsible for the murders of him and his girlfriend.

Accomplished comic-book action which looks good but rarely takes flight, following an all-too-predictable pattern.

w David J. Schow, John Shirley comic book James O'Barr d Alex Proyas ph Dariusz Wolski m Graeme Revell pd Alex McDowell ed Dov Hoenig, Scott Smith visual effects Andrew Mason make-up Lance Anderson

☆ Brandon Lee, Ernie Hudson, Michael Wincott, Angel David, David Patrick Kelly, Rochelle Davis, Laurence Mason, Bai Ling, Tony Todd, Jon Polito

'A stunning work of visual style – the best version of a comic book universe I've seen.' – *Roger Ebert, Chicago Sun-Times*

'A seamless, pulsating, dazzlingly visual revenge fantasy that stands as one of the most effective live-actioners derived from a comic strip.' – *Todd McCarthy, Variety*

† Brandon Lee died in a shooting accident during filming. The film was completed using computer techniques of digital compositing, in which Lee's image was placed in scenes in which he did not appear, and his face substituted for that of his body double in some scenes. The sell-through video release included an on-camera interview with Lee made a few days before his death.

'Believe in the power of another…'

The Crow: City of Angels

GB/US   1996   86m   DeLuxe
Buena Vista/Bad Bird/Miramax/Dimension (Edward R. Pressman, Jeff Most)
▄▄ ▄▄ ◎ ◎ ◎～

A drowned man returns to life to revenge his, and his baby's, death at the hands of a gang of bikers.

Less sequel than a rehash of the original, but without its visual power or even narrative interest.

w David Goyer comic book James O'Barr d Tim Pope ph Jean Yves Escoffier m Graeme Revell pd Alex McDowell ed Michael N. Knue, Anthony Redman, Barry Dresner, Neil Eric Wenger

☆ Vincent Perez, Mia Kirshner, Richard Brooks, Vincent Castellanos, Ian Dury, Tracey Ellis, Thomas Jane, Iggy Pop

'Offers the usual fragmentary "visions" of apocalypse, all mashed together into an occult junkyard that makes an average horror-trash music video look like a model of coherence.' – *Owen Gleiberman, Entertainment Weekly*

† The British release had 20 feet of film cut.

The Crowd ***

US   1928   98m   bw   silent
MGM (King Vidor)
▄▄ ◎～

Episodes in the life of a city clerk.

A deliberately humdrum story, chosen to show that drama can exist in the lowliest surroundings, retains much of its original power, though some of the director's innovations have become clichés.

w King Vidor, John V. A. Weaver, Harry Behn d King Vidor ph Henry Sharp ad Cedric Gibbons, Arnold Gillespie ed Hugh Wynn

☆ James Murray, Eleanor Boardman, Bert Roach, Estelle Clark

'No picture is perfect, but this comes as near to reproducing reality as anything you have ever witnessed.' – *Photoplay*

⅋ King Vidor; Unique and Artistic Picture

The Crowd Roars *

US   1932   85m   bw
Warner

A star motor-racing driver tries to prevent his young brother from following in his footsteps.

Typical early Cagney vehicle, still spectacularly pacy but dated in its dialogue scenes.

w Kubec Glasmon, John Bright, Niven Busch d Howard Hawks ph Sid Hickox, John Stumar md Leo Forbstein

☆ James Cagney, Joan Blondell, Ann Dvorak, Eric Linden, Guy Kibbee, Frank McHugh, Regis Toomey

'A thin and uneventful story, but a majority of the footage is devoted to three stirring contests.' – *Variety*

'As so often Hawks seems bitter at the world men have created but respects those who have to attempt to live it to the full.' – *NFT, 1963*

'The story is not precisely exciting … the closing episode is the best, for it reveals a certain originality in having the injured automobile racers eager to continue the race in ambulances on the way to hospital.' – *Mordaunt Hall, New York Times*

† Remade in 1939 as *Indianapolis Speedway*.

The Crowd Roars *

US   1938   90m   bw
MGM (Sam Zimbalist)

A young boxer becomes involved with the underworld.

Standard star vehicle with efficient trimmings.

w Thomas Lennon, George Bruce, George Oppenheimer d Richard Thorpe ph John Seitz m Edward Ward

☆ Robert Taylor, Frank Morgan, Edward Arnold, Maureen O'Sullivan, William Gargan, Frank Craven, Jane Wyman, Lionel Stander, Nat Pendleton

'Exciting melodrama with plenty of ring action, some plausible romance and several corking good characterizations.' – *Variety*

† Remade as *Killer McCoy*.

The Crowded Day

GB   1954   82m   bw
Advance

Problems of five assistants in a department store during the Christmas rush.

Naïve little portmanteau which suited its purpose.

w Talbot Rothwell d John Guillermin

☆ Joan Rice, John Gregson, Freda Jackson, Patricia Marmont, Josephine Griffin, Sonia Holm, Rachel Roberts, Thora Hird, Dora Bryan, Edward Chapman, Sid James, Richard Wattis

The Crowded Sky

US   1960   104m   Technicolor
Warner (Michael Garrison)

As two planes fly unwittingly towards each other, the passengers muse on their personal problems. An emergency landing averts total disaster.

The format goes back as far as Friday the Thirteenth, and forward to Airport 75, but this was in fact a cut-rate rehash of The High and the Mighty, with dull characters and insufficiently tense handling, not to mention a second team cast.

w Charles Schnee d Joseph Pevney ph Harry Stradling m Leonard Rosenman

☆ Dana Andrews, Rhonda Fleming, Efrem Zimbalist Jnr, John Kerr, Anne Francis, Keenan Wynn, Troy Donahue, Joe Mantell, Patsy Kelly

Crows and Sparrows *

China   1949   113m   bw
Peak Film Industries (Xia Yunhu, Ren Zongde)
original title: *Wuya Yu Maque*

Preparing to flee from the victorious Red Army, a landlord decides to sell his house and evict his tenants.

Lively slice-of-Chinese-life, made just before the Communist revolution.

w Shen Fu, Xu Tao, Zhao Dan, Lin Gu, Chen Baichen, Zheng Junli d Zheng Junli ph Miao Zhenhua, Hu Zhenhua md Wang Yunjie

☆ Zhao Dan, Wu Yin, Sun Daoling, Shangguan Yunzhu, Wei Heling, Li Tianji, Huang Zongying, Wang Pei

'What Some Hearts Desire They Must Possess.'
'Arthur Miller's Timeless Tale Of Truth On Trial.'

The Crucible **

US   1996   123m   Technicolor
TCF (Robert A. Miller, David V. Picker)

In Salem in the 1690s, a young woman claims that the wife of the married man she loves is a witch.

Powerful historical drama of the power of superstition when allied to the processes of an inquisition, though it has lost some of its contemporary relevance along the way.

w Arthur Miller play Arthur Miller d Nicholas Hytner ph Andrew Dunn m George Fenton pd Lilly Kilvert ed Tariq Anwar

☆ Daniel Day-Lewis, Winona Ryder, *Paul Scofield*, Joan Allen, Bruce Davison, Rob Campbell, Jeffrey Jones, Peter Vaughan, Karron Graves, Charlaine Woodard, George Gaynes

'Still possesses the power to stir up wrenching emotion through its elemental crises and conflicts. But neither the establishing dramatic linchpin nor the final conversion of conscience is terribly convincing, leaving this pared-down rendition of the original work diminished in power and meaning as well.' – *Todd McCarthy, Variety*

⅋ Joan Allen; Arthur Miller
ⓥ Paul Schofield

Crucible of Terror

GB   1971   91m   Eastmancolor
Glendale (Tom Parkinson)
▄▄

An art dealer and his girlfriend visit a reclusive artist with a penchant for murdering his models and turning them into bronze statues.

Slow-moving and dreary drama, with cliché-ridden dialogue and dull direction.

w Ted Hooker, Tom Parkinson d Ted Hooker ph Peter Newbrook m Paris Rutherford ad Arnold Chapkis ed Maxine Julius

☆ Mike Raven, Mary Maude, James Bolam, Ronald Lacey, Melissa Stribling, John Arnatt, Beth Morris, Judy Matheson, Betty Alberge

'What You Can't Have, You Can't Resist.'

Cruel Intentions *

US   1999   95m   DeLuxe
Columbia/Original/Newmarket (Neal H. Moritz)
▄▄ ▄▄ ◎～

Annoyed at losing her boyfriend, a rich girl wagers that her stepbrother cannot seduce two virgins.

A teenage version of a novel about world-weary adults; the attitudes of ennui and malice are an awkward fit on the young cast (even though they look too old to be still at school), but it has a little more bite than most movies aimed at a teen audience.

wd Roger Kumble novel Les liaisons dangereuses by Choderlos de Laclos ph Theo Van de Sande m Edward Shearmur pd Jon Gary Steele ed Jeff Freeman

☆ Sarah Michelle Gellar, Ryan Phillippe, Reese Witherspoon, Selma Blair, Louise Fletcher, Joshua Jackson, Eric Mabius, Sean Patrick Thomas, Swoosie Kurtz, Christine Baranski

'Nasty, profane and wickedly entertaining for the most part.' – *Emanuel Levy, Variety*

† Other recent films based on the novel include *Dangerous Liaisons* and *Valmont* (qqv).

Cruel Passion

GB   1977   97m   Eastmancolor
Target International (Chris Boger)
▄▄

Two sisters are sent away from a convent school: one becomes an aristocrat's mistress, the other is raped by him.

Good-looking but tedious and downbeat period drama, which owes little to de Sade and more to the British sex film industry of the 70s; its scenes of lesbian nuns, brothels and rape are not likely to find favour with the dirty macintosh brigade, and there is little to interest anyone else.

w Ian Cullen, Chris Boger, Peter Delfgou novel Justine by the Marquis de Sade d Chris Boger ph Roger Deakins pd Tony Curtis ed Peter Delfgou

☆ Koo Stark, Martin Potter, Lydia Lisle, Katherine Kath, Hope Jackman, Louis Ife, Barry McGinn

The Cruel Sea **

GB 1953 126m bw
Ealing (Leslie Norman)
📀 ▤

Life and death on an Atlantic corvette during World War II.

Competent transcription of a bestselling book, cleanly produced and acted; a huge box-office success.

w Eric Ambler *novel* Nicholas Monsarrat d Charles Frend ph Gordon Dines m Alan Rawsthorne ad Jim Morahan ed Peter Tanner
☆ *Jack Hawkins*, Donald Sinden, Stanley Baker, John Stratton, Denholm Elliott, John Warner, Bruce Seton, Virginia McKenna, Moira Lister, June Thorburn, Alec McCowen

'This is a story of the battle of the Atlantic, a story of an ocean, two ships and a handful of men. The men are the heroes. The heroines are the ships. The only villain is the sea – the cruel sea – that man has made even more cruel.' – *opening narration*
'One is grateful nowadays for a film which does not depict war as anything but a tragic and bloody experience, and it is this quality which gives the production its final power to move.' – *John Gillett*
'Sensitivity, faithfulness, and almost inevitable tedium.' – *Time Out, 1984*
⚖ Eric Ambler

Cruise Missile

Germany/Italy/Spain 1978 90m colour
Noble Productions/Echberg Film (Ika Panajotovic)
An American and Russian agent team up with the local police to prevent a terrorist blowing up a peace conference in Iran.

Substandard thriller, in which the Iranian police are portrayed as wonderful.

w Clarke Reynolds, Elio Romano d Leslie H. Martinson ph Claudio Catozzo m Alberto Baldan ed Enzio Monachesi
☆ Peter Graves, Curt Jurgens, Michael Dante, John Carradine

Cruisin' Down the River

US 1953 79m colour
Columbia
A night-club singer inherits a riverboat.

Slim excuse for a musical variety bill.

w Blake Edwards, Richard Quine d Richard Quine
☆ Dick Haymes, Audrey Totter, Billy Daniels, Cecil Kellaway, the Bell Sisters, Erze Ivan

Cruising

US 1980 106m Technicolor
Lorimar (Jerry Weintraub)
📀 ▤

A New York cop becomes degraded in his search among homosexuals for a sadistic killer.

Alleged thriller with phoney pretensions and repellent detail.

wd William Friedkin ph James Contner m Jack Nitzsche
☆ Al Pacino, Paul Sorvino, Karen Allen, Richard Cox, Don Scardino, Joe Spinell

'Like any approach to the bizarre, it's fascinating for about fifteen minutes. After that, it suffers from the same boring repetition that makes porno so uninteresting generally.' – *Variety*

Crumb ***

US 1994 120m colour
Artificial Eye/Superior (Lynn O'Donnell, Terry Zwigoff)
📀 ▤ ◎. ⊚

Robert Crumb, celebrated underground cartoonist and creator of Fritz the Cat and Mr Natural, discusses his life and work and plays ragtime and jazz from his vast collection of 78 rpm records as he leaves California to settle in France; his mother and brother and other cartoonists are also interviewed.

Fascinating documentary on an artist called 'the Breughel of the 20th century' by one interviewee, critic Robert Hughes, seen in context with his somewhat dysfunctional brothers who, also talented, have failed to come to terms with society in the way that he has. (Charles, his older brother, committed suicide a year after being filmed.)

d Terry Zwigoff ph Maryse Alberti ed Victor Livingston

☆ Robert Crumb, Charles Crumb, Maxon Crumb, Aline Kominsky, Dana Crumb, Beatrice Crumb

'By turns gripping and appalling, *Crumb* is one of the most complete pictures of an artist ever made.' – *Clark Collis, Empire*

'Wonders to dazzle the human imagination – in a flaming love story set in titanic world conflict!'

The Crusades **

US 1935 127m bw
Paramount/Cecil B. de Mille
Spurred by his wife Berengaria, Richard the Lionheart sets off on his holy wars.

Heavily tapestried medieval epic, spectacular sequences being punctuated by wodges of uninspired dialogue. A true de Mille pageant.

w Harold Lamb, Waldemar Young, Dudley Nichols d Cecil B. de Mille ph Victor Milner m Rudolph Kopp sp Gordon Jennings
☆ Henry Wilcoxon, Loretta Young, C. Aubrey Smith, Ian Keith, Katherine de Mille, Joseph Schildkraut, Alan Hale, C. Henry Gordon, George Barbier, Montagu Love, Lumsden Hare, William Farnum, Hobart Bosworth, Pedro de Cordoba, Mischa Auer

'Mr de Mille's evangelical films are the nearest equivalent today to the glossy German colour prints which decorated mid-Victorian bibles. There is the same lack of a period sense, the same stuffy horsehair atmosphere of beards and whiskers, and, their best quality, a childlike eye for detail.' – *Graham Greene*
'Cinema addicts by now have some idea what to expect in a de Mille version of the Holy Wars. *The Crusades* should fulfil all expectations. As a picture it is historically worthless, didactically treacherous, artistically absurd. None of these defects impairs its entertainment value. It is a hundred-million-dollar sideshow which has at least three features to distinguish it from the long line of previous de Mille extravaganzas. It is the noisiest; it is the biggest; it contains no baths.' – *Time*
'Probably only de Mille could make a picture like this and get away with it. It's long, and slow, and the story is not up to some of his previous films, but the production has sweep and spectacle.' – *Variety*
⚖ Victor Milner

Crush

New Zealand 1992 96m colour
Metro/Hibiscus/NZFC/NFU/NZ On Air/Movie Partners (Bridget Ikin)
📀 ▤

While she is in hospital recovering from a car crash, a female journalist is angered to discover that her best friend has begun an affair with a novelist she planned to interview.

A bisexual revenge thriller that attempts to expose bourgeois values, but fails to convince.

w Alison Maclean, Anne Kennedy d Alison Maclean ph Dion Beebe m JPS Experience, Antony Partos pd Meryl Cronin ed John Gilbert
☆ Marcia Gay Harden, William Zappa, Donogh Rees, Caitlin Bossley, Pete Smith, Jon Brazier

'Often as murky as the bubbling New Zealand mud springs Maclean cuts to in order to underscore the otherworldly ambience.' – *Empire*

The Crush

US 1993 89m Technicolor
Warner/Morgan Creek (James G. Robinson)
📀 ▤ ◎.

A teenage girl develops a crush on her new neighbour, a writer, and becomes violent when he ignores her advances.

Predictable and unintelligent thriller, recycling familiar themes in an uninspired fashion.

wd Alan Shapiro ph Bruce Surtees m Graeme Revell pd Michael Bolton ed Ian Crafford
☆ Cary Elwes, Alicia Silverstone, Jennifer Rubin, Amber Benson, Kurtwood Smith, Gwynyth Walsh, Matthew Walker

'Another by-the-numbers thriller longer on suspense than brains. Silly and predictable.' – *Variety*

Crusoe *

US 1988 94m Technicolor
Virgin/Island Pictures (Andrew Braunsberg)
▤

A slave-owner, shipwrecked on a desert island, makes friends with a cannibal.

Deft variation on the original familiar story.

w Walon Green, Christopher Logue *novel* Robinson Crusoe by Daniel Defoe d Caleb Deschanel ph Tom Pinter m Michael Kamen pd Velco Despotovic ed Humphrey Dixon
☆ Aidan Quinn, Elvis Payne, Richard Sharp, Colin Bruce, William Hootkins, Shane Rimmer, Jimmy Nail, Patrick Monkton, Chris Pitt, Ade Sapara

The Cry: see Il Grido

Cry Baby Killer

US 1958 62m bw
Roger Corman/AA
A gunman on the run barricades himself and hostages in a storeroom.

Modest second feature which served its purpose.

w Leo Gordon, Melvin Levy d Jus Addiss
☆ Jack Nicholson, Harry Lauter, Carolyn Mitchell, Brett Halsey

Cry Danger *

US 1951 79m bw
RKO/Olympic (Sam Wiesenthal, W. R. Frank)
▤

After serving five years for robbery, a man gets out on parole and clears his name.

Slick little slice of thick ear, very lively all round.

w William Bowers *story* Jerome Cady d Robert Parrish ph Joseph F. Biroc m Emil Newman, Paul Dunlap ad Richard Day
☆ Dick Powell, Rhonda Fleming, Richard Erdman, William Conrad, Regis Toomey, Jay Adler

Cry for Happy

US 1961 110m Eastmancolor
Cinemascope
Columbia (William Goetz)
Four navy cameramen in Japan help geishas to found an orphanage.

As bad as it sounds, a repellent mixture of sentiment and knockabout.

w Irving Brecher d George Marshall ph Burnett Guffey m George Duning
☆ Glenn Ford, Donald O'Connor, Miiko Taka, James Shigeta, Miyoshi Umeki, Joe Flynn, Howard St John

'Any film which expends most of its energies on a protracted joke about how far you can go with a geisha could hardly fail to be as charmless and witless as this.' – *MFB*

Cry Freedom **

GB 1987 158m colour Panavision
Marble Arch/Universal (Richard Attenborough)
📀 ▤ ◎. ⊚

South African journalist Donald Woods is forced to flee the country after attempting to investigate the death in custody of his friend the black activist Steve Biko.

Part thriller, part social conscience tract, the film has magnificent set-pieces typical of the director's work. However, it failed to satisfy either opponents or supporters of apartheid.

w John Briley d Richard Attenborough ph Ronnie Taylor m George Fenton, Jonas Gwangwa pd Stuart Craig
☆ Kevin Kline, Penelope Wilton, Denzel Washington, Alec McCowen, Kevin McNally, Zakes Mokae
⚖ Denzel Washington; music; song 'Cry Freedom' (m/ly George Fenton, Jonas Gwangwa)

A Cry from the Streets

GB 1958 100m bw
Film Traders (Ian Dalrymple)
📀

Episodes from the work of child welfare officers.

Mildly pleasing but unconvincing semi-documentary, with children competing with the star at scene-stealing.

w Vernon Harris *novel* The Friend in Need by Elizabeth Coxhead d Lewis Gilbert ph Harry Gilliam m Larry Adler
☆ Max Bygraves, Barbara Murray, Colin Petersen, Dana Wilson, Kathleen Harrison, Eleanor Summerfield, Mona Washbourne

Cry Havoc

US 1943 97m bw
MGM (Edwin Knopf)
War nurses are caught up in the Bataan retreat.

An all-woman cast adequately handles a stagey melodrama about a tragic situation.

w Paul Osborn *play* Proof thro' the Night by Allen R. Kenward d Richard Thorpe ph Karl Freund m Daniele Amfitheatrof
☆ Margaret Sullavan, Joan Blondell, Ann Sothern, Fay Bainter, Marsha Hunt, Ella Raines, Frances Gifford, Diana Lewis, Heather Angel, Connie Gilchrist

'A sincere fourth-rate film made from a sincere fifth-rate play.' – *James Agee*
'Its popularity will stem less from its probably factual record of nurses starving, sweating and dying in the beleaguered Philippine jungle than from the impressive all-woman cast which MGM has rounded up for the occasion.' – *Newsweek*

A Cry in the Dark *

Australia 1988 121m colour
Pathé/Evil Angels/Cannon International (Verity Lambert)
📀 ▤ ◎. ⊚ ⊙

A woman is tried for the murder of her baby daughter, who was carried off by a wild dog during a family camping expedition.

Skilful reconstruction of a sensational true-life court case.

w Robert Caswell, Fred Schepisi *book* Evil Angels by John Bryson d Fred Schepisi ph Ian Baker m Bruce Smeaton pd Wendy Dickson, George Liddle ed Jill Bilcock
☆ Meryl Streep, Sam Neill, Dale Reeves, David Hoflin, Jason Reason, Michael Wetter, Kane Barton, Trent Roberts, Brian Jones, Dorothy Alison

'May be the most quietly uncondescending film ever made about religious fundamentalists.' – *Peter Rainer, Los Angeles Herald Examiner*
⚖ Meryl Streep

A Cry in the Night

US 1956 75m bw
Warner/Jaguar (George C. Bertholon)
A peeping Tom, caught by a teenage couple, abducts the girl and threatens rape.

Odd little domestic thriller, with parents and police working together. Watchable, but a bit over the top.

w David Dortort *novel* Whit Masterson d Frank Tuttle ph John Seitz m David Buttolph
☆ Edmond O'Brien, Brian Donlevy, Natalie Wood, Raymond Burr, Richard Anderson, Irene Hervey, Anthony Caruso

Cry of the Banshee

GB 1970 87m Movielab
AIP (Gordon Hessler)
▤ ◎. ⊙

A 16th-century magistrate is cursed by a witch, who sends a devil in the form of a young man to destroy him.

Modest horror film which fails to do justice to its interesting plot.

w Tim Kelly, Christopher Wicking d Gordon Hessler ph John Coquillon m Les Baxter
☆ Vincent Price, Elisabeth Bergner, Patrick Mower, Essy Persson, Hugh Griffith, Hilary Dwyer, Sally Geeson

The Cry of the Black Wolves

West Germany 1972 90m colour
Hillenbrand (Gunter Eulan)
In Alaska, a fur-trapper is accused of killing the man who stole his dog-team.

Standard Western in an icy setting, complete with the bad guys in black hats.

w Kurt Nachmann, Rolf Olsen *story* Jack London d Harald Reinl ph Franz X. Lederle m Gerhard Heinz ad Rolf Zehetbauer, Herbert Strabel ed Eva Zeyn
☆ Ron Ely, Raimund Harmstorf, Gila von Weitershausen, Heinrich Schweiger

Cry of the City **

US 1948 96m bw
TCF (Sol C. Siegel)
A ruthless gangster on the run is pursued by a policeman who was once his boyhood friend.

Very well produced but relentlessly miserable New York thriller on the lines of Manhattan Melodrama and Angels with Dirty Faces.

w Richard Murphy *novel* The Chair for Martin Rome by Henry Helseth d Robert Siodmak ph Lloyd Ahern m Alfred Newman
☆ Victor Mature, Richard Conte, Mimi Aguglia, Shelley Winters, Tommy Cook, Fred Clark, Debra Paget

'When the city cries in a movie, it's with the desolate wail of police sirens and with rain-streaked sidewalks; but most of all with poetic justification.' – *Paul Taylor, Time Out, 1980*

The Cry of the Owl: see *Le Cri de Hibou*

Cry Terror **
US   1958   96m   bw
MGM/Andrew Stone, Virginia Stone
As security against ransom money being delivered, an airline bomber kidnaps a family.
Unabashed suspenser which screws panic situations as far as they will go and farther.
wd Andrew Stone *ph* Walter Strenge *m* Howard Jackson *m* Virginia Stone
☆ James Mason, Rod Steiger, Inger Stevens, Neville Brand, Angie Dickinson, Kenneth Tobey, Jack Klugman, Jack Kruschen
'The story is launched with dizzying speed and suspenseful pursuit that hardly relaxes until the final frame.' – *Variety*

Cry the Beloved Country *
GB   1951   96m   bw
London Films (Alan Paton)
⬛
US title: *African Fury*
In South Africa, a white farmer and a black preacher find friendship through linked family tragedies.
Well-intentioned, earnest, rather high-flown racial drama.
w Alan Paton *novel* Alan Paton *d* Zoltan Korda *ph* Robert Krasker *m* Raymond Gallois-Montbrun
☆ Canada Lee, Sidney Poitier, Charles Carson, Charles McRae, Joyce Carey, Geoffrey Keen, Michael Goodliffe, Edric Connor

Cry Vengeance
US   1954   81m   bw
Allied Artists (Lindsley Parsons)
⬛
An innocent man is released from jail and seeks vengeance against the man who framed him and killed his wife and child.
Adequate toughie with no particular flair.
w Warren Douglas, George Bricker *d* Mark Stevens *ph* William Sickner *m* Paul Dunlap
☆ Mark Stevens, Martha Hyer, Skip Homeier, Joan Vohs, Douglas Kennedy

Cry Wolf
US   1947   83m   bw
Warner (Henry Blanke)
A widow claims her husband's estate and finds his mysterious uncle very difficult to deal with…
Rather obvious old dark house mystery with a not very interesting solution, all relying too heavily on star performances.
w Catherine Turney *novel* Marjorie Carleton *d* Peter Godfrey *ph* Carl Guthrie *m* Franz Waxman
☆ Barbara Stanwyck, Errol Flynn, Geraldine Brooks, Richard Basehart, Helene Thimig

Cry Wolf
GB   1980   31m   bw
Picture Partnership/Paramount
A scientist accidentally imbibes a canine serum and turns into a werewolf.
Flattish comedy which is mainly indistinguishable from the low-budget British shockers it satirizes, but manages a few good moments.
w Stan Hey *d* Leszek Burzynski *ph* Robert Krasker
☆ Paul Maxwell, Rosalind Ayres, Stephen Greif

Cry-Baby
US   1990   85m   DeLuxe
UIP/Imagine Entertainment (Rachel Talalay)
⬛ ▬ ⬳ 🎧
A delinquent rock 'n' roll singer falls in love with an upper-class girl.
Kitsch celebration of the early 60s that soon grows tedious.
wd John Waters *ph* David Insley *m* Patrick Williams *pd* Vincent Peranio *ad* Delores Deluxe *ed* Janice Hampton
☆ Johnny Depp, Amy Locane, Susan Tyrrell, Polly Bergen, Iggy Pop, Ricki Lake, Traci Lords, Kim McGuire, Darren E. Burrows

Crying Freeman
France/Canada   1995   101m   CFI color
Davis/Ozla/Brian Yuzna/Toei (Samuel Hadida, Brian Yuzna)
⬛
An enigmatic hitman, who weeps for his victims, travels to Vancouver to eliminate a Japanese

gangster and a female artist who witnessed his murders.
Slick transfer to live action of a comic-book hero, with some stylish action sequences.
w Christophe Gans, Thierry Casals *comic book* Kazuo Koike, Ryoichi Ikegami *d* Christophe Gans *ph* Thomas Burstyn *m* Pat O'Hearn *pd* Douglas Higgins, Alex McDowell *ed* David Wu, Chris Roth
☆ Mark Dacascos, Julie Condra Douglas, Tcheky Karyo, Rae Dawn Chong, Byron Mann, Masaya Kato, Yoko Shimada, Mako
'A satisfying mix of smooth Asian chop-socky and smooth Western tech wizardry.' – *Variety*

Crying Freeman, Chapter One: Portrait of a Killer (dubbed)
Japan   1992   50m   colour
Toei (Shoko Takahashi, Akira Sasaki, Tomirou Kuriyama)
⬛
A 29-year-old Japanese artist who witnessed a Japanese assassin, working for the Chinese Mafia, kill three people awaits her own death at his hands.
A gore-filled cartoon for an adult audience that enjoys indifferent animation, sex and violence.
w Higashi Shimizu *d* Daisuke Nishio *ph* Hisao Shirai *m* Hiroaki Yoshino *ad* Mitsutaka Nakamura *ed* Shigeru Nishiyama
☆ Featuring Voices of Stephen Tremblay, Edita Brychta, Vincent Marzello, Bob Sherman, Burt Kwouk

Crying Freeman, Chapter Three: Retribution (dubbed)
Japan   1992   50m   colour
Toei (Akira Sasaki, Tomirou Kuriyama)
⬛
Crying Freeman finds himself confronting a group of African terrorists, while his wife gains a mystical sword.
The mixture as before: rudimentary animation and comic strip heroics, featuring much sudden and bloody death.
w Kazuo Koike, Toichi Ikegami *d* Johei Matsuura *ph* Yoichi Takanashi *m* Hiroaki Yoshino *ad* Tomoshi Urushibana *ed* Shigeru Nishiyama
☆ Featuring Voices of Stephen Tremblay, Edita Brychta, John Baddeley, Rosemary Miller, Deborah Weston

Crying Freeman, Chapter Two: The Enemy Within (dubbed)
Japan   1992   50m   colour
Toei (Shoko Takahashi, Akira Sasaki, Tomirou Kuriyama)
⬛
A Japanese hitman, who cries whenever he kills, suspects that the élite corps of killers he commands for the Chinese Mafia contains a traitor.
Another gore-filled cartoon for an adult audience that enjoys indifferent animation, sex and violence.
w Kazuo Koike, Toichi Ikegami *d* Nishizawa Nobukata *ph* Yoshijuki Tamagawa *m* Hiroaki Yoshino *ed* Shigeru Nishiyama
☆ Featuring Voices of Stephen Tremblay, Edita Brychta, Vincent Marzello, John Baddeley

'Desire Is A Danger Zone.'

The Crying Game ***
GB   1992   112m   Metrocolor   Panavision
Palace/Channel 4/Eurotrustees/NDF/British Screen (Stephen Woolley)
⬛ ▬ ⬳ 🎧
An IRA gunman makes friends with a black British soldier who is taken hostage and, after the soldier's death, goes to London where he falls for the man's lover.
Complex and brilliantly successful examination of matters of identity and gender.
wd Neil Jordan *m* Ian Wilson *m* Anne Dudley *pd* Jim Clay *ed* Kant Pan
☆ Stephen Rea, Miranda Richardson, Forest Whitaker, Jim Broadbent, Ralph Brown, Adrian Dunbar, Jaye Davidson, Tony Slattery
'An astonishingly good and daring film.' – *Variety*
'Every so often, a "little" film hits the collective heart. *The Crying Game* is one of these, because it shows that a man is never so naked as when he reveals his secret self.' – *Richard Corliss, Time*
🏆 Neil Jordan (as writer)
🏆 best picture; Neil Jordan (as director); Kant Pan; Stephen Rea; Jaye Davidson

Crypt of the Living Dead
US   1972   83m   Metrocolor   Scope
Golden Era/Coast Industries (Lou Shaw)
GB title: *Vampire Woman*
A female vampire comes back to life after her tomb is opened.
Uninteresting low-budget horror that fails to raise a shiver.
w Lou Shaw *d* Ray Danton *ph* Juan Gelpi *m* Phillip Lambro *ad* Juan Alberto *ed* David Rawlins
☆ Andrew Prine, Mark Damon, Patty Sheppard, Teresa Gimpera, Ihsan Genik, Mariano Rey, Frank Brana
'A dismal sortie into sanguineous legend.' – *Sight and Sound*

The Crystal Ball *
US   1943   82m   bw
UA/Richard Blumenthal
A failed beauty contestant becomes a fortune teller and is involved in a land swindle.
Pleasant comedy with fanciful moments, ending with a pie-throwing contest.
w Virginia Van Upp *d* Elliott Nugent *ph* Leo Tover *m* Victor Young
☆ Paulette Goddard, Ray Milland, Gladys George, Virginia Field, Cecil Kellaway, William Bendix, Ernest Truex

Crystal Heart
US   1987   103m   Technicolor
New World/Izaro/Eagle (Carlosa Vasallo)
⬛
A young musician, who has to live isolated in a plastic bubble, falls in love with a rock singer.
Dull and sentimental romantic drama intercut with a succession of uninspired music videos of routine songs; its chief interest is in observing Tawny Kitaen's succession of curious hairstyles and outfits.
w Linda Shayne *story* Alberto Vazquez-Figueroa *d* Gil Bettman *ph* Alexander Ulloa *m* Joel Goldsmith *pd* Jose Maria Alarcon *ed* Nicholas Wentworth
☆ Tawny Kitaen, Lee Curreri, Lloyd Bochner, Simon Andreu, May Heatherly, Lagena Lookabill, Marina Saura

Cuba
US   1979   122m   Technicolor
UA/Alex Winitsky, Arlene Sellers
▬
Upper-crust characters are caught in Havana when the Castro revolution starts.
Aimless romantic melodrama which gets absolutely nowhere and might have been better played in the Casablanca vein.
w Charles Wood *d* Richard Lester *ph* David Watkin *m* Patrick Williams *pd* Gil Parrando
☆ Sean Connery, Brooke Adams, Jack Weston, Hector Elizondo, Denholm Elliott, Martin Balsam, Chris Sarandon

Cuba Si! *
France   1961   58m   bw
Films de la Pléiade
A documentary on the Cuban revolution and Castro's rise to power.
Remarkable and influential at the time for its use of techniques which are now the commonplaces of television, this documentary still has its flashes of interest.
m E. G. Mantici, J. Calzada *ed* Eva Zora *wd/ph* Chris Marker
'An eloquent, personal record of history in the making.' – *Georges Sadoul*

Cuban Love Song
US   1931   86m   bw
MGM (Albert Lewin)
A marine on leave in Cuba falls in love; years later he returns to retrieve his illegitimate child, whose mother has died.
Pathetic musical melodrama which did not advance its singing star's film career.
w John Lynch *d* W. S. Van Dyke *ph* Harold Rosson *m* Charles Maxwell *m/ly* various
☆ Lawrence Tibbett, Lupe Velez, Jimmy Durante, Ernest Torrence, Karen Morley, Louise Fazenda
'Tibbett may be a sensation on the concert stage, but it's not the same in pictures.' – *Variety*

Cuban Pete
US   1946   61m ·bw
Universal (Will Cowan)
A Cuban orchestra leader comes to New York.
Flatfooted second feature.
w Robert Presnell Snr, M. Coates Webster *d* Jean Yarbrough
☆ Desi Arnaz, Joan Fulton, Beverly Simmons, Don Porter
'Dull pace and few chuckles.' – *Variety*

Cube *
Canada   1997   90m   colour
Trimark/Cineplex Odeon/Cube Libre (Mehra Meh, Betty Orr)
⬛ ⬳
Six people find themselves lost in a dangerous maze of interlocking metal boxes.
Teasing low-budget science-fiction movie that makes the most of its puzzling qualities.
w Vincenzo Natali, Andre Bijelic, Graeme Manson *d* Vincenzo Natali *ph* Derek Rogers *m* Mark Korven *pd* Jasna Stefanovic *ed* John Sanders *sp* CORE Digital Pictures
☆ Maurice Dean, Nicole deBoer, Nicky Guadagni, David Hewlett, Wayne Robson, Andrew Miller, Julian Richings
'Brilliant set design and smart plotting are let down by pedestrian dialogue.' – *Ken Eisner, Variety*

A Cuckoo in the Nest *
GB   1933   85m   bw
Gaumont (Ian Dalrymple, Angus MacPhail)
A newlywed husband is forced to spend a night at an inn with an old flame pretending to be his wife.
Classic Aldwych farce with the stage company in excellent form; directorial style on the stagey side.
w Ben Travers, A. R. Rawlinson *play* Ben Travers *d* Tom Walls *ph* Glen MacWilliams *ad* Alfred Junge *ed* Helen Lewis
☆ Ralph Lynn, Tom Walls, Yvonne Arnaud, Mary Brough, Veronica Rose, Gordon James, Cecil Parker, Roger Livesey, Robertson Hare
† Remade 1955 as *Fast and Loose*.

The Cuckoos
US   1930   90m   bw (Technicolor sequences)
RKO
Two tramps become fortune tellers.
The most ambitiously staged, and probably the most popular of this team's gag marathons.
w Cy Woods *musical comedy* The Ramblers by Guy Bolton, Harry Ruby, Bert Kalmar *d* Paul Sloane
☆ Bert Wheeler, Robert Woolsey, Jobyna Howland, June Clyde, Hugh Trevor, Dorothy Lee
'It holds little between the laughs and doesn't need anything else.' – *Variety*

Cujo
US   1983   91m   CFI color
ITC/Sunn Classic/Taft (Daniel H. Blatt)
▬ ⬳ 🎧
A St Bernard dog is bitten by a rabies-infected bat, and becomes a vicious killer.
Not much of a basis for a horror film, and this is not much of a horror film.
w Don Carlos Dunaway, Lauren Currier *novel* Stephen King *d* Lewis Teague *ph* Jan de Bont *m* Charles Bernstein *pd* Guy Comtois *ed* Neil Travis
☆ Dee Wallace, Daniel Hugh Kelly, Danny Pintauro, Ed Lauter, Christopher Stone

Cul de Sac
GB   1966   111m   bw
Compton-Tekli (Gene Gutowski)
⬛ ▬
Two gangsters on the run take refuge in an old castle on a desolate Northumbrian island, but find their nemesis in the effeminate owner and his voluptuous wife.
Overlong, eccentric black comedy, more perplexing than entertaining.
w Roman Polanski, Gerard Brach *d* Roman Polanski *ph* Gilbert Taylor *m* Komeda
☆ Lionel Stander, Donald Pleasence, Jack MacGowran, Françoise Dorléac, William Franklyn, Robert Dorning, Renée Houston
'A voyeur's wallow in schizophrenia and murder to no point beyond sensation – but one could not deny the creative talent at work.' – *Judith Crist*

The Culpeper Cattle Company *
US 1972 92m DeLuxe
TCF (Paul A. Helmick)

A 16-year-old would-be cowboy joins a cattle trail but is shocked at the harsh realities of Western life.
Excellent moody photography helps to convince us that the old west was really like this, but the story is more brutal than interesting.
w Eric Bercovici, Gregory Prentiss d Dick Richards ph *Lawrence Edward Williams*, Ralph Woolsey m Tom Scott, Jerry Goldsmith
☆ Gary Grimes, Billy 'Green' Bush, Luke Askew, Bo Hopkins, Geoffrey Lewis, Wayne Sutherlin

Cult of the Cobra
US 1955 79m bw
Universal-International

Six GIs are cursed by the high priest of an Indian cobra cult. Back in New York, a mysterious woman brings about their deaths, and when the survivor kills a cobra, it turns into her.
Glossy but wholly unconvincing and unexciting non-horror potboiler.
w Jerry Davis, Cecil Maiden, Richard Collins d Francis D. Lyon
☆ Faith Domergue, Richard Long, Marshall Thompson, Kathleen Hughes, Jack Kelly

'No Winners In This Game.'
'A soldier from Israel, captured in the Lebanon, but his goal was to be at the...'
Cup Final
Israel 1992 110m colour
(Michael Sharfshstein)

original title: *G'mar Giviya*
An Israeli soldier finds common ground with his PLO captors in talk of football.
A story of coexistence that may mean more to Israeli audiences than others. It points out the similarities that exist between enemies, but does little else to advance one's understanding.
w Eyal Halfon d Eran Riklis ph Amnon Salomon m Raviv Gazit ed Anat Lubarsky
☆ Moshe Ivgi, Muhammed Bakri, Suheil Haddad
'Exciting, touching and politically even-handed.' – *Empire*

A Cup of Kindness
GB 1934 81m bw
Gaumont (Michael Balcon)

Young lovers marry despite parental disapproval on both sides.
Farcical updating of Romeo and Juliet; it hasn't worn too well, but the stars are at their peak.
w Ben Travers *play* Ben Travers d Tom Walls ph Phil Tannura ad Alfred Junge ed A. W. Roome
☆ Tom Walls, Ralph Lynn, Robertson Hare, Claude Hulbert, Dorothy Hyson, Eva Moore

Curdled
US 1996 88m DeLuxe
Miramax/A Band Apart/Tinderbox (John Maass, Raul Puig)

A maid, who works for a service that cleans up after murders, discovers the identity of a serial killer.
Interminable comedy thriller with a script that is too thin to sustain the joke for long.
w John Maass, Reb Braddock d Reb Braddock ph Steven Bernstein m Joseph Julian Gonzalez pd Sherman Williams ed Mallory Gottlieb
☆ William Baldwin, Angela Jones, Bruce Ramsay, Mel Gorham, Lois Chiles, Daisy Fuentes, Barry Corbin
'Would have been better off remaining the short film it was to begin with.' – *Variety*
† The film began life as a short whose subject matter then inspired part of Tarantino's *Pulp Fiction*; in turn, Tarantino backed its reworking as a feature.

The Cure ****
US 1917 20m bw silent
Mutual/Charles Chaplin

A dipsomaniac sent to a spa gets his booze mixed up with the spa water.
One of the funniest of the Chaplin shorts, with no pathos intervening (nor come to that much plot); it is simply a succession of balletic slapstick scenes of the highest order.
wd *Charles Chaplin* ph William C. Foster, Rollie Totheroh
☆ Charles Chaplin, Edna Purviance, Eric Campbell, Henry Bergman

The Cure *
GB 1950 18m bw
Richard and Betty Massingham

A health nut tries every possible remedy for lumbago.
Richard Massingham huffs and puffs in his endearing way through a short which is too long by far to be effective in his particular vein; but it does identify his particular persona.
wd Richard and Betty Massingham

The Cure
US 1995 98m DeLuxe
Polygram/Universal/Island (Mark Burg, Eric Eisner)

Two young boys go in search of a cure for AIDS, which one of them contracted through a blood transfusion.
An earnest, well-acted narrative of childhood friendship that is sabotaged by the implausibilities of its plot.
w Robert Kuhn d Peter Horton ph Andrew Dintenfass m David Grusin pd Armin Ganz ed Anthony Sherin, Saar Klein
☆ Joseph Mazzello, Brad Renfro, Bruce Davison, Annabella Sciorra, Diana Scarwid, Aeryk Egan
'Reeks of staple television dramatic fare and, even if it represents the zenith of the form, it's very much rooted in small-screen, earnest, low-key human emotion.' – *Leonard Klady, Variety*

The Cure for Love
GB 1949 98m bw
London Films (Robert Donat)

An ex-soldier goes home and tries to get married.
Thin Lancashire comedy which seemed an astonishing choice for Robert Donat, whose acting and direction are equally ill at ease.
w Robert Donat, Alexander Shaw, Albert Fennell *play* Walter Greenwood d Robert Donat ph Jack Cox m William Alwyn
☆ Robert Donat, Renée Asherson, Dora Bryan, Marjorie Rhodes, Charles Victor, Thora Hird, Gladys Henson
'Antediluvian regional farce.' – *MFB*

The Cure Show
GB 1993 96m bw/colour
Rank/Fiction/Polygram Video (Steve Swartz)

Documentary on the British rock group The Cure performing at two concerts in Detroit in July 1992.
A concert recording strictly for fans of the group, with the cameras staying at a distance from the on-stage action, revealing nothing more than could be seen from the auditorium.
d Aubrey Powell, Leroy Bennett ph Jeff Zimmerman ed Ian Mallett, Liam Hall
'So depressingly ordinary – it could fill a late night TV slot and attract no reaction – that it is hard to see why it was made at all.' – *Sight and Sound*

The Curious Doctor Humpp (dubbed)
Argentina 1967 87m bw
Forbes/Unistar (Orestes Trucco)

original title: *La Venganza Del Sexo*
A mad scientist kidnaps couples and drugs them to engage in sexual activity so that he can create eternal life and dominate the world.
Risible, crudely-made, extremely low-budget mix of horror and soft-core porn, some of which was added by its American distributor.
wd Emilio Vieyra *story* Raul Zorrilla ph Anibal Paz m Victor Buchino ed Jacinto Cascales
☆ Richard Bauleo, Gloria Prat, Aldo Barbero, Susan Beltran, Justin Martin, Michel Angel, Mary Albano, Al Bigatti

'Big laughs come in small packages.'
Curly Sue
US 1991 101m Technicolor
Warner (John Hughes)

A con man and a nine-year-old orphan win the heart of a successful woman lawyer.
Gruesomely sentimental and manipulative comedy.
wd John Hughes ph Jeffrey Kimball m Georges Delerue pd Doug Kraner ed Peck Prior, Harvey Rosenstock
☆ James Belushi, Kelly Lynch, Alisan Porter, John Getz

'With its mix of childish gags and shameless melodrama, *Curly Sue* could make off with a tidy box-office take.' – *Variety*
'John Hughes here graduates from the most successful comedy in film history to scripting and directing a large piece of non-biodegradable tosh.' – *Nigel Andrews, Financial Times*
'Lacks the charm, good jokes or vigour to hide its contrivances.' – *Geoff Brown, The Times*

Curly Top *
US 1935 78m bw
Fox (Darryl F. Zanuck, Winfield Sheehan)

An orphan waif is adopted by a playboy, and not only sets his business right but fixes his romantic interest in her sister.
Archetypal Temple vehicle, a loose remake of Daddy Longlegs.
w Patterson McNutt, Arthur Beckhard d Irving Cummings ph John Seitz m/ly Ray Henderson, Ted Koehler, Edward Heyman, Irving Caesar
☆ Shirley Temple, John Boles, Rochelle Hudson, Jane Darwell, Rafaela Ottiano, Esther Dale, Arthur Treacher, Etienne Girardot
'Cinch b.o. for almost any house.' – *Variety*

Curry and Pepper
Hong Kong 1990 96m colour
Movie Impact (Ho-Sun Chan)

Two irresponsible cops fall out as partners when both fall for a glamorous TV reporter.
Crudely comic and violent action movie, which is closer to the Three Stooges or Police Academy than to John Woo, and all the worse for that.
w James Yuen d Blacky Ko (Ko Shuo Liang) ph Andrew Lau m Richard Lo ad Ben Luk ed Chan Ki Hop
☆ Jacky Cheung, Ann Bridgewater, Eric Tsang, Blacky Ko, Chow Mei-Yan, Barry Wong

The Curse: see *Xala*

Curse of Dark Shadows: see *House of Dark Shadows*

'The creature created by man is forgotten by nature!'
The Curse of Frankenstein **
GB 1957 83m Eastmancolor
Warner/Hammer (Anthony Hinds)

A lurid revamping of the 1931 *Frankenstein*, this time with severed eyeballs and a peculiarly unpleasant and uncharacterized creature, all in gory colour.
It set the trend in nasty horrors from which we have all suffered since, and launched Hammer Studios on a long and profitable career of charnelry. But it did have a gruesome sense of style.
w Jimmy Sangster d Terence Fisher ph Jack Asher m James Bernard ad Ted Marshall ed James Needs
☆ Peter Cushing, Christopher Lee, Hazel Court, Robert Urquhart, Valerie Gaunt, Noel Hood
'Among the half-dozen most repulsive films I have encountered in the course of some 10,000 miles of film reviewing. Indeed, at the moment, I can only think of two which sickened me more.' – *C. A. Lejeune*

'A tender tale of terror!'
The Curse of the Cat People *
US 1944 70m bw
RKO (Val Lewton)

A child is haunted by the spirit of the cat people.
A gentle film ordered by the studio as a sequel to Cat People but turned by Lewton into a fantasy of childhood. Slow to start but finally compelling, it's a pleasing and unusual film in a minor key.
w De Witt Bodeen d Robert Wise, Gunther von Fritsch ph Nicholas Musuraca m Roy Webb
☆ Kent Smith, Simone Simon, Jane Randolph, Julia Dean, Ann Carter, Elizabeth Russell
'Full of the poetry and danger of childhood.' – *James Agee*
'A clumsy coming together of unrealized ideas, gothic effects, and stiff, dull acting.' – *New Yorker, 1979*

Curse of the Crimson Altar
GB 1968 89m Eastmancolor
Tigon/AIP (Tony Tenser)

aka: *The Crimson Cult*
Witchcraft, diabolism and mystery in an English country house.
A derivative, muddled scribble of a horror film, making no sense and wasting much talent.
w Mervyn Haisman, Henry Lincoln d Vernon Sewell ph John Coquillon m Peter Knight
☆ Boris Karloff, Christopher Lee, Rupert Davies, Mark Eden, Barbara Steele, Michael Gough

Curse of the Demon: see *Night of the Demon*

The Curse of the Ellanbys: see *She Wolf of London*

'Entombed for eons – turned to stone – seeking women, women, women!'
Curse of the Faceless Man
US 1958 67m bw
Vogue/United Artists

An encrusted man, found in the earth near Pompeii, is revived and goes on the rampage, but is eventually dissolved by water.
Absurd chiller with the saving grace of not taking itself seriously.
w Jerome Bixby d Edward L. Cahn
☆ Richard Anderson, Elaine Edwards, Adele Mara, Gar Moore, Felix Locher

Curse of the Living Corpse
US 1963 78m bw
TCF (Del Tenney)

A millionaire vows to return and kill all his relatives if he is buried alive, which he is...
Gothic cheapie made in Stamford, Connecticut, where they have little experience of such things.
wd Del Tenney
☆ Roy Scheider, Candace Hilligoss

'Half bone, half bandage ... all bloodcurdling terror!'
Curse of the Mummy's Tomb
GB 1964 80m Technicolor Techniscope
Columbia/Swallow/Hammer (Michael Carreras)

An Egyptian mummy taken to London goes on the rampage, and meets its own wicked brother who has been cursed to eternal life.
Absurd farrago which takes too long to set up its plot and then finds little to do with its monster.
w Henry Younger (Michael Carreras) d Michael Carreras ph Otto Heller m Carlo Martelli ad Bernard Robinson ed James Needs, Eric Boyd-Perkins
☆ Ronald Howard, Terence Morgan, Fred Clark, Jeanne Roland, George Pastell, Jack Gwillim, John Paul

Curse of the Pink Panther
GB 1983 110m Technicolor Panavision
MGM-UA/Titan/Jewel (Blake Edwards, Gerald T. Nutting)

Inspector Clouseau has disappeared, and Dreyfus selects the world's worst detective to replace him.
Unspeakably awful attempt at prolonging a series whose star died two episodes ago. Crude, tasteless and unfunny throughout.
w Blake Edwards, Geoffrey Edwards d Blake Edwards ph Dick Bush m Henry Mancini pd Peter Mullins
☆ Ted Wass, Joanna Lumley, Herbert Lom, David Niven, Robert Wagner, Capucine, Harvey Korman, Burt Kwouk
'Another bout of film-making as grave robbing.' – *Sight and Sound*
'The ultimate version of deadpan humour ... the most tedious of the whole series.' – *Richard Combs, MFB*

Curse of the Undead
US 1959 79m bw
Universal-International

A black-clad stranger in a Western town turns out to be a vampire of Spanish origin.
Abysmal attempt to substitute Wyoming for Transylvania; more skill and sensitivity were required.
wd Edward Dein
☆ Michael Pate, Eric Fleming, Kathleen Crowley, John Hoyt

'He had but one body – yet lived with two souls!'

The Curse of the Werewolf
GB   1961   92m   Technicolor
U-I/Hotspur/Hammer (Anthony Hinds)
▦ ◖

A beggar rapes a servant girl and their offspring grows up to be a werewolf.
Doleful Hammer horror in a Spanish setting, with an absurd but predictable plot and a lack of sympathy for its fancy, hairy hero.
w John Elder (Anthony Hinds) *novel The Werewolf of Paris* by Guy Endore d Terence Fisher ph Arthur Grant m Benjamin Frankel ad Bernard Robinson ed James Needs, Alfred Cox
☆ Oliver Reed, Clifford Evans, Catherine Feller, Yvonne Romain, Anthony Dawson, Richard Wordsworth, Warren Mitchell, Peter Sallis

The Curse of the Wraydons
GB   1946   94m   bw
Bushey
The Victorian story of Spring-heeled Jack, here depicted as a mad inventor out for revenge.
Too long and stagey to be one of its star's better barnstormers, especially as by this time his girth made the notion of his springing about somewhat hilarious.
w Michael Barringer d Victor M. Gover
☆ Tod Slaughter, Bruce Seton, Gabriel Toyne

Curtain Call *
US   1940   63m   bw
RKO
Two Broadway producers buy an awful play in order to get even with a temperamental star, but she likes it.
Amusing second feature, a kind of flashforward to The Producers. A reprise the following year, Footlight Fever, did not work.
w Dalton Trumbo d Frank Woodruff ph Russell Metty m Roy Webb
☆ Alan Mowbray, Donald MacBride, Helen Vinson, Barbara Read, John Archer

Curtain Call at Cactus Creek *
US   1949   83m   Technicolor
U-I (Robert Arthur)
GB title: *Take the Stage*
A travelling repertory company in the old west exposes a gang of bank robbers.
Cheerful minor comedy with good pace and amusing burlesques of old melodramas.
w Oscar Brodney d Charles Lamont ph Russell Metty m Walter Scharf
☆ Donald O'Connor, Gale Storm, Eve Arden, Vincent Price, Walter Brennan, Chick Chandler

Curtain Up *
GB   1952   85m   bw
Rank/Constellation (Robert Garrett)
A seaside repertory company runs into trouble when the producer is at loggerheads with the author of next week's play.
Fairly amusing farce which has now acquired historical value for the light it throws on the old weekly reps.
w Michael Pertwee, Jack Davies *play On Monday Next* by Philip King d Ralph Smart ph Stanley Pavey m Malcolm Arnold
☆ Margaret Rutherford, Robert Morley, Olive Sloane, Joan Rice, Charlotte Mitchell, Kay Kendall, Liam Gaffney, Michael Medwin

Curucu, Beast of the Amazon
⋔ US   1956   76m   colour
Universal
Amazon explorers set out to find a man masquerading as a monster.
Rubbishy hokum, for tolerant kids.
wd Curt Siodmak
☆ John Bromfield, Beverly Garland, Tom Payne

Custer of the West
US   1967   146m   Technicolor   Super Technirama 70
Cinerama/Security (Louis Dolivet, Philip Yordan, Irving Lerner)
◉
After the Civil War, Custer is offered a cavalry command, becomes disillusioned, and is massacred with his troops at Little Big Horn.
Gloomily inaccurate spectacular with pauses for Cinerama carnival thrills and dour bits of melodrama.
w Bernard Gordon, Julian Halevy d Robert Siodmak ph Cecilio Paniagua m Bernardo Segall
☆ Robert Shaw, Mary Ure, Robert Ryan, Jeffrey Hunter, Ty Hardin, Lawrence Tierney, Kieron Moore

---

A Cut Above: see *Gross Anatomy*

Cutter and Bone
US   1981   109m   Technicolor
United Artists/Gurian
▦
GB title: *Cutter's Way*
A California failure witnesses the aftermath of murder, and with a crippled ex-Vietnam veteran turns detective.
Heavy-going melodrama which tries very hard to be something more than a thriller, and manages only to imply that the world stinks; so it might as well have stuck to Philip Marlowe.
w Jeffrey Alan Fiskin *novel* Newton Thornburg d Ivan Passer ph Jordan Cronenweth m Jack Nitzsche ed Caroline Ferriol
☆ Jeff Bridges, John Heard, Lisa Eichhorn, Ann Dusenberry, Stephen Elliott, Nina Van Pallandt

Cutter's Way: see *Cutter and Bone*

CutThroat Island
US   1995   93m   Technicolor   Panavision, Technovision
Guild/Carolco/Forge/Canal (Renny Harlin, Joel B. Michaels, Laurence Mark, James Gorman)
▦ ◖ ⌂ ◖
Determined to beat her dastardly uncle, a female pirate goes in search of buried treasure with the aid of a literate slave.
Dull and confused action film that swiftly sinks with all hands lost.
w Robert King, Marc Norman *story* Michael Frost Beckner, James Gorman, Bruce A. Evans, Raynold Gideon d Renny Harlin ph Peter Levy m John Debney pd Norman Garwood ed Frank J. Urioste, Ralph E. Winters
☆ Geena Davis, Matthew Modine, Frank Langella, Maury Chaykin, Patrick Malahide, Stan Shaw, Rex Linn, Harris Yulin
'This sort of film gives excitement a bad name.' – *Derek Malcolm, Guardian*
'A hoary pastiche of pirate movies of old, tricked out in cast-off clichés (inscrutable maps, monkey sidekicks, quicksand) and groaning under the strain of being driven so hard (breathless chases, an endless final battle), it is a sorry hulk of a film.' – *Leslie Felperin, Sight and Sound*

'The King Of The Rink Is About To Meet America's Ice Queen.'
The Cutting Edge
US   1992   110m   DeLuxe
UIP/MGM/Interscope (Ted Field, Karen Murphy, Robert W. Cort)
▦ ▦
A tough former ice-hockey player becomes the partner of a spoiled and wealthy figure-skater.
Predictable romantic teen movie of winning against the odds.
w Tony Gilroy d Paul M. Glaser ph Elliot Davis m Patrick Williams pd David Gropman ed Michael E. Polakow
☆ D. B. Sweeney, Moira Kelly, Roy Dotrice, Terry O'Quinn, Dwier Brown, Chris Benson, Kevin Peeks, Barry Flatman

Cybèle ou les Dimanches de Ville d'Avry: see *Sundays and Cybèle*

Cyberjack
Canada/Japan   1995   96m   colour
Catalyst/Fuji Eight (John A. Curtis)
▦ ▦
US title: *Virtual Assassin*
An ex-cop turned janitor foils a criminal's attempt to steal a super-virus.
Routine low-budget science fiction, substituting action for characterization.
w Eric Poppen, John A. Curtis d Robert Lee ph Allan Trow m George Blondheim pd Richard Paris, Linda del Rosario ed Derek Whelan sp Paller Special Effects, Magic Camera Co.
☆ Michael Dudikoff, Brion James, Suki Kaiser, Jon Cuthbert, James Thom
'The acting's not much, and the script is notably lacking in wit, but the set-in-the-near-future saga looks way better than its $2 million budget.' – Ken Eisner, *Variety*
† The movie was released direct to video.

'He's the first hero of the 21st century.'
Cyborg
US   1989   85m   colour
Cannon/Golan-Globus
▦ ▦ ⌂ ◖
A martial arts expert accompanies a female cyborg, holding information to save mankind, across post-apocalyptic America.
Charmless, cliché-packed action movie, carrying the explicit message that violence is good for you.
w Kitty Chalmers d Albert Pyun ph Philip Alan Waters m Kevin Bassinson pd Douglas Leonard ed Rozanne Zingale, Scott Stevenson
☆ Jean-Claude Van Damme, Deborah Richter, Vincent Klyn, Alex Daniels, Rolf Muller, Jackson Pinckney, Dayle Haddon

'He was programmed to kill ... Nobody can stop him.'
Cyborg Cop
US   1993   93m   colour
Nu Image/Nu World (Danny Lerner)
▦
An ex-cop goes to the rescue of his brother, who has been captured and turned into a killer cyborg by a mad millionaire drug dealer on a Caribbean island.
Dim standard robot action fodder, remarkable only for its violent, cliché-ridden plot and dialogue.
w Greg Latter d Sam Firstenberg ph Joseph Wein m Paul Fishman pd John Rosewarne ed Alan Patillo
☆ David Bradley, Todd Jensen, Alonna Shaw, Rufus Swart, John Rhys-Davies
'Some effective special effects make this watchable trash' – *Sight and Sound*

Cyborg Cop II
US   1994   97m   colour
New World
▦
A cop battles with a pyschotic killer who is turned into a cyborg and decides to wipe out the world.
A remake with a similar plot to the original film, and even less watchable this time around.
w Jon Stevens d Sam Firstenberg ph Joseph Wein m Bob Mithoff ed Marcus Manton
☆ David Bradley, Morgan Hunter, Jill Pierce
'Low budget schlock, directed without grace and displaying the offensive sexist exploitation which gave the horror genre such a bad reputation in the 70s.' – *Sight and Sound*

Cyclo **
France/Vietnam   1995   129m   colour
Entertainment/Lazannec/Lumière/La Sept/La SFP (Christophe Rossignon)
▦ ◖
original title: *Xich Lo*
After a pedicab driver has his vehicle stolen, his employer recruits him as a member of a criminal gang involved in robbery and drug-dealing.
A lovingly detailed drama of street life and the way in which old cultural values are eroded by modern commercial pressures.
w Nguyen Trung Binh, Tran Anh Hung d Tran Anh Hung ph Benoit Delhomme m Ton That Tiet ad Daniel Zalay ed Nicole Dedieu, Claude Ronzeau
☆ Le Van Loc, Tony Leung, Tran Nu Yen Khe, Nguyen Nhu Quynh, Nguyen Hoang Phuc, Ngo Vu Quang Hai
'A remarkable film, superbly performed, shot and designed with real distinction.' – *Derek Malcolm, Guardian*
† It won the Golden Lion as best film at the 1995 Venice Film Festival.

The Cyclops
US   1956   65m   bw
B and H (Bert I. Gordon)
Explorers in Mexico find animals turned by radiation into monsters, plus a one-eyed 25-foot-tall human.
Modest monster movie, quite palatable of its kind.
wd Bert I. Gordon ph Ira Morgan m Albert Glasser
☆ James Craig, Lon Chaney Jnr, Gloria Talbott, Tom Drake

Cynara **
US   1932   78m   bw
Samuel Goldwyn
A London barrister has an affair with a young girl who commits suicide when he goes back to his wife.

Solidly carpentered, effective star vehicle of the old school, now dated but preserving its dignity.
w Frances Marion, Lynn Starling *novel An Imperfect Lover* by Robert Gore Brown *play Cynara* by H. M. Harwood, Robert Gore Brown d King Vidor ph Ray June md Alfred Newman ad Richard Day
☆ Ronald Colman, Kay Francis, Phyllis Barry, Henry Stephenson, Paul Porcasi
'The values it involves are wholly unlike those which US audiences are usually called upon to comprehend.' – *Time*
† The film's title comes from Ernest Dowson's lines: 'I have been faithful to thee, Cynara, in my fashion.'

Cynthia
US   1947   98m   bw
MGM (Edwin H. Knopf)
GB title: *The Rich Full Life*
An over-protected girl finds an outlet in music and her parents finally allow her to lead her own life.
An overlong domestic drama in which thin writing and acting are backed by unsound psychology.
w Harold Buchman, Charles Kaufman *play* Vina Delmar d Robert Z. Leonard ph Charles Schoenbaum m Bronislau Kaper
☆ Elizabeth Taylor, George Murphy, Mary Astor, S. Z. Sakall, James Lydon, Gene Lockhart, Spring Byington

Cynthia's Secret: see *Dark Delusion*

Cyrano de Bergerac *
US   1950   112m   bw
Stanley Kramer
▦ ▦ ⌂
In the 17th century a long-nosed poet, philosopher and buffoon writes letters enabling a friend to win the lady he loves himself.
The classic romantic verse play does not take kindly to a hole-in-corner black-and-white production, but at the time it was lapped up as a daring cultural breakthrough.
w Brian Hooker *play* Edmond Rostand d Michael Gordon ph Franz Planer m Dimitri Tiomkin
☆ José Ferrer, Mala Powers, William Prince, Morris Carnovsky, Ralph Clanton, Virginia Farmer, Edgar Barrier, Elena Verdugo
'Vigorous, respectful, full of lively movement, and pictorially well-composed.' – *C. A. Lejeune*
♟ José Ferrer

Cyrano de Bergerac ***
France   1990   138m   colour
Hachette Première/Camera One/Films A2/D.D. Productions/UGC (Rene Cleitman, Michael Seydoux)
▦ ▦ ⌂ ◖ ◖
A dashing soldier and noted duellist, handicapped by his long nose, helps a handsome friend make love to the woman he adores from afar.
Exuberant version of the romantic French classic, using the rhymed couplets of the original. The English subtitles, in a rhyming translation by Anthony Burgess, are a distraction, though.
w Jean-Paul Rappeneau, Jean-Claude Carrière *play* Edmond Rostand d Jean-Paul Rappeneau ph Pierre Lhomme m Jean-Claude Petit ad Ezio Frigerio ed Noëlle Boisson
☆ Gérard Depardieu, Anne Brochet, Vincent Perez, Jacques Weber, Roland Bertin, Philippe Morier-Genoud, Philippe Volter, Pierre Maguelon
'A near-perfect balance of verbal and visual flamboyance.' – *Variety*
'Cyrano? Bravo!' – *Le Monde*
♟ Gérard Depardieu; best foreign film; best art direction; best costume design; best make-up
♟ Pierre Lhomme; Jean-Claude Petit

Czar of the Slot Machines: see *King of Gamblers*

Czarina: see *A Royal Scandal*

Czlowiek Z Marmur: see *Man of Marble*

Czlowiek Z Zelaza: see *Man of Iron*

D. C. Cab
US 1983 99m Technicolor
RKO-Universal (Topper Carew)

GB title: *Street Fleet*
Cab drivers for a run-down Washington company capture kidnappers.
Brainless extravaganza with aspirations somewhere between Taxi *and* Carry On.
wd Joel Schumacher *ph* Dean Cundey, Ron Van Nostrand *m* Giorgio Moroder *pd* John Lloyd *ed* David Blewitt
☆ Mr T, Max Gail, Adam Baldwin, Charlie Barnett, Gary Busey, Gloria Gifford
'Artificial energy used to bolster wretched material.' – *Steve Jenkins, MFB*

D.O.A. **
US 1950 83m bw
UA/Leo C. Popkin

The victim of a slow poison tracks down his own killer.
Semi-classic suspense drama, sufficiently original to be remembered though the plot details become hazy.
w Russel Rouse, Clarence Greene (partly from a 1931 German film* Der Mann der seinen Mörder Sucht*) *d* Rudolph Maté *ph* Ernest Laszlo *m* Dimitri Tiomkin
☆ *Edmond O'Brien, Pamela Britton, Luther Adler, Neville Brand, Beverly Campbell*
† The title is a police abbreviation for 'dead on arrival'
†† Remade as *Colour Me Dead* (qv) and see below.

D.O.A.
US 1988 97m CFI color
Warner/Touchstone/Silver Screen Partners III (Ian Sander, Laura Ziskin)

A college professor, discovering that he has been poisoned, and with less than 48 hours to live, solves the mystery of his murder.
Ambitious but inept remake, lacking in suspense.
w Charles Edward Pogue *story* Charles Edward Pogue, Russel Rouse, Clarence Greene *d* Rocky Morton, Annabel Jankel *ph* Yuri Neyman *m* Chaz Jankel *pd* Richard Amend *ed* Michael R. Miller, Raja Gosnell
☆ Dennis Quaid, Meg Ryan, Charlotte Rampling, Daniel Stern, Jane Kaczmarek, Christopher Neame, Robin Johnson, Rob Knepper, Jay Patterson

D2: The Mighty Ducks
US 1994 106m Astrocolor
Walt Disney (Jon Avnet, Jordan Kerner)

A coach gathers together a group of misfits and moulds them into an ice-hockey team to compete in the Junior Goodwill Games.
A lacklustre sequel of little interest to anyone.
w Steven Brill *d* Sam Weisman *ph* Mark Irwin *m* J. A. C. Redford *ed* John F. Link, Eric A. Sears
☆ Emilio Estevez, Kathryn Erbe, Michael Tucker, Jan Rubes, Carsten Norgaard, Maria Ellingsen, Joshua Jackson
'A pretty sorry follow-up.' – *Variety*
† It is a sequel to *The Mighty Ducks* (qv).

D3: Mighty Ducks
US 1996 104m Technicolor
Buena Vista/Disney (Jordan Kerner, Jon Avnet)

A hockey team gain scholarships to a snobbish private school.
Slight and sentimental comedy in which tedium sets in early.
w Steven Brill, Jim Burnstein *d* Ron Lieberman *ph* David Hennings *m* J. A. C. Redford *pd* Steven Storer *ed* Patrick Lussier, Colleen Halsey

☆ Emilio Estevez, Jeffrey Nordling, David Selby, Heidi Kling, Joshua Jackson, Joss Ackland
'This amazingly resilient film franchise continues to be entertaining in a shamelessly manipulative way.' – *Leonard Klady, Variety*

Da **
US 1988 102m colour
Premier/Film Dallas/A. J. Corman-Sheen/Greenblatt/Auerbach (Julie Corman)

A playwright, returning to Ireland for his father's funeral, finds himself discussing life with his father's ghost.
An autobiographical work which runs deep with emotion.
w Hugh Leonard *play* Hugh Leonard *d* Matt Clark *ph* Alar Kivilo *m* Elmer Bernstein *pd* Frank Conway *ed* Nancy Nuttal Beyda
☆ *Barnard Hughes*, Martin Sheen, William Hickey, Doreen Hepburn, Karl Hayden, Hugh O'Conor, Ingrid Craigie, Joan O'Hara, Jill Doyle

Da Uomo a Uomo: see *Death Rides a Horse*

Da Yuebing: see *The Big Parade* (1986)

Daayraa: see *The Square Circle*

Dad
US 1989 118m DeLuxe
UIP/Universal/Amblin Entertainment (Joseph Stern, Gary David Goldberg)

A son helps his father face up to death.
Excessively sentimental family drama.
wd Gary David Goldberg *novel* William Wharton *ph* Jan Kiesser *m* James Horner *pd* Jack DeGovia *ed* Eric Sears
☆ Jack Lemmon, Ted Danson, Olympia Dukakis, Kathy Baker, Kevin Spacey, Ethan Hawke, Zakes Mokae, J. T. Walsh, Peter Michael Goetz
'Emotional exploitation at its most objectionable.' – *MFB*

Dad Rudd films: see *On Our Selection*

Dad Savage
GB 1997 104m Technicolor Super 35
Polygram/Sweet Child/Dad Savage (Gwynneth Lloyd, Robert Jones)

In Norfolk, a gangster attempts to discover which of his accomplices killed his son and tried to steal his buried loot.
Derivative, brutal thriller that would seem more at home in the United States than rural England; its narrative overload gets in the way of any suspense.
w Steven Williams *d* Betsan Morris Evans *ph* Gavin Finney *pd* Michael Carlin *ed* Guy Bensley
☆ Patrick Stewart, Kevin McKidd, Helen McCrory, Joe McFadden, Marc Warren, Jake Wood
'Truly awful … another nail in the British Film Industry's revival coffin.' – *Alan Jones, Film Review*

Daddy Longlegs *
US 1931 80m bw
Fox

An orphan girl grows up to fall in love with her mysterious benefactor.
Cinderella-like romance, adequately adapted from a novel which became the classic American version of the January–May romance.
w Sonya Levien *novel* Jean Webster *d* Alfred Santell *ph* Lucien Andriot
☆ Janet Gaynor, Warner Baxter, Una Merkel, John Arledge, Claude Gillingwater, Louise Closser Hale

'A smash … one of those rare talkers with universal appeal.' – *Variety*
† Other versions were made in 1919 with Mary Pickford and Mahlon Hamilton, directed by Marshall Neilan; in 1935 disguised as *Curly Top* (qv) and in 1955 (see below).

Daddy Longlegs *
US 1955 126m Technicolor Cinemascope
TCF (Samuel G. Engel)

Overlong and unsuitably wide-screened musical version of a popular story (see above).
Generally clumsy and dispirited, but Astaire is always worth watching and a couple of the dances are well staged.
w Phoebe and Henry Ephron *d* Jean Negulesco *ph* Leon Shamroy *m* Alfred Newman *m/ly* Johnny Mercer
☆ *Fred Astaire*, Leslie Caron, *Fred Clark*, Thelma Ritter, Terry Moore, Charlotte Austin, Larry Keating
♫ Alfred Newman; song 'Something's Gotta Give'

Daddy Nostalgie **
France 1990 106m Eastmancolor
Clea/Little Bear/Solyfic Eurisma (Adolphe Viezzi)

aka: *These Foolish Things*
A screenwriter returns home to be close to her invalid father.
Gently understated domestic drama.
w Colo Tavernier O'Hagan *d* Bertrand Tavernier *ph* Denis Lenoir *m* Antoine Duhamel *pd* Jean-Louis Poveda *ed* Ariane Boeglin
☆ *Dirk Bogarde*, Jane Birkin, Emmanuelle Bataille, Charlotte Kady, Michele Minns
'A miniature jewel of a film … acted and directed with great subtlety.' – *Variety*

Daddy's Dyin', Who's Got the Will?
US 1990 95m DeLuxe
Palace/Propaganda Films/Artist Circle Entertainment (Sigurjon Sighvatsson, Steve Golin, Monty Montgomery)

Children gather at home after their father has a stroke.
Raucous comedy of family relationships that ends in sentimentality.
w Del Shores *play* Del Shores *d* Jack Fisk *ph* Paul Elliot *m* David McHugh *pd* Michelle Minch *ed* Edward A. Warschilka Jnr
☆ Beau Bridges, Beverly D'Angelo, Tess Harper, Judge Reinhold, Amy Wright, Patrika Darbo, Bert Remsen, Molly McClure, Keith Carradine, Newell Alexander

Daddy's Gone A-Hunting
US 1969 108m Technicolor
Warner/Red Lion (Mark Robson)

A child and its mother are threatened by her deranged ex-husband.
Unpleasant and protracted suspenser with the emphasis on sex rather than thrills.
w Larry Cohen, Lorenzo Semple Jnr *d* Mark Robson *ph* Ernest Laszlo *m* John Williams
☆ Carol White, Paul Burke, Scott Hylands, Mala Powers, Andrea King

Dad's Army **
GB 1971 95m Technicolor
Columbia/Norcon (John R. Sloan)

Misadventures of a number of elderly gents in Britain's wartime Home Guard.
Expanded big-screen version of the long-running TV series, a pleasant souvenir but rather less effective than was expected because everything is shown – the town, the Nazis, the wives – and thus the air of gentle fantasy

disappears, especially in the face of much coarsened humour.
w Jimmy Perry, David Croft *d* Norman Cohen *ph* Terry Maher *m* Wilfred Burns
☆ Arthur Lowe, John Le Mesurier, John Laurie, James Beck, Ian Lavender, *Arnold Ridley*, Liz Fraser, Clive Dunn, Bill Pertwee, Frank Williams, Edward Sinclair

Daens *
Belgium/France/Netherlands 1992 138m colour
Mayfair/Favourite/Investco/Kredietbank Luxembourg/Films Dérive/Titane/Shooting Star/BRTN/KRO (Dick Impens)

At the turn of the century, a Catholic priest champions the half-starved, underpaid workers in the city of Aalst.
Dogged biopic celebrating a remarkable man, but without much flair in its telling.
w François Chevallier, Stijn Coninx *novel* Pieter Daens by Louis Paul Boon *d* Stijn Coninx *ph* Wather Vanden Ende *m* Dirk Brossé *pd* Allan Starski *ed* Ludo Troch
☆ Jan Decleir, Gérard Desarthe, Antje de Boeck, Michael Pas, Johan Leysen, Idwig Stéphane, Wim Meuwissen
'A bit of a pudding, and long with it. It says all the right things … But it says them so slowly and deliberately that your patience is at times sorely tested.' – *Derek Malcolm, Guardian*
'A bit of a plod. But it does have dramatic force, a passionate central performance and the great virtue of clarity.' – *Adam Mars-Jones, Independent*
♫ best foreign film

Dahong Denglong Gaogao Gua: see *Raise The Red Lantern*

Daisies **
Czechoslovakia 1966 80m colour
Bohumil Smida (Lasislav Fikar)

original title: *Sedmikrásky*
Bored by their lives, two girls go in search of decadence.
Witty, playful, visually exuberant attack on conformity and a materialistic society that the Czech authorities banned for a time.
w Ester Krumbachova, Vera Chytilova *d* Vera Chytilova *ph* Jaroslav Kucera *pd* Ester Krumbachova
☆ Jitka Cerhova, Ivana Karbanova, Julius Albert
'What makes this film particularly distasteful is its idiot yearning for Western beatnikdom, its slobbering (and, I suspect, lesbian) adulation of its ghastly heroines.' – *John Simon*

Daisy Kenyon
US 1947 99m bw
TCF (Otto Preminger)

A fashion designer has two men in her life.
Adequate woman's picture which hardly justifies its cast.
w David Hertz *novel* Elizabeth Janeway *d* Otto Preminger *ph* Leon Shamroy *m* David Raksin
☆ Joan Crawford, Henry Fonda, Dana Andrews, Ruth Warrick, Martha Stewart, Peggy Ann Garner

Daisy Miller *
US 1974 92m Technicolor
Paramount/Copa de Oro (Peter Bogdanovich)

In the 19th century, an American girl tourist in Europe falls in love but dies of the Roman fever.
Curious attempt to film a very mild and uneventful Henry James story, with careful production but inadequate leads. The first sign that Bogdanovich was getting too big for his boots.

w Frederic Raphael *story* Henry James *d* Peter Bogdanovich *ph* Alberto Spagnoli *m* classical themes *ad* Ferdinando Scarfiotti

☆ Cybill Shepherd, Barry Brown, Cloris Leachman, Mildred Natwick, Eileen Brennan, James MacMurtry

'A historical film bereft of any feeling for history, and a literary adaptation which reveals a fine contempt for literary subtlety.' – *Jan Dawson*

'Appallingly crass ... directed with all the subtlety of a sledgehammer.' – *Michael Billington, Illustrated London News*

'Trying to make that little thing he's with into Daisy Miller was hilarious. God almighty couldn't do that. She's so coy.' – *Henry Hathaway*

Dakota

US   1945   82m   bw
Republic (Joseph Kane)
▦ ▤ ℺

The daughter of a railroad tycoon elopes with a cowboy and becomes involved in a land war.
Adequate star Western.
w Lawrence Hazard *story* Carl Foreman *d* Joseph Kane *ph* Jack Marta *m* Walter Scharf
☆ John Wayne, Vera Hruba Ralston, Walter Brennan, Ward Bond, Ona Munson, Hugo Haas, Mike Mazurki, Paul Fix, Grant Withers, Jack La Rue

Dakota Incident

US   1956   88m   bw
Republic
▤

Strangers take cover when they are attacked by Indians.
A formula older than Stagecoach is played out to humdrum results.
w Frederic Louis Fox *d* Lewis R. Foster
☆ Linda Darnell, Dale Robertson, Regis Toomey, John Lund, Ward Bond, Skip Homeier, Irving Bacon, John Doucette, Whit Bissell

Dakota Road

GB   1990   89m   colour
Mayfair/Dakota Road/Working Title/Film Four/British Screen (Donna Grey)
In East Anglia a 15-year-old girl suffers from her father's suicide, her family's eviction from their home and an unsatisfactory love affair with a local youth.
Rural melodrama so unrelievedly tragic that it hovers on the edge of parody.
wd Nick Ward *ph* Ian Wilson *m* Paul Stacey *pd* Careen Hertzog *ed* William Diver
☆ Charlotte Chatton, Jason Carter, Rachel Scott, Amelda Brown, Matthew Scurfield, Alan Howard, David Warrilow

'A melodrama with the *angst* button set to full volume, all the way through.' – *Sheila Johnston, Independent*

'Though the film is splendidly shot by Ian Wilson, making the most of the exposed landscape and its patches of unexpected lushness, it founders on a relentless rural miserabilism.' – *Hugo Davenport, Daily Telegraph*

Dal Polo all'Equatore: see *From The Pole to The Equator*

Daleks: Invasion Earth 2150 AD: see *Dr Who and the Daleks*

Dallas *

US   1950   94m   Technicolor
Warner (Anthony Veiller)
A renegade ex-Confederate colonel is pardoned for bringing law and order to Dallas.
Routinely competent top-of-the-bill Western.
w John Twist *d* Stuart Heisler *ph* Ernest Haller *m* Max Steiner
☆ Gary Cooper, Ruth Roman, Raymond Massey, Steve Cochran, Barbara Payton, Leif Erickson, Antonio Moreno, Jerome Cowan

Dallas Doll

Australia   1994   104m   Eastmancolor
Metro Tartan/Dallas Doll/ABC/BBC (Ross Matthews)
▦

A female American golf instructor causes dissension in an Australian family by seducing the husband, wife and son.
Dim would-be satirical comedy, a variation on Pasolini's Theorem, which falls very flat.

---

wd Ann Turner *ph* Paul Murphy *m* David Hirschfelder *pd* Marcus North *ed* Michael Honey
☆ Sandra Bernhard, Frank Gallacher, Victoria Longley, Jake Blundell, Rose Byrne, Jonathon Leahy, Douglas Hedge, Melissa Thomas

'An out-of-control mess.' – *Independent*

The Daltons Ride Again

US   1945   72m   bw
Universal (Howard Welsch)
An outlaw gang's last raid is complicated when one of them falls in love.
Unhistorical action Western with B-feature appeal.
w Roy Chanslor, Paul Gangelin *d* Ray Taylor
☆ Alan Curtis, Kent Taylor, Lon Chaney Jnr, Noah Beery Jnr, Martha O'Driscoll, Thomas Gomez, Milburn Stone, John Litel

The Dam Busters **

GB   1954   125m   bw
ABPC (Robert Clark)
▦ ▤

In 1943 the Ruhr dams are destroyed by Dr Barnes Wallis's bouncing bombs.
Understated British war epic with additional scientific interest and good acting and model work, not to mention a welcome lack of love interest.
w R. C. Sherriff *books* Guy Gibson and Paul Brickhill *d* Michael Anderson *ph* Erwin Hillier *m* Leighton Lucas, Eric Coates *sp* George Blackwell
☆ Michael Redgrave, Richard Todd, Basil Sydney, Derek Farr, Patrick Barr, Ernest Clark, Raymond Huntley, Ursula Jeans

A dama do cine Shanghai: see *The Lady from the Shanghai Cinema*

Dama sSobachkoi: see *The Lady with the Little Dog*

'Desire. Deceit.'

Damage

GB/France   1992   111m   Technicolor
Entertainment/Skreba/NEF/Canal (Louis Malle)
▦ ▤ ℺ ♫

A Conservative minister is destroyed by his obsessive love for his son's girlfriend.
Disappointingly thin tale that carries very little conviction.
w David Hare *novel* Josephine Hart *d* Louis Malle *ph* Peter Biziou *m* Zbigniew Preisner *pd* Brian Morris *ed* John Bloom
☆ Jeremy Irons, Juliette Binoche, *Miranda Richardson*, Rupert Graves, Leslie Caron, Ian Bannen, Gemma Clarke, Julian Fellowes, Tony Doyle, Benjamin Whitrow

'A cold, brittle film about raging, traumatic emotions.' – *Variety*

'A carefully controlled picture about uncontrollable passion, in which precise camera movements and unobtrusive editing subtly complement the immaculate acting.' – *Philip French, Observer*

♙ Miranda Richardson
♛ Miranda Richardson

Damaged Goods

US   1937   56m   bw
Grand National
A young man infects his wife and child with syphilis.
An 'awful warning' which seemed naïve even at the time; there had been a silent version in 1914.
w Upton Sinclair *play* Eugene Brieux *d* Phil Stone
☆ Pedro de Cordoba, Douglas Walton, Arletta Duncan, Esther Dale, Phyllis Barry

Damaged Lives

US   1937   61m   bw
Weldon
A young man infects his wife with syphilis.
One of a rival pair of moral tales (see above); both had trouble with the censors on subject matter alone. Not otherwise notable.
w Donald Davis, Edgar G. Ulmer *d* Edgar G. Ulmer
☆ Diane Sinclair, Lyman Williams, Cecilia Parker, George Irving, Jason Robards

La Dame aux Camélias: see *The Lady of the Camelias*

Dames **

US   1934   90m   bw
Warner (Robert Lord)
▤ ℺

A millionaire purity fanatic tries to stop the opening of a Broadway show.
Typical Warner musical of the period: its real raison d'être is to be found in the splendidly imaginative numbers at the finale, but it also gives very full rein to the roster of comic actors under contract at the time.
w Delmer Daves *d* Ray Enright *ph* Sid Hickox, George Barnes *m* various *ch* Busby Berkeley
☆ Joan Blondell, Hugh Herbert, Guy Kibbee, ZaSu Pitts, Dick Powell, Ruby Keeler

'That Warners was able to fashion so zestful an entertainment under post-Haysian restrictions is a credit to the collective ingenuities of the studio artificers ... Swell entertainment, no matter how you slice it.' – *Variety*
† Originally intended as *Gold Diggers of 1934*.

Les Dames du Bois de Boulogne *

France   1946   90m   bw
Consortium du Film (Raoul Ploquin)
▤

US title: *Ladies of the Park*
A woman revenges herself on her faithless lover by inveigling him into a marriage with a nightclub dancer-cum-prostitute.
An austerely directed romantic melodrama that fails to satisfy.
w Jean Cocteau, Robert Bresson *story* Diderot *d* Robert Bresson *ph* Philippe Agostini *m* Jean-Jacques Grunenwald *pd* Max Douy
☆ Paul Bernard, Maria Casarès, Elina Labourdette, Lucienne Bogaert, Jean Marchat

'The first time was only a warning!'

Damien: Omen Two

US   1978   109m   DeLuxe   Panavision
TCF (Harvey Bernhard)
▦ ▤ ℺ ♫

The antichrist who got rid of the entire cast of *The Omen* now, as a teenager, starts in on his foster parents.
Once was enough.
w Stanley Mann, Michael Hodges *d* Don Taylor *ph* Bill Butler *m* Jerry Goldsmith
☆ William Holden, Lee Grant, Jonathan Scott-Taylor, Robert Foxworth, Lucas Donat, Lew Ayres, Sylvia Sidney, Elizabeth Shepherd
† It was followed by *The Final Conflict* (qv).

Damn the Defiant: see *HMS Defiant*

Damn Yankees **

US   1958   110m   Technicolor
Warner (George Abbott, Stanley Donen)
▦ ▤ ℺ ♫

GB title: *What Lola Wants*
The devil interferes in the fortunes of a failing baseball team.
Smartly-styled but very American musical based on Faust; brilliant moments but some tedium.
w George Abbott *novel* Douglass Wallop *d* George Abbott, Stanley Donen *ph* Harold Lipstein *m/ly* Richard Adler, Jerry Ross *md* Ray Heindorf
☆ Gwen Verdon, Tab Hunter, Ray Walston, Russ Brown, Shannon Bolin
♛ Ray Heindorf

Damnation Alley

US   1977   95m   DeLuxe
TCF/Hal Landers, Bobby Roberts, Jerome M. Zeitman
Four survivors from World War Three try to reach a colony of fellow-survivors in New York.
Feeble attempt at a low-budget blockbuster.
w Alan Sharp, Lukas Heller *novel* Roger Zelazny *d* Jack Smight *ph* Harry Stradling Jnr *m* Jerry Goldsmith *pd* Preston Ames
☆ Jan-Michael Vincent, George Peppard, Dominique Sanda, Paul Winfield

The Damned *

France   1947   105m   bw
Speva Film
original title: *Les Maudits*
In 1945 fanatical Nazis escape in a submarine but make the mistake of stopping to sink a freighter.
Unusual melodrama with a brilliant sense of claustrophobia, good characterization and much suspense.

---

w Jacques Remy, René Clément, Henri Jeanson *d* René Clément *ph* Henri Alekan *m* Yves Baudrier
☆ Paul Bernard, Henri Vidal, Marcel Dalio, Michel Auclair, Florence Marly

The Damned *

GB   1963   87m   bw   HammerScope
Columbia/Hammer-Swallow (Anthony Hinds)
US title: *These Are the Damned*
A scientist keeps radioactive children in a cliff cave, sealed off from the world's corruption.
Absurdly pompous, downcast and confused sci-fi melodrama set in Weymouth, with a secondary plot about motor-cycling thugs.
w Evan Jones *novel The Children of Light* by H. L. Lawrence *d* Joseph Losey *ph* Arthur Grant *m* James Bernard *pd* Bernard Robinson
☆ Macdonald Carey, Shirley Anne Field, Alexander Knox, Viveca Lindfors, Oliver Reed, Walter Gotell, James Villiers

'A folie de grandeur.' – *Tom Milne*

'Out of this wild mishmash some really magnificent images loom.' – *John Coleman*

The Damned **

West Germany/Italy   1969   164m   Eastmancolor
Praesidens/Pegaso
▦ ▤ ℺ ♫

original title: *Götterdämmerung*
A family of German industrialists divides and destroys itself under Nazi influence.
A film which has been called baroque, Wagnerian, and just plain unpleasant; it is also rather a strain to watch, with exaggerated colour and make-up to match the rotting theme.
w Nicola Badalucco, Enrico Medioli, Luchino Visconti *d* Luchino Visconti *ph* Armando Nannuzzi, Pasquale de Santis *m* Maurice Jarre *ad* Enzo del Prato, Pasquale Romano
☆ Dirk Bogarde, Ingrid Thulin, Helmut Berger, Renaud Verley, Helmut Griem, René Kolldehoff, Albrecht Schönhals, Umberto Orsini

'One is left lamenting that such a quondam master of realism as Visconti is making his films look like operas from which the score has been inexplicably removed.' – *MFB*

'The ludicrous flailings of puny puppets in inscrutable wooden frenzies.' – *John Simon*
♘ script

'The private lady of a public enemy!'

The Damned Don't Cry

US   1950   103m   bw
Warner (Jerry Wald)
A middle-class housewife leaves her husband for a gambler, and becomes involved with gangsters, but eventually reforms.
Rather dreary stimulation for female audiences who like safe dreams of danger.
w Harold Medford, Jerome Weidman *novel Case History* by Gertrude Walker *d* Vincent Sherman *ph* Ted McCord *m* Daniele Amfitheatrof
☆ Joan Crawford, Kent Smith, David Brian, Steve Cochran, Hugh Sanders, Selena Royle, Morris Ankrum, Richard Egan

'Mad adventure! Daring deeds! White hot love with music!'

A Damsel in Distress *

US   1937   101m   bw
RKO (Pandro S. Berman)
▤ ℺

An American dancing star falls for an aristocratic young Englishwoman.
Astaire without Rogers, but the style is the same and there are some very good numbers.
w P. G. Wodehouse, S. K. Lauren, Ernest Pagano *d* George Stevens *ph* Joseph H. August *m/ly* George and Ira Gershwin *ch* Hermes Pan *ad* Carroll Clark
☆ Fred Astaire, George Burns, Gracie Allen, Joan Fontaine, Reginald Gardiner, Constance Collier, Ray Noble, Montagu Love

'Plenty for the b.o. – dancing, comedy, marquee values, the usual sumptuous investiture accorded by Pandro Berman, and those Gershwin songs.' – *Variety*
† Rogers had demanded a break from musicals, so she was replaced by the demure Miss Fontaine, who was generally thought disappointing.
♙ Hermes Pan
♘ Carroll Clark

Dance Academy

Italy/US   1988   117m   colour
RAI/TPI

An exclusive ballet school is transformed into a jazz dance academy.

Cheap rip-off of Fame, with forgettable songs sung by a cast that it is impossible to remember.

wd Ted Mather ph Dennis Peters m Guido and Maurizio de Angelis ch Dennon and Sayhber Rawles ed Rebecca Ross

☆ Tony Dean Fields, Gaylyn Görg, Scott Grossman, Eliska Krupka, Steve La Chance, Paula Nichols, Julie Newmar

Dance Band

GB   1935   75m   bw
BIP (Walter Mycroft)

A band leader who croons falls for the boss of an all-ladies orchestra.

Fairly slick light musical fare of its period.

w Roger Burford, Jack Davies, Denis Waldock d Marcel Varnel ph Bryan Langley md Harry Acres ad David Rawnsley ed Sidney Cole

☆ Buddy Rogers, June Clyde, Fred Duprez, Richard Hearne, Steve Geray, Magda Kun

'Popular entertainment from start to finish, cut to a point where there is hardly a draggy moment.' – *Variety*

Dance Fools Dance

US   1931   82m   bw
MGM

A lady reporter in Chicago proves her worth.

Bizarrely-titled gangster thriller based on the Jake Lingle killing. Very moderate of its kind.

w Richard Schayer, Aurania Rouverol d Harry Beaumont ph Charles Rosher

☆ Joan Crawford, Lester Vail, Cliff Edwards, William Bakewell, William Holden (the other one), Clark Gable, Earle Foxe, Joan Marsh

'It will rock the b.o … sex, romance, punch, suspense, and everything a deluxer can sell.' – *Variety*

Dance, Girl, Dance *

US   1940   88m   bw
RKO (Erich Pommer)

Private problems of the members of a night-club dance troupe.

Competent and sometimes interesting formula drama with a harder edge than usual.

w Tess Slesinger, Frank Davis story Vicki Baum d Dorothy Arzner ph Russell Metty m Edward Ward

☆ Maureen O'Hara, Louis Hayward, Lucille Ball, Maria Ouspenskaya, Ralph Bellamy, Virginia Field, Mary Carlisle, Walter Abel, Edward Brophy, Harold Huber

The Dance Goes On

Canada   1991   103m   colour
Quest (Paul Almond)

A brash young man learns to appreciate rustic values after he travels from Malibu to the family farm in Quebec with the ashes of his uncle.

Amiable family drama of a familiar kind, dealing with tensions between father and son.

wd Paul Almond ph Peter Benison m Claude Léveillée, James Smith pd Reuben Freed

☆ James Keach, Matthew James Almond, Geneviève Bujold, Leslie Hope, Bryan Hennessy, Deborah Freeland, Cary Lawrence

Dance Hall *

GB   1950   80m   bw
Ealing (Michael Balcon, E. V. H. Emmett)

Four factory girls seek relaxation and various kinds of romance at the local palais.

Untypically flat Ealing slice of life, now watchable only with a smile as musical nostalgia.

w E. V. H. Emmett, Diana Morgan, Alexander Mackendrick d Charles Crichton ph Douglas Slocombe m Joyce Cochran md Ernest Irving ed Seth Holt

☆ Natasha Parry, Donald Houston, Diana Dors, Bonar Colleano, Jane Hylton, Petula Clark, Gladys Henson, Sydney Tafler, Geraldo and his band, Ted Heath and his band

'Not a film that will please everyone. Its story is tiresome and not varied enough for the length of the picture.' – *A. Jympson Harman*

Dance Little Lady

GB   1954   87m   Eastmancolor
George Minter/Renown

An ambitious man tries to turn his balletomane daughter into a film star.

Artless melodrama in poor colour.

w Val Guest, Doreen Montgomery d Val Guest

☆ Terence Morgan, Mai Zetterling, Mandy Miller, Guy Rolfe, Eunice Gayson

Dance Me Outside *

Canada   1994   84m   colour
Yorktown/Shadow Shows (Brian Dennis, Bruce McDonald)

In Ontario, an 18-year-old Indian, compelled to write a story in order to get into mechanics school, recalls events following the rape and murder of an Indian girl by a white man.

Effective drama of racial tensions and resentment that touches with humour and insight on many other aspects of life.

w Bruce McDonald, Don McKellar, John Frizzell novel W. P. Kinsella d Bruce McDonald ph Miroslaw Baszak m Mychael Danna pd John Dondertman ed Michael Pacek

☆ Ryan Rajendra Black, Adam Beach, Lisa LaCroix, Michael Greyeyes, Kevin Hicks, Jennifer Podemski, Sandrine Holt

'Bolstered by a winning, youthful cast, the film is a droll ensemble piece that makes its serious points skillfully and effortlessly.' – *Leonard Klady, Variety*

The Dance of Death *

GB   1968   149m   Technicolor
BHE/National Theatre (John Brabourne)

Edgar and Alice live alone on an island, their marriage having become a constant war.

Too-literal film transcription of an applauded theatrical production, with the camera anchored firmly in the middle of the stalls.

w August Strindberg (translation C. D. Locock) d David Giles ph Geoffrey Unsworth

☆ Laurence Olivier, Geraldine McEwan, Robert Lang, Carolyn Jones

Dance of the Vampires: see The Fearless Vampire Killers

Dance of the Wind *

Germany/GB/France/Netherlands/India/Switzerland
1997   86m   colour
Artificial Eye/Pandora/Elephant Eye/Illumination/JBA/Filmcompany/NFDC (Karl Baumgartner)

In New Delhi, a singer of classical Hindustani music loses her voice when her mother dies, and goes to find the guru who was her mother's teacher.

A fable about individuality within a culture, accessible to a sympathetic Western audience.

w Robin Mukherjee d Rajan Khosa ph Piyush Shah pd Amardeep Behl ed Emma Matthews

☆ Kitu Gidwani, Bhaveen Gossain, B. C. Sanyal, Roshan Bano, Kapila Vatsyayan, Vinod Nagpal, Punamava Mehta, Ami Arora, Bhunvar Lal

'A little gem.' – *Empire*

Dance Pretty Lady

GB   1932   64m   bw
British Instructional (H. Bruce Woolfe)

Ballerina loves artist but settles unwisely for respectability.

Stilted early talkie from Compton Mackenzie's Carnival, qv under its own title.

wd Anthony Asquith ph Jack Parker m John Reynders ad Ian Campbell-Gray

☆ Ann Casson, Carl Harbord, Michael Hogan

Dance Team

US   1931   80m   bw
Fox

Struggles of a couple to become top ballroom dancers.

Easy-going star fare which needed tightening.

w Edwin Burke novel Sarah Addington d Sidney Lanfield

☆ James Dunn, Sally Eilers, Minna Gombell, Ralph Morgan

'Its comedy overcomes drawn-out sequences laden with sentimentality.' – *Variety*

Dance with a Stranger *

GB   1985   101m   Technicolor
Goldcrest/NFFC/First Picture Co (Roger Randall-Cutler)

Ex-prostitute Ruth Ellis, infatuated with a worthless sponger, shoots him dead rather than lose him.

Muddled account of the last woman to hang in Great Britain; no sympathies are aroused and no clear viewpoint taken.

w Shelagh Delaney d Mike Newell ph Peter Hannan m Richard Hartley pd Andrew Mollo ed Mick Audsley

☆ Miranda Richardson, Rupert Everett, Ian Holm, Matthew Carroll, Stratford Johns

Dance with Me

US   1998   126m   CFI color
Columbia/Mandalay (Lauren C. Weissman, Shinya Egawa, Randa Haines)

A young Cuban travels to the United States to find his father and a partner for a Las Vegas dance competition.

Lively romantic drama, with most of the action taking place on the dance-floor, but it is both forgettable and predictable.

w Daryl Matthews d Randa Haines ph Fred Murphy m Michael Convertino pd Waldemar Kalinowski ed Lisa Fruchtman

☆ Vanessa L. Williams, Chayanne, Kris Kristoffersen, Joan Plowright, Jane Krakowski, Beth Grant, William Marquez

'Flashdance for the 1990s, for good and ill.' – *Variety*

Dancers

US   1987   99m   colour
Cannon/Hera/Baryshnikov/Golan/Globus

On tour in Italy, a leading dancer recovers his inspiration when a young ballerina joins the company.

Trite script, dull romance and moments of exciting dance.

w Sarah Kernochan d Herbert Ross ph Ennio Guarnieri m Pino Donnagio pd Gianni Quaranta ed William Reynolds

☆ Mikhail Baryshnikov, Alessandra Ferri, Leslie Browne, Thomas Rall, Lynn Seymour, Victor Barbee, Julie Kent

Dancers in the Dark

US   1932   76m   bw
Paramount

A nightclub dancer with a shady past tries to prove that she's really in love.

Banal show business melodrama with authentic-seeming night-club background.

w Herman J. Mankiewicz d David Burton

☆ Miriam Hopkins, Jack Oakie, George Raft, William Collier Jnr, Lyda Roberti, Eugene Pallette

'Only fair for Times Square, looks surefire in the hinterland.' – *Variety*

Dances with Wolves **

US   1990   180m   DeLuxe Panavision
Guild/Tig Productions/Jim Wilson, Kevin Costner

A cavalry officer is adopted by the Sioux Indians.

A liberal Western – the Indians (or Native Americans) are the good guys – sentimental and over-long, but nonetheless affecting. A version of 'the director's cut' was promised for videocassette, with a running time of 240 minutes.

w Michael Blake novel Michael Blake d Kevin Costner ph Dean Semler m John Barry pd Jeffrey Beecroft ad William Ladd Skinner ed Neil Travis

☆ Kevin Costner, Mary McDonnell, Graham Greene, Rodney A. Grant, Floyd Red Crow Westerman, Tantoo Cardinal, Robert Pastorelli, Charles Rocket, Maury Chaykin, Jimmy Herman, Nathan Lee Chasing His Horse

'Dances with Wolves would be easier to love if screenwriter Blake had resisted the temptation to plug every positive stereotype about Native Americans. The characters, alternately stoic, are ecologically aware and brave. Even Hollywood Indians don't have to be like this.' – *Michael Dorris, Premiere*

'Long, simplistic and lacking in irony, though not in pawky humour. The action set-pieces (two ambushes, two pitched battles, a grand buffalo hunt) are dynamically handled. But the picture lacks the visual and dramatic authority of the best Westerns.' – *Philip French, Observer*

'Costner has feathers in his hair and feathers in his head.' – *Pauline Kael*

† A special edition of the film with an extra 53 minutes added was given a London cinema release in 1991 and later released on video.

▲ best film; Kevin Costner (as director); Michael Blake; John Barry; Dean Semler; Neil Travis; best sound

△ Kevin Costner (as actor); Mary McDonnell; Graham Greene; best costume design; best art direction

Dancin' thru the Dark **

GB   1990   95m   colour
Palace/BBC Films/Formost Films (Andre Molyneux)

On the night before her wedding, a woman goes out with her girl-friends for a celebration at a night-club, only to meet there her former lover, now a successful rock singer, and her fiancé, drunk from his stag-night party.

High-spirited and witty domestic drama.

w Willy Russell play Stags and Hens by Willy Russell d Mike Ockrent ph Philip Bonham-Carter m Willy Russell pd Paul Joel

☆ Claire Hackett, Con O'Neill, Angela Clarke, Mark Womack, Julia Deakin, Simon O'Brien, Louise Duprey, Andrew Naylor, Sandy Hendrickse, Peter Watts

'A satisfying and enjoyable work.' – *Variety*

'Five sisters embrace the spirit of a people.'

Dancing at Lughnasa

Ireland/GB/US   1998   92m   Rank Colour
Ferndale/Capitol/Sony/Channel 4 Films (Noel Pearson)

Five unmarried sisters contemplate their future in rural Donegal in the mid-30s.

A dull transfer of an atmospheric play about Irish identity to the screen; only the landscape holds the interest.

w. Frank McGuinness play Brian Friel d Pat O'Connor ph Kenneth MacMillan m Bill Whelan pd Mark Geraghty ed Humphrey Dixon

☆ Meryl Streep, Michael Gambon, Catherine McCormack, Kathy Burke, Sophie Thompson, Brid Brennan, Rhys Ifans, Darrell Johnston, Lorcan Cranitch, Peter Gowen

'Middlebrow, bland film, lacking in emotional or intellectual bite.' – *Claire Monk, Sight and Sound*

Dancing Co-ed

US   1939   90m   bw
MGM (Edgar Selwyn)
GB title: Every Other Inch a Lady

A college girl makes it in show business as well as the groves of academe.

Mindless vehicle for a 19-year-old star.

w Albert Mannheimer story Albert Treynor d S. Sylvan Simon ph Alfred Gilks m David Snell, Edward Ward

☆ Lana Turner, Richard Carlson, Artie Shaw, Leon Errol, Ann Rutherford, Lee Bowman, Monty Woolley, Roscoe Karns, June Preisser, Walter Kingsford

'Better than average programme entertainment.' – *Variety*

Dancing Fool: see Harold Teen

Dancing in the Dark *

US   1949   92m   Technicolor
TCF (George Jessel)

A silent movie idol makes a comeback as a talent scout, and spots his own daughter.

Thin but unusual Hollywood drama with music; in the long run too sentimental.

w Mary C. McCall Jnr play The Band Wagon by George S. Kaufman, Howard Dietz, Arthur Schwartz d Irving Reis ph Harry Jackson m Alfred Newman

☆ William Powell, Adolphe Menjou, Mark Stevens, Betsy Drake, Hope Emerson, Lloyd Corrigan, Walter Catlett, Jean Hersholt

Dancing in the Dark

Canada   1986   98m   colour
Brightstar/Film Arts/Film House/CBC (Anthony Kramreither)

A housewife recalls the events that led to her breakdown and the murder of her husband.

Virtually a monologue, well performed by Henry, of a woman who thoughtfully follows a conventional life with a conventional husband and begins to wonder why it is so unfulfilling; the theme has been worked so often that its appeal has begun to pall.
wd Leon Marr novel Joan Barfoot ph Vic Sarin pd Lillian Sarafinchan ed Tom Berner
☆ Martha Henry, Neil Munro, Rosemary Dunsmore, Richard Monette

Dancing Lady *
US 1933 94m bw
MGM (David O. Selznick)
▣ ◎⌐
A successful dancer chooses between a playboy and her stage manager.
Routine backstage semi-musical with interesting talent applied rather haphazardly.
w Allen Rivkin, P. J. Wolfson novel James Warner Bellah d Robert Z. Leonard ph Oliver T. Marsh m various md Louis Silvers
☆ Joan Crawford, Clark Gable, Fred Astaire, Franchot Tone, May Robson, Ted Healy and his Stooges (the Three Stooges), Winnie Lightner, Robert Benchley, Nelson Eddy
'Very potent b.o. in the screen musical cycle.' – Variety

The Dancing Masters
↟↟ US 1943 63m bw
TCF (Lee Marcus)
▣
Laurel and Hardy run a ballet school, and get involved with gangsters and inventors.
Insubstantial star comedy featuring reworkings of old routines, and a back-projected runaway bus climax.
w Scott Darling story George Bricker d Mal St Clair ph Norbert Brodine m Arthur Lange ad James Basevi, Chester Gore ed Norman Colbert
☆ Stan Laurel, Oliver Hardy, Trudy Marshall, Bob Bailey, Margaret Dumont, Matt Briggs, Robert Mitchum

Dancing with Crime
GB 1947 83m bw
Coronet-Alliance (James Carter)
A dance hall is the front for black marketeers, who are exposed by a resourceful taxi driver.
Tolerable post-war melodrama aping Hollywood.
w Brock Williams story Peter Fraser d John Paddy Carstairs
☆ Richard Attenborough, Barry K. Barnes, Sheila Sim, Garry Marsh, John Warwick, Barry Jones

The Dancing Years
GB 1949 97m Technicolor
ABPC (Warwick Ward)
A composer loves a singer who leaves him after a misunderstanding but later bears his son ... all in the Alps pre-1914.
Lamentable transcription of an operetta; precisely the ingredients which worked so well on stage seem embarrassing on film, and the performances and direction do not help.
w Warwick Ward, Jack Whittingham operetta Ivor Novello d Harold French ph Stephen Dade m Ivor Novello
☆ Dennis Price, Gisèle Préville, Patricia Dainton, Anthony Nicholls, Grey Blake, Muriel George, Olive Gilbert

Dandin **
France 1988 110m colour
Films du Losange/Selena Audiovisuel/Sept/A2 (Margaret Menegoz)
A rich peasant faces constant humiliation when he marries the daughter of an aristocrat; she refuses to consummate the marriage and her parents treat him with snobbish disdain.
A sumptuous-looking but tough and exhilaratingly uncompromising approach to a classic comedy of greed and desire so that, for all its period setting, it has a contemporary bite.
wd Roger Planchon play Georges Dandin by Molière ph Bernard Lutic
☆ Claude Brasseur, Zabou, Nelly Borgeaud, Evelyne Buyle, Jean-Claude Adelin, Daniel Gélin, Marco Bisson, Vincent Garanger

Dandy Dick
GB 1935 72m bw
BIP (Walter Mycroft)
A country vicar becomes innocently involved with racehorse doping.

Flatly-handled farce which helped to introduce Will Hay to the screen, though not in his accustomed role.
w William Beaudine, Frank Miller, Clifford Grey, Will Hay play Sir Arthur Wing Pinero d William Beaudine ph Jack Parker ad Duncan Sutherland ed A. C. Hammond
☆ Will Hay, Nancy Burne, Esmond Knight, Davy Burnaby

'His mission is murder! His victim – himself!'

A Dandy in Aspic
GB 1968 107m Technicolor Panavision
Columbia (Anthony Mann)
▣ ◎⌐
A double agent in Berlin is given orders to kill himself.
Muddled, pretentious spy thriller; flat, nebulous and boring.
w Derek Marlowe novel Derek Marlowe d Anthony Mann ph Christopher Challis m Quincy Jones
☆ Laurence Harvey, Tom Courtenay, Lionel Stander, Mia Farrow, Harry Andrews, Peter Cook, Per Oscarsson
† Anthony Mann died during shooting, and Laurence Harvey completed the direction.

Dandy the All-American Girl
US 1976 90m Metrocolor Panavision
MGM
GB title: Sweet Revenge
A much convicted woman car thief determines to become the legitimate owner of a Dino Ferrari.
The American dream gone sour again, this time offering in its wake a curious stream of moral values.
w B. J. Perla, Marilyn Goldin d Jerry Schatzberg
☆ Stockard Channing, Sam Waterston, Richard Doughty, Franklyn Ajaye

Danger by My Side
GB 1962 63m bw
Butchers (John I. Phillips)
US title: Danger on My Side
The sister of a murdered detective tracks down his killers.
Dreary little thriller, lacking even a touch of originality, and taken at a somnambulistic pace.
w Ronald Liles, Aubrey Cash d Charles Saunders ph Walter J. Harvey m Martin Slavin ad Harold Watson ed Jim Connock
☆ Anthony Oliver, Maureen Connell, Alan Tilvern, Bill Nagy, Sonya Cordeau, Tom Naylor, Brandon Brady, Richard Klee, Wally Patch

Danger: Diabolik
Italy/France 1967 105m Technicolor
Dino de Laurentiis/Marianne (Bruno Todini)
▣
International police bait a golden trap for a master criminal.
Superior Batman-type adventures with a comic strip hero-villain.
w Dino Maiuri, Adriano Baracco, Mario Bava d Mario Bava ph Antonio Rinaldi m Ennio Morricone
☆ John Phillip Law, Marisa Mell, Michel Piccoli, Adolfo Celi, Terry-Thomas

Danger Lights *
US 1930 87m bw
RKO (William LeBaron)
▣
Railroad owners face various problems.
Routine would-be thriller intended to show off a wide screen system called Spoor-Bergen Natural Vision; it failed owing to cost and the thin quality of the film.
w James Ashmore Creelman d George B. Seitz ph Karl Struss
☆ Louis Wolheim, Robert Armstrong, Jean Arthur, Hugh Herbert

Danger List
GB 1957 22m bw
Exclusive/Hammer (Anthony Hinds)
At a hospital dispensary, three out-patients are given a fatal drug by mistake.
Uneventful programme filler with predictable twists in its little tales.
w J. D. Scott d Leslie Arliss ph Arthur Grant m Edwin Astley ad Ted Marshall ed James Needs
☆ Philip Friend, Honor Blackman, Mervyn Johns, Alexander Field, Constance Fraser, Muriel Zillah

Danger, Love at Work *
US 1937 84m bw
TCF (Harold Wilson)
A young lawyer needs the signature of a rich crazy family to conclude a land sale.
The title doesn't suggest it, but this is a not inconsiderable comedy in the tradition of My Man Godfrey and You Can't Take It With You. A highly competent cast does its best.
w James Edward Grant, Ben Markson d Otto Preminger ph Virgil Miller md David Buttolph
☆ Ann Sothern, Jack Haley, Edward Everett Horton, Mary Boland, Walter Catlett, John Carradine, Maurice Cass, Alan Dinehart, E. E. Clive
'Not important enough to be a main feature but a very good dualler.' – Variety

Danger on My Side: see Danger by My Side

Danger Patrol
US 1937 58m bw
RKO
Life among 'soup handlers' – lorry drivers who deliver nitro-glycerine to oil wells.
An interesting notion slackly handled, with suspense losing out to romance.
w Sy Bartlett story Helen Vreeland, Hilda Vincent d Lew Landers ph Nicholas Musuraca ad Van Nest Polglase ed Ted Cheesman
☆ Sally Eilers, John Beal, Harry Carey, Frank M. Thomas, Crawford Weaver, Lee Patrick, Edward Gargan

Danger Route
GB 1967 92m DeLuxe
UA/Amicus (Max J. Rosenberg, Milton Subotsky)
An 'eliminator' for the British secret service finds after a series of adventures that he must dispose of his own girlfriend.
Dour sub-Bondian thriller with little to commend it.
w Meade Roberts novel The Eliminator by Andrew York d Seth Holt ph Harry Waxman m John Mayer
☆ Richard Johnson, Diana Dors, Sylvia Syms, Carol Lynley, Barbara Bouchet, Gordon Jackson, Sam Wanamaker, Maurice Denham, Harry Andrews

Danger Signal
US 1945 77m bw
Warner (William Jacobs)
A smooth heel implicated in murder charms a modest stenographer and her mother.
Tedious and less than competent melodrama.
w Adele Comandini, Graham Baker novel Phyllis Bottome d Robert Florey
☆ Faye Emerson, Zachary Scott, Dick Erdman, Rosemary de Camp, Bruce Bennett, Mona Freeman

'Four hundred plan to escape – one plans to betray!'

Danger Within **
GB 1958 101m bw
British Lion/Colin Lesslie
US title: Breakout
Escape plans of officers in a prisoner-of-war camp are threatened by an informer.
Familiar comedy and melodrama with an added whodunnit element, smartly handled and very entertaining.
w Bryan Forbes, Frank Harvey novel Michael Gilbert d Don Chaffey ph Arthur Grant m Francis Chagrin
☆ Richard Todd, Bernard Lee, Michael Wilding, Richard Attenborough, Dennis Price, Donald Houston, William Franklyn, Vincent Ball, Peter Arne

Danger Zone
US 1995 92m Foto-Kem
Nu Image (Danny Lerner, Elie Samaha)
▣▣ ▣
In East Africa, a disgraced American mining engineer, blamed for poisoning communities with toxic waste, goes to find his friend who was involved and discovers that the real purpose of his search has been kept from him.
Deplorable and ludicrous thriller that condemns ignorance about Africa, while at the same time exploiting its more exotic aspects, and revelling in violence; you might feel sympathy towards Billy Zane for being involved in such garbage if he were not also one of the movie's co-producers.

w Jeff Albert story Danny Lerner d Allan Eastman ph Yossi Wein m Daniel Pelfrey pd Leith Ridley, David Varod ed Alain Jakubowicz
☆ Billy Zane, Ron Silver, Cary-Hiroyuki Tagawa, Robert Downey Jnr, Lisa Collins

Dangerous *
US 1935 78m bw
Warner (Harry Joe Brown)
▣▣
An alcoholic actress is rehabilitated.
Unconvincing and only adequately handled melodrama which won the star her first Oscar, presumably from sympathy at her losing it the previous year for Of Human Bondage.
w Laird Doyle d Alfred E. Green ph Ernest Haller
☆ Bette Davis, Franchot Tone, Margaret Lindsay, Alison Skipworth, John Eldredge, Dick Foran
'Well-acted and directed drama with femme appeal.' – Variety
† Remade 1941 as Singapore Woman.
♟ Bette Davis

Dangerous Afternoon
GB 1961 92m bw
Bryanston/Theatrecraft
The owner of a boarding house for elderly criminals is blackmailed by an ex-convict who knows her true identity.
An interesting notion—a retirement home for genteel female crooks—becomes mired in an uninteresting story of blackmail and murder.
w Brandon Fleming play Gerald Anstruther d Charles Saunders
☆ Ruth Dunning, Nora Nicholson, Joanne Dunham, Howard Pays, May Hallatt, Gwenda Wilson, Ian Colin, Gladys Henson, Barbara Everest, Jerold Wells

Dangerous Beauty
US 1998 111m Technicolor Panavision
Warner/Regency/Bedford Falls (Arnon Milchan, Marshall Herskovitz, Edward Zwick, Sarah Kaplan)
▣▣ ▣ ◎
GB title: The Honest Courtesan
In 16th-century Venice, a woman becomes a celebrated courtesan when the man she loves marries for money.
Sumptuous historical romance, which is based on fact but plays as if it were invented by a sentimental novelist.
w Jeannine Dominy biography The Honest Courtesan by Margaret Rosenthal d Marshall Herskovitz ph Bojan Bazelli m George Fenton pd Norman Garwood ed Steven Rosenblum, Arthur Coburn
☆ Catherine McCormack, Rufus Sewell, Jacqueline Bisset, Oliver Platt, Moira Kelly, Fred Ward, Naomi Watts, Jeroen Krabbe, Joanna Cassidy, Peter Eyre
'An odd mix of high-toned intentions and cornball romance that works in fits and bursts.' – Leonard Klady, Variety

Dangerous Blondes
US 1943 81m bw
Columbia (Samuel Bischoff)
A detective story writer and his wife solve a real life murder.
More Thin Man imitations, rather tepid this time.
w Richard Flournoy, Jack Henley d Leigh Jason
☆ Allyn Joslyn, Evelyn Keyes, John Hubbard, Edmund Lowe, Anita Louise, Frank Craven, William Demarest

Dangerous Corner *
US 1934 67m bw
RKO
▣▣
After dinner conversation reveals what might have been if friends had spoken the truth about a long-ago suicide.
A fascinating trick play makes interesting but scarcely sparkling cinema.
w Anne Morrison Chapin, Madeleine Ruthven play J. B. Priestley d Phil Rosen ph J. Roy Hunt m Max Steiner
☆ Melvyn Douglas, Conrad Nagel, Virginia Bruce, Erin O'Brien Moore, Ian Keith, Betty Furness, Henry Wadsworth, Doris Lloyd
'Confusing mixture of a mystery and problem play ... doubtful as to general fan appeal.' – Variety

---

↟↟ film suitable for family viewing　　▣▣ VHS video-cassette for the British PAL system　　▣▣ VHS video-cassette for the British PAL system in wide screen-format　　✧ Video cassette in a computer-colourised version　　▣ American NTSC video-cassette　　◎⌐ Laser disc

Dangerous Crossing *

US 1953 75m bw

TCF (Robert Bassler)

At the start of an Atlantic sea voyage a woman's husband disappears, and she is assured that he never existed. He does, and is trying to murder her.

Adequately handled twist on the vanishing lady story: grade A production covers lapses of grade B imagination.

w Leo Townsend *story* John Dickson Carr d Joseph M. Newman *ph* Joseph LaShelle *md* Lionel Newman

☆ Jeanne Crain, Michael Rennie, Carl Betz, Casey Adams, Mary Anderson, Willis Bouchey

Dangerous Curves

US 1929 75m bw

Paramount

A bareback rider loves a high wire artist.

Obvious circus melodrama, a modest star vehicle.

w Donald Davis, Florence Ryerson d Lothar Mendes *ph* Harry Fischbeck

☆ Clara Bow, Richard Arlen, Kay Francis, David Newell, Anders Randolf

Dangerous Days: see *Wild Boys of the Road*

Dangerous Exile

GB 1957 90m Eastmancolor Vistavision

Rank (George H. Brown)

After the French Revolution, the young would-be Louis XVII is brought across the Channel and hidden in Pembrokeshire, where enemies attack him.

Historical romance, ineptly plotted but quite well produced.

w Robin Estridge *novel* Vaughan Wilkins d Brian Desmond Hurst *ph* Geoffrey Unsworth *m* Georges Auric

☆ Louis Jourdan, Belinda Lee, Keith Michell, Richard O'Sullivan, Martita Hunt, Finlay Currie, Anne Heywood, Jacques Brunius

Dangerous Female: see *The Maltese Falcon (1931)*

Dangerous Game: see *Snake Eyes (1993)*

A Dangerous Game

US 1941 61m bw

Universal

Various weird characters converge on a lunatic asylum where a fortune is hidden.

Failed attempt at black farce: the actors are game, but the material doesn't hold water.

w Larry Rhine, Ben Chapman, Maxwell Shane d John Rawlins

☆ Richard Arlen, Andy Devine, Jeanne Kelly, Edward Brophy, Marc Lawrence, Andrew Tombes, Tom Dugan

'For all its frantic, deafening slapstick it remains stubbornly humourless … if there's such a thing as a Class D picture, this is it.' – *Variety*

Dangerous Ground

South Africa/US 1996 96m DeLuxe

Entertainment/Investec/New Line (Gillian Gorfil, Darrell Roodt)

Returning to his home after a dozen years in America, a South African goes in search of his missing brother and discovers that he is involved with drug dealers.

Trite tale of revenge, a dreary gangster movie that gains nothing from its South African setting.

w Greg Latter, Darrell Roodt d Darrell Roodt *ph* Paul Gilpin *m* Stanley Clarke *pd* Dimitri Repanis *ed* David Heitner

☆ Ice Cube, Elizabeth Hurley, Sechaba Morojele, Eric 'Waku' Miyeni, Ving Rhames, Thokozani Nkosi, Ron Smerczak

'Don't see this film.' – *Film Review*

Dangerous Liaisons **

US 1988 120m Eastmancolor

Warner/Lorimar/NFH (Norma Heyman, Hank Moonjean)

Two jaded French aristocrats play games of sexual politics.

A cool dissection of sexual feeling.

w Christopher Hampton *play* Christopher Hampton *novel* Choderlos de Laclos d Stephen Frears *ph* Philippe Rousselot *m* George Fenton *pd* Stuart Craig *ed* Mick Audsley

☆ Glenn Close, John Malkovich, Michelle Pfeiffer, Swoosie Kurtz, Keanu Reeves, Mildred Natwick, Uma Thurman

'Beautifully acted (by Glenn Close in particular), elegantly phrased, carefully shot on location in an appropriate selection of chateaux, directed with a limpidly formalised serenity, it's a handsome and intelligent piece of work.' – *Tom Milne, MFB*

🎗 Christopher Hampton; Stuart Craig

🏆 best picture; Glenn Close; Michelle Pfeiffer; George Fenton

🎬 adapted screenplay; Michelle Pfeiffer

Dangerous Millions

US 1946 69m bw

TCF

GB title: *The House of Tao Ling*

Eight would-be inheritors of a millionaire's estate find themselves at the mercy of a warlord in the Chinese mountains.

Odd little second feature confusion of The Cat and the Canary *and* Shanghai Express; *quite watchable.*

w Irving Cummings Jnr, Robert G. North d James Tinling

☆ Kent Taylor, Dona Drake, Tala Birell, Leonard Strong, Konstantin Shayne

Dangerous Minds

US 1995 99m Technicolor

Buena Vista/Hollywood (Don Simpson, Jerry Bruckheimer)

An ex-marine becomes an English teacher at a tough inner-city school where she confronts raucous students who don't want to learn.

Despite its basis in fact, this comes across as bland and unbelievable wish-fulfilment, just another feel-good fantasy about tough, restive delinquents being tamed by poetry.

w Ronald Bass *book* My Posse Don't Do Homework by LouAnne Johnson d John N. Smith *ph* Pierre Letarte *m* Wendy & Lisa *pd* Donald Graham Burt *ed* Tom Rolf

☆ Michelle Pfeiffer, George Dzundza, Courtney B. Vance, Robin Bartlett, Bruklin Harris, Renoly Santiago, John Neville

'This earnest, sweet-natured inspirational drama almost seems like something from another, more innocent era.' – *Variety*

'This is one of those sham inspirational-teacher fables that worships the idea of knowledge without actually bothering to put any on screen. We're supposed to clasp our hands to our hearts when the kids learn a few lines of Dylan Thomas.' – *Owen Gleiberman, Entertainment Weekly*

† Andy Garcia's role as Michelle Pfeiffer's boyfriend was left on the cutting-room floor.

Dangerous Mission

US 1954 75m Technicolor 3-D

RKO (Irwin Allen)

In Montana's Glacier National Park, a policeman tries to protect an innocent girl witness from big city gangsters.

Tolerable routine double-bill thriller with a predictable cable car climax.

w Horace McCoy, W. R. Burnett, Charles Bennett, James Edmiston d Louis King *ph* William Snyder *m* Roy Webb

☆ Victor Mature, Piper Laurie, Vincent Price, William Bendix, Betta St John, Dennis Weaver

'The scenery received the best notices.' – *James Robert Parish, 1976*

'This is your melody – you gave it to me. I'll never play it again without thinking of you!'

Dangerous Moonlight *

GB 1941 98m bw

RKO (William Sistrom)

US title: *Suicide Squadron*

A Polish pianist escapes from the Nazis and loses his memory after flying in the Battle of Britain.

Immensely popular wartime romance which introduced Richard Addinsell's Warsaw Concerto. Production values and script somewhat below par.

w Shaun Terence Young, Brian Desmond Hurst, Rodney Ackland d Brian Desmond Hurst *ph* Georges Périnal, Ronald Neame *m* Richard Addinsell

☆ Anton Walbrook, Sally Gray, Derrick de Marney, Cecil Parker, Percy Parsons, Keneth Kent, Guy Middleton, John Laurie, Frederick Valk

Dangerous Moves *

Switzerland 1985 100m colour

Enterprise/Spectrafilm (Arthur Cohn)

The world championship chess showdown is between the Soviet title holder and an exiled dissident challenger.

Interesting, rather specialized actor's piece with political overtones.

wd Richard Dembo *ph* Raoul Coutard *m* Gabriel Yared *ad* Ivan Maussion *ed* Agnès Guillemot

☆ Michel Piccoli, Leslie Caron, Liv Ullmann, Alexandre Arbatt

🏆 best foreign film

Dangerous Number

US 1937 71m bw

MGM

A showgirl is confused by her husband's rich relations.

Rather tedious comedy drama which never really gets anywhere.

w Carey Wilson *story* Leona Dalrymple d Richard Thorpe

☆ Robert Young, Ann Sothern, Reginald Owen, Cora Witherspoon, Dean Jagger, Barnett Parker

'A compact piece of entertainment, though pretty shallow on the drama end.' – *Variety*

Dangerous Partners

US 1945 74m bw

Arthur J. Field/MGM

Nazi agents trying to get out of America are converted to democracy.

Bewildering mixture of propaganda and melodrama: nothing seems to mesh.

w Marion Parsonnet, Edmund L. Hartmann *story* Oliver Weld Bayer d Edward L. Cahn

☆ James Craig, Signe Hasso, Edmund Gwenn, Audrey Totter, Mabel Paige

A Dangerous Profession

US 1949 79m bw

RKO

An ex-detective tries to help a beautiful woman and becomes involved in murder and the bail bond racket.

Undistinguished crime melodrama providing a satisfactory vehicle for its stars.

w Martin Rackin, Warren Duff d Ted Tetzlaff

☆ Pat O'Brien, George Raft, Ella Raines, Jim Backus, Bill Williams

A Dangerous Summer

Australia 1982 94m colour Panavision

McElroy and McElroy

In a Blue Mountain resort, a partner decides to burn down the buildings for the insurance.

Modest melodrama with spectacular fire sequences.

w David Ambrose, Quentin Masters *novel* Kit Denton d Quentin Masters

☆ James Mason, Tom Skerritt, Ian Gilmour, Wendy Hughes, Kim Deacon

Dangerous to Know *

US 1938 70m bw

Paramount

A ruthless Chicago gangster comes a cropper when his Chinese mistress discovers he has fallen for a socialite.

Flatly handled but mildly interesting adaptation of a highly successful play, the potential of which seems to have been thrown away.

w William R. Lippman, Horace McCoy *play* On the Spot by Edgar Wallace d Robert Florey *ph* Theodor Sparkuhl

☆ Akim Tamiroff, Anna May Wong, Gail Patrick, Lloyd Nolan, Harvey Stephens, Anthony Quinn, Porter Hall

Dangerous When Wet **

US 1953 95m Technicolor

MGM (George Wells)

An entire Arkansas family is sponsored to swim the English Channel.

A bright and lively vehicle for an aquatic star, who in one sequence swims with Tom and Jerry. Amusing sequences give opportunities to a strong cast.

w Dorothy Kingsley d Charles Walters *ph* Harold Rosson *m/ly* Johnny Mercer, Arthur Schwartz *md* George Stoll

☆ Esther Williams, Charlotte Greenwood, William Demarest, Fernando Lamas, Jack Carson, Denise Darcel, Barbara Whiting

'The truth hurts. But a lie can kill.'

A Dangerous Woman *

US 1993 101m Eastmancolor

First Independent/Amblin/Island World/Gramercy/Rollercoaster (Naomi Foner)

An ungainly woman who finds it impossible to lie is faced with a situation where telling the truth will mean her imprisonment.

An unusual and sometimes affecting drama, dealing with moral dilemmas and skewed relationships, but heavy-handed in its methods.

w Naomi Foner *novel* Mary McGarry Morris d Stephen Gyllenhaal *ph* Robert Elswit *m* Carter Burwell *pd* David Brisbin *ed* Harvey Rosenstock

☆ Debra Winger, Barbara Hershey, Gabriel Byrne, David Strathairn, John Terry, Chloe Webb

'Pic will register deeply with some viewers, especially women, but it's the kind of odd and muted tale for which it is difficult to drum up theatrical interest these days.' – *Todd McCarthy, Variety*

'At times something of a ponderous bore and has enough characters and plots to keep a soap opera going for a few months.' – *Kim Newman, Empire*

Dangerous Youth: see *These Dangerous Years*

Dangerously They Live

US 1941 77m bw

Warner (Ben Stoloff)

American Nazi agents try to get a secret memorized by a British girl agent injured in a car crash.

Watchable, routine spy propaganda fare.

w Marion Parsonnet d Robert Florey *ph* William O'Connell

☆ John Garfield, Raymond Massey, Nancy Coleman, Moroni Olsen, Lee Patrick, Christian Rub, Frank Reicher

Dangerously Yours

US 1937 60m bw

TCF (Sol M. Wurtzel)

On board ship a detective captures a lady jewel thief but reforms her.

Very tolerable programme filler with watchable performances.

w Lou Breslow, John Patrick d Mal St Clair *ph* Harry Davis *md* Samuel Kaylin

☆ Cesar Romero, Phyllis Brooks, Jane Darwell, Alan Dinehart, Douglas Wood, Leon Ames

'Fox is turning out a pretty good quality of B product.' – *Variety*

Daniel

US 1983 129m Technicolor

World Film Services (John Van Eyssen)

The children of executed spies are traumatized by the past.

Patchwork vision of thirties America, with Jewishness thrown in for added weight. Not easy to watch.

w E. L. Doctorow *novel* The Book of Daniel by E. L. Doctorow d Sidney Lumet *ph* Andrzej Bartkowiak *m* Bob James *pd* Philip Rosenberg

☆ Timothy Hutton, Mandy Patinkin, Lindsay Crouse, Ed Asner, Ellen Barkin, Tovah Feldshuh

'Only with the last scene does one realize that it has collapsed into an empty liberal squeak.' – *Tom Milne, MFB*

Daniel and the Devil: see *All that Money Can Buy*

Daniel Boone, Trail Blazer

US 1956 76m Trucolor

Republic (Albert C. Gannaway)

Daniel Boone, battling against the Indians, makes the wilderness safe for settlers.

Stolidly acted story of the pioneer days of America, dully directed.

w Tom Hubbard, Jack Patrick d Albert C. Gannaway, Ismael Rodriguez *ph* Jack Draper *m* Raul Lavista *ed* Fernando A. Martinez

☆ Bruce Bennett, Lon Chaney, Faron Young, Kem Dibbs, Damian O'Flynn, Jacqueline Evans, Nancy Rodman, Freddy Fernandez

---

Danny Boy: see *Angel (1982)*

Danny Boy

GB   1941   80m   bw
Butcher's

A singer searches for her estranged husband and small son who have become street entertainers.
Sentimental drama with music; not for the critical.
w Oswald Mitchell, A. Barr-Carson d Oswald Mitchell
☆ Ann Todd, Wilfrid Lawson, Grant Tyler, John Warwick, David Farrar

Danny the Champion of the World *

🎬   GB   1989   99m   colour
Portobello Productions (Eric Abraham)
📼

A poacher's son devises a plan to discomfit the obnoxious squire.
Pleasant film aimed at a family audience, if it still exists.
w John Goldsmith *novel* Roald Dahl d Gavin Millar ph Oliver Stapleton m Stanley Myers pd Don Homfray ed Peter Tanner, Angus Newton
☆ Jeremy Irons, Robbie Coltrane, Samuel Irons, Cyril Cusack, Michael Hordern, Lionel Jeffries, Ronald Pickup, Jean Marsh, Jimmy Nail, William Armstrong, John Woodvine

Dans la Poussière du Soleil: see *Lust in the Sun*

Dans la Ville Blanche: see *In the White City*

'It Will Burn Itself Into Your Memory Forever!'
Dante's Inferno *

US   1935   89m   bw
Fox (Sol M. Wurtzel)

A ruthless carnival owner gets too big for his boots, and has a vision of hell induced by one of his own attractions.
Curiously unpersuasive melodrama with a moral, but the inferno sequence is one of the most unexpected, imaginative and striking pieces of cinema in Hollywood's history.
w Philip Klein, Robert Yost d Harry Lachman ph Rudolph Maté m Hugo Friedhofer, Samuel Kaylin, R. H. Bassett, Peter Brunelli sp Fred F. Sersen, Ralph Hammeras sets Willy Pogany, from drawings by Gustav Doré
☆ Spencer Tracy, Claire Trevor, Henry B. Walthall, Alan Dinehart, Scotty Beckett, Rita Hayworth
'A pushover for vigorous exploitation ... accentuate the inferno sequence and forget the rest, including the story.' – *Variety*
'We depart gratefully, having seen papier mâché photographed in more ways than we had thought possible.' – *Robert Herring*
'One of the most unusual and effectively presented films of the thirties.' – *John Baxter, 1968*
'The spectacle is shattering.' – *Sunday Times*
'Immediately following the 10-minute picturization of Hell, the story reverts to its native dullness.' – *Variety*
† Rita Hayworth's performance, as a dancer, was her first on the screen.

'The most awesome sight you'll ever see may be your last.'
Dante's Peak

US   1997   108m   DeLuxe   Panavision
Universal/Western Pacific (Gale Anne Hurd, Joseph M. Singer)
📼 ⬛ 🖥 ⚙ ⊚ ◉ 🎧

A vulcanologist warns an unheeding town of an impending disaster.
Disaster movie that follows a familiar narrative of a lone voice crying out against ignorance and complacency before the inevitable catastrophe; the eruption is spectacular, but hardly worth waiting for.
w Leslie Bohem d Roger Donaldson ph Andrzej Bartkowiak m John Frizzell, John Newton Howard pd Dennis Washington ed Howard Smith, Conrad Buff, Tina Hirsch sp Digital Domain
☆ Pierce Brosnan, Linda Hamilton, Charles Hallahan, Grant Heslov, Elizabeth Hoffman, Jamie Renee Smith, Jeremy Foley, Arabella Field
'Thanks to its predictable plot and boneheaded dialogue ("It's just like riding a bicycle," Brosnan assures a long-abstemious Hamilton about sex), Peak never reaches a peak among disaster films.' – *Leah Rozen, People Weekly*

Danton *

France/Poland   1982   136m   colour
Losange/Group X (for Gaumont/TFI)
📼 ⬛ 🖥

Robespierre quarrels with his colleague Danton, who hopes for a new spirit of tolerance.
Vivid historical re-creation which finally exhausts the spectator and is a little too concerned to make political points.
w Jean-Claude Carrière *play* The Danton Affair by Stanlislawa Przybyszewska d Andrzej Wajda ph Igor Luther m Jean Prodromides
☆ Gérard Depardieu, Wojciech Pszoniak, Anne Alvaro, Roland Blanche
'The temptation to see it in terms of Solidarity is unavoidable.' – *Philip Strick, MFB*
'By any reasonable standard, terrible.' – *New Yorker*
🎥 best foreign-language film

Danzón *

Spain   1991   96m   colour
Metro/Instituto Mexicano Cinematografia/Macondo Cine Video/Fondo de Fomento a la Calidad Cinematografia/Televisión Española/Tabasco/Gobierno del Estado de Veracruz (Jorge Sanchez)
📼 🖥

A telephone operator goes in search of her ballroom dancing partner, who has fled Mexico City after being accused of a crime, and finds new friends and excitement before returning home.
Slight but charming film of a woman finding herself.
w Beatriz Navaro, Maria Novaro d Maria Novaro ph Rodrigo Garcia ad Marisa Pecarlins, Noberto Sanchez-Mejorada ed Nelson Rodriguez, Maria Novaro
☆ Maria Rojo, Carmen Salinas, Blanca Guerra, Tito Vasconcelos, Victor Carpinteiro, Margarita Isabel
'Despite its lack of pace, and sometimes because of it, this is a lovely film which will remain in the memory longer than most.' – *Derek Malcolm, Guardian*

Darby O'Gill and the Little People *

🎬   US   1959   90m   Technicolor
Walt Disney
⬛ ⚙

An Irish caretaker falls down a well and is captured by leprechauns, who allow him three wishes to rearrange his life.
Pleasantly barmy Irish fantasy with brilliant trick work but some tedium in between.
w Lawrence Edward Watkin *stories* H. T. Kavanagh d Robert Stevenson ph Winton C. Hoch m Oliver Wallace ad Carroll Clark ed Stanley Johnson sp Peter Ellenshaw, Eustace Lycett, Joshua Meador
☆ Albert Sharpe, Jimmy O'Dea, Sean Connery, Janet Munro, Kieron Moore, Estelle Winwood, Walter Fitzgerald, Denis O'Dea, J. G. Devlin, Jack MacGowran
'One of the best fantasies ever put on film.' – *Leonard Maltin*

Darby's Rangers

US   1957   121m   bw
Warner (Martin Rackin)
⬛

GB title: The Young Invaders
A tough American commando unit is trained in Britain before seeing action in Africa and Sicily.
Standard World War II actioner, adequately executed.
w Guy Trosper *book* Major James Altieri d William Wellman ph William H. Clothier m Max Steiner
☆ James Garner, Etchika Choureau, Jack Warden, Edd Byrnes, Venetia Stevenson, Torin Thatcher, Stuart Whitman, Andrea King, Frieda Inescort, Reginald Owen, Adam Williams

D'Ardenelle: see *Harem*

The Daring Game

US   1967   101m   Eastmancolor
Paramount/Tors (Gene Levitt)
⬛

A commercial group experiments with airborne and underwater inventions, and rescues a scientist from a police state.
Well photographed but haphazardly assembled adventures, aimed at TV.

w Andy White d Laslo Benedek ph Edmund Gibson m George Bruns
☆ Lloyd Bridges, Nico Minardos, Joan Blackman, Michael Ansara

The Dark: see *The Haunted House of Horror* (1969)

The Dark

US   1979   92m   DeLuxe   Panavision
Film Ventures International (Dick Clark, Edward L. Montoro)
⬛

A homicidal alien stalks Los Angeles, ripping off people's heads.
Unconsidered shocker with nothing to it but the shocks.
w Stanford Whitmore d John Cardos ph John Morrill m Roger Kellaway ad Rusty Rosene ed Martin Dreffke
☆ William Devane, Cathy Lee Crosby, Richard Jaeckel, Keenan Wynn, Vivian Blaine

'Good Cop. Bad Alien. Big Trouble.'
Dark Angel *

US   1990   93m   DeLuxe
Vision/Damon/Saunders (Jeff Young)
📼 ⬛ 🖥

US title: I Come in Peace
A maverick cop and the FBI chase after a killer from another planet.
A cut above the usual aliens-on-the-rampage action, thanks to occasional wit and a narrative with unexpected twists.
w Jonathan Tydor, Leonard Maas Jnr d Craig R. Baxley ph Mark Irwin m Jan Hammer pd Phillip M. Leonard ad Nino Candido ed Mark Helfrich
☆ Dolph Lundgren, Brian Benben, Betsy Brantley, Matthias Hues, Jay Bilas, Jim Haynie, David Ackroyd, Sherman Howard, Sam Anderson
'This undemanding cinematic comic book may come in peace but doesn't seem likely to go all that quietly.' – *Variety*

The Dark Angel *

US   1925   83m   bw   silent
First National (Samuel Goldwyn)

During World War I, a blinded officer tries to persuade his fiancée to marry another man, without her knowing of his own infirmity.
Vilma Banky's first American film, her first teaming with Colman and a mid-twenties hit of colossal proportions.
w Frances Marion *play* Guy Bolton d George Fitzmaurice ph George Barnes
☆ Ronald Colman, Vilma Banky, Wyndham Standing, Frank Elliott, Charles Lane, Florence Turner, Helen Jerome Eddy

The Dark Angel *

US   1935   105m   bw
Samuel Goldwyn

Tearstained melodrama from another age (see above), neatly packaged for the romantic 1935 public.
w Lillian Hellman, Mordaunt Shairp d Sidney Franklin ph Gregg Toland m Alfred Newman ad Richard Day
☆ Merle Oberon, Fredric March, Herbert Marshall, Janet Beecher, John Halliday, Henrietta Crosman, Frieda Inescort, George Breakston, Claud Allister
'A sockaroo woman's picture.' – *Variety*
'A highly literate screen adaptation, telling the story with feeling and good taste.' – *New York Times*
'It makes a systematic and skilful appeal to those untrustworthy emotions which may suddenly cause the most hardened intellects to dissolve before the most obvious sentimentality.' – *The Times*
🏆 Richard Day
🏆 Merle Oberon

'Every time a woman turns her face away because she's tired or unwilling, there's someone waiting like me...'
The Dark at the Top of the Stairs *

US   1960   124m   Technicolor
Warner (Michael Garrison)
⬛

Twenties small town drama about a young boy's awakening to the sexual tensions around him.
Archetypal family drama set in that highly familiar American street. The perfect essence of this playwright's work, with high and low spots, several

irrelevancies, but a real feeling for the people and the place.
w Harriet Frank Jnr, Irving Ravetch *play* William Inge d Delbert Mann ph Harry Stradling m Max Steiner
☆ Robert Preston, Dorothy McGuire, Angela Lansbury, Eve Arden, Shirley Knight, Frank Overton, Lee Kinsolving, Robert Eyer
† The curious title turns out to be a synonym for life, which one should never be afraid of.
🏆 Shirley Knight

The Dark Avenger *

🎬   GB   1955   85m   Eastmancolor   Cinemascope
Allied Artists (Vaughan N. Dean)
⬛

US title: The Warriors
The Black Prince quells some French rebels.
Good-humoured historical romp with the ageing star in his last swashbuckling role, helped by a good cast and brisk pace.
w Daniel B. Ullman d Henry Levin ph Guy Green m Cedric Thorpe Davie
☆ Errol Flynn, Peter Finch, Joanne Dru, Yvonne Furneaux, Patrick Holt, Michael Hordern, Moultrie Kelsall, Robert Urquhart, Noel Willman

Dark City

US   1950   97m   bw
Paramount/Hal B. Wallis
⬛

A bookmaker finds himself on the run from a revenge-seeking psychopath.
Unattractive and heavily-handled underworld melodrama, a disappointment from the talents involved.
w John Meredyth Lucas, Larry Marcus d William Dieterle ph Victor Milner m Franz Waxman
☆ Charlton Heston, Lizabeth Scott, Viveca Lindfors, Dean Jagger, Don Defore, Jack Webb, Ed Begley, Henry Morgan, Mike Mazurki
'A jaded addition to a type of thriller which has become increasingly tedious and unreal.' – *MFB*

'They built a city to see what makes us tick. Last night one of us went off.'
Dark City *

US   1998   101m   DeLuxe   Panavision
Polygram/New Line/Mystery Clock (Andrew Mason)
📼 ⬛ 🖥

An amnesiac man in a strange night-time city discovers that aliens are carrying out an experiment by manipulating his life and that of its other inhabitants.
Paranoid fantasy that owes its visual style to graphic novels such as The Crow, and its tone to film noir; its narrative, though, is more muddled and, ultimately, somewhat forgettable.
w Alex Proyas, Lem Dobbs, David S. Goyer d Alex Proyas ph Dariusz Wolski m Trevor Jones pd George Liddle, Patrick Tatopolous ed Dov Hoenig
☆ Rufus Sewell, Kiefer Sutherland, Jennifer Connelly, William Hurt, Richard O'Brien, Ian Richardson, Colin Friels, Bruce Spence, John Bluthal
'Engaging mostly in the degree to which it creates and sustains a visually startling alternate universe.' – *Todd McCarthy, Variety*

Dark Command *

US   1940   92m   bw
Republic (Sol C. Siegel)
⬛

In pre-Civil War Kansas, an ambitious ex-schoolteacher named Cantrill organizes guerrilla bands to pillage the countryside.
Semi-historical hokum, quite well done with a good cast.
w Grover Jones, Lionel Houser, F. Hugh Herbert *novel* W. R. Burnett d Raoul Walsh ph Jack Marta m Victor Young ad John Victor Mackay
☆ John Wayne, Claire Trevor, Walter Pidgeon, Roy Rogers, George 'Gabby' Hayes, Porter Hall, Marjorie Main
'It's the highest budgeter for Republic to date, running in neighbourhood of 700,000 dollars in negative cost. In the family and action houses, it's a natural to roll up good grosses.' – *Variety*
🏆 Victor Young; art direction

🎬 film suitable for family viewing   📼 VHS video-cassette for the British PAL system   🖥 VHS video-cassette for the British PAL system in wide screen-format   ♻ Video cassette in a computer-colourised version   ⬛ American NTSC video-cassette   ⚙ Laser disc

The Dark Corner *
US 1946 98m bw
TCF (Fred Kohlmar)

A private eye with a criminal record thinks he is being menaced by an old adversary, but the latter is found murdered.
Moody, brutish, well-made thriller with a plot put together from bits and pieces of older, better movies, notably Clifton Webb's reprise of his Laura performance and William Bendix ditto The Glass Key.
w Jay Dratler, Bernard Schoenfeld *story* Leo Rosten d Henry Hathaway ph Joe MacDonald m Cyril Mockridge
☆ Mark Stevens, Clifton Webb, Lucille Ball, William Bendix, Kurt Kreuger, Cathy Downs, Reed Hadley, Constance Collier
CATHCART (CLIFTON WEBB): 'I hate the dawn. The grass always looks as though it's been left out all night.'
BRAD (MARK STEVENS): 'There goes my last lead. I feel all dead inside. I'm backed up in a dark corner, and I don't know who's hitting me.'
'Not so much a whodunwhat as a whodunnwhat … all seem bent on "getting" each other and their internecine plottings add up to an alpha thriller.' – *Daily Mail*

The Dark Crystal **
GB 1982 94m Technicolor
Panavision
Universal/AFD/ITC (David Lazer)

Two young people defeat the evil creatures who have taken over the world by replacing a shard which has been taken from the Dark Crystal.
Surprisingly effective piece of mysticism performed entirely by puppets from the Muppet stable.
w David Odell d Jim Henson, Frank Oz ph Oswald Morris pd Harry Lange ed Ralph Kemplen *conceptual designer* Brian FroudMD0
'A dazzling technological and artistic achievement … could teach a lesson in morality to youngsters at the same time as it is entertaining their parents.' – *Variety*

Dark Delusion
US 1947 90m bw
MGM
GB title: *Cynthia's Secret*
A neurotic girl may have to be committed to an asylum.
Last episode of the Dr Gillespie series; not a sensation on its own account.
w Jack Andrews, Harry Ruskin d Willis Goldbeck
☆ Lionel Barrymore, James Craig, Lucille Bremer, Edward Arnold, Keye Luke

Dark Eyes: see *Black Eyes*

Dark Eyes of London *
GB 1939 75m bw
Pathé/Argyle (John Argyle)

US title: *The Human Monster*
The proprietor of a home for the blind uses a mute giant to drown insured victims.
Reasonably effective British horror, a rarity at the time.
w John Argyle, Walter Summers, Patrick Kirwan *novel* Edgar Wallace d Walter Summers ph Bryan Langley m Guy Jones ad Duncan Sutherland ed E. G. Richards
☆ Bela Lugosi, Hugh Williams, Greta Gynt, Wilfrid Walter, Edmon Ryan
'Though it creaks a bit and some of the performances are stilted, this is actually one of Lugosi's better vehicles.' – *The Dark Side*
† It was the first British film to be given an H (for Horror) certificate.

Dark Forces: see *Harlequin*

Dark Habits
Spain 1983 100m colour
Metro/Tesauro (Luis Calvo)

original title: *Entre Tinieblas*
A drug-addicted singer takes refuge from the police in a convent full of decadent nuns.
High spirited, but for the easily amused only.
wd Pedro Almodóvar ph Angel L. Fernandez m Cam España pd Pin Morales, Roman Arango ed José Salcedo

☆ Cristina S. Pascual, Marisa Paredes, Mari Carrillo, Lina Canalejas, Manuel Zarzo, Carmen Maura, Chus Lampreave
'A rather labored series of jokes.' – *Pauline Kael, New Yorker*

The Dark Half
US 1991 122m DeLuxe
Orion/Dark Half (Declan Baldwin)

A writer has two personalities – one an unsuccessful novelist, the other a disreputable bestselling author who is also a killer.
A literary twist on Dr Jekyll and Mr Hyde, but only of minor interest; it neither shocks nor thrills.
wd George A. Romero *novel* Stephen King ph Tony Pierce-Roberts m Christopher Young pd Cletus Anderson ed Pasquale Buba sp *make-up:* John Vulich, Everett Burrell; *visual effects:* VCE/Peter Kuran; Video Image
☆ Timothy Hutton, Amy Madigan, Michael Rooker, Julie Harris, Robert Joy, Kent Broadhurst, Beth Grant, Chelsea Field, Royal Dano
'Features enough gruesome killings and special effects to satisfy hardcore horror fans, but also has sufficient narrative and thematic substance to keep more mainstream viewers interested.' – *Variety*
'A classy psychological horror movie, this delivers its share of visual shock moments, but relies for the most part on a controlled build-up of cumulative tension.' – *Nigel Floyd, The Dark Side*

Dark Hazard
US 1934 72m bw
Warner (Robert Lord)
A compulsive gambler loses his wife as well as his money.
Modest star drama, remade in 1937 as Wine, Women and Horses.
w Ralph Block, Brown Holmes *novel* W. R. Burnett d Alfred E. Green
☆ Edward G. Robinson, Glenda Farrell, Robert Barrat, Hobart Cavanaugh

The Dark Horse
US 1932 75m bw
Warner
A nitwit runs for governor and nearly makes it.
Mild political satire; closer to farce, really.
w Joseph Jackson, Wilson Mizner d Alfred E. Green
☆ Guy Kibbee, Bette Davis, Warren William, Frank McHugh

Dark Journey *
GB 1937 82m bw
London Films/Victor Saville

In 1915 Stockholm, a French woman spy masquerading as a traitor falls in love with her German spy contact.
Unconvincing but entertaining romantic adventure with good star performances.
w Lajos Biro, Arthur Wimperis *play* Lajos Biro d Victor Saville ph Georges Périnal, Harry Stradling m Richard Addinsell ad Andrei Andreiev ed William Hornbeck, Hugh Stewart
☆ Conrad Veidt, Vivien Leigh, Joan Gardner, Anthony Bushell, Ursula Jeans, Eliot Makeham, Austin Trevor, Edmund Willard
'An exceptional quantity of carefully thought out direction … the financial success will depend on whether the general public will understand and keep pace with the plot.' – *Variety*

The Dark Light
GB 1951 66m bw
Exclusive/Hammer (Michael Carreras)
A lonely lighthouse 20 miles off the South Coast goes dark and the captain of a passing ship investigates.
Dull and stolid thriller, which develops into a character study of uninteresting people.
wd Vernon Sewell ph Moray Grant md Frank Spencer ad France Bodie
☆ Albert Lieven, David Greene, Norman MacOwan, Martin Benson, Catherine Blake, Jack Stewart, Joan Carol, John Harvey

The Dark Man
GB 1950 91m bw
Rank/Independent Artists (Julian Wintle)
A mysterious murderer haunts a seaside resort.
Limp, disappointing location police thriller, with too much chat and generally mishandled moments of suspense.
wd Jeffrey Dell ph Eric Cross m Hubert Clifford
☆ Maxwell Reed, Edward Underdown, Natasha Parry, Barbara Murray, William Hartnell, Cyril Smith, Geoffrey Summer
'The contrivances of the script are not helped by stilted dialogue.' – *MFB*

'One twin loves – and one twin loves to kill!'
The Dark Mirror **
US 1946 85m bw
Universal

A police detective works out which of identical twin girls is a murderer.
Unconvincing but highly absorbing thriller with all credits plus; the best brand of Hollywood moonshine.
w Nunnally Johnson *story* Vladimir Pozner d Robert Siodmak ph Milton Krasner m Dimitri Tiomkin
☆ Olivia de Havilland, Lew Ayres, Thomas Mitchell, Garry Owen
'Smooth and agreeable melodrama … the detective work involves inkblot and word association tests and an amusingly sinister tandem of oscillating pens which register concealed emotions as one of the sisters talks.' – *James Agee*
⚷ Vladimir Pozner

Dark Obsession: see *Diamond Skulls*

Dark of the Night: see *Mr Wrong*

Dark of the Sun: see *The Mercenaries*

The Dark Page: see *Scandal Sheet*

Dark Passage **
US 1947 106m bw
Warner (Jerry Wald)

A convicted murderer escapes from jail and proves his innocence.
Loosely assembled, totally unconvincing star thriller which succeeds because of its professionalism, some good cameos, and a number of narrative tricks including subjective camera for the first half hour.
w Delmer Daves *novel* David Goodis d Delmer Daves ph Sid Hickox m Franz Waxman
☆ Humphrey Bogart, Lauren Bacall, Agnes Moorehead, Bruce Bennett, Tom D'Andrea, Houseley Stevenson
'An almost total drag.' – *New Yorker, 1977*

The Dark Past **
US 1948 75m bw
Columbia (Buddy Adler)

A psychiatrist turns the tables on convicts who break into his home.
Tense, economical remake of Blind Alley (qv); a fresh look at a familiar situation (The Small Voice, The Desperate Hours, etc.) helped by excellent performances.
w Philip Macdonald, Malvin Wald, Oscar Saul d Rudolph Maté ph Joseph Walker m George Duning
☆ William Holden, Lee J. Cobb, Nina Foch, Adele Jergens, Stephen Dunne
'A picture so packed with skill and imagination that every minute is absorbing.' – *Richard Mallett, Punch*

The Dark Road
GB 1948 70m bw
Exclusive/Marylebone-Hammer (Henry Halsted)
An American hack writer spins to his editor the story of the rise and fall of an English petty thief.
Mundane thriller that unabashedly revels in its own mediocrity.
d Alfred Goulding ph Stanley Clinton
☆ Charles Stuart, Joyce Linden, Farnham Baxter, Cyril Chamberlain, Sydney Bromley, Gale Douglas, Veronica Rose, Michael Ripper

Dark Sands: see *Jericho*

The Dark Side of Love
Italy 1985 88m colour
Globe/Dania/Filmes International (Pietro Innocenzi)

original title: *Fotografando Patrizia*
A sickly, isolated teenager is introduced to sex by his promiscuous sister.
Slick, glossily presented soft-core porn.
w Riccardo Ghione, Edith Bruck, Salvatore Samperi, Lewis E. Cianelli, Massimo di Luzio d Salvatore Samperi ph Dante Spinotti m Fred Bongusto pd Maria Chiara Gamba ed Sergio Montanari
☆ Monica Guerritore, Lorenzo Lena, Gianfranco Manfredi, Gilla Novak, Saverio Vallone
'Surprisingly well shot, boasting first rate interiors, lighting and cinematography in the style of Tony Scott.' – *Sight and Sound*

The Dark Side of the Moon
Denmark 1986 94m colour
Cannon/Film-Cooperative Denmark (Per Arman)
original title: *Manden I Manen*
A wife murderer, released from prison, tries to effect a reconciliation with his daughter.
Ponderously slow and introverted, with darkly expressionistic camerawork.
wd Eric Clausen ph Morten Bruus m John Hoybe pd Leif Sylvester ed Ghita Beckendorff
☆ Peter Thiel, Catherine Poul Dupont, Christina Bengtsson, Kim Jansson, Yavuzer Cetinkaya, Royt Richards, Berthe Qvistgaard, Erik Truxa

'The mission of the Strangelove generation!'
Dark Star ***
US 1974 83m Metrocolor
Jack H. Harris (John Carpenter)

In the 22nd century, the bored crew of a starship on an intergalactic mission become prey to their own phobias and to the alien mascot they are taking back to Earth.
A semi-professional film which turned out to be one of the screen's neatest low-budget entries in the pulp science fiction genre. That doesn't make it wholly entertaining, but its credentials are impeccable.
w John Carpenter, Dan O'Bannon d John Carpenter ph Douglas Knapp m John Carpenter pd/ed Dan O'Bannon
☆ Brian Narelle, Dre Pahich, Cal Kuniholm, Dan O'Bannon

Dark Summer
GB 1994 85m colour CinemaScope
2C/Activate (Charles Teton)
In Liverpool, a black youth turns professional boxer, only to lose his first fight and his wife.
An ambitious first feature in which style triumphs over content.
wd Charles Teton ph Charles Teton m Clive Chin pd Elouise Attwood ed Charles Teton
☆ Steve Ako, Joeline Garnier-Joel, Chris Darwin, Bernie Deasy, Wayne Ako, Sylvia Amon, Tom Williamson
'Despite the difficulties put in front of your average impatient viewer, who may wonder why the film is so painfully slow without looking under its surface, Teton is very clearly a film-maker to watch. Whether many will watch Dark Summer is more open to question.' – *Derek Malcolm, Guardian*

The Dark Tower
GB 1943 93m bw
Warner (Max Milder)
A circus hypnotist possessively controls a girl trapezist.
Heavy-handed but quite effective melodrama.
w Brock Williams, Reginald Purdell *play* Alexander Woollcott, George S. Kaufman d John Harlow ph Otto Heller
☆ Ben Lyon, Anne Crawford, David Farrar, Herbert Lom, William Hartnell, Frederick Burtwell, Josephine Wilson

'Never a love so exquisite! She smiled at the cost, and bravely paid the reckoning when her heart's happy dancing was ended!'
Dark Victory **
US 1939 106m bw
Warner (David Lewis)

A good-time society girl discovers she is dying of a brain tumour.

A highly commercial tearjerker of its day, this glutinous star vehicle now works only fitfully.
w Casey Robinson play George Brewer Jnr, Bertram Bloch d Edmund Goulding ph Ernest Haller m Max Steiner
☆ Bette Davis, George Brent, Humphrey Bogart, Ronald Reagan, Geraldine Fitzgerald, Henry Travers, Cora Witherspoon, Dorothy Peterson
JUDITH (BETTE DAVIS): 'Nothing can hurt us now. What we have can't be destroyed. That's our victory – our victory over the dark. It is a victory because we're not afraid.'
'If it were an automobile, it would be a Rolls-Royce with the very best trimmings.' – Time
'Will turn in a good account of itself at the box office, though not rating socko proportions.' – Variety
'A completely cynical appraisal would dismiss it all as emotional flim-flam ... but it is impossible to be that cynical about it.' – Frank S. Nugent
'A gooey collection of clichés, but Davis slams through them in her nerviest style.' – New Yorker, 1976
† Remade 1963 as Stolen Hours, with Susan Hayward; 1975 as Dark Victory (TV movie) with Elizabeth Montgomery.
ℛ best picture; Bette Davis; Max Steiner

Dark Water *
GB 1980 28m colour
Dragonfly/ITC
A girl locked in a swimming pool is terrorized by a mad killer.
Agreeably watchable thriller full of shadows and shocks.
w Andrew Bogle, Tony Grisoni d Andrew Bogle
☆ Phil Davis, Gwyneth Strong, David Beames

Dark Waters **
US 1944 90m bw
Benedict Bogeaus
▣ ◷
Recovering from being torpedoed, an orphan girl visits her aunt and uncle in Louisiana and has some terrifying experiences.
Competent frightened-lady melodrama helped by its bayou surroundings. Possibly discarded by Hitchcock, but with sequences well in his manner.
w Joan Harrison, Marian Cockrell d André de Toth ph John Mescall m Miklos Rozsa
☆ Merle Oberon, Franchot Tone, Thomas Mitchell, Fay Bainter, John Qualen, Elisha Cook Jnr, Rex Ingram

Dark Wind *
US 1991 111m Technicolor
Guild/Carolco/North Face Motion Picture Company (Patrick Markey)
▣ ◷
Hassled by corrupt FBI agents, a Navajo cop investigates drugs-related murders.
Despite its unusual hero, a disappointingly mundane thriller.
w Neal Jimenez, Eric Bergren, Mark Horowitz novel Tony Hillerman d Errol Morris ph Stefan Czapsky m Michel Colombier pd Ted Bafaloukos ed Susan Crutcher, Freeman Davies
☆ Lou Diamond Phillips, Gary Farmer, Fred Ward, Guy Boyd, John Karlen, Jane Loranger, Gary Basaraba, Blake Clark
'A smooth genre piece, well acted, slickly written and benefiting from the natural beauty of the setting.' – Kim Newman, Empire

Darker than Amber
US 1970 96m Technicolor
Cinema Center/Major Films (Walter Seltzer)
▣
A Florida private eye rescues a girl who is subsequently murdered and turns out to be part of a confidence racket.
Routine suspenser from the Travis McGee books; not very stimulating.
w Ed Waters novel John D. MacDonald d Robert Clouse ph Frank Phillips m John Parker
☆ Rod Taylor, Suzy Kendall, Theodore Bikel, James Booth, Jane Russell, Janet McLachlan, William Smith

Darklands
GB 1996 90m Sohoimages
Metrodome/Darklands/Lluniau Lliw Cyf (Paul Brooks)
▣▣
A journalist investigating the murder of a steelworker in South Wales uncovers a pagan cult involved in human sacrifice.
Dire, cheapskate Gothic horror movie, in thrall to the cult The Wicker Man (qv).
wd Julian Richards ph Zoran Djordjevic m John Murphy, David Hughes pd Hayden Pearce ed Mark Talbot-Butler
☆ Craig Fairbrass, Rowena King, Jon Finch, David Duffy, Richard Lynch, Nicola Branson, Beth Morris, William Thomas
'The acting fails to rise above a creaking script, and the visual style would shame a 30-year-old Look at Life.' – Richard Williams, Guardian

Darkman
US 1990 91m DeLuxe
UIP/Universal (Robert Tapert)
▣▣ ◷ ◷ ⌂
A hideously deformed scientist invents a synthetic skin that makes him a master of disguise.
Relentlessly silly horror movie full of extravagantly pointless camera movements.
w Chuck Pfarrer, Sam Raimi, Ivan Raimi, Daniel Goldin, Joshua Goldin d Sam Raimi ph Bill Pope m Danny Elfman pd Randy Ser ed David Stiven
☆ Liam Neeson, Frances McDormand, Colin Friels, Larry Drake, Nelson Mashita, Jesse Lawrence Ferguson, Rafael H. Robledo, Danny Hicks, Theodore Raimi

Darkness Falls
GB 1998 96m colour
Downtown/Vine International/Hoseplace (Alan Latham, Clifford Haydn-Tovey)
▣▣
A businessman has problems: he has 24 hours to repay a £10m loan, and he is confronted by a gunman accusing him of adultery.
An uninteresting thriller about uninteresting people.
w John Howlett play Dangerous Obsession by N. J. Crisp d Gerry Lively ph Adam Santelli m Guy Farley pd Edward Thomas ed David Spiers
☆ Sherilyn Fenn, Ray Winstone, Tim Dutton, Anita Dobson, Bryan Pringle, Robin McCaffrey, Michael Praed, Oliver Tobias
'A nasty, common little film.' – Danny Leigh, Sight and Sound

Darkness in Tallinn **
Finland/USA/Sweden/Estonia 1993 99m
bw/Eastmancolor
Metro/FilmZolfo/Upstream/FilmLance/Teknik/EXITfilm (Lasse Saarinen)
▣▣
original title: Tallinn Pimeduses
In 1991, ruthless gangsters decide to grab $970m in gold being returned to Tallinn, the capital of newly independent Estonia, from Paris, where it had been hidden for 50 years; but their plan depends on persuading a reluctant electrician to fix a city-wide power-cut at the time of the theft.
A deft and intriguing thriller, set against wider themes of freedom and responsibility. Järvilaturi builds the suspense to a tense climax while still allowing space for his actors to create individual characters.
w Paul Kolsby d Ilkka Järvilaturi ph Rein Kotov m Mader pd Toomas Hörak ed Christopher Tellefsen
☆ Ivo Uukkivi, Milena Gulbe, Enn Klooren, Jüri Järvet, Väino Laes, Peeter Dja, Monika Mäger
'A modest but quite ingenious genre pic with an unusual setting and plenty of atmosphere.' – Variety
'A compelling and densely plotted heist movie.' – Sight and Sound
'When she was good she was very very good. When she was bad, she was...'

Darling **
GB 1965 127m bw
Anglo-Amalgamated/Vic/Appia (Joseph Janni, Victor Lyndon)
▣▣ ◷ ◷
An ambitious young woman deserts her journalist mentor for a company director, an effeminate photographer and an Italian prince.
Fashionable mid-sixties concoction of smart swinging people and their amoral doings. Influential, put over with high style, and totally tiresome in retrospect.

w Frederic Raphael d John Schlesinger ph Ken Higgins m John Dankworth pd Ray Simm
☆ Julie Christie, Dirk Bogarde, Laurence Harvey, Roland Curram, Alex Scott, Basil Henson, Pauline Yates
BOGARDE TO CHRISTIE: 'Your idea of being fulfilled is having more than one man in bed at the same time.'
'As empty of meaning and mind as the empty life it's exposing.' – Pauline Kael
'A cool, clear and devastating look at the glossy success set.' – Judith Crist
♟ Frederic Raphael; Julie Christie
ℛ best picture; John Schlesinger
⏚ Frederic Raphael; Ray Simm; Dirk Bogarde; Julie Christie

Darling How Could You
US 1951 96m bw
Paramount (Harry Tugend)
GB title: Rendezvous
Children long separated from their parents have fantasies about them.
Faded-looking Edwardian comedy which does not quite have the style or the cast for success. (Or the title, come to that.)
w Dodie Smith, Lesser Samuels play Alice Sit by the Fire by J. M. Barrie d Mitchell Leisen ph Daniel L. Fapp m Frederick Hollander
☆ Joan Fontaine, John Lund, Mona Freeman, Peter Hanson, David Stollery, Lowell Gilmore, Robert Barrat, Gertrude Michael

Darling I am Growing Younger: see Monkey Business

Darling Lili *
US 1970 136m Technicolor Panavision
Paramount/Geoffrey (Owen Crump)
▣ ⌂
During World War I, an American air ace falls for a German lady spy, and waits till the war is over to marry her.
Farce and romance mix oddly with aerial acrobatics in this expensive and dull extravaganza which bore the sub-title Where Were You the Night I Shot Down Baron von Richthofen? (which probably sums up its aims and its failure). A coffee table film, good to look at and with occasional striking moments.
w Blake Edwards, William Peter Blatty d Blake Edwards ph Russell Harlan, Harold E. Wellman m Henry Mancini pd Fernando Carrere
☆ Julie Andrews, Rock Hudson, Jeremy Kemp, Lance Percival, Michael Witney, Jacques Marin, André Maranne
ℛ Henry Mancini; song 'Whistling Away the Dark' (m Henry Mancini, ly Johnny Mercer)

D'Artagnan's Daughter *
France 1994 130m colour
Artificial Eye/CiBy 2000/Little Bear/TF1 (Véronique Bousselon)
▣▣ ▣ ◷
original title: La Fille de D'Artagnan
D'Artagnan's daughter sets out to revenge the murder of a nun, an act which brings back into action the ageing three musketeers, who foil a plot to kill the king.
An enjoyable romp that does not take history or itself too seriously.
w Michel Leviant, Jean Cosmos, Bertrand Tavernier idea Riccardo Freda, Eric Poindrom d Bertrand Tavernier ph Patrick Blossier m Philippe Sarde ad Geoffroy Larcher ed Ariane Boeglin
☆ Sophie Marceau, Philippe Noiret, Claude Rich, Sami Frey, Jean-Luc Bideau, Raoul Billerey, Charlotte Kady, Nils Tavernier
'In an era where comedy wears hob-nailed boots, Tavernier's gentle, almost inconsequential touch gladdens the heart.' – Geoff Brown, The Times
† Italian Riccardo Freda, whose original idea it was, was set to direct, but a week before shooting began Sophie Marceau refused to work with him and he was replaced by the producer, Bertrand Tavernier.

The Darwin Adventure *
GB 1971 91m Eastmancolor
TCF/Palomar (Joseph Strick, Irving Lerner)
In 1831, Charles Darwin becomes ship's naturalist on the Beagle and studies wildlife in South America.

Rather naïve biopic of Darwin which tries to cover too much with too slender resources but makes a pleasant introduction to the subject.
w William Fairchild d Jack Couffer ph Denys Coop, Jack Couffer m Marc Wilkinson
☆ Nicholas Clay, Susan Macready, Ian Richardson, Christopher Martin, Robert Flemyng, Aubrey Woods, Hugh Morton
'The biopic plague, which has ravaged the screen lives of Pasteur, Juarez, Cole Porter and countless others, has now struck down the memory of famed naturalist Charles Darwin. The filmgoing public's own version of Darwin's natural selection theory will immediately weed out this inferior species.' – Variety

D.A.R.Y.L.
↟↟ US 1985 99m TVC Color Panavision
Columbia (Burt Harris, Gabrielle Kelly)
▣▣ ▣ ◷
A mysterious young man is really a robot, 'data analysing robot youth lifeform'; but he begins to have feelings...
Muddled sentimental fantasy which doesn't seem to know where it's going.
w David Ambrose, Allan Scott, Jeffrey Ellis d Simon Wincer ph Frank Watts m Marvin Hamlisch pd Alan Cassie ed Adrian Carr
☆ Mary Beth Hurt, Michael McKean, Kathryn Walker, Colleen Camp
'The kind of project that must have looked great on paper.' – Variety

A Date with a Lonely Girl: see T.R. Baskin (1971)

A Date with Destiny: see The Mad Doctor (1941)

A Date with Destiny: see The Return of October (1948)

A Date with Judy
US 1948 113m Technicolor
MGM (Joe Pasternak)
▣ ◷
A teenager wrongly suspects her friend of an illicit affair.
Ambitious but flat comedy musical which neatly wraps up all kinds of forties people and institutions: teenagers, small towns, families, Carmen Miranda and Miss Taylor, not to mention the producer.
w Dorothy Cooper, Dorothy Kingsley d Richard Thorpe ph Robert Surtees m/ly various md George Stoll
☆ Wallace Beery, Elizabeth Taylor, Jane Powell, Carmen Miranda, Xavier Cugat, Robert Stack, Selena Royle, Scotty Beckett, Leon Ames

A Date with the Falcon
US 1941 63m bw
RKO (Howard Benedict)
The Falcon attempts to save his forthcoming marriage and find a missing scientist with a formula for synthetic diamonds.
Slick comic thriller with a few amusing moments.
w Lynn Root, Frank Fenton character created by Michael Arlen d Irving Reis ph Robert de Grasse m Paul Sawtell ad Albert D'Agostino, Al Herman ed Harry Marker
☆ George Sanders, Wendy Barrie, James Gleason, Allen Jenkins, Mona Maris

Daughter of Darkness
GB 1947 91m bw
Kenilworth-Alliance (Victor Hanbury)
A murderous Irish servant girl has a fatal flair for men.
Absurd melodrama, almost Grand Guignol, louringly set on the Yorkshire moors but lethargically handled all round.
w Max Catto play They Walk Alone by Max Catto d Lance Comfort ph Stanley Pavey
☆ Siobhan McKenna, Anne Crawford, Maxwell Reed, George Thorpe, Barry Morse, Honor Blackman, Liam Redmond, David Greene

Daughter of Dr Jekyll
US 1957 74m bw
Allied Artists
An evil doctor tells his ward that she is the daughter of the unfortunate Dr Jekyll and therefore responsible for a series of werewolf killings.
Bathetic cheapie with risible views of England and a tendency to mix up several myths in one package.

---

w Jack Pollexfen d Edgar G. Ulmer
☆ Arthur Shields, John Agar, Gloria Talbott, John Dierkes

Daughter of Luxury: see *Five and Ten*

The Daughter of Rosie O'Grady *
US 1950 104m Technicolor
Warner (William Jacobs)
A girl determines to follow in her dead mother's musical comedy footsteps against the wishes of her still-grieving father.
Absolutely standard period musical, quite pleasantly handled but with below-par musical numbers.
w Jack Rose, Mel Shavelson, Peter Milne d David Butler ph Wilfred M. Cline md David Buttolph
☆ June Haver, Gordon MacRae, *James Barton*, S. Z. Sakall, Gene Nelson, Debbie Reynolds, Sean McClory, Jane Darwell

Daughter of Shanghai *
US 1937 63m bw
Paramount
The daughter of a wealthy merchant revenges herself on smugglers who kill him.
Pacy lower-berth melodrama packed with good talent.
w Gladys Unger, Garnett Weston d Robert Florey
☆ Anna May Wong, Charles Bickford, Philip Ahn, Larry Crabbe, Cecil Cunningham, Anthony Quinn, J. Carrol Naish, Evelyn Brent
'Meaningless title to a routine crime meller … downstairs dualler, but not half bad.' – *Variety*

Daughter of the Dragon
US 1931 70m bw
Paramount
📺
Fu Manchu continues to seek revenge on Dr Petrie for the loss of his wife in the Boxer rebellion.
Muddled thriller with too much plot and too little action.
w Lloyd Corrigan, Monte Katterjohn d Lloyd Corrigan
☆ Warner Oland, Anna May Wong, Sessue Hayakawa, Bramwell Fletcher, Holmes Herbert
'Chinese blunderings, murders, and silly acting. Best for the combos where the kids may get a kick out of it.' – *Variety*

Daughter of the Nile *
Taiwan 1988 91m colour
Artificial Eye/Fu Film Productions (Li Xianchang)
original title: *Nilouhe, Nuer*
A lovesick schoolgirl on the fringes of gangster society escapes from her workaday chores by reading a comic, *Daughter of the Nile*.
Impressively controlled direction and well observed characters flesh out a minimal story.
w Zhu Tianwen d Hou Hsiao-Hsien ph Chen Huai'en m Chen Zhiyuan, Zhang Hongyi pd Liu Zhihua, Lin Ju ed Liao Qingsong, Chen Liyu
☆ Yang Lin, Gao Jie, Yang Fan, Xin Shufen, Li Tianlu, Cui Fusheng
'By far the most achieved and mature of the cycle of "young criminal" films in recent Taiwanese cinema.' – *Tony Rayns, MFB*

'Twice in a Lifetime: A Motion Picture Like This…'
Daughters Courageous *
US 1939 107m bw
Warner (Hal B. Wallis)
A prodigal father returns to his family and sorts out their problems.
Following the success of Four Daughters *(qv) the cast was reassembled to make this amiable rehash about a different family.*
w Julius and Philip Epstein play *Fly Away Home* by Dorothy Bennett, Irving White d Michael Curtiz ph James Wong Howe m Max Steiner ad John Hughes ed Ralph Dawson
☆ *Claude Rains*, John Garfield, Jeffrey Lynn, Fay Bainter, Priscilla Lane, Rosemary Lane, Lola Lane, Gale Page, Donald Crisp, May Robson, Frank McHugh, Dick Foran, Berton Churchill
'Suited to the family trade anywhere … but there's something to be said against a running time of an hour and 47 minutes.' – *Variety*
'For its intelligent use of small town locations, its skilled acting, fine camerawork and evenly paced, sympathetic direction, it surpasses everything of its type.' – *John Baxter, 1968*
'Attractive people, good dialogue and camerawork, and skilful direction can work wonders.' – *Richard Mallett, Punch*

Daughters of Darkness *
Belgium/France/Germany 1970 96m colour
Roxy/Showking/Cinevog/Maya (Paul Collet, Alain Guillaume)
📼 📺 ⊚
original title: *Le Rouge aux Lèvres*
A seaside hotel in the dead season is visited by an elegant lesbian countess and her companion.
Surrealist and gory horror, stylishly directed and often visually intriguing.
w Harry Kumel, Pierre Drouot d Harry Kumel ph Eddy van der Enden m François de Roubiax ad Françoise Hardy ed Gust Verscheuren
☆ Delphine Seyrig, John Karlen, Daniele Ouimet, Andrea Rau, Paul Esser, Georges Jamin, Joris Collet, Fons Rademakers

Daughters of Destiny: see *Love, Soldiers and Women*

Daughters of the Dust *
US 1991 112m colour
BFI/American Playhouse/WMG/Geechee Girls (Julie Dash)
📼 📺 ⊚
At the turn of the century, a family of Gullahs, descendants of African slaves living on islands off South Carolina, prepare to make a journey to the mainland to travel to the North.
A commemoration and celebration of black experience in America and its African roots, told in overlapping voices of the old and the unborn, and shot with an eye for beauty.
wd Julie Dash ph A. Jaffa Fielder m John Barnes pd Kerry Marshall ed Amy Carey, Joseph Burton
☆ Adisa Anderson, Barbara-O, Cheryl Lynn Bruce, Cora Lee Day, Geraldine Dunston, Vertamae Grosvenor, Tommy Hicks, Trula Hoosier, Kaycee Moore, Eartha D. Robinson, Alva Rodgers, Cornell Royal, Catherine Tarver, Bahni Turpin
'This is balletic, operatic cinema, and a celebration of cinema itself.' – *Lizzie Francke, Sight and Sound*

'In a country where anybody can become President, anybody just did.'
Dave *
US 1993 110m colour
Warner (Luaren Schuler-Donner, Ivan Reitman)
📼 📺 ⊚ ⊚ ⊚ 🎧
After the President of the United States has a stroke, a Baltimore businessman is recruited by the White House to impersonate him.
A slight but amusing comedy of political life that nevertheless manages to evade most of the issues it raises.
w Gary Ross d Ivan Reitman ph Adam Greenberg m James Newton Howard pd J. Michael Riva ed Sheldon Kahn
☆ Kevin Kline, Sigourney Weaver, Frank Langella, Kevin Dunn, Ben Kingsley, Charles Grodin, Ving Rhames, Faith Prince, Laura Linney
'A dear and funny movie.' – *Richard Corliss, Time*
'A delightful, buoyant new take on an old theme that will win at the polls because it never strikes a false note.' – *Variety*
⅛ Gary Ross

'For this woman – he broke God's own commandments! The fire and tempest of their love still flames across 3000 years!'
David and Bathsheba *
US 1951 116m Technicolor
TCF (Darryl F. Zanuck)
📺 ⊚
King David loves the wife of one of his captains, and ensures that the latter is killed in battle.
Deliberately sober bible-in-pictures, probably intended as a riposte to Cecil B. de Mille. Somewhat lacking in excitement, but you can't call it gaudy.
w Philip Dunne d Henry King ph Leon Shamroy m Alfred Newman ad Lyle Wheeler, George Davis
☆ Gregory Peck, Susan Hayward, James Robertson Justice, Raymond Massey, Kieron Moore, Jayne Meadows, John Sutton, Dennis Hoey, Francis X. Bushman, George Zucco
'Hardly a single unintentional laugh.' – *Richard Mallett, Punch*
⅛ Philip Dunne; Leon Shamroy; Alfred Newman; art direction

David and Lisa *
US 1962 94m bw
Continental (Paul M. Heller)
📺 ⊚
Two disturbed adolescents at a special school fall in love.
Case history drama, earnest and well meaning rather than exciting.
w Eleanor Perry book Theodore Isaac Rubin d Frank Perry ph Leonard Hirschfield m Mark Lawrence
☆ Keir Dullea, Janet Margolin, Howard da Silva, Neva Patterson, Clifton James, Richard McMurray
'It recognises and probes the wounds of the mind and the heart and the power of love to penetrate even the most private of worlds.' – *Judith Crist*
† Made for 180,000 dollars, it took more than one million dollars in its first run in the States.
⅛ Eleanor Perry; Frank Perry

'One of the greatest stories of love and adventure ever told is brought to the screen as Dickens himself would wish it!'
David Copperfield ****
👪 US 1934 132m bw
MGM (David O. Selznick)
📼 📺 ⊚
Disliked by his cruel stepfather and helped by his eccentric aunt, orphan David grows up to become an author and eventually to marry his childhood sweetheart.
Only slightly faded after sixty years, this small miracle of compression not only conveys the spirit of Dickens better than the screen has normally managed but is a particularly pleasing example of Hollywood's handling of literature and of the deployment of a great studio's resources. It also overflows with memorable character cameos, and it was a box-office giant.
w Hugh Walpole, Howard Estabrook novel Charles Dickens d George Cukor ph Oliver T. Marsh m Herbert Stothart ad Cedric Gibbons ed Robert J. Kern montage Slavko Vorkapich
☆ Freddie Bartholomew, Frank Lawton, W. C. Fields, Roland Young, Edna May Oliver, Lennox Pawle, Basil Rathbone, Violet Kemble Cooper, Maureen O'Sullivan, Madge Evans, Elizabeth Allan, *Jessie Ralph*, Lionel Barrymore, Hugh Williams, Lewis Stone and also *Herbert Mundin* (Barkis), Elsa Lanchester (Clickett), Jean Cadell (Mrs Micawber), Una O'Connor (Mrs Gummidge), John Buckler (Ham), Hugh Walpole (the Vicar), Arthur Treacher (donkey man)
'One of the best ensembles ever … unusually good production which will win general approval.' – *Variety*
'Though half the characters are absent, the whole spectacle of the book, Micawber always excepted, is conveyed.' – *James Agee*
'The most profoundly satisfying screen manipulation of a great novel that the camera has ever given us.' – *André Sennwald*
'Perhaps the finest casting of all time.' – *Basil Wright, 1972*
† Charles Laughton was originally cast as Micawber, but resigned from the role after two days of shooting. It was said at the time that 'he looked as though he were about to molest the child'.
⅛ best picture; editing

David Harum *
US 1934 83m bw
Fox
A wily old rancher plays matchmaker.
Simple, pleasing small-town comedy-drama, ably fashioned for its star.
w Walter Woods play Edward Westcott d James Cruze m Hal Mohr m Louis de Francesco
☆ Will Rogers, Evelyn Venable, Kent Taylor, Louise Dresser, Stepin Fetchit, Charles Middleton, Noah Beery
'Looks like a sugar picture.' – *Variety*

Davy *
GB 1957 84m Technirama
Ealing (Basil Dearden)
A member of a family music hall act auditions at Covent Garden.
Curiously unsuccessful vehicle for a popular singing comic; the script and continuity are simply poor, and swamped by the wide screen.
w William Rose d Michael Relph ph Douglas Slocombe m various classics

☆ Harry Secombe, Ron Randell, George Relph, Alexander Knox, Susan Shaw, Bill Owen

Davy Crockett *
👪 US 1955 93m Technicolor
Walt Disney
Episodes in the career of the famous Tennessee hunter and Indian scout who died at the Alamo.
Disjointed and naïve but somehow very fresh and appealing adventures; made for American television (as 3 50m episodes) but elsewhere an enormous hit in cinemas.
w Tom Blackburn d Norman Foster ph Charles Boyle m George Bruns
☆ *Fess Parker*, Buddy Ebsen, Basil Ruysdael, William Bakewell, Hans Conried, Kenneth Tobey, Nick Cravat
† 1956 sequel on similar lines: *Davy Crockett and the River Pirates*

Dawandeh: see *The Runner*

Dawn *
GB 1928 90m bw silent
British and Dominions (Herbert Wilcox)
In 1914 Brussels, Nurse Edith Cavell helps 210 English soldiers to escape before the Germans catch and execute her.
Inspirational piece, totally dated now; remade by the same producer in 1939 as Nurse Edith Cavell, *with Anna Neagle.*
w Herbert Wilcox, Robert J. Cullen play Reginald Berkeley d Herbert Wilcox
☆ Sybil Thorndike, Marie Ault, Mary Brough, Haddon Mason

Dawn!
Australia 1979 115m colour
Aquataurus/SAFC (Joy Cavill)
Dawn Fraser reflects on her career as a swimmer which took her from a working-class Sydney suburb to international success and the winning of three Olympic gold medals.
A biopic that celebrates a bloody-minded heroine, forever at war with authority, but, with an inexperienced actress in the title role and a style that smooths away the rough edges, the result is too bland to engage the interest for long.
w Joy Cavill d Ken Hannam ph Russell Boyd m Michael Carlos pd Ross Major ed Max Lemon
☆ Bronwyn Mackay-Payne, Ron Haddrick, Bunney Brooke, Tom Richards, John Diedrich, Gabrielle Hartley

Dawn at Socorro
US 1954 80m Technicolor
Universal-International
A gunfighter is trapped into one last duel.
Moderate Western programmer.
w George Zuckerman d George Sherman
☆ Rory Calhoun, David Brian, Alex Nicol, Piper Laurie, Edgar Buchanan

'When there's no more room in Hell, the dead will walk the earth…'
Dawn of the Dead
US 1979 127m Technicolor
Target International/Laurel Group/Dawn Associates (Richard P. Rubinstein)
📼 📺 ⊚ ⊚ ⊚ 🎧
GB title: *Zombies*
America is filled by legions of carnivorous zombies.
Seemingly endless horror comic with absurd pretensions to be an allegory of something or other; occasionally laughable, otherwise sickening or boring.
wd George A. Romero ph Michael Gornick m The Goblins, Dario Argento ad Josie Caruso, Barbara Lifsher ed George A. Romero sp Tom Savini
☆ David Emge, Ken Foree, Scott H. Reiniger, Gaylen Ross

'Roaring into the blood-red dawn – fighting for women they had never seen – for love they might never know!'
'Forty youngsters sporting with fate!'
The Dawn Patrol **
US 1930 90m bw
Warner
In France during World War I, flying officers take their turn to leave on missions which may mean death.

The second version (see below) is more watchable today, but this early talkie was highly effective in its time, and much of its aerial footage was re-used.
w John Monk Saunders d Howard Hawks
ph Ernest Haller
☆ Richard Barthelmess, Douglas Fairbanks Jnr, Neil Hamilton, William Janney, James Finlayson, Clyde Cook, Edmund Breon, Frank McHugh
'No women and few laughs, so needs good surrounding comedy shorts.' – *Variety*
'Bare, cleancut, uncluttered technique, a stark story line, terse dialogue … and a pervasive atmosphere of hopelessness captured with economy and incisiveness.' – *Andrew Sarris, 1963*
† TV title is *Flight Commander*, which was the title of Saunders's original story.
🧍 John Monk Saunders

'There's no chance for a flight to get through, but one man – flying low, hedgehopping – might make it!'

The Dawn Patrol **
US 1938 103m bw
Warner (Hal B. Wallis)
😎
A remarkably early but trim and competent remake of the above, using much of the same aerial footage.
w Seton I. Miller, Dan Totheroh story John Monk Saunders d Edmund Goulding ph Tony Gaudio m Max Steiner
☆ Errol Flynn, Basil Rathbone, David Niven, Melville Cooper, Donald Crisp, Barry Fitzgerald, Carl Esmond
'A powerful, red-corpuscled drama … geared for top grosses.' – *Variety*
'A great deal of self-pity and romanticism have gone into the making of this excellent ham sandwich.' – *Graham Greene*

The Dawn Rider
US 1935 56m bw
Lone Star (Paul Malvern)
🎞
A cowboy revenges the murder of his father.
Standard quickie Western with little to recommend it.
wd Robert N. Bradbury ph Archie Stout
☆ John Wayne, Marion Burns, Yakima Canutt, Reed Howes, Denny Meadows, Bert Dillard

The Dawning *
GB 1988 97m colour
Enterprise/TVS (Sarah Lawson)
🎞 📀
In the 1920s in Southern Ireland, at the beginning of the Troubles between the Irish and the English, a teenage girl becomes involved with a mysterious stranger, to the annoyance of her English fiancé.
A small-scale but affecting film of the end of innocence.
w Moira Williams novel The Old Jest by Jennifer Johnson d Robert Knights ph Adrian Biddle m Simon May pd Mike Porter ed Max Lemon
☆ Trevor Howard, Hugh Grant, Anthony Hopkins, Rebecca Pidgeon, Jean Simmons, Adrian Dunbar, Tara MacGowran

The Day
GB 1960 26m bw
Peter Finch
A young Ibizan travels a long way to collect his relatives for the celebration of the birth of a baby.
Vivid and yet rather boring short which could have done with a twist in the tail.
wd Peter Finch

A Day at the Races ****
👫 US 1937 109m bw/blue-tinted ballet sequence
MGM (Lawrence Weingarten)
😎 🎞 📀
The Marxes help a girl who owns a sanatorium and a racehorse.
Fashions in Marxism change, but this top quality production, though lacking their zaniest inspirations, does contain several of their funniest routines and a spectacularly well integrated racecourse climax. The musical and romantic asides are a matter of taste but delightfully typical of their time.
w Robert Pirosh, George Seaton, George Oppenheimer d Sam Wood ph Joseph Ruttenberg m Franz Waxman ch Dave Gould

☆ Groucho, Chico, Harpo, Margaret Dumont, Maureen O'Sullivan, Allan Jones, Douglass Dumbrille, Esther Muir, Sig Rumann
'The money is fairly splashed about; the capitalists have recognized the Marx Brothers; ballet sequences, sentimental songs, amber fountains, young lovers. Easily the best film to be seen in London, but all the same I feel a nostalgia for the old cheap rickety sets.' – *Graham Greene*
🧍 Dave Gould

Day for Night ****
France/Italy 1973 116m Eastmancolor
Films du Carrosse/PECF/PIC (Marcel Bébert)
😎 📀
original title: *La Nuit Américaine*
Frictions and personality clashes beset the making of a romantic film in Nice.
Immensely enjoyable, richly detailed, insider's-eye-view of the goings-on in a film studio. A fun film with melodramatic asides.
w François Truffaut, Jean-Louis Richard, Suzanne Schiffman d François Truffaut ph Pierre-William Glenn m Georges Delerue
☆ Jacqueline Bisset, Valentina Cortese, Jean-Pierre Aumont, Jean-Pierre Léaud, Dani, Alexandra Stewart, Jean Champion, François Truffaut, David Markham
'I thought I'd had my last dram of enjoyment out of the Pagliacci theme and studio magic, and Truffaut shows there's life in the old whirl yet.' – *Stanley Kauffmann*
'Made with such dazzling craftsmanship and confidence that you can never quite believe Truffaut's point that directing a movie is a danger-fraught experience.' – *Michael Billington, Illustrated London News*
† Graham Greene, as Henry Graham, played an insurance representative.
🏆 best foreign film
🧍 script; François Truffaut (as director); Valentina Cortese
🎬 best picture; François Truffaut; Valentina Cortese

A Day in the Country: see Une Partie de Campagne

A Day in the Death of Joe Egg ***
GB 1971 106m Eastmancolor
Columbia/Domino (David Deutsch)
🎞
A teacher and his wife are frustrated by their own inability to cope with the problem of their spastic daughter.
A well-filmed version of a sincerely human play, with humour and fantasy sequences leavening the gloom.
w Peter Nichols play Peter Nichols d Peter Medak ph Ken Hodges m Elgar
☆ Alan Bates, Janet Suzman, Peter Bowles, Sheila Gish, Joan Hickson
'It's unsatisfying, and it's not to be missed.' – *Stanley Kauffmann*

A Day of Fury
US 1956 70m Technicolor
Universal (Robert Arthur)
A marshal is reluctant to shoot a wandering gunman who once saved his life.
Fair little Western with more tension than usual.
w James Edmiston, Oscar Brodney d Harmon Jones
☆ Dale Robertson, Jock Mahoney, Mara Corday, Carl Benton Reid

The Day of the Animals
US 1976 98m DeLuxe Todd-AO 35
Film Ventures International (Edward L. Montoro)
🎞 📀
In the Californian High Sierras, animals of all kinds suddenly turn on human beings, but a day later are all found dead.
Irritatingly pointless horror fable borrowing heavily from The Birds; basically an exploitation shocker, most efficient when most unpleasant.
w William and Eleanor Norton d William Girdler ph Tom McHugh m Lalo Schifrin
☆ Christopher George, Lynda Day George, Leslie Nielsen, Robert Sorrentino, Richard Jaeckel, Michael Ansara, Ruth Roman, Paul Mantee, Gil Lamb

Day of the Badman
US 1957 82m Eastmancolor Cinemascope
Universal-International
A circuit judge stands up against threatening outlaws.
Uninvolving Western which can't fill the wide screen.
w Irving Glassberg d Harry Keller
☆ Fred MacMurray, Joan Weldon, John Ericson, Robert Middleton, Edgar Buchanan

The Day of the Beast
Spain/Italy 1995 104m colour
Metro Tartan/Sogetel/Iberoamericana/M.G. SRL/Canal (Antonio Saura, Claudio Gaeta)
😎
original title: *El Dia de la Bestia*
With the aid of a heavy metal fan and a fake Satanist, a priest acts uncharitably in order to be able to track down the Anti-Christ, who is about to be born in Madrid.
Exuberant horror movie with a political subtext – the Devil finds work for idle fascists – and a blackly comic tone, but it fails to cohere into a satisfactory whole.
w Alex de la Iglesia, Jorge Guerricaechevarria d Alex de la Iglesia ph Flavio Martinez Labiano m Battista Lena pd José Luis Arrizabilaga ed Teresa Font sp make-up: José Antonio Sanchez
☆ Alex Angulo, Armando de Razza, Santiago Segura, Terele Pavez, Nathalie Sesaña, Jaime Blanch
'A rough piece that shows how low the New Spanish Cinema is prepared to grovel in its post-Franco search for international box-office.' – *Alexander Walker, London Evening Standard*
'The funniest Spanish film of the decade is also one of the most serious.' – *Sight and Sound*

Day of the Dead
US 1985 102m colour
Laurel/United (Richard P. Rubinstein)
😎 📀 🎞
Zombies outnumber normal humans by 400,000 to one, but a doctor is trying to domesticate them.
Gory but very talkative successor to Dawn of the Dead; not for regular audience consumption.
wd George A. Romero ph Michael Gornick m John Harrison pd Cletus Anderson ed Pasquale Buba
☆ Lori Cardille, Terry Alexander, Jarlath Conroy, Joseph Pilato

The Day of the Dolphin *
👫 US 1973 104m Technicolor
Panavision
Avco-Embassy/Icarus (Robert E. Relyea)
😎 📀
A marine biologist researching dolphins off the Florida coast discovers they are being used in a plot to blow up the President's yacht.
A strangely unexpected and unsuccessful offering from the talent involved: thin and repetitive as scientific instruction (the dolphins' language in any case topples it into fantasy), and oddly childlike as spy adventure.
w Buck Henry novel Robert Merle d Mike Nichols ph William A. Fraker m Georges Delerue pd Richard Sylbert
☆ George C. Scott, Trish Van Devere, Paul Sorvino, Fritz Weaver
'The whole thing seems to have been shoved through the cameras as glibly as possible, so that everyone concerned could grab the money and run.' – *Stanley Kauffmann*
'An eight and a half million dollar Saturday afternoon special for sheltered nine-year-olds.' – *Judith Crist*
'Dolphins may live in a state of ecstasy, but the cast of this film seems lost in a state of confusion, wondering whether they are in an enlightened documentary, juvenile fantasy, or lurid soap opera.' – *Les Keyser, Hollywood in the Seventies*
'The most expensive Rin Tin Tin movie ever made.' – *Judith Crist*
🧍 Georges Delerue

The Day of the Evil Gun *
US 1968 93m Metrocolor Panavision
MGM (Jerry Thorpe)
Returning home after three years, a rancher finds that his wife and child have been carried off by Indians.
Competent standard Western which resolves itself into a duel of wits between the hero and his rival.
w Charles Marquis Warren, Eric Bercovici d Jerry Thorpe ph W. Wallace Kelley m Jeff Alexander

☆ Glenn Ford, Arthur Kennedy, Dean Jagger, Paul Fix, John Anderson, Nico Minardos

The Day of the Jackal ***
GB/France 1973 142m Technicolor
Universal/Warwick/Universal France (John Woolf, David Deutsch)
😎 🎞 📀 📀
British and French police combine to prevent an OAS assassination attempt on de Gaulle by use of a professional killer.
An incisive, observant and professional piece of work based on a rather clinical bestseller. Lack of a channel for sympathy, plus language confusions, are its main drawbacks.
w Kenneth Ross novel Frederick Forsyth d Fred Zinnemann ph Jean Tournier m Georges Delerue ed Ralph Kemplen
☆ Edward Fox, Michel Lonsdale, Alan Badel, Eric Porter, Cyril Cusack, Delphine Seyrig, Donald Sinden, Tony Britton, Timothy West, Olga Georges-Picot, Barrie Ingham, Maurice Denham, Anton Rodgers
'Before Jackal is five minutes old, you know it's just going to be told professionally, with no flavour and no zest.' – *Stanley Kauffmann*
'All plot, with scarcely a character in sight.' – *Michael Billington, Illustrated London News*
'A better than average thriller for those who haven't read the book.' – *Judith Crist*
'A rare lesson in film-making in the good old grand manner.' – *Basil Wright, 1972*
🧍 Ralph Kemplen

'It happened in Hollywood – but it could have happened in Hell!'

The Day of the Locust **
US 1974 143m Technicolor
Paramount/Long Road (Jerome Hellman, Sheldon Shrager)
🎞 📀
In Hollywood in the 1930s, a novice is bewildered by the eccentricities of life and an innocent man is martyred by the crowd.
A curious and interesting work from a savagely satirical novel; full of stimulating scenes and characters, it barely succeeds as a whole and was a disaster at the box-office.
w Waldo Salt novel Nathanael West d John Schlesinger ph Conrad Hall m John Barry pd Richard MacDonald ed Jim Clark
☆ Donald Sutherland, William Atherton, Karen Black, Burgess Meredith, Geraldine Page, Richard A. Dysart, Bo Hopkins, Lelia Goldoni, Billy Barty
'The sense of horror which the film excites is all the sharper because the monstrosities of action are man-produced. In this brilliantly devised film it is the human heart, not some freak of an indifferent nature, which kills.' – *Dilys Powell*
🧍 Conrad Hall, Burgess Meredith

The Day of the Outlaw **
US 1958 96m bw
UA/Security Pictures (Sidney Harmon)
Two rival cattlemen forget their differences to fight six outlaws who ride into town.
Bleak and wintry Western, well done and sufficiently unusual to stick in the mind.
w Philip Yordan novel Lee Wells d André de Toth ph Russell Harlan m Alexander Courage
☆ Robert Ryan, Burl Ives, Tina Louise, Nehemiah Persoff, David Nelson, Venetia Stevenson, Jack Lambert, Lance Fuller
'In the best William S. Hart tradition.' – *MFB*

'Spine Chilling Terror!'

The Day of the Triffids *
GB 1962 95m Eastmancolor Cinemascope
Philip Yordan (George Pitcher)
😎 🎞 📀
Almost everyone in the world is blinded by meteorites prior to being taken over by intelligent plants.
Rough and ready adaptation of a famous sci-fi novel, sometimes blunderingly effective and with moments of good trick work.
w Philip Yordan novel John Wyndham d Steve Sekely ph Ted Moore m Ron Goodwin
☆ Howard Keel, Nicole Maurey, Kieron Moore, Janette Scott, Alexander Knox

---

Day of Wrath ***
Denmark 1943 105m bw
Palladium
⊞ ▦

original title: *Vredens Dag*
In a 17th-century village an old woman is burned as a witch and curses the pastor who judged her. He dies and his mother accuses her daughter-in-law, in love with another man, of using witchcraft to kill him.
Harrowing, spellbinding melodrama with a message, moving in a series of Rembrandtesque compositions from one horrifying sequence to another. Depressing, but marvellous.
w Carl Dreyer, Poul Knudsen, Mogens Skot-Hansen *play* Anne Pedersdotter by Hans Wiers Jenssen d Carl Dreyer ph Carl Andersson m Poul Schierbeck ad Erik Ases, Lis Fribert
☆ Thorkild Roose, Lisbeth Movin, Sigrid Neiiendam, Preben Lerdoff Rye, Anna Svierkier
  'An exceptional piece of cinema … the film will, I think, be remembered for its realistic treatment of the incredible; for its vicious tension; for the unrivalled horror of its picture of human callousness.' – *Dilys Powell*

The Day the Earth Caught Fire **
GB 1961 99m bw with filters Dyaliscope
British Lion/Pax (Val Guest)
▦

Nuclear tests knock the world off its axis and send it careering towards the sun.
A smart piece of science fiction told through the eyes of Fleet Street journalists and showing a sharp eye for the London scene. Rather exhaustingly talkative, but genuinely frightening at the time.
w Wolf Mankowitz, Val Guest d Val Guest ph Harry Waxman m Monty Norman
☆ Edward Judd, Janet Munro, Leo McKern, Arthur Christiansen (ex-editor of the Daily Express), Michael Goodliffe, Bernard Braden, Reginald Beckwith, Austin Trevor, Renée Asherson, Edward Underdown
† A remake went into production in 1995.
♔ screenplay

'From out of space – a warning and an ultimatum!'
The Day the Earth Stood Still **
US 1951 92m bw
TCF (Julian Blaustein)
⊞ ▦ ⊛ ☊

A flying saucer arrives in Washington and its alien occupant, aided by a robot, demonstrates his intellectual and physical power, warns the world what will happen if wars continue, and departs.
Cold-war wish-fulfilment fantasy, impressive rather than exciting but very capably put over with the minimum of trick work and the maximum of sober conviction. 'Klaatu barada nikto', the command given to the robot, has achieved cult status.
w Edmund H. North d Robert Wise ph Leo Tover m Bernard Herrmann
☆ Michael Rennie, Patricia Neal, Hugh Marlowe, Sam Jaffe, Billy Gray
  'Quite wry and alarmingly smooth.' – *New Yorker, 1977*

The Day the Fish Came Out
GB/Greece 1967 109m DeLuxe
TCF/Michael Cacoyannis
Atomic material contaminates a Mediterranean island.
Addle-pated, would-be satirical mod fantasy with establishment figures cast as world villains.
wd Michael Cacoyannis ph Walter Lassally m Mikis Theodorakis
☆ Tom Courtenay, Colin Blakely, Sam Wanamaker, Candice Bergen, Ian Ogilvy, Patricia Burke

The Day the Hot Line Got Hot
US 1968 92m Eastmancolor
Commonwealth United
▦
Russian and American agents are outwitted by their go-between.
Feeble espionage comedy teaming two big stars at the end of their careers.
w Paul Jarrico, Dominique Fabre, M. Trueblood d Etienne Périer
☆ Charles Boyer, Robert Taylor, George Chakiris, Marie Dubois

The Day the Sun Turned Cold *
Hong Kong 1994 100m colour
Artificial Eye/Pineast (Cherie Wong)
☊

original title: *Tianguo Niezi*
In China, a young man recalls to the police his troubled childhood, which ended with his mother poisoning his father.
Bleak and angry story of familial betrayal, which gains interest from its exoticism.
w Wang Xing Dong, Wang Zhe Bin d Yim Ho ph Hou Yong, Shang Yong m Otomo Yoshihide ad Gong Ming Hui ed Wong Yee-shun, Zhou Ying Wu, Yun Jiang Chun
☆ Si Ching Gao Wa, Tao Chung Wa, Ma Jing Wu, Wu'ai Zi, Shu Zi'ong, Li Hu
  'A haunting film, magnificently filmed and perfectly scored, a splendid example of the new Eastern cinema.' – *Nigel Robinson, Film Review*

'A new high in naked shrieking terror.'
Day the World Ended
US 1955 82m bw Superscope
AIP/Golden State (Roger Corman)
▦
Survivors of the nuclear war take refuge in a mountain hideout where they are attacked by three-eyed, cannibalistic mutants.
Small-scale, paranoid science-fiction thriller from what the film calls 'the age of anxiety'.
w Lou Rusoff d Roger Corman ph Jock Feindel m Ronald Stein ed Ronald Sinclair
☆ Richard Denning, Lori Nelson, Adele Jurgens, Touch Connors, Paul Birch, Raymond Hatton

The Day They Gave Babies Away: see *All Mine to Give*

The Day They Robbed the Bank of England *
GB 1960 85m bw
MGM/Summit (Jules Buck)
In 1901 Irish patriots plan a coup against the British government…
Small-scale, well-detailed period caper story, marred by a slow-starting script and unsympathetic acting.
w Howard Clewes, Richard Maibaum *novel* John Brophy d John Guillermin ph Georges Périnal m Edwin Astley
☆ Peter O'Toole, Aldo Ray, Elizabeth Sellars, Kieron Moore, Albert Sharpe, Hugh Griffith, John Le Mesurier, Joseph Tomelty, Miles Malleson, Colin Gordon

A Day to Remember
GB 1953 92m bw
Rank/Box-Thomas/GFD
A darts team takes a day trip to France.
Pleasant compendium of mini-stories with an agreeable cast.
w Robin Estridge *novel* The Hand and Flower by Jerrard Tickell d Ralph Thomas ph Ernest Steward m Clifton Parker ed Gerald Thomas
☆ Stanley Holloway, Donald Sinden, Joan Rice, Odile Versois, James Hayter, Edward Chapman, Harry Fowler, Peter Jones, Bill Owen

The Day Will Dawn *
GB 1942 98m bw
Niksos (Paul Soskin)
▦
US title: *The Avengers*
Norwegian freedom fighters destroy a U-boat base and are saved by commandos.
Dated propaganda piece with an interesting cast.
w Terence Rattigan, Anatole de Grunwald, Patrick Kirwan d Harold French ph Bernard Knowles m Richard Addinsell
☆ Ralph Richardson, Deborah Kerr, Hugh Williams, Griffith Jones, Francis L. Sullivan, Roland Culver, Niall MacGinnis, Finlay Currie, Bernard Miles, Patricia Medina

Daybreak: see *Le Jour Se Lève (1939)*

Daybreak *
US 1931 85m bw
MGM
An Austrian guardsman falls in love out of his class.
Elegant romantic fable comparable with Letter From an Unknown Woman; equally unpopular and quite forgotten.

w Ruth Cummings, Zelda Sears, Cyril Hume *play* Arthur Schnitzler d Jacques Feyder ph Merritt B. Gerstad
☆ Ramon Novarro, Helen Chandler, C. Aubrey Smith, Karen Morley, Kent Douglass, Jean Hersholt, Glenn Tryon
  'One of those pictures that won't draw after opening … pretty flat all the way … good only insofar as Novarro will draw anywhere.' – *Variety*

Daybreak
GB 1948 81m bw
GFD/Triton (Sydney Box)
A barber and part-time hangman marries a destitute girl, loses her to a Swedish seaman, and kills himself in such a way as to implicate the other man.
Dockside melodrama of extraordinary pretentious gloominess; laughable in most respects. A curious follow-up from the Seventh Veil team.
w Muriel and Sydney Box *play* Monckton Hoffe d Compton Bennett ph Reg Wyer
☆ Ann Todd, Eric Portman, Maxwell Reed, Edward Rigby, Bill Owen, Jane Hylton, Maurice Denham
† The film was made in 1946 but its release was delayed by censorship problems. When it was released, Sydney Box complained that the censor had ruined it by insisting on numerous cuts.

Daydream Believer
Australia 1991 82m colour
Beyond/Ben Gannon
☊
A scatterbrained actress with a fellow feeling for horses falls for a Cockney show-business entrepreneur with a stud farm.
Fluffy romantic comedy that is occasionally amusing but more often irritating, with its concentration on a charmless couple.
w Saturday Rosenberg d Kathy Mueller ph Andrew Lesnie m Todd Hunter, Johanna Pigott pd Roger Ford ed Robert Gibson
☆ Miranda Otto, Martin Kemp, Gia Carides, Anne Looby, Bruce Venables, Peter Hehir

'Hold Your Breath.'
Daylight
US 1996 115m DeLuxe
Universal/Davis Entertainment/Joseph M. Singer
⊞ ▦ ⊛ ⊚ ⊙ ☊
A diverse group of people is trapped in Manhattan's Holland Tunnel.
Stolid and claustrophobic disaster movie, in which Stallone flexes his muscles to little effect.
w Leslie Bohem d Rob Cohen ph David Eggby m Randy Edelman pd Benjamin Fernandez ed Peter Amundson
☆ Sylvester Stallone, Amy Brenneman, Viggo Mortensen, Dan Hedaya, Jay O. Sanders, Karen Young, Claire Bloom
  'Just too limited in scope, imagination and excitement.' – *Variety*
† The film cost more than $80m to make, and took around $33m at the US box-office and a further $111m worldwide.
♫ sound effects editing

The Days
China 1993 80m bw
ICA/Yinxiang Dianying Gongzuoshi (Liu Jie, Zhang Hongtao)
original title: *Dongchun De Rizi*
Two thirtysomething art teachers, bored with life and each other, decide to part.
A doom-laden study of a dysfunctional couple in which the most interesting things happen off-screen and are described in a voice-over; its interest and novelty lie in the fact that it is the first Chinese film to show aimless characters, alienated from their society but too indifferent to what is happening to them to rebel.
wd Wang Xiaoshuai ph Liu Jie, Wu Di m Liang Heping ed Qingqing
☆ Yu Hong, Liu Xiadong
  'The net impression is of inertia; the characters are bored with each other and we're bored with them.' – *Sheila Johnston, Independent*
† The film was made on a budget of $10,000 which the director raised from his friends and his savings.

Days and Nights in the Forest ***
India 1969 115m bw
Contemporary/Priya (Nepal Dutta, Ashim Dutta)
original title: *Aranyer Din Ratri*
A group of friends leave Calcutta to spend a few days in the country.
Episodic drama of four middle-class idlers forced to re-examine their lives in an unfamiliar environment, comic in tone, with an underlying seriousness.
wd Satyajit Ray *novel* Sunil Ganguli ph Soumendu Roy, Purnendu Bose m Satyajit Ray ad Bansi Chandragupta ed Dulal Dutta
☆ Soumitra Chatterjee, Subhendu Chatterjee, Samit Bhanja, Rabi Ghose, Pahari Sanyal, Sarmila Tagore, Kaveri Bose, Simi Garewal, Aparna Sen
  'One would rate this lucid, ironic and superlatively graceful film among the very best of his work.' – *Penelope Huston, MFB*
  'A major film by one of the great film artists.' – *Pauline Kael*
  'Pretentious, short on plot but striving to be long on character, stylistically awkward as a sign of sincere emotions, and all of it held together by a title that is more poetic than anything in the movie itself.' – *William Paul, Village Voice*

Days of Being Wild **
Hong Kong 1991 93m Agfacolor
Made in Hong Kong/In-Gear (Rover Tang)
original title: *Ahfei Zhenjuang*
In 1960, the lives of a womanizing playboy searching for his real mother, the abandoned girlfriend who pursues him, and a cop who realizes his ambition of becoming a sailor, cross in Hong Kong and Manila.
A stylish account of the disaffected and rootless young which eschews straightforward narrative for a more complex approach, strong on atmosphere and period re-creation.
wd Wong Kar-Wai ph Christopher Doyle pd William Chang ed Kai Kit-Wai
☆ Leslie Cheung, Maggie Cheung, Andy Lau, Carina Lau, Jacky Cheung, Rebecca Pan, Tony Leung
  'As an existential account of solitary souls in random orbits, the film blows away the entire body of recent French "designer cinema". As a touchstone for Hong Kong's specific identity and psyche, it's close to sublime.' – *Tony Rayns, Sight and Sound*
† This version was the director's cut following the film's original release in 1990, when despite winning the Hong Kong Film Awards for best film, best director, best actor (Leslie Cheung) and best art direction, it flopped at the local box-office.

Days of Glory
US 1944 86m bw
RKO (Casey Robinson)
▦
Russian peasants fight the invading Nazis.
Lower-berth wartime propaganda piece chiefly notable for introducing Gregory Peck to the screen.
w Casey Robinson *story* Melchior Lengyel d Jacques Tourneur ph Tony Gaudio m Daniele Amfitheatrof
☆ Tamara Toumanova, Gregory Peck, Alan Reed, Maria Palmer, Lowell Gilmore, Hugo Haas

'Your eyes – your ears – your senses will be overwhelmed!'
Days of Heaven ****
US 1978 95m Metrocolor
Paramount/OP (Bert and Harold Schneider)
⊞ ▦ ⊛ ⊚
In the early 20th century, three young immigrants leave Chicago for the wheatfields.
Visually a superb slice of period life, it has an emotional force that emerges slowly from the conjunction of the vast landscape and its reticent intruders, who have fled from the dark of the city to find no peace in the country.
wd Terrence Malick ph Nestor Almendros m Ennio Morricone
☆ Richard Gere, Brooke Adams, Sam Shepard, Linda Manz
  'It's serious, yes, very solemn, but not depressing.' – *Roger Ebert*
  'Superbly directed and acted; see it for a second time and its hold is still more relentless.' – *Dilys Powell, Punch*
  'One of the great cinematic achievements of the 1970s.' – *Variety*

⊚ Digital Video Disc Region 2　⊚ Digital Video Disc Region 1　☊ Soundtrack released on compact disc　☆ Cast in approximate order of importance　† Points of interest　♫ Notable songs　♔ Academy Award　♕ Academy Award nomination　♖ BAFTA

'Terrence Malick's innocently convoluted parable of love lost and found, and reconciliation achieved and then fatally broken, is superbly counterpointed, thanks to Nestor Almendros' photography, by the burgeoning expansiveness of Texas during the First War.' – *Sight and Sound*

🎞 Nestor Almendros
🎵 Ennio Morricone
🏆 Ennio Morricone

Days of Hope: see *Espoir*

Days of Thrills and Laughter ***
👪 US 1961 93m bw
TCF (Robert Youngson)
▦

Appealing if rather miscellaneous silent film compilation with the accent on action and thrills as well as comedy.
Like the other Youngson histories, a boon to film archivists despite a facetious commentary.
m Max Shaindlin *narrator* Jay Jackson
☆ Stan Laurel, Oliver Hardy, Snub Pollard, Douglas Fairbanks, Charles Chaplin, Pearl White, Houdini, Harry Langdon, Ben Turpin, Charlie Chase, Boris Karloff, Warner Oland, Fatty Arbuckle, Keystone Kops

Days of Thunder
US 1990 107m Technicolor Panavision
Paramount (Don Simpson, Jerry Bruckheimer)
⬚ ▦ 🎧

An eager young stock car driver challenges the champion. Guess who wins.
An over-familiar story rendered no more interestingly than usual. Despite its star, it flopped at the box-office.
w Robert Towne *story* Robert Towne, Tom Cruise d Tony Scott ph Ward Russell m Hans Zimmer ad Benjamin Fernandez, Thomas E. Sanders ed Billy Weber, Chris Lebenzon
☆ Tom Cruise, Robert Duvall, Nicole Kidman, Randy Quaid, Michael Rooker, Cary Elwes, Fred Dalton Thompson, John C. Reilly, J. C. Quinn, Don Simpson
'Simply a flashy, noisy star vehicle for Tom Cruise, one which – like the stock cars he drives – goes around in circles getting nowhere.' – MFB

'They Will Let Him Up Soon And He Will Look For His Wife And He May Pray That He Doesn't Find Her...'
Days of Wine and Roses **
US 1962 117m bw
Warner (Martin Manulis)
▦ 🎧

A PR man becomes an alcoholic; his wife gradually reaches the same state, but he recovers and she does not.
Smart satirical comedy confusingly gives way to melodrama, then sentimentality; quality is evident throughout, but all concerned are happiest with the first hour.
w J. P. Miller d Blake Edwards ph Philip Lathrop m Henry Mancini
☆ Jack Lemmon, Lee Remick, Charles Bickford, Jack Klugman, Alan Hewitt, Debbie Megowan, Jack Albertson
'The film fails. The fault is not an upbeat ending, but the mere fact that there is any ending at all. The ending, here, denatures the alcoholism, turning it from grim reality to dramatic device, and escaping from the battle of the bottle into a more manageable battle of the sexes.' – *Newsweek*
♪ title song (m Henry Mancini, ly Johnny Mercer)
🏆 Jack Lemmon; Lee Remick

A Day's Pleasure *
👪 US 1919 20m bw silent
First National/Charles Chaplin
⬚

Mishaps of a family picnic.
Very mild Chaplin, reaching for but not achieving a kind of lyric quality. Amusing bits rather than scenes.
wd Charles Chaplin ph Rollie Totheroh
☆ Charles Chaplin, Edna Purviance, Jackie Coogan, Henry Bergman, Babe London

Daytime Wife
US 1939 71m bw
TCF

A young wife finds that her husband is still dating his secretary, and retaliates by dating his colleague.
Hollywood version of a French farce; not terrific, but watchable.

w Art Arthur, Robert Harari d Gregory Ratoff
☆ Tyrone Power, Linda Darnell, Warren William, Binnie Barnes, Wendy Barrie, Joan Davis, Leonid Kinskey
'Will give a good account of itself in the key runs.' – *Variety*

Dayton's Devils
US 1968 103m Eastmancolor
Madison/Harold Goldman (Robert W. Stabler)
▦

A former USAF colonel assembles a group of misfits and adventurers to steal an army payroll.
Overlong, routine caper film with a surprisingly crisp climax (when it comes).
w Fred de Gorter d Jack Shea ph Brick Marquard m Marlin Skiles
☆ Leslie Nielsen, Rory Calhoun, Lainie Kazan, Hans Gudegast

'What a day. What a trip.'
The Daytrippers **
US 1996 87m colour
Metrodome/Fiasco/Trick Films (Nancy Tenenbaum, Steven Soderbergh)
⬚ ▦

The adventures of a wronged wife and her family as she drives from Long Island to confront her husband in Manhattan.
Clever road movie, which wittily dissects troubled relationships.
wd Greg Mottola ph John Inwood m Richard Martinez pd Bonnie J. Brinkley ed Anne McCabe
☆ Hope Davis, Pat McNamara, Anne Meara, Parker Posey, Liev Schreiber, Stanley Tucci, Campbell Scott, Marcia Gay Harden, Andy Brown
'Has more wit than countless studio movies.' – *Sunday Times*

Dazed and Confused **
US 1993 102m DeLuxe
Feature/Universal/Gramercy/Alphaville (James Jacks, Sean Daniel, Richard Linklater)
⬚ ▦ 🎧 🎧

In 1976, a group of high school students celebrate their last day by victimizing younger kids.
Enjoyable and truthful comedy of adolescents trying to avoid facing up to the inevitable future.
wd Richard Linklater ph Lee Daniel pd John Frick ed Sandra Adair
☆ Jason London, Wiley Wiggins, Milla Jovovich, Rory Cochrane, Shawn Andrews, Adam Goldberg, Anthony Rapp, Sasha Jenson, Matthew McConaughey, Ben Affleck
'A very clever piece of retro 70s anti-nostalgia which scrupulously avoids sentimentality. It just wants to tell us how genuinely strange the 70s were.' – *Steve Beard, Empire*

D-Day the Sixth of June
US 1956 106m Eastmancolor
Cinemascope
TCF (Charles Brackett)
▦

On the way to invade France in 1944, a British colonel and an American captain reminisce about their love for the same woman.
Turgid war romance with some good action scenes and the usual hilarious Hollywood view of London.
General effect very wooden.
w Ivan Moffat, Harry Brown *novel* Lionel Shapiro d Henry Koster ph Lee Garmes m Lyn Murray
☆ Robert Taylor, Richard Todd, Dana Wynter, Edmond O'Brien, John Williams, Jerry Paris, Richard Stapley
'Reminiscent of Mrs Miniver in style and feeling.' – *MFB*

De eso no se habla: see *We Don't Want to Talk about It*

'He made evil an art, vice a virtue and pain a pleasure!'
De Sade *
US/Germany 1969 113m Movielab
AIP/CCC/Transcontinental (Louis M. Heyward, Artur Brauner)
The unbalanced Marquis de Sade is tormented by his wicked uncle with thoughts of his past.
Mildly interesting attempt by AIP at European debauchery, with a good theatrical framework for the fantasies but too much flailing about by all concerned, especially in the slow motion orgy sequences, which are relentlessly boring, as is the film.

w Richard Matheson d Cy Endfield ph Heinz Pehlke m Billy Strange ad Jurgen Kiebach
☆ Keir Dullea, John Huston, Lilli Palmer, Senta Berger, Anna Massey, Uta Levka

The Dead ****
GB 1987 83m Foto-Kem
Vestron/Zenith/Liffey Films (Wieland Schulz-Keil, Chris Sievernich)
⬚ ▦

Two Irish spinster sisters throw a winter dinner for their relatives and friends.
Its director's last film is a warm and somehow invigorating reminiscence of things past.
w Tony Huston *book* Dubliners by James Joyce d John Huston ph Fred Murphy m Alex North pd Stephen Grimes, Dennis Washington cos Dorothy Jeakins
☆ Anjelica Huston, Donal McCann, Rachel Dowling, Cathleen Delany, Dan O'Herlihy, Helena Carroll, Donal Donnelly
'A delicate coda in a minor key to an illustrious 46-year career.' – *Daily Variety*
'A small masterpiece, perfectly achieved.' – *Time Out*
🏆 best adapted screenplay; Dorothy Jeakins

'How many times can you die for love?'
Dead Again *
US 1991 108m Technicolor/bw
UIP/Paramount/Mirage (Lindsay Doran, Charles H. Maguire)
⬚ ▦ 🎧 🎧

A private detective is hired to investigate an amnesiac who can only remember a past life as a concert pianist murdered by her husband.
Tricksy thriller, switching between past and present, which is frequently too clever for its own good.
w Scott Frank d Kenneth Branagh ph Matthew F. Leonetti m Patrick Doyle pd Tim Hervey ed Peter E. Berger
☆ Kenneth Branagh, Emma Thompson, Andy Garcia, Derek Jacobi, Robin Williams, Wayne Knight, Hanna Schygulla
'Briskly entertaining enough to generate mostly positive word of mouth among mature audiences.' – *Variety*
'A monstrous cinematic folly.' – *Geoff Brown, Sight and Sound*

Dead Alive: see *Braindead*

Dead and Buried *
US 1981 95m colour
GTO/Avco Embassy (Ronald Shusett, Robert Fentress)
⬚ ▦

A sheriff investigates killings in a small town where the locals are not what they seem.
Cheap horror movie along familiar and predictable lines.
w Ronald Shusett, Dan O'Bannon *story* Jeff Millar, Alex Stern d Gary A. Sherman ph Steve Poster m Joe Renzetti ad Bill Sandell, Joe Aubel ed Alan Balsam
☆ James Farentino, Melody Anderson, Jack Albertson, Dennis Redfield, Nancy Locke Hauser, Lisa Blount, Robert Englund, Bill Quinn
'The gratuitously explicit death-dealing mounts up, the reductive echoes of superior ventures into similar territory grow stronger, and it all peters out in a welter of speciously manufactured hysteria.' – *Tim Pulleine, MFB*

The Dead and the Deadly **
Hong Kong 1982 95m colour
Raymond Chow
original title: Ren Xia Ren
Murdered by his greedy colleagues after faking his own death to inherit a fortune, a wastrel returns as a ghost to seek his revenge.
Engaging black kung-fu comedy in which the humour and the conventions of the spirit world are more accessible than usual to Western audiences.
w Sammo Hung, Barry Wong d Wu Ma
☆ Sammo Hung, Wu Ma, Lam Ching-ying, Cherie Chung, Chung Fat

Dead Calm *
Australia 1988 96m colour
Warner/Kennedy Miller Productions (Terry Hayes, Doug Mitchell, George Miller)
⬚ ▦ 🎧 🎧

A couple bring a dangerous stranger aboard their yacht.
Effectively suspenseful.

w Terry Hayes *novel* Charles Williams d Phillip Noyce ph Dean Semler m Graeme Revell pd Graham 'Grace' Walker ed Richard Francis-Bruce
☆ Nicole Kidman, Sam Neill, Billy Zane, Rod Mulliner, Joshua Tilden, George Shevtsov, Michael Long

The Dead Can't Lie
US 1988 97m colour
Cannon/Showtime (David Latt)
A private eye is hired to prevent a millionaire being harassed by his dead wife.
Silly supernatural thriller, dead from the neck up.
wd Lloyd Fonvielle ph Michael Chapman m George Clinton pd Carol Spier ed Evan Lottman
☆ Tommy Lee Jones, Virginia Madsen, Colin Bruce, Kevin Jarre, Frederic Forrest

Dead Cert
GB 1974 99m DeLuxe
UA/Woodfall (Neil Hartley)
A gentleman jockey investigates the death of his friend, a horse owner and fellow amateur rider, during a steeplechase.
Dull and implausible thriller, not helped by its uncharismatic hero, though the climax, at the Grand National, generates a little excitement.
w Tony Richardson, John Oaksey *novel* Dick Francis d Tony Richardson ph Freddie Cooper m John Addison ad David Brockhurst ed John Glen
☆ Scott Anthony, Judi Dench, Michael Williams, Nina Thomas, Julian Glover, Mark Dignam, John Bindon, Ian Hogg, Bill Fraser
'Unfortunately, wonderful reads don't necessarily make wonderful scripts.' – *Tony Richardson*

The Dead Don't Dream
US 1947 62m bw
UA/Hopalong Cassidy Productions (Lewis J. Rachmil)
Hoppy goes to be best man at a wedding and instead solves the mystery of multiple murders at an inn.
Slow-paced, amiable but unremarkable Western with the emphasis on detection.
w Francis Rosenwald d George Archainbaud ph Mack Stengler m Darrell Calker ad Jerome Pycha Jnr ed Fred W. Berger
☆ William Boyd, Andy Clyde, Rand Brooks, John Parrish, Leonard Penn, Mary Tucker

'You may not like these people, nor pity them, but you'll never forget this picture!'
Dead End ***
👪 US 1937 92m bw
Samuel Goldwyn
▦ 🎧

A slice of life in New York's east side, where slum kids and gangsters live in a river street next to a luxury apartment block.
Highly theatrical film of a highly theatrical play, more or less preserving the single set and overcoming the limitations of the script and setting by sheer cinematic expertise. It is chiefly remembered, however, for introducing the Dead End Kids to a delighted world.
w Lillian Hellman *play* Sidney Kingsley d William Wyler ph Gregg Toland m Alfred Newman ad Richard Day
☆ Joel McCrea, Sylvia Sidney, Humphrey Bogart, Wendy Barrie, Claire Trevor, Allen Jenkins, Marjorie Main, James Burke, Ward Bond, The Dead End Kids (Billy Halop, Leo Gorcey, Bernard Punsley, Huntz Hall, Bobby Jordan, Gabriel Dell)
'Tense and accurate transcription, but sordid and depressing … in for a disappointing career.' – *Variety*
🏆 best picture; Gregg Toland; Claire Trevor; Richard Day

The Dead End Kids
The films in which the original gang of young 'hooligans' (see above) appeared were as follows:
1937 Dead End
1938 Crime School, Angels with Dirty Faces
1939 They Made Me a Criminal, Hell's Kitchen, Angels Wash Their Faces, On Dress Parade
Subsequently they broke up into the LITTLE TOUGH GUYS, the EAST SIDE KIDS, and the BOWERY BOYS (all qv).

👪 film suitable for family viewing   ⬚ VHS video-cassette for the British PAL system   ⬚ VHS video-cassette for the British PAL system in wide screen-format   🔄 Video cassette in a computer-colourised version   ▦ American NTSC video-cassette   🎧 Laser disc

Dead Fire

Canada/Czechoslovakia 1996 96m colour
North American/Do or Die (Lloyd A. Simandl)

In 2060 AD, after the world has been laid waste, a maverick security man on an orbiting space station is the only person who can defeat a criminal conspiracy to rule the future.

Cliché-ridden science fiction, with risible hard-boiled dialogue ('You've got big balls, Brody. I'll give you that. But you just tripped over them for the last time.') and performances to match.

w Christopher Hyde, Andrew McEvoy, Nicholas Racz d Robert Lee ph Dave Pelletier m Peter Allen ed Richard Benwick
☆ Matt Frewer, C. Thomas Howell, Colin Cunningham, Monika Schnarre, Rachel Hayward, Robert Russel, Jim Thorburn, Lucie Zednickova, Gerard Whelan

Dead Heart *

Australia 1996 103m colour
AFFC/New Town (Bryan Brown, Helen Watts)

A police constable in an isolated aboriginal community finds himself caught between upholding the law and conforming to the demands of tribal custom.

Interesting but muddled drama of a clash between cultures and between attitudes within cultures; it just fails to cohere into a satisfying experience.

wd Nick Parsons ph James Bartle m Stephen Rae pd Brian Edmonds ed Henry Dangar
☆ Bryan Brown, Ernie Dingo, Angie Milliken, Gnarnayarrahe Waitaire, Aaron Pedersen, John Jarratt, Lewis Fitz-Gerald, Anne Tenney, Lafe Charlton, David Gulpilil

Dead Heat

US 1988 83m Technicolor
Entertainment/New World Pictures (Michael Meltzer, David Helpern)

Two zombie cops track down their killer.
Asinine comic combination of DOA and The Night of the Living Dead.

w Terry Black d Mark Goldblatt ph Robert D. Yeoman m Ernest Troost pd Craig Stearns ed Harvey Rosenstock
☆ Treat Williams, Joe Piscopo, Lindsay Frost, Darren McGavin, Vincent Price, Clare Kirkconnell, Keye Luke, Ben Mittleman

Dead Heat on a Merry Go Round

US 1967 · 108m Technicolor
Columbia (Carter de Haven)

An ex-con breaks parole and plans to rob Los Angeles Airport.
Boringly arty caper comedy-melodrama, concentrating less on the robbery than on its hero's sexual prowess. All very superficially flashy, and what the title means is anybody's guess.

wd Bernard Girard ph Lionel Lindon m Stu Phillips
☆ James Coburn, Camilla Sparv, Aldo Ray, Nina Wayne, Robert Webber, Rose Marie, Todd Armstrong, Marian Moses, Severn Darden
'Just fills the space between a frisky title and a tricky TV-comedy ending, but doesn't fill it with any revels that require a viewer's complete attention.' – *Time*

Dead Image: see *Dead Ringer*

Dead Innocent

Canada 1996 92m colour
Blackwatch/Mariani (Michael Doherty, William R. Mariani)

A workaholic lawyer returns home late to discover her maid and daughter murdered.
A thriller that sets up an intriguing situation, but then fails to develop it satisfactorily.

w Dolores Payne, Mort Pattigo d Sarah Botsford ph Rodney Gibbons m David Findlay pd Donna Noonan ed Michael Doherty
☆ Genevieve Bujold, Nancy Beatty, Graham Greene, Emily Hampshire, Jonathan Scarfe, Neil Kroetsch, Benz Antoine

Dead Letter Office

Australia 1998 95m colour
BBC/AFFC/Artist Services/Film Victoria (Denise Patience)

Impelled by memories of her father, who left home when she was small, a young woman gets a job at the dead letter office, where she forms an uneasy relationship with her boss, a Chilean émigré.
Muted, elegiac movie about loss, given to over-heavy symbolism.

w Deb Cox d John Ruane ph Ellery Ryan m Roger Mason pd Chris Kennedy ed Denise Haratzis
☆ Miranda Otto, George DelHoyo, Nicholas Bell, Syd Brisbane, Georgina Naidu, Jane Hall, Barry Otto

'No One Can Survive Becoming A Legend.'
Dead Man **

US/Germany 1996 121m bw
Electric/12-Gauge/Pandora (Demetra J. MacBride)

An unemployed accountant goes into the lawless West and becomes a hunted man and a killer.
Enjoyable existential Western, slow-moving but providing an interesting and eccentric ride on the trail from civilization to savagery.

wd Jim Jarmusch ph Robby Müller m Neil Young pd Robert Ziembicki ed Jay Rabinowitz
☆ Johnny Depp, Gary Farmer, Lance Henriksen, Robert Mitchum, Crispin Glover, Gabriel Byrne, John Hurt, Alfred Molina, Michael Wincott, Mili Avital, Iggy Pop, Jared Harris, Billy Bob Thornton
'Only a few script drafts or some ruthless re-editing away from being rather good.' – *Adam Mars-Jones, Independent*

'The Drop-Dead Funniest Movie Of The Decade!'
Dead Man on Campus

US 1998 93m colour
Paramount/MTV/Pacific Western (Gale Anne Hurd)

Two partying medical students, on the verge of being expelled, discover that they will be awarded perfect grades if a room-mate commits suicide, and go in search of a suitable candidate.
Limp comedy that is too eager not to offend, and so fails to come to terms with its subject-matter.

w Michael Traeger, Mike White story Anthony Abrams, Adam Larson Broder d Alan Cohn ph John Thomas m Mark Mothersbaugh pd Carol Winstead Wood ed Debra Chiate
☆ Tom Everett Scott, Mark-Paul Gosselaar, Poppy Montgomery, Lochlyn Munro, Randy Pearlstein, Corey Page, Alyson Hannigan, Mari Morrow, Dave Ruby
'A modestly amusing trifle that merits a passing grade as lightweight entertainment.' – *Joe Leydon, Variety*
† A similar starting point was used in the movie *Dead Man's Curve* (qv).

Dead Man Walking **

US 1995 122m DuArt
Polygram/Working Title/Havoc (John Kilik, Tim Robbins, Rudd Simmons)

A murderer on Death Row repents of his crime after visits from a Catholic nun.
A tense and gripping meditation on death and the taking of lives, handled with sensitivity and an avoidance of sensationalism.

wd Tim Robbins book Sister Helen Prejean ph Roger A. Deakins m David Robbins pd Richard Hoover ed Lisa Zeno Churgin
☆ Susan Sarandon, Sean Penn, Robert Prosky, Raymond J. Barry, R. Lee Ermey, Celia Weston, Lois Smith, Scott Wilson
'As drama, *Dead Man Walking* is dead on its feet.' – *Tom Shone, Sunday Times*
'A film that carefully eschews the usual Hollywood sentimentality.' – *Derek Malcolm, Guardian*
♟ Susan Sarandon
♟ Sean Penn; song 'Dead Man Walking' (m/ly Bruce Springsteen)

Dead Man's Curve

US 1998 90m colour
Hope Street Entertainment/Mount Royal (Michael Amato, Theodore Schipper, Jeremy Lew)

Two college students discover that they can get a perfect grade if their room-mate kills himself; so

they decide to murder him and make it look like suicide.
Black thriller on the theme that winners take all; but there is an unpleasant, gloating tone to it, and its twists are predictable.

wd Dan Rosen ph Joey Forstyte m Shark pd Robert Harbour ed William Mercer
☆ Matthew Lillard, Michael Vartan, Randall Batinkoff, Keri Russell, Tamara Craig Thomas, Anthony Griffin, Bo Dietle, Kevin Huff, Henry Strozier, Dana Delany
'Isn't clever enough to hit the mark as an intended diabolical black comedy.' – *Dennis Harvey, Variety*
† A similar plot device was used in the comedy *Dead Man on Campus* (qv).

Dead Man's Evidence

GB 1967 62m bw
Bayford/RCM (Francis Searle)

A secret agent investigates the mystery of a diver's body found on an Irish beach.
Dreary thriller, with both script and direction below par, and acting that is, at best, perfunctory.

w Arthur La Bern d Francis Searle ph Ken Hodges m Ken Thorne md Phillip Martell ad Duncan Sutherland ed Jim Connock
☆ Conrad Phillips, Jane Griffiths, Veronica Hurst, Ryck Rydon, Alex Mackintosh, Godfrey Quigley, Bruce Seton, Harry Webster

Dead Man's Eyes

US 1944 64m bw
Universal

In order to trap a murderer, a blind artist pretends to have recovered his sight.
Cheerless lower-case thriller from the disappointing Inner Sanctum series.

w Dwight V. Babcock d Reginald LeBorg
☆ Lon Chaney Jnr, Jean Parker, Paul Kelly

Dead Man's Shoes

GB 1939 67m bw
Associated British (Walter Mycroft)

A wealthy Paris manufacturer is accused of being a criminal who once disappeared.
Sufficiently absorbing courtroom/amnesia melodrama, with British actors in a French setting.

w Hans Kafka, Nina Jarvis d Thomas Bentley ph Gunther Krampf ad Ian White ed Monica Kimmick
☆ Leslie Banks, Joan Marion, Geoffrey Atkins, Wilfrid Lawson, Judy Kelly, Nancy Price, Peter Bull, Walter Hudd, Ludwig Stossel
'Goes straight into tense situations, and there are unexpected twists … should do well.' – *Variety*

Dead Men Don't Die

US 1991 94m colour
Trans Atlantic/Waymar (Wayne Marmorstein)

After he is killed by drug dealers, a TV newscaster is brought back to life as a zombie.
Terrible, heavy-handed comedy, stuffed with ham acting.

☆ Elliott Gould, Melissa Anderson, Mark Moses, Mabel King, Philip Bruns, Jack Betts, Robert Dryer, Robert Covarrubias, Phil Shipko

Dead Men Don't Wear Plaid *

US 1982 88m bw
Universal/Aspen Film Society (David V. Picker, William E. McEuen)

A private eye is hired by a beautiful girl to find her father's murderer.
Ingenious but overstretched prank in which the hero apparently (by intercutting) gets involved with famous crime stars of the forties: Bogart, Ladd, Bacall, Stanwyck, etc. The basic script is simply not funny enough to support the superstructure, though the selection of lines from the oldies is often ingenious.

w Carl Reiner, George Gipe, Steve Martin d Carl Reiner ph Michael Chapman m Miklos Rozsa pd John DeCuir ed Bud Molin
☆ Steve Martin, Rachel Ward, Carl Reiner, Reni Santoni
'The content is undergraduate facetiousness at its worst, but at least the excerpts themselves provide a pleasant noir anthology.' – *Sight and Sound*

Dead Men Tell No Tales

GB 1938 80m bw
British National (John Corfield)

The matron of a school for boys is murdered after winning a lottery.
Reasonably intriguing mystery.

w Walter Summers, Stafford Dickens, Emlyn Williams novel The Norwich Victims by Francis Beeding d David MacDonald ph Bryan Langley md W. L. Trytel ed James Corbett
☆ Emlyn Williams, Hugh Williams, Marius Goring, Lesley Brook, Sara Seegar

Dead Men Walk

US 1943 64m bw
PRC

A vampire returns from death to destroy his twin brother.
Incompetent chiller partly sustained by its star performance.

w Fred Myton d Sam Newfield
☆ George Zucco, Mary Carlisle

'Like Nothing In This World You've Ever Thrilled To Before.'
Dead of Night ****

GB 1945 104m bw
Ealing (Sidney Cole, John Croydon)

An architect is caught up in an endless series of recurring dreams, during which he is told other people's supernatural experiences and finally murders the psychiatrist who is trying to help him.
Chillingly successful and influential compendium of the macabre, especially effective in its low-key handling of the linking sequence with its circular ending.

w John Baines, Angus MacPhail, based on stories by themselves, H. G. Wells, E. F. Benson d Cavalcanti, Charles Crichton, Robert Hamer, Basil Dearden ph Douglas Slocombe, Stan Pavey m Georges Auric ad Michael Relph
☆ Mervyn Johns, Roland Culver, Mary Merrall, Judy Kelly, Anthony Baird, Sally Ann Howes, Frederick Valk, Googie Withers, Ralph Michael, Esmé Percy, Basil Radford, Naunton Wayne, Miles Malleson, Michael Redgrave, Hartley Power and also Elizabeth Welch
'In a nightmare within a nightmare are contained five separate ghost stories … they have atmosphere and polish, they are eerie, they are well acted.' – *Richard Winnington*
'One of the most successful blends of laughter, terror and outrage that I can remember.' – *James Agee*
'The five ghost stories accumulate in intensity until the trap closes in the surrealist climax.' – *Pauline Kael, 1968*

Dead of Winter

US 1986 100m Metrocolor
UIP/MGM-UA (John Bloomgarden, Marc Shmuger)

An actress finds herself cast for a role which involves her being trapped in a country house with two villains.
Oddball suspenser with talent which seems to have expected something better.

w Marc Shmuger, Mark Malone d Arthur Penn ph Jan Weincke m Richard Einhorn pd Bill Brodie ed Rick Shaine
☆ Mary Steenburgen, Roddy McDowall, Jan Rubes, William Russ

Dead on Sight

US 1994 96m Foto-Kem
MCEG Sterling (Roxanne Messina Captor)

A university professor, trying to find the serial killer who murdered his wife, enlists the aid of a student who sees future murders in her dreams.
Extremely dull and silly thriller, remarkable only for its lack of suspense.

w Lewis Green d Ruben Preuss ph Levie Isaacks m Harry Manfredini pd Jo-Ann Chorney ed David Kern
☆ Jennifer Beals, Daniel Baldwin, Kurtwood Smith, William H. Macy, Kent Williams, Ed Beechner

---

Dead or Alive
Italy/US   1967   89m   Eastmancolor
Documento/Selmur (Albert Band)

US title: *A Minute to Pray, a Second to Die*
A gunman with a paralysed right arm helps a state governor rid a town of bandits.
Semi-spaghetti Western with a strong cast and violent action scenes.
w Ugo Liberatore, Louis Garfinkle d Franco Giraldi ph Aiace Parolin m Carlo Rustichelli
☆ Robert Ryan, Arthur Kennedy, Alex Cord, Nicoletta Machiavelli

Dead Pigeon on Beethoven Street
West Germany   1972   103m   DeLuxe
Bavaria Atelier
An American private eye is shot dead in Germany by an international extortion gang, and his partner arrives to seek revenge.
Cheapskate thriller of interest only to addicts of the director.
wd Samuel Fuller
☆ Glenn Corbett, Christa Lang, Anton Diffring

Dead Poets Society **
US   1989   129m   Metrocolor
Warner/Touchstone/Silver Screen Partners IV/Witt-Thomas Productions (Steven Haft, Paul Junger Witt, Tony Thomas)

A new English teacher subverts tradition by encouraging his students to enjoy life.
Heartfelt, but a little too manipulative to be totally successful.
w Tom Schulman d Peter Weir ph John Seale m Maurice Jarre pd Wendy Stites ed William Anderson, Lee Smith, Priscilla Nedd
☆ Robin Williams, Robert Sean Leonard, Ethan Hawke, Josh Charles, Gale Hansen, Dylan Kussman, Allelon Ruggiero, James Waterston, Norman Lloyd
🎘 Tom Schulman
⬥ best picture; Robin Williams; Peter Weir
⬥ best picture; Maurice Jarre

The Dead Pool
US   1988   91m   Technicolor
Warner/Malpaso (David Valdes)

Inspector Callahan investigates a murder and the game of Dead Pool, in which people bet on certain celebrities dying within a specified time.
Fifth and worst in the series involving a tough cop that began with Dirty Harry.
w Steve Sharon story Steve Sharon, Durk Pearson, Sandy Shaw d Buddy Van Horn ph Jack N. Green m Lalo Schifrin pd Edward C. Carfagno ed Ron Spang
☆ Clint Eastwood, Patricia Clarkson, Liam Neeson, Evan C. Kim, David Hunt, Michael Currie, Michael Goodwin, Darwin Gillett, Anthony Charnota

Dead Presidents *
US   1995   119m   Technicolor
Buena Vista/Hollywood/Caravan/Underworld (Allen Hughes, Albert Hughes)

After serving in Vietnam, a black man turns to crime to support himself, his girlfriend and child.
Downbeat thriller that struggles to marry social comment with the familiar form of a gangster movie; the union is not a happy one.
w Michael Henry Brown story *Specialist No. 4 Haywood T. 'The Kid' Kirkland* by Wallace Terry d Allen Hughes, Albert Hughes ph Lisa Rinzler m Danny Elfman pd David Brisbin ed Dan Lebental
☆ Larenz Tate, Keith David, Chris Tucker, Freddy Rodriguez, Rose Jackson, N'Bushe Wright, Bokeem Woodbine, Martin Sheen (uncredited)
'The outlook is bleak, the pessimism and the fatalism show that political consciousness without social outlets only leads to blanket nihilism.' – *Alexander Walker*

Dead Reckoning *
US   1947   100m   bw
Columbia (Sidney Biddell)

Two war veterans are on their way to be decorated in Washington when one disappears.
Dour, complexly plotted thriller, a typical Hollywood film noir of the post-war years but a long way behind
Gilda in likeability. The hero confesses the plot to a priest, and all the way it is more glum than fun.
w Oliver H. P. Garrett, Steve Fisher d John Cromwell ph Leo Tover m Marlin Skiles md Morris Stoloff
☆ Humphrey Bogart, Lizabeth Scott, Morris Carnovsky, Charles Cane, William Prince, Marvin Miller, Wallace Ford, James Bell
'The atmosphere is fraught with sinister suggestion.' – *Sunday Express*

Dead Ringer *
US   1964   116m   bw
Warner (William H. Wright)

GB title: *Dead Image*
A woman shoots her rich twin sister and assumes her identity.
High camp star vehicle, full of memories of long ago but rather drearily assembled and far too long, though Miss Davis as ever is in fighting form.
w Albert Beich, Oscar Millard d Paul Henreid ph Ernest Haller m André Previn
☆ Bette Davis, Karl Malden, Peter Lawford, Philip Carey, Jean Hagen, Estelle Winwood, George Chandler, Cyril Delevanti

Dead Ringers *
Canada   1988   115m   colour
Rank/The Mantle Clinic II/Morgan Creek Productions (David Cronenberg, Marc Boyman)

Identical twins, top gynaecologists, indulge in confusing their identities.
Downbeat and grisly, though possessing a certain elegance of style.
w David Cronenberg, Norman Snider book *Twins* by Barry Wood d David Cronenberg ph Peter Suschitzky m Howard Shore pd Carol Spier ed Ronald Sanders
☆ Jeremy Irons, Geneviève Bujold, Heidi von Palleske, Barbara Gordon, Shirley Douglas, Stephen Lack, Nick Nicholas, Lynne Cormack
'Its disturbing impact derives from a laying bare of male fantasies in such a way that masculinity itself is revealed as fragile, unstable, even impossible.' – *Pam Cook, MFB*

Dead Run
France   1967   100m   colour
SNC (René Picneres)
original title: *Deux Billets pour Mexico*
A pickpocket steals top-secret papers and is chased across Europe by the CIA and a ruthless freelance espionage outfit.
Lightweight thriller, with performances to match, and of little interest, even on the level of a travelogue.
w Christian-Jaque, Michael Levine, Pascal Jardin novel *Dead Run* by Robert Sheckley d Christian-Jaque ph Pierre Petit m Gerard Calvi ad Jurgen Kiebach ed Jacques Desagneaux
☆ Peter Lawford, Ira Furstenberg, Georges Geret, Maria Bucella, Werner Peters, Wolfgang Kieling, Horst Frank

The Dead that Walk: see The Zombies of Mora Tau

The Dead Zone *
US   1983   103m   Technicolor
Lorimar/Dino de Laurentiis (Debra Hill)

The survivor of a road accident discovers that he has psychic powers.
Glum thriller with a fairly predictable outcome but some well-staged episodes.
w Jeffrey Boam novel Stephen King d David Cronenberg ph Mark Irwin m Michael Kamen pd Carol Spier
☆ Christopher Walken, Brooke Adams, Tom Skerritt, Herbert Lom, Anthony Zerbe, Colleen Dewhurst

Dead-Bang
US   1989   102m   Metrocolor
Warner/Lorimar (Steve Roth)

A detective, hunting a killer, uncovers a white racist organization.
Loud and undistinguished thriller.
w Robert Foster d John Frankenheimer ph Gerry Fisher m Gary Chang, Michael Kamen pd Ken Adam ed Robert F. Shugrue
☆ Don Johnson, Penelope Ann Miller, William Forsythe, Bob Balaban, Frank Military, Tate
Donovan, Antoni Stutz, Mickey Jones, Ron Campbell
'John Frankenheimer's boldest, most enjoyable, and at least partially successful attempt both to recreate the halcyon days of his early 60s reputation, and to adapt them to changing times.' – *Richard Coombs, MFB*

Deadbolt
US   1992   95m   colour
Allegro/Image (Tom Berry, Franco Battista)

A divorced woman finds herself sharing an apartment with a manipulative homicidal maniac.
Risible, violent, dreary thriller on a threadbare theme; in order for the narrative to work, it requires intelligent people to behave stupidly.
w Mara Trafficante, Frank Rehwaldt d Douglas Jackson ph Rodney Gibbons m Milan Kymlicka pd Perri Gorrara ed Yves Langlois
☆ Justine Bateman, Adam Baldwin, Michelle Scarabelli, Chris Mulkey, Anthony Sherwood, Ellen Cohen, Colin Fox, Cyndi Pass
† The film was released direct to video in the US.

Deadfall
GB   1968   120m   DeLuxe
TCF/Salamanda (Paul Monash, Jack Rix)

Robbery turns sour when a cat burglar falls in love with the wife of his homosexual partner.
Drearily fashionable romantic melodrama with far too few high spots and generally dull performances.
wd Bryan Forbes novel Desmond Cory ph Gerry Turpin m John Barry
☆ Michael Caine, Eric Portman, Giovanna Ralli, Nanette Newman, David Buck
'Exhausted no doubt by their past passions and childhood traumas, the principal protagonists move like so many somnambulists through the turgid labyrinth … whatever the intention, *Deadfall* merely falls flat on its somewhat ludicrous face.' – *MFB*

Deadlier than the Male
GB   1966   101m   Techniscope
Rank/Sydney Box (Betty E. Box)
Bulldog Drummond traces the death of oil company executives to a master criminal using glamorous female assassins.
Just about tolerable recreation of Drummond in the modern world, with too little style, too much violence and sex, and an almost total lack of self-mockery. A sequel Some Girls Do *(qv) was an unmitigated disaster.*
w Jimmy Sangster, David Osborn, Liz Charles-Williams d Ralph Thomas ph Ernest Steward m Malcolm Lockyer ad Alex Vetchinsky
☆ Richard Johnson, Nigel Green, Elke Sommer, Sylva Koscina, Suzanna Leigh, Zia Mohyeddin, Steve Carlson
'The original Drummond would have found the whole thing rather distasteful.' – *MFB*

Deadline: see Deadline USA

Deadline at Dawn
US   1946   82m   bw
RKO (Adrian Scott)
A sailor on leave passes out, finds the girl he was with has been murdered, and is helped by a philosophical taxi driver and a girl.
This could have been another Crossfire, but is smothered by pretentious writing and uncertain direction. The credits are interesting, though.
w Clifford Odets novel William Irish (Cornell Woolrich) d Harold Clurman ph Nicholas Musuraca m Hanns Eisler
☆ Paul Lukas, Bill Williams, Susan Hayward, Osa Massen, Lola Lane

Deadline Midnight: see –30–

Deadline USA *
US   1952   87m   bw
TCF (Sol C. Siegel)
GB title: *Deadline*
Despite threats and the killing of a witness, a crusading newspaper goes ahead with a story about the crimes of a powerful gangster.
Watchable newspaper melodrama with nothing much to say except that America must wake up to the enemy within. Smooth production, but too much semi-pretentious talk.
wd Richard Brooks ph Milton Krasner m Cyril Mockridge
☆ Humphrey Bogart, Kim Hunter, Ethel Barrymore, Ed Begley, Paul Stewart, Warren Stevens, Martin Gabel, Joe de Santis, Audrey Christie, Jim Backus

Deadlock: see Wedlock

Deadly
Australia   1990   99m   colour
Beyond/AFFC/Moirstorm (Richard Moir)
A city cop in trouble goes to a small town to cover up the killing of an aborigine artist, found hanged in a police cell.
An angry drama of institutionalized racism and bigotry, but genuine emotion is soon submerged in the slickly melodramatic contrivances of the narrative.
w Esben Storm, Richard Moir, Ranald Allan d Esben Storm ph Geoffrey Simpson m Graeme Revell pd Peta Lawson ed Ralph Strasser
☆ Jerome Ehlers, Frank Gallacher, Lydia Miller, John Moore, Alan David Lee, Caz Lederman, Tony Barry, Julie Nihill, Martin Vaughan, Bill Hunter

Deadly Advice
GB   1994   90m   colour
Mayfair/Zenith (Nigel Stafford-Clark)

An unhappy woman has visions of famous murderers of the past, who advise her on how to kill her domineering mother and others who annoy her.
Flat attempt at a black comedy; it lacks the necessary style and wit and succeeds only in being depressing.
w Glenn Chandler d Mandie Fletcher ph Richard Greatrex m Richard Harvey pd Christopher Hobbs ed John Jarvis
☆ Jane Horrocks, Brenda Fricker, Jonathan Pryce, Imelda Staunton, Edward Woodward, Billie Whitelaw, Hywel Bennett, John Mills, Eleanor Bron, Jonathan Hyde
'Squanders a gaggle of British character actors on a nothing script that's desperately in need of a laugh track.' – *Derek Elley, Variety*

The Deadly Affair **
GB   1966   106m   Technicolor
Columbia/Sidney Lumet
A Foreign Office man apparently commits suicide; his colleague is unconvinced and finally uncovers a spy ring.
Compulsive if heavy-going thriller from the sour-about-spies era, deliberately glum, photographed against the shabbiest possible London backgrounds in muddy colour. Solidly entertaining for sophisticated grown-ups.
w Paul Dehn novel *Call for the Dead* by John Le Carré d Sidney Lumet ph Frederick A. Young m Quincy Jones
☆ James Mason, Simone Signoret, Harry Andrews, Maximilian Schell, Harriet Andersson, Kenneth Haigh, Max Adrian, Robert Flemyng, Roy Kinnear, Lynn Redgrave
'The whole film is a most skilful organisation of action, motive and character.' – *Dilys Powell*

The Deadly Bees
GB   1966   83m   Technicolor
Amicus
A pop singer goes on holiday to a remote farm and finds herself menaced by killer bees.
Flat little thriller with one very obvious twist and no monster: just those bees.
w Robert Bloch, Anthony Marriott d Freddie Francis
☆ Frank Finlay, Guy Doleman, Suzanna Leigh, Catherine Finn

'To the valley of mystery came the shadow of death!'
Deadly Blessing
US   1981   102m   Metrocolor
Polygram/Interplanetary (William Gilmore)

A strict Hittite sect in Pennsylvania is disrupted by the murderous activities of an incubus.
Further developments from the school of Alien, Omen and The Exorcist; basically a succession of well-engineered shocks punctuated by long periods of boredom.
w Glenn M. Benest, Matthew Barr, Wes Craven d Wes Craven ph Robert Jessup m James Horner sp Jack Bennett
☆ Maren Jensen, Susan Buckner, Jeff East, Ernest Borgnine, Lisa Hartman, Lois Nettleton

---

The Deadly Companions *
US 1961 90m Pathécolor Panavision
Warner/Pathé America (Charles B. Fitzsimmons)

An army sergeant, a deserter, a trigger-happy gunman and a saloon hostess join forces to rob a bank.
Disjointed but rather attractive little Western let down by corny moments in the script.
w A. S. Fleischman *novel* A. S. Fleischman
d Sam Peckinpah *ph* William H. Clothier
m Marlin Skiles, Raoul Kraushaar
☆ Brian Keith, Maureen O'Hara, Chill Wills, Steve Cochran, Strother Martin

Deadly Force
US 1983 95m CFI color
Hemdale/Sandy Howard

An ex-cop returns to Los Angeles to hunt a serial killer, to the annoyance of local police, gangsters and his estranged wife.
Tacky, dim-witted thriller, never less than implausible and hardly watchable.
w Ken Barnett, Barry Schneider, Robert Vincent O'Neil d Paul Aaron *ph* Norman Leigh, David Myers m Gary Scott *pd* Alan Roderick-Jones
ed Roy Watts
☆ Wings Hauser, Joyce Ingalls, Paul Shenar, Al Ruscio, Arlen Dean Snyder, Lincoln Kilpatrick

Deadly Friend
US 1986 99m Technicolor
Warner/Pan Arts Layton (Robert M. Sherman)

A bright kid robotizes a victimized girl and helps her get her revenge.
Silly but nasty horror flick of the Elm Street genre.
w Bruce Joel Rubin *novel* Friend by Diana Henstell d Wes Craven *ph* Philip Lathrop
m Charles Bernstein *pd* Daniel Lomino
ed Michael Eliot
☆ Matthew Laborteaux, Kristy Swanson, Michael Sharrett, Anne Twomey

Deadly Game: see *The Manhattan Project* (1986)

Deadly is the Female: see *Gun Crazy*

'See a 1000-ton insect monster hungering for human prey!'
The Deadly Mantis
US 1957 78m bw
Universal-International

A 'prehistoric' mantis escapes from Arctic ice and travels rapidly towards New York.
Absurd and poorly crafted monster movie.
w Martin Berkeley d Nathan Juran
☆ Craig Stevens, Alix Talton, William Hopper

Deadly Peacemaker: see *Man with the Gun*

Deadly Pursuit: see *Shoot to Kill*

Deadly Strangers
GB 1974 93m Eastmancolor
Rank/Silhouette (Peter Miller)

A girl accepts a lift from a motorist at a time when a mad strangler is on the loose.
Sub-Hitchcock melo-thriller with enough red herrings to sink a ship. Smartly enough done, but the grisliness needed balancing by humour.
w Philip Levene d Sidney Hayers *ph* Graham Edgar m Ron Goodwin
☆ Hayley Mills, Simon Ward, Sterling Hayden, Ken Hutchison, Peter Jeffrey

The Deadly Trackers
US 1973 104m Technicolor
Warner/Cine Film (Ed Rosen, Fouad Said)

A sheriff stalks the bandits who killed his wife and son.
Lurid and ludicrous Western started, and abandoned, by Samuel Fuller; the challenge need not have been taken up.
w Lukas Heller d Barry Shear *ph* Gabriel Torres
m various
☆ Rod Taylor, Richard Harris, Al Lettieri, Neville Brand, William Smith
'It is no more than the outline of a shadow.' – *Tony Rayns*

'An incoherent, blood-soaked chase story.' – *New Yorker, 1977*

The Deadly Trap
France/Italy 1971 100m Eastmancolor
Corona/Pomereu/Oceania

The children of an American couple in Paris are kidnapped.
Smoothly made thriller which spends rather too much time being chic.
w Sidney Buchman, Eleanor Perry *novel* The Children are Gone by Arthur Cavanaugh d René Clément
☆ Faye Dunaway, Frank Langella, Barbara Parkins

Deadwood '76
US 1965 97m Technicolor Techniscope
Ember/Fairway (Nicholas Meriwether)
In Deadwood, a young man who is mistaken for Billy the Kid finds himself at odds with the townspeople.
Poor acting and production values do nothing to aid an incoherent and convoluted narrative.
w Arch Hall Jnr d James Landis *ph* William Zsigmond, Lewis Guinn m Manuel Francisco
ad D. Reed III ed Anthony M. Lanza
☆ Arch Hall Jnr, Jack Lester, Melissa Morgan, William Watters, Robert Dix, La Donna Cottier
'It looks like a carbon copy of the worst of the Italian Westerns.' – *David McGillivray, MFB*
† Unshown in its home country, the film received a British release six years after it was made.

Deadwood Dick
US 1940 bw serial: 15 eps
Columbia

A crusading editor in disguise takes on a gang of renegades led by The Skull.
Mildly hilarious Western serial, under the gun of Laurel and Hardy's old director.
d James W. Horne
☆ Don Douglas, Lane Chandler, Harry Harvey

Deal of the Century
US 1983 98m Technicolor
Warner (Bud Yorkin)

An arms dealer is urged not to sell a new weapon to a warmongering dictator.
Complex comedy, descending into farce when the visiting general is bribed by the availability of American women. Not a success.
w Paul Brickman d William Friedkin *ph* Richard H. Kline m Arthur B. Rubinstein *pd* Bill Malley
ed Bud Smith
☆ Chevy Chase, Sigourney Weaver, Gregory Hines, Vince Edwards, William Jarvis, William Marquez

Dealers
GB 1989 91m colour
Rank/Euston Films (William P. Cartlidge)

An ambitious young dealer in the City makes good.
An admiring look at the unacceptable face of capitalism.
w Andrew MacLear d Colin Bucksey *ph* Peter Sinclair m Richard Hartley *pd* Peter J. Hampton
ed Jon Costelloe
☆ Paul McGann, Rebecca de Mornay, Derrick O'Connor, John Castle, Paul Guilfoyle, Rosalind Bennett, Adrian Dunbar, Nicholas Hewetson

Dear Brigitte
US 1965 100m DeLuxe Cinemascope
TCF (Henry Koster)

The small son of an American professor writes a love letter to Brigitte Bardot, and when they finally go to Paris he is charming to them.
Mild family comedy quaintly set around a decaying Mississippi riverboat home; despite assured performances, it all gets a bit icky at times.
w Hal Kanter *novel* Erasmus with Freckles by John Haase d Henry Koster *ph* Lucien Ballard
m George Duning
☆ James Stewart, Glynis Johns, Fabian, Cindy Carol, Billy Mumy, John Williams, Jack Kruschen, Brigitte Bardot, Ed Wynn, Alice Pearce

Dear Diary ***
Italy 1994 100m colour
Artificial Eye/Sacher/Banfilm/La Sept/Canal (Angelo Barbagallo, Nanni Moretti, Nella Banfi)

original title: *Caro Diario*
A filmed diary in three chapters: the first involves a trip around Rome on a scooter, a chance meeting with actress Jennifer Beals and a visit to the place where Pasolini was killed; the second an island-hopping trip with a friend who stopped watching television in the 60s but becomes obsessed by it again; the third hospital treatment for a form of cancer.
A brilliant essay in autobiography, often bordering on the inconsequential but always interesting, full of charm and humour which remains even when deepening into a confrontation with the likelihood of imminent death.
wd Nanni Moretti *ph* Giuseppe Lanci m Nicola Piovani *pd* Marta Maffucci ed Mirco Garrone
☆ Nanni Moretti, Jennifer Beals, Alexandre Rockwell, Renato Carpentieri, Antonio Neiwiller
'The film seems slight and a little slapdash until the final episode, when Moretti faces mortality with a deadpan humanism that, under the circumstances, is bracing, even heroic.' – *Time*
'Appearing to be about nothing very much, it manages to encompass an awful lot, and it would be a strange viewer who didn't, somewhere in the film, identify with its major concern, which is how to survive in an increasingly frustrating and impersonal world.' – *Derek Malcolm, Guardian*

Dear God
US 1996 112m DeLuxe
Paramount/Rysher (Steve Tisch)
A repentant con man answers letters addressed to God at the post office's dead letter office.
Soft-centred, extraordinarily sentimental hokum, enough to make you wish for a little curdling of the milk of human kindness.
w Warren Leight, Ed Kaplan d Garry Marshall *ph* Charles Minsky m Jeremy Lubbock, James Patrick Dunne *pd* Albert Brenner ed Debra Neil-Fisher
☆ Greg Kinnear, Laurie Metcalf, Tim Conway, Maria Pitillo, Roscoe Lee Browne, Jon Seda, Anna Maria Horsford, Hector Elizondo
'Plays very much like a good first draft for a much better movie than the one on view.' – *Leonard Klady, Variety*

Dear Heart *
US 1964 114m bw
Warner (Martin Manulis)
At a postmasters' convention in New York, two middle-aged delegates fall in love.
Charming, understated, overlong romantic drama in the Marty tradition; all quite professional and satisfying.
w Tad Mosel d Delbert Mann *ph* Russell Harlan m Henry Mancini
☆ Glenn Ford, Geraldine Page, Angela Lansbury, Michael Anderson Jnr, Barbara Nichols, Patricia Barry, Charles Drake, Ruth McDevitt, Neva Patterson, Alice Pearce, Richard Deacon
♫ title song (m Henry Mancini, ly Jay Livingston, Ray Evans)

Dear Inspector *
France 1977 105m Eastmancolor
Ariane/Mondex (Alexander Mnouchkine)

original title: *Tendre Poulet*
A female detective chases a murderer, helped by her professor boyfriend.
Very likeable comedy-thriller with neat performances. Popular in America, it was translated into a series for television, but didn't run.
w Michel Audiard, Philippe de Broca *novel* Jean-Paul Rouland, Claude Olivier d Philippe de Broca *ph* Jean-Paul Schwartz m Georges Delerue
☆ Annie Girardot, Philippe Noiret, Catherine Alric, Hubert Deschamps

Dear John *
Sweden 1964 111m bw
Sandrew (Bo Jonsson)
original title: *Kare John*
An unmarried mother in a seaside village falls for a seaman.

A slight story effectively tricked out with all manner of cinematic devices including multiple of flashbacks. *Very watchable if a little self-conscious.*
wd Lars Magnus Lindgren *novel* Olle Lansburg *ph* Rune Ericson m Bengt-Arne Wallin
☆ Jarl Kulle, Christina Schollin, Helena Nilsson, Morgan Anderson
'It shines with the cool clear light of the Swedish summer, and despite its glossy surface manages also to convey strong sensual pleasure.' – *Brenda Davies*
⚿ best foreign film

Dear Mr Prohack
GB 1949 91m bw
GFD/Wessex (Ian Dalrymple, Dennis Van Thal)

A treasury official copes admirably with public money but is helpless when he comes into a private fortune.
Flat little comedy in which the minor amusements are incidental to the story.
w Ian Dalrymple, Donald Bull *novel* Arnold Bennett d Thornton Freeland *ph* H. E. Fowle
m Temple Abady
☆ Cecil Parker, Hermione Baddeley, Dirk Bogarde, Sheila Sim, Glynis Johns, Heather Thatcher, Henry Edwards, Judith Furse

Dear Murderer
GB 1947 94m bw
GFD/Gainsborough (Betty E. Box)

Plot and counterplot among an adulterous triangle.
Thoroughly artificial pattern play set among the unreal rich, from one of those unaccountable West End successes, here boringly filmed.
w Muriel and Sydney Box, Peter Rogers *play* St John L. Clowes d Arthur Crabtree *ph* Stephen Dade
☆ Eric Portman, Greta Gynt, Dennis Price, Maxwell Reed, Jack Warner, Hazel Court, Andrew Crawford, Jane Hylton
'A quite alarming little picture.' – *Alan Dent, News Chronicle*

Dear Octopus **
GB 1943 86m bw
GFD/Gainsborough (Edward Black)
US title: *The Randolph Family*
Members of a well-to-do British family reunite for Golden Wedding celebrations.
Traditional upper-class British comedy drama, and very well done too, with opportunities for excellent character acting.
w R. J. Minney, Patrick Kirwan *play* Dodie Smith d Harold French *ph* Arthur Crabtree
☆ Margaret Lockwood, Michael Wilding, Helen Haye, Frederick Leister, Celia Johnson, Roland Culver, Athene Seyler, Basil Radford, Nora Swinburne, Jean Cadell, Kathleen Harrison, Ann Stephens, Muriel George, Antoinette Cellier, Graham Moffatt

'The screen's gayest love story!'
Dear Ruth *
US 1947 95m bw
Paramount (Paul Jones)
A schoolgirl causes confusion when she writes love letters to a soldier using her elder sister's photograph.
Smoothly amusing family comedy from a Broadway success.
w Arthur Sheekman *play* Norman Krasna d William D. Russell *ph* Ernest Laszlo m Robert Emmett Dolan
☆ Joan Caulfield, William Holden, Mona Freeman, Billy de Wolfe, Edward Arnold, Mary Philips, Virginia Welles
'It is unlikely that 1947 will bring an more satisfying comedy … so many surprising and funny twists.' – *John Thompson, New York Mirror*
† Two less amusing sequels were made using virtually the same cast: *Dear Wife* (1949, 88m †† d[/KW]Richard Haydn); *Dear Brat* (1951, 82m ††† d[/KW]William A. Seiter).

Dearest Love: see *Le Souffle au Coeur*

'Tonight, mercy will be buried with the past.'

Death and the Maiden **

GB/US/France 1995 103m colour
Electric/Capitol/Channel 4/Flach/Canal (Thom Mount,
Josh Kramer)

In a South American country, a woman realizes
that her neighbour is the man who raped and
tortured her in prison during a previous regime and
decides to try him for his crimes.
*Electrifying debate on matters of morality, with acting
and directing tightening the sense of unease and
suspense to the end.*
w Rafael Yglesias, Ariel Dorfman play Ariel
Dorfman d Roman Polanski ph Tonino delli Colli
m Wojciech Kilar pd Pierre Guffroy ed Herve de
Luze
☆ *Sigourney Weaver*, Ben Kingsley, Stuart Wilson,
Krystia Mova
'A tense, taut exercise in psychological menace
that offers the audience barely a moment's
respite.' – *Colin Brown, Screen International*

Death at Broadcasting House *

GB 1934 71m bw
ABFD/Phoenix (Hugh Perceval)
A radio actor is murdered during a broadcast.
*Intriguing little murder mystery with an unusual
background.*
w Basil Mason novel Val Gielgud d Reginald
Denham ph Gunther Krampf md Geoffrey
Goodhardt ad R. Holmes Paul
☆ Ian Hunter, Austin Trevor, Mary Newland,
Henry Kendall, Val Gielgud, Peter Haddon, Betty
Ann Davies, Jack Hawkins, Donald Wolfit

'Your basic black comedy.'

Death Becomes Her

US 1992 104m colour
UIP/Universal (Robert Zemeckis, Steve Starkey)

An ageing Broadway star and a novelist, both
rivals for the same man, take an elixir that gives
eternal life.
*A small comedy overwhelmed by its impressive special
effects and suffering from its director's belief that louder
and faster is funnier.*
w Martin Donovan, David Koepp d Robert
Zemeckis ph Dean Cundey m Alan Silvestri
pd Rick Carter ed Arthur Schmidt sp Industrial
Light and Magic
☆ Meryl Streep, Goldie Hawn, Bruce Willis,
Isabella Rossellini, Ian Ogilvy, Adam Storke,
Nancy Fish, Alaina Reed Hall, Michelle Johnson,
Mary Ellen Trainor
'A black comedy that is so pleased with its own
blackness that it frequently forgets to be funny.'
– *Kenneth Turan, Los Angeles Times*
⚱ Visual effects

Death before Dishonor

US 1986 95m DeLuxe
Kubik/MPI/RIMA/New World

The Marines fight terrorists in an Arab country.
*Violent exploitation actioner which will satisfy its
audience.*
w Frank Capra Jnr, Lawrence Kubik, John Gatliff
d Terry J. Leonard m Brian May
☆ Fred Dryer, Brian Keith, Paul Winfield, Joanna
Pacula

Death by Hanging ***

Japan 1968 117m bw VistaVision
Academy/Connoisseur/Sozosha (Masayuki Nakajima,
Takuji Yamaguchi, Nagisa Oshima)
original title: *Koshikei*
A Korean student survives being hanged for the
rape and killing of two Japanese girls but loses his
memory and refuses to accept responsibility for his
past actions.
*A complex, challenging and blackly comic examination
of racism, guilt and justice, filmed as a succession of re-
enacted episodes, complete with chapter headings, in
the life of the central character.*
w Tsutomu Tamura, Mamoru Sasaki, Michinori
Faukao, Nagisa Oshima d Nagisa Oshima
ph Yasuhiro Yoshioka m Hikaru Hayashi
ad Jusho Toda ed Sueko Shiraishi
☆ *Nagisa Oshima*, Yun-Do Yun, Kei Sato, Fumio
Watanabe, Toshiro Ishido, Masao Adachi,
Mutsuhiro Toura
'For three-quarters of its length, the film can be
read as a brilliantly, insolently witty Brechtian
parable; an alienation effect taking one away

from the appalling realities of death by hanging,
the better to make one understand the
implications of those realities.' – *Tom Milne*

Death Drums along the River

GB 1963 83m Technicolor Technoscope
Big Ben Films/Hallam
US title: *Sanders*
In Africa, a police commissioner foils a murderous
diamond smuggler.
*Stilted, often facetious cut-price version of the old
warhorse, and one that should have been put out to
grass.*
novel *Sanders of the River* by Edgar Wallace
d Lawrence Huntington ph Bob Huke ed Allan
Morrison
☆ Richard Todd, Marianne Cook, Albert Lieven,
Walter Rilla, Jeremy Lloyd, Robert Arden, Vivi
Bach, Bill Brewer, Simon Sabela

Death from a Distance

US 1936 73m bw
Chesterfield (Maury M. Cohen)
A murderer is trapped in a planetarium.
*Modest second feature which benefits from its unusual
setting.*
w John Krafft d Frank Strayer
☆ Russell Hopton, Lola Lane, George Marion Snr,
Lee Kohlmar

Death Hunt

US 1981 97m Technicolor
Golden Harvest (Murray Shostak)

In 1931 Yukon, a reclusive trapper turns to
violence when goaded by other wanderers and
drunken mounties.
*An arctic cross between Straw Dogs and Death
Wish, and not even so good as either.*
w Michael Grais, Mark Victor d Peter Hunt
ph James Devis m Jerrold.Immel
☆ Charles Bronson, Lee Marvin, Angie
Dickinson, Andrew Stevens, Ed Lauter, Carl
Weathers, Henry Beckman

Death in a French Garden *

France 1985 101m Eastmancolor
Artificial Eye/Gaumont (Emmanuel Schlumberger)

original title: *Péril en la Demeure*
aka: *Péril*
A music teacher, seduced by the mother of his
pupil, finds himself embroiled in other sexual
entanglements and murder.
Elegantly stylish thriller.
w Michel Deville, Rosalinde Damamme novel *Sur
la Terre Comme au Ciel* by Rene Belletto d Michel
Deville ph Martial Thury ad Philippe Combastel
ed Raymonde Guyot
☆ Michel Piccoli, Nicole Garcia, Anemone,
Christophe Malavoy, Richard Bohringer, Anaïs
Jeanneret, Jean-Claude Jay

Death in Brunswick **

Australia 1990 109m Eastmancolor
Meridian/Film Victoria/Australian Film Finance Corp
(Timothy White)

The new cook in a sleazy night-club accidentally
kills his drunken assistant and asks an old friend to
help him get rid of the body.
*Witty black comedy of losers adrift in a world they
cannot control.*
w John Ruane, Boyd Oxlade novel Boyd Oxlade
d John Ruane ph Ellery Ryan m Philip Judd
pd Chris Kennedy ed Neil Thumpston
☆ Sam Neill, Zoe Carides, John Clarke, Yvonne
Lawley, Deborah Kennedy
'An unusual, intelligent black comedy. Some
will find the film outrageous, but word-of-mouth
should give the pic legs on the international art-
house circuit.' – *Variety*

Death in Venice ***

Italy 1971 128m Technicolor Panavision
Warner/Alfa (Mario Gallo)

original title: *Morte a Venezia*
In a lush Venetian hotel one summer in the early
years of the century, a middle-aged German
composer on holiday falls for the charms of a silent
young boy, and stays in the city too long to escape
the approaching plague.
*Incredibly extended and rather pointless fable enriched
by moments of great beauty and directorial style; these*

do not quite atone for the slow pace or the muddled
storyline.' – *Tom Milne*
w Luchino Visconti, Nicola Badalucco
novel Thomas Mann d Luchino Visconti
ph Pasquale de Santis m Gustav Mahler
md Franco Mannino ad Ferdinando Scarfiotti
☆ Dirk Bogarde, Bjorn Andresen, Silvana
Mangano, Marisa Berenson, Mark Burns
'Maybe a story as elusive as *Death in Venice*
simply can't be filmed. Visconti has made a
brave attempt, always sensitive to the original;
but it's finally not quite the same thing.' – *David
Wilson, MFB*
'Camp and miscalculated from start to finish …
a prime contender for the title Most Overrated
Film of All Time.' – *Time Out, 1985*
⚱ costumes (Piero Tosi)
🏆 Pasquale de Santis; Ferdinando Scarfiotti

Death is My Trade **

West Germany 1977 145m colour
Contemporary/WDR/Iduna (Fred Ilgner)
original title: *Aus Einem Deutschen Leben*
A working class man rises through the Nazi
hierarchy to become commandant at Auschwitz.
*Dispassionate and chilling account of the banality of
evil.*
wd Theodor Kotulla novel Robert Merle
ph Dieter Naujeck m Eberhard Weber
ad Wolfgang Schunke ed Wolfgang Richter
☆ Gotz George, Kai Taschner, Elisabeth Schwartz,
Kurt Hubner, Hans Korte, Sigurd Fitzek, Peter
Franke, Wilfried Elste, Matthias Fuchs

Death Japanese Style **

Japan 1984 124m colour/bw
Yashushi Tamaoki, Yutaka Okada
original title: *Ososhiki*
aka: *The Funeral*
An actress arranges the three-day wake and funeral
of her father.
Witty and well-observed account of domestic dramas.
wd Juzo Itami ph Yonezo Yuasa ad Hiroshi
Tokuda ed Akira Suzuki
☆ Nobuko Miyamoto, Tsutomu Yamazaki, Kin
Sugai, Shuji Otaki, Ichiro Zaitsu

The Death Kiss

US 1932 74m bw
KBS/World Wide

During the making of a film an actor is murdered.
*Promising murder mystery which becomes more and
more muddled as it progresses; it wasn't helped by
advertising suggesting that Lugosi was again playing a
vampire instead of a red herring.*
w Barry Barringer, Gordon Kahn novel Madelon
St Dennis d Edwin L. Marin
☆ David Manners, Adrienne Ames, Bela Lugosi,
John Wray, Vince Barnett, Edward Van Sloan

Death Line

GB 1972 87m Technicolor
Rank/Jay Kanter-Alan Ladd Jnr (Paul Maslansky)
aka: *Raw Meat*
Police investigating missing persons at a London
underground station discover the existence of
cannibals living in abandoned tunnels.
*Tightly constructed thriller, unpleasant but effective,
and revelling in violence and decaying flesh.*
w Ceri Jones story Gary Sherman d Gary
Sherman ph Alex Thomson m Jeremy Rose
ad Denis Gordon-Orr ed Geoffrey Foot sp John
Horton
☆ Donald Pleasence, Christopher Lee, Norman
Rossington, David Ladd, Sharon Gurney, Hugh
Armstrong, Clive Swift, James Cossins
'The film, a coherent whole in which the parts
inter-relate suggestively rather than
schematically, and rich in mythological
overtones, represents one of the most remarkable
debuts of recent years.' – *Robin Wood, MFB*

'Man's Deadliest Invention Is About To Show Its
Metal.'
'In subterranean level 10 of the Chaank Corporation
Building there are 23.2 billion dollars of bonds …
And in vault No. 10…'

Death Machine *

US 1994 111m Eastmancolor
Entertainment/JVC Victor/Fugitive (Dominic Anciano)

After he is fired, a hi-tech armament company's
mad scientist sets the Warbeast, an unstoppable
killer robot, after his former boss and a gang of

activists, who are trapped in the headquarters
building.
*Knowing, blackly humorous, extremely gory science-
fiction thriller that borrows from Blade Runner,
Robocop and Terminator, among others, but does so
with more style than might have been expected.*
wd Stephen Norrington ph John de Borman
m Crispin Merrell pd Chris Edwards ed Paul
Endacott sp Peter Hutchinson; make-up: Dave
Elsey, Creature FX; animatronics: Nik Williams,
Animated Extras
☆ Brad Dourif, Ely Pouget, William Hootkins,
John Sharian, Martin McDougall, Andreas
Wisniewski, Richard Brake
'Great fun.' – *Film Review*
† The film features characters called John
Carpenter, Sam Raimi and Scott Ridley, and the
credits include, after a long list of Special Thanks,
the line 'No Thanks to They Know Who They
Are'.

Death of a Bureaucrat **

Cuba 1966 84m bw
ICAIC
original title: *La muerte de un burocrata*
When the widow of a stonemason discovers that to
obtain her state pension she needs his work card,
which has been buried with him, her nephew
decides to take action.
*Witty and irreverent satire at the expense of all
bureaucracies and jobsworths, directed with a light
hand and in a style that owes much to silent comedy.*
w Alfredo L. del Cueto, Ramón F. Suárez, Tomás
Guitiérrez Alea story Tomás Gutiérrez Alea
d Tomás Gutiérrez Alea ph Ramón F. Suárez
m Leo Brower md Manuel Duchesne Cuzán
ad Luis Márquez ed Mario González
☆ Salvador Wood, Silvia Planas, Manuel
Estanillo, Gaspar de Santelices, Carlos Ruiz de la
Tejera
† The film is dedicated to 'Luis Buñuel, Oliver
Hardy, Stan Laurel, Ingmar Bergman, Harold
Lloyd, Akira Kurosawa, Orson Wells [sic], Juan
Carlos Tabio, Elia Kazan, Buster Keaton, Jean
Vigo, Marilyn Monroe and all those who, in one
way or another, have taken part in the film
industry since the days of Lumière.'

Death of a Cyclist *

Spain/Italy 1955 85m bw
Guion-Suevia/Trionfalcine
original title: *Muerte de un Ciclista*
An accident – a cyclist is knocked down and killed
by an adulterous couple – tragically affects the lives
of many people.
*Rather like a politically conscious version of An
Inspector Calls, this mannered and unemotional film
was most interesting because of its almost
Hollywoodian self-assurance.*
wd Juan Antonio Bardem story Luis de Igoa
ph Alfredo Fraile m Isrido Maiztegui
☆ Lucia Bose, Alberto Closas, Otello Toso, Carlos
Casaravilla
'I can remember no other film which succeeds
without either jealousy or absurdity in presenting
a serious convincing picture of sophisticated
European society.' – *Dilys Powell*

'Is it love or guilt that's making you marry me after
all these years?'

Death of a Gunfighter *

US 1969 100m Technicolor
Universal (Richard E. Lyons)

An unpopular marshal refuses to resign, and the
situation leads to gunplay.
*Downcast character Western set in the early years of
the century.*
w Joseph Calvelli d Robert Totten, Don Siegel
ph Andrew Jackson m Oliver Nelson
☆ Richard Widmark, Lena Horne, John Saxon,
Carroll O'Connor, Larry Gates, Kent Smith

'A salesman's got to dream – it comes with the
territory!'
'One mistake – seen by his son – unleashes with
overwhelming power the great drama of our day!'

Death of a Salesman ***

US 1951 112m bw
Columbia (Stanley Kramer)
An ageing travelling salesman recognizes the
emptiness of his life and commits suicide.
*A very acceptable screen version of a milestone play
which has become an American classic; stage
conventions and tricks are cleverly adapted to cinematic*

---

use, especially when the hero walks from the present into the past and back again.

w Stanley Roberts play Arthur Miller d Laslo Benedek ph Franz Planer m Alex North md Morris Stoloff

☆ Fredric March, Kevin McCarthy, Cameron Mitchell, Mildred Dunnock, Howard Smith, Royal Beal, Jesse White

MRS LOMAN: 'Attention must finally be paid to such a man. He's not to be allowed to fall into his grave like an old dog.'

WILLY LOMAN: 'A salesman is somebody way up there in the blue, riding on a smile and a shoeshine…'

'Its time shifts with light, which were poetic in the theatre, seemed shabby in a medium that can dissolve time and space so easily.' – *Stanley Kauffmann*

⚜ Franz Planer; Alex North; Fredric March; Kevin McCarthy; Mildred Dunnock

Death of a Scoundrel *

US 1956 119m bw
RKO/Charles Martin
🔲 ⊙~

A Czech in New York becomes rich by fraud.
Unconvincing but intermittently entertaining melodrama, a vehicle for a male Bette Davis.
wd Charles Martin ph James Wong Howe m Max Steiner

☆ George Sanders, Yvonne de Carlo, Coleen Gray, Victor Jory, Zsa Zsa Gabor, Nancy Gates, John Hoyt, Tom Conway

'Vague moralizing and some attempts at social comment scarcely enliven this protracted study in megalomania.' – *MFB*

Death of a Soldier

Australia 1986 93m colour Panavision
Suatu/Scotti
🔲

The story of Edward J. Leonski, a psychopathic GI hanged in 1942 for the murders of three women.
Case history, most interesting for its re-creation of a period.
w William Nagle d Philippe Mora ph Louis Irving ad Geoff Richardson

☆ James Coburn, Reb Brown, Bill Hunter, Maurie Fields, Michael Pate, Terence Donovan

The Death of Mario Ricci *

Switzerland/France/West Germany 1983 101m
Eastmancolor
Pegase/TSR/Swanie/FR3/Tele München

A Swiss TV journalist arrives in a remote village to record an interview with a malnutrition expert, and finds himself in the middle of a mystery about the death of an Italian immigrant worker.
A rather uncontrolled drama which begins by suggesting Bad Day at Black Rock but becomes less interesting as it proceeds.
w Claude Goretta, Georges Haldas d Claude Goretta ph Hans Liechti m Arie Dzierlatka

☆ Gian-Maria Volonte, Magali Noel, Mimsy Farmer, Heinz Bennent, Jean-Michael Dupuis

Death on the Diamond

US 1934 69m bw
MGM

Murder during a baseball game.
The story isn't much, so the picture's appeal depends on one's addiction to baseball.
w Harvey Thew, Joseph Sherman, Ralph Spence, Cortland Fitzsimmons d Edward Sedgwick

☆ Robert Young, Madge Evans, Nat Pendleton, Ted Healy, C. Henry Gordon, Paul Kelly, Edward Brophy, Mickey Rooney, David Landau

'Due to plot, miscasting and some minor league technical preparation, it was two strikes to the bad before the cameras started to grind.' – *Variety*

Death on the Nile *

GB 1978 140m Technicolor
EMI (John Brabourne, Richard Goodwin)
🔲 🔲 ⊙~ ♫

Hercule Poirot solves the mystery of who killed the spoilt heiress on a steamer cruising down the Nile.
A pleasant thirties atmosphere and the travel poster backgrounds are the chief assets of this rather hesitant whodunnit which plays fair enough with the audience but gives its popular cast too little to do, while its constant repetitions of the crime become rather ghoulish. On the whole, though, a very passable

representation of an old-fashioned genre, and a few points up on Murder on the Orient Express.
w Anthony Shaffer novel Agatha Christie d John Guillermin ph Jack Cardiff m Nino Rota pd Peter Murton ad Malcolm Cooke

☆ Peter Ustinov, Bette Davis, Mia Farrow, Angela Lansbury, Jane Birkin, David Niven, George Kennedy, Jack Warden, Simon MacCorkindale, Lois Chiles, Jon Finch, Maggie Smith, Olivia Hussey, Harry Andrews, I. S. Johar

👗 costumes (Anthony Powell)

Death Race 2000 *

US 1975 79m colour
New World (Roger Corman)
🔲

In the year 2000, the world's most popular sport involves motor racers who compete for the highest total of human casualties.
Cheaply made macabre satire, quite well enough made to please addicts of the blackest of black comedy.
w Robert Thom, Charles Griffith, Ib Melchior d Paul Bartel ph Tak Fujimoto m Paul Chihara

☆ David Carradine, Simone Griffeth, Sylvester Stallone, Mary Woronov

'The script is hardly Swiftian and therefore treads a thin delicate line between mockery and exploitation.' – *Michael Billington, Illustrated London News*

Death Rides a Horse

Italy 1967 115m Technicolor Techniscope
PEC (Alfonso Sansone, Henryk Chroscicki)
🔲

original title: *Da Uomo a Uomo*

After his family is massacred, a young gunfighter tracks down the killers with the aid of a bandit who has his own reasons for seeking revenge.
Spaghetti Western that sticks close to the usual formula of over-dramatic gunfights.
w Luciano Vincenzoni, Giulio Petroni d Giulio Petroni ph Carlo Carlini m Ennio Morricone ad Franco Bottari, Rosa Sansone ed Eraldo Da Roma

☆ Lee Van Cleef, John Phillip Law, Anthony Dawson (Antonio Margheriti), Mario Brega, Luigi Pistilli, Jose Torres, Carlo Cassola

† The plot was used again in 1971 as the basis of *Viva Django*.

Death Ship

Canada 1980 91m CFI color
Astral Bellevue Pathé/Bloodstar

Survivors of a shipwreck take refuge on a mysterious empty ship which sets about killing them one by one.
Yes, that's the synopsis, in the wake of Killdozer and The Car, and this film is stupider than either.
w John Robins d Alvin Rakoff

☆ George Kennedy, Richard Crenna, Nick Mancuso, Sally Ann Howes, Kate Reid

'No woman ever loved such a man! The whole world waited while he made love!'
Death Takes a Holiday *

US 1934 78m bw
Paramount (E. Lloyd Sheldon)

In the form of a mysterious prince, Death visits an Italian noble family to see why men fear him so.
A somewhat pretentious classic from a popular play of the twenties: interesting handling and performances, but a slow pace by modern standards.
w Maxwell Anderson, Gladys Lehman, Walter Ferris plays Maxwell Anderson and Alberto Casella d Mitchell Leisen ph Charles Lang m Bernhard Kaun, Sigmund Krumgold ad Ernst Fegte

☆ Fredric March, Evelyn Venable, Sir Guy Standing, Katherine Alexander, Gail Patrick, Helen Westley, Kathleen Howard, Henry Travers, Kent Taylor

'Highly fantastic, but well done … likely to have greater appeal among the intelligentsia.' – *Variety*

† It was remade in 1998 as *Meet Joe Black* (qv).

Death Trap: see *Deathtrap* (1982)

Death Trap

US 1976 89m colour
Mars (Mohammed Rustam)
🔲

The proprietor of a motel on the edge of a swamp is a maniac who murders his guests and feeds them to his pet crocodile.

Pretty sick rip-off of Psycho, with no holds barred; a typical and regrettable example of the so-called Gothic horrors of the independent American cinema in the late seventies.
w Alvin L. Fast, Mardi Rustam d Tobe Hooper ph Jack Beckett m Tobe Hooper, Wayne Bell

☆ Neville Brand, Mel Ferrer, Carolyn Jones, Marilyn Burns, William Finley, Stuart Whitman

'Not even a scream escapes!'
Death Valley

US 1981 88m Technicolor
Universal (Elliott Kastner)
🔲

A boy on vacation in Arizona finds himself being chased by a murderer.
Tedious shocker with little in the way of scenic background to relieve the unpleasant monotony.
w Richard Rothstein d Dick Richards ph Stephen H. Burum m Dana Kaproff ed Joel Cox

☆ Paul Le Mat, Catherine Hicks, Stephen McHattie, A. Wilford Brimley, Edward Herrmann

Death Vengeance: see *Fighting Back*

Death Warrant

US 1990 89m DeLuxe
UIP/MGM/Pathé (Mark DiSalle)

A Canadian Mounted Policeman goes undercover to discover who is responsible for a series of prison murders.
An implausible thriller, given little sense of reality but affording opportunities, readily taken, for violence.
w David S. Goyer d Deran Sarafian ph Russell Carpenter m Gary Chang pd Curtis Schnell ed G. Gregg McLaughlin, John A. Barton

☆ Jean-Claude Van Damme, Robert Guillaume, Cynthia Gibb, George Dickerson, Art LaFleur, Patrick Kilpatrick, Joshua Miller

'Unusually sadistic even by genre standards, this well-made exploitation yarn unravels under the weight of its dim-witted carnage.' – *Variety*

'It began with a rape. It ended with a massacre'
Death Weekend

Canada 1976 94m Eastmancolor
Panavision
Reitman/Dunning/Link (Ivan Reitman)

Four louts take revenge on a lady driver by following her to a secluded country house.
Hoary shocker chiefly concerned with rape, the threat of rape, and various unpleasant methods of murder.
wd William Fruet ph Robert Saad ad Roy Forge Smith ed Jean Lafleur, Debbie Karjala

☆ Brenda Vaccaro, Don Stroud, Chuck Shamata

'Exploitation of the emptiest and most blatant kind.' – *MFB*

'Vigilante, city style … judge, jury and executioner!'
Death Wish *

US 1974 94m Technicolor
Paramount/Dino de Laurentiis (Hal Landers, Bobby Roberts, Michael Winner)
🔲 ⊙~ ♫

When his wife dies and his daughter becomes a vegetable after an assault by muggers, a New York businessman takes the law into his own hands.
After a highly unpleasant and sensational opening, this curious and controversial film settles down into what amounts to black comedy, with the audience well on the vigilante's side. It's not very good, but it keeps one watching.
w Wendell Mayes novel Brian Garfield d Michael Winner ph Arthur J. Ornitz m Herbie Hancock

☆ Charles Bronson, Hope Lange, Vincent Gardenia, Stuart Margolin, Steven Keats, William Redfield

'This urban version of Walking Tall transcends its violence to satisfy every base instinct that "we liberals" are heir to.' – *Judith Crist*

Death Wish 2

US 1981 95m colour
Golan-Globus/Landers-Roberts
🔲 🔲 ⊙~

His maid gang-raped and killed, his handicapped daughter driven to her death, Paul Kersey resumes his stalking of urban thugs.
A badly made exercise in the exploitation of the most repellent aspects of violence, without the first film's saving grace of slickness and humour.

w David Engelbach d Michael Winner ph Richard L. Kline, Tom Del Ruth m Jimmy Page

☆ Charles Bronson, Jill Ireland, Vincent Gardenia, J. D. Cannon, Anthony Franciosa

'Bad art is one thing, but Death Wish II is ludicrous.' – *Variety*

'The sort of sequel which makes you realize that the original wasn't half so bad as you thought.' – *Margaret Hinxman, Daily Mail*

'It doesn't contain an ounce of life. It slinks onto the screen and squirms for a while, and is over.' – *Roger Ebert*

Death Wish 3

US 1985 90m colour
Cannon (Menahem Golan, Yoram Globus)
🔲 🔲 ⊙~

Paul Kersey, the urban vigilante, eliminates a gang of thugs terrorizing an apartment block.
The killing sprees have become routine, and there's nothing else of interest in this boring sequel to a sequel.
w Michael Edmonds d Michael Winner ph John Stanier m Jimmy Page pd Peter Mullins ed Arnold Crust

☆ Charles Bronson, Deborah Raffin, Ed Lauter, Martin Balsam, Gavan O'Herlihy

Death Wish 4: The Crackdown

US 1987 99m colour
Cannon (Pancho Kohner)
🔲 🔲 ⊙~

The ageing vigilante attacks drug dealers in Los Angeles.
Repetitious violence, with little narrative, other than villains being set up so that they can be mown down.
w Gail Morgan Hickman d J. Lee-Thompson ph Gideon Porath m Paul McCallum, Valentine McCallum, John Bisharat ad Whitney Brooke Wheeler ed Peter Lee Thompson

☆ Charles Bronson, Kay Lenz, John P. Ryan, Perry Lopez, Soon-Teck Oh, George Dickerson, Dana Barron, Jesse Dabson

'The Vigilante Is Back…'
Death Wish 5: The Face of Death

US 1993 90m colour
21st Century (Damian Lee)
🔲 🔲 ⊙ ⊙~ ♫

A university professor seeks revenge after his girlfriend is first disfigured and then killed by her former lover, a gangster.
A rerun of the original movie, adding little that is new and nothing that is interesting.
wd Allan A. Goldstein ph Curtis Petersen m Terry Plumeri pd Csaba A. Kertesz ed Patrick Rand

☆ Charles Bronson, Lesley-Anne Down, Michael Parks, Saul Rubinek, Kenneth Welsh

'Comes off as a flat-footed, by-the-numbers programmer that, judging from what's on-screen, failed to spark much enthusiasm among the people who made it.' – *Variety*

† The film was released direct to video in Britain.

Deathcheaters

Australia 1976 96m colour
Australian Film Commission/Roadshow/D. L. Taffner/Trenchard Productions (Brian Trenchard Smith)

Two Vietnam veterans turned stuntmen are hired to infiltrate a Filipino fortress guarded by 150 men.
Jocular romp that provides an excuse for a succession of low-cost stunts, from car crashes to hang gliding.
w Michael Cove story Brian Trenchard Smith d Brian Trenchard Smith ph John Seale m Peter Martin ad Darrell Lass ed Ron Williams

☆ John Hargreaves, Grant Page, Margaret Gerard, Noel Ferrier, Judith Woodroffe

The Deathmaster

US 1973 88m DeLuxe
RF World Entertainment/AIP

California surfers cheerfully adopt a local mystic, not knowing that he is a vampire.
Modestly budgeted teenage screamer, competently made but of interest only to avid bibliographers of Count Dracula.
w R. L. Grove d Ray Danton

☆ Robert Quarry, Brenda Dickson, Bill Ewing, John Fiedler

Deathsport

US   1978   83m   Metrocolor
New World (Roger Corman)

📼

A popular game of the future involves gladiators willing to lose their lives against lethal motorcyclists.
Low-budget shocker for teenagers, by Rollerball out of Death Race. Of no possible interest except as exploitation.
w Henry Suso, Donald Stewart d Henry Suso, Allan Arkush ph Gary Graver m Andrew Stein
☆ David Carradine, Claudia Jennings, Richard Lynch, William Smithers

Deathstalker

Argentina   1984   80m   colour
New World (James Sbardellati)

📼

original title: *El Cazador de la Muerte*
A muscular hero battles against an evil wizard.
Low-budget, low-intelligence sword and sorcery, lacking any imagination, but offering a plethora of female nudity. It surprisingly spawned several sequels.
w Howard R. Cohen d John Watson (James Sbardellati) ph Leonardo Rodriguez Solis m Oscar Cardozo Ocampo ad Emilio Basaldua ed John Adams, Silvia Ripoli
☆ Richard Hill, Barbi Benton, Richard Brooker, Victor Bo, Lana Clarkson, Bernard Erhard

Deathstalker 2

US   1987   77m   colour
New Horizons (Frank Isaac)

📼

aka: *Deathstalker 2: Duel of the Titans*
Deathstalker goes to the aid of an exiled princess who has been robbed of her throne.
Sword-and-sorcery action played for laughs, which makes it no more entertaining.
w Neil Ruttenberg, R. J. Robertson d Jim Wynorski ph Leonard Solis m Oscar Cardozo Campo, Christopher Young ad Marta Albert ed Steve Barnett
☆ John Terlesky, Monique Gabrielle, John Lazar, Toni Naples, Maria Socas, Queen Kong

Deathstalker and the Warriors from Hell

US   1989   86m   colour
Concorde/New Horizons/Triana (Alfonso Corona, Antonio de Noriega)

📼 📼

aka: *Deathstalker III*
The outlaw Deathstalker honours the wish of a dying princess to search for a fabled city made of precious jewels and metals.
Tongue-in-cheek sword and sorcery, workmanlike but unimaginative and generally tedious.
w Howard Cohen d Alfonso Corona ph Xavier Cruz m Israel Torres, Alejandro Rulfo ad Francisco Magallon ed Ernesto Guillen
☆ John Allen Nelson, Carla Herd, Terri Treas, Thom Christopher, Aaron Hernan, Roger Cudney, Claudia Inchaurregui
† *Deathstalker IV: Match of the Titans*, produced, written and directed by Howard Cohen, followed in 1989.

Deathtrap *

US   1982   116m   Technicolor
Warner/LAH (Burtt Harris)

📼 📼

A playwright past his best conceives a plan to murder an upcoming rival and steal his script.
This thriller on the lines of Sleuth was enjoyable enough on stage, but on the screen, despite pretensions to style, it takes far too long to unravel its very few twists, the last of which is badly fumbled.
w Jay Presson Allen play Ira Levin d Sidney Lumet ph Andrzej Bartkowiak m Johnny Mandel pd Tony Walton
☆ Michael Caine, Christopher Reeve, Dyan Cannon, Irene Worth, Henry Jones
'It plays absolutely fair, more or less, and yet fools us every time, more or less.' – Roger Ebert

Deathwatch **

France/West Germany   1980   128m   Fujicolour
Panavision
Contemporary/Quartet (Gabriel Boustiani, Janine Rubeiz)

📼 📀

In the future, a TV documentary producer has a cameraman, who has the apparatus implanted in his brain, follow every moment in the life of a dying woman.
Grim fable of media manipulation and sensationalist pressures on popular entertainment that retains its resonance.
w Bertrand Tavernier, David Rayfiel novel *The Continuous Katherine Mortenhoe* by David Compton d Bertrand Tavernier ph Pierre-William Glenn m Antoine Duhamel ad Tony Pratt ed Armand Psenay, Michael Ellis
☆ Romy Schneider, Harvey Keitel, Harry Dean Stanton, Max von Sydow, Therese Liotard

'Some debts can never be paid'
The Debt Collector **

GB   1999   110m   Eastmancolor
Film4/GFF/Dragon (Graham Broadbent, Damian Jones)

📼

A bitter policeman is determined that an artist and writer shall not live down his violent past as a loan shark and murderer.
Violent, intensely-acted melodrama of hatred, rivalry and obsession that also casts an ironic sidelight on the current cult of the gangster as celebrity.
wd Anthony Neilson ph Dick Pope m Adrian Johnston pd Mark Geraghty ed John Wilson
☆ Billy Connolly, Ken Stott, Francesca Annis, Iain Robertson, Annette Crosbie, Alastair Galbraith
'Hardly a note rings false in this tightly paced, scorching thriller.' – Marianne Gray, Film Review

'Degenerate, disgusting, and ... deliciously funny!'
Decadence

GB/Germany   1993   108m   colour
Mayfair/Vendetta (Lance W. Reynolds, Christoph Meyer-Weil)

📼

A newly rich, upwardly mobile couple indulge in affairs: the husband with an upper-class woman, the wife with an investigator she has hired to spy on her husband.
An intensely theatrical work transfers unsuccessfully to film, with Berkoff playing a philandering husband and a private eye who mixes sex and business, and Collins as both a wealthy and a nouveau-riche woman; its stylized, over-the-top acting seems merely grotesque on the big screen and its satire on the get-rich-quick decade of the 80s is without bite.
wd Steven Berkoff ph Denis Lenoir m Stewart Copeland pd Yolanda Sonnabend, Simon Holland ed John Wilson
☆ Steven Berkoff, Joan Collins, Christopher Biggins, Michael Winner, Marc Sinden
'A ripe, belching, heaving, power-drill satire of 1980s Thatcherite Britain that's as full of excesses as the passé targets it parodies.' – Variety
'This offers very little to keep you glued to your seat for what is, in reality, two rather uncomfortable hours.' – Kim Newman, Empire

The Decameron *

Italy/France/W. Germany   1971   111m   colour
UA/PEA/Artemis (Franco Rossellini)

📼 📼 📀 📀

original title: *Il Decamerone*
Eight of the bawdier stories from Boccaccio's cycle.
The first of Pasolini's excursions into folk-tales, emphasizing their earthiness and sexuality.
wd Pier Paolo Pasolini book *The Decameron* by Giovanni Boccaccio ph Tonino delli Colli m Ennio Morricone, Pier Paolo Pasolini pd Dante Ferretti ed Nino Baragli, Tatiana Morigi
☆ Franco Citti, Ninetto Davoli, Angela Luce, Patrizia Capparelli, Pier Paolo Pasolini, Jovan Jovanovic, Gianni Rizzo
'A film which finds comedy and beauty in all aspects of human vitality.' – MFB
† It was followed by similar adaptations of The Canterbury Tales and Arabian Nights (qqv).

Decameron Nights

GB   1952   94m   Technicolor
Film Locations (M. J. Frankovich)
Young Boccaccio entertains a glamorous widow and her three guests with stories.
Feeble costume charade with all the cuckolding off-screen: insipid and artificial.
w George Oppenheimer d Hugo Fregonese ph Guy Green m Antony Hopkins
☆ Louis Jourdan, Joan Fontaine, Binnie Barnes, Joan Collins, Godfrey Tearle, Eliot Makeham, Noel Purcell

'The sort of hybrid international production of which experience has made one mistrustful.' – Gavin Lambert

Deceived

US   1991   108m   Eastmancolor
Warner/Touchstone/Silver Screen Partners IV (Michael Finnell, Wendy Dozoretz, Ellen Collett)

📼 📼 📀

A happily married New York art dealer discovers that her husband is not the person he claims to be.
An interesting premise is ignored in preference to an increasingly predictable narrative.
w Mary Agnes Donoghue, Derek Saunders d Damian Harris ph Jack N. Green m Thomas Newman pd Andrew McAlpine ed Neil Travis, Lisa M. Citron
☆ Goldie Hawn, John Heard, Ashley Peldon, Robin Bartlett, Tom Irwin, Amy Wright, Jan Rubes, Kate Reid
'A visually interesting but essentially made-to-order thriller.' – Sight and Sound

Deceiver: see Liar

The Deceivers

GB/India   1988   112m   colour
Merchant-Ivory/Michael White/Cinecom/Film Four (Ismail Merchant, Tim Van Rellim)

📼 📀 🎧

An English army officer serving in India in the 1820s infiltrates the cult of Thuggee, a secret society of murderers.
Muddled melodrama that fails to carry any conviction.
w Michael Hirst novel John Masters d Nicholas Meyer ph Walter Lassally m John Scott pd Ken Adam ed Richard Trevor
☆ Pierce Brosnan, Saeed Jaffrey, Shashi Kapoor, Helena Michell, Keith Michell, David Robb

'Two men loved her ... she loved them both'
December Bride *

GB   1990   90m   colour
BFI/Film Four/CTE/British Screen/Little Bird (Jonathan Cavendish)

📼

A servant girl with an illegitimate daughter defies local and religious feeling when she refuses to marry either of the two brothers who might be the father.
Engaging drama of individual struggle.
w David Rudkin novel Sam Hanna Bell d Thaddeus O'Sullivan ph Bruno de Keyzer m Jurgen Knieper pd Adrian Smith ed Rodney Holland
☆ Donal McCann, Saskia Reeves, Ciaran Hinds, Patrick Malahide, Brenda Bruce, Michael McKnight, Geoffrey Golden, Dervla Kirwan

Deception **

US   1947   112m   bw
Warner (Henry Blanke)

📼

A European cellist returning to America after the war finds that her former girlfriend has a rich and jealous lover.
Downcast melodrama made when its star was beginning to slide; today it seems irresistible bosh with a background of classical music, done with intermittent style especially by Claude Rains as the egomaniac lover.
w John Collier play Monsieur Lamberthier by Louis Verneuil d Irving Rapper ph Ernest Haller m Erich Wolfgang Korngold
☆ Bette Davis, Claude Rains, Paul Henreid, John Abbott, Benson Fong
'It's like grand opera, only the people are thinner ... I wouldn't have missed it for the world.' – Cecelia Ager
'Exquisitely foolish: a camp classic.' – New Yorker, 1977
† Previously filmed in 1929 as Jealousy, with Fredric March and Jeanne Eagels.

Decision Against Time: see The Man in the Sky

Decision at Sundown

US   1957   77m   Technicolor
Columbia (Harry Joe Brown)

📼

A cowboy tracks down the badman who has seduced his wife.
Routine small-town Western, efficiently done.
w Charles Lang Jnr d Budd Boetticher ph Burnett Guffey m Heinz Roemheld
☆ Randolph Scott, John Carroll, Karen Steele, Valerie French, Noah Beery Jnr, Andrew Duggan

Decision before Dawn *

US   1951   119m   bw
TCF (Anatole Litvak, Frank McCarthy)
In 1944, anti-Nazi German POWs are parachuted into Germany to obtain information.
Meticulous, well made but unexciting spy story which seldom comes vividly to life.
w Peter Viertel novel Call It Treason by George Howe d Anatole Litvak ph Franz Planer m Franz Waxman ed Dorothy Spencer
☆ Oskar Werner, Richard Basehart, Gary Merrill, Hildegarde Neff, Dominique Blanchar, Helene Thimig, O. E. Hasse, Hans Christian Blech
♬ best picture; editing

The Decision of Christopher Blake

US   1948   75m   bw
Warner (Ranald MacDougall)
A 12-year-old boy reunites his divorcing parents.
Sentimental slop, surprisingly ill done, but with a few good lines.
w Ranald MacDougall play Moss Hart d Peter Godfrey ph Karl Freund m Max Steiner
☆ Alexis Smith, Robert Douglas, Cecil Kellaway, Ted Donaldson, Harry Davenport, John Hoyt, Mary Wickes, Art Baker, Lois Maxwell

The Decks Ran Red

US   1958   84m   bw
MGM/Andrew and Virginia Stone
Unscrupulous sailors plan to murder the entire crew of a freighter and claim the salvage money.
Solidly crafted but basically uninteresting melodrama.
w Andrew and Virginia Stone d Andrew Stone ph Meredith M. Nicholson
☆ James Mason, Broderick Crawford, Dorothy Dandridge, Stuart Whitman

Decline and Fall

GB   1968   113m   DeLuxe
TCF/Ivan Foxwell
aka: *Decline and Fall of a Birdwatcher*
An innocent, accident-prone Oxford undergraduate is expelled and after various adventures in high and low society is convicted as a white slaver.
Flabby, doomed attempt to film a satirical classic which lives only on the printed page. Odd moments amuse.
w Ivan Foxwell novel Evelyn Waugh d John Krish ph Desmond Dickinson m Ron Goodwin
☆ Robin Phillips, Donald Wolfit, Genevieve Page, Robert Harris, Leo McKern, Colin Blakely, Felix Aylmer, Donald Sinden, Griffith Jones
'The British Graduate.' – New Yorker
'Literate, lavishly furnished, tastefully faithful.' – Observer

Decline and Fall of a Birdwatcher: see Decline and Fall

Decline of the American Empire ***

Canada   1986   101m   colour
Malofilm/National Film Board Of Canada (Rene Malo, Roger Frappier)

📼 📼

original title: *Le Déclin de l'Empire Américain*
A group of intellectuals discuss their attitudes to gender, sex and love.
Witty, perceptive conversation piece that won the Film Critics' award at the Cannes Film Festival in 1986.
wd Denys Arcand ph Guy Dufaux md François Dompierre, based on themes by Handel ad Gaudeline Sauriol ed Monique Forcier
☆ Dorothée Berryman, Louise Portal, Pierre Curzi, Rémy Girard, Yves Jacques, Genevieve Rioux, Daniel Briere, Gabriel Arcand
'Arcand isn't out to expose these people as spiritually empty; he's trying to present a truthful look at how they live. There's nothing weighty in his approach; it's a lovely, very unassuming picture, yet there is enough drama so that by the end a subtle shift in all the relationships is necessary.' – New Yorker
♬ foreign film

The Decline of Western Civilization *

US 1981 100m colour
Nu-Image (Penelope Spheeris)

⬛ ▣ 🎧

A documentary of punk rock in Los Angeles in the late 70s, with disenchanted and alienated teenagers both as performers and audience.

Quirky and fascinating study of some of the unlovelier aspects of youthful rebellion; it makes an interesting companion piece to the director's first feature film, Suburbia.

d Penelope Spheeris ph Steve Conant, Bill Muerer, Penelope Spheeris m Fear, Black Flag, Germs, X, Alice Bag Band, The Circle Jerks, Catholic Discipline ed Charles Mullin, Peter Wiehl, David Colburn

The Decline of Western Civilization Part II: The Metal Years *

US 1988 90m colour
New Line (Jonathan Dayton, Valerie Faris)

⬛ ▣ 🎧

Documentary on the bands and personalities of heavy metal rock.

Lively documentary of one of the noisier forms of popular entertainment, including interviews with some of its wilder practitioners.

d Penelope Spheeris ph Jeff Zimmerman, Julio Macat ed Earl Ghaffari

☆ Aerosmith, Alice Cooper, Kiss, Ozzy Osborne, Megadeath

'Harry Block Wrote A Bestseller About His Friends. Now, His Best Friends Are About To Become His Worst Enemies.'

Deconstructing Harry **

US 1997 96m DuArt
Fine Line (Jean Doumanian)

⬛ ▣ 🎥 🎧

A writer, who makes use of the lives of his friends and family in his novels, goes to a ceremony in his honour at his old school.

Witty, discursive comedy, shuttling between the realities of a novelist's life and the fictions he makes from them; it has some excellent jokes and moments of hilarious farce, but there is no centre to hold it all together.

wd Woody Allen ph Carlo DiPalma pd Santo Loquasto ed Susan E. Morse

☆ Woody Allen, Caroline Aaron, Kirstie Alley, Bob Balaban, Richard Benjamin, Eric Bogosian, Billy Crystal, Judy Davis, Hazelle Goodman, Mariel Hemingway, Amy Irving, Julie Kavner, Julia Louis-Dreyfus, Tobey Maguire, Demi Moore and also Elisabeth Shue, Stanley Tucci, Robin Williams

'Abrasive, complex, lacerating and self-revelatory. It's also very funny, most of the time.' – David Strattan, Variety

𝄞 Woody Allen (script)

Decoy: see Mystery Submarine (1962)

Decoy

US 1947 76m bw
Monogram

The girlfriend of an executed gangster tries to get her hands on his buried loot.

Surprisingly tough little co-feature of its day; even more surprisingly, the leading lady is British.

w Nedrick Young d Jack Bernhard

☆ Jean Gillie, Edward Norris, Herbert Rudley, Robert Armstrong

Dédée: see Dédée d'Anvers

Dédée d'Anvers *

France 1948 95m bw
Sacha Gordine (André Paulvé)
aka: Woman of Antwerp
aka: Dédée

A dockside prostitute falls for a sailor and arouses the jealousy of her protector.

Seamy low life melodrama, presented con brio, but rather like a tenth copy of Quai des Brumes.

w Yves Allégret, Jacques Sigurd d Yves Allégret
ph Jean Bourgoin m Jacques Besse

☆ Simone Signoret, Marcel Pagliero, Bernard Blier, Marcel Dalio, Jane Marken

The Deep

US 1977 124m Metrocolor Panavision
Columbia/EMI/Casablanca (Peter Guber)

⬛ ▣ 🎥 🎧

Underwater treasure seekers off Bermuda clash with black villains seeking a lost consignment of morphine.

An expensive action picture which is singularly lacking in action and even in plot, but oozes with brutality and overdoes the splendours of submarine life, forty per cent of it taking place under water.

w Peter Benchley, Tracy Keenan Wynn novel Peter Benchley d Peter Yates ph Christopher Challis, Al Giddings, Stan Waterman m John Barry pd Tony Masters

☆ Jacqueline Bisset, Robert Shaw, Nick Nolte, Lou Gossett, Eli Wallach

'The ultimate disco experience ... it dances on the spot for two hours, taking voodoo, buried treasure, morphine, violence and sea monsters in its stride.' – Time Out

'Peter Yates has knocked himself out doing masterly underwater action sequences in the service of a woefully crummy book.' – Russell Davies, Observer

Deep Blue Sea

US 1999 105m Technicolor Super 35
Warner/Village Roadshow/Groucho III (Alan Riche, Tony Ludwig, Akiva Goldsman)

⬛ ▣ 🎧

Sharks with enhanced intelligence threaten the staff of an underwater research facility.

Basically a B movie on steroids, this delivers all the expected, and more than familiar, thrills and spills, but lacks surprise.

w Duncan Kennedy, Donna Powers, Wayne Powers d Renny Harlin ph Stephen Windon m Trevor Rabin pd William Sandell, Joseph Bennett ed Frank J. Urioste, Derek G. Brechin, Dallas S. Puett sp ILM; Hammerhead

☆ Thomas Jane, Saffron Burrows, Samuel L. Jackson, Jacqueline McKenzie, Michael Rapaport, Stellan Skarsgard, LL Cool J, Aida Turturro

'Leave your brain at the popcorn concession stand and you'll just cope with this ridiculous but intermittently pleasurable waterlogged action thriller.' – Charles Gant, Heat

The Deep Blue Sea *

GB 1955 99m Eastmancolor Cinemascope
TCF/London Films (Anatole Litvak)

A judge's wife attempts suicide when jilted by her ex-RAF lover.

Undistinguished adaptation of a very good play, hampered by wide screen and muddy colour, helped by thoughtful performances.

w Terence Rattigan play Terence Rattigan d Anatole Litvak ph Jack Hildyard m Malcolm Arnold

☆ Vivien Leigh, Kenneth More, Eric Portman, Emlyn Williams, Moira Lister, Arthur Hill, Dandy Nichols, Jimmy Hanley, Miriam Karlin

'He'd be the perfect criminal if he wasn't the perfect cop.'

Deep Cover **

US 1992 112m DeLuxe
First Independent/Image Organisation (Pierre David)

⬛ ▣ 🎥 🎧

A cop finds himself in trouble when he is recruited to infiltrate the operation of a Los Angeles drug dealer with powerful South American connections.

Vigorous, intelligent thriller that offers more complexity than most of its type.

w Michael Tolkin, Henry Bean d Bill Duke ph Bojan Bazelli m Michel Colombier pd Pam Warner ed John Carter

☆ Larry Fishburne, Jeff Goldblum, Victoria Dillard, Charles Martin Smith, Gregory Sierra, Clarence Williams III, Sydney Lassick

'Deeply cynical, almost despairing second feature from Bill Duke features enough promotable hard action, rough violence and bad attitude to make a small spring stash.' – Variety

'A formulaic police thriller with a hip-hop musical tail that constantly wags the cinematic dog.' – Philip French, Observer

Deep Crimson **

Mexico/France/Spain 1996 115m colour
Metro/Tartan/Ivania/MCINE/MK2/Wanda (Miguel Necoechea, Pablo Barbachano)

⬛

original title: Profundo Carmesi
aka: Carmin Profond

In Mexico in the late 40s, a fat nurse and a con man join forces to cheat lonely widows of their money.

Slick, slightly camp, deeply romantic account of a couple of ruthless serial killers.

w Paz Alicia Garciadiego d Arturo Ripstein ph Guillermo Granillo m David Mansfield ad Mónica Chirinos, Patricia Nava ed Rafael Castanedo

☆ Daniel Gimenez Cacho, Regina Orozco, Marisa Paredes, Veronica Merchant, Julieta Egurrola, Rosa Furman

'It's not a comfortable watch, but it is a compelling one.' – Kim Newman, Empire

† The same true story was also the basis of The Honeymoon Killers (qv), directed by Leonard Kastle, to whom this film is dedicated.

Deep End *

West Germany/USA 1970 88m Eastmancolor
Maran/Kettledrum/Bavaria Atelier (Judd Bernard)

Sexual problems of two young people on the staff of a London municipal bathhouse.

Interestingly made but rather dreary and vaguely symbolic modern fable.

w Jerzy Skolimowski, Jerzy Gruza, Boleslaw Sulik d Jerzy Skolimowski ph Charly Steinberger m Cat Stevens

☆ Jane Asher, John Moulder-Brown, Diana Dors, Karl Michael Vogler, Christopher Sandford

'A study in the growth of obsession that is both funny and frighteningly exact.' – Nigel Andrews, MFB

The Deep End of the Ocean **

US 1999 105m Technicolor
Columbia/Mandalay/Via Rosa (Kate Guinzberg, Steve Nicolaides)

⬛ ▣ 🎧

A family struggles to survive the sudden disappearance of their three-year-old son.

Engrossing domestic drama exploring the meaning of family values which is elevated out of the ordinary by its central performances.

w Stephen Schiff novel Jacquelyn Mitchard d Ulu Grosbard ph Stephen Goldblatt m Elmer Bernstein pd Dan Davis ed John Bloom

☆ Michelle Pfeiffer, Treat Williams, Whoopi Goldberg, Jonathan Jackson, Ryan Merriman, John Kapelos, Michael McElroy, Cory Buck, Alexa Vega, Michael McGrady, Brenda Strong, Rose Gregorio

'Restrained and unsentimental, this astute drama deals thoughtfully with the chasm between real and idealized family lives.' – Janet Maslin, New York Times

'Oceans Rise. Cities Fall. Hope Survives.'

Deep Impact *

US 1998 125m DeLuxe 'Scope
Paramount/DreamWorks (Richard D. Zanuck, David Brown)

⬛ ▣ 🎥 🎧

When a huge asteroid is spotted on a collision course for Earth, astronauts are sent to try to destroy it while contigency plans are made to save the lives of a few.

Something of a feel-bad disaster movie, in which the world is almost destroyed, while the audience is slowly drowned in the sticky syrup of sentimentality. What is truly striking is the poverty of imagination: the end of all life is a theme worth more than the trivial psycho-dramas on display.

w Bruce Joel Rubin, Michael Tolkin d Mimi Leder ph Dietrich Lohmann m James Horner pd Leslie Dilley ed David Rosenbloom sp Industrial Light and Magic

☆ Robert Duvall, Téa Leoni, Elijah Wood, Vanessa Redgrave, Maximilian Schell, Morgan Freeman, James Cromwell, Ron Eldard, Jon Favreau

'This devastating, deadly-serious glimpse at the emotional impact of Earth's possible destruction is a bold experiment, superbly realized – a gripping, thoughtful big-budget Summer movie about real people.' – Jason Caro, Film Review

'Spectacular enough in its cataclysmic scenes of the planet being devastated by an unstoppable fireball, but proves far from thrilling in the down time spent with a largely dull assortment of troubled human beings.' – Todd McCarthy, Variety

Deep in My Heart *

US 1954 132m Eastmancolor
MGM (Roger Edens)

⬛ ▣ 🎥 🎧

Sigmund Romberg, a composer-waiter in New York, is helped by writer Dorothy Donnelly and showman Florenz Ziegfeld to become a famous writer of musicals.

Standard fictionalized biopic with plenty of good turns and a sharper script than usual.

w Leonard Spigelgass d Stanley Donen ph George Folsey m Sigmund Romberg ch Eugene Loring ad Cedric Gibbons, Edward Carfagno

☆ José Ferrer, Merle Oberon, Paul Henreid, Walter Pidgeon, Helen Traubel, Doe Avedon, Tamara Toumanova, Paul Stewart, Isobel Elsom, David Burns, Jim Backus and also Gene Kelly, Fred Kelly, Rosemary Clooney, Jane Powell, Ann Miller, Cyd Charisse, James Mitchell, Howard Keel, Tony Martin, Joan Weldon

'When was the last time you were really scared!!!?'
'You will never forget it!!!'

Deep Red **

Italy 1975 120m Eastmancolor
Rizzoli Film/SEDA Spettacoli/Salvatore Argento

⬛ ▣ 🎧

original title: Profondo Rosso
aka: The Hatchet Murders

A jazz pianist who witnesses a horrific murder obsessively and ineffectually tracks down the killer.

Slick, stylish, decadent, suspenseful thriller, with a disquieting atmosphere that continually puts its audience, like its victims, off-balance. Hemmings's character owes much to his role in Antonioni's Blow Up.

w Dario Argento, Bernardino Zapponi d Dario Argento ph Luigi Kuveiller m Giorgio Gaslini, Goblin ad Giuseppe Bassan ed Franco Fraticelli sp Germano Nobile, Carlo Rambaldi

☆ David Hemmings, Daria Nicolodi, Gabriele Lavia, Macha Meril, Eros Pagni, Giuliana Calandra, Glauco Mauri, Clara Calamai

'An Argento movie to treasure.' – The Dark Side
'A director of incomparable incompetence.' – Vincent Canby, New York Times

† The current British video release is of the subtitled original version. The film has also been released in an inferior dubbed version cut to 98m, which robs it of much of its narrative structure. The shorter version has been available on video.

Deep Rising

US 1998 106m Technicolor Panavision
Buena Vista/Hollywood Pictures (Laurence Mark, John Baldecchi)

⬛ ▣ 🎥 🎥 🎧

Pirates rescue a few survivors from a luxury liner that has been attacked by a gigantic octopus-like creature.

Glossy monster movie, with most of the budget going on special effects; the script appears to have been cobbled together after a hasty viewing of 50s horror movies.

wd Stephen Sommers ph Howard Atherton m Jerry Goldsmith pd Holger Gross ed Bob Ducsay, John Wright sp creature design: Rob Bottin

☆ Treat Williams, Famke Janssen, Anthony Heald, Kevin J. O'Connor, Wes Studi, Derrick O'Connor, Jason Flemying, Djimon Hounsou, Cliff Curtis, Clifton Powell

'An old-fashioned B movie with A-budget effects, but the quality sheen can't disguise the cheap-thrills hokum.' – Leonard Klady, Variety

The Deep Six

US 1958 110m Warnercolor
Jaguar (Martin Rackin)

⬛

A Quaker is unhappy at being drafted into the navy, but after initial unpopularity becomes a hero.

An ageing star contends with many hazards: slipshod production, poor colour, a dull script, and an unplayable part.

---

w John Twist, Martin Rackin, Harry Brown novel Martin Dibner d Rudolph Maté ph John Seitz m David Buttolph
☆ Alan Ladd, William Bendix, Efrem Zimbalist Jnr, Dianne Foster, Keenan Wynn, James Whitmore, Joey Bishop, Jeanette Nolan

Deep Valley

US 1947 104m bw
Warner (Henry Blanke)
The daughter of a poor California farmer falls for a convict on a work gang.
Downright peculiar melodrama, a cross between Tobacco Road and Cold Comfort Farm, with touches of High Sierra. For collectors.
w Salka Viertel, Stephen Morehouse Avery novel Dan Totheroh d Jean Negulesco ph Ted McCord m Max Steiner
☆ Ida Lupino, Dane Clark, Wayne Morris, Henry Hull, Fay Bainter, Willard Robertson

Deep Waters

🏃🏃 US 1948 85m bw
TCF
A problem orphan boy is content when adopted by a lobster fisherman.
Forgettable family film, smoothly directed and photographed.
w Richard Murphy d Henry King ph Joseph LaShelle m Cyril Mockridge
☆ Jean Peters, Dana Andrews, Dean Stockwell, Cesar Romero, Anne Revere

Deepstar Six *

US 1989 100m Technicolor
Tri-Star (Sean S. Cunningham, Patrick Markey)
📼 ▤ ℚ ∩
Underwater workers blow a hole in the sea-floor that releases a monster from the depths.
Modest, moderately suspenseful thriller with an excess of gore.
w Lewis Abernathy, Geoff Miller d Sean S. Cunningham ph Mac Ahlberg m Harry Manfredini pd John Reinhart ed David Handman
☆ Taurean Blacque, Nancy Everhard, Greg Evigan, Miguel Ferrer, Matt McCoy, Nia Peeples, Cindy Pickett, Marius Weyers

The Deer Hunter *

US 1978 182m Technicolor Panavision
Universal/EMI (Barry Spikings, Michael Deeley, Michael Cimino, John Peverall)
📼 ▤ ▤ ℚ ◎ ∩
Three friends from a small Pennsylvania town go to fight in Vietnam.
The three-hour running time is taken up with crosscutting of a wedding, a deer hunt and a game of Russian roulette. Presumably the audience has to guess the point, if any; meanwhile it may be repelled by this long and savage if frequently engrossing film.
w Deric Washburn story Michael Cimino, Louis Garfinkle, Quinn K. Redeker and Deric Washburn d Michael Cimino ph Vilmos Zsigmond m Stanley Myers
☆ Robert DeNiro, John Cazale, John Savage, Christopher Walken, Meryl Streep
'A hollow spectacle, less about war than its effect on a community, full of specious analogies, incoherent sentimentality and belief in its own self-importance.' – Time Out
🏅 best picture; direction; Christopher Walken
⬥ Deric Washburn; Vilmos Zsigmond; Robert DeNiro; Meryl Streep
🎬 Vilmos Zsigmond

Def by Temptation

US 1990 95m Technicolor
BFI/Troma/Orpheus/Bonded Filmworks (James Bond III)
📼 ▤ ℚ ◎
A young black man, intent on becoming a preacher, meets a woman possessed by a demon.
Slow-moving, low-budget occult thriller, more concerned with male/female relationships than horror, and showing promise of better movies to come from its first-time writer-director.
wd James Bond III ph Ernest Dickerson m Paul Laurence pd David Carrington ed Li-Shin Yu sp Rob Benevides
☆ James Bond III, Kadeem Hardison, Bill Nunn, Samuel L. Jackson, Minnie Gentry, Rony Clanton, Melba Moore, Stephen Van Cleef
'An instant addition to the canon of so-bad-it's-good classics and, inadvertently, a fascinating

glimpse into the contradictions of contemporary American black culture.' – John Lyttle, Independent
'Sharp, funny and borderline creepy socio-sexual horror story.' – Kim Newman, Sight and Sound

Def Jam's How to Be a Player: see How to Be a Player

Defcon-4

Canada 1984 90m colour
New World/Salter Street (B. A. Gillian, Maura O'Connell, Paul Donovan)
📼 ▤ ℚ ∩
aka: Ground Zero
Astronauts from an orbiting defence system return to Earth after a nuclear war to discover that savage tribes are fighting for control of the world.
Post-apocalyptic science-fiction of a familiar kind, but done with a certain unlovely intensity.
wd Paul Donovan ph Doug Connell, Les Krizsan m Chris Young ad J. W. Walsh, Emanuel Jannasch ed Todd Ramsay
☆ Lenore Zann, Maury Chaykin, Kate Lynch, Tim Choate, Kevin King, John Walsch, Jeff Pustil, Donna King

The Defector

France/West Germany 1966 101m
Eastmancolor
PECF/Rhein Main (Raoul Lévy)
original title: L'Espion
An American physicist in East Germany gets involved in the spy game.
Disenchanted espionage 'realism', not very well styled and hampered by a star at the end of his tether.
w Robert Guenette, Raoul Lévy novel The Spy by Paul Thomas d Raoul Lévy ph Raoul Coutard m Serge Gainsbourg
☆ Montgomery Clift, Hardy Kruger, Macha Meril, Roddy McDowall, David Opatoshu, Christine Delaroche, Jean-Luc Godard
'All that we're finally left with is the cliché, a relatively new one, along with the triple-viced hero, that spying is not a nice profession but the good guys have to go in and win for our team. Well, East, West, or Western, what this country needs, moviewise, is a good cliché-breaker – and hang the expense.' – Judith Crist

Defence of the Realm **

GB 1985 96m colour
(Rank) Enigma/NFFC (David Puttnam) (Linda Miles)
📼 ▤ ℚ ◎
A journalist tries to check the relationship between an MP and a Russian agent.
Efficient political melodrama, basically too old-fashioned to start a cult.
w Martin Stellman d David Drury ph Roger Deakins m Richard Hartley pd Roger Murray-Leach ed Michael Bradsell
☆ Gabriel Byrne, Greta Scacchi, Denholm Elliott, Ian Bannen, Fulton Mackay, Bill Paterson
🎬 best supporting actor, Denholm Elliott

Defenceless

US 1991 104m colour
New Visions (Renee Missel, David Bombyk)
📼 ▤ ℚ
A female attorney is hired to defend the wife of her lover, who is accused of his murder.
Moderately engaging thriller, in which the acting is better than the plot.
w James Hicks story James Hicks, Jeff Burkhart d Martin Campbell ph Phil Meheux m Curt Sobel pd Curtis A. Schnell ed Lou Lombardo, Chris Wimble
☆ Barbara Hershey, Sam Shepard, Mary Beth Hurt, J. T. Walsh, Kellie Overbey, Sheree North, Randy Brooks
'Effective (if somewhat predictable) thriller … Tense and engrossing.' – Sight and Sound
'A trite whodunnit dressed up with some good performances and an unusually emotional finale.' – Empire
† The film was released direct to video in Britain.

Defending Your Life **

US 1991 111m Technicolor
Warner/Geffen (Michael Grillo)
📼 ▤ ℚ
Killed in a car crash, an advertising executive finds himself in Judgement City where he must defend what he did with his life in a trial to decide his ultimate fate.

Enjoyable comedy of modern manners, less concerned with the afterlife than with the here-and-now.
wd Albert Brooks ph Allen Daviau m Michael Gore pd Ida Random ed David Finfer, Spencer Gross
☆ Albert Brooks, Meryl Streep, Rip Torn, Lee Grant, Buck Henry, Michael Durrell, James Eckhouse, Gary Beach, Julie Cobb
'Original in concept, funny in spasms and pretty good about the American propensity to examine themselves in such minute detail that Judgement Day is likely to seem like just another spell on the analyst's couch.' – Derek Malcolm, Guardian

Defiance

US 1980 102m Movielab
AIP
A young seaman staying in New York fights back against the power of an urban gang.
Belated and unnecessary addition to the gang cycle; violent nonsense.
w Thomas Michael Donnelly d John Flynn
☆ Jan Michael Vincent, Theresa Saldana, Danny Lopez

The Defiant Ones **

US 1958 96m bw
UA/Stanley Kramer
📼 ▤ ▤ ℚ
A black and a white convict escape from a chain gang, still linked together but hating each other.
Schematic melodrama with a moral, impeccably done and with good performances.
w Nathan E. Douglas, Harold Jacob Smith d Stanley Kramer ph Sam Leavitt m Ernest Gold ed Frederic Knudtson
☆ Tony Curtis, Sidney Poitier, Theodore Bikel, Charles McGraw, Lon Chaney Jnr, King Donovan, Claude Akins, Lawrence Dobkin, Whit Bissell, Carl 'Alfalfa' Switzer, Cara Williams
'Probably Kramer's best picture. The subject matter is relatively simple, though "powerful"; the action is exciting; the acting is good. But the singleness of purpose behind it all is a little offensive.' – Pauline Kael
† Nathan E. Douglas was a pseudonym for the blacklisted writer Ned Young.
👤 Nathan E. Douglas, Harold Jacob Smith; Sam Leavitt
🏅 best picture; Stanley Kramer; Tony Curtis; Sidney Poitier; Theodore Bikel; Cara Williams; editing
🎬 Sidney Poitier

Le Défroqué *

France 1953 111m bw
SFC/SNEG
A defrocked priest performs a gallant action which persuades an acquaintance to become a priest himself and try to draw his friend back into the fold.
Curious but holding moral melodrama embellished by good acting.
w Leo Joannon, Denys de la Patellière d Leo Joannon ph Nicolas Torporkoff m Jean-Jacques Grunenwald
☆ Pierre Fresnay, Pierre Trabaud, Nicole Stéphane, Marcelle Geniat, Guy Decomble, Leo Joannon, René Blancard

Déjà Vu

GB 1985 90m colour
Cannon (Michael Kagan)
Lovers discover that they are reincarnations of a couple who perished 50 years ago in a fire.
Muddling, over-talkative supernatural thriller with dollops of sex.
w Ezra D. Rappaport, Anthony Richmond book Trevor Meldal-Johnsen d Anthony Richmond
☆ Jaclyn Smith, Nigel Terry, Claire Bloom, Shelley Winters

'Sometimes your head has to listen to your heart.'

Déjà Vu

US 1997 115m DeLuxe
UIP/Rainbow/Revere/Jagtoria (John Goldstone)
A chance encounter leads to an American woman abandoning her fiancé for a new lover.
An involved and rarely believable tale of passion, in the style of a superior home movie; it may be enjoyed by those who believe that passion excuses bad behaviour.
w Henry Jaglom, Victoria Foyt d Henry Jaglom ph Hanania Baer m Gaili Schoen pd Helen Scott ed Henry Jaglom

☆ Stephen Dillane, Victoria Foyt, Vanessa Redgrave, Glynis Barber, Michael Brandon, Vernon Dobtcheff, Graydon Gould, Noel Harrison, Rachel Kempson, Aviva Marks, Anna Massey
'Ludicrously contrived and monumentally indulgent.' – Guardian

Déjeuner sur l'Herbe: see Lunch on the Grass

The Delavine Affair

GB 1954 64m bw
John Croydon/Monarch
US title: Murder Is News
A reporter is framed for killing an informer.
Routine British second feature.
w George Fisher story Winter Wears a Shroud by Robert Chapman d Douglas Pierce
☆ Honor Blackman, Peter Reynolds, Gordon Jackson, Michael Balfour

A Delicate Balance *

US 1975 134m colour
American Express/Ely Landau/Cinevision
▤
A quarrelsome Connecticut family is dominated by an ageing matriarch, and tensions mount to a climax of fear and threats.
Honourable but slightly boring film version of an essentially theatrical play: the acting is the thing.
w Edward Albee play Edward Albee d Tony Richardson ph David Watkin m none
☆ Katharine Hepburn, Paul Scofield, Joseph Cotten, Lee Remick, Kate Reid, Betsy Blair

The Delicate Delinquent

🏃🏃 US 1956 101m bw Vistavision
Paramount/Jerry Lewis
▤ ℚ
A New York policeman tries to make friends with an eccentric youth who mixes with thugs; the boy decides to train as a policeman.
Jerry Lewis's first film without Dean Martin: a sobering experience combining zany comedy, sentiment, pathos and social comment. The mixture fails to rise.
wd Don McGuire ph Haskell Boggs m Buddy Bregman
☆ Jerry Lewis, Darren McGavin, Martha Hyer, Robert Ivers, Horace McMahon

Delicatessen ***

France 1990 99m colour
Electric/Constellation/UGC/Hachette Première (Claudie Ossard)
📼 ▤ ℚ ∩
In a decaying city of the future, a butcher, who flourishes by killing his workers and selling their flesh, is attacked by underground vegetarian terrorists.
A gruesome theme given exuberant, witty, cartoon-like treatment.
wd Jean-Pierre Jeunet, Marc Caro ph Darius Khondji m Carlos D'Alessio ad Marc Caro ed Hervé Schneid
☆ Dominique Pinon, Marie-Laure Dougnac, Jean-Claude Dreyfus, Karin Viard, Ticky Holgado, Anne-Marie Pisani, Jacques Mathou
'Beautifully textured, cleverly scripted and eerily shot … a zany little film that should get terrific word of mouth.' – Variety
'An impressive achievement and extremely funny.' – Philip French, Observer

Delicious

US 1931 106m bw
Fox
An Irish girl in New York falls for a rich man.
Early musical, very thin, but an agreeable museum piece for collectors.
w Guy Bolton, Sonya Levien d David Butler ph Ernest Palmer m/ly George and Ira Gershwin
☆ Janet Gaynor, Charles Farrell, El Brendel, Lawrence O'Sullivan, Virginia Cherrill, Mischa Auer
'Cream puffs, applesauce, and plenty of nuts … should do the team's business on its name strength.' – Variety

Delightfully Dangerous

US 1945 93m bw
UA (Charles R. Rogers)
A straitlaced girl discovers that her eldest sister is a burlesque dancer.
Mild family comedy with music.

w Walter de Leon, Arthur Phillips d Arthur Lubin
☆ Jane Powell, Constance Moore, Ralph Bellamy, Arthur Treacher

The Delinquents
Australia 1989 101m colour
Warner/Village Roadshow (Alex Cutler, Michael Wilcox)
📼 ♫
Two teenagers ignore adult disapproval and fall in love.
Tiresome account of adolescent angst.
w Mac Gudgeon, Clayton Frohman novel Criena Rohan d Chris Thomson ph Andrew Lesnie m Miles Goodman pd Laurence Eastwood ed John Scott
☆ Kylie Minogue, Charlie Schlatter, Angela Punch McGregor, Bruno Lawrence, Todd Boyce, Desiree Smith, Melissa Jaffer

Deliverance ****
US 1972 109m Technicolor Panavision
Warner/Elmer Enterprises (John Boorman)
📼 📼 ▤ @ ♫
Four men spend a holiday weekend canoeing down a dangerous river, but find that the real danger to their lives comes from themselves and other humans.
Vigorous, meaningful, almost apocalyptic vision of man's inhumanity, disguised as a thrilling adult adventure.
w James Dickey novel James Dickey d John Boorman ph Vilmos Zsigmond m Eric Weissberg
☆ Burt Reynolds, Jon Voight, Ned Beatty, Ronny Cox, James Dickey
  'There is fundamentally no view of the material, just a lot of painful grasping and groping.' – Stanley Kauffmann
  ⬩ best picture; John Boorman

Dellamorte Dellamore: see Cemetery Man

'The distance between two men is … The Delta.'
The Delta *
US 1996 85m colour
Charlie Guidance (Margot Bridger)
In Memphis, a male prostitute, a Vietnamese immigrant of mixed race, involves a white, middle-class teenager in his seedy world of hustling for a living.
A gritty, documentary-style drama of disillusionment and alienated youth that just about overcomes its cheap production values.
wd Ira Sachs ph Benjamin P. Speth m Michael Rohatyn pd Bernhard Blythe ed Alfonso Goncalves
☆ Shayne Gray, Thang Chan, Rachel Zan Huss
  'Confronts issues of race and sexuality with a frankness rarely seen in the cinema, marrying a minimalist, almost intrusive, style to a naturalistic dialogue.' – James Mottram, Film Review

Delta Force
US 1986 129m colour
Cannon (Menahem Golan)
📼 ▤ @ ♫
A TWA plane is hijacked in Athens and rescued by an elite force.
What starts more or less as a recapitulation of fact turns at the half-way point into macho fantasy. Oddly enough, the paying customers rejected the mix.
w James Bruner, Menahem Golan d Menahem Golan ph David Gurfinkel m Alan Silvestri
☆ Chuck Norris, Lee Marvin, Martin Balsam, Joey Bishop, Shelley Winters, Robert Forster, Lainie Kazan, George Kennedy, Hanna Schygulla, Susan Strasberg, Bo Svenson, Robert Vaughn
  'An exercise in wish fulfilment … it's easy to get off on all this, as millions surely will, so long as you are willing to put your brain in hibernation for more than two hours.' – Variety

Delta Force 2
US 1990 111m colour
UIP/Cannon (Yoram Globus, Christopher Pearce)
📼 ▤ @ ♫
US commandos go into action against a South American drug baron.
Ridiculous action film with a superhuman hero and a high body-count.
w Lee Reynolds d Aaron Norris ph João Fernandes m Frederic Talgorn pd Ladislav Wilheim ed Michael J. Duthie, Daniel Candib

☆ Chuck Norris, Billy Drago, John P. Ryan, Richard Jaeckel, Begonia Plaza, Paul Perri

'When A Hollywood Cop Teams Up With A Detective From The Swamps Of New Orleans … All Hell Is About To Break Loose.'
Delta Heat
US 1992 91m colour
Harkham/Karen/Sawmill Entertainment (Richard L. Albert, Rudy Cohen)
📼 ▤
A Los Angeles detective goes to New Orleans to track down the killer of his partner with the help of a one-armed renegade ex-cop.
Energetic and occasionally amusing thriller providing some engaging, if mindless, entertainment.
w Sam A. Scribner d Michael Fischa ph Avi Karpik m Christopher Tyng, Rockin' Dopsie pd Don Day ed Robert Edwards, Robert Gordon
☆ Anthony Edwards, Lance Henriksen, Betsy Russell, Linda Doná, Rod Masterson, John 'Spud' McConnell, Clyde R. Jones
  'Nothing special, but not an ordeal.' – Empire

Delta of Venus
US 1994 100m Foto-Kem
New Line/Alliance/Evzen Kolar
▤
After an unhappy love affair, an American woman, who has come to Paris to write in 1940, begins to invent erotic stories for a private collector.
Trivial soft-core porn from a director whose notion of sophistication is accompanying sexual activity with classical music.
w Elisa Rothstein, Louisianna Knop novel Anaïs Nin d Zalman King ph Eagle Egilsson m George S. Clinton pd Zdenek Flemming ed James Gavin Bedford, Marc Grossman
☆ Audie England, Costas Mandylor, Eric Da Silva, Marek Vasut, Zette, Emma Louise Moore, Raven Snow, Rory Campbell
† The film was made in Prague.

Delusion *
US 1991 100m CFI color
Cineville/Seth M. Willenson (Daniel Hassid)
▤ ♫
aka: Mirage
An ambitious businessman, driving to Reno with $240,000 stolen from his employers, picks up a psychotic hitman and his girlfriend along the way.
Deft thriller, a little short on narrative twists, but filled with some enjoyably quirky characters.
w Carl Colpaert, Kurt Voss d Carl Colpaert ph Geza Sinkovics m Barry Adamson pd Ildiko Toth ed Mark Allan Kaplan
☆ Jim Metzler, Jennifer Rubin, Kyle Secor, Tracey Walter, Robert Costanzo, Jerry Orbach

Demasiado Miedo a la Vida, O Plaff: see Plaff! Or Too Afraid Of Life

Dementia 13 *
US/Eire 1963 81m bw
Filmgroup/AIP (Roger Corman)
▤ @
GB title: The Haunted and the Hunted
An axe murderer attacks members of a noble Irish family at their lonely castle.
Nastily effective macabre piece with interesting credits.
wd Francis Ford Coppola ph Charles Hannawalt m Ronald Stein
☆ Luana Anders, William Campbell, Bart Patton, Mary Mitchell, Patrick Magee, Eithne Dunn

Demetrius and the Gladiators **
👫 US 1954 101m Technicolor
Cinemascope
TCF (Frank Ross)
📼 ▤ @
A Greek slave who keeps Christ's robe after the crucifixion is sentenced to be one of Caligula's gladiators and becomes involved in Messalina's wiles.
Lively, efficient sequel to The Robe, with emphasis less on religiosity than on the brutality of the arena and our hero's sexual temptations and near-escapes. Good Hollywood hokum.
w Philip Dunne d Delmer Daves ph Milton Krasner m Franz Waxman ed Dorothy Spencer, Robert Fritch
☆ Victor Mature, Susan Hayward, Michael Rennie, Debra Paget, Anne Bancroft, Jay

Robinson, Barry Jones, William Marshall, Richard Egan, Ernest Borgnine
  'An energetic attempt to fling the mantle of sanctity over several more millions of the entertainment dollar.' – The Times

The Demi-Paradise *
GB 1943 114m bw
Two Cities (Anatole de Grunwald)
▤
US title: Adventure for Two
In 1939, a Russian inventor is sent to observe the British way of life.
Pleasant, aimless little satirical comedy in which this blessed plot seems to be peopled entirely by eccentrics.
w Anatole de Grunwald d Anthony Asquith ph Bernard Knowles m Nicholas Brodszky
☆ Laurence Olivier, Penelope Dudley Ward, Margaret Rutherford, Leslie Henson, Marjorie Fielding, Felix Aylmer, Guy Middleton, Michael Shepley, George Thorpe, Edie Martin, Muriel Aked, Joyce Grenfell
  'A backhanded way of showing us poor juvenile-minded cinemagoers that the England of Mr Punch and Mrs Malaprop lives forever.' – Richard Winnington

Demobbed
GB 1943 96m bw
Butcher/Mancunian (F. W. Baker, John E. Blakeley)
Four incompetent ex-servicemen prevent a crooked manager from robbing a factory. .
A rudimentary comedy from one of Britain's regional film companies that retains a slight interest by showcasing the performances of once popular variety theatre and radio performers.
w Roney Parsons, Anthony Toner d John E. Blakeley ph Geoffrey Faithfull, G. Gibbs md Percival Mackey ad Jim Carter ed Ted Richards
☆ Norman Evans, Nat Jackley, Dan Young, Betty Jumel, Webster Booth, Anne Ziegler, Tony Dalton, James Plant

The Democratic Terrorist *
Sweden/Norway 1992 98m colour
Sonet (Hans Iveberg)
original title: Den Demokratiske Terroristen
Carl Hamilton, a left-wing, CIA-trained Swedish naval officer, goes undercover in Hamburg to infiltrate a terrorist group.
A tough, and ultimately tense, thriller featuring Sweden's answer to James Bond, only bleaker, more brutal (and probably more realistic), and with less sex; Skarsgard makes a somewhat glum hero.
w Hans Iveberg novel Jan Guillou d Pelle Berglund m Erling Thurmann-Andersen m Björn J:son Lindh ad Rainer Schaper ed Sylvia Ingmarsson, Christin Loman
☆ Stellan Skarsgard, Katja Flint, Burkhard Driest, Heikko Deutschmann, Karl Heinz Maslo, Susanne Lothar, May Buchgraber

Les Demoiselles de Rochefort: see The Young Girls of Rochefort

Demolition Man **
US 1993 115m Technicolor
Warner/Silver Pictures (Joel Silver, Michael Levy, Howard Kazanjian)
📼 ▤ @ ◉ ◉ ♫
In the non-violent, politically correct world of the 21st century, a violent criminal from the 1990s escapes after being thawed out from his cryo-prison – and his arch-enemy, a cop framed on a murder charge, is brought back to life to catch him.
An exciting adventure, clever and violent, that has fun at the expense of a sanitized future, complete with the President Schwarzenegger Memorial Library, and also indulges in self-parody without compromising the action.
w Daniel Waters, Robert Reneau, Peter M. Lenkov d Marco Brambilla ph Alex Thomson m Elliot Goldenthal pd David L. Snyder ed Stuart Baird
☆ Sylvester Stallone, Wesley Snipes, Sandra Bullock, Nigel Hawthorne, Benjamin Bratt, Bob Gunton, Denis Leary
  'A noisy, soulless, self-conscious pastiche that mixes elements of sci-fi, action-adventure and romance, then pours on a layer of comedy replete with Hollywood in-jokes.' – Variety
  'Decently constructed, almost witty at times and a genuine attempt to make an action thriller

that's halfway intelligent.' – Derek Malcolm, Guardian

The Demolitionist
US 1995 93m CFI color
A-Pix/Planet/Le Monde (Donald P. Borchers)
▤ @ ◉
After she is killed by a violent criminal, an undercover cop is brought back to life as an unstoppable crime fighter.
Cheap and nasty exploitation flick; it borrows heavily from Robocop, but never rises above the level of sadistic and unoriginal trash.
w Brian DiMuccio, Dino Vindeni story Robert Kurtzman, Anne Kurtzman d Robert Kurtzman ph Marcus Hahn m Shawn Patterson pd Charley Cabrera ed Paolo Mazzucato sp John Hartigan, KNB EFX, Flash Film Works
☆ Nicole Eggert, Richard Grieco, Bruce Abbott, Susan Tyrrell, Peter Jason, Heather Langenkamp, Jack Nance, Tom Savini, Bruce Campbell (uncredited)

Demon: see God Told Me To

Demon Seed
US 1977 95m Metrocolor Panavision
MGM (Herb Jaffe)
A scientist invents too perfect a computer: it locks up his wife, rapes her, and incubates a child…
Science fiction at the end of its tether, all very smart and self-conscious, but at this length very tasteless. Hitchcock would have got it into a television half-hour.
w Robert Jaffe, Roger O. Hirson novel Dean R. Koontz d Donald Cammell ph Bill Butler m Jerry Fielding pd Edward Carfagno
☆ Julie Christie, Fritz Weaver, Gerrit Graham, Berry Kroeger, Lisa Lu

Demons
Italy 1985 89m colour
Dacfilm (Dario Argento)
📼 ▤ @ ◉
original title: Demoni
Members of an audience watching a horror movie about demons ravaging the world are themselves transformed into murderous monsters.
Gore-filled horror, derivative of modern American zombie movies.
w Lamberto Bava, Dario Argento, Dardano Sacchetti, Franco Ferrini d Lamberto Bava
☆ Urbano Barberini, Natasha Harvey, Karl Zinny, Fiore Argento, Paolo Cozzo, Fabiola Toledo

The Demons (dubbed)
Portugal/France 1972 116m Eastmancolor
Interfilme/Comptoir (Victor de Costa)
📼 ▤
original title: Os Demonios
Two nuns, the daughters of a witch burned at the stake, revenge their mother's death.
Bizarre and low-budget horror, exploiting sex and violence.
w Jesús Franco novel David Kuhne (Jesús Franco) d Clifford Brown (Jesús Franco) ph Raoul Artigot m Jean-Bernard Raiteux
☆ Anne Libert, Britt Nichols, Doris Thomas, John Foster, Michael Vernon, Karin Field, Alberto Dalbes
† The film was cut to 97m for its British release.

Demons 2
Italy 1987 91m colour
Avatar (Dario Argento)
📼 ▤ @ ◉ ♫
original title: Demoni 2
The occupants of an apartment block, watching a TV documentary about demons, are turned into rampaging monsters.
A sequel that repeats, with a slight twist, the events of the original and also its gore-filled content with less effect.
w Lamberto Bava, Dario Argento, Franco Ferrini, Dardano Sacchetti d Lamberto Bava ph Gianlorenzo Battaglia pd Davide Bassan ed Franco Fraticelli, Pietro Bozza
☆ David Knight, Nancy Brilli, Coralina Cataldi Tassoni, Bobby Rhodes, Asia Argento, Virginia Bryant

---

Demons of the Mind

GB   1972   89m   Technicolor
Hammer (Frank Godwin)
📺
aka: *Black Evil*
aka: *Nightmare of Terror; Blood Will Have Blood*
Crazed by the suicide of his wife, a Victorian aristocrat believes that his children are possessed by evil.
Lurid psychological thriller, with a rather better cast than it deserves.
w Christopher Wicking d Peter Sykes ph Arthur Grant m Harry Robinson ad Michael Stringer ed Chris Barnes
☆ Paul Jones, Patrick Magee, Gillian Hills, Robert Hardy, Michael Hordern, Yvonne Mitchell, Shane Briant, Kenneth J. Warren, Thomas Heathcote

Demons of the Swamp: see *Attack of the Giant Leeches*

Den Goda Viljan: see *The Best Intentions*

Den Sedmy – Osma Noc: see *Seventh Day, Eighth Night*

Denise Calls Up

US   1995   80m   colour
Artificial Eye/Off the Hook/Davis/Skyline/Dark Matter (J. Todd Harris)
📺 🖥 💿
A pregnant woman phones the man who provided the sperm for her baby.
A clever notion, of a group of people who fail to meet face to face but are linked by the technology of telephone and e-mail, is here stretched well beyond its limits, so that it fails to communicate much at all.
wd Hal Salwen ph Michael Mayers pd Susan Bolles ed Gary Sharfin
☆ Tim Daly, Caroleen Feeney, Dan Gunther, Dana Wheeler Nicholson, Liev Schreiber, Aida Turturro, Alanna Ubach
'Alas, with only one idea, the film soon has nowhere to go, and the cast, each acting in isolation with only a telephone to talk to, cannot give depth to the characters.' – *George Perry*

Dennis the Menace

👫 US   1993   96m   Technicolor
Warner (John Hughes, Richard Vane)
📺 🖥 💿 🎧
GB title: *Dennis*
A mischievous six-year-old boy makes his neighbours' life a misery.
Dull and saccharine comedy, indulging in the broadest slapstick and with Matthau going through his grumpiest grimaces.
w John Hughes, based on characters created by Hank Ketchum d Nick Castle ph Thomas Ackerman m Jerry Goldsmith pd James Bissell ed Alan Heim
☆ Walter Matthau, Mason Gamble, Joan Plowright, Christopher Lloyd, Lea Thompson, Robert Stanton, Amy Sakasitz, Kellen Hathaway, Paul Winfield
'Very young children may find the numbskull, by-the-numbers gags here amusing, but teens will consider this kids' stuff and adults will be pained.' – *Variety*

La Dentellière: see *The Lacemaker*

The Dentist **

US   1932   19m   bw
Paramount/Sennett
Classic star short with W. C. Fields working up briskly to a dentist sketch in which he deals summarily with a variety of patients.
d Leslie Pearce

The Dentist

US   1996   89m   colour
Trimark (Pierre David)
📺 🖥 💿 🎧
A marital break-up propels a dentist into madness and some unconventional surgery.
Macabre and gory horror that plays expertly on a common phobia.
w Dennis Paoli, Stuart Gordon, Charles Finch d Brian Yuzna ph Levie Isaacks m Alan Howarth pd William V. Ryder ed Christopher Roth
☆ Corbin Bernsen, Linda Hoffman, Molly Hagen, Michael Stadvec, Ken Foree, Tony Noakes, Patty Toy

---

'Sweet Dreams.'
The Dentist 2

US   1998   94m   colour
Trimark (Pierre David)
📺 🖥 💿 🎧
Escaping from a mental institution, a mad dentist settles down in a small town and gets to work on the locals.
An unsettling, unpleasant sequel that extracts more gruesome horror from teeth.
w Dennis Paoli, Stuart Gordon, Charles Finch d Brian Yuzna ph Levie Isaacks m Alan Howarth pd William B. Ryder ed Christopher Roth sp make-up fx: Anthony C. Ferrante
☆ Corbin Bernsen, Jillian McWhirter, Linda Hoffman, Jeff Douchette, Suzanne Wright, Jim Antonio
'How this mild-mannered and softly spoken filmmaker handles the material puts him head and shoulders above almost everybody working in the field today, from the past-it Argento to the unfulfilled Anthony Hickox.' – *Martyn Carroll, Dark Side*

Dentist in the Chair

GB   1960   88m   bw
Briand (Bertram Ostrer)
📺
Students at a dental college discover that the instruments they have sold to their colleagues were stolen and try to recover them with the aid of a burglar.
Routine and dispiriting farce, much in the manner of the Carry On and Doctor series.
w Val Guest, Bob Monkhouse, George Wadmore novel Matthew Finch d Don Chaffey ph Reginald Wyer m Ken Jones ad Bill Andrews ed Bill Lenny
☆ Bob Monkhouse, Peggy Cummins, Kenneth Connor, Eric Barker, Ronnie Stevens, Vincent Ball, Eleanor Summerfield, Reginald Beckwith, Stuart Saunders
† It was followed by a less amusing sequel, *Dentist on the Job*, directed by C. M. Pennington-Richards in 1961.

Dentist on the Job

GB   1961   88m   bw
Bertram Ostrer
US title: *Get On with It!*
Two incompetent, freshly graduated dentists are hired to promote a new toothpaste and decide to create their own superior brand.
Tired slapstick comedy that will not raise many smiles.
w Hazel Adair, Hugh Woodhouse, Bob Monkhouse d C. M. Pennington-Richards ph Stephen Dade m Ken Jones ad Tony Masters ed Bill Lenny
☆ Bob Monkhouse, Kenneth Connor, Shirley Eaton, Eric Barker, Richard Wattis, Ronnie Stevens, Reginald Beckwith, Charles Hawtrey, Graham Stark, Jeremy Hawk

Denver and Rio Grande

US   1952   89m   Technicolor
Nat Holt/Paramount
📺
Railroad companies compete to lay track through a narrow gorge.
Adequate Western thick ear.
w Frank Gruber d Byron Haskin
☆ Edmond O'Brien, Sterling Hayden, Dean Jagger, Laura Elliott, ZaSu Pitts, Lyle Bettger, J. Carrol Naish

Deported

US   1950   88m   bw
Universal-International
A gangster is sent back to his native Italy and tries to smuggle in his stolen money, but is finally redeemed.
Slightly unusual from this studio at this time, but not very interesting.
w Robert Buckner d Robert Siodmak
☆ Jeff Chandler, Marta Toren, Claude Dauphin, Marina Berti, Richard Rober

The Depraved

GB   1957   63m   bw
The Danzigers
An American officer helps his beloved kill her unattractive husband.
Shades of Double Indemnity, but only shades.
w Brian Clemens d Paul Dickson

☆ Anne Heywood, Robert Arden, Carroll Levis, Basil Dignam

Derby Day

GB   1952   84m   bw
British Lion/Wilcox-Neagle (Maurice Cowan)
US title: *Four Against Fate*
Intercut comic and melodramatic stories of four people who go to the Derby.
Quietly efficient, class-conscious entertainment on the lines of Friday the 13th and The Bridge of San Luis Rey. No surprises, but plenty of familiar faces.
w John Baines, Monckton Hoffe, Alan Melville d Herbert Wilcox ph Max Greene m Anthony Collins
☆ Anna Neagle, Michael Wilding, Googie Withers, Gordon Harker, John McCallum, Peter Graves, Suzanne Cloutier, Gladys Henson, Ralph Reader, Alfie Bass, Edwin Styles, Nigel Stock
'Excessive loyalty to a formula has produced far from happy results.' – *Penelope Houston, MFB*

Derelict

US   1930   73m   bw
Paramount
Two sea dogs battle over a ship and a girl.
Well-filmed melodrama, with plenty of location work.
w Max Marcin, William Slavens McNutt, Grover Jones d Rowland V. Lee
☆ George Bancroft, William Boyd, Jessie Royce Landis, Donald Stuart
'One of the best sea pictures filmed … a cinch for the deluxers.' – *Variety*

Le Dernier Combat: see *The Last Battle*

Le Dernier Milliardaire *

France   1934   100m   bw
Pathé-Natan
The queen of a small principality invites a financial wizard to pay court to her daughter. The girl elopes with a bandleader, the financier is engaged to the queen, and is then revealed as a sham.
Rather too determined to be satirical, this comedy sadly lacks the pace and flair of the director's best work but there are several sequences of interest.
wd René Clair ph Rudolph Maté, Louis Née m Maurice Jaubert
☆ Max Dearly, Renée Saint-Cyr, Marthe Mellot, Raymond Cordy
'This film is so unpopular here that the crowd is rioting against it nightly – partly because they think it's rotten and partly because they don't like the way it kids the State … despite flop here, American specialized houses should do well with it.' – *Variety, Paris*

Le Dernier Tournant *

France   1939   90m   bw
Lux
A French version of *The Postman Always Rings Twice*, qv for plot.
Interesting but not remarkable.
w Charles Spaak, Henry Torres novel James M. Cain d Pierre Chenal
☆ Fernand Gravet, Corinne Luchaire, Michel Simon, Marcel Vallée, Florence Marly
'Class B at best.' – *Variety*

Les Dernières Vacances *

France   1947   95m   bw
Pathé
During a country house holiday in the twenties, the last before the house is sold, old friends conduct amorous intrigues and so do their teenage progeny.
A moderately charming little fable making a rather obscure social point.
w R. Breuil, Roger Leenhardt d Roger Leenhardt ph Philippe Agostini
☆ Berthe Bovy, Renée Devillers, Pierre Dux, Jean d'Yd, Odile Versois, Michel François

Derrière la Façade *

France   1939   90m   bw
Filmsonor
A judge, his son, a soldier and a prostitute are involved in a night of attempted and actual murders.
Complex puzzle drama which made its mark.
d Yves Mirade, Georges Lacombe

☆ Lucien Baroux, Jacques Baumer, Jules Berry, Gaby Morlay, Michel Simon, Betty Stockfeld, Erich von Stroheim, Carette, André Lafaur

Dersu Uzala *

USSR/Japan   1975   140m   colour
Mosfilm/Toho
📺
A Russian surveyor mapping Siberian wastes becomes friendly with a wily Mongolian hunter.
Magnificent vistas punctuate an essentially plodding propaganda piece which does not rank with its director's best work.
w Yuri Nagibin, Akira Kurosawa d Akira Kurosawa
☆ Maxim Munzuk, Juri Solomine
🏆 best foreign film

Desert Attack: see *Ice Cold in Alex*

Desert Bloom

US   1985   104m   Metrocolor
Columbia/Carson/Delphi IV (Michael Hausman)
📺 🖥 💿
In 1950 Las Vegas, an ex-GI runs a gas station, illtreats his stepdaughters and falls for his sister-in-law.
Why do paying customers need to know all this? A downbeat enterprise which never got released.
wd Eugene Corr story Linda Remy ph Reynaldo Villalobos m Brad Fiedel
☆ Jon Voight, JoBeth Williams, Ellen Barkin, Allen Garfield, Annabeth Gish
'Viewers looking for sensitive, discreetly handled fare will be amply rewarded.' – *Variety*

The Desert Fox **

US   1951   88m   bw
TCF (Nunnally Johnson)
GB title: *Rommel, Desert Fox*
Rommel returns, disillusioned, to Hitler's Germany after his North African defeat, and is involved in the July plot.
Vivid but scrappy account of the last years of a contemporary hero. At the time it seemed to show a new immediacy in film-making, and was probably the first film to use an action sequence to arrest attention before the credit titles.
w Nunnally Johnson book Rommel by Desmond Young d Henry Hathaway ph Norbert Brodine m Daniele Amfitheatrof ad Lyle Wheeler, Maurice Ransford ed James B. Clark
☆ James Mason, Jessica Tandy, Cedric Hardwicke, Luther Adler, Everett Sloane, Leo G. Carroll, George Macready, Richard Boone, Eduard Franz, Desmond Young

'Two men wanted her love – the third wanted her life!'
Desert Fury

US   1947   96m   Technicolor
Paramount (Hal B. Wallis)
Against advice, a girl is attracted to a neurotic gambler who may have murdered his first wife.
Muddled melodrama slightly helped by Arizona colour settings; unconvincing characters mouth unspeakable lines in an airless tedium.
w Robert Rossen novel Desert Town by Ramona Stewart d Lewis Allen ph Charles Lang, Edward Cronjager m Miklos Rozsa
☆ Lizabeth Scott, Wendell Corey, Burt Lancaster, John Hodiak, Mary Astor, Kristine Miller
'The only fury I could sense was in my corner of the balcony.' – *C. A. Lejeune*

The Desert Hawk

👫 US   1950   77m   Technicolor
Universal-International
Against an Arabian Nights background, a cheerful outlaw abducts a princess.
Tolerable cloak-and-sandal action comedy.
w Aubrey Wisberg, Jack Pollexfen, Gerald Drayson Adams d Frederick de Cordova
☆ Richard Greene, Yvonne de Carlo, Jackie Gleason, George Macready, Rock Hudson, Carl Esmond

Desert Hearts

US   1985   91m   colour
Desert Heart Productions (Donna Deitch)
📺 🖥 💿
A would-be divorcée in Reno becomes a lesbian.

A fairly accessible piece of special pleading, nicely made and good to look at.

w Natalie Cooper *novel Desert of the Heart* by Jane Rule *d* Donna Deitch *ph* Robert Elswit *m* various *pd* Jeannine Oppewall *ed* Robert Estrin

☆ Helen Shaver, Patricia Charbonneau, Audra Lindley, Andra Akers

Desert Law

👫 Italy 1990 155m Eastmancolor
Titanus/Reteitalia/International Dean Film (Rossella Angeletti, David Pash)
▦

A New York businesswoman hires an ex-CIA agent to rescue her son, who has been kidnapped by his Arab grandfather to become the future leader of a tribe of desert warriors.

Glossy and competent thriller, most likely to appeal to 10-year-olds who can identify with the central character of a young boy.

w Adriano Bolzoni, Sergio Donati, Luigi Montefiori *d* Duccio Tessari *ph* Giorgio Di Battista *m* Ennio Morricone *pd* Luciano Sagoni *ed* Maria Morra

☆ Rutger Hauer, Carol Alt, Omar Sharif, Elliott Gould, Kabir Bedi, Brett Halsey, Peter Sands

'The Legion's my life. A girl doesn't fit into it. Especially a girl like you!'

Desert Legion

US 1953 86m Technicolor
Universal (Ted Richmond)

A Foreign Legion captain rids a lost city of menacing bandits.

Schoolboy stuff, impudent in its silly story and its unconvincing Shangri-La, but quite entertaining for those prepared to let their hair down.

w Irving Wallace, Lewis Meltzer *d* Joseph Pevney *ph* John Seitz *m* Frank Skinner

☆ Alan Ladd, Richard Conte, Arlene Dahl, Akim Tamiroff, Leon Askin

Desert Mice

GB 1959 83m bw
Artna/Welbeck/Sydney Box (Michael Relph, Basil Dearden)

Adventures of a concert party sent to entertain the troops in North Africa during World War II.

A most promising idea is wasted on a singularly unfunny script which leaves its actors all at sea.

w David Climie *d* Michael Relph *ph* Ken Hodges *m* Philip Green *pd* Peter Froud *ed* Reginald Beck

☆ Alfred Marks, Sid James, Patricia Bredin, Dick Bentley, Dora Bryan, Irene Handl, Kenneth Fortescue, Reginald Beckwith, Joan Benham, Marius Goring

Desert Passage

US 1952 60m bw
RKO (Herman Schlom)

A paroled bank robber hires a stagecoach owner to take him over the border with his recovered loot, while being chased by five other crooks.

Slow-moving Western, made near the end of Holt's long career; he seems as tired as his audience is likely to feel.

w Norman Houston *d* Lesley Selander *ph* J. Roy Hunt *m* Paul Sawtell *ad* Albert D'Agostino, Feild Gray *ed* Paul Weatherwax

☆ Tim Holt, Richard Martin, Joan Dixon, Walter Reed, Dorothy Patrick, John Dehner, Clayton Moore, Denver Pyle

Desert Patrol: see *Sea of Sand*

The Desert Rats *

US 1953 88m bw
TCF (Robert L. Jacks)
▦ ▦

An English captain commands an Australian detachment in the siege of Tobruk, and survives an encounter with Rommel.

Actioner made to cash in on the success of The Desert Fox (qv). Stars and battle scenes survive a studio look.

w Richard Murphy *d* Robert Wise *ph* Lucien Ballard *m* Leigh Harline *md* Nathaniel Finston *ad* Lyle Wheeler, Addison Hehr *ed* Barbara McLean

☆ James Mason, Richard Burton, Robert Newton, Robert Douglas, Torin Thatcher, Chips Rafferty, Charles Tingwell, Charles Davis
⚐ Richard Murphy

The Desert Song

US 1929 106m bw (Technicolor sequences)
Warner

A romantic and mysterious figure leads North African natives against evil Arabs.

Primitive sound version of the highly successful 1926 operetta.

w Harvey Gates *play* Otto Harbach, Lawrence Schwab, Frank Mandel *d* Roy del Ruth *ph* Barney McGill *m/ly* Sigmund Romberg, Oscar Hammerstein II

☆ John Boles, Carlotta King, Louise Fazenda, Johnny Arthur, Edward Martindel, Jack Pratt

The Desert Song

US 1943 96m Technicolor
Warner (Robert Florey)

Updated version with Nazis as the real villains.

w Robert Buckner *d* Robert Florey *ph* Bert Glennon *m* Heinz Roemheld

☆ Dennis Morgan, Irene Manning, Bruce Cabot, Lynne Overman, Gene Lockhart, Victor Francen, Faye Emerson, Curt Bois, Jack La Rue, Marcel Dalio, Nestor Paiva, Gerald Mohr

The Desert Song

US 1953 110m Technicolor
Warner (Rudi Fehr)
▦

Well staged straight version of the musical, with full score.

w Roland Kibbee *d* Bruce Humberstone *ph* Robert Burks *md* Max Steiner

☆ Gordon MacRae, Kathryn Grayson, Steve Cochran, Raymond Massey, Dick Wesson, Allyn McLerie, Ray Collins, Paul Picerni, William Conrad

Desert Tanks: see *The Battle of El Alamein*

The Desert Trail

US 1935 54m bw
Lone Star (Paul Malvern)

A cowboy and a womanizing gambler hunt down the man who framed them for the murder of a rodeo owner in Rattlesnake Gulch.

Sub-standard semi-comic Western.

w Lindsley Parsons *d* Cullen Lewis *ph* Archie Stout *ed* Carl Pierson

☆ John Wayne, Mary Kornman, Paul Fix, Eddy Chandler, Carmen LaRoux, Lafe McKee, Al Ferguson, Henry Hall

Desert Victory ***

GB 1943 60m bw
Ministry of Information/British Army Film Unit
▦

Montgomery's army chases the Nazis through Tripoli.

Classic war documentary.

w anonymous *d* David MacDonald *m* William Alwyn *ed* A. Best, F. Clarke *narrator* James Langdale Hodson

'The greatest battle film of the war … it puts the audience right in the middle … Americans who see this film will be anxiously waiting for the next – and a US equivalent.' – *Variety*
'A first rate work of art.' – *Time*
'The finest factual film ever made.' – *Daily Telegraph*
'Profoundly moving, and fierce in its impact upon imagination, eye and ear.' – *Scotsman*
† A few shots were reconstructed in the studio.
⚐ documentary feature

The Deserter

Italy/Yugoslavia/USA 1970 99m Technicolor Panavision
Dino de Laurentiis/Jadran/Heritage (Norman Baer, Ralph Serpe)

original title: La Spina Dorsale del Diavolo

In the South-west in 1886, a cavalry captain tracks down the Apaches who tortured his wife to death.

Brutal revenge Western, as muddled as its international credits would suggest.

w Clair Huffaker *d* Burt Kennedy *ph* Aldo Tonti *m* Piero Piccione *pd* Mario Chiari

☆ Bekim Fehmiu, John Huston, Richard Crenna, Chuck Connors, Ricardo Montalban, Ian Bannen, Brandon de Wilde, Slim Pickens, Albert Salmi, Woody Strode, Patrick Wayne, Fausto Tozzi

Il Deserto Rosso: see *The Red Desert*

'Three people who loved each other very much!'
Design for Living **

US 1933 88m bw
Paramount (Ernst Lubitsch)

Two friends love and are loved by the same worldly woman, and they set up house together.

Elegant but miscast version of a scintillating play, with all the sex and the sting removed (at the insistence of the Legion of Decency, then coming into power). Ben Hecht claimed to have removed all but one line of Coward's dialogue: 'For the good of our immortal souls!'

w Ben Hecht *play* Noël Coward *d* Ernst Lubitsch *ph* Victor Milner *m* Nathaniel Finston *ad* Hans Dreier

☆ Gary Cooper, Fredric March, Miriam Hopkins, Edward Everett Horton, Franklin Pangborn, Isabel Jewell

'Can't miss because it holds plenty … an improvement on the original.' – *Variety*
'A delightfully smart, crisp piece of entertainment, cleverly conceived and delightfully executed.' – *New York American*
'A partial cleansing for the screen of a stage story notorious for its wealth and variety of moral code infractions.' – *Martin Quigley*

Design for Lust: see *Confessions of a Sex Maniac*

Design for Scandal

US 1941 85m bw
MGM

A reporter is assigned by his boss to get a lady judge disbarred.

Mechanical star comedy.

w Lionel Houser *d* Norman Taurog

☆ Rosalind Russell, Walter Pidgeon, Edward Arnold, Guy Kibbee, Lee Bowman

The Designated Mourner *

GB 1997 94m colour
First Look/Greenpoint/BBC (Donna Grey, David Hare)
▦ ▦

Living under a repressive regime, a man, his wife and her father, a poet whose political views are not liked, discuss their relationships.

No attempt has been made to open up this stage play, which mainly consists of static monologues, and it does not transfer easily to the screen, though it will reward patient audiences.

w Wallace Shawn *play* Wallace Shawn *d* David Hare *ph* Oliver Stapleton *m* Richard Hartley *pd* Bob Crowley *ed* George Akers

☆ Mike Nichols, Miranda Richardson, David de Keyser

'Insidiously superb.' – *Stanley Kauffmann, New Republic*

Designing Woman *

US 1957 118m Metrocolor Cinemascope
MGM (Dore Schary)
▦ ▦

A sports reporter marries a dress designer and finds that their common interests are few.

Lumbering comedy which aims for sophistication but settles for farce: tolerable for star watchers who have dined well.

w George Wells *d* Vincente Minnelli *ph* John Alton *m* André Previn

☆ Gregory Peck, Lauren Bacall, Dolores Gray, Sam Levene, Tom Helmore, Mickey Shaughnessy, Jesse White, Chuck Connors, Jack Cole
⚐ George Wells

Desire **

US 1936 89m bw
Paramount (Ernst Lubitsch)

In Spain, an American car designer falls for a glamorous jewel thief.

Romantic comedy which the producer should have worked on longer: it begins brilliantly and keeps its style, but the pace and wit ebb away.

w Edwin Justus Mayer, Waldemar Young, Samuel Hoffenstein, from a German film *Die schönen Tage von Aranjuez* *play* Hans Szekely, R. A. Stemmle *d* Frank Borzage *ph* Charles Lang, Victor Milner *m* Frederick Hollander *ad* Hans Dreier, Robert Usher

☆ Marlene Dietrich, Gary Cooper, John Halliday, William Frawley, Ernest Cossart, Akim Tamiroff, Alan Mowbray, Zeffie Tilbury

'It sparkles and twinkles … one of the most engaging pictures of the season.' – *Frank S. Nugent, New York Times*

'A sure, beautifully written piece about the usual Lubitsch trifles, about crooks and fake countesses breathless before the dawn of romance.' – *Alistair Cooke*
'Brilliant treatment, superb staging and inspiring acting. Irresistible entertainment.' – *CEA Film Report*

Desire in the Dust

US 1960 102m bw Cinemascope
TCF/Associated Producers (William F. Claxton)

A wealthy Southern aristocrat is involved in a fatal car crash and persuades a young farmhand to take the blame.

Derivative hothouse drama, a little better than its title, with a cast breathing heavily in imitation of refugees from Tennessee Williams or William Faulkner.

w Charles Lang *novel* Harry Whittington *d* William F. Claxton *ph* Lucien Ballard *m* Paul Dunlap

☆ Raymond Burr, Martha Hyer, Joan Bennett, Ken Scott, Brett Halsey, Anne Helm, Jack Ging, Edward Binns

Desire Me

US 1947 91m bw
MGM (Arthur Hornblow Jnr)

The wife of a Normandy villager hears that he has died in a concentration camp. She marries the bearer of the news, who turns out to be a psychotic who has left her husband for dead … but he is not.

Dreary drama, troubled during production and offering little for the actors to chew on.

w Marguerite Roberts, Zoë Akins, Casey Robinson *novel* Leonhard Frank *d* not credited, but mostly by George Cukor, Mervyn Le Roy, Jack Conway *ph* Joseph Ruttenberg *m* Herbert Stothart

☆ Greer Garson, Robert Mitchum, Richard Hart, George Zucco, Morris Ankrum

'The supporting cast includes a number of characters who give the appearance of having come out of a dusty cupboard marked "French Types – Assorted".' – *MFB*
† Robert Montgomery shot a few scenes before bowing out to be replaced by Richard Hart.

Desire under the Elms

US 1958 111m bw Vistavision
Paramount (Don Hartman)
▦ ▦

A New England farmer brings home a young bride and causes friction with his son.

This bid for culture turns out like a hoary and very slow melodrama, not exactly risible but annoying because it teeters between several styles.

w Irwin Shaw *play* Eugene O'Neill *d* Delbert Mann *ph* Daniel L. Fapp *m* Elmer Bernstein

☆ Sophia Loren, Burl Ives, Anthony Perkins, Frank Overton, Pernell Roberts, Anne Seymour

'The film is consistently and unhappily out of its depth.' – *Penelope Houston*
'A challenging and inspiring picture.' – *News of the World*
⚐ Daniel L. Fapp

'Their story is not in the history books. It has never been seen on the screen – until now!'
Desirée

US 1954 110m DeLuxe Cinemascope
TCF (Julian Blaustein)
▦ ▦

Fictionalized biopic of one of Napoleon's mistresses.

Heavy-going costume piece, with all contributors distinctly uncomfortable.

w Daniel Taradash *novel* Annemarie Selinko *d* Henry Koster *ph* Milton Krasner *m* Alex North *ad* Lyle Wheeler, Leland Fuller

☆ Jean Simmons, Marlon Brando, Merle Oberon, Michael Rennie, Cameron Mitchell, Elizabeth Sellars, Cathleen Nesbitt, Isobel Elsom
⚐ art direction

Desk Set **

US 1957 103m Eastmancolor Cinemascope
TCF (Henry Ephron)
▦ ▦

GB title: His Other Woman

Ladies in a broadcasting company's reference section are appalled when an electronics expert is sent to improve their performance.

Thin comedy, altered from a Broadway success; patchy as a whole, but with several splendid dialogue scenes for the principals.

⊘ Digital Video Disc Region 2   ⊘ Digital Video Disc Region 1   ♫ Soundtrack released on compact disc   ☆ Cast in approximate order of importance   † Points of interest   ♪ Notable songs   ⚐ Academy Award   ⚐ Academy Award nomination   Ⓦ BAFTA w Phoebe and Henry Ephron *play* William Marchant *d* Walter Lang *ph* Leon Shamroy *m* Cyril Mockridge

☆ *Spencer Tracy, Katharine Hepburn,* Joan Blondell, Gig Young, Dina Merrill, Neva Patterson

'They lope through this trifling charade like, a couple of oldtimers who enjoy reminiscing with simple routines.' – *Bosley Crowther, New York Times*

Despair *

West Germany/France   1978   119m
Eastmancolor
NF Geria/Bavaria/SFP (Peter Märthesheimer)

▤

West German title: *Eine Reise ins Licht*

In 1930 Berlin, a Russian immigrant businessman leads a fantasy life which drives him to murder and insanity.

Filmed in English, this curious cross between Lolita *and* Repulsion *found surprisingly little critical favour, considering its participants.*

w Tom Stoppard *novel* Vladimir Nabokov *d* Rainer Werner Fassbinder *ph* Michael Ballhaus *m* Peer Raben *pd* Rolf Zehetbauer

☆ Dirk Bogarde, Andrea Ferreol, Volker Spengler, Klaus Löwitsch, Bernhard Wicki

'It begins magnificently, remains sporadically brilliant throughout, but grows heavier and heavier until it finally sinks into inertia.' – *Tom Milne, MFB*

'He came back to settle the score with someone. Anyone. Everyone.'

Desperado

US   1995   105m   Technicolor
Columbia/Los Hooligans (Bill Borden, Robert Rodriguez)

▥ ▤ ▤ ⊕. ◉ ◉ ◠

A man carrying a guitar case full of weapons walks into a small Mexican town and starts shooting.

This is more or less an expensive remake of El Mariachi, *and a disappointing one in its failure to develop the original in any significant way; it is one long gun battle, filmed in a style that owes much to the balletic tradition of John Woo and other Hong Kong film-makers.*

wd Robert Rodriguez *ph* Guillermo Navarro *m* Los Lobos *pd* Cecilia Montiel *ed* Robert Rodriguez

☆ Antonio Banderas, Salma Hayek, Joaquin de Almeida, Cheech Marin, Steve Buscemi, Carlos Gomez, Quentin Tarantino, Tito Larriva, Carlos Gallardo

'A film so insanely unambitious, so childishly unheeding of the normal rigours of film-making, it's almost cheering. It's got the crazed, obsessive squint of one of Roy Lichtenstein's immaculate dot paintings of a single explosion – it's pop art Peckinpah.' – *Tom Shone, Sunday Times*

† Its DVD release also includes its low-budget predecessor *El Mariachi* (qv).

Desperadoes

US   1943   85m   Technicolor
Columbia (Harry Joe Brown)

A gunman rides into town to cause trouble, but finds romance and renews an old friendship.

Lively star Western of its day.

w Max Brand, Robert Carson *d* Charles Vidor

☆ Randolph Scott, Glenn Ford, Evelyn Keyes, Edgar Buchanan, Claire Trevor, Guinn Williams

† This was Columbia's first film in colour.

'Hang on to your money, your woman, and your life!'

The Desperados

US   1968   90m   Technicolor
Columbia/Meadway (Irving Allen)

▤

After the Civil War, a fanatic 'parson' leads a tribe of violent outlaws including his three sons.

Rough-and-tumble Western in the modern savage manner; made in Spain.

w Walter Brough *d* Henry Levin *ph* Sam Leavitt *m* David Whitaker

☆ Vince Edwards, Jack Palance, George Maharis, Neville Brand, Sylvia Syms, Christian Roberts, Kate O'Mara, Kenneth Cope, John Paul

Desperate *

US   1947   73m   bw
RKO (Michel Kraike)

A trucker becomes innocently involved in a robbery and goes on the run.

Lively second feature from the studio's best period, with plenty of burgeoning talent.

w Harry Essex, Martin Rackin *story* Dorothy Atlas, Marston Mann *d* Anthony Mann *ph* George E. Diskant *m* Paul Sawtell

☆ Steve Brodie, Audrey Long, Raymond Burr, Jason Robards Snr, Douglas Fowley, William Challee, Ilka Gruning

'Amazingly watchable within its formulary limits.' – *Tom Milne, MFB, 1982*

Desperate Characters *

US   1971   106m   colour
ITC/TDJ (Frank D. Gilroy)

Residents of New York's east side find the rigours of life hard to take.

Curious but interesting suburban drama, a kind of deglamorized and updated City for Conquest.

wd Frank D. Gilroy *novel* Paula Fox *ph* Urs Furrer *m* Lee Konitz, Ron Carter, Jim Hall

☆ Shirley MacLaine, Gerald S. O'Loughlin, Kenneth Mars, Sada Thompson, Jack Somack

'The most blistering indictment of New York City since *Midnight Cowboy*.' – *Rex Reed*

'A film of authenticity, of delicately realized intangibles.' – *Stanley Kauffmann*

Desperate Hours

US   1990   105m   Technicolor
TCF/Dino de Laurentiis (Michael Cimino)

▥ ▤ ⊕. ◠

An armed robber on the run with two friends takes a family hostage.

A failure, even by the standards of the 1955 version.

w Lawrence Konner, Mark Rosenthal, Joseph Hayes *novel* Joseph Hayes *d* Michael Cimino *ph* Doug Milsome *m* David Mansfield *pd* Victoria Paul *ed* Peter Hunt

☆ Mickey Rourke, Anthony Hopkins, Mimi Rogers, Lindsay Crouse, Kelly Lynch, Elias Koteas, David Morse, Shawnee Smith

'A coldly mechanical and uninvolving remake.' – *Variety*

The Desperate Hours *

US   1955   112m   bw   Vistavision
Paramount (William Wyler)

▤ ⊕.

Three escaped convicts take over a suburban house but are finally outwitted by the family.

Ponderous treatment of an over-familiar situation with only the acting and an 'A' picture look to save it.

w Joseph Hayes *play* Joseph Hayes *novel* Joseph Hayes *d* William Wyler *ph* Lee Garmes *m* Gail Kubik

☆ *Fredric March,* Humphrey Bogart, Martha Scott, Arthur Kennedy, Gig Young, Dewey Martin, Mary Murphy, Robert Middleton, Richard Eyer

'A solid, deliberate and long-drawn-out exercise in the mechanics of suspense.' – *Penelope Houston*

† Bogart's role had been played on stage by Paul Newman. March's role had been offered to Spencer Tracy, but he wouldn't take second billing.

Desperate Journey **

US   1942   109m   bw
Warner (Hal B. Wallis)

▥ ▤

Three POWs in Nazi Germany fight their way back to freedom.

When you pit Errol Flynn against the Nazis, there's no doubt who wins; and the last line is 'Now for Australia and a crack at those Japs!' Exhilarating adventure for the totally uncritical; professional standards high.

w Arthur Horman *d* Raoul Walsh *ph* Bert Glennon *m* Max Steiner

☆ *Errol Flynn, Alan Hale,* Ronald Reagan, Nancy Coleman, Raymond Massey, Arthur Kennedy, Ronald Sinclair, Albert Basserman, Sig Rumann, Ilka Gruning, Pat O'Moore

'Yarn is an extreme strain on anyone's credulity, and yet it's so exciting that the preposterousness of it all is only something to be thought about on the way home from the theatre.' – *Variety*

'A 1942 treatment of *The Three Musketeers*, packed with action, shorn of romance, and utilizing the Third Reich for terrain. Folks who sacrifice reason for fast action and the joy of seeing Nazis foiled, will find it entirely gratifying.' – *New York Times*

Desperate Living

US   1977   95m   colour
New Line/Charm City (John Waters)

A paranoid housewife kills her husband with the aid of her maid and flees to a community of murderers and degenerates.

A typical Waters work, concerned with obesity, transvestism, transsexuality and nudity. It also features bad acting, uninspired direction, unimaginative camera-work and adolescent notions of what is shocking.

wd John Waters *ph* Thomas Loizeaux *m* Chris Lobinger *ad* Vincent Peranio *ed* Charles Roggero

☆ Mink Stole, Susan Lowe, Edith Massey, Mary Vivian Pearce, Jean Hill

'Detective Frank Connor is forced to choose between the badge he wears and the son he loves … no contest.'

Desperate Measures

US   1998   100m   Technicolor
Entertainment/Mandalay (Barbet Schroeder, Susan Hoffman, Gary Foster, Lee Rich)

▥ ▤ ⊕. ◉ ◠

A policeman is desperate to keep alive a violent escaped criminal because he needs him as a bone-marrow donor for his dying son.

Risible action movie, in which two uninteresting characters interminably stalk one another.

w David Klass *d* Barbet Schroeder *ph* Luciano Tavoli *m* Trevor Jones *pd* Geoffrey Kirkland *ed* Lee Percy

☆ Michael Keaton, Andy Garcia, Brian Cox, Marcia Gay Harden, Erik King, Efrain Figueroa, Joseph Cross

'As hackneyed and instantly forgettable as its title.' – *Variety*

Desperate Moment

GB   1953   88m   bw
GFD/Fanfare (George H. Brown)

In Poland, a man imprisoned for murder finds he didn't do it, escapes, and tracks down the real criminal, his best friend.

Cliché-ridden melodrama climaxing in a car chase; poor in all departments.

w Patrick Kirwan, George H. Brown *novel* Martha Albrand *d* Compton Bennett *ph* C. Pennington-Richards *m* Ronald Binge

☆ Dirk Bogarde, Mai Zetterling, Philip Friend, Albert Lieven, Carl Jaffe, Gerard Heinz

Desperate Remedies *

New Zealand   1993   93m   colour
Electric/NFU Studios/NZ on Air/New Zealand Film Commission/James Wallace

▤

In the 19th century, a bisexual wealthy woman finds herself involved in deceit and murder when she attempts to buy a husband for her sex- and drug-addicted sister.

A swooning parody of period romances, deliberately larger than life (more, in fact, similar to an imitation of Life) *and over-elaborate in its approach to costume and plot, enjoyable if you're in the mood for tongue-in-cheek melodrama.*

wd Stewart Main, Peter Wells *ph* Leon Narbey *m* Peter Scholes *pd* Michael Kane *ed* David Coulson

☆ Jennifer Ward-Lealand, Kevin Smith, Lisa Chappell, Cliff Curtis, Michael Hurst, Kiri Mills, Bridget Armstrong, Timothy Raby

'An extravagant, opulent and mostly enjoyable exercise in high camp (or low kitsch).' – *Variety*

'The cumulative effect is to make costume melodrama's classic preoccupations with strict social hierarchy and sexual propriety seem hilariously gratuitous, irrational and redundant.' – *Claire Monk, Sight and Sound*

Desperate Search

US   1952   73m   bw
MGM (Matthew Rapf)

A divorced pilot's search for his two children lost in a wilderness is hampered by the rivalry of his ex-wife.

Routine thriller that tries hard but remains unenlivening and lacking in suspense.

w Walter Doniger *novel* Arthur Mayse *d* Joseph Lewis *ph* Harold Lipstein *md* Rudolph G. Kopp *ad* Cedric Gibbons, Eddie Imazu *ed* Joseph Dervin

☆ Howard Keel, Jane Greer, Patricia Medina, Keenan Wynn, Robert Burton, Lee Aaker

Desperate Siege: see *Rawhide*

Desperately Seeking Susan *

US   1985   104m   DeLuxe
Orion/Sarah Pillsbury, Midge Sanford

▥ ▤ ⊕. ◠

A bored housewife causes confusion and mayhem when out of curiosity she tracks down what's behind some intriguing ads in the personal column.

Mildly diverting romantic mystery which could have been both funnier and more thrilling.

w Leona Barish *d* Susan Seidelman *ph* Edward Lachman *m* Thomas Newman *pd* Santo Loquasto *ed* Andrew Mondshein

☆ Rosanna Arquette, Madonna, Aidan Quinn, Mark Blum, Robert Joy

'Simply easy entertainment, with a lively cast caught up in a silly situation.' – *Variety*

🏆 Rosanna Arquette

'Roaring across the land of Marco Polo and Genghis Khan come Uncle Sam's sailors on camels!'

Destination Gobi *

US   1953   90m   Technicolor
TCF (Stanley Rubin)

American sailors get Mongol help against the Japanese in the Gobi desert.

A curious war adventure, a kind of camel opera, apparently based on fact; mildly enjoyable, though the outlandish is gradually replaced by the predictable.

w Everett Freeman *d* Robert Wise *ph* Charles G. Clarke *m* Sol Kaplan

☆ Richard Widmark, Don Taylor, Casey Adams, Murvyn Vye, Darryl Hickman, Martin Milner, Ross Bagdasarian, Rodolfo Acosta

Destination Moon *

US   1950   91m   Technicolor
Universal/George Pal

▤ ⊕. ◉ ◉ ◠

An American inventor gets private backing to build a rocket so that the US can reach the moon before the Russians.

Semi-documentary prophecy with impressive gadgetry encased in a tedious and totally unsurprising script.

w Rip Van Ronkel, Robert Heinlein, James O'Hanlon *d* Irving Pichel *ph* Lionel Lindon *m* Leith Stevens

☆ Warner Anderson, John Archer, Tom Powers, Dick Wesson

'Heavy-handed, unimaginative and very badly acted.' – *MFB*

Destination Murder

US   1950   70m   bw
RKO (Edward L. Cahn, Maurie M. Suess)

A college girl investigates the murder of her father by dating the man she thinks is responsible.

An unimaginative second feature, of no lasting interest.

w Don Martin *d* Edward L. Cahn *ph* Jackson J. Rose *m* Irving Gertz *ad* Boris Leven *ed* Philip Cahn

☆ Joyce MacKenzie, Stanley Clements, Hurd Hatfield, Albert Dekker, Myrna Dell, James Flavin, John Dehner

Destination Tokyo *

US   1943   135m   bw
Warner (Jerry Wald)

▥ ▤

A US submarine is sent into Tokyo harbour.

Solid, well acted war suspenser, but overlong.

w Delmer Daves, Albert Maltz *story* Steve Fisher *d* Delmer Daves *ph* Bert Glennon *m* Franz Waxman

☆ Cary Grant, John Garfield, Alan Hale, John Ridgely, Dane Clark, Warner Anderson, William Prince, Robert Hutton, Tom Tully, Peter Whitney, Faye Emerson, John Forsythe

'We don't say it is credible; we don't even suggest that it makes sense. But it does make a pippin of a picture from a purely melodramatic point of view.' – *Bosley Crowther*

'Even moviegoers who have developed a serious allergy for service pictures should find it high among the superior films of the war.' – *Newsweek*

𝄞 Steve Fisher

Destination Unknown

US   1933   69m   bw
Universal

Bootleggers, in a crippled ship with a mutinous crew, are saved by a mysterious stranger.

Curious melodrama which turns halfway through into
The Passing of the Third Floor Back.
w Tom Buckingham d Tay Garnett
☆ Pat O'Brien, Ralph Bellamy, Alan Hale, Russell
Hopton, Tom Brown, Betty Compson, Noel
Madison
'Good sea melodrama ruined by change of
intent.' – Variety

Destinées: see Love, Soldiers and Women

Destiny *
Germany   1921   100m   bw   silent
Decla-Bioscop
original title: Der Müde Tod
In the 19th century a young woman tries to save
her lover from the presence of Death, who shows
her that whatever she does it is inevitable.
A solemn fantasy on the lines of Appointment in
Samarra, the framing story being more effective
than the 'illustrations'.
w Thea von Harbou, Fritz Lang d Fritz Lang
ph Fritz Arno Wagner, Erich Nitschmann,
Hermann Saalfrank
☆ Lil Dagover, Rudolf Klein-Rogge, Bernhard
Götzke, Walter Janssen

Destiny *
US   1944   65m   bw
Universal (Roy William Neill)
An escaped convict on the run finds refuge with a
blind girl on a lonely farm.
Curious second feature, interesting because it began as
a story eliminated from Flesh and Fantasy (qv); extra
footage was added to bring it up to the required length.
The original footage is mainly the nightmare suffered by
the girl. Curtis died in the original, but survives here.
w Roy Chanslor (F and F Ernest Pascal)
d Reginald Le Borg (F and F Julien Duvivier)
ph George Robinson (F and F Paul Ivano)
m Frank Skinner
☆ Gloria Jean, Alan Curtis, Frank Craven, Grace
McDonald

Destiny of a Man *
USSR   1959   98m   bw
Sovexportfilm/Mosfilm (G. Kuznetsov)
original title: Sudba Cheloveka
During World War II a Russian is captured by
Nazis but escapes and returns home only to find his
family dead.
Strikingly styled sob story whose very glumness
prevented it from being hailed as a masterpiece; in
technique however it is in the best Russian tradition.
w Y. Lukin, F. Shakhmagonov story Mikhail
Sholokhov d Sergei Bondarchuk ph Vladimir
Monakhov m V. Basnov
☆ Sergei Bondarchuk, Zinaida Kirienko, Pavlik
Boriskin
'Of all Soviet post-war films, this will be looked
on as the greatest and most original work of the
period.' – MFB

'The craziest, wackiest journey you'll ever take!'
'A romantic adventure of mystical proportion.'
Destiny Turns on the Radio
US   1995   101m   CFI color
Entertainment/Savoy (Gloria Zimmerman)
A bank robber gets out of jail and goes to a Las
Vegas motel to find his partner and the loot, but
discovers that the money has been stolen by a
mysterious stranger.
Oddball movie that obstinately refuses to come to life;
it just lies there, leaving its cast and director stranded.
w Robert Ramsey, Matthew Stone d Jack Baran
ph James L. Carter m Steve Soles pd Jean-
Philippe Carp ed Raul Davalos
☆ James LeGros, Dylan McDermott, Quentin
Tarantino, Nancy Travis, James Belushi, Janet
Carroll, David Cross, Bobcat Goldthwait
'The plot is incomprehensible and the dialogue
cheapjack. This piece of cod-pulp fiction is
neither credible nor incredible. It's just dull.'–
Derek Malcolm, Guardian
'The intended tone of romantic, magical comedy
is spectacularly misjudged.' – Independent

'What nation will survive?'
Destroy all Monsters
ff   Japan   1968   89m   colour
Toho/AIP
Moon invaders gain control of Godzilla and his
friends.

Typically inept Japanese monster rally full of men in
rubber suits.
w Kaoru Mabuchi d Inoshiro Honda ph Taiichi
Kankura m Akira Ifukube
☆ Akira Kubo, Jun Tazaki, Kyoko Ai

'Her only rival is his ship!'
Destroyer
US   1943   99m   bw
Columbia (Louis F. Edelmann)
An old sea dog talks himself into a job on a World
War II destroyer but works his men too hard.
Flat propaganda piece, not too well made.
w Frank Wead, Lewis Meltzer, Borden Chase
d William A. Seiter ph Franz Planer m Anthony
Collins
☆ Edward G. Robinson, Glenn Ford, Marguerite
Chapman, Edgar Buchanan, Leo Gorcey, Regis
Toomey, Ed Brophy

The Destructors: see The Marseilles Contract

Destry *
US   1954   95m   Technicolor
U-I (Stanley Rubin)
Almost scene-for-scene remake of Destry Rides
Again (qv).
Well enough made and tolerably acted, but it doesn't
have the sparkle, despite employing the same director.
w Edmund H. North, D. D. Beauchamp d George
Marshall ph George Robinson m Joseph
Gershenson
☆ Audie Murphy, Mari Blanchard, Lyle Bettger,
Thomas Mitchell, Edgar Buchanan, Wallace Ford,
Lori Nelson, Alan Hale Jnr, Mary Wickes
'The impression is of a school revival of the
original production.' – MFB

'They make the fighting sinful west blaze into action
before your eyes!'
Destry Rides Again **
US   1939   94m   bw
Universal (Joe Pasternak)
A mild-mannered sheriff finally gets mad at local
corruption and straps on his guns.
Classic Western which manages to encompass
suspense, comedy, romance, tenderness, vivid
characterization, horseplay, songs and standard
Western excitements, without moving for more than a
moment from a studio main street set. It starts with a
sign reading 'Welcome to Bottleneck' and an outburst
of gunfire; it ends with tragedy followed by a running
joke. Hollywood expertise at its very best.
w Felix Jackson, Gertrude Purcell, Henry Myers
novel Max Brand d George Marshall ph Hal Mohr
m Frank Skinner m/ly Frederick Hollander, Frank
Loesser
☆ James Stewart, Marlene Dietrich, Brian Donlevy,
Charles Winninger, Samuel S. Hinds, Mischa Auer,
Irene Hervey, Jack Carson, Una Merkel, Allen
Jenkins, Warren Hymer, Billy Gilbert
'Makes the b.o. grade in a big way … just plain,
good entertainment.' – Variety
'I think it was Lord Beaverbrook who said that
Marlene Dietrich standing on a bar in black net
stockings, belting out See What the Boys in the
Back Room Will Have, was a greater work of art
than the Venus de Milo.' – Richard Roud
† An early sound version in 1932 starred Tom
Mix; Frenchie (1950) was a slight variation. See
also Destry.

Det Regnar Pa Var Kärlek: see It Rains on
Our Love

Detective *
France   1985   98m   colour
Sara/JLG
Four groups of people find their paths intersecting
in a Paris hotel while the hotel detective tries to
solve a murder.
Eccentric Grand Hotel-style compendium with many
baffling asides presumably attributable to the director.
One suspects that the audience is expected to be a
detective too.
w Alain Sarde, Philippe Setbon, Anne-Marie
Mieville, Jean-Luc Godard d Jean-Luc Godard
☆ Claude Brasseur, Nathalie Baye, Johnny
Hallyday, Laurent Terzieff, Jean-Pierre Léaud,
Alain Cuny

The Detective: see Father Brown (1954)

The Detective *
US   1968   114m   DeLuxe   Panavision
TCF/Arcola/Millfield (Aaron Rosenberg)
A New York police detective fights crime and
corruption.
Determinedly sleazy and 'frank' cop stuff, quite
arrestingly narrated and with something to say about
police methods. Good violent entertainment, with just
a shade too many homosexuals and nymphomaniacs for
balance.
w Abby Mann novel Roderick Thorp d Gordon
Douglas ph Joseph Biroc m Jerry Goldsmith
☆ Frank Sinatra, Lee Remick, Jacqueline Bisset,
Ralph Meeker, Jack Klugman, Horace MacMahon,
Lloyd Bochner, William Windom, Tony Musante,
Al Freeman Jnr, Robert Duvall
'It vacillates uncertainly between murder
mystery, political allegory, and a psychological
study of the hero.' – Jan Dawson

'A man whose wife was more woman than angel!'
Detective Story *
US   1951   103m   bw
Paramount (William Wyler)
A day in a New York precinct police station,
during which a detective of almost pathological
righteousness discovers a stain on his family and
himself becomes a victim of violence.
Clever, fluent transcription of a Broadway play with
some of the pretensions of Greek tragedy; it could have
been the negation of cinema, but professional handling
makes it the essence of it.
w Philip Yordan, Robert Wyler play Sidney Kingsley
d William Wyler ph Lee Garmes
☆ Kirk Douglas, Eleanor Parker, William Bendix,
Cathy O'Donnell, George Macready, Horace
MacMahon, Gladys George, Joseph Wiseman, Lee
Grant, Gerald Mohr, Frank Faylen, Luis Van
Rooten
'The admirably directed interaction of
movement and talk all over the big room is what
gives the thing its satisfying texture.' – Richard
Mallett, Punch
† No music was used.
ℶ Philip Yordan, Robert Wyler; William Wyler;
Eleanor Parker; Lee Grant

Detour *
US   1945   68m   bw
PRC (Leon Fromkess)
On his way to Hollywood to meet a girlfriend, a
night-club pianist assumes the identity of a dead
man.
A minor cult movie with as much doomladen dialogue
and film noir angles as could be shovelled into a
Poverty Row 'B' at the time. On the whole, less than
meets the eye.
w Martin Goldsmith d Edgar G. Ulmer
ph Benjamin H. Kline m Leo Erdody
☆ Tom Neal, Ann Savage, Claudia Drake,
Edmund MacDonald, Tim Ryan

Detroit Rock City
US   1999   95m   DeLuxe   Super 35
Entertainment/New Line/Takoma/Base-12/Kissnation
(Gene Simmons, Barry Levine, Kathleen Haase)
In the late 70s, four highschool students overcome
numerous problems in order to see their favourite
rock group Kiss give a concert in Detroit.
Sex, drugs and rock are all mixed together in a slight
drama that is only likely to be enjoyed by Kiss's fans.
w Carl V. Dupré d Adam Rifkin ph John R.
Leonetti m J. Peter Robinson ed Mark Goldblatt
☆ Edward Furlong, Giuseppe Andrews, James
DeBello, Sam Huntington, Gene Simmons, Paul
Stanley, Ace Frehley, Peter Criss, Melanie Lynskey,
Nick Scotti, Shannon Tweed
'Cruel, fast-paced, slapstick fun with an ace rock
soundtrack.' – Andrew Collins, Empire

'He's not very good-looking. But when the lights go
out... he's still not very good-looking.'
Deuce Bigalow: Male Gigolo
US   1999   88m   Technicolor
Buena Vista/Touchstone/Happy Madison/Out of the
Blue (Sid Ganis, Barry Bernardi)
After he trashes a gigolo's expensive aquarium, a
dim-witted fish fancier is forced to become a 'man-
whore', servicing unattractive women.

With Adam Sandler among the executive producers, no
one should be surprised that this is a gross, no-brow
comedy lacking wit and sense, consisting merely of a
series of crudely-done gags on bodily functions.
w Harris Goldberg, Rob Schneider d Mike
Mitchell ph Peter Lyons Collister m Teddy
Castellucci pd Alan Au ed George Bowers,
Lawrence Jordan
☆ Rob Schneider, William Forsythe, Eddie
Griffin, Arija Bareikis, Oded Fehr, Gail O'Grady,
Richard Riehle, Jacqueline Obradors
'The pic is a sign that the Sandler comedy
empire is expanding and reaching new depths of
pure gross-out stupidity.' – Robert Koehler, Variety

Deus e o Diabo na Terra do Sol: see Black
God, White Devil

Les Deux Anglaises et le Continent: see
Anne and Muriel

Deux ou trois choses que je sais d'elle:
see Two or Three Things I Know about Her

Devi *
India   1960   93m   bw
Satyajit Ray Productions
aka: The Goddess
While his son is away at university, a farmer
persuades his daughter-in-law that she is a goddess,
and the events which follow, including the death
of her son, are too much for her reason.
A curious, 'foreign' story which does not have the
usual Ray tempo or feeling for character, but wins one's
attention by its very strangeness.
wd Satyajit Ray story Prabhat Kumar Mukherjee
ph Subrata Mitra m Ali Akbar Khan ad Bansi
Chandragupta ed Dulal Dutta
☆ Chhabi Biswas, Sharmila Tagore, Soumitra
Chatterjee, Karuna Banerjee

The Devil and Daniel Webster: see All That
Money Can Buy

The Devil and Max Devlin
ff   US   1981   95m   Technicolor
Walt Disney (Jerome Courtland)
An unscrupulous apartment manager is knocked
down by a bus. Finding himself in hell, he is offered
freedom if he can buy three young souls within two
months.
Frowsty Freudian comedy, a very unhappy indication
of the depths to which Disney productions have sunk
since Walt's death. To carry this kind of thing off
requires a hundred times more style than is evidenced
here.
w Mary Rodgers d Steven Hilliard Stern
ph Howard Schwartz m Buddy Baker
☆ Elliott Gould, Bill Cosby, Susan Anspach,
Adam Rich, Charles Shamata, Ronnie Schell

The Devil and Miss Jones *
US   1941   97m   bw
RKO/Frank Ross, Norman Krasna
A millionaire masquerades as a clerk in his own
department store to investigate worker complaints.
Attractive comedy with elements of the crazy thirties
and the more socially conscious forties.
w Norman Krasna d Sam Wood ph Harry
Stradling m Roy Webb
☆ Jean Arthur, Charles Coburn, Robert
Cummings, Spring Byington, S. Z. Sakall, William
Demarest
ℶ Norman Krasna; Charles Coburn

'Her sin – their death?'
Devil and the Deep *
US   1932   73m   bw
Paramount (Emmanuel Cohen)
A submarine commander goes mad with jealousy of
his faithless wife.
A turgid melodrama notable for its stars.
w Benn Levy d Marion Gering ph Charles Lang
☆ Tallulah Bankhead, Charles Laughton, Gary
Cooper, Cary Grant, Paul Porcasi
'Of femme interest despite lukewarm
performance of Tallulah Bankhead … a fair
commercial release.' – Variety

The Devil and the Nun *

Poland   1960   108m   bw
Kadr

original title: Matka Joanna od Aniolow
aka: Mother Joan of the Angels

In a 17th-century convent nuns are possessed by
devils. A priest who tries to help is burned at the
stake; another becomes possessed himself.
*Reasonably dispassionate and fairly stylized version of
the same facts that were treated so hysterically by Ken
Russell in The Devils.*

w Tadeusz Konwicki, Jerzy Kawalerowicz
novel Jaroslav Iwaszkiewicz d Jerzy Kawalerowicz
ph Jerzy Wojcik m Adam Walacinski
☆ Lucyna Winnicka, Mieczyslaw Voit, Anna
Ciepielewska

The Devil at Four o'Clock

US   1961   126m   Eastmancolor
Columbia/Leroy/Kohlmar (Fred Kohlmar)

A drunken missionary and three convicts save a
colony of leper children from a South Seas
volcano.
*Muddled adventure melodrama with a downbeat
ending long delayed.*

w Liam O'Brien novel Max Catto d Mervyn Le
Roy ph Joseph Biroc m George Duning
☆ Spencer Tracy, Frank Sinatra, Kerwin Mathews,
Jean-Pierre Aumont, Grégoire Aslan, Alexander
Scourby, Barbara Luna

The Devil Bat

US   1941   70m   bw
PRC

A crazed scientist trains bats to kill at the scent of
a certain perfume.
Horror comic hokum from the bottom of the barrel.

w John Neville d Jean Yarbrough
☆ Bela Lugosi, Suzanne Kaaren, Dave O'Brien
† The DVD release also included Scared to Death
(qv).

Devil Bat's Daughter

US   1946   67m   bw
PRC

A girl who thinks she is the daughter of a vampire
consults a psychiatrist, who encourages her to
murder his wife.
Tolerable, potboiling shocker.

w Griffin Jay story Frank Wisbar, Ernst Jaeger
d Frank Wisbar
☆ Rosemary La Planche, John James, Michael
Hale, Nolan Leary

The Devil Came from Akasava

West Germany   1970   85m   colour
CCC Films/Fenix Films (Karl-Heinz Mannchen)

Rival groups attempt to control a stone with mystic
powers.
*Nonsensical adventure, barely competent in all
departments.*

w Paul Andre, Lladislas Fedor d Jess Frank (Jesús
Franco) ph Manuel Merino m Manfred Hubler,
Siegfried Schwab
☆ Fred Williams, Susann Korda, Horst Tappert,
Ewa Stroemberg, Siefried Schurenberg, Walter
Rilla, Paul Muller

The Devil Commands *

US   1941   65m   bw
Columbia (Wallace MacDonald)

An electrical scientist tries to communicate with
his dead wife through a medium.
*Modestly effective horror thriller, though rather too
deliberately paced.*

w Robert D. Andrews, Milton Gunzberg
story The Edge of Running Water by William Sloane
d Edward Dmytryk ph Allan G. Siegler
md Morris Stoloff
☆ Boris Karloff, Richard Fiske, Amanda Duff,
Anne Revere, Ralph Penney

Devil Dogs of the Air *

US   1935   86m   bw
Warner (Lou Edelman)

Rivalry and romance in the Marine Flying Corps.
*Standard, lively vehicle for Cagney and O'Brien, with
excellent stunt flying sequences.*

w Malcolm Stuart Boylan, Earl Baldwin
novel John Monk Saunders d Lloyd Bacon
ph Arthur Edeson md Leo F. Forbstein
☆ James Cagney, Pat O'Brien, Margaret Lindsay,
Frank McHugh, Helen Lowell, Ann Arledge,
Robert Barrat, Russell Hicks, Ward Bond
'Exhibs should have no squawks and may even
cheer if they put a little steam behind their
selling.' – Variety
'A loud and roughneck screen comedy, both
amusing and exciting.' – André Sennwald

'What Is The Strange Terrifying Evil Secret Of The
Dummy ... and why is it locked in a cage every
night?'
'Can You Keep The Secret Of The Most Diabolical
Ending Ever Filmed?'

Devil Doll

GB   1963   70m   bw
Galaworld/Gordon (Lindsay Shonteff)

A hypnotist and ventriloquist uses his doll,
containing the trapped soul of a human, to carry
out his evil purposes.
*Competent but uninspired thriller, too silly to be
effective and too obviously indebted to the much
superior Dead of Night (qv).*

w George Barclay (Ronald Kinnoch), Lance Z.
Hargreaves (Charles Vetter) story Frederick
Escreet Smith d Lindsay Shonteff ph Gerald
Gibbs ad Stan Shields ed Ernest Bullingham
☆ William Sylvester, Bryant Halliday, Yvonne
Romain, Sandra Dorne, Nora Nicholson, Alan
Gifford, Karel Stepanek, Francis de Wolff

'Earth menaced by fantastic powers!'

Devil Girl from Mars

GB   1954   76m   bw
Edward J. and Harry Lee Danziger

A female Martian is sent to Earth to bring back a
stock of men for breeding purposes.
*Absurd attempt to cash in on the new space fiction
craze. The budget matches the imagination.*

w John C. Maher, James Eastwood d David
MacDonald ph Jack Cox m Edwin Astley
☆ Patricia Laffan, Hugh McDermott, Joseph
Tomelty, Adrienne Corri, Peter Reynolds, Hazel
Court, John Laurie, Sophie Stewart
'There is really no fault in this film that one
would like to see eliminated. Everything, in its
way, is quite perfect.' – Gavin Lambert, Sight and
Sound

'Private detective Easy Rawlins has been caught on
the wrong side of the most dangerous secret in
town.'

Devil in a Blue Dress **

US   1995   102m   Technicolor
TriStar/Clinica Estetico/Mundy Lane (Jesse Beaton,
Gary Goetzman)

In Los Angeles in the late 40s, private eye Easy
Rawlins is hired to find a missing woman.
*Deft and engrossing thriller of corrupt politics and racial
and sexual tensions, well acted, and directed with
economy and style.*

wd Carl Franklin novel Walter Mosley ph Tak
Fujimoto m Elmer Bernstein pd Gary Frutkoff
ed Carole Kravetz
☆ Denzel Washington, Tom Sizemore, Jennifer
Beals, Don Cheadle, Maury Chaykin, Terry
Kinney, Mel Winkler, Albert Hall
'The most enjoyable private-eye film in a long
time: a modest, skillful, unfussy genre film that
tells an exciting story and lets its more serious
concerns remain just below the surface.' –
Terrence Rafferty, New Yorker

Devil in the Flesh: see Le Diable au Corps

The Devil Is a Sissy

US   1936   92m   bw
MGM (Frank Davis)

aka: The Devil Takes the Count

The young son of divorcing parents gets into bad
company.
Adequate juvenile melodrama.

w John Lee Mahin, Richard Schayer, Rowland
Brown d W. S. Van Dyke ph Harold Rosson,
George Schneiderman m Herbert Stothart
☆ Freddie Bartholomew, Jackie Cooper, Mickey
Rooney, Ian Hunter, Peggy Conklin, Katherine
Alexander, Gene Lockhart, Dorothy Peterson

'Men are my slaves – and glad to be!'

The Devil Is a Woman *

US   1935   82m   bw
Paramount

In Seville in the 1890s, a femme fatale has several
admirers.
*The last Dietrich vehicle to be directed by von
Sternberg, and rather splendid in its highly decorative
and uncommercial way; a treat for addicts.*

w John Dos Passos, S. K. Winston novel La
Femme et le Pantin by Pierre Louÿs d Josef von
Sternberg ph Josef von Sternberg, Lucien Ballard
m from Rimsky-Korsakov ad Hans Dreier
☆ Marlene Dietrich, Lionel Atwill, Cesar
Romero, Edward Everett Horton, Alison
Skipworth, Don Alvarado, Morgan Wallace,
Tempe Piggott
'A somewhat monotonous picture ...
sophisticated audiences are its best bet.' – Variety
'One of the most sophisticated films ever
produced in America.' – André Sennwald, New
York Times
'Light and shadow are splashed liberally around
over the white-painted sets; cafés, tobacco
factories, stairs and balconies are decorated with
every conceivable device and camera-level.' –
Peter John Dyer, 1964
'A clever, perversely dehumanized picture said to
be one of von Sternberg's favourites.' – New
Yorker, 1977

The Devil Is Driving

US   1937   69m   bw
Columbia

An attorney protects a friend's son from a drunk
driving charge, but finally indicts himself for
perjury.
Standard moral melodrama with the star in good form.

w Jo Milward, Richard Blake d Harry Lachman
☆ Richard Dix, Joan Perry, Nana Bryant, Frank C.
Wilson, Ian Wolfe, Elisha Cook Jnr, Henry Kolker,
Ann Rutherford, Walter Kingsford
'Carries a good deal of punch, but not enough to
lug it above the moderate biz bracket.' – Variety

The Devil Makes Three

US   1952   90m   bw
MGM (Richard Goldstone)

An American intelligence officer in post-war
Germany becomes involved with neo-Nazis.
*A curious break from dancing for Gene Kelly, this
obscurely titled thriller has little to commend it but
authentic locations.*

w Jerry Davis story Lawrence Bachmann
d Andrew Marton ph Vaclav Vich m Rudolph
G. Kopp
☆ Gene Kelly, Pier Angeli, Richard Rober,
Richard Egan, Claus Clausen

The Devil Never Sleeps: see Satan Never
Sleeps

Devil on Horseback

GB   1954   89m   bw
Group 3 (John Grierson, Isobel Pargiter)

A teenage jockey gets to the top the hard way.
*Highly resistible compendium of racetrack clichés and
sentiment, not at all what one expected from Group 3.*

w Neil Paterson, Montagu Slater d Cyril Frankel
ph Denny Densham m Malcolm Arnold
☆ Googie Withers, John McCallum, Jeremy
Spenser, Meredith Edwards, Liam Redmond, Sam
Kydd

The Devil, Probably *

France   1977   95m   Eastmancolor
Sunchold/GMF (Stéphane Tchalgadchieff)

original title: Le Diable, Probablement

A young Parisian goes to the devil and arranges to
have himself shot.
*A despairing vision of an arid world, seen through
unpleasant details of city life. A fascinating but
enervated film very typical of its director.*

wd Robert Bresson ph Pasqualino de Santis
m Philippe Sarde pd Eric Simon
☆ Antoine Monnier, Tina Irissari, Henri de
Maublanc

The Devil Rides Out *

GB   1968   95m   Technicolor
Warner/Hammer (Anthony Nelson-Keys)

US title: The Devil's Bride

The Duc de Richleau rescues a friend from a group
of Satanists.
*Rather stodgy adaptation of a frightening novel;
moments of suspense.*

w Richard Matheson novel Dennis Wheatley
d Terence Fisher ph Arthur Grant m James
Bernard ad Bernard Robinson ed James Needs,
Spencer Reeve
☆ Christopher Lee, Charles Gray, Leon Greene,
Patrick Mower, Gwen Ffrangcon-Davies

Devil Ship Pirates

GB   1964   96m   Technicolor   Hammerscope
ABP/Hammer (Anthony Nelson-Keys)

At the time of the Armada, Spanish privateers
terrorize a Cornish seaside village.
*Lacklustre pirate yarn with not much action and some
elements of Hammer horror.*

w Jimmy Sangster d Don Sharp ph Michael
Reed m Gary Hughes ad Bernard Robinson, Don
Mingaye ed James Needs
☆ Christopher Lee, John Cairney, Barry Warren,
Ernest Clark, Andrew Keir, Duncan Lamont

The Devil Takes the Count: see The Devil Is a
Sissy

The Devil Thumbs a Ride

US   1947   63m   bw
RKO

A commercial traveller gives a lift to a man who
turns out to be wanted for murder.
*Predictable suspenser without much entertainment
value.*

wd Felix Feist
☆ Ted North, Lawrence Tierney, Nan Leslie

The Devil to Pay *

US   1930   72m   bw
Samuel Goldwyn

The prodigal son of a snooty English family returns
to cheer them all up.
*Agreeably lighthearted star comedy in the drawing-
room tradition.*

w Frederick Lonsdale d George Fitzmaurice
ph Gregg Toland, George Barnes m Alfred
Newman
☆ Ronald Colman, Loretta Young, Myrna Loy,
Frederick Kerr
'Snappy British comedy that should please
everywhere ... a set-up for femmes.' – Variety
'Six reels of Mr Colman being charming ... a
polished, tasteful and entirely likeable screen
comedy.' – New York Herald Tribune

The Devil with Hitler

US   1942   44m   bw
Hal Roach

Hell's board of directors want to sack Satan and
bring in Hitler.
*Somewhat infantile war farce, one of this producer's
very few successful medium-length 'screenliners'.*

w Cortland FitzSimmons, Al Martin d Gordon
Douglas
☆ Alan Mowbray, Bobby Watson, George E.
Stone, Joe Devlin
† The Hays Office gave special permission, in a
just cause, for the use of the word 'Hell'.

A Devil with Women

US   1930   76m   bw
Fox (George Middleton)

Soldiers of fortune in a banana republic end the
regime of a notorious bandit and compete for a fair
señorita.
Primitive Flagg-and-Quirt style knockabout.

w Dudley Nichols, Henry M. Johnson novel Dust
and Sun by Clements Ripley d Irving Cummings
ph Arthur Todd m Peter Brunelli
☆ Victor McLaglen, Humphrey Bogart, Mona
Maris, Michael Vavitch
'No real plot or continuity, but has some laughs.
Best for neighbourhood grinds.' – Variety

Devil within Her (dubbed)
Italy 1974 109m Technicolor
UA/AR Cinematografica (Ovisio Assonitis, Giorgio C. Rossi)
🔲 ⬛
original title: *Chi Sei?*
US title: *Beyond the Door*
The Devil gives a black magician ten days to obtain the unborn child of his former mistress.
An unoriginal and unexciting variation on The Exorcist, repeating to lesser effect that film's tricks.
w Sonia Molteni, Antonio Troisio, Giorgio Marini, Aldo Crudo, Robert D'Ettore Piazzoli d Oliver Hellman ph Robert D'Ettore Piazzoli m Franco Micalizzi ad Piero Filippone, Franco Pellecchia Velchi ed Angelo Curi
☆ Juliet Mills, Richard Johnson, Gabriele Lavia, Barbara Fiorini, David Colin Jnr, Joan Acti
'A disastrous foray into the fashionable area of demonic possession, unencumbered with any trace of subtlety or conviction.' – *Verina Glaessner*

The Devil within Her: see *I Don't Want to Be Born (1975)*

Devil-Doll **
US 1936 79m bw
MGM (E. J. Mannix)
🔲
A refugee from Devil's Island disguises himself as an old lady who sells human dolls which murder those responsible for his imprisonment.
Interesting rather than exciting tall tale with a Paris backdrop; despite impressive moments it does not quite have the right frisson.
w Tod Browning, Garrett Fort, Erich von Stroheim, Guy Endore novel *Burn Witch Burn* by A. A. Merritt d Tod Browning ph Leonard Smith m Franz Waxman ad Cedric Gibbons
☆ Lionel Barrymore, Maureen O'Sullivan, Frank Lawton, Henry B. Walthall, Rafaela Ottiano, Grace Ford, Arthur Hohl
'Grotesque, slightly horrible and consistently interesting.' – *Frank Nugent, New York Times*

'Hell holds no surprises ... for them!'
The Devils **
GB 1970 111m Technicolor Panavision
Warner/Russo (Robert H. Solo, Ken Russell)
🔲 ⬛ 🎧
An account of the apparent demoniacal possession of the 17th-century nuns of Loudun, climaxing in the burning of their priest as a sorcerer.
Despite undeniable technical proficiency this is its writer-director's most outrageously sick film to date, campy, idiosyncratic and in howling bad taste from beginning to end, full of worm-eaten skulls, masturbating nuns, gibbering courtiers, plague sores, rats and a burning to death before our very eyes ... plus a sacrilegious dream of Jesus.
wd Ken Russell play John Whiting book *The Devils of Loudun* by Aldous Huxley ph David Watkin m Peter Maxwell Davies ad Robert Cartwright
☆ Vanessa Redgrave, Oliver Reed, Dudley Sutton, Max Adrian, Gemma Jones, Murray Melvin, Michael Gothard, Graham Armitage
'Ken Russell doesn't report hysteria, he markets it.' – *New Yorker, 1976*
'Russell's swirling multi-colored puddle ... made me glad that both Huxley and Whiting are dead, so that they are spared this farrago of witless exhibitionism.' – *Stanley Kauffmann*
'A garish glossary of sado-masochism ... a taste for visual sensation that makes scene after scene look like the masturbatory fantasies of a Roman Catholic boyhood.' – *Alexander Walker*

'Evil Has Its Winning Ways.'
Devil's Advocate
US 1997 144m Technicolor Panavision
Warner (Arnon Milchan, Arnold Kopelson, Anne Kopelson)
🔲 ⬛ 🎬 ⊙ ⊙ 🎧
A successful young lawyer is tempted to join a big New York firm that is run by the Devil.
A perfunctory thriller that seems mainly designed to provide Al Pacino with an opportunity to overact, which he accepts with relish.
w Jonathan Lemkin, Tony Gilroy novel Andrew Neiderman d Taylor Hackford ph Andrzej Bartkowiak m James Newton Howard pd Bruno Rubeo ed Mark Warner

☆ Keanu Reeves, Al Pacino, Charlize Theron, Jeffrey Jones, Judith Ivey, Connie Neilsen, Craig T. Nelson, Delroy Lindo (uncredited)
'A fairly entertaining supernatural potboiler that finally bubbles over with a nearly operatic sense of absurdity and excess.' – *Todd McCarthy, Variety*

The Devil's Advocate
West Germany 1977 109m colour
Geria (Lutz Hengst)
A dying priest is summoned to Rome to investigate the cult of a dead partisan nominated for sainthood.
Well-meaning but rather tepid and inconclusive adaptation of a bestseller which presumably made its points more firmly.
w Morris West novel Morris West d Guy Green ph Billy Williams m Bert Grund
☆ John Mills, Stéphane Audran, Jason Miller, Timothy West, Patrick Mower, Paola Pitagora, Daniel Massey, Leigh Lawson, Raf Vallone, Jack Hedley

The Devil's Agent
GB 1962 77m bw
British Lion/Emmet Dalton
A wine salesman in Germany is duped by Soviet agents.
Scrappy cold war adventures which look as though they were originally intended as episodes in a TV series.
w Robert Westerby d John Paddy Carstairs ph Gerald Gibbs m Philip Green
☆ Peter Van Eyck, Marianne Koch, Macdonald Carey, Christopher Lee, Billie Whitelaw, David Knight, Marius Goring, Helen Cherry, Colin Gordon, Niall MacGinnis, Eric Pohlmann, Peter Vaughan

Devil's Bait
GB 1959 58m bw
Rank/Independent Artists
A baker accidentally bakes a loaf containing poison.
B-feature thriller of minimal interest.
w Peter Johnson, Diana K. Watson d Peter Graham Scott ph Michael Reed m William Alwyn md Muir Mathieson ad Eric Saw ed John Trumper
☆ Geoffrey Keen, Jane Hylton, Gordon Jackson, Rupert Davies, Dermot Kelly

The Devil's Bride: see *The Devil Rides Out*

The Devil's Brigade
US 1968 132m DeLuxe Panavision
UA/David L. Wolper
🔲 🎬
For combat in Norway and Italy during World War II a US officer assembles a platoon of thugs and misfits to work with crack Canadian commandos.
Flagrant but routine imitation of The Dirty Dozen, quite undistinguished.
w William Roberts book Robert H. Adleman, George Walton d Andrew V. McLaglen ph William Clothier m Alex North
☆ William Holden, Cliff Robertson, Vince Edwards, Andrew Prine, Claude Akins, Carroll O'Connor, Richard Jaeckel
'After nearly three decades of World War II films, it is hardly surprising that Hollywood is beginning to suffer from combat fatigue.' – *Time*

The Devil's Brother: see *Fra Diavolo*

Devil's Canyon
US 1953 92m Technicolor 3-D
RKO/Edmund Grainger
🔲
Life in a notorious Arizona prison in the 1880s; a marshal is unjustly convicted but wins his pardon.
Fairly brutal Western, quite unmemorable.
w Frederick Hazlitt Brennan d Alfred Werker ph Nicholas Musuraca m Daniele Amfitheatrof
☆ Dale Robertson, Virginia Mayo, Stephen McNally, Arthur Hunnicutt, Robert Keith, Jay C. Flippen, Whit Bissell

The Devil's Disciple *
GB 1959 82m bw
UA/Hecht-Hill-Lancaster/Brynaprod (Harold Hecht)
🔲
In 1777 an American ne'er-do-well almost allows himself to be hanged by the British in mistake for a rebel pastor.
Star-studded but indifferently staged adaptation of a minor Shavian frolic. Patchy, with good moments.
w John Dighton, Roland Kibbee play Bernard Shaw d Guy Hamilton ph Jack Hildyard m Richard Rodney Bennett ad Terence Verity, Edward Carere
☆ Burt Lancaster, Kirk Douglas, Laurence Olivier, Eva Le Gallienne, Janette Scott, Harry Andrews, Basil Sidney, George Rose, Neil McCallum, David Horne, Mervyn Johns

Devil's Doorway
US 1950 84m bw
MGM (Nicholas Nayfack)
A Shoshone Indian fights valiantly in the Civil War but on his return to Wyoming finds himself hated and threatened by his former colleagues.
Dull pro-Indian Western with a most unsuitable star.
w Guy Trosper d Anthony Mann ph John Alton m Daniele Amfitheatrof
☆ Robert Taylor, Louis Calhern, Paula Raymond, Marshall Thompson, James Mitchell, Edgar Buchanan, Rhys Williams, Spring Byington

The Devil's Eight
US 1968 98m Pathécolor
AIP/Burt Topper
A federal agent on the trail of a moonshine gang recruits a gang of hardened convicts and arranges for them to escape.
The Dirty Dozen all over again, and not good.
w James Gordon White, Willard Huyck, John Milius d Burt Topper ph Richard C. Glouner m Mike Curb
☆ Christopher George, Ralph Meeker, Fabian, Tom Nardini, Leslie Parrish, Ross Hagen

The Devil's Envoys: see *Les Visiteurs du Soir*

The Devil's Eye *
Sweden 1960 90m bw
Svensk Filmindustri
🔲
An old proverb says that a woman's chastity is a stye in the devil's eye. So when Satan has a sore eye he comes down to earth to put things right.
Surprisingly shoddily-made comedy with just a few of the sharpnesses of technique and mystifications of plot which one had come to expect from this maestro.
wd Ingmar Bergman ph Gunnar Fischer m Domenico Scarlatti
☆ Jarl Kulle, Bibi Andersson, Nils Poppe, Stig Järrel, Gunnar Björnstrand

The Devil's General
West Germany 1955 121m bw
Ryal (Gyula Trebitsch)
In 1941 a German air ace becomes estranged from the high command and is tortured by the Gestapo. On release he helps a Jewish couple ...
Heavy-going melodrama which nevertheless paints a convincing picture of Berlin during the war.
w George Hurdalek, Helmut Kautner play Carl Zuckmayer d Helmut Kautner ph Albert Benitz
☆ Curt Jurgens, Victor de Kowa, Karl John, Eva-Ingeborg Scholz

The Devil's Hairpin
US 1957 83m Technicolor Vistavision
Paramount/Cornel Wilde
A former motor racing champion makes a comeback, and redeems his past boorish behaviour.
Efficient routine melodramatics with good action sequences.
w James Edmiston, Cornel Wilde d Cornel Wilde ph Daniel Fapp m Van Cleave
☆ Cornel Wilde, Jean Wallace, Arthur Franz, Mary Astor, Paul Fix

Devil's Holiday *
US 1930 80m bw
Paramount
A mercenary lady repents her life on the make.
Very dated moral story which at the time was showered with praise.
wd Edmund Goulding

☆ Nancy Carroll, Phillips Holmes, James Kirkwood, Hobart Bosworth, Ned Sparks, Jed Prouty, Paul Lukas, ZaSu Pitts
'It is pictures such as this which revive the drooping confidence in the screen as a mirror of things as they really are.' – *Variety*
ȣ Nancy Carroll

The Devil's Impostor: see *Pope Joan*

The Devil's in Love
US 1933 70m bw
Fox
At a French Foreign Legion post, an outcast doctor falls in love with the niece of a mission father.
Old-fashioned and predictable romantic drama.
w Howard Estabrook story Harry Hervey d William Dieterle
☆ Victor Jory, Loretta Young, Vivienne Osborne, David Manners, C. Henry Gordon, Herbert Mundin, J. Carrol Naish
'Given any kind of a break returns should be fair.' – *Variety*

Devil's Island *
US 1939 63m bw
Warner (Bryan Foy)
A surgeon is sent to Devil's Island for aiding an escaped convict.
Sharply-made exposé of the notorious French penal colony; commendable pace and vigour all round.
w Kenneth Gamet, Don Ryan d William Clemens
☆ Boris Karloff, James Stephenson, Nedda Harrigan, Adia Kuznetzoff, Robert Warwick, Pedro de Cordoba
'It is being touted as an "uncensored" version. But there is nothing in it that could startle a well-protected child of seven or give pause even to a censor.' – *Variety*

Devil's Island **
Iceland/Norway/Germany/Denmark 1996 103m colour
Theatrical Experience/IFC/Zentropa (Fridrik Thor Fridricksson, Egil ödergaard, Peter Rommel)
original title: *Djöflaeyjan*
In Iceland in the 50s, a man returns from America to live with his poverty-striken family in an abandoned US military barracks.
Engaging, episodic domestic drama, an effective mix of comedy and tragedy, among society's misfits.
w Einar Kárason d Fridrik Thor Fridriksson ph Ari Kristinsson m Hilmar örn Hilmarsson pd Arni Páll Jóhansson ed Steingrimur Karlsson, Skule Eriksen
☆ Baltasar Kormakur, Sveinn Geirsson, Gisli Halldorsson, Sigurveig Jonsdottir, Halldora Geirhardsdottir

The Devil's Kiss (dubbed)
Spain/Andorra 1974 104m colour
Andros
original title: *La Perversa Caricia De Satan*
With the aid of a telepath, a woman uses occult powers to seek revenge on those who wronged her and caused the death of her husband.
Dull horror movie, taken at a plodding pace; the music, dialogue, and acting are its true terrors.
wd Georges Gigo (Jorge Luis Gigo) ph Julio Peréz de Rozas m Albert Argudo ed Albert Gasset Nicolau
☆ Silvia Solar, Oliver Matthau (Olivier Mathot), Evelyne Scott, Daniel Martin, Jose Nieto, Ronnie Harp, Wendy Asher

The Devil's Mask
US 1946 66m bw
Columbia
An unclaimed parcel containing a shrunken head is found after a plane crash; murder follows.
Involved but amusing entry in the I Love a Mystery series.
w Charles O'Neal d Henry Levin
☆ Jim Bannon, Anita Louise, Michael Duane, Mona Barrie, Byron Foulger

The Devil's Nightmare
Belgium/France 1971 95m colour
Delfino/Cetelci
🔲
original title: *La Plus Longue Nuit du Diable*
Seven stranded travellers take shelter in a mansion occupied by a cursed family.

Predictable horror in which one murder follows another, whenever one of the seven deadly sins is committed; the overemphatic direction kills any suspense.

w Jean Brismée, Charles Lecocq, Patrice Rhomm, André Hunnebelle d Jean Brismée ph André Goeffers

☆ Erika Blanc, Jean Servais, Jacques Monseau, Lucien Raimbourg, Daniel Emilfork, Ivana Novak, Shirley Corrigan

Devils of Darkness

GB   1964   90m   Eastmancolor
Planet (Tom Blakeley)

A writer discovers that mysterious deaths in Brittany are caused by Count Sinistre and his gypsy bride, vampires who are protected by the locals.
Lacklustre low-budget horror, given a modern setting apart from its prologue; the script pits English rectitude against French perversity.

w Lyn Fairhurst d Lance Comfort ph Reg Wyer m Bernie Fenton ad John St John Earl ed John Trumper

☆ William Sylvester, Hubert Noel, Carole Gray, Tracy Reed, Diana Decker, Rona Anderson, Eddie Byrne, Gerard Heinz, Peter Illing, Brian Oulton

'Flat direction and cheap sets and camerawork make this one of the least atmospheric British horror movies of all time.' – *The Dark Side*

The Devil's Own: see The Witches (1966)

'One man trapped by destiny, and another bound by duty. They're about to discover what they're willing to live, to fight, and to die for.'

The Devil's Own

US   1997   110m   Technicolor   Panavision
Columbia (Lawrence Gordon, Robert F. Colesberry)

An IRA hitman goes to America to buy missiles and lodges with a New York cop who hates violence.
Dull glamorization of thuggery and male bonding.

w David Aaron Cohen, Vincent Patrick, Kevin Jarre d Alan J. Pakula ph Gordon Willis m James Horner pd Jane Musky ed Tom Rolf, Dennis Virkler

☆ Harrison Ford, Brad Pitt, Margaret Colin, Ruben Blades, Treat Williams, George Hearn, Mitchell Ryan, Natascha McElhone

'From the opening caterwauling … you can tell this film is going to be rubbish, and it is.' – *Andrew Harrison, Neon*

† The film cost some $95m and grossed around $42.9m in the US.

The Devil's Playground

US   1946   66m   bw
UA/Hopalong Cassidy (Lewis J. Rachmil)

Hoppy and his friends save a girl and stolen gold from a crooked judge and his gang.
Pleasant 'B' Western that mixes comedy and action to amiable effect.

w Ted Wilson d George Archainbaud ph Mack Stengler m David Chudnow ad Harvey T. Gillett ed Fred W. Berger

☆ William Boyd, Andy Clyde, Rand Brooks, Elaine Riley, Robert Elliott, Joseph J. Greene, Francis McDonald, Ned Young

The Devil's Playground *

Australia   1976   107m   Eastmancolor
The Feature Film House (Fred Schepisi)

Tensions between masters and boys in a Catholic seminary in the fifties.
Well made but rather dislikeable intrusion into Mr Perrin and Mr Traill country with the addition of modern frankness.

wd Fred Schepisi ph Ian Baker m Bruce Smeaton
☆ Arthur Dignam, Nick Tate, Simon Burke, Charles McCallum, John Frawley

The Devil's Rain

US   1975   86m   colour   Todd-AO 35
Rank/Sandy Howard (James V. Cullen, Michael S. Glick)

Witchcraft in the modern west causes victims to melt; the son of one of them takes arms against the leading Satanist.
Interestingly cast example of the low-budget seventies exploitation picture, with more nastiness than logic.

---

w Gabe Essoe, James Ashton, Gerald Hopman d Robert Fuest ph Alex Phillips Jnr m Al de Lory

☆ Ernest Borgnine, Ida Lupino, Eddie Albert, William Shatner, Keenan Wynn, Tom Skerritt

The Devil's Wanton *

Sweden   1949   80m   bw
Terrafilm

original title: *Fängelse*
aka: *Prison*

Film-makers discuss some rather unpleasant projects but put them aside as unsatisfactory.
A bit of a Scandinavian wallow, with heavy expressionism and low-life themes.

wd Ingmar Bergman ph Göran Strindberg m Erland von Koch

☆ Doris Svedlund, Birger Malmsten, Eva Henning, Hasse Ekman

'It employs all the paraphernalia associated with Scandinavian angst.' – *John Gillett, MFB*

The Devil's Widow: see Tam-Lin

Devlin

US   1992   106m   colour
Viacom (Paula de Oliviera, Craig Roessler)

A cop fights back when he discovers he is being framed for the murder of his brother-in-law, a leading politician.
An unoriginal movie that is acted and directed with enough pace and energy to make it enjoyable.

w David Taylor novel Roderick Thorp d Rick Rosenthal ph Neil Roach m John Altman pd Barbara Dunphy ed Tony Gibbs

☆ Bryan Brown, Roma Downey, Lloyd Bridges, Whip Hubley, Lawrence Dane, Lisa Eichhorn, Carole Shelley, Jan Rubes, Frances Fisher

'A slick thriller that really does thrill.' – *Alan Frank, Movies*

Devotion

US   1931   84m   bw
RKO-Pathé

A woman falls in love with a barrister and takes a job as governess to his son.
Rather winsome tear-jerker entirely dependent on its stars.

w Graham John, Horace Jackson novel A Little Flat in the Temple by Pamela Wynne d Robert Milton

☆ Ann Harding, Leslie Howard, Robert Williams, O. P. Heggie, Louise Closser Hale, Dudley Digges

'Much talk and little action. Star's name is best chance of rating more than mild financially.' – *Variety*

'It tells ALL about those Brontë sisters! … They didn't dare call it love – they tried to call it devotion!'

Devotion **

US   1946   107m   bw
Warner (Robert Buckner)

A highly romanticized account of the lives of the Brontë sisters and their brother Branwell.
An enjoyable bad example of a big-budget Hollywood production which tampers with things it cannot understand; in this case life in a Yorkshire parsonage in Victorian times. An excuse is found to give the curate an Austrian accent to fit the available actor, but this and other faux pas are atoned for by the vividness of Emily's recurrent dream of death as a silhouetted man on horseback. In general, an interesting period piece in more senses than one.

w Keith Winter d Curtis Bernhardt ph Ernest Haller m Erich Wolfgang Korngold

☆ Ida Lupino, Olivia de Havilland, Nancy Coleman, Arthur Kennedy, Montagu Love, Paul Henreid, Ethel Griffies, Sydney Greenstreet, Eily Malyon, Forrester Harvey, Victor Francen

'I found it painless. It never got nearer to the subject than names and consequently didn't hurt. But I would like to know who was devoted to whom and why.' – *Richard Winnington*

† More items from the extraordinary publicity campaign devised by Warner for this placid Victorian museum:
Emily: she ruled in that strange quiet house! None could resist the force of her will!
The man in black (i.e. the Revd Nicholls): he fled from her demands into her sister's arms!
Charlotte: the sweetness of love and the meaning of torment – she learned them both together!

The 'friend' – the furious fat man (i.e. William Makepeace Thackeray): they couldn't fool him – they couldn't trust him!
Dialogue includes the celebrated exchange between two celebrated London literary figures:
dickens: 'Morning, Thackeray.'
thackeray: 'Morning, Dickens.'
†† Made in 1943, but not released until later.

Dharmaga Tongjoguro Kan Kkadalgun?: see Why Did Bodhi-Dharma Leave for the East?

The DI

US   1957   106m   bw
Warner/Mark VII (Jack Webb)

A tough marine drill instructor takes a special interest in a backward member of his platoon.
Noisy recruiting poster heroics in which the producer gives himself a loud but boring part. The drill sequences are well done, but the film is overlong and repetitive.

w James Lee Barrett d Jack Webb ph Edward Colman m David Buttolph

☆ Jack Webb, Don Dubbins, Jackie Loughery, Lin McCarthy, Monica Lewis

El Dia de la Bestia: see The Day of the Beast

Le Diable au Corps *

France   1947   110m   bw
Transcontinental
US title: *Devil in the Flesh*

When her husband is away at war, a young married woman falls for a college student and dies bearing his child.
A love story of World War I; a great commercial success, but tending to be slow and dreary.

w Jean Aurenche, Pierre Bost novel Raymond Radiguet d Claude Autant-Lara ph Michel Kelber m René Cloërc

☆ Micheline Presle, Gérard Philipe, Jean Debucourt, Denise Grey, Jacques Tati

Le Diable, Probablement: see The Devil, Probably

Diabolique: see Les Diaboliques

Diabolique

US   1996   107m   Technicolor
Warner/Morgan Creek/Marvin Worth/ABC (Marvin Worth, James G. Robinson)

The wife and mistress of an unpleasant schoolmaster conspire to murder him, with unexpected results.
An appalling remake of Henri-Georges Clouzot's masterly Les Diaboliques; it is boring, badly made and miserably acted.

w Don Roos novel Celle qui n'était plus by Pierre Boileau and Thomas Narcejec d Jeremiah Chechik ph Peter James m Randy Edelman pd Leslie Dilley ed Carol Littleton

☆ Sharon Stone, Isabelle Adjani, Chazz Palminteri, Kathy Bates, Spalding Gray, Shirley Knight, Allen Garfield

'As mouldy as anything ever laid before an audience.' – *Tom Hutchinson, Film Review*
'While the original grabbed you by the synapses and shook hard, this amounts to watchable nonsense enacted by unbelievable people in a preposterous scenario.' – *Ian Nathan, Empire*
'The filmmakers have turned silk into a sow's ear, giving people new reason to fear Hollywood remakes of quality foreign films.' – *Variety*

Les Diaboliques ***

France   1954   114m   bw
Filmsonor (Henri-Georges Clouzot)

aka: *Diabolique*
GB title: *The Fiends*

A sadistic headmaster's wife and mistress conspire to murder him; but his body disappears and evidence of his presence haunts them.
Highly influential, suspenseful and scary thriller with a much-copied twist typical of its authors. Slow to start and shabby-looking as befits its grubby school setting, it gathers momentum with the murder and turns the screw with fine professionalism.

w Henri-Georges Clouzot, G. Geronimi novel The Woman Who Was by Pierre Boileau and Thomas Narcejac d Henri-Georges Clouzot ph Armand Thirard m Georges Van Parys

☆ Simone Signoret, Vera Clouzot, Charles Vanel, Paul Meurisse

---

'Scary, but so calculatedly sensational that it's rather revolting.' – *New Yorker, 1978*
'It depends very much on the intimate details of the seedy fourth-rate school, with its inadequate education and uneatable food, its general smell of unwashed children, hatred and petty perversions.' – *Basil Wright, 1972*
† Remade in 1976 as a TV movie, *Reflections of Murder.*

Diagnosis: Murder

GB   1974   90m   Eastmancolor
Silhouette (Patrick Dromgoole, Peter Miller)

A psychiatrist's wife disappears, and the police suspect her husband.
Well-upholstered but sadly old-fashioned domestic crime thriller; one is vaguely surprised to see it in colour, having seen it so often in black-and-white.

w Philip Levene d Sidney Hayers ph Bob Edwards m Laurie Johnson

☆ Jon Finch, Judy Geeson, Christopher Lee, Tony Beckley, Dilys Hamlett, Jane Merrow, Colin Jeavons

Dial 1119 *

US   1950   75m   bw
MGM (Richard Goldstone)
GB title: *The Violent Hour*

An assortment of people are held up in a bar by a maniac.
Suspenseful thriller when it sticks to its central theme; dullish when it tries characterization. A good second feature.

w John Monks Jnr d Gerald Mayer ph Paul Vogel m André Previn

☆ Marshall Thompson, Virginia Field, Andrea King, Leon Ames, Keefe Brasselle, Richard Rober, James Bell, William Conrad

'If a woman answers – hang on for dear life!'

Dial M For Murder **

US   1954   105m   Warnercolor   3-D
Warner (Alfred Hitchcock)

An ageing tennis champion tries to arrange the death of his wife so that he will inherit, but his complex plan goes wrong.
Hitchcock did not try very hard to adapt this highly commercial play for the cinema, nor did he exploit the possibilities of 3-D. But for a one-room film with a not very exciting cast the film holds its grip pretty well.

w Frederick Knott play Frederick Knott d Alfred Hitchcock ph Robert Burks m Dimitri Tiomkin ed Rudi Fehr

☆ Ray Milland, John Williams, Grace Kelly, Robert Cummings, Anthony Dawson

'All this is related with Hitchcock's ghoulish chic but everyone in it seems to be walking around with tired blood.' – *Pauline Kael, 1968*
† Although shot in 3-D, it was never released in that form.

The Diamond

GB   1954   83m   bw   3D
Gibraltar Films (Stephen Pallos)
US title: *The Diamond Wizard*

An American agent in London investigates a million-dollar treasury robbery involving a process for making synthetic diamonds.
Leaden cops-and-robbers which went out on the bottom of a bill instead of being shown in three dimensions.

w John C. Higgins story The Bowstring Murders by Maurice Proctor d Montgomery Tully m Matyas Seiber

☆ Dennis O'Keefe, Margaret Sheridan, Philip Friend, Alan Wheatley, Francis de Wolff

Diamond City

GB   1949   90m   bw
GFD/Gainsborough (A. Frank Bundy)

Law and order is maintained during the working of a South African diamond field.
British imitation of a Wyatt Earp Western; very milk-and-water.

w Roger Bray, Roland Pertwee d David MacDonald ph Reginald Wyer m Clifton Parker

☆ David Farrar, Honor Blackman, Diana Dors, Niall MacGinnis, Andrew Crawford, Mervyn Johns, Bill Owen, Phyllis Monkman

Diamond Frontier

US   1940   72m   bw
Universal

An honest diamond dealer is framed and sent to prison.

Co-feature action stuff, with South Africa standing in for the west.
w Edmund L. Hartmann, Stanley Rubin d Harold Schuster
☆ Victor McLaglen, Anne Nagel, John Loder, Philip Dorn, Cecil Kellaway

Diamond Head
US 1962 107m Eastmancolor Panavision
Columbia (Jerry Bresler)
▄▄ ⊙~
A domineering Hawaiian landowner almost ruins the lives of his family.
Predictable, heavy-going transcription of a bestseller.
w Marguerite Roberts novel Peter Gilman d Guy Green ph Sam Leavitt m Johnny Williams
☆ Charlton Heston, Yvette Mimieux, George Chakiris, France Nuyen, James Darren, Aline MacMahon, Elizabeth Allen, Richard Loo

Diamond Horseshoe
US 1945 104m Technicolor
TCF (William Perlberg)
▄▄
aka: *Billy Rose's Diamond Horseshoe*
A night-club singer gives up her career for a medical student.
Lavish but humourless star vehicle with standard numbers.
wd George Seaton play The Barker by Kenyon Nicholson ph Ernest Palmer m/ly Mack Gordon, Harry Warren
☆ Betty Grable, Dick Haymes, William Gaxton, Phil Silvers, Beatrice Kay, Carmen Cavallero, Margaret Dumont

Diamond Jim *
US 1935 93m bw
Universal (Edmund Grainger)
A fantasia on the life of the 1890s millionaire who sailed pretty close to the wind in business, adored Lillian Russell, and developed a gargantuan appetite.
Cheerful period comedy drama with plenty of gusto.
w Preston Sturges d A. Edward Sutherland ph George Robinson m Ferde Grofe, Franz Waxman
☆ Edward Arnold, Jean Arthur, Binnie Barnes, Cesar Romero, Eric Blore
'Good picture and title. Lacks real pull names.' – *Variety*

The Diamond Mercenaries
Switzerland/Ireland/South Africa 1975 101m colour
Michelangelo (Nat Wachsberger)
aka: *Killer Force*
A patrol guard joins a group of mercenaries to steal diamonds from a mine where there is a ruthless head of security.
Muddled and routine action movie which lacks a clear focus.
w Michael Winder, Gerald Sanford, Val Guest d Val Guest ph David Millin m Georges Garvarentz ad Peter Church ed Bill Butler
☆ Peter Fonda, Telly Savalas, Hugh O'Brian, Christopher Lee, Maud Adams, O. J. Simpson, Ian Yule
'Disappointingly fails to gel.' – *MFB*

The Diamond Queen
US 1953 80m Supercinecolor
Warner/Melson (Frank Melford, Edward L. Alperson Jnr)
Frenchmen journey to India to bring back a diamond for the crown of Louis XIV.
The adventures are basically lively enough to warrant a better production.
w Otto Englander d John Brahm ph Stanley Cortez m Paul Sawtell
☆ Fernando Lamas, Arlene Dahl, Gilbert Roland, Sheldon Leonard, Michael Ansara

Diamond Skulls
GB 1989 87m Technicolor
Virgin Vision/Working Title/British Screen/Channel 4 (Tim Bevan)
▄▄
US title: *Dark Obsession*
An aristocrat kills a woman in a hit-and-run accident and lets his friend take the blame.
Confused melodrama of sex and the old boy network that seems uncertain of what kind of film it wants to be.

w Tim Rose Price d Nick Broomfield ph Michael Coulter m Hans Zimmer pd Jocelyn James ed Rodney Holland
☆ Gabriel Byrne, Amanda Donohoe, Michael Hordern, Judy Parfitt, Douglas Hodge, Sadie Frost, Matthew Marsh, Ian Carmichael
'All in all, a promising portrait of aristocratic thuggery in changing times, yet ultimately too diffuse to deliver its punch with the force it needs.' – *Julian Petley, MFB*

The Diamond Wizard: see *The Diamond*

Diamonds
US 1975 108m Eastmancolor
Avco Embassy/AmeriEuro (Menahem Golan)
⊙
A London diamond merchant sets himself up to be robbed so that he can blackmail the culprits into a raid on the Tel Aviv diamond repository.
Cheerful but unremarkable caper movie with an upbeat ending.
w David Paulsen, Menahem Golan d Menahem Golan ph Adam Greenberg m Roy Budd
☆ Robert Shaw, Richard Roundtree, Barbara Seagull, Shelley Winters

Diamonds Are Forever *
♠♠ GB 1971 120m Technicolor Panavision
UA/Eon/Danjaq (Harry Saltzman, Albert R. Broccoli)
▄▄ ▄▄ ⊙~
Seeking a diamond smuggler, James Bond has adventures in Amsterdam, a Los Angeles crematorium, various Las Vegas gambling parlours, and a secret installation in the desert.
Campy, rather vicious addition to a well-worn cycle, with an element of nastiness which big-budget stunts cannot conceal. Panavision does not help, and Connery's return to the role is disappointing.
w Richard Maibaum, Tom Mankiewicz novel Ian Fleming d Guy Hamilton ph Ted Moore m John Barry pd Ken Adam
☆ Sean Connery, Jill St John, Charles Gray, Lana Wood, Jimmy Dean, Bruce Cabot, Bernard Lee, Lois Maxwell
'It has been claimed that the plot is impossible to describe, but I think I could if I wanted to. I can't think why anyone would want to, though.' – *Roger Ebert*

Diamonds for Breakfast
GB 1968 102m Eastmancolor
Paramount/Bridge Films (Carlo Ponti, Pierre Rouve)
An impoverished Russian aristocrat decides to retrieve from a museum the crown jewels of his ancestors, and seduces seven female accomplices.
Yawning caper yarn embellished with sex and slapstick.
w N. F. Simpson, Pierre Rouve, Ronald Harwood d Christopher Morahan ph Gerry Turpin m Norman Kay
☆ Marcello Mastroianni, Rita Tushingham, Elaine Taylor, Warren Mitchell, Nora Nicholson, Bill Fraser, Leonard Rossiter

Diane
US 1956 110m Eastmancolor Cinemascope
MGM (Edwin H. Knopf)
▄▄
Diane de Poitiers becomes a consultant to the king and falls in love with his son.
Solidly boring slice of Hollywood history, with all concerned out of their depth.
w Christopher Isherwood d David Miller ph Robert Planck m Miklos Rozsa
☆ Lana Turner, Roger Moore, Cedric Hardwicke, Pedro Armendariz, Marisa Pavan

Diary for My Children ***
Hungary 1982 107m bw
Artificial Eye/Mafilm/Hungarofilm
original title: *Napló Gyermekeimnek*
An orphan, returning to Budapest in 1947, recalls her happy childhood while dealing with a less enjoyable present.
Three generations of a family encapsulate the modern history of Hungary in a gripping film. Withheld from the West for two years, it won a special jury prize at the Cannes Film Festival in 1984.
w Márta Mészáros, Balàzs Fakan, András Szeredás d Márta Mészáros ph Miklós Jancsó Jnr m Zsolt Döme
☆ Zsuzsa Czinkóczi, Anna Polony, Jan Nowicki, Mari Szémes, Pàl Zolnay

Diary for My Father and Mother **
Hungary 1990 93m colour/bw
Budapest Film Studio/Hungarofilm
original title: *Napló Apámnak Anyámnak*
In 1956, a woman film-maker returns to Budapest from Moscow at a time of recrimination and betrayal, just after the Russians crush the Hungarian revolution.
Moving and emotional finale to an impressive, semi-autobiographical trilogy, tracing Hungary's changing fortunes through the experience of one woman; even if more recent events have made it seem like ancient history, it retains its power and interest through its emphasis on individual lives and feelings, though it will be most enjoyed by those familiar with the earlier films in the sequence.
w Márta Mészáros, éva Pataki d Márta Mészáros ph Nyika Jancsó m Zsolt Döme ed Éva Kármentö
☆ Zsuzsa Czinkóczi, Jan Nowicki, Anna Polony, Mari Töröcsik, Ildiko Bánsági

Diary for My Loves **
Hungary 1987 130m bw
Artificial Eye/Mafilm/Hungarofilm/Magyar Film/Zespoly Filmowe
original title: *Napló Szerelmeimnek*
An eighteen-year-old Hungarian girl goes to Moscow to become a film-maker and to search for her father.
Absorbing sequel to Diary for my Children, tracing the end of Stalinism.
w Márta Mészáros, éva Pataki d Márta Mészáros ph Nyika Jancsó pd Éva Martin ed Éva Kármentö
☆ Zsuzsa Czinkóczi, Anna Polony, Jan Nowicki, Irina Kouberskaya, László Szabó, Pál Zolnay, Adél Kováts, Erzsébet Kútvölgyi

A Diary for Timothy ***
GB 1945 40m bw
Basil Wright/Crown Film Unit
A baby is born as the war ends, and the narrator ponders its future.
Brilliant sentimental documentary, a summing up of the aims and feelings of Britain at the time.
w E. M. Forster d Humphrey Jennings narrator Michael Redgrave

Diary of a Bride: see *I, Jane Doe*

The Diary of a Chambermaid *
US 1946 86m bw
Benedict Bogeaus (Burgess Meredith, Paulette Goddard)
▄▄
A 19th-century serving girl causes sexual frustration and other troubles in two households.
Hollywood notables were all at sea in this wholly artificial and unpersuasive adaptation of a minor classic.
w Burgess Meredith novel Octave Mirbeau d Jean Renoir ph Lucien Andriot m Michel Michelet pd Eugene Lourié
☆ Paulette Goddard, Burgess Meredith, Hurd Hatfield, Francis Lederer, Judith Anderson, Florence Bates, Irene Ryan, Reginald Owen, Almira Sessions
'I do not mean to disparage Renoir's direction of the piece; erratic and with a curious element of flippancy and even vulgarity at the start, it advances with the melodramatic development of the plot to a fine climax of excitement, movement, terror. But the theme is incurably novelettish.' – *Dilys Powell*

The Diary of a Chambermaid *
France/Italy 1964 98m bw Franscope
Speva/Ciné Alliance/Filmsonor/Dear (Serge Silberman, Michel Sabra)
▄▄ ▄▄ ⊙~
original title: *Le Journal d'une Femme de Chambre*
Interesting but not especially successful Buñuel version: the subject is certainly up his street, but the novel seems to restrict him and the visual quality is unattractive.
w Luis Buñuel, Jean-Claude Carrière d Luis Buñuel ph Roger Fellous m none
☆ Jeanne Moreau, Georges Géret, Michel Piccoli, Françoise Lugagne
'The film remains notable but inconclusive: a half-Buñuel.' – *Dilys Powell*

Diary of a Cloistered Nun: see *Story of a Cloistered Nun*

The Diary of a Country Priest ***
France 1950 120m bw
Union Générale Cinématographique (Léon Carré)
▄▄
original title: *Journal d'un Curé de Campagne*
A lonely young priest fails to make much impression in his first parish; and, falling ill, he dies alone.
Striking, depressing, slow and austere, with little dialogue but considerable visual beauty; a very typical work of its director.
wd Robert Bresson novel Georges Bernanos ph L. Burel m Jean-Jacques Grunenwald
☆ Claude Laydu, Jean Riveyre, Armand Guibert, Nicole Ladmiral

'Nothing personal, purely business.'

Diary of a Hitman
US 1992 91m Technicolor
Vision International/Continental (Amin Q. Chaudhri)
▄▄ ▄▄ ⊙~
A hired killer begins to have doubts when a husband pays him to murder his wife and baby.
A wordy, claustrophobic thriller that betrays its stage origins and strains credulity.
w Kenneth Pressman play Insider's Price by Kenneth Pressman d Roy London ph Yuri Sokol m Michel Colombier pd Stephen Hendrickson ed Brian Smedley-Aston
☆ Forest Whitaker, John Bedford-Lloyd, James Belushi, Seymour Cassel, Lois Chiles, Lewis Smith, Sharon Stone, Sherilyn Fenn

Diary of a Lost Girl **
Germany 1929 110m bw silent
G. W. Pabst Film
▄▄ ▄▄ ⊙~
original title: *Tagebuch einer Verlorenen*
A rich man's daughter is seduced, has an illegitimate child, is placed in a house of correction and finds herself later in a brothel.
Heavily Germanic Road to Ruin, superbly mounted in best cinematic style, with several memorable sequences. Heavily mutilated by censors; according to the screenwriter the film ends just after the middle of his script.
w Rudolf Leonhardt novel Margaret Böhme d G. W. Pabst ph Sepp Allgeier
☆ Louise Brooks, Fritz Rasp, Josef Ravensky
† A previous version had been made in 1918, written and directed by Richard Oswald.

Diary of a Mad Housewife **
US 1970 95m Technicolor
Universal/Frank Perry
▄▄
The bored and repressed wife of a lawyer tries an affair, walks out on her husband, and opts for group therapy.
An agreeably mordant view of the contemporary American scene, with good dialogue and performances, but the little bits of satire do not really add up to a satisfactory film.
w Eleanor Perry novel Sue Kaufman d Frank Perry ph Gerald Hirschfeld
☆ Carrie Snodgress, Richard Benjamin, Frank Langella, Lorraine Cullen, Frannie Michel
'A prototypical contemporary American artifact … all its assorted talents and technological smartness are turned to the varnishing of mediocrity.' – *Stanley Kauffmann*
⅄ Carrie Snodgress

Diary of a Madman
US 1962 96m Technicolor
UA/Admiral (Robert E. Kent)
A murderer explains to a magistrate that he was possessed by an evil spirit.
Ponderous transcription of Maupassant stories with a few moments of horror.
w Robert E. Kent d Reginald Le Borg ph Ellis W. Carter m Richard La Salle ad Daniel Haller
☆ Vincent Price, Nancy Kovack, Chris Warfield, Stephen Roberts

The Diary of a Married Woman
Germany 1953 83m bw
Magna
original title: *Tagebuch einer Verliebten*
A wife divorces her adulterous husband, but their small son brings them together again.

One long Hollywood cliché, assembled with some spirit; notable only as one of the rare post-war German films to get distribution in English-speaking countries.
w Emil Burri, Johann Mario Simmel d Josef von Baky ph Oskar Snirch m Alois Melichar
☆ Maria Schell, O. W. Fischer, Franco Andrei

Diary of a Shinjuku Thief *
Japan 1969 94m bw/Eastmancolor
Sozosha (Masayuki Nakajima)
original title: *Shinjuku Dorobo Nikki*
A minor theft in a bookstore brings a young man into contact with a mysterious girl who leads him into various sexual experiments.
Inexplicable but quite fascinating piece of oriental mystification in which sex equates to some extent with revolution.
w Tsutomu Tamura and others d Nagisa Oshima ph Yasuhiro Yamaguchi m none
☆ Tadanori Yokoo, Rie Yokoyama, Moichi Tanabe

The Diary of Anne Frank **
US 1959 170m bw Cinemascope
TCF/George Stevens
In 1942, a Jewish family hides from the Nazis in an Amsterdam attic; just before the war ends, they are betrayed and sent to concentration camps.
Based on the diaries of a girl who died at Bergen-Belsen, this solemn adaptation is elephantine in its length, its ponderousness and its use of Cinemascope when the atmosphere is supposed to be claustrophobic.
w Frances Goodrich, Albert Hackett from their play based on Anne Frank's diaries d George Stevens ph William C. Mellor m Alfred Newman ad Lyle R. Wheeler, George W. Davis
☆ Millie Perkins, Joseph Schildkraut, Shelley Winters, Ed Wynn, Richard Beymer, Gusti Huber, Lou Jacobi, Diane Baker
🎗 William C. Mellor; Shelley Winters; art direction
🏆 best picture; George Stevens; Alfred Newman; Ed Wynn

The Diary of Lady M
Switzerland/Belgium/Spain/France 1993 112m colour
Filmograph/Nomad/Messidor/Lazennec (Alain Tanner, Jacques de Clercq, Dimitri de Clercq, Gerardo Herrero, Marta Esteban, Christophe Rossignon)
original title: *Le Journal de Lady M*
A Parisian singer begins a passionate affair with a Spanish painter and, discovering that he is married, invites his wife and family to join them.
Supposedly based on the star's diaries, this is a throwback to the sad sex films of the 60s, a drearily egocentric, uninteresting drama.
w Myriam Mézières d Alain Tanner ph Denis Jutzeler m Arie Dzierlatka ad Jordi Canora, Alain Chennaux ed Monica Goux
☆ Myriam Mézières, Juanjo Puligcorbé, Félicité Wouassi, Antoine Basler, Makeda, Marie Peyrucq-Yamiou, Gladys Gambie
'A preposterously clichéd, would-be (but not-at-all) titillating film that charts the sad decline of Alain Tanner … I started noting down the worst lines but soon gave up; I was transcribing the script.' – *Sheila Johnston, Independent*
'Pic's extremely frank sex scenes have a shocking realism and seem a natural outgrowth of Mézières' honesty in recounting her feelings. A scene in which Lady M shaves her pubic hair and dances for her lover clothed only in a long, dangling earring must set some kind of art-film precedent.' – *Variety*

The Diary of Major Thompson
France 1955 83m bw
SNE Gaumont/Paul Wagner
original title: *Les Carnets de Major Thompson*
US title: *The French They Are a Funny Race*
An Englishman married to a Frenchwoman keeps notes on the French way of life.
Tatty filming of a mildly amusing book; it falls away into a number of badly-timed and presented gags, and one can't believe that its creator was once the top comedy genius of Hollywood.
wd Preston Sturges ph Maurice Barry, Christian Matras m Georges Van Parys
☆ Jack Buchanan, Martine Carol, Noel-Noel, Genevieve Brunet
'Even allowing for the appalling editing and the frequently incomprehensible dubbed soundtrack, there is little evidence to suggest that this film

could ever have been anything but a shambles.'
– *Peter John Dyer, MFB*

Il Diavolo e il Morto: see *Lisa and The Devil*

Dice Rules
US 1991 83m Foto-Kem
Seven Arts/Fleebin Dabble (Fred Silverstein)
A 20-minute short on the emergence of the comedian is followed by footage of a concert performance in Madison Square Gardens.
Like strychnine, an acquired and less than enjoyable taste.
w Lenny Shulman, Andrew Dice Clay d Jay Dubin ph Michael Negrin d Mitchell Sinoway
☆ Andrew Dice Clay, Eddie Griffin, Sylvia Harman, Lee Lawrence, Noodles Levenstein, Maria Parkinson
'A pretty accurate snapshot of the comedian's standup act – crude, sexist, racist, homophobic and designed to shock.' – *Variety*

'A humorous look at man's greatest asset … and liability.'

Dick *
US 1990 13m bw
Island (Jo Menell)
Documentary in which photographs of multifarious flaccid male organs are flashed on screen to the accompaniment of women's voices answering such questions as 'Would you want one?'
Amusing novelty, although one that was denied a television showing in Britain.
d Jo Menell, B. Moel ph Paul Latoures m John Cale
'Menell's liberating, wholly unprurient film should put an end to Freud's theory of penis envy.' – *Philip French, Observer*

Dick Barton
The radio detective was created by Edward J. Mason in the mid-forties, and three rough-and-ready film versions were subsequently made by Hammer/Exclusive. They were *Dick Barton Special Agent* (1948); *Dick Barton Strikes Back* (1949); and *Dick Barton at Bay* (1950); all with Don Stannard. *Critical comment would be irrelevant.*

Dick Deadeye, or Duty Done
GB 1975 81m Technicolor
Bill Melendez Productions (Leo Rost)
A naval officer is commissioned by Queen Victoria to retrieve the Ultimate Secret from the Wicked Sorcerer.
Fairly joyless animated amalgam of several Gilbert and Sullivan operas, fussily designed by Ronald Searle and with modernized lyrics. Sure to infuriate G and S devotees and to bewilder everyone else.
w Robin Miller, Leo Rost d Bill Melendez animation d Dick Horn

Dick Tracy
US 1945 61m bw
RKO (Herman Schlom)
GB title: *Splitface*
The jut-jawed detective routs a disfigured criminal named Splitface.
Vigorous second feature from the comic strip.
w Eric Taylor comic strip Chester Gould d William Berke ph Frank Redman m Roy Webb
☆ Morgan Conway, Jane Greer, Mike Mazurki, Anne Jeffreys, Lyle Latell, Joseph Crehan, Trevor Bardette
† Sequels: *Dick Tracy vs Cueball* (1946) with Morgan Conway,
†† John Rawlins; *Dick Tracy Meets Gruesome* (1947) with Ralph Byrd, Boris Karloff,

Dick Tracy *
US 1990 103m Technicolor
Touchstone/Silver Screen Partners IV (Warren Beatty)
Detective Dick Tracy tangles with a master criminal.
A limp narrative is bolstered by a lavish and stylized production design, using comic-book primary colours, and by the careful re-creation of the bizarre appearance of the gangsters from the original newspaper strip-cartoon.
w Jim Cash, Jack Epps Jnr comic strip Chester Gould d Warren Beatty ph Vittorio Storaro m Danny Elfman m/ly Stephen Sondheim

pd Richard Sylbert ad Harold Michelson ed Richard Marks sp character make-up by John Caglione Jnr, Doug Drexler
☆ Warren Beatty, Charlie Korsmo, Glenne Headly, Madonna, Al Pacino, Dustin Hoffman, William Forsythe, Charles Durning, Mandy Patinkin, Paul Sorvino, R. G. Armstrong, Dick Van Dyke
'This is no ready-to-wear movie; it's the work of a cinematic couturier. Take it for what it is: a simple gift, consummately wrapped.' – *David Ansen, Newsweek*
'A charming and beautifully designed work of American popular art.' – *David Denby, New York Magazine*
'A grand exercise in cinema imagination and wit for their own sake.' – *Vincent Canby, New York Times*
'A major disappointment.' – *Variety*
🎗 best art direction; best song 'Sooner or Later'; best make-up
🏆 Al Pacino; Vittorio Storaro; best costume design; best sound
📼 Richard Sylbert

Dick Tracy Meets Gruesome
US 1947 65m bw
RKO (Herman Schlom)
Tracy tracks down a criminal who robs a bank with the aid of a paralysing gas.
Effective little thriller, once you accept the implausibilities of the plot.
w Robertson White, Eric Taylor story William H. Graffis, Robert E. Kent cartoon strip Chester Gould d John Rawlins ph Frank Redman m Paul Sawtell md C. Bakaleinikoff ad Albert S. D'Agostino, Walter E. Keller ed Elmo Williams
☆ Boris Karloff, Ralph Byrd, Anne Gwynne, Edward Ashley, June Clayworth, Lyle Latell, Skelton Knaggs, Lex Barker
'Employs almost serial-type action … with surprisingly good results.' – *Variety*
† The script's in-joke: one cop says of Gruesome, the character played by Karloff, 'He's weird. I tell you that if I didn't know better I swear we were doing business with Boris Karloff.'

Dick Tracy vs Cueball
US 1946 62m bw
RKO (Herman Schlom)
Dick Tracy solves the murder of a diamond dealer by a bald-headed crook.
Occasionally entertaining 'B' feature with a few colourful characters to compensate for Conway's blandness, though Tracy's detective skills seem limited to tailing suspects and arriving at the scene a few minutes after a crime has been committed.
w Dane Lussier, Robert E. Kent story Luci Ward cartoon strip Chester Gould d Gordon M. Douglas ph George E. Diskant m Phil Ohman md C. Bakaleinikoff ad Albert S. D'Agostino, Lucius O. Croxton ed Philip Martin Jnr
☆ Morgan Conway, Anne Jeffreys, Lyle Latell, Rita Corday, Ian Keith, Dick Wessel

Dick Tracy's Dilemma
US 1947 60m bw
RKO (Herman Schlom)
Dick Tracy investigates a murder at a fur warehouse and uncovers an insurance scam.
Enjoyable little thriller, with quirkier characters than are usually found in such low-budget excursions.
w Robert Stephen Brode cartoon strip Chester Gould d John Rawlins ph Frank Redman m Paul Sawtell md C. Bakaleinikoff ad Albert S. D'Agostino, Lucius O. Croxton ed Marvin Coil
☆ Ralph Byrd, Lyle Latell, Kay Christopher, Jack Lambert, Ian Keith, Bernadene Hayes, Jimmy Conlin, William B. Davidson, Tony Barrett, Richard Powers

Dick Turpin
GB 1933 79m bw
Stoll-Stafford (Clyde Cook)
In this version the highwayman's ride to York is to prevent an enforced marriage.
Mild British costume piece which sent its star to Hollywood.
w Victor Kendall novel *Rookwood* by Harrison Ainsworth d Victor Hanbury, John Stafford ph Desmond Dickinson ad Wilfred Arnold

☆ Victor McLaglen, Jane Carr, Frank Vosper, James Finlayson, Gillian Lind

Dick Turpin's Ride: see *The Lady and the Bandit*

The Dictator *
GB 1935 86m bw
Toeplitz
aka: *For Love of a Queen*
aka: *The Loves of a Dictator*
In 18th-century Denmark, a country doctor falls in love with his queen and overthrows the mad king.
Stiff-backed middle-class romance, an interesting example of English-German co-production at the time.
w Benn Levy, Hans Wilhelm, H. G. Lustig, Michael Hogan d Victor Saville, Alfred Santell ph Franz Planer m Karol Rathaus ad Andrei Andreiev ed Paul Weatherwax
☆ Clive Brook, Madeleine Carroll, Helen Haye, Emlyn Williams, Isabel Jeans, Alfred Drayton, Frank Cellier
'One of the most lavish costume pictures that has yet come out of England: supposed to have cost 500,000 dollars. It's great pictorially, but not moving enough.' – *Variety*

Did You Hear the One about the Traveling Saleslady?
US 1967 96m Technicolor
Universal (Si Rose)
In a Kansas town in 1910 an eccentric saleslady offers pianolas which tend to go berserk.
Cornbelt comedy vehicle for an unappealing star.
w John Fenton Murray d Don Weis ph Bud Thackery m Vic Mizzy
☆ Phyllis Diller, Bob Denver, Joe Flynn, Jeanette Nolan

Die! Die! My Darling: see *Fanatic*

Die Hard **
US 1988 132m DeLuxe Panavision
Fox/Gordon Company/Silver Pictures (Lawrence Gordon, Joel Silver)
A cop battles with terrorists who have taken over the building while his wife is among the hostages.
Powerful, suspenseful action movie, with splendid special effects, although it goes on rather too long.
w Jeb Stuart, Steven E. de Souza novel *Nothing Lasts Forever* by Roderick Thorp d John McTiernan ph Jan de Bont m Michael Kamen pd Jackson DeGovia ed Frank J. Urioste, John F. Link
☆ Bruce Willis, Bonnie Bedelia, Reginald VelJohnson, Paul Gleason, De'Voreaux White, William Atherton, Hart Bochner, James Shigeta, Alan Rickman, Alexander Godunov

Die Hard 2 *
US 1990 124m DeLuxe Panavision
Fox/Gordon Co /Silver Pictures (Lawrence Gordon, Joel Silver, Charles Gordon)
A cop, going to meet his wife at an airport, discovers that terrorists have taken it over.
Frenetically unsubtle, and very bloody, action movie.
w Steven E. de Souza, Doug Richardson novel *58 Minutes* by Walter Wager d Renny Harlin ph Oliver Wood m Michael Kamen pd John Vallone ad Christiaan Wagener ed Stuart Baird, Robert A. Ferretti
☆ Bruce Willis, Bonnie Bedelia, William Atherton, Reginald VelJohnson, Franco Nero, William Sadler, John Amos, Dennis Franz, Art Evans, Fred Dalton Thompson
† The film was advertised with the title *Die Hard 2: Die Harder.*

'It's Boomtime In The Big Apple.'

Die Hard with a Vengeance
US 1995 128m Technicolor
Buena Vista/Cinergi (Michael Tadross, John McTiernan)
A mad bomber plays explosive games with a New York detective and his black aide.
A sequel that abandons the formula of a lone cop battling against overwhelming odds in an isolated situation, substituting something closer to the Lethal Weapon films, with an edgy, racially tinged relationship at its centre, a convoluted, confusing, schematic narrative, and lots of big bangs.

🙆 film suitable for family viewing   📼 VHS video-cassette for the British PAL system   📼 VHS video-cassette for the British PAL system in wide screen-format   📀 Video cassette in a computer-colourised version   📼 American NTSC video-cassette   💿 Laser disc w Jonathan Hensleigh d John McTiernan ph Peter Menzies m Michael Kamen pd Jackson DeGovia ed John Wright

☆ Bruce Willis, Jeremy Irons, Samuel L. Jackson, Graham Greene, Colleen Camp, Larry Bryggman, Sam Phillips

'After a frenetic, razzley-dazzley first half hour, the film quickly fizzles into formula … with a vengeance.' – Andy Webster, Premiere

† The film took more than $353m at the box-office worldwide.

Die Laughing
US 1980 108m Technicolor
Orion/Warner (Jon Peters)

📀

After the murder of a nuclear scientist, a young musician who knows too much is chased by the murderers and the FBI.
Witless black comedy rehash of The 39 Steps.
w Jerry Segal, Robby Benson, Scott Parker d Jeff Werner

☆ Robby Benson, Linda Grovenor, Charles Durning, Elsa Lanchester, Bud Cort

Dieu A Besoin des Hommes *
France 1950 100m bw
Transcontinental (Paul Graetz)
aka: Isle of Sinners
aka: God Needs Men
The priest of a Breton island leaves in horror at the sinfulness of his flock, and the fisherfolk appoint one of their number as priest.
Cold, gloomy, rather pointless fable, often a pleasure to look at.
w Jean Aurenche, Pierre Bost novel Un Recteur de l'Ile de Sein by H. Queff'lec d Jean Delannoy ph Robert Le Fèbvre m René Cloërc

☆ Pierre Fresnay, Madeleine Robinson, Daniel Gélin, Andrée Clément, Sylvie, Jean Brochard

Diexue Shuang Xiong: see The Killer

'He's not half the man she used to be.'

Different for Girls *
GB 1996 97m colour
NTFC/X Pictures/BBC (John Chapman)
📀 ⓟ
A motorcycle courier falls in love with a schoolboy friend who has changed sex.
A heady and gritty mix of transsexual romance, police corruption and social comment, it at least ventures into new territory.
w Tony Marchant d Richard Spence ph Sean Van Hales m Stephen Warbeck pd Grenville Horner ed David Gamble

☆ Rupert Graves, Steven MacKintosh, Saskia Reeves, Neil Dudgeon, Charlotte Coleman, Miriam Margolyes, Ian Dury

'One of the best British films of the decade.' – Andy Medhurst, Sight and Sound
'Would be infinitely more likeable if it wasn't for some irritatingly unreal plot development.' – Rob Driscoll, Empire

A Different Story
US 1978 106m CFI color
Avco/Alan Belkin
A homosexual falls in love with a lesbian.
One supposes it had to come, but one doesn't really have to watch it.
w Henry Olek d Paul Aaron ph Philip Lathrop m David Frank

☆ Perry King, Meg Foster, Valerie Curtin, Peter Donat

'There's something in A Different Story to turn off audiences of every sexual persuasion – and movie lovers most of all.' – Richard Schickel, Time

La Diga sul Pacifico: see This Angry Age

Digby: the Biggest Dog in the World
🏃 GB 1973 88m Technicolor
TCF/Walter Shenson
📀
An old English sheepdog accidentally eats a chemical intended to increase the size of vegetables…
Nice to see this kind of gimmick used for comedy instead of horror, but the result is rather tame and old-fashioned, though for several years it made a pleasant television offering for Christmas.
w Michael Pertwee d Joseph McGrath ph Harry Waxman m Edwin T. Astley sp Tom Howard

☆ Jim Dale, Spike Milligan, Angela Douglas, Milo O'Shea, Dinsdale Landen, Garfield Morgan, Victor Spinetti, Bob Todd

Digging to China
US 1998 98m colour
Moonstone/David/Ministry of Film (Alan Mruvka, Marilyn Vance, John Davis, J. Todd Harris)
📀 📺
In the 60s, a mentally retarded man forms a friendship with an unhappy young girl whose mother runs a rural motel.
Soft-centred character study that skims the surface of things.
w Karen Janszen d Timothy Hutton ph Jorgen Persson m Cynthia Miller pd Robert de Vico ed Dana Congdon, Alain Jakubowicz

☆ Kevin Bacon, Mary Stuart Masterson, Cathy Moriarty, Even Rachel Wood, Marian Seldes

'Will ultimately move only those inclined to cry on cue.' – Variety

Diggstown *
US 1992 98m DeLuxe
UIP/MGM/Electric (Robert Schaffel)
📀 📺 📀 🎧
GB title: Midnight Sting
Two con men journey to a town noted for unofficial prize fights and take a $1 million bet that their boxer can beat 10 local fighters in a period of 24 hours.
Enjoyable enough caper, though it risks monotony with its repeated fights; it flopped at the box-office.
w Steven McKay novel The Diggstown Ringers by Leonard Wise d Michael Ritchie ph Gerry Fisher m James Newton Howard pd Steve Hendrickson ed Don Zimmerman

☆ James Woods, Louis Gossett Jnr, Bruce Dern, Oliver Platt, Heather Graham, Randall 'Tex' Cobb, Thomas Wilson Brown, Duane Davis, Willie Green

'This crowd-pleaser mixes it up with boxing, revenge and salty one-liners that should satisfy audiences.' – Variety

Dilemma
GB 1962 90m bw
Bryanston/ACT (Ted Lloyd)
On returning home from school, a teacher finds his wife missing and a dying man in his bathroom.
An interesting concept, of a man being continually interrupted as he tries to get rid of a corpse, that is given lacklustre treatment; it might have worked better as a black comedy.
wd Peter Maxwell story Pip and Janet Baker ph Gerald Moss ad Wilfred Arnold ed Tom Simpson

☆ Peter Halliday, Ingrid Hafner, Patricia Burke, Joan Heath, Patrick Jordan, Barbara Lott, William Sherwood

Dillinger *
US 1945 70m bw
Monogram (Frank and Maurice King)
📺
The life of American public enemy number one who was shot by the police in 1934.
Slick, speedy gangster thriller, possibly the most tolerable movie to come from this low-budget studio.
w Philip Yordan d Max Nosseck ph Jackson Rose m Dimitri Tiomkin

☆ Lawrence Tierney, Edmund Lowe, Anne Jeffreys
ℬ Philip Yordan

Dillinger *
US 1973 107m Movielab
AIP (Buzz Feitshans)
📀 📺 📀
Violence-soaked version, with black comedy touches, of the last year of Dillinger's life.
Not badly done, with a style reminiscent of Bonnie and Clyde.
wd John Milius ph Jules Brenner m Barry Devorzon ad Trevor Williams ed Fred R. Feitshans Jnr

☆ Warren Oates, Ben Johnson, Michelle Phillips, Cloris Leachman, Harry Dean Stanton, Richard Dreyfuss

Dim Sum: a Little Bit of Heart *
US 1985 89m colour
CIM (Tom Sternberg, Wayne Wang, Danny Yung)
📀 📺 📀
Convinced that she will soon die, a Chinese widow living in San Francisco tries to persuade her daughter to marry.
Domestic drama full of a gentle, rambling charm.
w Terrel Seltzer d Wayne Wang ph Michael Chin m Todd Boekelheide ad Danny Yung ed Ralph Wikke

☆ Lauren Chew, Kim Chew, Victor Wong, Ida F. O. Chung, Cora Miao, John Nishio

Un Dimanche à la Campagne: see Sunday in the Country

Dimension 5
US 1966 88m colour
United Pictures Corporation
CIA agents use a time converter to jump ahead three weeks and prevent the Chinese from bombing Los Angeles.
Silly spy fantasy with inadequate effects.
w Arthur C. Pierce d Franklin Adreon

☆ Jeffrey Hunter, France Nuyen, Harold Sakata, Donald Woods

Dimples **
🏃 US 1936 82m bw
TCF (Darryl F. Zanuck, Nunnally Johnson)
📺
In the New York Bowery in pre-Civil War days, a child and her reprobate grandfather win the hearts of high society.
Excellent Temple vehicle with good period flavour.
w Arthur Sheekman, Nat Perrin d William A. Seiter ph Bert Glennon m Louis Silvers m/ly Jimmy McHugh, Ted Koehler

☆ Shirley Temple, Frank Morgan, Helen Westley, Berton Churchill, Robert Kent, Delma Byron, Astrid Allwyn

'What they wanted most wasn't on the menu'

Diner **
US 1982 110m Technicolor
MGM/SLM (Jerry Weintraub)
📀 📺 📀
In 1959 Baltimore, college students congregate at their old meeting place and find themselves more occupied by adult problems than of yore.
Generally amusing group character study, an awkward attempt to divine the meaning of life through the accumulation of detail. A little masterpiece of observation, for those with ears to hear; but not necessarily a great film.
wd Barry Levinson ph Peter Sova m Bruce Brody, Ivan Kral pd Leon Harris ed Stu Linder

☆ Steve Guttenberg, Daniel Stern, Mickey Rourke, Kevin Bacon, Timothy Daly, Ellen Barkin, Paul Reiser, Kathryn Dowling, Michael Tucker, Jessica James

'A terrific movie – a gentle, lyrical, magically funny portrait of the games young men play to keep from growing up, and of the oddly childish society that encourages them.' – Stephen Schiff
ℬ original screenplay

Le Diner de Cons **
France 1998 80m colour
Pathé/Gaumont/Efve/TFI (Alain Poiré)
📀
A publisher attends a weekly dinner to which he and his friends invite the most boring people they encounter; but he becomes incapacitated and is trapped in his flat with a man who makes models of buildings out of matchsticks.
Enjoyable, expertly constructed, cruel farce of misunderstandings in which a sophisticated man's life is unravelled by a well-meaning fool.
wd Francis Veber play Francis Veber ph Luciano Tovoli m Vladimir Cosma ad Hugues Tissandier ed Georges Klotz

☆ Jacques Villeret, Thierry Lhermitte, Francis Huster, Alexandra Vandernoot, Daniel Prévost, Catherine Frot, Edgar Givry, Christian Pereira

'Veber delivers a marvellously wrought plot at exactly the length it can sustain, and manages consistently to pull out situations that provoke laughter and astonishment.' – Kim Newman, Empire

Dingaka
South Africa 1965 97m Technicolor
Cinemascope
Embassy (Jamie Uys)
Tribal antagonisms cause a simple native to seek revenge in the city.
Unconvincing and now very dated melodrama with rather too much local colour.
wd Jamie Uys ph Manie Botha m Bertha Egnos, Eddie Domingo, Basil Gray

☆ Ken Gampu, Stanley Baker, Juliet Prowse, Siegfried Mynhardt, Paul Makgoba

Dinky
US 1935 65m bw
Warner
The mother of a military school cadet is framed into a prison term.
Sentimental drama of little interest.
w Harry Sauber d D. Ross Lederman, Howard Bretherton

☆ Jackie Cooper, Mary Astor, Roger Pryor, Henry Armetta, Henry O'Neill, Edith Fellows

'A rapidly maturing Jackie Cooper is revealed here as lacking the strength to stand alone.' – Variety

Dinner at Eight ***
US 1933 113m bw
MGM (David O. Selznick)
📀 📺 📀
Guests at a society dinner party all find themselves in dramatic circumstances.
Artificial but compelling pattern play from a Broadway success.
w Frances Marion, Herman J. Mankiewicz play George S. Kaufman, Edna Ferber d George Cukor ph William Daniels m William Axt

☆ Marie Dressler, John Barrymore, Lionel Barrymore, Billie Burke, Wallace Beery, Jean Harlow, Lee Tracy, Edmund Lowe, Madge Evans, Jean Hersholt, Karen Morley, Louise Closser Hale, Phillips Holmes, May Robson, Grant Mitchell and also Elizabeth Patterson

KITTY (JEAN HARLOW): 'You know, I read a book the other day. It's all about civilization or something – a nutty kind of a book. Do you know that the guy said machinery is going to take the place of every profession?'

CARLOTTA (MARIE DRESSLER): 'Oh, my dear. That's something you need never worry about!'
'Marquee speaks for itself. It spells money, and couldn't very well be otherwise.' – Variety

Dinner at the Ritz
GB 1937 77m bw
New World (Robert T. Kane)
A French girl exposes swindlers who faked her father's suicide.
Once-diverting comedy melodrama with an international cast.
w Roland Pertwee, Romney Brent d Harold Schuster ph Philip Tannura m Lee Sims ed James B. Clark

☆ Annabella, Paul Lukas, David Niven, Romney Brent, Stewart Rome, Francis L. Sullivan, Nora Swinburne, Frederick Leister

'Slow and shoddily made British product.' – Variety
'It moves with old world decorum and occasional touches of gout.' – New York Times

Dino
US 1957 93m bw
AA/Bernice Block
A juvenile delinquent released from prison has trouble reforming.
Adequately made social drama with good credentials.
w Reginald Rose play Reginald Rose d Thomas Carr

☆ Sal Mineo, Brian Keith, Susan Kohner, Frank Faylen, Joe DeSantis

Dinosaurus!
US 1960 85m DeLuxe Cinemascope
Jack H. Harris, Irvin S. Yeaworth Jnr
Workers on a tropical island bring up from the seabed a frozen Neanderthal man and two dinosaurs, who promptly thaw out.
Risible monster movie with effects that are more comic than horrific.
w Dan E. Weisburd, Jean Yeaworth d Irvin S. Yeaworth Jnr ph Stanley Cortez m Ronald Stein

ad Jack Senter *ed* John A. Bushelman *sp* Tim Baar, Wah Chang, Gene Warren
☆ Ward Ramsey, Paul Lukather, Kristina Hanson, Alan Roberts, Gregg Martell

The Dion Brothers: see *The Gravy Train*

Diplomaniacs
US   1933   59m   bw
RKO
▦   ◎⌐
Two halfwits are offered a fortune to go to Geneva and make the peace delegates stop fighting.
Fatuous comedy which never gets going.
w Joseph Mankiewicz, Henry Meyers *d* William Seiter
☆ Bert Wheeler, Robert Woolsey, Hugh Herbert, Marjorie White, Phyllis Barry, Louis Calhern
  'A baddie; rhymed dialogue no help for inane plot.' – *Variety*

The Diplomatic Corpse
GB   1958   65m   bw
Rank/ACT Films (Francis Searle)
A crime reporter, investigating the identity of a corpse found in the Thames, uncovers a drug-smuggling ring.
Programme filler of a thriller, involving a great deal of talk and not much action.
w Sidney Nelson, Maurice Harrison *d* Montgomery Tully *ph* Philip Grindrod *ad* Joseph Bato *ed* James Connock
☆ Robin Bailey, Susan Shaw, Liam Redmond, Harry Fowler, André Mikhelson, Bill Shine, Charles Farrell

Diplomatic Courier *
US   1952   98m   bw
TCF (Casey Robinson)
▦
American and Russian agents clash on a train between Salzburg and Trieste; an unexpected master spy is revealed after several chases.
Lively cold war intrigue, well produced and played with relish.
w Casey Robinson, Liam O'Brien *novel* Sinister Errand by Peter Cheyney *d* Henry Hathaway *ph* Lucien Ballard *m* Sol Kaplan *md* Lionel Newman
☆ Tyrone Power, Patricia Neal, Stephen McNally, Hildegarde Neff, Karl Malden, James Millican, Herbert Berghof
  'A reversion to the oldest tradition of spy fiction.' – *Penelope Houston*

Dirigible *
US   1931   102m   bw
Columbia
The story of an airship disaster.
Economical epic with a few Capra touches.
w Jo Swerling, Dorothy Howell *story* Frank 'Spig' Wead *d* Frank Capra *ph* Joe Wilbur, Elmer Dyer, Joseph Walker
☆ Jack Holt, Fay Wray, Ralph Graves, Hobart Bosworth, Roscoe Karns
  'Plenty of everything expected in a flying film spectacle.' – *Variety*

The Dirt Bike Kid
♔♔   US   1985   90m   colour
Cinema/Concorde (Julie Corman)
▦   ◎⌐
A boy acquires a motor-bike with magical powers and defeats the plans of a wicked banker.
Trivial and predictable film, intended for a childish audience.
w Lewis Colick, David Brandes *d* Hoite C. Caston *ph* Daniel Lacambre *m* Bill Bowersock *ad* Betty Block *ed* Jeff Freeman
☆ Peter Billingsley, Stuart Pankin, Anne Bloom, Patrick Collins, Sage Parker, Chad Sheets, Daniel Breen

Dirty Dancing *
US   1987   97m   colour
Vestron (Linda Gottlieb)
▦   ▦   ◎⌐   ◉   ♫
In 1963, kids go dance crazy at a borscht belt resort.
Mildly agreeable variant on Saturday Night Fever, almost equally successful at the box-office.
w Eleanor Bergstein *d* Emile Ardolino *ph* Jeff Jur *m* John Morris *pd* David Chapman *ed* Peter C. Frank

☆ Jennifer Grey, Patrick Swayze, Jerry Orbach, Cynthia Rhodes, Jack Weston
♟ song 'I've Had the Time of My Life' (Franke Previte, John DeNicola, Donald Markowitz)

Dirty Dingus Magee
US   1970   91m   Metrocolor   Panavision
MGM (Burt Kennedy)
▦▦
A likeable Western outlaw crosses swords with an old enemy.
Fair burlesque Western often stooping to vulgarity.
w Tom Waldman, Frank Waldman, Joseph Heller *novel* David Markson *d* Burt Kennedy *ph* Harry Stradling *m* Jeff Alexander
☆ Frank Sinatra, George Kennedy, Anne Jackson, Lois Nettleton, Jack Elam, John Dehner, Henry Jones, Harry Carey Jnr, Paul Fix
  'Skittish burlesque, scripted in the brash and undisciplined style of a TV show … heavily reliant on the *Carry On* brand of humour.' – *David McGillivray*

'Damn them or praise them – you'll never forget them!'
The Dirty Dozen **
US/Spain   1967   150m   Metrocolor   70mm
MGM/Kenneth Hyman
▦▦   ▦   ▦   ◎⌐   ♫
In 1944, twelve convicts serving life sentences are recruited for a commando suicide mission.
Professional, commercial but unlikeable slice of wartime thick ear; pretensions about capital punishment are jettisoned early on in favour of frequent and violent bloodshed. Much imitated, e.g. by The Devil's Brigade, A Reason to Live, a Reason to Die, etc.
w Nunnally Johnson, Lukas Heller *novel* E. M. Nathanson *d* Robert Aldrich *ph* Edward Scaife *m* Frank de Vol
☆ Lee Marvin, Ernest Borgnine, Robert Ryan, Charles Bronson, Jim Brown, John Cassavetes, George Kennedy, Richard Jaeckel, Trini Lopez, Telly Savalas, Ralph Meeker, Clint Walker, Robert Webber, Donald Sutherland
♟ John Cassavetes

Dirty Hands: see *Les Mains Sales*

'You don't assign him to murder cases – you just turn him loose!'
Dirty Harry ***
US   1971   103m   Technicolor   Panavision
Warner/Malpaso (Don Siegel)
▦▦   ▦   ◎⌐   ◉   ♫
A violently inclined San Francisco police inspector is the only cop who can bring to book a mad sniper. When the man is released through lack of evidence, he takes private revenge.
A savage cop show which became a cult and led to a spate of dirty cop movies, including four sequels, Magnum Force, The Enforcer, Sudden Impact and The Dead Pool (qqv). Well done for those who can take it.
w Harry Julian Fink, Rita M. Fink, Dean Riesner *d* Don Siegel *ph* Bruce Surtees *m* Lalo Schifrin
☆ Clint Eastwood, Harry Guardino, Reni Santoni, John Vernon, Andy Robinson, John Larch, John Mitchum
  HARRY CALLAHAN (CLINT EASTWOOD): 'I know what you're thinking, punk. You're thinking, "Did he fire six shots or only five?" Now, to tell you the truth I've forgotten myself in all this excitement. But being this is a .44 Magnum, the most powerful handgun in the world, and will blow your head clean off, you've gotta ask yourself a question, "Do I feel lucky?" Well, do ya, punk?'

Dirty Little Billy
US   1972   92m   Eastmancolor
Columbia/WRG/Dragoti (Jack L. Warner)
The violent young life of Billy the Kid.
Squalid little Western with few attractive aspects except that it presents its hero as the mentally retarded delinquent which history says he was.
w Charles Moss, Stan Dragoti *d* Stan Dragoti *ph* Ralph Woolsey *m* Sascha Burland
☆ Michael J. Pollard, Lee Purcell, Richard Evans, Charles Aidman
  'The gap between its ostensible aims and its manner of realizing them continually leaves the film bogged down in its own scrupulously realistic mud.' – *Tony Rayns*

Dirty Mary, Crazy Larry
US   1974   92m   DeLuxe
Academy Pictures Corporation (Norman T. Herman)
▦
Two racing drivers and a kooky groupie rob a supermarket and almost elude their police pursuers.
Elaborately stunted chase film, agreeable enough to watch if the characters were not so disagreeable.
w Leigh Chapman, Antonio Santean *novel* The Chase by Richard Unekis *d* John Hough *ph* Mike Margulies *m* Jimmie Haskell
☆ Peter Fonda, Susan George, Adam Roarke, Vic Morrow, Kenneth Tobey, Roddy McDowall, Eugene Daniels
  'The film's general delight in destruction and despoilation makes one wonder if it is the cinema that reflects the ugliness of modern society or the ugliness of modern society that reflects trends in the cinema.' – *Michael Billington, Illustrated London News*

Dirty Money (dubbed) *
France/Italy   1972   98m   Eastmancolor
Columbia-Warner/Corona/Oceania/Euro (Robert Dorfmann)
original title: *Un Flic*
While investigating a drug-running operation, a police inspector solves a robbery and discovers that his mistress is double-crossing him.
Glum investigation of betrayal in which atmosphere is all, but not enough to sustain interest.
wd Jean-Pierre Melville *ph* Walter Wottitz *m* Michel Colombier *pd* Théo Muerisse *ed* Patricia Renaut
☆ Alain Delon, Catherine Deneuve, Richard Crenna, Riccardo Cucciolla, Michael Conrad, André Pousse
  'It is curiously fitting that Melville's last feature should reaffirm the genre's hardiest conventions in a context of disenchantment and failure; and happy that this final, equivocal embrace of the genre should be distinguished by the director's most adventurous experiments with form.' – *Tony Rayns, MFB*

Dirty Rotten Scoundrels
US   1988   110m   DeLuxe
Rank/Orion (Bernard Williams)
▦▦   ▦   ◎⌐   ◉
Two con men compete in a contest of skills.
Heavy-handed remake of Ralph Levy's Bedtime Story, made in 1964.
w Dale Launer, Stanley Shapiro, Paul Henning *d* Frank Oz *ph* Michael Ballhaus *m* Miles Goodman *pd* Roy Walker *ed* Stephen A. Rotter, William Scharf
☆ Steve Martin, Michael Caine, Glenne Headly, Anton Rodgers, Barbara Harris, Ian McDiarmid, Dana Ivey, Meagen Fay, Frances Conroy, Nicole Calfan

Dirty Weekend
GB   1993   103m   colour
UIP/Scimitar (Michael Winner, Robert Earl)
▦▦   ♫
A woman, harassed by a succession of lecherous males, decides to kill them.
A sleazy little tale of a female vigilante, directed and acted in a perfunctory, over-emphatic manner.
w Michael Winner, Helen Zahavi *novel* Helen Zahavi *d* Michael Winner *ph* Alan Jones *m* David Fanshawe *pd* Crispian Sallis *ed* Arnold Crust
☆ Lia Williams, Rufus Sewell, Michael Cule, David McCallum, Christopher Ryan, Sean Pertwee, Ian Richardson
  'Michael Winner aims low and half misses.' – *Variety*
  'The film is uniquely awful … sheer murder to watch.' – *Nick James, Sight and Sound*

Dirty Work ***
♔♔   US   1933   20m   bw
Hal Roach
Chimney sweeps cause havoc in the house of an eccentric scientist.
Hilarious star comedy with splendid timing and comedy touches.
w H. M. Walker *d* Lloyd French *ph* Kenneth Peach *ed* Bert Jordan
☆ Laurel and Hardy, Lucien Littlefield, Sam Adams

Dirty Work
GB   1934   78m   bw
Gaumont (Michael Balcon)
Shop assistants pose as crooks in order to catch thieves.
Rather thin Ben Travers farce with some authentic moments.
w Ben Travers *play* Ben Travers *d* Tom Walls *ph* Phil Tannura *md* Louis Levy *ad* Alfred Junge *ed* Alfred Roome
☆ Ralph Lynn, Gordon Harker, Robertson Hare, Lillian Bond, Basil Sydney, Cecil Parker, Margaretta Scott, Gordon James, Peter Gawthorne

The Disappearance
GB/Canada   1977   102m   Eastmancolor
Trofar/Tiberius (David Hemmings)
An international hit man finds that his wife has disappeared.
Confusing and pretentious thriller which spends more time on introspection than action and ends up not satisfying anybody.
w Paul Mayersberg *novel* Echoes of Celandine by Derek Marlowe *d* Stuart Cooper *ph* John Alcott *m* Robert Farnon
☆ Donald Sutherland, Francine Racette, David Hemmings, John Hurt, David Warner, Peter Bowles, Virginia McKenna, Christopher Plummer

The Disappearance of Finbar
Ireland/GB/Sweden/France   1997   102m   colour
Film Four/Pandora/First City/Samson/Victoria (Bertil Ohlsson, Martin Bruce-Clayton)
A detective and his best friend go looking for an unsettled Irish teenager who disappears from his home.
An aimless road movie that gets lost in Scandinavia.
w Dermot Bolger, Sue Clayton *novel* The Disappearance of Rory Brophy by Carl Lombard *d* Sue Clayton *ph* Eduardo Serra *m* Davy Spillane *ad* Ned McLoughlin, Connor Devlin, Bengt Froderberg *ed* J. Patrick Duffner, Alan Strachan
☆ Jonathan Rhys Meyers (credited as Rhys-Myers), Luke Griffin, Fanny Risberg, Lorraine Pilkington, Eleanor Methven, Sean Lawlor, Sean McGinley
  'Ambitious and sloppy, yet occasionally likeable, cross-European fable.' – *Caroline Westbrook, Empire*

'The Movie Hollywood Doesn't Want You To See.'
Disappearance of Kevin Johnson *
US   1995   106m   Foto-Kem
Bedford/Makani Kai/Wobblyscope (Scott Richard Wolf)
A British documentary team, who are making a feature on expatriates in Hollywood, investigate the disappearance of a missing producer on the brink of the big time.
An amusing look at the seedier side of the dream factory, done in the muck-raking style of the sleazier television documentaries.
wd Francis Megahy *ph* John C. Newby *m* John Coda *ad* Sandy Grass *ed* Hudson Legrand
☆ Alexander Folk, Bridget Baiss, Carl Sundstrom, Michael Brandon, Keely Sims, Hector Elias, Pierce Brosnan, James Coburn, Dudley Moore
  'This exercise in witty Hollywood-bashing is subtler than most.' – *Kim Newman*

Disbarred
US   1938   58m   bw
Paramount
A lady lawyer is paid by a crime czar to defend a gangster.
Slick mini-melo of the kind at which this studio excelled at the time.
w Lillie Hayward, Robert Presnell *d* Robert Florey
☆ Otto Kruger, Gail Patrick, Robert Preston, Sidney Toler, Charles D. Brown
  'Moderately entertaining drama; nicely fills the lower brackets.' – *Variety*

'Sex is power.'
Disclosure *
US   1994   127m   Technicolor   Panavision
Warner/Baltimore/Constant c (Barry Levinson, Michael Crichton)
▦▦   ▦   ▦   ◎⌐   ◉   ♫
A female executive in a computer company accuses a male colleague of sexual harassment after he rejects her advances.

Entertaining nonsense, abandoning all pretence to be ostensibly exploring matters of social concern in favour of sensationalism and the trappings of a computer thriller; it is a movie of virtual unreality.
w Paul Attanasio *novel* Michael Crichton d Barry Levinson *ph* Anthony Pierce-Roberts m Ennio Morricone *pd* Neil Spisak *ed* Stu Linder *sp* visual effects: Industrial Light and Magic
☆ Michael Douglas, Demi Moore, Donald Sutherland, Caroline Goodall, Dylan Baker, Roma Maffia, Dennis Miller, Allan Rich
'This is the kind of well-made and highly professional entertainment which relies as much on techno-babble, a virtual reality encounter between the two principals and screens which tell you how to run your lives than on the moral dilemma.' – Derek Malcolm, *Guardian*
'If the viewer can get past the stupidity of *Disclosure*'s plot and casting, the movie isn't all that bad.' – Joe Queenan

The Discreet Charm of the Bourgeoisie ****

France/Spain/Italy 1972 105m Eastmancolor
Greenwich (Serge Silberman)
📀 💿 🎧
original title: Le Charme Discret de la Bourgeoisie
The efforts of a group of friends to dine together are continually frustrated.
A frequently hilarious, sometimes savage surrealist fable which makes all its points beautifully and then goes on twenty minutes too long. The performances are a joy.
w Luis Buñuel, Jean-Claude Carrière d Luis Buñuel *ph* Edmond Richard *ad* Pierre Guffroy *ed* Hélène Plemiannikov
☆ Fernando Rey, Delphine Seyrig, Stéphane Audran, Bulle Ogier, Jean-Pierre Cassel, Paul Frankeur, Julien Bertheau
'A perfect synthesis of surreal wit and blistering social assault.' – Jan Dawson, *MFB*
♟ best foreign film
♟ Luis Buñuel, Jean-Claude Carrière (script)
▽ Stéphane Audran; script

The Disembodied

US 1957 73m bw
Allied Artists
In the tropics, a doctor's wife is really a voodoo queen who is trying to kill him by supernatural means.
Verbose rubbish with more yawns than thrills.
w Jack Townley d Walter Grauman
☆ Allison Hayes, Paul Burke, John Wengraf

Dishonored **

US 1931 91m bw
Paramount
An officer's widow turned streetwalker is hired by the German government as a spy.
Rather gloomy melodrama which helped to establish its star as a top American attraction; but the heavy hand of her Svengali, von Sternberg, was already evident.
w Daniel N. Rubin *story* Josef von Sternberg d Josef von Sternberg *ph* Lee Garmes m Karl Hajos
☆ Marlene Dietrich, Victor McLaglen, Lew Cody, Gustav von Seyffertitz, Warner Oland, Barry Norton, Wilfred Lucas
'Miss Dietrich rises above her director … should make the money grade of an A1 draw talker.' – *Variety*
'The most exciting movie I have seen in several months … yet I hope I may die young if I ever again have to listen to a manuscript so full of recusant, stilted, outmoded theatrical mouthings.' – Pare Lorentz
'The whole film has a kind of magnificent grandeur embellished, of course, by its shining central performance.' – John Gillett, 1964

'She insulted her soul!'

Dishonored Lady

US 1947 85m bw
Mars Film (Hedy Lamarr)
📀
A girl with a past is cleared of a murder charge by her psychiatrist.
Melodramatic showpiece designed for herself by a glamorous star; OK for the silly season.
w Edmund H. North *play* Edward Sheldon, Margaret Ayer Barnes d Robert Stevenson *ph* Lucien Andriot m Carmen Dragon

☆ Hedy Lamarr, John Loder, Dennis O'Keefe, Paul Cavanagh, William Lundigan, Natalie Schafer, Morris Carnovsky

Dishonour Bright *

GB 1936 82m bw
GFD/Cecil (Herman Fellner, Max Schach)
An ageing playboy is blackmailed about a past affair.
Interesting semi-smart comedy of the period, tailored for its star.
w Ben Travers d Tom Walls *ph* Phil Tannura
☆ Tom Walls, Eugene Pallette, Betty Stockfeld, Diana Churchill, Arthur Wontner, Cecil Parker, George Sanders, Henry Oscar, Basil Radford

Disorderly Conduct

US 1932 82m bw
Fox
A cop turns crook after being demoted.
Heavy-going melodrama apparently intended as a tribute to the New York police.
w William Anthony McGuire d John W. Considine Jnr
☆ Spencer Tracy, Sally Eilers, El Brendel, Dickie Moore, Ralph Bellamy, Ralph Morgan, Alan Dinehart
'Good entertainment … mother-love sentiment with some kid atmosphere.' – *Variety*

The Disorderly Orderly

US 1964 89m Technicolor
Paramount/York (Paul Jones)
📀
A hospital orderly creates havoc by his inefficiency and his sympathy for other people's predicaments.
Spasmodic farce with far too much pathos between its highlights.
wd Frank Tashlin *ph* W. Wallace Kelley m Joseph Lilley
☆ Jerry Lewis, Glenda Farrell, Everett Sloane, Kathleen Freeman, Karen Sharpe, Susan Oliver, Alice Pearce

Disorganized Crime

US 1989 98m Metrocolor
Touchstone/Silver Screen Partners IV (Lynn Bigelow)
📀 🎧
A gang of incompetent crooks await the arrival of their leader, who has escaped from prison, so that they can attempt the perfect bank robbery.
Dull and uninteresting crime caper with stereotyped characters that flopped at the box-office.
wd Jim Kouf *ph* Ron Garcia m David Newman *pd* Waldemar Kalinowski *ed* Frank Morriss, Dallas Puett
☆ Hoyt Axton, Corbin Bernsen, Ruben Blades, Fred Gwynne, Ed O'Neill, Lou Diamond Phillips, Daniel Roebuck, William Russ

Les Disparus de St Agil *

France 1938 95m bw
Vog Films
Students disappear in a school whose headmaster is a forger and murderer.
Curious black comedy: a half-success.
w J. H. Blanchon *novel* Pierre Véry d Christian-Jaque
☆ Michel Simon, Erich von Stroheim, Aimé Clariond, Armand Bernard

A Dispatch from Reuters **

US 1940 90m bw
Warner (Henry Blanke)
GB title: *This Man Reuter*
The story of the man who provided Europe's first news service.
Acceptable if slightly dull addition to Warner's prestige biopics; well made and acted.
w Milton Krims d William Dieterle *ph* James Wong Howe m Max Steiner
☆ Edward G. Robinson, Edna Best, Eddie Albert, Albert Basserman, Gene Lockhart, Otto Kruger, Montagu Love, Nigel Bruce, James Stephenson

Disputed Passage *

US 1939 90m bw
Paramount (Harlan Thompson)
A young scientist who wants to marry meets resistance from his mentor.
Adequate screen version of a bestseller.
w Anthony Veiller, Sheridan Gibney *novel* Lloyd C. Douglas d Frank Borzage *ph* William C. Mellor m Frederick Hollander, James Leopold

☆ Dorothy Lamour, John Howard, Akim Tamiroff, Judith Barrett, William Collier Snr, Victor Varconi, Keye Luke, Elizabeth Risdon
'Fine drama of medical science: a top-of-the-bill attraction.' – *Variety*
'I should describe the flavour as a rather nauseating blend of iodine and glucose.' – Graham Greene

'It dwarfs the stage!'

Disraeli *

US 1929 89m bw
Warner
🎧
Fictionalized episodes in the life of the Victorian statesman, including his activities as a matchmaker.
Very early star talkie, of primarily archival interest; Arliss had appeared in a silent version in 1921.
w Julien Josephson *play* Louis N. Parker d Alfred E. Green *ph* Lee Garmes *md* Louis Silvers
☆ George Arliss, Joan Bennett, Florence Arliss, Anthony Bushell, David Torrence, Ivan Simpson, Doris Lloyd
'Those seeking a fuller assessment of the man and his work would have been better off in a library.' – Clive Hirschhorn, 1982
♟ George Arliss
♟ best picture; Julian Josephson

'The rescue … the throbbing jungle drums … the man-devouring marsh wilderness aflame with unseen menace!'

Distant Drums

US 1951 101m Technicolor
United States Pictures (Milton Sperling)
🎧 🎵
In 1840 Florida, an army officer rescues prisoners from an Indian fort and decimates the Seminoles who threaten their return journey.
Overlong action saga, with dull stretches compensated by a dominating star and some lively incident.
w Niven Busch, Martin Rackin d Raoul Walsh *ph* Sid Hickox m Max Steiner
☆ Gary Cooper, Mari Aldon, Richard Webb, Ray Teal, Arthur Hunnicutt, Robert Barrat
'Don't look for surprises. Mr Cooper is kept steady and laconic throughout, the action is serio-comic, and the pace is conventionally maintained.' – Bosley Crowther, *New York Times*

Distant Thunder ***

India 1973 100m colour
Balaka (Sarbani Bhattacharya)
🎧
original title: Asani Sanket
In 1943 a Brahmin teacher-priest and his wife experience in their small village the beginnings of a famine in Bengal.
A potent account of the breakdown of traditional values under the pressure of terrible events.
wd Satyajit Ray *novel* Bibhutibhusan Banerjee *ph* Soumendu Ray m Satyajit Ray *ad* Asok Bose *ed* Dulal Dutta
☆ Soumitra Chatterjee, Babita, Ramesh Mukherjee, Chitra Banerjee, Gobinda Chakravarti, Sandhya Roy
'I don't know when I've been so moved by a picture that I knew was riddled with flaws. It must be that Ray's vision comes out of so much hurt and guilt and love that the feeling pours over all the cracks in *Distant Thunder* and fills them up.' – Pauline Kael, *New Yorker*
† It won the Golden Bear award for Best Film at the Berlin Film Festival in 1973.

Distant Thunder

US/Canada 1988 114m Technicolor
Paramount (Robert Schaffel)
📀 🎧
A Vietnam veteran who, after his wartime experiences, lives on the fringes of society renews contact with the 18-year-old son he abandoned years before.
Soft-centred drama of male bonding through violence which might have been made for television; it is small in scale and scope, despite its melodramatic climax.
w Robert Stitzel, Deedee Wehle d Rick Rosenthal *ph* Ralf Bode m Maurice Jarre *ed* Dennis Virkler
☆ John Lithgow, Ralph Macchio, Kerrie Keane, Reb Brown, Janet Margolin, Denis Arndt, Jamey Sheridan, Tom Bower

A Distant Trumpet

US 1964 116m Technicolor Panavision
Warner (William H. Wright)
The new commander of a cavalry outpost tightens up discipline, which serves him well when Indian trouble erupts.
Moderate Western, quite well staged but with a second team cast.
w John Twist *novel* Paul Horgan d Raoul Walsh *ph* William Clothier m Max Steiner
☆ Troy Donahue, Suzanne Pleshette, James Gregory, Diane McBain, William Reynolds, Claude Akins, Kent Smith, Judson Pratt

Distant Voices, Still Lives *

GB 1988 84m colour
BFI/Film Four International (Colin MacCabe)
📀 🎧
Working-class family life in Liverpool in the 40s and 50s.
Low-budget labour of love filmed at intervals over two years, succeeding through close, unsentimental observation and excellent performances by a cast of unknowns.
wd Terence Davies *ph* William Diver, Patrick Duval *pd* Miki van Zwanenberg
☆ Freda Dowie, Pete Postlethwaite, Angela Walsh
'While its pacing and structure may exasperate some, should envelop receptive audiences with its special magic.' – *Variety*

The Distinguished Gentleman *

US 1992 112m Technicolor
Buena Vista/Hollywood Pictures (Leonard Goldberg, Michael Peyser)
📀 🎧 🎧
A con man decides that the best place for his talents is in government.
Enjoyable, broad comedy, which gives Murphy a good opportunity to display his fast-talking talents.
w Marty Kaplan d Jonathan Lynn *ph* Gabriel Beristain m Randy Edelman *pd* Leslie Dilley *ed* Tony Lombardo, Barry B. Leirer
☆ Eddie Murphy, Lane Smith, Sheryl Lee Ralph, Joe Don Baker, Victoria Rowell, Grant Shaud, Kevin McCarthy
'A lazily slung together collection of clichés, mixing diet politics with laughter-free comedy.' – Kim Newman, *Empire*

Disturbing Behavior

US 1998 84m DeLuxe
MGM/Village Roadshow/Hoyts/Beacon Communications (Armyan Bernstein, Jon Shestack)
🎧 🎧
A new high-school student discovers something odd about the school's athletic élite, who are able to get away with murder.
A somewhat dumb variation on The Stepford Wives (qv), played as a comedy and designed for a teenage audience.
w Scott Rosenberg d David Nutter *ph* John S. Bartley m Mark Snow *pd* Nelson Coates *ed* Randy Jon Morgan
☆ James Marsden, Katie Holmes, Nick Stahl, Steve Railsback, Bruce Greenwood, William Sadler, Chad E. Donella, Ethan Embry, Katherine Isabelle
'Brisk, slick, sloppily plotted, cliché-ridden script pic won't win many critical allies.' – Dennis Harvey, *Variety*

Ditte, Child of Man *

Denmark 1946 106m bw
Nordisk
original title: Ditte Menneskebarn
An unmarried mother abandons her daughter, who grows up to be a servant and to be seduced in her turn.
Impressive, doom-laden Scandinavian saga, highly thought of on its release.
wd Astrid and Bjarne Henning-Jensen *novel* Martin Andersen *ph* Werner Jenssen m Herman Koppel
☆ Tove Maes, Rasmus Ottesen, Karen Poulsen

Ditte Menneskebarn: see Ditte, Child of Man

Diva *

France 1981 117m Eastmancolor
Galaxie/Greenwich/Antenne 2 (Irene Silberman)
🎧 🎧 🎧
A black prima donna in Paris becomes accidentally involved in drug smuggling and murder.

A curious hybrid of violence and surrealism which doesn't seem to know what effect it's aiming at, or at least doesn't let the viewer in on the secret, being content to entertain in a flashy and sometimes shocking way.

w Jean-Jacques Beineix, Jean Van Hamme novel Delacorta d Jean-Jacques Beineix ph Philippe Rousselot m Vladimir Cosma pd Hilton McConnico

☆ Frederic Andrei, Roland Bertin, Richard Bohringer, Wilhelmenia Wiggins Fernandez, Jean-Jacques Moreau, Chantal Deruaz

'It's a mixture of style and chic hanky-panky, but it's genuinely sparkling.' – New Yorker

The Dive

GB/Norway   1989   95m   colour
Filmeffekt/Millennium/British Screen (Dag Alveberg, Patrick Cassavetti)

Deep-sea divers are trapped underwater while attempting to repair a pipeline.
Standard rescue melodrama, more lethargically directed than most.

w Leidulv Risan, Carlos Wiggen d Tristan de Vere Cole ph Harald Paalgard m Geir Bihren, Bent Aserud pd Jarle Blesvik ed Russell Lloyd

☆ Björn Sundquist, Frank Grimes, Eindride Eidsvold, Marika Lagercrantz, Nils Ole Oftebro, Michael Kitchen, Sverre Anker Ousdal

Dive Bomber *

US   1941   133m   Technicolor
Warner (Hal B. Wallis)
🎬

Aviation scientists work to eliminate pilot blackout.
Somewhat rarefied propaganda piece with too many reels of romantic banter but tense climactic scenes and good star performances.

w Frank 'Spig' Wead, Robert Buckner d Michael Curtiz m Bert Glennon, Winton C. Hoch m Max Steiner md Leo F. Forbstein

☆ Errol Flynn, Fred MacMurray, Ralph Bellamy, Alexis Smith, Regis Toomey, Robert Armstrong, Allen Jenkins, Craig Stevens, Moroni Olsen, Gig Young, William Hopper, Charles Drake, Russell Hicks, Addison Richards, Ann Doran and also Herbert Anderson

♯ Bert Glennon, Winton C. Hoch

The Divided Heart **

GB   1954   89m   bw
Ealing (Michael Truman)

A boy believed to be a war orphan is lovingly brought up by foster parents; then his real mother turns up and wants him back.
Effective 'woman's picture' set in Europe and giving a genuine sense of post-war feelings and problems.

w Jack Whittingham d Charles Crichton ph Otto Heller m Georges Auric

☆ Cornell Borchers, Yvonne Mitchell, Armin Dahlen, Alexander Knox, Geoffrey Keen, Michel Ray, Liam Redmond, Eddie Byrne

🅥 Yvonne Mitchell; Cornell Borchers

The Dividing Line: see The Lawless

The Divine Lady *

US   1929   100m   bw
Warner

The adventures of Emma, Lady Hamilton.
Historical charade which titillated at the time.

w Agnes Christine Johnston, Forrest Halsey d Frank Lloyd ph John Seitz

☆ Corinne Griffith, Victor Varconi, H. B. Warner, Montagu Love, Marie Dressler

👤 Frank Lloyd

♯ John Seitz; Corinne Griffith

Divine Madness

US   1980   93m   Technicolor   Panavision
Ladd Company/Warner
🎬   ◎

A record of a Bette Midler concert performance.
'Since this is the time capsule version of my show, I may as well do everything I know.'
It certainly isn't a movie.

d Michael Ritchie ph William A. Fraker

The Divine Woman *

US   1927   95m   bw   silent
MGM

The loves of Sarah Bernhardt.
Garbo's first star role; a typical Hollywood melodramatization of facts.

w Dorothy Farnum play Starlight by Gladys Unger d Victor Sjostrom

☆ Greta Garbo, Lars Hanson, Lowell Sherman, John Mack Brown, Polly Moran

Divorce

US   1945   71m   bw
Monogram/Jeffrey Bernerd/Kay Francis

A much-married woman tries to break up another happy family.
This somewhat elementary tract was the star's first independent production, and not a success.

w Sidney Sutherland, Harvey Gates d William Nigh

☆ Kay Francis, Bruce Cabot, Helen Mack, Jonathan Hale, Jerome Cowan

'A lacklustre script grooves it for the duals.' – Variety

'In America the ring costs two dollars to put on – and a fortune to take off!'

Divorce American Style **

US   1967   109m   Technicolor
Columbia/Tandem (Norman Lear)

Well-heeled Los Angeles suburbanites toy with divorce but eventually resume their domestic bickering.
Rather arid and patchy but often sharply sardonic comedy about a society in which people can't afford to divorce.

w Norman Lear d Bud Yorkin ph Conrad Hall m David Grusin pd Edward Stephenson

☆ Dick Van Dyke, Debbie Reynolds, Jean Simmons, Jason Robards Jnr, Van Johnson, Joe Flynn, Shelley Berman, Martin Gabel, Lee Grant, Tom Bosley, Dick Gautier

♯ Norman Lear

A Divorce in the Family

US   1932   78m   bw
MGM

A boy is affected by his parents' divorce.
Dated drama, an odd choice of vehicle for a boy star fresh from The Champ.

w Delmer Daves, Maurice Rapf d Charles Reisner

☆ Jackie Cooper, Conrad Nagel, Lois Wilson, Lewis Stone, Jean Parker, Lawrence Grant

'Not more than medium box office; Cooper fans will not be attracted by the title.' – Variety

'A delightfully daring plan to give marriage a surprise ending!'

Divorce Italian Style **

Italy   1961   108m   bw
Lux/Vides/Galatea (Franco Cristaldi)
🎬

original title: Divorzio all'Italiana

A Sicilian nobleman explains how, wishing to be rid of his wife, he arranged for her to be seduced and later shot by a jealous lover.
Sardonic, stylized comedy which, rather in the manner of Kind Hearts and Coronets, manages while retailing a black comedy plot to satirize Italian manners and institutions.

w Ennio de Concini, Pietro Germi, Alfredo Giannetti d Pietro Germi ph Leonida Barboni m Carlo Rustichelli

☆ Marcello Mastroianni, Daniela Rocca, Stefania Sandrelli, Leopoldo Trieste

👤 script

♯ Pietro Germi; Marcello Mastroianni

🅥 Marcello Mastroianni

The Divorce of Lady X **

GB   1938   92m   Technicolor
London Films (Alexander Korda)
📼   ◎

A nobleman's daughter wins a barrister by posing as a divorce client.
Pleasing comedy with high production standards of its time, deftly performed by a distinguished cast.

w Lajos Biro, Arthur Wimperis, Ian Dalrymple play Counsel's Opinion by Gilbert Wakefield d Tim Whelan ph Harry Stradling m Miklos Rozsa ad Lazare Meerson, Paul Sheriff ed William Hornbeck

☆ Laurence Olivier, Merle Oberon, Binnie Barnes, Ralph Richardson, Morton Selten, J. H. Roberts

'Her sin was no greater than his, but she was a woman! If the world permits the husband to philander – why not the wife?'

The Divorcee *

US   1930   83m   bw
MGM (Robert Z. Leonard)
🎬

Would-be liberal young marrieds divorce when she puts up with his affairs but he can't tolerate hers. She falls in love with another married man but sends him back to his wife.
Rather wan illustration of the double standard which was being much discussed in society at the time.

w John Meehan, Nick Grinde, Zelda Sears novel Ex-Wife by Ursula Parrott d Robert Z. Leonard ph Norbert Brodine ad Cedric Gibbons

☆ Norma Shearer, Chester Morris, Conrad Nagel, Robert Montgomery, Florence Eldridge

'Shearer's specialty was sexy suffering in satin gowns by Adrian; here, she almost seems to want to abandon herself to naughtiness, but one line after another stops her.' – Pauline Kael, 70s

👤 Norma Shearer

♯ best picture; Robert Z. Leonard; John Meehan, Nick Grinde, Zelda Sears

Divorcing Jack **

GB/France   1998   100m   Rank Colour
BBC/Winchester/Scala (Robert Cooper)

In an independent Northern Ireland, a journalist goes on the run after being framed for a murder, and is hunted by Loyalists and the IRA.
Tense, tough thriller that thumbs its nose at gunmen of all persuasions, served up with some wit and a gun-toting stripper-nun.

w Colin Bateman novel Colin Bateman d David Caffrey ph James Welland m Adrian Johnston pd Claire Kenny ed Nick Moore

☆ David Thewlis, Rachel Griffiths, Robert Lindsay, Jason Isaacs, Laura Fraser, Richard Gant, Bronagh Gallagher

'An out-and-out chase movie, stuffed with visual gags and boasting a fine comedy script which bends the ear with delight.' – Jake Hamilton, Empire

Divorzio all'Italiana: see Divorce Italian Style

Dixiana

US   1930   100m   bw (Technicolor sequences)
RKO
🎬   ◎

A Dutchman from Pennsylvania tries to run a plantation in Louisiana.
Lavish but utterly witless musical comedy which just lies there and dies there.

wd Luther Reed play Ann Caldwell

☆ Bebe Daniels, Bert Wheeler, Robert Woolsey, Everett Marshall, Joseph Cawthorn, Jobyna Howland, Dorothy Lee, Bill Robinson

'Not much but bigness for exploiting.' – Variety

Dixie *

US   1943   90m   Technicolor
Paramount (Paul Jones)

The life of old-time minstrel man Dan Emmett.
Lighter-than-air fictionalized biography with pleasing mid-19th-century settings.

w Karl Tunberg, Darrell Ware d A. Edward Sutherland ph William C. Mellor m Robert Emmett Dolan m/ly Johnny Burke, Jimmy Van Heusen

☆ Bing Crosby, Dorothy Lamour, Marjorie Reynolds, Lynne Overman, Eddie Foy Jnr, Billy de Wolfe, Raymond Walburn, Grant Mitchell

Dixie Dugan

US   1943   63m   bw
TCF (Walter Morosco)

A secretary with a screwball family gets a government job in Washington.
Fairly feeble adaptation from a popular comic strip.

w Lee Loeb, Harold Buckman d Otto Brower

☆ Lois Andrews, James Ellison, Charlie Ruggles, Charlotte Greenwood, Raymond Walburn, Eddie Foy Jnr

Django **

Italy/Spain   1966   95m   colour
BRC/Tecisa (Manolo Bolognini)
📼   ◎

A gunfighter who carries a machine-gun in a coffin rids a town of its gangs of Mexican bandits and the Ku Klux Klan.

One of the earliest, most notorious and influential of spaghetti Westerns, marked by a high level of violence but nevertheless watchable for its operatic style.

w Sergio Corbucci, Bruno Corbucci, Franco Rossetti, José G. Naesso, Piero Vivarelli d Sergio Corbucci ph Enzo Barboni m Luis Enrique Bacalov

☆ Franco Nero, Eduardo Fajardo, Loredana Nusciak, José Bodalo, Angel Alvarez

'After Leone, Corbucci was the genius of the spaghettis.' – Empire

Django against Sartana (dubbed)

Italy   1970   90m   Telecolor
P.A.C./B.C.R. (Roberto Bessi)

original title: Django Sfida Sartana

Django avenges the death of his brother, hanged for a crime he did not commit.
Mundane spaghetti Western, a sequel lacking the excesses of the original and content to provide the minimum in interest or excitement.

wd William Redford (Pasquale Squitteri) ph Eugenio Bentivoglio m Piero Umiliani

☆ George Ardisson, Tony Kendall, José Torres, Bernard Faber, Adler Gray, John Alvar

Django, Kill! (dubbed)

Italy/Spain   1967   120m   colour
GIA/Hispamer (Alex J. Rascal)

original title: Sei Sei Vivo, Spara!
aka: If You Live Shoot!

A vengeful gunman, who was among Mexicans double-crossed and shot down by American bandits, tracks the gang to a town controlled by Zorro, a homosexual bandit, and his followers.
Sprawling, decadent spaghetti Western in a rococo style, given over to brutal deaths; it is not often screened uncut.

w Franco Arcalli, Giulio Questi, Benedetto Benedetti idea Ma del Carmen, M. Roman d Giulio Questi ph Franco delli Colli m Ivan Vandor ed Franco Arcalli

☆ Tomas Milian, Marilu Tolo, Piero Lulli, Milo Quesada, Roberto Camardiel, Patrizia Valturri, Raymond Lovelock

† The film exists in several other, shorter versions, cut for reasons of violence or length.

Django Sfida Sartana: see Django against Sartana

Django Spara per Primo

Italy   1966   95m   Technicolor   Techniscope
Gala/Fida (Edmondo Amati)

aka: He Who Shoots First

Django is framed for a bank robbery by the man who murdered his father.
Tedious re-run of the usual theme of vengeance, done without style or originality.

w Sandro Continenza, Massimiliano Capriccoli, Florenzo Carpi, Vincenzo Flamini, Alberto de Martino d Alberto de Martino ph Ricardo Pallottini m Bruno Nicolai ad Pier Vittorio Marchi ed Otello Colangeli

☆ Glenn Saxon, Fernando Sancho, Evelyn Stewart (Ida Galli), Nando Gazzolo, Lee Burton (Guido Lollobrigida)

'A lifeless Italian Western … plods wearily through the required rituals.' – MFB

En Djunselsaga: see The Flute and the Arrow

DNA

US   1996   93m   colour
InterLight (Patrick D. Choi, Nile Niami)
🎬

A doctor's discovery in Borneo is stolen by a power-crazed genetic scientist who uses it to bring back to life a long-dead mutant.
Undemanding action fare in a jungle setting, with borrowings from many horrors, from King Kong to Alien and Predator.

w Nick Davis d William Mesa ph Gerry Lively m Christopher L. Stone pd Charles Wood ed Edward R. Abroms

☆ Mark Dacascos, Jürgen Prochnow, Robin McKee, Roger Aaron Brown, John H. Brennan, Thomas Taus Jnr

The Do It Yourself Cartoon Kit **

GB   1961   6m   Eastmancolor
Biographic

A commercial for the kit in question, poking fun at all comers in a Monty Pythonish way.

Great stuff for those who like zany humour well controlled.

w Colin Pearson d Bob Godfrey

'What should a girl do when opportunity knocks ... twice?'

Do Not Disturb

US 1965 102m DeLuxe Cinemascope
TCF/Melcher/Arcola (Aaron Rosenberg, Martin Melcher)

An American wool executive is posted to London; his dizzy wife makes him jealous by flirting with a French antique dealer.

Silly farce which paints a lunatic picture of English and French life but occasionally raises a wild laugh or two. Thin script and production.

w Milt Rosen, Richard Breen *play* William Fairchild d Ralph Levy ph Leon Shamroy m Lionel Newman

☆ Doris Day, Rod Taylor, Sergio Fantoni, Reginald Gardiner, Hermione Baddeley, Leon Askin

Do the Right Thing ***

US 1989 120m colour
UIP/Forty Acres And A Mule Filmworks/Spike Lee
📼 🎬 ⊚ ⊙ 🎧

A white pizza parlour owner in a black neighbourhood sparks off a riot.

Complex, witty, street-wise and passionate film about racism.

w Spike Lee d Spike Lee ph Ernest Dickerson m Bill Lee pd Wynn Thomas ed Barry Alexander Brown

☆ Danny Aiello, Ossie Davis, Ruby Dee, Richard Edson, Giancarlo Esposito, Spike Lee, Bill Nunn, John Turturro, John Savage, Rosie Perez

'A very unusual movie experience – two hours of bombardment with New York-style stimuli.' – *Terrence Rafferty, New Yorker*

🔔 best original screenplay; Danny Aiello

Do You Like Women?

France/Italy 1964 100m bw
Francoriz/Number One/Federiz (Pierre Kalfon)
original title: *Aimez-Vous Les Femmes?*

Secret rival sects of woman-eaters cause an outbreak of murders in Paris.

Bizarre black comedy that doesn't quite work but provides ghoulish fun along the way.

w Roman Polanski, Gérard Brach *novel* Georges Bardawil d Jean Léon ph Sacha Vierny m Ward Swingle

☆ Sophie Daumier, Guy Bédos, Edwige Feuillère, Grégoire Aslan, Roger Blin

'It has the provoking quality of a carefully-prepared firework display which, due to faulty timing or bad connections, is never actually ignited.' – *MFB*

Do You Love Me?

US 1946 91m Technicolor
TCF (George Jessel)

The lady dean of a music school gets herself glamorized.

Thin, mildly agreeable but forgettable musical.

w Robert Ellis, Helen Logan d Gregory Ratoff ph Edward Cronjager m/ly various

☆ Maureen O'Hara, Dick Haymes, Harry James and his Orchestra, Reginald Gardiner, Richard Gaines, Stanley Prager

The Doberman Gang

US 1972 87m Eastmancolor
Fox-Rank/Rosamond (David Chudnow)
📼

After his accomplices bungle a robbery, a crook trains six Dobermans to rob a bank.

The dogs run away with the picture, but invention and budget are both on too tight a leash to offer much more than the equivalent of an over-long pet-food commercial.

w Louis Garfinkle, Frank Ray Perilli d Byron Ross Chudnow ph Robert Caramico m Bradford Craig, Alan Silvestri ad Budd Costello ed Herman Freedman

☆ Byron Mabe, Hal Reed, Julie Parrish, Simmy Bow, Jojo D'Amore

'The film hovers uncertainly between straight thriller and comedy.' – *MFB*

† It was followed by two sequels with similar plots, *The Daring Dobermans*, 1973, and the bigger-budget *The Amazing Dobermans*, 1976 (qv), in which the dogs were on the side of the law.

Dobermann *

France 1997 103m colour 'Scope
Polygram/Noé/La Chauve Souris/Tawak/Canal+/France 3/Comstock (Frederique Dumas, Eric Neve)
📼

A violent bank-robber, his deaf girlfriend and psychotic gang are hunted down by a brutal and sadistic cop.

Frenetic, black thriller, a fast-moving romp in the manner of an exuberant comic strip; its style almost compensates for its unremitting violence.

w Joel Houssin *novels* Joel Houssin d Jan Kounen ph Michel Amathieu m Schyzomaniac pd Michel Barthelemy ed Benedicte Brunet sp Mac Guff Ligne

☆ Vincent Cassel, Monica Belluci, Tcheky Karyo, Antoine Basler, Dominique Bettenfeld, Chick Ortéga, Stephane Metzger

'Ultraviolent, sexist, scatological and drug-drenched... Astoundingly high-voltage entertainment.' – *Stephen O'Shea, Variety*

Doc *

US 1971 96m DeLuxe
UA/Frank Perry

Doc Holliday goes to Tombstone to die of TB, but is drawn into the feud between the Clantons and his friend Wyatt Earp, whose motives are not of the highest.

A somewhat glum debunking of the west's most heroic myth, backing dour character study with grubby pictures. The result lacks excitement but maintains interest.

w Pete Hamill d Frank Perry ph Gerald Hirschfeld m Jimmy Webb

☆ Stacy Keach, Harris Yulin, Faye Dunaway, Mike Witney, Denver John Collins, Dan Greenberg

'The physical realism that *Doc* is at pains to establish becomes simply a convention of its own.' – *Richard Combs*

Doc Hollywood *

US 1991 103m Technicolor
Warner (Susan Solt, Deborah D. Johnson)
📼 🎬 ⊚ ⊙ 🎧

On the way to a new job as a plastic surgeon in Hollywood, a young doctor crashes his car in a small town and is sentenced to work at the local hospital.

Amiable, inoffensive comedy in a familiar vein.

w Jeffrey Price, Peter S. Seaman, Daniel Pyne *novel What?* ... *Dead Again* by Neil B. Shulman d Michael Caton-Jones ph Michael Chapman m Carter Burwell pd Lawrence Miller ed Gregg London

☆ Michael J. Fox, Julie Warner, Barnard Hughes, Woody Harrelson, David Ogden Stiers, Frances Sternhagen, George Hamilton, Bridget Fonda, Mel Winkler, Helen Martin, Roberts Blossom

'This serving of recycled Capracorn has no real taste of its own, but, in its mildness and predictability, offers the reassurance of a fast-food or motel chain.' – *Variety*

'Have no fear, Doc Savage is here!'

Doc Savage, Man of Bronze

👪 US 1975 100m Technicolor
Warner (George Pal)
📼

A thirties superman and his assistants the Amazing Five fly to South America to avenge the death of Doc's father.

Stolid, humourless adaptation from a comic strip, totally lacking in the necessary panache.

w George Pal, Joe Morhaim *stories* Kenneth Robeson d Michael Anderson ph Fred Koenekamp m John Philip Sousa

☆ Ron Ely, Paul Gleason, Bill Lucking, Michael Miller, Eldon Quick

'A slick, ultra-self-conscious camp that denies the material its self-respect.' – *Colin Pahlow*

'Nothing in this unfortunate enterprise is likely to please anyone: former Savage fans will be enraged, newcomers bored, and children will probably feel superior to the whole mess...' – *New Yorker*

The Dock Brief

GB 1962 88m bw
MGM/Dimitri de Grunwald
📼
US title: *Trial and Error*

An incompetent barrister defends his client on a murder charge. The client is found guilty but the

sentence is quashed on the grounds of inadequate defence.

Flat filming of a TV play which was a minor milestone; the film is twice the length and half as funny, and both stars quickly become tiresome.

w John Mortimer, Pierre Rouve *play* John Mortimer d James Hill ph Ted Scaife m Ron Grainer

☆ Peter Sellers, Richard Attenborough, Beryl Reid, David Lodge, Frank Pettingell

Docks of New York **

US 1928 80m bw silent
Paramount

A stoker marries a girl he has saved from suicide. Further unfortunate incidents result in his going to prison, but she waits for him.

Glum melodrama chiefly remarkable for its sets and lighting, reminiscent of the later Quai des Brumes.

w Jules Furthman *story The Dock Walloper* by John Monk Saunders d Josef von Sternberg ph Harold Rosson ad Hans Dreier

☆ George Bancroft, Betty Compson, Olga Baclanova, Clyde Cook, Gustav von Seyffertitz

'One comes away with the memory of a film impregnated with a life whose essential is in its energy and force.' – *Louis Chavance*

Docks of New York

US 1945 61m bw
Pathé/Monogram/Banner (Sam Katzman, Jack Dietz)

Mugs and Glimpy become involved in espionage and skulduggery when they try to help two refugees, who turn out to be European royalty being hunted by secret foreign agents.

Average programmer, broadly acted and with a patriotic propaganda message. It was one of the last films in the East Side Kids series (qv).

w Harvey Gates d Wallace Fox ph Ira Morgan md Edward Kay ed William Austin

☆ Leo Gorcey, Huntz Hall, Billy Benedict, Gloria Pope, Carlyle Blackwell Jnr, Betty Blythe, Cyrus Kendall, George Meeker

The Doctor **

US 1991 125m Technicolor
Buena Vista/Touchstone/Silver Screen Partners IV (Laura Ziskin)
📼 🎬 ⊚

A repressed surgeon alters his attitudes after he becomes a cancer patient at his own hospital.

Well-made drama of personal redemption.

w Robert Caswell *book A Taste of My Own Medicine* by Ed Rosenbaum d Randa Haines ph John Seale m Michael Convertino pd Ken Adam ed Bruce Green, Lisa Fruchtman

☆ William Hurt, Christine Lahti, Elizabeth Perkins, Mandy Patinkin, Adam Arkin, Charlie Korsmo, Wendy Crewson, Bill Macy

'Grapples powerfully with themes seldom faced in today's escapist marketplace: mortality, compassion, social responsibility.' – *Variety*

The Doctor and the Debutante: see *Dr Kildare's Victory*

The Doctor and the Devils

GB 1985 93m Rank Colour Panavision
Brooksfilm (Jonathan Sanger)
📼

In the late 18th century an Edinburgh surgeon starts to pay for bodies as specimens, and doesn't ask their provenance.

Yet another version (see The Body Snatcher, The Flesh and the Fiends, Burke and Hare*) of the tale of Dr Knox, and this time a pretty poor one, justified by the use of Dylan Thomas's script.*

w Ronald Harwood, from Dylan Thomas d Freddie Francis ph Gerry Turpin, Norman Warwick m John Morris pd Robert Laing

☆ Timothy Dalton, Jonathan Pryce, Twiggy, Julian Sands, Lewis Fiander, Stephen Rea

'Unrelentingly serious treatment of a gruesome subject is unlikely to attract many warm bodies to the box office.' – *Variety*

The Doctor and the Girl

US 1949 98m bw
MGM (Pandro S. Berman)

A young doctor renounces specialization to help the poor.

Antediluvian medical romance full of the nicest people. Technically very competent.

w Theodore Reeves, from 'a literary work' by Maxene Van Der Meersch d Curtis Bernhardt ph Robert Planck m R. G. Kopp

☆ Glenn Ford, Charles Coburn, Gloria de Haven, Janet Leigh, Bruce Bennett, Warner Anderson

Doctor at Large

👪 GB 1957 104m Eastmancolor
Rank (Betty E. Box)
📼

Simon Sparrow tries two country practices, but returns at last to St Swithin's.

Hit-or-miss medical comedy with honours about even.

w Nicholas Phipps *novel* Richard Gordon d Ralph Thomas ph Ernest Steward m Bruce Montgomery

☆ Dirk Bogarde, Muriel Pavlow, James Robertson Justice, Donald Sinden, Shirley Eaton, Derek Farr, Michael Medwin, Edward Chapman, Barbara Murray, Gladys Henson, Lionel Jeffries, A. E. Matthews, Athene Seyler, George Coulouris

Doctor at Sea *

👪 GB 1955 93m Technicolor VistaVision
Rank/Group Films (Betty E. Box)
📼

Simon Sparrow becomes medical officer on a cargo steamer.

Reasonably lively comedy of errors with nice seascapes and predictable jokes.

w Nicholas Phipps, Jack Davies d Ralph Thomas ph Ernest Steward m Bruce Montgomery

☆ Dirk Bogarde, Brigitte Bardot, Brenda de Banzie, James Robertson Justice, Maurice Denham, Michael Medwin, Hubert Gregg, Raymond Huntley, Geoffrey Keen, George Coulouris, Jill Adams, James Kenney

'Brisk professional humour has given way to the more elementary business of traditional British farce.' – *Penelope Houston, MFB*

Doctor Blood's Coffin

GB 1960 92m Eastmancolor
UA/Caralan (George Fowler)
📼

A disbarred doctor sets up in a Cornish tin mine and begins to emulate Dr Frankenstein.

Lurid horror piece which makes no sort of sense.

w Jerry Juran, Nathan Juran d Sidney J. Furie ph Stephen Dade m Buxton Orr

☆ Kieron Moore, Hazel Court, Ian Hunter, Gerald C. Lawson, Kenneth J. Warren, Fred Johnson

'It lacks style, suspense and imagination and will scarcely satisfy even the most naive necrophiliac.' – *MFB*

'He's the main stem's specialist in heart trouble – and lead poisoning!'

Dr Broadway

US 1942 75m bw
Paramount

A young medico gets involved with guns, girls and gangsters.

Adequate filler which failed to spawn the intended series.

w Art Arthur *story* Borden Chase d Anthony Mann

☆ Macdonald Carey, Jean Phillips, J. Carrol Naish, Richard Lane, Eduardo Ciannelli

Dr Bull

US 1933 75m bw
Fox

A genial country doctor triumphs over his own lack of medical knowledge.

Rather lumpy star vehicle which paid its way.

w Paul Green *novel The Last Adam* by James Gould Cozzens d John Ford

☆ Will Rogers, Vera Allen, Marian Nixon, Berton Churchill, Louise Dresser, Andy Devine, Ralph Morgan

'Drips with human interest and can scarcely miss.' – *Variety*

Dr Christian

Following the success of THE COUNTRY DOCTOR (qv), a rival studio (RKO) made a series of second features about a fictional country doctor, the rights to Dr Dafoe's life story being unavailable. Jean Hersholt again played the leading role and the films were immensely popular in small towns. A TV series followed in the fifties, starring Macdonald Carey.
1939 Meet Dr Christian

1940 The Courageous Dr Christian, Dr Christian Meets the Women, Remedy for Riches
1941 Melody for Three, They Meet Again

Dr Crippen *

GB 1962 98m bw
ABP/John Clein
◙

A quiet doctor murders his wife and elopes with a typist.
Straightforward account of a famous and rather unsurprising Edwardian murder case; well enough made but with no special raison d'être.
w Leigh Vance d Robert Lynn ph Nicolas Roeg m Kenneth Jones
☆ Donald Pleasence, Coral Browne, Samantha Eggar, Donald Wolfit

'Diabolical dictator ... devastating discoverer of the most frightening invention in the history of civilized man!'
'The picture made behind locked doors!'

Dr Cyclops *

US 1940 76m Technicolor
Paramount (Merian C. Cooper)
◙ ◠

Jungle travellers are captured and miniaturized by a mad scientist.
Splendid special effects and an appropriately sombre atmosphere are hampered by a slow-paced narrative in this minor horror classic.
w Tom Kilpatrick d Ernest Schoedsack ph Henry Sharp, Winton Hoch m Ernst Toch, Gerard Carbonara, Albert Hay Malotte
☆ Albert Dekker, Janice Logan, Victor Kilian, Thomas Coley, Charles Halton

Doctor Death: Seeker of Souls

US 1973 89m Movielab
Fox-Rank/Freedom Arts (Eddie Saeta)
▦

Doctor Death, who has the power to pass his and others' souls into the bodies of those he kills, attempts to re-animate a woman at the request of her grieving husband.
Bizarre low-budget horror which, judging from a brief turn by one of the Three Stooges, is presumably meant to amuse, though, seeing its general ineptitude, it is hard to be sure.
w Sal Ponti d Eddie Saeta ph Kent Wakeford, Emil Oster m Richard LaSalle ad Ed Graves ed Tony DiMarco
☆ John Considine, Barry Coe, Cheryl Miller, Stewart Moss, Leon Askin, Jo Morrow, Moe Howard
'The spectator who brings a properly black frame of mind to it may well be entertained.' – Jonathan Rosenbaum, MFB

Dr Dolittle

👫 US 1967 152m DeLuxe Todd-AO
TCF/APJAC (Arthur P. Jacobs)
In a Victorian English village, Dr Dolittle is a veterinary surgeon who talks to his patients; escaping from a lunatic asylum, he travels with friends to the South Seas in search of the Great Pink Sea Snail.
Lumpish family spectacular with no imagination whatever, further handicapped by charmless performances and unsingable songs.
novels Hugh Lofting d Richard Fleischer ph Robert Surtees md Lionel Newman, Alex Courage pd Mario Chiari w/songs Leslie Bricusse
☆ Rex Harrison, Anthony Newley, Samantha Eggar, Richard Attenborough, William Dix, Peter Bull
🎵 song 'Talk to the Animals'; special effects (L. B. Abbott)
& best picture; Robert Surtees; Lionel Newman, Alex Courage; Leslie Bricusse (m)

Dr Dolittle

👫 US 1998 85m DeLuxe
TCF (John Davis, Joseph M. Singer, David T. Friendly)
◙ ▦ ◠

A doctor who can talk to animals is put in an asylum by jealous colleagues.
The second unsuccessful attempt to make a movie of Hugh Lofting's creation; this time, there's talking animatronic animals and crude jokes, but it lacks charm.
w Nat Mauldin, Larry Levin stories Hugh Lofting d Betty Thomas ph Russell Boyd m Richard

---

Gibbs pd William Elliott ed Peter Teschner sp animatronics: Jim Henson's Creature Shop
☆ Eddie Murphy, Ossie Davis, Oliver Platt, Peter Boyle, Richard Schiff, Kristen Wilson, Jeffrey Tambor, Kyla Pratt, Raven-Symoné, Steven Gilborn and also the voices of: Norm Macdonald, Albert Brooks, Chris Rock, Reni Santoni, John Leguizamo, Julie Kavner, Garry Shandling
'This is as self-conscious and iconoclastic as story-telling gets. What kids will make of it, is anyone's guess.' – Charlotte O'Sullivan, Sight and Sound
'Slim on story and rife with scatological jokes, the film may strike a chord with pre-teens but misses for an older crowd despite some nifty effects and broad humor.' – Leonard Klady, Variety

Dr Ehrlich's Magic Bullet ***

US 1940 103m bw
Warner (Wolfgang Reinhardt)
aka: The Story of Dr Ehrlich's Magic Bullet
A German scientist develops a cure for venereal disease.
Excellent period biopic: absorbing, convincing and extremely well put together.
w John Huston, Heinz Herald, Norman Burnside d William Dieterle ph James Wong Howe m Max Steiner
☆ Edward G. Robinson, Ruth Gordon, Otto Kruger, Donald Crisp, Maria Ouspenskaya, Montagu Love, Sig Rumann, Donald Meek, Henry O'Neill, Albert Basserman, Edward Norris, Harry Davenport, Louis Calhern, Louis Jean Heydt
'A superb motion picture.' – Pare Lorentz
Ⴘ John Huston, Heinz Herald, Norman Burnside

Dr Faustus

GB 1967 93m Technicolor
Columbia/Oxford University Screen Productions/Nassau Films/Venfilms (Richard Burton, Richard McWhorter)
A medieval scholar conjures up Mephistopheles and offers his soul in exchange for a life of voluptuousness.
Marlowe's play has been adapted and 'improved', and there is some good handling of the poetry, but the production is flat, dingy and uninspired, as well as ludicrous when Miss Taylor makes her silent appearances.
w Nevill Coghill play Christopher Marlowe d Richard Burton, Nevill Coghill ph Gabor Pogany m Mario Nascimbene pd John DeCuir
☆ Richard Burton, Andreas Teuber, Ian Marter, Elizabeth Donovan, Elizabeth Taylor
'It is of an awfulness that bends the mind. The whole enterprise has the immense vulgarity of a collaboration in which academe would sell its soul for a taste of the glamour of Hollywood, and the stars are only too happy to appear a while in academe.' – John Simon
'It turns out to be the story of a man who sold his soul for Elizabeth Taylor.' – Judith Crist

Doctor from Seven Dials: see Corridors of Blood

'A new prescription for terror.'

Dr Giggles

US 1992 95m DeLuxe
Universal (Stuart M. Besser)
◙ ▦ ◠ ◈ 🎧

A mad doctor takes his revenge on those who lynched his equally murderous father.
Predictably grisly horror played for laughs.
w Manny Coto, Graeme Whifler d Manny Coto ph Robert Draper m Brian May pd Bill Malley ed Debra Neil sp Phil Cory Special EFX, Digital Fantasy
☆ Larry Drake, Holly Marie Combs, Cliff de Young, Glenn Quinn, Keith Diamond, Richard Bradford, Michelle Johnson
'Picture is aimed at the low end of the shock audience.' – Variety
'A piece of excrement.' – Nigel Floyd
'What this project really needs is major script surgery.' – The Dark Side

Dr Gillespie's Criminal Case

US 1943 89m bw
MGM
GB title: Crazy to Kill
The elderly doctor solves a murder for which an innocent man is in prison.

Skilled programme filler with beloved characters.
w Martin Berkeley, Harry Ruskin, Lawrence Bachmann d Willis Goldbeck
☆ Lionel Barrymore, Margaret O'Brien, Donna Reed, Van Johnson, Keye Luke, Marilyn Maxwell
† See also Dr Kildare.

Dr Gillespie's New Assistant

US 1942 88m bw
MGM
Shorn of young Dr Kildare, Gillespie chooses a new support from three interns, and meanwhile concentrates on an amnesia case.
Slick series entry which played widely as top of the bill.
w Willis Goldbeck, Harry Ruskin, Lawrence Bachmann d Willis Goldbeck
☆ Lionel Barrymore, Van Johnson, Keye Luke, Richard Quine, Susan Peters
† See also Dr Kildare.

Dr Goldfoot and the Bikini Machine

US 1965 90m Pathécolor Panavision
AIP (Anthony Carras)
Dr G. makes girl robots programmed to lure wealthy men into their clutches.
Way-out farce for the jaded end of the teenage market; a few lively touches and a climactic chase partly atone for the general tastelessness.
w Elwood Ullman, Robert Kaufman d Norman Taurog ph Sam Leavitt m Les Baxter ad Daniel Haller
☆ Vincent Price, Fred Clark, Frankie Avalon, Dwayne Hickman, Susan Hart, Jack Mullaney

'Meet the girls with the thermo-nuclear navels! The most titillating time bombs you've ever been tempted to trigger!'

Dr Goldfoot and the Girl Bombs

US/Italy 1966 86m colour
AIP
The evil mastermind teams up with Red China to cause trouble between Russia and the USA.
Inane teenage nonsense, almost enough to make one swear off movies.
w Louis M. Heyward, Robert Kaufman d Mario Bava
☆ Vincent Price, Fabian Forte, Franco Franchi, Laura Antonelli

Dr Heckyl and Mr Hype

US 1980 99m Metrocolor
Golan-Globus
▦

An ugly scientist is transformed into a handsome young sadist.
Would-be comic variation on a well-worn theme; the level of comedy is indicated by the title.
wd Charles B. Griffith
☆ Oliver Reed, Sunny Johnson, Mel Wells, Maia Danziger

Doctor in Clover

👫 GB 1966 101m Eastmancolor
Rank/Betty E. Box-Ralph Thomas
Grimsdyke goes back to his old hospital for a refresher course and finds a rejuvenating drug useful in his philandering.
Depressing mixture of smut and slapstick.
w Jack Davies novel Richard Gordon d Ralph Thomas ph Ernest Steward m John Scott
☆ Leslie Phillips, James Robertson Justice, Shirley Anne Field, Joan Sims, John Fraser, Arthur Haynes, Fenella Fielding, Noel Purcell, Jeremy Lloyd, Eric Barker, Terry Scott, Alfie Bass
'Everything is reduced to clichés and stereotypes.' – Ken Russell

Doctor in Distress

👫 GB 1963 102m Eastmancolor
Rank/Betty E. Box-Ralph Thomas
▦

Simon Sparrow goes back to work for Sir Lancelot Spratt and finds his old mentor in love.
Tedious flummery whose characters fail to perform with the old pizazz.
w Nicholas Phipps, Ronald Scott Thorn d Ralph Thomas ph Ernest Steward m Norrie Paramor
☆ Dirk Bogarde, James Robertson Justice, Mylene Demongeot, Samantha Eggar, Barbara Murray, Donald Houston, Jessie Evans, Ann Lynn, Leo McKern, Dennis Price

---

Doctor in Love

GB 1960 97m Eastmancolor
Rank/Betty E. Box-Ralph Thomas
Dr Burke and Dr Hare have various adventures, mostly amorous, in city and country practices.
Virtually plotless collection of weak sketches based on schoolboy smut.
w Nicholas Phipps novel Richard Gordon d Ralph Thomas ph Ernest Steward m Bruce Montgomery
☆ Michael Craig, Leslie Phillips, James Robertson Justice, Virginia Maskell, Nicholas Phipps, Reginald Beckwith, Joan Sims, Liz Fraser, Ambrosine Philpotts, Irene Handl

Doctor in the House **

👫 GB 1954 91m Eastmancolor
Rank (Betty E. Box)
◙ ▦

Amorous and other misadventures of medical students at St Swithin's Hospital.
A comedy with much to answer for: several sequels and an apparently endless TV series. The original is not bad, as the students, though plainly over age, constitute a formidable mass of British talent at its peak.
w Nicholas Phipps novel Richard Gordon d Ralph Thomas ph Ernest Steward m Bruce Montgomery
☆ Dirk Bogarde, Kenneth More, Donald Sinden, Donald Houston, Kay Kendall, Muriel Pavlow, James Robertson Justice, Geoffrey Keen
'Works its way with determined high spirits through the repertoire of medical student jokes.' – MFB
'An uproarious, devil-may-care, almost wholly ruthless picture.' – Dilys Powell
† Sequels, of increasing inanity and decreasing connection with the original characters, were: Doctor at Sea, Doctor at Large, Doctor in Love, Doctor in Distress, Doctor in Clover and Doctor in Trouble. Carry on Doctor and Carry on Again Doctor were horses of a different colour.
Ⴘ Kenneth More

Doctor in the Village *

Holland 1958 92m bw
Nationale Filmproductie Maatschappij (Bobby Roosenboom)
original title: Dorp aan de Rivier
Stories are recalled of an eccentric but respected country doctor at the turn of the century.
Tragi-comic incidents in the vein of Pagnol, a little too rich in farce and melodrama to be convincingly human.
w Hugo Claus novel Antoon Coolen d Fons Rademakers ph Eduard J. R. van der Enden m Jurriaan Andriessen
☆ Max Croiset, Mary Dresselhuys, Bernhard Droog, Jan Teulings
'Scenes which should have had disturbing power seemed run upon one another with an almost repellent relish which falls over into parody.' – Peter John Dyer, MFB

Doctor in Trouble

👫 GB 1970 90m Technicolor
Rank/Betty E. Box
Dr Burke inadvertently becomes a stowaway on an Atlantic cruise.
Witless tailpiece to the Doctor saga, like a half-hearted wrapping-up of discarded jokes from the other episodes.
w Jack Davies novel Doctor on Toast by Richard Gordon d Ralph Thomas ph Ernest Steward m Eric Rogers
☆ Leslie Phillips, Harry Secombe, Angela Scoular, Irene Handl, Robert Morley, Simon Dee, Freddie Jones, James Robertson Justice, Joan Sims, John Le Mesurier, Fred Emney
'The cinematic equivalent of an end-of-the-pier summer show.' – Films and Filming

Doctor Jack *

US 1922 72m bw silent
Pathé/Rolin
A quack country doctor does more good than the licensed medicos.
Pleasing but not hilariously funny star vehicle.
w Sam Taylor, Jean Havez d Fred Newmeyer
☆ Harold Lloyd, Mildred Davis, John Prince, Eric Mayne

'The greatest drama of dual identity ever written!'

Dr Jekyll and Mr Hyde **

US 1921 63m bw silent
Paramount Artcraft

▭ 𝒬 ⌕

A respected London physician experiments with a drug which separates out the evil part of his soul.
A lively star vehicle which renewed John Barrymore's popularity with film audiences. Some scenes still grip, and Barrymore accomplished some transformations in full view of the camera, by facial contortions.
w Clara S. Beranger novel Robert Louis Stevenson d John S. Robertson
☆ John Barrymore, Nita Naldi, Martha Mansfield, Louis Wolheim

'Strange desires! Loves and hates and secret yearnings ... hidden in the shadows of a man's mind!'

Doctor Jekyll and Mr Hyde ****

US 1931 98m bw
Paramount (Rouben Mamoulian)

▭ 𝒬 ⌕

A Victorian research chemist finds a formula which separates the good and evil in his soul; when the latter predominates, he becomes a rampaging monster.
The most exciting and cinematic version by far of the famous horror story; the make-up is slightly over the top, but the gas-lit London settings, the pace, the performances and clever camera and sound tricks make it a film to enjoy over and over again. Subjective camera is used at the beginning, and for the first transformation the actor wore various layers of make up which were sensitive to different colour filters and thus produced instant change.
w Samuel Hoffenstein, Percy Heath novel Robert Louis Stevenson d Rouben Mamoulian ph Karl Struss ad Hans Dreier
☆ Fredric March, Miriam Hopkins, Rose Hobart, Holmes Herbert, Halliwell Hobbes, Edgar Norton
'Promises abundant shocks and returns now that the fan public is horror conscious. Probably loses something on popular appeal by highbrow treatment.' – Variety
'As a work of cinematic imagination this film is difficult to fault.' – John Baxter, 1968
† The screenplay with 1,400 frame blow-ups was published in 1976 in the Film Classics Library (editor Richard J. Anobile).
†† The film was subsequently edited down to 80m, and this is the only version remaining.
🏆 Fredric March
& Samuel Hoffenstein, Percy Heath; Karl Struss

'A romantic gentleman by day – a love-mad beast at night!'

Dr Jekyll and Mr Hyde **

US 1941 122m bw
MGM (Victor Saville, Victor Fleming)

▭ 𝒬

Curiously misconceived, stately, badly cast version with elaborate production including Freudian dream sequences.
Always worth watching, but not a success.
w John Lee Mahin d Victor Fleming ph Joseph Ruttenberg m Franz Waxman ed Harold F. Kress
☆ Spencer Tracy, Ingrid Bergman, Lana Turner, Ian Hunter, C. Aubrey Smith, Donald Crisp, Sara Allgood
'Not so much evil incarnate as ham rampant ... more ludicrous than dreadful.' – New York Times
† Other versions: The Two Faces of Dr Jekyll (1960), I Monster (1970). Variations: Daughter of Dr Jekyll (1957), Abbott and Costello Meet Dr Jekyll and Mr Hyde (1954), Son of Dr Jekyll (1951), The Ugly Duckling (1960), House of Dracula (1945), The Nutty Professor (1963), Dr Jekyll and Sister Hyde (1971).
& Joseph Ruttenberg; Franz Waxman; Harold F. Kress

Dr Jekyll and Ms Hyde

US 1995 89m Technicolor
Rank/Rastar/Savoy/Leider-Shapiro

▭ ▭ 𝒬 ⌕

An under-achieving chemist experiments on a formula he finds in his grandfather's scientific journals, which turns him into an ambitious, seductive woman.
A concept that first surfaced in Hammer's Dr Jekyll and Sister Hyde; time has not lent it any enchantment, even when it is played for laughs as it is here - unfortunately few are forthcoming.

w Tim John, Oliver Butcher, William Davies, William Osborne story David F. Price d David F. Price ph Tom Priestley m Mark McKenzie pd Gregory Melton ed Tony Lombardo sp make-up: Kevin Yagher; visual effects: Dream Quest Images
☆ Sean Young, Tim Daly, Lysette Anthony, Stephen Tobolowsky, Harvey Fierstein, Polly Bergen, Stephen Shellen
'A typical thesaurus includes some 350 synonyms for the word bad – an alarming number of which apply to this thoroughly misbegotten outing.' – Premiere
'The film is littered with embarrassingly ham-fisted farce.' – Kim Newman, Sight and Sound

Dr Jekyll and Sister Hyde *

GB 1971 97m Technicolor
MGM-EMI/Hammer (Albert Fennell, Brian Clemens)

▭ ▭ 𝒬

A twist: Jekyll now turns into a young and beautiful woman, and kills prostitutes so that he can continue his research.
Half-successful attempt to link the legend with Jack the Ripper, killed by gore and overlength.
w Brian Clemens d Roy Ward Baker ph Norman Warwick m David Whitaker pd Robert Jones ed James Needs
☆ Ralph Bates, Martine Beswick, Gerald Sim, Lewis Fiander, Dorothy Alison

Dr Kildare

This long-running screen hero was a young intern at Blair Hospital, under the cranky tutelage of old Dr Gillespie. Created by Max Brand in a series of novels, he first appeared on the screen in a 1937 Paramount double-biller called INTERNS CAN'T TAKE MONEY, played by Joel McCrea with Barbara Stanwyck, no less, providing the love interest. Kildare came up against gangsters; Gillespie did not appear. MGM then took over the property and went to town with it, making fifteen films in ten years. They were as follows:
1938 Young Dr Kildare
1939 Calling Dr Kildare, The Secret of Dr Kildare
1940 Dr Kildare's Strange Case (qv), Dr Kildare Goes Home (qv), Dr Kildare's Crisis (qv)
1941 The People vs Dr Kildare
1942 Dr Kildare's Wedding Day (qv)
1942 Dr Kildare's Victory (qv), Calling Dr Gillespie, Dr Gillespie's New Assistant (qv)
1943 Dr Gillespie's Criminal Case (qv)
1944 Three Men in White, Between Two Women
1947 Dark Delusion (qv)
Lew Ayres played Kildare, but in 1942 declared himself a conscientious objector and was dropped. The emphasis shifted to Gillespie, played by Lionel Barrymore from a wheelchair, and he proceeded to deal with a whole series of interns. The films were well enough made on medium budgets; nine were directed by Harold S. Bucquet and the last five by Willis Goldbeck, one by W. S. Van Dyke. In 1961 a TV series began with Richard Chamberlain and Raymond Massey, and ran for seven years.

Dr Kildare Goes Home

US 1940 79m bw
MGM

Young Dr Kildare temporarily deserts Blair Hospital to help his father establish a small-town clinic.
Rather below par episode with obvious outcome.
w Willis Goldbeck, Harry Ruskin d Harold S. Bucquet
☆ Lew Ayres, Lionel Barrymore, Laraine Day, Samuel S. Hinds, Gene Lockhart

Dr Kildare's Crisis

US 1940 75m bw
MGM

Dr Kildare's fiancée may have epilepsy in the family.
The series at its peak.
w Willis Goldbeck, Harry Ruskin d Harold S. Bucquet
☆ Lew Ayres, Lionel Barrymore, Robert Young, Laraine Day, Nat Pendleton, Marie Blake

Dr Kildare's Strange Case

US 1940 77m bw
MGM

The young doctor cures a mental patient by the newest methods.
Crisp series episode.

w Willis Goldbeck, Harry Ruskin d Harold S. Bucquet
☆ Lew Ayres, Lionel Barrymore, Laraine Day, Shepperd Strudwick, Samuel S. Hinds

Dr Kildare's Victory

US 1942 92m bw
MGM
GB title: The Doctor and the Débutante
Back at Blair, Dr Kildare fights ambulance zoning regulations.
Rather heavy-going episode, its star's last before becoming a conscientious objector and leaving Hollywood for the duration.
w Harry Ruskin, Willis Goldbeck d W. S. Van Dyke
☆ Lew Ayres, Lionel Barrymore, Ann Ayars, Robert Sterling

Dr Kildare's Wedding Day

US 1941 83m bw
MGM
GB title: Mary Names the Day
Dr Kildare's fiancée is killed in a road accident.
Rather deliberately downbeat episode, well enough assembled.
w Lawrence Bachmann, Ormond Ruthven d Harold S. Bucquet
☆ Lew Ayres, Lionel Barrymore, Laraine Day, Red Skelton, Nils Asther

Dr Knock *

France 1936 74m bw
Pathé-Natan
A sly young doctor takes over a country practice and turns the townsfolk into hypochondriacs.
Amusing version of a modern French comedy classic.
w Jules Romains play Jules Romains d Louis Jouvet, Roger Goupillières
☆ Louis Jouvet, Palau, Le Vigan, Moor, Alexandre Rignault
'Once under way it scoots along like a Bermuda sloop, and holds right till the surprise fadeout.' – Variety

'Death is the ultimate vacation.'

Dr M

West Germany/France/Italy 1989 116m colour
Hobo/NEF/Ellepi Film/Clea Productions (Ingrid Windisch)

▭ ▭

US title: Camp Extinction
A doctor indoctrinates holidaymakers with the desire to commit suicide.
Limp thriller.
w Sollace Mitchell story Thomas Bauermeister d Claude Chabrol ph Jean Rabier m Paul Hindemith pd Wolfgang Hundhammer, Dante Ferretti ed Monique Fardoulis
☆ Alan Bates, Jennifer Beals, Jan Niklas, Hanns Zischler, Benoit Regent, William Berger, Alexander Radszun, Peter Fitz, Daniela Poggi

Doctor Mabuse the Gambler ***

Germany 1922 101m bw silent
UFA (Erich Pommer)

▭ ▭

original title: Doktor Mabuse, der Spieler
A criminal mastermind uses hypnotism and blackmail in his efforts to obtain world domination, but when finally cornered is discovered to be a raving maniac.
A real wallow in German post-war depression and melodrama, in the form of a Fu Manchu/Moriarty type thriller. Fascinating scene by scene, but by now a slightly tiresome whole.
w Thea von Harbou, Fritz Lang novel Norbert Jacques d Fritz Lang ph Carl Hoffman ad Otto Hunte, Stahl-Urach, Erich Kettelhut, Karl Vollbrecht
☆ Rudolf Klein-Rogge, Alfred Abel, Gertrude Welcker, Lil Dagover, Paul Richter
† Originally issued in Germany in two parts, Der Grosse Spieler and Inferno, adding up to a much longer running time
†† See sequels, The Testament of Dr Mabuse and The Thousand Eyes of Dr Mabuse.

Dr Monica

US 1934 80m bw
Warner (Henry Blanke)
A lady doctor allows her husband to fall for another woman.

Heavy-handed 'woman's picture' which did well at the time.
w Charles Kenyon play Marja Morozowicz d William Keighley
☆ Kay Francis, Warren William, Jean Muir, Verree Teasdale, Philip Reed, Emma Dunn

Doctor No ***

♟♟ GB 1962 111m Technicolor
UA/Eon (Harry Saltzman, Albert R. Broccoli)

▭ ▭ ▭ 𝒬 ⌕ ⌕

A British secret service agent foils a master criminal operating in the West Indies.
First of the phenomenally successful James Bond movies, mixing sex, violence and campy humour against expensive sets and exotic locales. Toned down from the original novels, they expressed a number of sixties attitudes, and proved unstoppable box-office attractions for nearly twenty-five years. The first was, if not quite the best, reasonably representative of the series.
w Richard Maibaum, Johanna Harwood, Berkely Mather novel Ian Fleming d Terence Young ph Ted Moore m Monty Norman
☆ Sean Connery, Ursula Andress, Jack Lord, Joseph Wiseman, John Kitzmiller, Bernard Lee, Lois Maxwell, Zena Marshall, Eunice Gayson, Anthony Dawson
† The subsequent titles, all qv, were From Russia with Love (1963), Goldfinger (1964), Thunderball (1965), You Only Live Twice (1967), On Her Majesty's Secret Service (1969), Diamonds Are Forever (1971), Live and Let Die (1973), The Man with the Golden Gun (1974), The Spy Who Loved Me (1977), Moonraker (1979), For Your Eyes Only (1981), Octopussy (1983), A View To A Kill (1985), The Living Daylights (1987), Licence To Kill (1989), Golden Eye (1995). Never Say Never Again (1984) was not part of the series, though it brought back Sean Connery as Bond. Casino Royale (1967) was a Bond spoof made by other hands.

Dr O'Dowd

GB 1940 70m bw
Warner
A drunken doctor redeems himself.
Somewhat woebegone tearjerker with an interesting cast.
w Derek Twist, Austin Melford story L. A. G. Strong d Herbert Mason
☆ Shaun Glenville, Peggy Cummins, Mary Merrall, Liam Gaffney, Patricia Roc, Walter Hudd, Irene Handl

Dr Petiot

France 1990 102m colour/bw
Electric/MS/Sara/Cine 5 (Alain Sarde, Philippe Chapelier-Dehesdin)

▭

In wartime Paris, a doctor who claims to help Jews to escape the Nazis kills them instead.
An unflinching examination of a serial killer, filmed in the style of an old-fashioned horror movie.
w Dominique Garnier, Christian de Chalonge d Christian de Chalonge ph Patrick Blossier m Michel Portal ad Yves Brover ed Anita Fernandez
☆ Michel Serrault, Pierre Romans, Zbigniew Horoks, Berangere Bonvoisin, Aurore Prieto, André Chaumeau, Axel Bogousslavski

'The sting's in the tale!'

Dr Phibes Rises Again *

GB 1972 89m DeLuxe
AIP (Richard Dalton)

▭ 𝒬

The immortal Phibes and his wife rise from the dead to seek an Egyptian elixir of life, and cross swords with a satanic Egyptologist.
Uncertainly paced but generally zippy comic strip for adults, with all concerned entering gleefully into the evil spirit of the thing. See prequel, The Abominable Dr Phibes.
w Robert Fuest, Robert Blees d Robert Fuest ph Alex Thomson m John Gale ad Brian Eatwell
☆ Vincent Price, Robert Quarry, Valli Kemp, Fiona Lewis, Peter Cushing, Beryl Reid, Terry-Thomas, Hugh Griffith, Peter Jeffrey, Gerald Sim, John Thaw, John Cater, Lewis Fiander
'It's refreshing to find a sequel which is better than its prototype.' – Philip Strick, MFB

◉ Digital Video Disc Region 2   ◉ Digital Video Disc Region 1   ⌕ Soundtrack released on compact disc   ☆ Cast in approximate order of importance   † Points of interest   🎵 Notable songs   🏆 Academy Award   & Academy Award nomination   🏛 BAFTA

Dr Renault's Secret

US 1942 58m bw
TCF

A scientist turns an ape into a semi-human, which runs amok.

Fairly well done horror support.

w William Bruckner, Robert F. Metzler d Harry Lachman

☆ George Zucco, J. Carrol Naish, John Shepperd, Lynne Roberts

Dr Rhythm *

US 1938 80m bw
Paramount

A veterinary surgeon goes into show business.

Easy-going star musical with pleasant songs.

w Jo Swerling, Richard Connell story O. Henry d Frank Tuttle

☆ Bing Crosby, Beatrice Lillie, Mary Carlisle, Andy Devine, Laura Hope Crews, Rufe Davis

'Armed with a doctor's kit, he fought a thousand killers!'

Dr Socrates *

US 1935 70m bw
Warner (Robert Lord)

A small-town doctor is forced to help wounded gangsters, and becomes involved.

Good star melodrama.

w Robert Lord novel W. R. Burnett d William Dieterle ph Tony Gaudio md Leo F. Forbstein

☆ Paul Muni, Ann Dvorak, Barton MacLane, Robert Barrat, John Eldredge, Hobart Cavanaugh, Mayo Methot, Samuel S. Hinds, Henry O'Neill

'Arriving at the tail end of the G-man and gangster cycle, *Dr Socrates* is a graceful valedictory.' – *Variety*

'Rapid, strong and exciting.' – *Sunday Times*

† Remade as *King of the Underworld* and *Bullet Scars*.

'The hot line suspense comedy!'

Dr Strangelove; or, How I Learned to Stop Worrying and Love the Bomb ****

GB 1963 93m bw
Columbia/Stanley Kubrick (Victor Lyndon)

A mad USAF general launches a nuclear attack on Russia, and when recall attempts fail, and retaliation is inevitable, all concerned sit back to await the destruction of the world.

Black comedy resolving itself into a series of sketches, with the star playing three parts (for no good reason): the US president, an RAF captain, and a mad German-American scientist. Historically an important film in its timing, its nightmares being those of the early sixties, artistically it clogs its imperishable moments by untidy narrative.

w Stanley Kubrick, Terry Southern, Peter George novel Red Alert by Peter George d Stanley Kubrick ph Gilbert Taylor m Laurie Johnson ad Ken Adam

☆ Peter Sellers, George C. Scott, Peter Bull, Sterling Hayden, Keenan Wynn, Slim Pickens, James Earl Jones, Tracy Reed

GENERAL (GEORGE C. SCOTT): 'I don't say we wouldn't get our hair mussed, but I do say no more than ten to twenty million people killed.'

'Scarcely a picture of relentless originality; seldom have we seen so much made over so little.' – *Joan Didion*

'The double-face of the story – serious events broken up into farcical incidents – is expressed in double-face acting of a high order.' – *Dilys Powell*

'Irreverent to the point of savagery; it is funny and it is engrossing. And it's heady stuff for moviegoers, for Kubrick, boy genius that he is, assumes that we're grown-up enough to share his bitter laughter.' – *Judith Crist*

† *Fail Safe* (qv), which took the same theme more seriously, was released almost simultaneously.

⧓ best picture; script; Stanley Kubrick (as director); Peter Sellers

▽ best picture; best British film; Ken Adam

Dr Syn *

GB 1937 80m bw
Gaumont (Michael Balcon)

The vicar of Dymchurch in 1780 is really a pirate believed dead.

This now obscure, lively pirate yarn was its star's last film.

w Michael Hogan, Roger Burford novel Russell Thorndike d Roy William Neill ph Jack Cox

md Louis Levy ad Vetchinsky ed R. E. Dearing, Alfred Roome

☆ George Arliss, Margaret Lockwood, John Loder, Roy Emerton, Graham Moffatt, Frederick Burtwell, Meinhart Maur, George Merritt

'With Arliss in the name part it doesn't ring true.' – *Variety*

Dr Syn Alias the Scarecrow

†† GB 1963 98m Technicolor
Walt Disney (Bill Anderson)

The vicar of Dymchurch is really a smuggler who manages to outwit a rascally general and save a prisoner from Dover Castle.

Oddly released the same year as another version of the story, Captain Clegg, this rather set-bound adventure yarn turns its hero into a Robin Hood figure. It was originally made to be shown in three parts on American TV.

w Robert Westerby novel Christopher Syn by Russell Thorndike, William Buchanan d James Neilson ph Paul Beeson m Gerard Schurmann

☆ Patrick McGoohan, George Cole, Tony Britton, Geoffrey Keen, Kay Walsh, Patrick Wymark, Alan Dobie, Eric Pohlmann, Michael Hordern

The Doctor Takes a Wife *

US 1940 89m bw
Columbia (William Perlberg)

A young doctor has to pretend to be the husband of a socialite.

Typical high life comedy of its period, quite brisk and diverting.

w George Seaton, Ken Englund d Alexander Hall ph Sid Hickox m Frederick Hollander md Morris Stoloff

☆ Loretta Young, Ray Milland, Edmund Gwenn, Reginald Gardiner, Gail Patrick, Frank Sully, George Metaxa, Charles Halton, Chester Clute

Dr Terror's House of Horrors

GB 1965 98m Technicolor Techniscope
Amicus (Milton Subotsky, Max J. Rosenberg)

An eccentric, who turns out to be Death himself, tells the fortunes of five men in a railway carriage.

One of the first Amicus horror compendiums and a weak one, not helped by wide screen, a couple of naïve scripts and ho-hum acting. The book-ends are quite pleasant, though.

w Milton Subotsky d Freddie Francis ph Alan Hume m Elisabeth Lutyens, Tubby Hayes ad Bill Constable ed Thelma Connell sp Ted Samuels

☆ Peter Cushing, Ursula Howells, Max Adrian, Roy Castle, Alan Freeman, Bernard Lee, Jeremy Kemp, Kenny Lynch, Christopher Lee, Michael Gough, Donald Sutherland

† Later collections from the same stable include *Torture Garden, Tales from the Crypt, Vault of Horror* and *Asylum*.

Dr Who and the Daleks

†† GB 1965 83m Techniscope
British Lion/Regal/Aaru (Milton Subotsky, Max J. Rosenberg)

Three children and their grandfather accidentally start his time machine and are whisked away to a planet where villainous robots rule.

Junior science fiction from the BBC series. Limply put together, and only for indulgent children.

w Milton Subotsky d Gordon Flemyng ph John Wilcox m Malcolm Lockyer

☆ Peter Cushing, Roy Castle, Jennie Linden, Roberta Tovey, Barrie Ingham

† A sequel, no better, emerged in 1966: *Daleks: Invasion Earth 2150 AD*, with similar credits except that Bernard Cribbins instead of Roy Castle provided comic relief.

'A full moon was his signal to kill!'

Doctor X **

US 1932 82m Technicolor
Warner (Hal Wallis)

A reporter investigates a series of moon murders and narrows his search to one of several doctors at a medical college.

Fascinating, German-inspired, overblown and generally enjoyable horror mystery whose armless villain commits murders by growing limbs from 'synthetic flesh'.

w Earl Baldwin, Robert Tasker play Howard W. Comstock, Allen C. Miller d Michael Curtiz ph Richard Towers md Leo Forbstein

☆ Lee Tracy, Lionel Atwill, Preston Foster, Fay Wray, George Rosener, Mae Busch, Arthur Edmund Carewe, John Wray

'The settings, lighting and final battle with the man-monster are quite stunning.' – *NFT, 1974*

'It almost makes Frankenstein seem tame and friendly.' – *New York Times*

Doctor You've Got to be Kidding

US 1967 93m Metrocolor Panavision
MGM/Trident (Douglas Laurence)

A girl arrives at a maternity hospital chased by three prospective husbands.

Wild and wacky farce which leaves little impression.

w Phillip Shuken novel Patte Wheat Mahan d Peter Tewkesbury ph Fred Koenekamp m Kenyon Hopkins

☆ Sandra Dee, George Hamilton, Celeste Holm, Bill Bixby, Dwayne Hickman, Dick Kallman, Mort Sahl, Allen Jenkins

'A love caught in the fire of revolution!'

Doctor Zhivago ***

US 1965 192m Metrocolor Panavision 70
MGM/David Lean/Carlo Ponti

A Moscow doctor is caught up in World War I, exiled for writing poetry, forced into partisan service and separated from his only love.

Beautifully photographed and meticulously directed, this complex epic has been so reduced from the original novel that many parts of the script simply do not make any kind of sense. What remains is a collection of expensive set-pieces, great for looking if not listening.

w Robert Bolt novel Boris Pasternak d David Lean ph Frederick A. Young m Maurice Jarre pd John Box ed Norman Savage

☆ Omar Sharif, Julie Christie, Rod Steiger, Alec Guinness, Rita Tushingham, Ralph Richardson, Tom Courtenay, Geraldine Chaplin, Siobhan McKenna, Noel Willman, Geoffrey Keen, Adrienne Corri

'A long haul along the road of synthetic lyricism.' – *MFB*

'David Lean's *Doctor Zhivago* does for snow what his *Lawrence of Arabia* did for sand.' – *John Simon*

'It isn't shoddy (except for the music); it isn't soap opera; it's stately, respectable, and dead. Neither the contemplative Zhivago nor the flow of events is intelligible, and what is worse, they seem unrelated to each other.' – *Pauline Kael*

⧓ Robert Bolt; Frederick A. Young; Maurice Jarre

▽ best picture; David Lean; Tom Courtenay

A Doctor's Diary

US 1937 77m bw
Paramount

The resident physician of a privately-endowed hospital is impatient with the niceties of procedure.

Unsurprising medical drama which adequately filled half a bill.

w Sam Ornitz, Joseph Anthony d Charles Vidor

☆ George Bancroft, John Trent, Helen Burgess, Ruth Coleman, Charles Waldron, Ra Hould, Sidney Blackmer

'Packs enough drama to hold attention.' – *Variety*

The Doctor's Dilemma *

GB 1958 99m Metrocolor
MGM/Anatole de Grunwald

Eminent Harley Street surgeons debate the case of a devoted wife and her tubercular artist husband.

Well acted but curiously muffled filming of Shaw's Edwardian play about ethics and human values.

w Anatole de Grunwald play Bernard Shaw d Anthony Asquith ph Robert Krasker m Joseph Kosma ad Paul Sheriff

☆ Leslie Caron, Dirk Bogarde, John Robinson, Alastair Sim, Felix Aylmer, Robert Morley, Michael Gwynn, Maureen Delany, Alec McCowen

Doctor's Orders

GB 1934 68m bw
BIP (Walter Mycroft)

A peddler of patent medicines tries to conceal his occupation from his son, who is training to be a doctor.

Mild comedy that is unlikely to make an audience feel good.

w Clifford Grey, Syd Courtenay, Lola Harvey d Norman Lee ph Brian Langley ad Cedric Dawe ed John Neil Brown

☆ Leslie Fuller, Mary Jerrold, John Mills, Marguerite Allan, Ronald Shiner, Georgie Harris, Felix Aylmer, William Kendal

Doctors' Wives

US 1970 102m Eastmancolor
Columbia/M. J. Frankovich

When Dr Dellman shoots his unfaithful wife, his colleagues reconsider their sex lives.

Adult soap opera from talents who at other times have found better things to do. In the sensational circumstances, two sanguinary operation sequences are tastelessly irrelevant.

w Daniel Taradash novel Frank G. Slaughter d George Schaefer ph Charles B. Lang m Elmer Bernstein

☆ Richard Crenna, Janice Rule, Gene Hackman, John Colicos, Dyan Cannon, Diana Sands, Rachel Roberts, Carroll O'Connor, Cara Williams, Ralph Bellamy, Richard Anderson

'Crisis follows hard on crisis to breathlessly ludicrous effect.' – *Tom Milne*

Dodes'ka-den **

Japan 1970 140m Eastmancolor
Essential Cinema/Yonki-No-Kai/Toho (Akira Kurosawa, Keisuke Kinoshita, Kon Ichikawa, Masaki Kobayashi)

In a shanty town on the outskirts of Tokyo, a group of down-and-outs go about the daily business of surviving.

Fascinating, detailed portrait of ordinary and eccentric lives in the lower depths.

w Akira Kurosawa, Hideo Orguni, Shinobu Hashimoto novel Kisetsu No Nai Machi by Shugoro Yamamoto d Akira Kurosawa ph Takao Saito, Yasumichi Fukusawa m Toru Takemitsu ad Yoshiro Muraki, Shinobu Muraki ed Reiko Keneko

☆ Yoshitaka Zushi, Kin Sugai, Kaou Kato, Junzaburo Ban, Kiyoko Tange, Michiko Hino, Tatsuhei Shimokawa

⛊ Foreign language film

'West of Chicago there was no law! West of Dodge City there was no God!'

Dodge City ***

US 1939 104m Technicolor
Warner (Robert Lord)

An ex-soldier and trail boss helps clean up the west's great railroad terminus.

Standard, satisfying big-scale Western with all clichés intact and very enjoyable, as is the soft, rich early colour. The story is plainly inspired by the exploits of Wyatt Earp.

w Robert Buckner d Michael Curtiz ph Sol Polito, Ray Rennahan m Max Steiner

☆ Errol Flynn, Olivia de Havilland, Ann Sheridan, Bruce Cabot, Alan Hale, Frank McHugh, John Litel, Victor Jory, William Lundigan, Henry Travers, Henry O'Neill, Guinn Williams, Gloria Holden

'A lusty Western, packed with action, including some of the dandiest mêlée stuff screened.' – *Variety*

'It looks programmed and underpopulated, though in an elegantly stylized way.' – *New Yorker, 1980*

Dodsworth ***

US 1936 101m bw
Samuel Goldwyn

An American businessman takes his wife on a tour of Europe, and their lives are changed.

Satisfying, well-acted drama from a bestselling novel; production values high.

w Sidney Howard novel Sinclair Lewis d William Wyler ph Rudolph Maté m Alfred Newman ad Richard Day

☆ Walter Huston, Mary Astor, Ruth Chatterton, David Niven, Paul Lukas, Gregory Gaye, Maria Ouspenskaya, Odette Myrtil, Spring Byington, John Payne

'No one, I think, will fail to enjoy it, in spite of its too limited and personal plot, the sense it leaves behind of a very expensive, very contemporary, Bond Street vacuum flask.' – *Graham Greene*

'William Wyler has had the skill to execute it in cinematic terms, and a gifted cast has been able to bring the whole alive to our complete satisfaction.' – *New York Times*

'A smoothly flowing narrative of substantial interest, well-defined performances and good talk.' – *New York Times*

'An offering of dignity and compelling power to provide you with a treat you can rarely experience in a picture house.' – *Hollywood Spectator*

🏋 Richard Day
👤 best picture; Sidney Howard; William Wyler; Walter Huston; Maria Ouspenskaya

The Does: see *Les Biches*

Dog Day Afternoon ***
US 1975 130m Technicolor
Warner/AEC (Martin Bregman, Martin Elfand)
▣▣ ⊛ 🎧
Two incompetent robbers are cornered in a Brooklyn bank.
Recreation of a tragi-comic episode from the newspaper headlines; for half its length a fascinating and acutely observed film which then bogs itself down in a surplus of talk and excessive sentiment about homosexuality.
w Frank Pierson book Patrick Mann d Sidney Lumet m Victor J. Kemper m none
☆ Al Pacino, John Cazale, *Charles Durning*, Sully Boyar, James Broderick, Chris Sarandon
'There is plenty of Lumet's vital best here in a film that at least glancingly captures the increasingly garish pathology of our urban life.' – *Jack Kroll*
'Scattered moments of wry humour, sudden pathos and correct observation.' – *John Simon*
'The mask of frenetic cliché doesn't spoil moments of pure reporting on people in extremity.' – *New Yorker*
'A long and wearying case history of the beaten, sobbing, despairing and ultimately powerless anti-hero.' – *Karyn Kay, Jump Cut*
'Full of galvanic mirth rooted in human desperation.' – *Michael Billington, Illustrated London News*
'Brisk, humorous and alive with urban energies and angers fretting through the 92 degree heat.' – *Sight and Sound*
🏋 Frank Pierson
👤 best picture; Sidney Lumet; Al Pacino; Chris Sarandon
🎬 Al Pacino

A Dog of Flanders
🏋🏋 US 1959 97m DeLuxe Cinemascope
TCF/Associated Producers (Robert B. Radnitz)
▦
A small boy wants to be an artist; when he runs away in frustration, his shaggy dog, formerly a stray, leads his family to him.
Old-fashioned tear-jerker for well-brought-up children, previously filmed as a silent; quite accomplished in presentation.
w Ted Sherdeman novel Ouida d James B. Clark ph Otto Heller m Paul Sawtell, Bert Shefter
☆ David Ladd, Donald Crisp, Theodore Bikel, Max Croiset, Monique Ahrens

Dog Soldiers: see *Who'll Stop the Rain?*

'Get "touched" by an angel.'

Dogma **
US 1999 135m DeLuxe Panavision
Miramax/View Askew (Scott Mosier)
▣▣ ▦
Two fallen angels plan to take advantage of a theological loophole to re-enter heaven by passing through the entrance to a New Jersey cathedral, an act that will bring the world to an end.
A bizarre comedy that is on the side of the angels (the heavenly host, that is). In part an attack on the dumbing down of religious faith, it is also a hodge-podge of cinematic genres and styles, taking in road and chase movies, surreal and comic encounters, and theological musings.
wd Kevin Smith ph Robert Yeoman m Howard Shore pd Robert 'Ratface' Holtzman ed Kevin Smith, Scott Mosier sp Bellissimo, Belardinelli Effects; Vincent Guastini; Station X Studios
☆ Ben Affleck, Matt Damon, Linda Fiorentino, Salma Hayek, Jason Lee, Jason Mewes, Alan Rickman, Chris Rock, George Carlin, Bud Cort, Alanis Morissette, Kevin Smith, Janeane Garofalo

'Mr Smith enjoys shock value, but this time he makes it mercilessly funny and places it in the context of an obviously devout, enlightened parable.' – *Janet Maslin, New York Times*
† The film caused controversy among Catholic organisations, as a result of which Miramax sold the film to distributor Lion's Gate.

Dogpound Shuffle
🏋🏋 Canada 1974 97m Eastmancolor
Elliott Kastner/Bulldog
▦
aka: *Spot*
An old Irish hobo lives on the earnings of his dancing dog.
Dog-eared 'family film' which didn't seem to entertain many families.
wd Jeffrey Bloom
☆ Ron Moody, David Soul, Ray Stricklyn

Dogs In Space *
Australia 1986 108m colour
Recorded Releasing/Skouras/Atlantic (Glenys Rowe)
▦
Punks and hippies gather in a squat in Melbourne in the late 1970s.
Episodic, rambling film with a raucous rock soundtrack, but with an engaging affection for its lost tribe of teenagers.
wd Richard Lowenstein ph Andrew de Groot m Iggy Pop, Dogs In Space and others ad Jody Borland ed Jill Bilcock
☆ Michael Hutchence, Saskia Post, Nique Needles, Deanna Bond, Tony Helou, Chris Haywood, Peter Walsh, Laura Swanson

A Dog's Life: see *Mondo Cane* (1961)

A Dog's Life *
🏋🏋 US 1918 30m bw silent
First National/Charles Chaplin
⊛
A tramp and a stray mongrel help each other towards a happy ending.
Threatening sentiment is kept at bay by amusing sight gags in this pleasing star featurette.
wd Charles Chaplin ph Rollie Totheroh
☆ Charles Chaplin, Edna Purviance, Chuck Riesner, Henry Bergman, Albert Austin, Scraps

The Dogs of War
GB 1980 118m Technicolor
UA/Silverwold (Larry De Waay)
▣▣ ▦ ⊛
A disenchanted mercenary becomes involved in a plot to take over an impoverished West African state.
Tough but seemingly dated modern irony, somewhat lacking in action and surprise.
w Gary DeVore, George Malko novel Frederick Forsyth d John Irvin ph Jack Cardiff m Geoffrey Burgon pd Peter Mullins ed Antony Gibbs
☆ Christopher Walken, Tom Berenger, Colin Blakely, Hugh Millais, Paul Freeman, Robert Urquhart

Doing Time: see *Porridge*

Doktor Mabuse, der Spieler: see *Doctor Mabuse*

La Dolce Vita ****
Italy/France 1960 173m bw Totalscope
Riama/Pathé Consortium (Giuseppe Amato)
▣▣ ▦ ⊛ 🎧
aka: *The Sweet Life*
A journalist mixes in modern Roman high society and is alternately bewitched and sickened by what he sees.
Episodic satirical melodrama, a marathon self-indulgent wallow with a wagging finger never far away. Full of choice moments such as a statue of Christ being flown by helicopter over the city.
w Federico Fellini, Tullio Pinelli, Ennio Flaiano, Brunello Rondi d Federico Fellini ph Otello Martelli m Nino Rota ad Piero Gherardi
☆ Marcello Mastroianni, Anita Ekberg, Anouk Aimée, Alain Cuny, Yvonne Furneaux, Magali Noel, Nadia Gray, Lex Barker
'Its personification of various familiar symbols – love, death, purity, sin, reason and so on – never succeeds in reflecting human values or creating intellectual excitement ... Its actual significance rests in the way its (albeit specious) social attack has stirred the imagination of other Italian film-

makers, as well as public interest in their work.' – *Robert Vas, MFB*
'An awesome picture, licentious in content but moral and vastly sophisticated in its attitude and what it says.' – *Bosley Crowther, New York Times*
'One of the few films that one feels can be seen with increasing enjoyment a second or third time.' – *Paul V. Backley, New York Herald Tribune*
👤 script; Federico Fellini

Doll Face
US 1945 80m bw
TCF (Bryan Foy)
GB title: *Come Back to Me*
A burlesque queen goes to Broadway.
Lower case musical of minimal interest.
w Leonard Praskins d Lewis Seiler ph Joseph LaShelle m/ly Harold Adamson, Jimmy McHugh
☆ Vivian Blaine, Dennis O'Keefe, Carmen Miranda, Perry Como, Martha Stewart, Michael Dunne, Reed Hadley, George E. Stone, Donald McBride, Edgar Norton

The Doll Squad
US 1973 101m Eastmancolor
Nationwide/Feature-Faire (Ted V. Mikels)
A female team of CIA agents track down the man who sabotaged an American space project.
Badly made, poorly scripted and acted comedy thriller.
w Jack Richesin, Pam Eddy, Ted V. Mikels d Ted V. Mikels ph Anthony Salinas m Nicholas Carras pd Mike McCloskey ed Ted V. Mikels
☆ Michael Ansara, Francine York, Anthony Eisley, John Carter, Rafael Campos, William Bagdad, Lillian Garrett
'The endless running, jumping and kicks-to-the-groin stunts of this bevy of Emma Peels are conceived and executed with about as much conviction as knockabout comedy.' – *David Pirie, MFB*

Dollar
Sweden 1938 80m bw
Svensk Filmindustri
An American millionairess upsets the lives of three married couples.
A sour and brittle little comedy of romantic misunderstandings.
w Stina Bergman play Hjalmar Bergman d Gustaf Molander ph Åke Dahlquist
☆ Ingrid Bergman, Georg Rydeberg, Tutta Rolfe, Kotti Chave, Birgit Tengroth, Håkan Westergren, Edvin Adolphson, Elsa Burnett

The Dollar Bottom
GB 1981 33m Eastmancolor
Rocking Horse Films/Paramount
A sharp-witted public schoolboy sells his friends insurance against being beaten.
Ingenious but thinly acted short, with the added hazard of impenetrable accents.
w Shane Connaughton story James Kennaway d Roger Christian
☆ Rikki Fulton, Robert Urquhart, Jonathan McNeil

Dollars *
US 1971 120m Technicolor
Columbia/M. J. Frankovich
▦ ⊛
GB title: *The Heist*
An American security expert installs an electronic system in a Hamburg bank which he plans to rob himself.
Overlong caper comedy-drama which is quite good to watch when it starts moving, though the quick cutting, short takes and deliberately obscure narrative leave one breathless.
wd Richard Brooks ph Petrus Schloemp m Quincy Jones
☆ Warren Beatty, Goldie Hawn, Gert Frobe, Robert Webber, Scott Brady, Arthur Brauss
'An essay in virtuoso film construction ... rather as if one were watching a perfect machine in full throttle but with nowhere to go.' – *John Gillett*

Dolls
US 1986 77m colour
Empire Pictures/Taryn Productions (Brian Yuzna)
▦ ⊛
On a dark and stormy night, stranded travellers take refuge in an old house inhabited by an elderly couple and their killer dolls.
Risible, low-budget horror with more clichés than corpses.

w Ed Naha d Stuart Gordon ph Mac Ahlberg m Fuzzbee Morse, Victor Spiegel pd Giovanni Natalucci ed Lee Percy
☆ Stephen Lee, Guy Rolfe, Hilary Mason, Ian Patrick Williams, Carolyn Purdy-Gordon, Cassie Stuart, Bunty Bailey, Carrie Lorraine

A Doll's House *
GB 1973 95m Eastmancolor
Elkins/Freeward (Hillard Elkins)
▦
A wife begins to resist her husband's will. Ibsen's feminist play was always good value; set in Norway in the 1890s, it was taken up eighty years later as a precursor of women's lib, which accounts for two film versions in one year.
This one is simply staged and well performed, but suffers from a bad translation.
w Christopher Hampton play Henrik Ibsen d Patrick Garland ph Arthur Ibbetson m John Barry
☆ Claire Bloom, Anthony Hopkins, Ralph Richardson, Denholm Elliott, Anna Massey, Edith Evans

A Doll's House
GB/France 1973 106m Eastmancolor
World Film Services/Les Films de la Boétie (Joseph Losey)
▦
Opened out but less effective version of the above, with too much solemnity and the central part miscast.
w David Mercer play Henrik Ibsen d Joseph Losey ph Gerry Fisher m Michel Legrand
☆ Jane Fonda, David Warner, Trevor Howard, Edward Fox, Delphine Seyrig, Anna Wing

The Dolly Sisters **
US 1945 114m Technicolor
TCF (George Jessel)
The lives of a Hungarian sister act in American vaudeville.
Fictionalized biographical musical, only fair in the script department but glittering to look at in superb colour, and enriched by splendid production values. Undoubtedly among the best of its kind.
w John Larkin, Marian Spitzer d Irving Cummings ph Ernest Palmer m/ly various md Alfred Newman, Charles Henderson ch Seymour Felix ad Lyle Wheeler, Leland Fuller
☆ Betty Grable, June Haver, John Payne, S. Z. Sakall, Reginald Gardiner, Frank Latimore, Gene Sheldon, Sig Rumann, Trudy Marshall
🎵 song 'I Can't Begin to Tell You' (m James Monaco, ly Mack Gordon)

'They Were Separated By A Death ... And Reunited By A Murder.'

Dolores Claiborne **
US 1995 131m Technicolor
Rank/Castle Rock (Taylor Hackford, Charles Mulvehill)
▣▣ ▣▣ ▦ ⊛ 🎧
When an elderly woman dies, her housekeeper, who had earlier been acquitted of killing her husband, is arrested for her murder, an event that brings home her estranged daughter, whom she has not seen for 15 years.
Effective melodrama with feminist overtones: all the women are abused or misunderstood, all the men are abusers; what saves it from too much over-simplification is the revelation of the reasons for the edgy relationship between mother and daughter.
w Tony Gilroy novel Stephen King d Taylor Hackford ph Gabriel Beristain m Danny Elfman pd Bruno Rubeo ed Mark Warner
☆ Kathy Bates, Jennifer Jason Leigh, Judy Parfitt, Christopher Plummer, David Strathairn, Eric Bogosian
'Highly engrossing psychological study that manages to be both raw and finally tender in its treatment.' – *Lizzie Franke*
'The sensible formality of Taylor Hackford's direction has the effect of cooling the film's narrative frenzies and helping the actors dig some simple, truthful stuff out of the hubbub.' – *Richard Schickel, Time*

Dom Za Vesanje: see *Time Of the Gypsies*

Domani è Troppo Tardi
Italy   1950   101m   bw
Rizzoli (Giuseppe Amato)
GB title: *Tomorrow Is Too Late*
Inquisitive pupils and repressive teachers at a co-educational school almost cause a tragedy.
Possibly well intentioned, but in effect an old-fashioned melodrama which works well enough on its level.
w Alfred Machard, Leonide Moguy d Leonide Moguy ph Mario Craveri, Renato del Frate m Alessandro Cicognini
☆ Vittorio de Sica, Lois Maxwell, Gabrielle Dorziat, Anna Maria Pierangeli, Gino Leurini

Domenica d'Agosto **
Italy   1950   75m   bw
Colonna (Sergio Amidei)
GB title: *Sunday in August*
Various Romans enjoy Sunday by the sea at Ostia.
Fragmented comedy-drama which succeeds in being charming throughout, every detail being freshly observed through an inquisitive eye.
w Franco Brusati, Luciano Emmer, Giulio Macchi, Cesare Zavattini d Luciano Emmer ph Domenico Scala, Leonida Barboni, Ubaldo Marelli m Roman Vlad ad Jolanda Benvenuti
☆ Anna Baldini, Franco Interlenghi, Elvy Lissiak, Massimo Serato, Marcello Mastroianni, Corrado Verga

Domicile Conjugal: see *Bed and Board*

The Dominant Sex
GB   1937   71m   bw
BIP (Walter Mycroft)
A woman demands the right to her own individuality after marriage.
Tepid comedy drama from a popular stage play.
w Vina de Vesci, John Fernald play Michael Egan d Herbert Brenon ph J. J. Cox, Roy Clark ad Cedric Dawe
☆ Phillips Holmes, Diana Churchill, Carol Goodner, Romney Brent, Hugh Miller, Billy Milton

Dominick and Eugene: see *Nicky and Gino*

Dominion Tank Police Acts I & II (dubbed)
Japan   1989   80m   colour
Masamune Shirow/Hakusensha/Agent 21/Toshiba Video (Ritsuko Kakita, Kazuhiko Inomata, Tomaki Harada)
A girl who joins the Tank Police in its fight against crime accidentally destroys a large tank and builds a smaller, cute one.
Japanese animated comic-book fare, revealing a debt to American strip cartoons, done with less violence and more humour than usual. The story, such as it is, is continued in Dominion Tank Police Acts III & IV.
w Kouichi Mashimo story Masamune Shirow d Kouichi Mashimo ad Matsuharu Miyamae
☆ Featuring the voices of Toni Barry, Stephen Graf, Sean Barrett, Jesse Vogel, Bill Armstrong, John Bull, Marc Smith
† The film was released direct to video.

Dominion Tank Police Acts III & IV (dubbed)
Japan   1989   70m   colour
Masamune Shirow/Hakusensha/Agent 21/Toshiba Video (Kazuhiko Inomata, Tomaki Harada)
An android criminal and his two cat-like female accomplices who steal a priceless painting and kidnap a policewoman are hunted down by the Tank Police and a private security organization.
Bizarre animated movie, mixing comedy, violence, science fiction and mysticism in a manner that is unlikely to engage the interest of occidental audiences, despite its slick, cartoon-like style.
w Dai Kohno story Masamune Shirow d Takaaki Ishiyama ph Kazushi Torigoe m Brown Eyes ad Osamu Honda
☆ Featuring the voices of Toni Barry, Stephen Graf, Sean Barrett, Jesse Vogel, Bill Armstrong, John Bull, Marc Smith, Alison Dowling, Garrick Hagon
† The film was released direct to video.

'Dominique will make you shriek!'
Dominique
GB   1978   100m   colour
Grand Prize/Melvin Simon (Milton Subotsky, Andrew Donally)
A woman who was convinced that her husband was deliberately driving her mad is found dead, and buried, but seemingly returns…
The old Diabolique syndrome revamped in a very parsimonious production with little to hold the interest.
w Edward and Valerie Abraham novel *What Beckoning Ghost* by Harold Lawlor d Michael Anderson ph Ted Moore m David Whitaker
☆ Cliff Robertson, Jean Simmons, Jenny Agutter, Simon Ward, Ron Moody, Judy Geeson, Michael Jayston, Flora Robson, David Tomlinson, Jack Warner

The Domino Killings: see *The Domino Principle*

'Trust no one. No one!'
The Domino Principle
US   1977   100m   CFI color
Associated General Films (Lew Grade, Martin Starger)
GB title: *The Domino Killings*
A murderer is offered his freedom if he will assassinate a national figure.
Fashionable, complex and rather boring political thriller.
w Adam Kennedy novel Adam Kennedy d Stanley Kramer ph Fred Koenekamp, Ernest Laszlo m Billy Goldenberg
☆ Gene Hackman, Richard Widmark, Candice Bergen, Mickey Rooney, Edward Albert, Eli Wallach, Ken Swofford, Neva Patterson
'Terrible movies tend to start with a preposterous premise and then laboriously work their way to an impossible conclusion. This one however starts with an arrant impossibility and works its way to whatever lies beyond and below that.' – John Simon

Don Camillo e l'Onorevolo Peppone: see *Don Camillo's Last Round*

Don Camillo's Last Round *
Italy   1955   98m   bw
Rizzoli
original title: *Don Camillo e l'Onorevole Peppone*
The village Catholic priest tries to stop the re-election of the communist mayor.
Pleasant third collection of encounters with familiar characters.
w Giovanni Guareschi and others books Giovanni Guareschi d Carmine Gallone ph Anchise Brizzi m Alessandro Cicognini
☆ Fernandel, Gino Cervi, Claude Silvain, Leda Gloria
'The episodic narrative is full of mildly amusing incident.' – *MFB*

Don Giovanni
France-Italy-Germany   1979   184m   colour
Gaumont-Opera-Camera One (Michel Seydoux)
Grandiose but artistically somewhat hesitant version of Mozart's opera; little here for film buffs.
d Joseph Losey ph Gerry Fisher ad Alexander Trauner cinematic conception Rolf Lieberman
☆ Ruggero Raimondi, John Macurdy, Edda Moser, Kiri Te Kanawa

The Don Is Dead
US   1973   117m   Technicolor
Universal/Hal B. Wallis (Paul Nathan)
Cross and double cross among Mafia families.
A failed attempt to cash in on The Godfather, this endless melodrama is boringly violent and totally predictable.
w Marvin H. Albert novel Marvin H. Albert d Richard Fleischer ph Richard H. Kline m Jerry Goldsmith
☆ Anthony Quinn, Frederic Forrest, Robert Forster, Al Lettieri, Angel Tompkins, Charles Cioffi

Don Juan **
US   1926   126m   bw
Warner
Exploits of the famous lover and adventurer at Lucretia Borgia's court.
Lithe swashbuckler in the best silent tradition, but with a synchronized score (by William Axt) which made it a sensation and led directly to the talkie revolution.
w Bess Meredyth d Alan Crosland ph Byron Haskin
☆ John Barrymore, Mary Astor, Warner Oland, Estelle Taylor, Myrna Loy, Phyllis Haver, Willard Louis, Montagu Love

'The story of a man who thought he was the greatest lover in the world … and the people who tried to cure him of it!'
Don Juan de Marco *
US   1995   90m   colour
Entertainment/New Line/American Zoetrope (Francis Ford Coppola, Fred Fuchs, Patrick Palmer)
A young man wearing a mask and cape who claims to be a legendary lover is examined by a psychiatrist.
A dashingly romantic, modern-day variation on the old swashbuckling movies, enabling audiences to enjoy the fantasy while it is being explained away.
wd Jeremy Leven pd Ralf Bode m Michael Kamen pd Sharon Seymour ed Tony Gibbs
☆ Marlon Brando, Johnny Depp, Faye Dunaway, Geraldine Pailhas, Bob Dishy, Rachel Ticotin, Talisa Soto, Richard Sarafian
'Great Lover spoof is a long-winded bore.'– Alexander Walker, *London Evening Standard*
'Romantic without being super-sweet and avoids the heaviness of most Hollywood attempts to spring a tear.' – Derek Malcolm, *Guardian*
♫ song 'Have You Ever Really Loved A Woman' (m/ly Michael Kamen, Bryan Adams, Robert John Lange)

Don Juan Quilligan
US   1945   76m   bw
TCF
A would-be romantic bargee becomes engaged to two girls simultaneously, one on each side of the Hudson.
Thin comedy of bigamy, similar to The Captain's Paradise, which came later.
w Arthur Kober, Frank Gabrielson d Frank Tuttle
☆ William Bendix, Phil Silvers, Joan Blondell, Mary Treen, Anne Revere, George Macready

'The finest adventure tale ever screened!'
Don Q Son of Zorro *
US   1925   170m   bw   silent
United Artists
Further adventures in the manner of the star's 1920 hit (see *The Mark of Zorro*).
w Jack Cunningham novel K. and H. Prichard d Donald Crisp ph Henry Sharp
☆ Douglas Fairbanks, Mary Astor, Donald Crisp, Jack McDonald, Jean Hersholt

Don Quixote *
France   1933   82m   bw
Vandor/Nelson/Webster
♫
An adequate potted version starring Fedor Chaliapin and in the English version George Robey (French version: Dorville).
w Paul Morand, Alexandre Arnoux, from Cervantes d G. W. Pabst ph Nikolas Farkas, Paul Portier m Jacques Ibert ad Andrei Andreiev
'Strictly for the arty clientele … for general consumption tedious and dull … Americans in general may feel that the story scarcely rates retelling.' – *Variety*

Don Quixote **
USSR   1957   105m   Agfacolor   Sovscope
Lenfilm
An extremely handsome version with a commanding star performance.
w E. Schwarz d Grigori Kozintsev ph Andrei Moskvin, Apollinari Dudko m Kara-Karayev ad Yevgeny Yenei
☆ Nikolai Cherkassov, Yuri Tolubyev
† Other versions came from France in 1902 and 1908, Italy in 1910, France in 1911, USA in 1915, Britain in 1923, Denmark in 1926, Spain in 1947,

Britain in 1972, and Britain (ballet version with Nureyev) in 1975.

Dona Flor and Her Two Husbands
Brazil   1976   110m   Eastmancolor
Carnaval (Luis Carlos Barreto)
A young widow remarries, and has to share her bed with her late husband's ghost.
Semi-pornographic comedy which achieved some fashionable success.
wd Bruno Barreto novel Jorge Amado ph Maurito Salles m Chico Buarque de Holanda
☆ Sonia Braga, Jose Wilker, Mauro Mendonca

Dona Herlinda and Her Son *
Mexico   1986   90m   colour
Clasa Films Mondiales (Manuel Barbachano Ponce)
original title: *Doña Herlinda y Su Hijo*
A mother insists that her homosexual son, a doctor, get married, whereupon he sets up home with his wife and boyfriend.
An amusing comedy of manners, on how to remain gay in a masculine society.
wd Jaime Humberto Hermosillo ph Miguel Erhenberg ed Luis Kelly
☆ Arturo Meza, Marco Antonio Treviño, Leticia Lupercio, Guadalupe Del Toro, Angelica Guerrero, Donato Casteñeda, Guillermina Alba

Dondi
US   1960   80m   bw
Allied Artists
GIs in Italy adopt an orphan boy, who stows away to be with them in America.
Glutinous, sentimental comedy-drama.
w Albert Zugsmith, Gus Edson, from a comic strip d Albert Zugsmith
☆ David Janssen, Patti Page, Walter Winchell, Mickey Shaughnessy, Robert Strauss, Arnold Stang, Gale Gordon

Dongchun De Rizi: see *The Days*

La Donna del Fiume: see *Woman of the River*

Donna Donna
Holland   1987   90m   colour
Movies Film (Chris Brouwer, Haig Balian)
Distressed by his inability to attract a girlfriend, a bright but inept student falls in love with a girl on a poster.
A small-scale, lackadaisical comedy, amiable enough in its casual way.
w Luc Van Beek d Hans Van Beek, Luc Van Beek ph Peter de Bont m Bert Hermelink ad Harry Ammerlaan ed Wim Louwrier
☆ René Van 'Thof, Simone Walraven, Glenn Durfort, Guusje Van Tilborgh, Bridget George, Joke Tjalsma, Lou Landré, Heleen Van Meurs

'1978. The US Government Waged A War Against Organised Crime. One Man Was Left Behind The Lines.'
Donnie Brasco ***
US   1997   126m   Technicolor   Panavision
Entertainment/Mandalay/Baltimore (Mark Johnson, Barry Levinson, Louis DiGiaimo, Gail Mutrux)
After he successfully infiltrates the Mafia, an undercover agent for the FBI finds himself torn between duty and friendship for the gangster who vouched for him.
A Mob movie, based on a true story, that takes an almost academic interest in the rituals and manners of its denizens, concerned less with their actions than their characters, which gives it an effectively tragic intensity as two different sets of loyalties collide.
w Paul Attanasio book Joseph D. Pistone with Richard Woodley d Mike Newell ph Peter Sova m Patrick Doyle pd Donald Graham Burt ed Jon Gregory
☆ Al Pacino, Johnny Depp, Michael Madsen, Bruno Kirby, James Russo, Anne Heche, Zeljko Ivanek, Gerry Becker, Zach Grenier
'One of the best gangster movies you'll see this year, bursting with tension and filled with rewarding moments.' – John Patterson, *Neon*
♫ Paul Attanasio

The Donor

Canada 1994 94m colour
MCEG Sterling (Damian Lee)

🖾

A stuntman spends the night with an attractive woman and wakes up to find that he is missing a kidney.

Part action film, part psychological thriller: neither works – the action sequences include a bicycle chase, and script and acting aren't up to emotional depth.

w Neal Dobrofsky, Tippi Dobrofsky d Damian Lee ph Gerald R. Goozee m Ronald J. Weiss pd John Gillespie ed David Ransley

☆ Jeff Wincott, Michelle Johnson, Gordon Thomson, Richard Zeppieri, Joseph Scorsiani, Amanda Tapping, Geza Kovacs

Donovan's Brain *

US 1953 81m bw
UA/Dowling (Tom Gries)

🖾 ⊕

An unscrupulous tycoon is fatally injured, but his brain is kept alive by a surgeon who finds himself dominated by it.

Modest competence marks this version of a much filmed novel, with quiet suspense and a firm central performance.

wd Felix Feist novel Curt Siodmak ph Joseph Biroc m Eddie Dunstedter

☆ Lew Ayres, Gene Evans, Nancy Davis, Steve Brodie, Lisa K. Howard

† It was a remake of *The Lady and the Monster* (qv).

Donovan's Reef

US 1963 108m Technicolor
Paramount (John Ford)

🖾 ⊕

War veterans settle down on a South Sea island; when the daughter of one of them comes to visit, his reputation must be protected.

Good-humoured but finally enervating mixture of rough-house and slapstick, with the appearance of an old friends' benefit and the director in familiar sub-standard form.

w Frank Nugent, James Edward Grant d John Ford ph William H. Clothier m Cyril Mockridge

☆ John Wayne, Lee Marvin, Jack Warden, Elizabeth Allen, Dorothy Lamour, Cesar Romero, Mike Mazurki

Don's Party *

Australia 1976 90m Eastmancolor
Miracle/Double Head/AFC (Philip Adams)

🖾 🖾

In suburban Sydney, a political celebration party turns into a pretence of wife-swapping.

Fairly acute observation of middle-class antipodean mores, interrupted with predictable bouts of antipodean crudeness.

w David Williamson play David Williamson d Bruce Beresford

☆ Ray Barrett, Clare Binney, Pat Bishop, Graeme Blundell, John Hargreaves

Don't Be a Menace to South Central While Drinking Your Juice in the Hood

US 1996 88m DeLuxe
Miramax/Island/Ivory Way (Keenen Ivory Wayans, Eric L. Gold)

🖾 ⊕ ⊚

A son moves in with his irresponsible father and gun-toting cousin.

Broad-humoured satire that sends up socially conscious movies of black experience; the jokes are usually coarse and sometimes funny.

w Shawn Wayans, Marlon Wayans, Phil Beauman d Paris Barclay ph Russ Brandt m John Barnes pd Aaron Osborne ed William Young

☆ Shawn Wayans, Marlon Wayans, Tracey Cherelle Jones, Chris Spencer, Suli McCullough, Darrell Heath, Keenen Ivory Wayans

'Full of obvious spoofery and funnier in the concept than in execution.' – *Variety*

Don't Bother to Knock *

US 1952 76m bw
TCF (Julian Blaustein)

🖾

A deranged girl gets a baby-sitting job in a hotel and terrifies all concerned by threatening to kill her charge.

Curious vehicle for the emergent Monroe, who is not up to it, as who would be? Technical credits par, but entertainment value small.

w Daniel Taradash novel Charlotte Armstrong d Roy Baker ph Lucien Ballard m Lionel Newman

☆ Marilyn Monroe, Richard Widmark, Anne Bancroft, Donna Corcoran, Jeanne Cagney, Lurene Tuttle, Jim Backus, Elisha Cook Jnr

Don't Bother to Knock

GB 1961 89m Technicolor Cinemascope
ABP/Haileywood (Frank Godwin)

🖾

US title: Why Bother to Knock

A Casanova travel agent gives each of his girlfriends a key to his Edinburgh flat.

Poorly developed and self-conscious sex farce.

w Denis Cannan, Frederic Gotfurt, Frederic Raphael novel Clifford Hanley d Cyril Frankel ph Geoffrey Unsworth m Elisabeth Lutyens

☆ Richard Todd, Judith Anderson, Elke Sommer, June Thorburn, Nicole Maurey, Rik Battaglia, Eleanor Summerfield, John Le Mesurier

Don't Drink the Water

US 1969 100m Berkeley-Pathé
Avco Embassy (Jack Rollins, Charles H. Joffe)

🖾

Americans, visiting Europe for the first time, are stranded in Bulgaria, where they are mistaken for spies and forced to take refuge in the American embassy staffed by incompetents.

Frenetic and stagey version of the play, with broad acting that diminishes what is left of the comedy.

w R. S. Allen, Harvey Bullock play Woody Allen d Howard Morris ph Harvey Genkins m Pat Williams ad Robert Gundlach ed Ralph Rosenblum

☆ Jackie Gleason, Estelle Parsons, Ted Bessell, Joan Delaney, Michael Constantine, Howard St John, Danny Meehan

Don't Ever Leave Me

GB 1949 85m bw
Triton/Rank

🖾

A kidnapped teenager falls for her abductor.

No Orchids for Miss Blandish played as a family comedy; quite unmemorable.

w Robert Westerby novel *The Wide Guy* by Anthony Armstrong d Arthur Crabtree

☆ Jimmy Hanley, Petula Clark, Edward Rigby, Hugh Sinclair, Linden Travers, Anthony Newley

Don't Get Me Started

GB/Germany 1994 76m colour
BFI/TiMe Medienvertriebs/Skyline (Steve Clark-Hall)

A murderer who has got away with his crime finds the strain of giving up smoking too much for him.

A strange, unenthralling thriller that suggests repression is bad for you; it certainly doesn't do much for the film.

wd Arthur Ellis ph Gil Taylor m Roger Bolton pd Caroline Amies ed Mike Bradsell

☆ Trevor Eve, Steve Waddington, Marion Bailey, Ralph Brown, Marcia Warren, Alan David, Patrick O'Connell, Lorna Heilbron

'A neat idea on paper that doesn't survive its journey to the screen.' – *Variety*

† It was first shown at Cannes in 1993 under the title *Psychotherapy* in a version that ran for 98m. It was withdrawn, re-cut, and some additional scenes added, under the direction of Paul Cowan and Martin Walsh.

Don't Give Up the Ship

US 1959 89m bw
Hal Wallis (Paramount)

🖾

A dim-witted naval lieutenant is accused of stealing a destroyer.

Feeble American service farce.

w Herbert Baker, Edmund Beloin, Henry Garson d Norman Taurog ph Haskell Boggs

☆ Jerry Lewis, Dina Merrill, Diana Spencer, Mickey Shaughnessy, Robert Middleton, Gale Gordon

Don't Go Breaking My Heart

GB 1998 94m colour
Polygram/Bill Kenright

🖾 🖾

As the result of a hypnotic suggestion going wrong, a widow with teenage children falls for an American sports therapist.

Dire romantic comedy; it is slick and glossy, and also clumsy and dull.

w Geoff Morrow d Willi Patterson ph Vernon Lawton m Rolfe Kent pd Tony Noble ed Peter Beston

☆ Anthony Edwards, Jenny Seagrove, Charles Dance, Jane Leeves, Tom Conti, Linford Christie, Ben Reynolds, Ace Ryan, Amanda Holden

'One of those little British films that is so mind-bogglingly bad you will weep with boredom and frustration and beg for mercy – and that's even before the opening credits are over.' – *Cosmo Landesman, Sunday Times*

Don't Go in the House

US 1980 90m DeLuxe
Film Ventures/Turbine (Ellen Hammill)

🖾 ⊙

In revenge for being burned as a child, a mother-dominated man incinerates women to whom he is attracted.

Extraordinarily unpleasant horror movie, influenced for the bad by Psycho.

w Joseph Ellison, Ellen Hammill, Joseph R. Masefield d Joseph Ellison ph Oliver Wood m Richard Einhorn ad Sarah Wood ed Jane Kurson

☆ Dan Grimaldi, Robert Osth, Ruth Dardick, Charles Bonet, Bill Ricci, Dennis M. Hunter

Don't Go Near the Water *

US 1957 107m Metrocolor Cinemascope
MGM/Avon (Lawrence Weingarten)

The US Navy sets up a public relations unit on a South Pacific island.

*Loosely cemented service farce full of fumbling lieutenants and bumbling commanders, a more light-hearted M*A*S*H. Boring romantic interludes separate some very funny farcical sequences.*

w Dorothy Kingsley, George Wells novel William Brinkley d Charles Walters ph Robert Bronner m Bronislau Kaper

☆ Glenn Ford, Fred Clark, Gia Scala, Romney Brent, Mickey Shaughnessy, Earl Holliman, Anne Francis, Keenan Wynn, Eva Gabor, Russ Tamblyn, Jeff Richards, Mary Wickes

'Drop everything! And see the cheekiest comedy of the year!'

Don't Just Lie There, Say Something!

GB 1973 91m Eastmancolor
Comocroft/Rank

By a strange chapter of accidents, a politician finds himself in bed with his under-secretary and a lady not his wife.

Stupefying from-the-stalls rendering of a successful stage farce; in this form it simply doesn't work.

w Michael Pertwee play Michael Pertwee d Bob Kellett

☆ Brian Rix, Leslie Phillips, Joan Sims, Joanna Lumley, Derek Royle, Peter Bland

Don't Just Stand There

US 1967 99m Techniscope
Universal (Stan Margulies)

A mild-mannered watch smuggler gets himself involved with kidnapping, murder, and finishing a sex novel.

Frantic but ineffective farce which keeps on the move but does not arrive anywhere.

w Charles Williams novel *The Wrong Venus* by Charles Williams d Ron Winston ph Milton Krasner m Nick Perito

☆ Mary Tyler Moore, Robert Wagner, Barbara Rhoades, Glynis Johns, Harvey Korman

'Paris locations might have helped, but we're stuck with the San Fernando Valley.' – *Robert Windeler*

'The Kings of Rock are rollin' back to the screen in their biggest!'

Don't Knock the Rock *

US 1956 84m bw
Columbia/Clover (Sam Katzman)

A singer returns to his home town to show adults that rock is harmless fun.

Cheap exploitation movie, most notable for Little Richard's performances of 'Long Tall Sally', 'Rip It Up' and 'Tutti Frutti'.

w Robert E. Kent, James B. Gordon d Fred F. Sears ph Benjamin H. Kline ad Paul Palmentola ed Edwin Bryant, Paul Borofsky

☆ Alan Dale, Alan Freed, Bill Haley and the Comets, Jimmy Ballard, Little Richard, the Treniers, Dave Appell and his Applejacks

Don't Look Now ****

GB 1973 110m Technicolor
BL/Casey/Eldorado (Peter Katz)

🖾 ⊕ ⊕ 🎧

After the death of their small daughter, the Baxters meet in Venice two old sisters who claim mediumistic connection with the dead girl. The husband scorns the idea, but repeatedly sees a little red-coated figure in shadowy passages by the canals. Then he confronts it…

A macabre short story has become a pretentious and puzzling piece of high cinema art full of vague suggestions and unexplored avenues. Whatever its overall deficiencies, it is too brilliant in surface detail to be dismissed. Depressingly but fascinatingly set in wintry Venice, it has to be seen to be appreciated.

w Allan Scott, Chris Bryant story Daphne du Maurier d Nicolas Roeg ph Anthony Richmond m Pino Donaggio ad Giovanni Soccol

☆ Donald Sutherland, Julie Christie, Hilary Mason, Clelia Matania, Massimo Serrato

'The fanciest, most carefully assembled enigma yet seen on the screen.' – *New Yorker*

'A powerful and dazzling visual texture.' – *Penelope Houston*

🎬 Anthony Richmond

Don't Look Now … We're Being Shot At! *

France 1966 130m Eastmancolor Panavision
Les Films Corona (Robert Dorfmann)

original title: *La Grande Vadrouille*

During World War II three members of a British bomber crew bale out over Paris and make a frantic escape to the free zone by means of various wild disguises.

Freewheeling star farce, a shade lacking in control, but with some funny sequences.

wd Gérard Oury d Claude Renoir m Georges Auric

☆ Terry-Thomas, Bourvil, Louis de Funès, Claudio Brook, Mike Marshall

'Both the sight gags and the characters evoke pale echoes of Laurel and Hardy, but it is not familiarity that breeds contempt here so much as the debasement of the familiar.' – *MFB*

Don't Lose Your Head: see Carry On – Don't Lose Your Head

Don't Make Waves

US 1967 97m Metrocolor Panavision
MGM/Filmways (John Calley, Martin Ransohoff)

A swimming-pool salesman attempts to get his own back on an impulsive young woman who has wrecked his car.

Malibu beach farce for immature adults, made by professionals helpless in the face of a weak script, but boasting a funny climax with a house teetering on the edge of a cliff.

w Ira Wallach, George Kirgo novel *Muscle Beach* by Ira Wallach d Alexander Mackendrick ph Philip Lathrop m Vic Mizzy

☆ Tony Curtis, Claudia Cardinale, Robert Webber, Joanna Barnes, Sharon Tate, Jim Backus, Mort Sahl

Don't Move, Die and Rise Again!: see Zamri, Umri, Voskresni!

Don't Open the Window: see The Living Dead at the Manchester Morgue

Don't Open till Christmas

GB 1983 86m colour
21st Century

A maniac goes about killing Father Christmases.

Tawdry horror film of marginal interest because of subject and cast.

w Derek Ford, Al McGoohan d Edmund Purdom

☆ Edmund Purdom, Alan Lake, Gerry Sundquist, Belinda Mayne, Mark Jones

Don't Panic, Chaps!

GB 1959 85m bw
Columbia/Hammer/ACT (Teddy Baird)

British and German units are sent to set up observation posts on the same Adriatic island, and agree to sit out the war in comfort.

An ingenious idea is ill-served by a poorly written script and a rather bored cast.

w Jack Davies story Michael Corston, Ronald Holroyd d George Pollock ph Arthur Graham m Philip Green ad Scott MacGregor ed Harry Aldous

☆ Dennis Price, George Cole, Thorley Walters, Harry Fowler, Nicholas Phipps, Percy Herbert, Nadja Regin

Don't Raise the Bridge, Lower the River

🏋🏋 GB 1967 100m Technicolor
Columbia/Walter Shenson
📺

An American turns his English wife's home into a discotheque.
Dreary comedy apparently intent on proving that its star can be just as unfunny abroad as at home.
w Max Wilk d Jerry Paris ph Otto Heller m David Whitaker
☆ Jerry Lewis, Terry-Thomas, Jacqueline Pearce, Bernard Cribbins, Patricia Routledge, Nicholas Parsons, Michael Bates

Don't Take it to Heart *

GB 1944 90m bw
GFD/Two Cities (Sydney Box)
A genial castle ghost is unleashed by a bomb and affects the love affair of a researcher with the daughter of the house.
Amiably lunatic British-upper-class extravaganza with eccentric characters and some felicitous moments.
wd Jeffrey Dell ph Eric Cross m Mischa Spoliansky
☆ Richard Greene, *Edward Rigby*, Patricia Medina, Alfred Drayton, Richard Bird, Wylie Watson, Moore Marriott, Brefni O'Rorke, Amy Veness, Claude Dampier, Joan Hickson, Joyce Barbour, Ronald Squire, Ernest Thesiger
'A cheerful and rewarding entertainment.' – *Richard Mallett, Punch*
'Not funny accidental but funny deliberate, and nine times out of ten the joke comes off.' – *Observer*

Don't Talk to Strange Men

GB 1962 65m bw
British Lion-Bryanston/Derick Williams
A girl begins a romance via a telephone call-box with a man she has never met.
Undramatic little warning to the young about the dangers of accepting lifts from strange men.
w uncredited story Gwen Cherrell d Pat Jackson ph Stephen Dade ad Brian Herbert ed Helen Wiggins
☆ Christina Gregg, Cyril Raymond, Gillian Lind, Conrad Phillips, Janina Faye, Dandy Nichols, Gwen Nelson

Don't Tell Her It's Me

US 1990 102m CFI color
Rank/Sovereign (George Braunstein, Ron Hamady)
📺 ▦ ⚉
A romantic novelist persuades her wimpish brother, who is recovering from radiation treatment, to pretend to be a biker in order to get a girlfriend.
Trivial, depressingly unsubtle comedy with matching performances.
w Sarah Bird novel *The Boyfriend School* by Sarah Bird d Malcolm Mowbray ph Reed Smoot m Michael Gore pd Linda Pearl, Daryl Kerrigan ed Marshall Harvey
☆ Shelley Long, Steve Guttenberg, Jami Gertz, Kyle MacLachlan, Madchen Amick, Kevin Scannell
'Takes the germ of an amusing notion about the division between realistic and fantastic romantic hero and hammers it painfully into the ground.' – *Kim Newman, Sight and Sound*
'Grotesquely unfunny comedy.' – *Variety*

Don't Tell Mom the Babysitter's Dead

US 1991 105m DeLuxe
Warner/HBO/Cinema Plus/Outlaw/Mercury/Douglas (Robert Newmyer, Brian Reilly, Jeffrey Silver)
📺 ▦ ⚉ 🎧
A young girl supports her siblings while their mother is away on holiday.
Lamentably silly comedy.
w Neil Landau, Tara Ison d Stephen Herek ph Tim Suhrstedt m David Newman, Brian Nazarian pd Stephen Marsh ed Larry Bock
☆ Christina Applegate, Joanna Cassidy, John Getz, Josh Charles, Keith Coogan, Concetta Tomei, David Duchovny, Kimmy Robertson

Don't Trust Your Husband

US 1948 90m bw
James Nasser/United Artists
An executive conceals from his wife the sex of the client with whom he has to spend a lot of time.
Ho-hum comedy with a laborious plotline and a flagging cast.
w Lou Breslow, Joseph Hoffman d Lloyd Bacon
☆ Fred MacMurray, Madeleine Carroll, Charles Rogers

The Doolins of Oklahoma

US 1949 90m bw
Columbia (Harry Joe Brown)
📺
GB title: *The Great Manhunt*
When his old gang claims his return to lawlessness, Bill Doolin walks into the sheriff's guns rather than cause his wife unhappiness.
Moderate Western with an unusually less-than-sympathetic role for its star.
w Kenneth Gamet d Gordon Douglas ph George Lawton m Paul Sawtell, George Duning
☆ Randolph Scott, George Macready, Louise Allbritton, John Ireland, Noah Beery Jnr, Dona Drake

The Doom Generation

US/France 1995 83m colour
Metro Tartan/Union Générale/Teen Angst/Desperate/Blurco/Why Not (Andresa Sperling, Gregg Araki)
📺 ▦
A young drifter involves two teenagers in sex, robbery and murder.
Randomly violent road movie, which seems to be deliberately devoid of meaning.
wd Gregg Araki ph Jim Fealy pd Therese Deprez ed Gregg Araki
☆ James Duval, Rose McGowan, Johnathon Schaech, Cress Williams, Skinny Puppy, Parker Posey, Heidi Fleiss
'A stunning film with superlative production values … pic is bold not only in its art design, but also in its narrative and tone, a mixture of satire and horror.' – *Emanuel Levy, Variety*

Doomed: see *Ikiru*

The Doomed Battalion *

US/Germany 1932 74m bw
Universal
Austrians fight Italians high in the Alps.
Interesting but not very effective attempt to internationalize a German 'bergfilm'.
w Luis Trenker, Carl Harth d Cyril Gardner
☆ Luis Trenker, Tala Birell, Victor Varconi, Albert Conti, C. Henry Gordon, Gibson Gowland, Henry Armetta
'Beaucoup snow and ice stuff for hot weather appeal … capable of sustaining bally.' – *Variety*

Doomed Cargo: see *Seven Sinners*

Doomed to Die: see *Mr Wong*

Doomwatch

GB 1972 92m colour
Tigon (Tony Tenser)
An investigator of coastal pollution discovers a village in which dumped chemicals have given all the inhabitants a distorting disease called acromegaly.
An unsatisfactory horror film is drawn from a moderately serious TV series about ecology.
w Clive Exton d Peter Sasdy ph Kenneth Talbot m John Scott
☆ Ian Bannen, Judy Geeson, John Paul, Simon Oates, George Sanders, Percy Herbert, Geoffrey Keen, Joseph O'Conor

The Door in the Wall *

GB 1956 29m Technicolor Vistavision
AB Pathé/BFI/Lawrie (Howard Thomas)
A man is obsessed by a childhood dream of a green door which leads into a beautiful garden.
The story is chosen to experiment with Dynamic Frame, a system in which the picture changes shape and size according to the subject matter. In this case the results are entertaining enough.
wd Glenn H. Alvey Jnr ph Jo Jago m James Bernard
☆ Stephen Murray, Ian Hunter

The Door with Seven Locks

GB 1940 89m bw
Rialto (John Argyle)
📺 ⚉
US title: *Chamber of Horrors*
A mad doctor abducts an heiress in the hope of gaining her wealth.
Old-fashioned barnstormer, ineptly made.
w Norman Lee, John Argyle, Gilbert Gunn novel Edgar Wallace d Norman Lee ph Desmond Dickinson
☆ Leslie Banks, Lilli Palmer, Romilly Lunge, Gina Malo, Richard Bird, David Horne, Cathleen Nesbitt

'The Ceremony Is About To Begin.'

The Doors **

US 1991 134m DeLuxe Panavision
Guild/Carolco/Imagine (Bill Graham, Sasha Harari, A. Kitman Ho)
📼 ▦ ⚉ ◉ 🎧
A film school drop-out and poet becomes a drug-abusing, self-destructive rock star.
Despite the title, the focus of this grandiose biopic is The Door's singer Jim Morrison. Fans will enjoy it most; others are likely to find it noisy, overlong and over-busy.
w J. Randal Johnson, Oliver Stone d Oliver Stone ph Robert Richardson m The Doors pd Barbara Ling ed David Brenner, Joe Hutching
☆ Val Kilmer, Frank Whaley, Kevin Dillon, Meg Ryan, Kyle MacLachlan, Billy Idol, Dennis Burkley, Josh Evans, Michael Madsen, Michael Wincott, Kathleen Quinlan
'It is folly to lavish $40 million (that's $10 million a Door!) and 2hr 15 min. of your time on a proposition – some guys can't handle fame – that was evident two decades ago. Maybe it was fun to bathe in decadence back then. But this is no time to wallow in that mire.' – *Richard Corliss, Time*

Doorway to Hell

US 1930 79m bw
Warner
GB title: *A Handful of Clouds*
A young gangster tries to go straight but is driven back into crime.
Vividly written but dramatically evasive crime-does-not-pay story, trying to eat its cake and have it.
w George Rosener story *A Handful of Clouds* by Rowland Brown d Archie Mayo ph Barney McGill md Leo Forbstein
☆ Lew Ayres, Charles Judels, James Cagney, Dorothy Matthews, Leon Janney, Robert Elliott
'Swell gang picture, handled so as to just slip by the censors.' – *Variety*
🎵 original story

Dop Bey Kuan Wan: see *One Armed Boxer*

Doppelganger: see *Journey to the Far Side of the Sun*

Doro No Kawa: see *Muddy River*

Dorp aan de Rivier: see *Doctor in the Village*

Dosshouse *

GB 1933 53m bw
MGM/Sound City (John Baxter)
An escaped convict is captured by a reporter and detective posing as tramps.
Low-budget featurette which deserves a footnote in film history for its social consciousness, rare at the time, especially in the dosshouse scenes.
w Herbert Ayres d John Baxter ph George Stretton md Colin Wark ad D. W. L. Daniels ed R. Gardener, R. Swan
☆ Frank Cellier, Arnold Bell, Herbert Franklyn, J. Hubert Leslie

Dou San: see *God of Gamblers*

The Double: see *Kagemusha*

Double Bunk

GB 1960 92m bw
British Lion/Bryanston (George H. Brown)
Newlyweds live in an old houseboat.
Thin comedy which turns out not to be leakproof.
wd C. M. Pennington-Richards ph Stephen Dade m Stanley Black

☆ Ian Carmichael, Janette Scott, Liz Frazer, Sid James, Dennis Price, Reginald Beckwith, Irene Handl, Noel Purcell, Naunton Wayne

Double Confession

GB 1950 85m bw
ABP/Harry Reynolds
At a seaside resort, a man finds his wife dead and tries to frame her lover, but becomes confused with two real murderers with a different purpose.
Confused and unlikely melodrama which signally lacks the ancient mariner's eye.
w William Templeton novel *All on a Summer's Day* by John Garden d Ken Annakin ph Geoffrey Unsworth m Benjamin Frankel
☆ Derek Farr, Peter Lorre, William Hartnell, Joan Hopkins, Naunton Wayne, Ronald Howard, Kathleen Harrison, Leslie Dwyer, Edward Rigby

Double Deal

Australia 1981 90m colour Panavision
Rychemond Film Productions (Brian Kavanagh, Lynn Barker)
A wealthy businessman plans an elaborate scheme to rid himself of his disenchanted wife.
Silly thriller in the style of Sleuth.
wd Brian Kavanagh ph Ross Berryman m Bruce Smeaton ad Jill Eden ed Tim Lewis
☆ Louis Jourdan, Angela Punch McGregor, Diane Craig, Warwick Comber, Peter Cummins, Bruce Spence, June Jago, Kerry Walker

'Frankenstein, Dracula and other screen monsters pale by comparison with this fiendish, decadent woman!'

Double Door

US 1934 75m bw
Paramount
A selfish, wealthy Fifth Avenue spinster takes a dislike to her brother's girlfriend and locks her up in a vault.
Silly, rather boring melodrama which may have worked on the stage but did not take to the screen.
w Gladys Lehman, Jack Cunningham play Elizabeth McFadden d Charles Vidor
☆ Mary Morris, Evelyn Venable, Kent Taylor, Sir Guy Standing, Anne Revere, Colin Tapley, Halliwell Hobbes
'Not likely to get anywhere at the b.o … dull, drab and incredible.' – *Variety*

Double Dragon

US 1994 95m CFI color
Gramercy/Imperial Entertainment/Scanbox/Greenleaf (Sunil R. Shah, Ash R. Shah, Alan Schechter, Jan Heald, Don Murphy)
📼 ▦ 🎧
In the future, when Los Angeles has been reduced to rubble by an earthquake, two brothers fight an evil ruler who wants to control the world.
Martial arts mayhem based on a successful video game, consisting only of endless noisy fights.
w Michael Davis, Peter Gould d James Yukich ph Gary Kibbe m Jay Ferguson pd Mayne Berke ed Florent Retz
☆ Robert Patrick, Mark Dacascos, Scott Wolf, Kristina Malandro Wagner, Julia Nickson, Alyssa Milano
'Even kids won't get much of a kick out of this high-energy, low-IQ futuristic slugfest.' – *Brian Lowry, Variety*

Double Dynamite

US 1951 80m bw
RKO (Irving Cummings Jnr)
📺
aka: *It's Only Money*
A bank teller wins a fortune at the race track but is afraid his winnings will be thought the proceeds of a bank robbery.
Insultingly mild comedy, nearly saved by a few quips from Groucho.
w Melville Shavelson, Harry Crane, Leo Rosten d Irving Cummings ph Robert de Grasse m Leigh Harline
☆ Frank Sinatra, Jane Russell, Groucho Marx, Don McGuire, Howard Freeman
† Made in 1948.

'What Starts With A Kiss Will End With A Killing...'
Double Exposure
US 1993 93m CFI color
New Age/Falcon Arts & Entertainment/Joey Walker
(Joanne Watkins)

A jealous husband, who suspects his wife of having
an affair, hires a private detective with troubles of
his own to investigate.
*Exceedingly dull and trivial thriller, acted and directed
without conviction.*
w Claudia Hoover, Bridget Hoffman
story Christine Colfer d Claudia Hoover ph John
Connor m Paolo Rustichelli pd Tim Keating
ed Tom Meshelski
☆ Ron Perlman, Ian Buchanan, Jennifer Gatti,
Dedee Pfeiffer, William R. Moses, James
McEachin, Bridget Hoffman

Double Harness
US 1933 70m bw
RKO
A girl sets out to trick a rich man into marriage.
*Mildly amusing comedy which in its time was
considered risqué.*
w Jane Murfin play Edward Montgomery d John
Cromwell
☆ Ann Harding, William Powell, Henry
Stephenson, Lillian Bond, Reginald Owen, George
Meeker, Kay Hammond
'Managed with such reticence that at no time is
there a note of offence ... this class actress again
triumphs over her surroundings, and the picture
will please her large following.' – *Variety*

'Twin brothers torn apart by violence. On a mission
of revenge. One packs a punch. One packs a piece.
Together they deliver...'
Double Impact
US 1991 109m DeLuxe
Columbia TriStar/Stone Group (Ashok Amritaj, Jean-
Claude Van Damme)

Twin brothers, separated when young, get together
when grown up to avenge their parents' murder by
gangsters.
*Two Van Dammes for the price of one merely doubles
the incoherence of this otherwise ordinary martial arts
movie.*
w Sheldon Lettich, Jean-Claude Van Damme
story Sheldon Lettich, Jean-Claude Van Damme,
Steve Meerson, Peter Krikes d Sheldon Lettich
ph Richard Kline m Arthur Kempel pd John Jay
Moore ed Mark Conte, Brent White
☆ Jean-Claude Van Damme, Geoffrey Lewis, Alan
Scarfe, Alonna Shaw, Cory Everson, Philip Can
Yan Kin, Bolo Yeung, Sarah-Jane Varley
'Turns on a typically lame revenge plot while
dragging out unimaginatively shot action
sequences until no one will give a good Van
Damme. Tedious story-telling should mute the
pic's b.o. impact.' – *Variety*

Double Indemnity: see *The River's Edge (1956)*

'You can't kiss away a murder!'
Double Indemnity ****
US 1944 107m bw
Paramount (Joseph Sistrom)

An insurance agent connives with the glamorous
wife of a client to kill her husband and collect.
*Archetypal film noir of the forties, brilliantly filmed
and incisively written, perfectly capturing the decayed
Los Angeles atmosphere of a Chandler novel but using
a simpler story and more substantial characters. The
hero/villain was almost a new concept.*
w Billy Wilder, Raymond Chandler novel James M.
Cain d Billy Wilder ph John Seitz m Miklos Rozsa
☆ Fred MacMurray, Barbara Stanwyck, Edward G.
Robinson, Tom Powers, Porter Hall, Jean Heather,
Byron Barr, Richard Gaines
'The sort of film which revives a critic from the
depressive effects of bright epics about the big
soul of America or the suffering soul of Europe
and gives him a new lease of faith.' – *Richard
Winnington*
'The most pared-down and purposeful film ever
made by Billy Wilder.' – *John Coleman, 1966*
'Profoundly, intensely entertaining.' – *Richard
Mallett, Punch*
'One of the highest summits of film noir ...
without a single trace of pity or love.' – *Charles
Higham, 1971*

best picture; script, direction; John Seitz; Miklos
Rozsa; Barbara Stanwyck

'Murder Isn't Always A Crime.'
Double Jeopardy
US 1999 105m DeLuxe Panavision
Paramount (Leonard Goldberg)

Sentenced to prison for killing her husband, a wife
discovers he framed her and that, when she gets
out, she can kill him with impunity because she
cannot be tried twice for the same offence.
*Idiotically implausible thriller; if you can accept its
premise, there are mild pleasures to be had.*
w David Weisberg, Douglas S. Cook d Bruce
Beresford ph Peter James m Normand Corbeil
pd Howard Cummings ed Mark Warner
☆ Tommy Lee Jones, Ashley Judd, Bruce
Greenwood, Annabeth Gish, Roma Maffia,
Davenia McFadden, Jay Brazeau, Gillian Barber,
Benjamin Weir, Spencer Treat Clark
'It will hold your attention, but it does nothing
to win your admiration.' – *Cosmo Landesman,
Sunday Times*
† The film was a hit, taking more than $100m at
the US box-office.

'This woman inspired him – this woman feared him!'
A Double Life **
US 1947 103m bw
Universal/Kanin Productions (Michael Kanin)

An actor playing Othello is obsessed by the role
and murders a woman he imagines to be
Desdemona.
*An old theatrical chestnut (cf Men Are Not Gods) is
decked out with smartish backstage dialogue but despite
a pleasant star performance remains unrewarding if
taxing, and the entertainment value of the piece is on
the thin side considering the mighty talents involved.*
w Ruth Gordon, Garson Kanin d George Cukor
ph Milton Krasner m Miklos Rozsa
☆ Ronald Colman, Shelley Winters, Signe Hasso,
Edmond O'Brien, Millard Mitchell
'As a piece of film story-telling it is generally
skilled. Yet the central situation is artificial.' –
Dilys Powell
♟ Miklos Rozsa; Ronald Colman
⚖ Ruth Gordon, Garson Kanin; George Cukor

The Double Life of Véronique **
France/Poland 1991 98m colour
Gala/Sidéral/Canal Plus/TOR/Norsk Film (Leonardo de
la Fuente)

original title: *La Double Vie de Véronique*
Two young women, one Polish, the other French,
seem to share a single existence.
*A complex, finely acted and directed puzzle of a film,
but one that grips the attention throughout.*
w Krzysztof Kieślowski, Krzysztof Piesiewicz
d Krzysztof Kieślowski ph Slawomir Idziak
m Zbigniew Preisner pd Patrice Mercier, Halina
Dobrowolska ed Jacques Witta
☆ Irène Jacob, Halina Gryglaszewska, Kalina
Jedrusik, Aleksander Bardini, Wladyslaw Kowalski,
Jerzy Gudejko
'Despite pic's many-splendoured outbursts of
filmic creativity and intense emotion, final result
remains a head-scratching cipher with blurred
edges.' – *Variety*

The Double Man *
GB 1967 105m Technicolor
Warner/Hal E. Chester
A CIA agent investigates the death of his son on a
Swiss skiing holiday and finds the murder was a
lure to get him there so that an enemy lookalike
can substitute for him.
*Rather ruthless but good-looking and generally
watchable spy melodrama.*
w Frank Tarloff, Alfred Hayes novel Henry S.
Maxfield d Franklin Schaffner ph Denys Coop
m Ernie Freeman
☆ Yul Brynner, Clive Revill, Anton Diffring, Britt
Ekland, Moira Lister

The Double McGuffin
👫 US 1979 100m colour
Mulberry Square/Joe Camp

Kids turn into amateur detectives when they find
that a visiting foreign leader is to be assassinated.

*Barely tolerable lightweight mystery for an audience
which probably doesn't exist.*
wd Joe Camp ph Don Reddy m Euel Box
pd Harland Wright
☆ Ernest Borgnine, George Kennedy, Elke
Sommer, Rod Browning

Double Negative
Canada 1980 96m colour
Quadrant

A photo journalist tries to find the murderer of his
wife, and discovers he's an amnesiac and did it
himself.
*Ho-hum mystery thriller centring on an ancient
wheeze; treatment resolutely plodding.*
w Thomas Hedley Jnr, Janis Allen, Charles Dennis
novel *The Three Roads* by Ross Macdonald
d George Bloomfield
☆ Michael Sarrazin, Susan Clark, Anthony
Perkins, Howard Duff, Kate Reid

Double or Nothing
US 1937 90m bw
Paramount
Inheritors under a trick will must double their
bequests or lose them.
*Flat comedy with music; none of the elements are
really up to scratch.*
w Charles Lederer and others d Theodore Reed
☆ Bing Crosby, Martha Raye, Andy Devine,
William Frawley, Mary Carlisle, Benny Baker
'Due for big openings and tapering-off business.
Will squeeze through.' – *Variety*

Double Team
US 1997 91m Technicolor Panavision
Columbia/Mandalay/Moshe Diamant/One Story

A top agent who wants to quit the game discovers
that his wife and unborn child are threatened by
the terrorist he failed to kill.
*Frenetic action movie that throws in everything but the
towel and the kitchen sink.*
w Don Jacoby, Paul Mones d Tsui Hark ph Peter
Pau m Gary Chang pd Marek Dobrowolski
ed Bill Pankow
☆ Jean-Claude Van Damme, Dennis Rodman,
Mickey Rourke, Paul Freeman, Natacha Lindinger,
Valeria Cavalli, Jay Benedict, Rob Diem
'Action-packed, often campy and colorful
amusement park of a movie.' – *Variety*

Double Wedding
US 1937 87m bw
MGM (Joseph L. Mankiewicz)
A bohemian artist makes a play for the lady of his
choice by romancing her sister.
Zany star comedy which doesn't quite come off.
w Jo Swerling play *Great Love* by Ferenc Molnar
d Richard Thorpe ph William Daniels m Edward
Ward
☆ William Powell, Myrna Loy, John Beal,
Florence Rice, Jessie Ralph, Edgar Kennedy, Sidney
Toler, Barnett Parker, Katherine Alexander,
Donald Meek
'OK for topflight business ... would be funnier if
it were shorter.' – *Variety*

Double Whoopee **
US 1928 20m bw silent
Hal Roach
Incompetent doormen at a swank hotel cause
havoc.
Simple-minded but pleasing star farce.
w Leo McCarey, H. M. Walker d Lewis R. Foster
ph George Stevens, Jack Roach ed Richard
Currier
☆ Laurel and Hardy, Jean Harlow, Charlie Hall

Double X
GB 1991 97m Technicolor
Feature/String of Pearls (Shani S. Grewal)

A reformed safebreaker asks a former Chicago cop-
turned-hitman to help him rescue his kidnapped
daughter from a vicious gangleader.
*Dismal thriller, with a dreary plot and uninspired
direction and acting, which suggests that the British film
industry is bent on committing ritual suicide.*
wd Shani S. Grewal story *Vengeance* by David
Fleming ph Dominique Grosz m Raf Ravenscroft
pd Colin Pocock ed Michael Johns

☆ Simon Ward, William Katt, Norman Wisdom,
Bernard Hill, Gemma Craven, Leon Herbert,
Derren Nesbitt, Vladek Sheybal, Chloe Annett
'An inept low-budget suspenser. Reliable cast is
double-crossed by a laughable script and clumsy
helming. Result, which hardly cuts it even as a
TV pic, should expire fast.' – *Variety*

Doubting Thomas
US 1935 78m bw
Fox
Small-town 'society' puts on an amateur show.
Slight but attractive star vehicle.
w William Conselman, Bartlett Cormack
novel *The Torch Bearers* by George Kelly d David
Butler
☆ Will Rogers, Billie Burke, Alison Skipworth,
Sterling Holloway, Andrew Tombes, Gail Patrick
'There is one thing that Rogers knows, and that
is how to get laughs with any sort of a situation,
and he didn't learn that just from reading the
papers.' – *Variety*

Douce *
France 1943 106m bw
Société Parisienne de l'Industrie Cinématographique
In 1887 Paris a sheltered young rich girl falls for a
steward and encounters family opposition.
*A charming old-fashioned story which provides a well-
taken opportunity for a portrait of the old bourgeoisie.*
w Jean Aurenche, Pierre Bost d Claude Autant-
Lara ph Gaston Thonnart m René Cloërc
☆ Odette Joyeux, Jean Debucourt, Marguerite
Moreno, Roger Pigaut, Madeleine Robinson
'Direction and camerawork constantly reveal
touches of felicity.' – *MFB*

Doucement Les Basses: see *Take It Easy*

Doughboys *
👫 US 1930 80m bw
MGM/Buster Keaton (Lawrence Weingarten)

GB title: *Forward March*
A young eccentric joins the army.
*Simple-minded farce with a few good routines for the
star.*
w Richard Schayer d Edward Sedgwick
ph Leonard Smith
☆ Buster Keaton, Sally Eilers, Cliff Edwards,
Edward Brophy
'Keaton's first talker is comedy with a kick.' –
Variety

The Doughgirls *
US 1944 102m bw
Warner (Mark Hellinger)
In a crowded wartime Washington hotel, a
honeymoon is frustrated by constant interruption,
not to mention the discovery that the wedding was
not legal.
*Frantic farce, generally well adapted, and certainly
played with gusto.*
w James V. Kern, Sam Hellman play Joseph Fields
d James V. Kern ph Ernest Haller m Adolph
Deutsch
☆ Alexis Smith, Jane Wyman, Jack Carson, Ann
Sheridan, Irene Manning, Eve Arden, Charlie
Ruggles, John Alexander, John Ridgely, Craig
Stevens, Alan Mowbray, Donald MacBride
'There's nothing so good in it that you must
attend, just as there is nothing bad enough to
keep you away.' – *Archer Winsten*

Doug's 1st Movie
👫 US 1999 77m Technicolor
Buena Vista/Walt Disney/Jumbo (Jim Jenkins, David
Campbell, Melanie Grisanti, Jack Spillum)

Schoolfriends discover a monster, created from
pollutants, in their local lake.
*A spinoff from a long-running US TV series, this is a
leisurely, adequately animated movie of minimal
appeal.*
w Ken Scarborough characters created by Jim
Jenkins d Maurice Joyce m Mark Watters
ed Alysha Nadine Cohen, Christopher K. Gee
☆ Featuring voices: Thomas McHugh, Fred
Newman, Chris Phillips, Constance Shulman,
Frank Welker, Doug Preis, Guy Hadley
'I can't believe kids will tolerate this boring
ET/Free Willy knock-off.' – *Peter Bradshaw,
Guardian*

The Dove *

US   1968   15m   bw
Coe/Davis Ltd
Back in the countryside of his childhood, a Nobel prize winner recalls the events of a summer…
Elaborate Ingmar Bergman spoof complete with subtitles and pidgin Swedish. Hilarious at the time for those who had just seen Wild Strawberries.
w Sidney Davis d George Coe, Anthony Lover ph Anthony Lover
☆ David Zirlin, George Coe, Pamela Burrell, Madeline Kahn

The Dove *

👫👫 US   1974   104m   Technicolor Panavision
St George Productions (Gregory Peck)
🖫
Yachtsman Robin Lee Graham makes a five-year voyage around the world.
Bland, rather stolid adventure story for boat-niks, based on real incidents; good to look at.
w Peter Beagle, Adam Kennedy book Robin Lee Graham, Derek Gill d Charles Jarrott ph Sven Nykvist m John Barry
☆ Joseph Bottoms, Deborah Raffin, John McLiam, Dabney Coleman
'Postcard views flick by to the strains of a saccharine score.' – David McGillivray

The Dover Road: see Where Sinners Meet

Down among the Sheltering Palms

US   1952   86m   Technicolor
TCF (Fred Kohlmar)
An American army unit takes over a South Sea island, but fraternization is forbidden.
Tolerable comedy-musical with familiar jokes and situations.
w Claude Binyon, Albert Lewin, Burt Styler d Edmund Goulding ph Leon Shamroy m Leigh Harline m/ly Harold Arlen, Ralph Blane
☆ William Lundigan, Jane Greer, Mitzi Gaynor, David Wayne, Gloria de Haven, Gene Lockhart, Jack Paar, Billy Gilbert

Down among the Z Men

GB   1952   71m   bw
New Realm (E. J. Fancey)
🖭 🖫 📀
US title: *Stand Easy*
A detective turned soldier keeps an atomic formula out of enemy hands.
A missed opportunity to transfer the appeal of The Goons from their successful radio show to the screen; it was not helped by the conventional script, the dancing girls and Secombe's straight role.
w Jimmy Grafton, Francis Charles d Maclean Rogers ph Geoffrey Faithfull m Jack Jordan ed Peter Mayhew
☆ Peter Sellers, Michael Bentine, Harry Secombe, Spike Milligan, Carole Carr, Andrew Timothy, Graham Stark, Miriam Karlin, Eunice Gayson, The Television Toppers

Down and Out in Beverly Hills *

US   1985   97m   Technicolor
Touchstone (Paul Mazursky)
🖭 🖫 📀
A wandering con artist is taken in by an insecure Beverly Hills family.
Somewhat bumbling but sporadically effective rehash of Renoir's Boudu Sauvé des Eaux (qv), with a few modern jabs and effectively eccentric performances.
w Paul Mazursky, Leon Capetanos play René Fauchois d Paul Mazursky ph Donald McAlpine m Andy Summers pd Pato Guzman
☆ Nick Nolte, Richard Dreyfuss, Bette Midler, Little Richard, Tracy Nelson, Elizabeth Pena
'What makes this picture so enjoyable is not the exaggerations of its narrative but the richness of its texture. Every inch of every frame is utilized. While, in the foreground, the actors are doing or saying one thing, behind them a television screen is telling us something else. The audience is completely embroiled in every incident.' – Quentin Crisp

Down Argentine Way *

US   1940   94m   Technicolor
TCF (Harry Joe Brown)
🖫 📀
A wealthy American girl falls in love with an Argentinian horse-breeder.
A very moderate musical which happened to bring both Grable and Miranda to star stature and set Fox off on their successful run of forties extravaganzas, reasonably pleasant to look at but empty-headed.
w Karl Tunberg, Darrell Ware d Irving Cummings ph Ray Rennahan, Leon Shamroy m/ly Harry Warren, Mack Gordon ad Richard Day, Joseph C. Wright
☆ Betty Grable, Carmen Miranda, Don Ameche, Charlotte Greenwood, J. Carrol Naish, Henry Stephenson, Leonid Kinskey, The Nicholas Brothers
'I dislike Technicolor in which all pinks resemble raspberry sauce, reds turn to sealing wax, blues shriek of the washtub, and yellows become suet pudding.' – James Agate
'So outrageous – that it's hard to believe it isn't at least partly intentional – but why would anybody make this picture on purpose.' – New Yorker, 1976
🎕 Ray Rennahan, Leon Shamroy; title song (m Harry Warren, ly Mack Gordon); art direction

Down by Law *

US   1986   107m   bw
Island Pictures/Black Snake/Grokenburger Films (Alan Kleinberg)
🖭 🖫
A disc jockey and a pimp, framed for crimes they did not commit, escape from jail with an Italian who has a minimal grasp of English.
Engaging lowlife comedy.
wd Jim Jarmusch ph Robby Müller m John Lurie, Tom Waits ed Melody London
☆ Tom Waits, John Lurie, Roberto Benigni, Ellen Barkin, Billie Neal, Rockets Redglare, Vernel Bagneris, Nicoletta Braschi

Down Memory Lane *

US   1949   70m   bw
Aubrey Schenck
A kaleidoscope of Mack Sennett comedy shorts, linked by Steve Allen as a disc jockey. Much Bing Crosby; Fields in *The Dentist*; an appearance by Sennett himself.
d Phil Karlson

Down Periscope

US   1996   93m   DeLuxe
TCF (Robert Lawrence)
🖭 🖫
A submarine commander is given a broken-down ship, crewed by misfits, with which to prove his abilities.
Low comedy that sends up submarine movies, but sinks under the weight of some leaden jokes.
w Hugh Wilson, Andrew Kurtzman, Eliot Wald d David S. Ward ph Victor Hammer m Randy Edelman, Mark McKenzie pd Michael Corenblith ed William Anderson, Armen Minasian
☆ Kelsey Grammer, Lauren Holly, Rob Schneider, Harry Dean Stanton, Bruce Dern, William H. Macy, Ken Hudson Campbell, Rip Torn
'A curiously sterile effort which, although by no means unwatchable, still manages to reinvent good old-fashioned bland.' – Bob McCabe, Empire

Down Three Dark Streets *

US   1954   85m   bw
UA/Edward Small (Arthur Gardner, Jules V. Levy)
An FBI agent is shot on duty, and his friend avenges him in the course of clearing up three cases in which he was involved.
Competent, enjoyable police film with three cases for the price of one.
w The Gordons, Bernard C. Schoenfeld book Case File FBI by the Gordons d Arnold Laven ph Joseph Biroc m Paul Sawtell
☆ Broderick Crawford, Ruth Roman, Martha Hyer, Marisa Pavan, Casey Adams, Kenneth Tobey
† One of the first collaborations of the prolific production company Laven-Gardner-Levy.

Down to Earth

US   1932   79m   bw
Nouveau riche Americans return from Europe and find themselves misfits at home.

Thin sequel to They Had to See Paris.
w Edwin Burke story Homer Croy d David Butler
☆ Will Rogers, Dorothy Jordan, Irene Rich, Matty Kemp, Mary Carlisle
'Will need support … the least powerful in draw of all Rogers' pictures.' – Variety

Down to Earth *

US   1947   101m   Technicolor
Columbia (Don Hartman)
🖭 🖫
The muse Terpsichore comes down to help a Broadway producer fix a new show in which she is featured.
Pleasant but undistinguished musical fantasy, a sequel to Here Comes Mr Jordan. The heavenly sequences promise more amusement than they produce.
w Edwin Blum, Don Hartman d Alexander Hall ph Rudolph Maté m Heinz Roemheld
☆ Rita Hayworth, Larry Parks, Roland Culver, Edward Everett Horton, Marc Platt, James Gleason
'Just the film to make the spectator forget the troubles of life.' – MFB
'Celestial whimsy musical, with arch acting and a dull score.' – New Yorker, 1977
† Rita Hayworth's singing was dubbed by Anita Ellis.

Down to the Sea in Ships *

US   1948   120m   bw
TCF (Elmer Clifton)
🖫
An old whaling skipper wants his grandson to follow in his footsteps.
Seagoing spectacle with strong characters; all concerned show Hollywood in its most professional form, but the film somehow fails to catch the imagination or live in the memory.
w John Lee Mahin, Sy Bartlett d Henry Hathaway ph Joe MacDonald m Alfred Newman
☆ Lionel Barrymore, Dean Stockwell, Richard Widmark, Cecil Kellaway, Gene Lockhart

Down Went McGinty: see The Great McGinty

Downhill

GB   1927   80m   bw   silent
Gainsborough (Michael Balcon)
US title: *When Boys Leave Home*
A sixth-form schoolboy, accused of theft, is expelled and goes to the bad in Marseilles before being found innocent.
Absurd novelette with only marginal glimpses of the director's emerging talent.
w Eliot Stannard play David Lestrange (Ivor Novello, Constance Collier) d Alfred Hitchcock ph Claude McDonnell ed Ivor Montagu
☆ Ivor Novello, Ben Webster, Robin Irvine, Sybil Rhoda, Lilian Braithwaite, Isabel Jeans, Ian Hunter
FAMOUS LINE: 'Does this mean, sir, that I shall not be able to play for the Old Boys?'

Downhill Racer *

US   1969   101m   Technicolor
Paramount/Wildwood (Richard Gregson)
🖭 📀
An ambitious American skier gains a place on the team competing in Europe.
Virtually plotless, casually assembled study of a man and a sport, good to look at, often exciting, but just as frequently irritating in its throwaway style.
w James Salter novel Oakley Hall d Michael Ritchie ph Brian Probyn m Kenyon Hopkins
☆ Robert Redford, Gene Hackman, Camilla Sparv, Joe Jay Jalbert, Timothy Kirk, Dabney Coleman
🎬 Robert Redford

Downstairs

US   1932   77m   bw
MGM
A villainous chauffeur blackmails the other servants.
Failed attempt by a falling star to do something different.
w Melville Baker, Lenore Coffee story John Gilbert d Monta Bell
☆ John Gilbert, Virginia Bruce, Paul Lukas, Hedda Hopper, Reginald Owen, Olga Baclanova

'Next Time Take The Stairs.'

Downtime **

GB/France   1997   91m   colour
Film Four/Scala/Channel 4/Arts Council/Moving Image/Pandora (Richard Johns)
🖭
A former police psychologist is trapped in a lift in a gang-ridden tower block on a run-down housing estate with the suicidal woman he fancies, her young son and an epileptic old man.
A low-budget thriller grounded in a slum-ridden social reality which delivers on downbeat suspense, apart from its unconvincing ending.
w Caspar Berry d Bharat Nalluri ph Tony Imi m Simon Boswell pd Chris Townsend ed Les Healey
☆ Paul McGann, Susan Lynch, Tom Georgeson, David Roper, Denise Bryson, Adam Johnston, David Horsefield, Stephen Graham, Birdy Sweeney
'It's a game try with some splendid moments.' – Variety

Downtown

US   1990   96m   DeLuxe
TCF (Charles H. Maguire)
🖭 🖫 📀
An idealistic young white cop is transferred from a genteel suburb to a tough black inner-city neighbourhood.
Unarresting buddy movie that is an uneasy mix of broad comedy, violence and far too many narrative clichés.
w Nat Mauldin d Richard Benjamin ph Richard H. Kline m Alan Silvestri pd Charles Rosen ed Jacqueline Cambas, Brian Chambers
☆ Anthony Edwards, Forest Whitaker, Penelope Ann Miller, Joe Pantoliano, David Clennon, Art Evans

Drachenfutter: see Dragon's Food

Dracula: see Bram Stoker's Dracula (1992)

'The strangest love a woman has ever known … a livid face bent over her in the ghostly mist!'

Dracula ***

US   1931   84m   bw
Universal (Carl Laemmle Jnr)
🖫 📀
A Transylvanian vampire count gets his comeuppance in Yorkshire.
A film which has much to answer for. It started its star and its studio off on horror careers, and it launched innumerable sequels (see below). In brief, after two eerie reels, it becomes a pedantic and slow transcription of a stage adaptation, and its climax takes place offscreen; but for all kinds of reasons it remains full of interest.
w Garrett Fort play Hamilton Deane, John Balderston novel Bram Stoker d Tod Browning ph Karl Freund m Tchaikovsky
☆ Bela Lugosi, Helen Chandler, David Manners, Dwight Frye, Edward Van Sloan
'Must have caused much uncertainty as to the femme fan reaction … as it turns out the signs are that the woman's angle is all right and that sets the picture for better than average money … it comes out as a sublimated ghost story related with all surface seriousness and above all with a remarkably effective background of creepy atmosphere.' – Variety
'A too literal adaptation of the play (not the book) results in a plodding, talkative development, with much of the vital action taking place off-screen.' – William K. Everson
'The mistiest parts are the best; when the lights go up the interest goes down.' – Ivan Butler
'It'll chill you and fill you with fears. You'll find it creepy and cruel and crazed.' – New York Daily News
† Later advertising variations concentrated on the horror element: 'In all the annals of living horror one name stands out as the epitome of evil! So evil, so fantastic, so degrading you'll wonder if it isn't all a nightmare! Innocent girls lured to a fate truly worse than death!'
†† Lugosi was not the first choice for the role of the Count. Ian Keith and William Powell were strongly favoured
††† Sequels include *Dracula's Daughter* (qv), *Son of Dracula* (qv); the later Hammer sequence consists of *Dracula* (see below), *Brides of Dracula* (qv), *Dracula Prince of Darkness* (qv), *Dracula Has Risen From the Grave* (qv), *Taste the Blood of Dracula*

(qv), *Scars of Dracula* (qv), *Dracula AD 1972* (qv),
The Satanic Rites of Dracula (qv). Other associated
films in which the Count or a disciple appears
include (all qv) *Return of the Vampire* (1944),
House of Frankenstein (1945), *House of Dracula*
(1945), *Abbott and Costello Meet Frankenstein*
(1948), *The Return of Dracula* (1958), *Kiss of the
Vampire* (1963), *The Fearless Vampire Killers* (1967),
Count Yorga Vampire (1969), *Countess Dracula*
(1970), *Vampire Circus* (1970), *The House of Dark
Shadows* (1970), *Vampire Lovers* (1971), *Blacula*
(1972), *Dracula* (1974), *Martin* (1978), *Dracula*
(1979), *Salem's Lot* (1979), *Nosferatu The Vampyre*
(1979), *The Hunger* (1983), *The Lost Boys* (1987),
Bram Stoker's Dracula (1992). Minor potboilers are
legion.

'Who will be his bride tonight?'
Dracula ***
GB 1958 82m Technicolor
Rank/Hammer (Anthony Hinds)
▣ ⊜~ ⌒
US title: *Horror of Dracula*
A remake of the 1931 film.
*Commendably brief in comparison with the later
Hammer films, this was perhaps the best horror piece
they turned out as well as the most faithful to its
original. Decor and colour were well used, and the
leading performances are striking.*
w Jimmy Sangster novel Bram Stoker d Terence
Fisher ph Jack Asher m James Bernard ad Bernard
Robinson ed James Needs, Bill Lenny
☆ Peter Cushing, *Christopher Lee*, Melissa Stribling,
Carol Marsh, Michael Gough, John Van Eyssen,
Valerie Gaunt, Miles Malleson

Dracula
Italy 1974 93m colour
Andrew Braunsberg
▣ ⊚
aka: *Andy Warhol's Dracula*
aka: *Blood for Dracula*
In this sick and gory version, Dracula becomes ill if
he feasts on anything but pure virgin's blood. The
hero saves the heroine in the predictable way.
Not for the squeamish.
wd Paul Morrissey
☆ Udo Kier, Arno Juerging, Vittorio de Sica,
Maxime McEmory, Joe Dallesandro

Dracula *
GB 1979 112m Technicolor Panavision
Universal/Mirisch (Marvin Mirisch/Tom Pevsner)
▣ ▣ ⊜~ ⌒
A lush, expensive and romantic version which
presents the count as a matinee idol and spends too
much time on the romantic scenes to distract
attention from an old old story.
w W. D. Richter d John Badham ph Gilbert
Taylor m John Williams pd Peter Murton
☆ Frank Langella, Laurence Olivier, Donald
Pleasence, Kate Nelligan, Trevor Eve
'*A triumphantly lurid creation that seems bound
to be either under-valued for its circus effects or
over-valued for the stylishness with which it
steers between the reefs of camp and theatrical
indulgence.*' – Richard Combs, MFB

Dracula 71: see *Bram Stoker's Count Dracula*

'The Count is back, with an eye for London's hot
pants, and a taste for everything!'
Dracula AD 1972
GB 1972 95m Eastmancolor
Warner/Hammer (Josephine Douglas)
▣
Dracula reappears among Chelsea teenagers
practising black magic.
*Depressed attempt to update a myth; the link with
modern sin makes it seem not only tarnished but
tasteless, and the film itself is lamentably short on
excitement.*
w Don Houghton d Alan Gibson ph Richard
Bush m Michael Vickers pd Don Mingaye
ed James Needs
☆ Peter Cushing, Christopher Lee, Stephanie
Beacham, Michael Coles, Christopher Neame,
William Ellis

Dracula contra Frankenstein: see *Dracula –
Prisoner of Frankenstein*

'You'll die laughing. Then you'll rise from the dead
and laugh once more.'
Dracula: Dead and Loving It
US 1995 90m Technicolor
Polygram/Castle Rock/Gaumont/Brooksfilms (Mel
Brooks)
▣ ▣ ⊜~ ⌒
Dracula comes to London to seek fresh blood.
*A feeble comedy, poking fun at British repression while
sticking surprisingly closely to the plot of the original
novel.*
w Mel Brooks, Rudy de Luca, Steve Haberman
d Mel Brooks ph Michael D. O'Shea m Hummie
Mann pd Roy Forge Smith ed Adam Weiss
☆ Leslie Nielsen, Peter MacNicol, Steven Weber,
Amy Yasbeck, Lysette Anthony, Harvey Korman,
Mel Brooks, Anne Bancroft, Clive Revill
'*As thin as bat wing.*' – Sunday Times

'You just can't keep a good man down!'
Dracula Has Risen from the Grave
GB 1968 92m Technicolor
Hammer (Aida Young)
▣ ▣ ⊜~
Dracula again terrorizes the village in the shadow
of his castle, and is routed by a bishop.
*Tedious, confined and repetitive shocker with little
conventional action and an unusual emphasis on sex.*
w John Elder (Anthony Hinds) d Freddie Francis
ph Arthur Grant m James Bernard ad Bernard
Robinson ed James Needs, Spencer Reeve
☆ Christopher Lee, Rupert Davies, Veronica
Carlson, Barbara Ewing, Barry Andrews, Ewan
Hooper
'*A bloody bore.*' – Judith Crist

**Dracula is Alive and Well and Living in
London:** see *The Satanic Rites of Dracula*

Dracula Prince of Darkness
GB 1966 90m Techniscope
Warner/Hammer/Seven Arts (Anthony Nelson-Keys)
▣ ▣ ⊜~ ⊚
Stranded travellers are made welcome at the late
count's castle by his sinister butler, who proceeds to
use the blood of one of them to revivify his master.
*Ingenious rehash of incidents from the original story,
largely dissipated by poor colour and unsuitable wide
screen.*
w John Sansom story John Elder d Terence
Fisher ph Michael Reed m James Bernard
pd Bernard Robinson ed James Needs, Chris
Barnes
☆ Christopher Lee, *Philip Latham*, Barbara Shelley,
Thorley Walters, Andrew Keir, Francis Matthews,
Suzan Farmer, Charles Tingwell
'*Run-of-the-coffin stuff … only for ardent fang-
and-cross fans.*' – Judith Crist

Dracula – Prisoner of Frankenstein
(dubbed)
Spain/France 1972 90m Telecolor
Interfilme/Fenix/Prodif ETS
original title: *Dracula contra Frankenstein*
aka: *The Screaming Dead*
Frankenstein revives Dracula in order to create an
army of vampires to take over the world.
*Horrendous not for its subject matter but for its total
incompetence, including an incoherent narrative and a
directorial style that consists of meaningless zooms and
out-of-focus close-ups. An ailing Price plays
Frankenstein as a somnambulistic zombie and the
acting honours go to a rubber bat.*
w Jess Franco, Paul D'Ales d Jess Franco (Jesús
Franco) ph José Climent m Bruno Nicolai ed R.
Aventer
☆ Howard Vernon (Mario Lippert), Dennis Price,
Genevieve Deloir, Josiane Gilbert, Albert D'Albes,
Mary Francis

Dracula versus Frankenstein (dubbed)
Spain/West Germany/Italy 1971 87m
Eastmancolor Totalvision
Monarch/Eichberg/International Jaguar/Jaime Prades
aka: *El Hombre que Vino de Ummo*
Aliens attempt to conquer Earth by reviving
Dracula, Frankenstein's monster, the Mummy and
a werewolf.
*Dire mix of horror and science fiction, cheaply and
unimaginatively made.*
w Jacinto Molina Alvarez d Tulio Demicheli
ph Godofredo Pachecho m Franco Salina
ad Adolfo Cofiño ed Emilio Rodriguez
sp Antonio Molna

☆ Michael Rennie, Karin Dor, Craig Hill, Patty
Sheppard, Paul Naschi
'*The film's sole claim on anyone's attention is
the unabashed sadism of several sequences … As
for the English title, Dracula and Frankenstein
are never in the same shot together, let alone in
conflict.*' – Tony Rayns

'More sensational than her unforgettable father!'
Dracula's Daughter **
US 1936 70m bw
Universal (E. M. Asher)
▣ ⊜~
The daughter of the old count follows his remains
to London.
*Lively sequel which develops in the manner of a
Sherlock Holmes story.*
w Garrett Fort d Lambert Hillyer ph George
Robinson m Heinz Roemheld
☆ Otto Kruger, Marguerite Churchill, Edward Van
Sloan, Gloria Holden, Irving Pichel, Nan Grey,
Hedda Hopper, Gilbert Emery, Claud Allister, E. E.
Clive, Halliwell Hobbes, Billy Bevan

'There's more to the legend than meets the throat!'
Dracula's Dog
US 1977 88m DeLuxe
Vic (Albert Band, Frank Ray Perelli)
▣ ▣
GB title: *Zoltan, Hound of Dracula*
The resurrected servant of Dracula tries to use his
vampire dog to create a new master.
*Ingenious but unattractive addition to the saga, with
dogs as chief villains; the style varies between spoof and
rather nasty horror.*
w Frank Ray Perelli d Albert Band ph Bruce
Logan m Andrew Belling
☆ José Ferrer, Reggie Nalder, Michael Pataki, Jan
Shutan

Draegerman Courage
US 1937 59m bw
Warner
Problems of a Nova Scotian gold mine cave-in.
*Adequate action fare inspired by a real event.
(Draegermen are burrowers.)*
w Anthony Coldeway d Louis King
☆ Jean Muir, Barton MacLane, Henry O'Neill,
Robert Barrat. Addison Richards, Gordon Oliver
'*Vivid and often thrilling.*' – Variety

Dragao da Maldade contra o Santo
Guerreiro: see *Antonio das Mortes*

Dragnet *
US 1954 93m Warnercolor
Mark VII (Stanley Meyer)
▣ ▣
Sgt Joe Friday solves the murder of an ex-convict.
*Moderately interesting but overlong attempt to transfer
television techniques to the big screen; laconic dialogue,
question and answer, cheap sets, close-ups and
convenient Los Angeles locations.*
w Richard Breen d Jack Webb ph Edward
Colman m Walter Schumann
☆ Jack Webb, Ben Alexander, Richard Boone,
Stacy Harris, Ann Robinson, Virginia Gregg

Dragnet
US 1987 106m DeLuxe
Universal/Applied Action/Bernie Brillstein
▣ ▣ ⊜~ ⊚ ⌒
The nephew of Sgt Joe Friday gets involved in a
murder case.
*Overlong parody with some obvious amusements before
the whole thing becomes tiresome.*
w Dan Aykroyd, Alan Zweibel, Tom Mankiewicz
d Tom Mankiewicz ph Matthew F. Leonetti
m Ira Newborn pd Robert F. Boyle
☆ Dan Aykroyd, Tom Hanks, Christopher
Plummer, Harry Morgan, Alexandra Paul,
Elizabeth Ashley, Dabney Coleman

The Dragnet *
US 1928 77m bw silent
Paramount
▣
When his buddy is killed, a detective resigns from
the force and takes to the bottle.
*Obviously interesting sequel to Underworld. It can't
be evaluated because no print is known to exist.*
w Jules and Charles Furthman story *Night Stick* by
Oliver H. P. Garrett d Josef von Sternberg
ph Harold Rosson ad Hans Dreier

☆ George Bancroft, Evelyn Brent, William
Powell, Fred Kohler, Francis McDonald, Leslie
Fenton

Dragon Seed *
US 1944 144m bw
MGM (Pandro S. Berman)
▣
Chinese peasants fight the Japanese.
*Ill-advised attempt to follow the success of The Good
Earth; badly cast actors mouth propaganda lines in a
mechanical script which provokes more boredom and
unintentional laughter than sympathy.*
w Marguerite Roberts, Jane Murfin novel Pearl S.
Buck d Jack Conway, Harold S. Bucquet
ph Sidney Wagner m Herbert Stothart
☆ Katharine Hepburn, Walter Huston, Turhan
Bey, Aline MacMahon, Akim Tamiroff, Hurd
Hatfield, Frances Rafferty, Agnes Moorehead,
Henry Travers, J. Carrol Naish
'*A kind of slant-eyed North Star. Often awkward
and pretentious, it nevertheless has moments of
moral and dramatic grandeur.*' – Time
'*A fine film in anybody's sweepstakes. It'll wow
'em at the box office.*' – Variety (It didn't.)
⊗ Sidney Wagner; Aline MacMahon

'The Mystery. The Life. The Love. The Legend.'
Dragon: The Bruce Lee Story *
US 1993 120m DeLuxe Panavision
Universal (Raffaella de Laurentiis)
▣ ▣ ⊜~ ⊚ ⌒
A boy who trains in martial arts grows up to
become a star of kung-fu movies, haunted by a
vision of a dragon representing his inner fears, and
dies young.
*Enjoyable, if unenlightening, biopic of Bruce Lee that
does little to explain why he became the genre's most
famous performer, but notable for starring an
interesting actor, the unrelated Jason Scott Lee.*
w Edward Khmara, John Raffo, Rob Cohen
book *Bruce Lee: The Man Only I Knew* by Linda
Lee Cadwell d Rob Cohen ph David Eggby
m Randy Edelman pd Robert Ziembicki ed Peter
Amundson
☆ Jason Scott Lee, Lauren Holly, Robert Wagner,
Michael Learned, Nancy Kwan, Kay Tong Lim, Ric
Young, John Cheung
'*Seemingly contrary elements and styles
nonetheless mesh into an entertaining whole
and the result provides extremely touching and
haunting material.*' – Variety
'*It's less about daring deeds than about Lee's
triumph over adversity.*' – Vincent Canby, New
York Times
'*Cheerful, downmarket hagiography.*' – Derek
Malcolm, Guardian

Dragonfly: see *One Summer Love*

Dragonheart *
⇈ UIP 1996 103m DeLuxe Panavision
UIP/Universal (Raffaella de Laurentiis)
▣ ▣ ⊜~ ⊚ ⌒
In the late 900s, a knight forms an alliance with
the last dragon to rid Britain of a tyrant.
*A thin medieval fantasy saved from mediocrity by its
splendid dragon, voiced by Connery.*
w Charles Edward Pogue d Rob Cohen ph David
Eggby m Randy Edelman pd Benjamin Fernandez
ed Peter Amundson sp Industrial Light and
Magic; Tippett Studio
☆ Dennis Quaid, Sean Connery (voice), David
Thewlis, Pete Postlethwaite, Dina Meyer, Jason
Isaacs, Julie Christie, John Gielgud (voice)
'*A blunted sword-and-sorcery fantasy which
never gets it together.*' – Tom Hutchinson, Film
Review
⊗ visual effects

Dragon's Food **
West Germany 1987 75m bw
Novoskop Film Jan Schutte/Probst Film (Eric
Nellessen)
original title: *Drachenfutter*
aka: *Spicy Rice*
A Pakistani and a Chinese immigrant struggle to
open their own restaurant in Hamburg.
*The dialogue mixes half-a-dozen languages, but
succeeds in communicating its message of lives wasted
by prejudice and intolerance.*
w Jan Schutte, Thomas Strittmatter d Jan Schutte
ph Lutz Konermann m Claus Bantzer ed Andreas
Schreitmiller

⊙ Digital Video Disc   ⊚ Digital Video Disc   ⌒ Soundtrack released   ☆ Cast in approximate   † Points of interest   ♫ Notable songs   ▮ Academy Award   ⊗ Academy Award nomination   ▼ BAFTA
  Region 2   Region 1   on compact disc   order of importance

☆ Bhaskar, Ric Young, Buddy Uzzaman, Wolf-Dieter Springer, Ulrich Wildgruber

Dragons Forever (dubbed)

Japan 1988 90m colour
Golden Harvest (Leonard K. C. Ho)

A lawyer discovers, when he falls in love, that he is on the wrong side in a case involving pollution and drug-dealing.
Comic martial arts adventure with romantic overtones and spectacular combat, for the undemanding.
w Szeto Cheuk-Hon story Gordon Chan, Leung Yiu Ming d Samo Hung ph Jimmy Leung, Cheung Yiu Tso m James Wong pd Oliver Wong ed Peter Cheung, Josephy Chiang
☆ Jackie Chan, Samo Hung, Yuen Biao, Deannie Yip, Pauline Yeung, Crystal Kwok

'Only sorcery can destroy it!'

Dragonslayer

US 1981 110m Metrocolor
Panavision
Walt Disney/Paramount (Howard W. Koch, Hal Barwood)

A sorcerer's apprentice uses his master's magic amulet to ward off various dangers.
Heavy-going sword-and-sorcery fable, not helped at all by slow plotting and dark photography. The dragons, however, are genuinely fierce.
w Hal Barwood, Matthew Robbins d Matthew Robbins ph Derek Vanlint m Alex North pd Elliot Scott sp Thomas Smith
☆ Peter MacNicol, Caitlin Clarke, Ralph Richardson, John Hallam, Peter Eyre, Albert Salmi
'Verges on the nasty for the nippers; sails too close to déjà vu for fantasy fans.' – Time Out
§ Alex North; visual effects (Dennis Muren and others)

Dragonwyck *

US 1946 103m bw
TCF (Darryl F. Zanuck)
In the 1840s a farmer's daughter marries her rich cousin, not knowing that he has poisoned his first wife.
Good-looking but rather tedious romance of the Jane Eyre/Rebecca school: tyrannical recluse, mystery upstairs, spooky house, etc. Heavy going.
wd Joseph L. Mankiewicz novel Anya Seton ph Arthur Miller m Alfred Newman
☆ Gene Tierney, Vincent Price, Glenn Langan, Walter Huston, Anne Revere, Spring Byington, Henry Morgan, Jessica Tandy

Dragoon Wells Massacre *

US 1957 88m DeLuxe CinemaScope
Allied Artists (Lindsley Parsons)
A group of travellers are stranded in hostile Indian territory.
Moderately suspenseful Western on a familiar theme.
w Warren Douglas story Oliver Drake d Harold Schuster ph William Clothier m Paul Dunlap ed Maurice Wright
☆ Barry Sullivan, Dennis O'Keefe, Mona Freeman, Katy Jurado, Sebastian Cabot, Jack Elam

'Car crazy, speed crazy, boy crazy!'

Dragstrip Girl

US 1957 69m bw
AIP/Golden State (Alex Gordon)
Two young hot-rodders are rivals for a new girl in town.
Stalled low-budget drive-in movie, requiring minimal attention from its audience.
w Lou Rusoff d Edward L. Cahn ph Frederick E. West m Ronald Stein ad Don Ament ed Ronald Sinclair
☆ Fay Spain, Steve Terrell, John Ashley, Frank Gorshin, Russ Bender, Tommy Ivo

Drake of England

GB 1935 104m bw
BIP (Walter C. Mycroft)
US title: Drake the Pirate
US title: Elizabeth of England
Sir Francis Drake is knighted by Queen Elizabeth for his seafaring exploits, and defeats the Spanish Armada.
Stiffly moving historical pageant; you can smell the mothballs.
w Clifford Grey, Akos Tolney, Marjorie Deans, Norman Watson play Drake by Louis N. Parker

d Arthur Woods ph Claude Friese-Greene, Ronald Neame, Jack Parker m G. H. Clutsam ad Duncan Sutherland, Clarence Elder ed E. B. Jarvis
☆ Matheson Lang, Athene Seyler, Jane Baxter, Donald Wolfit, Henry Mollison, George Merritt, Amy Veness, Sam Livesey, Ben Webster

Drake the Pirate: see *Drake of England*

A Drama of Jealousy: see *Jealousy Italian Style*

'Yearning Youth – Behind the Scenes of a Parisian Dramatic School.'

Dramatic School *

US 1938 80m bw
MGM (Mervyn Le Roy)
Young actresses compete for success.
Another, less lively, Stage Door; tolerable but not exciting.
w Ernst Vajda, Mary McCall Jnr play School of Drama by Hans Szekely, Zoltan Egyed d Robert B. Sinclair Jnr ph William Daniels m Franz Waxman
☆ Luise Rainer, Paulette Goddard, Alan Marshal, Lana Turner, Anthony Allan (later John Hubbard), Henry Stephenson, Genevieve Tobin, Gale Sondergaard, Melville Cooper, Erik Rhodes, Ann Rutherford, Margaret Dumont, Virginia Grey, Hans Conried
'A disappointing effort which arouses little interest in its unfolding.' – Variety

Dramma della Gelosia – Tutti i Particolari in Cronaca: see *Jealousy Italian Style*

Drango

US 1957 92m bw
UA/Hall Bartlett
After the Civil War, a Union Army officer is assigned to bring law and order to a Georgia community.
Eccentric, downbeat semi-Western with aspirations to be some kind of film noir; does not come off.
w Hall Bartlett d Hall Bartlett, Jules Bricken ph James Wong Howe m Elmer Bernstein
☆ Jeff Chandler, Ronald Howard, Joanne Dru, Julie London, Donald Crisp, John Lupton, Morris Ankrum

The Draughtsman's Contract **

GB 1982 108m colour
BFI/Channel 4 (David Payne)

In 1694 a young draughtsman receives a curious commission from a country gentlewoman, his rewards to include bed and bawd.
Pleasantly unusual, stylized puzzle film which involves both sex and murder while maintaining a detached attitude to both. The period costumes help to give it an air of fantasy which was presumably intended.
wd Peter Greenaway ph Curtis Clark m Michael Nyman ed John Wilson
☆ Anthony Higgins, Janet Suzman, Anne Louise Lambert, Neil Cunningham, Hugh Fraser, Dave Hill
'Mannered and idiosyncratic, the speeches are so arch and twitty that they seem to be pitched higher than a dog whistle.' – Pauline Kael, New Yorker
'Perhaps the four-hour version which may one day become available is clearer if not more concise.' – Guardian
'Best enjoyed as a sly piece of double bluff, a puzzle without a solution, an avant garde hoax in the spirit of Dada and the surrealists.' – Observer

Dream Demon

GB 1988 89m colour
Palace (Paul Webster)
A woman begins to have horrific nightmares before her marriage to a hero of the Falklands War.
A moderately effective psychological thriller, though over-reliant on shock effects.
w Harley Cokliss, Christopher Wicking d Harley Cokliss ph Ian Wilson m Bill Nelson pd Hugo Luczyc-Wyhowski ed Ian Crafford, David Martin
☆ Jemma Redgrave, Jimmy Nail, Timothy Spall, Kathleen Wilhoite, Annabelle Lanyon, Susan Fleetwood, Nickolas Grace
'One of this, or any year's, worst … proof of the low levels the genre can sink to.' – Stefan Jaworzyn, Shock Xpress

Dream Girl

US 1947 86m bw
Paramount (P. J. Wolfson)
A girl revels in her own romantic dreams, one of which nearly comes true.
Potentially pleasant comedy about a female Walter Mitty does not work because the director has run out of ideas, the star is miscast and Hollywood has insisted on making the girl rich to begin with, which robs the dreams of any point.
w Arthur Sheekman play Elmer Rice d Mitchell Leisen ph Daniel L. Fapp m Victor Young
☆ Betty Hutton, Macdonald Carey, Walter Abel, Patric Knowles, Virginia Field, Peggy Wood, Lowell Gilmore

Dream Lover

US 1986 104m Technicolor
MGM-UA/Alan J. Pakula, Jon Boorstin
A dream researcher is assigned to the case of a girl who has fatally stabbed an intruder.
Flabby and overlong case history with no very interesting conclusion.
w Jon Boorstin d Alan J. Pakula . ph Sven Nykvist m Michael Small
☆ Kristy McNichol, Ben Masters, Paul Shenar, John McMartin, Gayle Hunnicutt, Justin Deas

Dream Lover

US 1994 103m DeLuxe
Rank/Polygram/Propaganda/Nicita/Lloyd/Edward R. Pressman (Sigurjon Sighvatsson, Wallis Nicita, Lauren Lloyd)

An architect begins to suspect that his model wife is not who she claims to be.
An uninvolving drama of identity, exploring interesting territory but making no new discoveries.
wd Nicholas Kazan ph Jean-Yves Escoffier m Christopher Young pd Richard Hoover ed Jill Savitt, Susan Crutcher
☆ James Spader, Mädchen Amick, Bess Armstrong, Larry Miller, Frederic Lehne, William Shockley
'Looks more like the thing you might get out of the video store but would balk at paying for in the cinema. It's a bit basic really, playing one tune over and over again.' – Derek Malcolm, Guardian

Dream Machine

US 1991 86m Hawk
DM (Lyman Dayton)

A college student is given a Porsche by a wealthy, vengeful wife; unknown to either, her philandering husband's body is hidden in its boot, and his murderer wants it back.
Inane wish-fulfilment for teenage drivers: a love story about a boy and his car, though a comedy thriller was intended.
w Eric Hendershot d Lyman Dayton m T. C. Christenson m Lex de Azevedo pd Michael C. Ayers ed Steve Johnson
☆ Corey Haim, Evan Richards, Jeremy Slate, Randall England, Tracy Fraim, Brittney Lewis, Susan Seaforth Hayes

The Dream of a Rarebit Fiend *

US 1906 4m bw silent
Early trick film depicting a nightmare resulting from overeating.
w Winsor McCay d Edwin S. Porter

A Dream of Kings

US 1969 110m Technicolor
National General (Jules Schermer)

Episodes in the life of an improvident, lusty, poetical Chicago Greek with a dying son.
The part screamed for Anthony Quinn and got him, with the result that it has all been seen before, too frequently. Well made, with strong appeal to Chicago Greeks.
w Harry Mark Petrakis, Ian Hunter novel Harry Mark Petrakis d Daniel Mann ph Richard H. Kline m Alex North
☆ Anthony Quinn, Irene Papas, Inger Stevens, Sam Levene, Val Avery, Tamara Daykarhanova

A Dream of Life: see *Life Begins*

The Dream of Light: see *The Quince Tree Sun*

The Dream of Olwen: see *While I Live*

A Dream of Passion

Greece 1978 110m Eastmancolor
Branfilm/Melinafilm (Jules Dassin)

A woman who, Medea-like, has killed her children is drawn into an eccentric relationship with an actress playing Medea on the stage.
Weird and ineffective character drama which badly needs discipline.
wd Jules Dassin ph George Arvanitis m Ionnis Markopoulos
☆ Melina Mercouri, Ellen Burstyn, Andreas Voutsinas, Despo Diamantidou

Dream Street *

US 1921 89m bw silent
D. W. Griffith Inc

Three Limehouse folk, torn between good and evil, act out their dreams.
Trilogy of moral tales, fancifully and often charmingly assembled by the master director who often reminds one of a Victorian lace maker.
wd D. W. Griffith stories Thomas Burke ph Henrik Sartov
☆ Carol Dempster, Ralph Graves, Charles Emmett Mack, Edward Peil, Tyrone Power Snr, W. J. Ferguson

The Dream Team *

US 1989 113m DeLuxe Panavision
UIP/Imagine Entertainment (Christopher W. Knight)

On a day trip to New York, four inmates of a psychiatric hospital foil a murder plot.
Enjoyable sentimental comedy that avoids most of the pitfalls of its subject matter.
w Jon Connolly, David Loucka d Howard Zieff ph Adam Holender m David McHugh pd Todd Hallowell ad Christopher Nowak ed C. Timothy O'Meara
☆ Michael Keaton, Christopher Lloyd, Peter Boyle, Stephen Furst, Dennis Boutsikaris, Lorraine Bracco, Milo O'Shea, Philip Bosco, James Remar
'Sharp and punchily acted.' – John Pym, MFB

Dream Wife

US 1953 99m bw
MGM (Dore Schary)
An executive leaves his ambitious wife for a sheik's daughter schooled in the art of pleasing men, but naturally finds drawbacks.
Very moderate comedy with strained situations and few laughs. The stars work hard.
w Sidney Sheldon, Herbert Baker, Alfred L. Levitt d Sidney Sheldon ph Milton Krasner m Conrad Salinger
☆ Cary Grant, Deborah Kerr, Walter Pidgeon, Betta St John, Eduard Franz, Buddy Baer, Les Tremayne

Dream with the Fishes *

US 1997 97m Foto-Kem
Columbia TriStar/3 Ring Circus (Johnny Wow, Mitchell Stein)

A terminally ill man offers to help a would-be suicide kill himself in return for financing some of his fantasies, which include nude bowling and public drug-taking.
Sometimes engaging, somewhat schematic celebration of life that harks back to the style of 70s movies.
wd Finn Taylor ph Barry Stone m Tito Larriva pd Justin McCartney ed Nick LeCompte
☆ David Arquette, Brad Hunt, Kathryn Erbe, Cathy Moriarty, J. E. Freeman, Allyce Beasley
'Refreshing, unexpectedly profound comedy.' – Variety

Dreamboat *

US 1952 83m bw
TCF (Sol C. Siegel)
A romantic star of the silent film era is embarrassed when his old movies turn up on television.
Hollywood rather blunderingly makes fun of its arch enemy in this sometimes sprightly but often disappointing comedy which should have been a bull's-eye.
wd Claude Binyon ph Milton Krasner m Cyril Mockridge

☆ Clifton Webb, Ginger Rogers, Anne Francis, Jeffrey Hunter, Elsa Lanchester, Fred Clark, Ray Collins, Paul Harvey

'A merry comedy filled with uproarious laughter from beginning to end.' – *Hollywood Reporter*

Dreamchild **

GB 1985 94m Technicolor
Thorn EMI/PFH (Rick McCallum, Kenith Trodd)
📽

Travelling to New York for the centenary of Lewis Carroll's birth, Alice Hargreaves, the original of his Alice, remembers her relationship with him.
Complex and intriguing drama of a woman coming to terms with her past and present.
w Dennis Potter d Gavin Millar ph Billy Williams m Stanley Myers pd Roger Hall ed Angus Newton sp Jim Henson's Creature Shop
☆ Coral Browne, Peter Gallagher, Ian Holm, Jane Asher, Nicola Cowper, Caris Corfman, Amelia Shankley

'Not a movie for a wide audience: it simply isn't conceived in the broad narrative patterns that please most moviegoers. Yet it's very enjoyable; it has a twinkling subtext, and in some scenes it achieves levels of feeling that the new mainstream films don't get near.' – *Pauline Kael, New Yorker*

'Ambitious but unsatisfying and gimmicky.' – *Variety*

Dreamer

US 1979 86m Eastmancolor
TCF (Michael Lobell)
📽

A young man dreams of becoming a professional bowling champion.
Faced with the impossible task of making tenpin bowling visually or dramatically interesting, the makers focus instead on a stormy romance and a sentimental relationship with an elderly mentor; they are no more effective in gaining an audience's attention.
w James Proctor, Harry Bischof d Noel Nosseck ph Bruce Surtees m Bill Conti ad Archie Sharp ed Fred Chulack
☆ Tim Matheson, Susan Blakely, Jack Warden

Dreaming

GB 1944 78m bw
Ealing

A soldier on leave gets a bump on the head, and dreams ...
Rather elementary series of sketches with a few good laughs and interesting guest appearances.
w Bud Flanagan, Reginald Purdell d John Baxter
☆ Flanagan and Allen, Hazel Court, Dick Francis, Philip Wade, Teddy Brown, Reginald Foort, Gordon Richards, Alfredo Campoli

Dreaming Lips *

GB 1936 94m bw
Trafalgar (Max Schach, Paul Czinner)

The wife of an invalid musician has an affair with another man and commits suicide.
Standard star fare, possibly Miss Bergner's most notable film, also available in a German version.
w Margaret Kennedy, Lady Cynthia Asquith, Carl Mayer play Melo by Henry Bernstein d Paul Czinner, Lee Garmes ph Roy Clark m William Walton ad Andrei Andreiev, Tom Morahan ed David Lean
☆ Elisabeth Bergner, Romney Brent, Raymond Massey, Joyce Bland, Sydney Fairbrother, Felix Aylmer, Donald Calthrop

'In many respects one of the finest productions ever made in England ... made in Hollywood, the story would be whitewashed and much of its strength weakened.' – *Variety*

'Even with her eyes wide open, she never stopped...'

Dreaming of Joseph Lees

US/GB 1999 92m Technicolor
TCF/Midsummer/IoMFC (Chris Milburn)

In Somerset in the 1950s, a young woman is obsessed by her one-legged cousin.
Unhappy, underwritten rural melodrama that fails to sustain its attempt at a romantic tragedy.
w Catherine Linstrum d Eric Styles ph Jimmy Dibling m Zbigniew Preisner pd Humphrey Jaeger ed Caroline Limmer cos Maggie Chappellow
☆ Samantha Morton, Lee Ross, Rupert Graves, Holly Aird, Miriam Margolyes, Frank Finlay, Nick Woodeson, Lauren Richardson, Felix Billson

---

'A humourless symphony of false notes.' – *Philip French, Observer*

The Dreamlife of Angels ***

France 1998 113m colour
Bagheera/Diaphana/France3 (François Marquis)
📼

original title: *La Vie Rêvée des Anges*

Two young women, trying to survive in Lille, form an uneasy friendship with each other and with two bouncers at rock concerts.
Engrossing and frequently surprising narrative of French working-class life, with two protagonists with contrasting personalities: one happy to take life as it comes, the other striving for material success.
w Erick Zonca, Roger Bohbot d Erick Zonca ph Agnes Godard m Yann Thiersen pd Jimmy Vansteenkiste ed Yannick Kergoat
☆ Elodie Bouchez, Natacha Regnier, Gregoire Colin, Jo Prestia, Patrick Mercado

'A passionate and unpretentious gem.' – *Film Review*

† In France, it won the Prix Méliès as the best French film of the year. Elodie Bouchez and Natacha Regnier were joint winners of the best actress award at the 1998 Cannes Film Festival.

Dreams That Money Can Buy *

US 1946 81m Technicolor
Art of the Century (Hans Richter, Peggy Guggenheim, Kenneth MacPherson)

A young itinerant sells dreams to people who need them.
Semi-underground surrealist film, momentarily of interest, but disjointed and with no real apparent purpose.
wd Hans Richter ph Arnold Eagle md Louis Applebaum

'Arch, snobbish and sycophantic, about as genuinely experimental as a Chemcraft set.' – *James Agee*

† The individual dreams are Max Ernst, Man Ray, Fernand Leger, Marcel Duchamp and Alexander Calder as well as Richter.

Dreamscape

US 1984 99m CFI color
Thorn-EMI/Zuplein-Curtis/Bella (Bruce Cohn Curtis)
📼 📽 📀 ♫

Experiments prove that it is possible for a dreamer to enter the dreams of others, and a subject finds himself being used for a plot against the president of the US.
Complex fantasy melodrama with a cold war basis; neither exciting nor praiseworthy.
w David Loughery, Joseph Ruben, Chuck Russell d Joseph Ruben ph Brian Tufano, Kevin Kutchaver m Maurice Jarre ad Jeff Stags ed Richard Halsey
☆ Dennis Quaid, Max von Sydow, Christopher Plummer, Eddie Albert, Kate Capshaw

Drei von der Tankstelle *

Germany 1930 80m bw
UFA

Three penniless young men find happiness as petrol station attendants.
Light-hearted operetta of the Depression era, well received at the time.
w Franz Schultz, Paul Frank d William Thiele ph Franz Planer m Werner Heymann
☆ Willy Fritsch, Lilian Harvey, Oskar Karlweis, Heinz Ruhmann, Olga Tchekhova

'When leaving this charming talker operetta, one feels in good humour, humming the catchy hits of its talented composer ... constant laughter and enthusiasm.' – *Variety*

† Remade 1955 by Hans Wolff, with a cast still led by Willy Fritsch.

Die Dreigroschenoper **

Germany 1931 114m bw
Warner/Tobis/Nero
📼 📽

US title: *The Threepenny Opera*

In turn-of-the-century London, Mack the Knife marries the daughter of the beggar king and runs into trouble.
Heavy-footed but interesting updating of The Beggar's Opera, with splendid sets.
w Bela Balazs, Leo Lania, Ladislas Vajda play Bertolt Brecht d G. W. Pabst ph Fritz Arno Wagner m Kurt Weill ad Andrei Andreiev

---

☆ Lotte Lenya, Rudolf Forster, Fritz Rasp, Caroline Neher, Reinhold Schunzel, Valeska Gert, Vladimir Sokoloff

† Brecht disliked the film and sued the makers, but lost

†† A French version was also released under the title *L'Opéra de Quat'sous*, with Albert Préjean.

Dressage (dubbed)

France 1985 90m Eastmancolor
Samourai
📼

A woman sets out to corrupt her father's 17-year-old daughter while her friend attempts to ruin a would-be politician by seducing him and his son.
Glossy soft-core porn, slickly done but uninteresting.
w Jean-Philippe Berger, J. C. Roy d Pierre B. Reinhard ph Denis Lenoir m Philippe Brejean ad Jean-Claude Roy
☆ Véronique Catanzaro, Patrick Guillemin, Marc Henry, Henri-Jacques Huet, André Nader, Sylvie Novak, Katya Strambi, Cornélia Wilms

Dressed to Kill

US 1946 72m bw
Universal (Roy William Neil)
📼 📽

aka: *Sherlock Holmes: Dressed to Kill*

Sherlock Holmes pits his wits against a murderous gang searching for the location of printing plates stolen from the Bank of England.
Unremarkable end to an enjoyable series, with some barely adequate performances, apart from the central duo of Rathbone and Bruce.
w Frank Gruber, Leonard Lee d Roy William Neil ph Maury Gertsman m Milton Rosen ad Jack Otterson, Martin Obzina ed Saul A. Goodkind
☆ Basil Rathbone, Nigel Bruce, Patricia Morison, Edmund Breon, Frederick Worlock, Carl Harbord, Mary Gordon, Anita Glyn

'Every nightmare has a beginning. This one never ends!'

Dressed to Kill **

US 1980 105m Technicolor
Filmways/Samuel Z. Arkoff/Cinema 77 (George Litto)
📼 📽 📀 ♫

A sexually disturbed matron under analysis is murdered by a transvestite slasher, who then goes after a witness.
Occasionally brilliant, generally nasty suspenser clearly derived from many viewings of Psycho. Certainly not for the squeamish.
wd Brian de Palma ph Ralf Bode m Pino Donaggio pd Gary Weist
☆ Michael Caine, Angie Dickinson, Nancy Allen, Keith Gordon, Dennis Franz

'De Palma goes right for the audience jugular ... it fully milks the boundaries of its "R" rating.' – *Variety*

'By casting a halo of excitement around killing, a glow of degradation around living, and linking the two in a queasy, guilty partnership, de Palma is asking us to celebrate the joys of barbarism in a world already drunk on rape, torture, murder and war.' – *Sunday Times*

'De Palma earns the title of master, all right ... but Hitch remains the grand master.' – *Roger Ebert*

The Dresser ***

GB 1983 118m colour
Columbia/Goldcrest/World Film Services (Peter Yates)
📽 📀

An exhausted Shakespearean actor-manager has a wild last day on tour, comforted and restrained by his homosexual dresser.
A strained film, but a valuable record of a play based on the touring career of Donald Wolfit, whose dresser the author was.
w Ronald Harwood play Ronald Harwood d Peter Yates ph Kelvin Pike m James Horner pd Stephen Grimes
☆ Albert Finney, Tom Courtenay, Edward Fox, Zena Walker, Eileen Atkins, Michael Gough, Betty Marsden, Lockwood West

'The best sort of drama, fascinating us on the surface with colour and humour and esoteric detail, and then revealing the truth underneath.' – *Roger Ebert*

'It is not an American picture; it is not like *42nd Street*. It is British and therefore tells a tale not of effortless overnight success but of day by day humiliation and defeat ... It is utterly joyless. I

---

can only claim that it tells its grim tale with sparks of humor and in merciless detail.' – *Quentin Crisp*

& best picture; Tom Courtenay; Albert Finney; Peter Yates as director; Ronald Harwood (adaptation)

The Dressmaker *

GB 1988 91m colour
Rank/Film Four International/British Screen (Ronald Shedlo)
📼 📽 📀

Tensions arise in wartime within a puritanical working-class family with the arrival of American GIs.
Well acted, but depressing.
w John McGrath novel Beryl Bainbridge d Jim O'Brien ph Michael Coulter m George Fenton pd Caroline Amies ed William Diver
☆ Joan Plowright, Billie Whitelaw, Jane Horrocks, Tim Ransom, Peter Postlethwaite, Pippa Hinchley, Rosemary Martin, Tony Haygarth

'A masterpiece of minimalist compression.' – *Hal Hinson, Washington Post*

Dreyfus *

GB 1931 80m bw
BIP (F. W. Kraemer)

US title: *The Dreyfus Case*

In 1894 France, a Jewish officer is accused of spying.
Primitive version of a much-filmed story (cf The Life of Emile Zola, I Accuse).
w Reginald Berkeley, Walter C. Mycroft play *The Dreyfus Case* by Hans Rehfisch, Wilhelm Herzog d F. W. Kraemer, Milton Rosmer ph Willy Minterstein ed Langford Reed, Betty Spiers
☆ Cedric Hardwicke, George Merritt, Charles Carson, Sam Livesey, Garry Marsh, Randle Ayrton, George Zucco

'A picture of the documentary class, well out of the ordinary.' – *Variety*

Drifters *

GB 1929 40m bw
Empire Marketing Board (John Grierson)

A documentary of the North Sea fishing fleet.
A highly influential documentary, made at a time when British films were totally unrealistic and studio-bound. Unfortunately it now seems extremely dull.
wd John Grierson ph Basil Emmott ed John Grierson

Drifting Clouds **

Finland 1996 93m Eastmancolor
Metro/Tartan/Sputnik Oy/YLE TV-1/Pandora/Pyramide (Aki Kaurismäki)
📼

original title: *Kauas Pilvet Karkaavat*

A tram-driver and his wife, a head waiter, face difficulties when they lose their jobs and decide to try to open their own restaurant.
A bleakly humorous account of domestic difficulties with, for a change, a feel-good ending; it all has an inconsequential charm.
wd Aki Kaurismäki ph Timo Salminen ad Markku Pätilä, Jukka Salmi ed Aki Kaurismäki
☆ Kati Outinen, Kari Väänänen, Elina Salo, Sakari Kuosmanen, Matti Onnismaa, Markku Peltola

'There are small quirky pleasures to cherish from this warm, comical and optimistic tribute to the human spirit.' – *Caroline Rees, Empire*

† The film is dedicated to Matti Pellonpää, an actor who died in 1995 and appeared in many of Kaurismäki's movies; he appears here as the child in a photograph.

Driftwood

🎬 US 1947 90m bw
Republic

An orphan is adopted by a kindly doctor.
Lavender-scented family yarn with pleasant backgrounds and expert performances.
w Mary Loos, Richard Sale d Allan Dwan ph John Alton m Nathan Scott
☆ Natalie Wood, Ruth Warrick, Walter Brennan, Dean Jagger, Charlotte Greenwood

---

'An erotic dream of obsession.'
Driftwood
Ireland/GB   1996   100m   Technicolor
Blue Dolphin/Goldcrest/Deadwood/Setanta (Mary Breen-Farrelly)
🎧

A French sculptor discovers an injured man on a remote beach in Ireland and takes him home to keep.
A cliché-ridden situation and a script that is beyond redemption.
w Richard M. N. Waring d Ronan O'Leary ph Billy Williams m John Cameron pd Tim Hutchinson ed Malcolm Cooke
☆ James Spader, Anne Brochet, Barry McGovern, Anna Massey, Aiden Grenell, Kevin McHugh
'Banal and dreary.' – *Sight and Sound*

'The blood runs in rivers, and the drill keeps tearing through flesh and bone.'
The Driller Killer
US   1979   85m   colour
Navaron (Rochelle Weisberg)
📼 🎦

A disturbed artist murders vagrants with an electric drill.
Gruesome movie of frustration and sordid city life; it was among the first so-called 'video nasties' to be banned in Britain, until its re-release in 1999.
w Nicholas St John, Louis Mascolo d Abel Ferrara ph Ken Kelsch m Joseph Delia ad Louis Mascolo ed Orlando Gallini, Bonnie Constant, Michael Constant, Jimmy Laine (Abel Ferrara) sp David Smith
☆ Jimmy Laine (Abel Ferrara), Carolyn Marz, Baybi Day, Harry Schultz, Alan Wynroth, Maria Helhoski, Bob DeFrank
'Ferrara's films may be rough, but there's no denying the cheapskate proficiency with which he puts them together, or the painful accuracy of his probing for the unhealthy nerve.' – *Kim Newman, MFB*

Drive
US/Japan   1997   99m   CFI
Overseas/Neo
📼 🎦 🎦

A Chinese man, who has been fitted with a bio-mechanical device that increases his physical abilities, is hunted by gangsters after he flees to the US.
Frenetic, stunt-crammed, tongue-in-cheek, over-the-top martial arts thriller with an invincible hero and gun-toting bad guys who couldn't a barn door at three paces; it is the sort of film where a gang of killers burst through the windows of a nightclub on motorbikes, while firing automatic weapons, in order to take out one man.
w Scott Phillips d Steve Wang ph Michael G. Wojciechowski m Walter Werzowa pd Terrence Foster ed Ivan Ladizinsky
☆ Mark Dacascos, Kadeem Hardison, ohn Pyper-Ferguson, Brittany Murphy, Tracey Walter, James Shigeta, Masaya Kato

'She needed the money – and I needed her!'
Drive a Crooked Road
US   1954   82m   bw
Columbia (Jonie Taps)
A garage mechanic falls in with bank robbers.
Terse crime melodrama, quite watchable.
w Blake Edwards d Richard Quine ph Charles Lawton Jnr md Ross di Maggio
☆ Mickey Rooney, Kevin McCarthy, Dianne Foster

Drive He Said
US   1970   90m   colour
Columbia/Drive Productions/BBS (Steve Blauner)
An easygoing college basketball star is helped by an eccentric rebel to ensure his own unfitness for military service. Both run into trouble.
Flabby celebration of against-the-government attitudes, expressed partly through sex and bad language. Defiantly hard to like.
w Jeremy Larner, Jack Nicholson d Jack Nicholson ph Bill Butler m David Shire
☆ Michael Margotta, William Tepper, Bruce Dern, Karen Black, Robert Towne, Henry Jaglom

Drive-in
US   1976   96m   Technicolor
Columbia (George Litto)
📼

In Texas, various illicit activities find their climax at a drive-in movie.
Mild sex-and-destruction comedy which raises few laughs and makes little sense.
w Bob Peete d Rod Amateau ph Robert Jessup m various
☆ Lisa Lemole, Glenn Morshower, Gary Cavagnaro, Billy Milliken, Lee Newsome, Regan Kee

The Driver ****
US   1978   91m   DeLuxe
TCF/EMI/Lawrence Gordon
📼 🎦

A detective determines to catch an old enemy, a getaway driver.
Deft and clever thriller that has been stripped of all redundancies and reduced to its core, of two obsessional men on different sides of the law locked in deadly conflict. It is a simple, spare story of bleak lives, brilliantly told.
wd Walter Hill ph Philip Lathrop m Michael Small
☆ Ryan O'Neal, Bruce Dern, Isabelle Adjani, Ronee Blakley
'Comic book cops and robbers existentialism.' – *Pauline Kael*
'Because of the quiet and mysterious mood of this picture, it has a pretentious quality to it.' – *Variety*

Driving Force
Australia/US/Philippines   1989   90m
J & M/Eastern (Howard Grigsby, Rod Confesor)
📼 🎦

In a future post-industrial world, an honest trucker battles with a violent gang of scavengers.
Incoherent action film that fails in its recreation of a believable future (although virtually all goods are recycled or secondhand, petrol is plentiful), and is not helped by having an uncharismatic star.
w Patrick Edgeworth d A. J. Prowse ph Kevan Lind, Richard Michalak m Paul Schutze pd Toto Castillo ed Tony Paterson
☆ Sam Jones, Catherine Bach, Don Swayze, Gerald Gordon, Angel Cook, Renata Scott, Robert Marius, Billy Blanks

Driving Me Crazy: see Dutch

Driving Miss Daisy *
US   1989   99m   Technicolor   Panavision
Warner/Zanuck Company/Richard Zanuck, Lili Fini Zanuck
📼 🎦 🎦 🎦 🎦 🎧

A elderly rich Jewish widow at first resists, and then succumbs to, the obsequious attentions of her black chauffeur.
Old-fashioned and charming, but slight to the point of inconsequentiality.
w Alfred Uhry play Alfred Uhry d Bruce Beresford ph Peter James m Hans Zimmer pd Bruno Rubeo ed Mark Warner
☆ Morgan Freeman, Jessica Tandy, Dan Aykroyd, Patti LuPone
🏆 best picture; best makeup; Alfred Uhry; Jessica Tandy
🏅 Morgan Freeman; Dan Aykroyd; best art direction; best costume design
🎬 Jessica Tandy

Le Droit d'Aimer: see Brainwashed

Drôle de Drame *
France   1936   100m   bw
aka: Bizarre, Bizarre (84m American version)
A complicated chain of bizarre events is set in motion when a botanist pretends not to be a detective story writer, a bishop tries to be a detective, and a murderer seeks revenge for libel.
A curious satirical comedy which is never quite as funny as it seems about to be, but should be seen for its downright peculiar London sets and its array of actors in top form.
w Jacques Prévert novel The Lunatic at Large by J. Storer Clouston d Marcel Carné ph Eugene Schufftan m Maurice Jaubert pd Alexandre Trauner
☆ Françoise Rosay, Michel Simon, Louis Jouvet, Jean-Louis Barrault, Jean-Pierre Aumont

'Art theatres and foreign-language houses will do fair business.' – *Variety*
'No one with any taste for nonsense should miss it.' – *Richard Mallett, Punch*

Drôle d'endroit pour une Rencontre *
France   1988   98m   colour
Artificial Eye/Hachette/A2/DD/Deneuve/Orly/Editions Sidonie (Patrick Bordier)
📼

GB title: *A Strange Place to Meet*
A doctor falls in love with an abandoned wife, who is waiting for her husband to return.
An unconvincing romance, full of longueurs.
w François Dupreyron, Dominique Faysse d François Dupreyron ph Charlie Van Damme ad Carlos Conti ed Françoise Collin
☆ Catherine Deneuve, Gérard Depardieu, André Wilms, Nathalie Cardone, Jean-Pierre Sentier, Alain Rimoux, Vincent Martin

Drop Dead Darling
GB   1966   100m   Technicolor   Panavision
Seven Arts (Ken Hughes)
US title: *Arrivederci Baby*
A con man who marries and murders rich women meets a con lady with similar intentions.
Loud, restless black comedy which squanders its moments of genuine inventiveness among scenes of shouting, confusion and action for action's sake.
wd Ken Hughes story The Careful Man by Richard Deming ph Denys Coop m Dennis Farnon
☆ Tony Curtis, Rosanna Schiaffino, Lionel Jeffries, Zsa Zsa Gabor, Nancy Kwan, Fenella Fielding, Anna Quayle, Warren Mitchell, Mischa Auer

'He creates the havoc. She takes the blame.'
Drop Dead Fred
US   1991   99m   colour
Rank/Working Title/Polygram (Paul Webster)
📼 🎦 🎦

A young woman in difficulties is revisited by her imaginary, destructive childhood friend.
Singularly tasteless comedy, lacking any vestige of wit or even humour.
w Carlos Davis, Anthony Fingleton story Elizabeth Livingston d Ate de Jong ph Peter Deming m Randy Edelman pd Joseph T. Garrity ed Marshall Harvey
☆ Phoebe Cates, Rik Mayall, Marsha Mason, Tim Matheson, Bridget Fonda, Carrie Fisher, Keith Charles, Ashley Peldon, Daniel Gerroll
'Harvey reimagined for the Beetlejuice generation, with strident gags standing in for magic and relentless obviousness overriding the disturbing ambiguity that might have made the film work.' – *Kim Newman, Sight and Sound*
'This celebration of mental retardation is where the nadirs of two current Hollywood cycles – the regression to childhood/life swap movie and the ghost/revenant picture – intersect.' – *Philip French, Observer*

'If Looks Could Kill...'
'The Battle Between The Good And The Bad Is About To Get Ugly.'
Drop Dead Gorgeous
US/Germany   1999   98m   DeLuxe
New Line/Capella/KC Medien (Gavin Pallone, Judy Hofflund)
📼 🎦 🎦

A documentary film crew follow the events leading up to a beauty contest, which the town's wealthiest woman is determined that her daughter will win.
Heavy-handed satire on small town life and the beauty business; the narrative becomes too contrived to provide much satisfaction.
w Lona Williams d Michael Patrick Jann ph Michael Spiller m Mark Mothersbaugh pd Ruth Ammon ed David Codron, Janice Hampton
☆ Kirsten Dunst, Ellen Barkin, Allison Janney, Denise Richards, Kirstie Alley, Sam McMurray, Amy Adams, Tara Redepenning, Shannon Nelson, Sarah Stewart, Michael McShane
'Crude mockery that thinks it's satire.' – *Lisa Schwarzman, Entertainment Weekly*

Drop Squad
US   1994   86m   colour
Universal/Gramercy/40 Acres & A Mule (Shelby Stone, Butch Robinson)
📼 🎦

A group of black vigilantes – Deprogramming and Restoration of Pride – kidnap people to bring them back to a sense of community.
A satire aimed at those who forget their roots and adopt attitudes that destroy ethnic communities, but one that is too slapdash and crude to convince.
w David C. Johnson, Butch Robinson story David Taylor d D. Clark Johnson ph Ken Kelsch m Michael Bearden pd Ina Mayhew ed Kevin Lee
☆ Eriq LaSalle, Vondie Curtis-Hall, Ving Rhames, Kasi Lemmons, Leonard Thomas, Vanessa Williams, Nicole Powell, Eric A. Payne, Spike Lee

'Something Dangerous Is In The Air.'
Drop Zone
US   1994   101m   DeLuxe
UIP/Nicita/Lloyd
📼 🎦 🎦 🎦

A discredited US marshal goes undercover to expose a gang of skydiving crooks who killed his brother, kidnapped his prisoner and escaped from a 747 jet in mid-flight.
A stunt-driven thriller, in which breathtaking aerial acrobatics do not make up for the absence of a suspenseful narrative.
w Peter Barsocchini, John Bishop, Tony Griffin, Guy Manos d John Badham ph Roy. H. Wagner m Hans Zimmer pd Joe Alves ed Frank Morriss
☆ Wesley Snipes, Gary Busey, Yancy Butler, Michael Jeter, Corin Nemec, Kyle Secor, Luca Bercovici, Grace Zabriskie
'Little more than a by-the-numbers programmer, reasonably diverting and briskly paced but thinly written and utterly predictable.' – *Variety*
'Skydiving may be spectacular, but one hopes its participants are less rip-roaringly boorish than they appear in *Drop Zone*. I kept hoping their parachutes wouldn't open.' – *Derek Malcolm, Guardian*

Drowning by Numbers **
GB   1988   119m   Kodak Color
Film Four International/Elsevier Vendex
📼 🎦 🎦 🎦

Three women (all with the same name) murder their respective husbands with the collusion of the local coroner.
Cynical black comedy, beautifully played and more accessible than this director's earlier work, although with some obscure formalism.
wd Peter Greenaway ph Sacha Vierny m Michael Nyman pd Ben Van Os, Jan Roelfs
☆ Bernard Hill, Joan Plowright, Juliet Stevenson, Joely Richardson, Jason Edwards

The Drowning Pool
US   1975   108m   Technicolor   Panavision
Warner/Coleytown (Lawrence Turman, David Foster)
📼 🎦

Private eye Lew Harper goes to New Orleans to investigate an anonymous letter which ends in murder.
Dreary sequel to Harper (qv), full of boring characters uninventively deployed.
w Tracy Keenan Wynn, Lorenzo Semple Jnr, Walter Hill novel John Ross MacDonald d Stuart Rosenberg ph Gordon Willis m Michael Small
☆ Paul Newman, Joanne Woodward, Coral Browne, Tony Franciosa, Murray Hamilton, Gail Strickland, Linda Hayes, Richard Jaeckel
'The impenetrable mystery is not particularly gripping; and the general air of pointlessness is only intensified by the sudden rush of clarifications at the end.' – *Tom Milne*
'It recycles every private eye cliché known to civilized man as it crawls through Louisiana talking all the way.' – *Paul D. Zimmermann*
'All the clichés of cheapjack TV private eye capers have been added to MacDonald's book; whatever separates him from the paperback hacks has been deleted.' – *Judith Crist*

Drugstore Cowboy **
US   1989   100m   colour
Avenue Pictures (Nick Wechsler, Karen Murphy)
📼 🎦 🎦

A drug-addict, his wife and two friends travel across America, robbing drug-stores to support their habit.

Low-key, effective melodrama with an unconvincing ending.
w Gus Van Sant, Daniel Yost *novel* James Fogle *d* Gus Van Sant *ph* Robert Yeoman *m* Elliot Goldenthal *pd* David Brisbin *ed* Curtiss Clayton
☆ Matt Dillon, Kelly Lynch, James Remar, James Le Gros, Heather Graham, William S. Burroughs
'A rather thoughtless and unenlightening film about drug addiction.' – *MFB*

Drum

US 1976 100m Metrocolor Panavision
Dino de Laurentiis (Ralph Serpe)
🖼
In 1860 New Orleans, a bordello house slave faces all manner of sexual predators.
Tediously single-minded sequel to the appalling Mandingo.
w Norman Wexler *novel* Kyle Onstott *d* Steve Carver *ph* Lucien Ballard *m* Charles Smalls
☆ Warren Oates, Ken Norton, Isela Vega, Yaphet Kotto, John Colicos, Royal Dano
'Shamelessly it exploits the factors which explain the success of the prototype: a feeble pretence at outraged historical exposé of the abuses of the slave trade provides the excuse for an orgy of wish dreams, of sadism, flagellation, domination, sexuality of all tastes, popular fantasies of negro potency.' – *David Robinson, The Times*

The Drum *

GB 1938 96m Technicolor
UA/London Films (Alexander Korda)
🖼
US title: Drums
The British army helps an Indian prince to resist his usurping uncle.
Reasonably entertaining story of the Raj, with adequate excitement after a meandering start.
w Lajos Biro, Arthur Wimperis, Patrick Kirwan, Hugh Gray *novel* A. E. W. Mason *d* Zoltan Korda *ph* Georges Périnal, Osmond Borradaile *m* John Greenwood, Miklos Rozsa *ad* Vincent Korda *ed* William Hornbeck, Henry Cornelius
☆ Sabu, Roger Livesey, Raymond Massey, Valerie Hobson, Desmond Tester, David Tree, Francis L. Sullivan, Roy Emerton, Edward Lexy
'Looks like a 100% commercial bet.' – *Variety*

Drum Beat

US 1954 111m Warnercolor CinemaScope
Jaguar (no producer credited)
🖼
An Indian fighter sets out to make peace with a renegade.
Long, dull Western, stolid all round.
wd Delmer Daves *ph* J. Peverell Marley *m* Victor Young
☆ Alan Ladd, Audrey Dalton, Marisa Pavan, Robert Keith, Rodolfo Acosta, Charles Bronson, Warner Anderson, Elisha Cook Jnr, Anthony Caruso

Drum Crazy: see *The Gene Krupa Story*

Drums: see *The Drum*

Drums Across the River

US 1954 78m Technicolor
Universal-International (Melville Tucker)
🖼
A young Westerner who hates Indians finally helps them to overthrow a white crook.
Slick little Western with almost every familiar ingredient.
w John K. Butler, Lawrence Roman *d* Nathan Juran *ph* Harold Lipstein *m* Joseph Gershenson
☆ Audie Murphy, Walter Brennan, Lyle Bettger, Lisa Gaye, Hugh O'Brian, Jay Silverheels, Emile Meyer

Drums Along the Amazon: see *Angel on the Amazon*

Drums Along the Mohawk **

US 1939 103m Technicolor
TCF (Raymond Griffith)
🖼
Colonists survive Indian attacks in upstate New York during the Revolutionary War.
Patchy, likeable period adventure story with domestic and farming interludes; in its way a key film in the director's canon.

w Lamar Trotti, Sonya Levien *novel* Walter Edmonds *d* John Ford *ph* Bert Glennon, Ray Rennahan *m* Alfred Newman
☆ Claudette Colbert, Henry Fonda, *Edna May Oliver*, Eddie Collins, John Carradine, Dorris Bowdon, Jessie Ralph, Arthur Shields, Robert Lowery, Roger Imhof, Ward Bond
'Outdoor spec, a top-bracketer, though not in the smash division.' – *Variety*
'No one appears to know why the picture is being made, or what its point is, exactly.' – *Pauline Kael, 70s*
& Edna May Oliver

Drums in the Deep South

US 1951 87m Supercinecolor
RKO/King Brothers
🖼
A Confederate officer finds himself fighting a lonely battle with his best friend from West Point.
Barely stimulating semi-Western in appalling colour.
w Philip Yordan, Sidney Harmon *d* William Cameron Menzies *pd* William Cameron Menzies
☆ James Craig, Barbara Payton, Guy Madison, Barton MacLane, Craig Stevens, Tom Fadden, Taylor Holmes

Drums of Fu Manchu *

US 1940 bw serial: 15 eps
Republic
The Yellow Peril seeks the long-lost sceptre of Genghis Khan, which will allow him to rule the eastern hordes.
Spirited rendering of an ideal serial theme.
d William Witney, John English
☆ Henry Brandon, William Royle, Robert Kellard, Gloria Franklin, Olaf Hytten, Luana Walters, Dwight Frye

'A volcano erupts! A hurricane strikes! A man ... a woman ... discover passion in each other's arms!'
Drums of Tahiti

US 1953 73m Technicolor 3D
Columbia (Sam Katzman)
In 1877 an American helps the queen of Tahiti, who doesn't want to become a French possession.
Cheapskate potboiler with an extended volcanic climax (courtesy of older, better movies).
w Douglas Heyes, Robert E. Kent *d* William Castle
☆ Dennis O'Keefe, Patricia Medina, Francis L. Sullivan, Sylvia Lewis

Drunken Angel **

Japan 1948 102m bw
Toho
🖼
original title: Yoidore Tenshi
A gruff, hot-tempered, alcoholic doctor befriends a young gangster who is dying of tuberculosis.
Moving drama of sacrifice and redemption, filmed in an understated, realistic style.
w Keinosuke Uekusa, Akira Kurosawa *d* Akira Kurosawa *ph* Takeo Ito *m* Fumio Hayasaka
☆ Takashi Shimura, *Toshiro Mifune*, Reizaburo Yamamoto, Chieko Nakakita, Michiyo Kogure

Dry Rot

GB 1956 87m bw
Romulus (Jack Clayton)
Three bookmakers plot to make a fortune by substituting a doped horse for the favourite.
Flat filming of a long-running theatrical farce.
w John Chapman *play* John Chapman *d* Maurice Elvey *ph* Arthur Grant *m* Peter Akister
☆ Ronald Shiner, Brian Rix, Sid James, Michael Shepley, Joan Haythorne, Joan Sims, Heather Sears, Lee Patterson, Peggy Mount

A Dry White Season *

US 1989 107m DeLuxe
UIP/MGM/Star Partners II (Paula Weinstein)
🖼
A white South African is transformed into a radical after investigating the death of his gardener at the hands of the police.
Filmed with a passion that does not always communicate to the audience.
w Colin Welland, Euzhan Palcy *novel* André Brink *d* Euzhan Palcy *ph* Kelvin Pike, Pierre William Glenn *pd* John Fenner *ed* Sam O'Steen, Glenn Cunningham
☆ Donald Sutherland, Janet Suzman, Zakes Mokae, Jurgen Prochnow, Susan Sarandon, Marlon

Brando, Winston Ntshona, Thoko Ntshinga, Leonard Maguire
& Marlon Brando

Du Barry, Woman of Passion

US 1930 88m bw
United Artists (Talmadge)
Incidents in the life of the mistress of Louis XV.
Tedious early talkie which marked the virtual end of its star's career.
play David Belasco *d* Sam Taylor *ph* Oliver T. Marsh
☆ Norma Talmadge, William Farnum, Hobart Bosworth, Conrad Nagel, Alison Skipworth
'Wholly unimpressive ... nix for kids and the sticks.' – *Variety*

Du Rififi chez les Hommes: see *Rififi*

Du Skal Aere Din Hustru: see *Master of the House*

Dual Alibi

GB 1947 81m bw
British National (Louis H. Jackson)
Twin trapezists fall out over a lottery ticket and a worthless woman, but later extract a unique revenge.
Sprightly circus melodrama, shot on a shoestring.
w Alfred Travers, Stephen Clarkson *d* Alfred Travers *ph* James Wilson
☆ Herbert Lom, Phyllis Dixey, Ronald Frankau, Terence de Marney, Abraham Sofaer, Eugene Deckers

Dubarry Was a Lady

US 1943 101m Technicolor
MGM (Arthur Freed)
🖼
A New Yorker imagines himself back at the court of Louis XIV.
Dull, stiff adaptation of a Broadway musical comedy, with changed songs.
w Irving Brecher *book* B. G. de Sylva, Herbert Fields *d* Roy del Ruth *ph* Karl Freund *m/ly* Cole Porter *md* George Stoll
☆ Gene Kelly, Lucille Ball, Red Skelton, Virginia O'Brien, Zero Mostel, Rags Ragland, Tommy Dorsey and his Orchestra

'If the rustlers didn't get you ... the hustlers did!'
The Duchess and the Dirtwater Fox

US 1976 104m DeLuxe Panavision
TCF (Melvin Frank)
🖼
A Barbary Coast con man and a saloon singer have various hectic adventures.
Wild and woolly spoof Western which fires off aimlessly in a variety of styles and becomes merely tiresome despite good scenes.
w Melvin Frank, Barry Sandler *d* Melvin Frank *ph* Joseph Biroc *m* Charles Fox
☆ George Segal, Goldie Hawn, Conrad Janis, Thayer David, Roy Jenson, Bob Hoy, Bennie Dobbins
'The classic Western has now been shot to death by Sam Peckinpah, laughed to death by Mel Brooks and pondered to death by Arthur Penn, and Frank is like a scavenger picking up stray relics from its body.' – *Newsweek*
'The relentless vulgarity of the enterprise suggests that Mr Frank, having been so long constrained by the Hollywood Production Code when churning out vehicles for Bob Hope and Danny Kaye, is still making up for lost time.' – *Philip French*

The Duchess of Idaho

US 1950 98m Technicolor
MGM (Joe Pasternak)
Romantic misunderstandings among candidates for Miss Idaho Potato.
Lightweight musical, quite pleasant if routine, with guest spots.
w Dorothy Cooper, Jerry Davis *d* Robert Z. Leonard *ph* Charles Schoenbaum *md* Georgie Stoll
☆ Esther Williams, Van Johnson, John Lund, Paula Raymond, Clinton Sundberg, Eleanor Powell, Lena Horne, Red Skelton

Duck Soup ****

US 1933 68m bw
Paramount
🖼
An incompetent becomes President of Fredonia and wages war on its scheming neighbour.
The satirical aspects of this film are fascinating but appear to have been unintentional. Never mind, it's also the most satisfying and undiluted Marx Brothers romp, albeit the one without instrumental interludes. It does include the lemonade stall, the mirror sequence, and an endless array of one-liners and comedy choruses.
w Bert Kalmar, Harry Ruby, Arthur Sheekman, Nat Perrin *d* Leo McCarey *ph* Henry Sharp *m/ly* Bert Kalmar, Harry Ruby *ad* Hans Dreier, Wiard Ihnen *ed* LeRoy Stone
☆ Groucho Marx, Chico Marx, Harpo Marx, Zeppo Marx, *Margaret Dumont*, Louis Calhern, Edgar Kennedy, Raquel Torres
'Practically everybody wants a good laugh right now, and this should make practically everybody laugh.' – *Variety*
'So much preliminary dialogue is necessary that it seems years before Groucho comes on at all; and waiting for Groucho is agony.' – *E. V. Lucas, Punch*
'The most perfect of all Marxist masterpieces.' – *Time Out, 1984*
♫ Hail, Hail Freedonia; His Excellency is Due; Just Wait 'til I Get Through With It; Freedonia's Going to War.

Duck, You Sucker: see *A Fistful of Dynamite*

Dudes

US 1987 90m colour
Recorded Releasing/New Century/Vista (Herbert Jaffe, Miguel Tejada Flores)
🖼
Three punk rockers, on their way to California, fall foul of a gang of murderous rednecks.
Haphazard, absurdist account of a violent culture clash.
w John Randall Johnson *d* Penelope Spheeris *ph* Robert Richardson *m* Charles Bernstein *pd* Robert Ziembicki *ed* Andy Horvitch
☆ Jon Cryer, Daniel Roebuck, Flea, Catherine Mary Stewart, Lee Ving

Due Soldi di Speranza *

Italy 1952 98m bw
Universalcine (Sandro Ghenzi)
GB title: Two Pennyworth of Hope
Demobilized after World War II, Antonio finds life in his native village hard to take.
Neo-realist comedy-melodrama full of gesticulating rustics; good for those who like this sort of thing.
w Renato Castellani, Titina de Filippo *d* Renato Castellani *ph* Arturo Gallea *m* Alessandro Cicognini
☆ Vincenzo Musolino, Maria Fiore, Filumena Russo, Luigi Astarita

Le Due Vite di Mattia Pascal: see *The Two Lives of Mattia Pascal*

Duel **

US 1971 90m colour
Universal (George Eckstein)
🖼
A travelling salesman discovers that the driver of the petrol tanker following him is determined to kill him.
Tense, suspenseful drama that made Spielberg's name as a bright young director.
w Richard Matheson *story* Richard Matheson *d* Steven Spielberg
☆ Dennis Weaver, Jacqueline Scott, Eddie Firestone, Lou Frizzell
† Made for television, the film received a UK release in 1972, but was not seen in American cinemas until 1983.

Duel at Diablo *

US 1966 103m DeLuxe
UA/Nelson/Engel/Cherokee/Rainbow/Brien
🖼
White and black man fight together as Apaches attack.
Well-paced, old-fashioned, shoot-'em-up star Western.
w Marvin H. Albert, Michel M. Grilikhes *d* Ralph Nelson *ph* Charles F. Wheeler *m* Neal Hefti

☆ Sidney Poitier, James Garner, Bibi Andersson, Bill Travers, William Redfield, John Hoyt, John Hubbard

Duel at Silver Creek

US 1952 77m Technicolor
U-I (Leonard Goldstein)

An honest man is murdered by claim jumpers, and the Silver Kid is suspected.
Modest, efficient Western.
w Gerald Drayson Adams, Joseph Hoffman d Don Siegel ph Irving Glassberg m Hans Salter
☆ Audie Murphy, Stephen McNally, Faith Domergue, Susan Cabot, Gerald Mohr, Eugene Iglesias, Lee Marvin, Walter Sande

Duel at the Rio Grande: see *The Mark of Zorro (1963)*

Duel in the Jungle

GB 1954 101m Technicolor
ABP/Marcel Hellman
An African explorer intends to defraud an insurance company and sets traps for the investigator who pursues him.
Lackadaisical romp in the studio jungle, none of it with much style or film sense.
w Sam Marx, T. J. Morrison d George Marshall ph Erwin Hillier m Mischa Spoliansky
☆ Dana Andrews, Jeanne Crain, David Farrar, Patrick Barr

Duel in the Sun **

US 1946 138m Technicolor
David O. Selznick

A half-breed girl causes trouble between two brothers.
Massive Western, dominated and fragmented by its producer, who bought the best talent and proceeded to interfere with it, so that while individual scenes are marvellous, the narrative has little flow. The final gory shoot-up between two lovers was much discussed at the time.
w David O. Selznick, Oliver H. P. Garrett novel Niven Busch d King Vidor (and others) ph Lee Garmes, Harold Rosson, Ray Rennahan m. Dimitri Tiomkin pd J. McMillan Johnson ad James Basevi second unit B. Reeves Eason, Otto Brower
☆ Jennifer Jones, Joseph Cotten, Gregory Peck, Lionel Barrymore, Lillian Gish, Walter Huston, Herbert Marshall, Charles Bickford, Tilly Losch, Joan Tetzel, Harry Carey, Otto Kruger, Sidney Blackmer
'A knowing blend of oats and aphrodisiac.' – *Time*
'Cornographic is a word that might have been coined for it.' – *Daily Mail*
'As sexual melodrama with a spectacular background it is in its way remarkable.' – *New Statesman*
'A razzmatazz of thunderous naïvety simmering into a kind of majestic dottiness.' – *Basil Wright, 1972*
'A lavish, sensual spectacle, so heightened it becomes a cartoon of passion.' – *Pauline Kael, 70s*
† The uncredited directors included Josef von Sternberg, William Dieterle, B. Reeves Eason, and Selznick himself.
⟁ Jennifer Jones; Lillian Gish

Duel on the Mississippi

US 1955 72m Technicolor
Columbia (Sam Katzman)
A river planter owes money to pirates.
Standard second feature excitements with romantic interludes.
w Gerald Drayson Adams d William Castle
☆ Patricia Medina, Lex Barker, Craig Stevens, Warren Stevens

The Duellists *

GB 1977 101m colour
Scott Free/NFFC/David Puttnam

In the early 1800s, two Hussar Officers challenge each other to a series of duels; after sixteen years an ironic truce is called.
A singularly pointless anecdote; its main virtue is that it is coldly attractive to look at.

w Gerald Vaughan-Hughes story *The Point of Honour* by Joseph Conrad d Ridley Scott ph Frank Tidy m Howard Blake pd Peter J. Hampton
☆ Keith Carradine, Harvey Keitel, Albert Finney, Edward Fox, Cristina Raines, Tom Conti, Robert Stephens, John McEnery

Duet for One

GB 1987 107m Rank Colour
Cannon (Menahem Golan, Yoram Globus)

A leading lady violinist contracts multiple sclerosis.
Lamentable opening out of a two-character play, all gloom and doom and overstatement.
w Tom Kempinski, Jeremy Lipp, Andrei Konchalovsky play Tom Kempinski d Andrei Konchalovsky ph Alex Thomson pd John Graysmark ed Henry Richardson
☆ Julie Andrews, Alan Bates, Max von Sydow, Rupert Everett, Margaret Courtenay

'Some helpful hints for those who are very rich, very beautiful, very hip, elaborately oversexed, tuned in, turned on and bored to death!'

Duffy

GB 1968 101m Technicolor
Columbia/Martin Manulis
Two half-brothers plan to rob their millionaire father.
Would-be with-it caper film, all flashy fragments and pop art, like sitting through a feature-length commercial. Exasperating.
w Donald Cammell, Harry Joe Brown Jnr d Robert Parrish ph Otto Heller m Ernie Freeman
☆ James Coburn, James Mason, James Fox, Susannah York, John Alderton, Guy Deghy, Tutte Lemkow, Carl Duering, Marne Maitland

Duffy of San Quentin

US 1953 78m bw
Allied Artists (Berman Swartz, Walter Doniger)
GB title: *Men Behind Bars*
An elderly warden institutes prison reforms which cause him problems.
Semi-true melodrama with standard excitements and too much talk.
wd Walter Doniger ph John Alton m Paul Dunlap
☆ Paul Kelly, Louis Hayward, Maureen O'Sullivan, Joanne Dru, George Macready, Horace MacMahon

Duffy's Tavern

US 1945 97m bw
Paramount (Danny Dare)
The owner of a bar is helped by Hollywood stars.
Flat comedy based on a radio show and not helped by dismal guest star appearances.
w Melvin Frank, Norman Panama d Hal Walker ph Lionel Lindon m Robert Emmett Dolan
☆ Ed Gardner, Victor Moore, Marjorie Reynolds, Barry Sullivan, Bob Hope, Bing Crosby, Betty Hutton, Alan Ladd, Dorothy Lamour, Veronica Lake, William Bendix, Joan Caulfield

'Two thousand men and a girl!'

The Duke of West Point *

US 1938 112m bw
Edward Small
An extrovert army cadet finds the going tough.
Dated romantic flagwaver which pleased at the time.
w George Bruce d Alfred E. Green ph Robert Planck
☆ Louis Hayward, Joan Fontaine, Tom Brown, Richard Carlson, Alan Curtis, Don Barry, Gaylord Pendleton, Jed Prouty, Marjorie Gateson
'Fairly good entertainment. Much human interest, but the comedy relief is rather light.' – *Variety*

The Duke Wore Jeans

♟♟ GB 1958 89m bw
Insignia (Peter Rogers)
An aristocrat persuades his Cockney double to woo a princess on his behalf.
Moderately lively comedy with songs, tailored for Britain's new musical star.
w Norman Hudis story Lionel Bart, Michael Pratt d Gerald Thomas ph Otto Heller m Bruce Montgomery

☆ Tommy Steele, June Laverick, Michael Medwin, Alan Wheatley, Eric Pohlmann

Dulcima

GB 1971 98m Technicolor
EMI (Basil Rayburn)
A farmer's daughter reluctantly moves in with a persistent, lecherous old miser.
Weird sex melodrama from Cold Comfort Farm country, more risible than interesting.
wd Frank Nesbitt story H. E. Bates ph Tony Imi m Johnny Douglas ad Ray Sim
☆ John Mills, Carol White, Stuart Wilson, Bernard Lee, Dudley Foster

Dulcimer Street: see *London Belongs to Me*

'For Harry And Lloyd Every Day Is A No-Brainer.'
Dumb & Dumber

♟♟ US 1994 106m Film House colour
First Independent/New Line/MPCA (Charles B. Wessler, Brad Krevoy, Steve Stabler)

A dim-witted chauffeur travels across America with his dimmer-witted friend in order to return a briefcase to someone who does not want it back.
In comparison with Jerry Lewis, the comedian he most resembles, there is something sweetly innocent about the personality of the relentlessly mugging Jim Carrey, which can wear down resistance to what is no more than a succession of bad jokes on such matters as farting. It makes the most basic Carry On movie look sophisticated and was among the most successful releases of the year.
w Peter Farrelly, Bennett Yellin, Bobby Farrelly d Peter Farrelly ph Mark Irwin m Todd Rundgren pd Sidney Bartholomew Jnr ed Christopher Greenbury
☆ Jim Carrey, Jeff Daniels, Lauren Holly, Karen Duffy, Teri Garr, Mike Starr, Charles Rocket, Victoria Rowell
'*D and D* – in comparison with which Jim Carrey's other pictures look as if they were scripted by Oscar Wilde – makes you laugh out loud for almost its entire running time.' – *Richard Schickel, Time*
'A flat-out celebration of stupidity, bodily functions and pratfalls … ideal fare for those who want to laugh themselves sick' – *Variety*

Dumbo ****

♟♟ US 1941 64m Technicolor
Walt Disney

A baby circus elephant finds that his big ears have a use after all.
Delightful cartoon feature notable for set-pieces such as the drunken nightmare and the crows' song.
w various d Ben Sharpsteen m Frank Churchill, Oliver Wallace
☆ Featuring the voices of Sterling Holloway, Edward Brophy, Verna Felton, Herman Bing, Cliff Edwards
♪ music
♫ song, 'Baby Mine' (m Frank Churchill, ly Ned Washington)

The Dummy Talks

GB 1943 85m bw
British National
A ventriloquist turns to blackmail and is murdered backstage.
Curious, oddly cast murder mystery, not unentertaining at the time.
w Michael Barringer d Oswald Mitchell
☆ Jack Warner, Claude Hulbert, Beryl Orde, G. H. Mulcaster, Ivy Benson, Manning Whiley

Dune

US 1984 140m Technicolor Todd-AO
Dino de Laurentiis (Raffaella de Laurentiis)
Armies from several planets descend on another which has valuable spice guarded by monster worms.
A basically simple space fiction plot is immensely complicated by a welter of characters who are not properly introduced and who indeed are mostly irrelevant. The result, which cost nearly 50 million dollars, is inaudible, invisible (because of dim lighting) and unentertaining: a disaster of the very first order.
wd David Lynch novel Frank Herbert ph Freddie Francis m Toto pd Anthony Masters ed Antony Gibbs

☆ Francesca Annis, Jose Ferrer, Sian Phillips, Brad Dourif, Dean Stockwell, Freddie Jones, Linda Hunt, Kenneth McMillan, Richard Jordan, Kyle MacLachlan, Silvana Mangano, Jurgen Prochnow, Max Von Sydow, Sting
'Huge, hollow, imaginative and cold.' – *Variety*
'This movie is a real mess, an incomprehensible, ugly, unstructured, pointless excursion into the murkier realms of one of the most confusing screenplays of all time.' – *Roger Ebert*

Dunkirk **

GB 1958 135m bw
MGM/Ealing (Michael Balcon)
In 1940 on the Normandy beaches, a small group gets detached from the main force.
Sober, small-scale approach to an epic subject; interesting but not inspiring, with performances to match.
w W. P. Lipscomb, David Divine d Leslie Norman ph Paul Beeson m Malcolm Arnold
☆ John Mills, Richard Attenborough, Bernard Lee, Robert Urquhart, Ray Jackson

Dunston Checks In *

♟♟ Canada 1996 88m DeLuxe
TCF (Joe Wizan, Todd Black)

An aristocratic hotel burglar has an unusual accomplice: an orang-utan, who prefers the company of the manager's two young sons.
Enjoyable, smartly written farce that also charms; the laughs keep coming.
w John Hopkins, Bruce Graham d Ken Kwapis ph Peter Collister m Miles Goodman pd Rusty Smith ed Jon Poll
☆ Jason Alexander, Faye Dunaway, Eric Lloyd, Rupert Everett, Graham Sack, Paul Reubens, Glenn Shadix, Sam
'It all works very smoothly, mostly because the sight gags are just predictable enough for comfort, and partly because of a cast who gamely suffer simian-inflicted indignities.' – *Guardian*

'Men invoke its horror! Women invite its shame!'
The Dunwich Horror *

US 1970 90m Movielab
AIP (Roger Corman, Jack Bohrer)

A young warlock plans to use his girlfriend in a fertility rite.
Bookish horror story, quite well done against a village background.
w Curtis Lee Hanson, Henry Rosenbaum, Ronald Silkosky story H. P. Lovecraft d Daniel Haller ph Richard C. Glouner m Les Baxter
☆ Dean Stockwell, Sandra Dee, Ed Begley, Sam Jaffe, Lloyd Bochner
'A bit psychedelic in places, but with a real feeling for sinister rites and strange manifestations.' – *Sight and Sound*

Duoluo Tianshi: see *Fallen Angels*

Duped Till Doomsday *

East Germany 1957 97m bw
DEFA (Adolf Fischer)
original title: *Betrogen bis zum Jungsten Tag*
Three Nazi NCOs go to the bad.
Propagandist anti-Nazi war melodrama, very well made in parts.
w Kurt Bortfeldt novel Kameraden by Franz Fuhmann d Kurt Jung-Alsen ph Walter Fehdmer
☆ Wolfgang Kieling, Rudolph Ulrich, Hans-Joachim Martens

During One Night

GB 1961 80m bw
Galaworldfilm
During World War II, a country girl helps a USAAF deserter dispel his fear of impotence.
Glum sex drama, a curious and unsuccessful attempt.
wd Sidney J. Furie ph Norman Warwick m Bill McGuffie
☆ Don Borisenko, Susan Hampshire, Sean Sullivan, Joy Webster, Jackie Collins

Dust

Belgium/France 1985 87m Fujicolour
Mans/Daska/Flach/FR3

On an isolated South African farm, a girl murders her adulterous father.

Doomladen saga redeemed by strong pictorial style.
wd Marion Hansel *novel In the Heart of the Country by J. M. Coetzee*
☆ Jane Birkin, Trevor Howard, John Matshikiza

Dust Be My Destiny *
US   1939   88m   bw
Warner (Lou Edelman)
A young misfit tries to find himself in the country.
Dated but well made social melodrama.
w Robert Rossen *story* Jerome Odlum d Lewis Seiler ph James Wong Howe m Max Steiner
☆ John Garfield, Priscilla Lane, Alan Hale, Frank McHugh, John Litel, Charles Grapewin, Billy Halop, Bobby Jordan, Stanley Ridges
'Strong programmer, though overlong and episodic.' – *Variety*
'You can tell from the title that John Garfield has his usual part – the angry, bitter, tough poor young man with slight persecution mania.' – *Richard Mallett, Punch*
† Remade 1942 as *I Was Framed*, with Michael Ames.

Dust Devil: The Final Cut
GB   1992   103m   Technicolor
Polygram/Palace/Film Four/Richard Stanley
▣ ▤ ◌
An alien, which has to kill in order to return to its own world, journeys to a ghost town, where he is attracted by two people with a death-wish: a battered wife fleeing her husband and a black cop who has lost his wife and son.
Confused science-fiction thriller that never quite comes to life; whatever message the director is striving to impart, it remains obscure.
wd Richard Stanley ph Steven Chivers m Simon Boswell pd Joseph Bennett ed Derek Trigg, Paul Carlin sp The Dream Machine, Rick Cresswell
☆ Robert Burke, Chelsea Field, Zakes Mokae, John Matshikiza, Marianne Sagebrecht, William Hootkins, Rufus Swart
'Overflowing with ideas, visual invention and genre references but saddled by a weak, unfocused script.' – *Variety*
'In any of its several versions, this is a considerable and remarkable film.' – *Kim Newman*
† The film exists in several versions. The above is the director's preferred version, which he restored with his own money. A shorter version, cut by its

American distributor, was released in Europe under the title *Demonica*. The US version of the film was re-dubbed and had a new voice-over added.

Dust in the Wind *
Taiwan   1987   100m   colour
ICA/Central Motion Picture (Ling Deng Fei, Xu Guo Liang)
original title: Lien-lien feng-ch'en
Instead of going to high school, a youth leaves his mining village to seek work in the big city, where his girlfriend joins him.
A leisurely, intermittently insightful examination of the tensions and pleasures of family life and the problems of surviving without much education in an unsympathetic urban environment.
w Wu Nien-jen, Chu Tien-wen d Hou Hsiao-hsien ph Li Ping-pin pd Zhao Qi Bin
☆ Wang Ching-Wen, Hsing Shu-fen, Ch'en Shu-fang, Li Tien-lu

Dusty
♟♟   Australia   1982   85m   colour
Panavision
Kestrel Films/Dusty Productions (Gil Brealey)
▤
An old shepherd takes to the bush to save his half-wild dog from being shot by sheep farmers.
Sentimental tale with pleasant landscape photography.
w Sonia Berg *novel* Frank Dalby Davison d John Richardson ph Alex McPhee m Frank Strangio pd Robbie Perkins ad Ivana Perkins ed David Greig
☆ Bill Kerr, Noel Trevarthen, Carol Burns, John Stanton, Nicholas Holland

Dusty Ermine
GB   1938   74m   bw
Julius Hagen/Twickenham
US title: Hideout in the Alps
Scotland Yard chases counterfeiters to Switzerland, and the hunt ends in a ski chase.
Modestly effective melodrama with dated romantic leads.
w Paul Hervey Fox *play* Neil Grant d Bernard Vorhaus
☆ Jane Baxter, Anthony Bushell, Ronald Squire, Margaret Rutherford, Athole Stewart, Katie Johnson, Austin Trevor, Felix Aylmer
'The humour is of the British kind – not too hilarious but still tickling.' – *Variety*

Dutch
♟♟   US   1991   107m   DeLuxe
TCF (John Hughes, Richard Vane)
▣ ▤ ◌
GB title: Driving Me Crazy
An arrogant and snobbish twelve-year-old boy is reformed by his divorced mother's working-class boyfriend.
Inert comedy of class warfare, part of the cycle of buddy-buddy movies in which antagonists at the beginning become friends by the end.
w John Hughes d Peter Faiman ph Charles Minsky m Alan Silvestri pd Stan Jolley ed Paul Hirsch, Adam Bernardi
☆ Ed O'Neill, Ethan Randall, Christopher McDonald, Ari Meyers, E. G. Daily, L. Scott Caldwell, Kathleen Freeman

Dutchman *
GB   1966   56m   bw
Gene Persson
On a New York subway train a woman humiliates a black man and finally knifes him.
An allegory for addicts who can ferret out the meaning; on the surface, vaguely Pinterish and mainly boring.
w LeRoi Jones *play* LeRoi Jones d Anthony Harvey ph Gerry Turpin m John Barry
☆ Shirley Knight, Al Freeman Jnr

D'Ye Ken John Peel?
GB   1935   81m   bw
AP&D/Twickenham (Julius Hagen)
US title: Captain Moonlight
In the early 1800s, an army officer prevents a villain from marrying the girl he loves.
A muddled melodrama of highwaymen and skulduggery with musical interludes; it provided Stanley Holloway with an opportunity to perform one of his best-known monologues, 'Sam, Pick Up Thy Musket', and also contains the English equivalent of cavalry riding to the rescue with a charge of fox-hunters.
w H. Fowler Mear *story* Charles Cullum d Henry Edwards ph Sydney Blythe, William Luff m W. L. Trytel ad James A. Carter ed Jack Harris, Lister Laurence
☆ John Garrick, Winifred Shotter, Stanley Holloway, John Stuart, Leslie Perrins, Mary Lawson, Charles Carson

'Just when she'd given up on love, she fell for a guy who'd given up on life.'

Dying Young
US   1991   111m
TCF/Fogwood (Sally Field, Kevin McCormick)
▣ ▤ ◌ ◌
A man suffering from leukaemia falls in love with the nurse he hires to look after him.
Inane romance, meandering and glossily sentimental, and coming to the conclusion that death is nothing to worry about if you've Julia Roberts by your side.
w Richard Friedenberg *novel* Marti Leimbach d Joel Schumacher ph Juan Ruiz Anchia m James Newton Howard ad Guy J. Comtois, Richard Johnson ed Robert Brown, Jim Prior
☆ Julia Roberts, Campbell Scott, Vincent D'Onofrio, Colleen Dewhurst, David Selby, Ellen Burstyn, Dion Anderson, George Martin
'Starpower should carry this rather thin and maudlin weeper through some heated weeks, but the only real legs likely to be shown are those amply exposed by the femme lead.' – *Variety*

Dynamite **
US   1929   129m   bw
MGM (Cecil B. de Mille)
In order to gain an inheritance, a socialite marries a man about to be executed … but he is reprieved.
Dated but still dynamic social melodrama of the early talkie period.
w Jeanie Macpherson d Cecil B. de Mille ph Peverell Marley m Herbert Stothart ad Mitchell Leisen
☆ Kay Johnson, Charles Bickford, Conrad Nagel, Julia Faye, Joel McCrea
'A pot-pourri of all previous de Mille efforts crammed into one picture.' – *Variety*
'Exuberant, wonderfully vigorous, the film skilfully evokes the look and character of the Jazz Age.' – *Charles Higham*
'An astonishing mixture, with artificiality vying with realism and comedy hanging on the heels of grim melodrama.' – *Mordaunt Hall, New York Times*
♪ Mitchell Leisen

Dynamite Man from Glory Jail: see *Fools Parade*

Dyrygent: see *The Conductor*

E la Nave Va: see *And the Ship Sails On*

...E Poi Lo Chiamarono Il Magnifico: see *Man of the East*

E.T. The Extra-Terrestrial **
👪 US 1982 115m DeLuxe
Universal (Steven Spielberg, Kathleen Kennedy)
📼 📼 🖾 📀 🎧
When an alien spacecraft is disturbed in a Los Angeles suburb, one of its crew members is left behind and befriended by a small boy.
Stupefyingly successful box-office fairy tale by the current wonder kid Spielberg, taken to the world's heart because he dares to make films without sex, violence or bad language. This one could hardly be simpler, but it works; and the ailing cinema would love to know how to repeat the trick several times a year.
w *Melissa Mathison* d *Steven Spielberg* ph *Allen Daviau* m *John Williams* pd *James D. Bissell* sp *Creator of E.T.: Carlo Rambaldi*
☆ Dee Wallace, Henry Thomas, Peter Coyote, Robert MacNaughton, Drew Barrymore, K. C. Martel
'The most moving science-fiction movie ever made on earth.' – *Pauline Kael, New Yorker*
'E.T. is the closest film to my own sensibilities, my own fantasies, my own heart.' – *Steven Spielberg*
† E.T. – extra-terrestrial.
🏆 visual effects; music; sound
⚜ best picture; direction; original screenplay; cinematography; editing
⎊ best score

E Tornato Sabata ... Hai Chiuso un'Altra Volta: see *Return of Sabata*

Each Dawn I Die *
US 1939 84m bw
Warner (David Lewis)
📼 🖾 📀
original title: *Killer Meets Killer*
A crusading reporter is framed for manslaughter and becomes a hardened prisoner.
Efficient, vigorous yet slightly disappointing star vehicle; the talents are in the right background, but the script is wobbly.
w *Norman Reilly Raine, Warren Duff, Charles Perry* novel *Jerome Odlum* d *William Keighley* ph *Arthur Edeson* m *Max Steiner* ad *William Cameron Menzies*
☆ James Cagney, George Raft, Jane Bryan, George Bancroft, Maxie Rosenbloom, Stanley Ridges, Alan Baxter, Victor Jory
'Rich in horror and brutality.' – *New York Sunday Mirror*
'In addition to its crackling screenplay, it is made memorable by the easy mastery of its two principals.' – *Time*
'Towards the end of the thirties Warners' underworld pictures began to get hazy and high-minded, and in this one the pre-Second World War spiritual irradiation blurs the conventions of the prison genre.' – *Pauline Kael, 70s*

Eadie was a Lady
US 1945 90m bw
Columbia (Michel Kraike)
An upper-crust co-ed leads a double night life as a burlesque dancer.
Modestly effective minor musical.
w *Monte Brice* d *Arthur Dreifuss*
☆ Ann Miller, Joe Besser, William Wright, Jeff Donnell

The Eagle **
US 1925 80m bw silent
United Artists/Joseph M. Schenck
📼 🖾 📀
A Cossack lieutenant turns masked outlaw when his father's lands are annexed.
Enjoyable romp in the wake of Robin Hood, the Scarlet Pimpernel and Zorro; the eye-flashing star is somewhere near his best.
w *Hans Kraly* story *Dubrowsky* by Alexander Pushkin d *Clarence Brown* ph *George Barnes*
☆ Rudolph Valentino, Vilma Banky, Louise Dresser

The Eagle and the Hawk **
US 1933 72m bw
Paramount
In 1918 France, two American army flyers dislike each other but come together before the death of one of them.
Dawn Patrol melodrama, well done with unusually vivid dialogue and acting.
w *Bogart Rogers, Seton I. Miller* story *John Monk Saunders* d *Stuart Walker* ph *Harry Fischbeck*
☆ Fredric March, Cary Grant, Carole Lombard, Sir Guy Standing, Jack Oakie, Forrester Harvey
'Will make good with those it attracts, but is handicapped by the mass of earlier flight pictures.' – *Variety*

The Eagle and the Hawk
US 1949 86m bw
(Paramount)
During the Mexican wars, a US government agent tracks down a traitor who is supplying arms to the rebel Juarez.
Stolid adventure yarn, energetically played.
w *Geoffrey Homes, Lewis R. Foster* d *Lewis R. Foster* ph *James Wong Howe* m *David Chudnow*
☆ John Payne, Dennis O'Keefe, Rhonda Fleming, Thomas Gomez, Fred Clark, Frank Faylen, Eduardo Noriega

The Eagle Has Landed *
GB 1976 135m Eastmancolor Panavision
ITC/Associated General (Jack Wiener, David Niven Jnr)
📼 🖾 📀
During World War II, enemy aliens infiltrate an English village in the hope of killing Churchill.
Elaborately plotted but uninvolving spy melodrama, lethargically directed, muddily coloured and too concerned to create some good Germans.
w *Tom Mankiewicz* novel *Jack Higgins* d *John Sturges* ph *Anthony Richmond* m *Lalo Schifrin*
☆ Michael Caine, Donald Sutherland, Robert Duvall, Jenny Agutter, Donald Pleasence, Anthony Quayle, Jean Marsh, Sven-Bertil Taube, John Standing, Judy Geeson, Larry Hagman, Maurice Roeves

Eagle in a Cage *
GB 1970 103m Eastmancolor
Group W/Ramona (Millard Lampell, Albert Schwarz)
In 1815, a professional soldier becomes governor of St Helena and jailer to Napoleon.
Talkative, anecdotal, heavily serious historical reconstruction with good acting but little control.
w *Millard Lampell* d *Fielder Cook* ph *Frano Vodopivec* m *Marc Wilkinson*
☆ John Gielgud, Ralph Richardson, Kenneth Haigh, Billie Whitelaw, Moses Gunn, Ferdy Mayne, Lee Montague

Eagle Squadron
US 1942 102m bw
Universal (Walter Wanger)
During World War II, American flyers join the RAF.
Studio-bound air epic, leavened with conventional romance but little humour or sympathy.
w *Norman Reilly Raine* story *C. S. Forester* d *Arthur Lubin* ph *Stanley Cortez* m *Frank Skinner*
☆ Robert Stack, Diana Barrymore, John Loder, Eddie Albert, Nigel Bruce, Leif Erickson, Edgar Barrier, Jon Hall, Evelyn Ankers, Isobel Elsom, Alan Hale Jnr, Don Porter, Frederick Worlock, Gladys Cooper

Eagle's Wing
GB 1979 111m Eastmancolor Panavision
Rank/Peter Shaw (Ben Arbeid)
📼 🖾
A Comanche chief pursues a white man who has stolen a prize Indian horse.
Would-be poetic Western which emerges as very pretty but stultifyingly dull; an odd thing indeed to come from a moribund British studio.
w *John Briley* d *Anthony Harvey* ph *Billy Williams* m *Marc Wilkinson* pd *Herbert Westbrook*
☆ Martin Sheen, Sam Waterston, Harvey Keitel, Stephane Audran, John Castle

The Ear *
Czechoslovakia 1970 93m bw
Barrandov (Erich Svabik, Jan Prochazka)
original title: *Ucho*
An unhappily married couple return to their bugged home from an official reception, at which the husband, a government minister, has discovered that he is to be purged.
A skilled but claustrophobic domestic and political drama, which is partly filmed in semi-darkness to emphasize its atmosphere of betrayal, guilt and general malaise; though when characters emerge into the light it is for a sinister purpose.
w *Jan Prochazka, Karel Kachyna* d *Karel Kachyna* ph *Joseph Illik* m *Svatopluk Havelka* ed *Stansikav Petrek*
☆ Jirina Bohdalova, Radoslav Brzobohaty, Gustav Opecensky, Miroslav Holub, Lubor Tokos, Borivoj Navratil, Jiri Cisler
† Russian authorities suppressed the film for 20 years.

Earl Carroll Sketchbook *
US 1946 90m bw
Republic
GB title: *Hats Off to Rhythm*
A songwriter gives up and sells radio jingles.
Modest follow-up to Earl Carroll Vanities, a background for half-a-dozen songs.
w *Frank Gill Jnr, Parke Levy* d *Albert S. Rogell* ph *Jack Marta*
☆ Constance Moore, William Marshall, Bill Goodwin, Edward Everett Horton, Vera Vague, Johnny Coy, Hillary Brooke

Earl Carroll Vanities *
US 1945 91m bw
Republic (Albert J. Cohen)
A Ruritanian princess in need of a loan becomes the singing star of a New York night-club.
Nit-witted musical with no style but an engaging cast.
w *Frank Gill Jnr* d *Joseph Santley* ph *Jack Marta* m/ly *Walter Kent, Kim Gannon* md *Walter Scharf*
☆ Constance Moore, Dennis O'Keefe, Alan Mowbray, Eve Arden, Otto Kruger, Pinky Lee, Mary Forbes, Stephanie Bachelor, Parkyakarkus, Leon Belasco, Robert Greig
⎊ song 'Endlessly'

The Earl of Chicago *
US 1939 87m bw
MGM (Victor Saville)
An American gangster accedes to an English earldom but is tried for murder.
Unusual but unsatisfactory comedy-drama which rambles to a dismal conclusion but has entertaining passages.
w *Lesser Samuels* novel *Brock Williams* d *Richard Thorpe* ph *Ray June* m *Werner Heymann*
☆ Robert Montgomery, Edward Arnold, Reginald Owen, Edmund Gwenn
† This had been planned as a British production, but the war intervened.

The Early Bird
👪 GB 1965 98m Eastmancolor
Rank/Hugh Stewart
📼
A milkman gets involved in an inter-company war.
Star farcical comedy; not the worst of Wisdom, but overlong and mainly uninventive.
w *Jack Davies, Norman Wisdom, Eddie Leslie, Henry Blyth* d *Robert Asher* ph *Jack Asher* m *Ron Goodwin*
☆ Norman Wisdom, Edward Chapman, Jerry Desmonde, Paddie O'Neil, Bryan Pringle, Richard Vernon, John Le Mesurier, Peter Jeffrey

Early Frost
Australia 1982 90m colour
Filmco (David Hannay)
A private investigator discovers that a series of apparently accidental deaths are the work of a serial killer who hates mothers.
A psychological horror story that tries hard to scare, but becomes more ludicrous the longer it lasts.
w *Terry O'Connor* d uncredited ph *David Eggby* m *Mike Harvey* ad *Bob Hilditch* ed *Tim Street*
☆ Diana McLean, Jon Blake, Jan Kingsbury, Kit Taylor, David Franklin, Joanne Samuel, Danny Adcock, Daniel Cumerford, Guy Doleman

Early Spring *
Japan 1956 108m bw
Shochiku
original title: *Soshun*
The marriage of an office worker breaks down when he begins an affair with a typist.
A slight, unengaging tale of the dreariness of domestic and office life.
w *Kogo Noda, Yasujiro Ozu* d *Yasujiro Ozu* ph *Yuharu Atsuta* m *Kojun Saito* ad *Tatsuo Hamada* ed *Yoshiyasu Hamamura*
☆ Chikage Awajima, Ryo Ikebe, Keiko Kishi, Teiji Takahashi, Chishu Ryu, So Yamamura, Haruko Sugimura, Takako Fujino

Early Summer *
Japan 1951 125m bw
Shochiku
🖾
original title: *Bakushu*
A family breaks up when the daughter rejects the man chosen as her husband and marries someone else.
A complex, compassionate, beautifully observed study of family tensions, traced over three generations living together.
w *Kogo Noda, Yasujiro Ozu* d *Yasujiro Ozu* ph *Yuharu Atsuta* m *Senji Ito* ad *Toshio Hamada* ed *Yoshiyasu Hamamura*
☆ Setsuko Hara, Chishu Ryu, Chikage Awajima, Kuniko Miyake, Ichiro Sugai, Chieko Higashiyama, Haruko Sugimura

Early to Bed
👪 US 1928 20m bw silent
Hal Roach
Stan becomes Ollie's butler but rebels when his friend's fortune goes to his head.
One of the most untypical and seldom seen of the stars' comedies, with both prankishly out of character. On its own account however it is mainly very funny.

w H. M. Walker d Emmett Flynn ph George Stevens ed Richard Currier
☆ Stan Laurel, Oliver Hardy

The Earrings of Madame De: see *Madame De*

Earth ***
USSR 1930 63m bw silent
VUFKU
◉ ▤
original title: *Zemlya*
Trouble results in a Ukrainian village when a landowner refuses to hand over his land for a collective farm.
The melodramatic little plot takes second place to lyrical sequences of rustic beauty, illustrating life, love and death in the countryside.
wd Alexander Dovzhenko ph Danylo Demutsky ed Alexander Dovzhenko
☆ Semyon Svashenko, Stephan Shkurat, Mikola Nademsky, Yelena Maximova
'Stories in themselves do not interest me. I choose them in order to get the greatest expression of essential social forms.' – *Dovzhenko*
'A picture for filmgoers who are prepared to take their cinema as seriously as Tolstoy took the novel.' – *James Agate*

Earth Girls Are Easy
⋔⋔ US 1988 100m colour Panavision
Fox/De Laurentiis/Kestrel Films (Tony Garnett)
◉ ▤ ⌒
Three aliens crashland on Earth and learn to enjoy disco dancing.
Ineffectual teenage musical.
w Julie Brown, Charlie Coffey, Terrence E. McNally d Julien Temple ph Oliver Stapleton md Nile Rodgers pd Dennis Gassner ed Richard Halsey
☆ Geena Davis, Jeff Goldblum, Jim Carrey, Damon Wayans, Julie Brown, Michael McKean, Charles Rocket, Larry Linville, Rick Overton

Earth Versus the Flying Saucers
⋔⋔ US 1956 83m bw
Columbia (Charles H. Schneer)
◉ ▤ ⌒
Saucermen from another planet try to disintegrate the Earth.
Elementary science fiction with special effects in a similar if enthusiastic vein.
w George Worthing Yates, Raymond T. Marcus story Curt Siodmak d Fred F. Sears ph Fred Jackman Jnr sp Ray Harryhausen
☆ Hugh Marlowe, Joan Taylor, Donald Curtis, Morris Ankrum

Earth vs The Spider
US 1958 72m bw
AIP (Bert I. Gordon)
◉ ▤
A seemingly dead giant spider is brought back to life by the playing of a high-school rock 'n' roll group.
Ineffably silly horror movie with poor special effects.
w Laszlo Gorog, George Worthing Yates story Bert I. Gordon d Bert I. Gordon ph Jack Marta m Albert Glasser ad Walter Keller ed Ronald Sinclair sp Bert I. Gordon
☆ Ed Kemmer, June Kenney, Gene Persson

Earthbound *
US 1940 67m bw
TCF (Sol M. Wurtzel)
The ghost of a murdered man helps his widow to bring the murderer to justice.
Curious attempt at Topper without laughs, nicely done once you get used to the idea.
w John Howard Lawson, Samuel Engel story Basil King d Irving Pichel
☆ Warner Baxter, Lynn Bari, Andrea Leeds, Charles Grapewin, Henry Wilcoxon, Elizabeth Patterson

Earthquake *
US 1974 123m Technicolor Panavision
Universal/Jennings Lang/Mark Robson
◉ ▤ ⌒ ⌒
Various personal stories intertwine in a Los Angeles earthquake.
Dreary drama with very variable special effects, gimmicked up by Sensurround. A box-office bonanza.
w George Fox, Mario Puzo d Mark Robson ph Philip Lathrop m John Williams

pd Alexander Golitzen, E. Preston Ames ed Dorothy Spencer sp Albert Whitlock, Frank Brendel, Glen Robinson
☆ Charlton Heston, Ava Gardner, Lorne Greene, Marjoe Gortner, Barry Sullivan, George Kennedy, Richard Roundtree, Geneviève Bujold, Walter Matuschanskayasky (Walter Matthau), Lloyd Nolan, Victoria Principal
'The picture is swell, but it isn't a cheat. It's an entertaining marathon of Grade A destruction effects, with B-picture stock characters spinning through it.' – *Pauline Kael*
🔊 sound; visual effects
✧ Philip Lathrop; Alexander Golitzen, E. Preston Ames; Dorothy Spencer

Earthworm Tractors
US 1936 69m bw
Warner
GB title: *A Natural Born Salesman*
A salesman whose fiancée wants him to think big turns to tractors.
One of the star's livelier comedies.
w Richard Macaulay, Joe Traub, Hugh Cummings d Ray Enright
☆ Joe E. Brown, June Travis, Guy Kibbee, Dick Foran

'The frank fearless drama of a woman who sinned!'
The Easiest Way
US 1931 86m bw
MGM
A hard-working slum girl falls into the lap of luxury but her easy virtue finally causes her to be rejected.
Familiar moral melodrama which got past the Hays Office only after some heavy deletions.
w Edith Ellis play Eugene Walter d Jack Conway ph John Mescall
☆ Constance Bennett, Robert Montgomery, Adolphe Menjou, Anita Page, Marjorie Rambeau, J. Farrell MacDonald, Clark Gable, Clara Blandick
'Gilded wickedness played by flawless cast: will entice.' – *Variety*

East End Chant: see *Limehouse Blues*

'A Comedy Of Families, A Chip Shop... And A Very Randy Dog.'
East is East ***
GB 1999 96m DeLuxe
FilmFour/Assassin/BBC (Leslee Udwin)
◉
The children of a strict Pakistani father, who is married to an Englishwoman, rebel when he arranges marriages for them.
Often broad but always enjoyable comedy that, for all its use of stereotypical characters and situations, manages to be truthful about family relationships.
w Ayub Khan-Din play Ayub Khan-Din d Damien O'Donnell ph Brian Tufano m Deborah Mollison pd Tom Conroy ed Michael Parker
☆ Om Puri, Linda Bassett, Jordan Routledge, Archie Panjabi, Emil Marwa, Chris Bisson, Jimi Mistry, Raji James, Ian Aspinall, Lesley Nicol, Gary Damer, John Bardon, Emma Rydal, Ruth Jones
† It is the most successful fully-funded British film so far.
🎦 British film

East Is West
US 1930 72m bw
Universal
Half-caste Big Time Charlie Young lords it over San Francisco's Chinatown.
Muddled melodrama reminiscent of many silent films.
w Tom Reed play Sam Shipman, John Hymer d Monta Bell ph Jerome Ash
☆ Edward G. Robinson, Lupe Velez, Lew Ayres, Henry Kolker, Mary Forbes, Edgar Norton
'Good daily change grind meller.' – *Variety*

East L.A.: see *My Family*

East Lynne
US 1931 102m bw
Fox
A Victorian lady is unjustly divorced by her husband, and later loses both her lover and her sight.
Much caricatured melodrama, here presented in stolidly acceptable form.

w Bradley King, Tom Barry novel Mrs Henry Wood d Frank Lloyd ph John Seitz m Richard Fall
☆ Ann Harding, Clive Brook, O. P. Heggie, Conrad Nagel, Cecilia Loftus, Beryl Mercer, Flora Sheffield
'A lavish production, some corking direction, and the elemental appeal of all dramatic hokum.' – *Variety*
† Previous versions had been made by Fox, in 1916 with Theda Bara and in 1925 with Alma Rubens.
✧ best picture

East Lynne on the Western Front
GB 1931 85m bw
Gaumont-Welsh-Pearson (T. A. Welsh)
War rookies produce *East Lynne* to relieve boredom.
Slapstick army farce which tickled a few fancies at the time.
w Donovan Parsons, Mary Parsons story George Pearson d George Pearson ph Percy Strong
☆ Herbert Mundin, Wilfred Lawson, Mark Daly, Harold French
'Recording is not good and the production shoddy, but it's crammed with hoke and will do good business for juvenile matinées and in the neighbourhoods.' – *Variety*

East Meets West
GB 1936 74m bw
Gaumont
◉
A proud sultan learns that his son is having an affair with the wife of a crook.
Derivative star vehicle, very stagey even then.
w Maude Howell play The Lake of Life by Edwin Greenwood d Herbert Mason ph Bernard Knowles m John Greenwood ad Oscar Werndorff
☆ George Arliss, Godfrey Tearle, Lucie Mannheim, Romney Brent, Ballard Berkeley, John Laurie
'Avoid like the plague.' – *Graham Greene*

'Of what a boy did ... what a girl did ... of ecstasy and revenge!'
'The most shocking revenge a girl ever let one brother take on another!'
East of Eden **
US 1955 115m Warnercolor Cinemascope
Warner (Elia Kazan)
◉ ▤ ⌒ ⌒
In a California farming valley in 1917 a wild adolescent rebels against his stern father and discovers that his mother, believed dead, runs a nearby brothel.
Turgid elaboration of Genesis with strong character but nowhere to go. Heavily over-directed and rousingly acted.
w Paul Osborn novel John Steinbeck d Elia Kazan m Ted McCord m Leonard Rosenman ad James Basevi, Malcolm Bert
☆ Raymond Massey, James Dean, Julie Harris, Dick Davalos, Jo Van Fleet, Burl Ives, Albert Dekker
'The first distinguished production in Cinemascope.' – *Eugene Archer*
🏆 Jo Van Fleet
✧ Paul Osborn; Elia Kazan; James Dean

East of Elephant Rock
GB 1976 92m colour
Boyd's Company/Kendon (Don Boyd)
▤
In 1948 Malaya a womanizing civil servant is shot by his jealous mistress.
Style-less and quite uncredited re-hash of The Letter, striving vainly to recreate the spirit of Somerset Maugham.
wd Don Boyd ph Keith Goddard m Peter Skellern
☆ Judi Bowker, Jeremy Kemp, John Hurt, Christopher Cazenove, Anton Rodgers, Vajira, Tariq Yunus
'Punishingly inept in every department.' – *David Badder, MFB*

East of Java: see *South Sea Sinner (1949)*

East of Java
US 1935 72m bw
Universal
After a shipwreck, menagerie animals take refuge along with the passengers on a tropic island.
The synopsis says it all; the production is sub-standard.

w James Ashmore Creelman, Paul Perez story Tiger Island by Gouverneur Morris d George Melford ph Norbert Brodine m Franz Waxman
☆ Charles Bickford, Elizabeth Young, Frank Albertson, Sig Rumann
'Highly thrilling, weak on names.' – *Variety*

East of Piccadilly
GB 1940 79m bw
ABPC (Walter C. Mycroft)
US title: *The Strangler*
A novelist and a girl reporter catch a silk stocking murderer.
Adequate lower case mystery with good atmosphere.
w Lesley Storm, J. Lee-Thompson novel Gordon Beckles d Harold Huth ph Claude Friese-Greene
☆ Sebastian Shaw, Judy Campbell, Henry Edwards, Niall MacGinnis, George Pughe, Martita Hunt, George Hayes, Cameron Hall, Edana Romney

East of Shanghai: see *Rich and Strange*

East of Sudan
GB 1964 94m Techniscope
Columbia/Ameran (Charles H. Schneer)
A trooper, a governess and others escape downriver from one of General Gordon's outposts.
Shameless borrowing of plot from The African Queen and footage from The Four Feathers. The purest hokum.
w Jud Kinberg d Nathan Juran ph Wilkie Cooper m Laurie Johnson
☆ Anthony Quayle, Sylvia Syms, Jenny Agutter
'Nathan Juran could direct this kind of thing blindfold, and for once would appear to have done so.' – *MFB*

East of Sumatra *
US 1953 82m Technicolor
U-I (Albert J. Cohen)
A mining engineer has trouble with the ruthless chief of a Pacific island.
A good example of routine Hollywood hokum, efficiently staged and acted.
w Frank Gill Jnr novel Louis L'Amour d Budd Boetticher ph Clifford Stine md Joseph Gershenson
☆ Jeff Chandler, Anthony Quinn, Marilyn Maxwell, John Sutton

East of the Rising Sun: see *Malaya*

The East Side Kids
US 1940 62m bw
Monogram (Sam Katzman)
▤
Street kids reform after helping to catch counterfeiters.
See entry for The Dead End Kids; this is the first attempt at a splinter group, and one that did not suggest longevity.
Later, the East Side Kids were boosted by the addition of members of the original Dead End Kids, Leo Gorcey and Bobby Jordan, soon followed by Huntz Hall and Gabriel Dell. They made the following movies before the group was re-formed as The Bowery Boys (qv):
1940 Boys of the City, That Gang of Mine
1941 Pride of the Bowery, Spooks Run Wild
1942 Mr Wise Guy, Let's Get Tough!, Smart Alecks, 'Neath Brooklyn Bridge
1943 Kid Dynamite, Clancy Street Boys (qv), Ghosts on the Loose, Mr Muggs Steps Out, Million Dollar Kid
1944 Follow the Leader, Block Busters (qv), Bowery Champs
1945 Docks of New York, Mr Muggs Rides Again, Come Out Fighting (qv)
w Robert Lively d Bob Hill
☆ Leon Ames, Dave O'Brien, Joyce Bryant, Harris Burger, Frankie Burke, Donald Haines, David Durand, Hally Chester (later Hal E. Chester, producer)
'An absurdly poor picture that will command little interest even from the vast army of Dead End Kids devotees.' – *Variety*

East Side of Heaven
US 1939 85m bw
Universal
A singing taxi driver looks after an abandoned baby.
Modestly pleasing comedy with music and sentiment; Baby Sandy subsequently starred in her own series.

---

w William Conselman d David Butler
☆ Bing Crosby, Joan Blondell, Mischa Auer, C. Aubrey Smith, Irene Hervey, Baby Sandy
'A grand package of entertainment that will play a merry tune at the b.o.' – *Variety*

East Side West Side *
US   1949   108m   bw
MGM (Voldemar Vetluguin)
📺

A New York businessman is torn between his wife and another woman.
High-class soap opera with all the production stops pulled out; generally well acted and reasonably entertaining.
w Isobel Lennart novel Marcia Davenport d Mervyn Le Roy ph Charles Rosher m Miklos Rozsa
☆ James Mason, Barbara Stanwyck, Van Heflin, Ava Gardner, Gale Sondergaard, Cyd Charisse, Nancy Davis, William Conrad
'No company is quite so adept as MGM at presenting basically uninteresting material with such style, and such a strong cast, that it cannot fail to entertain.' – *Penelope Houston*

Easter Parade **
👪 US   1948   109m   Technicolor
MGM (Arthur Freed)
📼 📺 🔵 🎧

A song and dance man quarrels with one partner but finds another.
A musical which exists only in its numbers, which are many but variable. All in all, an agreeable lightweight entertainment without the style to put it in the top class.
w Sidney Sheldon, Frances Goodrich, Albert Hackett d Charles Walters ph Harry Stradling m/ly Irving Berlin md Roger Edens, Johnny Green
☆ Fred Astaire, Judy Garland, Ann Miller, Peter Lawford, Clinton Sundberg, Jules Munshin
'The important thing is that Fred Astaire is back, with Irving Berlin calling the tunes.' – *Newsweek*
† Fred Astaire was actually second choice, replacing Gene Kelly who damaged an ankle.
👤 Roger Edens, Johnny Green

Easy Come, Easy Go
US   1947   78m   bw
Paramount (Kenneth MacGowan)
An old Irishman gambles away the money his daughter earns.
Whimsical sentimental comedy with an unattractive central character.
w Francis Edward Faragoh, John McNulty, Anne Froelick d John Farrow ph Daniel L. Fapp m Roy Webb
☆ Barry Fitzgerald, Diana Lynn, Sonny Tufts, Dick Foran, Frank McHugh, Allen Jenkins, John Litel, Arthur Shields

Easy Come, Easy Go
US   1966   97m   Technicolor
Paramount/Wallis-Hazen
📼
A frogman tries to salvage a treasure from a wreck off the California coast.
Empty-headed star vehicle, almost indistinguishable from many of the others.
w Allan Weiss, Anthony Lawrence d John Rich ph William Margulies m Joseph J. Lilley
☆ Elvis Presley, Dodie Marshall, Pat Priest, Pat Harrington, Skip Ward, Frank McHugh, Elsa Lanchester

'Where there's smoke, there must be somebody smoking!'

Easy Living **
US   1937   91m   bw
Paramount (Arthur Hornblow Jnr)
📺 🔵
A fur coat is thrown out of a window and lands on a typist…
Amusing romantic comedy with farcical trimmings; it now stands among the semi-classic crazy comedies of the thirties.
w Preston Sturges d Mitchell Leisen ph Ted Tetzlaff md Boris Morros
☆ Jean Arthur, Ray Milland, Edward Arnold, Luis Alberni, Mary Nash, Franklin Pangborn, William Demarest, Andrew Tombes
'Slapstick farce which does not fulfil the box office possibilities of its stars.' – *Variety*

'Secretaries, millionaires, jokes, sight gags, furies, attacks of cool sense – there are always three things going on at once.' – *New Yorker, 1977*

Easy Living
US   1949   77m   bw
RKO (Robert Sparks)
📼 📺
An ageing football star wants to retire but has to satisfy the living standards of his ambitious wife.
Dim drama.
w Charles Schnee story Education of the Heart by Irwin Shaw d Jacques Tourneur ph Harry J. Wild m Roy Webb
☆ Victor Mature, Lucille Ball, Lizabeth Scott, Sonny Tufts, Lloyd Nolan, Paul Stewart, Jack Paar, Jeff Donnell

Easy Money
GB   1948   93m   bw
GFD/Gainsborough (A. Frank Bundy)
Four people win big prizes on the football pools.
Short story compendium; very average.
w Muriel and Sydney Box play Arnold Ridley d Bernard Knowles ph Jack Asher m Temple Abady
☆ Edward Rigby, Greta Gynt, Dennis Price, Jack Warner, Mervyn Johns, Petula Clark, Marjorie Fielding, Bill Owen, Raymond Lovell

Easy Money
US   1983   100m   bw
Orion
📺 🔵
A baby photographer is left a fortune provided that he totally reforms.
Overlong and increasingly feeble comedy with a star who quickly outstays his welcome.
w Rodney Dangerfield, Michael Endler, P. J. O'Rourke, Dennis Blair d James Signorelli
☆ Rodney Dangerfield, Joe Pesci, Geraldine Fitzgerald, Candy Azzara, Val Avery

'A man went looking for America and couldn't find it anywhere!'
Easy Rider ****
US   1969   94m   Technicolor
Columbia/Pando/Raybert (Peter Fonda)
📼 📺 🔵 🎧
Two drop-outs ride across America on motorcycles.
Happening to please hippies and motor-cycle enthusiasts as well as amateur politicians, this oddball melodrama drew freakishly large audiences throughout the world and was much imitated though never equalled in its casual effectiveness.
w Peter Fonda, Dennis Hopper, Terry Southern d Dennis Hopper ph Laszlo Kovacs m various recordings
☆ Peter Fonda, Dennis Hopper, Jack Nicholson
'Cinéma-vérité in allegory terms.' – *Peter Fonda*
'Ninety-four minutes of what it is like to swing, to watch, to be fond, to hold opinions and to get killed in America at this moment.' – *Penelope Gilliatt*
👤 script; Jack Nicholson

Easy Street ****
👪 US   1917   22m   bw   silent
Mutual/Charles Chaplin
In a slum street, a tramp is reformed by a dewy-eyed missionary, becomes a policeman, and tames the local bully.
Quintessential Chaplin, combining sentimentality and social comment with hilarious slapstick.
wd Charles Chaplin ph William C. Foster, Rollie Totheroh
☆ Charles Chaplin, Edna Purviance, Albert Austin, Eric Campbell

Easy to Love *
US   1933   62m   bw
Warner
A pair of couples get into a romantic mix-up.
Innocent predecessor of Bob and Carol and Ted and Alice; come to think of it, quite sophisticated for its year.
w Carl Erickson, Manuel Seff play Thompson Buchanan d William Keighley
☆ Adolphe Menjou, Genevieve Tobin, Mary Astor, Edward Everett Horton, Guy Kibbee, Patricia Ellis, Hugh Herbert
'Adaptation, direction and able performances make an old story amusing entertainment.' – *Variety*

Easy to Love
US   1953   96m   Technicolor
MGM (Joe Pasternak)
📺
The romances of an aqua-queen in Florida's Cypress Gardens.
Thin, humourless and forgettable musical vehicle sustained by spectacular water ballets.
w Laslo Vadnay, William Roberts d Charles Walters ph Ray June md Lennie Hayton, George Stoll ch Busby Berkeley
☆ Esther Williams, Tony Martin, Van Johnson, John Bromfield, Carroll Baker

Easy to Wed *
US   1946   110m   Technicolor
MGM (Jack Cummings)
A socialite threatens a newspaper with libel; he postpones his own wedding and sets a friend to compromise her.
Bright but tasteless remake of Libelled Lady, with a second team cast trying hard.
w Dorothy Kingsley, Maurine Watkins, Howard Emmett Rogers, George Oppenheimer d Edward Buzzell ph Harry Stradling m Johnny Green
☆ Van Johnson, Esther Williams, Lucille Ball, Keenan Wynn, Cecil Kellaway, Carlos Ramirez, Ben Blue, Ethel Smith

Easy Virtue
GB   1927   73m   bw   silent
Gainsborough (Michael Balcon)
A drunkard's wife falls for a young man who kills himself. Her past then prevents her attempts to lead a respectable life.
Vapid social melodrama with minimal points of interest despite its credits.
w Eliot Stannard play Noël Coward d Alfred Hitchcock ph Claude McDonnell ed Ivor Montagu
☆ Isabel Jeans, Franklin Dyall, Eric Bransby Williams, Ian Hunter, Violet Farebrother, Robin Irvine

The Easy Way: see **Room for One More**

Eat a Bowl of Tea **
US   1989   104m   DeLuxe   Panavision
Artificial Eye/American Playhouse Theatre (Tom Sternberg)
📼 📺 🔵
A young Chinese-American brings back to New York a Chinese-born bride, but finds that family pressures to produce children make him impotent.
Sharply observed, witty domestic drama, set in the 1940s when Chinese immigrants were first allowed to bring their wives to America.
w Judith Rascoe novel Louis Chu d Wayne Wang ph Amir Mokri m Mark Adler pd Bob Ziembicki ed Richard Candib
☆ Cora Miao, Russell Wong, Victor Wong, Lau Siu Ming, Eric Tsang Chi Wai
'An engaging and welcome picture. Good-humoured, sincere, it is nothing more than it modestly aspires to be.' – *MFB*

Eat and Run
US   1985   86m   colour
New World (Jack Briggs)
📼 📺
A cop investigates when an obese alien lands on earth and begins to eat Italians.
A send-up of science-fiction and police movies, but done with little style and overusing its one joke – a voice-over narration spoken out loud by the characters.
w Stan Hart, Christopher Hart d Christopher Hart ph Dyanna Taylor m Scott Harper pd Robert Kracik, Anne C. Patterson ed Pamela Scott Arnold
☆ Ron Silver, Sharon Schlarth, R. L. Ryan, John J. Fleming, Derek Murcott, Robert Silver
† The British video release runs for 80m.

'A comedy to arouse your appetite.'
Eat Drink Man Woman **
Taiwan   1994   124m   DuArt
Buena Vista/Central Motion Picture/Good Machine/Ang Lee (Li-Kong Hsu)
📼 📺 🔵
original title: *Yinshi Nan Nu*
A widowed chef who has lost his sense of taste recovers it once he gets his three daughters off his hands.
Gentle comedy of food and family life, reasserting primary needs over more ephemeral desires.

w Hui-Ling Wang, Ang Lee, James Schamus d Ang Lee ph Jong Lin m Mader pd Fu-Hsiung Lee ed Tim Squyres
☆ Sihung Lung, Kuei-Mei Yang, Chien-Lien Wu, Yu-Wen Wang, Winston Chao, Ah-Leh Gua, Sylvia Chang, Lester Chen
'The movie is more likeable than memorable; you come out running for the nearest restaurant.' – *Terrence Rafferty, New Yorker*
'A feel-good movie, to be sure – but is that a stigma when so many young film-makers seem hell-bent on making us feel bad?' – *Sheila Johnston, Independent*
👤 Best Foreign Film

Eat the Peach *
Eire   1986   95m   Technicolor
Strongbow/Film Four International (David Collins)
📼 📺
Out-of-work Irish devise a mad scheme to construct a motorcycle Wall of Death.
Fairly amusing comedy, like an Irish version of an Ealing movie.
w Peter Ormrod, John Kelleher d Peter Ormrod ph Arthur Wooster m Donal Lunny
☆ Stephen Brennan, Eamon Morrissey, Catherine Byrne, Niall Toibin, Joe Lynch, Tony Doyle

Eating Raoul *
US   1982   83m   Pacific Color
Bartel Film (Anne Kimmel)
📼 📺
A restaurateur kills a drunken swinger, and finds that he has a profitable sideline on his hands…
Black comedy with insufficient humour to offset tastelessness.
w Richard Blackburn, Paul Bartel d Paul Bartel ph Gary Thieltges m Arlon Ober
☆ Paul Bartel, Mary Woronov, Robert Beltran, Susan Saiger, Richard Blackburn
'I wanted to make a film about two greedy, uptight people who are at the same time not so unlike you and me and Nancy and Ronnie, to keep it funny and yet communicate something about the psychology and perversity of these values … My movie touches on many things: the perversion of middle class values, the resurgence of Nixonism, machismo versus WASP fastidiousness, film noir…' – *Paul Bartel*

L'Eau Froide
France   1994   92m   colour
Ima/La Sept/Arte/SPF (Georges Benayoun, Paul Rozenberg)
aka: *Cold Water*
On the outskirts of Paris in the early 70s, two unhappy teenagers seek solace with each other after abrasive confrontations with parents and teachers.
A muted study in alienation and misery, much of it shot with a handheld camera to provide a sense of immediacy and intimacy; adult sympathies may be moderated by its youthful delight in unmotivated delinquency.
wd Olivier Assayas ph Denis Lenoir ad Gilbert Gagneux ed Luc Barnier
☆ Virginie Ledoyen, Cyprien Fouquet, Laszlo Szabo, Jean-Pierre Darroussin, Dominique Faysse, Smail Mekki, Jackie Berroyer
'Delivers a sustained emotional pummeling, underscored by a steady whisper of despair.' – *David Rooney, Variety*

'The story of a man who thought he was God!'
Ebb Tide **
US   1937   92m   Technicolor
Paramount (Lucien Hubbard)
Sailors are stranded with a dangerous fanatic on a South Sea island.
Interesting adaptation of Stevenson, notable both for its early colour and its genuinely sour, anti-romantic mood; almost unique for Hollywood in this period.
w Bertram Millhauser novel R. L. Stevenson, Lloyd Osbourne d James Hogan ph Leo Tover m Victor Young
☆ Ray Milland, Frances Farmer, Oscar Homolka, Barry Fitzgerald, Lloyd Nolan
'More pretentious as to production than dramatically. Does not suggest big b.o.' – *Variety*
† Remade 1946 as *Adventure Island.*

👪 film suitable for family viewing   📼 VHS video-cassette for the British PAL system   📺 VHS video-cassette for the British PAL system in wide screen-format   🔄 Video cassette in a computer-colourised version   ▦ American NTSC video-cassette   🔵 Laser disc

Ebbtide

Australia 1994 90m colour
Ambroco/Genesis (Craig Lahiff, Paul Davies, Helen Leake)

A lawyer, who takes over the clients of his dead partner, finds himself mixed up in murder when he investigates a case involving toxic waste.

Glossy, melodramatic and implausible thriller, with rather too much time spent on shots of Hamlin staring moodily into the far distance.

w Robert Ellis, Peter Goldsworthy, Warwick Hind
idea Craig Lahiff, Helen Leake d Craig Lahiff
ph Steve Arnold m Peter Best pd Ross Major
ed Peter Carrodus

☆ Harry Hamlin, Judy McIntosh, John Waters, Susan Lyons, John Gregg, Frankie J. Holden

Ebirah, Horror of the Deep

🎦 Japan 1966 85m Eastmancolor
Tohoscope
Toho (Tomoyuki Tanaka)

Scientists creating nuclear weapons on an island guarded by a giant lobster are foiled with the aid of Godzilla.

The usual hokum, enlivened by fight sequences that have Godzilla heading rocks with the aplomb of a football striker, and a giant moth that looks as if it has been made from an old carpet.

w Shinichi Sekizawa d Jun Fukuda ph Kazuo Yamada ad Takeo Kita sp Eiji Tsuburaya

☆ Akira Takarada, Kumi Mizuno, Akihiko Hirata, Jun Tazaki, Hideo Sunazuka, Chotaro Togin, Toru Watanabe

The Echo Murders

GB 1945 80m bw
British National

Sexton Blake conquers Nazi spies.

Feebly made addition to the short Blake cycle.

wd John Harlow

☆ David Farrar, Dennis Price, Pamela Stirling, Julien Mitchell

'About as modern as a reissue of *The Perils of Pauline*.' – *Variety*

Echo of Barbara

GB 1958 58m bw
Independent Artists

A stripper poses as the daughter of an ex-con in a plot to retrieve hidden loot.

Taut little crime support, not bad at all.

w John Kruse novel Jonathan Burke d Sidney Hayers ph Michael Reed m David Lee

☆ Mervyn Johns, Maureen Connell, Paul Stassino, Ronald Hines, Tom Bell

Echo of Diana

GB 1963 61m bw
Butcher's (John I. Phillips)

A journalist friend investigates when the wife of a missing pilot discovers that her husband seems to have had a mistress.

Stolidly directed spy drama that will keep an audience just about awake.

w Reginald Hearne d Ernest Morris ph Walter J. Harvey m Martin Slavin ad Elliott Scott ed David Hawkins

☆ Vincent Ball, Betty McDowall, Geoffrey Toone, Clare Owen, Marianne Stone, Peter Illing, Dermot Walsh, Arthur English, Leon Cortez

Echo Park *

Austria 1985 92m colour
Sasha Wein/Walter Shenson
📀 ⊙.

In a rundown area of Los Angeles, three unsuccessful youngsters await the big break.

Vaguely entertaining slice-of-life drama with good observational touches.

w Michael Ventura d Robert Dornhelm ph Karl Kofler m David Rickets

☆ Susan Dey, Thomas Hulce, Michael Bowen, Christopher Walker

Echoes of a Summer

US/Canada 1975 98m Eastmancolor
Beata/Castle/Astral/Bryanston (Robert L. Joseph)

An 11-year-old girl dying of heart disease spends her last summer with her parents on holiday in a Nova Scotian village.

Excruciating.

w Robert L. Joseph d Don Taylor ph John Coquillon m Terry James

☆ Jodie Foster, Richard Harris, Lois Nettleton, Geraldine Fitzgerald, William Windom, Brad Savage

'The only honest thing about this movie is its desire to make a buck.' – *Frank Rich, New York Post*

Eclipse *

Canada/Germany 1994 95m colour/bw
Pagemedia/Fire Dog/Time Medienvertieb (Camelia Frieberg, Jeremy Podeswa)

As a solar eclipse approaches in Toronto, ten people are linked through their various sexual encounters.

A stylish exercise in voyeurism and abortive relationships, in which pleasure is swiftly followed by disillusionment.

wd Jeremy Podeswa ph Miroslaw Baszak m Ernie Tollar ad Tamara Deverell ed Susan Maggi

☆ Von Flores, John Gilbert, Pascale Montpetit, Manuel Aranguiz, Maria Del Mar, Greg Ellwand, Matthew Ferguson, Earl Pastko, Daniel MacIvor, Kirsten Johnson

'Don't go near this film. It's about as interesting as watching a sunbather peel.' – *Tom Shone, Sunday Times*

'Powerful blend of casual sex, eye-catching, arty camera work and witty, sophisticated dialogue.' – *Variety*

The Eclipse **

Italy/France 1962 125m bw
Interopa-Cineriz/Paris Film (Robert and Raymond Hakim)
📀

original title: *L'Eclisse*

A young Roman woman breaks off one affair and begins another.

A portrait in depth, rather tiresomely long and with at least one totally irrelevant stock-market sequence; but superbly done for connoisseurs.

wd Michelangelo Antonioni, Tonino Guerra, Elio Bartolini, Ottiero Ottieri ph Gianni di Venanzo m Giovanni Fusco

☆ Monica Vitti, Alain Delon, Francisco Rabal

'The first time I saw the film I thought it magnificent but chill, played glitteringly ... At a second visit the passion breaks through.' – *Dilys Powell*

L'Eclisse: see The Eclipse

L'école Buissonière *

France 1948 89m bw
UGC/CGCF

US title: *I Have a New Master*

At a provincial village school, a new teacher introduces new methods and takes a while to win over the locals.

Rustic comedy-drama of a kind the French do well.

w Jean-Paul Le Chanois, Elise Freinet d Jean-Paul Le Chanois ph Marc Fossard, Maurice Pecqueux, André Dumaître m Joseph Kosma

☆ Bernard Blier, Juliette Fabre, Edouard Delmont

L'école des Facteurs **

France 1947 14m bw
Cady (Fred Orain)
📀

A village postman puts into practice what he has learned at training school.

Amusing short, full of a humane humour, which was to blossom a year later into the wonderful Jour de Fête.

wd Jacques Tati m Jean Yatove ed Marcel Moreau

☆ Jacques Tati, Paul Demange

† It was released on video together with *Cours du Soir* and *Soigne Ton Gauche* as *Tati Shorts*.

Ecologia del Delitto: see A Bay of Blood

Ecstasy: see Extase

Ed

🎦 US 1996 94m DeLuxe
Universal/Longview (Rosalie Swedlin)
📀 ⊙.

An unsuccessful baseball player discovers a chimpanzee with a talent for the game.

A sporting comedy so thin that the most human and engaging character is an animatronic ape.

w David Mickey Evans d Bill Couturie ph Alan Caso m Stephen D. Endelman pd Curtis A. Schnell ed Robert K. Lambert

☆ Matt LeBlanc, Jayne Brook, Bill Cobbs, Jack Warden, Doren Fein, Patrick Kerr, Charlie Schlatter

'Almost painfully modest in its ambition and accomplishment, this slow-pitch offering might tolerably amuse the under-10 crowd, but will prove borderline intolerable for everyone else.' – *Todd McCarthy, Variety*

Ed Wood **

US 1994 124m bw
Buena Vista/Touchstone (Denise di Novi, Tim Burton)
📀 📀 ⊙.

Biopic of the film director who has become posthumously notorious for writing and directing some of the worst movies ever made (most of which, ironically, are now available on video and laser disc).

A delightful, charming, straight-faced account of a hopelessly obsessive film-maker and transvestite which turns his ineffectual life and career into some sort of triumphant celebration of the American dream, making a success of failure; its appeal, though, may be limited to those who have experienced Wood's films.

w Scott Alexander, Larry Karaszewski book Nightmare of Ecstasy: The Life and Art of Edward D. Wood by Rudolph Grey d Tim Burton ph Stefan Czapsky m Howard Shore pd Tom Duffield ed Chris Lebenzon

☆ Johnny Depp, *Martin Landau*, Sarah Jessica Parker, Patricia Arquette, Jeffrey Jones, Vincent D'Onofrio, Bill Murray, Lisa Marie, George 'The Animal' Steele, G. D. Spradlin

'There's a strong whiff of pointlessness to the whole enterprise.' – *Terrence Rafferty, New Yorker*

'Wood was an obsessive without taste, an artist without art, and Burton, forgoing irony, celebrates the innocence, the energy, the perfection of ineptitude.' – *New York*

† Edward D. Wood Jnr (1922–1978) is best known for making *Plan 9 from Outer Space* (qv). His other films include *Bride of the Monster, Glen or Glenda?* and *Night of the Ghouls* (qqv).

🏆 Martin Landau; make-up (Rick Baker, Ve Neill, Yolanda Toussieng)

Eddie

US 1996 100m Technicolor
Buena Vista/Hollywood (David Permut, Mark Burg)
📀 📀 ⊙. ⊙

A female baseball fan is made coach of the New York Knicks by the team's new owner.

Dumb comedy of minor interest, and one that fails to exploit its central fantasy.

w Jon Connolly, David Loucka, Eric Champnella, Keith Mitchell, Steve Zacharias, Jeff Buhai d Steve Rash ph Victor Kemper m Stanley Clarke pd Dan Davis ed Richard Halsey

☆ Whoopi Goldberg, Frank Langella, Dennis Farina, Richard Jenkins, Lisa Ann Walter, John Benjamin Hickey

'Especially uninspired.' – *Variety*

Eddie and the Cruisers

US 1983 95m Technicolor
Embassy/Aurora (Joseph Brooks, Robert K. Lifton)
📀 📀 ⊙.

A high-school teacher recalls his days as a member of a 60s rock group, prompted by a journalist investigating the suicide of its charismatic lead singer.

A dully nostalgic drama, interspersed with some energetic rock and hampered by a convoluted narrative that leads nowhere; it toys with themes of change and decay but fails to develop them.

w Martin Davidson, Arlene Davidson novel P. F. Kluge d Martin Davidson ph Fred Murphy m John Cafferty ad Gary Weist ed Priscilla Nedd

☆ Tom Berenger, Michael Paré, Joe Pantoliano, Matthew Laurance, Helen Schneider, David Wilson, Michael Antunes, Ellen Barkin

† It was followed by an even less successful sequel in 1989, *Eddie and the Cruisers II: Eddie Lives*, directed by Jean-Claude Lord, with Michael Paré reprising his role as Eddie.

'It's big and bright as those banjo eyes!'

The Eddie Cantor Story

US 1953 116m Technicolor
Warner (Sidney Skolsky)

After a tough childhood on New York's east side, Israel Iskowitz becomes a famous entertainer.

Deliberately patterned after the success of The Jolson Story, this is an unhappy example of how close are

success and failure; the elements are the same, but this film suffers from unsure timing, lack of humour, rather apologetic numbers, a really dismal script and a caricature performance in the lead.

w Jerome Weidman, Ted Sherdeman, Sidney Skolsky d Alfred E. Green ph Edwin DuPar m/ly various md Ray Heindorf ch Le Roy Prinz

☆ Keefe Brasselle, Marilyn Erskine, Aline MacMahon, Arthur Franz, Alex Gerry, Gerald Mohr, William Forrest, Will Rogers Jnr, Eddie Cantor

'When I saw the rushes, I realized there was something wrong. When I read the reviews, I knew what it was: everything.' – *Keefe Brasselle*

'If that's my life, I didn't live.' – *Eddie Cantor*

† Eddie Cantor sings the songs off screen.

Eddie Holm's Second Life **

Denmark 1985 95m colour
Scenograf (Poul Arnt Thomsen)

original title: *Eddie Holms Andet Liv*

A suicidal musician is taken back through his life to discover what drove him to end it.

Witty, black comedy of love, death and family life.

w Bjarne Henriksen, Gert Henriksen d Esben Hüilund Carlsen ph Ole Schultz m Bo Lykke Jürgensen ed Jetter Allarp

☆ Kristian Halken, Pernille Hansen, Lisbet Lundquist, Claus Nissen, Holger Boland, Karen Marie Lowert, Frederik Esbensen

Eddie Macon's Run

US 1983 95m Technicolor
Universal/Martin Bregman (Louis A. Stroller)
📀 ⊙.

A man innocently convicted escapes and hotfoots it back home.

Old-style chase film marred by passages of sex and crude backwoods violence.

wd Jeff Kanew novel James McLendon ph James A. Contner m Norton Buffalo ed Jeff Kanew

☆ John Schneider, Kirk Douglas, Lee Purcell, Leah Ayres

The Eddy Duchin Story

US 1956 123m Technicolor Cinemascope
Columbia (Jonie Taps, Jerry Wald)
📀 📀 ⊙. ⊙

The success story of a pianist who died of leukemia.

Predictable, glossy, sentimental musical biopic.

w Samuel Taylor story Leo Katcher d George Sidney ph Harry Stradling m George Duning piano Carmen Cavallero

☆ Tyrone Power, Kim Novak, Victoria Shaw, James Whitmore, Shepperd Strudwick, Frieda Inescort, Gloria Holden, Larry Keating

🎵 Leo Katcher; Harry Stradling; George Duning

Eden Valley

GB 1994 95m colour
Amber/Channel 4/NDR/Northern Arts

A youth, arrested for theft, is given six months to redeem himself, and goes to stay with his father on some isolated fields where he breeds trotting horses.

An austere slice-of-life drama, closer to the British documentary traditions than to normal features; the narrative ends at the point where it begins to get interesting.

☆ Brian Hogg, Darren Bell, Mike Elliott, Jimmy Killeen, Wayne Buck, Kevin Buck, Rose Laidler, Brian Laidler

'The major investment here has been made in terms of time and energy rather than money and the dividend – a self-contained, distinctive film which eschews clichés and sentimentality – pays off.' – *Jo Comino, Sight and Sound*

† Amber Films is a collective and does not provide individual production credits. Its team was: Richard Grassick, Ellen Hare, Sirkka Lisa Konttinen, Murray Martin, Pat McCarthy, Lorna Powell, Pete Roberts.

Edes Emma, Draga Böbe – Vazlatok, Aktok: see Dear Emma, Sweet Böbe

Edgar Wallace

Between 1960 and 1966 no fewer than 46 second features emerged from Jack Greenwood's production unit at the London suburban studios of Merton Park, under the Edgar Wallace banner and prefaced by a sinister revolving bust of the author (though few had very much to do with his original stories).

All maintained a better standard than any other crime second features of the period, and a few were seized on with delight by the critics. They were subsequently popular on television, though the Independent Broadcasting Authority banned repeats on the grounds that they were without merit. In this complete list, details are given for the more interesting items:

The Clue of the Twisted Candle
A Marriage of Convenience
The Man Who Was Nobody
The Clue of the New Pin*, w Philip Mackie, d Allan Davis, with Paul Daneman, Bernard Archard
Partners in Crime
The Fourth Square
The Man at the Carlton Tower
The Clue of the Silver Key
Attempt to Kill
The Sinister Man*, w Philip Mackie , d Clive Donner, with Patrick Allen, John Bentley
Never Back Losers
Man Detained
Ricochet
The Double
The Rivals
To Have and to Hold
The Partner
Five to One
Accidental Death
We Shall See
Downfall
The Verdict
Who Was Maddox?*, w Roger Marshall , d Geoffrey Nethercott, with Bernard Lee, Finlay Currie
Act of Murder*, w Lewis Davidson , d Alan Bridges, with John Carson, Anthony Bate
Face of a Stranger
Never Mention Murder*, w Robert Banks Stewart , d John Nelson Burton, with Maxine Audley, Dudley Foster
The Main Chance
Game for Three Losers
Dead Man's Chest
Change Partners
Strangler's Web*, w George Baxt , d John Moxey, with Griffith Jones, Gerald Harper
Backfire
Candidate for Murder*, w Lukas Heller , d David Villers, with Michael Gough, John Justin
Flat Two
The Share-Out
Number Six
Time to Remember
Playback*, w Robert Banks Stewart , d Quentin Lawrence, with Barry Foster, Dinsdale Landen
Margit Saad
Solo for Sparrow
Locker 69
Death Trap
The Set-Up
On the Run
The £20,000 Kiss
Incident at Midnight
Return to Sender

'They were fighting over a woman until the plane went down. Now, their only chance for survival is each other.'

The Edge *
US   1997   117m   DeLuxe   Panavision
TCF (Art Linson)
When their plane crashes, a billionaire and a fashion photographer, whom he suspects of lusting after his wife, a fashion model, are stranded in an Alaskan wilderness inhabited by a ferocious bear.
Enjoyable hokum amidst splendid scenery, concentrating on the battle for supremacy between two very different men.
w David Mamet d Lee Tamahori ph Donald M. McAlpine m Jerry Goldsmith pd Wolf Kroeger ed Neil Travis
☆ Anthony Hopkins, Alec Baldwin, Elle Macpherson, Harold Perrineau, L. Q. Jones, Kathleen Wilhoite
'A tense, pleasurably visceral battle-of-wits thriller played out against a spectacular wilderness background.' – Todd McCarthy, Variety

Edge of Darkness *
US   1943   124m   bw
Warner (Henry Blanke)
Norwegian village patriots resist the Nazis.
High-intentioned, ambitiously cast but ultimately bathetic resistance melodrama, high principled down to its tragic finale but compromised by backlot shooting and the presence of Errol Flynn.
w Robert Rossen d Lewis Milestone ph Sid Hickox m Franz Waxman
☆ Errol Flynn, Ann Sheridan, Walter Huston, Judith Anderson, Ruth Gordon, Nancy Coleman, Helmut Dantine, Morris Carnovsky, Charles Dingle, John Beal, Richard Fraser, Helene Thimig
'It is not a tea party. It is an icy shower turned loose on audiences in the hope of driving home what this war is about.' – Motion Picture Herald

Edge of Divorce: see Background

Edge of Doom
US   1950   97m   bw
Samuel Goldwyn
GB title: Stronger than Fear
A desperate youth kills a priest and struggles with his conscience.
A sanctimonious weirdie, extremely odd coming from this producer, and unhappily re-edited before release. Someone was interested enough to want to make it, but it seems to have been killed by the cast and the front office.
w Philip Yordan novel Leo Brady d Mark Robson ph Harry Stradling m Hugo Friedhofer
☆ Dana Andrews, Farley Granger, Joan Evans, Robert Keith, Paul Stewart, Mala Powers, Adele Jergens, Harold Vermilyea, Mabel Paige

Edge of Eternity *
US   1959   80m   Technicolor   Cinemascope
Columbia/Thunderbird (Kendrick Sweet)
A Grand Canyon sheriff traces three murders to an ownership struggle over a disused mine.
Routine but suspenseful thriller with splendid locations.
w Knut Swenson, Richard Collins d Don Siegel ph Burnett Guffey m Daniele Amfitheatrof
☆ Cornel Wilde, Victoria Shaw, Edgar Buchanan, Mickey Shaughnessy, Jack Elam

Edge of Hell
US   1956   76m   bw
Universal-International (Hugo Haas)
In a slummy rooming house, a beggar who lives by his dog's talents falls for the new lodger.
Self-parodying sub-Jannings melodrama with an unlikely star.
wd Hugo Haas ph Edward Fitzgerald m Ernest Gold
☆ Hugo Haas, Francesca de Scaffa, Ken Carlton, June Hammerstein

Edge of Honor *
US   1991   92m   Western Cine colour
Merit Badge/Guerilla Film Unit (Jay B. Davis, Peter Garrity, David O'Malley)
Scouts are attacked by a gang of ruthless arms smugglers after they discover a cache of weapons hidden in a forest.
A violent but effective action adventure intended for a teenage audience.
w Mark Rosenbaum, Michael Spence, David O'Malley d Michael Spence ph Billy Dickson m William Stromberg pd Charles Armstrong ed Ellen Keneshea
☆ Corey Feldman, Meredith Salenger, Scott Reeves, Ken Jenkins, Don Swayze, Christopher Neame
'A great action movie with a gung-ho performance by Don Swayze.' – Sight and Sound

Edge of Sanity
GB   1988   90m   Eastmancolor
Palace/Allied Vision (Edward Simons, Harry Alan Towers)
Dr Jekyll, under the influence of drugs, becomes Jack the Ripper.
Dire variation on Robert Louis Stevenson's classic.
w J. P. Felix, Ron Raley d Gerard Kikoine ph Tony Spratling m Frederic Talgorn pd Jean Charles Dedieu ed Malcolm Cooke

☆ Anthony Perkins, Glynis Barber, Sarah Maur-Thorp, David Lodge, Ben Cole, Ray Jewers, Jill Melford

Edge of the City **
US   1957   85m   bw
MGM/Jonathan (David Susskind, Jim di Ganci)
GB title: A Man is Ten Feet Tall
Racial tensions lead to tragedy in the railroad yards of New York's waterfront.
Tense, brutal melodrama, which has historical interest as an effective opening-up in cinematic terms of a TV play, in its imitation of On the Waterfront, and in its rebel hero and relaxed black friend.
w Robert Alan Aurthur play Robert Alan Aurthur d Martin Ritt ph Joseph Brun m Leonard Rosenman
☆ Sidney Poitier, John Cassavetes, Jack Warden, Kathleen Maguire, Ruby Dee, Robert Simon, Ruth White

The Edge of the Horizon *
France/Portugal/Spain   1993   90m   colour
Films do Principe Real/CTN/Origen (António da Cunha Telles)
original title: Le Fil de l'Horizon
A Lisbon mortuary worker is puzzled to discover that the body of a murdered 25-year-old man resembles him as he was 30 years ago.
Intriguing, slow-paced psychological and philosophical mystery, heavily reliant on the melancholy charm of Brasseur's performance as a man who feels he should not be alive.
w Christopher Frank, Jean Nachbaur novel Il Fillo dell'Orizonte by Antonio Tabucchi d Fernando Lopes ph Javier Aguirresarobe m Zbigniew Preisner ad Jasmim de Matos ed Jacques Witta
☆ Claude Brasseur, Andrea Ferreol, Antonio Valero, Ana Padrão, Miguel Guilherme

Edge of the World **
GB   1937   80m   bw
GFD/Rock (Joe Rock)
Life, love and death on Foula, a remote Shetland island.
Rare for its time, a vigorous location drama in the Flaherty tradition; sometimes naïve, usually exhilarating.
wd Michael Powell ph Ernest Palmer, Monty Berman, Skeets Kelly m Lambert Williamson ed Derek Twist
☆ Niall MacGinnis, Belle Chrystal, John Laurie, Finlay Currie, Eric Berry
'Scant of plot and unlikely to be hailed by the public at large.' – Variety

'The love of a woman ... the courage of a fighting America ... lifted him from obscurity to thrilling fame!'

Edison the Man **
US   1940   107m   bw
MGM (John W. Considine Jnr)
Edison struggles for years in poverty before becoming famous as the inventor of the electric light bulb.
Standard, well-made biopic following on from Young Tom Edison; reasonably absorbing, but slightly suspect in its facts.
w Dore Schary, Talbot Jennings, Bradbury Foote, Hugo Butler d Clarence Brown ph Harold Rosson m Herbert Stothart
☆ Spencer Tracy, Rita Johnson, Lynne Overman, Charles Coburn, Gene Lockhart, Henry Travers, Felix Bressart
§ Dore Schary, Hugo Butler (original story)

Edith and Marcel *
France   1984   140m   Eastmancolor
Gala/Cannon/Film 13/Parafrance/Miramax (Tania Zazulinsky)
Two French idols indulge in a tragic love affair.
Effective biopic based on the affair between singer Edith Piaf and boxer Marcel Cerdan.
wd Claude Lelouch ph Jean Boffety m Francis Lai ed Hugues Darmois
☆ Evelyne Bouix, Jacques Villeret, Francis Huster, Jean-Claude Brialy, Jean Bouise, Charles Gérard, Marcel Cerdan Jnr

Edouard et Caroline **
France   1951   99m   bw
UGC/CICC
A young pianist and his wife quarrel while preparing for an important recital.
Gay, slight, charming comedy, a two-hander taking place within the course of a few hours.
w Annette Wademant, Jacques Becker d Jacques Becker ph Robert Le Fèbvre m Jean-Jacques Grunenwald
☆ Daniel Gélin, Anne Vernon, Jacques François, William Tubbs, Jean Galland, Elina Labourdette, Betty Stockfeld
'It lifts its weighty trivialities into a world of enchantment.' – Sunday Times

Ed's Next Move
US   1996   88m   DeLuxe
Orion/Ed's Films (Sally Roy)
A young, socially inept scientist moves from Wisconsin to New York and falls in love with a singer.
Slight romantic comedy that tries too hard to charm; it most resembles a situation comedy stretched slowly beyond its limits.
wd John Walsh ph Peter Nelson m Benny Golson pd Kristin Vallow ed Pamela Martin
☆ Matt Ross, Callie Thorne, Kevin Carroll, Ramsey Faragallah, Nina Sheveleva
'A delightful, sweet first film.' – Variety

'The Story Of A Nobody Everybody Is Watching!'

EdTV *
US   1999   122m   DeLuxe
Universal/Imagine (Brian Grazer, Ron Howard)
A video-store clerk becomes a star when his life is shown on cable television 24 hours a day.
Mildly amusing comedy about modern-day celebrity and the public fascination with people who are famous for being famous.
w Lowell Ganz, Babaloo Mandel screenplay Louis XIX: Roi des ondes by Emile Gaudreault, Sylvie Bouchard d Ron Howard ph John Schwartzman m Randy Edelman pd Michael Corenblith ed Mike Hill, Dan Hanley
☆ Matthew McConaughey, Jenna Elfman, Woody Harrelson, Ellen DeGeneres, Sally Kirkland, Martin Landau, Rob Reiner, Dennis Hopper, Elizabeth Hurley, Clint Howard
'Good humored, deceptively easygoing satire.' – Janet Maslin, New York Times

Educated Evans
GB   1936   bw
Warner (Irving Asher)
A racetrack bookie becomes a trainer.
Rather unexciting vehicle for a star who 'arrived' too suddenly to be prepared for it.
w Frank Launder and Robert Edmunds story Edgar Wallace d William Beaudine ph Basil Emmott ad Peter Proud
☆ Max Miller, Nancy O'Neil, Clarice Mayne, Albert Whelan, Hal Walters
† A sequel followed in 1938: Thank Evans

Educating Rita *
GB   1983   110m   Technicolor
Rank/Acorn (Lewis Gilbert)
A cheerful young hairdresser improves her knowledge of English Literature by enrolling on an Open University course.
Rather dismal, thinly characterized and ill-lit variation on Pygmalion, with endless talk leading nowhere (it was originally a two-character play). Due to its Liverpudlian modishness it achieved surprising box-office success.
w Willy Russell play Willy Russell d Lewis Gilbert ph Frank Watts m David Hentschel
☆ Michael Caine, Julie Walters, Michael Williams, Maureen Lipman
'If only I'd been able to believe they were actually reading the books, everything else would have fallen into place.' – Roger Ebert
§ Michael Caine; Julie Walters; Willy Russell
▼ best picture; Michael Caine; Julie Walters

Edvard Munch *
Norway/Sweden   1976   215m   colour
New Yorker/SR
The life of the 19th-century Norwegian expressionist painter.

A yawn for the majority but a delight for connoisseurs of a certain kind; with a wholly non-professional cast.
wd Peter Watkins
☆ Geir Westby, Gro Fraas, Johan Halsborg, Lotte Teig

Edward II **

GB 1991 90m colour
Palace/Edward II/Working Title/British Screen/BBC (Steve Clark-Hall, Antony Root)
⬚ ▤ ⌒

Edward II's love for Piers Gaveston leads to his downfall.
An explicitly homosexual reworking of Marlowe's play, done in modern dress and given a contemporary twist.
w Derek Jarman, Stephen McBride, Ken Butler play Christopher Marlowe d Derek Jarman ph Ian Wilson m Simon Fisher Turner pd Christopher Hobbs ed George Akers
☆ Steven Waddington, Kevin Collins, Andrew Tiernan, John Lynch, Dudley Sutton, Tilda Swinton, Jerome Flynn, Jody Graber, Nigel Terry, Annie Lennox
'Provocative and challenging ... likely will be the director's most commercial production to date.' – *Variety*
'Through the miracle of cinema, two sensibilities and centuries become wondrously fused. Bold, passionate and savagely beautiful.' – *Geoff Brown, The Times*

Edward My Son

GB 1949 112m bw
MGM (Edwin H. Knopf)

A rich, unscrupulous man remembers the people he has made unhappy, and the son to whom he never behaved as a father should.
Unsatisfactory, rather ugly-looking adaptation of a gripping piece of theatre, with casting and direction remarkably uncertain from such professionals.
w Donald Ogden Stewart play Robert Morley d George Cukor ph F. A. Young m John Wooldridge, Malcolm Sargent
☆ Spencer Tracy, Deborah Kerr, Ian Hunter, James Donald, Leueen McGrath, Mervyn Johns
⚇ Deborah Kerr

Edward Scissorhands **

⬚⬚ US 1990 98m colour
Fox (Denise de Novi, Tim Burton)
⬚ ⬚ ▤ ⌒ ⌒

A boy with artificial hands upsets the community in which he lives.
Bizarre fairy-tale with a good deal of charm.
w Caroline Thompson story Tim Burton d Tim Burton ph Stefan Czapsky m Danny Elfman pd Bo Welch ad Tom Duffield ed Richard Halsey
☆ Johnny Depp, Winona Ryder, Dianne Wiest, Anthony Michael Hall, Alan Arkin, Kathy Baker, Robert Oliver, Conchata Ferrell, Vincent Price
'A delightful and delicate comic fable.' – *Variety*
⚇ best makeup
🏆 Bo Welch

The Eel **

Japan 1996 117m colour
Artificial Eye/KSS/Eisei Gekijo/Groove/Shochiku (Hisa Iino)

When he is released from prison, an introverted wife-murderer opens a barber's shop and takes an unstable woman as his assistant.
Enigmatic, though simple-seeming, drama of a man coming to terms with himself and his actions; the narrative takes on a dream-like quality.
w Motofumi Tomikawa, Daisuke Tengan, Shohei Imamura story Glittering in the Dark by Akira Yoshimura d Shohei Imamura ph Shigeru Komatsubara m Shinichiro Ikebe pd Hisao Inagaki ed Hajime Okayasu
☆ Koji Yakusho, Misa Shimizu, Fujio Tsuneta, Mitsuko Baisho, Makoto Sato, Akira Emoto, Sho Aihara, Ken Kobayashi, Sabu Kawahara, Etsuko Ichihara
'What starts out as intriguing turns into simply baffling.' – *Empire*
'It's too early to be sure whether The Eel is a great Imamura film or merely a good one.' – *Tony Rayns, Sight and Sound*
† The film won the Palme d'Or at the 1997 Cannes Film Festival.

The Effect of Gamma Rays on Man-in-the-Moon Marigolds

US 1972 101m DeLuxe
Newman-Foreman (Paul Newman)

A slatternly middle-aged woman dreams of better times for herself and her children.
Well-written but essentially banal and pretentious domestic drama, the kind of film that only gets made when powerful stars see in it a juicy role.
w Alvin Sargent play Paul Zindel d Paul Newman ph Adam Holender m Maurice Jarre
☆ Joanne Woodward, Nell Potts, Roberta Wallach, Judith Lowry

Effi Briest *

West Germany 1974 140m bw
Tango Film (Rainer Werner Fassbinder)
⬚ ▤

original title: Fontane Effi Briest
A teenage girl is married to a rich baron, but fails to understand what is expected of her.
Overlong but often fascinating picture of a vanished society in which not the slightest weakening of structure is permitted.
wd Rainer Werner Fassbinder novel Theodor Fontane ph Jürgen Jürges, Dietrich Lohmann m from Saint-Saëns
☆ Hanna Schygulla, Wolfgang Schenck, Ulli Lommel, Karl-Heinz Böhm, Ursula Strätz
'Beautiful. It renders the book as fully and texturally as could be possible in 140 minutes, and it's a work, in and of itself, intrinsically cinematic.' – *Stanley Kauffmann*

The Efficiency Expert: see Spotswood

L'Effrontée: see The Impudent Girl

The Egg and I *

US 1947 104m bw
U-I (Chester Erskine)
▤ ⌒

A city couple try to become gentleman farmers.
Mild, pleasant comedy notable chiefly for introducing a hillbilly couple, Ma and Pa Kettle, who went on, in the personae of Main and Kilbride, to make several later features. (See under Kettles.)
w Chester Erskine, Fred Finklehoffe novel Betty Macdonald d Chester Erskine ph Milton Krasner m Frank Skinner
☆ Claudette Colbert, Fred MacMurray, Marjorie Main, Percy Kilbride, Louise Allbritton, Richard Long, Billy House, Ida Moore, Donald MacBride
'Marjorie Main, in an occasional fit of fine, wild comedy, picks the show up and brandishes it as if she were wringing its neck. I wish to God she had.' – *James Agee*
⚇ Marjorie Main

Egon Schiele: Excess and Punishment

(dubbed)
Austria/Germany/France 1980 90m colour
Gamma/Stand'Art/Cineproduction/Profinanz/Jadran/V-Film/Dieter Geissler
⬚

original title: Egon Schiele: Exzess und Bestrafung
In prison awaiting trial for corrupting a minor, an artist recalls his past, while his model attempts to obtain his release.
Uninvolving biopic of the Austrian Expressionist artist Egon Schiele (1890–1918), which gives the impression that he never painted anything other than naked women.
w Herbert Vesely, Leo Tichat d Herbert Vesely ph Rudolf Blahaček m Brian Eno, Anton von Webern, Felix Mendelssohn-Bartholy
☆ Mathieu Carrière, Jane Birkin, Nina Fallenstein, Kristina Van Eyck, Marcel Ophuls
† The British video release runs for 81m.

Egymásra Nézve: see Another Way

'10,965 pyramids! 5,337 dancing girls! One million swaying bulrushes! 802 sacred bulls!'

The Egyptian *

US 1954 140m DeLuxe Cinemascope
TCF (Darryl F. Zanuck)
▤ ⌒

In ancient Egypt an abandoned baby grows up to be physician to the pharaoh.
More risible than reasonable, sounding more like a parody than the real thing, this pretentious epic from a bestseller flounders helplessly between its highlights but has moments of good humour and makes an excellent

example of the pictures they don't make 'em like any more.
w Philip Dunne, Casey Robinson novel Mika Waltari d Michael Curtiz ph Leon Shamroy m Bernard Herrmann, Alfred Newman ad Lyle Wheeler, George W. Davis
☆ Edmund Purdom, Victor Mature, Peter Ustinov, Bella Darvi, Gene Tierney, Michael Wilding, Jean Simmons, Judith Evelyn, Henry Daniell, John Carradine, Carl Benton Reid
'The novel ... supplied the reader with enough occurrences and customs of Akhnaton's time ... to hide some of the more obvious contrivances of the story. The film does not do this.' – *Carolyn Harrow, Films in Review*
⚇ Leon Shamroy

Die Ehe der Maria Braun: see The Marriage of Maria Braun

Ehi, Amico ... C'è Sabata, Hai Chiuso: see Sabata

The Eiger Sanction *

US 1975 125m Technicolor Panavision
Universal/Malpaso (Jennings Lang)
⬚ ▤ ⊘ ⊘ ⌒

An art teacher returns to the CIA as an exterminator, and finds himself in a party climbing the Eiger.
Silly spy melodrama with some breathtaking mountain sequences.
w Warren B. Murphy, Hal Dresner, Rod Whitaker novel Trevanian d Clint Eastwood ph Frank Stanley, John Cleare, Jeff Schoolfield, Peter Pilafian, Pete White m John Williams
☆ Clint Eastwood, George Kennedy, Vonetta McGee, Jack Cassidy, Heidi Bruhl, Thayer David
'All the villains have been constructed from prefabricated Bond models.' – *Richard Combs*

'You can't prepare for where the truth will take you.'

8mm

US 1999 119m Technicolor
Columbia (Gavin Polone, Judy Hofflund, Joel Schumacher)
⬚ ⊘ ⊘ ⌒

A wealthy widow discovers among her dead husband's possessions a videocassette showing the apparent murder of a teenage girl, and hires an investigator to find out the girl's identity.
A gloating, exploitative thriller about pornography in Los Angeles; it develops a hectoring tone that cannot be justified by script, direction or acting.
w Andrew Kevin Walker d Joel Schumacher ph Robert Elswit m Mychael Danna pd Gary Wissner ed Mark Stevens
☆ Nicolas Cage, Joaquin Phoenix, James Gandolfini, Peter Stormare, Anthony Heald, Chris Bauer, Catherine Keener, Myra Carter, Amy Morton
'Loathsome crap ... Coming generations of late-night video hounds may recognize it, along with Oliver Stone's The Doors, as one of the most unintentionally hilarious attempts at serious filmmaking in cinema history.' – *Andrew O'Hehir, Salon*
'Delves into the perverse underworld of the pornography business, shocking audiences with the realization that sex and violence can be so dull.' – *Janet Maslin, New York Times*

Eight and a Half ****

Italy 1963 138m bw
Cineriz (Angelo Rizzoli)
⬚ ▤ ⌒

original title: Otto e Mezzo
A successful film director on the verge of a nervous breakdown has conflicting fantasies about his life.
A Fellini self-portrait in which anything goes.
w Federico Fellini, Ennio Flaiano, Tullio Pinelli, Brunello Rondi d Federico Fellini ph Gianni di Venanzo m Nino Rota ad Piero Gherardi
☆ Marcello Mastroianni, Claudia Cardinale, Anouk Aimée, Sandra Milo, Rossella Falk, Barbara Steele, Madeleine Lebeau
'The whole may add up to a magnificent folly, but it is too singular, too candid, too vividly and insistently alive to be judged as being in any way diminishing.' – *Peter John Dyer, MFB*
'Fellini's intellectualizing is not even like dogs dancing; it is not done well, nor does it surprise us that it is done at all. It merely palls on us, and finally appals us.' – *John Simon*

'A de luxe glorification of creative crisis, visually arresting but in some essential way conventional-minded.' – *Pauline Kael, 70s*
⚇ best foreign film
🏆 script; direction

8 Heads in a Duffell Bag

US 1997 95m DeLuxe
Rank/Orion (Brad Krevoy, Steve Stabler, John Bertolli)
⬚⬚

A gangster attempts to find his bag, containing the heads of his boss's enemies, after it is mixed up with one belonging to a medical student.
Gruesome and tasteless comedy that hasn't even the saving grace of being amusing.
wd Tom Schulman ph Adam Holender m Andrew Gross pd Paul Peters ed David Holden
☆ Joe Pesci, Kristy Swanson, David Spade, George Hamilton, Dyan Cannon, Andy Comeau, Todd Luiso
'A charmless mess.' – *Richard Williams, Guardian*
'About as funny as being a guest at the St Valentine's Day Massacre.' – *Philip French, Observer*

Eight Iron Men

US 1952 80m bw
Columbia/Stanley Kramer

In the ruins of an Italian village, eight American infantrymen wait for relief.
Quickie war film in which everyone talks a lot and they all survive; from the time when Kramer was discovering how fast he could turn 'em out.
w Harry Brown play A Sound of Hunting by Harry Brown d Edward Dmytryk ph Roy Hunt m Leith Stevens pd Rudolph Sternad
☆ Bonar Colleano, Lee Marvin, Arthur Franz, Richard Kiley, Nick Dennis, James Griffith, Dick Moore, George Cooper

Eight Men Out ***

US 1988 119m colour
Rank/Orion (Sarah Pillsbury, Midge Sandford)
⬚ ▤ ⊘ ⌒

In 1919 members of the great Chicago White Sox baseball team take bribes to lose the World Series.
Absorbing drama, excellently filmed, with good ensemble acting.
w John Sayles book Eliot Asinof d John Sayles ph Robert Richardson m Mason Daring pd Nora Chavooshian ed John Tintori
☆ John Cusack, Clifton James, Michael Lerner, Christopher Lloyd, John Mahoney, Charlie Sheen, David Strathairn, D. B. Sweeney

8 Million Ways to Die

US 1986 115m bw
Tri-Star/PSO (Steve Roth)
▤

An alcoholic ex-cop tries to discover the killer of a prostitute who had asked him to protect her.
Dreary thriller of redemption from the low life; its pace is numbingly slow, despite the insistent score trying to impose a faster rhythm.
w Oliver Stone, David Lee Henry novel Lawrence Block d Hal Ashby ph Stephen H. Burum m James Newton Howard pd Michael Haller ed Stuart Pappé, Robert Lawrence
☆ Jeff Bridges, Rosanna Arquette, Alexandra Paul, Andy Garcia, Randy Brooks

Eight O'Clock Walk

GB 1953 87m bw
British Lion/George King
⬚

A young barrister proves a taxi driver innocent of murder.
Minor-league courtroom stuff, an adequate time-passer.
w Katherine Strueby, Guy Morgan story Jack Roffey, Gordon Harbord d Lance Comfort ph Brendan Stafford m George Melachrino
☆ Richard Attenborough, Derek Farr, Cathy O'Donnell, Ian Hunter, Maurice Denham, Bruce Seton, Harry Welchman

Eight on the Lam

US 1966 107m DeLuxe
United Artists/Hope Enterprises (Bill Lawrence)
GB title: *Eight on the Run*
A bank teller is suspected of embezzlement and goes on the run with his seven children.
Feeble comedy punctuated by even feebler chases; the star had lost his comic character.

w Albert E. Lewin, Burt Styler, Bob Fisher, Arthur Marx d George Marshall ph Alan Stensvold m George Romanis
☆ Bob Hope, Phyllis Diller, Jonathan Winters, Shirley Eaton, Jill St John

Eight on the Run: see *Eight on the Lam*

'The sport made him a Legend. His heart made him a Hero.'
8 Seconds
US   1994   105m   Film House colour
First Independent/New Line/Jersey Films (Michael Shamberg)
The former world bull-riding champion wins back his title and his wife after losing both to booze.
Based on the life of Lane Frost, this is a mundane biopic of limited interest.
w Monte Merrick d John G. Avildsen ph Victor Hammer m Bill Conti pd William J. Cassidy ed J. Douglas Seelig
☆ Luke Perry, Stephen Baldwin, James Rebhorn, Red Mitchell, Ronnie Claire Edwards, Linden Ashby, Cynthia Geary, Carrie Snodgress
'Never more than occasionally diverting, and in spite of some spirited playing is strictly for Luke Perry fans and rodeo nuts.' – *Anwar Brett, Film Review*

18 Again!
US   1988   100m   DeLuxe
Entertainment/New World (Walter Coblenz)
After a car crash, the mind of an 81-year-old grandfather is switched into the body of his 18-year-old grandson.
Feeblest of the body-swap cycle of films, with little to entertain.
w Josh Goldstein, Jonathan Prince d Paul Flaherty ph Stephen M. Katz m Billy Goldenberg pd Dena Roth ed Danford B. Greene
☆ George Burns, Charlie Schlatter, Tony Roberts, Anita Morris, Miriam Flynn, Jennifer Runyon, Red Buttons

The Eighth Day *
France   1996   114m   colour
Polygram/Pan-Européene/Home Made/TF1/RTL/TVI/Working Title/DA (Philippe Godeau)
original title: *Le Huitième Jour*
A salesman brefriends a young runaway with Downs syndrome.
Accomplished and sentimental comedy, with an unpleasant shock ending, of one man's redemption, in which emotional manipulation predominates.
wd Jaco Van Dormael ph Walther Van Ende m Pierre Van Dormael ad Hubert Pouille ed Susana Rossberg
☆ Daniel Auteuil, Pascal Duquenne, Miou-Miou, Isabelle Sadoyan, Henri Garcin, Michele Maes
'The result is a European film aiming at sophistication that becomes more and more like a Hollywood epic about idiots savants.' – *Derek Malcolm, Guardian*
† Daniel Auteuil and Pascal Duquenne shared the best actor award at the 1996 Cannes Film Festival.

84 Charing Cross Road **
GB   1986   97m   Rank Colour
Columbia/Brooksfilm (Geoffrey Helman)
A New York woman conducts a long correspondence with an antiquarian bookseller in London.
Pleasant picturization of a now famous book which had already been seen on TV and stage.
w Hugh Whitemore book Helene Hanff d David Jones ph Brian West m George Fenton pd Eileen Diss, Edward Pisoni
☆ Anne Bancroft, Anthony Hopkins, Judi Dench, Maurice Denham, Jean de Baer, Eleanor David
ʊ Anne Bancroft

84 Charlie Mopic *
US   1989   95m   colour
Charlie Mopic Company (Michael Nolin)
An army cameraman and an inexperienced officer accompany a reconnaissance patrol in Vietnam.
A documentary-style account of war as it affects the individual, as seen from the subjective viewpoint of the cameraman.

wd Patrick Duncan ph Alan Casco m Donovan ad Douglas Dick ed Stephen Purvis
☆ Jonathan Emerson, Nicholas Cascone, Jason Tomlins, Christopher Burgard, Glenn Morshower, Richard Brooks, Byron Thames

80,000 Suspects *
GB   1963   113m   bw   Cinemascope
Rank/Val Guest
A smallpox epidemic terrorizes the city of Bath.
Predictable melodrama which adequately passes the time.
wd Val Guest novel *The Pillars of Midnight* by Elleston Trevor ph Arthur Grant m Stanley Black ad Geoffrey Tozer ed Bill Lenny
☆ Claire Bloom, Richard Johnson, Yolande Donlan, Cyril Cusack, Michael Goodliffe, Mervyn Johns, Kay Walsh, Basil Dignam, Ray Barrett

Einmal Ku'damm und Zurück: see *Girl In a Boot*

Él **
Mexico   1952   91m   bw
Nacional Film (Oscar Dancigers)
aka: *This Strange Passion*
aka: *Torments*
A middle-aged aristocrat marries a beautiful young girl and falls victim to insane jealousy.
A tragi-comic case history with chilling and memorable details; not one of its director's great works, but an engaging minor one.
w Luis Buñuel, Luis Alcoriza novel *Pensamientos* by Mercedes Pinto d *Luis Buñuel* ph Gabriel Figueroa m Luis Hernandez Breton
☆ Arturo de Cordova, Delia Garces, Luis Beristain, Aurora Walker

El Chucho, Quién Sabe?: see *A Bullet for the General*

El Cid *
╫╫   US/Spain   1961   184m   Super Technirama
Samuel Bronston
A legendary 11th-century hero drives the Moors from Spain.
Endless glum epic with splendid action sequences as befits the high budget.
w Fredric M. Frank, Philip Yordan, Ben Barzman d Anthony Mann ph Robert Krasker m Miklos Rozsa
☆ Charlton Heston, Sophia Loren, Raf Vallone, Genevieve Page, John Fraser, Gary Raymond, Herbert Lom, Hurd Hatfield, Massimo Serato, Andrew Cruickshank, Michael Hordern, Douglas Wilmer, Frank Thring
'A Lone Ranger liberation tale.' – *Judith Crist*
† Ben Barzman, a screenwriter who was blacklisted in the 50s, had his name restored to the credits in 1999.
♫ Miklos Rozsa; song 'The Falcon and the Dove' (mMiklos Rozsa, lyPaul Francis Webster)

El Condor
US   1970   102m   Technicolor
National General/Carthay Continental (André de Toth)
An escaped convict and a con man seek a fortune in gold believed to be hidden in a fortress in the Mexican desert.
Blood and guts Western with few moments of interest.
w Larry Cohen, Steven Carabatsos d John Guillermin ph Henri Persin m Maurice Jarre
☆ Jim Brown, Lee Van Cleef, Patrick O'Neal, Marianna Hill, Iron Eyes Cody, Elisha Cook Jnr
'The kind of fun you can find at your friendly neighbourhood abattoir.' – *Judith Crist, 1977*

'The big one with the big two!'
El Dorado *
US   1967   126m   Technicolor
Paramount/Laurel (Howard Hawks)
A gunfighter and a drunken sheriff tackle a villainous cattle baron.
Easy-going, semi-somnolent, generally likeable but disappointing Western ... an old man's movie all round.
w Leigh Brackett novel *The Stars in Their Courses* by Harry Joe Brown d Howard Hawks ph Harold Rosson m Nelson Riddle ad Hal Pereira, Carl Anderson ed John Woodcock

☆ John Wayne, Robert Mitchum, James Caan, Charlene Holt, Michele Carey, Ed Asner, Arthur Hunnicutt, R. G. Armstrong, Paul Fix, Christopher George
'A rumbustious lament for the good days of the bad old west.' – *Tom Milne*
'A claustrophobic, careless and cliché-ridden thing, wavering constantly between campy self-deprecation and pretentious pomposity.' – *Richard Schickel*
'Wayne and Mitchum, parodying themselves while looking exhausted.' – *Pauline Kael, 70s*

El Dorado *
France/Spain   1988   123m   colour
Palace/Iberoamericana/Chrysalide/UGC-Top1/FR3/Canal Plus (Victor Albarran)
Conquistadores set out from Peru to find El Dorado, the fabled land of gold.
Ambitious but flawed epic, handicapped by its ponderous approach.
d Carlos Saura ph Teo Escamilla md Alejandro Masso ad Terry Pritchard ed Pedro del Rey
☆ Omero Antonutti, Eusebio Poncela, Lambert Wilson, Gabriela Roel, Jose Sancho, Feodor Atkine, Patxi Bisquert, Francisco Algora, Francisco Merino

El Greco
Italy/France   1964   94m   Eastmancolor Cinemascope
(TCF) Artistiche Internazionale/Arco-Films du Siècle (Alfredo Bini, Mel Ferrer)
In the 16th century, a Greek-Italian painter finds favour in Spain and falls in love with an aristocratic girl.
Heavily embellished history with a few good scenes.
w Guy Elmes, Massimo Franciosa, Luigi Magni, Luciano Salce d Luciano Salce ph Leonida Barboni m Ennio Morricone
☆ Mel Ferrer, Rosanna Schiaffino, Adolfo Celi, Angel Aranda

El Mariachi **
US   1992   81m   Technicolor
Columbia/Los Hooligans (Robert Rodriguez, Carlos Gallardo)
In a small Mexican town a wandering musician with his guitar-case is mistaken for a hitman.
Witty, visually inventive low-budget thriller, cleverly taking apart the conventions of Westerns and reassembling them in a quirky and individual way.
wd Robert Rodriguez ph Robert Rodriguez m Marc Trujillo, Alvaro Rodriguez, Chris Knudson, Cecilio Rodriguez, Eric Guthrie ed Robert Rodriguez
☆ Carlos Gallardo, Consuelo Gómez, Reinol Martinez, Peter Marquardt, Jaime de Hoyos, Ramiro Gómez, Jesus Lopez, Luis Baro
'Uses a broad genre to make subtle points: about change and tradition, about Mexicans and Chicanos with separate values and voices. Despite its superficial sense of low-budget genre-as-usual, this project offers something truly new for American film.' – *Sight and Sound*
'Has an exhilarating rawness that works for, rather than against it, its kinetic pacing, visceral editing and bravura camerawork revealing the presence of a director with unbridled visual panache. A minor masterpiece.' – *Empire*
† The film, by a 24-year-old director born in Texas, is said to have cost $7,000 (coming in $2,000 under budget) to shoot in 14 days and became the cheapest movie to be given international distribution by Columbia. He was signed to remake the film with a budget of $6m.
†† It was released on DVD together with its bigger budget remake *Desperado* (qv).

El Paso
US   1949   92m   Cinecolor
Paramount/Pine-Thomas
After the civil war, a young lawyer brings a corrupt township to its senses by learning to outshoot the badmen.
Lively, fairly tough Western with all the familiar ingredients.
wd Lewis R. Foster ph Ellis Carter m Darrell Calker
☆ John Payne, Gail Russell, Dick Foran, Sterling Hayden, George 'Gabby' Hayes

El Topo *
Mexico   1971   124m   Eastmancolor
Producciones Panic
An evil gunfighter rides through the old west and has various encounters, after which he sets himself on fire.
Curious, perverse, powerful surrealist allegory which takes in the life of Christ and the fate of man among some exceedingly unpleasant violence. A treat for connoisseurs of the unpleasantly absurd.
ph Raphael Corkidi wd/m/ad Alejandro Jodorowsky
☆ Alejandro Jodorowsky, Brontis Jodorowsky, Mara Lorenzio, David Silva

'Reading. Writing. Revenge.'
Election ***
US   1999   103m   DeLuxe
Paramount/MTV/Bonafide (Albert Berger, Ron Yerxa, David Gale, Keith Samples)
The star pupil at a Midwest high school is determined to become president of the student government; a disgruntled teacher is determined that she should fail.
Witty, inventive satire that, although given a high-school setting, makes telling points about the politics and underhand methods involved in all kinds of power struggles.
w Alexander Payne, Jim Taylor novel Tom Perrotta d Alexander Payne ph James Glennon m Rolfe Kent pd Jane Ann Stewart ed Kevin Tent
☆ Matthew Broderick, Reese Witherspoon, Chris Klein, Jessica Campbell, Mark Harelik, Phil Reeves, Molly Hagan, Delaney Driscoll, Colleen Camp
'If Billy Wilder had been assigned to make a teen comedy, he might well have come up with a film as sour and witty as this.' – *Geoffrey Macnab, Sight and Sound*
'Pertinent, fiendishly funny... A modern classic.' – *Peter Bradshaw, Guardian*
ℬ script (Alexander Payne, Jim Taylor)

'He's a good cop on a big bike on a bad road!'
Electra Glide in Blue *
US   1973   113m   DeLuxe   Panavision
UA/James William Guercio/Rupert Hitzig
A small-town motor-cycle cop becomes disillusioned.
Agreeable desert melodrama in the wake of Easy Rider, freshly observed with mordant humour, marred by a fashionable downbeat ending.
w Robert Boris m Conrad Hall m James William Guercio d/m James William Guercio
☆ Robert Blake, Billy Green Bush, Mitch Ryan, Jeannine Riley, Elisha Cook Jnr, Royal Dano

Electric Dreams
╫╫   GB   1984   112m   Metrocolor
Virgin/MGM-UA (Rusty Lemorande, Larry de Waay)
A computer becomes jealous of its owner's love affair.
Gruesomely extended revue sketch which totally fails to develop its characters and offers instead a very sparing amount of cleverness.
w Rusty Lemorande d Steve Barron ph Alex Thomson m Giorgio Moroder pd Richard MacDonald
☆ Lenny von Dohlen, Virginia Madsen, Maxwell Caulfield, Bud Cort, Don Fellows

The Electric Horseman *
╫╫   US   1979   120m   Technicolor Panavision
Columbia/Universal (Ray Stark/Wildwood)
A horseman advertising breakfast cereal in Las Vegas suddenly tires of it all and heads for the wilderness.
Pretty but slightly sheepish moral saga with too much technique for its own good.
w Robert Garland d Sydney Pollack ph Owen Roizman m Dave Grusin pd Stephen Grimes
☆ Robert Redford, Jane Fonda, Valerie Perrine, Willie Nelson, John Saxon, Nicolas Coster
'Overlong, talky and diffused.' – *Variety*

The Electric Man: see *Man Made Monster*

Electric Moon

GB 1991 103m Technicolor
Winstone/Grapevine Media/Channel 4/Times
Television (Sundeep Singh Bedi)

Rivalry between an Indian hotelier, a former
Maharajah, and the director of the national park in
which the hotel is situated causes problems for a
group of Western tourists.

*Uncertain comedy that mocks the expectations and
preconceptions of tourists in India.*

w Arundhati Roy d Pradip Krishen ph Giles
Nuttgens m Basaya Khan, Zakab Khan, Deepak
Castelino, Sanjee Saith pd Arundhati Roy
ed Pradip Krishen

☆ Roshan Seth, Naseeruddin Shah, Leela Naidu,
Gerson Da Cunha, Raghubir Yadav, Alice Spivak,
Frances Helm, James Fleet, Francesca Brill

'Loses its shine early on. This amiable, good-
humored satire on cultural stereotypes on both
sides of the Indian tourist fence is too low-
voltage to create much of a theatrical buzz.' –
Variety

Elementary School **

Czechoslovakia 1991 97m colour
Barrandov (Jaromir Lukas)

original title: *Obecna Skola*

Episodes in the life of a 10-year-old boy at home
and with his unruly school-friends, just after the
end of the Second World War.

*A gently comic, nostalgic, semi-autobiographical
movie; it has a quiet charm, enhanced by its romantic
visual style.*

w Zdenek Sverak d Jan Sverak ph F. A. Brabec
m Jiri Traxler ad Vladimir Labsky, Gabriella
Kubenove ed Alois Fisarek

☆ Jan Triska, Rudolf Hrusinsky, Zdenek Sverak,
Libuse Safrankova, Vaclav Jakoubek, Daniela
Kolarova, Boleslav Polivka, Petr Cepek

& foreign-language film

Eleni

US 1985 117m colour
CBS/Vanoff/Pick/Gage

▦ &

A journalist back in Greece investigates his
mother's death in the civil war of the late 1940s.

*Deadeningly boring true life drama with flashbacks
which fail to communicate the author's sense of
revenge.*

w Steve Tesich book Nicholas Gage d Peter
Yates ph Billy Williams m Bruce Smeaton
pd Roy Walker ed Ray Lovejoy

☆ Kate Nelligan, John Malkovich, Linda Hunt,
Oliver Cotton, Ronald Pickup, Rosalie Crutchley

'As lofty in ambition as it is deficient in
accomplishment.' – *Variety*

Elenya *

GB 1992 82m colour
Frankfurter Film/S4C/BFI/Ffilmian/ZDF (Heidi Ulmke)

▦

An elderly woman remembers how, as a young girl
living in Wales in 1940, she tried to hide and care
for a German pilot she discovered wounded in a
wood.

*Pleasant low-budget feature, but lacking in any
particular individuality or originality.*

wd Steve Gough ph Patrick Duval m Simon
Fisher Turner pd Hayden Pearce ed Alan
Smithee

☆ Margaret John, Pascale Delafouge Jones, Seirol
Tomos, Sue Jones Davies, Iago Wynn Jones, Lilo
Milward, Catrin Llwyd, Edward Elwyn Jones, Ioan
Meredith, Klaus Behrendt

'Very quiet, acutely sensitive in some areas and a
debut from which much could spring.' – *Derek
Malcolm, Guardian*

The Elephant and the Bicycle **

Cuba 1995 85m colour/bw
ICAIC/Channel 4 (Rafael Rey)

original title: *El Elefante y la Bicicleta*

In 1925, a former prisoner returns to his island
village with a movie projector and a film of Robin
Hood which, as the villagers watch it every night,
becomes a film about their own oppression by the
local landowner.

*A charming, sophisticated fable of the transforming
power of art, or the ability of people to read into it what
they want; in one witty scene, the villagers, in critical
mode, debate whether cinema should be escapist or
reflect reality – this manages to do both.*

w Eliseo Alberto Diego, Juan Carlos Tabio d Juan
Carlos Tabio, Rapi Diego ph Julio Valdes m Jose
Vitier ad Onelio Larralde ed Lina Baniela

☆ Luis Alberto Garcia, Lilian Vega, Martha Farre,
Raul Pomares, Daisy Granados, Adolfo Llaurado,
Patricio Wood, Fidelio Torres

Elephant Boy **

👫 GB 1937 91m bw
London Films (Alexander Korda)

▦ ▤

In India, a boy elephant keeper helps government
conservationists.

*Documentary drama which seemed fresh and
extraordinary at the time, has dated badly since, but
did make an international star of Sabu.*

w John Collier, Akos Tolnay, Marcia de Sylva
novel *Toomai of the Elephants* by Rudyard Kipling
d Robert Flaherty, Zoltan Korda ph Osmond
Borradaile m John Greenwood ed William
Hornbeck, Charles Crichton

☆ Sabu, Walter Hudd, Allan Jeayes, W. E.
Holloway, Wilfrid Hyde-White

'Should draw anywhere in the world.' – *Variety*

'This is a fractured film, its skeleton is awry, its
bones stick out through the skin.' – *Richard
Griffith, 1941*

'It has gone the way of *Man of Aran*: enormous
advance publicity, director out of touch with the
press for months, rumours of great epics sealed in
tins, and then the disappointing diminutive
achievement.' – *Graham Greene*

Un Eléphant ça Trompe Enormément:
see *Pardon Mon Affaire*

Elephant Gun: see *Nor the Moon by Night*

The Elephant Man ***

US 1980 124m bw Panavision
EMI/Brooksfilms (Stuart Cornfeld)

▦ ▦ ▦ & 🎧

In 1884 London, a penniless man deformed by a
rare illness is rescued by a doctor from a fairground
freak show, and becomes a member of fashionable
society.

*A curious story which happens to be true; the film sets
its scene superbly, has splendid performances and a
fascinating make-up. Yet it fails to move quite as it
should, perhaps because the central figure is treated as
a horrific come-on, like the hunchback of Notre Dame.*

w Christopher de Vore, Eric Bergren, David
Lynch, from various memoirs d David Lynch
ph Freddie Francis m John Morris pd Stuart
Craig

☆ *Anthony Hopkins, John Hurt*, John Gielgud,
Anne Bancroft, Freddie Jones, Wendy Hiller,
Michael Elphick, Hannah Gordon

'If there's a wrong note in this unique movie – in
performance, production design, cinematography
or anywhere else – I must have missed it.' – *Paul
Taylor, Time Out*

'In an age of horror movies this is a film which
takes the material of horror and translates it into
loving kindness.' – *Dilys Powell, Punch*

& best film; screenplay; David Lynch; editing
(Anne V. Coates); art direction (Stuart Craig, Bob
Cartwright, Hugh Scaife); John Morris; costume
design (Patricia Norris); John Hurt

🎭 best film; production design; John Hurt

Elephant Walk *

US 1954 103m Technicolor
Paramount (Irving Asher)

▦

The owner of a Ceylon tea plantation takes back
an English wife who finds the atmosphere strange
and turns to a friendly overseer for comfort.

*Echoes of Jane Eyre and Rebecca, with stampeding
elephants instead of a mad or dead wife.*

w John Lee Mahin novel Robert Standish
d William Dieterle ph Loyal Griggs m Franz
Waxman

☆ Elizabeth Taylor, Peter Finch, Dana Andrews,
Abraham Sofaer

'The climactic elephant stampede's a rouser – if
you're still awake.' – *Judith Crist*

Elephants Never Forget: see *Zenobia*

Eleven Harrowhouse *

GB 1974 108m DeLuxe Panavision
TCF/Harrowhouse (Elliott Kastner)

▤

An American diamond merchant is robbed of a
valuable jewel, and finds himself in the middle of
an ingenious plot.

*Amusing caper story marred by sudden changes of
mood.*

w Jeffrey Bloom novel Gerald A. Browne
d Aram Avakian ph Arthur Ibbetson m Michael
J. Lewis

☆ Charles Grodin, *James Mason*, Trevor Howard,
John Gielgud, Candice Bergen, Peter Vaughan,
Helen Cherry, Jack Watson, Jack Watling

'This lackadaisical caper comedy is inoffensive,
but the comic ideas don't build or erupt, and
since the director fails to get any suspense going,
it becomes a bumbling and stupid romp.' –
Pauline Kael

Elinor Norton

US 1935 71m bw
Fox

A wife has a jealous husband and a South
American lover.

*Unfortunate triangle drama which never comes to
boiling point.*

w Rose Franken, Philip Klein novel *The State
versus Elinor Norton* by Mary Roberts Rinehart
d Hamilton McFadden

☆ Claire Trevor, Gilbert Roland, Hugh Williams,
Henrietta Crosman, Norman Foster

'No cast for b.o. and results look mild.' – *Variety*

Elisa *

France 1994 114m colour
Gala/Christian Fechner/Solo/TF1 (Henri Brichetti)

▦

A street-smart teenager, whose mother committed
suicide when she was a baby, blames the father who
.abandoned them for the tragedy and sets out to
find him.

*A vehicle designed to establish Paradis as film star as
well as a singer, in which it succeeds: she is convincing
as an amoral flirt, and more interesting than the film
itself.*

w Jean Becker, Fabrice Carazo d Jean Becker
ph Etienne Becker m Zbigniew Preisner
ad Thérèse Ripaux ed Jacques Witta

☆ Vanessa Paradis, Gérard Depardieu, Clothilde
Courau, Sekkou Sall, Florence Thomassin

'A subtly structured, often whimsical personal
odyssey.' – *Empire*

† The title is taken from a song by Serge
Gainsbourg, to whom the film is dedicated.

Eliza Fraser

Australia 1976 127m colour
Hexagon (Tim Burstall)

A shipwrecked couple have to live with
Aborigines; later she becomes a fairground
attraction.

*Would-be bawdy historical romp on the lines of Tom
Jones; it seldom works.*

w David Williamson d Tim Burstall

☆ Susannah York, Trevor Howard, Noel Ferrier,
John Waters, Charles Tingwell

'Declared Illegitimate Aged 3. Tried For Treason Aged
21. Crowned Queen Aged 25.'
'Absolute Power Demands Absolute Loyalty.'

Elizabeth ***

GB 1998 121m colour
Polygram/Channel 4/Working Title (Alison Owen, Eric
Fellner, Tim Bevan)

▦ ▤ & 📀 📀 🎧

Amid plots and counter-plots, the hatred of her
Catholic sister, Queen Mary, and the loss of her
lover, Elizabeth survives to become absolute ruler
of England.

*Fast-moving drama which, while it rearranges historical
events, seems accurate in spirit to the political
upheavals of the time; against the background of
religious persecution and overweening ambitions, it
charts Elizabeth's emotional life, as she moves from
frightened and passionate girl to a frightening and
passionless queen.*

w Michael Hirst d Shekhar Kapur ph Remi
Adefarasin m David Hirschfelder pd John Myhre
ed Jill Bilcock

☆ *Cate Blanchett, Geoffrey Rush*, Christopher
Eccleston, Joseph Fiennes, Richard Attenborough,
Fanny Ardant, Kathy Burke, Eric Cantona, James

Frain, Vincent Cassel, Daniel Craig, John Gielgud,
Angus Deayton, Edward Hardwicke, Terence Rigby

'The very model of a successful historical drama
– imposingly beautiful, persuasively resonant,
unfailingly entertaining. – *Richard Williams,
Guardian*

'A horror film masquerading as a historical
pageant.' – *David Denby, New Yorker*

🏆 Jenny Shircore (make-up)

& best picture; Cate Blanchett; Remi Adefarasin;
David Hirschfelder; John Myhre; Alexandre Byrne
(costumes)

🎭 best British film; Cate Blanchett; Remi
Adefarasin; David Hirschfelder; Jenny Shircore
(make-up)

Elizabeth and Essex: see *The Private Lives of
Elizabeth and Essex*

Elizabeth of England: see *Drake of England*

Elizabeth of Ladymead

GB 1948 97m Technicolor
BL/Imperadio (Herbert Wilcox)

Four husbands of different generations come home
from war (1854, 1903, 1919, 1946) to find their
wives altered.

*Thin star vehicle turns into an amateur-night
compendium with a few funny moments.*

w Frank Harvey play Frank Harvey d Herbert
Wilcox ph Max Greene md Robert Farnon

☆ Anna Neagle, Hugh Williams, Bernard Lee,
Michael Laurence, Nicholas Phipps, Isabel Jeans,
Michael Shepley, Jack Allen

Elizabeth the Queen: see *The Private Lives of
Elizabeth and Essex*

Ella Cinders **

US 1926 83m bw silent
First National

▤

A servant girl wins a trip to Hollywood.

*Famous and still pleasing comedy from the comic strip
Cinderella in the Movies.*

w Frank Griffin, Mervyn Le Roy d Alfred E.
Green ph Arthur Martinelli

☆ Colleen Moore, Lloyd Hughes, Vera Lewis,
Doris Baker

Ellen: see *The Second Woman*

Ellery Queen

The debonair detective created by Manfred B. Lee
and Frederic Dannay was seen in several
unremarkable second features, usually with his
secretary Nikki and his police inspector father. The
first two were made for Republic, the rest for
Columbia.

1935 The Spanish Cape Mystery with Donald
Cook
1936 The Mandarin Mystery (Eddie Quillan)
1940 Ellery Queen Master Detective (Ralph
Bellamy)
1941 Ellery Queen's Penthouse Mystery, Ellery
Queen and the Perfect Crime, Ellery Queen and
the Murder Ring (all Bellamy)
1942 A Close Call for Ellery Queen, A Desperate
Chance for Ellery Queen, Enemy Agents Meet
Ellery Queen (all William Gargan)
In 1971 Peter Lawford starred in a TV pilot, *Don't
Look Behind You*, and in 1975 a one-season series
starred Jim Hutton. The books, pseudonymously
authored by Ellery Queen, were far more popular
than any of the movies.

Ellery Queen, Master Detective

US 1940 66m bw
Columbia

Searching for the missing daughter of a dying
health food tycoon, Ellery Queen finds the wrong
girl and solves the mystery of a murder in a locked
room.

*A slow-moving mystery, bland and uninteresting, with
a great deal of talk and very little action, being mainly
confined to a couple of interior sets.*

w Eric Taylor story Ellery Queen d Kurt
Neumann ph James S. Brown Jnr m Lee Zahler
ed Dwight Caldwell

☆ Ralph Bellamy, Margaret Lindsay, Charley
Grapewin, James Burke, Michael Whalen

Elles n'oublient pas: see *Love in the Strangest
Way*

Elmer and Elsie
US   1934   65m   bw
Paramount
A wife harbours big ideas for her meek-and-mild husband.
Unsuccessful attempt to find a change of pace for a fading star.
w Humphrey Pearson *play* To the Ladies *by* George S. Kaufman, Marc Connelly d Gilbert Pratt
☆ George Bancroft, Frances Fuller, Roscoe Karns, George Barbier, Nella Walker
'Screen version has not only removed most of the verve, pace and bite but has loaded itself down with a couple of maladroit cases of miscasting.' – Variety

'From a book that shook a nation with its sledgehammer theme ... From a Nobel Prize-winning author ... comes the raging story of the man who used the Holy Bible and broke every rule in it!'
**Elmer Gantry **
US   1960   146m   Eastmancolor
UA/Bernard Smith
◉◉ ▬ ◎~ ◠
The exploits of an American evangelist in the twenties.
Mainly gripping but overlong exposé of commercialized small-town religion.
wd Richard Brooks *novel* Sinclair Lewis *ph* John Alton *m* André Previn *ad* Edward Carrere
☆ Burt Lancaster, Jean Simmons, Arthur Kennedy, Shirley Jones, Dean Jagger, Edward Andrews, Patti Page, John McIntire
♟ Richard Brooks (as writer); Burt Lancaster; Shirley Jones
♟ best picture; André Previn

Elmer the Great
US   1933   74m   bw
Warner (Ray Griffith)
A country hick turns out to be a great baseball hitter.
Best and most farcical version of a play also filmed in 1929 as Fast Company *and in 1939 as* The Cowboy Quarterback.
w Tom Geraghty *play* Ring Lardner, George M. Cohan d Mervyn Le Roy
☆ Joe E. Brown, Patricia Ellis, Frank McHugh, Claire Dodd, Sterling Holloway, Emma Dunn, Douglass Dumbrille, Jessie Ralph, J. Carrol Naish

Elmore Leonard's Gold Coast
US   1997   105m   DuArt
Paramount/Chanticleer/Mancat/Richard Maynard
◉◉ ▬
In Florida, a petty crook falls for the widow of a Mafia boss, who is being threatened by a hired killer.
Tart, spare thriller, slickly made but underpowered.
w Harley Peyton *novel* Elmore Leonard d Peter Weller *ph* Jacek Laskus *m* Peter Harris *pd* Maria Caso *ed* Dean Goodhill
☆ David Caruso, Marg Helgenberger, Jeff Kober, Barry Primus, Wanda de Jesus, Richard Bradford, Rafael Baez, Melissa Raven
† The film was made for cable television.

'A picture that goes beyond what men think about ... because no man ever thought about it in quite this way!'
Elopement
US   1951   82m   bw
TCF (Fred Kohlmar)
A girl student eloping with her professor is chased by her father.
Unconvincing domestic comedy with some lively chase sequences.
w Bess Taffel d Henry Koster *ph* Joseph LaShelle *m* Cyril Mockridge
☆ Clifton Webb, Charles Bickford, Anne Francis, William Lundigan, Margalo Gillmore, Evelyn Varden, Reginald Gardiner

Elstree Calling *
GB   1930   95m   bw/Pathécolour
Wardour/BIP (John Maxwell)
A film studio mounts a television show.
Slender excuse for an all-star revue which luckily preserves much light entertainment talent of the time.
w Adrian Brunel, Walter C. Mycroft, Val Valentine d Adrian Brunel, Alfred Hitchcock, Jack Hulbert, André Charlot, Paul Murray *ph* Claude Friese-Greene *m* Reg Casson, Vivian

Ellis, Chick Endor, Ivor Novello, Jack Strachey *ed* émile de Ruelle, A. C. Hammond
☆ Tommy Handley, Jack Hulbert, Cicely Courtneidge, Will Fyffe, Lily Morris, Teddy Brown, Anna May Wong, Gordon Harker, Donald Calthrop, John Longden, Jameson Thomas, Bobbie Comber

The Elstree Story *
GB   1952   61m   bw
ABPC (Gilbert Gunn)
A compilation drawn from 25 years of filmmaking at Elstree Studios.
Highlights include Hitchcock's Number Seventeen; The White Sheik; Piccadilly; Bulldog Drummond; Arms and the Man; The Informer; Blossom Time; *and* Poison Pen. *Commentary and presentation are adequate.*
d Gilbert Gunn *m* Philip Green

The Elusive Pimpernel *
GB   1950   109m   Technicolor
BL/London Films (Michael Powell, Emeric Pressburger)
◉◉ ▬
US title: *The Fighting Pimpernel*
A foppish 18th-century London dandy is actually the hero who rescues French aristocrats from the guillotine.
Expensive remake of The Scarlet Pimpernel *which fails to please, apparently because the talents were not congenial to the subject. Interesting detail, though.*
wd Michael Powell, Emeric Pressburger *novel* Baroness Orczy *ph* Hein Heckroth *m* Brian Easdale
☆ David Niven, Margaret Leighton, Cyril Cusack, Jack Hawkins, David Hutcheson, Robert Coote
'The quality of excitement which should carry the film is quite lost. The Elusive Pimpernel is highly – often too highly – coloured, and has an artificiality quite different in character from that of the original.' – Penelope Houston
'I never thought I should feel inclined to leave a Powell and Pressburger film before the end; but I did here.' – Richard Mallett, Punch
'Niven plays the Scarlet Pimpernel with the sheepish lack of enthusiasm of a tone deaf man called upon to sing solo in church. His companions lumber through their parts like schoolboys afraid to go down with mumps.' – Daily Express

Elvira Madigan *
Sweden   1967   95m   Eastmancolor
Europa Film (Waldemar Bergendahl)
◉◉ ▬ ◎~ ◠
A married army officer runs off with a tightrope dancer; when they run out of money they live in the woods and finally commit suicide rather than part.
A simple Victorian romantic idyll, based on a true incident; a director's and photographer's piece which entrances the eyes and ears while starving the mind.
ph Jörgen Persson *m* Mozart *ed/ed* Bo Widerberg
☆ Thommy Berggren, Pia Degermark

Elvira, Mistress of the Dark
US   1988   96m   CFI color
Entertainment/New World/NBC/Queen B (Eric Gardner, Mark Pierson)
◉◉ ▬ ◎~
The hostess of a TV horror show discovers that she has magic powers.
Camp nonsense, limply performed.
w Sam Egan, John Paragon, Cassandra Peterson d James Signorelli *ph* Hanania Baer *m* James Campbell *pd* John DeCuir Jnr *ed* Battle Davis
☆ Cassandra Peterson, W. Morgan Sheppard, Daniel Greene, Susan Kellermann, Jeff Conaway, Edie McClurg, Kurt Fuller, Pat Crawford Brown

**Elvis! Elvis! **
Sweden   1977   100m   colour
Moviemakers/SF1/SR-TV2 (Bert Sundberg)
A sensitive seven-year-old boy tries to cope with a mother obsessed by Elvis Presley.
Unimaginative family drama.
w Maria Gripe, Kay Pollak *novel* Maria Gripe d Kay Pollak *ph* Mikael Salomon *m* Ralph Lundsten *ed* Lasse Lundberg
☆ Lele Dorazio, Lena-Pia Bernhardsson, Fred Gunnarsson, Elisaveta, Allan Adwall

Embassy *
US   1972   90m   colour
Hemdale/Triad/Weaver (Mel Ferrer)
At the US Embassy in Beirut, a Soviet official seeking asylum is in danger from a KGB killer.
Goodish suspenser with reasonably literate dialogue and several Hitchcockian sequences.
w William Fairchild d Gordon Hessler *ph* Raoul Coutard *m* Jonathan Hodge
☆ Richard Roundtree, Chuck Connors, Max von Sydow, Broderick Crawford, Ray Milland

Embryo
US   1976   104m   colour
Cine Artists (Arnold H. Orgolini, Anita Doohan)
A researcher experiments on foetuses with growth hormones, and lives to regret it.
Rather unpleasant mixture of science fiction and old-fashioned horror; slickness can't conceal a total lack of taste.
w Anita Doohan, Jack W. Thomas d Ralph Nelson *ph* Fred Koenekamp *m* Gil Melle
☆ Rock Hudson, Diane Ladd, Barbara Carrera, Roddy McDowall

The Emerald Forest *
GB   1985   113m   Technicolor   Panavision
Embassy/John Boorman
◉◉ ▬ ◎~ ◠
An American engineer sets off to find his lost son in the jungles of Brazil.
Heavy-going, dazzling to look at, finally uncomforting dalliance with themes originally explored in Tarzan the Ape Man, *e.g. would man do better to return to nature?*
w Rospo Pallenberg d John Boorman *ph* Philippe Rousselot *m* Junior Homrich, Brian Gascoyne *pd* Simon Holland
☆ Powers Boothe, Meg Foster, Charley Boorman
'Begins as a breathtaking fable and ends as a routine action movie. Somewhere along the way, there was a failure of the imagination.' – Roger Ebert

Emergency!: see *Emergency Call* (1952)

Emergency
GB   1962   63m   bw
Butcher's (Francis Searle)
While her parents quarrel, police search for three blood donors who can save the life of a little girl.
Domestic drama that manages to encompass an absconding spy, a murderer and an international football match; not bad of its forgettable kind.
w Don Nicholl, James O'Connolly d Francis Searle *ph* Ken Hodges *m* John Veale *md* Philip Martell *ad* Duncan Sutherland *ed* Jim Connock
☆ Glyn Houston, Zena Walker, Dermot Walsh, Colin Tapley, Garard Green, Anthony Dawn, Patrick Jordan, Candy Pibworth

Emergency Call *
GB   1952   90m   bw
Butcher's/Nettlefold (Ernest G. Roy)
US title: *Emergency*
Inspector Lane tracks down several people who share a rare blood group needed to save a life.
Now a boringly predictable collection of mild anecdotes, but then a rather smart idea, much better executed than one would normally expect of Britain's Poverty Row.
w Vernon Harris, Lewis Gilbert d Lewis Gilbert *ph* Wilkie Cooper *m* Wilfred Burns
☆ Jack Warner, Joy Shelton, Anthony Steel, Sidney James, Freddie Mills, Earl Cameron, John Robinson, Thora Hird

The Emigrants *
Sweden   1970   191m   Technicolor
Svensk Filmindustri (Bengt Forslund)
original title: *Utvandrarna*
A family of farmers leaves famine-stricken 19th-century Sweden for America, and builds a homestead in Minnesota.
Solemn, forceful, overlong epic which while full of trial and tribulation is sufficiently well made to cast a hypnotic spell and was a major hit among Swedish-Americans.
w Jan Troell, Bengt Forslund *novels* Vilhelm Moberg *m* Erik Nordgren *ed* Jan Troell *d/ph/ed* Jan Troell
☆ Max von Sydow, Liv Ullmann, Eddie Axberg, Svenolof Bern

'A Fordian canvas without the Fordian warmth.' – Sight and Sound
† A sequel, *The New Land*, shortly appeared, and this was also the title of a short-lived TV series on the subject.
♟ best picture; best foreign film; Jan Troell (direction and script); Liv Ullmann

Emil and the Detectives *
Germany   1931   80m   bw
UFA
City children discover and chase a crook, who is finally arrested.
A pleasing fable for children which has survived several subsequent versions; the original is probably the best.
w Billy Wilder *novel* Erich Kästner d Gerhard Lamprecht *ph* Werner Brandes *m* Allan Grey
☆ Fritz Rasp, Kathe Haack
† Other versions: Britain 1935, directed by Milton Rosmer, with George Hayes; West Germany 1954, directed by R. A. Stemmle, with Kurt Meisel; US 1964 (Walt Disney), directed by Peter Tewkesbury, with Walter Slezak.

Emma *
US   1932   73m   bw
MGM
A servant marries into the family.
Predictably cosy family drama tailored for its star.
w Frances Marion, Leonard Praskins, Zelda Sears d Clarence Brown *ph* Oliver T. Marsh
☆ Marie Dressler, Richard Cromwell, Jean Hersholt, Myrna Loy, John Miljan, Purnell E. Pratt
'A hoke story saved by the star.' – Variety
♟ Marie Dressler

'A new comedy from Jane Austen's timeless classic.'
Emma *
GB/US   1996   120m   Eastmancolor
Buena Vista/Matchmaker/Miramax/Haft (Patrick Cassavetti, Steven Haft)
◉◉ ▬ ◎~ ◉ ◠
A rich young woman's matchmaking goes amiss, but she finds happiness where she least expects it.
Pleasant but stolid adaptation that skates lightly over the moral concerns of the original.
wd Douglas McGrath *novel* Jane Austen *ph* Ian Wilson *m* Rachel Portman *pd* Michael Howells *ed* Lesley Walker
☆ Gwyneth Paltrow, Toni Collette, Jeremy Northam, Alan Cumming, Ewan McGregor, Greta Scacchi, Juliet Stevenson, Polly Walker, Sophie Thompson, Phyllida Law
'Jane Austen cooked up a full-banquet romantic comedy in her happiest, best-known masterpiece; writer-director Douglas McGrath offers a light, sunny, American-style tea party.' – Lisa Schwarzbaum, Entertainment Weekly
'Pretty and pleasing, but there are less patronising ways of opening your time.' – Tom Shone, Sunday Times
♟ Rachel Portman
♟ Ruth Myers (costumes)

Emmanuelle *
France   1974   91m   Eastmancolor
Trinacra/Orphée (Yves Rousset-Rouard)
◉◉ ◉ ◠
The bored bride of a French Embassy official in Siam is initiated by well-meaning friends into various forms of sexual activity.
Not much sexier than a Sunday colour supplement, this fashionable piece of suberoticism took off like a bomb and spawned half-a-dozen so-called sequels. Future students may well wonder why.
w Jean-Louis Richard *novel* Emmanuelle Arsan d Just Jaeckin *ph* Richard Suzuki, Marie Saunier *m* Pierre Bachelet
☆ Sylvia Kristel, Marika Green, Daniel Sarky, Alain Cuny
'Much hazy, soft-focus coupling in downtown Bangkok.' – Michael Billington, Illustrated London News

Emma's War
Australia   1985   96m   colour
Curzon/Belinon (Clytie Jessop, Andrena Finlay)

In the 40s, a 14-year-old girl befriends a runaway conscientious objector, after her mother takes her away from the dangers of wartime Sydney to live in a cottage in the mountains.
Mundane domestic drama of life's little disappointments.

🏠 film suitable for family viewing   ◉◉ VHS video-cassette for the British PAL system   ▭ VHS video-cassette for the British PAL system in wide screen-format   ✧ Video cassette in a computer-colourised version   ▬ American NTSC video-cassette   ◎~ Laser disc w Peter Smalley, Clytie Jessop *d* Clytie Jessop *ph* Tom Cowan *m* John Williams *ad* Jane Norris *ed* Sonia Hofmann

☆ Lee Remick, Miranda Otto, Mark Lee, Terence Donovan, Donal Gibson

L'Emmerdeur **
France/Italy   1973   84m   Eastmancolor
Miracle/Les Films Ariane/Mondex/OPIC (George Dancigers)
aka: *A Pain in the A–*
A hit-man, waiting in a Paris hotel to kill a witness, befriends a suicidal husband and is unable to get rid of him.
Amusing character comedy of a strong, silent man and a chattering weakling.
w Edouard Molinaro, Francis Veber *play Le Contrat* by Francis Veber *d* Edouard Molinaro *ph* Raoul Coutard *m* Jacques Brel, François Gabuber *ad* Jacques Brizzio *ed* Robert Isnardon, Monique Isnardon
☆ Lino Ventura, Jacques Brel, Caroline Cellier, Nino Castelnuovo, Jean-Pierre Darras, André Vallardy
'A black comedy par excellence. All that really need be said about it is that it begins well, sustains its chosen mood efficiently, builds to a satisfying climax and is in other words a delight from start to finish.' – *David McGillivray, Films and Filming*
† The film was remade by Billy Wilder as *Buddy Buddy*.

The Emperor Jones *
US   1933   72m   bw
UA
A train porter becomes king of the Haitian jungle.
Stagey transcript of a stagey play, with acting of some interest at the time.
w DuBose Heyward *play* Eugene O'Neill *d* Dudley Murphy *ph* Ernest Haller *m* Frank Tours
☆ Paul Robeson, Dudley Digges, Frank Wilson
'For the classes rather than the masses, and questionable commercially.' – *Variety*

Emperor of the North: see *Emperor of the North Pole*

Emperor of the North Pole *
US   1973   119m   DeLuxe
TCF/Inter Hemisphere (Robert Aldrich)
GB title: *Emperor of the North*
In 1933 Oregon, freeloading hobos are brutally attacked by a sadistic train guard.
Unlikely melodrama with vicious but exhilarating high spots separating acres of verbiage.
w Christopher Knopf *d* Robert Aldrich *ph* Joseph Biroc *m* Frank de Vol
☆ Lee Marvin, Ernest Borgnine, Keith Carradine, Charles Tyner, Malcolm Atterbury, Elisha Cook Jnr
'It's hard, contrived, pointless in its thesis, repulsive in its people, and it's singularly joyless and contemptible in its glorification of the bum and freeloader.' – *Judith Crist*

'The biggest thing that ever happened to Bing – or to you!'
The Emperor Waltz
US   1948   106m   Technicolor
Paramount (Charles Brackett)
In 1901 Austria, a countess falls for an American phonograph salesman.
Thin to the point of emaciation, this witless comedy with music, dully set-bound, proved its director's strangest and most unsatisfactory choice.
w Charles Brackett, Billy Wilder *d* Billy Wilder *ph* George Barnes *m* Victor Young *m/ly* Johnny Burke, Jimmy Van Heusen *ad* Hans Dreier, Franz Bachelin
☆ Bing Crosby, Joan Fontaine, Roland Culver, Lucile Watson, Richard Haydn, Harold Vermilyea, Sig Rumann, Julia Dean
♫ Victor Young

The Emperor's Candlesticks *
US   1937   89m   bw
MGM (John Considine Jnr)
In old Russia, spies on opposite sides fall in love.
Lavish romantic comedy drama, generally well handled; superior Hollywood moonshine.

w Monckton Hoffe, Herman J. Mankiewicz, Harold Goldman *novel* Baroness Orczy *d* George Fitzmaurice *ph* Harold Rosson *m* Franz Waxman
☆ William Powell, Luise Rainer, Maureen O'Sullivan, Robert Young, Frank Morgan, Douglass Dumbrille
'It's about international spies in evening dress during that long ago period when Russia had a Czar, Vienna was the scene of brilliant *valasques*, and the favour of royalty was something to get excited over … it's acted with unusual seriousness midst settings of unusual extravagance.' – *Variety*

L'Empire des Sens: see *Ai No Corrida*

Empire of Passion: see *Ai No Borei*

Empire of the Ants
US   1977   89m   Movielab
AIP/Cinema 77 (Bert I. Gordon)
Giant ants menace a stretch of the Florida coast.
A long way behind Them, but as exploitation it could be worse.
w Jack Turley *story* H. G. Wells *d* Bert I. Gordon *ph* Reginald Morris *m* Dana Kaproff
☆ Joan Collins, Robert Lansing, John David Carson, Albert Salmi, Jacqueline Scott

Empire of the Passions: see *Ai No Corrida*

Empire of the Sun ***
US   1987   152m   Technicolor
Robert Shapiro/Amblin (Steven Spielberg, Kathleen Kennedy, Frank Marshall)
Semi-autobiographical story of an 11-year-old English boy learning to grow up in a Japanese internment camp during World War II.
Intelligent and thought-provoking movie about the loss of childhood innocence through the horrors of war. Bale, as the boy, gives an extraordinarily believable performance
w Tom Stoppard *novel* J. G. Ballard *d* Steven Spielberg *ph* Allen Daviau *m* John Williams *pd* Norman Reynolds *ed* Michael Kahn
☆ Christian Bale, John Malkovich, Miranda Richardson, Nigel Havers, Joe Pantoliano
'A masterpiece of popular cinema.' – *MFB*
�హ Allen Daviau; editing; Norman Reynolds; John Williams; costumes (Bob Ringwood); sound
⚑ Allen Daviau; John Williams

'Selling records but not selling out.'
Empire Records
US   1995   91m   colour
Warner/New Regency (Tony Ludwig, Alan Riche, Michael Nathanson, Arnon Milchan)
A day in the life of the staff of a record shop as they fight off an attempt to buy the business.
Drearily inane comedy, with uncertain performers enunciating unspeakable dialogue on an overpowering soundtrack.
w Carol Heikkinen *d* Allan Moyle *ph* Walt Lloyd *m* Mitchell Leib *pd* Peter Jamison *ed* Michael Chandler
☆ Anthony LaPaglia, Liv Tyler, Johnny Whitworth, Rory Cochrane, Renee Zellweger, Robin Tunney, Ethan Randall, Maxwell Caulfield, Debi Mazar
'A soundtrack in search of a movie.' – *Variety*

Empire State
GB   1987   104m   colour
Miracle/Virgin (Norma Heyman)
An American gangster tries to infiltrate London's East End.
Over-the-top melodrama with an irritating pictorial style.
w Ron Peck, Mark Ayres *d* Ron Peck *ph* Tony Imi *m* Steve Parsons *pd* Adrian Smith *ed* Chris Kelly
☆ Cathryn Harrison, Jason Hoganson, Elizabeth Hickling, Jamie Foreman, Martin Landau, Ray McAnally

The Empire Strikes Back ***
US   1980   124m   Eastmancolor
Panavision
TCF/Lucasfilm (Gary Kurtz)
The Rebel Alliance takes refuge from Darth Vader on a frozen planet.

More exhilarating interplanetary adventures, as mindless as Star Wars but just as enjoyable for aficionados.
w Leigh Brackett, Lawrence Kasdan *story* George Lucas *d* Irvin Kershner *ph* Peter Suschitzky *m* John Williams *pd* Norman Reynolds
☆ Mark Hamill, Harrison Ford, Carrie Fisher, Billy Dee Williams
'Slightly encumbered by some mythic and neo-Sophoclean overtones, but its inventiveness, humour and special effects are scarcely less inspired than those of its phenomenally successful predecessor.' – *New Yorker*
⚑ John Williams; art direction
⚏ music

Employees' Entrance *
US   1933   75m   bw
Warner
A ruthless department store manager gets his come-uppance.
Smart comedy-melodrama with solidly familiar cast.
w Robert Presnell *play* David Boehm *d* Roy del Ruth
☆ Warren William, Loretta Young, Alice White, Wallace Ford, Allen Jenkins, Marjorie Gateson
'Here's one that calls for preferred dating … plenty to sell for the mobs.' – *Variety*

The Empty Beach
Australia   1985   100m   Eastmancolor
Jethro (John Edwards, Timothy Read)
A private eye searches around Bondi Beach for a businessman who went missing in mysterious circumstances two years earlier.
A conventional and, for the most part, unsurprising thriller with the occasional witty line of dialogue; its hero is beaten up so often that it is clear he is in the wrong business.
w Keith Dewhurst *novel* Peter Corris *d* Chris Thomson *ph* John Seale *m* Martin Armiger, Red Symons *pd* Lawrence Eastwood *ed* Lindsay Frazer
☆ Bryan Brown, Anna Maria Monticelli, Ray Barrett, John Wood, Belinda Giblin, Peter Collingwood, Nick Tate, Kerry Mack

The Empty Canvas
Italy/France   1964   118m   bw
CC Champion/Concordia (Joseph E. Levine, Carlo Ponti)
original title: *La Noia*
A young painter, obsessed by his own spiritual emptiness, becomes paranoically jealous of his promiscuous young mistress.
An extraordinarily boring film version of a novel which needed Buñuel, if anybody, to handle it.
w Tonino Guerra, Ugo Liberatore, Damiano Damiani *novel* Alberto Moravia *d* Damiano Damiani *ph* Roberto Gerardi *m* Luis Enriquez Bacalov
☆ Horst Buchholz, Catherine Spaak, Bette Davis, Isa Miranda, Lea Padovani

The Empty Table
Japan   1985   142m   colour
Electric Pictures/Marugen Building Group/Haiyu-za Film/Herald Ace (Ginichi Kishimoto, Kyoto Oshima)
original title: *Shokutaku No Nai Ie*
A family disintegrates when the eldest son is arrested for terrorism.
Slow and ponderous, without much to interest a Western audience.
wd Masaki Kobayashi *story* Fumiko Enji *ph* Kozo Okazaki *md* Toru Takemitsu *pd* Shigemasha Toda *ed* Nobuo Ogawa
☆ Tatsuya Nakadai, Mayumi Ogawa, Kie Nakaj, Kiichi Nakai, Takeyuki Takemoto, Shima Iwashita

En Cas de Malheur *
France/Italy   1958   120m   bw
Iena/UCIL/Incom
aka: *Love Is My Profession*
A wealthy, middle-aged lawyer leaves his wife for a worthless young wanton whom he is defending on a robbery charge.
Good solid melodrama with excellent credits: it caught all concerned on top form and had international success, but the theme is not in itself very interesting.
w Jean Aurenche, Pierre Bost *novel* Georges Simenon *d* Claude Autant-Lara *ph* Jacques Natteau *m* René Cloërc
☆ Jean Gabin, Edwige Feuillère, Brigitte Bardot, Franco Interlenghi

En Compagnie de Max Linder: see *Laugh with Max Linder*

En Effeuillant la Marguerite: see *Plucking the Daisy*

En Kille Och En Tjej: see *A Lover and His Lass*

En Rade *
France   1927   60m   bw   silent
Neofilm
A Marseilles docker dreams of escaping his pent-in existence and fleeing with his mistress to the South Seas.
More realistic than Pagnol's Marius trilogy, which used the same setting, this remains an interesting slice of romantic realism, with good attention to detail.
w Alberto Cavalcanti, Claude Heymann *d* Alberto Cavalcanti *ph* Jimmy Rogers, A. Fairli, P. Enberg
☆ Catherine Hessling, Philippe Heriat, Georges Charlia

Enchanted April
US   1935   66m   bw
RKO
A woman becomes lonely when her husband turns into a successful novelist.
Thin marital comedy-drama for fans of the star.
w Samuel Hoffenstein, Ray Harris *novel* Elizabeth von Arnim *d* Harry Beaumont
☆ Ann Harding, Frank Morgan, Katharine Alexander, Reginald Owen, Jane Baxter, Jessie Ralph
'Very British in background and proceeding at all times with a lifted eyebrow.' – *Variety*

'Escaping From Winter In London, They Planned A Holiday In Paradise … Everything Was Going Perfectly, Until The Men Arrived.'
Enchanted April
GB   1991   99m   colour
Curzon/Miramax/BBC/Greenpoint (Ann Scott)
In the 1920s four Englishwomen, bored with their lives, take a holiday in Italy.
Stilted period movie that is pretty to look at but has little to engage the mind.
w Peter Barnes *novel* Elizabeth von Arnim *d* Mike Newell *ph* Rex Maidment *m* Richard Rodney Bennett *pd* Malcolm Thornton *ed* Dick Allen
☆ Miranda Richardson, Josie Lawrence, Polly Walker, Joan Plowright, Alfred Molina, Michael Kitchen, Jim Broadbent
'A slim comedy of manners about Brits discovering their emotions in Italy … Strong cast's reliable playing is undercut by a script that dawdles over well-trod territory.' – *Variety*
'Crude, fussy, bland stuff gauged to please American anglophiles who watch Masterpiece Theatre.' – *Philip French, Observer*
⚑ Joan Plowright; Peter Barnes; costumes (Sheena Napier)

The Enchanted Cottage *
US   1945   92m   bw
RKO (Harriet Parsons)
A plain girl and a disfigured man are beautiful to each other.
Wartime updating of a sentimental old play; insufficiently well considered to be more than tolerable.
w De Witt Bodeen, Herman J. Mankiewicz *play* Sir Arthur Wing Pinero *d* John Cromwell *ph* Ted Tetzlaff *m* Roy Webb *ad* Albert D'Agostino, Carroll Clark *ed* Joseph Noriega
☆ Dorothy McGuire, Robert Young, Herbert Marshall, Mildred Natwick, Spring Byington, Hillary Brooke
'A silly film with considerable charm. It will be liked by millions, who are fully aware of its silliness while being captivated by its charm. It will be liked for the best of reasons; because it is based on a solid and humane truth.' – *C. A. Lejeune*
† A silent version in 1924 starred Richard Barthelmess and May McAvoy.
⚑ Roy Webb

The Enchanted Forest *

US 1945 77m Cinecolor
PRC
▤

Old John the Hermit talks to trees and animals, and rescues a lost child.
Surprising piece of Victorian whimsy, remarkably effective in its unambitious way, especially as a product of this studio. The best known example of Cinecolor.
w Robert Lee Johnson, John Le Bar, Lou Brock d Lew Landers ph Marcel Le Picard m Alfred Hay Malotte
☆ Harry Davenport, Edmund Lowe, Brenda Joyce, Billy Severn

Enchanted Island

US 1958 94m Technicolor
Waverly (Benedict Bogeaus)

In the 1840s two sailors jump ship and settle on what they later discover to be a cannibal island.
Tame adaptation of a minor classic, with the actors all at sea. Powell makes an unconvincing Polynesian.
w James Leicester, Harold Jacob Smith novel Typee by Herman Melville d Allan Dwan ph George Stahl m Raul Lavista
☆ Jane Powell, Dana Andrews, Don Dubbins, Arthur Shields, Ted de Corsia, Friedrich Ledebur

Enchantment *

US 1948 101m bw
Samuel Goldwyn
▣

A London house tells the story of three generations.
Yes, a house tells the story, and the leading characters are called Rollo and Lark, but this is a very appealing piece of period romantic nonsense, with the highest possible gloss upon it.
w John Patrick novel A Fugue in Time by Rumer Godden d Irving Reis ph Gregg Toland m Hugo Friedhofer ed Daniel Mandell
☆ David Niven, Teresa Wright, Evelyn Keyes, Farley Granger, Jayne Meadows, Leo G. Carroll
'Deliberate in pace, and artfully contrived as an emotional holiday, yet genuinely moving on its own terms.' – *Newsweek*
'Genuinely moving on its own terms, produced with a careful good taste that should disarm the critics of lachryma and old lace.' – *Newsweek*

Encino Man

♠♠ US 1992 88m Technicolor
Warner/Hollywood Pictures/Touchwood Pacific Partners 1 (George Zaloom)
▣ ▤ ◎ ♫
GB title: California Man
Two high-school students revive a frozen prehistoric youth who quickly adapts to the prevailing life-style.
A depressing youth comedy, though those with a Neanderthal sense of humour may be amused.
w Shawn Schepps story George Zaloom, Shawn Schepps d Les Mayfield ph Robert Brickmann m J. Peter Robinson pd James Allen ed Eric Sears, Jonathan Siegel
☆ Sean Astin, Brendan Fraser, Pauly Shore, Megan Ward, Robin Tunney, Michael DeLuise, Patrick Van Horn, Dalton James, Rick Ducommun
'Mindless would-be comedy ... insulting even within its own no-effort parameters.' – *Variety*
'Less funny than your own funeral.' – *Washington Post*

Encore *

GB 1951 88m bw
GFD/Two Cities (Antony Darnborough)
▤

Three more Somerset Maugham short stories introduced by the author.
The final follow-up to the success of Quartet and Trio; television playlets quickly made this kind of short story seem old-fashioned, but the standard here was high.
w T. E. B. Clarke, Arthur Macrae, Eric Ambler stories The Ant and the Grasshopper by Somerset Maugham d Pat Jackson, Anthony Pelissier, Harold French ph Desmond Dickinson m Richard Addinsell
☆ Nigel Patrick, Roland Culver, Kay Walsh, Noel Purcell, Ronald Squire, John Laurie, Glynis Johns, Terence Morgan, David Hutcheson

Encounter: see *Stranger On the Prowl*

Encounter at Raven's Gate

Australia 1989 93m colour
Castle Premier/Hemdale/FGH/International Film Management (Rolf de Heer, Marc Rosenberg)
▣ ◎~

A strange scientist appears to orchestrate a series of bizarre happenings at an isolated farming community.
Low budget science fiction non-thriller that rarely explains what is happening but staggers from one spooky event to the next.
w Rolf de Heer, Marc Rosenberg screenplay James Michael Vernon d Rolf de Heer ph Richard Michalak m Graham Tardif, Roman Kronen pd Judith Russell ed Suresh Ayyar
☆ Steven Vidler, Celine Griffin, Ritchie Singer, Vince Gil, Saturday Rosenberg, Max Cullen, Terry Camilleri

'A comedy for you and your next of kin!'

The End

US 1978 100m DeLuxe
UA/Lawrence Gordon (Hank Moonjean)
▤ ◎~

A selfish man finds he is dying and unsuccessfully tries to change what remains of his life.
Presumably intended as an ironic black comedy, this comes over as tasteless ham; nobody involved, least of all the director-star, has any idea how to handle it.
w Jerry Belson d Burt Reynolds ph Bobby Byrne m Paul Williams pd Jan Scott
☆ Burt Reynolds, Dom DeLuise, Sally Field, Strother Martin, David Steinberg, Joanne Woodward, Norman Fell, Myrna Loy, Pat O'Brien, Robby Benson, Carl Reiner

End as a Man: see *The Strange One*

The End of August *

US 1981 107m Metrocolor
Sewanee (Martin Jurow)
In 1900, a bored young wife takes a lover beneath her station.
Unexpectedly nostalgic wallow in days gone by, the background detail seeming more important than the personal story, and certainly very good to look at.
w Eula Seaton, Leon Heller novel The Awakening by Kate Chopin d Bob Graham ph Robert Elswit m Shirley Walker pd Warren Jacobson, Erin Jo Jurow
☆ Sally Sharp, Lilia Skala, David Marshall Grant, Kathleen Widdoes, Paul Roebling, Paul Shenar
'Reminiscent of nothing so much as the turning of pages in a family album.' – *Jo Imeson, MFB*

End of Days

US 1999 120m DeLuxe Panavision
Universal/Beacon (Armyan Bernstein, Bill Borden)
▣ ▤ ◎
In the final moments before the new millennium, an alcoholic ex-cop must prevent Satan from impregnating a young woman and bringing about the end of days, as foretold in the Book of Revelation.
As pumped-up as its hero, this is a riotous, over-the-top mish-mash of religiosity and shock effects, like The Omen on steroids.
w Andrew W. Marlowe d Peter Hyams ph Peter Hyams m John Debney pd Richard Holland ed Steve Kemper sp creature fx: Stan Winston; makeup fx: Kurtzman, Nicotero & Berger EFX Group
☆ Arnold Schwarzenegger, Gabriel Byrne, Kevin Pollak, Robin Tunney, CCH Pounder, Rod Steiger, Derrick O'Connor, Miriam Margolyes, Udo Kier, Victor Varnado
'Pointlessly nasty would-be thriller. The material is so derivative that it amounts to a tag sale of used parts from better apocalyptic movies.' – *Janet Maslin, New York Times*
'Dreadful enough to make most viewers consider gouging out their eyes in order to avoid seeing a second time the spectacle of the world's most wooden actor pretending to undergo a spiritual crisis.' – *Mark Kermode, Sight and Sound*
'A fun, all-out action movie with a sexy millennial edge.' – *Bob McCabe, Empire*

The End of St Petersburg **

USSR 1927 110m bw silent
Mezhrabpom-Russ
▣

original title: *Konyets Sankt-Peterburga*
A peasant comes to live in St Petersburg in 1914, understands the workers' problems, and joins in the revolution.
Exhilarating propaganda, reprehensible but superbly conceived, with an especially rousing climax.
w Nathan Zarkhi d V. I. Pudovkin ph Anatoli Golovnya, K. Vents ad S. Kozlovsky
☆ Ivan Chuvelov, Vera Baranovskaya, A. P. Christiakov
† The film was officially commissioned as part of the 10th anniversary celebrations.

The End of the Affair

GB 1954 106m bw
Columbia/Coronado (David Lewis)
◎ ♫
In wartime London, a repressed wife has an affair with a writer but develops religious guilt which leads indirectly to her death.
Glum sinning in Greeneland; over-ambitious, miscast, and poor-looking.
w Lenore Coffee novel Graham Greene d Edward Dmytryk ph Wilkie Cooper m Benjamin Frankel
☆ Deborah Kerr, Van Johnson, Peter Cushing, John Mills, Stephen Murray, Nora Swinburne, Charles Goldner

'The end was just the beginning'

The End of the Affair *

GB 1999 109m Technicolor
Columbia (Stephen Woolley, Neil Jordan)
▣ ◎ ♫
In 1946, a writer tries to understand why his wartime affair with a married woman came to a sudden end.
On one level, this is an effective movie of love among the emotionally repressed; but the changes made to Greene's novel negate its original purpose, in demonstrating the power and purpose of religious faith.
wd Neil Jordan novel Graham Greene ph Roger Pratt m Michael Nyman pd Anthony Pratt ed Tony Lawson
☆ Ralph Fiennes, Julianne Moore, Stephen Rea, Ian Hart, Samuel Bould, Jason Isaacs, James Bolam, Deborah Findlay
'An awkward, edgy, tormented novel has been upholstered for comfort.' – *Philip Kemp, Sight and Sound*
'A movie to make you think and to feel and to live another life for nearly two hours alongside as compelling, flawed and real a group of characters as any movie can offer.' – *Anwar Brett, Film Review*
⚱ Julianne Moore; Roger Pratt
Ⓥ Neil Jordan (screenplay)

End of the Game *

US/West Germany 1976 104m colour
TCF/Maximilian Schell
A retiring police inspector intensifies his vendetta against the crooked industrialist who thirty years earlier killed the woman they both loved.
Chess-like revenge melodrama very typical of its author, with no light relief and a few existentialist touches added for general confusion. Well made and sometimes fascinating, but finally annoying.
w Maximilian Schell, Friedrich Dürrenmatt novel The Judge and his Hangman by Friedrich Dürrenmatt d Maximilian Schell ph Ennio Guarnieri, Klaus Koenig, Roberto Gerardi
☆ Jon Voight, Robert Shaw, Martin Ritt, Jacqueline Bisset
'A more addled, overreaching, misjudged, ill-made, wasteful, posturing, uninteresting and tedious little epic has not toddled into town in years.' – *Charles Champlin, Los Angeles Times*

The End of the Golden Weather

♠♠ New Zealand 1992 103m colour
Blue Dolphin/South Pacific/New Zealand Film Commission/TV New Zealand (Christina Milligan, Ian Mune)
▣
During a summer holiday a lonely boy becomes friendly with a retarded youth with Olympic ambitions.
A slight and uninvolving movie of the dawning of maturity.
w Ian Mune, Bruce Mason play Bruce Mason d Ian Mune ph Alun Bollinger m Stephen McCurdy pd Ron Highfield ed Michael Horton
☆ Stephen Fulford, Stephen Papps, Paul Gittins, Gabrielle Hammond, David Taylor, Alexandra Marshall
'An intimate and gentle coming-of-age comedy drama.' – *Variety*

End of the Rainbow: see *Northwest Outpost*

The End of the River *

♠♠ GB 1947 83m bw
GFD/The Archers (Michael Powell, Emeric Pressburger)
A South American Indian boy flees to the outside world and finds life in the city as dangerous as in the jungle.
Strange but oddly impressive departure for British film-makers at this time. A commercial and critical disaster.
w Wolfgang Wilhelm novel Desmond Holdridge d Derek Twist ph Christopher Challis m Lambert Williamson
☆ Sabu, Esmond Knight, Bibi Ferreira, Robert Douglas, Antoinette Cellier, Raymond Lovell, Torin Thatcher, James Hayter

End of the Road *

US 1970 110m Eastmancolor
Contemporary/Allied Artists (Stephen F. Kesten, Terry Southern)
▤
Released from a sanitarium, a teacher takes a job at a local university and impregnates a professor's wife.
Determinedly offbeat, intermittently successful movie that was very much of its time, with the mad being regarded as truly sane.
w Aram Avakian, Dennis McGuire, Terry Southern novel John Barth d Aram Avakian ph Gordon Willis m Teo Macero pd John K. Wright ed Robert Q. Lovett
☆ Stacy Keach, Harris Yulin, Dorothy Tristan, James Earl Jones, Grayson Hall, Ray Brock, James Coco
'The cinematography by Gordon Willis is often beautiful, the optical effects are sometimes elegant, and the sets and details are often remarkably fine, but the absurdist point of view has too self-congratulatory a tone.' – *Pauline Kael*

The End of the Road *

GB 1954 77m bw
Group Three (Alfred Shaughnessy)
A retired engineer becomes frustrated by idleness, and his family contemplate sending him to an old people's home.
Reasonably absorbing study of old age, suffering from a contrived end.
w James Forsyth, Geoffrey Orme d Wolf Rilla ph Arthur Grant m John Addison
☆ Finlay Currie, Duncan Lamont, Naomi Chance, David Hannaford

End of the World *

France 1930 105m bw
Erran d'Art (Abel Gance)
original title: *La Fin du Monde*
Social and economic panic is caused when a comet is about to hit the Earth.
Massive attempt by Gance to rival his Napoleon in scope. Made in German, French and English, it cost a phenomenal sum which it never regained; Gance found work hard to get in future, especially since he set himself up as a prophet.
wd Abel Gance
☆ Abel Gance, Colette Darfeuil, Sylvia Grenade, Victor Francen
'A megalomaniac's effort turned out without consideration for financial results, and containing a strange mixture of crazy stuff, with successfully directed spectacular sequences.' – *Variety*
† The full title is The End of the World as Seen, Heard and Rendered by Abel Gance.

The End of the World (in our usual bed in a night full of rain)

Italy 1978 104m colour
Gil Shiva/Liberty/Warner
▤
aka: *Night Full of Rain*
An American lady photographer has a bumpy romance with an Italian communist journalist with expensive tastes.

'The first story of the double-fisted DA who tore apart the evil dynasty that peddled murder for a price!'

The Enforcer ***
US   1950   87m   bw
United States Pictures (Milton Sperling)
▣ ▣ ◎
GB title: *Murder, Inc*
A crusading District Attorney tracks down the leader of a gang which murders for profit.
Extremely suspenseful and well-characterized police yarn based on fact. One of the very best of its kind.
w Martin Rackin & Bretaigne Windust ph Robert Burks m David Buttolph ed Fred Allen
☆ Humphrey Bogart, Everett Sloane, Zero Mostel, Ted de Corsia, Roy Roberts, King Donovan
'A tough, very slickly-made thriller with a host of fine character parts.' – *NFT, 1969*
'Absorbing and exciting, with little of the violence that so often disfigures films of this kind.' – *Richard Mallett, Punch*
'The first fifteen minutes is as powerful and rapid a sketch of tension as I can recall for seasons. The last fifteen might make Hitch weep with envy.' – *Observer*
† Raoul Walsh directed much of the film, uncredited.

The Enforcer
US   1976   96m   DeLuxe   Panavision
Warner/Malpaso (Robert Daley)
▣ ▣ ◎
Brutal Inspector Callahan of the San Francisco police redeems himself by rounding up a group of psychopathic hoodlums.
Dirty Harry, phase three: for hardened veterans only.
w Stirling Silliphant, Dean Riesner d James Fargo ph Richard Glouner m Jerry Fielding
☆ Clint Eastwood, Tyne Daly, Harry Guardino, Bradford Dillman, John Mitchum, DeVeren Bookwalter, John Crawford
'A new low in mindless violence is reached in this film, which is so bad it would be funny if it were not for the gut-thumping killings from beginning to end.' – *William F. Fore, Film Information*

The Engagement *
GB   1970   44m   Technicolor
Memorial (David Barber)
A young executive spends a devastating afternoon trying to borrow money to pay for an engagement ring which cost more than he expected.
Brisk little comedy which doesn't wear out its welcome.
w Tom Stoppard d Paul Joyce ph Tony Spratling m John Dankworth
☆ David Warner, Michael Bates, George Innes, Juliet Harmer, Paul Curran, Barbara Couper, Peter Copley

England Made Me ***
GB   1972   100m   Eastmancolor   Panavision
Hemdale/Atlantic (Jack Levin)
In 1935 a sponging Englishman becomes involved through his sister with a German financier.
Somewhat altered from the novel, this unusual film remains a lively, intelligent character melodrama.
w Desmond Cory, Peter Duffell novel Graham Greene d Peter Duffell ph Ray Parslow m John Scott
☆ Peter Finch, Michael York, Hildegarde Neil, Michael Hordern, Joss Ackland

'In memory, love lies forever.'
The English Patient **
US   1996   162m   DeLuxe
Buena Vista/Tiger Moth/Miramax (Saul Zaentz)
▣ ▣
Tended by a devoted nurse in a deserted Italian villa at the end of the Second World War, a dying Austrian count recalls his doomed affair with the English wife of a colleague.
Those who believe that love excuses any behaviour will succumb to this glossy romance, made on an epic scale and in that Hollywood tradition where heroes emerge from a three-day walk across the desert looking slightly tousled, and derelict pianos remain miraculously in tune; others, despite the skills on display, may find its celebration of betrayal less entrancing.
wd Anthony Minghella novel Michael Ondaatje ph John Seale m Gabriel Yared pd Stuart Craig ed Walter Murch
☆ Ralph Fiennes, Juliette Binoche, Willem Dafoe, Kristin Scott-Thomas, Naveen Andrews, Colin Firth, Julian Wadham, Jürgen Prochnow

'A respectable, intelligent, but less-than-stirring adaptation of an imposingly dense and layered novel.' – *Todd McCarthy, Variety*
'A *tour de force* so haunting that other films can't exorcise the memory of its radiant cast, exquisite craftsmanship or complex system of metaphors.' – *Rita Kempley, Washington Post*
† Juliette Binoche won the best actress award for her performance at the Berlin Film Festival in 1997.
🏆 Best picture; Anthony Minghella (as director); Juliette Binoche; John Seale; Walter Murch; Gabriel Yared; Ann Roth (costumes); Stuart Craig; sound
🏆 Kristin Scott-Thomas; Ralph Fiennes; Anthony Minghella (as adaptor)
🏆 Best film; Anthony Minghella (best adapted screenplay); Juliette Binoche; John Seale; Gabriel Yared; Walter Murch

English without Tears *
GB   1944   89m   bw
GFD/Two Cities (Anatole de Grunwald, Sydney Box)
US title: *Her Man Gilbey*
During World War II a rich ATS girl falls for her butler who has become a lieutenant.
Wispy satirical comedy with amusing moments, chiefly interesting for the pre-war League of Nations sequences.
w Terence Rattigan, Anatole de Grunwald d Harold French ph Bernard Knowles
☆ Lilli Palmer, Michael Wilding, Margaret Rutherford, Penelope Dudley Ward, Albert Lieven, Roland Culver, Peggy Cummins

The Englishman Who Went Up a Hill But Came Down a Mountain *
🎬 GB   1995   99m   colour
Buena Vista/Parallax (Sarah Curtis)
▣ ▣ ◎
In 1917, two English surveyors working in a Welsh village discover that the highest local point cannot be classified as a mountain because it is 16 feet short of the necessary 1,000 feet; the outraged villagers decide to make good the discrepancy.
Amiable comedy in a quaintly English tradition, with shrewd rural characters outwitting smarter urban outsiders; inevitably, it suggests Ealing comedies, but the best of those avoided period settings.
wd Chris Monger story Ifor David Monger, Ivor Monger & Vernon Layton m Stephen Endelman pd Charles Garrad ed David Martin
☆ Hugh Grant, Tara Fitzgerald, Colm Meaney, Ian McNeice, Ian Hart, Kenneth Griffith, Tudor Vaughn, Hugh Vaughn
'Certainly a charming piece of work, a film that fits in tidily with our pseuding national cinema.' – *Adam Mars-Jones, Independent*

An Englishman's Home
GB   1939   79m   bw
UA/Aldwych (Neville E. Neville, Sidney Harrison)
US title: *Madmen of Europe*
An English family plays unwitting host to a foreign spy.
Hilarious clinker, far too unintentionally funny to make the effective propaganda intended.
w (catch them all) Dennis Wheatley, Edward Knoblock, Ian Hay, Robert Edmunds, Dora Nirva, Clifford Grey, Richard Llewellyn, Rodney Ackland play Guy du Maurier d Albert de Courville ph Mutz Greenbaum, Henry Harris ed Lister Laurence
☆ Edmund Gwenn, Mary Maguire, Paul Henreid, Geoffrey Toone, Richard Ainley, Desmond Tester
'There is nothing to be said for this film – though it might prove useful propaganda in enemy countries, purporting to illustrate the decadence of English architecture and taste.' – *Graham Greene*

Enid Is Sleeping
US   1989   102m   DeLuxe
First Independent/Vestron/Davis (John A. Davis, Howard Malin)
▣ ▣
GB title: *Over Her Dead Body*
Having accidentally killed her sister, who discovered her in bed with her husband, a woman tries to dispose of the body without arousing suspicion.
Unoriginal attempt at a black comedy, lacking wit and timing; Hitchcock did it far better with The Trouble With Harry.

w Maurice Phillips, A. J. Tipping, James Whaley d Maurice Phillips ph Affonso Beato m Craig Safan pd Paul Peters ed Malcolm Campbell
☆ Elizabeth Perkins, Judge Reinhold, Jeffrey Jones, Rhea Perlman, Michael J. Pollard, Brion James, Charles Tyner
'Neither farcical enough nor sufficiently outrageous to justify the sterling efforts of the cast to inject some much-needed energy into the flatly directed scenes.' – *Nigel Floyd, Sight and Sound*

Enigma
GB/France   1982   101m   colour
Embassy/Filmcrest/Peter Shaw
▣ ▣ ◎
An East German refugee is recruited by the CIA to return to East Berlin.
Threadbare spy stuff with an indecipherable plot.
w John Briley novel Michael Barak d Jeannot Szwarc ph Jean-Louis Picavet m Marc Wilkinson
☆ Martin Sheen, Brigitte Fossey, Sam Neill, Derek Jacobi, Michel Lonsdale, Frank Finlay, Michael Williams, Warren Clarke
'Well made but insufficiently exciting.' – *Variety*
'The mystery is why they bothered.' – *Guardian*

The Enigma of Kaspar Hauser ****
West Germany   1974   110m   colour
Contemporary/Zud Deutscher Rudfunk/Werner Herzog
▣
original title: *Jeder für sich und Gott gegen alle*
aka: *The Mystery of Kaspar Hauser; Every Man for Himself and God against All*
In the 1820s, a 16-year-old boy, who has spent his life isolated from others, is found abandoned in the town square of Nuremberg.
Based on a true story, a disturbing and affecting account of an untouched mind confronting humanity at its best and worst and exposing the limitations of society's response, with a fiercely convincing performance in the title role.
wd Werner Herzog ph Jörg Schmidt-Reitwein m Pachelbel, Albinoni and others ad Henning V. Gierke ed Beate Mainke-Jellinghaus
☆ Bruno S., Walter Ladengast, Brigitte Mira, Willy Semmelrogge, Gloria Dör, Volker Prechtel, Hans Musaus
'A double fable, intermingling the stultifying effects of bourgeois society and the cruelty of a demonic universe.' – *Pauline Kael*
'Herzog's direction is not free of the hallmarks of contemporary German film-making, an estheticism, a slow pace, an arrogance toward dramatic concept that almost supply an imaginary soundtrack accompanying the picture saying: "You can see that this film was made by an intellectual, can't you?"' – *Stanley Kauffmann*
† The film was awarded the Special Jury Prize at the Cannes Film Festival in 1975.

Ensayo de un Crimen: see *The Criminal Life of Archibaldo de la Cruz*

Ensign Pulver
US   1964   104m   Technicolor   Panavision
Warner (Joshua Logan)
▣
Further naval misadventures of the character from *Mr Roberts*.
Threadbare naval comedy with every expected cliché.
w Joshua Logan, Peter S. Feibleman play Joshua Logan, Thomas Heggen & Joshua Logan ph Charles Lawton m George Duning
☆ Robert Walker, Burl Ives, Walter Matthau, Tommy Sands, Millie Perkins, Kay Medford, Larry Hagman, James Farentino, James Coco, Al Freeman Jnr

Entebbe: Operation Thunderbolt: see *Operation Thunderbolt*

Entente Cordiale *
France   1939   95m   bw   Max Glass
A history of relations between England and France from Victorian times to the present day.
Ambitious pageant from the French point of view.
w Steve Passeur, Max Glass book Edward VII and His Times by André Maurois d Marcel l'Herbier ph Ted Pahle, Marc Fossard m Darius Milhaud
☆ Victor Francen, Gaby Morlay, André Lefaur, Jean Perier, Jean d'Yd, Jean Worms
'One of the most outstanding productions of its type ever made in France.' – *Variety*

Enter Arsène Lupin
US   1944   72m   bw
Universal (Ford Beebe)
A master thief protects a beautiful girl's emerald.
Stiff little second which failed to bring forth a series.
w Bertram Millhauser d Ford Beebe
☆ Charles Korvin, Ella Raines, J. Carrol Naish, George Dolenz, Gale Sondergaard, Miles Mander

Enter Inspector Duval
GB   1961   64m   bw
Bill Luckwell
A French detective helps Scotland Yard solve the murder of a socialite.
Dim mystery with no hope of becoming a series.
w J. Henry Piperno d Max Varnel ph Stephen Dade m Wilfred Burns
☆ Anton Diffring, Diane Hart, Mark Singleton

Enter Laughing *
US   1966   111m   Technicolor
Columbia/Acre/Sajo (Carl Reiner, Joseph Stein)
▣
In New York in the thirties, a young man about to train as a pharmacist decides to become an actor instead.
Strident Jewish comedy based on the writer-director's own youthful experiences, which might have been more effectively strained by another hand. The talent is there, though.
w Joseph Stein, Carl Reiner play Carl Reiner d Carl Reiner ph Joseph Biroc m Quincy Jones
☆ Reni Santoni, José Ferrer, Shelley Winters, Elaine May, Jack Gilford, Janet Margolin, David Opatoshu, Michael J. Pollard, Rob Reiner

Enter Madame
US   1934   83m   bw
Paramount
A millionaire is humbled when he marries a glamorous opera singer.
Modest comedy operetta, with the star's voice dubbed by Nina Koshetz.
w Charles Brackett, Gladys Lehman play Gilda Varesi Archibald, Dorothea Donn-Byrne d Elliott Nugent
☆ Elissa Landi, Cary Grant, Lynne Overman, Sharon Lynne, Paul Porcasi

Enter the Dragon *
US/Hong Kong   1973   99m   Technicolor   Panavision
Warner/Concord (Fred Weintraub, Paul Heller)
▣ ▣ ◎ ◎ ◎
A master of martial arts is enlisted by British intelligence to stop opium smuggling.
The first Hollywood-based Kung Fu actioner; not bad, on the lines of a more violent James Bond.
w Michael Allin d Robert Clouse ph Gilbert Hubbs m Lalo Schifrin
☆ Bruce Lee, John Saxon, Shih Kien, Jim Kelly, Bob Wall
'A good-natured example of the pleasures of schlock art.' – *Pauline Kael*

The Entertainer *
GB   1960   96m   bw
BL/Bryanston/Woodfall/Holly (John Croydon)
▣ ▣
A faded seaside comedian reflects on his failure as an entertainer and as a man.
Even with Olivier repeating his stage triumph, or perhaps because of it, this tragi-comedy remains defiantly theatrical and does not take wing on film.
w John Osborne, Nigel Kneale play John Osborne d Tony Richardson ph Oswald Morris m John Addison
☆ Laurence Olivier, Joan Plowright, Brenda de Banzie, Roger Livesey, Alan Bates, Shirley Anne Field, Albert Finney, Thora Hird, Daniel Massey
'No amount of deafening sound effects and speciously busy cutting can remove one's feeling that behind this distracting façade of heightened realism lurks a basic lack of confidence.' – *Peter John Dyer*
† A 1975 version for television starred Jack Lemmon.
🏆 Laurence Olivier

Pretentious talk-piece which slowly gets nowhere.
wd Lina Wertmuller
☆ Candice Bergen, Giancarlo Giannini

The End of Violence *
US/Germany/France 1997 122m DeLuxe
Otto Nemenz Cameras
Artificial Eye/CiBy 2000/Road Movies/Kintop (Deepak Nayar, Wim Wenders, Nicholas Klein)
▢ ▤

A Hollywood producer of violent action movies goes into hiding after being kidnapped and nearly killed by incompetent hitmen.
A stylish, enigmatic, paranoid thriller that touches on themes of movie violence and real-life surveillance without being particularly illuminating about either.
w Nicholas Klein d Wim Wenders ph Pascal Rabaud m Ry Cooder pd Patricia Norris ed Peter Przygodda
☆ Bill Pullman, Andie MacDowell, Gabriel Byrne, Loren Dean, Traci Lind, Daniel Benzali, K. Todd Freeman, Pruitt Taylor Vince, Peter Horton, Udo Kier, Samuel Fuller
'A cool, contemplative consideration of a hot contemporary topic.' – *Variety*

Endangered Species
US 1982 97m Metrocolor
MGM/Alive Enterprises (Carolyn Pfeiffer)
Citizens of a small Wyoming town discover that their cattle are being systematically murdered.
Curious melodrama which never really explains itself but seems to be carrying a message about chemical warfare. With a proper ending it could have been a good suspenser.
w Alan Rudolph, John Binder story Judson Klinger, Richard Woods d Alan Rudolph ph Paul Lohmann m Gary Wright pd Trevor Williams
☆ Robert Urich, JoBeth Williams, Paul Dooley, Hoyt Axton, Peter Coyote

'It's not over ... it's not over!'
Endless Love
US 1981 110m Technicolor
Polygram (Keith Barish)
▤ ℚ

A high school student's love for a 15-year-old girl is thwarted by circumstance and accident.
Overheated melodrama with unbelievable and unlikeable characters. Why this director should choose to make it is mysterious.
w Judith Rascoe novel Scott Spencer d Franco Zeffirelli ph David Watkin m Jonathan Tunick pd Ed Wittstein
☆ Brooke Shields, Martin Hewitt, Shirley Knight, Don Murray, Richard Kiley, Beatrice Straight
♫ title song (m/ly Lionel Richie)

Endless Night *
GB 1971 99m Eastmancolor
BL/EMI (Leslie Gilliat)
▤ ℚ

An American girl buys an English stately home and marries a chauffeur, but is later frightened to death.
Bumpy British thriller, structurally weak and peopled by the dullest conceivable characters, but with watchably scary sequences.
wd Sidney Gilliat novel Agatha Christie ph Harry Waxman m Bernard Herrmann
☆ Hayley Mills, Hywel Bennett, George Sanders, Britt Ekland, Per Oscarsson, Lois Maxwell

The Endless Summer
👫 US 1966 95m Technicolor
Bruce Brown Films/Columbia
▤ ℚ

A study of surfing round the world.
A documentary which became a cult for those influenced by this Californian obsession; smashing photography hardly atones for an approach so naïve as to become fatuous.
wd/ph/ed Bruce Brown

'When Was The Last Time You Stood Up And Cheered At A Movie?'
Endurance *
US 1998 83m DeLuxe Super 35
Buena Vista/Hollywood/La Junta/Film Four/Helkon (Edward R. Pressman, Terrence Malick, Max Palevsky)
A biopic of the Ethiopian long distance runner Haile Gebrselassie.
Framed by his winning performance over 10,000 metres at the 1996 Olympics, Haile Gebrselassie's life is told in flashback in a mix of documentary and

dramatic re-creation, revealing him as a natural athlete who has rarely stopped running and has managed to outpace the poverty in which he began.
wd Leslie Woodhead ph Ivan Strasburg m John Powell ed Saar Klein, Oral Norrie Ottey
☆ Haile Gebrselassie, Shawananness Gebrselassie, Yonas Zergaw, Tedesse Haile, Gebrselassie Bekele, Alem Tellahun
'Its mixture of biographical hype and social studies quickly curdles.' – *Stephen Holden, New York Times*
† The producers signed up eight runners in the 10,000 metres at the Atlanta Olympics so that they could make a documentary about the winner.

Enemies, a Love Story *
US 1989 120m colour
Fox/Morgan Creek Productions (Paul Mazursky)
▤ ℚ

The life of a Jew who survived the concentration camps becomes tragically entangled with that of three women: his first wife, whom he thought was dead, his second wife and his mistress.
Rushed in its telling, despite its length, and lacking in conviction.
w Roger L. Simon, Paul Mazursky novel Isaac Bashevis Singer d Paul Mazursky ph Fred Murphy m Maurice Jarre pd Pato Guzman ed Stuart Pappe
☆ Anjelica Huston, Ron Silver, Lena Olin, Margaret Sophie Stein, Judith Malina, Alan King, Rita Karin, Phil Leeds
♟ Anjelica Huston, Lena Olin; screenplay

Enemies of the Public: see The Public Enemy

Enemy Agent: see British Intelligence (1940)

Enemy Agent
US 1940 64m bw
Universal
An aircraft worker is framed as a spy.
Nifty little topical support with not much sense but plenty of zest.
w Sam Robbins, Edmund L. Hartmann d Lew Landers
☆ Richard Cromwell, Philip Dorn, Helen Vinson, Marjorie Reynolds, Robert Armstrong, Vinton Haworth, Abner Biberman, Jack Carson, Jack La Rue

Enemy Agents Meet Ellery Queen
US 1942 64m bw
Columbia (Ralph Cohn)
Sailors and marines help Ellery to rout Nazi spies.
Uncoordinated extravaganza which signalled the end of the Queen series.
w Eric Taylor d James Hogan
☆ William Gargan, Margaret Lindsay, Charley Grapewin, Gale Sondergaard, Gilbert Roland, Sig Rumann

The Enemy Below *
US 1957 98m Technicolor Cinemascope
TCF (Dick Powell)
▢

During World War II an American destroyer in the South Atlantic is involved in a cat-and-mouse operation with a U-boat.
Well-staged, unsurprising naval thriller with good pace and a pat let's-not-be-nasty-to-each-other ending.
w Wendell Mayes novel Commander D. A. Rayner d Dick Powell ph Harold Rosson m Leigh Harline
☆ Robert Mitchum, Curt Jurgens, Theodore Bikel, David Hedison

Enemy from Space: see Quatermass II

The Enemy General
US 1960 74m bw
Columbia (Sam Katzman)
An American officer takes revenge on the German general who executed his fiancée.
Routine World War II heroics with a plot deserving a rather better production.
w Dan Pepper, Burt Picard d George Sherman ph Basil Emmott md Mischa Bakaleinikoff
☆ Van Johnson, Jean-Pierre Aumont, John Van Dreelen, Dany Carrel, Françoise Prévost

Enemy Mine
US 1985 108m DeLuxe Amiflex Widescreen
Kings Road/TCF (Stephen Friedman)
▢ ▤ ℚ ◎

A space pilot goes down on Dracon and makes friends with his lizard-like captor.
All talk and little action, this is a way-out piece of do-goodery which tests the patience.
w Edward Khmara story Barry Longyear d Wolfgang Petersen ph Tony Imi m Maurice Jarre pd Rolf Zehetbauer ed Hannes Nikel
☆ Dennis Quaid, Lou Gossett Jnr, Brion James, Richard Marcus, Carolyn McCormick

An Enemy of the People *
US 1977 103m Metrocolor
First Artists (George Schaefer)
A small-town doctor discovers that for commercial reasons his colleagues propose to conceal the fact that the local spa is contaminated by tannery waste.
Ibsen's plot is well intentioned but well worn – it more or less served as the starting point for Jaws – so in any modern version the acting is all. Here it isn't enough, though the star so badly wanted to do it that arguments and sulks kept him off the screen for three years.
w Alexander Jacobs play Arthur Miller's version of the play by Henrik Ibsen d George Schaefer ph Paul Lohmann m Leonard Rosenman
☆ Steve McQueen, Charles Durning, Bibi Andersson, Eric Christmas, Richard Bradford, Richard A. Dysart
'The main thing I was shooting for was not to make bucks but to have something I could believe in.' – *Steve McQueen*

An Enemy of the People *
India 1989 100m Eastmancolor
Contemporary/Electric/National Film Development Corp of India (Anil Gupta)
▢
original title: *Ganashatru*
A doctor encounters local hostility when he complains of polluted water supplies.
Less than successful transfer of Ibsen's play to modern-day India, in a studio-bound production.
wd Satyajit Ray play Henrik Ibsen ph Barun Raha m Satyajit Ray ad Ashok Bose ed Dulal Dutta
☆ Soumitra Chatterjee, Dhritiman Chatterjee, Ruma Guhathakurta, Mamata Shankar, Dipankar Dey, Subhendu Chatterjee

Enemy of the State
US 1998 127m Technicolor Panavision
Buena Vista/Touchstone/Scott Free (Don Simpson/Jerry Bruckheimer)
▢ ▤ ◎ ◎ ℚ

Government agents target a lawyer who inadvertently has incriminating evidence against them.
Energetic, paranoid thriller preoccupied with surveillance methods; its narrative becomes increasingly implausible and substitutes speed for sense.
w David Marconi d Tony Scott ph Dan Mindel m Trevor Rabin, Harry Gregson-Williams pd Benjamin Fernandez ed Chris Lebenzon
☆ Will Smith, Gene Hackman, Jon Voight, Lisa Bonet, Regina King, Stuart Wilson, Tom Sizemore, Loren Dean, Barry Pepper, Ian Hurt, Jake Busey, Scott Caan, Jason Lee, Gabriel Byrne, James Le Gros
'The movie goes like the wind, but it's more a technological exercise than anything else.' – *David Denby, New Yorker*

L'Enfance Nue **
France 1968 80m colour
Stephan Films (Mag Bodard, François Truffaut, Claude Berri, Jo and Samy Siritzky)
aka: *Naked Childhood*
US title: *Me*
Rejected by his foster parents because of his difficult behaviour, a 10-year-old boy finds temporary refuge with an elderly couple.
A restrained, unsentimental account of a troubled and troublesome childhood, shot in a naturalistic style with a non-professional cast.
w Maurice Pialat, Arlette Langmann d Maurice Pialat ph Claude Beausoleil m Wagner
☆ Michel Tarrazon, Rene Thierry, Marie-Louis Thierry, Henri Puff, Maurice Coussoneau, Marie Marc, Michel Soulé

L'Enfant Sauvage *
France 1970 84m bw
UA/Films du Carrosse (Marcel Berbert)
US title: *The Wild Child*
In 1797, a scientist tames and studies a young boy who has mysteriously been living wild in the forest.
Slightly flat but generally interesting reconstruction of a true event, the same one which subsequently inspired TV projects such as Stalk the Wild Child and Lucan.
w François Truffaut, Jean Gruault d François Truffaut ph Nestor Almendros m Vivaldi
☆ Jean-Pierre Cargol, François Truffaut, Jean Dasté, Françoise Seigner

Les Enfants du Paradis ****
France 1945 195m bw
Pathé (Fred Orain, Raymond Borderic)
▢ ▤ ℚ
US title: *Children of Paradise*
In the 'theatre street' of Paris in the 1840s, a mime falls in love with the elusive Garance, but her problems with other men keep them apart.
A magnificent evocation of a place and a period, this thoroughly enjoyable epic melodrama is flawed only by its lack of human warmth and of a real theme. It remains nevertheless one of the cinema's most memorable films.
w Jacques Prévert d Marcel Carné ph Roger Hubert m Maurice Thiriet, Joseph Kosma, G. Mouque ad Alexandre Trauner, Léon Barsacq, Raymond Gabutti
☆ Arletty, Jean-Louis Barrault, Pierre Brasseur, Marcel Herrand, Maria Casarès, Louis Salou, Pierre Renoir, Gaston Modot, Jane Marken
'A magnificent scenario ... Prévert is as adept with wit as with poignancy ... I don't believe a finer group of actors was ever assembled on film' – *John Simon*
♟ Jacques Prévert

Les Enfants Terribles *
France 1950 100m bw
Jean-Pierre Melville
▢
aka: *The Strange Ones*
The hothouse relationship of an adolescent brother and sister leads to tragedy.
Rough-edged, stage-bound but occasionally quite powerful exploration into familiar Cocteau territory.
wd Jean-Pierre Melville novel Jean Cocteau ph Henri Decaë m Bach, Vivaldi
☆ Nicole Stéphane, Edouard Dermithe, Renée Cosima, Jacques Bernard

L'Enfer **
France 1993 100m Eastmancolor
Mayfair/MK2/CED/France 3/Cinemanuel/Canal (Marin Karmitz)
▢ ▤ ◎
aka: *Torment*
A hotelier becomes insanely jealous of his wife and imagines that she is having affairs with locals and the guests.
Chilling study of a disintegrating marriage, and a husband's descent into a mad hell of his own making, though the ambiguous ending is not entirely satisfactory.
w Henri-Georges Clouzot, Jose-Andre Lacour, Claude Chabrol d Claude Chabrol ph Bernard Zitzermann m Matthieu Chabrol ad Emile Ghigo ed Monique Fardoulis
☆ Emmanuelle Béart, François Cluzet, Nathalie Cardone, André Wilms, Marc Lavoine, Christiane Minazzoli, Dora Doll, Mario David, Jean-Pierre Cassel
'Under the film's sunny surface and vacational locations this is a winter's tale about the long autumn of love that has a casebook darkness to it.' – *Tom Hutchinson, Film Review*
† Director Henri-Georges Clouzot began making the film from his script in 1964, with Romy Schneider and Serge Reggiani, but had to stop when Reggiani became ill. He was rehearsing with a new star, Jean-Louis Trintignant, when he suffered a heart attack and had to abandon the production; he never tried again, despite living for another 13 years.

Entertaining Angels: The Dorothy Day Story

US 1996 111m DeLuxe
Warner/Paulist (Ellwood E. Kieser)

A left-wing journalist and intellectual becomes a Catholic, founds the crusading *The Catholic Worker* newspaper and establishes soup kitchens and shelters for the homeless.

A bland biopic about an interesting woman, short on conflict, but big on uplift.

w John Wells d Michael Ray Rhodes ph Michael Fash m Bill Conti, Ashley Irwin ed George Folsey Jnr, Geoffrey Rowland

☆ Moira Kelly, Heather Graham, Melinda Dillon, Martin Sheen, Lenny von Dohlen, Paul Lieber, Boyd Kestner, James Lancaster, Brian Keith

'A stultifying bore.' – *Film Review*

† The film's production company is a branch of the Paulist Fathers, 'dedicated to the communication of spiritual values through modern media'.

Entertaining Mr Sloane *

GB 1969 94m Technicolor
Pathé/Canterbury (Douglas Kentish)

A lodger attracts the amorous attention of both the middle-aged daughter and older son of the house.

A Gothic tour de force of bad taste which worked better on the stage but has its moments.

w Clive Exton play Joe Orton d Douglas Hickox ph Wolfgang Suschitzky m Georgie Fame

☆ Beryl Reid, Harry Andrews, Peter McEnery, Alan Webb

'What works as an offbeat comedy in the theatre fails to grip in the cinema where the darkness is made light. The direction becomes as brash as the dayglo colours of Beryl Reid's see-through mini-dress.' – *Ken Russell, Fire over England*

The Entity

US 1981 125m Technicolor Panavision
TCF/Pelleport Investors/American Cinema (Harold Schneider)

A young mother is attacked and raped by an invisible entity which may come from her own id.

Unpleasant nonsense, way overlong but with the occasional well-staged scene for those who can stay the course.

w Frank DeFelitta novel Frank DeFelitta d Sidney J. Furie ph Stephen H. Burum m Charles Bernstein pd Charles Rosen ed Frank J. Urioste

☆ Barbara Hershey, Ron Silver, David Labiosa, George Coe, Jacqueline Brookes

Entr'acte **

France 1924 20m bw silent
Ballets Suédois

Various eccentric characters become involved in a crazy chase.

Hilarious nonsense short, devised originally to be shown between the acts of a Dadaist ballet. Very clearly the start of a famous directorial career.

w Francis Picabia ph J. Berliet d/ed René Clair

☆ Jean Borlin, Inge Fries, Francis Picabia, Man Ray, Georges Auric, Marcel Achard, Marcel Duchamp

'The trap is set.'

Entrapment *

US/Germany 1999 110m DeLuxe Panavision
TCF/New Regency/Fountainbridge (Michael Hertzberg, Sean Connery, Rhonda Tollefson)

A female insurance investigator sets a trap for the world's greatest thief by asking him to steal a Chinese mask worth millions.

A thriller-cum-romantic-comedy with the emphasis on glamour; it has little else to offer.

w Ron Bass, William Broyles d Jon Amiel ph Phil Meheux m Christopher Young pd Norman Garwood ed Terry Rawlings

☆ Sean Connery, Catherine Zeta-Jones, Ving Rhames, Will Patton, Maury Chaykin, Kevin McNally, Terry O'Neill, David Yip

'No need to believe the outlandish details of the story; there's enough verve and charisma to the stars to make the escapade easy on the eyes.' – *Janet Maslin, New York Times*

'Preposterous whimsy that sort of gets by thanks to lustrous settings, slick production values and,

---

especially, its ultra-attractive stars.' – *Todd McCarthy, Variety*

Entre Nous: see *Coup de Foudre*

Entre Onze Heures et Minuit *

France 1948 103m bw
Francinex (Jacques Roitfeld)

A police detective solves his case by impersonating one of the victims.

Twisty, elaborate murder mystery, very competently performed but a little overlong.

w Henri Decoin, Marcel Rivet novel *Le Sosie de la Morgue* by Claude Luxel d Henri Decoin ph Nicolas Hayer m Henri Saguet

☆ Louis Jouvet, Madeleine Robinson, Robert Arnoux, Gisèle Casadesus

Entre Tinieblas: see *Dark Habits*

Entrée des Artistes *

France 1938 100m bw
Regina

Jealousies among the students at the Paris Conservatory lead to murder.

Predictable but well-made audience pleaser.

w Henri Jeanson, André Cayatte d Marc Allegret

☆ Louis Jouvet, Odette Joyeux, Claude Dauphin, Janine Darcy, Carette, Dalio, Sylvie

'Everyone Has A Dark Side. Henry's About To Meet His.'

Equinox *

US 1992 110m colour Panavision
Metro Tartan/SC Entertainment (David Blocker)

A shy and timid garage mechanic discovers that he has a twin brother who is a killer.

Quirky, stylized but insubstantial tale of people damaged by, or fearful of, life; but it cannot bear as much weight as its director intended.

wd Alan Rudolph ph Elliot Davis m Rachmaninov and others pd Steven Legler ed Michael Ruscio

☆ Matthew Modine, Lara Flynn Boyle, Marisa Tomei, Fred Ward, Tyra Ferrell, Kevin J. O'Connor, Tate Donovan, Lori Singer, M. Emmet Walsh, Gailard Sartain

'A film which needs several viewings to be appreciated. Although the battle between dark and light is obvious, the finer touches are buried in a visual tapestry to be discovered by the devoted (perhaps obsessive) viewer.' – *Sight and Sound*

L'Equipage *

France 1935 107m bw
Pathé-Natan

A World War 1 flyer finds that the love of his life is the wife of his colleague.

Tense romantic drama with aerial sequences, subsequently remade in Hollywood as The Woman I Love.

story Joseph Kessel d Anatole Litvak

☆ Charles Vanel, Jean-Pierre Aumont, Annabella

'A gripping human story, beautifully told.' – *Variety*

Equus *

GB 1977 137m colour
UA/Winkast (Denis Holt)

A middle-aged psychiatrist tries to find out why a 17-year-old boy blinded six horses.

Overlong film version of a play which was a succès d'estime; it makes the fatal mistake of showing the tragic events realistically instead of stylistically as was done on the stage, and as a study in abnormal psychology it is scarcely gripping or revealing.

w Peter Shaffer play Peter Shaffer d Sidney Lumet ph Oswald Morris m Richard Rodney Bennett pd Tony Walton

☆ Richard Burton, Peter Firth, Colin Blakely, Joan Plowright, Harry Andrews, Eileen Atkins, Jenny Agutter, Kate Reid

'It sets Peter Shaffer's worst ideas on a pedestal.' – *Pauline Kael*

Ⅰ Peter Shaffer; Richard Burton; Peter Firth

Ⓥ Jenny Agutter

'He will erase your past to protect your future.'

Eraser

US 1996 115m Technicolor Panavision
Warner (Arnold Kopelson, Anne Kopelson)

An agent for the Federal Witness Protection Program discovers that he can trust no one.

Predictable recycling of the themes of modern paranoid thrillers, punctuated by the furious sound of monstrous gun battles.

w Tony Puryear, Walon Green d Charles Russell ph Adam Greenberg m Alan Silvestri pd Bill Kenney ed Michael Tronick

☆ Arnold Schwarzenegger, James Caan, Vanessa Williams, James Coburn, Robert Pastorelli, James Cromwell, Andy Romano, Danny Nucci

'If *Mission: Impossible* failed to make any sense to you, you could look on *Eraser* as the world's fastest remake, since its plot, its characters and its big set pieces are exactly the same.' – *Mark Steyn, Spectator*

'Filmgoers may feel that they've been there, seen that: fans will still flock.' – *Alexander Walker*

† It was a box-office success in 1996, grossing around $234m worldwide.

Ⅱ sound effects editing

Eraserhead

US 1976 89m bw
David Lynch

A nondescript man has a number of increasingly nightmarish experiences including becoming pregnant and being consumed by a planet.

Tediously elongated piece of schlock surrealism. At least Buñuel and Dali didn't take so long about their nonsense.

wd David Lynch ph David Elmes, Herbert Cardwell

☆ John Nance, Charlotte Stewart, Allen Joseph

'A compulsive hybrid mix of punk surrealism and B picture.' – *Time Out*

Erbin des Dracula: see *Vampyros Lesbos*

Ercole e la Regina di Lidia: see *Hercules Unchained*

L'Erdita Ferramonti: see *The Inheritance*

Erendira *

France/Mexico/Germany 1982 105m colour
Les Films du Triangle/A2/Cine Qua Non/Atlas Saskia Film (Alain Queffelean)

An intolerant woman tries to restore the family fortune by prostituting her young granddaughter after she accidentally burns down their home.

Bizarre, surrealist fable of thwarted love and domination.

w Gabriel García Marquez d Ruy Guerra ph Denys Clerval m Maurice Lecoeur pd Pierre Cadiou ed Kenout Peltier

☆ Irene Papas, Claudia Ohana, Michel Lonsdale, Oliver Wehe, Rufus, Blanca Guerra, Ernesto Gomez Cruz

Erik the Viking

GB 1989 108m Technicolor
UIP/Erik The Viking Productions/Prominent Features/AB Svensk Filmindustri (Terry Glinwood)

A Viking sails on an expedition to wake the Gods.

Uneasy mix of fantasy and humour.

wd Terry Jones novel Terry Jones ph Ian Wilson m Neil Innes pd John Beard ed George Akers

☆ Tim Robbins, Mickey Rooney, Eartha Kitt, Terry Jones, Imogen Stubbs, John Cleese, Tsutomu Sekine, Antony Sher, Gary Cady, Charles McKeown, Tim McInnerny, John Gordon Sinclair

'A thunderous, unfunny jumble.' – *MFB*

'She brought a small town to its feet and a huge corporation to its knees.'

Erin Brockovich ***

US 2000 131m CFI
Columbia TriStar/Universal/Jersey (Danny DeVito, Michael Shamberg, Stacey Sher)

A working-class mother, who talks her way into a job in a law firm, organises a winning investigation into industrial pollution that has devastated a community.

Unexpectedly lively and amusing movie of a heartening true story, one that gives Julia Roberts her best and

---

most convincing role so far, as a feisty but vulnerable mother who refuses to be intimidated by anyone.

w Susannah Grant d Steven Soderbergh ph Ed Lachman m Thomas Newman pd Phil Messina ed Anne V. Coates cos Jeffrey Kurland

☆ Julia Roberts, Albert Finney, Aaron Eckhart, Marg Helgenberger, Cherry Jones, Veanne Cox, Conchata Ferrell, Tracey Walter, Peter Coyote, Scotty Leavenworth, Gemmenne De la Pena, Jamie Harrold

'A movie that is both intensely funny and emotionally satisfying.' – *Ian Nathan, Empire*

† Erin Brockovich herself appears briefly as a waitress in a coffee shop.

Ermo ***

China/Hong Kong 1994 98m colour
ICA/Ocean/Shanghai Studio (Jimmy Tan, Chen Kunming)

A wife with an elderly and impotent husband works hard in order to buy a big-screen television set to impress the neighbours.

Biting comedy of village and peasant life, which also asks some tough questions on what gives meaning and purpose to a person's existence.

w Lang Yun story Xu Baoqi d Zhou Xiaowen ph Lu Gengxin m Zhoi Xiaowen ad Zhang Daqian ed Zhong Furong

☆ Ailiya, Liu Peiqi, Ge Zhijun, Zhang Haiyan, Zan Zhenguo

'A lively, constantly diverting film: it was amusing, colourful characters, a generous dash of humour and not a jot of sentimentality.' – *Independent*

Ernest Rides Again

US 1994 92m CFI color
Emsell (Stacy Williams)

Ernest discovers that a cannon contains the British Crown Jewels.

There are few experiences more depressing than attempting to sit through an Ernest movie: it's not just that the jokes are poor, the comic timing is off and its hero has all the charm of an over-ripe skunk; it is just the pervasive feeling that no one is having fun, on either side of the camera.

w John Cherry, William M. Akers d John Cherry ph David Geddes m Bruce Arntson ed Craig Bassett

☆ Jim Varney, Ron James, Linda Kash, Tom Butler, Xuke Ernsberger, Jeff Pillars

Ernest Saves Christmas

US 1988 91m Metrocolor
Warner/Touchstone/Silver Screen Partners III (Stacy Williams, Doug Claybourne)

Santa Claus goes to America to find someone to take over his job.

Inept and witless from start to finish.

w B. Kline, Ed Turner d John Cherry ph Peter Stein m Mark Snow ad Ian Thomas ed Sharyn L. Ross

☆ Jim Varney, Douglas Seale, Oliver Clark, Noelle Parker, Gailard Sartain, Billie Bird, Bill Byrge, Robert Lesser, Key Howard

L'Eroe di Babylon: see *The Hero of Babylon*

Eroica *

Poland 1957 83m bw
Kadr
aka: *Heroism*

Two ironic episodes of war; in the 1944 Warsaw uprising and in a POW camp.

Nicely-judged little stories with a sting.

w Jerzy Stefan Stawinski novels Jerzy Stefan Stawinski d Andrzej Munk ph Jerzy Wojcik m Jan Krenz

☆ Barbara Polomska, L. Niemszyk, Edward Dziewonski, K. Rudzki, Roman Klosowski, Josef Nowak

The Erotic Dreams of Cleopatra (dubbed)

Italy/France 1983 85m colour
2T/Naja (Victor Beniard)

Cleopatra, a captive in Rome, becomes caught up in the power struggle to control the Empire.

An oddity: a risible, would-be erotic exploitation movie that opens with a quote from Cicero, followed by the assassination of Julius Caesar in a thick fog (a dream by Cleopatra) and then departs from known history

---

with its cast simultaneously engaging in energetic couplings and banal political discussions.
w Rino di Silvestro d Cesar Todd ph Giovanni Bergamini m Romuald ad Mario Ambrosino ed Adriano Tagliavia
☆ Marcella Petrelli, Rita Silva, Jacques Stany, Andrea Coppola, Maurizio Faraoni

Erotikon *
Sweden 1920 85m bw silent
Svensk Filmindustri
When a professor discovers that his wife is unfaithful, he consoles himself with his young niece.
Sophisticated comedy drama filled with material which might later have appealed to Lubitsch; a little faded now, but it still has charm.
w Gustav Molander, Mauritz Stiller play Franz Herzeg d Mauritz Stiller ph Henrik Jaenzon
☆ Lars Hanson, Karin Molander, Tora Teje, Anders de Wahl

Erotikon *
Czechoslovakia 1929 85m bw silent
Gem Film
A stationmaster's daughter takes a rich lover.
Atmospheric little sex drama which sufficiently justified its title to be a big international success.
wd Gustav Machaty ph Vaclav Vich
☆ Ita Rina, Karel Schleichert, Olaf Fjord, Theo Pistek

The Errand Boy
🎏 US 1961 92m bw
Paramount/Jerry Lewis (Ernest D. Glucksman)
■ ▦ ⌖
A dimwit paperhanger causes havoc in a Hollywood studio but is eventually signed up as a comic to rival Jerry Lewis.
Feeble comedy with the star at his self-satisfied worst.
wd Jerry Lewis ph W. Wallace Kelley m Walter Scharf
☆ Jerry Lewis, Brian Donlevy, Sig Rumann, Fritz Feld, Isobel Elsom, Iris Adrian

Es Geschah am 20 Juli: see Jackboot Mutiny

Escapade: see Robinson Crusoeland (1950)

Escapade
US 1935 87m bw
MGM (Bernard Hyman)
Affairs of a Viennese artist.
Turgid romantic drama copied from the more successful German film Maskerade.
w Herman J. Mankiewicz original Walter Reisch d Robert Z. Leonard ph Ernest Haller m Bronislau Kaper, Walter Jurmann
☆ William Powell, Luise Rainer, Virginia Bruce, Mady Christians, Reginald Owen, Frank Morgan, Laura Hope Crews, Henry Travers
'A triumph of studio slickness.' – Variety

Escapade *
🎏 GB 1955 87m bw
Pinnacle (Daniel Angel)
▦
Parents row with a headmaster when their three sons steal an aeroplane, but all is well when it turns out that they are on a peace mission.
Whimsical comedy-drama with a rather foolish point; the cast however can hardly fail to provide entertaining moments.
w Gilbert Holland (Donald Ogden Stewart) play Roger MacDougall d Philip Leacock ph Eric Cross m Bruce Montgomery
☆ John Mills, Alastair Sim, Yvonne Mitchell, Colin Gordon, Marie Lohr

Escapade in Florence
🎏 US 1962 80m Technicolor
Walt Disney (Bill Anderson)
Two American students in Florence uncover art thefts.
Cheerful adventure for children, well enough produced on location, but quite unmemorable.
w Maurice Tombragel novel The Golden Doors by Edward Fenton d Steve Previn ph Kurt Grigoleit m Buddy Baker
☆ Ivan Desny, Tommy Kirk, Annette Funicello, Nino Castelnuovo

Escapade in Japan
US 1957 93m Technirama
RKO (Arthur Lubin)
▦
An American boy survives a plane crash in Tokyo and the crisis reunites his parents.
Nicely photographed travelogue with a thread of plot; pleasant but hardly sustaining.
w Winston Miller d Arthur Lubin ph William Snyder m Max Steiner
☆ Cameron Mitchell, Teresa Wright, Jon Prevost, Philip Ober

Escape
GB 1930 69m bw
ATP (Basil Dean)
An escaped convict on Dartmoor is helped and hindered by various chance encounters.
Episodic, unsatisfactory drama from a stilted play.
wd Basil Dean play John Galsworthy ph Jack Mackenzie, Robert Martin md Ernest Irving ad Clifford Pember ed Jack Kitchin
☆ Gerald du Maurier, Edna Best, Madeleine Carroll, Gordon Harker, Horace Hodges, Mabel Poulton, Lewis Casson, Ian Hunter, Felix Aylmer
'A more careful work than most of the British talker product, but as an entertainment proposition it doesn't mean much.' – Variety

'There is a love from which no man can escape!'
Escape **
US 1940 104m bw
MGM (Lawrence Weingarten)
reissue title: When the Door Opened
An American gets his mother out of a Nazi concentration camp before World War II.
Ingenious but somewhat slow-moving melodrama with an exciting climax and good production values.
w Arch Oboler, Marguerite Roberts novel Ethel Vance d Mervyn Le Roy ph Robert Planck m Franz Waxman
☆ Norma Shearer, Robert Taylor, Conrad Veidt, Nazimova, Felix Bressart, Albert Basserman, Philip Dorn, Bonita Granville
'It takes an hour to get started and makes just another feeble fable from headlines.' – Otis Ferguson
'Far and away the most dramatic and hair-raising picture yet made on the sinister subject of persecution in a totalitarian land.' – Bosley Crowther, New York Times
'One of the most poignant dramatic films of the year.' – Modern Screen
'The director takes forever to set up the manoeuvres, and the villain is so much more attractive than the hero that the whole thing turns into a feeble, overproduced joke.' – Pauline Kael, 70s

'Some men are born to spoilled adventure! Some women are drawn to the most dangerous of loves!'
Escape
GB 1948 79m bw
TCF (William Perlberg)
Wholly artificial, predictable and uninteresting remake of the 1930 film.
w Philip Dunne d Joseph L. Mankiewicz ph Frederick A. Young m William Alwyn
☆ Rex Harrison, Peggy Cummins, William Hartnell, Norman Wooland, Jill Esmond

The Escape Artist *
🎏 US 1982 93m Technicolor
Zoetrope Studios (Doug Claybourne, Buck Houghton)
▦
A young boy justifies his descent from 'the world's greatest escape artist'.
Curiously unfulfilled fable, too vague to satisfy the family audience it seems to aim at, but with pleasant moments.
w Melissa Mathison, Stephen Zito. novel David Wagoner d Caleb Deschanel ph Stephen H. Burum m Georges Delerue pd Dean Tavoularis
☆ Griffin O'Neal, Raul Julia, Teri Garr, Joan Hackett, Gabriel Dell, Desi Arnaz

Escape by Night
GB 1953 79m bw
Tempean (Robert S. Baker, Monty Berman)
A tough reporter tries to get the inside story on a vice ring.
Formula thick ear with what now seems the world's most unlikely villain – Sid James.
wd John Gilling ph Monty Berman m Stanley Black

☆ Bonar Colleano, Andrew Ray, Sidney James, Ted Ray, Simone Silva, Avice Landone, Patrick Barr

Escape from Alcatraz *
US 1979 112m DeLuxe
Paramount/Malpaso (Don Siegel)
■ ▦ ⌖ ⌖
The allegedly true story of a 1960 escape from the prison on a rock in San Francisco Bay.
A dour, terse, depressing prison movie which makes an uncomfortable star vehicle and not very much of an entertainment, but does preserve a certain integrity right to its ambiguous ending.
w Richard Tuggle book J. Campbell Bruce d Don Siegel ph Bruce Surtees m Jerry Fielding pd Allen Smith
☆ Clint Eastwood, Patrick McGoohan, Roberts Blossom, Jack Thibeau, Larry Hankin
'An almost entirely interior film masquerading as an exterior one.' – Tom Milne, MFB

Escape from Dartmoor *
GB 1930 77m bw
Pro Patria
A barber murders his wife's lover.
Stilted melodrama, of interest only as an early British part-talkie. (The only words heard are from a film in a cinema which the characters visit.)
w Herbert Price d Anthony Asquith
☆ Norah Baring, Uno Henning, Hans Schlettow
'Morbid material, interesting only because of clever direction.' – Variety

Escape from East Berlin
Germany/US 1962 94m bw
MGM/Walter Wood/Hans Albin
aka: Tunnel 28
An East German chauffeur is persuaded to help an escape attempt by digging and tunnelling under the Berlin Wall.
Cheerless escape melodrama, thinly based on fact but without much suspense.
w Gabrielle Upton, Peter Berneis, Millard Lampell d Robert Siodmak ph Georg Krause m Hans-Martin Majewski
☆ Don Murray, Christine Kaufmann, Werner Klemperer, Ingrid van Bergen

Escape from Fort Bravo *
US 1953 98m Anscocolor
MGM (Nicholas Nayfack)
A girl helps her Confederate lover to escape from a Yankee fort in Arizona; the commander then tries to save them from Indians.
Grade A Western, effectively shot in Death Valley.
w Frank Fenton d John Sturges ph Robert Surtees m Jeff Alexander
☆ William Holden, Eleanor Parker, John Forsythe, William Demarest

'Snake is Back.'
Escape from L.A.
US 1996 100m DeLuxe Panavision
Paramount/Rysher (Kurt Russell, Debra Hill)
■ ▦ ⌖
aka: John Carpenter's Escape from L.A.
In 2013, an outlaw is sent to the island of Los Angeles to eliminate the President's daughter, who has stolen a device to shut down the world's power sources and joined a revolution against her father's right-wing government.
No more than a weary rehash of Carpenter's Escape from New York; the plot has aged in the 15-year gap between the two movies, and one might have hoped that its star and director would have moved on to something less stale.
w John Carpenter, Debra Hill, Kurt Russell d John Carpenter ph Gary B. Kibbe m Shirley Walker, John Carpenter pd Lawrence G. Paull ed Edward Warschilka
☆ Kurt Russell, Stacy Keach, Steve Buscemi, Peter Fonda, George Corraface, Valeria Golino, Pam Grier, Michelle Forbes, Cliff Robertson
'Easily the crappiest-looking, cheesiest FX-toting, shoddiest excuse for a $50 million action epic ever foisted on unsuspecting audiences.' – Guardian
† The film took $25m at the US box-office.

Escape from New York *
US 1981 99m Metrocolor Panavision
Avco Embassy/International Film Investors/Goldcrest (Larry Franco, Debra Hill)
■ ▦ ⌖ ⌖ ⌖ ⌖ ◠
In 1997 the whole of Manhattan Island has become a vast security prison; a president has to bale out over it and is taken hostage.
Inventive but too complex melodrama with unattractive detail; its director's biggest production but not his most rewarding.
w John Carpenter, Nick Castle d John Carpenter ph Jim Lucas m John Carpenter pd Joe Alves
☆ Kurt Russell, Lee Van Cleef, Ernest Borgnine, Donald Pleasence, Isaac Hayes, Season Hubley, Adrienne Barbeau, Harry Dean Stanton

Escape from the Dark
🎏 GB 1976 104m Technicolor
Walt Disney (Ron Miller)
In 1909 Yorkshire, two boys save pit ponies from the slaughterhouse.
Efficient family fare with plenty of suspense and good character cameos.
w Rosemary Anne Sisson d Charles Jarrott ph Paul Beeson m Ron Goodwin
☆ Alastair Sim, Peter Barkworth, Maurice Colbourne, Susan Tebbs, Geraldine McEwan, Prunella Scales, Leslie Sands, Joe Gladwin

'A New Generation Of Incredible Apes In The Most Exciting Suspense Film Of Them All.'
Escape from the Planet of the Apes
US 1971 97m DeLuxe Panavision
TCF/APJAC (Arthur P. Jacobs, Frank Capra Jnr)
■ ▦ ⌖ ◠
Three educated apes travel back from the disaster-strewn future to warn mankind of what lies ahead. Mankind naturally misunderstands.
Predictable third in the series, with infantile humour alternating with a downbeat trend.
w Paul Dehn d Don Taylor ph Joseph Biroc m Jerry Goldsmith
☆ Roddy McDowall, Kim Hunter, Bradford Dillman, Ricardo Montalban, Natalie Trundy, Eric Braeden, William Windom, Sal Mineo
† See also Planet of the Apes.

Escape from Zahrain
US 1961 93m Technicolor Panavision
Paramount (Ronald Neame)
Prisoners escape across the desert from an oil sheikdom.
Slow, boring adventure film; good to look at, with James Mason unbilled in a tiny part.
w Robin Estridge d Ronald Neame ph Ellsworth Fredricks m Lyn Murray
☆ Yul Brynner, Sal Mineo, Madlyn Rhue, Jack Warden, Jay Novello

Escape If You Can: see St Benny the Dip

Escape in the Desert
US 1945 81m bw
Warner (Alex Gottlieb)
An American flyer outwits renegade Nazis.
Oddball remake of The Petrified Forest, with Nazis sitting in for gangsters. Of no interest in itself.
w Thomas Job play Robert E. Sherwood d Edward A. Blatt ph Robert Burks m Adolph Deutsch
☆ Philip Dorn, Helmut Dantine, Alan Hale, Jean Sullivan, Irene Manning, Samuel S. Hinds

Escape in the Fog
US 1945 65m bw
Columbia
A nurse sees a man attacked in a dream, and helps to save him when the events recur in real life.
Muddy little spy story with premonition used as a book-end.
w Aubrey Wisberg d Budd Boetticher
☆ Nina Foch, Otto Kruger, William Wright

Escape Me Never *
GB 1935 95m bw
B and D (Herbert Wilcox)
The mother of an illegitimate baby marries a composer who loves someone else.
Archetypal romantic weepie which has probably the star's most memorable and likeable performance.
w Carl Zuckerman, Robert Cullen play Margaret Kennedy d Paul Czinner ph Georges Périnal

---

☆ *Elisabeth Bergner*, Hugh Sinclair, Griffith Jones, Penelope Dudley Ward, Irene Vanbrugh, Leon Quartermaine, Lyn Harding

'Story stirs audience resentment, yet its able presentation commands attention.' – *Variety*

'That it is a thoroughly British film is proved by the fact that among the staff one can see names like Andrejiev, Allgeier and Strassner, that the principal actress is German, and the producer is German too.' – *James Agate*

⚮ Elisabeth Bergner

Escape Me Never

US 1947 104m bw
Warner (Henry Blanke)

Muddled remake of the above with shifted emphasis.

So ill-conceived it's like watching through frosted glass.

w Thomas Williamson d Peter Godfrey ph Sol Polito m Erich Wolfgang Korngold

☆ Errol Flynn, Ida Lupino, Eleanor Parker, Gig Young, Reginald Denny, Isobel Elsom, Albert Basserman, Ludwig Stossel, Helene Thimig

The Escape of Mechagodzilla: see *Monsters from an Unknown Planet*

Escape of the Amethyst: see *Yangtse Incident*

Escape Route

GB 1952 79m bw
Banner/Eros
US title: *I'll Get You*

Man on the run turns out to be FBI agent on the spy trail.

A moderate co-feature, as unremarkable as its plot.

w John Baines, Nicholas Phipps d Seymour Friedman, Peter Graham Scott ph Eric Cross m Hans May

☆ George Raft, Sally Gray, Clifford Evans, Reginald Tate

Escape to Athena

GB 1979 117m Eastmancolor Panavision
ITC/Pimlico (David Niven Jnr, Jack Wiener)

Prisoners-of-war on a Greek island during World War II recruit the aid of their sympathetic camp commandant in harassing the SS.

Expensive but not very involving thick ear, hampered by tediously typecast actors and an uninventive script.

w Edward Anhalt, Richard S. Lochte d George Pan Cosmatos ph Gil Taylor m Lalo Schifrin

☆ Roger Moore, David Niven, Elliott Gould, Sonny Bono, Telly Savalas, Claudia Cardinale, Stefanie Powers, Richard Roundtree, Anthony Valentine

'Performing as though they had met up by chance on holiday … the clutch of box office stars do what they can in a situation where they are the stand-ins and the stuntmen (especially the motorcyclists) dominate the screen.' – *Martyn Auty, MFB*

Escape to Burma

US 1955 88m Technicolor Superscope
Benedict Bogeaus

An adventurer suspected of murder hides out on the tea plantation of an indomitable American woman.

Far Eastern hokum in which the heroine has a way with elephants.

w Talbot Jennings, Herbert Donovan d Allan Dwan ph John Alton m Louis Forbes

☆ Barbara Stanwyck, Robert Ryan, David Farrar, Murvyn Vye, Reginald Denny

Escape to Danger

GB 1943 92m bw
RKO (William Sistrom)

A British schoolmistress becomes a spy.

Adequate propaganda hokum.

w Wolfgang Wilhelm, Jack Whittingham d Lance Comfort ph Max Greene m William Alwyn

☆ Eric Portman, Ann Dvorak, Karel Stepanek, Ronald Ward, Ronald Adam, Lily Kann, David Peel, Felix Aylmer, A. E. Matthews

Escape to Glory

US 1940 74m bw
Columbia (Sam Bischoff)
aka: *Submarine Zone*

A merchant ship with a variety of passengers is stalked by a Nazi submarine.

Minor Grand Hotel afloat: quite brisk and watchable.

w P. J. Wolfson d John Brahm ph Franz Planer

☆ Pat O'Brien, Constance Bennett, John Halliday, Alan Baxter, Melville Cooper, Edgar Buchanan, Marjorie Gateson

Escape to Happiness: see *Intermezzo*

Escape to Victory: see *Victory*

Escape to Witch Mountain *

👥 US 1974 97m Technicolor
Walt Disney (Jerome Courtland)

Two mysterious orphan children have extraordinary powers, are chased by a scheming millionaire, and prove to come from another planet.

Mildly ingenious story frittered away by poor scripting and special effects. A stimulating change in children's films, however.

w Robert Malcolm Young novel Alexander Key d John Hough ph Frank Phillips m Johnny Mandel sp Art Cruickshank, Danny Lee

☆ Ray Milland, Donald Pleasence, Eddie Albert, Kim Richards, Ike Eisenmann, Walter Barnes, Reta Shaw, Denver Pyle

Escapement

GB 1957 72m bw
Anglo Amalgamated/Merton Park Studios (Alec C. Snowden)

An insurance investigator traces some mysterious deaths in France to a health clinic where doctors are experimenting with mind-altering techniques.

Efficient and slightly unconventional low-budget thriller.

w Charles Eric Maine, J. Maclaren-Ross d Montgomery Tully ph Bert Mason, Teddy Catford m Soundrama md Richard Taylor ad Wilfred Arnold ed Geoffrey Muller

☆ Rod Cameron, Mary Murphy, Meredith Edwards, Peter Illing, Carl Jaffé, Kay Callard, Carl Duering, Roberta Huby

The Escapist

US 1983 87m colour
Mid-American Promotions (Ron Hostetler, Eddie Beverly Jnr)

A small-time radio owner tries to emulate Houdini's feats in order to prevent a take-over by a big corporation.

Bizarre low-budget drama, featuring bad actors enunciating a worse script.

w Stephen Meyers d Eddie Beverly Jnr ph Stephen Posey m Jeffrey Boze pd Charles Largent ed Ron Hostetler

☆ Bill Shirk, Milbourne Christopher, Peter Lupus, Dick The Bruiser, Gary Todd, Cynthia Johns, Terri Mann

The Escort: see *La Scorta*

Escort Girls

GB 1974 95m Eastmancolor
Variety/Donwin (Donovan Winter)

Six stories of encounters between clients and escorts hired for the night from an agency, which frequently end in rape or seduction.

Glossily made but empty sexploitation movie, hampered by a script that never deviates from the obvious.

wd Donovan Winter ph Gus Coma, Austin Parkinson ed Donovan Winter

☆ David Dixon, Maria O'Brien, Marika Mann, Gil Barber, Helen Christie, Richard Wren

Escort West

US 1958 75m bw Cinemascope
Batjac/Romina/UA

An ex-Confederate soldier helps the survivors of a Union wagon train attack.

Watchable lower-berth Western.

w Leo Gordon, Fred Hartsook d Francis D. Lyon ph William H. Clothier m Henry Vars

☆ Victor Mature, Elaine Stewart, Faith Domergue, Noah Beery Jnr, Rex Ingram, John Hubbard

Eskimo *

US 1933 120m bw
MGM

The life of an Eskimo hunter and his family.

Curious fated attempt by a major studio to do a northern version of the successful White Shadows in the South Seas. Despite a melodramatic plot and gripping documentary sequences, the locale chilled audiences to the marrow.

w John Lee Mahin, Peter Freuchen d W. S. Van Dyke ed Conrad Nervig

☆ Mala, Peter Freuchen

'Igloo whoopee variations not sufficiently hotcha to spell b.o.' – *Variety*

🏆 editing

L'Espion: see *The Defector*

Espionage *

US 1937 67m bw
MGM (Harry Rapf)

Spies and counter spies mingle on the Orient Express.

Lively second feature on familiar lines.

w Manuel Seff, Leonard Lee, Ainsworth Morgan play Walter Hackett d Kurt Neumann ph Ray June m William Axt

☆ Edmund Lowe, Madge Evans, Paul Lukas, Ketti Gallian, Skeets Gallagher, Leonid Kinskey, Barnett Parker, Frank Reicher

'Quite some laughs but chiefly for the duals.' – *Variety*

Espionage Agent

US 1939 83m bw
Warner (Louis F. Edelmann)

An American diplomat falls in love with a spy.

Anti-isolationist, semi-documentary exposé, a rather sketchy cross between Foreign Correspondent and Confessions of a Nazi Spy.

w Warren Duff, Michael Fessier, Frank Donaghue, Robert Buckner d Lloyd Bacon ph Charles Rosher

☆ Joel McCrea, Brenda Marshall, Jeffrey Lynn, George Bancroft, Stanley Ridges, James Stephenson, Nana Bryant

'War headlines dramatized. Lots of openings for exploitation.' – *Variety*

Les Espions

France 1957 136m bw
Cinedis (L. de Mazure)
aka: *The Spies*

Spies from all sides converge on a psychiatric clinic where an atomic scientist is being hidden.

Unsatisfactory thriller with some aims to be both a whimsy and a parable. Not one of its director's successes.

w Henri-Georges Clouzot, Gerome Geronomi d Henri-Georges Clouzot ph Christian Matras m Georges Auric

☆ Martita Hunt, Peter Ustinov, Sam Jaffe, Vera Clouzot, Gabrielle Dorziat, Curt Jurgens, Gerard Sety, O. E. Hasse

El Espiritu de la Colmene: see *The Spirit of the Beehive*

Espoir *

France/Spain 1938 73m bw
Cornignion/Moligniec
aka: *Days of Hope*
aka: *Man's Hope*

Events of the Spanish Civil War, recreated by surviving combatants.

Anti-fascist propaganda which seems a good deal less inspiring than on its first release, but has some vivid cinematic ideas.

wd André Malraux ph Louis Page m Darius Milhaud

☆ Mejuto, Nicolas Rodriguez, Jose Lado

Esprit d'Amour

Hong Kong 1983 100m colour
Cinema City (Dean Shek, Raymond Wong)

A hen-pecked insurance investigator is haunted by the spirit of a young girl who died in an accidental fall.

Insubstantial and heavy-handed comedy, though attractive to look at.

w Ko Chi Sum, Lo Kin, Raymond Fung story Raymond Wong d Ringo L. T. Lam m Tang Siu Lam pd Nansun Shi, Raymond Fung ed Tony Chow

☆ Alan Tam, Cecilia Chan, Ni Shu Chun

'And it was written – gather together all the fair young virgins unto the palace – and let the maiden which pleaseth the king be queen.'

Esther and the King

US 1960 109m Technicolor Cinemascope
TCF/Galatea (Raoul Walsh)

A Persian king selects a new bride who helps defend him from his enemies.

Tedious biblical hokum with a muddled script and the usual co-production deficiencies.

w Raoul Walsh, Michael Elkins d Raoul Walsh ph Mario Bava m Francesco Lavagnino, Roberto Nicolosi

☆ Richard Egan, Joan Collins, Denis O'Dea, Sergio Fantoni, Rik Battaglia

Esther Waters

GB 1947 108m bw
GFD/Wessex (Ian Dalrymple)

In the 1870s, a maid is seduced by a squire but insists on bringing up her child without help.

Faded costumer with tentative performances and little else to recommend it.

w Michael Gordon, William Rose, Gerard Tyrrell novel George Moore d Ian Dalrymple, Peter Proud ph C. Pennington-Richards, H. E. Fowle m Gordon Jacob

☆ Kathleen Ryan, Dirk Bogarde, Cyril Cusack, Ivor Barnard, Fay Compton, Mary Clare, Morland Graham

Et Dieu Créa la Femme: see *And God Created Woman*

Et Mourir de Plaisir: see *Blood and Roses*

L'Eté Meurtrier: see *One Deadly Summer*

The Eternal Sea

US 1955 96m bw
Republic (John H. Auer)

The career of an aircraft carrier captain in World War II and Korea.

Solemn biopic of John Hoskins: competent but quite uninspired.

w Allen Rivkin d John H. Auer ph John L. Russell Jnr m Elmer Bernstein

☆ Sterling Hayden, Alexis Smith, Dean Jagger, Virginia Grey

Eternally Yours *

US 1939 95m bw
Walter Wanger

A magician's wife thinks he is too interested in his tricks.

Slightly scatty romantic comedy, amiable if not quite good enough to stand the test of time, but with a great cast.

w Gene Towne, Graham Baker d Tay Garnett ph Merritt Gerstad m Werner Janssen

☆ Loretta Young, David Niven, Broderick Crawford, Hugh Herbert, Billie Burke, C. Aubrey Smith, Raymond Walburn, ZaSu Pitts, Virginia Field, Eve Arden, Herman the Rabbit

'Will have to depend on the name power to get it by.' – *Variety*

'An amusing and irresponsible picture, though on the whole more irresponsible than amusing.' – *New York Times*

⚮ Werner Janssen

L'Eternel Retour: see *Love Eternal*

Eternity and a Day **

Greece/France/Italy 1998 134m colour
Theo Angelopoulos/Greek Film Centre/ERT/Paradis/La Sept/Intermedias (Theo Angelopoulos, Eric Heumann, Giorgio Silvagni, Amedeo Pagani)

original title: *Mia Eoniotita Ke Mia Mera*

A dying Greek writer ponders on the past while attempting to return an Albanian boy to his homeland.

Lyrical, elegiac meditation on the purpose of life; a slow-moving, deeply felt journey into the soul of man.

w Theo Angelopoulos, Tonino Guerra, Petros Markaris, Giorgio Silvagni d Theo Angelopoulos *ph* Giorgos Arvanitis, Andreas Sinani *m* Eleni Karaindrou *pd* Giorgos Patsos, Giorgos Ziakas *ed* Yannis Tsitsopoulos

☆ Bruno Ganz, Isabelle Renauld, Achileas Skevis, Despina Bebedeli, Iris Chatziantoniou, Helene Gerasimidiou, Fabrizio Bentivoglio, Vassilis Siemenis

'Give it time and Theo Angelopolous's sedate but eloquent tone-poem will reward your patience.' – *Nigel Cliff, The Times*

† The film won the Palme d'Or at the Cannes Film Festival in 1998.

Ethan Frome

US 1993 99m DuArt
American Playhouse/Richard Price/BBC (Stan Wlodkowski)

The new minister in a small and repressive Massachusetts community hires a crippled farmer to be his driver and discovers the story of love and hate that lies behind the man's injury.
A somewhat inert version of a rural tragedy, a grim tale of requited love, though it is strikingly photographed.
w Richard Nelson *novel* Edith Wharton *d* John Madden *ph* Bobby Bukowski *m* Rachel Portman *pd* Andrew Jackness *ed* Katherine Wenning
☆ Liam Neeson, Patricia Arquette, Joan Allen, Tate Donovan, Katharine Houghton, Stephen Mendillo
'Careful, literary, restrained, nicely acted and more than a bit dry.' – *Variety*

L'étoile du Nord *

France 1982 124m Fujicolour
Gala/Sara Films/Antenne 2 (Alain Sarde)
A lodger entrances his landlady with stories of his Egyptian adventures, neglecting to mention his involvement in a murder there.
Two well-dovetailed performances lift this odd little thriller above the ordinary.
w Jean Aurenche, Michel Grisolia, Pierre Granier-Deferre *novel* Le Locataire by Georges Simenon *d* Pierre Granier-Deferre *ph* Pierre-William Glenn *m* Philippe Sarde *ad* Dominique André *ed* Jean Revel
☆ *Simone Signoret, Philippe Noiret*, Fanny Cottençon, Julie Jezequel, Liliana Gerace, Gamil Ratib

Eureka

GB/USA 1982 129m Technicolor
MGM/UA/RPC/JF (Jeremy Thomas)

An immensely rich gold striker becomes a recluse and is murdered by Mafia hoods.
Unpleasant in detail and obscure in meaning, this is the sort of film of which the fact that it was financed at all is the most interesting thing about it.
w Paul Mayersberg *book* Who Killed Sir Harry Oakes? by Marshall Houts *d* Nicolas Roeg *ph* Alex Thomson *m* Stanley Myers *pd* Michael Seymour
☆ Gene Hackman, Theresa Russell, Rutger Hauer, Jane Lapotaire, Mickey Rourke, Ed Lauter
'A Roeg elephant film.' – *Variety*
'Between them Roeg and Mayersberg have worked an astonishing alchemy through which an abstraction of the basic patterns of human intercourse is rendered wholly concrete. Embodying Vico's cyclical theory of history, it expounds the despair of humanity's vicious circle from ecstasy to agony, as the impulse to love and possession leads inevitably to loss and destruction.' – *Tom Milne, Monthly Film Bulletin*
'I've a feeling it will become a cult movie, but no one will convince me that it isn't just the poshest kind of tosh.' – *Margaret Hinxman, Daily Mail*

Eureka Stockade

GB 1948 103m bw
Ealing (Leslie Norman)
US title: *Massacre Hill*
In 1854, Australian gold miners revolt against a harsh governor.
Unconvincingly made historical actioner from Ealing's antipodean period.
w Harry Watt, Walter Greenwood, Ralph Smart *d* Harry Watt *ph* Gerald Heath *m* John Greenwood
☆ Chips Rafferty, Jane Barrett, Gordon Jackson, Jack Lambert, Peter Illing, Ralph Truman, Peter Finch

Europa **

Denmark 1991 114m bw/colour Scope
Electric/Nordisk/Eurimages (Peter Aalbaek Jensen, Bo Christensen)

US title: *Zentropa*
In Germany in 1945, an idealistic young American finds work as a sleeping-car attendant and falls in love with a Nazi sympathizer.
Witty and exuberant tragi-comedy of the clash between New World innocence and European sophistication.
w Lars von Trier, Niels Vorsel, Tomas Gislason *d* Lars von Trier *ph* Henning Bendtsen, Jean-Paul Meurisse, Edward Klosinsky *m* Joakim Holbek *pd* Henning Bahs *ed* Herve Schneid
☆ Jean-Marc Barr, Barbara Sukowa, Udo Kier, Ernst-Hugo Järegård, Erik Mörk, Jörgen Reenberg, Henning Jensen, Eddie Constantine, Max von Sydow

Europa 51 *

Italy 1952 110m bw
Ponti/de Laurentiis
An American society woman living in Rome seeks vainly for truth in the chaotic post-war world and is committed to an asylum by her husband.
A despairing, ironic comment on a period which unfortunately does not convince on the personal level.
w Roberto Rossellini and others *d* Roberto Rossellini *ph* Aldo Tonti *m* Renzo Rossellini
☆ Ingrid Bergman, Alexander Knox, Ettore Giannini, Giulietta Masina

Europa Europa **

France/Germany 1991 110m Eastmancolor
Les Films du Losange/CCC Filmkunst/Perspektywa (Margaret Menegoz, Artur Brauner)

A young Polish Jew, captured by the Germans, pretends to be a loyal Nazi in order to stay alive.
A fascinating true story with the qualities of a thriller, filmed with sensitivity.
wd Agnieszka Holland *book* Salomon Perel *ph* Jacek Petrycki *m* Zbigniew Priesner *pd* Allan Starski *ed* Ewa Smal
☆ Marco Hofschneider, Julie Delpy, André Wilms, Aschley Wanninger, Hanns Zischler, Klaus Kowatsch, Hanna Labornaska
'Filled with suspense and touches of humour, pic brings a fresh approach to familiar themes and should find an appreciative arthouse audience in many parts of the world.' – *Variety*
† Controversy erupted over the German committee's failure to nominate the film for an Oscar for best foreign film. Most leading German directors signed a letter protesting about its decision.
♫ Agnieszka Holland (screenplay adaptation)

European Nights *

France/Italy 1959 79m Technicolor
Avers Film (Fabio Jegher)

A collection of cabaret acts from various European cities are seen in live performances.
A film of some historical interest, showing the sort of entertainment that once flourished in big cities. The highlight is the immaculate magic of Channing Pollock, effortlessly producing doves out of thin air. Also on show are The Platters, Italian singer-songwriter Domenico Modugno, French ventriloquist Robert Lamouret, and some lesser acts, such as Belgium's junior xylophone champion and Colin Hicks (Tommy Steele's less successful brother).
w Ennio de Concini, Gualtiero Jacopetti, Richard Wadleigh *d* Alessandro Blasetti *ph* Gabor Pogany *m* Carlo Savina *ad* Flavio Mogherini *ed* Mario Serandrei
☆ Carmen Sevilla, Henry Salvador, Domenico Modugno, The Platters, Channing Pollock, Robert Lamouret, Colin Hicks, The Rastellis, Le Charley Ballet, Ukrainian Orlyck Dance Group, Eddie Gray, The Three Monarchs

The Europeans *

GB 1979 83m colour
Merchant Ivory (Ismail Merchant)

In 1850, a European baroness arrives in Boston in search of a husband.
Charming if rather tentative period mood piece, probably the most professional and judicious of all the overpraised Merchant Ivory offerings.

w Ruth Prawer Jhabvala *novel* Henry James *d* James Ivory *ph* Larry Pizer *m* Richard Robbins *ad* Jeremiah Rusconi
☆ Lee Remick, Robin Ellis, Tim Woodward, Wesley Addy, Lisa Eichhorn
'A film of astonishing delicacy and richness in which the tiniest gesture or intonation reverberates with a world of meanings.' – *Tom Milne, MFB*

Eva

France/Italy 1962 135m bw
Paris/Interopa (Robert and Raymond Hakim)
A raw Welsh novelist in Venice is humiliated by a money-loving Frenchwoman who erotically ensnares him.
Foolish story of a femme fatale; elegantly Freudian at moments, it long outstays its welcome.
w Hugo Butler, Evan Jones *novel* James Hadley Chase *d* Joseph Losey *ph* Gianni di Venanzo *m* Michel Legrand
☆ Stanley Baker, Jeanne Moreau, Virna Lisi, James Villiers
'They don't hardly make 'em like Joseph Losey's *Eva* anymore, not even in Hollywood, not since Elinor Glyn passed from the script scene and Theda Bara quit as head vamp.' – *Judith Crist*

Eve Knew Her Apples

US 1945 64m bw
Wallace McDonald/Columbia
A radio singer sets off incognito for a vacation.
Mild musical support whose plot owes something to It Happened One Night.
w E. Edwin Moran *d* Will Jason
☆ Ann Miller, William Wright, Robert Williams, Ray Walker

The Eve of St Mark

US 1944 96m bw
TCF (William Perlberg)
A small-town boy goes to war and his sweetheart waits for him.
Poetic propaganda based on a sticky play which however had a tragic ending that the film eschews. Smartly made is all one can say.
w George Seaton *play* Maxwell Anderson *d* John M. Stahl *ph* Joseph LaShelle *m* Cyril Mockridge
☆ William Eythe, Anne Baxter, Michael O'Shea, Vincent Price, Ruth Nelson, Ray Collins, Stanley Prager, Henry Morgan

Eve Wants to Sleep *

Poland 1957 98m bw
Film Polski (Wislaw Mincer)
An innocent country girl arrives in a city overrun by subversives.
Curious yet sympathetic black farce, like a cross between Hellzapoppin and Mr Bru on In.
wd Tadeusz Chmielewski *ph* Stefan Matyjaskiewicz *m* Henryk Czyz
☆ Barbara Kwiatkowska, Stanislaw Mikulski, Ludwik Benoit

Evel Knievel

US 1971 90m Metrocolor
(MGM) Fanfare (George Hamilton)

Episodes from the life of a motor-cycle stuntman.
Mildly entertaining ragbag of action sequences and fragments of philosophy which might have been more tolerable had EK played himself.
w Alan Caillou, John Milius *d* Marvin Chomsky *ph* David Walsh *m* Pat Williams
☆ George Hamilton, Sue Lyon, Bert Freed, Rod Cameron

Evelyn Prentice

US 1934 80m bw
MGM (John W. Considine Jnr)
The wife of a criminal lawyer has an affair with a man who blackmails her.
Moderate domestic-cum-courtroom melodrama, heavily reliant on its popular stars.
w Lenore Coffee *novel* W. E. Woodward *d* William K. Howard *ph* Charles G. Clarke *md* Oscar Radin
☆ Myrna Loy, William Powell, Una Merkel, Harvey Stephens, Isabel Jewell, Rosalind Russell, Henry Wadsworth, Edward Brophy
'Uneven film but extra heavy cast and strong femme sob yarn will put it in the money class.' – *Variety*

'There have been many great drivers, but only one great passenger.'
Even Cowgirls Get the Blues

US 1993 96m Alpha Cine
Rank/New Line/Fourth Vision (Laurie Parker)

The adventures of the world's greatest hitchhiker, a woman with large thumbs and a penchant for dressing as a cowgirl.
A cult novel of the 70s fails to become a cult film of the 90s; the world has moved on and stranded its characters in some whimsical no-man's land.
wd Gus Van Sant *novel* Tom Robbins *ph* John Campbell, Eric Alan Edwards *m* k. d. lang, Ben Mink *pd* Missy Stewart *ed* Curtiss Clayton
☆ Uma Thurman, Lorraine Bracco, Angie Dickinson, Noriyuki 'Pat' Morita, Keanu Reeves, John Hurt, Rain Phoenix, Roseanne Arnold, Ed Begley Jnr, Crispin Glover, Buck Henry, Carol Kane, Sean Young
'Result is at best amusing; at worst, uninvolving, often confusing and sometimes a little boring.' – *Variety*
'A mess, but a fitfully interesting one.' – *Sheila Johnston, Independent*

Even Dwarfs Started Small

West Germany 1970 96m bw
Werner Herzog

original title: *Auch Zwerge Haben Klein Angefangen*
Dwarfs in a prison settlement on a volcanic island stage an unsuccessful revolt.
Bizarre and off-putting movie that attempts to say something about the human condition but muddles its message.
wd Werner Herzog *ph* Thomas Mauch *m* Florian Fricke *ed* Beate Mainka-Jellinghaus
☆ Helmut Doring, Paul Glauer, Gisela Hertwig, Hertel Minkner, Gertraud Piccini, Marianne Saar, Brigitte Saar
'There is little arresting in the visual images and the determined obliqueness of treatment is finally unsatisfying.' – *Films and Filming*

Evening Dress: see Tenue de Soirée

'A story about friends, family and other natural disasters.'
The Evening Star

US 1996 128m DeLuxe
Paramount/Rysher (David Kirkpatrick, Polly Platt, Keith Samples)

In the 80s, a grandmother tries to cope with the lives and loves of her three adult grandchildren.
Routine soap opera, which lacks the spice of the first instalment, though the actors are again encouraged to go over the top in their performances.
wd Robert Harling *novel* Larry McMurtry *ph* Don Burgess *m* William Ross *pd* Bruno Rubeo *ed* Priscilla Nedd-Friendly, David Moritz
☆ Shirley MacLaine, Bill Paxton, Juliette Lewis, Miranda Richardson, Ben Johnson, Scott Wolf, George Newbern, Marion Ross, Mackenzie Astin, Donald Moffat, Jack Nicholson
'A vastly disappointing sequel to a superlative original.' – *Variety*
† It is a sequel to *Terms of Endearment* (qv).

Evenings

Netherlands 1989 126m colour
Concorde/Praxino (René Solleveld, Peter Weijdeveld)
original title: *De Avonden*
In 1946 in Amsterdam a young man, unhappy at home and work, contemplates his unsatisfactory life before deciding to write about it.
Tiresome account of an obsessive adolescent's refusal to grow up.
w Jean Ummels, Rudolf van den Berg *novel* Gerard Reve *d* Rudolf van den Berg *ph* Willy Stassen *m* Bob Zimmerman *ad* Freek Bissiot *ed* Maria Steenburgen
☆ Thom Hoffman, Rijk de Gooijer, Viviane de Muynck, Sylvia de Leur, Leen Jongewaard, Kees Coolen Pierre Bokma, Eljer Pelgrom, Jobet Schnibbe, Gija Scholten-van Aschat

Evenings for Sale

US 1932 68m bw
Paramount
An impoverished count becomes a dancing master.
Scented Viennese romance intended to extend the star's success in Trouble in Paradise.

🎞️ film suitable for family viewing   📼 VHS video-cassette for the British PAL system   📼 VHS video-cassette for the British PAL system in wide screen-format   💿 Video cassette in a computer-colourised version   ⬛ American NTSC video-cassette   💿 Laser disc

w S. K. Lauren, Agnes Brand Leahy *novel* I. A. R. Wylie *d* Stuart Walker
☆ Herbert Marshall, Sari Maritza, Mary Boland, Charles Ruggles
'Fair entertainment but extremely doubtful on the draw.' – *Variety*

Evensong *
GB 1934 84m bw
Gaumont (Michael Balcon)
At the turn of the century, an Austrian prima donna gives up her career for love.
Well-made romantic drama of its type, notable as the best of its star's few films.
w Edward Knoblock, Dorothy Farnum *play* Beverley Nichols, Edward Knoblock *novel* Beverley Nichols *d* Victor Saville *ph* Max Greene *m/ly* Mischa Spoliansky, Edward Knoblock *ad* Alfred Junge *ed* Otto Ludwig
☆ Evelyn Laye, Fritz Kortner, Carl Esmond, Alice Delysia, Emlyn Williams, Muriel Aked
'A highly absorbing and intelligently produced musical … looks like money.' – *Variety*

Event Horizon
US 1997 95m Rank Colour Panavision
Paramount/Golar/Impact (Lawrence Gordon, Lloyd Levin, Jeremy Bolt)
In 2047, the crew of a spaceship, who go to the rescue of an apparently lifeless experimental ship, experience terrible hallucinations.
Creepy horror movie in outer space that delivers the requisite shocks; a little less predictability would have been welcome, though.
w Philip Eisner *d* Paul Anderson *ph* Adrian Biddle *m* Michael Kamen *pd* Joseph Bennett *ed* Martin Hunter
☆ Laurence Fishburne, Sam Neill, Kathleen Quinlan, Joely Richardson, Richard T. Jones, Jack Noseworthy, Jason Isaacs, Sean Pertwee
'A muddled and curiously uninvolving sci-fi horror show.' – *Joe Leydon, Variety*
'Essentially *The Old Dark House* in outer space.' – *George Perry*

'Desire. Defy. Escape.'
Ever After: A Cinderella Story *
US 1998 122m Technicolor Panavision
TCF (Mireille Soria, Tracey Trench)
A prince falls in love with a beautiful girl who disguises her true identity.
A swooningly romantic version of Cinderella, done as a period drama.
w Susannah Grant, Andy Tennant, Rick Parks *d* Andy Tennant *ph* Andrew Dunn *m* George Fenton *pd* Michael Howells *ed* Roger Bondelli
☆ Drew Barrymore, Anjelica Huston, Dougray Scott, Patrick Godfrey, Megan Dodds, Melanie Lynskey, Jeanne Moreau, Timothy West, Judy Parfitt, Jeroen Krabbe
'A rather pompous, overlong, only thinly charming love story.' – *Ian Nathan, Empire*

Ever in My Heart
US 1933 70m bw
Warner
A Daughter of the American Revolution finds that her husband is a German spy.
Heavy romantic drama with a tragic finish.
w Bertram Millhauser *story* Beulah Marie Dix *d* Archie Mayo
☆ Barbara Stanwyck, Otto Kruger, Ralph Bellamy, Ruth Donnelly, Frank Albertson
'A clean picture, more for the nabes than the first runs.' – *Variety*

'She'd say yes, but she no's him too well!'
Ever Since Eve
US 1937 80m bw
Warner (Earl Baldwin)
A publisher falls for a pretty girl, not realizing that she is his own plain secretary in disguise.
Silly romantic comedy which sadly lacks wit, style and believability.
w Lawrence Riley, Earl Baldwin, Lillie Hayward *d* Lloyd Bacon *ph* George Barnes *m* Heinz Roemheld
☆ Marion Davies, Robert Montgomery, Frank McHugh, Patsy Kelly, Louise Fazenda, Barton MacLane, Mary Treen
'A highly incredible script, and badly handled … it just doesn't jell.' – *Variety*
† It was Marion Davies's last film.

Ever Since Venus
US 1944 74m bw
Columbia
The inventors of a new lipstick formula can't get production facilities.
Modestly effective wartime comedy with good talent not ill-used.
w Arthur Dreifuss, McElbert Moore *d* Arthur Dreifuss
☆ Hugh Herbert, Billy Gilbert, Ina Ray Hutton, Glenda Farrell, Ann Savage, Ross Hunter, Alan Mowbray, Fritz Feld, Thurston Hall, Marjorie Gateson

Evergreen **
GB 1934 90m bw
Gaumont (Michael Balcon)
A star's daughter takes her mother's place, with romantic complications.
Pleasant musical with more wit and style than might be expected.
w Emlyn Williams, Marjorie Gaffney *play* Ever Green by Benn W. Levy *d* Victor Saville *ph* Glen Mac Williams *m/ly* Rodgers and Hart ('Dancing on the Ceiling', 'Dear Dear'); all other songs Harry Woods *md* Louis Levy *ad* Alfred Junge, Peter Proud *ed* Ian Dalrymple
☆ Jessie Matthews, Sonnie Hale, Betty Balfour, Barry Mackay, Ivor McLaren, Hartley Power

Eversmile New Jersey
US/Argentina 1989 103m Technicolor
J&M Entertainment/Los Films del Camino (Oscar Kramer)
A cavity-obsessed Irish dentist travelling around Patagonia acquires a female assistant en route.
An extraordinarily dreary attempt at a comic road movie, impossible to enjoy without anaesthetic.
w Jorge Goldenberg, Roberto Scheuer, Carlos Sorin *d* Carlos Sorin *ph* Esteban Courtalon *m* Steve Levine *ad* Coca Oderigo, Maria Julia Bertotto *ed* Bryan Oates
☆ Daniel Day-Lewis, Mirjana Jokovic, Gabriela Acher, Julio de Grazia, Ignacio Quiros

Every Day's a Holiday *
US 1937 79m bw
Paramount (Emmanuel Cohen)
A confidence girl in the old Bowery sells Brooklyn Bridge to suckers.
The most satisfactory example of post-Legion of Decency Mae West, the smut being replaced by a lively cast of comedians.
w Mae West *d* A. Edward Sutherland *ph* Karl Struss *m/ly* various *ad* Wiard Ihnen
☆ Mae West, Edmund Lowe, Charles Butterworth, Charles Winninger, Walter Catlett, Lloyd Nolan, Herman Bing, Roger Imhof, Chester Conklin
'A lively, innocuously bawdy, and rowdy entertainment.' – *Variety*
§ Wiard Ihnen

Every Girl Should Be Married
US 1948 84m bw
RKO (Don Hartman, Dore Schary)
A determined girl sets her cap at a bachelor pediatrician.
Woefully thin star comedy with few laughs.
w Stephen Morehouse Avery, Don Hartman *d* Don Hartman *ph* George E. Diskant *m* Leigh Harline
☆ Cary Grant, Betsy Drake, Franchot Tone, Diana Lynn, Alan Mowbray, Elizabeth Risdon, Richard Gaines
'In the past, Cary Grant has shown a talent for quietly underplaying comedy. In this picture, he has trouble finding comedy to play.' – *Time*

Every Home Should Have One
GB 1970 94m Eastmancolor
British Lion/Example (Ned Sherrin)
An advertising man goes berserk when he tries to think up an erotic way of selling porridge.
Tiresomely frenetic star comedy with the emphasis on smut.
w Marty Feldman, Barry Took, Denis Norden *d* James Clark *ph* Ken Hodges *m* John Cameron
☆ Marty Feldman, Shelley Berman, Judy Cornwell, Julie Ege, Patrick Cargill, Jack Watson, Patience Collier, Penelope Keith, Dinsdale Landen

Every Little Crook and Nanny
US 1972 92m Metrocolor
MGM (Leonard J. Ackerman)
A Mafia chief finds his child's new nanny has a grudge against him.
Sporadically amusing farce.
w Cy Howard, Jonathan Axelrod, Robert Klane *d* Cy Howard *ph* Philip Lathrop *m* Fred Karlin
☆ Victor Mature, Lynn Redgrave, Paul Sand, Maggie Blye, Austin Pendleton, John Astin, Dom DeLuise

Every Man for Himself: see Sauve Qui Peut (La Vie)

Every Man for Himself and God against All: see The Enigma of Kasper Hauser

Every Minute Counts: see Count the Hours

Every Night at Eight
US 1935 80m bw
Paramount (Walter Wanger)
Three sisters become a successful radio singing team.
Forgettable comedy musical with a mildly interesting cast.
w Gene Towne, Graham Baker *d* Raoul Walsh *ph* James Van Trees *m/ly* Dorothy Fields, Jimmy McHugh
☆ George Raft, Alice Faye, Frances Langford, Patsy Kelly, The Radio Rogues, Walter Catlett, Herman Bing
'Looks like another case of missed opportunity … a routine show world romance.' – *Variety*

Every Other Inch a Lady: see Dancing Co-Ed

Every Saturday Night: see The Jones Family

Every Second Counts: see Les Assassins du Dimanche

Every Time We Say Goodbye
US 1986 95m colour
Tri-Star (Jacob Kotzky, Sharon Harel)
In 1942 Jerusalem, an American pilot falls for a Sephardic Jewish girl.
Patchy and spasmodically developed story of love across the cultures: TV movie stuff.
w Moshe Mizrahi, Rachel Fabien, Leah Appet *d* Moshe Mizrahi *ph* Giuseppe Lanci *m* Philippe Sarde *ad* Micky Zahar *ed* Mark Burns
☆ Tom Hanks, Cristina Marsillach, Benedict Taylor, Anat Atzmon

Every Which Way but Loose
US 1978 114m DeLuxe
Warner/Malpaso (Robert Daley)
A Los Angeles trucker wins an orang-utan in a prize fight and becomes involved in sundry brawls and chases.
Easy-going, shambling star vehicle which was liked by nobody but the public.
w Jeremy Joe Kronsberg *d* James Fargo *ph* Rexford Metz *md* Steve Dorff
☆ Clint Eastwood, Sondra Locke, Ruth Gordon, Geoffrey Lewis, Walter Barnes
† The 1980 sequel, almost indistinguishable, was *Any Which Way You Can* (qv).

Every Woman's Man: see The Prizefighter and the Lady

Everybody Dance
GB 1936 74m bw
Gaumont/Gainsborough (Michael Balcon)
A night-club singer is forced to pose as a rural do-gooder.
Thin comedy vehicle.
w Stafford Dickens, Ralph Spence, Leslie Arliss *d* Charles Riesner *ph* J. J. Cox *m/ly* Mack Gordon, Harry Revel *md* Louis Levy *ad* Vetchinsky *ed* R. E. Dearing
☆ Cicely Courtneidge, Ernest Truex, Charles Riesner Jnr, Billie de la Volta, Percy Parsons

Everybody Does It
US 1949 98m bw
TCF (Nunnally Johnson)
A stage-struck wife is chagrined to see her dull husband accidentally become an opera singer.
Very mild remake of Wife, Husband and Friend; everyone tries to be zany, but the result is often just silly.
w Nunnally Johnson *story* James M. Cain *d* Edmund Goulding *ph* Joseph LaShelle *md* Alfred Newman
☆ Paul Douglas, Celeste Holm, Linda Darnell, Charles Coburn, Millard Mitchell, Lucile Watson, John Hoyt, George Tobias, Leon Belasco
'For sheer momentary enjoyment it would be hard to beat.' – *Richard Mallett, Punch*

Everybody Sing *
US 1937 80m bw
MGM (Harry Rapf)
An eccentric theatrical family is upstaged by its servants, who put on a Broadway show.
Agreeably zany comedy with music.
w Florence Ryerson, Edgar Allan Woolf *d* Edwin L. Marin *ph* Joseph L. Ruttenberg *m* William Axt
☆ Allan Jones, Fanny Brice, Judy Garland, Reginald Owen, Billie Burke, Lynne Carver, Monty Woolley, Reginald Gardiner, Henry Armetta
'Excellent film musical with fresh ideas and a corking cast … for the top spots.' – *Variety*

Everybody Wins
GB 1990 97m DuArt
Virgin/Recorded Picture Company (Jeremy Thomas)
A private eye is seduced by the unstable woman who has hired him to clear a youth of a murder charge.
Old-fashioned, unsubtle and wordy exploration of small-town corruption.
w Arthur Miller *d* Karel Reisz *ph* Ian Baker *m* Leon Redbone *pd* Peter Larkin *ed* John Bloom
☆ Debra Winger, Nick Nolte, Will Patton, Judith Ivey, Jack Warden, Kathleen Wilhoite, Frank Converse
'For a brief period in the late sixties and early seventies, moviegoers seemed willing to be guided through a movie by their intuition and imagination; if this slyly funny movie about the spread of corruption had been released then, it might have been considered a minor classic.' – *Pauline Kael, New Yorker*

Everybody's All-American: see When I Fall In Love

Everybody's Cheering: see Take Me Out to the Ball Game

Everybody's Fine: see Stanno Tutti Bene

Everyone Says I Love You **
US 1996 101m DuArt
Sweetland/Jean Doumanian (Robert Greenhut)
A teenager observes the year-long romantic entanglements of her mother, her divorced father, and her half-brothers and -sisters.
A slightly sour romantic comedy, and a musical for people who don't like musicals, with its cast warbling and dancing in an amateurish manner; it has a certain charm, though, even if the old songs deserve better.
wd Woody Allen *ph* Carlo Di Palma *m* Dick Hyman *ch* Graciela Daniele *pd* Santo Loquasto *ed* Susan E. Morse
☆ Woody Allen, Alan Alda, Drew Barrymore, Goldie Hawn, Julia Roberts, Tim Roth, Lukas Haas, Gaby Hoffman, Edward Norton, Natalie Portman, David Ogden Stiers, Natasha Lyonne
'A cinematic oxymoron – complex, bold and audacious and simultaneously simple, guileless and sublime.' – *Leonard Klady, Variety*
'Perhaps it isn't only the musical that is a highly artificial form, but Allen's particular blend of romanticism, therapy, middlebrow comedy and undemanding art film.' – *Adam Mars-Jones, Independent*

Everything But the Truth
US 1956 83m Technicolor
U-I (Howard Christie)
A small boy embarrasses his family by telling the truth at all times.
Dum-dum formula comedy made with jaded professionalism.
w Herb Meadow *d* Jerry Hopper *ph* Maury Gertsman *m* Milton Rosen

☆ Maureen O'Hara, John Forsythe, Tim Hovey, Frank Faylen, Barry Atwater

Everything Happens at Night

US 1939 77m bw
TCF (Harry Joe Brown)

Two reporters fall for the daughter of a Nobel Peace Prize winner on the run from the Gestapo.
The star's sixth American film plays down the music and skating in favour of rather jaded spy comedy. Modest entertainment.

w Art Arthur, Robert Harari d Irving Cummings ph Edward Cronjager m various
☆ Sonja Henie, Ray Milland, Robert Cummings, Maurice Moscovich, Leonid Kinskey, Alan Dinehart, Fritz Feld, Victor Varconi
'At no time does very much happen that is of interest.' – *Variety*

Everything Happens to Us: see *Hi Ya Chum*

Everything I Have Is Yours

US 1952 92m Technicolor
MGM (George Wells)

A song and dance team is disrupted when the wife decides to become a mother.
Uninventive but lively musical vehicle for the Champions.

w George Wells d Robert Z. Leonard ph William V. Skall md David Rose ch Nick Castle, Gower Champion
☆ Marge and Gower Champion, Dennis O'Keefe, Eduard Franz

Everything Is Rhythm

GB 1936 73m bw
Joe Rock

A dance band leader wins a European princess.
Modest programme filler remarkable only for its record of a top band of its time.

w Syd Courtenay, Jack Byrd, Stanley Haynes story Tom Geraghty d Alfred Goulding ph Ernest Palmer ad A. L. Mazzei, George Provis
☆ Harry Roy and his Band, Princess Pearl, Ivor Moreton, Dave Kaye

Everything Is Thunder *

GB 1936 76m bw
Gaumont British (S. C. Balcon)

A German girl helps a British prisoner of war to escape.
Tolerable let's-not-be-beastly melodrama, quite unusual in its time.

w Marion Dix, John Orton novel Jocelyn L. Hardy d Milton Rosmer ph Gunther Krampf ad Alfred Junge
☆ Constance Bennett, Douglass Montgomery, Oscar Homolka, Roy Emerton, Frederick Lloyd, George Merritt
'Very good entertainment of a kind, the kind that deals with disguises and pursuits and incredible resourcefulness, with policemen on the stairs and hunted men in bathrooms.' – *Graham Greene*

Everything You Always Wanted to Know about Sex *

US 1972 87m DeLuxe
UA (Charles H. Joffe)

Seven sketches on sexual themes.
Dishevelled revue with a reasonable number of laughs for broadminded audiences.

wd Woody Allen book Dr David Reuben ph David M. Walsh m Mundell Lowe pd Dale Hennesy
☆ Woody Allen, Lynn Redgrave, Anthony Quayle, John Carradine, Lou Jacobi, Louise Lasser, Tony Randall, Burt Reynolds, Gene Wilder

Everything's Ducky

US 1961 81m bw
Barboo/Columbia

Two naval ratings adopt a talking duck.
Anything-goes service farce, with material below the standard of the talent available.

w John Fenton Murray, Benedict Freedman d Don Taylor ph Carl Guthrie m Bernard Green
☆ Mickey Rooney, Buddy Hackett, Jackie Cooper, Joanie Summers, Roland Winters

Eve's Bayou **

US 1997 108m colour
Alliance/Trimark (Caldecot Chubb, Samuel L. Jackson)

In the early 60s, a 10-year-old girl with psychic powers vows to kill her philandering father for sexually assaulting her sister.
A family saga seen through the distancing eyes of a child; it is an intriguing story of shifting memories and blame, as the truth of situations changes.

wd Kasi Lemmons d Amy Vincent m Terence Blanchard pd Jeff Howard ed Terilyn A. Shropshire
☆ Jurnee Smollett, Megan Good, Samuel L. Jackson, Lynn Whitfield, Debi Morgan, Jake Smollett, Diahann Carroll, Ethel Ayler, Vondie Curtis Hall
'If it's not nominated for Academy Awards then the Academy is not paying attention.' – *Roger Ebert, Chicago Sun-Times*

The Evictors

US 1979 92m Movielab Panavision
AIP (Charles B. Pierce)

Axe murders abound when a young couple move into an old house with a history.
Old-hat horror, out of Psycho and The Amityville Horror: strictly for drive-ins.

w Charles B. Pierce, Gary Rusoff, Paul Fisk d Charles B. Pierce ph Chuck Bryant m Jaime Mendoza-Nava ed Shirak Khojayan
☆ Michael Parks, Jessica Harper, Vic Morrow, Sue Ane Langdon

The Evil

US 1978 89m Movielab
New World/Rangoon (Ed Carlin)

A psychologist takes a team to investigate a haunted house, and is soon sorry he meddled.
Another variation on the theme of The Haunting and The Legend of Hell House; more this time on the horror comic level, but reasonably effective.

w Donald G. Thompson d Gus Trikonis ph Mario Di Leo m Johnny Harris
☆ Richard Crenna, Joanna Pettet, Andrew Prine, Cassie Yates, Victor Buono, Lynne Moody

The Evil Dead

US 1983 85m DuArt
Palace/Renaissance (Robert G. Tapert)

Five youngsters in a remote cabin find an old book which helps them summon up dormant demons from a nearby forest.
Semi-professional horror rubbish, blown up from 16mm and looking it. When released in England, it was prosecuted as unsuitable for public showing and gained a cult following. It was released on video in a cut version.

wd Sam M. Raimi ph Tim Philo m Joe LoDuca ed Edna Ruth Paul
☆ Bruce Campbell, Ellen Sandweiss, Betsy Baker, Hal Delrich
'The ne plus ultra of low-budget gore and shock effects.' – *Variety*
† Originally made in 1980, but not released publically for 3 years.

Evil Dead 2: Dead by Dawn

US 1987 85m Technicolor
Renaissance/De Laurentiis (Robert G. Tapert)

Trapped in a lonely cabin, a couple fight off ferocious hordes of the spirits of the dead.
Fast-moving horror movie with flashy camerawork and an exuberant taste in sick jokes.

w Sam Raimi, Scott Spiegel d Sam Raimi ph Peter Deming m Joseph LoDuca ad Philip Duffin, Randy Bennett ed Kaye Davis sp make-up: Mark Shostrom
☆ Bruce Campbell, Sarah Berry, Dan Hicks, Kassie Wesley, Theodore Raimi, Denise Bixler
'More an absurdist comedy than a horror film.' – *Variety*
† It was followed by a sequel, *Army of Darkness* (qv).

Evil Ed (dubbed) *

Sweden 1995 90m colour/bw
Evil Ed Productions (Göran Lundström)

A mild-mannered film editor becomes increasingly deranged after he goes to work in his studio's

splatter-and-gore department to remove excessive violence from the company's movies.
Exuberant, over-the-top satire of bloody horror flicks, done with some wit; but the lashings of gore overwhelm whatever serious intentions may have been lurking beneath its surface.

w Anders Jacobsson, Göran Lundström, Christer Ohlsson d Anders Jacobsson ph Anders Jacobsson m Henriksson & Lindh ed Anders Jacobsson
☆ Johan Rudebeck, Per Löfberg, Olof Rhodin, Camela Leierth, Gert Fylking, Cecilia Ljung

Evil Fingers: see *The Fifth Cord*

'The monster's back and no one can stop him!'
The Evil of Frankenstein

GB 1964 94m Eastmancolor
Rank/Hammer (Anthony Hinds)

Frankenstein returns to his derelict castle and finds the Monster preserved in a glacier.
For their third Frankenstein film Hammer made a distribution deal with Universal and thus for the first time were able to use fragments of the old plots as well as something approximating to the Karloff make-up. Production and writing, however, are sadly dispirited except when relying on sadism.

w John Elder (Anthony Hinds) d Freddie Francis ph John Wilcox m Don Banks ad Don Mongaye ed James Needs
☆ Peter Cushing, Peter Woodthorpe, Sandor Eles, Kiwi Kingston, Duncan Lamont, Katy Wild, David Hutcheson

Evil Senses (dubbed)

Italy 1986 90m colour
DMV/Globe/Dania/Filmes International/National Cinematografica (Pietro Innocenzi)

A hitman on the run from other killers takes refuge in a high-class brothel and begins an obsessive relationship with a mysterious part-time prostitute.
Glossy but unremarkable thriller, with a flimsy plot and some ludicrous sexual interludes.

w Gianfranco Clerici, Gabriele Lavia, Vincenzo Mannino, Dardano Sacchetti d Gabriele Lavia ph Mario Vulpiani m Fabio Frizzi ad Giovanni Agostinucci ed Daniele Alabiso
☆ Monica Guerritore, Gabriele Lavia, Mimsy Farmer, Lewis Eduard Ciannelli, Dario Mazzoli, Gioia Maria Scola, Jean René Masrevery, Ragnhild Aslaksen
'Sleekly shot, and has enough narrative twists to maintain a modicum of interest despite the risibly melodramatic sex scenes.' – *Sight and Sound*

The Evil that Men Do

US 1984 90m CFI color
ITC/Capricorn/Zuleika Farms (Pancho Kohner)

A professional killer is asked to eliminate a sadistic political torturer in Guatemala.
More than usually turgid and unpleasant vehicle for a star who is now too old for this kind of thing.

w David Lee Henry, John Crowther novel R Lance Hill d J. Lee-Thompson ph Javier Ruvalcaba Cruz m Ken Thorne
☆ Charles Bronson, Theresa Saldana, Joseph Maher, José Ferrer, René Enriquez, John Glover, Raymond St Jacques

Evil under the Sun

GB 1982 117m Technicolor Panavision
EMI/Mersham/Titan (John Brabourne, Richard Goodwin)

Hercule Poirot solves the murder of a film star on an Adriatic holiday island.
Very competent but somehow too bland package in the Agatha Christie series, not quite so lively as Death on the Nile.

w Anthony Shaffer novel Agatha Christie d Guy Hamilton ph Christopher Challis m Cole Porter pd Elliot Scott
☆ Peter Ustinov, James Mason, Diana Rigg, Maggie Smith, Colin Blakely, Jane Birkin, Nicholas Clay, Roddy McDowall, Sylvia Miles, Denis Quilley
'They have swapped elegant English menace for a splurge of theatrical camp.' – *Time Out*
'Temperance beverage Noël Coward.' – *Sunday Times*

Evils of Chinatown: see *Confessions of an Opium Eater*

Evita *

US 1996 134m Eastmancolor
Entertainment/Cinergi/Robert Stigwood/Dirty Hands (Alan Parker, Andrew G. Vajna, Robert Stigwood)

The progress to fame and political power of Eva Duarte, who rises from poverty to become a model, film actress and wife of the president of Argentina.
Epic version of the stage musical with a star performance in the title role, and providing some sweep and power, while still retaining the clumsy narrative and uninteresting music of the original.

w Alan Parker, Oliver Stone musical Andrew Lloyd Webber, Tim Rice d Alan Parker ph Darius Khondji m/ly Andrew Lloyd Webber, Tim Rice md John Mauceri ch Vincent Paterson pd Brian Morris ed Gerry Hambling
☆ Madonna, Antonio Banderas, Jonathan Pryce, Jimmy Nail, Victoria Sus, Julian Littman, Olga Merediz
'No effort or expense has been spared in transforming the stage musical into a Hollywood spectacular. As such, the film is, as the hype would have it, a triumph. The problems start, however, as soon as one has lost interest in the sumptuous clothes, virtuoso tango-dancing and necrophiliac display. There is very little dramatic tension.' – *Linda Holt, TLS*
† The film was one of the few to be subtitled in non-English speaking countries. Even such musicals as The Sound of Music have been dubbed in the past for most Spanish- and Italian-speaking countries.
♪ song 'You Must Love Me' (mAndrew Lloyd-Webber, lyTim Rice)
⌘ Darius Khondji; Brian Morris; Gerry Hambling; sound

'Forged by a god! Foretold by a wizard! Found by a king!'
'No mortal could possess it! No kingdom could command it!'
Excalibur *

US 1981 140m Technicolor
Warner/Orion (John Boorman)

The story of King Arthur, Merlin, Uther Pendragon, the Holy Grail and the Lady of the Lake.
Curiously pointless retelling of a legend with unexplained flashes of realism and bouts of gore alternating with romance and modern wisecracks. Of mainly visual interest.

w Rospo Pallenberg, John Boorman d John Boorman ph Alex Thomson m Trevor Jones pd Anthony Pratt ed John Merritt
☆ Nigel Terry, Helen Mirren, Nicol Williamson, Nicholas Clay, Cherie Lunghi, Paul Geoffrey, Liam Neeson, Patrick Stewart
'Left entirely to his own devices, Boorman seems to run in self-defeating circles.' – *Richard Combs, MFB*
'It tries overhard to be simultaneously critical and credulous, magical and earthy, inspiring and entertaining.' – *Sunday Times*
'A record of the comings and goings of arbitrary, inconsistent, shadowy figures who are not heroes but simply giants run amok.' – *Roger Ebert*
⌘ Alex Thomson

Excess Baggage

US 1997 98m Technicolor
Columbia/First Kiss (Bill Borden, Carolyn Kessler)

A bored rich girl who fakes her own kidnapping becomes involved with a car thief, who is being hunted by crooked debt-collectors.
Trivial comedy that is about nothing in particular, and has no particular place to go.

w Max D. Adams, Dick Clement, Ian La Frenais d Marco Brambilla ph Jean Yves Escoffier m John Lurie pd Missy Stewart ed Stephen Rivkin
☆ Alicia Silverstone, Benicio del Toro, Christopher Walken, Jack Thompson, Harry Connick Jnr, Nicholas Turturro, Michael Bowen, Sally Kirkland
'A film so airy that viewers will forget about it even while they're watching it.' – *Timothy M. Gray, Variety*

Excessive Force
US 1993 90m DeLuxe
New Line/3 Arts/Ian Page (Oscar L. Costo, Thomas Ian Griffith, Erwin Stoff)

A maverick Chicago cop finds himself framed for the murder of a gangster.
Excessively violent, cliché-ridden movie with no redeeming qualities.
w Thomas Ian Griffith d Jon Hess ph Donald M. Morgan m Charles Bernstein pd Michael Z. Hanan ed Alan Baumgarten
☆ Thomas Ian Griffith, Lance Henriksen, Tom Hodges, James Earl Jones, Charlotte Lewis, Tony Todd, Burt Young, Earl Brown
  'The only surprising thing about this by-the-numbers effort is the talent squandered in supporting roles.' – *Joe Leydon, Variety*
† It was followed in 1995 by *Excessive Force 2: Force on Force*, an equally violent but otherwise unconnected film set in Los Angeles.

Ex-Champ
US 1939 72m bw
Universal
A retired boxer works as a doorman and has trouble with his ungrateful and semi-criminal son.
Father-love weepie, rather hard to take.
w Alex Gottlieb, Edmund L. Hartmann, Gordon Kahn d Phil Rosen
☆ Victor McLaglen, Tom Brown, Nan Grey, William Frawley, Constance Moore
  'Pathos and sentiment expertly mixed for satisfactory dualler.' – *Variety*

'Racket rule sweeps midwest city!'
Exclusive
US 1937 76m bw
Paramount
Journalist sacrifices himself for daughter whose views he despises.
Solid newspaper drama jinxed by the excellent tragic performance of a star too long regarded as a comedian.
w John C. Moffitt, Sidney Salkow, Rian James d Alexander Hall
☆ Charles Ruggles, Fred MacMurray, Frances Farmer, Lloyd Nolan
  'Hokey newspaper-gangster yarn of old-fashioned meller calibre.' – *Variety*
  'In the tough race it falls behind – it can't make the 1937 speed in murder, and the result, like lavender, is not unagreeable.' – *Graham Greene*

Exclusive Story
US 1934 75m bw
MGM
A newspaperman has a go at the numbers racket.
Tolerable anti-gangster crusade.
w Michael Fessier, Martin Mooney d George B. Seitz
☆ Franchot Tone, Madge Evans, *Joseph Calleia*, Stuart Erwin, J. Carrol Naish
  'Publicity possibilities should put this one over, but it also has plenty of excitement to sell.' – *Variety*

Excuse My Dust *
US 1951 82m Technicolor
MGM (Jack Cummings)
The inventor of a horseless carriage loves the daughter of a livery stable owner.
Innocuous small-town 1890s comedy with a race climax. Quite pleasant.
w George Wells d Roy Rowland ph Alfred Gilks m Arthur Schwartz
☆ Red Skelton, Sally Forrest, Macdonald Carey, William Demarest

'Every day he loves, somebody else dies!'
The Executioner *
GB 1970 107m Technicolor Panavision
Columbia/Ameran (Charles H. Schneer)

A British spy suspects a colleague of being a double agent.
Dour espionage thriller with a reasonably holding narrative and predictable performances.
w Jack Pulman d Sam Wanamaker ph Denys Coop m Ron Goodwin
☆ George Peppard, Nigel Patrick, Joan Collins, Judy Geeson, Oscar Homolka, Charles Gray, Keith Michell, George Baker, Alexander Scourby, Peter Bull, Ernest Clark, Peter Dyneley

'Does not escape from the well-worn shallow groove in which the contemporary spy film is in danger of becoming stuck.' – *Russell Campbell*

Executioner of Venice
Italy 1963 90m colour
Liber (Ottavio Poggi)
original title: Il Boia di Venezia
On the day of his marriage the son of the Doge of Venice discovers that his true father was a pirate and is arrested for treason on the orders of the power-hungry Grand Inquisitor.
Standard swashbuckler with glossy production values.
d Luigi Capuano ph Alvardo Mancori ed Antonietta Zita
☆ Lex Barker, Guy Madison, Alessandro Panaro, Alberto Farnese, Mario Petri, Giulio Marchetti

Executive Action *
US 1973 91m colour
EA Enterprises/Wakefield Orloff (Edward Lewis)

An imaginative version of the facts behind the 1963 assassination of President Kennedy.
Interesting but rather messy mixture of fact and fiction; makes one sit up while it's unreeling.
w Dalton Trumbo story Mark Lane, Donald Freed d David Miller ph Robert Steadman m Randy Edelman
☆ Burt Lancaster, Robert Ryan, Will Geer, Gilbert Green, John Anderson
  'A dodo bird of a movie, the winner of the *Tora Tora Tora* prize.' – *Variety*

Executive Decision
US 1996 132m Technicolor
Warner/Silver Pictures (Joel Silver)

An élite team of commandos goes into action when Islamic militants, carrying a nerve gas that could kill everyone in Washington, hijack an aeroplane and demand a $50m ransom.
This is everything you would expect from a movie produced by Joel Silver: glossy, loud, fast and empty, but at least Steven Seagal disappears halfway through the action.
w Jim Thomas, John Thomas d Stuart Baird ph Alex Thomson m Jerry Goldsmith pd Terence Marsh ed Dallas Pruitt, Frank J. Urioste, Stuart Baird
☆ Kurt Russell, Halle Berry, John Leguizamo, Steven Seagal, Oliver Platt, Joe Morton, David Suchet, B. D. Wong, Len Cariou, Whip Hubley, J. T. Walsh
  'The acting is all first base, the script a laughable stream of gung ho-isms, the action merely solid and the effects indifferent. Yet, you still stroll out with a grin a mile wide.' – *Ian Nathan*

'High up in the skyscraper beauty and power clash in conflict!'
Executive Suite **
US 1954 104m bw
MGM (John Houseman)

When the president of a big company dies, the boardroom sees a battle for control.
First of the boardroom films of the fifties, a calculatedly commercial mixture of business ethics and domestic asides, with an all-star cast working up effective tensions.
w Ernest Lehman novel Cameron Hawley d Robert Wise ph George Folsey m none ad Cedric Gibbons, Edward Carfagno
☆ Fredric March, William Holden, June Allyson, *Barbara Stanwyck*, Walter Pidgeon, Shelley Winters, Paul Douglas, *Louis Calhern*, Dean Jagger, Nina Foch, Tim Considine
  'Not a classic, not a milestone in movie making, but it does suggest a standard of product that could bring back to the box office those vast audiences long alienated by trivia.' – *Arthur Knight*
  'The only trouble with all these people is that they are strictly two-dimensional. They give no substantial illusion of significance, emotion or warmth.' – *Bosley Crowther, New York Times*
† A TV series followed in 1976.
♟ George Folsey; Nina Foch; art direction

Ex-Flame
US 1930 68m bw
Liberty
A modernized version of *East Lynne*.
With so many American accents attached to the British peerage, this is mainly for laughs – unintentional ones.
wd Victor Halperin

☆ Neil Hamilton, Marian Nixon, Norman Kerry, Roland Drew, Snub Pollard
  'Old-fashioned mush stuff for the woman.' – *Variety*

The Exile *
US 1948 90m bw
U-I (Douglas Fairbanks Jnr)
The man who is to return to the English throne as Charles II hides in Holland, receives his friends and despatches his enemies.
Curious, talkative swashbuckler with only a few moments of action; the available talents are simply not used, though the director imposes a nice pictorial style.
w Douglas Fairbanks Jnr novel His Majesty the King by Cosmo Hamilton d Max Ophüls ph Franz Planer m George Parrish
☆ Douglas Fairbanks Jnr, Maria Montez, Paula Corday, Henry Daniell, Nigel Bruce, Robert Coote
† Originally released in sepia.

Exile Express
US 1939 70m bw
Grand National
A lab assistant is innocently involved in the murder of her boss by a spy gang.
Lumpy comedy thriller taking place mainly on a train; very forgettable.
w Edwin Justus Mayer, Ethel La Blanche d Otis Garrett ph John Mescall m George Parrish
☆ Anna Sten, Alan Marshal, Jerome Cowan, Jed Prouty, Stanley Fields, Walter Catlett, Leonid Kinskey, Harry Davenport, Irving Pichel
  'Both story and direction take it up all sorts of dull and impossible alleys.' – *Variety*

'Play It. Live It. Kill For It.'
'Plug Into The Most Dangerous Fantasy Ever Created.'
eXistenZ *
US 1999 97m DeLuxe
Miramax/Alliance Atlantis/Serendipity Point/Natural Nylon (Robert Lantos, Andras Hamori, David Cronenberg)

A leading video-game designer, demonstrating her latest creation, is threatened with death by a group who object to artificial realities.
The problem here is that the video game is one that you can imagine only Cronenberg wanting to play, and underneath the hi-tech trimmings, which look like leftovers from his Naked Lunch, are themes on the relativity of truth that were handled rather better by Pirandello 70 years ago; but perhaps that is to take the movie more seriously than was intended.
wd David Cronenberg ph Peter Sushitzky m Howard Shore pd Carol Spier ed Ronald Sanders sp Jim Isaac
☆ Jennifer Jason Leigh, Jude Law, Willem Dafoe, Ian Holm, Don McKellar, Callum Keith Rennie, Sarah Polley, Christopher Eccleston
  'Unquestionably Cronenberg Lite, but there is plenty of fun to be had from the absurdities and convoluted plotting, and a solid cast lends stature to the far-fetched fantasies.' – *David Stratton, Variety*

Exit Smiling **
US 1926 71m bw silent
MGM (Sam Taylor)
The worst actress in a stock company saves the show.
Amusing comedy for a star who never quite made it in films: this is the best of her vehicles.
w Sam Taylor, Tim Whelan play Marc Connelly d Sam Taylor ph André Barlatier
☆ Beatrice Lillie, Jack Pickford, Harry Myers, Doris Lloyd, DeWitt Jennings, Louise Lorraine, Franklin Pangborn

Exit to Eden
US 1994 113m Technicolor
Guild/Savoy (Alex Rose, Garry Marshall)

Undercover detectives track a diamond smuggler to a holiday island devoted to gratifying sado-masochistic sexual fantasies.
Drear, unbelievably bad comedy; the actors seem embarrassed, as well they might, and the director is obviously uncomfortable with any fantasy more explicit than his Pretty Woman.
w Deborah Amelon, Bob Brunner novel Anne Rice d Garry Marshall ph Theo Van de Sande m Patrick Doyle pd Peter Jamison ed David Finfer
☆ Dana Delany, Paul Mercurio, Rosie O'Donnell, Dan Aykroyd, Hector Elizondo, Stuart Wilson, Iman

'The film is awful.' – *Derek Malcolm, Guardian*
'It has the sophistication of an adolescent bathroom joke indifferently told.' – *Variety*

'We don't dare tell you how daring it is!'
Ex-Lady *
US 1933 70m bw
Warner

A lady artist has ultra-modern views on sex and marriage, but turns conventional when she falls in love.
Mildly shocking in its day, this romantic drama was one of the contributing factors to the onslaught of the Legion of Decency which transformed Hollywood output in the following year.
w David Boehm story Edith Fitzgerald, Robert Riskin d Robert Florey
☆ Bette Davis, Gene Raymond, Frank McHugh, Monroe Owsley, Claire Dodd
† Previously filmed in 1931 as *Illicit*.

The Ex-Mrs Bradford *
US 1936 87m bw
RKO (Edward Kaufman)

A doctor's scatty ex-wife involves him in solving a murder plot.
Amusing crime comedy, just a little way behind The Thin Man.
w Anthony Veiller, James Edward Grant d Stephen Roberts ph J. Roy Hunt m Roy Webb
☆ William Powell, Jean Arthur, James Gleason, Eric Blore, Robert Armstrong, Lila Lee, Grant Mitchell, Ralph Morgan

Exodus *
US 1960 220m Technicolor Super Panavision 70
UA/Carlyle/Alpha (Otto Preminger)

The early years of the state of Israel, seen through various eyes.
Heavy-going modern epic, toned down from a passionate novel.
w Dalton Trumbo novel Leon Uris d Otto Preminger ph Sam Leavitt m Ernest Gold
☆ Paul Newman, Eva Marie Saint, Ralph Richardson, Peter Lawford, Lee J. Cobb, Sal Mineo, John Derek, Hugh Griffith, Gregory Ratoff, Felix Aylmer, David Opatoshu, Jill Haworth, Alexandra Stewart, Martin Benson, Martin Miller
  'Professionalism is not enough – after three and a half hours the approach seems more exhausting than exhaustive.' – *Penelope Houston*
† Jewish comedian Mort Sahl, invited by the director to a preview, is said to have stood up after three hours and said: 'Otto – let my people go!'
♟ Ernest Gold
♟ Sam Leavitt; Sal Mineo

The Exorcist *
US 1973 122m Metrocolor
Warner/Hoya (William Peter Blatty)

A small girl is unaccountably possessed by the devil and turned into a repellent monster who causes several violent deaths before she is cured.
Spectacularly ludicrous mishmash with uncomfortable attention to physical detail and no talent for narrative or verisimilitude. Its sensational aspects, together with a sudden worldwide need for the supernatural, assured its enormous commercial success.
w William Peter Blatty novel William Peter Blatty d William Friedkin ph Owen Roizman m Jack Nitzsche pd Bill Malley ed Jordan Leandopoulos, Evan Lottman, Norman Gay, Bud Smith
☆ Ellen Burstyn, Max von Sydow, Jason Miller, Linda Blair, Lee J. Cobb, Kitty Winn, Jack MacGowran
  'No more nor less than a blood and thunder horror movie, foundering heavily on the rocks of pretension.' – *Tom Milne*
  'The Exorcist makes no sense, [but] if you want to be shaken, it will scare the hell out of you.' – *Stanley Kauffmann*
  'It exploits the subject of diabolic possession without telling you anything about it ... just a stylistic exercise.' – *Michael Billington, Illustrated London News*
  'There is a little exposition, some philosophy and theology, a quiet interlude, and then pandemonium reigns: rooms shake, heads turn full circle on bodies, wounds fester, vomit spews forth in bilious clouds besmirching a saintly

priest, a possessed adolescent girl masturbates bloodily on a crucifix as she barks blasphemies and obscenities, and hoary demons freeze the soul.' – *Les Keyser, Hollywood in the Seventies*

'I know how to do it. I just throw everything at the audience and give them a real thrill. That's what they want. They don't want to go into a theater and treat it like a book. They don't even read books!' – *William Peter Blatty*

'This one was scheduled for 105 days. It wound up 200 days. We were plagued by strange and sinister things from the beginning.' – *William Peter Blatty*

'…raw and painful experience. Are people so numb that they need movies of this intensity in order to feel anything at all?' – *Roger Ebert*

† Published 1974: *The Story Behind the Exorcist* by Peter Travers and Stephanie Reiff.

♟ William Peter Blatty; sound (Robert Knudson, Chris Newman)

⦾ best picture; William Friedkin; Owen Roizman; Ellen Burstyn; Jason Miller; Linda Blair; Bill Malley; editing

'It's four years later. What does she remember?'
Exorcist II: The Heretic
US   1977   117m   Technicolor
Warner (Richard Lederer, John Boorman)
▦ ◫

Father Lamont, investigating the case related in *The Exorcist*, finds that the evil in Regan, apparently exorcized, is only dormant.
Highly unsatisfactory psychic melodrama which, far from the commercial route of the shocker followed by its predecessor, falls flat on its face along some wayward path of metaphysical and religious fancy. A commercial disaster, it was released in two versions and is unintelligible in either.
w William Goodhart d John Boorman
ph William A. Fraker m Ennio Morricone
pd Richard MacDonald
☆ Richard Burton, Linda Blair, Louise Fletcher, Kitty Winn, Max von Sydow, Paul Henreid, James Earl Jones, Ned Beatty

'Do You Dare Walk These Steps Again?'
The Exorcist III
US   1990   110m   DeLuxe
Fox/Morgan Creek/Carter DeHaven (James G. Robinson, Joe Roth)
▦ ▦ ◫

A cop investigates a series of strange killings with the aid of an exorcist.
Unexciting and confused sequel that follows on from the first film in the series.
wd William Peter Blatty novel *Legion* by William Peter Blatty ph Gerry Fisher m Barry DeVorzon pd Leslie Dilley ed Tom Ramsay, Peter-Lee Thompson
☆ George C. Scott, Ed Flanders, Brad Dourif, Jason Miller, Nicol Williamson, Scott Wilson, Nancy Fish, George DiCenzo, Don Gordon

Exotica **
Canada   1994   104m   colour
Artificial Eye/Alliance/Ego (Atom Egoyan, Camelia Frieberg)
▦ ▦ ◠

A murder and an attempt to smuggle eggs bring together five disparate people in a club specializing in striptease and lap-dancing.
Elegantly devious drama about sex and voyeurism and the unexpected connections between people, told in a deliberately enigmatic way, gradually revealing the secrets that link one person to the next.
wd Atom Egoyan ph Paul Sarossy m Mychael Danna pd Linda del Rosario, Richard Paris ed Susan Shipton
☆ Bruce Greenwood, Elias Koteas, Don McKellar, Mia Kirshner, Arsinée Khanjian, Sarah Polley
'Egoyan promises us a sleazy tabloid sex thriller, then gives us an altogether sobering psychological thriller.' – *Jonathan Romney, Guardian*
† The film won a Genie award as the best Canadian film of 1994.

Experiment in Terror **
US   1962   123m   bw
Columbia/Geoffrey-Kate Productions (Blake Edwards)
▦ ◫

GB title: *The Grip of Fear*
An asthmatic stranger threatens the life of a bank teller and her sister if she does not help him commit a robbery.

Detailed, meticulous police thriller with San Francisco locations. Good stuff, a bit long.
w The Gordons novel *Operation Terror* by The Gordons d Blake Edwards ph Philip Lathrop m Henry Mancini
☆ Glenn Ford, Lee Remick, Ross Martin

Experiment Perilous *
US   1944   91m   bw
RKO (Warren Duff)
▦

A wealthy husband becomes insanely jealous of his wife.
Enjoyable mystery melodrama which takes itself with a pinch of salt.
w Warren Duff novel Margaret Carpenter d Jacques Tourneur ph Tony Gaudio m Roy Webb ad Albert S. D'Agostino, Jack Okey
☆ Hedy Lamarr, Paul Lukas, George Brent, Albert Dekker, Margaret Wycherly
⦾ art direction

'It's time to enter the new dragon.'
Expert Weapon
US   1993   90m   colour
Silver Screen/Cine Excel (David Hue, K. Y. Lim)
▦ ▦

A convicted killer is offered freedom if he turns assassin for a secret government organization.
Incoherent action flick, made on a minuscule budget, and with talents to match.
w Steven Austin, Henry Clay d Steven Austin ph Dwight F. Lay m H. Schuyler Collins ed James Fletcher
☆ Joe Estevez, Ian Jacklin, Sam J. Jones, Judy Landers, Julie Merrill, Mel Novak

The Experts
US   1989   83m   Alpha Cine
Paramount (James Keach)
▦ ◫

Two trendy New Yorkers think they have been hired to open a night-club in Nebraska; in reality, they are transported to the USSR to teach American manners to Russian spies living in a replica of a US town.
Feeble and simple-minded comedy that is almost enough to restart the Cold War.
w Nick Thiel, Stephen Greene, Eric Alter d Dave Thomas ph Ronnie Taylor m Marvin Hamlisch pd David Fischer ed Bud Molin
☆ John Travolta, Arye Gross, Kelly Preston, Deborah Foreman, James Keach, Jan Rubes, Brian Doyle Murray, Mimi Maynard, Eve Brent, Charles Martin Smith

The Exploits of Elaine *
US   1914   bw   silent
Pathé/Wharton
Detective Craig Kennedy helps his girlfriend avenge her father's murder.
Archetypal cliffhanger serial in 14 episodes, each 20 minutes long, following on the success of The Perils of Pauline. It was itself followed within a year by The New Exploits of Elaine and The Romance of Elaine. Chapter headings included such now familiar clichés as 'The Clutching Hand', 'The Vanishing Jewels', 'The Poisoned Room', 'The Death Ray' and 'The Devil Worshippers'. The films were much praised by critics for their pace and inventiveness.
w Charles W. Goddard, George B. Seitz stories Arthur B. Reeve d Louis Gasnier, George B. Seitz
☆ Pearl White, Creighton Hale, Sheldon Lewis, Arnold Daly

Explorers
👪   US   1985   109m   Technicolor
Paramount/Edward S. Feldman/Industrial Light and Magic
▦ ◫ ◠

Two boys make off in a space craft and encounter an alien race whose culture consists of intercepted American television programmes.
Slightly interesting but overlong fantasy spoof, probably not for popular consumption.
w Eric Luke d Joe Dante ph John Hora m Jerry Goldsmith pd Robert F. Boyle
☆ Ethan Hawke, River Phoenix, Jason Presson, Amanda Peterson
'One of the weirdest and most endearingly offbeat alien pix to have surfaced in recent years.' – *Variety*

Exposed
US   1983   99m   Metrocolor
MGM-UA (James Toback)
▦

A fashion model falls for a concert violinist who turns out to be a notorious terrorist.
A glossy absurdity confected from reading too many indigestible headlines.
wd James Toback ph Henri Decae m Georges Delerue pd Brian Eatwell ed Robert Lawrence, Annie Charvein
☆ Nastassja Kinski, Rudolf Nureyev, Harvey Keitel, Ian McShane, Bibi Andersson, Ron Randell, Pierre Clementi
'It often seems to be working out of a tension between sophisticated ambition and the capabilities of a tyro director, a kind of neo-primitivism (with a hint, perhaps, of Fuller, especially in its cultural name-dropping – Bach, Bosch, Dostoievsky, Heifetz, Perlman, Stern, to name a few).' – *Richard Combs, MFB*

'Johnny never had it so good – or lost it so fast!'
Expresso Bongo *
👪   GB   1959   111m   bw   Dyaliscope
BL/Britannia/Conquest (Val Guest)
▦ ◫

A Soho agent turns a nondescript teenage singer into an international star.
Heavily vulgarized version of a stage skit on the Tommy Steele rock phenomenon, divested of most of its satirical barbs and only intermittently amusing.
w Wolf Mankowitz play Wolf Mankowitz d Val Guest ph John Wilcox m/ly David Heneker, Monty Norman md Robert Farnon
☆ Laurence Harvey, Sylvia Syms, Yolande Donlan, Cliff Richard, Meier Tzelniker, Gilbert Harding, Ambrosine Philpotts, Eric Pohlmann, Wilfrid Lawson, Hermione Baddeley, Reginald Beckwith, Martin Miller
'What the cinema offers is a sardonic rattle with music … The approach may be satirical or flippant; and yet one finds oneself half-beginning to believe in the subject; even minding about it.' – *Dilys Powell*

The Exquisite Sinner
US   1926   80m   bw   silent
MGM
A young French industrialist becomes bored with his society and takes off with a band of gypsies.
Curious and unsatisfactory farrago with extensive retakes by Phil Rosen (who also took credit the following year for an almost exactly similar film with a different title, Heaven on Earth, but featuring the same stars).
w Josef von Sternberg, Alice Duer Miller d Josef von Sternberg, Phil Rosen ph Max Fabian ad Cedric Gibbons
☆ Conrad Nagel, Renee Adoree, Myrna Loy

Exquisite Tenderness
Germany/US   1994   100m   CFI color
Guild/Connexion (Alan Beattie, Chris Chesser, Willi Baer)
A mad doctor runs amok in a hospital, killing patients in order to obtain the ingredients for his miracle cure
Bizarre horror movie that gives the impression that the participants improvised the increasingly risible plot; it runs out of originality within minutes.
w Patrick Cirillo, based on a screenplay by Bernard Sloane d Carl Schenkel ph Thomas Burstyn m Christopher Franke pd Douglas Higgins ed Jimmy B. Frazier sp Gary Paller; make-up: Steve Johnson
☆ Isabel Glasser, James Remar, Sean Haberle, Peter Boyle, Malcolm McDowell, Charles Dance
'A slick, sadistic horror film which is about as exquisite and tender as a medical textbook.' – *Tom Shone, Sunday Times*
'Over-excited camerawork barely dispels one's impression that the script and indeed the movie were thrown together in five minutes.' – *Independent*

Extase *
Czechoslovakia   1932   90m   bw
Universal Elektra Film
▦ ◫

aka: *Ecstasy*
A country girl takes a lover.
Simple love story with Freudian sequences, quite successfully and cinematically done. It caused a sensation at the time and was issued in various censored versions; the star's husband later tried to destroy all the copies.

wd Gustav Machaty story Viteslav Nezval ph Jan Stallich m Giuseppe Becce
☆ Hedy Kiesler (later Hedy Lamarr), Aribert Mog
'The first important film to come out of Czechoslovakia since *Erotikon*, and what a hornet's nest it has stirred up! Critics and public are divided into two camps. Some proclaim it the world's worst, others rank it among the best productions of the year. It would never get by the censor in America.' – *Variety*

The Exterminating Angel ***
Mexico   1962   95m   bw
Uninci Films 59 (Gustavo Alatriste)
▦ ▦

original title: *El Angel Exterminador*
High society dinner guests find themselves unable to leave the room, stay there for days, and go totally to the bad before the strange spell is broken; when they go to church to give thanks, they find themselves unable to leave.
Fascinating surrealist fantasia on themes elaborated with even more panache in The Discreet Charm of the Bourgeoisie. Nevertheless, one of its director's key films.
wd Luis Buñuel (story assistance from Luis Alcoriza) ph Gabriel Figueroa ad Jesus Bracho
☆ Silvia Pinal, Enrique Rambal, Jacqueline Andere, Jose Baviera
'An unsound and unsightly mixture of spurious allegory and genuine craziness.' – *John Simon*

The Exterminator
US   1980   102m   Movielab
Interstar (Mark Buntzman)
▦ ▦ ◠

An ex-Vietnam vet goes berserk when his friend is killed by a street gang, and vows revenge.
Vigilante movie with aspects of the modern horror-comic tradition; not much doubt that its real purpose is exploitation. It aroused some anger in America when a murder seemed to be based on its methods, but it was quickly succeeded by even more violent films.
wd James Glickenhaus ph Robert M. Baldwin m Joe Renzetti
☆ Robert Ginty, Christopher George, Samantha Eggar, Steve James
'Glickenhaus has plundered the iconographic treasury of recent American cinema, wrenching the images of war, sexuality and street crime out of their contexts and deploying them portentously so as to lend spurious significance to his film.' – *Martyn Auty, MFB*

Exterminator 2
US   1984   90m   TVC Color
Cannon
▦ ▦

An unemployed Vietnam veteran in New York eliminates punks with a flame thrower.
Violence fantasy, an extreme form of Death Wish; quite reprehensible, and not for the squeamish.
w Mark Buntzman, William Sachs d Mark Buntzman
☆ Robert Ginty, Deborah Geffner, Mario Van Peebles, Frankie Faison

The Extra Day
GB   1956   83m   Eastmancolor
British Lion/William Fairchild (E. M. Smedley Aston)
The personal problems of five film extras who are recalled when a scene has to be reshot.
Thin excuse for portmanteau drama, only amusing in its depiction of a British movie being made with mostly foreign talent.
wd William Fairchild ph Arthur Grant m Philip Green
☆ Richard Basehart, Simone Simon, Sid James, Josephine Griffin, George Baker, Colin Gordon, Laurence Naismith, Charles Victor, Olga Lindo, Beryl Reid, Dennis Lotis

The Extra Girl *
US   1923   69m   bw   silent
Mack Sennett
▦ ◠

A small town girl wins a beauty contest and goes to Hollywood.
A comparatively restrained comedy with slapstick interludes, this charming film shows its star at her best and admirably illustrates Hollywood in the early twenties.
w Bernard McConville d Mack Sennett ph Homer Scott, Eric Crockett
☆ Mabel Normand, Max Davidson, Ralph Graves, George Nicholls

👪 film suitable for family viewing   ▦ VHS video-cassette for the British PAL system   ▦ VHS video-cassette for the British PAL system in wide screen-format   ⟳ Video cassette in a computer-colourised version   ▬ American NTSC video-cassette   ◠ Laser disc

The Extraordinary Seaman
US 1968 80m Metrocolor Panavision
MGM/John Frankenheimer/Edward Lewis (John H. Cushingham, Hal Dresner)
Four stranded sailors come upon the ghostly Royal Navy captain of a ghostly World War II ship.
Curious sixties attempt at forties fantasy; obviously, from its short running time and fragmented style, something went sadly adrift during its making, and the wide screen does not help, but there are scattered funny moments.
w Philip Rock, Hal Dresner d John Frankenheimer ph Lionel Lindon m Maurice Jarre
☆ David Niven, Faye Dunaway, Alan Alda, Mickey Rooney, Jack Carter, Juano Hernandez, Barry Kelley
'A cleverly made curiosity, not so much produced as manufactured.' – Marjorie Bilbow

Extreme Justice
US 1993 96m Foto-Kem
Reflective/Arica (Frank Sacks)
⬚ ▤ ⚊ ◎ ♫
aka: S.I.S. Extreme Justice
A young cop joins the Special Investigations Section of the Los Angeles police, a secret unit that tracks known dangerous criminals, but becomes concerned about their methods of shooting first and not bothering to ask questions later.
Despite its claim to be based on fact (which annoyed the LAPD), the movie sticks to the familiar exploitation routines of young idealistic recruit versus older cynical cop, car chases, violence and gratuitous gore.
w Frank Sacks, Robert Boris d Mark L. Lester ph Mark Irwin m David Michael Frank pd Richard L. Johnson ed Donn Aron
☆ Lou Diamond Phillips, Scott Glenn, Chelsea Field, Yaphet Kotto, Andrew Divoff, Richard Grove, William Lucking, Ed Lauter
'Lester's direction is leaden and the script, while raising some intriguing moral questions, lacks subtlety or grace.' – Sight and Sound
† Originally intended for cinema release, it was first shown on cable TV, and was released direct to video in Britain.

Extreme Measures
GB/US 1996 117m Technicolor
Columbia/Castle Rock/Simian (Elizabeth Hurley)
⬚ ▤ ⚊ ◎ ♫
A doctor working in a New York hospital discovers that unethical experiments are being carried out on patients.
An unsuccessful medical thriller about a mad scientist, notable mainly as an attempt to broaden Grant's appeal to encompass action.
w Tony Gilroy novel Michael Palmer d Michael Apted m John Bailey m Danny Elfman pd Doug Kramer ed Rick Shaine
☆ Hugh Grant, Gene Hackman, Sarah Jessica Parker, David Morse, Bill Nunn, John Toles-Bey, Paul Guilfoyle, Debra Monk
'Can never quite make up its mind whether it's a horror movie, an action thriller, or a reasonably serious medical drama. In fact, it is not quite any of these things and its screenplay betrays a fundamental lack of confidence.' – Derek Malcolm, Guardian
† The first production from Hugh Grant and Elizabeth Hurley's company, the film was a box-office flop, grossing just over $17m in the US.

Extreme Prejudice
US 1987 104m Technicolor
Carolco/Tri-Star (Buzz Feitshans)
⬚ ▤ ⚊ ♫
A Texas Ranger pins down a drug trafficker.
Ordinary urban thriller with overplayed violence.
w Deric Washburn, Harry Kleiner story Jim Milius, Fred Rexer d Walter Hill ph Matthew F. Leonetti m Jerry Goldsmith pd Albert Heschong ed Freeman Davies
☆ Nick Nolte, Powers Boothe, Michael Ironside, Rip Torn, Clancy Brown, Maria Conchita Alonso

Extremities
US 1986 90m colour
Atlantic Releasing (Burt Sugarman)
⬚ ▤ ⚊
A girl takes revenge on the man who raped her.
Unpleasant when it's not verbose; anything but entertaining.
w William Mastrosimone play William Mastrosimone d Robert M. Young ph Curtis

Clark m J. A. C. Redford pd Chester Kaczenski ed Arthur Coburn
☆ Farrah Fawcett, James Russo, Diana Scarwid, Alfre Woodard

'What do you do when justice fails?'
Eye for an Eye
US 1996 101m DeLuxe
Paramount (Michael I. Levy)
⬚ ▤ ⚊
When the rapist and killer of her teenage daughter is freed on a legal technicality, a mother decides to kill him herself.
Contrived and unpleasant little pro-vigilante movie that loads the scales of justice while providing Sally Field with an opportunity to display prolonged hysteria.
w Amanda Silver, Rick Jaffa novel Erika Holzer d John Schlesinger ph Amir M. Mokri m James Newton Howard pd Stephen Hendrickson ed Peter Honess
☆ Sally Field, Kiefer Sutherland, Ed Harris, Beverly D'Angelo, Charlaine Woodard, Joe Mantegna, Olivia Burnette, Alexandra Kyle
'A virtually worthless piece of film-making. It's a crude and paranoid scare story dressed up as moral sensitivity.' – Tom Shone, Sunday Times

An Eye for an Eye
France/Italy 1956 93m Technicolor VistaVision
UGC/Jolly (André Cayatte)
A doctor finds himself trekking across the desert with a demented man whose wife has died in his care.
Initially striking melodrama which becomes increasingly unconvincing and has a tendency to harp on unpleasant detail.
wd André Cayatte novel Vahe Katcha ph Christian Matras m Louiguy
☆ Curt Jurgens, Folco Lulli, Lea Padovani

An Eye for an Eye
US 1981 104m CFI color
Avco Embassy/Adams Apple/South Street/Westcom (Frank Capra Jnr)
▤
An undercover cop resigns from the force but uncovers a drug ring.
Tedious and violent actioner with a martial arts champion for hero.
w William Gray, James Bruner d Steve Carver ph Roger Shearman m William Goldstein ad Vance Lorenzini ed Anthony Redman
☆ Chuck Norris, Christopher Lee, Richard Roundtree, Matt Clark, Mako, Maggie Cooper, Rosalind Chao, Toru Tanaka

'Terror that tears the scream right out of your throat!'
Eye of the Cat *
US 1969 102m Technicolor
Universal/Joseph M. Schenck (Bernard Schwarz, Philip Hazelton)
A young man who hates cats goes to stay with his crippled aunt who keeps a house full of them.
Odd, Psycho-like thriller (from the same screen writer) with plenty of scary sequences but an inadequate resolution.
w Joseph Stefano d David Lowell Rich ph Russell Metty, Ellsworth Fredricks m Lalo Schifrin cat trainer Ray Berwick
☆ Eleanor Parker, Michael Sarrazin, Gayle Hunnicutt, Tim Henry, Laurence Naismith
'Not so much a good film as an extravagantly enjoyable one.' – MFB

Eye of the Devil *
GB 1967 92m bw
MGM/Filmways (John Calley, Ben Kadish)
A French nobleman is obsessed by a family tradition of pagan self-sacrifice.
Diabolical goings-on in a spooky castle, not really helped by a glittering supporting cast any more than by miscast stars, sluggish direction or a general atmosphere of gloom rather than suspense.
w Robin Estridge, Dennis Murphy novel Day of the Arrow by Philip Loraine d J. Lee-Thompson ph Erwin Hillier m Gary McFarland
☆ David Niven, Deborah Kerr, Emlyn Williams, Flora Robson, Donald Pleasence, Edward Mulhare, David Hemmings, Sharon Tate, John Le Mesurier, Donald Bisset

'It is hard to say why the total effect is so constantly hilarious.' – MFB
† The film had a chequered career. The first attempt to make it was abandoned because of Kim Novak's inadequacy; it then went through three titles and a lot of trouble with the censor.

'To love a stranger is easy … to kill a lover is not!'
Eye of the Needle
GB 1981 113m Technicolor
UA/Kings Road (Stephen Friedman)
▤
In London in 1940 a German agent murders his landlady but is eventually cornered by a girl on a Scottish island.
Listless espionage narrative with very little drive or interest: the shape of the story defies suspense.
w Stanley Mann novel Ken Follett d Richard Marquand ph Alan Hume m Miklos Rozsa
☆ Donald Sutherland, Kate Nelligan, Christopher Cazenove, Ian Bannen, Alex McCrindle

Eye of the Tiger
US 1986 90m United Color
Scotti Brothers (Tony Scotti)
⬚ ▤ ⚊
A vigilante avenges his wife's murder.
Predictable thriller with video in mind.
w Michael Montgomery d Richard Sarafian ph Peter Collister ad Wayne Springfield ed Greg Prange
☆ Gary Busey, Yaphet Kotto, Seymour Cassel, Bert Remsen, William Smith

Eye Witness: see Your Witness (1950)

Eye Witness
GB 1956 82m bw
Rank/Sydney Box
A maniacal burglar pursues a witness of his crime into the emergency ward of a busy hospital.
Naïve but adequate suspenser with too many character cameos getting in the way of the plot.
w Janet Green d Muriel Box ph Reg Wyer m Bruce Montgomery
☆ Donald Sinden, Muriel Pavlow, Belinda Lee, Michael Craig, Nigel Stock, Susan Beaumont, David Knight, Ada Reeve

Eyes in the Night *
US 1942 80m bw
MGM (Jack Chertok)
A blind detective sets out to discover whether a mysterious man engaged to an heiress is really a Nazi spy.
Tolerable wartime puzzler.
w Guy Trosper, Howard Emmett Rogers novel Odor of Violets by Baynard Kendrick d Fred Zinnemann ph Robert Planck, Charles Lawton m Lennie Hayton
☆ Edward Arnold, Ann Harding, Donna Reed, Allen Jenkins, John Emery, Stephen McNally, Reginald Denny, Rosemary de Camp, Stanley Ridges
'They have converted a basically humdrum yarn into a tense and tingling little thriller.' – New York Times
† Edward Arnold appeared once more as Duncan Maclain, in The Hidden Eye (1944) (qv).

Eyes of Laura Mars *
US 1978 104m Metrocolor
Columbia/Jon Peters (Jack H. Harris)
⬚ ▤ ⚊
A fashion photographer has violent premonitions about a series of murders.
Silly and often unpleasant suspenser which despite its chic appearance never bothers to explain itself.
w John Carpenter, David Zelag Goodman d Irvin Kershner ph Victor J. Kemper m Artie Kane
☆ Faye Dunaway, Tommy Lee Jones, Brad Dourif, René Auberjonois, Raul Julia, Frank Adonis
'Long on trendy settings, high-priced actors and vicious murders, but devoid of narrative thrills.' – Richard Schickel, Time
'Perhaps the most austerely elegant horror film ever made.' – New Yorker

Eyes of the Underworld
US 1942 61m bw
Universal
A crusading lawyer exposes an auto theft ring.

Efficient little support which was smart enough to play top on its original release.
w Michael L. Simmons, Arthur Strawn d Roy William Neill
☆ Richard Dix, Lon Chaney Jnr, Wendy Barrie, Don Porter, Billy Lee, Lloyd Corrigan

Eyes Wide Shut **
US/GB 1999 159m DeLuxe
Warner/Pole Star/Hobby (Stanley Kubrick)
⬚ ▤ ⚊
Distressed by his wife's account of a sexual fantasy, a New York doctor goes on an erotic odyssey through the city.
An atmospheric account of sexual jealousy, temptation and fidelity, meticulously made and with an oddly dreamlike quality about it; but, while being faithful to its slim source, it is also overlong and much too portentous.
w Stanley Kubrick, Frederic Raphael novella Dream Story/Traumnovelle by Arthur Schnitzler ph Larry Smith m Jocelyn Pook pd Les Tomkins, Roy Walker ed Nigel Galt
☆ Tom Cruise, Nicole Kidman, Sydney Pollack, Marie Richardson, Rade Sherbedgia, Todd Field, Vinessa Shaw, Alan Cumming, Sky Dumont, Fay Masterson, Leelee Sobieski, Thomas Gibson, Madison Eginton
'An uncanny masterpiece.' – Glenn Kenny, Premiere
'This musty tale feels exactly what it is: a small-scale arthouse movie way past its sell-by date, exhumed from a bygone era of Freudian fascination.' – Matt Mueller, Total Film
'The batsqueak of hysteria and absurdity is essential to this fable of erotic paranoia and erotic discontent within a bourgeois marriage.' – Peter Bradshaw, Guardian
† The film took $31m in its first week at the US box-office, after which audiences fell away; its final take was $55.7m.

Eyes without a Face *
France/Italy 1959 90m bw
Champs Elysées/Lux (Jules Borkon)
⬚ ▤
original title: Les Yeux sans Visage
US title: The Horror Chamber of Dr Faustus
When his daughter is mutilated in a car accident, a mad professor murders young girls in the process of grafting their faces onto hers.
Unpleasant horror film which its director seems to have made as a joke; the years have made it a cult.
w Jean Redon novel Jean Redon d Georges Franju ph Eugen Schüfftan m Maurice Jarre
☆ Pierre Brasseur, Alida Valli, Edith Scob, François Guérin

Eyewitness *
GB 1970 91m Technicolor
ITC/ABP (Paul Maslansky)
⬚ ▤
aka: Sudden Terror
A boy is the sole witness to an assassination, but no one believes him except the assassins.
The Window all over again, the standard clichés being tricked out with fancy photography, sub-Hitchcock set-ups and Mediterranean locations, which make it all very tolerable.
w Ronald Harwood novel Mark Hebden d John Hough ph David Holmes m Fairfield Parlour, David Whitaker
☆ Mark Lester, Lionel Jeffries, Susan George, Tony Bonner, Jeremy Kemp, Peter Vaughan, Peter Bowles, Betty Marsden

Eyewitness
US 1981 108m Technicolor
TCF (Peter Yates)
▤ ⚊
GB title: The Janitor
A bashful janitor with a crush on a TV star finds himself hunted down by a murderer afraid of identification.
Odd little character thriller which despite pleasant touches never really seems to have its mind on its plot.
w Steve Tesich d Peter Yates ph Matthew F. Leonetti m Stanley Silverman pd Philip Rosenberg
☆ William Hurt, Christopher Plummer, Sigourney Weaver, Irene Worth, James Woods, Kenneth McMillan, Steven Hill

---

⊚ Digital Video Disc Region 2   ⊚ Digital Video Disc Region 1   ♫ Soundtrack released on compact disc   ☆ Cast in approximate order of importance   † Points of interest   ♪ Notable songs   ▌ Academy Award   ♙ Academy Award nomination   �BAFTA

F

F for Fake *

France/Iran/West Germany 1973 85m colour
Astrophore/Saco/Janus (Dominique Antoine, François Reichenbach)

French title: *Vérités et Mensonges*

Orson Welles, at a railway station, lectures the audience in truth and falsehood, in art, in films and in life.

A ragbag of an entertainment, cannibalizing as it does more than one unsold documentary, shredded at the editing table to match the narrator's illusionist style. Despite the raptures of some critics, this is an irritating effusion, and Welles now looks more like a clever charlatan than a master film-maker.

w Orson Welles, Oja Palinkas d Orson Welles ph Gary Graver, Christian Odasso m Michel Legrand

'Welles stretches his material and his legend just about as thin as possible in this tedious treatise on truth and illusion.' – *Kevin Thomas, Los Angeles Times*
† Joseph Cotten, Paul Stewart and Laurence Harvey make fleeting appearances.

F.P.1 *

GB/Germany 1933 93m bw
Gaumont/UFA (Erich Pommer)

Financiers try to destroy the first floating aerodrome.

'*Futuristic*' *melodrama about an aircraft carrier. Very well done, and shot in two languages, but now dated in most respects.*

w Curt Siodmak, Walter Reisch, Robert Stevenson, Peter Macfarlane d Karl Hartl ph Gunther Rittau, Konstantin Tochet
☆ Conrad Veidt, Leslie Fenton, Jill Esmond, George Merritt, Donald Calthrop, Nicholas Hannen, Francis L. Sullivan

F/X

US 1985 106m Technicolor
Orion (Dodi Fayed, Jack Wiener)

GB title: *Murder by Illusion*

A special effects man is paid to stage a phony assassination, then finds himself the target of hit men.

Initially mysterious premise settles down into a long chase, which of its kind isn't badly done but goes on forever.

w Robert T. Megginson, Gregory Fleeman d Robert Mandel ph Miroslav Ondricek m Bill Conti pd Mel Bourne ed Terry Rawlings
☆ Bryan Brown, Brian Dennehy, Diane Venora, Cliff DeYoung, Mason Adams, Jerry Orbach

'Delivers high-gear excitement from start to finish.' – *Bruce Williamson, Playboy*

'Outgunned by the mob, outmanned by the cops ... their effects had better be special!'

F/X2: The Deadly Art of Illusion

US 1991 108m DeLuxe
Columbia TriStar/Orion (Jack Wiener, Dodi Fayed)

A former special effects man and a private eye team up to recover some stolen Michelangelo medallions.

Virtually a repeat of the first movie, but done with much less panache and little attempt at plausibility.

w Bill Condon d Richard Franklin ph Victor J. Kemper, David M. Walsh, Tonino Delli Colli m Lalo Schifrin pd John Jay Moore ed Andrew London, Michael Tronick sp Eric Allard
☆ Bryan Brown, Brian Dennehy, Rachel Ticotin, Joanna Gleason, Philip Bosco, Kevin J. O'Connor, Tom Mason

'With all the ingenuity that went into toys and gadgetry in this five-years-removed sequel, it's a shame no-one bothered to hook up a brain to the plot.' – *Variety*

The Fabulous Adventures of Marco Polo

France/Italy/Yugoslavia/Egypt/Afghanistan 1964
115m Eastmancolor Franscope
Ittac/Prodi/Avala/Mounir Rafla/Italaf Kaboul (Raoul Lévy)

aka: *Marco the Magnificent*

In 1271 Marco Polo carries a message of peace to Kubla Khan.

Curious mixture of melodrama and pantomime, with a star cast half playing for laughs.

w Raoul Lévy, Denys de la Patellière d Denys de la Patellière, Noel Howard ph Armand Thirard m George Garvarentz
☆ Horst Buchholz, Anthony Quinn, Orson Welles, Akim Tamiroff, Robert Hossein, Omar Sharif, Elsa Martinelli, Grégoire Aslan, Massimo Girotti, Folco Lulli

The Fabulous Baker Boys *

US 1989 113m colour
Rank/Gladden (Paula Weinstein, Sydney Pollack, Mark Rosenberg)

Two piano-playing brothers hire a female singer to enliven their night-club act.

Enjoyable excursion into the lower depths of showbusiness.

wd Steve Kloves ph Michael Ballhaus m Dave Grusin pd Jeffrey Townsend ed Bill Steinkamp
☆ Jeff Bridges, Michelle Pfeiffer, Beau Bridges, Ellie Raab, Jennifer Tilly
& Michelle Pfeiffer; Michael Ballhaus; Dave Grusin; Bill Steinkamp

The Fabulous Dorseys

US 1947 91m bw
UA (Charles R. Rogers)

Two quarrelling bandleader brothers are reunited on the death of their father.

Slight, comedic biopic with the Dorseys playing well and trying hard.

w Richard English, Art Arthur, Curtis Kenyon d Alfred E. Green ph James Van Trees m Leo Shuken
☆ Tommy Dorsey, Jimmy Dorsey and their bands, Janet Blair, Paul Whiteman, William Lundigan

The Fabulous Texan

US 1947 97m bw
Republic

Confederate officers after the Civil War return home to find Texas overrun by carpetbaggers and despotic state police.

Fairly handsome Western which gets by without ever being memorable.

w Lawrence Hazard, Horace McCoy d Edward Ludwig
☆ William Elliott, John Carroll, Catherine McLeod, Andy Devine, Albert Dekker, Ruth Donnelly, Harry Davenport, Douglass Dumbrille

Faccia a Faccia: see *Face to Face (1967)*

'The blag to kill for. Only one of them meant it for real.'

Face *

GB 1997 103m colour
UIP/BBC/Distant Horizon (David M. Thompson, Elinor Day)

A thief who sets up a robbery with four others tries to discover which of them is a traitor.

A streetwise thriller with political overtones, too old-fashioned and heavy-handed to carry much conviction.

w Ronan Bennett d Antonia Bird ph Fred Tamms pd Chris Townsend ed St John O'Rorke
☆ Robert Carlyle, Ray Winstone, Steven Waddington, Philip Davis, Damon Albarn, Lena Headey, Peter Vaughan, Sue Johnston, Gerry Conlon

'The soundtrack is full of blurred and sombre beats, while the yellow overalls worn by the gang for the raid make the job look designed as much as planned. But this is only top dressing when the script is full of howling clichés.' – *Adam Mars-Jones, Independent*

The Face ***

Sweden 1958 100m bw
Svensk Filmindustri (Allan Ekelund)
original title: *Ansiktet*
US title: *The Magician*

In 19th-century Sweden, a mesmerist and his troupe are halted at a country post to be examined by three officials. Partly exposed as a fraud, he takes a frightening revenge.

A virtually indecipherable parable which may be about the survival of Christianity (and may not), this wholly personal Bergman fancy has to be enjoyed chiefly for its surface frissons, for its acting and its look, which are almost sufficient compensation.

wd Ingmar Bergman ph Gunnar Fischer m Erik Nordgren ad P. A. Lundgren ed Oscar Rosander
☆ Max von Sydow, Ingrid Thulin, Gunnar Björnstrand, Naima Wifstrand, Uke Fridell, Lars Ekborg, Bengt Ekerot

The Face at the Window *

GB 1939 65m bw
Pennant/Ambassador (George King)

In 1880 Paris, a murderer uses his moronic half-brother to distract his victims but is foiled when a dead man apparently incriminates him.

Roistering melodrama which provided Tod Slaughter with one of his juiciest roles and is here effectively presented, which is more than can be said for the screen treatments of most of his other vehicles.

w A. R. Rawlinson, Ronald Fayre play F. Brooke Warren d George King ph Hone Glendining md Jack Beaver ad Philip Bawcombe ed Jack Harris
☆ Tod Slaughter, Marjorie Taylor, John Warwick, Leonard Henry, Aubrey Mallalieu

'One of the best English pictures I have seen ... leaves the American horror films far behind.' – *Graham Greene*

The Face behind the Mask *

US 1941 69m bw
Columbia (Wallace MacDonald)

When his face is disfigured in a fire, an immigrant turns to a life of crime.

Effective second feature melodrama with a good star performance.

w Allen Vincent, Paul Jarrico play Thomas O'Connell d Robert Florey ph Franz Planer md Sidney Cutner
☆ Peter Lorre, Evelyn Keyes, Don Beddoe, George E. Stone

A Face in the Crowd ***

US 1957 126m bw
(Warner) Newton (Elia Kazan)

A small-town hick becomes a megalomaniac when television turns him into a cracker-barrel philosopher.

Brilliantly cinematic melodrama of its time which only flags in the last lap and paints a luridly entertaining picture of modern show business.

w Budd Schulberg story Your Arkansas Traveller by Budd Schulberg d Elia Kazan ph Harry Stradling, Gayne Rescher m Tom Glazer
☆ Andy Griffith, Lee Remick, Walter Matthau, Patricia Neal, Anthony Franciosa, Percy Waram, Marshall Neilan

'Savagery, bitterness, cutting humour.' – *Penelope Houston*
'If Kazan and Schulberg had been content to make their case by implication, it might have been a completely sophisticated piece of movie-

making. Instead, everything is elaborately spelled out, and the film degenerates into preposterous liberal propaganda.' – *Andrew Sarris*
'Some exciting scenes in the first half, but the later developments are frenetic, and by the end the film is a loud and discordant mess.' – *Pauline Kael, 70s*

A Face in the Rain *

US 1963 80m bw
Filmways/Calvic (John Calley)

During World War II an American spy in Italy bungles his mission, and hides in the apartment of a professor's wife.

Offbeat, talkative melodrama with a few neat touches.

w Hugo Butler, Jean Rouverol d Irvin Kershner ph Haskell Wexler m Richard Markowitz
☆ Rory Calhoun, Marina Berti, Niall MacGinnis

Face in the Sky

US 1933 68m bw
Fox

A sign painter falls for a farmer's daughter.

Curious, whimsical comedy romance which didn't work at any level.

w Humphrey Pearson story Myles Connolly d Harry Lachman
☆ Spencer Tracy, Marian Nixon, Stuart Erwin, Sam Hardy, Lila Lee

'Why it was considered feature-length picture material is hard to understand.' – *Variety*

Face of a Fugitive *

US 1959 81m Eastmancolor
Columbia/Morningside

A man falsely accused of murder makes a new life in a frontier town.

Lively Western melodrama with good atmosphere.

w David T. Chantler d Paul Wendkos ph Wilfrid M. Cline m Jerry Goldsmith
☆ Fred MacMurray, Lin McCarthy, Alan Baxter, James Coburn

Face of a Stranger: see *The Promise*

The Face of Fu Manchu **

GB 1965 96m Techniscope
Anglo EMI/Hallam (Harry Alan Towers)

In the twenties, Nayland Smith of Scotland Yard links an oriental crime wave with evil mastermind Fu Manchu.

A splendidly light touch and attention to detail make this entertaining spoof like a tuppenny blood come to life.

w Peter Welbeck (Harry Alan Towers) d Don Sharp ph Ernest Steward m Chris Whelan ad Frank White
☆ Nigel Green, Christopher Lee, Tsai Chin, Howard Marion Crawford

The Face of Marble

US 1946 70m bw
Monogram (Jeffrey Bernard)

A scientist revives the dead through voodoo.

Grade Z shocker with entertaining moments.

w Michel Jacoby d William Beaudine
☆ John Carradine, Robert Shayne, Claudia Drake, Maris Wrixon

Face/Off **

US 1997 138m DeLuxe Panavision
Buena Vista/Douglas/Reuther/WCG (David Permut, Barrie M. Osborne, Terence Chang, Christopher Godsick)

In order to discover the location of a bomb planted in Los Angeles, an FBI man assumes a false identity by having his own face replaced by that of a criminal.

🏃 film suitable for family viewing   📼 VHS video-cassette for the British PAL system   📼 VHS video-cassette for the British PAL system in wide screen-format   📀 Video cassette in a computer-colourised version   📼 American NTSC video-cassette   💿 Laser disc

Delirious thriller, in which the two male stars play each other as well as themselves in a pas de deux of elaborately choreographed violence.

w Mike Werb, Michael Colleary d John Woo ph Oliver Wood m John Powell pd Neil Spisak ed Christian Wagner, Steven Kemper

☆ John Travolta, Nicolas Cage, Joan Allen, Alessandro Nivola, Gina Gershon, Dominique Swain, Nick Cassavetes, Harve Presnell, Colm Feore

'Woo clearly thinks he's onto something big and mythic about male identity but, in truth, the film never really rises above the shin-kicking level of a pubescent bun fight – like the surgery itself, the film only goes skin deep.' – *Tom Shone, Sunday Times*

'It takes a lot of patience and stamina to watch more than two hours of this brazen rubbish.' – *Geoff Brown, The Times*

† The film was originally written as a vehicle for Arnold Schwarzenegger and Sylvester Stallone

†† It was the tenth most commercially successful movie of the year, grossing some $112m in the US, and another $115m elsewhere.

⅄ sound effects editing

Face the Music

GB   1954   84m   bw
Exclusive/Hammer (Michael Carreras)
US title: *The Black Glove*
An American musician in London solves the murder of a night-club singer.
Minor thriller in a sub-Chandler manner, improved by its music featuring the trumpet-playing of Kenny Baker.
w Ernest Borneman *novel* Ernest Borneman d Terence Fisher ph Jimmy Harvey m Kenny Baker's Dozen ad J. Elder Wills ed Maurice Rootes
☆ Alex Nicol, Eleanor Summerfield, John Salew, Paul Carpenter, Geoffrey Keen, Ann Hanslip

Face to Face

US   1952   89m   bw
RKO/Huntington Hartford
Two stories of confrontation, artificially presented by an independent company: *The Secret Sharer* by Joseph Conrad and *The Bride Comes to Yellow Sky* by Stephen Crane.
w Aeneas Mackenzie, James Agee d John Brahm, Bretaigne Windust ph Karl Struss, George Diskant
☆ James Mason, Gene Lockhart, Michael Pate; Robert Preston, Marjorie Steele, Minor Watson

Face to Face *

Italy/Spain   1967   110m   Technicolor
Techniscope
PEA/Arturo Gonzalez (Alberto Grimaldi)
original title: *Faccia a Faccia*
A consumptive university professor goes to Texas for a cure and becomes the ruthless leader of a gang of outlaws.
Political spaghetti Western that can be taken as an allegory for the rise of fascism and the doctrine that ten violent men are bandits, but hundreds are an army and thousands are history.
w Sergio Donati, Sergio Sollima d Sergio Sollima ph Raphael Pacheco m Ennio Morricone ad Carlo Simi ed Eugenio Alabiso
☆ Gian Maria Volonte, Tomas Milian, William Berger, Jolanda Modio, Gianni Rizzo, Carol André, Lidya Alfonsi

Face to Face ****

Sweden   1976   136m   Eastmancolor
Ingmar Bergman/De Laurentiis/Sveriges Radio (Ingmar Bergman, Lars-Owe Carlberg)
▦
A psychiatrist staying with her grandparents finds herself in need of guidance.
Fascinating material edited down from a TV series; too long as a film.
wd Ingmar Bergman ph Sven Nykvist m Mozart ad Anne Terselius-Hagegård, Anna Asp, Maggie Strindberg ed Siv Lundgren
☆ Liv Ullmann, Erland Josephson, Gunnar Björnstrand, Aino Taube-Henrikson
'After one has detailed its shortcomings, a wonderful fact remains: it's a work possible only to a first-class artist who has invested his life with other artists.' – *Stanley Kauffmann*
⅄ Ingmar Bergman (as director); Liv Ullmann

The Faceless Monster: see *Night of the Doomed*

Faces *

US   1968   130m   bw
Maurice McEndree
▦ ▤
A discontented Los Angeles executive tries but fails to go through with a divorce.
A personal, probing study of middle-aged loneliness, made with the director's usual long-winded relentlessness but quite frequently compelling.
wd John Cassavetes m Jack Ackerman ph/ed Al Ruban
☆ John Marley, Gena Rowlands, Lynn Carlin, Fred Draper, Seymour Cassel
'The cast are all painfully and overpoweringly real.' – *Jan Dawson*
⅄ John Cassavetes (as writer); Lynn Carlin; Seymour Cassel

Faces in the Dark *

GB   1960   85m   bw
Rank/Welbeck/Penington Eady (Jon Penington)
A blind man survives a plot against his life.
Unlikely but watchable puzzler, betrayed by lifeless handling. Hitchcock could have worked wonders with such a plot.
w Ephraim Kogan, John Tulley *novel* Pierre Boileau, Thomas Narcejac d David Eady ph Ken Hodges m Edwin Astley
☆ John Gregson, Mai Zetterling, Michael Denison, John Ireland, Tony Wright, Nanette Newman

The Facts of Life *

US   1960   103m   bw
UA/HLP (Norman Panama)
Two middle-aged married suburbanites have an abortive affair.
Star comedy with muted slapstick and earnest acting, a good try, but less effective than their normal pratfalls.
w Norman Panama, Melvin Frank d Melvin Frank ph Charles Lang Jnr m Leigh Harline ad Joseph McMillan Johnson, Kenneth A. Reid
☆ Bob Hope, *Lucille Ball*, Ruth Hussey, Don Defore, Louis Nye, Philip Ober
'Random shots of mockery aimed effectively at the American middle-class way of life.' – *Peter John Dyer*
⅄ Norman Panama, Melvin Frank (script); Charles Lang Jnr; title song (*m/ly* Johnny Mercer); art direction

The Faculty *

US   1998   102m   colour
Dimension/Los Hooligans (Elizabeth Avellan)
▦ ▤ ☺ ◉ ♫
High-school students notice that teachers and classmates are behaving oddly.
An adolescent variation on Invasion of the Body Snatchers, done with immense energy and a little wit.
w Kevin Williamson *story* David Wechter, Bruce Kimmel d Robert Rodriguez ph Enrique Chediak m Marco Beltrami pd Cary White ed Robert Rodriguez sp make-up and creature fx: Robert Kurtzman, Gregory Nicotero, Howard Berger, KNB EFX
☆ Jordana Brewster, Clea DuVall, Laura Harris, Josh Harnett, Shawn Hatosy, Salma Hayek, Famke Janssen, Piper Laurie, Chris McDonald, Bebe Neuwirth, Robert Patrick, Usher Raymond, Jon Stewart, Daniel von Bargen, Elijah Wood
'A rip-snorting hunk of giddy, self-aware genre trash.' – *Dennis Harvey, Variety*
'It isn't the least bit scary or particularly involving, but that seems to be the point.' – *Peter Matthews, Sight and Sound*

Fade to Black

US   1980   100m   colour
Compass International/Leisure Investment/Movie Ventures (George Braunstein, Ron Hamady)
▦ ▤
A film buff becomes known as the 'Celluloid Killer' for murdering his victims while disguised as his favourite movie characters.
Violent, off-beat thriller that makes black jokes at the expense of movies.
wd Vernon Zimmerman *story* Irving Yablans ph Alex Phillips Jnr ed Howard Kunin sp James Wayne
☆ Dennis Christopher, Linda Kerridge, Tim Thomerson, Morgan Paull, Hennen Chambers, Marya Small, Mickey Rourke
† The film won the Critics' Prize at the Avoriaz Festival of Fantastic Films in 1981.

Fahrenheit 451 *

GB   1966   112m   Technicolor
Rank/Anglo Enterprise/Vineyard (Lewis M. Allen)
▦ ▤ ☺ ◉ ♫
In a fascist future state, a fireman's job is to burn books.
1984 stuff, a little lacking in plot and rather tentatively directed, but with charming moments.
w François Truffaut, Jean-Louis Richard *novel* Ray Bradbury d François Truffaut ph Nicolas Roeg m Bernard Herrmann *design consultant* Tony Walton
☆ Oskar Werner, Julie Christie, Cyril Cusack, Anton Diffring, Jeremy Spenser
'He barely dramatizes the material at all, and though there are charming, childlike moments, the performers seem listless, and the whole enterprise is a little drab.' – *Pauline Kael*
† All the credits in this film are spoken.

'It will have you sitting on the brink of eternity!'

Fail Safe ***

US   1964   111m   bw
Columbia/Max E. Youngstein/Sidney Lumet
▤ ☺
An American atomic bomber is accidentally set to destroy Moscow, and the president has to destroy New York in retaliation.
Despite a confusing opening, this deadly earnest melodrama gets across the horror of its situation better than the contemporaneous Dr Strangelove which treated the same plot as black comedy. Here the details are both terrifying and convincing.
w Walter Bernstein *novel* Eugene Burdick, Harvey Wheeler d Sidney Lumet ph Gerald Hirschfeld m none
☆ Henry Fonda, Walter Matthau, Dan O'Herlihy, Frank Overton, Fritz Weaver, Edward Binns, Larry Hagman, Russell Collins

Fair Game: see *Mamba (1988)*

Fair Game

US   1995   90m   Technicolor
Warner/Silver Pictures (Joel Silver)
▦ ▤ ☺ ◉
A Miami lawyer is targeted by a former KGB killer.
A star vehicle built around Cindy Crawford: as long as she's in motion, it works as a low-level, senseless action film; when she stops, not even the many loud explosions can hide her lack of acting ability.
w Charles Fletcher *novel* Paula Gosling d Andrew Sipes ph Richard Bowen m Mark Mancina pd James Spencer ed David Finfer, Christian Wagner, Steven Kemper
☆ William Baldwin, Cindy Crawford, Steven Berkoff, Christopher McDonald, Miguel Sandoval, Johann Carlo, Salma Hayek
'Notable only for its jaw-dropping stupidity, the sort of action yarn that hopes nonstop mayhem will help cloud just how nonsensical it is.' – *Brian Lowry, Variety*
'A thriller primarily about the movement of Cindy Crawford's breasts beneath a succession of ever-smaller T-shirts.' – *Entertainment Weekly*
† The novel was first filmed in 1986 as *Cobra* (qv), starring Sylvester Stallone.

Fair Warning

US   1937   70m   bw
TCF
A sheriff solves the murder of a Death Valley miner.
Very watchable little second feature.
wd Norman Foster *story* Philip Wylie
☆ J. Edward Bromberg, Betty Furness, John Howard Payne, Victor Kilian, Gavin Muir, Andrew Tombes
'Stereotype whodunit comedy.' – *Variety*
'An hour of genuine entertainment and taut suspense.' – *Film Daily*

Fair Wind to Java

US   1952   92m   Trucolor
Republic (Joseph Kane)
A sailor with a mutinous crew seeks a South Sea treasure.
Routine adventure culminating in a volcanic explosion.
w Richard Tregaskis *novel* Garland Roark d Joseph Kane ph Jack Marta m Victor Young
☆ Fred MacMurray, Vera Hruba Ralston, Robert Douglas, Victor McLaglen

'Believe.'

Fairytale – A True Story

US   1997   99m   DeLuxe
Warner/Icon (Wendy Finerman, Bruce Davey)
▦ ▤ ☺ ♫
Two young girls cause a sensation by taking photographs of fairies.
Sentimental drama that swoons into fantasy and stays there, limp and apparently lifeless.
w Ernie Contreras *story* Albert Ash, Tom McLoughlin d Charles Sturridge ph Michael Coulter m Zbigniew Preisner pd Michael Howells ed Peter Coulson sp Tim Webber
☆ Florence Hoath, Elizabeth Earl, Paul McGann, Phoebe Nicholls, Peter O'Toole, Harvey Keitel, Anton Lesser, Bill Nighy, Bob Peck, Tim McInnerny, Mel Gibson (uncredited)
† The film is based on the true story of the Cottingley Fairies, when two young girls faked photographs of fairies in 1917, which was also the basis of another film, *Photographing Fairies*.

Faithful *

US   1996   88m   Technicolor
Miramax/Savoy/Tribeca (Jane Rosenthal, Robert DeNiro)
▤
While waiting for a signal to kill the wife of a philandering husband, a hitman chats to his victim.
A profane conversation piece that shows its stage origins too obviously, but the dialogue has an amusing bite about it.
w Chazz Palminteri *play* Chazz Palminteri d Paul Mazursky ph Fred Murphy m Philip Johnston pd Jeffrey Townsend ed Nicholas C. Smith
☆ Cher, Chazz Palminteri, Ryan O'Neal, Paul Mazursky, Amber Smith, Elisa Leonetti
'This determinedly offbeat comedy drama too often seems talky and static.' – *Variety*

Faithful in My Fashion

US   1946   81m   bw
MGM
A soldier on leave causes havoc in a department store where his girlfriend is manager.
Sentimental comedy, forgettable for itself but containing endearing performances by a number of favourite character actors.
w Lionel Houser d Sidney Salkow
☆ Tom Drake, Donna Reed, Edward Everett Horton, Spring Byington, Harry Davenport, Sig Rumann, Margaret Hamilton, Hobart Cavanaugh

Faithless

US   1932   76m   bw
MGM
A spoiled rich girl and her beau both descend to working-class level and almost further.
Would-be sensational drama ruined by censorship and miscasting.
w Carey Wilson *novel* Tinfoil by Mildred Cram d Harry Beaumont ph Oliver T. Marsh
☆ Tallulah Bankhead, Robert Montgomery, Hugh Herbert, Maurice Murphy, Louise Closser Hale, Lawrence Grant, Henry Kolker
'They pile the suffering on so thick that any but the most naive theatregoers are going to revolt and scoff.' – *Variety*

The Fake

GB   1953   81m   bw
Pax (Steven Pallos)
The Tate Gallery hires an American investigator who discovers that one of their da Vincis is a substitute.
Very standard co-feature mystery with pleasant touches.
w Patrick Kirwan d Godfrey Grayson ph Cedric Williams m Matyas Seiber
☆ Dennis O'Keefe, Coleen Gray, Hugh Williams, John Laurie, Guy Middleton, Dora Bryan, Billie Whitelaw

The Falcon

A debonair solver of crime puzzles allegedly created by Michael Arlen but owing much to The Saint and resulting from a need by RKO for more of the same. Helped by a tough/comic manservant, he flourished during the forties in sixteen second features (the last three for Film Classics). After three episodes George Sanders tired of the role and was written out by being 'shot' and having his real-life brother Tom Conway take over as his fictional one. The performances of these two actors are

pleasant, though the films are now fairly unwatchable, but John Calvert who took over for the last three was not a success.
1941 The Gay Falcon, A Date with the Falcon
1942 The Falcon Takes Over (the plot was borrowed from Raymond Chandler's Farewell My Lovely) (qv), The Falcon's Brother (qv)
1943 The Falcon Strikes Back (qv), The Falcon and the Co-Eds (qv), The Falcon in Danger
1944 The Falcon in Hollywood (qv), The Falcon in Mexico (qv), The Falcon Out West
1945 The Falcon in San Francisco (qv)
1946 The Falcon's Alibi (qv), The Falcon's Adventure
1948 The Devil's Cargo, Appointment with Murder, Search for Danger

The Falcon and the Co-Eds
US   1943   68m   bw
RKO (Maurice Geraghty)
The Falcon is called to a girl's school to investigate the murder of a teacher, forecast by a psychic student.
Flimsy programmer, with less wit and more implausibility than usual.
w Ardel Wray, Gerald Geraghty d William Clemens ph Roy Hunt md C. Bakaleinikoff ad Albert S. D'Agostino ed Theron Warth
☆ Tom Conway, Jean Brooks, Rita Corday, Amelita Ward, Isabel Jewell, George Givot, Cliff Clark, Ed Gargan

The Falcon and the Snowman
US   1984   123m   DeLuxe
Orion/Gabriel Katzka, John Schlesinger (John Daly)
A college dropout and a drug pusher sell secrets to the Russians.
A true case is made to seem not merely impossible but uninteresting by flaccid cinematic treatment.
w Steven Zaillian book Robert Lindsey d John Schlesinger ph Allen Daviau m Pat Metheny, Lyle Mays pd James D. Bissell ed Richard Marden
☆ Timothy Hutton, Sean Penn, David Suchet, Lori Singer, Pat Hingle, Dorian Harewood

The Falcon in Hollywood
US   1944   67m   bw
RKO (Maurice Geraghty)
Holidaying in Hollywood, the Falcon reluctantly investigates an actor's murder.
Light thriller, well enough done in its low-budget way, with a narrative device that prefigures The Producers.
w Gerald Geraghty d Gordon Douglas ph Nicholas Musuraca m C. Bakaleinikoff
ad Albert S. D'Agostino ed Gene Milford
☆ Tom Conway, Barbara Hale, Veda Ann Borg, John Abbott, Sheldon Leonard, Rita Corday

The Falcon in Mexico
US   1944   70m   bw
RKO (Maurice Geraghty)
The Falcon, suspected of murdering an art dealer and stealing a valuable painting, goes to Mexico to solve the mystery.
Moderate thriller, though the Falcon's capacity for being knocked unconscious at inopportune moments seems inexhaustible.
w George Worthing Yates, Gerald Geraghty d William Berke ph Frank Redmon md C. Bakaleinikoff ad Albert S. D'Agostino ed Joseph Noriega
☆ Tom Conway, Mona Maris, Martha MacVicar, Nestor Paiva, Mary Currier, Joseph Vitale

The Falcon in San Francisco
US   1945   66m   bw
RKO (Maurice Geraghty)
The Falcon goes to the rescue of a small girl and uncovers a smuggling ring.
One of the best of the series, an entertaining mix of thriller and comedy.
w Robert Kent, Ben Markson d Joseph H. Lewis ph Virgil Miller, William Sickner m Paul Sawtell ad Albert S. D'Agostino, Charles Pyke ed Ernie Leadlay
☆ Tom Conway, Rita Corday, Edward S. Brophy, Sharyn Moffett, Fay Helm, Robert Armstrong, Carl Kent

The Falcon Strikes Back
US   1943   66m   bw
RKO (Maurice Geraghty)
The Falcon, framed for stealing war bonds and shooting a bank messenger, tracks down the real culprit.
Thriller that tries rather too hard to be amusing, although it occasionally succeeds.
w Edward Dein, Gerald Geraghty story Stuart Palmer d Edward Dmytryk ph Jack Mackenzie md Roy Webb ad Albert S. D'Agostino, Walter E. Keller ed George Crone
☆ Tom Conway, Harriet Hilliard, Jane Randolph, Edgar Kennedy, Cliff Edwards, Cliff Clark, Ed Gargan

The Falcon Takes Over *
US   1942   62m   bw
RKO (Howard Benedict)
The Falcon goes after a killer and finds himself vamped by a femme fatale with his death on her mind.
The best of the Falcon series, taking Chandler's complex plot and compressing it into a fast-moving little thriller with comic elements.
w Lynn Root, Frank Fenton novel Farewell My Lovely by Raymond Chandler d Irving Reiss ph George Robinson md C. Bakaleinikoff ad Albert S. D'Agostino, Feild M. Gray ed Harry Marker
☆ George Sanders, Lynn Bari, James Gleason, Allen Jenkins, Helen Gilbert, Ward Bond, Edward Gargan
† Chandler's novel was refilmed in 1944 as the classic Farewell My Lovely (aka Murder, My Sweet) and again in 1975.

The Falcon's Alibi
US   1946   62m   bw
RKO (William Berke)
The Falcon foils a gang of jewel thieves.
Dull episode that lacks the usual comedy and provides very little mystery.
w Paul Yawitz story Dane Lussier, Manny Seff d Ray McCarey ph Frank Redman md C. Bakaleinikoff ad Albert S. D'Agostino, Lucius Croxton ed Phillip Martin Jnr
☆ Tom Conway, Rita Corday, Vince Barnett, Jane Greer, Elisha Cook Jnr, Emory Parnell, Al Bridge, Jason Robards

The Falcon's Brother
US   1942   63m   bw
RKO (Maurice Geraghty)
The Falcon's brother helps him bring to justice a Nazi spy-ring in America.
One of the dullest films in the series, with Sanders in a coma for most of the time and Conway not yet into his stride or his stroll.
w Stuart Palmer, Craig Rice d Stanley Logan ph Russell Metty m Roy Webb ad Albert S. D'Agostino, Walter E. Keller ed Mark Robson
☆ George Sanders, Tom Conway, Jane Randolph, Don Barclay, Cliff Clark, Edward Gargan, Eddie Dunn, Charlotte Wynters, Keye Luke
† Sanders was persuaded to make the fourth in the Falcon series only because a part was written for his brother Tom Conway, who took over as the Falcon. To RKO's surprise, Conway was a success in the role.

The Fall *
Argentina   1958   86m   bw
Argentine Sono (Leopoldo Torre Nilsson)
original title: La Caida
A strictly brought-up college girl lodges with an eccentric family whose strange world comes to mean more to her than the love of a young lawyer.
Odd, claustrophobic melodrama from a very personal film-maker.
w Beatriz Guido, Leopoldo Torre Nilsson novel Beatriz Guido d Leopoldo Torre Nilsson ph Alberto Etchebehere m Juan Carlos Paz
☆ Elsa Daniel, Duilio Marzia, Lydia Lamaison, Carlos Lopez Monet

Fall In
US   1943   48m   bw
Hal Roach
Two army sergeants resent each other.
Very mild farce, another of Hal Roach's middle-length 'screenliners'.
w Eugene Conrad, Edward E. Seabrook d Kurt Neumann

☆ William Tracy, Joe Sawyer, Robert Barrat, Jean Porter, Arthur Hunnicutt

The Fall of Berlin *
USSR   1949   160m   Agfacolor
Mosfilm
A steel worker turns soldier, sees all the major Russian battles of World War II, and has his hand shaken by Stalin.
Out-and-out propaganda, with caricatures of famous people and magnificently staged battles.
w M. Chiaureli, P. A. Pavlenko d M. Chiaureli ph L. V. Kosmatov m Dmitri Shostakovich
☆ B. Andreyev, M. Gelovani, V. Stanitsine, M. Kovaleva

The Fall of the House of Usher: see House of Usher (1960)

The Fall of the House of Usher
France   1928   48m   bw   silent
Roderick Usher's sister, prone to catalepsy, is buried alive; her unexpected return to life is instrumental in setting the house ablaze.
The original story is not so much stated as inferred in this very impressionistic version, of limited interest only to art movie buffs.
wd Jean Epstein, Luis Buñuel story Edgar Allen Poe ad Pierre Kefer
☆ Marguerite Gance, Jean Debucourt, Charles Lamy

The Fall of the House of Usher
GB   1950   70m   bw
GIB (Ivan Barnett)
Dismally inept low-budgeter, a pain to sit through.
w Kenneth Thompson, Dorothy Catt d Ivan Barnett
☆ Gwen Watford, Kay Tendeter, Irving Steen

The Fall of the Roman Empire **
US/Spain   1964   187m   Technicolor   Ultra Panavision 70
Samuel Bronston
After poisoning the Emperor Marcus Aurelius his mad son Commodus succumbs to dissipation and allows Rome to be ravaged by pestilence and the Barbarians.
Would-be distinguished epic with an intellectual first hour; unfortunately the hero is a priggish bore, the villain a crashing bore, the heroine a saintly bore, and the only interesting character is killed off early. A chariot race, a javelin duel, some military clashes and a mass burning at the stake keep one watching, and the production values are high indeed.
w Ben Barzman, Basilio Franchina, Philip Yordan d Anthony Mann ph Robert Krasker m Dimitri Tiomkin pd Veniero Colasanti, John Moore ed Robert Lawrence
☆ Alec Guinness, Christopher Plummer, Stephen Boyd, James Mason, Sophia Loren, John Ireland, Eric Porter, Anthony Quayle, Mel Ferrer, Omar Sharif
CHRISTOPHER PLUMMER TO SOPHIA LOREN: 'Sister! And I thought you'd retired as a vestal virgin!'
'The film works from a restricted palette, and the result is weirdly restraining and severe, a dignified curb on absurdities.' – John Coleman
'You have to hand it to Bronston for thinking and making it big – both in spectacle and silliness.' – Judith Crist
† The forum set in this film is said to be the largest ever built.
⅄ Dimitri Tiomkin

'Today ... innocence is about to die.'
Fall Time **
US   1994   88m   colour
Polygram/Capitol (Edward Bates)
Three teenagers who stage a fake murder in a small town as a prank find themselves caught up with vicious bank robbers.
Clever, darkly ironic thriller that moves from a pastiche of such movies and its clichés into something more real and frightening.
w Steve Alden, Paul Skemp d Paul Warner ph Mark J. Gordon m Hummie Mann pd Andrew Precht ed Steve Nevius

☆ Mickey Rourke, Stephen Baldwin, Sheryl Lee, Jason London, David Arquette, Jonah Blechman, J. Michael Hunter
'Wry, witty and unsettling ... takes on major themes without ever slowing its pace or loosening its dramatic grip.' – Philip Kemp, Sight and Sound
'Nasty, mean-spirited and leaden. The only point of interest is that it marks another stage in the weird decline of Mickey Rourke.' – Jonathan Romney, Guardian

'Don't Trust A Soul.'
Fallen
US   1998   124m   Technicolor   Panavision
Warner/Turner/Atlas (Charles Roven, Dawn Steel)
A police detective discovers that the serial killer he is tracking is a demon with the ability to transfer its soul from one person to another.
A supernatural thriller that offers little in the way of frisson; the Devil may have the best tunes, but he still has the worst films.
w Nicholas Kazan d Gregory Hoblit ph Newton Thomas Sigel m Tan Dun pd Terence Marsh ed Lawrence Jordan
☆ Denzel Washington, John Goodman, Donald Sutherland, Embeth Davidtz, James Gandolfini, Elias Koteas, Gabriel Casseus, Michael J. Pagan
'A convoluted picture that's only intermittently suspenseful and not very engaging emotionally or intellectually.' – Emanuel Levy, Variety

'Even now she stood between us – the taunt of her smile like a black curse on our love!'
Fallen Angel *
US   1945   97m   bw
TCF (Otto Preminger)
A man plans to get rid of his wife and marry another woman, but it is the latter who is murdered.
Oddly sleazy melodrama, not more successful then because it was unexpected than now because it is miscast. Some good sequences, though.
w Harry Kleiner novel Marty Holland d Otto Preminger ph Joseph LaShelle m David Raksin
☆ Dana Andrews, Alice Faye, Linda Darnell, Charles Bickford, Anne Revere, Bruce Cabot, John Carradine, Percy Kilbride
'It holds you by its undertones of small-town life and frustration.' – Richard Winnington
'It isn't in the class of Laura, but it's tolerable, in a tawdry sort of way.' – Pauline Kael, 70s

Fallen Angels **
Hong Kong   1995   96m   colour
Electric/Jet Tone (Jeff Lau)
original title: Duoluo Tianshi
A hitman and a former convict look for love.
A stylish, elliptical romance about lonely people veering from doom-laden despair to loud comedy; probably an acquired taste, but an interesting and unusual one.
wd Wong Kar-Wai ph Christopher Doyle m Frankie Chan, Roel A. Garcia pd William Chang ed William Chan, Wong Ming-Lam
☆ Leon Lai, Michele Reis, Takeshi Kaneshiro, Charlie Young, Karen Mong
'Takes every risk known to film-making, and succeeds triumphantly a whole lot more often than it fails.' – Tony Rayns, Sight and Sound

The Fallen Idol ***
GB   1948   94m   bw
British Lion/London Films (Carol Reed)
US title: The Lost Illusion
An ambassador's small son nearly incriminates his friend the butler in the accidental death of his shrewish wife.
A near-perfect piece of small-scale cinema, built up from clever nuances of acting and cinematic technique.
w Graham Greene story The Basement Room by Graham Greene d Carol Reed ph Georges Périnal m William Alwyn
☆ Ralph Richardson, Michèle Morgan, Bobby Henrey, Sonia Dresdel, Jack Hawkins
'A short story has become a film which is compact without loss of variety in pace and shape.' – Dilys Powell
'It's too deliberate and hushed to be much fun ... you wait an extra beat between the low-key lines of dialogue.' – Pauline Kael, 70s

---

♟ Graham Greene; Carol Reed
🏆 best British film

The Fallen Sparrow *
US 1943 93m bw
RKO (Robert Fellows)
📼 ▤ ◎~

An American veteran of the Spanish Civil War finds himself hounded in New York by Nazis seeking the Spanish flag of freedom.
Obscure melodrama, very good to look at but hardly worth unravelling; a precursor of Hollywood's post-war films noirs.
w Warren Duff *novel* Dorothy B. Hughes d Richard Wallace ph Nicholas Musuraca md Roy Webb, Constantin Bakaleinikoff
☆ John Garfield, Maureen O'Hara, Walter Slezak, Martha O'Driscoll, Patricia Morison, Bruce Edwards, John Banner, John Miljan
'One of the uncommon and provocatively handled melodramas of recent months.' – *New York Times*
♟ Roy Webb, Constantin Bakaleinikoff

Falling Down **
US 1992 112m Technicolor
Warner (Arnold Kopelson, Herschel Weingrod, Timothy Harris)
📼 ▤ ◎~

A redundant defence worker abandons his car on the Los Angeles freeway and attempts to make his way to the home of his former wife and their daughter. Confronted with the problems of urban life, from recalcitrant shopkeepers to unnecessary roadworks and would-be muggers, his behaviour becomes increasingly violent.
A fascinating movie on urban life, with a protagonist who is both hero and villain. It can be seen as a vigilante film, an attempt to claim a position for White Anglo-Saxon Protestants as among the victims of modern society, or a satire on over-reaction to city living. It remains a slightly queasy but enjoyable experience.
w Ebbe Roe Smith d Joel Schumacher ph Andrzej Bartkowiak m James Newton Howard pd Barbara Ling ed Paul Hirsch
☆ Michael Douglas, *Robert Duvall*, Barbara Hershey, Rachel Ticotin, Tuesday Weld, Frederic Forrest, Lois Smith
'At first comes across like a mean-spirited black comedy and then snowballs into a reasonably powerful portrait of social alienation.' – *Variety*
'Glitzy, casually cruel, hip and grim. It's something very funny, and often nasty in the way it manipulates one's darkest feelings.' – *Vincent Canby, New York Times*
'It's hard to decide whether it's a fascist movie made by a liberal or a liberal film made by a fascist. Sometimes it's hard to tell the difference between a hawk on good behaviour or a dove on steroids.' – *Adam Mars-Jones*

Falling for You *
GB 1933 88m bw
Gainsborough (Michael Balcon)
Fleet Street journalists in Switzerland try to outsmart each other.
Dated comedy very typical of the stars' extremely casual style, with immaculate set-pieces.
w Jack Hulbert, Douglas Furber, Robert Stevenson *story* Sidney Gilliat d Jack Hulbert, Robert Stevenson ph Bernard Knowles m/ly Vivian Ellis, Douglas Furber ad Vetchinsky ed R. E. Dearing
☆ Jack Hulbert, Cicely Courtneidge, Tamara Desni, Garry Marsh, Alfred Drayton, O. B. Clarence, Morton Selten

Falling From Grace
US 1992 100m Technicolor
Columbia (Harry Sandler)
▤ ◎~

A country singer returns home with his wife and child and begins an affair with his first girlfriend, who is now married to his brother and having an affair with his father.
Dull domestic drama of an Oedipal conflict that leads nowhere interesting, accompanied by a soundtrack of country songs.
w Larry McMurtry d John Mellencamp ph Victor Hammer pd George Corsillo ed Dennis Virkler
☆ John Mellencamp, Mariel Hemingway, Claude Akins, Dub Taylor, Kay Lenz, Larry Crane, Kate

---

Noonan, Deirdre O'Connell, John Prine, Brent Huff

Falling in Love *
US 1984 107m Technicolor
Paramount/Marvin Worth
▤ ◎~

Meeting as commuters, Frank and Molly, each married to someone else, think about having an affair.
Rather tedious rehash of Brief Encounter, with no real interest in the characters or their backgrounds.
w Michael Cristofer d Ulu Grosbard ph Peter Suschitzky m Dave Grusin pd Santo Loquasto ed Michael Kahn
☆ Robert DeNiro, Meryl Streep, Harvey Keitel, Jane Kaczmarek, George Martin
'The effect of this talented pair acting in such a lightweight vehicle is akin to having Horowitz and Rubinstein improvise a duet on the theme of Chopsticks.' – *Variety*

Falling in Love Again *
US 1980 103m colour
International Picture Show of Atlanta (Steven Paul)
▤ ◎~

A middle-aged New Yorker remembers his young romances and his dreams of success.
Warm little independent production harking back to the days of H. M. Pulham Esquire and none the worse for that.
w Steven Paul, Ted Allan, Susannah York d Steven Paul ph Michael Mileham, Dick Bush, Wolfgang Suschitzky m Michel Legrand
☆ Elliott Gould, Susannah York, Stuart Paul, Kaye Ballard

Die Fälschung: see *Circle of Deceit*

False Faces: see *Let 'Em Have It*

False Witness: see *Zigzag*

Falstaff: see *Chimes at Midnight*

Fame *
US 1980 133m Metrocolor
MGM (David de Silva, Alan Marshall)
📼 ▤ ◎~ 🎧

Assorted teenagers attend Manhattan's High School for the Performing Arts.
Cleverly shot and edited slice of life which unfortunately features people whose language and personalities are fairly repellent. The result is like A Chorus Line without the music.
w Christopher Gore d Alan Parker ph Michael Seresin m Michael Gore pd Geoffrey Kirkland ed Gerry Hambling
☆ Irene Cara, Lee Curreri, Laura Dean, Paul McCrane, Barry Miller, Gene Anthony Ray
'Our film, I hope, will be a microcosm of New York … a dozen races pitching in and having their own crack at the American dream.' – *Alan Parker*
'Its soft-centred view of human relationships is periodically undercut by what can only be described as the grotesque.' – *John Pym*
🏅 Michael Gore; song 'Fame' (mMichael Gore, lyDean Pitchford)
♟ screenplay; song 'Out Here On My Own' (mMichael Gore, lyLesley Gore); editing

Fame Is the Spur *
GB 1947 116m bw
GFD/Two Cities/Charter Films (John Boulting)
The rise to political eminence of a working-class socialist.
Disappointingly flat historical drama from a novel allegedly based on the career of Ramsay MacDonald. Interesting moments.
w Nigel Balchin *novel* Howard Spring d Roy Boulting ph Gunther Krampf, Harry Waxman m Alan Rawsthorne
☆ Michael Redgrave, Rosamund John, Bernard Miles, Carla Lehmann, Hugh Burden, Marjorie Fielding, Seymour Hicks
'The picture is not merely a misfortune, it is a symbol of something mislaid. But for an absence of aplomb and background choruses it might have been made by an average Hollywood director.' – *Richard Winnington*

La Famiglia: see *The Family* (1987)

The Family: see *Violent City* (1970)

The Family **
Italy/France 1987 127m colour
Maasfilm/Cinecittà/Cinemax/Ariane (Franco Committeri)
original title: *La Famiglia*
A man of 80 recalls the events of his long life, centred on the Rome apartment where he and his family still live.
An intriguing family saga of love, laughter and disappointment that is both a character and a social study.
w Ruggero Maccari, Furio Scarpelli, Ettore Scola d Ettore Scola ph Ricardo Aronovich m Armando Trovajoli ad Luciano Ricceri ed Ettore Scola
☆ Vittorio Gassman, Fanny Ardant, Stefania Sandrelli, Andrea Occhipinti, Jo Champa

A Family Affair *
↟↟ US 1937 69m bw
MGM (Lucien Hubbard)
A small-town judge faces a few family problems.
The second feature that started the highly successful Hardy family series (qv under Hardy). In this case the judge and his wife were played by actors who did not persevere into the series, but the stage was otherwise set for a long run, and the town of Carvel came to mean home to many Americans abroad.
w Kay Van Riper *play* Skidding by Aurania Rouverol d George B. Seitz ph Lester White m David Snell
☆ Lionel Barrymore, Spring Byington, Mickey Rooney, Eric Linden, Cecilia Parker, Sara Haden, Charles Grapewin, Julie Haydon
'Family trade and tops in dual locations.' – *Variety*

Family Business
US 1989 110m colour
Palace/Tri-Star (Lawrence Gordon)
📼 ▤ ◎~

Three generations of crooks take part in a robbery.
Dull comedy that never convinces and certainly doesn't amuse.
w Vincent Patrick *novel* Vincent Patrick d Sidney Lumet ph Andrzej Bartkowiak m Cy Coleman pd Philip Rosenberg ed Andrew Mondshein
☆ Sean Connery, Dustin Hoffman, Matthew Broderick, Rosana DeSoto, Janet Carroll, Victoria Jackson, Bill McCutcheon, Deborah Rush, Marilyn Cooper

Family Doctor: see *RX Murder*

Family Honeymoon
US 1948 90m bw
U-I (John Beck, Z. Wayne Griffin)
A college professor marries a widow whose three children join them on their Grand Canyon honeymoon.
Very ordinary and predictable star comedy.
w Dane Lussier, Homer Croy d Claude Binyon ph William Daniels m Frank Skinner
☆ Claudette Colbert, Fred MacMurray, Rita Johnson, Gigi Perreau, Peter Miles, Jimmy Hunt, Hattie McDaniel, Chill Wills

The Family Jewels
US 1965 100m Technicolor
Paramount/York/Jerry Lewis
▤

A child heiress chooses a new father from among her five uncles.
Unfunny star farce with multiple impersonations.
w Jerry Lewis, Bill Richmond d Jerry Lewis ph W. Wallace Kelley m Pete King
☆ Jerry Lewis, Donna Butterworth, Sebastian Cabot, Robert Strauss

Family Life ***
GB 1971 108m Technicolor
EMI/Kestrel (Tony Garnett)
A 19-year-old girl is driven into a mental collapse by emotional and family problems.
A slice of suburban life and an indictment of it, put together with unknown actors and probing TV techniques. Somewhat too harrowing for fiction, but extraordinarily vivid.
w David Mercer *play* In Two Minds by David Mercer d Ken Loach ph Charles Stewart m Marc Wilkinson
☆ Sandy Ratcliff, Bill Dean, Grace Cave

'There's no body in the family plot!'

Family Plot **
US 1976 126m Technicolor
Universal (Alfred Hitchcock)
📼 ▤ ◎~

A fake medium tries for easy money by producing a lost heir.
Talkative, complex, patchy, low-key but always interesting Hitchcock suspenser in an unusually friendly vein.
w Ernest Lehman *novel* The Rainbird Pattern by Victor Canning d Alfred Hitchcock ph Leonard J. South m John Williams pd Henry Bumstead
☆ Karen Black, Bruce Dern, Barbara Harris, William Devane, Ed Lauter, Cathleen Nesbitt
'Full of benign mischief, beautiful craftsmanship and that elusive sense of cinematic rhythm that has always been Hitchcock's trump card.' – *Michael Billington, Illustrated London News*
'The picture bogs down in one talky, undramatic sequence after another, and the plot, with all its exposition and loose ends, is involved beyond belief.' – *De Witt Bodeen, Films in Review*

Family Portrait **
GB 1950 24m bw
Festival of Britain/Wessex (Ian Dalrymple)
A study of the English tradition and spirit through history.
The last work of a director-poet; not his most vivid movie, yet an accurate distillation of the themes which concerned him and of a dreamlike patriotism which now seems lost.
wd Humphrey Jennings ph Martin Curtis ed Stewart MacAllister *commentary* Michael Goodliffe
'Perhaps the most polished in style of all Jennings' films … continuously fascinating, sharp and evocative.' – *MFB*

Family Resemblances: see *Un Air de Famille*

The Family Secret
US 1951 85m bw
Columbia/Santana (Robert Lord, Henry S. Kesler)
▤

The son of a suburban family kills his best friend in a brawl, and his mother insists he conceal the truth even when another man is charged.
Television-style pattern play, not even very interesting at the time.
w Francis Cockrell, Andrew Solt d Henry Levin ph Burnett Guffey m George Duning
☆ John Derek, Lee J. Cobb, Erin O'Brien Moore, Jody Lawrance, Henry O'Neill, Carl Benton Reid
'The general atmosphere is one of outward torment unbacked by inner emotion.' – *MFB*

A Family Thing
US 1996 109m DeLuxe
United Artists/Butcher's Run (Todd Black, Randa Haines, Robert Duvall)
📼 ▤ ◎~

A white Arkansas man discovers that he has a black half-brother, a Chicago cop.
Despite the best efforts of its cast, an uninvolving, melodramatic family drama that skirts around the issue of race.
w Billy Bob Thornton, Tom Epperson d Richard Pearce ph Fred Murphy m Charles Gross ed Mark Warner pf Linda DeScenna
☆ Robert Duvall, James Earl Jones, Michael Beach, *Irma P. Hall*, Grace Zabriskie, Regina Taylor

Family Viewing
Canada 1988 86m colour
The Other Cinema/Ego Film (Atom Egoyan)
A television- and video-obsessed family live lives of quiet desperation.
Interesting low-budget film, originally shot on video, and as obsessed as its characters with electronic media.
wd Atom Egoyan ph Robert Macdonald m Michael Danna ad Linda del Rosario ed Atom Egoyan, Bruce Macdonald
☆ David Hemblen, Aidan Tierney, Gabrielle Rose, Arsinee Khanjian, Selma Keklikian, Rose Sarkisyan, Jeanne Sabourin
'There are streaks of filmmaking talent visible through the pretentious murk of this disjointed story.' – *Variety*

The Family Way *
GB   1966   115m   Eastmancolor
BL/Jambox (John Boulting)
There is consternation in a Lancashire family when the son cannot consummate his marriage.
Overstretched domestic farce-drama. Good scenes and performances, but it was all much sharper as a one-hour TV play.
w Bill Naughton *play* Honeymoon Deferred by Bill Naughton d Roy Boulting ph Harry Waxman m Paul McCartney
☆ John Mills, Marjorie Rhodes, Hywel Bennett, Hayley Mills, Avril Angers, Murray Head, Wilfred Pickles, Barry Foster, Liz Fraser

The Famous Ferguson Case
US   1932   80m   bw
Warner
Reporters on a small town paper expose their own hang-ups as they argue over the outcome of a current murder trial.
Generally unsuccessful attempt to do something mildly different.
w Harvey Thew *story* Courtenay Terrett, Granville Moore d Lloyd Bacon
☆ Joan Blondell, Tom Brown, Adrienne Dore, Walter Miller, Leslie Fenton, J. Carrol Naish, Grant Mitchell
'Dull, trite, talky exposé of yellow journalism.' – *Variety*

The Fan *
US   1949   79m   bw
TCF (Otto Preminger)
GB title: *Lady Windermere's Fan*
Scandal almost results when Lady Windermere loses her fan.
Reasonably polished, rather dull version of an old play, not really helped by modern bookends.
w Walter Reisch, Dorothy Parker, Ross Evans *play* Lady Windermere's Fan by Oscar Wilde d Otto Preminger ph Joseph LaShelle m Daniele Amfitheatrof
☆ George Sanders, Madeleine Carroll, Jeanne Crain, Richard Greene, Martita Hunt, John Sutton, Hugh Dempster, Richard Ney

The Fan
US   1981   95m   Technicolor
Paramount/Robert Stigwood/Filmways
A Broadway actress is threatened by a disturbed admirer.
Ruthless, witless thriller with no suspense cliché unturned.
w Priscilla Chapman, John Hartwell d Edward Bianchi ph Dick Bush m Pino Donaggio pd Santo Loquasto
☆ Lauren Bacall, James Garner, Maureen Stapleton, Hector Elizondo, Michael Biehn, Anna Maria Horsford
'Horror comic mechanics … the theatrical milieu fails to register, either individually or collectively.' – *Gilbert Adair, MFB*

The Fan
US   1996   115m   Technicolor   Panavision
Entertainment/TriStar/Mandalay/Scot Free (Wendy Finerman)
An unemployed, frustrated baseball fan kidnaps the son of a star player and threatens to kill him.
A hyperactive thriller that makes little effort to investigate the fraught relationship between fan and hero; the emphasis here is on shock and sensation.
w Phoef Sutton *novel* Peter Abrahams d Tony Scott ph Dariusz Wolski m Hans Zimmer pd Ida Random ed Christian Wagner, Claire Simpson
☆ Robert DeNiro, Wesley Snipes, Ellen Barkin, John Leguizamo, Benicio del Toro, Patti D'Arbanville, Chris Mulkey
'Fails even as pulp. It's all urgency and no pace, and the climax is an insult.' – *Tom Shone, Sunday Times*

Fanatic *
GB   1965   96m   Technicolor
Hammer/Seven Arts (Anthony Hinds)
US title: *Die! Die! My Darling*
An American girl in England visits the mother of her dead fiancé and finds herself the prisoner of a religious maniac.

Boringly overlong Grand Guignol which even defeats its gallantly unmade-up and deathly-looking star; mildly notable however as a record of one of her last performances.
w Richard Matheson *novel* Nightmare by Anne Blaisdell d Silvio Narizzano ph Arthur Ibbetson m Wilfrid Josephs pd Peter Proud ed James Needs, John Dunsford
☆ Tallulah Bankhead, Stefanie Powers, Peter Vaughan, Yootha Joyce, Donald Sutherland

The Fanatics *
France   1957   92m   bw
Cinégraphe-Regent (Pierre Lévy)
Patriots quarrel over the assassination by bomb of a South American dictator when he travels by public plane.
Suspense melodrama with many artificial twists, but slick and well acted.
w Alex Joffé, Jean Levitte d Alex Joffé ph L. H. Burel m Paul Misraki
☆ Pierre Fresnay, Michel Auclair, Grégoire Aslan, Betty Schneider

Fancy Pants **
US   1950   92m   Technicolor
Paramount (Robert Welch)
A British actor stranded in the far west poses as a butler.
Lively Western comedy remake of Ruggles of Red Gap (qv), one of the star's better vehicles.
w Edmund Hartmann, Robert O'Brien d George Marshall ph Charles Lang Jnr m Van Cleave
☆ Bob Hope, Lucille Ball, Bruce Cabot, Jack Kirkwood, Lea Penman, Eric Blore, John Alexander, Norma Varden

Fandango
US   1984   91m   Technicolor
Warner/Amblin (Tim Zinnemann)
In the early 1970s, a group of college friends drive across Texas for a final weekend of fun before graduation and army service in Vietnam looms.
Slight but enjoyable movie that began life as a small student film before being expanded under the auspices of Steven Spielberg's production company.
wd Kevin Reynolds ph Thomas Del Ruth m Alan Silvestri ad Peter Lansdown Smith ed Arthur Schmidt, Stephen Semel
☆ Kevin Costner, Judd Nelson, Sam Robards, Chuck Bush, Brian Cesak, Marvin J. McIntyre, Suzy Amis, Glenne Headly

Fanfan la Tulipe *
France   1951   98m   bw
Filmsonor/Ariane/Amato (Alexandre Mnouchkine)
Recruited into the army of Louis XV by a prophecy that he will marry the king's daughter, a young braggart does everything he can to live up to it.
Rather like a spoof Errol Flynn effort, this likeable swashbuckler can't quite summon up enough buckle or swash to be the minor classic it clearly intends.
w Christian-Jaque, Henri Jeanson, René Wheeler *story* René Wheeler, René Fallet d Christian-Jaque ph Christian Matras m Georges Van Parys, Maurice Thiriet ad Robert Gys ed Jacques Desagneaux
☆ Gérard Philipe, Gina Lollobrigida, Marcel Herrand, Olivier Hussenot, Henri Rollan, Nerio Bernardi, Jean Marc Tennberg, Jean Parédès, Noël Roquevert, Geneviève Page, Sylvia Pelayo
'A daring and delightful piece of work.' – *The Times*
† The film won Christian-Jaque the award for best director at the Cannes Film Festival in 1952.

Fängelse: see *The Devil's Wanton*

Fanny ***
France   1932   128m   bw
Les Films Marcel Pagnol/Braunberger-Richebé
After her lover returns to sea, Fanny discovers that she is pregnant and agrees to marry a wealthy widower.
The second instalment of Pagnol's trilogy of Marseilles life, suffused with acute observation, warmth and humanity.
w Marcel Pagnol *play* Marcel Pagnol d Marc Allégret ph Nicolas Toporkoff, André Dantan, Roger Hubert, Georges Benoit, Coutelain m Vincent Scotto ed Raymond Lamy

☆ Raimu, Orane Demazis, Pierre Fresnay, Fernand Charpin, Alida Rouffe, Robert Vattier, Auguste Mouriès, Milly Mathis, Maupi, Edouard Delmont
† This was the first film Pagnol made as his own producer. After its success he was able to build his own studio. An Italian version, directed by Mario Almirante, was made in 1933 and a German version starring Emil Jannings in 1934. It followed on from Marius and was followed by a sequel, César (qqv).

'There are three men in her life. The one she married … the young adventurer … and the baby they all shared!'

Fanny *
US   1961   133m   Technicolor
Warner/Mansfield (Joshua Logan)
Life on the Marseilles waterfront, and in particular the story of two old men and two lovers.
Lumbering adaptation of three Pagnol films of the thirties (Marius, Fanny, César – see Marius) previously seen as a 1938 Hollywood film (Port of Seven Seas) and later as a Broadway musical. This is the dullest version despite fine photography and a couple of good performances.
w Julius J. Epstein *play* S. N. Behrman, Joshua Logan *films* Marcel Pagnol d Joshua Logan ph Jack Cardiff m Harold Rome md Morris Stoloff, Harry Sukman
☆ Charles Boyer, Maurice Chevalier, Leslie Caron, Horst Buchholz, Georgette Anys, Salvatore Baccaloni, Lionel Jeffries, Raymond Bussières, Victor Francen
† The film was proudly advertised as 'Joshua Logan's Fanny' until the press pointed out the double meaning.
⯃ best picture; Jack Cardiff; Morris Stoloff, Harry Sukman; Charles Boyer

Fanny and Alexander ****
Sweden/France/West Germany   1982   188m   Eastmancolor
AB Cinematograph/Swedish Film Institute/Swedish TV One/Gaumont/Persona Film/Tobis (Jörn Donner)
A well-to-do Uppsala family comes together to celebrate Christmas 1907.
An interesting mixture of Dear Octopus and Wild Strawberries turns into something more akin to The Face or The Night Comers. A kind of Bergman compendium, and impossible to describe exactly for those who have not seen it.
wd Ingmar Bergman ph Sven Nykvist m Daniel Bell pd Anna Asp
☆ Gunn Walgren, Ewa Fröling, Jarl Kulle, Erland Josephson, Börje Ahlstedt, Mona Malm, Gunnar Björnstrand, Jan Malmsjö
'It's as if Bergman's neuroses had been tormenting him for so long that he cut them off and went sprinting back to Victorian health and domesticity.' – *New Yorker*
⯃ cinematography; best foreign-language film; art direction; costume
⯃ direction; screenplay
▽ cinematography

Fanny by Gaslight **
GB   1944   108m   bw
GFD/Gainsborough (Edward Black)
US title: *Man of Evil*
The illegitimate daughter of a cabinet minister is saved from a lustful lord.
Highly-coloured Victorian romantic melodrama, enjoyably put over with no holds barred and a pretty high budget for the time.
w Doreen Montgomery, Aimée Stuart *novel* Michael Sadleir d Anthony Asquith ph Arthur Crabtree m Cedric Mallabey
☆ James Mason, Phyllis Calvert, Stewart Granger, Wilfrid Lawson, John Laurie, Margaretta Scott, Stuart Lindsell, Jean Kent
'Seldom have I seen a film more agreeable to watch, from start to finish.' – *William Whitebait*
'Mr Asquith does not seem to have made much effort to freshen it by interesting treatment, so that the rare unusual device seems quite out of key among so much that is simple, obvious, hackneyed.' – *Richard Mallett, Punch*
† One of several costume melodramas patterned after the success of The Man in Grey (qv).

Fanny Hill
West Germany   1965   104m   bw
Albert Zugsmith/Pan World
Adventures of an 18th-century woman of pleasure.
Tacky exploitation piece half-spoofing a suddenly fashionable piece of pornography.
w Robert Heel d Russ Meyer
☆ Miriam Hopkins, Leticia Roman, Walter Giller, Alex D'Arcy, Helmut Weiss

Fanny (Pagnol): see *Marius*

Fantasia ****
US   1940   135m   Technicolor
Walt Disney
A concert of classical music is given cartoon interpretations.
Brilliantly inventive for the most part, the cartoons having become classics in themselves. The least part (the Pastoral Symphony) can be forgiven.
The pieces are:
Bach: Toccata and Fugue in D Minor
Tchaikovsky: The Nutcracker Suite
Dukas: The Sorcerer's Apprentice
Stravinsky: The Rite of Spring
Beethoven: The Pastoral Symphony
Ponchielli: Dance of the Hours
Moussorgsky: Night on a Bald Mountain
Schubert: Ave Maria
md Edward H. Plumb *supervisor* Ben Sharpsteen
☆ Leopold Stokowski, the Philadelphia Orchestra, Deems Taylor
'Dull as it is towards the end, ridiculous as it is in the bend of the knee before Art, it is one of the strange and beautiful things that have happened in the world.' – *Otis Ferguson*
'It is ambitious, and finely so, and one feels that its vulgarities are at least unintentional.' – *James Agate*
'Disney sometimes at his worst, often at his very best; and the best is on a level which no other cinematographic designer has reached. It takes over two hours, but somehow or other I'm afraid you will have to find the time.' – *Dilys Powell*
† Multiplane cameras, showing degrees of depth in animation, were used for the first time. The film was re-released in a print restored to its original freshness in 1990.
⯃ Special Award to Walt Disney, Leopold Stokowski

The Fantasist
Ireland   1987   98m   colour
Blue Dolphin (Mark Forstater)
A psychopathic killer stalks a young country girl who goes to work in Dublin.
Occasionally suspenseful thriller, but it offers little out of the ordinary and is muddled in its intentions, attempting to be a more serious film than it actually is.
wd Robin Hardy *novel* Goosefoot by Patrick McGinley ph Frank Gell m Stanislas Syrewicz ed Thomas Schwalm
☆ Moira Harris, Christopher Cazenove, Timothy Bottoms, John Kavanagh, Mick Lally

The Fantastic Disappearing Man: see *The Return of Dracula*

Fantastic Invasion of Planet Earth: see *The Bubble*

Fantastic Planet **
France/Czechoslovakia   1970   72m   colour
Armorial/Ceskoslovensky Filmexport (S. Damiani, A. Valio-Cavaglione)
original title: *La Planète Sauvage*
On a distant planet, a race of meditating giants use humans as slaves and playthings.
A witty fable of the worth of liberty, elegantly animated in a semi-surrealist style.
w Roland Topor, Rene Laloux *novel* Oms en Serie by Stefan Wul d Rene Laloux ph Lubomir Rejthar, Boris Baromyk m Alain Goraguer pd Roland Topor ed Rich Harrison, Dick Elliott
☆ Featuring the voices of: Cynthia Adler, Barry Bostwick, Mark Gruner, Nora Heflin, Marvin Miller
† The film was shot in the animation studios of Jiri Trnka in Prague.

Fantastic Voyage *

US 1966 100m DeLuxe
Cinemascope
TCF (Saul David)

When a top scientist is shot and suffers brain damage, a team of doctors and a boat are miniaturized and injected into his blood stream ... but one is a traitor.
Engagingly absurd science fiction which keeps its momentum but is somewhat let down by its décor.
w Harry Kleiner d Richard Fleischer ph Ernest Laszlo m Leonard Rosenman ad Dale Hennesy, Jack Martin Smith sp L. B. Abbott, Art Cruickshank, Emil Kosa Jnr
☆ Stephen Boyd, Raquel Welch, Edmond O'Brien, Donald Pleasence, Arthur Kennedy, Arthur O'Connell, William Redfield
'The process shots are so clumsily matted ... that the actors look as if a child has cut them out with blunt scissors.' – *Pauline Kael*
🏆 art direction; special visual effects (Art Cruickshank)
🏅 Ernest Laszlo

Fantomas *

France/Italy 1964 104m bw
SNEG

A master crook is also a master of disguise.
One of several films made in the sixties in affectionate imitation of a French silent serial.
w Jean Halain, Pierre Foucaud d André Hunebelle m Marcel Grignon m Michel Magne
☆ Jean Marais, Louis de Funes, Mylene Demongeot, Jacques Dynam

Le Fantôme de la Liberté: see *The Phantom of Liberty*

Far and Away

US 1992 140m DeLuxe Panavision Super 70
UIP/Universal/Imagine (Brian Grazer, Ron Howard)

A young Irish woman, daughter of a landowner, runs away to America, taking one of her father's tenants with her as an unwilling servant.
A romance conceived on an epic scale, but still-born; an uninteresting molehill of a movie.
w Bob Dolman story Bob Dolman, Ron Howard d Ron Howard ph Mikael Salomon m John Williams pd Jack T. Collis, Allan Cameron ed Michael Hill, Daniel Hanley
☆ Tom Cruise, Nicole Kidman, Thomas Gibson, Robert Prosky, Barbara Babcock, Cyril Cusack, Eileen Pollock, Colm Meaney, Niall Toibin
'A doddering bloated bit of corn, and its characters and situations so obviously hackneyed, that we can't give in to the story and allow ourselves to be swept away.' – *Washington Post*
'The plot and characters sometimes seem to have been borrowed from a picture storybook for teenage girls.' – *Iain Johnstone, Sunday Times*
'Unrepentant and vapid nonsense, celebrated with inappropriate splendour.' – *Philip Strick, Sight and Sound*

The Far Country *

US 1954 97m Technicolor
U-I (Aaron Rosenberg)

Two cowboys on their way to the Alaska goldfields are beset by swindlers.
Sturdy star Western with good production values.
w Borden Chase d Anthony Mann ph William Daniels m Hans Salter
☆ James Stewart, Walter Brennan, Ruth Roman, Corinne Calvet, John McIntire

Far East

Australia 1982 100m colour
Filmco Australia/Alfred Road (Richard Mason)

An American bar owner in an Asian city rampant with violence is confronted by a girl from his past.
A disappointing attempt to redo Casablanca without the wit or style.
wd John Duigan ph Brian Probyn m Sharon Calcraft pd Ross Major ed Henry Dangar
☆ Bryan Brown, Helen Morse, John Bell, Raina McKeon, Henry Duval, Sinan Leong, Bill Hunter

Far from Home

US 1989 86m CFI color
Vestron/Lightning (Donald P. Borchers)

While on holiday with her father, an adolescent girl is stalked by a serial killer.
Drear little film that follows the standard pattern for the over-familiar genre.
w Tommy Lee Wallace story Ted Gershuny d Meiert Avis ph Paul Elliott m Jonathan Elias ed Marc Grossman
☆ Matt Frewer, Drew Barrymore, Richard Masur, Karen Austin, Susan Tyrrell, Anthony Rapp, Jennifer Tilly, Dick Miller

Far from Home: The Adventures of Yellow Dog *

US 1994 81m colour
TCF (Peter O'Brian)

After being shipwrecked, a 14-year-old boy survives a fortnight in the wilderness of British Columbia with the help of his labrador.
Enjoyable, if simple-minded, adventure story in imposing landscapes which should set a few tails wagging.
wd Phillip Borsos ph James Gardner m John Scott pd Mark S. Freeborn ed Sidney Wolinsky
☆ Mimi Rogers, Bruce Davison, Jesse Bradford, Tom Bower, Joel Palmer, Josh Wanamaker, Dakotah
'Predictability doesn't overshadow the movie's appeal since it is deftly handled by Borsos, striking such a basic emotional chord that you'd have to have a heart of stone not to get pulled in. This really is miles better than you would expect.' – *Julie Stevens, Empire*

Far from the Madding Crowd *

GB 1967 175m Technicolor Panavision 70
EMI/Vic/Appia (Joseph Janni)

In Victorian Wessex a headstrong girl causes unhappiness and tragedy.
Good-looking but slackly handled version of a melodramatic and depressing novel.
w Frederic Raphael novel Thomas Hardy d John Schlesinger ph Nicolas Roeg m Richard Rodney Bennett pd Richard Macdonald
☆ Julie Christie, Peter Finch, Alan Bates, Terence Stamp, Prunella Ransome
'In this rather plodding film the insufficiency of the foreground is partly offset by the winsomeness of the backgrounds. The very sheep are so engaging as to entice our gaze into some extremely amiable woolgathering.' – *John Simon*
🏅 Richard Rodney Bennett

The Far Horizons

US 1955 108m Technicolor Vistavision
(Paramount)

The story of Lewis and Clark's 1803 expedition west through the Louisiana Purchase territory.
Flabbily-handled historical hokum; potential interest quickly dissipated.
w Winston Miller, Edmund H. North d Rudolph Maté ph Daniel L. Fapp m Hans Salter
☆ Fred MacMurray, Charlton Heston, Donna Reed, Barbara Hale, William Demarest

Far North

US 1988 89m colour
Rank/Alive Films/Nelson/Circle JS (Malcolm R. Harding, Carolyn Pfieffer)

A family squabbles around the bed of their sick father.
Inconsequential film that marked the directorial début of writer/actor Shepard.
wd Sam Shepard ph Robbie Greenberg m The Red Clay Ramblers, J. A. Deane pd Peter Jamison ed Bill Yahraus
☆ Jessica Lange, Tess Harper, Charles Durning, Donald Moffat, Ann Wedgeworth, Patricia Arquette, Nina Draxten

A Far Off Place *

US 1993 116m Technicolor
Buena Vista/Walt Disney/Amblin (Eva Monely, Elaine Sperber)

A teenage boy and girl, pursued by murderous ivory poachers, are guided across the Kalahari desert by a young bushman.

Old-fashioned children's movie about discovering maturity through an understanding of the natural world; the photography has charm.
w Robert Caswell, Jonathan Hensleigh, Sally Robinson book A Story Like the Wind and a Far Off Place by Laurens van der Post d Mikael Salomon ph Juan Ruiz-Anchia m James Horner pd Gemma Jackson ed Ray Lovejoy
☆ Reese Witherspoon, Ethan Randall, Jack Thompson, Sarel Bok, Robert Burke, Patricia Kalember, Maximilian Schell
'A coming-of-age yarn that should hold the attention of kids and patient adults.' – *Variety*
'Potential date movie material for environmentally aware 13-year-olds.' – *Matt Mueller, Empire*

Far Out Man

US 1990 85m Foto-Kem
New Line/CineTel (Lisa M. Hansen)

An ageing, permanently stoned hippie searches for his former girlfriend and their child.
A Chong family home movie inflicted upon a wider public, it is only worth watching if you are related to the writer/director and even then you must be prepared to be indulgent.
wd Tommy Chong ph Greg Gardiner, Eric Woster m Jay Chattaway ed Stephen Myers, Gilberto Costa Nunes
☆ Tommy Chong, C. Thomas Howell, Rae Dawn Chong, Shelby Chong, Paris Chong, Martin Mull, Bobby Taylor, Al Mancini, Judd Nelson, Cheech Marin, Paul Bartel
'Technically, pic is a mess. Two lensers are credited, so it may be that one held the camera while the other held the film and the director never came out of character long enough to tell them what to do with either.' – *Variety*

Faraway, So Close

Germany 1993 144m colour/bw
Columbia TriStar/Road Movies/Tobis (Wim Wenders)

original title: *In Weiter Ferne, So Nah!*
An angel watching over the citizens of Berlin decides to become human but finds that life is too difficult for him to survive.
A bungled and often sentimental sequel to Wings of Desire which suddenly switches into a confused thriller about arms dealing; it does have some superlative moments, but not enough.
w Wim Wenders, Ulrich Zieger, Richard Reitinger d Wim Wenders ph Jürgen Jürges m Laurent Petitgirard pd Albrecht Konrad ed Peter Przygodda
☆ Otto Sander, Peter Falk, Bruno Ganz, Horst Buchholz, Nastassja Kinski, Heinz Rühmann, Solveig Dommartin, Rudiger Vogler, Lou Reed, Willem Dafoe, Henri Alekan, Mikhail Gorbachev
'Occasionally veers into pretension, wavers between perfect black-and-white and striking washed-out colour, and discusses politics and eternity, but is filled with moments that will stay with you forever.' – *Kim Newman, Empire*

Farewell *

USSR 1981 126m colour
Artificial Eye/Mosfilm (A. Rasskazov, G. Sokolova)

original title: *Proshchanie*
A peasant community is resettled, against its will, into modern apartments to make way for a new dam.
Emotional and detailed look at the destruction of a community and its relationships.
w Lorisa Shepitko, Rudolf Tyurin, German Klimov novel Valentin Rasputin d Elem Klimov ph Alexei Rodionov, Yuri Skhirtladze, Sergei Taraskin m V. Artyomov ad V. Petrov ed V. Byelova
☆ Stefaniya Stayuta, Lev Durov, Alexei Petrenko, Leonid Kryuk, Vadim Yakovenko, Yuri Katin-Yartsev, Denis Luppov

Farewell Again **

GB 1937 85m bw
Pendennis/London Films (Erich Pommer)

US title: *Troopship*
Soldiers returning from India have six hours' shore leave to sort out their problems.
Dated but slackly made compendium drama, a solid success of its time.
w Clemence Dane, Patrick Kirwan story Wolfgang Wilhelm d Tim Whelan ph James

Wong Howe, Hans Schneeberger m Richard Addinsell ad Frederick Pusey ed Jack Dennis
☆ Flora Robson, Leslie Banks, Robert Newton, René Ray, Patricia Hilliard, Sebastian Shaw, Leonora Corbett, Anthony Bushell, Edward Lexy, Wally Patch, Edmund Willard, Martita Hunt, John Laurie

Farewell My Concubine ***

Hong Kong/China 1993 156m colour
Artificial Eye/Thomson/China Film/Beijing Film (Hsu Feng)

Two boys who train together at the Peking Opera form a lifelong relationship, both on-stage – one playing masculine roles, the other in feminine parts – and off, through the political upheavals from the 1930s onwards until their final performance in the 60s.
A beautiful and epic film that records the social changes of Chinese life with an unblinking eye and from the viewpoint of the endlessly persecuted.
w Lilian Lee, Lu Wei novel Lilian Lee d Chen Kaige ph Gu Changwei m Zhaao Jiping ad Chen Huaikai ed Pei Xiaonan
☆ Leslie Cheung, Zhang Fengyi, Gong Li, Lu Qi, Ying Da, Ge You, Lin Chun, Lei Han, Tong Di
'Chinese cinema ceases to be an acquired taste and becomes a required one ... Its vast running time contains some episodes of pleasure, pain, adventure, vice or instructive insight for every taste or brow – high and low.' – *Alexander Walker, London Evening Standard*
'Chen's attempt to reach a wider audience with a bigger, less ambiguous film is still a formidable success. It's a kind of opera in itself, conducted by a director whose visual power is matched by an emotional force that few others in world cinema can match.' – *Derek Malcolm*
'A big, eventful historical soap opera of the Doctor Zhivago school.' – *Terrence Rafferty, New Yorker*
† The film was joint winner of the Palme d'Or at the Cannes Film Festival in 1993.
🏅 best foreign-language film; Gu Changwei

Farewell My Lovely ***

US 1944 95m bw
RKO (Adrian Scott)

aka: *Murder My Sweet*
A private eye searches for an ex-convict's missing girlfriend.
A revolutionary crime film in that it was the first to depict the genuinely seedy milieu suggested by its author. One of the first films noirs of the mid-forties, a minor masterpiece of expressionist film making, and a total change of direction for a crooner who suddenly became a tough guy.
w John Paxton novel Raymond Chandler d Edward Dmytryk ph Harry J. Wild m Roy Webb
☆ Dick Powell, Claire Trevor, Anne Shirley, Mike Mazurki, Otto Kruger, Miles Mander, Douglas Walton, Ralf Harolde, Don Douglas, Esther Howard
MARLOWE (DICK POWELL): '"Okay Marlowe," I said to myself. "You're a tough guy. You've been sapped twice, choked, beaten silly with a gun, shot in the arm until you're crazy as a couple of waltzing mice. Now let's see you do something really tough – like putting your pants on."'
MARLOWE: 'I caught the blackjack right behind my ear. A black pool opened up at my feet. I dived in. It had no bottom.'
MARLOWE: 'My fingers looked like a bunch of bananas.'
'A nasty, draggled bit of dirty work, accurately observed.' – *C. A. Lejeune*

Farewell, My Lovely ***

US 1975 95m Technicolor
Avco Embassy/Elliott Kastner/ITC (George Pappas, Jerry Bruckheimer)

A pretty sharp remake of the above, with the plot slightly rewritten but tightened, and an excellent performance from a rather over-age star.
w David Zelag Goodman d Dick Richards ph John A. Alonzo m David Shire pd Dean Tavoularis
☆ Robert Mitchum, Charlotte Rampling, John Ireland, Sylvia Miles, Anthony Zerbe, Jack O'Halloran, Kate Murtagh
'A moody, bluesy, boozy recreation of Marlowe's tacky, neon-flashed Los Angeles of the early forties.' – *Judith Crist*

◎ Digital Video Disc Region 2   ◉ Digital Video Disc Region 1   🎧 Soundtrack released on compact disc   ☆ Cast in approximate order of importance   † Points of interest   🎵 Notable songs   🏆 Academy Award   🏅 Academy Award nomination   🏵 BAFTA

'A delicious remake with a nice, smoky 1940s atmosphere.' – *Michael Billington, Illustrated London News*
🎞 Sylvia Miles

A Farewell to Arms **
US   1932   78m   bw
(Paramount)
▦   ◉~   ◎

In World War I, a wounded American ambulance driver falls in love with his nurse.
Now very dated but important in its time, this romantic drama was one of the more successful Hemingway adaptations to be filmed.
w Benjamin Glazer, Oliver H. P. Garrett *novel* Ernest Hemingway d Frank Borzage *ph* Charles Lang m W. Franke Harling *ad* Hans Dreier, Roland Anderson
☆ Gary Cooper, *Helen Hayes*, Adolphe Menjou, Mary Philips, Jack La Rue, Blanche Frederici, Henry Armetta
  'Too much sentiment and not enough strength.' – *Mordaunt Hall, New York Times*
  'Borzage has invested the war scenes with a strange, brooding expressionistic quality … indeed, the overall visual style is most impressive.' – *NFT, 1974*
  'Corking femme film fare at any angle or price.' – *Variety*
† Remade as *Force of Arms* (qv) and see below.
🎥 Charles Lang
🎞 best picture; art direction

A Farewell to Arms
US   1957   150m   DeLuxe   Cinemascope
TCF/David O. Selznick
▦   ▦   ◉~

Elaborate ill-fated remake which tried to make an adventure epic out of a low-key war drama.
Its failure caused David O. Selznick to produce no more films.
w Ben Hecht d Charles Vidor *ph* Piero Portalupi, Oswald Morris m Mario Nascimbene *pd* Alfred Junge
☆ Rock Hudson, Jennifer Jones, Vittorio de Sica, Alberto Sordi, Kurt Kasznar, Mercedes McCambridge, Oscar Homolka, Elaine Stritch, Victor Francen
  'If there were a supreme Bad Taste Award for movies, *A Farewell to Arms* would win it hands down. This smutty version of Ernest Hemingway's novel will set thousands of stomachs to turning.' – *William K. Zinsser, New York Herald-Tribune*
† The film's original director, John Huston, was fired after clashing with Selznick. Cinematographer Oswald Morris quit after Selznick claimed that Hudson was being favoured over Jennifer Jones, his wife.
🎞 Vittorio de Sica

Farewell to the King
US   1988   117m   Technicolor
Vestron/Orion/Film Plan Financing Number 1 (Albert S. Ruddy, André Morgan)
▦   ▦   ◉~   ◎

In the Second World War, an American ruler of a tribe of headhunters in Borneo helps the British attack the Japanese.
Ineffectual Kiplingesque adventure with a confusing narrative.
wd John Milius *novel* L'Adieu au Roi *by* Pierre Schoendoerffer *pd* Dean Semler m Basil Poledouris *ed* Anne V. Coates, Timothy O'Meara
☆ Nick Nolte, Nigel Havers, Frank McRae, James Fox, Marilyn Tokuda, Marius Weyers, William Wise, John Bennett Perry, Elan Oberon, Gerry Lopez, Choy Chang Wing
  'Thematically speaking, the admixture of the *Heart of Darkness* and *The Man Who Would Be King* promises a heady brew, but what emerges, alas, is a cup of weak tea.' – *Tom Milne, MFB*

Fargo
US   1964   99m   Technicolor
Universal/Pennebaker (Al Ruddy)
aka: *Wild Seed*

A teenage girl hitch-hikes from New York to Los Angeles and is befriended by a young tramp.
Peripatetic romance in the modern manner, with no conclusions drawn and not much entertainment value beyond the scenery.
w Les Pine d Brian G. Hutton *ph* Conrad Hall m Richard Markowitz

☆ Michael Parks, Celia Kaye, Ross Elliott, Woodrow Chambliss, Eva Novak

'Small Town … Big Crime … Dead Cold.'

Fargo ****
US   1996   98m   DuArt
Polygram/Working Title (Ethan Coen)
▦   ◉~   ◎   ◉~   ◎

In a small Minnesota town, a car salesman with money troubles hires two criminals to kidnap his wife so that her wealthy father will pay a ransom.
Deft, witty and original thriller which pits a pregnant, rural police chief against two city slickers; the violence, when it comes, is properly shocking, but it's the humanity that you will remember.
w Joel and Ethan Coen d Joel Coen *ph* Roger Deakins m Carter Burwell *pd* Rick Heinrichs *ed* Roderick Jaynes (Joel and Ethan Coen)
☆ Frances McDormand, William H. Macy, Steve Buscemi, Peter Stormare, Harve Presnell, Kristin Rudrüd, Tony Denman
  'Written and directed with the verve, painstaking nuance and outrageously black humour that became the mainstay of a Coen movie.' – *Ian Nathan, Empire*
  'I came away feeling what a great film it was as it had managed to make the basically bland triumph of decency over evil a most rivetting affair.' – *Marianne Gray, Film Review*
† A subtitle claims that the film is based on a true story, but it is more likely an invention of its authors.
🎥 Frances McDormand; Ethan and Joel Coen (screenplay)
🎞 best picture; William H. Macy; Joel Coen (as director); Roger Deakins; Roderick Jaynes
🎬 Joel Coen (as director)

Farinelli Il Castrato *
Italy/Belgium   1994   111m   colour
Guild/Stephan/Alinea/Canal/France 2/Images/K2/RTL/TV1 (Vera Belmont)
▦   ◉~   ◎

Europe's most famous singer, a castrato who has a love-hate relationship with his more virile brother, becomes involved in a feud with Handel.
Enjoyably over-the-top biopic, made in a style that veers from high camp to low opera; it's good to look at and, sometimes, to listen to.
w André Corbiau, Gérard Corbiau, Marcel Beaulieu d Gérard Corbiau *ph* Walther Vanden Ende *md* Christophe Rousset *pd* Gianni Quaranta *ed* Joelle Hache
☆ Stéfano Dionisi, Enrico Lo Verso, Elsa Zylberstein, Caroline Cellier, Marianne Basler, Jeroen Krabbé, Graham Valentine, Omero Antonutti
  'Not since *Amadeus* has a film made classical music so accessible or yesteryear's people understandable.' – *Tom Hutchinson, Film Review*
† The unusual vocal sound of the castrated Farinelli was created by digitally combining the singing of counter-tenor Derek Lee Ragin and soprano Ewa Mallas-Godlewska.

The Farmer Takes a Wife *
US   1935   91m   bw
TCF (Winfield Sheehan)
▦

By the Erie Canal in the 1820s, a wandering girl finds security with a farmer.
Pleasantly 'different' romantic drama, quite ably executed and introducing Henry Fonda to the screen.
w Edwin Burke *play* Frank B. Elser, Marc Connelly *novel* Rome Haul *by* Walter D. Edmonds d Victor Fleming *ph* John Seitz m Arthur Lange
☆ Janet Gaynor, Henry Fonda, Charles Bickford, Slim Summerville, Andy Devine, Roger Imhof, Jane Withers, Margaret Hamilton, Sig Rumann, John Qualen
  'It will pull in the Gaynor fans, and do much to return her to favour.' – *Variety*

The Farmer Takes a Wife *
US   1953   81m   Technicolor
TCF (Frank P. Rosenberg)
▦

Musical remake with an agreeably stylized look, hampered by a slowish script and dull cast.
w Walter Bullock, Sally Benson, Joseph Fields d Henry Levin *ph* Arthur E. Arling m Cyril Mockridge *m/ly* Harold Arlen, Dorothy Fields *ad* Lyle Wheeler, Addison Hehr

☆ Betty Grable, Dale Robertson, Thelma Ritter, Eddie Foy Jnr, John Carroll

The Farmer's Daughter
US   1940   60m   bw
Paramount (William C. Thomas)
A stage struck country girl tries to horn in on a Broadway musical rehearsing nearby.
Feeble comedy for the sticks.
w Lewis R. Foster, Delmer Daves d James Hogan *ph* Leo Tover
☆ Martha Raye, Charles Ruggles, Richard Denning, Gertrude Michael, William Frawley, William Demarest, Jack Norton

'Now she's raising eyebrows instead of corn!'

The Farmer's Daughter **
US   1947   97m   bw
RKO (Dore Schary)
▦

The Swedish maid of a congressman becomes a political force.
Well-made Cinderella story with a touch of asperity and top notch production values and cast.
w Allen Rivkin, Laura Kerr d H. C. Potter *ph* Milton Krasner m Leigh Harline
☆ Loretta Young, Joseph Cotten, Ethel Barrymore, Charles Bickford, Rose Hobart, Rhys Williams, Harry Davenport, Tom Powers
  'Patricians, politicians, even peasants are portrayed with unusual perception and wit.' – *James Agee*
🎥 Loretta Young
🎞 Charles Bickford

The Farmer's Wife
GB   1928   67m   bw   silent
BIP (John Maxwell)
▦

A farmer seeks a wife and after three disappointments settles for his housekeeper.
A simple and not very interesting silent screen version of a stage success which depended largely on dialogue.
wd Alfred Hitchcock *play* Eden Philpotts *ph* Jack Cox *ed* Alfred Booth
☆ Jameson Thomas, Gordon Harker, Lilian Hall-Davis, Maud Gill
  'Some pleasant photography and a subtle impression of rural life rescued the picture from complete failure.' – *George Perry, 1966*

The Farmer's Wife
GB   1940   82m   bw
Associated British
Talkie remake of the above, a perfectly adequate photographed play.
w Norman Lee, Leslie Arliss, J. E. Hunter *play* Eden Philpotts d Norman Lee, Leslie Arliss
☆ Basil Sydney, Wilfrid Lawson, Nora Swinburne, Patricia Roc, Michael Wilding

Farrebique **
France   1947   85m   bw
L'Ecran Français/Les Films Etienne Lallier
Problems of a peasant family in central France.
Superbly-filmed semi-documentary, acted by a real family.
wd Georges Rouquier *ph* André Dantan m Henri Sauguet
  'Definitely a film for posterity.' – *MFB*

Fashions of 1934 *
US   1934   78m   bw
Warner (Henry Blanke)
A confidence trickster conquers the French fashion world.
Slight musical comedy with a couple of splendid Berkeley numbers.
w F. Hugh Herbert, Carl Erickson d William Dieterle *ph* William Rees *m/ly* Sammy Fain, Irving Kahal *ch* Busby Berkeley *ad* Jack Okey
☆ William Powell, Bette Davis, Verree Teasdale, Frank McHugh, Reginald Owen, Hugh Herbert, Henry O'Neill

Fast and Furious: see *Fast Company* (1938)

Fast and Loose
US   1930   70m   bw
Paramount
A spoiled rich girl falls in love with a car mechanic.
Tiresome melodrama, dully scripted.

w Doris Anderson, Jack Kirkland, Preston Sturges *play* The Best People *by* Avery Hopwood, David Gray d Fred Newmeyer *ph* William Steiner
☆ Miriam Hopkins, Carole Lombard, Frank Morgan, Charles Starrett, Henry Wadsworth, David Hutcheson, Ilka Chase

Fast and Loose *
US   1939   80m   bw
MGM (Frederick Stephani)
Married detectives and rare book experts solve the mystery of a missing Shakespeare manuscript.
Pleasing comedy mystery in the wake of The Thin Man.
w Harry Kurnitz d Edwin L. Marin *ph* George Folsey
☆ Robert Montgomery, Rosalind Russell, Ralph Morgan, Reginald Owen, Etienne Girardot, Alan Dinehart, Joan Marsh, Sidney Blackmer

Fast and Loose
GB   1954   75m   bw
Group Films/Rank
By a series of accidents, a married man has to spend a night at an inn with an old flame.
Spiritless and miscast remake of A Cuckoo in the Nest; all talents below form.
w A. R. Rawlinson, Ben Travers *play* Ben Travers d Gordon Parry
☆ Brian Reece, Stanley Holloway, Kay Kendall, Reginald Beckwith, Charles Victor, June Thorburn

Fast Company *
US   1938   75m   bw
MGM
A couple in the rare book business are implicated in the murder of a rival.
First of three whodunnits featuring Joel and Garda Page, whose style was not at all dissimilar from that of Nick and Nora Charles in the Thin Man series. A polished time-passer.
w Marco Page (Harry Kurnitz) d Edward Buzzell
☆ Melvyn Douglas, Florence Rice, Claire Dodd, Louis Calhern, George Zucco
† The follow-ups had different stars as the pair of sleuths. *Fast and Loose* (qv) featured Robert Montgomery and Rosalind Russell; Sidney Blackmer, Ralph Morgan and Reginald Owen supported. *Fast and Furious*, also released in 1939, starred Franchot Tone and Ann Sothern, with Ruth Hussey, Lee Bowman and Allyn Joslyn.

Fast Company
US   1953   67m   bw
MGM
A girl inherits a racing stable and discovers a little chicanery.
Ho-hum support wasting a good cast.
w William Roberts d John Sturges
☆ Howard Keel, Nina Foch, Polly Bergen, Marjorie Main

Fast Food
GB   1998   97m   colour
Optimum/Twin/Fast Food (Phil Hunt)
A telephone engineer gets together with his old gang to rob a criminal who keeps his money in a local sweetshop and be re-united with his former girlfriend.
Hapless thriller composed of the less interesting elements from every other gangster movie; the ending is simply silly.
wd Stewart Sugg *ph* Simon Reeves m Ben Lee-Delisle *pd* Katie Franklyn-Thompson *ed* Jeremy Gibbs
☆ Douglas Henshall, Emily Woof, Miles Anderson, Gerard Butler, Danny Midwinter, Stephen Lord
  'It takes a certain ingenuity to make a film as bad as this.' – *James Christopher, Times*

Fast Getaway
US   1991   90m   Foto-Kem
New Line/CineTel (Lisa M. Hansen, Paul Hertzberg)
▦   ◎

A father and son team of bank robbers is betrayed by the girlfriend the son abandoned.
Energetic though mindless action film, with Rothrock demonstrating her high-kicking abilities.
w James Dixon d Spiro Razatos *ph* Jacques Haitkin m Bruce Rowland *ed* David Kern
☆ Corey Haim, Cynthia Rothrock, Leo Rossi, Ken Lerner, Marcia Strassman, Shelli Lether, Richard Jewkes, Jeff Olsen

---

'Will appeal to video fans tired of overblown, hyped-up cinema.' – *Variety*

Fast Getaway II

US 1994 90m Foto-Kem
CineTel/Live Entertainment (Russell D. Markowitz)
🔲 🔳

A former thief hunts the female bank robber who frames him for her crimes.
Dull action film, with the emphasis on Haim's reformed crook and his relationships with his father and girlfriend, neither of which will interest anyone outside the immediate family.
w Mark Sevi d Oley Sassone ph Mark Parry m David Robbins pd Jeannie M. Lomma ed Glenn Garland
☆ Corey Haim, Cynthia Rothrock, Sarah Buxton, Leo Rossi, Peter Liapis
'Action buffs won't be busting down the doors for this one.' – *Variety*

The Fast Lady **

GB 1962 95m Eastmancolor
Rank/Group Films (Julian Wintle, Leslie Parkyn)
A bashful suitor buys an old Bentley, becomes a roadhog, passes his test, captures some crooks and gets the girl.
Spirited if aimless farcical comedy which crams in all the jokes about cars anyone can think of.
w Jack Davies, Henry Blyth d Ken Annakin ph Reg Wyer m Norrie Paramor
☆ Stanley Baxter, James Robertson Justice, Leslie Phillips, Julie Christie, Dick Emery

Fast Talking

Australia 1984 95m Eastmancolor
Ross Matthews/Oldata
The youngest son of a shiftless and semi-criminal Sydney family gets into trouble and finally drives off on his motor cycle to an uncertain future.
Depressingly downbeat comedy-drama about characters of whom any audience must quickly tire.
wd Ken Cameron ph David Gribble m Sharon Calcraft
☆ Rod Zuanic, Toni Allaylis, Chris Truswell, Gail Sweeny, Steve Bisley

Fast Times at Ridgemont High

US 1982 92m Technicolor
Universal/Refugee (C. O. Erickson)
🔳 📷

Students at a California high school aim to lose their virginity.
The tiresome content of this teen comedy is slightly offset by bright handling. But only slightly.
w Cameron Crowe book Cameron Crowe d Amy Heckerling ph Matthew F. Leonetti m/songs Rob Fahey
☆ Sean Penn, Jennifer Jason Leigh, Judge Reinhold, Phoebe Cates, Brian Backus, Robert Romanus, Ray Walston

Faster, Pussycat! Kill! Kill!

US 1966 84m bw
Eve (Russ and Eve Meyer)
🔲 🔳

Three homicidal exotic dancers drive around the Californian desert.
Meyer's best movie, with his usual ingredients of big-breasted women and lustful, ineffectual men.
w Jack Moran story Russ Meyer d Russ Meyer ph Walter Schenk m Paul Sawtell, Bert Shefter ed Russ Meyer
☆ Tura Satana, Haji, Stuart Lancaster, Lori Williams, Paul Trinka, Susan Bernard, Dennis Busch

The Fastest Guitar Alive

US 1968 87m Metrocolor
Sam Katzman/MGM
🔳

Inept Confederate soldiers are sent on a spy mission.
Ham-handed farce with music, unappealing on either count.
w Robert E. Kent d Michael Moore
☆ Roy Orbison, Sammy Jackson, Maggie Pierce, Joan Freeman, Lyle Bettger

The Fastest Gun Alive *

US 1956 89m bw
MGM (Clarence Greene)
🔲 🔳

A mild-mannered Western storekeeper proves to be the son of a famous gunfighter, and is put to the test.
Flimsily contrived mini-Western helped by good performances.
w Frank D. Gilroy, Russel Rouse d Russel Rouse ph George Folsey m André Previn
☆ Glenn Ford, Broderick Crawford, Jeanne Crain, Russ Tamblyn, Allyn Joslyn, Leif Erickson, John Dehner

Fast-Walking

US 1981 116m Metrocolor
Lorimar
🔳

Racial disharmony and violence prevail at a midwest state prison.
Curious black comedy dealing entirely with unpleasant types.
wd James B. Harris novel The Rap by Ernest Brawley
☆ James Woods, Tim McIntire, Kay Lenz, Robert Hooks, M. Emmet Walsh
'What do people think of when they write a script these days? Don't they have any sense of human values or human decency?' – *Arthur Knight*

Fat City **

US 1972 96m Eastmancolor
Columbia/Rastar (Ray Stark)
In a small Californian town, a has-been boxer tries to get back to the top, but loses his self respect and becomes a hobo.
Vivid but over-casual exploration of failure, with more interest in the characters than the sport.
w Leonard Gardner novel Leonard Gardner d John Huston ph Conrad Hall md Marvin Hamlisch pd James William Newport ed Don Zimmerman
☆ Stacy Keach, Jeff Bridges, Susan Tyrrell, Candy Clark
'Huston has confronted a piece of material and a milieu perfectly suited to his insights and talents. The result is his best film in years and one of the best he has ever done: a lean, compassionate, detailed, raucous, sad, strong look at some losers and survivors on the side streets of small-city Middle America.' – *Charles Champlin*
⧉ Susan Tyrrell

The Fat Man

US 1950 77m bw
U-I (Aubrey Schenck)
The murder of a dentist leads to the circus.
Dense murder mystery featuring a gourmet 17-stone detective; understandably, no series resulted.
w Harry Essex, Leonard Lee d William Castle ph Irving Glassberg m Bernard Green
☆ J. Scott Smart, Rock Hudson, Julie London, Clinton Sundberg, Jerome Cowan, Jayne Meadows

Fat Man and Little Boy: see Shadow Makers

Fatal Attraction

Canada 1980 88m colour
Greentree/Michael Grant
🔲 🔳
aka: Head On
In Toronto, after an academic psychologist has a head-on crash with a car driven by a married female psychiatrist, the two begin a torrid affair in which they act out their erotic desires.
Uninvolving drama, notable, given the protagonists' professions, for the banality of its sexual fantasies, concerning as they do nursery rhymes, shaving cream, sex in the office and playing at gangsters.
w James Sanderson, Paul Illidge d Michael Grant ph Anthony Richmond m Peter Mann pd Antonin Dimitrov ed Gary Oppenheimer
☆ Sally Kellerman, Stephen Lack, Lawrence Dane, John Peter Linton, John Huston

Fatal Attraction **

US 1987 119m Technicolor
Paramount/Jaffe-Lansing (Stanley Jaffe, Sherry Lansing)
🔲 🔳 📷 🎧
A married man finds it difficult to shed his nearly homicidal light of love.

A kind of rehash of Play Misty for Me, *and a sensational success at the box-office: the timing must have been right, even if the details aren't always persuasive.*
w James Dearden d Adrian Lyne ph Howard Atherton m Maurice Jarre pd Mel Bourne ed Michael Kahn, Peter E. Berger
☆ Michael Douglas, Glenn Close, Anne Archer, Fred Gwynne
'A predictable dog's dinner of thriller clichés – will appeal strongly to those who think women should be kept on a short leash.' – *Time Out*
'This shrewd film also touches on something deeper than men's fear of feminism: their fear of women, their fear of women's emotions, of women's hanging on to them. Fatal Attraction doesn't treat the dreaded passionate woman as a theme; she's merely a monster in a monster flick.' – *Pauline Kael*
† A video release of the movie included an alternative ending to the film.
⧉ Glenn Close; Anne Archer; Adrian Lyne; best picture; James Dearden; film editing

Fatal Beauty

US 1987 104m colour
Enterprise/MGM/CST Communications (Leonard Kroll)
🔲 🔳 📷 🎧
A female cop tracks down a drug dealer.
A violent formula film with nothing new to offer.
w Hilary Henkin, Dean Riesner story Bill Svanoe d Tom Holland ph David M. Walsh m Harold Faltermeyer pd James William Newport ed Don Zimmerman
☆ Whoopi Goldberg, Sam Elliott, Ruben Blades, Harris Yulin, John P. Ryan, Jennifer Warren, Brad Dourif, Mike Jolly, Charles Hallahan, David Harris

Fatal Bond

Australia 1991 89m colour
Avalon Films/Phillip Avalon
🔳
A hairdresser begins to suspect that her mysterious new boyfriend is killing and raping young girls.
Overblown, under-budgeted thriller, of interest only to followers of the declining career of Linda Blair.
w Phillip Avalon d Vincent Monton ph Ray Henman m Art Phillips ad Keith Holloway ed Ted ötton
☆ Linda Blair, Jerome Ehlers, Joe Bugner, Donal Gibson, Stephen Leeder, Caz Lederman, Teo Gerbert, Penny Pederson

The Fatal Glass of Beer *

US 1933 18m bw
Paramount/Sennett
The prodigal son returns to a snowbound cabin in the Yukon.
Absurd star comedy with appeal to addicts only: most of the humour consists of repeats of one line, "Taint a fit night out for man nor beast.'
w W. C. Fields d Clyde Bruckman
☆ W. C. Fields, Rosemary Theby, Rychard Cramer, George Chandler

'Torn between his wife, a seductress and a pet skunk … he's a private eye in danger of spreading himself too thin!'

Fatal Instinct

US 1993 88m DeLuxe
MGM (Katy Jacobs, Pierce Gardner)
🔲 🔳 📷
A double-crossing wife plans to murder her husband, a cop-cum-lawyer who is seduced by her twin sister and being chased by a tattooed ex-convict.
Clumsy farce that attempts to parody film noir and such modern thrillers as Fatal Attraction, Basic Instinct and Body Heat; about one joke in twenty raises a hint of a smile.
w David O'Malley d Carl Reiner ph Gabriel Beristain m Richard Gibbs pd Sandy Veneziano ed Bud Molin, Stephen Myers
☆ Armand Assante, Sherilyn Fenn, Kate Nelligan, Sean Young, Christopher McDonald, James Remar, Tony Randall
'The insane collision of plot climaxes is funny, but as collections of cinematic jests go, it's even thinner than most.' – *Angie Errigo, Empire*
† It was released direct to video in Britain.

Fatal Lady

US 1936 77m bw
Walter Wanger/Paramount
An opera singer has trouble with men and becomes involved with murder.
Lively melodrama with songs, very much of its period.
w Jules Furthman d Edward Ludwig ph Leon Shamroy
☆ Mary Ellis, Walter Pidgeon, John Halliday, Ruth Donnelly, Alan Mowbray, Edgar Kennedy

The Fatal Night *

GB 1948 49m bw
Anglofilm (Mario Zampi)
A joke haunting has unfortunate consequences.
A small, cheaply-made film which really thrilled.
w Gerald Butler story The Gentleman from America by Michael Arlen d Mario Zampi ph Cedric Williams m Stanley Black
☆ Lester Ferguson, Jean Short, Leslie Armstrong, Brenda Hogan, Patrick MacNee

Fate Is the Hunter

US 1964 106m bw Cinemascope
TCF/Arcola (Aaron Rosenberg)
An airline executive investigates the cause of a fatal crash in which his friend the pilot was a victim.
Watchable how-did-it-happen melodrama marred by pretentious dialogue.
w Harold Medford novel Ernest K. Gann d Ralph Nelson ph Milton Krasner m Jerry Goldsmith
☆ Glenn Ford, Rod Taylor, Nehemiah Persoff, Nancy Kwan, Suzanne Pleshette, Jane Russell
⧉ Milton Krasner

Father

Australia 1989 100m colour
Leftbank/Barron (Damien Parer, Tony Cavanaugh, Graham Hartley, Paul D. Barron)
In modern-day Australia, a grandfather is accused of being an SS officer who massacred an entire village in the Second World War.
Moderately engaging but overly manipulative drama, concentrating on family relationships rather than the larger issues it raises.
w Tony Cavanaugh, Graham Hartley d John Power m Dan Burstall m Peter Best pd Phil Peters ed Kerry Regan
☆ Max von Sydow, Carol Drinkwater, Julia Blake, Steve Jacobs, Simone Robertson, Kahli Sneddon
'Boasts a good screenplay, firm direction and a couple of very strong performances.' – *Variety*

Father and Master: see Padre Padrone

Father and Son

Hong Kong 1981 96m Eastmancolor
BFI/Feng Huang Motion Picture Company (Wong Kai-Chuen)
original title: Fuzi Qing
Returning home for his father's funeral, a film-maker reflects on his childhood.
A gently observant semi-autobiographical domestic drama, but lacking individuality.
w Chan Chiu, Cheung Kin-Ting, Lee Bik-Wah d Fong Yuk-Ping (Allen Fong) ph Patrick Wong m Violet Lam ad Wong Huk-Sun, Wong Kwai-Ping
☆ Shek Lui, Lee Yu-Tin, Cheng Yu-Or, Chan Sun, Cheung Kwok-Ming, Kung Yee, Yan Sin-Mei, Yung Wai-Man, Chung Hung, Lo Tai-Wai

Father Brown ***

GB 1954 91m bw
Columbia/Facet (Vivian A. Cox)
🔳
US title: The Detective
A Catholic clergyman retrieves a priceless church cross from master thief Flambeau.
Delightfully eccentric comedy based closely on the famous character, with a sympathetic if rather wandering script, pointed direction and some delicious characterizations. A thoroughly civilized entertainment.
w Thelma Schnee story The Blue Cross by G. K. Chesterton d Robert Hamer ph Harry Waxman m Georges Auric
☆ Alec Guinness, Joan Greenwood, Peter Finch, Sidney James, Cecil Parker, Bernard Lee, Ernest Thesiger, Marne Maitland
'It has wit, elegance, and kindly humour – all somewhat rare commodities in the 1954 cinema.' – *Star*

⊚ Digital Video Disc Region 2   ⊚ Digital Video Disc Region 1   🎧 Soundtrack released on compact disc   ☆ Cast in approximate order of importance   † Points of interest   🎵 Notable songs   ⧉ Academy Award   ⧉ Academy Award nomination   🎬 BAFTA

Father Brown Detective *
US   1934   67m   bw
Paramount
Flambeau, the thief, decides to steal Father Brown's blue cross.
Early attempt at the same story used in the 1954 Father Brown with Alec Guinness; quite pleasantly interesting.
story *The Blue Cross* by G. K. Chesterton
d Edward Sedgwick
☆ Walter Connolly, Paul Lukas, Gertrude Michael, Robert Loraine, Halliwell Hobbes, Una O'Connor, E. E. Clive
'Clean, but not strong enough to stand solo.' – *Variety*

Father Came Too
GB   1963   93m   Eastmancolor
Rank/Independent Artists
Honeymooners agree to live with her overbearing actor-manager father.
Less funny sequel to The Fast Lady, with comic household disasters striking every couple of minutes. Easy-going, and predictably amusing in spots.
w Jack Davies, Henry Blyth   d Peter Graham Scott   ph Reg Wyer   m Norrie Paramor
☆ Stanley Baxter, James Robertson Justice, Leslie Phillips, Sally Smith, Ronnie Barker, Timothy Bateson, Philip Locke

Father, Dear Father
GB   1972   99m   Eastmancolor   MultiVista
Sedgemoor-MM (Peter J. Thompson)
A divorced, middle-aged writer, who has problems with his two teenage daughters, decides he should get married.
Trivial comedy, based on a TV sitcom, and looking and sounding like it.
w Johnnie Mortimer, Brian Cooke   d William G. Stewart   ph Alan Hume   m Nachum Heiman   pd Michael Bastow   ed Timothy Gee
☆ Patrick Cargill, Natasha Pyne, Ann Holloway, Noël Dyson, Ursula Howells, Joyce Carey, Richard O'Sullivan, Joseph O'Conor, Jack Watling, Jill Melford, Beryl Reid, Donald Sinden

Father Goose *
US   1964   116m   Technicolor
U-I/Granox (Robert Arthur)
During World War II a South Seas wanderer is compelled by the Australian navy to act as sky observer on a small island, where he finds himself in charge of six refugee schoolchildren and their schoolmistress.
Eager-to-please but unsatisfactory film which wanders between farce, adventure and sex comedy, taking too long about all of it.
w Peter Stone, Frank Tarloff   d Ralph Nelson   ph Charles Lang Jnr   m Cy Coleman
☆ Cary Grant, Leslie Caron, Trevor Howard
CARY GRANT: 'Let me tell you I am not a father figure. I am not a brother figure or an uncle figure or a cousin figure. In fact, the only figure I intend being is a total stranger figure.'
'Reasoning would indicate a made-to-order Christmas package for the family trade. However, the more sophisticated may be bored and exasperated after some of the initial brightness wears off.' – *Cue*
'Cary Grant wrings what there is to be wrung from the role, but never quite enough to conceal the fact that *Father Goose* is a waste of his talent and the audience's time.' – *Arthur Knight*
⚲ Peter Stone, Frank Tarloff

Father Hood
US   1993   94m   Technicolor
Buena Vista/Hollywood (Nicholas Pileggi, Anant Singh, Gillian Gorfil)
A petty crook kidnaps his children from their foster home and takes them on a cross-country journey.
Inane and clumsy road movie, uninteresting to watch and with the explicit message that robbery is fun.
w Scott Spencer   d Darrell James Roodt   ph Mark Vicente   m Patrick O'Hearn   pd David Barkham   ed David Heitner
☆ Patrick Swayze, Halle Berry, Diane Ladd, Brian Bonsall, Sabrina Lloyd, Michael Ironside, Bob Gunton
'A train wreck from start to finish.' – *Variety*

Father Is a Bachelor
US   1950   85m   bw
Columbia (S. Sylvan Simon)
A young tramp cares for a family of orphaned children.
Boringly sentimental semi-Western.
w Aleen Leslie, James Edward Grant   d Norman Foster, Abby Berlin   ph Burnett Guffey   m Arthur Morton
☆ William Holden, Coleen Gray, Charles Winninger, Stuart Erwin, Sig Rumann
'Saccharine, paper thin. At least one spectator at the Palace yesterday couldn't take it – a tot of about four, wearing a cowboy suit, who aimed a toy pistol at the screen and popped off the cast one by one.' – *New York Times*

Father Is a Prince: see Big Hearted Herbert

'The bride gets the thrills! Father gets the bills!'
Father of the Bride **
US   1950   93m   bw
MGM (Pandro S. Berman)
A dismayed but happy father surveys the cost and chaos of his daughter's marriage.
Fragmentary but mainly delightful suburban comedy which finds Hollywood in its best light vein and benefits from a strong central performance.
w Frances Goodrich, Albert Hackett   novel Edward Streeter   d Vincente Minnelli   ph John Alton   m Adolph Deutsch
☆ Spencer Tracy, Joan Bennett, Elizabeth Taylor, Don Taylor, Billie Burke, Moroni Olsen, Leo G. Carroll, Taylor Holmes, Melville Cooper
'The idealization of a safe sheltered existence, the good life according to MGM: 24 carat complacency.' – *New Yorker, 1980*
† Jack Benny badly wanted the role but was thought unsuitable.
⚖ best picture; Frances Goodrich, Albert Hackett; Spencer Tracy

'Love is wonderful. Until it happens to your only daughter.'
Father of the Bride
US   1991   105m   Technicolor
Touchstone/Touchwood Pacific Partners I (Nancy Myers, Carol Baum, Howard Rosenman)
A father is upset by his daughter's announcement that she is engaged – and even more horrified by the arrangements for an expensive wedding.
Lacklustre remake with flat or exaggerated performances, few jokes and a great deal of sentimentality.
w Frances Goodrich, Albert Hackett, Nancy Myers, Charles Shyer   novel Edward Streeter   d Charles Shyer   ph John Lindley   m Alan Silvestri   pd Sandy Veneziano   ed Richard Marks
☆ Steve Martin, Diane Keaton, Kimberly Williams, Martin Short, Kieran Culkin, George Newbern, B. D. Wong, Peter Michael Goetz
'Little more than a mildly entertaining diversion.' – *Empire*

Father of the Bride 2
US   1995   106m   Technicolor
Buena Vista/Touchstone/Sandollar/Meyers/Shyer
As they are on the point of becoming grandparents, a couple find that they are also about to be parents again.
Broad and undistinguished comedy, though audiences that enjoyed the previous film will find this no worse, though no better either.
w Nancy Meyers, Charles Shyer   screenplay Albert Hackett, Frances Goodrich   d Charles Shyer   ph William A. Fraker   m Alan Silvestri   pd Linda DeScenna   ed Stephen A. Rotter
☆ Steve Martin, Diane Keaton, Martin Short, Kimberly Williams, George Newbern, Kieran Culkin, B. D. Wong, Peter Michael Goetz
'Pleasant enough, assuming a reasonably high tolerance for saccharine in one's diet.' – *Variety*
† The film is a remake of *Father's Little Dividend*.

Father Takes a Wife *
US   1941   80m   bw
RKO (Lee S. Marcus)
A famous actress marries a shipping magnate and runs into resentment from her children.
Disappointing comedy with a script too flat for the stars to make interesting.

w Dorothy and Herbert Fields   d Jack Hively   ph Robert de Grasse   m Roy Webb
☆ Gloria Swanson, Adolphe Menjou, Desi Arnaz, John Howard, Helen Broderick, Florence Rice, Neil Hamilton

Father Was a Fullback
US   1949   84m   bw
TCF (Fred Kohlmar)
The coach of a college football team has domestic problems.
Thin star comedy, strictly double bill.
w Aleen Leslie, Casey Robinson, Richard Sale, Mary Loos   play Clifford Goldsmith   d John M. Stahl   ph Lloyd Ahern   m Cyril Mockridge
☆ Fred MacMurray, Maureen O'Hara, Betty Lynn, Natalie Wood, Rudy Vallee, Jim Backus

'One kid. Two dads. A who done it?'
Fathers' Day
US   1997   98m   Technicolor   Panavision
Warner/Silver/Northern Lights (Joel Silver, Ivan Reitman)
Two men – one a suicidal writer, the other a successful lawyer – search for a missing 16-year-old youth, each believing that he is the boy's father.
Tiresome comedy, slick and soulless, with little evidence of life or interest from its cast.
w Lowell Ganz, Babaloo Mandel   film Les Compères by Francis Veber   d Ivan Reitman   ph Stephen H. Burum   m James Newton Howard   pd Thomas Sanders   ed Sheldon Kahn, Wendy Greene Bricmont
☆ Robin Williams, Billy Crystal, Julia Louis-Dreyfus, Nastassja Kinski, Charlie Hofheimer, Bruce Greenwood, Jared Harris, Louis Lombardi, Patti D'Arbanville
'A brainless feature-length sitcom with too much sit and no com.' – *Roger Ebert, Chicago Sun-Times*

Father's Doing Fine
GB   1952   83m   Technicolor
Marble Arch/ABP (Victor Skutezky)
An impoverished lady has trouble with her daughters, one of whom is pregnant.
Agreeable madcap farce from a long-running stage success (so why did they change the title?).
w Anne Burnaby   play *Little Lambs Eat Ivy* by Noel Langley   d Henry Cass   ph Erwin Hillier   ad Don Ashton
☆ Heather Thatcher, Richard Attenborough, Susan Stephen, Noel Purcell, George Thorpe

Father's Little Dividend
US   1951   81m   bw
MGM (Pandro S. Berman)
Sequel to *Father of the Bride*, in which the newlyweds have a baby.
A very flat follow-up, palatable enough at the time but quite unmemorable.
w Frances Goodrich, Albert Hackett   d Vincente Minnelli   ph John Alton   m Albert Sendrey
☆ Spencer Tracy, Joan Bennett, Elizabeth Taylor, Don Taylor, Billie Burke, Moroni Olsen, Frank Faylen, Marietta Canty, Russ Tamblyn

'The world's most uncovered undercover agent!'
Fathom
GB   1967   99m   DeLuxe   Franscope
TCF (John Kohn)
Adventures of a glamorous sky-diving spy.
Watchable romp with nothing memorable about it.
w Lorenzo Semple Jnr   novel Larry Forrester   d Leslie Martinson   ph Douglas Slocombe, Jacques Dubourg   m Johnny Dankworth
☆ Raquel Welch, Tony Franciosa, Clive Revill, Ronald Fraser, Greta Chi, Richard Briers, Tom Adams
'Belongs not in the category of High Camp but in that of Good Wholesome Fun.' – *MFB*

Le Fatiche di Ercole: see Hercules

Fatso
US   1980   93m   DeLuxe
TCF/Brooksfilms
A fat man fails to make much headway at slimming, and gives up.
Unappealing mixture of sentiment, satire, shouting and crude humour.
wd Anne Bancroft

☆ Dom DeLuise, Anne Bancroft, Ron Carey, Candice Azzara
'As bumbling and sluggish as its title might suggest, a lamentable affair which ricochets uncontrollably between attempts at hilarity and pathos.' – *Variety*

Fatto di Sarigine fra due vomini per causa di una vedora – si sospettano moventi politici: see Blood Feud

Faust **
Germany   1926   100m   bw   silent
UFA
A superbly stylish version of the legend about a man who sells his soul to the devil.
The best of many silent versions; see also All That Money Can Buy.
w Hans Kyser   d F. W. Murnau   ph Carl Hoffman
☆ Emil Jannings, Gosta Ekman, Camilla Horn, Yvette Guilbert, William Dieterle

'A magical tale of love, friendship and dreams that come true.'
Fausto
France   1992   81m   colour
Mayfair/Amorces/Lili/BBD/France 2 (Christine de Jekel)
In mid-60s Paris, a 17-year-old orphan falls in love and becomes a successful fashion designer.
Slight and frivolous first feature by an advertising director which is full of pretty images but has nothing of interest to sell; it gets by for a while on charm.
w Richard Morgiève, Rémy Duchemin   novel Richard Morgiève   d Rémy Duchemin   ph Yves Lafaye   m Denis Barbier   ad Fouillet & Wieber   ed Maryline Monthieux
☆ Florence Darel, Jean Yanne, Ken Higelin, François Hautesserre, Maite Nahyr, Maurice Bénichou, Bruce Myers
'Sadly, fragile whimsy cannot sustain a whole movie.' – *Kim Newman, Empire*

Faustrecht der Freiheit: see Fox

'Two Women. Three Men. One Secret.'
'An outrageous romantic comedy.'
The Favor
US   1994   97m   DeLuxe
Nelson (Lauren Shuler-Donner)
A bored but happily married woman asks a friend to make real her fantasy, by bedding her high school sweetheart.
Tiresome romantic drama that needed a lighter touch and a better script; it is heavy-handed and heavy-going.
w Sara Parriott, Josann McGibbon   d Donald Petrie   ph Tim Suhrstedt   m Thomas Newman   pd David Chapman   ed Harry Keramidas
☆ Elizabeth McGovern, Harley Jane Kozak, Bill Pullman, Brad Pitt, Ken Wahl, Larry Miller, Holland Taylor
'Delicate material, and unfortunately it's executed by comparative barbarians.' – *Variety*
† The film was made in 1991 and its release delayed by Orion's financial difficulties.

Les Favoris de la Lune: see Favourites of the Moon

'A romantic comedy beyond normal experience.'
The Favour, the Watch & the Very Big Fish
France/GB   1991   87m   colour
Rank/Sovereign/Ariane/Fildebroc/Umbrella (Michelle de Broca)
A religious photographer, who gets an ex-criminal to pose as Christ for him, falls in love with an actress who dubs pornographic films.
Flaccid farce in which most of the cast give the impression that they would rather be somewhere else.
wd Ben Lewin   story *Rue Saint-Sulpice* by Marcel Ayme   ph Bernard Zitzermann   m Vladimir Cosma   pd Carlos Conti   ed John Grover
☆ Bob Hoskins, Jeff Goldblum, Natasha Richardson, Michel Blanc, Jacques Villeret, Jean-Pierre Cassel, Angela Pleasence
'Mildy intriguing title, stultifyingly dull film.' – *Empire*

Favourites of the Moon *

France 1984 102m Eastmancolor
Philippe Dussart/FR3

original title: *Les Favoris de la Lune*

Characters in Paris find that their paths cross as they pursue their obsessions.

Buñuel-like surrealism without Buñuel's intensity of vision results in a film which sometimes pleases but eventually becomes tiresome.

w Otar Iosseliani, Gerard Brach d Otar Iosseliani ph Philippe Theaudiere

☆ Katia Rupe, Hans Peter Cloos, Alix de Montaigu, François Michel

FBI Code 98

US 1964 94m bw
Warner

G-men track down a mad bomber.

Thin action thriller originally intended for TV.

w Stanley Niss d Leslie H. Martinson ph Robert Hoffman m Max Steiner

☆ Jack Kelly, Ray Danton, Andrew Duggan, Philip Carey, William Reynolds

The FBI Story *

US 1959 149m Technicolor
Warner (Mervyn Le Roy)

An FBI agent thinks back on his career with the bureau.

Predictable mix of domestic sentimentality (very trying) and competent crime capsules: mad bomber, Ku Klux Klan, thirties hoodlums, Nazi spy rings and the cold war.

w Richard L. Breen, John Twist d Mervyn Le Roy ph Joseph Biroc m Max Steiner ad John Beckman

☆ James Stewart, Vera Miles, Larry Pennell, Nick Adams, Murray Hamilton

'Insufferably cosy.' – *MFB*

Fear

US 1946 68m bw
Monogram

A student kills his professor, and a detective taunts him to the point of confession.

Cheeky second feature version of Crime and Punishment, with a twist ending. Not too bad in its way.

w Alfred Zeisler, Dennis Cooper d Alfred Zeisler ph Jackson Rose

☆ Warren William, Peter Cookson, Anne Gwynne, Nestor Paiva

'Your First Impulse. Your Last Sensation.'

Fear

US 1989 95m CFI color
First Independent/Richard Kobritz-Rockne S. O'Bannon
🖭 🖵

A psychic detective discovers that the killer she is hunting is also a powerful psychic.

Mindless thriller that offers nothing new.

wd Rockne S. O'Bannon ph Robert Stevens m Henry Mancini pd Joseph Nemec III ed Kent Beyda

☆ Ally Sheedy, Pruitt Taylor Vince, Lauren Hutton, Michael O'Keefe, Stan Shaw, Dina Merrill, John Agar

'Treads an increasingly uninspiring road to nowhere.' – *MFB*

Fear

US 1996 96m DeLuxe Panavision
Universal/Imagine (Brian Grazer, Ric Kidney)
🖭 🟰 🖵 🔘

An architect's teenage daughter falls for a psychopath.

Uninteresting teen thriller, predictable from its opening to its closing moments.

w Christopher Crowe d James Foley ph Thomas Kloss m Carter Burwell pd Alex McDowell ed David Brenner

☆ Mark Wahlberg, Reese Witherspoon, William Petersen, Amy Brenneman, Alyssa Milano, Christopher Gray

'Stylishly crafted suspenser doesn't hold many surprises for those familiar with the genre.' – *Variety*

The Fear: see *City of The Living Dead*

Fear and Loathing in Las Vegas

US 1998 119m Rank Colour 'Scope
Universal/Rhino (Laila Nabulsi, Patrick Cassavetti)
🖭 🟰 🖵

In 1971, a journalist and his attorney binge on drugs in Las Vegas.

A surreal trip into bad drugs makes for a queasy film that is unlikely to attain the cult status of the original book.

w Terry Gilliam, Tony Grisoni, Tod Davies, Alex Cox book Hunter S. Thompson d Terry Gilliam ph Nicola Pecorini m Ray Cooper pd Alex McDowell ed Lesley Walker sp Kent Houston; make-up fx: Rob Bottin

☆ Johnny Depp, Benicio Del Toro, Craig Bierko, Ellen Barkin, Gary Busey, Cameron Diaz, Flea, Mark Harmon, Katherine Helmond, Michael Jeter, Penn Jillette, Lyle Lovett, Tobey Maguire, Christina Ricci, Harry Dean Stanton and also Tim Thomerson

'It's hard to imagine any segment of the public embracing this off-putting, unrewarding slog through the depths of the drug culture.' – *Todd McCarthy, Variety*

Fear City

US 1985 93m colour
Zupnik-Curtis Enterprises (Bruce Cohn Curtis)
🖭 🟰 🖵

A psychopathic killer terrorizes strippers working in the Times Square area of New York.

Sleazy, violent, low-life thriller, of minimal interest despite an interesting cast.

w Nicholas St John d Abel Ferrara ph James Lemmo m Dick Halligan ed Jack Holmes, Anthony Redman

☆ Tom Berenger, Billy Dee Williams, Jack Scalia, Melanie Griffith, Rossano Brazzi, Rae Dawn Chong, Joe Santos

Fear Eats the Soul *

West Germany 1974 92m colour
Tango Film (Christian Hohoff)
🖭

original title: *Angst essen Seele auf*

A Moroccan immigrant in Munich comes up against social and racial prejudice when he marries a sixty-year-old charwoman.

Unexceptionable moral tale which can hardly have been necessary in view of the infrequency of such cases.

wd Rainer Werner Fassbinder ph Jürgen Jürges ed Thea Eymèsz

☆ Brigitte Mira, El Hedi Ben Salem, Barbara Valentin, Irm Hermann, Rainer Werner Fassbinder

Fear in the Night **

US 1947 72m bw
Paramount (William H. Pine, William C. Thomas)
🟰

A man suffering from a strange nightmare discovers he has been hypnotized into committing a murder.

Intriguing small-scale puzzler later remade to less effect as Nightmare (qv). Adequate performances and handling, but the plot's the thing.

wd Maxwell Shane ph Jack Greenhalgh m Rudy Schrager

☆ Paul Kelly, DeForest Kelley, Ann Doran, Kay Scott

Fear in the Night *

GB 1972 85m Technicolor
MGM-EMI/Hammer (Jimmy Sangster)

A girl recovering from a nervous breakdown is deluded into committing a murder.

Yet another variant on Les Diaboliques, ingeniously worked out with good touches of detail to produce an air of general competence.

w Jimmy Sangster, Michael Syson d Jimmy Sangster ph Arthur Grant m John McCabe ad Don Picton ed Peter Weatherley

☆ Peter Cushing, Judy Geeson, Joan Collins, Ralph Bates

Fear Is the Key *

GB 1972 108m Technicolor Panavision
EMI/KLK (Alan Ladd Jnr, Elliott Kastner)
🖭 🔘

A man conceives an elaborate plot to track down those responsible for killing his wife and family in a plane crash.

Reasonably absorbing, surprise-plotted thriller.

w Robert Carrington novel Alistair MacLean d Michael Tuchner ph Alex Thomson m Roy Budd

☆ Suzy Kendall, Barry Newman, John Vernon, Dolph Sweet, Ben Kingsley, Ray McAnally

Fear o' God: see *The Mountain Eagle*

Fear of a Black Hat *

US 1993 86m colour
Oakwood (Darin Scott)

A mock documentary on the progress of a tough rap group, NWH (Niggas With Hats), and its members, Ice Cold, Taste Taste and Tone Def.

Witty demolition of rap's pretensions, in the style of This Is Spinal Tap, that hits the target more often than the similar, rival movie CB4.

wd Rusty Cundieff ph John Demps m Larry Robinson pd Stuart Blatt ed Karen Horn

☆ Larry B. Scott, Christopher Lawrence, Rusty Cundieff, Kasi Lemmons, Howie Gold, Barry Heins, Eric Laneuville

'A midnight movie. But wild irreverent humor and exuberant music may also help this spoof find a larger, hip public.' – *Variety*

Fear Strikes Out

US 1957 100m bw Vistavision
Paramount/Alan Pakula
🟰 🖵

A father wants his son to become a professional baseball player, and the son in consequence suffers a nervous breakdown.

Rather flat biopic of Jim Piersall; well-intentioned and careful in its psychological insights, but too often just plain dull.

w Ted Berkman, Raphael Blau d Robert Mulligan ph Haskell Boggs m Elmer Bernstein

☆ Anthony Perkins, Karl Malden, Norma Moore, Perry Wilson

Fearless **

US 1993 122m Technicolor
Warner/Spring Creek (Paula Weinstein, Mark Rosenberg)
🖭 🟰 🖵 🔘

The survivor of a plane crash loses all sense of fear in his everyday life, but also all feelings of responsibility to his wife and son.

A refreshingly different mainstream Hollywood film, tackling matters of life and death and individual freedom and obligation, but failing to resolve them satisfactorily.

w Rafael Yglesias d Peter Weir ph Allen Daviau m Maurice Jarre pd John Stoddart ed William Anderson

☆ Jeff Bridges, Isabella Rossellini, Rosie Perez, Tom Hulce, John Turturro, Deirdre O'Connell, Benicio del Toro

'It always feels like it could become a breathtaking, thought provoking film that does everything that the run-of-the-mill Hollywood drama so singularly fails to do. Unfortunately, and not a little ironically, about halfway through it gets cold feet and bottles out of saying anything remotely meaningful or even logical with regards to all that has gone before.' – *Anwar Brett, Film Review*

Fearless Fagan

US 1952 78m bw
MGM

A circus clown is enlisted and takes his pet lion along.

Rather silly comedy padded out with sentimentality.

w Charles Lederer d Stanley Donen ph Harold Lipstein

☆ Carleton Carpenter, Janet Leigh, Keenan Wynn, Richard Anderson, Ellen Corby

The Fearless Vampire Killers, or Pardon Me, Your Teeth Are in My Neck *

US 1967 124m Metrocolor Panavision
MGM/Cadre Films/Filmways (Gene Gutowski)
🖭 🟰 🖵

aka: *Dance of the Vampires*

A professor and his assistant stake a Transylvanian vampire.

Heavy, slow spoof of Dracula, most of which shows that sense of humour is very personal; a few effective moments hardly compensate for the prevailing stodge.

w Gerard Brach, Roman Polanski d Roman Polanski ph Douglas Slocombe m Krzystof Komeda pd Wilfrid Shingleton

☆ Jack MacGowran, Roman Polanski, Alfie Bass, Sharon Tate, Ferdy Mayne, Iain Quarrier, Terry Downes

'An engaging oddity ... long stretches might have been lifted intact from any Hammer horror.' – *Tom Milne*

† A credit ran: Fangs by Dr Ludwig von Krankheit.

Fearless Young Boxer: see *The Avenging Boxer*

The Fearmakers

US 1958 85m bw
Pacemaker (Martin H. Lancer)

A brainwashed Korean War veteran returns to Washington and finds that his PR firm has been taken over by communist racketeers.

Unusual but cheaply made anti-Red propaganda, too talkative to be very entertaining.

w Elliot West, Chris Appley novel Darwin Teilhet d Jacques Tourneur ph Sam Leavitt m Irving Gertz

☆ Dana Andrews, Dick Foran, Mel Tormé

A Feast at Midnight

GB 1995 106m colour
Entertainment/Kwai River (Yoshi Nishio)
🖭

A new boarder at a public school, where there is a regime of healthy eating, becomes popular by producing gourmet food and cakes.

Shades of Billy Bunter arise in this old-fashioned school story that is presumably someone's nostalgic fantasy of childhood, one that an audience is unlikely to share.

w Justin Hardy, Yoshi Nishio d Justin Hardy ph Tim Maurice-Jones m David Hughes, John Murphy pd Christiane Ewing ed Michael Johns

☆ Freddie Findlay, Christopher Lee, Aled Roberts, Andrew Lusher, Robert Hardy, Samuel West, Edward Fox, Carol Macready, Lisa Faulkner

'Nothing about it suggests that it should have been made for the big screen, so modest is its scope.' – *Empire*

'There is no escape from the past.'

Feast of July

GB/US 1995 113m Technicolor
Buena Vista/Touchstone/Merchant Ivory (Henry Herbert, Christopher Neame)
🖭 🟰

In the 1890s, a woman, abandoned by her lover, finds brief happiness with a simple-minded youth.

Glum tale of working-class suffering and loss that never comes fully to life, muting any emotional response.

w Christopher Neame novel H. E. Bates d Christopher Menaul ph Peter Sova m Zbigniew Preisner pd Christopher Robilliard ed Chris Wimble

☆ Embeth Davidtz, Tom Bell, Gemma Jones, James Purefoy, Ben Chaplin, Kenneth Anderson, Greg Wise, David Neal

'Sadly, script and direction give the actors little chance to develop their characters and they remain ciphers.' – *George Perry*

A Feather in Her Hat

US 1935 72m bw
Columbia

A London widow with delusions of grandeur tells her son that his real mother was a famous actress.

Outmoded mother-love drama, interestingly cast.

w Lawrence Hazard story I. A. R. Wylie d Alfred Santell ph Joseph Walker

☆ Pauline Lord, Basil Rathbone, Louis Hayward, Billie Burke, Wendy Barrie, J. M. Kerrigan, Victor Varconi, Nydia Westman, Thurston Hall

'Too British for general appeal, though well acted.' – *Variety*

Feather Your Nest *

🎞🎞 GB 1937 86m bw
ATP (Basil Dean)

A gramophone record technician substitutes his own voice for a star and becomes world famous.

The star in less farcical vein than usual; this is the one in which he sings 'Leaning on a Lamp-post'.

w Austin Melford, Robert Edmunds, Anthony Kimmins story Ivar and Sheila Campbell d William Beaudine ph Ronald Neame m Leslie Sarony, Leslie Holmes and others ad R. Holmes Paul ed Ernest Aldridge

☆ George Formby, Polly Ward, Enid Stamp Taylor, Val Rosing, Davy Burnaby

Fedora *
West Germany/France   1978   110m
Eastmancolor
Geria/SFP (Billy Wilder)
🎬 📺 🎧
An ageing star who seems miraculously to have
kept her beauty comes out of retirement.
*Sunset Boulevard revisited, with a less bitter approach
and less effectiveness; but any civilized film is welcome
in the late seventies.*
w I. A. L. Diamond, Billy Wilder *story* Crowned
Heads by Tom Tryon d Billy Wilder ph Gerry
Fisher m Miklos Rozsa
☆ William Holden, Marthe Keller, Hildegarde
Knef, José Ferrer, Mario Adorf, Henry Fonda,
Michael York
'Rife with Wilderean gallows humour and a
sumptuous sense of decay in never-never land.' –
Sight and Sound

Feds
US   1988   82m   colour
Warner (Ilona Herzberg, Len Blum)
🎬 📺 🎧 🔵
Two women – one academic, the other athletic –
meet masculine prejudice when they train to
become FBI agents.
*A mild, unaresting comedy, too predictable and
unmemorable to cause more than a very occasional
smile.*
w Len Blum, Dan Goldberg d Dan Goldberg
ph Timothy Suhrstedt m Randy Edelman
pd Randy Ser ed Donn Cambern
☆ Rebecca DeMornay, Mary Gross, Ken Marshall,
Fred Dalton Thompson, Larry Cedar, Raymond
Singer, James Luisi, Rex Ryon, Tony Longo

Feel the Motion (dubbed)
West Germany   1985   98m   colour
Atlas International/Solaris/Bavaria Atelier/Neue
Constantin (Peter Zenk)
🎬
A female car mechanic tries to persuade a
television pop show to listen to her demo tape.
*Trivial story of a pop romance interspersed with
forgettable songs and heavy-handed rock parodies.*
w Wolfgang Büld, Rochus Hahn, Peter Zemann
d Wolfgang Büld ph Roland Willaert pd Twyla
Weixl ed Inge Kuhnert
☆ Sissy Kelling, Frank Meyer-Brockmann, Ingolf
Lück, Dietmar Bär, Kurt Raab, Meatloaf, Falco,
The Flirts, Pia Zadora, Limahl, Die Toten Hosen

Feeling Minnesota *
US   1996   95m   DeLuxe
Entertainment/New Line/Jersey (Danny DeVito,
Michael Shamberg, Stacy Sher)
🎬 📺 🎧 ⊙ 🔵
An ex-convict goes on the run with his brother's
bride.
*Over-the-top, small-town, family melodrama of
double-dealing gangsters, less interesting than it sounds.*
wd Steven Baigelman ph Walt Lloyd pd Naomi
Shohan ed Martin Walsh
☆ Keanu Reeves, Vincent D'Onofrio, Cameron
Diaz, Delroy Lindo, Courtney Love, Tuesday Weld,
Dan Aykroyd, Levon Helm
'Suggests Sam Shepard trying to be Quentin
Tarantino. It makes even gun battles seem
pretentious.' – Owen Gleiberman, *Entertainment
Weekly*

'A thrill a minute! A laugh a second! A comedy
cyclone!'
Feet First **
👪 US   1930   88m   bw
Harold Lloyd
🎬 📺
A shoe salesman gets entangled with crooks and
has a narrow escape when hanging from the side of
a building.
*Very funny early talkie comedy, probably the
comedian's last wholly satisfactory film.*
w Lex Neal, Felix Adler, Paul Gerard Smith
d Clyde Bruckman ph Walter Lundin, Henry
Kohler
☆ Harold Lloyd, Robert McWade, Barbara Kent
'That Lloyd was a bit pressed for laughs may be
guessed from the fact that he is again dangling
from the front of a skyscraper.' – *Variety*

Feiying Gaiwak: see *Operation Condor*

Felicia's Journey **
GB/Canada   1999   116m   DeLuxe
Panavision
Icon/Marquis/Screen Ventures XLIII
🎬 📺
A pregnant Irish girl comes to England to search
for the father of her child, and is taken in by a
middle-aged catering manager who lives alone in
the family house once occupied by his mother, a
TV cook.
*Creepy drama of the unloved searching for redemption,
an unsettling insight into the mind of a serial killer.*
wd Atom Egoyan *novel* William Trevor ph Paul
Sarossy m Mychael Danna pd Jim Clay ed Susan
Shipton cos Sandy Powell
☆ Bob Hoskins, Elaine Cassidy, Arsinee Khanjian,
Peter McDonald, Gerard McSorley, Brid Brennan,
Danny Turner, Claire Benedict
'An altogether amazing work; it creates a world
and then leaves it with you, what's more, in a
manner that you might find difficult to forget.' –
Andrew O'Hagan, *Daily Telegraph*
'Very well-made, but cold and hollow at its core.'
– Stephen Farber, *Movieline*

Felix the Cat: The Movie
👪 US   1989   82m   colour
Transatlantic/Felix The Cat Creations/Productions Inc
(Don Oriolo, Christian Schneider, Janos Schenk)
🎬 📺
Felix rescues a princess from another dimension.
Laboured attempt to update the classic cartoon figure.
w Don Oriolo, Pete Brown d Tibor Hernadi
ph Laszlo Radocsay d Tibor A. Belay, Tibor
Hernadi
☆ Featuring the voices of Chris Phillips, Maureen
O'Connnell, Peter Neuman, Alice Playten, Susan
Montanaro, Don Oriolo, Christian Schneider,
David Kolin
'More likely to bury the ingratiating Felix
beyond revival than to stimulate fresh legions of
fans.' – Philip Strick, *MFB*

Fellini's Casanova: see *Casanova*

'The decline and fall of the Roman Empire,
1931–1972!'
Fellini's Roma **
Italy/France   1972   119m   Technicolor
Ultra/Artistes Associés (Turi Vasile)
🎬 📺 🎧 🔵
aka: *Roma*
A small boy learns about Rome at school and then
grows up to visit a city that does not resemble the
place of his imagination; later, as a film director, he
films the city of the 1970s in all its chaos and
confusion.
*Delightful mix of documentary and autobiography,
combining fantasy and reality, artifice and actuality; it
is a record of the director's love affair with Rome,
recalled with nostalgic affection for the past and distress
for its future.*
w Federico Fellini, Bernardino Zapponi
d Federico Fellini ph Giuseppe Rotunno m Nino
Rota ad Danilo Donati ed Ruggero Mastroianni
☆ Peter Gonzales, Fiona Florence, Britta Barnes,
Pia de Doses, Marne Maitland, Renato Giovannoli
'Fellini shows a Rome which reflects his own
feelings and experiences, in short himself. The
film is a huge dream, an offshoot of his *Satyricon*,
grotesque, horrible, beautiful.' – Dily Powell,
Sunday Times

Fellini's Satyricon: see *Satyricon*

Fellow Traveller **
GB/US   1989   97m   colour
BFI/BBC Films/HBO (Michael Wearing)
🎬 📺
A blacklisted American scriptwriter ponders the
suicide of his closest friend, a Hollywood star, and
the role played in it by their Marxist
psychotherapist.
*Intelligent political thriller, despite some melodramatic
moments.*
w Michael Eaton d Philip Saville ph John
Kenway m Colin Towns pd Gavin Davies
ed Greg Miller
☆ Ron Silver, Imogen Stubbs, Hart Bochner,
Daniel J. Travanti, Katherine Borowitz, Julian
Fellowes, Richard Wilson, Doreen Mantle, David
O'Hara
'Thought-provoking, entertaining and visually
pleasurable … one of the most original and

impressive British films of the 80s' – Julian
Petley, *MFB*
'One of the most politically sophisticated,
visually imaginative British pictures of the past
decade.' – Philip French, *Observer*

Female *
US   1933   60m   bw
Warner
🎬 🔵
A high-powered lady president of a motor car
company has a secret night life.
*Slick star vehicle reminiscent of Peg's Paper but
absorbing while on screen.*
w Gene Markey, Kathryn Scola *story* Donald
Henderson Clarke d Michael Curtiz, William
Dieterle
☆ Ruth Chatterton, George Brent, Johnny Mack
Brown, Ruth Donnelly, Douglass Dumbrille, Lois
Wilson
'The story is worthy neither of this actress nor of
the high-grade production.' – *Variety*

The Female Animal
US   1957   82m   bw   Cinemascope
U-I (Albert Zugsmith)
A beach bum becomes the lover of a film star, then
falls in love with her daughter.
*Dreary and humourless melodrama notable only for the
comeback appearance of one of the screen's legendary
glamour queens.*
w Robert Hill d Harry Keller ph Russell Metty
m Hans Salter
☆ Hedy Lamarr, Jan Sterling, Jane Powell, George
Nader, James Gleason

Female Jungle
US   1956   69m   bw
Burt Kaiser
🎬 📺
aka: *The Hangover*
An off-duty cop, too drunk to remember his
actions, begins to suspect that he might have been
guilty of the murder of an actress.
*Minor pulp thriller that attempts a hard-boiled tone,
but succeeds only in being corny, with overblown
dialogue.*
w Burt Kaiser, Bruno Ve Sota d Bruno Ve Sota
ph Elwood Bredell m Nicholas Carras pd Ben
Roseman ed Carl Pingitore
☆ Kathleen Crowley, Lawrence Tierney, John
Carradine, Jayne Mansfield, Burt Kaiser, James
Kodl, Rex Thorsen, Jack Hill, Bruno Ve Sota

'Once she was too hungry for love to be afraid – but
now – it was too late!'
The Female on the Beach
US   1955   97m   bw
U-I (Albert Zugsmith)
A wealthy widow visits her late husband's beach
house and falls for the gigolo next door, who later
seems intent on murdering her.
*Absurd and jaded melodrama, a rehash of Love from a
Stranger, enlivened by some hilarious love-hate
dialogue.*
w Robert Hill, Richard Alan Simmons d Joseph
Pevney ph Charles Lang m Joseph Gershenson
☆ Joan Crawford, Jeff Chandler, Jan Sterling,
Cecil Kellaway, Natalie Schafer
JOAN CRAWFORD TO JEFF CHANDLER: 'I wouldn't
have you if you were hung with diamonds, upside
down!'

Female Perversions
US/Germany   1996   113m   Foto-Kem
Feature/MAP/Trans Atlantic/Kinowelt/Degeto (Mindy
Affrime)
🎬 📺
An ambitious Los Angeles lawyer finds herself
facing a crisis about her sexuality and her
relationship with her academic sister, a compulsive
thief.
*Stylish but uninvolving feminist critique of male
attitudes towards women and women's attitudes
towards themselves, though its concentration on nudity,
underwear and erotic fantasies suggests that it is aimed
at the usual audience for the work of Zalman King, one
of its executive producers, who directed Red Shoe
Diaries (for cable TV) and Wild Orchid (qv).*
w Julie Herbert, Susan Streitfeld book Female
Perversions: The Temptations of Emma Bovary by
Louise J. Kaplan d Susan Streitfeld ph Teresa
Medina m Debbie Wiseman pd Missy Stewart
ed Curtiss Clayton, Leo Trombetta

☆ Tilda Swinton, Amy Madigan, Karen Sillas,
Frances Fisher, Laila Robins, Clancy Brown,
Paulina Porizkova, Lisa Jane Persky
'One of the most disturbing, intriguing feminist
films in years … unsettlingly recognisable and
often cynically funny.' – Claire Monk, *Sight and
Sound*

Female Vampire
France/Belgium   1973   101m   Technicolor
General Films/Eurocine (Marius Lesoeur)
🎬
aka: *Les Avaleuses*
aka: *The Bare Breasted Countess; La Comtesse Noire;
La Comtesse aux Seins Nus; Jacula; The Last Thrill;
Yacula*
Irina, a mute and frequently naked female vampire,
fellates her partners to death.
*An attempt to combine horror and soft-core porn,
marked by its prolific director's usual out-of-focus
zooms; the content is negligible when not risible.*
wd J. P. Johnson (Jesús Franco) ph Joan Vincent
(Jesús Franco) m Daniel White ed P. Querut
(Jesús Franco)
☆ Lina Romay, Jack Taylor, Alice Arno, Monica
Swin, Jess Franck (Jesús Franco)
'Even in its original version, one might have
grave doubts about a film which relies on such
gambits as the question put to Irina by a
journalist, "Do you feel ill at ease being
descended from a family of vampires?"' – David
McGillivray, *MFB*
† The movie exists in several versions, some
concentrating on its sexual content, others on
horror. The dubbed British video release runs for
94m, while the version shown in UK cinemas in
1978 ran for 59m.

The Feminine Touch
US   1941   97m   bw
MGM (Joseph L. Mankiewicz)
A professor gets into woman trouble when he
writes a book about jealousy.
*Matrimonial comedy rather less interesting than its
credits suggest.*
w George Oppenheimer, Edmund L. Hartmann,
Ogden Nash d W. S. Van Dyke m Franz Waxman
☆ Rosalind Russell, Don Ameche, Kay Francis,
Van Heflin, Donald Meek, Henry Daniell, Sidney
Blackmer

The Feminine Touch
GB   1956   91m   Technicolor
Ealing (Jack Rix)
US title: *The Gentle Touch*
Five young student nurses arrive at St Augustine's
Hospital.
Portmanteau soap opera of no absorbing interest.
w Ian McCormick *novel* A Lamp Is Heavy by
Sheila Mackay Russell d Pat Jackson ph Paul
Beeson m Clifton Parker
☆ George Baker, Belinda Lee, Delphi Lawrence,
Adrienne Corri, Henryetta Edwards, Barbara
Archer, Diana Wynyard, Mandy Miller

La Femme de l'Aviateur: see *The Aviator's
Wife*

La Femme de Mon Pote: see *My Best Friend's
Girl*

La Femme de Nulle Part *
France   1922   70m   bw   silent
aka: *The Woman from Nowhere*
A woman who feels that her life has been ruined
through love returns home and persuades a young
girl not to do the same.
*A minor atmospheric piece of some power, comparable
with Partie de Campagne and cinematically very
interesting.*
wd Louis Delluc ph Lucas Gibory ad F. Jourdain
☆ Eve Francis, Roger Karl, Gine Avril

Une Femme Disparait *
France   1944   104m   bw
Mayer-Burstyn
aka: *A Woman Disappeared*
aka: *Portrait of a Woman*
When a body is found, four people believe it to be
that of a loved one who has disappeared; their
stories are told in flashback.
*Virtually a short story portmanteau to accommodate
five performances by its star.*
wd Jacques Feyder *novel* Jacques Viot

☆ Françoise Rosay, Henri Guisol, Jean Nohain, Claire Gérard

Une Femme Douce **

France 1969 88m Eastmancolor
Academy/Parc/Marianne (Mag Bodard)
aka: *A Gentle Creature*

A husband attempts to explain to the maid the events of his married life which led to his wife's suicide.

A cool and subtle exploration of the gap between a person's understanding of life and reality.

wd Robert Bresson *story A Gentle Soul* by Fyodor Dostoevsky *ph* Ghislain Cloquet *m* Jean Wiener *ad* Pierre Charbonnier *ed* Raymond Lamy

☆ Dominique Sanda, Guy Frangin, Jane Lobre

'One of Bresson's big films, and, like all his others, it is really about confinement and flight – an account of a character pledged to escape.' – *New Yorker*

La Femme du Boulanger **

France 1938 110m bw
Marcel Pagnol
aka: *The Baker's Wife*

Villagers put a stop to the infidelity of the baker's wife because her husband no longer has the heart to make good bread.

Best-known of Pagnol's rustic fables, this rather obvious and long-drawn-out joke is important because international critics hailed it as a work of art (which it isn't) and because it fixed an image of the naughty bucolic French.

wd Marcel Pagnol *novel Jean Le Bleu* by Jean Giono *ph* Georges Benoit, R. Lendruz, N. Daries *m* Vincent Scotto *ed* Suzanne de Troeye

☆ Raimu, Ginette Leclerc, Charles Moulin, Charpin, Maximilienne

'It is a long film with a small subject, but the treatment is so authentic that it seems over far too soon, and the acting is superb.' – *Graham Greene*

Une Femme Est une Femme: see *A Woman Is a Woman*

'A secret life. A deadly passion.'

Femme Fatale

US 1991 96m Foto-Kem
Republic/Gibraltar Entertainment (Andrew Lane, Nancy Rae Stone)

After his wife leaves him at the start of their honeymoon, a husband discovers that she has more than one identity.

Anonymous thriller that stumbles to a lame conclusion.

w Michael Ferris, John D. Brancato *d* André Guttfreund *ph* Joey Forsyte *m* Parmer Fuller *pd* Pam Warner *ed* Richard Candib

☆ Colin Firth, Lisa Zane, Billy Zane, Scott Wilson, Lisa Blount, Suzanne Snyder

Une Femme Française *

France/GB/Germany 1995 98m Eastmancolor
UGC/TF1/Recorded Pictures/DA/Studio Babelsberg (Yves Marmion)

aka: *A French Woman*

During and after the Second World War, the wife of a French soldier has numerous affairs while her husband serves in Germany, Syria, Indochina and Algeria.

A glossy, highly charged, sometimes diverting, episodic account of an unhappy relationship over a period of 15 years; its restless, promiscuous heroine may be intended as a symbol of France during a period of social upheaval and, on this wider level, it fails to convince.

w Regis Wargnier, Alain Le Henry *d* Regis Wargnier *ph* François Catonné *m* Patrick Doyle *pd* Jacques Bufnoir *ed* Genevieve Winding, Agnes Schwab

☆ Emmanuelle Beart, Daniel Auteuil, Gabriel Barylli, Jean-Claude Brialy, Genevieve Casile, Michel Etcheverry, Heinz Bennent

'A painless slice of handsome moviemaking that offers goodly guilty pleasures.' – *Variety*

La Femme Infidèle **

France/Italy 1968 98m Eastmancolor
La Boëtie/Cinegay (André Génovès)

aka: *The Unfaithful Wife*

A middle-aged insurance broker, set in his ways, murders his wife's lover; when she suspects the truth, they are drawn closer together.

Almost a Buñuel-like black comedy, spare and quiet, with immaculate performances.

wd Claude Chabrol *ph* Jean Rabier *m* Pierre Jansen *ed* Jacques Gaillard

☆ Stéphane Audran, Michel Bouquet, Maurice Ronet

'On any level, this bizarre murder framed by whiskies emerges as Chabrol's most flawless work to date.' – *Jan Dawson, MFB*

Une Femme Mariée: see *A Married Woman*

La Femme Nikita: see *Nikita*

Une Femme ou Deux

France 1985 97m colour
AAA/Hachette/Philippe Dussart/FR3/DD (Michel Choquet)

aka: *One Woman or Two*

An advertising woman uses an archaeologist as basis for a new campaign, then falls in love with him.

Lighthearted, not to say light-headed, romantic comedy with silly asides: Doris Day and Rock Hudson, where are you?

w Daniel Vigne, Elizabeth Rappeneau *d* Daniel Vigne *ph* Carlo Varini *m* Kevin Mulligan, Evert Verhees, Toots Thielemans *ad* Jean-Pierre Kohut-Svelko *ed* Marie-Josèphe Yoyotte

☆ Gérard Depardieu, Sigourney Weaver, Michel Aumont, Dr Ruth Westheimer, Zabou, Jean-Pierre Bisson

'Unsatisfactory on all levels.' – *Quentin Crisp*

La Femme-flic *

France 1979 100m Eastmancolor
Sara/Antenne 2 (Alain Sarde)

aka: *The Lady Cop*

A female police inspector who becomes a political embarrassment is transferred to the provinces, where she is subjected to high-level interference when she uncovers a child pornography racket.

Tough and cynical political thriller which comes to the conclusion that honesty is far from the best policy.

w Claude Veillot *story* Claude Veillot, Yves Boisset *d* Yves Boisset *ph* Jacques Loiseleux *m* Philippe Sarde *pd* Maurice Sergent, Jimmy Vansteenkiste *ed* Albert Jurgenson, Nadine Muse, Martine Fleury

☆ Miou-Miou, Jean-Marc Thibault, Leny Escudero, Jean-Pierre Kalfon, François Simon, Alex Lacast, Niels Arestrup, Henri Garçin, Philippe Caubere

Femmes de Paris *

France 1954 85m Agfacolor
Optimax-Lux (Edgar Bacquet)

aka: *Ah! Les Belles Bacchantes*

A touring revue is almost run out of town for indecency.

A rather crude but quite valuable record of Dhéry's stage revue, which convulsed London in the fifties.

w Robert Dhéry *d* Jean Loubignac *ph* René Colas *m* Gérard Calvi

☆ Robert Dhéry, Colette Brosset, Louis de Funès, Raymond Bussières, the Bluebell Girls

The Fencing Master ***

Spain 1992 88m colour
Mayfair/Majestic/Origen/Altube Filmeak/ICAA (Antonio Cardenal, Pedro Olea)

original title: *El Maestro de Esgrima*

In Madrid in the 1860s, at a time of extreme political upheaval, a fencing master becomes involved with a beautiful woman and finds himself caught up in a situation he does not understand.

Elegant, erotically charged story of love and loyalty and of different codes of behaviour, told with subtlety, dash and elegance.

w Antonio Larreta, Francisco Prada, Arturo Pérez Reverte, Pedro Olea *novel* Arturo Pérez Reverte *d* Pedro Olea *ph* Alfredo Mayo *m* José Nieto *ad* Luis Valles *ed* José Salcedo

☆ Omero Antonutti, Assumpta Serna, Joaquim de Almeida, José Luis Lopez Vázquez, Alberto Closas, Miguel Rellán

'Stellar performances ... a distinguished and literate script, fine plot development and accomplished direction and lensing.' – *Variety*

'A deeply romantic Spanish thriller with two performances at its centre that do more than catch the eye. At times they catch the breath.' – *Derek Malcolm, Guardian*

Fengyue: see *Temptress Moon*

La Ferme du Pendu *

France 1946 90m bw
Corona

aka: *Hanged Man's Farm*

The lecherous son of a farming family brings tragedy to the lives of himself and his brothers and sister.

Cold Comfort Farm with a vengeance, appropriately played: arrant melodrama, but watchable.

w André-Paul Antoine *d* Jean Dréville *ph* André Thomas *m* Marcel Delannoy

☆ Alfred Adam, Charles Vanel, Arlette Merry

FernGully: The Last Rainforest

ⵟ Australia 1992 76m DeLuxe
TCF/FAI/Youngheart (Wayne Young, Peter Faiman)

A fairy, a fruit-bat and a miniaturized lumberjack save the rainforest from the evil spirit who would destroy it.

Moderately enjoyable animated feature with an ecological moral: be kind to trees.

w Jim Cox *story* Diana Young *d* Bill Kroyer *m* Alan Silvestri *ad* Susan Kroyer *ed* Gillian Hutshing

☆ Featuring the voices of: Tim Curry, Samantha Mathis, Christian Slater, Jonathan Ward, Robin Williams, Grace Zabriskie, Geoffrey Blake, Robert Pastorelli, Cheech Marin, Tommy Chong, Tone-Loc

'As lectures on the environment go, this one is less likely to induce adult narcolepsy than most.' – *Ian Johnstone, Sunday Times*

'Pic will amply entertain tykes while feeding them an environmental lesson, and features enough amusing jokes and clever songs to make it palatable for adults.' – *Variety*

Ferris Bueller's Day Off *

ⵟ US 1986 103m Metrocolor
Panavision
Paramount/John Hughes, Tom Jacobson

A teenage student enjoys an aimless day playing truant.

Aimless it is, and juvenile, but people have found pleasing things in it.

wd John Hughes *ph* Tak Fujimoto *m* Ira Newborn *pd* John W. Corso *ed* Paul Hirsch

☆ Matthew Broderick, Alan Ruck, Mia Sara, Jeffrey Jones, Cindy Pickett, Jennifer Grey

Ferry to Hong Kong

GB 1958 113m Eastmancolor
Cinemascope
Rank (George Maynard)

An Austrian layabout can land at neither of the Hong Kong ferry's ports of call, but shows his true worth when a typhoon strikes.

Silly storyline and rampant bad acting ruin the Rank Organization's first attempt at an international epic.

w Vernon Harris, Lewis Gilbert *d* Lewis Gilbert *ph* Otto Heller *m* Kenneth V. Jones

☆ Curt Jurgens, Sylvia Syms, Orson Welles, Jeremy Spenser, Noel Purcell

Festen ***

Denmark 1998 105m colour
October/Nimbus/DR TV/SVT Drama (Brigitte Hald)

aka: *The Celebration*

At a formal dinner to celebrate a patriarch's 60th birthday, his eldest son makes a speech claiming that his father sexually abused him as a child, and drove his twin sister to kill herself.

Unsettling, nervy drama, in which the edgy acting and twitchy camera combine to give a raw, emotional power to the narrative.

w Thomas Vinterberg, Mogens Rukov *d* Thomas Vinterberg *ph* Anthony Dod Mantle *ed* Valdis Oskarsdottir

☆ Ulrich Thomsen, Henning Moritzen, Thomas Bo Larsen, Paprika Steen, Birthe Neumann, Trine Dyrholm, Helle Dolleris, Therese Glahn, Klaus Bondam, Bjarne Henriksen, Gbatokai Dakinah

'As smart, sharp and stinging as a slap around the face.' – *Tom Shone, Sunday Times*

† The film was made under the dictates of Dogma 95, of which Vinterberg was a signatory; its conditions laid down for film-making include location shooting, direct sound, and hand-held camerawork.

La Fête à Henriette *

France 1952 113m bw
Regina-Filmsonor
aka: *Holiday for Henrietta*

Two screenwriters disagree whether or not to give their hero and heroine a happy ending.

A rather heavy-handed romantic joke which does have its moments and was later – fatally – Americanized as Paris When It Sizzles.

w Julien Duvivier, Henri Jeanson *d* Julien Duvivier *ph* Roger Hubert *m* Georges Auric

☆ Dany Robin, Henri Auclair, Hildegarde Neff, Michel Roux, Saturnin Fabre, Julien Carette

Le Feu Follet ***

France 1963 107m bw
Lux/Nouvelles éditions (Jean Pieuchot)

US title: *The Fire Within*

aka: *Will-O'-The-Wisp; A Time to Live and a Time to Die*

A recovering alcoholic, urged to be positive, visits his old friends and, horrified by the compromises they have made, kills himself.

A compassionate and fascinating film, shot in an understated way; though, with its downbeat ending, it is not easy viewing.

wd Louis Malle *novel* Pierre Drieu La Rochelle *ph* Ghislain Cloquet *m* Erik Satie *ad* Bernard Evein *ed* Suzanne Baron, Monique Nana

☆ Maurice Ronet, Léna Skerla, Jeanne Moreau, Yvonne Clech, Hubert Deschamps, Alexandra Stewart

'An epitaph for all the beautiful young men, the semi-intellectual "gilded mediocrities" who skim through their days to their doom unchanged save for a surface tarnish. A latter-day parable of a Dorian Gray, superbly acted and beautifully filmed.' – *Judith Crist*

Feudin', Fussin' and A-fightin'

US 1948 78m bw
Universal-International

A fast-running travelling salesman is kidnapped by a hillbilly town which needs him in its annual sports.

Unpretentious lower-berth comedy for middle America.

w D. D. Beauchamp *d* George Sherman

☆ Donald O'Connor, Marjorie Main, Percy Kilbride, Penny Edwards, Joe Besser

A Fever in the Blood

US 1960 117m bw
Warner (Roy Huggins)

Candidates for governor sharpen their campaigns on a murder trial.

Interestingly-cast, flabbily-written melodrama.

w Roy Huggins, Harry Kleiner *novel* William Pearson *d* Vincent Sherman *ph* J. Peverell Marley *m* Ernest Gold

☆ Efrem Zimbalist Jnr, Angie Dickinson, Don Ameche, Herbert Marshall, Jack Kelly, Ray Danton, Jesse White, Rhodes Reason, Robert Colbert

Fever Pitch

US 1985 96m Metrocolor
MGM-UA/Freddie Fields

A compulsive Vegas gambler gets in deep with loan sharks.

You might think there was more to the plot than that, but no; and the whole thing is just glum.

wd Richard Brooks *ph* William Fraker *m* Thomas Dolby *pd* Raymond G. Storey

☆ Ryan O'Neal, Catherine Hicks, Giancarlo Giannini, Bridgette Andersen, Chad Everett, John Saxon

'The cards are stacked against it.' – *Variety*

'Life Gets Complicated When You Love One Woman and Worship Eleven Men.'

Fever Pitch *

GB   1996   102m   Rank Colour
Film Four/Wildgaze (Amanda Posey)

A soccer-mad London comprehensive school English teacher neglects his girlfriend in his obsession for Arsenal Football Club.
A small-scale attempt at a romantic comedy, which finds its climax in a real-life event – Arsenal's triumph in the last moment of their last game to win the league championship – but otherwise indulges in a fantasy of a man behaving badly and getting away with it.
w Nick Hornby *book* Nick Hornby d David Evans ph Chris Seager pd Michael Carlin ed Scott Thomas
☆ Colin Firth, Ruth Gemmell, Neil Pearson, Lorraine Ashbourne, Mark Strong, Holly Aird, Ken Stott, Stephen Rea
'Should do as well as Arsenal – though, like them, it is a little dull to watch.' – *Derek Malcolm, Guardian*

A Few Good Men **

US   1992   138m   Technicolor
Columbia TriStar/Castle Rock (David Brown, Rob Reiner, Andrew Scheinman)

A lawyer known for plea bargaining decides to defend two marines accused of killing a fellow marine, a case that depends on discrediting their martinet of a commanding officer.
Slick, engrossing courtroom drama, in which audiences can cheer the hero and hiss the villain, even though it seems little more than a more portentous re-run of The Caine Mutiny.
w Aaron Sorkin *play* Aaron Sorkin d Rob Reiner m Robert Richardson m Marc Shaiman pd J. Michael Riva ed Robert Leighton
☆ Tom Cruise, Jack Nicholson, Demi Moore, Kevin Bacon, Kiefer Sutherland, Kevin Pollak, James Marshall, J. T. Walsh, Christopher Guest, J. A. Preston
'A big-time, mainstream Hollywood movie par excellence.' – *Variety*
'A slick, entertaining, flashily-acted courtroom drama replete with all the standard ingredients.' – *Philip French, Observer*
& Best picture; Jack Nicholson; Robert Leighton

ffoulkes: see *North Sea Hijack*

Fiddler on the Roof **

US   1971   180m   Technicolor
Panavision 70
UA/Mirisch (Norman Jewison)

In a pre-revolutionary Russian village, Tevye the Jewish milkman survives family and political problems and when the pogroms begin cheerfully emigrates to America.
Self-conscious, grittily realistic adaptation of the stage musical, with slow and heavy patches in its grossly overlong celebration of a vanished way of life. The big moments still come off well though the songs tend to be thrown away and the photography is unnecessarily murky.
w Joseph Stein *play* Joseph Stein *story* Tevye and his Daughters by Sholom Aleichem d Norman Jewison ph Oswald Morris m/ly Jerry Bock, Sheldon Harnick md John Williams pd Robert Boyle
☆ Topol, Norma Crane, Leonard Frey, Molly Picon
'Jewison hasn't so much directed a film as prepared a product for world consumption.' – Stanley Kauffmann
& Oswald Morris; John Williams
& best picture; Norman Jewison (as director); Topol; Leonard Frey

Fiddlers Three *

GB   1944   87m   bw
Ealing (Robert Hamer)

Sailors struck by lightning on Salisbury Plain are transported back to ancient Rome.
Sequel to Sailors Three; despite a harsh and unattractive look, every conceivable joke about old Romans is deftly mined and the good humour flows free.
w Diana Morgan, Angus Macphail d Harry Watt ph Wilkie Cooper m Spike Hughes
☆ Tommy Trinder, Sonnie Hale, Frances Day, Francis L. Sullivan, Ernest Milton, Diana Decker, Elisabeth Welch, Mary Clare, Kay Kendall

'It Owns Him. It Possesses Him. It Could Even Destroy Him.'

The Field *

GB   1990   110m   colour
Granada (Noel Pearson)

A farmer is prepared to kill in order to keep a rented field which his family has farmed for generations and which an American wishes to buy.
Melodramatic domestic drama trying for a tragic dimension it cannot quite encompass.
wd Jim Sheridan *play* John B. Keane ph Jack Conroy m Elmer Bernstein pd Frank Conway ad Frank Hallinan Flood ed J. Patrick Duffner
☆ Richard Harris, John Hurt, Tom Berenger, Sean Bean, Frances Tomelty, Brenda Fricker
'Superb acting and austere visual beauty are offset by a somewhat overheated screenplay.' – *Variety*
& Richard Harris

Field of Dreams **

US   1989   106m   DeLuxe
Guild/Universal/Carolco (Lawrence Gordon, Charles Gordon)

A farmer builds a baseball pitch to summon the ghosts of past players.
A gentle fantasy with the power to charm.
wd Phil Alden Robinson *book* Shoeless Joe by W. P. Kinsella ph John Lindley m James Horner pd Dennis Gassner ed Ian Crafford
☆ Kevin Costner, Amy Madigan, James Earl Jones, Timothy Busfield, Ray Liotta, Burt Lancaster, Gaby Hoffman, Frank Whaley, Dwier Brown
& best film; best adapted screenplay; best original score

'Don't be ashamed to scream! Everyone in the theatre will be screaming with you!'

The Fiend Who Walked the West

US   1958   101m   bw   Cinemascope
TCF (Herbert B. Swope Jnr)

A sadistic killer released from prison tracks down the associates of a cellmate and terrorizes the district.
Western remake of Kiss of Death, with babyface Robert Evans in the Widmark role. Violent and dull.
w Harry Brown, Philip Yordan d Gordon Douglas ph Joe MacDonald m Leon Klatzkin
☆ Hugh O'Brian, Dolores Michaels, Robert Evans, Linda Cristal, Stephen McNally, Edward Andrews

'New Horrors! Mad Science Spawns Evil Fiends!'

Fiend without a Face

GB   1957   75m   bw
Eros/Producers Associates (John Croydon)

A scientist working on materialized thought produces monsters from his own id.
Tepid shocker with well-organized mobile brains.
w Herbert J. Leder *story* Amelia Reynolds Long d Arthur Crabtree ph Lionel Banes m Buxton Orr md Frederic Lewis ad John Elphick ed R.O. McNaughton sp Ruppel & Nordhoff, Peter Neilson
☆ Marshall Thompson, Kynaston Reeves, Terence Kilburn, Kim Parker, Stanley Maxted, James Dyrenforth, Robert MacKenzie, Michael Balfour

The Fiendish Plot of Dr Fu Manchu

US   1980   108m   Technicolor
Warner/Orion/Playboy (Hugh Hefner)

The 'yellow peril' returns to the western world to mastermind diamond thefts.
Feeble spoof with a history of production troubles; clearly the only thing in anybody's mind was to get it over with.
w Jim Moloney, Rudy Dochtermann d Piers Haggard ph Jean Tournier m Marc Wilkinson pd Alexander Trauner
☆ Peter Sellers, Helen Mirren, David Tomlinson, Sid Caesar, Simon Williams, Steve Franken, Stratford Johns, John Le Mesurier, Clive Dunn

The Fiends: see *Les Diaboliques*

'Don't Pet Them.'

Fierce Creatures *

GB/US   1997   95m   Rank Colour   Panavision
Universal/Fish Productions/Jersey Films (Michael Shamberg, John Cleese)

A megalomaniacal tycoon puts an incompetent ex-policeman in charge of running an English zoo.
A floundering comedy that never gets its act together; its running jokes are lame, and the satire is heavy-handed.
w John Cleese, Ian Johnstone d Robert Young, Fred Schepisi ph Adrian Biddle, Ian Baker m Jerry Goldsmith pd Roger Murray-Leach ed Robert Gibson
☆ John Cleese, Jamie Lee Curtis, Kevin Kline, Michael Palin, Ronnie Corbett, Carey Lowell, Robert Lindsay
'A distracting little comedy with an Ealing-esque theme and a clutch of star names giving their all to a script which they know is beneath them.' – *Independent*
† After previews in December 1995, the film's release was delayed by more than a year so that new scenes could be shot, in which Kline, as the tycoon's son, does not die. It took six months to reassemble the cast, by which time director Robert Young was busy elsewhere. So Fred Schepisi replaced him for the three weeks, filming additional material.

The Fiercest Heart

US   1961   90m   DeLuxe   Cinemascope
TCF (George Sherman)

A British army deserter joins a Boer trek into South Africa.
Pioneer 'Western', poorly done but with novelty value.
w Edmund H. North *novel* Stuart Cloete d George Sherman ph Ellis Carter m Irving Gertz
☆ Stuart Whitman, Juliet Prowse, Raymond Massey, Ken Scott, Geraldine Fitzgerald, Rafer Johnson

Fiesta

US   1947   102m   Technicolor
MGM (Jack Cummings)

A young Mexican wants to be a musician though his father insists he should be a bullfighter.
An extremely boring idea for a musical which at best is a tedious time-passer.
w George Bruce, Lester Cole d Richard Thorpe ph Sidney Wagner, Charles Rosner, William Cline m Aaron Copland md John Green
☆ Esther Williams, Ricardo Montalban, Cyd Charisse, Mary Astor, John Carroll, Akim Tamiroff, Hugo Haas
& John Green

Fièvre *

France   1921   50m   bw   silent
Alhambra

A brawl in a Marseilles bar ends in murder.
A dramatic sketch, filmed with remarkable detail and artistry.
wd Louis Delluc ph A. Gibory ad Bécan
☆ Eve Francis, Edmond Van Daele, Gaston Modot

Fifi la Plume

France   1964   80m   bw
Les Films Montsouris (Albert Lamorisse)

A burglar becomes a circus bird-man, learns to fly, and is everywhere mistaken for an angel.
A likeable fantasy idea which doesn't quite come off, alternating uneasily between slapstick and sentiment.
wd Albert Lamorisse ph Pierre Petit m Jean-Michel Defaye
☆ Philippe Avron, Mireille Nègre, Henri Lambert, Raoul Delfosse

Fifth Avenue Girl *

US   1939   83m   bw
RKO (Gregory La Cava)

An unemployed girl is persuaded by a millionaire to pose as a gold digger and annoy his avaricious family.
Brightish comedy of the Cinderella kind.
w Allan Scott d Gregory La Cava ph Robert de Grasse
☆ Ginger Rogers, Walter Connolly, Verree Teasdale, Tim Holt, James Ellison, Franklin Pangborn, Kathryn Adams, Louis Calhern

'Substantial comedy drama for top grosses.' – *Variety*

The Fifth Chair: see *It's in the Bag*

The Fifth Cord (dubbed)

Italy   1971   100m   Eastmancolor
Jumbo/BRC/Dario (Manolo Bolognini)

original title: Giornata Nera per L'Ariete
aka: Evil Fingers

A journalist investigating a crime becomes a murder suspect when people he questions are murdered.
Uninteresting thriller with cardboard characters and a teasing narrative.
w Mario di Nardo, Mario Fenelli, Luigi Bazzoni *novel* D. M. Devine d Luigi Bazzoni ph Vittorio Storaro m Ennio Morricone ad Gastone Carsetti ed Eugenio Alabiso
☆ Franco Nero, Silvia Monti, Wolfgang Preiss, Ira Furstenberg, Edmund Purdom, Maurizio Bonuglia, Pamela Tiffin, Renato Romano
'Shoals of red herrings do little to make up for … meagre characterisation, the scrambled course of its plot, or its shamefully deceptive ending.' – *David McGillivray, MFB*
† The British release in 1973 was cut by the censor to 80m. The UK video release runs for 89m.

The Fifth Element *

France   1997   127m   Technicolor
Columbia/Gaumont (Patrice Ledoux)

original title: Le Cinquième Elément

In 2214, a taxi driver, a monk and a supreme being (a willowy blonde with garishly dyed red hair) save the world from total destruction.
Juvenile space hokum that derives from pulp writing of the 30s; its visual style and simple action narrative attracted a mass audience, presumably hungering for mindless entertainment, since that is what it successfully delivers.
w Luc Besson, Robert Mark Kamen d Luc Besson ph Thierry Arbogast m Eric Serra pd Dan Weil ed Sylvie Landra sp Digital Domain
☆ Bruce Willis, Gary Oldman, Ian Holm, Milla Jovovich, Chris Tucker, Luke Perry, Brion James, John Neville, John Bluthal, Mathieu Kassovitz, Lee Evans
'This mishmash of half-baked futuristic, mythological, quasi-religious, big-scale action and would-be romantic motifs. Despite the hefty production coin, there is something left to be desired about nearly every aspect of the picture, from the narrative line and vision of the future to the score and execution of the special effects, that will combine to turn off all but the most avid teen sci-fi fans long before the pic comes in for its final landing.' – *Todd McCarthy, Variety*
'A massively bad, massively stupid film.' – *Jim Schembri, Melbourne Age*
† The film, at a cost of around $89m, was the most expensive so far made in France, and had its origins in a script Besson wrote at the age of 16. It took around $63m at the US box-office and more than $200m elsewhere in the world.
& sound effects editing

The Fifth Musketeer *

Austria   1978   106m   Eastmancolor
Sascha-Wien Film/Ted Richmond

aka: Behind the Iron Mask

Louis XIII and his twin brother Philippe vie for the crown of France.
Virtually a remake of The Man in the Iron Mask, with patchy style and a few excisable sex scenes added. The 1939 version was better.
w David Ambrose d Ken Annakin ph Jack Cardiff m Riz Ortolani
☆ Beau Bridges, Sylvia Kristel, Ursula Andress, Cornel Wilde, Lloyd Bridges, Alan Hale Jnr, José Ferrer, Rex Harrison, Olivia de Havilland, Ian McShane, Helmut Dantine

55 Days at Peking *

US/Spain   1963   154m   Super Technirama 70
Samuel Bronston

In 1900 Peking, Boxer fanatics are encouraged by the Empress to take over the city and besiege the international diplomatic quarter; an American major leads the defence.

Spasmodically lively action spectacular weighed down by romantic stretches.

w Philip Yordan, Bernard Gordon d Nicholas Ray, Andrew Marton ph Jack Hildyard, Manuel Berenguer m Dimitri Tiomkin ad Venerio Colasanti, John Moore

☆ Charlton Heston, David Niven, Ava Gardner, Flora Robson, Robert Helpmann, Leo Genn, Paul Lukas, John Ireland, Harry Andrews, Elizabeth Sellars, Massimo Serrato, Jacques Sernas, Geoffrey Bayldon

'An open-air western in Chinese.' – *David Niven*
'Pictorially this is a beautiful film, but the characters are conventional siege figures.' – *Sunday Times*

♫ Dimitri Tiomkin; song 'So Little Time' (mDimitri Tiomkin, lyPaul Francis Webster)

'The Story That Seduced The World Is Now The Most Provocative Film Of The Year.'

54
US 1998 92m DeLuxe
Miramax/Redeemable Features/Dollface/Film Colony (Richard N. Gladstein, Dolly Hall, Ira Deutchman)
▦▦ ▦▦ ♫

In the late 70s, a working-class youth gets a job in New York's most fashionable disco, where he observes the decadent, drug-fuelled lifestyle of the wealthy.
Tame, inhibited biopic of club-owner Steve Rubell, entrepreneur of the disco culture of the 70s; the real thing must have been more interesting, otherwise no one would ever have gone to Studio 54.

wd Mark Christopher ph Alexander Gruszynski m Marco Beltrami pd Kevin Thompson ed Lee Percy

☆ Ryan Phillippe, Salma Hayek, Neve Campbell, Mike Myers, Sela Ward, Breckin Meyer, Sherry Stringfield, Ellen Albertini Dow, Heather Matarazzo, Skipp Sudduth, Aemillia Robinson, Lauren Hutton, Michael York

'Those expecting any real insight into the 70s club scene will come away hugely disappointed.' – *Caroline Westbrook, Empire*

Fifty Million Frenchmen
US 1931 68m Technicolor
Warner

A rich American in Paris tries to prove that he was able to win a blonde without the aid of his bankroll.
Much changed and enfeebled version of a Broadway musical, with the Broadway talent transplanted.

w Al Boasberg, Eddie Welch, Joseph Jackson d Lloyd Bacon

☆ Olsen and Johnson, William Gaxton, John Halliday, Helen Broderick, Claudia Dell, Lester Crawford

'Will have to depend mostly on its title for b.o. attraction.' – *Variety*

Fifty Roads to Town *
US 1937 80m bw
TCF

Mistaken identities abound in a snowbound cabin.
Fairly funny minor comedy.

w George Marion Jnr, William Conselman d Norman Taurog

☆ Don Ameche, Ann Sothern, Slim Summerville, Jane Darwell, John Qualen, Douglas Fowley, Stepin Fetchit

'Just about right for summer audiences ... pleasant light romantic comedy demanding a minimum of concentration.' – *Variety*

52 Pick-up
US 1986 114m TVC Color
Cannon (Henry T. Weinstein)
▦▦ ▦

A businessman rounds on blackmailers who take films of his sex life.
Uninteresting melodrama based on the same novel as The Ambassador, released two years earlier by the same company.

w Elmore Leonard, John Steppling novel Elmore Leonard d John Frankenheimer ph Jost Vacano m Gary Chang

☆ Roy Scheider, Ann-Margret, Vanity, John Glover, Robert Trebor, Lonny Chapman

'There is no rush of energy to propel the film past its improbability.' – *Variety*

52nd Street
US 1937 83m bw
Walter Wanger

A strictly-brought-up young woman shocks her family by falling for a singer.
Tame romantic comedy with musical items.

w Grover Jones d Harold Young

☆ Kenny Baker, Ella Logan, Ian Hunter, ZaSu Pitts, Leo Carrillo

'It may have been a good idea to make a film about the metamorphosing of 52nd Street into a lane of niteries, but the conception doesn't come through ... filmgoers are likely to wonder what it's all about, and why.' – *Variety*

'Mischief. Mayhem. Soap.'

Fight Club *
US 1999 139m Technicolor Panavision
TCF/Fox 2000/Regency (Art Linson, Cean Chaffin, Ross Grayson Bell)

Tired of his life as a cog in a corporate and consumer society, an insomniac businessman sets up secret clubs where men indulge in bare-knuckle fighting and anarchist activities.
It is impossible to take seriously the film's sado-masochistic posturing, its insistence that inflicting and suffering pain is redemptive; but as a blackly comic updating of Dr Jekyll and Mr Hyde, a sick fantasy of a man in two minds, it has its moments.

w Jim Uhls novel Chuck Palahniuk d David Fincher ph Jeff Cronenweth m Dust Brothers pd Alex McDowell ed James Haygood

☆ Brad Pitt, Edward Norton, Helena Bonham Carter, Meat Loaf, Jared Leto

'There are sequences in this film I never thought I would see on a screen; ideas I never believed a responsible Hollywood corporation would permit to be voiced as popular entertainment.' – *Alexander Walker, London Evening Standard*
'A fascist rhapsody posing as a metaphor of liberation... a laborious and foolish waste of time.' – *David Denby, New Yorker*
'Witless mishmash of whiny, infantile philosophising and bone-crunching violence' – *Kenneth Turan*

† The BBFC cut eight seconds from the film for its UK release.
♫ sound effects editing (Ren Klyce, Richard Hymns)

Fight for Your Lady *
US 1937 67m bw
RKO

A jilted tenor is helped by a wrestling trainer.
Odd little comedy which contrives to amuse.

w Ernest Pagano, Harry Segall, Harold Kusell story Jean Negulesco, Isabel Leighton d Ben Stoloff ph Jack MacKenzie

☆ John Boles, Jack Oakie, Ida Lupino, Margot Grahame, Erik Rhodes, Billy Gilbert

'This picture is going to entertain whether it sells or not.' – *Variety*

The Fighter
US 1952 78m bw
GH (Alex Gottlieb)
▦▦

A Mexican fisherman whose family is murdered by government troops becomes a prizefighter to earn money for the rebels.
A rather glum attempt to turn a few ringside clichés.

w Aben Kandel, Herbert Kline story The Mexican by Jack London d Herbert Kline ph James Wong Howe m Vincente Gomez

☆ Richard Conte, Vanessa Brown, Lee J. Cobb, Frank Silvera

Fighter Attack
US 1953 80m bw
Allied Artists
▦▦

Exploits of an American air base in Corsica.
Routine war action efficiently dispensed.

w Simon Wincelberg d Lesley Selander

☆ Sterling Hayden, J. Carrol Naish, Joy Page, Kenneth Tobey, Anthony Caruso

Fighter Squadron
US 1948 96m Technicolor
Warner (Seton I. Miller)

In World War II, a dedicated flyer risks his friends' lives.
Routine aerial actioner.

w Seton I. Miller d Raoul Walsh ph Sid Hickox, Wilfrid M. Cline m Max Steiner

☆ Edmond O'Brien, Robert Stack, John Rodney, Tom D'Andrea, Henry Hull, Walter Reed, Shepperd Strudwick, Rock Hudson

The Fighting 69th *
US 1940 89m bw
Warner (Hal B. Wallis)
▦▦

During World War I in the trenches, a cocky recruit becomes a hero and loses his life in the process.
Recruiting poster stuff, all well enough done but bewildering in its changes of mood.

w Norman Reilly Raine, Fred Niblo Jnr, Dean Franklin d William Keighley ph Tony Gaudio m Adolph Deutsch

☆ James Cagney, Pat O'Brien, George Brent, Jeffrey Lynn, Alan Hale, Frank McHugh, Dennis Morgan, Dick Foran, William Lundigan, Guinn Williams, John Litel, Henry O'Neill

'The picture is better if you can manage to forget the plot and think of it instead as the human, amusing and frequently gripping record of a regiment marching off to war.' – *Frank Nugent, New York Times*

'Enough is enough!'

Fighting Back
US 1982 98m Technicolor
Dino de Laurentiis (D. Constantine Conte)
▦▦

GB title: *Death Vengeance*

After his wife and mother are both injured in crimes of violence, a delicatessen owner forms a vigilante group and is backed to some extent by police and businessmen.
Smartly made but ethically muddled urban shocker.

w Tom Hedley, David Zelag Goodman d Lewis Teague ph Franco DiGiacomo m Piero Piccioni

☆ Tom Skerritt, Michael Sarrazin, Patti LuPone, Yaphet Kotto, David Rasche

Fighting Father Dunne
US 1948 93m bw
RKO (Phil L. Ryan)

A clergyman looks after unfortunate boys.
A slum melodrama which all concerned could have made with their eyes closed, and probably did.

w Martin Rackin, Frank Davis d Ted Tetzlaff ph George E. Diskant m Roy Webb

☆ Pat O'Brien, Darryl Hickman, Charles Kemper, Una O'Connor

The Fighting Guardsman
US 1945 84m bw
Columbia

Under the tyrannical reign of Louis XVI a young nobleman leads a peasants' revolt.
Stiff swashbuckler in which the actors appear to have been only recently introduced to their clothes.

w Franz Spencer, Edward Dein d Henry Levin

☆ Willard Parker, Anita Louise, George Macready, John Loder

Fighting Justice: see *True Believer*

The Fighting Kentuckian
US 1949 100m bw
Republic (John Wayne)
▦▦

In 1810 a farmer combats land-grabbing criminals.
Standard star Western for the family.

wd George Waggner ph Lee Garmes m George Antheil

☆ John Wayne, Vera Ralston, Oliver Hardy, Philip Dorn, Marie Windsor, Mae Marsh

Fighting Mad
US 1976 90m DeLuxe
TCF/Santa Fe (Roger Corman)
▦▦

A rancher and his son are murdered by a local industrialist who wants their land, and the rancher's city-bred son takes revenge.
Another vigilante Western in modern dress, very laborious and violent without being very exciting.

wd Jonathan Demme ph Bill Birch m Bruce Langhorne

☆ Peter Fonda, Lynn Lowry, John Doucette, Philip Carey, Scott Glenn

'Demme has allowed violence to outweigh ideas to such a degree that the picture becomes a turnoff, little more than a blatantly obvious play to the yahoo mentality.' – *Kevin Thomas, Los Angeles Times*

The Fighting O'Flynn
US 1949 94m bw
U-I (Douglas Fairbanks Jnr)
▦▦

In 18th-century Ireland, a penniless young adventurer abets Napoleon's plan for invasion.
Lively minor-league adventure.

w Douglas Fairbanks Jnr, Robert Thoeren novel Justin Huntly McCarthy d Arthur Pierson ph Arthur Edeson m Frank Skinner

☆ Douglas Fairbanks Jnr, Helena Carter, Richard Greene, Patricia Medina, Arthur Shields, J. M. Kerrigan

'Fairbanks plays the irrepressible O'Flynn with unflagging energy and tongue in cheek good humour; the rest of the cast stolidly refuses to see the joke.' – *MFB*

The Fighting Pimpernel: see *Pimpernel Smith*

The Fighting Prince of Donegal
↟ GB 1966 104m Technicolor
Walt Disney (Bill Anderson)
▦▦

Adventures of an Irish rebel in the reign of Elizabeth I.
Adequate Boys' Own Paper romp.

w Robert Westerby novel Red Hugh, Prince of Donegal by Robert T. Reilly d Michael O'Herlihy ph Arthur Ibbetson m George Bruns

☆ Peter McEnery, Susan Hampshire, Tom Adams, Gordon Jackson, Andrew Keir, Norman Wooland, Richard Leech

The Fighting Seabees
US 1944 100m bw
Republic (Albert J. Cohen)
▦▦ ▦▦

During World War II in the Pacific, construction workers attack the Japanese.
Routine, studio-staged war melodrama, heavily fleshed out with love interest.

w Borden Chase, Aeneas Mackenzie d Edward Ludwig ph William Bradford m Walter Scharf, Roy Webb

☆ John Wayne, Susan Hayward, Dennis O'Keefe, William Frawley, Duncan Renaldo, Addison Richards, Leonid Kinskey, Paul Fix

♫ Walter Scharf, Roy Webb

The Fighting Seventh: see *Little Big Horn*

Fighting Stock
GB 1935 68m bw
Gaumont/Gainsborough (Michael Balcon)

The family gets together to save a girl from a blackmailer.
Fair example of the Aldwych farces, with the trio in good form.

w Ben Travers d Tom Walls ph Phil Tannura

☆ Tom Walls, Ralph Lynn, Robertson Hare, Marie Lohr, Lesley Waring

The Fighting Sullivans: see *The Sullivans*

The Figurehead *
GB 1952 8m Technicolor

A carved saint is turned into a figurehead and can't respond when a mermaid falls in love with him.
Pleasant whimsy, one of the better jobs from this team of animators.

poem Crosbie Garstin pd John Halas, Joy Batchelor animation John Halas, Joy Batchelor

☆ Robert Beatty

Figures in a Landscape
GB 1970 110m Technicolor Panavision
Cinecrest (John Kohn)

Two men on the run are pursued by soldiers and helicopters; only one crosses the frontier.
Portentous Pinterish parable, very long-winded and relentlessly boring though good to look at. Everything is symbolic, nothing is specific, not even the country.

w Robert Shaw novel Barry England d Joseph Losey ph Henri Alekan m Richard Rodney Bennett

☆ Robert Shaw, Malcolm McDowell

Le Fil de l'Horizon: see *The Edge of the Horizon*

The File of the Golden Goose

GB   1969   109m   DeLuxe
UA/Theme/Caralan/Dador (David E. Rose)
An American agent works with Scotland Yard to track down counterfeiters.
Incredibly predictable spy thriller which almost makes an eccentricity out of collecting so many clichés and so many tourist views of London. Like ten TV episodes cut together.
w John C. Higgins, James B. Gordon d Sam Wanamaker ph Ken Hodges m Harry Robinson
☆ Yul Brynner, Edward Woodward, Charles Gray, John Barrie, Bernard Archard, Ivor Dean, Adrienne Corri, Graham Crowden, Karel Stepanek
'The film plods wearily homewards through an exceptionally uninteresting batch of fights, intrigues and sinister encounters.' – *MFB*

The File on Thelma Jordon *

US   1949   100m   bw
Paramount (Hal B. Wallis)
aka: *Thelma Jordon*
A district attorney falls for a murder suspect and has her acquitted by losing the case.
Stylishly made, murkily plotted melodrama and a superior star vehicle of its time.
w Ketti Frings d Robert Siodmak ph George Barnes m Victor Young
☆ Barbara Stanwyck, Wendell Corey, Paul Kelly, Joan Tetzel, Stanley Ridges, Richard Rober, Minor Watson, Barry Kelley

La Fille de D'Artagnan: see *D'Artagnan's Daughter*

'An Ordinary Woman. An Extraordinary Love. A Daring Adventure.'
La Fille de l'Air **

France   1992   106m   colour
Ciby 2000/TF1 (Farid Chaouche)
A woman learns to fly a helicopter so that she can help her husband to break out of a Paris prison.
An unusual romantic drama, celebrating a wife's fierce and determined love and ignoring her dubious morality and that of her friends; it is nevertheless an extraordinary story, based on fact and told with conviction.
w Florence Quentin, Maroun Bagdadi, Dan Franck book Nadine Vaujour d Maroun Bagdadi ph Thierry Arbogast m Gabriel Yared ad Michael Vandestien ed Luc Barnier
☆ Beatrice Dalle, Thierry Fortineau, Hippolyte Girardot, Roland Bertin, Jean-Claude Dreyfus, Catherine Jacob, Liliane Rovere, Jean-Paul Roussillon, Louis-Laure Mariani
'Delivers on action and suspense.' – *Variety*

La Fille du Puisatier *

France   1946   131m   bw
Marcel Pagnol
aka: *The Well-Digger's Daughter*
A stern old well-digger feels bound to send his daughter away when she becomes pregnant.
More matters than from Pagnol, this time with an East Lynne type plot getting in the way of some fine acting. Not much comedy.
wd Marcel Pagnol m Vincent Scotto
☆ Raimu, Fernandel, Charpin, Josette Day
'There is a feeling in France that such films are made for the foreigner and exploit the eccentricities of French rural life rather than the realities.' – *MFB*

Film

GB   1979   26m   Eastmancolor
BFI
No synopsis is possible for this speechless parable about a poor old man fighting (presumably) against personal obscurity, but its credits make it interesting; it was originally written for Buster Keaton.
w Samuel Beckett d David Rayner Clark ph Mike Tomlinson pd Ariane Gastambide
☆ Max Wall, Patricia Hayes

Film ohne Titel *

West Germany   1947   100m   bw
Camera Film (Erwin Gitt)
aka: *Film without Title*
Scriptwriters discuss how it is possible to make a comedy film in post-war Germany, and evolve a story with alternative endings.
Elegantly conceived but rather humourlessly executed, this interesting film was one of the first post-war German exports, but failed to start a trend. It has similarities to La Fête à Henriette and Rashomon.
w Helmut Kautner, Ellen Fechner, Rudolf Jugert d Rudolf Jugert ph Igor Oberberg m Bernard Eichhorn
☆ Hans Söhnker, Hildegarde Knef, Irene von Meyendorff, Willy Fritsch

Film without Title: see *Film ohne Titel*

Filofax: see *Taking Care of Business*

Fin Août, Début Septembre: see *Late August, Early September*

Fin de Semana para los Muertos: see *The Living Dead at the Manchester Morgue*

La Fin du Jour **

France   1939   106m   bw
Filmsonor/Regina
Tensions mount in a home for retired actors.
Fascinating opportunity for three fine actors to play off each other.
w Charles Spaak, Julien Duvivier d Julien Duvivier ph Christian Matras m Maurice Jaubert
☆ Michel Simon, Louis Jouvet, Victor Francen, Gabrielle Dorziat, Madeleine Ozeray, Sylvie

La Fin du Monde: see *End of the World*

'A psychiatrist and two beautiful sisters playing the ultimate mind game. Someone was seduced. Someone was set up. And before it was over ... someone was dead.'
'Hot-blooded passion. Cold-blooded murder.'
Final Analysis

US   1992   124m   Technicolor
Warner/Roven-Cavallo (Charles Roven, Paul Junger Witt, Anthony Thomas)
A psychiatrist begins a passionate affair with a patient's married sister, with the result that she decides she no longer wants her husband around.
Drearily derivative thriller that fails to engage the attention.
w Wesley Strick story Robert Berger, Wesley Strick d Phil Joanou ph Jordan Cronenweth m George Fenton pd Dean Tavoularis ed Thom Noble
☆ Richard Gere, Kim Basinger, Uma Thurman, Eric Roberts, Paul Guilfoyle, Keith David, Robert Harper
'A crackling good melodrama in which star power and slick surfaces are used to potent advantage.' – *Variety*
'Nothing rings very true in this slick, vacuous Hitchcockian thriller.' – *Newsday*

Final Appointment

GB   1954   61m   bw
Monarch/Unit (Francis Searle)
A reporter discovers that members of an army court-martial are being killed off one by one.
Mildly intriguing little thriller with a cast of expert character actors.
w Kenneth Hayles play *Death Keeps a Date* by Sidney Nelson, Maurice Harrison d Terence Fisher ph Jonah Jones ad C. P. Norman ed John Ferris
☆ John Bentley, Eleanor Summerfield, Hubert Gregg, Liam Redmond, Meredith Edwards, Jean Lodge, Sam Kydd, Charles Farrell, Arthur Lowe

Final Combination

US   1993   92m   Foto-Kem
Rank/Polygram/Propaganda (Steve Golin, Gregg Fienberg)
A cop tracks down an ex-boxer turned serial killer.
Mundane thriller that makes all the expected moves in a clumsy fashion.
w Larry Golin story Jonathan Tydor d Nigel Dick ph David Bridges m Rolfe Kent pd Gary Steele ed Henry Richardson, Jonathan Shaw
☆ Michael Madsen, Lisa Bonet, Gary Stretch, Damian Chapa, Tim Russ, Clarence Landry, Carmen Argenziano, Susan Byun, Alan Toy
'Dim.' – *Observer*

'Any time, any place, at any game – Samson Shillitoe can outfox them all!'
'The power of evil is no longer in the hands of a child!'
The Final Conflict

US   1981   108m   DeLuxe   Panavision
TCF/Mace Neufeld (Harvey Bernhard)
The Antichrist, now head of Thorn Industries, arranges to become US Ambassador in London.
The devil as an adult proves somehow less chilling than the devil as a child, and all the elaborate mayhem seems decidedly old hat in this sequel to The Omen and Damien: Omen II.
w Andrew Birkin d Graham Baker ph Robert Paynter, Phil Meheux m Jerry Goldsmith pd Herbert Westbrook
☆ Sam Neill, Rossano Brazzi, Don Gordon, Lisa Harrow, Mason Adams, Robert Arden
'If Armageddon is as boring as this movie, we'll need a program to tell the players.' – *Roger Ebert*

The Final Countdown *

US   1980   105m   TVC Color   Panavision
UA/Bryna (Peter Vincent Douglas)
An aircraft carrier on manoeuvres near Hawaii passes through a strange storm and finds itself back at Pearl Harbor.
Quite an enjoyable bit of schoolboy science fiction, but containing no more body than an episode of Twilight Zone. The ending, as so often, is impenetrable.
w David Ambrose, Gerry Davis, Thomas Hunter, Peter Powell d Don Taylor ph Victor J. Kemper m John Scott pd Fernando Carrere
☆ Kirk Douglas, Martin Sheen, Katharine Ross, James Farentino, Ron O'Neal, Charles Durning

'Have you ever wondered about your wife? Jude did. so he decided to find out, and now... Jude Is Dead.'
Final Cut

GB   1998   93m   colour
Downtown/Fugitive (Dominic Anciano, Ray Burdis)
Gathering at a wake for a dead actor, guests watch a video he made secretly of them indulging in drugs, sex and petty mischief.
Narcissistic, semi-improvised, trivial thriller that resembles one of those home movies, of a game of charades, that is better left unseen.
wd Dominic Anciano, Ray Burdis ph John Ward m Feelybooth, Thierry Lang pd Sabina Sattar ed Sam Sneade
☆ Ray Winstone, Sadie Frost, Jude Law, Holly Davidson, John Beckett, Mark Burdis, Perry Benson, Lisa Marsh, William Scully, Ray Burdis, Dominic Anciano
'A contrived and ultimately preposterous film, redeemed by its voracious cynicism.' – *Steve Grant, Sunday Times*
'Regrettable, self-indulgent mush that skirts the odd telling insight into the two-facedness of close friendships in favour of the worst kind of verite arse.' – *Ian Nathan, Empire*

'No Accidents. No Coincidences. No Escapes.'
'I'll See You Soon.'
Final Destination

US   2000   97m   DeLuxe
New Line (Warren Zide, Craig Perry, Glen Morgan)
After saving his friends from a plane crash in which there were no survivors, a psychic student discovers that it is difficult to cheat death.
Intriguing and gory horror that begins well but finally runs out of control.
w Glen Morgan, James Wong, Jeffrey Reddick d James Wong ph Robert McLachlan m Shirley Walker pd John Willet ed James Coblentz sp Ariel Velasco Shaw; Terry Sonderhoff
☆ Devon Sawa, Ali Larter, Kerr Smith, Kristen Cloke, Daniel Roebuck, Roger Guenveur Smith, Chad E. Donella, Seann William Scott, Tony Todd, Amanda Detmer
'As subtle as a brick, but sometimes obvious silly, shrieky fun is all you want from a film. This one will have you laughing all the way to the end.' – *Cam Winstanley, Total Film*
† Many of the characters' names derive from participants in classic horror movies, including Tod Browning, Lon Chaney, Alfred Hitchcock, Val Lewton, Max Schreck, George Waggner, and Robert Wiene.

Final Impact

US   1992   102m   Foto-Kem
PM (Richard Pepin, Joseph Merhi)
A former kick-boxing champion trains his protégé to fight the new champion.
Undistinguished action flick, with the same moves and narrative that have been seen dozens of times before.
w Stephen Smoke d Joseph Merhi, Stephen Smoke m John Gonzalez pd Richard Dearborn ed Geraint Bell, John Weidner
☆ Lorenzo Lamas, Kathleen Kinmont, Jeff Langton, Kathrin Lautner, Mike Toney, Michael Worth

The Final Option: see *Who Dares Wins*

'The future is cancelled!'
The Final Programme

GB   1973   89m   Technicolor
Goodtimes/Gladiole (John Goldstone, Sanford Lieberson)
US title: *The Last Days of Man on Earth*
In the future, when the world is torn by famine and war, a scientist awaits a new messiah.
Intellectualized sci-fi, hard to take as entertainment but very glossy.
wd Robert Fuest novel Michael Moorcock ph Norman Warwick m Paul Beaver, Bernard Krause
☆ Jon Finch, Jenny Runacre, Sterling Hayden, Hugh Griffith
'Clumsy and almost incomprehensible.' – *Sight and Sound*

The Final Test

GB   1953   90m   bw
Rank/ACT (R. J. Minney)
A cricketer looks forward to his last game but is out for a duck; he is however cheered by the crowd and comforted by his son.
Flat character study some way below the author's best style, cluttered up with real cricketers and stymied by lack of action.
w Terence Rattigan d Anthony Asquith ph Bill McLeod m Benjamin Frankel
☆ Jack Warner, Robert Morley, George Relph

Finally, Sunday *

France   1983   111m   bw
Films du Carrosse/Films A2/Soprofilms (Armand Barbault)
French title: *Vivement Dimanche*
When his friend is murdered, a small-town estate agent becomes a prime suspect.
Agreeable Hitchcock parody which goes on too long and runs out of steam.
w François Truffaut, Suzanne Schiffman, Jean Aurel novel *The Long Saturday Night* by Charles Williams d François Truffaut ph Nestor Almendros m Georges Delerue pd Hilton McConnico
☆ Fanny Ardant, Jean-Louis Trintignant, Philippe Laudenbach, Caroline Sihol
'Devoid of interest or distinction, a comedy-thriller that is not funny and most emphatically not thrilling. Ardant and Trintignant fancy themselves as Carole Lombard and Fredric March, an illusion not likely to be shared by anyone else...' – *Gilbert Adair, MFB*

Find the Blackmailer

US   1943   55m   bw
Warner
A private eye seeks a talking crow which may have evidence in a murder case.
Modest mystery filler.
w Robert E. Kent story G. E. Fleming-Roberts d D. Ross Lederman
☆ Jerome Cowan, Faye Emerson, Gene Lockhart, Marjorie Hoshelle, Robert Kent

Find the Lady

Canada/GB   1976   79m   colour   Panavision
Quadrant/Impact (Gerald Flint-Shipman, David Main, John Trent)
aka: *Call the Cops!*
aka: *Kopek and Broom*
Two incompetent cops go on the track of two bumbling crooks.
Coarse slapstick comedy that yields very few laughs.

🏵 film suitable for family viewing   📼 VHS video-cassette for the British PAL system   📼 VHS video-cassette for the British PAL system in wide screen-format   ♱ Video cassette in a computer-colourised version   ▦ American NTSC video-cassette   ◉ Laser disc

w David Main, John Trent d John Trent
ph Harry Waxman m Robert Sharples pd Karen Bromley ed Al Gell
☆ Lawrence Dane, John Candy, Dick Emery, Mickey Rooney, Peter Cook, Alexandra Bastedo, Richard Monette, Bob Vinci, Ed McNamara, Tim Henry

Finders Keepers
GB 1966 94m Eastmancolor
UA/Interstate (George H. Brown)
The Americans lose an atomic bomb off the Spanish coast, and it's found by a pop group.
Harmless youth musical without much style. Tunes poor, comedy rather too easy-going.
w Michael Pertwee d Sidney Hayers ph Alan Hume m The Shadows, Norrie Paramor
☆ Cliff Richard, The Shadows, Robert Morley, Peggy Mount, Viviane Ventura, Graham Stark, John Le Mesurier, Robert Hutton

Finders Keepers
US 1984 96m Technicolor
CBS (Sandra Marsh, Terence Marsh)
On a train from California to New York, various factions try to grab stolen money hidden in a coffin.
Yawnworthy comedy-thriller with a zany streak; all the elements have been better done in other movies.
w Ronny Graham, Charles Dennis, Terence Marsh novel The Next to Last Train Ride by Charles Dennis d Richard Lester ph Brian West m Ken Thorne pd Terence Marsh
☆ Michael O'Keefe, Beverly D'Angelo, Lou Gossett Jnr, Pamela Stephenson, Ed Lauter, David Wayne, Brian Dennehy, John Schuck

Finders Keepers, Lovers Weepers!
US 1968 71m Eastmancolor
Eve (Russ Meyer)
A brothel-keeper organizes the robbery of a club belonging to one of her lovers.
Typical Meyer fare, in which larger-breasted women get the better of less virile men, and a bad time is had by all.
w Richard Zachary story Russ Meyer d Russ Meyer ph Russ Meyer md Igor Kantor ed Russ Meyer, Richard Brummer
☆ Anne Chapman, Paul Lockwood, Gordon Westcourt, Duncan McLeod, Robert Rudelson, Lavelle Roby

'Not your ordinary fairy tale.'
Finding North
US 1997 95m colour
Millivres/SoNo (Steven A. Jones, Stephen Dyer)
A gay man, grieving over the death from AIDS of his lover, forms a friendship with a lonely woman looking for love.
Slight sentimental tale of a self-obsessed man finding an unlikely redemption.
w Kim Powers d Tanya Wexler ph Michael Barrett m Café Noir pd James B. Smythe ed Thom Zimny
☆ Wendy Makkena, John Benjamin Hickey, Anne Bobby, Rebecca Creskoff, Angela Pietropinto, Freddie Roman, Molly McClure
'It glibly uses gay men's experience of bereavement as an easy passport to the touchy-feely values of empathy.' – Peter Bradshaw, Guardian

Fine and Dandy: see West Point Story

A Fine Madness *
US 1966 104m Technicolor
Warner Seven Arts (Jerome Hellman)
A frustrated New York poet has outbursts of violence.
Patchy, interesting, with-it comedy which suffers from too many changes of mood.
w Elliott Baker novel Elliott Baker d Irvin Kershner ph Ted McCord m John Addison
☆ Sean Connery, Jean Seberg, Joanne Woodward, Patrick O'Neal, Colleen Dewhurst, Clive Revill
'Straddling a no man's land somewhere between the nouvelle vague and the crazy comedies of Old Hollywood.' – Tom Milne

A Fine Mess
US 1985 88m DeLuxe Panavision
Columbia/BEE/Delphi V (Tony Adams)
Two private eyes who accidentally know too much are chased by gangsters.
Not enough plot for a feature, and not enough comedy talent for a comedy, despite the dedication to Laurel and Hardy.
wd Blake Edwards ph Harry Stradling m Henry Mancini pd Rodger Maus ed John F. Burnett
☆ Ted Danson, Howie Mandel, Richard Mulligan, Stuart Margolin, Paul Sorvino
'Word of mouth is unlikely to be favourable … mechanically contrived funny business, most of which falls pretty flat.' – Variety
'The plot needn't be the thing, but then the gags and setpieces aren't much either.' – Sight and Sound

A Fine Pair
Italy 1968 115m Technicolor Panavision
Vides (Franco Cristaldi)
original title: Ruba al Prossimo Tua
A New York detective falls for an Italian girl jewel thief.
Tedious, meandering comedy-thriller with nothing to offer apart from a good robbery sequence.
w Francesco Maselli, Luisa Montagnana, Larry Gelbart, Virgil C. Leone d Francesco Maselli ph Alfio Contino m Ennio Morricone
☆ Rock Hudson, Claudia Cardinale, Tomas Milian, Leon Askin, Ellen Corby

The Finest Hour
US 1991 105m colour
21st Century (Menahem Golan)
Two tough Navy SEALS, who are rivals for the same woman, are sent on a dangerous assignment in the Gulf War.
Gung-ho tedium, full of noisy, macho posturing.
w Shimon Dotan, Stuart Schoffman d Shimon Dotan ph Avi Karpik m Walter Christian Rothe pd Avi Avivi ed Netaya Anbar, Bob Ducsay
☆ Rob Lowe, Gale Hansen, Tracy Griffith, Eb Lottimer
'Just ignore the boisterous propaganda, suspend disbelief and enjoy the roller-coaster ride.' – Empire

The Finest Hours *
GB 1964 116m Technicolor
(Jack Le Vien)
The life of Winston Churchill is built up from newsreels plus a few feature film clips and some original location shooting.
Generally excellent documentary, a handy introduction to Churchill's own writing and rather more entertaining than the later Young Winston.
w Victor Wolfson d Peter Baylis
⚜ best documentary

Finger of Guilt: see The Intimate Stranger

The Finger Points
US 1931 88m bw
Warner
A crime reporter succumbs to pressures from the underworld.
Humourless and low-geared exposé-style melodrama.
w John Monk Saunders, W. R. Burnett, Robert Lord d John Francis Dillon
☆ Richard Barthelmess, Clark Gable, Fay Wray, Regis Toomey

Fingers *
US 1977 90m Technicolor
Gala/Brut (George Barrie)
A would-be concert pianist gets involved with his father's gangster friends, and violence results.
Lively and interesting skirmish with an overworked and essentially downbeat subject.
wd James Toback ph Mike Chapman pd Gene Rudolf ed Robert Lawrence
☆ Harvey Keitel, Tisa Farrow, Jim Brown, Marian Seldes, Danny Aiello

Fingers at the Window
US 1942 90m bw
MGM (Irving Asher)
A stage magician hypnotizes lunatics into murdering all those who stand between him and an inheritance.

Slow-starting thriller which never achieves top gear.
w Rose Caylor, Lawrence P. Bachmann d Charles Lederer ph Harry Stradling, Charles Lawton m Bronislau Kaper
☆ Basil Rathbone, Lew Ayres, Laraine Day, Walter Kingsford, Miles Mander, Russell Gleason
'The kind of picture actors do when they need work.' – Lew Ayres

Finian's Rainbow *
US 1968 140m Technicolor
Panavision 70
Warner Seven Arts (Joseph Landon)
A leprechaun tries to retrieve a crock of gold from an old wanderer who has taken it to America.
Musical whimsy-whamsy, a long way after a 1947 Broadway success; in this overlong and overblown screen version the elements and the style do not jell and there is too much sentimental chat, but moments of magic shine through.
w E. Y. Harburg, Fred Saidy play E. Y. Harburg, Fred Saidy d Francis Ford Coppola m/ly Burton Lane, E. Y. Harburg md Ray Heindorf pd Hilyard M. Brown
☆ Fred Astaire, Petula Clark, Tommy Steele, Don Francks, Keenan Wynn, Barbara Hancock, Al Freeman Jnr
♫ Ray Heindorf

Finis Terrae *
France 1929 90m bw silent
Société Générale des Films
A re-enacted account of the lives of fishermen on remote Brittany islands.
A feature documentary which was impressive at the time; very similar to Flaherty's Man of Aran.
wd Jean Epstein ph Joseph Barth, Joseph Kottula

Finishing School
US 1934 73m bw
RKO (Kenneth MacGowan)
A girl at an exclusive school falls for an intern.
Modest pap for the teenage audience.
w Wanda Tuchock, Laird Doyle d George Nicholls Jnr ph J. Roy Hunt m Max Steiner
☆ Frances Dee, Ginger Rogers, Billie Burke, Bruce Cabot, John Halliday, Beulah Bondi, Sara Haden

The Finishing Touch *
US 1928 20m bw silent
Hal Roach
Stan and Ollie accidentally destroy the house they are building.
Excellent early star slapstick with predictable but enjoyable gags.
w H. M. Walker d Clyde Bruckman ph George Stevens ed Richard Currier
☆ Stan Laurel, Oliver Hardy, Edgar Kennedy, Dorothy Coburn

Finn and Hattie
US 1930 77m bw
Paramount
A newly rich American takes his family to Paris.
Dodsworth-like comedy, fairly well regarded in its time but now looking very thin.
w Sam Mintz, Joseph L. Mankiewicz story Donald Ogden Stewart d Norman Taurog, Norman McLeod
☆ Leon Errol, ZaSu Pitts, Mitzi Green, Jackie Searl, Regis Toomey, Lilyan Tashman

Finyé: see The Wind

Fiorile **
Italy/France/Germany 1993 122m colour
Arrow/Filmtre-Gierre/Pemnta/Flordia/La Sept/Canal/Roxy/KS (Grazia Volpi, Jean-Claude Cecile, Luggi Waldleitner, Karl Spiehs)
On a car journey, a father tells his children the story of a curse on the family that began more than two hundred years before, when their peasant forebears became rich with the theft of a chest of gold belonging to Napoleon's army.
A compelling tale of unfulfilled love and political expediency, and of past events influencing the future, delivered by master storytellers.
w Sandro Petraglia, Paolo and Vittorio Taviani d Paolo and Vittorio Taviani ph Giuseppe Lanci m Nicola Piovani ad Gianni Sbarra ed Roberto Perpignani
☆ Claudio Bigagli, Galatea Ranzi, Michael Vartan, Renato Carpentieri, Lino Capolicchio,

Costanze Engelbrecht, Chiara Caselli, Athina Cenci
'Remains worth seeing, as an example of how it is still possible to make a film that means to do no more than just entertain. I wish I could say, however, that it was more like the best of the Tavianis' work than it actually is.' – Derek Malcolm, Guardian

Fire and Ice
US 1982 82m colour
Fox/PSO (Ralph Bakshi, Frank Frazetta)
Evil Lord Nekron uses black magic to subdue the good King Jarol.
Fair cartoon feature, using rotoscoping, in the mould of Conan the Barbarian.
w Roy Thomas, Gerry Conway d Ralph Bakshi m William Kraft ed E. Davis Marshall
☆ Featuring the voices of Susan Tyrrell, Maggie Rosewell, William Ostrander, Stephen Mendel, Clare Nono, Alan Koss

'Three of the biggest in one of the best!'
Fire Down Below
GB 1957 116m Technicolor Cinemascope
Columbia/Warwick (Irving Allen, Albert Broccoli)
Partners in a Caribbean fishing and smuggling business fall out over a woman.
Overheated melodrama with thin characters, predictable incident and ill-advised casting.
w Irwin Shaw novel Max Catto d Robert Parrish ph Desmond Dickinson m Arthur Benjamin
☆ Rita Hayworth, Robert Mitchum, Jack Lemmon, Herbert Lom, Bonar Colleano, Bernard Lee, Edric Connor, Peter Illing
'A fast-paced adventure yarn laced around a taut interlude of high drama.' – Time

Fire Down Below
US 1997 105m Technicolor
Warner (Steven Seagal, Julius Nasso)
An environmental protection agent investigates the dumping of toxic waste in the Kentucky hills.
Self-regarding action movie with moments of moralizing; neither makes much impact.
w Jeb Stuart d Felix Enriquez Alcala ph Tom Houghton m Nick Glennie-Smith pd Joe Alves ed Robert A. Ferretti
☆ Steven Seagal, Marg Helgenberger, Harry Dean Stanton, Stephen Lang, Kris Kristofferson, Levon Helm, Ed Bruce, Richard Masur
'Slick, shallow good-guy/bad-guy stuff interrupted from time to time with some ill-conceived sermonizing. It tries hard to generate heat but is actually no more substantive than a puff of smoke.' – Leonard Klady, Variety

Fire Festival
Japan 1985 120m Eastmancolor
Recorded Releasing/Gunro/Seibu/Cine Saison (Kazuo Shimizu)
original title: Himatsuri
A nature-loving lumberjack turns killer after observing the effects of pollution on the locality.
Fairly impenetrable to Western audiences, despite its ecological message.
w Kanji Nakagami d Mitsuo Yanagimachi ph Masaki Tamura m Toru Takemitsu ad Takeo Kimura ed Sachiko Yamaji
☆ Kinya Kitaoji, Kiwako Taichi, Ryota Nakamoto, Norihei Miki, Rikiya Yasuoka, Seiji Kurasaki, Maiko Kawakami

A Fire Has Been Arranged
GB 1935 70m bw
Twickenham (Julius Hagen)
Ex-convicts find a building in the field where they buried the loot.
Modest star comedy. Was this the first use of this well-worn plot?
w H. Fowler Mear, Michael Barringer, James Carter d Leslie Hiscott ph Sydney Blythe
☆ Bud Flanagan, Chesney Allen, Alastair Sim, Robb Wilton, Mary Lawson, Harold French, C. Denier Warren
'Is meant to be funny and is very, very dreary.' – Graham Greene

Fire in the Sky
US 1993 109m DeLuxe Panavision
Paramount (Joe Wizan, Todd Black)
📼 📼 ⊞ 🔎

A lumberjack is suspected of murder when a friend goes to investigate a flying saucer and disappears.
A close encounter of the boring kind, in which small-town values are made to seem even more alien than tadpoles from outer space.
w Tracy Tormé book *The Walton Experience* by Travis Walton d Robert Lieberman ph Bill Pope m Mark Isham pd Laurence Bennett ed Steve Mirkovich sp Industrial Light and Magic
☆ D. B. Sweeney, Robert Patrick, Craig Sheffer, Peter Berg, Henry Thomas, Bradley Gregg, Noble Willingham, James Garner
'This unappealing pic is likely to attract only a few curiosity seekers.' – *Variety*

The Fire in the Stone
👫👫 Australia 1983 100m colour
South Australian Film Corp (Pamela H. Vanneck)
A teenager foils a murderer, finds some opals and re-unites his parents.
Unexceptional and undemanding entertainment.
w Graeme Koetsveld novel Colin Thiele d Gary Conway ph Ross Berryman m Garry and Anita Hardman ad Derek Mills ed Philip Reid
☆ Alan Cassell, Paul Smith, Ray Meagher, Linda Hartley, Leo Taylor, Andrew Gaston, Theo Pertsinidis

'A world of women seeking male partners to carry on their race!'
Fire Maidens from Outer Space
GB 1956 80m bw
Criterion Films/Eros (George Fowler)
📼
Space explorers find that the thirteenth moon of Jupiter is inhabited solely by sixteen beautiful girls and an aged patriarch.
A strong contender for the title of worst movie ever made, with diaphanously clad English gals striking embarrassed poses against cardboard sets. Must be seen to be believed.
wd Cy Roth ph Ian Struthers
☆ Susan Shaw, Anthony Dexter, Harry Fowler, Sydney Tafler, Owen Berry, Paul Carpenter
'Even the most dedicated connoisseurs of the artless are likely to find this something of a strain on their patience.' – *MFB*

Fire over Africa: see *Malaga*

Fire over England ***
GB 1937 92m bw
London Films/Pendennis (Erich Pommer)
📼 📼 🔎
Elizabeth I and her navy overcome the Spanish Armada.
Though the film has a faded air and the action climax was always a bath-tub affair, the splendid cast keeps this pageant afloat and interesting.
w Clemence Dane, Sergei Nolbandov novel A. E. W, Mason d William K. Howard ph James Wong Howe m Richard Addinsell ad Lazare Meerson, Frank Wells ed Jack Dennis
☆ Flora Robson, Laurence Olivier, Leslie Banks, Vivien Leigh, Raymond Massey, Tamara Desni, Morton Selten, Lyn Harding, James Mason
'Should bring much artistic acclaim but, outside of the urban class spots, business will be stubborn … if it had marquee strength it would stand an excellent chance.' – *Variety*
'Pommer and Howard have done one remarkable thing: they have caught the very spirit of an English public schoolmistress's vision of history.' – *Graham Greene*
'Swashbuckling nonsense, but with a fine spirit.' – *Pauline Kael, 70s*

Fire over Rome
Italy 1968 94m colour
GMC (Giorgio Marzelli)
original title: *L'incendio di Roma*
aka: *Revenge of the Gladiators*
A Roman consul defies Nero's order to massacre Christians.
One of Italy's interminable gladiatorial epics of the period, consisting mainly of a series of sword fights, although Jesus gets a walk-on role right at the end.
d Guido Malatesta ph Aldo Greci ad Oscar D'Amico ed Enzo Alfonsi
☆ Lang Jeffries, Cristina Gaioni, Moira Orfei, Mario Feliciani, Luciano Marin, Evi Maltagliati

Fire Sale *
US 1977 88m DeLuxe
TCF (Marvin Worth)
Misadventures of a frantic, eccentric New York-Jewish family who own a department store.
Frenzied black farce for ethnic audiences.
w Robert Klane novel Robert Klane d Alan Arkin ph Ralph Woolsey m Dave Grusin
☆ Alan Arkin, Rob Reiner, Vincent Gardenia, Anjanette Comer, Kay Medford, Sid Caesar, Alex Rocco
'It moves fast enough to carry the occasional lapses from its own high standards of tastelessness.' – *Jan Dawson, MFB*

Fire with Fire
US 1986 103m Metrocolor
Paramount (Gary Nardino)
📼 📼
aka: *Captive Hearts*
A girl at an expensive Catholic boarding school falls in love with a boy at a nearby parole camp.
Sluggish teen romance that not even its melodramatic finale can save.
w Bill Phillips, Warren Skaaren, Paul and Sharon Boorstin d Duncan Gibbins ph Hiro Narita m Howard Shore pd Norman Newberry ed Peter E. Berger
☆ Virginia Madsen, Craig Sheffer, Kate Reid, Jeffrey Jay Cohen, Jon Polito, Jean Smart, David Harris

The Fire Within: see *Le Feu Follet*

The Fireball
US 1950 84m bw
Thor/TCF
A juvenile delinquent becomes a ruthless roller-skating champion.
Predictable and unattractive star character drama with sporting asides.
w Tay Garnett, Horace McCoy d Tay Garnett ph Lester White m Victor Young
☆ Mickey Rooney, Pat O'Brien, Beverly Tyler, Glenn Corbett

The Firebird
US 1934 75m bw
Warner
An actor with the reputation of a Lothario is murdered.
Well cast but rather disappointing murder mystery.
w Charles Kenyon play Lajos Zilahy d William Dieterle
☆ Verree Teasdale, Ricardo Cortez, Lionel Atwill, C. Aubrey Smith, Anita Louise, Dorothy Tree, Hobart Cavanaugh
'Padding in late reels keeps it from ace rating.' – *Variety*

Firecreek
US 1967 104m Technicolor Panavision
Warner Seven Arts (Philip Leacock)
The people of Firecreek protect themselves from wandering gunmen.
Dour, predictable little Western which does not show its stars at their best.
w Calvin Clements d Vincent McEveety ph William Clothier m Alfred Newman
☆ James Stewart, Henry Fonda, Inger Stevens, Gary Lockwood, Dean Jagger, Ed Begley, Jay C. Flippen, Jack Elam, James Best, Barbara Luna
'This cramped and clumsy western grinds to a standstill in its attempts to give Firecreek symbolic status … while the gunmen roister like mad and the townsfolk rhubarb glumly in the background.' – *MFB*

Fired Wife
US 1943 75m bw
Universal
A radio actress has to keep her marriage a secret in order to preserve her job.
Decidedly humdrum comedy.
w Michael Fessier, Ernest Pagano d Charles Lamont
☆ Louise Allbritton, Diana Barrymore, Robert Paige, Walter Abel, George Dolenz, Walter Catlett, Ernest Truex, Rex Ingram, Richard Lane

'It will make 1937 remembered always as the year of the first romantic dramatic musical film!'
The Firefly *
US 1937 131m bw
MGM (Hunt Stromberg)
📼
Adventures of a Spanish lady spy during the Napoleonic war.
Solid production of a romantic operetta; splendid stuff for connoisseurs.
w Frances Goodrich, Albert Hackett, Ogden Nash original book/ly Otto Harbach d Robert Z. Leonard ph Oliver Marsh m/ly Rudolf Friml, Otto Harbach, Gus Kahn md Herbert Stothart ch Albertina Rasch
☆ Jeanette MacDonald, Allan Jones, Warren William, Billy Gilbert, Henry Daniell, George Zucco, Douglass Dumbrille
'The sepia tint is monotonous … the length will seriously militate against popularity.' – *Variety*
'A lavish musical monstrosity.' – *New Yorker, 1978*
'The musical film par excellence … resplendent and gorgeous.' – *Evening News*
🎵 Love is Like a Firefly; The donkey Serenade; Giannina Mia; He Who Loves and Runs Away; Sympathy; When a Maid Comes Knocking at Your Heart

Firefox
US 1982 136m DeLuxe Panavision
Warner/Malpaso (Clint Eastwood)
📼 📼 🔎
An American pilot is disguised as a businessman and sent to Moscow to steal a new supersonic Soviet fighter.
Dreary melodrama with doleful acting and very little action or suspense.
w Alex Lasker, Wendell Willman novel Craig Thomas d Clint Eastwood ph Bruce Surtees m Maurice Jarre sp John Dykstra
☆ Clint Eastwood, Freddie Jones, David Huffman, Warren Clarke, Ronald Lacey, Kenneth Colley, Nigel Hawthorne
'What is most curious about this farrago is that Eastwood, the actor and the director, should have walked through it all with scarcely a thought for each other.' – *Richard Combs, MFB*
'Despite the tense mission being depicted, there's no suspense, excitement or thrills to be had, and lackadaisical pacing gives the viewer plenty of time to ponder the gaping implausibilities that skilful execution could have rendered irrelevant.' – *Variety*
'Immensely long, unfailingly dull, and not even silly enough to be funny.' – *Sunday Times*

'Passion has no limits.'
Firelight
US/GB 1997 103m colour 'Scope
Miramax/Capitol/Wind Dancer/Carnival (Brian Eastman)
📼 📼 🔎
In the 1840s, a Swiss governess goes in search of the child she had by an English aristocrat.
Unconvincing romantic melodrama, a poor man's Jane Eyre.
wd William Nicholson ph Nic Morris m Christopher Gunning pd Rob Harris ed Chris Wimble
☆ Sophie Marceau, Stephen Dillane, Kevin Anderson, Joss Ackland, Lia Williams, Dominique Belcourt
'First time director and veteran screenwriter never puts a foot wrong in this powerful and moving story of forbidden love and all-consuming passion.' – *Nick Briggs, Film Review*

Fireman Save My Child
US 1932 67m bw
Warner/First National
A fireman is more interested in baseball but becomes a hero all the same.
Thin star comedy.
w Ray Enright, Robert Lord, Arthur Caesar d Lloyd Bacon
☆ Joe E. Brown, Evalyn Knapp, Lillian Bond, Guy Kibbee

Fireman Save My Child
👫👫 US 1954 80m bw
U-I (Howard Christie)
In 1910 San Francisco, incompetent firemen accidentally catch a gang of crooks.

Slapstick farce intended for Abbott and Costello, taken over by a new team which did not catch on, played like the Keystone Kops. Mildly funny during the chases.
w Lee Loeb, John Grant d Leslie Goodwins ph Clifford Stine m Joseph Gershenson
☆ Buddy Hackett, Spike Jones and the City Slickers, Hugh O'Brian, Adèle Jergens

The Firemen's Ball *
Czechoslovakia/Italy 1967 73m Eastmancolor
Barrandov/Carlo Ponti
📼 📼 🔎
original title: *Hori, Ma Panenko*
In a small provincial town, arrangements for the firemen's annual ball go wrong at every turn.
Vaguely amusing Tati-esque comedy with not quite enough funny moments and a prevailing atmosphere of pessimism.
w Milos Forman, Ivan Passer, Jaroslav Papousek d Milos Forman ph Miroslav Ondricek m Karel Mares
☆ Jan Vostrcil, Josef Kolb, Josef Svet, Frantisek Debelka
'A compendium of superb items.' – *Philip Strick*
🏅 best foreign film

Firepower
GB 1979 104m Technicolor
ITC/Michael Winner
📼 📼
A chemist about to expose contaminated drugs is murdered; his widow persuades the US Justice Department to hire her ex-lover, a gangster, to track down his killers.
Globe-trotting kaleidoscope of the familiar patterns of violence; tolerable for those who haven't been here a hundred times before.
w Gerald Wilson d Michael Winner ph Robert Paynter, Dick Kratina m Gato Barbieri md Jay Chattaway pd John Blezard, Robert Gundlach ed Arnold Crust
☆ Sophia Loren, James Coburn, Anthony Franciosa, O. J. Simpson, Eli Wallach, George Grizzard, Vincent Gardenia, Victor Mature
'The nearest thing yet to film-making by numbers, with identikit characters jet-setting across a travel brochure landscape to an orchestration of gunfire, car smashes and colourful explosions.' – *Clyde Jeavons, MFB*

Fires on the Plain **
Japan 1959 108m bw
Daiei (Masaichi Nagata)
📼
original title: *Nobi*
In the Philippines during World War II, a half-demented Japanese private takes to the hills, becomes a cannibal, and is shot by the Americans when he tries to surrender.
Stomach-turning anti-war epic with fine scenes and performances but dubious intent.
w Natto Wada novel Shohei O-oka d Kon Ichikawa ph Setsuo Kobayashi m Yasushi Akatagawa
☆ Eiji Funakoshi, Osamu Takizawa, Micky Curtis

Fires Were Started **
GB 1943 63m bw
Crown Film Unit (Ian Dalrymple)
aka: *I Was a Fireman*
One day and night in the life of a National Fire Service unit during the London blitz.
Thoughtful, slow-moving, poetic documentary originally intended as a training film but generally released to boost morale. Not its director's finest work, but perhaps his most ambitious.
wd Humphrey Jennings ph C. Pennington-Richards m William Alwyn
'An astonishingly intimate portrait of an isolated and besieged Britain … an … unforgettable piece of human observation, affectionate, touching, and yet ironic.' – *Georges Sadoul*
'It transforms its observation into a personal, epic celebration of the courage and dignity of ordinary people in times of stress.' – *Time Out, 1984*
† The firemen were real firemen, but the scenes were re-enacted.

Fires Within
US 1991 87m colour Panavision
MGM/Pathé (Wallis Nicita, Lauren Lloyd)
📼 📼 🔎
In Miami, a Cuban woman is forced to choose between her husband, returning to her after eight

years as a political prisoner, and the man she has come to love.

Lacklustre drama, mixing romance and politics, but with little conviction; the emphasis is on local colour and music.

w Cynthia Cidre d Gillian Armstrong ph David Gribble m Maurice Jarre pd Robert Ziembicki ed John Scott

☆ Jimmy Smits, Greta Scacchi, Vincent D'Onofrio, Luis Avalos, Bertila Damas, Raul Davila

'A cold narrative that never lingers on any situation long enough to generate either suspense or romance.' – *Variety*

Firestarter
US 1984 114m Technicolor
Universal (Frank Capra Jnr)
A young girl is capable of starting fires by pyrokinesis, and the government wants to use her as a weapon.

Complicated and dislikeable piece of political science fiction.

w Stanley Mann novel Stephen King d Mark L. Lester ph Giuseppe Ruzzolini m Tangerine Dream

☆ Drew Barrymore, George C. Scott, David Keith, Martin Sheen, Freddie Jones, Heather Locklear, Art Carney, Louise Fletcher, Moses Gunn

'The most astonishing thing in the movie is how boring it is.' – *Roger Ebert*

Firestorm
US 1998 89m DeLuxe
TCF (Joseph Loeb III, Matthew Weisman, Thomas H. Hammel)
A fire-fighter is parachuted into a forest to fight a blaze set by a group of hardened criminals in order to break out of prison.

A lacklustre thriller, which tries in vain to breathe a little life into disaster movies.

w Chris Soth d Dean Semler ph Stephen F. Windon m J. Peter Robinson pd Richard Paris, Linda del Rosario ed Jack Hofstra

☆ Howie Long, Scott Glenn, William Forsythe, Suzy Amis, Christianne Hirt, Garwin Sanford, Sebastian Spence

'A half-baked B movie.' – *Variety*

Firewalker
US 1986 104m TVC Color
Cannon (Menahem Golan, Yoram Globus)
Adventurers seek gold in an Aztec temple.

Old hat heroics and violence in the wake of Raiders of the Lost Ark. Not a happy outcome.

w Robert Gosnell d J. Lee-Thompson ph Alex Phillips m Gary Chang pd Jos Rodriguez ed Richard Marx

☆ Chuck Norris, Lou Gossett Jnr, Melody Anderson, John Rhys-Davies, Will Sampson

The Firm *
US 1993 154m DeLuxe
Paramount (Sydney Pollack, Scott Rudin, John Davis)
A bright young lawyer finds himself trapped between becoming an informant for the FBI and being killed by the ruthless Mafia gangsters who control his firm.

An attention-holding thriller for the most part, though its conclusion, diverging from the tougher stance of the novel, is unsatisfactory.

w David Rabe, Robert Towne, David Rayfiel novel John Grisham d Sydney Pollack ph John Seale m David Grusin pd Richard Macdonald ed William Steinkamp, Frederic Steinkamp

☆ Tom Cruise, Jeanne Tripplehorn, Gene Hackman, Hal Holbrook, Terry Kinney, Wilford Brimley, Ed Harris, Holly Hunter, David Strathairn, Gary Busey, Steven Hill, Tobin Bell

'A vacuous upper-middle-class success story about a fresh-faced lad outwitting both sides of the law while securing wealth and safety for his family.' – *Michael Sragow, New Yorker*

'There is sufficient conviction from everyone before and behind the camera to provide an absorbing, pulpy, old-fashioned movie experience.' – *Variety*

♫ Holly Hunter; Dave Grusin

First a Girl
GB 1935 94m bw
Gaumont (Michael Balcon)
A messenger girl attracts attention by posing as a boy, and becomes a star.

Moderate light star vehicle.

w Marjorie Gaffney play Viktor und Viktoria by Reinhold Schunzel d Victor Saville ph Glen MacWilliams md Louis Levy ad Oscar Werndorff ed Al Barnes

☆ Jessie Matthews, Sonnie Hale, Griffith Jones, Anna Lee, Alfred Drayton, Martita Hunt, Eddie Gray

† Julie Andrews starred in a remake entitled *Victor/Victoria* in 1982.

The First and the Last: see *Twenty-One Days*

First Blood
US 1982 94m Technicolor Panavision
Carolco (Buzz Feitshans)
A former Green Beret gets into trouble in a small Californian community and sets himself against the forces of law.

Pure blood and thunder with some decent action sequences.

w Michael Kozoll, William Sackheim, Sylvester Stallone novel David Morell d Ted Kotcheff ph Andrew Laszlo m Jerry Goldsmith

☆ Sylvester Stallone, Richard Crenna, Brian Dennehy, David Caruso, Jack Starrett

'Socially irresponsible … there are enough nuts out there without giving them a hero to cheer for.' – *Variety*

† It was followed by two sequels: *Rambo: First Blood II* and *Rambo III*.

First Comes Courage
US 1943 88m bw
Columbia (Harry Joe Brown)
During World War II, a Norwegian girl appears to be a Quisling but is really a spy getting information from the Nazis by fraternizing with them.

Doleful war drama with little to commend it except propaganda.

w Lewis Meltzer, Melvin Levy novel The Commandos by Elliott Arnold d Dorothy Arzner ph Joseph Walker m Ernst Toch

☆ Merle Oberon, Brian Aherne, Carl Esmond, Fritz Leiber, Erik Rolf, Reinhold Schunzel, Isobel Elsom

'When we see a beautiful women being shunned by her fellow-townsmen in Norway we know that because we are film-goers and we are familiar with that look of acute self-sacrifice and abnegation accompanying the exquisitely designed clothes and perfect make-up and because she is Merle Oberon.' – *Richard Winnington*

The First Deadly Sin
US 1980 112m TVC Color
Filmways/Artanis/Cinema Seven (Elliott Kastner)
A police lieutenant tracks down a homicidal lunatic but is unable to save his own wife who is dying in hospital from an obscure ailment.

The two halves of this depressing cop show don't seem to relate, and it offers little in the way of entertainment value beyond the traditional tracking down of the murderer.

w Mann Rubin novel Lawrence Sanders d Brian G. Hutton ph Jack Priestley m Gordon Jenkins

☆ Frank Sinatra, Faye Dunaway, David Dukes, George Coe, Brenda Vaccaro, Martin Gabel, Anthony Zerbe, James Whitmore

'An odd collection of pretensions seem to be rattling round in an overlength TV film.' – *Mark Lefanu, MFB*

'Mystery without meaning, despite a froth of intercutting and religious iconography.' – *Sight and Sound*

The First Gentleman
GB 1948 111m bw
Columbia (Joseph Friedman)
US title: *Affairs of a Rogue*
The affairs and foibles of the Prince Regent.

Dullish adaptation of a successful West End play about 18th-century court life; script and performances still entertain.

w Nicholas Phipps, Reginald Long play Norman Ginsbury d Cavalcanti ph Jack Hildyard

☆ Cecil Parker, Jean-Pierre Aumont, Joan Hopkins, Margaretta Scott, Jack Livesey, Ronald Squire, Athene Seyler, Hugh Griffith

The First Great Train Robbery *
GB 1978 108m Technicolor Panavision
UA/Starling (John Foreman)
US title: *The Great Train Robbery*
In 1855, an elegant but ruthless crook picks out a gang to help him rob the Folkestone express of gold bullion.

Patchy but generally very likeable period crime story, with just a few lapses of pace and taste.

wd Michael Crichton novel Michael Crichton ph Geoffrey Unsworth m Jerry Goldsmith pd Maurice Carter

☆ Sean Connery, Donald Sutherland, Lesley-Anne Down, Alan Webb, Robert Lang, Malcolm Terris

'My dream was that the historical world was going to be lovingly recreated, and then I was going to shoot *The French Connection* inside it.' – *Michael Crichton*

The First Hundred Years
US 1938 75m bw
MGM
A self-supporting wife is reluctant to give up her career.

Tolerable matrimonial comedy resolved by pregnancy.

w Melville Baker story Norman Krasna d Richard Thorpe

☆ Robert Montgomery, Virginia Bruce, Warren William, Binnie Barnes, Alan Dinehart, Harry Davenport, Nydia Westman

First Kid
US 1996 101m Continental Color
Buena Vista/Walt Disney/Caravan (Roger Birnbaum, Riley Kathryn Ellis)
An agent is given the task of guarding the US President's bored teenage son.

Occasionally amusing, sentimental comedy of the bonding of two misfits.

w Tim Kelleher d David Mickey Evans ph Anthony Richmond m Richard Gibbs pd Chester Kaczenski ed Harry Keramidas

☆ Sinbad, Robert Guillaume, Timothy Busfield, Brock Pierce, Blake Boyd, Art La Fleur, Lisa Eichhorn, James Naughton

'The film has a lot of heart and humor.' – *Variety*

'Their greatest battle would be for her love.'
First Knight
US 1995 134m Technicolor
Columbia/Zucker Brothers (Jerry Zucker, Hunt Lowry)
Guinevere marries King Arthur to protect her lands and finds herself torn between her love for Lancelot and her respect for her husband.

This is less the medieval epic it attempts to be, and closer in spirit to A Yankee in King Arthur's Court, thanks to Gere's American gigolo masquerading as Lancelot; it lacks passion and there is no feeling that anything is worth fighting or dying for.

w William Nicholson d Jerry Zucker ph Adam Greenberg m Jerry Goldsmith pd John Box ed Walter Murch

☆ Sean Connery, Richard Gere, Julia Ormond, Ben Cross, Liam Cunningham, Christopher Villiers, Valentine Pelka, John Gielgud

'It is not often that the genuine Hollywood vulgarian adds a new chapter to our national heritage. The event should be commemorated somehow. But I do not believe this will be achieved at the historic site called a box-office.' – *Alexander Walker, London Evening Standard*

'May look impressive on the surface; inside it is a mediocrity de luxe.' – *Geoff Brown, The Times*

† The film cost $60m and took $37m at the US box-office.

First Lady *
US 1937 82m bw
Warner (Hal B. Wallis)
The President's wife is a power behind the scenes.

Solidly entertaining Washington comedy.

w Rowland Leigh play George S. Kaufman, Katherine Dayton d Stanley Logan ph Sid Hickox m Max Steiner

☆ Kay Francis, Preston Foster, Anita Louise, Walter Connolly, Verree Teasdale, Victor Jory, Marjorie Rambeau, Louise Fazenda

'Smart stuff but generally palatable.' – *Variety*

The First Legion *
US 1951 86m bw
Sedif (Douglas Sirk)
Priests are bewildered when one of their number is the centre of an apparent miracle.

Talkative religious drama of a peculiarly American kind which likes to have its cake and eat it; watchable for the performances.

w Emmet Lavery play Emmet Lavery d Douglas Sirk ph Robert de Grasse m Hans Sommer

☆ Charles Boyer, William Demarest, Lyle Bettger, Barbara Rush, Leo G. Carroll, Walter Hampden, George Zucco, Taylor Holmes

First Love *
US 1939 84m bw
Universal (Joe Pasternak)
An orphaned teenager goes to live with her uncle and his snobbish family, and falls for a local bigwig's son.

A vehicle carefully conceived to introduce its star to grown-up romance. The compromises show, but it's palatable enough.

w Bruce Manning, Lionel Houser d Henry Koster ph Joseph Valentine m Frank Skinner md Charles Previn ad Jack Otterson, Martin Obzina

☆ Deanna Durbin, Robert Stack, Eugene Pallette, Helen Parrish, Lewis Howard, Leatrice Joy

'A top-bracketer for general audiences in keys and subsequents.' – *Variety*

'The most obvious Cinderella story I ever met with, apart from *Cinderella*.' – *Richard Mallett, Punch*

'There is nothing at all to resent in the picture: it is admirably directed, amusingly written, and acted with immense virtuosity by a fine cast.' – *Graham Greene*

♫ Charles Previn; art direction

First Love
US 1977 92m Metrocolor
Paramount (Lawrence Turman, David Foster)
A romantic, inhibited student falls in love with a girl who is involved with an older, married man.

Dull, unoriginal and uninvolving drama that spends a great deal of time spelling out the obvious.

w Jane Stanton Hitchcock, David Freeman story Sentimental Education by Harold Brodkey d Joan Darling ph Bobby Byrne pd Robert Luthardt ed Frank Morriss

☆ William Katt, Susan Dey, John Heard, Beverly D'Angelo, Robert Loggia, Tom Lacy, Swoosie Kurtz

First Man into Space
GB 1958 78m bw
Producers' Associates (John Croydon)
An astronaut runs into a cloud of meteor dust and returns to Earth a vampirish killer.

Quatermass-like shocker with modest budget but firm control.

w John C. Cooper, Lance Z. Hargreaves d Robert Day ph Geoffrey Faithfull m Buxton Orr

☆ Marshall Thompson, Marla Landi, Bill Edwards

First Men in the Moon *
GB 1964 103m Technicolor Panavision
Columbia/Ameran (Charles H. Schneer)
A Victorian eccentric makes a voyage to the moon and is forced to stay there.

Rather slack in plot development, but an enjoyable schoolboy romp with a good eye for detail and tongue firmly in cheek.

w Nigel Kneale, Jan Read novel H. G. Wells d Nathan Juran ph Wilkie Cooper m Laurie Johnson sp Ray Harryhausen

☆ Lionel Jeffries, Edward Judd, Martha Hyer

† Uncredited, Peter Finch played the bit part of a process server.

'In the Supreme Court, there are only eight of them against all of her!'

First Monday in October
US   1981   99m   Metrocolor   Panavision
Paramount (Paul Heller, Martha Scott)
📼 📀

Ruth Loomis becomes the first woman to be appointed to the US Supreme Court, and wins over her severest critic.
Fairly yawnworthy comedy which has nowhere to go from its initial situation, and has detail too complex for any but politically minded Americans.
w Jerome Lawrence, Robert E. Lee *play* Jerome Lawrence, Robert E. Lee d Ronald Neame ph Fred J. Koenekamp m Sousa, Handel, arr. Ian Fraser pd Philip M. Jefferies
☆ Jill Clayburgh, Walter Matthau, Barnard Hughes, Jan Sterling, James Stephens, Joshua Bryant
   'Any attempts to inject a little healthy subversion or a few dangerous thoughts are soon smothered by the plot demands of middle-aged romantic whimsy.' – *Sunday Times*

First Name Carmen *
France   1983   85m   colour
Sara/A2/JLG Films (Alain Sarde)
📼 📀
original title: Prénom Carmen
The niece of a mad film director pretends to be making a film in order to organize an armed robbery.
A quirky film, in which Godard enjoys himself playing a film director at the end of his tether, but which is otherwise disorganized and disjointed.
w Jean-Luc Godard, Anne-Marie Miéville d Jean-Luc Godard ph Raoul Coutard m Beethoven
☆ Maruschka Detmers, Jacques Bonnaffé, Myriem Roussel, Christophe Odent, Pierre-Alain Chapuis, Bertrand Liebert, Jean-Luc Godard
   'From the way this new film is made, it appears that Godard feels hurt on some deep level and he thinks the movies did it to him – and he's not going to let himself be hurt again. He won't throw himself into this project. He gives the story a dry, flat treatment and entertains himself with Beethoven and the rolling surf and with a limited palette – soft, somber tones and subdued golden ones – that suggest the classics (but not of movies).' – *Pauline Kael*

The First of the Few **
GB   1942   117m   bw
Melbourne/British Aviation (Leslie Howard, George King, Adrian Brunel, John Stafford)
📼
US title: Spitfire
The story of R. J. Mitchell who saw World War II coming and devised the Spitfire.
Low-key but impressive biopic with firm acting and good dialogue scenes. Production values slightly shaky.
w Anatole de Grunwald, Miles Malleson, Henry C. James, Katherine Strueby d Leslie Howard ph Georges Perinal m William Walton
☆ Leslie Howard, David Niven, Rosamund John, Roland Culver, David Horne
   'Full of action, Schneider Trophy races, test flying and flashes from the Battle of Britain.' – *Sunday Times*

The First Power
US   1990   98m   DeLuxe
Castle Premier/Nelson Entertainment/Interscope Communications (David Madden)
📼 📀
A serial killer comes back from the dead to continue his murders.
Silly, predictable tale of the supernatural.
wd Robert Resnikoff ph Theo Van de Sande pd Joseph T. Garrity ed Michael Bloecher
☆ Lou Diamond Phillips, Tracy Griffith, Jeff Kober, Mykel T. Williamson, Elizabeth Arlen, Dennis Lipscomb, Carmen Argenziano, Julianna McCarthy

The First Rebel: see Allegheny Uprising

First Strike: see *Jackie Chan's First Strike*

The First Texan
US   1956   82m   Technicolor   Cinemascope
Allied Artists (Walter Mirisch)
The Governor of Tennessee helps Texas win its independence.

Generally well done biopic of Sam Houston, with the usual Western excitements.
w Daniel B. Ullman d Byron Haskin ph Wilfrid Cline m Roy Webb
☆ Joel McCrea, Felicia Farr, Jeff Morrow, Wallace Ford, Abraham Sofaer

The First Time
US   1968   90m   DeLuxe
UA/Mirisch/Rogallan (Roger Smith, Allan Carr)
📼
GB title: You Don't Need Pajamas at Rosie's
Three teenage boys who fantasize about sex help a stranded girl under the impression that she is a prostitute.
Embarrassingly sentimental teenage sex comedy, all the more irritating by its restraint. Not a patch on Summer of '42.
w Jo Heims, Roger Smith d James Nielson ph Ernest Laszlo m Kenyon Hopkins
☆ Jacqueline Bisset, Wes Stern, Rick Kelman, Wink Roberts, Sharon Acker

First to Fight
US   1967   97m   Technicolor   Panavision
Warner (William Conrad)
A World War II hero is taken home and fêted, but on returning to the front he loses his nerve.
War film in the guise of a psychological study; competently done but very American in its sentiments and a bit shaky on period detail.
w Gene L. Coon d Christian Nyby ph Harold Wellman m Fred Steiner
☆ Chad Everett, Gene Hackman, Dean Jagger, Marilyn Devin, Claude Akins

The First Traveling Saleslady
US   1956   92m   Technicolor
RKO (Arthur Lubin)
Two women set out to sell barbed wire in the old west.
Strained comedy with very few effective moments.
w Devery Freeman, Stephen Longstreet d Arthur Lubin ph William Snyder m Irving Gertz
☆ Ginger Rogers, Carol Channing, Barry Nelson, James Arness, David Brian, Clint Eastwood

'Don't get mad. Get Everything.'
The First Wives Club *
US   1996   96m   DeLuxe
UIP/Paramount (Scott Rudin)
📼 📀 🎧
Three women, dumped by their husbands for younger women, decide to get their own back.
Old-fashioned, brightly played, sugar-coated, sitcom-styled farce of marital revenge.
w Robert Harling *novel* Olivia Goldsmith d Hugh Wilson ph Donald Thorin m Marc Shaiman pd Peter Larkin ed John Bloom
☆ Goldie Hawn, Bette Midler, Diane Keaton, Maggie Smith, Dan Hedaya, Victor Garber, Bronson Pinchot, Marcia Gay Harden, Eileen Heckart, Philip Bosco, Elizabeth Berkley
   'Whisks us along. But then the dumb revenge plot takes over, and the comedy leaks out of the movie like helium from a balloon.' – *Owen Gleiberman, Entertainment Weekly*
   ♫ Marc Shaiman

First Yank into Tokyo
US   1945   82m   bw
RKO (J. Robert Bren)
📼
An army pilot undergoes plastic surgery so that he can infiltrate the Japanese lines.
Highly unconvincing spy fiction ripped off from the headlines as the war ended.
w J. Robert Bren d Gordon Douglas ph Harry J. Wild m Leigh Harline
☆ Tom Neal, Richard Loo, Marc Cramer, Barbara Hale, Keye Luke

The First Year *
US   1932   80m   bw
Fox
Problems of a couple in their first year of married life.
Pleasant sun vehicle.
w Lynn Starling *play* Frank Craven d William K. Howard
☆ Janet Gaynor, Charles Farrell, Minna Gombell, Dudley Digges, Leila Bennett
   'Gaynor and Farrell in a story that's as close to perfection for them as any piece of screenwriting could be.' – *Variety*

Firstborn
US   1984   100m   Technicolor
Paramount (Paul Junger Witt, Tony Thomas)
📼 📀
A divorced woman's children defend her against her malevolent second husband.
Heavy-handed melodrama with no clue to what inspired its making.
w Ron Koslow d Michael Apted ph Ralf D. Bode m Michael Small pd Paul Sylbert ed Arthur Schmidt
☆ Teri Garr, Peter Weller, Christopher Collet, Corey Haim, Sarah Jessica Parker

A Fish Called Wanda **
US   1988   108m   Technicolor
MGM (Michael Shamberg)
📼 📀 📀 🎧
Diamond-heist comedy depending on Anglo-American rivalries for its laughs.
Deft, blackish comedy with a little romance thrown in; its humour relied too much on Cleese's familiar, if expert, performance as an overbearing, uptight buffoon.
w John Cleese, Charles Crichton d Charles Crichton ph Alan Hume m John Du Prez pd Roger Murray-Leach
☆ John Cleese, Jamie Lee Curtis, Kevin Kline, Michael Palin, Maria Aitken
⚑ Kevin Kline
⚐ Charles Crichton; best original screenplay
⚑ John Cleese (as actor); Michael Palin (supporting actor)

The Fish that Saved Pittsburgh
US   1979   104m   colour
United Artists (David Dashev, Gary Stromberg)
📼
An inept baseball team improves its performance by recruiting players born under the sign of Pisces.
Uninteresting comedy to a disco beat.
w Jaison Starkes, Edmond Stevens d Gilbert Moses m Frank Stanley m Thom Bell ad Herbert Spencer Deverill ed Peter Zinner
☆ Julius Erving, Jonathan Winters, Meadowlark Lemon, Jack Kehoe, Margaret Avery, James Bond III, Michael V. Gazzo, M. Emmet Walsh, Stockard Channing, Flip Wilson

'A Modern Day Tale About The Search For Love, Sanity, Ethel Merman And The Holy Grail.'
The Fisher King **
US   1991   137m   Technicolor
Columbia TriStar (Debra Hill, Linda Obst)
📼 📼 📀 📀 🎧
A former disc jockey seeking salvation becomes involved in the mystic quest of a tramp who was once a medieval historian.
Enjoyable more for its director's extravagances than for its attempt at modern myth-making, and finally too diffuse to be taken seriously.
w Richard LaGravenese d Terry Gilliam ph Roger Pratt m George Fenton pd Mel Bourne ed Lesley Walker
☆ Robin Williams, Jeff Bridges, Amanda Plummer, Mercedes Ruehl, Michael Jeter
   'Has all the ingredients of a major critical and commercial event: two actors at the top of their form, and a compelling, well-directed and well-produced story.' – *Variety*
   'At heart, the film is no different from a whole string of Hollywood movies centering on mysterious madmen who may be legendary heroes … A peculiarly irritating failure – a leaden piece of uplift.' – *New Yorker*
⚑ Mercedes Ruehl
⚐ Robin Williams; Richard LaGravenese; George Fenton; Mel Bourne

Fisherman's Wharf
US   1939   72m   bw
Sol Lesser/RKO
The relationship of a boy and his foster father is upset by the arrival of relations on their fishing boat.
Family fare for addicts of the singing boy star.
w Bernard Schubert, Ian McLellan Hunter, Herbert Clyde Lewis d Bernard Vorhaus
☆ Bobby Breen, Leo Carrillo, Lee Patrick, Henry Armetta, Tommy Bupp
   'Lightweight entertainment which will find its level in the duals.' – *Variety*

F.I.S.T. *
US   1978   145m   Technicolor
UA/Norman Jewison (Gene Corman)
📼 📼 📀
The rise and fall of a union boss.
Reminiscent of All the King's Men and On the Waterfront, this much overlong melodrama has compelling passages, but the star is not quite equal to it and parts are both repetitive and obscure.
w Joe Eszterhas, Sylvester Stallone d Norman Jewison ph Laszlo Kovacs m Bill Conti pd Richard MacDonald
☆ Sylvester Stallone, Rod Steiger, Peter Boyle, Melinda Dillon, David Huffman, Tony Lo Bianco, Cassie Yates, Peter Donat, Henry Wilcoxon
   'Stallone exerts the same compulsive presence we saw in *Rocky* – and this time there is the added bonus that you can understand what he's saying.' – *Variety*

Fist of Fury (dubbed)
Hong Kong   1972   106m   Eastmancolor   Dyaliscope
Cathay/Golden Harvest (Raymond Chow)
📼 📼 📀
aka: The Chinese Connection
aka: The Iron Hand
A kung-fu fighter revenges himself on a gang of Japanese karate experts who have murdered his old teacher.
Violent martial arts movie, enlivened by Lee's style in the frequent fight scenes.
wd Lo Wei ph Chen Ching Cheh m Joseph Koo pd Lo Wei ed Chang Yao Chung
☆ Bruce Lee, Nora Miao, James Tien, Robert Baker

Fist of the North Star (dubbed)
Japan   1986   110m   colour
Tohi (Shoji Kishimoto)
📼 📀
In a world after a nuclear holocaust, grotesquely muscled thugs with mystic powers battle for supremacy.
Repellently violent animated feature, full of exploding heads, popping eyeballs and gushers of blood; as if that were not bad enough, it also lacks any narrative coherence.
w Buronson, Tetsuo Hara *graphic novel* Buronson, Tetsuo Hara d Toyoo Ashida ph Tamiyo Hosoda m Katsuhisa Haltori ad Shiko Tanaka
☆ Featuring the voices of John Vickery, Michael McConnohie, Melodee Spivack, Dan Woren, Tony Oliver, Wally Burr, Gregory Snegoff
† The film was released direct to video.

Fist of the North Star
US/Japan   1995   88m   Foto-Kem
Overseas/First Look/Ozla/Zeta/Neo (Mark Yellen, Aki Komine)
📼 🎧
The last champion of a martial arts studio battles against a ruthless dictator who plans to rule a post-apocalyptic world.
A live-action remake of the animated film which simplifies the narrative but retains the unpleasantly over-the-top comic-book violence with gouts of blood and exploding heads; the acting is resolutely one-dimensional.
w Peter Atkins, Tony Randel *graphic novels* Buronson, Tetsuo Hara d Tony Randel ph Jacques Haitkin m Christopher L. Stone pd Clark Hunter ed Sonny Baskin
☆ Gary Daniels, Costas Mandylor, Chris Penn, Malcolm McDowell, Isako Washio, Melvin Van Peebles, Downtown Julie Brown
   'This ludicrously cramped nonsense, which presents the regulation post-Apocalypse wasteland on what is obviously a very small sound stage.' – *Sight and Sound*

A Fistful of Dollars ***
Italy/Germany/Spain   1964   100m   Techniscope
UA/Jolly/Constantin/Ocean (Arrigo Colombo, Georgio Papi)
📼 📼 📀 📀 🎧
original title: Per un Pugno di Dollari
An avenging stranger, violent and mysterious, cleans up a Mexican border town.
A film with much to answer for: it began the craze for 'spaghetti Westerns', took its director to Hollywood, and made a TV cowboy into a world star. It turned the Western into a brutal baroque opera, a violent clash between individuals.

w Sergio Leone, Duccio Tessari d *Sergio Leone*
ph Massimo Dallamano m Ennio Morricone
☆ Clint Eastwood, Gian Maria Volonte, Marianne Koch

'A film with no purpose beyond its ninety-five-minute Technicolor close-up portrayals of men being shot, gouged, burned, beaten and stomped to death.' – *Judith Crist*

† Direct sequels by Leone, apart from numerous imitations, are *For a Few Dollars More* and *The Good, the Bad and the Ugly*.

A Fistful of Dynamite

Italy 1971 150m Techniscope
UA/Rafran/San Marco/Miura (Fulvio Morsella)
▦ ◎ ⌂

original title: *Giù la Testa*
aka: *Duck, You Sucker*

In 1913 a Mexican bandit and an ex-IRA explosives expert join forces to rob a bank.
Overblown action spectacular, far too long to be sustained by its flashes of humour and excitement. A good instance of what happens to a small talent when success goes to its head.

wd *Sergio Leone* ph Giuseppe Ruzzolini m Ennio Morricone

☆ Rod Steiger, James Coburn, Romolo Valli, Maria Monti

'The greatest Western ever made ... in Somerset.'

A Fistful of Fingers *

GB 1995 81m Rank Colour
Blue Dolphin/Wrightstuff (Daniel Figuero)

A gunman, No-Name, and his Red Indian sidekick, Running Sore, go looking for a bad man called Squint.
A fun-packed Western, sending up the style and conventions of the spaghetti Western; the cowboys ride pantomime horses and the jokes may be old but there are plenty of them.

wd Edgar Wright ph Alvin Leong m François Evans pd Simon Bowles ed Giles Harding

☆ Graham Low, Martin Curtis, Oliver Evans, Quentin Green, William Cornes, Edward Scotland, Jeremy Beadle

'Shows more wit and invention than most of its no-budget Brit saddlemates.' – *Variety*
'Has more than its tongue in its cheek. It has wit, brains and a touch of the Monty Pythons, too.' – *Alexander Walker*

† The film's 20-year-old director made the film on a budget of around 7,500.

Fists in the Pocket *

Italy 1965 113m bw
Doria (Ezio Passadore)
▦

original title: *I Pugni in Tasca*

One of a family of epileptics murders most of the others in order to help his normal eldest brother.
Complex black melodrama which makes its points, if it has any, with great style.

wd Marco Bellocchio ph Alberto Marrama m Ennio Morricone

☆ Lou Castel, Paola Pitagora, Liliana Gerace
'There have been few débuts as exciting as this in recent years.' – *Tom Milne, MFB*

Fists of Fury: see The Big Boss

Fit for a King

US 1937 73m bw
RKO

A cub reporter falls for a princess.
Standard star comedy with action climax.

w Richard Flournoy d Edward Sedgwick

☆ Joe E. Brown, Helen Mack, Halliwell Hobbes, Paul Kelly, Harry Davenport, John Qualen

Fitzcarraldo ****

West Germany 1982 158m colour
Werner Herzog/ProjectFilmproduktion/Zweite Deutsches Fernsehen/Wildlife Films, Peru (Werner Herzog, Lucki Stipetic)
▣ ▣

In Peru at the turn of the century, an eccentric Irishman succeeds against all odds in establishing an opera house in the jungle.
A strange and brilliant film centring on the hero's successful attempt to drag his massive boat from one river to another.

wd *Werner Herzog* ph Thomas Mauch m Popol Vuh

☆ *Klaus Kinski*, Claudia Cardinale, Jose Lewgoy, Paul Hittscher

† 'Fitzcarraldo' is the nearest the natives can get to 'Fitzgerald'.

Fitzwilly *

US 1967 102m DeLuxe Panavision
UA/Dramatic Features Inc/Walter Mirisch
⌂

GB title: *Fitzwilly Strikes Back*

A New York butler, in order to keep his lady in style, has to organize the staff into a crime syndicate.
Moderately inventive, good-looking comedy with rather too much plot and not enough funny lines.

w Isobel Lennart *novel* A Garden of Cucumbers by Poyntz Tyler d Delbert Mann ph Joseph Biroc m Johnny Williams

☆ Dick Van Dyke, Edith Evans, Barbara Feldon, John McGiver, Harry Townes, John Fiedler, Norman Fell, Cecil Kellaway, Anne Seymour, Sam Waterston, Billy Halop

Fitzwilly Strikes Back: see Fitzwilly

Five

US 1951 89m bw
Columbia (Arch Oboler)

There are only five survivors of an atomic holocaust, and their political and racial tensions soon reduce the number to two.
Gutless talkfest which becomes interesting only when the camera moves out of doors; otherwise, too pretentious and dull by half.

wd Arch Oboler m Lou Stoumen, Ed Spiegel, Sid Lubow m Henry Russell

☆ William Phipps, Susan Douglas, James Anderson, Charles Lampkin, Earl Lee
'The talk leaves one with a strong impression that in this case the fittest did not survive.' – *Penelope Houston*

Five Against the House

US 1955 84m bw
Columbia (Stirling Silliphant, John Barnwell)

College students try to rob a casino.
Meandering caper melodrama with too much flabby dialogue.

w Stirling Silliphant, John Barnwell *novel* Jack Finney d Phil Karlson ph Leslie White m George Duning

☆ Guy Madison, Kim Novak, Brian Keith, Kerwin Mathews, William Conrad

Five and Ten

US 1931 88m bw
MGM

GB title: *Daughter of Luxury*

A chain store heiress elopes with a married man, but is tamed by family misfortune.
Solid star drama which maintains points of interest.

w A. P. Younger, Edith Fitzgerald *novel* Fannie Hurst d Robert Z. Leonard

☆ Marion Davies, Leslie Howard, Richard Bennett, Irene Rich, Kent Douglass, Halliwell Hobbes

Five Angles on Murder: see The Woman in Question

Five Boys from Barska Street *

Poland 1953 115m Agfacolor
Film Polski

original title: *Piatka z Ulicy Barskiej*

Five city boys are placed on probation and gradually change their attitudes towards life and society.
Rather dated propaganda piece with a plot which surprisingly follows Western models.

wd Aleksander Ford *novel* Kazimierz Kozniewski ph Jaroslav Tuzar m Kazimierz Serocki

☆ Tadeusz Janczar, Aleksandra Slaska, Andrzej Kozak

Five Branded Women

Italy/US 1960 100m bw
Paramount/Dino de Laurentiis

Five Yugoslav girls have their heads shaved for associating with German soldiers, and after various adventures join the partisans.
Rough, tough war adventure which makes a few boring points about love and war.

w Ivo Perelli *novel* Ugo Pirro d Martin Ritt ph Giuseppe Rotunno m Francesco Lavagnino

☆ Silvana Mangano, Van Heflin, Vera Miles, Barbara Bel Geddes, Jeanne Moreau, Richard Basehart, Harry Guardino, Steve Forrest, Alex Nicol

'For the most part the film is devoted to unexciting guerrilla action and uninviting partisan life ... obstinately unreal despite lashings of blood, mutilation, childbirth and death.' – *MFB*

Five Came Back **

US 1939 75m bw
RKO (Robert Sisk)
▦ ◎

A passenger plane crashlands in the jungle. It can carry back only five survivors, and headhunters are coming closer...
A minor film which gradually achieved cult status and was remade as Back to Eternity as well as being the starting point for many variations. Still gripping in its dated way.

w Jerry Cady, Dalton Trumbo, Nathanael West d John Farrow ph Nicholas Musuraca m Roy Webb

☆ Chester Morris, Lucille Ball, C. Aubrey Smith, Elizabeth Risdon, Wendy Barrie, John Carradine, Joseph Calleia, Allen Jenkins, Kent Taylor, Patric Knowles
'Exceptionally well-made adventure yarn, out of the B category and almost rates A ... looks like a solid click.' – *Variety*

Five Card Stud

US 1968 103m Technicolor
Paramount/Hal. B. Wallis
▦

Members of a lynching party are murdered one by one.
Would-be nonchalant murder mystery Western: the stars just about hold it together, but it's an uphill fight.

w Marguerite Roberts *novel* Ray Gaulden d Henry Hathaway ph Daniel L. Fapp m Maurice Jarre

☆ Dean Martin, Robert Mitchum, Inger Stevens, Roddy McDowall, Katherine Justice, John Anderson, Yaphet Kotto
'Marginally watchable ... but destined to sink without trace minutes after one leaves the cinema.' – *Gavin Millar*
'So mediocre you can't get mad at it.' – *Judith Crist*

Five Corners *

US 1988 93m colour
Handmade Films (Tony Bill, Forest Murray)
▦ ⌂

Four old friends meet again when one of them is released from prison.
Set in the 1960s, a perceptive period piece that unhappily segues into an unconvincing melodrama.

w John Patrick Shanley d Tony Bill m Fred Murphy m James Newton Howard ed Andy Blumenthal

☆ Jodie Foster, Tim Robbins, Todd Graff, John Turturro, Elizabeth Berridge, Rose Gregorio, Gregory Rozakis, John Seitz

Five Days One Summer *

US 1982 108m Technicolor
Warner/Ladd (Fred Zinnemann)
▦

In 1932 a middle-aged Scots doctor takes his young mistress on an Alpine climbing holiday, and she falls for the guide.
Superbly photographed and crafted mountain movie, akin to the German epics of the early thirties. Alas, the content is very thin.

w Michael Austin *story* Maiden Maiden by Kay Boyle d Fred Zinnemann ph Giuseppe Rotunno m Elmer Bernstein pd Willy Holt ed Stuart Baird

☆ Sean Connery, Betsy Brantley, Lambert Wilson, Jennifer Hilary, Isabel Dean, Anna Massey
'Dawdling and eventually silly, though the veteran director's tenacity and craftsmanship provide muted applause.' – *Variety*

Five Dolls for an August Moon (dubbed)

Italy 1970 88m colour
PAC
▣

original title: *Cinque Bambole per la Luna d'Agosto*

A group of wealthy industrialists and their entourages are murdered one by one when they go to an island mansion to bid for the rights to a valuable formula.
Although the plot is based on Agatha Christie's Ten Little Indians, Bava shows little interest in its thriller
aspects, preferring to concentrate on fashionable gloss, flashy photography and the occasional grisly image.

w Mario Di Nardo d Mario Bava ph Antonio Rinaldi m Piero Umiliani ad Giuseppe Aldobranc

☆ William Berger, Ira Furstenberg, Edwige Fenech, Howard Ross (Renato Rossini), Helena Ronée, Teodoro Corrá, Maurice Poli
'A pleasure to watch even when the plot flags and the zooms proliferate.' – *Tom Milne*

† The British video release runs for 80m.

Five Easy Pieces **

US 1970 98m Technicolor
Columbia/Bert Schneider (Bob Rafelson, Richard Wechsler)
▦ ▣ ◎ ◎ ◎

A middle-class drifter jilts his pregnant mistress for his brother's fiancée, but finally leaves both and hitches a ride to nowhere in particular.
Echoes of Easy Rider, The Graduate and Charlie Bubbles abound in this generally likeable but insubstantial modern anti-drama which at least takes place in pleasant surroundings and is firmly directed.

w Adrien Joyce d Bob Rafelson ph Laszlo Kovacs m various

☆ *Jack Nicholson*, Karen Black, Susan Anspach, Lois Smith, Billy 'Green' Bush, Fannie Flagg

⚯ best picture; Adrien Joyce; Jack Nicholson; Karen Black

'There are many kinds of love, but are there any without guilt?'

Five Finger Exercise

US 1962 109m bw
Columbia/Sonnis (Frederick Brisson)

A snobbish wife falls in love with a young house guest, with dire effect on her husband and son.
This West End study of a neurotic family is probably not good film material, certainly not adaptable to California, and above all not suitable to this star's whizzbang dramatics. Numbing hysteria arrives early and stays till the end.

w Frances Goodrich, Albert Hackett *play* Peter Shaffer d Daniel Mann ph Harry Stradling m Jerome Moross

☆ Rosalind Russell, Jack Hawkins, Maximilian Schell, Richard Beymer

Five Fingers **

US 1952 108m bw
TCF (Otto Lang)
▦ ⌂

The valet of the British ambassador in Ankara sells military secrets to the Germans, who pay him but never use the information.
Absorbing, lightweight film adaptation of a true story of World War II; civilized suspense entertainment with all talents contributing nicely.

w Michael Wilson *book* Operation Cicero by L. C. Moyzisch d Joseph L. Mankiewicz ph Norbert Brodine m Bernard Herrmann ad Lyle Wheeler, George W. Davis

☆ James Mason, Danielle Darrieux, Michael Rennie, Walter Hampden, Oscar Karlweis, Herbert Berghof, John Wengraf, Michael Pate
'One of the highest, fastest and most absorbing spy melodramas since Hitchcock crossed the Atlantic.' – *Arthur Knight*

⚯ Michael Wilson; Joseph L. Mankiewicz

Five Gates to Hell

US 1959 98m bw Cinemascope
TCF

A Vietcong warlord carries off a nun and seven nurses; the latter escape by brutal means.
Unpleasant shocker showing no signs of talent in any department.

wd James Clavell ph Sam Leavitt m Paul Dunlap

☆ Dolores Michaels, Patricia Owens, Neville Brand, Kevin Scott, Nobu McCarthy, Nancy Kulp, Shirley Knight, Irish McCalla
'This grimly amateurish war film exploits sex and violence with an emotional arrest bordering on paranoia.' – *MFB*

Five Golden Dragons

GB 1965 92m Techniscope
Harry Alan Towers
▣ ▣

An American playboy in Hong Kong becomes involved in the affairs of five master criminals preparing to sell out to the Mafia.
Anything-goes comedy-thriller, patchy at best, unintelligible at worst, and filled with ageing stars.

w Harry Alan Towers d Jeremy Summers
☆ Robert Cummings, Rupert Davies, Margaret Lee, Maria Perschy, Klaus Kinski, Dan Duryea, Brian Donlevy, Christopher Lee, George Raft

Five Golden Hours

GB/Italy   1960   90m   bw
Columbia/Anglofilm/Fabio Jegher (Mario Zampi)
📺

A con man tries to murder three widows who have invested money in one of his schemes.
Ill-judged black comedy, sadly lacking style.
w Hans Wilhelm d Mario Zampi ph Christopher Challis m Stanley Black
☆ Ernie Kovacs, Cyd Charisse, Kay Hammond, George Sanders, Dennis Price, Reginald Beckwith, Martin Benson, Ron Moody, Finlay Currie, Avice Landone, Sydney Tafler, John Le Mesurier, Clelia Matania

Five Graves to Cairo ***

US   1943   96m   bw
Paramount (Charles Brackett)

During the North Africa campaign, British spies try to destroy Rommel's secret supply dumps.
Intriguing spy melodrama set in a desert hotel, a notable example of Hollywood's ability to snatch polished drama from the headlines.
w Charles Brackett, Billy Wilder play Lajos Biro d Billy Wilder ph John Seitz m Miklos Rozsa ad Hans Dreier, Ernst Fegte ed Doane Harrison
☆ Franchot Tone, Anne Baxter, Erich von Stroheim, Akim Tamiroff, Peter Van Eyck, Miles Mander
   'Von Stroheim has all the other movie Huns backed completely off the screen.' – *Variety*
   'Billy Wilder must have had something a little grander in mind: the cleverness lacks lustre.' – *New Yorker, 1978*
   'A fabulous film fable, but it has been executed with enough finesse to make it a rather exciting pipe dream.' – *Howard Barnes, New York Herald Tribune*
† Locations representing the African desert include California's Salton Sea and Yuma, Arizona.
⅋ John Seitz; art direction; editing

Five Guns West

US   1955   78m   Pathécolor
Palo Alto (Roger Corman)

Five criminals are recruited into the Southern army to catch a traitor and some Union gold.
Western trial run for The Dirty Dozen; cheapjack actioner, quite tolerable of its kind.
w R. Wright Campbell d Roger Corman ph Floyd Crosby m Buddy Bregman ed Ronald Sinclair
☆ John Lund, Dorothy Malone, Chuck Connors, Paul Birch

The Five Heartbeats *

US   1991   121m   DeLuxe
TCF (Loretha C. Jones)
📺 🎞 🔍 🔊

The ups and downs of a vocal group in the 1960s and 70s.
A dramatic and witty account of the tribulations of a black group fighting for recognition in a world controlled by whites.
w Robert Townsend, Keenen Ivory Wayans d Robert Townsend ph Bill Dill m Stanley Clarke pd Wynn Thomas ed John Carter
☆ Robert Townsend, Michael Wright, Leon, Harry J. Lennix, Tico Wells, Diahann Carroll, Harold Nicholas, Tressa Thomas, John Canada Terrell
   'Convincing only in its sweet and dazzling musical sequences, this overly sincere effort otherwise misses its mark.' – *Variety*

Five Little Peppers and How They Grew

US   1939   58m   bw
Columbia

While Mrs Pepper is out working, eldest daughter Polly must take care of the other children.
Sentimental second feature which quickly spawned two others, Five Little Peppers at Home and Five Little Peppers in Trouble.
w Nathalie Bucknall, Jefferson Parker novel Margaret Sidney d Charles Barton
☆ Edith Fellows, Clarence Kolb, Dorothy Peterson, Ronald Sinclair, Tommy Bond

Five Miles to Midnight *

France/Italy   1962   110m   bw
UA/Filmsonor/Dear Film (Anatole Litvak)

A neurotic believed dead forces his terrified wife to collect his life insurance.
Hysterical melodrama, smoothly made with all the familiar expressionist devices, but far too long for its content.
w Peter Viertel, Hugh Wheeler d Anatole Litvak ph Henri Alekan m Mikis Theodorakis
☆ Sophia Loren, Anthony Perkins, Gig Young, Jean-Pierre Aumont, Yolande Turner, Tommy Norden
   'From the polished immediacy of the cars, streets, shop windows and café tables to the off-focus vertigo shots of panic, from the overhead view of neighbours on stairs … to the close-ups of hands in filing trays touching off the details of fear and guilt, there is a thread of colour to keep you watching.' – *MFB*
   'One of those movies without a country that are becoming as fixed a part of the international scene as the Duke and Duchess of Windsor.' – *Arthur Schlesinger Jnr, Show*

Five Million Years to Earth: see Quatermass and the Pit

Five of a Kind

US   1938   83m   bw
TCF

Two reporters compete for the best stories about the Dionne Quintuplets.
Third effort to exploit the famous quins, then four years old. Not otherwise remarkable.
w Lou Breslow, John Patrick d Herbert I. Leeds
☆ Jean Hersholt, Claire Trevor, Cesar Romero, Slim Summerville, Henry Wilcoxon, John Qualen, Jane Darwell
   'Will find difficulty in generating much audience enthusiasm except in spots where women patronage predominates.' – *Variety*

The Five Pennies *

US   1959   117m   Technicolor Vistavision
Paramount/Dena (Jack Rose)
📺

The rags-to-riches success story of cornet player Red Nichols.
The only touch of originality in this biopic is that the subject is given touches of irascibility. Production values reach a good standard.
w Jack Rose, Melville Shavelson d Melville Shavelson ph Daniel L. Fapp m cornet solos: Red Nichols m/ly Sylvia Fine m Leith Stevens ad Hal Pereira, Tambi Larsen
☆ Danny Kaye, Barbara Bel Geddes, Louis Armstrong, Bob Crosby, Harry Guardino, Tuesday Weld, Ray Anthony
⅋ Daniel L. Fapp; Leith Stevens; title song

Five Savage Men: see The Animals

Five Star Final **

US   1931   89m   bw
Warner

A sensation-seeking newspaper causes tragedy.
Dated but still powerful melodrama which set the pattern for all the newspaper films of the thirties.
w Robert Lord, Byron Morgan play Louis Weitzenkorn d Mervyn Le Roy ph Sol Polito md Leo F. Forbstein
☆ Edward G. Robinson, H. B. Warner, Marian Marsh, Anthony Bushell, George E. Stone, Ona Munson, Aline MacMahon, Boris Karloff
   'All the elements to make a hit attraction.' – *Variety*
† Remade in 1936 with Humphrey Bogart, as *Two Against the World.*
⅋ best picture

Five Steps to Danger

US   1956   80m   bw
UA (Henry S. Kesler)

A girl possessing secret information from her dead scientist brother has a mental breakdown, and is pursued by spies.
Lively if cliché-ridden espionage melodrama, like an old-time serial.
wd Henry S. Kesler novel Donald Hamilton ph Kenneth Peach m Paul Sawtell, Bert Shefter
☆ Sterling Hayden, Ruth Roman, Werner Klemperer, Richard Gaines

The Five Thousand Fingers of Doctor T *

👪 US   1953   88m   Technicolor
Columbia (Stanley Kramer)

A boy who hates piano lessons dreams of his teacher as an evil genius who keeps five hundred boys imprisoned in a castle of musical instruments.
Badly scripted fantasy with gleaming sophisticated dream sequences which deserve a better frame. A real oddity to come from Hollywood at this time, even though Dr Seuss's books were and are bestsellers.
w Dr Seuss (Theodore Geisel), Allan Scott d Roy Rowland ph Franz Planer m Frederick Hollander ch Eugene Loring pd Rudolph Sternad ly Dr Seuss
☆ Hans Conried, Tommy Rettig, Peter Lind Hayes, Mary Healy
⅋ Frederick Hollander

Five Weeks in a Balloon

👪 US   1962   101m   DeLuxe
Cinemascope
TCF (Irwin Allen)
📺

In 1862 a professor is financed on a balloon trip into central Africa.
Would-be humorous semi-fantasy which strives to equal Journey to the Center of the Earth but unfortunately falls flat on its face despite the interesting talent available. Limp comedy situations, poor production values.
w Charles Bennett, Irwin Allen, Albert Gail novel Jules Verne d Irwin Allen ph Winton Hoch m Paul Sawtell ad Jack Martin Smith, Alfred Ybarra
☆ Cedric Hardwicke, Peter Lorre, Red Buttons, Fabian, Richard Haydn, Billy Gilbert, Herbert Marshall, Reginald Owen, Henry Daniell

The 5th Monkey

US   1990   93m   Rank Colour
21st Century (Menahem Golan)
📺

In Brazil, a snake hunter finds four chimpanzees and travels across country in search of a buyer for them so that he can earn enough to get married.
Pleasant but inconsequential drama; the exotic setting appears to have interested its makers more than the episodic and clichéd narrative, though Kingsley brings his customary intensity to his role in an attempt to prevent the apes from stealing the film.
wd Eric Rochat novel Le Cinquième Singe by Jacques Zibi ph Gideon Porath m Robert O. Ragland ad Pedro Nanni ed Alain Jakubowicz, Fabien D. Tordjmann
☆ Ben Kingsley, Mika Lins, Silvia de Carvalho, Vera Fischer, Carlos Kroeber, Julio Levy

Fixed Bayonets! *

US   1951   93m   bw
TCF (Jules Buck)

An American platoon in Korea fights a rearguard action.
Downbeat war melodrama of a familiar kind, with more characterization than action.
wd Samuel Fuller ph Lucien Ballard m Roy Webb
☆ Richard Basehart, Gene Evans, Michael O'Shea, Richard Hylton, Craig Hill

The Fixer

US   1968   130m   Metrocolor
MGM/Edward Lewis, John Frankenheimer

A Jew in Tsarist Russia denies his race but becomes a scapegoat for various crimes and is imprisoned without trial until he becomes a cause célèbre.
Worthy but extremely dreary realist melodrama.
w Dalton Trumbo novel Bernard Malamud d John Frankenheimer ph Marcel Grignon m Maurice Jarre
☆ Alan Bates, Dirk Bogarde, Georgia Brown, Jack Gilford, Hugh Griffith, Elizabeth Hartman, Ian Holm, David Warner, Carol White, Murray Melvin, Peter Jeffrey, Michael Goodliffe
   'The kind of film in which one has to admire much of the acting simply because it is all there is to admire.' – *David Pirie*
   'A totally false film, devoid of a breath of human life or truth.' – *Arthur Schlesinger Jnr*
   'Alan Bates's bare posterior, known to us from Georgy Girl and King of Hearts, makes another timely appearance here, thus becoming one of the most exposed arses in cinematic annals.' – *John Simon*
⅋ Alan Bates

The Fixer Uppers

👪 US   1935   20m   bw
Hal Roach
📺

Christmas card salesmen try to help a bored wife, but her jealous husband challenges Ollie to a duel.
Rather flat comedy marking a tailing-off from the stars' best period.
w uncredited d Charles Rogers ph Art Lloyd ed Bert Jordan
☆ Stan Laurel, Oliver Hardy, Mae Busch, Charles Middleton, Arthur Housman, Noah Young
† A remake of an early silent, *Slipping Wives.*

Fixing the Shadow

US   1992   101m   Technicolor
Columbia TriStar/Polar/Capitol (John Fiedler, Mark Tarlov)
📺

A sacked cop is recruited by the FBI to infiltrate a violent gang of drug-pushing bikers.
Dreary action picture that runs through all the clichés of the genre without any conviction.
wd Larry Ferguson d Robert Stevens m Cory Lerios, John D'Andrea pd James L. Schoppe ed Robert C. Jones, Don Brochu
☆ Charlie Sheen, Linda Fiorentino, Michael Madsen, Courtney B. Vance, Rip Torn
   'Trashy dialogue, indifferent performances and shoddy construction make it strictly minor league stuff.' – *Film Review*

The Flag Lieutenant

GB   1933   85m   bw
British and Dominions (Herbert Wilcox)

A naval lieutenant, thought to be a coward, shows his true courage when a fort is beleaguered.
Boy's Own Paper stuff from a popular play previously filmed in 1919 (with George Wynn) and 1926 (with Henry Edwards).
w Joan Wentworth Wood play W. P. Drury, Leo Tover d Henry Edwards ph Stanley Rodwell m Harris Weston ad Wilfred Arnold ed Michael Hankinson
☆ Henry Edwards, Anna Neagle, Joyce Bland, Peter Gawthorne, Sam Livesey, O. B. Clarence, Abraham Sofaer

The Flame

US   1947   97m   bw
Republic (John H. Auer)

A nurse marries for money, but her ailing spouse recovers and she falls in love with him.
Turgid melodrama, ineptly presented.
w Lawrence Kimble d John H. Auer ph Reggie Lanning m Heinz Roemheld
☆ Vera Hruba Ralston, John Carroll, Robert Paige, Broderick Crawford, Henry Travers, Blanche Yurka, Constance Dowling, Hattie McDaniel, Sen Yung
   'A good picture to stay away from, with or without a good book.' – *Cue*

The Flame and the Arrow *

👪 US   1950   88m   Technicolor
Warner/Norma (Harold Hecht, Frank Ross)
📺 🔍 🎧

In medieval Italy, a rebel leader seeks victory over a tyrant.
Good-humoured Robin Hood stuff with the star at his most acrobatic.
w Waldo Salt d Jacques Tourneur ph Ernest Haller m Max Steiner ad Edward Carrere
☆ Burt Lancaster, Virginia Mayo, Robert Douglas, Aline MacMahon, Frank Allenby, Nick Cravat
   'I never found a Technicolor costume picture so entertaining.' – *Richard Mallett, Punch*
⅋ Ernest Haller; Max Steiner

The Flame and the Flesh

US   1954   104m   Technicolor
MGM (Joe Pasternak)

An unscrupulous American woman in Naples has a fatal fascination for the local menfolk.
Dreary remake of Naples au Baiser du Feu (France 1937), with the dullest possible handling all round.
w Helen Deutsch novel Auguste Bailly d Richard Brooks ph Christopher Challis m Nicholas Brodszky
☆ Lana Turner, Carlos Thompson, Bonar Colleano, Pier Angeli, Charles Goldner, Peter Illing

---

A Flame In My Heart
France/Switzerland 1987 110m bw
Mainline/Garance/Le Sept/Filmograph (Paulo Branco)
original title: *Une Flamme dans Ma Coeur*
An actress ditches her working-class Arab lover for a journalist.
Pretentious and tasteless, always straining for the arty effect.
w Myriam Mezières, Alain Tanner d Alain Tanner ph Acacio de Almeida m Bach ed Laurent Uhler
☆ Myriam Mezières, Benoit Regent, Aziz Kabouche, André Marcon, Jean-Gabriel Nordman, Jean-Yves Berteloot, Anne Rucki, Douglas Ireland

Flame in the Streets
GB 1961 93m colour Cinemascope
Rank/Somerset (Roy Baker)
A liberal-minded union man erupts when his daughter proposes to marry a black man.
Predictable East End problem picture, unconvincingly set and acted and boring into the bargain.
w Ted Willis *play* Hot Summer Night by Ted Willis d Roy Baker ph Christopher Challis m Phil Green
☆ John Mills, Brenda de Banzie, Sylvia Syms, Earl Cameron, Johnny Sekka, Ann Lynn, Wilfrid Brambell
'Its methods belong more to the writer's study than to life.' – *John Gillett*

The Flame of New Orleans *
US 1941 79m bw
Universal (Joe Pasternak)
A European adventuress settles in America.
Fluffy comedy romance with the exiled director scarcely in top form.
w Norman Krasna d René Clair ph Rudolph Maté m Frank Skinner ad Martin Obzina, Jack Otterson
☆ Marlene Dietrich, Roland Young, Bruce Cabot, Mischa Auer, Andy Devine, Frank Jenks, Eddie Quillan, Laura Hope Crews, Franklin Pangborn
† Remade as Scarlet Angel.
Ⓧ art direction

Flame of the Barbary Coast
US 1945 97m bw
Republic (Joseph Kane)
In old San Francisco, a cowboy becomes involved with a night-club queen, and their fortunes are resolved by the earthquake.
Tolerable period melodrama, and the one in which Wayne played a character named Duke: the nickname stuck.
w Borden Chase d Joseph Kane ph Robert de Grasse m Dale Butts sp Howard and Theodore Lydecker
☆ John Wayne, Ann Dvorak, Joseph Schildkraut, William Frawley, Virginia Grey, Russell Hicks, Jack Norton, Paul Fix, Marc Lawrence
Ⓧ Dale Butts

Flame of the Islands
US 1955 90m Trucolor
Republic (Edward Ludwig)
A girl invests a bequest in a Bahamas night-club, and there becomes involved with four men.
Barely competent time-filler.
w Bruce Manning d Edward Ludwig ph Bud Thackery m Nelson Riddle
☆ Yvonne de Carlo, Howard Duff, Zachary Scott, Kurt Kasznar, Barbara O'Neil, James Arness, Frieda Inescort

Flame Over India: see *Northwest Frontier*

The Flame Within
US 1935 73m bw
MGM
A lady psychiatrist falls for the husband of one of her patients.
Decent star melodrama.
wd Edmund Goulding
☆ Ann Harding, Maureen O'Sullivan, Louis Hayward, Henry Stephenson, Herbert Marshall

Flaming Brothers
Hong Kong 1988 117m colour
In-Gear/Rover K. C. Tang (Alan Tang)
Two orphans, lifelong friends who grow up to be successful crooks in Macao, run into problems: one

wishes to go straight so that he can marry, the other provokes a war with the local gang boss.
Romantic comedy, religiosity and the extreme violence on view here make for a gruesome mix; the abrupt changes from sentimentality to brutality will be hard to take for all but devout aficionados of the genre.
w Kelvin Wang d Tony Velesco ph Ma Chor Shing m Lam Mun Ye ad William Cheung ed Poon Hung
☆ Chow Yun-Fat, Alan Tang, Jenny Yen, Pat Ha, Tse Yin, Philip Chan, Kent Tsui

Flaming Feather
US 1951 78m Technicolor
Paramount (Nat Holt)
Arizona is harassed by an outlaw called The Sidewinder who leads a troupe of pillaging Indians.
Spot-the-villain Western; not much to detain one.
w Gerald Drayson Adams d Ray Enright ph Ray Rennahan
☆ Sterling Hayden, Forrest Tucker, Barbara Rush, Richard Arlen, Victor Jory, Edgar Buchanan

Flaming Star *
US 1960 92m DeLuxe Cinemascope
TCF (David Weisbart)
A half-breed family is torn between two loyalties.
Solemn, unusual Civil War Western with a downbeat ending.
w Clair Huffaker, Nunnally Johnson *novel* Clair Huffaker d Don Siegel ph Charles G. Clarke m Cyril Mockridge
☆ Elvis Presley, Dolores del Rio, Steve Forrest, Barbara Eden, John McIntire, Rodolfo Acosta
'Despite familiar absurdities, it has more than its share of good moments.' – *MFB*

The Flaming Torch: see *The Bob Mathias Story*

The Flamingo Kid
US 1984 100m DeLuxe
Palace/Mercury/ABC (Michael Phillips)
In 1963, a teenager comes of age while working at a beach club.
Innocent but unexciting comedy-drama about matters which scarcely concern grown-ups.
w Neal Marshall, Garry Marshall (no relation) d Garry Marshall ph James A. Contner pd Lawrence Miller ed Priscilla Nedd
☆ Matt Dillon, Richard Crenna, Hector Elizondo, Jessica Walter, Fisher Stevens

'A wrong girl from the right side of the tracks!'
Flamingo Road *
US 1949 94m bw
Warner (Jerry Wald)
A tough carnival dancer is stranded in a small town and soon affects the lives of the local politicians.
Standard melodrama from a bestseller, absurd but well performed.
w Robert Wilder *play* Robert Wilder, Sally Wilder d Michael Curtiz ph Ted McCord m Max Steiner
☆ Joan Crawford, David Brian, Sydney Greenstreet, Zachary Scott, Gladys George, Virginia Huston, Fred Clark

Une Flamme Dans Mon Coeur: see *A Flame In My Heart*

The Flanagan Boy
GB 1953 81m bw
Exclusive/Hammer (Anthony Hinds)
US title: *Bad Blonde*
A young merchant seaman becomes a boxer and is corrupted by a hard-boiled blonde.
Competent British imitation of an American B movie.
w Guy Elmes, Richard Landau *novel* Max Catto d Reginald LeBorg ph Walter Harvey m Ivor Slaney ad Wilfred Arnold ed James Needs
☆ Tony Wright, Barbara Payton, Sidney James, John Slater, Frederick Valk, Marie Burke

Flap
US 1970 106m Technicolor Panavision
Warner (Jerry Adler)
GB title: *The Last Warrior*
A drunken Indian on a dilapidated modern reservation starts a public relations war and leads a march on the city.

Unendearing comedy with a tragic end tacked on, not very entertaining as whimsy, farce or social conscience.
w Clair Huffaker *novel* Nobody Loves a Drunken Indian by Clair Huffaker d Carol Reed ph Fred Koenekamp m Marvin Hamlisch
☆ Anthony Quinn, Claude Akins, Tony Bill, Victor Jory, Shelley Winters

Flare Up
US 1969 98m Metrocolor
MGM/GMF (Leon Fromkes)
A man kills his wife and threatens her friends who he feels are responsible for the break-up of his marriage.
Sensationally violent melodrama with a plot that goes back to Sudden Fear and further. Adequately made.
w Mark Rodgers d James Neilson ph Andrew J. McIntyre m Les Baxter
☆ Raquel Welch, James Stacy, Luke Askew, Don Chastain, Ron Rifkin

Flash Gordon *
The hero of the 25th century was created in comic strip form by Alex Raymond and his chief claims to film fame are three wild and woolly serials made by Universal: *Flash Gordon* (1936), *Flash Gordon's Trip to Mars* (1938), and *Flash Gordon Conquers the Universe* (1940), all starring Buster Crabbe with Charles Middleton as the wily Emperor Ming.
Their cheap and cheerful futuristic sets and their non-stop action have kept them popular with film buffs through the years. In 1974 a semi-porno spoof, Flesh Gordon, appeared.

Flash Gordon
GB 1980 115m Technicolor Todd-AO
EMI/Famous/Starling (Dino de Laurentiis)
A football hero, his girlfriend, and Dr Zarkov have adventures on the planet Mongo.
Lively comic strip addition to the increasing numbers of such things being restaged at enormous expense fifty years after their prime.
w Lorenzo Semple Jnr, from characters created by Alex Raymond d Michael Hodges ph Gil Taylor m Queen pd Danilo Donati
☆ Sam J. Jones, Melody Anderson, Topol, Max von Sydow, Timothy Dalton, Brian Blessed, Peter Wyngarde
'An expensively irrelevant gloss on its sources.' – *Richard Combs, MFB*

Flashback *
US 1990 108m colour
Paramount (Marvin Worth)
An uptight young FBI agent is chosen to escort to prison a hero of the counter-culture who has been caught after 20 years on the run.
A lightweight comedy of a culture clash, but too contrived to afford lasting amusement, particularly as everyone ends up on the same side.
w David Loughery d Franco Amurri ph Stefan Czapsky m Barry Goldberg pd Vincent Cresciman ed C. Timothy O'Meara
☆ Dennis Hopper, Kiefer Sutherland, Carol Kane, Paul Dooley, Cliff de Young, Richard Masur, Michael McKean, Kathleen York, Tom O'Brien

'Don't you understand? When you give up the dream, you die!'
Flashdance *
US 1983 98m Movielab
Paramount/Polygram (Don Simpson, Jerry Bruckheimer)
A female welder in a Pittsburgh factory has ambitions to be a ballet dancer.
Slickly-made, disco-style but dramatically empty entertainment.
w Tom Hedley, Joe Eszterhas d Adrian Lyne ph Don Peterman m Giorgio Moroder ed Bud Smith, Walt Mulconery
☆ Jennifer Beals, Michael Nouri, Lilia Skala, Sunny Johnson, Kyle T. Heffner, Belinda Bauer
'It resembles an extended video for a record album.' – *Observer*
'A preposterous success.' – *Guardian*
'Basically, a series of rock videos.' – *New Yorker*
♪ song, 'Flashdance ... What a Feeling' (mGiorgio Moroder, lyKeith Forsey, Irene Cara)
Ⓧ cinematography; editing; song, 'Maniac' (m/lyMichael Sembello, Dennis Matkosky)

'You never know anything about anybody until they're dead.'
Flashfire
US 1994 90m colour
Silver Lion/Avondale (Lance Hool)
Police detectives investigate the activities of an arsonist.
Unoriginal paranoid thriller, about corruption in high places; it offers nothing new or interesting.
w John Warren, Dan York d Elliot Silverstein ph Bert Dunk m Sylvester Lay pd Gregory Melton ed Mark Conte
☆ Billy Zane, Louis Gossett Jnr, Kristin Minter, Tom Mason
'Pleasant and inoffensive, but decidedly unexciting.' – *Variety*

Flashpoint
US 1984 94m Metrocolor
Home Box Office/Silver Screen (Skip Short)
Border patrolmen discover treasure and decide to make off with it.
Competent action melodrama which doesn't quite hang together in the later stretches but has plenty of lively moments.
w Dennis Shryack, Michael Butler *novel* George La Fountaine d William Tannen ph Peter Moss m various, performed by Tangerine Dream
☆ Kris Kristofferson, Treat Williams, Rip Torn, Kevin Conway, Miguel Ferrer

Flatliners
US 1990 114m DeLuxe Panavision
Columbia-Tri-Star/Stonebridge (Michael Douglas, Rick Bieber)
Medical students experiment to discover whether there is life after death.
Hectic fantasy, filmed in a restless manner.
w Peter Filardi d Joel Schumacher ph Jan de Bont m James Newton Howard ed Robert Brown
☆ Kiefer Sutherland, Julia Roberts, Kevin Bacon, William Baldwin, Oliver Platt, Kimberly Scott, Joshua Rudoy, Benjamin Mouton
'Filmed like an epic, packed with crisis, shock and suspense, it's a small tale that has been spectacularly escalated into a tall one.' – *Philip Strick, MFB*

Flavia Priestess of Violence: see *Flavia the Heretic*

Flavia the Heretic (dubbed)
Italy/France 1974 97m Technicolor
Eagle/PAC/ROC
original title: *Flavia la Monaca Musulmana*
aka: *Flavia la Nonne Musulmana; Flavia Priestess of Violence; The Rebel Nun*
Forced to become a nun by her father and appalled by the violence of masculine society, a young woman takes her revenge by joining a force of invading Muslims.
An unpleasant mixture of religiosity and sadism, masquerading as a feminist tract. Some images are extraordinary – a naked woman crawling into the hanging carcase of a cow – but hardly compensate for its general lack of narrative drive.
w Fabrizio Onofri, Gianfranco Mingozzi, Bruno Di Geronimo, Sergio Tau *story* Raniero Di Giovanbattista, Sergio Tau, Francesco Vietri d Gianfranco Mingozzi ph Alfio Contini m Nicola Piovani ad Guido Josia ed Ruggero Mastroianni
☆ Florinda Bolkan, Maria Casares, Claudio Cassinelli, Anthony Corlan, Spiros Focas

Flaxy Martin
US 1948 86m bw
Warner (Saul Elkins)
A lawyer falls for a racketeer's girlfriend and finds himself framed for murder.
Flatly-handled melodrama with unsympathetic characters.
w David Lang d Richard Bare ph Carl Guthrie
☆ Zachary Scott, Virginia Mayo, Dorothy Malone, Tom d'Andrea, Elisha Cook Jnr

A Flea in Her Ear *
US/France 1968 94m DeLuxe Panavision
TCF (Fred Kohlmar)
Various suspicious wives and husbands converge on the notorious Hotel Coq d'Or.

Disappointing filming of a Feydeau farce, which needs to be much more cleverly handled to come over with its full theatrical force.

w John Mortimer *play* La Puce à l'Oreille *by* Georges Feydeau *d* Jacques Charon *ph* Charles Lang *m* Bronislau Kaper *pd* Alexander Trauner
☆ Rex Harrison, Rachel Roberts, Rosemary Harris, Louis Jourdan, John Williams, Grégoire Aslan, Edward Hardwicke, Frank Thornton, Victor Sen Yung

'The plunge into madness never comes, and one is left with the sight of a group of talented players struggling with alien material.' – *Michael Billington, Illustrated London News*

Fled

US   1996   105m   DeLuxe
MGM (Frank Mancuso Jnr)
📼 ▪️ ⚪
Two convicts escape, chased by a hitman hired by a gangster, who wants to get back incriminating evidence that one of them possesses.
Chase thriller that borrows heavily from predecessors, consisting of a sequence of shoot-outs, none of them of any particular interest.
w Preston A. Whitmore II *d* Kevin Hooks *ph* Matthew F. Leonetti *m* Graeme Revell *pd* Charles Bennett *ed* Richard Nord, Joseph Gutowski
☆ Laurence Fishburne, Stephen Baldwin, Will Patton, Robert John Burke, Robert Hooks, Victor Rivers, David Dukes, Salma Hayek

'Devotes itself to one mindless macho bang-bang sequence after another.' – *Ty Burr, Entertainment Weekly*

'Gobs of glee! A boatload of beauties! A shipful of songs!'

The Fleet's In *

US   1942   93m   bw
Paramount (Paul Jones)
A sailor on leave in San Francisco takes a bet that he can kiss the glamorous singer at a swank night-club.
Mindless wartime musical which happened to set the seal of success on a number of young talents.
w Walter de Leon, Sid Silvers, Ralph Spence *play* Sailor Beware *by* Kenyon Nicholson *story* Monte Price, J. Walter Ruben *d* Victor Schertzinger *ph* William Mellor *m/ly* Victor Schertzinger, Johnny Mercer *ed* Paul Weatherwax
☆ Dorothy Lamour, William Holden, *Eddie Bracken, Betty Hutton,* Cass Daley, Gil Lamb, Leif Erickson, Betty Jane Rhodes

'A slim and obvious comedy with some good tunes. Much of the film is a roughhouse; several reels towards the end are turned over to straight vaudeville.' – *Eileen Creelman, New York Sun*

† Previously a Clara Bow vehicle, it was later remade as *Sailor Beware* starring Dean Martin and Jerry Lewis

🎵 'I Remember You'; 'When You Hear the Time Signal'; 'The Fleet's In'; 'Tomorrow You Belong to Uncle Sam'; 'Arthur Murray Taught Me Dancing in a Hurry'; 'If You Build a Better Mousetrap'; 'Tangerine'; 'Conga from Honga'

The Flemish Farm

GB   1943   82m   bw
Two Cities (Sydney Box)
An attempt is made to retrieve a buried flag from occupied Belgium.
Tolerable wartime flagwaver.
w Jeffrey Dell, Jill Craigie *d* Jeffrey Dell *ph* Eric Cross *m* Ralph Vaughan Williams
☆ Clive Brook, Clifford Evans, Jane Baxter, Philip Friend, Brefni O'Rorke

'He sacrificed his career for the sake of a woman's lying lips!'

Flesh *

US   1932   95m   bw
MGM
A German wrestler in the US falls for a street waif.
Unusual, rather unattractive, but vivid melodrama.
w Leonard Praskins, Edgar Allan Woolf, Moss Hart *story* Edmund Goulding *d* John Ford *ph* Arthur Edeson *ed* William S. Gray
☆ Wallace Beery, Ricardo Cortez, Karen Morley, John Miljan, Jean Hersholt, Herman Bing, Edward Brophy

'Not bad, could have been better ... that it takes 95 minutes to get home is the big fault.' – *Variety*

Flesh *

US   1968   105m   colour
Vaughn/Score Movies (Andy Warhol)
📼 ⚪
aka: *Andy Warhol's Flesh*
A day in the life of a male prostitute.
A revelation at the time, for putting New York street life and unabashed sexuality on the screen. It wears better than most underground movies of its time.
wd Paul Morrissey
☆ Joe Dallesandro, Geraldine Smith, Patti D'Arbanville, Candy Darling, Jackie Curtis, Geri Miller

'With this strangely kindly and sympathetic film obscenity is only in the beholder's eye.' – *David Robinson, Financial Times*
'Totally obscene from the conventional point of view.' – *John Weightman, Encounter*

Flesh and Blood

GB   1951   102m   bw
BL/Harefield (Anatole de Grunwald)
Three generations of a family suffer from the effects of heredity.
Fragmented Scottish period piece which never settles down long enough to make an impact with any group of characters.
w Anatole de Grunwald *play* A Sleeping Clergyman *by* James Bridie *d* Anthony Kimmins *ph* Otto Heller *m* Charles Williams
☆ Richard Todd, Glynis Johns, Joan Greenwood, André Morell, Ursula Howells, Freda Jackson, George Cole, James Hayter, Ronald Howard, Muriel Aked

Flesh & Blood

US   1985   126m   DeLuxe   Technovision
Riverside/Impala (Gys Versluys)
📼 ▪️ ⚪
In a dark medieval world, a young bride-to-be is kidnapped and raped, but grows to like it.
Unpleasant wallow in a decadent world of the imagination.
w Gerard Soeteman, Paul Verhoeven *d* Paul Verhoeven *ph* Jan de Bont *m* Basil Poledouris *ad* Felix Murcia *ed* Ine Schenkkan
☆ Rutger Hauer, Jennifer Jason Leigh, Tom Burlinson, Jack Thompson, Susan Tyrrell, Ronald Lacey

The Flesh and Blood Show

GB   1972   96m   Eastmancolor
Tigon/Peter Walker
📼
Actors rehearsing a play in a derelict seaside theatre are killed off one by one.
A low-budget horror-cum-whodunnit, with a few interesting moments before it succumbs to banality.
w Alfred Shaughnessy *d* Peter Walker *ph* Peter Jessop *m* Cyril Ornadel *ed* Ron Pope
☆ Jenny Hanley, Ray Brooks, Luan Peters, Judy Matheson, Candace Glendenning, Robin Askwith, Patrick Barr, Jess Conrad

'Has an unexpectedly pleasing, old-fashioned quality about it.' – *David Pirie, MFB*
† The film was partly made in 3D
†† The 1997 video release runs for 86m.

Flesh and Bone *

US   1993   124m   DeLuxe
Paramount/Mirage/Spring Creek (Mark Rosenberg, Paula Weinstein)
📼 ▪️ ⚪ 🎧
A vending machine operator realizes that the woman he meets on the road is the only survivor of a family killed by his crooked father 30 years earlier.
Tense, intriguing psychological drama of love and betrayal, although its conclusion is not altogether satisfactory.
wd Steve Kloves *ph* Philippe Rousselot *m* Thomas Newman *pd* Jon Hutman *ed* Mia Goldman
☆ Dennis Quaid, Meg Ryan, James Caan, Gwyneth Paltrow, Scott Wilson, Christopher Rydell

'Offbeat but emotionally stunted piece ... Trying to shoehorn a cute romance of temperamental opposites into an essentially somber, violent format.' – *Variety*

Flesh and Fantasy *

US   1943   94m   bw
Universal (Charles Boyer, Julien Duvivier)
A club bore tells three strange stories.
A portmanteau with ingredients of varying interest, attempting to emulate the success of Tales of Manhattan. The fourth episode planned was deleted and turned up as Destiny *(qv). All quite stylish, the best section being Lord Arthur Savile's Crime.*
w Ernest Pascal, Samuel Hoffenstein, Ellis St Joseph *story* Ellis St Joseph, Oscar Wilde, Laslo Vadnay *d* Julien Duvivier *ph* Paul Ivano, Stanley Cortez *m* Alexandre Tansman
☆ Robert Benchley, Edward G. Robinson, Barbara Stanwyck, Charles Boyer, Betty Field, Robert Cummings, *Thomas Mitchell*, C. Aubrey Smith, Dame May Whitty, Edgar Barrier, David Hoffman

Flesh and the Devil *

US   1926   109m   bw   silent
MGM
📼 ▪️
A temptress toys with three men.
Hokey but good-looking star melodrama, climaxing with death on an ice floe. A huge commercial success because of the off-screen Garbo-Gilbert romance.
w Benjamin Glazer *novel* The Undying Past *by* Hermann Sudermann *d* Clarence Brown *ph* William Daniels
☆ Greta Garbo, John Gilbert, Lars Hanson, Marc McDermott, Barbara Kent

'A film of more than passing cleverness ... the theme is sheer undiluted sex, and Brown uses a series of close-ups to get this across with considerable effect.' – *Paul Rotha, The Film Till Now*

The Flesh and the Fiends

GB   1959   97m   bw   Dyaliscope
Regal/Triad (Robert Baker, Monty Berman)
▪️
US title: *Mania*
In 1820 Edinburgh, 'resurrection men' commit murders to keep anatomists supplied.
Dr Robert Knox rides again, in a version more bloody but less entertaining than The Body Snatcher.
w John Gilling, Leon Griffiths *d* John Gilling *ph* Monty Berman *m* Stanley Black
☆ Peter Cushing, June Laverick, George Rose, Donald Pleasence, Renée Houston, Billie Whitelaw, Dermot Walsh

The Flesh Is Weak

GB   1957   88m   bw
Eros (Raymond Stross)
A girl goes from bad to worse when she finds that her boyfriend is head of a vice ring.
Road to Ruin, fifties style; competently made, but neither shocking nor entertaining, just an exploitation piece.
w Leigh Vance *d* Don Chaffey *ph* Stephen Dade *m* Tristram Cary
☆ John Derek, Milly Vitale, William Franklyn, Martin Benson, Freda Jackson, Norman Wooland, Harold Lang, Patricia Jessel, John Paul

The Flesh of the Orchid

France/Italy/Germany   1974   100m
Eastmancolor
VMP/Paris Cannes Productions/F. Meric/L'Astrophone/ORTF/Oceana/TIT (Vincent Malle)
original title: *La Chair de l'Orchidée*
A young heiress, incarcerated in a mental institution by her aunt who wants her fortune, goes on the run with a man being hunted by contract killers.
A baroque and overwrought stew of sex and death, likely to be too rich for most tastes.
w Jean-Claude Carrière, Patrice Chéreau *novel* James Hadley Chase *d* Patrice Chéreau *ph* Pierre Lhomme *m* Fiorenzo Carpi *ad* Richard Peduzzi *ed* Pierre Gillette
☆ Charlotte Rampling, Bruno Cremer, Edwige Feuillère, Alida Valli, Hans Christian Blech, François Simon, Hugues Quester, Simone Signoret

Fletch *

US   1985   96m   Technicolor
Universal/Douglas/Greisman
📼 ▪️ ⚪
A newspaper columnist with a penchant for disguise tracks down a nefarious con man.
A lightness of touch unusual for the eighties makes this comedy mystery more welcome than most.
w Andrew Bergman *novel* Gregory McDonald *d* Michael Ritchie *ph* Fred Schuler *m* Harold Faltermeyer
☆ Chevy Chase, Dana Wheeler-Nicholson, Tim Matheson, Joe Don Baker, Richard Libertini, Kenneth Mars, M. Emmet Walsh

Fletch Lives

US   1989   95m   colour
UIP/Universal/Greisman/Douglas
📼 ▪️ ⚪
An investigative reporter inherits trouble along with a Southern mansion.
Dire comedy with nothing to recommend it.
w Leon Capetanos *d* Michael Ritchie *ph* John McPherson *m* Harold Faltermeyer, Buckwheat Zydeco *ed* Richard A. Harris
☆ Chevy Chase, Hal Holbrook, Julianne Phillips, R. Lee Ermey, Richard Libertini, Randall 'Tex' Cobb, Cleavon Little

Les Fleurs Sauvages

Canada   1982   153m   bw/colour
Cinegate/Cinak (Marguerite Duparc)
A seventy-year-old widow visits her married daughter for a holiday.
Excessively drawn-out and introspective view of family relationships that loses interest long before the end.
wd Jean Pierre Lefèbvre *ph* Guy Dufaux *m* Raoul Duguay, Jean Corriveau *ed* Marguerite Duparc
☆ Marte Nadeau, Michell Magny, Pierre Curzi, Claudia Aubin, Eric Beausejour, Georges Belisle, Sarah Mills

Un Flic: see Dirty Money

'What would you do if the man you loved wanted you to love his pal?'
'The first all-talking drama of the air!'

Flight

US   1929   110m   bw
Columbia (Harry Cohn)
Two rival flyers join a mission to rescue US Marines ambushed in Nicaragua.
Pale stuff now, but in its time an ambitious action movie showing a new suppleness in its young director.
w Frank Capra, Ralph Graves *d* Frank Capra *ph* Joseph Walker *ad* Harrison Wiley
☆ Jack Holt, Lila Lee, Ralph Graves, Alan Roscoe, Harold Goodwin, Jimmy de la Cruze

Flight Angels

US   1940   74m   bw
Edmund Grainger/Warner
Airline stewardesses compete for the favours of a romantic pilot.
An efficient potboiler, now most interesting for its depiction of 1939 air travel.
w Maurice Leo *d* Lewis Seiler
☆ Virginia Bruce, Dennis Morgan, Wayne Morris, Ralph Bellamy, Jane Wyman, John Litel

Flight Command

US   1940   116m   bw
MGM (J. Walter Ruben)
A cocky recruit makes good in the naval air arm.
Routine flagwaver.
w Wells Root, Cmdr Harvey Haislip *d* Frank Borzage *ph* Harold Rosson *m* Franz Waxman
☆ Robert Taylor, Ruth Hussey, Walter Pidgeon, Paul Kelly, Nat Pendleton, Red Skelton, Shepperd Strudwick, Dick Purcell

Flight Commander: see The Dawn Patrol (1930)

Flight for Freedom

US   1943   101m   bw
RKO (David Hempstead)
Biography of an intrepid aviatrix and her husband.
Patchy job based on the life of Amelia Earhart, suggesting that her final disappearance was in a government mission. Dull production.
w Oliver H. P. Garrett, S. K. Lauren *story* Horace McCoy *d* Lothar Mendes *ph* Lee Garmes *m* Roy Webb *ad* Albert S. D'Agostino, Carroll Clark
☆ Rosalind Russell, Fred MacMurray, Herbert Marshall, Eduardo Ciannelli, Walter Kingsford
Ꝗ art direction

Flight from Ashiya *
US/Japan 1963 102m Eastmancolor
Panavision
UA/Harold Hecht/Daiei

When a cargo vessel sinks off the coast of Japan during a typhoon, the helicopter rescue service springs into action.
Conventional Grade A action thriller with flashbacks to earlier disasters in the lives of its heroes.
w Elliott Arnold, Waldo Salt d Michael Anderson ph Joe MacDonald, Burnett Guffey m Frank Cordell pd Eugène Lourié
☆ Yul Brynner, Richard Widmark, George Chakiris, Shirley Knight, Daniele Gaubert, Suzy Parker

Flight from Destiny
US 1941 74m bw
Warner

An elderly professor with six months to live determines on one good deed … which includes murder.
Likeable minor melodrama, well put together.
w Barry Trivers play Anthony Berkeley d Vincent Sherman
☆ Thomas Mitchell, Geraldine Fitzgerald, Jeffrey Lynn, Mona Maris

Flight from Folly
GB 1944 93m bw
Warner

A chorus girl cures a playwright's amnesia.
Leadenly-titled and played variation on Random Harvest, with dreary musical numbers.
w Basil Woon, Lesley Storm, Katherine Strueby d Herbert Mason
☆ Pat Kirkwood, Hugh Sinclair, Sydney Howard, Marian Spencer, Tamara Desni, Jean Gillie, A. E. Matthews

Flight from Glory *
US 1937 66m bw
Robert Sisk/RKO
▥

Tensions mount among flyers who cross the Andes daily between secluded mines and their supply base.
Tense 'B' picture which looks like a trial run for Only Angels Have Wings.
w David Silverstein, John Twist d Lew Landers
☆ Chester Morris, Whitney Bourne, Onslow Stevens, Van Heflin, Richard Lane, Paul Guilfoyle
'Better than the average programmer and worth strong exhibitor plugging. In tone the picture may be fairly described as semi-sophisticated, which for rank and file purposes is probably just the right amount of sophistication.' – *Variety*

Flight Lieutenant
US 1942 80m bw
Columbia (B. P. Schulberg)

A careless pilot crashes a plane, but atones heroically for his former misdeeds.
Inept wartime flagwaver.
w Michael Blankfort d Sidney Salkow
☆ Glenn Ford, Pat O'Brien, Evelyn Keyes, Minor Watson, Jonathan Hale

Flight Nurse
US 1953 90m bw
Republic

An air force nurse is on the front line during the Korean War.
Routine mix of love and action.
w Alan LeMay d Allan Dwan
☆ Joan Leslie, Forrest Tucker, Arthur Franz, Jeff Donnell, Ben Cooper

Flight of the Doves *
👫 US 1971 101m colour
Columbia/Rainbow (Ralph Nelson)
🎧

Two children run away from their bullying stepfather to join their Irish grandmother, but are chased by a wicked uncle who knows they are heirs to a fortune.
Pantomimish whimsy which works in fits and starts, but has little real humour or charm.
w Frank Gabrielson, Ralph Nelson novel Walter Macken d Ralph Nelson ph Harry Waxman m Roy Budd
☆ Ron Moody, Dorothy McGuire, Helen Raye, Dana, Jack Wild, Stanley Holloway, William Rushton

The Flight of the Dragon
👫 US 1982 98m colour
Rankin/Bass Productions (Arthur Rankin Jnr, Jules Bass)

An author is plucked from modern times back into a mythic past to help save magic in the world.
Children's cartoon with an ecological message. By modern standards, the animation is above average.
w Romeo Muller book The Flight of Dragons by Peter Dickinson d Arthur Rankin Jnr, Jules Bass m Maury Laws pd Wayne Anderson
☆ Featuring the voices of Victor Buono, James Gregory, James Earl Jones, Harry Morgan, John Ritter

Flight of the Innocent
Italy 1993 105m Technicolor
Buena Vista/Cristaldi/Fandango/Raitre/Fildebroc (Franco Cristaldi, Domenico Procacci)
▥ ▤ 🔍 🎧

original title: *Corsa dell'Innocente*

A 10-year-old boy, witness to a gang killing, goes on the run followed by killers.
An unoriginal and violent chase movie with a sickly ending, done with skill but hardly worth the doing; it represents the neo-realist tradition at its most decadent.
w Carlo Carlei, Gualtiero Rosella d Carlo Carlei ph Raffaele Mertes m Carlo Siliotto pd Franco Ceraolo ed Carlo Fontana, Claudio di Mauro
☆ Manuel Colao, Federico Pacifici, Nicola di Pinto, Francesca Neri, Jacques Perrin
'Carlei has a strong eye for comic book images but he doesn't know when to stop, and the whole thing soon turns into a shapeless, hysterical melodrama.' – *Derek Malcolm, Guardian*
'This despicable docuthriller … the film's only agenda is finding pretexts to photograph people lifted out of their shoes and blown across the room, farmyard, or plaza by a shotgun blast to the chest, preferably in gold-suffused backlight.' – *Richard T. Jameson, Film Comment*

'The only thing they can count on is each other.'
Flight of the Intruder
US 1991 113m Technicolor Panavision
Paramount/Mace Neufeld, Robert Rehme
▥ ▤ 🔍

Pilots aboard an aircraft carrier during the Vietnam war decide to bomb Hanoi.
Dated and dull, with nothing to recommend it.
w Robert Dillon, David Shaber novel Stephen Coonts d John Milius m Fred J. Koenekamp m Basil Poledouris pd Jack T. Collis ad E. Albert Heschong ed C. Timothy O'Mears, Steve Mirkovich, Peck Prior
☆ Danny Glover, Willem Dafoe, Brad Johnson, Rosanna Arquette, Tom Sizemore, J. Kenneth Campbell

Flight of the Navigator *
👫 US 1986 90m colour
Buena Vista/Walt Disney (Robby Wald, Dimitri Villard)
▤ 🔍 🎧

Kidnapped by aliens, a 12-year-old boy returns home after an eight-year absence without having grown any older.
Science fiction aimed at a family audience and providing blandly innocuous, occasionally amusing entertainment.
w Michael Burton, Matt Macmanus story Mark H. Baker d Randal Kleiser ph James Glennon m Alan Silvestri pd William J. Creber ed Jeff Gourson
☆ Joey Cramer, Veronica Cartwright, Cliff DeYoung, Sarah Jessica Parker, Matt Adler, Howard Hesseman, Paul Mall (Paul Reubens), Robert Small

The Flight of the Phoenix *
US 1965 149m DeLuxe
TCF/Associates and Aldrich
▥ 🔍

A cargo passenger plane crashes in the desert, and the survivors try to avert disaster.
Achingly slow character adventure; an all-star cast works desperately hard but the final flight of the rebuilt plane seems almost an anticlimax after the surfeit of personal melodramatics.
w Lukas Heller novel Elleston Trevor d Robert Aldrich ph Joseph Biroc m Frank de Vol
☆ James Stewart, Richard Attenborough, Hardy Kruger, Peter Finch, Dan Duryea, Ernest Borgnine,
Ian Bannen, Ronald Fraser, Christian Marquand, George Kennedy
🏆 Ian Bannen

The Flight of the White Stallions: see The Miracle of the White Stallions

The Flight that Disappeared
US 1961 73m bw
UA/Harvard (Robert E. Kent)

Atomic scientists on an airliner find themselves in 'heaven' being tried by people of the future.
Eccentric anti-bomb curiosity, a second feature Outward Bound.
w Ralph Hart, Judith Hart, Owen Harris d Reginald Le Borg ph Gilbert Warrenton m Richard La Salle
☆ Gregory Morton, Addison Richards, Craig Hill, Paula Raymond, Dayton Lummis

Flight to Hong Kong
US 1956 88m bw
UA

A syndicate boss tries to two-time the mob.
Co-feature hokum which barely justifies its length.
w Leo Townsend, Edward G. O'Callaghan d Joseph M. Newman
☆ Rory Calhoun, Barbara Rush, Dolores Donlon, Soo Yong, Pat Conway, Werner Klemperer

Flight to Mars
US 1951 75m Cinecolor
Monogram
▥

After a rocket flight, four scientists discover that the inhabitants of Mars speak perfect American, learned by radio.
Pioneering science-fiction entry with nothing going for it but being first: writing, production and acting are alike abysmal.
w Arthur Strawn d Lesley Selander ph Harry Newman m Marlin Skiles
☆ Cameron Mitchell, Marguerite Chapman, Arthur Franz, Virginia Huston, John Litel

Flight to Tangier
US 1953 90m Technicolor 3-D
Paramount (Nat Holt)

A female FBI agent chases a three million dollar letter of credit.
Forced and boring action romance without much of either element.
wd Charles Marquis Warren ph Ray Rennahan m Paul Sawtell
☆ Joan Fontaine, Jack Palance, Corinne Calvet, Robert Douglas, Marcel Dalio, Jeff Morrow, Murray Matheson, John Doucette

The Flim Flam Man *
US 1967 104m DeLuxe Panavision
TCF/Lawrence Turman
▥

GB title: *One Born Every Minute*
An army deserter joins forces with an elderly con man.
Folksy comedy in a small-town setting; none of it really comes to the boil after a couple of early chase sequences.
w William Rose novel Guy Owen d Irvin Kershner, Yakima Canutt ph Charles Lang m Jerry Goldsmith
☆ George C. Scott, Michael Sarrazin, Sue Lyon, Harry Morgan, Jack Albertson, Alice Ghostley, Albert Salmi

'Yabba Dabba Do!'
The Flintstones
👫 US 1994 93m DeLuxe
Universal/Amblin/Hanna-Barbera (Bruce Cohen)
▥ ▤ 🔍 🎧

In the Stone Age town of Bedrock, quarry worker Fred Flintstone is promoted to vice-president so that he can be the fall guy for his boss's crooked schemes.
The only appeal of this live-action version of Hanna-Barbera's dated, animated TV sitcom lies in the actual re-creation of a cartoon environment and creatures. In the absence of anything approaching wit or humour, that soon palls; but the film found favour with the public, who flocked to see it.
w Tom S. Parker, Jim Jennewein, Steven E. de Souza d Brian Levant ph Dean Cundey m David Newman pd William Sandell ed Kent Beyda sp Industrial Light and Magic
☆ John Goodman, Elizabeth Perkins, Rick Moranis, Rosie O'Donnell, Elizabeth Taylor, Kyle MacLachlan, Halle Berry, Jonathan Winters, Sam Raimi
'Yabba Dabba Doo-doo.' – *Philadelphia Inquirer*
'Yabba Dabba Don't.' – *USA Today*
'Yabba Dabba Dud.' – *New York Daily Post*
'Yabba Dabba Poo!' – *Empire*
† The film's script was worked on by more than 30 writers, many of them in 'round table' sessions, in the style of TV sitcom scriptwriting.

Flipper
👫 US 1963 87m Metrocolor
(MGM)
▥▥

A fisherman's son on the Florida Keys befriends a dolphin.
Harmless boy-and-animal adventure which spawned two sequels and a TV series.
w Arthur Weiss d James B. Clark ph Lamar Boren, Joseph Brun m Henry Vars
☆ Chuck Connors, Luke Halpin, Kathleen Maguire, Connie Scott
† *Flipper's New Adventure* followed in 1964.

Flipper
👫 US 1996 96m DeLuxe
Universal/Bubble Factory/American Film (James J. McNamara, Perry Katz)
▥ ▤ 🔍

A 14-year-old boy, staying with his uncle on a Florida island, makes friends with a young dolphin.
Lacklustre movie in which nothing much happens very slowly; even dolphin lovers will be disappointed.
wd Alan Shapiro ph Bill Butler m Joel McNeely pd Thomas A. Walsh ed Peck Prior
☆ Paul Hogan, Elijah Wood, Chelsea Field, Isaac Hayes, Jonathan Banks, Jason Fuchs, Jessica Wesson
'You just can't get away with this sort of lack of invention any more.' – *Empire*

Flirtation Walk *
US 1934 97m bw
Warner (Frank Borzage)
▥

Love affairs of West Point cadets.
Light musical very typical of its period, with a few agreeable numbers.
w Delmer Daves d Frank Borzage ph Sol Polito, George Barnes m/ly Allie Wrubel, Mort Dixon ch Bobby Connolly
☆ Dick Powell, Ruby Keeler, Pat O'Brien, Ross Alexander, John Arledge, Henry O'Neill, Guinn Williams
'A rousing recruiting poster … and a splendid laboratory specimen of the adolescent cinema.' – *André Sennwald, New York Times*
🏆 best picture

Flirting *
Australia 1989 99m colour
Warner/Kennedy Miller (George Miller, Doug Mitchell, Terry Hayes)
▥ ▤ 🔍

A 17-year-old Australian schoolboy falls in love with a Ugandan girl at a neighbouring school.
A less effective, though occasionally affecting, sequel to The Year My Voice Broke.
wd John Duigan ph Geoff Burton pd Roger Ford ed Robert Gibson, Marcus D'Arcy
☆ Noah Taylor, Thandie Newton, Nicole Kidman, Bartholomew Rose, Felix Nobis, Josh Picker, Kiri Paramore
'Such rites of passage movies are common currency nowadays, but Duigan's ability to summon up the past with conviction, get good performances from his cast and to apply a sense of humour as well as a feeling of horror at what Australians did to their young circa 1965, makes the film universal in its appeal.' – *Derek Malcolm, Guardian*

The Flirting Widow
US 1930 70m bw
First National

A girl invents a lover, then kills him off … but his friend shows up.
Whimsical comedy which outstays its welcome.
w John F. Goodrich story Green Stockings by A. E. W. Mason d William A. Seiter
☆ Dorothy Mackaill, Basil Rathbone, Leila Hyams, Claude Gillingwater, William Austin

'Slim for the key houses and really built for neighbourhoods.' – *Variety*

Flirting with Disaster **
US   1996   92m   DeLuxe
Buena Vista/Miramax (Dean Silvers)
🎬 ▦ ⊙
After his wife gives birth to their son, the new father decides it is time to find his biological parents.
Witty road movie about a search for identity and new possibilities.
wd David O. Russell *ph* Eric Edwards *m* Stephen Endelman *pd* Kevin Thompson *ed* Christopher Tellefsen
☆ Ben Stiller, Patricia Arquette, Téa Leoni, Mary Tyler Moore, George Segal, Alan Alda, Lily Tomlin, Richard Jenkins, Josh Brolin
'Packed to the roof with genuinely chucklesome humour … manages to keep you laughing for at least two-thirds of its running time.' – *Total Film*

Flood Tide
US   1958   82m   bw   'Scope
Universal
A boy is jealous of his widowed mother's interest in a neighbour.
Modest melodrama, typical of its studio at the time.
w Dorothy Cooper *d* Abner Biberman
☆ George Nader, Cornell Borchers, Michel Ray, Judson Pratt, Joanna Moore

Floods of Fear *
GB   1958   84m   bw
Rank/Sydney Box
Two escaped convicts, a warder, and a pretty girl are trapped by floods in a lonely house.
Adequate melodrama with impressively gloomy production and performances but not many surprises.
wd Charles Crichton *novel* John and Ward Hawkins *ph* Christopher Challis *m* Alan Rawsthorne
☆ Howard Keel, Anne Heywood, Harry H. Corbett, Cyril Cusack

Floodtide
GB   1949   90m   bw
Aquila/Rank
A Clydebank apprentice becomes a ship designer.
Boring inspirational drama hindered by the Independent Frame method.
w Donald B. Wilson, George Blake *d* Frederick Wilson
☆ Gordon Jackson, Rona Anderson, John Laurie, Jack Lambert, Elizabeth Sellars

La flor de mi secreto: see *The Flower of My Secret*

The Floradora Girl
US   1930   75m   bw   (Technicolor sequence)
MGM
GB title: The Gay Nineties
The romance of the last remaining Floradora girl.
Not a musical but a period farce which laughs at rather than with the fashions of 1900. It doubtless succeeded with the audiences of its time.
w Gene Markey, Ralph Spence, Al Boasberg, Robert Hopkins *d* Harry Beaumont
☆ Marion Davies, Lawrence Gray, Walter Catlett, Ilka Chase, Vivian Oakland, Jed Prouty
'Good hoke entertainment … an all-type audience picture with no limitations.' – *Variety*

The Florentine Dagger
US   1935   69m   bw
Warner
A mysterious Borgia influence is brought to bear on the murder of an art dealer.
Vaguely unsatisfactory whodunnit with some intriguing and some pretentious elements.
w Brown Holmes, Tom Reed *novel* Ben Hecht *d* Robert Florey
☆ Margaret Lindsay, Donald Woods, C. Aubrey Smith, Robert Barrat, Henry O'Neill

Florian
US   1940   91m   bw
MGM (Winfield Sheehan)
In 1910 Austria, a poor boy and a rich girl are united by their love of a Lippizaner stallion.
Not kinky, but strangely dull.
w Noel Langley, Geza Herczeg, James K. McGuinness *d* Edwin L. Marin *ph* Karl Freund, Richard Rosson *m* Franz Waxman

---

☆ Robert Young, Helen Gilbert, Charles Coburn, Lee Bowman, Reginald Owen, S. Z. Sakall, Lucile Watson, Irina Baronova

Flower Drum Song *
US   1961   133m   Technicolor   Panavision
U-I/Rodgers and Hammerstein/Joseph Fields (Ross Hunter)
▦ ⊙
Romantic problems among the immigrants in San Francisco's Chinatown.
A Broadway musical which on the screen seems old-fashioned, remorselessly cute, and even insulting to the Chinese characters. Within its limits, however, it is well enough staged and performed.
w Joseph Fields *d* Henry Koster *ph* Russell Metty *m/ly* Richard Rodgers, Oscar Hammerstein II *md* Alfred Newman, Ken Darby *ch* Hermes Pan *ad* Alexander Golitzen, Joseph Wright *cos* Irene Sharaff
☆ Nancy Kwan, James Shigeta, Juanita Hall, Miyoshi Umeki, Jack Soo, Sen Yung, Kam Tong, Reiko Sato
† Nancy Kwan's singing was dubbed by B. J. Baker, Kam Tong's by John Dodson, and Reiko Sato's by Marilyn Horne.
🎭 Alfred Newman, Ken Darby; Russell Metty

The Flower of My Secret *
Spain/France   1995   107m   Eastmancolor
Electric/CiBy 2000/El Deseo (Esther Garcia)
▦
original title: La flor de mi secreto
A best-selling romantic novelist has a mid-life crisis: she takes to drink, tries a different kind of fiction, and rids herself of her quarrelsome husband.
Rather like his heroine, Almodóvar abandons his camp frivolities for something more mundane; it is sometimes effective, but as artificial as ever and not entirely convincing.
wd Pedro Almodóvar *ph* Affonso Beato *m* Alberto Iglesias *ad* Wolfgang Burmann *ed* José Salcedo
☆ Marisa Paredes, Juan Echanove, Imanol Arias, Carmen Elias, Rossy de Palma, Chus Lampreave, Joaquin Cortes
'From a director whose wackiness had begun to seem irritatingly predictable, it's a thoughtful and provocative new departure.' – *Sheila Johnston, Independent*

Flowers in the Attic
US   1987   92m   colour
Entertainment/New World (Sy Levin, Thomas Fries)
🎬 ▦ ⊙ ⌾
Four children are kept locked in an attic by their deranged grandmother.
Tame melodrama that tones down the horrors of the novel and settles for a soporific approach to its sensational material.
wd Jeffrey Bloom *novel* Virginia C. Andrews *ph* Frank Byers, Gil Hubbs *m* Christopher Young *pd* John Muto *ed* Gregory F. Plotts
☆ Louise Fletcher, Victoria Tennant, Jeb Stuart Adams, Ben Granger, Lindsay Parker, Marshall Colt, Nathan Davis

The Flowers of St Francis: see *Francis, God's Jester*

Flowing Gold
US   1940   82m   bw
Warner
A fugitive from justice finds himself in a Western oilfield.
Routine melodrama with climactic heroics and nothing to remember next day.
w Kenneth Gamet *d* Alfred E. Green
☆ John Garfield, Pat O'Brien, Frances Farmer, Raymond Walburn, Cliff Edwards

Flubber
🎬 US   1997   93m   Technicolor   Panavision
Buena Vista/Walt Disney/Great Oaks (John Hughes, Ricardo Mestres)
▦ ⊙ ⌾ ⊙
An absent-minded scientist accidentally invents a substance that is lighter than air.
The change of title in this sequel reflects the altered emphasis, which is now firmly on special effects that suggest Hughes should be making animated films.

Playing stooge to a green jelly, Williams lacks gravity and also humour.
w John Hughes, Bill Walsh *story* Samuel W. Taylor *d* Les Mayfield *ph* Dean Cundey *m* Danny Elfman *pd* Andrew McAlpine *ed* Harvey Rosenstock, Michael A. Stevenson *sp* Industrial Light and Magic
☆ Robin Williams, Marcia Gay Harden, Christopher McDonald, Raymond J. Barry, Clancy Brown, Ted Levine, Wil Wheaton, Edie McClurg
'Old-fashioned family entertainment.' – *The Times*
† It is a remake of the 1961 movie *The Absent-Minded Professor* (qv), starring Fred MacMurray, which was followed by a sequel, *Son of Flubber*.

Fluffy
🎬 US   1964   92m   Eastmancolor
U-I/Scarus (Gordon Kay)
A biologist manages to tame a lion.
Mindless, cheerful animal comedy.
w Samuel Rocca *d* Earl Bellamy *ph* Clifford Stine *m* Irving Gertz
☆ Tony Randall, Shirley Jones, Edward Andrews, Ernest Truex, Howard Morris, Jim Backus, Frank Faylen

'Have you ever met someone you felt you already knew?'
Fluke
US   1995   96m   colour
MGM/Rocket (Paul Maslansky, Lata Ryan)
🎬 ▦ ⊙ ⌾
After dying in a car crash, a man is reincarnated as a dog and tries to find his way home.
Doggedly sentimental fantasy; it sits up and begs to be liked, but lacks bite.
w Carlo Carlei, James Carrington *novel* James Herbert *d* Carlo Carlei *ph* Raffaele Mertes *m* Carlo Siliotto *pd* Hilda Stark *ed* Mark Conte
☆ Matthew Modine, Nancy Travis, Eric Stoltz, Jon Polito, Tom Coleman

The Flute and the Arrow *
Sweden   1957   75m   Technicolor   Agascope
Sandrews (Arne Sucksdorff)
original title: En Djungelsaga
The story of a remote Indian tribe and a prowling leopard thought to be possessed by a demon.
Superbly photographed but rather dull: Sucksdorff failed to provide enough story for a feature.
m Ravi Shankar *wd/ph* Arne Sucksdorff

'Once it was human … even as you and I … this monster created by atoms gone wild!'
The Fly
US   1958   94m   Eastmancolor   Cinemascope
TCF (Kurt Neumann)
🎬 ▦ ⊙
A scientist invents a method of transmitting and reassembling atoms. He transmits himself and does not notice a fly in the compartment…
Unpleasant horror film which becomes ludicrous but not funny.
w James Clavell *story* George Langelaan *d* Kurt Neumann *ph* Karl Struss *m* Paul Sawtell
☆ David Hedison, Patricia Owens, Herbert Marshall, Vincent Price
'It might be possible, I suppose, to take this preposterous piece of merchandise as a monstrous joke. Even so, it would be a joke in deplorably bad taste.' – *C. A. Lejeune*
† Sequels were *Return of the Fly* (1959) and *Curse of the Fly* (1965), neither worth noting in detail. And see below.

'Be afraid. Be very afraid.'
The Fly *
US   1986   100m   DeLuxe
TCF/Brooksfilm (Stuart Cornfeld)
🎬 ▦ ⊙ ⌾
A deliberately gruesome update of the above, with much unpleasant detail carried along by a certain style.
w Charles Edward Pogue, David Cronenberg *d* David Cronenberg *ph* Mark Irwin *m* Howard Shore *pd* Carol Spier *ed* Ronald Sanders
☆ Jeff Goldblum, Geena Davis, John Getz
'One does not have to be totally warped to appreciate this film, but it does take a particular sensibility to embrace it.' – *Variety*
'Stylish acrobatics, cowgum gore.' – *Sight and Sound*
🎭 make-up (Chris Walas, Stephen Dupuis)

Fly Away Home **
🎬 US   1996   106m   Technicolor
Columbia/Sandollar (John Veitch, Carol Baum)
▦ ⊙ ⌾
After her mother dies, a 13-year-old goes to Canada to live with her estranged father and adopts a family of motherless goslings.
Charming, understated film about loss and love, which reaches a splendid climax as the young girl teaches geese to migrate to their winter haunts.
w Robert Rodat, Vince McKewin *autobiography* Bill Lishman *d* Carroll Ballard *ph* Caleb Deschanel *m* Mark Isham *pd* Seamus Flannery *ed* Nicholas C. Smith *sp* CORE Digital
☆ Jeff Daniels, Anna Paquin, Dana Delany, Terry Kinney, Holter Graham, Jeremy Ratchford
'It's a genuine delight, and a definite thumbs aloft for kids of about six upwards.' – *Philip Thomas, Empire*
🎭 Caleb Deschanel

'Action that makes every pulse beat sound like thunder!'
Fly by Night *
US   1942   74m   bw
Paramount
GB title: Secrets of G32
A doctor, accused of murdering a scientist, goes on the run and uncovers a Nazi spy ring.
Hoary 39 Steps imitation, commendably done on a low budget to furnish wartime propaganda.
w Jay Dratler, F. Hugh Herbert *d* Robert Siodmak
☆ Richard Carlson, Nancy Kelly, Albert Basserman, Walter Kingsford, Martin Kosleck, Miles Mander

'Like father. Like son.'
The Fly II
US   1989   105m   colour
Fox/Brooksfilms (Steven-Charles Jaffe)
🎬 ▦ ⊙ ⌾
The precocious son of The Fly takes his revenge on the scientist who exploits him.
An uneasy mix of sentimentality and gore, but otherwise a standard monster movie.
w Mick Garris, Jim and Ken Wheat, Frank Darabont *d* Chris Walas *ph* Robin Vidgeon *m* Christopher Young *pd* Michael S. Bolton *ed* Sean Barton *sp* Chris Walas
☆ Eric Stoltz, Daphne Zuniga, Lee Richardson, Harley Cross, Gary Chalk, Ann Marie Lee, Frank C. Turner, John Getz
'Constructed with a refreshing intricacy and visual panache.' – *Philip Strick, MFB*

The Flying Circus: see *Flying Devils*

The Flying Deuces *
🎬 US   1939   67m   bw
Boris Morros
🎬 ▦ ⊙
Laurel and Hardy join the Foreign Legion.
Patchy comedy from the end of the comedians' period of glory, and showing signs of decline.
w Ralph Spence, Harry Langdon, Charles Rogers, Alfred Schiller *d* Edward Sutherland *ph* Art Lloyd, Elmer Dyer *m* Leo Shuken *md* Edward Paul *ed* Jack Dennis
☆ Stan Laurel, Oliver Hardy, Jean Parker, James Finlayson, Reginald Gardiner, Charles Middleton
'Mechanical stuff … seemed like *Beau Hunks* and *Bonnie Scotland* all over again.' – *William K. Everson*

Flying Devils
US   1933   62m   bw
RKO
GB title: The Flying Circus
Three war veteran pilots join a flying circus.
Smart little programmer which certainly provided money's worth and has no axe to grind.
w Byron Morgan, Louis Stevens *d* Russell Birdwell *ph* Nicholas Musuraca *m* Max Steiner
☆ Arline Judge, Bruce Cabot, Ralph Bellamy, Eric Linden, Cliff Edwards

Flying Down to Rio **
US   1933   89m   bw
RKO (Merian C. Cooper, Lou Brock)
🎬
A dance band is a big success in Rio de Janeiro.
A thin musical electrified by the finale in which girls dance on the wings of moving airplanes, and by the

---

teaming of Astaire and Rogers for the first time. Now an irresistible period piece.

w Cyril Hume, H. W. Hanemann, Erwin Gelsey play Anne Caldwell story Louis Brock
d Thornton Freeland ph J. Roy Hunt
m/ly Vincent Youmans, Edward Eliscu, Gus Kahn md Max Steiner ch Dave Gould ad Van Nest Polglase, Carroll Clark ed Jack Kitchin
☆ Dolores del Rio, Gene Raymond, Raul Roulien, Ginger Rogers, Fred Astaire, Blanche Frederici, Walter Walker, Franklin Pangborn, Eric Blore
'Its main point is the screen promise of Fred Astaire ... the others are all hoofers after him.' – Variety
♫ 'Music Makes Me'; 'Orchids in the Moonlight'; 'Flying Down to Rio'
♫ song 'The Carioca'

Flying Elephants
👬 US 1927 20m bw silent
Hal Roach

A caveman has the toothache.
Fragmentary and generally unsatisfactory comedy starring Laurel and Hardy before they properly teamed, but released after their joint success.
w Hal Roach, H. M. Walker d Frank Butler sp Roy Seawright
☆ Stan Laurel, Oliver Hardy, James Finlayson, Viola Richard, Dorothy Coburn
† According to Hal Roach, he directed the film, with Butler only doing a day's work on retakes.

The Flying Fontaines
US 1959 73m Eastmancolor
Columbia

Jealousy on the big top trapeze.
Old hat circus melodrama, not especially well presented.
w Donn Mullally, Lee Ewin d George Sherman
☆ Michael Callan, Evy Norlund, Joan Evans, Rian Garrick, Joe DeSantis

Flying Fortress
GB 1942 110m bw
Warner (Max Milner)

A Canadian becomes a hero of bombing missions over Berlin.
Cardboard propaganda with silly love interest and a hilarious climax in which the hero does his stuff on the wing of a flying plane.
w Brock Williams, Gordon Wellesley, Edward Dryhurst d Walter Forde ph Gus Drisse, Basil Emmott
☆ Richard Greene, Carla Lehmann, Betty Stockfeld, Donald Stewart, Charles Heslop, Sidney King, Basil Radford, John Stuart

Flying High
US 1931 80m bw
MGM
GB title: Happy Landing

A zany inventor breaks a long-distance flight record because he doesn't know how to land.
Primitive comedy musical with inept dialogue and a static camera, partially salvaged by two early Busby Berkeley routines.
w Robert Hopkins, A. P. Younger, Charles Riesner d Charles Riesner
☆ Bert Lahr, Charlotte Greenwood, Pat O'Brien, Charles Winninger, Guy Kibbee, Hedda Hopper

'Marine air-devils in hot pursuit ... Blood-red trails streak the sky!'
'Bares the hearts of women who wait!'

Flying Leathernecks
US 1951 102m Technicolor
RKO (Edmund Grainger)
👓 📼 📷

Two marine officers fight the Japs and each other on Guadalcanal.
Empty, violent war actioner full of phoney heroics.
w James Edward Grant d Nicholas Ray ph William E. Snyder m Roy Webb
☆ John Wayne, Robert Ryan, Janis Carter, Don Taylor, Jay C. Flippen, William Harrigan, James Bell
'Ray's treatment is depressingly second rate and does nothing to alleviate the unpleasant impression of this disturbingly violent production.' – Penelope Houston

The Flying Missile
US 1950 92m bw
Columbia (Jerry Bresler)

A submarine commander defies authority to prove that rockets can be launched from the deck of a submarine.
Dated semi-documentary melodrama which was pretty flat on first viewing.
w Richard English, James Gunn d Henry Levin ph William Snyder m George Duning
☆ Glenn Ford, Viveca Lindfors, Henry O'Neill, Carl Benton Reid, Joe Sawyer, John Qualen

Flying Saucer
US 1949 60m bw
Film Classics (Mikel Conrad)

Russians try to steal the secret of a flying saucer from its inventor.
A film whose title brought the term into general use; otherwise it is a standard paranoid Cold War thriller.
w Mikel Conrad, Howard Irving Young d Mikel Conrad ph Phil Tannura m Darrell Calker ed Robert Crandall
☆ Mikel Conrad, Pat Garrison, Lester Sharpe, Russell Hicks, Frank Draper, Virginia Hewitt, Hantz von Teuffen

The Flying Scotsman
GB 1929 63m bw
Warner/BIP

An ex-employee tries to wreck a crack train.
Fairly presentable example of an early talkie film originally shot silent; one or two climactic thrills.
w Victor Kendall, Garnett Weston story Joe Grossman d Castleton Knight ph Theodor Sparkuhl m Idris Lewis, John Reynders ad T. H. Gibbins ed A. C. Hammond
☆ Moore Marriott, Pauline Jameson, Ray Milland, Alec Hurley, Dino Galvani

The Flying Serpent
US 1945 59m bw
PRC (Sigmund Neufeld)
📼

A crazed archaeologist uses a rare bird as a murder instrument.
Ineffective low-key horror despite an always interesting star.
w John T. Neville d Sherman Scott (Sam Newfield)
☆ George Zucco, Ralph Lewis, Hope Kramer, Eddie Acuff

'A bomber squadron wouldn't get through ... but one ship might make it!'
Flying Tigers
US 1942 100m bw
Republic (Edmund Grainger)
👓 📼 📷 🎧

American airmen fight the Japs over World War II China.
More mock heroics with noisy but unconvincing action sequences.
w Kenneth Gamet, Barry Trivers d David Miller ph Jack Marta m Victor Young
☆ John Wayne, John Carroll, Anna Lee, Paul Kelly, Mae Clarke
♫ Victor Young

FM
US 1978 104m Technicolor
CIC/Universal (Rand Holston)
📼 📷
aka: Citizens' Band

Problems of a commercial radio station whose disc jockeys seek integrity above commerce.
Footling cause-pleading is all this 'with-it' movie has to offer apart from its picture of commercial radio in the late seventies, which should be of interest to social historians.
w Ezra Sacks d John A. Alonzo ph David Myers m Steely Dan, Linda Ronstadt, Jimmy Buffett and others pd Lawrence G. Paull ed Jeff Gourson
☆ Michael Brandon, Eileen Brennan, Alex Karras, Cleavon Little, Martin Mull

Fog
US 1933 70m bw
Columbia

Three murders occur on an ocean liner enveloped in fog.
Promising but increasingly inept mystery with an unconvincing solution.

w Ethel Hill, Dore Schary story Valentine Williams, Dorothy Rice Sims d Albert Rogell
☆ Donald Cook, Mary Brian, Reginald Denny, Robert McWade, Maude Eburne
'Ably directed but deficient on casting and story.' – Variety

The Fog *
US 1979 91m Metrocolor Panavision
Rank/Avco Embassy (Debra Hill)
📼 📼 📷 🎧

A small Californian town is invaded by the leprous ghosts of mariners wrecked on the coast a hundred years before.
Silly but beguiling horror film with shock effects typical of its director.
w John Carpenter, Debra Hill d John Carpenter ph Dean Cundey m John Carpenter pd Tommy Lee Wallace ed Tommy Lee Wallace, Charles Bornstein
☆ Adrienne Barbeau, Hal Holbrook, John Houseman, Janet Leigh, Jamie Lee Curtis, Tom Atkins
'An uneasy venture down a blind alley.' – Tom Milne, MFB

Fog Island
US 1945 70m bw
PRC (Leon Fromkess)
📼

A wealthy ex-convict gathers on a foggy island all the people he considers responsible for his downfall.
Very tolerable minor mystery lifted without permission from Agatha Christie's And Then There Were None.
w Pierre Gendron d Terry Morse
☆ George Zucco, Lionel Atwill, Jerome Cowan, Sharon Douglas, Veda Ann Borg, Ian Keith

Fog over Frisco ***
US 1934 68m bw
Warner (Henry Blanke)

A San Francisco heiress gets herself murdered.
Silly whodunnit highly notable for its cinematic style, all dissolves, wipes and quick takes. Probably the fastest moving film ever made, and very entertaining despite its plot inadequacy.
w Robert N. Lee novel George Dyer d William Dieterle ph Tony Gaudio md Leo F. Forbstein ed Harold McLernon
☆ Bette Davis, Donald Woods, Margaret Lindsay, Lyle Talbot, Hugh Herbert, Arthur Byron, Robert Barrat, Douglass Dumbrille, Henry O'Neill, Irving Pichel, Alan Hale
'Another racketeering story, mild in entertainment. No marked names of strength.' – Variety
'It reveals those qualities of pace and velocity and sharpness which make the Hollywood product acceptable even when the shallow content of ideas makes you want to scream.' – Robert Forsythe
'Its speed is artificially created by pacing, wipes, opticals, overlapping sound, camera movement and placing of characters, and by its habit of never having time really to begin or end scenes.' – William K. Everson
† Remade 1942 as Spy Ship, a second feature.

Folies Bergère ***
US 1935 84m bw
Twentieth Century (William Goetz, Raymond Griffith)
GB title: The Man from the Folies Bergère

A Parisian banker persuades a music hall artist to impersonate him, but the wife and girlfriend become involved in the confusion.
Amusing star vehicle with inventive Berkeleyish numbers and some remarkably sexy dialogue.
w Bess Meredyth, Hal Long play The Red Cat by Rudolph Lothar, Hans Adler d Roy del Ruth ph Barney McGill, Peverell Marley md Alfred Newman ch Dave Gould
☆ Maurice Chevalier, Merle Oberon, Ann Sothern, Eric Blore
† Remade as That Night in Rio, with Don Ameche, and On the Riviera, with Danny Kaye (both qv).
👤 Dave Gould

The Folies of Elodie (dubbed)
France 1981 90m Fujicolour
AGC/MMP
📼
aka: Naughty Blue Knickers

A pair of satin panties tells the story of the adventures of its owner with her lover, maid, godson, her godson's mother and a truck driver.
Trite comic erotica, despite its high-powered scriptwriters, done with no style, merely soft-focus photography of banal images.
w Paul Gegauff, Gerard Croce, Andre Genoves novel Les Mémoires d'une Culotte by Aymé Dubois-Jolly d Andre Genoves ph Jean G. Charruyer m C. Pimper ad Michel Debats ed Aline Asseo
☆ Marcha Grant, Andre Genoves, Caroline Aguilar, Bruno Du Louvat, Charlotte Walior, Yves Massard, Marthe Mercadier

Folks!
US 1992 106m Technicolor
First Independent/Penta (Victor Drai, Malcolm R. Harding)
📼 📼 📷

At his ailing mother's suggestion, a businessman tries to kill her and his senile father for the insurance money.
Embarrassingly bad comedy, not merely tasteless but, what is worse, devoid of humour.
w Robert Klane d Ted Kotcheff ph Larry Pizer m Michel Colombier pd William J. Creber ed Joan E. Chapman
☆ Tom Selleck, Don Ameche, Anne Jackson, Christine Ebersole, Wendy Crewson, Robert Pastorelli, Michael Murphy
'Marking severe career setbacks for Ameche and Selleck, Folks! obviously miscalculates the low intelligence of the mass audience.' – Variety

Follies Girl
US 1943 71m bw
PRC

An army private visits the forces canteen but falls for the burlesque dancer next door.
Feebly developed romance with music, mostly notable for its specialities.
w Marcy Klauber, Charles Robinson d William Rowland
☆ Wendy Barrie, Doris Nolan, Gordon Oliver, Anne Barrett, Cora Witherspoon

Follow a Star
👬 GB 1959 104m bw
Rank (Hugh Stewart)

A shy amateur singer allows a fading star to mime to his voice.
Star comedy with an antique plot and a superfluity of pathos.
w Jack Davies, Henry Blyth, Norman Wisdom d Robert Asher ph Jack Asher m Philip Green
☆ Norman Wisdom, Jerry Desmonde, June Laverick, Hattie Jacques, Richard Wattis, John Le Mesurier, Fenella Fielding, Ron Moody
'Such comedy as there is is mostly muffed by the lack of any sense of comic timing.' – MFB

Follow Me
GB 1971 93m Technicolor Panavision
Universal/Hal B. Wallis (Paul Nathan)
🎧
US title: The Public Eye

An eccentric private eye is hired to follow an accountant's wife, and she finds him fascinating.
Dullish, whimsical rendering of a dullish, whimsical one-act play; it never springs to life or interest.
w Peter Shaffer play Peter Shaffer d Carol Reed ph Christopher Challis m John Barry
☆ Topol, Michael Jayston, Mia Farrow
'An uneasy mixture of broad comedy and high romance.' – Sight and Sound

Follow Me Boys
👬 US 1966 132m Technicolor
Walt Disney (Winston Hibler)

The domestic trials and tribulations of a smalltown schoolmaster.
Sentimental family saga full of patriotic fervour.
w Louis Pelletier novel God and My Country by Mackinlay Kantor d Norman Tokar ph Clifford Stine m George Bruns
☆ Fred MacMurray, Vera Miles, Lillian Gish, Charlie Ruggles, Elliott Reid, Kurt Russell, Luana Patten, Ken Murray
'Demands an extremely strong stomach.' – MFB

'One of the worst films to emanate from the Disney studios, a near parody of all the lowbrow small-townery that has given Disney's features a bad name among intellectuals who never go to Disney movies. It is unworthy of the Disney trademark.' – *Judith Crist*

Follow Me Quietly *
US   1949   60m   bw
RKO (Herman Schlom)
Police track down a killer who strangles whenever it rains.
Effective little urban thriller with nice sense of detail.
w Lillie Hayward d Richard Fleischer ph Robert de Grasse
☆ William Lundigan, Dorothy Patrick, Jeff Corey, Nestor Paiva, Charles D. Brown, Paul Guilfoyle

Follow That Camel: see *Carry On – Follow That Camel*

Follow That Dream
US   1962   110m   DeLuxe   Panavision
UA/Mirisch (David Weisbart)
◙▤ ▣ ◠
A wandering family sets up house on a Florida beach.
Tiresomely cute comedy vehicle for a resistible star.
w Charles Lederer novel *Pioneer Go Home* by Richard Powell d Gordon Douglas ph Leo Tover m Hans Salter
☆ Elvis Presley, Arthur O'Connell, Joanna Moore, Anne Helm, Jack Kruschen

Follow That Guy with the One Black Shoe: see *Le Grand Blond avec une Chaussure Noire*

Follow the Band
US   1943   60m   bw
Universal (Paul Malvern)
A farm worker on his first visit to New York becomes a trombonist in a night-club.
Minor musical filler which packs in a surprising range of talent.
w Warren Wilson, Dorothy Bennett d Jean Yarbrough
☆ Eddie Quillan, Leon Errol, Mary Beth Hughes, Samuel S. Hinds, Robert Mitchum, Frances Langford, Leo Carrillo, Hilo Hattie, the King Sisters, Skinnay Ennis and his band

Follow the Boys *
US   1944   109m   bw
Universal (Charles K. Feldman)
A song and dance man organizes entertainment for the US troops during World War II.
Scrappy, unattractive propaganda tribute by the stars to the stars, enlivened only by a few guest spots.
w Lou Breslow, Gertrude Purcell d A. Edward Sutherland ph David Abel m Leigh Harline and others
☆ George Raft, Vera Zorina, Charley Grapewin, Grace MacDonald, Charles Butterworth, George Macready, Elizabeth Patterson; and Orson Welles, Marlene Dietrich, Jeanette MacDonald, Dinah Shore, Donald O'Connor, Peggy Ryan, W. C. Fields, the Andrews Sisters, Artur Rubinstein and also Sophie Tucker, Ted Lewis and his band, etc
♫ song 'I'll Walk Alone' (mJule Styne, lySammy Cahn)

Follow the Boys
US   1963   95m   Metrocolor   Panavision
MGM/Franmet (Lawrence P. Bachmann)
An American warship is diverted from Cannes to Santa Margarita, and the waiting wives have to follow by road.
Harmless star comedy musical.
w David T. Chantler, David Osborn d Richard Thorpe ph Ted Scaife
☆ Connie Francis, Paula Prentiss, Dany Robin, Russ Tamblyn, Richard Long

Follow the Fleet **
US   1936   110m   bw
RKO (Pandro S. Berman)
▤ ◠
Sailors on shore leave romance a couple of girl singers.
Amiable star musical which makes heavy weather of a listless and overlong script, but has good numbers for those who can wait.

w Dwight Taylor play *Shore Leave* by Hubert Osborne, Allan Scott d Mark Sandrich ph David Abel m/ly Irving Berlin md Max Steiner
☆ Fred Astaire, Ginger Rogers, Randolph Scott, Harriet Hilliard, Astrid Allwyn, Harry Beresford, Lucille Ball, Betty Grable, Tony Martin
'The running time is way overboard … dialogue is good and can be depended on for laughs, with the Astaire-Rogers dancing sure to do the rest. But cutting it would have helped a lot more.' – *Variety*
♫ 'I'm Putting All My Eggs in One Basket'; 'We Saw the Sea'; 'Let's Face the Music and Dance'; 'Let Yourself Go'; 'But Where Are You?'; 'I'd Rather Lead a Band'; 'Get Thee Behind Me Satan'; 'With a Smile on My Face'.

Follow the Leader
US   1930   76m   bw
Paramount
A saucy understudy replaces a kidnapped leading lady.
Broadway spoof rather tediously designed as a vehicle for the star's face-pulling.
w Sid Silvers, Gertrude Purcell from the Broadway musical *Manhattan Mary* d Norman Taurog
☆ Ed Wynn, Ginger Rogers, Ethel Merman, Lou Holtz, Stanley Smith
'First-run material and above average.' – *Variety*

Follow the Leader
US   1944   64m   bw
Monogram/Banner (Sam Katzman, Jack Dietz)
Muggs, unhappy at being unable to stay in the Army, escapes a murder rap and exposes a thief robbing Army stores.
Despite a violent death, this is a sentimental addition to the East Side Kids series, substituting flag-waving and mother-love for the more usual comedy.
w William X. Crowley, Beryl Sachs story Ande Lamb d William Beaudine ph Marcel LePicard md Edward Kay ad Ernest Hickson ed Carl Pierson
☆ Leo Gorcey, Huntz Hall, Gabriel Dell, Billy Benedict, Joan Marsh, Jack LaRue, Dave Durand, Gene Austin, Sherrill Sisters

Follow the Sun
US   1951   93m   bw
TCF (Samuel G. Engel)
Ben Hogan, a professional golfer, recovers slowly and painfully from a car crash and for the first time gains the affection of the crowd.
Modest sporting biopic, generally watchable but rising to no great heights.
w Frederick Hazlitt Brennan d Sidney Lanfield ph Leo Tover m Cyril Mockridge
☆ Glenn Ford, Anne Baxter, Dennis O'Keefe, June Havoc, Larry Keating, Nana Bryant, Roland Winters

Follow Thru
US   1930   93m   Technicolor
Paramount
Two women are after the same pro golfer.
Flat film version of a Broadway show.
w De Sylva, Brown, Henderson, from their show d Laurence Schwab, Lloyd Corrigan
☆ Charles Rogers, Nancy Carroll, Zelma O'Neal, Jack Haley, Eugene Pallette, Thelma Todd
'Paramount has tossed away a heavy money picture.' – *Variety*
♫ 'Button Up Your Overcoat'; 'You Wouldn't Fool Me Would You'; 'I'm Hard to Please'; 'A Peach of a Pair'; 'It Must be You'.

Folly to be Wise *
GB   1952   91m   bw
London Films/Launder and Gilliat
A brains trust at an army unit starts off a battle of the sexes.
Typical James Bridie comedy which starts brightly and whimsically, then peters out and is saved by the acting.
w Frank Launder, John Dighton play *It Depends What You Mean* by James Bridie d Frank Launder ph Jack Hildyard m Temple Abady
☆ Alastair Sim, Roland Culver, Elizabeth Allan, Martita Hunt, Colin Gordon
'It seems to get funnier the longer it's spun out.' – *Pauline Kael, 70s*

Fong Sai Yuk *
Hong Kong/China   1993   112m   colour
Eastern (Chui Po Chu)
aka: *The Legend of Fong Sai Yuk*
With the help of his fighting mother, a martial arts expert wins a bride and joins a revolution to overthrow the Manchu dynasty.
Exuberant mix of broad comedy and acrobatic martial arts, encompassing mistaken identity, gender confusion and romance.
w Kay On, Chan Kim Chung d Corey Yuen ph Jingle Ma m James Wong pd Ann Hui ed Cheung Yim Chung
☆ Jet Li, Josephine Siao, Michele Reis, Adam Cheng, Sibelle Hu, Paul Chu Kong

Fong Sai Yuk II
Hong Kong   1993   colour
Eastern
aka: *The Legend of Fong Sai Yuk II*
Fong Sai Yuk defeats a traitor's attempt to rule a triad opposed to the Manchu dynasty, while two women battle for his love.
A lively though scrappy sequel with the emphasis on comedy and romantic passion and disappointment; it climaxes with some spectacular, acrobatic fight sequences, including Jet Li's blindfolded sword-wielding and a battle with benches to prevent his mother's death by hanging.
☆ Jet Li, Michelle Reis, Amy Kwok, Josephine Siao, Adam Cheng

Fontan **
USSR   1988   101m   colour
BFI/Lenfilm (Boris Pavlov-Silvanski)
aka: *The Fountain*
The eccentric inhabitants of a Leningrad apartment block take matters into their own hands when their water and electricity are cut off.
Satirical comedy poking fun at most aspects of Gorbachev's Russia.
w Vladimir Vardunas d Yuri Mamin ph Anatoli Lapshov m Aleksei Zalivalow ad Yuri Pugach ed O. Adrianova
☆ Asankul Kuttubaev, Sergei Dontsov, Zhanna Kerimtaeva, Viktor Mikhailov, Anatoli Kalmikov, Liudmila Samokhvalova

Fontane Effi Briest: see *Effi Briest*

The Food of the Gods
US   1976   88m   Movielab
AIP (Bert I. Gordon)
A curious substance which oozes out of the ground turns common beasts into monsters.
Rather crude horror movie which has little affinity with its literary original.
wd Bert I. Gordon story H. G. Wells ph Reginald Morris m Elliot Kaplan
☆ Marjoe Gortner, Pamela Franklin, Ida Lupino, Ralph Meeker, John McLiam
'Not only sick, but sickening.' – *Arthur Knight*
'I wish I hadn't seen the movie, so I could avoid it like the plague.' – *John Simon*
'More plot holes than any movie in recent memory, and enough dopey lines to make a Saturday night audience howl in all the wrong places.' – *David Sterritt, Christian Science Monitor*

Food of the Gods II
Canada   1989   91m   colour
Rose & Ruby (David Mitchell, Damian Lee)
◙▤ ▤ ◠
Giant man-eating rats are let loose on a college campus.
Risibly bad horror with a catch-penny title; it was not a sequel to the first film nor does it in any way resemble Wells's original story.
w Richard Bennett, E. Kim Brewster d Damian Lee ph Curtis Petersen ed David Mitchell sp Ted Rae
☆ Paul Coufos, Lisa Schrage, Colin Fox, Frank Moore, Real Andrews, Jackie Burroughs

The Fool **
GB   1990   140m   colour
Hobo/Sands Films/Richard Goodwin, Christine Edzard
A Victorian clerk enjoys a double life as a businessman moving in the best social circles.
Its meticulous evocation of Victorian life, drawing on the books of Henry Mayhew, sometimes overwhelms the slender plot, but it is never less than watchable.

w Christine Edzard, Olivier Stockman d Christine Edzard ph Robin Vidgeon m Michael Sanvoisin ed Olivier Stockman
☆ Derek Jacobi, Cyril Cusack, Ruth Mitchell, Maria Aitken, Irina Brook, Paul Brooke, Richard Caldicot, James Cairncross, Jim Carter, Jonathan Cecil, Maria Charles

Fool for Love
US   1985   106m   colour
Cannon/Golan-Globus
▤
In a decaying motel, a half-brother and sister pick over the scab of their unsatisfactory, incestuous relationship.
Basically a filmed play, claustrophobic and taken at an excessively slow tempo.
w Sam Shepard play *Sam Shepard* d Robert Altman ph Pierre Mignot m George Burt pd Stephen Altman ed Luce Grunenwaldt, Steve Dunn
☆ Sam Shepard, Kim Basinger, Randy Quaid, Harry Dean Stanton

The Fool Killer
US   1964   100m   bw
Landau/AA
An orphan suspects his friend is an axe murderer.
Post-Civil War fable with good performances but not much point.
w David Friedkin, Morton Fine novel Helen Eustis d Servando Gonzalez
☆ Anthony Perkins, Edward Albert, Dana Elcar, Henry Hull, Salome Jens

A Fool There Was *
US   1915   67m   bw   silent
William Fox
A financier in Europe forsakes all for a *femme fatale*, and dies in her arms.
Antediluvian moral melodrama which made a star of Bara and added the word 'vamp' to the language.
wd Frank Powell play Porter Emerson Browne suggested by Rudyard Kipling's poem *The Vampire*
☆ Theda Bara, Edward Jose, Mabel Frenyer, May Allison

Foolin' Around
US   1979   101m   DeLuxe
Columbia/Arnold Kopelson
A country bumpkin wins a runaway heiress.
Uneasy harkback to the innocence of It Happened One Night, with willing performers in search of a script and setting.
w Mike Kane, David Swift d Richard T. Heffron ph Philip Lathrop m Charles Bernstein
☆ Gary Busey, Annette O'Toole, John Calvin, Eddie Albert, Cloris Leachman, Tony Randall

Foolish Wives **
US   1921   85m   bw   silent
Universal
◠
In Monte Carlo, a fake count seduces and blackmails rich women.
Weird melodrama with memorable moments and a vast set; Stroheim's most vivid star performance and one of his most lavish productions.
wd Erich von Stroheim ph Ben Reynolds, William Daniels ad Erich von Stroheim, Richard Day
☆ Erich von Stroheim, Mae Busch, Maude George, Cesare Gravina
'A very superior piece of photoplay craftsmanship, original in ideas and treatment and deserving of higher rating than *Orphans of the Storm, Loves of Pharaoh, The Storm* and other second-class material which however brought forth applause and bravos from screen public and scribes.' – *Tamar Lane, What's Wrong with the Movies*
† The film was released in Latin America at a length of 6hrs 48m.

Fools
US   1970   93m   Eastmancolor
Translor
▤
An unsuccessful actor has an idyllic love affair with a girl he meets in a park; but her jealous millionaire husband shoots her dead.
Foolish is the word for those who concocted this tedious parable about the innocence of love and the sickness of society.
w Robert Rudelson d Tom Gries

☆ Jason Robards Jnr, Katharine Ross, Scott Hylands

Fools for Scandal *
US 1938 81m bw
Warner (Mervyn Le Roy)
A Hollywood movie star falls in love with a French nobleman.
Disappointingly leaden romantic comedy.
w Herbert and Joseph Fields *play* Return Engagement by Nancy Hamilton, Rosemary Casey, James Shute d Mervyn Le Roy ph Ted Tetzlaff m/ly Richard Rodgers, Lorenz Hart
☆ Carole Lombard, Fernand Gravet, Ralph Bellamy, Allen Jenkins, Isabel Jeans, Marie Wilson, Ottola Nesmith
'Many diverting moments … will do average business.' – *Variety*

Fools of Fortune *
GB 1990 109m Technicolor
Palace/Polygram/Working Title/Film Four International (Sarah Radclyffe)
▭ ▭ ◎ ∿
An Anglo-Irish family becomes caught up in the troubles of the 1920s.
Understated story of family tragedy, with a quiet appeal.
w Michael Hirst *novel* William Trevor d Pat O'Connor ph Jerzy Zielinski m Hans Zimmer pd Jamie Leonard ed Michael Bradsell
☆ Iain Glen, Mary Elizabeth Mastrantonio, Julie Christie, Michael Kitchen, Niamh Cusack, Tom Hickey, John Kavanagh, Mick Lally, Niall Toibin
'A piece of classically-British film-making in the television style: restrained, elliptical, curiously reticent.' – *David Wilson, MFB*

Fools Parade **
US 1971 98m Eastmancolor
Columbia/Stanmore/Penbar (Andrew V. McLaglen)
GB title: *Dynamite Man from Glory Jail*
An ex-con has trouble cashing a cheque for his prison savings, especially as outlaws are after it.
Curious admixture of comedy, adventure and violence with a thirties setting, from the author of Night of the Hunter; generally gripping entertainment.
w James Lee Barrett *novel* Davis Grubb d Andrew V. McLaglen ph Harry Stradling Jnr m Henry Vars ad Alfred Sweeney ed David Bretherton, Robert Simpson
☆ James Stewart, George Kennedy, Strother Martin, Anne Baxter, Kurt Russell, William Windom, Mike Kellin
'A quintessentially American tribute to the quiet heroism of the self-made man.' – *Nigel Andrews*

Fools Rush In
GB 1949 82m bw
Rank/Pinewood
A girl changes her mind on her wedding day, and causes repercussions through the family.
Thin, flat film version of a successful play.
w Geoffrey Kerr *play* Kenneth Horne d John Paddy Carstairs
☆ Sally Ann Howes, Guy Rolfe, Nora Swinburne, Nigel Buchanan, Raymond Lovell, Thora Hird

'An impulsive love story'
Fools Rush In
US 1997 108m Technicolor
Columbia (Doug Draizin)
▭ ▭ ◎
Boy meets girl, boy loses girl, boy gets girl and a baby.
Unexciting, formulaic romantic comedy of minimal interest.
w Katherine Reback d Andy Tennant ph Robbie Greenberg m Alan Silvestri pd Edward Pisoni ed Roger Bondelli
☆ Matthew Perry, Salma Hayek, Jon Tenney, Carlos Gomez, Tomas Milian, Siobhan Fallon, John Bennett Perry, Jill Clayburgh
'The intended humorous moments aren't very funny, while the scenes stressing pathos and drama seem tentative and unconvincing.' – *Todd McCarthy, Variety*

Football Crazy
Italy 1974 106m colour
Documento Films (Gianni Hecht Lucara)
A small-town football referee, who dreams of making the big time, has an affair with a glamorous journalist.

An ineffectual comedy that requires an audience to believe that referees are heroes in their community and that Joan Collins offers erotic promise.
w G. Scarniaci, R. Vianello, S. Continenza, Luigi Filipo D'Amico d Luigi Filipo D'Amico ph Sergio D'Offizi m Guido and Maurizio de Angelis pd Walter Patriarca ed Marisa Mengoli
☆ Lando Buzzanca, Joan Collins, Gabriella Pallotta, Ignazio Leone, Daniele Vargas

'Can you even think of missing it?'
'1,000 surprises! 300 beauties! 20 big stars!'
Footlight Parade ***
US 1933 104m bw
Warner (Robert Lord)
▭ ▭ ◎
A determined producer of cine-variety numbers gets the show going despite great difficulty.
Classic putting-on-a-show musical distinguished by rapid-fire dialogue, New York setting, star performances and some of the best Busby Berkeley numbers.
w Manuel Seff, James Seymour d Lloyd Bacon ph George Barnes m/ly Harry Warren, Al Dubin, Sammy Fain, Irving Kahal ch Busby Berkeley ad Anton Grot, Jack Okey ed George Amy
☆ James Cagney, Joan Blondell, Ruby Keeler, Dick Powell, Frank McHugh, Guy Kibbee, Ruth Donnelly, Hugh Herbert, Claire Dodd, Herman Bing
'Bevies of beauty and mere males disport themselves in a Honeymoon Hotel, by (and in) a Waterfall, and over several acres of Shanghai.' – C. A. Lejeune
† The Chester Kent studio was a take-off of Fanchon and Marco, who had just such a studio on Sunset Boulevard
♫ 'By a Waterfall'; 'Ah, the Moon Is Here'; 'Sittin' on a Backyard Fence'; 'Shanghai Lil'; 'Honeymoon Hotel'

Footlight Serenade
US 1942 80m bw
TCF (William LeBaron)
▭
A boxer romances a showgirl.
Indifferent star musical.
w Robert Ellis, Helen Logan, Lynn Starling d Gregory Ratoff ph Lee Garmes m/ly Ralph Rainger, Leo Robin md Charles Henderson
☆ Betty Grable, John Payne, Victor Mature, James Gleason, Phil Silvers, Jane Wyman, Cobina Wright Jnr, June Lang, Mantan Moreland

'He's A Big-City Kid In A Small Town. They Said He'd Never Win. He Knew He Had To.'
Footloose
US 1984 107m Movielab
Paramount/Indieprod (Lewis J. Rachmil, Craig Zadan)
▭ ◎ ∩
The domination of an old-fashioned local preacher is slackened by a young newcomer who insists on arranging a dance.
Odd fable which seeks to combine Flashdance with Rebel without a Cause, and misses out on both.
w Dean Pitchford d Herbert Ross ph Ric Waite m various pd Ron Hobbs
☆ Kevin Bacon, Lori Singer, John Lithgow, Dianne Wiest, Christopher Penn
'The celebration of teenage frustration as dance reduces the issues to the level of platitude.' – *Donald Greig, MFB*
♫ title song (m/ly Kenny Loggins, Dean Pitchford); song 'Let's Hear It for the Boy' (m/ly Dean Pitchford, Tom Snow)

Footsteps in the Dark
US 1941 96m bw
Warner (Robert Lord)
A would-be detective novelist on the lookout for story material finds himself solving a murder.
Lethargic modern vehicle for Flynn between his swashbucklers, a poor imitation of the Thin Man style.
w Lester Cole, John Wexley *play* Blondie White by Ladislas Fodor d Lloyd Bacon ph Ernest Haller m Frederick Hollander
☆ Errol Flynn, Brenda Marshall, Ralph Bellamy, Alan Hale, Lucile Watson, Allen Jenkins, Lee Patrick, William Frawley, Roscoe Karns, Grant Mitchell
'The footsteps were those of restless patrons on their way out to buy popcorn.' – *Clive Hirschhorn*

'When he comes to her room at midnight, is it to kiss or kill?'
Footsteps in the Fog *
GB 1955 90m Technicolor
Film Locations/Mike Frankovich (Maxwell Setton)
A Victorian murderer plans to eliminate a blackmailing maid.
This variation on Gaslight turns into a black comedy without laughs, but it has effective moments and is efficiently if charmlessly made.
w Dorothy Reid, Lenore Coffee *story* The Interruption by W. W. Jacobs d Arthur Lubin ph Christopher Challis m Benjamin Frankel ad Wilfrid Shingleton
☆ Stewart Granger, Jean Simmons, Bill Travers, Ronald Squire, Finlay Currie, Peter Bull

For a Few Dollars More **
Italy/Spain/West Germany 1965 130m Techniscope
PEA/Gonzales/Constantin (Alberto Grimaldi)
▭ ▭ ◎ ⊘ ⊘ ∩
original title: *Per Qualche Dollari in Più*
Bounty hunters in El Paso agree to work together.
Vague, inflated, sometimes good-looking sequel to A Fistful of Dollars, with customary violence and predictably mean performances.
wd Sergio Leone ph Massimo Dallamano m Ennio Morricone
☆ Clint Eastwood, Lee Van Cleef, Gian Maria Volonte, Klaus Kinski

For Better, For Worse: see *Zandy's Bride* (1974)

For Better For Worse
GB 1954 84m Eastmancolor
Kenwood (Kenneth Harper)
US title: *Cocktails in the Kitchen*
Tribulations of a young married couple.
Undernourished comedy with an agreeable cast but no surprises.
wd J. Lee-Thompson *play* Arthur Watkyn ph Guy Green m Wally Stott
☆ Dirk Bogarde, Susan Stephen, Cecil Parker, Dennis Price, Athene Seyler, Eileen Herlie, Thora Hird, James Hayter, Pia Terri, Sid James, Charles Victor

For Freedom
GB 1940 88m bw
GFD/Gainsborough (Edward Black, Castleton Knight)
Events surrounding the Battle of the River Plate and the sinking of the *Graf Spee*.
Economical wartime potboiler with much use of newsreel.
w Miles Malleson, Leslie Arliss d Maurice Elvey, Castleton Knight ph Arthur Crabtree
☆ Will Fyffe, Anthony Hulme, E. V. H. Emmett, Guy Middleton, Albert Lieven

For Heaven's Sake
US 1950 92m bw
TCF (William Perlberg)
Two angels are sent to earth to mend a Broadway producer's marriage.
Silly, flat whimsy of the Here Comes Mr Jordan school, and originating from the same author. Stale beer, but historically interesting.
wd George Seaton *play* Harry Segall ph Lloyd Ahern m Alfred Newman
☆ Clifton Webb, Edmund Gwenn, Robert Cummings, Joan Bennett, Joan Blondell, Gigi Perreau, Jack La Rue

For Keeps: see *Maybe Baby*

For Love of a Queen: see *The Dictator*

For Love of Ivy
US 1968 100m Perfectcolor
Cinerama/Palomar (Edgar J. Scherick, Jay Weston)
An invaluable coloured maid gives notice, and the family blackmails a likeable black ne'er-do-well to make love to her so that she will stay.
Unhappy whimsy with an extremely laboured script and no jokes, notable only as Hollywood's first bow towards a black love affair.
w Robert Alan Aurthur *story* Sidney Poitier d Daniel Mann ph Joseph Coffey m Quincy Jones
☆ Sidney Poitier, Abbey Lincoln, Beau Bridges, Carroll O'Connor, Nan Martin, Lauri Peters
♫ title song (m Quincy Jones, ly Bob Russell)

For Love or Money
US 1963 108m Technicolor
U-I (Robert Arthur)
A rich widow hires a lawyer to look after the affairs of her three wayward daughters; he picks the eldest for himself.
Slow, thin, overlong comedy with a surfeit of witless chat.
w Larry Marks, Michael Morris d Michael Gordon ph Clifford Stine m Frank de Vol
☆ Kirk Douglas, Mitzi Gaynor, Thelma Ritter, William Bendix, Gig Young

For Love or Money
US 1993 96m DeLuxe
Universal (Brian Grazer)
▭ ▭ ◎
GB title: *The Concierge*
A concierge's dreams of owning his own hotel come true.
A dim romantic comedy that wastes a likeable star.
w Mark Rosenthal, Lawrence Konner d Barry Sonnenfeld ph Oliver Wood m Bruce Broughton pd Peter Larkin ed Jim Miller
☆ Michael J. Fox, Gabrielle Anwar, Anthony Higgins, Michael Tucker, Bob Balaban, Isaac Mizrahi, Udo Kier, Dan Hedaya
'No amount of good humor can deter the thin tale from evaporating before the final clinch.' – *Variety*
'A faceless bit of professionalism, occasionally sparked by incidental bits of business, which coasts too heavily on Fox's boyish charm.' – *Kim Newman*

For Me and My Gal ***
US 1942 104m bw
MGM (Arthur Freed)
▭ ◎
Just before World War I, a girl vaudevillian chooses between two partners.
A routine musical romance at the time of its production, this film now stands out because of its professional execution, its star value, and the fact that they don't make 'em like that any more.
w Richard Sherman, Sid Silvers, Fred Finklehoffe d Busby Berkeley ph William Daniels md Georgie Stoll, Roger Edens
☆ Judy Garland, Gene Kelly, George Murphy, Marta Eggerth, Ben Blue, Richard Quine, Stephen McNally
'A touch of imagination and a deal more than a touch of energy.' – *The Times*
♫ 'Oh, You Beautiful Doll'; 'For Me and My Gal'; 'When You Wore a Tulip'; 'After You've Gone'; 'Till We Meet Again'; 'Ballin' the Jack'.
& Georgie Stoll, Roger Edens

For Men Only
US 1952 95m bw
Lippert
A college professor is shocked when a death ensues from a freshman 'hazing' ceremony.
Weird exploitation study of supposed college rites.
w Lou Morheim, Herbert Margolies d Paul Henreid
☆ Paul Henreid, Robert Sherman, Russell Johnson, Margaret Field, Vera Miles
'Henreid allots himself an over-generous proportion of screen time – walking in and out of doors, smiling at the camera, being charming.' – *MFB*

For Pete's Sake *
US 1974 90m Eastmancolor
Columbia/Rastar/Persky-Bright-Barclay (Martin Erlichmann, Stanley Shapiro)
▭
A New York taxi driver's wife borrows money and finds herself heavily committed to work off the debt.
Involved farcical comedy with amusing passages.
w Stanley Shapiro, Martin Richlin d Peter Yates ph Laszlo Kovacs m Artie Butler
☆ Barbra Streisand, Michael Sarrazin, Estelle Parsons, William Redfield, Molly Picon
'Revives memories of how much more inventively they used to do it thirty years ago.' – *Sight and Sound*

For Queen and Country
GB/US 1988 106m Eastmancolor
UIP/Zenith/Atlantic/Working Title (Tim Bevan)
A black soldier returns to a squalid civilian life in Britain.

Turgid political drama that alienates the sympathies it attempts to arouse.

w Martin Stellman, Trix Worrell d Martin Stellman ph Richard Greatrex m Michael Kamen, Geoff MacCormack, Simon Goldenberg pd Andrew McAlpine ed Stephen Singleton
☆ Denzel Washington, Dorian Healy, Amanda Redman, Sean Chapman, Bruce Payne, Geff Francis, George Baker

For Roseanna: see *Roseanna's Grave*

'For The Laughter. For The Tears. For The Boys.'
For the Boys
US   1991   145m   DeLuxe
TCF/All Girl (Bette Midler, Bonnie Bruckheimer, Margaret South)
🎞 ▤ 🎬 🎧
A singer reminisces about her forty years in showbusiness and her partnership with a song-and-dance man.
Designed mainly as a showcase for Bette Midler, it becomes instead a sentimental wallow in cheap emotions.
w Marshall Brickman, Neal Jimenez, Lindy Laub d Mark Rydell m Stephen Goldblatt m Dave Grusin pd Assheton Gorton ed Jerry Greenberg, Jere Huggins
☆ Bette Midler, James Caan, George Segal, Patrick O'Neal, Christopher Rydell, Arye Gross, Norman Fell, Rosemary Murphy, Bud Yorke
'Strong on period décor, weak and dishonest on social history. What it makes you loathe is the ethos of show business.' – *Philip French, Observer*
🏆 Bette Midler

For the Defense *
US   1930   62m   bw
Paramount
Exploits of a New York criminal lawyer.
Slick programme picture of its day; it gave a lift to its star's career.
w Oliver H. P. Garrett (based on the career of William J. Fallon) d John Cromwell
☆ William Powell, Kay Francis, Scott Kolk, Thomas E. Jackson, William B. Davidson
'Certain to hold its head up on grosses.' – *Variety*

For the First Time
US   1959   97m   Technirama
MGM/Corona/Orion (Alexander Gruter)
A famous tenor slips off incognito to Capri and falls in love with a deaf girl.
Slipshod co-production (with West Germany) with a heavy sentimental plot, a fat star, and some agreeable picture postcard views.
w Andrew Solt d Rudolph Maté ph Aldo Tonti md Georgie Stoll
☆ Mario Lanza, Johanna von Koczian, Kurt Kasznar, Zsa Zsa Gabor, Hans Sohnker

For the Love of Ada
GB   1972   88m   Eastmancolor
LMG/Tigon (Peter J. Thompson)
An elderly grave-digger and his wife celebrate their first wedding anniversary.
A mild comedy, consisting of a series of tiny jokes, stretched well beyond its ability to amuse or entertain.
w Harry Driver, Vince Powell TV serial Harry Driver, Vince Powell d Ronnie Baxter ph Alan Hume m Frank Barber pd Bill Palmer ed Anthony Palk
☆ Irene Handl, Wilfred Pickles, Barbara Mitchell, Jack Smethurst, Arthur English, Patsy Kensit
'A boneless jelly of a film, setting up pointless little heartbreaks so that it can dissolve them in a flood of coy sentimentality.' – *Tom Milne, MFB*
† It was a spin-off from a TV sitcom that ran from 1970 to 1971.

For the Love of Benji
👫 US   1977   84m   colour
Mulberry Square
▤ ◎
A small dog gets lost in the Greek islands.
Adequate follow-up to Benji; what more can one say?
w Ben Vaughn, Joe Camp d Joe Camp
☆ Patsy Garrett, Cynthia Smith, Peter Bowles, Ed Nelson

For the Love of Mary
US   1948   90m   bw
Universal (Robert Arthur)
A White House switchboard operator gets tangled up in politics when the president helps cure her hiccups.
Tedious comedy with music, a hasty vehicle for a star past her peak.
w Oscar Brodney d Frederick de Cordova ph William Daniels m Frank Skinner
☆ Deanna Durbin, Edmond O'Brien, Harry Davenport, Don Taylor, Jeffrey Lynn, Ray Collins, Hugo Haas
'A warning to all interfering presidents.' – *MFB*

For the Love of Mike
US   1927   74m   bw   silent
First National
Three bachelors adopt an abandoned baby boy, who nearly (but not quite) lets them down when he grows up.
Sentimental comedy most notable now as the leading lady's first movie.
w Leland Hayward, J. Clarkson Miller story Hell's Kitchen by John Moroso d Frank Capra ph Ernest Haller
☆ Claudette Colbert, Ben Lyon, George Sidney, Ford Sterling, Hugh Cameron, Skeets Gallagher

For the Love of Mike *
👫 US   1960   84m   DeLuxe   Cinemascope
TCF/Shergari (George Sherman)
GB title: *None But the Brave*
An Indian boy in New Mexico is helped by a priest to care for sick animals.
Sentimental outdoor film for young people with a pleasantly light touch.
w D. D. Beauchamp d George Sherman ph Alex Phillips m Raul Lavista
☆ Richard Basehart, Stuart Erwin, Arthur Shields, Armando Silvestre

For Them That Trespass
GB   1948   93m   bw
ABP (Victor Skutezky)
A man proves himself innocent of the crime for which he has served fifteen years in prison.
Tedious melodrama which served to introduce Richard Todd to the screen.
w J. Lee-Thompson d Alberto Cavalcanti ph Derick Williams m Philip Green
☆ Richard Todd, Stephen Murray, Joan Dowling, Patricia Plunkett, Michael Laurence, Rosalyn Boulter

For Those in Peril
GB   1944   67m   bw
Ealing
Exploits of the air/sea rescue service.
Standard semi-documentary morale-raiser.
w Harry Watt, J. O. C. Orton, T. E. B. Clarke d Charles Crichton ph Douglas Slocombe
☆ David Farrar, Ralph Michael, Robert Wyndham, John Slater

For Those Who Think Young
US   1964   96m   Techniscope
UA/Aubrey Schenck-Howard W. Koch (Hugh Benson)
College students save their favourite club from closure.
Tedious beach party frolic, very typical of its day, with some odd cameo appearances.
w James and George O'Hanlon, Dan Beaumont d Leslie H. Martinson ph Harold E. Stine m Jerry Fielding
☆ James Darren, Pamela Tiffin, Woody Woodbury, Nancy Sinatra, Tina Louise, Paul Lynde, Bob Denver, Jack La Rue, George Raft, Allen Jenkins, Robert Armstrong, Roger Smith

For Valour *
GB   1937   95m   bw
GFD/Capitol (Max Schach)
Adventures in two wars of a major, his shady friend, and their sons.
Agreeable adult farce with the stars each playing father and son.
w Ben Travers d Tom Walls ph Phil Tannura md Van Phillips ad Oscar Werndorff ed E. B. Jarvis
☆ Tom Walls, Ralph Lynn, Veronica Rose, Joan Marion, Hubert Harben
'A very pleasant antidote to the Coronation, though a little marred by its inability to remain wholly flippant.' – *Graham Greene*

'168 minutes of breathless thrills and romance!'
For Whom the Bell Tolls **
US   1943   168m   Technicolor
Paramount (Sam Wood)
🎞 ▤ ◎ 🎧
An American joins partisan fighters in the Spanish Civil War and falls in love with a refugee girl before going on a suicide mission.
Portentous, solemn adventure story based on a modern classic but without much cinematic impetus despite careful handling and useful performances. It looks expensive, though.
w Dudley Nichols novel Ernest Hemingway d Sam Wood ph Ray Rennahan m Victor Young pd William Cameron Menzies ed Sherman Todd, John Link
☆ Gary Cooper, Ingrid Bergman, Akim Tamiroff, Arturo de Cordova, Katina Paxinou, Vladimir Sokoloff, Mikhail Rasumny, Victor Varconi, Joseph Calleia, Alexander Granach
MARIA (INGRID BERGMAN): 'I do not know how to kiss, or I would kiss you. Where do the noses go?'
'Everybody must have thought they were making a classic … but what with the typical Hollywood compromises, plus the political pressures from Spain and from Catholics – or the fears of such pressures – the whole thing became amorphous and confused.' – *Pauline Kael, 70s*
'The rhythm of this film is the most defective I have ever seen in a super-production … colour is very nice for costume pieces and musical comedies, and has a great aesthetic future in films, but it still gets fatally in the way of any serious imitation of reality.' – *James Agee*
🏆 Katina Paxinou
🏆 best picture; Ray Rennahan; Victor Young; Gary Cooper; Ingrid Bergman; Akim Tamiroff; Sherman Todd, John Link

For You Alone: see *When You're in Love (1937)*

For You Alone
GB   1944   98m   bw
Butcher's
Romance of a naval officer and a vicar's daughter.
Sentimental drama with music; you can smell the lavender a mile off, but it was probably the most ambitious production of this indefatigable Poverty Row production company.
w Montgomery Tully d Geoffrey Faithfull
☆ Lesley Brook, Jimmy Hanley, Dinah Sheridan, G. H. Mulcaster, Manning Whiley

For Your Eyes Only *
👫 GB   1981   127m   Technicolor
Panavision
UA/Eon (Albert R. Broccoli)
🎞 🎞 ▤ 🎬
James Bond traces a top secret device sunk in a surveillance vehicle off the Greek coast.
Lively set-pieces can't quite redeem this wholly uninventive addition to the Bond canon. Fun while it's on, but next morning there's nothing left to remember.
w Richard Maibaum, Michael G. Wilson d John Glen ph Alan Hume m Bill Conti pd Peter Lamont
☆ Roger Moore, Carole Bouquet, Topol, Lynn-Holly Johnson, Julian Glover, Jill Bennett, Jack Hedley, Lois Maxwell, Desmond Llewelyn, Geoffrey Keen
'Roger Moore fronts for a succession of stunt men with all the relaxed, lifelike charm of a foyer poster of himself.' – *Sunday Times*
'Pretty boring between the stunts, as if the director isn't interested in actors, and Broccoli forgot to commission a screenplay.' – *Guardian*
† The first Bond in which original author Ian Fleming doesn't even rate a credit.
🏆 title song (mBill Conti, lyMick Leeson)

Forbidden
US   1953   85m   bw
Universal-International
A detective falls in love with the woman a mobster has hired to find.
Would-be intense film noir; talent does not enable it to register.
w William Sackheim, Gil Doud d Rudolph Maté
☆ Tony Curtis, Joanne Dru, Lyle Bettger, Marvin Miller, Sen Yung

Forbidden Alliance: see *The Barretts of Wimpole Street (1934)*

The Forbidden Dance: see *Lambada: Forbidden Dance*

Forbidden Fruit *
France   1952   103m   bw
Gray Film
original title: *Le Fruit Défendu*
A widowed doctor marries again, then falls for a prostitute.
One of the rather solemn romantic melodramas in which the star insisted from time to time in becoming involved.
w Jacques Companeez, Henri Verneuil, Jean Manse novel Lettre à Mon Juge by Georges Simenon d Henri Verneuil ph Henri Alekan m Paul Durand
☆ Fernandel, Claude Nollier, Françoise Arnoul, Sylvie

Forbidden Games: see *Jeux Interdits*

Forbidden Music: see *Land without Music*

Forbidden Paradise
US   1924   60m   bw   silent
Paramount
GB title: *Czarina*
The amorous intrigues of Catherine the Great of Russia.
Seldom seen these days, this was judged at the time a scintillating satire, with its sly innuendo and modern references such as motor cars and bobbed hair. Remade, more or less, as A Royal Scandal.
w Hans Kraly, Agnes Christine Johnston play The Czarina by Melchior Lengyel, Lajos Biro d Ernst Lubitsch ph Charles Van Enger ad Hans Dreier
☆ Pola Negri, Adolphe Menjou, Rod La Rocque, Pauline Starke, Fred Malatesta
'Lubitsch's most brilliant film' – *Paul Rotha, 1949*

'More than a year in production!'
Forbidden Planet **
US   1956   98m   Eastmancolor   Cinemascope
MGM (Nicholas Nayfack)
🎞 🎞 ▤ 🎬 ◎ 🎧
In AD 2200 a space cruiser visits the planet Altair Four to discover the fate of a previous mission.
Intriguing sci-fi with a plot derived from The Tempest and a Prospero who unwittingly creates monsters from his own id. High spirits and suspense sequences partially cancelled out by wooden playing from the younger actors and some leaden dialogue.
w Cyril Hume d Fred M. Wilcox ph George Folsey m Louis and Bebe Barron ad Cedric Gibbons, Arthur Lonergan
☆ Walter Pidgeon, Anne Francis, Leslie Nielsen, Warren Stevens, Jack Kelly, Richard Anderson, Earl Holliman
'It's a pity they didn't lift some of Shakespeare's language.' – *New Yorker, 1977*

Forbidden Relations
Hungary   1983   92m   Eastmancolor
Cinegate/Objektiv Filmstudio/Mafilm (Jozsef Marx)
original title: *Visszaesök*
In a peasant community, a step-brother and sister fall in love.
Relentless account of an uninteresting incest.
wd Zsolt Kézdi-Kovacs ph János Kende ad Tamas Banovich ed Andrasne Karmento
☆ Lili Monori, Miklós B. Székely, Mari Töröcsik, József Horváth, József Tóth, Tibor Molnar

The Forbidden Street: see *Britannia Mews*

Forbidden Valley
US   1938   67m   bw
Universal
After the death of a rancher, who lived in hiding after being accused of murder, his son vows to find the real killer.
Melodramatic Western with stilted dialogue and clumsy direction. (Gittens was a writer-director of silents, and has an overemphatic style.)
wd Wyndham Gittens novel The Mountains Are My Kingdom by Stuart Hardy ph Elwood Bredell md Charles Previn ad Jack Otterson ed Frank Gross
☆ Noah Beery Jnr, Frances Robinson, Robert Barrat, Fred Kohler, Alonzo Price, Samuel S. Hinds, Stanley Andrews
† It was remade as *Sierra* in 1950.

The Forbin Project **

US 1969 100m Technicolor Panavision
Universal (Stanley Chase)
GB title: *Colossus, The Forbin Project*

An enormous computer takes over the defence of the western world; but it goes into collaboration with the Russian one.
Good-looking sci-fi for intellectual addicts.
w James Bridges *novel* Colossus by D. F. Jones
d Joseph Sargent ph Gene Polito m Michel Colombier
☆ Eric Braeden, Gordon Pinsent, Susan Clark, William Schallert

Force Majeure *

France 1989 85m colour
CAPAC/Fildebroc/Investimage (Paul Claudon, Michelle de Broca)

Two Frenchmen are faced with a dilemma: to continue with their lives or face imprisonment in South-East Asia, where a casual acquaintance has been sentenced to death for being in possession of drugs that they gave to him.
Intriguing, though slightly plodding, drama of conscience and commitment.
w Pierre Jolivet, Olivier Schatzky d Pierre Jolivet ph Bertrand Chatry m Serge Perathoner, Jannick Top ad Eric Simon
☆ Patrick Bruel, François Cluzet, Kristin Scott-Thomas, Alan Bates, Thom Hoffman, Sabine Haudepin

Force of Arms *

US 1951 100m bw
Warner (Anthony Veiller)

A soldier in the Italian campaign falls in love with his nurse.
Routine variation on A Farewell to Arms, adequately but unexcitingly mounted.
w Orin Jannings *story* Richard Tregaskis
d Michael Curtiz ph Ted McCord m Max Steiner
☆ William Holden, Nancy Olson, Frank Lovejoy, Gene Evans, Dick Wesson, Paul Picerni
'The romance rings true and the battle scenes are dangerously alive.' – *Variety*

The Force of Destiny: see *La Forza del Destino*

Force of Evil **

US 1948 80m bw
MGM/Enterprise (Bob Roberts)

A lawyer is corrupted by the easy money provided by his clients, gangsters who are opposed by his brother in their plans to take over the city's numbers racket.
Bleak and powerful melodrama, an attack on capitalism that is here personified by racketeers.
w Abraham Polonsky, Ira Wolfert *novel* Tucker's People by Ira Wolfert d Abraham Polonsky
ph George Barnes m David Raksin ad Richard Day ed Art Seid
☆ John Garfield, Thomas Gomez, Beatrice Pearson, Roy Roberts, Marie Windsor, Howland Chamberlain, Barry Kelley, Paul Fix

A Force of One

US 1979 90m colour
American Cinema (Alan Belkin)

A karate expert tackles drug pushers in California.
Standard undistinguished action fare.
w Ernest Tidyman *story* Pat Johnson, Ernest Tidyman d Paul Aaron ph Roger Shearman m Dick Halligan ad Norman Baron ed Bert Lovitt
☆ Chuck Norris, Jennifer O'Neill, Clu Gulager, Ron O'Neal, James Whitmore Jnr, Clint Ritchie, Pepe Serna
† A sequel to *Good Guys Wear Black* (qv).

Force Ten from Navarone

GB 1978 118m Technicolor Panavision
Columbia/AIP/Guy Hamilton (Oliver A. Unger)

During World War II, commandos are detailed to blow up a vital bridge separating the Germans and partisans in Yugoslavia.
Routine war hokum with plenty of explosions and sudden death, but not much sense. Nothing, really, to do with The Guns of Navarone.
w Robin Chapman *novel* Alistair MacLean
d Guy Hamilton ph Chris Challis m Ron Goodwin pd Geoffrey Drake

☆ Robert Shaw, Edward Fox, Franco Nero, Harrison Ford, Barbara Bach, Richard Kiel

Forced Vengeance

US 1982 90m colour
MGM (John B. Bennett)

In Hong Kong, a casino security chief seeks revenge when his boss is shot and his girlfriend raped and killed by gangsters who want to take over the business.
The modern equivalent of the second-feature Western of the 40s, as the Stetson-wearing Norris stomps woodenly through an uninteresting narrative, dispensing rough justice and preferring fists to guns; the main difference is the gloating here over the scenes of violence.
w Franklin Thompson d James Fargo ph Rexford Metz m William Goldstein pd George B. Chan ed Irving C. Rosenblum
☆ Chuck Norris, Mary Louise Weller, Michael Cavanaugh, David Opatoshu, Camila Griggs, Seiji Sakaguchi, Frank Michael Liu

Forces of Nature

US 1999 104m Technicolor Panavision
DreamWorks (Susan Arnold, Donna Arkoff Roth, Ian Bryce)

Attempting to get to his wedding through catastrophic accidents and bad weather, an uptight man becomes involved with a free-spirited woman.
Trivial attempt at a screwball comedy, one that lacks any kind of sparkle or wit despite its engaging stars.
w Marc Lawrence d Bronwen Hughes ph Elliot Davis m John Powell pd Lester Cohen ed Craig Wood
☆ Sandra Bullock, Ben Affleck, Maura Tierney, Steve Zahn, Blythe Danner, Ronny Cox, Michael Fairman, Janet Carroll, Richard Schiff, David Strickland, Meredith Scott Lynn
'Who on earth left the handbrake on?' – *Empire*

A Foreign Affair **

US 1948 116m bw
Paramount (Charles Brackett)

A deputation of American politicians goes to visit post-war Berlin and a congresswoman finds herself in an emotional triangle with a captain and his German mistress.
Bleakly sophisticated comedy from this team's headline-grabbing period; full of interest and amusement, it never quite sparkles enough to remove the doubtful taste.
w Charles Brackett, Billy Wilder, Richard Breen *story* David Shaw d Billy Wilder ph Charles Lang Jnr m Frederick Hollander
☆ Jean Arthur, Marlene Dietrich, John Lund, Millard Mitchell, Peter von Zerneck, Stanley Prager
'This deliberately cynical political farce ... often seems on the verge of being funny, but the humour is too clumsily forced.' – *New Yorker, 1980*
'What really shocks me about this Hollywood film is the attitude towards life that it reflects; the casual acceptance of irresponsibility and bad manners, of lawlessness and boorishness and mischief-making.' – *C. A. Lejeune*
⚖ script; Charles Lang Jnr

Foreign Affaires

GB 1935 71m bw
Gainsborough (Michael Balcon, Tom Walls)

A gambler and a car salesman get mixed up with a phoney casino.
Mild star farce.
w Ben Travers d Tom Walls ph Roy Kellino md Louis Levy ad Vetchinsky ed Alfred Roome
☆ Tom Walls, Ralph Lynn, Robertson Hare, Norma Varden, Marie Lohr, Diana Churchill, Cecil Parker
'A well-*written* film in which Mr Tom Walls gives a really lovely performance.' – *Graham Greene*

Foreign Correspondent ****

US 1940 120m bw
Walter Wanger

An American journalist is sent to Europe in 1938 and becomes involved with spies.

Thoroughly typical and enjoyable Hitchcock adventure with a rambling script which builds up into brilliantly managed suspense sequences: an assassination, a windmill, an attempted murder in Westminster Cathedral, a plane crash at sea. The final speech was an attempt to encourage America into the war.
w Charles Bennett, Joan Harrison, James Hilton, Robert Benchley *novel* Personal History by Vincent Sheean d Alfred Hitchcock ph Rudolph Maté m Alfred Newman pd William Cameron Menzies ad Alexander Golitzen sp Lee Zavitz
☆ Joel McCrea, Laraine Day, Herbert Marshall, Albert Basserman, Edmund Gwenn, George Sanders, Eduardo Ciannelli, Robert Benchley, Harry Davenport, Martin Kosleck
HAVERSTOCK (JOEL McCREA): 'I've been watching a part of the world blown to pieces! I can't read the rest of the speech I had because the lights have gone out. It is as if the lights were out everywhere, except in America. Keep those lights burning there! Cover them with steel! Ring them with guns! Build a canopy of battleships and bombing planes around them! Hello, America! Hang on to your lights, they're the only lights left in the world!'
'If you have any interest in the true motion and sweep of pictures, watching that week of work is like listening to music ... If you would like a seminar in how to make a movie travel the lightest and fastest way, in a kind of beauty that is peculiar to movies alone, you can see this once, and then again to see what you missed, and then study it twice.' – *Otis Ferguson*
'The most excitingly shot and edited picture of the year.' – *Basil Wright*
'A masterpiece of propaganda, a first class production which no doubt will make a certain impression upon the broad masses of the people in enemy countries.' – *Joseph Goebbels*
'This juxtaposition of outright melodramatics with deadly serious propaganda is eminently satisfactory ... Hitchcock uses camera tricks, cinematic rhythm and crescendo to make his points.' – *Howard Barnes, New York Herald Tribune*
'Easily one of the year's finest pictures.' – *Time*
⚖ best picture; script; Rudolph Maté; Albert Basserman; Alexander Golitzen

Foreign Intrigue *

US 1956 100m Eastmancolor
UA/Sheldon Reynolds

A press agent investigates the death of a man who had been blackmailing potential traitors.
Location espionage melodrama of the cold war fifties, quite well done in a rather dismal vein, but a long way from Foreign Correspondent.
wd Sheldon Reynolds ph Bertil Palmgren m Paul Durand
☆ Robert Mitchum, Genevieve Page, Ingrid Thulin, Eugene Deckers

Foreign Student

US 1994 96m colour
Universal/Carthago/Libra/Featherstone (Mark Lombardo)

In the mid-50s, a French student goes to study at an American university in Virginia, where he falls in love with a local black teacher and maidservant.
Rose-coloured, nostalgic view of material – involving culture clash and colour prejudice – that might have benefited from a tougher treatment; even abrasive blues singer Howling Wolf, in a brief appearance, appears to have succumbed to the all-enveloping mellowness.
w Menno Meyjes *novel* Philippe Labro d Eva Sereny ph Franco Di Giacomo m Jean-Claude Petit pd Howard Cummings ed Peter Hollywood
☆ Marco Hofschneider, Robin Givens, Rick Johnson, Charlotte Ross, Anthony Herrera, Jack Coleman, Hinton Battle, Charles Dutton, Edward Herrmann

The Foreman Went to France **

GB 1941 87m bw
Ealing (Alberto Cavalcanti)
US title: *Somewhere in France*

Before Dunkirk, a Welsh foreman is sent on a mission to salvage secret French machinery.
Fresh, appealing comedy drama based on a true incident of World War II.
w John Dighton, Angus Macphail, Leslie Arliss, Roger Macdougall, Diana Morgan *story* J. B.

Priestley d Charles Frend ph Wilkie Cooper m William Walton
☆ Tommy Trinder, Constance Cummings, Clifford Evans, Robert Morley, Gordon Jackson, Ernest Milton

'The thrilling story of women who play with fire, and men who fight it!'

The Forest Rangers *

US 1942 85m Technicolor
Paramount (Robert Sisk)

A socialite marries a district ranger and rescues her disgruntled rival during a forest blaze.
Routine, competent, box-office actioner of its time, with popular stars, adequate plot, but precious little inventiveness.
w Harold Shumate d George Marshall ph Charles Lang m Victor Young
☆ Fred MacMurray, Paulette Goddard, Susan Hayward, Lynne Overman, Albert Dekker, Eugene Pallette, Regis Toomey, Rod Cameron
'Another tale of the tall timbers, complete with conflagrations, he-men, and women like cats.' – *New York Times*

Forever Amber *

US 1947 137m Technicolor
TCF (William Perlberg)

Adventures of a desirable young lady during the reign of Charles II.
Much-bowdlerized version of a sensational novel of the forties; pretty but rather thin, with a colourless cast, saved by lively action sequences.
w Philip Dunne, Ring Lardner Jnr *novel* Kathleen Winsor d Otto Preminger ph Leon Shamroy m David Raksin ad Lyle Wheeler
☆ Linda Darnell, Cornel Wilde, George Sanders, Richard Greene, Glenn Langan, Richard Haydn, Jessica Tandy, Anne Revere, Robert Coote, John Russell, Leo G. Carroll
⚖ David Raksin

Forever and a Day **

US 1943 104m bw
RKO (Herbert Wilcox, Victor Saville)

The history of a London house from 1804 to the blitz of World War II.
Made for war charities by a combination of the European talents in Hollywood, this series of sketches was unavoidably patchy but gave good opportunities to several familiar performers and stands as a likeable quick reference to their work at this period.
w Charles Bennett, C. S. Forester, Lawrence Hazard, Michael Hogan, W. P. Lipscomb, Alice Duer Miller, John Van Druten, Alan Campbell, Peter Godfrey, S. M. Herzig, Christopher Isherwood, Gene Lockhart, R. C. Sherriff, Claudine West, Norman Corwin, Jack Hartfield, James Hilton, Emmet Lavery, Frederick Lonsdale, Donald Ogden Stewart, Keith Winter d René Clair, Edmund Goulding, Cedric Hardwicke, Frank Lloyd, Victor Saville, Robert Stevenson, Herbert Wilcox ph Robert de Grasse, Lee Garmes, Russell Metty, Nicholas Musuraca m Anthony Collins ad Albert D'Agostino, Lawrence Williams, Al Herman
☆ Anna Neagle, Ray Milland, Claude Rains, C. Aubrey Smith, Dame May Whitty, Gene Lockhart, Edmund Gwenn, Ian Hunter, Jessie Matthews, Charles Laughton, Montagu Love, Cedric Hardwicke, Reginald Owen, Buster Keaton, Wendy Barrie and also Ida Lupino, Brian Aherne, Edward Everett Horton, June Duprez, Eric Blore, Merle Oberon, Una O'Connor, Nigel Bruce, Roland Young, Gladys Cooper, Robert Cummings, Richard Haydn, Elsa Lanchester, Sara Allgood, Robert Coote, Donald Crisp, Ruth Warrick, Kent Smith, Herbert Marshall, Victor McLaglen, and many others in bit parts
'One of the most brilliant casts of modern times has been assembled to bolster up one of the poorest pictures.' – *James Agate*
'It is holding and entertaining ... a production of outstanding quality.' – *CEA Film Report*
† The film is notable for having the longest-ever list of credited co-writers.

Forever Darling

US 1956 91m Eastmancolor
MGM/Zanra (Desi Arnaz)

A couple's matrimonial difficulties are solved by her guardian angel.

Cutesy-pie comedy with all concerned embarrassed by their material.
w Helen Deutsch d Alexander Hall ph Harold Lipstein m Bronislau Kaper
☆ Lucille Ball, Desi Arnaz, James Mason, John Emery, Louis Calhern, John Hoyt, Natalie Schafer

Forever England: see Brown on Resolution

Forever Female

US 1953 93m bw
Paramount (Pat Duggan)
A young writer sells his play to a Broadway producer who wants to transform it into a vehicle for his ex-wife; she falls for the writer but eventually discourages him.
Talky romantic comedy without much style or sense of Broadway; a long way from All About Eve.
w Julius J. Epstein, Philip G. Epstein play Rosalind by J. M. Barrie d Irving Rapper ph Harry Stradling m Victor Young
☆ Ginger Rogers, William Holden, Paul Douglas, James Gleason, Pat Crowley

Forever in Love: see Pride of the Marines

Forever Lulu

US/Germany 1986 90m Precision colour
Lulu/TV60/TV-80/Bayerischer Rundfunk/Dieter Geissler (Amos Kollek)
🎦 ▦ ◷
US video title: Crazy Streets
In New York, a struggling German-born writer finds fame and fortune when she becomes inadvertently involved in murder.
An experience as depressing as the life of its protagonist: the script is implausible when it is not ridiculous, the direction dull and the performances mostly inadequate.
wd Amos Kollek ph Lisa Rinzler pd Stephen McCabe ed Jay Freund
☆ Hanna Schygulla, Deborah Harry, Alec Baldwin, Paul Gleason, Annie Golden, Dr Ruth Westheimer, Amos Kollek

Forever Mary: see Mery per sempre

Forever Young

GB 1984 84m colour
Goldcrest (Chris Griffin)
Father Michael finds himself influenced by sexual tensions among his flock.
Rather slight drama chiefly concerning a twelve-year-old boy who idolizes his fallible priest.
w Ray Connolly d David Drury ph Norman Langley md Anthony King
☆ James Aubrey, Nicholas Gecks, Alec McCowen, Karen Archer

'Fifty years ago he volunteered for a dangerous experiment. All in the name of love.'
'Time waits for no man, but true love waits forever.'
Forever Young *

US 1992 102m Technicolor
Warner/Icon (Bruce Davey)
🎦 ▦ ◷ ◷ ◷
A pilot, who is frozen in an experiment in 1939, wakes up to find that it is 1992.
Pleasant, light-hearted romantic movie, a throwback to the past.
w Jeffrey Abrams d Steve Miner ph Russell Boyd m Jerry Goldsmith pd Gregg Fonseca ed Jon Poll
☆ Mel Gibson, Jamie Lee Curtis, Elijah Wood, Isabel Glasser, George Wendt, Joe Morton, Nicholas Surovy, David Marshall Grant, Robert Hy Gorman, Millie Slavin
'A big, rousing, old-fashioned romance ... A perfect "women's picture" alternative to action fare and kid-oriented sequels.' – Variety

Forever Yours: see Forget Me Not

Forfaiture: see The Cheat

Forget Me Not

GB 1936 72m bw
UA/Itala/London Films (Alberto Giacolone, Alexander Korda)
🎦
US title: Forever Yours
On the rebound from a shipboard romance, a young girl marries a widowed tenor.
Bland romance, notable only for the star's singing.

w Hugh Gray, Arthur Wimperis d Zoltan Korda, Stanley Irving d Hans Schneeberger m Mischa Spoliansky ed O. H. Cornelius
☆ Beniamino Gigli, Joan Gardner, Ivan Brandt, Hugh Wakefield
'As a larynx exercise it possesses an appeal for those audiences which go for singing.' – Variety

'A Comedy About Love ... After Marriage.'
Forget Paris

US 1995 101m
Rank/Castle Rock/Face (Billy Crystal)
🎦 ▦ ◷ ◷
An on-and-off romance of a basketball referee and the married woman he meets in Paris, when he goes there to bury his father.
Dreary romantic comedy, with the focus on Crystal's unlovable character, who is meant to be charmingly offbeat, but is just irritating; forget to watch it.
w Billy Crystal, Lowell Ganz, Babaloo Mandel d Billy Crystal ph Don Burgess m Marc Shaiman pd Terence Marsh ed Kent Beyda
☆ Billy Crystal, Debra Winger, Joe Mantegna, Julie Kavner, Richard Masur, Cathy Moriarty, William Hickey, Cynthia Stevenson
'Lots of big laughs and a sweet if sometimes sticky take on love amongst the regular folks will satisfy the date-night crowd.' – Variety

Forgotten Commandments *

US 1932 75m bw
Paramount
In a Russia which has renounced Christianity, a scientist who considers himself above emotion is led by jealousy into the murder of his mistress.
Vague, feeble and absurd modern parable which takes in its stride a 20-minute excerpt from de Mille's 1923 The Ten Commandments.
w J. B. Fagan, Agnes Brand Leahy d Louis Gasnier, William Schoor ph Karl Struss
☆ Gene Raymond, Sari Maritza, Irving Pichel, Marguerite Churchill, Edward Van Sloan, Harry Beresford
'Hardly a single dramatic sequence and not over three laughs at the New York opening – and one of them at, not with, the picture.' – Variety

Forgotten Faces

US 1936 70m bw
Paramount
Jailed for killing his wife's lover, a man escapes to thwart his wife's further plans.
Slightly unusual melodrama which was remade as A Gentleman After Dark.
w Marguerite Roberts, Robert Yost, Brian Marlow d E. A. Dupont
☆ Herbert Marshall, Gertrude Michael, James Burke, Robert Cummings

Forgotten Girls

US 1940 68m bw
Republic (Robert North)
A girl is convicted for a murder committed by her stepmother.
Minor saga of prison life, with an absurd method of proving the heroine's innocence.
w Joseph March, F. Hugh Herbert, Frank McDonald d Phil Rosen
☆ Louise Platt, Donald Woods, Wynne Gibson, Robert Armstrong, Eduardo Ciannelli, Jack La Rue

Forgotten Woman

US 1939 68m bw
Universal (Edmund Grainger)
A woman wrongfully imprisoned has a baby in prison and emerges embittered.
Heavygoing tearjerker.
w Lionel Houser, Harold Buchman, John Kobler d Harold Young
☆ Sigrid Gurie, Eve Arden, Donald Briggs, William Lundigan, Elizabeth Risdon

The Formula

US 1980 117m Metrocolor
MGM/CIP (Steve Shagan)
A cop follows a murder trail to West Germany and finds that it all hinges on a secret formula for turning coal into petrol.
Convoluted thriller which is all McGuffin and no interest.
w Steven Shagan novel Steven Shagan d John G. Avildsen ph James Crabe m Bill Conti
☆ George C. Scott, Marlon Brando, Marthe Keller, John Gielgud, Beatrice Straight, Richard Lynch
𝄞 James Crabe

Forrest Gump **

👪 US 1994 142m colour Panavision
🎦 ▦ ◷
A retarded boy grows up to become an All-American footballer, a Vietnam hero, champion ping-pong player and a millionaire, while the woman he loves finds that her progress is mostly downhill.
A slick comedy as simple-minded as its hero, worth watching for the clever manner in which it slots Gump into the same historical frame as Kennedy, Johnson and Nixon. He remains a blank on which an audience can project any feelings it chooses, while the film's opprobrium is vented on the less conservative values represented by the woman he loves, whose fate is a lingering death. The movie's point is obscure, unless it is to suggest that you have to be an idiot to believe in the American dream, and its success took even its makers by surprise.
w Eric Roth novel Winston Groom d Robert Zemeckis ph Don Burgess m Alan Silvestri pd Rick Carter ed Arthur Schmidt
☆ Tom Hanks, Robin Wright, Gary Sinise, Sally Field, Mykelti Williamson, Michael Conner Humphreys, Hanna R. Hall
'Warm, wise and wearisome as hell.' – New Yorker
'An unembarrassed celebration of stupidity.' – Gilbert Adair, Sunday Times
'Marred by sentiment and cant and much flattery of the audience.' – David Denby, New York
'A film which would make saccharine taste sour. It goes beyond the further shores of the glutinous, with just enough historical wit to dampen the nausea.' – Martin Walker, Sight and Sound
† A book of the sayings of Forrest Gump was published following the film's success, of which the best-known (as well as the most banal) is 'Life is like a box of chocolates. You never know what you're gonna get.'
†† It is the third-most successful film so far, having taken more than $325m at the US box-office and a total of more than $635m worldwide. The video sold more than 15 million copies in the United States.
🏆 best picture; Robert Zemeckis; Tom Hanks; Eric Roth; Arthur Schmidt; visual effects (Ken Ralston, George Murphy, Stephen Rosenblum, Allen Hall)
🏅 Gary Sinise; Alan Silvestri; art direction; cinematography; sound; sound effects editing; make-up

Forsaking All Others *

US 1934 84m bw
MGM (Bernard H. Hyman)
A woman almost marries the wrong man twice.
Star power carries this thin comedy drama.
w Joseph L. Mankiewicz play Edward Barry Roberts, Frank Morgan Cavett d W. S. Van Dyke ph Gregg Toland, George Folsey m William Axt
☆ Clark Gable, Joan Crawford, Robert Montgomery, Charles Butterworth, Billie Burke, Frances Drake, Rosalind Russell, Arthur Treacher
'Stock romantic comedy despite some messy hokum.' – Variety
'Contrary to expectation, sophistication is at a minimum.' – Time

The Forsyte Saga: see That Forsyte Woman

'Where a woman meant more to a man than anywhere else in the world!'
Fort Algiers

US 1953 85m bw
Erco/UA
A female French agent loves a fellow spy who turns up as a Foreign Legionnaire, working against an evil Emir.
Quite lively old-fashioned hokum, satisfactory on its level.
w Theodore St John d Lesley Selander ph John Seitz ad Boris Leven
☆ Yvonne de Carlo, Carlos Thompson, Raymond Burr, Leif Erickson, Anthony Caruso

Fort Apache **

US 1948 127m bw
RKO/Argosy (John Ford, Merian C. Cooper)
🎦 ▦ ◷
In the old west, a military martinet has trouble with his family as well as the Indians.

Rather stiff and unsatisfactory epic Western which yet contains sequences in its director's best manner.
w Frank S. Nugent story Massacre by James Warner Bellah d John Ford ph Archie Stout m Richard Hageman ad James Basevi ed Jack Murray
☆ Henry Fonda, John Wayne, Shirley Temple, Pedro Armendariz, Ward Bond, Irene Rich, George O'Brien, John Agar, Victor McLaglen, Anna Lee, Dick Foran, Guy Kibbee
'A visually absorbing celebration of violent deeds.' – Howard Barnes
'The whole picture is bathed in a special form of patriotic sentimentality: scenes are held so that we cannot fail to appreciate the beauty of the American past.' – New Yorker, 1976
'Shirley Temple and her husband handle the love interest as though they were sharing a soda fountain special, and there is enough Irish comedy to make me wish Cromwell had done a more thorough job.' – James Agee

Fort Apache, the Bronx

US 1980 123m DeLuxe
Time Life/Producer Circle (Martin Richards, Tom Fiorello)
▦ ◷
A veteran policeman deals with various violent crimes in New York.
This instantly forgettable movie unspools like an ultra-violent Dixon of Dock Green, but Newman is no Jack Warner.
w Heywood Gould d Daniel Petrie ph John Alcott m Jonathan Tunick pd Ben Edwards
☆ Paul Newman, Ed Asner, Ken Wahl, Danny Aiello, Rachel Ticotin, Pam Grier, Kathleen Beller

Fort Defiance

US 1951 81m Cinecolor
Ventura/UA
Ben Shelby comes back from the Civil War to avenge his brother's death.
Complicated lower-berth Western, crudely executed.
w Louis Lantz d John Rawlins
☆ Dane Clark, Ben Johnson, Peter Graves, Tracey Roberts, George Cleveland

Fort Dobbs

US 1957 90m bw
Warner
Man on the run rescues widow from Comanches and clears his name.
Very routine medium-scale Western showcasing a TV star.
w George W. George, Burt Kennedy d Gordon Douglas
☆ Clint Walker, Virginia Mayo, Brian Keith, Richard Eyer

Fort Massacre

US 1958 80m DeLuxe Cinemascope
Mirisch/UA
A cavalry sergeant becomes reckless when he has to lead to safety the survivors of an Indian attack.
Psychological Western without the skill necessary to realize its pretensions.
w Martin M. Goldsmith d Joseph Newman
☆ Joel McCrea, Forrest Tucker, Susan Cabot, John Russell

Fort Ti

US 1953 73m Technicolor 3-D
Columbia (Sam Katzman)
In 1759 a platoon of Rogers' Rangers marches north to defend their territory against Indians.
Cheap and feeble Western memorable only for the amount of miscellaneous objects thrown at the audience via 3-D photography.
w Robert E. Kent d William Castle ph Lester E. White, Lathrop B. Worth md Ross di Maggio
☆ George Montgomery, Joan Vohs, Irving Bacon, James Seay
'The lack of restraint is remarkable. To the injury of tomahawks, rifle shots, cannon balls, flaming arrows, broken bottles and blazing torches is added the insult of grubby redskins hurled judo style into one's lap.' – David Robinson

Fort Utah

US 1967 84m Technicolor Techniscope
Paramount (A. C. Lyles)
Crazed killers take over a cavalry fort.
Muddled Western with the producer's usual roster of familiar old faces.

---

w Steve Fisher, Andrew Craddock d Lesley Selander

☆ John Ireland, Virginia Mayo, Scott Brady, John Russell, Robert Strauss, James Craig, Richard Arlen, Jim Davis, Don Barry

Fort Vengeance

US 1953 75m Cinecolor
Allied Artists (Walter Wanger)

A new Mountie recruit is an Indian killer.
Uninteresting Western with stock cast and situations.
w Dan Ullman d Lesley Selander
☆ James Craig, Rita Moreno, Keith Larsen, Reginald Denny, Morris Ankrum

Fort Worth

US 1951 80m Technicolor
Warner
⊞

A newspaper editor combats a would-be dictator.
Satisfying slick Western.
w John Twist d Edwin L. Marin ph Sid Hickox
☆ Randolph Scott, Phyllis Thaxter, David Brian, Dick Jones, Paul Picerni

Fort Yuma

US 1955 78m colour
UA (Howard W. Koch)

Indians steal army uniforms and attack a fort.
Minor but efficient co-feature Western.
w Danny Arnold d Lesley Selander ph Gordon Avil m Paul Dunlap
☆ Peter Graves, Joan Vohs, John Hudson, Joan Taylor, Addison Richards

Fortress

Australia/US 1993 89m CFI color
Village Roadshow/Davis Entertainment (John Davis, John Flock)
⊞ ▦ ◎. ◎.

In the future, a couple who break the law by having more than one child are incarcerated in a huge underground prison, run by a harsh private corporation.
An efficient action film in a science-fiction setting, but one that is unable to escape from its own over-familiar scenario.
w Steve Feinberg, Troy Neighbors, Terry Curtis Fox d Stuart Gordon ph David Eggby m Frederic Talghorn pd David Copping ed Timothy Wellburn sp Tad Pride, Paul Gentry
☆ Christopher Lambert, Kurtwood Smith, Loryn Locklin, Lincoln Kilpatrick, Clifton Gonzalez Gonzalez, Jeffrey Combs, Tom Towles, Vernon Wells

'A grim, sometimes bloody, futuristic prison picture that has been well produced and directed within the limitations of a predictable, uninspired screenplay.' – *Variety*

The Fortune

US 1975 88m Technicolor Panavision
Columbia (Hank Moonjean)

A twenties heiress elopes with her lover and his dim-witted friend but discovers that they mean to murder her for her money.
Bungled black comedy with top talent over-confident of carrying it.
w Adrien Joyce (Carol Eastman) d Mike Nichols ph John A. Alonzo m various songs pd Richard Sylbert
☆ Jack Nicholson, Warren Beatty, Stockard Channing, Florence Stanley, Richard B. Shull, John Fiedler

'Like the ill-assorted styles of the film generally, the stars themselves frequently seem to belong in different movies.' – *Richard Combs*
'A silly, shallow, occasionally enjoyable comedy trifle ... classy 20's production values often merit more attention than the plot.' – *Variety*

Fortune and Men's Eyes

Canada/US 1971 102m Metrocolor
MGM/Cinemex/CFD (Lester Persky, Lewis M. Allen)
▦

Life among homosexuals in a Canadian jail.
A welter of sensational incident outweighs any point the author may have had; this prison seems to be beyond reform.
w John Herbert play John Herbert d Harvey Hart ph Georges Dufaux m Galt McDermot
☆ Wendell Burton, Michael Greer

The Fortune Cookie *

US 1966 125m bw Panavision
UA/Mirisch/Phalanx/Jalem (Billy Wilder)
⊞ ◎.

GB title: Meet Whiplash Willie

A crooked lawyer forces his slightly injured client to sue for a million dollars.
Flat, stretched-out, only occasionally effective comedy which relies too much on mordant attitudes and a single star performance.
w Billy Wilder, I. A. L. Diamond d Billy Wilder ph Joseph LaShelle m André Previn
☆ Walter Matthau, Jack Lemmon, Ron Rich, Cliff Osmond, Lurene Tuttle

'A jackhammer of a film savagely applied to those concrete areas of human spirit where cupidity and stupidity have been so long entrenched.' – *Richard Schickel*
♟ Walter Matthau
♟ Billy Wilder, I. A. L. Diamond (script); Joseph LaShelle

Fortune Is a Woman *

GB 1957 95m bw
Columbia/Frank Launder, Sidney Gilliat
US title: She Played with Fire

An insurance assessor investigates a fire, finds a murder, marries the victim's widow, and is blackmailed...
Slackly-handled mystery thriller, a disappointment from the talents involved.
w Frank Launder, Sidney Gilliat novel Winston Graham d Sidney Gilliat ph Gerald Gibbs m William Alwyn
☆ Jack Hawkins, Arlene Dahl, Dennis Price, Geoffrey Keen, Violet Farebrother, John Robinson, Bernard Miles, Greta Gynt

Fortunes of Captain Blood

US 1950 91m bw
Columbia (Harry Joe Brown)

The famous Caribbean pirate eludes his pursuers by taking over their own ship.
Lethargic adventures on a low budget; the cast was there for something better.
w Michael Hogan, Robert Libbott, Frank Burt d Gordon Douglas
☆ Louis Hayward, Patricia Medina, George Macready, Dona Drake, Alfonso Bedoya

Forty Carats *

US 1973 109m Metrocolor
Columbia/M. J. Frankovich
◎.

A 40-year-old divorcee on holiday in Greece has a brief affair with a 22-year-old man.
Curiously miscast and mishandled comedy for the smart set; scores a laugh or two but never really takes off.
w Leonard Gershe play Pierre Barillet, Jean-Pierre Gredy d Milton Katselas ph Charles Lang Jnr m Michel Legrand
☆ Liv Ullmann, Edward Albert, Gene Kelly, Billy 'Green' Bush, Binnie Barnes, Nancy Walker, Deborah Raffin, Don Porter, Natalie Schafer, Rosemary Murphy

Forty Eight Hours: see Went the Day Well? (1942)

48 Hours

US 1982 96m Movielab
Paramount/Lawrence Gordon
⊞ ▦ ◎.

A cop and a criminal on parole combine to track down the latter's former associates.
Reasonable action melodrama with comedy asides and San Francisco locations; but too violent for its own good.
w Roger Spottiswoode, Walter Hill, Larry Gross, Steven E. de Souza d Walter Hill ph Ric Waite m James Horner pd John Vallone
☆ Nick Nolte, Eddie Murphy, Annette O'Toole, Frank McRae

'It's like *The French Connection*, *Dirty Harry* and *Butch Cassidy* all put in a compactor and pressed into cartoon form.' – *New Yorker*
† It was followed, after a long gap, by a sequel *Another 48 Hours* (qv).

The Forty First *

USSR 1927 80m bw silent
Mezhrabpom
original title: Sorok Pervyi

During the Civil War in Turkestan, a girl sniper for the Reds becomes the companion in adventure of a White lieutenant. But in the end he becomes her 41st victim.
Strong action melodrama which found an international audience.
w Boris Lavrynov novel Boris Lavrynov d Yakov Protazanov ph Pyotr Yermolov
☆ Ada Voitsik, Ivan Kovan-Samborsky
† Remade in 1956 by Grigori Chukrai, in colour.

Forty Guns *

US 1957 80m bw Cinemascope
TCF/Globe (Samuel Fuller)

A powerful ranchwoman protects her hoodlum brother.
Heavily melodramatic and slow-moving Western with a few effective moments.
wd Samuel Fuller ph Joseph Biroc m Harry Sukman
☆ Barbara Stanwyck, Barry Sullivan, Dean Jagger, Gene Barry, John Ericson

Forty Guns to Apache Pass

US 1966 95m Technicolor
Admiral/Columbia

A cavalry captain protects homesteaders when Cochise attacks.
Flat and overlong star Western compounded of excessively familiar elements.
w Willard and Mary Willingham d William Witney ph Jacques R. Marquette m Richard La Salle
☆ Audie Murphy, Michael Burns, Kenneth Tobey, Laraine Stephens

Forty Little Mothers

US 1940 90m bw
MGM (Harry Rapf)

A teacher in a girls' school finds himself in charge of a baby.
Ill-advised star vehicle composed largely of whimsy ... and no musical numbers.
w Dorothy Yost, Ernest Pagano d Busby Berkeley ph Charles A. Lawton Jnr
☆ Eddie Cantor, Judith Anderson, Bonita Granville, Rita Johnson, Diana Lewis, Nydia Westman, Martha O'Driscoll

Forty Naughty Girls

US 1937 68m bw
RKO (William Sistrom)

Hildegarde Withers solves a murder backstage.
Weak addition to a faltering series.
w John Grey, Stuart Palmer d Edward Cline
☆ ZaSu Pitts, James Gleason, Marjorie Lord, George Shelley, Joan Woodbury

'Decidedly tame, and won't cause much ripple on nether side of duals, where it'll undoubtedly land.' – *Variety*

49th Parallel ***

GB 1941 123m bw
GFD/Ortus (John Sutro, Michael Powell)
⊞ ▦ ◎.

US title: The Invaders

In Canada, five stranded U-boat men try to escape into the US.
Episodic, effective propaganda piece which develops some nice Hitchcockian touches and allows a range of star actors to make impact.
w Emeric Pressburger, Rodney Ackland d Michael Powell ph F. A. Young m Ralph Vaughan Williams ad David Rawnsley ed David Lean
☆ Eric Portman, Laurence Olivier, Anton Walbrook, Leslie Howard, Raymond Massey, Glynis Johns, Niall MacGinnis, Finlay Currie, Raymond Lovell, John Chandos

'Some of the plotting and characterization look rather rusty at this remove, but the sense of landscape and figures passing through it remains authoritatively dynamic.' – *Tony Rayns, Time Out, 1979*
'An admirable piece of work from every point of view.' – *MFB*
♟ original story (Emeric Pressburger)
♟ best picture; script

The Forty Niners

US 1954 70m bw
Allied Artists

A marshal tracks down three men who were accomplices to a murder.
Very tolerable minor Western.
w Dan Ullman d Thomas Carr
☆ Wild Bill Elliott, Virginia Grey, Henry Morgan, John Doucette, Lane Bradford

Forty Pounds of Trouble *

US 1963 105m Eastmancolor Panavision
U-I/Curtis Enterprises (Stan Margulies)

A casino manager is chased by his ex-wife's detective for alimony payments, and also has to look after an abandoned six-year-old girl.
Standard sentimental comedy with some verve and a lively climactic chase through Disneyland.
w Marion Hargrove d Norman Jewison ph Joe MacDonald m Mort Lindsey
☆ Tony Curtis, Phil Silvers, Suzanne Pleshette, Edward Andrews

Forty Thousand Horsemen

Australia 1940 100m bw
Famous Feature Films (Charles Chauvel)

The story of the Australian Light Horse in Palestine during World War I.
One of the first Australian bids for the world market; in itself, just a competent little war movie, and too long.
w Charles Chauvel, Elsa Chauvel d Charles Chauvel
☆ Chips Rafferty, Betty Bryant, Grant Taylor, Pat Twohill

'Almost unbelievably primitive in these days of stream-lined talkies. It is also most uncannily exciting. I don't remember enjoying a film quite in this way since the first cowboys rode the range.' – *C. A. Lejeune*

'Mightier than Broadway ever beheld.'
'Most important entertainment event since Warner Bros gave you Vitaphone!'

42nd Street ***

US 1933 89m bw
Warner (Hal B. Wallis)
⊞ ▦ ◎.

A Broadway musical producer has troubles during rehearsal but reaches a successful opening night.
Archetypal Hollywood putting-on-a-show musical in which the leading lady is indisposed and a chorus girl is told to get out there and come back a star. The clichés are written and performed with great zest, the atmosphere is convincing, and the numbers when they come are dazzlers.
w James Seymour, Rian James novel Bradford Ropes d Lloyd Bacon ph Sol Polito m/ly Al Dubin, Harry Warren ch Busby Berkeley
☆ Warner Baxter, Ruby Keeler, Bebe Daniels, George Brent, Una Merkel, Guy Kibbee, Dick Powell, Ginger Rogers, Ned Sparks, George E. Stone, Allen Jenkins

(WARNER BAXTER): 'Sawyer, you listen to me, and you listen hard. Two hundred people, two hundred jobs, two hundred thousand dollars, five weeks of grind and blood and sweat depend upon you. It's the lives of all these people who've worked with you. You've got to go on, and you've got to give and give and give. They've got to like you. Got to. Do you understand? You can't fall down. You can't because your future's in it, my future and everything all of us have is staked on you. All right, now I'm through, but you keep your feet on the ground and your head on those shoulders of yours and go out, and Sawyer, you're going out a youngster but you've got to come back a star!'
'The story has been copied a hundred times since, but never has the backstage atmosphere been so honestly and felicitously caught.' – *John Huntley, 1966*
'It gave new life to the clichés that have kept parodists happy.' – *New Yorker, 1977*
♫ 'Forty-Second Street'; 'It Must Be June'; 'Shuffle Off to Buffalo'; 'Young and Healthy'; 'You're Getting to Be a Habit with Me'
♟ best picture

Forty-Five Fathers

US 1937 71m bw
TCF (John Stone)

A show business orphan becomes the personal ward of the Gun and Spear Club.
Palatable vehicle for a growing child star.

w Frances Hyland, Albert Ray, Mary Bickel
d James Tinling
☆ Jane Withers, Paul and Grace Hartman, Thomas Beck, Louise Henry, Richard Carle, Nella Walker, Andrew Tombes

The Forty-Ninth Man

US   1953   73m   bw
Columbia (Sam Katzman)
Spies try to infiltrate a big bomb into the US.
Tolerable low-berth security thriller on semi-documentary lines.
w Harry Essex story Ivan Tors d Fred F. Sears
☆ John Ireland, Richard Denning, Suzanne Dalbert, Touch Connors

Forward March: see *Doughboys*

La Forza del Destino *

Italy   1950   100m   bw
Union Film Gallone (Ottavio Poggi)
The Duke of Rivas, a political prisoner, is inspired by an 18th-century manuscript to write a play about the doomed love affair between Don Alvaro and Leonora.
A voice-over narration is used to compress and contain Verdi's sprawling melodrama, in which those of the principals are pretending to be someone else. It has been effectively opened up and framed within the story of how Saavedra's original came to be written, but remains of interest mainly for Tito Gobbi, the bass of Giulio Neri and as an example of Italian opera of its time.
w Mario Corsi, Ottavio Poggi, Lionello de Felice
play Angelo Saavedra d Carmine Gallone
ph Aldo Giordani m Giuseppe Verdi
md Gabriele Santini ad Gastone Medin
ed Nicolo Lazzari
☆ Nelly Corradi, Tito Gobbi, Gino Sinimberghi, John Kitzmiller, Giulio Neri, Vito de Taranto
† The singers are: Tito Gobbi, Caterina Mancini, Fausto Tomei, Galliano Masini, Giulio Neri

Foul Play *

US   1978   116m   Movielab
Paramount/Thomas L. Miller, Edward K. Milkis
Two innocents in San Francisco get involved in a plot to assassinate the visiting pope.
Sometimes sprightly, sometimes tired rehash of Hitchcock elements, rather on the level of the similar Silver Streak.
wd Colin Higgins ph David M. Walsh m Charles Fox
☆ Goldie Hawn, Chevy Chase, Burgess Meredith, Rachel Roberts, Eugene Roche, Dudley Moore, Billy Barty
♫ song 'Ready to Take a Chance Again' (mCharles Fox, lyNorman Gimbel)

The Fountain: see *Fontan*

The Fountain

US   1934   84m   bw
RKO (Pandro S. Berman)
During World War I a British woman is tempted to forsake her mangled German air ace husband for her childhood sweetheart.
A slice of impenetrable gloom from an intractable novel.
w Jane Murfin, Samuel Hoffenstein novel Charles Morgan d John Cromwell ph Henry W. Gerrard m Max Steiner
☆ Ann Harding, Brian Aherne, Paul Lukas, Jean Hersholt, Ralph Forbes, Violet Kemble-Cooper, Sara Haden
 'One of the talkiest talkies yet.' – Variety
 'Long and solemn and wonderfully empty.' – Otis Ferguson

The Fountainhead **

US   1949   114m   bw
Warner (Henry Blanke)
An idealistic architect clashes with big business.
Overripe adaptation of a rather silly novel, full of Freudian symbols and expressionist techniques with which the star really can't cope; but an enjoyable field day for the director and the rest of the cast.
w Ayn Rand novel Ayn Rand d King Vidor
ph Robert Burks m Max Steiner
☆ Gary Cooper, Patricia Neal, Raymond Massey, Kent Smith, Robert Douglas, Henry Hull, Ray Collins, Moroni Olsen, Jerome Cowan

 'If you like deep thinking, hidden meanings, plus pure modern architecture, then this is something for which you have been waiting a long time.' – Screenland
 'The most bizarre movie in both Vidor's and Cooper's filmographies, this adaptation mutes Ms Rand's neo-Nietzschian philosophy of "objectivism" but lays on the expressionist symbolism with a "free enterprise" trowel.' – Time Out, 1980

Four Adventures of Reinette and Mirabelle **

France   1986   99m   colour
Artificial Eye/CER/Les Films du Losange (Eric Rohmer)
original title: *Quatre Aventures de Reinette et Mirabelle*
Four stories involving two contrasted students, one from the country, the other from the city.
Charming small-scale work, full of incidental pleasures.
wd Eric Rohmer ph Sophie Maintigneux
m Ronan Girre, Jean-Louis Valero ed Marie-Luisa Garcia
☆ Joëlle Miquel, Jessica Forde, Philippe Laudenbach, Yasmine Haury, Marie Rivière, Beatrice Romand, Gérard Courant, David Rocksavage

Four Against Fate: see *Derby Day*

Four Clowns **

US   1970   96m   bw
Robert Youngson Productions (Herb Gelbspan)
Studies of four silent comedians. Laurel and Hardy in excerpts from *Putting Pants on Philip*, *The Second Hundred Years*, *Their Purple Moment*, *Big Business*, *Two Tars* and *Double Whoopee*; Charley Chase in *Us*, *What Price Goofy*, *Fluttering Hearts*, *The Family Group* and *Limousine Love*; Buster Keaton in *Seven Chances*.
An essential compendium, especially for the Charley Chase revaluation which was long overdue.
w Robert Youngson m Manny Alban
☆ Jay Jackson

Four Dark Hours: see *The Green Cockatoo*

Four Daughters ***

US   1938   90m   bw
Warner (Henry Blanke)
Domestic and romantic adventures of a small-town family.
Standard small-town hearth-fire hokum, impeccably done and really quite irresistible. Garfield is a sensation in his first role.
w Julius Epstein, Lenore Coffee novel Sister Act by Fannie Hurst d Michael Curtiz ph Ernest Haller m Max Steiner ad John Hughes ed Ralph Dawson
☆ Claude Rains, John Garfield, Priscilla Lane, Rosemary Lane, Lola Lane, Gale Page, Jeffrey Lynn, Frank McHugh, May Robson, Dick Foran
 'It may be sentimental, but it's grand cinema.' – New York Times
 'It simply, yet powerfully, brings into focus a panorama of natural but startling events.' – Motion Picture Herald
† An immediate sequel was required, but the Garfield character had been killed off, so to accommodate him a variation was written under the title *Daughters Courageous*; then came two proper sequels without him, *Four Wives* and *Four Mothers*. In 1955 the original was remade as *Young at Heart* (qv).
♫ best picture; script; Michael Curtiz; John Garfield

The Four Days of Naples *

Italy   1962   119m   bw
Titanus-Metro (Goffredo Lombardo)
A reconstruction of the 1943 city battle in which the Nazis were driven out by civilian fury.
A kind of update of Open City: much admired, but a little ill-timed.
w Nanni Loy and others d Nanni Loy
ph Marcello Gatti m Carlo Rustichelli
☆ Lea Massari, Frank Wolff, Domenico Formato, Raffaele Barbato
♫ best foreign film; script

Four Desperate Men: see *The Siege of Pinchgut*

The Four Dimensions of Greta

GB   1972   89m   Eastmancolor/bw
Hemdale/Peter Walker
A reporter from Berlin comes to London to investigate the disappearance of a German au pair girl.
Flat soft-core sex flick; its only novelty is the inclusion of some uninteresting 3-D sequences in black and white, in which characters hold objects at arm's length close to the lens. In an attempt to disarm criticism, one character remarks, 'This is just like a very cheap British sex film!', and so it is.
w Murray Smith d Peter Walker ph Peter Jessop
m Harry South ed Matt McCarthy
☆ Tristan Rogers, Karen Boyes, Alan Curtis, Robin Askwith, Leena Skoog, Kenneth Hendel, John Clive, Godfrey Kenton, Pearl Hackney, Bill Maynard, Myna Bird
 'Tepid and tedious sexploitation picture.' – Nigel Andrews, MFB

Four Faces West

US   1948   90m   bw
Enterprise (David Loewe, Charles Einfeld)
aka: *They Passed This Way*
A young man turns bandit to save his father's ranch.
Thoughtful minor Western, nicely made.
w Graham Baker, Teddi Sherman novel Paso por aqui by Eugene Rhodes d Alfred E. Green
ph Russell Harlan m Paul Sawtell
☆ Joel McCrea, Frances Dee, Charles Bickford, Joseph Calleia

The Four Feathers **

US   1929   83m   bw
Paramount (David O. Selznick)
During the Sudan campaign of the 1890s, a stay-at-home receives four white feathers as a symbol of cowardice; but he goes undercover, becomes a hero, and rescues his best friend.
Ambitious early talkie based on a famous adventure novel, partly filmed in Africa; interesting but now very stilted.
w Howard Estabrook novel A. E. W. Mason
d Lothar Mendes, Merian C. Cooper, Ernest Schoedsack ph Robert Kurrle, Merian C. Cooper, Ernest Schoedsack m William F. Peters
☆ Richard Arlen, Fay Wray, Clive Brook, William Powell, George Fawcett, Theodore Von Eltz, Noah Beery

The Four Feathers ****

GB   1939   130m   Technicolor
London (Alexander Korda, Irving Asher)
The standard version of the above, perfectly cast and presented, with battle scenes which have since turned up in a score of other films from *Zarak* to *Master of the World*; also a triumph of early colour.
w R. C. Sherriff, Lajos Biro, Arthur Wimperis
d Zoltan Korda ph Georges Périnal, Osmond Borradaile, Jack Cardiff m Miklos Rozsa
ad Vincent Korda ed William Hornbeck, Henry Cornelius
☆ John Clements, Ralph Richardson, C. Aubrey Smith, June Duprez, Allan Jeayes, Jack Allen, Donald Gray, Henry Oscar, John Laurie
 'It cannot fail to be one of the best films of the year ... even the richest of the ham goes smoothly down, savoured with humour and satire.' – Graham Greene
 'Keeps the screen packed with movement, spectacle, and excitement. Beyond these box-office virtues, however, it has another quality. It tells a thumping good personal story.' – C. A. Lejeune
† Remade 1956 as *Storm over the Nile* (qv). An effective TV movie, *The Four Feathers*, was made in 1977, directed by Don Sharp and starring Beau Bridges, Robert Powell, Simon Ward, Richard Johnson, Jane Seymour and Harry Andrews.

Four for Texas

US   1963   124m   Technicolor
Warner/Sam Company (Robert Aldrich)
Two survivors of a stagecoach raid doublecross each other for the loot and become rival saloon owners.
Flabby Western comedy, tediously directed and casually performed.

w Teddi Sherman, Robert Aldrich d Robert Aldrich ph Ernest Laszlo m Nelson Riddle
☆ Dean Martin, Frank Sinatra, Anita Ekberg, Ursula Andress, Charles Bronson, Victor Buono, the Three Stooges
 'The major laughs come from the Three Stooges doing an ancient routine and an old lady falling out of her wheelchair. Zowie.' – Judith Crist
 'One suspects that the most amusing antics were those that went on off-screen.' – Films and Filming

Four Friends

US   1981   115m   Technicolor
Filmways/Cinema 77/Geria (Arthur Penn, Gene Lasko)
GB title: *Georgia's Friends*
A Yugoslavian boy grows up in Indiana and is influenced by the adult behaviour of his three friends.
Mildly interesting semi-autobiographical nostalgia movie, a vein which has been mined twice too often.
w Steve Tesich d Arthur Penn ph Ghislain Cloquet m Elizabeth Swados pd David Chapman
☆ Craig Wasson, Jodi Thelen, Michael Huddleston, Jim Metzler

 'They threw away conventions with their tattered clothes!'

Four Frightened People *

US   1934   78m   bw
Paramount/Cecil B. de Mille
A bubonic plague outbreak on board ship causes four survivors to escape via a lifeboat and trek through dangerous jungle.
Studio-bound but interesting action melodrama, of a type unusual from this director.
w Bartlett Cormack, Lenore Coffee novel E. Arnot Robertson d Cecil B. de Mille ph Karl Struss m Karl Hajos and others
☆ Claudette Colbert, Herbert Marshall, William Gargan, Mary Boland, Leo Carrillo, Nella Walker, Tetsu Komai, Ethel Griffies
 'The adventures are episodic and disjointed, running the gamut from stark tragedy to unbelievable farce.' – Variety
 'A cumbersome sort of melodrama ... despite some mildly entertaining jungle scenes.' – Literary Digest

Four Girls in Town

US   1956   85m   Technicolor   Cinemascope
U-I (Aaron Rosenberg)
Girls from various countries are chosen for Hollywood screen tests.
Formula romantic comedy adequately exposing young talent.
wd Jack Sher ph Irving Glassberg m Alex North
☆ George Nader, Julie Adams, Marianne Cook, Elsa Martinelli, Gia Scala, Sydney Chaplin, Grant Williams, John Gavin

Four Girls in White

US   1938   88m   bw
MGM (Nat Levine)
Drama among the student nurses.
Standard hospital fare designed as a try-out for budding talent.
w Dorothy Yost story Nathalie Bucknall, Endre Bohem d S. Sylvan Simon
☆ Florence Rice, Alan Marshal, Ann Rutherford, Una Merkel, Buddy Ebsen, Mary Howard, Kent Taylor, Jessie Ralph, Sara Haden, Philip Terry, Tom Neal

Four Guns to the Border

US   1954   83m   Technicolor
Universal-International
Things go wrong for four bank robbers after a raid.
Rather downbeat Western with insufficient excitement.
w George Van Marter, Franklin Coen d Richard Carlson ph Russell Metty
☆ Rory Calhoun, Walter Brennan, Colleen Miller, George Nader, Nina Foch, John McIntire, Charles Drake

The Four Horsemen of the Apocalypse **

US   1921   150m   bw   silent
Metro
A young Argentinian fights for his father's country, France, in World War I.
Highly derivative dramatic spectacle, almost a pageant, from a fairly unreadable novel. Despite its variable if exotic style, it made a star of Rudolph Valentino.

---

w June Mathis *novel* Vicente Blasco-Ibanez
d *Rex Ingram* ph John F. Seitz
☆ *Rudolph Valentino*, Alice Terry, Nigel de Brulier, Alan Hale, Jean Hersholt, Wallace Beery
'A blend of exotic settings, striking composition, dramatic lighting, and colourful if sordid atmosphere.' – *Lewis Jacobs*
'Not only was it marvellously effective in its appeal to the eye, but the logical and dramatic unfolding of the basic story was a striking revelation of the valuable service that an expert scenario-writer may render to the professional writer of novels.' – *Edward S. Van Zile, That Marvel the Movie*

The Four Horsemen of the Apocalypse *
US 1961 153m Metrocolor Cinemascope
MGM (Julian Blaustein)
▦
In this ill-fated modernization, the idle grandson of an Argentinian beef tycoon finds his manhood at last as a member of the French resistance during World War II.
The visionary skyriding figures of death and pestilence simply do not fit in with bombs and concentration camps. Glum acting by a too elderly company, ugly colour and the usual hindrances of Cinemascope.
w Robert Ardrey, John Gay d Vincente Minnelli ph Milton Krasner m André Previn
☆ Glenn Ford, Ingrid Thulin, Charles Boyer, Paul Henreid, Lee J. Cobb, Paul Lukas, Karl Boehm, Yvette Mimieux
'An elephantine helping of hysteria and hokum.' – *Judith Crist, 1973*

Four Hours to Kill **
US 1935 74m bw
Paramount (Arthur Hornblow Jnr)
A psychopathic gangster gets loose during an evening at the theatre.
Tense, well-handled melodrama making full use of its setting.
w Norman Krasna *play Small Miracle* by Norman Krasna d Mitchell Leisen ph Theodor Sparkuhl
☆ Richard Barthelmess, Ray Milland, Gertrude Michael, Joe Morrison, Helen Mack, Dorothy Tree, Roscoe Karns, Henry Travers
'It fails to grip and isn't long on laughs.' – *Variety*

The Four Hundred Blows **
France 1959 94m bw Dyaliscope
Films du Carrosse/SEDIF (Georges Charlot)
▦ ▦ ⊘ ⊙
original title: *Les Quatre Cents Coups*
A 12-year-old boy, unhappy at home, finds himself in a detention centre but finally escapes and keeps running.
Little more in plot terms than a piece of character observation, this engaging film is so controlled and lyrical as to be totally refreshing, and it gives a very vivid picture of the Paris streets.
wd François Truffaut ph Henri Decaë m Jean Constantin ad Bernard Evein ed Marie-Josèph Yoyotte
☆ Jean-Pierre Léaud, Claire Maurier, Albert Rémy
'The narrative is boldly fluent. Sympathetic, amused, reminded, occasionally puzzled, you are carried along with it. I don't think you will get away before the end.' – *Dilys Powell*
† The film is said to be based on Truffaut's own childhood.
⅄ script

Four in a Jeep *
Switzerland 1951 96m bw
Praesensfilm (Lazar Wechsler)
▦
In the post-war international zone of Vienna, the four nationals of a police patrol come to blows over the cases they encounter.
Historically interesting but rather bland illustration of an untenable and even tragic political situation which was treated more melodramatically in The Third Man.
w Richard Schweizer d Leopold Lindtberg ph Emil Barna m Robert Blum
☆ Viveca Lindfors, Ralph Meeker, Yoseph Yadin, Michael Medwin

Four in the Morning *
GB 1965 94m bw
West One (John Morris)
Four personal stories are intercut during one London night.

Attractive minor effort which takes the eye without engaging the mind.
wd Anthony Simmons ph Larry Pizer m John Barry
☆ Ann Lynn, Judi Dench, Norman Rodway, Brian Phelan, Joe Melia
🏆 Judi Dench

Four Jacks and a Jill
US 1941 68m bw
RKO (John Twist)
Four struggling musicians adopt a down-and-out girl.
Flimsy remake of That Girl from Paris; the talent is given little opportunity to rise.
w John Twist d Jack Hively ph Russell Metty m/ly Mort Greene, Harry Revel
☆ Anne Shirley, Ray Bolger, Desi Arnaz, Jack Durant, June Havoc, Eddie Foy Jnr, Fritz Feld

Four Jills in a Jeep
US 1944 89m bw
TCF (Irving Starr)
Four Hollywood glamour girls entertain the troops.
Condescending, dispirited 'semi-documentary' war musical.
w Robert Ellis, Helen Logan, Snag Werris d William A. Seiter ph Peverell Marley md Emil Newman
☆ Kay Francis, Martha Raye, Carole Landis, Mitzi Mayfair, Jimmy Dorsey and his band, John Harvey, Phil Silvers, Dick Haymes, Betty Grable, Carmen Miranda, George Jessel, Alice Faye
'It gives the painful impression of having been tossed together in a couple of hours.' – *Bosley Crowther*

The Four Just Men *
GB 1939 85m bw
Ealing-Capad (Michael Balcon, S. C. Balcon)
US title: *The Secret Four*
To save the Empire, four stalwart Britishers agree to murder a villainous MP.
Bright, unusual but dated thriller from a popular novel.
w Roland Pertwee, Angus Macphail, Sergei Nolbandov *novel* Edgar Wallace d Walter Forde ph Ronald Neame m Ernest Irving ad Wilfred Shingleton ed Charles Saunders
☆ Hugh Sinclair, Francis L. Sullivan, Frank Lawton, Griffith Jones, Anna Lee, Basil Sydney, Alan Napier, Athole Stewart, Edward Chapman, Garry Marsh, Ellaline Terriss, Lydia Sherwood, George Merritt
† The TV series of the late fifties restrained its heroes from criminal acts; the men were Jack Hawkins, Richard Conte, Dan Dailey, Vittorio de Sica.

Four Men and a Prayer *
US 1938 85m bw
TCF (Kenneth MacGowan)
Four young Englishmen set out to clear the name of their dishonoured father.
Pleasantly performed mystery which improves after a slowish start.
w Richard Sherman, Sonya Levien, Walter Ferris *novel* David Garth d John Ford ph Ernest Palmer md Louis Silvers
☆ Loretta Young, Richard Greene, George Sanders, David Niven, William Henry, C. Aubrey Smith, J. Edward Bromberg, John Carradine, Alan Hale, Reginald Denny, Barry Fitzgerald, Berton Churchill, John Sutton
'Better cast than story … the pace is so uneven that the general effect at times is bewildering.' – *Variety*
'Energetically told, compactly presented.' – *New York Times*

Four Mothers
US 1940 86m bw
Warner (Henry Blanke)
The four Lemp sisters, all happily married, have financial problems.
Third and last in the Four Daughters trilogy; quite attractively made but very routine.
w Stephen Morehouse Avery d William Keighley m Heinz Roemheld
☆ Priscilla Lane, Rosemary Lane, Lola Lane, Gale Page, Claude Rains, Dick Foran, Frank McHugh, Jeffrey Lynn, Eddie Albert, Vera Lewis

---

'What has eight legs, feathers, and is usually seen coming to the rescue?'
The Four Musketeers (The Revenge of Milady) *
🏆🏆 Panama 1974 103m Technicolor
TCF/Film Trust/Este (Alexander Salkind, Michael Salkind)
▦ ⊘ ⊙
Athos, Porthos, Aramis and D'Artagnan have a final battle with Rochefort.
Perfunctory sequel to the same team's The Three Musketeers; allegedly the two films were intended as one, but if so the first ten reels were by far the best, though this section has its regulation quota of high spirits and lusty action.
w George MacDonald Fraser d Richard Lester ph David Watkin m Lalo Schifrin pd Brian Eatwell
☆ Michael York, Oliver Reed, Frank Finlay, Richard Chamberlain, Raquel Welch, Faye Dunaway, Charlton Heston, Christopher Lee, Simon Ward, Geraldine Chaplin, Jean-Pierre Cassel, Roy Kinnear
'The whole sleek formula has rolled over to reveal a very soft, very flabby underside.' – *Tony Rayns*

Four Rooms
US 1995 97m DeLuxe
Buena Vista/Miramax (Lawrence Bender)
⊞ ▦ ⊘ ⊙ ⊙
On New Year's Eve, the bell-hop at a run-down hotel deals with customers in four rooms: in the first, he is asked to supply some semen for witches attempting to bring the goddess Diana back to life (*The Missing Ingredient*); in the second, he deals with a gun-toting, drug-taking husband who has tied up his wife (*The Wrong Man*); in the third, he baby-sits some young delinquents (*The Misbehavers*); in the fourth, some movie executives are recreating a moment from a Hitchcock television story, in which Peter Lorre bet Steve McQueen his car against McQueen's little finger that McQueen could not light his cigarette lighter ten times in a row (*The Man from Hollywood*).
One of those occasions where the film-makers may have enjoyed themselves, but audiences won't. Four feeble anecdotes suffer from sloppy writing and unfocused acting; it should have remained a home movie.
w Tim Roth, Jennifer Beals, David Proval, Antonio Banderas, Kathy Griffin, Marc Lawrence, Marisa Tomei, Sammi Davis, Amanda de Cadenet, Valeria Golino, Madonna, Quentin Tarantino, Lawrence Bender
'This showcase folly by four of Hollywood's "hottest" stars plumbs new depths.' – *Mark Kermode, Sight and Sound*

'Here's to our friends – and the strength to put up with them!'
The Four Seasons **
US 1981 108m Technicolor
Universal (Martin Bregman)
▦ ⊘
Three married couples take seasonal holidays together, and remain united despite various tensions.
Rueful sexual comedy which maintains considerable momentum and actually makes us laugh at its sympathetic characters.
wd Alan Alda ph Victor J. Kemper m Antonio Vivaldi
☆ Alan Alda, Carol Burnett, Len Cariou, Sandy Dennis, Rita Moreno, Jack Weston, Bess Armstrong
'An odd mingling of perspicuity and histrionics … a real middle-of-the-road film.' – *Geoff Brown, MFB*
'Unfailingly amusing, touchingly honest, and in the end refreshingly decent.' – *Margaret Hinxman, Daily Mail*

'See! a strange and beautiful woman created before your eyes!'
Four Sided Triangle
GB 1953 81m bw
Exclusive/Hammer (Michael Carreras, Alexander Paàl)
When a scientist's girlfriend marries another, he creates a clone but finds that it has the same preferences.
A very early entry in this field; not too well done, but faithful to its silly theme.

---

w Paul Tabori, Terence Fisher *novel* William F. Temple d Terence Fisher ph Reg Wyer m Malcolm Arnold ad J. Elder Wills ed Maurice Rootes
☆ Stephen Murray, Barbara Payton, James Hayter, John Van Eyssen, Percy Marmont, Kynaston Reeves

The Four Skulls of Jonathan Drake
US 1959 70m bw
UA/Vogue (Robert E. Kent)
A family is cursed by a head-hunting Equadorian medicine man.
Cheaply made but full-blooded occult horror, rather effectively done by a cast that knows how.
w Orville H. Hampton d Edward L. Cahn ph Maury Gertsman m Paul Dunlap
☆ Henry Daniell, Eduard Franz, Valerie French, Grant Richards, Paul Cavanagh
'Amazonian Indians may find the plot a shade far-fetched.' – *MFB*

Four Sons *
US 1940 89m bw
TCF (Darryl F. Zanuck)
A Czech family is divided when the Nazis take over.
Predictable po-faced anti-Hitler melodrama released to an indifferent public well before America entered the war. A remake of a silent film set during World War I.
w John Howard Lawson d Archie Mayo ph Leon Shamroy m David Buttolph
☆ Don Ameche, Eugenie Leontovich, Mary Beth Hughes, Alan Curtis, George Ernest, Robert Lowery, Sig Rumann, Lionel Royce, Ludwig Stossel
'It partakes more of sentimental melodrama than of tragedy … Neither in its performance nor its writing does the film ever rise to any passion.' – *New York Times*

Four Steps in the Clouds *
Italy 1942 90m bw
Cines Amato
original title: *Quattro Passi fra le Nuvole*
A travelling salesman on a bus gets involved with the problems of a pregnant girl, but misunderstandings are finally cleared up to general satisfaction.
A comedy on the American model which was a great success in wartorn Italy. Not particularly remarkable in itself, it was remade in 1957, as The Virtuous Bigamist, with Fernandel. It does show the lighter side of Italian neo-realism.
w Cesare Zavattini, Giuseppe Amato, Piero Tellini, Aldo de Benedetti d Alessandro Blasetti ph Vaclav Vich m Alessandro Cicognini
☆ Gino Cervi, Adriana Benetti, Giuditta Rissone
'A gay tender ironic story of a brief encounter; a small film with an effervescent belief in life.' – *Richard Winnington*

Four Times That Night (dubbed)
Italy/Germany 1972 90m colour
Delfino/Hape (Zeljko Kunkera, Claudio Rainis)
original title: *Quante Volte... Quella Notte*
Four people tell what happened after a playboy picked up a girl.
Italian fluff that copies Rashomon with its central conceit of the same event seen from differing viewpoints, but is mainly concerned with undressing its female star, a former Miss Italy.
w Mario Moroni, Carl Ross, Guido Leoni d Mario Bava ph Antonio Rinaldi m Lallo Gori pd Andrea Crisanti ed Otello Colangeli
☆ Daniela Giordano, Brett Halsey, Dick Randall, Valeria Sabel, Michael Hinz, Rainer Basedow, Pascale Petit, Brigitte Skay, Calisto Calisti

'Five Good Reasons To Stay Single.'
Four Weddings and a Funeral ***
GB 1994 117m Eastmancolor
Rank/Polygram/Channel 4/Working Title (Duncan Kenworthy)
⊞ ▦ ⊘ ⊙ ⊙
A confirmed bachelor chases the woman of his dreams from one wedding to another.
Enjoyable, episodic comedy with expert comic performances, occasionally hindered by its lapses into broad farce and ancient jokes.
w Richard Curtis d Mike Newell ph Michael Coulter m Richard Rodney Bennett pd Maggie Gray ed Jon Gregory
☆ Hugh Grant, Andie MacDowell, *Kristin Scott Thomas*, Simon Callow, James Flett, David Bower, Charlotte Coleman, John Hannah, Anna

---

Chancellor, Robert Lang, Jeremy Kemp, Rosalie Crutchley, Rowan Atkinson

'Old-fashioned in its essence, and highly conservative: there will certainly be some British viewers who find the languid mating rites of the moneyed upper-middle-classes less than compulsive.' – *Sheila Johnston, Independent*

'Highly expert and entertaining comedy.' – *Derek Malcolm, Guardian*

† The film is the most successful British movie so far, having taken more than £130m at the box-office worldwide. Its British video release was available for sale for five weeks only

†† Following the recitation of one of his poems in the film, a slim paperback of love poems by W. H. Auden became a best-seller.

ℇ best picture; Richard Curtis

Ⓡ best film; most popular film; Mike Newell; Hugh Grant; Kristin Scott Thomas

Four Wives *

US   1939   110m   bw
Warner (Henry Blanke)

Three of the Lemp girls find a new husband for their widowed sister.

Lively and thickly textured sequel to Four Daughters; *predecessor of the less interesting* Four Mothers.

w Julius J. and Philip G. Epstein, Maurice Hanline novel *Sister Act* by Fannie Hurst d Michael Curtiz ph Sol Polito m Max Steiner

☆ Claude Rains, Priscilla Lane, Rosemary Lane, Lola Lane, Gale Page, Jeffrey Lynn, Eddie Albert, May Robson, Frank McHugh, Dick Foran, John Garfield

'Will ride along on momentum to excellent box office.' – *Variety*

The Four-Poster

US   1952   103m   bw
Columbia/Stanley Kramer

The history of a marriage told in a series of bedroom scenes.

Hastily shot and rather tatty looking version of a stage play; unfortunately film can't contrast the comedy of the opening and the tragedy of the close within one small set, and the UPA cartoon bridges, though smart in themselves, are merely an irritation.

w Allan Scott play Jan de Hartog d Irving Reis ph Hal Mohr m Dimitri Tiomkin

☆ Rex Harrison, Lilli Palmer

℥ Hal Mohr

Four's a Crowd

US   1938   91m   bw
Warner (Hal B. Wallis/David Lewis)

A public relations man has the job of promoting a mean-spirited millionaire, and falls in love with his daughter.

Floppy comedy, neither very witty nor as crazy as might have been expected. However, it ambles along quite engagingly.

w Casey Robinson, Sig Herzig d Michael Curtiz ph Ernest Haller m Heinz Roemheld, Ray Heindorf

☆ Errol Flynn, Rosalind Russell, Olivia de Havilland, Patric Knowles, Walter Connolly, Hugh Herbert, Melville Cooper, Franklin Pangborn, Herman Bing, Margaret Hamilton

'Goofy click comedy that moves along to a whirlwind laugh finish.' – *Variety*

Fourteen Hours ***

US   1951   92m   bw
TCF (Sol C. Siegel)

A man stands on the ledge of a tall building and threatens to jump.

Well-made documentary drama based on a true occurrence but given a happy ending. First class detail gives an impression of realism.

w John Paxton article Joel Sayre d Henry Hathaway ph Joe MacDonald m Alfred Newman ad Lyle Wheeler, Leland Fuller

☆ Richard Basehart, Paul Douglas, Barbara Bel Geddes, Grace Kelly, Debra Paget, Agnes Moorehead, Robert Keith, Howard da Silva, Jeffrey Hunter, Martin Gabel, Jeff Corey

'A model of craftsmanship in all departments.' – *Penelope Houston*

'A highly enjoyable small scale picture, with a strength immensely greater than its size would suggest.' – *Richard Mallett, Punch*

℥ art direction

The Fourth Man **

Netherlands   1983   102m   colour
Mainline/De Verenigde Nederlandsche Filmcompagnie/Spectrafilm (Rob Houwer)

📼   ⚲

original title: *De Vierde Man*

A novelist makes love to a widow as the first step to seducing her boyfriend.

Inventive, exuberant black comedy.

w Gerard Soeteman novel Gerard Reve d Paul Verhoeven ph Jan de Bont m Loek Dikker ad Roland de Groot ed Ine Schenkkan

☆ Jeroen Krabbé, Renee Soutendijk, Thom Hoffman, Dolf de Vries, Geert de Jong, Hans Veerman, Hero Muller, Caroline de Beus

'A highbrow debauch of depravity, destruction, sex and blasphemy.' – *Quentin Crisp*

The Fourth Protocol *

GB   1987   119m   Rank Colour
Rank (Timothy Burrill)

🔀   📼   ⚲

Vying masterspies narrowly avert nuclear disaster.

Very competent but somehow old hat espionage thriller, from a best seller.

w Frederick Forsyth novel Frederick Forsyth d John Mackenzie ph Phil Meheux m Lalo Schifrin pd Alan Cameron

☆ Michael Caine, Pierce Brosnan, Joanna Cassidy, Ned Beatty, Betsy Brantley, Ray McAnally, Ian Richardson, Anton Rodgers

'There is an uneasy feeling that the whole affair could have been better made into an excellent miniseries.' – *Daily Variety*

'It's no longer East vs West … Just two proud heroes with no one to fight … but each other.'

The Fourth War

US   1990   91m   DeLuxe
Kodiak (Wolf Schmidt)

🔀   📼   ⚲

A violent feud develops between an American and a Soviet colonel, each in charge of a border post between Czechoslovakia and East Germany.

Moderate thriller, somewhat overtaken by events.

w Stephen Peters, Kenneth Ross novel Stephen Peters d John Frankenheimer ph Gerry Fisher m Bill Conti pd Alan Manzer ed Robert F. Shugrue

☆ Roy Scheider, Jürgen Prochnow, Tim Reid, Lara Harris, Harry Dean Stanton, Dale Dye, Bill MacDonald

'A simple moral story, directly told without adornment and relying on old-fashioned effects.' – *MFB*

The Fourth Wish

Australia   1976   105m   colour
Galaxy/South Australian Film Corp (John Morris)

A single father sets out to grant three wishes to his 12-year-old son, who is dying from leukaemia.

Effective domestic drama, cut down from a three-part television series, held together by Meillon's strong central performance.

w Michael Craig d Don Chaffey ph Geoff Burton m Tristram Cary ad David Copping ed G. Turney Smith

☆ John Meillon, Robert Bettles, Michael Craig, Anne Haddy, Ron Haddrick, Robyn Nevin

Les Fous de Bassan: see In the Shadow of the Wind

Fox *

West Germany   1975   123m   Eastmancolor
Tango Film (Rainer Werner Fassbinder)

🔀   📼

original title: *Faustrecht der Freiheit*

aka: *Fox and His Friends*

The decline of a homosexual sideshow performer.

Ironic, semi-autobiographical melodrama in the Blue Angel tradition, with sidelong glances at Hollywood glamour. In its way very memorable, but overlong.

w Rainer Werner Fassbinder, Christian Hohoff d Rainer Werner Fassbinder ph Michael Ballhaus m Peer Raben

☆ Rainer Werner Fassbinder, Karl-Heinz Boehm, Peter Chatel, Harry Bär, Adrian Hoven, Ulla Jacobsson

'Between Ellen and Jill came Paul…'

The Fox *

US/Canada   1968   110m   DeLuxe
Warner/Raymond Stross/Motion Pictures International (Howard Koch)

On an isolated farm, two lesbians are disturbed by the arrival of a wandering seaman.

Rather obvious sexual high jinks full of symbolism and heavy breathing.

w Lewis John Carlino, Howard Koch novel D. H. Lawrence d Mark Rydell ph Bill Fraker m Lalo Schifrin

☆ Anne Heywood, Sandy Dennis, Keir Dullea

℥ Lalo Schifrin

Fox and His Friends: see Fox

The Fox and the Hound *

🔀   US   1981   83m   Technicolor
Walt Disney (Wolfgang Reitherman, Art Stevens)

🔀   📼   ⚲

A fox cub makes friends with a hound puppy, but their friendship is tested when they grow up.

Not unpleasant but somewhat heavy-going for a feature cartoon, made with some of the old Disney style but none of the old inventiveness.

w various novel Daniel P. Mannix d Art Stevens, Ted Berman, Richard Rich

☆ Featuring the voices of Mickey Rooney, Kurt Russell, Pearl Bailey, Jack Albertson, Sandy Duncan, Jeanette Nolan

'Laughs are few and far between … the whole enterprise lacks vitality.' – *Brenda Davies, MFB*

Fox Movietone Follies of 1929

US   1929   82m   bw (colour sequences)
Fox

GB title: *Movietone Follies of 1929*

An all-star review.

Every studio had its early talkie musical using up its contract stars; this was perhaps the least interesting.

wd David Butler, William K. Wells ph Charles Van Enger m Con Conrad, Sidney Mitchell, Archie Gottlieb md Arthur Kay

☆ Sue Carol, Lola Lane, Dixie Lee, Sharon Lynn, Stepin Fetchit

Foxes

US   1980   106m   Technicolor
UA/Polygram (David Puttnam, Gerald Ayres)

📼

Four teenage girls battle with sex, drugs and life in general.

Well-meaning but entirely resistible melodrama from behind the headlines.

w Gerald Ayres d Adrian Lyne ph Leon Bijou m Giorgio Moroder ad Michael Levesque ed Jim Coblentz

☆ Jodie Foster, Scott Baio, Sally Kellerman, Randy Quaid, Adam Faith

'Almost nil adult appeal.' – *Variety*

The Foxes of Harrow

US   1947   117m   bw
TCF (William A. Bacher)

In 1820 New Orleans, a philanderer seeks advancement by breaking up his marriage.

Tolerable but rather flat adaptation of a bestseller, stultified by central miscasting.

w Wanda Tuchock novel Frank Yerby d John M. Stahl ph Joseph LaShelle m Alfred Newman

☆ Rex Harrison, Maureen O'Hara, Richard Haydn, Victor McLaglen, Vanessa Brown, Patricia Medina, Gene Lockhart, Hugo Haas

† Rex Harrison's role had been turned down by Tyrone Power.

'I don't care what they call you! I only care that you are all man – and all mine!'

Foxfire

US   1955   92m   Technicolor
U-I (Aaron Rosenberg)

A rich New York girl on holiday in Arizona is attracted to a half-Apache miner.

Romantic melodrama with action asides; watchable for those who like that sort of thing.

w Ketti Frings novel Anya Seton d Joseph Pevney ph William Daniels m Frank Skinner

☆ Jane Russell, Jeff Chandler, Frieda Inescort, Dan Duryea

Foxhole in Cairo

GB   1960   80m   bw
Omnia (Steven Pallos, Donald Taylor)

A German agent in Libya is allowed to get back to Rommel with false information.

Interesting true spy story deflated by muddled handling.

w Leonard Mosley novel *The Cat and the Mice* by Leonard Mosley d John Moxey ph Desmond Dickinson m Wolfram Rohrig, Douglas Gamley, Ken Jones

☆ James Robertson Justice, Adrian Hoven, Albert Lieven, Niall MacGinnis, Peter Van Eyck, Robert Urquhart, Fenella Fielding

Foxtrot

Mexico/Switzerland   1977   91m   Technicolor
New World (Gerald Green)

📼

Rich people retreat to a desert island to avoid World War II, but their servants revolt.

A more or less direct attempt to remake La Règle du Jeu; it sinks into boredom.

w Arturo Ripstein, José Emilio Pacheco, H. A. L. Craig d Arturo Ripstein

☆ Peter O'Toole, Charlotte Rampling, Max von Sydow, Jorge Luke, Helena Rojo, Claudio Brook

Fra Diavolo **

US   1933   90m   bw
MGM/Hal Roach

🔀   📼   ⚲

aka: *The Devil's Brother*

Two incompetent bandits are hired as manservants by a real bandit.

Auber's 1830 operetta becomes a vehicle for Laurel and Hardy, setting a pattern they followed with Babes in Toyland and The Bohemian Girl. They have excellent sequences, but overall the film lacks pace.

w Jeanie Macpherson d Hal Roach, Charles Rogers ph Art Lloyd, Hap Depew m LeRoy Shield ed Bert Jordan, William Terhune

☆ Stan Laurel, Oliver Hardy, Dennis King, James Finlayson, Thelma Todd

'An early 19th-century comic opera doesn't make for particularly good film fare despite its hoking.' – *Variety*

La Fracture du Myocarde: see Cross My Heart

Fragment of an Empire *

USSR   1929   100m   bw   silent
Sovkino

A young man who lost his memory in World War I regains it in 1928 and surveys the changed social order.

Mildly satirical propaganda piece with a vivid impression of Leningrad at the time.

w Friedrich Ermler, Katerina Vinogradskaya d Friedrich Ermler ph Yevgeni Schneider

☆ Fyodor Nikitin, Yakov Gudkin, Ludmila Semyonova

Fragment of Fear *

GB   1970   95m   Technicolor
Columbia (John R. Sloan)

A young writer investigates the murder of his aunt, but finds that he may himself be mad.

What appears to be a whodunnit turns into a flashy, fashionable, sub-Antonioni puzzle with no ending, but despite the considerable irritation this causes, the details and character cameos are excellent.

w Paul Dehn novel John Bingham d Richard C. Sarafian ph Oswald Morris m Johnny Harris

☆ David Hemmings, Gayle Hunnicutt, Roland Culver, Daniel Massey, Flora Robson, Wilfrid Hyde-White, Adolfo Celi, Mona Washbourne

Framed

US   1947   82m   bw
Columbia

GB title: *Paula*

A drunken out-of-work engineer is used as fall guy by two thieves planning an elaborate coup.

Lugubrious mixture of puzzle, character drama and gloomy philosophizing, complete with femme fatale who is handed over to the cops at the end.

w Ben Maddow d Richard Wallace

☆ Glenn Ford, Janis Carter, Barry Sullivan

🔀 film suitable for family viewing   🔀 VHS video-cassette for the British PAL system   📼 VHS video-cassette for the British PAL system in wide screen-format   ⚲ Video cassette in a computer-colourised version   📼 American NTSC video-cassette   ⚲ Laser disc

Framed

US 1974 106m Metrocolor
Paramount

A Tennessee gambler inadvertently kills a sheriff, is sent to prison, gets out on parole and wreaks revenge on those who framed him.

Violent thick-ear update of The Count of Monte Cristo, of interest only to connoisseurs of gratuitous nastiness.

w Mort Briskin d Phil Karlson
☆ Joe Don Baker, Conny Van Dyke, Gabriel Dell, Brock Peters, John Marley, John Larch

Frances

US 1982 140m Technicolor
EMI/Brooksfilm (Jonathan Sanger)

The downhill career of 30s actress Frances Farmer.

Long, glum, and not particularly convincing in its inferences, this exhaustive study of a person who didn't deserve all this fuss is illuminated only by a strong star performance.

w Eric Bergren, Christopher Devore, Nicholas Kazan d Graeme Clifford ph Laszlo Kovacs m John Barry pd Richard Sylbert
☆ Jessica Lange, Kim Stanley, Sam Shepard, Bart Burns, Jeffrey de Munn
♪ Jessica Lange; Kim Stanley

Francesco, Giullare di Dio: see *Francis, God's Jester*

The Franchise Affair *

GB 1950 88m bw
ABP (Robert Hall)

A young girl accuses two gentlewomen of kidnapping and ill-treating her.

Unusual and absorbing mystery based on a true 18th-century case; the treatment however is rather too mild.

w Robert Hall, Lawrence Huntington novel Josephine Tey d Lawrence Huntington ph Gunther Krampf m Philip Green
☆ Michael Denison, Dulcie Gray, Anthony Nicholls, Marjorie Fielding, Athene Seyler, Ann Stephens, Hy Hazell, John Bailey, Kenneth More

Francis *

↑↑ US 1949 90m bw
U-I (Robert Arthur)

An army private makes friends with a talking mule who causes him some embarrassment.

Simple-minded, quite agreeable if rather slow-moving fantasy farce which was popular enough to spawn several sequels and later a TV series called Mister Ed.

Sequels (the first six with Donald O'Connor):
1951 Francis Goes to the Races
1952 Francis Goes to West Point
1953 Francis Covers Big Town
1954 Francis Joins the WACS
1955 Francis in the Navy
1956 Francis in the Haunted House (with Mickey Rooney)

w David Stern novel David Stern d Arthur Lubin ph Irving Glassberg m Frank Skinner
☆ Donald O'Connor, Patricia Medina, ZaSu Pitts, Ray Collins, John McIntire, Eduard Franz, Robert Warwick, Chill Wills

Francis, God's Jester **

Italy 1950 75m bw
Cineriz (Giuseppe Amato)
original title: *Francesco, Giullare di Dio*
aka: *The Flowers of St Francis*

An anecdotal and episodic account of the beginnings of the Franciscan order and its first members as they go to preach their faith.

Using mainly non-professional actors, and with Franciscan monks playing the founders of their order, Rossellini, with compassion and humour, affirms that the great virtues are innocence and simplicity.

w Roberto Rossellini, Federico Fellini book The Little Flowers of St Francis and The Life of Brother Ginepro d Roberto Rossellini ph Otello Martelli m Renzo Rossellini, Father Enrico Buondonno ed Jolanda Benvenuti
☆ Aldo Fabrizi, Arabella Lemaitre, Brother Nazario Gerardi

Francis of Assisi

US 1961 107m DeLuxe Cinemascope
TCF/Perseus (Plato A. Skouras)

The son of a medieval cloth merchant takes a vow of poverty, cares for animals and dies a hermit.

Tedious biopic.

w Eugene Vale, Jack Thomas, James Forsyth d Michael Curtiz ph Piero Portalupi m Mario Nascimbene
☆ Bradford Dillman, Dolores Hart, Stuart Whitman, Eduard Franz, Pedro Armendariz, Cecil Kellaway, Finlay Currie, Mervyn Johns, Athene Seyler

Françoise Steps Out: see *Rue de l'Estrapade*

'A Terrifying Tale Of Sluts And Bolts.'
'Where Sex Can Cost You An Arm And A Leg.'

Frankenhooker

US 1990 90m colour
Shapiro/Glickenhaus (Edgar Levens)

A mad scientist uses the bodies of prostitutes to rebuild his girlfriend, cut to pieces in a lawnmower accident.

Odd mix of uninventive comedy and gore, relying on its tastelessness to amuse.

w Robert Martin, Frank Henenlotter d Frank Henenlotter ph Robert M. Baldwin m Joe Renzetti sp Kevin Tent sp Gabe Bartalos
☆ James Lorintz, Patty Mullen, Charlotte Helmkamp, Shirley Stoler, Louise Lasser
† The film was cut to 81m on its British video release.

'To have seen it is to wear a badge of courage!'
'A monster science created but could not destroy!'

Frankenstein ****

US 1931 71m bw
Universal (Carl Laemmle Jnr)

A research scientist creates a living monster from corpses, but it runs amok.

Whole books have been written about this film and its sequels. Apart from being a fascinating if primitive cinematic work in its own right, it set its director and star on interesting paths and established a Hollywood attitude towards horror (mostly borrowed from German silents such as The Golem). A seminal film indeed, which at each repeated viewing belies its age.

w Garrett Fort, Francis Edwards Faragoh, John L. Balderston play Peggy Webling novel Mary Wollstonecraft Shelley d James Whale m Arthur Edeson m David Broekman ad Charles D. Hall
☆ Boris Karloff, Colin Clive, Mae Clarke, John Boles, Edward Van Sloan, Frederick Kerr, Dwight Frye

'Still the most famous of all horror films, and deservedly so.' – *John Baxter, 1968*
'The horror is cold, chilling the marrow but never arousing malaise.' – *Carlos Clarens*
† Direct sequels by the same studio (all qv) include *The Bride of Frankenstein, Son of Frankenstein, Ghost of Frankenstein, Frankenstein Meets the Wolf Man, House of Frankenstein, House of Dracula, Abbott and Costello Meet Frankenstein*. The later Hammer series, which told the story all over again in gorier vein, includes (all qv) *The Curse of Frankenstein, The Revenge of Frankenstein, The Evil of Frankenstein, Frankenstein Created Woman, Frankenstein Must be Destroyed, Horror of Frankenstein, Frankenstein and the Monster from Hell*. Other Frankenstein films date from as early as 1908, and scores have been made in various languages. *Young Frankenstein* (qv) is a partly effective spoof on the Hollywood series; *The Munsters* was a sixties comedy series for TV which used the monster as its leading character in a domestic setting.
Robert Florey is said to have contributed to the script, having been the first choice for director.

Frankenstein '70

US 1958 83m bw Cinemascope
Allied Artists (Aubrey Schenck)

Television film-makers descend on Castle Frankenstein; the current Count needs the money to finance some monster making of his own.

Boringly talkative and very silly 'futuristic' blot on an honourable name, apart from a rather frightening pre-credits sequence.

w Richard Landau, G. Worthing Yates d Howard W. Koch ph Carl Guthrie m Paul Dunlap
☆ Boris Karloff, Tom Duggan, Jana Lund, Mike Lane

Frankenstein and the Monster from Hell

GB 1973 99m Technicolor
Hammer/Avco (Roy Skeggs)

The Baron turns an injured lunatic into a hairy ape man.

Cheaply made and very ghoulish horror comic in the unattractive setting of an asylum; very little entertainment is provided.

w John Elder (Anthony Hinds) d Terence Fisher ph Brian Probyn ad Scott MacGregor ed James Needs
☆ Peter Cushing, Shane Briant, Madeleine Smith, John Stratton, Bernard Lee, Dave Prowse, Patrick Troughton

'A beautiful woman with the soul of a devil!'

Frankenstein Created Woman

GB 1966 86m Technicolor
Warner/Hammer-Seven Arts (Anthony Nelson-Keys)

The Baron invests the body of a dead girl with the soul of her dead lover, and a murder spree results.

Crude and gory farrago, with the central laboratory sequence apparently excised at the last moment.

w John Elder (Anthony Hinds) d Terence Fisher ph Arthur Grant m James Bernard pd Bernard Robinson ad Don Mingaye ed James Needs, Spencer Reeve
☆ Peter Cushing, Thorley Walters, Susan Denberg, Robert Morris, Duncan Lamont

'Titans of terror, clashing in mortal combat!'

Frankenstein Meets the Wolf Man **

US 1943 73m bw
Universal (George Waggner)

Lawrence Talbot, the wolf man, travels to Vasaria in the hope of a cure, and finds the Frankenstein monster being reactivated.

Once one recovered from the bargain basement combination of two monsters in one picture, this was a horror comic with stylish sequences, weakened by cuts in the script and a miscast Bela Lugosi.

w Curt Siodmak d Roy William Neill ph George Robinson m Hans Salter
☆ Lon Chaney Jnr, Ilona Massey, Bela Lugosi, Patric Knowles, Maria Ouspenskaya

Frankenstein Must Be Destroyed

GB 1969 96m Technicolor
Warner-Pathé/Hammer (Anthony Nelson-Keys)

The Baron transplants the brain of one colleague into the body of another.

Spirited but decidedly unpleasant addition to the cycle, made more so by a genuine note of pathos.

w Bert Batt d Terence Fisher ph Arthur Grant m James Bernard ad Bernard Robinson ed Gordon Hales
☆ Peter Cushing, Freddie Jones, Veronica Carlson, Simon Ward, Thorley Walters, Maxine Audley

Frankenstein Unbound

US 1990 85m DeLuxe
Fox/Mount Company (Roger Corman, Thom Mount, Kabi Jaeger)

A scientist is transported back in time to Switzerland in the 1800s where he meets Mary Godwin, Byron, Shelley and Dr Frankenstein and his monster.

Odd mix of science fiction and horror that fails to cohere.

w Roger Corman, F. X. Feeney novel Brian Aldiss d Roger Corman ph Armando Nannuzzi, Michael Scott m Carl Davis pd Enrico Tovaglieri ed Jay Cassidy, Mary Bauer
☆ John Hurt, Raul Julia, Bridget Fonda, Nick Brimble, Catherine Rabett, Jason Patric, Michael Hutchence
'Competent but uninspired.' – *Variety*

Frankie and Johnny *

US 1966 87m Technicolor
UA/F and J (Edward Small)

On a Mississippi riverboat, a gambling singer is the despair of his lady partner.

Mildly amusing pastiche both of the old song and the various riverboat dramas.

w Alex Gottlieb d Frederick de Cordova ph Jacques Marquette m Fred Karger

☆ Elvis Presley, Donna Douglas, Sue Ane Langdon, Harry Morgan, Nancy Kovack, Audrey Christie, Jerome Cowan

'He's no knight in shining armor. She's no princess. But who says life is a fairytale anyway?'

Frankie and Johnny *

US 1991 118m Technicolor
UIP/Paramount (Garry Marshall)

A short-order cook ardently woos a reluctant waitress.

Soft-centred romance with its stars trying hard to persuade an audience that they are damaged and unlovable until the final clinch.

w Terrence McNally play Frankie and Johnny in the Clair de Lune by Terrence McNally d Garry Marshall ph Dante Spinotti m Marvin Hamlisch pd Albert Brenner ed Battle Davis, Jacqueline Cambas
☆ Al Pacino, Michelle Pfeiffer, Hector Elizondo, Nathan Lane, Jane Morris, Greg Lewis, Al Fann, Glenn Plummer, Sean O'Bryan, Kate Nelligan
'The layers of artifice are just too thick for the film's warm glow to last long.' – *Geoff Brown, The Times*
'This is a vehicle of Pacino and Pfeiffer, and they're more glamorous than the characters they're playing, but, in a weird way, their star power is perfectly appropriate here: it's the meat-and-potatoes stuff of big-budget movie entertainment.' – *New Yorker*
♪ Kate Nelligan

Frankie Starlight *

US 1995 100m colour
Film Four/Ferndale (Noel Pearson)

A dwarf becomes a successful author with an autobiographical novel about his French mother, who arrived in Ireland in the late 40s, pregnant by a GI.

Offbeat romantic drama about the power of dreams.

w Chet Raymo, Ronan O'Leary novel The Dork of Cork by Chet Raymo d Michael Lindsay-Hogg ph Paul Laufer m Elmer Bernstein pd Frank Conway ed Ruth Foster
☆ Anne Parillaud, Matt Dillon, Gabriel Byrne, Corban Walker, Rudi Davies, Georgina Cates, Alan Pentony, Niall Toibin, Dearbhla Molloy
'A noble effort whose ambitious, unorthodox approach limits it to a rarefied crowd.' – *Variety*

Frantic: see *Lift to the Scaffold* (1957)

Frantic *

US 1988 120m colour
Warner/Mount (Thom Mount, Tim Hampton)

An American cardiologist in Paris hunting for his kidnapped wife becomes embroiled with Arab terrorists.

Amiable thriller with Hitchcockian touches, quite untypical of this director.

w Roman Polanski, Gérard Brach d Roman Polanski ph Witold Sobocinski m Ennio Morricone pd Pierre Guffroy ed Sam O'Steen
☆ Harrison Ford, Betty Buckley, Emmanuelle Seigner, John Mahoney, Jimmy Ray Weeks, Yorgo Voyagis, David Huddleston
'Disappointingly conventional mystery.' – *Variety*

Fratelli e Sorelle

Italy 1992 101m colour Technovision
Duea/Filmauro/RAI-1 (Antonio Avati, Luigi and Aurelio De Laurentiis)

Leaving her adulterous husband, an Italian woman takes her teenage sons and goes to St. Louis to visit her sister, who lives with an Italian and his two American daughters.

Dysfunctional families meet in an enclosed Italian community; the result resembles an overlong soap opera episode.

wd Pupi Avati ph Roberto D'Ettorre Piazzoli m Riz Ortolani ad Carlo Simi ed Amedeo Salfa
☆ Franco Nero, Paola Quattrini, Anna Bonaiuto, Lino Capolicchio, Luciano Federico, Stefano Accorsi, Kelly Evinston, Barbara Wilder
'Phony, contrived and awkward.' – *Variety*

Fraternally Yours: see *Sons of the Desert*

Fraternity Row *
US 1977 101m colour
Paramount (Charles Gary Allison)
In the early 1950s, students indulge in dangerous fraternity initiations at an exclusive Eastern university.
Efficient, well-acted drama of college life.
w Charles Gary Allison d Thomas J. Tobin ph Peter Gibbons m Michael Corner, Don McLean ad James Sbardellati ed Eugene A. Fournier
☆ Peter Fox, Gregory Harrison, Scott Newman, Nancy Morgan, Wendy Phillips, Robert Emhardt, Robert Matthews, Bernard R. Kantor, Cliff Robertson

Frau im Mond: see *The Woman in the Moon*

'He's No Ordinary Insurance Man. You Can Bet Your Life On It!'
Frauds
Australia 1992 94m colour
First Independent/Latent Image/AFFC (Andrena Finlay, Stuart Quin)
A manic practical-joke-playing insurance agent, who tosses dice to decide his next action, torments a couple who decide to play him at his own game.
A frantic comedy that remains unsympathetic viewing; it is simply not funny, despite the strenuous efforts of everyone involved.
wd Stephan Elliott ph Geoff Burton m Guy Gross pd Brian Thomson ed Frans Vandenburg
☆ Phil Collins, Hugo Weaving, Josephine Byrnes, Peter Mochrie, Helen O'Connor, Rebel Russell, Colleen Clifford
'Chronically over-designed and over-directed, each angle containing something cute and clever.' – *Sheila Johnston, Independent*
'A comedy designed to set teeth on edge.' – *Sight and Sound*

Fräulein
US 1958 100m Eastmancolor
Cinemascope
TCF (Walter Reisch)
During World War II an American prisoner of war escapes and is helped by the daughter of a German professor.
Studio-bound war heroics with little conviction achieved or aimed at.
w Leo Townsend novel James McGowan d Henry Koster ph Leo Tover m Daniele Amfitheatrof
☆ Dana Wynter, Mel Ferrer, Margaret Hayes, Dolores Michaels, Theodore Bikel, Helmut Dantine

Fräulein Doktor
Italy/Yugoslavia 1968 104m Technicolor
(Paramount)
In World War I, a German lady spy outwits British intelligence.
Rather glum international action melodrama.
w Duilio Coletti, H. A. L. Craig, Stanley Mann, Vittoriano Petrilli, Alberto Lattuada d Alberto Lattuada ph Luigi Kuveiller m Ennio Morricone
☆ Suzy Kendall, Kenneth More, James Booth, Capucine, Alexander Knox, Nigel Green, Roberto Bisacco
† A similar story was filmed in 1936 as *Mademoiselle Docteur*.

Freaked
US 1993 79m DeLuxe
TCF/Tommy (Harry Ufland, Mary Jane Ufland)
A glib spokesman for a polluting chemical company is turned into a monster by a freak-show proprietor.
A comic horror movie, in which most of the energy and imagination went into the creation of a succession of bizarre characters.
w Tim Burns, Tom Stern, Alex Winter d Tom Stern, Alex Winter ph Jamie Thompson m Kevin Kiner pd Catherine Hardwicke ed Malcolm Campbell sp Thomas Rainone
☆ Alex Winter, Megan Ward, Randy Quaid, Brooke Shields, Mr T, Michael Stoyanov, William Sadler, Alex Zuckerman, Derek McGrath
'An anarchic mix of hip comedy, vague, socially correct, eco politics and overstated make-up effects ... disproves the old saw that brevity is the soul of wit.' – *Leonard Klady, Variety*

† Keanu Reeves makes a brief, uncredited appearance as a Dog Boy.

Freaks **
US 1932 64m bw
MGM (Tod Browning)
A lady trapeze artist marries a midget, then attempts to poison him; his abnormal friends take revenge by turning her into a freak.
Made but disowned by MGM after accusations of tastelessness, this strident and silly melodrama has dated badly but has sequences of great power, especially the final massing of the freaks, slithering to their revenge in a rainstorm. It would have been better as a silent; the dialogue kills it.
w Willis Goldbeck, Leon Gordon novel Spurs by Tod Robbins d Tod Browning ph Merritt B. Gerstad
☆ Wallace Ford, Olga Baclanova, Leila Hyams, Roscoe Ates, Johnny Eck, Daisy Hilton, Violet Hilton
'Either too horrible or not sufficiently so.' – *Variety*
'It is a skilfully presented production but of a character which in consideration of the susceptibilities of mass audiences should be avoided.' – *Martin Quigley*
'For pure sensationalism it tops any picture yet produced.' – *Louella Parsons*
'I want something that out-horrors Frankenstein.' – *Irving Thalberg*
'Touching and funny and made with a miraculous delicacy.' – *Evening Standard, 1964*

Freaky Friday
☆☆ US 1976 100m Technicolor
Walt Disney (Ron Miller)
A 13-year-old and her mother, each discontented with their lot, express a wish to change places – and do.
A trendy update of Vice Versa, padded out with Disney irrelevancies and long outstaying its welcome.
w Mary Rodgers novel Mary Rodgers d Gary Nelson ph Charles F. Wheeler m Johnny Mandel
☆ Jodie Foster, Barbara Harris, John Astin, Patsy Kelly, Dick Van Patten, Sorrell Booke, Marie Windsor

Freckles
☆☆ US 1935 69m bw
RKO (Pandro S. Berman)
A mild teenager gets a job as a timber guard.
Unsensational version of a rustic classic.
w Dorothy Yost novel Gene Stratton-Porter d Edward Killy, William Hamilton
☆ Tom Brown, Carol Stone, Virginia Weidler, Lumsden Hare, James Bush, Addison Richards, George Lloyd
'The novel, published in 1875, is shown to have sold 2,000,000 copies. It will have a tough time making the same grade as a picture ... its appeal is of a past generation.' – *Variety*
† A 1960 remake for Fox starred Martin West.

Freddie as F.R.0.7
☆☆ GB 1992 91m colour
Rank/Hollywood Road Films
A human-sized frog, a French secret agent, investigates the disappearance of such British institutions as Buckingham Palace and the Tower of London.
Dated, animated parody of James Bond. It was intended as the first of a series starring Freddie, but its box-office failure led to a sequel being abandoned.
w Jon Acevski, David Ashton d Jon Acevski ph Rex Neville m/ly David Dundas, Rick Wentworth, Don Black, Jon Acevski, David Ashton ad Paul Shardlow ed Alex Rayment, Mick Manning
☆ Featuring the voices of Ben Kingsley, Jenny Agutter, Brian Blessed, Nigel Hawthorne, Michael Hordern, Edmund Kingsley, Phyllis Logan, Victor Maddern, Jonathan Pryce, Prunella Scales, John Sessions, Billie Whitelaw
'This likeable enough saga of a super-agent frog looks unlikely to hop into the big time.' – *Variety*

'They saved the best ... for last.'
Freddy's Dead: The Final Nightmare
US 1991 90m DeLuxe Part 3-D
Guild/New Line (Robert Shaye, Aron Warner)
With the aid of some disturbed teenagers, Freddy Krueger's daughter ends her father's life.
Sixth and, with luck, the last of the Nightmare On Elm Street series, which has little to offer other than the gimmick of an ineffectual 3-D climax.
w Michael DeLuca story Rachel Talalay d Rachel Talalay ph Declan Quinn m Brian May pd C. J. Strawn ed Janice Hampton
☆ Robert Englund, Lisa Zane, Shon Greenblatt, Leslie Deane, Ricky Dean Logan, Breckin Meyer, Yaphet Kotto, Roseanne Arnold, Tom Arnold, Alice Cooper
'Delivers enough violence, black humor and even a final reel in 3-D to hit paydirt with horror-starved audiences.' – *Variety*
'The dream logic of Wes Craven's ground-breaking original has been reduced to sloppy plotting and a string of unrelated special-effects set-pieces. It is sadly apt therefore that the manner of Freddy's passing should be as unimaginative as the enervated sequels themselves.' – *Sight and Sound*
† It was followed by *Wes Craven's New Nightmare* (qv)

Free and Easy
US 1930 75m bw
MGM (Edward Sedgwick)
A beauty contest winner is taken to Hollywood by her accident-prone manager.
Primitive talkie showing a great silent comedian all at sea with the new techniques, and the MGM studio offering entertainment on the level of a very bad school concert.
w Al Boasberg, Richard Schayer d Edward Sedgwick ph Leonard Smith
☆ Buster Keaton, Anita Page, Robert Montgomery, Trixie Friganza

Free and Easy
US 1941 56m bw
MGM
In British high society, father and son both seek rich wives.
A remarkable cast is all at sea in a potted version of Ivor Novello's The Truth Game.
w Marvin Borowsky d George Sidney
☆ Nigel Bruce, Robert Cummings, Ruth Hussey, Judith Anderson, C. Aubrey Smith, Reginald Owen, Tom Conway, Forrester Harvey
'This one must have slipped through the Metro wringer while the brains department was out to lunch.' – *Variety*

Free for All
US 1949 83m bw
U-I (Robert Buckner)
A young inventor finds a way of turning water into petrol.
Scatty comedy with mildly amusing moments.
w Robert Buckner d Charles T. Barton ph George Robinson m Frank Skinner
☆ Robert Cummings, Ann Blyth, Percy Kilbride, Ray Collins, Donald Woods, Mikhail Rasumny

A Free Soul *
US 1931 91m bw
MGM
An unconventional lawyer regrets allowing his daughter to consort with a gangster.
Heavy melodrama with outdated attitudes, but an impressive example of the studio's style in the early thirties.
w John Meehan novel Adela Rogers St Johns d Clarence Brown ph William Daniels m William Axt
☆ Lionel Barrymore, Norma Shearer, Leslie Howard, Clark Gable, Lucy Beaumont, James Gleason
'An ungainly, rambling and preposterous theme, awkwardly brought to the screen.' – *Variety*
† Remade 1953 as *The Girl Who Had Everything*.
🏆 Lionel Barrymore (who had a 14-minute speech)
🏆 Clarence Brown; Norma Shearer

Free to Live: see *Holiday (1938)*

'A 12 Year Old Street Kid. A 3 Ton Killer Whale. A Friendship You Could Never Imagine. An Adventure You'll Never Forget.'
Free Willy *
☆☆ US 1993 112m Technicolor
Panavision
Warner/Canal/Regency/Alcor (Jennie Lew Tugend, Lauren Shuler-Donner)
A young, disturbed boy forms a friendship with a killer whale threatened with death.
Sentimental animal story with a little charm and some appeal to the under-10s, but no more than a damp update of Lassie.
w Keith A. Walker, Corey Blechman d Simon Wincer ph Robbie Greenberg m Basil Poledouris pd Charles Rosen ed O. Nicholas Brown
☆ Jason James Richter, Lori Petty, Jayne Atkinson, August Schellenberg, Michael Madsen, Michael Ironside, Keiko
'An exhilarating drama of boy and nature that unabashedly pulls at the heart-strings. Thankfully, its creators know just what to do emotionally and technically to pull off this old-fashioned sentimental yarn.' – *Variety*
'The movie hits every emotional button with a firm fist.' – *Richard Corliss, Time*

Free Willy 2: The Adventure Home
US 1995 96m Technicolor Panavision
Warner (Lauren Shuler-Donner, Jennie Lew Tugend)
A teenage boy and his young brother save a family of whales from an oil spillage and those who plan to exploit them.
Mundane sequel, using animatronic whales, which settles for simple thrills together with familiar teenage problems of growing up.
w Karen Janszen, Corey Blechman, John Mattson d Dwight Little ph Laszlo Kovacs m Basil Poledouris pd Paul Sylbert ed Robert Brown, Dallas Puett
☆ Jason James Richter, August Schellenberg, Michael Madsen, Jayne Atkinson, Mary Kate Schellhardt, Francis Capra, Jon Tenney, Elizabeth Pena, M. Emmet Walsh
'Somebody set us straight on this: When did killer whales become the stuff of cute and cuddly animal-buddy movies? Last we checked, Orca was noshing on Bo Derek's leg.' – *Premiere*

'A new friend. A new threat. A new adventure that will capture your heart.'
Free Willy 3: The Rescue
☆☆ US 1997 86m Technicolor
Warner/Regency (Jennie Lew Tugend)
A friendship between a 17-year-old youth and a 10-year-old boy, whose father is illegally hunting whales, saves Willy and his pregnant mate from death.
The mixture much as before, with a killer whale acting as the unwitting saviour of unhappy kids; those who enjoyed the earlier episodes should gain an equal amount of pleasure this time around.
w John Mattson d Sam Pillsbury ph Tobias Schliesser m Cliff Eidelman pd Brent Thomas ed Margie Goodspeed
☆ Jason James Richter, August Schellenberg, Annie Corley, Vincent Berry, Patrick Kilpatrick, Tasha Simms
'Whether Willy can fuel any more screen vehicles remains in serious doubt. But if he's to be put out to pasture, he couldn't have asked for a better bon voyage.' – *Leonard Klady, Variety*
'This may well be the worst sequel of all time.' – *Mark Steyn, Spectator*
† The two leading whales, Willy and Nikki, were animatronic creations and not real animals.

'Today they demolished 23 cars, four motor cycles and one apartment building. But don't call the cops. They are the cops!'
Freebie and the Bean *
US 1974 113m Technicolor Panavision
Warner (Richard Rush)
Two vaguely incompetent cops try to link a mobster with the numbers racket.
Violent comedy melodrama with a high mortality rate, amoral outlook, and the usual seventies reliance on incoherent plot, bumbled dialogue and excessive background noise. Occasionally funny all the same.
w Richard Kaufman d Richard Rush ph Laszlo Kovacs m Dominic Frontière

---

🏠 film suitable for family viewing   📼 VHS video-cassette for the British PAL system   📼 VHS video-cassette for the British PAL system in wide screen-format   ✇ Video cassette in a computer-colourised version   ◼ American NTSC video-cassette   ◎~ Laser disc

☆ Alan Arkin, James Caan, Loretta Swit, Jack Kruschen, Mike Kellin

'It summarizes Hollywood's favourite thematic elements of the early seventies: platonic male love affair, police corruption, comic violence, cynicism in high places, San Francisco, gay villains, the car chase. A return to the Keystone Kops, with character trimmings and lashings of sado-masochistic mayhem.' – *Clyde Jeavons*

'A tasteless film from a spitball script.' – *Variety*

'There is a beating or a killing, or at least a yelling scene, every couple of minutes.' – *New Yorker, 1980*

Freedom Is Paradise: see SER

Freedom Radio

GB   1941   95m   bw

Columbia/Two Cities (Mario Zampi)

US title: *A Voice in the Night*

In Vienna during World War II, the husband of a Nazi actress runs a secret radio transmitter for Allied propaganda.

Moderate wartime flagwaver.

w Basil Wood, Gordon Wellesley, Louis Golding, Anatole de Grunwald, Jeffrey Dell, Bridget Boland, Roland Pertwee d Anthony Asquith ph Bernard Knowles

☆ Diana Wynyard, Clive Brook, Raymond Huntley, Joyce Howard, Derek Farr, Howard Marion Crawford, Morland Graham

Freejack

US   1992   108m   Technicolor

Warner/Morgan Creek (Ronald Shusett, Stuart Oken)

A racing-car driver on the point of death is taken eighteen years into the future so that his body can house the mind of a terminally ill millionaire.

Predictable science fiction about a sleazy future that lacks the wit and originality of the novel on which it is based.

w Steven Pressfield, Ronald Shusett, Dan Gilroy *novel Immortality Inc* by Robert Sheckley d Geoff Murphy ph Amir Mokri m Trevor Jones pd Joe Alves ed Dennis Virkler sp Richard Hoover

☆ Emilio Estevez, Mick Jagger, René Russo, Anthony Hopkins, Jonathan Banks, David Johansen, Amanda Plummer

'Chalk it up as one of life's little ironies that a pic about mind transfers would be so mindless.' – *Variety*

Freeway

US   1996   108m   DeLuxe

Kushner-Locke/Samuel Hadida/August/Davis/Illusion (Chris Hanley, Brad Wyman)

On the run after her mother, a drug-addicted prostitute, is arrested, an illiterate 15-year-old girl is picked up by a serial killer.

The opening credits, showing a sex-obsessed wolf chasing Red Riding Hood, suggest some sort of satire is intended; but what follows is a sleazily violent, unsubtle melodrama.

wd Matthew Bright ph John Thomas m Danny Elfman, Tito Larriva pd Pam Warner ed Maysie Hoy

☆ Kiefer Sutherland, Reese Witherspoon, Wolfgang Bodison, Dan Hedaya, Amanda Plummer, Brooke Shields, Michael T. Weiss, Bokeem Woodbine

'A thoroughly nasty piece of work, the product of a filmmaker with a ludicrously misplaced confidence in his own cleverness. Pic is so cartoonish and mean-spirited, it is impossible to work up any sympathy for anyone on screen.' – *Joe Leydon, Variety*

Freeze Frame

US   1989   78m   colour

Film Indiana/Creative Edge (Martin Wiley)

aka: *The Homeroom News*

A high-school reporter exposes a crooked would-be politician.

Uninteresting and silly drama, written, directed and acted without noticeable flair and with little to interest any audience.

wd William Bindley ph Craig Somers m John Cascella ad Todd Hatfield ed Jeffrey Neuman

☆ Shannen Doherty, Charles Haid, Ryan Lambert, Adam Carl, Robyn Douglass, Seth Michaels

French Can-Can **

France/Italy   1955   105m   Technicolor

Franco-London/Jolly (Louis Wipf)

How the can-can was launched in Paris night-clubs.

A dramatically thin vehicle splendidly evoking a vision of vanished Paris: a feast for the eyes.

w André-Paul Antoine d Jean Renoir ph Michel Kelber m Georges Van Parys

☆ Jean Gabin, Françoise Arnoul, Maria Félix, Jean-Roger Caussimon, Edith Piaf, Patachou

'Doyle is bad news ... but a good cop!'

The French Connection ****

US   1971   104m   DeLuxe

TCF/Philip D'Antoni

New York police track down a consignment of drugs entering the country in a car.

Lively semi-documentary based on the true exploits of a tough cop named Eddie Egan who liked to break a few rules. Most memorable for a car chase scene involving an elevated railway, for showing the seamy side of New York more or less as it is.

w Ernest Tidyman *book* Robin Moore d William Friedkin ph Owen Roizman m Don Ellis ad Ben Kazaskow ed Jerry Greenberg

☆ Gene Hackman, Roy Scheider, Fernando Rey, Tony Lo Bianco, Marcel Bozzufi

'The only thing this movie believes in is giving the audience jolts, and you can feel the raw, primitive responses in the theater.' – *Pauline Kael, New Yorker*

🏆 best picture; Ernest Tidyman; William Friedkin; Gene Hackman

♞ Owen Roizman; Roy Scheider

🏵 Gene Hackman

French Connection II

US   1975   119m   DeLuxe

TCF (Robert L. Rosen)

The New York cop who in *The French Connection* smashed most of a drug ring arrives in Marseilles to track down its elusive leader.

Sleazy, virtually plotless and unattractive sequel which rises to a few good action moments but is bogged down by bad language, unconvincing characterization and an interminable and irrelevant 'cold turkey' sequence.

w Robert Dillon, Laurie Dillon, Alexander Jacobs d John Frankenheimer ph Claude Renoir m Don Ellis pd Jacques Saulnier ed Tom Rolf

☆ Gene Hackman, Fernando Rey, Bernard Fresson, Jean-Pierre Castaldi, Charles Millot, Cathleen Nesbitt

'Visually as well as morally the film makes you uncertain where its feet are.' – *New Yorker*

French Dressing

GB   1963   86m   bw

ABP/Kenwood (Kenneth Harper)

A deckchair attendant and a local reporter believe that what Bardot can do for St Tropez they can do for Gormleigh-on-Sea.

Cinema's enfant terrible directs this his first theatrical film at breakneck speed with echoes of Tati, Keaton and the Keystone Kops. Alas, lack of star comedians and firm control make its exuberance merely irritating.

w Peter Myers, Ronald Cass, Peter Britt d Ken Russell ph Ken Higgins m Georges Delerue

☆ James Booth, Roy Kinnear, Marisa Mell, Bryan Pringle

'Saddled with lousy dialogue and a director who seems more concerned with composition than content ... I actually heard the director compare his film with Jacques Tati's *Monsieur Hulot's Holiday*. What arrogance! Dream on, Mr Director, dream on.' – *Ken Russell*

The French Key

US   1946   67m   bw

Republic

Private eyes, locked out of their hotel room for non-payment of rent, use the fire escape and find a body inside.

Minor mystery which seemed passable at the time.

w Frank Gruber *novel* Frank Gruber d Walter Colmes

☆ Albert Dekker, Mike Mazurki, Evelyn Ankers, John Eldredge, Frank Fenton

'Kate's stuck in a place where anything can happen with a guy who'll make sure that it does.'

French Kiss

US   1995   111m   DeLuxe

Polygram/TCF/Working Title/Prufrock (Tim Bevan, Eric Fellner, Meg Ryan, Kathryn F. Galan)

An American woman goes to Paris, in search of her fiancé who has fallen for a Frenchwoman, and becomes romantically involved with a French thief.

A tourist trip around the more photogenic parts of Paris, providing a background to a lacklustre love story between two incompatible people, which offers nothing that hasn't been done rather better before.

w Adam Brooks d Lawrence Kasdan ph Owen Roizman m James Newton Howard pd Jon Hutman ed Joe Hutshing

☆ Meg Ryan, Kevin Kline, Timothy Hutton, Jean Reno, François Cluzet, Susan Anbeh, Renee Humphrey

'A romantic comedy that's neither very romantic nor very comic.' – *Derek Malcolm, Guardian*

French Leave

GB   1930   100m   bw

D and H (Louis Zimmerman)

In order to be near her husband, a British girl pretends to be French and goes behind the trenches.

Flat picturization of a popular stage farce of the twenties.

w W. P. Lipscomb, Reginald Berkeley *play* Reginald Berkeley d Jack Raymond ph Bernard Knowles ad G. T. Stoneham

☆ Madeleine Carroll, Sydney Howard, Arthur Chesney, Haddon Mason, Henry Kendall

† Remade in 1937 with Betty Lynne, Norman Lee, for Welwyn.

'She was lost from the moment she saw him...'

The French Lieutenant's Woman *

GB   1981   123m   Technicolor

UA/Juniper (Leon Clore)

In 1867 Lyme Regis, a man forsakes his fiancée for the abandoned mistress of a French seaman.

Vaguely unsatisfactory and muddily coloured adaptation of a novel which set its thin story against the entire social background of the Victorian age as related to our own. The attempt to replace this by an equally thin modern story about actors playing the Victorian roles fails rather dismally; but the enterprise supplies points of interest along the way.

w Harold Pinter *novel* John Fowles d Karel Reisz ph Freddie Francis m Carl Davis pd Assheton Gorton

☆ Jeremy Irons, Meryl Streep, Leo McKern, Patience Collier, Peter Vaughan, Hilton McRae

'Pinter's reduction not only shears away the sliding historical perspective, but robs the narrative of its Victorian charisma.' – *Tom Milne, MFB*

'There are some lovely moments, and a few have magical undertones, but most of the picture might be taking place in a glass case.' – *Pauline Kael*

'If you see the movie, the book will still surprise you, and that's as it should be.' – *Roger Ebert*

♞ Harold Pinter; editing (John Bloom); Meryl Streep

🏵 best sound; Carl Davis; Meryl Streep

The French Line

US   1953   102m   Technicolor   3-D

RKO (Edmund Grainger)

A cheery Texas oil heiress finds a husband while travelling to France.

Very thinly plotted but quite attractive light musical with a good-humoured star wearing costumes once thought censorable.

w Mary Loos, Richard Sale d Lloyd Bacon ph Harry J. Wild m Walter Scharf md Lionel Newman ch Jack Cole

☆ Jane Russell, Gilbert Roland, Arthur Hunnicutt, Mary McCarty

'A slouching Amazon, her clothes appear to stay put just as long as she agrees not to burst out of them; essentially a good sort, she has an ever-

annihilating sneer for the false, the pretentious and the fresh.' – *MFB*

A French Mistress

GB   1960   98m   bw

British Lion/Charter (John Boulting)

An attractive new mistress causes havoc at a boys' school.

Sloppy, predictable comedy with practised performers getting a few easy laughs. The producers tried to excuse its imperfections by promoting it as 'a romp'.

w Roy Boulting, Jeffrey Dell *play* Robert Monro (Sonnie Hale) d Roy Boulting ph Max Greene m John Addison ad Albert Witherick ed John Jympson

☆ James Robertson Justice, Cecil Parker, Raymond Huntley, Ian Bannen, Agnes Laurent, Thorley Walters, Edith Sharpe, Athene Seyler, Kenneth Griffith, Irene Handl

The French They Are a Funny Race: see *The Diary of Major Thompson*

French Twist **

France   1995   107m   colour

Guild/Renn/TF1/Les Films Flam (Claude Berri)

original title: *Gazon Maudit*

A lesbian musician forms a *menage à trois* with a married couple.

An enjoyable comedy at the expense of male philandering, performed with excellent comic timing; it was, perhaps surprisingly, a box-office success in France.

wd Josiane Balasko ph Gérard de Battista m Manuel Malou ad Carlos Conti ed Claudine Merlin

☆ Victoria Abril, Josiane Balasko, Alain Chabat, Ticky Holgado, Miguel Bosé, Catherine Hiegel, Catherine Samie

'Funny, breezy, erotic, and so matter-of-fact about the infinite variety of human sexuality, it could only be baked in France.' – *Lisa Schwarzbaum, Entertainment Weekly*

A French Vampire in America: see *Innocent Blood*

French without Tears **

GB   1939   85m   bw

Paramount/Two Cities (David E. Rose)

Young Britons at a French crammer fall for the young sister of one of their number.

Pleasant light comedy from a successful West End play.

w Terence Rattigan, Anatole de Grunwald, Ian Dalrymple *play* Terence Rattigan d Anthony Asquith ph Bernard Knowles, Jack Hildyard m Nicholas Brodszky ad Paul Sheriff, Carmen Dillon ed David Lean

☆ Ray Milland, Ellen Drew, Guy Middleton, Roland Culver, David Tree, Jim Gerald, Janine Darcy, Kenneth Morgan

'There is always something a little shocking about English levity. The greedy exhilaration of these blithe young men when they learn that another fellow's girl is to join them at the establishment where they are learning French, the scramble over her luggage, the light-hearted badinage, the watery and libidinous eye – that national mixture of prudery and excitement – would be unbearable if it were not for Mr Asquith's civilized direction.' – *Graham Greene*

† Incredibly, Paramount had purchased the property as a vehicle for Marlene Dietrich.

Frenchie

US   1950   80m   Technicolor

U-I (Michel Kraike)

A saloon queen sets up shop in Bottleneck, her real aim being to track down her father's murderers.

Modest Western of the Destry Rides Again school.

w Oscar Brodney d Louis King ph Maury Gertsman m Hans Salter

☆ Shelley Winters, Joel McCrea, Paul Kelly, Elsa Lanchester, Marie Windsor, John Emery, George Cleveland, John Russell

'For 24 reckless hours she embraced her – and she knew the thrill of true love!'

Frenchman's Creek *

US   1944   112m   Technicolor

Paramount (B. G. de Sylva)

In Restoration England, a lady flees from a lascivious nobleman to her family home in

Cornwall, where she falls in love with a French pirate.

Enjoyable Girls' Own Paper romance, dressed to kill and entertaining despite its many palpable absurdities.

w Talbot Jennings *novel* Daphne du Maurier d Mitchell Leisen *ph* George Barnes *m* Victor Young *ad* Hans Dreier, Ernst Fegte

☆ Joan Fontaine, Arturo de Cordova, Basil Rathbone, Nigel Bruce, Cecil Kellaway, Ralph Forbes, Moyna McGill

'Masturbation fantasy triple distilled.' – *James Agee*

🎨 art direction

Frenzy: see *Latin Quarter* (1945)

Frenzy *

Sweden 1944 101m bw
Svensk Filmindustri
🔲 🔲

original title: *Hets*
aka: *Torment*

A sadistic Latin teacher and his sensitive pupil find themselves competing for the same girl.

Hothouse melodrama of the Blue Angel school: it seemed pretty powerful at the time.

w Ingmar Bergman d Alf Sjöberg *ph* Martin Bodin *m* Hilding Rosenberg

☆ Stig Jarrel, Alf Kjellin, Mai Zetterling

'In spite of being always moving and sincere and pictorially satisfying, the film seems to miss the revelation it strives for. The lack – of passion, of inspiration – is inherent in the picture, and that is judging it by those very high standards it fails by so narrow a margin to reach.' – *Richard Winnington*

'From the master of shock, a shocking masterpiece!'

Frenzy *

GB 1972 116m Technicolor
Universal/Alfred Hitchcock
🔲 🔲 🔍

A disillusioned and aggressive ex-RAF officer is suspected through circumstantial evidence of being London's 'necktie murderer'.

Has-been, unconvincing, cliché-ridden thriller, an old man's sex suspenser, which would have been derided if anyone but Hitchcock had made it. As it is, a few comic and suspenseful touches partly atone for the implausibilities and lapses of taste.

w Anthony Shaffer *novel Goodbye Piccadilly, Farewell Leicester Square* by Arthur La Bern d Alfred Hitchcock *ph* Gilbert Taylor *m* Ron Goodwin *pd* Syd Cain *ed* John Jympson

☆ Jon Finch, Alec McCowen, Barry Foster, Vivien Merchant, Anna Massey, Barbara Leigh-Hunt, Billie Whitelaw

'Hitchcock's most stodgy piece since *Dial M for Murder* and possibly his least interesting film from any period.' – *William S. Pechter*

'There is suspense, and local colour, and always, Hitchcock smacking his lips and rubbing his hands and delighting in his naughtiness.' – *Roger Ebert*

Fresa y Chocolate: see *Strawberry and Chocolate*

'In a world where criminals make the rules, one kid is out to beat them at their own game.'

Fresh **

US/France 1994 112m DeLuxe
Entertainment/Lumière (Randy Ostrow, Lawrence Bender)
🔲 🔲 🔍

In Brooklyn, a 12-year-old black youth, who divides his time between drug-running for local dealers and attending to his schoolwork, devises a desperate plan to obtain a better life for himself and his addicted sister.

A tough tale of street life lived on the edge, violent, foul-mouthed and full of casual slaughter, told with a raw authenticity; it is a brutal urban tragedy that touches on real emotions of loss and despair.

wd Boaz Yakin *ph* Adam Holender *m* Stewart Copeland *pd* Dan Leigh *ed* Dorian Harris

☆ Sean Nelson, Giancarlo Esposito, Samuel L. Jackson, N'Bushe Wright, Ron Brice, Jean LaMarre

'This taut little thriller is brutal and unformulaic, a real surprise.' – *Alexander Walker, London Evening Standard*

'This portrait of a childhood both incredibly resourceful and tragically deprived is memorable.' – *Variety*

Fresh Horses

US 1988 103m colour
Columbia TriStar/Weintraub Entertainment (Dick Berg)
🔲 🔲 🔍

A wealthy student falls in love with a married 16-year-old girl.

Insignificant romance, no more than adequate.

w Larry Ketron *play* Larry Ketron d David Anspaugh *ph* Fred Murphy *m* David Foster, Patrick Williams *pd* Paul Sylbert *ed* David Rosenbloom

☆ Molly Ringwald, Andrew McCarthy, Patti D'Arbanville, Ben Stiller, Leon Russom, Molly Hagen, Viggo Mortensen, Doug Hutchinson, Chiara Peacock

The Freshman **

US 1925 75m bw silent
Harold Lloyd
🔲 🔲

An awkward college student accidentally becomes a star football player.

A rather slow but striking star vehicle with assured set-pieces. The football game climax was later used as the first reel of Mad Wednesday.

w Sam Taylor, Ted Wilde, Tim Whelan, John Grey d Fred Newmeyer, Sam Taylor *ph* Walter Lundin, John Kohler

☆ Harold Lloyd, Jobyna Ralston, Brooks Benedict

'Next time they make you an offer you can't refuse ... refuse!'

The Freshman **

👪 US 1990 102m Technicolor
Tri-Star/Mike Lobell, Andrew Bergman
🔲 🔲 🔍

A student of gangster movies goes to work for a real-life criminal.

A genial spoof of The Godfather films, with Brando parodying his own performance as an ageing patriarch of crime.

wd Andrew Bergman *ph* William A. Fraker *m* David Newman *ed* Barry Malkin

☆ Marlon Brando, Matthew Broderick, Bruno Kirby, Penelope Ann Miller, Frank Whaley, Jon Polito, Paul Benedict, Richard Gant, Kenneth Welsh, Pamela Payton-Wright

Freud **

GB 1962 140m bw
U-I (Wolfgang Reinhardt)
🎧

Vienna 1885; Dr Sigmund Freud, a neurologist, uses hypnotism to treat hysteria, and finds new interest in the case of a boy whose hatred of his father springs from incestuous love of his mother, a failing which Freud finds in himself.

Earnest and competent biopic harking back to Warner's similar films of the 30s, with the addition of franker language. Generally absorbing, but undeniably hard work.

w Charles Kaufman, Wolfgang Reinhardt d John Huston *ph* Douglas Slocombe *m* Jerry Goldsmith

☆ Montgomery Clift, Larry Parks, Susannah York, Eileen Herlie, Susan Kohner, David McCallum

'The dream sequences, photographed mostly in negative or overexposure, belong not on the couch of Dr Freud but in the Cabinet of Dr Caligari.' – *John Simon*

'It is impossible, I would think, for any educated person to sit through *Freud* without bursting into laughter at least once.' – *Ernest Callenbach, Film Quarterly*

🎵 script; Jerry Goldsmith

Die Freudlose Gasse: see *Joyless Street*

Fric Frac *

France 1939 95m bw
Maurice Lehmann

A provincial jeweller's assistant falls in with underworld characters.

Well-prized French comedy with dialogue entirely in thieves' slang.

w Michel Duran *play* Edouard Bourdet d Maurice Lehmann

☆ Michel Simon, Fernandel, Arletty, Helene Robert

Friday

US 1995 89m Foto-Kem
Entertainment/New Line/Priority (Patricia Charbonnet)
🔲 🔲 🔍 🎧

Two friends, one unemployed, the other having problems with his drug dealer, watch the neighbourhood go by in South Central Los Angeles.

A sort of extended sitcom with an improvised air, this consists of idle gossip interspersed with moments of brisker action; despite being written and performed by rappers, it has little sense of urgency or aggression apart from that supplied by its soundtrack.

w Ice Cube, DJ Pooh d F. Gary Gray *ph* Gerry Lively *m* Hidden Faces *pd* Bruce Bellamy *ed* John Carter

☆ Ice Cube, Chris Tucker, Nia Long, Tiny 'Zeus' Lister Jnr, John Witherspoon, Anna Maria Horsford

'A crudely made, sometimes funny bit of porchfront humor from the 'hood.' – *Variety*

'Broad, unsophisticated, appallingly sexist stuff.' – *Independent*

† It was followed by a sequel *Next Friday* (qv).

Friday the 13th

US 1980 95m colour
Georgetown (Sean S. Cunningham)
🔲 🔲 🔍

When a summer camp is reopened after many years, the grisly murders which closed it down begin again.

Horror suspense story with no raison d'être but a series of inventively gory shock moments, which were enough for it to ring the box-office bell.

w Victor Miller d Sean S. Cunningham *ph* Barry Abrams *m* Harry Manfredini *ad* Virginia Field *ed* Bill Freda

☆ Betsy Palmer, Adrienne King, Jeannine Taylor, Robbi Morgan

'An oversexed couple makes love in the bottom bunk, there's a dead body in the top bunk and the rest of the bunk is in the television commercials.' – *Variety*

Friday the 13th Part II

US 1981 87m DeLuxe
CIC/Georgetown (Steve Miner, Dennis Murphy)
🔲 🔲 🔍

The sole survivor of the massacre at Camp Crystal Lake is murdered, and five years later the mayhem begins again, the villain being the son of the woman who committed the former killings.

Virtually a remake of the first film, starting with a long flashback to it; short sharp shocks punctuate slabs of tedium.

w Ron Kurz d Steve Miner *ph* Peter Stein *m* Harry Manfredini *pd* Virginia Field *ed* Susan E. Cunningham

☆ Amy Steel, John Furey, Adrienne King, Kirsten Baker, Stu Charno

Friday the 13th Part III

US 1982 95m Movielab 3D
UIP/Jason Productions (Frank Mancuso Jnr)
🔲 🔲 🔍

Crazy Jason is still murdering kids up at Crystal Lake.

No better than its predecessors for being in three dimensions; in fact, half as bad again.

w Martin Kitrosser, Carol Watson d Steve Miner *ph* Gerald Feil *m* Harry Manfredini *ad* Robb Wilson *ed* George Hively

☆ Dana Kimmell, Paul Kratka, Catherine Parks, Paul Kratka

'The first was dreadful and took seventeen million. The second was just as bad and took more than ten million. No doubt the distributor will be happy to learn that the third is terrible too.' – *Variety*

Friday the 13th Part V – A New Beginning

US 1985 92m colour
UIP/Paramount (Timothy Silver)
🔲 🔲 🔍

A mass murderer stalks a private hospital, killing the inmates.

Gory return of a series that could only offer a repetition of its previous killings, poverty-stricken in imagination and everything else.

w Martin Kitrosser, David Cohen, Danny Steinmann d Danny Steinmann *ph* Stephen L.

Posey *m* Harry Manfredini *pd* Robert Howland *ed* Bruce Green

☆ John Shepard, Shavar Ross, Melanie Kinnaman, Richard Young, Corey Feldman, Corey Parker

Friday the 13th Part VI – Jason Lives

US 1986 87m Metrocolor
Paramount (Don Behrns)
🔲 🔲 🔍

The corpse of the exhumed Jason is brought to life after being hit by lightning and, to the surprise only of the cast, begins killing teenagers yet again.

Tedious re-run of previous movies in the series without even a hint of originality to be discovered.

wd Tom McLoughlin *ph* Jon Kranhouse *m* Harry Manfredini *pd* Joseph T. Garrity *ed* Bruce Green *sp* Martin Becker

☆ Thom Mathews, Jennifer Cooke, David Kagen, Renee Jones, C. J. Graham, Tony Goldwyn

'Jason Is Back. But This Time Someone's Waiting.'

Friday the 13th Part VII – The New Blood

US 1988 90m Technicolor
Paramount/Friday Four (Iain Paterson)
🔲 🔲 🔍

A woman with telekinetic powers attempts to stop the axe-wielding Jason continuing his killing spree.

Lacklustre continuation, still offering no variation on its basic theme of killing teenagers, especially those who display any sexual feelings. There is, though, less gore than usual; perhaps make-up was in as short supply as imagination.

w Daryl Haney, Manuel Fidello d John Carl Buechler *ph* Paul Elliott *m* Harry Manfredini, Fred Mollin *pd* Richard Lawrence *ed* Barry Zetlin, Maureen O'Connell, Martin Jay Sadoff

☆ Lar Park Lincoln, Kevin Blair, Susan Blu, Terry Kiser, Kane Hodder

Friday the 13th Part VIII – Jason Takes Manhattan

US 1989 96m Technicolor
Paramount/Horror, Inc. (Randolph Cheveldave)
🔲 🔲 🔍

An underwater electrical accident re-animates the corpse of Jason, who clambers aboard the cruise ship Lazarus to murder its young passengers.

The interminable story retold in the standard manner, though with less gore than usual; fans of the series, if any remain, are likely to be disappointed at the way the film cuts away from the action at the many moments of teenage death.

wd Rob Hedden *ph* Bryan England *m* Fred Mollin *pd* David Fischer *ed* Steve Mirkovich *sp* make-up effects: Jamie Brown; mechanical effects: Martin Becker

☆ Jensen Daggett, Scott Reeves, Barbara Bingham, Peter Mark Richman, Kane Hodder, Sharlene Martin

Friday the 13th: The Final Chapter

US 1984 91m Movielab
Paramount (Frank Mancuso Jnr)
🔲 🔲 🔍

Supposedly dead Jason escapes from cold storage at the morgue and goes on another rampage.

The awful mixture as before: would that the title meant what it says.

w Barney Cohen d Joseph Zito *ph* Joao Fernandes *m* Harry Manfredini *pd* Shelton H. Bishop III *ed* Joel Goodman

☆ E. Erich Anderson, Judie Aronson, Peter Barton, Kimberly Beck

'Yet another catalogue of mindless slaughter which doesn't even offer the courtesy of a story.' – *Daily Mail*

'The censor says you have to be 18 to see it. I would suggest you merely have to be daft.' – *Sunday Times*

Friday the Thirteenth ***

GB 1933 84m bw
Gainsborough (Michael Balcon)

Several people are involved in a bus crash, and we turn back the clock to see how they came to be there.

Highly competent compendium of comedies and dramas looking back to The Bridge of San Luis Rey and forward to the innumerable all-star films of the forties.

w G. H. Moresby-White, Sidney Gilliat, Emlyn Williams d Victor Saville *ph* Charles Van Enger *ad* Alfred Junge, Vetchinsky *ed* R. E. Dearing

---

☆ Sonnie Hale, Cyril Smith, *Eliot Makeham*, Ursula Jeans, *Emlyn Williams*, Frank Lawton, Belle Chrystal, *Max Miller*, Alfred Drayton, Edmund Gwenn, Mary Jerrold, Gordon Harker, *Robertson Hare*, Martita Hunt, Leonora Corbett and also Jessie Matthews, Ralph Richardson

'The secret of life? The secret's in the sauce.'

Fried Green Tomatoes at the Whistle Stop Café *

US 1991 130m DeLuxe
Rank/Act III/Electric Shadow (Jordan Kerner, Jon Avnet)

▣ ▦ ◎ ⊘ ⊘ ◠

A middle-aged housewife is encouraged to be more self-assertive after listening to an old woman recalling her past.

A pleasant wallow in nostalgia for a less complicated age.

w Fannie Flagg, Carol Sobieski *novel* Fannie Flagg d Jon Avnet ph Geoffrey Simpson m Thomas Newman pd Barbara Ling ed Debra C. Neil

☆ Kathy Bates, Jessica Tandy, Mary-Louise Parker, Mary Stuart Masterson, Cicely Tyson, Gailard Sartain, Stan Shaw

'Absorbing and life-affirming quality fare.' – *Variety*

⅄ Jessica Tandy; Fannie Flagg, Carol Sobieski

'Would you take Frieda into *your* home?'

Frieda *

GB 1947 97m bw
Ealing (Michael Relph)

An RAF officer marries and takes home a girl who helped him escape from a POW camp.

Stuffy and dated drama about how one English family learned to love one particular German. Timely when it appeared, however, and well made within its conventions.

w Angus MacPhail, Ronald Millar *play* Ronald Millar d Basil Dearden ph Gordon Dines m John Greenwood

☆ Mai Zetterling, David Farrar, Glynis Johns, Flora Robson, Albert Lieven

'Something of a cinema rarity – a film which stimulates intelligent thought and argument.' – *Dick Richards, Sunday Pictorial*

Friendly Enemies

US 1925 70m bw silent
PDC

Two German immigrants are divided when the United States enters the war.

Curious comedy-drama for two vaudevillians, based on a topical play of the time.

w Alfred A. Cohn *play* Samuel Shipman, Aaron Hoffman d George Melford ph Charles Clarke

☆ Joe Weber, Lew Fields, Virginia Brown Faire, Jack Mulhall

† Remade in 1942 with Charles Winninger.

Friendly Persuasion **

US 1956 139m DeLuxe
AA (William Wyler)

▦ ▦

At the outbreak of the Civil War, a family of Quakers has to consider its position.

Sentimental, homespun Western fare, well done without being especially engrossing.

w Michael Wilson *novel* Jessamyn West d William Wyler ph Ellsworth Fredericks m Dimitri Tiomkin

☆ Gary Cooper, Dorothy McGuire, Anthony Perkins, Marjorie Main, Richard Eyer, Robert Middleton, Walter Catlett

'The material is a little tenuous ... but Wyler's sure-handed direction constantly illuminates it with a humour, a gentle charm and a feeling for fundamental values that are rare indeed.' – *Moira Walsh, America*

† It was successfully remade as a TV movie in 1975, directed by Joseph Sargent and starring Richard Kiley and Shirley Knight.

⅄ best picture; Michael Wilson; William Wyler; Anthony Perkins; song 'Thee I Love' (*m*Dimitri Tiomkin, *ly*Paul Francis Webster)

'Who needs the world when you own the moon and stars?'

Friends

GB 1971 102m Technicolor
Paramount (Lewis Gilbert)

▦

Teenage lovers run away to a country cottage and have a child.

Peculiar idyll given corny 'poetic' treatment: a real non-starter.

w Jack Russell, Vernon Harris d Lewis Gilbert ph Andreas Winding m Elton John

☆ Sean Bury, Anicee Alvina, Toby Robbins, Ronald Lewis

'In a world ripped apart friends are all you can trust.'

Friends *

GB/France 1993 109m Technicolor
Metro Tartan/Friends/Chrysalide/Rio/Channel 4 (Judith Hunt)

▦

Three friends from university – two white, one black – follow divergent paths in the political life of South Africa in the 1980s.

A complex film of an impossible situation and personal responses to it, although a schematic approach – the three female protagonists are an Afrikaner, a wealthy white who turns to terrorism, and a poor black – lessens its impact.

wd Elaine Proctor ph Dominique Chapuis m Rachel Portman pd Carmel Collins ed Tony Lawson

☆ Kerry Fox, Dambisa Kente, Michele Burgers, Marius Weyers, Tertius Meintjes, Dolly Rathebe, Wilma Stockenstrom

'This powerful, moving and uplifting film uses its unfailingly human story to convey its anti-apartheid message without a hint of the righteousness which so often accompanies such statements. Intelligent, affecting and thoroughly thought-provoking cinema.' – *Yvette Huddleston, Empire*

Friends and Husbands **

West Germany 1982 106m colour
Miracle/Bioskop/Les Films du Losange/Westdeutscher Rundfunk (Eberhard Junkersdorf)
original title: *Heller Wahn*

Two women engage in a friendship that destroys them both.

Slow-moving, but intense and absorbing.

wd Margarethe von Trotta ph Michael Ballhaus m Nicolas Economou ad Jurgen Henze, Werner Mink ed Dagmar Hirtz

☆ Hanna Schygulla, Angela Winkler, Peter Striebeck, Christine Fersen, Franz Buchrieser, Jochen Striebeck, Therese Affolter, Werner Eichhorn

Friends and Lovers

US 1931 67m bw
RKO (William Le Baron)

◎~

A society wife causes several hearts to flutter illicitly.

Unsatisfactory comedy-drama which lurches along from one mood to another and may have been intended as satire.

w Wallace Smith *novel The Sphinx Has Spoken* by Maurice Dekobra d Victor Schertzinger ph J. Roy Hunt m Victor Schertzinger, Max Steiner

☆ Adolphe Menjou, Laurence Olivier, Lili Damita, Erich von Stroheim, Hugh Herbert, Frederick Kerr, Blanche Friderici

'Dumb sentimental romance ... the people never once display motives that are understandable or reasonable.' – *Variety*

The Friends of Eddie Coyle *

US 1973 102m Technicolor
Paramount (Paul Monash)

An ageing hoodlum agrees to become a police informer and is hunted down by his former associates.

Dour gangster melodrama held together by its central performance.

w Paul Monash *novel* George V. Higgins d Peter Yates ph Victor J. Kemper m Dave Grusin

☆ Robert Mitchum, Peter Boyle, Richard Jordan, Steven Keats, Mitch Ryan, Alex Rocco

Friends of Mr Sweeney *

US 1934 68m bw
Warner

A brow-beaten reporter gets drunk, faces life, and changes his personality.

Amusing minor comedy of a kind no longer made.

w Warren Duff, Sidney Sutherland *novel* Elmer Davis d Edward Ludwig

☆ Charles Ruggles, Eugene Pallette, Berton Churchill, Robert Barrat, Ann Dvorak

'Old situations given a new comedy coating ... positive all-round fun for every family.' – *Variety*

Fright

GB 1971 87m Eastmancolor
Fantale/British Lion (Harry Fine, Michael Style)

▦

A babysitter is menaced by a psychotic.

Unattractive screamer which starts on a hysterical note and never lets up.

w Tudor Gates d Peter Collinson

☆ Susan George, Ian Bannen, Dennis Waterman, Honor Blackman, John Gregson, Maurice Kaufmann

Fright Night

US 1985 105m Metrocolor
Columbia/Vista (Herb Jaffe)

▣ ▦ ◎~ ⊘

A vampire moves in next door to a teenage horror film buff.

Fairly agreeable mixture of modest comedy and genuine scares; but no classic.

wd Tom Holland ph Jan Kiesser m Brad Fiedel pd John DeCuir Jnr ed Kent Beyda

☆ Chris Sarandon, William Ragsdale, Amanda Bearse, Roddy McDowall

Fright Night Part 2

US 1988 104m DeLuxe Panavision
Columbia TriStar/Vista (Herb Jaffe, Mort Engelberg)

▣ ▦ ◎~ ⊘

A college student is attacked by vampires.

Virtually a remake of the first film, and much less effective the second time around.

w Tim Metcalfe, Miguel Tejada-Flores, Tommy Lee Wallace d Tommy Lee Wallace ph Mark Irwin ed Jay Lash Cassidy, Jonathan P. Shaw, Duwayne Dunham

☆ Roddy McDowall, William Ragsdale, Traci Lin, Julie Carmen, Jonathan Gries, Russell Clark, Brian Thompson

'Strictly an identikit remake of Tom Holland's already derivative original.' – *Kim Newman, MFB*

The Frightened Bride: see *The Tall Headlines*

Frightened City: see *The Killer That Stalked New York (1950)*

Frightened City

GB 1961 98m bw
Anglo Amalgamated/Zodiac (John Lemont)

▣

Gangsters fall out over a protection racket.

Reasonably terse racketeer melodrama rather surprisingly set in London.

w Leigh Vance d John Lemont ph Desmond Dickinson m Norrie Paramor

☆ Herbert Lom, Sean Connery, John Gregson, Alfred Marks, Yvonne Romain, Kenneth Griffith

The Frightened Lady

GB 1932 87m bw
Gainsborough/British Lion (Michael Balcon)
US title: *Criminal at Large*

A mad young lord is protected by his mother.

Modest chiller remade later as The Case of the Frightened Lady (qv).

w Angus MacPhail, Bryan Edgar Wallace *play The Case of the Frightened Lady* by Edgar Wallace d T. Hayes Hunter ph Bernard Knowles, Alex Bryce ad Norman Arnold ed Ralph Kemplen

☆ Norman McKinnel, Cathleen Nesbitt, Emlyn Williams, Gordon Harker, Belle Chrystal, Finlay Currie

The Frightened Man

GB 1952 69m bw
Eros/Tempean (Robert S. Baker, Monty Berman)

An antique dealer's ambitious plans for his son go wrong after he is sent down from university.

Crisp, competent drama, nominally a thriller but less interested in action than in the relationships between its characters.

wd John Gilling ph Monty Berman m John Lanchbery md Eric Robinson ad Andrew Mazzei ed Jack Slade

☆ Dermot Walsh, Barbara Murray, Charles Victor, John Blythe, Michael Ward, Thora Hird, Ballard Berkeley

The Frighteners *

New Zealand/US 1996 109m colour
UIP/Universal/Wingnut (Jamie Selkirk, Peter Jackson)

▣ ▦ ◎~ ⊘ ◠

Accompanied by three ghosts, a dubious psychic investigator turns himself into a spirit so he can discover what evil is killing the inhabitants of a small town.

An odd horror movie that mixes jokes and shocks in a special-effects extravaganza; at its best it is unsettling, but it too often borders on the incoherent.

w Fran Walsh, Peter Jackson d Peter Jackson ph Alun Bolinger, John Blick m Danny Elfman pd Grant Major sp Jamie Selkirk sp WETA *creature & make-up design* Richard Taylor

☆ Michael J. Fox, Trini Alvarado, Peter Dobson, John Astin, Jeffrey Combs, Dee Wallace Stone

'A smart, subtle movie disguised as a dumb, noisy one ... a rare horror film that gets better as it proceeds.' – *Ken Tucker, Entertainment Weekly*

Fringe Dwellers

Australia 1986 98m colour
Virgin/Damien Nolan/Ozfilm (Sue Milliken)

▦ ◎~

Two sisters of an aboriginal family persuade their parents to move from their shantytown to a house on a new estate, where they encounter prejudice and miss the community they have left.

A sharp look at racism that avoids simple-mindedness – the young black woman at the centre of the action resents allowances being made for her, and her father is a lazy, feckless drunk – but fails to energize its subject, becoming bogged down in petty detail.

w Bruce Beresford, Rhoisin Beresford *novel* Nene Gare d Bruce Beresford ph Donald McAlpine m George Dreyfus pd Herbert Pinter ed Tim Wellburn

☆ Justine Saunders, Kristina Nehm, Bob Maza, Kylie Belling, Ernie Dingo, Malcom Silva, Kath Walker, Denis Walker, Bill Sandy

Frisco Jenny

US 1933 73m bw
Warner

A Barbary Coast lady is prosecuted for murder by her own son.

Antediluvian melodramatic plot, borrowed from Madame X, *provides an adequate star vehicle.*

w Wilson Mizner, Robert Lord d William A. Wellman

☆ Ruth Chatterton, Donald Cook, Louis Calhern, J. Carrol Naish, James Murray

The Frisco Kid *

US 1935 77m bw
Warner (Samuel Bischoff)

A Shanghaied sailor rises to power among the riff raff of the Barbary Coast in the 1860s.

Fair melodrama with the star in action and (less interestingly) in love.

w Warren Duff, Seton I. Miller d Lloyd Bacon ph Sol Polito md Leo F. Forbstein

☆ James Cagney, Margaret Lindsay, Ricardo Cortez, Lili Damita, Donald Woods, Barton MacLane, George E. Stone, Addison Richards

'So similar to *Barbary Coast* as almost to be its twin ... nevertheless, good entertainment.' – *Variety*

The Frisco Kid

US 1979 108m Technicolor
Warner (Howard W. Koch Jnr)

▣ ▦

In the old west, a rabbi heading for San Francisco makes friends with an outlaw.

Unsuccessful episodic comedy, unreasonably alternating farce with sentimentality.

w Michael Elias, Frank Shaw d Robert Aldrich ph Robert B. Hauser m Frank de Vol

☆ Gene Wilder, Harrison Ford, Ramon Bieri, Leo Fuchs, Penny Peyser

'A very forced comedy, made all the worse by the fact that Aldrich seems to time and edit comedy as though it were a melodrama only played a little slower.' – *Richard Combs, MFB*

Frisco Lil

US 1942 62m bw
Universal
A girl law student traps a killer and clears her dad.
Formula second feature, quite adequate in its way.
w George Bricker, Michel Jacoby d Erle C. Kenton
☆ Irene Hervey, Kent Taylor, Minor Watson, Jerome Cowan

Frisco Sal

US 1945 63m bw
Universal
A New England girl goes to California to avenge her brother's murder.
Minor musical vehicle for a star being groomed as a rival to Deanna Durbin.
w Curt Siodmak, Gerald Geraghty d George Waggner
☆ Susanna Foster, Turhan Bey, Alan Curtis, Andy Devine, Thomas Gomez, Samuel S. Hinds

Frisk

US 1995 83m colour
Dangerous to Know/Strand/Industrial Eye (Marcus Hu, Jon Gerrans)
An adult homosexual acts out his youthful fantasies of killing his sexual partners.
A story of sado-masochistic lust somewhat unimaginatively handled; had it been better, it would have probably been even less watchable.
w Jim Dwyer, George LaVoo novel Dennis Cooper d Todd Verow m Greg Watkins m Coil et al pd Jennifer Graber ed Todd Verow
☆ Michael Gunther, Craig Chester, Parker Posey, James Lyons, Alexis Arquette, Raoul O'Connell, Jaie Laplante, Michael Stock
'Though intelligent and daring in its own right, does little to disprove the adage that great novels rarely make great films.' – *José Arroyo, Sight and Sound*

Le Frisson des Vampires (dubbed)

France 1970 90m colour
Films ABC/Filmes Modernes (Jean Rollin)
aka: *Sex and the Vampire*
aka: *The Terror of the Vampires; Vampire Thrills*
A newly married couple break their journey to stay at an ancient chateau, where a vampire errant has changed its two owners from vampire hunters into bourgeois vampires.
A ridiculous, high-camp horror, which consists mainly of actresses removing their clothes, usually to indulge in a little lesbian lovemaking. An attempt at a crepuscular atmosphere, all guttering candles and flaming torches against old stone, is not helped by a rock music soundtrack or by the trance-like acting and banal dialogue.
wd Jean Rollin ph Jean-Jacques Renon m Acanthus ad Michel Delesalles ed Olivier Grégoire
☆ Sandra Julien, Jean-Marie Durand, Jacques Robiolles, Michel Delahaye, Marie-Pierre, Kuelan Herce, Nicole Nancel, Dominique
'It combines the triteness of a typical Hammer plot with stretches of decidedly unerotic skinflick writhing, but is redeemed by Rollin's quirky descent into surrealist imagery.' – *Empire*

Fritz the Cat **

US 1971 78m DeLuxe
Fritz Productions/Aurica (Steve Krantz)
An alleycat student in New York seeks new and varied experience.
Cartoon feature which applies the old anthropomorphism to the contemporary scene, and whips up more obscenity and violence than Disney ever dreamed of. A fast-moving orgy of outrage which could never have got by in live form.
comic strip R. H. Crumb m Ed Bogas, Ray Shanklin wd/animator Ralph Bakshi
'A bitter and snarling satire that refuses to curl up in anyone's lap.' – *Bruce Williamson*

The Frog *

GB 1937 75m bw
Herbert Wilcox
The mysterious leader of a criminal organization is unmasked.
Lively old-fashioned mystery melodrama.

w Ian Hay, Gerald Elliott novel *The Fellowship of the Frog* by Edgar Wallace d Jack Raymond ph Frederick A. Young
☆ Gordon Harker, Carol Goodner, Noah Beery, Jack Hawkins, Richard Ainley, Esmé Percy, Felix Aylmer
'Badly directed, badly acted, it is like one of those plays produced in country towns by stranded actors. It has an old-world charm: Scotland Yard is laid up in lavender.' – *Graham Greene*
† Sequel 1938: *The Return of the Frog.*

The Frog Prince *

GB 1984 90m Eastmancolor
Warner/Goldcrest/Enigma (Iain Smith)
In Paris in the early 1960s an English girl studying at the Sorbonne decides to lose her virginity to a handsome young Frenchman.
Quietly charming, though unmemorable, romantic drama.
w Brian Gilbert, Posy Simmonds d Brian Gilbert ph Clive Tickner m Enya Ni Bhraonain pd Anton Furst ed Jim Clark
☆ Jane Snowden, Alexandre Sterling, Diana Blackburn, Oystein Wiik

The Frogmen

US 1951 96m bw
TCF (Samuel G. Engel)
Underwater demolition experts pave the way for the invasion of a Japanese-held island.
Standard, efficient war fare.
w John Tucker Battle d Lloyd Bacon ph Norbert Brodine m Cyril Mockridge
☆ Richard Widmark, Dana Andrews, Gary Merrill, Jeffrey Hunter, Warren Stevens, Robert Wagner, Harvey Lembeck
'Competent, unpretentious and free from jingoism.' – *MFB*
Å original story (Oscar Millard); Norbert Brodine

'Frogs lay millions and millions of eggs each year! What if they all hatched? Today the pond – tomorrow the world!'

Frogs *

US 1972 91m Movielab
AIP (George Edwards, Peter Thomas)
A remote, inhabited island in the southern States is overtaken by amphibians.
As Hitchcock might have said, the frogs is coming; instead of monsters, ordinary creepy-crawlies in their thousands devour most of the cast. Well enough done for those with strong stomachs.
w Robert Hutchison, Robert Blees d George McCowan ph Mario Tosi m Les Baxter
☆ Ray Milland, Joan Van Ark, Sam Elliott, Adam Roarke, Judy Pace
'One of the most remarkable and impressive onslaughts since *King Kong*.' – *David Pirie*

'A mind is a terrible thing to waste.'

From Beyond *

US 1986 85m colour
Empire (Brian Yuzna)
aka: *H. P. Lovecraft's From Beyond*
A physicist's experiment to stimulate the pineal gland and create a sixth sense summons man-eating monsters from another dimension.
Slickly directed, and extremely gory, horror that comes closer than most to recreating the nauseating, tentacled nightmares of Lovecraft's decadent imagination and an addiction to the search for forbidden knowledge.
w Dennis Paoli story H. P. Lovecraft, adapted by Brian Yuzna, Dennis Paoli, Stuart Gordon d Stuart Gordon ph Mac Ahlberg m Richard Band pd Giovanni Natalucci ed Lee Percy sp John Buechler, Mark Shostrom, John Naulin, Anthony Doublin
☆ Jeffrey Combs, Barbara Crampton, Ken Foree, Ted Sorel, Carolyn Purdy-Gordon, Bunny Summers, Bruce McGuire

From Beyond the Grave *

GB 1973 98m Technicolor
Warner/Amicus (Milton Subotsky)
The proprietor of an East End antique shop involves his customers in horrific situations.
Reasonably lively portmanteau of tall tales from a familiar stable.

w Robin Clarke, Raymond Christodoulou d Kevin Connor ph Alan Hume m David Gamley pd Maurice Carter
☆ David Warner, Donald Pleasence, Ian Bannen, Diana Dors, Margaret Leighton, Ian Carmichael, Nyree Dawn Porter, Ian Ogilvy

From Dusk till Dawn *

US 1995 198m Technicolor
Dimension/Los Hooligans/A Band Apart (Gianni Nunnari, Meir Teper)
Two ruthless robbers take a preacher and his children hostage and drive with them to Mexico, where they stumble into a den of vampires.
Extraordinarily gory horror that begins, and might have been better advised to have continued, as a tense, hyper-kinetic thriller; even so, it has a power and energy that put it a cut above most movies of its kind.
w Quentin Tarantino story Robert Kurtzman d Robert Rodriguez ph Guillermo Navarro m Graeme Revell pd Cecilia Montiel ed Robert Rodriguez make-up fx Kurtzman, Nicotero & Berger EFX
☆ Harvey Keitel, George Clooney, Quentin Tarantino, Juliette Lewis, Salma Hayek, Brenda Hillhouse, Marc Lawrence, Cheech Marin, Michael Parks, Kelly Preston, Fred Williamson, John Saxon, Tom Savini, Ernest Liu
'Pure juvenilia that should have remained true to its origins as a straight-to-video low-budget project.' – *Lizzie Franke, Sight and Sound*

From Headquarters

US 1933 63m bw
Warner (Sam Bischoff)
The police solve a murder by scientific methods.
Efficient, rather boring programmer.
w Robert N. Lee, Peter Milne d William Dieterle ph William Reese
☆ George Brent, Margaret Lindsay, Eugene Pallette, Hugh Herbert, Hobart Cavanaugh, Robert Barrat, Henry O'Neill, Edward Ellis

From Hell It Came

US 1957 71m bw
Milner Brothers/Allied Artists
An executed native of Kalai returns to life in the form of a vengeful tree stump.
Absolute rubbish, just about worth sitting through for the unintentional laughs.
w Richard Bernstein d Dan Milner ph Brydon Baker
☆ Tod Andrews, Tina Carver, Linda Watkins

From Hell to Heaven

US 1933 67m bw
Paramount
Stories of a racetrack hotel.
Very minor Grand Hotel, neatly made for its time.
w Percy Heath, Sidney Buchman story Lawrence Hazard d Erle C. Kenton
☆ Carole Lombard, Jack Oakie, Sidney Blackmer, Adrienne Ames, David Manners

From Hell to Texas

US 1958 100m Eastmancolor
Cinemascope
TCF (Robert Buckner)
GB title: *Manhunt*
After accidentally killing a man, a cowboy is vengefully pursued by the victim's father.
Competent chase Western with a stand against violence.
w Robert Buckner, Wendell Mayes d Henry Hathaway ph Wilfrid Cline m Daniele Amfitheatrof
☆ Don Murray, Diane Varsi, Chill Wills, Dennis Hopper, R. G. Armstrong, Margo, Jay C. Flippen

'The Boldest Book Of Our Time ... Honestly, Fearlessly On The Screen!'

From Here to Eternity ***

US 1953 118m bw
Columbia (Buddy Adler)
Life in a Honolulu barracks at the time of Pearl Harbor.
Cleaned up and streamlined version of a bestseller in which the mainly sexual frustrations of a number of unattractive characters are laid bare. As a production, it is Hollywood in good form, and certainly took the public fancy as well as establishing Sinatra as an acting force.

w Daniel Taradash novel James Jones d Fred Zinnemann ph Burnett Guffey m George Duning ed William Lyon
☆ Burt Lancaster, Deborah Kerr, Frank Sinatra, Donna Reed, Ernest Borgnine, Montgomery Clift, Philip Ober, Mickey Shaughnessy
'This is not a theme which one would expect Zinnemann to approach in the hopeful, sympathetic mood of his earlier films; but neither could one expect the negative shrug of indifference with which he seems to have surrendered to its hysteria.' – *Karel Reisz, Sight and Sound*
† The story was remade for TV in 1979 as a six-hour mini-series
†† Frank Sinatra got his key role after Eli Wallach dropped out.
Å best picture; Daniel Taradash; Fred Zinnemann; Burnett Guffey; Frank Sinatra; Donna Reed; William Lyon
Ä George Duning; Burt Lancaster; Deborah Kerr; Montgomery Clift

From Hollywood to Deadwood *

US 1988 102m DuArt
Island/Night Film (Jo Peterson)
Two impecunious tough-talking private detectives are hired by a Hollywood production company to find an actress who has gone missing.
Entertaining dark-toned thriller in a pulp fiction style, with hard-boiled private eyes cracking wise when they are not being set up.
wd Rex Pickett ph Peter Deming m Alex Gibson, Gregory Kuehn ad Tori Nourafchan ed Steve Adrianson, Robert Erickson
☆ Scott Paulin, Jim Haynie, Barbara Schock, Chris Mulkey, Jurgen Doeres, Michael Genovese, Norbert Weisser, Tom Dahlgren, Campbell Scott

From Noon Till Three

US 1976 99m DeLuxe
UA/Frankovich-Self
A bank robber becomes a local legend when he interrupts a raid to dally with an attractive widow. Later, when someone else is shot in mistake for him, he is reduced to penury, unable to prove his identity or live up to his own legend.
Curious, shapeless, lumpy Western satire, difficult to synopsize or analyse. Despite effort all round, it's just plain unsatisfactory.
wd Frank D. Gilroy novel Frank D. Gilroy ph Lucien Ballard m Elmer Bernstein
☆ Charles Bronson, Jill Ireland, Douglas Fowley, Stan Haze, Damon Douglas
'It squanders its early sparkle for a pot of message.' – *Michael Billington, Illustrated London News*
'The main thing – hell, the only thing – worth noting about *From Noon Till Three* is that it's profoundly weird, which is not quite the same thing as being good.' – *Frank Rich, New York Post*

From Russia with Love ***

GB 1963 118m Technicolor
UA/Eon (Harry Saltzman, Albert Broccoli)
A Russian spy joins an international crime organization and develops a plan to kill James Bond and steal a coding machine.
The second Bond adventure and possibly the best, with Istanbul and Venice for backdrops and climaxes involving a speeding train and a helicopter. Arrant nonsense with tongue in cheek, on a big budget.
w Richard Maibaum, Johanna Harwood novel Ian Fleming d Terence Young ph Ted Moore m John Barry titles Robert Brownjohn
☆ Sean Connery, Robert Shaw, Pedro Armendariz, Daniela Bianchi, Lotte Lenya, Bernard Lee, Eunice Gayson, Lois Maxwell
Ö Ted Moore

From Soup to Nuts *

US 1928 20m bw silent
Hal Roach
Two temporary waiters wreck a dinner party.
Very funny slapstick which the stars subsequently reworked into A Chump at Oxford.
w H. M. Walker story Leo McCarey d Edgar Kennedy ph Len Powers ed Richard Currier
☆ Laurel and Hardy, Anita Garvin, Tiny Sandford

From the Earth to the Moon

US 1958 100m Technicolor
Waverley (Benedict Bogeaus)

📀 📹

In the 1880s an armaments millionaire finances a trip to the moon in a projectile fired by his own invention.
Cardboard science fiction, with an imposing cast at sea in an unspeakable script and an unseaworthy production.
w Robert Blees, James Leicester *novel* Jules Verne d Byron Haskin *ph* Edwin DuPar *m* Louis Forbes *ad* Hal Wilson Cox
☆ Joseph Cotten, George Sanders, Henry Daniell, Carl Esmond, Melville Cooper, Don Dubbins, Debra Paget, Patric Knowles

From the Hip

US 1987 112m Technicolor
De Laurentiis Entertainment Group/Indian Neck (René Dupont, Bob Clark)

📀 📹

An ambitious and unscrupulous young lawyer defends an academic accused of murder.
An unfortunate mix of courtroom drama and romantic comedy that fails on all levels.
w David E. Kelley, Bob Clark d Bob Clark *ph* Dante Spinotti *m* Paul Zaza *pd* Michael Stringer *ed* Stan Cole
☆ Judd Nelson, Elizabeth Perkins, John Hurt, Darren McGavin, Dan Monahan, David Alan Grier, Ray Walston

From the Life of the Marionettes *

West Germany 1980 104m colour/bw
ITC/Personafilm (Horts Wendlandt, Ingrid Bergman, Richard Brick)

📀 📹

original title: Aus Dem Leben Der Marionetten
An inquiry into the killing of a prostitute by a rich businessman.
A film somehow very typical of its director, but far from his most interesting work.
wd Ingmar Bergman *ph* Sven Nykvist *m* Rols Wilhelm *pd* Rolf Zehetbauer *ed* Petra von Oelffen, Geri Ashur
☆ Robert Atzorn, Christine Buchegger, Martin Benrath

'In its unalloyed pessimism, its complete negation of hope, the film, stripped of the incidents, the excitements which have illumined the director's earlier work, is the purest of Bergman. He can go no farther.' – *Dilys Powell, Punch*

From the Mixed-Up Files of Mrs Basil E. Frankweiler

👫 US 1973 105m colour
Cinema 5

Two children hide out in New York's Metropolitan Museum of Art and befriend a rich woman.
An unusual idea makes ho-hum entertainment for well-brought-up children.
w Blanche Hanalis *novel* E. L. Konigsberg d Fielder Cook *ph* Victor J. Kemper *m* Donald Devor
☆ Ingrid Bergman, Sally Prager, Johnny Doran, George Rose, Richard Mulligan

From The Pole to The Equator *

W. Germany/Italy 1986 96m bw/colour
ZDF (Gianikian & Ricci Lucchi)

📀

original title: Dal Polo all'Equatore
Deteriorating documentary footage, taken in the early 1900s by a forgotten pioneer, the much-travelled Luca Comerio (died 1940), was rescued, reprinted, tinted, speeded up and slowed down to recreate a psychedelic vision of the past.
A curiosity, a silent film, with electronic musical accompaniment, of images from another age; they flicker, fade and disintegrate as you watch, though the memories they contain are often less than nostalgic. Yesterday has seldom seemed so remote.
wd Gianikian & Ricci Lucchi *ph* Luca Comerio *m* Keith Ullrich, Charles Anderson

From the Terrace

US 1960 144m DeLuxe Cinemascope
TCF/Linebrook (Mark Robson)

📀

Life among Pennsylvania's idle rich.
Heavy-going family melodrama from a bestseller peopled with boorish characters.
w Ernest Lehman *novel* John O'Hara d Mark Robson *ph* Leo Tover *m* Elmer Bernstein
☆ Paul Newman, Joanne Woodward, Myrna Loy, Ina Balin, Leon Ames, Felix Aylmer, George Grizzard, Patrick O'Neal, Elizabeth Allen

From This Day Forward ***

US 1946 95m bw
RKO (William L. Pereira)

After World War II, a New York couple think back to their early years in the poverty-stricken thirties.
Effective sentimental realism coupled with Hollywood professionalism made this film more memorable than it may sound.
w Hugo Butler, Garson Kanin *novel* All Brides Are Beautiful by Thomas Bell d John Berry *ph* George Barnes *m* Leigh Harline
☆ Joan Fontaine, Mark Stevens, Rosemary de Camp, Henry Morgan, Wally Brown, Arline Judge, Bobby Driscoll, Mary Treen

'Distinguished from the usual film about Young Love and Young Marriage by irony, poetry and realism.' – *Richard Winnington*

The Front *

US 1976 95m Metrocolor
Columbia/Persky-Bright, Devon (Martin Ritt, Charles H. Joffe)

📀 🇺🇸 📹

For a small commission, a bookmaker puts his name to scripts by blacklisted writers.
Rather bland satire on the communist witch hunts of the fifties; interesting, but neither funny nor incisive enough.
w Walter Bernstein d Martin Ritt *ph* Michael Chapman *m* Dave Grusin
☆ Woody Allen, Zero Mostel, Herschel Bernardi, Michael Murphy, Andrea Marcovicci, Lloyd Gough

'The pacing is off, the sequences don't flow, and the film seems sterile, unpopulated and flat.' – *New Yorker*
'A light comedy forged out of dark and authentic pain.' – *Frank Rich, New York Post*
'It catches the anguish of America's creative community with wit and feeling.' – *Sunday Express*
♟ Walter Bernstein

The Front Page ***

US 1931 101m bw
Howard Hughes

📀

A Chicago reporter wants to retire and marry, but is tricked by his scheming editor into covering one last case.
Brilliant early talkie perfectly transferring into screen terms a stage classic of the twenties. Superficially a shade primitive now, its essential power remains.
w Bartlett Cormack, Charles Lederer *play* Charles MacArthur, Ben Hecht d Lewis Milestone *ph* Glen MacWilliams
☆ Adolphe Menjou, Pat O'Brien, Mary Brian, Edward Everett Horton, Walter Catlett, George E. Stone, Mae Clarke, Slim Summerville, Matt Moore, Frank McHugh

'Sure money-getter … it will universally entertain and please.' – *Variety*
'The most riproaring movie that ever came out of Hollywood.' – *Pare Lorentz*
'It excelled most of the films of its day by sheer treatment. The speedy delivery of lines and business and the re-emphasis upon cutting as a prime structural element made the film a model of mobility for confused directors who did not know yet how to handle sound.' – *Lewis Jacobs, The Rise of the American Film*
† Remade in 1940 as *His Girl Friday* (qv) and in 1988 as *Switching Channels* (qv). And see below.
♟ best picture; Lewis Milestone; Adolphe Menjou

'It's the hottest story since the Chicago fire … and they're sitting on it.'

The Front Page **

US 1974 105m Technicolor Panavision
U-I (Paul Monash)

📀 📹 📀

Disappointing Billy Wilder remake, relying overmuch on bad language and farcical intrusions, while tending to jettison the plot in the latter half. Some laughs nevertheless.
w Billy Wilder, I. A. L. Diamond d Billy Wilder *ph* Jordan S. Cronenweth *m* Billy May *ad* Henry Bumstead *ed* Ralph E. Winters

Front Page Story *

GB 1953 99m bw
British Lion/Jay Lewis

📺

A day in the life of a Fleet Street newspaper, when the editor is torn between several big stories and nearly loses his wife.
Dogged 'slice of life' drama with few excitements but some incidental entertainment and a production of routine competence.
w Jay Lewis, Jack Howells *novel* Final Night by Robert Gaines d Gordon Parry *ph* Gilbert Taylor *m* Jackie Brown
☆ Jack Hawkins, Elizabeth Allan, Derek Farr, Michael Goodliffe, Martin Miller

Front Page Woman **

US 1935 82m bw
Warner (Samuel Bischoff)

Rival reporters try to outshine each other.
Lively comedy-melodrama very typical of its style and time.
w Laird Doyle, Lillie Hayward, Roy Chanslor d Michael Curtiz *ph* Tony Gaudio *m* Heinz Roemheld *md* Leo Forbstein
☆ Bette Davis, George Brent, Roscoe Karns, Wini Shaw, J. Carrol Naish, Walter Walker

'Completely screwy but will get fair b.o.' – *Variety*
'A swift-moving, unsensational, unsentimental, honest piece of cynicism which is really good value for money.' – *MFB*

La Frontera *

Chile/Spain 1991 115m colour
Metro Tartan/Cine XXI (Eduardo Larrain S., Ricardo Larrain P.)

Because of his outspokenness, a Santiago schoolteacher is exiled to a remote seaside town in the mid-80s.
An interesting look back at Chile's recent political past from a left-wing standpoint; it was a big hit in Chile, but unlikely to mean as much outside the country, other than as an indication of a revitalized cinema.
w Jorge Goldenberg, Ricardo Larrain d Ricardo Larrain *ph* Hector Rios *m* Jaime de Aguirre *ad* Juan Carlos Castillo *ed* Claudio Martinez
☆ Patricio Contreras, Gloria Laso, Hector Noguera, Alonso Venegas, Aldo Bernales, Patricio Bunster

'Despite the extraordinary wild scenery and unhistrionic performances, the movie tends to get bogged down in its melancholy mood and ends up rather cheerless and dull.' – *Caroline Rees, Empire*

Frontier: see *Aerograd*

Frontier Badmen

US 1943 74m bw
Ford Beebe Universal

Texas ranchers try to break a cattle-buying monopoly.
The good guys and the bad guys at it again, with fair results.
w Gerald Geraghty, Morgan B. Cox d William McGann
☆ Robert Paige, Anne Gwynne, Lon Chaney Jnr, Noah Beery Jnr, Diana Barrymore, Leo Carrillo, Andy Devine, Thomas Gomez, William Farnum

Frontier Gal

US 1945 84m Technicolor
Universal (Michael Fessier, Ernest Pagano)
GB title: *The Bride Wasn't Willing*

An outlaw weds a saloon girl at pistol point; emerging five years later from prison, he finds he has a daughter.
Rambling Western with some pretensions to humour and sentiment; not a success, but it established de Carlo as a star.
w Michael Fessier, Ernest Pagano d Charles Lamont *ph* George Robinson, Charles Boyle *m* Frank Skinner
☆ Yvonne de Carlo, Rod Cameron, Sheldon Leonard, Andy Devine, Fuzzy Knight, Andrew Tombes, Clara Blandick

Frontier Marshal *

US 1933 66m bw
Fox

A marshal cleans up Tombstone.
Interesting trial run for the 1939 film, which was subsequently done over as My Darling Clementine.
w William Conselman, Stuart Anthony *book* Stuart N. Lake d Lew Seiler
☆ George O'Brien, Irene Bentley, George E. Stone, Ruth Gillette
† For legal reasons in this version the marshal is called Michael Wyatt instead of Wyatt Earp.

Frontier Marshal *

US 1939 70m bw
TCF (Sol M. Wurtzel)

Wyatt Earp cleans up Tombstone.
Simple-minded, pleasing Western, later worked over by Ford as My Darling Clementine.
w Sam Hellman *book* Stuart N. Lake d Allan Dwan *ph* Charles Clarke *m* Samuel Kaylin
☆ Randolph Scott, Nancy Kelly, Cesar Romero, Binnie Barnes, John Carradine, Joe Sawyer, Lon Chaney Jnr, Ward Bond, Edward Norris, Eddie Foy Jnr

'Strong programme western, in-betweener for key duals, but a top biller in subsequents.' – *Variety*
† Eddie Foy Jnr appeared as his father, who historically did perform in Tombstone at the time. The equivalent in *My Darling Clementine* was the Shakespearean actor played by Alan Mowbray.

Frou Frou: see *The Toy Wife*

'At First Family Sperm Bank, she banks on babies, he banks on bucks.'

Frozen Assets

US 1992 93m Eastmancolor
RKO (Don Klein)

📀 📹 🎧

A financial expert takes a job in a small town and discovers that he's expected to run a sperm bank.
A coy and extremely predictable comedy that treats its subject-matter with sniggers.
w Don Klein, Tom Kartozian d George Miller *ph* Ron Lautore, Geza Sinkovics *m* Michael Tavera *pd* Dorian Vernacchio *ed* Larry Bock
☆ Shelley Long, Corbin Bernsen, Larry Miller, Dody Goodman, Matt Clark, Jeanne Cooper, Paul Sand, Gloria Camden, Teri Copley

'Yet another waste of the talents of Shelley Long, but she's the film's one real asset.' – *Variety*
† It was released direct to video in Britain.

The Frozen Dead

GB 1966 95m Eastmancolor
Goldstar/Seven Arts

In an English laboratory, a scientist is trying to revive the frozen corpses of Nazi leaders.
Flatfooted horror piece providing very little of interest to pass the time.
wd Herbert J. Leder
☆ Dana Andrews, Anna Palk, Philip Gilbert, Karel Stepanek, Kathleen Breck

The Frozen Ghost *

US 1945 61m bw
Universal

When a drunk dies while under his influence, a hypnotist fears he has the will and power to kill.
Absurdly titled and insufficiently vigorous entry in the Inner Sanctum series.
w Bernard Schubert, Luci Ward d Harold Young
☆ Lon Chaney Jnr, Evelyn Ankers, Martin Kosleck, Milburn Stone, Tala Birell, Douglass Dumbrille

The Frozen Limits *

👫 GB 1939 84m bw
Gainsborough (Edward Black)

Six impecunious comedians hear of the Yukon gold rush, and join it … forty years too late.
The Crazy Gang not quite at its best, but working hard, with a few hilarious moments and a special assist from Moore Marriott.
w Marriott Edgar, Val Guest, J. O. C. Orton d Marcel Varnel *ph* Arthur Crabtree *md* Louis Levy *ad* Vetchinsky *ed* R. E. Dearing, Alfred Roome

---

☆ Bud Flanagan, Chesney Allen, Jimmy Nervo, Teddy Knox, Charlie Naughton, Jimmy Gold, *Moore Marriott*, Eileen Bell, Anthony Hulme, Bernard Lee, Eric Clavering

'The funniest English picture yet produced … it can bear comparison with *Safety Last* and *The General*.' – *Graham Greene*

Frühlingssinfonie: see *Spring Symphony*

Le Fruit Défendu: see *Forbidden Fruit*

The Fruit Machine
GB   1988   103m   colour
Vestron/Granada/Ideal (Steve Morrison)
🎞 ▦ ◷ ⌢

Two mixed-up teenagers run away after witnessing a murder.
Unsuccessful mixture of fantasy and thriller.
w Frank Clarke d Philip Saville ph Dick Pope m Hans Zimmer pd David Brockhurst ed Richard Bedford
☆ Emile Charles, Tony Forsyth, Robert Stephens, Clare Higgins, Bruce Payne, Robbie Coltrane, Kim Christie, Julie Graham

Fu Manchu
The Yellow Peril, or evil Oriental master criminal, was created by Sax Rohmer in a 1911 novel, which led to 13 more plus some short stories.
A long series of British two-reelers was made in the twenties, and talking films are as follows:
1929 The Mysterious Dr Fu Manchu, with Warner Oland (Paramount)
1930 The Return of Dr Fu Manchu (ditto)
1931 Daughter of Fu Manchu (ditto)
1932 The Mask of Fu Manchu (qv) with Boris Karloff (MGM)
1939 Drums of Fu Manchu, with Henry Brandon (Republic serial)
The remainder are British productions by Harry Alan Towers, with Christopher Lee:
1965 The Face of Fu Manchu (qv)
1966 Brides of Fu Manchu
1968 The Vengeance of Fu Manchu
1969 The Blood of Fu Manchu
1970 The Castle of Fu Manchu

Fucking Åmål ★★
Sweden/Denmark   1998   89m   colour
Alliance/Memfis (Lars Jönsson)
aka: *Show Me Love*
In a dull Swedish suburb of Åmål, an unhappy 16-year-old has a secret crush on her school's most popular girl.
Gentle, believable story of adolescent ennui and trauma which retains its interest despite its lack of action.
wd Lukas Moodysson ph Ulf Brantas ed Lina Strand, Heidi Saikkonen ed Michal Leszczylowski, Bernhard Winkler
☆ Alexandra Dahlström, Rebecca Liljeberg, Mathias Rust, Erica Carlson, Stefan Hörberg, Josefin Nyberg, Ralph Carlsson, Maria Hedborg, Axel Widegren, Jill Ung

'I've never been so moved by the loneliness of growing pains.' – *James Christopher, Times*
'I urge everyone who likes good film-making to go and see this film.' – *Mike Figgis*

Fuddy Duddy Buddy ★★
🏃 US   1952   7m   Technicolor
UPA
Mr Magoo mistakes a walrus for his friend the colonel.
Top drawer Magoo adventure climaxing with the celebrated line: 'I don't care if he is a walrus. I like him. I like him!'
wd John Hubley m William Lava

The Fugitive: see *On the Night of the Fire* (1939)

The Fugitive ★
US   1947   104m   bw
Argosy (Merian C. Cooper, John Ford)
🎞 ▦ ◷

In an anti-clerical country, a priest is on the run.
Ford's attempt to do a Mexican Informer *is slow and rather boring, but the pictures are nice to look at even though the original novel has been totally emasculated.*
w Dudley Nichols novel *The Power and the Glory* by Graham Greene d John Ford ph Gabriel Figueroa m Richard Hageman ad Alfred Ybarra ed Jack Murray

☆ Henry Fonda, Dolores del Rio, Pedro Armendariz, J. Carrol Naish, Leo Carrillo, Ward Bond, Robert Armstrong, John Qualen
'A symphony of light and shade, of deafening din and silence, of sweeping movement and repose.' – *Bosley Crowther*
'The most pretentious travesty of a literary work since *For Whom the Bell Tolls*.' – *Richard Winnington*

'A murdered wife. A one-armed man. An obsessed detective. The chase begins.'
The Fugitive ★★★
US   1993   127m   Technicolor
Warner (Keith Barish, Arnold Kopelson)
🎞 ▦ ◷ ◵ ◷ ⌢

A surgeon, unjustly accused of his wife's murder, goes on the run to find the real killer, while being hunted by a ruthless cop.
Tense and exciting thriller that sticks closely to the plot of the original television series and, despite its many improbabilities, remains compulsively watchable.
w Jeb Stuart, David Twohy story David Twohy based on characters created by Roy Huggins (for the TV series) d Andrew Davis ph Michael Chapman m James Newton Howard pd Dennis Washington ed Dennis Virkler, David Finfer, Dean Goodhill, Don Brochu, Richard Nord, Dov Hoenig
☆ Harrison Ford, *Tommy Lee Jones*, Sela Ward, Joe Pantoliano, Jeroen Krabbé, Andreas Katsulas, Julianne Moore
'A consummate nail-biter that never flags, it leaves you breathless from the chase yet anxious for the next bit of mayhem or clever plot twist.' – *Variety*
'A remarkably successful Hollywood product, with a brilliantly contrived star double act pursuing different paths through the central plot.' – *Kim Newman, Sight and Sound*
† The TV series ran from 1963 to 1967 and starred David Janssen.
🏆 Tommy Lee Jones
🅱 best picture; Michael Chapman; James Newton Howard; editing; sound; sound effects editing

The Fugitive Kind
US   1960   121m   bw
UA/Martin Jurow/Richard A. Shepherd/Pennebaker
▦

A Mississippi drifter in a small strange town runs into trouble with women.
Doom-laden melodrama, almost a parody of the author's works, full of cancer patients, nympho-dipsos, and cemetery seductions; we are however spared the final castration.
w Tennessee Williams, Meade Roberts play *Orpheus Descending* by Tennessee Williams d Sidney Lumet ph Boris Kaufman m Kenyon Hopkins pd Richard Sylbert
☆ Marlon Brando, Anna Magnani, Joanne Woodward, Victor Jory, Maureen Stapleton, R. G. Armstrong
'A series of mythological engravings, determined by a literary text and a lurid concept of hell on earth.' – *Peter John Dyer*
'Sidney Lumet is usually clever at least part of the time – an acquisitive magpie who has picked up, along with the selly trash, a few small gems. This time he brings us nothing but bits of coloured glass.' – *Stanley Kauffmann*

Fugitive Lovers
US   1934   74m   bw
MGM
▦

A convict escapes on a transcontinental bus.
Unsatisfactory comedy drama with a miscast star; chiefly interesting for showing the form of travel, but It Happened One Night *did it better in the following year.*
w Ferdinand Reyher, Frank Wead d Richard Boleslawski
☆ Robert Montgomery, Madge Evans, Ted Healy and the Three Stooges, Nat Pendleton, C. Henry Gordon
'Acceptable for lesser houses but not de luxe quality.' – *Variety*

Full Circle
GB/Canada   1976   97m   Eastmancolor
Paramount/Fetter-Classic (Peter Fetterman, Alfred Parisier)
▦ ⌢

After the death of her small daughter, a woman leaves home to live in an old house which is

haunted by the malevolent spirit of another dead child.
Unpleasant and incompetent supernatural nonsense, seeking a niche somewhere between Don't Look Now *and* The Exorcist.
w Dave Humphries novel *Julia* by Peter Straub d Richard Loncraine ph Peter Hannan m Colin Towns
☆ Mia Farrow, Keir Dullea, Tom Conti, Jill Bennett, Robin Gammell, Cathleen Nesbitt, Mary Morris, Edward Hardwicke

Full Confession
US   1939   73m   bw
RKO
A priest bound by the sanctity of confession urges a murderer to give himself up.
Neat little melodrama with a plot much copied subsequently.
wd John Farrow
☆ Victor McLaglen, Barry Fitzgerald, Sally Eilers, Joseph Calleia
'Rather interesting, but not strong enough for the upper bracket.' – *Variety*

Full Contact
Hong Kong   1992   97m   colour
Made in Hong Kong/Golden Princess (Ringo Lam)
original title: *Xia Dao Gao Fei*
Two friends fall out over guns and the wife of one of them.
Violent, action-packed drama of revenge of a familiar kind.
w Nam Yin d Ringo Lam ph Lau Hung Chun, Joe Chan m Teddy Robin Kwan ad Ray Lam ed Tony Chow
☆ Chow Yun-Fat, Simon Yam, Ann Bridgewater, Anthony Wong, Bonnie Fu, Lee Kin-Sang, Frankie Chin
'The movie is such a catalogue of inventively inflicted bodily harm and casual sordid behaviour, it's almost like watching a sustained piece of Theatre of Cruelty.' – *David Tse, Sight and Sound*

A Full Day's Work ★
France   1973   90m   Eastmancolor
President/Cinetel/Euro International (Jacques-Eric Strauss)
original title: *Une Journée Bien Remplie*
A baker sets out to kill in one day the jurors who found his son guilty of murder.
Mildly amusing black comedy, though it is too self-conscious for its own good.
wd Jean-Louis Trintignant ph William Lubtchansky m Bruno Nicolai ed Nicole Lubtchansky
☆ Jacques Dufilho, Luce Marquand, Denise Peron, Antoine Marin, Jacques Doniol-Valcroze, Vittorio Caprioli

Full Eclipse
US   1993   93m   colour
HBO/Citadel (Peter Abrams, Robert L. Levy)
🎞

A detective discovers that an élite group of cops, concerned about 'animals ruling the streets', become werewolves in order to deal with them outside the law.
Daft thriller that begins as if the director had overdosed on John Woo's shoot-outs and then becomes like any other cheap horror movie.
w Richard Christian Matheson, Michael Reaves d Anthony Hickox ph Sandi Sissel m Gary Chang pd Gregory Melton ed Peter Amundson sp make-up effects: Alterian Studios
☆ Mario Van Peebles, Patsy Kensit, Anthony John Denison, Jason Beghe, Paula Marshall, John Verea, Dean Norris, Willie C. Carpenter, Bruce Payne
'Daft but pleasurable.' – *Sight and Sound*

Full House: see *O. Henry's Full House*

'In Vietnam The Wind Doesn't Blow. It Sucks.'
Full Metal Jacket ★★
GB   1987   116m   Rank Colour
Warner/Stanley Kubrick
🎞 ▦ ◷ ⌢

After rigorous training, US marines land in Vietnam.
Smartly ordered but rather ordinary and predictable war film to come from one of the cinema's acknowledged masters after seven years of silence.

w Stanley Kubrick, Michael Herr, Gustav Hasford novel *The Short Timers* by Gustav Hasford d Stanley Kubrick ph Douglas Milsome m Abigail Mead pd Anton Furst
☆ Matthew Modine, Adam Baldwin, Vincent D'Onofrio, R. Lee Ermey, Dorian Harewood, Arliss Howard
🅱 best adapted screenplay

'The year's most revealing comedy.'
The Full Monty ★★★
GB/US   1997   91m   Metrocolor
TCF/Redwave (Uberto Pasolini)
🎞 ▦ ◷ ⌢

A group of unemployed Sheffield steelworkers decide to become male strippers in order to raise some money.
Clever, enjoyable comedy about salvaging self-respect and baring all, emotionally as well as physically; it struck a chord not only in Britain, but around the world.
w Simon Beaufoy d Peter Cattaneo ph John de Borman m Anne Dudley pd Max Gottlieb ed David Freeman, Nick More
☆ Robert Carlyle, Tom Wilkinson, Mark Addy, Lesley Sharp, Emily Woof, Steve Huison, Paul Barber, Hugo Speer, Deirdre Costello
'The particular magic of the film is the way in which it draws credible characters in a recognizable setting but elevates them and their story into crowd-pleasing fare without losing sight of the big social picture.' – *Derek Elley, Variety*
'The fault of the film is not that it deals in wishful thinking but that its style of wishful thinking – assertive, benignly narcissistic, dedicated to overcoming fear – is imported, a graft job. The people in the film would be much more likely to see success as a form of class betrayal and defeat than as a badge of solidarity.' – *Adam Mars-Jones, Independent*
† The film cost $3.5m and grossed $35m in the US, and another $132m elsewhere. It was, briefly, the biggest-grossing film at the British box-office, and is now second only to *Titanic*.
†† Two origins are given for the title phrase. 'Monty' was the nickname given to Field Marshal Montgomery. The Full Monty is either slang to describe the three-piece suits provided to soldiers on demobilization at the end of the Second World War, or to the Field Marshal's insistence on being served with a full English breakfast on the battlefield.
🎵 Anne Dudley
🅱 best film; Peter Cattaneo; Simon Beaufoy
🆃 best film; Robert Carlyle; Tom Wilkinson

Full Moon High
US   1981   94m   colour
Filmways/Larco (Larry Cohen)
After a visit to Romania, a high-school student turns into a werewolf and ceases to age.
Tame and trivial teen comedy.
wd Larry Cohen ph Daniel Pearl m Gary William Friedman ad Robert Burns ed Armond Lebowitz
☆ Adam Arkin, Roz Kelly, Ed McMahon, Joanne Nail, Elizabeth Hartman, Louis Nye, Kenneth Mars, Alan Arkin, Tom Aldredge, Pat Morita

Full Moon in Blue Water
US   1988   95m   Technicolor
Entertainment/Trans World Entertainment (Lawrence Turman, David Foster, John Turman)
▦ ◷

A Texan restaurateur foils plans by property developers to buy his diner.
Weak and sentimental comedy, resembling a TV sitcom.
w Bill Bozzone d Peter Masterson ph Fred Murphy m Phil Marshall ed Jill Savitt
☆ Gene Hackman, Teri Garr, Burgess Meredith, Elias Koteas, Kevin Cooney, David Doty, Gil Glasgow, Becky Gelke, Marietta Marich, Lexie Masterson
'A comedy as soft-centred as they come … just about insufferable' – *MFB*

Full Moon in Paris ★
France   1984   102m   colour
🎞 ▦
original title: *Les Nuits de la Pleine Lune*
Striving for independence, a girl divides her time between her boyfriend in the suburbs and a flat in Paris.

One of Rohmer's talkier Comedies and Proverbs, taking as its epigraph 'He who has two women loses his soul. He who has two houses loses his mind.'
w Eric Rohmer ph Renato Berta m Elli and Janco ed Cecile Decugis
☆ Pascale Ogier, Tcheky Karyo, Fabrice Luchini, Virginie Thevenet, Christian Vadim, Laszlo Szabo

Full of Life *
US   1956   91m   bw
Columbia (Fred Kohlmar)
A poor New York/Italian couple expect a baby.
Domestic comedy drama with good scenes but fatally uncertain mood.
w John Fante novel John Fante d Richard Quine ph Charles Lawton Jnr m George Duning
☆ Judy Holliday, Richard Conte, Esther Minciotti, Salvatore Baccaloni

Full Speed
France   1996   85m   colour
Dangerous to Know/Magouric/Téléma/France2/Rhône-Alpes (Laurent Bénégui)
original title: A Toute Vitesse
After his lover is killed in a racist attack, an Algerian falls for a novelist whose only interest is using the incident for his next book.
Slick but uninvolving account of treating others as objects.
w Gaël Morel, Catherine Corsini d Gaël Morel ph Jeanne Lapoirie m various ad Frédérique Hurpeau ed Catherine Schwartz
☆ élodie Bouchez, Pascal Cervo, Stéphane Rideau, Meziane Bardadi, Romain Auger, Salim Kechiouche, Mohammed Dib
'While beautiful to look at, its themes of prejudice and sexuality makes this film, overall, a bleak one.' – Terry Richards, Film Review

'A new experience in screen suspense!'
The Full Treatment
GB   1960   109m   bw   Megascope
Columbia/Hilary/Falcon (Val Guest)
US title: Stop Me Before I Kill
A racing driver crashes and subsequently tries to murder his wife; psychiatric help leads to further gruesome goings-on.
Variation on Les Diaboliques, with very little mystery and too much talk from boring characters.
w Val Guest, Ronald Scott Thorn novel Ronald Scott Thorn d Val Guest ph Gilbert Taylor m Stanley Black
☆ Ronald Lewis, Diane Cilento, Claude Dauphin, Françoise Rosay, Bernard Braden

The Fuller Brush Girl *
US   1950   85m   bw
Columbia (S. Sylvan Simon)
▤ ◎
GB title: Affairs of Sally
A cosmetics saleslady gets involved in murder.
Fairly amusing slapstick mystery with the star in good form.
w Frank Tashlin d Lloyd Bacon ph Charles Lawton m Heinz Roemheld
☆ Lucille Ball, Eddie Albert, Carl Benton Reid, Gale Robbins, Jeff Donnell, John Litel, Jerome Cowan, Lee Patrick

The Fuller Brush Man *
US   1948   93m   bw
Columbia (S. Sylvan Simon)
▤ ◎
GB title: That Mad Mr Jones
A door-to-door salesman gets involved in homicide.
Bright star comedy with slow patches.
w Frank Tashlin, Devery Freeman d S. Sylvan Simon ph Lesley White m Heinz Roemheld
☆ Red Skelton, Janet Blair, Don McGuire, Adele Jergens

Fun
US   1994   105m   DeLuxe/bw
Metro Tartan/Prerogative/Lighthouse/Neo Modern (Rafal Zielinski)
Two teenage girls become friends and enjoy themselves by killing an old lady.
A voyeuristic look at the lives of amoral youngsters, providing little in the way of insight and too keen to shock.
w James Bosley play James Bosley d Rafal Zielinski ph Jens Sturup m Marc Tschanz pd Vally Mestroni ed Monika Lightstone

☆ Alicia Witt, Renee Humphrey, William R. Moses, Leslie Hope, Ania Suli
'A queasy contribution to the current "bad seed" exploitation flicks.' – Alexander Walker, London Evening Standard

Fun and Fancy Free *
👥👥 US   1947   73m   Technicolor
Walt Disney (Ben Sharpsteen)
Cartoon stories told by and to Jiminy Cricket and Edgar Bergen.
Variable Disney ragbag including Bongo the Bear, and a lengthy version of Jack and the Beanstalk.
w various d various

Fun Down There
US   1988   88m   colour
Metro/Angelina/Stigliano
A young homosexual leaves home to enjoy life in New York.
Full of grainy, low-budget sincerity, but slight to the point of boredom.
w Roger Stigliano, Michael Waite d Roger Stigliano ph Peggy Ahwesh ed Roger Stigliano, Keith Sanbourn
☆ Michael Waite, Nickolas Nagurney, Martin Goldin, Jeanne Sobkowski, Gretschen Somerville, Elizabeth Waite, Harold Waite
'Low-budget Woody Allen without the angst and wit.' – MFB

Fun in Acapulco
US   1963   97m   Technicolor
Paramount/Hal B. Wallis
▤
A trapeze artist becomes a lifeguard and is pursued by a lady bullfighter.
Dim comedy musical.
w Allan Weiss d Richard Thorpe ph Daniel Fapp m Joseph J. Lilley
☆ Elvis Presley, Ursula Andress, Paul Lukas

Fun on a Weekend
US   1947   93m   bw
United Artists
A girl with self-confidence persuades a penniless man to pose as a millionaire.
Weakish comedy with good moments.
wd Andrew Stone
☆ Eddie Bracken, Priscilla Lane, Tom Conway, Allen Jenkins, Arthur Treacher, Clarence Kolb

Fun with Dick and Jane
US   1976   100m   Metrocolor
Columbia/Peter Bart, Max Pelevsky
When an aerospace executive is fired, in order to keep up with the Joneses he and his wife embark on a life of crime.
This being a 1970s satire, they actually get away with it, providing some, but not enough, fun on the way.
w David Giler, Jerry Belson, Mordecai Richler story Gerald Gaiser d Ted Kotcheff ph Fred J. Koenekamp m Ernest Gold
☆ George Segal, Jane Fonda, Ed McMahon, Dick Gautier, Alan Miller
'A nitwit mixture of counterculture politics, madcap comedy and toilet humour.' – New Yorker
† The sequence in which the heroine discusses the family predicament while sitting on a toilet was later deleted, reducing the running time by two minutes.

The Funeral: see Death Japanese Style

The Funeral
US   1996   100m   DuArt
Guild/October/MDP/C&P (Mary Kane)
▤ ▤
In New York in the 30s, the psychopathic brothers of a murdered gangster hunt his killer.
A brutal movie with pretensions, mixing windy philosophizing with sudden violence.
w Nicholas St John d Abel Ferrara ph Ken Kelsch m Joe Delia pd Charles M. Lagola ed Mayin Lo, Bill Pankow
☆ Christopher Walken, Chris Penn, Annabella Sciorra, Isabella Rossellini, Vincent Gallo, Benicio del Toro
'A dull, unimpressive experience.' – George Perry

Funeral in Berlin *
GB   1967   .102m   Technicolor
Paramount/Harry Saltzman (Charles Kasher)
▤ ◎
Harry Palmer is sent to Berlin to check a story that a Russian colonel wants to defect.
Initially intriguing, finally confusing, always depressing spy yarn in the sixties manner, i.e. with every character devious and no one a hero. Good production.
w Evan Jones novel Funeral in Berlin by Len Deighton d Guy Hamilton ph Otto Heller m Konrad Elfers pd Ken Adam
☆ Michael Caine, Oscar Homolka, Eva Renzi, Paul Hubschmid, Hugh Burden, Guy Doleman, Rachel Gurney
'So many twists that even Sherlock Holmes might have been baffled ... before long it becomes difficult to remember who is watching whom and why, or indeed whether anybody was watching anybody at any given moment.' – Tom Milne
† Second in the Harry Palmer series, of which the first was The Ipcress File and the third Billion Dollar Brain (both qv).

The Funhouse
US   1981   96m   Technicolor   Panavision
Universal/Mace Neufeld (Derek Power, Steven Bernhardt)
▤ ▤ ◎
aka: Carnival of Terror
Four teenagers decide to spend the night in the Haunted House of a travelling fair.
A violent, freak-show horror that tries for black humour but misses most of the time; it sticks to the usual equation: teenage sex equals gruesome death.
w Larry Block d Tobe Hooper m Andrew Laszlo m John Beal pd Morton Rabinowitz ed Jack Hofstra sp Rick Baker, Craig Reardon
☆ Elizabeth Berridge, Shawn Carson, Jeanne Austin, Jack McDermott, Cooper Huckabee, Largo Woodruff, David Carson, Sylvia Miles

The Funniest Man in the World *
👥👥 US   1967   102m   bw
Funnyman Inc
Moderately intelligent compilation of sequences from the films of Charlie Chaplin, including Making a Living, Kid Auto Races at Venice, Tillie's Punctured Romance, The Tramp, A Night Out, The Rink, The Immigrant and Easy Street. The later shorts and features, on which Chaplin himself claimed full copyright, are not included.
wd Vernon P. Becker

Funny about Love
US   1990   101m   colour
Paramount (John Avnet, Jordan Kerner)
▤ ▤
A cartoonist and his wife experience marital problems when they fail to have a child.
Misconceived and mawkish romantic comedy which fails to extract much humour from its treatment of infertility.
w Norman Steinberg, David Frankel story Bob Greene d Leonard Nimoy m Fred Murphy m Miles Goodman pd Stephen Storer ed Peter E. Berger
☆ Gene Wilder, Christine Lahti, Mary Stuart Masterson, Robert Prosky, Stephen Tobolowsky, Anne Jackson, Susan Ruttan

'Beware. Comic geniuses at work.'
Funny Bones *
GB   1995   126m   Technicolor
Buena Vista/Hollywood Pictures (Simon Fields, Peter Chelsom)
▤ ▤ ◎
A failing American comedian, son of a successful comic, goes to Blackpool, where he spent his childhood, to rediscover the truth about his father and the difference between his comedy and that of his English half-brother, a natural clown.
The adventuresomeness of the film and the refusal by its director to play safe are to be applauded, as is his investigation of the nature of comedy; unfortunately there is a problem: it simply isn't ever funny, not even when it is intended to be.
w Peter Chelsom, Peter Flannery d Peter Chelsom ph Eduardo Serra m John Altman pd Caroline Hanania ed Martin Walsh

☆ Oliver Platt, Lee Evans, Richard Griffiths, Oliver Reed, George Carl, Leslie Caron, Jerry Lewis
'A complex saga of vaudeville and schtick, pathos and absurdity. One can only quarrel with the density of the effort, which stuffs far too much story and sideshow into its modest frame.' – Leonard Klady, Variety
'A nostalgic homage to the art of slapstick, its nostalgia somehow feels closer to a disinterment, its homage more of an autopsy. It's comedy on the slab.' – Tom Shone, Sunday Times

A Funny Dirty Little War *
Argentina   1983   79m   Eastmancolor
ICA/Aries Cinematografica Argentina (Fernando Ayala, Luis Osvaldo)
Small town rebels defy the army as Perón is returned to power in 1974.
A brutal black farce of civilians succumbing to military terror, it won the special jury prize at the Berlin Film Festival in 1984.
w Roberto Cossa, Hector Olivera novel Osvaldo Soriano d Hector Olivera ph Leonardo Rodriguez m Oscar Cadoza Ocampo ed Eduaro Lopez
☆ Federico Luppi, Hector Bidonde, Victor Laplace, Rodolfo Ranni, Miguel Angel Sola, Julio de Grazia, Lautaro Murua

Funny Face: see Bright Lights (1935)

Funny Face **
US   1956   103m   Technicolor   Vistavision
Paramount (Roger Edens)
▤ ▤ ◎
A fashion editor and photographer choose a shy bookstore attendant as their 'quality woman'.
Stylish, wistful musical with good numbers but drawn-out dialogue; finally a shade too sophisticated and a whole lot too fey.
w Leonard Gershe d Stanley Donen ph Ray June m/ly George and Ira Gershwin ad Hal Pereira, George W. Davis art consultant Richard Avedon
☆ Fred Astaire, Audrey Hepburn, Kay Thompson, Michel Auclair, Robert Flemyng
& Leonard Gershe; Ray June; art direction

Funny Farm
US   1988   101m   colour
Warner/Cornelius-Pan Arts (Robert L. Crawford)
▤ ▤ ◎
A New York sports writer moves to live in the country, and regrets it.
Leisurely comedy, in which old jokes are recycled slowly.
w Jeffrey Boam book Jay Cronley d George Roy Hill ph Miroslav Ondricek m Elmer Bernstein pd Henry Bumstead ed Alan Heim
☆ Chevy Chase, Madolyn Smith, Joseph Maher, Jack Gilpin, Brad Sullivan, Macintyre Dixon, Audrie Neenan, Kevin O'Morrison, Caris Corfman

Funny Games **
Germany   1997   108m   colour
Metro Tartan/Wega (Veit Heiduschka)
▤
A wealthy family in their holiday home are terrorized by two strangers.
A disturbing film, intended as a polemic against film-makers and audiences who enjoy gratuitous violence; the violence here is presented in a way to make it seem painful rather than thrilling.
wd Michael Haneke ph Jurgen Jurges pd Christoph Kanter ed Andreas Prochaska
☆ Susanne Lothar, Ulrich Muhe, Frank Giering, Arno Frisch, Stefan Clapczynski
'Why would anyone stay when the film so explicitly challenges them to leave?' – Mark Kermode, Sight and Sound

Funny Girl **
US   1968   169m   Technicolor   Panavision 70
Columbia/Rastar (Ray Stark)
▤ ▤ ◎
Fanny Brice, an ugly Jewish girl from New York's east side, becomes a big Broadway star but loses her husband in the process.
Interminable cliché-ridden musical drama relieved by a few good numbers, high production gloss and the unveiling of a new powerhouse star.
w Isobel Lennart play Isobel Lennart d William Wyler ph Harry Stradling m/ly Jule Styne, Bob Merrill md Walter Scharf pd Gene Callahan

☆ *Barbra Streisand*, Omar Sharif, Walter Pidgeon, Kay Medford, Anne Francis, Lee Allen, Gerald Mohr, Frank Faylen

🎭 Barbra Streisand

🏆 best picture; Harry Stradling; Walter Scharf; Kay Medford; title song

Funny Lady *
US 1975 138m Eastmancolor Panavision
Columbia/Rastar/Persky-Bright/Vista (Ray Stark)
📼 ⊙ꟲ

Fanny Brice marries Billy Rose.
Unnecessary sequel to the above, entirely predictable and far from the truth, but with the occasional pleasures that a high budget brings.
w Jay Presson Allen, Arnold Schulman d Herbert Ross ph James Wong Howe m/ly various md Peter Matz pd George Jenkins
☆ Barbra Streisand, James Caan, *Ben Vereen*, Omar Sharif, Roddy McDowall, Larry Gates
'The plot line is as slackly handled as the milieu.' – *Geoff Brown*
'As Fanny Brice, Streisand is no longer human; she's like a bitchy female impersonator imitating Barbra Streisand.' – *New Yorker*
🏆 James Wong Howe; Peter Matz; song 'How Lucky Can You Get' (*m/ly* Fred Ebb, John Kander)

Funny Man
GB 1994 93m Technicolor
Feature/Nomad (Nigel Odell)
📼 ⊙ꟲ

A record producer and his friends are killed one by one when they visit the stately home he won in a poker game.
Gruesome, low-budget, jokey horror that features a killer who resembles Punch but which has an incoherent narrative that lacks impact.
wd Simon Sprackling ph Tom Ingle Jnr m Parsons/Haines pd David Endley ed Ryan L. Driscoll sp Neill Gorton, Jim Francis
☆ Tim James, Christopher Lee, Benny Young, Pauline Chan, Ingrid Lacey, Matthew Devitt, Chris Walker
'Isn't half as funny as it thinks it is, but has enough chuckles to draw the six-pack and frozen-dinner contingent.' – *Derek Elley, Variety*

A Funny Thing Happened on the Way to the Forum **
👨‍👩‍👧 GB 1966 99m DeLuxe
UA/Quadrangle (Melvin Frank)
📼 ꟲ ⊙ꟲ

In ancient Rome, a conniving slave schemes to win his freedom.
Bawdy farce from a Broadway musical inspired by Plautus but with a New York Jewish atmosphere. The film pays scant attention to the comic numbers that made the show a hit, but adds some style of its own, including a free-for-all slapstick climax.
w Melvin Frank, Michael Pertwee musical comedy Burt Shevelove, Larry Gelbart d Richard Lester ph Nicolas Roeg m/ly Stephen Sondheim md Ken Thorne pd Tony Walton titles Richard Williams
☆ Zero Mostel, Phil Silvers, Michael Crawford, Jack Gilford, Michael Hordern, Buster Keaton, Patricia Jessel, Leon Greene, Beatrix Lehmann
'Actors have to be very fast and very sly to make themselves felt amid the flash and glitter of a characteristic piece of Lester film-mosaic.' – *John Russell Taylor*
'He proceeds by fits and starts and leaves jokes suspended in mid-air … like coitus interruptus going on forever.' – *Pauline Kael*
🎭 Ken Thorne

Funnyman
US 1967 100m bw/colour
Korty Films (Hugh McGraw, Stephen Schmidt)
A satirical comedian seeks some better occupation in life, but finally agrees he's best as a comic.

One suspects Korty has seen Sullivan's Travels several times; but even though his film tries hard, it finally provides more yawns than appreciative chuckles.
w John Korty, Peter Bonerz d John Korty ph John Korty m Peter Schickele
☆ Peter Bonerz, Sandra Archer, Carol Androsky, Gerald Hiken
'It has its dull patches, but it made me laugh louder and more often than any other film this year.' – *Michael Billington, Illustrated London News*

The Furies *
US 1950 109m bw
Paramount/Hal B. Wallis
A cattle baron feuds with his tempestuous daughter.
Interesting but heavy-going Western, more solemn than stimulating despite its Freudian excesses.
w Charles Schnee novel Niven Busch
d Anthony Mann ph Victor Milner m Franz Waxman
☆ Barbara Stanwyck, *Walter Huston*, Wendell Corey, Judith Anderson, Gilbert Roland, Thomas Gomez, Beulah Bondi, Wallace Ford, Albert Dekker, Blanche Yurka
'An immoral saga, capably mounted, with some pretentious psychological trimmings.' – *MFB*
🎭 Victor Milner

The Further Adventures of Tennessee Buck
US 1988 90m colour
Sarlui/Diamant/Sri Lanka Film Location Services (Gideon Amir)
📼 ꟲ ⊙ꟲ

A big white hunter in Borneo leads a rich couple into cannibal country.
Charmless action adventure with a leering emphasis on the female body.
w Barry Jacobs, Stuart Jacobs, Paul Mason d David Keith ph Avraham Karpick m John Debney pd Errol Kelly ed Anthony Redman
☆ David Keith, Kathy Shower, Brant Van Hoffmann, Sydney Lassick

A Further Gesture
GB/German/Ireland/Japan 1997 101m
Metrocolor
Film Four/Channel 4/NDF/Pony Canyon/Zephyr/Samson/Road Movies (Chris Curling)
📼

An IRA prisoner escapes to America, falls in love, and agrees to assassinate the dictator who killed his girlfriend's father.
Melancholy tale of a violent man who cannot escape his past; it offers little that is new or interesting.
w Ronan Bennett idea Stephen Rea d Robert Dornhelm ph Andrzej Sekula m John Keane pd Kalina Ivanov, Tom McCullagh ed Masahiro Hirakubo
☆ Stephen Rea, Rosana Pastor, Alfred Molina, Brendan Gleeson, Jorge Sanz, Pruitt Taylor Vince, Maria Doyle Kennedy
'Mostly fires from only one barrel.' – *Variety*

The Further Perils of Laurel and Hardy ***
👨‍👩‍👧 US 1967 99m bw
TCF/Robert Youngson
📼

A compilation of longish extracts from the stars' silent comedies, including *Early to Bed, The Second Hundred Years, Should Married Men Go Home, You're Darn Tootin', Habeas Corpus, That's My Wife*, and *Leave 'Em Laughing*. The producer is to be congratulated on refurbishing so many deteriorating negatives, though the commentary leaves much to be desired.
m John Parker w/ed Robert Youngson
☆ Stan Laurel, Oliver Hardy

Fury ***
US 1936 94m bw
MGM (Joseph L. Mankiewicz)
📼

A traveller in a small town is mistaken for a murderer and apparently lynched; he escapes in a fire but determines to have his persecutors hanged for his murder.
Powerful drama which becomes artificial in its latter stages but remains its director's best American film.
w Bartlett Cormack, Fritz Lang story Norman Krasna d Fritz Lang ph Joseph Ruttenberg m Franz Waxman
☆ Spencer Tracy, Sylvia Sidney, Bruce Cabot, Walter Abel, Edward Ellis, Walter Brennan, Frank Albertson
'The surface of American life has been rubbed away: Fury gets down to the bones of the thing and shows them for what they are.' – *C. A. Lejeune*
'Since the screen began to talk, no other serious film except *The Front Page* has so clearly shown that here is a new art and what this new art can do.' – *John Marks*
'Everyday events and people suddenly took on tremendous and horrifying proportion; even the most insignificant details had a pointed meaning.' – *Lewis Jacobs*
'For half its length a powerful and documented piece of fiction about a lynching, and for the remaining half a desperate attempt to make love, lynching and the Hays Office come out even.' – *Otis Ferguson*
'Astonishing, the only film I know to which I have wanted to attach the epithet of *great*.' – *Graham Greene*
🎭 Norman Krasna

The Fury *
US 1978 117m DeLuxe
TCF/Frank Yablans (Ron Preissman)
📼 ⊙ꟲ 🎧

The head of a government institute for psychic research finds that his own son is wanted by terrorists who wish to use his lethal psychic powers.
Flashy, kaleidoscopic nonsense which never even begins to make sense but is used as the basis for the director's showing-off, which is occasionally worth a glance for those with hardened stomachs.
w John Farris novel John Farris d Brian de Palma ph Richard H. Kline m John Williams
☆ Kirk Douglas, John Cassavetes, Carrie Snodgress, Charles Durning, Andrew Stevens, Amy Irving, Fiona Lewis
'A conception of cinema that is closer to Ken Russell than Alfred Hitchcock.' – *Richard Combs, MFB*

Fury at Furnace Creek *
US 1948 88m bw
TCF
A Westerner clears the name of his father, a general accused of diverting a wagon train into hostile Indian territory.
Adequate old-fashioned Western with a good story line and standard excitements.
w Charles G. Booth d H. Bruce Humberstone ph Harry Jackson m David Raksin md Alfred Newman
☆ Victor Mature, Coleen Gray, Glenn Langan, Reginald Gardiner

Fury at Smugglers' Bay
GB 1960 96m Eastmancolor Panascope
Regal/Mijo (Michael Green, Joe Vegoda)
The squire of a Cornish village is being blackmailed by the vicious leader of a gang of wreckers.
Watchable, then forgettable variation on Jamaica Inn.
wd John Gilling ph Harry Waxman m Harold Geller

☆ Peter Cushing, John Fraser, Bernard Lee, William Franklyn, June Thorburn, Miles Malleson, Michele Mercier, George Coulouris

Fuss over Feathers: see *Conflict of Wings*

Futtock's End *
GB 1969 49m Eastmancolor
Paradine/Gannet/British Lion
Adventures of a weekend in an English country mansion.
A collection of visual gags, rather thinly spread, with dialogue replaced by squeaks and mumblings. Like all Barker's subsequent comedies on similar lines (The Picnic, By the Sea, etc) one chuckles in constant anticipation of guffaws which never come.
w Ronnie Barker d Bob Kellett
☆ Ronnie Barker, Michael Hordern, Roger Livesey, Julian Orchard, Kika Markham, Mary Merrall, Richard O'Sullivan

Future Cop: see *Trancers*

The Future of Emily
France/West Germany 1984 116m colour
Mainline/Les Films du Losange/Helma Sanders/Literarisches Colloquium/ZDF/BMI/FFA/Berliner Film (Nicole Flipo, Ursula Ludwig)
original title: *L'Avenir D'Emilie*
Mother and daughter (a film star) discuss their attitudes to life.
Conversation piece of limited interest.
wd Helma Sanders-Brahms ph Sacha Vierney m Jürgen Knieper ad Jean-Michel Hugon, Rainer Schaper ed Ursula West
☆ Brigitte Fossey, Hildegarde Knef, Ivan Desny, Herman Treusch, Camille Raymond, Mathieu Carrière

Futureworld *
US 1976 107m Metrocolor
AIP (James T. Aubrey Jnr, Paul Lazarus III)
📼

The robot factory seen in *Westworld* (qv) now aims at world domination by duplicating influential figures.
Amusing and fairly suspenseful fantasy with a bigger budget than its predecessor.
w Mayo Simon, George Schenck d Richard T. Heffron ph Howard Schwartz, Gene Polito m Fred Karlin
☆ Peter Fonda, Blythe Danner, Arthur Hill, Yul Brynner, John Ryan, Stuart Margolin, Jim Antonio

Fuzi Qing: see *Father and Son*

Fuzz *
US 1972 93m DeLuxe
UA/Filmways/Javelin (Jack Farren)
📼

Detectives of Boston's 87th precinct try to catch a rapist.
A black farce devoted to police incompetence, though taken from a straight 'Ed McBain' story. Brisk and sometimes funny.
w Evan Hunter ('Ed McBain') d Richard A. Colla ph Jacques Marquette m Dave Grusin
☆ Burt Reynolds, Raquel Welch, Jack Weston, Yul Brynner, Tom Skerritt, James McEachin

The Fuzzy Pink Nightgown
US 1957 88m bw
UA/Russ-Field (Robert Waterfield)
A glamorous film star falls in love with her kidnapper.
Unendurable cheap romantic farce.
w Richard Alan Simmons novel Sylvia Tate d Norman Taurog ph Joseph LaShelle m Billy May
☆ Jane Russell, Ralph Meeker, Keenan Wynn, Fred Clark, Adolphe Menjou, Una Merkel

---

'Failure Is Not an Option.'
G.I. Jane
US 1997 124m Technicolor Panavision
Buena Vista/Hollywood/Scott Free/Largo (Roger Birnbaum, Demi Moore, Suzanne Todd)
In the face of much male hostility, a female intelligence officer attempts to become the first woman to join the élite Navy SEALS, which involves a gruelling training programme.
Noisy, incoherent and thuggish movie that finds something redemptive in pain and violence.
w David Twohy, Danielle Alexandra d Ridley Scott ph Hugh Johnson m Trevor Jones pd Arthur Max ed Pietro Scalia
☆ Demi Moore, Viggo Mortensen, Anne Bancroft, Jason Beghe, Scott Wilson, Lucinda Jenney, Morris Chestnut, Daniel von Bargen
'A very entertaining get-tough fantasy with political and feminist underpinnings.' – *Todd McCarthy, Variety*
'It indulges the drive for physical perfection that Moore has so consistently mistaken for screen acting.' – *Tom Shone, Sunday Times*

G Man's Wife: see *Public Enemy's Wife*

'Time starts here...'
'G' Men ***
US 1935 85m bw
Warner (Lou Edelman)
A young lawyer becomes a G-man to avenge the murder of his best friend, and finds himself tracking down another old friend who is a gangster.
In the face of mounting criticism of their melodramas making heroes of gangsters, Warner pulled a clever switch by showing the same crimes from a different angle, that of the law enforcer. As an action show it became pretty good after a slow start.
w Seton I. Miller d William Keighley ph Sol Polito md Leo F. Forbstein
☆ James Cagney, Ann Dvorak, Margaret Lindsay, Robert Armstrong, Barton MacLane, Lloyd Nolan, William Harrigan
'Cagney joins the government and cleans up the gangsters. Just loads of action, knocked off in bing-bang manner. Strong b.o.' – *Variety*
'The gangster is back, racing madly through one of the fastest melodramas ever made.' – *New York Sun*
'The headiest dose of gunplay that Hollywood has unleashed in recent months.' – *André Sennwald, New York Times*
'It is not violence alone which is in the air; there is also a skilfully contrived and well-maintained suspense, and throughout a feeling of respect for the men who are paid to die in the execution of necessary work.' – *The Times*
'A swell show: the construction is swift and staccato.' – *New York World Telegraph*
'Not for the kiddies, but see it if your nerves are good.' – *Photoplay*

'Time starts here...'
G:MT Greenwich Mean Time
GB 1998 118m DeLuxe
Icon/Anvil/GMT (Taylor Hackford)
Three members of a London rock group fall out over the type of music they should play.
Slick and confused account of would-be musicians becoming involved with drugs and gangsters as they try to hold on to their integrity, a quality nowhere evident in the movie itself.
w Simon Mirren d John Strickland ph Alan Almond m Guy Sigsworth pd Luana Hanson ed Patrick Moore
☆ Alec Newman, Melanie Gutteridge, Georgia MacKenzie, Chiwetel Ejiofor, Steve John Shepherd, Alicya Eyo, Benjamin Waters, Anjela Lauren Smith
'This must be the worst coming-of-age/life-in-a-band yoof film ever made, with a rare and ruthless power to irritate and embarrass.' – *Cosmo Landesman, Sunday Times*

Gabbeh **
Iran 1995 74m colour
MK2/Sanayeh Dasti (Khalil Daroudchi, Khalil Mahmoudi)
A young woman tells the story of her frustrated love for a mysterious horseman, and her father's reluctance to let her marry, to an elderly woman, whom she resembles, and her querulous husband.
Set among a nomadic tribe of carpet weavers, this fable mixes magic realism with a documentary approach; its power derives from its ambiguous narrative, which may be a ghost story and from the exotic beauty of its images, especially of figures dwarfed by the landscapes through which they move.
wd Mohsen Makhmalbaf ph Mahmoud Kalari m Houssein Alizadeh
☆ Abbas Sayah, Shaghayegh Djodat, Hossein Moharami, Rogheih Moharami, Parvaneh Ghalandari, Hassen Kermi, Zineb Kermi

'They had more than love ... they had fame!'
Gable and Lombard
US 1976 131m Technicolor
Universal (Harry Korshak)
After Carole Lombard's death in a 1942 air crash, Clark Gable recalls their years together.
Vulgar and inaccurate representation of two Hollywood stars of the thirties; it fails even as titillation.
w Barry Sandler d Sidney J. Furie ph Jordan S. Cronenweth m Michel Legrand pd Edward Carfagno ed Argyle Nelson
☆ James Brolin, Jill Clayburgh, Allen Garfield, Red Buttons, Joanne Linville
'A limply raunchy, meaningless movie with nothing to say about the movies, about love, or about stardom.' – *New Yorker*
'An uneven combination of smut and sentimentality.' – *Les Keyser, Hollywood in the Seventies*

'It comes like a marching army to thrill the nation!'
'The picture that will make 1933 famous!'
Gabriel over the White House *
US 1933 87m bw
MGM/Walter Wanger
A crook becomes president and mysteriously reforms.
Pleasing, dated New Deal fantasy.
w Carey Wilson, Bertram Bloch novel *Rinehard* by T. F. Tweed d Gregory La Cava ph Bert Glennon m William Axt
☆ Walter Huston, Karen Morley, Franchot Tone, C. Henry Gordon, Samuel S. Hinds, Jean Parker, Dickie Moore
'Flag-waving flapdoodle, shrewdly dished up for the man in the street and his best girl. Beautifully produced, cannily hoked, and looks like money all round.' – *Variety*

Gabriela
Brazil 1983 99m colour
Sultana
In a coastal town in 1925, the sensual Gabriela marries a bar owner but becomes involved again with her old gangster cronies.
Ethnic melodrama of familiar type, a spin-off from an immensely popular Brazilian TV series.
w Leopoldo Serran, Bruno Barreto novel *Jorge Amada* d Bruno Barreto
☆ Sonia Braga, Marcello Mastroianni, Antonio Cantafora

Gaby
US 1956 97m Eastmancolor Cinemascope
MGM (Edwin H. Knopf)
Flabby remake of *Waterloo Bridge* (qv); saccharine, fussy and outmoded, despite updated settings and a happy ending.
w Albert Hackett, Frances Goodrich, Charles Lederer d Curtis Bernhardt ph Robert Planck m Conrad Salinger
☆ Leslie Caron, John Kerr, Cedric Hardwicke, Taina Elg, Margalo Gillmore

Gaby – A True Story *
US 1987 114m colour
Columbia TriStar (Pinchas Perry)
A Mexican girl suffering from cerebral palsy struggles to overcome her disabilities.
Well-acted and touching.
w Martin Salinas, Michael James Love d Luis Mandoki ph Lajos Koltai m Maurice Jarre ad Alejandro Luna ed Garth Craven
☆ Liv Ullmann, Norma Aleandro, Robert Loggia, Rachel Levin, Lawrence Monoson, Robert Beltran, Beatriz Sheridan, Tony Goldwyn
♀ Norma Aleandro

Gadael Lenin: see *Leaving Lenin*

Gaiety George
GB 1946 98m bw
Embassy (George King)
US title: *Showtime*
The career in the London theatre of Irish impresario George Howard in the early part of the century.
Tepid musical biopic.
w Katherine Strueby d George King ph Otto Heller md Jack Beaver
☆ Richard Greene, Ann Todd, Peter Graves, Hazel Court, Leni Lynn, Ursula Jeans, Morland Graham, Frank Pettingell

Gaiety Girls: see *Paradise for Two*

Gaily, Gaily **
US 1969 117m DeLuxe
UA/Mirisch/Cartier (Norman Jewison)
GB title: *Chicago, Chicago*
The early life on a Chicago newspaper of Ben Hecht.
Busy, farcical, melodramatic, always interesting biopic of the formative years of a celebrated literary figure.
w Abram S. Ginnes book *Ben Hecht* d Norman Jewison ph Richard Kline m Henry Mancini pd Robert Boyle
☆ Beau Bridges, Melina Mercouri, Brian Keith, George Kennedy, Hume Cronyn, Margot Kidder, Wilfrid Hyde-White, Melodie Johnson, John Randolph

The Gal Who Took the West
US 1949 84m Technicolor
Universal-International
In 1890, an opera singer travels west and is the object of romantic rivalry.
Lame attempt to equal the splendid idiocy of Salome Where She Danced.
w William Bowers, Oscar Brodney d Frederick de Cordova ph William H. Daniels m Frank Skinner
☆ Yvonne de Carlo, Charles Coburn, Scott Brady, John Russell, James Millican

'The Show Was Cancelled..But The Adventure Has Only Begun.'
Galaxy Quest *
US 1999 104m Technicolor Panavision
DreamWorks (Mark Johnson, Charles Newirth)
The fading stars of a cult TV science-fiction series are approached by gullible aliens who need help in defeating an extraterrestrial terrorist.
Enjoyable comedy at the expense of space operas such as Star Trek and the trivia-obsessed fans of the genre.
w David Howard, Robert Gordon d Dean Parisot ph Jerzy Zielinski m David Newman pd Linda DeScenna ed Don Zimmerman sp make and creature fx: Stan Winston cos Albert Wolsky
☆ Tim Allen, Sigourney Weaver, Alan Rickman, Tony Shalhoub, Sam Rockwell, Daryl Mitchell, Enrico Colantoni, Robin Sachs, Patrick Breen, Missi Pyle
'A mischievously clever and slickly commercial sci-fi comedy with strong cross-generational appeal.' – *Joe Leydon, Variety*

Galileo *
GB 1974 145m Eastmancolor
Ely Landau/Cinevision
In the 17th century, a poor Italian mathematics teacher has trouble establishing his 'heretical' astronomical theories.
Overlong play-on-celluloid for the American Film Theatre: very decently made and acted, it lacks inspiration.
w Barbara Bray, Joseph Losey play Bertolt Brecht d Joseph Losey ph Michael Reed m Hanns Eisler
☆ Topol, Edward Fox, Michel Lonsdale, Richard O'Callaghan, Tom Conti, Judy Parfitt, Patrick Magee, Michael Gough, John Gielgud, Colin Blakely, Margaret Leighton, Clive Revill
'The whole feeling is something like a modestly produced star touring-show. Without the star.' – *Stanley Kauffmann*

Gallant Bess
US 1946 99m Cinecolor
MGM
A soldier's horse saves his life and becomes his peacetime friend.
Boy-and-horse story with a wartime setting; good for small towns.
w Jeanne Bartlett d Andrew Marton
☆ Marshall Thompson, George Tobias, Clem Bevans, Donald Curtis

The Gallant Blade
US 1948 81m Cinecolor
Columbia
In France in 1648, a dashing young lieutenant rescues his general from the plot of a would-be revolutionary.
Pinchpenny swashbuckler which maintains a commendable verve.
w Walter Ferris, Morton Grant d Henry Levin
☆ Larry Parks, Marguerite Chapman, Victor Jory, George Macready

The Gallant Hours *
US 1959 115m bw
UA/James Cagney/Robert Montgomery
Episodes in the career of Admiral William F. Halsey.
Adulatory but physically restrained biopic which covers World War II with barely a scene outside control room sets: interesting but finally too talky.
w Beirne Lay Jnr, Frank D. Gilroy d Robert Montgomery ph Joe MacDonald m Roger Wagner
☆ James Cagney, Dennis Weaver, Richard Jaeckel, Ward Costello, Carl Benton Reid
'Imaginatively conceived but erroneously realized.' – *Robert Vas*

◎ Digital Video Disc Region 2　　◎ Digital Video Disc Region 1　　⌒ Soundtrack released on compact disc　　☆ Cast in approximate order of importance　　† Points of interest　　♪ Notable songs　　♟ Academy Award　　♟ Academy Award nomination　　℗ BAFTA

Gallant Journey

US 1946 86m bw
Columbia (William A. Wellman)

The life of an early American aviation pioneer.

Curious biopic, very tentatively done, about an inventor so obscure as to be virtually fictitious. Sentimental, artificial, but harmless.

w Byron Morgan, William A. Wellman
d William A. Wellman ph Burnett Guffey
m Marlin Skiles

☆ Glenn Ford, Janet Blair, Charles Ruggles, Henry Travers, Arthur Shields

Gallant Lady

US 1933 84m bw
UA/Twentieth Century (Darryl F. Zanuck)

A woman allows her illegitimate son to be adopted, but years later marries his stepfather.

A tearjerker very typical of its time, moderately well assembled; later remade as Always Goodbye (qv).

w Sam Mintz story Gilbert Emery, Doug Doty
d Gregory La Cava ph Peverell Marley m Alfred Newman

☆ Ann Harding, Clive Brook, Otto Kruger, Tullio Carminati, Dickie Moore, Janet Beecher

The Gallant Legion

US 1948 86m bw
Republic

The Texas Rangers are formed but have to prove themselves.

Acceptable second-string Western with plenty of action and a strong cast.

w Gerald Drayson Adams d Joseph Kane ph Jack Marta

☆ William Elliott, Adrian Booth, Joseph Schildkraut, Bruce Cabot, Andy Devine, Jack Holt, Grant Withers, Adele Mara

Gallant Sons

US 1940 71m bw
MGM

Schoolboys club together to get the father of one of them off a murder charge.

Unlikely and undemanding but pleasant filler.

w William R. Lipman, Marion Parsonnet
d George B. Seitz

☆ Jackie Cooper, Bonita Granville, Gene Reynolds, Gail Patrick, Ian Hunter, June Preisser, Leo Gorcey, William Tracy, El Brendel

'From a place you may never have heard of, a story you'll never forget!'

Gallipoli *

Australia 1981 111m Eastmancolor
Panavision
Associated R and R (Martin Cooper, Ben Gannon)

In 1915, two friends trek from Perth across the desert to join up, and one dies in the Dardanelles.

Consistently interesting aspects of the 1914–18 war, but rather broken-backed as a story.

w David Williamson d Peter Weir ph Russell Boyd md Brian May

☆ Mark Lee, Mel Gibson, Bill Hunter, Robert Grubb, Tim McKenzie, Bill Kerr

'Like so many of Weir's films it promises more than it delivers.' – Time Out, 1984

Gallivant **

GB 1996 104m colour
Electric/Tall Stories/BFI/Channel 4 (Ben Woolford)

A director travels around the coast of Britain in a camper van with his 85-year-old grandmother and seven-year-old daughter, who suffers from Joubert's Syndrome, a condition that restricts her ability to speak.

Quirky documentary on a 10-week tour of Britain, including interviews with a variety of everyday eccentrics met on the way; but the concentration is on the relationship between the generations of a family, particularly between the busily signalling young girl and her great-grandmother.

wd Andrew Kötting ph N. G. Smith m David Burnand ed Cliff West

☆ Gladys Morris, Eden Kötting

'That rare thing, a celebratory film that never turns sugary or mawkish.' – Philip Kemp, Sight and Sound

The Galloping Major *

GB 1951 82m bw
British Lion/Romulus (Monja Danischewsky)

A group of suburbanites form a syndicate to buy a racehorse.

Rather contrived and imitative sub-Ealing comedy which fails to generate much steam.

w Monja Danischewsky, Henry Cornelius
d Henry Cornelius ph Stan Pavey m Georges Auric

☆ Basil Radford, Janette Scott, Hugh Griffith, Jimmy Hanley, René Ray, Joyce Grenfell, Sydney Tafler, Charles Victor, A. E. Matthews

Gambit **

US 1966 109m Techniscope
Universal (Leo L. Fuchs)

A Cockney thief conspires with a Eurasian girl to rob a multi-millionaire of a prize statue.

An enjoyably light pattern of cross and double cross is well sustained to the end.

w Jack Davies, Alvin Sargent story Sidney Carroll
d Ronald Neame ph Clifford Stine m Maurice Jarre

☆ Michael Caine, Shirley MacLaine, Herbert Lom, John Abbott, Roger C. Carmel, Arnold Moss

'He's been bruised, blackmailed, sliced and slammed. But nothing can stop him from going after the big money!'

The Gambler *

US 1975 111m Eastmancolor
Paramount (Irwin Winkler, Robert Chartoff)

A compulsive gambler has a will to lose.

Flashily made but basically uninteresting sub-Freudian study, vaguely based on Dostoievsky.

w James Toback d Karel Reisz ph Victor J. Kemper m Mahler md Jerry Fielding

☆ James Caan, Paul Sorvino, Lauren Hutton, Morris Carnovsky, Jacqueline Brookes, Burt Young

'The script is pretentious and empty. Reisz's quality, apparent in his early films and writings, seems to have atrophied with disuse and tension.' – Stanley Kauffmann

'In The Grip Of Obsession, Reason Is Suspended.'

The Gambler

GB/Netherlands/Hungary 1997 97m colour
Film Four/Channel 4/Image/Hungry Eye/KRO (Charles Cohen, Marc Vlessing)

As an ageing Dostoyevsky struggles to complete a novel before his deadline, his young stenographer becomes fascinated by him and the story he tells, of a man who gambles to save those he loves.

A complex tale that intertwines life and art but illuminates neither.

w Katharine Ogden, Charles Cohen, Nick Dear
d Karoly Makk ph Jules van den Steenhoven
m Brian Lock, Gerard Schurmann pd Ben van Os
ed Kevin Whelan

☆ Michael Gambon, Jodhi May, Polly Walker, Dominic West, Luise Rainer, John Wood, Johan Leysen, Angeline Ball, Tom Jansen

'To put it bluntly, the gloomy Russian scribe isn't the sexiest subject for a frock movie.' – Derek Elley, Variety

The Gambler and the Lady

GB 1952 74m bw
Exclusive/Hammer (Anthony Hinds)

A tough American gambler and club-owner in London is ruined by his attempt to move in aristocratic circles.

Enjoyable if routine thriller with its contrast between a streetwise American losing his way among the upper-class English.

w uncredited d Patrick Jenkins ph Walter Harvey m Ivor Slaney ad J. Elder Wills
ed Maurice Rootes

☆ Dane Clark, Kathleen Byron, Naomi Chance, Meredith Edwards, Anthony Forwood, Eric Pohlmann, Julian Somers, Thomas Gallagher, Max Bacon, Mona Washbourne

Gambler from Natchez

US 1954 88m Technicolor
TCF (Leonard Goldstein)

A professional gambler returns to New Orleans to avenge his father's murder, and disposes of his enemies one by one.

Mildly watchable semi-Western with a plot borrowed from The Count of Monte Cristo.

w Gerald Drayson Adams, Irving Wallace
d Henry Levin ph Lloyd Ahern md Lionel Newman

☆ Dale Robertson, Debra Paget, Thomas Gomez, Kevin McCarthy

Gambling *

US 1934 82m bw
Fox/Harold B. Franklin

A professional gambler ferrets out the killer of his ward.

Transcript of a George M. Cohan play, with the star in good form; but the presentation is uncinematic and tedious.

w Garrett Graham play George M. Cohan
d Rowland V. Lee

☆ George M. Cohan, Wynne Gibson, Dorothy Burgess, Theodore Newton

'It moves too slowly towards an intelligent but almost wholly mental climax.' – Variety

Gambling Lady *

US 1934 66m bw
Warner (Henry Blanke)

The daughter of a gambling suicide follows in father's footsteps and becomes involved in murder.

Fast-paced melodrama with a happy ending: smart entertainment of its time.

w Ralph Block, Doris Malloy d Archie Mayo
ph George Barnes

☆ Barbara Stanwyck, Joel McCrea, Pat O'Brien, Claire Dodd, C. Aubrey Smith, Robert Barrat, Philip Reed

Gambling on the High Seas

US 1940 56m bw
Warner

A reporter proves that a gambling ship owner is a murderer.

Unsurprising filler.

w Robert E. Kent d George Amy

☆ Wayne Morris, Jane Wyman, Gilbert Roland, William Pawley, John Litel

Gambling Ship

US 1933 70m bw
Paramount

A big shot gambler annoys rivals by opening a gambling ship off Long Beach.

Any freshness this once had wore off long ago.

w Max Marcin, Seton I. Miller d Max Marcin
☆ Cary Grant, Benita Hume, Roscoe Karns, Glenda Farrell, Jack La Rue

'A fair flicker ... but in toto it's a familiar formula of mob vs mob.' – Variety

'Are You Ready To Play?'

The Game ***

US 1997 128m Technicolor Panavision
Polygram/Propaganda (Steve Golin, Cean Chaffin)

A middle-aged workaholic millionaire is, for his birthday, given a gift that casts him as a participant in a mysterious game that turns his life upside down.

A high-energy paranoid thriller that plunges its protagonist, and the audience, into a world where nothing is to be trusted; the result is some dazzling sleight-of-hand.

w John Brancato, Michael Ferris d David Fincher
ph Harris Savides m Howard Shore pd Jeffrey Beecroft ed James Haygood

☆ Michael Douglas, Sean Penn, Deborah Kara Unger, James Rebhorn, Peter Donat, Carroll Baker, Anna Katarina, Armin Mueller-Stahl

'A high-toned mind-game of a movie.' – Variety

A Game for Vultures

GB 1979 106m colour
Columbia

In Rhodesia, a sanctions-buster comes to understand a black freedom fighter.

After a lot of violence and attitudinizing, that is, in this unattractively pretentious piece of bloodthirsty hokum.

w Phillip Baird novel Michael Hartmann
d James Fargo

☆ Richard Harris, Richard Roundtree, Ray Milland, Joan Collins, Sven Bertil Taube, Denholm Elliott

A Game of Death

US 1945 72m bw
RKO

Cheap remake of The Most Dangerous Game (qv); excitement dissipated by poor handling.

w Norman Houston d Robert Wise ph J. Roy Hunt m Paul Sawtell

☆ John Loder, Audrey Long, Edgar Barrier, Russell Wade, Russell Hicks

Games *

US 1967 100m Techniscope
Universal (George Edwards)

A sophisticated New York couple play complex games, one of which turns out to have a deadly effect.

Tedious variation on Les Diaboliques, with interesting moments.

w Gene Kearney d Curtis Harrington ph William A. Fraker m Samuel Matlovsky

☆ Simone Signoret, James Caan, Katharine Ross, Don Stroud, Kent Smith, Estelle Winwood, Marjorie Bennett

'A cheap-jack mélange of Angel Street and Diabolique in a New York brownstone.' – Judith Crist

The Games *

GB 1970 97m DeLuxe Panavision
TCF (Lester Linsk)

Four men in various parts of the world prepare to take part in the marathon at the Rome Olympics.

Tepid multi-drama with good locations and a well-shot and exciting climactic race.

w Erich Segal novel Hugh Atkinson d Michael Winner ph Robert Paynter m Francis Lai

☆ Stanley Baker, Michael Crawford, Ryan O'Neal, Charles Aznavour, Jeremy Kemp, Elaine Taylor, Kent Smith, Mona Washbourne

'Dramatically captures the tension, the physical agony and the almost religious fervour of the Olympics.' – Daily Mail

The Gamma People

GB 1955 79m bw
Warwick/Columbia

Journalists in a Balkan state uncover a plot by a mad scientist to control the minds of children by gamma rays.

Artless serial-like thriller with little suspense.

w John Gilling, John Gossage d John Gilling

☆ Paul Douglas, Leslie Phillips, Eva Bartok, Walter Rilla, Philip Leaver

Gamyuk Muntong: see The Chinese Feast

Ganashatru: see An Enemy of the People

'His goal was freedom ... his strategy was peace ... his weapon was his humanity!'

Gandhi ***

GB 1982 188m Technicolor Panavision
Columbia/Goldcrest/Indo-British/International Film Investors/National Film Development Corporation of India (Richard Attenborough)

The life of the young Indian advocate who became a revolutionary, a saint and a martyr.

A straightforward treatment with the odd twist and turns expected of this director; but the remarkable things about the film are first, that it was made at all in an age which regards inspirational epics as very old hat; and secondly, that it has brought into life so splendid a leading performance. Beside these factors the sluggish pace and the air of schoolbook history seem comparatively unimportant.

w John Briley d Richard Attenborough ph Billy Williams, Ronnie Taylor m George Fenton
pd Stuart Craig ed John Bloom

☆ Ben Kingsley, Candice Bergen, Edward Fox, John Mills, John Gielgud, Trevor Howard, Martin Sheen, Ian Charleson, Athol Fugard, Saeed Jaffrey

'It reminds us that we are, after all, human, and thus capable of the most extraordinary and wonderful achievements, simply through the use of our imagination, our will, and our sense of right.' – Roger Ebert

† Opening dedication: 'No man's life can be encompassed in one telling ... what can be done is to be faithful in spirit to the record and try to find one's way to the heart of the man.'

🏆 best picture; Ben Kingsley; Richard Attenborough as director; John Briley; cinematography; costume design (John Mollo, Bhanu Athalya); art direction (Stuart Craig, Bob Laing); editing (John Bloom)

♫ music

📺 best film; best direction; best actor; best supporting actress (Rohini Hattangady); outstanding newcomer (Ben Kingsley)

Gang Buster *
US   1931   65m   bw
Paramount
A small-town sap defeats gangsters by accident.
Lively comedy which scored in the middle of the first gangster cycle.
w Joseph L. Mankiewicz *story* Percy Heath d A. Edward Sutherland
☆ Jack Oakie, Jean Arthur, William Boyd, Wynne Gibson, Tom Kennedy
'First-rate week-stander … inlaid with surefire comic devices.' – *Variety*

'The best place to hide is behind a badge.'
Gang Related *
US   1997   122m   DeLuxe
MGM/Orion (John Bertolli, Brad Krevoy, Steven Stabler)
▣ ▤
Two crooked cops frame a vagrant for their murder of an undercover agent.
Familiar fare of police corruption, drugs and inner-city deprivation, enlivened by its direction and dry wit.
wd Jim Kouf ph Brian H. Reynolds m Mickey Hart pd Charles Breen ed Todd C. Ramsay
☆ James Belushi, Tupac Shakur, Lela Rochon, Dennis Quaid, James Earl Jones, David Paymer, Wendy Crewson, Gary Cole
'Little more than a TV movie with a bad mouth.' – *James Cameron-Wilson, Film Review*

The Gang That Couldn't Shoot Straight
US   1971   96m   Metrocolor
MGM (Robert Chartoff, Irwin Winkler)
Members of the New York Mafia organize a cycle race and start antagonisms that end in mass murder.
Unfunny black comedy with all concerned gesticulating wildly.
w Waldo Salt *novel* Jimmy Breslin d James Goldstone ph Owen Roizman m Dave Grusin
☆ Jerry Orbach, Leigh Taylor-Young, Jo Van Fleet, Lionel Stander, Robert DeNiro, Herve Villechaize, Joe Santos

Gang War: see *Odd Man Out (1946)*

Gang War *
US   1958   75m   bw   RegalScope
Fox (Harold E. Knox)
When his wife is killed by gangsters a reluctant witness seeks revenge.
Minor prototype for Death Wish and the star's other vehicles in similar vein.
w Louis Vittes *novel The Hoods Take Over* by Ovid Demaris d Gene Fowler Jnr
☆ Charles Bronson, Kent Taylor, Jennifer Holden, John Doucette, Gloria Henry

The Gang's All Here *
GB   1939   77m   bw
ABPC/Jack Buchanan (Walter C. Mycroft)
US title: *The Amazing Mr Forrest*
An insurance investigator goes undercover among gangsters.
Lively comedy-melodrama.
w Ralph Spence d Thornton Freeland ph Claude Friese-Greene ad John Mead, Cedric Dawe ed E. B. Jarvis
☆ Jack Buchanan, Googie Withers, Edward Everett Horton, Syd Walker, Otto Kruger, Jack La Rue, Walter Rilla
† Buchanan played the same character in *Smash and Grab.*

The Gang's All Here **
US   1943   103m   Technicolor
TCF (William Le Baron)
GB title: *The Girls He Left Behind*
A serviceman is caught between a fiery entertainer and a Park Avenue socialite.
Frenetic wartime musical with some of Busby Berkeley's most outré choreography (e.g. 'The Lady in the Tutti Frutti Hat') and gleamingly effective Technicolor.
w Walter Bullock ph Edward Cronjager m/ly Leo Robin, Harry Warren md Alfred Newman ad James Basevi, Joseph C. Wright d/ch Busby Berkeley
☆ Alice Faye, Carmen Miranda, James Ellison, Phil Baker, Benny Goodman, Charlotte Greenwood, Eugene Pallette, Edward Everett Horton

'Those who consider Berkeley a master consider this film his masterpiece.' – *New Yorker, 1976*
'Mainly made up of Busby Berkeley's paroxysmic production numbers, which amuse me a good deal.' – *James Agee*
⅄ art direction

Gangs of New York *
US   1938   67m   bw
Republic
A cop infiltrates the mob and impersonates a tough gangster.
Highly unlikely but entertaining programmer, a good shot for a B studio.
w Wellyn Totman, Sam Fuller, Charles Francis Royal d James Cruze
☆ Charles Bickford, Ann Dvorak, Alan Baxter, Wynne Gibson, Harold Huber, Willard Robertson, Maxie Rosenbloom, John Wray
'Rapid-fire gangster meller … sure to be a strong entry.' – *Variety*

Gangs of the Waterfront
US   1945   55m   bw
Republic
When his brother is killed, a taxidermist who looks like a gang leader assumes the leader's place and rounds up the mob.
Serial-like action antics; a reliable second feature.
w Albert Beich d George Blair
☆ Robert Armstrong, Stephanie Batchelor, Martin Kosleck, Marion Martin

The Gangster *
US   1947   84m   bw
Monogram/King Bros (Maurice King)
▤
Rival gangs rub each other out.
Shoddy-looking Poverty Row melodrama with little rhyme, reason or interest.
w Daniel Fuchs *novel* Daniel Fuchs d Gordon Wiles ph Paul Ivano m Louis Gruenberg
☆ Barry Sullivan, Akim Tamiroff, Belita, John Ireland

The Gangster's Moll: see *Minbo No Onna*

Gangway *
GB   1937   89m   bw
GFD/Gaumont (Michael Balcon)
A girl reporter poses as a star's maid and is accused of theft.
Mildly pleasing star vehicle.
w Lesser Samuels, Sonnie Hale d Sonnie Hale ph Glen MacWilliams
☆ Jessie Matthews, Barry Mackay, Nat Pendleton, Noel Madison, Alastair Sim

Gangway for Tomorrow
US   1943   69m   bw
RKO
Five defence workers with problematical pasts unite in the cause of war.
Naïve but oddly stirring little propaganda piece.
w Arch Oboler d John H. Auer
☆ Robert Ryan, Margo, John Carradine

Gaolbreak
GB   1962   61m   bw
Butcher's (Francis Searle, Ronald Liles)
A safe-breaker is sprung from jail so that he can help his brother carry out a jewel robbery on behalf of a crooked antique dealer.
Undistinguished thriller with occasional touches of originality, such as its motherly master criminal, but not enough to sustain interest for long.
w A. R. Rawlinson d Francis Searle ph Ken Hodges m John Gregory ad Duncan Sutherland ed Jim Connock
☆ Peter Reynolds, Avice Landone, Carol White, David Kernan, John Blythe, David Gregory

Garbo Talks *
US   1984   103m   Technicolor
MGM-UA/Elliott Kastner (Burtt Harris)
▤ ⍟
A dying woman's last obsession is to meet her idol Greta Garbo.
New York wry comedy which doesn't seem entirely clear of its point but is smartly acted and produced.
w Larry Grusin d Sidney Lumet ph Andrzej Bartkowiak m Cy Coleman pd Philip Rosenberg ed Andrew Mondshein
☆ Anne Bancroft, Ron Silver, Carrie Fisher, Catherine Hicks, Steven Hill, Howard Da Silva,

Harvey Fierstein, Dorothy Loudon, Hermione Gingold
'A sweet and sour film clearly not for all tastes.' – *Variety*

La Garce: see *The Bitch (1984)*

Garde à Vue *
France   1981   88m   Eastmancolor
Ariane/TF1 (Georges Dancigers, Alexandre Mnouchkine)
GB title: *The Inquisitor*
In a French provincial town a wealthy lawyer is interrogated by police, who think he may be implicated in a rape case.
Basically a talk-piece, though with a twist ending, this is a smart little film which would undoubtedly have its best effect when not understood through sub-titles.
w Claude Miller, Jean Herman *novel Brainwash* by John Wainwright d Claude Miller ph Bruno Nuytten m Georges Delerue
☆ Lino Ventura, Michel Serrault, Guy Marchand, Romy Schneider
'Not unlike a *Twelve Angry Men* from which all comfortable certainties have been withdrawn.' – *Tom Milne, MFB*

The Garden *
GB   1990   90m   colour
Artificial Eye/Basilisk/Channel 4/British Screen/ZDF/Uplink (James McKay)
▣ ▤
A sequence of images – of Jesus, the Last Supper, the director tending his garden, and a homosexual couple being persecuted – create the effect of a series of semi-religious tableaux.
AIDS and homosexual suffering are the main themes of an intensely personal film most likely to find favour with those who share the director's preoccupations or who can admire his visual flair.
wd Derek Jarman ph Christopher Hughes m Simon Fisher Turner pd Derek Brown, Christopher Hobbs ed Peter Cartwright
☆ Kevin Collins, Roger Cook, Jody Graber, Pete Lee-Wilson, Philip Macdonald, Johnny Mills, Tilda Swinton

'Dangerous love in a desert paradise!'
The Garden of Allah **
US   1936   80m   Technicolor
David O. Selznick
▣ ▤ ⍟
A disenchanted socialite falls in love with a renegade monk in the Algerian desert.
Arty old-fashioned romantic star vehicle; great to look at, and marking a genuine advance in colour photography, but dramatically a bit of a drag.
w W. P. Lipscomb, Lynn Riggs *novel* Robert Hichens d Richard Boleslawski ph W. Howard Greene, Harold Rosson m Max Steiner ad Sturges Carne, Lyle Wheeler, Edward Boyle
☆ Marlene Dietrich, Charles Boyer, Basil Rathbone, Tilly Losch
'The last word in colour production, but a pretty dull affair.' – *Variety*
'Hopelessly dated folderol.' – *J. R. Parish*
'The juiciest tale of woe ever, produced in poshly lurid colour, with a Max Steiner score poured on top.' – *Judith Crist*
'Alas! my poor church, so picturesque, so noble, so superhumanly pious, so intensely dramatic. I really prefer the *New Statesman* view, shabby priests counting pesetas on their dingy fingers before blessing tanks.' – *Graham Greene*
† Previous, silent, versions had been made in 1917, with Tom Santschi and Helen Ware, and in 1927 with Ivan Petrovich and Alice Terry.
🎖 special award for colour cinematography
⅄ Max Steiner

Garden of Evil *
US   1954   100m   Technicolor   Cinemascope
TCF (Charles Brackett)
⌒
En route to the Californian goldfields an ex-sheriff and a gambler help a woman to rescue her husband from a mine, but are trapped by Indians.
High-flying Western melodrama with the principals glowering at each other. Stock situations quite skilfully compiled.
w Frank Fenton d Henry Hathaway ph Milton Krasner m Bernard Herrmann
☆ Susan Hayward, Gary Cooper, Richard Widmark, Hugh Marlowe, Cameron Mitchell

The Garden of the Finzi-Continis **
Italy/West Germany   1970   95m   Eastmancolor
Documento Film/CCC Filmkunst (Gianni Hecht Lucari, Arthur Cohn)
▤ ⍟ ⌒
In 1938, a family of wealthy Italian Jews sees its world collapse, with a concentration camp as the next destination.
A dreamlike, poignant, and very beautiful film.
w Tullio Pinelli, Valerio Zurlini, Franco Brusati, Ugo Pirro, Vittorio Bonicelli, Alain Katz *novel* Giorgio Bassani d Vittorio de Sica ph Ennio Guarnieri m Manuel de Sica
☆ Dominique Sanda, Lino Capolicchio, Helmut Berger, Romolo Valli, Fabio Testi
'I lived through the period. The same feelings I experienced in life I transposed to the picture: that is the definition of the artist.' – *Vittorio de Sica*
'This extraordinary film, with its melancholy glamour, is perhaps the only one that records the halfhearted anti-Jewish measures of the Mussolini period.' – *New Yorker*
🎖 best foreign film
⅄ script

Garden of the Moon
US   1938   94m   bw
Warner (Lou Edelman)
A night-club owner vies with his bandleader for the affections of his leading singer.
Pleasant talent can't turn this script into anything but a tedious small-scale musical, especially since both director and songwriters are operating below par.
w Jerry Wald, Richard Macaulay d Busby Berkeley m/ly Al Dubin, Harry Warren
☆ Pat O'Brien, Margaret Lindsay, John Payne, Melville Cooper, Isabel Jeans

Gardens of Stone
US   1987   111m   DeLuxe
Tri-Star/ML Delphi (Michael I. Levy, Francis Coppola)
▣ ▤ ⌒
A soldier trains youngsters for the Vietnam War despite his conviction that the war is wrong.
Muddled talk-piece which fails to make any point.
w Ronald Bass *novel* Nicholas Proffitt d Francis Coppola ph Jordan Cronenweth m Carmine Coppola pd Dean Tavoularis ed Barry Malkin
☆ James Caan, Anjelica Huston, James Earl Jones, D. B. Sweeney, Dean Stockwell, Mary Stewart Masterson, Dick Anthony Williams

Garm Hava *
India   1973   136m   Eastmancolor
Unit 3 MM/Film Finance Corp. (Abu Siwani, Ishan Arya, M. S. Sathyu)
aka: *Hot Winds*
aka: *Scorching Winds*
After India's independence and partition, some members of a prosperous Muslim family leave to live in Pakistan while others choose to remain in India, where they face hostility and prejudice.
Sprawling family drama, engrossing, despite its occasional clumsinesses, in exploring the impact of public events on private lives.
w Kaifi Azmi, Shama Zaidi *story* Ismat Chugtai d M. S. Sathyu ph Ishan Arya md Ustad Bahadur Khan ed S. Chakraborty, Herman Topno
☆ Balraj Sahni, Jalal Agha, Jamal Hashmi, Gita, A. K. Hangal, Yunus Parwaiz, Shaukat Kalfi, Vikas Anand, Rajendra Raghuvanshi

The Garment Jungle *
US   1957   88m   bw
Columbia (Harry Kleiner)
Union and gangster problems abound for a family in the New York clothing business.
Reasonably powerful melodrama fashioned from familiar material in the wake of On the Waterfront.
w Harry Kleiner d Robert Aldrich, Vincent Sherman ph Joseph Biroc m Leith Stevens
☆ Lee J. Cobb, Kerwin Mathews, Gia Scala, Richard Boone, Valerie French, Robert Loggia, Joseph Wiseman

Gas Food Lodging **
US   1991   101m   DeLuxe
Mainline/Cineville Partners (Daniel Hassid, Seth M. Willenson, William Ewart)
▣ ▤ ⌒ ⍟
A mother and her two disaffected daughters look for love in a small town.

Engrossing domestic drama of three women struggling to survive and searching for something to make life worthwhile.

wd Allison Anders novel Don't Look and It Won't Hurt by Richard Peck ph Dean Lent m J. Mascis pd Jane Ann Stewart ed Tracy S. Granger
☆ Brooke Adams, Ione Skye, Fairuza Balk, James Brolin, Robert Knepper, David Lansbury, Jacob Vargas, Donovan Leitch, Chris Mulkey
'Anders's film is sometimes stilted, at times over-contrived, but it invariably rings true both socially and psychologically.' – Philip French, Observer

Gas House Kids
US   1946   71m   bw
PRC
Young New Yorkers help a crippled veteran buy a chicken ranch.
First of three forgotten attempts to stretch out the Dead End Kids genre; not good. (The other titles, both in 1947, were Gas House Kids Go West and Gas House Kids in Hollywood.)
w Raymond Schrock, George and Elsie Bricker d Sam Newfield ph Jack Greenhalgh
☆ Billy Halop, Alfalfa Switzer, Robert Lowery, Teala Loring, Rex Downing, David Reed

Gas! or It Became Necessary to Destroy the World in Order to Save It
US   1970   79m   Movielab
AIP/San Jacinto (Roger Corman)
A gas which speeds up the ageing process is accidentally released and kills everyone over twenty-five.
Psychedelic sci-fi for the Easy Rider set. Very mildly diverting.
w Graham Armitage d Roger Corman ph Ron Dexter m Country Joe and the Fish
☆ Robert Corff, Elaine Giftos, Pat Patterson, Graham Armitage, Alex Wilson, Ben Vereen, Bud Cort

Gasbags *
GB   1940   77m   bw
Gainsborough (Edward Black)
Airmen stranded in Germany by a barrage balloon return in a captured secret weapon.
Fast-moving knockabout from the Crazy Gang; often inventive despite reach-me-down script and production.
w Val Valentine, Val Guest, Marriott Edgar d Marcel Varnel ph Arthur Crabtree md Louis Levy ad Vetchinsky ed R. E. Dearing
☆ Bud Flanagan, Chesney Allen, Jimmy Nervo, Teddy Knox, Charlie Naughton, Jimmy Gold, Moore Marriott, Wally Patch, Peter Gawthorne, Frederick Valk

Gaslight ****
GB   1940   88m   bw
British National (John Corfield)
US title: Angel Street
A Victorian schizophrenic drives his wife insane when she seems likely to stumble on his guilty secret of an old murder and hidden rubies.
Modest but absolutely effective film version of a superb piece of suspense theatre.
w A. R. Rawlinson, Bridget Boland play Patrick Hamilton d Thorold Dickinson ph Bernard Knowles m Richard Addinsell
☆ Anton Walbrook, Diana Wynyard, Frank Pettingell, Cathleen Cordell, Robert Newton, Jimmy Hanley
'For one who has seen the stage play, much of the tension is destroyed by the insistence on explaining everything rather than hinting at it.' – Dilys Powell
'The electric sense of tension and mid-Victorian atmosphere are entirely cinematic.' – Sequence, 1950
† MGM is said to have tried to destroy the negative of the film when it made its version four years later. See below.

'A melodrama of a strange love!'
'This is love ... clouded by evil ... darkened by a secret no one dared to guess! The strange drama of a captive sweetheart!'

Gaslight **
US   1944   114m   bw
MGM (Arthur Hornblow Jnr)
GB title: The Murder in Thornton Square
Grossly overblown and less effective version of the above, but with moments of power, effective performances and superior production.
w John Van Druten, Walter Reisch, John L. Balderston play Patrick Hamilton d George Cukor ph Joseph Ruttenberg m Bronislau Kaper ad Cedric Gibbons, William Ferrari
☆ Charles Boyer, Ingrid Bergman, Joseph Cotten, Dame May Whitty, Barbara Everest, Angela Lansbury, Edmund Breon, Halliwell Hobbes
† Irene Dunne and Hedy Lamarr were previously offered the Ingrid Bergman part, and turned it down.
♦ Ingrid Bergman; art direction
♢ best picture; script; Joseph Ruttenberg; Charles Boyer; Angela Lansbury

Gasoline Alley
US   1951   76m   bw
Columbia (Milton Feldman)
Young marrieds open a diner.
Placid comedy-drama from a 30-year-old comic strip; the intended series did not materialize.
wd Edward Bernds comic strip Frank O. King ph Lester H. White
☆ Scotty Beckett, Jimmy Lydon, Susan Morrow, Don Beddoe, Dick Wessel, Gus Schilling

The Gate
Canada   1987   92m   colour
Vista (John Kemeny)
Two young boys dig a hole in their back yard which opens a gate to hell.
Enjoyable low-budget horror, with some amusing moments.
w Michael Nankin d Tibor Takacs ph Thomas Vamos m Michael Hoenig, J. Peter Robinson pd William Beeton ed Rit Wallis sp Randall William Cook
☆ Stephen Dorff, Christa Denton, Louis Tripp, Kelly Rowan, Jennifer Irwin, Scott Denton
'Sort of an Evil Dead for pre-teen nerds.' – Stefan Jaworzyn, Shock Xpress

Gate II
Canada   1992   95m   Film House colour
Alliance/Andras Hamori
A teenager and his two friends summon demons who possess them.
Predictable horror aimed at teen audiences, but too tame to attract them.
w Michael Nankin d Tibor Takacs ph Brian England m George Blondheim pd William Beeton ed Ronald Sanders sp Randall William Cook
☆ Louis Tripp, Simon Reynolds, Pamela Segall, James Villemaire, Neil Munro
'An idiotic horror film boasting good monster effects.' – Variety

Gate of Hell *
Japan   1953   90m   Eastmancolor
Daiei (Masaichi Nagata)
original title: Jigokumon
After a 12th-century war, a soldier demands as his prize a woman who has helped him; but she is married.
Curious traditional Japanese saga, its emphases strange to western eyes and ears. Its colour, however, is devastatingly beautiful.
wd Teinosuke Kinugasa novel Kan Kikuchi ph Kohei Sugiyama m Yasushi Akutagawa
☆ Machiko Kyo, Kazuo Hasegawa, Isao Yamagata
♦ best foreign film

Gate of Lilacs: see Porte des Lilas

Gates of Hell: see City of The Living Dead

Gates of Night: see Les Portes de la Nuit

Gates of Paris: see Porte des Lilas

Gateway *
US   1938   75m   bw
TCF (Darryl F. Zanuck)
An Irish girl emigrating to the US is helped on board ship by a war correspondent.
Brisk romantic drama which provides an interesting recreation of the Ellis Island procedures still effective in the thirties.
w Lamar Trotti d Alfred Werker ph Edward Cronjager m Arthur Lange, Charles Maxwell
☆ Don Ameche, Arleen Whelan, Gregory Ratoff, Raymond Walburn, Binnie Barnes, Gilbert Roland, John Carradine, Harry Carey
'Grand Hotel treatment applied to Ellis Island ... should look to fair b.o.' – Variety

A Gathering of Eagles
US   1963   115m   Eastmancolor
U-I (Sy Bartlett)
A colonel becomes unpopular when he strives to improve the efficiency of a Strategic Air Command base.
Tame revamp of Twelve O'clock High without the justification of war; all strictly routine and perfectly dull.
w Robert Pirosh d Delbert Mann ph Russell Harlan m Jerry Goldsmith
☆ Rock Hudson, Mary Peach, Rod Taylor, Barry Sullivan, Kevin McCarthy

'Come and get him!'
Gator
US   1976   116m   DeLuxe   Todd-AO 35
UA/Levy-Gardner-Laven
A convicted moonshiner is blackmailed into becoming a government undercover man in the organization of a hoodlum.
Shambling mixture of action, violence, and raw humour.
w William Norton d Burt Reynolds ph William A. Fraker m Charles Bernstein
☆ Burt Reynolds, Jack Weston, Lauren Hutton, Jerry Reed, Alice Ghostley, Dub Taylor, Mike Douglas
'The relentless violence, the sentimentality, the raucous stag party humour, the inability to cut off a scene once it has made its point, attest to the influence of Robert Aldrich.' – Philip French

'There Is No Gene For The Human Spirit.'
Gattaca
US   1997   106m   Technicolor   Super 35
Columbia TriStar/Jersey (Danny DeVito, Michael Shamberg, Stacey Sher)
In the future, when genetically engineered people control the world, an ordinary person takes another's identity to succeed.
Glossy science fiction with a very soft centre under its hard surface.
wd Andrew Niccol ph Slawomir Idziak m Michael Nyman pd Jan Roelfs ed Lisa Zeno Churgin
☆ Ethan Hawke, Uma Thurman, Alan Arkin, Jude Law, Loren Dean, Gore Vidal, Ernest Borgnine, Blair Underwood, Xander Berkeley, Tony Shalhoub
'For all its style and promise, Gattaca is far easier to look at than actually watch.' – Neil Jeffries, Empire
♢ Jan Roelfs

Il Gatto Dogli Occhi Di Gioda: see The Cat's Victims

Il Gatto Nero: see The Black Cat (1981)

Il Gattopardo: see The Leopard

The Gaucho *
US   1928   115m   bw   silent
Douglas Fairbanks
An outlaw reforms when he falls for the Girl of the Shrine.
Subdued star swashbuckler leading up to a fine climax.
w Lotta Woods story Douglas Fairbanks d F. Richard Jones
☆ Douglas Fairbanks, Lupe Velez, Geraine Greer, Gustav von Seyffertitz

The Gaunt Stranger *
GB   1938   73m   bw
Northwood/Capad (Ealing) (Michael Balcon, S. C. Balcon)
US title: The Phantom Strikes
A criminal master of disguise threatens to kill a much more despicable criminal at an appointed hour ... and does so despite police protection.
A highly reliable suspenser of which this is perhaps the best film version.
w Sidney Gilliat play and novel The Ringer by Edgar Wallace d Walter Forde ph Ronald Neame ad Oscar Werndorff ed Charles Saunders
☆ Sonnie Hale, Wilfrid Lawson, Alexander Knox, Louise Henry, Patricia Roc, Patrick Barr, John Longden, George Merritt
'Dialogue, humour and suspense are effectively alternated ... the film is in fact capital crime fiction.' – Kine Weekly
† Other versions, as The Ringer, appeared in 1931 and 1953.

The Gauntlet *
US   1977   109m   DeLuxe   Panavision
Warner/Malpaso (Robert Daly)
A disreputable cop is assigned to escort a foul-mouthed prostitute to a courtroom across country, through the gauntlet of baddies who want them both dead.
The epitome of seventies violence, with no excuse except to stage one detailed shoot-up or explosion after another. Well done for those who like this sort of thing.
w Michael Butler, Dennis Shryack d Clint Eastwood ph Rexford Metz m Jerry Fielding
☆ Clint Eastwood, Sondra Locke, Pat Hingle, William Prince
'At times the whole world seems to be firing at them. Buildings and cars are turned to lace. You look at the screen even though there's nothing to occupy your mind...' – Pauline Kael
† This was the first film to give a credit for first aid.

Gawain and the Green Knight *
GB   1973   93m   Technicolor   Panavision
UA/Sancrest (Philip Breen)
The medieval legend of a supernatural knight who challenges the king's men to kill him.
Enterprising if unsuccessful low-budget attempt to create a medieval world; too long by half.
w Philip Breen, Stephen Weeks d Stephen Weeks ph Ian Wilson m Ron Goodwin ad Anthony Woollard
☆ Murray Head, Ciaran Madden, Nigel Green, Anthony Sharp, Robert Hardy, Murray Melvin

The Gay Bride
US   1934   80m   bw
MGM (John Considine Jnr)
A gold-digging chorus girl marries a racketeer but soon becomes a widow.
Misfiring satirical melodrama which quickly becomes tedious.
w Bella and Samuel Spewack story Repeal by Charles Francis Coe d Jack Conway ph Ray June
☆ Carole Lombard, Chester Morris, ZaSu Pitts, Nat Pendleton, Leo Carrillo
'Gangster pictures are gone, and this won't do anything to bring them back.' – Variety

The Gay Deception *
US   1935   79m   bw
Fox (Jesse L. Lasky)
A Ruritanian prince becomes a doorman at a swank New York hotel, and marries a secretary.
Lightly-handled Cinderella story showing most of its director's accomplishment.
w Stephen Morehouse Avery, Don Hartman d William Wyler ph Joseph Valentine m Louis de Francesco
☆ Francis Lederer, Frances Dee, Benita Hume, Alan Mowbray, Akim Tamiroff, Lennox Pawle, Richard Carle, Lionel Stander
'Doesn't lean too much to sophistication to miss appreciation in the hamlet houses.' – Variety
♢ story

The Gay Desperado **
US   1936   85m   bw
Mary Pickford
An heiress is held for ransom by a romantic bandit.

Very light, quite amusing, sometimes irritatingly skittish musical spoof sparked by the director's ideas.
w Wallace Smith *story* Leo Birinski *d* Rouben Mamoulian *ph* Lucien Andriot *m* Alfred Newman
☆ Ida Lupino, Nino Martini, Leo Carrillo, Harold Huber, Mischa Auer
'Fairly diverting Mexican western ... it'll do spotty trade, depending on locale.' – *Variety*
'One of the best light comedies of the year ... Mr Mamoulian's camera is very persuasive.' – *Graham Greene*
'While some of the show is fetching, the ideas mostly misfire and the spell is fitful and unsure.' – *Otis Ferguson*
'It has the lightness of touch which goes into the making of the perfect meringue.' – *Basil Wright*

The Gay Diplomat
US 1931 66m bw
RKO
A Russian officer is sent to Bucharest to combat a woman superspy.
Thoroughly confused and inane mixture of romance, presumed sophistication and dark doings.
w Doris Anderson *story* Benn W. Levy *d* Richard Boleslawski
☆ Ivan Lebedeff, Genevieve Tobin, Ilka Chase, Betty Compson
'A picture almost without a merit.' – *Variety*

The Gay Divorce: see *The Gay Divorcee*

'The gayest of mad musicals!'
'The dance-mad musical triumph of two continents!'
The Gay Divorcee **
US 1934 107m bw
RKO (Pandro S. Berman)
GB title: *The Gay Divorce*
A would-be divorcee in an English seaside hotel mistakes a dancer who loves her for a professional co-respondent.
Wildly and hilariously dated comedy musical with splendidly archaic comedy routines supporting Hollywood's great new dance team in their first big success. Not much dancing, but 'The Continental' is a show-stopper.
w George Marion Jnr, Dorothy Yost, Edward Kaufman *play* Dwight Taylor, J. Hartley Manners *musical comedy* Samuel Hoffenstein, Kenneth Webb, Cole Porter *d* Mark Sandrich *ph* David Abel *m/ly* various *md* Max Steiner *ad* Van Nest Polglase, Carroll Clark *ed* William Hamilton *sp* Vernon Walker
☆ Fred Astaire, Ginger Rogers, Edward Everett Horton, Alice Brady, Erik Rhodes, Eric Blore, Lillian Miles, Betty Grable
'Cinch box office anywhere and certain of big foreign grosses.' – *Variety*
'The plot is trivial French farce, but the dances are among the wittiest and most lyrical expressions of American romanticism on the screen.' – *New Yorker, 1977*
† 'Night and Day' was the only Cole Porter song to survive from the stage musical.
♪ song 'The Continental' (*m*Con Conrad, *ly*Herb Magidson)
♟ best picture; musical score (Ken Webb, Samuel Hoffenstein); art direction

The Gay Dog
GB 1954 87m bw
Coronet/Eros
A miner trains a pet greyhound to win races.
Modest, set-bound regional comedy.
w Peter Rogers *play* Joseph Colton *d* Maurice Elvey *ph* James Wilson *m* Edwin Astley
☆ Wilfred Pickles, Petula Clark, Megs Jenkins, John Blythe

The Gay Duellist: see *Meet Me at Dawn*

The Gay Imposters: see *Gold Diggers in Paris*

The Gay Intruders
US 1948 68m bw
TCF
Quarrelling stage marrieds consult psychiatrists, who end up more confused than the patients.
Unusual second feature comedy with a few good laughs; allegedly based on Tallulah Bankhead.
w Francis Swann *d* Ray McCarey
☆ Tamara Geva, John Emery, Leif Erickson, Virginia Gregg

The Gay Lady: see *Trottie True*

The Gay Mrs Trexel: see *Susan and God*

The Gay Nineties: see *The Floradora Girl*

Gay Purree *
♟♟ US 1962 85m Technicolor
UPA (Henry Saperstein)
▣ ⊚
A country cat goes to Paris and is Shanghaied.
Feature cartoon similar to Disney's later The Aristocats and about as good, i.e. not quite up to the best standards.
w Dorothy and Chuck Jones *d* Abe Levitow *m/ly* Harold Arlen, E. Y. Harburg *md* Mort Lindsey
☆ Featuring the voices of Judy Garland, Robert Goulet, Hermione Gingold

The Gay Sisters *
US 1942 110m bw
Warner (Henry Blanke)
Three sisters refuse to sell their aristocratic New York mansion to make way for development.
Slowish but quite interesting family drama with Chekhovian touches.
w Lenore Coffee *novel* Stephen Longstreet *d* Irving Rapper *ph* Sol Polito *m* Max Steiner
☆ Barbara Stanwyck, George Brent, Geraldine Fitzgerald, Donald Crisp, Gig Young, Nancy Coleman, Gene Lockhart, Larry Simms, Donald Woods, Grant Mitchell
† Gig Young took his name from his part in this film; he was formerly Byron Barr.

The Gazebo *
US 1959 102m bw
MGM/Avon (Lawrence Weingarten)
A TV writer kills a blackmailer (he thinks) and hides his body in the garden.
Frenetic black comedy which must have worked better on the stage but produces a few laughs.
w George Wells *play* Alec Coppel *d* George Marshall *ph* Paul C. Vogel *m* Jeff Alexander
☆ Glenn Ford, Debbie Reynolds, Carl Reiner, John McGiver, Mabel Albertson, Doro Merande, ZaSu Pitts, Martin Landau

Gazon Maudit: see *French Twist*

The Geisha Boy
♟♟ US 1958 98m Technicolor
Vistavision
Paramount (Jerry Lewis)
▣
A third-rate magician joins a USO entertainment tour in Japan.
Disconnected farce which amuses only fitfully, and actively displeases when it becomes sentimental with the star drooling over a baby.
wd Frank Tashlin *ph* Haskell Boggs *m* Walter Scharf
☆ Jerry Lewis, Marie MacDonald, Barton MacLane, Sessue Hayakawa, Suzanne Pleshette

The Gene Krupa Story
US 1959 101m bw
Columbia (Philip A. Waxman)
▣ ⊚
GB title: *Drum Crazy*
A successful jazz drummer is convicted on a drugs charge and falls from grace.
Dreary biopic with the expected music track.
w Orin Jannings *d* Don Weis *ph* Charles Lawton Jnr *m* Leith Stevens
☆ Sal Mineo, Susan Kohner, James Darren, Susan Oliver, Yvonne Craig, Lawrence Dobkin, Celia Lovsky, Shelly Manne, Buddy Lester, Red Nichols

'Everybody laughs but Buster!'
The General **
♟♟ US 1926 80m bw silent
UA/Buster Keaton (Joseph M. Schenck)
▣ ▤ ⊚ ⊙ ⊚
A confederate train driver gets his train and his girl back when they are stolen by Union soldiers.
Slow-starting, then hilarious action comedy, often voted the one of the best ever made. Its sequence of sight gags, each topping the one before, is an incredible joy to behold.
w Al Boasberg, Charles Smith *d* Buster Keaton, Clyde Bruckman *ph* J. Devereux Jennings, Bert Haines
☆ Buster Keaton, Marion Mack, Glen Cavander

'It has all the sweet earnestness in the world. It is about trains, frontier America, flower-faced girls.' – *New Yorker, 1977*
'The production itself is singularly well mounted, but the fun is not exactly plentiful ... here he is more the acrobat than the clown, and his vehicle might be described as a mixture of cast iron and jelly.' – *Mordaunt Hall, New York Times*
† The story is based on an actual incident of the Civil War, treated more seriously in *The Great Locomotive Chase* (qv).
†† The screenplay with 1,400 freeze frames was issued in 1976 in the Film Classics Library (editor, Richard Anobile).

The General *
Ireland/GB 1998 123m bw Panavision
Warner/Merlin Films/J&M (John Boorman)
▣ ⊚
In Dublin of the early 90s, Martin Cahill, a charming and brutal gangster, pulls off a succession of daring robberies until he betrays himself and is killed by an IRA gunman.
A knowing, witty throwback to the street-smart, socially aware gangster films of the 30s. Although 'torn from today's headlines', it follows a classic tragic trajectory, of a man taking on the world until he is undone by his own overweening pride.
wd John Boorman *ph* Seamus Deasy *m* Richie Buckley *pd* Derek Wallace *ed* Ron Davis
☆ Brendan Gleeson, Adrian Dunbar, Sean McGinley, Maria Doyle Kennedy, Angeline Ball, Jon Voight
'Both challenges and entertains the audience at a variety of levels, as well as reviving the vitality and freshness of the helmer's earliest, mid-'60s pics.' – *Derek Elley, Variety*
† John Boorman won the prize for best director at the 1998 Cannes Film Festival.

General Della Rovere **
Italy 1959 130m bw
Gaumont/Zebra (Morris Ergas)
original title: *Il Generale Della Rovere*
A petty thief, forced by the Nazis to pose as a Resistance leader to flush out the real leaders, begins to take the role seriously.
De Sica's bravura performance saves a slickly made but emotionally hollow film, one that its director seems not to have liked.
w Sergio Amidei, Diego Fabbri, Indro Montanelli, Roberto Rossellini *d* Roberto Rossellini *ph* Carlo Carlini *m* Renzo Rossellini *ad* Piero Zuffi *ed* Cesare Cavagna
☆ Vittorio de Sica, Hannes Messemer, Sandra Milo, Giovanna Ralli
† The film was co-winner of the Golden Lion at the Venice Film Festival in 1959.
♟ story and screenplay

'Gary goes to town for the best-looking gal in China!'
The General Died at Dawn **
US 1936 93m bw
Paramount (William le Baron)
▣
A mercenary in China overcomes an evil warlord and falls in love with a spy.
Heavy-going but very decorative studio-bound intrigue which seems to take place on the old Shanghai Express sets with an extra infusion of dry ice. An intellectual's picture of its day.
w Clifford Odets *novel* Charles Booth *d* Lewis Milestone *ph* Victor Milner *m* Werner Janssen, Gerard Carbonara
☆ Gary Cooper, Madeleine Carroll, Akim Tamiroff, Dudley Digges, Porter Hall, William Frawley
'If it were not for a rather ludicrous ending, this would be one of the best thrillers for some years.' – *Graham Greene*
'In terms of cinematic invention, a fascinating technical exercise.' – *John Baxter, 1968*
'A curious study in exoticism.' – *NFT, 1974*
'In direction and photography it has undeniable class ... but like most movies, it is empty of any ideas or characters that stay with you longer than it takes to reach the nearest subway entrance.' – *Brooklyn Daily Eagle*
♟ Victor Milner; Werner Janssen; Akim Tamiroff

The General Line **
USSR 1929 90m bw silent
Sovkino
▣▣
original title: *Staroye i Novoye*
aka: *Old and New*
A country woman helps to start a village co-operative.
A slight piece of propaganda, put together with all of Eisenstein's magnificent cinematic resources: the cream separator demonstration is one of the most famous montage sequences in cinema history.
w Sergei Eisenstein *d* Sergei Eisenstein, Grigori Alexandrov *ph* Edouard Tissé
☆ Marta Lapkina and a cast of non-professionals

General Spanky
♟♟ US 1936 73m bw
MGM/Hal Roach
▣ ⊚
A small boy is instrumental in a famous Civil War victory.
Uneasy sentimental melodrama vehicle for one of the moppet stars of 'Our Gang'.
w Richard Flournoy, Hal Yates, John Guedel *d* Gordon Douglas, Fred Newmeyer
☆ Spanky McFarland, Phillips Holmes, Hobart Bosworth, Ralph Morgan, Irving Pichel
'Desultory, overlong ... built for the lesser family trade.' – *Variety*

General Suvorov
USSR 1941 90m bw
Mosfilm
The career of the general who turned back Napoleon at the gates of Moscow.
Competent propaganda piece, but not one of the Russian classics.
w G. Grebner *d* V. I. Pudovkin
☆ N. P. Cherkasov, A. Yachnitscki, S. Kiligin

'To Find The Truth, Follow the Lies.'
'Her Murder Was Just The Beginning.'
General's Daughter
US/Germany 1999 116m DeLuxe Panavision
Paramount (Mace Neufeld)
▣▣ ⊚
A detective has 36 hours in which to solve the rape and murder of a general's daughter.
Ponderous, loquacious whodunnit, with an involved narrative that becomes more unbelievable, and less involving, by the minute.
w Christopher Bertolini, William Goldman *novel* Nelson DeMille *d* Simon West *ph* Peter Menzies Jnr *m* Carter Burwell *pd* Dennis Washington *ed* Glen Scantlebury
☆ John Travolta, Madeleine Stowe, James Cromwell, Timothy Hutton, Leslie Stefanson, Daniel von Bargen, Clarence Williams III, James Woods, Peter Weireter, Mark Boone Jnr
'Misogynist nonsense' – *Guardian*
'The cinematic equivalent of a disposable airplane read, a hokey, kinky military thriller that's twisty and compelling enough to hook viewers in the mood for a trashy good time.' – *Variety*
† It grossed more than $102m at the US box-office.

Generation *
Poland 1954 90m bw
Film Polski
▣▣ ▤
original title: *Pokolenie*
In occupied Warsaw in 1942 a teenager becomes hardened by life and joins the resistance.
Heavy-going but quite striking propaganda piece, amply demonstrating its director's talents.
w Bohdan Czeszko *novel* Bohdan Czeszko *d* Andrzej Wajda *ph* Jerzy Lipman *m* Andrzej Markowski
☆ Tadeusz Lomnicki, Urszula Modrzynska, Roman Polanski, Zbigniew Cybulski

Generation
US 1969 104m Technicolor
Avco Embassy/Frederick Brisson
▣
GB title: *A Time for Giving*
A Denver advertising executive is horrified by his daughter's ideas of modern marriage.
Lame generation-gap comedy centring on a couple who intend to deliver their own baby.

---

w William Goodhart *play* William Goodhart d George Schaefer *ph* Lionel Lindon *m* Dave Grusin

☆ David Janssen, Kim Darby, Carl Reiner, Pete Duel, Andrew Prine, James Coco, Sam Waterston, Don Beddoe

'Slightly too sticky for comfort.' – MFB

Genevieve ****

GB 1953 86m Technicolor
GFD/Sirius (Henry Cornelius)

Two friendly rivals engage in a race on the way back from the Brighton veteran car rally.
One of those happy films in which for no very good or expected reason a number of modest elements merge smoothly to create an aura of high style and memorable moments. A charmingly witty script, carefully pointed direction, attractive actors and locations, an atmosphere of light-hearted British sex and a lively harmonica theme turned it, after a slowish start, into one of Britain's biggest commercial hits and most fondly remembered comedies.
w William Rose *d* Henry Cornelius *ph* Christopher Challis *m* Larry Adler (who also played it) *md* Muir Mathieson *ad* Michael Stringer
☆ Dinah Sheridan, John Gregson, Kay Kendall, Kenneth More, Geoffrey Keen, Joyce Grenfell, Reginald Beckwith, Arthur Wontner

'One of the best things to have happened to British films over the last five years.' – Gavin Lambert

† On American prints, Muir Mathieson was credited as the composer and with the Oscar nomination rather than Larry Adler, who was blacklisted at the time.
☿ William Rose; Larry Adler
♼ best British film

'In the eight centuries since he ruled the world, no man has matched the magnificence of his adventure!'

Genghis Khan *

US 1964 126m Technicolor Panavision
Columbia/Irving Allen/CCC/Avala

Temujin raises a Mongol army and revenges himself on his old enemy Jamuga.
Meandering epic in which brutality alternates with pantomimish comedy and bouts of sex. Necessarily patchy but reasonably watchable.
w Clarke Reynolds, Beverley Cross *d* Henry Levin *ph* Geoffrey Unsworth *m* Ducan Radic
☆ Omar Sharif, Stephen Boyd, Françoise Dorléac, James Mason, Robert Morley, Telly Savalas, Woody Strode, Eli Wallach, Yvonne Mitchell

Genius at Work

US 1946 61m bw
RKO (Herman Schlom)
Radio detectives expose a killer.
Rackety vehicle for a comedy team which never even approached Abbott and Costello.
w Robert E. Kent, Monte Brice *d* Leslie Goodwins *ph* Robert De Grasse
☆ Wally Brown, Alan Carney, Anne Jeffreys, Bela Lugosi, Lionel Atwill

A Genius in the Family: see *So Goes My Love*

Genou de Claire: see *Claire's Knee*

Les Gens de la Rizière: see *Rice People*

Les Gens du Voyage *

France 1938 123m bw
Tobis
Trials and tribulations of circus people on the road.
Interesting but overlong multi-drama.
w Jacques Feyder, Jacques Viol *d* Jacques Feyder
☆ Françoise Rosay, André Brule, Fabien Loris, Marie Glory, Sylvia Bataille

'Boredom is unavoidably the impression.' – Variety

Gente di rispetto: see *The Masters*

Gentle Annie

US 1944 80m bw
MGM
A marshal deals with a lady rancher who sees no harm in an occasional bank robbery to augment her income.
Tidy MGM second-string Western, originally intended for Robert Taylor.

w Lawrence Hazard *novel* Mackinlay Kantor *d* Andrew Marton
☆ James Craig, Marjorie Main, Donna Reed, Henry Morgan, Paul Langton, Barton MacLane

A Gentle Creature: see *Une Femme Douce*

The Gentle Giant

US 1967 93m Eastmancolor
Ivan Tors/Paramount

A small boy in Florida befriends a bear, which later saves his disapproving father's life.
Lumbering family movie which provided the impetus for a TV series.
w Edward J. Lakso, Andy White *novel* Gentle Ben by Walt Morey *d* James Neilson *ph* Howard Winner
☆ Dennis Weaver, Clint Howard, Vera Miles, Ralph Meeker, Huntz Hall

The Gentle Gunman

GB 1952 88m bw
GFD/Ealing (Michael Relph)

Tensions mount in an IRA family where one brother believes in peace.
Stilted and unconvincing pattern play which wouldn't have done at all once the Troubles restarted.
w Roger MacDougall *play* Roger MacDougall *d* Basil Dearden *ph* Gordon Dines *m* John Greenwood *ed* Peter Tanner
☆ John Mills, Dirk Bogarde, Elizabeth Sellars, Barbara Mullen, Robert Beatty, Eddie Byrne, Joseph Tomelty, Gilbert Harding, Liam Redmond, Jack MacGowran

The Gentle Sergeant: see *Three Stripes in the Sun*

The Gentle Sex **

GB 1943 93m bw
Rank/Two Cities/Concanen (Leslie Howard, Derrick de Marney)
Seven girls from different backgrounds are conscripted into the ATS.
Unassuming war propaganda, quite pleasantly done and historically very interesting.
w Moie Charles, Aimée Stuart, Phyllis Rose, Roland Pertwee *d* Leslie Howard, Maurice Elvey *ph* Robert Krasker *m* John Greenwood
☆ Rosamund John, Joan Greenwood, Joan Gates, Jean Gillie, Lilli Palmer, Joyce Howard, Barbara Waring, John Justin, Frederick Leister, Mary Jerrold, Everley Gregg
† Leslie Howard is heard as narrator and recognizably glimpsed in two scenes photographed from behind.

The Gentle Trap

GB 1960 59m bw
Butcher's (Jack Parsons)
A first-time jewel thief falls among double-crossing bigger crooks.
Risible attempt at a tough-guy thriller, cliché-ridden and barely competent.
w Brock Williams, Alan Osborne *story* Guido Coen *d* Charles Saunders *ph* Ken Hodges *m* William Davies *ad* John Earl *ed* Peter Pitt
☆ Spencer Teakle, Felicity Young, Martin Benson, Dorinda Stevens, Dawn Brooks, Alan Edwards, Hugh Latimer

A Gentleman after Dark

US 1942 74m bw
Edward Small
A jewel thief comes out of prison to pay back his vindictive wife for shopping him.
Efficient melodrama of a dated kind.
w Patterson McNutt, George Bruce *story* A Whiff of Heliotrope by Richard Washburn Child *d* Edwin L. Marin *ph* Milton Krasner *m* Dimitri Tiomkin
☆ Brian Donlevy, Miriam Hopkins, Preston Foster, Harold Huber, Philip Reed, Gloria Holden, Douglass Dumbrille, Ralph Morgan
† Previously filmed in 1920 as *Heliotrope* with Fred Burton; in 1928 as *Forgotten Faces* with Clive Brook; and in 1936 as *Forgotten Faces* with Herbert Marshall.

A Gentleman at Heart

US 1942 66m bw
TCF (Walter Morosco)
A racetrack bookie has aspirations to the art business but finds there are crooks there too.

Fairly lively second feature.
w Lee Loeb, Harold Buchman *story* Paul Hervey Fox *d* Ray McCarey *ph* Charles Clarke *md* Emil Newman *ad* Richard Day, Nathan Juran *ed* J. Watson Webb Jnr
☆ Cesar Romero, Carole Landis, Milton Berle, J. Carrol Naish, Rose Hobart, Jerome Cowan, Elisha Cook Jnr, Steve Geray, Richard Derr, Francis Pierlot

Gentleman for a Day: see *Union Depot*

The Gentleman in Room 6 *

US 1951 11m bw
Meteor Films (George Brest)
In a seedy room in South America, a man we can't see gives orders to old associates. As he finally goes to shave, we see in the mirror that he is – Adolf Hitler!
A fairly sensational novelty at the time, and historically interesting still.
w Sidney Carroll *d* Alexander Hammid

Gentleman Jim **

US 1942 104m bw
Warner (Robert Buckner)
The rise to fame of boxer Jim Corbett.
Cheerful biopic of an 1890s show-off, mostly played for comedy.
w Vincent Lawrence, Horace McCoy *book* The Roar of the Crowd by James J. Corbett *d* Raoul Walsh *ph* Sid Hickox *m* Heinz Roemheld
☆ Errol Flynn, Alan Hale, Alexis Smith, John Loder, Jack Carson, Ward Bond, William Frawley, Rhys Williams, Arthur Shields

'Good-natured enough, but it lacks flavour.' – New Yorker, 1976

A Gentleman of Paris

GB 1931 76m bw
Stoll/Gaumont
A philandering French judge knows that the girl before him is innocent of murder, but dare not say so.
Tolerable melodrama of its time.
w Sinclair Hill, Sidney Gilliat, Sewell Collins *novel* His Honour the Judge by Niranjan Pal *d* Sinclair Hill *ph* Mutz Greenbaum *ad* A. L. Mazzei
☆ Arthur Wontner, Hugh Williams, Vanda Greville, Phyllis Konstam, Sybil Thorndike

'Now! It comes to the screen with nothing left unsaid and no emotion unstressed!'

Gentleman's Agreement **

US 1947 118m bw
TCF (Darryl F. Zanuck)
A journalist poses as a Jew in order to write about anti-semitism.
Worthy melodrama which caused a sensation at the time but as a film is alas rather dull and self-satisfied.
w Moss Hart *novel* Laura Z. Hobson *d* Elia Kazan *ph* Arthur Miller *m* Alfred Newman *ed* Harmon Jones
☆ Gregory Peck, Dorothy McGuire, John Garfield, Celeste Holm, Anne Revere, June Havoc, Albert Dekker, Jane Wyatt, Dean Stockwell
♼ best picture; Elia Kazan; Celeste Holm
☿ Moss Hart; Gregory Peck; Dorothy McGuire; Anne Revere; editing

Gentleman's Fate

US 1931 90m bw
MGM
A man goes to the bad after his wife walks out on him.
Dismal early talkie, one of several which killed off its star's career.
w Leonard Praskins *story* Ursula Parrott *d* Mervyn Le Roy
☆ John Gilbert, Louis Wolheim, Leila Hyams, Anita Page, John Miljan, Marie Prevost

'It got a laugh at the Strand Saturday afternoon, where all of the audience probably thought the same thing, that Gilbert died too late as the picture had been dying since its start.' – Variety

A Gentleman's Gentleman

GB 1939 70m bw
Warner (Jerome Jackson)
A valet thinks his master is a murderer, and tries a little blackmail.

Uneasy serio-comic vehicle for a London stage character who had made his name in Hollywood.
w Austin Melford, Elizabeth Meehan *play* Philip MacDonald *d* Roy William Neill *ph* Basil Emmott
☆ Eric Blore, Peter Coke, Marie Lohr, David Hutcheson

Gentlemen Are Born

US 1934 74m bw
Warner
College graduates find it hard to get jobs.
Tedious and uninventive quartet of linked stories.
w Eugene Solow, Robert Lee Johnson *d* Alfred E. Green
☆ Franchot Tone, Ross Alexander, Dick Foran, Robert Light, Jean Muir, Margaret Lindsay, Ann Dvorak, Charles Starrett

Gentlemen Don't Eat Poets: see *The Grotesque*

Gentlemen Marry Brunettes

US 1955 95m Technicolor Cinemascope
UA/Russ-Field (Richard Sale, Robert Waterfield)
Two American shopgirls seek rich husbands in Paris, and find that their aunts were notorious there.
Jaded sequel to Gentlemen Prefer Blondes; it barely raises a smile and the numbers are dismal.
w Mary Loos, Richard Sale *d* Richard Sale *ph* Desmond Dickinson *m* Robert Farnon *ch* Jack Cole *ad* Paul Sheriff
☆ Jane Russell, Jeanne Crain, Alan Young, Scott Brady, Rudy Vallee
† Jeanne Crain's vocals were dubbed by Anita Ellis.

Gentlemen Prefer Blondes *

US 1953 91m Technicolor
TCF (Sol C. Siegel)
A dumb blonde and a showgirl go to Paris in search of rich husbands.
Musicalized and updated version of the twenties satire; no real vigour, but not too bad.
w Charles Lederer *novel* Anita Loos *d* Howard Hawks *ph* Harry J. Wild *m/ly* Jule Styne, Leo Robin *md* Lionel Newman *ch* Jack Cole
☆ Jane Russell, Marilyn Monroe, Charles Coburn, Tommy Noonan, Norma Varden, Elliott Reid, George Winslow

Geordie *

GB 1955 99m Technicolor
British Lion/Argonaut (Sidney Gilliat, Frank Launder)
US title: Wee Geordie
A weakly Scottish boy takes a physical culture course and becomes an Olympic hammer-thrower.
Slight comic fable, good to look at but without the necessary style to follow it through.
w Sidney Gilliat, Frank Launder *novel* David Walker *d* Frank Launder *ph* Wilkie Cooper *m* William Alwyn
☆ Bill Travers, Alastair Sim, Norah Gorsen, Raymond Huntley, Brian Reece, Miles Malleson, Stanley Baxter

George and Margaret

GB 1940 77m bw
Warner
The frictions of a suburban family come to boiling point.
Fairly spruce film version of a stage comedy in which the title pair were much talked of but never seen.
w Brock Williams, Rodney Ackland *play* Gerald Savory *d* George King
☆ Judy Kelly, Marie Lohr, Oliver Wakefield, Noel Howlett, Ann Casson, Arthur Macrae

George and Mildred

GB 1980 93m colour
Chips/ITC (Roy Skeggs)
A suburban husband on a weekend package holiday is mistaken for a hired killer.
Abysmal TV spinoff, seeming even more lugubrious since it was released after the death of the female star.
w Dick Sharples *d* Peter Frazer Jones *ph* Frank Watts *m* Philip Martell *ad* Carolyn Scott *ed* Peter Weatherley
☆ Yootha Joyce, Brian Murphy, Stratford Johns, Norman Eshley, Sheila Fearn, Kenneth Cope

'Flaccid entertainment even by routine sit-com standards.' – Martyn Auty, MFB

George in Civvy Street

GB 1946 79m bw
Columbia (Marcel Varnel, Ben Henry)

A soldier returns to his country pub and finds himself in the middle of a beer war.

The star's last film was oddly lacklustre and compared very badly with his earlier successes.

w Peter Fraser, Ted Kavanagh, Max Kester, Gale Pedrick d Marcel Varnel ph Phil Grindrod
☆ George Formby, Rosalyn Boulter, Ronald Shiner, Ian Fleming, Wally Patch

George of the Jungle *

↟↟ US 1997 91m colour
Buena Vista/Walt Disney/Mandeville (David Hoberman, Jordan Kerner, Jon Avnet)
⊟⊟ ⊚ ⊙. ⊘ ⊕

A dim-witted ape-man meets his first humans and falls in love.

An affectionate send-up of Tarzan, with a talking ape and a puppy-like elephant; Fraser, too, has a puppy-dog manner that gives this juvenile stuff a slight charm.

w Dana Olsen, Audrey Wells *characters developed by* Jay Ward d Sam Weisman ph Thomas Ackerman m Marc Shaiman pd Stephen Marsh ed Stuart Pappé, Roger Bondelli
☆ Brendan Fraser, Leslie Mann, Thomas Haden Church, Richard Roundtree, Greg Cruttwell, John Cleese

'Sporadically playful, it ends up wearing as thin as any film geared to a pre-teen sense of humor is bound to.' – *Kenneth Turan, Los Angeles Times*
† The film was based on an animated series for television that ran from 1967 to 1970.
†† It grossed $105m at the US box-office, and $35m elsewhere.

The George Raft Story

US 1961 105m bw
Allied Artists (Ben Schwab)
GB title: *Spin of a Coin*

In twenties New York, a dancer falls in with gangsters, but eludes them when he goes to Hollywood, where his acting career is harmed by temperament.

Tepid, unconvincing biopic, rather shoddily made but with flashes of interest.

w Crane Wilbur d Joseph M. Newman ph Carl Guthrie m Jeff Alexander
☆ Ray Danton, Julie London, Jayne Mansfield, Frank Gorshin, Neville Brand

George Washington Slept Here

US 1942 93m bw
Warner (Jerry Wald)
⊟

A New York couple move to a dilapidated country house.

Disappointingly stiff and ill-timed version of a play that should have been a natural.

w Everett Freeman *play* George Kaufman, Moss Hart d William Keighley ph Ernest Haller m Adolph Deutsch ad Max Parker, Mark-Lee Kirk
☆ Jack Benny, Ann Sheridan, Percy Kilbride, Charles Coburn, Hattie McDaniel, William Tracy, Lee Patrick, John Emery, Charles Dingle
⅄ art direction

George White's 1935 Scandals *

US 1935 83m bw
Fox (Winfield Sheehan)

A small-town star is discovered by a Broadway producer.

Again, basic plot serves to introduce some pretty good acts.

w Jack Yellen, Patterson McNutt d George White ph George Schneiderman m/ly various
☆ George White, Alice Faye, James Dunn, Eleanor Powell, Ned Sparks, Lyda Roberti, Cliff Edwards, Arline Judge

George White's Scandals *

US 1934 79m bw
Fox (Winfield Sheehan)

Romance blossoms backstage during the production of a big musical.

Revue with minimum plot and some impressive numbers.

w Jack Yellen, from the Broadway show directed by George White d Thornton Freeland, Harry Lachman, George White ph Lee Garmes, George Schneiderman m/ly various

☆ George White, Rudy Vallee, Alice Faye, Jimmy Durante, Dixie Dunbar, Adrienne Ames, Cliff Edwards, Gertrude Michael, Gregory Ratoff

George White's Scandals *

US 1945 95m bw
RKO (Jack J. Gross, Nat Holt, George White)
⊟

Ex-Scandals girls get together, and one disappears.

Lively comedy-musical with vaudeville orientations.

w Hugh Wedlock, Parke Levy, Howard Green d Felix E. Feist ph Robert de Grasse m Leigh Harline m/ly various
☆ Joan Davis, Jack Haley, Philip Terry, Martha Holliday, Ethel Smith, Margaret Hamilton, Glenn Tryon, Jane Greer, Fritz Feld, Rufe Davis

Georgia

Australia 1988 93m colour
Jethro (Bob Weis)

A tough tax investigator tries to find out the truth about how her mother died when she was a baby.

Implausible and uninteresting thriller that comes to no satisfactory conclusion.

w Ben Lewin, Joanna Murray-Smith, Bob Weis *story* Mac Gudgeon d Ben Lewin ph Yuri Sokol m Paul Grabowsky pd Jon Dowding ed Edward McQueen-Mason
☆ Judy Davis, John Bach, Julia Blake, Alex Menglet, Marshall Napier, Lewis Fiander

'A rather silly piece of hokum.' – *Scott Murray, Australian Cinema*

Georgia *

US/France 1995 117m Technicolor
CiBy 2000 (Ulu Grosbard, Barbara Turner, Jennifer Jason Leigh)
⊟ ⊘

A self-destructive woman with ambitions, but not the talent, to be a rock performer envies her elder sister who is a successful singer.

Intense study of family tensions within the life of an unhappy alcoholic who cannot come to terms with her own failings; it is affecting and irritating in equal measure.

w Barbara Turner d Ulu Grosbard ph Jan Kiesser pd Lester Cohen ed Elizabeth Kling
☆ Jennifer Jason Leigh, Mare Winningham, Ted Levine, John Doe, John C. Reilly, Jimmy Witherspoon

'A nearly perfect movie about a nearly total screw-up.' – *Entertainment Weekly*
'Performed to maximum effect by a host of top-flight actors.' – *Variety*
⅄ Mare Winningham

Georgia's Friends: see Four Friends

Georgy Girl *

GB 1966 100m bw
Columbia/Everglades (Otto Plaschkes, Robert A. Goldston)
⊟⊟ ⊟ ⊚.

An unattractive girl is fancied by her middle-aged employer but escapes to look after the illegitimate baby of her ungrateful friend.

Frantic black farce which seems determined to shock, but has a few good scenes once you get attuned to the mood. A censorship milestone.

w Margaret Forster, Peter Nichols *novel* Margaret Forster d Silvio Narizzano ph Ken Higgins m Alexander Faris
☆ James Mason, Lynn Redgrave, Charlotte Rampling, Alan Bates, Bill Owen, Clare Kelly, Rachel Kempson

'Another swinging London story filled with people running through London late at night, dancing madly in the rain, and visiting deserted children's playgrounds to ride on the roundabouts.' – *MFB*
'So glib, so clever, so determinedly kinky that everything seems to be devalued.' – *Pauline Kael*
'Its barrage of fashionable tricks proves exhausting.' – *Sight and Sound*
⅄ Ken Higgins; James Mason; Lynn Redgrave; title song (m Tom Springfield, ly Jim Dale)

Gerald McBoing Boing ***

↟↟ US 1951 7m Technicolor
UPA

A small boy becomes famous because he can't speak words: 'he goes boing-boing instead'.

Highly influential cartoon in what was then a new style; told with a light touch which is still extremely

funny. *Followed less successfully by* Gerald McBoing Boing's Symphony *and* Gerald McBoing Boing On Planet Moo.

w Dr Seuss (*Theodore Geisel*) d Robert Cannon m Gail Kubik pd John Hubley
⅄ best cartoon

The German Sisters *

West Germany 1981 107m Fujicolour
Bioskop Film/ (Eberhard Junkersdorf)
original title: *Die Bleierne Zeit*

Based on a real-life case, this is a suppositional account of how two well-brought-up girls can develop so differently.

wd Margarethe von Trotta ph Franz Rath m Nicolas Economou ed Dagmar Hirtz
☆ Jutta Lampe, Barbara Sukowa, Rudiger Vogler, Doris Schade, Verenice Rudolph

'Beautifully acted and strikingly shot, it all has a calculated, crowd-pleasing fervour.' – *Tom Milne, MFB*

Germany Year Zero *

France/Italy 1947 78m bw
Union Générale Cinématographique/DEFA
⊟

original title: *Germania Anno Zero*

Life in post-war Germany is so appalling that a boy kills his father and then himself.

Both realistic and pessimistic, this depressing film has a savage power of its own but totally fails to be constructive.

w Roberto Rossellini, Carlo Lizzani, Max Kolpet d Roberto Rossellini ph Robert Juillard m Renzo Rossellini ad Piero Filippone ed Eraldo Da Roma
☆ Edmund Moeschke, Ernst Pittschau, Franz Krüger, Ingetraud Hintze

'Sloppy, over-hasty and careless without even appearing to be informed by sincerity.' – *Paul Dehn*
'A film of inescapable irony and pity.' – *William Whitebait*

Germinal ***

France/Italy 1993 158m colour Panavision
AMLF/Renn/France 2/DD/Alternative Films/Nuova Artisti (Claude Berri)
⊟⊟ ⊚ ⊚. ⊘

In the 1870s, an unemployed railroad engineer finds work as a miner and joins a strike against poverty and appalling working conditions; the result is tragedy as the workers are starved, soldiers are called in, and the mine is sabotaged.

Detailed and sweeping epic evocation of Zola's novel, an impassioned portrait of exploitation and a plea for a more just society that retains much of the force of the original.

w Claude Berri, Arlette Langmann *novel* Emile Zola d Claude Berri ph Yves Angelo m Jean-Louis Roques ad Thanh At Hoang, Christian Marti ed Hervé de Luze
☆ Gérard Depardieu, Miou-Miou, Renaud, Jean Carmet, Judith Henry, Jean-Roger Milo, Laurent Terzieff

'One of those truly great examples of European filmmaking, a monumental statement of a movie about the fundamental struggles for life, love, freedom and the pursuit of even the most fragile happiness.' – *Phillipa Bloom, Empire*
'Strangely flat and matter-of-fact, this earnest depiction of class struggle will be a struggle for many viewers as well.' – *Variety*
† It was the most expensive film so far made in France, at a cost of 172m francs ($30m).

'Ten thousand red raiders roar into battle!'
Geronimo!

US 1939 89m bw
Paramount

The seventh cavalry gives the Indians a run for their money.

Muddled Western of no discernible merit.

wd Paul H. Sloane ph Henry Sharp m Gerard Carbonara
☆ Ellen Drew, Preston Foster, Andy Devine, Gene Lockhart, Ralph Morgan, William Henry

'Lusty and actionful melodrama geared to hit popular appeal.' – *Variety*

Geronimo

US 1962 101m Technicolor Panavision
UA/Laven-Gardner-Levy
⊟

In 1883 Geronimo and his remaining Apaches seek peace but are betrayed.

Moderate Western held back by script and performances.

w Pat Fielder d Arnold Laven ph Alex Phillips m Hugo Friedhofer
☆ Chuck Connors, Ross Martin, Kamala Devi

'A Warrior. A Leader. A Legend.'
Geronimo: An American Legend *

US 1994 115m Technicolor Panavision
Columbia (Walter Hill, Neil Canton)
⊟⊟ ⊟ ⊚. ⊘ ⊕
GB title: *Geronimo*

A young cavalry officer is assigned to a patrol to track down Geronimo, after the Chiricahua Apache leader breaks out of a reservation and defies attempts to recapture him and his small band of warriors.

Handsome, moderately gripping Western, although the story, told often in voice-over from the viewpoint of a white Texan participant, distances the audience from its central character, treating him from the start as mythic, and also provides for a degree of self-congratulation in the making of a comparatively Indian-free America.

w John Milius, Larry Gross d Walter Hill ph Lloyd Ahern m Ry Cooder pd Joe Alves ed Freeman Davies, Carmel Davies, Donn Aron
☆ Wes Studi, Gene Hackman, Jason Patric, Robert Duvall, Matt Damon, Rodney A. Grant, Kevin Tighe, Steve Reevis

'A physically impressive, well-acted picture whose slightly stodgy literary quality holds it back from even greater impact.' – *Todd McCarthy, Variety*

Gert and Daisy's Weekend

GB 1941 79m bw
Butcher's

Gert and Daisy accompany a crowd of Cockney children who are being evacuated to a stately home in the country.

Low-budget wartime comedy starring a popular double-act from the radio; their humour has lost its appeal, and the script and direction lack polish and style.

w Kathleen Butler, Maclean Rogers, H. F. Maltby d Maclean Rogers ph Stephen Dade md Percival Mackey ad W. J. Hemsley
☆ Elsie Waters, Doris Waters, Iris Vandeleur, Elizabeth Hunt, John Slater, Wally Patch, Annie Esmond, Aubrey Mallalieu, Gerald Rex

Gertrud *

Denmark 1966 115m bw
Pathé Contemporary/Palladium

A lawyer's wife leaves him for an unhappy affair with a young musician.

Austere psychological drama, better to look at than to listen to.

wd Carl Theodor Dreyer *play* Hjalmar Soderberg
☆ Nina Pens Rode, Bendt Rothe, Ebbe Rode, Axel Strobye

Gervaise *

France 1956 116m bw
Agnès Delahaye-Silver Films-CLCC

In 19th-century Paris, a laundrymaid is deserted by her lover, settles with another man and is able to open her own laundry, but they both take to drink.

The French equivalent of David Lean's Dickens films, superbly detailed and wonderful to look at, but with a plot which finally seems worthless and depressing.

w Jean Aurenche, Pierre Bost *novel* L'Assommoir *by* Emile Zola d René Clément ph René Juillard m Georges Auric ad Paul Bertrand
☆ Maria Schell, François Périer, Suzy Delair, Mathilde Casadesus

'A tremendous *tour de force* of literal realism ... a piece for the admiration of technicians, or for those whose consciences are purged and hands kept clean by the vicarious contemplation of how the other half lived – once upon a time.' – *David Robinson, MFB*
† Other French versions were made in 1902, 1909, 1911 and 1933.
⅄ best foreign film
⅊ best picture; François Périer

Gestapo: see Night Train to Munich

Get Back

↟↟ GB 1991 89m colour/bw
Entertainment/Allied Filmmakers/Front Page/MPL (Henry Thomas, Philip Knatchbull)

Documentary of a world tour by Paul McCartney and his band.

An extended music video that is a far cry from Lester's exuberant earlier treatment of the Beatles; he and McCartney are obviously older and staider.

d Richard Lester ph Jordan Cronenweth, Robert Paynter ed John Victor Smith

'Heavy on nostalgia and light on visual zap. Low-tech item will score limited biz in specialized play-off … By MTV standards, this is somewhere in a stone age.' – *Variety*

Get Carter **
GB 1971 112m Metrocolor
MGM/Mike Klinger
◧ ▣

A racketeer goes to Newcastle to avenge his brother's death at the hands of gangsters. He kills those responsible but is himself shot by a sniper.
Brutal British crime melodrama with faint echoes of Raymond Chandler. Sex and thuggery unlimited.
wd Mike Hodges *novel Jack's Return Home* by Ted Lewis ph Wolfgang Suschitzky m Roy Budd
☆ Michael Caine, John Osborne, Ian Hendry, Britt Ekland

'TV on the big screen – more sex, more violence, but no more attention to motivation or plot logic.' – *Arthur Knight*
'So calculatedly cool and soulless and nastily erotic that it seems to belong to a new era of virtuoso viciousness.' – *Pauline Kael*
'A cracking good movie.' – *Ken Russell*

Get Charlie Tully: see Ooh, You Are Awful

Get Cracking *
🏶 GB 1942 96m bw
Columbia (Ben Henry)
George joins the home guard.
Adequate star comedy.
w L. DuGarde Peach d Marcel Varnel ph Stephen Dade md Harry Bidgood
☆ George Formby, Edward Rigby, Frank Pettingell, Dinah Sheridan, Ronald Shiner, Wally Patch, Irene Handl

Get Hep to Love
US 1942 79m bw
Universal
GB title: She's My Lovely
A child concert prodigy is overworked by a mercenary aunt and goes off alone for a vacation.
Uninspired musical vehicle for young studio talents.
w Jay Dratler, M. M. Musselman d Charles Lamont
☆ Gloria Jean, Donald O'Connor, Peggy Ryan, Jane Frazee, Robert Paige, Nana Bryant, Edith Barrett, Cora Sue Collins

Get Off My Back: see Synanon

Get Off My Foot
GB 1935 83m bw
Warner (Irving Asher)
A Smithfield porter becomes a butler, and later finds himself heir to a fortune.
The nearest Max Miller came to being a genuine film star was in this first of eight Warner comedies, but the screen simply couldn't contain him.
w Frank Launder, Robert Edmunds *play Money By Wire* by Edward Paulton d William Beaudine ph Basil Emmott ad Peter Proud
☆ Max Miller, Chili Bouchier, Morland Graham, Jane Carr, Norma Varden, Reginald Purdell, Wally Patch

Get On the Bus **
US 1996 120m Technicolor
Columbia/40 Acres & A Mule (Reuben Cannon, Bill Borden, Barry Rosenbush)
◧ ▣

A varied group of black men travel to Washington together for the Million Man March, called by the Black Muslim leader Louis Farrakhan, in October 1995.
An effective, talky movie that overcomes the schematic problems of its representative passengers – ranging from the elderly to the delinquent young, from a cop to a killer, gay to heterosexual – to engage in a worthwhile debate on the difficulties of masculinity which transcends race.
w Reggie Rock Blythewood d Spike Lee ph Elliot Davis m Terence Blanchard pd Ina Mayhew ed Leander T. Sales
☆ Richard Belzer, DeAundre Bonds, Andre Braugher, Thomas Jefferson Byrd, Gabriel Casseus, Albert Hall, Ossie Davis, Charles S. Dutton

'Will prove enormously entertaining to black audiences and should get many former Lee fans of all stripes back on board.' – *Todd McCarthy, Variety*
† The film was shot on a budget of $2.5m raised from 15 black men: Larkin Arnold, Jheryl Busby, Reggie Rock Blythewood, Reuben Cannon, Johnnie L. Cochran Jnr, Lemuel Daniels, Danny Glover, Calvin Grigsby, Robert Guillaume, Robert Johnson, Olden Lee, Spike Lee, Charles D. Smith, Will Smith, and Wesley Snipes.

Get Out Your Handkerchiefs **
France 1978 108m Eastmancolor
Les Films Ariane/CAPAC/Belga/SODEP (Georges Dancigers, Alexandre Mnouchkine, Paul Claudon)
◧ ▣

original title: *Préparez Vos Mouchoirs*
A frigid wife is provided with a handsome lover by her doting husband but finds satisfaction only when she meets a bright 13-year-old boy.
Mildly amusing comedy, helped by some deft performances from the leading actors.
wd Bertrand Blier ph Jean Penzer m Georges Delerue ad Eric Moulard ed Claudine Merlin
☆ Gérard Depardieu, Patrick Dewaere, Carole Laure, Michel Serrault, Eleonore Hirt, Jean Rougerie, Sylvie Jolly, Riton

'Flagrantly funny in a slangy, buoyant, unpredictable way.' – *New Yorker*
🏆 best foreign film

'What if you can't avoid sexuality virginity bigotry stupidity insecurity hormones heavies prats liars rumours confusion and big big trouble? Don't get angry…'

Get Real *
GB/South Africa 1999 110m Rank Colour
Panavision
Paramount/Distant Horizon/Graphite (Stephen Taylor)
▤ 🎧

A gay sixth-former begins a covert relationship with the school's star athlete.
Earnest coming-of-age and coming-out drama, effectively written and acted for the most part, but a little glib.
w Patrick Wilde *play What's Wrong with Angry* by Patrick Wilde d Simon Shore ph Alan Almond m John Lunn pd Bernd Lepel ed Barrie Vince
☆ Ben Silverstone, Brad Gorton, Charlotte Brittain

'Ends up being merely likable and rather quaint.' – *José Arroyo, Sight and Sound*

Get Shorty **
US 1995 105m DeLuxe
MGM/Jersey
◧ ▤ 🔍 ⚙ ⊙ 🎧

A Miami debt collector for the Mob goes to Las Vegas after a defecting client and discovers that his talents fit him to become a successful film producer.
Enjoyable thriller that makes fun of Hollywood's hustlers and pretentions, but its impact is lessened by dull direction.
w Scott Frank *novel Elmore Leonard* d Barry Sonnenfeld ph Don Peterman m John Lurie pd Peter Larkin ed Jim Miller
☆ John Travolta, Gene Hackman, René Russo, Danny DeVito, Dennis Farina, Delroy Lindo, James Gandolfini, Jon Gries, David Paymer

'The pleasures of *Get Shorty* are genuine, but they remain stubbornly on the surface.' – *Entertainment Weekly*
† Bette Midler and Harvey Keitel appear uncredited.

Get to Know Your Rabbit
US 1972 91m Technicolor
Warner/Bernhardt-Gaer
A bored businessman enrols in a school of magic.
Whimsical satire which never takes off.
w Jordon Crittenden d Brian DePalma
☆ Tom Smothers, John Astin, Suzanne Zenor, Orson Welles, Samantha Jones, Allen Garfield, Katharine Ross

The Getaway
US 1941 89m bw
MGM
A lawman goes to jail, gets to know an imprisoned mob leader, and breaks out with him.
Routine rehash of 1935's Public Hero Number One.
w Wells Root, W. R. Burnett d Edward Buzzell

☆ Robert Sterling, Dan Dailey, Donna Reed, Charles Winninger, Henry O'Neill

'It takes two to make it. The big two!'

The Getaway **
US 1972 122m Technicolor Todd-AO 35
Solar/First Artists (David Foster, Mitchell Brower)
◧ ⊙

A convict leaves jail and promptly joins his wife in a bank robbery.
Violent, amoral, terse and fast-moving action melodrama which generally holds the interest despite its excesses.
w Walter Hill *novel Jim Thompson* d Sam Peckinpah ph Lucien Ballard m Quincy Jones
☆ Steve McQueen, Ali MacGraw, Ben Johnson, Sally Struthers, Al Lettieri, Slim Pickens

'This pair have no mission or "meaning". As in all romances, *The Getaway* simply extracts one element of reality and dwells on it. Nor is the violence "American". Pictures like this don't fail overseas.' – *Stanley Kauffmann*

The Getaway *
US 1994 115m DeLuxe Panavision
Warner/Largo/JVC (David Foster, Lawrence Turman, John Alan Simon)
◧ ▤ 🔍 ⊙

A crook, released from jail with the help of a gangster, promises his wife that their next robbery will be their last.
Slick, fast-moving thriller, an involved tale of duplicity and deception, but no improvement on the original and hardly worth re-making.
w Walter Hill, Amy Jones *novel Jim Thompson* d Roger Donaldson ph Peter Menzies Jnr m Mark Isham pd Joseph Nemec III ed Conrad Buff
☆ Alec Baldwin, Kim Basinger, Michael Madsen, James Woods, David Morse, Jennifer Tilly, James Stephens, Richard Farnsworth

'A pretty good remake of a pretty good action thriller.' – *Variety*
'Like a digitally remastered CD of a Top Forty hit that you never much cared for.' – *Terrence Rafferty, New Yorker*

Getting Away with Murder
US 1996 92m Technicolor
Rank/Peter V. Miller/Savoy (Penny Marshall, Frank Price)
◧ ▤

An ethics professor discovers that his kindly next-door neighbour is a Nazi war criminal who ran a concentration camp, and decides to poison him.
Feeble sitcom treatment of the Holocaust; it is a mystery why it was even made, or ever released. If it has a moral, it appears to be that murder is good for your sex life.
wd Harvey Miller ph Frank Tidy m John Debney pd John Jay Moore ed Richard Nord
☆ Dan Aykroyd, Lily Tomlin, Jack Lemmon, Bonnie Hunt, Brian Kerwin, Jerry Adler, Andy Romano

'A distasteful affair that should embarrass all concerned.' – *Daniel M. Kimmel, Variety*
† The film was released direct to video in Britain. In the US it took under $198,000 at the box-office.

Getting Even with Dad
🏶 US 1994 108m DeLuxe
MGM (Katie Jacobs, Pierce Gardner)
◧ ▤ 🔍 🎧

An 11-year-old hides the proceeds of his father's latest robbery and refuses to return it unless he promises to give him a good time and then return the money.
Crushingly dull comedy of father–son bonding and role reversal, in which the infant phenomenon that is Macaulay Culkin turns in a smug and charmless performance.
w Tom S. Parker, Jim Jennewein d Howard Deutch ph Tim Suhrstedt m Miles Goodman pd Virginia L. Randolph ed Richard Halsey
☆ Macaulay Culkin, Ted Danson, Glenne Headly, Gailard Sartain, Saul Rubinek, Hector Elizondo, Sam McMurray, Kathleen Wilhoite

'A dim affair, lacking even the gooey conviction of Hollywood's usual efforts to make one the better convinced of family values.' – *Derek Malcolm, Guardian*

Getting Gertie's Garter
US 1945 73m bw
UA (Edward Small)
A businessman tries all manner of wiles to retrieve an incriminating garter.
Silly variation on Up in Mabel's Room, with similar team and cast. A few laughs are inevitable.
w Allan Dwan, Karen de Wolf *play Wilson Collison, Avery Hopwood* d Allan Dwan ph Charles Lawton Jnr
☆ Dennis O'Keefe, Marie McDonald, Binnie Barnes, Barry Sullivan, J. Carrol Naish

Getting It Right
US 1989 102m Fujicolour
▤ 🔍

A hairdresser becomes involved with three contrasting women.
Mildly amusing, old-fashioned, romp.
w Elizabeth Jane Howard *novel Elizabeth Jane Howard* d Randal Kleiser ph Clive Tickner pd Caroline Amies ad Frank Walsh ed Chris Kelly
☆ Jesse Birdsall, Helena Bonham Carter, Peter Cook, John Gielgud, Jane Horrocks, Lynn Redgrave, Shirley Anne Field, Pat Heywood, Bryan Pringle, Nan Munro

'A contemporary London romance that vacillates between the relishable and the acutely embarrassing.' – *Kim Newman, MFB*

Getting It Up: see Les Valseuses

The Getting of Wisdom **
Australia 1977 101m Eastmancolor
Southern Cross/AFC/Victorian Film Corporation/9 Television Network (Phillip Adams)
◧ ▤

In 1897 a backwoods girl is sent to an exclusive Melbourne ladies' college and eventually wins a music scholarship.
Praiseworthy period piece which thankfully seems to have no axe to grind and is all the better for it.
w Eleanor Witcombe *novel Henry Handel Richardson (Ethel Richardson)* d Bruce Beresford ph Donald McAlpine m various pd John Stoddart
☆ Susannah Fowle, Sheila Helpmann, Patricia Kennedy, John Waters, Barry Humphries, Kerry Armstrong

Getting Straight *
US 1970 125m Eastmancolor
Columbia/The Organization (Richard Rush)
▤

A political activist returns to college in order to teach and discovers the foolishness of most contemporary attitudes.
Modish comedy, too long, far too pleased with itself, and now irrevocably dated.
w Robert Kaufman *novel Ken Kolb* d Richard Rush ph Laszlo Kovacs m Ronald Stein
☆ Elliott Gould, Candice Bergen, Robert F Lyons, Jeff Corey, Max Julien, Cecil Kellaway

'Witness History.'
'In The Tradition Of "Gone With The Wind".'

Gettysburg **
US 1993 254m Foto-Kem
Mayfair/Turner (Robert Katz, Moctesuma Esparza)
◧ ▤ 🔍 ⊙

In July 1863, during three days of fighting that left more than 50,000 dead, Confederate General Robert E. Lee's troops are defeated at Gettysburg in the decisive battle in the American Civil War.
A stirring and epic historical re-creation of the event as seen from the point of view of the commanders and their officers, concentrating on strategy as well as the actual bloody fighting; it ignores the wider causes of the war and does little to explain how such slaughter could come about among men of apparent goodwill.
wd Ronald F. Maxwell *novel The Killer Angels* by Michael Shaara ph Kees van Oostum m Randy Edelman pd Cary White ed Corky Ehlers
☆ Tom Berenger, Martin Sheen, Stephen Lang, Richard Jordan, Jeff Daniels, Sam Elliott, C. Thomas Howell, Kevin Conway, Andrew Prine, Maxwell Caulfield, James Lancaster, Royce Applegate, Brian Mallon, Buck Taylor, Patrick Stuart

'Succeeds as a motion picture event, and as a re-creation of a pivotal chapter of American history.' – *Variety*
† The film was shown on TV in a longer version as a three-part mini-series and also released on

---

🏶 film suitable for family viewing   ◧ VHS video-cassette for the British PAL system   ▤ VHS video-cassette for the British PAL system in wide screen-format   ⊡ Video cassette in a computer-colourised version   ▤ American NTSC video-cassette   🔍 Laser disc video in a version that runs for just under six hours.

Ghare-Baire: see *The Home and the World*

Ghost **
US   1990   127m   Technicolor
UIP/Paramount/Howard W. Koch (Lisa Weinstein)

◎ ▤ ⊙ ♫

A murdered stockbroker returns as a ghost to hunt down his killers.
Deftly made, romantic, sentimental, sometimes silly thriller that was the surprise hit of 1990, either because of its fundamentalist view of heaven and hell or its underlying theme that revenge is good for the soul.
w Bruce Joel Rubin d Jerry Zucker pd Adam Greenberg pd Jane Musky ed Walter Murch sp Industrial Light and Magic
☆ Patrick Swayze, Demi Moore, Tony Goldwyn, Whoopi Goldberg, Stanley Lawrence, Christopher J. Keene, Susan Breslau, Martina Degnan
'Amiable entertainment, even for those not looking for reassurances that the afterlife still permits use of the subway.' – David Robinson, *The Times*
♟ Whoopi Goldberg; Bruce Joel Rubin
⅋ best picture; best score; best film editing
🏆 Whoopi Goldberg

The Ghost and Mr Chicken
US   1965   90m   Technicolor/Techniscope
Universal (Edward J. Montagne)
An incompetent small-town reporter finds ghosts in a local murder mansion.
Old-fashioned scare comedy starring a highly resistible comic. A big hit in American small towns.
w James Fritzell, Everett Greenbaum d Alan Rafkin ph William Margulies m Vic Mizzy
☆ Don Knotts, Skip Homeier, Joan Staley, Liam Redmond, Dick Sargent, Reta Shaw

'Doin' what comes supernaturally … it's the man-woman affair that's like nothing on earth!'

The Ghost and Mrs Muir *
US   1947   104m   bw
TCF (Fred Kohlmar)
A widow refuses to be frightened away from her seaside home by the ghost of a sea captain, with whom she falls in love.
Charming sentimental fable in Hollywood's best style.
w Philip Dunne novel R. A. Dick d Joseph L. Mankiewicz ph Charles Lang m Bernard Herrmann ad Richard Day, George Davis
☆ Gene Tierney, Rex Harrison, George Sanders, Edna Best, Vanessa Brown, Anna Lee, Robert Coote, Natalie Wood, Isobel Elsom
'A not at all disagreeable piece of whimsy.' – *News Chronicle*
'A jolly caper, gently humorous and often sparkling.' – *New York Times*
† A half-hour TV series followed in 1968.
⅋ Charles Lang

The Ghost and the Darkness
US   1996   109m   DeLuxe   Panavision
Paramount/Constellation (Gale Anne Hurd, Paul Radin, A. Kitman Ho)

◎ ▤ ⊙ ♫

In the 1890s, an engineer and a big-game hunter stalk two man-eating lions who are terrorizing the locals and preventing the building of a railway across Africa.
A stilted, curiously old-fashioned colonial adventure, broadly acted and dully written.
w William Goldman d Stephen Hopkins ph Vilmos Zsigmond m Jerry Goldsmith pd Stuart Wurtzel ed Robert Brown, Steve Mirkovich sp Stan Winston Studio
☆ Michael Douglas, Val Kilmer, Bernard Hill, John Kani, Tom Wilkinson, Brian McCardie, Henry Cele, Om Puri
'A blatantly trashy film that marks time until its climax.' – *Kim Newman, Sight and Sound*
♟ sound effects editing (Bruce Stambler)

The Ghost and the Guest
US   1943   59m   bw
PRC (Arthur Alexander)
A honeymooning couple find no peace in an eerie country house with hidden ghosts and gangsters.
Predictable, mildly amusing second feature comedy-thriller.
w Morey Amsterdam story Milt Gross d William Nigh

☆ James Dunn, Florence Rice, Mabel Todd, Sam McDaniel, Robert Dudley

The Ghost Breakers ***
US   1940   85m   bw
Paramount (Arthur Hornblow Jnr)

▤ ⊙

A girl inherits a West Indian castle and finds herself up to her neck in ghosts, zombies and buried treasure.
Archetypal comedy horror, very well done; a follow-up to the success of The Cat and the Canary, and just about as entertaining.
w Walter de Leon play Paul Dickey, Charles W. Goddard d George Marshall ph Charles Lang m Ernst Toch ad Hans Dreier, Robert Asher
☆ Bob Hope, Paulette Goddard, Paul Lukas, Willie Best, Richard Carlson, Lloyd Corrigan, Anthony Quinn, Noble Johnson, Pedro de Cordoba
'Bob Hope can joke, apparently, even with a risen corpse.' – MFB
'Paramount has found the fabled formula for making audiences shriek with laughter and fright at one and the same time.' – New York Times
† Previously filmed in 1914 with H. B. Warner; in 1922 with Wallace Reid; and remade in 1953 as *Scared Stiff*.

The Ghost Camera
GB   1933   68m   bw
H & S Films/Real Art (Julius Hagen)

▤

A chemist investigates how a camera containing film of a murder came into his possession.
Mundane, stagey thriller with much talk and little action.
w H. Fowler Mear story Jefferson Farjeon d Bernard Vorhaus ph Ernest Palmer ad James A. Carter ed David Lean
☆ Ida Lupino, Henry Kendall, John Mills, S. Victor Stanley, George Merritt, Felix Aylmer

Ghost Catchers
US   1944   68m   bw
Universal
A Southern colonel and his beautiful daughters have spooks in their mansion – or bats in the belfry.
Lower-case farce made when the stars' contract was being allowed to run out.
w Edmund L. Hartmann story Milt Gross, Edward Cline d Edward Cline
☆ Ole Olsen, Chic Johnson, Gloria Jean, Leo Carrillo, Martha O'Driscoll, Andy Devine, Lon Chaney Jnr, Walter Catlett, Henry Armetta

Ghost Chase
🎬 West Germany   1987   89m   colour
Medusa/Contropolis/pro-ject Film/Hessischer Rundfunk (Dean Heyde)

▤

Horror movie-makers summon a ghost to help them find treasure.
Its convoluted plot seems designed to confuse the young audience at which it is presumably aimed, though it misses the target anyway.
w Roland Emmerich, Thomas Kubisch story Roland Emmerich, Oliver Eberle d Roland Emmerich ph Karl Walter Lindenlaub pd Ekkehard Schroeer, Sonja B. Zimmer ed Brigitte Pia Fritsche sp Joachim Grueninger, Hubert Bartholomae
☆ Jason Lively, Jill Whitlow, Tim McDaniel, Paul Gleason, Chuck Mitchell, Leonard Lansink, Ian McNaughton, Toby Kaye, Cynthia Frost, Julian Curry

The Ghost Comes Home
US   1940   79m   bw
MGM
The return of a long-lost father causes embarrassment to his family.
Hoary hide-in-the-closet farce with all concerned straining at the leash.
w Richard Maibaum, Harry Ruskin d William Thiele
☆ Frank Morgan, Billie Burke, Ann Rutherford, John Shelton, Reginald Owen, Donald Meek, Nat Pendleton

Ghost Dad
US   1990   84m   DeLuxe
Universal/SAH (Terry Nelson)

◎ ▤ ⊙ ♫

A frantic businessman, killed in a traffic accident, is given three days to sort out his affairs and see that his orphaned children are provided for.
A sentimental comedy dependent on its special effects for laughs; otherwise the jokes are so thin as to be almost invisible.
w Chris Reese, Brent Maddock, S. S. Wilson d Sidney Poitier ph Andrew Laszlo m Henry Mancini pd Henry Bumstead ed Pembroke Herring
☆ Bill Cosby, Kimberly Russell, Denise Nicholas, Ian Bannen, Christine Ebersole, Barry Corbin, Salim Grant, Brooke Fontaine

'All assassins live beyond the law. Only one follows the code.'

Ghost Dog: The Way of the Samurai ***
US/Japan/France/Germany   1999   116m   DeLuxe
Film4/JVC/Bac Films/Canal+/Pandora/ARD/Degeto/Plywood (Richard Guay, Jim Jarmusch)
A reclusive, pigeon-fancying hitman, who leads his life as if he were a samurai warrior, becomes a target for assassination after killing a member of a Mafia gang.
A film that is likely to divide audiences: some will find its literary structure pretentious, others will enjoy a slyly comic movie about a clash between two different codes of honour.
wd Jim Jarmusch ph Robby Muller m RZA pd Ted Berner ed Jay Rabinowitz
☆ Forest Whitaker, John Tormey, Cliff Gorman, Henry Silva, Isaach de Bankolé, Tricia Vessey, Victor Argo, Gene Ruffini, Richard Portnow, Camille Winbush
'A playful but exceedingly wispy piece of doodling.' – Todd McCarthy, Variety

The Ghost Goes West ***
GB   1935   85m   bw
London Films (Alexander Korda)

◎ ▤

When a millionaire buys a Scottish castle and transports it stone by stone to America, the castle ghost goes too.
Amusing whimsy which is always pleasant but never quite realizes its full potential; fondly remembered for its star performance.
w Robert E. Sherwood, Geoffrey Kerr story Eric Keown d René Clair ph Harold Rosson m Mischa Spoliansky
☆ Robert Donat, Jean Parker, Eugene Pallette, Elsa Lanchester, Ralph Bunker, Patricia Hilliard, Morton Selten
'Fine business likely in the keys, but not for the tanks.' – Variety
'Although the film is not cast in the fluid, rapidly paced style of Clair's typical work, it has a sly wit and an adroitness of manner that make it delightful.' – André Sennwald, New York Times
'It is typical of the British film industry that M. René Clair should be brought to this country to direct a Scottish film full of what must to him be rather incomprehensible jokes about whisky and bagpipes, humorous fantasy without any social significance, realistic observation, or genuine satire.' – Graham Greene

The Ghost in the Invisible Bikini
US   1966   82m   Pathécolor
American International
A motor cycle gang gets mixed up with a rejuvenated corpse in a haunted mansion.
Mindless beach party stuff suffering under one of Hollywood's most inane titles.
w Louis M. Heyward, Elwood Ullman d Don Weis
☆ Boris Karloff, Basil Rathbone, Patsy Kelly, Tommy Kirk, Deborah Walley, Aron Kincaid, Quinn O'Hara, Jesse White

'They said the killer was better off dead. They were wrong.'

Ghost in the Machine
US   1993   95m   DeLuxe
TCF (Paul Schiff)

◎ ▤ ⊙ ♫

The spirit of a serial killer escapes into cyber-space at the moment of his death, so that he can continue his killing spree.

Paranoid fantasy about computers aimed at a teenage audience; it is a familiar and silly horror story that is dependent upon some gruesome moments to maintain interest.
w William Davies, William Osborne d Rachel Talalay ph Phil Meheux m Graeme Revell pd James Spencer ed Janice Hampton, Erica Huggins sp make-up: Alterian Studios; visual effects: VIFX
☆ Karen Allen, Chris Mulkey, Ted Marcoux, Wil Horneff, Jessica Walter, Brandon Quintin Adams, Rick Ducommun, Nancy Fish, Jack Laufer
'The film's social statement may be hopelessly muddy, but its adroit sense of fun and thrills cannot be discounted.' – Variety
† The film was released direct to video in Britain.

Ghost in the Shell
Japan/GB   1995   83m   Eastmancolor
Straight/Kodansha/Bandai/Manga

◎ ▤ ⊚ ♫

aka: Kokaku Kidotai
In Tokyo in 2029, a cyborg cop investigates a master criminal and discovers that he is a government-controlled entity that is trying to escape and become human.
Spectacular-looking Japanese animated film, but one that, like so many of its kind, involves a confusing narrative and peculiar metaphysics that reduce interest in its depiction of a corrupt future.
w Kazunori Ito graphic novel Shirow Masamune d Mamoru Oshii ph Hisao Shirai m Kenji Kawai ad Hiromasa Ogura sp Shuichi Kakesu
☆ Featuring the voices of: Richard George, Mimi Woods, William Frederick, Abe Lasser, Christopher Joyce, Mike Sorich, Ben Isaacson
'This is exactly the kind of film that James Cameron would make if Disney ever let him through the front gates.' – Empire

'You can't keep a good monster down!'

The Ghost of Frankenstein
US   1942   67m   bw
Universal (George Waggner)

▤ ⊙ ♫

Frankenstein's second son implants evil shepherd Igor's brain into the monster.
The rot sets in with this flatly-handled potboiler, which had none of the literary mood or cinematic interest of Bride or Son which preceded it, and suffered from a particularly idiotic script.
w W. Scott Darling story Eric Taylor d Erle C. Kenton ph Milton Krasner, Woody Bredell m Charles Previn md Hans J. Salter
☆ Cedric Hardwicke, Lon Chaney Jnr, Bela Lugosi, Lionel Atwill, Evelyn Ankers, Ralph Bellamy
† See Frankenstein for other episodes in the series.

The Ghost of St Michael's **
🎬 GB   1941   82m   bw
Ealing (Basil Dearden)
A school is evacuated to the Isle of Skye, and the local ghost turns out to be an enemy agent.
The star's schoolmaster character is here at its seedy best, and he is well supported in a comedy-thriller plot.
w Angus Macphail, John Dighton d Marcel Varnel ph Derick Williams
☆ Will Hay, Claude Hulbert, Felix Aylmer, Raymond Huntley, Elliot Mason, Charles Hawtrey, John Laurie, Hay Petrie, Roddy Hughes, Manning Whiley

Ghost Ship
GB   1952   74m   bw
Anglo Amalgamated

▤

A motor yacht proves to be haunted by the previous owner's murdered wife.
Mildly unusual second feature.
wd Vernon Sewell
☆ Dermot Walsh, Hazel Court, Hugh Burden, John Robinson

The Ghost Ship
US   1943   69m   bw
RKO (Val Lewton)

⊙

The captain of a merchant ship is driven mad by isolation.
Long unavailable because of legal problems, this very minor Val Lewton thriller inevitably disappoints because it has no supernatural elements and must compare unfavourably with both The Caine Mutiny

and The Sea Wolf, *which plotwise it closely resembles.*
w Donald Henderson Clarke d Mark Robson ph Nicholas Musuraca m Roy Webb
☆ Richard Dix, Russell Wade, Edith Barrett, Ben Bard, Edmund Glover, Skelton Knaggs

'She'll never rest till her tale is told!'

Ghost Story *
GB   1974   89m   Fujicolour
Stephen Weeks
▤

Former college acquaintances spend a weekend at a country house, and one of them is drawn into tragic events of forty years before.
Overlong chiller, ingeniously shot in India but very variably acted; aims for the M. R. James style and sometimes achieves it, but badly needs cutting.
w Rosemary Sutcliff, Stephen Weeks d Stephen Weeks ph Peter Hurst m Ron Geesin
☆ Murray Melvin, Larry Dann, Vivian Mackerall, Marianne Faithfull, Anthony Bate, Leigh Lawson, Barbara Shelley

Ghost Story
US   1981   110m   Technicolor
Universal (Ronald G. Smith)
▤ ◎ ⊚ ⌖

Four old men tell each other ghost stories, but are haunted by a guilty secret of their own.
Bizarre vehicle for four welcome old actors, ruined by the director's insistence on frequent shock cuts to the rotting spectre. A subtler treatment akin to that of The Uninvited might have produced a little masterpiece.
w Lawrence D. Cohen novel Peter Straub d John Irvin ph Jack Cardiff m Philippe Sarde
☆ Fred Astaire, Melvyn Douglas, John Houseman, Douglas Fairbanks Jnr, Craig Wasson, Patricia Neal, Alice Krige, Jacqueline Brookes

The Ghost that Never Returns *
USSR   1929   80m   bw   silent
Sovkino
original title: *Prividenie, Kotoroe ne Vozvrashchaetsya*
After ten years' imprisonment for leading a strike, a South American worker is given a day's leave which may result in his death.
Unsatisfactory communist propaganda of its time, probably rescued from obscurity by its title. A few strikingly visual moments stand out, but the narrative is needlessly obscure.
w Valentin Turkin story Henri Barbusse d Abram Room ph Dmitri Feldman
☆ B. Ferdinandov, Olga Zhizneva, Maxime Straukh

The Ghost that Walks Alone
US   1943   63m   bw
Columbia
Honeymooners find a dead radio producer in their suite.
Ho-hum second feature mystery.
w Doris Shattuck, Clarence Upson Young d Lew Landers ph L. William O'Connell
☆ Arthur Lake, Janis Carter, Frank Sully, Lynne Roberts

Ghost Town
US   1956   72m   bw
Bel Air/UA
Stagecoach passengers are forced to spend the night in a ghost town beset by Indians.
Thin Western second with a few effectively restrained moments.
w Jameson Brewer d Allen Miner
☆ Kent Taylor, John Smith, Marian Carr, John Doucette

The Ghost Train **
👫   GB   1931   72m   bw
Gainsborough (Michael Balcon)
Passengers stranded at a haunted station in Cornwall include a detective posing as a silly ass in order to trap smugglers.
Excellent early sound version of a comedy-thriller play which has not only been among the most commercially successful ever written but also provided the basic plot for many another comedy: Oh Mr Porter, The Ghost of St Michael's, Back Room Boy, Hold That Ghost, *etc. Previously filmed as a silent in 1927, with Guy Newall.*
w Angus MacPhail, Lajos Biro play Arnold Ridley d Walter Forde ph Leslie Rowson ad Walter Murton ed Ian Dalrymple

☆ Jack Hulbert, Cicely Courtneidge, Donald Calthrop, Ann Todd, Cyril Raymond, Angela Baddeley, Allan Jeayes

The Ghost Train *
👫   GB   1941   85m   bw
Gainsborough (Edward Black)
Adequate remake with the lead split into two characters, which doesn't work quite so well.
w Marriott Edgar, Val Guest, J. O. C. Orton d Walter Forde ph Jack Cox
☆ Arthur Askey, Richard Murdoch, Kathleen Harrison, Morland Graham, Linden Travers, Peter Murray Hill, Herbert Lomas

Ghostbusters *
👫   US   1984   105m   Metrocolor Panavision
Columbia/Delphi (Ivan Reitman)
▦ ▤ ◎ ⊚ ⊚ ⌖

Unemployed academic parapsychologists set themselves up as ghostbusters and destroy several monstrous apparitions on the streets of New York.
Crude farce with expensive special effects. It took more money – millions more – than Indiana Jones and the Temple of Doom, *which must say something about the age we live in.*
w Dan Aykroyd, Harold Ramis d Ivan Reitman ph Laszlo Kovacs, Herb Wagreitch m Elmer Bernstein pd John DeCuir ed Sheldon Kahn, David Blewitt
☆ Bill Murray, Dan Aykroyd, Harold Ramis, Sigourney Weaver, Rick Moranis, Annie Potts, William Atherton
𝄢 title song (m/ly Ray Parker)

Ghostbusters II
👫   US   1989   108m   DeLuxe   Panavision
Columbia TriStar (Ivan Reitman)
▦ ▤ ◎ ⊚ ⌖

The disbanded Ghostbusters reform to deal with supernatural threats to New York.
Rambling, disjointed sequel of little amusement.
w Harold Ramis, Dan Aykroyd d Ivan Reitman ph Michael Chapman m Randy Edelman pd Bo Welch ed Sheldon Kahn, Donn Cambern
☆ Bill Murray, Dan Aykroyd, Sigourney Weaver, Harold Ramis, Rick Moranis, Ernie Hudson, Annie Potts, Peter MacNicol, Harris Yulin, David Margulies

Ghostly Love
Hong Kong   1990   92m   colour
Kam Chung Kuey
▦

A man's love for the spirit of a dead girl brings her back to life.
A ghost story that mixes crude sex and cruder acting in an incomprehensible plot which is rendered in confusing subtitles: 'I counted something is happening recently. You better watch out lately,' *says one character in an attempt to explain events.*
d Wu Kwo Rem
☆ Emily Chu, Hui Tien Chee, Lam Wei, Mark Long

Ghosts from the Past: see *Ghosts of Mississippi*

The Ghosts of Berkeley Square *
GB   1947   89m   bw
British National (Louis H. Jackson)
Two 18th-century ghosts are doomed to haunt a London house until royalty visits.
Thin, skittish whimsy with pleasant moments.
w James Seymour novel *No Nightingales* by S. J. Simon, Caryl Brahms d Vernon Sewell ph Ernest Palmer
☆ Robert Morley, Claude Hulbert, Felix Aylmer, Yvonne Arnaud, Abraham Sofaer, Ernest Thesiger, Marie Lohr, Martita Hunt, A. E. Matthews, John Longden, Ronald Frankau, Wilfrid Hyde-White, Esmé Percy, Mary Jerrold, Wally Patch and also Martin Miller

Ghosts of Mississippi
US   1996   130m   Technicolor   Panavision
Rank/Castle Rock (Frederick Zollo, Nicholas Paleologos, Andrew Scheinman, Rob Reiner)
▦ ▤ ◎
GB title: *Ghosts from the Past*
In the 80s, an assistant district attorney decides to reopen the case of a racist who killed black civil

rights activist Medgar Evans in 1963 and was exonerated by two all-white juries.
A Hollywood re-creation of a real trial, in which all the participants, save the murderer Beckwith, are reduced to stereotypes; Woods's intense performance as the killer overwhelms the surrounding, self-congratulatory blandness.
w Lewis Colick d Rob Reiner ph John Seale m Marc Shaiman pd Lilly Kilvert ed Robert Leighton
☆ Alec Baldwin, Whoopi Goldberg, James Woods, Craig T. Nelson, Susanna Thompson, Lucas Black, William H. Macy, Virginia Madsen
'Tepid and two dimensional in the manner of many telepics.' – *Godfrey Cheshire, Variety*

Ghosts ... of the Civil Dead
Australia   1988   93m   colour
Electric/Correctional Services/Outlaw Values (Evan English)
▦ ⌖
Prisoners react violently against a repressive regime.
A confused narrative weakens a brutal drama, filmed in a documentary style.
w Gene Conkie, John Hillcoat, Evan English, Nick Cave, Hugo Race d John Hillcoat ph Paul Goldman, Graham Wood m Nick Cave, Mick Harvey, Blixa Bargeld pd Chris Kennedy ed Stewart Young
☆ Dave Field, Mike Bishop, Chris de Rose, Nick Cave, Freddo Dierck, Vincent Gil, Bogdan Koca, Kevin Mackey, Dave Mason

The Ghoul **
GB   1933   79m   bw
Gaumont (Michael Balcon)
▦
An Egyptologist returns from the tomb to uncover stolen jewels and a murderer.
Fascinating minor horror piece reminiscent of The Old Dark House, *with many effective moments and a ripe cast.*
w Frank King, Leonard Hines, L. DuGarde Peach, Roland Pertwee, John Hastings Turner, Rupert Downing novel Frank King d T. Hayes Hunter ph Gunther Krampf make-up Heinrich Heitfeld
☆ Boris Karloff, Cedric Hardwicke, Ralph Richardson, Kathleen Harrison, Ernest Thesiger, Dorothy Hyson, Anthony Bushell, D. A. Clarke-Smith
'Lacks general US appeal because of bad plot mechanics, mostly bad acting, and colourless camerawork.' – *Variety*
† Remade after a fashion as *What A Carve Up* (1961).

The Ghoul
GB   1975   87m   Eastmancolor
Tyburn (Kevin Francis)
In the twenties, a group of stranded travellers is reduced in number when they take shelter in the house of a former clergyman.
The build-up is too slow, the revelation too nasty, and the whole thing is a shameless rip-off of the structure of Psycho.
w John Elder (Anthony Hinds) d Freddie Francis ph John Wilcox m Harry Robinson
☆ Peter Cushing, Alexandra Bastedo, John Hurt, Gwen Watford, Veronica Carlson, Don Henderson
'Peter Cushing brings out his violin for a soothing spot of the classics, the local copper mutters veiled warnings before trundling off on his bike, and thick fog swirls round the exterior sets at the drop of a canister.' – *Geoff Brown*

Ghoulies
US   1985   88m   colour
Empire (Jefery Levy)
▦ ▤
After a youth invokes a Satanic ritual, vicious imp-like creatures are loosed on the world.
Cheap and nasty rip-off of Gremlins, *lacking wit and style and even failing at slapstick comedy.*
w Luca Bercovici, Jefery Levy d Luca Bercovici ph Mac Ahlberg m Richard Band, Shirley Walker
☆ Peter Liapis, Lisa Pelikan, Michael Des Barres, Jack Nance, Peter Risch, Tamara de Treaux
† It was followed by *Ghoulies 2*, directed by Albert Band, in 1988, and *Ghoulies 3: Ghoulies Go to College*, directed by John Carl Buechler, in 1991, both conforming to the usual law of diminishing returns. Both were also released direct to video.

Ghoulies 4 (1993), directed by Jim Wynorski, continued the downward trend.

GI Blues
US   1960   104m   Technicolor
Paramount/Hal B. Wallis (Paul Nathan)
▦ ▤ ⊚
A guitar-playing gunner with the American army in West Germany falls for a cabaret dancer.
Routine star vehicle marking Presley's return from military service.
w Edmund Beloin, Henry Garson d Norman Taurog ph Loyal Griggs m Joseph J. Lilley
☆ Elvis Presley, Juliet Prowse, Robert Ivers, Letitia Roman, Arch Johnson

Giant **
US   1956   197m   Warnercolor
Warner (George Stevens, Henry Ginsburg)
▦ ▤ ◎ ⊚
The life of a Texas cattle rancher through two generations.
Sprawling, overlong family saga with unconvincing acting but good visual style.
w Fred Guiol, Ivan Moffat novel Edna Ferber d George Stevens ph William C. Mellor, Edwin DuPar m Dimitri Tiomkin ad Boris Leven ed William Hornbeck, Philip W. Anderson, Fred Bohanan
☆ Rock Hudson, Elizabeth Taylor, James Dean, Mercedes McCambridge, Carroll Baker, Chill Wills, Jane Withers, Dennis Hopper, Sal Mineo, Rod Taylor, Judith Evelyn, Earl Holliman, Alexander Scourby, Paul Fix
‡ George Stevens
𝄢 best picture; script; Dimitri Tiomkin; Rock Hudson; James Dean; Mercedes McCambridge; art direction; editing

The Giant Behemoth
GB   1959   70m   bw
Artistes Alliance/Stratford
aka: *Behemoth the Sea Monster*
A radioactive palaeosaurus menaces London.
Underfed monster, undercast melodramatics.
w Eugene Lourie d Eugene Lourie, Douglas Hickox
☆ Gene Evans, André Morell, Leigh Madison, John Turner, Jack MacGowran

The Giant Claw
US   1957   71m   bw
Clover (Sam Katzman)
▦ ▤
A monstrous bird threatens New York.
Incompetent horror item: the bird is mostly talons and sound track.
w Samuel Newman, Paul Gangelin d Fred F. Sears
☆ Jeff Morrow, Mara Corday, Morris Ankrum

'A giant among men in a gigantic color spectacle.'
The Giant of Marathon (dubbed) *
Italy/France   1960   92m   Eastmancolor
Dyaliscope
MGM/Titanus/Galatea/Lux (Bruno Vailati)
▤
original title: *La Battaglia di Maratona*
Philippides, an Olympic athlete, encourages the Spartans to fight the invading Persian army at Marathon and goes to Athens to organize a sea battle against the invaders.
Inaccurate history, but enjoyable as a lively example of an Italian epic.
w Ennio de Concini, Augusto Frassonetti, Bruno Vailati idea Alberto Barsanti, Raffaelo Pacini d Jacques Tourneur ph Mario Bava, Massimo Terzano m Roberto Nicolosi ad Marcello Del Prato ed Mario Serandrei
☆ Steve Reeves, Mylène Demongeot, Sergio Fantoni, Alberto Lupo, Ivo Garrani, Philippe Hersent, Daniella Rocca
† Tourneur directed only the main dialogue scenes, with the rest of the film being shot by Bava and Vailati.

The Giant Spider Invasion
US   1975   76m   Eastmancolor
Hemdale/Transcentury/Cinema Group 75 (Bill Rebane, Richard L. Huff)
▤
Nuclear fall-out causes giant spiders to breed and go on the rampage.
Thinly scripted reprise of one of those small-town horror thrillers of the fifties.

👫 film suitable for family viewing   ▦ VHS video-cassette for the British PAL system   ▤ VHS video-cassette for the British PAL system in wide screen-format   ⊚ Video cassette in a computer-colourised version   ▤ American NTSC video-cassette   ◎ Laser disc

w Richard L. Huff, Robert Easton d Bill Rebane
☆ Barbara Hale, Steve Brodie, Leslie Parrish, Alan Hale

Gideon of Scotland Yard: see *Gideon's Day*

Gideon's Day *
GB 1958 91m Technicolor
Columbia/John Ford (Michael Killanin)
US title: *Gideon of Scotland Yard*
A Scotland Yard Inspector has an eventful but frustrating day.
Pleasant, ordinary little TV style police yarn showing no evidence of its director's particular talents.
w T. E. B. Clarke *novel* John Creasey d John Ford ph Frederick C. Young m Douglas Gamley ad Ken Adam
☆ Jack Hawkins, Dianne Foster, Anna Lee, Andrew Ray, Anna Massey, Frank Lawton, John Loder, Cyril Cusack

Gidget
♠♠ US 1959 95m Eastmancolor Cinemascope
Columbia (Lewis J. Rachmil)
A 16-year-old girl falls for a surfer; her parents disapprove until he turns out to be the son of their best friend.
Commercial mixture of domestic comedy and beach athletics, for nice teenagers and their moms and pops.
w Gabrielle Upton *novel* Frederick Kohner d Paul Wendkos ph Burnett Guffey m George Duning md Morris Stoloff ad Ross Bellah ed William A. Lyon
☆ Sandra Dee, Cliff Robertson, James Darren, Arthur O'Connell
† Sequels include *Gidget Goes Hawaiian* (V*, 1961) with Deborah Walley; *Gidget Goes to Rome* (V*, 1962) with Cindy Carol; and two TV movies.

A Gift for Heidi
♠♠ US 1962 71m Eastmancolor
RKO/Chabert (Robert Goodstein)
A young girl learns about faith, hope and charity.
An excruciatingly sentimental family film, based on the character created by Johanna Spyri, which is given to plodding moralistic homilies and features one of the least endearing of child actresses.
w Eugene Vale, David Dortort d George Templeton ph Bruno Stephan m Bert Grund ad Hans Berthel, Willi Schatz ed Jack Ogilvie
☆ Sandy Descher, Douglas Fowley, Peter Capell, Van Dyke Parks, Eric Jelde, Rolf Wanka

The Gift Horse *
GB 1952 100m bw
British Lion/Molton (George Pitcher)
US title: *Glory at Sea*
In 1940 an old US destroyer is given to Britain, and an officer reluctantly takes charge of it.
Conventional, popular seafaring war adventure.
w William Fairchild, Hugh Hastings, William Rose *story* Ivan Goff, Ben Roberts d Compton Bennett ph Harry Waxman m Clifton Parker
☆ Trevor Howard, Richard Attenborough, Sonny Tufts, James Donald, Joan Rice, Bernard Lee, Dora Bryan, Hugh Williams, Robin Bailey

The Gift of Gab
US 1934 71m bw
Universal
A conceited radio announcer gets his comeuppance.
Odd little comedy drama notable only for its long list of stars making cameo appearances.
w Rian James, Lou Breslow d Karl Freund m Albert von Tilzer, Con Conrad, Charles Tobias
☆ Edmund Lowe, Gloria Stuart, Ruth Etting, Phil Baker, Alexander Woollcott, Ethel Waters, Victor Moore, Boris Karloff, Bela Lugosi, Paul Lukas, Chester Morris, Binnie Barnes, Douglass Montgomery, Wini Shaw
'A hodge-podge, an elongated short.' – *Variety*

The Gift of Love
US 1958 105m Eastmancolor Cinemascope
TCF (Charles Brackett)
A dying wife adopts an orphan girl so that her husband will not be lonely.
Incredibly cloying and miscast remake of Sentimental Journey (qv).
w Luther Davis d Jean Negulesco ph Milton Krasner m Cyril Mockridge

☆ Lauren Bacall, Robert Stack, Evelyn Rudie, Lorne Greene

The Gig
US 1985 92m colour
McLaughlin, Piven, Vogel (Norman I. Cohen)
A group of amateur Dixieland musicians take a professional job at a holiday resort, which is not quite as they had imagined.
Gently humorous drama of the male menopause; it has some charm and avoids easy resolutions, but is a little thin.
wd Frank D. Gilroy ph Jeri Sopanen md Warren Vaché ed Rick Shaine
☆ Wayne Rogers, Cleavon Little, Andrew Duncan, Jerry Matz, Daniel Nalbach, Joe Silver, Warren Vaché

Gigi *
France 1948 109m bw
Codo Cinema (Claude Dolbert)
In Paris in the 1890s, a young girl is trained by her aunt to be a cocotte, but when married off to a rake she reforms him.
Charming, overlong, non-musical version of a famous story, chiefly memorable for its local colour.
w Pierre Laroche *novel* Colette d Jacqueline Audry ph Gérard Perrin m Marcel Landowski
☆ Daniele Delorme, Gaby Morlay, Yvonne de Bray, Frank Villard, Jean Tissier, Madeleine Rousset

Gigi ***
US 1958 119m Metrocolor Cinemascope
MGM (Arthur Freed)
Laundered and musicalized version; delightfully set, costumed and performed, but oddly lacking dance numbers.
w Alan Jay Lerner d Vincente Minnelli ph Joseph Ruttenberg m/ly Frederick Loewe, Alan Jay Lerner md André Previn ed Adrienne Fazan pd/cos Cecil Beaton
☆ Leslie Caron, Louis Jourdan, Maurice Chevalier, Hermione Gingold, Isabel Jeans, Jacques Bergerac, Eva Gabor, John Abbott
'It has the sureness expected when a group of the most sophisticated talents are able to work together on material entirely suited to them.' – *Penelope Houston*
† Leslie Caron's vocals were dubbed by Betty Wand.
‡ best picture; Alan Jay Lerner; Vincente Minnelli; Joseph Ruttenberg; André Previn; Cecil Beaton; editing; Preston Ames and William A. Horning (art directors); title song; Maurice Chevalier (special award)

Gigot
US 1962 104m DeLuxe
TCF/Seven Arts (Kenneth Hyman)
The mute caretaker of a Montmartre boarding house looks after an ailing prostitute and her child.
From Paris, Hollywood, comes a grotesque piece of self-indulgence, the arch example of the clown who wanted to play Hamlet. Plotless, mawkish and wholly unfunny.
w John Patrick, Jackie Gleason d Gene Kelly ph Jean Bourgoin m Jackie Gleason md Michael Magne ad Auguste Capelier
☆ Jackie Gleason, Katherine Kath, Gabrielle Dorziat, Jean Lefebvre, Jacques Marin
'Chaplinesque pretensions have proved fatal before to artists who will not accept their own limitations.' – *Gavin Lambert*
♪ Michael Magne

'There never was a woman like Gilda!'
Gilda ***
US 1946 110m bw
Columbia (Virginia Van Upp)
A gambler in a South American city resumes a love-hate relationship with an old flame ... but she is now married to his dangerous new boss.
Archetypal Hollywood film noir, wholly studio-bound and the better for it, with dialogue that would seem risible if it did not happen to be dealt with in this style and with these actors, who keep the mood balanced between suspense and irony.
w Marion Parsonnet *story* E. A. Ellington d Charles Vidor ph Rudolph Maté m Hugo Friedhofer md Morris Stoloff, Marlin Skiles

☆ Rita Hayworth, Glenn Ford, George Macready, Steve Geray, Joseph Calleia, Joe Sawyer, Gerald Mohr, Ludwig Donath
'From a quietly promising opening the film settles into an intractable obscurity of narrative through which as in a fog three characters bite off at each other words of hate.' – *Richard Winnington*
† Rita Hayworth's singing was dubbed by Anita Ellis.

The Gilded Cage
GB 1955 72m bw
Tempean/Eros (Robert S. Baker, Monty Berman)
In London a US airforce officer hunts for the killer of his brother's girlfriend.
Routine thriller, slow and predictable.
w Brock Williams *story* Paul Erickson d John Gilling ph Monty Berman md Stanley Black ad Wilfred Arnold ed Jim Connock
☆ Alex Nichol, Veronica Hurst, Clifford Evans, Ursula Howells, Elwyn Brook-Jones, John Stuart

'He fed her popcorn and kisses on a park bench!'
The Gilded Lily *
US 1935 85m bw
Paramount (Albert Lewis)
A poor stenographer who meets her reporter boyfriend on a park bench is wooed by a British peer.
Good depression era romantic comedy with the heroine inevitably choosing poverty.
w Claude Binyon d Wesley Ruggles ph Victor Milner
☆ Claudette Colbert, Fred MacMurray, Ray Milland, C. Aubrey Smith, Luis Alberni, Donald Meek
'Breezy romance ... should carry box-office draught.' – *Variety*

'Altamont changed a lot of people's heads.'
Gimme Shelter ***
US 1970 90m colour
Cinema 5 (Ronald Schneider)
Documentary of the Rolling Stones' free concert at Altamont Speedway in December 1969, when a member of the audience was killed by Hell's Angels who had been hired as security for the event.
An excellently photographed concert film that unexpectedly turned out to be the obverse of Woodstock, revealing the darker side of rock and the revolutionary fervour that once accompanied it.
d Albert Maysles, David Maysles, Charlotte Zwerin
☆ The Rolling Stones, Ike and Tina Turner, Jefferson Airplane, The Flying Burrito Brothers

Ginger and Fred ***
Italy/France/West Germany 1986 126m colour
PEA/Revcom/Stella/RAI (Alberto Grimaldi)
An ageing pair of dancers is brought out of retirement to appear on a TV show.
Melancholy comedy with resonances, chiefly taking the side of age against youth, with 'Fred' as an image of Fellini himself.
w Federico Fellini, Tonino Guerra, Tullio Pinelli d Federico Fellini ph Tonino Delli Colli, Ennio Guarnieri m Nicola Piovani pd Dante Ferretti
☆ Giulietta Masina, Marcello Mastroianni, Franco Fabrizi, Frederick von Ledebur

The Gingerbread Man
US 1997 113m CFI color
Polygram/Island/Enchanter (Jeremy Tannenbaum)
A lawyer is accused of murdering his girlfriend's father, a cult leader who kidnapped his children.
Routine thriller, in which the director's usual quirkiness has been reined in by the script.
w Al Hayes *story* John Grisham d Robert Altman ph Changwei Gu m Mark Isham pd Stephen Altman ed Geraldine Peroni
☆ Kenneth Branagh, Embeth Davidtz, Robert Downey Jnr, Daryl Hannah, Robert Duvall, Tom Berenger, Famke Janssen, Clyde Hayes, May Whitman
'A thoroughly run-of-the-mill thriller.' – *Stephen Amidon, Sunday Times*
'Superbly visualised, broodingly atmospheric, blessed with emotional and moral resonances far beyond the squeaks expected from Grisham's

usual band of lawyers in trouble.' – *Geoff Brown, The Times*

Giornata Nera per L'Ariete: see *The Fifth Cord*

The Gipsy: see *Le Gitan*

Girl
US 1998 94m Foto-Kem
Feature Film/Kushner-Locke/HSX Films/Muse (Jeff Most, Brad Wyman, Chris Hanley)
In her last year in high school, a girl from a wealthy family is determined to lose her virginity to the local rock star.
Routine rites-of-passage movie, most likely to interest a teen audience, and given an occasional fillip by the contrast between our heroine's voice-over commentary, which swings between naivety and perceptiveness, and her wilder actions.
w David E. Tolchinsky *novel* Blake Nelson d Jonathan Kahn ph Tami Reiker m Michael Tavera pd Magda Lavandez-Berliner ed Gillian Hutshing
☆ Dominique Swain, Sean Patrick Flanery, Summer Phoenix, Tara Reid, Selma Blair, Channon Roe, Portia Di Rossi, Christopher Masterson, David Moslow, Rosemary Forsyth, James Karen
'A well-cast, modestly effective pic aimed squarely at the younger set.' – *David Stratton, Variety*
'Trite, clichéd and thoroughly condescending.' – *Sight and Sound*

'Six Is For Sex...'
Girl 6 *
US 1996 108m DeLuxe
TCF/Fox Searchlight/40 Acres and a Mule (Spike Lee)
An unsuccessful actress finds employment providing sex chats on the phone, and begins to enjoy her work too much until she is threatened by a man whose fantasies are about killing prostitutes.
A curious soft-centred movie that begins with confident satire, but tends to exploit what it also condemns, though its inclusion of fantasy sequences involving stereotyped roles in popular entertainment, from Carmen Jones to blaxploitation movies and sitcoms, suggests Lee wants to make some wider point. He moves away from his documentary style to something that attempts, without great success, to incorporate the self-referential and the surreal; what holds the disparate parts together is the performance of Theresa Randle.
w Suzan-Lori Parks d Spike Lee ph Malik Hassan Sayeed m Prince pd Ina Mayhew ed Sam Pollard
☆ Theresa Randle, Isaiah Washington, Spike Lee, Jenifer Lewis, Debi Mazar, Peter Berg, Michael Imperioli, Naomi Campbell, Quentin Tarantino, Madonna, John Turturro, Ron Silver
'Lee's film both has its cheesecake and eats it.' – *Sunday Times*

A Girl, a Guy and a Gob
US 1941 91m bw
RKO/Harold Lloyd
GB title: *The Navy Steps Out*
A secretary and her sailor boyfriend teach her stuffy boss how to enjoy life.
Did producer Lloyd intend himself for the role played by O'Brien? If so, he would have needed a stronger script to prevent this Capraesque comedy from falling flat.
w Frank Ryan, Bert Granet d Richard Wallace ph Russell Metty m Roy Webb
☆ Lucille Ball, Edmond O'Brien, George Murphy, George Cleveland, Henry Travers, Franklin Pangborn, Marguerite Churchill, Lloyd Corrigan

The Girl and the General
Italy/France 1967 113m Technicolor
MGM/Champion/Corcordia (Carlo Ponti)
During World War I, a captured Austrian general escapes with a girl partisan.
Turgid epic veering from melodrama to comedy.
w Luigi Malerba, Pasquale Festa Campanile d Pasquale Festa Campanile ph Ennio Guarnieri m Ennio Morricone
☆ Rod Steiger, Virna Lisi, Umberto Orsini

A Girl Called Katy Tippel: see *Keetje Tippel*

The Girl Can't Help It *

ↀ US 1956 97m Eastmancolor
Cinemascope
TCF (Frank Tashlin)

A theatrical agent grooms a gangster's dumb girlfriend for stardom.

Scatty, garish pop scene spoof with a plot borrowed from Born Yesterday and a lot of jokes about its new star's superstructure. Some scenes are funny, and it puts the first rock and roll stars in pickle for all time.

w Frank Tashlin, Herbert Baker story *Do Re Mi* by Garson Kanin d Frank Tashlin ph Leon Shamroy md Lionel Newman

☆ Jayne Mansfield, Tom Ewell, Edmond O'Brien, Henry Jones, John Emery; and Julie London, Ray Anthony, Fats Domino, Little Richard, The Platters

'Add to this shimmering example of fifties femininity a massive dose of rock 'n' roll, a crazy plot, mix it up with swirling style and colour, fast humour and neat timing, and you get a bundle of joy whichever way you look at it.' – *Judith Williamson, City Limits*

Girl Crazy

US 1932 75m bw
RKO

Romance at a desert college.

Early talkie version of the musical comedy (see below), here redesigned as a weak vehicle for two comedy stars.

w Tim Whelan, Herman J. Mankiewicz
d William A. Seiter

☆ Bert Wheeler, Robert Woolsey, Eddie Quillan, Dorothy Lee, Mitzi Green, Arline Judge

'A weak sister ... after a while it all becomes too silly.' – *Variety*

Girl Crazy *

US 1943 99m bw
MGM (Arthur Freed)

aka: *When the Girls Meet the Boys*

Romance at a desert college.

Predictable star musical with good tunes.

w Fred Finklehoffe play Guy Bolton, Jack McGowan d Norman Taurog ph William Daniels, Robert Planck m/ly George and Ira Gershwin md Georgie Stoll

☆ Judy Garland, Mickey Rooney, Guy Kibbee, Gil Stratton, Robert E. Strickland, Rags Ragland, June Allyson, Nancy Walker, Tommy Dorsey and his band

† Busby Berkeley was replaced as director during filming. Remade 1965 as *When the Boys Meet the Girls*.

The Girl Downstairs

US 1938 77m bw
MGM

A rich bachelor in Europe chooses the maid instead of the mistress.

Feeble rewrite of Cinderella.

w Harold Goldman, Felix Jackson, Karl Noti
d Norman Taurog

☆ Franchot Tone, Franciska Gaal, Walter Connolly, Rita Johnson, Reginald Owen, Reginald Gardiner, Franklin Pangborn, Robert Coote

'Keen direction and fine performances highlight moderate programmer.' – *Variety*

The Girl Friend

US 1935 67m bw
Columbia

An actor and two songwriters become rural con men.

Thin comedy with music.

w Gertrude Purcell, Benny Rubin d Eddie Buzzell
ph Joseph Walker

☆ Ann Sothern, Jack Haley, Roger Pryor, Thurston Hall, Victor Kilian

'Enough hoke to make it a welcome laugh picture for lesser towns.' – *Variety*

The Girl Friends: see *Le Amiche*

The Girl from Avenue A

US 1940 73m bw
Sol M. Wurtzel/TCF

A slum brat is picked up by an author, who takes her home to use for reference.

Pygmalion did this far better, but the star was adolescent and the studio didn't know what else to do with her.

w Frances Hyland play *The Brat* by Maude Fulton
d Otto Brower

☆ Jane Withers, Kent Taylor, Katharine Aldridge, Elyse Knox, Laura Hope Crews, Jessie Ralph, Harry Shannon, Ann Shoemaker

The Girl from Jones Beach

US 1949 78m bw
Warner

A commercial artist meets a schoolteacher who is the real-life counterpart of his 'perfect girl'.

Predictable comedy with only the dimmest professional sparkle.

w I. A. L. Diamond d Peter Godfrey ph Carl Guthrie m David Buttolph

☆ Ronald Reagan, Virginia Mayo, Eddie Bracken, Dona Drake, Henry Travers, Florence Bates

A Girl from Lorraine

France 1980 112m colour
Gala/Phoenix/Gaumont/FR3/SSR (Yves Peyrot, Raymond Pousaz)

aka: *La Provinciale*

A woman from the country finds heartbreak in Paris.

Over-solemn in its determination to discover the disillusion of city life.

w Claude Goretta, Jacques Kirsner, Rosine Rochette d Claude Goretta ph Philippe Rousselot m Arié Dzierlatka ad Jacques Bufnoir ed Joele Van Effenterre

☆ Nathalie Baye, Angela Winkler, Bruno Ganz, Pierre Vernier, Patrick Chesnais, Dominique Paturel, Roland Monod

The Girl from Manhattan

US 1948 81m bw
UA/Benedict Bogeaus

A model returns home to help her uncle with his mortgaged boarding house.

Mouldy comedy-drama full of kind thoughts, charming failures and worldly priests. Interesting for cast.

w Howard Estabrook d Alfred E. Green
ph Ernest Laszlo m Heinz Roemheld md David Chudnow

☆ Dorothy Lamour, Charles Laughton, George Montgomery, Ernest Truex, Hugh Herbert, Constance Collier, Sara Allgood, Frank Orth, Howard Freeman, Adeline de Walt Reynolds, George Chandler, Maurice Cass

The Girl from Maxim's

GB 1933 79m bw
UA/London Films (Alexander Korda, Ludovico Toeplitz)

Circumstances force a doctor to pass off a singer as his wife.

Tolerable period farce.

w Arthur Wimperis, Harry Graham play Georges Feydeau d Alexander Korda ph Georges Périnal m Kurt Schroeder ad Vincent Korda ed Harold Young, R. Bettinson

☆ Leslie Henson, Frances Day, George Grossmith, Lady Tree, Stanley Holloway

† A French version, not released until 1934, was made simultaneously with a French cast in the leading roles; Odette Florelle replaced Frances Day and André Lefaur took the part played by Leslie Henson.

The Girl from Mexico: see *Mexican Spitfire*

The Girl from Missouri *

US 1934 75m bw
MGM (Bernard H. Hyman)

aka: *100% Pure*

original titles: *Born to be Kissed; Eadie was a Lady*

A chorus girl determines to remain virtuous until the right millionaire comes along.

Smart, amusing comedy very typical of its period.

w Anita Loos, John Emerson d Jack Conway
ph Ray June m William Axt

☆ Jean Harlow, Franchot Tone, Lionel Barrymore, Lewis Stone, Patsy Kelly, Alan Mowbray, Clara Blandick, Henry Kolker

'It's going to be in the money ... one that plenty of purity crusaders will see and like.' – *Variety*
'Noisily defiant, rip-roaring and raucous in spots ... fast and furious adult fare.' – *Photoplay*

The Girl from Petrovka

US 1974 103m Technicolor
Universal/Richard Zanuck, David Brown

An American correspondent in Moscow falls for a Russian girl.

Lugubrious and lethargic romantic comedy-drama.

w Allan Scott, Chris Bryant d Robert Ellis Miller
m Henry Mancini

☆ Goldie Hawn, Hal Holbrook, Anthony Hopkins, Grégoire Aslan, Anton Dolin

The Girl from Scotland Yard

US 1937 61m bw
Paramount

A female agent tracks down the cause of mysterious explosions.

Lacklustre second feature.

w Doris Anderson, Dore Schary d Robert Vignola
ph Robert Pittack m George Stoll

☆ Karen Morley, Robert Baldwin, Katherine Alexander, Eduardo Ciannelli

'Weak thriller ... only for the back seat in duals.' – *Variety*

The Girl from Tenth Avenue

US 1935 69m bw
Warner (Robert Lord)

GB title: *Men on Her Mind*

A jilted attorney drowns his sorrows and marries on the rebound.

Watchable 'woman's picture'.

w Charles Kenyon play Hubert Henry Davies
d Alfred E. Green ph James Van Trees

☆ Bette Davis, Ian Hunter, Colin Clive, Alison Skipworth, Katherine Alexander, John Eldredge, Philip Reed

'Bette Davis' first starring venture ... she should pull the picture through to good returns.' – *Variety*

The Girl Habit

US 1931 77m bw
Paramount

A mild Lothario tries to get arrested as protection from the gangster husband who has threatened him.

Easy-going farce which established Ruggles in Hollywood.

w Owen Davis, Gertrude Purcell play A. E. Thomas, Clayton Hamilton d Eddie Cline

☆ Charles Ruggles, Tamara Geva, Margaret Dumont, Allen Jenkins, Donald Meek, Sue Conroy

'Hardly a dynamic b.o. prospect but nice entertainment.' – *Variety*

Girl Happy

ↀ US 1965 96m Metrocolor
Panavision
MGM/Euterpe (Joe Pasternak)

A pop singer in Florida is forced to chaperone a group of college girls including a gangster's daughter.

Standard star vehicle, quite professionally made and totally forgettable.

w Harvey Bullock, R. S. Allen d Boris Sagal
ph Philip Lathrop m George Stoll

☆ Elvis Presley, Harold J. Stone, Shelley Fabares, Gary Crosby, Nita Talbot

The Girl He Left Behind

US 1956 103m bw
Warner (Frank P. Rosenberg)

The army makes a man of a spoiled youth.

Platitudinous recruiting comedy for dim American teenagers.

w Guy Trosper book Marion Hargrove d David Butler ph Ted McCord m Roy Webb

☆ Tab Hunter, Natalie Wood, Jessie Royce Landis, Jim Backus, Henry Jones, Murray Hamilton, Alan King, James Garner, David Janssen

The Girl Hunters

GB 1963 100m bw Panavision
Present Day (Robert Fellows)

Private eye Mike Hammer solves a few murders plus the disappearance of his own ex-secretary.

Comic strip thuggery with the author playing his own slouchy hero; the general incompetence gives this cheap production an air of Kafkaesque menace.

w Mickey Spillane, Roy Rowland, Robert Fellows
d Roy Rowland ph Ken Talbot m Phil Green

☆ Mickey Spillane, Shirley Eaton, Lloyd Nolan

Girl in a Boot

West Germany 1983 96m colour
Cannon/Cinecom/Neue Filmproduktion/Sender Freies (Axel Bar, Franz Thies)

aka: *Einmal Ku'damm Und Zurück*

An East Berlin woman falls in love with a Swiss cook but opts to stay her side of the Wall.

Soberly shot romance which has dated more than somewhat.

w Jurgen Engert d Herbert Ballman ph Ingo Hamer m Jurgen Knieper ed Hans Otto Kruger, Ruth Kusche

☆ Ursula Monn, Christian Kohlund, Evelyn Meyka, Peter Schiff

A Girl in a Million

GB 1946 90m bw
Boca/British Lion (Sydney Box)

Having divorced a nagging wife, a chemist marries a dumb girl, but when he cures her...

Thin comedy which must have seemed funnier on the page than it does on the screen.

w Muriel and Sydney Box d Francis Searle

☆ Joan Greenwood, Hugh Williams, Basil Radford, Naunton Wayne, Wylie Watson, Yvonne Owen

The Girl in Black

Greece 1955 93m bw
Hermes

original title: *To Koritsi me ta Mavra*

A writer holidaying on a remote fishing island causes tension and tragedy when he falls for a local maiden.

Watchable mood piece benefiting from its star female performance.

wd Michael Cacoyannis ph Walter Lassally
m Argyris Kounadis, Manos Hadji Bredkis

☆ Ellie Lambetti, Georges Foundas, Dimitri Horna

The Girl in Black Stockings

US 1957 71m bw
Bel Air/UA

Suspects abound when a young woman is killed in a Utah hotel.

Tolerable murder mystery.

w Richard Landau story *Wanton Murder* by Peter Godfrey d Howard W. Koch

☆ Anne Bancroft, Lex Barker, Mamie Van Doren, John Dehner, Ron Randell, Marie Windsor

Girl in Distress: see *Jeannie*

A Girl in Every Port *

US 1928 62m bw silent
Fox

Two sailors brawl over women.

Adventure comedy with themes typical of its director.

w Seton Miller, James K. McGuinness
story Howard Hawks d Howard Hawks ph R. J. Bergquist, L. William O'Connell ed Ralph Dixon

☆ Victor McLaglen, Robert Armstrong, Natalie Joyce, Dorothy Matthews, Maria Casajuana, Louise Brooks, Francis McDonald

'Brief and essentially anecdotal, it now looks more than anything else like a preliminary sketch for concerns which Hawks would later elaborate.' – *Tim Pulleine, MFB*

A Girl in Every Port

US 1951 87m bw
RKO (Irwin Allen, Irving Cummings Jnr)

Two accident-prone sailors have trouble with a racehorse.

Dismally mechanical farce.

wd Chester Erskine ph Nicholas Musuraca
m Roy Webb

☆ Groucho Marx, William Bendix, Marie Wilson, Don Defore, Gene Lockhart

The Girl in Overalls: see *Maisie (Swing Shift Maisie)*

The Girl in Pawn: see *Little Miss Marker (1934)*

The Girl in Room 17: see *Vice Squad*

The Girl in the Headlines *
GB   1963   93m   bw
Bryanston/Viewfinder (John Davis)
US title: The Model Murder Case
Scotland Yard investigates the murder of a model.
Standard police mystery, well enough done.
w Vivienne Knight, Patrick Campbell novel The Nose on My Face by Laurence Payne d Michael Truman w Stan Pavey m John Addison ad Alan Withy ed Frederick Wilson
☆ Ian Hendry, Ronald Fraser, Margaret Johnston, Natasha Parry, Jeremy Brett, Kieron Moore, Jane Asher, Rosalie Crutchley

The Girl in the Kremlin
US   1957   81m   bw
Universal
An OSS agent infiltrates the Iron Curtain to assist a plot to overthrow Stalin.
Boring cold war nonsense with the leading lady for some reason playing three parts.
w Gene L. Coon, Robert Hill d Russell Birdwell ph Carl Guthrie ad Alexander Golitzen
☆ Lex Barker, Zsa Zsa Gabor, Jeffrey Stone, Maurice Manson, William Schallert

The Girl in the News *
GB   1940   78m   bw
TCF (Edward Black)
A nurse is framed for the death of her employer.
Easy-going British mystery of the Agatha Christie school.
w Sidney Gilliat novel Roy Vickers d Carol Reed ph Otto Kanturek md Louis Levy
☆ Margaret Lockwood, Barry K. Barnes, Emlyn Williams, Margaretta Scott, Roger Livesey, Basil Radford, Wyndham Goldie, Irene Handl, Mervyn Johns, Kathleen Harrison, Richard Bird, Michael Hordern, Roland Culver, Edward Rigby

The Girl in the Painting: see Portrait from Life

The Girl in the Red Velvet Swing *
US   1955   109m   DeLuxe   Cinemascope
TCF (Charles Brackett)
👓
In New York at the turn of the century, a rich unstable man shoots his mistress's former lover.
Plushy but not very interesting recounting of a celebrated murder case in which the victim was a famous architect, Stanford White.
w Walter Reisch, Charles Brackett d Richard Fleischer ph Milton Krasner m Leigh Harline ad Lyle R. Wheeler, Maurice Ransford
☆ Ray Milland, Farley Granger, Joan Collins, Glenda Farrell, Luther Adler, Cornelia Otis Skinner, Philip Reed, John Hoyt
'A needlessly long-winded piece of lush sensationalism.' – Penelope Houston

The Girl in the Taxi
GB   1937   72m   bw
ABFD/British Unity (Eugene Tuscherer, Kurt Bernhardt)
The head of the purity league is drawn into an adulterous flirtation.
Moderately piquant comedy shot in English and French versions.
w Austin Melford, Val Valentine and Fritz Gottfurcht play Georg Okonowsky d André Berthomieu ph Roy Clark md Jean Gilbert ad D'Eaubonne ed Ray Pitt
☆ Frances Day, Henri Garat, Lawrence Grossmith, Jean Gillie, Mackenzie Ward, Helen Haye, Albert Whelan

The Girl in White *
US   1952   93m   bw
MGM (Armand Deutsch)
GB title: So Bright the Flame
The story of Dr Emily Dunning, the first woman to become an intern in one of New York's hospitals.
Bland biopic, modestly produced, with predictable plot crises.
w Irmgard von Cube, Allen Vincent book Bowery to Bellevue by Emily Dunning Barringer d John Sturges ph Paul C. Vogel m David Raksin
☆ June Allyson, Arthur Kennedy, Gary Merrill, Mildred Dunnock, Jesse White, Marilyn Erskine

Girl, Interrupted *
US   1999   127m   DeLuxe
Columbia/Red Wagon/Global (Douglas Wick, Cathy Konrad)
🎬   🎧
In the mid-60s, a teenage girl is wrongly institutionalized in a hospital for the mentally ill.
An only occasionally interesting rites-of-passage drama, contrasting two young women, one vulnerable, the other out-of-control; but it says little of interest about the times or the use of such institutions to dump those who did not accept the way things were.
w James Mangold, Lisa Loomer, Anna Hamilton Phelan book Susanna Kaysen d James Mangold ph Jack Green m Mychael Danna pd Richard Hoover ed Kevin Tent cos Arianne Phillips
☆ Winona Ryder, Angelina Jolie, Clea Duvall, Brittany Murphy, Elisabeth Moss, Jared Leto, Jeffrey Tambor, Vanessa Redgrave, Whoopi Goldberg, Mary Kay Place
'A lopsided, often dull movie.' – Variety
🏆 Angelina Jolie

Girl Loves Boy
US   1937   77m   bw
ABFD/Grand National (B. F. Zeidman)
In the early 1900s, a rich, spoilt young man, after being tricked into marriage by a crooked woman, finds true love.
A sickly mix of sentimentality and heavy-handed humour, hardly watchable.
w Duncan Mansfield, Carroll Graham story Karl Brown, Hinton Smith d Duncan Mansfield ph Edward Snyder md Abe Meyer ad Edward Jewell ed Edward Schroeder
☆ Eric Linden, Cecilia Parker, Roger Imhof, Dorothy Peterson, Pedro de Cordoba, Bernadene Hayes

The Girl Most Likely
US   1958   98m   Technicolor   RKOscope
RKO (Stanley Rubin)
🎬   📀
A girl finds herself engaged to three men at the same time, and envisions marriage with each.
Dully cast, quite brightly handled remake of Tom, Dick and Harry, with modest songs and dances.
w Devery Freeman d Mitchell Leisen ph Robert Planck m Nelson Riddle m/ly Ralph Blane, Hugh Martin
☆ Jane Powell, Cliff Robertson, Keith Andes, Tommy Noonan, Kaye Ballard, Una Merkel
† For Mitchell Leisen and RKO studios, their last film.

A Girl Must Live **
GB   1939   92m   bw
Gainsborough-20th Century (Edward Black)
A runaway schoolgirl falls among chorus girls planning to marry into the nobility.
Light, peppery comedy with a strong cast.
w Frank Launder, Michael Pertwee novel Emery Bonnet d Carol Reed ph Jack Cox m/ly Eddie Pola, Manning Sherwin md Louis Levy ad Vetchinsky ed R. E. Dearing
☆ Margaret Lockwood, Renée Houston, Lilli Palmer, George Robey, Hugh Sinclair, Naunton Wayne, Moore Marriott, Mary Clare, David Burns, Kathleen Harrison, Martita Hunt, Helen Haye
'An unabashed display of undressed femininity, double-meaning dialogue alternating between piquancy and vulgarity, and hearty knockabout involving scantily attired young viragos who fight furiously in a whirligig of legs and lingerie.' – Kine Weekly

'He was half-oriental ... but he used the women of two continents without shame or guilt!'

A Girl Named Tamiko
US   1962   119m   Technicolor   Panavision
Paramount/Hal B. Wallis (Paul Nathan)
A Eurasian photographer uses his women in an attempt to get American nationality.
Humdrum romantic melodrama with dim performances.
w Edward Anhalt novel Ronald Kirkbride d John Sturges ph Charles Lang Jnr m Elmer Bernstein
☆ Laurence Harvey, France Nuyen, Martha Hyer, Michael Wilding, Miyoshi Umeki

The Girl Next Door
US   1953   92m   Technicolor
TCF (Robert Bassler)
🎬   📀
A Broadway musical star falls for her suburban neighbour.
Mild musical linked by UPA cartoon sequences.
w Isobel Lennart d Richard Sale ph Leon Shamroy m/ly Josef Myrow, Mack Gordon md Lionel Newman ch Richard Barstow
☆ Dan Dailey, June Haver, Natalie Schafer, Dennis Day, Cara Williams

The Girl of the Golden West
US   1930   81m   bw
Warner (Robert North)
A gun-toting, saloon-owning girl marries an outlaw and saves him from the sheriff.
Straight version of a dusty old Broadway success, later musicalized under the same title (see below).
w Waldemar Young play David Belasco d John Francis Dillon ph Sol Polito
☆ Ann Harding, James Rennie, Harry Bannister, Ben Hendricks Jnr, J. Farrell MacDonald
† A silent version was made in 1923 by First National, with Sylvia Breamer and J. Warren Kerrigan, directed by Edwin Carewe.

The Girl of the Golden West
US   1938   121m   bw/sepia release
MGM (William Anthony McGuire)
🎬
In backwoods Canada, a girl loves a bandit who is being chased by the Mounties.
Solemn musical melodrama in which the stars seem miscast and a bit of pep is badly needed. Taken from a hoary David Belasco spectacular, and looks it.
w Isabel Dawn, Boyce DeGaw d Robert Z. Leonard ph Oliver Marsh m/ly Sigmund Romberg, Gus Kahn
☆ Jeanette MacDonald, Nelson Eddy, Walter Pidgeon, Leo Carrillo, Buddy Ebsen, Olin Howland
'This musical mustanger finds the stars not only out of their element, but hemmed in by a two-hour mélange of the great outdoors, Mexican bandits, early Spanish-Californian atmosphere and musical boredom ... a spotty entry.' – Variety

Girl of the Limberlost
👫 US   1934   86m   bw
Monogram
A girl of the swamps becomes a high school graduate.
Tearful rehash of an old sentimental warhorse.
w Adele Comandini novel Gene Stratton Porter d Christy Cabanne
☆ Louise Dresser, Ralph Morgan, Marian Marsh, Henry B. Walthall, Helen Jerome Eddy, Betty Blythe
'Wholesome to a fault. A family film good enough for anybody to see, but the fault lies in that not everybody will want to see it.' – Variety

Girl of the Night
US   1960   93m   bw
Vanguard/Warner
A streetwalker confesses all to her psychiatrist.
Stalwart exploitation picture of its time.
w Ted Berkman, Raphael Blau book The Call Girl by Dr Harold Greenwald d Joseph Cates
☆ Anne Francis, Lloyd Nolan, Kay Medford, John Kerr, Arthur Storch, James Broderick

Girl of the Year: see The Petty Girl

The Girl on a Motorcycle
GB/France   1968   91m   Technicolor
Mid Atlantic/Ares (William Sassoon)
🎬   📀
US title: Naked under Leather
French title: La Motocyclette
A married woman leaves her husband, zooms off on her motorcycle to see her lover, and crashes to her death while indulging in sexual reverie.
An incredibly plotless and ill-conceived piece of sub-porn claptrap, existing only as a long series of colour supplement photographs.
w Ronald Duncan novel La Motocyclette by André Pieyre de Mandiargues d Jack Cardiff ph Jack Cardiff, René Guissart m Les Reed
☆ Marianne Faithfull, Alain Delon, Roger Mutton, Marius Goring

Girl on Approval
GB   1962   75m   bw
Bryanston/Eyeline (Harold Orton)
A couple foster a difficult teenager whose mother is in prison.
Competent domestic drama of family tensions.
w Kathleen White d Charles Frend ph John Coquillon m Clifton Parker ad Herbert Smith, Malcolm Pride ed John Bloom
☆ Rachel Roberts, James Maxwell, Annette Whiteley, Ellen McIntosh, John Dare, Michael Clarke

The Girl on the Boat
GB   1962   91m   bw
UA/Knightsbridge (John Bryan)
In the 20s, a shipboard romance develops between an upper-class Englishman and an American girl.
A misfiring attempt at a satirical comedy with a miscast star, who looks unhappy in its period setting.
w Reuben Ship novel P. G. Wodehouse d Henry Kaplan ph Denys Coop m Kenneth Jones ad Tony Masters ed Noreen Ackland
☆ Norman Wisdom, Millicent Martin, Richard Briers, Sheila Hancock, Bernard Cribbins, Athene Seyler, Philip Locke, Reginald Beckwith, Peter Bull, Ronald Fraser

The Girl on the Canal: see Painted Boats

The Girl on the Front Page
US   1936   74m   bw
Universal
The lady owner of a newspaper gets a job on it under an assumed name, and helps the editor solve a mystery.
Fairly pleasing programmer.
w Austin Parker, Albert R. Perkins, Alice Duer Miller d Harry Beaumont
☆ Edmund Lowe, Gloria Stuart, Spring Byington, Reginald Owen

The Girl Rosemarie
West Germany   1958   100m   bw
Roxy
original title: Das Mädchen Rosemarie
Corrupt industrialists and investigators alike are relieved when a girl who had been the mistress of all of them is murdered.
Slick melodrama based on an actual case; almost a documentary exposé.
w Erich Kuby, Rolf Thiele, Joe Herbst, Rolf Urich d Rolf Thiele ph Klaus von Rautenfeld m Norbert Schultze
☆ Nadja Tiller, Peter Van Eyck, Carl Raddatz, Gert Frobe, Mario Adorf, Horst Frank

The Girl Rush
US   1955   85m   Technicolor   Vistavision
Paramount (Frederick Brisson, Robert Alton)
A gambler's daughter inherits a half share in a Las Vegas hotel.
Dull charmless semi-musical vehicle for a star who can't quite carry it.
w Phoebe and Henry Ephron d Robert Pirosh ph William Daniels m Herbert Spencer, Earle Hagen ch Robert Alton
☆ Rosalind Russell, Eddie Albert, Fernando Lamas, James Gleason, Gloria de Haven, Marion Lorne

Girl Shy **
US   1924   65m   bw   silent
Pathé/Harold Lloyd
🎬   📀
A bashful, stuttering apprentice tailor in a small town writes a book on love-making, despite being terrified of girls.
A comedy of character that only comes to life in its final slapstick chase sequence, one that has few rivals for invention and complexity as Lloyd transfers from car to horse, fire-engine, tram, speeding car, motorcycle and collapsing horse and cart in order to get to the church on time.
story Sam Taylor, Ted Wilde, Tim Whelan d Fred Newmeyer, Sam Taylor ph Walter Ludin ad Liell K. Vedder ed Allen McNeil
☆ Harold Lloyd, Jobyna Ralston, Richard Daniels, Carlton Griffin
† The film was the first of Lloyd's own productions.

Girl Stroke Boy

GB 1971 88m Eastmancolor

Hemdale/Virgin (Ned Sherrin, Terry Glinwood)

A well-to-do couple try to find out whether their son's house guest is male or female.

Initially funny but appallingly extended one-joke comedy which many will find merely embarrassing.

w Caryl Brahms, Ned Sherrin *play Girlfriend* by David Percival d Bob Kellett ph Ian Wilson m John Scott

☆ Joan Greenwood, Michael Hordern, Clive Francis, Patricia Routledge, Peter Bull, Rudolph Walker, Elizabeth Welch

Girl Trouble

US 1942 82m bw

TCF (Robert Bassler)

A South American in New York rents the apartment of a socialite who pretends to be his maid.

Thin romantic comedy with half-hearted screwball touches.

w Ladislas Fodor, Robert Riley Crutcher d Harold Schuster

☆ Don Ameche, Joan Bennett, Billie Burke, Frank Craven, Alan Dinehart

A Girl Was Young: see Young and Innocent

The Girl Who Couldn't Quite

GB 1950 85m bw

Argyle

Smile, that is. A tramp cures a teenager's amnesia and she fails to recognize him afterwards.

Sentimental bosh from a mildly popular play of its time.

w Norman Lee, Marjorie Deans *play* Leo Marks d Norman Lee

☆ Bill Owen, Iris Hoey, Elizabeth Henson, Betty Stockfeld

The Girl Who Couldn't Say No

Italy 1968 104m Techniscope

INC/PC/Fulcro

original title: *Il Suo Modo di Fari*

A medical assistant has an on-off relationship with an eccentric girl.

Downright peculiar romantic comedy with an American star all at sea in the Mediterranean.

w Franco Brusati, Ennio de Concini d Franco Brusati

☆ George Segal, Virna Lisi, Lila Kedrova

The Girl Who Had Everything

US 1953 69m bw

MGM (Armand Deutsch)

🎬

The daughter of a wealthy criminal lawyer falls in love with one of her father's crooked clients.

Glossy melodrama of purely superficial interest.

w Art Cohn *novel* Adela Rogers St Johns d Richard Thorpe ph Paul Vogel m André Previn

☆ Elizabeth Taylor, William Powell, Fernando Lamas, Gig Young

† Remake of *A Free Soul.*

The Girl with Brains in Her Feet

GB 1997 98m Metrocolor

Alliance/Lexington (Don Boyd)

🎬

In the early 70s, an athletic teenage girl discovers sex with a Leicestershire farmworker.

Low-budget movie about the pains and pleasures of growing up that will probably seem more watchable on the small screen.

w Jo Hodges d Robert Bangura ph Peter Butler m Rob Lane pd Lynn Bird ed Adam Ross

☆ Amanda Mealing, Joanna Ward, Jamie McIntosh, Jodie Smith, Richard Claxton, John Thompson, Garth Tudor-Price, Samantha Wheatley

Girl with Green Eyes **

GB 1963 91m bw

UA/Woodfall (Oscar Lewenstein)

🎬

An artless young Dublin girl falls for a middle-aged writer.

Lyrical romance which just about preserves its charm by good location sense.

w Edna O'Brien *novel The Lonely Girl* by Edna O'Brien d Desmond Davis ph Manny Wynn m John Addison

☆ Peter Finch, Rita Tushingham, Lynn Redgrave

'A beautiful and eloquent first directorial effort … embodies all that is naive and silly and noble and wonderful and heartbreaking and funny about being young.' – *Judith Crist*

A Girl with Ideas

US 1937 70m bw

Universal

A rich girl takes control of a daily paper which libelled her.

Lively comedy on familiar lines.

w Bruce Manning, Robert T. Shannon d S. Sylvan Simon

☆ Wendy Barrie, Walter Pidgeon, Kent Taylor, George Barbier, Dorothea Kent, Samuel S. Hinds

'Bright and original comedy, suitable for the more important first runs.' – *Variety*

The Girl with Red Hair

Netherlands 1981 116m Fujicolour

Blue Dolphin/Movies Filmproductions/VNU/Trio/Vara TV/Querido/Meteor (Chris Brouwer, Haig Balian)

original title: *Het Meisje Met Het Rode Haar*

The life and death of a member of the Dutch resistance at the hands of the Nazis is recalled by a friend.

Muddled attempt to explain actions from a feminist point of view.

w Ben Verbong, Peter de Vos *novel* Theun de Vries d Ben Verbong ph Theo Van de Sande m Nicola Piovani ad Dorus Van Der Linden ed Ton de Graff

☆ Renee Soutendijk, Peter Tuinman, Loes Luca, Johan Leysen, Robert Delhez, Ada Bouwman, Lineke Rijxman, Maria de Booy

The Girlfriend: see La Amiga

Girlfriends *

US 1978 86m DuArt

Cyclops (Claudia Weill, Jan Saunders)

A Jewish girl photographer in New York is ditched by her girlfriend and considers men.

Mild, amusing, well-observed little comedy-drama which goes nowhere in particular and slightly outstays its welcome.

w Vicki Polon d Claudia Weill ph Fred Murphy m Michael Small

☆ Melanie Mayron, Eli Wallach, Anita Skinner, Bob Balaban

'A quiet triumph … There is no tedium, there is realization; involvement; pleasure. The more I think about this film, the warmer I feel.' – *Stanley Kauffmann*

The Girl-Getters: see The System (GB)

Les Girls *

US 1957 114m Metrocolor Cinemascope

MGM (Sol. C. Siegel)

🎬 🎬 🎬

One member of a dancing troupe sues another over her memoirs.

Disappointing, talent-laden comedy-musical with a Rashomon-like flashback plot and a curious absence of the expected wit and style.

w John Patrick *novel* Vera Caspary d George Cukor ph Robert Surtees m/ly Cole Porter md Adolph Deutsch ch Jack Cole

☆ Gene Kelly, Kay Kendall, Mitzi Gaynor, Taina Elg, Jacques Bergerac, Leslie Phillips, Henry Daniell, Patrick MacNee

The Girls: see Les Bonnes Femmes

Girls about Town

US 1931 80m bw

Paramount

Gold diggers find true love.

A laugh, a tear and a wisecrack in the big city: very dated, but may have seemed fresh at the time.

w Raymond Griffith, Brian Marlow *story* Zoë Akins d George Cukor

☆ Kay Francis, Joel McCrea, Lilyan Tashman, Eugene Pallette, Alan Dinehart, George Barbier

'Generally only fair b.o. as ultra sophistication may be small-town setback.' – *Variety*

Girls' Dormitory *

US 1936 66m bw

TCF

A college girl falls for her headmaster.

Old-fashioned romance for nice young people, smoothly produced in the Fox mid-30s manner.

---

w Gene Markey *story* Ladislaus Fodor d Irving Cummings ph Merritt B. Gerstad m Arthur Lange

☆ Herbert Marshall, *Simone Simon*, Ruth Chatterton, Constance Collier, J. Edward Bromberg, Dixie Dunbar, Tyrone Power

'The picture, dewy as it is, has merit even apart from Mlle Simon (it is well directed and the performance of Mr Edward Bromberg as a cruel, warped pedagogic type is admirable), but I am afraid its concentrated atmosphere of young innocence (even the bathing-costumes are white like the nightdresses) defeats its own purpose.' – *Graham Greene*

'The Swingin'-est Elvis! The Fastest-Movin' Fun'n'Music! And The World's Curviest Girls! Girls! Girls!'

Girls! Girls! Girls!

US 1962 106m Technicolor

Wallis-Hazen (Hal B. Wallis)

🎬

A night-club singer runs a fishing boat as a hobby.

Empty-headed, lighter than air vehicle for star fans.

w Edward Anhalt, Allan Weiss d Norman Taurog ph Loyal Griggs m Joseph J. Lilley

☆ Elvis Presley, Stella Stevens, Laurel Goodwin, Jeremy Slate

The Girls He Left Behind: see The Gang's All Here (1943)

Girls in the Night

US 1953 82m bw

Universal

GB title: *Life After Dark*

The son of a New York tenement family falls under suspicion of murder.

Very mildly sensational low-life melodrama, like a citified Tobacco Road.

w Ray Buffum d Jack Arnold ph Carl Guthrie ad Alexander Golitzen

☆ Glenda Farrell, Harvey Lembeck, Joyce Holden, Glen Roberts, Don Gordon

Girls in the Street: see London Melody

Girls in Uniform: see Maedchen in Uniform

Girls Just Want to Have Fun

US 1985 87m CFI color

New World/James G. Robinson (Chuck Russell)

🎬

A new girl at high school defies her strict father to take part in a TV dance contest.

High-spirited but vapid comedy; of minimal interest outside its target audience of girls in their early teens.

w Amy Spies d Alan Metter ph Thomas Ackerman m Thomas Newman *tvl* Jeffrey Staggs ed David Rawlins, Lorenzo Destefano

☆ Sarah Jessica Parker, Lee Montgomery, Helen Hunt, Morgan Woodward, Ed Lauter, Jonathan Silverman, Holly Gagnier, Shannen Doherty

Girls Never Tell: see Her First Romance

Girls Night

GB/US 1997 102m Technicolor

Granada/Showtime (Bill Boyes)

🎬

Two sisters-in-law, one dying of cancer, take off for Las Vegas to spend their bingo winnings.

Derivative movie of terminal illness that has all the attractions, and most of the emotions, of a television soap opera.

w Kay Mellor d Nick Hurran ph David Odd m Ed Shearmur pd Taff Batley ed John Richards

☆ Brenda Blethyn, Julie Walters, Kris Kristofferson, George Costigan, James Gaddas, Philip Jackson, Sue Cleaver, Myra Syal

'A film so forcibly aimed at a particular audience it becomes offensive.' – *Gaby Wood, Guardian*

The Girls of Pleasure Island

US 1953 96m Technicolor

Paramount (Paul Jones)

In 1945 the Marines land on a tiny Pacific island, disturbing the life of an English gentleman and his three inexperienced but beautiful daughters.

Tedious and wholly artificial comedy with a leaden touch, devised as a try-out for young talent.

w F. Hugh Herbert d F. Hugh Herbert, Alvin Ganzer ph Daniel Fapp m Lyn Murray

---

☆ Leo Genn, Gene Barry, Don Taylor, Elsa Lanchester, Dorothy Bromiley, Audrey Dalton, Joan Elan

The Girls of Summer: see Satisfaction

Girls on Probation

US 1938 63m bw

Warner

A lawyer falls in love with a young girl in trouble.

Formula B picture that was re-released a few years later when its two stars were more familiar to the public.

w Crane Wilbur d William McGann ph Arthur Todd ad Hugh Reticker ed Frederick Richards

☆ Jane Bryan, Ronald Reagan, Sheila Bromley, Anthony Averill, Henry O'Neill, Elisabeth Risdon

'A creditable job.' – *Variety*

Girls Town

US 1996 89m DuArt

Metrodome/AC Hundred/Boomer (Lauren Zalaznick)

Three high-school friends take action when another friend kills herself because she was raped.

A confrontational drama, worked out in improvisational workshops before it was shot, that has some effective moments, but lacks a solid narrative base.

w Jim McKay, Denise Casano, Anna Grace, Bruklin Harris, Lili Taylor d Jim McKay ph Russell Lee Fine m Guru pd David Doernberg ed Jim McKay, Alex Hall

☆ Lili Taylor, Brucklin Harris, Anna Grace, Aunjanue Ellis, Ramya Pratt, Asia Minor, Carl Kwaku Ford, Guillermo Diaz

'This indie's attraction lies in its raw, unpredictable plot.' – *Jessica Mellor, Empire*

Girly: see Mumsy, Nanny, Sonny and Girly

Giro City *

GB 1982 102m colour

Silvarealm/Rediffusion/Channel 4 (Sophie Balhetchet, David Payne)

A television documentary team tries to present honest programmes about Ireland and about local government corruption.

Smartly made if somewhat predictably and stridently left-wing slice of so-called realism.

wd Karl Francis ph Curtis Clark m Alun Francis ed Kent Pan

☆ Glenda Jackson, Jon Finch, Kenneth Colley, James Donnelly, Emrys James, Simon Jones

Le Gitan

France/Italy 1975 94m Eastmancolor

Lara/Adel (Raymond Danon, Alain Delon)

aka: *The Gipsy*

On the run from the police, an alienated gypsy commits a series of daring robberies with the aid of two accomplices.

A tired, plodding thriller-cum-protest about society's persecution of gypsies that settles for making its murderous hero into a figure of alluring glamour.

wd José Giovanni *novel Histoire de Fou* by José Giovanni ph Jean-Jacques Tarbes m Django Reinhardt, Claude Bolling, Lick ad Willy Holt ed Jacqueline Thiedot

☆ Alain Delon, Annie Girardot, Paul Meurisse, Marcel Bozzuffi, Maurice Barrier, Maurice Giraud, Bernard Giraudeau, Renato Salvatori

Giulietta degli Spiriti: see Juliet of the Spirits

Giuseppina *

GB 1960 32m Technicolor

British Petroleum

The daughter of an Italian petrol station proprietor has an amusing afternoon watching customers.

Pleasing little Tatiesque sponsored comedy.

wd James Hill

Give a Girl a Break *

US 1953 84m Technicolor

MGM (Jack Cummings)

🎬 🎬

A Broadway star walks out on a show and three girls audition as replacements.

Minor musical vehicle for the Champions; an agreeable time-passer.

w Frances Goodrich, Albert Hackett d Stanley Donen ph William Mellor m/ly Burton Lane, Ira Gershwin md André Previn ch Stanley Donen, Gower Champion

---

☆ Marge and Gower Champion, Debbie Reynolds, Bob Fosse, Kurt Kasznar

Give Her a Ring
GB 1934 79m bw
BIP (Walter Mycroft)
A telephonist falls for her employer.
Curious romantic comedy attempting to woo continental audiences.
w Clifford Grey, Ernst Wolff, Marjorie Deans, Wolfgang Wilhelm *play* H. Rosenfeld *d* Arthur Woods *ph* Claude Friese-Greene, Ronald Neame *m/ly* Clifford Grey, Hans May *md* Harry Acres *ad* Duncan Sutherland *ed* E. B. Jarvis
☆ Clifford Mollison, Wendy Barrie, Zelma O'Neal, Erik Rhodes, Bertha Belmore, Stewart Granger (cameo)
'Delightful and unassuming' – *National Film Theatre, 1970*

Give Me a Break: see Life with Mikey

Give Me a Sailor
US 1938 80m bw
Paramount (Jeff Lazarus)
An ugly girl envies her sister her beaux, but ends up winning a competition for beautiful legs.
One of the double bill comedies which got Bob Hope's career off to a shaky start.
w Doris Anderson, Frank Butler *play* Anne Nichols *d* Elliott Nugent *ph* Victor Milner *m/ly* Leo Robin, Ralph Rainger *md* Boris Morros
☆ Martha Raye, Bob Hope, Betty Grable, Jack Whiting, Clarence Kolb
'Not so funny farce.' – *Variety*

Give Me the Stars
GB 1944 90m bw
British National (Friedrich Zelnik)
An American girl takes charge of her Scottish grandfather.
Half-hearted comedy of the music halls.
w Maclean Rogers, Austin Melford *d* Maclean Rogers *ph* James Wilson
☆ Will Fyffe, Leni Lynn, Jackie Hunter, Olga Lindo, Stanelli, Ronald Chesney

Give My Regards to Broad Street *
♫♫ GB 1984 108m colour
TCF/MPL (Andros Epimanondas)
▤ ◎◟
An international rock star fears that the priceless tapes of his new album have been stolen, and searches London for them.
An absurdly thin premise even for a musical which is essentially an ego trip for Paul McCartney, who at least squandered his own money on it and not the bank's. Some of the numbers have merit but the mood never connects.
w Paul McCartney *d* Peter Webb *ph* Ian McMillan *m* Paul McCartney *pd* Anthony Pratt
☆ Paul McCartney, Bryan Brown, Ringo Starr, Barbara Bach, Tracey Ullman, Ralph Richardson, George Martin, John Bennett

Give My Regards to Broadway *
US 1948 89m Technicolor
TCF (Walter Morosco)
◎◟
An old-time vaudevillian yearns to get back into show business.
Pleasantly performed, sentimental family comedy with familiar tunes.
w Samuel Hoffenstein, Elizabeth Reinhardt *d* Lloyd Bacon *ph* Harry Jackson
☆ Dan Dailey, *Charles Winninger*, Fay Bainter, Charles Ruggles, Nancy Guild
'Vaudeville is dead. I wish to God someone would bury it.' – *James Agee*

Give Out, Sisters
US 1942 65m bw
Universal
For reasons of pure plot, the Andrews Sisters pose as wealthy old maids.
One of scores of musical seconds produced by Universal at this time; this one has an unusually strong cast.
w Paul Gerard Smith, Warren Wilson *d* Edward F. Cline
☆ The Andrews Sisters, Grace McDonald, Dan Dailey, Charles Butterworth, Walter Catlett, William Frawley, Donald O'Connor, Peggy Ryan

Give Us the Moon
GB 1944 95m bw
GFD/Gainsborough (Edward Black)
In post-war London a club is opened for idle members only.
Whimsical comedy which fell with a dull thud.
wd Val Guest *novel* The Elephant is White by Caryl Brahms, S. J. Simon
☆ Margaret Lockwood, Vic Oliver, Peter Graves, Max Bacon, Roland Culver, Frank Cellier, Jean Simmons

Give Us This Day
GB 1949 120m bw
Plantagenet (Rod E. Geiger, N. A. Bronsten)
US title: *Salt to the Devil*
Depression struggles of an Italian immigrant family in New York.
An unconvincing, self-pitying wallow, a very curious enterprise for a British studio.
w Ben Barzman *story* Christ in Concrete by Pietro di Donato *d* Edward Dmytryk *ph* C. Pennington Richards *m* Benjamin Frankel
☆ Sam Wanamaker, Lea Padovani, Kathleen Ryan, Charles Goldner, Bonar Colleano, William Sylvester, Karel Stepanek, Sidney James
'Dmytryk insisted on cutting the film himself and he has left in at least three spare reels.' – *Richard Winnington*
'Worth making and worth seeing, but cramped by its symbolism and its language.' – *Richard Mallett, Punch*

Give Us Wings
US 1941 60m bw
Universal
City boys become pilots in the Army Air Corps.
Undistinguished combining of the Dead End Kids with the East Side Kids.
w Arthur T. Horman, Robert Lee Johnson *d* Charles Lamont
☆ Billy Halop, Huntz Hall, Gabriel Dell, Bernard Punsley, Bobby Jordan, Wallace Ford, Anne Gwynne, Victor Jory, Shemp Howard

Gladiator *
US 1992 102m Technicolor
Columbia TriStar/Columbia/Price Entertainment (Frank Price, Steve Roth)
▤ ▤ ◎◟ ◠
A white teenage amateur boxer is forced to turn professional by a crooked promoter and forms a friendship with a young black fighter.
Enjoyable boxing movie that nevertheless sticks to all the usual moves; it could never have been a contender but on its modest level it holds the interest.
w Lyle Kessler, Robert Mark Kamen *story* Djordje Milicevic, Robert Mark Kamen *d* Rowdy Herrington *ph* Tak Fujimoto *m* Brad Fiedel *pd* Gregg Fonseca *ed* Peter Zinner, Harry B. Miller III
☆ James Marshall, Cuba Gooding Jnr, Brian Dennehy, Robert Loggia, Ossie Davis, Jon Seda, Cara Buono, Lance Slaughter
'An exercise in audience manipulation that probably will get a thumbs-down from the targetted younger audience.' – *Variety*

'What We Do In Life Echoes In Eternity.'
Gladiator ***
US 2000 154m Technicolor Panavision
Universal/DreamWorks/Scott Free (Douglas Wick, David Franzoni, Branko Lustig)
◠
Condemned to die by a power-mad Emperor, a Roman general escapes to become a slave and a gladiator before he gains an opportunity for vengeance.
Lavish, spectacular, action-packed epic that re-invigorated a moribund genre, though in contrast to its predecessors it is somewhat glum in its approach; in its attempt at a tragic dimension, it eschews the camp decadence and fun of previous excursions into ancient Rome.
w David Franzoni, John Logan, William Nicholson *d* Ridley Scott *ph* John Mathieson *m* Hans Zimmer, Lisa Gerrard *pd* Arthur Max *ed* Pietro Scalia *sp* Neil Corbould; John Nelson; Mill Film *cos* Janty Yates
☆ Russell Crowe, Joaquin Phoenix, Connie Nielsen, *Oliver Reed*, Derek Jacobi, Djimon Hounsou, Richard Harris, David Schofield, John Shrapnel, Tomas Arana, Ralf Moeller, Spencer Treat Clark, David Hemmings

'So entertaining and carried off with such chutzpah, you forgive the odd absurdity and wonder where this genre has been all your life.' – *Peter Bradshaw, Guardian*
'A muscular and bloody combat picture, a compelling revenge drama and a truly transporting trip back nearly 2,000 years.' – *Todd McCarthy, Variety*

The Gladiator
US 1938 70m bw
Columbia
▤
A poor boy wins a prize and becomes a college football hero.
Elementary star farce.
w Charles Melson, Arthur Sheekman *novel* Philip Wylie *d* Edward Sedgwick
☆ Joe E. Brown, Man Mountain Dean, June Travis, Dickie Moore, Lucien Littlefield
'Goofy but a lot of fun.' – *Variety*

Glamorous Night
GB 1937 81m bw
BIP/ABP (Walter C. Mycroft)
An opera singer and her gypsy friends save a Ruritanian king from his scheming prime minister.
Modest transcription of a popular stage musical.
w Dudley Leslie, Hugh Brooke, William Freshman *play* Ivor Novello *d* Brian Desmond Hurst *ph* Fritz Arno Wagner *m/ly* Ivor Novello, Christopher Hassall *md* Harry Acres *ad* Cedric Dawe *ed* Flora Newton
☆ Mary Ellis, Otto Kruger, Victor Jory, Barry Mackay, Trefor Jones, Finlay Currie, Felix Aylmer
† Although several of the original songs are either sung or heard, much of the background music is not Novello's.

Glamour
US 1934 74m bw
Universal
A day in the life of a Broadway star.
Competent minor entertainment.
w Doris Anderson *story* Edna Ferber *d* William Wyler *ph* George Robinson
☆ Constance Cummings, Paul Lukas, Philip Reed, Joseph Cawthorn, Doris Lloyd, Olaf Hytten
'A good b.o. number with special pull for the femmes.' – *Variety*

Glamour Boy *
US 1941 79m bw
Colbert Clark/Paramount
GB title: *Hearts in Springtime*
An ex-child star finds himself tutoring his successor.
Quite an appealing peep inside Hollywood, and especially wry at the time because the star was still a household word.
w Bradford Ropes, Val Burton *d* Ralph Murphy
☆ Jackie Cooper, Susanna Foster, Walter Abel, Darryl Hickman, Ann Gillis, William Demarest
'One of the happiest "idea" pictures turned out by Hollywood in a long time.' – *Variety*

'Underwater ... undercover ... under any circumstances ... you must see the wildest, funniest new comedy!'
The Glass Bottom Boat
US 1966 110m Metrocolor Panavision
MGM/Arwin-Reame (Martin Melcher)
▤ ◎◟
A young widow gets involved with spies.
Frantic spy spoof, pleasantly set on the Californian coast, but overflowing with pratfalls, messy slapstick and pointless guest appearances.
w Everett Freeman *d* Frank Tashlin *ph* Leon Shamroy *m* Frank de Vol
☆ Doris Day, Rod Taylor, Arthur Godfrey, Paul Lynde, John McGiver, Edward Andrews, Eric Fleming, Dom DeLuise

The Glass Cage
GB 1954 59m bw
Exclusive/Hammer (Anthony Hinds)
US title: *The Glass Tomb*
A freak-show promoter solves the murder of a circus girl.
Moderate programmer with an interesting cast.
w Richard Landau *novel* The Outsiders by A. E. Martin *d* Montgomery Tully *ph* Walter Harvey *m* Leonard Salzedo *md* John Hollingsworth *ad* J. Elder Wills *ed* James Needs

☆ John Ireland, Honor Blackman, Geoffrey Keen, Eric Pohlmann, Sidney James, Liam Redmond, Sydney Tafler, Sam Kydd, Ferdy Mayne, Tonia Bern

'He carries his love in his iron fists!'
The Glass Key **
US 1935 87m bw
Paramount (E. Lloyd Sheldon)
A slightly corrupt but good-natured politician is saved by his henchman from being implicated in a murder.
Lively transcription of a zesty crime novel.
w Kathryn Scola, Kubec Glasmon, Harry Ruskin *novel* Dashiell Hammett *d* Frank Tuttle *ph* Henry Sharp
☆ Edward Arnold, George Raft, Claire Dodd, Rosalind Keith, Guinn Williams, Ray Milland
'Will have to struggle to strike above average grosses.' – *Variety*

The Glass Key **
US 1942 85m bw
Paramount (Fred Kohlmar)
▤ ◎◟
Nifty remake of the above which finds some limited talents in their best form, helped by a plot which keeps one watching.
w Jonathan Latimer *d* Stuart Heisler *ph* Theodor Sparkuhl *m* Victor Young
☆ Brian Donlevy, Alan Ladd, Veronica Lake, Bonita Granville, William Bendix, Richard Denning, Joseph Calleia, Moroni Olsen
MADVIG (BRIAN DONLEVY): 'I'm going to society. He's practically given me the key to his house.'
BEAUMONT (ALAN LADD): 'Yeah, a glass key. Be sure it doesn't break up in your hand.'

The Glass Menagerie **
US 1950 107m bw
Warner/Charles K. Feldman (Jerry Wald)
A shy crippled girl seeks escape from the shabby reality of life in St Louis and from her mother's fantasies.
Pleasantly moody version of one of its author's lighter and more optimistic plays; fluent and good-looking production, memorable performances.
w Tennessee Williams, Peter Berneis *play* Tennessee Williams *d* Irving Rapper *ph* Robert Burks *m* Max Steiner
☆ Gertrude Lawrence, Jane Wyman, Kirk Douglas, Arthur Kennedy
† An excellent TV movie of the play, directed by Anthony Harvey and starring Katharine Hepburn, was made in 1973.

The Glass Menagerie *
US 1987 135m DuArt
Cineplex (Burtt Harris)
▤ ◎◟
A son longs to escape from his stifling home, where his genteel mother worries about the future prospects of his lame, shy sister.
Well-acted and faithful to the original stage play, this version still obstinately refuses to come to life on the screen.
w Tennessee Williams *play* Tennessee Williams *d* Paul Newman *ph* Michael Ballhaus *m* Henry Mancini *pd* Tony Walton *ed* David Ray
☆ Joanne Woodward, John Malkovich, Karen Allen, James Naughton

The Glass Mountain
GB 1949 98m bw
Victoria (John Sutro, Joseph Janni, Fred Zelnik)
In the Dolomites, a married composer loves an Italian girl who saved his life during the war.
Tedious sudser, ineptly produced; an enormous British box-office success because of its theme music.
w Joseph Janni, John Hunter, Emery Bonnet, Henry Cass, John Cousins *d* Henry Cass *ph* Otello Martelli, William McLeod *m* Nino Rota
☆ Michael Denison, Dulcie Gray, Valentina Cortese, Tito Gobbi, Sebastian Shaw

The Glass Shield *
US 1995 108m Foto-Kem
CiBy 2000 (Tom Byrnes, Carolyn Schroeder)
▤ ▤ ◎◟
The first black cop at a Los Angeles station is tempted to collude in the framing of a black man for murder.

Intense study of the corruption of a police force within a violent society, but too heavy-handed to be entirely successful.
wd Charles Burnett *screenplay* One of Us by Ned Welsh *ph* Elliot Davis *m* Stephen Taylor *pd* Penny Barrett *ed* Curtiss Clayton
☆ Michael Boatman, Lori Petty, Richard Anderson, Ice Cube, Michael Ironside, Bernie Casey, Elliott Gould, M. Emmet Walsh
'A powerful moral drama that tries to deal with the racism at the root of many problems in contemporary American society.' – Todd McCarthy, Variety

The Glass Slipper
US 1954 94m Eastmancolor
MGM (Edwin H. Knopf)
The story of Cinderella.
To those used to the pantomime version this is dull, dreary, high-flown stuff: limbo sets, ballets, psychological rationalization and virtually no comedy.
d Charles Walters *ph* Arthur E. Arling *m* Bronislau Kaper *ch* Roland Petit *w/ly* Helen Deutsch
☆ Leslie Caron, Michael Wilding, Elsa Lanchester, Barry Jones, Estelle Winwood

The Glass Sphinx
Spain/Italy 1968 98m colour
AIP (Fulvio Lucisano)
An archaeologist is in danger because of his discoveries.
Multi-national mish-mash only notable as one of the last films of its star.
w Adriano Bolzoni, Louis M. Heyward *d* Luigi Scattini
☆ Robert Taylor, Anita Ekberg, Gianna Serra, Jack Stuart

The Glass Tomb: see The Glass Cage

The Glass Web
US 1953 81m bw 3-D
U-I (A. J. Cohen)
A TV executive kills a blackmailing actress and allows a young scriptwriter to be accused.
Boring thriller set in a TV studio.
w Robert Blees, Leonard Lee *d* Jack Arnold *ph* Maury Gertsman *m* Joseph Gershenson
☆ Edward G. Robinson, John Forsythe, Marcia Henderson, Richard Denning

Glastonbury The Movie
GB 1996 92m colour
Starlight/GTM/Space Baby/Arts Council
Documentary of three rock music festivals staged at Glastonbury in the late 80s and early 90s.
A film that goes with the flow, not imposing much editorial control over a collage of images of a festival noted for its slightly mystical, New Age slant; the emphasis is rarely on performances by the various groups involved.
d Robin Mahoney, Matthew Salkeld, William Beaton *et al ph* Aubrey Fagon, Robin Mahoney, William Beaton *et al ed* Robin Mahoney, Matthew Salkeld, William Beaton

Gleaming the Cube
US 1988 105m Deluxe
Rank/Gladden Entertainment (Lawrence Turman)
A teenage skateboarder tracks down the killers of his adopted Vietnamese brother.
Likely to appeal only to those who know what the film's title means.
w Michael Tolkin *d* Graeme Clifford *ph* Reed Smoot *m* Jay Ferguson *pd* John Muto *ed* John Wright
☆ Christian Slater, Steven Bauer, Richard Herd, Le Tuan, Min Luong, Art Chudabala, Ed Lauter, Micole Mercurio, Peter Kwong

Glen or Glenda?
US 1953 61m bw
Edward D. Wood Jnr
aka: I Changed My Sex
aka: He or She; The Transvestite; I Led Two Lives
A doctor relates stories about transvestites and sex-change operations.
Notorious grade Z exploitation piece, often counted among the worst films ever made. See for yourself.
wd Edward D. Wood Jnr *ph* William C. Thompson *ad* Jack Miles *ed* Bud Schelling

☆ Lyle Talbot, Timothy Farrell, Bela Lugosi, Dolores Fuller

'A Story For Everyone Who Works For A Living.'
Glengarry Glen Ross **
US 1992 100m Eastmancolor
Rank/Zupnik Enterprises (Jerry Tokofsky, Stanley R. Zupnik)
Four real-estate salesmen are in competition to see who can sell the most, with the sack facing the two losers.
A brilliant stage play seems a little claustrophobic on its transfer to the screen, but provides opportunities for some excellent acting.
w David Mamet *play* David Mamet *d* James Foley *ph* Juan Ruiz Anchia *m* James Newton Howard *pd* Jane Musky *ed* Howard Smith
☆ Al Pacino, Jack Lemmon, Alec Baldwin, Ed Harris, Alan Arkin, Kevin Spacey, Jonathan Pryce
'The prize-winning comedy of outrage is brought to the screen, intact and enhanced.' – Time
'An entertaining but slightly uncomfortable marriage both of different stage traditions and of movie ways of dealing with them.' – Richard Combs, Sight and Sound
† Jack Lemmon won the best actor award at the 1992 Venice Film Festival for his performance.
⍟ Al Pacino

The Glenn Miller Story **
US 1953 116m Technicolor
U-I (Aaron Rosenberg)
The life of the unassuming trombonist and bandleader whose plane disappeared during World War II.
Competent musical heartwarmer with a well-cast star and successful reproduction of the Miller sound. A big box-office hit.
w Valentine Davies, Oscar Brodney *d* Anthony Mann *ph* William Daniels *md* Henry Mancini, Joseph Gershenson *ad* Bernard Herzbrun, Alexander Golitzen *ed* Russell Schoengarth
☆ James Stewart, June Allyson, Harry Morgan, Charles Drake, Frances Langford, Louis Armstrong, Gene Krupa
† Jimmy Stewart's trombone playing was dubbed by Murray MacEachern and Joe Yukl.
⍟ sound recording
⍟ script; music direction

Gli Occhi, La Bocca: see Those Eyes, That Mouth

The Glimmer Man
US 1996 91m Technicolor Panavision
Warner (Steven Seagal, Julius R. Nasso)
A cop and a martial arts expert, who team up to catch a serial killer who crucifies his victims, discover that the murders are part of a larger conspiracy.
Unoriginal and ever-predictable action movie; isn't it time someone thought up a slightly better plot than this paranoid nonsense?
w Kevin Brodbin *d* John Gray *ph* Rick Bota *m* Trevor Rabin *pd* William Sandell *ed* Donn Cambern
☆ Steven Seagal, Keenen Ivory Wayans, Bob Gunton, Brian Cox, John M. Jackson, Michelle Johnson, Stephen Tobolowsky
'The clichés pile up as fast as the bodies.' – George Perry

A Global Affair
US 1963 84m bw
Seven Arts/Hall Bartlett
A United Nations official has to look after an abandoned baby.
Flat sentimental farce which embarrassingly tries to say something about the UN.
w Arthur Marx, Bob Fisher, Charles Lederer *d* Jack Arnold *ph* Joseph Ruttenberg *m* Dominic Frontiere
☆ Bob Hope, Lilo Pulver, Michèle Mercier, Yvonne de Carlo
'Squaresville incarnate, with a side trip into Leersville.' – Judith Crist, 1973

La Gloire de Mon Père *
France 1990 110m Eastmancolor
Palace/Gaumont International/La Guéville/TF1 (Marc Goldstaub, Guy Azzi)
aka: My Father's Glory
A young city boy goes on holiday to Provence with his family and falls in love with the countryside.
Charm and nostalgia are laid on thickly in a movie based on the childhood of Marcel Pagnol, who grew up to become an influential film-maker.
w Jérôme Tonnerre, Louis Nucera, Yves Robert *autobiography* Marcel Pagnol *d* Yves Robert *ph* Robert Alazraki *m* Vladimir Cosma *ad* Jacques Dugied *ed* Pierre Gillette
☆ Philippe Caubère, Nathalie Roussel, Didier Pain, Thérèse Liotard, Julien Ciamaca, Victorien Delamare, Joris Molinas, Paul Crauchet, Jean-Pierre Darras
'The weave of inner drama, family album, and discursive sceneries is gentle and lightly enchanting.' – Raymond Durgnat, Sight and Sound
† The story is continued in a sequel, Le Château de Ma Mère (qv).

Gloria *
US 1980 121m Technicolor
Columbia (Sam Shaw)
In the Bronx, an innocent woman finds she has to meet violence with violence in order to protect a small boy from the mob.
Overlong but lively and oddly entertaining; however, one is never quite sure what if anything it is getting at.
wd John Cassavetes *ph* Fred Schuler *m* Bill Conti *ad* Rene D'Auriac *ed* George C. Villasenor
☆ Gena Rowlands, John Adames, Buck Henry, Julie Carmen, Tony Knesich, Gregory Cleghorn
⍟ Gena Rowlands

'Gloria. Big mouth. Big attitude. But who knew she had a big heart.'
Gloria
US 1998 108m Technicolor
Entertainment/Mandalay/Eagle Point (Gary Foster, Lee Rich)
A woman flees from her gangster boyfriend, taking with her a young child, the sole survivor of a mob hit, and an incriminating computer disc.
A lacklustre chase movie that plods towards total inertia and ennui; the only suspense it provides is wondering whether one will still be awake at the end.
w Steven Antin *d* Sidney Lumet *ph* David Watkin *m* Howard Shore *pd* Mel Bourne *ed* Tom Swartwout *cos* Dona Granata
☆ Sharon Stone, Jean-Luke Figueroa, Jeremy Northam, Cathy Moriarty, George C. Scott, Mike Starr, Barry McEvoy, Don Billett, Jerry Dean, Tony DiBenedetto, Bonnie Bedelia, Teddy Atlas
'A travesty trying to be a Sharon Stone vehicle, this wooden crime yarn easily qualifies as the most tired, unexciting mob movie in recent memory.' – Godfrey Cheshire, Variety
† Although there is no mention of it in the credits, the movie is a remake of John Cassavetes' Gloria (qv).

Glorifying the American Girl *
US 1929 87m bw (colour sequence)
Paramount (Florenz Ziegfeld)
A chorus girl rejects her boyfriend for the sake of stardom.
Archetypal show-must-go-on musical.
w J. P. McEvoy, Millard Webb *d* Millard Webb, John Harkrider *ph* George Folsey *md* Frank Tours
☆ Mary Eaton, Edward Crandall, Helen Morgan, Rudy Vallee, Florenz Ziegfeld, Adolph Zukor, Otto Kahn, Texas Guinan, Mayor Jimmy Walker, Ring Lardner, Noah Beery, Johnny Weissmuller, Eddie Cantor

The Glorious Adventure *
GB 1921 100m Prizmacolor silent
Stoll/J.Stuart Blackton
Various lives are affected by the Great Fire of London in 1666.
Stagey costume drama, notable only as the first British film in colour.
w Felix Orman *d* J. Stuart Blackton *ph* William T. Crespinal

☆ Lady Diana Manners, Victor McLaglen, Gerald Lawrence, Cecil Humphreys, Alex Crawford, Lennox Pawle

Glorious Betsy
US 1928 90m bw silent
Warner
Napoleon's younger brother loves an American girl.
Popular period romance of its day.
w Anthony Coldeway *play* Rida Johnson Young *d* Alan Crosland
☆ Conrad Nagel, Dolores Costello, John Miljan, Betty Blythe
† The happy ending is not historical. It was remade in 1936 as Hearts Divided (qv).
⍟ Anthony Coldeway

Glory **
US 1989 122m Technicolor Panavision
Columbia TriStar (Freddie Fields)
A young and inexperienced Union officer is given command of the first black regiment recruited to fight in the Civil War.
Moving, if sometimes sanitised, account of the stirrings of black freedom.
w Kevin Jarre *book* Lay This Laurel by Lincoln Kirstein, One Gallant Rush by Peter Burchard, the letters of Robert Gould Shaw *d* Edward Zwick *ph* Freddie Francis *m* James Horner *pd* Norman Garwood *ed* Steven Rosenblum
☆ Matthew Broderick, Denzel Washington, Cary Elwes, Morgan Freeman, Jihmi Kennedy, Andre Braugher, John Finn, Donovan Leitch, John David Cullum
⍟ Freddie Francis; Denzel Washington
⍟ art direction; editing

Glory Alley
US 1952 79m bw
MGM (Nicholas Nayfack)
A sullen young boxer has trouble with his girl, her father and the demon rum.
Flat, boring second feature with musical interludes.
w Art Cohn *d* Raoul Walsh *ph* William Daniels *md* Georgie Stoll
☆ Leslie Caron, Ralph Meeker, Kurt Kasznar, Gilbert Roland, John McIntire, Louis Armstrong, Jack Teagarden
'This is the kind of film that contains bits of everything. New Orleans night life and an episode of the Korean war; an arty French ballet sequence and jazz from Louis Armstrong; a boxer who acquired a neurosis in childhood when his father hit him over the head and a blind old father with a French accent, who knows all about everything.' – MFB

Glory at Sea: see The Gift Horse

The Glory Brigade
US 1953 82m bw
TCF (William Bloom)
Greek soldiers fight in Korea alongside the Americans.
Modest war adventure with predictable racial tensions.
w Franklin Coen *d* Robert D. Webb *ph* Lucien Andriot *md* Lionel Newman
☆ Victor Mature, Alexander Scourby, Lee Marvin, Richard Egan

The Glory Guys *
US 1965 112m DeLuxe Panavision
UA/Levy-Gardner-Laven
Officers of the US cavalry disagree about dealing with the Indians.
Standard big-budget Western.
w Sam Peckinpah *novel* The Dice of God by Hoffman Birney *d* Arnold Laven *ph* James Wong Howe *m* Riz Ortolani
☆ Tom Tryon, Harve Presnell, Senta Berger, Andrew Duggan, James Caan, Slim Pickens, Michael Anderson Jnr

G'mar Giviya: see Cup Final

The Gnome-Mobile *
US 1967 90m Technicolor
Walt Disney (James Algar)
A millionaire and his family go for a forest picnic and help a colony of gnomes.

Cheerful adventures for small children, with good trick work.
w Ellis Kadison novel Upton Sinclair d Robert Stevenson ph Edward Colman m Buddy Baker
☆ Walter Brennan, Matthew Garber, Karen Dotrice, Richard Deacon, Sean McClory, Ed Wynn, Jerome Cowan, Charles Lane

'A weekend wasted is never a wasted weekend.'

Go **
US 1999 103m DeLuxe Panavision
Columbia/Banner/Saratoga (Paul Rosenberg, Mickey Liddell, Matt Freeman)

The lives of a supermarket checkout girl, four friends on a weekend in Vegas, two actors and a drug dealer collide with one another.
Enjoyably hectic caper with three interlocking stories of rave-ups and drug deals going wrong, deftly done with just enough wit and style.
w John August d Doug Liman ph Doug Liman m BT pd Tom Wilkins ed Stephen Mirrione
☆ Desmond Askew, Taye Diggs, William Fichtner, J.E. Freeman, Katie Holmes, Breckin Meyer, Jay Mohr, Timothy Olyphant, Sarah Polley, Scott Wolf
'An overly calculated concoction that nonetheless delivers a pretty good rush.' – Variety

Go Fish *
US 1994 83m bw
Mainline/Islet/Can I Watch Pictures/KVPI (Rose Troche, Guinevere Turner)

A young lesbian would-be writer looks for love and finds it.
Wry, witty and sometimes charming account of a community of lesbians, though their interests rarely stray from talk of sex, and gossip about who is making it with whom.
w Guinevere Turner, Rose Troche d Rose Troche ph Ann T. Rossetti m Brendan Dolan, Jennifer Sharpe ed Rose Troche
☆ V. S. Brodie, Guinevere Turner, T. Wendy McMillan, Migdalia Melendez, Anastasia Sharp
'A low-budget When Sally Met Sally.' – Sight and Sound
'By turns charming and tedious, this proves that no matter what your sexual preferences may be, we are all faced with the same problems in life.' – Empire

Go for a Take
GB 1972 90m colour
Rank/Century Films (Roy Simpson)

Two waiters in debt to a gangster take refuge in a film studio.
Painful British farce.
w Alan Hackney d Harry Booth ph Mark McDonald m Glen Mason
☆ Reg Varney, Norman Rossington, Sue Lloyd, Dennis Price, Julie Ege, Patrick Newell, David Lodge

Go for Broke
US 1951 93m bw
MGM (Dore Schary)

World War II exploits of Japanese-American soldiers.
Absolutely unsurprising war film with all the anti-Japs converted by the end. Production quite good.
wd Robert Pirosh ph Paul C. Vogel m Alberto Colombo
☆ Van Johnson, Lane Nakano, George Miki, Akira Fukunaga, Warner Anderson, Don Haggerty
& Robert Pirosh (as writer)

Go Into Your Dance **
US 1935 89m bw
Warner (Sam Bischoff)

GB title: Casino de Paree
A big-headed star gets his come-uppance and finds happiness.
Moderate backstage musical notable for the only teaming of Jolson and Keeler, who were then married.
w Earl Baldwin story Bradford Ropes d Archie Mayo ph Tony Gaudio, Sol Polito m/ly Harry Warren, Al Dubin ch Bobby Connolly
☆ Al Jolson, Ruby Keeler, Glenda Farrell, Benny Rubin, Phil Regan, Barton MacLane, Helen Morgan, Patsy Kelly
'It has everything for the box office.' – Variety
& Bobby Connolly

Go, Johnny Go!
US 1958 75m bw
Hal Roach (Alan Freed)

A former choirboy becomes a rock singer.
Typical teen fare of its time; if it retains any interest, it is due to Berry singing the title song, 'Little Queenie' and 'Memphis Tennessee', and to Ritchie Valens's only film performance.
w Gary Alexander d Paul Landres
☆ Alan Freed, Chuck Berry, Jimmy Clanton, Sandy Stewart, Herb Vigran, Eddie Cochrane, Ritchie Valens

Go Man Go
US 1954 82m bw
Alfred Palca (Anton M. Leader)

How Abe Saperstein moulded and trained the Harlem Globetrotters basketball team.
Not so much a film as an athletic demonstration with some actors round the edges.
w Arnold Becker d James Wong Howe ph Bill Steiner m Alex North
☆ Dane Clark, Sidney Poitier, Pat Breslin, Edmon Ryan

Go Naked in the World
US 1960 103m Metrocolor Cinemascope
MGM/Arcola (Aaron Rosenberg)

A prostitute causes a rift between son and millionaire father.
Antediluvian melodrama with overblown performances.
wd Ranald MacDougall novel Tom Chamales ph Milton Krasner m Adolph Deutsch
☆ Gina Lollobrigida, Tony Franciosa, Ernest Borgnine, Luana Patten, Will Kuluva, Philip Ober
'A good example of how the increased liberation of Hollywood can be misused.' – MFB

Go Tell the Spartans
US 1978 114m CFI color
Spartan Company (Allan F. Bodoh, Mitchell Cannold)

In Vietnam, a seasoned commander tries to get a platoon of raw soldiers out of a Vietcong ambush.
We have been here before, in other wars, and since there is little heroism to be had from Vietnam it is difficult to see why we are invited again.
w Wendell Mayes story Daniel Ford d Ted Post ph Harry Stradling Jnr m Dick Halligan
☆ Burt Lancaster, Craig Wasson, Jonathan Goldsmith, Marc Singer
'No earth-shaking masterpieces, but in its small-scale way it's strong, hard, forthright.' – Stanley Kauffmann
'Has the virtues of its defects. It is understated, lacking in powerful dramatic incidents and high human emotion, and rather flatly written and directed. As a result, it has about it a realistically antiheroic air that is rare enough in any movie about any war.' – Richard Schickel, Time

Go to Blazes
GB 1961 84m Technicolor Cinemascope
ABP (Kenneth Harper)

Ex-convicts become firemen, intending to use the engine for smash and grab raids.
Mild comedy ruined by wide screen.
w Patrick Campbell, Vivienne Knight d Michael Truman ph Erwin Hillier m John Addison
☆ Dave King, Daniel Massey, Norman Rossington, Wilfrid Lawson, Maggie Smith, Robert Morley, Coral Browne

'Laughter is what it has nothing else but!'

Go West *
US 1925 70m bw silent
Metro-Goldwyn/Buster Keaton (Joseph M. Schenck)

A tenderfoot makes friends with a cow and takes it everywhere.
Disappointingly slow star comedy with splendid moments.
w Raymond Cannon d Buster Keaton ph Bert Haines, E. Lessley
☆ Buster Keaton, Howard Truesdall, Kathleen Myers

Go West **
US 1940 82m bw
MGM (Jack Cummings)

Three zanies tackle a Western villain.

Minor Marx comedy with a good start (the ticket office sketch) and a rousing finale as they take a moving train to bits, but some pretty soggy stuff in between.
w Irving Brecher d Edward Buzzell ph Leonard Smith m Bronislau Kaper md George Stoll
☆ Groucho Marx, Harpo Marx, Chico Marx, John Carroll, Diana Lewis, Robert Barrat

Go West Young Lady
US 1940 70m bw
Columbia

A lawless Western town expects a sheriff who turns out to be a girl.
Mildly pleasing variation on Destry Rides Again.
w Karen de Wolf, Richard Flournoy d Frank Strayer
☆ Glenn Ford, Penny Singleton, Charles Ruggles

'How you gonna keep 'em down on the farm, after they've seen Mae West?'

Go West Young Man
US 1936 80m bw
Paramount (Emanuel E. Cohen)

A movie star has a car breakdown in Pennsylvania and falls for a local lad.
Cleaned-up Mae West vehicle, all rather boring.
w Mae West play Personal Appearance by Lawrence Riley d Henry Hathaway ph Karl Struss m George Stoll
☆ Mae West, Randolph Scott, Warren William, Lyle Talbot, Alice Brady, Isabel Jewell, Elizabeth Patterson
'On the way to snug profits.' – Variety
'Quite incredibly tedious, as slow and wobbling in its pace as Miss West's famous walk. The wisecracks lack the old impudence, and seldom have so many feet of film been expended on a mere dirty look.' – Graham Greene

The Goalie's Anxiety at the Penalty Kick: see The Goalkeeper's Fear of the Penalty Kick

The Goalkeeper's Fear of the Penalty Kick **
West Germany 1971 101m colour
Filmverlag der Autoren/Osterreichischer Telefilm (Thomas Schamoni, Peter Genee)

original title: Die Angst des Tormanns beim Elfmeter
Sent off during a game, an ageing goalkeeper commits a motiveless murder.
Disturbing film of the failure of communication; difficult but rewarding for the patient.
wd Wim Wenders story Peter Handke ph Robby Muller m Jurgen Knieper ed Peter Przygodda
☆ Arthur Brauss, Kai Fischer, Erika Pluhar, Libgart Schwartz, Rudiger Vogler, Marie Bardischewski

The Go-Between ***
GB 1970 116m Technicolor
EMI/World Film Services (John Heyman, Norman Priggen)

Staying at a stately home around the turn of the century, 12-year-old Leo carries love letters from a farmer to his friend's sister.
A rather tiresome plot sustains a rich picture of the Edwardian gentry, a milieu with which however the director is not at home and treats far too slowly and tricksily.
w Harold Pinter novel L. P. Hartley d Joseph Losey ph Geoffrey Fisher m Michel Legrand ad Carmen Dillon
☆ Alan Bates, Julie Christie, Michael Redgrave, Dominic Guard, Michael Gough, Margaret Leighton, Edward Fox
'It's an almost palpable recreation of a past environment, and that environment is the film's real achievement, not the drama enacted within it.' – Stanley Kauffmann
& Margaret Leighton
▼ Harold Pinter; Edward Fox; Margaret Leighton; Dominic Guard

God Gave Him a Dog: see The Biscuit Eater (1940)

God Is My Partner
US 1957 82m bw Regalscope
TCF (Sam Hersh)

A surgeon retires and begins to give his money away to religious causes; members of his family file suit against him.
Rather obvious fable in the Mr Deeds tradition.

w Charles Francis Royal d William F. Claxton
☆ Walter Brennan, John Hoyt, Marion Ross, Jesse White

God Needs Men: see Dieu a Besoin des Hommes

God of Gamblers
Hong Kong 1990 120m colour
Wins (Charles Heung)

original title: Dou San
A successful globe-trotting gambler loses his intelligence in an accident and becomes involved with petty crooks.
Over-long thriller with its emphasis on broad comedy, although it livens up for the last half-hour. The subtitling is sub-standard, getting every idiom wrong, as in 'Let's be frankly', 'I'll put him dead' and 'I was self-defencing'.
d Wong Ching
☆ Chow Yun-Fat, Andy Leung
'The action is great and the gambling scenes are crazy. Recommended.' – Sight and Sound
† The film was a big local success and gave a boost in Hong Kong to movies about gambling.

God Told Me To
US 1976 89m colour
Larco

GB title: Demon
A detective investigates the death of a mad sniper and finds it to be a case of demonic possession.
Unsavoury mix of several genres, insufficiently well written to compel.
wd Larry Cohen ph Paul Glickman m Frank Cordell
☆ Tony Lo Bianco, Deborah Raffin, Sandy Dennis, Sylvia Sidney, Sam Levene, Robert Drivas, Richard Lynch, Harry Bellaver

The Goddess: see Devi (1960)

The Goddess *
US 1958 105m bw
Columbia/Carnegie (Milton Perlman)

A small-town girl becomes a Hollywood sex symbol and lives to regret it.
Savage attack on the Marilyn Monroe cult, a bit lachrymose and compromised by miscasting, but with interesting detail.
w Paddy Chayefsky d John Cromwell ph Arthur J. Ornitz m Virgil Thomson
☆ Kim Stanley, Lloyd Bridges, Steven Hill, Betty Lou Holland
& Paddy Chayefsky

The Godfather ****
US 1972 175m Technicolor
Paramount/Alfran (Albert S. Ruddy)

When, after ruling for two generations, the Mafia's New York head dies of old age, his son takes over reluctantly but later learns how to kill.
A brilliantly-made film with all the fascination of a snake pit: a warm-hearted family saga except that the members are thieves and murderers. Cutting would help, but the duller conversational sections do heighten the cunningly judged moments of suspense and violence.
w Francis Ford Coppola, Mario Puzo novel Mario Puzo d Francis Ford Coppola ph Gordon Willis m Nino Rota pd Dean Tavoularis
☆ Marlon Brando, Al Pacino, Robert Duvall, James Caan, Richard Castellano, Diane Keaton, Talia Shire, Richard Conte, John Marley
'The immorality lies in his presentation of murderers as delightful family men – the criminal is the salt of the earth – and to our shame we rub it into the wounds of our Watergate-world mortality and even ask for more.' – Judith Crist, 1974
'They have put padding in Brando's cheeks and dirtied his teeth, he speaks hoarsely and moves stiffly, and these combined mechanics are hailed as great acting ... Like star, like film, the keynote is inflation. The Godfather was made from a big bestseller, a lot of money was spent on it, and it runs over three hours. Therefore it's important.' – Stanley Kauffmann
'The greatest gangster picture ever made.' – Pauline Kael
■ best picture; script; Marlon Brando

👤 Francis Ford Coppola (as director); Al Pacino; Robert Duvall; James Caan
🎬 Nino Rota

The Godfather of Harlem: see *Black Caesar*

The Godfather Part II ****

US 1974 200m Technicolor
Paramount/the Coppola Company (Francis Ford Coppola)

📼 🖥 📀 🎧

In 1958, Michael Corleone reflects on the problems of himself and his father before him.
Complex gangster movie, explaining the present in terms of the past and providing a comprehensive view of American society, full of good scenes and performances.

w Francis Ford Coppola, Mario Puzo d Francis Ford Coppola ph Gordon Willis m Nino Rota, Carmine Coppola pd Dean Tavoularis
☆ Al Pacino, *Robert DeNiro*, Diane Keaton, Robert Duvall, John Cazale, Lee Strasberg, Michael V. Gazzo, Talia Shire, Troy Donahue

'The daring of Part II is that it enlarges the scope and deepens the meaning of the first film … It's an epic vision of the corruption of America.' – *Pauline Kael, New Yorker*

† The two films were eventually combined and extended for television into a ten-hour serial, *The Godfather Saga*.

🏆 best picture; script; Francis Ford Coppola (as director); Nino Rota, Carmine Coppola; Robert DeNiro
👤 Al Pacino; Lee Strasberg; Michael V. Gazzo; Talia Shire
🎬 Al Pacino

'Real Power Can't Be Given. It Must Be Taken.'
The Godfather Part III **

US 1990 161m Technicolor
Paramount/Zoetrope (Francis Ford Coppola)

📼 🖥 📀 🎧

Michael Corleone attempts to become a legitimate businessman while grooming his brother's violent and illegitimate son as his successor.
Overlong, often confusing to those who cannot remember the earlier films, and hampered by at least one wretched performance, it fails to reach the standard of the first two movies in the series. But for all that it retains one's interest most of the time.

w Mario Puzo, Francis Ford Coppola d Francis Ford Coppola ph Gordon Willis m Carmine Coppola, Nino Rota pd Dean Tavoularis ad Alex Tavoularis ed Barry Malkin, Lisa Fruchtman, Walter Murch
☆ Al Pacino, Diane Keaton, Talia Shire, Andy Garcia, Eli Wallach, Joe Mantegna, George Hamilton, Bridget Fonda, Sofia Coppola, Raf Vallone, Franc D'Ambrosio, Donal Donnelly, Richard Bright, Helmut Berger, Don Novello

'While certain flaws may prevent it from being regarded as the full equal of its predecessors … it nonetheless matches them in narrative intensity, epic scope, sociopolitical analysis, physical beauty and deep feeling for its characters and milieu.' – *Variety*

'This engrossing movie is conceived and executed on a grand scale. In these inflationary times, the numbers of killings and the sums of money under discussion are much greater than before. But, oddly enough, Michael seems to shrink in stature as the picture proceeds and the *Lear*-like tragedy at which Coppola aims is not realised.' – *Philip French, Observer*

'As in the second film, a fearful price is paid for power, and Michael is left alone to consider the cost. It is here, in the ruined face of such a man, that *The Godfather Part III* locates an emotional gravity rare in American movies. The film is a slow fuse with a big bang – one that echoes through every family whose own tragedy is an aching for things past and loved ones lost.' – *Richard Corliss, Time*

👤 best picture; Francis Ford Coppola; Andy Garcia; best song 'Promise Me You'll Remember'; best art direction; best cinematography, best film editing

'Sometimes It's Hard To Tell Them Apart.'
Gods and Monsters **

US 1998 105m colour/bw
Regent (Paul Colichman, Gregg Fienberg, Mark Harris)

📼 🖥 📀

Ailing film director James Whale looks back on his life while attempting a seduction of his young gardener.
Enjoyable, if fictional, account of the last days of a director who reinvented himself in America as a middle-class Englishman and a master of horror; if the material is sometimes a little thin, the acting carries it through.

wd Bill Condon novel *Father of Frankenstein* by Christopher Bram ph Stephen M. Katz m Carter Burwell pd Richard Sherman ed Virginia Katz
☆ *Ian McKellen*, Brendan Fraser, Lynn Redgrave, Lolita Davidovich, Kevin J. O'Connor, David Dukes, Brandon Kleyla, Jack Plotnick

'Beautifully acted, witty and heart-tugging film.' – *Janet Maslin, New York Times*

'I dare say some people will find it all touchingly affectionate. To me, its posthumous libelling of James Whale, without a shred of evidence for most of its fictions, proves that death is not the last thing one has to fear.' – *Alexander Walker, London Evening Standard*

🏆 Bill Condon (script)
👤 Ian McKellen; Lynn Redgrave

God's Army: see *The Prophecy*

God's Country and the Woman

US 1936 80m Technicolor
Warner (Lou Edelman)
The junior partner of a lumber company goes to work undercover in an opponent's camp, causes trouble, and falls in love.
Adequate outdoor melodrama in early colour.

w Norman Reilly Raine novel James Oliver Curwood d William Keighley ph Tony Gaudio m Max Steiner
☆ George Brent, Beverly Roberts, Barton MacLane, Robert Barrat, Alan Hale, Addison Richards, El Brendel, Roscoe Ates, Billy Bevan

'Great outdoors in Technicolor, but not likely for much b.o.' – *Variety*

God's Gun

Italy/Israel 1976 94m colour
Cannon/Rovi/Golan/Globus

🖥

aka: *Pistola di Dio*

When bandits kill a priest, a young boy goes to find the man's brother, a gunfighter, so that he can seek revenge.
Dull and violent Western, in which Lee Van Cleef plays two roles, indistinguishable one from the other, and neither cast nor director displays any enthusiasm for the tired material.

wd Frank Kramer (Gianfranco Parolini) story John Fonseca ph Sandro Mancori m Sante Maria Romitelli pd Claudio Desantis ed Manlio Camastro
☆ Jack Palance, Lee Van Cleef, Richard Boone, Sybil Danning, Leif Garrett, Robert Lipton, Cody Palance, Ian Sander

'The story that no one dared film till now becomes the most adult motion picture ever made!'
God's Little Acre *

US 1958 110m bw
Security (Sidney Harmon)

🖥

A poor white farmer in Georgia neglects his land in a fruitless search for gold.
Tobacco Road under another name, and not so lively: bowdlerized and eventually tedious despite a welter of sensational incident and depraved characters.

w Philip Yordan novel Erskine Caldwell d Anthony Mann ph Ernest Haller m Elmer Bernstein
☆ Robert Ryan, Aldo Ray, Tina Louise, Buddy Hackett, Jack Lord, Vic Morrow, Rex Ingram

The Gods Must Be Crazy

👨‍👩‍👧 South Africa 1980 109m colour
Panavision
New Realm/Mimosa/CAT (Jamie Uys)

📼 🖥 📀

A Coca-Cola bottle falls from a plane and becomes a religious object to Kalahari bushmen.
Unexpected throwback farce with the blacks behaving almost as stupidly as Mantan Moreland in an old

Charlie Chan movie. One for the Race Relations Board.

wd Jamie Uys ph Jamie Uys, Buster Reynolds m John Boshoff ad Caroline Burls
☆ N'xau, Marius Weyers, Sandra Prinsloo, Nic de Jager, Michael Thys

The Gods Must Be Crazy II

South Africa 1988 98m colour
Fox/Elrina Investment Corp (Boet Troskie)

📼 🖥 📀

A bushman searching for his lost children finds a New York lawyer in the desert.
Implausible tale, as condescending as the first film to its black cast.

wd Jamie Uys ph Buster Reynolds m Charles Fox ed Renee Engelbrecht, Ivan Hall
☆ N'xau, Lena Farugia, Hans Strydom, Eiros, Nadies, Erick Bowen, Treasure Tshabalala, Pierre Van Pletzen, Lournes Swanepoel, Richard Loring

The Godson: see *The Samurai*

'The gospel according to today!'
Godspell *

👨‍👩‍👧 US 1973 102m TVC Color
Columbia/Lansbury/Duncan/Beruh (Edgar Lansbury)

🖥 📀

The Gospel according to St Matthew played out musically by hippies in the streets of New York.
Wild and woolly film version of the successful theatrical fantasy, surviving chiefly by virtue of its gleaming photography.

w David Greene, John Michael Tebelak play John Michael Tebelak d David Greene ph Richard G. Heimann m/ly Stephen Schwartz
☆ Victor Garber, David Haskell, Jerry Sroka, Lynne Thigpen, Robin Lamont

'A patch of terra incognita somewhere between *Sesame Street* and the gospel according to *Laugh-In*.' – *Bruce Williamson*

Godzilla

👨‍👩‍👧 Japan 1955 80m bw
Toho (Tomoyuki Tanaka)

🖥 📀

original title: *Gojira*

A prehistoric monster is awakened by H-bomb tests and menaces Tokyo.
Tepid forerunner of scores of Japanese monster movies peopled by men in rubber suits.

w Takeo Murato, Inoshiro Honda d Inoshiro Honda ph Masao Tamai m Akira Ifukube
☆ Raymond Burr, Takashi Shimura, Momoko Kochi

† Sequels included *Godzilla vs the Thing*, *King Kong vs Godzilla*, *Godzilla vs the Sea Monster*, *Godzilla vs the Smog Monster*, *Destroy All Monsters*. Other monstrous creations included *Rodan*, *Manda* and *Mothra*.

'Size Does Matter.'
Godzilla

US 1998 138m Technicolor
Columbia TriStar/Centropolis/Fried/Independent (Dean Devlin)

📼 🖥 📀 📀 💿 🎧

The result of French nuclear tests in the Pacific, a giant lizard invades Manhattan to lay its eggs.
An expensive, but dull, remake of the first Godzilla movie, in which the monster is a baddie; unlike the Japanese original, the lizard king is here created by computer graphics; it is the remainder of the cast who seem to be played by men in rubber suits.

w Dean Devlin, Roland Emmerich, Ted Elliott, Terry Rossio d Roland Emmerich ph Ueli Steiger m David Arnold pd Oliver Scholl ed Peter Amundson, David J. Siegel
☆ Matthew Broderick, Jean Reno, Maria Pitillo, Hank Azaria, Kevin Dunn, Michael Lerner, Harry Shearer, Arabella Field, Vicki Lewis

'Despite all the flash and filigree, this monster movie is curiously – and conspicuously – lacking in heart.' – *Joe Leydon, Variety*

'An overblown action montrosity with no surprises, no exhilaration and no thrills.' – *Mick LaSalle, San Francisco Chronicle*

'To many, Godzilla has become the ultimate example of a marketing campaign in search of a movie. The movie was seemingly made, not to entertain audiences, but to help sell tacos and T-shirts.' – *Peter Bart, Variety*

Godzilla on Monster Island: see *Godzilla versus Gigan*

Godzilla versus Gigan

👨‍👩‍👧 Japan 1972 89m colour
Toho Productions (Tomoyuki Tanaka)
aka: *Godzilla on Monster Island*
With the aid of Godzilla and his friends, a comic-book artist foils a plot by giant alien cockroaches to take over the world.
The usual nonsense, with the novelty of talking monsters, although their dialogue is no more interesting than that of the humans.

w Shinichi Sekizawa d Jun Fukuda m Akira Ifukube pd Yoshifumi Honda ed Yoshio Tamura sp Akiyoshi Nakano
☆ Hiroshi Ishikawa, Tomoko Umeda, Yuriko Hishimi, Minora Takashima, Zan Fujita, Toshiaki Nishizawa, Kunio Murai

Godzilla versus Mechagodzilla

Japan 1974 84m colour
Toho (Tomoyuki Tanaka)
original title: *Gojira Tai Mekagojira*
Aliens from the Third Planet of the Black Hole build a mechanical Godzilla from space titanium to destroy the world; in order to save it, Godzilla needs the help of a royal monster.
Vapid fantasy, with an often incoherent narrative and not much action.

w Hiroyasu Yamaura, Jun Fukuda story Shinichi Sekizawa, Masatoyo Fukushima d Jun Fukuda ph Jo Aizawa m Masaru Sato ad Kazuo Satsuya sp Teruyoshi Nakano
☆ Masaaki Daimon, Kazuya Aoyama, Reiko Tajima, Bellbella Leen, Hiromi Matsushita, Akihiko Hirata, Mamoru Kusumi, Isami Zushi, Issei Mori

Godzilla versus Megalon

👨‍👩‍👧 Japan 1976 80m colour
Toho Studios (Tomoyuki Tanaka)

Angered by nuclear tests, the ruler of an underwater world sends a monster, a sort of winged lobster, to destroy Tokyo.
Most ridiculous, and, for that reason, the most enjoyable of the Godzilla series, notable for the Seatopians, a submarine race given to wearing togas with knee-length boots, and the tag-team wrestling style of the monster combats.

w Shinichi Sekizawa d Jun Fukuda ph Yuzuru Aizawa m Riichiro Manabe ad Yoshibumi Honda ed Michiko Ikeda sp Akiyoshi Nakano
☆ Katsuhiko Sasaki, Yutaka Hayashi, Hiroyuki Kawase

Godzilla versus Monster Zero: see *Invasion of the Astro-Monsters*

Godzilla vs King Ghidorah

Japan 1998 100m colour
Toho (Shogo Tomiyama)

Time-travelling aliens try to prevent Godzilla from interfering with the monster King Ghidorah which they create to take over the world.
This attempt to re-create Godzilla in a more modern style has a bigger budget than usual, but the narrative and acting remain perfunctory.

wd Kazuki Omori ph Yoshinori Sekiguchi m Akira Ifukube ed Michiko Ikeda sp Koichi Kawakita
☆ Anna Nakagawa, Isao Toyohara, Megumi Odaka, Chuck Wilson, Yoshio Tsuchiya, Katsuhiko Sasaki, Richard Berger

Gog *

US 1954 85m Color Corporation 3D
Ivan Tors
In an underground laboratory in New Mexico, a giant computer controls two robots, and a spy programs it to kill.
Brisk, imaginative low-budget sci-fi in gleaming colour, well staged and developed.

w Tom Taggart d Herbert L. Strock ph Lothrop B. Worth m Harry Sukman
☆ Richard Egan, Constance Dowling, Herbert Marshall

The Go-Getter

US 1937 90m bw
Warner (Sam Bischoff)
A one-legged navy veteran is determined that his injury will not prevent him from becoming a success.
Moderate comedy-drama, agreeably played.

---

w Delmer Daves, Peter B. Kyne d Busby Berkeley ph Arthur Edeson md Leo F. Forbstein
☆ George Brent, Charles Winninger, Anita Louise, John Eldredge, Henry O'Neill, Willard Robertson, Eddie Acuff
'A fair amount of comedy within a story bordering on the ridiculous.' – Variety

Goha
France/Tunisia 1957 90m Agfacolor
Films Franco-Africains
A young Arab helps a blind musician and falls in love with a wise man's young bride.
Curiously winning, good-looking little romance which, apart from an unexpected sad ending, plays like an update of the Arabian Nights.
w Georges Schéhadé novel Le Livre de Goha le Simple by A. Ades, A. Jospiovici d Jacques Baratier ph Jean Bourgoin m Maurice Ohana
☆ Omar Chérif (later Sharif), Zina Bouzaiane, Lauro Gazzolo

'Saved from the hangman for a fate worse than death!'
Goin' South
US 1978 101m Metrocolor
Paramount (Henry Gittes, Harold Schneider)
An unwashed outlaw is saved from the rope when a young girl promises to marry and reform hiim, for no very good reason
Curious semi-comic Western which might have made a good two-reeler.
w John Herman Shaner, Al Ramrus, Charles Shyer, Alan Mandel d Jack Nicholson ph Nestor Almendros m Van Dyke Parks, Perry Botkin Jnr
☆ Jack Nicholson, Mary Steenburgen, Christopher Lloyd, John Belushi, Veronica Cartwright, Richard Bradford

'Mae's a lady now and she'll lick anyone in the house who says she ain't!'
Goin' to Town *
US 1935 74m bw
Paramount (William Le Baron)
A Western oil heiress moves into society.
Reasonably satisfactory Mae West vehicle, but not in the old bawdy style.
w Mae West d Alexander Hall ph Karl Struss m/ly Sammy Fain, Irving Kahal md Andrea Setaro
☆ Mae West, Paul Cavanagh, Ivan Lebedeff, Tito Coral, Marjorie Gateson, Fred Kohler Snr, Monroe Owsley
'No amount of epigrammatic hypoing can offset the silly story.' – Variety

Going All the Way *
US 1997 103m Foto-Kem
Polygram/Lakeshore/Gramercy (Tom Gorai, Sigurjon Sighvatsson)
In the mid-50s, two young GIs – one sexually shy, the other confident – become friends.
Amiable rites-of-passage drama that looks back on the period with regretful nostalgia.
w Dan Wakefield novel Dan Wakefield d Mark Pellington ph Bobby Bukowski m Tomandandy pd Thérèse DuPrez ed Leo Trombetta
☆ Jeremy Davies, Ben Affleck, Amy Locane, Rose McGowan, Rachel Weisz, John Lordan, Bob Swan, Jill Clayburgh, Lesley Ann Warren
'Has charm, but it certainly doesn't linger in the mind.' – Edward Porter, Sunday Times

Going Bye Bye **
US 1934 20m bw
Hal Roach
A violent convict escapes to take vengeance on the two innocents whose evidence sent him up.
Splendid star comedy displaying most of the team's most endearing aspects.
w Stan Laurel, Charles Rogers, Frank Terry d Charles Rogers ph Francis Corby ed Bert Jordan
☆ Stan Laurel, Oliver Hardy, Walter Long, Mae Busch

Going Highbrow
US 1935 68m bw
Warner
Two nouveaux riches people try to trick their way into society.
Agreeably cast farce that outstays its welcome.

w Edward Kaufman, Sy Bartlett, Ralph Spence d Robert Florey
☆ Edward Everett Horton, Guy Kibbee, ZaSu Pitts, Ross Alexander, Judy Canova
'So-so flicker for the lesser spots.' – Variety

Going Hollywood *
US 1933 80m bw
MGM
A crooner is pursued by a girl who poses as a French maid.
Lively comedy with a studio setting; anything goes.
w Donald Ogden Stewart d Raoul Walsh
☆ Bing Crosby, Marion Davies, Patsy Kelly, Stuart Erwin
'Lavishly produced musical with everything but a story.' – Variety

Going Home
US 1971 98m colour
MGM (Herbert B. Leonard)
An ex-convict who killed his wife while drunk assumes an ambivalent relationship with his son.
Thoroughly uninteresting melodrama which was barely released.
w Lawrence Marcus d Herbert B. Leonard ph Fred Jackman m Bill Walker
☆ Robert Mitchum, Jan-Michael Vincent, Brenda Vaccaro

Going in Style
US 1979 97m Technicolor
Warner/Tony Bill
Three bored elderly men decide to plan a bank robbery.
Curiously aimless sentimental comedy-drama which is simply neither funny enough, thrilling enough or moving enough to hold the interest.
wd Martin Brest ph Billy Williams m Michael Small
☆ George Burns, Art Carney, Lee Strasberg

Going My Way **
US 1944 126m bw
Paramount (Leo McCarey)
A young priest comes to a New York slum parish and after initial friction charms the old pastor he is to succeed.
Sentimental comedy which got away with it wonderfully at the time, largely through careful casting, though it seems thin and obvious now.
w Frank Butler, Frank Cavett, Leo McCarey d Leo McCarey ph Lionel Lindon m Robert Emmett Dolan m/ly Johnny Burke, James Van Heusen, J. R. Shannon ed Leroy Stone
☆ Bing Crosby, Barry Fitzgerald, Rise Stevens, Frank McHugh, James Brown, Gene Lockhart, Jean Heather, Porter Hall
'I should not feel safe in recommending it to anyone but a simple-hearted sentimentalist with a taste for light music.' – Richard Mallett, Punch
'The lessons, if I read them right, are that leisureliness can be excellent, that if you take a genuine delight in character the universe is opened to you, and perhaps above all that a movie, like any other genuine work of art, must be made for love. But I am willing to bet that the chief discernible result of Going My Way will be an anxiety-ridden set of vaudeville sketches about Pat and Mike in cassocks.' – James Agee
† Father O'Malley reappeared in The Bells of St Mary's and Say One for Me (both qv).
🏆 best picture; script; original story (Leo McCarey); Leo McCarey (direction); Bing Crosby; Barry Fitzgerald (best supporting actor); song, 'Swinging on a Star' (mJames Van Heusen, lyJohnny Burke)
👤 Lionel Lindon; Barry Fitzgerald (best actor); Leroy Stone

Going Places: see Les Valseuses (1974)

Going Places
US 1938 84m bw
Warner (Hal Wallis)
A sporting goods salesman poses as a jockey and has to ride a horse to victory.
Thin musical spurred by the hit song 'Jeepers Creepers', here sung by Louis Armstrong to the race horse.
w Jerry Wald, Sig Herzig, Maurice Leo play The Hottentot by Victor Mapes, William Collier d Ray

Enright ph Arthur L. Todd md Leo F. Forbstein ad Hugh Reticker ed Clarence Kolster
☆ Dick Powell, Anita Louise, Ronald Reagan, Louis Armstrong, Allen Jenkins, Walter Catlett
'Satisfactory but not smash.' – Variety
👤 song 'Jeepers Creepers' (mHarry Warren, lyJohnny Mercer)

Going Undercover: see Yellow Pages

Gold *
GB 1974 124m Technicolor Panavision
Hemdale/Avton (Michael Klinger)
A South African mining engineer falls for the boss's granddaughter and exposes a conspiracy.
Old-fashioned thick ear with spectacular underground sequences and a rousing finale.
w Wilbur Smith, Stanley Price novel Goldmine by Wilbur Smith d Peter Hunt ph Ousama Rawi m Elmer Bernstein
☆ Roger Moore, Susannah York, Ray Milland, Bradford Dillman, John Gielgud, Tony Beckley
👤 song 'Wherever Love Takes Me' (mElmer Bernstein, lyDon Black)

The Gold and the Glory
Australia 1984 112m colour Panavision
Alpine/Noble (John Weiley)
aka: The Coolangatta Gold
A son defies his father by challenging his elder brother in the Iron Man marathon race.
A film of Oedipal conflict that never quite escapes from its parochial concerns.
w Peter Shreck, Ted Robinson idea Max Oldfield d Igor Auzins ph Keith Wagstaff m Bill Conti pd Bob Hill ed Tim Wellburn
☆ Josh McWilliam, Nick Tate, Robyn Nevin, Josephine Smulders, Grant Kenny, Colin Friels

'Here They Come On A Million Dollar Spree To Wake and Make and Take Paree!'
Gold Diggers in Paris *
US 1938 95m bw
Warner (Sam Bischoff)
GB title: The Gay Imposters
Three girls chase rich husbands abroad.
A thin end to the series, saved by an agreeable cast.
w Earl Baldwin, Warren Duff d Ray Enright ph Sol Polito, George Barnes m/ly Harry Warren, Al Dubin, Johnny Mercer ch Busby Berkeley
☆ Rudy Vallee, Rosemary Lane, Hugh Herbert, Allen Jenkins, Gloria Dickson, Melville Cooper, Fritz Feld, Ed Brophy, Curt Bois

'Your dream of perfect beauty come true!'
Gold Diggers of 1933 ***
US 1933 96m bw
Warner (Robert Lord)
Cheerful, competent, well-cast remake of the above; numbers include 'My Forgotten Man', 'We're in the Money' and 'Pettin' in the Park'.
w Erwin Gelsey, James Seymour, David Boehm, Ben Markson play The Gold Diggers by Avery Hopwood d Mervyn Le Roy ph Sol Polito m/ly Harry Warren, Al Dubin ch Busby Berkeley
☆ Warren William, Joan Blondell, Aline MacMahon, Ruby Keeler, Dick Powell, Guy Kibbee, Ned Sparks, Ginger Rogers, Clarence Nordstrom
'It sums up what is meant by the phrase "pure thirties": electrically wired chorus girls singing "In the Shadows Let Me Come and Sing to You" merge to form a big illuminated violin.' – New Yorker, 1979
'It is memorable chiefly because Busby Berkeley created a mad geometry of patterned chorines … The innocent vulgarity of the big numbers is charming and uproarious, and aesthetically preferable to the pretentious ballet finales of fifties musicals like An American in Paris. Even those of us who were children at the time did not mistake Gold Diggers for art – and certainly no one took it for life.' – Pauline Kael, 1968

Gold Diggers of 1935 **
US 1934 95m bw
Warner (Robert Lord)
A socialite puts on a Broadway show at her country home, and is taken in by a swindler.

Heavy-handed but laugh-provoking comedy with familiar faces of the day, climaxed by big numbers including 'Lullaby of Broadway'.
w Manuel Seff, Peter Milne, Robert Lord ph George Barnes m/ly Harry Warren, Al Dubin md Ray Heindorf d/ch Busby Berkeley
☆ Dick Powell, Adolphe Menjou, Gloria Stuart, Alice Brady, Hugh Herbert, Glenda Farrell, Frank McHugh, Grant Mitchell, Wini Shaw
'Busby Berkeley, the master of scenic prestidigitation, continues to dazzle the eye and stun the imagination.' – André Sennwald, New York Times
'A decidedly heady mixture.' – Pare Lorentz
🏆 song 'Lullaby of Broadway'
👤 choreography

Gold Diggers of 1937 *
US 1936 100m bw
Warner (Hal B. Wallis)
A group of insurance salesmen back a show.
Mild tailing-off of the Gold Diggers series, though with the accustomed production polish.
w Warren Duff play Richard Maibaum, Michael Wallach, George Haight d Lloyd Bacon ph Arthur Edeson m/ly Harry Warren, Al Dubin, E. Y. Harburg, Harold Arlen ch Busby Berkeley
☆ Dick Powell, Joan Blondell, Glenda Farrell, Victor Moore, Lee Dixon, Osgood Perkins, Charles D. Brown
👤 Busby Berkeley

'Exceeds in pretentiousness and beauty anything which has yet appeared on the screen!'
Gold Diggers of Broadway *
US 1929 98m Technicolor
Warner
Three Broadway chorus girls seek rich husbands.
Fascinating primitive musical that includes the songs 'Tiptoe Through the Tulips' and 'Painting the Clouds With Sunshine'.
w Robert Lord play The Gold Diggers by Avery Hopwood d Roy del Ruth ph Barney McGill, Ray Rennahan m/ly Al Dubin, Joe Burke
☆ Nancy Welford, Conway Tearle, Winnie Lightner, Ann Pennington, Lilyan Tashman, William Bakewell, Nick Lucas
† Other versions of the play include The Gold Diggers (1923), Gold Diggers of 1933 (qv), Painting the Clouds with Sunshine (qv).

Gold Dust Gertie
US 1931 66m bw
Warner
GB title: Why Change Your Husband?
A tough divorcee tries to sponge on her former spouses.
Silly and unattractive comedy.
w W. K. Wells, Ray Enright play The Life of the Party by Len D. Hollister d Lloyd Bacon
☆ Winnie Lightner, Chic Johnson, Ole Olsen, Dorothy Carlisle, Claude Gillingwater
'Roughest kind of comedy dialogue; in need of careful surgery.' – Variety

Gold Is Where You Find It *
US 1938 90m Technicolor
Warner (Sam Bischoff)
Gold rush miners settle as California farmers.
Agreeable Western in excellent early colour.
w Warren Duff, Clements Ripley, Robert Buckner d Michael Curtiz ph Sol Polito m Max Steiner
☆ George Brent, Olivia de Havilland, Claude Rains, Margaret Lindsay, John Litel, Marcia Ralston, Barton MacLane, Tim Holt, Sidney Toler
'It's jam but good jam – with a few better moments you don't often find in films like this.' – Graham Greene

Gold of Naples
Italy 1955 135m bw
Ponti-de Laurentiis
original title: L'Oro di Napoli
Six sketches, comic and tragic, give an impression of Naples today.
A variable collection, mainly shown around the world in abridged versions.
w Cesare Zavattini, Vittorio de Sica, Giuseppe Marotta d Vittorio de Sica ph Otello Martelli m Alessandro Cicognini
☆ Vittorio de Sica, Eduardo de Filippo, Toto, Sophia Loren, Paolo Stoppa, Silvana Mangano

Gold of the Seven Saints
US   1961   89m   bw   Warnerscope
Warner (Leonard Freeman)
Cowboys compete in a search for lost gold.
Adequate minor Western using TV stars.
w Leigh Brackett, Leonard Freeman d Gordon
Douglas ph Joseph Biroc m Howard Jackson
☆ Clint Walker, Roger Moore, Letitia Roman,
Robert Middleton, Chill Wills, Gene Evans

The Gold Rush ***
👫 US   1925   72m   bw
Charles Chaplin
📼 ▤ ⌕ ～
A lone prospector in the Yukon becomes rich after
various adventures.
*Essentially a succession of slowly but carefully built
visual gags, this is Chaplin's finest example of comedy
drawn from utter privation; as such it appealed vastly
to the poor of the world. As a clown, Chaplin himself is
near his best, though as usual there is rather too much
straining for pathos.*
ph Rollie Totheroh md Max Terr (1942 version)
ad Charles D. Hall ed Harold McGhean (1942
version) wd/p/m Charles Chaplin
☆ Charles Chaplin, Georgia Hale, Mack Swain,
Tom Murray
🎵 Max Terr

The Golden Age of Buster Keaton **
👫 US   1975   97m   bw
Jay Ward (Raymond Rohauer)
A useful introductory package to the shorts and
features of Buster Keaton, with most of the great
silent scenes present.
commentary Bill Scott

The Golden Age of Comedy ****
👫 US   1957   78m   bw
Robert Youngson Productions
▤ ⌕
First of the scholarly compilations of silent comedy
which saved many negatives from destruction, this
is a fast-paced general survey which despite a
facetious sound track does provide a laugh a
minute.
*It particularly brought Laurel and Hardy back into
public notice, and includes sections from Two Tars and
The Battle of the Century.*
wd Robert Youngson m George Steiner
narrators Dweight Weist, Ward Wilson
☆ Stan Laurel, Oliver Hardy, Harry Langdon, Ben
Turpin, Will Rogers, Billy Bevan, Charley Chase,
Andy Clyde

Golden Arrow
US   1936   68m   bw
Warner
An heiress tricks a newspaper reporter into a
marriage of convenience.
Dull, schematic romantic comedy.
w Charles Kenyon, Michael Arlen d Alfred E.
Green
☆ Bette Davis, George Brent, Eugene Pallette,
Dick Foran

Golden Arrow
GB   1952   82m   bw
Anatole de Grunwald
US title: *The Gay Adventure*
On a transcontinental train, three men have
different daydreams about the same girl.
Transparent portmanteau comedy which didn't click.
w Paul Darcy, Sid Colin d Gordon Parry ph Otto
Heller
☆ Jean Pierre Aumont, Paula Valenska, Burgess
Meredith, Richard Murdoch, Kathleen Harrison,
Karel Stepanek, Edward Lexy

Golden Balls *
Spain   1993   95m   colour
UIP/Lolafilms/Oviedo/Filmauro/Hugo/Lumiere (Marivi
de Villanueva)
📼
original title: *Huevos de Oro*
An entrepreneur who regards the erection of the
tallest skyscraper in Benidorm as an extension of
his own virility is ruined by the complications of
his sexual involvement with four women.
*Engaging comedy, much concerned with sex, death,
food, and the limitations of machismo, and a satire at
the expense of Spanish icons, from Salvador Dali to
Julio Iglesias.*

w Cuca Canals, Bigas Luna d Bigas Luna ph José
Luis Alcaine m Nicola Piovani ad Antxón
Gómez ed Carmen Frias
☆ Javier Bardem, Maria de Medeiros, Maribel
Verdú, Elisa Touati, Raquel Bianca, Maria Martin,
Francisco Casares
'It will doubtless find a following among the
designer raincoat brigade who don't mind
subtitles over bedroom scenes, but slobberers
would probably enjoy it more without the
jamón-fisted analysis of the crisis of Spanish
masculinity and the huevos-up Luna makes of
telling his story.' – *Kim Newman, Empire*
'Script is weak, with numerous false leads that
are never followed up. The sex scenes may help
pic chalk up some sales for this meretricious and
ultimately non-erotic film.' – *Variety*

'His blade of gold, a legend in battle – her kiss of
surrender, the prize of victory!'

The Golden Blade
👫 US   1953   80m   Technicolor
U-I (Richard Wilson)
With the help of a magic sword, Harun saves a
princess and captures a rebel.
*Standard cut-rate Arabian Nights adventure, very
typical of its studio during the fifties.*
w John Rich d Nathan Juran ph Maury
Gertsman m Joseph Gershenson
☆ Rock Hudson, Piper Laurie, George Macready,
Gene Evans, Kathleen Hughes

Golden Boy *
US   1939   101m   bw
Columbia (William Perlberg)
A poor boy is torn between two absorbing
interests: prizefighting and the violin.
*Personalized version of a socially conscious play;
moderately effective with smooth production and good
cast.*
w Lewis Meltzer, Daniel Taradash, Sarah Y.
Mason, Victor Heerman play Clifford Odets
d Rouben Mamoulian ph Nicholas Musuraca, Karl
Freund m Victor Young md Morris Stoloff
ad Lionel Banks ed Otto Meyer
☆ Barbara Stanwyck, William Holden, Adolphe
Menjou, Joseph Calleia, Lee J. Cobb, Sam Levene,
Edward Brophy, Don Beddoe
'Strong entertainment with general audience
appeal.' – *Variety*
'A slick, swift, exciting but insensitive movie.' –
Gordon Sager
'Interesting, entertaining, dramatic, but scarcely
first-rate.' – *Frank Nugent, New York Times*
🎵 Victor Young

Golden Braid *
Australia   1990   91m   colour
Artificial Eye/Illumination/Australian Film
Commission/Film Victoria (Paul Cox, Paul Ammitzboll,
Santhana Naidu)
📼
A clock restorer, obsessed by death and time, falls
in love with a braid of hair he discovers in the
secret drawer of an antique cabinet.
*Slow-paced account of a man trying to decide between
fantasy and reality that at times comes near to showing
that one man's obsession is another's tedium.*
w Paul Cox, Barry Dickens story La Chevelure by
Guy de Maupassant d Paul Cox ph Nino G.
Marinetti pd Neil Angwin ed Russell Hurley
☆ Chris Haywood, Gosia Dobrowolska, Paul
Chubb, Norman Kaye, Marion Heathfield, Monica
Maughan, Robert Menzies, Jo Kennedy

The Golden Child
👫 US   1986   93m   Metrocolor
Paramount/Feldman-Meeker/Eddie Murphy
📼 ▤ ⌕ ～
A social worker is assigned to look for a mystic
child who will bring peace to the Earth.
Astonishingly inept fantasy.
w Dennis Feldman d Michael Ritchie ph Donald
E. Thorin m Michel Colombier
☆ Eddie Murphy, Charles Dance, Charlotte Lewis,
Victor Wong

The Golden Coach
Italy/France   1953   100m   Technicolor
Hoche/Panaria (Valentine Brosio, Giuseppe
Bordognoi)
▤ ⌕
original title: *Le Carrosse d'Or*
In Spanish South America in the 18th century, the
leading lady of a band of strolling players turns all
heads including that of the viceroy, who
scandalizes all by making her a present of his
official golden coach.
*The director seems to have been chiefly interested in the
colour and the backgrounds: the story is a bore and the
leading lady ill-chosen.*
w Jean Renoir, Jack Kirkland, Renzo Avanzo,
Giulio Macchi play Prosper Merimée d Jean
Renoir ph Claude Renoir m Vivaldi
☆ Anna Magnani, Duncan Lamont, Paul
Campbell, Ricardo Rioli, William Tubbs

The Golden Disc
GB   1958   78m   bw
Butchers (W. G. Chalmers)
An unsuccessful singer helps her aunt transform a
rundown coffee bar and start a record company,
making a star of a stagehand.
*Tired British second feature, aimed at a young audience
at a time when Gaggia espresso machines and juke
boxes playing rock and skiffle were the height of
fashion; the music is bland and the guitars are acoustic.*
w Don Nicholl, Don Sharp story Gee Nicholl
d Don Sharp ph Geoffrey Faithfull md Philip
Green ad John Jones ed Eily Boland
☆ Lee Patterson, Mary Steele, Terry Dene, Linda
Gray, Ronald Adam, Peter Dyneley, David Jacobs
† Apart from Dene, artists featured are Nancy
Whiskey, Dennis Lotis, the Sonny Stewart Skiffle
Kings, Terry Kennedy Group, Murray Campbell,
Sheila Buxton, Les Hobeaux and the Phil Seamen
(misspelt Seamon on the credits) Jazz Group

'Now you know the way a gypsy loves!'

Golden Earrings *
US   1947   95m   bw
Paramount (Harry Tugend)
A British Intelligence officer is helped by a gypsy
to sneak a poison gas formula out of Nazi Germany.
*One of the silliest stories of all time, despite the
presence of Quentin Reynolds asserting that he believed
it; also lacking in the humour which might have saved
it, but produced with polish and interesting for the two
stars at this stage in their careers.*
w Abraham Polonsky, Frank Butler, Helen
Deutsch novel Yolanda Foldes d Mitchell Leisen
ph Daniel L. Fapp m Victor Young
☆ Ray Milland, Marlene Dietrich, Murvyn Vye,
Bruce Lester, Dennis Hoey, Reinhold Schunzel,
Ivan Triesault
'A good deal of torso work goes on which I can't
help feeling they're a bit old for.' – *Richard
Winnington*

The Golden Falcon (dubbed)
Italy   1955   90m   colour
Ottavio Poggi
original title: *Il Falco d'Oro*
Rivalry between two powerful Italian families
becomes more intense when plans go wrong over
an arranged marriage to end the fighting.
*Comic swashbuckler, performed without much panache
and not helped by unsympathetic dubbing.*
d Carlo Ludovico Bragaglia ph Alvaro Mancori
☆ Anna Maria Ferrero, Nadia Gray, Massimo
Serato

The Golden Fleecing
US   1940   68m   bw
MGM (Edgar Selwyn)
A timid insurance salesman becomes embroiled
with gangsters.
Modestly effective double-bill comedy.
w S. J. and Laura Perelman d Leslie Fenton
☆ Lew Ayres, Lloyd Nolan, Virginia Grey, Leon
Errol, Rita Johnson, Nat Pendleton, William
Demarest, Marc Lawrence

Golden Gate
US   1993   90m   colour
American Playhouse (Michael Brandman)
📼 ▤ ～
An FBI agent, feeling guilty over the suicide of an
innocent Chinese laundry worker, whom he put in
prison for 10 years, seduces the man's daughter.
*Confused, heavy-handed, tendentious drama that gets
itself into a moral muddle with its crass characterizations.*

w David Henry Hwang d John Madden
ph Bobby Bukowski m Elliot Goldenthal
pd Andrew Jackness ed Sean Barton
☆ Matt Dillon, Joan Chen, Bruno Kirby, Teri
Polo, Tzi Ma, Stan Egi, Jack Shearer, Peter
Murnick, George Guidall

Golden Girl *
US   1951   108m   Technicolor
TCF (George Jessel)
The story of Lotta Crabtree, who after the Civil
War determined to become a great musical star.
Harmless semi-Western biopic with good tunes.
w Walter Bullock, Charles O'Neal, Gladys
Lehman d Lloyd Bacon ph Charles G. Clarke
md Lionel Newman ch Seymour Felix
☆ Mitzi Gaynor, Dale Robertson, Dennis Day,
James Barton, Una Merkel, Raymond Walburn,
Gene Sheldon
🎵 song 'Never' (mLionel Newman, lyEliot Daniel)

The Golden Hawk
👫 US   1952   83m   Technicolor
Columbia (Sam Katzman)
A pirate determines to avenge his mother's death
at the hands of the governor of Cartagena.
*Clean-cut period romp for boys who don't demand
realism.*
w Robert E. Kent novel Frank Yerby d Sidney
Salkow ph William B. Skall md Mischa
Bakaleinikoff
☆ Sterling Hayden, Rhonda Fleming, John
Sutton, Helena Carter, Paul Cavanagh

The Golden Head
US/Hungary   1964   115m   Technirama 70
Cinerama/Hungarofilm (Alexander Paal)
Passengers on a Danube pleasure boat become
involved in the theft of the golden head of St Laszlo.
*Travelogue with a thin plot, somewhat slow moving but
suitable for children.*
w Stanley Boulder, Ivan Boldizsar d Richard
Thorpe ph Istvan Hildebrand m Peter Fenyes
☆ George Sanders, Buddy Hackett, Douglas
Wilmer, Jess Conrad, Robert Coote

The Golden Heist: see *Inside Out*

The Golden Horde
👫 US   1951   76m   Technicolor
U-I (Howard Christie)
aka: *The Golden Horde of Genghis Khan*
Crusaders meet Mongols in Samarkand, and Sir
Guy wins a princess.
*Rather priceless idiocies are perpetrated in this variation
on the studio's favourite Arabian Nights theme, but
somehow they fail to make one laugh, which should be
the only possible response to such a farrago.*
w Gerald Drayson Adams d George Sherman
ph Russell Metty m Hans Salter
☆ David Farrar, Ann Blyth, George Macready,
Henry Brandon, Richard Egan, Marvin Miller

The Golden Horde of Genghis Khan: see
The Golden Horde

The Golden Hour: see *Pot o' Gold*

The Golden Madonna
GB   1949   88m   bw
IFP/Pendennis (John Stafford)
Two young people search Italy for a religious
painting stolen by thieves.
*Stilted but eager to please, this romantic comedy-drama
seemed a bit lacking in drive.*
w Akos Tolnay d Ladislas Vajda ph Anchise Brizzi
☆ Phyllis Calvert, Michael Rennie, Tullio
Carminati, David Greene, Aldo Silvani

Golden Marie: see *Casque d'Or*

The Golden Mask: see *South of Algiers*

The Golden Mistress *
US   1954   80m   Technicolor
UA/RK (Richard Kay, Harry Rybnick)
An American and his girlfriend search the sea bed
for the forbidden treasure of a Haitian tribe.
*Curious independent production, an adventure in the
style of silent serials; amateur in many ways, yet with a
freshness of photography and location plus some
powerful voodoo scenes.*
wd Joel Judge (Abner Biberman) ph William C.
Thompson m Raoul Kraushaar
☆ John Agar, Rosemarie Bowe, Abner Biberman

👫 film suitable for
family viewing   📼 VHS video-cassette for
the British PAL system   ▤ VHS video-cassette for the British
PAL system in wide screen-format   ⌕ Video cassette in a computer-
colourised version   ▤ American NTSC video-cassette   ⌕～ Laser disc

'Whoever owns them can rule the world!'
Golden Needles
US 1974 92m Movielab Panavision
AIP/Sequoia (Fred Weintraub, Paul Heller)
Various factions seek a Hong Kong statue showing seven miraculous acupuncture points.
Youth/sex/Kung Fu/James Bond action amalgam.
w S. Lee Pogostin, Sylvia Schneble d Robert Clouse ph Gilbert Hubbs m Lalo Schifrin
☆ Joe Don Baker, Elizabeth Ashley, Jim Kelly, Burgess Meredith, Ann Sothern

Golden Rendezvous
US 1977 109m colour
Film Trust/Milton Okun (Andre Pieterse)
📀
Murderous mercenaries take over a freighter, but reckon without the courageous first officer.
Blood-and-thunder hokum with many casualties but not much sense.
w Stanley Price novel Alistair MacLean
d Ashley Lazarus ph Ken Higgins m Jeff Wayne
☆ Richard Harris, Ann Turkel, David Janssen, Burgess Meredith, John Vernon, Gordon Jackson, Keith Baxter, Dorothy Malone, John Carradine, Robert Flemyng, Leigh Lawson, John Beatty

The Golden Seal *
🏃🏃 US 1983 94m Metrocolor
Samuel Goldwyn Jnr (Russell Thatcher)
📀
On a bleak Aleutian island a boy stops hunters from killing a seal once thought mythical.
Rather chilling and thinly plotted moral fable for children, who may, however, be bored. The seals, the scenery and the music just about save it.
w John Groves novel A River Ran out of Eden by James Vance Marshall d Frank Zuniga ph Eric Saarinen m Dana Kaproff, John Barry
☆ Steve Railsback, Michael Beck, Penelope Milford, Torquil Campbell

The Golden Virgin: see The Story of Esther Costello

The Golden Voyage of Sinbad *
🏃🏃 GB 1973 105m Eastmancolor
Columbia/Morningside (Charles H. Schneer)
📀 ▦ 📀
Sinbad finds a strange map and crosses swords with a great magician.
Routine, rather uninspired fantasy enlivened by grotesque trick effects.
w Brian Clemens, Ray Harryhausen d Gordon Hessler ph Ted Moore m Miklos Rozsa pd John Stoll sp Ray Harryhausen
☆ John Phillip Law, Caroline Munro, Tom Baker, Douglas Wilmer, Grégoire Aslan

'No limits. No fears. No substitutes.'
GoldenEye **
US 1995 130m DeLuxe Panavision
UIP/United Artists/Danjaq/Eon (Michael G. Wilson, Barbara Broccoli)
📀 ▦ ▦ 📀 ◎ ◎ ◎ 🎧
Bond goes to Russia to defeat a criminal mastermind who controls a secret satellite that can disable the world's electronic devices.
The mixture much as before, except that the makers give a few nods and winks to the audience so that everyone is in on the joke of this suave agent saving the world yet again; the stunts are spectacular, Brosnan well conveys a slightly weary sophistication, and the jokes are familiar, which should be enough to keep its new audience happy.
w Jeffrey Caine, Bruce Feirstein story Michael France d Martin Campbell ph Phil Meheux m Eric Serra pd Peter Lamont ed Terry Rawlings
☆ Pierce Brosnan, Sean Bean, Izabella Scorupco, Famke Janssen, Joe Don Baker, Judi Dench, Robbie Coltrane, Tcheky Karyo, Gottfried John, Alan Cumming, Desmond Llewelyn, Samantha Bond, Michael Kitchen
'The very definition of escapist fare.' – *Variety*
'At last, you think, somebody has had the courage to make a Bond film as it should be made nowadays: as period drama.' – *Tom Shone, Sunday Times*
'Proves that the dinosaur can change its spots.' – *Adam Mars-Jones, Independent*
'Fast cars! Exotic games of baccarat! Double entendres that might have been cribbed from a 20-year-old copy of Playboy! Are we having fun now or what?' – *Owen Gleiberman, Entertainment Weekly*

† The film took more than $219m at the box-office worldwide.

Goldengirl
US 1979 104m colour
Avco Embassy (Danny O'Donovan)
▦
A scientist uses experimental drugs on his daughter to turn her into an Olympic champion runner.
Ridiculous and overblown fantasy with a cast busily distancing themselves from the script.
w John Kohn novel Peter Lear d Joseph Sargent ph Steven Larner m Bill Conti ad Syd Litwack ed George Nicholson
☆ Susan Anton, James Coburn, Curt Jurgens, Leslie Caron, Robert Culp, James A. Watson Jnr, Harry Guardino, Ward Costello, Michael Lerner

'James Bond 007 Back In Action!'
Goldfinger ***
🏃🏃 GB 1964 112m Technicolor
UA/Eon (Harry Saltzman, Albert R. Broccoli)
📀 📀 ▦ 📀 🎧
James Bond prevents an international gold smuggler from robbing Fort Knox.
Probably the liveliest and most amusing of the Bond spy spoofs, with a fairly taut plot between the numerous highlights. The big budget is well used.
w Richard Maibaum, Paul Dehn novel Ian Fleming d Guy Hamilton ph Ted Moore m John Barry pd Ken Adam titles Robert Brownjohn
☆ Sean Connery, Honor Blackman, Gert Frobe, Harold Sakata, Shirley Eaton, Bernard Lee, Lois Maxwell, Desmond Llewelyn
'A dazzling object lesson in the principle that nothing succeeds like excess.' – *Penelope Gilliatt*
'A diverting comic strip for grown-ups.' – *Judith Crist*

Goldie
US 1931 58m bw
Fox
A carnival girl causes a rift between two sailors.
Curious comedy-drama notable only for its stars.
w Gene Towne, Paul Perez d Ben Stoloff
☆ Spencer Tracy, Jean Harlow, Warren Hymer, Lina Basquette, Maria Alba

The Goldwyn Follies **
US 1938 115m Technicolor
Samuel Goldwyn
▦
A Hollywood producer seeks the average girl to test his scripts.
Goldwyn's failure to become Ziegfeld, chiefly due to a lack of humour in the script, still has a soupçon of effective Hollywood satire and some excellent numbers.
w Ben Hecht d George Marshall ph Gregg Toland m Alfred Newman ch George Balanchine ad Richard Day
☆ Kenny Baker, Vera Zorina, the Ritz Brothers, Adolphe Menjou, Edgar Bergen and Charlie McCarthy, Helen Jepson, Phil Baker, Ella Logan, Bobby Clark, Jerome Cowan, Nydia Westman, Andrea Leeds
'An advance glimpse at next Sunday's amusement section from any metropolitan newspaper.' – *Variety*
'The bizarre in musical pretentiousness.' – *Commonweal*
'Many features to suit all tastes and not enough of them to suit anybody's.' – *Time*
⚗ Alfred Newman; Richard Day

The Golem ***
Germany 1920 75m bw silent
UFA
In 16th-century Prague a Jewish rabbi constructs a man of clay to defend his people against a pogrom.
There were several versions of this story (Germany 1913, sequel 1917; Czechoslovakia 1935 and 1951), but this is almost certainly the best, its splendid sets, performances and certain scenes all being clearly influential on later Hollywood films, especially Frankenstein.
w Paul Wegener, Henrik Galeen d Paul Wegener, Carl Boese ph Karl Freund, Guido Seeber ad Hans Poelzig
☆ Paul Wegener, Albert Steinruck, Ernst Deutsch

The Golem *
Czechoslovakia 1936 95m bw
AB
GB title: *The Legend of Prague*
Rather disappointing remake with entirely French crew.
w André Paul Antoine, Julien Duvivier novel Gustav Meyrinck d Julien Duvivier ph Vaclav Vich, Jan Stallich m Joseph Kumok
☆ Harry Baur, Roger Karl, Ferdinand Hart, Charles Dorat
'Sequences are scattered; there's no build-up, and no human interest is created.' – *Variety*
'It is all rich and spacious, and rather exquisite, and the big scene at the end should do nicely. If one can forget that Wegener once did it so much better, with nothing but a robot, a child and a flower.' – *C. A. Lejeune*

Golem – The Wandering Soul
France/Germany/Netherlands/Italy/GB 1992 colour
Agav (Laurent Truchot)
original title: *Golem – L'Esprit de l'Exil*
An Israeli woman living in Paris suffers after her husband dies in an accident and her two sons are killed by racists.
Dully experimental movie on the theme of narrow chauvinism, mainly composed of uninteresting images combined with dialogue taken from the Old Testament, but all is vanity.
wd Amos Gitai ph Henri Alekan m Simon Stockhausen, Markus Stockhausen ad Thierry François m Anna Ruiz
☆ Hanna Schygulla, Opra Shemesh, Mireille Perrier, Sotigui Kouyate, Samuel Fuller, Bernardo Bertolucci, Fabienne Babe, Bernard Eisenschitz, Antonio Carallo, Bernard Levy

The Golf Specialist **
US 1930 18m bw
RKO
A film version of a classic vaudeville golfing sketch (also reprised in *You're Telling Me*).
d Monte Brice
☆ W. C. Fields

Golgotha *
France 1935 100m bw
D'Agular
🎧
The trial and passion of Jesus Christ.
Impressive version made at a time when the portrayal of Christ was still virtually taboo.
wd Julien Duvivier m Jacques Ibert
☆ Harry Baur, Jean Gabin, Robert le Vigan, Charles Granval, Edwige Feuillère
'An accomplishment that should bring world-wide prestige to the French film industry.' – *Variety*

'A Thousand And One Women Dream Of His Embrace.'
Goliath and the Barbarians (dubbed)
Italy/US 1959 88m Eastmancolor Totalscope Standard/AIP (Emimmo Salvi)
original title: *Il Terrore dei Barbari*
In AD 568, a man vows vengeance and disguises himself as a monster when barbarian hordes, invading northern Italy, massacre his father and other villagers.
A garish Italian epic adapted for an American audience with a voice-over narration, and concentrating on spectacle and action.
w Gino Mangini, Carlo Campogalliani, Nino Stresa, Giuseppe Taffarel, Emimmo Salvi d Carlo Campogalliani ph Alberto Albertini m Les Baxter, Carlo Innocenzi ad Camillo del Signore, Emilio D'Andria ed Franco Fraticelli
☆ Steve Reeves, Chelo Alonso, Bruce Cabot, Giulia Rubini, Luciano Marin, Livio Lorenzon

Goliath, King of Slaves: see The Hero of Babylon

Golpes a Mi Puerta: see Knocks at My Door

Gomar the Human Gorilla: see Night of the Bloody Apes

Gone Fishin'
US 1997 94m Technicolor
Buena Vista/Hollywood/Caravan (Roger Birnbaum, Julie Bergman Sender)
📀 ▦
Two slow-witted friends win a trip to the Everglades, where everything goes wrong.
A dim and ever dimmer comedy, in which stupidity substitutes for wit.
w Jill Mazursky Cody, Jeffrey Abrams d Christopher Cain ph Dean Semler m Randy Edelman pd Lawrence Miller ed Jack Hofstra
☆ Joe Pesci, Danny Glover, Rosanna Arquette, Lynn Whitfield, Willie Nelson, Nick Brimble, Gary Grubbs, Carol Kane
'Comes across as an unwitting tribute to the films of Huntz Hall.' – *Variety*
† Louise Fletcher and Maury Chaykin appear uncredited.

Gone to Earth
GB 1950 110m Technicolor
London Films/David O. Selznick (Michael Powell, Emeric Pressburger)
US title: *The Wild Heart*
In the 1890s, a wild Shropshire girl is desired by the local squire.
Unintentionally funny film version of an intractable novel.
wd Michael Powell, Emeric Pressburger novel Mary Webb ph Christopher Challis m Brian Easdale pd Hein Heckroth
☆ Jennifer Jones, David Farrar, Cyril Cusack, Esmond Knight, Sybil Thorndike, Edward Chapman, George Cole, Hugh Griffith, Beatrice Varley
'It tries hard to be a powerful work of art, but it is intrinsically artificial and pretentious.' – *Richard Mallett, Punch*
† For the version shown in US, additional scenes were directed by Rouben Mamoulian.

'The most magnificent picture ever!'
Gone with the Wind ****
US 1939 220m Technicolor
MGM/Selznick International (David O. Selznick)
📀 ▦ 📀 ◎ 🎧
An egotistic Southern girl survives the Civil War but finally looses the only man she cares for.
The only film in history which could be profitably revived for forty years: 'still pure gold', said the Daily Mirror in 1975. Whole books have been written about it; its essential appeal is that of a romantic story with strong characters and an impeccable production. The widescreen version produced in the late sixties ruined its composition and colour, but it is to be hoped that the original negative still survives.
w Sidney Howard (and others) novel Margaret Mitchell d Victor Fleming (and George Cukor, Sam Wood) ph Ernest Haller, Ray Rennahan m Max Steiner pd William Cameron Menzies ad Lyle Wheeler ed Hal C. Kern, James E. Newcom sp Jack Cosgrove, Fred Albin, Arthur Johns
☆ Clark Gable, Vivien Leigh, Olivia de Havilland, Leslie Howard, Thomas Mitchell, Barbara O'Neil, Hattie McDaniel, Butterfly McQueen, Victor Jory, Evelyn Keyes, Ann Rutherford, Laura Hope Crews, Harry Davenport, Jane Darwell, Ona Munson and also Ward Bond
'A major event in the history of the industry but only a minor event in motion picture art. There are moments when the two categories meet on good terms, but the long stretches between are filled with mere spectacular efficiency.' – *Franz Hoellering, The Nation*
'Shakespeare's The Taming of the Shrew seems to have got mixed up with one of the novels of Ethel M. Dell.' – *James Agate*
'Perhaps the key plantation movie.' – *Time Out, 1980*
'Forget it, Louis, no Civil War picture ever made a nickel.' – *Irving Thalberg to Louis B. Mayer, 1936*
† The best account of the film's making is in Gavin Lambert's 1975 book, *GWTW*.
🎵 In the early seventies a stage musical version toured the world, with music by Harold Rome.
⚗ best picture; Sidney Howard; Victor Fleming; best cinematography; Lyle Wheeler; Vivien Leigh; Hattie McDaniel; best film editing; William Cameron Menzies (special award)
⚖ Max Steiner; Clark Gable; Olivia de Havilland; special effects

---

The Gong Show Movie

US   1980   89m   colour

Chuck Barris Productions (Bud Granoff)

The trials and tribulations of the host of a TV talent show for untalented amateurs.

A once-successful television show transfers unsuccessfully to the screen.

w Chuck Barris, Robert Downey d Chuck Barris ph Richard C. Glouner m Milton Delugg ad Robert J. Kinoshita ed James Mitchell

☆ Chuck Barris, Robin Altman, Brian O'Mullin, Mabel King, James B. Douglas, Jaye P. Morgan

Good Burger

US   1997   95m   DeLuxe

Paramount/Nickelodeon (Mike Tollin, Brian Robbins)

⬚⬚ ▬ ꕀ

A tiny fast-food restaurant is faced with overwhelming competition from a corporate giant.

Developed from a series of comedy sketches on cable television, this inept slapstick will not satisfy comic appetites outside the United States.

w Dan Schneider, Kevin Kopelow, Heather Seifert d Brian Robbins ph Mac Ahlberg m Stewart Copeland pd Steven Jordan ed Anita Brandt-Burgoyne

☆ Kel Mitchell, Kenan Thompson, Sinbad, Abe Vigoda, Shar Jackson, Dan Schneider, Jan Schweiterman

'This winning comedy serves up a hearty helping of fun and wholesome values.' – *Leonard Klady, Variety*

'When this movie was screened to a selection of 15 hardened filmic hacks, a record total of nine walked out … this episode is beyond help.' – *Bob McCabe, Empire*

The Good Companions **

GB   1933   113m   bw

Gaumont/Welsh-Pearson (Michael Balcon, George Pearson)

Three ill-assorted people take to the road and in various capacities join the Dinky Doos pierrot troupe.

Gallant, mini-budgeted version of Priestley's popular picaresque novel. A little faded now, it retains some of its vigour, and the performances please.

w W. P. Lipscomb, Angus MacPhail, Ian Dalrymple play J. B. Priestley, Edward Knoblock novel J. B. Priestley d Victor Saville ph Bernard Knowles m/ly George Posford, Douglas Furber md Louis Levy ad Alfred Junge ed Frederick Y. Smith

☆ Edmund Gwenn, Mary Glynne, John Gielgud, Jessie Matthews, Percy Parsons, A. W. Baskcomb, Dennis Hoey, Richard Dolman, Frank Pettingell, Finlay Currie, Max Miller, Jack Hawkins, George Zucco

'Has come to the screen just as it was written, honest and sentimental and splendid, with the smell of the tarmac and the railway buffet, the tinny rapture of the pavilion piano, the jostling pageantry of insignificant faces.' – *C. A. Lejeune*

The Good Companions *

GB   1956   104m   Technicolor   Cinemascope

ABP (Hamilton Inglis, J. Lee-Thompson)

Faint-hearted remake of the above, unwisely Cinemascoped and leaving no impression.

w T. J. Morrison d J. Lee-Thompson ph Gilbert Taylor m Laurie Johnson

☆ Eric Portman, Celia Johnson, John Fraser, Janette Scott, Hugh Griffith, Bobby Howes, Rachel Roberts, John Salew, Thora Hird

† A stage musical version (m André Previn, ly Johnny Mercer) had moderate success in London in 1974.

†††.

Good Dame

US   1934   77m   bw

Paramount

GB title: *Good Girl*

A penniless chorus girl falls for a cardsharp.

Unsurprising pattern play for two miscast stars.

w William R. Lipman, Vincent Lawrence, Frank Partos, Sam Hellman d Marion Gering

☆ Sylvia Sidney, Fredric March, Jack La Rue, Noel Francis, Russell Hopton

Good Day for a Hanging

US   1959   85m   Columbia Color

Columbia

A young outlaw is arrested and seems destined to be lynched; the marshal tries to see fair play.

Moody Western in which the protected hero turns out to be very guilty after all.

w Daniel B. Ullman, Maurice Zimm d Nathan Juran

☆ Fred MacMurray, Robert Vaughn, Maggie Hayes, Joan Blackman, James Drury

The Good Die Young *

GB   1954   98m   bw

Remus (Jack Clayton)

Four crooks, all with private problems, set out to rob a mail van.

Glum all-star melodrama which set a pattern for such things; worth waiting for is the climactic chase through underground stations.

w Vernon Harris, Lewis Gilbert d Lewis Gilbert ph Jack Asher m Georges Auric

☆ Laurence Harvey, Margaret Leighton, Gloria Grahame, Richard Basehart, Joan Collins, John Ireland, René Ray, Stanley Baker, Robert Morley

'To the memory of Irving Grant Thalberg we dedicate this picture – his last great achievement!'

The Good Earth ***

US   1937   138m   bw

MGM (Irving Thalberg)

▬ ꔪ

A Chinese peasant grows rich but loses his beloved wife.

A massive, well-meaning and fondly remembered production which is nevertheless artificial, unconvincing and pretty undramatic in the second half. The star performances impress to begin with, then wear thin, but the final locust attack is as well done as it originally seemed. Historically valuable as a Hollywood prestige production of the thirties.

w Talbot Jennings, Tess Schlesinger, Claudine West play Owen and Donald Davis novel Pearl S. Buck d Sidney Franklin ph Karl Freund m Herbert Stothart ad Cedric Gibbons ed Basil Wrangell montage Slavko Vorkapich

☆ Paul Muni, Luise Rainer, Walter Connolly, Tilly Losch, Jessie Ralph, Charley Grapewin, Keye Luke, Harold Huber

'A true technical achievement with names enough to send it across. But it's not going to be easy to get the three-million-dollar investment back. And if it does come back it's going to take a long time.' – *Variety*

'Performances, direction and photography are of a uniform excellence, and have been fused perfectly into a dignified, beautiful, but soberly dramatic production.' – *New York Times*

'One of the superb visual adventures of the period.' – *John Baxter, 1968*

'Prestigious boredom, and it goes on for a very long time.' – *New Yorker, 1977*

⏚ Karl Freund; Luise Rainer

Å best picture; Sidney Franklin; Basil Wrangell

The Good Fairy *

US   1935   90m   bw

Universal (Henry Henigson)

A beautiful but naïve cinema usherette ensnares three rich men.

Unusual, rather lumpy romantic comedy using top talent.

w Preston Sturges play Ferenc Molnar d William Wyler ph Norbert Brodine

☆ Margaret Sullavan, Herbert Marshall, Frank Morgan, Reginald Owen, Alan Hale, Beulah Bondi, Cesar Romero, Eric Blore, Al Bridge

'It's rather slapsticking a master but it's for the box office. Will not please those who cherish memories of the play but it will please a more important audience.' – *Variety*

† Remade as *I'll Be Yours* (qv).

The Good Father **

GB   1986   90m   Technicolor

Channel 4/Greenpoint (Ann Scott)

Two divorced men become bitter about the way their marriages ended, estranging them from their children.

An astringent study of masculine rage and emotional impotence, and of the difficulty of maintaining honest relationships.

w Christopher Hampton novel Peter Prince d Mike Newell ph Michael Coulter m Richard Hartley pd Adrian Smith ed Peter Hollywood

☆ Anthony Hopkins, Jim Broadbent, Harriet Walter, Frances Viner, Simon Callow, Miriam Margolyes, Joanne Whalley-Kilmer, Michael Byrne, Jennie Stoller, Stephen Fry

'Though the emotional perceptions might speak to a wider audience, its practical concerns are those of that newly-important consumer class, the well-meaning, hard-done-by professionals.' – *Judith Williamson, New Statesman*

The Good Fellows

US   1943   70m   bw

Paramount

A family man spends too much time with his fraternal order.

Mild, pleasant family comedy.

w Hugh Wedlock Jnr, Howard Snyder play George S. Kaufman, Herman Mankiewicz d Jo Graham

☆ Cecil Kellaway, Helen Walker, James Brown, Mabel Paige

Good Girl: see Good Dame

Good Girls Go to Paris *

US   1939   75m   bw

Columbia (William Perlberg)

After several zany adventures, a Greek professor marries a gold digger.

Amusingly crazy comedy, one of the last of its type.

w Gladys Lehman, Ken Englund d Alexander Hall ph Henry Freulich md Morris Stoloff

☆ Melvyn Douglas, Joan Blondell, Walter Connolly, Alan Curtis, Joan Perry, Isabel Jeans, Alexander D'Arcy, Clarence Kolb

'It can't stand analysis much, but it pleases while you're there.' – *Variety*

The Good Guys and the Bad Guys *

US   1969   90m   Technicolor   Panavision

Warner (Ronald M. Cohen, Dennis Shryack)

An ageing sheriff and a train robber have one last showdown.

Good-humoured, black-flavoured Western set in the early days of automobiles.

w Ronald M. Cohen, Dennis Shryack d Burt Kennedy ph Harry Stradling Jnr m William Lava

☆ Robert Mitchum, George Kennedy, David Carradine, Tina Louise, Douglas Fowley, Martin Balsam, Lois Nettleton, John Davis Chandler, John Carradine, Marie Windsor

Good Guys Wear Black

US   1977   95m   CFI color

Enterprise/Mar Vista/Action One Film Partners (Allan F. Bodoh)

⬚⬚ ▬

The former leader of a commando raid into North Vietnam sets out to discover who in Washington betrayed him and his men.

Lacklustre martial arts action in an unsuccessful American attempt to create a local star to replace Bruce Lee.

w Bruce Cohn, Mark Medoff story Joseph Fraley, d Ted Post ph Bob Steadman m Craig Safan ad B. B. Neal ed William and Millie Moore

☆ Chuck Norris, Anne Archer, James Franciscus, Lloyd Haynes, Dana Andrews, Jim Backus

† The film was followed by a sequel, *A Force of One* (qv).

Good Little Girls: see Les Petites Filles Modèles

'Deep In The Heart Of Africa The British Practise Bizarre Rituals. They Call It Diplomacy.'

A Good Man in Africa

US   1994   95m   Technicolor

UIP/Polar/Capitol/Southern Sun (John Fiedler, Mark Tarlov)

⬚⬚ ▬ ꔪ

A British diplomat in Africa decides, after dubious political and sexual manoeuvres, that he will try to be a better man.

A flaccid comedy satirizing colonial corruption and the lessons learnt by local politicians, acted and directed without distinction.

w William Boyd novel William Boyd d Bruce Beresford ph Andrzej Bartkowiak m John du Prez pd Herbert Pinter ed Jim Clark

☆ Colin Friels, Joanne Whalley-Kilmer, Sean Connery, Louis Gossett Jnr, John Lithgow, Diana Rigg, Maynard Eziashi, Sarah Jane Fenton

'Has a good cast, and that's all that can be claimed for it.' – *Alexander Walker, London Evening Standard*

'Stumbles its way through a series of comic mishaps and manages to upturn every cliché in its path.' – *Screen International*

A Good Marriage: see Le Beau Mariage

Good Morning Babylon *

Italy/France   1987   115m   colour

Filmtre/MK2/Pressman/RAI/Films A2 (Giuliani G. de Negri)

⬚⬚ ▬ ꔪ ꕀ ꗳ

Italian film-makers set out for Hollywood to restore the family fortunes.

Likeable but sometimes inept fantasia on Hollywood's early silent days.

wd Paolo and Vittorio Taviani ph Giuseppe Lanci m Nicola Piovani ad Gianni Shara ed Roberto Perpignanni

☆ Vincent Spano, Joaquim de Almeida, Greta Scacchi, Desiree Becker, Charles Dance

'They have made a molehill of a picture out of a mountain of an idea.' – *Daily Variety*

Good Morning Boys **

👪 GB   1937   79m   bw

GFD/Gainsborough (Edward Black)

A schoolmaster takes his troublesome pupils to Paris and becomes involved in an art theft.

Sprightly vehicle for the star's seedy schoolmaster persona: it established him as a major draw in British films.

w Marriott Edgar, Val Guest, Anthony Kimmins d Marcel Varnel m Arthur Crabtree md Louis Levy ad Vetchinsky ed R. E. Dearing, Alfred Roome

☆ Will Hay, Graham Moffatt, Lilli Palmer, Mark Daly, Peter Gawthorne, Martita Hunt, Charles Hawtrey, Will Hay Jnr

† Remade with Ronald Shiner as *Top of the Form*.

Good Morning, Doctor: see You Belong to Me

Good Morning, Judge

US   1943   66m   bw

Paul Malvern/Universal

A music publisher falls for the lady lawyer suing him for plagiarism.

Light, predictable comedy for double billing.

w Maurice Geraghty, Warren Wilson d Jean Yarbrough

☆ Dennis O'Keefe, Louise Allbritton, J. Carrol Naish, Mary Beth Hughes, Louise Beavers, Samuel S. Hinds

Good Morning, Miss Dove

US   1955   107m   Eastmancolor   Cinemascope

TCF (Samuel G. Engel)

While recovering from an operation, a small-town schoolmistress looks back on her career.

A fairly spirited weepie with a happy ending and a strong sense of cynicism behind the scenes.

w Eleanore Griffin novel Frances Gray Patton d Henry Koster ph Leon Shamroy m Leigh Harline

☆ Jennifer Jones, Robert Stack, Robert Douglas, Kipp Hamilton, Peggy Knudsen, Marshall Thompson, Chuck Connors, Mary Wickes

'Mr Chips has changed sex and habitat while preserving intact his ability to provoke epidemics of sentimentality.' – *MFB*

Good Morning, Vietnam *

US   1987   120m   DeLuxe

Touchstone (Mark Johnson, Larry Brezner)

⬚⬚ ▬ ꔪ

Exploits of an Armed Forces Radio disc-jockey in Saigon at the height of the Vietnam War.

Largely a vehicle for the frenetic irreverence of Robin Williams, enjoyed by many for the 60s hits used copiously on the soundtrack.

w Mitch Markowitz d Barry Levinson ph Peter Sova m Alex North pd Roy Walker

☆ Robin Williams, Forest Whitaker, Tung Thanh Tran, Chintara Sukapatana, Bruno Kirby

Å Robin Williams

The Good Mother

US   1988   103m   colour

Warner/Touchstone/Silver Screen Partners IV (Arnold Glimcher)

⬚⬚ ▬ ꔪ

GB video title: *The Price of Passion*

A separated husband claims his daughter has been sexually abused by his wife's lover.

Dull domestic drama.

---

w Michael Bortman *novel* Sue Miller *d* Leonard Nimoy *m* Elmer Bernstein *pd* Stan Jolley *ed* Peter Berger

☆ Diane Keaton, Liam Neeson, Jason Robards, Ralph Bellamy, Teresa Wright, James Naughton, Asia Vieira, Joe Morton, Katey Sagal, Margaret Bard, Nancy Beatty

'An over-simplified addendum to a series of recent works in which mothers are taken to task and sometimes pilloried.' – *MFB*

'It's All About That Laff-Whopping' Eye Poppin' Suburban Switcheroo!'
Good Neighbour Sam
US   1964   130m   Eastmancolor
Columbia/David Swift
▤

A prissy suburban advertising man becomes innocently involved in a pretence to be the husband of the divorcee next door.
A promising comic idea is here ruined by lengthiness, lack of funny lines, and no apparent idea of how to film a farce. The actors are driven to repeating every trick a dozen times.

w James Fritzell, Everett Greenbaum, David Swift *novel* Jack Finney *d* David Swift *ph* Burnett Guffey *m* Frank de Vol

☆ Jack Lemmon, Romy Schneider, Dorothy Provine, Senta Berger, Edward G. Robinson, Mike Connors, Edward Andrews, Louis Nye

'Lemmon and company breathlessly toss gags from bedrooms to advertising offices with verve and vigor.' – *New York Times*

Good News
US   1930   85m   bw
MGM

Fraternity tensions are sorted out in time for the big football game.
Spirited early talkie musical.

w Frances Marion, Joe Farnham *d* Nick Grinde, Edgar McGregor *m* Percy Hilburn *m/ly* De Sylva, Brown, Henderson and others *md* Abe Lyman

☆ Bessie Love, Stanley Smith, Gus Shy, Mary Lawlor, Lola Lane, Dorothy McNulty (aka Penny Singleton), Cliff Edwards

'Not the smash hit the show was. Too fast, too peppy, too entertaining to flop, though.' – *Variety*

♫ 'He's a Ladies' Man'; 'The Best Things in Life Are Free'; 'Varsity Drag'; 'Good News'; 'Tait Song'; 'Students Are We'; 'If You're Not Kissing Me'; 'Football'; 'I Feel Pessimistic'; 'I'd Like to Make You Happy'

Good News *
US   1947   83m   Technicolor
MGM (Arthur Freed)
▤ ▦ ◉〜

Bright, good-humoured remake of the above.
w Betty Comden, Adolph Green *d* Charles Walters *ph* Charles Schoenbaum *m/ly* De Sylva, Brown, Henderson and others *md* Lennie Hayton *ad* Cedric Gibbons, Edward Carfagno *ed* Albert Akst

☆ June Allyson, Peter Lawford, Patricia Marshall, Joan McCracken, Mel Tormé

🎵 song 'Pass that Peace Pipe' (*m/ly* Ralph Blane, Hugh Martin, Roger Edens)

The Good Old Days
GB   1939   79m   bw
Warner (Jerome Jackson)

A noble child is kidnapped by a chimney sweep and saved by strolling players.
Curious Victorian vehicle for a snappy 20th-century star.

w Austin Melford, John Dighton *story* Ralph Smart *d* Roy William Neill *ph* Basil Emmott

☆ Max Miller, Hal Walters, Kathleen Gibson, H. F. Maltby, Martita Hunt, Allan Jeayes, Roy Emerton

Good Old Schooldays: see Those Were the Days

Good Old Soak
US   1937   67m   bw
MGM

A small-town drunk beats a teetotal banker guilty of a shady transaction.
Amiable star comedy.

w A. E. Thomas *play* The Old Soak by Don Marquis *d* J. Walter Ruben

---

☆ Wallace Beery, Una Merkel, Eric Linden, Judith Barrett, Betty Furness, Janet Beecher, Robert McWade, Margaret Hamilton

'A melodramatic sentimentality that will probably okay.' – *Variety*

Good Sam
US   1948   114m   bw
Rainbow (Leo McCarey)

A small-town business man is so charitable that he finds himself bankrupt.
Poor, disjointed, overlong and obvious comedy in the Capra style.

w Ken Englund *d* Leo McCarey *ph* George Barnes *m* Robert Emmett Dolan

☆ Gary Cooper, Ann Sheridan, Ray Collins, Edmund Lowe, Joan Lorring, Ruth Roman, Clinton Sundberg

'A bit too long, but in its incidentals often very enjoyable.' – *Richard Mallett, Punch*

The Good Son
US   1993   87m   DeLuxe   Panavision
TCF (Mary Anne Page, Joseph Ruben)
▦ ◫ ◉〜 ⌂

A sweet-seeming 10-year-old boy is actually an amoral, murderous child.
A slick but uninvolving updating of the themes of The Bad Seed

w Ian McEwan *d* Joseph Ruben *ph* John Lindley *m* Elmer Bernstein *pd* Bill Groom *ed* George Bowers

☆ Macaulay Culkin, Elijah Wood, Wendy Crewson, David Morse, Daniel Hugh Kelly, Jacqueline Brooks, Quinn Culkin

'This rather peculiar thriller doesn't deliver enough jolts to leave the audience screaming.' – *Variety*

'If this film were a teenager, it would be the one who always did his homework, never pranged the family car, and then one day quietly shot everyone with a rifle made in his metalwork class.' – *Leslie Felperin Sharman, Sight and Sound*

The Good, the Bad and the Ugly ***
Italy   1966   180m   Techniscope
PEA (Alberto Grimaldi)
▦ ◫ ◉〜 ◉ ⌂

original title: *Il Buono, il Brutto, il Cattivo*
During the American Civil War, three men seek hidden loot.
Intermittently lively, very violent, and interminably drawn-out Western with a number of rather hilarious stylistic touches.

w Age Scarpelli, Luciano Vincenzoni, Sergio Leone *d* Sergio Leone *ph* Tonino delli Colli *m* Ennio Morricone

☆ Clint Eastwood, Eli Wallach, Lee Van Cleef

Good Time Girl
GB   1948   93m   bw
Triton/Rank (Sydney Box)

A girl escapes from a remand home and starts on the road to ruin.
Risible vehicle for a rising star; at the time it set the box-offices clicking.

w Muriel and Sydney Box, Ted Willis *novel* Night Darkens the Street by Arthur La Bern *d* David MacDonald *ph* Stephen Dade *m* Lambert Williamson *ad* George Provis

☆ Jean Kent, Dennis Price, Flora Robson, Griffith Jones, Diana Dors, Herbert Lom, Bonar Colleano, Michael Hordern

Good Times
US   1967   92m   DeLuxe
Motion Picture International

A singing duo in Hollywood imagines starring in films of various types.
Mildly agreeable light fantasy.

w Tony Barrett *d* William Friedkin

☆ Sonny and Cher, George Sanders, Norman Alden, Larry Duran

Good to Go
US   1986   91m   Technicolor
Island Visual Arts (Doug Dilge, Sean Ferrer)
▦ ◫ ◉〜

aka: *Short Fuse*
An alcoholic journalist begins to acquire a social conscience as he watches a cop hunt down an innocent black man accused of rape and murder.
Little more than a failed attempt to market Go-Go groups, a music that failed to find an audience outside

---

Washington: a coarse-toned and uninteresting drama, in which any narrative momentum is lost in order to showcase the music.

wd Blaine Novak *ph* Peter Sinclair *m* Trouble Funk, Redds & The Boys, Chuck Brown and the Soul Searchers *ad* Ron Downing *ed* Gib Jaffe, Kimberly Logan, D. C. Stringer

☆ Art Garfunkel, Robert Doqui, Harris Yulin, Reginald Daughtry, Richard Brooks, Richard Bauer, Paula Davis, Michael White, Hattie Winston, Anjelica Huston

The Good Wife
Australia   1987   92m   Eastmancolor
Entertainment/Laughing Kookaburra (Jan Sharp, Helen Watts)

Australian title: *The Umbrella Woman*
In 1939, a wife is bored with her backwater life, and takes a lover.
Heavy-going domestic drama with an interesting setting.

w Peter Kenna *d* Ken Cameron *ph* James Bartle *m* Cameron Allan *pd* Sally Campbell *ed* John Scott

☆ Rachel Ward, Bryan Brown, Sam Neill, Steven Vidler

Good Will Hunting **
US   1997   126m   colour
Miramax (Lawrence Bender)
▦ ◫ ◉〜 ◉ ◉ ⌂

A delinquent working-class youth with a gift for mathematics has a difficult choice to make: continue working as a janitor, and drinking and brawling with his friends, or become a highly paid resident genius with a powerful corporation.
The analogue to the narrative on the screen is one about an unknown actor who dreams of being admired, and writes a script with a star part for himself about a boy who is loved by all, however he behaves; in Matt Damon's case, the wish fulfilment worked.

w Matt Damon, Ben Affleck *d* Gus Van Sant *ph* Jean Yves Escoffier *m* Danny Elfman *pd* Melissa Stewart *ed* Pietro Scalia

☆ Matt Damon, Robin Williams, Ben Affleck, Minnie Driver, Stellan Skarsgard, Casey Affleck, Cole Hauser

'To see it is to fall under its spell. Never do you doubt that everybody connected with this film cares. It works – satisfyingly, urgently and richly – because it comes to us as felt knowledge.' – *Jay Carr, Boston Globe*

'Schematic, predictable and somewhat tedious.' – *Alexander Walker, London Evening Standard*

'Robin Williams, disproving optimistic predictions that he might be back on track, plays not just restrained, but restrained and noble. At the same time.' – *Emma Forrest, Guardian*

🏆 Matt Damon, Ben Affleck (as writers); Robin Williams

🎗 best picture; Matt Damon (as actor); Minnie Driver; Gus Van Sant; Pietro Scalia; Danny Elfman; song 'Miss Misery' (*m/ly* Elliott Smith)

Goodbye Again
US   1933   66m   bw
Warner

An author's secretary is jealous of his rekindled interest in an old flame.
Unassuming star comedy which entertained at the time.

w Ben Markson *play* George Haight, Allan Scott *d* Michael Curtiz

☆ Warren William, Joan Blondell, Genevieve Tobin, Hugh Herbert, Helen Chandler, Ruth Donnelly

† *Honeymoon for Three* in 1941 (qv) was a leaden remake.

Goodbye Again *
US   1961   120m   bw
UA/Mercury/Argus/Anatole Litvak
▤

A woman of forty swaps her rich lover for a young law student.
Melancholy romantic drama, well produced and staged on Paris locations.

w Samuel Taylor *novel* Aimez-vous Brahms by Françoise Sagan *d* Anatole Litvak *ph* Armand Thirard *m* Georges Auric

☆ Ingrid Bergman, Anthony Perkins, Yves Montand, Jessie Royce Landis, Jackie Lane

'A grey-toned Sagan novella, spread wide and lush over two hours of screen time.' – *MFB*

'The kind of "woman's picture" that gives women a bad name.' – *Judith Crist, 1973*

Goodbye Charlie *
US   1964   116m   DeLuxe   Cinemascope
TCF/Venice (David Weisbart)

A philandering gangster, shot dead by an irate husband, is reincarnated in his friend's house as a dishy blonde.
Overlong but amusing Broadway comedy for wisecrackers, uninventively adapted.

w Harry Kurnitz *play* George Axelrod *d* Vincente Minnelli *ph* Milton Krasner *m* André Previn

☆ Debbie Reynolds, Pat Boone, Walter Matthau, Tony Curtis

'Every father's daughter is a virgin!'
Goodbye Columbus **
US   1969   105m   Technicolor
Paramount/Willow Tree (Stanley Jaffe)
▤   ◫ ◉〜   ⌂

A young Jewish librarian has an affair with the wilful daughter of a *nouveau riche* family.
An amusing and well-observed delineation of two kinds of Jewish life in New York; the story, despite its frank talk of penises and diaphragms, leaves much to be desired, and the style is post-Graduate.

w Arnold Schulman *novel* Philip Roth *d* Larry Peerce *ph* Gerald Hirschfeld *m* Charles Fox

☆ Richard Benjamin, Ali MacGraw, Jack Klugman, Nan Martin, Michael Meyers, Lori Shelle

🎗 Arnold Schulman

Goodbye Gemini
GB   1970   colour
Cinerama/Josef Shaftel (Peter Snell)

A 20-year-old brother and sister share a world of petulant fantasy which leads to murder.
Abysmally over-the-top melodrama with a swinging London backdrop. Its immaculate appearance only makes matters worse.

w Edmund Ward *novel* Ask Agamemnon by Jenni Hall *d* Alan Gibson *ph* Geoffrey Unsworth *m* Christopher Gunning *pd* Wilfrid Shingleton

☆ Judy Geeson, Martin Potter, Michael Redgrave, Alexis Kanner, Mike Pratt, Freddie Jones, Peter Jeffrey

'Every man she ever loved thought a permanent relationship was a three-day weekend!'
The Goodbye Girl *
US   1977   110m   Metrocolor
Warner/Rastar (Ray Stark)
▦ ◫ ▤ ◉〜

A misunderstanding about the lease of an apartment results in a girl dancer agreeing to share it with a would-be actor.
A very moderate script assisted by excellent acting and the usual array of Neil Simon one-liners. Nothing at all new, but enjoyable.

w Neil Simon *d* Herbert Ross *ph* David M. Walsh *m* Dave Grusin

☆ Richard Dreyfuss, Marsha Mason, Quinn Cummings, Paul Benedict, Barbara Rhoades

🏆 Richard Dreyfuss

🎗 best picture; Neil Simon; Marsha Mason; Quinn Cummings

🏆 Richard Dreyfuss

Goodbye Lover
US/Germany   1998   101m   Technicolor
Panavision
Warner/Arnon Milchan/Gotham/Lightmotive (Alexandra Milchan, Patrick McDarrah, Joel Roodman, Chris Daniel)
▦ ▤

A Los Angeles advertising executive plots with his wife to collect millions on his brother's life.
Convoluted, comic thriller of double-cross and deception that is heavy-handed and obtuse.

w Ron Peer, Joel Cohen, Alec Sokolow *d* Roland Joffé *ph* Dante Spinotti *m* John Ottman *pd* Stewart Starkin *ed* William Steinkamp

☆ Patricia Arquette, Dermot Mulroney, Ellen DeGeneres, Mary-Louise Parker, Don Johnson, Ray McKinnon, Alex Rocco, André Gregory, John Neville

'Once the thud of its wooden dialogue has settled into a deadly mechanical clomp – about 10 minutes into the film – you wonder why this risible movie didn't go straight to video.' – *Stephen Holden, New York Times*

'Unmitigated ordure.' – *Peter Bradshaw, Guardian*

Goodbye Mr Chips ✱✱✱
GB   1939   114m   bw
MGM (Victor Saville)
📺 ▦ ⌕

The life of a shy schoolmaster from his first job to his death.
Sentimental romance in MGM's best style, a long-standing favourite for its performances and humour; but the production seems slightly unsatisfactory these days.
w R. C. Sherriff, Claudine West, Eric Maschwitz *novel* James Hilton d Sam Wood ph Frederick A. Young m Richard Addinsell ed Charles Frend
☆ Robert Donat, Greer Garson, Paul Henreid, Lyn Harding, Austin Trevor, Terry Kilburn, John Mills, Milton Rosmer, Judith Furse
'Charming, quaintly sophisticated … more for the big situations than the smaller towns.' – *Variety*
'The whole picture has an assurance, bears a glow of popularity like the face of a successful candidate on election day. And it is wrong to despise popularity in the cinema.' – *Graham Greene*
'The picture has no difficulty in using two hours to retell a story that was scarcely above short story length. Mr Chips is worth its time.' – *New York Times*
'The novel became an American best seller when that old sentimentalist Alexander Woollcott touted it on the radio … the movie clogs the nose more than necessary.' – *Pauline Kael, 70s*
🏆 Robert Donat
🏆 best picture; script; Sam Wood; Greer Garson; editing

'He is a shy schoolmaster. She is a music hall star. They marry and immediately have 283 children – all boys!'
Goodbye Mr Chips ✱
GB   1969   147m   Metrocolor   Panavision 70
MGM/APJAC (Arthur P. Jacobs)
📺 ▦ ⌕

Elaborate musical remake of the above.
Slow and slushy, with no improvement visible whatever; but a few of the trimmings please.
w Terence Rattigan d Herbert Ross ph Oswald Morris m Leslie Bricusse md John Williams pd Ken Adam
☆ Peter O'Toole, Petula Clark, Michael Bryant, Michael Redgrave, George Baker, Jack Hedley, Sian Phillips, Alison Leggatt
'The sum total is considerably less than the parts.' – *Variety*
'An overblown version with songs where they are not needed (and Leslie Bricusse's songs are never needed).' – *Pauline Kael, New Yorker*
† Originally sought for the title role, in order of preference, were Richard Burton and Rex Harrison; for the female lead, Samantha Eggar and Lee Remick.
🏆 Leslie Bricusse, John Williams; Peter O'Toole

Goodbye My Fancy
US   1951   107m   bw
Warner (Henry Blanke)
A congresswoman returns to her old college for an honorary degree, and falls in love.
Tolerable romantic flim-flam.
w Ivan Goff, Ben Roberts *play* Fay Kanin d Vincent Sherman ph Ted McCord m Daniele Amfitheatrof
☆ Joan Crawford, Robert Young, Frank Lovejoy, Eve Arden, Janice Rule

Goodbye My Lady ✱
🏃 US   1956   95m   bw
Warner/Batjac (William Wellman)
▦ ⌕

A Mississippi swamp boy finds a valuable dog but eventually returns it to its owner.
Reliable, slightly unusual family film.
w Sid Fleischman *novel* James Street d William Wellman ph William H. Clothier, Archie Stout m Laurindo Almeida, George Field
☆ Brandon de Wilde, Walter Brennan, Phil Harris, Sidney Poitier, William Hopper, Louise Beavers

Goodbye New York
US/Israel   1985   90m   colour
Kole-Hill (Amos Kollek)
📺 ▦ ⌕

An accident-prone New York businesswoman, who decides her life lacks adventure, sets out for Paris and ends up in Israel.
Pleasant but unremarkable comedy of cultural misunderstandings; it sinks under its own weightlessness.
wd Amos Kollek ph Amnon Salomon m Michael Abene ed Alan Heim
☆ Julie Hagerty, Amos Kollek, David Topaz, Aviva Ger, Shmuel Shiloh, Jennifer Babtist, Christopher Goutman

The Goodbye People
US   1984   104m   DeLuxe
Embassy/Coney Island (David V. Picker)
▦ ⌕

Middle-aged eccentrics meet on a beach.
Saroyanesque talk piece which never quite comes off, and will probably be seen only at festivals.
wd Herb Gardner ph John Lindley pd Tony Walton ed Rick Shaine
☆ Martin Balsam, Judd Hirsch, Pamela Reed, Ron Silver, Michael Tucker, Gene Saks

Goodbye Pork Pie ✱
New Zealand   1980   105m   Eastmancolor
NZ Film Commission/NZ United Corporation/Nigel Hutchinson, Geoff Murphy
📺 ⌕

Three young people go on an illegal road spree and are arrested one by one.
Familiar high jinks with a moral conclusion. Fun up to a point, and good to look at.
w Geoff Murphy, Ian Mune d Geoff Murphy ph Alun Bollinger m John Charles
☆ Tony Barry, Kelly Johnson, Claire Oberman
'Displays encouraging physical flair in its cross-country sweep of action.' – *Tim Pulleine, MFB*

'Three Decades of Life in the Mafia.'
GoodFellas ✱✱✱✱
US   1990   146m   Technicolor
Warner (Irwin Winkler)
📺 ▦ ⌕ ⊙ ⊙ ⌒

An Irish-Italian boy grows up to become a gangster.
Brilliant, unsparing delineation of the sub-culture of crime and the corruption of the spirit it entails.
w Martin Scorsese, Nicholas Pileggi *novel* Wiseguy by Nicholas Pileggi d Martin Scorsese ph Michael Ballhaus pd Kristi Zea ad Maher Ahmad ed Thelma Schoonmaker
☆ Robert DeNiro, Ray Liotta, Joe Pesci, Lorraine Bracco, Paul Sorvino, Frank Sivero, Tony Darrow, Mike Starr, Frank Vincent, Chuck Low
'Simultaneously fascinating and repellent.' – *Variety*
'In its own narrow, near-claustrophobic perspective, however, driven along by a classic soundtrack and with no shortage of master directorial brush strokes, it is hard to imagine a bigger picture than this.' – *Empire*
🏆 Joe Pesci
🏆 Martin Scorsese; Lorraine Bracco; best adapted screenplay; best film editing; best picture
🏆 best picture; adapted screenplay; Martin Scorsese

Goodnight Vienna
GB   1932   76m   bw
British and Dominions (Herbert Wilcox)
US title: *Magic Night*
In 1913 Vienna, a general's son falls for a shopgirl.
Already dated when it was made, this thin musical romance nevertheless made a star of Anna Neagle and re-established Jack Buchanan on the screen.
w Holt Marvel, George Posford *play* Holt Marvel, George Posford d Herbert Wilcox ph F. A. Young m George Posford, Eric Maschwitz ad L. P. Williams ed E. Aldridge
☆ Jack Buchanan, Anna Neagle, Gina Malo, Clive Currie, William Kendall

A Goofy Movie
🏃 US   1995   78m   Technicolor
Buena Vista/Walt Disney (Dan Rounds)
📺 ▦

Goofy takes his slacker son on holiday and ends up in Los Angeles.
Minor animated feature; it may be of some social interest that Goofy is a single parent, but this tale of male bonding otherwise has little to offer.
w Jymn Magon, Chris Matheson, Brian Pimental d Kevin Lima m Carter Burwell pd Fred Warter ed Gregory Perler, Catherine Rascon
☆ Featuring the voices of: Bill Farmer, Jason Marsden, Jim Cummings, Kellie Martin, Rob Paulsen, Wallace Shawn
'The strength lies in the storytelling, and while this is slight, it's still a lot of fun.' – *Empire*

The Goonies
🏃 US   1985   111m   Technicolor
Panavision
Warner/Steven Spielberg
📺 ▦ ⌕ ⌒

Kids discover a pirate map and set out on a fantasy treasure hunt.
The bottomless pit of the Spielberg genre, a silly tale which takes forever to get going and is acted by children who have not studied elocution. The trick effects when they come are OK, but it's a long annoying haul to that point.
w Chris Columbus *story* Steven Spielberg d Richard Donner ph Nick McLean m Dave Grusin pd J. Michael Riva ed Michael Kahn
☆ Sean Astin, Josh Brolin, Jeff Cohen, Corey Feldman, Kerri Green, Martha Plimpton, Ke Huy Kwan

The Goose and the Gander
US   1935   65m   bw
Warner
A divorcee can't leave her ex-husband's life alone.
Tolerable farcical goings-on which just fail to come to the boil.
w George Kenyon d Alfred E. Green
☆ Kay Francis, George Brent, Genevieve Tobin, John Eldredge, Claire Dodd
'Well-played little farce with too much story for its own good.' – *Variety*

The Goose Steps Out ✱
🏃 GB   1942   79m   bw
Ealing (S. C. Balcon)
To steal a secret weapon, an incompetent teacher is sent into Germany in place of his Nazi double.
Quite amusing star vehicle, not up to his best standards.
w Angus Macphail, John Dighton d Will Hay, Basil Dearden ph Ernest Palmer m Bretton Byrd
☆ Will Hay, Charles Hawtrey, Frank Pettingell, Julien Mitchell, Peter Croft, Jeremy Hawk, Peter Ustinov, Raymond Lovell, Barry Morse

The Goose Woman
US   1925   90m   bw   silent
Universal
A young actress falls for the son of an embittered old one.
Interesting character melodrama of which prints have survived.
w Melville Brown *story* Rex Beach d Clarence Brown m Milton Moore
☆ Louise Dresser, Jack Pickford, Constance Bennett, James Barrows

The Gorbals Story
GB   1949   75m   bw
Eros/New World (Ernest Gartside)
A successful artist remembers his unhappy youth in a tenement in the slums of Glasgow.
Well-meaning, low-budget proletarian melodrama, featuring actors from the Glasgow Unity theatre. Set mainly in a couple of tenement rooms, it would have benefited from opening up with more exterior scenes; as it is, it remains a photographed stage play.
w David MacKane *play* Robert McLeish d David MacKane ph Stanley Clinton m John Bath ad George Haslam ed Helen Wiggins
☆ Russell Hunter, Betty Henderson, Howard Connell, Marjorie Thomson, Roddy McMillan, Isobel Campbell, Carl Williamson, Lothar Lewinsohn, Andrew Keir

Gordon's War
US   1973   90m   TVC Color
TCF/Palomar (Robert L. Schaffel)
A black Vietnam veteran returns to Harlem and avenges the death of his wife.
Violent vigilante melodrama with vivid locations.
w Howard Friedlander, Ed Spielman d Ossie Davis ph Victor J. Kemper m Andy Bodale, Al Ellis
☆ Paul Winfield, Carl Lee, David Downing

A Gorgeous Bird Like Me: see *Une Belle Fille comme Moi*

'An unbeatable cast in an unequalled drama! Metro's successor to The Great Ziegfeld!'
The Gorgeous Hussy ✱
US   1936   105m   bw
MGM (Joseph L. Mankiewicz)
The love life of Peggy O'Neal, protégée of President Andrew Jackson.
Bowdlerized all-star historical drama; the production values are better than the script.
w Ainsworth Morgan, Stephen Morehouse Avery *novel* Samuel Hopkins Adams d Clarence Brown ph George Folsey m Herbert Stothart
☆ Joan Crawford, Lionel Barrymore, Franchot Tone, Melvyn Douglas, Robert Taylor, James Stewart, Alison Skipworth, Louis Calhern, Beulah Bondi, Melville Cooper, Sidney Toler, Gene Lockhart
† A foreword read: 'This story of Peggy Eaton and her times is not presented as a precise account of either, rather as fiction founded upon historical fact.'
🏆 George Folsey; Beulah Bondi

'This is the big one! Two years in the making!'
Gorgo
🏃 GB   1960   78m   Technicolor
King Brothers (Wilfred Eades)
▦ ⌕

A prehistoric monster is caught in Irish waters and brought to London, but rescued by its mother.
Amiable monster hokum with a happy ending but not much technical resource.
w John Loring, Daniel Hyatt d Eugene Lourié ph Frederick A. Young m Angelo Lavagnino sp Tom Howard
☆ Bill Travers, William Sylvester, Vincent Winter, Christopher Rhodes, Joseph O'Conor, Bruce Seton, Martin Benson

The Gorgon ✱
GB   1964   83m   Technicolor
Columbia/Hammer (Anthony Nelson-Keys)
📺 ▦ ⌕

A castle ruin near a German village is infested by Megaera, the gorgon of ancient myth, whose gaze turns people to stone and who can take over the form of an unknowing villager.
Writhing snakes in the hair-do being too great a challenge to the make-up man, the monster is barely glimpsed and the film becomes a who-is-it, all quite suspenseful despite the central idea being too silly for words.
w John Gilling *story* J. Llewellyn Devine d Terence Fisher ph Michael Reed m James Bernard ad Bernard Robinson ed James Needs, Eric Boyd-Perkins
☆ Peter Cushing, Christopher Lee, Barbara Shelley, Richard Pasco, Patrick Troughton, Michael Goodliffe, Jack Watson

The Gorilla ✱
US   1939   66m   bw
TCF (Harry Joe Brown)
▦ ⌕

A murderer blames an escaped gorilla for his crimes.
Spooky house mystery comedy revamped as a Ritz Brothers vehicle; not much suspense, but it all looks good and the cast is highly satisfactory.
w Rian James, Sid Silvers *play* Ralph Spence d Allan Dwan ph Edward Cronjager md David Buttolph
☆ The Ritz Brothers, Bela Lugosi, Lionel Atwill, Patsy Kelly, Joseph Calleia, Anita Louise, Edward Norris, Wally Vernon
'A good programmer that will get by for normal biz where the Ritzes can attract.' – *Variety*
† There were two previous versions, in 1927 with Charlie Murray and 1931 with Joe Frisco.

'Get out of the way – before it's too late!'
Gorilla at Large
US   1954   93m   Technicolor   3-D
TCF/Panoramic (Robert L. Jacks)
A circus gorilla is used as a cover for murder.
Silly thriller with the gorilla as unconvincing as the story.
w Leonard Praskins, Barney Slater d Harmon Jones ph Lloyd Ahern m Lionel Newman
☆ Anne Bancroft, Lee J. Cobb, Cameron Mitchell, Lee Marvin, Raymond Burr, Charlotte Austin, Peter Whitney, Warren Stevens

---

🏃 film suitable for family viewing   📺 VHS video-cassette for the British PAL system   ▦ VHS video-cassette for the British PAL system in wide screen-format   ⊙ Video cassette in a computer-colourised version   ▥ American NTSC video-cassette   ⌕ Laser disc

The Gorilla Man
US 1942 63m bw
Warner
A wounded commando discovers that his hospital is run by Nazis, who then try to prove him insane so that he won't be believed.
There must have been less laborious ways, one assumes, but at least this farrago is good for a few unintentional laughs.
w Anthony Coldeway d D. Ross Lederman
☆ John Loder, Ruth Ford, Richard Fraser, Paul Cavanagh, John Abbott

Gorillas in the Mist *
US 1988 129m Technicolor
UIP/Warner (Arnold Glimcher, Terence Clegg)
▣ ▤ ◎ ◯
Researching into the lives of gorillas, a reclusive female scientist antagonizes local poachers.
Respectful, unenlightening biopic.
w Anna Hamilton Phelan story Anna Hamilton Phelan, Tab Murphy book Dian Fossey (article by Harold T. P. Hayes) d Michael Apted ph John Seale m Maurice Jarre pd John Graysmark ed Stuart Baird sp Rick Baker
☆ Sigourney Weaver, Bryan Brown, Julie Harris, John Omirah Miluwi, Iain Cuthbertson, Constantin Alexandrov, Waigwa Wachira, Iain Glen, David Lansbury
⚬ Sigourney Weaver; Maurice Jarre; Anna Hamilton Phelan; Stuart Baird; best sound

Gorky Park *
US 1983 128m Technicolor
Orion/Eagle (Gene Kirkwood, Howard W. Koch Jnr)
▣ ▤ ◎ ◯
The Moscow police link murders with a sable-smuggling operation.
Bleak thriller which doggedly makes its way through a conventional plot but fails to convey the book's detail of life in Moscow today. (The film was shot in Helsinki.)
w Dennis Potter novel Martin Cruz Smith d Michael Apted ph Ralf D. Bode m James Horner pd Paul Sylbert
☆ Lee Marvin, William Hurt, Brian Dennehy, Ian Bannen, Joanna Pacula, Michael Elphick, Richard Griffiths, Alexander Knox

The Gospel According to St Matthew *
Italy/France 1964 142m bw
Arco/Lux (Alfredo Bini)
original title: Il Vangelo Secondo Matteo
The life of Christ seen almost as a ciné-vérité documentary.
The tone is realist but not notably iconoclastic.
wd Pier Paolo Pasolini ph Tonino delli Colli m Bach, Mozart, Prokofiev, Webern md Luis Enrique Bacalov ad Luigi Scaccianoce ed Nino Baragli
☆ Enrique Irazoqui, Susanna Pasolini, Mario Socrate
⚬ Luis Enrique Bacalov

The Gospel According to Vic: see Heavenly Pursuits

Gösta Berlings Saga: see The Atonement of Gösta Berling

Una Gota De Sangre Para Morir Amando: see Murder in a Blue World

Gothic
GB 1986 90m Eastmancolor
Virgin Visions (Penny Corke)
▣ ▤ ◎ ◯
Byron, the Shelleys and Dr Polidori spend a weekend thinking up ghost stories.
Somewhat unhinged version of a famous occurrence in 1816, full of nauseous detail typical of its director.
w Stephen Volk d Ken Russell ph Mike Southon m Thomas Dolby pd Christopher Hobbs
☆ Gabriel Byrne, Julian Sands, Natasha Richardson, Miriam Cyr, Timothy Spall
'The thinking man's *Nightmare on Elm Street.*' – *Daily Variety*

Götterdämmerung: see The Damned (1969)

Goupi Mains Rouges *
France 1943 95m bw
Minerva
US title: It Happened at the Inn
A French village is largely populated by members of the same family, and one of them murders another.
An odd little black comedy which strengthened its director's reputation.
w Pierre Véry, Jacques Becker novel Pierre Véry d Jacques Becker ph Pierre Montazel, Jean Bourgoin m Jean Alfaro
☆ Fernand Ledoux, Georges Rollin, Blanchette Brunoy, Robert Le Vigan

The Governess
GB/France 1997 114m colour Super 35
Alliance/Pandora/Parallax (Sarah Curtis)
▣ ▤
In the 1840s, a Jewish woman, who disguises her origins, becomes governess to a Scottish family.
A feminist variation on Jane Eyre that says little that is new or interesting.
wd Sandra Goldbacher ph Ashley Rowe m Edward Shearmur pd Sarah Greenwood ed Isabel Lorente
☆ Minnie Driver, Tom Wilkinson, Harriet Walter, Florence Hoath, Bruce Myers, Jonathan Rhys Meyers, Arlene Cockburn, Emma Bird
'Pictorially, the movie is never less than sophisticated; only on a dramatic level is it silly.' – *Peter Matthews, Sight and Sound*

Government Girl
US 1943 94m bw
RKO
War Department secretaries find their love lives confused in wartime Washington, where rooms have to be shared.
Thin variation on a theme curiously dear to Hollywood at the time.
wd Dudley Nichols story Adela Rogers St Johns, Budd Schulberg
☆ Olivia de Havilland, Sonny Tufts, Anne Shirley, James Dunn, Paul Stewart, Agnes Moorehead, Harry Davenport, Una O'Connor, Sig Rumann, Jane Darwell

Le Graal: see Lancelot du Lac

The Grace Moore Story: see So This Is Love

Grace of my Heart *
US 1996 115m CFI color
Universal/Gramercy/Cappa (Ruth Charny, Daniel Hassid)
▣ ▤ ◎ ◯
A would-be singer becomes a successful songwriter in New York's Brill Building in the 50s and 60s.
Amiable trot through the pop music styles of the period in a movie that is loosely based on the career of Carole King; it is enjoyable, but as evanescent as the music it celebrates.
wd Allison Anders ph Jean-Yves Escoffier m Larry Klein, Elvis Costello, Burt Bacharach pd François Seguin ed Thelma Schoonmaker, James Kwei, Harvey Rosenstock
☆ Illeana Douglas, John Turturro, Eric Stoltz, Patsy Kensit, Bridget Fonda, Matt Dillon, Bruce Davison, Lucinda Jenney, Jennifer Leigh Warren, Christina Pickles
'Art with heart and rhythm, this is irresistibly wonderful. We're unlikely to see many films that are more entertaining all year.' – *Angie Errigo, Empire*
† Illeana Douglas's singing is dubbed by Kristen Vigard.

Grace Quigley
US 1984 95m colour
Cannon/Northbrook (Menahem Globus, Yoram Globus)
▤
aka: The Ultimate Solution of Grace Quigley
An aged widow blackmails a hit man into performing his services for all her elderly and miserable friends.
Yukky black comedy which ill befits its star and is an embarrassment from start to finish.
w A. Martin Zweiback d Anthony Harvey ph Larry Pizer m John Addison
☆ Katharine Hepburn, Nick Nolte, Elizabeth Wilson, Walter Abel, Kit Le Fever, Chip Zuen

† The *Grace Quigley* version has a contrived happy ending. In the original, Grace walks into the sea and the hit man is drowned trying to save her.

The Gracie Allen Murder Case *
US 1939 74m bw
George K. Arthur/Paramount
Gracie Allen helps Philo Vance solve the murder of an escaping convict.
At the time of Gracie Allen's radio eminence, this was a cute comedy idea.
w Nat Perrin novel S. S. Van Dine d Alfred E. Green
☆ Gracie Allen, Warren William, Ellen Drew, Kent Taylor, Jed Prouty, Jerome Cowan, Donald McBride, H. B. Warner, William Demarest
'Smacko for general audiences ... one of the top comedies of the season.' – *Variety*

Gracious Living: see La Vie de Château

'This is Benjamin ... he's a little worried about his future!'

The Graduate ****
US 1967 105m Technicolor Panavision
UA/Embassy (Lawrence Turman)
▣ ▤ ◎ ◎ ◎ ◯
A rich Californian ex-student is led into an affair with the wife of his father's friend, then falls in love with her daughter.
Richly reflecting the anything-goes mood of the late sixties, this lushly-filmed sex comedy opened a few new doors, looked ravishing, was well acted and had a popular music score. A comedy of its time, it has also stood the test of time.
w Calder Willingham, Buck Henry novel Charles Webb d Mike Nichols ph Robert Surtees m Dave Grusin m/ly Paul Simon (sung by Simon and Art Garfunkel) pd Richard Sylbert
☆ Dustin Hoffman, Anne Bancroft, Katharine Ross, Murray Hamilton, William Daniels, Elizabeth Wilson
BENJAMIN: 'Mrs Robinson, if you don't mind my saying so, this conversation is getting a little strange.'
'Seeing *The Graduate* is a bit like having one's most brilliant friend to dinner, watching him become more witty and animated with every moment, and then becoming aware that what one may really be witnessing is the onset of a nervous breakdown.' – *Renata Adler*
'Yes, there are weaknesses ... But in cinematic skill, in intent, in sheer connection with us, *The Graduate* is a milestone in American film history.' – *Stanley Kauffmann*
♟ Mike Nichols
⚬ best picture; script; Robert Surtees; Dustin Hoffman; Anne Bancroft; Katharine Ross
Ⓑ best picture; Mike Nichols; Calder Willingham, Buck Henry; Dustin Hoffman

Graffiti Bridge
US 1990 95m colour
Warner/Paisley Park (Arnold Stiefel, Randy Phillips)
▣ ▤
Two clubowners quarrel over the type of music they should be featuring.
Little more than an excuse for Prince to perform his songs, and strictly for fans.
wd Prince ph Bill Butler m Prince pd Vance Lorenzini ed Rebecca Rose
☆ Prince, Ingrid Chavez, Morris Day, Jerome Benton, Mavis Staples

The Grail: see Lancelot du Lac

Le Grand Blond avec une Chaussure Noire (dubbed) *
France 1972 89m Eastmancolor
Fox-Rank/Gaumont International/Productions de la Guéville/Madeleine (Alain Poiré, Yves Robert)
▣ ▤
aka: Follow That Guy with the One Black Shoe
aka: The Tall Blond Man with One Black Shoe
A disaster-prone violinist is the victim of a set-up by the head of the secret service who is attempting to discredit his second-in-command.
Mildly amusing comedy that makes fun of spies and their suspicious attitudes, though it suffers from being dubbed.
w Yves Robert, Francis Véber d Yves Robert ph René Mathelin m Vladimir Cosma ed Ghislaine Desjonquères

☆ Pierre Richard, Bernard Blier, Jean Rochefort, Mireille Darc, Jean Carmet, Colette Castel

Grand Canary
US 1934 76m bw
Fox (Jesse Lasky)
In the Canary Islands, a missionary girl tries to reform a derelict doctor, who finds true love elsewhere.
Curiously slack adaptation; one feels that something grandly philosophical was attempted and failed.
w Ernest Pascal novel A. J. Cronin d Irving Cummings
☆ Warner Baxter, H. B. Warner, Madge Evans, Marjorie Rambeau, Juliette Compton, Zita Johann
'Essentially dull and slow ... nothing very much happens.' – *Variety*

Grand Canyon *
US 1991 134m DeLuxe Panavision
TCF (Lawrence Kasdan, Charles Okun, Michael Grillo)
▣ ▤ ▤ ◎ ◯
After a black truck driver comes to the aid of a white lawyer, the two men form a friendship despite the disparity between them.
A sentimental account of urban unease, and one that offers glib answers to the questions it raises, but at least it does raise questions.
w Meg and Lawrence Kasdan d Lawrence Kasdan ph Owen Roizman m James Newton Howard pd Bo Welch ed Carol Littleton
☆ Danny Glover, Kevin Kline, Steve Martin, Mary McDonnell, Mary-Louise Parker, Alfre Woodard
'As a study of survival strategies in a disintegrating metropolis, pic brings a welcome seriousness and maturity to subject matter too often treated with flippancy and mindless romanticism.' – *Variety*
'It is hard to think of another American movie that has so directly, even naively, confronted the basic source of our existential unease.' – *Richard Schickel, Time*
⚬ Meg and Lawrence Kasdan (screenplay)

Grand Central Murder
US 1942 72m bw
MGM (B. F. Zeidman)
A murder is solved in New York's giant railway station.
Very moderate time-filler with a rather lethargic script.
w Peter Ruric novel Sue McVeigh d S. Sylvan Simon ph George F. Folsey m David Snell
☆ Van Heflin, Cecilia Parker, Sam Levene, Connie Gilchrist, Millard Mitchell, Tom Conway, Virginia Grey, Samuel S. Hinds

Le Grand Chemin **
France 1987 107m colour
Warner/Flach/Selena Audio Visuel/TFI (Pascal Hommais, Jean-François Lepetit)
◯
A nine-year-old boy spends the summer with a childless couple.
Charming account of a child trying to cope with the adult world which was a big hit in France.
wd Jean-Loup Hubert ph Claude Lecomte m Georges Granier pd Farid Chaouche ed Raymonde Guyot
☆ Anemone, Richard Bohringer, Antoine Hubert, Vanessa Guedi, Christine Pascal, Raoul Billerey, Pascale Roberts, Marie Matheron, Daniel Railet

The Grand Duchess and the Waiter *
US 1926 90m bw silent
Famous Players
A millionaire becomes a servant in order to win the heart of a titled lady.
Sophisticated silent comedy with a good reputation.
w Pierre Collings, John Lynch play Alfred Savoir d Malcolm St Clair ph Lee Garmes
☆ Adolphe Menjou, Florence Vidor, Lawrence Grant, Andre Beranger

Grand Exit
US 1935 68m bw
Columbia
An insurance company sleuth traps an arson fiend.
Lively co-feature mystery.
w Gene Towne, Graham Baker, Bruce Manning, Lionel Houser d Erle C. Kenton
☆ Edmund Lowe, Ann Sothern, Onslow Stevens, Robert Middlemass, Selmer Jackson, Edward Van Sloan

---

'Novel story, crisp dialogue, distinguished direction.' – *Variety*

'The greatest cast in stage or screen history!'
Grand Hotel **
US   1932   115m   bw
MGM (Irving Thalberg)
🔲 ⌾~
The lives of various hotel guests become intertwined and reach their climaxes.
It's a little faded now, but much of the magic still works in this first of the portmanteau movies; the production is opulent yet somehow stiff, and the performances have survived with varying success.
w William A. Drake *novel* Vicki Baum
d Edmund Goulding *ph* William Daniels
ad Cedric Gibbons
☆ Greta Garbo, John Barrymore, Lionel Barrymore, Joan Crawford, Wallace Beery, Jean Hersholt, Lewis Stone
  DOCTOR (LEWIS STONE): 'Grand Hotel. Always the same. People come, people go. Nothing ever happens.'
  GRUSINSKAYA (GRETA GARBO): 'I want to be alone … I think I have never been so tired in my life.'
† Remade as *Weekend at the Waldorf* (qv).
🏆 best picture

Le Grand Jeu *
France   1934   115m   bw
Films de France
A young man joins the Foreign Legion to forget a woman, meets another who reminds him of her, and is condemned to death for murdering the second woman's lover.
Hokey melodrama whose great interest lay in its picture of life in the Legion.
w Charles Spaak, Jacques Feyder d Jacques Feyder
ph Harry Stradling, Maurice Forster m Hanns Eisler
☆ Pierre-Richard Wilm, Marie Bell, Françoise Rosay, Charles Vanel
  'At last a good French film.' – *Variety*
† A remake appeared in 1953, directed by Robert Siodmak and starring Jean-Claude Pascal, Gina Lollobrigida and Arletty. Sometimes known as *Card of Fate*, it is of little interest.

Le Grand Meaulnes **
France   1967   110m   Eastmancolor
Techniscope
Fair Enterprises/Madeleine/Awa (Gilbert de Goldschmidt)
aka: *The Wanderer*
An adolescent's frantic search for a beautiful young girl he met by chance ends in tragedy.
A bitter-sweet romance that is faithful to the original but, for all its limitations, lacks imagination in its transfer to the screen.
w Isabelle Rivière, Jean-Gabriel Albicocco
novel Alain-Fournier d Jean-Gabriel Albicocco
ph Quinto Albicocco m Jean-Pierre Bourtayre
ad Daniel Louradour ed Georges Klotz
☆ Brigitte Fossey, Jean Blaise, Alain Libolt, Alain Noury, Juliette Villard, Christian de Tillière
  'Photographed for the most part in unforgettable scenery, and acted with convincing delicacy and charm, it carries a real poetic power and retains an amazing amount of the original's intensely romantic quality of loss and fragile innocence.' – *David Pirie, MFB*

Le Grand Méliès *
France   1952   30m   bw
Armor Films (Fred Orain)
The life of Georges Méliès, conjuror and pioneer film maker, is told in a series of vignettes separated by clips from his films.
An interesting documentary reconstruction.
wd Georges Franju
☆ André Méliès

Grand National Night
GB   1953   80m   bw
Talisman (George Minter)
US title: *The Wicked Wife*
A stable owner accidentally kills his drunken wife, but fate and a complex series of events clear him.
Slightly dubious morally, but otherwise an adequate detective story with the outcome hinging on train timetables and the like.
w Dorothy and Campbell Christie *play* Dorothy and Campbell Christie d Bob McNaught ph Jack Asher m John Greenwood

☆ Nigel Patrick, Moira Lister, Beatrice Campbell, Betty Ann Davies, Michael Hordern, Noel Purcell, Leslie Mitchell, Barry Mackay, Colin Gordon

Grand Prix *
US   1966   179m   Metrocolor   Super Panavision
MGM/Douglas and Lewis (Edward Lewis)
🔲 ⌾~
Motor racers converge on Monte Carlo and other European centres.
Seemingly endless montage, mostly in multisplit screens, of motor races, with some very jaded personal footage between. It looks a dream but quickly becomes a bore.
w Robert Alan Aurthur d John Frankenheimer
ph Lionel Lindon m Maurice Jarre pd Richard Sylbert
☆ James Garner, Eva Marie Saint, Brian Bedford, Yves Montand, Toshiro Mifune, Jessica Walter, Françoise Hardy, Adolfo Celi, Claude Dauphin, Genevieve Page
  'The same old story with the same types we've seen flying planes and riding horses in dozens of fast, cheap, hour-and-a-quarter movies.' – *Pauline Kael*
  'Nothing more nor less than a paean to the racing car … off the track, though, the film is firmly stuck in bottom gear.' – *MFB*

Grand Rue: see *Calle Mayor*

Il Grand Silencio: see *The Big Silence*

Grand Slam
US   1933   65m   bw
Warner
A Russian waiter is called in to make a fourth at bridge and proves to be an expert.
Able spoof of the bridge craze then sweeping America; precise knowledge unnecessary.
w David Boehm, Ernest Gelsey *novel* B. Russell Herts d William Dieterle
☆ Paul Lukas, Loretta Young, Frank McHugh, Glenda Farrell, Helen Vinson, Walter Byron, Ferdinand Gottschalk
  'It just about makes three spades doubled, which isn't bad when you're vulnerable, and that should be enough to show a profit.' – *Variety*

Grand Slam
Italy/Spain/West Germany   1967   120m
Techniscope
Paramount/Jolly-Coral-Constantin (Harry Columbo, George Papi)
original title: *Ad Ogni Costo*
A retired professor has a plan for a diamond robbery, but recruits his aides unwisely.
Long drawn-out caper melodrama with good sequences but nothing at all new; a very poor man's Rififi.
w Mino Roli, Caminito, Marcello Fondato, Antonio de la Loma d Giuliano Montaldo
ph Antonio Macasoli m Ennio Morricone
☆ Janet Leigh, Edward G. Robinson, Klaus Kinski, Robert Hoffman, Georges Rigaud, Adolfo Celi

La Grande Bouffe: see *Blow-Out*

La Grande Illusion ***
France   1937   117m   bw
Réalisations d'Art Cinématographique (Frank Rollmer, Albert Pinkovitch)
🔲 ⌾~
During World War I, three captured French pilots have an uneasy relationship with their German commandant.
Celebrated mood piece with much to say about war and mankind; more precisely, it is impeccably acted and directed and has real tragic force.
w Jean Renoir, Charles Spaak d Jean Renoir
ph Christian Matras m Joseph Kosma
m/ly Vincent Telly, Albert Valsien ad Eugène Lourie ed Marguerite Renoir, Marthe Huguet
☆ Pierre Fresnay, Erich von Stroheim, Jean Gabin, Julien Carette, Marcel Dalio, Gaston Modot, Jean Dasté, Dita Parlo
  'The story is true. It was told to me by my friends in the war … notably by Pinsard who flew fighter planes. I was in the reconnaissance squadron. He saved my life many times when the German fighters became too persistent. He himself was shot down seven times. His escapes are the basis for the story.' – *Jean Renoir*
  'Artistically masterful.' – *Variety*

'One of the true masterpieces of the screen.' – *Pauline Kael, 70s*
🏆 best picture

La Grande Vadrouille: see *Don't Look Now … We're Being Shot At!*

Les Grandes Manoeuvres *
France/Italy   1955   106m   Eastmancolor
Filmsonor/Rizzoli
aka: *Summer Manoeuvres*
In 1913, an army lieutenant takes a bet that he can win any woman in the town in which his regiment is quartered during manoeuvres.
An elegant, but surprisingly unwitty film from this director, saddled with a well-worn and very predictable plot.
wd René Clair ph Robert Le Fèbvre, Robert Juillard m Georges Van Parys
☆ Gérard Philipe, Michèle Morgan, Brigitte Bardot, Yves Robert, Jean Desailly, Pierre Dux

Grandma's Boy *
👫 US   1922   50m   bw   silent
Associated Exhibitors (Hal Roach)
Inspired by the heroism of his own grandpa, a meek and mild young fellow subdues a terrifying tramp.
Modest second-feature-length comedy of a burgeoning star, no great shakes by his later standards.
w Harold Lloyd, Sam Taylor, Jean Havez d Fred Newmeyer
☆ Harold Lloyd, Dick Sutherland, Anna Townsend

Granny Get Your Gun
US   1939   56m   bw
Warner
An indomitable old lady gets sheriff to get her granddaughter off the hook for murder.
Energetic second feature comedy mystery from a Perry Mason story; pleasant performances.
w Kenneth Gamet d George Amy
☆ May Robson, Harry Davenport, Margot Stevenson, Hardie Albright

'The thousands who have read the book will know why WE WILL NOT SELL ANY CHILDREN TICKETS to see this picture!'
The Grapes of Wrath ****
US   1940   128m   bw
TCF (Darryl Zanuck, Nunnally Johnson)
🔲 ⌾~
After the dust-bowl disaster of the thirties, Oklahoma farmers trek to California in the hope of a better life.
A superb film which could scarcely be improved upon. Though the ending is softened from the book, there was too much here for filmgoers to chew on. Acting, photography, direction combine to make this an unforgettable experience, a poem of a film.
w Nunnally Johnson *novel* J. Steinbeck d John Ford ph Gregg Toland m Alfred Newman
ad Richard Day, Mark Lee Kirk ed Robert Simpson
☆ Henry Fonda, Jane Darwell, John Carradine, Charley Grapewin, Dorris Bowdon, Russell Simpson, Zeffie Tilbury, O. Z. Whitehead, John Qualen, Eddie Quillan, Grant Mitchell
  TOM (HENRY FONDA) READING GRAVE MARKER: 'This here's William James Joad, died of a stroke, old, old man. His fokes bured him because they got no money to pay for funerls. Nobody kilt him. Just a stroke and he died.'
  MA (JANE DARWELL): 'Rich fellas come up, an' they die, an' their kids ain't no good, an' they die out. But we keep a-comin'. We're the people that live. Can't lick us. We'll go on forever, Pa, because we're the people.'
  MA: 'Well, Pa, woman can change bettern a man. Man lives – well, in jerks. Baby born or somebody dies, that's a jerk. Gets a farm or loses one, an' that's a jerk. With a woman, it's all one flow, like a stream – little eddies, little waterfalls – but the river, it goes right on. Woman looks at it that way.'
  'A genuinely great motion picture which makes one proud to have even a small share in the affairs of the cinema.' – *Howard Barnes*
  'The most mature motion picture that has ever been made, in feeling, in purpose, and in the use of the medium.' – *Otis Ferguson*
  'A sincere and searing indictment of man's cruel indifference to his fellows.' – *Basil Wright*
🏆 John Ford; Jane Darwell

🏆 best picture; Nunnally Johnson; Henry Fonda; Robert Simpson

Grass *
US   1925   50m   bw   silent
Famous Players-Lasky
🔲
Nomadic Iranian tribes make an annual migration in search of fresh pasture.
Striking early documentary marred by facetious subtitles.
wd/ph Merian C. Cooper, Ernest Schoedsack
titles Terry Ramsaye

The Grass Harp *
US   1995   106m   colour
Pathé/Grass Harp/Fine Line (Charles Matthau, Jerry Tokofsky, John Davis, James J. Davis)
🔲 ⌾~ 🎧
In America in the 30s, a teenage boy goes to live with his two aunts whose quarrel splits the neighbourhood.
Slight, ineffectual, anecdotal account of small-town life; its pleasures, too, are small.
w Sterling Silliphant, Kirk Ellis *novel* Truman Capote d Charles Matthau ph John A. Alonzo m Patrick Williams pd Paul Sylbert ed Sidney Levin, C. Timothy O'Leary
☆ Piper Laurie, Sissy Spacek, Walter Matthau, Edward Furlong, Nell Carter, Jack Lemmon, Mary Steenburgen, Sean Patrick Flanery, Joe Don Baker, Charles Durning, Roddy McDowall, Mia Kirshner
  'A tale steeped in tragic loss tempered with a wit that engages and meanders to almost equal effect.' – *Bob McCabe, Empire*

The Grass Is Greener *
GB   1960   104m   Technirama
Grandon (Stanley Donen)
🔲 ⌾~
The wife of an English earl falls for an American millionaire tourist.
Heavy-going and unsuitably widescreened version of an agreeable piece of West End fluff. Performances just about save it.
w Hugh and Margaret Williams *play* Hugh and Margaret Williams d Stanley Donen
ph Christopher Challis m/ly Noël Coward
md Muir Mathieson
☆ Cary Grant, Deborah Kerr, Robert Mitchum, Jean Simmons, Moray Watson
  'It's too bad Coward couldn't have written the wisecracks too.' – *Philip T. Hartung*
  'The stars do not glitter or even glow. Instead of being liberated and propelled by the screenplay, they are chained and sunk. It is one of the year's most disappointing films.' – *James Powers, Hollywood Reporter*

The Grasshopper
US   1970   98m   Technicolor
NGP (Jerry Belson, Garry Marshall)
A small-town girl goes from man to man in Los Angeles and Las Vegas, finally becoming a call girl.
The road to ruin in modern dress; nicely made and quite entertaining in its gaudy way.
w Jerry Belson *novel* The Passing of Evil by Mark MacShane d Jerry Paris ph Sam Leavitt m Billy Goldenberg
☆ Jacqueline Bisset, Jim Brown, Joseph Cotten, Corbett Monica

Grave Indiscretions: see *The Grotesque*

'4 kids. 3 bodies. 2 fights. 1 night. No $!*'
Gravesend *
US   1997   85m   Technicolor
Manga/Island/Brooklynwood/Gravesend (Salvatore Stabile)
🔲 🔲 ⊚ 🎧
Four Brooklyn layabouts attempt to dispose of the body when one accidentally shoots his friend's brother.
Oliver Stone endorsed this slice of street life, which has an authenticity, as well as a touch of slickness, about its account of losers losing what little they have.
wd Salvatore Stabile ph Joseph Dell'Olio m Bill Laswell ed Miranda Davin
☆ Tony Tucci, Michael Parducci, Tom Malloy, Thomas Brandise, Sean Quinn, Macky Aquilino
  'This is about as cutting edge as movies get.' – *Ian Freer, Empire*

---

† Stabile shot his film on the streets of New York with the aid of a $5,000 inheritance, though it cost another $60,000 to bring it to its final polish.

The Graveyard: see *Persecution*

Graveyard Shift
US   1990   86m   DeLuxe
Columbia TriStar/Graveyard Inc (William J. Dunn, Ralph S. Singleton)
📀 ▥ ⊚
Workers in a rat-infested, run-down mill investigate a mysterious killer beast in the cellars.
Dreary, badly made horror movie that fails on every level.
w John Esposito *story* Stephen King d Ralph S. Singleton ph Peter Stein m Anthony Marinelli, Brian Banks pd Gary Wissner ed Jim Gross, Randy Jon Morgan
☆ David Andrews, Kelly Wolf, Stephen Macht, Andrew Divoff, Vic Polizos, Brad Dourif, Robert Alan Beuth, Ilona Margolis
   'Miserably inept.' – *Sight and Sound*

The Gravy Train *
US   1974   96m   Eastmancolor
Columbia-Warner/Tomorrow Entertainment (Jonathan T. Taplin)
aka: *The Dion Brothers*
Two working-class brothers throw up their jobs and take to crime with bloody results.
Moderately entertaining caper, which manages to mix comedy and mayhem with some success.
w Bill Kerby, David Whitney (Terrence Malick) d Jack Starrett ph Jerry Hirshfeld pd Stan Jolley ed Jim Horger
☆ Stacy Keach, Frederic Forrest, Margot Kidder, Barry Primus, Richard Romanus, Denny Miller

Gray Lady Down
US   1978   111m   Technicolor   Panavision
Universal/Mirisch (Walter Mirisch)
▥
After a collision, an American submarine lodges in the neck of an underwater canyon.
A rather boring update of Morning Departure *with added technology.*
w James Whittaker, Howard Sackler *novel Event 1000* by David Levallee d David Greene ph Stevan Larner m Jerry Fielding
☆ Charlton Heston, David Carradine, Stacy Keach, Ned Beatty, Stephen McHattie, Ronny Cox, Dorian Harewood, Rosemary Forsyth
   'The crew eventually reach the surface, but the film deserves to sink without trace.' – Nicholas Wapshott, *The Times*

Grayeagle
US   1977   104m   Movielab   Panavision
Orion/AIP (Charles B. Pierce)
▥
In Montana in the 1840s, a settler tracks the Indian who kidnapped his daughter.
Overlong Western, which owes something to The Searchers, *though it is less complex and not hung up on matters of race; the acting, for the most part, and for most parts, is so ripe that it is almost rotten.*
wd Charles B. Pierce story Brad White, Mike Sajbel ph Jim Roberson m Jaime Mendoza-Nava ed Jim Roberson
☆ Ben Johnson, Iron Eyes Cody, Lana Wood, Jack Elam, Paul Fix, Alex Cord, Jacob Daniels, Jimmy Clem, Charles B. Pierce

Gray's Anatomy *
US/GB   1996   80m   colour
Independent Film Channel/BBC (John Hardy)
Spalding Gray describes his medical experiences, conventional and alternative, when he discovered that he had a problem with the vision in his left eye.
Moderately engaging monologue, with some distracting direction and ineffectual vox pop interviews. It has about it an air of contrivance, as if the various therapies were tried in order to provide good material for an amusing monologue.
w Spalding Gray d Steven Soderbergh ph Elliot Davies m Cliff Martinez pd Adele Plauché ed Susan Littenberg
☆ Spalding Gray

Grease **
👪 US   1978   110m   Metrocolor
Panavision
Paramount/Robert Stigwood, Allan Carr
📀 ▥ ▥ ⊚ ⌾
The path of true love in a fifties high school does not run smoothly.
Amiable 'period' musical for teenagers: a highly fashionable exploitation of the new star John Travolta, its commerciality was undeniable, and it carefully built in appeal to older age groups.
w Bronte Woodard stage musical Jim Jacobs, Warren Casey d Randal Kleiser ph Bill Butler m/ly Jim Jacobs, Warren Casey md Louis St Louis ch Patricia Birch pd Phil Jefferies ed John F. Burnett titles John Wilson
☆ John Travolta, Olivia Newton-John, Stockard Channing, Eve Arden, Frankie Avalon, Joan Blondell, Edd Byrnes, Sid Caesar, Alice Ghostley, Sha Na Na, Jeff Conaway, Barry Pearl, Michael Tucci
   'A bogus, clumsily jointed pastiche of late fifties high school musicals, studded with leftovers from *West Side Story* and *Rebel Without A Cause*.' – *New Yorker*
♫ song, 'Hopelessly Devoted to You' (m/ly John Farrar)

Grease 2
👪 US   1982   114m   Metrocolor
Panavision
Paramount (Robert Stigwood, Allan Carr)
📀 ▥ ▥ ⊚ ⌾
In 1961 an English boy causes emotional problems when he joins the senior class of Rydell High School.
Despite the mixture as before, this sequel was a resounding flop in all departments, perhaps proving that the success of the original was only a fluke of timing.
w Ken Finkleman d Patricia Birch ph Frank Stanley md Louis St Louis songs various
☆ Maxwell Caulfield, Michelle Pfeiffer, Adrian Zmed, Lorna Luft, Eve Arden, Sid Caesar, Tab Hunter, Connie Stevens
   'It's like being cooped up for two hours inside a combination of juke box and pinball machine, with you as the ball.' – *Daily Mail*

Greased Lightning
US   1977   96m   Movielab
Third World (Hannah Weinstein)
A black Virginian moonshiner becomes a famous stock car racer.
Fashionable action hokum based on a real character.
w Kenneth Vose, Lawrence DuKore, Melvin Van Peebles, Leon Capetanos d Michael Schultz ph George Bouiller m Fred Karlin
☆ Richard Pryor, Beau Bridges, Pam Grier, Cleavon Little, Vincent Gardenia

The Great Adventure: see *The Adventurers (1950)*

The Great Adventure **
👪 Sweden   1953   73m   bw
Arne Sucksdorff
▥
Two boys on a farm rescue an otter and keep it as a pet.
Superbly photographed wildlife film featuring a variety of small animals.
m Lars Erik Larsson wd/ed/ph Arne Sucksdorff
☆ Anders Norberg, Kjell Sucksdorff, Arne Sucksdorff

The Great Alaskan Mystery *
US   1944   bw   serial: 13 eps
Universal
Dr Miller invents a defence weapon called the Peratron, and goes to Alaska, followed by evil fascists, in search of the one element which will make it work.
Good serial stuff with a remarkably recognizable cast, and Ralph Morgan for once not the villain.
d Ray Taylor, Lewis D. Collins
☆ Milburn Stone, Marjorie Weaver, Edgar Kennedy, Ralph Morgan, Samuel S. Hinds, Martin Kosleck, Joseph Crehan, Fuzzy Knight, Harry Cording

The Great American Broadcast *
US   1941   90m   bw
TCF (Kenneth MacGowan)
A romantic triangle set against the burgeoning years of the radio industry.
Pleasant musical, amusing if historically inaccurate.
w Don Ettlinger, Edwin Blum, Robert Ellis, Helen Logan d Archie Mayo ph Leon Shamroy, Peverell Marley m/ly Mack Gordon, Harry Warren
☆ Alice Faye, John Payne, Jack Oakie, Cesar Romero, The Ink Spots, The Nicholas Brothers, The Wiere Brothers

The Great American Pastime
US   1956   89m   bw
MGM (Henry Berman)
A mild lawyer takes over a junior baseball team but incurs parental jealousy.
Thin lower-bracket comedy.
w Nathaniel Benchley d Herman Hoffman ph Arthur E. Arling m Jeff Alexander
☆ Tom Ewell, Anne Francis, Ann Miller, Dean Jones, Raymond Bailey

The Great Awakening: see *New Wine*

The Great Balloon Adventure: see *Olly Olly Oxen Free*

Great Balls of Fire!
US   1989   107m   colour
Rank/Orion (Adam Fields)
📀 ▥ ⌾
Biopic of the country rock singer Jerry Lee Lewis.
Unimaginative, unfactual treatment that conveys little of the performer's qualities.
w Jack Baran, Jim McBride book Myra Lewis, Murray Silver d Jim McBride ph Affonso Beato pd David Nichols ed Lisa Day, Pembroke Herring, Bert Lovitt
☆ Dennis Quaid, Winona Ryder, John Doe, Joe Bob Briggs, Stephen Tobolowsky, Trey Wilson, Alec Baldwin, Steve Allen, Lisa Blount, Joshua Sheffield

The Great Bank Robbery *
US   1969   98m   colour   Panavision
Warner (Malcolm Stuart)
Would-be bank robbers turn up in a Western town disguised as priests.
Western spoof without the courage of its convictions, but easy enough to watch.
w William Peter Blatty novel Frank O'Rourke d Hy Averback ph Fred J. Koenekamp m Nelson Riddle
☆ Kim Novak, Zero Mostel, Clint Walker, Claude Akins, Akim Tamiroff, Larry Storch, John Anderson, Sam Jaffe, Ruth Warrick, Elisha Cook Jnr

The Great Barrier
GB   1937   85m   bw
Gaumont British (Gunther Stapenhorst)
US title: *Silent Barriers*
A professional cardplayer gets involved in the building of the Canadian Pacific Railway.
Forgotten epic which has scenes of some grandeur.
w Ralph Spencer, Michael Barringer, Milton Rosmer novel The Great Divide by Alan Sullivan d Milton Rosmer, Geoffrey Barkas ph Glen MacWilliams, Robert Martin, Sidney Bonnett m Hubert Bath md Louis Levy ad Walter Murton ed Charles Frend
☆ Richard Arlen, Antoinette Cellier, Lilli Palmer, Barry Mackay, Roy Emerton
   'Authentic history done sensitively … ranks with the best made anywhere … will certainly achieve commercial and artistic success throughout the world.' – *Variety*

The Great Caruso **
US   1951   109m   Technicolor
MGM (Joe Pasternak)
📀 ▥ ⌾
Semi-fictional biography of the Italian tenor.
Dramatically flat but opulently staged biopic, turned into a star vehicle and a huge commercial success.
w Sonya Levien, William Ludwig d Richard Thorpe ph Joseph Ruttenberg md Johnny Green, Peter Herman Adler
☆ Mario Lanza, Ann Blyth, Dorothy Kirsten, Jarmila Novotna, Carl Benton Reid, Eduard Franz, Richard Hageman, Ludwig Donath, Alan Napier
   'Sounds like a recorded programme of excerpts from "Operas You Have Loved" which indeed it is.' – C. A. Lejeune
♫ Johnny Green, Peter Herman Adler

Great Catherine
GB   1968   98m   Technicolor
Warner/Keep Films (Jules Buck)
An English captain visits the court of Catherine the Great.
Chaos results from the attempt to inflate an ill-considered Shavian whimsy into a feature film: the material is simply insufficient and the performances flounder in irrelevant production values.
w Hugh Leonard play Bernard Shaw d Gordon Flemyng ph Oswald Morris m Dimitri Tiomkin pd John Bryan
☆ Jeanne Moreau, Peter O'Toole, Zero Mostel, Jack Hawkins, Marie Lohr, Akim Tamiroff, Marie Kean, Kenneth Griffith
   'All Shaw's jokes work very well, but the film has been padded out with Cossack dances, frantic chases, and unfunny slapstick.' – Michael Billington, *Illustrated London News*

The Great Chase
👪 US   1963   82m   bw
Continental
▥
A compendium of chase sequences from silent films.
w Harvey Kort, Paul Killiam, Saul Turrell
☆ William S. Hart, Douglas Fairbanks Snr, Buster Keaton

The Great Commandment
US   1940   78m   bw
John T. Coyle
In AD 30, with Judaea still under Roman rule, a village scholar preaches the teachings of Jesus.
Thin little religious fable, independently produced and without much going for it.
w Dana Burnet d Irving Pichel
☆ John Beal, Albert Dekker, Maurice Moscovich, Marjorie Cooley, Lloyd Corrigan

The Great Dan Patch
US   1949   92m   bw
United Artists (W. R. Frank)
▥
The career of a famous racehorse at the turn of the century.
Modest small-town crowd-pleaser.
w John Taintor Foote d Joseph Newman
☆ Dennis O'Keefe, Gail Russell, Ruth Warrick, Charlotte Greenwood, Henry Hull, John Hoyt, Arthur Hunnicutt

Great Day
GB   1945   79m   bw
RKO British (Victor Hanbury)
A village Women's Institute prepares for a visit by Mrs Roosevelt.
Modestly pleasing little drama from a successful play.
w Wolfgang Wilhelm, John Davenport play Lesley Storm d Lance Comfort ph Erwin Hillier
☆ Eric Portman, Flora Robson, Sheila Sim, Isabel Jeans, Walter Fitzgerald, Philip Friend, Marjorie Rhodes, Maire O'Neill, Beatrice Varley

A Great Day in Harlem **
US   1995   bw/colour
Flo-Bert/NYFA (Jean Bach)
📀 ▥ ▥ ⌾
The story of the day in 1958 when Art Kane gathered more than 50 leading jazz musicians together to take a now-famous photograph for *Esquire*, as remembered by some of those involved.
A heart-warming documentary, using still photography, by Dizzy Gillespie, Mary Lou Williams, Mike Lipskin and others, and 8mm colour film shot by bassist Milt Hinton and his wife Mona, and performances from the television documentary The Sound of Jazz. *What comes through most strongly is the participants' respect and affection for one another; it is essential viewing for anyone interested in jazz or in the pleasure artists can take in the abilities of their peers.*
w Jean Bach, Susan Peehl, Matthew Seig d Jean Bach ph Steve Petropoulos ed Susan Peehl

☼ Quincy Jones
'A likeable, intelligently original and moving documentary.' – *Sight and Sound*

Great Day in the Morning

US   1955   92m   Technicolor   Superscope
RKO/Edmund Grainger

At the outbreak of the Civil War, Denver has divided loyalties.
Solemn semi-Western without much excitement.
w Lesser Samuels *novel* Robert Hardy Andrews d Jacques Tourneur *ph* William Snyder *m* Leith Stevens
☼ Robert Stack, Virginia Mayo, Ruth Roman, Alex Nicol, Raymond Burr, Regis Toomey

The Great Diamond Robbery

US   1953   69m   bw
MGM (Edward Knopf)

Crooks convince a dumb jewellery apprentice to help them.
Tedious second feature comedy, the star's last for the studio.
w Laslo Vadnay d Robert Z. Leonard *ph* Joseph Ruttenberg
☼ Red Skelton, Cara Williams, James Whitmore, Kurt Kasznar, Reginald Owen

The Great Dictator **

US   1940   129m   bw
United Artists/Charles Chaplin
⊞ ▆ ℚ～ ⌕

A Jewish barber is mistaken for dictator Adenoid Hynkel.
Chaplin's satire on Hitler has a few funny moments, but the rest is heavy going, the production is cheeseparing, and the final speech to the world is a grave mistake.
wd Charles Chaplin *ph* Karl Struss, Rollie Totheroh *m* Meredith Willson *ad* J. Russell Spencer *ed* Willard Nico
☼ Charles Chaplin, Paulette Goddard, Jack Oakie, Reginald Gardiner, Henry Daniell, Billy Gilbert, Maurice Moscovich

'For this film he takes on more than a mimed representation of common humanity; he states, and accepts, the responsibility of being one of humanity's best and most widely-known representatives.' – *Basil Wright*
'The last impassioned speech about peace and serenity still wrecks everything that has gone before: Chaplin mawkish can always overrule Chaplin the innocent mime.' – *New Yorker, 1978*
'You must go back to *Intolerance* for another motion picture that is so completely one man's personal expression of his attitude on something about which he feels deeply and passionately.' – *James Shelley Hamilton, National Board of Review*
'No time for comedy? Yes, I say, time for comedy. Time for Chaplin comedy. No time ever for Chaplin to preach as he does in those last six minutes, no matter how deeply he may feel what he wrote and says. He is not a good preacher. Indeed, he is frighteningly bad.' – *John O'Hara*
'Some moments actually work, but they are very few and far between.' – *Time Out, 1984*
⌕ best picture; Charles Chaplin (as writer and actor); Meredith Willson; Jack Oakie

The Great Escape **

US   1963   173m   DeLuxe   Panavision
UA/Mirisch/Alpha (John Sturges)
⊞ ▆ ℚ～ ⌕ ⌕

Allied prisoners plan to escape from a German prison camp.
Pretty good but overlong POW adventure with a tragic ending that gave Steve McQueen his defining role.
w James Clavell, W. R. Burnett *book* Paul Brickhill d John Sturges *ph* Daniel Fapp *m* Elmer Bernstein
☼ James Garner, Steve McQueen, Richard Attenborough, James Donald, Charles Bronson, Donald Pleasence, James Coburn, David McCallum, Gordon Jackson, John Leyton, Nigel Stock

Great Expectations

US   1934   100m   bw
Universal
⊞ ▆ ℚ～ ⌕

A poor boy becomes unexpectedly rich and mistakes the source of his good fortune.

Solidly carpentered but never inspired version of a sprawling novel later tackled with much more style by David Lean. *See below.*
w Gladys Unger *novel* Charles Dickens d Stuart Walker *m* Edward Ward
☼ Phillips Holmes, Jane Wyatt, Henry Hull, Florence Reed, Alan Hale, Rafaela Ottiano, Francis L. Sullivan

'First half represents a fine achievement ... and then it all falls apart.' – *Variety*

Great Expectations ****

GB   1946   118m   bw
Rank/Cineguild (Anthony Havelock-Allan)
⊞ ▆ ⌕

A boy meets an escaped convict on the Romney Marshes, with strange consequences for both of them.
Despite the inevitable simplifications, this is a superbly pictorial rendering of a much-loved novel, with all the famous characters in safe hands and masterly judgement in every department.
w Ronald Neame, David Lean, Kay Walsh, Cecil McGivern, Anthony Havelock-Allan d David Lean *m* Guy Green *m* Walter Goehr *ad* John Bryan
☼ John Mills, Bernard Miles, Finlay Currie, Martita Hunt, Valerie Hobson, Jean Simmons, Alec Guinness, Francis L. Sullivan, Anthony Wager, Ivor Barnard, Freda Jackson, Hay Petrie, O. B. Clarence, George Hayes, Torin Thatcher and also Eileen Erskine

'The first big British film to have been made, a film that sweeps our cloistered virtues out into the open.' – *Richard Winnington*
'The best Dickens adaptation, and arguably David Lean's finest film.' – *NFT, 1969*
'It does for Dickens what *Henry V* did for Shakespeare. That is, it indicates a sound method for translating him from print to film ... almost never less than graceful, tasteful and intelligent, and some of it better than that.' – *James Agee*
† It was remade as a less than memorable TV movie in 1974, directed by Joseph Hardy and starring Michael York, Sarah Miles and James Mason.
†† Robert Krasker was the original cinematographer, but was replaced after Lean found his photography flat and uninteresting.
♟ Guy Green; John Bryan
⌕ best picture; script; David Lean (as director)

'She'll only break your heart – yet you'll still pursue her.'

Great Expectations

US   1998   111m   DeLuxe   Panavision
TCF (Art Linson)
⊞ ▆ ℚ～ ◠

In Florida, an orphan helps an escaped convict and his life is transformed.
A modern version of Charles Dickens's novel, with its hero turned into a brooding artist; despite the care lavished upon it, the picture is devoid of life.
w Mitch Glazer *novel* Charles Dickens d Alfonso Cuaron *ph* Emmmanuel Lubezki *m* Patrick Doyle *pd* Tony Burrough *ed* Steven Weisberg
☼ Ethan Hawke, Gwyneth Paltrow, Hank Azaria, Chris Cooper, Ann Bancroft, Robert de Niro, Josh Mostel, Kim Dickens, Nell Campbell

'Despite the dream-team production, despite the star-packed cast and its strong back-up characters, despite some ravishing camera-work, the film *Great Expectations* is a turkey. The actors can't get inside their characters.' – *John Sutherland, Guardian*

The Great Flamarion

US   1945   78m   bw
Republic
▆

A jealous vaudeville sharpshooter hunts down and kills the woman he loves because she prefers another.
Heavy-handed melodrama reminiscent of German silents but without their flair.
w Heinz Harald, Ann Wigton, Richard Weil d Anthony Mann
☼ Erich von Stroheim, Dan Duryea, Mary Beth Hughes

The Great Flirtation

US   1934   71m   bw
Paramount

An actor is jealous of his wife's stardom.
Would-be sophisticated comedy with far too many loose ends.
w Humphrey Pearson *story* Gregory Ratoff d Ralph Murphy
☼ Adolphe Menjou, Elissa Landi, David Manners, Lynne Overman, Raymond Walburn, Paul Porcasi, Akim Tamiroff

'Hardly a picture of strong audience appeal.' – *Variety*

The Great Gabbo

US   1929   88m   bw
Sono Art

A ventriloquist's personality is taken over by that of his dummy.
Yes, that old chestnut, here in tedious and primitive early talkie form.
w F. Hugh Herbert *story* Ben Hecht d James Cruze
☼ Erich von Stroheim, Betty Compson, Margie Kane

The Great Gambini

US   1937   70m   bw
Paramount

A mindreader's efforts to solve a murder only point to his own guilt.
Talkative twister which doesn't quite work.
w Frederick Jackson, Frank Partos, Howard Irving Young d Charles Vidor
☼ Akim Tamiroff, John Trent, Marian Marsh, Genevieve Tobin, Reginald Denny, William Demarest, Edward Brophy

'Not enough punch to produce better than ordinary entertainment.' – *Variety*

The Great Game

GB   1952   80m   bw
Advance

A football club chairman gets involved in crooked deals.
Dismal comedy drama which gives few opportunities to anybody.
w Wolfgang Wilhelm *play* Shooting Star by Basil Thomas d Maurice Elvey
☼ James Hayter, Diana Dors, Thora Hird, Sheila Shand Gibbs, John Laurie, Glyn Houston

The Great Garrick **

US   1937   91m   bw
Warner (Mervyn Le Roy)

When Garrick goes to act in Paris, members of the Comédie Française take over a wayside inn and try to teach him a lesson, but the plan goes awry.
A pleasant unhistorical conceit makes a rather literary film to have come from Hollywood, but it is all very winning and cast and director keep the fun simmering happily.
w Ernest Vajda d James Whale *ph* Ernest Haller *m* Adolph Deutsch
☼ Brian Aherne, Edward Everett Horton, Olivia de Havilland, Lionel Atwill, Melville Cooper, Luis Alberni, étienne Girardot, Marie Wilson, Lana Turner, Albert Dekker, Fritz Leiber, Dorothy Tree, Chester Clute

'Finely made period romantic comedy, but its reception at the paygate is extremely problematical.' – *Variety*
'As elegantly witty as anything Whale ever did.' – *Tom Milne*
'A jestful and romantic piece.' – *Frank S. Nugent, New York Times*

The Great Gatsby *

US   1949   90m   bw
Paramount (Richard Maibaum)

Events leading to the death of a retired gangster and mysterious Long Island plutocrat.
Rather bland and uninteresting attempt to accommodate a unique author to a formula star.
w Richard Maibaum *novel* F. Scott Fitzgerald d Elliott Nugent *ph* John Seitz *m* Robert Emmett Dolan
☼ Alan Ladd, Macdonald Carey, Betty Field, Barry Sullivan, Howard da Silva
† A silent version in 1926 had starred Warner Baxter.

The Great Gatsby **

US   1974   146m   Eastmancolor
Paramount/Newdon (David Merrick)
⊞ ▆ ℚ～

Plush version with lavish production values and pleasing period sense but not much grip on the story or characters. Overlong footage is not made to seem shorter by snail's pace and dull performances.
w Francis Ford Coppola d Jack Clayton *ph* Douglas Slocombe *m* Nelson Riddle *pd* John Box
☼ Robert Redford, Mia Farrow, Karen Black, Scott Wilson, Sam Waterston, Lois Chiles

'Pays its creator the regrettable tribute of erecting a mausoleum over his work.' – *Richard Combs*
'Leaves us more involved with six-and-a-half-million dollars' worth of trappings than with human tragedy.' – *Judith Crist*
'A total failure of every requisite sensibility.' – *Stanley Kauffmann*
'Profoundly unfilmable: a poetic and ultimately pessimistic comment on the American dream is transformed by cinematic realism into pure prose.' – *Michael Billington, Illustrated London News*
♟ Nelson Riddle; costumes (Theoni V. Aldredge)
♟ Douglas Slocombe; John Box

The Great Gilbert and Sullivan: see *The Story of Gilbert and Sullivan*

The Great Gildersleeve

US   1942   61m   bw
RKO (Herman Schlom)

A small town loudmouth is always in hot water.
Unremarkable film début for a radio character from Fibber McGee and Molly. Three more second features followed.
w Jack Townley, Joseph Josephson d Gordon Douglas
☼ Harold Peary, Jane Darwell, Nancy Gates, Charles Arnt, Thurston Hall

Great Guns *

US   1941   74m   bw
TCF (Sol M. Wurtzel)
⊞ ▆

A young millionaire's retainers join the army with him.
Disappointing Laurel and Hardy comedy, their first for Fox and the beginning of their decline. A few good jokes, but no overall control or inventiveness.
w Lou Breslow d Monty Banks *ph* Glen MacWilliams *m* Emil Newman *ed* Al de Gaetano
☼ Stan Laurel, Oliver Hardy, Sheila Ryan, Dick Nelson, Edmund Macdonald, Charles Trowbridge, Ludwig Stossel, Mae Marsh

Great Guy *

US   1936   73m   bw
Grand National (Douglas Maclean)
▆

GB title: Pluck of the Irish

An ex-prizefighter joins the bureau of weights and measures and fights corruption.
Rather tame racket film, Cagney's first independent venture away from Warner. He atones for rather thin production values.
w Henry McCarthy, Henry Johnson, James Edward Grant, Harry Ruskin d John G. Blystone *ph* Jack McKenzie *m* Marlin Skiles
☼ James Cagney, Mae Clarke, James Burke, Edward Brophy, Henry Kolker

'It's all typical Cagney stuff, and that's the trouble with it. Cagney apparently is doing the things he likes best, but they're repetitious and apt to disappoint a public anticipating something finer from this star after his quite lengthy absence.' – *Variety*

The Great Hospital Mystery

US   1937   59m   bw
TCF

The lady superintendent of a hospital has a busy night including impersonation and murder.
Confused but watchable second feature.
w Bess Meredyth, William Conselman, Jerry Cady *novel* Mignon G. Eberhart d James Tinling
☼ Jane Darwell, Joan Davis, Sig Rumann, Sally Blane, Thomas Beck, William Demarest

---

The Great Hotel Murder

US   1934   70m   bw
TCF

Rival sleuths find the truth about a murder less important than being first to find it out.

Lively programme filler of its day, with the stars still doing their Flagg and Quirt act.

w Arthur Kober *story* Vincent Starrett d Eugene Forde

☆ Edmund Lowe, Victor McLaglen, Rosemary Ames, Mary Carlisle

The Great Impersonation *

US   1935   81m   bw
Universal (Edmund Grainger)

During World War I, a German murders an English nobleman and, being his double, takes over.

Reliable espionage melodrama with atmospheric country house asides, from a sturdily compelling novel.

w Frank Wead, Eve Greene *novel* E. Phillips Oppenheim d Alan Crosland ph Milton Krasner m Franz Waxman

☆ Edmund Lowe, Valerie Hobson, Wera Engels, Henry Mollison, Lumsden Hare, Spring Byington, Charles Waldron, Dwight Frye

'They giggled a bit when Lowe went to bed with candles, and an hour later a sliding panel attempt on his life has him pushing an electric light switch ... probably doesn't matter that the 1914 characters are dressed throughout in 1935 modishness and drive around in streamlined automobiles.' – *Variety*

† It was previously filmed in 1921 with James Kirkwood.

The Great Impersonation *

US   1942   71m   bw
Universal (Paul Malvern)

Okay quickie updating of the above, serviceable rather than inventive.

w W. Scott Darling d John Rawlins ph George Robinson m Hans Salter

☆ Ralph Bellamy, Evelyn Ankers, Aubrey Mather, Edward Norris, Karen Verne, Henry Daniell, Ludwig Stossel

The Great Imposter *

US   1961   112m   bw
U-I (Robert Arthur)
▣

The career of Ferdinand Waldo Demara, a marine and Trappist monk who also impersonated a Harvard research fellow, a prison warden, a naval doctor and a schoolteacher.

Uncertain mood hampers this biopic of a likeable fantasist.

w Liam O'Brien *book* Robert Crichton d Robert Mulligan ph Robert Burks m Henry Mancini

☆ Tony Curtis, Raymond Massey, Karl Malden, Edmond O'Brien, Arthur O'Connell, Gary Merrill, Frank Gorshin, Joan Blackman, Robert Middleton

Great – Isambard Kingdom Brunel *

�” GB   1975   28m   Eastmancolor
British Lion

A musical, animated biography of the great Victorian engineer.

Quite unexpected, and therefore the more delightful.

w Bob Godfrey d Bob Godfrey

The Great Jasper

US   1933   83m   bw
RKO

An Irish motorman becomes a fortune teller, and has his way with lots of women.

Curious comedy-melodrama which never quite hits the right style.

w Sam Ornitz, H. W. Hanemann *novel* Fulton Oursler d J. Walter Ruben

☆ Richard Dix, Wera Engels, Edna May Oliver, Florence Eldridge, Bruce Cabot

'Okay as a critics' film but looks like an in-and-outer.' – *Variety*

The Great Jesse James Raid

US   1953   70m   Anscocolor
Lippert

Jesse James comes out of retirement for one last haul.

Boring two-bit Western, all preparation and no action.

w Richard Landau d Reginald Le Borg

☆ Willard Parker, Barbara Payton, Tom Neal, Wallace Ford, Jim Bannon

The Great Jewel Robber

US   1950   91m   bw
Warner

The exploits of real-life society thief Gerald Graham Dennis.

Surprisingly acceptable and entertaining reconstruction.

w Borden Chase d Peter Godfrey

☆ David Brian, Marjorie Reynolds, John Archer, Jacqueline de Wit

The Great John L.

US   1945   96m   bw
UA/Bing Crosby Productions (Frank Mastroly, James Edward Grant)

GB title: *A Man Called Sullivan*

Women in the life of prizefighter John L. Sullivan.

Very mild period biopic without the zest of Gentleman Jim.

w James Edward Grant d Frank Tuttle ph James Van Trees m Victor Young

☆ Greg McClure, Linda Darnell, Barbara Britton, Lee Sullivan, Otto Kruger, Wallace Ford, Robert Barrat

'Sometimes there's a terrible penalty for telling the truth...'

The Great Lie ***

US   1941   107m   bw
Warner (Hal B. Wallis, Henry Blanke)
▣   ◎▿

A determined girl loses the man she loves, believes him dead in a plane crash, and takes over the baby which his selfish wife does not want.

Absurd melodrama becomes top-flight entertainment with all concerned in cracking form and special attention on the two bitchy female leads, splendidly played. Classical music trimmings, too.

w Lenore Coffee *novel* January Heights by Polan Banks d Edmund Goulding ph Tony Gaudio m Max Steiner

☆ Bette Davis, Mary Astor, George Brent, Lucile Watson, Hattie McDaniel, Grant Mitchell, Jerome Cowan

♦ Mary Astor

The Great Locomotive Chase *

🏛 US   1956   76m   Technicolor
Cinemascope
Walt Disney (Lawrence Edward Watkin)
▣   ◉

During the Civil War, Union spies steal a train and destroy track and bridges behind them.

A serious version of Buster Keaton's The General, based on a true incident; good sequences but no overall pace.

w Lawrence Edward Watkin d Francis D. Lyon ph Charles Boyle m Paul Smith

☆ Fess Parker, Jeffrey Hunter, Jeff York, John Lupton, Kenneth Tobey

The Great Lover

US   1931   77m   bw
MGM

Capers of a philandering opera star.

Satisfactory drama-comedy vehicle for a durable star.

w Gene Markey d Harry Beaumont

☆ Adolphe Menjou, Irene Dunne, Neil Hamilton, Olga Baclanova

'Appeal limited to the mature fan.' – *Variety*

The Great Lover *

US   1949   80m   bw
(Paramount) Hope Enterprises (Edmund Beloin)
▣

On a transatlantic liner, a timid scoutmaster catches a strangler.

Amusing suspense comedy, a good star vehicle.

w Edmund Beloin, Melville Shavelson, Jack Rose d Alexander Hall ph Charles Lang m Joseph J. Lilley

☆ Bob Hope, Rhonda Fleming, Roland Young, Jim Backus, Roland Culver, George Reeves

The Great Man **

US   1956   92m   bw
U-I (Aaron Rosenberg)

A memorial programme to a much-loved TV personality turns into an exposé.

Patchy melodrama with a Citizen Kane framework; the best bits are very effective.

w José Ferrer, Al Morgan *novel* Al Morgan d José Ferrer ph Harold Lipstein m Herman Stein

☆ José Ferrer, Dean Jagger, Keenan Wynn, Julie London, Joanne Gilbert, Ed Wynn, Jim Backus

The Great Man Votes *

US   1938   72m   bw
RKO (Cliff Reid)

A drunken professor turns out to have the casting vote in a local election.

Slow-starting but progressively funny political comedy with some favourite talents in good form.

w John Twist *story* Gordon Malherbe Hillman d Garson Kanin ph Russell Metty m Roy Webb

☆ John Barrymore, Virginia Weidler, Peter Holden, William Demarest, Donald MacBride

'It will be hailed by class audiences as a fine example of the film art, yet carrying sock appeal for mass patronage.' – *Variety*

The Great Manhunt: see *The Doolins of Oklahoma* (1949)

The Great Manhunt: see *State Secret* (1950)

The Great Man's Lady *

US   1941   90m   bw
Paramount (William A. Wellman)

A Western pioneer is inspired and encouraged by his wife.

Adequate but unsurprising flashback family drama starting with its star as a lady of 109.

w W. L. Rivers *story* Vina Delmar d William A. Wellman ph William C. Mellor m Victor Young

☆ Barbara Stanwyck, Joel McCrea, Brian Donlevy, Katharine Stevens, Thurston Hall, Lloyd Corrigan

'He'll give you the biggest heart sock, laugh shock you ever thrilled to!'

The Great McGinty **

US   1940   83m   bw
Paramount (Paul Jones)
▣   ◎▿

GB title: *Down Went McGinty*

A hobo and a crook have a hectic political career.

Lively comedy-drama which signalled the arrival as director of a new and stimulating Hollywood talent.

wd Preston Sturges ph William C. Mellor m Frederick Hollander

☆ Brian Donlevy, Akim Tamiroff, Muriel Angelus, Louis Jean Heydt, Arthur Hoyt

PROLOGUE: 'This is the story of two men who met in a banana republic. One of them never did anything dishonest in his life except for one crazy minute. The other never did anything honest in his life except for one crazy minute. They both had to leave the country.'

'This is his first directing job and where has he been all our lives? He has that sense of the incongruous which makes some of the best gaiety.' – *Otis Ferguson*

'The tough dialogue is matched by short, snappy scenes; the picture seems to have wasted no time, no money.' – *Gilbert Seldes*

'A director as adroit and inventive as any in the business ... it starts like a five-alarm fire and never slackens pace for one moment until its unexpected conclusion.' – *Pare Lorentz*

'Sturges takes the success ethic and throws it in the face of the audience.' – *James Orsini*

'Capra with the gloves off.' – *Raymond Durgnat*

♠ script

The Great McGonagall

GB   1974   89m   Eastmancolor
Darlton

An unemployed Scot aims to become Queen Victoria's Poet Laureate.

Appalling tribute to a minor figure of sub-literature.

w Joe McGrath, Spike Milligan d Joe McGrath

☆ Spike Milligan, Peter Sellers, Julia Foster, Julian Chagrin, John Bluthal, Valentine Dyall, Victor Spinetti

The Great Meadow

US   1931   80m   bw
MGM

Early settlers from Virginia walk to Kentucky.

Dim pioneering fable, without even a covered wagon.

w Edith Ellis, Charles Brabin *novel* Elizabeth Madox Roberts d Charles Brabin

☆ John Mack Brown, Eleanor Boardman, Lucille La Verne, Anita Louise, Gavin Gordon, Guinn Williams

'Rather a sorry mess ... cannot be depended on for an average gross.' – *Variety*

The Great Missouri Raid

US   1950   81m   Technicolor
Nat Holt/Paramount
▣

Jesse and Frank James are seen as Civil War guerrillas, subsequently forced into crime by a vengeful officer.

Unsuccessful whitewash job, tediously told.

w Frank Gruber d Gordon Douglas

☆ Macdonald Carey, Wendell Corey, Ward Bond, Ellen Drew, Bruce Bennett, Bill Williams, Anne Revere, Edgar Buchanan

'They booed him to greatness!'

The Great Moment **

US   1944   83m   bw
Paramount
▣

How anaesthetics may have been invented.

Curious biopic of Dr W. T. G. Morgan, poised somewhere between utter seriousness and pratfall farce. The beginning of its director's decline, but always interesting in itself.

wd Preston Sturges *book* Triumph over Pain by René Fulop-Miller ph Victor Milner m Victor Young

☆ Joel McCrea, Betty Field, William Demarest, Harry Carey, Franklin Pangborn, Porter Hall, Grady Sutton

'Mr Sturges has triumphed over stiffness in screen biography.' – *New York Times*

'The careless, careful authority is there ... the contrivance is smart enough.' – *Sunday Times*

Great Moments in Aviation

GB   1994   92m   colour
BBC Films (Phillippa Giles)

En route to London, a young West Indian woman begins a shipboard romance with a mysterious Scotsman who is accused of theft and murder by a fellow passenger.

Incoherent and arcane romantic drama with leaden dialogue that not even its talented cast can make meaningful.

w Jeanette Winterson d Beeban Kidron ph Remi Adefarasin m Rachel Portman pd Tony Burrough ed John Stothart

☆ Vanessa Redgrave, John Hurt, Jonathan Pryce, Dorothy Tutin, Rakie Ayola

'Damaged beyond repair by a mannered scripting style and evident recutting, this wingless relic looks commercially to stay confined to its hangar.' – *David Rooney, Variety*

The Great Mouse Detective *

🏛 US   1986   80m   Technicolor
Walt Disney/Silver Screen Partners II (Burny Mattinson)
▣◻   ▣   ◎▿   ◠

GB title: *Basil, The Great Mouse Detective*

A mouse who has studied Sherlock Holmes solves the mystery of a missing mouse toymaker and outwits the evil Professor Rattigan.

One of the better recent Disney cartoon features, but the texture will probably never again be so rich as in the days of Pinocchio and Bambi.

w Pete Young, Steve Hulett, John Musker, Matthew O'Callaghan, Dave Michener, Vance Gerry, Ron Clements, Bruce M. Morris, Melvin Shaw, Burney Mattinson *novel* Basil of Baker Street by Eve Titus d John Musker, Ron Clements, Dave Michener, Burney Mattinson ph Ed Austin m Henry Mancini pd Guy Vasilovich ed Roy M. Brewer Jnr, James Melton

☆ Featuring the voices of Barrie Ingham, Vincent Price, Val Bettin, Alan Young

The Great Mr Handel *

🏛 GB   1942   103m   Technicolor
Rank/GHW (James B. Sloan)
▣◻

How the 18th-century composer came to write the Messiah.

Earnest, unlikely biopic, naïve but rather commendable.

w Gerald Elliott, Victor MacClure *play* L. DuGarde Peach d Norman Walker ph Claude Friese-Greene, Jack Cardiff md Ernest Irving

---

☆ Wilfrid Lawson, Elizabeth Allan, Malcolm Keen, Michael Shepley, Hay Petrie, A. E. Matthews

'A graceful addition to the ranks of prestige pictures.' – *Kine Weekly*

The Great Mr Nobody

US   1941   71m   bw
Warner
A classified ad salesman is too prone to let colleagues take the credit for his ideas.
Thin character comedy which did nobody concerned any good.
w Ben Markson, Kenneth Gamet d Ben Stoloff
☆ Eddie Albert, Joan Leslie, Alan Hale, William Lundigan, John Litel

The Great Muppet Caper **

👫👫   GB   1981   97m   Technicolor
ITC (David Lazer, Frank Oz)
📼 ▦ ◉ ⌒
Kermit and Fozzie are reporters sent to solve a jewel robbery.
Considerably livelier than The Muppet Movie but a badly timed flop at the box-office, this genial caper has a pleasant collection of guest stars as well as showing the familiar puppets at their most typical.
w Tom Patchett, Jay Tarses, Jerry Juhl, Jack Rose
d Jim Henson ph Oswald Morris m Joe Raposo
pd Harry Lange
☆ Diana Rigg, Charles Grodin, John Cleese, Robert Morley, Trevor Howard, Peter Ustinov, Jack Warden

'Large chunks are pleasingly daft.' – *Sight and Sound*
♫ song 'The First Time It Happened' (*m/ly* Joe Raposo)

The Great Northfield Minnesota Raid *

US   1971   91m   Technicolor
Universal/Robertson and Associates/Jennings Lang
▦
In 1876 a gang of bandits, technically pardoned, plan a bank robbery.
'Realistic' Western in which the settings and photography have an impressively rough look but the script leaves much to be desired.
wd Philip Kaufman ph Bruce Surtees m Dave Grusin
☆ Cliff Robertson, Robert Duvall, Luke Askew, Elisha Cook Jnr

The Great O'Malley

US   1937   77m   bw
Warner (Harry Joe Brown)
An overzealous cop cares for the wife and child of a petty criminal whom he has sent to prison.
Considering the talent involved, an astonishingly routine programmer.
w Milton Krims, Tom Reed story *The Making of O'Malley* by Gerald Beaumont d William Dieterle
ph Ernest Haller m Heinz Roemheld
☆ Pat O'Brien, Humphrey Bogart, Ann Sheridan, Sybil Jason, Frieda Inescort, Donald Crisp, Henry O'Neill, Hobart Cavanaugh, Mary Gordon

'Familiar sentimental police theme: little action or appeal.' – *Variety*
† Previously filmed in 1923 with Milton Sills, as *The Making of O'Malley.*

The Great Outdoors

👫👫   US   1988   90m   CFI color   Panavision
Universal/Hughes Entertainment (Arne L. Schmidt)
📼 ▦ ◉ ◉
A family's holiday in the woods is disrupted by a surprise visit from their wealthy in-laws.
Broad and tiresome comedy in which its participants flail around noisily to no particular purpose.
w John Hughes d Howard Deutch ph Ric Waite
m Thomas Newman pd John W. Corso ed Tom Rolf, William Gordean, Seth Flaum
☆ Dan Aykroyd, John Candy, Stephanie Faracy, Annette Bening, Chris Young, Ian Giatti, Hilary Gordon, Rebecca Gordon, Robert Prosky

The Great Profile *

US   1940   82m   bw
TCF (Raymond Griffith)
A dissipated actor disgraces his family and becomes an acrobat.
Shapeless farce in which a great talent on his last legs parodies himself.
w Milton Sperling, Hilary Lynn d Walter Lang
ph Ernest Palmer m Cyril Mockridge

☆ John Barrymore, Mary Beth Hughes, Gregory Ratoff, Anne Baxter, John Payne, Lionel Atwill, Edward Brophy, Willie Fung

'The greatest comedy ever made!'
The Great Race ***

👫👫   US   1965   163m   Technicolor   Super Panavision
Warner/Patricia/Jalem/Reynard (Martin Jurow)
📼 ▦ ◉ ⌒
In 1908, the Great Leslie and Professor Fate are leading contenders in the first New York to Paris car race.
Elaborate comedy spectacular with many good moments, notably the early disasters, a Western saloon brawl, and a custard pie fight. Elsewhere, there is more evidence of an oversize budget than of wit or finesse, and the entire Prisoner of Zenda spoof could have been omitted. Excellent production detail and general good humour.
w Arthur Ross d Blake Edwards ph Russell Harlan m Henry Mancini pd Fernando Carrere
☆ Jack Lemmon, Tony Curtis, Peter Falk, Natalie Wood, George Macready, Ross Martin, Vivian Vance, Dorothy Provine

'The most expensive comedy ever filmed; but there the superlatives end: it is not exactly the worst.' – *Time*
♫ Russell Harlan; song 'The Sweetheart Tree' (*m* Henry Mancini, *ly* Johnny Mercer)

The Great Rupert

👫👫   US   1950   87m   bw
Eagle Lion (George Pal)
▦
A family of impoverished acrobats are assisted by a pet squirrel which proves lucky in more ways than one.
Modest whimsical comedy which outstays its welcome.
w Laslo Vadnay d Irving Pichel
☆ Jimmy Durante, Terry Moore, Tom Drake, Sara Haden, Frank Orth
† The squirrel was part puppet.

The Great Santini *

US   1979   115m   Technicolor
Warner/Orion/Bing Crosby Productions (Charles A. Pratt)
▦ ◉
A crack fighter pilot has difficulty adjusting to peacetime domestic life.
Overlong but generally absorbing star character drama.
wd Lewis John Carlino novel Pat Conroy
ph Ralph Woolsey m Elmer Bernstein pd Jack Poplin
☆ Robert Duvall, Blythe Danner, Michael O'Keefe, Lisa Jane Persky, Julie Anne Haddock
♫ Robert Duvall; Michael O'Keefe (supporting actor)

'They were not forgotten by history – they were left out on purpose!'
The Great Scout and Cathouse Thursday

US   1976   102m   Technicolor
AIP (Jules Buck and David Korda)
▦
reissue title: *Wildcat*
While trying to revenge himself on an absconding partner, an old cowboy falls for a young prostitute.
Downright peculiar comedy Western which never seems to make up its mind what it's trying to be, and too often is merely embarrassing.
w Richard Shapiro d Don Taylor ph Alex Phillips Jnr m John Cameron pd Jack Martin Smith
☆ Lee Marvin, Oliver Reed, Kay Lenz, Robert Culp, Elizabeth Ashley, Strother Martin, Sylvia Miles

'It takes more than a dollop or two of sentiment and acres of dirty talk to make a movie.' – *Michael Billington, Illustrated London News*
'It sounds like the latest in the cute twosome series launched by *Butch Cassidy and the Sundance Kid.* In fact it features not two but seven wacky westerners who all seem addicted to stealing, hee-hawing, falling into puddles and punching each other in the privates.' – *Janet Maslin, Newsweek*

The Great Sinner *

US   1949   110m   bw
MGM (Gottfried Reinhardt)
A serious young writer becomes a compulsive gambler.

Rather pointless and heavy-handed but extremely good-looking and splendidly cast period drama vaguely based on Dostoievsky.
w Ladislas Fodor, Christopher Isherwood
d Robert Siodmak ph George Folsey m Bronislau Kaper ad Cedric Gibbons, Hans Peters
☆ Gregory Peck, Walter Huston, Ava Gardner, Agnes Moorehead, Ethel Barrymore, Melvyn Douglas, Frank Morgan

The Great Sioux Massacre

US   1965   93m   Eastmancolor   Cinemascope
Columbia/FF (Leon Fromkess)
Two officers are court-martialled after Custer's last stand.
Fragmentary flashback Western let down by production and performances.
w Fred C. Dobbs d Sidney Salkow ph Irving Lippman m Emil Newman, Edward B. Powell
☆ Joseph Cotten, Darren McGavin, Phil Carey, Nancy Kovack, Julie Sommars, Michael Pate

The Great Sioux Uprising

US   1953   80m   Technicolor
U-I (Albert J. Cohen)
Indians rebel when their horses are stolen for sale to the commander of Fort Laramie.
Moderate Western programmer.
w Richard Breen, Gladys Atwater d Lloyd Bacon
ph Maury Gertsman m Joseph Gershenson
☆ Jeff Chandler, Faith Domergue, Lyle Bettger

The Great Smokey Roadblock

US   1976   106m   colour
Marvista (Ingo Preminger, Allan F. Bodoh)
▦
original title: *The Last Of The Cowboys*
A truckdriver avoiding the finance company picks up an assortment of eccentrics and starts on a wild chase.
What possessed Henry Fonda to appear in this hick action melodrama will be forever unclear.
wd John Leone ph Ed Brown Snr m Craig Safan
ed Corky Ehlers
☆ Henry Fonda, Eileen Brennan, John Byner, Dub Taylor, Susan Sarandon, Dana House, Robert Englund, Melanie Mayron, Valerie Curtin

The Great Spy Mission: see *Operation Crossbow*

The Great St Trinian's Train Robbery

👫👫   GB   1966   94m   Eastmancolor
British Lion/Braywild (Leslie Gilliat)
📼 ▦
The staff of St Trinian's is infiltrated by would-be train robbers.
Flat-footed farce with a sense of strain evident from first to last shot.
w Frank Launder, Ivor Herbert d Frank Launder, Sidney Gilliat ph Ken Hodges m Malcolm Arnold
☆ Frankie Howerd, Dora Bryan, Reg Varney, Desmond Walter-Ellis, Raymond Huntley, Richard Wattis, George Benson, Eric Barker, Godfrey Winn, George Cole, Colin Gordon, Barbara Couper, Elspeth Duxbury

The Great Stone Face *

US   1968   93m   bw
Funnyman Productions
A very acceptable biography of Buster Keaton, with unusual emphasis on the very early films.
wd Vernon P. Becker

The Great Train Robbery: see *The First Great Train Robbery (1978)*

The Great Train Robbery ***

US   1903   10m   bw   silent
Edison
Bandits tie up a telegraph operator and rob a train, but are arrested.
In its day this was a real pioneer. It was among the longest films then made, it had the most complicated story line, it was the first Western and it used new technical tricks such as the pan and the close-up. Needless to say, it must now be viewed with sympathy.
wd Edwin S. Porter
☆ Marie Murray, Broncho Billy Anderson, George Barnes

'The grandest of love stories told to the tunes of the grandest musical score ever written!'
The Great Victor Herbert *

US   1939   91m   bw
Paramount (Andrew L. Stone)
At the turn of the century a famous composer plays cupid to two young singers.
Pleasant minor musical with excellent songs and an infectious cheerfulness.
w Russel Crouse, Robert Lively d Andrew L. Stone ph Victor Milner md Phil Boutelje, Arthur Lange
☆ Walter Connolly, Allan Jones, Mary Martin, Susanna Foster, Lee Bowman

'Elaborately produced, visually effective ... but audiences will learn from it very little about Victor Herbert.' – *Variety*
'Not highbrow, not lowbrow, but strictly on the beam for both mass and class audiences.' – *Motion Picture Herald*
♫ Phil Boutelje, Arthur Lange

'What do you do when the war is over and you're the second best pilot in the world?'
The Great Waldo Pepper *

👫👫   US   1975   108m   Technicolor   Todd-AO 35
Universal (George Roy Hill)
📼 ▦ ◉ ◉
In the twenties, a World War I flyer becomes an aerial stuntman.
Whimsical spectacular which concentrates less on the mystique of flying than on a series of splendid stunts.
w William Goldman d George Roy Hill ph Robert Surtees m Henry Mancini
☆ Robert Redford, Bo Svenson, Bo Brundin, Susan Sarandon, Geoffrey Lewis

'Charged with enthralling balletic precision.' – *Tom Milne*
'One hundred per cent pure plastic adolescent male fantasy.' – *New Yorker*

A Great Wall

US   1987   102m   colour
Mainline/W and S/Nanhai (Shirley Sun)
📼 ▦ ◉
A Chinese-American executive takes his family to visit China and the sister he has not seen for twenty years.
The first American film to be made in China since the revolution turns out to be a small and pleasant comedy of cultural misunderstandings.
w Peter Wang, Shirley Sun d Peter Wang
ph Peter Stein, Robert Primes m David Laing, Ge Ganru ad Wing Lee, Feng Yuan, Moing Ming Cheung ed Graham Weinbren
☆ Peter Wang, Sharon Iwai, Kelvin Han Yee, Li Qinqin, Hu Xiaoguang, Shen Guanglan

'Miliza Korjus – rhymes with gorgeous!'
The Great Waltz ***

US   1938   103m   bw
MGM (Bernard Hyman)
▦
Young Johann Strauss becomes Vienna's waltz king.
Exhilarating old-fashioned studio-set musical located in Hollywood's enduring vision of Old Vienna, assisted by streamlined production and excellent cast. Musical schmaltz.
w Walter Reisch, Samuel Hoffenstein
story Gottfried Reinhardt d Julien Duvivier
ph Joseph Ruttenberg m Dimitri Tiomkin
ed Tom Held
☆ Fernand Gravet, Luise Rainer, Miliza Korjus, Lionel Atwill, Hugh Herbert, Herman Bing, Curt Bois

'Should click nicely, but in these swingaroo days the waltz part may slow down anticipated b.o. enthusiasm.' – *Variety*
'A film to set the feet itching, and to make you want to grab a partner and join in.' – *Film Weekly*
♫ Joseph Ruttenberg
♫ Miliza Korjus; Tom Held

The Great Waltz *

US   1972   134m   Metrocolor   Panavision 70
MGM (Andrew L. Stone)
Heavy-going remake set on real locations and hampered by them, styled in the manner of the same director's *Song of Norway*, i.e. with no real style at all.
The music survives.
wd Andrew L. Stone ph David Boulton m the Strauss family, adapted by Robert Wright, Chet

---

Forrest ch Onna White ad William Albert
Havenmeyer ed Ernest Walter
☆ Horst Buchholz, Nigel Patrick, Mary Costa,
Rossano Brazzi, Yvonne Mitchell
'Take a box of chocolates – soft-centred, of
course.' – *Michael Billington, Illustrated London
News*

'He could beat any white man in the world. He just
couldn't beat all of them!'

The Great White Hope **
US 1970 103m DeLuxe Panavision
TCF (Lawrence Turman)
▤

In 1910, a black boxer becomes world heavyweight
champ but has trouble through his affair with a
white girl.
*Vivid, slightly whitewashed biopic of Jack Johnson
(called Jefferson). Dramatic deficiencies outweighed by
excellent period detail and a spellbinding central
performance.*
w Howard Sackler *play* Howard Sackler d Martin
Ritt ph Burnett Guffey md Lionel Newman
pd John DeCuir
☆ James Earl Jones, Jane Alexander, Lou Gilbert,
Joel Fluellen, Chester Morris, Robert Webber, Hal
Holbrook
♕ James Earl Jones; Jane Alexander

'If you can't find the perfect contender ... make one.'

The Great White Hype
US 1996 91m DeLuxe
TFC/Atman (Fred Berner, Joshua Donen)
▨▤

Worried about falling revenues for fights featuring
his black heavyweight champion, a fraudulent
promoter builds up an inept white boxer as a
leading contender.
*While boxing is certainly ripe for a hard-hitting exposé
of its behind-the-scenes machinations, this movie isn't
it, settling instead for some inoffensive comedy.*
w Tony Hendra, Ron Shelton d Reginald Hudlin
ph Ron Garcia m Marcus Miller pd Charles
Rosen ed Earl Watson
☆ Samuel L. Jackson, Jeff Goldblum, Peter Berg,
Jon Lovitz, Damon Wayans, Corbin Bernsen,
Cheech Marin, John Rhys-Davies, Salli
Richardson, Jamie Foxx
'Thin, uneven scripting and unfocused direction
create the impression of a TV sketch stretched
to feature length.' – *Godfrey Cheshire, Variety*

The Great Ziegfeld **
US 1936 179m bw
MGM (Hunt Stromberg)
▤ ◉

The growth and Broadway fame of impresario
Florenz Ziegfeld.
*Mammoth biopic which despite a few show-stopping
numbers never takes off dramatically and becomes
something of an endurance test; interesting, however,
as a spectacular of its time.*
w William Anthony McGuire d Robert Z.
Leonard ph Oliver T. Marsh, Ray June, George
Folsey, Karl Freund m/ly Irving Berlin, Walter
Donaldson, Harold Adamson md Arthur Lange
ch Seymour Felix ad Cedric Gibbons, Eddie
Imazu, Edwin B. Willis ed William S. Gray
cos Adrian
☆ William Powell, Luise Rainer, Myrna Loy,
Frank Morgan, Reginald Owen, Nat Pendleton,
Virginia Bruce, Ray Bolger, Harriet Hoctor, Ernest
Cossart, Fanny Brice, Robert Greig, Gilda Gray,
Leon Errol, Stanley Morner
'This huge inflated gas-blown object bobs into
the critical view as irrelevantly as an airship
advertising somebody's toothpaste at a south
coast resort. It lasts three hours. That is its only
claim to special attention.' – *Graham Greene*
'Everything should have been tightened – not in
the team job of cutting those miles of negative,
but in boiling down the script, saving a line
here, combining two scenes into one.' – *Otis
Ferguson*
♛ best picture; Luise Rainer; Seymour Felix
♕ William Anthony McGuire; Robert Z. Leonard;
art direction

The Greatest
US/GB 1977 101m Metrocolor
Columbia/EMI (John Marshall)
The life and times of Muhammed Ali.
*Bland confection of rags to riches in the boxing ring, its
only plus being that Ali plays himself and offers a
predictable array of enjoyable one-liners.*

w Ring Lardner Jnr book The Greatest by
Muhammed Ali d Tom Gries ph Harry Stradling
m Michael Masser
☆ Muhammad Ali, Ernest Borgnine, Roger E.
Mosley, Lloyd Haynes, Malachi Throne, John
Marley, Robert Duvall, David Huddleston, Ben
Johnson, James Earl Jones, Dina Merrill, Paul
Winfield

The Greatest Attack
France 1978 96m colour
Adel Productions/Films 21/Eota Films/Antenne 2
original title: *Le Toubib*
An introspective surgeon falls for a sickly nurse
during a European war in the 1980s.
Moodily self-indulgent melodrama.
w Pascal Jardin, Pierre Granier-Deferre
novel *Harmonie ou les horreurs de la guerre* by Jean
Freustie d Pierre Granier-Deferre ph Claude
Renoir m Phillipe Sarde ad Maurice Sargent
ed Jean Revel
☆ Alain Delon, Veronique Jannot, Bernard
Giraudeau, Bernard Le Coq, Catherine Lachens,
Francine Berge, Michel Auclair

The Greatest Show on Earth *
♟♟ US 1952 153m Technicolor
Paramount/Cecil B. de Mille (Henry Wilcoxon)
▨▤ ◉

Various dramas come to a head under the big top.
*Moribund circus drama with bad acting, stilted
production, an irrelevant train crash climax and a few
genuinely spectacular and enjoyable moments.*
w Fredric M. Frank, Theodore St John, Frank
Cavett, Barre Lyndon d Cecil B. de Mille
ph George Barnes, Peverell Marley, Wallace Kelley
m Victor Young ad Hal Pereira, Walter Tyler
ed Anne Bauchens
☆ Betty Hutton, Cornel Wilde, James Stewart,
Charlton Heston, Dorothy Lamour, Gloria
Grahame, Lyle Bettger, Henry Wilcoxon, Emmett
Kelly, Lawrence Tierney, John Kellogg, John
Ringling North
♛ best picture; original story (Fredric M. Frank,
Theodore St John, Frank Cavett)
♕ Cecil B. de Mille (as director); editing

The Greatest Story Ever Told **
US 1965 225m Technicolor Ultra
Panavision 70
UA/George Stevens
▨▤ ◉ ♫

Solemn spectacular with an elephantine pace, shot
in Utah because allegedly it looked more like
Palestine than Palestine did.
*All frightfully elegant and reverent, but totally
unmoving, partly because of the fatal casting of stars in
bit parts. (John Wayne looks in merely to say 'Truly
this man was the son of God.')*
w James Lee Barrett, George Stevens d George
Stevens ph William C. Mellor, Loyal Griggs
m Alfred Newman ad Richard Day, William Creber
☆ Max von Sydow, Dorothy McGuire, Claude
Rains, José Ferrer, David McCallum, Charlton
Heston, Sidney Poitier, Donald Pleasence, Roddy
McDowall, Gary Raymond, Carroll Baker, Pat
Boone, Van Heflin, Sal Mineo, Shelley Winters
and also Ed Wynn, John Wayne, Telly Savalas,
Angela Lansbury, Joseph Schildkraut, Victor
Buono, Nehemiah Persoff
'George Stevens was once described as a water
buffalo of film art. What this film more precisely
suggests is a dinosaur.' – *MFB*
'God is unlucky in The Greatest Story Ever Told.
His only begotten son turns out to be a bore ...
the photography is inspired mainly by Hallmark
Cards ... as the Hallelujah Chorus explodes
around us stereophonically and stereotypically it
becomes clear that Lazarus was not so much
raised from the tomb as blasted out of it. As for
pacing, the picture does not let you forget a
single second of its four hours.' – *John Simon*
'No more than three minutes have elapsed
before we suspect that Stevens' name and fame
have been purchased by the Hallmark Greeting
Card Company, and that what we are looking at
is really a lengthy catalogue of greeting cards for
1965 – for Those Who Care Enough to Send the
Very Best.' – *Stanley Kauffmann*
'Who but an audience of diplomats could sit
through this thing? As the picture ponderously
unrolled, it was mainly irritation that kept me
awake.' – *Shana Alexander, Life*
'If the subject-matter weren't sacred, we would
be responding to the picture in the most

charitable way by laughing at it from start to
finish.' – *Brendan Gill, New Yorker*
'A big windy bore.' – *Bruce Williamson, Playboy*
† The film was originally released at 4 hours 20
minutes. Subsequent versions were at 3 hours 58
minutes, 3 hours 17 minutes, 2 hours 27 minutes
and 2 hours 7 minutes.
♫ William C. Mellor, Loyal Griggs; Alfred
Newman

Greed ***
US 1924 110m bw silent
MGM/Goldwyn Company (Erich von Stroheim, Irving
Thalberg)
▨▤ ◉

An ex-miner dentist kills his avaricious wife. Later
in Death Valley he also kills her lover, but is bound
to him by handcuffs.
*This much-discussed film is often cited as its director's
greatest folly: the original version ran eight hours. Re-
edited by June Mathis, it retains considerable power
sequence by sequence, but is necessarily disjointed in
development. However, it must be seen to be
appreciated.*
wd Erich von Stroheim novel McTeague by Frank
Norris ph Ben Reynolds, William Daniels
ad Richard Day, Cedric Gibbons, Erich von
Stroheim ed Erich Von Stroheim, Rex Ingram,
June Mathis, Jos W. Farnham
☆ Gibson Gowland, ZaSu Pitts, Jean Hersholt,
Chester Conklin, Dale Fuller
'The end leaves one with an appalling sense of
human waste, of futility, of the drabness and
cruelty of lives stifled by genteel poverty. Every
character in the film is overwhelmed by it.' –
Gavin Lambert
'Von Stroheim is a genius – Greed established
that beyond all doubt – but he is badly in need
of a stopwatch.' – *Robert E. Sherwood*
'Nothing more morbid and senseless, from a
commercial picture standpoint, has been seen on
the screen for a long time ... Never has there
been a more out-and-out box-office flop.' –
Variety
† In 1972 Herman G. Weinberg published a
complete screenplay with 400 stills.
†† The original length at the première is said to
have been 420m.

The Greed of William Hart
GB 1948 78m bw
Bushey (Gilbert Church)
In old Edinburgh, grave robbers procure corpses for
an anatomist.
*Cheapie version of a much filmed subject. This
scenario was refurbished eleven years later by the same
writer as The Flesh and the Fiends; see also The
Body Snatcher, Burke and Hare.*
w John Gilling d Oswald Mitchell ph S. D.
Onions
☆ Tod Slaughter, Henry Oscar, Aubrey Woods,
Arnold Bell

Greedy *
US 1994 113m DeLuxe
Imagine
▨▤ ◉ ◎

A family waiting for their aged millionaire uncle to
die begins to worry when he hires an attractive
young nurse.
*A heartless black comedy that might have been funnier
had it been taken at a brisker pace; the compensations
include Kirk Douglas as the hard-hearted invalid.*
w Lowell Ganz, Babaloo Mandel d Jonathan
Lynn ph Gabriel Beristain m Randy Edelman
pd Victoria Paul ed Tony Lombardo
☆ Michael J. Fox, Kirk Douglas, Nancy Travis,
Olivia D'Abo, Bob Balaban, Ed Begley Jnr, Phil
Hartman, Jere Burns, Colleen Camp, Kevin
McCarthy, Austin Pendleton, Jonathan Lynn
'Nicely nasty farce succeeds by humiliating all its
characters.' – *Sight and Sound*
† The family is named McTeague, after the one in
Erich von Stroheim's Greed, while the plot owes a
debt to Charles Dickens's Martin Chuzzlewit.

The Greek Tycoon
US 1978 106m Technicolor Panavision
Universal/ABKCO (Allan Klein, Ely Landau)
▤

A billionaire shipping tycoon marries the widow of
an American president.
*Rather messy 'faction' based on Onassis and Jacqueline
Kennedy; entirely uninteresting save for glossy

backgrounds and the relentlessness with which the
characters swear at each other.*
w Mort Fine d J. Lee-Thompson ph Tony
Richmond m Stanley Myers pd Michael Stringer
☆ Anthony Quinn, Jacqueline Bisset, Raf
Vallone, Edward Albert, James Franciscus, Camilla
Sparv
† Among its other idiocies, this is the first film to
credit 'Assistant to the assistant to the Unit
Publicist'.

The Greeks Had a Word for Them *
US 1932 77m bw
UA/Samuel Goldwyn
Adventures of three New York gold diggers.
*Smart early talkie which helped launch the Gold
Diggers series and TCF's parallel Three Little
Mice/Moon over Miami/How to Marry a
Millionaire series.*
w Sidney Howard play Zoe Akins d Lowell
Sherman ph George Barnes m Alfred Newman
☆ Joan Blondell, Madge Evans, Ina Claire, David
Manners, Lowell Sherman, Phillips Smalley, Betty
Grable
'Grand rowdy comedy ... a revel in femme
clothes and a picture calculated to fascinate
women. Backwater clienteles questionable.' –
Variety

'Their badge of honour was a green beret, and it said
they had lived it all ... the night jumps, the
ambushes, the hand-to-hand combat, and the long
nights of terror they filled with courage!'

The Green Berets
US 1968 141m Technicolor Panavision
Warner/Batjac (Michael Wayne)
▨▤ ◉ ◎ ♫

After extensive training, two tough army
detachments see service in Vietnam.
*Overlong actioner criticized for unquestioningly
accepting the Vietnam cause; in itself, violent,
exhausting and dull.*
w James Lee Barrett novel Robin Moore d John
Wayne, Ray Kellogg ph Winton C. Hoch
m Miklos Rozsa
☆ John Wayne, David Janssen, Jim Hutton, Aldo
Ray, Raymond St Jacques, Jack Soo, Bruce Cabot,
Patrick Wayne, Irene Tsu, Jason Evers, Luke Askew
'Propaganda as crude as this can only do damage
to its cause.' – *David Wilson*
'A film best handled from a distance and with a
pair of tongs.' – *Penelope Gilliatt*

Green Card *
Australia/France 1990 108m Technicolor
Touchstone (Peter Weir)
▨▤ ◉ ♫

A Frenchman marries a New Yorker in order to
stay in the United States.
Amiable romantic tale of an odd couple.
wd Peter Weir ph Geoffrey Simpson m Hans
Zimmer pd Wendy Stites ad Christopher Nowak
ed William Anderson
☆ Gérard Depardieu, Andie MacDowell, Bebe
Neuwirth, Gregg Edelman, Robert Prosky, Jessie
Keosian, Ethan Phillips, Mary Louise Wilson, Lois
Smith, Conrad McLaren
♕ Peter Weir (as writer)

The Green Cockatoo
GB 1940 65m bw
TCF/New World (Robert T. Kane)
aka: *Four Dark Hours*
aka: *Race Gang*
A man seeks revenge on the gangsters who killed
his brother.
*Sleazy little Soho-set thriller, mainly remarkable for
cast and credits.*
w Edward O. Berkman, Arthur Wimperis
story Graham Greene d William Cameron
Menzies ph Osmond Borradaile m Miklos Rozsa
☆ John Mills, Robert Newton, Rene Ray, Bruce
Seton, Charles Oliver
† The film was made in 1937 but not shown for
three years.

◎ Digital Video Disc   ◉ Digital Video Disc   ♫ Soundtrack released   ☆ Cast in approximate   † Points of interest   ♫ Notable songs   ♛ Academy Award   ♕ Academy Award nomination   ♖ BAFTA
   Region 2   Region 1   on compact disc   order of importance

'A fiery girl dares the dangers of the sea and a strange land – fighting for the love of a bold adventurer!'

Green Dolphin Street

US   1947   141m   bw
MGM (Carey Wilson)
▤   ◎~

A Channel Islander emigrates to New Zealand and sends home for the wrong bride.

Silly 19th-century romance climaxed by rather a good earthquake. Expensively but falsely produced.

w Samson Raphaelson *novel* Elizabeth Goudge d Victor Saville ph George Folsey m Bronislau Kaper ed George White

☆ Lana Turner, Richard Hart, Edmund Gwenn, Van Heflin, Donna Reed

'The actors in this stupefyingly flimsy epic seem to be in competition for booby prizes.' – *Pauline Kael, 70s*

ß George Folsey; George White

Green Eyed Woman: see Take a Letter Darling

Green Fingers

GB   1946   83m   bw
British National (Louis H. Jackson)

An unqualified osteopath tries to achieve respectability.

Unsurprising and flatly made drama of eventual success against all odds.

w Jack Whittingham *novel* Persistent Warrior by Edith Arundel d John Harlow m Hans May

☆ Robert Beatty, Carol Raye, Nova Pilbeam, Felix Aylmer, Moore Marriott, Edward Rigby

Green Fire

US   1954   100m   Eastmancolor
Cinemascope
MGM (Armand Deutsch)

Two engineers disagree over their mining of Colombia emeralds.

Routine adventure story with good action highlights including landslide, flood and storm, all deadened by dull dialogue and romantic complications.

w Ivan Goff, Ben Roberts d Andrew Marton ph Paul Vogel m Miklos Rozsa

☆ Stewart Granger, Paul Douglas, Grace Kelly

Green for Danger ***

GB   1946   93m   bw
Rank/Individual (Frank Launder, Sidney Gilliat)
▤   ◎~

A mysterious murderer strikes on the operating table at a wartime emergency hospital.

Classic comedy-thriller, with serious detection balanced by excellent jokes and performances, also by moments of fright.

w Sidney Gilliat, Claud Guerney *novel* Christianna Brand d Sidney Gilliat ph Wilkie Cooper m William Alwyn pd Peter Proud ed Thelma Myers

☆ Alastair Sim, Sally Gray, Rosamund John, Trevor Howard, Leo Genn, Megs Jenkins, Judy Campbell, Ronald Ward, Moore Marriott

'Slick, witty and consistently entertaining.' – *Daily Telegraph*

'Launder and Gilliat have told an exciting story excitingly.' – *Times*

The Green Glove

US/France   1952   89m   bw
UA/Benagoss (George Maurer)
▤

A paratrooper against all odds returns a jewelled relic to its proper place in a French church.

An unsatisfactory concoction by people who have clearly seen The Maltese Falcon as well as lots of Hitchcock films, this interestingly cast and credited independent production never really takes off.

w Charles Bennett d Rudolph Maté ph Claude Renoir m Joseph Kosma

☆ Glenn Ford, Cedric Hardwicke, Geraldine Brooks, George Macready, Gaby André, Roger Treville

The Green Goddess *

US   1930   80m   bw
Warner

An Indian potentate holds Britishers prisoner.

Early talkie star vehicle which was also successful on the stage and as a silent but has little appeal now.

w Julien Josephson *play* William Archer d Alfred E. Green ph James Van Trees

☆ George Arliss, Alice Joyce, H. B. Warner, Ralph Forbes, David Tearle

'Nice programme fare, but it suggests too many synthetic thrillers that have gone before.' – *Variety*

† Remade 1942 as *Adventure in Iraq.*

ß George Arliss

Green Grass of Wyoming

↑↑ US   1948   88m   Technicolor
TCF

A rancher captures his runaway white stallion and wins the local trotting races.

Predictable, good-looking family film shot on location; a second sequel to My Friend Flicka.

w Martin Berkeley *novel* Mary O'Hara d Louis King ph Charles G. Clarke m Cyril Mockridge

☆ Peggy Cummins, Charles Coburn, Robert Arthur, Lloyd Nolan

ß Charles G. Clarke

Green Grow the Rushes

GB   1951   77m   bw
ACT Films (John Gossage)
▤

Civil servants discover that a Kentish village is devoted to smuggling.

Amiable but disappointingly feeble imitation of Ealing comedy by a company formed from the technicians' union; it simply hasn't got the right snap in any department.

w Derek Twist, Howard Clewes *novel* Howard Clewes d Derek Twist ph Harry Waxman m Lambert Williamson

☆ Roger Livesey, Richard Burton, Honor Blackman, Frederick Leister, John Salew, Colin Gordon, Geoffrey Keen, Harcourt Williams, Vida Hope

Green Hell *

US   1940   87m   bw
Universal (Harry Edington)

Explorers seek Inca treasure in the South American jungle.

Studio-bound potboiler unworthy of its director but mainly enjoyable as a romp.

w Frances Marion d James Whale ph Karl Freund

☆ Douglas Fairbanks Jnr, Joan Bennett, George Sanders, Vincent Price, Alan Hale, Gene Garrick, George Bancroft, John Howard

'It's the old nickelodeon mellerdrammer, at higher prices.' – *Picture Play*

'It was one of the funniest films ever shot anywhere in the world. About five of the worst pictures ever made are all in that picture.' – *Vincent Price*

† The temple set was re-used the same year in *The Mummy's Hand.*

The Green Helmet

GB   1961   88m   bw
MGM (Charles Francis Vetter)

A race driver with shattered nerves makes his last job the introduction of an American car of new design.

Totally conventional motor racing thriller. Most of the work could just as effectively have been phoned in.

w Jon Cleary *novel* Jon Cleary d Michael Forlong ph Geoffrey Faithfull m Ken Jones

☆ Bill Travers, Ed Begley, Sidney James, Nancy Walters, Ursula Jeans, Megs Jenkins

Green Ice

GB   1981   116m   colour
ITC/Lew Grade (Jack Wiener)
▤   ◎~

An aimless American in Mexico becomes involved with emerald thieves.

Dismally routine punch-ups and car chases are enlivened by a mildly original theft by balloon, but the overall effect is soporific.

w Edward Anhalt, Ray Hassett, Anthony Simmons, Robert de Laurentiis *novel* Gerald Browne d Ernest Day ph Gilbert Taylor m Bill Wyman

☆ Ryan O'Neal, Anne Archer, Omar Sharif, Philip Stone

'It should not tempt anyone away from doubtlessly superior versions of the same material on television.' – *Geoff Brown, MFB*

Green Light *

US   1935   85m   bw
Warner (Henry Blanke)

A dedicated doctor gives up his practice when a patient dies.

Adequate star melodrama.

w Milton Krims *novel* Lloyd C. Douglas d Frank Borzage ph Byron Haskin m Max Steiner

☆ Errol Flynn, Anita Louise, Margaret Lindsay, Cedric Hardwicke, Henry O'Neill, Spring Byington

'Customer lure in the title and the player names … it will carry a weak sister nicely.' – *Variety*

The Green Man *

GB   1956   80m   bw
BL/Grenadier (Frank Launder, Sidney Gilliat)
◉◉

A professional assassin stalks a pompous politician.

Cheerful but not very subtle black comedy, suffering from the attempt to make a star part out of a very minor character.

w Sidney Gilliat, Frank Launder *play* Meet a Body by Sidney Gilliat, Frank Launder d Robert Day ph Gerald Gibbs m Cedric Thorpe Davie

☆ Alastair Sim, George Cole, Jill Adams, Terry-Thomas, Avril Angers, John Chandos, Dora Bryan, Colin Gordon, Raymond Huntley

Green Mansions

US   1959   104m   Metrocolor   Cinemascope
MGM/Avon (Edmund Grainger)

In a remote Amazon forest an adventurer encounters Rima, a child of nature who takes him on a quest for truth.

Absurd studio-bound Shangri-La story based on an Edwardian fantasy that may well have suited the printed page, but not the wide screen. Dismally photographed in shades of green, with all concerned looking acutely uncomfortable.

w Dorothy Kingsley *novel* W. H. Hudson d Mel Ferrer ph Joseph Ruttenberg m Bronislau Kaper, Heitor Villa-Lobos

☆ Anthony Perkins, Audrey Hepburn, Lee J. Cobb, Henry Silva

'Paul Edgecomb did not believe in miracles...until he met one.'

The Green Mile **

US   1999   187m   Technicolor
Warner/Castle Rock (David Valdes, Frank Darabont)
◉◉   ▤   ◎~

A retired prison warden recalls how his life dealing with prisoners condemned to die in the electric chair was changed by a giant convict with mystical healing powers.

Immaculately done, well-acted fantasy of redemption, suffused with a sickly religiosity; it fails to justify its inordinate length.

wd Frank Darabont *novel* Stephen King ph David Tattersall m Thomas Newman pd Terence Marsh ed Richard Francis-Bruce

☆ Tom Hanks, David Morse, Bonnie Hunt, Michael Clarke Duncan, James Cromwell, Michael Jeter, Graham Greene, Doug Hutchison, Sam Rockwell, Barry Pepper, Jeffrey DeMunn, Harry Dean Stanton, Gary Sinise

'A well-populated drama with a relatively simple story, one that could have been told with more economy and fewer talky bits of business around the cellblock.' – *Janet Maslin, New York Times*

'If you can stand this three-hour-plus stretch of saccharine gibberish and patronising racial politics, you've got a stronger stomach than me.' – *Peter Bradshaw, Guardian*

† The film was a commercial success, taking more than 132m at the US box-office.

ß picture; Michael Clarke Duncan; Frank Darabont (as writer); sound (Robert J. Litt, Elliot Tyson, Michael Herbick, Willie D. Burton).

The Green Pastures ***

↑↑ US   1936   93m   bw
Warner (Henry Blanke)

Old Testament stories as seen through simple-minded negro eyes.

Though recently attacked as setting back the cause of black emancipation, this is a brilliantly sympathetic and humorous film, very cunningly adapted for the screen in a series of dramatic scenes which make the material work even better than it did on the stage.

w Marc Connelly *play* Marc Connelly stories Roark Bradford d William Keighley, Marc Connelly ph Hal Mohr m Erich Wolfgang Korngold

☆ Rex Ingram, Oscar Polk, Eddie Anderson, Frank Wilson, George Reed

'I imagine God has a sense of humour, and I imagine that He is delighted with The Green Pastures.' – *Don Herold*

'That disturbance around the Music Hall yesterday was the noise of shuffling queues in Sixth Avenue and the sound of motion picture critics dancing in the street.' – *Bosley Crowther, New York Times*

'This is as good a religious play as one is likely to get in this age from a practised New York writer.' – *Graham Greene*

Green Promise

US   1949   88m   bw
RKO/Glenn McCarthy (Robert Paige, Monty F. Collins)
▤

GB title: *Raging Waters*

A farmer refuses to move from the dust bowl area, and a landslide causes a flood.

Curiously stilted independent production which doesn't really bear comparison with The Grapes of Wrath.

w Monty F. Collins d William D. Russell ph John Russell m David Chudnow

☆ Marguerite Chapman, Walter Brennan, Robert Paige, Natalie Wood, Ted Donaldson, Connie Marshall

The Green Ray **

France   1986   98m   colour
Les Films du Losange (Margaret Menegoz)
◉◉

original title: *Le Rayon Vert*
aka: *Summer*

A lonely secretary goes on holiday alone and, after days of tedium, falls in love.

With its improvised dialogue and less than sympathetic heroine, the movie lacks the precision and interest of Rohmer's best work, even if the theme remains the same.

w Eric Rohmer, Marie Rivière d Eric Rohmer ph Sophie Maintigneux m Jean-Louis Valero ed Marie-Luisa Garcia

☆ Marie Rivière, Lisa Heredia, Béatrice Romand, Vincent Gautier, Eric Hamm, Rosette, Vanessa Leleu, Irene Skobline, Carita

The Green Scarf

GB   1954   96m   bw
B and A (Bertram Ostrer, Albert Fennell)

An elderly French lawyer takes on the defence of a blind, deaf and dumb murder suspect.

Plodding courtroom drama with familiar faces in unconvincing French guise.

w Gordon Wellesley *novel* The Brute by Guy des Cars d George More O'Ferrall ph Jack Hildyard m Brian Easdale

☆ Michael Redgrave, Ann Todd, Leo Genn, Kieron Moore

The Green Years *

↑↑ US   1946   127m   bw
MGM (Leon Gordon)

A young boy brought up strictly in Ireland makes friends with his mischievous grandfather.

Period family film in familiar style, sparked only by its scene-stealing star performance.

w Robert Ardrey, Sonya Levien *novel* A. J. Cronin d Victor Saville ph George Folsey m Herbert Stothart ad Cedric Gibbons, Hans Peters

☆ Charles Coburn, Dean Stockwell, Tom Drake, Beverly Tyler, Hume Cronyn, Gladys Cooper, Selena Royle, Jessica Tandy, Richard Haydn, Andy Clyde

'It has been described in the ads as "wonderful" by everyone within Louis B. Mayer's purchasing power except his horses, so I hesitate to ask you to take my word for it: the picture is awful.' – *James Agee*

ß George Folsey; Charles Coburn

The Greengage Summer *

GB   1961   99m   Technicolor
Columbia/PKL (Victor Saville, Edward Small)
US title: *Loss of Innocence*

A young girl staying at a hotel falls in love with a jewel thief but is accidentally responsible for his capture.

Old-fashioned and not very interesting story with an appeal, one supposes, to young well-brought-up young women. Decently made.

w Howard Koch *novel* Rumer Godden d Lewis Gilbert ph Frederick A. Young m Richard Addinsell

☆ Kenneth More, Danielle Darrieux, Susannah York, Claude Nollier, Jane Asher, Elizabeth Dear, Maurice Denham

---

Greenwich Village *

US 1944 82m Technicolor
TCF (William Le Baron)

In the twenties, a hick composer in New York allows his concerto to be used in a jazz musical.

Lightweight musical romp.

w Michael Fessier, Ernest Pagano d Walter Lang ph Leon Shamroy, Harry Jackson m/ly Leo Robin, Nacio Herb Brown

☆ Carmen Miranda, Don Ameche, William Bendix, Vivian Blaine, Felix Bressart, Tony and Sally de Marco, Adolph Green, Betty Comden, Alvin Hammer, Judy Holliday

Greetings *

US 1968 88m Eastmancolor
West End Films

A draftee tries every which way to be exempted, then subjects himself to a whirl of physical experience.

Kaleidoscopic stringing together of fleeting satirical bits; talent undeniable but equally uncontrolled.

w Charles Hirsch, Brian de Palma d Brian de Palma ed Brian de Palma

☆ Jonathan Warden, Robert DeNiro, Gerrit Graham, Megan McCormick

Gregorio

Peru 1985 95m colour
Grupo Chaski (Maria Barea)

The young son of a peasant farmer turns to crime in the big city.

The documentary-style work of a film collective, well-meaning but only intermittently interesting.

w Maria Barea, Fernando Espinoza, Stefan Kaspar, Alejandro Legaspi, Margreth Noth, Susi Pastor d Alejandro Legaspi m Arturo Ruiz del Pozo ad Rafael Hernandez ed Alejandro Legaspi, Stefan Kasper, Gaby Faura

☆ Marino Leon de La Torre, Vetzy Perez-Palma, Augusto Varillas, Manuel Acosta Ojeda, Rafael Hernandez

Gregory's Girl ***

GB 1980 91m colour
Lake/NFFC/STV (Davina Belling, Clive Parsons)

In a Scottish new town, a school footballer becomes aware of sex.

Curiously diverting comedy peopled by dreamers but handicapped by impenetrable accents. An unexpected world-wide success.

wd Bill Forsyth ph Michael Coulter m Colin Tully ad Adrienne Coulter ed John Gow

☆ Gordon John Sinclair (later John Gordon Sinclair), Dee Hepburn, Jake D'Arcy, Claire Grogan

♕ best script

Gregory's Two Girls

GB 1999 116m DeLuxe
FilmFour/SAC/NLF/Kinowelt/Young Lake (Christopher Young)

A left-wing English teacher at a Scottish school muddles through life, lusting after a schoolgirl and ignoring the maturer love offered by a colleague.

Disappointing sequel from a director who seems to have lost much of his interest in people; the narrative veers from an observant study of the life of a hapless teacher into an unlikely, ill-handled story of industrial espionage and illegal immigration.

wd Bill Forsyth ph John de Borman m Michael Gibbs pd Andy Harris ed John Gow

☆ John Gordon Sinclair, Carly McKinnon, Dougray Scott, Maria Doyle Kennedy, Kevin Anderson, Martin Schwab, Fiona Bell, Hugh McCue, John Murtagh, Matt Costello, Jane Stabler

'A perfect example of why well-loved nostalgia should never be updated.' – *Sarah Cohen, Heat*

Gremlins *

↟↟ US 1984 106m Technicolor
Warner/Amblin (Michael Finnell)

Small furry creatures called mogwais prove to be immensely prolific and dangerous when wet.

Juvenile horror comic, a kind of deliberate inversion of E.T. Slow to start, and a little too knowingly nasty, with variable special effects; but a pretty hot commercial success.

w Chris Columbus d Joe Dante ph John Hora m Jerry Goldsmith ed Tina Hirsch sp Gremlin designer: Chris Walas

☆ Zach Galligan, Phoebe Cates, Hoyt Axton, Polly Holliday, Keye Luke, Scott Brady, Edward Andrews

'Don't go if you still believe in Santa Claus.' – *Roger Ebert*

Gremlins 2: The New Batch **

↟↟ US 1990 105m Technicolor
Warner/Amblin (Michael Finnell)

A mogwai, captured by mad research scientists, produces hundreds of violent gremlins who run amuck in a megalomaniac property developer's skyscraper.

A sequel more entertaining than the original, stuffed with in-jokes for movie buffs.

w Charlie Haas d Joe Dante ph John Hora m Jerry Goldsmith pd James Spencer ad Joe Lucky ed Kent Beyda sp Gremlin and mogwai effects: Rick Baker

☆ Zach Galligan, Phoebe Cates

'An hilarious sequel featuring equal parts creature slapstick and satirical barbs for adults.' – *Variety*

The Grey Fox *

Canada 1982 91m Eastmancolor
Mercury (Peter O'Brian)

The more or less true story of a turn-of-the-century stagecoach bandit who in 1901 was released from a long prison term, genially committed more crimes, and disappeared.

Likeable semi-Western with an excellent sense of place and time.

w John Hunter d Phillip Borsos ph Frank Tidy m Michael Conway

☆ Richard Farnsworth, Jackie Burroughs, Ken Pogue, Wayne Robson

Greyfriars Bobby *

↟↟ GB 1961 91m Technicolor
Walt Disney (Hugh Attwooll)

A Skye terrier keeps persistent vigil over his master's grave and is made a freeman of the city of Edinburgh.

Adequately produced film of a charming old Victorian story.

w Robert Westerby book Eleanor Atkinson d Don Chaffey ph Paul Beeson m Francis Chagrin

☆ Donald Crisp, Laurence Naismith, Alexander Mackenzie, Kay Walsh, Andrew Cruickshank, Vincent Winter, Moultrie Kelsall, Duncan Macrae

'The better Disney qualities of exact period detail and childlike directness are apparent.' – *MFB*

† The story was previously filmed as *Challenge to Lassie*.

Greystoke: The Legend of Tarzan, Lord of the Apes

↟↟ GB 1984 130m Eastmancolor
Panavision
Warner/WEA Records (Hugh Hudson, Stanley S. Canter)

In the 1880s, an English lord and lady are killed in Africa, and their son is brought up by apes.

An absurd attempt to treat the story seriously after 70 years of hokum, this meandering chronicle, cut down from something much longer and even less endurable, has men in ape suits, an eye for unpleasant detail, and Ralph Richardson sliding down the stairs on a tray. The attempt to moralize at the end is emetic.

w P. H. Vazak (Robert Towne), Michael Austin novel Tarzan of the Apes by Edgar Rice Burroughs d Hugh Hudson ph John Alcott m John Scott pd Stuart Craig

☆ Ralph Richardson, Ian Holm, James Fox, Christopher Lambert, Andie MacDowell, Cheryl Campbell, Paul Geoffrey, John Wells, Nigel Davenport, Ian Charleson, John Griffiths

'A unique mixture of pomposity and ineptitude … in the second half the movie simply loses its mind, and dribbles to a pathetically indecisive conclusion.' – *Pauline Kael, New Yorker*

† Andie MacDowell's voice was dubbed by Glenn Close.

♕ Ralph Richardson (supporting actor); adapted screenplay

Gridlock'd *

US 1997 91m DeLuxe
Polygram/Interscope/DEF/Webster and Dragon (Damian Jones, Paul Webster, Erica Huggins)

After their singer suffers from an overdose, her two drug-addicted accompanists try to kick the habit.

Engaging streetwise narrative which depends for its moderate success on the interaction between its two leads.

wd Vondie Curtis-Hall ph Bill Pope m Stewart Copeland, The Angel pd Dan Bishop ed Charles Koefoed

☆ Tim Roth, Tupac Shakur, Thandie Newton, Charles Fleischer, Howard Hesseman, James Pickens Jnr, John Sayles

'There is the nagging feeling that the film has neither been quite as funny or as truly involving as it might have been.' – *Todd McCarthy, Variety*

Il Grido *

Italy 1957 102m bw
SPA Cinematografica/Robert Alexander
aka: The Cry

A man whose wife has left him travels across the Po Valley with his daughter in search of new happiness, but fails to find it and commits suicide.

Watchable but rather aimlessly depressing character drama.

w Michelangelo Antonioni, Elio Bartolini, Ennio de Concini d Michelangelo Antonioni ph Gianni di Venanzo m Giovanni Fusco

☆ Steve Cochran, Alida Valli, Dorian Gray, Betsy Blair, Lynn Shaw

Grief *

US 1993 87m colour
ICA/Grief (Ruth Charny, Yoram Mandel)

Romantic entanglements and power struggles during a week at a TV production company creating sensational drama set in a divorce court.

Enjoyable, often comic drama which begins as a gay soap opera and develops into an exploration of friendship.

wd Richard Glatzer ph David Dechant m Tom Judson pd Don Diers ed Robin Katz, William W. Williams

☆ Craig Chester, Jackie Beat, Illeana Douglas, Alexis Arquette, Carlton Wilborn, Shawn Hoffman, Lucy Gutteridge

'Isn't a dazzling debut technique-wise, but its drollery and genuine warmth are of another, perhaps deeper stripe. As "feel-good" sleepers go, this one is funny, smart and sweet.' – *Dennis Harvey, Variety*

La Grieta

Spain 1989 83m colour
Warner/Dister (Jose Escriva, Francesca de Laurentiis)

aka: The Rift

Submariners discover mutated monsters under the sea.

Feeble fantasy with poor special effects.

w J. P. Simon, Mark Klein d J. P. Simon ph Manuel Rojas m Joel Goldsmith pd Gonzalo Gonzalo ed Isaac Sehayek, Earl Watson

☆ Jack Scalia, R. Lee Ermey, Ray Wise, Deborah Adair, John Toles Bey, Ely Pouget, Emilio Linder, Tony Isbert, Alvaro Labra, Luis Lorenzo

'The characterisation is predictably shallow and the romantic interest distinctly soggy, while the model work and creature effects plumb new depths of ineptitude.' – *Nigel Floyd, MFB*

Grievous Bodily Harm *

Australia 1988 96m colour
International Film Management/Smiley/FGH (Richard Brennan)

A teacher goes on a killing spree in an attempt to discover the whereabouts of his missing wife, tracked by an unscrupulous journalist and a crooked cop.

Clever, slick thriller that maintains its momentum despite its shallow characterization.

w Warwick Hind d Mark Joffe ph Ellery Ryan m Chris Neal pd Roger Ford ed Marc Van Buren

☆ Colin Friels, John Waters, Bruno Lawrence, Shane Briant, Caz Lederman, Sandy Gore, Kerry Armstrong, Joy Bell

'Just another day of lying, cheating and stealing.'

The Grifters ***

US 1990 110m CFI color
Palace/Cineplex Odeon (Martin Scorsese, Robert Harris)

A mother, who is robbing her gangster boss, is reunited with her son and his girlfriend, both confidence tricksters.

Bleakly invigorating vision of the underside of the American dream.

w Donald Westlake novel Jim Thompson d Stephen Frears ph Oliver Stapleton m Elmer Bernstein pd Dennis Gassner ed Mick Audsley

☆ Anjelica Huston, John Cusack, Annette Bening, Pat Hingle, Henry Jones, Michael Laskin, Eddie Jones, J. T. Walsh, Charles Napier

'A brilliant, immensely seductive mix of Kammerspiel, film noir and naturalistic slice-of-life.' – *Tom Milne, MFB*

♕ Anjelica Huston; Stephen Frears; Annette Bening; Donald Westlake

Grim Prairie Tales *

US 1990 94m colour
East West Film Partners (Richard Hahn)

Two drifters, who meet by chance on the prairie, pass the night by telling each other stories.

A clever compendium movie, a mix of Western and atmospheric horror, which is stylish and imaginative enough to rise above its low-budget limitations, helped by strong performances from its two leads.

wd Wayne Coe ph Janusz Kaminski m Steve Dancz pd Anthony Zierhut ed Earl Ghaffari

☆ James Earl Jones, Brad Dourif, William Atherton, Lisa Eichhorn, Marc McClure, Scott Paulin, Will Hare, Michelle Joyner, Wendy Cooke

The Grim Reaper *

Italy 1962 100m bw
Cineriz/Compagnia/Cervi (Antonio Cervi)

original title: La Commare Secca

After a prostitute is found murdered in a park, a series of suspects account for their movements to the police.

Intermittently interesting drama of restricted lives, with an emotional impact that is dulled by its repetitious structure.

w Bernardo Bertolucci, Sergio Citti story Pier Paolo Pasolini d Bernardo Bertolucci ph Gianni Narzisi m Piero Piccioni ed Nino Baragli

☆ Francesco Ruiu, Giancarlo de Rosa, Vincenzo Ciccora, Alfredo Leggi, Gabriella Giorgelli, Marisa Solinas, Romano Labate, Alvaro D'Ercole

'At once a gritty documentary-style drama about life on the streets and a dewy-eyed evocation of adolescence, this ranks alongside its director's best work.' – *Sight and Sound*

The Grip of Fear: see Experiment in Terror

Grip of the Strangler *

GB 1958 78m bw
Producers' Associates (John Croydon)

US title: The Haunted Strangler

A novelist investigating an old murder case finds that he was himself the murderer.

Moderate thriller with a predictable but efficient plot.

w Jan Read d Robert Day ph Lionel Banes m Buxton Orr

☆ Boris Karloff, Elizabeth Allan, Jean Kent, Vera Day, Anthony Dawson

Grissly's Millions

US 1945 71m bw
Republic

An heiress is in danger from less successful relations.

Watchable co-feature.

w Muriel Roy Bolton d John English

☆ Paul Kelly, Virginia Grey, Don Douglas, Elisabeth Risdon, Robert Barrat, Clem Bevans

The Grissom Gang

US 1971 128m Metrocolor
Associates and Aldrich/ABC

In 1931, a New York heiress is kidnapped by gangsters and comes to like it.

Unpleasant remake of No Orchids for Miss Blandish (previously filmed under that title, incredibly badly, in GB in 1948), with too much footage of lush blonde

---

being slobbered over by psychotic thug, and an inevitable emphasis on violence.
w Leon Griffiths *novel* James Hadley Chase
d Robert Aldrich *ph* Joseph Biroc *m* Gerald Fried *ad* James Dowell Vance
☆ Scott Wilson, Kim Darby, Tony Musante, Robert Lansing, Irene Dailey, Connie Stevens, Wesley Addy
'Offensive, immoral and perhaps even lascivious.' – *Vincent Canby*

Gritos en la Noche: see *The Awful Dr Orloff*

'18 feet of towering fury! The most dangerous jaws on land!'
Grizzly
US   1976   91m   Movielab   Todd-AO 35
Film Ventures International (David Sheldon, Harvey Flaxman)

▦

aka: *Killer Grizzly*
A mammoth bear preys upon campers in a national park.
Inept and boring shocker in the wake of Jaws.
w Harvey Flaxman, David Sheldon d William Girdler *ph* William Asman *m* Robert O. Ragland
☆ Christopher George, Andrew Prine, Richard Jaeckel, Joan McCall

The Groom Wore Spurs
US   1951   81m   bw
Universal (Howard Welsch)
A supposed tough cowboy star gets into trouble in Las Vegas.
Tedious star comedy.
w Robert Carson *novel Legal Bride* by Robert Carson d Richard Whorf
☆ Ginger Rogers, Jack Carson, Joan Davis, Stanley Ridges, James Brown

Gross Anatomy
US   1989   107m   Technicolor
Touchstone/Silver Screen Partners IV (Howard Rosenman, Debra Hill)

▦   ▦   ◎

aka: *A Cut Above*
A fisherman's son, who becomes a medical student because he wants to be rich, discovers compassion and love in his first year.
A light romantic comedy that cannot encompass the darker moments it attempts, relying too heavily on the charm of its star to compensate for the conceited brat he plays.
w Ron Nyswaner, Mark Spragg *story* Mark Spragg, Howard Rosenman, Alan Jay Glueckman, Stanley Isaacs d Thom Eberhardt *ph* Steve Yaconelli *m* David Newman *pd* William F. Matthews *ed* Bud Smith, Scott Smith
☆ Matthew Modine, Daphne Zuniga, Christine Lahti, Todd Field, John Scott Clough, Alice Carter, Robert Desiderio, Zakes Mokae

'Even A Hit Man Deserves A Second Shot.'
Grosse Pointe Blank *
US   1997   108m   Technicolor
Buena Vista/Hollywood/Caravan/New Crime (Susan Arnold, Donna Arkoff Roth, Roger Birnbaum)

▦   ▦   ◎   ◉   ◯

A professional killer with work problems goes to his old school reunion.
Slick romantic comedy with added violence; it has a few amusing moments amid the bloodshed.
w Tom Jankiewicz, D. V. DeVincentis, Steve Pink, John Cusack d George Armitage *ph* Jamie Anderson *m* Joe Strummer *pd* Stephen Altman *ed* Brian Berdan
☆ John Cusack, Minnie Driver, Alan Arkin, Dan Aykroyd, Joan Cusack, Jeremy Piven, Hank Azaria, Barbara Harris, Mitchell Ryan
'Very enjoyable. It is also very insubstantial … Strategically, the film has been conceived as a vehicle to advance Cusack's career.' – *John Sutherland, TLS*

'Beneath the surface of respectability lies the shadow of our darker side.'
The Grotesque
GB   1996   98m   Technicolor
Starlight/Xingu (Trudie Styler)

▦   ▦   ◯

US title: *Gentlemen Don't Eat Poets*
US video title: *Grave Indiscretions*
In the late 40s, a new, devious butler and his alcoholic wife bring death and destruction to the household of an eccentric, aristocratic palaeontologist.
Limp social satire that never touches on any sort of reality, which may be why its cast resorts to mannered performances.
w Patrick McGrath, John-Paul Davidson *novel The Grotesque* by Patrick McGrath d John-Paul Davidson *ph* Andrew Dunn *m* Anne Dudley *pd* Jan Roelfs, Michael Seirton *ed* Tariq Anwar
☆ Alan Bates, Theresa Russell, Sting, Lena Headey, Jim Carter, Anna Massey, Trudie Styler, Maria Aitken, James Fleet, Steven Mackintosh, John Mills
'The genre props – thunderstorms, marshes, family retainers both *compos* and *non-compos mentis* – ensure that it's closer to a game of Cluedo than a genuinely engaging drama.' – *Adam Mars-Jones, Independent*
'This bizarre shambles of a film.' – *George Perry, Sunday Times*

Ground Zero *
Australia   1987   109m   Eastmancolor
Panavision
BDB/Pattinson-Burrowes

▦   ◎

A cinematographer stumbles on dangerous secrets when investigating his father's death 30 years previously.
Smart contemporary thriller with a political theme.
w Jan Sardi, Mac Gudgeon d Michael Pattinson, Bruce Myles
☆ Colin Friels, Jack Thompson, Donald Pleasence, Natalie Bate

'He's having the day of his life … over and over again.'
Groundhog Day ***
US   1993   101m   Technicolor   Panavision
Columbia TriStar/Columbia (Trevor Albert, Harold Ramis)

▦   ▦   ◎   ◉   ◯

A cynical weatherman, sent to cover an annual small-town Groundhog ceremony, finds himself reliving his day over and over again until he becomes a better person.
A 90s version of It's A Wonderful Life: *tougher, smarter, more knowing and successfully avoiding corn to provide an unexpectedly witty and warming comedy.*
w Danny Rubin, Harold Ramis d Harold Ramis *ph* John Bailey *m* George Fenton *pd* David Nichols *ed* Pembroke J. Herring
☆ Bill Murray, Andie MacDowell, Chris Elliott, Stephen Tobolowsky, Brian Doyle-Murray, Marita Geraghty, Angela Paton, Rick Ducommun
'A major studio Hollywood comedy that both delights and surprises.' – *Sight and Sound*
'Something of a comedy classic, and a film which, for sheer entertainment value, you'd be hard pushed to beat.' – *Empire*
𝖚 best original screenplay

Grounds for Marriage
US   1950   90m   bw
MGM (Samuel Marx)
A divorced couple meet again and find they have strange effects on each other.
Stolid romantic comedy with second team talent.
w Allen Rivkin, Laura Kerr *story* Samuel Marx d Robert Z. Leonard *ph* John Alton *m* Johnny Green
☆ Van Johnson, Kathryn Grayson, Paula Raymond, Lewis Stone, Reginald Owen, Barry Sullivan

'We challenge you to guess the ending!'
The Groundstar Conspiracy *
US   1972   96m   Technicolor   Panavision
Universal/Hal Roach International (Trevor Wallace)

▦

An explosion rips apart a top secret space project, and the surviving scientist loses his memory.
Gimmicky but generally compulsive sci-fi mystery yarn, with an effective though predictable climax.
w Matthew Howard *novel The Alien* by L. P. Davies d Lamont Johnson *ph* Michael Reed *m* Paul Hoffert
☆ George Peppard, Michael Sarrazin, James Olson, Christine Belford, Tim O'Connor, James McEachin

The Group ***
US   1966   152m   DeLuxe
UA/Famous Artists (Sidney Buchman)
The subsequent love lives of a group of girls who graduate from Vassar in 1933.
Patchy but generally fascinating series of interwoven sketches and character studies, with mainly tragic overtones; good attention to period detail, and dazzling array of new talent.
w Sidney Buchman *novel* Mary McCarthy d Sidney Lumet *m* Boris Kaufman *m* Charles Gross *pd* Gene Callahan
☆ Joanna Pettet, Candice Bergen, Jessica Walter, Joan Hackett, Elizabeth Hartman, Mary Robin-Redd, Kathleen Widdoes, Shirley Knight, Larry Hagman, Hal Holbrook, Robert Emhardt, Richard Mulligan, James Congdon, James Broderick
'Although it is a strange, inclusive, no-holds-barred movie that runs the gamut from scenes that are almost soap-operaish, to amusing scenes that are almost satire, to outrageously frank scenes that are almost voyeuristic, it is still greatly exhilarating while it provokes thought and pushes the viewer into examining his own conscience.' – *Philip T. Hartung, Commonweal*

Grumpier Old Men
US   1995   100m   Technicolor
Warner/John Davis/Lancaster Gate

▦   ▦   ◎   ◯

Two elderly rivals intensify their feud when an Italian widow and her daughter move into the neighbourhood.
A sequel that is a virtual rerun of the original movie, with Lemmon and Matthau showing surprising enthusiasm for the familiar material.
w Mark Steven Johnson d Howard Deutch *ph* Tak Fujimoto *m* Alan Silvestri *pd* Gary Frutkoff *ed* Billy Weber, Seth Flaum, Maryann Brandon
☆ Jack Lemmon, Walter Matthau, Ann-Margret, Sophia Loren, Kevin Pollak, Daryl Hannah, Burgess Meredith
'Lazily scripted and crude in every sense of the word, without the two wily leads it would be nothing. With them it's a double tonic.' – *Sight and Sound*
† The film was released direct to video in Britain.

Grumpy
US   1930   74m   bw
Paramount
A very elderly gentleman is still in control of his family.
Interesting but not exciting transcript of a production which was having surprising success on Broadway with English players, though a very musty vehicle even then.
w Doris Anderson *play* Horace Hodges, Thomas Wigney Percyval d George Cukor, Cyril Gardner
☆ Cyril Maude, Phillips Holmes, Paul Cavanagh, Frances Dade, Halliwell Hobbes, Paul Lukas
'Its box office fate is in the balance.' – *Variety*

Grumpy Old Men
US   1993   104m   Technicolor
Warner/Lancaster Gate (John Davis, Richard C. Berman)

▦   ▦   ◎   ◉

A long feud between two ageing neighbours is intensified when an attractive widow moves into the neighbourhood.
Mildy amusing comedy, providing an opportunity for Lemmon, Matthau and Meredith to do their party pieces, which they do as well as their somewhat thin material will allow.
w Mark Steven Johnson d Donald Petrie *ph* Johnny E. Jensen *m* Alan Silvestri *pd* David Chapman *ed* Bonnie Koehler
☆ Jack Lemmon, Walter Matthau, Ann-Margret, Burgess Meredith, Daryl Hannah, Kevin Pollak, Ossie Davis, Buck Henry, Christopher McDonald
'Light, reasonably pleasant and undoubtedly sappy holiday entertainment.' – *Variety*

Gruppo di Famiglia in un Interno: see
Conversation Piece

Guadalcanal Diary *
US   1943   93m   bw
TCF (Bryan Foy)
Marines fight for a vital Pacific base.
Standard war propaganda, with good action scenes.
w Lamar Trotti *book* Richard Tregaskis d Lewis Seiler *ph* Charles G. Clarke *m* David Buttolph
☆ Preston Foster, Lloyd Nolan, William Bendix, Richard Conte, Anthony Quinn, Richard Jaeckel, Roy Roberts, Minor Watson, Ralph Byrd, Lionel Stander, Miles Mander, Reed Hadley

'A Comedy About Life, Death, Cars And … Cuba!'
Guantanamera
Cuba/Spain/Germany   1995   102m   colour
Film Four/Tornasol/Alta/CAICICAA (Gerardo Herrero)
A bureaucrat gets the opportunity to test his scheme for transporting dead bodies around the island when his aunt dies.
Disappointing comedy of red tape and bungled chances, too tame to be effective.
w Eliseo Alberto Diego, Tomás Gutiérrez Alea, Juan Carlos Tabío d Tomás Gutiérrez Alea, Juan Carlos Tabío *ph* Hans Burmann *m* José Nieto *pd* Onelio Larralde *ed* Carmen Frias
☆ Carlos Cruz, Mirtha Ibarra, Jorge Perugorria, Raul Eguren, Pedro Fernández, Luis Alberto Garcia
'While the obscure humour takes time to weave its magic, this is a film to be cherished for its ingenious plot and its sheer mischievousness.' – *Empire*

'Tonight, while the world is asleep … an ancient evil is about to awaken.'
The Guardian
US   1990   93m   Technicolor
UIP/Universal (Joe Wizan)

▦   ▦   ◎

A nanny sacrifices her charges to a tree.
Ridiculous horror of no discernible interest.
w Stephen Volk, Dan Greenburg *novel The Nanny* by Dan Greenburg d William Friedkin *m* Jack Hues *pd* Gregg Fonseca *ed* Seth Flaum *sp* Phil Cory, Ray Svedin, Hans Metz
☆ Jenny Seagrove, Dwier Brown, Carey Lowell, Brad Hull, Miguel Ferrer, Natalia Nogulich, Pamela Brull, Gary Swanson
'An ill-conceived, simple-minded horror flick' – *Variety*

'The Mission: Protect The Former President's Wife. The Danger: The Former President's Wife.'
'A Comedy Beyond The Call Of Duty.'
Guarding Tess *
US   1994   96m   Technicolor
TriStar/Channel (Ned Tanen, Nancy Graham Tanen)

▦   ▦   ◎   ◉

A secret service agent engages in a battle of wills with a temperamental former First Lady.
Likeable comedy of conflicting personalities, played with a lightness and charm by its two leads; its later plunge into melodrama is a mistake.
w Hugh Wilson, Peter Torokvei d Hugh Wilson *ph* Brian Reynolds *m* Michael Convertino *pd* Peter Larkin *ed* Sidney Levin
☆ Shirley MacLaine, Nicolas Cage, Austin Pendleton, Edward Albert, James Rebhorn, Richard Griffiths, John Roselius, David Graf
'Comedy, pathos and thrills alternately collide, creating problems in both pacing and developing a consistent tone. Ultimately, its thinness works against it.' – *Leonard Klady, Variety*

The Guardsman *
US   1931   83m   bw
MGM (Albert Lewin)
A jealous actor tests his wife's fidelity.
Theatrically effective comedy filmed for the sake of its stars; later remade as a musical, The Chocolate Soldier (qv).
w Ernest Vajda, Claudine West *play* Ferenc Molnar d Sidney Franklin *ph* Norbert Brodine
☆ Alfred Lunt, Lynn Fontanne, Roland Young, ZaSu Pitts, Maude Eburne, Herman Bing, Ann Dvorak
'Looks like a smash engagement on Broadway and less than moderate returns on general release.' – *Variety*
⚖ Alfred Lunt; Lynn Fontanne

Guelwaar **
Senegal/France   1992   115m   colour
Domireew/Galatee/FR3 (Ousmane Sembène, Jacques Perrin)
A Catholic family discover when they come to bury their father that his corpse has disappeared and he has been given a Muslim funeral by mistake.

A comic and ironic tone pervades an engaging tale of bureaucratic bungling, chauvinism, parochial intransigence and civic and national corruption.
wd Ousmane Sembène ph Dominique Gentil m Baaba Mall pd François Laurent Sulva ed Marie-Aimée Debril
☆ Omar Seck, Ndiawar Diop, Mame Ndoumbe Diop, Isseu Niang, Thierno Niaye, Joseph Baloma Sane, Abou Camara, Samba Wane, Moustapha Diop
'One of the more accessible African films to emerge in the last couple of years.' – *Variety*
† Sample dialogue: Man to young widow, 'For you, I'll divorce my four wives.'

Les Guerisseurs
Ivory Coast/France   1988   90m   colour
Afriki Projection/Cote d'Ivoire Films/DEA/Alain Depardieu (Ayala Bakaba)
aka: *Aduefue, Lords of the Street*
In order to get money to finance his extravagant lifestyle, a black businessman plans a robbery with the aid of a French pimp.
A rambling, ill-constructed narrative on corruption, semi-satirical in tone and influenced for the worse by American action movies.
wd Sijiri Bakaba ph Mohammed Soudani m Serge Franklin ad Alama Kanate ed Olivier Morel
☆ Pierre Loup Rajot, Georges T. Benson, Nayanka Bell, Mory Traore, Sijiri Bakaba, Alpha Blondy, Salifou Keita

La Guerra di Troia: see *The Trojan War*

La Guerre Est Finie
France/Sweden   1966   122m   bw
Sofracima/Europa Film
⊡
aka: *The War Is Over*
A Spanish revolutionary maintains his ideals even though he is warned that he will be sold out.
Dreary drama with romantic interludes and a fussy technique involving what appears to be the first use of flashforwards.
w Jorge Semprun d Alain Resnais ph Sacha Vierny m Giovanni Fusco
☆ Yves Montand, Ingrid Thulin, Geneviève Bujold, Michel Piccoli
'The most sophisticated work Alain Resnais has yet provided us, perfecting his technique in dealing cinematically with the interrelation of time and place, and never before has he brought such lyricism to the harshness of everyday living or given such scope to the probing of the inner man – all this within the framework of a suspense thriller.' – *Judith Crist*
👤 Jorge Semprun

Guess Who's Coming to Dinner **
US   1967   112m   Technicolor
Columbia/Stanley Kramer
⊡ ▤ ⌕ ◉
A well-to-do San Francisco girl announces that she is going to marry a black man, and her parents find they are less broad-minded than they thought.
The problem picture that isn't really, since everyone is so nice and the prospective bridegroom is so eligible. It looks like a photographed play, but isn't based on one; the set is unconvincing; but the acting is a dream.
w William Rose d Stanley Kramer ph Sam Leavitt md Frank de Vol pd Robert Clatworthy
☆ Spencer Tracy, Katharine Hepburn, Katharine Houghton, Sidney Poitier, Cecil Kellaway, Roy E. Glenn Snr, Beah Richards, Isabel Sanford, Virginia Christine
'Suddenly everybody's caught up in a kind of integrated drawing-room comedy, and unable to decide whether there's anything funny in it or not.' – *Ann Birstein, Vogue*
'A load of embarrassing rubbish. In the circumstances there is little that director Stanley Kramer can do but see that his camera plod from room to room and make the most of people sitting down and getting up again.' – *Penelope Mortimer*
'What Rose and Kramer have done is to create a number of elaborate Aunt Sallies, arrange them in attractive patterns, and dispose of them with the flick of a feather.' – *Basil Wright, 1972*
'Mendacious and sanctimonious drivel.' – *John Simon*
† Katharine Houghton is the niece of Katharine Hepburn.
👤 William Rose; Katharine Hepburn

best picture; Stanley Kramer; Frank de Vol; Spencer Tracy; Cecil Kellaway; Beah Richards
🏆 Spencer Tracy; Katharine Hepburn

The Guest: see *The Caretaker*

Guest House Paradiso
GB   1999   89m   colour
UIP/Universal (Phil McIntyre)
Two manic, light-fingered sadists run a seedy boarding house near a nuclear power station.
Gross and excessively aggressive comedy, mainly concerned with vomit and violent assaults on the more delicate parts of the human anatomy; banging your head hard against a brick wall would be considerably more entertaining, and would also capture the spirit of the movie.
w Adrian Edmondson, Rik Mayall d Adrian Edmondson ph Alan Almond m Colin Towns pd Tom Brown ed Sean Barton
☆ Rik Mayall, Adrian Edmondson, Vincent Cassel, Hélène Mahieu, Bill Nighy, Simon Pegg, Fenella Fielding, Lisa Palfrey, Kate Ashfield, Steve O'Donnell
'Years of barrel-scraping could not produce a film more hackneyed and lacklustre than this celluloid toilet paper.' – *James Christopher, Times*
'Horrifyingly unfunny, it is naff, smug, cynical, ugly and charmless.' – *Peter Bradshaw, Guardian*

Guest in the House *
US   1944   121m   bw
Hunt Stromberg
A seemingly pleasant young woman is invited to stay with a family and brings tragedy and hatred to them.
Theatrical and rather unconvincing melodrama.
w Ketti Frings play *Dear Evelyn* by Dale Eunson, Hagar Wilde d John Brahm ph Lee Garmes m Werner Janssen pd Nicolai Remisoff
☆ Anne Baxter, Ralph Bellamy, Aline MacMahon, Ruth Warrick, Scott McKay, Jerome Cowan, Marie McDonald, Percy Kilbride, Margaret Hamilton
👤 Werner Janssen

Guest Wife
US   1945   90m   bw
UA/Greentree (Jack H. Skirball)
▤ ⌕
For business purposes a man allows his wife to pretend to be the wife of another.
Stereotyped star farce which seemed tolerable at the time.
w Bruce Manning, John Klorer d Sam Wood ph Joseph Valentine md Daniele Amfitheatrof
☆ Claudette Colbert, Don Ameche, Dick Foran, Charles Dingle, Grant Mitchell
'Mr Wood is a big gun to be trained on so trivial a target, but the result justifies the choice.' – *Richard Mallett, Punch*
👤 Daniele Amfitheatrof

'For the married man who's thinking single – or the single man who's just thinking!'

A Guide for the Married Man **
US   1967   91m   DeLuxe   Panavision
TCF (Frank McCarthy)
▤
A practised wolf explains to a perfect husband how to be unfaithful.
Generally funny revue with as many hilarious moments as flat spots.
w Frank Tarloff m Gene Kelly ph Joe Macdonald m Johnny Williams
☆ Walter Matthau, Inger Stevens, *Robert Morse*, Sue Ane Langdon, Lucille Ball, Art Carney, Jack Benny, Polly Bergen, Joey Bishop, Sid Caesar, Wally Cox, Jayne Mansfield, Carl Reiner, Phil Silvers, Jeffrey Hunter and also Terry-Thomas, Ben Blue
'One of the funniest films of the last several seasons … it has sense enough to sit down when it's through.' – *Robert Windeler*

Guilt Is My Shadow
GB   1950   86m   bw
ABPC (Ivan Foxwell)
A girl kills her villainous husband and is helped by a farmer.
Tedious melodrama, stiffly told and not helped by rural surroundings.

w Ivan Foxwell, Roy Kellino, John Gilling novel *You're Best Alone* by Peter Curtis d Roy Kellino
☆ Patrick Holt, Elizabeth Sellars, Peter Reynolds, Lana Morris, Avice Landone

The Guilt of Janet Ames *
US   1947   83m   bw
Columbia
A paralysed war widow seeks to discover whether her husband's sacrifice was worthwhile.
Embarrassing attempt by a comedienne to play Hamlet.
w Louella Macfarlane, Allen Rivkin, Devery Freeman story Lenore Coffee d Henry Levin ph Joseph Walker m Morris Stoloff
☆ Rosalind Russell, Melvyn Douglas, Sid Caesar, Betsy Blair, Nina Foch, Harry von Zell, Arthur Space
'If you're willing to swallow the hypnotic idea, the substance of the film is lively and entertaining, and includes a gem of a cabaret turn by Sid Caesar.' – *Fred Majdalany, Daily Mail*

Guilty?
GB   1956   93m   bw
Grand National/Gibraltar (Charles A. Leeds)
An ex-resistance heroine is on trial for murder at the Old Bailey; her young solicitor goes to Avignon to prove her innocence.
Solidly cast old-fashioned mystery with a courtroom climax.
w Maurice J. Wilson novel *Death Has Deep Roots* by Michael Gilbert d Edmond Greville ph Stan Pavey m Bruce Montgomery
☆ John Justin, Barbara Laage, Donald Wolfit, Stephen Murray, Norman Wooland, Frank Villard, Sydney Tafler, Betty Stockfeld

Guilty as Charged
US   1991   95m   Foto-Kem
Copeland/Colichman (Randolph Gale)
▤
A mad tycoon turned vigilante sets up his own electric chair to execute murderers who escape the law.
Over-the-top performances help distract attention from the predictable events.
w Charles Gale d Sam Irvin ph Richard Michalak m Steve Bartek pd Byrnadette DiSanto ed Kevin Tent
☆ Rod Steiger, Lauren Hutton, Heather Graham, Lyman Ward, Isaac Hayes, Zelda Rubinstein, Irwin Keyes, Michael Beach

Guilty as Hell *
US   1932   82m   bw
Paramount
A doctor commits what he hopes is the perfect murder.
Smart murder story with two points of interest: the audience knows who done it from the start, and the detective and reporter roles are worked over to fit the actors who played Flagg and Quirt. It certainly pleased at the time.
w Arthur Kober, Frank Partos play *Riddle Me This* by Daniel Rubin d Erle C. Kenton
☆ Edmund Lowe, Victor McLaglen, Richard Arlen, Ralph Ince, Adrienne Ames, Henry Stephenson, Elizabeth Patterson
'Excellent entertainment and should do a good business where the title does not hurt.' – *Variety*
† It was remade in 1937 as *Night Club Scandal*, with John Barrymore in the lead as the doctor.

Guilty as Sin
US   1993   107m   Technicolor
Buena Vista/Hollywood (Martin Ransohoff)
⊡ ▤ ⌕ ◉ ◉
An ambitious lawyer agrees to defend a man accused of murdering his wife and discovers that he is a serial killer.
Elegant but empty thriller, taken at too easy a tempo to create any suspense or tension.
w Larry Cohen d Sidney Lumet ph Andrzej Bartkowiak m Howard Shore pd Philip Rosenberg ed Evan Lottman
☆ Rebecca DeMornay, Don Johnson, Stephen Lang, Jack Warden, Dana Ivey, Ron White
'This has the empty, varnished vacuity of any old American TV movie, masquerading as one of those lesser Hitchcock courtroom sagas. The director is Sidney Lumet. I have absolutely no idea why he dunnit.' – *Derek Malcolm, Guardian*

'All it took was a whisper.'

Guilty by Suspicion *
US   1990   105m   DeLuxe
Warner (Arnon Milchan)
⊡ ▤ ⌕ ◉
In the 1950s, a successful film director finds himself without work after refusing to co-operate with the House Un-American Activities Committee investigating 'communist subversion' in Hollywood.
A weak, if well-meaning, attempt to deal with the period of blacklisting in Hollywood, but one that comes close to ignoring the complicity of the majority of studios in HUAC's activities. Martin Scorsese makes a brief appearance playing Joe Lesser, a director based on Joseph Losey, who fled to Europe to avoid testifying to the committee.
wd Irwin Winkler ph Michael Ballhaus m James Newton Howard pd Leslie Dilley ed Priscilla Nedd
☆ Robert DeNiro, Annette Bening, George Wendt, Patricia Wettig, Sam Wanamaker
'Once again, a producer has confused earnestness with seriousness, and felt that displaying good intentions could serve as a substitute for the low cunning of entertainment.' – *Sight and Sound*

Guilty Hands
US   1931   60m   bw
MGM
A district attorney commits murder and tries to frame a girl, but is killed when rigor mortis makes the gun go off in his victim's hand.
Risible melodrama which might with better writing have been effective.
w Bayard Veiller d W. S. Van Dyke
☆ Lionel Barrymore, Kay Francis, Madge Evans, William Bakewell, C. Aubrey Smith, Polly Moran, Alan Mowbray
'Someone missed here, and plenty.' – *Variety*

Guilty of Treason
US   1950   86m   bw
Eagle Lion
GB title: *Treason*
An account of the trial by the Russians of the Hungarian primate Cardinal Mindzenty.
Gutter press version of real events, with cheap production and fictional frills.
w Emmet Lavery d Felix Feist
☆ Charles Bickford, Paul Kelly, Bonita Granville, Richard Derr, Berry Kroeger, Elisabeth Risdon

The Guinea Pig **
GB   1948   97m   bw
Pilgrim (John Boulting)
⊡
US title: *The Outsider*
The first poor boy to win a scholarship to a famous public school has a hard time.
Enjoyable though unrealistic school drama with chief interest centring on the staff. A rude word ('kick up the arse') ensured its popularity.
w Bernard Miles, Warren Chetham Strode play Warren Chetham Strode d Roy Boulting ph Gilbert Taylor m John Wooldridge
☆ Richard Attenborough, *Robert Flemyng*, Cecil Trouncer, Sheila Sim, Bernard Miles, Joan Hickson

Guling Jie Shaonian Sha Ren Shijian: see *A Brighter Summer Day*

Gulliver's Travels **
👥 US   1939   74m   Technicolor
Paramount/Max Fleischer
▤ ⌕
Animated cartoon version which invents a Romeo-Juliet romance between Lilliput and Blefuscu and has the usual trouble with romantic humans.
At the time it represented a genuine challenge to Disney, but has not worn well in terms of pace or inventiveness. Fleischer made one more feature cartoon, Mr Bug Goes to Town.
d Dave Fleischer m Victor Young m/ly Ralph Rainger, Leo Robin
☆ Featuring the voices of Lanny Ross, Jessica Dragonette
'Effective entertainment, but may not reach the grosses of Snow White.' – *Variety*
🎵 song 'Faithful Forever'; Victor Young

Gulliver's Travels
ᛁᛁ   GB   1976   81m   Eastmancolor
EMI/Valeness-Belvision (Josef Shaftel)

An ineffective treatment, again aimed at children, in which Gulliver is the only human element and all the Lilliputians are cartooned.

w Don Black d Peter Hunt ph Alan Hume
m Michel Legrand pd Michael Stringer
☆ Richard Harris, Catherine Schell, Norman Shelley

'Bonelessly inoffensive.' – Sight and Sound

The Gumball Rally
ᛁᛁ   US   1976   107m   Technicolor
Warner/First Artists (Chuck Bail)
▤

A variety of vehicles take part in a crazy race from New York to Long Beach.
The stuntmen are the real stars of this good-looking but dramatically deficient chase and destruction extravaganza.

w Leon Capetanos d Chuck Bail ph Richard Glouner m Dominic Frontière stunt coordinator Eddie Donno
☆ Michael Sarrazin, Norman Burton, Gary Busey, John Durren, Susan Flannery

Gummo
US   1997   88m   DeLuxe
Entertainment/Fine Line (Cary Woods)
▥▤ ▤ ▦

Unhappy adolescents search for ways of passing the time in a dull Ohio town devastated by a tornado.
Deliberately haphazard account of fractured lives which seems intended as a freak show for idle minds.

wd Harmony Korine ph Jean Yves Escoffier
pd Dave Doernberg ed Christopher Tellefsen
☆ Jacob Reynolds, Nick Sutton, Jacob Sewell, Darby Dougherty, Chloe Sevigny, Carisa Bara, Linda Manz, Max Perlich

'A puzzlingly idiosyncratic, and not entirely effective, feature.' – Variety
'On one level Gummo represents a high watermark of 90s White Trash Chic, on another its resurrection and flagrant deforming of the neo-realist impulse harbours a longing to invent a Cinema of Abjection.' – Gavin Smith, Sight and Sound

Gumshoe **
GB   1971   85m   Eastmancolor
Columbia/Memorial (David Barber)
▥▤ ▤

A Liverpool bingo caller dreams of becoming a Bogart-like private eye and finds himself in the middle of a murder case.
A likeable spoof which is never quite as funny as it means to be. Billy Liar did it better, but there's plenty of amusing detail.

w Neville Smith d Stephen Frears ph Chris Menges m Andrew Lloyd Webber
☆ Albert Finney, Billie Whitelaw, Fulton Mackay, Frank Finlay, Janice Rule

Gun Crazy *
US   1949   87m   bw
King Brothers/Universal-International
▤

reissue title: Deadly Is the Female

A boy and girl set off on a trail of armed robbery and murder.
Modernized Bonnie and Clyde story which has become a minor cult film.

w Dalton Trumbo story Mackinlay Kantor
d Joseph H. Lewis ph Russell Harlan m Victor Young
☆ John Dall, Peggy Cummins, Morris Carnovsky, Berry Kroeger, Annabel Shaw, Harry Lewis, Russ Tamblyn

Gun for a Coward
US   1956   88m   Technicolor   Cinemascope
U-I (William Campbell)

Three brothers join forces on a cattle drive, but one is killed.
Slightly pretentious Western co-feature.

w R. Wright Campbell d Abner Biberman
ph George Robinson
☆ Fred MacMurray, Jeffrey Hunter, Dean Stockwell, Chill Wills, Janice Rule

Gun Fury
US   1953   80m   Technicolor   3-D
Columbia (Lewis J. Rachmil)
▤ ▦

Outlaws rob a stagecoach and abduct a girl; her fiancé follows and takes revenge.
Adequate Western programmer.

w Irving Wallace, Roy Huggins novel Ten Against Caesar by Kathleen, George and Robert Granger d Raoul Walsh ph Lester H. White md Mischa Bakaleinikoff
☆ Rock Hudson, Donna Reed, Phil Carey, Lee Marvin, Neville Brand

Gun Glory
US   1957   89m   Metrocolor   Cinemascope
MGM (Nicholas Nayfack)

A gunfighter returns home to settle down, but finds his wife dead and his son resentful.
Dull, unexciting star Western.

w William Ludwig novel Man of the West by Philip Yordan d Roy Rowland ph Harold J. Marzorati m Jeff Alexander
☆ Stewart Granger, Rhonda Fleming, Chill Wills, Steve Rowland, James Gregory

'She Was Nobody Until Somebody Found…'

The Gun in Betty Lou's Handbag
US   1992   89m   Technicolor
Buena Vista/Touchstone/Interscope/Nomura Babcock & Brown (Scott Kroopf)
▥▤ ▤ ▦

An unassertive librarian, tired of being ignored by everyone, confesses to a murder she did not commit.
Drear and dim-witted comedy, short on laughs, long on longueurs and with a few moments of unpleasant violence to ensure its failure as entertainment.

w Grace Cary Bickley d Allan Moyle ph Charles Minsky m Richard Gibbs pd Michael Corenblith ed Janice Hampton, Erica Huggins
☆ Penelope Ann Miller, Eric Thal, William Forsythe, Cathy Moriarty, Julianne Moore, Alfre Woodard

'Figures to fire a blank into the box-office till' – Variety

The Gun Runner: see Santiago

The Gun Runners *
US   1958   82m   bw
UA/Seven Arts (Clarence Greene)

The owner of a Florida motor cruiser innocently rents it to a gun merchant.
Modestly effective action melodrama, the third version of To Have and Have Not (qv).

w Daniel Mainwaring, Paul Monash d Don Siegel ph Hal Mohr m Leith Stevens
☆ Audie Murphy, Eddie Albert, Patricia Owens, Everett Sloane

Gun Smoke
US   1931   64m   bw
Paramount

Cowboys defeat a gang of big city crooks who plan to ransack a small town.
Odd little western, in which the crooks are defined as 'capitalists', modernity is mocked, and the good guys are even more ruthless than the gangsters, arguing that 'the only thing to do with killers is to kill 'em.'

w Grover Jones, William McNutt d Edward Sloman ph Archie Stout
☆ Richard Arlen, Mary Brian, Eugene Pallette, Louise Fazenda, Charles Winninger, Guy Oliver, James Durkin, Brooks Benedict, William 'Stage' Boyd, J. Carrol Naish

Gunbus
aka: Sky Bandits

Guncrazy
US   1992   93m   Foto-Kem
Zeta/First Look (Zane W. Levitt, Diane Firestone)
▥▤ ▤ ▦

A parentless 16-year-old marries a paroled murderer and the two take to the road, robbing and killing as they go.
An uninvolving thriller set in a depressed and depressing red-neck community; it may interest for the light it sheds on the darker edges of American society, but it is hardly entertaining.

w Matthew Bright d Tamra Davis ph Lisa Rinzler m Ed Tomney ed Kevin Tent

☆ Drew Barrymore, James LeGros, Billy Drago, Rodney Harvey, Joe Dallesandro, Michael Ironside, Ione Skye

'A shoot-'em-up exploitationer with a few interesting ideas … settles into a surprisingly somber mood that suppresses the possibilities latent in the story and actors.' – Variety

Guney's The Wall: see The Wall

'In the bullring at Bajo Rio, Mexico, on Saturday at 4 pm, they'll pay to see two men kill each other!'

A Gunfight *
US   1970   94m   Technicolor
Harvest/Thoroughbred/Bryna (Ronnie Lubin, Harold Jack Bloom)
▤

Two famous gunfighters on their uppers stage a duel for money.
Austere and anti-climactic Western supposedly against popular blood lust.

w Harold Jack Bloom d Lamont Johnson
ph David M. Walsh m Laurence Rosenthal
☆ Kirk Douglas, Johnny Cash, Karen Black, Raf Vallone, Jane Alexander

Gunfight at Comanche Creek
US   1963   90m   DeLuxe   Panavision
Allied Artists (Ben Schwalb)

In 1875 a detective goes undercover to unmask the brains behind a robber gang with complex methods.
Ingenious but over-emphatic Western programmer.

w Edward Bernds d Frank McDonald ph Joseph Biroc m Marlin Skiles ad Edward Jewell ed William Austin
☆ Audie Murphy, Ben Cooper, Colleen Miller, John Hubbard, DeForest Kelley
† It was a remake of Last of the Badmen (qv).

Gunfight at Dodge City
US   1958   81m   DeLuxe   Cinemascope
UA/Mirisch

After various problems, Bat Masterson is elected sheriff of Dodge City.
Fair standard Western with emphasis on plot and character.

w Daniel B. Ullman, Martin M. Goldsmith
d Joseph M. Newman ph Carl Guthrie m Hans Salter
☆ Joel McCrea, Julie Adams, John McIntire, Richard Anderson, Nancy Gates

Gunfight at the OK Corral **
US   1957   122m   Technicolor   Vistavision
Paramount/Hal Wallis
▥▤ ▤ ▦

Wyatt Earp and Doc Holliday defeat the Clanton gang.
Watchable, ambitious, but vaguely disappointing super-Western.

w Leon Uris d John Sturges ph Charles B. Lang m Dimitri Tiomkin
☆ Burt Lancaster, Kirk Douglas, Jo Van Fleet, Rhonda Fleming, John Ireland, Frank Faylen, Kenneth Tobey, Earl Holliman

'Carefully and lavishly mounted, but overlong and overwrought.' – John Cutts
† The legendary gunfight was tackled again in the 1994 Western Tombstone (qv).

Gunfight in Abilene
US   1967   86m   Technicolor
Universal

After the Civil War, an officer goes home to find strife between farmers and cattlemen.
Fairly sensible and pleasing lower-berth Western.

w Berne Giler, John D. F. Black d William Hale
☆ Bobby Darin, Emily Banks, Leslie Nielsen, Donnelly Rhodes, Don Galloway, Michael Sarrazin

'His only friend was his gun – his only refuge, a woman's heart!'

The Gunfighter **
US   1950   84m   bw
TCF (Nunnally Johnson)
▥▤ ▤ ▦

A gunfighter fails to shake off his past.
Downbeat, small-scale but very careful adult Western set in a believable community.

w William Bowers, William Sellers d Henry King ph Arthur Miller m Alfred Newman

☆ Gregory Peck, Helen Westcott, Millard Mitchell, Jean Parker, Karl Malden, Skip Homeier, Mae Marsh

'Preserves throughout a respectable level of intelligence and invention.' – Lindsay Anderson
'Not merely a good western, a good film.' – Richard Mallett, Punch
'The movie is done in cold, quiet tones of gray, and every object in it – faces, clothing, a table, the hero's heavy moustache – is given an air of uncompromising authenticity, suggesting those dim photographs of the nineteenth-century west…' – Robert Warshow, The Immediate Experience
β original story (William Bowers, André de Toth)

Gunfighters
US   1947   87m   Cinecolor
Columbia
GB title: The Assassin

A retired gunfighter is suspected of the murder of his best friend.
Presentable star Western.

w Alan Le May novel Twin Sombreros by Zane Grey d George Waggner
☆ Randolph Scott, Barbara Britton, Dorothy Hart, Bruce Cabot, Forrest Tucker

Gunfire: see China 9, Liberty 37

Gung Ho!
US   1943   88m   bw
Universal/Walter Wanger

Adventures of the Marines in the Pacific War.
Trite flagwaver, popular at the time.

w Lucien Hubbard, based on the experiences of Captain W. S. LeFrançois USMC d Ray Enright ph Milton H. Krasner m Frank Skinner, Hans Salter
☆ Randolph Scott, Grace MacDonald, Alan Curtis, Noah Beery Jnr, J. Carrol Naish, David Bruce, Peter Coe, Robert Mitchum

Gung Ho
US   1986   111m   Technicolor   Panavision
Paramount (Tony Ganz, Deborah Blum)
▤ ▦

Japanese management takes over an American small town.
Basically old-fashioned hands-across-the-sea stuff, without any very clear attitude except gentle fun. It rapidly led to a TV series, which folded, and that's about its level.

w Lowell Ganz, Babaloo Mandel d Ron Howard ph Don Peterman m Thomas Newman pd James Schoppe ed Daniel Hanley, Michael Hill
☆ Michael Keaton, Gedde Watanabe, George Wendt, Mimi Rogers, John Turturro

'A film that's not much of anything except two hours long.' – People

'Thrills for a thousand movies plundered for one mighty show!'
'Romance aflame through dangerous days and nights of terror! In a land where anything can happen – most of all to a beautiful girl alone!'

Gunga Din ***
ᛁᛁ   US   1939   117m   bw
RKO (George Stevens)
▤ ▦

Three cheerful army veterans meet adventure on the North-West Frontier.
Rousing period actioner with comedy asides, one of the most entertaining of its kind ever made.

w Joel Sayre, Fred Guiol, Ben Hecht, Charles MacArthur poem Rudyard Kipling d George Stevens ph Joseph H. August m Alfred Newman ad Van Nest Polglase
☆ Cary Grant, Victor McLaglen, Douglas Fairbanks Jnr, Sam Jaffe, Eduardo Ciannelli, Joan Fontaine, Montagu Love, Robert Coote, Cecil Kellaway, Abner Biberman, Lumsden Hare

'One of the big money pictures this year … will recoup plenty at the box office window.' – Variety
'One of the most enjoyable nonsense-adventure movies of all time.' – Pauline Kael, 1968
'Bravura is the exact word for the performances, and Stevens' composition and cutting of the fight sequences is particularly stunning.' – NFT, 1973

Gunhed (dubbed)
Japan 1989 99m colour
Manga/Toho/Sunrise (Yoshishige Shimatani, Tetsuhisha Yamada)
⬚
In 2039, engineers patch up warrior-robots to disarm a super-computer that is trying to take over the world.
Comic-book science fiction, frequently risible and always over the top.
w Masato Harada, James Bannon d Masato Harada ph Jinichi Fujisawa m Toshiyuki Honda ed Yoshitami Kuroiwa sp Koichi Kawakita, Imagica Group
☆ Masahiro Takashima, Brenda Bakke, Yujin Harada, Kaori Mizushima, Aya Enyoji, Mickey Curtis, James B. Thompson, Doll Nguyen, Landy Leyes
'A hokey slab of Nipponese sci-fi that's OK for buffs but not high-key enough to break into wider markets.' – *Variety*
'This is the computer game as cinema.' – *Derek Malcolm, Guardian*

Gunman's Walk *
US 1958 97m Technicolor Cinemascope
Columbia (Fred Kohlmar)
A tough Westerner has two sons, one of whom follows too literally in his footsteps.
Competent action melodrama with good characterization.
w Frank Nugent d Phil Karlson ph Charles Lawton m George Duning
☆ Van Heflin, Tab Hunter, James Darren, Kathryn Grant

Gunmen
US 1992 90m DeLuxe
Dimension/Davis (Laurence Mark, John Davis, John Flock)
⬚ ▤ ⚊ ⌒
Ruthless killers search for a fortune of $400m stolen from a powerful South American drug dealer and hidden on a boat.
Ludicrously overheated and violent thriller with some moments of sanctimonious moralizing that only emphasize its inherent sleaziness.
w Stephen Sommers d Deran Sarafian ph Hiro Narita m John Debney pd Michael Seymour ed Bonnie Koehler
☆ Christopher Lambert, Mario Van Peebles, Denis Leary, Kadeem Hardison, Sally Kirkland, Richard Sarafian, Robert Harper, Brenda Bakke, Patrick Stewart, Deran Sarafian
'A routine, vacuous actioner that tries to mix thrills with humor.' – *Variety*
'Charmless.' – *Empire*

Gunn *
US 1967 95m Technicolor
Paramount/Geoffrey (Owen Crump)
⌒
A private eye is hired to find a gangster's killer.
Tongue-in-cheek violence from the television series, with Craig Stevens doing a Cary Grant imitation.
w Blake Edwards, William Peter Blatty d Blake Edwards ph Philip Lathrop m Henry Mancini
☆ Craig Stevens, Laura Devon, Ed Asner, Sherry Jackson, Helen Traubel, J. Pat O'Malley, Regis Toomey
'Falters between parody and straight action.' – *MFB*

Gunpoint: see *At Gunpoint*

Gunpoint
US 1965 86m Technicolor
Universal
⬚
A Colorado sheriff goes after train robbers.
Simple-minded but quite professional and good-looking Western programmer.
w Mary and Willard Willingham d Earl Bellamy ph William Margulies m Hans Salter
☆ Audie Murphy, Joan Staley, Warren Stevens, Edgar Buchanan, Denver Pyle, Royal Dano

Guns at Batasi *
GB 1964 103m bw Cinemascope
TCF/George H. Brown
▤
The headquarters of an Anglo-African regiment is threatened by rebels.
Basically the old chestnut about a group of disparate types trapped in a dangerous situation, this is given

shape and stature by the star's lively performance as the martinet of an RSM.
w Robert Holles *novel The Siege of Battersea* by Robert Holles d John Guillermin ph Douglas Slocombe m John Addison
☆ Richard Attenborough, Flora Robson, Mia Farrow, Jack Hawkins, Cecil Parker, Percy Herbert, Errol John, John Leyton, Earl Cameron
🎖 Richard Attenborough

Guns for San Sebastian
France/Mexico/Italy 1967 111m Metrocolor
Franscope
MGM/Cipra/Filmes/Ernesto Eniques (Jacques Bar)
⌒
In Mexico in 1746, a rebel on the run stays to defend a besieged village.
Multi-national actioner, violent but quite undistinguished.
w James R. Webb *book A Wall for San Sebastian* by William B. Flaherty d Henri Verneuil ph Armand Thirard m Ennio Morricone
☆ Anthony Quinn, Charles Bronson, Sam Jaffe, Anjanette Comer, Silvia Pinal, Fernand Gravet

Guns in the Afternoon: see *Ride the High Country*

Guns in the Heather
🎪 US 1968 90m Technicolor
Walt Disney
An American schoolboy in Ireland finds that his elder brother is a CIA agent.
Tolerable kiddie-fodder from the Disney treadmill; later desiccated for TV.
w Herman Groves *novel Lockhart Amerman* d Robert Butler ph Michael Reed m Buddy Baker
☆ Glenn Corbett, Alfred Burke, Kurt Russell, Patrick Barr

Guns of Darkness
GB 1962 102m bw
ABP/Cavalcade (Thomas Clyde)
A British plantation boss in Latin America escapes with his wife when rebels strike.
Chase/escape film with a few tiny comments about violence.
w John Mortimer *novel Act of Mercy* by Francis Clifford d Anthony Asquith ph Robert Krasker m Benjamin Frankel
☆ David Niven, Leslie Caron, James Robertson Justice, David Opatoshu

The Guns of Fort Petticoat
US 1957 79m Technicolor
Columbia/Brown-Murphy (Harry Joe Brown)
During the Civil War, a wandering Texan trains townswomen into a fighting force.
Unlikely Western which passes the time.
w Walter Doniger d George Marshall ph Ray Rennahan m Mischa Bakaleinikoff
☆ Audie Murphy, Kathryn Grant, Hope Emerson, Jeff Donnell, Isobel Elsom

The Guns of Loos *
GB 1927 89m bw silent
Stoll/New Era
A blinded hero of the war returns home to run an industrial empire and is confronted by a strike.
One of the better British silents, with a strong plot and an interesting cast.
w L. H. Gordon, Reginald Fogwell, Sinclair Hill d Sinclair Hill ph Desmond Dickinson
☆ Henry Victor, Madeleine Carroll, Bobby Howes, Hermione Baddeley

The Guns of Navarone **
GB 1961 157m Technicolor Cinemascope
Columbia/Open Road/Carl Foreman (Cecil F. Ford)
⬚ ▤ ⚊
In 1943 a sabotage team is sent to destroy two giant guns on a Turkish island.
Ambitiously produced Boy's Own Paper heroics, with lots of noise and self-sacrifice; intermittently exciting but bogged down by philosophical chat.
w Carl Foreman *novel Alistair MacLean* d J. Lee-Thompson *novel Oswald Morris* m Dimitri Tiomkin ad Geoffrey Drake
☆ Gregory Peck, David Niven, Stanley Baker, Anthony Quinn, Anthony Quayle, James Darren, Gia Scala, James Robertson Justice, Richard Harris, Irene Papas, Bryan Forbes

'A desperate imbalance: the moral arguments cut into the action without extending it.' – *Penelope Houston*
🎖 best picture; Carl Foreman; J. Lee-Thompson; Dimitri Tiomkin; special effects (Bill Warrington, Vivian C. Greenham)

Guns of the Magnificent Seven
US 1969 106m DeLuxe Panavision
UA/Mirisch (Vincent M. Fennelly)
▤
Seven mercenaries rescue a Mexican Robin Hood.
Stale, flat and unprofitable third serving of this particular hash.
w Herman Hoffman d Paul Wendkos ph Antonio Macasoli m Elmer Bernstein
☆ George Kennedy, Monte Markham, Joe Don Baker, James Whitmore, Bernie Casey, Scott Thomas, Reni Santoni, Michael Ansara, Wende Wagner, Fernando Rey, Frank Silvera

Guns of the Timberland
US 1960 91m Technicolor
Jaguar (Aaron Spelling)
Loggers are opposed by cattle interests.
Routine star Western with tolerable production values.
w Joseph Petracca, Aaron Spelling *novel Louis L'Amour* d Robert D. Webb ph John Seitz m David Buttolph
☆ Alan Ladd, Jeanne Crain, Gilbert Roland, Frankie Avalon, Lyle Bettger, Noah Beery Jnr

Guns of Wyoming: see *Cattle King*

Gunsmoke
US 1953 79m Technicolor
Universal (Aaron Rosenberg)
A cowboy befriends the rancher he has been hired to kill.
Moderate Western with too many pauses for sentiment.
w D. D. Beauchamp d Nathan Juran ph Charles P. Boyle
☆ Audie Murphy, Paul Kelly, Susan Cabot, Mary Castle, Charles Drake

The Guru
US/India 1969 112m DeLuxe
TCF/Arcadia (Ismail Merchant)
In India, an English pop singer succumbs to the local atmosphere.
Pleasant, affectionate but forgettable anecdote of modern India.
w Ruth Prawer Jhabvala, James Ivory d James Ivory ph Subrata Mitra m Ustad Vilayat Khan
☆ Michael York, Rita Tushingham, Utpal Dutt, Aparna Sen, Barry Foster

Guru in Seven
GB 1997 107m colour
Ratpack/Balhar (Shani Grewal)
After his girlfriend leaves him, an artist bets his friends that he can bed seven women in a week.
Familiar sex comedy routine, given a little twist by being set within a Punjabi community in Britain; it tries, but fails, to be an Alfie for the 90s.
wd Shani Grewal ph James Bishop m Matthew Best, Neil Hourigan, Sean Maher, Sunny Sehgal ed Shani Grewal
☆ Saeed Jaffrey, Jacqueline Pearce, Nitin Chandra Ganatra, Lea Rochelle, Lynne Michelle, Elle Lewis, Amanda Pointer
'Definitely worth seeking out.' – *Empire*

Gus
🎪 US 1976 96m Technicolor
Walt Disney (Ron Miller)
▤ ⚊
A football team co-opts a mule which can kick a hundred yard ball.
Predictable Disney fantasy comedy with a direct line back to The Absent Minded Professor.
w Arthur Alsberg, Don Nelson d Vincent McEveety ph Frank Phillips m Robert F. Brunner
☆ Ed Asner, Don Knotts, Gary Grimes, Tim Conway, Liberty Williams, Bob Crane, Harold Gould, Tom Bosley, Dick Van Patten
'In the current comedy climate, when humour so often hinges on a four-letter word or its lengthier variant, a light-hearted football game spoof is a breath of fresh air.' – *Tatiana Balkoff Lipscomb, Films in Review*

The Guv'nor
GB 1935 88m bw
Gaumont (Michael Balcon)
US title: *Mr Hobo*
By chance a tramp becomes a bank director.
Predictable star vehicle with Arliss a most unlikely tramp.
w Maude Howell, Guy Bolton d Milton Rosmer ph Max Greene md Louis Levy
☆ George Arliss, Gene Gerrard, Viola Keats, Patric Knowles, Frank Cellier, Mary Clare, George Hayes
'His admirers need not fear that he has lost any of his usual refinement or sentiment, his cultured English accent, his Universal certificate.' – *Graham Greene*

Guy
GB/Germany 1996 94m colour
Polygram/Pandora (Renée Missel)
⬚
A documentary photographer stalks a car salesman with her camera.
An anecdote of surveillance that goes on for far too long.
w Kirby Dick d Michael Lindsay-Hogg ph Arturo Smith m Jeff Beal pd Kara Lindstrom ed Dody Dorn
☆ Vincent D'Onofrio, Hope Davis, Kimber Riddle, Diane Salinger, Richard Portnow, Valente Rodriguez, Michael Massee, John O'Donohue
'Lacks enough imagination to make it more than a smart, postgraduate film-making exercise.' – *Liese Spencer, Sight and Sound*

A Guy Named Joe *
US 1944 120m bw
MGM (Everett Riskin)
▤
A flyer is killed but comes back as a ghost to supervise his ex-girl's new romance.
Icky romantic comedy-drama with strong propaganda intent; the stars make it tolerable.
w Dalton Trumbo d Victor Fleming ph George Folsey, Karl Freund m Herbert Stothart
☆ Spencer Tracy, Irene Dunne, Ward Bond, Van Johnson, James Gleason, Lionel Barrymore, Barry Nelson, Don Defore, Henry O'Neill
'As far as I could judge, the audience loved it: melodrama, farce, fake philosophy, swimming eyes and all.' – *Richard Mallett, Punch*
'It neatly obtunds death's sting as ordinary people suffer it by not only assuming but photographing a good, busy, hearty hereafter.' – *James Agee*
† The title was explained by one of the characters who observed that 'in the Army Air Corps, any fellow who is a right fellow is called Joe'.
†† It was remade in 1989 as *Always* (qv).
🎖 original story (David Boehm, Chandler Sprague)

The Guy Who Came Back
US 1951 92m bw
TCF
A pro football player hates the thought of retiring.
Sentimental sporting drama without much life in it.
w Allan Scott d Joseph Newman
☆ Paul Douglas, Joan Bennett, Linda Darnell, Don Defore, Zero Mostel

Guys and Dolls *
US 1955 149m Eastmancolor
Cinemascope
Samuel Goldwyn
⬚ ▤ ⚊ ◎
A New York gangster takes a bet that he can romance a Salvation Army lady.
The artifices of Runyonland are made more so by a defiantly studio-bound production and thoroughly flat handling; but the songs and sometimes the performances survive.
wd Joseph L. Mankiewicz *musical* Jo Swerling, Abe Burrows ph Harry Stradling m/ly Frank Loesser md Cyril Mockridge, Jay Blackton ch Michael Kidd pd Oliver Smith ad Joseph Wright
☆ Frank Sinatra, Marlon Brando, Jean Simmons, Vivian Blaine, Stubby Kaye, B. S. Pully, Robert Keith, Sheldon Leonard, George E. Stone
'Quantity has been achieved only at the cost of quality.' – *Penelope Houston*
🎖 Harry Stradling; Cyril Mockridge, Jay Blackton; art direction

Gycklarnas Afton: see *Sawdust and Tinsel*

Gymkata
US 1985 90m Metrocolor
MGM/UA (Fred Weintraub)
An American gymnast trains to win a contest of skill and strength in a small Asian country, mainly populated by ninjas, in order that the US can install a spy satellite there.
Disagreeable and ridiculous gung-ho martial arts nonsense.
w Charles Robert Carner *novel The Terrible Game* by Dan Tyler Moore d Robert Clouse *ph* Godfrey Godar *m* Alfi Kabiljo *pd* Veljko Despotovic *ed* Robert A. Ferretti
☆ Kurt Thomas, Tetchie Agbayani, Richard Norton, Edward Bell, John Barrett, Conan Lee

Gypsy
GB 1936 78m bw
Warner (Irving Asher)
An ageing playboy marries a gypsy but gives her back to her true love.
Hard-to-swallow drama with insufficient comedy relief for its star.
w Brock Williams, Terence Rattigan *novel Tsigane* by Lady Eleanor Smith d Roy William Neill
☆ Roland Young, Chili Bouchier, Hugh Williams, Frederick Burtwell

'The girl who became the greatest show in show business!'
Gypsy *
US 1962 149m Technirama
Warner (Mervyn Le Roy)
The early days of stripteaser Gypsy Rose Lee, and the exploits of her ambitious mother.
A vaudeville musical that is nowhere near raucous enough, or brisk enough, for its subject, and is miscast into the bargain. The songs are great, but not here: Miss Russell is as boring as an electric drill in a role that should have been reserved for Ethel Merman.
w Leonard Spigelgass *play* Arthur Laurents d Mervyn Le Roy *ph* Harry Stradling *m/ly* Jule Styne, Stephen Sondheim *md* Frank Perkins *ad* John Beckman
☆ Rosalind Russell, Natalie Wood, *Karl Malden*, James Millhollin
† Natalie Wood's singing was dubbed by Marni Nixon.
†† A TV version was made in 1993 directed by Emile Ardolino and starring Bette Midler.
♫ Harry Stradling; Frank Perkins

The Gypsy and the Gentleman
GB 1957 107m Eastmancolor
Rank (Maurice Cowan)
A penniless Regency rake marries a tempestuous gypsy, with melodramatic and tragic results.
Expensive and typically mistimed Rank attempt to re-

do The Man in Grey; *a barnstormer notable only for waste of talent.*
w Janet Greene *novel Darkness I Leave You* by Nina Warner Hooke d Joseph Losey *ph* Jack Hildyard *m* Hans May *ad* Ralph Brinton
☆ Melina Mercouri, Keith Michell, Patrick McGoohan, June Laverick, Flora Robson, Helen Haye, Mervyn Johns

Gypsy Colt
US 1954 72m Anscocolor
MGM (William Grady Jnr, Sidney Franklin Jnr)
A cherished colt has to be sold, but makes its way back home.
Disguised second feature remake of Lassie Come Home; good for children.
w Martin Berkeley *story* Eric Knight d Andrew Marton *ph* Harold Lipstein *m* Rudolph G. Kopp *ad* Cedric Gibbons
☆ Donna Corcoran, Ward Bond, Frances Dee, Larry Keating, Lee Van Cleef

Gypsy Girl: see *Sky West and Crooked*

The Gypsy Moths *
US 1969 110m Metrocolor
MGM/Frankenheimer-Lewis (Hal Landers, Bobby Roberts)
Sky-diving stuntmen find love and death on a small-town tour.
Brilliantly breathtaking actioner which too frequently gets grounded, and does not find a reason for being so glum.

w William Hanley *novel* James Drought d John Frankenheimer *ph* Philip Lathrop *m* Elmer Bernstein *aerial ph* Carl Boenisch
☆ Burt Lancaster, Deborah Kerr, Gene Hackman, Scott Wilson, William Windom, Bonnie Bedelia, Sheree North
'A Bergmanesque world of inner emotions and ambiguous means … As in many of Frankenheimer's films it rains, and the wind in the trees in the park and the sound of traffic all contribute to the realism that makes his work so satisfying.' – *Gerald Pratley*

Gypsy Wildcat
US 1944 77m Technicolor
Universal (George Waggner)
A Transylvanian gypsy girl is really a long lost countess.
Universal's Frankenstein sets are put to lighter use in a quite incredible piece of downright hokum.
w James Hogan, Gene Lewis, James M. Cain d Roy William Neill *ph* George Robinson, W. Howard Greene *m* Edward Ward
☆ Maria Montez, Jon Hall, Leo Carrillo, Gale Sondergaard, Douglass Dumbrille, Nigel Bruce, Peter Coe, Curt Bois
'The picture's so bad, it's bound to make money.' – *Cue*
'Never rises to the wild camp of *Cobra Woman*; it's just *opéra bouffe* without music.' – *Pauline Kael, 70s*

H.M. Pulham Esquire **

US 1940 120m bw

MGM (King Vidor)

A moderately successful Bostonian businessman looks back over his rather stuffy life and has a fling.

Solidly upholstered drama which does not quite do justice to the book on which it is based.

w King Vidor, Elizabeth Hill *novel* John P. Marquand *d* King Vidor *ph* Ray June *m* Bronislau Kaper

☆ Robert Young, Ruth Hussey, Hedy Lamarr, Charles Coburn, Van Heflin, Fay Holden, Bonita Granville

H. P. Lovecraft's From Beyond: see *From Beyond*

H. P. Lovecraft's The Unnamable Returns: see *The Unnamable Returns*

Habeas Corpus *

♟♟ US 1928 20m bw silent

Hal Roach

A mad professor sends two vagabonds out to look for a body.

Unusual star comedy, more grotesque and pantomimish than any of the others.

w H. M. Walker *story* Leo McCarey *d* James Parrott *ph* Len Powers *ed* Richard Currier

☆ Stan Laurel, Oliver Hardy, Richard Carle, Charley Rogers

† It was the pair's first sound film, but the discs on which the soundtrack of music and effects were recorded have been lost.

Hachigatsu-no-Kyoshikyoku: see *Rhapsody in August*

Hackers

US 1995 104m colour

United Artists (Michael Peyser, Ralph Winter)

⬚ ▤ @ ⊚ ⊚ ⌾

A teenage hacker and his friends thwart a man attempting a sophisticated and large-scale computer fraud.

A film for 'teens who may enjoy seeing themselves as heroes while adults are portrayed as invariably mean-spirited and nasty; it's childish stuff, with little understanding of how computers actually work.

w Rafael Moreu *d* Ian Softley *ph* Andrzej Sekula *m* Simon Boswell *pd* John Beard *ed* Christopher Blunden, Martin Walsh

☆ Jonny Lee Miller, Angelina Jolie, Jesse Bradford, Matthew Lillard, Laurence Mason, Fisher Stevens, Alberta Watson, Renoly Santiago

'A dismal mess.' – *Entertainment Weekly*

Hadaka no Shima: see *The Island*

Hail the Conquering Hero ***

US 1944 101m bw

Paramount (Preston Sturges)

▤

An army reject is accidentally thought a hero when he returns to his small-town home.

Skilfully orchestrated Preston Sturges romp, slightly marred by an overdose of sentiment but featuring his repertory of comic actors at full pitch.

wd Preston Sturges *ph* John Seitz *m* Werner Heymann

☆ Eddie Bracken, William Demarest, Ella Raines, Franklin Pangborn, Elizabeth Patterson, Raymond Walburn, Alan Bridge, Georgia Caine, Freddie Steele, Jimmy Conlin, Torben Meyer

'Mob scenes, rough-houses and sharply serious passages are played for all the pantomime they are worth … one of the happiest, heartiest comedies in a twelvemonth.' – *Otis L. Guernsey Jnr*

'First rate entertainment, a pattern of film making, not to be missed.' – *Richard Mallett, Punch*

'The energy, the verbal density, the rush of Americana and the congestion seen periodically in *The Miracle of Morgan's Creek* stagger the senses in this newest film.' – *James Ursini*

'It tells a story so touching, so chock-full of human frailties and so rich in homely detail that it achieves a reality transcending the limitations of its familiar slapstick.' – *James Agee*

'He uses verbal as well as visual slapstick, and his comic timing is so quirkily effective that the dialogue keeps popping off like a string of firecrackers.' – *New Yorker, 1977*

⅋ Preston Sturges (as writer)

'The Morning After Was Just The Beginning…'

La Haine **

France 1995 97m bw

Metro Tartan/Lazennec/Canal/La Sept/Kaso (Christophe Rossignon)

⬚

aka: *Hate*

A day in the life of three unemployed youths, one black, one Jewish, one Arab, as they join a riot on their rundown suburban housing estate against the brutalities of the police.

Passionate and angry movie, on the side of the dispossessed, filmed in a documentary style that adds authenticity to its account of urban affliction.

wd Mathieu Kassovitz *ph* Pierre Aïm *ad* Giuseppe Ponturo *ed* Mathieu Kassovitz, Scott Stevenson

☆ Vincent Cassel, Hubert Kounde, Saïd Taghmaoui, Karim Belkhadra, Edouard Montoute, Françoise Levantal, Solo, Marc Duret

'It is hugely energetic, totally convinced of the rightness of its case and pretty angry about everything. It can't possibly be ignored, since it is not about France alone, but about urban and suburban problems almost everywhere in the West.' – *Derek Malcolm, Guardian*

'An exhilarating, thought-provoking triumph.' – *Sunday Times*

† The film caused a sensation in France, with the Prime Minister insisting that his Cabinet watch it. Kassovitz won the best director prize at the Cannes Film Festival in 1995, and the film also won Europe's Felix as the Best Young Film.

Hair *

US 1979 121m Technicolor Panavision

UA/CIP (Lester Persky, Michael Butler)

⬚ ▤

An Oklahoman on his way to enlist for Vietnam service stops off in New York and becomes embroiled with the flower people.

Slick, vigorous but eventually unsatisfying version of a quickly dated musical frolic with some obvious points to make.

w Michael Weller *musical play* Galt MacDermot (music) *and* Gerome Ragni/James Rado (book) *d* Milos Forman *ph* Miroslav Ondricek, Richard Kratina, Jean Talvin *m/ly* Galt MacDermot, Gerome Ragni, James Rado

☆ John Savage, Treat Williams, Beverly D'Angelo, Annie Golden, Dorsey Wright

'The makers of *Hair* have given us some high-spirited reminders of splendid things that film can do and, these days, isn't often asked to.' – *Stanley Kauffmann*

The Hairdresser's Husband **

France 1990 80m colour Panavision

Palace/Lambart/TFI/Investimage 2 and 3/Sofica (Thierry de Ganay)

⬚ ⌾

original title: *Le Mari de la Coiffeuse*

A middle-aged man fulfils his childhood erotic fantasy of marrying a hairdresser.

Quirky, witty drama of an obsessive relationship.

w Claude Klotz, Patrice Leconte *d* Patrice Leconte *ph* Eduardo Serra *m* Michael Nyman *ad* Ivan Maussion *ed* Joëlle Hache

☆ Jean Rochefort, Anna Galiena, Roland Bertin, Maurice Chevit, Philippe Clevenot, Jacques Mathou, Claude Aufaure, Henry Hocking

Hairspray

US 1988 90m colour

Palace (Rachel Talalay)

⬚ ▤ @ ⌾

A fat teenager becomes the star of a local TV dance show.

Drear and campy comedy, set in the early days of rock and beehive hair-styles.

wd John Waters *ph* David Insley *m* Kenny Vance *pd* Vincent Peranio *ed* Janice Hampton

☆ Sonny Bono, Ruth Brown, Divine, Colleen Fitzpatrick, Jo Ann Havrilla, Michael St Gerard, Debbie Harry, Ricki Lake, Leslie Ann Powers

The Hairy Ape

US 1944 91m bw

Jules Levy

▤

A ship's stoker aims to kill a socialite who has insulted him.

Patchy treatment of an intractable and dated play.

w Jules Levy *play* Eugene O'Neill *d* Alfred Santell *ph* Lucien Andriot *m* Michel Michelet, Edward Paul

☆ William Bendix, Susan Hayward, John Loder, Dorothy Comingore, Roman Bohnen, Alan Napier

⅋ Michel Michelet, Edward Paul

Hakayitz Shel Aviya: see *The Summer of Aviya*

Half a Hero

US 1953 71m bw

MGM (Matthew Rapf)

A timid journalist has problems with wife, baby, boss and new house.

Aimless comedy quite unsuited to its star.

w Max Shulman *d* Don Weis *ph* Paul C. Vogel *m* Paul Sawtell

☆ Red Skelton, Jean Hagen, Charles Dingle, Mary Wickes, Polly Bergen

Half a Sinner

US 1934 70m bw

Universal

A cheerful elderly cardsharp masquerades as a deacon.

Midwestern pleaser not too well made here, but later remade under its original title as a Bob Burns vehicle.

w Earle Snell, Clarence Marks *play* Alias the Deacon by John B. Hymer and LeRoy Clemens *d* Kurt Neumann

☆ Berton Churchill, Joel McCrea, Sally Blane, Mickey Rooney, Spencer Charters

'Little marquee strength, but sufficient punch to please 'em once they're in.' – *Variety*

'It's everything a motion picture can be!'

Half a Sixpence *

♟♟ GB 1967 148m Technicolor Panavision

Paramount/Ameran (Charles H. Schneer, George Sidney)

⬚ ▤

A draper's assistant inherits a fortune and moves into society.

Mildly likeable but limp and overlong musical which would have benefited from more intimate, sharper treatment than the wide screen can give. The period decor and lively numbers seem insufficient compensation for the longueurs.

w Beverley Cross *play* Beverley Cross *novel* Kipps by H. G. Wells *d* George Sidney *ph* Geoffrey Unsworth *m/ly* David Heneker *ch* Gillian Lynne *pd* Ted Haworth

☆ Tommy Steele, Julia Foster, Cyril Ritchard, Penelope Horner, Elaine Taylor, Hilton Edwards, Pamela Brown, James Villiers

'The confessions of a female sleepwalker!'

Half Angel

US 1951 80m Technicolor

TCF

A prim and proper nurse has a more forthright personality when she sleepwalks.

Silly romantic comedy with amusing moments.

w Robert Riskin *d* Richard Sale

☆ Loretta Young, Joseph Cotten, Cecil Kellaway, Basil Ruysdael, Jim Backus, Irene Ryan

Half Baked

US 1998 80m DeLuxe

Universal (Robert Simonds)

Stoned friends become drug dealers to raise money to get a friend out of prison.

A modern update of the sort of comedies Cheech and Chong used to make, likely to appeal to ageing hippies.

w Dave Chappelle, Neal Brennan *d* Tamra Davis *ph* Steven Bernstein *m* Alf Clausen *pd* Perry Andelin Blake *ed* Don Zimmerman

☆ Dave Chappelle, Guillermo Diaz, Jim Breuer, Harland Williams, Rachel True, Clarence Williams III

'A couple of hash brownies short of a satisfying cinematic picnic.' – *Variety*

Half Moon Street

US 1986 90m Technicolor

RKO/Edward R. Pressman (Geoffrey Reeve)

⬚ ▤

A lady PhD turns to prostitution to augment her income, and becomes involved in Middle Eastern schemes.

Totally muddled compromise between thriller and exploitation piece; its message seems to have got left on the cutting room floor.

w Bob Swaim, Edward Behr *novel* Dr Slaughter by Paul Theroux *d* Bob Swaim *ph* Peter Hannan *m* Richard Harvey *pd* Anthony Curtis *ed* Richard Marden

☆ Sigourney Weaver, Michael Caine, Patrick Kavanagh, Keith Buckley

'A half-baked excuse for a film.' – *Variety*

The Half Naked Truth *

US 1932 67m bw

RKO (David O. Selznick)

A publicity agent has trouble with a temperamental actress whose schemes are always over the top.

Amusing wisecracking comedy.

w Bartlett Cormack, Corey Ford *d* Gregory La Cava *ph* Bert Glennon *m* Max Steiner

☆ Lee Tracy, Lupe Velez, Eugene Pallette, Frank Morgan, Bob McKenzie

Half Shot at Sunrise

US 1930 78m bw

Radio (William LeBaron)

▤

In 1918, two American soldiers go absent without leave and chase the girls while they are chased by military police.

Breezily inconsequential comedy, little more than a succession of vaudeville routines, but undemandingly amusing at times.

w Anne Caldwell, Ralph Spence *story* James Ashmore Creelman *d* Paul Sloane *ph* Nick Musuraca *m* Harry Tierney *ad* Max Rée *ed* Arthur Roberts

☆ Bert Wheeler, Robert Woolsey, Dorothy Lee, George McFarlane, Edna May Oliver, Leni Stengel

---

Half Way to Shanghai
US   1942   61m   bw
Universal (Paul Malvern)
Spies are included among the passengers on a
Burma night train before the Japanese invasion.
*Watchable if muddled mystery with a good cast;
Shanghai is neither relevant nor mentioned.*
w Stuart Palmer   d John Rawlins
☆ Kent Taylor, Irene Hervey, Henry Stephenson,
J. Edward Bromberg, George Zucco, Alexander
Granach, Lionel Royce

Halfaouine
Tunisia/France   1990   98m   colour
Cine Tele/France Media/Scarabee/RTT/La Sept/WDR
(Ahmed Attia, Hassen Daldoul, Elaine Stutterheim)
aka: *The Rooftop Hopper*
In Tunis, a young boy begins to discover sex, a
subject that also obsesses his elders.
Slight, episodic narrative of minor interest.
w Férid Boughedir, Maryse Léon Garcia, Nouri
Bouzid, Taoufik Jebali   d Férid Boughedir
ph George Barsky   m Anouar Braham   ed Moufida
Tlatli
☆ Mohamed Driss, Mustafa Adueni, Rabia Ben
Abdallah, Fatma Ben Saidane, Helène Catazaras,
Fathi Al Hadawi, Sélim Boughedir
   'Boughedir is a director of broad ideas more than
   a stylist, yet the pic manages to capture and hold
   viewers from start to finish.' – *Variety*

The Half-Breed
US   1952   81m   Technicolor
RKO
▦
A gambler helps a half-breed and wins the respect
of the Apaches.
*Half-hearted Western which could never be more than
the bottom half of a double bill.*
w Harold Shumate, Richard Wormser   d Stuart
Gilmore   ph William V. Skall   m Paul Sawtell
☆ Robert Young, Jack Buetel, Janis Carter, Barton
MacLane, Reed Hadley, Porter Hall, Connie
Gilchrist

The Halfway House *
GB   1944   99m   bw
Ealing (Cavalcanti)
Overnight guests at an inn find it was bombed a
year before and they have all been given a
supernatural chance to reconsider their lives.
*Interesting pattern play which would have benefited
from lighter handling.*
w Angus MacPhail, Diana Morgan *play Peaceful
Inn* by Denis Ogden   d Basil Dearden   ph Wilkie
Cooper   m Lord Berners   ad Michael Relph
☆ Françoise Rosay, Tom Walls, Alfred Drayton,
Sally Ann Howes, Mervyn Johns, Glynis Johns,
Esmond Knight, Richard Bird, Guy Middleton

Hallelujah! **
US   1929   106m   bw
MGM (King Vidor)
▦ ◎
A black cotton worker accidentally kills a man and
decides to become a preacher.
*Hollywood's unique black melodrama now seems stilted
because of its early talkie technique, but at the time its
picture of negro life had a freshness and truth which
was not reached again for thirty years.*
w Wanda Tuchock, King Vidor   d King Vidor
ph Gordon Avil   md Eva Jessye
☆ Daniel Haynes, Nina Mae McKinney, William
Fountaine, Fannie Belle de Knight, Harry Gray
   'The central theme became swamped by the
   forty or so singing sequences of folk songs,
   spirituals, baptism wails, love songs and blues.' –
   Peter Noble, The Negro in Films
♫ King Vidor

Hallelujah, I'm a Bum **
US   1933   80m   bw
Lewis Milestone
▦
GB titles: *Hallelujah I'm a Tramp*
aka: *Lazy Bones*
The leader of a group of Central Park tramps
smartens himself up for love of a lady who lost her
memory. When she recovers it, he becomes a
tramp again.
*Curious whimsy expressed mainly in recitative, with
embarrassing stretches relieved by moments of visual
and verbal inspiration. Very typical of the Depression,
with the tramps knowing best how life should be lived.*

w S. N. Behrman, Ben Hecht   d Lewis Milestone
ph Lucien Andriot   ad Richard Day
rhymes/m/ly Richard Rodgers, Lorenz Hart
☆ Al Jolson, Harry Langdon, Madge Evans, Frank
Morgan, Chester Conklin
   'It must rise or fall by Al Jolson's rep … it won't
   bore, once in, but it's not a mass play picture.' –
   Variety
   'Given a scene or two of high sentiment, he still
   has you wrapped round his little finger.' – *The
   Times, 1973*
♫ 'Hallelujah I'm a Bum'; 'You Are Too Beautiful';
'I'll Do It Again'; 'What Do You Want with
Money?'; 'I've Got to Get Back to New York'

Hallelujah, I'm a Tramp: see *Hallelujah, I'm a Bum*

The Hallelujah Trail
US   1965   167m   Technicolor   Ultra
Panavision 70
UA/Mirisch/Kappa (John Sturges)
▦ ▦ ◎ ⌒
In 1867 a wagonload of whisky bound for Denver is
waylaid by Indians, temperance crusaders and the
civilian militia.
*Absurdly inflated, prolonged, uninventive comedy
Western with poor narrative grip; all dressed up and
nowhere to go.*
w John Gay *novel* Bill Gulick   d John Sturges
ph Robert Surtees   m Elmer Bernstein
☆ Burt Lancaster, Lee Remick, Brian Keith, Jim
Hutton, Donald Pleasence, Martin Landau

The Halliday Brand *
US   1956   78m   bw
UA/Collier Young
A tough farmer/sheriff conflicts with his son over
his attitude to Indians.
Dour, reliable Western melodrama with a good cast.
w George W. George, George F. Slavin   d Joseph
H. Lewis   ph Ray Rennahan   m Stanley Wilson
☆ Joseph Cotten, Viveca Lindfors, Ward Bond,
Betsy Blair, Bill Williams, Jay C. Flippen

Halloween *
US   1978   91m   Metrocolor   Panavision
Falcon International (Irwin Yablans)
▦ ▦ ◎ ⌒
In a small Illinois town, a mad killer escapes from
the asylum.
*Single-minded shocker with virtually no plot, just a
succession of bloody attacks in semi-darkness. Very
well done if you like that kind of thing, though the final
suggestion of the supernatural is rather baffling.*
w John Carpenter, Debra Hill   d John Carpenter
ph Dean Cundey   m John Carpenter   pd Tommy
Wallace
☆ Donald Pleasence, Jamie Lee Curtis, Nancy
Loomis, P. J. Soles
   'One of the cinema's most perfectly engineered
   devices for saying Boo!' – *Richard Combs, MFB*

Halloween Five: The Revenge of Michael Myers
US   1989   96m   CFI color
Magnum (Ramsey Thomas)
▦ ▦ ◎ ◎ ⌒
A small girl senses when the Halloween killer is
going to strike again.
*Lacklustre sequel that goes to some lengths to set up a
further instalment of mindless killings at its end.*
w Michael Jacobs, Dominique Othenin-Girard,
Shem Bitterman   d Dominique Othenin-Girard
ph Robert Draper   m Alan Howarth, John
Carpenter   pd Steven Lee   ed Jerry Brady
☆ Donald Pleasence, Danielle Harris, Wendy
Kaplan, Ellie Cornell, Donald L. Shanks, Jeffrey
Landman, Beau Starr
   'Pretty stupid and boring fare.' – *Variety*

Halloween Four: The Return of Michael Myers
US   1988   88m   colour   Panavision
Fox/Trancas International/Halloween 4 Partnership
(Paul Freeman)
▦ ▦ ◎ ◎ ⌒
The motiveless murderer emerges from a coma to
kill again, and again, and again.
A further unnecessary sequel, poorly made.
w Alan B. McElroy *story* Dhani Lipsius, Larry
Rattner, Benjamin Ruffner   d Dwight H. Little
ph Peter Lyons Collister   m Alan Howarth
ad Roger S. Crandall   ed Curtiss Clayton

☆ Donald Pleasence, Ellie Cornell, Danielle
Harris, Michael Pataki, Beau Starr, Kathleen
Kinmont, Sasha Jenson, George P. Wilbur, Gene
Ross, Carmen Filpi

Halloween H20
US   1998   85m   colour   Panavision
Dimension/Nightfall (Paul Freeman)
▦ ▦
A homicidal maniac discovers the whereabouts of
the sister he terrorized on the night of Halloween
20 years before, and goes after her.
*There's not much that's new here in the recycling of a
familiar series; the movie is more knowing than its
predecessors, in the style of modern horror, and delivers
the requisite shocks.*
w Robert Zappia, Matt Greenberg   d Steve Miner
ph Daryn Okada   m John Ottman   pd John Willet
ed Patrick Lusser
☆ Jamie Lee Curtis, Adam Arkin, Josh Hartnett,
Michelle Williams, Adam Hann-Byrd, Jodi Lyn
O'Keefe, Janet Leigh, LL Cool J, Joseph Gordon
Levitt, Nancy Stephens, Branden Williams, Chris
Durand
   'Given how dreary the Michael Myers sequels
   are, it is hardly much of an achievement that
   H20 is the best of them.' – *Kim Newman, Empire*

Halloween: The Curse of Michael Myers
US   1995   88m   CFI color
Nightfall (Paul Freeman)
▦ ▦ ◎ ⌒
Michael Myers murders the surviving relatives of
families he butchered in the past.
*Tired and, at times, incomprehensible sequel that adds
black magic rituals to the familiar mix but without
making it any more interesting.*
w Daniel Farrands   d Joe Chappelle   ph Billy
Dickson   m Alan Howarth   pd Bryan Ryman
ed Randy Bricker   sp John Carl Buechler
☆ Donald Pleasence, Mitch Ryan, Marianne
Hagan, Paul Rudd, Leo Geter, George P. Wilbur,
Devin Gardner, Mariah O'Brien
   'The producers should take the advice of one of
   the characters in the film, "Enough of this
   Michael Myers bullshit!"' – *Shivers*
† The six Halloween films cost in total less than
$20m to make. So far they have taken more than
$200m at the box-office.

Halloween Three: Season of the Witch
US   1983   98m   Technicolor   Panavision
Dino de Laurentiis (Debra Hill, John Carpenter)
▦ ▦ ◎ ◎ ⌒
A malicious toy maker intends to restore
Halloween to its witch cult origins through magic
masks made at his Santa Mira factory. The
Halloween zombie-killer makes no appearance: this
is a fresh story inspired by *Invasion of the Body
Snatchers.*
Alas, its good intentions flounder in a bath of gore.
wd Tommy Lee Wallace   ph Dean Cundey
m John Carpenter, Alan Howarth   pd Peter
Jamison
☆ Tom Atkins, Stacey Nelkin, Dan O'Herlihy,
Ralph Strait, Michael Currie
† Nigel Kneale wrote the original script but asked
to have his name removed from the credits.

Halloween Two
US   1981   92m   Metrocolor   Panavision
Dino de Laurentiis (Debra Hill, John Carpenter)
▦ ▦ ◎ ⌒
The motiveless murderer from *Halloween* escapes
from the asylum fifteen years later.
*A totally unnecessary sequel which seems merely an
excuse for assorted mayhem at close quarters.*
w John Carpenter, Debra Hill   d Rick Rosenthal
ph Dean Cundey   m John Carpenter, Alan
Howarth
☆ Donald Pleasence, Jamie Lee Curtis, Charles
Cyphers, Jeffrey Kramer

Halls of Anger
US   1969   20m   DeLuxe
UA/Mirisch (Herbert Hirschman)
A black basketball star goes to teach in his home
town and faces segregation problems.
Schematic melodrama, as well meaning as it is boring.
w John Shaner, Al Ramrus   d Paul Bogart
ph Burnett Guffey   m Dave Grusin
☆ Calvin Lockhart, Janet MacLachlan, Jeff Bridges

Halls of Montezuma *
US   1950   113m   Technicolor
TCF (Robert Bassler)
▦ ▦
Marines fight World War II in the Pacific.
Well-mounted, simple-minded actioner.
w Michael Blankfort   d Lewis Milestone
ph Winton C. Hoch, Harry Jackson   m Sol Kaplan
md Lionel Newman
☆ Richard Widmark, Jack Palance, Reginald
Gardiner, Robert Wagner, Karl Malden, Richard
Hylton, Richard Boone, Skip Homeier, Jack Webb,
Bert Freed, Neville Brand, Don Hicks, Martin
Milner
   'By far the noisiest war film I ever encountered.'
   – *Richard Mallett, Punch*

Ham and Eggs at the Front
US   1927   70m   bw   silent
Warner
Two black soldiers have adventures in the
trenches.
*Irresistibly-titled war farce with our heroes played by
whites in blackface.*
w Darryl F. Zanuck   d Roy Del Ruth
☆ Tom Wilson, Charlie Conklin, Myrna Loy

Hamam *
Italy/Spain/Turkey   1997   101m   Cinecitta
Sorpasso/Promete Film/Asbrell (Marco Risi, Maurizio
Tedesco)
aka: *The Turkish Bath*
An unhappily married Italian designer moves to
Istanbul after he inherits from his aunt a rundown
Turkish bath.
*Engaging drama of cultural differences, of traditional
ways opposed to modern commerce, of dysfunctional
families and functioning communities.*
w Stefano Tummolini, Ferzan Ozpetek   d Ferzan
Ozpetek   ph Pasquale Mari   m Pivio, Aldo de
Scalzi   ad Virginia Vianello, Mustafa Ziya
Ulgenciler   ed Mauro Bonanni
☆ Alessandro Gassman, Francesca d'Aloja, Carlo
Cecchi, Halil Ergun, Serif Sezer, Mehmet Gunsur,
Basak Koklukaya, Alberto Molinari
   'An intelligent and attractive take on cross-
   cultural confusion and attraction.' – *Paul Julian
   Smith, Sight and Sound*

Hambone and Hillie
↟↟ US   1983   90m   colour   Panavision
Sandy Howard/Adams Apple (Gary Gillingham)
▦
A small dog is lost at New York airport and tracks
his aged mistress on foot to California.
*Basically a revamp of Lassie Come Home, with a
cute dog and some attractive exteriors, but made
unsuitable for its presumably intended family audience
by the death of a second dog and a horrific pitchfork
sequence in which a heavily pregnant woman is
attacked by multipliers.*
w Sandra K. Bailey, Michael Murphey, Joel
Soisson   d Roy Watts   ph Jon Kranhouse
m George Garvarentz
☆ Lillian Gish, Timothy Bottoms, Candy Clark,
Robert Walker, O. J. Simpson, Jack Carter, Alan
Hale

Hamburger Hill *
US   1987   110m   Technicolor
Paramount/RKO (Marcia Nasatir, Jim Carabatsos)
▦ ▦ ◎ ⌒
An untried squad goes into action in Vietnam.
*One of several Vietnam pics released almost
simultaneously; neither the worst nor the best.*
w Jim Carabatsos   d John Irvin   ph Peter
MacDonald   m Philip Glass   pd Austen Spriggs
ed Peter Tanner
☆ Anthony Barrie, Michael Patrick Boatman,
Don Cheadle, Michael Dolan, Don James
   'Had the filmmakers resisted the temptation to
   politicise their material they might have made a
   great war movie. They might also have thought
   to give us some indication of the strategic
   significance of the hill. As it is, they've managed
   to create a deeply affecting, highly accomplished
   film.' – *Hal Hinson, Washington Post*

Hamlet **
GB   1948   142m   bw
Rank/Two Cities (Laurence Olivier)
▦ ▦ ◎
Prince Hamlet takes too long making up his mind
to revenge his father's death.

↟↟ film suitable for   ▦ VHS video-cassette for   ▦ VHS video-cassette for the British   ◎ Video cassette in a computer-   ▦ American NTSC video-cassette   ◎ Laser disc
family viewing   the British PAL system   PAL system in wide screen-format   colourised version

The play is sharply cut, then time is wasted having the camera prowl pointlessly along gloomy corridors ... but much of the acting is fine, some scenes compel, and the production has a splendid brooding power.
w Alan Dent play William Shakespeare d Laurence Olivier ph Desmond Dickinson m William Walton pd Roger Furse ad Carmen Dillon

☆ *Laurence Olivier, Eileen Herlie, Basil Sydney, Jean Simmons, Felix Aylmer, Norman Wooland, Terence Morgan, Stanley Holloway, Peter Cushing, Esmond Knight, Anthony Quayle, Harcourt Williams, John Laurie, Niall MacGinnis, Patrick Troughton*
'Be you 9 or 90, is this Joe, *Hamlet* is the movie of the year.' – *Washington Times*
'By the end one no longer thinks of the piece as filmed Shakespeare, but accepts it simply as a splendid production of a masterpiece.' – *Dilys Powell*

♟ best picture; Laurence Olivier (as actor)
♟ Laurence Olivier (as director); William Walton; Jean Simmons; art direction
🎖 best picture

Hamlet *
USSR 1964 150m bw Sovscope
Lenfilm
A Russian version of the play, with lowering sets, brooding photography and strong acting.
play William Shakespeare (translation Boris Pasternak) d Grigori Kozintsev ph I. Gritzys m Dmitri Shostakovich
☆ *Innokenti Smoktunovsky, Mikhail Nazvanov, Elsa Radzin, Anastasia Vertinskaya, Yuri Tolubeyev*
'An opportunity almost deliberately missed.' – *Basil Wright, 1972*

Hamlet *
GB 1969 119m Technicolor
Woodfall/Filmways/Columbia (Neil Hartley)
🖭
A version which has its moments but fails to impress as a whole.
d Tony Richardson ph Gerry Fisher m Patrick Gowers ad Jocelyn Herbert
☆ *Nicol Williamson, Anthony Hopkins, Gordon Jackson, Judy Parfitt, Marianne Faithfull, Mark Dignam, Roger Livesey*

Hamlet *
US 1991 135m colour
Warner/Nelson Entertainment/Icon (Dyson Lovell)
🖭 🖳 📽 🎧
A son, inspired by his father's ghost, vows to kill his murdering uncle, who has married his mother and usurped the throne of Denmark.
Decent, unadventurous adaptation that does not challenge Olivier's version.
w Christopher de Vore, Franco Zeffirelli play William Shakespeare d Franco Zeffirelli ph David Watkin m Ennio Morricone pd Dante Ferretti ad Michael Lamont ed Richard Marden
☆ *Mel Gibson, Glenn Close, Alan Bates, Paul Scofield, Ian Holm, Helena Bonham Carter, Stephen Dillane, Nathaniel Parker, Sean Murray, Michael Maloney, Trevor Peacock, John McEnery*
'A generally flat-footed production, an illustrated gloss on the full Shakespearean text.' – *Variety*
'Funny thing is, Hamlet almost is perfect for Gibson, with his neurotic physicality and urgent baritone ... Zeffirelli goes for the grand. His aim here – nicely realised in a sumptuous production – is to make *Hamlet* so vigorous that the kids will forget it's poetry.' – *Richard Corliss, Time*
♟ best art direction; best costume design

Hamlet **
US 1996 242m Technicolor 70mm
Rank/Castle Rock (David Barron)
🖭 🖳 📽 🎧
In the 1800s, a Danish prince is slow to take revenge when he discovers that his uncle and stepfather has usurped his father's throne.
Sumptuous version of Shakespeare's play which is notable for presenting an uncut text, though Branagh's vigorous, well-spoken performance makes Hamlet's delay even more inexplicable than usual. Billy Crystal is an excellent gravedigger; some of the other star turns in minor roles would have been better buried.
wd Kenneth Branagh play William Shakespeare ph Alex Thomson m Patrick Doyle pd Tim Harvey ed Neil Farrell
☆ *Kenneth Branagh, Derek Jacobi, Julie Christie, Kate Winslet, Richard Briers, Nicholas Farrell,*

Michael Maloney, Brian Blessed, Jack Lemmon, Billy Crystal, Robin Williams, Gérard Depardieu, Charlton Heston, Rosemary Harris, Judi Dench and also John Gielgud (Priam), Rufus Sewell (Fortinbras), Ken Dodd (Yorick)
'A greatly flawed project – not so much the curate's egg as the curate's 1,000 egg omlette, with good and bad ideas scrambled together on a huge scale.' – *Adam Mars-Jones, Independent*
♟ Kenneth Branagh (as writer); Patrick Doyle; Tim Harvey; Alex Byrne (costumes)

Hamlet Goes Business **
Finland 1987 86m bw
Electric/Villealfa Productions/Aki Kaurismäki
🖭
original title: *Hamlet Liikemaailmassa*
A son whose father is murdered takes revenge on the killer.
Bizarre and enjoyable modern-day version of Shakespeare's play, which is treated as black comedy and set in the world of business, with company directors attempting to control the rubber duck industry.
wd Aki Kaurismäki ph Tino Salminen m Shostakovich, Tchaikovsky, Elmore James and others ed Raija Talvio
☆ *Pirkka-Pekka Petelius, Esko Salminen, Kati Outinen, Elina Salo, Esko Nikkari, Kari Vaananen, Hannu Valtonen, Mari Rantasila*

Hamlet Liikemaailmassa: see Hamlet Goes Business

Hammerhead
GB 1968 99m Technicolor
Columbia (Irving Allen)
An American secret agent captures a master criminal.
Jaded James Bond imitation, full of would-be fashionable detail.
w William Best, Herbert Baker novel James Mayo d David Miller ph Kenneth Talbot m David Whitaker
☆ *Vince Edwards, Peter Vaughan, Judy Geeson, Diana Dors, Michael Bates, Beverly Adams, Patrick Cargill, Patrick Holt*

Hammersmith Is Out *
US 1972 114m DuArt
Cinerama/J. Cornelius Cream (Alex Lucas)
🖳
With the help of a male nurse, a homicidal mental inmate escapes and becomes the most influential man in the country.
Pretentious updating of Faust into a kind of black farce that seldom amuses but is interesting in fits and starts.
w Stanford Whitmore d Peter Ustinov ph Richard Kline m Dominic Frontière
☆ *Richard Burton, Elizabeth Taylor, Peter Ustinov, Beau Bridges, Leon Ames, John Schuck, George Raft*

Hammett *
US 1982 97m Technicolor
Orion/Zoetrope (Francis Coppola)
🖭
San Francisco 1928: Dashiell Hammett is asked to locate a missing Chinese girl and gets involved in sinister goings-on which provide the basis for another mystery book.
Careful and interesting crime thriller in which, however, the rather pretentious framework is largely irrelevant, leaving a detective story slightly off-beat in treatment but otherwise indistinguishable from many others.
w Ross Thomas, Dennis O'Flaherty novel Joe Gores d Wim Wenders ph Philip Lathrop, Joseph Biroc m John Barry pd Dean Tavoularis, Eugene Lee ed Barry Malkin, Marc Laub, Robert Q. Lovett, Randy Roberts
☆ *Frederic Forrest, Peter Boyle, Marilu Henner, Roy Kinnear, Elisha Cook Jnr, R. G. Armstrong, Richard Bradford, Sylvia Sidney, Royal Dano, Samuel Fuller*
'A symbolic liquidation by Wenders of the massive, but ambivalent patrimony of the American cinematic and cultural tradition that has increasingly dominated his work.' – *Sheila Johnston, MFB*
† The film was actually in pre-production from 1975, though shooting did not begin until 1980. This version was abandoned in rough cut and two-thirds of it was shot again in 1981 with a different

---

crew. Sylvia Miles and Brian Keith were in the first version and not the second.

The Hammond Mystery: see The Undying Monster

Hamnstad: see Port of Call

Hana-Bi **
Japan 1997 103m colour
Office Kitano/Bandai/Television Tokyo/Tokyo FM (Masayuki Mori, Yasushi Tsuge, Takio Yoshida)
🖭
A tough cop, who leaves the force to look after his dying wife and the family of a dead colleague, turns to crime to get the money he needs.
An unusual drama, with dialogue pared to the mimimum and a protagonist whose emotions are kept under strict control, except when they flare into violence; it requires the audience to fill in the gaps in leaves.
wd Takeshi Kitano ph Hideo Yamamoto m Joe Hisaishi ad Norihiro Isoda ed Takeshi Kitano, Yoshinori Ota
☆ *Beat Takeshi (aka Takeshi Kitano), Kayoko Kishimoto, Ren Osugi, Susumu Terajima, Tetsu Watanabe*
'An intriguing and curiously engaging movie.' – *Bob McCabe, Empire*

The Hand
GB 1960 60m bw
Bill and Michael Luckwell/Butcher's
🖳
When an old man has his hand severed and is subsequently murdered, the trail leads to a doctor who subsequently commits suicide.
Confused second feature which seems to have been badly edited but might otherwise have been quite entertaining.
w Ray Cooney, Tony Hilton d Henry Cass ph Walter J. Harvey md Wilfred Burns
☆ *Derek Bond, Ronald Leigh-Hunt, Reed de Rouen, Ray Cooney, Harold Scott*

The Hand
US 1981 104m Technicolor
Warner/Orion (Edward R. Pressman)
🖳 📽
A cartoonist loses his hand, which takes on a life of its own to wreak vengeance on his enemies.
Pale imitation of The Beast with Five Fingers, which wasn't all that good to begin with.
wd Oliver Stone novel *The Lizard's Tail* by Oliver Stone ph King Baggot m James Horner pd John Michael Riva ed Richard Marks sp Carlo Rambaldi
☆ *Michael Caine, Andrea Marcovicci, Viveca Lindfors, Rosemary Murphy, Bruce McGill*

Hand in Hand *
👫 GB 1960 80m bw
ABP (Helen Winston)
The friendship of two 7-year-olds is affected by racial prejudice because one is Catholic and the other Jewish; but after misunderstandings their friendship is confirmed by priest and rabbi.
Pleasant, well-meaning drama apparently intended for older children.
w Diana Morgan d Philip Leacock ph Frederick A. Young m Stanley Black
☆ *Loretta Parry, Phillip Needs, Sybil Thorndike, John Gregson, Finlay Currie*

The Hand of Night
GB 1966 73m Technicolor
Associated British Pathé (Harry Field)
US title: *Beast of Morocco*
In order to recover from the death of his wife and children, an architect holidays in Morocco, where a vampire princess sets out to seduce him.
A psychological horror film, long on talk and short on action.
w Bruce Stewart d Frederic Goode ph William Jordan m Joan Shakespeare ad Peter Moll ed Frederick Ives
☆ *William Sylvester, Diane Clare, William Dexter, Alizia Gur, Edward Underdown, Terence de Marney*
'Relies heavily on old Hammer production tricks without contributing any original variations of its own.' – *MFB*

The Hand that Rocks the Cradle *
US 1991 110m Alpha Cine
Buena Vista/Hollywood Pictures/Interscope/Nomura, Babcock & Brown (David Madden)
🖭 🖳 📽 📀 📀 🎧
After her husband's suicide and her miscarriage, a woman becomes nanny to the family she blames for her misfortunes.
A predictable thriller that just manages to hold an audience's interest.
w Amanda Silver d Curtis Hanson ph Robert Elswit m Graeme Revell pd Edward Pisoni ed John F. Link
☆ *Annabella Sciorra, Rebecca de Mornay, Matt McCoy, Ernie Hudson, Julianne Moore, Madeline Zima, John de Lancie, Kevin Skousen*
'Diagrammatic script channels the action in a predictable direction toward an inevitable climax, but fine performances and a refusal to pander to the audience's grosser instincts raise this a notch or two above the norm.' – *Variety*
'A rabble-rousing hit, so adept is the movie at exploiting the sinister potential in ordinary domestic surroundings.' – *Gary Arnold, Washington Times*

A Handful of Clouds: see Doorway to Hell

A Handful of Dust **
GB 1988 118m colour
Premier (Derek Granger)
🖭 🖳 🎧
An aristocratic wife, frustrated by the old-fashioned habits of her stately home-owning husband, begins an affair with a young man-about-town.
Glossy production, impeccably acted, although it loses some of the satire of the original.
w Charles Sturridge, Tim Sullivan, Derek Granger novel Evelyn Waugh d Charles Sturridge ph Peter Hannan m George Fenton pd Eileen Diss ed Peter Coulson
☆ *James Wilby, Kristin Scott Thomas, Rupert Graves, Anjelica Huston, Judi Dench, Alec Guinness, Stephen Fry, Graham Crowden*
♟ best costume design (Jane Robinson)
🎖 Judi Dench

Handgun *
US 1982 101m DuArt
EMI/Kestrel (Tony Garnett)
A schoolmistress, raped at gunpoint, takes her revenge.
Novel, feminist revenge drama with a neat twist at the end.
wd Tony Garnett ph Charles Stewart m Mike Post pd Lilly Kilvert
☆ *Karen Young, Clayton Day, Suzie Humphreys, Helena Humann*

Handgun
US 1994 90m colour
Workin' Man/Odessa/Shooting Gallery (Bob Gosse, Larry Meistrich)
🖭
After their father dies, having hidden away half a million stolen dollars, his two crooked sons join forces to find the money before anyone else.
Enjoyably quirky comedy of the low life, slickly written and well acted.
d Whitney Ransick ph Michael Spiller m Douglas J. Cuomo pd Andras Kanegson ed Tom McCardle
☆ *Treat Williams, Seymour Cassel, Paul Schulze, Toby Huss, Angel Caban, Frank Vincent*
'Exhibits an unmistakably alert intelligence and cinematic sensibility that announce the arrival of an original American filmmaker.' – *Emanuel Levy, Variety*

Handle with Care *
US 1958 82m bw
MGM (Morton Fine)
Small-town college students stage a mock trial and come up with some embarrassing answers.
Interesting melodrama with a disappointing ending; a well done second feature.
w Morton Fine, David Friedkin d David Friedkin ph Harold J. Marzorati m Alexander Courage
☆ *Dean Jones, Joan O'Brien, Thomas Mitchell, Walter Abel, John Smith*

Handle with Care *

US   1977   98m   colour
Paramount (Paul Brickman)
aka: Citizens Band
An enthusiast of Citizen's Band radio tries to prevent it being abused in his home town.
Lively and often sharp comedy, but one that failed to find an audience at the time.
w Paul Brickman d Jonathan Demme ph Jordan Cronenweth m Bill Conti pd Bill Malley ed John F. Link II
☆ Paul LeMat, Candy Clark, Ann Wedgeworth, Bruce McGill, Marcia Rodd, Charles Napier, Alix Elias, Roberts Blossom, Ed Begley Jnr
'A palmy, elegantly deadpan comedy; the jokes aren't pushed, so it takes viewers a few minutes to settle into the comic style, which has the mellow, light touch of thirties Renoir.' – *Pauline Kael, New Yorker*
'For once, the intelligentsia are right about an American genre film; this one is worth serious consideration.' – *Richard Schickel, Time*

The Handmaid's Tale

US/Germany   1990   109m   colour
Virgin/Cinecom/Bioskop Film (Daniel Wilson)
In the near future, a woman revolts against her role as child-bearer for the controlling elite.
Barren feminist fantasy.
w Harold Pinter novel Margaret Atwood d Volker Schlondorff ph Igor Luther m Ryuichi Sakamoto pd Tom Walsh ed David Ray
☆ Natasha Richardson, Robert Duvall, Faye Dunaway, Aidan Quinn, Elizabeth McGovern, Victoria Tennant, Blanche Baker, Traci Lind, David Dukes

Hands across the Table *

US   1935   81m   bw
Paramount (E. Lloyd Sheldon)
A manicurist determines to marry a rich man.
Lively romantic comedy, smoothly made and typical of its time.
w Norman Krasna, Vincent Lawrence, Herbert Fields d Mitchell Leisen ph Ted Tetzlaff m Sam Coslow, Frederick Hollander
☆ Carole Lombard, Fred MacMurray, Ralph Bellamy, Astrid Allwyn, Ruth Donnelly, Marie Prévost, William Demarest, Ed Gargan
'Snappy comedy that should satisfy all over.' – *Variety*
'A happy mixture of brainwork and horseplay and a reminder that when intelligence goes for a walk among even the oldest props, the props may come to life.' – *Otis Ferguson*
† Ray Milland was originally cast, but bowed out saying that he couldn't play comedy.

The Hands of Orlac: see *Mad Love (1935)*

The Hands of Orlac

GB/France   1960   105m   bw
Riviera/Pendennis (Steven Pallos, Don Taylor)
A concert pianist's hands are crushed in an accident, and a mad surgeon grafts on those of an executed murderer.
Flatulent remake of the 1926 German silent and the 1935 American Mad Love. Stilted, hammy, threadbare and overlong.
w John Baines, Edmond T. Gréville novel Maurice Renard d Edmond T. Gréville ph Desmond Dickinson m Claude Bolling
☆ Mel Ferrer, Donald Wolfit, Christopher Lee, Dany Carrel, Felix Aylmer, Basil Sydney, Donald Pleasence

Hands of the Ripper

GB   1971   85m   Technicolor
Rank/Hammer (Aida Young)
Jack the Ripper stabs his wife to death in view of his small daughter, who grows up a sexually repressed murderess.
Gory Hammer horror with well done scenes.
w L. W. Davidson story Edward Spencer Shew d Peter Sasdy ph Kenneth Talbot m Christopher Gunning ed Roy Stannard ed Christopher Barnes
☆ Angharad Rees, Eric Porter, Dora Bryan, Jane Merrow, Derek Godfrey

Hands off the Loot: see *Touchez pas au Grisbi*

Hands over the City

Italy   1963   105m   bw   Galatea
original title: *Le Mani sulla Città*
A property tycoon wangles local politicians so that he gets development on the property he controls.
An angry political film which is too strident to have much entertainment value.
w Enzo Provenzale, Enzo Forcella, Raffaele La Capria, Francesco Rosi d Francesco Rosi ph Gianni di Venanzo m Piero Piccioni
☆ Rod Steiger, Salvo Randone, and non-professionals

Hands Up *

US   1926   65m   bw   silent
Paramount
General Lee assigns a spy to prevent a Union man from getting his hands on a gold cache.
Pleasant Civil War comedy with a curious Mormon happy ending.
w Monte Brice, Lloyd Corrigan d Clarence Badger
☆ Raymond Griffith, Marian Nixon, Virginia Lee Corbin, Mack Swain, Montagu Love

Handsome Antonio: see *Il Bell'Antonio*

Handy Andy

US   1934   82m   bw
Fox
A midwestern druggist is married to a snob.
Competent star vehicle overflowing with crackerbarrel philosophy.
w William Conselman, Henry Johnson play Merry Andrew by Lewis Beach d David Butler ph Arthur Miller
☆ Will Rogers, Peggy Wood, Conchita Montenegro, Mary Carlisle, Roger Imhof, Robert Taylor, Paul Harvey

'They made two mistakes – they hanged the wrong man, and they didn't finish the job!'

Hang 'em High

US   1967   114m   DeLuxe
UA/Malpaso/Leonard Freeman
A cowboy is rescued from lynching and takes revenge on his persecutors.
Hollywood's first attempt to imitate the gore and brutality of spaghetti Westerns and to take back its own errant star. Emetic and interminable.
w Leonard Freeman, Mel Goldberg d Ted Post ph Leonard South, Richard Kline m Dominic Frontière
☆ Clint Eastwood, Inger Stevens, Ed Begley, Pat Hingle, James MacArthur, Arlene Golonka, Charles McGraw, Ben Johnson, L. Q. Jones

Hangar 18

US   1980   97m   Technicolor
Sunn Classic
A UFO crashlands and is cared for in secret by the American government.
A cinematic equivalent to the yellow press, supposing villainous behaviour by all concerned but eager only to provide low grade thriller entertainment.
w Steven Thornley d James L. Conway ph Paul Hipp m John Cavacas
☆ Darren McGavin, Robert Vaughn, Gary Collins, Philip Abbott

Hanged Man's Farm: see *La Ferme du Pendu*

'It's gonna be one hell of a night.'

Hangin' with the Homeboys **

US   1991   89m   Metrocolor
Palace/New Line (Richard Brick)
In the Bronx, four youths get together for an eventful night out on the town and end up in the unfamiliar surroundings of Manhattan.
Acute and humorous portrait of the immature discovering the beginnings of maturity and self-knowledge.
wd Joseph B. Vasquez ph Anghel Decca ad Isabel Bau Madden ed Michael Schweitzer
☆ Doug E. Doug, Mario Joyner, John Leguizamo, Nestor Serrano, Kimberly Russell, Mary B. Ward, Reggie Montgomery, Christine Claravall, Rosemary Jackson

The Hanging Garden *

Canada   1997   91m   colour
Triptych/Galafilm/Emotion (Louise Garfield, Arnie Gelbart, Thom Fitzgerald)
After a decade away, a gay 25-year-old man returns home to Nova Scotia for his sister's wedding.
Slightly surreal domestic drama with a blackly comic edge.
wd Thom Fitzgerald ph Daniel Jobin m John Roby, Ashley MacIsaac, Heather Rankin, Mary Jane Lamond ad Taavo Soodor ed Susan Shanks
☆ Chris Leavins, Kerry Fox, Seana McKenna, Peter MacNeill, Christine Dunsworth, Troy Veinotte, Sarah Polley, Joel S. Keller
'A strange, utterly original look at a seriously dysfunctional family.' – *Variety*

The Hanging Tree *

US   1959   106m   Technicolor
Warner/Baroda (Martin Jurow, Richard Shepherd)
Life is tough in a Montana gold-mining camp, especially for a doctor who has killed his unfaithful wife.
Lowering Western with a feeling for place and period, plus a welter of melodramatic incident.
w Wendell Mayes, Halsted Welles novel Dorothy M. Johnson d Delmer Daves ph Ted McCord m Max Steiner
☆ Gary Cooper, Maria Schell, Karl Malden, Ben Piazza, George C. Scott
♫ title song (m Jerry Livingston, ly Mack David)

'Every family has a few hang-ups.'

Hanging Up

US   2000   93m   DeLuxe
Columbia (Nora Ephron, Laurence Mark)
After their grumpy old father goes into hospital, three middle-aged sisters indulge in sibling rivalries.
Slick, soft-centred soap-opera with the emphasis on glamour and easy sentimentality.
w Delia Ephron, Nora Ephron book Delia Ephron d Diane Keaton ph Howard Atherton m David Hirschfelder pd Waldemar Kalinowski ed Julie Monroe cos Bobbie Read
☆ Meg Ryan, Diane Keaton, Lisa Kudrow, Walter Matthau, Adam Arkin, Duke Moosekian, Ann Bortolotti, Cloris Leachman, Maree Cheatham, Myndy Crist, Jesse James
'An unspeakably bad film.' – *Guardian*

The Hangman

US   1959   86m   bw
Paramount (Frank Freeman Jnr)
A marshal with a reputation for getting his man deliberately allows one to escape.
Dour, low-key Western, competent but rather flat and uninteresting.
w Dudley Nichols d Michael Curtiz ph Loyal Griggs m Harry Sukman
☆ Robert Taylor, Jack Lord, Fess Parker, Tina Louise, Mickey Shaughnessy

Hangman's House

US   1928   72m   bw   silent
Fox
To please her dying father, an Irish girl marries a wastrel instead of the man she loves, but her husband is killed in a duel.
Blarney-filled melodrama, like a sober Quiet Man. John Wayne can be glimpsed as an extra.
w Marion Orth story Brian Oswald Donn-Byrne d John Ford ph George Schneiderman
☆ June Collyer, Larry Kent, Earle Foxe, Victor McLaglen, Hobart Bosworth

Hangman's Knot

US   1952   81m   Technicolor
Columbia (Harry Joe Brown)
Confederate soldiers returning home with Union booty are waylaid at a way station by renegades.
Adequate suspense Western.
wd Roy Huggins ph Charles Lawton Jnr ad George Brooks ed Gene Havlick
☆ Randolph Scott, Donna Reed, Claude Jarman Jnr, Frank Faylen, Glenn Langan, Richard Denning, Lee Marvin, Jeanette Nolan

Hangmen Also Die! *

US   1943   131m   bw
Arnold Pressburger/Fritz Lang (T. W. Baumfield)
reissue title: *Lest We Forget*
The Nazis take revenge for the killing of Heydrich.
Disappointingly heavy-handed, though deeply felt war propaganda set in Hollywood's idea of Czechoslovakia. Only moments of interest remain.
w John Wexley story Fritz Lang, Bertolt Brecht d Fritz Lang ph James Wong Howe m Hanns Eisler
☆ Brian Donlevy, Anna Lee, Walter Brennan, Gene Lockhart, Dennis O'Keefe, Alexander Granach, Margaret Wycherly, Nana Bryant, Hans von Twardowski, Jonathan Hale, Lionel Stander
'Lang, working with American actors on an American theme, has produced Fury. Lang trying to recreate his own Central Europe on a Hollywood set is completely at sea.' – *Paul Rotha, 1949*
'Directed with a skill which excites and delights … brilliant use of the tiny, shocking detail.' – *Dilys Powell*
'They have chosen to use brutality, American gangster idiom, and middle high German cinematic style to get it across, and it is rich with clever melodrama, over-*maestoso* directional touches, and the sort of Querschnitt sophistication for detail which Lang always has.' – *James Agee*
† Working titles included *The Silent City* and *Never Surrender.*
♫ Hanns Eisler

The Hangover: see *Female Jungle*

Hangover Square *

US   1945   77m   bw
TCF (Robert Bassler)
In 1903 London, a psychopathic composer murders pretty women.
This rather empty melodrama has almost nothing to do with the book from which it is allegedly taken, but the Hollywoodian evocation of gaslit London is richly entertaining and good to look at.
w Barre Lyndon novel Patrick Hamilton d John Brahm ph Joseph LaShelle m Bernard Herrmann ad Lyle Wheeler, Maurice Ransford
☆ Laird Cregar, Linda Darnell, George Sanders, Glenn Langan, Faye Marlowe, Alan Napier, Frederick Worlock
'Cregar lumbers around with a Karloffian glare in the spacious mists which happily blur the architectural decor.' – *Richard Winnington*
'Distinguished photography gets the last glint of fancy fright out of the pomps and vanities of the turn of the century.' – *Time*
'A half-chewed collection of reminiscences of *Dr Jekyll and Mr Hyde* and *The Lodger*.' – *Richard Mallett, Punch*
'The worst betrayal of a first class novel that I can remember.' – *James Agate*
'A better than average horror picture up to, but not including, its wildly overloaded climax.' – *James Agee*
† Tragically, Laird Cregar died after slimming for this role, to which he was in any case unsuited.

Hanky Panky

US   1982   107m   Metrocolor
Columbia (Martin Ransohoff)
A girl on a spy mission is pursued by assassins and enlists the reluctant aid of an architect she meets in a taxi.
Frantic spoof of North by Northwest, which was itself as spoofy as all get out. This strained effort lacks wit, substituting shouting, violence and an exasperating hero.
w Henry Rosenbaum, David Taylor d Sidney Poitier ph Arthur Ornitz m Tom Scott pd Ben Edwards ed Harry Keller
☆ Gene Wilder, Gilda Radner, Kathleen Quinlan, Richard Widmark
'The plot, rather like Mr Wilder, rushes hither and yon at the slightest excuse without ever adding up to very much. Even McGuffins are supposed to make more sense than this.' – *Richard Combs, MFB*
'A comedy thriller designed solely as a vehicle for Wilder's uninhibited hysteria is bad enough; one that so thoroughly submerges everyone else is so much worse.' – *Sight and Sound*
'One long screech.' – *Ibid.*

Hannah and Her Sisters ***

US 1986 106m Technicolor
Orion/Charles R. Joffe, Jack Rollins (Robert Greenhut)

📀 🇺🇸 🎧

Relationships intermingle for a New York family over a two-year period between Thanksgiving dinners.

Even though it has nowhere in particular to go, and certain scenes are over the top, this is a brilliantly assembled and thoroughly enjoyable mélange of fine acting and New Yorkish one-liners, with particularly sharp editing and a nostalgic music score.

wd Woody Allen ph Carlo di Palma m popular and classical extracts pd Stuart Wurtzel ed Susan E. Morse

☆ Woody Allen, Mia Farrow, Dianne Wiest, Michael Caine, Carrie Fisher, Barbara Hershey, Maureen O'Sullivan, Lloyd Nolan, Max von Sydow, Daniel Stern, Sam Waterston, Tony Roberts

'A loosely knit canvas of Manhattan interiors and exteriors.' – Sight and Sound

'One of Woody Allen's great films.' – Variety

🏆 best original screenplay; Dianne Wiest; Michael Caine

🏵 best picture; Woody Allen (as director); Susan E. Morse; art direction

🎖 best original screenplay; direction

Hanna's War

US 1988 148m colour
Cannon (Menahem Golan, Yoram Globus)

📀 🇺🇸 🎧

A Jewish poetess, working for the British secret service, is parachuted into Yugoslavia, captured and, after being taken to Budapest, is tortured and executed.

A true and tragic story diminished by its clumsy telling.

wd Menahem Golan books The Diaries of Hanna Senesh by Hanna Senesh; A Great Wind Cometh by Yoel Palgi ph Elemer Ragalyi m Dov Seltzer pd Kuli Sander ed Alain Jakubowicz

☆ Ellen Burstyn, Maruschka Detmers, Anthony Andrews, Donald Pleasence, David Warner, Vincenzo Ricotta, Christopher Fairbank

Hannibal

👫 Italy 1959 103m Technicolor
Superscinescope
Liber Film (Ottavio Poggi)

Hannibal crosses the Alps and falls for the daughter of a Roman senator.

Unhistorical farrago which totally fails to entertain on any level.

w Mortimer Braus d Carlo Ludovico Bragaglia, Edgar G. Ulmer ph Raffaele Masciocchi m Carlo Rustichelli

☆ Victor Mature, Rita Gam, Gabriele Ferzetti, Milly Vitale, Rik Battaglia

'Not even the elephants emerge with dignity.' – MFB

Hannibal Brooks

GB 1968 102m DeLuxe
UA/Scimitar (Michael Winner)

A British POW in Germany escapes over the Alps with an elephant.

Curious action adventure which seems undecided whether to take itself seriously. Some passable sequences.

w Dick Clement, Ian La Frenais d Michael Winner ph Robert Paynter m Francis Lai

☆ Oliver Reed, Michael J. Pollard, Wolfgang Preiss, Karin Baal

Hannie Caulder

GB 1971 85m colour Panavision
Tigon/Curtwel (Tony Tenser)

📀 🇺🇸 🎧

Raped by three outlaws who murdered her husband, a Western woman takes revenge.

Unintentionally comical action melodrama with the star defeating all comers.

w Z. X. Jones (Burt Kennedy, David Haft) d Burt Kennedy ph Ted Scaife m Ken Thorne

☆ Raquel Welch, Robert Culp, Ernest Borgnine, Strother Martin, Jack Elam, Christopher Lee, Diana Dors

Hanover Street

GB 1979 108m Technicolor Panavision
Columbia (Paul N. Lazarus III)

📀 🎧

In 1943, an American bomber pilot meets a Red Cross nurse in a bus queue.

Wartime romance of a rather sticky sort, which turns with little warning into escape adventure, with our hero rescuing his loved one's husband from certain death.

wd Peter Hyams ph David Watkin m John Barry pd Philip Harrison

☆ Harrison Ford, Lesley-Anne Down, Christopher Plummer, Alec McCowen, Richard Masur, Michael Sacks, Max Wall

Hans Christian Andersen *

👫 US 1952 112m Technicolor
Samuel Goldwyn

📀 🇺🇸 🎧

A storytelling cobbler leaves his village to make shoes for the prima ballerina in Copenhagen.

Artificial, sugary confection with little humour and far too little magic of any kind; the star carries it nicely, but he is on his own apart from the songs.

w Moss Hart d Charles Vidor ph Harry Stradling m/ly Frank Loesser md Walter Scharf ch Roland Petit ad Richard Day

☆ Danny Kaye, Zizi Jeanmaire, Farley Granger, John Qualen, Joey Walsh

'I found it such a charming entertainment, full of happiness and pathos, expert in interpretation yet swinging along with a gay holiday spirit that, when it was all over, I wanted to sit still for a minute and think about it, and then go away and sing its praises.' – C. A. Lejeune

† 16 screenplays were written before this one was chosen. Moira Shearer was signed for the role of ballerina but became pregnant. Gary Cooper was thought of for the lead, with William Wyler as director

🎵 'The King's New Clothes'; 'I'm Hans Christian Andersen'; 'Wonderful Copenhagen'; 'The Ugly Duckling'; 'Anywhere I Wander'; 'The Inch Worm'; 'No Two People'.

🏵 Harry Stradling; Walter Scharf; song 'Thumbelina'

Hanussen *

Hungary/West Germany 1988 117m
Eastmancolor
Columbia TriStar/Objektiv/Mafilm/CCC Filmkunst/ZDF (Arthur Brauner)

📀 🇺🇸 🎧

An Austrian clairvoyant's predictions are used as Nazi propaganda.

Unusual, if somewhat insubstantial, political drama.

w István Szabó, Péter Dobai d István Szabó ph Lajos Koltai m György Vukan ed Zsuzsa Csákány, Eva Szentandrási, Brigitta Kajdácsi, Bettina Rekuc

☆ Klaus Maria Brandauer, Erland Josephson, Ildikó Bánsági, Walter Schmidinger, Károly Eperjes

🏵 best foreign film

The Happening

US 1967 101m Technicolor
Columbia/Horizon/Dover (Jud Kinberg)

Four young hippies kidnap a wealthy businessman and don't know what to do with him; he turns the tables.

Freewheeling irresponsible comedy which even at the time of swinging cities seemed very irritating.

w Frank R. Pierson, James D. Buchanan, Ronald Austin d Elliot Silverstein ph Philip Lathrop m Frank de Vol pd Richard Day

☆ Anthony Quinn, George Maharis, Michael Parks, Faye Dunaway, Robert Walker, Oscar Homolka, Martha Hyer, Milton Berle, Jack Kruschen

'A wacky comedy à la mode, oddly mixed and only spasmodically effective.' – Variety

Happidrome

GB 1943 87m bw
Aldwych

A play intended seriously becomes a comedy hit.

A theme later used by The Producers forms the background for this naïve screen version of a wartime radio series.

w Tom Arnold, James Seymour d Phil Brandon

☆ Harry Korris, Robbie Vincent, Cecil Frederick, Bunty Meadows, Lisa Lee, 'Hutch', the Cairoli Brothers

The Happiest Days of Your Life ***

👫 GB 1950 81m bw
British Lion/Individual (Frank Launder)

📀

A ministry mistake billets a girls' school on a boys' school.

Briskly handled version of a semi-classic postwar farce, with many familiar talents in excellent form.

w Frank Launder, John Dighton play John Dighton d Frank Launder ph Stan Pavey m Mischa Spoliansky

☆ Alastair Sim, Margaret Rutherford, Joyce Grenfell, Richard Wattis, Edward Rigby, Guy Middleton, Muriel Aked, John Bentley, Bernadette O'Farrell

'Absolutely first rate fun.' – Richard Mallett, Punch

'Launder couldn't have knocked another laugh out of the situation if he'd used a hockey stick.' – Sunday Express

'The best mixed comedy pairing since Groucho Marx and Margaret Dumont.' – Sunday Chronicle

The Happiest Millionaire

👫 US 1967 159m Technicolor
Walt Disney (Bill Anderson)

📀

In 1916, a sporting millionaire has several surprising interests but finds time to sort out family problems.

Drearily inept family entertainment with a couple of good songs and an amusing alligator sequence but acres of yawning boredom in between.

w A. J. Carothers play Kyle Crichton book My Philadelphia Father by Cornelia Drexel Biddle d Norman Tokar ph Edward Colman m/ly Richard M. and Robert B. Sherman md Jack Elliott

☆ Fred MacMurray, Tommy Steele, Greer Garson, John Davidson, Gladys Cooper, Lesley Ann Warren, Geraldine Page, Hermione Baddeley

Happiness ***

US 1998 139m DuArt
October/Good Machine/Killer Films (Ted Hope, Christine Vachon)

📀

A group of suburbanites seek, but do not find, fulfilment.

A bleak drama, verging on the misanthropic but lightened by a cutting wit, on the unsuccessful pursuit of happiness, and the subsequent discovery of the joylessness of sex and the damage that people can do to one another in unsatisfactory relationships.

wd Todd Solondz ph Maryse Alberti m Robbie Kondor pd Therese Deprez ed Alan Oxman

☆ Jane Adams, Dylan Baker, Lara Flynn Boyle, Ben Gazzara, Jared Harris, Philip Seymour Hoffman, Jon Lovitz, Marla Maples, Cynthia Stevenson, Elizabeth Ashley, Louise Lasser

'A disturbing black comedy that, at bottom, is about all the trouble sex causes people ... Controversy and critical support will create want-see among discerning and adventurous specialty audiences, but breakout to a wider public will be difficult.' – Todd McCarthy, Variety

The Happiness of Three Women

GB 1954 78m bw
Advance

A village postman and busybody adopts various subterfuges to improve the future happiness of his clients.

Minor Welsh waffle which pleased naïve audiences at the time.

w Eynon Evans play Wishing Well by Eynon Evans d Maurice Elvey ph Stan Pavey m Edwin Astley

☆ Brenda de Banzie, Eynon Evans, Petula Clark, Donald Houston, Patricia Burke, Patricia Cutts

Happy

GB 1934 84m bw
ABPC/BIP (Fred Zelnik)

Two musicians find fortune and love in Paris.

Amiable musical, using revue and music-hall talents of the time, although the atmosphere remains resolutely Cockney despite its French setting.

w Austin Melford, Stanley Lupino, Frank Launder d Fred Zelnik ph Claude Friese-Greene m Fred Schwarz m/ly Stanley Lupino, Noel Gay and others md Harry Acres ad Clarence Elder and A. S. Bates

☆ Stanley Lupino, Laddie Cliff, Will Fyffe, Dorothy Hyson, Renee Gadd, Harry Tate, Bertha Belmore, Gus McNaughton

† The script was adapted from French and German films written by Jacques Bachrach, Alfred Halm and Karl Noti.

†† Stanley Lupino and Laddie Cliff formed a notable partnership in several successful stage musicals.

Happy Anniversary

US 1959 83m bw
UA/Ralph Fields

A television set causes family trouble.

Marital farce designed to take a few sideswipes at TV.

w Joseph Fields, Jerome Chodorov play Anniversary Waltz by Joseph Fields, Jerome Chodorov d David Miller ph Lee Garmes m Sol Kaplan, Robert Allan

☆ David Niven, Mitzi Gaynor, Carl Reiner, Loring Smith, Patty Duke, Phyllis Povah

Happy Anniversary *

France 1961 13m bw
Capac

A husband is late for his anniversary dinner because of a traffic jam.

Amusing gag comedy, virtually silent and all the better for it.

wd Pierre Etaix

☆ Pierre Etaix, Loriot, Nono Zammit

Happy Birthday to Me

Canada 1980 111m Metrocolor
Birthday/CFDC/Famous Players (John Dunning, Andre Link)

📀 🎧

Members of the senior class at Crawford Academy are killed off one at a time by one of their number.

Abysmal teenage shocker which grinds on relentlessly for nearly two hours.

w Timothy Bond, Peter Jobin, John Saxton d J. Lee-Thompson ph Miklos Lente m Bo Harwood, Lance Rubin

☆ Melissa Sue Anderson, Glenn Ford, Lawrence Dane, Sharon Acker, Frances Hyland

Happy Birthday Wanda June *

US 1971 105m Technicolor
Columbia (Lester Goldsmith)

An adventurer believed dead returns just as his wife is about to choose one of two suitors.

A farcical situation becomes in this writer's hands an investigation of the hero cult, with many zany jokes, episodes in heaven, and bad language. Interesting in spots, but it would have worked better with a more fluent cinematic technique.

w Kurt Vonnegut Jnr play Kurt Vonnegut Jnr d Mark Robson ph Fred J. Koenekamp

☆ Rod Steiger, Susannah York, George Grizzard, Don Murray

'We can only assume that Mr Robson deserted the filmic instincts that brought him commercial success because here he was, finally, in the presence of Art.' – Hollis Alpert

'Nothing more than a miscast film record of the dialogue and plot outline of the stage work.' – Judith Crist

Happy Days

US 1930 86m bw Grandeur
Fox

A showboat singer is a hit in New York and helps her old friends.

Virtually a revue, with spectacular effects on the giant screen.

w Sidney Lanfield, Edwin Burke d Benjamin Stoloff ph Lucien Andriot and others m Hugo Friedhofer m/ly various

☆ Marjorie White, Janet Gaynor, Charles Farrell, Victor McLaglen, Edmund Lowe, El Brendel, Walter Catlett, James J. Corbett, Tom Patricola, Dixie Lee, Sharon Lynn, Whispering Jack Smith

'We don't love. We just make love. And damn little of that!'

The Happy Ending *

US 1969 112m Technicolor Panavision
UA/Pax Films (Richard Brooks)

📀

A middle-aged woman reflects over sixteen years of unhappy marriage.

Sometimes glum, sometimes trenchant sophisticated drama with enough interesting scenes to make it more than merely a 'woman's picture'.

wd Richard Brooks ph Conrad Hall m Michel Legrand

☆ Jean Simmons, John Forsythe, Shirley Jones, Lloyd Bridges, Teresa Wright, Dick Shawn, Nanette Fabray, Bobby Darin, Tina Louise

'Packed with punchy little epigrams floating in a vacuum of glossy superficiality.' – David Wilson

'The truth about the process of ageing is what binds this film together like cement.' – Alexander Walker

---

📀 Digital Video Disc Region 2   📀 Digital Video Disc Region 1   🎧 Soundtrack released on compact disc   ☆ Cast in approximate order of importance   † Points of interest   🎵 Notable songs   🏆 Academy Award   🏵 Academy Award nomination   🎖 BAFTA

♫ Jean Simmons; song 'What Are You Doing the Rest of Your Life' (mMichel Legrand, lyAlan and Marilyn Bergman)

Happy Ever After

GB/Germany 1932 86m bw

UFA (Erich Pommer)

Window-cleaners put a young actress on the way to stardom.

Cheerful comedy, set and made in Germany by mainly British talent.

w Jack Hulbert, Douglas Furber story Walter Reisch, Billy Wilder d Paul Martin, Robert Stevenson

☆ Lilian Harvey, Jack Hulbert, Cicely Courtneidge, Sonnie Hale, Edward Chapman

Happy Ever After *

GB 1954 87m Technicolor

ABP/Mario Zampi

▦

US title: *Tonight's the Night*

Irish villagers draw lots for the privilege of murdering their rascally squire.

Fairly hilarious black comedy with a good cast entering into the spirit of the thing.

w Jack Davies, Michael Pertwee, L. A. G. Strong d Mario Zampi ph Stan Pavey m Stanley Black

☆ David Niven, Yvonne de Carlo, A. E. Matthews, Michael Shepley, George Cole, Barry Fitzgerald

Happy Family: see *The Merry Frinks (1934)*

The Happy Family

GB 1952 86m bw

London Independent (William McQuitty)

US title: *Mr Lord Says No*

A shopkeeper refuses to move and provide a site for the Festival of Britain.

Pale Ealing imitation with amiable cast.

w Muriel and Sydney Box play Michael Clayton Hutton d Muriel Box ph Reginald Wyer m Francis Chagrin

☆ Stanley Holloway, Kathleen Harrison, Naunton Wayne, George Cole, Dandy Nichols, Miles Malleson

Happy Gilmore

US 1996 92m DeLuxe

Universal (Robert Simonds)

▦ ▦ ▣

A bad-tempered ice hockey player, in need of quick money, discovers that he has a talent for golf.

Crude and clumsy slapstick comedy, bone-crunchingly boring.

w Adam Sandler, Tim Herlihy d Dennis Dugan ph Arthur Albert m Mark Mothersbaugh pd Perry Andelin Blake ed Jeff G———

☆ Adam Sandler, Christopher McDonald, Julie Bowen, Frances Bay, Carl Weathers, Alan Covert, Robert Smigel, Richard Kiel, Dennis Dugan

'The laughs come from inflicting injury on anything animate and the hero's answer to every setback lie suffers is a bone-crunching punch, a head butt, a kick in the ribs or groin, all gratifyingly amplified on the soundtrack. Maybe the damage this might do to impressionable kids is unproven. But the damage it does to wit, character and story-telling is demonstrable.' – *Alexander Walker*

Happy Go Lovely

GB 1950 97m Technicolor

Excelsior (Marcel Hellman)

▦

A chorus girl meets a millionaire during the Edinburgh Festival.

For a semi-official contribution to the Festival of Britain this is a lamentably unspontaneous musical with no use of cinema techniques or natural locales. Even allowing for the flat handling, it is tedious.

w Val Guest d Bruce Humberstone ph Erwin Hillier m Mischa Spoliansky

☆ David Niven, Vera-Ellen, Cesar Romero, Bobby Howes, Diane Hart, Gordon Jackson, Barbara Couper, Gladys Henson, Joyce Carey

† A remake of *Paradise for Two.*

Happy Go Lucky

US 1942 81m Technicolor

Paramount (Harold Wilson)

A cigarette girl chases a millionaire to a Caribbean island.

Flimsy musical for those who like the stars.

w Walter de Leon, Melvin Frank, Norman Panama d Curtis Bernhardt ph Karl Struss, Wilfrid Cline m/ly Frank Loesser, Jimmy McHugh

☆ Mary Martin, Dick Powell, Betty Hutton, Rudy Vallee, Eddie Bracken, Mabel Paige, Eric Blore, Clem Bevans

Happy Gypsies *

Yugoslavia 1967 90m Eastmancolor

Avala

US title: *I Even Met Happy Gypsies*

A handsome, cruel-natured gypsy and his wife have violent adventures and find themselves on the run from the police.

The first film in the gypsy language does not make one too sympathetic to their cause, but some scenes are well managed and the colour is fine.

wd Alexander Petrovic ph Tomislav Pinter m gypsy melodies

☆ Bekim Fehmiu, Olivera Vuco, Bata Zivojinovic

♟ best foreign film

The Happy Hooker

US 1975 98m Movielab

Double H/Cannon-Happy (Fred Caruso)

▦ ▣

A Dutch girl in New York starts a career as a prostitute and finds she enjoys it.

Glum sex comedy based on the supposed exploits of a real madam; crude and not very funny. If this is emancipation, Shirley Temple seems more attractive by the minute.

w William Richert book Xaviera Hollander d Nicholas Sgarro ph Dick Kratina m Don Elliott

☆ Lynn Redgrave (hilariously miscast), Jean-Pierre Aumont, Lovelady Powell, Nicholas Pryor, Elizabeth Wilson, Tom Poston, Conrad Janis, Richard Lynch

† Follow-ups: *The Happy Hooker Goes to Washington* (1977), *The Happy Hooker Goes to Hollywood* (1980).

Happy Is the Bride *

GB 1957 84m bw

Panther/Paul Soskin

A couple planning a quiet summer wedding reckon without the intervention of her parents.

Tame remake of Quiet Wedding; the right spirit but not much sparkle.

w Jeffrey Dell, Roy Boulting play Esther McCracken d Roy Boulting ph Ted Scaife m Benjamin Frankel

☆ Ian Carmichael, Janette Scott, Cecil Parker, Joyce Grenfell, Terry-Thomas, John Le Mesurier, Eric Barker, Edith Sharpe, Athene Seyler

Happy Land *

US 1943 75m bw

TCF (Kenneth MacGowan)

Grandfather's ghost comes back to comfort a family which has lost its son at war.

Sentimental flagwaver very typical of its time; well made, it ensured not a dry eye in the house.

w Kathryn Scola, Julien Josephson novel Mackinlay Kantor d Irving Pichel ph Joseph LaShelle m Cyril Mockridge

☆ Don Ameche, Frances Dee, Harry Carey, Ann Rutherford, Cara Williams, Henry Morgan, Richard Crane, Dickie Moore

Happy Landing: see *Flying High (1931)*

Happy Landing *

US 1938 102m bw

TCF (David Hempstead)

A Norwegian girl falls for an American flyer who crashes near her home.

Lightweight skating musical, well put together.

w Milton Sperling, Boris Ingster d Roy del Ruth ph John Mescall md Louis Silvers

☆ Sonja Henie, Don Ameche, Cesar Romero, Ethel Merman, Jean Hersholt, Billy Gilbert, Wally Vernon, El Brendel

'Just about everything to ensure entertainment value, shrewdly blended.' – *Variety*

Happy New Year *

France/Italy 1973 115m Eastmancolor

Films 13/Rizzoli (Claude Lelouch)

▦

original title: *La Bonne Année*

A thief is paroled on New Year's Eve in the hope that he will lead police to his confederates. In fact he learns a lot about the world and himself.

Bitter comedy apparently intended to distance the director from the romantic fervour of A Man and a Woman, a clip from which is screened for the convicts at the beginning.

m Francis Lai wd/ph Claude Lelouch

☆ Lino Ventura, Françoise Fabian, Charles Gérard, André Falcon

Happy New Year *

US 1987 85m DeLuxe

Columbia/Delphi IV (Jerry Weintraub)

Two middle-aged jewel thieves head for a big score in Florida.

Loose remake of Lelouch's La Bonne Année, quite watchable in its familiar way.

w Warren Lane d John G. Avildsen ph James Crabe m Bill Conti pd William J. Cassidy ed Jane Kuson

☆ Peter Falk, Charles Durning, Wendy Hughes, Tom Courtenay, Joan Copeland

The Happy Road *

👪 US/France 1956 100m bw

MGM/Thor (Gene Kelly)

Two children run away from a Swiss school and are pursued by the American father of one of them.

Whimsical peripatetic comedy which fails to come off despite charming passages.

w Arthur Julian, Joseph Morhaim, Harry Kurnitz d Gene Kelly ph Robert Juillard m George Van Parys

☆ Gene Kelly, Barbara Laage, Michael Redgrave, Bobby Clark, Brigitte Fossey

'Happy, Texas. Where even people on the run find a moment to be fabulous.'

Happy, Texas **

US 1999 104m Foto-Kem

Marked Entertainment (Mark Illsley, Rick Montgomery, Ed Stone)

▦ ▦ ▣

Two escaped convicts are mistaken for a gay couple who have been hired to stage a beauty pageant in a small town.

Enjoyably eccentric comedy of mistaken identity and sexual confusion.

w Mark Illsley, Ed Stone, Phil Reeves d Mark Illsley ph Bruce Douglas Johnson m Peter Harris pd Maurin Scarlata ed Norman Buckley

☆ Jeremy Northam, Steve Zahn, William H. Macy, Ally Walker, Illeana Douglas, M.C. Gainey, Ron Perlman, Tim Bagley, Michael Hitchcock, Paul Dooley

'A film that, although bright and likeable, is otherwise a touch good-natured for its own good.' – *Philip Kemp, Sight and Sound*

The Happy Thieves

US 1962 88m bw

UA/Hillworth (James Hill, Rita Hayworth)

A gentleman thief and his accomplice become unwittingly involved in murder.

Dreary comedy which turns into equally dreary drama and makes its European backgrounds look ugly.

w John Gay novel The Oldest Confession by Richard Condon d George Marshall ph Paul Beeson m Mario Nascimbene

☆ Rex Harrison, Rita Hayworth, Grégoire Aslan, Joseph Wiseman, Alida Valli

'Absolute rubbish.' – *Rex Harrison*

The Happy Time ***

US 1952 94m bw

Columbia/Stanley Kramer (Earl Felton)

Domestic misadventures of a family of French Canadians during the twenties.

Basically concerned with adolescent sexual stirrings, this very agreeable film has a light touch and is most deftly directed and acted.

w Earl Felton play Samuel A. Taylor d Richard Fleischer ph Charles Lawton Jnr m Dimitri Tiomkin pd Rudolph Sternad

☆ Charles Boyer, Louis Jourdan, Bobby Driscoll, Marsha Hunt, Marcel Dalio, Kurt Kasznar, Linda Christian, Jeanette Nolan, Jack Raine, Richard Erdman

Happy Times: see *The Inspector General*

Happy Together

US 1990 96m Metrocolor

Seymour Borde (Jere Henshaw)

▦ ▦ ▣

Due to a mix-up, a prudish college student finds himself sharing a room with an attractive girl.

Predictable teenage wish-fulfilment comedy unlikely to interest anyone over school-going age.

w Craig J. Nevius d Mel Damski ph Joe Pennella m Robert Folk pd Marcia Hinds ed O. Nicholas Brown

☆ Patrick Dempsey, Helen Slater, Dan Schneider, Kevin Hardesty, Marius Weyers, Barbara Babcock

Happy Together *

Hong Kong 1997 97m bw/colour

Artificial/Block 2/Prenom H/Seawoo/Jet Tone (Wong Kar-Wai)

▦ ▦ ♫

original title: *Chunguang Zhaxie*

In Argentina, two Chinese male lovers quarrel and part.

An intense and claustrophobic study of jealousies and passion, done with an excess of style.

wd Wong Kar-Wai novel The Buenos Aires Affair by Manuel Puig ph Christopher Doyle m Danny Chung pd William Chang Suk-ping ed William Chang Suk-ping, Wong Ming-Lam

☆ Leslie Cheung, Tony Leung, Chang Chen

'In the absence of any genuine emotional wallop, it is the directorial pizzazz that pulls you through. Just about.' – *Ian Freer, Empire*

† The film won Wong Kar-Wai the prize as best director at the 1997 Cannes Film Festival

Happy We *

Sweden 1983 111m colour

AB Svenski Filmindustri

original title: *Tv Killar Och en Tjej*

A dentist recalls how he met his second wife, renewing a friendship begun in student days with her and her former husband.

Pleasantly nostalgic comedy of love and marriage, mainly roses all the way with the occasional thorn of sharp observation.

w Brasse Brännström, Lasse Hallström, Magnus Härenstam d Lasse Hallström ph Roland Lundin, Torbjörn Andersson m Anders Berglund ad Lasse Westfelt ed Lasse Hallström, Jan Persson

☆ Brasse Brännström, Magnus Härenstam, Lars Amble, Ivan Oljelund, Pia Green

The Happy Years

US 1950 86m bw

MGM (Carey Wilson)

The taming of an unruly pupil at a turn-of-the-century American school.

A curiously unrealized piece of Americana, with only moments to suggest what was being aimed at.

w Harry Ruskin novel The Lawrenceville School Stories by Owen Johnson d William Wellman ph Paul C. Vogel m Leigh Harline

☆ Dean Stockwell, Leo G. Carroll, Darryl Hickman, Scotty Beckett, Leon Ames, Margalo Gillmore

Hara Kiri: see *The Battle (1934)*

Hara Kiri *

Japan 1962 135m bw Grandscope

Shochiku (Tatsuo Hosoya)

original title: *Seppuku*

17th-century samurai often pretend to commit hara kiri so that a grand lord will have sympathy and take them on. One of them is forced to go through with it.

Strange, traditional, slow and explicitly brutal costume piece, for specialized western eyes only.

w Shinobu Hashimoto d Masaki Kobayashi ph Yoshio Miyajima m Toru Takemitsu ad Junichi Ozumi

☆ Tatsuya Nakadai, Shima Iwashita, Akira Isahama

'As a cop, he has brains, brawn and an instinct to kill.'

Hard Boiled *

Hong Kong 1992 126m colour

Golden Princess/Milestone (Linda Kuk, Terence Chang)

▦ ▦ ▦ ▣ ▣ ♫

original title: *Lashou Shentan*

A gun-happy cop smashes a smuggling ring.

👪 film suitable for family viewing   ▦ VHS video-cassette for the British PAL system   ▦ VHS video-cassette for the British PAL system in wide screen-format   ✧ Video cassette in a computer-colourised version   ▦ American NTSC video-cassette   ▣ Laser disc

Spectacularly violent gangster movie, with a body-count in the hundreds and stylishly choreographed, slow-motion deaths and stunts; possibly the best example of John Woo's particular talents for large-scale mayhem.

w Barry Wong *story* John Woo d John Woo ph Wang Wing-Heng m Michael Gibbs, James Wong ad James Leung, Joel Chong ed John Woo, David Wu, Kai Kit-Wai

☆ Chow Yun-Fat, Tony Leung, Teresa Mo, Philip Chan, Philip Kwok, Anthony Wong, Kwan Hoi-Shan, Tung Wai, Y. Yonemura

'Superbly choreographed violence … Pic delivers ample ammunition with a good dose of humor.' – *Variety*

'A vivid cartoon version of the kinetics and twisted-loyalty themes of Sam Peckinpah.' – *Michael Sragow, New Yorker*

† The film was released on video in a subtitled wide-screen and a dubbed version.

The Hard Boiled Canary
US   1941   80m   bw
Paramount (Andrew Stone)
GB title: *There's Magic in Music*

A young burlesque singer is softened at a summer music school.
Another Pygmalion enterprise, but the story is only a slim vehicle for the songs.
w Frederick Jackson *story* Andrew L. Stone, Robert Lively, Ann Ronell d Andrew Stone
☆ Susanna Foster, Allan Jones, Margaret Lindsay, Lynne Overman, William Collier Snr

Hard Contract
US   1969   106m   DeLuxe   Panavision
TCF (Marvin Schwarz)

A professional killer has sexual hang-ups.
Heavy-going modern thriller with lively scenes separated by too much self-analytical chat, not to mention a tour of Europe.
wd S. Lee Pogostin ph Jack Hildyard m Alex North
☆ James Coburn, Lilli Palmer, Lee Remick, Burgess Meredith, Patrick Magee, Sterling Hayden, Helen Cherry, Karen Black, Claude Dauphin

'Behind it one glimpses a much better film than its surface suggests.' – *MFB*
'Like a flat-footed James Bond story that soaked its feet in a hot bath of existentialism.' – *John Simon*

Hard Country
US   1981   104m   CFI color
AFD (David Greene, Mack Bing)
▦ ⊛

An urban cowboy has no ambitions until he falls in love.
Simple modern Western with music, not at all bad but with a scant potential audience.
w Michael Kane d David Greene ph Dennis Dalzell m Michael Martin Murphey, Jimmie Haskell pd Edward Richardson ed John A. Martinelli
☆ Jan-Michael Vincent, Kim Basinger, Michael Parks, Tanya Tucker, Gailard Sartain

A Hard Day's Night ****
👫   GB   1964   85m   bw
UA/Proscenium (Walter Shenson)
▦ ▤ ⊛ ⊚ ♫

Harassed by their manager and Paul's grandpa, the Beatles embark from Liverpool by train for a London TV show.
Comic fantasia with music; an enormous commercial success with the director trying every cinematic gag in the book, it led directly to all the kaleidoscopic swinging London spy thrillers and comedies of the later sixties, and so has a lot to answer for; but at the time it was a sweet breath of fresh air, and the Beatles even seemed willing and likeable.
w Alun Owen d Richard Lester ph Gilbert Taylor m/ly The Beatles md George Martin
☆ The Beatles, Wilfrid Brambell, Norman Rossington, Victor Spinetti

'A fine conglomeration of madcap clowning … with such a dazzling use of camera that it tickles the intellect and electrifies the nerves.' – *Bosley Crowther*
'All technology was enlisted in the service of the gag, and a kind of nuclear gagmanship exploded.' – *John Simon*
'The *Citizen Kane* of Jukebox movies' – *Andrew Sarris*

† It has also been released on CD-ROM for Apple Macintosh computers, together with the script and an essay on the movie.
⌕ Alun Owen; George Martin

Hard Driver: see *The Last American Hero*

Hard Eight *
US   1996   101m   DeLuxe   Super 35
Entertainment/Rysher/Green Parrot (Robert Jones, John Lyons)
▦ ▤ ⊚

A con man has a private reason for taking as a protégé an unsuccessful young gambler.
Tough-talking, low-budget thriller with an atmosphere both claustrophobic and menacing.
wd Paul Thomas Anderson ph Robert Elswit m Michael Penn, Jon Brion pd Nancy Deren ed Barbara Tulliver
☆ Philip Baker Hall, John C. Reilly, Gwyneth Paltrow, Samuel L. Jackson, F. William Parker, Philip Seymour Hoffman

'Modern *film noir* of sure touch pivoting round a remarkable performance given by Philip Baker Hall.' – *Richard Williams, Guardian*

Hard, Fast and Beautiful
US   1951   76m   bw
RKO/The Filmmakers (Collier Young)

A girl tennis player is influenced by her ambitious mother.
Unusual but not very effective melodrama.
w Martha Wilkerson *novel* John R. Tunis d Ida Lupino ph Archie Stout m Roy Webb
☆ Claire Trevor, Sally Forrest, Carleton Young, Robert Clarke, Kenneth Patterson, Joseph Kearns

Hard Men
GB/France   1996   87m   colour
Entertainment/Venture/Dacia (J. K. Amalou, Georges Benayoun)
▦

A London gangster orders two of his enforcers to kill a colleague.
Low-budget movie of a second-hand kind, fashionably violent.
wd J. K. Amalou ph Nick Sawyer pd Simon Elliott ed Victoria Boydell
☆ Vincent Regan, Ross Boatman, Lee Ross, 'Mad' Frankie Fraser, Ken Campbell, Mirella D'Angelo

'A game attempt at a British Tarantino that has its moments but is deep-sixed by lackluster dialogue and uninvolving characters.' – *Derek Elley, Variety*

Hard Promises
US   1991   95m   DeLuxe
Columbia/Stone/High Horse (Cindy Chvatal, William Petersen)
▦ ⊚

An absentee husband, discovering that his wife has divorced him, returns home to prevent her remarriage.
Drear domestic comedy in which it is hard to sympathize with any of the main characters.
w Jule Selbo d Martin Davidson ph Andrzej Bartkowiak m Kenny Vance pd Dan Leigh ed Bonnie Koehler
☆ Sissy Spacek, William Petersen, Brian Kerwin, Mare Winningham, Jeff Perry, Olivia Burnette, Peter MacNicol

Hard Rain
US   1998   96m   DeLuxe   Panavision
Paramount/Mutual (Mark Gordon, Gary Levinsohn, Ian Bryce)
▦ ▤ ⊛ ⊚ ⊚ ♫

In a flooded town, a bank robber and an unscrupulous sheriff battle to get their hands on a fortune in stolen notes.
A mix of disaster movie and thriller; the result is a disastrous thriller.
w Graham Yost d Mikael Salomon ph Peter Menzies Jnr m Christopher Young pd J. Michael Riva ed Paul Hirsch
☆ Morgan Freeman, Christian Slater, Randy Quaid, Minnie Driver, Ed Asner, Richard Dysart, Betty White, Mark Rolston

'A waterlogged would-be thriller deep-sixed by its misguided notion of high concept.' – *Todd McCarthy, Variety*
† The film was made in 1996 and then, according to reports, altered to make less a disaster movie and more a thriller.

Hard Steel
GB   1942   86m   bw
GFD/GHW (James B. Sloan)
reissue title: *What Shall It Profit*

A steel worker is promoted and loses his humanity, but comes to his senses when his wife leaves him.
Modest moral drama from the uplift side of the Rank empire.
w Lydia Hayward *novel* Steel Saraband by Roger Dataller d Norman Walker ph Claude Friese-Greene
☆ Wilfrid Lawson, Betty Stockfeld, John Stuart, George Carney, Joan Kemp-Welch, Hay Petrie

'Don't hunt what you can't kill.'
Hard Target
US   1993   97m   DeLuxe
UIP/Alphaville/Renaissance (James Jacks, Sean Daniel)
▦ ▤ ⊛ ⊚ ♫

In New Orleans, a wealthy man organizes the hunting and killing of men for sport.
John Woo, Hong Kong's influential director of action films, makes his American debut with yet another re-make of The Most Dangerous Game; *the experience seems not to have been a happy one for him, or for his audience.*
w Chuck Pfarrer d John Woo ph Russell Carpenter m Graeme Revell pd Phil Dagort ed Bob Murawski
☆ Jean-Claude Van Damme, Lance Henriksen, Yancy Butler, Arnold Vosloo, Kasi Lemmons, Wilford Brimley, Chuck Pfarrer

'A thuggish, badly scripted thriller.' – *Philip French, Observer*
'Giggles seem as appropriate as shocked gasps. For this film has nothing to do with real life or real violence.' – *Nigel Andrews, Financial Times*

Hard Times *
US   1975   93m   Metrocolor   Panavision
Columbia (Lawrence Gordon)
▦ ▤ ⊛
GB title: *The Streetfighter*

In New Orleans in the Depression-hit thirties, a prizefighter and a promoter help each other.
Interesting, atmospheric melodrama on the lone stranger theme.
w Walter Hill, Bryan Gindorff, Bruce Henstell d Walter Hill ph Philip Lathrop m Barry DeVorzon
☆ Charles Bronson, James Coburn, Jill Ireland, Strother Martin, Maggie Blye

Hard Times *
Portugal/GB   1988   96m   bw
Artificial Eye/Joã Botelho
original title: *Tempos dificeis, este tempo*

A circus child is brought up in the loveless household of a pedant who teaches his children to revere facts.
Dickens is scaled down, but effectively translated to modern-day Portugal.
wd Joã Botelho *novel* Charles Dickens ph Elso Roque m António Pinho Vargas ad Jasmin Matos ed Joã Botelho
☆ Luis Estreka, Julia Britton, Isabel de Castro, Ruy Furtado, Inês Medeiros, Henrique Viana, Lia Gama, Joaquim Mendes, Isabel Ruth

Hard to Get
US   1938   80m   bw
Warner

An architect is reduced to working at a gas station; here he meets and falls in love with a millionairess.
Arch romantic comedy which failed to enhance its stars.
w Jerry Wald, Maurice Leo, Richard Macaulay d Ray Enright ph Charles Rosher
☆ Dick Powell, Olivia de Havilland, Charles Winninger, Thurston Hall, Isabel Jeans, Penny Singleton, Allen Jenkins

'Will carry in top brackets mainly due to selling names.' – *Variety*

Hard to Handle **
US   1933   75m   bw
Warner (Robert Lord)

The success story of a cheerful public relations man.
Punchy star comedy with interesting sidelights on the social fads of the early thirties including marathon dancing, get-rich-quick schemes and grapefruit diets.
w Wilson Mizner, Robert Lord d Mervyn Le Roy ph Barney McGill

☆ James Cagney, Ruth Donnelly, Mary Brian, Allen Jenkins, Claire Dodd

'Hokum this time instead of the realism that boosted him to stardom.' – *Variety*
'A violent, slangy, down-to-the-pavement affair which has many a mirthful moment.' – *Mordaunt Hall*

Hard to Kill
US   1989   96m   Technicolor
Warner/Lee Rich Productions/Adelson-Todman-Simon
▦ ▤ ⊚

Reviving from a seven-year coma, a former cop and martial arts expert seeks revenge for the massacre of his family.
Formula action film.
w Steve McKay d Bruce Malmuth ph Matthew F. Leonetti m David Michael Frank pd Robb Wilson King ed John F. Link
☆ Steven Seagal, Kelly Le Brock, Bill Sadler, Frederick Coffin, Bonnie Burroughs, Andrew Bloch, Branscombe Richmond, Charles Boswell

'There are two sides to every story – and every woman!'
The Hard Way *
US   1942   109m   bw
Warner (Jerry Wald)

A strong-willed girl pushes her reluctant sister to the heights of show business.
Unconvincing but well-mounted drama.
w Daniel Fuchs, Peter Viertel d Vincent Sherman ph James Wong Howe m Heinz Roemheld md Leo F. Forbstein
☆ Ida Lupino, Joan Leslie, Dennis Morgan, Jack Carson, Gladys George, Faye Emerson, Paul Cavanagh, Roman Bohnen

The Hard Way *
US   1991   111m   DeLuxe
UIP/Universal/Badham/Cohen (William Sackheim)
▦ ▤ ⊛ ⊚ ♫

A Hollywood actor who plans to play a cop in his new film teams up with a real-life New York policeman who is obsessed with catching a serial killer.
Amusing comedy that pokes fun at buddy-buddy and cop movies while being both itself.
w Daniel Pyne, Lem Dobbs *story* Lem Dobbs, Michael Kozoll d John Badham ph Robert Primes, Don McAlpine m Arthur B. Rubinstein pd Philip Harrison ed Frank Morriss
☆ Michael J. Fox, James Woods, Stephen Lang, Annabella Sciorra, Delroy Lindo, Luis Guzman, Mary Mara, Penny Marshall

'Proves that sometimes the system, fuelled here by self-mocking jibes, can turn out films appreciable and enjoyable without adding anything to the cinema.' – *Kim Newman, Sight and Sound*

'Hi-Octane Hi-Calibre Hi-Body Count!'
Hard-Boiled 2: The Last Blood
Hong Kong   1994   89m   colour
Movie Impact (Wallace Cheung, Eric Tsang)
▦

In Singapore, a Hong Kong security expert fights to prevent an army of Japanese terrorists killing the one man who can save the life of a visiting Buddhist religious leader (variously called Takka Lama and Daka Lama, and who forgets his principles for long enough to slit the throat of a would-be assassin).
Deliriously silly, over-the-top action thriller, not helped by the poor subtitling (as in: 'Drop that pistol, and let us fight it bear-handed' and 'Many people have bet less but they want it to loss well'); the movie lacks both a coherent narrative and John Woo's panache in its scenes of indiscriminate slaughter, as hostages and bystanders are mown down without compunction.
d Wong Ching (action director: Blackie Ko) ph Jingle Ma ad Fong Ying ed Chang Kwok Kuen
☆ Andy Lau, Alan Tam, Leung Ka Yan, May Lo, Eric Tsang, Chan Pak Cheung

'Tightly-directed set pieces, slow-motion photography and superbly choreographed fights elevate this shaggy dog thriller.' – *Sight and Sound*

† Apart from the title, the film has no connection with John Woo's original.

Hardcore

GB 1977 82m Technicolor
Norfolk/Assay (Brian Smedley-Aston)

A vicar's daughter recounts her sexual experiences to a stranger.

Billed as 'the frankly sensational adventures of a liberated lady', it is neither frank nor sensational, but coy, witless and dull, with its cast of familiar character actors giving their worst performances on film, as they try to match the standard set by its star.

w James Kenelm Clarke, Michael Robson
d James Kenelm Clarke ph Mike Molloy
m James Kenelm Clarke md Syd Dale ad Roger King ed Jim Connock

☆ Fiona Richmond, Anthony Steel, Victor Spinetti, Graham Stark, Graham Crowden, Ronald Fraser, Percy Herbert, Roland Curram, Harry H. Corbett, Jeremy Child, John Clive, Michael Feast

'A disaster, this is yet another unamusing British sex comedy which misuses all the talents involved.' – *Scott Meek, MFB*

Hardcore ***

US 1979 108m Metrocolor
Columbia/A-Team (John Milius)
■ ⊚

GB title: *The Hardcore Life*

A religious man from Michigan journeys to Los Angeles in search of his daughter, who has taken to acting in porno films.

Intense and solemn treatment of a situation that could have gone over the top, and very nearly does; the acting saves it.

wd Paul Schrader ph Michael Chapman m Jack Nitzsche

☆ George C. Scott, Peter Boyle, Season Hubley, Dick Sargent, Leonard Gaines

'Flawed and uneven, it contains moments of pure revelation.' – *Roger Ebert*

The Hardcore Life: see Hardcore

The Harder They Come **

Jamaica 1972 110m Metrocolor
International Films (Perry Henzell)
■■ ▦ ⊚

A country boy comes to the city to make it as a reggae singer but finds success only when he turns to crime.

Lively, tough drama of drugs and corruption in which the action is matched by the vigour of the music, which did much to give reggae an international appeal.

w Perry Henzell, Trevor D. Rhone d Perry Henzell ph David MacDonald, Peter Jessop, Franklyn St Juste m Jimmy Cliff, Toots and the Maytalls, Desmond Dekker, The Slickers ad Sally Henzell ed John Victor Smith, Richard White, Reicland Anderson

☆ Jimmy Cliff, Janet Bartley, Carl Bradshaw, Ras Daniel Hartman, Basil Keane, Robert Charlton, Winston Stona

'The film itself is a mess, but the music is redeeming, and Jimmy Cliff's joy in music, along with the whole culture's, stays with you.' – *Pauline Kael*

'No Punches Pulled!'
'If you thought "On the Waterfront" hit hard ... wait till you see this one!'
'This Is A Fighting-Mad Motion Picture!'

The Harder They Fall *

US 1956 109m bw
Columbia (Philip Yordan)

A press agent exposes the crooked fight game.

Wearily efficient sporting melodrama.

w Philip Yordan novel Budd Schulberg d Mark Robson ph Burnett Guffey m Hugo Friedhofer

☆ Humphrey Bogart, Rod Steiger, Jan Sterling, Mike Lane, Max Baer, Edward Andrews, Harold J. Stone

† It was Bogart's last performance.
⌥ Burnett Guffey

Hardware *

GB/US 1990 92m colour
Palace/Miramax/British Screen/BSB/Wicked Films (Joanne Sellar, Paul Trybits)
■■ ▦ ⊚

Scavengers in a radioactive wasteland unknowingly recover a killer robot.

A low-budget science-fiction horror story, filmed in the style of a rock music video.

wd Richard Stanley story SHOK! by Steve McManus, Kevin O'Neill ph Steven Chivers

m Simon Boswell pd Joseph Bennett ed Derek Trigg sp Image Animation

☆ Dylan McDermott, Stacey Travis, John Lynch, William Hootkins, Iggy Pop

'A cacophonic, nightmarish variation on the postapocalyptic cautionary genre.' – *Variety*

The Hardy Family
👫

America's favourite fictional characters just before and during World War II were the family of a small-town judge, who seemed to personify all that everyone was fighting for, especially as the young son was always getting into amusing scrapes. Designed by a delighted MGM as low-budgeters, they paid for many an expensive failure, and introduced, as young Andy's girlfriends, a series of starlets who went on to much bigger things. The basic family was Lewis Stone, Fay Holden, Mickey Rooney, Cecilia Parker and Sara Haden (as the spinster aunt); but in the very first episode Lionel Barrymore and Spring Byington played the judge and his wife. MGM was given a special Academy Award in 1942 'for representing the American Way of Life' in the films.

1937 A Family Affair (qv); 69m, d George B. Seitz w Kay Van Riper play Aurania Rouverol
1938 You're Only Young Once; 78m d George B. Seitz w Kay Van Riper; introducing Ann Rutherford (who became a regular)
1938 Judge Hardy's Children; 78m d George B. Seitz w Kay Van Riper; with Ruth Hussey
1938 Love Finds Andy Hardy; 90m d George B. Seitz w William Ludwig; with Judy Garland, Lana Turner
1938 Out West with the Hardys; 90m d George B Seitz w Kay Van Riper, Agnes Christine Johnston, William Ludwig
1939 The Hardys Ride High; 81m d George B. Seitz w as above
1939 Andy Hardy Gets Spring Fever; 85m d W. S. Van Dyke II w Kay Van Riper
1939 Judge Hardy and Son; 90m d George B. Seitz w Carey Wilson; with June Preisser, Maria Ouspenskaya
1940 Andy Hardy Meets a Debutante; 89m d George B. Seitz w Annalee Whitmore, Thomas Seller; with Judy Garland
1941 Andy Hardy's Private Secretary; 101m d George B. Seitz w Jane Murfin, Harry Ruskin; with Kathryn Grayson, Ian Hunter
1941 Life Begins for Andy Hardy; 100m d George B. Seitz w Agnes Christine Johnston; with Judy Garland
1942 The Courtship of Andy Hardy; 93m d George B. Seitz w Agnes Christine Johnston; with Donna Reed
1942 Andy Hardy's Double Life; 92m d George B. Seitz w Agnes Christine Johnston; with Esther Williams, Susan Peters
1944 Andy Hardy's Blonde Trouble; 107m d George B. Seitz w Harry Ruskin, William Ludwig, Agnes Christine Johnston; with Bonita Granville, Jean Porter, Herbert Marshall, the Wilde twins
1946 Love Laughs at Andy Hardy; 94m d Willis Goldbeck w Harry Ruskin, William Ludwig; with Bonita Granville
1958 Andy Hardy Comes Home; 80m d Howard Koch w Edward Everett Hutshing, Robert Morris Donley; without Lewis Stone

Harem

France 1985 113m colour Panavision
Sara (Alain Sarde)
■■ ▦ ⊚

aka: *D'Ardenelle*

A New York stockbroker is kidnapped by an Arab prince as an addition to his harem, and she likes it. *Glossy but vacuous drama, in which high-priced talents fight against a script devoid of interest, though some swiftly give up the struggle; even by the standards of Valentino's The Sheik, which it resembles in a retrograde way, it is junk.*

w Arthur Joffé, Tom Rayfiel d Arthur Joffé ph Pasqualino De Santis m Philippe Sarde pd Alexandre Trauner ed Françoise Bonnot, Ruggero Mastroianni

☆ Nastassja Kinski, Ben Kingsley, Dennis Goldson, Michel Robin, Zohra Segal, Julette Simpson

† The British video release ran for 94m.

Harem Girl

US 1952 70m bw
Columbia

The secretary to a princess vanquishes her employer's Arab ill-wishers.

Dispirited pratfall farce, its star's last movie.

w Edward Bernds, Elwood Ullman d Edward Bernds

☆ Joan Davis, Peggie Castle, Arthur Blake, Paul Marion

Harem Holiday: see Harum Scarum

Harlem Nights

US 1989 116m Technicolor
UIP/Paramount/Eddie Murphy Productions (Robert D. Wachs, Mark Lipsky)
■■ ▦

Two night-club owners fight off a takeover bid by gangsters.

Witless display of self-indulgence by its overparted director-author-star.

wd Eddie Murphy ph Woody Omens m Herbie Hancock pd Lawrence G. Paull ed George Bowers, Alan Balsam

☆ Eddie Murphy, Richard Pryor, Redd Foxx, Danny Aiello, Michael Lerner, Della Reese, Berlinda Tolbert, Stan Shaw, Jasmine Guy, Vic Polizos

⌥ best costume design (Joe I. Tompkins)

Harlequin

Australia 1980 93m Eastmancolor
Panavision
FG Films/Far Flight (Anthony Ginnane)
■■

US title: *Dark Forces*

A faith healer cures a politician's son, seduces his wife, and proves to be of supernatural origin.

Muddled and unsatisfactory fantasy in the manner of The Passing of the Third Floor Back; in this case far too much is left unexplained, and the film is scarcely entertaining despite effort all round.

w Everett de Roche d Simon Wincer ph Gary Hanson m Brian May

☆ Robert Powell, David Hemmings, Carmen Duncan, Broderick Crawford

Harley Davidson and the Marlboro Man

US 1991 98m DeLuxe
UIP/MGM (Jere Henshaw)
■■ ■ ⊚ ♫

In the near future, two drifters rob a bank to save their favourite bar from being re-developed.

Tiresome action film on the side of lawlessness and disorder.

w Don Michael Paul d Simon Wincer ph David Eggby m Basil Poledouris pd Paul Peters ed Corky Ehlers

☆ Mickey Rourke, Don Johnson, Chelsea Field, Daniel Baldwin, Giancarlo Esposito, Vanessa Williams, Robert Ginty, Tia Carrere, Julius Harris, Eloy Casados

'Bone-headed biker Western.' – *Variety*

'She was famous for light dresses, loose living, and trips to the bottom between pictures!'

Harlow

US 1965 125m Technicolor Panavision
Paramount/Embassy/Prometheus (Joseph E. Levine)
■■

In 1929, starlet Jean Harlow is shot to fame by her agent Arthur Landau.

Absurdly whitewashed and excruciatingly boring rags-to-riches yarn with most of the characters fictitious and little to do with the real Jean Harlow. Only the studio scenes are mildly interesting.

w John Michael Hayes d Gordon Douglas ph Joseph Ruttenberg m Neal Hefti ad Hal Pereira, Roland Anderson cos Edith Head

☆ Carroll Baker, Peter Lawford, Mike Connors, Red Buttons, Raf Vallone, Angela Lansbury, Martin Balsam

'Hollywood once again succeeds in reducing one of its few fascinating realities to the sleazy turgid level of its more sordid fictions.' – *Judith Crist*

† A rather better television tape drama of the same title, starring Carol Lynley and Ginger Rogers, was made almost simultaneously. It was converted to film ('Electronovision') but had few bookings.

Harmony Heaven *

GB 1930 61m bw/colour
BIP

A composer becomes famous with the help of his girlfriend.

Unbelievably naïve musical, notable only as British and in colour. Not tolerable today as entertainment.

w Arthur Wimperis, Randall Faye d Thomas Bentley ph Theodor Sparkuhl m/ly Edward Brandt, Eddie Pola md John Reynders ad John Mead ed Sam Simmonds

☆ Polly Ward, Stuart Hall, Trilby Clark, Jack Raine

Harmony Lane

US 1935 85m bw
Mascot (Colbert Clark)

The life of Stephen Foster.

Heavygoing biopic from an independent studio; for rural audiences only.

wd Joseph Santley story Milton Krims

☆ Douglass Montgomery, Evelyn Venable, Adrienne Ames, Joseph Cawthorn, William Frawley, Clarence Muse

Harmony Parade: see Pigskin Parade

Harold and Maude *

US 1971 92m Technicolor
Paramount/Mildred Lewis/Colin Higgins
■■ ⊚

A repressed young man, fixated on death and funerals, has an affair with an 80-year-old woman. *Often hilarious black comedy for those who can stand it; the epitome of bad taste, splashed around with wit and vigour, it became a minor cult.*

w Colin Higgins d Hal Ashby ph John A. Alonzo m Cat Stevens

☆ Bud Cort, Ruth Gordon, Vivian Pickles, Cyril Cusack

Harold Lloyd's Funny Side of Life ***

👫 US 1963 99m bw
Harold Lloyd (Duncan Mansfield)

Excerpts from twenties comedies plus a shortened version of *The Freshman* (1925).

Excellent compilation, though the mini-feature makes it a little unbalanced.

w Arthur Ross m Walter Scharf

☆ Harold Lloyd

Harold Lloyd's World of Comedy ****

👫 US 1962 97m bw
Harold Lloyd
♫

Generous clips from the comic climaxes of Lloyd's best silent and sound comedies including *Safety Last*, *The Freshman*, *Hot Water*, *Why Worry*, *Girl Shy*, *Professor Beware*, *Movie Crazy* and *Feet First*. *As Lloyd's work lends itself well to extract, this can hardly fail to be a superb anthology capsuling the appeal of one of America's greatest silent comedians. The timing is just perfect.*

w Walter Scharf

☆ Art Ross

Harold Teen

US 1934 66m bw
Warner

GB title: *Dancing Fool*

A young reporter saves a small-town bank from collapse.

Teenage romantic comedy.

w Paul Gerard Smith, Al Cohn comic strip Carl Ed d Murray Roth

☆ Hal Le Roy, Rochelle Hudson, Patricia Ellis, Guy Kibbee, Hobart Cavanaugh

† Previously filmed in 1928 (with Arthur Lake and Mary Brian, directed by Mervyn Le Roy) and here reduced to second feature status.

The Harp of Burma: see The Burmese Harp

Harper *

US 1966 121m Technicolor Panavision
Warner/Gershwin-Kastner
■■

GB title: *The Moving Target*

A Los Angeles private eye is hired by a rich woman to find her missing husband.

Formula Californian detection distinguished by its cast rather than by any special talent in the writing or presentation. It seemed likely to produce a new Chandleresque school, but imitations proved very

---

sporadic; the star repeated the role less successfully in The Drowning Pool *(qv).*

w William Goldman *novel The Moving Target* by John Ross Macdonald d Jack Smight ph Conrad Hall m Johnny Mandel

☆ Paul Newman, Lauren Bacall, Shelley Winters, Arthur Hill, Julie Harris, Janet Leigh, Pamela Tiffin, Robert Wagner, Robert Webber, Strother Martin

'It isn't a bad try, but it never really slips into overdrive.' – *Penelope Houston*
'Nothing needs justification less than entertainment; but when something planned only to entertain fails, it has no justification. A private-eye movie without sophistication and style is ignominious.' – *Pauline Kael, 1968*

Harper Valley P.T.A.

US   1978   93m   colour
April Fools (George Edwards)
▦

An independent woman takes her revenge on those who disapprove of her free-wheeling ways.
A feeble-minded comedy that cannot sustain interest for any longer than the hit song of the 1960s on which it is based.

w George Edwards, Barry Schneider d Richard Bennett ph Willy Kurant m Nelson Riddle ed Michael Economu

☆ Barbara Eden, Ronny Cox, Nanette Fabray, Susan Swift, Louis Nye, Pat Paulsen

The Harrad Experiment

US   1973   97m   Eastmancolor
Cinerama/Cinema Arts (Dennis F. Stevens)
▦

A college professor conducts a series of tests on sexual relationships.
Low-keyed Kinsey Report for the seventies, pleasantly made but not very stimulating.

w Michael Werner, Ted Cassidy *novel* Robert H. Rimmer d Ted Post ph Richard Kline m Artie Butler

☆ James Whitmore, Tippi Hedren, Don Johnson, Laurie Walters, Robert Middleton

'Ludicrously sober-sided amalgam of nude yoga and extra-curricular groping, which should set sex educational theory back ten years.' – *Sight and Sound*

Harrad Summer

US   1974   105m   colour
Cinerama (Dennis F. Stevens)
▦

Students at a sex-education college return home to put their knowledge into practice.
Dull, if inoffensive, drama that never rises above the level of an average soap opera.

w Morth Thaw, Steven Zacharias d Steven Hilliard Stern ph Richard Kline m Pat Williams ed Bill Brame

☆ Robert Reiser, Laurie Walters, Richard Doran, Victoria Thompson, Emaline Henry, Bill Dana

† A sequel to *The Harrad Experiment* (qv).

Harriet Craig

US   1950   94m   bw
Columbia (William Dozier)
A wife's only real love is her meticulously kept and richly appointed house.
Ho-hum remake of a sturdy thirties film Craig's Wife (qv).

w Anne Froelick, James Gunn *play Craig's Wife* by George Kelly d Vincent Sherman ph Joseph Walker m George Duning md Morris Stoloff

☆ Joan Crawford, Wendell Corey, Allyn Joslyn, Lucile Watson, William Bishop, K. T. Stevens, Raymond Greenleaf

Harriet the Spy *

👫   US   1996   101m   DeLuxe
Paramount/Nickelodeon/Rastar (Marykay Powell)
▦ ▦

An 11-year-old girl, who writes down misleading observations on friends and neighbours, learns the error of her ways.
Entertaining family movie with a moral, told with a light touch.

w Douglas Petrie, Theresa Rebeck *novel* Louise Fitzhugh d Bronwen Hughes ph Francis Kenny m Jamshied Sharifi pd Lester Cohen ed Debra Chiate

☆ Michelle Trachtenberg, Rosie O'Donnell, Vanessa Lee Chester, Gregory Smith, J. Smith-Cameron, Robert Joy, Eartha Kitt, Don Francks

'Thankfully, what could easily have been mawkish claptrap turns out to be smart, good natured and fun.' – *Empire*

'They're two men with nothing in common – they're father and son!'

Harry and Son

US   1984   117m   Technicolor
Orion/Paul Newman
▦

An ageing construction worker is at odds with his twenty-one-year-old son, who lives with him.
One can't imagine why Paul Newman wanted to make this boring shouting match between people no one can care for.

w Ronald L. Buck, Paul Newman *novel A Lost King* by Raymond DeCapite d Paul Newman ph Donald McAlpine m Henry Mancini

☆ Paul Newman, Robby Benson, Ellen Barkin, Wilford Brimley

Harry and the Hendersons

👫   US   1987   110m   DeLuxe
Universal/Amblin (Richard Vane, William Dear)
▦

GB title: *Big Foot and the Hendersons*
A camping family meets a docile Big Foot.
Elementary kiddie/family pic in the wake of E.T.

w William Dear, William E. Martin, Ezra D. Rappaport d William Dear m Bruce Broughton pd James Bissell ed Donn Cambern sp Harry designed by Rick Baker

☆ John Lithgow, Melinda Dillon, David Suchet, Don Ameche, Margaret Langrick, Joshua Rudoy

🏆 best make-up

Harry and Tonto *

US   1974   115m   DeLuxe
TCF (Paul Mazursky)
▦

An elderly New York widower and his cat are evicted and trek to Chicago.
Amiable character study, very watchable but rather pointless.

w Paul Mazursky, Josh Greenfeld d Paul Mazursky ph Michael Butler m Bill Conti

☆ Art Carney, Ellen Burstyn, Chief Dan George, Geraldine Fitzgerald, Larry Hagman, Arthur Hunnicutt, Herbert Berghof

'A vivacious and affectionate folk tale.' – *New Yorker*
'It has a life-affirming quality as welcome contrast to the destructive delirium of most modern movies.' – *Michael Billington, Illustrated London News*

🏆 Art Carney
🏅 Paul Mazursky (as writer)

Harry and Walter Go to New York

US   1976   120m   Metrocolor   Panavision
Columbia (Don Devlin, Harry Gittes)
▦ ▦

In oldtime New York, two carnival entertainers get involved with suffragettes and a safecracker.
Extended period romp in which the high humour soon palls and a general lack of talent makes itself felt.

w John Byrum, Robert Kaufman d Mark Rydell ph Laszlo Kovacs m David Shire pd Harry Horner

☆ James Caan, Elliott Gould, Michael Caine, Diane Keaton, Charles Durning, Lesley Ann Warren, Jack Gilford

'A charmless mishmash.' – *Sight and Sound*
'This film fails to work as a light comedy, as a period piece, as a jigsaw puzzle … mainly, it just sits there and dies.' – *Frank Rich, New York Post*
'Strictly for those who'll laugh at anything.' – *Kevin Thomas, Los Angeles Times*

'The woman or the tiger? He can't have them both!'

Harry Black

GB   1958   117m   Technicolor   Cinemascope
Mersham (John Brabourne)
▦

US title: *Harry Black and the Tiger*
A famous tiger hunter allows his best friend to prove himself a hero, and falls in love with the friend's wife.
Lethargic melodrama with good Indian backgrounds.

w Sydney Boehm *novel* David Walker d Hugo Fregonese ph John Wilcox m Clifton Parker

☆ Stewart Granger, Anthony Steel, Barbara Rush, I. S. Johar

Harry Black and the Tiger: see *Harry Black*

Harry in Your Pocket

US   1973   103m   DeLuxe   Panavision
UA/Cinema Video (Bruce Geller)
Adventures of a young, a middle-aged and an old pickpocket.
Partly pleasant but rather aimless comedy drama, agreeably set in Seattle and Salt Lake City.

w Ron Austin, James Buchanan d Bruce Geller ph Fred Koenekamp m Lalo Schifrin

☆ James Coburn, *Walter Pidgeon*, Michael Sarrazin, Trish Van Devere

Harry Munter **

Sweden   1969   101m   Eastmancolor
Gala/Sandrew (Göran Lindgren)
A schoolboy inventor rejects the opportunity to move to America with his discontented parents and make his fortune because he feels a responsibility to help the people around him.
Affecting and witty account of the difficulties of adolescent idealism.

wd Kjell Grede ph Lars Björne m Dvorak ed Lars Hagström

☆ Jan Nielsen, Carl-Gustaf Lindstedt, Gun Jönsson, Georg Adelly, Al Simon, Elina Salo

'Some kind of personal vision does emerge to save the film from undiluted monotony.' – *Films and Filming*

Harum Scarum

US   1965   95m   Metrocolor
MGM (Sam Katzman)
▦ ▦

GB title: *Harem Holiday*
An American star on the way to the Middle Eastern première of his latest film is kidnapped by assassins.
Flavourless comedy with music; before dull backgrounds the star performs adequately.

w Gerald Drayson Adams d Gene Nelson ph Fred H. Jackman

☆ Elvis Presley, Mary Ann Mobley, Fran Jeffries, Michael Ansara, Theo Marcuse, Jay Novello, Billy Barty

Harvest

France   1937   122m   bw
Marcel Pagnol
original title: *Regain*
A poacher and an itinerant girl set up house in a deserted village and bring it back to life.
Somewhat charming but interminably slow rustic parable.

wd Marcel Pagnol *novel* Jean Giono ph Willy Ledru, Roger Ledru m Arthur Honegger

☆ Gabriel Gabrio, Fernandel, Orane Demazis, E. Delmont

The Harvest *

US   1993   97m   CFI color
Feature Film/Curb Mustfilm/Ron Stone (Morgan Mason, Jason Clark)
▦ ▦

A Hollywood screenwriter goes to Mexico to research a script and is kidnapped by a local gang which specializes in selling body parts.
A clever little thriller dealing with many kinds of betrayal: from male–female relationships to Hollywood's way with reality, the arrogance of privilege and the compromises made by hack writers.

wd David Marconi ph Emmanuel Lubezki m Dave Allen, Rick Boston pd Rae Fox ed Carlos Puente

☆ Miguel Ferrer, Leilani Sarelle Ferrer, Henry Silva, Anthony John Denison, Tim Thomerson, Harvey Fierstein, Mike Vendrell, George Clooney

'Stylish and satisfying low-budget noir thriller, with a cleverly constructed can-this-really-be-happening-to-me plot that goes on producing surprising twists to the last frame.' – *George Perry*

Harvest of Hate

Australia   1979   80m   colour
South Australian Film Corp./Nine Network/Australian Film Commission (Jane Scott)
In the Australian desert Arab guerrillas training to attack Israel take prisoner a couple visiting an isolated house.
Tepid thriller with a ridiculous plot, not helped by its percussive, over-insistent score which attempts to suggest excitement where there is none.

w uncredited d Michael Thornhill ph David Sanderson m uncredited ad David Copping ed G. Turney Smith

☆ Dennis Grosvenor, Kris McQuade, Richard Meikle, Michael Atkins, Leon Cosak, Moshe Kedein, John Oresik

Harvey ***

👫   US   1950   104m   bw
U-I (John Beck)
▦ ▦ ▦

A middle-aged drunk has an imaginary white rabbit as his friend, and his sister tries to have him certified.
An amiably batty play with splendid lines is here transferred virtually intact to the screen and survives superbly thanks to understanding by all concerned, though the star is as yet too young for a role which he later made his own.

w Mary Chase (with Oscar Brodney) *play* Mary Chase d Henry Koster ph William Daniels m Frank Skinner

☆ James Stewart, Josephine Hull, Victoria Horne, Peggy Dow, Cecil Kellaway, Charles Drake, Jesse White, Nana Bryant, Wallace Ford

VETA LOUISE (JOSEPHINE HULL): 'Myrtle Mae, you have a lot to learn, and I hope you never learn it.'

ELWOOD (JAMES STEWART): 'I've wrestled with reality for 35 years, and I'm happy, doctor, I finally won out over it.'

ELWOOD: 'Harvey and I have things to do … we sit in the bars … have a drink or two … and play the juke box. Very soon the faces of the other people turn towards me and they smile. They say: "We don't know your name, mister, but you're all right." Harvey and I warm ourselves in these golden moments. We came as strangers – soon we have friends. They come over. They sit with us. They drink with us. They talk to us. They tell us about the great big terrible things they've done and the great big wonderful things they're going to do. Their hopes, their regrets. Their loves, their hates. All very large, because nobody ever brings anything small into a bar. Then I introduce them to Harvey, and he's bigger and grander than anything they can offer me. When they leave, they leave impressed. The same people seldom come back.'

ELWOOD (DESCRIBING HIS FIRST MEETING WITH HARVEY): 'I'd just helped Ed Hickey into a taxi. Ed had been mixing his drinks, and I felt he needed conveying. I started to walk down the street when I heard a voice saying: "Good evening, Mr Dowd". I turned, and there was this big white rabbit leaning against a lamp-post. Well, I thought nothing of that! Because when you've lived in a town as long as I've lived in this one, you get used to the fact that everybody knows your name…'

🏆 Josephine Hull
🏅 James Stewart

The Harvey Girls **

US   1946   101m   Technicolor
MGM (Arthur Freed)
▦ ▦ ▦

A chain of 19th-century restaurants hires young ladies to go out west as waitresses.
Sprightly if overlong musical based on fact; a good example of an MGM middle-budget extravaganza.

w Edmund Beloin, Nathaniel Curtis d George Sidney ph George Folsey m/ly Johnny Mercer, Harry Warren md Lennie Hayton

☆ Judy Garland, Ray Bolger, John Hodiak, Preston Foster, Virginia O'Brien, Angela Lansbury, Marjorie Main, Chill Wills, Kenny Baker, Selena Royle

'Anybody who did anything at all in America up to 1900 is liable to be made into a film by MGM.' – *Richard Winnington*
'An abundance of chromatic spectacle and an uncommonly good score.' – *New York Times*
'A perfect example of what Hollywood can do with its vast resources when it wants to be really showy.' – *New York Herald Tribune*

🎵 song 'On the Atcheson, Topeka and the Santa Fe'

🏅 Lennie Hayton

Harvey Middleman Fireman *

US   1965   76m   Eastmancolor
Columbia (Robert L. Lawrence)
A frustrated middle-aged fireman begins an affair; the resulting guilt complex drives him to a psychiatrist.
Grotesque satirical comedy from one of the sixties' most fashionable cartoonists. Mild, quite pleasing, occasionally crude.

---

wd Ernest Pintoff *ph* Karl Malkames *m* Bernard Green
☆ Gene Troobnick, Hermione Gingold, Pat Harty

Has Anybody Seen My Gal? **
US   1952   89m   Technicolor
U-I (Ted Richmond)

A multi-millionaire pretends to be poor and moves in with distant relatives to test their worthiness.
Very agreeable comedy set in the twenties and centring on a satisfying star performance.
w Joseph Hoffman *d* Douglas Sirk *ph* Clifford Stine *m* Joseph Gershenson *ad* Bernard Herzbrun, Hilyard Brown
☆ Charles Coburn, Piper Laurie, Rock Hudson, Gigi Perreau, Lynn Bari, Larry Gates, William Reynolds, Skip Homeier, James Dean

Hasards Ou Coincidences: see *Chance or Coincidence*

Hasta Morir
Mexico   1994   90m   colour
Imcine/FFCC/Ocixem/Vida (Fernando Sariñana)
aka: *'Til Death*

Two petty crooks fall out after one shoots a cop and is forced to flee; the other assumes his identity for a property swindle.
Lurid melodrama set in an urban wasteland, in which flashy camerawork attempts to compensate for the halting narrative; it has a fashionable gloss, but not much substance.
w Marcela Fuentes-Berain *d* Fernando Sariñana *ph* Guillermo Granillo *m* Enrique Quezadas *ad* Gloria Carrasco *ed* Carlos Bolado
☆ Demian Bichir, Juan Manuel Bernal, Veronica Merchant, Vanessa Bauche, Dolores Beristain, Montserrat Ontiveros, Alfreda Sevilla, Dino Garcia
'Admirably manages to conjure up this marginal world of violence and street gangs.' – *Variety*

The Hasty Heart *
GB   1949   104m   bw
ABP (Vincent Sherman)

At an army hospital in Burma, attitudes to an arrogant young Scot change when it is learned that he has only a few weeks to live.
Flat, adequate filming of a successful sentimental stage play.
w Ranald MacDougall *play* John Patrick *d* Vincent Sherman *ph* Wilkie Cooper *m* Jack Beaver
☆ Richard Todd, Patricia Neal, Ronald Reagan, Orlando Martins, Howard Marion-Crawford
⟡ Richard Todd

Hat Check Honey
US   1911   66m   bw
Universal (Will Cowan)

A veteran comic wants his son to click, but is not so sure when the boy gets a Hollywood contract.
Lightweight musical filler with more numbers than plot.
w Maurice Leo, Stanley Davis, Al Martin *d* Edward F. Cline
☆ Leon Errol, Grace McDonald, Richard Davis, Walter Catlett, Milburn Stone

Hat, Coat and Glove
US   1934   64m   bw
RKO

A New York lawyer accidentally kills an old flame.
Tiresome courtroom melodrama, told in a rather stilted manner.
w Francis Faragoh *play* Wilhelm Speyer *d* Worthington Miner *ph* J. Roy Hunt *md* Max Steiner
☆ Ricardo Cortez, Barbara Robbins, John Beal, Margaret Hamilton, Sara Haden, Samuel S. Hinds

Hatari! *
US   1962   158m   Technicolor
Paramount/Malabar (Howard Hawks)

International hunters in Tanganyika catch game to send to zoos.
Plotless adventure film with good animal sequences but no shape or suspense; a typical folly of its director, whose chief interest is seeing smart men and women in tough action. The elephants steal this overlong show.
w Leigh Brackett *d* Howard Hawks *ph* Russell Harlan *m* Henry Mancini
☆ John Wayne, Elsa Martinelli, Red Buttons, Hardy Kruger

'Hawks was taking his friends and cast and crew on a trip he wanted to make personally, and the film is both the incidental excuse for and the record of that experience.' – *Joseph Gelmis, 1970*
⟡ Russell Harlan

Hatchet Man
US   1994   100m   Foto-Kem
Overseas/Itasca (Daniel Grodnik, Robert Snukal, John Tarnoff)

aka: *The Nature of the Beast*

Two psychopaths meet on the road.
An effective thriller, if you ignore its pretensions to say something significant about the human condition.
wd Victor Salva *ph* Levie Isaacks *m* Bennett Salvay *pd* Stephen Greenberg *ed* W. Peter Miller
☆ Eric Roberts, Lance Henriksen, Brion James, Sasha Jenson, Ana Gabriel, Eloy Casados
† Lance Henriksen is also credited as 'creative consultant'.

'A beautiful butterfly broken on the wheel of life!'
The Hatchet Man
US   1932   74m   bw
Warner
GB title: *The Honourable Mr Wong*

The executioner of a San Francisco tong dutifully kills his best friend but promises to care for his daughter.
Unconvincing Chinese-American melodrama.
w J. Grubb Alexander *play* The Honourable Mr Wong by Achmed Abdullah, David Belasco *d* William A. Wellman *ph* Sid Hickox
☆ Edward G. Robinson, Loretta Young, Dudley Digges, Leslie Fenton, Edmund Breese, Tully Marshall, J. Carrol Naish, Noel Madison, Blanche Frederici
'Mild gang stuff in oriental trappings … dynamic action or high voltage drama is missing.' – *Variety*

The Hatchet Murders: see *Deep Red*

A Hatful of Rain *
US   1957   108m   bw   Cinemascope
TCF/ (Buddy Adler)

A war veteran becomes a drug addict and upsets his wife and family.
One of the first drug dramas: straightforward, well acted, and quite powerful.
w Michael V. Gazzo, Alfred Hayes *play* Alfred Hayes *d* Fred Zinnemann *ph* Joe Macdonald *m* Bernard Herrmann
☆ Eva Marie Saint, Don Murray, Anthony Franciosa, Lloyd Nolan, Henry Silva
⟡ Anthony Franciosa

'Are you shockproof? Then you will dare to see this famous drama of violence – of hate – of men who teach women the terror of cruelty and mad obsession!'
Hatter's Castle **
GB   1941   102m   bw
Paramount British (Isadore Goldsmith)

In the 1890s, a megalomaniac Scottish hatter ruins the lives of his wife and daughter.
Enjoyable period melodrama with a rampant star performance and pretty good detail.
w Rodney Ackland *novel* A. J. Cronin *d* Lance Comfort *ph* Max Greene *m* Horace Shepherd
☆ Robert Newton, Deborah Kerr, James Mason, Beatrice Varley, Emlyn Williams, Henry Oscar, Enid Stamp-Taylor, Brefni O'Rorke

Haunted
GB/US   1995   107m   colour
Entertainment/Double 'A'/American Zoetrope/Lumière (Anthony Andrews, Lewis Gilbert)

An academic who debunks psychic phenomena is invited by an old lady to visit a house which she claims is haunted.
Tedious and stultifyingly old-fashioned horror movie whose effect on an audience is more likely to be sedative than scary.
w Tim Prager, Lewis Gilbert, Bob Kellett *novel* James Herbert *d* Lewis Gilbert *ph* Tony Pierce Roberts *m* Debbie Wiseman *pd* John Fenner, Brian Ackland-Snow *ed* Johnny Jympson *sp* Peter Hutchinson
☆ Aidan Quinn, Kate Beckinsale, Anthony Andrews, John Gielgud, Anna Massey, Simon Lowe, Geraldine Somerville, Liz Smith

'Its makers seem to have decided, not to reinvent the horror film, but to deinvent it, to strip it back down to the crude constituent elements from which it was first pieced together: haunted houses, creaking doors, blown-out candles, self-playing pianos, even bumps in the night, if you can believe that, which is more than the characters manage.' – *Tom Shone, Sunday Times*

The Haunted and the Hunted: see *Dementia 13*

Haunted Gold
US   1932   57m   bw
Warner (Leon Schlesinger)

A cowboy prevents bandits from taking over a gold mine with the aid of a mysterious rider.
Warner played safe with Wayne's first Western for the studio, remaking The Phantom City, directed in 1929 by Albert Rogell and starring Ken Maynard and his horse Tarzan; the result is unexciting.
w Adele Buffington *d* Mack V. Wright *ph* Nicholas Musuraca *m* Leo F. Forbstein *ed* William Clemens
☆ John Wayne, Sheila Terry, Erville Alderson, Harry Wood, Otto Hoffman, Martha Mattox, Blue Washington, Duke

Haunted Honeymoon: see *Busman's Honeymoon (1940)*

Haunted Honeymoon
US   1986   82m   Rank Colour
Orion/Susan Ruskin

A radio actor takes his fiancee to the family's gloomy country estate, where werewolves and transvestites are some of the creatures which abound.
Mainly unfunny spoof: all concerned should have taken a closer look at The Cat and the Canary.
w Gene Wilder, Terence Marsh *d* Gene Wilder *ph* Fred Schuler *m* John Morris *pd* Terence Marsh *ed* Christopher Greenbury
☆ Gene Wilder, Gilda Radner, Dom DeLuise, Jonathan Pryce, Peter Vaughan, Bryan Pringle
'Faintly amusing but singularly uncompelling.' – *Variety*

The Haunted House of Horror
GB/US   1969   90m   Eastmancolor
Tigon/AIP (Tony Tenser)
US title: *The Horror House*
aka: *The Dark*

A group of young people try to cover up the murder of one of their number, killed during a night spent at a haunted house.
Wretched attempt to combine a youth movie of swinging London and low-budget horror; neither element works.
w Michael Armstrong, Peter Marcus *d* Michael Armstrong *ph* Jack Atcheler *m* Reg Tilsley *ad* Haydon Pearce *ed* Peter Pitt
☆ Frankie Avalon, Jill Haworth, Dennis Price, George Sewell, Gina Warwick, Richard O'Sullivan, Carol Dilworth, Julian Barnes, Mark Wynter

The Haunted Palace
US   1963   85m   Pathécolor   Panavision
AIP/Alta Vista (Roger Corman)

In 1875 a New Englander claims an old mansion as his inheritance and is haunted by his vicious ancestor.
Plodding horror comic, too slow to give opportunities to its stalwart cast.
w Charles Beaumont, from material by H. P. Lovecraft and Edgar Allan Poe *d* Roger Corman *ph* Floyd Crosby *m* Ronald Stein
☆ Vincent Price, Lon Chaney Jnr, Debra Paget, Frank Maxwell, Leo Gordon, Elisha Cook Jnr, John Dierkes
'For those of ghoulish bent, or lovers of the perfectly awful.' – *Judith Crist*

The Haunted Strangler: see *Grip of the Strangler*

Haunted Summer
US   1988   106m   colour
Pathé/Cannon (Martin Poll)

Byron, Shelley, Mary Godwin and others indulge in drugs and sex in Switzerland.
Unconvincing as history or cinema.
w Lewis John Carlino *novel* Anne Edwards *d* Ivan Passer *ph* Giuseppe Rotunno *m* Christopher Young *pd* Stephen Grimes *ed* Cesare D'Amico, Richard Fields, Steve Peck
☆ Philip Anglim, Laura Dern, Alice Krige, Eric Stoltz, Alexander Winter, Peter Berling, Don Hodson

'You may not believe in ghosts, but you cannot deny terror!'
The Haunting *
GB   1963   112m   bw   Panavision
MGM/Argyle (Robert Wise)

An anthropologist, a sceptic and two mediums spend the weekend in a haunted Boston mansion.
Quite frightening but exhausting and humourless melodrama with a lot of suspense, no visible spooks, and not enough plot for its length. The wide screen is a disadvantage.
w Nelson Gidding *novel* The Haunting of Hill House by Shirley Jackson *d* Robert Wise *ph* David Boulton *m* Humphrey Searle *pd* Elliot Scott *ed* Ernest Walter
☆ Richard Johnson, Claire Bloom, Russ Tamblyn, Julie Harris, Lois Maxwell, Valentine Dyall

The Haunting
US   1999   113m   Technicolor   Panavision
DreamWorks (Susan Arnold, Donna Arkoff Roth, Colin Wilson)

A doctor studies the effects of fear by gathering together a group of unhappy adults in a haunted house.
Tepid, effects-stuffed horror in which the cast is out-acted by the decor; Neeson wanders through it looking as though he has been hit over the head with a very blunt instrument, such as the script.
w David Self *novel* The Haunting of Hill House by Shirley Jackson *d* Jan De Bont *ph* Karl Walter Lindenlaub *m* Jerry Goldsmith *pd* Dean Tavoularis *ed* Michael Kahn *sp* Phil Tippett, Craig Hayes
☆ Liam Neeson, Catherine Zeta-Jones, Owen Wilson, Lili Taylor, Bruce Dern, Marian Seldes, Alix Koromzay, Todd Field, Virginia Madsen
'Worse than awful: desperate. It's a horror flick afraid of its own audience.' – *Lisa Schwarzbaum, Entertainment Weekly*

Havana
US   1990   145m   DeLuxe
UIP/Universal/Mirage (Sydney Pollack, Richard Roth)

An American gambler becomes involved in left-wing Cuban politics in the last days of the Batista regime.
Inconsequential, rambling tale with no perceptible point.
w Judith Rascoe, David Rayfiel *d* Sydney Pollack *ph* Owen Roizman *m* Dave Grusin *pd* Terence Marsh *ad* George Richardson *ed* Frederic Steinkamp, William Steinkamp
☆ Robert Redford, Lena Olin, Alan Arkin, Tomas Milian, Raul Julia, Daniel Davis, Tony Plana, Betsy Brantley
'A hollow, handsomely designed reworking of Casablanca.' – *Philip French, Observer*
⟡ Dave Grusin

Havana Widows *
US   1933   63m   bw
First National

Gold diggers seek millionaires in Havana.
Lively second feature with the Warner repertory company.
w Stanley Logan, Earl Baldwin *d* Ray Enright
☆ Joan Blondell, Glenda Farrell, Guy Kibbee, Lyle Talbot, Allen Jenkins, Frank McHugh, Ruth Donnelly, Hobart Cavanaugh
'Hasn't been a picture in weeks with the same content of rapid-fire laughs, all legitimately gained and inescapable.' – *Variety*

Have a Heart

US　1934　75m　bw
MGM

A dancing instructress becomes a cripple and is deserted by her boyfriend.

Family drama with comedy asides, plus a dog and a mystery element.

w Florence Ryerson, Edgar Allan Woolf　d David Butler

☆ Jean Parker, James Dunn, Una Merkel, Stuart Erwin, Willard Robertson

'Such a barrage of sobbing hokum is a novelty in itself in this supposedly sophisticated age.' – *Variety*

Having a Wild Weekend: see *Catch Us If You Can*

Having Wonderful Crime

US　1945　70m　bw
RKO

Three amateur detectives solve the mystery of a disappearing magician.

Easy-going comedy thriller.

w Howard J. Green, Stewart Sterling, Parke Levy　d Eddie Sutherland

☆ Pat O'Brien, Carole Landis, George Murphy

Having Wonderful Time

US　1938　70m　bw
RKO (Pandro S. Berman)

A New York girl falls in love at a summer camp.

Mild comedy which, robbed of its original Jewish milieu, falls resoundingly flat.

w Arthur Kober *play* Arthur Kober　d Alfred Santell　ph Robert de Grasse　m Roy Webb

☆ Ginger Rogers, Douglas Fairbanks Jnr, Peggy Conklin, Lucille Ball, Lee Bowman, Eve Arden, Red Skelton, Donald Meek, Jack Carson

Hawaii *

US　1966　186m　DeLuxe　Panavision
UA/Mirisch (Lewis J. Rachmil)

In 1820 a pious Yale divinity student becomes a missionary to the Hawaiian islands.

Ambitious attempt to contrast naïve dogma with native innocence, ruined by badly handled sub-plots, storms, a childbirth sequence and other distractions, all fragments of an immense novel. Heavy going.

w Daniel Taradash, Dalton Trumbo *novel* James A. Michener　d George Roy Hill　ph Russell Harlan　m Elmer Bernstein　pd Cary Odell *second unit* Richard Talmadge

☆ Max von Sydow, Julie Andrews, Richard Harris, Jocelyn La Garde, Carroll O'Connor, Torin Thatcher, Gene Hackman

'Consistently intelligent humanism gives it a certain stature among the wide screen spectacles.' – *Brenda Davies*

⅋ cinematography; Elmer Bernstein; Jocelyn La Garde; song 'My Wishing Doll' (*m*Elmer Bernstein, *ly*Mack David)

Hawaii Calls

US　1938　73m　bw
RKO (Sol Lesser)

Boy stowaways catch a steamer from San Francisco to Hawaii.

Slight vehicle for a singing star.

w Wanda Tuchock *novel* Stowaways in Paradise by Don Blanding　d Edward F. Cline

☆ Bobby Breen, Ned Sparks, Irvin S. Cobb, Warren Hull, Gloria Holden, Pua Lani

'Okay musically but light on romance.' – *Variety*

The Hawaiians

US　1970　132m　DeLuxe　Panavision
UA/Mirisch (Walter Mirisch)
GB title: *Master of the Islands*

A young scion of a shipping business leaves after an argument and strikes oil in terrain supposedly barren.

More fragments from Michener, covering 1870 to 1900 and comprising an absolutely uninteresting family chronicle with moments of spectacle.

w James R. Webb　d Tom Gries　ph Philip Lathrop　m Henry Mancini　pd Cary Odell

☆ Charlton Heston, Tina Chen, Geraldine Chaplin, John Phillip Law, Alec McCowen, Mako, Ann Knight, Lyle Bettger, Keye Luke

'A quickfire succession of corruption, revolution, plague, fire and questions of moral responsibility.' – *MFB*

'Total relaxation – preferably of the brain – is recommended.' – *Judith Crist*

The Hawk: see *Ride Him Cowboy (1932)*

'The First Person You Want To Trust. The Last Person You Want To Suspect.'

The Hawk

GB　1992　86m　Rank Colour
Feature Film/BBC/Initial (Ann Wingate, Eileen Quinn)

A wife begins to suspect that her husband is a serial killer.

A thriller that fails to grip the attention and provides little insight.

w Peter Ransley *novel* Peter Ransley　d David Hayman　ph Andrew Dunn　m Nick Bicat　pd David Myerscough-Jones　ed Justin Krish

☆ Helen Mirren, George Costigan, Rosemary Leach, Owen Teale, Christopher Madin, Marie Hamer, Melanie Hill, Helen Ryan

'A small film without too much ambition.' – *Derek Malcolm, Guardian*

Hawk the Slayer

⋔⋔　GB　1980　93m　colour
ITC/Chips (Harry Robertson)

Good and evil brothers compete for possession of a magical flying sword.

Curiously unexciting and rather gloomy sword-and-sorcery epic.

w Terry Marcel, Harry Robertson　d Terry Marcel　ph Paul Beeson　m Harry Robertson

☆ Jack Palance, John Terry, Bernard Bresslaw, Ray Charleson, Annette Crosbie, Cheryl Campbell, Peter O'Farrell

Hawks

GB　1988　109m　colour
Rank (Stephen Lanning, Keith Cavele)

Two terminal cancer patients escape from hospital to have a final fling.

Black comedy that lacks the courage of its convictions.

w Roy Clarke　d Robert Ellis Miller　ph Doug Milsome　m Barry Gibb, John Cameron　pd Peter Howitt　ed Malcolm Cooke

☆ Timothy Dalton, Anthony Edwards, Janet McTeer, Camille Coduri, Jill Bennett, Robert Lang, Pat Starr, Bruce Boa, Sheila Hancock, Geoffrey Palmer

Hawks and Sparrows **

Italy　1966　88m　bw
Arco (Alfredo Bini)

original title: *Uccellacci e Uccellini*

A father and son set out on a quest, accompanied by a talkative crow, a left-wing bird who tells them stories.

A comic fable of a search for faith, sometimes reminiscent of Chaplin in its slapstick identification with the poor and dispossessed, of innocents abroad in a cynical world.

wd Pier Paolo Pasolini　ph Mario Bernardo, Tonino delli Colli　m Ennio Morricone　ad Luigi Scaccianoce　ed Nino Baragli

☆ Totò, Ninetto Davoli, Femi Benussi, Umberto Bevilacqua, Renato Capogna, Alfredo Leggi, Renato Montalbano

'A fantasy, mixing in equal measure frivolity and satire, and for the first half it works well enough or better.' – *John Simon*

† The credits at the beginning of the film are sung as well as shown.

Hawmps

⋔⋔　US　1976　127m　colour
Mulberry Square

The Texas cavalry experiments with the use of camels in the South-western desert.

Incredibly overstretched and tedious period comedy with some bright patches.

w William Bickley, Michael Warren　d Joe Camp

☆ James Hampton, Christopher Connelly, Slim Pickens, Denver Pyle, Jennifer Hawkins, Jack Elam

Häxan: see *Witchcraft Through the Ages*

Hazard

US　1948　95m　bw
Paramount (Mel Epstein)

A compulsive lady gambler agrees to marry the winner of a dice game, but runs away and is chased by a private detective.

Silly, unamusing romantic comedy-drama.

w Arthur Sheekman, Roy Chanslor　d George Marshall　ph Daniel L. Fapp　m Frank Skinner

☆ Paulette Goddard, Macdonald Carey, Fred Clark, Stanley Clemens, Maxie Rosenbloom, Charles McGraw

'A good bit this side of inspired.' – *New York Times*

He Found a Star

GB　1941　88m　bw
John Corfield

A theatrical agent loses his star singer and thinks again about his secretary.

A strong contender for the Golden Turkey Award (British Division); the ineptitude has to be sampled to be believed.

w Austin Melford, Bridget Boland　d John Paddy Carstairs

☆ Vic Oliver, Sarah Churchill, Joan Greenwood, Evelyn Dall, Robert Atkins

He Got Game *

US　1998　134m　Technicolor
Buena Vista/Touchstone/40 Acres and a Mule (Jon Kilik, Spike Lee)

A wife-killer is given a week's clandestine parole so that he can persuade his basketball-playing son to sign up for the prison warden's old college.

Drama of a father–son relationship that seems too schematic to carry much conviction.

wd Spike Lee　ph Malik Hassan Sayeed　m Aaron Copland, Public Enemy (songs)　pd Wynn Thomas　ed Barry Alexander Brown

☆ Denzel Washington, Ray Allen, Milla Jovovich, Rosario Dawson, Hill Harper, Zelda Harris, Jim Brown, Joseph Lyle Taylor, Ned Beatty, Bill Nunn, Michele Shay, Thomas Jefferson Byrd, Lonette McKee, John Turturro

'Demonstrates that Lee sits in the first rank of American film-makers.' – *Anwar Brett, Film Review*

He Knows You're Alone

US　1980　92m　Metrocolor
MGM (Lansbury-Beruh)

A sex-starved maniac attacks teenage girls.

Cheapjack horror comic full of fashionable slashing and screaming; of no cinematic interest whatever.

w Scott Parker　d Armand Mastroianni　ph Gerald Feil　m Alexander Peskanov

☆ Don Scardino, Elizabeth Kemp, Caitlin O'Heaney, Tom Hanks

'At this point in the killer-with-a-knife sweepstakes, every company in Hollywood is getting into the act … more ingenuity is going into the titles and campaigns than into the films.' – *Variety*

He Laughed Last *

US　1956　77m　Technicolor
Columbia (Jonie Taps)

In the twenties, New York gangsters battle for control of a night-club.

Small-scale gangster burlesque which comes off rather better than its credits suggest.

wd Blake Edwards　ph Henry Freulich　m Arthur Morton

☆ Frankie Laine, Lucy Marlow, Anthony Dexter, Jesse White

He Married His Wife

US　1940　83m　bw
TCF (Raymond Griffith)

A divorced wife falls back in love with her husband.

Pleasant minor comedy with screwball touches.

w Sam Hellman, Darrell Ware, Lynn Starling, John O'Hara *story* Erna Lazarus, Scott Darling　d Roy Del Ruth　ph Ernest Palmer　m David Buttolph

☆ Joel McCrea, Nancy Kelly, Roland Young, Mary Boland, Cesar Romero, Lyle Talbot, Elisha Cook Jnr

He or She: see *Glen or Glenda?*

'Dynamite fills the screen with their kind of love!'

He Ran All the Way *

US　1951　78m　bw
UA/Bob Roberts

A hoodlum on the run from the police virtually picks up a girl and hides in her family's apartment.

Uninteresting situation melodrama helped by intelligent acting and handling.

w Guy Endore, Hugo Butler *novel* Sam Ross　d John Berry　ph James Wong Howe　m Franz Waxman

☆ John Garfield, Shelley Winters, Wallace Ford, Selena Royle, Gladys George, Norman Lloyd, Bobby Hyatt

'Good production values keep a routine yarn fresh and appealing. Film is scripted, played and directed all the way with little waste motion, so that the suspense is steady and interest constantly sustained.' – *Variety*

He Rides Tall

US　1964　84m　bw
Universal

A marshal postpones his marriage after being forced to kill his stepbrother.

Semi-adult Western, of no particular consequence.

w Charles W. Irwin, Robert Creighton　d R. G. Springsteen　ph Ellis Carter　m Irving Gertz

☆ Tony Young, Dan Duryea, Madlyn Rhue, Jo Morrow, R. G. Armstrong

He Said, She Said

US　1991　115m　Technicolor
Paramount (Frank Mancuso Jnr)

A couple of TV journalists break up during a programme.

An unusual idea – the story is told first from the man's point of view and then from the woman's – fails to work, owing to a script that provides neither insight nor humour.

w Brian Hohlfeld　d Ken Kwapis, Marisa Silver　ph Stephen H. Burum　m Miles Goodman　pd Michael Corenblith　ed Sidney Levin

☆ Kevin Bacon, Elizabeth Perkins, Nathan Lane, Anthony LaPaglia, Sharon Stone, Stanley Anderson, Charlaine Woodard, Danton Stone

'Two awful films rolled into one.' – *Variety*

He Snoops to Conquer

GB　1944　103m　bw
Columbia (Ben Henry, Marcel Varnel)

A local handyman exposes a corrupt council.

Spotty star comedy with insufficient zest for its great length.

w Stephen Black, Howard Irving Young, Norman Lee, Michael Vaughan, Langford Reed　d Marcel Varnel　ph Roy Fogwell

☆ George Formby, Robertson Hare, Elizabeth Allan, Aubrey Mallalieu

He Stayed for Breakfast

US　1940　89m　bw
Columbia (B. P. Schulberg)

A Parisian communist waiter hides out in the apartment of American capitalists, and learns from them.

Post-Ninotchka comedy, not bad but somehow rather uninteresting and mechanical.

w P. J. Wolfson, Michael Fessier, Ernest Vajda *play* Liberté Provisoire by Michel Duran　d Alexander Hall　ph Joseph Walker　m Werner Heymann

☆ Melvyn Douglas, Loretta Young, Alan Marshal, Eugene Pallette, Una O'Connor, Curt Bois, Leonid Kinskey

He Walked by Night *

US　1948　80m　bw
Eagle-Lion/Bryan Foy

A burglar becomes a cop-killer and is hunted down by the police.

Interesting if rather flatly handled documentary melodrama in clear imitation of Naked City.

w John C. Higgins, Crane Wilbur　d Alfred Werker　ph John Alton　m Leonid Raab

☆ Richard Basehart, Scott Brady, Roy Roberts, Whit Bissell

He Was Her Man

US　1934　70m　bw
Warner

A safecracker goes straight in order to get even with old rivals.

Sassy comedy-drama, not quite smart enough to match its star.
w Niven Busch, Tom Buckingham d Lloyd Bacon
☆ James Cagney, Joan Blondell, Victor Jory, Frank Craven, Harold Huber
'No help will be President Roosevelt's pronunciamento of last Saturday (May 19) in which he decried the public penchant for romanticizing crime.' – *Variety*

He Who Gets Slapped *
US   1924   80m   bw   silent
MGM
A scientist starts a new life as a circus clown.
Odd poetic tragedy, Metro-Goldwyn-Mayer's very first production; the public took to it surprisingly well.
w Victor Sjostrom, Carey Wilson play Leonid Andreyev d Victor Sjostrom
☆ Lon Chaney, Norma Shearer, John Gilbert, Tully Marshall, Ford Sterling
'For dramatic value and a faultless adaptation of a play, this is the finest production we have yet seen.' – *New York Times*

He Who Must Die *
France/Italy   1957   126m   bw   Cinemascope
Indusfilms
original title: *Celui Qui Doit Mourir*
In a Greek village in 1921, preparations for a passion play are interrupted by the arrival of refugees from the mountains.
Occasionally striking, but mainly arty and pretentious parable; however well meant, a bore to watch.
w Ben Barzman, Jules Dassin novel Nikos Kazantzakis d Jules Dassin ph Jacques Natteau m Georges Auric
☆ Jean Servais, Carl Mohner, Pierre Vaneck, Melina Mercouri, Fernand Ledoux

He Who Rides a Tiger
GB   1965   103m   bw
British Lion/David Newman
A feckless burglar comes out of prison and returns to the old life.
Cliché crime yarn which tries rather desperately after fresh detail but bogs down in romantic asides.
w Trevor Peacock d Charles Crichton ph John von Kotze m Alexander Faris
☆ Tom Bell, Judi Dench, Paul Rogers, Kay Walsh, Ray McAnally, Jeremy Spenser

He Who Shoots First: see *Django Spara per Primo*

Head *
👫👫 US   1968   85m   Technicolor
Columbia (Bert Schneider)
📼 🖥 ⊘
Fantasia on the life of a sixties pop group.
A psychedelic trip of a movie which does for the Monkees what A Hard Day's Night and Yellow Submarine did for the Beatles, and what Monty Python did for us all. Sometimes funny, slick and clever; often just plain silly.
w Jack Nicholson, Bob Rafelson d Bob Rafelson ph Michel Hugo m Ken Thorne sp Chuck Gaspar
☆ The Monkees, Victor Mature, Annette Funicello, Timothy Carey
'Random particles tossed around in some demented jester's wind machine.' – *Richard Combs, MFB, 1978*
'A mind-blowing collage of mixed media, a free-for-all freakout of rock music and psychedelic splashes of colour.' – *Daily Variety*

'Murder just became a water sport.'
Head above Water
US/GB   1996   92m   colour
Warner/Head above Water/Firmjewel/InterMedia/Fine Line (Jim Wilson, John M. Jacobsen)
📼 🖥
A judge's wife tells a passing cop the series of misunderstandings that led to the deaths of her husband and two friends.
Frenetic farce of mounting catastrophes, fatally flawed by its slow pace and broad style.
w Theresa Marie screenplay Geir Eriksen, Eirik Ildahl d Jim Wilson ph Richard Bowen m Christopher Young pd Jeffrey Beecroft ed Michael R. Miller
☆ Harvey Keitel, Cameron Diaz, Craig Sheffer, Billy Zane, Shay Duffin

'The director may have been told he was doing a comedy. But the cast act as if they think they're doing a drama. A total breakdown in communication is the only explanation for a film of such calamitous ineptitude.' – *Alexander Walker, London Evening Standard*

Head On: see *Fatal Attraction* (1980)

Head On *
Australia   1997   104m   colour
Millivres/AFFC/Head On/Film Victoria (Jane Scott)
An unhappy Greek-Australian youth decides it is time to leave home and come to terms with his homosexuality.
A powerful film of drug-filled alienation and self-destruction, given energy not only by its performances but by the disjointed rhythms of its camerawork.
w Andrew Bovell, Ana Kokkinos, Mira Robinson book Loaded by Christos Tsiolkas d Ana Kokkinos ph Jaems Grant m Ollie Olsen pd Nikki Di Falco ed Jill Bilcock
☆ Alex Dimitriades, Paul Capsis, Julian Garner, Elena Mandalis, Tony Nikolakopolous, Damien Fotiou, Eugenia Fragos, Dora Kaskanis
'Makes all sexual encounters seem futile and banal, and its final message of nihilistic defiance is shrill and unconvincing.' – *Peter Bradshaw, Guardian*

Head over Heels *
GB   1937   81m   bw
Gaumont (S. C. Balcon)
US title: *Head Over Heels in Love*
A singing star can't make up her mind between two men.
Interestingly dated light star vehicle.
w Dwight Taylor, Fred Thompson, Marjorie Gaffney play Pierre ou Jack by François de Croisset d Sonnie Hale ph Glen McWilliams m/ly Harry Revel, Mack Gordon md Louis Levy ad Alfred Junge
☆ Jessie Matthews, Robert Flemyng, Louis Borell, Romney Brent, Helen Whitney Bourne, Eliot Makeham
'The dialogue has a moral earnestness for which it would be hard to find a parallel even in the Victorian Age.' – *Graham Greene*

Head over Heels
US   1980   97m   Technicolor
UA/Triple Play (Mark Metcalf, Amy Robinson, Griffin Dunne)
🖥
aka: *Chilly Scenes of Winter*
A government office worker thinks back on his on-again off-again relationship with the woman he loves.
Quirky comedy drama without the zest of Annie Hall, which it much resembles; too much like a television play for box-office success.
wd Joan Micklin Silver novel Chilly Scenes of Winter by Ann Beattie ph Bobby Byrne m Ken Lauber pd Peter Jamison ed Cynthia Scheider
☆ John Heard, Mary Beth Hurt, Peter Riegert, Kenneth McMillan, Gloria Grahame

Head over Heels in Love: see *Head over Heels* (1937)

Heads Up
US   1930   76m   bw
Paramount
A coastguard ensign is assigned to a private yacht under suspicion of rum-running.
Tedious, flat musical, only interesting for starring the 'boop boop a doop girl', who soon outstays her welcome.
w Jack McGowan, Jack Kirkland d Victor Schertzinger
☆ Charles Rogers, Helen Kane, Victor Moore, Margaret Breen
'Holds nothing to pull above average grosses and will slide many a house below that mark.' – *Variety*

Health *
US   1979   102m   DeLuxe
TCF/Robert Altman
Complications result when a health foods convention is staged in a Florida hotel.
Zany satirical all-star romp on the lines of A Wedding but by no means as likeable or laughable, considering its cast, as it should be.

w Robert Altman, Paul Dooley, Frank Barhydt d Robert Altman ph Edmond L. Koons m Joseph Byrd
☆ Lauren Bacall, Glenda Jackson, James Garner, Dick Cavett, Carol Burnett, Paul Dooley, Henry Gibson, Donald Moffat

Hear My Song **
GB   1991   105m   Fujicolour
Palace/Film Four/Vision/Limelight/British Screen/Windmill Lane (Alison Owen-Allen)
📼 🖥 ⊘ ⊙
To revive his flagging business, a 1980s Liverpudlian night-club manager hires a singer who may, or may not, be Joseph Locke, a romantic tenor who was once a variety theatre headliner and fled to Ireland to avoid charges of tax evasion.
A small-scale delight, a film of charm and wit.
w Peter Chelsom, Adrian Dunbar d Peter Chelsom ph Sue Gibson m John Altman pd Caroline Hanania ed Martin Walsh
☆ Ned Beatty, Adrian Dunbar, Shirley Anne Field, Tara Fitzgerald, William Hootkins, Harold Berens, David McCallum, John Dair, Stephen Marcus
'One of the year's most delightful films.' – *Kevin Thomas, Los Angeles Times*
'Far from making an innovative contribution to British cinema, Hear My Song relies for the most part on nostalgia, whimsy and sleight of hand.' – *Tom Charity, Sight and Sound*

Hear No Evil
US   1993   97m   Technicolor
TCF/Great Movie Ventures (David Matalon)
📼 🖥 ⊘
A deaf fitness trainer becomes a target for crooks trying to recover a stolen priceless coin.
Dull and pointless thriller that looks as if it's been made to be sandwiched between television commercials.
w R. M. Badat, Kathleen Rowell d Robert Greenwood ph Steven Shaw m Graeme Revell pd Bernt Capra ed Eva Gardos
☆ Marlee Matlin, D. B. Sweeney, Martin Sheen, John C. McGinley, Christina Carlisi, Greg Elam, Charley Lang
'This is filming by numbers, the algebra of the inane.' – *Sight and Sound*

The Hearse
US   1980   95m   Metrocolor
Crown International/Marimark (Mark Tenser)
🖥
A woman moves into a house that is reputed to be haunted.
Tedious and interminable, lacking suspense and interest.
w Bill Bleich d George Bowers ph Mori Kawa m Webster Lewis ad Keith Michl ed George Berndt
☆ Trish Van Devere, Joseph Cotten, David Gautreaux, Donald Hotton, Med Flory, Donald Petrie, Christopher McDonald, Perry Lang

Heart
US   1987   90m   TVC Color
New World (Randy Jurgensen)
🖥
An ageing boxer has one last chance to make the big time, not knowing that his sleazy manager has agreed to throw the fight.
Uninvolving drama that is always predictable; the story has often been told before, and much better than it is here.
w James Lemmo, Randy Jurgensen d James Lemmo ph Jacek Laskus m Geoff Levin, Chris Many pd Vicki Paul ed Lorenzo Marinelli
☆ Brad Davis, Jesse Doran, Steve Buscemi, Robinson Frank Adu, Sam Gray, Billy Costello, Frances Fisher

'Warning: Jealousy Seriously Damages Your Health.'
Heart *
GB   1998   83m   Technicolor
Feature Film/Granada/MFPF (Nicola Shindler)
📼
A mother becomes engrossed with the man, an obsessively jealous husband, who is given her son's heart in a transplant operation.
Intense drama of sex and death that grips the attention, though, on reflection, its melodramatic conclusion teeters on the edge of absurdity.
w Jimmy McGovern d Charles McDougall ph Julian Court m Stephen Warbeck pd Stuart Walker, Chris Roope ed Edward Mansell

☆ Christopher Eccleston, Saskia Reeves, Kate Hardie, Rhys Ifans, Anna Chancellor, Bill Paterson, Matthew Rhys
'A bizarre and riveting sexual melodrama.' – *Peter Bradshaw, Guardian*

Heart and Souls
US   1993   104m   DeLuxe
Universal/Alphaville/Stampede (Nancy Roberts, Sean Daniel)
📼 🖥 ⊘ ⊙ ⊙
Passengers killed in a car and coach crash become guardian angels to the child born of a couple who survive the accident, but he grows up to become a sleazy banker.
Curious and uninvolving movie of obscure intentions.
w Brent Maddock, S. S. Wilson, Gregory and Erik Hansen d Ron Underwood ph Michael Watkins m Marc Shaiman pd John Muto ed O. Nicholas Brown
☆ Robert Downey Jnr, Charles Grodin, Alfre Woodard, Kyra Sedgwick, Tom Sizemore, David Paymer, Elisabeth Shue
'That the effort is at all watchable is a tribute largely to its performers.' – *Variety*

Heart Beat
US   1979   109m   Technicolor
Orion/Warner (Alan Greisman, Michael Shamberg)
The literary career of Jack Kerouac is paralleled with his curious sex life. Hesitant and generally unsatisfactory analysis of the so-called beat generation.
w John Byrum ph Laszlo Kovacs m Jack Nitzsche pd Jack Fisk ed Eric Jenkins
☆ John Heard, Nick Nolte, Sissy Spacek, Ray Sharkey, Tony Bill

Heart Condition
US   1990   95m   DeLuxe
Enterprise/New Line Cinema (Steve Tisch)
📼 🖥 ⊘
A bigoted white cop who has a heart transplant is haunted by the organ's donor, a suave black lawyer.
Dire comedy, despite likeable performances by its stars.
wd James D. Parriott ph Arthur Albert m Patrick Leonard pd John Muto ed David Finfer
☆ Bob Hoskins, Denzel Washington, Chloe Webb, Robert Apisa, Jeffrey Meek, Frank R. Roach, Kieran Mulroney, Lisa Stahl, Ray Baker, Eva Larue, Roger E. Mosley

A Heart in Winter: see *Un Coeur en Hiver*

The Heart Is a Lonely Hunter *
US   1968   123m   Technicolor
Warner Seven Arts (Joel Freeman)
📼 🖥 ⊙
Incidents in the life of a gentle deaf mute in a small Southern town.
Wispy film of a wistful novel; quite well done but overlong and hard to cheer at.
w Thomas C. Ryan novel Carson McCullers d Robert Ellis Miller ph James Wong Howe m Dave Grusin
☆ Alan Arkin, Sondra Locke, Stacy Keach, Laurinda Barrett, Chuck McCann, Biff McGuire, Percy Rodriguez, Cicely Tyson
𝄞 Alan Arkin; Sondra Locke

Heart Like a Wheel *
US   1983   113m   CFI color
Aurora (Charles Rovin)
🖥 ⊘
The wife of a service station owner stops at nothing to become a racing driver.
Well-made study of an obsession, with the usual racing thrills.
w Ken Friedman d Jonathan Kaplan ph Tak Fujimoto m Laurence Rosenthal pd James William Newport
☆ Bonnie Bedelia, Beau Bridges, Leo Rossi, Hoyt Axton, Bill McKinney
'An Americanized Chariots of Fire for the drive-in market.' – *Observer*

Heart of a Nation **
France   1940   111m   bw
Paul Graetz
original title: *Untel Père et Fils*
The story of a Paris family from the Franco-Prussian war to 1939.
Uneven and episodic but consistently interesting piece completed just as the Nazis moved into Paris and

suppressed by them, but later released from America with linking narrative by Charles Boyer.

w Charles Spaak d Julien Duvivier ph Jules Kruger m Jean Wiener

☆ Louis Jouvet, Raimu, Suzy Prim, Lucien Nat, Michèle Morgan

Heart of Dixie

US   1989   105m   DeLuxe

Orion (Steve Tisch)

The civil rights movement impinges on the lives of three friends at a college in Alabama in the 1950s.
Trivial stuff, presumably aimed at a teen audience that no longer exists for such mild and inoffensive drama.

w Tom McCown novel *Heartbreak Hotel* by Anne Rivers Siddons d Martin Davidson ph Robert Elswit m Kenny Vance, Phillip Namanworth pd Glenda Ganis ed Bonnie Koehler

☆ Ally Sheedy, Virginia Madsen, Phoebe Cates, Treat Williams, Don Michael Paul, Kyle Secor, Francesca Roberts

'A messy goo of nostalgia, rites of passage and clumsy social conscience with an almost exclusive emphasis on Sheedy's eager smile and breathless enthusiasm.' – *Empire*

Heart of Glass *

West Germany   1976   94m   Eastmancolor

Werner Herzog

original title: *Herz aus Glas*

A wandering herdsman with special powers supplies a factory owner with the secret of making a very precious glass.
Apocalyptic visionary parable which may mean everything, or nothing, but amuses fitfully while it's on the screen.

w Werner Herzog, Herbert Achternbusch d Werner Herzog ph Jörg Schmidt-Reitwin, Michael Gast m Popol Vuh ed Beate Mainka-Jellinghaus

☆ Josef Bierbichler, Stefan Güttler, Clemens Scheitz, Sonja Skiba

Heart of Midnight

US   1988   105m   TVC Color

Vestron/AG Productions (Jon Kurtis)

An emotionally disturbed woman uncovers the dark secrets of a night-club left to her by her uncle.
Unattractive psychological horror.

wd Matthew Chapman ph Ray Rivas m Yanni pd Gene Rudolph ed Penelope Shaw

☆ Jennifer Jason Leigh, Denise Dummont, Gale Mayron, James Rebhorn, Sam Schacht, Frank Stallone, Brenda Vaccaro, Peter Coyote, Jack Hallett, Nick Love

Heart of New York *

US   1932   74m   bw

Warner

A plumber invents a washing machine and becomes a millionaire.
Ethnic farce set in New York's Jewish quarter; of considerable curiosity value.

w Arthur Caesar, Houston Branch play *Mendel Inc* by David Freedman d Mervyn Le Roy

☆ Joe Smith, Charles Dale, George Sidney, Anna Apfel, Aline MacMahon, Donald Cook

'Gabby to an extreme … too much dialect and too little animation.' – *Variety*

† Smith and Dale were a famous vaudeville act.

The Heart of the Matter *

GB   1953   105m   bw

British Lion/London Films (Ian Dalrymple)

In 1942 in an African colony a police officer has an affair while his wife is away, is blackmailed, and plans suicide despite his staunch Catholic belief.
Rather stodgy attempt to film Graham Greene; perhaps everyone tries a little too hard, and in any case the ending is compromised.

w Ian Dalrymple, Lesley Storm novel Graham Greene d George More O'Ferrall ph Jack Hildyard m Brian Easdale

☆ Trevor Howard, Maria Schell, Elizabeth Allan, Denholm Elliott, Peter Finch, Gérard Oury, George Coulouris, Earl Cameron, Michael Hordern, Colin Gordon, Cyril Raymond, Orlando Martins

'A curious choice for commercial filming.' – *Lindsay Anderson*

Heart of the North

US   1938   74m   Technicolor

Warner (Bryan Foy)

The Canadian Mounties chase after gold and fur thieves.
Routine adventure utilizing early developments in colour processing.

w Lee Katz, Vincent Sherman novel William Byron Mowery d Lew Seiler

☆ Dick Foran, Gloria Dickson, Gale Page, Allen Jenkins, Patric Knowles, James Stephenson

Heartbeat

US   1946   102m   bw

RKO/Robert and Raymond Hakim

A French gamin released from reform school becomes a professional pickpocket.
Unamusing remake of Battement de Coeur, with script and most performances very strained.

w Hans Wilhelm, Max Kolpe, Michel Duran, Morrie Ryskind d Sam Wood ph Joe Valentine m Paul Misraki

☆ Ginger Rogers, Jean-Pierre Aumont, Adolphe Menjou, Basil Rathbone, Mikhail Rasumny, Melville Cooper, Mona Maris, Henry Stephenson

'The heartbeat is irregular and sadly ailing.' – *Photoplay*

Heartbreak Hotel

US   1988   93m   colour

Buena Vista/Touchstone (Lyda Obst, Debra Hill)

In 1972, a teenager kidnaps Elvis Presley to please his divorced mother, a long-time fan who runs a run-down hotel bereft of guests.
For the most part this is a risible, deeply sentimental fantasy, though there are a few relishable comic moments, including a parody of early rock movies, a German accordion band serenading Elvis, and his redecoration of the hotel in the style of Graceland.

wd Chris Columbus ph Stephen Dobson m Georges Delerue pd John Muto ed Raja Gosnell

☆ David Keith, Tuesday Weld, Charlie Schlatter, Angela Goethals, Chris Mulkey, Karen Landry

The Heartbreak Kid *

US   1972   106m   DeLuxe

(TCF) Palomar (Edgar J. Scherick)

Disappointed with his honeymoon, a sporting goods salesman promptly sets his cap at a richer, prettier prospective spouse.
Heartless modern comedy reminiscent of The Graduate; quite well done but unsympathetic and somehow too American to export satisfactorily.

w Neil Simon story *A Change of Plan* by Bruce Jay Friedman d Elaine May ph Owen Roizman m Garry Sherman

☆ Charles Grodin, Cybill Shepherd, Jeannie Berlin, Eddie Albert, Audra Lindley, William Prince, Art Metrano

'The latest in a relatively new kind of American film – glittery trash.' – *Stanley Kauffmann*

⚿ Jeannie Berlin; Eddie Albert

Heartbreak Ridge

US   1986   130m   Technicolor

Warner/Malpaso/Jay Weston (Clint Eastwood)

An ageing gunnery sergeant transforms raw recruits into fighting men who become heroes in Grenada.
Dismayingly predictable potboiler with nothing but foul language to pass the time.

w James Carabatsos d Clint Eastwood ph Jack N. Green m Lennie Niehaus

☆ Clint Eastwood, Marsha Mason, Everett McGill, Moses Gunn, Eileen Heckart, Bo Svenson

'Now looking increasingly like an Easter Island statue, he has a voice pickled in Bourbon, a tongue like razor wire and a body so full of shrapnel he can't walk through airport metal detectors.' – *Time Out*

Heartbreakers

US   1984   98m   DeLuxe

Orion/Jethro Films (Bob Weis, Bobby Roth)

Two old friends, one an artist, the other a businessman, worry about their relationship, their careers and their love-life.
Mundane drama of male bonding.

wd Bobby Roth ph Michael Ballhaus m Tangerine Dream pd David Nichols ed John Carnochan

☆ Peter Coyote, Nick Mancuso, Carole Laure, Max Gail, James Laurenson, Carol Wayne, Jamie Rose, Kathryn Harrold

Heartburn *

US   1986   108m   Technicolor

Paramount/Mike Nichols, Robert Greenhut

Romantic problems of a busy professional couple.
Rather ordinary and overstretched scripting is enlivened by star playing, but the overall feeling is one of disappointment.

w Nora Ephron novel Nora Ephron d Mike Nichols ph Nestor Almendros m Carly Simon pd Tony Walton ed Sam O'Steen

☆ Meryl Streep, Jack Nicholson, Jeff Daniels, Maureen Stapleton, Stockard Channing, Richard Masur, Steven Hill, Milos Forman, Catherine O'Hara

'A movie of colossal inconsequence. Heartburn? No, just a bad attack of wind.' – *Time Out*

Heartland *

US   1979   96m   DuArt

Wilderness Women Productions/Filmhaus (Annick Smith)

In 1910 Wyoming, a woman with a small daughter takes up her arduous duties as housekeeper to a dour rancher.
Impressive if not very likeable semidocumentary which certainly rubs one's nose in the unfairness of life.

w Beth Ferris, from the papers of Elmore Randall Stewart d Richard Pearce ph Fred Murphy m Charles Gross

☆ Conchata Ferrell, Rip Torn, Barry Primus, Lilia Skala

Heart's Desire

GB   1935   82m   bw

BIP (Walter Mycroft)

In old Vienna, a tenor finds that a glamorous socialite wants him for his voice rather than himself.
Dated operetta, but the star still reigns supreme.

w L. DuGarde Peach, Jack Davies, Roger Burford, Bruno Frank story Lioni Pickard d Paul Stein ph Jack Cox m Schumann and others md Idris Lewis, Stanford Robinson ad Clarence Elder ed Leslie Norman

☆ Richard Tauber, Leonora Corbett, Diana Napier, Frank Vosper

Hearts Divided

US   1936   76m   bw

Warner

Napoleon's brother weds a Baltimore beauty.
Uneasy remake of Glorious Betsy (qv) with a couple of musical numbers added; a splendid cast retires defeated.

w Laird Doyle, Casey Robinson d Frank Borzage

☆ Marion Davies, Dick Powell, Edward Everett Horton, Claude Rains, Charles Ruggles, Arthur Treacher, Henry Stephenson

Hearts in Springtime: see *Glamour Boy*

Hearts of Darkness: A Filmmaker's Apocalypse **

US   1991   96m   colour

Blue Dolphin/Zaloom Mayfield/Zoetrope (George Zaloom, Les Mayfield)

A documentary on the making of Francis Ford Coppola's *Apocalypse Now* in 1976.
Fascinating glimpse not only of filmmaking on a troubled location with oversized egos in collision, but also of Hollywood attitudes of the time. It bears out Coppola's own summation, 'We had access to too much money, too much equipment, and little by little we went insane.'

wd Fax Bahr, George Hickenlooper ph Larry Carney, Eleanor Coppola, Bill Neal, Doug Ryan, Les Blank and others m Todd Boekelheide ed Michael Hreer, Jay Miracle

Hearts of Fire

US   1987   95m   colour   J-D-C Scope

UKFD/Lorimar/Phoenix Entertainment/Fox (Richard Marquand, Jennifer Miller, Jennifer Alward)

A female rock singer succeeds with the aid of a reclusive star and a weary British rocker.

Tedious exposé of the world of rock music, lacking in excitement and a sad end to the career of Marquand, who died soon after finishing it.

w Scott Richardson, Joe Eszterhas d Richard Marquand ph Alan Hume m John Barry pd Roger Murray-Leach ed Sean Barton

☆ Fiona Flanagan, Bob Dylan, Everett Everett, Lesley Donaldson, Barbara Barnes-Hopkins, Maury Chaykin, Ian Dury, Richie Havens, Julian Glover

Hearts of the West *

US   1975   103m   Metrocolor

MGM/Bill-Zieff (Tony Bill)

GB title: *Hollywood Cowboy*

In the early thirties a naïve midwesterner almost accidentally becomes a Hollywood star.
Overstretched comedy poking gentle fun at old Hollywood: likeable but finally disappointing, as it obviously needed a Buster Keaton.

w Rob Thompson d Howard Zieff ph Mario Tosi m Ken Lauber

☆ Jeff Bridges, Alan Arkin, Andy Griffith, Blythe Danner, Donald Pleasence, Richard B. Shull, Herb Edelman

Hearts of the World *

US   1918   80m   bw   silent

Artcraft (David Wark Griffith)

Of various people involved in World War I, the patriotic and dutiful ones come out best.
Rather dim patriotic propaganda made by Griffith at the request of the British government and using a good deal of newsreel as well as reconstruction. The personal stories are on the predictable side.

wd David Wark Griffith ph Billy Bitzer ed James Smith

☆ Lillian Gish, Dorothy Gish, Robert Harron, Josephine Crowell, Erich von Stroheim, Noël Coward

'Here we have an art of pure emotion which can go beneath thought, beneath belief, beneath ideals, down to the brute fact of emotional psychology, and make a man or a woman who has hated war, all war, even this war, feel the surge of group emotion, group loyalty and group hate.' – *Kenneth MacGowan, The New Republic (1918)*

† For the screenplay credit Griffith used the pseudonym of Gaston de Tolignac.

Heat *

US   1972   100m   colour

Score/Sarx (Andy Warhol)

aka: *Andy Warhol's Heat*

An out-of-work television actor and singer moves into a run-down Los Angeles motel and begins an affair with an older, fading actress.
Perverse variation on Sunset Boulevard, casually presented but offering amusement along the way.

wd Paul Morrissey idea John Hallowell ph Paul Morrissey m John Cale ed Lan Jokel, Jed Johnson

☆ Joe Dallesandro, Sylvia Miles, Andrea Feldman, Pat Ast, Ray Vestal, P. J. Lester, Eric Emerson

'An unsavoury piece of work, laced with sex, lesbianism, self-abuse and perversion.' – *Daily Record, Glasgow*

'Succeeds in being both funny and effortlessly truthful.' – *Derek Malcolm, Guardian*

Heat

US   1987   101m   Technicolor

Vista/New Century (Keith Rotman, George Pappas)

A Las Vegas gambler gets into trouble with gangsters.
Unremarkable toughie with the star at his most predictable.

w William Goldman novel William Goldman d R. M. Richards ph James Contner m Michael Gibbs ed Jeffrey Wolf

☆ Burt Reynolds, Karen Young, Peter MacNicol, Howard Hesseman, Diana Scarwid

Heat **

US   1995   172m   Technicolor   Panavision

Warner/Monarchy/Forward Pass/Regency (Michael Mann, Art Linson)

A streetwise Los Angeles cop with marital problems comes to respect the ruthless leader of a gang of armed robbers.
A highly polished, lovingly crafted thriller, but overlong, portentous and padded with irrelevant

---

subplots, and one that finally gives birth to a mouse of an idea: that cops and robbers are much alike. Its true subject-matter is no more than male bonding between two boastful and unlovely characters, and its real purpose seems to have been to bring together on-screen Pacino and de Niro. De Niro, perhaps remembering Bogart's not dissimilar duel with Rod Steiger in The Harder They Fall, goes for a minimalist approach; Pacino shouts a lot.

wd Michael Mann ph Dante Spinotti m Elliot Goldenthal pd Neil Spisak ed Dov Hoenig, Pasquale Buba, William Goldenberg, Tom Rolf
☆ Al Pacino, Robert DeNiro, Val Kilmer, Jon Voight, Tom Sizemore, Diane Venora, Amy Brenneman, Ashley Judd, Wes Studi, Natalie Portman

'Stands apart from other films of its type by virtue of its extraordinarily rich characterizations and its thoughtful, deeply melancholy take on modern life.' – Todd McCarthy, Variety
'Proves one thing absolute. If you put great actors and a great script together with a great visionary director, you get a great movie.' – Empire
'What is surprising is that the movie is 2 hours and 52 minutes long, and that neither character is entertaining enough to fill the time. Mann's action scenes have an existential, you-are-there jitteriness, but when the characters are just sitting around hatching schemes, Heat is a dry, talky movie.' – Owen Gleiberman, Entertainment Weekly
† It was based on a TV movie (L.A. Takedown), made by Michael Mann in 1989, which has been released on video

Heat and Dust **
GB   1982   130m   colour
Merchant Ivory (Ismail Merchant)
📼 ▬ 📷 🎧

A woman discovers India's past through her great-aunt's letters.
Much praised by those who admire the work of this team, but found (as usual) mildly bewildering by others, this has at least a large enough budget to produce interest in its historically re-created backgrounds if not its complex plot structure.
w Ruth Prawer Jhabvala novel Ruth Prawer Jhabvala d James Ivory ph Walter Lassally m Richard Robbins
☆ Julie Christie, Christopher Cazenove, Shashi Kapoor, Greta Scacchi, Nickolas Grace, Jennifer Kendal, Julian Glover, Susan Fleetwood
'A likeable patchwork of concepts and cameos.' – Philip Strick, MFB
Ⓤ screenplay

Heat and Sunlight
US   1987   98m   bw
Stutz/Snowball/New Front Alliance (Steve Burns, Hildy Burns)
▬

A photographer becomes confused when he discovers that his love affair with a dancer is coming to an end.
An improvised low-budget study in neurosis, of interest mainly to its participants.
wd Rob Nilsson ph Tomas Tucker m David Byrne, Brian Eno pd Hildy Burns, Steve Burns ed Henk Van Eeghen
☆ Rob Nilsson, Don Bejema, Consuelo Faust, Ernie Fosselius

Heat Lightning
US   1934   63m   bw
Warner
A lady gas station attendant in the hot South-west becomes involved with two murderers on the run.
Cautionary tale which does not quite gel despite effort all round.
w Brown Holmes, Warren Duff play George Abbott, Leon Abrams d Mervyn Le Roy
☆ Aline MacMahon, Ann Dvorak, Preston Foster, Lyle Talbot, Glenda Farrell, Frank McHugh, Ruth Donnelly
'Drab background, little sex appeal and not enough tension. It's a sluffo for deluxers, but can get by elsewhere.' – Variety
† Remade in 1941 as Highway West.

Heathers
US   1988   103m   DeLuxe
Premier Releasing/New World/Cinemarque Entertainment (Denise Di Novi)
📼 ▬ 📷 🎧

A high-school student begins to systematically murder his fellow students.
Black joke that rapidly runs out of interest.
w Daniel Waters d Michael Lehmann ph Francis Kenny m David Newman pd Jon Hutman ed Norman Hollyn
☆ Winona Ryder, Christian Slater, Shannen Doherty, Lisanne Falk, Kim Walker, Penelope Milford, Glenn Shadix
'The film is not seriously a comedy about high school as a metaphor for society – its false values, its power-hungry cliques, its emotional exploitation.' – Richard Coombs, MFB

The Heat's On
US   1943   79m   bw
Columbia (Milton Carter)
GB title: Tropicana
A star seeks financial backing from an elderly angel whose sister runs the Legion of Purity.
Dim musical vehicle for a fading star; her last film for twenty-seven years.
w Fitzroy Davis, George S. George, Fred Schiller d Gregory Ratoff ph Franz Planer m John Leipold md Yasha Bunchuk
☆ Mae West, Victor Moore, William Gaxton, Almira Sessions, Lester Allen, Mary Roche, Hazel Scott, Alan Dinehart, Lloyd Bridges, Xavier Cugat and his Orchestra
'A stale-ale musical in which a lot of good people apathetically support the almost equally apathetic Mae West.' – James Agee

Heatwave *
Australia   1982   95m   Eastmancolor
M and L Enterprises/Preston Crothers (Hilary Linstead)
📼 ▬

Community activists move to prevent the schemes of a Sydney developer.
Rather like an Ealing drama descending into melodrama; a polished piece of committed film journalism masquerading as fiction.
w Marc Rosenberg, Phillip Noyce d Phillip Noyce ph Vincent Monton m Cameron Allan pd Ross Major
☆ Judy Davis, Richard Moir, Chris Haywood, Bill Hunter, John Meillon, John Gregg
† A similarly themed Australian film, The Killing of Angel Street, came out almost simultaneously.

Heaven *
US   1987   80m   colour
Island Pictures/RVP Productions (Joe Kelly)
Interviews with a variety of people about death, after-life and heaven are interspersed with clips from old Hollywood movies and TV programmes that illustrate or contradict the statements made.
Documentary demonstrating the optimism and vagueness of our views on the subject, entertaining in its offbeat fashion despite the manner in which the interviewees are photographed in distracting patterns of light and shade.
d Diane Keaton ph Frederick Elmes, Joe Kelly m Howard Shore ad Barbara Ling ed Paul Barnes

'From Vietnam to America, one woman's journey from hope, to love, to discovery.'
Heaven & Earth *
US   1993   140m   Technicolor   Panavision
Warner/Regency/Canal/Alcor (Oliver Stone, Arnon Milchan, Robert Kline, A. Kitman Ho)
📼 ▬ 📷 🎧

A Vietnamese peasant woman endures hardships and torment from both sides in the war, and life is slow to improve after she goes to America as the wife of a US marine.
An ambitious and epic film, but too strident to be successful and one that, although ostensibly dealing with the life of a Vietnamese woman, still manages to make the subject-matter that of the American experience in Vietnam and its aftermath; the balance shifts from the moment Tommy Lee Jones's damaged marine enters the picture.
wd Oliver Stone books When Heaven and Earth Changed Place by Le Ly Hayslip, Jay Wurts; Child of War, Woman of Peace by Le Ly Hayslip, James Hayslip ph Robert Richardson m Kitaro

pd Victor Kempster ed David Brenner, Sally Menke
☆ Tommy Lee Jones, Joan Chen, Haing S. Ngor, Hiep Thi Le, Debbie Reynolds, Supak Pititam, Thuan K. Nguyen
'The sledgehammer approach to storytelling merely results in audience numbness and distance from the potentially moving material.' – Variety
'Thematically grotesque but visually gorgeous … if Stone simplifies and distorts, he often does so brilliantly, like a cartoonist with a Fauvist's eye for the drama in color and character.' – Richard Corliss, Time
'Cry? I could have wept with boredom.' – Alexander Walker

Heaven Can Wait ***
US   1943   112m   Technicolor
TCF (Ernst Lubitsch)
▬ 📷

On arrival in Hades, an elderly playboy reports his peccadilloes to Satan, who sends him Upstairs.
Charming period piece with fantasy bookends; the essence of the piece is its evocation of American society in the 1890s, and in its director's waspish way with a funny scene.
w Samson Raphaelson play Birthday by Lazlo Bus-Fekete d Ernst Lubitsch ph Edward Cronjager m Alfred Newman ad James Basevi, Leland Fuller
☆ Don Ameche, Gene Tierney, Laird Cregar, Charles Coburn, Marjorie Main, Eugene Pallette, Allyn Joslyn, Spring Byington, Signe Hasso, Louis Calhern
'It was so good I half believed Lubitsch could still do as well as he ever did, given half a chance.' – James Agee
⚜ best picture; Ernst Lubitsch; Edward Cronjager

Heaven Can Wait *
US   1978   100m   Movielab
Paramount/Warren Beatty (Howard W. Koch Jnr, Charles H. McGuire)
A football star finds himself accidentally in heaven after a car accident; when he is allowed to return, his body has been cremated, so he has to find another.
Unexpectedly commercially successful (the late seventies clearly needed religion) remake of 1941's Here Comes Mr Jordan. It lacks the sharpness and style of its predecessor, and despite amusing moments is often merely tacky.
w Warren Beatty, Elaine May play Harry Segall d Warren Beatty, Buck Henry ph William A. Fraker m Dave Grusin pd Paul Sylbert, Edwin O'Donovan ed Robert C. Jones
☆ Warren Beatty, Julie Christie, James Mason, Jack Warden, Charles Grodin, Dyan Cannon, Buck Henry, Vincent Gardenia, Joseph Maher
'Script and direction are … providing a rich mix of visual and verbal humor that is controlled and avoids the extremes of cheap vulgarity and overly esoteric whimsy.' – Variety
'It lifts the spirits and makes you feel good about life on earth and even beyond.' – Rex Reed
⚜ art direction
⚜ best picture; script; direction; photography; music; Warren Beatty (as actor); Jack Warden; Dyan Cannon

Heaven Fell That Night
France/Italy   1958   90m   Eastmancolor   Cinemascope
IENA/CEIAP (Raoul Levy)
original title: Les Bijoutiers du Clair de Lune
A young girl becomes involved in a revenge plot and finds herself on the run with a killer.
Heavy going sex-and-violence hokum.
w Roger Vadim, Peter Viertel novel Albert Vidalie d Roger Vadim ph Armand Thirard m Georges Auric
☆ Brigitte Bardot, Alida Valli, Stephen Boyd, Pepe Nieto

Heaven Help Us **
US   1985   104m   colour
HBO/Silver Screen Partners (Mark Carliner, Dan Wigutow)
📼 ▬ 📷
GB title: Catholic Boys
A new boy discovers friendship, love and tough treatment at a Catholic high school in Brooklyn in the mid-60s.

Engrossing story of adolescent strivings, done with some wit and style.
w Charles Purpura d Michael Dinner ph Miroslav Ondricek m James Horner pd Michael Molly ed Stephen A. Rotter
☆ Andrew McCarthy, Mary Stuart Masterson, Kevin Dillon, Malcolm Danare, Jennie Dundas, Kate Reid, Wallace Shawn, Jay Patterson, John Heard, Donald Sutherland

Heaven Is Round the Corner
GB   1943   94m   bw
British National/Fred Zelnick
A war veteran is helped to find his long-lost love.
Sentimental tosh with music, a second team effort which went down well enough in wartime.
w Austin Melford d Maclean Rogers
☆ Will Fyffe, Leni Lynn, Austin Trevor, Magda Kun, Peter Glenville

Heaven Knows Mr Allison *
US   1957   105m   Technicolor   Cinemascope
TCF (Buddy Adler, Eugene Franks)
▬

Marooned on a small Pacific island during World War II, a marine and a nun, antagonistic to each other, combine to outwit the Japs.
Silly adventure story with predictably well-handled action sequences separated by even more predictable dialogue, lots of it.
w John Lee Mahin, John Huston novel Charles Shaw d John Huston ph Oswald Morris m Georges Auric ad Stephen Grimes ed Russell Lloyd
☆ Robert Mitchum, Deborah Kerr
⚜ script; Deborah Kerr

Heaven on Earth: see The Exquisite Sinner (1927)

Heaven on Earth
US   1931   78m   bw
Universal
Mississippi steamship owners feud with the shanty houseboaters who line the riverbank.
Oddly titled melodrama with a conscience; it doesn't really work.
w Ray Doyle novel Mississippi by Ben Lucian Burman d Russell Mack
☆ Lew Ayres, Anita Louise, Harry Beresford, Elizabeth Patterson, Slim Summerville
'Needs strong stage support wherever chanced.' – Variety

Heaven Only Knows
US   1947   98m   bw
UA (Seymour Nebenzal)
An angel is sent to the old west to reform a bad man.
Whimsical comedy-drama which doesn't work at all, even as a distant cousin of Here Comes Mr Jordan.
w Art Arthur, Rowland Leigh d Albert S. Rogell ph Karl Struss m Heinz Roemheld
☆ Robert Cummings, Brian Donlevy, Marjorie Reynolds, Bill Goodwin, John Litel, Stuart Erwin

Heaven with a Barbed Wire Fence
US   1939   61m   bw
TCF (Sol M. Wurtzel)
A New York clerk hitch-hikes his way to Arizona, where he has bought a piece of land.
Subdued flagwaver with everybody behaving just swell in God's own country.
w Dalton Trumbo, Leonard Hoffman, Ben Grauman Kohn d Ricardo Cortez ph Edward Cronjager md Samuel Kaylin
☆ Glenn Ford, Jean Rogers, Richard Conte, Marjorie Rambeau, Raymond Walburn, Eddie Collins, Ward Bond
'A slightly clouded title, with little possibility of propelling many customers through the front door.' – Variety
† It was Glenn Ford's first film.

Heaven with a Gun
US   1969   101m   Metrocolor   Panavision
MGM (King Brothers)
The determined new preacher of a small Western town is an ex-gunfighter.
Solidly carpentered half-a-bill Western.
w Richard Carr d Lee Katzin ph Fred J. Koenekamp m Johnny Mandel
☆ Glenn Ford, Carolyn Jones, David Carradine, J. D. Cannon, Barbara Hershey, Noah Beery Jnr

---

Heavenly Bodies

Canada 1985 89m Medallion
Alliance/PSO/RSL/Playboy (Robert Lantos, Stephen J.Roth)

Rivalries between two aerobic instructors lead to a marathon workout contest.
Absurd and trivial musical, with all the depth of characterization and narrative interest of a pop video; even those who enjoy watching young women jumping up and down in leotards will tire of it long before it ends.

w Lawrence Dane, Ron Base d Lawrence Dane ph Thomas Burstyn md Paul Hoffert ch Brian Foley pd Lindsey Goddard
☆ Cynthia Dale, Richard Rebiere, Walter George Alton, Laura Henry, Stuart Stone, Patrica Idlette, Pam Henry

The Heavenly Body

US 1943 93m bw
MGM (Arthur Hornblow Jnr)

An astronomer is too busy to notice his wife, so she takes up astrology and meets a dark handsome stranger as predicted.
Thin romantic comedy which despite crazy touches never actually makes one laugh.

w Michael Arlen, Walter Reisch d Alexander Hall ph Robert Planck m Bronislau Kaper
☆ William Powell, Hedy Lamarr, James Craig, Fay Bainter, Henry O'Neill, Spring Byington, Morris Ankrum, Connie Gilchrist

'Not all angels are innocent.'
'The True Story Of A Crime That Shocked A Nation.'
Heavenly Creatures ***

New Zealand 1994 98m Eastmancolor
Buena Vista/Wingnut/Fontana/NZFC (Jim Booth)

In New Zealand, two schoolgirls, who form a close relationship, based on a shared fantasy world, decide to kill the mother of one of them to prevent their separation.
Chilling, sensitively directed account of the dangerous mixture of fantasy and reality that precipitated a tragic and violent death. It is a considerable achievement and an unexpected advance from a director hitherto known for slapdash, gore-filled horror movies such as Braindead.

w Frances Walsh, Peter Jackson d Peter Jackson ph Alun Bollinger m Peter Dasent pd Grant Major ed Jamie Selkirk
☆ Melanie Lynskey, Kate Winslet, Sarah Peirse, Diana Kent, Clive Merrison, Simon O'Connor, Jed Brophy
'The sad creatures who Pauline and Juliet must have been in real life are alchemized into figures of horror and beauty. They become the stuff of thrilling popular art.' – Richard Corliss, Time
'A striking addition to the cinema of folie à deux, the madness for two that is either a perversion of true love or its purest manifestation.' – Adam Mars-Jones, Independent
† The real-life Juliet now lives in Scotland and writes, under the name of Anne Perry, mystery novels set in Victorian times.
⚷ Frances Walsh, Peter Jackson (screenplay)

Heavenly Days

US 1944 72m bw
RKO (Robert Fellows)

Fibber McGee and Molly go to Washington.
Extension of a radio comedy series about a man who simply can't tell the truth; amusing at the time, but with topical references which mean little today.

wd Howard Estabrook ph J. Roy Hunt m Leigh Harline
☆ Jim Jordan, Marion Jordan, Eugene Pallette, Gordon Oliver, Raymond Walburn, Barbara Hale, Don Douglas, Frieda Inescort

Heavenly Pursuits

GB 1986 91m colour
Island Films/Skreba/Film Four (Michael Relph)

US title: The Gospel According to Vic
A sceptical Scottish teacher is involved with seemingly miraculous happenings at a Catholic school.
Well acted, ineffectual satire on education and religion.

wd Charles Gormley ph Michael Coulter m B. A. Robinson pd Rita McGurn ed John Gow
☆ Tom Conti, Helen Mirren, Brian Pettifer, David Hayman, Dave Anderson, Jennifer Black

Heavens Above *

GB 1963 118m bw
British Lion/Charter (Roy Boulting)

A northern parson with proletarian sympathies is accidentally appointed to a snobby village where he converts the dowager aristocrat to works of absurd charity. Eventually he has the whole country in an uproar and takes the place of an astronaut.
Patchy satirical comedy which takes unsteady aim at too many targets but scores some predictable laughs.

w Frank Harvey, John Boulting d John Boulting ph Max Greene m Richard Rodney Bennett
☆ Peter Sellers, Isabel Jeans, Cecil Parker, Brock Peters, Ian Carmichael, Irene Handl, Eric Sykes, Bernard Miles

'What one loves about life are the things that fade...'
'The most talked-about film of the decade!'
'The only thing greater than their passion for America ... was their passion for each other!'
Heaven's Gate

US 1980 219m Technicolor Panavision
UA (Joann Carelli)

1890 Wyoming: established cattlemen fight immigrants.
Totally incoherent, showy Western which was lambasted by the critics and quickly withdrawn. A vital turning point in Hollywood policy, hopefully marking the last time a whiz kid with one success behind him is given a blank cheque to indulge in self-abuse.

wd Michael Cimino ph Vilmos Zsigmond m David Mansfield ad Tambi Larsen ed Tom Rolf, William Reynolds, Lisa Fruchtman, Gerald Greenberg
☆ Kris Kristofferson, Christopher Walken, John Hurt, Sam Waterston, Brad Dourif, Isabelle Huppert, Joseph Cotten, Jeff Bridges
'The trade must marvel that directors now have such power that no one, in the endless months since work on the picture began, was able to impose some structure and sense.' – Variety
'All too much and not enough.' – Sunday Times
'A film which John Ford would have brought in on time and on budget with quite as much social, critical and political comment – and much more entertainment value.' – Margaret Hinxman, Daily Mail
'It fails so completely that you might suspect Mr Cimino sold his soul to the devil to obtain the success of The Deer Hunter, and the devil has just come around to collect.' – Vincent Canby, New York Times
† The film was budgeted at $7.5 million and cost $36 million. The story of what happened is told in Stephen Bach's Final Cut: Dreams and Disaster in the Making of Heaven's Gate, published in 1985.
⚷ Tambi Larsen

'Trusting the wrong woman can be a deadly choice.'
Heaven's Prisoners

US 1996 132m colour
Rank/New Line/Savoy (Albert S. Ruddy, Andre E. Morgan, Leslie Greif)

A former New Orleans cop is drawn into the world of drugs and mob violence after he rescues a young girl from a crashed aeroplane.
Revenge thriller of no particular distinction; competent is as good as it gets.

w Harley Peyton, Scott Frank novel James Lee Burke d Phil Joanou ph Harris Savides m George Fenton pd John Stoddart ed William Steinkamp
☆ Alec Baldwin, Mary Stuart Masterson, Kelly Lynch, Teri Hatcher, Eric Roberts, Vondie Curtis-Hall, Badja Djola
'An overlong plod, justifying the oxymoronic description a boring thriller.' – George Perry
† The film flopped at the US box-office, taking $5m.

Heavy *

US 1995 103m DuArt
Artificial Eye/Mayfair/Available Light (Richard Miller)

A reclusive, overweight, mother-dominated pizza chef falls for a teenage waitress.
A small-scale, slow-moving drama of an unexamined life being sparked into awareness of the world.

wd James Mangold ph Michael Barrow m Thurston Moore pd Michael Shaw ed Meg Reticker
☆ Pruitt Taylor Vince, Shelley Winters, Liv Tyler, Deborah Harry, Joe Grifasi, Evan Dando
'Well-acted pic dawdles long enough to lose viewers with short attention spans, but delivers modest rewards to those who get in tune with its peculiar rhythms and concerns.' – Variety

'A step beyond science fiction!'
Heavy Metal *

US 1981 90m Metrocolor
Columbia/Ivan Reitman, Leonard Vogel

A complicated comic strip/science fiction story, with soft core jokes in the modern manner, is told by international teams of animators each working on an episode.
The experiment is interesting rather than successful.

w Dan Goldberg, Len Blum story Richard Corben, Angus McKie, Dan O'Bannon, Thomas Warkentin, Berni Wrightson d Gerald Potterton m Elmer Bernstein and others pd Michael Gross ed Janice Brown
☆ Featuring voices of: Roger Bumpass, Jackie Burroughs, John Candy, Joe Flaherty, Don Francks, Eugene Levy, Harold Ramis
'Something of a hodge-podge ... the script is a skeletal, whimsically mystical affair...' – John Pym, MFB

Heavy Petting *

US 1988 80m bw/colour
ICA/Fossil (Obie Benz, Carol Noblitt)

An examination of the sexual customs and habits of the 1950s as seen in films of the time and as recalled by interviews with celebrities. It includes excerpts from Highschool Hellcats, Blackboard Jungle, Because They're Young and Rebel Without a Cause and from educational films.
An entertaining documentary, although many of the interviews are less revealing than the films of the time.

d Obie Benz, Josh Waletzky ph Sandi Sissel ed Josh Waletzky, Judith Sobol, Edith Becker
☆ Laurie Anderson, Sandra Bernhard, William Burroughs, Allen Ginsberg, David Byrne, Spalding Gray, Abbie Hoffman, Josh Mostel

Heavyweights

US 1995 97m Technicolor
Buena Vista/Walt Disney/Caravan (Joe Roth, Roger Birnbaum)

A keep-fit fanatic takes over a holiday camp for overweight children.
Tasteless and inane comedy, a clumsy anthology of bad jokes.

w Judd Apatow, Steven Brill d Steven Brill ph Victor Hammer m J. A. C. Redford pd Stephen Storer ed C. Timothy O'Meara
☆ Tom McGowan, Aaron Schwartz, Ben Stiller, Shaun Weiss, Tom Hodges, Leah Lail, Paul Feig
'The fat gags merely serve to perpetuate offensive and unhelpful stereotypes. It's depressing to think Disney could sink so low.' – Film Review

Hedd Wyn *

Wales 1992 125m colour
S4C (Shân Davis)

A Welsh farmer wins a prize for his poetry after he is killed in the First World War.
Glossy period piece, well done but too long for comfort.

w Alan Llwyd d Paul Turner m John E. R. Hardy pd Jane Roberts, Martin Morley ed Chris Lawrence
☆ Huw Garmon, Sue Roderick, Judith Humphreys, Nia Dryhurst, Gwen Ellis, Grey Evans, Emlyn Gomer
'With its emphasis on veracity and immaculate production design and costuming, pic lacks enough dramatic smarts to go the two-hour-plus distance.' – Variety
⚷ best foreign-language film

Hedda

GB 1975 102m Technicolor
Brut (Robert Enders)

A selfish pregnant woman is bored by her husband and revolted at the idea of carrying his child. She takes an opportunity to revenge herself on an old lover, but the scheme rebounds on herself.

Rather flat rendering of a play which has received more than its due share of approbation.

wd Trevor Nunn play Henrik Ibsen ph Douglas Slocombe m Laurie Johnson
☆ Glenda Jackson, Peter Eyre, Timothy West, Jennie Linden, Patrick Stewart
⚷ Glenda Jackson

Heidi *

US 1937 88m bw
TCF (Raymond Griffith)

An orphan is sent to stay with her crusty grandfather in a mountain village.
Star-tailored version of a favourite children's story; just what the box-office ordered at the time.

w Walter Ferris, Julien Josephson novel Johanna Spyri d Allan Dwan ph Arthur Miller md Louis Silvers
☆ Shirley Temple, Jean Hersholt, Arthur Treacher, Helen Westley, Pauline Moore, Mary Nash, Thomas Beck, Sidney Blackmer, Mady Christians, Sig Rumann, Marcia Mae Jones, Christian Rub
'Good for the average Temple draw or better.' – Variety

Heimat ***

West Germany 1984 924m bw/colour
Edgar Reitz/WDR/SFB
aka: Homeland

An epically conceived story of life in a German village between 1919 and 1982.
Essentially a superior soap opera with pretensions of grandeur, this beautifully photographed serial has moments of magic amid much that is merely pretentious and unexplained. Despite the symbolism and the irony (a village idiot is ever present), an eager if arty audience found that it had much to say, though no one could explain its lapses from colour to black-and-white and back again.

w Edgar Reitz, Peter Steinbach d Edgar Reitz ph Gernot Roll m Nikos Mamangakis
☆ Marita Breuer, Michael Lesch, Dieter Schaad, Karin Kienzler, Eva Maria Bayerswaltes, Rüdiger Weigang, Karin Rasenach

The Heir to Genghis Khan: see Storm Over Asia

'She was taught to love and hate – by masters!'
The Heiress **

US 1949 115m bw
Paramount (William Wyler)

A plain but rich young woman takes revenge on her fortune-seeking lover.
Richly-decorated and generally pleasing version of a stage success based on a Henry James story set in the 1890s.

w Ruth and Augustus Goetz play Washington Square by Ruth and Augustus Goetz novel Washington Square by Henry James d William Wyler ph Leo Tover m Aaron Copland ad John Meehan
☆ Olivia de Havilland, Ralph Richardson, Montgomery Clift, Miriam Hopkins, Vanessa Brown, Mona Freeman, Ray Collins
'Wyler is that rarest of craftsmen who can take such a drama, already completely fulfilled in theatre terms, and convert it to film without ever permitting the play-form to dominate the screen.' – Hermione Isaacs, Films in Review
▲ Aaron Copland; Olivia de Havilland; John Meehan
⚷ best picture; William Wyler; Leo Tover; Ralph Richardson

The Heist: see Dollars

'No star ever climbed higher – no woman ever fell lower!'
The Helen Morgan Story

US 1957 118m bw Cinemascope
Warner (Martin Rackin)

GB title: Both Ends of the Candle
A young singer rises from vaudeville to Broadway but becomes an alcoholic.
Moderately truthful biopic with effective 20s trimmings.

w Oscar Saul, Dean Riesner, Stephen Longstreet, Nelson Gidding d Michael Curtiz ph Ted McCord m various ad John Beckman

☆ Ann Blyth, Paul Newman, Richard Carlson, Gene Evans, Alan King, Cara Williams, Walter Woolf King

† Ann Blyth's vocals were sung by Gogi Grant.

'All the tumultuous wonder and tremendous drama in the story of history's most famous runaway lovers! Soon the whole world will know of its greatness!'

Helen of Troy

US/Italy 1955 118m Warnercolor
Cinemascope
Warner (Robert Wise)
Helen is kidnapped by Paris and regained by use of the Trojan Horse.
Dingy historical spectacular, stultifyingly boring until the final spectacle, with the actors obviously wishing themselves doing anything but mouthing the doggerel dialogue.
w John Twist, Hugh Gray d Robert Wise
ph Harry Stradling m Max Steiner
☆ Rossana Podesta, Jacques Sernas, Cedric Hardwicke, Niall MacGinnis, Stanley Baker, Nora Swinburne, Robert Douglas, Torin Thatcher, Harry Andrews, Janette Scott, Ronald Lewis, Brigitte Bardot

The Helicopter Spies

US 1967 90m Metrocolor
MGM/Arena (Anthony Spinner)
Spies recruit an expert criminal to open a safe containing a thermal prism, or heat ray, that can destroy the world.
The usual comic-strip mad-scientist scenario with two mad scientists, but entertaining in its undemanding way.
w Dean Hargrove d Boris Sagal ph Fred Koenekamp m Richard Shores ad George W. Davis, James W. Sullivan ed Joseph Dervin, John B. Rogers
☆ Robert Vaughn, David McCallum, Carol Lynley, Bradford Dillman, Lola Albright, John Dehner, John Carradine, Leo G. Carroll, Julie London, H. M. Wynant

Hell and High Water *

US 1954 103m Technicolor Cinemascope
TCF (Raymond A. Klune)
A privately-financed anti-Red scientific expedition sets off for Alaska to prevent a Chinese anti-American plot.
Early scoper which mixes deviously plotted schoolboy fiction with submarine spectacle and cold war heroics.
wd Samuel Fuller ph Joe MacDonald m Alfred Newman
☆ Richard Widmark, Bella Darvi, Victor Francen, David Wayne, Cameron Mitchell, Gene Evans

'Out of the warm arms of women ... into the cold grip of the sea!'
Hell Below
US 1933 105m bw
MGM
Tensions mount at a Mediterranean submarine base during World War I.
Adequate war actioner with appropriate trimmings of heroism, tragedy, comedy and romance.
w John Lee Mahin, John Meehan, Laird Doyle, Raymond Schrock novel Pigboats by Commander Edward Ellsberg d Jack Conway ph Harold Rosson
☆ Robert Montgomery, Walter Huston, Madge Evans, Jimmy Durante, Eugene Pallette, Robert Young, Edwin Styles, John Lee Mahin, Sterling Holloway
'Not a two dollar picture, but will be more than oke in the grinds.' – Variety

Hell below Zero

GB 1954 91m Technicolor
Columbia/Warwick (Irving Allen, Albert Broccoli)
An American adventurer accompanies the daughter of a whaling captain to the Antarctic to discover who killed her father.
Adequate outdoor thick ear with an unusual setting and lively cast.
w Alec Coppel, Max Trell novel The White South by Hammond Innes d Mark Robson ph John Wilcox m Clifton Parker
☆ Alan Ladd, Joan Tetzel, Basil Sydney, Stanley Baker, Jill Bennett, Niall MacGinnis

Hell Bent for Glory: see Lafayette Escadrille

Hell Bent for Leather

US 1960 82m Eastmancolor Cinemascope
Universal (Gordon Kay)
An innocent cowboy is accused of murder.
Energetic but unimaginative Western of a man on the run, relying heavily on star appeal.
w Christopher Knopf novel Ray Hogan d George Sherman ph Clifford Stine m William Lava, Irving Gertz ed Milton Carruth
☆ Audie Murphy, Felicia Farr, Stephen McNally, Robert Middleton, Rad Fulton, Jan Merlin, Herbert Rudley, Malcolm Atterbury, John Qualen, Bob Steele

Hell Boats

GB 1970 95m Technicolor
UA/Oakmont
An American commander with the British navy is assigned to blockade Malta.
Decently made small-scale war epic.
w Anthony Spinner, Donald and Derek Ford d Paul Wendkos ph Paul Beeson m Frank Cordell
☆ James Franciscus, Elizabeth Shepherd, Ronald Allen, Inigo Jackson

Hell Comes to Frogtown

US 1987 82m Technicolor
New World Entertainment (Donald G. Jackson, Randall Frakes)

In the future, one of the few potent men is sent on a mission to rescue women captured by mutants and impregnate them to provide cannon-fodder for another world war.
Adolescent, misogynistic comedy not helped by having a slob as its hero.
w Donald G. Jackson, Randall Frakes d R. J. Kizer, Donald G. Jackson ph Donald G. Jackson, Enrico Picard m David Shapiro ed James Metheny, R. J. Kizer
☆ Roddy Piper, Sandahl Bergman, William Smith, Rory Calhoun, Nicholas Worth, Kristi Somers, Cec Verrell

Hell Divers *

US 1931 113m bw
MGM
Friendly rivalry exists between two officers in the Naval Air Force.
Routine romantic melodrama with action highlights; a crowdpuller of its day.
w Harvey Gates, Malcolm Stuart Boylan story Frank 'Spig' Wead d George Hill ph Harold Wenstrom
☆ Wallace Beery, Clark Gable, Conrad Nagel, Dorothy Jordan, Marjorie Rambeau, Marie Prévost, Cliff Edwards
'Fine technical naval aviation display, and no story ... unusually long on footage and short on entertainment.' – Variety
'It's a matter of squadron after squadron of planes, the mechanics attached thereto, the cutting in and around newsreel material, which Metro does so well, and Beery's excellent personal performance.' – Hollywood Reporter

Hell Drivers *

GB 1957 108m bw Vistavision
Rank/Aqua (Ben Fisz)
Fast driving on death-trap roads is required of rival lorry drivers for a cheapjack haulage firm.
Absurd, violent, hilarious and constantly surprising melodrama with the silliest of premises backed by a good cast and well handled thrill sequences.
w John Kruse, C. Raker Endfield d C. Raker Endfield ph Geoffrey Unsworth m Hubert Clifford
☆ Stanley Baker, Patrick McGoohan, Herbert Lom, Peggy Cummins, William Hartnell, Wilfrid Lawson, Sidney James, Jill Ireland, Alfie Bass, Gordon Jackson
'This extraordinary film may interest future historians for its description of road haulage and masculine social behaviour in the mid-20th century ... though produced with efficiency and assurance it is disagreeable and occasionally vicious.' – MFB

Hell Harbor

US 1930 90m bw
United Artists
Derelicts congregate in a Caribbean harbour.
Low-life dramatics and scenery, but not much story interest.

w Clarke Silvernail story Rida Johnson Young d Henry King
☆ Lupe Velez, Jean Hersholt, Gibson Gowland, John Holland, Al St John
'Production of great beauty retarded by a story which fails to retain interest.' – Variety

Hell, Heaven and Hoboken: see I Was Monty's Double

Hell in Korea: see A Hill in Korea

Hell in the Heavens

US 1934 79m bw
Fox
In the 1918 air war, an American helps a French unit to get an ace German flyer.
Routine Dawn Patrol stuff which somehow fails to make an impact.
w Byron Morgan, Ted Parsons play The Ace by Herman Rossmann d John G. Blystone
☆ Warner Baxter, Conchita Montenegro, Herbert Mundin, Russell Hardie, Andy Devine, Ralph Morgan
'Interesting but probably too familiar at this date.' – Variety

Hell in the Pacific *

US 1969 104m Technicolor Panavision
Cinerama/Selmur (Reuben Bercovitch)

During World War II, an American pilot and a Japanese naval officer who are stranded on the same tiny Pacific island almost become friends.
Highly artificial and pretentious allegorical two-parter which is occasionally well acted and good to look at.
w Alexander Jacobs, Eric Bercovici d John Boorman ph Conrad Hall m Lalo Schifrin
☆ Lee Marvin, Toshiro Mifune
'No real reverberation and no real excitement, intellectual or physical.' – Tom Milne

Hell Is a City *

GB 1959 93m bw Hammerscope
ABP/Hammer (Michael Carreras)

A jewel thief breaks jail and is hunted by the Manchester police.
Lively semi-documentary, cameo-filled cop thriller filmed on location.
wd Val Guest novel Maurice Proctor ph Arthur Grant m Stanley Black
☆ Stanley Baker, John Crawford, Donald Pleasence, Maxine Audley, Billie Whitelaw, Joseph Tomelty, George A. Cooper, Vanda Godsell
'A hectic pace, with frequent scene changes, mobility of camera and performers, and much rapid, loud, intense dialogue.' – MFB

Hell Is for Heroes *

US 1962 90m bw
Paramount (Henry Blanke)

In 1944, embittered GIs fight and die while taking a German pillbox near the Siegfried line.
Fairly routine anti-war film with a strong cast and effectively-directed moments battling a generally artificial look.
w Robert Pirosh, Richard Carr d Don Siegel ph Harold Lipstein m Leonard Rosenman
☆ Steve McQueen, Bobby Darin, Fess Parker, James Coburn, Bob Newhart, Harry Guardino

Hell Is Sold Out

GB 1951 84m bw
Zelstro (Raymond Stross)
A novelist returns from the supposed dead to find that a glamorous woman is posing as his widow and issuing best-sellers under his name.
Downright peculiar comedy-drama which never jells for long enough to be enjoyable. ('Hell Is Sold Out' is the title of a book in the story.)
w Guy Morgan, Moie Charles d Michael Anderson ph Jack Anderson m Sonny Miller
☆ Herbert Lom, Mai Zetterling, Richard Attenborough

Hell Night

US 1981 101m Metrocolor
BLT (Irwin Yablans, Bruce Cohn Curtis)

As an initiation ceremony, four students spend a night in an old mansion where 12 years earlier a man murdered his demented wife and deformed

children and then committed suicide, witnessed by his mute son, who then disappeared.
Direly unimaginative teen horror, presumably made for the mentally challenged.
w Randolph Feldman d Tom de Simone ph Mac Ahlberg m Dan Wyman ad Steven C. Legler ed Tony Di Marco sp Court Wizard productions; make-up: Kenneth Horn, Tom Schwartz
☆ Linda Blair, Vincent Van Patten, Kevin Brophy, Jenny Neumann, Suki Goodwin, Jimmy Sturtevant, Peter Barton

Hell on Frisco Bay

US 1955 98m Warnercolor Cinemascope
Jaguar (George Berthelon)

An ex-cop sets out to find the man who framed him for manslaughter.
Tedious actioner enlivened by the character parts and a violent climax.
w Sydney Boehm, Martin Rackin novel William P. McGivern d Frank Tuttle ph John Seitz m Max Steiner
☆ Alan Ladd, Edward G. Robinson, Joanne Dru, Paul Stewart, William Demarest, Fay Wray

Hell to Eternity

US 1960 132m bw
Allied Artists/Atlantic (Irving H. Levin)
Marine Guy Gabaldon, brought up by Japanese foster parents, has divided loyalties after Pearl Harbor.
Battle-strewn biopic which after two hours seems to lose its point, if it ever had one, but is efficiently made.
w Ted Sherdeman, Walter Roeber Schmidt d Phil Karlson ph Burnett Guffey m Leith Stevens
☆ Jeffrey Hunter, David Janssen, Vic Damone, Patricia Owens, Richard Eyer, Sessue Hayakawa

Hell up in Harlem

US 1973 96m colour
AIP (Larry Cohen)

A gangster attempts to clean up Harlem by killing everyone.
Tediously violent exploitation movie, showing little of its director's usual quirky style.
wd Larry Cohen ph Fenton Hamilton m Fonce Mizell, Freddie Perren pd Larry Lurin ed Franco Guerri, Peter Holmes
☆ Fred Williamson, Julius W. Harris, Gloria Hendry, Margaret Avery, D'Urville Martin.
† A sequel to Black Caesar (qv).

'They all had something to sell – courage – sex – corruption!'
The Hell with Heroes
US 1968 102m Techniscope
Universal (Stanley Chase)
Air cargo experts find themselves unwittingly smuggling cigarettes into France, and American counter-intelligence steps in.
Unremarkable, totally predictable action melodrama.
w Halsted Welles, Harold Livingston d Joseph Sargent m Bud Thackery m Quincy Jones
☆ Rod Taylor, Claudia Cardinale, Harry Guardino, Kevin McCarthy, Pete Deuel, William Marshall

Hellbound

US/Canada/Israel 1993 95m colour
Cannon (Anthony Ridio, Dean Ferrandini)

In Chicago, two cops battle against the resurrected emissary of Satan, who has escaped from being entombed for eight hundred years to bring about the final confrontation between good and evil.
Unsuccessful attempt to broaden Chuck Norris's usual limited range, by mixing a conventional buddy movie with even more conventional moments of horror.
w Brent Friedman, Donald C. Thompson d Aaron Norris ph Joao Fernandes m George S. Clinton pd Kuly Sander ed Michael J. Duthie
☆ Chuck Norris, Calvin Levels, Sheree J. Wilson, Christopher Neame, David Robb, Cherie Franklin, Jack Adalist, Erez Atar

Hellbound: Hellraiser II

GB 1988 93m Technicolor
Premier Releasing/Film Futures/New World Pictures (Christopher Figg)

A crazed psychiatrist resurrects a dead woman and ventures into hell with her.
Confused and bloody sequel to Hellraiser (qv).

w Peter Atkins *story* Clive Barker *d* Tony Randel *ph* Robin Vidgeon *m* Christopher Young *pd* Mike Buchanan *ed* Richard Marden
☆ Clare Higgins, Ashley Laurence, Kenneth Cranham, Imogen Boorman, Sean Chapman, William Hope, Doug Bradley, Barbie Wilde, Simon Bamford, Nicholas Vince

Hellcamp: see *Opposing Force*

Hellcats of the Navy
US 1957 82m bw
Columbia (Charles H. Schneer)
Exploits of a daring submarine commander in the war against Japan.
Flimsy jingoistic potboiler.
w David Lang, Raymond Marcus *book* Charles A. Lockwood, Hans Christian Adamson *d* Nathan Juran *ph* Irving Lippman *md* Mischa Bakaleinikoff *ad* Rudi Feld *ed* Jerome Thoms
☆ Ronald Reagan, Nancy Davis, Arthur Franz, Robert Arthur

Helldorado
US 1934 75m bw
Fox (Jesse L. Lasky)
A penniless hitchhiker finds a ghost town with a gold mine.
Feeble fable unpersuasively presented.
w Frances Hyland, Rex Taylor *story* Frank M. Dazey *d* James Cruze
☆ Richard Arlen, Madge Evans, Henry B. Walthall, Ralph Bellamy, James Gleason, Helen Jerome Eddy
'Incredible story poorly cast and not at all likely at the b.o.' – *Variety*

Heller in Pink Tights *
US 1960 100m Technicolor Vistavision
Paramount (Carlo Ponti, Marcello Girosi)
Adventures of a dramatic company touring the west in the 1880s.
Genteel spoof Western which does not quite come off.
w Dudley Nichols, Walter Bernstein *novel Heller with a Gun* by Louis L'Amour *d* George Cukor *ph* Harold Lipstein *m* Daniele Amfitheatrof *ad* Hal Pereira, Eugene Allen
☆ Sophia Loren, Anthony Quinn, Steve Forrest, Eileen Heckart, Edmund Lowe, Margaret O'Brien, Ramon Novarro
'It has a welcome individuality which is never quite smothered by its lapses into convention.' – *Penelope Houston*

Heller Wahn: see *Friends and Husbands*

Hellfighters
US 1968 120m Technicolor Panavision
Universal (Robert Arthur)
Oil well fire-fighting specialists have problems among themselves and with their womenfolk.
Ham-fisted story line and performances are slightly, but only slightly, compensated by excellent special effects.
w Clair Huffaker *d* Andrew V. McLaglen *ph* William H. Clothier *m* Leonard Rosenman
☆ John Wayne, Jim Hutton, Katharine Ross, Vera Miles, Jay C. Flippen, Bruce Cabot, Barbara Stuart
'The overall effect is unpardonably tedious.' – *MFB*

The Hellfire Club *
GB 1960 93m Eastmancolor Dyaliscope
Regal/New World (Robert S. Baker, Monty Berman)
In the 18th century, a nobleman's child escapes from his degenerate father, joins a travelling circus, and later returns to claim his inheritance.
Sprightly historical romantic melodrama lightly based on the nefarious activities of the real Hellfire Club; energetic and entertaining if slightly too jokey.
w Leon Griffiths, Jimmy Sangster *m* Clifton Parker *d/ph* Robert S. Baker, Monty Berman
☆ Keith Michell, Peter Arne, Adrienne Corri, Kai Fischer, Bill Owen, Peter Cushing, David Lodge, Francis Matthews

The Hellhounds of Alaska *(dubbed)*
West Germany 1973 90m colour
A fur-trapper solves a mystery of a missing gold shipment and a lost child.
A snow- and cliché-bound Western, attempting the baroque style of the Italians and missing it entirely.
w Johannes Weiss *d* Harald Reinl *m* Heinz Hölscher *m* Bruno Nicolai *ad* Zeljko Senecic *ed* Eva Zeyn

☆ Doug McClure, Harald Leipnitz, Angelica Ott, Roberto Blanco, Kristina Nel, Klaus Löwitsch, Kurt Bülau, Heinz Reincke

The Hellions
GB 1961 80m Technirama
Columbia/Irving Allen, Jamie Uys (Harold Huth)
In the 1860s, a family of South African outlaws starts a reign of terror in a small village.
A British attempt to restage the OK Corral; it goes sadly awry.
w Harold Swanton, Patrick Kirwan, Harold Huth *d* Ken Annakin *ph* Ted Moore *m* Larry Adler
☆ Richard Todd, Lionel Jeffries, James Booth, Jamie Uys, Ronald Fraser, Anne Aubrey, Zena Walker, Marty Wilde, Colin Blakely
'Unconvincingly staged and plotted, tediously violent, uncertainly directed and very badly acted.' – *MFB*

Hello Again
US 1987 96m colour
Warner/Touchstone (Frank Perry)
A year after dying, a housewife is brought back by her sister, a medium, to discover that life has changed in her absence.
Moribund comedy that fails to get much mileage from its material.
w Susan Isaacs *d* Frank Perry *ph* Jan Weincke *m* William Goldstein *pd* Edward Pisoni *ed* Peter C. Frank, Trudy Ship
☆ Shelley Long, Judith Ivey, Thor Fields, Corbin Bernsen, Gabriel Byrne, Sela Ward, Austin Pendleton, Carrie Nye

Hello Beautiful: see *The Powers Girl*

Hello Dolly **
US 1969 129m DeLuxe Todd-AO
TCF/Chenault (Ernest Lehman)
In 1890 New York, a widowed matchmaker has designs on a wealthy grain merchant.
Generally agreeable but overblown musical based on a slight but much worked-over farce, fatally compromised by the miscasting of a too-young star. Some exhilarating moments.
w Ernest Lehman *play The Matchmaker* by Thornton Wilder *musical* Jerry Herman *d* Gene Kelly *ph* Harry Stradling *md* Lennie Hayton, Lionel Newman *ch* Michael Kidd *pd* John DeCuir *m/l* Michael Stewart *(book)*
☆ Barbra Streisand, Walter Matthau, *Michael Crawford*, Marianne McAndrew, E. J. Peaker, Tommy Tune, David Hurst
'The film leaves an oddly negative impression; a good deal of synthetic effervescence … but very little real vitality.' – *David Wilson*
† Carol Channing, Ginger Rogers and Betty Grable all fought to get the title role.
♫ music direction; art direction; sound (Jack Solomon, Murray Spivack)
⧫ best picture; photography

Hello Down There
US 1969 98m Eastmancolor
MGM (Ivan Tors)
The designer of an underwater house volunteers to live in it for a month.
Curious comedy with predictable obstacles to the happy ending.
w Frank Telford, John McGreevey *d* Jack Arnold *ph* Cliff Poland *m* Jeff Barry
☆ Tony Randall, Janet Leigh, Jim Backus, Roddy McDowall, Merv Griffin, Ken Berry, Richard Dreyfuss

'A lady bountiful with a ready song on her lips to hide the ache of emptiness in her own heart!'
Hello Everybody
US 1932 69m bw
Paramount
An overweight girl becomes a national radio celebrity.
Slim vehicle in which its star sings nine times.
w Dorothy Yost, Lawrence Hazard *story* Fannie Hurst *d* William Seiter
☆ *Kate Smith*, Randolph Scott, Sally Blane, Jerry Tucker, George Barbier
'Should do okay outside big cities.' – *Variety*

Hello Frisco Hello *
US 1943 98m Technicolor
TCF (Milton Sperling)
On the Barbary Coast, a girl singer becomes a star.
Moderately pleasing period musical with plenty going on but nothing very striking.
w Robert Ellis, Helen Logan, Richard Macaulay *d* Bruce Humberstone *ph* Charles Clarke, Allen Davey *m/ly* various *ad* James Basevi, Boris Leven
☆ Alice Faye, John Payne, Jack Oakie, Lynn Bari, Laird Cregar, June Havoc, Ward Bond, Aubrey Mather, George Barbier, Frank Orth
♫ song 'You'll Never Know' (*m*Harry Warren, *ly*Mack Gordon)
⧫ Charles Clarke, Allen Davey

Hello Goodbye
US 1970 101m DeLuxe
TCF (André Hakim)
A cheerful young Englishman falls for a mysterious Frenchwoman who turns out to be the wife of a Baron.
Modest, aimless, forgettable romantic comedy, full of old-fashioned clichés imperfectly remembered.
w Roger Marshall *d* Jean Negulesco *ph* Henri Decaë *m* Francis Lai *pd* John Howell *ad* Auguste Capelier
☆ Michael Crawford, Geneviève Gilles, Curt Jurgens, Ira Furstenberg

Hello Hemingway **
Cuba 1990 88m colour
Metro/ICAIC (Ricardo Guila)
In the 1950s a teenage girl from a poor Havana family enters an examination to win a scholarship to an American university.
Modest and enjoyable movie that marries Hemingway's The Old Man and the Sea to a narrative of adolescent striving.
w Maydo Royero *d* Fernando Perez *ph* Julio Valdes *m* Edesio Alejandro *ad* Onelio Larraldi *ed* Jorge Abello
☆ Laura de la Uz, Raul Paz, Herminia Sanchez, Caridad Hernandez, Enrique Molina, Maria Isabel Diaz, Marta Del Rio, Micheline Calvert
'A thoughtful, lovely little film.' – *Variety*

Hello Sister *
US 1933 62m bw
Fox (Winfield Sheehan)
aka: *Walking Down Broadway*
Boy meets girl in New York.
A mild little romance, only notable because it was edited down from an original by Erich von Stroheim, and touches of his work remain.
w Erich von Stroheim, Leonard Spigelgass *novel* Dawn Powell *d* Erich von Stroheim, Alfred Werker *m* James Wong Howe
☆ James Dunn, Boots Mallory, ZaSu Pitts, Minna Gombell

Hellraiser
GB 1987 93m Technicolor
Cannon/Film Futures/New World Entertainment (Christopher Figg)
A woman tries to bring back her lover from the tortures of hell.
Gloatingly sadistic and unnecessarily gory horror movie.
wd Clive Barker *novel The Hellbound Heart* by Clive Barker *ph* Robin Vidgeon *m* Christopher Young *ad* Jocelyn James *ed* Richard Marden
☆ Andrew Robinson, Clare Higgins, Ashley Laurence, Sean Chapman, Oliver Smith, Robert Hines, Antony Allen, Leon Davis, Michael Cassidy
† It was followed by a sequel, *Hellbound: Hellraiser II* (qv).

Hellraiser: Bloodline
US 1995 85m CFI color
Dimension/Trans Atlantic/Clive Barker (Nancy Rae Stone)
In the past, present and future, members of the same family exhibit the power to summon demons from hell.
A feeble horror movie that attempts to compensate for its many failings with an excess of gore; it is yet another example of a series that has lost its way, bereft of ideas and imagination.
w Peter Atkins *d* Alan Smithee (Kevin Yeager) *ph* Gary Lively *m* Daniel Licht *pd* Ivo Cristante

ed Ron Dean, Randolph K. Bricker *sp* Kevin Yeager; make-up: John Buechler
☆ Bruce Ramsay, Valentina Vargas, Doug Bradley, Kim Myers, Christine Harnos, Charlotte Chatton, Paul Perri, Mickey Cottrell
'Except for the most undiscriminating gorehound, pic is a pointless mess.' – *Variety*

'What Began In Hell Will End On Earth.'
Hellraiser III: Hell on Earth
US 1992 93m colour
Arrow/Nostradamus (Lawrence Mortorff)
A television journalist battles with Pinhead, a creature from hell.
Gore-filled horror, in which the main intention seems to be to create in Pinhead a demonic figure capable of sustaining a long-running series of such movies.
w Peter Atkins *story* Peter Atkins, Tony Randel *d* Anthony Hickox *ph* Gerry Lively *m* Randy Miller, Christopher Young *pd* Steve Hardie *ed* Christopher Cibelli, James D. R. Hickox *sp* Bob Keen; Cinema Research Corporation
☆ Terry Farrell, Doug Bradley, Paula Marshall, Kevin Bernhardt, Ken Carpenter, Peter Boynton, Aimee Leigh, Lawrence Mortorff
'Film's extremely grotesque gore effects and negative tone will turn off mainstream viewers but hold a hypnotic appeal for hardcore horror aficionados.' – *Variety*
'It is competent and accomplishes the small feat of being better than its predecessor.' – *Sheila Johnston, Independent*

Hell's Angels ***
US 1930 135m bw (colour sequences)
Howard Hughes
Two Americans become flyers in World War I.
Celebrated early talkie spectacular, with zeppelin and flying sequences that still thrill. The dialogue is another matter, but all told this expensive production, first planned as a silent, is a milestone of cinema history.
w Howard Estabrook, Harry Behn *d* Howard Hughes *ph* Tony Gaudio, Harry Perry, E. Burton Steene *m* Hugo Reisenfeld
☆ Ben Lyon, James Hall, Jean Harlow, John Darrow, Lucien Prival
'That it will ever pay off for its producer is doubtful … he's in so deep it can't really matter to him now. Minus blue nose interference, it can't miss, but it's up to the brim with sex.' – *Variety*
'It is not great, but it is as lavish as an eight-ring circus, and when you leave the theatre you will know you have seen a movie and not a tinny reproduction of a stage show.' – *Pare Lorentz*
† The film was reissued in 1940 in a 96m version which has not survived.
⧫ Tony Gaudio, Harry Perry, E. Burton Steene

Hells Angels on Wheels
US 1967 95m Eastmancolor
Fanfare (Joe Solomon)
A sacked petrol station attendant joins the Hells Angels for a violent ride across country.
Cheap biker movie, lacking plot and maintaining momentum with fights and parties; it employs actual Hells Angels but still achieves an ersatz feeling, perhaps because they cannot act, and Nicholson looks too old for his role as an inexperienced new recruit to the gang.
w R. Wright Campbell *d* Richard Rush *ph* Leslie Kovacs (Laszlo Kovacs) *m* Stu Phillips *ed* William Martin
☆ Adam Roarke, Jack Nicholson, Sabrina Scharf, Jana Taylor, Richard Anders, John Garwood, I. J. Jefferson, Jack Starrett, Sonny Barger
† The British video release was cut to 80m.

Hell's Five Hours
US 1958 75m bw
Allied Artists
A psychopath takes hostages and threatens to blow up a rocket fuel plant.
Standard suspense programmer; tolerable but entirely forgettable.
wd Jack L. Copeland
☆ Stephen McNally, Vic Morrow, Coleen Gray

Hell's Half Acre
US 1953 91m bw
Republic
A soldier missing after Pearl Harbor turns up years later in Hawaii under a different identity.

Complex melodrama ending in self-sacrifice; amusing bits don't make it hang together.

w Steve Fisher d John H. Auer

☆ Wendell Corey, Evelyn Keyes, Elsa Lanchester, Nancy Gates, Philip Ahn, Keye Luke

Hell's Heroes

US 1930 65m bw
Universal

Three cowboys find an abandoned baby.
Yet another version of Three Godfathers; *maybe not the best but the shortest.*

w Tom Reed *novel* Peter Kyne d William Wyler ph George Robinson

☆ Charles Bickford, Raymond Hatton, Fred Kohler, Fritzi Ridgeway

† Photographed in the Mojave and Panamint Deserts.

Hell's Highway *

US 1932 62m bw
RKO

A convict plans escape from a forced labour gang, under the threat of the lash and the sweatbox.
Well-made but heavy-going melodrama without light relief.

w Samuel Ornitz, Robert Tasker, Rowland Brown d Rowland Brown

☆ Richard Dix, Rochelle Hudson, Tom Brown, C. Henry Gordon, Louise Carter

'The story is too sodden to carry a general appeal.' – *Variety*

Hell's House

US 1932 72m bw
Capital Films

A boy is wrongly sentenced to a corrupt reform school.
Primitive cheapie notable only for the early appearance of Bette Davis.

w Paul Gangelin, B. Harrison Orkow d Howard Higgin ph Alan Siegler

☆ Bette Davis, Pat O'Brien, Junior Durkin, Junior Coghlan, Emma Dunn, Charley Grapewin

Hell's Island *

US 1955 84m Technicolor Vistavision
Paramount/Pine-Thomas

Crooks congregate on a Caribbean island in search of a famous ruby.
Cheeky rehash of The Maltese Falcon, *not bad in its own routine way.*

w Maxwell Shane d Phil Karlson ph Lionel Lindon md Irvin Talbot

☆ John Payne, Mary Murphy, Francis L. Sullivan, Arnold Moss

Hell's Kitchen

US 1939 82m bw
Warner (Mark Hellinger, Bryan Foy)

Boys revolt under the cruel headmaster of a reformatory.
Dreary vehicle for the Dead End Kids.

w Crane Wilbur, Fred Niblo Jnr d Lewis Seiler, E. A. Dupont ph Charles Rosher ad Hugh Reticker ed Clarence Kolster

☆ Billy Halop, Leo Gorcey, Bobby Jordan, Huntz Hall, Gabriel Dell, Bernard Punsley, Ronald Reagan, Margaret Lindsay, Stanley Fields, Grant Mitchell

'A quagmire of misplaced sentimentality hokum and general incredulousness.' – *Variety*

The Hellstrom Chronicle

👪 US 1971 90m CFI color
David Wolper

A scientist explains the range and variety of insect life.
Odd documentary in fictional bookends; smart and quite sensational for those with strong stomachs.

w David Seltzer d Walon Green

☆ Lawrence Pressman

🏆 best documentary

Hellzapoppin ***

👪 US 1942 84m bw
Universal/Mayfair (Glenn Tryon, Alex Gottlieb)

Two incompetent comics make a picture.
Zany modification of a smash burlesque revue; the crazy jokes are toned down and a romantic interest is added (and tentatively sent up). The result is patchy but often hilarious, and the whole is a handy consensus of forties humour and pop music.

w Nat Perrin, Warren Wilson d H. C. Potter ph Woody Bredell m Frank Skinner md Charles Previn

☆ Ole Olsen, Chic Johnson, Hugh Herbert, Martha Raye, Mischa Auer, Robert Paige, Jane Frazee, Shemp Howard, Elisha Cook Jnr, Richard Lane

'Alive with good gags, mechanical surprise effects, and novelty touches.' – *CEA Report*

† The Frankenstein monster and Man Who Falls into Pool were played by Dale Van Sickel.

Help! *

👪 GB 1965 92m Eastmancolor
UA/Walter Shenson/Suba Films

An oriental high priest chases the Beatles around the world because one of them has a sacred ring.
Exhausting attempt to outdo A Hard Day's Night *in lunatic frenzy, which goes to prove that some talents work better on low budgets. The humour is a frantic cross between* Hellzapoppin, *the* Goons, Bugs Bunny *and the shade of Monty Python to come. It looks good but becomes too tiresome to entertain.*

w Charles Wood, Marc Behm d Richard Lester ph David Watkin m Ken Thorne, The Beatles ad Ray Simm ed John Victor Smith

☆ John Lennon, Paul McCartney, George Harrison, Ringo Starr, Leo McKern, Eleanor Bron, Victor Spinetti, Roy Kinnear, John Bluthal, Patrick Cargill

Helpmates ***

👪 US 1932 20m bw
Hal Roach

Stan helps Ollie clean up after a wild party while the wife was away.
A brilliant succession of catastrophe gags in the stars' best tradition.

w H. M. Walker d James Parrott ph Art Lloyd ed Richard Currier

☆ Stan Laurel, Oliver Hardy, Blanche Payson, Robert Callahan

Helter Skelter

GB 1949 75m bw
GFD/Gainsborough (Anthony Darnborough)

An heiress with hiccups is helped by the staff of the BBC.
Scatty comedy which tries everything, from custard pies and guest stars to a clip from a silent Walter Forde *comedy. It isn't the British* Hellzapoppin *it sets out to be, but hardened buffs will find it worth a look.*

w Patrick Campbell d Ralph Thomas ph Jack Asher m Francis Chagrin

☆ Carol Marsh, David Tomlinson, Mervyn Johns, Peter Hammond, Jimmy Edwards, Richard Hearne, Jon Pertwee, Terry-Thomas

Helter Skelter

US 1976 92m Movielab
Hemdale/Lorimar (Tom Gries)

Charles Manson and his followers are charged with the murders of actress Sharon Tate and others.
Dull re-telling of a horrific series of killings from the viewpoint of the prosecutor.

w J. P. Miller *book* The Manson Murders *by* Vincent Bugliosi with Curt Gentry d Tom Gries ph Jules Brenner m Billy Goldenberg ad Phil Barber ed Bud S. Isaacs, Byron 'Buzz' Brandt

☆ George DiCenzo, Steve Railsback, Nancy Wolf, Marilyn Burns, Christina Hart, Cathey Paine

† The film was an edited version of an 194m TV mini-series.

Hemingway's Adventures of a Young Man *

US 1962 145m DeLuxe Cinemascope
TCF (Jerry Wald)

aka: *Adventures of a Young Man*

The son of a weak doctor and a religious mother breaks away from his family circle on a voyage of discovery.
Curious mélange of ill-assimilated Hemingway stories based on his Nick Adams character. The film has good intentions but no shape or style, and the guest stars don't help.

w A. E. Hotchner *stories* Ernest Hemingway d Martin Ritt ph Lee Garmes m Franz Waxman

☆ Richard Beymer, Diane Baker, Corinne Calvet, Fred Clark, Dan Dailey, James Dunn, Juano Hernandez, Arthur Kennedy, Ricardo Montalban, Susan Strasberg, Paul Newman, Jessica Tandy, Eli Wallach

'They had killed a woman and destroyed his life. Now he will kill a woman and destroy their nation!'

Hennessy

GB 1975 104m colour
AIP/Marseilles (Peter Snell)

Angered at the death of his family in the Belfast troubles, an Irish revolutionary hurries to London to blow up the Houses of Parliament.
Unattractive, uninventive thriller with a silly script and not an ounce of real suspense.

w John Gay *story* Richard Johnson d Don Sharp ph Ernest Steward m John Scott pd Ray Simm

☆ Rod Steiger, Richard Johnson, Lee Remick, Trevor Howard, Eric Porter, Peter Egan, David Collings

Henry Aldrich

Henry was originally a radio character created by Ezra Stone, an awkward small-town youth who like Andy Hardy was always getting into scrapes. Clifford Goldsmith wrote the original play which hit Broadway as well as the radio waves before starting a Hollywood series of amiable Paramount second features, most of them starring Jimmy Lydon with Charles Smith as his friend Dizzy.
1939 What a Life (with Jackie Cooper)
1941 Life with Henry (with Jackie Cooper), Henry Aldrich for President
1942 Henry and Dizzy, Henry Aldrich Editor
1943 Henry Aldrich Gets Glamour, Henry Aldrich Swings It, Henry Aldrich Haunts a House
1944 Henry Aldrich Boy Scout, Henry Aldrich Plays Cupid, Henry Aldrich's Little Secret

Henry and June *

US 1990 136m colour
UIP/Universal/Walrus & Associates (Peter Kaufman)

Anais Nin, married to a banker, has affairs with the writer Henry Miller and his wife.
Complex film of shifting relationships and their transmutation into literature, graphically portrayed.

w Philip Kaufman, Rose Kaufman *book* Anais Nin d Philip Kaufman ph Philippe Rousselot m Mark Adler pd Guy-Claude François ed Vivien Hillgrove, William S. Scharf, Dede Allen

☆ Fred Ward, Uma Thurman, Maria de Medeiros, Richard E. Grant, Kevin Spacey, Jean-Philippe Ecoffey, Bruce Myers, Jean-Louis Buñuel, Feodor Atkine

'It's like a well-wrapped and luxurious parcel that contains just what you don't want for Christmas.' – *Derek Malcolm, Guardian*

🏆 Philippe Rousselot

Henry Fool *

US 1997 141m DuArt
True Fiction/Shooting Gallery (Hal Hartley)

A stranger arrives in a small town and changes the life of a garbage collector and his sister.
Eccentric comedy of liberation that ends up nowhere in particular but provides pleasures along the way.

wd Hal Hartley ph Mike Spiller m Hal Hartley pd Steve Rosenzweig ed Steve Hamilton

☆ Thomas Jay Ryan, James Urbaniak, Parker Posey, Maria Porter, James Saito, Kevin Corrigan, Liam Aiken, Miho Nikaido, Gene Riffini, Nicholas Hope, Diana Ruppe

'Poetic, bawdy, contemplative, often side-wrenchingly funny and finally quite touching.' – *Derek Elley, Variety*

Henry Nine Till Five *

GB 1970 6m colour
British Lion

A commuter spends his working days fantasizing about sex.
Typical and very lively cartoon.

w Stan Heyward d Bob Godfrey

Henry: Portrait of a Serial Killer **

US 1990 83m colour
Electric/Maljack (John McNaughton, Lisa Dedmond, Steven A. Jones)

Documentary-style account of the life and methods of a motiveless mass murderer.
Oddly compelling, it is often hard to watch because of its violence and, perversely, hard not to watch.

w Richard Fire, John McNaughton d John McNaughton ph Charlie Lieberman m John McNaughton, Ken Hale, Steven A. Jones pd Rick Paul ed Elena Maganini

☆ Michael Rooker, Tom Towles, Tracy Arnold

'A film of clutching terror that's meant to heighten our awareness instead of dulling it ... This film gives off a dark chill that follows you all the way home.' – *Peter Travers, Rolling Stone*

Henry the Rainmaker

US 1948 64m bw
Monogram (Peter Scully)

A concerned citizen runs for mayor and calls in a rainmaker to solve a drought.
Pleasant homely comedy which ran to a brief series.

w Lane Beauchamp d Jean Yarbrough

☆ Raymond Walburn, Walter Catlett, William Tracy, Mary Stuart, Barbara Brown

Henry V ****

👪 GB 1944 137m Technicolor
Rank/Two Cities (Laurence Olivier)

Shakespeare's historical play is seen in performance at the Globe Theatre in 1603; as it develops, the scenery becomes more realistic.
Immensely stirring, experimental and almost wholly successful production of Shakespeare on film, sturdy both in its stylization and its command of more conventional cinematic resources for the battle.

w Laurence Olivier, Alan Dent *play* William Shakespeare d Laurence Olivier ph Robert Krasker m William Walton ad Paul Sheriff, Carmen Dillon ed Reginald Beck

☆ Laurence Olivier, Robert Newton, Leslie Banks, Esmond Knight, Renée Asherson, George Robey, Leo Genn, Ernest Thesiger, Ivy St Helier, Ralph Truman, Harcourt Williams, Max Adrian, Valentine Dyall, Felix Aylmer, John Laurie and also Roy Emerton, Michael Shepley, George Cole

'His production – it was his first time out as a director – is a triumph of colour, music, spectacle, and soaring heroic poetry, and, as actor, he brings lungs, exultation, and a bashful wit to the role.' – *Pauline Kael, 70s*

'What Shakespeare wrote in *Henry V*, and what the film has splendidly caught in its own fashion, is a fanfare; a flourish; a salute to high adventure; a kind of golden and perennially youthful exaltation of man's grim work.' – *C. A. Lejeune*

🏅 Special Award to Laurence Olivier

🏅 best picture; William Walton; Laurence Olivier (as actor); art direction

Henry V ***

GB 1989 137m Technicolor
Curzon/Renaissance Films (Bruce Sharman)

After his claim to the throne of France is refused, King Henry invades the country and wins a famous victory.
A darker film than Olivier's, with which it can stand comparison, stressing the brutality of war.

w Kenneth Branagh *play* William Shakespeare d Kenneth Branagh ph Kenneth MacMillan m Patrick Doyle pd Tim Harvey ed Mike Bradsell

☆ Kenneth Branagh, Derek Jacobi, Simon Shepherd, James Larkin, Brian Blessed, James Simmons, Paul Gregory, Charles Kay, Alec McCowen, Edward Jewesbury, Ian Holm, Michael Williams, Geoffrey Hutchings, Robert Stephens, Judi Dench and also Paul Scofield, Harold Innocent, Emma Thompson, Geraldine McEwan

'The film's visual tedium, vulgarity and musical mediocrity would be more bearable if Branagh himself were a more persuasive lead actor.' – *MFB*

'The more I thought about it, the more convinced I became that here was a play to be reclaimed from jingoism and its World War Two associations.' – *Kenneth Branagh*

🏅 best costume design (Phyllis Dalton)

🏅 Kenneth Branagh (as best actor and best director)

🏅 Kenneth Branagh (as director)

Henry VIII and His Six Wives *

GB 1972 125m Technicolor
EMI (Roy Baird)

Dullish historical account of the king's reign, staged as recollections from his deathbed but lacking any of the sparkle of *The Private Life of Henry VIII* made forty years previously.
Accurate sets and costumes fail to compensate for lack of film flair.

---

w Ian Thorne d Waris Hussein ph Peter Suschitzky m David Munro
☆ *Keith Michell*, Frances Cuka, Charlotte Rampling, Jane Asher, Jenny Bos, Lynne Frederick, Barbara Leigh-Hunt, Donald Pleasence
† The production was stimulated by a highly successful BBC TV series, *The Six Wives of Henry VIII*.

Her Adventurous Night
US 1946 75m bw
Universal (Marshall Grant)
An imaginative boy spreads a story which lands his headmaster in jail, but absolves himself by solving a murder mystery.
Agreeable minor comedy for the hinterlands.
w Jerry Warner d John Rawlins
☆ Dennis O'Keefe, Helen Walker, Tom Powers, Fuzzy Knight, Scotty Beckett

Her Alibi
US 1989 94m colour
Warner (Keith Barish)
▣ ◉. ◎.
A thriller writer provides a false alibi for a woman accused of murder.
A romantic comedy without laughs or much love.
w Charlie Peters d Bruce Beresford ph Freddie Francis m Georges Delerue pd Henry Bumstead ed Anne Goursaud
☆ Tom Selleck, Paulina Porizkova, William Daniels, James Farentino, Hurd Hatfield, Ronald Guttman, Victor Argo, Patrick Wayne, Tess Harper
  'Lacking a script able to go beyond the obvious, and direction able to make up for the lack of wit and sophistication.' – *MFB*

Her Cardboard Lover *
US 1942 93m bw
MGM (J. Walter Ruben)
A flirtatious lady hires a lover to make her fiancé jealous.
Paper-thin comedy previously filmed in 1932 with Buster Keaton. It did nobody any good, but preserves some style despite a witless script.
w Jacques Deval, John Collier, Anthony Veiller, William H. Wright play Jacques Deval d George Cukor ph Harry Stradling, Robert Planck m Franz Waxman
☆ Norma Shearer, Robert Taylor, George Sanders, Frank McHugh, Elizabeth Patterson, Chill Wills

Her Favourite Husband
GB 1950 79m bw
Orlux/Renown
US title: *The Taming of Dorothy*
A wife finds that her husband has been replaced by a gangster who aims to rob a bank.
Rather tiresome Italian-set comedy with funny moments.
w Noel Langley, W. F. Templeton play Pepine de Felipe d Mario Soldati ph Mario Bava m Nino Rota
☆ Jean Kent, Robert Beatty, Gordon Harker, Margaret Rutherford, Rona Anderson, Max Adrian

Her First Beau
US 1941 76m bw
Columbia (B. B. Kahane)
A teenage girl finds her childhood sweetheart is taking her for granted.
Mild family comedy, but the star did not easily take to semi-adult roles.
w Gladys Lehman, Karen DeWolf d Theodore Reed
☆ Jane Withers, Jackie Cooper, Edith Fellows, Josephine Hutchinson, William Tracy, Una O'Connor, Edgar Buchanan

Her First Romance
US 1951 73m bw
Columbia
GB title: *Girls Never Tell*
A schoolgirl pursues an older boy to a summer camp.
Flat little adolescent comedy which did no good for a star in her awkward age.
w Albert Mannheimer d Seymour Friedman
☆ Margaret O'Brien, Allen Martin Jnr, Jimmy Hunt, Sharyn Moffett

Her Highness and the Bellboy
US 1945 112m bw
MGM (Joe Pasternak)
A hotel bellboy forsakes his crippled sweetheart to woo a visiting princess.
Glutinous sentimental mishmash; one waits for musical numbers which never happen.
w Richard Connell, Gladys Lehman d Richard Thorpe ph Harry Stradling m Georgie Stoll
☆ Hedy Lamarr, Robert Walker, June Allyson, Rags Ragland, Agnes Moorehead, Carl Esmond, Warner Anderson, Ludwig Stossel

Her Husband Lies
US 1937 74m bw
Paramount
A New York gambler tries to ensure that his kid brother is not contaminated.
Adequate remake of Street of Chance.
w Wallace Smith, Eve Brown story O. H. P. Garrett d Edward Ludwig
☆ Ricardo Cortez, Gail Patrick, Akim Tamiroff, Tom Brown, Louis Calhern
  'Superb direction and expert acting.' – *Variety*

Her Husband's Affairs *
US 1947 83m bw
Columbia (Raphael Hakim)
▣
A husband and wife team of advertising agents promote a depilatory which turns out to grow hair instead.
Mildly amiable crazy comedy.
w Ben Hecht d S. Sylvan Simon ph Charles Lawton Jnr m George Duning
☆ Lucille Ball, Franchot Tone, Edward Everett Horton, Mikhail Rasumny, Gene Lockhart, Nana Bryant, Jonathan Hale, Mabel Paige

'See the mystical hypnotic rites of the white goddess of the jungle! See the plane crash in the tragic typhoon! See the ravening charge of the hundred sacred crocodiles!'

Her Jungle Love *
US 1938 81m Technicolor
Paramount (George M. Arthur)
An aviator crashlands in the jungle, where he is comforted by a lovely lady, a chimp and a lion but distressed by an earthquake, a volcano and assorted villains.
Second of Dorothy Lamour's jungle hokum shows, and the first in colour; despite its fair technical proficiency, the fact that it once packed 'em in is tribute to the changing tastes of mankind.
w Joseph M. March, Lillie Hayward, Eddie Welch d George Archainbaud ph Ray Rennahan m Gregory Stone
☆ Dorothy Lamour, Ray Milland, Lynne Overman, J. Carrol Naish, Dorothy Howe
  'Splendid colour job, but there's little more … only slightly varied from the type of a bygone era.' – *Variety*
† The Lynne Overman character wisecracks: 'Those *Esquire* cartoons must be right: there's always just one girl on a desert island.'
†† The lion cub in this case is called Meewa, the chimp Gaga.

Her Kind of Man
US 1946 78m bw
Warner
A singer finds a gangster irresistible but eventually settles for a newspaper columnist.
Shiny, nondescript forties copy of a thirties style; more yawns than thrills.
w Gordon Kahn, Leopold Atlas d Frederick de Cordova
☆ Dane Clark, Zachary Scott, Janis Paige, Faye Emerson, George Tobias, Sheldon Leonard

Her Majesty Love
US 1931 76m bw
Warner
A well-born Berliner finds it easier to court the barmaid he loves after she has married a baron.
Heavy-handed musical comedy worth excavating for the odd talents involved.
w Robert Lord, Arthur Caesar d William Dieterle
☆ Marilyn Miller, Ben Lyon, W. C. Fields, Leon Errol, Chester Conklin, Ford Sterling
  'An exceptionally dismal musical.' – *Clive Hirschhorn, 1983*

Her Man *
US 1930 85m bw
Pathé
The story of Frankie and Johnnie is transposed to a French apache setting.
Comedy melodrama which has its adherents.
w Tom Buckingham, Howard Higgin, Tay Garnett d Tay Garnett ph Edward Snyder
☆ Helen Twelvetrees, Ricardo Cortez, Marjorie Rambeau, James Gleason, Franklin Pangborn, Phillips Holmes, Thelma Todd
  'Looks like box office … full of action.' – *Variety*

Her Man Gilbey: see *English without Tears*

Her Master's Voice
US 1936 75m bw
Paramount (Walter Wanger)
Henpecked by his wife and her mother, a man makes a name for himself as a radio troubadour.
Mild comedy from a stage success.
w Dore Schary, Harry Sauber play Clare Kummer d Joseph Santley
☆ Edward Everett Horton, Peggy Conklin, Laura Hope Crews, Elizabeth Patterson, Grant Mitchell
  'Suitable because of frothy humour for family and nabe audiences solo.' – *Variety*

Her Panelled Door: see *The Woman with No Name*

Her Primitive Man
US 1944 87m bw
Universal
An author disguises himself as a savage in order to denounce a woman trying to prove his theories a fraud.
Very silly comedy partly salvaged by a few good lines.
w Michael Fessier, Ernest Pagano d Charles Lamont
☆ Robert Paige, Louise Allbritton, Robert Benchley, Edward Everett Horton, Helen Broderick, Ernest Truex, Walter Catlett, Nydia Westman

Her Sister's Secret
US 1946 86m bw
PRC (Henry Brash)
A pregnant girl hands over her child to her sister; but what will the sister's husband say?
Peg's Paper in modern dress, but an ambitious project for this Poverty Row company.
w Anne Green novel Dark Angel by Gina Kaus d Edgar G. Ulmer
☆ Nancy Coleman, Margaret Lindsay, Philip Reed, Felix Bressart, Regis Toomey, Henry Stephenson, Fritz Feld

Her Sweetheart: see *Christopher Bean*

Her Twelve Men
US 1954 91m Anscocolor
MGM (John Houseman)
A woman teacher in a boys' school reforms a difficult class.
Predictable, sugary and artificial school story with the star exuding sweetness and light.
w William Roberts, Laura Z. Hobson d Robert Z. Leonard ph Joseph Ruttenberg m Bronislau Kaper
☆ Greer Garson, Robert Ryan, Richard Haydn, Barry Sullivan

Her Wedding Night
US 1930 78m bw
Paramount
On the Italian riviera a man marries his friend's wife under the impression that they are only booking rooms for the night.
Spicy bedroom farce which crested the wave of its star's notoriety.
w Henry Myers play Avery Hopwood d Frank Tuttle
☆ Clara Bow, Charles Ruggles, Ralph Forbes, Skeets Gallagher
  'Deftly handled for smartness and taste … ought to make women talk.' – *Variety*

Herbie Goes Bananas
👫 US 1980 100m Technicolor
Walt Disney
▣ ▤
Two Americans take their magical Volkswagen on a South American holiday.

Listless addition to a series which has already gone on too long.
w Don Tait d Vincent McEveety
☆ Charles Martin Smith, Stephan W. Burns, Cloris Leachman, John Vernon

Herbie Goes to Monte Carlo
👫 US 1977 105m Technicolor
Walt Disney (Ron Miller)
▤
The Volkswagen with a mind of its own enters the Monte Carlo rally and routs a gang of thieves.
Utterly predictable, patchily made family comedy.
w Arthur Alsberg, Don Nelson d Vincent McEveety ph Leonard J. South m Frank de Vol
☆ Dean Jones, Don Knotts, Julie Sommars, Jacques Marin, Roy Kinnear, Bernard Fox
† Second sequel to *The Love Bug*.

Herbie Rides Again
👫 US 1974 88m Technicolor
Walt Disney (Bill Walsh)
▣ ▤ ◉.
A Volkswagen with a mind of its own helps an old lady to rout a property developer.
Acceptable sequel to The Love Bug.
w Bill Walsh d Robert Stevenson ph Frank Phillips m George Bruns
☆ Helen Hayes, Ken Berry, Stefanie Powers, John McIntire, Keenan Wynn, Huntz Hall

Hercules
👫 Italy 1959 105m Eastmancolor
Dyaliscope
Oscar/Galatea (Federico Teti)
▤ ◉.
original title: *Le Fatiche di Ercole*
Hercules helps Jason find the golden fleece.
The strong man epic which started a genre; of little interest in itself.
w Pietro Francisci, Ennio de Concini, Gaio Frattini d Pietro Francisci ph Mario Bava m Enzo Masetti
☆ Steve Reeves, Sylva Koscina, Gianna Maria Canale, Fabrizio Mione

'The man. The myth. The movie.'

Hercules *
👫 US 1997 92m Technicolor
Buena Vista/Walt Disney (Alice Dewey, John Musker, Ron Clements)
▣ ▤ ◉. ◎. 🎧
Hercules, son of Zeus, is kidnapped by the minions of Hades, ruler of the underworld, and brought up as a mortal; he can only become a god again if he proves himself a hero.
Those with a classical education, or a knowledge of Greek myths, will wince at the crassness of this cartoon feature, though it looks good and provides intermittent pleasures.
w Ron Clements, John Musker, Bob Shaw, Donald McEnery, Irene Mecchi d John Musker, Ron Clements m Alan Menken m/ly Alan Menken, David Zippel pd Gerald Scarfe ed Tom Finan, Jeff Jones, John K. Carr
☆ Featuring the voices of: Tate Donovan, Danny DeVito, James Woods, John Keaton, Roger Bart, Susan Egan, Bobcat Goldthwait, Matt Frewer, Rip Torn, Samantha Eggar, Barbara Barrie, Hal Holbrook, Charlton Heston (narrator)
  'A winning tale, cleverly told and wonderfully voiced.' – *Variety*
  'This is Disney's weakest score in a decade and, although the visual style of the picture has a rare distinction, that's not enough to damp down the feeling that the company's run of animated hits is coming to a close.' – *Mark Steyn, Spectator*
† The film grossed some $99m in the US and another $229m elsewhere.
🎵 song 'Go the Distance' (m/ly Alan Menken, David Zippel)

Hercules against Rome (dubbed)
France/Italy 1965 87m Eastmancolor
Totalscope
Romana/Regina (Fortunato Misiano)
original title: *Ercole contro Roma*
aka: *Hercules in Rome*
Hercules, a blacksmith, goes to the aid of the daughter of the Emperor, in the power of the commander of the Praetorian Guard.
Standard muscle-bound epic, with our hero fighting, not too convincingly, against state corruption.
w Piero Pierotti, Arpad de Riso story Arpad de Riso, Nino Scolaro d Piero Pierotti ph Augusto

Tiezzi m A. F. Lavagnino ad Salvatore Giancotti ed Iolanda Benvenuti d (US version) Robert Spafford

☆ Alan Steel, Wandisa Guida, Daniele Vargas, Livio Lorenzon, Andrea Aureli, Dina de Santis, Mimmo Palmara

Hercules Goes Bananas: see Hercules in New York

Hercules in New York

US 1969 91m Eastmancolor
RAF Industries (Aubrey Wisberg)

aka: Hercules Goes Bananas
aka: Hercules – the Movie

Hercules drops in on modern-day New York and becomes involved with wrestlers and gamblers.
Schwarzenegger's first film, a dim comedy – and one that no doubt returns to haunt him, particularly his dubbed all-American high tenor voice and the way his muscles do the acting.
w Aubrey Wisberg d Arthur A. Seidelman ph Leo Lebowitz m John Balamos ad Perry Watkins ed Donald Finamore
☆ Arnold Stang, Arnold Strong (later Schwarzenegger), Deborah Loomis, James Karen, Ernest Graves, Tanny McDonald, Taina Elg, Michael Lipton
'Schwarzenegger as Herc wrestled with a man in a bear suit and when I tell you that the suit was a better actor you will have some conception.' – Nancy Banks-Smith, Guardian

Hercules in Rome: see Hercules against Rome

Hercules Returns

Australia 1993 80m colour
Metro Tartan/Philm (Philip Jaroslow)

Film enthusiasts reopen a cinema with the last film it showed 30 years before, an Italian muscle-man epic, but, discovering the soundtrack is in Italian, they are forced to dub it in English as it is screened.
An opened-out movie version of an apparently popular live performance by Double Take (Des Mangan and Sally Patience), who improvise new dialogue to bad old films, a joke that requires more wit than is on display here.
w Des Mangan d David Parker ph David Connell m Philip Judd pd Jon Dowding ed Peter Carrodus
☆ David Argue, Mary Coustas, Michael Carman, Bruce Spence, Brendon Suhr and also the voices of Des Mangan, Sally Patience, Matthew King

Hercules – the Movie: see Hercules in New York

Hercules Unchained

🕇🕇 Italy/France 1960 105m Eastmancolor
Dyaliscope
Lux/Galatea (Bruno Vailati)

original title: Ercole e la Regina di Lidia

Hercules has problems with the king of Thebes and the queen of Lidia.
More comic-strip versions of old legends. This item had more spent on it in publicity than in production cost, and consequently was seen by vast audiences around the world. It isn't very good.
w Pietro Francisci, Ennio de Concini d Pietro Francisci ph Mario Bava m Enzo Masetti
☆ Steve Reeves, Sylva Koscina, Sylvia Lopez, Primo Carnera
† Many sequels followed, the hero sometimes being known as Ursus or Goliath.

Here Come the Coeds

US 1945 88m bw
Universal (John Grant)

Janitors help to forestall a mortgage foreclosure on a college for women.
Routine star vehicle with few highlights.
w Arthur T. Horman, John Grant d Jean Yarbrough ph George Robinson m/ly Jack Brooks, Edgar Fairchild
☆ Bud Abbott, Lou Costello, Lon Chaney Jnr, Peggy Ryan, Martha O'Driscoll, Donald Cook, June Vincent, Charles Dingle

Here Come the Girls *

US 1953 78m Technicolor
Paramount/Hope Enterprises (Paul Jones)

original title: Champagne for Everybody

In the 1890s an ageing chorus boy traps a mysterious murderer.
Spotty, ineptly titled star comedy with music; in fact among the last of his passable vehicles, with excellent production backing.
w Edmund Hartmann, Hal Kanter d Claude Binyon ph Lionel Lindon md Lyn Murray ad Hal Pereira, Roland Anderson
☆ Bob Hope, Rosemary Clooney, Tony Martin, Arlene Dahl, Millard Mitchell, Fred Clark, William Demarest, Robert Strauss

Here Come the Huggetts *

GB 1948 93m bw
Rank/Gainsborough (Betty Box)

A suburban family has its ups and downs.
Cosy domestic comedy drama, a presage of TV soap operas to come, or Britain's answer to the Hardys, depending how you look at it. Tolerable at the time.
w Mabel and Denis Constanduros, Muriel and Sydney Box, Peter Rogers d Ken Annakin ph Reg Wyer m Anthony Hopkins
☆ Jack Warner, Kathleen Harrison, Jane Hylton, Susan Shaw, Petula Clark, Jimmy Hanley, David Tomlinson, Diana Dors, Peter Hammond, John Blythe
† The Huggetts had actually originated in Holiday Camp the previous year, and appeared again in Vote for Huggett and The Huggetts Abroad; Warner and Harrison became an inseparable duo for many years.

Here Come the Nelsons

US 1951 76m bw
Universal

The sons of an advertising agent get involved with gangsters.
Empty-headed family comedy based on the long-running TV show The Adventures of Ozzie and Harriet.
w Ozzie Nelson, Donald Nelson, William Davenport d Frederick de Cordova ph Irving Glassberg
☆ Ozzie Nelson, Harriet Hilliard, David Nelson, Ricky Nelson, Rock Hudson, Barbara Lawrence, Ann Doran, Jim Backus

Here Come the Waves

US 1944 98m bw
Paramount (Mark Sandrich)

A sailor falls in love with identical twin Waves.
Empty-headed, professionally executed musical recruiting poster.
w Allan Scott, Ken Englund, Zion Myers d Mark Sandrich ph Charles Lang m/ly Harold Arlen, Johnny Mercer md Robert Emmett Dolan
☆ Bing Crosby, Betty Hutton, Sonny Tufts, Ann Doran, Gwen Crawford
'An almost totally negligible musical.' – James Agee
♫ song 'Accentuate the Positive'

Here Comes Cookie

US 1935 65m bw
Paramount (William Le Baron)

Gracie comes into money and opens a theatre-cum-hotel for vaudevillians.
Slight star comedy with its share of laughs.
w Sam Mintz, Don Hartman d Norman Z. McLeod
☆ George Burns, Gracie Allen, George Barbier, Betty Furness, Andrew Tombes
'Situation and gag pounding without an ounce of seriousness or sense.' – Variety

Here Comes Mr Jordan ***

US 1941 93m bw
Columbia (Everett Riskin)

A prizefighter who is also an amateur saxophonist crashes in his private plane and goes to heaven by mistake: he was supposed to survive and live another forty years. Unfortunately when he goes back for his body it has been cremated, so he has to find another one, recently deceased…
Weird heavenly fantasy which succeeded because of its novelty and because heaven in wartime was a comforting vision. As a movie taken on its own merits, it suffers from illogicalities, a miscast star and a wandering plot, but scene for scene there is enough

firmness and control to make it memorable. It certainly had many imitations, including Angel on My Shoulder, Down to Earth, A Guy Named Joe, Heaven Only Knows, The Horn Blows at Midnight and That's the Spirit.
w Seton I. Miller, Sidney Buchman play Halfway to Heaven by Harry Segall d Alexander Hall ph Joseph Walker m Frederick Hollander md Morris Stoloff
☆ Robert Montgomery, Evelyn Keyes, Rita Johnson, Claude Rains, James Gleason, Edward Everett Horton, John Emery, Donald MacBride, Halliwell Hobbes, Don Costello
'There is something about this original so sweet-spirited and earnest that it transcends its plot devices and shines through its comedic asides to become a true morality play without once becoming either preachy or mawkish.' – Kit Parker catalogue, 1980
'Audiences loved this chunk of whimsy … the slickly hammy Rains gives Mr Jordan a sinister gloss, as if he were involved in some heavenly racket, like smuggling Chinese.' – Pauline Kael, 70s
† Remade 1978 as Heaven Can Wait.
⚬ original story (Harry Segall); script
⚬ best picture; Alexander Hall; Joseph Walker; Robert Montgomery; James Gleason

Here Comes the Band

US 1935 82m bw
MGM

Buddies from an army band are stuck in the taxi business.
Shapeless comedy with interesting numbers. But not very.
w Paul Sloane, Ralph Spence, Victor Mansfield d Paul Sloane
☆ Ted Lewis and his Band, Ted Healy, Nat Pendleton, Virginia Bruce, Harry Stockwell, Donald Cook, Spanky McFarland
'Not punchy enough for the de luxe trade … best as second stringer.' – Variety

Here Comes the Groom *

US 1951 114m bw
Paramount (Frank Capra)

A journalist adopts war orphans and reforms his selfish fiancée.
Tired attempt by Capra to recapture his prewar mood; despite intermittent pleasures it has neither the right style nor the topical substance.
w Virginia Van Upp, Myles Connolly, Liam O'Brien story Robert Riskin d Frank Capra ph George Barnes m/ly Jay Livingston, Ray Evans md Joseph Lilley
☆ Bing Crosby, Jane Wyman, Franchot Tone, Alexis Smith, James Barton, Connie Gilchrist, Robert Keith, Anna Maria Alberghetti
'The general impression is of a loud, strident, rather vulgar comedy in which technique is used to disappointingly mechanical ends, and which a few bright lines of dialogue cannot rescue from tedium.' – Penelope Houston
⚬ song 'In the Cool Cool Cool of the Evening' (mHoagy Carmichael, lyJohnny Mercer)
⚬ Robert Riskin

Here Comes the Navy *

US 1934 86m bw
Warner (Lou Edelman)

An aggressive young naval rating fights with his former friend, now Petty Officer.
Breezy comedy melodrama teaming Cagney and O'Brien for the first time and offering star heroics as a sop to the Legion of Decency.
w Ben Markson, Earl Baldwin d Lloyd Bacon ph Arthur Edeson m Leo F. Forbstein
☆ James Cagney, Pat O'Brien, Dorothy Tree, Gloria Stuart, Frank McHugh, Robert Barrat
'It's a bit too masculine for matinée appeal and it'll have to be a case of the kids and men dragging the womenfolk along.' – Variety
'Rapid and reasonably authentic, a satisfactory addition to a series of cinema cartoons which, because their colour and mood are indigenous and timely, may be more interesting twenty years from now.' – Time
⚬ best picture

Here Comes the Sun

GB 1946 91m bw
Universal (John Baxter)

Racetrack touts help to breathe fresh life into a provincial newspaper.
Amiable comedy with a touch of do-goodery, very typical of this producer.
w Geoffrey Orme d John Baxter
☆ Bud Flanagan, Chesney Allen, Joss Ambler, Dick Francis, Horace Kenney

Here I Am a Stranger

US 1939 82m bw
TCF (Harry Joe Brown)

A rich woman tries to prevent her son being influenced by her once-drunken ex-husband.
Predictable family drama which was catnip to 1939 audiences.
w Sam Hellman and Milton Sperling story Gordon Malherbe Hillman d Roy del Ruth ph Arthur Miller md Louis Silvers
☆ Gladys George, Richard Dix, Richard Greene, Brenda Joyce, Roland Young, Russell Gleason, George Zucco
'Strong programme drama will catch many top key spots.' – Variety

Here Is a Man: see All That Money Can Buy

Here Is My Heart

US 1934 73m bw
Paramount

An American radio crooner on the riviera pretends to be a waiter in order to court a princess.
Musical remake of The Grand Duchess and the Waiter; not bad of its type.
w Edwin Justus Mayer, Harlan Thompson d Frank Tuttle m/ly Leo Robin, Ralph Rainger
☆ Bing Crosby, Kitty Carlisle, Roland Young, Alison Skipworth, Reginald Owen, Akim Tamiroff
'First-class entertainment … though it seems they adapted it by running it through the electric fan.' – Variety
♫ 'Love Is Just Around the Corner'; 'With Every Breath I Take'; 'June in January'; 'Here Is My Heart'; 'You Can't Make a Monkey of the Moon'.

Here We Go Again

US 1942 75m bw
RKO (Allan Dwan)

Various radio celebrities congregate at Silvertip Lodge.
Random excuse for a variety show, with top talent of its day; a sequel to Look Who's Laughing.
w Paul Gerard Smith, Joe Bigelow d Allan Dwan ph Frank Redman m Roy Webb m/ly Mort Greene, Harry Revel
☆ Jim Jordan, Marion Jordan (Fibber McGee and Molly), Edgar Bergen, Charlie McCarthy, Harold Peary (The Great Gildersleeve), Ginny Simms, Gale Gordon, Ray Noble and his orchestra

Here We Go Round the Mulberry Bush *

GB 1967 96m Technicolor
UA/Giant (Larry Kramer, Clive Donner)

A school-leaver is obsessed with sex and determines to lose his virginity.
Repetitive comedy which certainly opened new avenues in British humour and seemed pretty permissive at the time (pre-Graduate). In itself, however, more modish than sympathetic.
w Hunter Davies, Larry Kramer novel Hunter Davies d Clive Donner ph Alex Thomson m various groups
☆ Barry Evans, Judy Geeson, Angela Scoular, Adrienne Posta, Sheila White, Vanessa Howard, Denholm Elliott, Maxine Audley, Moyra Fraser, Michael Bates
'The only incongruity is that it should have been made by adults, so completely does it enter into the teenager's view of himself.' – MFB

Here's To Romance

US 1935 82m bw
TCF (Jesse L. Lasky)

A young tenor who finds a patron in Paris is pursued by the wealthy wife.
Amiable piece of musical froth which somehow failed to make a big singing star of Martini.
w Ernest Pascal, Arthur Richman d Alfred E. Green
☆ Nino Martini, Genevieve Tobin, Reginald Denny, Anita Louise, Mme Schumann-Heink, Maria Gambarelli

'Given a sturdier story he might have emerged as a Grace Moore for talkers.' – Variety

Hero *

US 1992 116m Technicolor
Columbia TriStar (Laura Ziskin)

🎬 📺 ⊚ 🎧

GB title: Accidental Hero
A drifter claims to be the saviour of a plane crash while the real hero, a petty crook, goes unrecognized.
An interesting central situation is inadequately developed and finally frittered away.
w David Webb Peoples story Laura Ziskin, Alvin Sargent d Stephen Frears ph Oliver Stapleton m George Fenton pd Dennis Gassner ed Mick Audsley
☆ Dustin Hoffman, Geena Davis, Andy Garcia, Joan Cusack, Kevin J. O'Connor, Maury Chaykin, Stephen Tobolowsky
'Peppered with occasional gems but one has to sift through a lot of wreckage to find them.' – Variety

The Hero: see Bloomfield

A Hero Ain't Nothing but a Sandwich

US 1977 107m CFI color
New World/Radnitz-Mattel (Robert B. Radnitz)

📺 ⊚

Problems for an urban family in the black ghetto.
Well-intentioned but ultimately wearisome and cliché-strewn melodrama.
w Alice Childress novel Alice Childress d Ralph Nelson ph Frank Stanley m Tom McIntosh
☆ Cicely Tyson, Paul Winfield, Larry B. Scott, Helen Martin, Glynn Turman
'The sort of dreaded wholesome film that cultural and societal groups heavily endorse but nobody pays money to go see.' – Variety

Hero at Large

US 1980 98m Metrocolor
UA/MGM (Stephen Friedman)

🎬

An unemployed actor's bravery while impersonating a comic-book hero is exploited for political gain.
Amiable small-town satire, watchable but forgettable too.
w A. J. Carothers d Martin Davidson ph David M. Walsh m Patrick Williams pd Albert Brenner ed Sidney Levin, David Garfield
☆ John Ritter, Anne Archer, Bert Convy, Kevin McCarthy, Harry Bellaver, Anita Dangler, Jane Hallaren, Kevin Bacon

The Hero of Babylon

Italy/France 1964 90m Eastmancolor
Euroscope
FIA/Gladiator Film (Albino Morandini)
original title: L'Eroe di Babylone
aka: Goliath, King of Slaves
Prince Nipur returns home to find that his cousin has usurped the throne of Babylon and is ruling as a tyrant.
Typical product of the Italian cycle of movies with an Old Testament setting, given over to sword fights.
w Gianpaolo Callegari, Siro Marcellini, Albert Valentin d Siro Marcellini ph Pierludovico Pavoni m Carlo Franzi pd Vittorio Marchi ed Nella Nannuzzi
☆ Gordon Scott, Moira Orfei, Geneviève Grad, Piero Lulli, Andrea Scotti, Mario Petri

Heroes

US 1977 113m Technicolor
Universal (David Foster, Lawrence Turman)

📺

A Vietnam veteran, made slightly kooky by his experiences, settles down after several adventures when he falls in love.
Just plain awful: a would-be star vehicle that doesn't work.
w James Carabatsos (David Freeman, uncredited) d Jeremy Paul Kagan ph Frank Stanley m Jack Nitzsche, Richard Hazard
☆ Henry Winkler, Sally Field, Harrison Ford, Val Avery

The Heroes

Italy/France/Spain 1972 110m Telecolor
Scope
Paladin/Gerico Sound/Finarco/Corona/Transinter/Atlantida (Alfredo Bini)
original title: Gli Eroi
In North Africa during the Second World War a former prostitute makes off with £2 million, pursued by German soldiers, a British officer and assorted allies.
Dull caper movie of predictable unoriginality.
w Luciano Vincenzoni, Sergio Donati novel Albert Kantof, René Harvard d Duccio Tessari ph Carlo Carlini m Riz Ortolani ad Walter Patriarca, Andrea Crisanti ed Mario Morra
☆ Rod Steiger, Rosanna Schiaffino, Rod Taylor, Claude Brasseur, Terry-Thomas
'Treads a well-worn path with a handful of stock characters.' – Tom Milne, MFB
† The film was cut to 99m for its British release.

The Heroes Are Tired

France 1955 101m bw
Cila-Terra
original title: Les Héros Sont Fatigués
Two ex-wartime pilots, one Free French and the other German, set up an air charter service in Liberia but come to grief over stolen diamonds.
Gloomy post-war film noir set in a peculiarly depressing atmosphere, and not really sharp enough to overcome its squalid plot.
w Yves Ciampi, Jacques-Laurent Bost novel Christine Garnier d Yves Ciampi ph Henri Alekan m Louiguy
☆ Yves Montand, Maria Félix, Jean Servais, Curt Jurgens, Gérard Oury

Heroes Die Hard: see Mister Kingstreet's War

Heroes for Sale

US 1933 73m bw
Warner

📺

A war veteran becomes in turn a drug addict, a millionaire and the central figure in a labour dispute.
Minor social-conscience melodrama with watchable elements.
w Robert Lord, Wilson Mizner d William A. Wellman
☆ Richard Barthelmess, Aline MacMahon, Loretta Young, Berton Churchill, Robert Barrat
'This attempted satire on unemployment conditions just prior to the Roosevelt election is not well told … b.o. doubtful.' – Variety

The Heroes of Telemark *

GB 1965 131m Technicolor Panavision
Rank/Benton (Ben Fisz)

🎬

Norwegian resistance workers in World War II help the Allies to smash a heavy water plant.
Ambling narrative with big action sequences which often seem irrelevant, so that the story as a whole fails to excite.
w Ivan Moffat, Ben Barzman d Anthony Mann ph Robert Krasker m Malcolm Arnold
☆ Kirk Douglas, Richard Harris, Ulla Jacobsson, Roy Dotrice, Anton Diffring, Michael Redgrave

Heroic Trio

Hong Kong 1992 88m colour
China Entertainment/Paka Hill (Ching-Siu Tung)

🎬

original title: Dongfang San Xia
Three superheroines – Wonder Woman, Thief Catcher and Invisible Woman – search for 18 babies that have been kidnapped as future Emperors of China.
Comic-book heroics with plenty of flashy action and some grisly scenes, including cannibalism and child murder.
w Sandy Shaw (Shao Liqiong) d Johnny To (Du Qifeng) ph Poon Hang-Sang, Tom Lau m William Hu (Hu Weili) ad Bruce Yu, Raymond Chan
☆ Maggie Cheung, Anita Mui, Michelle Yeoh, Damian Lau, Anthony Wong, Paul Chin
'A bravura mix of outrageous acrobatics, over-the-top stunts and superb special effects.' – Film Review

The Heroin Gang: see Sol Madrid

Heroism: see Eroica

Hero's Island *

US 1962 94m Technicolor Panavision
UA/Daystar/Portland (James Mason, Leslie Stevens)
In 1718 bondslaves settle on a Carolina island, are attacked by fishermen and protected by one of the aides of Blackbeard the Pirate.
An oddly personal, patchy, rather mysterious film with a rhetorical script and rather good action sequences.
wd Leslie Stevens ph Ted McCord m Dominic Frontière
☆ James Mason, Kate Manx, Neville Brand, Rip Torn

Les Héros Sont Fatigués: see The Heroes Are Tired

Un Héros Trés Discret: see A Self-Made Hero

Herr Puntila and His Servant Matti *

Austria 1955 95m Agfacolor
Bauerfilm
A rich landowner, usually drunk, is rescued from scrapes by his patient valet.
A cogent comedy which its author is said to have approved in this version.
w Alberto Cavalcanti, Vladimir Pozner, Ruth Wieden play Bertolt Brecht d Alberto Cavalcanti ph André Bac, Arthur Hämmerer m Hanns Eisler
☆ Curt Bois, Hans Engelmann, Maria Emo, Edith Prager

Hers to Hold

US 1943 94m bw
Universal (Felix Jackson)
A girl decides whether or not to marry a serviceman.
Limp star vehicle, a sequel to Three Smart Girls (qv).
w Lewis R. Foster d Frank Ryan ph Elwood Bredell m Frank Skinner md Charles Previn
☆ Deanna Durbin, Joseph Cotten, Charles Winninger, Nella Walker, Gus Schilling, Ludwig Stossel
♫ song 'Say a Prayer for the Boys Over There' (mJimmy McHugh, lyHerb Magidson)

Herz aus Glas: see Heart of Glass

He's a Cockeyed Wonder

US 1950 77m bw
Columbia (Rudolph C. Flotow)
An orange sorter goes into the magic business.
Energetic low-budget comedy vehicle for unsophisticated audiences.
w Jack Henley d Peter Godfrey ph Lester H. White
☆ Mickey Rooney, Terry Moore, William Demarest, Charles Arnt, Mike Mazurki

Hester Street *

US 1974 89m bw
Midwest Films (Raphael D. Silver)

🎬

How Jewish immigrants settled in East Side New York in the 1890s.
Modest, humorous, but not always smooth or dramatically emphatic chronicle of a familiar background; the detail however is excellent.
wd Joan Micklin Silver story Yekl by Abraham Cahan ph Kenneth Van Sickle m William Bolcom
☆ Steven Keats, Carol Kane, Mel Howard, Dorrie Kavanaugh, Doris Roberts
'A small, beautifully detailed, slightly shaggy independent film of charm and substance.' – Judith Crist
'For old diehards who still go to the cinema seeking humanity, tenderness and insight.' – Michael Billington, Illustrated London News
⚲ Carol Kane

Het Meisje Met Het Rode Haar: see The Girl with the Red Hair

Hets: see Frenzy

Hex

US 1973 93m DeLuxe
TCF (Clark Paylow)

📺 ⊚

aka: The Shrieking
In 1919, when their remote farm in Nebraska is invaded by a gang of bikers, one sister reacts by falling in love while the other uses her occult powers to destroy them.

Odd little adolescent fantasy given a slight twist by its period setting, although the characters' attitudes are strictly from the 60s.
w Leo Garen, Steve Katz story Doran William Cannon, Vernon Zimmerman ph Charles Rosher Jnr m Charles Bernstein ad Gary Weist, Frank Sylos ed Robert Belcher
☆ Tina Herazo (Cristina Raines), Keith Carradine, Hilarie Thompson, Scott Glenn, Gary Busey, Mike Combs, Dan Haggerty, John Carradine

Hexed

US 1993 90m colour
Columbia/Price Entertainment/Brillstein-Grey (Marc S. Fischer, Louis G. Friedman)

📺 ⊚

A fantasist of a hotel clerk becomes involved with a murderous model.
Curious black comedy that has the requisite streak of cruelty but not enough momentum to its narrative to entertain.
wd Alan Spencer ph James Chressanthis m Lance Rubin pd Brenton Swift ed Debra McDermott
☆ Arye Gross, Claudia Christian, Adrienne Shelly, Ray Baker, R. Lee Ermey, Michael Knight, Robin Curtis, Brandis Kemp, Norman Fell

Hexen geschändet und zu Tode gequält: see Mark of the Devil

Hey, Good-Lookin'

US 1982 76m Technicolor
Warner (Ralph Bakshi)
Life in 1953 Brooklyn centres round two young womanizers.
Enterprising attempt to use animation to tell a youth melodrama; interesting but not successful.
wd Ralph Bakshi
☆ Featuring the voices of Richard Romanus, David Proval, Jesse Welles, Tina Bowman

Hey! Hey! USA!

GB 1938 92m bw
Gainsborough (Edward Black)
An education expert sails to America, falls in with gangsters, and saves a boy from being kidnapped by them.
Misconceived star vehicle which provides some laughs, but not of the expected kind.
w J. O. C. Orton, Val Guest, G. Marriott Edgar story Howard Irving Young, Ralph Spence d Marcel Varnel ph Arthur Crabtree m Cecil Milner md Louis Levy ad Vetchinsky ed R. E. Dearing
☆ Will Hay, Edgar Kennedy, David Burns, Fred Duprez

Hey Rookie

US 1944 71m bw
Columbia (Irving Briskin)
A musical comedy producer in the army puts on a show.
Virtually a non-stop revue.
w Henry Myers, Edward Eliscu, Jay Gurney play K. B. and Doris Culvan d Charles Barton
☆ Ann Miller, Joe Besser, Larry Parks, Joe Sawyer, the Condos Brothers, Jack Gilford, the Hal McIntyre Orchestra
'Brief, to the point, and will do.' – Variety

Hi Buddy

US 1943 66m bw
Universal (Paul Malvern)
Soldiers stage a benefit show at a boys' club.
Luckily the sentiment does not get in the way of the numbers; ordinary modest musical filler.
w Warren Wilson d Harold Young
☆ Dick Foran, Harriet Hilliard, Robert Paige, Marjorie Lord, the King's Men, the Four Sweethearts, Dolores Diane

Hi Diddle Diddle *

US 1943 72m bw
UA/Andrew Stone
aka: Try and Find It
Young lovers are hampered by con artist parents.
Scatty comedy with amusing patches and some zest in the telling.
w Edmund L. Hartmann d Andrew L. Stone ph Charles Van Enger m Phil Boutelje
☆ Adolphe Menjou, Pola Negri, Dennis O'Keefe, Billie Burke, Martha Scott, June Havoc
♫ Phil Boutelje

Hi Gang

GB   1941   100m   bw
Rank/Gainsborough (Edward Black)
American expatriates in London get involved in a case of mistaken identity.
Icky farce based faintly on a wartime radio variety series, notable only for preserving the three stars involved.
w Val Guest, Marriott Edgar, J. O. C. Orton, Howard Irving Young d Marcel Varnel ph Jack Cox
☆ Bebe Daniels, Ben Lyon, Vic Oliver, Graham Moffatt, Moore Marriott, Felix Aylmer, Sam Browne

Hi, Mom! *

US   1969   86m   Movielab
West End Films
Adventures of a young porno film maker and of the eccentrics who live in the same building.
Busy comedy of the drop-out life, full of random satirical jabs and homages to other film makers.
wd Brian de Palma ph Robert Elfstrom m Eric Kaz
☆ Robert DeNiro, Allen Garfield, Gerrit Graham, Jennifer Salt, Charles Durning

Hi Nellie *

US   1934   79m   bw
Warner (Robert Presnell)
An ex-editor is demoted to advice to the lovelorn and gets involved in city rackets.
Minor, effective star comedy-melodrama.
w Abem Finkel, Sidney Sutherland d Mervyn Le Roy ph Sol Polito
☆ Paul Muni, Glenda Farrell, Ned Sparks, Robert Barrat, Hobart Cavanaugh, Berton Churchill, Donald Meek, Douglass Dumbrille, Edward Ellis
'Barely gets by as fair entertainment … it's a better Muni performance than a picture.' – *Variety*
† Remade in 1935 as *Front Page Woman*; 1937 as *Love Is on the Air*; 1942 as *You Can't Escape Forever*; 1949 as *The House across the Street*.

Hi Ya Chum

US   1943   61m   bw
Universal
GB title: *Everything Happens to Us*
On their way to Hollywood, variety performers are stranded in a small town.
Thin star comedy support.
w Edmund L. Hartmann d Harold Young
☆ The Ritz Brothers, Jane Frazee, Robert Paige, June Clyde

Hiawatha

US   1952   80m   Cinecolor
Allied Artists
A young brave prevents war between three Indian tribes.
Muddled actioner which has little to do with Longfellow's poem.
w Arthur Strawn, Dan Ullman d Kurt Neumann ph Harry Neumann m Marlin Skiles
☆ Vincent Edwards, Yvette Dugay, Keith Larsen, Morris Ankrum, Ian MacDonald

Hickey and Boggs

US   1972   111m   DeLuxe
UA/Film Guarantors Ltd (Fouad Said)
Two down and out private eyes, hired to find a girl, keep falling over dead bodies.
Extraordinarily confused thriller with moments of humour and well staged action sequences.
w Walter Hill d Robert Culp ph Wilmer Butler m Ted Ashford
☆ Robert Culp, Bill Cosby, Rosalind Cash

The Hidden

US   1988   97m   DeLuxe
Palace/New Line-Heron/Third Elm Street Venture (Robert Shaye, Gerald T. Olson, Michael Meltzer)
Detectives hunt down a murderous slug-like alien who possesses the bodies of humans.
Standard action fare, somewhat sillier than the norm.
w Bob Hunt d Jack Sholder m Michael Convertino ad C. J. Strawn, Mick Strawn ed Michael N. Knue
☆ Kyle MacLachlan, Michael Nouri, Claudia Christian, Clarence Felder, Clu Gulager, Ed O'Ross, William Boyett, Richard Brooks, Larry Cedar

Hidden Agenda **

GB   1990   108m   Eastmancolor
Enterprise/Hemdale (Eric Fellner)
A police officer discovers that members of the Royal Ulster Constabulary are responsible for murders of IRA sympathizers in Belfast.
Powerful political film, based in part on actual events, that sometimes descends into hectoring agit-prop. It won the Jury Prize at the Cannes Film Festival in 1990.
w Jim Allen d Ken Loach ph Clive Tickner m Stewart Copeland pd Martin Johnson ed Jonathan Morris
☆ Brian Cox, Frances McDormand, Brad Dourif, Mai Zetterling, Bernard Bloch, John Benfield, Jim Norton, Patrick Kavanagh, Bernard Archard
'*Hidden Agenda*, though it attempts to make an acceptable theatrical entertainment out of a complex political saga, lacks big-screen impact.' – *Variety*

Hidden City

GB   1988   107m   colour
Other Cinema/Hidden City/Film Four/ZDF (Irving Teitelbaum)
A writer, persuaded by an out-of-work researcher to investigate mysterious happenings caught on old government information films, finds himself the target of a security operation.
Paranoiac thriller of a cover-up which never achieves credibility.
wd Stephen Poliakoff ph Witold Stok m Michael Storey pd Martin Johnson ed Peter Coulson
☆ Charles Dance, Cassie Stuart, Bill Paterson, Richard E. Grant, Alex Norton, Tusse Silberg

The Hidden Eye

US   1945   69m   bw
MGM
A blind detective gets on the trail of a murderer who deliberately leaves confusing clues.
Thin successor to Eyes in the Night: no style at all.
w George Harmon Coxe, Harry Ruskin d Richard Whorf
☆ Edward Arnold, Frances Rafferty, William Phillips, Ray Collins, Thomas Jackson

Hidden Fear

US   1957   83m   bw
UA (St Aubrey-Kohn)
An American cop in Copenhagen clears his sister of a murder charge.
Patchy, tough thriller with some pretensions to style sabotaged by a muddled script.
w André de Toth, John Ward Hawkins d Paul de Toth
☆ John Payne, Anne Neyland, Alexander Knox, Conrad Nagel, Elsy Albiin

The Hidden Fortress **

Japan   1958   123m   bw   Tohoscope
Toho (Masumi Fujimoto)
original title: *Kakushi Toride No San-Akunin*
In medieval Japan, the heiress of a feudal lord is saved from a bandit by a samurai.
Roistering eastern Western.
w Ryuzo Kikushima, Hideo Oguni, Shinobu Hashimoto, Akira Kurosawa d Akira Kurosawa ph Ichio Yamazaki m Masaru Sato
☆ Toshiro Mifune, Misa Uehara, Minoru Chiaki
† George Lucas has said that the film was his inspiration for *Star Wars*.

The Hidden Room: see *Obsession* (1948)

Hide and Seek

GB   1963   90m   bw
British Lion/Albion/Spectrum (Hal E. Chester)
A research scientist is the centre of a kidnap plan designed to make it appear that he has defected.
Too many mysterious happenings with too little explanation sink this comedy-thriller from the start.
w David Stone d Cy Endfield ph Gilbert Taylor m Muir Mathieson, Gary Campbell
☆ Ian Carmichael, Janet Munro, Curt Jurgens, Hugh Griffith, George Pravda, Kieron Moore, Edward Chapman

Hide in Plain Sight

US   1980   92m   Metrocolor   Panavision
MGM (Robert Christiansen, Rick Rosenberg)
A factory worker searches for his children when his former wife is hidden by the government to protect her husband, an informer.
Unpersuasive melodrama with little more than its unusual plot to commend it.
w Spencer Eastman book Leslie Waller d James Caan ph Paul Lohmann m Leonard Rosenman
☆ James Caan, Jill Eikenberry, Robert Viharo

Hideaway

US   1995   103m   Technicolor   Panavision
TriStar/S/Q (Jerry Baerwitz, Agatha Hanczakowski, Gimel Everett)
An antiques dealer, resuscitated after a car crash, begins to share the experiences of a serial killer, who also has returned from death.
Ordinary horror flick, tricked out with some fancy effects in an attempt to make it watchable; the cast do what they can, but it's dull stuff.
w Andrew Kevin Walker, Neal Jimenez novel Dean R. Koontz d Brett Leonard ph Gale Tattersall m Trevor Jones pd Michael Bolton ed B. J. Sears
☆ Jeff Goldblum, Christine Lahti, Alicia Silverstone, Jeremy Sisto, Alfred Molina, Rae Dawn Chong
'Collapses into a mess of clunking dialogue and computer effects.' – *Sight and Sound*

Hideaway Girl

US   1936   71m   bw
Paramount (A. M. Botsford)
A girl suspected of stealing a necklace goes on the run.
Humdrum comedy melodrama with songs: a hotchpotch.
w Joseph Moncure March d George Archainbaud
☆ Martha Raye, Shirley Ross, Robert Cummings, Monroe Owsley
'Rowdy, nonsensical lightweight, geared for doubles.' – *Variety*

'Morocco 1972. It's not about escape, it's about discovery…'
Hideous Kinky

GB/France   1998   97m   colour   'Scope
Film Consortium/BBC/Arts Council/Greenpoint/L Films/AMLF (Ann Scott)
In the early 70s, an Englishwoman, who is living in Marrakesh with two young daughters, begins an affair with a local acrobat.
Episodic, colourful drama about the illusion of freedom, but a little lacking in substance.
w Billy MacKinnon novel Esther Freud d Gillies MacKinnon ph J. de Borman m John Keane pd Louise Marzaroli, Pierre Gompertz ed Pia Di Ciaula
☆ Kate Winslet, Said Taghmaoui, Bella Riza, Carrie Mullan, Pierre Clementi, Sira Stampe
'A pleasant evening in the cinema, but not a great deal more than that.' – *Derek Malcolm, Guardian*

The Hideous Sun Demon

US   1959   74m   bw
Clarke-King Enterprises/Robert Clarke
GB title: *Blood on His Lips*
Subjected to a high level of radiation, a scientist turns into a giant two-legged lizard when exposed to sunlight.
Simple-minded science fiction featuring the producer-director-star in an ill-fitting monster costume.
w E. S. Seeley Jnr, Doane Hoag d Robert Clarke, Tom Boutrous ph John Morrill, Vilis Lapenieks, Stan Follis m John Seely ad Gianbattista Cassarino ed Tom Boutrous
☆ Robert Clarke, Patricia Manning, Nan Peterson, Patrick White

Hideout

US   1934   83m   bw
MGM
An injured racketeer takes refuge with a farm family and is reformed by the simple life and true love.
Schematic eat-your-cake-and-have-it melodrama which pleased audiences at the time.
w Frances Goodrich, Albert Hackett story Mauri Grashin d W. S. Van Dyke
☆ Robert Montgomery, Maureen O'Sullivan, Mickey Rooney, Edward Arnold, C. Henry Gordon, Elizabeth Patterson, Edward Brophy, Herman Bing
§ original story

The Hideout: see *The Small Voice* (1948)

Hideout in the Alps: see *Dusty Ermine*

Hider in the House

US   1989   108m   CFI color
Vestron/Precision Films (Edward Teets, Michael Taylor)
A murderer, hiding in the attic of a house, spies on the family that lives there.
A thriller lacking in suspense and with nothing else to recommend it.
w Lem Dobbs d Matthew Patrick ph Jeff Jur m Christopher Young pd Victoria Paul ed Debra T. Smith
☆ Gary Busey, Mimi Rogers, Michael McKean, Kurt Christopher Kinder, Candy Hutson, Elizabeth Ruscio, Chuck Lafont, Bruce Glover

Hiding Out

US   1987   98m   Technicolor
DEG/Evenmore/Locomotion (Jeff Rothberg)
A stockbroker on the run from a hitman disguises himself as a high-school student.
Inane attempt at a comic thriller; it lacks suspense and fails to exploit its central situation of an adult trapped in an adolescent environment, concentrating instead on an unlikely love affair.
w Joe Menosky, Jeff Rothberg d Bob Giraldi ph Daniel Pearl m Anne Dudley pd Dan Leigh ed Edward Warschilka
☆ Jon Cryer, Keith Coogan, Annabeth Gish, Oliver Cotton, Claude Brooks, Tim Quill, Gretchen Cryer, Nancy Fish

Hifazaat: see *In Custody*

The Higgins Family

US   1938   65m   bw
Republic
An advertising man is driven almost to divorce when his wife becomes a radio personality.
Modest family comedy which ran to a short series.
w Paul Gerard Smith, Jack Townley, Richard English d Gus Meins
☆ James Gleason, Lucille Gleason, Russell Gleason, Lynne Roberts, Harry Davenport
'Shows fine promise.' – *Variety*

High and Dry: see *The Maggie*

High and Low **

Japan   1963   142m   bw   Tohoscope
Toho (Tomoyuki Tanaka)
A wealthy shoe manufacturer's chauffeur's son is kidnapped in mistake for his own, and he faces a moral dilemma.
Interesting, rather gloomy Japanese version of a light American thriller with all the style expected of the director.
w Hideo Oguni, Ryuzo Kikushima, Eijiro Hisaito, Akira Kurosawa novel *The King's Ransom* by Ed McBain d Akira Kurosawa ph Asakazu Nakai, Takao Saito m Masaru Sato
☆ Toshiro Mifune, Kyoko Kagawa, Tatsuya Nakadai
'A tapestry of crime, detection and punishment, with vivid vignettes of various strata of society, haunting moments on the waterfront, in an all-night saloon, in an opium den, right down to the confrontation between victim and criminal in the death cell.' – *Judith Crist*

The High and the Mighty *

US   1954   147m   Warnercolor   Cinemascope
Wayne – Fellows
A big passenger plane is in trouble over the Pacific, and its occupants react in various ways to the prospect of a crash landing.
Compendium fiction with even the pilot having a personal problem which could cloud his judgement. Tolerable, well made hokum.

---

w Ernest K. Gann *novel* Ernest K. Gann
d William Wellman *ph* William Clothier
m Dimitri Tiomkin
☆ John Wayne, Robert Newton, Robert Stack, Doe Avedon, Claire Trevor, Laraine Day, Jan Sterling, Phil Harris, Sidney Blackmer, John Howard
🎵 Dimitri Tiomkin
🗣 William Wellman; Claire Trevor; Jan Sterling; title song (*m*Dimitri Tiomkin, *ly*Ned Washington)

High Anxiety *
US　1977　94m　DeLuxe
TCF/Crossbow (Mel Brooks)
📀 📀 🎧
A psychologist taking up a new appointment suspects that his predecessor may have been murdered.
Elementary but somewhat entertaining spoof of various Hitchcock movies (Spellbound, North by Northwest, The Birds), with the level of humour as unsubtle and lavatorial as one has come to expect.
w Mel Brooks, Ron Clark, Rudy DeLuca, Barry Levinson *d* Mel Brooks *ph* Paul Lohmann *m* John Morris
☆ Mel Brooks, Madeline Kahn, Cloris Leachman, Harvey Korman, Ron Carey, Howard Morris, Dick Van Patten
　'It basically just shambles along, in search of the next big set-piece to send up.' – *Richard Combs, MFB*
　'Brooks has no idea of how to build a sequence, how to tell a story, when to leave well enough (or ill enough) alone.' – *Philip French, Observer*
　'A child's idea of satire – imitations, with a comic hat and a leer.' – *New Yorker*

'A story of ambition, sacrifice, seduction and other career moves.'
High Art *
US　1998　102m　colour
October Films (Dolly Hall, Jeff Levy-Hinte, Susan A. Stover)
🎧
A young magazine editor leaves her boyfriend for a once-famous, druggy female photographer, who lives with a heroin-addicted actress.
Innocence and experience meet in a not particularly compelling romantic melodrama.
wd Lisa Cholodenko *ph* Tami Reiker *m* Shudder to Think *pd* Bernhard Blythe *ed* Amy E. Duddleston
☆ Ally Sheedy, Radha Mitchell, Patricia Clarkson, Tammy Grimes, Gabriel Mann, Bill Sage, Ann Duong, David Thornton
　'Should be wholeheartedly embraced by the lesbian community and, with the right marketing, can cross over to a larger sophisticated audience.' – *Emanuel Levy, Variety*

High Barbaree
US　1947　91m　bw
MGM (Everett Riskin)
📀
A pilot crashlands in the Pacific and finds himself drifting towards a Utopian island fancifully described by his favourite uncle.
Thin Hollywood mysticism on Shangri-La lines but without the solid virtues of plot, dialogue and imagination.
w Anne Morrison Chapin, Whitfield Cook, Cyril Hume *d* Jack Conway *ph* Sidney Wagner *m* Herbert Stothart
☆ Van Johnson, June Allyson, Thomas Mitchell, Marilyn Maxwell

The High Bright Sun
GB　1965　114m　Technicolor
Rank (Betty Box)
📀
US title: *McGuire Go Home*
In 1957 Cyprus the British army is beleaguered by partisans, and an officer tries to contact a leading rebel.
Confused and boring attempt to make romantic drama out of an intractably sad situation.
w Ian Stuart Black *novel* Ian Stuart Black *d* Ralph Thomas *ph* Ernest Steward *m* Angelo Lavagnino
☆ Dirk Bogarde, Susan Strasberg, George Chakiris, Denholm Elliott

The High Command *
GB　1936　88m　bw
ABFD/Fanfare/Wellesley/ (Gordon Wellesley)
📀
The general of a West African garrison has a guilty secret known to his young medical officer.
Dated melodrama, rather interestingly performed and directed.
w Katherine Strueby, Walter Meade, Val Valentine *novel* The General Goes Too Far by Lewis Robinson *d* Thorold Dickinson *ph* Otto Heller, James Rogers *md* Ernest Irving *ad* R. Holmes Paul *ed* Sidney Cole
☆ James Mason, Lionel Atwill, Lucie Mannheim, Steve Geray, Leslie Perrins
　'Its avoidance of reality and its slowness make it a first-class soporific.' – *Sunday Times*
　'A film critic should be capable of distinguishing, from the faults due to a poor story, an uncertain script and mere poverty, the very high promise of the direction.' – *Graham Greene*
　† The cost of the film, including scenes shot in West Africa, was 30,000.

The High Commissioner: see *Nobody Runs Forever*

High Conquest
US　1947　79m　bw
Monogram (Irving Allen)
A young man tries to climb the Matterhorn, on which his father was killed.
Unsatisfactory and ill-edited drama filmed partly in Switzerland and Austria. A good cast is largely wasted.
w Max Troll, Aben Kandel *d* Irving Allen
☆ Anna Lee, Gilbert Roland, Warren Douglas, Beulah Bondi, C. Aubrey Smith, John Qualen, Helene Thimig

The High Cost of Loving *
US　1958　87m　bw　Cinemascope
MGM (Milo O. Frank Jnr)
A happily married middle class couple have doubts about their future.
Pleasant, mildly satirical romantic comedy which doesn't really get anywhere.
w Rip Van Ronkel *d* José Ferrer *ph* George J. Folsey *m* Jeff Alexander
☆ José Ferrer, Gena Rowlands, Joanne Gilbert, Jim Backus, Bobby Troup, Philip Ober, Edward Platt, Werner Klemperer

The High Country
Canada　1981　101m　colour　Panavision
Crown International/Gene Slott (Bruce Mallen)
An escaped convict heads for the mountains accompanied by a simple-minded girl on the run from home.
Tedious drama that will test the patience of the most tolerant; it has nothing to recommend it.
w Bud Townsend *d* Harvey Hart *ph* Robert Ryan *m* Eric Robertson *ad* Reuben Freed *ed* Ron Wisman
☆ Timothy Bottoms, Linda Purl, George Sims

High Encounters of the Ultimate Kind:
see *Cheech and Chong's Next Movie*

High Flight
GB　1957　102m　Technicolor　Cinemascope
Columbia/Warwick (Phil C. Samuel)
Cadets train at the Royal Air Force College.
Simple-minded peacetime flagwaver.
w Joseph Landon, Ken Hughes *d* John Gilling *ph* Ted Moore *m* Kenneth V. Jones, Douglas Gamley *md* Muir Mathieson *title march* Eric Coates
☆ Ray Milland, Bernard Lee, Kenneth Haigh, Anthony Newley, Kenneth Fortescue, Sean Kelly, Helen Cherry

High Flyers
US　1937　70m　bw
RKO (Lee Marcus)
Two incompetents are duped into smuggling contraband gems.
Feeble finale to the career of two comedians.
w Benny Rubin, Bert Granet *play* Victor Mapes *d* Edward Cline *ph* Jack Mackenzie *m* Roy Webb *m/ly* Herman Ruby, Dave Dreyer
☆ Bert Wheeler, Robert Woolsey, Lupe Velez, Marjorie Lord, Margaret Dumont, Jack Carson, Paul Harvey .

High Fury: see *White Cradle Inn*

'A mother, a daughter, a lover. Relationships can be murder.'
High Heels
Spain　1991　112m　Eastmancolor
El Deseo/Ciby 2000 (Agustín Almadóvar)
📀 📀 🎧
original title: *Tacones Lejanos*
A singer restarts an affair with a former lover, who is now married to her daughter.
Camp extravaganza of a showbiz mother-daughter relationship that tries too hard to shock and titillate.
wd Pedro Almodóvar *ph* Alfredo Mayo *m* Ryuichi Sakamoto *ad* Pierre-Louis Thevenet *ed* José Salcedo
☆ Victoria Abril, Marisa Paredes, Miguel Bosé, Feodor Atkine, Pedro Díez del Corral, Ana Lizarán
　'One of the finest, most high fashion portrayals of loss and mourning' – *Stuart Klawans, The Nation*
　'It's got mad love, a bad-seed child, acrobatic sex, an anchor-woman's on-air announcement of her own arrest for murder, a chorus line in a woman's prison and, of course, cross-dressing. It careers like a runaway circus train over the rickety trestle of melodrama. Yet it already has even true believers – Almodóvar's own camp followers – asking, "Is that all there is?"' – *Richard Corliss, Time*

High Hopes
GB　1988　112m　Eastmancolor
Palace/Portman/Film Four International/British Screen (Simon Channing-Williams, Victor Glynn)
📀
A family of contrasting types gather to celebrate their mother's birthday.
A comedy of caricatures.
wd Mike Leigh *m* Andrew Dixon *pd* Diana Charnley *ed* Jon Gregory
☆ Philip Davis, Ruth Sheen, Edna Dore, Philip Jackson, Heather Tobias, Lesley Manville, David Bamber, Jason Watkins, Judith Scott

High Lonesome
US　1950　80m　Technicolor
Eagle Lion
A young man believed to be crazed and homicidal flees into the desert and returns to establish his innocence.
Thinly stretched Western not helped by an exhibitionist star performance.
wd Alan Le May *ph* Howard Greene *m* Rudolph Schrager
☆ John Barrymore Jnr, Chill Wills, Kristine Miller, Lois Butler

'When the hands point up ... the excitement starts!'
High Noon ****
US　1952　85m　bw
Stanley Kramer
📀 📀 🎧 ⊚
A marshal gets no help when he determines to defend his town against revengeful badmen.
A minor Western with a soft-pedalled message for the world, this turned out to be a classic simply because it was well done, with every scene and performance clearly worked out. Cinematically it was pared to the bone, and the theme tune helped.
w Carl Foreman *story* The Tin Star by John W. Cunningham *d* Fred Zinnemann *ph* Floyd Crosby *m* Dimitri Tiomkin *ed* Elmo Williams, Harry Gerstad *singer* Tex Ritter
☆ Gary Cooper, Grace Kelly, Thomas Mitchell, Lloyd Bridges, Katy Jurado, Otto Kruger, Lon Chaney, Henry Morgan
　'The western form is used for a sneak civics lesson.' – *Pauline Kael, 70s*
　'Like nearly all the Kramer productions, this is a neat, well-finished and literate piece of work, though its limitations are more conventional than most.' – *Gavin Lambert*
　'A western to challenge Stagecoach for the all-time championship.' – *Bosley Crowther*
　'A series of crisp and purposeful scenes that interpret each other like the pins on a strategist's war map.' – *Robert L. Hatch*
　'It is astonishing how much of the simple western story is told visually by rapid cross-cutting.' – *Films in Review*
　'Few recent westerns have gotten so much tension and excitement into the classic struggle between good and evil.' – *Life*

　'The most un-American thing I've ever seen in my whole life.' – *John Wayne*
　† The leading role was turned down by John Wayne, Charlton Heston, Marlon Brando and Gregory Peck.
　🎖 Dimitri Tiomkin; Gary Cooper; title song (*m*Dimitri Tiomkin, *ly*Ned Washington); editing
　🗣 best picture; Carl Foreman; Fred Zinnemann

'They'll never forget the day he drifted into town!'
High Plains Drifter *
US　1972　105m　Technicolor　Panavision
Universal/Malpaso (Robert Daley)
📀 📀 🎧 ⊚
A mysterious stranger rides into town and terrifies the inhabitants.
Semi-supernatural, mystical revenge Western with an overplus of violence. Very watchable, but irritating.
w Ernest Tidyman *d* Clint Eastwood *ph* Bruce Surtees *m* Dee Barton *ad* Henry Bumstead
☆ Clint Eastwood, Verna Bloom, Marianna Hill, Mitch Ryan, Jack Ging
　'Ritualized violence and plodding symbolism make for heavy going.' – *Sight and Sound*
　'A nervously humorous, self-conscious near-satire on the prototype Eastwood formula.' – *Variety*

High Pressure *
US　1932　74m　bw
Warner
A would-be tycoon believes there's a fortune to be made in artificial rubber.
Amusing con man comedy with good work all round.
w Joseph Jackson *play* Hot Money by Aben Kandel *d* Mervyn Le Roy
☆ William Powell, Evelyn Brent, George Sidney, Guy Kibbee, Frank McHugh
　'Well acted, but lacks strength to attract much business.' – *Variety*

'Getting In Was Easy ... Getting Out Was War!!!'
High Risk
US　1981　94m　colour
American Cinema (Joe Raffill, Gerard Green)
📀
A documentary film-maker enlists three buddies to steal a million dollars from a South American drugs dealer.
Moderately entertaining caper movie which stops too often for action and occasionally for comedy.
wd Stewart Raffill *ph* Alex Phillips Jnr *m* Mark Snow *ed* Tom Walls Jnr
☆ James Brolin, Cleavon Little, Lindsay Wagner, Ernest Borgnine, Bruce Davison, Chick Vennera, Anthony Quinn, James Coburn

High Road to China
US　1983　105m　Technicolor
Golden Harvest/Pan Pacific (Fred Weintraub)
📀 📀 🎧
In the twenties, an American heiress in Afghanistan has adventures with a drunken flyer.
Abysmal attempt to mate James Bond with a cut-price Raiders of the Lost Ark. It comes up with nothing at all, and is on the lowest level for continuity, dialogue and direction.
w Sandra Weintraub Roland, S. Lee Pogostin *novel* Jon Cleary *d* Brian G. Hutton *ph* Ronnie Taylor *m* John Barry *pd* Robert Laing
☆ Tom Selleck, Bess Armstrong, Jack Weston, Robert Morley, Wilford Brimley, Brian Blessed
　'An attempt to revive the sort of comedy-adventure romance in which Clark Gable and Jean Harlow would squabble furiously but you knew they were really in love. But as scripted and abominably directed, the thing is as flat as a pancake.' – *Guardian*

High School Confidential!
US　1958　85m　bw　CinemaScope
MGM (Albert Zugsmith)
📀 🎧
A new and obnoxious student turns out to be an undercover narcotics policeman tracking down pot-smokers.
An engagingly silly period piece, with its hysteria about drugs, determination to be up to date with its teenage slang ('Tomorrow is dragsville, cats') and portentous final statement following a fight between students and gun-toting gangsters: 'You have just seen an authentic disclosure of conditions that unfortunately exist in some of our high schools today...'

⊚ Digital Video Disc Region 2　　⊚ Digital Video Disc Region 1　　🎧 Soundtrack released on compact disc　　☆ Cast in approximate order of importance　　† Points of interest　　🎵 Notable songs　　🎖 Academy Award　　🗣 Academy Award nomination　　🏆 BAFTA w Lewis Meltzer, Robert Blees d Jack Arnold ph Harold J. Marzorati ad William J. Horning, Hans Peters ed Ben Lewis

☆ Russ Tamblyn, Jan Sterling, John Drew Barrymore, Mamie Van Doren, Jerry Lee Lewis, Ray Anthony, Jackie Coogan, Charles Chaplin Jnr, Diane Jergens, Michael Landon, Burt Douglas

High School High

US 1996 86m Technicolor
Sony/TriStar (David Zucker, Robert LoCash, Gil Netter)
🔲 🔳 ⊘

An earnest and idealistic teacher joins the staff of a tough ghetto school.
A spoof of movies such as Dangerous Minds, *but without class; it limps along from one bad joke to another.*

w David Zucker, Robert LoCash, Pat Proft d Hart Bochner ph Vernon Layton m Ira Newborn pd Dennis Washington ad James R. Symons

☆ Jon Lovitz, Tia Carrere, Mekhi Phifer, Louise Fletcher, Guillermo Diaz, John Neville, Malinda Williams, Gil Espinoza, Brian Hooks

'The problem isn't that it always goes for the cheap laugh, but that it fails at getting it so often.' – *Variety*

High Season

GB 1987 92m colour
Curzon/British Screen/Film Four/Michael White/Hemdale (Clare Downs)
🔳 ⊘

A female photographer meets strange friends in Rhodes.
Spies, thieves and tourists make an odd lightweight mixture in a movie best suited to TV.

w Mark and Clare Peploe d Clare Peploe ph Chris Menges m Jason Osborn pd Andrew McAlpine ad Gabriella Cristiani

☆ Jacqueline Bisset, James Fox, Irene Papas, Sebastian Shaw, Kenneth Branagh, Robert Stephens

'The blazing mountain manhunt for Killer Mad-Dog Earle!'

High Sierra *

US 1941 96m bw
Warner (Hal. B. Wallis, Mark Hellinger)
🔳 ⊘

An ex-con gangster plans one last heist in the Californian mountains, but is mortally wounded through his involvement with two women.
Rather dreary action melodrama which gave Bogart his first real star part (after George Raft turned it down). Remade 1955 as I Died a Thousand Times *(qv); also in 1949 as a Western,* Colorado Territory.

w John Huston, W. R. Burnett novel W. R. Burnett d Raoul Walsh ph Tony Gaudio m Adolph Deutsch

☆ Humphrey Bogart, Ida Lupino, Joan Leslie, Alan Curtis, Arthur Kennedy, Henry Hull, Henry Travers, Jerome Cowan

'The last swallow, perhaps, of the gangsters' summer.' – *William Whitebait*
'Like it or not, I'll be damned if you leave before the end, or go to sleep.' – *Otis Ferguson*
'As gangster pictures go, this one has everything – speed, excitement, suspense, and that ennobling suggestion of futility which makes for irony and poetry.' – *New York Times*

High Society

US 1956 107m Technicolor Vistavision
MGM (Sol C. Siegel)
🔲 🔳 ⊘ ⌒

A haughty rich girl chooses between several suitors.
Cold, flat, dull musical reworking of The Philadelphia Story *(qv), with ill-cast performers and just a few bright moments.*

w John Patrick d Charles Walters ph Paul C. Vogel m/ly Cole Porter md Johnny Green, Saul Chaplin ad Cedric Gibbons, Hans Peters

☆ Bing Crosby, Grace Kelly, Frank Sinatra, Celeste Holm, Louis Armstrong, Sidney Blackmer, Margalo Gillmore, Louis Calhern, Lydia Reed, John Lund

'The principals perform, most of the time, with a kind of glum cheeriness.' – *Hollis Alpert*
'Simply not Top Drawer.' – *Time*
🎵 'Well, Did You Evah'; 'High Society'; 'Who Wants to be a Millionaire?'; 'I Love You, Samantha'; 'Now You Has Jazz'
🎜 Johnny Green, Saul Chaplin; song 'True Love'

High Society Blues

US 1930 102m bw
Fox

A girl ditches a French count in favour of an all-American hero.
Frothy musical romance which did nothing for its stars and is now unwatchable.

w Howard J. Green d David Butler ph Charles Van Enger m/ly Joe McCarthy, James Hanley

☆ Janet Gaynor, Charles Farrell, William Collier Snr, Hedda Hopper, Louise Fazenda, Lucien Littlefield, Joyce Compton

'Certain to please the average fan ... commercial product of the first programme grade.' – *Variety*

High Spirits

GB 1988 96m colour
Palace/Vision PDG (Stephen Woolley, David Saunders)
🔲 🔳 ⊘ ⌒

In order to attract tourists, the owner of an Irish castle fakes ghosts and then discovers that he has summoned up some real ones.
Insubstantial comedy that lurches unsuccessfully into supernatural romance.

wd Neil Jordan ph Alex Thomson m George Fenton pd Alex Furst ed Michael Bradsell

☆ Peter O'Toole, Donal McCann, Mary Coughlan, Liz Smith, Steve Guttenberg, Beverly D'Angelo, Jennifer Tilly, Peter Gallagher, Daryl Hannah, Liam Neeson, Ray McAnally

High Tension

US 1936 63m bw
TCF

Exploits of a cable layer in Hawaii.
Routine brawling comedy.

w Lou Breslow, Edward Eliscu, John Patrick d Allan Dwan

☆ Brian Donlevy, Norman Foster, Glenda Farrell, Helen Wood, Robert McWade

The High Terrace

GB 1956 82m bw
CIPA/Robert S. Baker

A theatrical producer is murdered, and members of the cast protect their leading lady; but she is guilty.
Rather solemn, enclosed little mystery which evokes no compulsion to go on watching.

w Alfred Shaughnessy, Norman Hudis d Henry Cass

☆ Lois Maxwell, Dale Robertson, Derek Bond, Eric Pohlmann, Mary Laura Wood, Lionel Jeffries

High Tide *

Australia 1987 104m colour
Ritzy/FGH/STL/Hemdale (Sandra Levy)
🔲 🔳 ⊘

An unsuccessful singer meets the teenage daughter she abandoned years before.
Unsentimental and well acted study of maternal stirrings.

w Laura Jones d Gillian Armstrong ph Russell Boyd m Peter Best pd Sally Campbell ed Nicholas Beauman

☆ Judy Davis, Jan Adele, Claudia Karvan, Colin Friels, John Clayton, Frankie J. Holden

'There have never been characters like Ally and her mom in movies, and there has never been a film like this emotional riptide.' – *Carrie Rickey, Philadelphia Inquirer*

High Time

US 1960 103m DeLuxe Cinemascope
TCF/Bing Crosby (Charles Brackett)

A middle-aged widower goes back to college.
Flaccid comedy-musical with some undergraduatish jokes.

w Tom and Frank Waldman d Blake Edwards ph Ellsworth Fredericks m Henry Mancini songs Jimmy Van Heusen, Sammy Cahn

☆ Bing Crosby, Tuesday Weld, Fabian, Richard Beymer, Nicole Maurey

🎜 song 'The Second Time Around'

High Treason

GB 1929 90m bw
Gaumont

In 1940, women unite to prevent a second world war.
Tired little prophetic fable with primitive techniques.

w L'Estrange Fawcett play Noel Pemberton-Billing d Maurice Elvey

☆ Jameson Thomas, Benita Hume, Basil Gill, Humberston Wright

High Treason *

GB 1951 93m bw
GFD/Conqueror (Paul Soskin)
Saboteurs are routed by the London police.
Unconvincing documentary melodrama which moves fast enough to be entertaining.

w Frank Harvey, Roy Boulting d Roy Boulting ph Gilbert Taylor m John Addison

☆ Liam Redmond, André Morell, Anthony Bushell, Kenneth Griffith, Patric Doonan, Joan Hickson, Anthony Nicholls, Mary Morris, Geoffrey Keen, Dora Bryan

High Vermilion: see *Silver City*

High Wall

US 1947 99m bw
MGM (Robert Lord)
A war veteran is put in an asylum after confessing to killing his wife, but later events prove that he was drugged into saying so.
Adequately entertaining, supremely unconvincing mystery melodrama.

w Sydney Boehm d Curtis Bernhardt ph Paul C. Vogel m Bronislau Kaper

☆ Robert Taylor, Herbert Marshall, Audrey Totter, Dorothy Patrick, H. B. Warner, Warner Anderson

High, Wide and Handsome *

US 1937 110m bw
Paramount (Arthur Hornblow Jnr)
Pennsylvania 1859: a travelling showgirl falls in love with a farmer.
Disappointingly stilted period musical with most of the talent ill at ease until the final reel.

w Oscar Hammerstein II d Rouben Mamoulian ph Victor Milner, Theodor Sparkuhl m/ly Jerome Kern, Oscar Hammerstein II md Boris Morros ch Le Roy Prinz ad Hans Dreier, John Goodman

☆ Irene Dunne, Randolph Scott, Dorothy Lamour, Raymond Walburn, Alan Hale, Elizabeth Patterson, Charles Bickford, William Frawley, Akim Tamiroff, Ben Blue, Irving Pichel, Lucien Littlefield

'Not a road show, but a big picture, and should get nice returns.' – *Variety*
'There are two hours of this long, dumb and dreary picture ... one is left with a few dim distressing memories.' – *Graham Greene*
'Irene Dunne at her cornball primmest, singing alongside a farmhouse when Randolph Scott isn't around.' – *Pauline Kael, 70s*

A High Wind in Jamaica *

👫 GB 1965 104m DeLuxe Cinemascope
TCF (John Croydon)
In Victorian days, English children en route home from Jamaica are captured by pirates and influence their lives.
Semi-serious adventure story with a highly unlikely ending in which the chief pirate allows himself to be executed for a murder committed by a child. There are however pleasures along the way.

w Stanley Mann, Ronald Harwood, Denis Cannan novel Richard Hughes d Alexander Mackendrick ph Douglas Slocombe m Larry Adler

☆ Deborah Baxter, Anthony Quinn, James Coburn, Isabel Dean, Nigel Davenport, Gert Frobe, Lila Kedrova

The High Window: see *The Brasher Doubloon*

High-Ballin'

US 1978 100m Movielab
AIP/Stanley Chase/Pando (Jan Slan)
🔳

An independent trucker battles hijackers as well as pressures from a giant trucking firm.
Routine action hokum, a long way behind 1948's Thieves' Highway *and even less entertaining than TV's* Movin' On.

w Paul Edwards d Peter Carter ph René Verzier m Paul Hoffert

☆ Peter Fonda, Jerry Reed, Helen Shaver, Chris Wiggins

Higher and Higher *

US 1943 90m bw
RKO (Tim Whelan)

Servants have an elaborate plan to restore the family fortune.

Unamusing musical which undernourishes several talents.

w Jay Dratler, Ralph Spence play Gladys Hurlbut, Joshua Logan d Tim Whelan ph Robert de Grasse m/ly Jimmy McHugh, Harold Adamson md Constantin Bakaleinikoff

☆ Michele Morgan, Jack Haley, Frank Sinatra, Leon Errol, Marcy McGuire, Victor Borge, Mary Wickes, Barbara Hale, Elizabeth Risdon

'There may be some folks who can't figure out the reasons for Sinatra's meteoric rise, or might be wondering whether he's here to stay or not, but in his first screen starring role he at least gets in no one's way.' – *Variety*
🎜 Constantin Bakaleinikoff; song 'I Couldn't Sleep a Wink Last Night'

Higher Learning *

US 1994 127m Technicolor
Columbia/New Deal (John Singleton, Paul Hall)
🔲 🔳

New students at a university campus find themselves in conflict with fellow students according to their colour.
Earnest drama on the complexities and inequalities of the education system, a little too schematic in its oppositions to be entirely persuasive, particularly in its melodramatic finale.

wd John Singleton ph Peter Lyons Collister m Stanley Clarke pd Keith Brian Burns ed Bruce Cannon

☆ Omar Epps, Kristy Swanson, Michael Rapaport, Jennifer Connelly, Ice Cube, Laurence Fishburne, Jason Wiles, Tyra Banks, Cole Hauser

'A thoughtful, angry film, but marred by stereotyping and a pervasive self-righteousness.' – *Sheila Johnston, Independent*

The Highest Honour

Australia 1982 143m colour
Southern International Films (Lee Robinson)
aka: *Southern Cross*
In 1942, an Australian spy befriends his captor and finally executioner.
Sombre true story, far too long in the telling.

w Lee Robinson d Peter Maxwell ph John McLean m Eric Jupp

☆ George Mallaby, Michael Aitkens, John Howard, Atsuo Nakamura, Stuart Wilson, Steve Bisley

'Largely fails to ignite.' – *Julian Petley, MFB*

Highlander

GB/US 1986 111m Technicolor
EMI/Highlander (Peter S. Davis, William N. Panzer)
🔲 🔳 ⊘

A 14th-century Scotsman apparently dies in battle but finds he is an immortal, and is still crossing swords with his enemy the Kurgan in 20th-century Manhattan.
Muddled, violent and noisy jamboree. The explanation doesn't come until most people will have given up.

w Gregory Widden, Peter Bellwood, Larry Ferguson d Russell Mulcahy m Gerry Fisher m Michael Kamen pd Allan Cameron ed Peter Honess

☆ Christopher Lambert, Roxanne Hart, Clancy Brown, Sean Connery

'While there are entertaining moments, total work is a mess.' – *Variety*
'A moody combination of *Blade Runner*, *The Terminator* and your last really good nightmare.' – *People*

'It's Time For A New Kind Of Magic.'
Highlander II – The Quickening

US 1990 100m Eastmancolor
Entertainment/Lamb Bear/Peter S. Davis, William Panzer
🔲 🔳 ⊘ ⊘ ⌒

Two immortal aliens join forces to defeat a dictator who controls the Earth.
Incoherent and inconsequential sequel.

w Peter Bellwood new Brian Clemens, William Panzer d Russell Mulcahy ph Phil Meheux m Stewart Copeland pd Roger Hall ed Hubert C. de la Bouillerie, Anthony Redman sp John Richardson

☆ Christopher Lambert, Sean Connery, Virginia Madsen, Michael Ironside, Allan Rich, John C. McGinley

'A terrible mess. The film's organization at all levels, from plot down to the cutting of individual action sequences, is so full of holes that there is nothing solid for it to adhere to.' – *Sight and Sound*

'Throughout time they have hunted each other, fulfilling the prophecy that there can be only one.' 'The final conflict.'

Highlander III: The Sorcerer

Canada/France/GB 1994 99m colour
Scope
Entertainment/Transfilm/Initial/Fallingcloud (Claude Léger)

The Highlander is menaced by a fellow immortal, released after being trapped inside a mountain for 400 years.

This third episode of an increasingly woebegone series is set in the time between the first and the second movie and merely adds some oriental trimmings to its unimaginative rerun of a similar narrative.

w Paul Ohl *story* William Panzer, Brad Mirman d Andy Morahan *ph* Steven Chivers *m* J. Peter Robinson *pd* Gilles Aird, Ben Morahan *ed* Yves Langlois *sp* make-up effects: Stephen Dupuis, Charles Carter

☆ Christopher Lambert, Mario Van Peebles, Deborah Unger, Mako, Michael Jayston, Martin Neufeld

'A breakneck, roller-coaster genre ride that's brainless fodder for undiscriminating auds.' – *Variety*

Highly Dangerous

GB 1950 88m bw
Rank/Two Cities (Anthony Darnborough)

A lady entomologist in a Balkan country is suspected of spying but manages to outwit her enemies.

Odd blend of straight adventure and spoof; it doesn't quite come off.

w Eric Ambler d Roy Baker *ph* Reg Wyer *m* Richard Addinsell

☆ Margaret Lockwood, Dane Clark, Marius Goring, Naunton Wayne, Eugene Deckers, Wilfrid Hyde-White, Michael Hordern, Gladys Henson

Highpoint

Canada 1984 88m Eastmancolor
Highpoint/New World

An industrialist is on the run from both the Mafia and the CIA.

Routine thriller with a finale atop Toronto's CN Tower.

w Richard Guttman, Ian Sutherland d Peter Carter

☆ Richard Harris, Christopher Plummer, Beverly D'Angelo, Kate Reid, Peter Donat

† Filmed in 1979.

Highway 301 *

US 1950 83m bw
Warner (Bryan Foy)

The Tri-State Gang is apprehended by police.

Actionful gangster melodrama of the Bonnie and Clyde type with plenty of suspenseful situations and slick camerawork.

wd Andrew Stone *ph* Carl Guthrie *m* William Lava

☆ Steve Cochran, Virginia Grey, Gaby Andre, Edmon Ryan, Richard Egan, Robert Webber

'Several good suspense sequences, some good comic observation, and many pleasing visual moments of the wet-streets-at-night category.' – *Richard Mallett, Punch*

Highway 61 *

Canada/GB 1991 102m colour
Shadow Shows/Telefilm Canada/Film Four International (Colin Brunton, Bruce McDonald)

A guileless small-town Canadian barber and jazz trumpeter travels to New Orleans with a delinquent fugitive rock roadie who has stolen her group's stash of drugs and hidden it in a corpse.

Quirky little movie about the exploited and the exploitative, and those who sell their souls too cheaply.

w Don McKellar d Bruce McDonald *ph* Miroslaw Baszak *m* Nash The Slash *ad* Ian Brock *ed* Michael Pacek

☆ Don McKellar, Valerie Buhagiar, Earl Pastko, Peter Breck, Art Bergmann

Highway Dragnet

US 1954 71m bw
Allied Artists (William F. Broidy)

A lady photographer gives a lift to an ex-marine who may or may not be a murderer.

Twisty lower-berth thriller in which all is not as it seems.

w Herb Meadow, Jerome Odlum *story* Roger Corman d Nathan Juran *ph* John Martin *md* Edward Kay

☆ Joan Bennett, Richard Conte, Wanda Hendrix, Reed Hadley, Mary Beth Hughes, Iris Adrian

Highway Patrolman *

Mexico 1991 104m colour
Metro Tartan/Cable Hogue/Together Brothers/Ultra (Lorenzo O'Brien)

original title: El Patrullero

A newly qualified, poorly paid highway cop finds that maintaining law and order is not as straightforward as he thought during his training, especially when he is offered bribes.

Entertaining, episodic account of low life in Mexico, filmed in a semi-documentary style and concentrating on the small happenings of an existence on the margins.

w Lorenzo O'Brien d Alex Cox *ph* Miguel Garzon *m* Zander Schloss *pd* Cecilia Montiel *ed* Carlos Puente

☆ Roberto Sosa, Bruno Bichir, Vanessa Bauche, Zaide Silvia Gutierrez, Pedro Armendariz Jnr, Ernesto Gomez Cruz, Jorge Russek, Karl Braun

'An enjoyable trip and Cox's most accomplished film for a decade.' – *Adam Mars-Jones, Independent*

'It is intelligent, caustic, ironic and humorous all at once, and shows that Cox is a director to match the best of them.' – *Steve Beard, Empire*

Highway to Freedom: see Joe Smith American

'Where the toll is your soul.'

Highway to Hell

US 1992 93m CFI color
Sovereign/Hemdale (Mary Anne Page, John Byers)

An eloping couple on the way to Las Vegas run into a demonic cop who abducts the girl.

Hell is an uninventive horror flick.

w Brian Helgeland d Ate de Jong *ph* Robin Vidgeon *m* Hidden Faces *pd* Phillip Dean Foreman *ed* Todd Ramsay, Randy Thornton

☆ Patrick Bergin, Adam Storke, Chad Lowe, Kristy Swanson, Pamela Gidley, Jarrett Lennon, C. J. Graham, Richard Farnsworth

'A failed horror comedy in search of a bigger budget and far better script.' – *Variety*

† Made in 1989.

The Highwayman

US 1951 82m Cinecolor
Allied Artists/Jack Dietz (Hal. E. Chester)

A 17th-century nobleman disguises himself as a Quaker and becomes a highwayman to right wrongs.

Curious Poverty Row period actioner with ideas generally above its station, not to mention an unexpected tragic ending.

w Jan Jeffries *poem* Alfred Noyes d Lesley Selander *ph* Harry Neumann *m* Herschel Burke Gilbert

☆ Philip Friend, Charles Coburn, Victor Jory, Wanda Hendrix, Cecil Kellaway, Scott Forbes, Virginia Huston, Dan O'Herlihy

Highways by Night

US 1942 62m bw
RKO

A millionaire drafts legal resources to round up hi-jackers.

Formula thick ear with romance.

w Lynn Root, Frank Fenton *story* Clarence Budington Kelland d Peter Godfrey

☆ Richard Carlson, Jane Randolph, Jane Darwell, Barton MacLane, Ray Collins

The Hi-Jackers

GB 1963 69m bw
Butcher's (John I. Phillips)

A driver and his girlfriend track down the criminal gang who steal his lorry and its valuable load.

Dull thriller with an occasional nice touch in the direction, but not enough to save it from mediocrity.

w Jim O'Connolly *ph* Walter J. Harvey *m* Johnny Douglas *ad* Duncan Sutherland *ed* Henry Richardson

☆ Anthony Booth, Jacqueline Ellis, Derek Francis, Patrick Cargill, Glynn Edwards, David Gregory, Harold Goodwin, Ronald Hines, Marianne Stone, Arthur English

'The true story of two sisters who shared a passion, a madness and a man.'

Hilary and Jackie **

GB 1998 124m DeLuxe Panavision
Intermedia/Film Four/British Screen/Arts Council/Oxford (Andy Paterson, Nicolas Kent)

The life and loves of cellist Jacqueline Du Pré, whose career ended when she was 27, owing to multiple sclerosis.

Some excellent acting gives an emotional power and rawness to this often conventional biopic, which concentrates on the relationship and rivalry between two sisters.

w Frank Cottrell-Boyce *book* A Genius in the Family by Hilary and Piers Du Pré d Anand Tucker *ph* David Johnson *m* Barrington Pheloung *pd* Alice Normington *ed* Martin Walsh

☆ Emily Watson, Rachel Griffiths, James Frain, David Morrissey, Charles Dance, Celia Imrie, Rupert Penry-Jones, Bill Paterson, Auriol Evans, Keeley Flanders, Nyree Dawn Porter, Vernon Dobtcheff

'Audiences will find the film an extremely moving and haunting – if ultimately gruelling – experience.' – *James Cameron-Wilson, Film Review*

♟ Emily Watson; Rachel Griffiths

'I want to live like a man – and still be a woman!'

Hilda Crane

US 1956 87m Technicolor Cinemascope
TCF (Herbert B. Swope Jnr)

An unhappy woman marries for the third time and convinces herself it won't work.

Emotional melodrama of the old school: very moderate in all departments.

wd Philip Dunne *play* Samson Raphaelson *ph* Joe MacDonald *m* David Raksin

☆ Jean Simmons, Guy Madison, Jean-Pierre Aumont, *Evelyn Varden*, Judith Evelyn, Peggy Knudsen

'They went up like men! They came down like animals!'

The Hill **

GB 1965 122m bw
MGM/Seven Arts (Kenneth Hyman)

Prisoners rebel against the harsh discipline of a British military detention centre in North Africa during World War II.

Lurid melodrama which descends fairly quickly into black farce with a number of sweaty actors outshouting each other. Enjoyable on this level when you can hear the dialogue through the poor sound recording.

w Ray Rigby *play* Ray Rigby, R. S. Allen d Sidney Lumet *ph* Oswald Morris *m* none *ad* Herbert Smith *ed* Thelma Connell

☆ Sean Connery, Harry Andrews, Michael Redgrave, Ian Bannen, Alfred Lynch, Ossie Davis, Roy Kinnear, Jack Watson, Ian Hendry

♟ Oswald Morris

Hill 24 Doesn't Answer

Israel 1954 101m bw
Sikor (Thorold Dickinson, Peter Frye)

Four friends defend Hill 24 against the Arabs on the eve of the cease-fire, and are all killed.

Israel's first feature film, a curious amalgam of the slick and the amateur, with long flashbacks which make it resemble The Bridge of San Luis Rey.

w Zvi Kolitz, Peter Frye, Joanna and Thorold Dickinson d Thorold Dickinson *ph* Gerald Gibbs *m* Paul Ben-Haim

☆ Michael Wager, Edward Mulhare, Haya Harareet, Arieh Lavi, Michael Shilo

A Hill in Korea

GB 1956 81m bw
British Lion/Wessex (Anthony Squire)

US title: Hell in Korea

During the Korean war, a small patrol guards a hill.

Minor war talk-piece, shot in Surrey and looking it.

w Ian Dalrymple, Anthony Squire, Ronald Spencer *novel* Max Catto d Julian Amyes *ph* Freddie Francis *m* Malcolm Arnold

☆ George Baker, Harry Andrews, Stanley Baker, Michael Medwin, Ronald Lewis, Stephen Boyd, Victor Maddern, Harry Landis

'Character is adequately sketched into a suitably laconic script.' – *MFB*

Hill's Angels: see The North Avenue Irregulars

The Hills Have Eyes

US 1977 90m Movielab
New Realm/Blood Relations (Peter Locke)

Holidaymakers are waylaid and killed by a family of desert cannibals.

Low-grade shocker which mysteriously achieved some cult status.

wd Wes Craven *ph* Eric Saarinen *m* Don Peake *ad* Robert Burns *ed* Wes Craven

☆ John Steadman, Janus Blythe, Arthur King, Russ Grieve, Virginia Vincent

'Simultaneously risible and nauseating.' – *Tim Pulleine, MFB*

The Hills of Home

⚦⚦ US 1948 95m Technicolor
MGM

GB title: Master of Lassie

A doctor returns to his Scottish village to practise medicine, and brings his faithful collie.

Adequate addition to the Lassie saga, with competent work all round.

w William Ludwig d Fred Wilcox

☆ Edmund Gwenn, Tom Drake, Donald Crisp, Rhys Williams, Reginald Owen

'A Land Without Boundaries. A Passion Without Limits.'

The Hi-Lo Country *

US 1999 114m colour
Universal/Polygram/Working Title/Cappa/De Fina (Barbara De Fina/Martin Scorsese/Eric Fellner/Tim Bevan)

In the late 40s, two cowboys, friends who are in love with the same woman, find it difficult to adapt to the changing ways of the modern world.

Elegiac, overlong movie of the decline of Western traditions that occasionally hints at more complex matters, of men trapped by their own situation, before settling for nostalgia.

w Walon Green *novel* Max Evans d Stephen Frears *ph* Oliver Stapleton *m* Carter Burwell *pd* Patricia Norris *ed* Masahiro Hirakubo

☆ Woody Harrelson, Billy Crudup, Patricia Arquette, Cole Hauser, Penelope Cruz, Darren Burrows, Jacob Vargas, James Gammon, Lane Smith, Katy Jurado, Sam Elliott

'A good stab at an American genre piece, a modern western.' – *Adam Mars-Jones, Times*

Himatsuri: see Fire Festival

Der Himmel über Berlin: see Wings of Desire

The Hindenburg *

US 1975 125m Technicolor Panavision
Universal/Filmmakers (Robert Wise)

In 1937, sabotage causes the airship Hindenburg to crash on arrival at New York.

An extremely uninteresting guess at the cause of this famous disaster. The plot and dialogue are leaden, and such actors as have more than a couple of lines look extremely glum. The special effects, however, are fine despite curious blue-rinse photographic processing.

w Nelson Gidding *novel* Michael M. Mooney d Robert Wise *ph* Robert Surtees *m* David Shire *pd* Edward Carfagno *sp* Albert Whitlock

☆ George C. Scott, Anne Bancroft, Burgess Meredith, William Atherton, Roy Thinnes, Gig Young, Charles Durning, Robert Clary, René Auberjonois

'The tackiest disaster movie yet – a cheap and chaotic collage of painted drops, wooden actors and not-so-special effects that manages to make one of this century's most sensational real-life catastrophes seem roughly as terrifying as a badly stubbed toe.' – *Frank Rich*

♟ Robert Surtees

Hindle Wakes

GB 1952 82m bw
Monarch
US title: *Holiday Week*
A Lancashire millgirl spends a week at Blackpool with the master's son but causes a scandal when she refuses to marry him.
Modestly competent version of a semi-classic play about class distinctions.
w John Baines *play* Stanley Houghton d Arthur Crabtree *ph* Geoffrey Faithfull m Stanley Black
☆ Lisa Daniely, Leslie Dwyer, Brian Worth, Sandra Dorne, Ronald Adam, Joan Hickson
† A probably better, but unavailable version was made in 1931 by Victor Saville for Gaumont, with Belle Chrystall, Edmund Gwenn, John Stuart, Ruth Peterson, Norman McKinnel and Sybil Thorndike.

Hips Hips Hooray

US 1934 68m bw
RKO
▤
Two salesmen pitch flavoured lipstick to a beauty parlour chain.
Tired star comedy.
w Harry Ruby, Bert Kalmar d Mark Sandrich
☆ Bert Wheeler, Robert Woolsey, Ruth Etting, Thelma Todd, Dorothy Lee, George Meeker
'Femme display chief asset.' – *Variety*

The Hired Hand

US 1971 93m Technicolor
Universal/Pando (William Hayward)
▤
Two Western drifters avenge the killing of their friend and settle down to work on a farm; but violence follows them.
A potentially enjoyable small-scale Western is spoiled by pretentious direction and effects which bore the spectator to death.
w Alan Sharp d Peter Fonda *ph* Vilmos Zsigmond m Bruce Langhorne
☆ Peter Fonda, Warren Oates, Verna Bloom, Severn Darden
'The first slow-motion western, with endless artsy photography not quite succeeding in obscuring the rambling plot.' – *Judith Crist, 1973*
'When a film begins with a "lyrical" shot, your heart has a right to sink.' – *Stanley Kauffmann*

Hired Wife

US 1940 96m bw
Universal
A secretary who loves her boss saves his company by marrying him so that it can be transferred to her name.
After which the plot has absolutely nowhere to go.
w Richard Connell, Gladys Lehman d William A Seiter
☆ Rosalind Russell, Brian Aherne, Virginia Bruce, Robert Benchley, John Carroll, Hobart Cavanaugh

The Hireling *

GB 1973 108m colour
Columbia/World Film Services (Ben Arbeid)
In the twenties, a lady's chauffeur falls in love with her.
Talkative drama, elegant but not much fun.
w Wolf Mankowitz *novel* L. P. Hartley d Alan Bridges *ph* Michael Reed m Marc Wilkinson *pd* Natasha Kroll
☆ Sarah Miles, Robert Shaw, Peter Egan, Elizabeth Sellars, Caroline Mortimer
Ⓥ Natasha Kroll; Peter Egan

Hiroshima Mon Amour *

France/Japan 1959 91m bw
Argos/Comei/Pathé/Daiei
▤ ▤
A French actress working in Hiroshima falls for a Japanese architect and remembers her tragic love for a German soldier during the occupation.
Jumbled mixture of flashbacks and flashforwards which can now be recognized as typical of this director and on its first appearance was hailed as a work of art in an innovative new style.
w Marguerite Duras d Alain Resnais *ph* Sacha Vierny, Takahashi Michio m Giovanni Fusco, Georges Delerue
☆ Emmanuele Riva, Eiji Okada
'Suddenly a new film. Really new, first-hand: a work which tells a story of its own in a style of its own. One is almost afraid to touch it.' – *Dilys Powell*
♟ Marguerite Duras

His Affair: see This Is My Affair

His and Hers

GB 1960 90m bw
Eros (Hal E. Chester)
An author gets lost with the Bedouin while on a research trip, and by the time he gets home his personality is transformed.
The thinnest of comedy ideas becomes a film of almost no substance at all.
w Stanley Mann, Jan and Mark Lowell d Brian Desmond Hurst
☆ Terry-Thomas, Janette Scott, Wilfrid Hyde-White, Nicole Maurey, Joan Sims, Kenneth Connor, Kenneth Williams, Meier Tzelniker, Joan Hickson, Colin Gordon, Oliver Reed, Francesca Annis

His Brother's Wife

US 1936 91m bw
MGM (Lawrence Weingarten)
A young scientist is helped out of trouble by his brother, on condition he disappears; the brother then weds the scientist's girlfriend.
Heavy romantic melodrama containing everything including jungle fever, flung together to take advantage of the stars' real-life romance.
w Leon Gordon, John Meehan *story* George Auerbach d W. S. Van Dyke II *ph* Oliver T. Marsh m Franz Waxman
☆ Robert Taylor, Barbara Stanwyck, Joseph Calleia, John Eldredge, Jean Hersholt, Samuel S. Hinds, Leonard Mudie, Jed Prouty

His Butler's Sister *

US 1943 94m bw
Universal (Felix Jackson)
A temporary maid falls for her sophisticated boss.
Pleasant comedy musical: no great shakes, but the principals give the air of enjoying themselves.
w Samuel Hoffenstein, Betty Reinhardt d Frank Borzage *ph* Elwood Bredell m Hans Salter
☆ Deanna Durbin, Franchot Tone, Pat O'Brien, Evelyn Ankers, Walter Catlett, Alan Mowbray, Akim Tamiroff, Elsa Janssen, Iris Adrian

His Double Life *

US 1933 63m bw
Paramount (Eddie Dowling)
▤
A famous painter, when his valet dies, takes his identity.
Adequate transcription of a novel later redone as Holy Matrimony.
w Arthur Hopkins, Clara Beranger *novel and play* Arnold Bennett d Arthur Hopkins *ph* Arthur Edeson
☆ Roland Young, Lillian Gish, Lumsden Hare, Lucy Beaumont
'Pleasant little film; big grosses unlikely.' – *Variety*

His Excellency

GB 1951 84m bw
Ealing (Michael Truman)
The Labour government sends a trade union official to govern a Mediterranean colony.
Disappointingly tacky-looking and stagebound version of an unpersuasive West End comedy.
w Robert Hamer, W. P. Lipscomb *play* Dorothy and Campbell Christie d Robert Hamer *ph* Douglas Slocombe m Handel *md* Ernest Irving
☆ Eric Portman, Cecil Parker, Helen Cherry, Susan Stephen, Edward Chapman, Clive Morton, Robin Bailey, Geoffrey Keen

His Family Tree

US 1935 59m bw
RKO
An Irishman migrates to America and gets involved in politics.
Lively second feature for the Irish halls.
w Joel Sayre, John Twist *play* Old Man Murphy by Patrick Kearney, Harry Wagstaff Gribble d Charles Vidor
☆ James Barton, Margaret Callahan, Maureen Delany, Addison Randall, William Harrigan
'With more care, this might have been much better.' – *Variety*

His Girl Friday ****

US 1940 92m bw
Columbia (Howard Hawks)
▤ ▤
A remake of *The Front Page* (qv), with Hildy Johnson turned into a woman.
Frantic, hilarious black farce with all participants at their best; possibly the fastest comedy ever filmed, and one of the funniest.
w Charles Lederer *play* The Front Page by Charles MacArthur, Ben Hecht d Howard Hawks *ph* Joseph Walker m Sydney Cutner *md* Morris Stoloff
☆ Rosalind Russell, Cary Grant, Ralph Bellamy, Gene Lockhart, Porter Hall, Ernest Truex, Cliff Edwards, Clarence Kolb, Roscoe Karns, Frank Jenks, Abner Biberman, John Qualen, Helen Mack, Billy Gilbert and also Alma Kruger
'The kind of terrific verbal slam-bang that has vanished from current film-making.' – *New Yorker, 1975*
'One of the fastest of all movies, from line to line and from gag to gag.' – *Manny Farber, 1971*
'Overlapping dialogue carries the movie along at breakneck speed; word gags take the place of the sight gags of silent comedy, as this vanished race of brittle, cynical, childish people rush around on corrupt errands.' – *Pauline Kael, 1968*
'The main trouble is that when they made *The Front Page* the first time, it stayed made.' – *Otis Ferguson*
† The Rosalind Russell role had first been turned down by Jean Arthur, Ginger Rogers, Claudette Colbert and Irene Dunne.

His Glorious Night

US 1929 85m bw
MGM
GB title: *Breath of Scandal*
A princess falls in love with a commoner.
Soporific early talkie, remade in 1960 as A Breath of Scandal. The movie which first exposed its star's high-pitched voice and is credited with killing his career.
w Willard Mack *play* Olimpia by Ferenc Molnar d Lionel Barrymore *ph* Percy Hilburn
☆ John Gilbert, Catherine Dale Owen, Hedda Hopper, Gustav von Seyffertitz, Nance O'Neil

His Kind of Woman *

US 1951 120m bw
RKO (Howard Hughes, Robert Sparks)
▤ ▤
At a remote Mexican ranch resort, a gangster on the run holds up residents including a fortune-hunting girl and a fading matinee idol.
Agreeable tongue-in-cheek melodrama which slightly outstays its welcome but is generally good fun.
w Frank Fenton d John Farrow *ph* Harry J. Wild m Leigh Harline *md* Constantin Bakaleinikov
☆ Robert Mitchum, Jane Russell, Vincent Price, Raymond Burr, Tim Holt, Charles McGraw, Marjorie Reynolds, Jim Backus

His Lordship *

GB 1936 71m bw
Gaumont (S. C. Balcon)
US title: *Man of Affairs*
A politician's twin takes his place to expose an old murder.
Comfortable star comedy-drama.
w Maude Howell, Edwin Greenwood, L. DuGarde Peach *play* The Nelson Touch by Neil Grant d Herbert Mason *ph* Gunther Krampf *md* Louis Levy *ad* Alfred Junge
☆ George Arliss, Rene Ray, Romilly Lunge, Jessie Winter, Allan Jeayes

His Majesty Bunker Bean: see Bunker Bean

His Majesty O'Keefe

GB 1954 90m Technicolor
Warner/Norma (Harold Hecht)
Native islanders are taught by an easygoing mariner how to exploit their natural resources and defend themselves against pirates.
Thin adventure romance with too little for its star to do.
w Borden Chase, James Hill *novel* Lawrence Kingman, Gerald Green d Byron Haskin *ph* Otto Heller m Robert Farnon
☆ Burt Lancaster, Joan Rice, André Morell, Abraham Sofaer, Benson Fong, Archie Savage

His Night Out

US 1935 74m bw
Universal
A henpecked office help saves the bonds from gangsters.
Typical star farce, a remake of The Mollycoddle.
w Doris Malloy, Harry Clork d William Nigh
☆ Edward Everett Horton, Irene Hervey, Robert McWade, Jack La Rue, Willard Robertson

His Other Woman: see Desk Set

His Private Secretary

US 1933 68m bw
Showmen's/Screencraft (Al Alt)
A wealthy playboy falls for minister's granddaughter, much to his father's annoyance.
A curiosity from Wayne's early career, in which he plays a sophisticated man-about-town.
w Lewis D. Collins, Jack Natteford d Philip H. Whitman *ph* Abe Scholtz *ed* Bobby Ray
☆ John Wayne, Evelyn Knapp, Alec B. Francis, Reginald Barlow, Natalie Kingston, Arthur Hoyt, Al 'Fuzzy' St John, Hugh Kidder

'From the ends of the earth ... a darling baby brings them together!'

His Woman

US 1931 80m bw
Paramount (Albert Kaufman)
The captain of a tramp freighter finds himself in charge of an abandoned baby and a runaway girl.
Slow, indifferent comedy drama, previously filmed in 1929 as Sal of Singapore.
w Adelaide Heilbron, Melville Baker *novel* The Sentimentalist by Dale Collins d Edward Sloman *ph* William Steiner, Arthur Ellis
☆ Gary Cooper, Claudette Colbert, Averill Harris, Richard Spiro, Douglass Dumbrille, Joseph Calleia, Harry Davenport
'Actionless picture ... too many barnacles cling to the script.' – *Variety*

Une Histoire D'Amour *

France 1951 95m bw
Jacques Roitfeld/Cité Films
GB title: *Love Story*
A police inspector discovers that a young couple killed themselves because of parental opposition.
A rather soggy little drama made watchable by its careful detail and immaculate leading performance.
w Michel Audiard d Robert Clavel *ph* Louis Page m Paul Misraki
☆ Louis Jouvet, Daniel Gélin, Dany Robin

Une Histoire Inventée: see An Imaginary Tale

Histoires Extraordinaires *

France/Italy 1968 120m Eastmancolor
Les Films Marceau/Cocinor/PEA (Raymond Eger)
▤
GB title: *Tales of Mystery and Imagination*
aka: *Spirits of the Dead*
Episodic film based on three stories by Edgar Allan Poe.
Only Fellini provides entertainment, and that by abandoning all pretence to be faithful to the original, with a story about a drunken English actor working in Rome.
w Metzengerstein: Roger Vadim, Pascal Cousin, Clement Biddlewood; William Wilson: Louis Malle, Clement Biddlewood; Toby Dammit: Federico Fellini, Bernardino Zapponi *stories* Edgar Allan Poe d Metzengerstein: Roger Vadim; William Wilson: Louis Malle; Toby Dammit: Federico Fellini *ph* Metzengerstein: Claude Renoir; William Wilson: Tonino Delli Colli; Toby Dammit: Guiseppe Rotundo m Metzengerstein: Jean Prodromides; William Wilson: Diego Masson; Toby Dammit: Nino Rota *ad* William Wilson: Carlo Leva; Toby Dammit: Fabrizio Clerici *ed* Metzengerstein: Helene Plemiannikov; William Wilson: Franco Arcalli, Susanne Baron; Toby Dammit: Ruggiero Mastroianni
☆ Metzengerstein: Jane Fonda, Peter Fonda, Carla Marlier, James Robertson Justice; William Wilson: Alain Delon, Brigitte Bardot, Katia Christina; Toby Dammit: Terence Stamp, Salvo Randone

---

History Is Made at Night *

US　1937　97m　bw

Walter Wanger

A divorcee and her new love have trouble from her ex-husband.

Atmospheric, artificial, generally entertaining romantic comedy-drama of a kind which went out of fashion long ago.

w Gene Towne, Graham Baker　d Frank Borzage ph Gregg Toland　m Alfred Newman

☆ Charles Boyer, Jean Arthur, Leo Carrillo, Colin Clive

'A weird and unbelievable melodrama … mildly entertaining with good scenes.' – *Variety*

'So souped up with demonic passions and tender glances and elegant photography that it's rather fun.' – *New Yorker, 1978*

'Frank Borzage, who could turn *Frankenstein Meets the Wolf Man* into a romantic reverie, is quite undeterred by the venality rampant in the script and interjects his vision of what Andrew Sarris called love over probability. Oh, there's an iceberg disaster too.' – *Kit Parker catalogue*

The History of Mr Polly *

GB　1948　94m　bw

GFD/Two Cities (John Mills)

A draper's assistant buys a small shop but tires of his nagging wife and decides the time has come for a change.

Patchy but generally amusing version of a popular comic novel, very English and rather appealingly done.

w Anthony Pelissier　novel H. G. Wells d Anthony Pelissier　ph Desmond Dickinson m William Alwyn

☆ John Mills, Sally Ann Howes, Megs Jenkins, Finlay Currie, Betty Ann Davies, Edward Chapman

History of the World Part One

US　1981　92m　DeLuxe　Panavision

Brooksfilms (Mel Brooks)

Episodes from world history are presented with the author's usual lack of taste or wit: a woeful collection of schoolboy scatology.

wd Mel Brooks　ph Woody Omens, Paul Wilson m John Morris

☆ Mel Brooks, Dom DeLuise, Madeline Kahn, Cloris Leachman, Harvey Korman, Ron Carey, Sid Caesar, Pamela Stephenson, Henny Youngman

'Most of the time it's just expensive sets sitting around waiting for Brooks to do something funny in front of them.' – *Roger Ebert*

Hit!

US　1973　134m　Technicolor　Panavision

Paramount (Harry Korshak)

A federal agent takes personal action against a drug ring which caused his daughter's death.

Black vigilante melodrama, very violent and interminably padded out with irrelevancies.

w Alan Trustman, David M. Wolf　d Sidney J. Furie　ph John A. Alonzo　m Lalo Schifrin

☆ Billy Dee Williams, Richard Pryor, Paul Hampton, Gwen Welles

'No more under-the-armpit shots, but obscurity is still the keynote of this Sidney Furie effort in the urban vigilante genre.' – *Sight and Sound*

The Hit

GB　1984　98m　Technicolor

Zenith/Central/The Recorded Picture Company (Jeremy Thomas)

A supergrass hiding in Spain is sought by two gang executioners.

Old hat thuggery shown in new-style detail. Violently suspenseful but not otherwise interesting.

w Peter Prince　d Stephen Frears　ph Mike Molloy m Paco de Lucia　pd Andrew Sanders

☆ John Hurt, Terence Stamp, Tim Roth, Laura del Sol, Fernando Rey, Bill Hunter

'Sensitive editing and seductive camerawork can't disguise that the exercise is heading nowhere, a road movie without fuel.' – *Philip Strick, MFB*

Hit Man

US　1972　90m　colour

MGM (Gene Corman)

A professional killer returns home to avenge his brother's death.

An ineffectual reworking of the superior Get Carter, with an American setting and a black cast.

wd George Armitage　novel *Jack's Return Home* by Ted Lewis　ph Andrew Davis　m H. B. Barnum ad Lynn Griffin　ed Morton Tubor

☆ Bernie Casey, Pam Grier, Lisa Moore, Bhetty Waldron, Sam Laws, Don Diamond

Hit Me

US　1996　123m　Foto-Kem

Slough Pond (Steven Shainberg)

An ambitious hotel worker succumbs to the attentions of a mysterious woman and a petty crook.

Plodding thriller of double dealing and double-cross, not helped by miscast leads.

w Denis Johnson　novel *A Swell-Looking Babe* by Jim Thompson　d Steven Shainberg　ph Mark J. Gordon　m Phillip Manning Robinson　pd Amy Danger　ed Donn Aron

☆ Elias Koteas, Laure Marsac, Jay Leggett, Bruce Ramsay, Kevin J. O'Connor, Philip Baker Hall, J. C. Quinn, Haing S. Ngor, William H. Macy

'A bleak, rewarding film noir.' – *Lawrence van Gelder, New York Sunday Times*

The Hit Parade

US　1937　77m　bw

Republic (Nat Levin)

An agent tries to get a new star into radio.

An excuse for a line-up of acts, some quite tolerable.

w Bradford Ropes, Sam Ornitz　d Gus Meins

☆ Frances Langford, Phil Regan, Louise Henry, Pert Kelton, Al Pearce, Ed Brophy, William Demarest, Duke Ellington and his Band, Eddy Duchin and his Band, Max Terhune, Monroe Owsley, Inez Courtney, the Tic Toc Girls

'Should gather plenty of de luxe dates … the tempo guarantees that the average fan will find it diverting.' – *Variety*

Hit Parade of 1941

US　1940　83m　bw

Republic (Sol C. Siegel)

The young owner of a radio station subs his singer girlfriend for the sponsor's daughter.

Moderate musical in need of a better script.

w Bradford Ropes, F. Hugh Herbert (no relation), Maurice Leo　d John H. Auer　m Cy Feuer

☆ Kenny Baker, Frances Langford, Hugh Herbert, Mary Boland, Ann Miller, Patsy Kelly, Phil Silvers, Sterling Holloway, Donald MacBride, Barnett Parker, Franklin Pangborn, Six Hits and a Miss, Borrah Minevitch and his Harmonica Rascals

♪ Cy Feuer; song 'Who Am I?' (mJule Styne, lyWalter Bullock)

Hit Parade of 1943

US　1943　90m　bw

Republic (Albert J. Cohen)

aka: *Change of Heart*

A plagiaristic songwriter becomes a model swain.

Lively comedy musical, third and best of the series.

w Frank Gill Jnr　d Albert S. Rogell　m Walter Scharf

☆ John Carroll, Susan Hayward, Gail Patrick, Eve Arden, Melville Cooper, Walter Catlett, Mary Treen, Tom Kennedy, Dorothy Dandridge, the Golden Gate Quartet, Count Basie and his orchestra

♪ Walter Scharf; song 'Change of Heart' (mJule Styne, lyHarold Adamson)

Hit Parade of 1947

US　1947　90m　bw

Republic (Frank McDonald)

A struggling songwriter tries in vain to become sophisticated.

Tolerable musical jamboree with too thin a storyline.

w Mary Loos, Parke Levy　d Frank McDonald

☆ Eddie Albert, Constance Moore, Joan Edwards, Gil Lamb, Bill Goodwin, William Frawley, Richard Lane, Roy Rogers and Trigger, Woody Herman and his orchestra

Hit the Deck

US　1930　93m　bw (colour sequences)

RKO

Navy recruits have girl trouble.

Lumpy production of a stage musical already well worn.

wd Luther Reed　play Herbert Fields

☆ Jack Oakie, Polly Walker, Roger Gray, Harry Sweet

'No reason why this one should run into trouble on week stands or less.' – *Variety*

Hit the Deck

US　1955　112m　Eastmancolor

Cinemascope

MGM (Joe Pasternak)

Romantic adventures of three sailors on shore leave in San Francisco.

Boring situations and performances reduce the temperature of this youth musical which is not another On the Town.

w Sonya Levien, William Ludwig　novel *Shore Leave* by Hubert Osborn　musical play *Herbert Fields*　d Roy Rowland　ph George Folsey m/ly Vincent Youmans, Leo Robin　md George Stoll　ch Hermes Pan

☆ Tony Martin, Jane Powell, Ann Miller, Debbie Reynolds, Walter Pidgeon, Vic Damone, Gene Raymond

The Hitcher *

US　1986　97m　Metrocolor　Panavision

Columbia-EMI-Warner/HBO (David Bombyk, Kip Ohman)

A hitchhiker murders all those he meets, implicating a teenage driver in his crimes.

Grim little fable, maintaining a sweaty suspense to the end.

w Eric Red　d Robert Harmon　ph John Seale m Mark Isham　pd Dennis Gassner　ed Frank J. Urioste

☆ Rutger Hauer, C. Thomas Howell, Jennifer Jason Leigh, Jeffrey DeMunn, Billy Greenbush, Jack Thibeau, John Jackson

'Superior exploitation picture.' – *Nigel Floyd, MFB*

Hitch-hike Lady

US　1935　77m　bw

Republic

An English housekeeper saves enough money to visit her son in the US, not aware that he is in San Quentin.

Easy-going sentimental comedy, shot on the road.

w Gordon Rigby, Lester Cole　story Wallace MacDonald　d Aubrey Scotto

☆ Alison Skipworth, Arthur Treacher, Mae Clarke, James Ellison, Warren Hymer, Beryl Mercer

'Happy intermingling of humour and heart tugs.' – *Variety*

Hitler

US　1961　107m　bw

Three Crown/E. Charles Straus

A sex-oriented, semi-fictional biopic of the German dictator, from the murder of his niece to his final madness and suicide.

Enterprising sensationalism which deserves a nod for sheer audacity.

w Sam Neuman　d Stuart Heisler　ph Joseph Biroc m Hans Salter

☆ Richard Basehart, Maria Emo, Martin Kosleck, John Banner

Hitler – Beast of Berlin

US　1939　87m　bw

PRC

aka: *Beasts of Berlin*

A spy among Hitler's storm troopers escapes to Switzerland.

Feeble exploitation item which succeeded only as propaganda. Hitler is not seen.

w Shepard Traube　story *Goose Step* by Shepard Traube　d Sherman Scott

☆ Roland Drew, Steffi Duna, Alan Ladd, Greta Granstedt, Lucien Prival

'There are doubtless powerful pictures to be made on the anti-Nazi theme, but this isn't one.' – *Variety*

Hitler – Dead or Alive

US　1942　72m　bw

Ben Judell/Charles House

Three Alcatraz graduates try to collect a prize for the capture of Hitler.

Silly mix of farce and propaganda.

w Sam Neumann, Karl Brown　d Nick Grinde

☆ Ward Bond, Dorothy Tree, Warren Hymer, Paul Fix, Russell Hicks, Bobby Watson

'More morphine for Herr Goering! The greatest gangster picture of all!'

'Did Hitler kill the one woman he loved? What was Hess to Hitler?'

The Hitler Gang **

US　1944　101m　bw

Paramount (B. G. de Sylva)

The rise to power of Hitler and his henchmen.

Though at the time it seemed rather like a serious cabaret turn, this fictionalization of historical fact has some good impersonations and dramatically effective scenes.

w Frances Goodrich, Albert Hackett　d John Farrow　ph Ernest Laszlo　m David Buttolph

☆ Robert Watson, Martin Kosleck, Victor Varconi, Luis Van Rooten, Alexander Pope, Roman Bohnen, Ivan Triesault, Helene Thimig, Reinhold Schunzel, Sig Rumann, Alexander Granach

Hitler – The Last Ten Days

GB/Italy　1973　104m　Technicolor

MGM/Wolfgang Reinhardt/Westfilm

With Adolf and Eva in the bunker.

Claustrophobic historical reconstruction with an uncomfortable star.

w Ennio de Concini, Maria Pia Fusco, Wolfgang Reinhardt, Ivan Moffat　d Ennio de Concini ph Ennio Guarnieri　m Mischa Spoliansky

☆ Alec Guinness, Simon Ward, Doris Kunstmann, Adolfo Celi, Diane Cilento, Eric Porter, Joss Ackland

'The truth about the Nazis from the cradle to the battlefront!'

Hitler's Children *

US　1943　83m　bw

RKO (Edward A. Golden)

A family reacts to Hitler and the Hitler Youth.

Artificial melodrama set in an unlikely Germany but successful at the time because of its topicality and its refusal to play the Nazis as idiots, which was the usual Hollywood line.

w Emmet Lavery　book *Education for Death* by Gregor Ziemer　d Edward Dmytryk　ph Russell Metty　m Roy Webb

☆ Tim Holt, Bonita Granville, Otto Kruger, Kent Smith, H. B. Warner, Lloyd Corrigan, Erford Gage, Gavin Muir, Hans Conried

'A curiously compromised production … strong anti-Nazi propaganda, it has not been woven into a defined and moving show.' – *Howard Barnes, New York Herald Tribune*

Hitler's Gold: see *Inside Out*

Hitler's Hangman: see *Hitler's Madman*

Hitler's Madman *

US　1943　84m　bw

MGM/PRC (Seymour Nebenzal)

aka: *Hitler's Hangman*

Heydrich is assassinated in Czechoslovakia and the Nazis take revenge on the village of Lidice.

Cheapjack sensationalism based on a horrifying incident of World War II; despite its imperfections it generates a certain raw power.

w Peretz Hirshbein, Melvin Levy, Doris Malloy d Douglas Sirk　m Karl Hajos

☆ Patricia Morison, John Carradine, Alan Curtis, Ralph Morgan, Ludwig Stossel, Edgar Kennedy, Al Shean, Jimmy Conlin, Blanche Yurka, Victor Kilian

'Newspaper accounts of the bombing of German cities will be pleasant antidotes for the unhappy feeling brought on by the final grim scenes of *Hitler's Madman*.' – *New York Herald Tribune*

'Even in its poorly depicted scenes of brutality, it inflames a common anger.' – *Theodore Strauss, New York Times*

HMS Defiant *

GB　1962　101m　Technicolor　Cinemascope

Columbia/GW (John Brabourne)

US title: *Damn the Defiant*

Mutiny erupts on an 18th-century British sailing ship.

Rather unpleasant and unenterprising sea fare reminiscent of the goings-on aboard the Bounty. *Well*

enough staged and acted but not very remarkable or memorable.

w Nigel Kneale, Edmund H. North *novel Mutiny* by Frank Tilsley d Lewis Gilbert ph Christopher Challis m Clifton Parker

☆ Alec Guinness, Dirk Bogarde, Anthony Quayle, Tom Bell, Nigel Stock, Murray Melvin, Victor Maddern, Maurice Denham, Walter Fitzgerald

'It authentically if superficially recreates the days of press gangs, maggots and the cat.' – *Peter John Dyer*

Ho! *(dubbed)*
France/Italy 1968 107m Eastmancolor
Golden Era/Filmsonor/Marceau/Cocinor/Mega Film
aka: *Criminal Face*

A racing driver turned crook decides to go straight. The title refers to the hero's nickname of Ho.
Ho-hum drama.

w Pierre Pelegri, Lucienna Hamon, Robert Enrico *novel* José Giovanni d Robert Enrico ph Jean Boffety m François de Roubaix *ad* Jacques Saulnier *ed* Jacqueline Meppiel

☆ Jean-Paul Belmondo, Joanna Shimkus, Paul Crauchet, Stéphane Fey, Tony Taffin, Sydney Chaplin

Hobson's Choice ***
GB 1953 107m bw
British Lion/London (Norman Spencer)
🔲 ▦ ◎~

In the 1890s a tyrannical Lancashire bootmaker is brought to heel by his plain-speaking daughter and her simple-minded husband.
Brilliantly played version of a famous working-class comedy, memorably set and photographed; one regrets only the slight decline of the predictable third act.

w Norman Spencer, Wynard Browne *play* Harold Brighouse d David Lean ph Jack Hildyard m Malcolm Arnold *ad* Wilfrid Shingleton

☆ Charles Laughton, Brenda de Banzie, John Mills, Richard Wattis, Helen Haye, Daphne Anderson, Prunella Scales

† Previously filmed in 1931 by Thomas Bentley for BIP from a screenplay by Frank Launder, with James Harcourt, Viola Lyel and Frank Pettingell.
▽ best British film

Hocus Pocus
🔾 US 1993 96m Technicolor
Buena Vista/Walt Disney (David Kirschner, Steven Haft)
🔲 ▦ ◎~ ⊚ ⊚ ଘ

In Salem, three children inadvertently conjure up three wicked witches.
A mildly comic vehicle for Bette Midler, though a kiddies' film is not the best setting for her talents.

w Mick Garris, Neil Cuthbert *story* David Kirschner, Mick Garris d Kenny Ortega ph Hiro Narita m John Debney *pd* William Sandell *ed* Peter E. Berger

☆ Bette Midler, Sarah Jessica Parker, Kathy Najimy, Omri Katz, Thora Birch, Vinessa Shaw, Amanda Shepherd

'The blend of witchcraft and comedy should divert kids without driving the patience of their parents to the boiling point.' – *Variety*

Hoffa
US 1992 140m colour Panavision
TCF/Jersey (Edward R. Pressman, Danny DeVito, Caldecot Chubb)
🔲 ▦ ◎~ ଘ

An aggressive agitator for the Teamster's Union accepts the aid of gangsters and becomes its leader before mysteriously vanishing.
A creakingly old-fashioned biopic that reaches few conclusions and makes no judgements.

w David Mamet d Danny DeVito ph Stephen H. Burum m David Newman *pd* Ida Random *ed* Lynzee Klingman, Ronald Roose

☆ Jack Nicholson, Danny DeVito, Armand Assante, J. T. Walsh, John C. Reilly, Frank Whaley, Kevin Anderson, John P. Ryan, Robert Prosky, Cliff Gorman

'As is so often the case with biopics that attempt to convey decades, something gets sacrificed. Here, it's a human drama one can relate to.' – *Variety*
▷ Stephen H. Burum

'Hope never dies for a man with a good dirty mind.'

Hoffman
GB 1970 113m Technicolor
ABP/Longstone (Ben Arbeid)
🔲

A middle-aged misfit blackmails a typist into spending a week with him.
Interminable sex comedy padded out from a short TV play; it quickly becomes claustrophobic, tasteless, and boring.

w Ernest Gebler *play* Ernest Gebler *novel* Ernest Gebler d Alvin Rakoff ph Gerry Turpin m Ron Grainer

☆ Peter Sellers, Sinead Cusack, Jeremy Bulloch, Ruth Dunning

Hog Wild ***
🔾 US 1930 20m bw
Hal Roach
🔲

Stan helps Ollie to put a radio aerial on the roof of his house.
Brilliantly sustained slapstick makes this one of the best star comedies of Laurel and Hardy.

w H. M. Walker, Leo McCarey d James Parrott ph George Stevens *ed* Richard Currier

☆ Stan Laurel, Oliver Hardy, Fay Holderness, Dorothy Granger

Hohenfeuer: see *Alpine Fire*

Hol Volt, Hol Nem Volt...: see *A Hungarian Fairy Tale*

The Holcroft Covenant
GB 1985 112m colour
EMI/Ely and Edie Landau
▦ ◎~ ⊚

One of the architects of Hitler's Third Reich leaves a bequest which may fall into the wrong hands.
Muddled political thriller which tends to provoke unintended laughs.

w George Axelrod, Edward Anhalt, John Hopkins *novel* Robert Ludlum d John Frankenheimer ph Gerry Fisher m Stanislas *pd* Peter Mullins

☆ Michael Caine, Anthony Andrews, Victoria Tennant, Lilli Palmer, Mario Adorf, Michael Lonsdale, Bernard Hepton

'A narrative deficient in thrills or plausibility.' – *Variety*

'Master of love! He is to all women what each desires him to be!'

Hold Back the Dawn *
US 1941 115m bw
Paramount (Arthur Hornblow Jnr)

A would-be immigrant into the US via Mexico marries a schoolteacher he does not love.
Surprisingly effective romantic melodrama with a nice style and some mordant lines in the script.

w Charles Brackett, Billy Wilder d Mitchell Leisen ph Leo Tover m Victor Young *ad* Hans Dreier, Robert Usher

☆ Charles Boyer, Olivia de Havilland, Paulette Goddard, Victor Francen, Walter Abel, Curt Bois, Rosemary de Camp, Nestor Paiva, Mitchell Leisen

'All those years with all the others I closed my eyes and thought of you.' – *sample dialogue spoken by Paulette Goddard*

'It has all the vitamins for mass popular appeal.' – *Variety*

† The story is told by Boyer to Mitchell Leisen on a film set where he has just shot a scene from *I Wanted Wings.*

⨂ best picture; Charles Brackett, Billy Wilder; Leo Tover; Victor Young; Olivia de Havilland; art direction

Hold Back the Night
US 1956 80m bw
Allied Artists

From World War II to Korea, a marine commander carries with him a lucky whisky bottle.
Pointlessly titled war heroics, competently mounted.

w John C. Higgins, Walter Doniger *novel* Pat Frank d Allan Dwan ph Ellsworth J. Fredricks m Hans Salter

☆ John Payne, Mona Freeman, Peter Graves, Chuck Connors, Audrey Dalton

---

'It's hard to keep yourself a secret.'

Hold Back the Night
GB/Italy 1999 104m DeLuxe
UIP/Film Consortium/Film4/Arts Council/BIM/Wave/Parallax (Sally Hibbin)

A teenage girl runs away from home and teams up with an environmental activist and a elderly lesbian who is dying from cancer.
A small-scale, gritty road movie with revelations of sexual abuse and parental estrangement along the way; it has nothing fresh to say.

w Steve Chambers d Phil Davis ph Cinders Forshaw m Peter John Vettese *pd* Chris Roope *ed* Adam Ross

☆ Christine Tremarco, Stuart Sinclair Blyth, Sheila Hancock, Richard Platt, Julie Ann Watson, Kenneth Colley, Tommy Tiernan, Andrew Livingstone

'Maladroit, and baffingly without the conviction, sophistication or production values you would expect from the most ordinary television drama.' – *Peter Bradshaw, Guardian*

Hold Back Tomorrow
US 1956 75m bw
Universal-International (Hugo Haas)

A convicted killer's last request is for a woman to spend his last night with him. They fall in love before he is executed.
A ripe example of the higher tosh, indifferently made and acted.

wd Hugo Haas

☆ Cleo Moore, John Agar, Frank de Kova, Dallas Boyd

Hold Everything
US 1930 78m Technicolor
Warner

A comedian becomes a prizefighter.
Pleasant comedy musical which established Joe E. Brown in Hollywood, as it had established Bert Lahr on stage.

w Robert Lord *play* B. G. De Sylva, John McGowan d Roy del Ruth

☆ Joe E. Brown, Winnie Lightner, Georges Carpentier, Sally O'Neil, Bert Roach

'Pip laugh picture, the best comedy Warners has turned out since talkers came in.' – *Variety*

Hold Me Thrill Me Kiss Me *
US 1992 92m Foto-Kem
Art House/Mad Dog (Travis Swords)
🔲 ▦ ◎~

A burglar, on the run from a shotgun marriage in which he accidentally shot the bride, ends up in a trailer park with a jealous stripper and her virginal sister.
This attempt by its director to add sex and violence to the screwball comedy genre is intermittently amusing, but needed defter comic timing from its cast to succeed.

wd Joel Hershman ph Kent Wakeford m Gerald Gouriet *pd* Dominic Wymark *ed* Kathryn Himoff

☆ Sean Young, Max Parrish, Diane Ladd, Adrienne Shelly, Andrea Naschak, Timothy Leary, Bela Lehoczky, Ania Suli

'Crazed, larger than life and great fun.' – *Empire*

Hold My Hand
GB 1938 76m bw
Associated British (Walter C. Mycroft)

A businessman is engaged to an aristocrat's daughter but marries his secretary instead.
Routine light comedy with a few songs that must have worked better on the stage. It ends with one of the most absurd dance sequences on film.

w Clifford Grey, Bert Lee, William Freshman *play* Stanley Lupino d Thornton Freeland ph Otto Kanturek *md* Harry Acres *ad* Ian White *ed* E. B. Jarvis

☆ Stanley Lupino, Fred Emney, Syd Walker, Barbara Blair, Sally Gray, Polly Ward, Bertha Belmore, Jack Melford, John Wood

Hold That Blonde
US 1945 75m bw
Paramount (Paul Jones)

A psychiatrist suggests that romance may cure a kleptomaniac, but the patient unfortunately chooses a jewel thief.
Thin comedy which erupts into frantic farce, with some energetic slapstick and a Harold Lloyd style finale.

w Walter de Leon, Earl Baldwin, E. Edwin Moran d George Marshall ph Daniel L. Fapp m Werner Heymann

---

☆ Eddie Bracken, Veronica Lake, Albert Dekker, Frank Fenton, George Zucco, Donald MacBride, Norma Varden, Willie Best

Hold That Co-Ed *
US 1938 80m bw
TCF (David Hempstead)
GB title: *Hold That Girl*

A girl dressed as a boy wins a university football match and thereby helps a governor get re-elected.
Intriguingly-cast crazy comedy which works up into a fine frenzy.

w Karl Tunberg, Don Ettlinger, Jack Yellen d George Marshall ph Robert Planck *md* Arthur Lange

☆ John Barrymore, Joan Davis, George Murphy, Marjorie Weaver, Jack Haley, George Barbier, Donald Meek, Johnny Downs, Guinn Williams

'On the wacky side and fairly amusing, but not quite making the big league.' – *Variety*

Hold That Ghost *
US 1941 86m bw
Universal (Burt Kelly, Glenn Tryon)
▦

A group of strangers are stranded in an apparently haunted house.
Long thought of as Abbott and Costello's best comedy, this now seems pretty strained and slow to start, but it has its classic moments.

w Robert Lees, Fred Rinaldo, John Grant d Arthur Lubin ph Elwood Bredell, Joe Valentine m Hans Salter

☆ Bud Abbott, Lou Costello, Joan Davis, the Andrews Sisters, Richard Carlson, Ted Lewis and his band, Evelyn Ankers, Marc Lawrence, Mischa Auer

Hold That Girl: see *Hold That Co-Ed*

Hold That Kiss
US 1938 75m bw
MGM

A man and woman each believe the other to be wealthy.
Elementary comedy of misunderstandings, of no abiding interest.

w Stanley Rauh d Edwin L. Marin

☆ Maureen O'Sullivan, Dennis O'Keefe, Mickey Rooney, George Barbier, Jessie Ralph, Ed Brophy

'Pleasant but undistinguished.' – *Variety*

Hold Your Man *
US 1933 89m bw
MGM (Sam Wood)

A hard boiled young woman falls for a confidence man, has his baby, and waits for him to emerge from prison.
Briskly-fashioned star comedy-drama with entertaining moments.

w Anita Loos, Howard Emmett Rogers d Sam Wood ph Harold Rosson *m/ly* Nacio Herb Brown, Arthur Freed

☆ Jean Harlow, Clark Gable, Stuart Erwin, Dorothy Burgess, Muriel Kirkland, Paul Hurst

'A real money picture … most promising box office prospect in months.' – *Variety*
'The sudden transition from wise-cracking romance to sentimental penitence provides a jolt.' – *Frank S. Nugent*

The Hole: see *Onibaba (1964)*

The Hole *
France/Italy 1959 123m bw
Play-Art/Filmsonor/Titanus (Serge Silberman)
original title: *Le Trou*

Four convicts in a Paris prison dig a tunnel to freedom and almost make it.
Meticulous escape drama nicely shot in very limited sets; hypnotic for those with the patience to adjust to its pace.

w Jacques Becker, José Giovanni, Jean Aurel *novel* José Giovanni d Jacques Becker ph Ghislain Cloquet

☆ Philippe Leroy, Marc Michel, Jean Kéraudy, Michel Constantin

---

A Hole in the Head *

US 1959 120m DeLuxe Cinemascope
UA/Sincap (Frank Sinatra)
🇺🇸

A Miami hotelier is threatened with foreclosure
and tries to raise the money from his provident
elder brother.
*Easy-going comedy without much point, but various
amusing facets artfully deployed.*
w Arnold Shulman *play* Arnold Shulman
d Frank Capra *ph* William H. Daniels *m* Nelson
Riddle
☆ Frank Sinatra, Edward G. Robinson, Eleanor
Parker, Edward Hodges, Carolyn Jones, Thelma
Ritter, Keenan Wynn, Joi Lansing
👤 song 'High Hopes' (mJimmy Van Heusen,
lySammy Cahn)

The Hole in the Wall

US 1929 73m bw
Paramount
A gangster falls for a phony fortune teller on a
revenge scheme.
*Involved melodrama, a primitive talkie notable chiefly
for its stars.*
w Pierre Collings *play* Fred Jackson *d* Robert
Florey *ph* George Folsey
☆ Edward G. Robinson, Claudette Colbert, David
Newell, Nelly Savage, Donald Meek, Louise
Closser Hale

Holiday *

US 1930 99m bw
Pathé (E. B. Derr)
A bright-minded rich girl steals her sister's fiancé, a
struggling young lawyer.
Competent early talkie version of a hit play.
w Horace Jackson *play* Philip Barry *d* Edward H.
Griffith *ph* Norbert Brodine *m* Josiah Zuro
☆ Ann Harding, Robert Ames, Mary Astor,
Edward Everett Horton, Hedda Hopper, Monroe
Owsley, William Holden
'A comedy of wide appeal in a finished style.' –
Variety
👤 Horace Jackson; Ann Harding

'So daring – so tender – so human – so true – that
everyone in love will want to see it!'

Holiday *

US 1938 93m bw
Columbia (Everett Riskin)
🎬 🇺🇸 📀
GB titles: *Free to Live*
aka: *Unconventional Linda*
A man becomes engaged to a millionaire's
daughter but discovers that he loves her
unconventional suster.
*Elegant, highly successful remake; still a stage play on
film, but subtly devised to make the very most of the
lines and performances. Horton played the same role in
both versions.*
w Donald Ogden Stewart *d* George Cukor *ph* Franz
Planer *m* Sidney Cutner *ad* Stephen Goosson,
Lionel Banks
☆ Katharine Hepburn, Cary Grant, Doris Nolan,
Edward Everett Horton, Ruth Donnelly, Lew Ayres,
Henry Kolker, Binnie Barnes
'Corking comedy ... exhibitors will pencil in
some extra days.' – *Variety*
'The comedy is full of the best of humour, edged
with pathos never allowed to drop into
sentimentality. It is played with the greatest
cheerfulness and a winning skill.' – *Arthur
Pollock, Brooklyn Daily Eagle*
'I suppose actually it is a neat and sometimes
elegant job, but under its surface of too much
brightness and too many words it seems so
deadly bored and weary. Hell, save your money
and yawn at home.' – *Otis Ferguson*
'Played with the greatest cheerfulness and a
winning skill.' – *Brooklyn Daily Eagle*
👤 art direction

Holiday Affair

US 1949 87m bw
RKO (Don Hartman)
A young widow falls for an easy-going boat builder.
Flimsy star-shaped romantic comedy with nice touches.
w Isobel Lennart *story* Christmas Gift by John D.
Weaver *d* Don Hartman *ph* Milton Krasner
m Roy Webb *ad* Albert D'Agostino, Carroll
Clark *ed* Harry Marker

☆ Robert Mitchum, Janet Leigh, Wendell Corey,
Griff Barnett, Esther Dale, Gordon Gebert, Henry
O'Neill, Harry Morgan

Holiday Camp *

GB 1947 97m bw
GFD/Gainsborough (Sydney Box)
At a summer holiday camp, a murderer on the
prowl affects people's enjoyment in various ways.
*Seminal compendium comedy drama, a bore in itself
but establishing several post-war norms of the British
cinema, including the Huggetts.*
w Muriel and Sydney Box, Ted Willis, Peter
Rogers, Mabel and Denis Constanduros
story Godfrey Winn *d* Ken Annakin *ph* Jack
Cox *m* Bob Busby
☆ Jack Warner, Kathleen Harrison, Flora Robson,
Dennis Price, Hazel Court, Emrys Jones, Yvonne
Owen, Esmond Knight, Jimmy Hanley, Peter
Hammond, Esma Cannon, John Blythe, Susan
Shaw
'It is real – and true – and it will be a smash at
the box office.' – *Sunday Chronicle*

Holiday for Henrietta: see *La Fête à Henriette*

Holiday for Lovers

US 1959 103m DeLuxe Cinemascope
TCF (David Weisbart)
To distract his teenage daughter from boys, a
Boston psychiatrist organizes a family holiday in
South America.
*Frail old-fashioned family comedy with entirely
predictable situations culminating in a drunk scene for
stuffy father.*
w Luther Davis *d* Henry Levin *ph* Charles G.
Clarke *m* Leigh Harline
☆ Clifton Webb, Jane Wyman, Paul Henreid,
Carol Lynley, Jill St John, Gary Crosby, José Greco

Holiday for Sinners

US 1952 72m bw
MGM (John Houseman)
In New Orleans during the Mardi Gras three old
friends meet crises in their lives.
*Slightly curious but not very interesting portmanteau
drama.*
w A. I. Bezzerides *novel* Hamilton Basso
d Gerald Mayer *ph* Paul Vogel *md* Alberto
Colombo
☆ Gig Young, Keenan Wynn, Janice Rule,
Richard Anderson, William Campbell, Michael
Chekhov, Sandro Giglio, Edith Barrett, Porter Hall
'It gives an impression of blurred, rather heavy-
going sincerity.' – *MFB*

Holiday in Mexico

US 1946 127m Technicolor
MGM (Joe Pasternak)
The daughter of the American Ambassador to
Mexico falls for Jose Iturbi.
*Travel brochure musical in which the occasional plums
do not redeem the sogginess of the pudding.*
w Isobel Lennart *d* George Sidney *ph* Harry
Stradling *m* André Previn
☆ Walter Pidgeon, Ilona Massey, Jane Powell, Jose
Iturbi, Roddy McDowall

Holiday in Spain: see *Scent of Mystery*

Holiday Inn **

US 1942 101m bw
Paramount (Mark Sandrich)
🎬 🇺🇸 📀
The joint proprietors of a roadhouse hotel love the
same girl.
*Plain, simple-minded musical which provided a peg for
pleasant performances and good numbers. It hit the
box-office spot, especially as it introduced 'White
Christmas'.*
w Claude Binyon, Elmer Rice *d* Mark Sandrich
ph David Abel *m/ly* Irving Berlin *md* Robert
Emmett Dolan
☆ Bing Crosby, Fred Astaire, Walter Abel,
Marjorie Reynolds, Virginia Dale, Louise Beavers,
Irving Bacon, James Bell
'The best musical drama of the year.' – *New York
Post*
† Marjorie Reynolds was dubbed by Martha Mears
👤 song 'White Christmas'
👤 original story (Irving Berlin); Robert Emmett
Dolan

Holiday on the Buses

GB 1973 85m Technicolor
MGM-EMI/Hammer (Ronald Wolfe, Ronald Chesney)
After losing their jobs on the buses, two drivers
and an inspector find work at a holiday camp.
*Tired sitcom spin-off in which the cast go half-heartedly
through their familiar, poorly timed slapstick routines.*
w Ronald Wolfe, Ronald Chesney from their TV
series *d* Bryan Izzard *ph* Brian Probyn *m* Denis
King *ad* Don Picton *ed* James Needs
☆ Reg Varney, Stephen Lewis, Doris Hare,
Michael Robbins, Anna Karen, Bob Grant, Wilfrid
Brambell, Arthur Mullard, Henry McGee
'The only concession Wolfe and Chesney have
made to avoid being accused of compiling the
entire scripts from old Carry On situations
involves a subsidiary romance between Doris
Hare and Wilfred Brambell. One could probably
conceive of a more revolting spectacle than
Brambell panting after Miss Hare and making
jokes about cutting notches on his walking stick,
but nothing comes immediately to mind.' –
David McGillivray, Films and Filming

Holidays on the River Yarra

Australia 1990 88m colour
Jungle Pictures/AFC/Film Victoria (Fiona Cochrane)
In Melbourne, two young petty thieves, one
violent and the other ineffectual, try to raise
money to join a group of white supremacists who
plan to overthrow the government of an African
island.
*The one live song – 'Defecate on My Face', performed
by TISM – sets the tone of this downbeat account of
alienated youth; it may have local resonance, but lacks
international appeal.*
wd Leo Berkeley *ph* Brendan Lavelle *m* Sam
Mallet *ad* Margaret Eastgate, Adele Flere *ed* Leo
Berkeley
☆ Craig Adams, Luke Elliot, Alexander Menglet,
Tahir Cambis, Claudia Karvan, Ian Scott, Sheryl
Munks, Angela McKenna

'Not All Marriages Are Made In Heaven.'

Hollow Reed

GB/Germany 1996 106m Rank Colour
Film Four/Scala/Senator/Channel 4 (Elizabeth Karlsen)
🎬 🇺🇸 🎧
A gay father, who discovers that his ex-wife's new
lover is physically abusing their son, attempts to
gain custody of the boy.
*Harsh-toned, old-fashioned problem film that muddles
its message.*
w Paula Milne *story* Neville Bolt *d* Angela Pope
ph Remi Adefarasin *m* Anne Dudley *pd* Stuart
Walker *ed* Sue Wyatt
☆ Martin Donovan, Joely Richardson, Ian Hart,
Jason Flemyng, Sam Bould, Edward Hardwicke,
Douglas Hodge, Annette Badland
'A truly disquieting experience because it packs
its punch in simple, formal fashion. One cannot
be unmoved by the pain at the story's center,
especially when it's caused by good intentions.' –
Leonard Klady, Variety

Hollow Triumph: see *The Scar*

The Holly and the Ivy *

GB 1952 83m bw
British Lion/London (Anatole de Grunwald)
Christmas brings family revelations in a remote
Norfolk rectory.
*A badly-filmed stage success which succeeds because of
its performances.*
w Anatole de Grunwald *play* Wynard Browne
d George More O'Ferrall *ph* Ted Scaife
m Malcolm Arnold
☆ Ralph Richardson, Celia Johnson, Margaret
Leighton, Denholm Elliott, John Gregson, Hugh
Williams, Margaret Halstan, Maureen Delany,
William Hartnell, Robert Flemyng, Roland Culver
'This type of direct translation to the screen,
using none of the cinema's resources, can only
do harm to the play itself.' – *Penelope Houston*

Hollywood and Vine

US 1945 59m bw
PRC (Leon Fromkess)
GB title: *Daisy Goes to Hollywood*
A New York writer is ordered to Hollywood to
script a film for a dog.
Mild satire which works in fits and starts.
w Edith Watkins, Charles Williams *d* Alexis
Thurn-Taxis

☆ James Ellison, Wanda McKay, June Clyde,
Ralph Morgan, Emmett Lynn, Franklin Pangborn,
Leon Belasco

Hollywood Boulevard *

US 1936 75m bw
Paramount (A. M. Botsford)
A washed-up Hollywood actor writes a sensational
memoir for publication, but lives to regret it.
*Entertaining melodrama with famous names in bit
parts.*
w Marguerite Roberts *d* Robert Florey *ph* Karl
Struss *m* Gregory Stone
☆ John Halliday, Marsha Hunt, Robert Cummings,
C. Henry Gordon, Frieda Inescort, Esther Dale;
and Gary Cooper, Francis X. Bushman, Maurice
Costello, Mae Marsh, Charles Ray, Jane Novak,
Bryant Washburn, Jack Mulhall, Creighton Hale,
Bert Roach
'A pretty hoary melodrama and a slight enough
excuse for a whole series of homilies upon the
uncertainty of fame and fortune in the glamour
city.' – *New York Times*

Hollywood Boulevard

US 1977 83m colour
New World (Jon Davison)
🇺🇸
An inexperienced actress goes to work for makers
of low-budget exploitation movies with violent
results.
*Bizarre action film spoof, with dialogue and a slim
narrative added to action sequences taken from
previous Roger Corman movies; it will mainly interest
fans of Corman or of the other talents involved.*
w Patrick Hobby *d* Allan Arkush, Joe Dante
ph Jamie Anderson *m* Andrew Stein *ad* Jack
DeWolfe *ed* Allan Arkush, Joe Dante, Amy Jones
☆ Candice Rialson, Mary Woronov, Rita George,
Jeffrey Kramer, Dick Miller, Paul Bartel, Jonathan
Kaplan, Charles B. Griffith
† The film began as a bet which Davison made
with Roger Corman that he could produce a
picture for $90,000, which was less than any other
New World movie, providing he could use stock
footage from other Corman productions. It was
shot in ten days at a cost of $80,000.

Hollywood Canteen *

US 1944 123m bw
Warner (Alex Gottlieb)
🇺🇸 📀
The stars give their evenings to entertaining
soldiers.
*Shoddily made but sociologically fascinating record of
Hollywood doing its bit in World War II.*
wd Delmer Daves *ph* Bert Glennon *m* Ray
Heindorf *md* Leo F. Forbstein
☆ Joan Leslie, Robert Hutton, Dane Clark, Janis
Paige; and The Andrews Sisters, Jack Benny, Joe E.
Brown, Eddie Cantor, Joan Crawford, Bette Davis,
John Garfield, Sydney Greenstreet, Paul Henreid,
Peter Lorre, Ida Lupino, Dennis Morgan and also
Roy Rogers, S. Z. Sakall, Alexis Smith, Barbara
Stanwyck, Jane Wyman, etc etc
'The corporal steps slowly backwards, in his eyes
that look of glazed ecstasy which Jennifer Jones
wore all through The Song of Bernadette. He has
just been kissed by Joan Leslie.' – *Richard
Winnington*
'To be perfectly blunt about it, this film seems a
most distasteful show of Hollywood's sense of its
own importance.' – *New York Times*
👤 Ray Heindorf; song 'Sweet Dreams, Sweetheart'
(mM. K. Jerome, lyTed Koehler)

'It does for the motion picture what Alexander's
Ragtime Band did for popular music!'

Hollywood Cavalcade *

US 1939 96m Technicolor
TCF (Harry Joe Brown)
The career of an old-time Hollywood producer.
*A lively first half with amusing re-staging of early
slapstick comedies gives way depressingly to personal
melodrama, but there is enough historical interest to
preserve the balance.*
w Ernest Pascal *d* Irving Cummings *ph* Allen M.
Davey, Ernest Palmer *m* David Raksin, David
Buttolph, Cyril Mockridge *md* Louis Silvers
ad Richard Day, Wiard B. Ihnen
☆ Don Ameche, Alice Faye, J. Edward Bromberg,
Alan Curtis, Stuart Erwin, Jed Prouty, Buster
Keaton, Donald Meek, and the original Keystone
Kops

◎ Digital Video Disc   ◉ Digital Video Disc   🎧 Soundtrack released   ☆ Cast in approximate   † Points of interest   🎵 Notable songs   🏆 Academy Award   👤 Academy Award nomination   🏆 BAFTA
Region 2   Region 1   on compact disc   order of importance

'Surefire ... should score heavily in theatres of every type.' – *Variety*

† Alice Faye did not sing. The Keystone Kops sequence was directed by Mal St Clair. The Ameche/Faye characters were supposedly based on Mack Sennett and Mabel Normand; Mack Sennett's appearance under his own name seemed to be an effort to throw people off the scent.

Hollywood Cowboy: see *Hearts of the West*

Hollywood Hotel
US   1938   109m   bw
Warner (Sam Bischoff)
A Hollywood radio show has its problems.
Half-hearted, overlong Warner musical with little of the expected zip.
w Jerry Wald, Maurice Leo, Richard Macaulay d Busby Berkeley ph Charles Rosher, George Barnes m/ly Johnny Mercer, Richard Whiting
☆ Dick Powell, Rosemary Lane, Lola Lane, Hugh Herbert, Ted Healy, Glenda Farrell, Louella Parsons, Alan Mowbray, Frances Langford, Allyn Joslyn, Benny Goodman, Edgar Kennedy

Hollywood or Bust
US   1956   95m   Technicolor   Vistavision
Paramount/Hal Wallis
Two halfwits win a car and drive across country to Hollywood.
Dopey comedy with more misses than hits; the last film of Martin and Lewis as a team.
w Erna Lazarus d Frank Tashlin ph Daniel Fapp m Walter Scharf
☆ Dean Martin, Jerry Lewis, Pat Crowley, Maxie Rosenbloom, Anita Ekberg

Hollywood Party
US   1934   68m   bw (Technicolor sequence)
MGM (Harry Rapf, Howard Dietz)
▦
A mad Russian throws a party which ends in disaster.
Dismal 'all-star' comedy relieved by guest appearances.
w Howard Dietz, Arthur Kober d (uncredited) Richard Boleslawski, Allan Dwan, Roy Rowland, George Stevens ph James Wong Howe m/ly Rodgers, Hart and others ed George Boemler
☆ Laurel and Hardy, Jimmy Durante, Lupe Velez, Charles Butterworth, Eddie Quillan, Ted Healy and the Stooges, Polly Moran
'A big short ... averagely passable screen divertissement.' – *Variety*
'The picture hardly rates the time and money that MGM has expended.' – *Hollywood Reporter*
† The film was dogged by disaster and was in production for a year. At least eight directors were involved, but no one wanted a credit on the finished film.

The Hollywood Revue of 1929 **
US   1929   116m   bw (part Technicolor)
MGM (Harry Rapf)
◎
A variety show featuring most of MGM's talent in slightly surprising acts, this is something of a bore to sit through but an archival must; and just occasionally it boasts surprising vitality.
w Al Boasberg, Robert E. Hopkins d Charles F. Reisner ph John Arnold, Irving Ries, Maximilian Fabian m/ly various ch Sammy Lee
☆ Jack Benny, Buster Keaton, Joan Crawford, John Gilbert, Norma Shearer, Laurel and Hardy, Marion Davies, Marie Dressler, William Haines, Lionel Barrymore, Conrad Nagel, Bessie Love, Cliff Edwards, Nils Asther
⚐ best picture

Hollywood Shuffle *
US   1987   82m   colour
Samuel Goldwyn Company/Conquering Unicorn (Robert Townsend)
▦ ▤ ◎
A young black actor looks for work in films.
A loosely connected series of satirical sketches that provide fun at the expense of current movie genres and the stereotyping of black actors as gangsters or pimps.
w Robert Townsend, Keenen Ivory Wayans d Robert Townsend ph Peter Deming m Patrice Rushen, Udi Harpaz ad Melba Katzman Farquhar ed W. O. Garrett
☆ Robert Townsend, Anne-Marie Johnson, Starletta Dupois, Helen Martin, Craigus R. Johnson, John Witherspoon, Keenen Ivory Wayans, Jimmy Woodard

'Scattershot humor misses as much as it hits.' – *Variety*

Hollywood Speaks
US   1932   71m   bw
Columbia
A Los Angeles columnist exposes Hollywood corruption.
Superficial exploitation piece of no interest apart from glimpses of studios.
w Norman Krasna, Jo Swerling d Eddie Buzzell
☆ Pat O'Brien, Genevieve Tobin, Lucien Prival, Rita Leroy
'Its field is really the split weeks ... good bet for the less educated clientele.' – *Variety*

Hollywood Story *
US   1951   76m   bw
U-I (Leonard Goldstein)
A young producer solves a 20-year-old studio murder mystery.
Adequate potboiler with a reasonably absorbing plot and glimpses of silent stars.
w Frederick Kohner, Fred Brady d William Castle ph Carl Guthrie m Joseph Gershenson
☆ Richard Conte, Julie Adams, Richard Egan, Henry Hull, Fred Clark, Jim Backus, Paul Cavanagh; and Francis X. Bushman, William Farnum, Betty Blythe, Helen Gibson, Joel McCrea

Holocaust 2000
GB/Italy   1977   102m   Technicolor Technovision
Rank/Aston/Embassy (Edmondo Amati)
▤
aka: *The Chosen*
The executive in charge of a thermonuclear plant in the Middle East is drawn into a legend about the rebirth of the anti-Christ, and discovers that the evil one is his own son.
Extraordinary mishmash of horror, religiosity and social conscience which scarcely works on any level.
w Sergio Donati, Alberto de Martino, Michael Robson d Alberto de Martino ph Erico Menczer m Ennio Morricone
☆ Kirk Douglas, Simon Ward, Agostina Belli, Anthony Quayle, Virginia McKenna, Spiros Focas, Alexander Knox, Adolfo Celi
'The wildest farrago yet to have come out of the demonology genre.' – *Richard Combs, MFB*

Holy Man
US   1998   114m   Technicolor   Panavision
Buena Vista/Touchstone/Caravan (Roger Birnbaum, Stephen Herek)
▦ ▤ ◎ ◯
A programmer for a TV shopping station discovers a guru who sends ratings and sales figures soaring.
Glib but toothless satire of rampant commercialism.
w Tom Schulman d Stephen Herek ph Adrian Biddle m Alan Silvestri pd Andrew McAlpine ed Trudy Ship
☆ Eddie Murphy, Jeff Goldblum, Kelly Preston, Robert Loggia, Jon Cryer, Eric McCormack, Sam Kitchin, Robert Small, Marc Macaulay, Morgan Fairchild, Nino Cerruti
'Pulls its punches and winds up caught up in the sort of half-truths it chastises.' – *Leonard Klady, Variety*

Holy Matrimony *
US   1943   87m   bw
TCF (Nunnally Johnson)
A famous painter comes back from exile for a knighthood; but when his valet dies of pneumonia, has him buried as himself in Westminster Abbey.
Slightly stilted but generally warmly amusing version of a favourite novel, with excellent star performances.
w Nunnally Johnson novel *Buried Alive* by Arnold Bennett d John Stahl ph Lucien Ballard m Cyril Mockridge
☆ Monty Woolley, Gracie Fields, Laird Cregar, Eric Blore, Una O'Connor
'A pleasant hour and a half, very well produced and acted.' – *James Agate*
⚐ Nunnally Johnson

Holy Matrimony
US   1994   93m   CFI color
Buena Vista/Interscope/Polygram/Aurora (William Stuart, David Madden, Diane Nabatoff)
▦ ▤ ◎
A woman on the run from a robbery takes refuge in a Hutterite community where her husband has

hidden the money and, after his death, marries his 12-year-old brother while she searches for the loot.
Mind-bogglingly silly comedy that is unlikely to appeal to any age group.
w David Weisberg, Douglas S. Cook d Leonard Nimoy ph Bobby Bukowski m Bruce Broughton pd Edward Pisoni ed Peter E. Berger
☆ Patricia Arquette, Joseph Gordon-Levitt, Armin Mueller-Stahl, Tate Donovan, Lois Smith, John Schuck, Courtney B. Vance
'An unfunny, unholy mess.' – *Guardian*

'Journey into temptation, but be sure you know your way back.'
Holy Smoke *
US   1999   114m   colour
Film4/Miramax (Jan Chapman)
◉
An American expert is hired to deprogram a young Australian woman who has become a member of a cult headed by an Indian guru.
A topical subject is explored in depth, with every approach to life equally questioned, but along the way, with its concentration on the relationship between Keitel and Winslet, the impetus is lost and most of the questions raised remain unanswered.
w Anna Campion, Jane Campion d Jane Campion ph Dion Beebe m Angelo Badalamenti pd Janet Patterson ed Veronika Jenet
☆ Kate Winslet, Harvey Keitel, Pam Grier, Julie Hamilton, Sophie Lee, Daniel Wyllie, Paul Goddard, Tim Robertson, George Mangos
'There's something persuasive about being in the hands of such an uncompromising filmmaker who refuses to take a predictable course or make things easy by over-explaining.' – *David Rooney, Variety*
'It is an immense, emotional, engrossing film that nevertheless wears its brilliance casually.' – *Stella Bruzzi, Sight and Sound*

Holy Terror: see *Communion (1978)*

The Holy Terror
👫 US   1937   66m   bw
TCF
A child is a mischief-maker at a naval air station.
Lightweight star vehicle for Shirley Temple's only competitor.
w Lou Breslow, John Patrick d James Tinling
☆ Jane Withers, Tony Martin, Leah Ray, Joan Davis, El Brendel, John Eldredge
'Nicely paced for laughs ... strong dual bill attraction.' – *Variety*

The Holy Virgin versus The Evil Dead
Hong Kong   1990   90m   colour
T & M
▦
A university professor is accused of murdering his students after they are attacked at a night-time picnic by a supernatural being, a worshipper of a moustachioed Cambodian goddess.
Gruesome horror-cum-martial arts movie in various cinematic styles, with a little time out for sex; it is unlikely to be found erotic by many, since the nudity is usually accompanied by violent death. The subtitles manage to mix idioms, as in 'You'll get into hot water if you fall into me, got it?'
d Choy Fat (Wang Zhen-Yi)
☆ Donnie Yen, Ken Lo, Pauline Wong, Hui Hoi Chung, Lam Wei Lan
'You'll probably need to lie down in a darkened room for half an hour after this one!' – *The Dark Side*
† It was one of the first films to be issued with Hong Kong's Category III rating (equivalent to the British 18 certificate) because of its sex and nudity.

Homage
US   1995   96m   Foto-Kem
Arrow/Skyline (Mark Medoff, Elan Sassoon)
▤
A postgraduate mathematician, working as a caretaker on a widow's small farm, begins an affair with her visiting daughter, a drug-addicted TV star.
Uninvolving domestic drama of three unlovely people: its documentary direct-to-camera approach of TV news broadcasts is at odds with the directorial style, full of flamboyant little distracting flourishes.
w Mark Medoff play *The Homage that Follows* by Mark Medoff d Ross Kagan Marks ph Tom Richmond m W. G. Snuffy Walden pd Amy B. Ancona ed Kevin Tent

☆ Blythe Danner, Frank Whaley, Sheryl Lee, Danny Nucci, Bruce Davison
'Story provides no rooting interest, and the creepiness of the material tries one's patience.' – *Variety*

Hombre **
US   1967   111m   DeLuxe   Panavision
TCF/Hombre Productions (Martin Ritt, Irving Ravetch)
▤ ◎
Stagecoach passengers at the mercy of a robber are helped by a despised half-caste.
Slow but suspenseful Western melodrama which works up to a couple of good climaxes but falls away in an unnecessary tragic ending.
w Irving Ravetch, Harriet Frank novel Elmore Leonard d Martin Ritt ph James Wong Howe m David Rose
☆ Paul Newman, Diane Cilento, Fredric March, Richard Boone, Martin Balsam, Barbara Rush, Cameron Mitchell
'A fine array of quirkish characters ... and some unusually literate dialogue.' – *Tom Milne*

Hombre Mirando al Sudeste *
Argentina   1986   100m   Eastmancolor
Cinequanon (Hugo E. Lauria)
A saxophone-playing psychiatrist is confronted by a patient who claims to come from another planet.
An interesting, if portentously told, fable of a Christ-like character meeting with incomprehension in the modern world.
wd Eliseo Subiela ph Ricardo de Angelis m Pedro Aznar pd Marta Albertinazzi ed Luis Cesar D'Angiolillo
☆ Lorenzo Quinteros, Hugo Soto, Ines Vernengo

El Hombre que Vino de Ummo: see *Dracula versus Frankenstein*

Home Alone *
👫 US   1990   102m   DeLuxe
TCF/John Hughes
▦ ▤ ◎ ◯
A young boy, inadvertently left behind at Christmas when his parents go on holiday, foils some inept house-breakers.
Swinging uneasily between heavy-handed slapstick and sentimental domestic comedy, this unpretentious movie was, inexplicably, the biggest box-office success of 1990.
w John Hughes d Chris Columbus ph Julio Macat m John Williams pd John Muto ed Raja Gosnell
☆ Macaulay Culkin, Joe Pesci, Daniel Stern, Catherine O'Hara, John Heard, Roberts Blossom, John Candy
'What is astonishing is that a cute family comedy which takes over an hour really to get going should have provoked such an enthusiastic audience response and gained such a phenomenal word-of-mouth reputation.' – *MFB*
⚐ John Williams; best song 'Somewhere In My Memory'

'He's Up Past His Bedtime In The City That Never Sleeps!'
Home Alone 2: Lost in New York
👫 US   1992   120m   colour
TCF (John Hughes)
▦ ▤ ◎ ◯
Separated from his family after boarding the wrong plane, a young boy alone in New York thwarts the same two robbers he met at home.
Virtually a re-make of the first film, though the humour has a far more unpleasantly sadistic edge to it. This undistinguished comedy was among the biggest box-office successes of 1992.
w John Hughes d Chris Columbus ph Julio Macat m John Williams pd Sandy Veneziano ed Raja Gosnell
☆ Macaulay Culkin, Joe Pesci, Daniel Stern, Catherine O'Hara, John Heard, Devin Ratray, Hillary Wolf, Maureen Elisabeth Shay, Brenda Fricker
'An interesting example of formula film-making, making use of a higher budget than before but even lower expectations.' – *Derek Malcolm, Guardian*

Home Alone 3

US 1997 102m DeLuxe
TCF (John Hughes, Hilton Green)
▢ ▦ ◉ ▦

Crooks attempt to recover from a small boy a toy in which a valuable computer chip is hidden.
A dispiriting continuation of the series, featuring much the same old routine of violent slapstick that, this time, borders on the sadistic.
w John Hughes d Raja Gosnell ph Julio Macat m Nick Glennie-Smith pd Henry Bumstead ed Bruce Green, Malcolm Campbell, David Rennie
☆ Alex D. Linz, Olek Krupa, Rya Kihlstedt, Lenny von Dohlen, David Thornton, Haviland Morris, Kevin Kilner
'A largely pointless experience.' – *Empire*

Home and the World **

India 1984 140m Eastmancolor
Artificial Eye/National Film Development Corp of India
▦

original title: Ghare-Baire
A wealthy landowner brings his wife out from purdah into the world, with fatal results.
Elegant and impressively acted, with an undercurrent of despair.
wd Satyajit Ray novel Rabindranath Tagore ph Soumendu Roy m Satyajit Ray ad Ashoke Bose ed Dulal Dutt
☆ Soumitra Chatterjee, Victor Banerjee, Swatilekha Chatterjee, Gopa Aich, Jennifer Kapoor, Manoj Mitra, Indrapramit Roy, Bimal Chatterjee

Home at Seven

GB 1952 85m bw
British Lion/London (Maurice Cowan)
▦

US title: Murder on Monday
A clerk suffers a 24-hour loss of memory and may have been involved in a murder.
Intriguing suburban mystery, well acted but all too flatly transferred from the stage, and with a weak solution.
w Anatole de Grunwald play R. C. Sherriff d Ralph Richardson ph Jack Hildyard, Edward Scaife m Malcolm Arnold
☆ Ralph Richardson, Margaret Leighton, Jack Hawkins, Campbell Singer, Michael Shepley, Margaret Withers, Meriel Forbes, Frederick Piper
'A film with a notable absence of imagination in conception, direction and acting is not vindicated because it was made very cheaply in fifteen days … it seems ominous that the technique closely resembles that of television.' – *MFB*

Home before Dark

US 1958 137m bw
Warner (Mervyn Le Roy)
A college professor brings his wife home after a year in a mental hospital, but trouble starts again as the circumstances are unchanged.
Overlong, heavygoing, well-made soap opera, quite unconvincing despite firm performances and a suitably gloomy mise-en-scène.
w Eileen and Robert Bassing d Mervyn Le Roy ph Joseph Biroc m Franz Waxman md Ray Heindorf
☆ Jean Simmons, Efrem Zimbalist Jnr, Dan O'Herlihy, Rhonda Fleming, Mabel Albertson

Home Fires Burning: see *The Turning*

'Meet the family that put the fun in dysfunctional!'
Home for the Holidays

US 1995 103m colour
Polygram/Egg (Peggy Rajski, Jodie Foster)
▢ ▦ ◉ ▦

A brother and sister reluctantly return home for a family celebration of Thanksgiving.
Frantic comedy, on the level of a TV sitcom and peopled by eccentrics, whose peculiarities barely raise a smile.
w W. D. Richter story Chris Radant d Jodie Foster ph Lajos Koltai m Mark Isham pd Andrew McAlpine ed Lynzee Klingman
☆ Holly Hunter, Robert Downey Jnr, Anne Bancroft, Charles Durning, Dylan McDermott, Geraldine Chaplin, Cynthia Stevenson, Steve Guttenberg, Claire Danes, Austin Pendleton, David Strathairn

'Likeable in that cosy, wet Sunday afternoon, family sort of way.' – *Empire*

Home from the Hill

US 1960 150m Metrocolor Cinemascope
MGM/Sol C. Siegel (Edmund Grainger)
▦ ◉

A Southern landowner with a voracious sexual appetite has trouble with his two sons, legitimate and illegitimate.
Shades of Cold Comfort Farm *and* Tobacco Road *… and this solemn family saga does go on a bit.*
w Irving Ravetch, Harriet Frank novel William Humphrey d Vincente Minnelli ph Milton Krasner m Bronislau Kaper
☆ Robert Mitchum, George Hamilton, George Peppard, Eleanor Parker, Luana Patten, Everett Sloane, Constance Ford, Ray Teal

Home in Indiana

US 1944 103m Technicolor
TCF (André Daven)
Farmers compete in trotting races and their progeny fall in love.
Archetypal homespun Americana, well enough made according to its lights, but now like something from another world … an innocent one.
w Winston Miller novel The Phantom Filly by George Agnew Chamberlain d Henry Hathaway ph Edward Cronjager m Hugo Friedhofer md Emil Newman
☆ Jeanne Crain, June Haver, Lon McCallister, Walter Brennan, Charlotte Greenwood, Ward Bond, Charles Dingle, Willie Best
† Remade as *April Love*.
◊ Edward Cronjager

A Home of Our Own

US 1993 104m DeLuxe
Rank/Polygram/A&M (Dale Pollock, Bill Borden)
▢ ▦ ◉

A widowed mother leaves Los Angeles to settle in the country with her six children in the hope of giving them a better life.
Sentimental, nostalgic drama of family togetherness that seems nearer to wish fulfilment than reality; it passes the time in an unmemorable fashion.
w Patrick Duncan d Tony Bill ph Jean Lepine m Michael Convertino pd James Schoppe ed Axel Hubert
☆ Kathy Bates, Edward Furlong, Tony Campisi, Soon-Teck Oh, Clarissa Lassig, Sarah Schaub, T. J. Lowther, Miles Feulner, Amy Sakasitz
'Audiences will likely find no particular reason to see such a family drama on the big screen, since in scope, scale and production values it perfectly befits TV, where similar inspirational country tales are often shown.' – *Variety*

Home of the Brave *

US 1949 86m bw
Stanley Kramer
▦ ◉

During World War II, a black man finds himself the butt of racist behaviour from the rest of his platoon.
One of the first films to touch the subject of anti-black bias, this now seems pretty tame and dated, and in fact never was much more than a filmed play (in which the butt was originally a Jew).
w Carl Foreman play Arthur Laurents d Mark Robson ph Robert de Grasse m Dimitri Tiomkin
☆ Frank Lovejoy, Lloyd Bridges, Douglas Dick, James Edwards, Steve Brodie, Jeff Corey, Cliff Clark
† When Arthur Laurents asked Stanley Kramer why the central character was no longer a Jew, Kramer replied, 'Because Jews have been done.'

A Home of Your Own *

🏃 GB 1965 44m bw
Dormar/British Lion
Calamities pile up on a building site.
Genuinely funny silent comedy, with bits from a variety of familiar faces.
w Jay Lewis, John Whyte d Bob Kellett ph Dennis Coop m Ron Goodwin
☆ Ronnie Barker, George Benson, Richard Briers, Janet Brown, Peter Butterworth, Bernard Cribbins, Fred Emney, Bill Fraser, Ronnie Stevens

Home Sweet Home

GB 1945 92m bw
Butcher Empire (F. W. Baker, John E. Blakeley)
A worker in a piano factory tries to cope with his fractious employer and his wife, who gives birth to four sons.
An odd confection: there are a few cherishable moments of Randle's anarchic comedy, with its mix of slapstick and surrealism, but there's also a sickly romance, and the action stops halfway through for an interlude of classical music provided by the then-popular Austrian pianists Rawicz and Landauer.
w Roney Parsons, Anthony Toner, Arthur Mertz d John E. Blakeley ph Geoffrey Faithfull md Percival Mackey ad Jim Carter ed V. Sagovsky
☆ Frank Randle, Nicolette Roeg, Tony Pendrell, H. F. Maltby, Cecil Frederick, Stan Little, Hilda Bayley, Donovan & Byl, Arnley & Gloria

Home Sweet Homicide

🏃 US 1946 90m bw
TCF
Children solve a murder mystery with the help of their mother, a detective novelist.
Mild family fare.
w F. Hugh Herbert novel Craig Rice d Lloyd Bacon ph John Seitz m David Buttolph
☆ Lynn Bari, Randolph Scott, Peggy Ann Garner, Connie Marshall, Dean Stockwell, Barbara Whiting

The Home Towners

US 1928 84m bw
Warner
A wealthy man falls for a girl half his age and is warned by a hometown friend that she may be a gold digger.
Fairly fluent early talkie which pleased at the time.
w Addison Burkhart play George M. Cohan d Bryan Foy
☆ Richard Bennett, Robert McWade, Doris Kenyon, Stanley Taylor
† Remakes include *Times Square Playboy* (1936) with Warren William, Gene Lockhart and June Travis, d William McGann; and *Ladies Must Live* (1940) with Wayne Morris, Priscilla Lane and Roscoe Karns; both for Warner.

Homebodies

US 1973 96m colour
Essential/Cinema Entertainment (Marshall Backlar)
Among the old people living in a tenement scheduled for redevelopment are homicidal maniacs.
Bizarre and tasteless horror of little visible merit.
w Larry Yust, Howard Kaminsky, Bennett Sims d Larry Yust ph Isidore Mankofsky m Bernardo Segall ad John Retsek ed Peter Parasheles
☆ Peter Brocco, Frances Fuller, William Hansen, Ruth McDevitt, Paula Trueman
'The film never finds its right level (and, incidentally, seems at a loss to know how to conclude itself).' – *David McGillivray*

Homeboy

US 1988 116m Technicolor
TCF/Homeboy Productions/Redruby (Alan Marshall, Elliott Kastner)
▢ ▦ ◉ ▦ ◉

A down-and-out boxer gets one last chance at the big time.
Dim melodrama of the low life.
w Eddie Cook story Mickey Rourke d Michael Seresin ph Gale Tattersall m Eric Clapton, Michael Kamen pd Brian Morris ed Ray Lovejoy
☆ Mickey Rourke, Christopher Walken, Debra Feuer, Thomas Quinn, Kevin Conway, Anthony Alda, Jon Polito, Bill Slayton, David Taylor, Joseph Ragno

Homecoming

US 1948 113m bw
MGM (Sidney Franklin)
▦

A ruthless society doctor is called up in World War II and has his life changed by a brief affair with a nurse who is killed in action.
Ho-hum romantic melodrama which stumbles most badly when it aims to be serious.
w Paul Osborn d Mervyn Le Roy ph Harold Rosson m Bronislau Kaper md Charles Previn
☆ Clark Gable, Lana Turner, Anne Baxter, John Hodiak, Ray Collins, Gladys Cooper, Cameron Mitchell, Marshall Thompson

'Its basic substance, like the base of a perfume, has a terrible smell; but to many moviegoers the end-product will seem quite pleasant.' – *Time*

The Homecoming *

GB 1973 114m colour
American Express/Ely Landau
Tensions mount and sexual revelations abound in the house of a retired London butcher.
Plain treatment of an anything-but-plain Pinter play. The result is a record of a performance rather than a film.
w Harold Pinter play Harold Pinter d Peter Hall ph David Watkin m Thelonious Monk pd John Bury
☆ Paul Rogers, Cyril Cusack, Michael Jayston, Ian Holm, Vivien Merchant, Terence Rigby
'Shocking in its own lucidity, and fascinating as an arrangement of mutually reflecting prisms … the remarkable control of Pinter's language guarantees that the dramatic situations are revealed to be even more abstract and diagrammatic as they steadily accumulate psychological density.' – *Jonathan Rosenbaum*

Homegrown

US 1998 101m DeLuxe
TriStar/Lakeshore/Rollercoaster (Jason Clark)
▢ ▦ ◉

In northern California, three marijuana growers decide to go into dope-dealing for themselves when their boss is unexpectedly murdered.
Laid-back, desultory thriller with a comic tone; interesting mainly in its depiction of the drug business away from its usual urban setting.
w Nicholas Kazan, Stephen Gyllenhaal d Stephen Gyllenhaal m Trevor Rabin pd Richard Sherman ed Michael Jablow
☆ Billy Bob Thornton, Hank Azaria, Kelly Lynch, Jon Bon Jovi, Ryan Phillippe, Ted Danson, Judge Reinhold, John Lithgow, Jamie Lee Curtis
'Serious, funny, sinister, sexy, silly and a lot more. But it isn't particularly good in any one of those departments.' – *Leonard Klady, Variety*

Homer

US 1970 91m colour
Palomar/Cinema VI (Terence Dene, Steven North)
As the Vietnam War begins, an 18-year-old would-be rock singer finds small-town life constricting.
An unoriginal plod through the usual teenage angst.
w Claude Harz d John Trent ph Laszlo G. George ad Jack McAdam ed M. C. Manne
☆ Don Scardino, Alex Nicol, Tisa Farrow, Lenka Peterson, Tim Henry, Tom Harvey

The Homeroom News: see *Freeze Frame*

The Homestretch

US 1947 97m Technicolor
TCF (Robert Bassler)
A racing enthusiast neglects his wife.
Thin romantic drama, handsomely photographed on various racecourses.
w Wanda Tuchock d H. Bruce Humberstone ph Arthur Arling m David Raksin
☆ Cornel Wilde, Maureen O'Hara, Glenn Langan, Helen Walker, James Gleason, Henry Stephenson

Homeward Bound II: Lost in San Francisco

🏃 US 1996 88m Technicolor
Buena Vista/Walt Disney (Barry Jossen)
▢ ▦ ◉ ◉

Two dogs and a cat, stranded in San Francisco, evade dog-nappers to find their way home.
A sequel, featuring animals with human voices and emotions, that treads much the same ground as its predecessor; enjoyable enough in its way, unless you like dumb animals.
w Chris Hauty, Julie Hickson d David R. Ellis ph Jack Conroy m Bruce Broughton pd Michael Bolton ed Peter E. Berger, Michael A. Stevenson
☆ Robert Hays, Kim Greist, Veronica Lauren, Kevin Chevalia, Benj Thall, Max Perlich, Michael Rispoli and also the voices of: Michael J. Fox, Sally Field, Ralph Waite, Jon Polito, Adam Goldberg, Sinbad
'Pic is funny enough to amuse adults who are willing to play along with it.' – *Variety*

◎ Digital Video Disc Region 2   ◎ Digital Video Disc Region 1   ◌ Soundtrack released on compact disc   ☆ Cast in approximate order of importance   † Points of interest   ♫ Notable songs   🏆 Academy Award   ◊ Academy Award nomination   ▽ BAFTA

Homeward Bound: The Incredible Journey

⋔⋔ US 1993 85m Technicolor

Buena Vista/Walt Disney/Touchwood Pacific Partners I (Franklin R. Levy, Jeffrey Chernov)

📼 ▤ ◕ ⊙ ⊙ 🎧

Two dogs and a cat, separated from their human family, run off to find them.

A remake of Disney's The Incredible Journey with human voices added for the animals, in the manner of the Look Who's Talking films; speech adds a feeling of unreality to the proceedings, but probably young audiences will not mind.

w Caroline Thompson, Linda Wolverton book *The Incredible Journey* by Sheila Burnford d Duwayne Dunham ph Reed Smoot m Bruce Broughton pd Roger Cain ed Jonathan P. Shaw, Jay Cassidy, Michael Kelly, Brian Berdan

☆ Featuring the voices of Michael J. Fox, Sally Field, Don Ameche

'A sprightly little entertainment that should enthrall tots without straining the patience of parents.' – *Variety*

Homework: see La Tarea

'Can your heart stand the challenge when the clock starts the countdown?'
'All those too timid to take the climax will be welcomed to the cowards' corner!'

Homicidal

US 1961 87m bw

Columbia/William Castle

📼

A murderous blonde and a very strange young man both live in the house of a paralysed old lady.

Transvestite horror comic allegedly based on a true case; made on a low budget and played for cheap shocks.

w Robb White d William Castle ph Burnett Guffey m Hugo Friedhofer

☆ Jean Arless, Glenn Corbett, Patricia Breslin, Eugenie Leontovich, Alan Bunce, Richard Rust

† The film was played with a 'fright break' during which faint-hearted members of the audience might leave before the final onslaught.

Homicide

US 1949 76m bw

Warner

A murder witness is intimidated by the killers.

Stiff little crime yarn which slowly recovers after a dull beginning.

w William Sackheim d Felix Jacoves ph J. Peverell Marley

☆ Robert Douglas, Robert Alda, Helen Westcott

'Bob Gold is a cop. A good cop. But tonight, he will betray his friends, disgrace the force, and commit an act of violence because he believes it is the only right thing to do.'

Homicide **

US 1991 102m colour

First Independent/J&M Entertainment/Cinehaus (Michael Hausman, Edward R. Pressman)

📼 ▤ ◕

A Jewish cop investigating the murder of a storekeeper suspects an anti-Semitic conspiracy.

Engrossing study of one man's disintegration.

wd David Mamet ph Roger Deakins m Alaric Jans pd Michael Merritt ed Barbara Tulliver

☆ Joe Mantegna, William H. Macy, Natalija Nogulich, Ving Rhames, Rebecca Pidgeon, J. J. Johnston, Jack Wallace

'Portrayed with a spell-binding skill and precision, the pace of an action-thriller off-set by unexpected patterns of colour and speech, part documentary, part theatrical melodrama.' – *Philip Strick, Sight and Sound*

Homicide Bureau

US 1938 56m bw

Columbia

A tough small-town cop deals with racketeers.

Routine programme filler.

w Earle Snell d C. C. Coleman Jnr

☆ Bruce Cabot, Rita Hayworth, Marc Lawrence, Moroni Olsen

'Hits new low … every department of production way below par.' – *Variety*

Un Homme Amoureux: see A Man in Love

L'Homme au Chapeau Rond *

France 1946 91m bw

Alcina

When his wife dies, a man becomes obsessed with causing the downfall of her two lovers.

Heavy-going melodrama without much in the way of light relief; chiefly memorable for its central performance.

w Charles Spaak, Jean Loubignac novel *The Eternal Husband* by Dostoevsky d Pierre Billon ph Nicolas Torporkoff m Maurice Thiriet

☆ *Raimu*, Aimé Clariond, Lucy Valnor

L'Homme de Ma Vie *

France/Canada 1992 104m colour

Optima/Cineroux/Ciné Cinq/Prodeve (Gabriel Boustani)

📼 📼

aka: *The Man of My Life*

Determined to find a rich husband, a young Parisian woman marries a bad-tempered restaurant critic and suffers in style before deciding that love is better than comfort.

A light and frothy account of male–female relationships.

wd Jean Charles Tacchella ph Dominique Le Rigoleur m Raymond Alessandrini ad Serge Douy ed Marie-Aimée Debril

☆ Maria de Medeiros, Thiérry Fortineau, Anne Letourneau, Ginette Garcin, Ginette Mathieu, Alain Doutey, Jean-Pierre Bacri

L'Homme de Rio: see That Man from Rio

Un Homme est Mort: see The Outside Man

Un Homme et une Femme: see A Man and a Woman

Hommes Femmes: Mode d'emploi: see Men Women: A User's Manual

Hondo *

US 1953 93m Warnercolor 3-D

Wayne-Fellows

In 1874 New Mexico a cavalry despatch rider stops to defend a lonely widow and her son against Indians.

Overwritten but pleasant-looking Western, clearly patterned after Shane.

w James Edward Grant novel Louis L'Amour d John Farrow ph Robert Burks, Archie Stout m Emil Newman, Hugo Friedhofer

☆ John Wayne, Geraldine Page, Ward Bond, Michael Pate

♫ Geraldine Page

The Honest Courtesan: see Dangerous Beauty

Honey

US 1930 75m bw

Paramount

A brother and sister rent out their Southern mansion and decide to become the butler and cook.

Comedy with music, a little heavier than it should have been.

w Herman J. Mankiewicz play *Come Out of the Kitchen* by Alice Duer Miller, A. E. Thomas d Wesley Ruggles

☆ Nancy Carroll, Skeets Gallagher, Stanley Smith, Lillian Roth, Harry Green, Mitzi Green, ZaSu Pitts

'Not worthy of a big rave but should satisfy the mob.' – *Variety*

Honey, I Blew Up the Kid

US 1992 89m Technicolor

Buena Vista/Walt Disney (Dawn Steel, Edward S. Feldman)

📼 ▤ ◕ 🎧

An inventor inadvertently exposes his two-year-old son to a ray that causes him to grow to 50 feet tall.

Predictable and dull comedy that fails to develop its central notion in interesting ways.

w Thom Eberhardt, Peter Elbling, Garry Goodrow d Randal Kleiser ph John Hora m Bruce Broughton pd Leslie Dilley ed Michael A. Stevenson, Harry Hitner, Tina Hirsch

☆ Rick Moranis, Marcia Strassman, Robert Oliveri, Daniel Shalikar, Joshua Shalikar, Lloyd Bridges, John Shea, Keri Russell, Ron Canada, Amy O'Neill

'A romp, escapism at its breeziest.' – *Variety*
'Proclaims in its every move that particular blend of crassness and technical expertise that is so often used for Hollywood's more down-market popular successes.' – *Derek Malcolm, Guardian*

Honey, I Shrunk the Kids *

US 1989 93m Metrocolor

Warner/Walt Disney/Doric (Penny Finkelman Cox)

📼 ▤ ◕ 🎧

An inventor inadvertently miniaturizes his children and dumps them in the garden.

Amusing comedy with Disney's winsomeness kept at bay for the most part, apart from a brave little ant.

w Ed Naha, Tom Schulman story Stuart Gordon, Brian Yuzna, Ed Naha d Joe Johnston ph Hiro Narita pd Gregg Fonseca ed Michael A. Stevenson

☆ Rick Moranis, Matt Frewer, Marcia Strassman, Kristine Sutherland, Thomas Brown, Jared Rushton, Amy O'Neill, Robert Oliveri, Carl Steven

'You are cordially invited to a perfectly elegant case of murder!'

The Honey Pot *

US 1966 150m Technicolor

UA/Famous Artists (Charles K. Feldman) (Joseph L. Mankiewicz)

▤

A millionaire pretends to be dying in order to trick three former mistresses; but one of them is murdered.

Uneasy variation, via two other variations, on Ben Jonson's Volpone; despite bright moments, the mood is fatally inconsistent, and a cloud of pseudo-sophisticated dialogue hangs over the whole thing like a pall.

wd Joseph L. Mankiewicz play Mr Fox of Venice by Frederick Knott novel *The Evil of the Day* by Thomas Sterling ph Gianni di Venanzo m John Addison pd John DeCuir

☆ Rex Harrison, Susan Hayward, *Maggie Smith*, Cliff Robertson, Capucine, Edie Adams, Adolfo Celi, Herschel Bernardi

'One of the talkiest pictures ever made.' – *Stephen Farber*

Honeychile

US 1951 89m Trucolor

Republic

A music publisher tries to cheat a country composer.

Hayseed shenanigans for small-town consumption.

w Jack Townley, Charles Roberts d R. G. Springsteen ph Jack Marta m Victor Young

☆ Judy Canova, Eddie Foy Jnr, Alan Hale Jnr, Walter Catlett, Claire Carleton, Leonid Kinskey

'Miss Glamorous and Mr Amorous in a gay elopement adventure that makes Mexico City blush!'

Honeymoon

US 1947 74m bw

RKO (Warren Duff)

GB title: *Two Men and a Girl*

An 18-year-old elopes to Mexico City with an army corporal but meets a sophisticated older man.

Emaciated comedy, one of the reasons for Shirley Temple's early retirement.

w Michael Kanin story Vicki Baum d William Keighley ph Edward Cronjager m Leigh Harline

☆ Shirley Temple, Franchot Tone, Guy Madison, Lina Romay, Gene Lockhart, Grant Mitchell

Honeymoon

Spain/GB 1959 109m Technicolor

Technirama/Dimension 180

Suevia/Everdene (Cesario Gonzalez, Michael Powell)

Spanish title: *Luna de Miel*

An ex-ballerina in Spain with her new husband is tempted to return to the boards.

Incredibly shapeless travel poster with some dancing and two interpolated ballets to provide moments of musical interest. An unbelievable disaster from the co-creator of The Red Shoes.

w Michael Powell, Luis Escobar d Michael Powell ph Georges Périnal, Gerry Turpin m Mikis Theodorakis

☆ Anthony Steel, Ludmilla Tcherina, Antonio, Leonide Massine

Honeymoon Deferred

US 1940 84m bw

Universal

An insurance investigator is called away from honeymoon when his boss is murdered.

Unremarkable star programmer.

w Roy Chanslor, Eliot Gibbons d Lew Landers

☆ Edmund Lowe, Margaret Lindsay, Elizabeth Risdon, Joyce Compton, Chick Chandler

Honeymoon Deferred

GB 1951 79m bw

Vic Films

A war veteran returns for his honeymoon to the Italian village he helped to liberate, but finds himself accused of ruining the crops.

Curious hybrid comedy which fails to jell on all levels.

w Suso d'Amico, A. Pietrangeli d Mario Camerini ph Geoffrey Faithfull, Otello Martelli m Nino Rota

☆ Griffith Jones, Sally Ann Howes, Kieron Moore, Lea Padovani

Honeymoon for Three

US 1941 77m bw

Warner

An author is protected from adoring females by his secretary.

Fairly flaccid romantic comedy, a remake of Goodbye Again (1933).

w Julius J. Epstein, Philip G. Epstein, Earl Baldwin d Lloyd Bacon

☆ George Brent, Ann Sheridan, Osa Massen, Charles Ruggles, Jane Wyman, Lee Patrick

Honeymoon Hotel

US 1964 98m Metrocolor Cinemascope

MGM/Avon (Lawrence Weingarten)

A jilted swain goes off with a philandering friend on what was to have been his honeymoon trip … only to be followed by his repentant fiancée.

Rather unattractive farce with insufficient funny moments.

w R. S. Allen, Harvey Bullock d Henry Levin ph Harold Lipstein m Walter Scharf

☆ Nancy Kwan, Robert Goulet, Robert Morse, Jill St John, Elsa Lanchester, Keenan Wynn

Honeymoon in Bali

US 1939 95m bw

Paramount (Jeff Lazarus)

GB title: *Husbands or Lovers?*

A department store head intends to pursue her career without marriage, but two swains try to prove her wrong.

Thin romantic comedy which got by on its stars.

w Virginia Van Upp d Edward H. Griffith

☆ Madeleine Carroll, Fred MacMurray, Allan Jones, Akim Tamiroff, Helen Broderick, Osa Massen

'Infectiously sparkling … will click substantially in the regular runs.' – *Variety*

† The original title, *Are Husbands Necessary?*, was discarded when Miss Carroll became involved in a divorce suit.

'A comedy about one bride, two grooms, and 34 flying Elvises.'

Honeymoon in Vegas *

US 1992 96m Technicolor

First Independent/Castle Rock/New Line/Lobell/Bergman (Mike Lobell)

📼 ▤ ◕ ⊙ 🎧

In a poker game a Las Vegas gambler wins a weekend with the fiancée of a New York detective.

Moderately enjoyable comedy, with an amusing running gag about Elvis impersonators.

wd Andrew Bergman ph William A. Fraker m David Newman pd William A. Elliott ed Barry Malkin

☆ James Caan, Nicolas Cage, Sarah Jessica Parker, Pat Morita, Johnny Williams, Anne Bancroft, Peter Boyle

'A virtually nonstop scream of benign delirium, pop entertainment as revivifying as anything you're likely to see this year.' – *Vincent Canby, New York Times*
'A very good comedy indeed, a dynamite throwback to those 40s screwball numbers.' – *Jeff Dawson, Empire*

The Honeymoon Killers *

US 1969 108m bw

Warren Steibel

📼 ▤ ◕

A gigolo and a nurse team up to prey upon women looking for a husband.

Unsparing low-budget film, based on a true story of multiple murderers, that has gained a cult following.

⋔⋔ film suitable for family viewing 📼 VHS video-cassette for the British PAL system 📼 VHS video-cassette for the British PAL system in wide screen-format ⟳ Video cassette in a computer-colourised version ▤ American NTSC video-cassette ◕ Laser disc *wd* Leonard Kastle *ph* Oliver Wood *ed* Stan Warnow

☆ Shirley Stoler, Tony Lo Bianco, Mary Jane Higby, Doris Roberts, Kip McArdle

The Honeymoon Machine

US 1961 91m Metrocolor Cinemascope
MGM/Avon (Lawrence Weingarten)

A naval lieutenant uses the ship's computer to break the bank at the Venice casino.
Stolid, expensive-looking comedy which barely raises a laugh.
w George Wells *play* The Golden Fleecing by Lorenzo Semple Jnr *d* Richard Thorpe *ph* Joseph LaShelle *m* Leigh Harline
☆ Steve McQueen, Brigid Bazlen, Jim Hutton, Paula Prentiss, Dean Jagger, Jack Weston, Jack Mullaney

Honeysuckle Rose

US 1980 119m Technicolor
Warner (Sydney Pollack)
▣ ◎. ◠
A happily married country and western star takes to the bottle whenever he goes on the road.
Glum modern drama with music, a semi-autobiographical star vehicle; for fans only.
w Carol Sobieski, William D. Wittliff, John Binder *d* Jerry Schatzberg *m* Robby Muller *m/ly* Willie Nelson *pd* Joel Schiller *ed* Aram Avakian, Norman Gay, Marc Laub, Evan Lottman
☆ Willie Nelson, Dyan Cannon, Amy Irving, Slim Pickens
♫ song 'On the Road Again'

Hong Gaoliang: see Red Sorghum

Hong Kong

US 1951 91m Technicolor
Paramount/Pine-Thomas

An ex-GI has various adventures with a Chinese orphan and a golden idol.
And a plot that seems to make itself up as they go along. Corn-fed hokum.
w Winston Miller *d* Lewis R. Foster *ph* Lionel Lindon *m* Lucien Cailliet *ad* Lewis H. Creber *ed* Howard Smith
☆ Ronald Reagan, Rhonda Fleming, Nigel Bruce, Marvin Miller, Lowell Gilmore

The Honkers

US 1972 102m DeLuxe
Levy-Gardner-Lavin

An ageing rodeo performer runs into trouble when he returns to his home town.
Mundane and predictable drama of middle-aged regrets and disappointments.
w Steve Ihnat, Stephen Lodge *d* Steve Ihnat *ph* James Crabe *m* Jimmie Haskell *ed* Tom Rolf
☆ James Coburn, Lois Nettleton, Slim Pickens, Anne Archer, Richard Anderson, Joan Huntington, Jim Davis, Ramon Bieri

Honky Tonk

US 1929 80m bw
Warner

A night-club entertainer sacrifices everything for her daughter's education.
Primitive cross between Applause and Imitation of Life, with spirited moments from Sophie Tucker the only plus.
w C. Graham Baker, Jack Yellen *d* Lloyd Bacon
☆ Sophie Tucker, Lila Lee, Audrey Ferris, George Duryea, Mahlon Hamilton

'Every kiss a thrill!'

Honky Tonk *

US 1941 104m bw
MGM (Pandro S. Berman)

A Western con man meets his match in the daughter of a fake judge.
Generally amusing comedy melodrama that ambles along between two styles but leaves a pleasant after-effect.
w Marguerite Roberts, John Sanford *d* Jack Conway *ph* Harold Rosson *m* Franz Waxman
☆ Clark Gable, Lana Turner, Frank Morgan, Claire Trevor, Marjorie Main, Albert Dekker, Henry O'Neill, Chill Wills, Betty Blythe
'A lively, lusty western that makes you wish you had been there.' – Variety

Honky Tonk Freeway

US 1981 107m Technicolor
EMI/Kendon/HTF Company (Don Boyd, Howard W. Koch Jnr)
◉◉
The mayor of a small Florida resort town has it painted pink to attract tourists ... but too many of the wrong kind come in.
Zany farce, rather like It's a Mad Mad Mad Mad World without a proper hook to the story. Not an audience-pleaser, and very expensive.
w Edward Clinton *d* John Schlesinger *ph* John Bailey *m* George Martin, Elmer Bernstein
☆ William Devane, Beau Bridges, Teri Garr, Beverly D'Angelo, Hume Cronyn, Jessica Tandy, Howard Hesseman, Geraldine Page, George Dzundza
'A shambles, and a more convincing one than the half-hearted affair which brings it to a close.' – Richard Combs, MFB
'A film for "now" which seems almost endearingly bereft of any real ideas about the messed-up contemporary world it inhabits.' – Guardian

Honkytonk Man

US 1982 122m Technicolor
Warner/Malpaso (Clint Eastwood)
◉◉ ▣ ◎. ◠
In the thirties, an ageing and alcoholic country singer turns to his rural family for help.
Yet another occasion when the star should have asked for help instead of doing all the chores himself. Not much real entertainment here, just a very few moments that amuse.
w Clancy Carlile *novel* Clancy Carlile *d* Clint Eastwood *ph* Bruce Surtees *m* Steve Dorff *pd* Edward Carfagno
☆ Clint Eastwood, Kyle Eastwood, John McIntire, Verna Bloom, Alexa Kenin, Matt Clark

Honolulu

US 1938 83m bw
MGM (Jack Cummings)

A movie star is mistaken for his double.
Sloppy comedy with a few musical numbers.
w Herbert Fields, Frank Partos *d* Edward Buzzell *ph* Ray June *m* Franz Waxman
☆ Robert Young, Eleanor Powell, George Burns, Gracie Allen, Rita Johnson, Ruth Hussey, Clarence Kolb, Sig Rumann, Eddie Anderson
'Fairly amusing comedy for top brackets in duals.' – Variety
'The whole thing seems to have been thrown together so that Eleanor Powell can do a frenetic hula.' – New Yorker, 1977

Honor Among Lovers

US 1931 76m bw
Paramount

A young businessman complicates his life when he decides to marry his secretary.
Smart comedy unfolding a complex plot, but slow by modern standards.
w Austin Parker, Gertrude Purcell *d* Dorothy Arzner
☆ Claudette Colbert, Fredric March, Monroe Owsley, Charlie Ruggles, Ginger Rogers
'A sweet piece of work hiding behind a faulty title.' – Variety

Honor Bound

US 1989 102m Technicolor
Pacific/FilmAccord (Tim Van Relim, Eric A. Weymueller)

Two American soldiers investigate a mysterious happening at a Soviet missile base in East Germany.
Cold War thriller of limited interest.
w Aiken Woodruff *novel* Recovery by Steven L. Thompson *d* Jeannot Szwarc *ph* Robert Stevens *m* Mark Shreeve *pd* John Graysmark *ed* John Jympson
☆ John Philbin, Tom Skerritt, Gabrielle Lazure, George Dzundza, Lawrence Pressman, Gene Davis

Honor of the Family

US 1931 66m bw
First National

The young mistress of an aged Budapest resident is after his money.
Tiresome comedy drama.
play Emil Fabre *story* Balzac *d* Lloyd Bacon
☆ Bebe Daniels, Warren William, Frederick Kerr, Alan Mowbray, Blanche Friderici

The Honorary Consul

GB 1983 104m Movielab
World Film Services (Norma Heyman)
US title: *Beyond the Limit*

In northern Argentina, a doctor is drawn into the kidnapping by activists of a drunken British consul.
Self-parodic visit to Greeneland, with everybody drunk or depressed. Bouts of explicit sex don't help much, if at all.
w Christopher Hampton *novel* Graham Greene *d* John MacKenzie *ph* Phil Meheux *m* Stanley Myers *pd* Allan Cameron
☆ Michael Caine, Richard Gere, Bob Hoskins, Elpidia Carrillo, Joaquim de Almeida
'Some very old friends: exhausted passion, moral betrayal and relics of religious faith.' – Sight and Sound
'All it takes is the character to decide he is a burnt-out case, sleeping with all women but capable of loving none, for all the familiar icons to be ranged in battle array.' – Tom Milne, MFB

Honour Among Thieves: see Touchez pas au Grisbi

The Honourable Mr Wong: see The Hatchet Man

An Honourable Murder *

GB 1959 70m bw
Warner/Danzigers (Edward J. Danziger, Harry Lee Danziger)

Boardroom executives scheme to be rid of their chairman.
Oddball, interesting attempt to play Julius Caesar in modern dress. Not entirely successful, but full marks for trying.
w Brian Clemens, Eldon Howard *d* Godfrey Grayson *ph* James Wilson
☆ Norman Wooland, Margaretta Scott, Lisa Daniely, Douglas Wilmer, Philip Saville, John Longden

'They had it all. It cost them everything.'

Hoodlum

US 1997 130m DeLuxe
MGM/UA (Frank Mancuso Jnr)
◉◉ ▣
In the 30s, black gangster Bumpy Johnson fights Dutch Schultz for control of the numbers racket in Harlem.
Tough gangster movie that is enjoyable without being memorable.
w Chris Brancato *d* Bill Duke *ph* Frank Tidy *m* Elmer Bernstein *pd* Charles Bennett *ed* Harry Keramidas
☆ Laurence Fishburne, Tim Roth, Andy Garcia, Vanessa L. Williams, Cicely Tyson, Chi McBride, William Atherton
'The film falls short of its aim for mythic proportion. Still, there's a vibrancy that's engrossing, if uneven.' – Leonard Klady, Variety
† The film was released direct to video in Britain.

The Hoodlum

US 1951 63m bw
Jack Schwarz Productions
▣
A convict is paroled but continues his criminal career.
Toughish crime support with interesting moments.
w Sam Neumann, Nat Tanchuck *d* Max Nosseck *ph* Clark Ramsey *m* Darrell Calker
☆ Lawrence Tierney, Lisa Golm, Edward Tierney, Allene Roberts

Hoodlum Empire

US 1952 98m bw
Republic (Joseph Kane)
▣
A Congressional committee investigates a racketeer.
Moderate semi-documentary potboiler inspired by the Kefauver investigations.
w Bruce Manning, Bob Considine *d* Joseph Kane *ph* Reggie Lanning *m* Nathan Scott
☆ Brian Donlevy, Forrest Tucker, Claire Trevor, Vera Ralston, Luther Adler, John Russell, Gene Lockhart, Grant Withers, Taylor Holmes
'Familiar gangster melodramatics and repentances, played out in a rigmarole of flashbacks.' – MFB

The Hoodlum Priest *

US 1961 100m bw
UA/Don Murray-Walter Wood

A Jesuit teacher tries to help young criminals, especially a condemned murderer.
Moderately well done, very depressing and downbeat chunk of social conscience based on the life of Charles Dismas Clark.
w Don Mankiewicz, Joseph Landon, 'Don Deer' (i.e. Don Murray) *d* Irvin Kershner *ph* Haskell Wexler *m* Richard Markowitz
☆ Don Murray, Keir Dullea, Larry Gates, Cindi Wood, Logan Ramsey

The Hoodlum Saint

US 1946 93m bw
MGM (Cliff Reid)

A cynical newspaperman turns to religion and succours thieves.
Hard-boiled sentimentality, a downright peculiar and doleful comedy drama in deflated post-war mood.
w Frank Wead, James Hill *d* Norman Taurog *ph* Ray June *m* Nathaniel Shilkret
☆ William Powell, Esther Williams, Angela Lansbury, James Gleason, Rags Ragland, Frank McHugh, Slim Summerville, Roman Bohnen, Louis Jean Heydt, Charles Arnt, Charles Trowbridge, Henry O'Neill

Hook *

♟♟ US 1991 144m DeLuxe Panavision
Columbia TriStar/Amblin (Kathleen Kennedy, Frank Marshall, Gerald R. Molen)
◉◉ ▣ ◎. ◠
Peter Pan, who has returned to the ordinary world to become a father and a corporate lawyer, returns to Neverland to fight Captain Hook.
Sprawling, overlong, often camp extravaganza with splendid special effects and settings that may appeal to the small child in most of us, even if it is time that Spielberg himself grew up.
w Jim V. Hart, Malia Scotch Marmo *play* Peter Pan by J. M. Barrie *story* Jim V. Hart, Nick Castle *d* Steven Spielberg *ph* Dean Cundey *m* John Williams *pd* Norman Garwood (John Napier was visual consultant) *ed* Michael Kahn *sp* Industrial Light and Magic
☆ Dustin Hoffman, Robin Williams, Julia Roberts, Bob Hoskins, Maggie Smith, Caroline Goodall, Charlie Korsmo, Amber Scott, Laurel Cronin, Phil Collins, David Crosby
'Spirited, rambunctious, often messy and undisciplined, this determined attempt to recast the Peter Pan story in contemporary terms splashes every bit of its megabudget (between $60 and $80 million) onto the screen; commercial elements overflow in such abundance that major hit status seems guaranteed.' – Variety
'Peel away the expensive, special effects surface and there's nothing but formula.' – Washington Post
† Glenn Close appears in an uncredited role as a bearded pirate.
♫ song 'When You're Alone' (*m*John Williams, *ly*Leslie Bricusse); Norman Garwood; visual effects

The Hook

US 1962 98m bw Panavision
MGM/Perlberg-Seaton

Three GIs escaping from Korea are ordered to execute a prisoner but cannot bring themselves to do it.
Predictable, claustrophobic drama which becomes a slick exercise in morality.
w Henry Denker *novel* L'Hameçon by Vahe Katcha *d* George Seaton *ph* Joe Ruttenberg *m* Larry Adler
☆ Kirk Douglas, Robert Walker, Nick Adams, Nehemiah Persoff

Hook Line and Sinker

US 1930 72m bw
RKO
◎.
Two insurance agents run a derelict hotel.
Feeble comedy vehicle.
w Tim Whelan, Ralph Spence *d* Eddie Cline
☆ Bert Wheeler, Robert Woolsey, Hugh Herbert, Dorothy Lee, Jobyna Howland, Ralf Harolde
'Will tickle most in those spots where the price is least.' – Variety

---

Hook, Line and Sinker

US 1968 92m Technicolor
Columbia/Jerry Lewis

A salesman who thinks he is dying goes on a spending spree; when he learns the truth, he has to disappear because of his huge debts.
Miserable comedy with frantic slapstick interludes. The plot might have served Preston Sturges.
w Rod Amateau d George Marshall ph W. Wallace Kelley m Dick Stabile
☆ Jerry Lewis, Peter Lawford, Anne Francis, Pedro Gonzales Gonzales

'The Film That Stunned A Nation!'

Hoop Dreams ***

US 1994 174m colour
Feature/FineLine/Kartemquin/KCTA-TV (Fred Marx, Steve James, Peter Gilbert)

Two black teenagers pursue their hopes of becoming professional basketball players.
A documentary that makes redundant all the recent fictional accounts of basketball heroics; here is the real thing, a brilliant documentary of the conjunction and conflict of the American Dream and the realities of life, following its two protagonists and their families through four years of success and failure.
d Steve James ph Peter Gilbert ed Fred Marx, Steve James, Bill Haugse
☆ William Gates, Arthur Agee, Emma Gates, Curtis Gates, Sheila Agee
'Has the crackle and density of that elusive beast, the Great American Novel.' – *Geoff Brown, The Times*
'A prodigious achievement that conveys the fabric of modern American life, aspirations and, incidentally, sport in close-up.' – *Todd McCarthy, Variety*
⅋ editing

Hooper *

US 1978 99m Metrocolor
Warner/Burt Reynolds, Lawrence Gordon (Hank Moonjean)

An ageing stunt man decides on one last sensational stunt before retiring.
There are some agreeably striking moments, but you can't make a movie out of stunts and loud camaraderie. This one palls half way through.
w Thomas Rickman, Bill Kerby d Hal Needham ph Bobby Byrne m Bill Justis
☆ Burt Reynolds, Sally Field, Brian Keith, Jan-Michael Vincent, John Marley, Robert Klein, James Best, Adam West
'Burt Reynolds's annual Kleenex of a movie: something to use and throw away without any thought beyond a certain gratitude for the convenience of the thing.' – *Richard Schickel, Time*

'Clara Bow ... red-headed warm-blooded dynamite ... again releases the torrent of her genius in the most colorful performance of her life.'

Hoopla

US 1933 85m bw
Fox

A hardboiled carnival dancer agrees to seduce the son of the show's manager, but ends by marrying him.
Strained melodrama with the star, in her last film, at the end of her tether.
w Bradley King, J. M. March play The Barker by Kenyon Nicholson d Frank Lloyd
☆ Clara Bow, Richard Cromwell, Preston Foster, Herbert Mundin, James Gleason, Minna Gombell, Roger Imhof
'Miss Bow seems ripe to come back strongly.' – *Variety*

Hooray for Love

US 1935 75m bw
RKO (Felix Young)

A rich college boy plays angel to a musical comedy.
Thin pot-pourri of familiar elements.
w Lawrence Hazard, Ray Harris story Marc Lachmann d Walter Lang ph Lucien Andriot m/ly Dorothy Fields, Jimmy McHugh md Albert Colombo ad Van Nest Polglase ed George Crone
☆ Ann Sothern, Gene Raymond, Bill Robinson, Thurston Hall, Pert Kelton, Lionel Stander, Fats Waller
'Trouble is entirely traceable to its terribly lethargic tempo and lack of any real production numbers.' – *Variety*

The Hoosegow **

†† US 1929 20m bw
Hal Roach

Stan and Ollie, in prison, contrive to fell a tree on the cook's tent and to smother the governor in boiled rice.
Splendid slapstick leading up to one of their best tit-for-tat routines.
w Leo McCarey, H. M. Walker d James Parrott ph George Stevens, Len Powers, Glenn Robert Kershner ed Richard Currier
☆ Stan Laurel, Oliver Hardy, James Finlayson, Tiny Sandford, Ellinor Vanderveer

Hoosier Schoolboy

US 1937 62m bw
Monogram (Ken Goldsmith)

A rural boy defends his drunken father, shell-shocked in the war.
Simple tale for rural audiences.
w Robert Lee Johnson novel Edward Eggleston d William Nigh
☆ Mickey Rooney, Anne Nagel, Frank Shields, Edward Pawley
'A compelling film which word of mouth might turn into a sleeper.' – *Variety*

Hoosiers

US 1986 114m CFI color
Orion/Hemdale/Carter de Haven

GB title: *Best Shot*
The training and triumph of an Indiana high school basketball team.
Expertise expended on a subject of very limited interest.
w Angelo Pizzo d David Anspaugh ph Fred Murphy m Jerry Goldsmith
☆ Gene Hackman, Barbara Hershey, Dennis Hopper, Sheb Wooley, Fern Persons
'Both rousing and too conventional.' – *Variety*
⅋ Jerry Goldsmith; Dennis Hopper

Hoots Mon *

GB 1939 77m bw
Warner

A Cockney comedian starts a popularity contest with a female impressionist.
Tolerable comedy whose value is that it preserves, albeit in cleaned-up form, portions of Max Miller's variety act. Florence Desmond isn't bad either.
w Roy William Neill, Jack Henley, John Dighton d Roy William Neill ph Basil Emmott md Bretton Byrd ad Norman Arnold ed Leslie Norman
☆ Florence Desmond, Max Miller, Hal Walters, Davina Craig, Garry Marsh

Hopalong Cassidy

††
Cassidy, a creation of Clarence E. Mulford, was a fictitious gentleman cowboy who oddly enough wore black; 26 books about him were published between 1912 and 1956 when Mulford died. 66 films were made starring William Boyd as Hoppy, with either George Gabby Hayes or Andy Clyde as comic sidekick: Harry Sherman produced them, first for Paramount and then for UA, and they were later edited down for TV, in which medium Boyd became a folk hero and eventually made a further series. The films were easy-going, slow-moving second features which always pointed an admirable moral for children; their main directors were Howard Bretherton, Nate Watt, Lesley Selander and George Archainbaud.
1935 Hopalong Cassidy, The Eagle's Brood, Bar 20 Rides Again
1936 Call of the Prairie, Three on the Trail, Heart of the West, Hopalong Cassidy Returns, Trail Dust
1937 Borderland, Hills of Old Wyoming, North of the Rio Grande, Rustlers' Valley, Hopalong Rides Again, Texas Trail
1938 Heart of Arizona, Bar 20 Justice, Pride of the West, In Old Mexico, Sunset Trail, The Frontiersman, Partners of the Plains, Cassidy of Bar 20
1939 Range War, Law of the Pampas, Silver on the Sage, Renegade Trail
1940 Santa Fe Marshal, The Showdown, Hidden Gold, Stagecoach War, Three Men from Texas
1941 Doomed Caravan, In Old Colorado, Border Vigilantes, Pirates on Horseback, Wide Open Town, Outlaws of the Desert, Riders of the Timberline, Secrets of the Wasteland, Stick to

Your Guns, Twilight on the Trail
1942 Undercover Man
1943 Colt Comrades, Bar 20, Lost Canyon, Hoppy Serves a Writ, Border Patrol, The Leather Burners, False Colours, Riders of the Deadline
1944 Mystery Man, Forty Thieves, Texas Masquerade, Lumberjack
1946 The Devil's Playground
1947 Fool's Gold, Hoppy's Holiday, Marauders, Unexpected Guest, Dangerous Venture
1948 Sinister Journey, Silent Conflict, Strange Gamble, Borrowed Trouble, The Dead Don't Dream, False Paradise

Hope and Glory **

GB 1987 113m Technicolor
Columbia/Goldcrest/Nelson (John Boorman)

Adventures of a small boy and his family during World War II in suburban London.
Generally appealing but not too accurate reminiscences of an exciting and emotional time.
wd John Boorman ph Philippe Rousselot m Peter Martin pd Anthony Pratt ad Don Dossett
☆ Sarah Miles, Susan Wooldridge, Ian Bannen, David Hayman, Derrick O'Connor, Sebastian Rice-Edwards
⅋ Philippe Rousselot; John Boorman as director; best picture; best original screenplay; best art direction – set decoration
🅥 Susan Wooldridge

'When life fell apart love fell into place.'

Hope Floats

US 1998 114m DeLuxe
TCF/Fortis (Lynda Obst)

After the revelation on a TV talkshow that her husband is having an affair with her best friend, a woman returns home to Texas and meets a childhood sweetheart.
Leaden, dull, slow-paced, overlong drama of small-town virtues and redemption.
w Steven Rogers d Forest Whitaker ph Caleb Deschanel m Dave Grusin pd Larry Fulton ed Richard Chew
☆ Sandra Bullock, Harry Connick Jnr, Gena Rowlands, Mae Whitman, Michael Paré, Cameron Finley, Kathy Najimy, Rosanna Arquette (uncredited)
'A by-the-numbers bit of emotional calculation without a single fresh, original or offbeat move in its system.' – *Todd McCarthy, Variety*

Hoppity Goes to Town: see *Mr Bug Goes to Town*

Hopscotch *

US 1980 104m Movielab
Avco/Edie and Ely Landau (Otto Plaschkes)

An ex-CIA man writes a revealing book and foils the consequent attempts on his life.
Genial but patchy spy comedy caper; a filler for all concerned.
w Brian Garfield, Bryan Forbes novel Brian Garfield d Ronald Neame ph Arthur Ibbetson m Ian Fraser
☆ Walter Matthau, Glenda Jackson, Ned Beatty, Sam Waterston, Herbert Lom, George Baker

Hori, Ma Panenko: see *The Firemen's Ball*

Horizons West

US 1952 81m Technicolor
U-I (Albert J. Cohen)

After the Civil War, a rancher builds an empire on greed and ruthlessness, and his brother has to bring him to trial.
Rather lugubrious Western with the usual quota of effective action scenes.
w Louis Stevens d Budd Boetticher ph Charles P. Boyle md Joseph Gershenson
☆ Rock Hudson, Robert Ryan, Julia Adams, John McIntire, Raymond Burr, Dennis Weaver, Judith Braun

The Horizontal Lieutenant

US 1962 90m Metrocolor Cinemascope
MGM/Euterpe (Joe Pasternak)

World War II Hawaii; an amorous intelligence officer accidentally captures a Japanese guerrilla.
Very moderate army farce of no great skill or memorability.

w George Wells d Richard Thorpe ph Robert Bronner m George Stoll
☆ Jim Hutton, Paula Prentiss, Jim Backus, Miyoshi Umeki, Jack Carter

L'Horloger de St Paul: see *The Watchmaker of St Paul*

The Horn Blows at Midnight *

US 1945 80m bw
Warner (Mark Hellinger)

An angel is sent to earth to destroy the planet with Gabriel's horn.
Wacky comedy inspired by Here Comes Mr Jordan, but on a broader slapstick level; much better than its star always pretended.
w Sam Hellman, James V. Kern d Raoul Walsh ph Sid Hickox m Franz Waxman
☆ Jack Benny, Alexis Smith, Dolores Moran, Allyn Joslyn, Guy Kibbee, Reginald Gardiner, Franklin Pangborn, John Alexander, Margaret Dumont

Hornet's Nest

US 1969 109m DeLuxe
UA/Triangle (Stanley S. Kanter)

In World War II Italy, a wounded US army demolitions expert is nursed back to health by child partisans, who help him destroy a German-held dam.
Overlong war exploits with the children used as a tiresome gimmick.
w S. S. Schweitzer d Phil Karlson ph Gabor Pogany m Ennio Morricone
☆ Rock Hudson, Sergio Fantoni, Sylva Koscina, Jacques Sernas

Horriplante Bestia Humana: see *Night of the Bloody Apes*

Horror Express *

GB/Spain 1972 88m Technicolor
Gala/Granada/Benmar (Bernard Gordon)

aka: *Panic on the Trans-Siberian Express*
Spanish title: *Pánico en el Transiberiano*
An alien intelligence, trapped in a humanoid fossil for centuries, escapes and goes on a killing spree in which it absorbs the memories of its victims.
Moderately effective and ingenious low-budget horror.
w Arnaud d'Usseau, Julian Halevy story Eugenio Martin d Gene Martin ph Alejandro Ulloa m John Cavacas ad Ramiro Gomez Guadiana ed Robert Dearberg sp Pablo Perez
☆ Christopher Lee, Peter Cushing, Telly Savalas, Silvia Tortosa, Jorge Rigaud, Alberta de Mondoza
'The script unwinds itself with sufficient cunning to keep interest alive, always one step ahead of the audience with a new revelation to come.' – *Tom Milne, MFB*

'Black Gloves Of Evil Lay Bare The Ultimate Horror!'

Horror Hospital

GB 1973 91m Eastmancolor
Noteworthy (Richard Gordon)

A songwriter goes to spend a week at a health hotel run by a mysterious crippled doctor, who gives a lobotomy to all his patients.
High-camp, macabre movie that opens with a double decapitation and relishes its recycling of familiar horrors.
w Antony Balch, Alan Watson d Antony Balch ph David McDonald m De Wolfe, Mystic ad David Bill ed Robert Dearberg
☆ Michael Gough, Robin Askwith, Vanessa Shaw, Dennis Price, Ellen Pollock, Skip Martin, Kurt Christian, Barbara Wendy, Kenneth Benda
'If Horror Hospital makes no serious attempt to replace the basic clichés, it at least celebrates their survival with a satirical relish seldom displayed on this side of the Atlantic.' – *Jan Dawson, MFB*

Horror Hotel: see *City of the Dead*

The Horror House: see *The Haunted House of Horror*

Horror Island

US 1941 60m bw
Universal

Various people travel to an island where buried treasure might be hidden.

Feeble little mystery with very little interest in who done what to whom.
w Maurice Tombragel, Victor McLeod d George Waggner
☆ Dick Foran, Leo Carrillo, Peggy Moran, Fuzzy Knight, John Eldredge, Walter Catlett, Hobart Cavanaugh

Horror of Dracula: see *Dracula* (1958)

The Horror of Frankenstein
GB 1970 95m Technicolor
EMI/Hammer (Jimmy Sangster)
Victor Frankenstein is not above murdering his acquaintances for the sake of his experiments in bringing the dead back to life.
Ill-advised attempt to remake the original story as a black comedy, with Frankenstein frankly villainous from the start. The last in the Hammer series.
w Jeremy Burnham, Jimmy Sangster d Jimmy Sangster ph Moray Grant m Malcolm Williamson ad Scott MacGregor ed Chris Barnes
☆ Ralph Bates, Kate O'Mara, Graham James, Veronica Carlson, Bernard Archard, Dennis Price, Joan Rice, Dave Prowse

Horror of Snape Island: see *Tower of Evil*

Horror Planet: see *Inseminoid*

The Horror Show
US 1989 95m DeLuxe
UA (Sean S. Cunningham)
aka: House III
A cop and his family become the target for a dead homicidal maniac, resurrected through electricity.
Muddled and confused horror that never sparks into life.
w Alan Smithee (Allyn Warner), Leslie Bohem d James Isaac ph Mac Ahlberg m Harry Manfredini pd Stewart Campbell ed Edward Anton
☆ Lance Henriksen, Brion James, Rita Taggart, Dedee Pfeiffer, Thom Bray, Matt Clark, Lawrence Tierney

Horrors of the Black Museum
GB 1959 81m Eastmancolor Cinemascope
Herman Cohen
A crime writer is fascinated by murder, and works out his own plots by practice beforehand.
Crude shocker.
w Aben Kandel, Herman Cohen d Arthur Crabtree ph Desmond Dickinson m Gerard Schurmann
☆ Michael Gough, Graham Curnow, Shirley Anne Field, Geoffrey Keen

Hors La Vie
French/Italian/German 1991 97m colour
Galatee/A2/Filmalpha/Lamy/Canal Plus/Raidue (Jacques Perrin)
A French photographer working in Beirut is taken hostage.
Based on fact, this is an unsensational but not illuminating account of what it is to be held prisoner.
w Maroun Bagdadi, Didier Decoin, Elias Khoury book Roger Auque, Patrick Forestier d Maroun Bagdadi ph Patrick Blossier m Nicola Piovani ad Dan Weil ed Luc Barnier
☆ Hippolyte Girardot, Rafic Ali Ahmad, Hussein Sbetty, Habib Hammoud, Magdi Machmouchi, Hassan Farhat, Hamzah Nasrullah, Nidal El Achkar
'Sober, uncompromising but never excessive treatment conveys the mental and physical horrors of detention while delineating delicate balance between captors and victim.' – *Variety*
'An assembly-kit political thriller. In a moment of madness the Cannes Jury gave it a Special Jury Prize. Perhaps they liked the telegraphic simplicity of the story.' – *Nigel Andrews, Financial Times*

'A scandalous record of low Marx at college – or life among the thirsty co-eds!'
Horse Feathers ***
US 1932 69m bw
Paramount (Herman J. Mankiewicz)
A college needs to win at football, and its corrupt new president knows just how to do it.
Possibly the Marxes' wildest yet most streamlined kaleidoscope of high jinks and irreverence, with at least one bright gag or line to the minute and lively musical interludes to boot. A classic of zany comedy.
w Bert Kalmar, Harry Ruby, S. J. Perelman, Will B. Johnstone d Norman Z. McLeod ph Ray June m/ly Bert Kalmar, Harry Ruby
☆ Groucho Marx, Chico Marx, Harpo Marx, Zeppo Marx, Thelma Todd, Robert Greig
GROUCHO: 'You have the brain of a four-year-old child, and I'll bet he was glad to get rid of it.'
CHICO: 'There's a man outside with a big black moustache.'
GROUCHO: 'Tell him I've got one.'
GROUCHO (TO ZEPPO): 'You're a disgrace to our family name of Wagstaff, if such a thing is possible.'
GROUCHO: 'For years before my son was born I used to yell from night till morn Whatever it is – I'm against it! And I've been yelling since I first commenced it – I'm against it!'
'The current Marx comedy is the funniest talkie since the last Marx comedy, and the record it establishes is not likely to be disturbed until the next Marx comedy comes along. As for comparisons, I was too busy having a good time to make any.' – *Philip K. Scheuer*

The Horse in the Grey Flannel Suit
US 1969 112m Technicolor
Walt Disney
A teenager's horse becomes the central figure in an advertising campaign for a stomach pill.
Interminable kiddie movie which in its virtual absence of plot or excitement is likely to bore kiddies to death.
w Louis Pelletier novel *The Year of the Horse* by Eric Hatch d Norman Tokar ph William Snyder m George Bruns
☆ Dean Jones, Fred Clark, Diane Baker, Lloyd Bochner, Morey Amsterdam

The Horse Soldiers *
US 1959 119m DeLuxe
UA/Mirisch (John Lee Mahin, Martin Rackin)
In 1863 a Union cavalry officer is sent three hundred miles into Confederate territory to demolish a railroad junction.
Typically sprawling John Ford cavalry Western with not too many high spots and more sombre ingredients than usual.
w John Lee Mahin, Martin Rackin d John Ford ph William Clothier m David Buttolph
☆ John Wayne, William Holden, Constance Towers, Hoot Gibson
HOLDEN: 'Look here, colonel, I didn't ask to be assigned to this mission…'
'Blemished as many of his films are blemished: patches of horseplay, too much manly chest-beating. But the blemishes proceed from the quality which gives his work its frequent splendours. The horseplay and the over-emphasised masculinity belong to his romantic vision.' – *Dilys Powell*

Horse Thief **
China 1986 88m colour
Xi'an Film Studio (Li Changqing)
Trying to feed his family, a peasant becomes a thief and outcast.
Its stunning visuals, of exotic rituals and broad landscapes, and exuberant style compensate for the slightness of narrative.
w Zhang Rui d Tian Zhuangzhuang ph Hou Yong, Zhao Fei m Qu Xiaosong ad Huo Jianqi ed Li Jingzhong
☆ Tseshang Rinzim, Dan Jiji, Jayang Jamco

The Horse Whisperer
US 1998 168m Technicolor Panavision
Buena Vista/Touchstone/Wildwood (Robert Redford, Patrick Markey)
When her daughter and horse are both traumatized by a riding accident, a New York magazine editor travels to Montana to seek the help of an equine expert.
Ponderous romantic drama, lushly photographed but never convincing on an emotional level.
w Eric Roth, Richard LaGravenese novel Nicholas Evans d Robert Redford ph Robert Richardson m Thomas Newman pd Jon Hutman ed Tom Rolf, Freeman Davies, Hank Corwin
☆ Robert Redford, Kristin Scott Thomas, Sam Neill, Dianne Wiest, Scarlett Johansson, Chris Cooper, Cherry Jones, Ty Hillman, Catherine Bosworth
'An exquisitely crafted, morally and thematically mature picture.' – *Todd McCarthy, Variety*
'Punishingly dull.' – *Newsweek*
'This stately, aggravating film is set in that hollow universe known only to popular middle-brow novels and Hollywood stars too cocooned by their own eminence to recognise the march of time.' – *Geoff Brown, The Times*
♫ song 'A Soft Place to Fall' (m/ly Allison Moorer, Gwil Owen)

The Horse without a Head **
GB 1963 89m Technicolor
Walt Disney (Hugh Attwooll)
Stolen money is hidden in an old toy horse, and crooks trying to get it back clash with police and children.
Excellent children's adventure with scenes on trains and in a toy factory.
w T. E. B. Clarke d Don Chaffey ph Paul Beeson m Eric Rogers
☆ Leo McKern, Jean-Pierre Aumont, Herbert Lom, Pamela Franklin, Vincent Winter

The Horseman on the Roof
France 1995 135m colour
Hachette/France2/CEC/Canal (René Cleitman)
original title: *Le Hussard sur le Toit*
An Italian hussar hides from his enemies in Provence, where he meets a young woman searching for her husband.
Sweepingly romantic, epic romance that delights the eye more than the mind; handsome is as handsome does, and it doesn't do enough to engage the attention for long.
w Jean-Paul Rappeneau, Nina Companeez, Jean-Claude Carrière novel Jean Giono d Jean-Paul Rappeneau ph Thierry Arbogast m Jean-Claude Petit ad François Hamel ed Noëlle Boisson
☆ Olivier Martinez, Juliette Binoche, Isabelle Carré, François Cluzet, Jean Yanne, Claudio Amendola, Pierre Arditi, Gérard Depardieu
† It was reportedly the most expensive French film yet made, at a cost of around 176m francs.

The Horsemen
US 1970 109m colour Super Panavision
Columbia/John Frankenheimer-Edward Lewis
An Afghan tribesman is determined to rival his father at horsemanship.
Rather tedious variant on Taras Bulba; plenty of action but not much characterization, or taste, or interest.
w Dalton Trumbo novel Joseph Kessel d John Frankenheimer ph Claude Renoir m Georges Delerue
☆ Omar Sharif, Jack Palance, Leigh Taylor-Young, Peter Jeffrey, Eric Pohlmann, Despo, David de Keyser

The Horse's Mouth *
GB 1958 93m Technicolor
UA/Knightsbridge (John Bryan)
An obsessive painter is a liability to his friends.
Thin but fitfully amusing light study of a social outcast, with a background of London river and streets. Too slight for real success.
w Alec Guinness novel Joyce Cary d Ronald Neame ph Arthur Ibbetson m K. V. Jones from Prokofiev paintings John Bratby
☆ Alec Guinness, Kay Walsh, Renée Houston, Robert Coote, Arthur Macrae, Michael Gough, Ernest Thesiger
'Immensely and joyously successful at what it sets out to do.' – *Evening Standard*
'A work of genius.' – *News of the World*
♟ Alec Guinness (as writer)

The Hospital ***
US 1971 101m DeLuxe Panavision
UA/Simcha (Howard Gottfried)
A city hospital is beset by weird mishaps, and it transpires that a killer is on the loose.
*Black comedy with the emphasis on sex and medical ethics; in the same genre as M*A*S*H, and very funny if you can take it.*
w Paddy Chayefsky d Arthur Hiller ph Victor Kemper m Morris Surdin
☆ George C. Scott, Diana Rigg, Barnard Hughes, Nancy Marchand, Richard Dysart
♟ Paddy Chayefsky
♟ George C. Scott

The Hostage
GB 1956 86m bw
Westridge/Eros
A South American president condemns a revolutionary to death; in London, sympathizers kidnap the president's daughter.
Tolerable support.
w Alfred Shaughnessy d Harold Huth ph Brendan Stafford m Bretton Byrd
☆ Ron Randell, Mary Parker, Carl Jaffe, Margaret Diamond, Cyril Luckham

'They're blasting the Nazis – from inside!'
Hostages
US 1943 88m bw
Paramount (Sol C. Siegel)
In occupied Prague, the Nazis seize a variety of hostages and threaten them with death as a reprisal for underground activities.
Modest morale-builder, unfortunately padded out with melodramatics and overacting.
w Lester Cole, Frank Butler novel Stefan Heym d Frank Tuttle ph Victor Milner m Victor Young
☆ Luise Rainer, Paul Lukas, William Bendix, Oscar Homolka, Arturo de Cordova, Katina Paxinou, Roland Varno

Hostile Guns
US 1967 91m Techniscope
Paramount (A. C. Lyles)
A marshal has to deliver four dangerous convicts to the penitentiary.
Rather crude addition to the A. C. Lyles series distinguished only by nostalgic casting.
w Steve Fisher, Sloan Nibley d R. G. Springsteen
☆ George Montgomery, Tab Hunter, Yvonne de Carlo, Brian Donlevy, Fuzzy Knight, John Russell, Leo Gordon, Robert Emhardt, Richard Arlen

Hostile Hostages: see *The Ref*

Hostile Witness
GB 1968 101m DeLuxe
UA/Caralan/Dador (David E. Rose)
A barrister suffers a nervous breakdown after the death of his daughter and finds himself accused of murder.
Complex courtroom thriller, filmed in a flatly boring way with stagey sets and performances. The plot is the only interest.
w Jack Roffey play Jack Roffey d Ray Milland ph Gerry Gibbs
☆ Ray Milland, Sylvia Sims, Felix Aylmer, Raymond Huntley, Geoffrey Lumsden, Norman Barrs, Percy Marmont, Ewan Roberts

'Be there when Jane Russell shakes her tambourines!'
'If you'd hit me and given me orders on our wedding night, I would have kissed your hand!'
Hot Blood
US 1955 85m Technicolor Cinemascope
Columbia (Howard Welsch)
A dying gypsy king wants his young brother to get married and succeed him.
What promises to be a boring musical proves to be a boring melodrama. Artificial Romany hokum.
w Jesse Lasky Jnr d Nicholas Ray ph Ray June m Les Baxter
☆ Cornel Wilde, Jane Russell, Joseph Calleia, Helen Westcott, Mikhail Rasumny

The Hot Box
US 1972 89m Metrocolor
New Realm/New World (Jonathan Demme)
Three American nurses are kidnapped by a revolutionary leader in Latin America.
Ridiculous exploitation film providing sex and violence.

w Joe Viola, Jonathan Demme d Joe Viola
ph Felipe Sacdalan m Resti Umali ad Ben Otico
ed Ben Barcelon

☆ Andrea Cagan, Margaret Markov, Rickey Richardson, Laurie Rose, Carmen Argenziano, Charles Dierkop

'The film emerges as an honourable solution to the problem of taking a left-wing position in an essentially capitalist industry.' – Tony Rayns, MFB

† The film was cut to 86m on its British release.

Hot Enough for June

GB 1963 98m Eastmancolor
Rank (Betty E. Box)
US title: Agent 8 3/4
A penniless writer is sent to Czechoslovakia on a goodwill mission and finds himself being used as a spy.
Very moderate spoof, neither very funny nor very thrilling.
w Lukas Heller novel The Night before Wenceslas by Lionel Davidson d Ralph Thomas ph Ernest Steward m Angelo Lavagnino
☆ Dirk Bogarde, Sylva Koscina, Robert Morley, Leo McKern, John Le Mesurier

Hot, Hard and Mean: see Black Mama, White Mama

Hot Lead

US 1951 60m bw
RKO (Herman Schlom)
Two cowboys set out to capture the train robbers who killed their friend.
Average supporting Western, with all the usual ingredients of gunfights, fistfights, chases, a cattle stampede, mistaken identity and a little romance and comedy.
w William Lively d Stuart Gilmore ph Nicholas Musuraca m Paul Sawtell ad Albert S. D'Agostino, Feild Gray ed Robert Golden
☆ Tim Holt, Joan Dixon, Richard Martin, Ross Elliott, John Dehner, Robert Wilke, Paul Marion

Hot Lead and Cold Feet

👫 US 1978 90m colour
Buena Vista (Ron Miller)
Twin brothers, one a tough gunfighter, the other a pacifist, compete in a race to inherit a Western town.
Comic Western showcasing Dale in three differing roles – as the father and his two sons – but with a script that runs out of ideas long before the end.
w Arthur Alsberg, Joe McEveety, Don Nelson story Rod Piffath d Robert Butler ph Frank Phillips m Buddy Baker ad John Mansbridge, Frank T. Smith ed Ray de Leuw
☆ Jim Dale, Karen Valentine, Don Knotts, Jack Elam, Darren McGavin, John Williams, Warren Vanders

Hot Millions *

US 1968 106m colour
MGM/Mildred Freed Alberg
A confidence trickster makes a fortune out of fictitious companies.
Elaborate, talky, overlong comedy with irresistible star performances.
w Ira Wallach, Peter Ustinov d Eric Till m Laurie Johnson
☆ Peter Ustinov, Maggie Smith, Bob Newhart, Karl Malden, Robert Morley, Cesar Romero
& Ira Wallach, Peter Ustinov (script)

Hot Money

Canada 1989 78m colour
Westfront (Zale Magder)
A million-dollar robbery causes problems to the inhabitants of a small town as state police and tax investigators move in.
Totally incoherent drama, with little in the way of narrative or continuity, but a great deal of windy philosophizing. It was Welles's last, and least, performance.
w Carl Desantis, Phyllis Camesano, Joel Cohen, Neil Cohen d Selig Usher ph Stan Mestel m John Jones pd C. M. Zaharuk ed Murray Jay
☆ Orson Welles, Michael Murphy, Michelle Finney, Henry Ramer, Kenneth Pogue, Bobby Pickett, Ann Lance, Thomas Kopache
† Made in 1986.

The Hot One: see Corvette Summer

Hot Pursuit

US 1987 93m Metrocolor
Paramount/RKO (Theodore R. Parvin, Pierre David)
Delayed at the start of a Caribbean holiday, a student tries to catch up with his girlfriend and her family who have gone on ahead.
Predictable and uninteresting teen comedy that veers into unexpected and unnecessary violence at its climax.
w Stephen Lisberger, Steven Carabatsos d Stephen Lisberger ph Frank Tidy m Rareview pd William J. Creber ed Mitchell Sinoway
☆ John Cusack, Robert Loggia, Wendy Gazelle, Jerry Stiller, Monte Markham, Shelley Fabares

The Hot Rock ***

US 1972 105m DeLuxe Panavision
TCF (Hal Landers, Bobby Roberts)
GB title: How to Steal a Diamond in Four Uneasy Lessons
Four crooks plan to rob the Brooklyn Museum of a priceless diamond.
Enjoyable variation on the caper theme, with relaxed comic performances and highly skilled technical back-up. It's refreshing to come across a film which hits its targets so precisely.
w William Goldman novel Donald E. Westlake d Peter Yates ph Ed Brown m Quincy Jones
☆ Robert Redford, George Segal, Zero Mostel, Paul Sand, Ron Leibman, Moses Gunn, William Redfield

'A funny, fast-paced, inventive and infinitely clever crime comedy, almost as if The French Connection had been remade as a piece of urban humour.' – Michael Korda

'Her lips offered what her heart denied!'
Hot Saturday

US 1932 73m bw
Paramount
Malicious gossip in a small town causes a girl to lose her job.
Small town, small potatoes; interesting chiefly for its two budding male stars.
w Seton I. Miller novel Harvey Ferguson d William A. Seiter
☆ Nancy Carroll, Cary Grant, Randolph Scott, Edward Woods, Lillian Bond, Jane Darwell, William Collier Snr

'Fairly agreeable as entertainment, but will not get preferred playing time.' – Variety

Hot Shot

US 1987 90m Precision colour
Arista (Steve Pappas)
A rich, cocky New Yorker, who upsets his faullily by insisting on playing professional soccer, goes to Brazil to ask Pelé to help him improve his game.
A standard revolting-teenager movie aimed at those who understand little about the sport; knowledgeable audiences are likely to find it unintentionally amusing and may be disappointed that Pelé's contribution is mainly restricted to some limited acting (he even cries at the end).
w Joe Sauter, Rick King, Ray Errol Fox, Bill Guttentag d Rick King ph Greg Andracke, Edgar Moura m William Orbit pd Ruth Ammon, Beata Segall ed Stan Salfas
☆ Jim Youngs, Pelé, Billy Warlock, Jeremy Green, Weyman Thompson, Mario Van Peebles, Penelope Miller, David Groh

'There's Something Funny In The Air.'
Hot Shots!

👫 US 1991 85m DeLuxe
TCF (Bill Badalato)
A young disturbed pilot joins an élite group to take part in a raid on a nuclear plant or, as secondary target, an accordion factory.
A hit-and-miss send-up of Top Gun and other Hollywood hits, in which most of the targets are missed.
w Jim Abrahams, Pat Proft d Jim Abrahams ph Bill Butler m Sylvester Levay pd William A. Elliott ed Jane Kurson, Eric Sears
☆ Charlie Sheen, Cary Elwes, Valeria Golino, Lloyd Bridges, Jon Cryer, Kevin Dunn, Bill Irwin, William O'Leary, Kristy Swanson, Efrem Zimbalist Jnr

'Re-Armed, Re-United ... Re-Diculous!'
Hot Shots!: Part Deux

US 1993 88m DeLuxe
TCF (Bill Badalato)
A special forces mission is sent to the Middle East to rescue a special forces mission whose mission it was to rescue hostages.
A send-up of Rambo, if that is possible, which also takes in references to dozens of other movies, but without providing much in the way of laughs.
w Jim Abrahams, Pat Proft d Jim Abrahams ph John R. Leonetti m Basil Poledouris pd William A. Elliott ed Malcolm Campbell
☆ Charlie Sheen, Lloyd Bridges, Valeria Golino, Richard Crenna, Brenda Bakke, Miguel Ferrer, Rowan Atkinson

'To truly enjoy it, the viewer must abandon his or her dignity for at least 90 minutes, and accept the inherent silliness.' – John Anderson, Newsday

Hot Spell *

US 1958 86m bw Vistavision
Paramount/Hal Wallis
In a small Southern town, a husband seeks to leave his wife and family for a 20-year-old girl.
Overwrought domestic drama slipping perilously close to farce at times, but a good theatrical vehicle for its stars.
w James Poe play Next of Kin by Lonnie Coleman d Daniel Mann ph Loyal Griggs m Alex North
☆ Anthony Quinn, Shirley Booth, Shirley MacLaine, Earl Holliman, Eileen Heckart

Hot Spot: see I Wake Up Screaming (1941)

The Hot Spot *

US 1990 130m colour
Rank/Orion (Paul Lewis)
A car dealer's wife seduces a drifter and petty crook who goes to work for her husband.
Effective melodrama, much in the manner of a 1940s film noir.
w Nona Tyson, Charles Williams novel Hell Hath No Fury by Charles Williams d Dennis Hopper ph Ueli Steiger m Jack Nitzsche pd Cary White ed Wende Phifer Mate
☆ Don Johnson, Virginia Madsen, Jennifer Connelly, Charles Martin Smith, William Sadler, Jerry Hardin, Barry Corbin, Leon Rippy, Jack Nance

Hot Stuff

US 1979 91m Metrocolor
Columbia/Rastar/Mort Engelberg
Members of a Burglary Task Force need convictions, so they set up fences in order to lure criminals, and are embarrassed by the results.
Slightly unusual but rather frantically assembled comedy which wears out its welcome long before the end.
w Michael Kane, Donald E. Westlake d Dom DeLuise m James Pergola m Patrick Williams
☆ Dom DeLuise, Suzanne Pleshette, Ossie Davis, Jerry Reed, Luis Avalos, Marc Lawrence

'Heavy farce in which a bright comedy is struggling to escape.' – Tom Milne, MFB

Hot Summer Night *

US 1957 85m bw
MGM (Morton S. Fine)
A foolhardy reporter determines on an interview with a notorious outlaw, and has to be rescued.
Interesting but disappointing low-budget experiment.
w Morton S. Fine, David Friedkin d David Friedkin ph Harold S. Marcorati m André Previn
☆ Leslie Nielsen, Colleen Miller, Edward Andrews, Jay C. Flippen, James Best, Paul Richards, Robert Wilke, Claude Akins

Hot Sweat: see Keetje Tippel

Hot Target

New Zealand 1985 90m colour
Crown International/Endeavour (John Barnett, Bryan Cook)
The bored wife of a ruthless and wealthy businessman begins an affair with a man she meets in a park – and discovers that he is a criminal.
Dull and unexciting thriller, in which even the twist in the tale is predictable.

wd Denis Lewiston story Gerry O'Hara ph Alec Mills m Gil Melle pd Jo Ford ed Michael Horton
☆ Simone Griffeth, Steve Marachuk, Bryan Marshall, Peter McCauley, Elizabeth Hawthorne, Ray Henwood, John Watson

Hot Water *

👫 US 1924 50m bw silent
Harold Lloyd
A young husband has trouble with a turkey, a new car and his in-laws.
Casually structured star comedy with brilliant sequences.
w Harold Lloyd, Sam Taylor d Fred Newmeyer, Sam Taylor
☆ Harold Lloyd, Jobyna Ralston, Josephine Crowell

Hot Winds: see Garm Hava

Hotel *

US 1967 124m Technicolor
Warner (Wendell Mayes)
Guests at a luxurious New Orleans hotel have various problems.
Old-fashioned omnibus drama from a bestseller, quite brightly done.
w Wendell Mayes novel Arthur Hailey d Richard Quine ph Charles Lang m Johnny Keating
☆ Rod Taylor, Catherine Spaak, Karl Malden, Melvyn Douglas, Merle Oberon, Michael Rennie, Kevin McCarthy, Alfred Ryder

Hotel Berlin *

US 1945 98m bw
Warner (Louis F. Edelman)
Various lives intertwine in a Berlin hotel towards the end of the war.
After five years of total war this view of life on the other side can hardly fail to be unconvincing, but the actors gleefully seize on moments of melodrama.
w Jo Pagano, Alvah Bessie novel Vicki Baum d Peter Godfrey ph Carl Guthrie m Franz Waxman
☆ Raymond Massey, Peter Lorre, Faye Emerson, Helmut Dantine, Andrea King, Alan Hale, George Coulouris, Henry Daniell, Helene Thimig, Kurt Kreuger, Steve Geray, Frank Reicher

'The most heavily routine of Warners' political melodramas, stuffed with sympathetic veterans.' – James Agee

'A comedy for the romantically confused.'
Hotel de Love *

Australia 1996 93m colour
Village Roadshow/Pratt (Michael Lake, David Parker)
Two brothers vie for the love of the same woman.
Kitsch romantic comedy with a modicum of wit.
wd Craig Rosenberg ph Steve Windon m Christine Woodruff pd Simon Dobbin ed Bill Murphy
☆ Simon Bossell, Aden Young, Saffron Burrows, Pippa Grandison, Ray Barrett, Julia Blake

'Stocked with enough solid laugh-lines and feel-good resolutions for a half-dozen romantic comedies.' – Ken Eisner, Variety

Hotel du Nord **

France 1938 110m bw
Sedif/Imperial
People with problems congregate at a small hotel.
Melancholy, studio-confined character drama which has its adherents but technically seemed a throwback to earlier standards. The acting rescues it.
w Henri Jeanson, Eugene Dabit d Marcel Carné ph Armand Thirard m Maurice Jaubert
☆ Annabella, Louis Jouvet, Jean-Pierre Aumont, Arletty, Jeanne Marken, Bernard Blier

'An outstander in this country and possesses good chance abroad.' – Variety (Paris)

Hotel du Paradis

GB/France 1986 113m Eastmancolor
Umbrella-Portman Films/Pierson/Film Four/London Trust/Antenne 2 (Simon Perry)
An ageing actor, planning a comeback in a one-man show, revisits a small Parisian hotel that he loves.
Slow, atmospheric but inconsequential drama.

---

wd Jana Bokova ph Gerard de Battista m Rodolfo Mederos pd Patrick Weibel ed Bill Shapter

☆ Fernando Rey, Fabrice Luchini, Berangere Bonvoisin, Hugues Quester, Marika Rivera, Carola Regnier, Raul Gimenez, Michael Medwin, Georges Geret

Hotel for Women

US 1939 83m bw
TCF (Raymond Griffith)

Young city gold diggers are encouraged by a matron.

Slight comedy drama notable for the acting debut of hostess Elsa Maxwell.

w Kathryn Scola, Darrell Ware d Gregory Ratoff ph Peverell Marley m David Buttolph

☆ Elsa Maxwell, Linda Darnell, Ann Sothern, James Ellison, John Halliday, Lynn Bari, Alan Dinehart

'Synthetic Cinderella story … fluffed up with a generous display of latest fashions.' – *Variety*

Hotel Haywire

US 1937 66m bw
Paramount (Harold Hurley)

An astrologer makes eyes at a dentist's wife, and causes much confusion in a hotel.

Frantic farce which might have been funnier if it had stuck to the original script and cast (it was intended for Burns and Allen).

w Preston Sturges (before studio revision) d George Archainbaud ph Henry Sharp

☆ Leo Carrillo, Lynne Overman, Mary Carlisle, Benny Baker, Spring Byington, George Barbier, Porter Hall, Lucien Littlefield, John Patterson

'Broad comedy applied with sufficient skill and effect to make the journey on the dual route fairly safe.' – *Variety*

'Flaming love drama of the war-torn Balkans!'
'Her beauty sent men marching to their death with a smile!'

Hotel Imperial

US 1939 78m bw
Paramount

Balkans, 1916: a Polish dancer suspects a Hungarian officer of being responsible for her sister's death.

Dim romantic melodrama with espionage trimmings.

w Gilbert Gabriel, Robert Thoeren play Lajos Biro d Robert Florey ph William Mellor md Boris Morros

☆ Ray Milland, Isa Miranda, Reginald Owen, Gene Lockhart, J. Carrol Naish, Curt Bois, Henry Victor, Albert Dekker

'Nothing much to be done about this one … a weak sister, dated and inconclusive … never seems to generate any interest.' – *Variety*
'A very competent rehash … for the unexacting the picture has its moments.' – *Graham Greene*
† Previously made in 1926 by Mauritz Stiller, with Pola Negri. This version was originally announced in 1936 as *I Loved a Soldier*, to star Marlene Dietrich (or Margaret Sullavan) and Charles Boyer.

The Hotel New Hampshire

US 1984 108m Technicolor
Orion/Woodfall (Neil Hartley, Pieter Kroonenburg, David Patterson)

A schoolmaster and his family are obsessed by the fantasy of living in a hotel, and this fantasy is performed with variations.

A parable of life in the manner of Thornton Wilder's The Skin of Our Teeth, and sometimes even more obscure, but generally quite entertaining along the way.

wd Tony Richardson novel John Irving ph David Watkin m Jacques Offenbach pd Jocelyn Herbert ed Robert K. Lambert

☆ Rob Lowe, Jodie Foster, Paul McCrane, Beau Bridges, Nastassja Kinski, Wallace Shawn, Wilford Brimley

Hotel Paradiso *

US 1966 99m Metrocolor Panavision
MGM (Peter Glenville)

Various romantic affairs come to a head one evening at a seedy hotel.

A famous boulevard farce seems jellied in aspic in this good-looking but very flatly handled film version, in which famous artists are left to caper about on an unsuitable wide screen with no help from the director.

w Peter Glenville, Jean-Claude Carrière play Georges Feydeau, Maurice Desvallières d Peter Glenville ph Henri Decaë m Laurence Rosenthal pd François de Lamothe

☆ Alec Guinness, Gina Lollobrigida, Robert Morley, Peggy Mount, Douglas Byng, Akim Tamiroff, Robertson Hare

Hotel Reserve

GB 1944 89m bw
RKO (Victor Hanbury)

An Austrian refugee in the south of France is asked by the police to track down a spy among his fellow hotel guests.

Slow, obvious and poorly made suspenser from a good novel.

w John Davenport novel Epitaph for a Spy by Eric Ambler d Victor Hanbury, Lance Comfort, Max Greene ph Max Greene

☆ James Mason, Lucie Mannheim, Raymond Lovell, Julien Mitchell, Martin Miller, Herbert Lom, Frederick Valk, Valentine Dyall

Hotel Sahara *

GB 1951 96m bw
GFD/Tower (George H. Brown)

In North Africa during World War II, a small hotel changes its loyalties to suit its occupiers.

Overstretched, studio-bound, fitfully amusing comedy.

w George H. Brown, Patrick Kirwan d Ken Annakin ph Jack Hildyard m Benjamin Frankel

☆ Peter Ustinov, Yvonne de Carlo, David Tomlinson, Roland Culver, Albert Lieven, Bill Owen, Sydney Tafler, Ferdy Mayne

'Cheerful, uncomplicated empty stuff … no more subtle than a music hall sketch.' – *Richard Mallett, Punch*

Hotel Sorrento

Australia 1994 112m Cinevex
Polygram/Bayside/Horizon/AFFC (Richard Franklin)

Three sisters quarrel at a family reunion over an autobiographical novel one of them has written.

Stolid adaptation of a theatrical success, which is little more than a staged debate on the cultural condition of Australia; on this evidence, it's in a bad way.

w Richard Franklin, Peter Fitzpatrick play Hannie Rayson d Richard Franklin ph Geoff Burton m Nerida Tyson-Chew pd Tracy Watt ed David Pulbrook

☆ Caroline Goodall, Caroline Gillmer, Tara Morice, Joan Plowright, Ray Barrett, Nicholas Bell, Ben Thomas, John Hargreaves

'A film which seems determined to shoot itself in the foot at every turn.' – *Sight and Sound*

The Hottentot

US 1929 77m bw
Warner

A horse lover is forced to masquerade as a champion jockey.

Early talkie version of a well-worn theme which had previously appeared as a silent in 1923 with Douglas MacLean; it later turned up as a Joe E. Brown vehicle and in 1938 became Going Places, a Dick Powell musical.

w Harvey Thew play Victor Mapes, Willie Collier d Roy del Ruth

☆ Patsy Ruth Miller, Douglas Gerrard

Houdini

US 1953 106m Technicolor
Paramount (George Pal)

In the 1890s a fairground magician shows a passionate talent for escapology and finally kills himself by undertaking increasingly impossible tricks.

Superficial biopic with more attention to romance than to interesting detail. Some zest in the playing is killed by claustrophobic studio sets.

w Philip Yordan d George Marshall ph Ernest Laszlo m Roy Webb

☆ Tony Curtis, Janet Leigh, Torin Thatcher, Sig Rumann, Angela Clarke

The Hound Dog Man

US 1959 87m DeLuxe Cinemascope
TCF/Company of Artists (Jerry Wald)

An irresponsible country boy gets his come-uppance.

Mild, competent backwoods comedy drama introducing a teenage rave.

w Fred Gipson, Winston Miller novel Fred Gipson d Don Siegel ph Charles G. Clarke

m Cyril Mockridge ad Lyle Wheeler, Walter M. Simonds ed Louis Loeffler

☆ Fabian, Stuart Whitman, Carol Lynley, Arthur O'Connell, Betty Field, Royal Dano, Jane Darwell, Edgar Buchanan, Claude Akins

The Hound of the Baskervilles **

👥 US 1939 80m bw
(TCF)
▦ ☍

Sherlock Holmes solves the mystery of a supernatural hound threatening the life of a Dartmoor baronet.

Basil Rathbone's first appearance as Sherlock Holmes is in a painstaking studio production which achieves good atmosphere and preserves the flavour if not the letter of the book but is let down by a curious lack of pace.

w Ernest Pascal novel Arthur Conan Doyle d Sidney Lanfield ph Peverell Marley m Cyril Mockridge ad Thomas Little

☆ Basil Rathbone, Nigel Bruce, Richard Greene, Wendy Barrie, Lionel Atwill, Morton Lowry, John Carradine, Barlowe Borland, Beryl Mercer, Ralph Forbes, E. E. Clive, Eily Malyon, Mary Gordon

'A startling mystery-chiller … will find many bookings on top spots of key duallers.' – *Variety*
'Lush dialogue, stagey sets and vintage supporting cast make it a delectable Hollywood period piece.' – *Judith Crist, 1980*
† For Rathbone's other appearances as Holmes see under *Sherlock Holmes*.

The Hound of the Baskervilles *

GB 1959 86m Technicolor
UA/Hammer (Anthony Hinds)
▦

Spirited remake let down by dogged Hammer insistence on promises of horror and sex; good atmosphere also let down by poor colour.

w Peter Bryan novel Arthur Conan Doyle d Terence Fisher ph Jack Asher m James Bernard ad Bernard Robinson ed James Needs

☆ Peter Cushing, André Morell, Christopher Lee, Marla Landi, Ewen Solon, Francis de Wolff, Miles Malleson, John Le Mesurier

The Hound of the Baskervilles

GB 1977 85m Technicolor
Hemdale/Michael White Ltd (John Goldstone)
▦

A pointless, pitiful and vulgar spoof of an enjoyable original.

w Dudley Moore, Peter Cook, Paul Morrissey d Paul Morrissey ph Dick Bush, John Wilcox m Dudley Moore

☆ Peter Cook, Dudley Moore, Denholm Elliott, Terry-Thomas, Joan Greenwood, Max Wall, Irene Handl, Kenneth Williams, Hugh Griffith, Roy Kinnear, Penelope Keith, Dana Gillespie, Prunella Scales, Jessie Matthews, Spike Milligan

Hounded: see *Johnny Allegro*

The Hounds of Zaroff: see *The Most Dangerous Game*

'As I held her in my arms, how could I know that she was as vicious as she was beautiful?'

The Hour before the Dawn

US 1944 75m bw
Paramount (William Dozier)

When a pacifist English nobleman discovers during World War II that he has married a Nazi spy, he strangles her and joins the forces.

Stultifyingly absurd, badly made and acted melodrama which its author clearly wished he had never written, as it was later withdrawn from his canon.

w Michael Hogan, Lesser Samuels novel W. Somerset Maugham d Frank Tuttle ph John F. Seitz m Miklos Rozsa

☆ Franchot Tone, Veronica Lake, John Sutton, Binnie Barnes, Henry Stephenson, Philip Merivale, Nils Asther, Edmund Breon

'Tedious and generally uneventful … a weak entry for the duals.' – *Variety*

The Hour of Decision

GB 1957 81m bw
Tempean/Eros
▦

A reporter is assigned to investigate the death of a columnist.

A familiar type of second feature whodunnit, with little about it to spark enthusiasm.

w Norman Hudis d C. Pennington-Richards

☆ Jeff Morrow, Hazel Court, Lionel Jeffries, Anthony Dawson, Mary Laura Wood

Hour of Glory: see *The Small Back Room*

'Wyatt Earp – hero with a badge, or cold-blooded killer?'

Hour of the Gun **

US 1967 101m DeLuxe Panavision
UA/Mirisch/Kappa (John Sturges)
▦ ☍

After the gunfight at the OK Corral, Wyatt Earp tracks down the rest of the Clanton gang.

Vividly set, slowly developed Western which makes an ambiguous but forceful figure of Earp. Generally confident and interesting.

w Edward Anhalt d John Sturges ph Lucien Ballard m Jerry Goldsmith ad Alfred Ybarra ed Ferris Webster

☆ James Garner, Jason Robards Jnr, Robert Ryan, Steve Ihnat, Michael Tolan, Frank Converse, Sam Melville, Monte Markham, Albert Salmi, Jon Voight, William Windom, Charles Aidman

'The case is a dog. The defendant is a pig. And the law is an ass.'

The Hour of the Pig *

GB/France 1993 117m colour
Mayfair/BBC/CiBy 2000 (David M. Thompson)
▦

In medieval France, a young city lawyer is sent to a backward, rural area, to defend a pig on the charge of murdering a Jewish boy.

An original film that manages to cram in comedy, traces of thriller, and high-level corruption in its depiction of the superstitious past; it doesn't work as well as it might, but at least it tries something a little different from the endless reworking of over-familiar material.

wd Leslie Megahey ph John Hooper m Alexandre Desplat pd Bruce Macadie ed Isabelle Dedieu

☆ Colin Firth, Ian Holm, Donald Pleasence, Amina Annabi, Nicol Williamson, Michael Gough, Harriet Walter, Jim Carter, Lysette Anthony

'The picture is an off-beat one. A pity that the mix is too rich and the cooking of it frequently too muddled and a lot of the acting is mummery dressed in drama-school accents.' – *Alexander Walker*

The Hour of the Wolf *

Sweden 1968 89m bw
Svensk Filmindustri (Lars-Owe Carlberg)

original title: *Vargtimmen*

A painter, at his summer island home with his wife, is terrorized by monstrous nightmares and by memories of his own adulterous past.

Rather like the gloomy side of Smiles of a Summer Night, this very typical Bergman melodrama doesn't quite flow as intended, and whatever its meaning may be, its surface is less entertaining than usual.

wd Ingmar Bergman ph Sven Nykvist m Lars Johan Werle ad Marik Vos-Lundh ed Ulla Ryghe

☆ Max von Sydow, Liv Ullmann, Ingrid Thulin, Georg Rydeberg, Erland Josephson

The Hour of Thirteen

GB 1952 78m bw
MGM (Hayes Goetz)

Edwardian London is shocked when policemen are stabbed one by one.

Jaded Hollywood-English thriller, a remake of The Mystery of Mr X (qv).

w Leon Gordon, Howard Emmett Rogers novel X vs Rex by Philip MacDonald d Harold French ph Guy Green m John Addison

☆ Peter Lawford, Dawn Addams, Roland Culver, Derek Bond, Leslie Dwyer, Michael Hordern, Colin Gordon, Heather Thatcher

† Originally to be called *T for Terror*.

The Hours and Times *

US 1991 60m bw
ICA/Antarctic Pictures
▦

On holiday in Spain with Beatle John Lennon, his manager Brian Epstein tries to get him into bed and is as unsuccessful in seducing a hotel bellboy. *Interesting, very low-budget feature exploring the ambivalent relationship of men divided by sex and class.*

---

wd Christopher Münch ph Christopher Münch
ed Christopher Münch
☆ David Angus, Ian Hart, Stephanie Pack, Robin McDonald, Sergio Moreno, Unity Grimwood
'A quality piece of film-making.' – *Derek Malcolm, Guardian*
'A touching, perceptive film and well worth seeing.' – *Philip French, Observer*

House
US   1986   93m   colour
New World/Sean Cunningham
📼 🟰 📀 💿 🔘 🎧
An old lady is found dead in her spooky house; her nephew moves in and endures various apparitions.
Silly film in which the creatures look ridiculous and the psychology makes no sense, especially when the whole thing attempts to be a protest about Vietnam.
w Ethan Wiley d Steve Miner ph Mac Ahlberg m Harry Manfredini pd Gregg Fonseca
☆ William Katt, George Wendt, Richard Moll, Kay Lenz

'Life's not about winning or losing, it's about crossing the line.'
House!
GB   1999   90m   colour
Pathé/House/Arts Council NL (Michael Kelk)
In Wales, the owner of a small bingo hall is threatened by competition from a bigger hall run by a large corporation.
A movie in the old Ealing comedy tradition of the little guy winning through; unfortunately, it lacks the Ealing touch, and also resorts to a feeble plot device to make its point.
w Jason Sutton d Julian Kemp ph Kjell Vassdal m David Alldridge, Craig Blake-Jones, Mark Thomas pd Kit Line ed Jonathon Rudd cos Leila Ransley
☆ Kelly MacDonald, Gwenllian Davies, Sue Hopkins, Eileen Edwards, Marlene Griffiths, Freddie Jones, Mossie Smith., Jason Hughes, Miriam Margolyes, Bruce Forsyth, Keith Chegwin
'Charismatic, audience-friendly film... thoroughly enjoyable from start to finish.' – *Emma Cochrane, Empire*

The House across the Bay
US   1940   88m   bw
UA/Walter Wanger
🟰
To protect her racketeer husband from his enemies, his wife has him convicted of income tax evasion.
Unpersuasive melodrama, a star potboiler.
w Kathryn Scola d Archie Mayo ph Merritt Gerstad m Werner Janssen
☆ Joan Bennett, George Raft, Lloyd Nolan, Walter Pidgeon, Gladys George, June Knight

The House across the Street
US   1949   69m   bw
Warner (Saul Elkins)
A racketeer brings pressure on a newspaper, and a crusading reporter is relegated to giving advice to the lovelorn.
Tepid remake of Hi Nellie.
w Russell Hughes, Roy Chanslor d Richard Bare ph William Snyder m William Lava
☆ Wayne Morris, Janis Paige, James Mitchell, Alan Hale, Bruce Bennett

House Arrest
US   1996   108m   DeLuxe
MGM/UA/Rysher (Judith A. Polone, Harry Winer)
Unhappy with their divorcing parents, children lock them in the basement until they agree to stay together.
Trivial comedy that makes poor jokes about a subject that deserves more serious treatment.
w Michael Hitchcock d Harry Winer ph Ueli Steiger m Bruce Broughton pd Peter Jamison ed Ronald Roose
☆ Jamie Lee Curtis, Kevin Pollak, Jennifer Tilly, Christopher McDonald, Wallace Shawn, Sheila McCarthy, Caroline Aaron, Jennifer Love Hewitt, Ray Walston
'A tepid and repetitious comedy that won't capture the attention of many ticketbuyers.' – *Variety*

House by the River *
US   1950   88m   bw
Republic/Fidelity (Howard Welsch)
A weak and lecherous writer murders his maid and persuades his brother to help cover up the deed.

Intriguing little thriller, atmospheric and suspenseful for the most part, until it topples into melodrama.
w Mel Dinelli novel A. P. Herbert d Fritz Lang ph Edward Cronjager m George Antheil ad Boris Leven ad Arthur D. Hilton
☆ Louis Hayward, Lee Bowman, Jane Wyatt, Dorothy Patrick, Ann Shoemaker, Jody Gilbert, Peter Brocco, Howland Chamberlin

House Calls *
US   1978   98m   Technicolor
Universal/Jennings Lang (Alex Winitsky, Arlene Sellers)
🟰 📀
A middle-aged doctor finds himself widowed and seeks a new mate.
Spotty comedy which tries to combine conventional romantic spats with medical satire, and comes off only in fits and starts.
w Max Shulman, Julius J. Epstein, Alan Mandel, Charles Shyer d Howard Zieff ph David M. Walsh m Henry Mancini
☆ Walter Matthau, Glenda Jackson, Art Carney, Richard Benjamin, Candice Azzara, Thayer David, Dick O'Neill

A House Divided *
US   1931   70m   bw
Universal (Paul Kohner)
A tough widowed fisherman seeks a new wife, but she falls in love with his son.
Glum variation on Desire under the Elms, interesting for early Wyler touches.
w John P. Clymer, Dale Van Every, John Huston story Heart and Hand by Olive Edens d William Wyler ph Charles Stumar
☆ Walter Huston, Kent Douglass, Helen Chandler, Vivian Oakland, Frank Hagney, Mary Foy

House II: The Second Story
US   1988   88m   colour
Entertainment/New World (Sean S. Cunningham)
📼 🟰 📀 🎧
A former Vietnam veteran moves into an old house where his parents were killed 25 years before and searches for a valuable Aztec skull buried with one of his ancestors.
A movie that has little relationship to the original, other than in its general silliness and incoherence.
wd Ethan Wiley ph Mac Ahlberg m Harry Manfredini pd Gregg Fonseca ed Marty Nicholson
☆ Arye Gross, Jonathan Stark, Royal Dano, Bill Maher, Lar Park Lincoln, John Ratzenberger
'Sluggish, nonsensical and a generally pointless venture, replete with animated monsters, unresolved plot convolutions and totally forgettable characters. Ridiculous.' – *Stefan Jaworzyn, Shock Xpress*

House III: see *The Horror Show*

The House in Nightmare Park *
GB   1973   95m   Technicolor
EMI/Associated London/Extension (Clive Exton, Terry Nation)
📼 🟰
US title: *Night of the Laughing Dead*
aka: *Crazy House*
In 1907, a ham actor is asked to perform at an old dark house in the country where an axe murderer prowls during the night.
Standard creepy house comedy thriller, well enough done though it would have been better with Bob Hope.
w Clive Exton, Terry Nation d Peter Sykes ph Ian Wilson m Harry Robinson
☆ Frankie Howerd, Ray Milland, Hugh Burden, Kenneth Griffith, John Bennett, Rosalie Crutchley, Ruth Dunning

The House in the Square *
GB   1951   91m   Technicolor (bw endpieces)
TCF (Sol C. Siegel)
US title: *I'll Never Forget You*
An American atomic chemist living in London becomes his own ancestor of two hundred years ago, and falls in love.
Slow-starting but thereafter quite acceptable remake of Berkeley Square (qv), with some interesting dialogue and a genuinely affecting fade-out.
w Ranald MacDougall play John L. Balderston d Roy Baker ph Georges Périnal m William Alwyn ad C. P. Norman

☆ Tyrone Power, Ann Blyth, Michael Rennie, Beatrice Campbell, Dennis Price, Raymond Huntley, Irene Browne, Robert Atkins

A House Is Not a Home
US   1964   98m   bw
Paramount/Embassy (Clarence Greene)
The life story of New York's most famous madam, Polly Adler.
Dismal, unappealing, laundered biopic, cheaply made in an unconvincing period setting.
w Russel Rouse, Clarence Greene d Russel Rouse ph Harold Stine m Joseph Weiss
☆ Shelley Winters, Robert Taylor, Cesar Romero, Ralph Taeger, Broderick Crawford

'Home Deadly Home.'
House IV
US   1992   93m   DeLuxe
Sean S. Cunningham Films
🟰 📀
A widow's brother-in-law attempts to frighten her into abandoning the family mansion.
An improvement over its predecessors, it maintains interest despite its unoriginality.
w Geof Miller, Deirdre Higgins story Jim Wynorski, R. J. Robinson d Lewis Abernathy ph James Mathers m Harry Manfredini ed Seth Gaven
☆ Terri Treas, William Katt, Scott Burkholder, Melissa Clayton, Denny Dillon, Dabbs Greer, Mark Gash
'The emphasis ... is on scares rather than comedy, and the result is satisfying.' – *Variety*
'Representing yet another in the seemingly endless parade of artistically-bankrupt genre sequels ... It's really sad that given the high-gloss resources afforded this production, the filmmakers couldn't have done any better.' – *Fangoria*

The House of a Thousand Candles
US   1936   54m   bw
Republic
A young man must live in an unfinished mansion to inherit under the terms of his grandfather's will.
Odd but basically unremarkable little mystery; the title is more interesting than the movie.
w H. W. Hanemann, Endre Bohem novel Meredith Nicholson d Arthur Lubin
☆ Phillips Holmes, Mae Clarke, Irving Pichel, Rosita Moreno

'On the road ... but going nowhere.'
House of America
GB/Netherlands   1997   96m   colour
First Independent/September/Bergen (Sheryl Crown)
📼 🟰
Living in an isolated house with their unbalanced mother, an incestuous brother and sister dream of being reunited in America with the father who abandoned them long ago.
Bleak and melodramatic drama of the hopeless, unable to escape their miserable fate, done in a Gothic, over-emphatic manner.
w Edward Thomas play Edward Thomas d Marc Evans ph Pierre Aim m John Cale pd Mark Tildesley ed Michael Reichwein
☆ Sian Phillips, Steven Mackintosh, Lisa Palfrey, Matthew Rhys, Pascal Laurent, Richard Harrington, Islwyn Morris
'Evans' debut direction is superb, consisting of a dazzling array of images, and the acting is sound. Yet despite its ironic humour there seems little on show for young filmgoers to connect with.' – *Jake Hamilton, Empire*

House of Angels **
Sweden   1992   119m   colour
Mayfair/Memfis/Sveriges Television/TV2/Svenska Filminstitute/Danmarks Radio/Nordisk Film and TV (Lars Jönsson, Lars Dahlquist)
📼 🟰
original title: *Änglagård*
Villagers are scandalized when a landowner dies and his farm is inherited by his hitherto unknown granddaughter, a night-club singer who has a bisexual boyfriend.
Highly enjoyable comedy of a culture clash, full of a generosity of spirit.
wd Colin Nutley ph Jens Fischer m Björn Isfält pd Ulla Herdin ed Perry Schaffer

☆ Helena Bergström, Rikard Wolff, Sven Wollter, Reine Brynolfsson, Ernst Gunter, Viveka Seldahl, Per Oscarsson, Tord Peterson, Ing-Marie Carlsson
'Nutley's achievement is in finding a delicate balance between satire and sentiment ... a surprising delight.' – *Angie Errigo, Empire*

'The story Tokyo couldn't hide, and Washington couldn't hold back!'
House of Bamboo **
US   1955   102m   DeLuxe   Cinemascope
TCF (Buddy Adler)
Japanese and American authorities move into undercover action against Tokyo gangsters.
Routine big-budget crime drama where a novel twist by its location and vaguely adapted from The Street with No Name (qv).
w Harry Kleiner, Samuel Fuller d Samuel Fuller ph Joe MacDonald m Leigh Harline pd Lyle R. Wheeler, Addison Hehr ed James B. Clark
☆ Robert Stack, Robert Ryan, Shirley Yamaguchi, Cameron Mitchell, Sessue Hayakawa

House of Cards
US   1968   100m   Techniscope
Universal/Westward (Dick Berg)
An American becomes tutor in the Paris household of a French general's widow, and finds himself a pawn in a high-powered game of international intrigue.
Good-looking location thriller which after an intricate opening settles into a 39 Steps-style chase, but makes little of it.
w James P. Bonner novel Stanley Ellin d John Guillermin ph Piero Portalupi m Francis Lai
☆ George Peppard, Inger Stevens, Orson Welles, Keith Michell, William Job, Maxine Audley, Peter Bayliss

House of Cards
US   1993   107m   Technicolor
Penta/A&M Films (Dale Pollock, Lianne Halfon, Wolfgang Glattes)
📼 🟰 📀 💿
After the sudden death of her husband, a woman struggles with the fact that her daughter has stopped talking and begun to act in strange ways.
Mundane domestic drama that veers unerringly towards the sentimental.
wd Michael Lessac ph Victor Hammer m James Horner pd Peter Larkin ad Walter Murch
☆ Kathleen Turner, Tommy Lee Jones, Asha Menina, Shiloh Strong, Esther Rolle, Park Overall, Michael Horse, Anne Pitoniak
'Plays like a top-of-the-line disease-of-the-week TV movie.' – *Variety*
† The film was released direct to video in Britain.

House of Connelly: see *Carolina*

House of Dark Shadows *
US   1970   97m   Metrocolor
MGM (Dan Curtis)
📼 🟰 📀 🎧
A 200-year-old vampire is released from the crypt of an old mansion and tries to find a cure for his affliction.
Effectively creepy little horror, done with some style.
w Sam Hall, Gordon Russell d Dan Curtis ph Arthur Ornitz m Robert Cobert pd Trevor Williams ed Arline Garson
☆ Jonathan Frid, Joan Bennett, Roger Davis, Grayson Hall, Kathryn Leigh Scott, Nancy Barrett, Thayer David
'Despite a few awkward moments in the photography and editing (betraying under-budgeting and hasty shooting), the result is the most satisfyingly convulsive traditional horror film in years.' – *Tony Rayns, MFB*

House of Doom: see *The Black Cat*

House of Dracula *
US   1945   67m   bw
Universal (Paul Malvern)
🟰 📀
As a result of being visited in one evening by Count Dracula, the Wolf Man and the Frankenstein monster, a sympathetic doctor goes on the rampage. Mind-boggling finale to the first Universal monster cycle, with a happy ending for the Wolf Man.
Cheaply made and not really inventive, but has to be seen to be believed.

w Edward T. Lowe d Erle C. Kenton ph George Robinson m Edgar Fairchild

☆ Onslow Stevens, John Carradine, Lon Chaney Jnr, Glenn Strange, Lionel Atwill, Martha O'Driscoll, Jane Adams

The House of Fear: see *The Last Warning* (1929)

The House of Fear
US 1939 65m bw
Universal
Murder in a haunted theatre: an actor dies and the corpse disappears.
Lively Crime Club whodunnit, a remake of The Last Warning (1929).
w Peter Milne d Joe May
☆ William Gargan, Irene Hervey, Dorothy Arnold, Alan Dinehart, Harvey Stephens, Walter Woolf King, Robert Coote, El Brendel, Tom Dugan
'Sufficient edge-of-seat suspense to catch lower-bracket bookings in the nabe duallers.' – *Variety*

The House of Fear *
US 1944 68m bw
Universal
💿 ⊙~
Members of a club are murdered one by one.
A knotty problem for Sherlock Holmes, but rather tediously unravelled. Despite the orange pips it owes virtually nothing to Conan Doyle.
w Roy Chanslor d Roy William Neill ph Virgil Miller md Paul Sawtell
☆ Basil Rathbone, Nigel Bruce, Dennis Hoey, Aubrey Mather, Paul Cavanagh, Holmes Herbert, Gavin Muir

'Mighty monsters, locked in mortal combat!'
House of Frankenstein *
US 1944 71m bw
Universal (Paul Malvern)
💿 ⊙~
A mad doctor thaws out the monster and the Wolf Man (frozen at the end of *Frankenstein Meets the Wolf Man*) but comes to a sticky end.
Originally called Chamber of Horrors, this was the studio's first attempt to package its monsters (the first two reels are about Dracula). It could have been pacier in view of the possibilities, but it has its interest.
w Edward T. Lowe, Curt Siodmak d Erle C. Kenton ph George Robinson m Hans Salter
☆ Boris Karloff, John Carradine, Lon Chaney Jnr, George Zucco, J. Carrol Naish, Anne Gwynne, Elena Verdugo, Lionel Atwill, Sig Rumann, Glenn Strange
'A chiller-diller meller.' – *Variety*

House of Fright: see *The Two Faces of Dr Jekyll*

House of Games *
US 1987 102m Du Art Color
Filmhaus/Orion (Michael Hausman)
💿 💿 ⊙~
A psychiatrist becomes involved with a confidence trickster.
Stylish directorial debut, playing dazzling tricks with its audiences' expectations, by a respected Broadway playwright.
wd David Mamet ph Juan Ruiz Anchia m Alaric Jans pd Michael Merritt ed Trudy Ship
☆ Lindsay Crouse, Joe Mantegna, Mike Nussbaum, Lilia Skala

House of Horrors
US 1946 65m bw
Universal
💿 ⊙~
GB title: *Joan Medford Is Missing*
An incompetent sculptor tricks a psychopathic killer into murdering his critics.
Grade Z thriller with a monster element; crude beyond belief.
w George Bricker d Jean Yarbrough
☆ Martin Kosleck, Rondo Hatton, Robert Lowery, Virginia Grey, Bill Goodwin

House of Long Shadows: see *House of the Long Shadows*

House of Menace: see *Kind Lady*

House of Mortal Sin
GB 1975 104m Technicolor
Columbia-Warner/Pete Walker
A sexually obsessed and murderous Catholic priest attempts to blackmail a young woman over her confession.
A horror film of some originality, but feebly directed and acted.
w David McGillivray story Pete Walker d Pete Walker ph Tony Imi m Stanley Myers ad Chris Burke ed Matt McCarthy
☆ Anthony Sharp, Susan Penhaligon, Stephanie Beacham, Norman Eshley, Sheila Keith, Mervyn Johns, Bill Kerr, Andrew Sachs

House of Mystery: see *Night Monster* (1942)

House of Mystery
GB 1961 56m bw
Anglo Amalgamated/Independent Artists (Julian Wintle, Leslie Parkyn)
A house-hunting couple hear from a mysterious woman why an apparently desirable cottage is being sold at a low price.
Effectively spooky little thriller, a story of jealousy and murder.
wd Vernon Sewell ph Ernest Steward m Stanley Black ad Jack Shampan ed John Trumper
☆ Jane Hylton, Peter Dyneley, Nanette Newman, Maurice Kaufmann, Colin Gordon, John Merivale, Ronald Hines, Colette Wilde

House of Numbers
US 1957 92m bw Cinemascope
MGM (Charles Schnee)
A man helps his thuggish twin brother escape from prison.
An original melodramatic idea is frittered away through slow pacing.
w Russel Rouse, Don M. Mankiewicz novel Jack Finney d Russel Rouse ph George J. Folsey m André Previn
☆ Jack Palance, Barbara Lang, Harold J. Stone, Edward Platt

The House of Rothschild *
US 1934 87m bw (Technicolor sequence)
Twentieth Century (William Goetz, Raymond Griffith)
The chronicles of the famous banking family at the time of the Napoleonic Wars.
Lavish historical pageant with interesting scenes and performances.
w Nunnally Johnson play George Humbert Westley d Alfred Werker ph Peverell Marley m Alfred Newman
☆ George Arliss, Loretta Young, Boris Karloff, Robert Young, C. Aubrey Smith, Arthur Byron, Helen Westley, Reginald Owen, Florence Arliss, Alan Mowbray, Holmes Herbert
'A fine picture on all counts … one of those occasional 100% smashes which Hollywood achieves.' – *Variety*
'A good dramatic photoplay, finely presented, packed with ripe incident and quite beautiful photography.' – C. A. *Lejeune*
♟ best picture

House of Secrets
GB 1956 97m Technicolor Vistavision
Rank/Julian Wintle (Vivian A. Cox)
US title: *Triple Deception*
A naval officer is asked to impersonate a lookalike counterfeiter and work undercover to expose the gang.
Old-hat Boys' Own Paper adventure story, mindlessly watchable.
w Robert Buckner, Bryan Forbes novel *Storm over Paris* by Sterling Noel d Guy Green ph Harry Waxman m Hubert Clifford
☆ Michael Craig, Julia Arnall, Brenda de Banzie, David Kossoff, Barbara Bates, Gerard Oury, Geoffrey Keen, Anton Diffring

House of Settlement: see *Mr Soft Touch*

The House of Seven Corpses
US 1973 90m colour
TCA (Paul Lewis, Paul Harrison)
A film crew, making a horror movie in a house where seven people met violent ends, decide to incorporate in the script an ancient ritual to raise the dead, with predictable results.
Atmospheric low-budget movie, which builds the tension slowly before its horrific climax.
w Paul Harrison, Thomas J. Kelly d Paul Harrison ph Don Jones
☆ John Ireland, Faith Domergue, John Carradine, Carole Wells, Jerry Strickler, Charles Macaulay

The House of Seven Gables
US 1940 89m bw
Universal (Burt Kelly)
In 17th-century New England, a jealous brother sends his sister's fiancé to prison.
Flat adaptation of a grim, brooding novel; it never grips.
w Lester Cole novel Nathaniel Hawthorne d Joe May ph Milton Krasner m Frank Skinner
☆ George Sanders, Margaret Lindsay, Vincent Price, Alan Napier, Nan Grey, Cecil Kellaway, Dick Foran, Miles Mander
♪ Frank Skinner

House of Strangers *
US 1949 101m bw
TCF (Sol C. Siegel)
💿
An Italian-American banker who rigidly controls his three sons is arrested for illegal practices, and the family ties slacken.
Interesting ethnic melodrama with good script and performances; much remade, e.g. as Broken Lance.
w Philip Yordan novel Jerome Weidman d Joseph L. Mankiewicz ph Milton Krasner m Daniele Amfitheatrof
☆ Edward G. Robinson, Richard Conte, Susan Hayward, Luther Adler, Paul Valentine, Efrem Zimbalist Jnr, Debra Paget, Hope Emerson, Esther Minciotti, Diana Douglas

The House of Tao Lin: see *Dangerous Millions*

The House of the Angel *
Argentina 1957 73m bw
Argentina Sono Film (Leopoldo Torre Nilsson)
original title: *La Casa del Angel*
A repressed girl is obsessed for life by the shame of her first love affair.
Fascinating minor classic in a heavily Wellesian style.
w Beatriz Guido, Leopoldo Torre Nilsson, Martin Rodriguez Mentasti novel Beatriz Guido d Leopoldo Torre Nilsson ph Anibal Gonzalez Paz m Juan Carlos Paz
☆ Elsa Daniel, Lautaro Murua, Guillermo Battaglia
'The first major work of a director of individual vision and strongly national style.' – *Robert Vas, MFB*

The House of the Arrow
GB 1940 66m bw
ABPC
US title: *Castle of Crimes*
A wealthy Frenchwoman is murdered and her English companion is under suspicion.
A case for Inspector Hanaud; very tolerable whodunnit.
w Doreen Montgomery novel A. E. W. Mason d Harold French
☆ Keneth Kent, Diana Churchill, Belle Chrystal, Peter Murray Hill, Clifford Evans, Catherine Lacey
† A previous version in 1930 starred Dennis Neilson Terry and was directed by Leslie Hiscott. A further version in 1953 with Oscar Homolka as Hanaud was directed by Michael Anderson for Associated British.

House of the Damned *
US 1963 63m bw
TCF/Associated Producers (Maury Dexter)
An architect is asked to make a survey of an old empty castle, but he and his wife find that someone or something is in hiding there.
Corny but mildly effective second feature with a few neat touches.
w Harry Spalding d Maury Dexter ph John Nickolaus Jnr m Henry Vars
☆ Ronald Foster, Merry Anders

House of the Long Shadows
GB 1983 101m colour
Cannon (Jenny Craven)
An author takes a bet to isolate himself in a dilapidated house and write a Gothic novel within 24 hours…
Semi-spoof variation on an old chestnut, with aged horror practitioners interrupting the silence. Too restricted in script and production to be really effective.
w Michael Armstrong play *Seven Keys to Baldpate* by George M. Cohan novel *Earl Derr Biggers* d Pete Walker ph Norman Langley m Richard Harvey
☆ Christopher Lee, Peter Cushing, Vincent Price, Desi Arnaz Jnr, John Carradine, Sheila Keith, Julie Peasgood, Richard Todd
'Golan and Globus seem to have inherited Lord Grade's habit of assembling advertising packages with movies appended as an afterthought.' – *Kim Newman, MFB*
'A horror flick which basks in the Hammer tradition without in any way understanding it.' – *Guardian*

House of the Seven Hawks
GB 1959 92m bw
MGM/David E. Rose
An American adventurer becomes involved in a search by criminals for buried Nazi loot.
Cliché-ridden thick ear, adequately produced but of no interest.
w Jo Eisinger novel *The House of Seven Flies* by Victor Canning d Richard Thorpe ph Ted Scaife m Clifton Parker
☆ Robert Taylor, Nicole Maurey, Linda Christian, Donald Wolfit, David Kossoff, Eric Pohlmann, Gerard Heinz

'Every Passion … Every Obsession … Caught In The Fire Of Revolution.'
The House of the Spirits
Germany/Denmark/Portugal 1993 138m
colour Panavision
Entertainment/Neue Constantin/Spring Creek/House of Spirits/Costa do Castelo (Bernd Eichinger)
💿💿 💿 ⊙~
In Chile, a saga of a family's rise to power and its fall is played out against a background of political upheaval.
Miscast and misconceived, this tale of magic realism is turned into a stolid drama of mundane fantasy; a disappointment.
wd Bille August novel Isabel Allende ph Jörgen Persson m Hans Zimmer pd Anna Asp ed Janus Billeskov Jansen
☆ Jeremy Irons, Meryl Streep, Glenn Close, Winona Ryder, Antonio Banderas, Vanessa Redgrave, Maria Conchita Alonso, Armin Mueller-Stahl
'Turgid, overlong, silly, hysterical (and that spells TOSH).' – *Adam Mars-Jones, Independent*
'What we get is a romantic drama set against the tide of history, that looks more and more like Latin-American melodrama traversed by a cast of talented strangers to the culture.' – *Derek Malcolm, Guardian*

House of Unclaimed Women: see *The Smashing Bird I Used to Know*

House of Usher *
US 1960 85m Eastmancolor Cinemascope
AIP/Alta Vista (Roger Corman)
💿 ⊙~
GB title: *The Fall of the House of Usher*
The last of the Usher line, prone to catalepsy, is buried alive by her brother and returns to wreak vengeance.
Stylish but grottily-coloured low-budget horror which started the Poe cycle of the sixties. A bit slow, it would have worked better in the standard screen ratio, but there is a tense and spectacular finale.
w Richard Matheson story Edgar Allan Poe d Roger Corman ph Floyd Crosby m Les Baxter ad Daniel Haller
☆ Vincent Price, Myrna Fahey, Mark Damon, Harry Ellerbe

House of Usher
US 1990 90m Rank Colour
21st Century/Breton (Harry Alan Towers)
💿 ⊙~
Roderick Usher attempts to force his nephew's girlfriend to bear his child.
Tedious version of the oft-filmed tale, lacking style and substance.
w Michael J. Murray story *The Fall of the House of Usher* by Edgar Allan Poe d Alan Birkinshaw ph Jossi Wein m George S. Clinton, Gary Chang pd Leonardo Coen Cagli ed Michael J. Duthie
☆ Oliver Reed, Donald Pleasence, Romy Windsor, Rufus Swart, Norman Coombes, Anne Stradi

---

'This remake offers no suspense and a very weak cast.' – *Variety*

'The most astounding motion picture since motion pictures began! Man turned monster stalking show-world beauties! The ultimate dimension in terror!'
'You've never been scared until you've been scared in 3-D!'

House of Wax **

US   1953   88m   Warnercolor   3-D
Warner (Bryan Foy)

🎦 📼 📀

Mutilated in a fire at his wax museum, a demented sculptor arranges a supply of dead bodies to be covered in wax for exhibition at his new showplace.
Spirited remake of The Mystery of the Wax Museum (qv); as a piece of screen narrative it leaves much to be desired, but the sudden shocks are well managed, perhaps because this is the first Grade-A 3-D film, packed with gimmicks irrelevant to the story and originally shown with stereophonic sound.
w Crane Wilbur *screenplay The Mystery of the Wax Museum by Don Mullaly, Carl Erickson play Charles S. Belden by The Wax Museum*
d André de Toth ph Bert Glennon m David Buttolph ad Stanley Fleischer ed Rudi Fehr
☆ Vincent Price, Carolyn Jones, Paul Picerni, Phyllis Kirk, Frank Lovejoy, Dabs Greer, Paul Cavanagh
† The director could not see the 3-D effect, being blind in one eye.
†† The film marked the beginning of Price's horror career.

House of Whipcord *

GB   1974   101m   Eastmancolor
Miracle/Peter Walker

🎦

An elderly couple and their son, who run their own private penal system, sentence to death a French model on charges of immorality.
Low-budget psychological horror that stylishly achieves its object: to disturb.
w David McGillivray *story* Peter Walker d Peter Walker ph Peter Jessop m Stanley Myers ad Mike Pickwood ed Matt McCarthy
☆ Barbara Markham, Patrick Barr, Ray Brooks, Ann Michelle, Penny Irving, Sheila Keith, Celia Imrie
'Shows that something worthwhile in the entertainment-horror market can be done for the tiny sum of £60,000.' – *Derek Elley, Films and Filming*

House of Women

US   1962   85m   bw
Warner

A pregnant woman is sent to prison for a robbery she didn't commit.
Loose remake of Caged, with very little sense or vigour.
w Crane Wilbur d Walter Doniger ph Harold Stine m Howard Jackson
☆ Shirley Knight, Andrew Duggan, Constance Ford, Barbara Nichols, Margaret Hayes

The House on 92nd Street ***

US   1945   88m   bw
TCF (*Louis de Rochemont*)

During World War II in New York, the FBI routs Nazi spies after the atomic bomb formula.
Highly influential documentary-style 'now it can be told' spy drama, which borrowed the feel of its producer's March of Time series and applied them to a fairly true story set on genuine locations though with a modicum of fictional mystery and suspense.
Highly effective in its own right, it looked forward to The Naked City three years later; the later film unaccountably got most of the credit for taking Hollywood out into the open air.
w Barre Lyndon, Charles G. Booth, John Monks Jnr d Henry Hathaway ph Norbert Brodine m David Buttolph
☆ William Eythe, Lloyd Nolan, Signe Hasso, *Leo G. Carroll*, Gene Lockhart, Lydia St Clair, Harry Bellaver
'Recommended entertainment for those who believe that naïve Americans are no match for wily Europeans in the spy trade, and for those who just like their movies to move.' – *Time*
'Imagine an issue of The March of Time. The hard agglomeration of fact; the road drill style; the voice. Prolong it to four times its usual length, throw in a fictional climax, and there you have

The House on 92nd Street.' – William Whitebait, New Statesman
🎖 original story (Charles G. Booth)

House on Bare Mountain

US   1962   62m   colour
Olympic International/B and M (David Andrew, Wes Don)

The elderly headmistress of a girl's school keeps a werewolf in her cellar, where she brews her own booze.
Very cheap exploitation movie – the lip movements and dialogue don't match — that consists mainly of the usual lingering on the bodies of young women, but also shows a modicum of cynical wit.
w Denver Scott d R. L. Frost ph Greg Sandor m Pierre Martel ed Gary Lindsay
☆ Bob Cresse, Leticia Cooper, Laine Carlin, Connie Hudson, Dan Hyland, John Nada, Betty Peters
† Credits include 'Casting Director (Deceased)', which, in the circumstances, must have seemed an excellent career move.

The House on Carroll Street *

US   1988   100m   colour
Rank/Orion (Peter Yates, Robert F. Colesberry)

🇺🇸 📀

A journalist, forced out of her job in McCarthyite America, uncovers a right-wing political conspiracy.
Moderately effective thriller, in a style close to Hitchcock.
w Walter Bernstein d Peter Yates ph Michael Ballhaus m Georges Delerue pd Stuart Wurtzel ed Ray Lovejoy
☆ Kelly McGillis, Jeff Daniels, Mandy Patinkin, Christopher Rhode, Jessica Tandy, Jonathan Hogan

House on Haunted Hill

US   1958   75m   bw
Allied Artists/William Castle

🎦 📀

An old house which has seen several murders is the setting for a millionaire's party.
Gimmick ghost story with some (unexplained) gruesome moments; the most outlandish of its producer's cheapjack trick films (Thirteen Ghosts, The Tingler, Macabre, etc), it was originally billed as being in Emergo, which meant that at an appropriately horrific moment an illuminated skeleton on wires was suddenly trundled over the heads of the audience.
w Robb White d William Castle m Carl Guthrie m Von Dexter
☆ Vincent Price, Richard Long, Carol Ohmart, Alan Marshal, Elisha Cook Jnr

'Five strangers have the chance to make $1,000,000 each. All they have to do is make it throught the night... Alive'
'Evil Loves to Party!'

House on Haunted Hill

US   1999   96m   Technicolor   Panavision
Warner/Dark Castle (Robert Zemeckis, Joel Silver, Gilbert Adler)

🇺🇸 📀

A multimillionaire offers a prize of $1m to any party guest who can last the night in a haunted house, a former asylum for the criminally insane.
Supernatural horror that is heavy on shocks and special effects, but otherwise offers little that is special, though Rush's Vincent Price impersonation provides a little fun.
w Dick Beebe *story* Robb White d William Malone ph Rick Bota m Don Davis pd David F. Klassen ed Anthony Adler
sp Bellissimo/Belardinelli; make-up fx: Robert Kurtzman, Gregory Nicotero, Howard Berger
☆ Geoffrey Rush, Famke Janssen, Taye Diggs, Peter Gallagher, Chris Kattan, Ali Larter, Bridgette Wilson, Max Perlich, Jeffrey Combs, Lisa Loeb
'"Hill" was pronounced junk in these pages in 1959. And it is still junk.' – *Lawrence Van Gelder, New York Times*

The House on Telegraph Hill

US   1951   93m   bw
TCF (Robert Bassler)

A woman in a concentration camp assumes her dead friend's identity so that on release she can be sent to America; but murder threatens there.
Modernized amalgam of Gaslight and Suspicion, not as good as either, but the complexities of the story hold adequate interest.

w Elick Moll, Frank Partos *novel* Dana Lyon d Robert Wise ph Lucien Ballard m Sol Kaplan ad Lyle Wheeler, John DeCuir
☆ Richard Basehart, Valentina Cortesa, William Lundigan, Fay Baker, Gordon Gebert, Steve Geray
🎖 art direction

House Party

US   1990   104m   Metrocolor
Enterprise/Hudlin Brothers/New Line (Gerald Olsen)

🎦 📼 📀

A teenager, whose parents are away, throws a party for his friends.
Low-budget youth movie, likeable enough but unlikely to rouse much enthusiasm on the adult side of the generation gap.
wd Reginald Hudlin ph Peter Deming m Marcus Miller pd Bryan Jones ed Earl Watson
☆ Christopher Reid, Robin Harris, Christopher Martin, Martin Lawrence, Tisha Campbell, A. J. Johnson, Paul Anthony

House Party 2

US   1991   94m   DeLuxe
New Line (Doug McHenry, George Jackson)

🎦 📼 📀

Two rappers leave high school and consider their future.
Dull sequel, as if no one was quite sure of what to do next.
w Rusty Cundieff, Daryl G. Nickens d Doug McHenry, George Jackson ph Francis Kenny m Vassal Benford pd Michelle Minch ed Joel Goodman
☆ Christopher Reid, Christopher Martin, Tisha Campbell, Iman, Martin Lawrence, D. Christopher Judge, Queen Latifah
'The crowd's the same, but the atmosphere's different in this disappointing followup.' – *Variety*

'Terror Waits For You In Every Room.'

The House that Dripped Blood *

GB   1970   102m   Eastmancolor
Amicus (Milton Subotsky)

🇺🇸

A Scotland Yard man investigating a disappearance is led to a house with a murderous history.
Quartet of stories in Dead of Night style, neatly made and generally pleasing despite a low level of originality in the writing.
w Robert Bloch d Peter John Duffell ph Robert Parslow m Michael Dress
☆ John Bennett, Christopher Lee, Peter Cushing, Denholm Elliott, Joanna Dunham, Nyree Dawn Porter, Jon Pertwee, Ingrid Pitt

Houseboat

US   1958   110m   Technicolor
Vistavision
Paramount/Scribe (Jack Rose)

🎦 📀

A widower with three children engages a maid who is really a socialite, and they all set up house on a boat.
Artificial sentimental comedy with A 1 credits but little style or bite.
w Melville Shavelson, Jack Rose d Melville Shavelson ph Ray June m George Duning
☆ Cary Grant, Sophia Loren, Martha Hyer, Eduardo Ciannelli, Harry Guardino
'The kind of picture to which you can take your stuffy maiden aunt, your wicked sophisticated uncle and your ten-year-old child, and they will all have a wonderful time.' – *Ruth Waterbury, Los Angeles Examiner*
🎖 script; song 'Almost In Your Arms' (m/ly Jay Livingston, Ray Evans)

The Housekeeper's Daughter *

US   1939   71m   bw
Hal Roach

A gangster's moll returns to mama for a visit and falls in love with the stuffy son of the household.
Zany crime farce which too often lets its zip fade, but atones in a crazy firework finale.
w Rian James, Gordon Douglas *novel* Donald Henderson Clarke d Hal Roach ph Norbert Brodine m Amedeo de Filippi
☆ Joan Bennett, John Hubbard, Adolphe Menjou, William Gargan, George E. Stone, Peggy Wood, Donald Meek, Marc Lawrence, Lillian Bond, Victor Mature, Luis Alberni

'A smacko laugh generator due for profitable biz up and down the line.' – *Variety*

Housekeeping *

🎦 US   1987   115m   colour
Columbia (Robert F. Colesberry)

Two orphaned sisters are brought up by their wayward aunt.
In his first American feature, Forsyth's pawky humour is overlaid with a bleaker view and his characters seem more conventional and less well-observed.
wd Bill Forsyth *novel* Marilynne Robinson ph Michael Coulter m Michael Gibbs pd Adrienne Atkinson ed Michael Ellis
☆ Christine Lahti, Sara Walker, Andrea Burchill, Anne Pitoniak, Barbara Reese, Bill Smillie, Margo Pinvidic, Wayne Robson
'I wouldn't call it a great film, but it comes very close to being a perfect one in everything that it sets out to do.' – *Jonathan Rosenbaum, Chicago Reader*

Housemaster *

GB   1938   95m   bw
ABPC (Walter Mycroft)

A schoolmaster sides with his boys against the new headmaster's dictatorial methods.
Pleasing photographed play with all concerned in good form.
w Dudley Leslie, Elizabeth Meehan *play Bachelor Born by Ian Hay d Herbert Brenon ph Otto Kanturek ad Cedric Dawe ed Flora Newton
☆ Otto Kruger, Diana Churchill, Phillips Holmes, Joyce Barbour, Kynaston Reeves, Rene Ray, Walter Hudd, John Wood, Cecil Parker, Michael Shepley, Jimmy Hanley

Housesitter

US   1992   102m   DeLuxe
UIP/Imagine/Universal (Brian Grazer)

🎦 📼 📀 🎧

After a one-night stand with an architect, a waitress decides to move into his new house, claiming to be his wife.
A farcical comedy that is too leisurely to provoke laughter.
w Mark Stein, Brian Grazer d Frank Oz ph John A. Alonzo m Miles Goodman pd Ida Random ed John Jympson
☆ Steve Martin, Goldie Hawn, Dana Delany, Julie Harris, Donald Moffat, Peter MacNicol, Richard B. Shull, Laurel Cronin
'A tediously unfunny screwball comedy … a career misstep both for Steve Martin and Goldie Hawn.' – *Variety*

Housewife

US   1934   69m   bw
Warner (Robert Lord)

For an advertising copywriter, success almost brings divorce.
Modestly efficient romantic programmer of its day.
w Manuel Seff, Lillie Hayward d Alfred E. Green ph William Rees m Leo. F. Forbstein
☆ Bette Davis, George Brent, Ann Dvorak, John Halliday, Ruth Donnelly, Hobart Cavanaugh, Robert Barrat, Phil Regan
'The dramatic punches are not merely telegraphed, but radioed.' – *Frank S. Nugent*

The Houston Story

US   1956   80m   bw
Columbia (Sam Katzman)

An oil worker has a plan for stealing oil, and is employed by the syndicate.
Racketeering melodrama of the least interesting kind.
w James B. Gordon d William Castle
☆ Gene Barry, Barbara Hale, Edward Arnold, Paul Richards, Frank Jenks

How Do I Love Thee

US   1970   109m   Metrocolor
ABC (Robert Enders, Everett Freeman)

A philosophy professor recalls the odd career of his atheist father.
Curious comedy about an eccentric and his family relationships, a kind of Cheaper by the Dozen with religion added. Not on in 1970.
w Everett Freeman *novel Let Me Count the Ways by Peter de Vries d Michael Gordon ph Russell Metty m Randy Sparks*
☆ Jackie Gleason, Maureen O'Hara, Shelley Winters, Rick Lenz, Rosemary Forsyth
'Nauseated embarrassment for participants and onlookers alike.' – *Judith Crist*

🎦 film suitable for family viewing   📼 VHS video-cassette for the British PAL system   📀 VHS video-cassette for the British PAL system in wide screen-format   🖥 Video cassette in a computer-colourised version   🇺🇸 American NTSC video-cassette   📀 Laser disc

'Rich is their humor! Deep are their passions! Reckless are their lives! Mighty is their story!'
"What are you? A man or a saint? I don't want him, I want you!" Her desire scorched both their lives with the vicious breath of scandal!'

How Green Was My Valley ***
US   1941   118m   bw
TCF (Darryl F. Zanuck)

Memories of childhood in a Welsh mining village.
Prettified and unconvincing but dramatically very effective tearjerker in the style which lasted from Cukor's David Copperfield to The Green Years. High production values here add a touch of extra class, turning the result into a Hollywood milestone despite its intrinsic inadequacies.
w Philip Dunne *novel* Richard Llewellyn d John Ford *ph* Arthur Miller m Alfred Newman ad Richard Day, Nathan Juran ed James B. Clark
☆ Walter Pidgeon, Maureen O'Hara, Roddy McDowall, Donald Crisp, Sara Allgood, Anna Lee, John Loder, Barry Fitzgerald, Patric Knowles, Morton Lowry, Arthur Shields, Frederic Worlock
'Perfection of cinematic narrative ... pure visual action, pictures powerfully composed, dramatically photographed, smoothly and eloquently put together.' – *James Shelley Hamilton*
† The unseen narrator was Irving Pichel.
🏆 best picture; John Ford; Arthur Miller; Donald Crisp; art direction
🏆 Philip Dunne; Alfred Newman; Sara Allgood; James B. Clark

How He Lied to Her Husband
GB   1930   33m   bw
BIP

An early film version of Shaw's playlet about a minor flirtation.
Of historical interest only.
w Frank Launder *play* George Bernard Shaw d Cecil Lewis *ph* J. J. Cox ad Gladys Calthrop ed Sam Simmonds
☆ Edmund Gwenn, Robert Harris, Vera Lennox

How I Got Into College
US   1989   89m   colour
TCF (Michael Shamberg)

Dim student applies to go to the same difficult-to-enter college as the girl he loves.
Mildly amusing teenage comedy.
w Terrel Seltzer d Savage Steve Holland m Joseph Vitarelli pd Ida Random ed Sonya Sones Tramer, Kaja Fehr
☆ Anthony Edwards, Corey Parker, Lara Flynn Boyle, Finn Carter, Charles Rocket, Christopher Rydell, Brian-Doyle Murray

How I Won the War
GB   1967   110m   Eastmancolor
UA/Petersham (Richard Lester)

During World War II an earnest young man becomes an officer and survives many tribulations including the death of his comrades.
Appalling kaleidoscope of black comedy and the director's own brand of uncontrolled cinematic zaniness, with echoes of Candide and Oh What a Lovely War! Just the way to alienate a paying audience.
w Charles Wood *novel* Patrick Ryan d Richard Lester ph David Watkin m Ken Thorne
☆ Michael Crawford, John Lennon, Roy Kinnear, Lee Montague, Jack MacGowran, Michael Hordern, Jack Hedley, Karl Michael Vogler, Ronald Lacey, James Cossins, Alexander Knox
'Pretentious tomfoolery.' – *John Simon*
'One feels that Lester has bitten off more than he can chew ... the ideas misfire, lost somewhere between the paper on which they were conceived and the celluloid on which they finally appear.' – *MFB*

How Stella Got Her Groove Back
US   1998   124m   DeLuxe
TCF (Deborah Schindler)

A middle-aged stockbroker begins an affair with an unemployed Jamaican half her age.
Bland, boring, glossy romantic drama that never attempts to treat its theme with even a pretence of reality.
w Terry McMillan, Ron Bass *novel* Terry McMillan d Kevin Rodney Sullivan ph Jeffrey Jur m Michel Colombier ed George Bowers
☆ Angela Bassett, Taye Diggs, Whoopi Goldberg, Regina King, Suzzanne Douglas, Michael J. Pagan, Sicily, Richard Lawson, Barry (Shabaka) Henley, Lee Weaver, Glynn Turman, Phyllis Yvonne Stickney
'A pretty horrendous experience. Indeed it's the sort of movie that might very well figure in some cynics' 10 worst lists of the year.' – *Derek Malcolm, Guardian*
'Slick production is an ideal girls-night-out attraction, as well as sure-fire date fare.' – *Todd McCarthy, Variety*

How Sweet It Is *
US   1968   98m   Technicolor   Panavision
Warner/Cherokee/National General (Garry Marshall, Jerry Belson)

Suspicious of their son's intentions towards his girlfriend on a European holiday, a middle-aged American couple decide to follow.
Good-looking, rather silly comedy, plain spoken in the modern manner but without much entertainment value except when farce gets the upper hand.
w Garry Marshall, Jerry Belson *novel* The Girl in the Turquoise Bikini by Muriel Resnik d Jerry Paris ph Lucien Ballard m Pat Williams
☆ James Garner, Debbie Reynolds, Maurice Ronet, Paul Lynde, Marcel Dalio, Terry-Thomas, Donald Losby, Hilarie Thompson
'One of those slender marital farces in which the behaviour of the adults is consistently more juvenile than that of the teenagers.' – *MFB*

How the West Was Won *
US   1962   162m   Technicolor   Cinerama
MGM/Cinerama (Bernard Smith)

Panoramic Western following the daughter of a pioneering family from youth (1830) to old age, with several half-relevant stories along the way.
Muddled spectacular with splendid set-pieces but abysmal dullness in between, especially if not seen in three-strip Cinerama (the Cinemascope prints are muddy and still show the dividing lines). An all-star fairground show of its time.
w James R. Webb d Henry Hathaway (first half), John Ford (Civil War), George Marshall (train) ph William Daniels, Milton Krasner, Charles Lang Jnr, Joseph LaShelle m Alfred Newman ad George W. Davis, William Ferrari, Addison Hehr
☆ Debbie Reynolds, Carroll Baker, Lee J. Cobb, Henry Fonda, Carolyn Jones, Karl Malden, Gregory Peck, George Peppard, Robert Preston, James Stewart, Eli Wallach, John Wayne, Richard Widmark, Brigid Bazlen, Walter Brennan and also David Brian, Andy Devine, Raymond Massey, Agnes Moorehead, Henry Morgan, Thelma Ritter, Russ Tamblyn, Spencer Tracy (narrator)
'That goddamned Cinerama ... do you know a waist shot is as close as you could get with that thing?' – *Henry Hathaway*
🏆 James R. Webb
🏆 best picture; photography; music

How to Be a Player
US   1997   94m   colour
Polygram/Island/Outlaw (Mark Burg, Todd Baker, Russell Simmons, Preston Holmes)

A womanizer gets his come-uppance from his six girlfriends.
Glossy, empty comedy of sexual stereotypes; it has a very limited appeal.
w Mark Brown, Demetria Johnson d Lionel C. Martin ph Ross Berryman m Darren Floyd pd Bruce Curtis ed William Young
☆ Bill Bellamy, Natalie Desselle, Lark Voorhies, Mari Morrow, Pierre, Jermaine 'Big Hugg' Hopkins
'An inept sexist comedy ... It is only too typical of mainstream black American cinema today and makes one feel nostalgic for the gutsy blaxploitation pictures of the early Seventies.' – *Philip French, Observer*

How to Be a Woman and Not Die in the Attempt *
Spain   1991   89m   colour
Mayfair/Iberoamericana/Atrium/Idea (Rafael Fernández)

original title: Como ser mujer y no morir en el intento

A three-times-married journalist grows tired of having to be a mother to her husband, his and her children, and her boss.
Pleasant comedy about the shifting relationships between the sexes, tame by feminist standards, but perceptive enough to bring smiles of recognition from most audiences.
w Carmen Rico-Godoy *novel* Carmen Rico-Godoy d Ana Belén ph Juan Amoros m Antonio Garcia de Diego, Pancho Verona, Mariano Diaz ad Gerardo Vera ed Carmen Frias
☆ Carmen Maura, Antonio Resines, Carmen Conesa, Juanjo Puigcorbe, Miguel Rellan, Tina Sainz, Asunción Balaguer, Enriqueta Carballeira, Paco Aguilar, José Ma Cañete
'A rather creaking middle-aged affair.' – *Empire*
'The script goes nowhere and the characters are drawn paper-thin.' – *Variety*

How to Be Very Very Popular
US   1955   89m   DeLuxe   Cinemascope
TCF (Nunnally Johnson)

Two belly dancers on the run from gangsters hide out in a co-ed college.
Wacky remake of She Loves Me Not (qv); tries hard for a vein of freewheeling lunacy but only occasionally achieves it. A few numbers might have helped.
wd Nunnally Johnson ph Milton Krasner m Cyril Mockridge
☆ Betty Grable, Sheree North, Charles Coburn, Robert Cummings, Orson Bean, Fred Clark, Tommy Noonan

How to Beat the High Cost of Living
US   1980   110m   Movielab
Filmways

Three middle-class women take to robbery when they can't make the housekeeping balance.
Undercast, reprehensible and almost totally unfunny alleged comedy.
w Robert Kaufman d Robert Scheerer
☆ Susan Saint James, Jane Curtin, Jessica Lange, Richard Benjamin, Fred Willard, Eddie Albert

How to Commit Marriage
US   1969   98m   Technicolor
Cinerama/Naho (Bill Lawrence)

A couple decide to divorce, with repercussions on their family and in-laws.
Tiresome generation-gap comedy.
w Ben Starr, Michael Kanin d Norman Panama ph Charles Lang m Joseph J. Lilley
☆ Bob Hope, Jackie Gleason, Jane Wyman, Leslie Nielsen, Maureen Arthur, Paul Stewart, Tina Louise

How to Get Ahead in Advertising
GB   1989   94m   colour
Virgin/HandMade Films (David Wimbury)

An advertising man, in revolt against salesmanship, grows a boil that turns into an alternative head.
Unsuccessful diatribe on the consumer society.
wd Bruce Robinson ph Peter Hannan m David Dundas, Rick Wentworth pd Michael Pickwood ed Alan Strachan
☆ Richard E. Grant, Rachel Ward, Richard Wilson, Jacqueline Tong, John Shrapnel, Susan Wooldridge, Mick Ford, Jacqueline Pearce, Roddy Maude-Roxby

How to Make a Monster
US   1958   74m   bw/colour
AIP (Herman Cohen)

A movie make-up man takes his revenge by turning his fake monsters into real ones after the new studio bosses sack him.
A tongue-in-cheek attempt to get more mileage out of I Was a Teenage Frankenstein and I Was a Teenage Werewolf, produced and directed by the same team, and to cash in on the popularity of rock; the result is uninspired.
w Kenneth Langtry, Herman Cohen d Herbert L. Strock ph Maury Gertsman m Paul Dunlap ad Leslie Thomas sp make-up: Philip Scheer
☆ Robert H. Harris, Paul Brinegar, Gary Conway, Gary Clarke, Malcolm Atterbury, Morris Ankrum, Walter Reed, Heather Ames, John Ashley

'There's beauty in the patterns of life.'
How to Make an American Quilt **
US   1995   117m   DeLuxe
Universal/Amblin (Sarah Pillsbury, Midge Sanford)

A graduate student learns about the loves of her grandmother and her women friends as they sew her wedding quilt.
A formulaic film that manages to be a humane and enjoyable celebration of feminism without being merely an exercise in nostalgia, illuminating the struggles and triumphs of its participants in their unexceptional lives.
w Jane Anderson *novel* Whitney Otto d Jocelyn Moorhouse ph Janusz Kaminski m Thomas Newman pd Leslie Dilley ed Jill Bilock
☆ Winona Ryder, Anne Bancroft, Ellen Burstyn, Kate Nelligan, Alfre Woodard, Kate Capshaw, Adam Baldwin, Dermot Mulroney, Maya Angelou, Lois Smith, Jean Simmons, Rip Torn, Derrick O'Connor, Johnathon Schaech, Samantha Mathis
'A quality movie that leisurely maps a muted, liberal feminism.' – *Sight and Sound*

How to Make It: see Target Harry

How to Marry a Millionaire **
US   1953   96m   Technicolor   Cinemascope
TCF (Nunnally Johnson)

Three girls rent an expensive New York apartment and set out to trap millionaires.
Cinemascope's first attempt at modern comedy was not quite as disastrous as might have been expected, largely because of the expensiveness of everything and the several stars still brightly twinkling, but the handling of this variation on the old Golddiggers theme, while entirely amiable, is dramatically very slack.
w Nunnally Johnson d Jean Negulesco ph Joe MacDonald m Cyril Mockridge md Alfred Newman
☆ Lauren Bacall, Marilyn Monroe, Betty Grable, William Powell, Cameron Mitchell, David Wayne, Rory Calhoun, Alex D'Arcy, Fred Clark
'Not only educational, but great fun.' – *Star*
† The film has an eight-minute pre-credits concert sequence, which is pretty unnerving when it unspools on TV.

'The last word in do-it-yourself!'
How to Murder a Rich Uncle
GB   1957   80m   bw   Cinemascope
Columbia/Warwick (Ronald Kinnoch)

An impoverished nobleman decides to murder his rich old uncle.
Feebly-handled black comedy which does not come off at all despite a highly talented cast.
w John Paxton *play* Il Faut Tuer Julie by Didier Daix d Nigel Patrick ph Ted Moore
☆ Nigel Patrick, Charles Coburn, Katie Johnson, Wendy Hiller, Anthony Newley, Athene Seyler, Michael Caine, Noel Hood, Kenneth Fortescue

'When Was The Last Time You Took The Wife To A Movie? (This could be it!)'
How to Murder Your Wife *
US   1964   118m   Technicolor
UA/Murder Inc (George Axelrod)

A strip cartoonist tests out his violent scenes in real life; when his wife disappears he finds himself accused of murder.
Amusing preliminaries give way to dreary plot complications and an overlong courtroom scene. Leave after the first hour.
w George Axelrod d Richard Quine ph Harry Stradling m Neal Hefti pd Richard Sylbert
☆ Jack Lemmon, Virna Lisi, Terry-Thomas, Eddie Mayehoff, Sidney Blackmer, Claire Trevor
'Decked out with gross gags and humorless witticisms, the film is infinitely more vulgar than a mere summary can convey.' – *John Simon*

How to Rob a Bank: see A Nice Little Bank That Should Be Robbed

---

How to Save a Marriage and Ruin Your Life

US 1968 102m Technicolor Panavision
Columbia/Nob Hill (Stanley Shapiro)

An attorney takes it upon himself to convince his friend of the infidelity of the friend's mistress…
Tedious sex antics without any sex; a few smiles are not enough to endear it.
w Stanley Shapiro, Nate Monaster d Fielder Cook ph Lee Garmes m Michel Legrand
☆ Dean Martin, Eli Wallach, Stella Stevens, Anne Jackson, Betty Field, Jack Albertson, Katharine Bard
  'Another variation on Hollywood's patent version of the Restoration comedy, which as usual abandons the lustiness of its 17th-century prototype in favour of guilt-ridden lechery and a fundamental respect for the married state.' – *MFB*

How to Steal a Diamond in Four Uneasy Lessons: see The Hot Rock

How to Steal a Million *

US 1966 127m DeLuxe Panavision
TCF/World Wide (Fred Kohlmar)

The daughter of an art forger mistakenly involves a private detective in a robbery.
High-class but rather boring romantic comedy; the credits promise much but interest wanes quickly owing to uncertain handling.
w Harry Kurnitz story George Bradshaw d William Wyler ph Charles Lang m Johnny Williams pd Alexandre Trauner
☆ Audrey Hepburn, Peter O'Toole, Charles Boyer, Hugh Griffith, Eli Wallach, Fernand Gravet, Marcel Dalio
  'Terribly wordy and slow … Wyler hasn't got the touch nowadays.' – *Sight and Sound*
  'The picture isn't offensive, and it's handsome enough, but it's just blah.' – *Pauline Kael, New Yorker*

How to Steal the World

US 1968 90m Metrocolor
MGM/Arena (Anthony Spinner)

A renegade American agent sets out to end war by kidnapping six leading scientists to create a special gas that will allow him to control the minds of everyone else.
Glossily vacuous spy caper, rarely rising above an atmosphere of genial stupidity amid mass slaughter.
w Norman Hudis d Sutton Roley ph Robert B. Hauser m Richard Shores ad George W. Davis, James W. Sullivan ed Joseph Dervin, Harry Knapp
☆ Robert Vaughn, David McCallum, Barry Sullivan, Eleanor Parker, Leslie Nielsen, Tony Bill, Mark Richman, Dan O'Herlihy, Leo G. Carroll
† The film was edited from an episode from the television series *The Man from U.N.C.L.E.* Its scriptwriter is better known for having written the first six *Carry On* movies.

How to Stuff a Wild Bikini

US 1965 93m Pathécolor Panavision
AIP (Samuel Z. Arkoff, James H. Nicholson)

Serving in the army in Tahiti, a youth asks a witch doctor to ensure that his girlfriend remains faithful to him.
A formula exhibiting tiredness, as a familiar plot and situations – a couple's bland jealousies, some blander vocalizing – are recycled for the umpteenth time.
w William Asher, Leo Townsend d William Asher ph Floyd Crosby m Les Baxter ad Howard Campbell ed Fred R. Feitshans, Eve Newman
☆ Annette Funicello, Dwayne Hickman, Brian Donlevy, Harvey Lembeck, Beverly Adams, Jody McCrea, John Ashley, Buster Keaton, Mickey Rooney, Brian Wilson, The Kingsmen

How to Succeed in Business without Really Trying **

US 1967 121m DeLuxe Panavision
UA/Mirisch (David Swift)

A window cleaner cajoles his way to the top of a New York company.
Cinematically uninventive but otherwise brisk and glowing adaptation of a sharp, slick Broadway musical.
wd David Swift book Shepherd Mead musical book Abe Burrows, Jack Weinstock, Willie Gilbert ph Burnett Guffey m/ly Frank Loesser md Nelson

Riddle ad Robert Boyle, Mary Blair ed Ralph E. Winters, Allan Jacobs
☆ Robert Morse, Rudy Vallee, Michele Lee, Anthony Teague, Maureen Arthur, Murray Matheson
  'Shows how taste and talent can succeed in bringing a stage musical to the screen with its virtues intact.' – *John Cutts*
† Credits include 'visual gags by Virgil Partch'.

Howard, a New Breed of Hero: see Howard the Duck

Howard the Duck

US 1986 111m DeLuxe
Universal/Gloria Katz/George Lucas

GB title: *Howard, a New Breed of Hero*

A duck from outer space comes to Earth and has various uncomfortable adventures.
Toned down from an adult comic strip, this peculiar film has nowhere to go because it's too sexy for kids and too stupid for adults.
w Willard Huyck, Gloria Katz from Steve Gerber's character d Willard Huyck ph Richard H. Kline m John Barry pd Peter Jamison
☆ Lea Thompson, Jeffrey Jones, Paul Guilfoyle

Howards End ***

GB 1992 140m Technicolor Super35 Widescreen
Merchant Ivory/Film Four (Ismail Merchant)

The fortunes of two middle-class families overlap and interlock.
The best of the adaptations of Forster's novels, in which the nostalgia is undercut by an examination of the moral bankruptcy of the ruling class.
w Ruth Prawer Jhabvala novel E. M. Forster d James Ivory ph Tony Pierce-Roberts m Richard Robbins pd Luciana Arrighi ed Andrew Marcus
☆ Anthony Hopkins, Vanessa Redgrave, Helena Bonham Carter, *Emma Thompson*, James Wilby, Sam West, Jemma Redgrave, Nicola Duffett, Prunella Scales, Simon Callow
  'A most compelling drama, perhaps the best film made during the 30-year partnership of Ismail Merchant and James Ivory.' – *Variety*
  'A handsome and intelligent piece of work: a faithful, well-paced, and carefully crafted dramatization of a very good story.' – *Terrence Rafferty, New Yorker*
♟ Emma Thompson; Ruth Prawer Jhabvala; Luciana Arrighi
♟ Best picture; James Ivory; Vanessa Redgrave; Tony Pierce-Roberts; Richard Robbins; Jenny Beavan, John Bright (costume design)
♟ best picture; Emma Thompson

The Howards of Virginia

US 1940 117m bw
Columbia (Frank Lloyd)

GB title: *The Tree of Liberty*

A Virginian surveyor finds himself involved in the Revolutionary War.
Historical cavalcade in which central miscasting seems to cast a shadow of artifice over the whole. Interesting but seldom stimulating.
w Sidney Buchman novel The Tree of Liberty by Elizabeth Page d Frank Lloyd ph Bert Glennon m Richard Hageman
☆ Cary Grant, Martha Scott, Cedric Hardwicke, Alan Marshal, Richard Carlson, Paul Kelly, Irving Bacon, Elizabeth Risdon
♟ Richard Hageman

'Imagine your worst fear a reality!'

The Howling *

US 1980 90m CFI color
Avco Embassy/International Film Investors/Wescom (Ron Bottin)

A lady newscaster discovers that the medical retreat at which she stays to recover from a nervous breakdown is likely to give her another.
A plethora of werewolves and a glut of in-jokes pale beside a gallery of convincing and horrifying special effects.
w John Sayles, Terence H. Winkless novel Gary Brandner d Joe Dante ph John Hora m Pino Donaggio make-up Rick Baker
☆ Dee Wallace, Patrick Macnee, Dennis Dugan, Christopher Stone, Kevin McCarthy, John Carradine, Slim Pickens

† Some of the character names: George Waggner, R. William Neill, Sam Newfield, Fred Francis, Terry Fisher, Erle Kenton, Charlie Barton, Lew Landers…

Howling II … Your Sister Is a Werewolf

US 1985 90m colour
Thorn-EMI /Granite/Hemdale (Steven Lane)

An expert goes to Transylvania to track down the werewolf queen.
Thin attempt at comedy-horror, which barely got released.
w Robert Sarno, Gary Brandner d Philippe Mora
☆ Christopher Lee, Annie McEnroe, Reb Brown, Ferdy Mayne, Sybil Danning
† The film, which was shot in Czechoslovakia, has no relation whatsoever to *The Howling*.

The Howling III

Australia 1987 94m colour
Baccanial (Charles Waterstreet, Philippe Mora)

A mad scientist goes in search of marsupial werewolves, which resemble fierce koala bears.
Bizarre horror spoof that somehow manages to incorporate the drag act of Barry Humphries as Australian super-housewife Dame Edna Everage – the result is below average.
wd Philippe Mora novel Gary Brandner ph Louis Irving m Allan Zavod pd Ross Major ed Lee Smith sp Bob McCarron
☆ Barry Otto, Imogen Annesley, Dasha Blahova, Max Fairchild, Ralph Cotterill, Barry Humphries, Michael Pate, Frank Thring

Howling IV: The Original Nightmare

GB 1988 92m colour
IVE (Harry Alan Towers)

A best-selling author has visions of a werewolf and goes to an isolated cottage for a rest cure.
Like the rest of this series, this movie bears little resemblance to its predecessors, other than in its low-budget mediocrity.
w Clive Turner, Freddie Rowe d John Hough ph Godfrey Godar m David George, Barrie Guard ed Claudia Finkle, Malcolm Burns-Errington sp Steve Johnson
☆ Romy Windsor, Michael T. Weiss, Anthony Hamilton, Suzanne Severeid, Lamya Derval, Norman Anstey, Kate Edwards, Clive Turner
  'Poor horror fare.' – *Films and Filming*

Howling V: The Rebirth

US 1989 99m colour
Allied Vision (Clive Turner)

A group of tourists are invited to spend a weekend in an ancient castle in Budapest – and discover that one of them is a werewolf.
Dismal horror that attempts to take the myth more seriously than other films in the series, but succeeds only in being a boring variation on Agatha Christie's Ten Little Indians.
w Clive Turner, Freddie Rowe novel The Howling 1–3 by Gary Brandner d Neal Sundstrom ph Arledge Armenaki m The Factory
☆ Ben Cole, William Shockley, Mark Siversen, Philip Davis, Elizabeth She, Victoria Catlin, Stephanie Faulkner, Mary Stavin, Clive Turner

The Howling VI: The Freaks

US 1991 102m Foto-Kem
Allied Lane Pringle

A wandering werewolf with kindly intentions arrives in a small Southern town and falls prey to the evil owner of a freak show.
Leisurely, affected and lacklustre horror, with pretensions above its budget and the ability of its cast and director.
w Kevin Rock novel The Howling 1–3 by Gary Brandner d Hope Perello ph Edward Pei m Patrick Gleeson pd Richard Reams ed Adam Wolfe sp Steve Johnson; make-up effects: Todd Masters
☆ Brendan Hughes, Michele Matheson, Sean Gregory Sullivan, Antonio Fargas, Carol Lynley, Jered Barclay, Bruce Martyn Payne
  'Tasteless but effective shocker.' – *Variety*
† During a sequence in which a sheriff is chased by a monster, also visible on-screen are the shadows thrown by the camera and crew.

Hsimeng Rensheng: see The Puppetmaster

Huang Tudi: see Yellow Earth

Huck and the King of Hearts

US 1993 94m Foto-Kem
Crystal Sky/Trimark (Steven Paul)

A young boy runs away from home to find his grandfather, and is befriended by a card-sharp fleeing from a hitman.
Charmless updating of Twain into a world of dysfunctional families, drug-dealing and guns.
w Christopher Sturgeon story Mark Twain d Michael Keusch ph Victor Goss m Chris Saranec pd Mary Patvaldnieks ed Jack Tucker
☆ Chauncey Leopardi, Joe Piscopo, Graham Greene, Dee Wallace Stone, Gretchen Becker, John Astin

Huckleberry Finn

US 1931 71m bw
Paramount

The river adventures of Mark Twain's scapegrace hero.
Adequate early talkie family film.
w Grover Jones, William Slavens McNutt d Norman Taurog ph David Abel
☆ Jackie Coogan, Junior Durkin, Mitzi Green, Jackie Searl, Eugene Pallette

Huckleberry Finn **

US 1939 90m bw
MGM (Joseph L. Mankiewicz)

Solidly competent remake with excellent production values and several entertaining sequences.
w Hugo Butler d Richard Thorpe ph John Seitz m Franz Waxman
☆ Mickey Rooney, Walter Connolly, William Frawley, Rex Ingram

Huckleberry Finn *

US 1960 107m Metrocolor Cinemascope
MGM (Samuel Goldwyn Jnr)
aka: *The Adventures of Huckleberry Finn*

Another patchy remake.
w James Lee d Michael Curtiz ph Ted McCord m Jerome Moross
☆ Eddie Hodges, Tony Randall, Archie Moore, Neville Brand, Judy Canova, Buster Keaton, Andy Devine

Huckleberry Finn

US 1974 118m DeLuxe Panavision
UA/Apjac/Readers Digest (Robert Greenhut)

Ambitious but lustreless version of the famous story, with songs.
d J. Lee-Thompson ph Laszlo Kovacs pd Philip Jefferies w/m/ly Richard M. Sherman, Robert B. Sherman
☆ Jeff East, Paul Winfield, David Wayne, Harvey Korman, Arthur O'Connell, Gary Merrill, Natalie Trundy
  'It expires in a morass of treacle.' – *Tom Milne*
  'It transforms a great work of fiction into something bland, boring and tasteless.' – *Michael Billington, Illustrated London News*

The Hucksters **

US 1947 115m bw
MGM (Arthur Hornblow Jnr)

Back from the war, an advertising executive finds it difficult to put up with his clients' tantrums.
Good topical entertainment which still entertains and gives a good impression of its period.
w Luther Davis novel Frederic Wakeman d Jack Conway ph Harold Rosson m Lennie Hayton
☆ Clark Gable, Deborah Kerr, Ava Gardner, Sydney Greenstreet, Adolphe Menjou, Keenan Wynn, Edward Arnold, Aubrey Mather
  'A good picture, quick and to the point.' – *Photoplay*

Hud ****

US 1963 112m bw Panavision
Paramount/Salem/Dover (Martin Ritt, Irving Ravetch)

Life is hard on a Texas ranch, and the veteran owner is not helped by his sexually arrogant ne'er-do-well son, who is a bad influence on the household.

Superbly set in an arid landscape, this incisive character drama is extremely well directed and acted.

w Irving Ravetch, Harriet Frank novel Horseman Pass By by Larry McMurtry d Martin Ritt ph James Wong Howe m Elmer Bernstein
☆ Paul Newman, Patricia Neal, Melvyn Douglas, Brandon de Wilde
'So uncompromising in its portrait of an amoral man and his impact upon three people that I am tempted to reach for that dangerous adjective "unique".' – Judith Crist
♟ James Wong Howe; Patricia Neal; Melvyn Douglas
♟ script; Martin Ritt; Paul Newman
♟ Patricia Neal

Huddle

US   1932   104m   bw
MGM
GB title: The Impossible Lover
A steel worker's son makes good at Harvard, and wants to marry out of his class.
Would-be serious class drama which fell over its own feet.
w Robert Johnson, C. Gardner Sullivan, Arthur Hyman, Walton Smith d Sam Wood
☆ Ramon Novarro, Madge Evans, Una Merkel, Conrad Nagel, Arthur Byron, Cliff Edwards
'Football film doing much to defeat its own purpose by extreme length … the Metro foreign production end is substituting soccer for the football portions for European screenings.' – Variety

'For the world's greatest cat burglar nine lives may just not be enough…'
Hudson Hawk

US   1991   100m   Technicolor
Columbia TriStar/Silver Pictures/Ace Bone (Joel Silver)
A cat burglar is hired to steal from the Vatican an alchemical formula for turning lead into gold.
Direly unsuccessful attempt at a comedy thriller that was a box-office flop.
w Steven E. de Souza, Daniel Waters story Bruce Willis, Robert Kraft d Michael Lehmann ph Dante Spinotti m Michael Kamen, Robert Kraft pd Jack DeGovia ed Chris Lebenzon, Michael Tronick
☆ Bruce Willis, Danny Aiello, Andie MacDowell, James Coburn, Richard E. Grant, Sandra Bernhard, Donald Burton, Don Harvey, David Caruso
'Ever wondered what a Three Stooges short would look like with a $40 million budget? Then meet Hudson Hawk, a relentlessly annoying clay duck that crash-lands in a sea of wretched excess and silliness.' – Variety
'Its utter failure can only be explained by some form of madness having overcome the people involved in its making.' – Philip French, Observer

Hudson's Bay **

US   1940   95m   bw
TCF (Kenneth MacGowan)
Pierre Radisson, a French Canadian trapper, opens up millions of acres of northern wilderness for England.
Well-made historical saga with good production and performances.
w Lamar Trotti d Irving Pichel ph Peverell Marley, George Barnes m Alfred Newman ad Richard Day, Wiard B. Ihnen
☆ Paul Muni, Laird Cregar, Gene Tierney, John Sutton, Virginia Field, Vincent Price, Nigel Bruce, Morton Lowry, Robert Greig, Frederic Worlock, Montagu Love

The Hudsucker Proxy **

US   1994   111m   colour
Warner/Polygram/Silver/Working Title (Ethan Coen)
In the 50s, a bright but gullible business school graduate rises from the mailroom to be president of a vast corporation overnight as the result of boardroom devilry and makes good against the odds.
Clever and enjoyable pastiche of Hollywood comedies of the 40s, close in spirit to Preston Sturges with an ending straight out of Frank Capra. It is stylized, stylish and civilized entertainment.
w Ethan Coen, Joel Coen, Sam Raimi d Joel Coen ph Roger Deakins m Carter Burwell, Aram Khachaturian pd Dennis Gassner ed Thom Noble

☆ Tim Robbins, Jennifer Jason Leigh, Paul Newman, Charles Durning, Jim True, John Mahoney, Bill Cobbs, Bruce Campbell
'Has little else but spasmodic entertainment value to commend it.' – Derek Malcolm, Guardian
'Seems like a wizardly but artificial synthesis of aspects of vintage fare, leaving a hole in the middle where some emotion and humanity ought to be.' – Todd McCarthy, Variety

Hue and Cry ***

GB   1946   82m
Ealing (Michael Balcon)
East End boys discover that their favourite boys' paper is being used by crooks to pass information.
The first 'Ealing comedy' uses vivid London locations as background for a sturdy comic plot with a climax in which the criminals are rounded up by thousands of boys swarming over dockland.
w T. E. B. Clarke d Charles Crichton ph Douglas Slocombe, John Seaholme m Georges Auric
☆ Alastair Sim, Jack Warner, Harry Fowler, Valerie White, Frederick Piper
'Refreshing, bloodtingling and disarming.' – Richard Winnington

Huey Long **

US   1985   88m   DuArt/bw
Ken Burns, Richard Kilberg
The life and death of the populist American politician Huey Long, who dominated the politics of Louisiana in the 30s and was murdered at a point when he might have gone on to become US President or even dictator.
Fascinating documentary not only on the rise of a politician but on the wider question of the corruption of power, told using archive footage and reminiscences of many of the people involved.
w Geoffrey C. Ward d Ken Burns ph Ken Burns, Buddy Squires md John Colby ed Amy Stechler Burns
☆ David McCullough

Hugo the Hippo

US   1975   78m   colour
Brut (Robert Halmi)
An independently-minded hippo combats a Zanzibar magician.
Uninventive cartoon feature, endearing neither in characterization nor in draughtsmanship.
w Thomas Baum d William Feigenbaum md Bert Keyes
☆ Featuring the voices of Burl Ives, Marie Osmond, Jimmy Osmond, Robert Morley, Paul Lynde

Hugs and Kisses *

Sweden   1966   96m   bw
Sandrews (Göran Lindgren)
original title: Puss och Kram
A destitute bohemian takes over the house and the wife of the old executive friend who shelters him out of pity.
Rather like a comedy version of the Dirk Stroeve section of The Moon and Sixpence, this sophisticated film came under censorship fire for depicting the first full frontal female.
wd Jonas Cornell ph Lars Swanberg m Bengt Ernryd
☆ Sven-Bertil Taube, Agneta Ekmanner, Hakan Serner
'The brilliance of the film lies in the way humour and sadness are kept in perfect equilibrium.' – MFB

Huis Clos *

France   1954   99m   bw
Films Marceau
Two women and a man die, go to hell, and are locked up for ever in an elegant room.
Rather flat intellectual fantasy from a play which made great waves when first performed.
w Pierre Laroche play Jean-Paul Sartre d Jacqueline Audry ph Robert Juillard m Joseph Kosma
☆ Arletty, Frank Villard, Gaby Sylvia
'Without the ecstasy, terror and poetic imagination of a Cocteau, the subject becomes a fatally stationary one.' – Peter John Dyer, MFB

Huk!

US   1956   83m   Eastmancolor
UA (Collier Young)
In 1951, an American fights Philippine guerrillas who murdered his father.
Crude action melodrama which served a purpose.
w Stirling Silliphant novel Stirling Silliphant d John Barnwell ph William Snyder m Albert Glasser
☆ George Montgomery, Mona Freeman, John Baer, James Bell

Hullabaloo

US   1940   77m   bw
MGM (Louis K. Sidney)
A veteran actor goes into radio and causes a furore with a broadcast about men from Mars.
Slim framework for a variety show encasing some young MGM talents.
w Nat Perrin d Edwin L. Marin
☆ Frank Morgan, Virginia Grey, Dan Dailey Jnr, Billie Burke, Nydia Westman, Donald Meek, Reginald Owen, Leni Lynn, Virginia O'Brien, Sara Haden

The Human Beast: see La Bête Humaine

The Human Comedy *

US   1943   117m   bw
MGM (Clarence Brown)
In a small town during the war, a telegram boy brings tragedy to others and is touched by it himself.
Gooey, sentimental morale booster in the best MGM tradition, a variant on the Hardy family series but with all the pretensions of its author.
w Howard Estabrook novel William Saroyan d Clarence Brown ph Harry Stradling m Herbert Stothart
☆ Mickey Rooney, Frank Morgan, James Craig, Marsha Hunt, Jackie Jenkins, Fay Bainter, Ray Collins, Van Johnson, Donna Reed
OPENING NARRATION BY RAY COLLINS: 'I am Matthew Macauley. I have been dead for two years. So much of me is still living that I know now the end is only the beginning. As I look down on my homeland of Ithaca, California, with its cactus, vineyards and orchards, I see that so much of me is still living there – in the places I've been, in the fields and streets and church and most of all in my home, where my hopes, my dreams, my ambitions still live in the daily life of my loved ones.'
'The dignity and simplicity of the ideas shade off into cheap pretentiousness.' – Bosley Crowther
'The best one can say of it … is that it tries on the whole to be "faithful" to Saroyan; not invariably a good idea.' – James Agee
'The Saroyan touch leaves nothing ordinary: the film is electric with the joy of life.' – Time
♟ original story
♟ best picture; Clarence Brown; Harry Stradling; Mickey Rooney

Human Desire

US   1954   90m   bw
Columbia (Lewis J. Rachmil)
A jealous railway official forces his wife to help him murder her suspected lover.
Drab and unattractive remake of La Bête Humaine.
w Alfred Hayes d Fritz Lang ph Burnett Guffey m Daniele Amfitheatrof
☆ Gloria Grahame, Glenn Ford, Broderick Crawford, Edgar Buchanan

The Human Factor

GB   1975   95m   Technicolor
Eton (Terry Lens)
The family of a NATO war planner in Italy is slaughtered by terrorists.
Violent revenge drama, of little interest.
w Tom Hunter, Peter Powell d Edward Dmytryk
☆ George Kennedy, John Mills, Raf Vallone, Arthur Franz, Rita Tushingham, Frank Avianca, Barry Sullivan

The Human Factor

GB   1979   114m   Technicolor   Panavision
Rank/Wheel/Sigma/Otto Preminger
An innocent man is suspected of being the 'mole' in the Foreign Office.
Quietly sardonic scenes of diplomatic chess are played far too broadly and literally in this ill-advised and

poorly executed foray into the serious spy scene, which despite its stars becomes merely risible before the end.
w Tom Stoppard novel Graham Greene d Otto Preminger ph Mike Malloy m Richard and Gary Logan
☆ Nicol Williamson, Richard Attenborough, Derek Jacobi, Robert Morley, John Gielgud, Ann Todd, Richard Vernon, Joop Doderer, Iman
'Unfortunately, Preminger stages it all as if he was just trying to get all the actors through their line readings in under two hours, allowing no breathing room or time for character nuance in a tale which resolutely calls for quiet moments.' – Variety

The Human Jungle

US   1954   82m   bw
Allied Artists
A new police captain cleans up a gangster-ridden slum district.
Adequate low-life actioner of the kind later taken over by TV.
w William Sackheim, Daniel Fuchs d Joseph M. Newman ph Ellis Carter m Hans Salter
☆ Gary Merrill, Jan Sterling, Paula Raymond, Emile Meyer, Regis Toomey, Lamont Johnson, Chuck Connors

The Human Monster: see Dark Eyes of London

The Human Side

US   1934   60m   bw
Universal
A philandering theatrical producer returns to his family.
Pleasant light comedy, instantly forgettable.
w Frank Craven, Ernest Pascal play Christine Ames d Eddie Buzzell
☆ Adolphe Menjou, Doris Kenyon, Charlotte Henry, Dickie Moore, Reginald Owen, Joseph Cawthorn
'Homely, wholesome domestic comedy that should find beaucoup favour with the family trade.' – Variety

Human Traffic **

GB/Ireland   1999   95m   Fujicolor
Metrodome/Irish Screen/Fruit Salad (Allan Niblo, Emer McCourt)
Five Welsh friends, high on Ecstasy, spend a weekend together in clubs and bedrooms, sorting out their sexual problems.
Energetic youth movie, using lurid fantasy sequences and stylistic excesses of one sort and another to duplicate the druggy experiences of its characters.
wd Justin Kerrigan ph David Bennett m Rob Mello, Mathew Herbert pd David Buckingham ed Patrick Moore
☆ John Simm, Lorraine Pilkington, Shaun Parkes, Danny Dyer, Nicola Reynolds, Dean Davies, Peter Albert, Jan Anderson
'The accuracy of Kerrigan's observations on rave culture are less in question than the absence of a definable narrative drive, the messily episodic structure, characters which hover above caricature or the film's fundamental validity as compelling cinema.' – Trevor Lewis, Empire

Humanoids from the Deep

US   1980   81m   Metrocolor
New World (Martin B. Cohen)
GB title: Monster
Gruesome amphibious creatures rise from the ocean to stalk and destroy the most nubile women in sight.
Lurid, nonsensical but very violent horror flick, with much rape and nudity; like a Corman quickie of the fifties but with added gore.
w Frederick James d Barbara Peeters ph Daniele Lacambre m James Horner cos Rob Bottin
☆ Vic Morrow, Doug McClure, Ann Turkel

Humoresque **

US   1946   125m   bw
Warner (Jerry Wald)
An ambitious violinist gets emotionally involved with his wealthy patroness.
Lush soaper about suffering in high society, complete with tragic end and lashings of classical music (Isaac Stern on the sound track).

w Clifford Odets, Zachary Gold *novel* Fannie Hurst *d* Jean Negulesco *ph* Ernest Haller *md* Franz Waxman

☆ Joan Crawford, John Garfield, Oscar Levant, J. Carrol Naish, Joan Chandler, Tom D'Andrea, Craig Stevens, Ruth Nelson

'This brilliantly executed but less well-conceived picture functions like a beautifully made piece of machinery, fascinating to watch in action, powerful, but cold and insensitive.' – *Jympson Harman, London Evening News*

♪ Franz Waxman

The Hunchback of Notre Dame **
US   1923   120m   bw   silent
Universal
📼 ▤

The deformed Notre Dame bellringer rescues a gypsy girl from the evil intentions of her guardian.
Victorian gothic version with a riveting star performance.
w Percy Poore Sheehan, Edward T. Lowe Jnr *novel* Notre Dame de Paris by Victor Hugo *d* Wallace Worsley *ph* Robert S. Newhard, Tony Kornman

☆ Lon Chaney, Patsy Ruth Miller, Norman Kerry, Ernest Torrence, Gladys Brockwell, Kate Lester, Brandon Hurst, Tully Marshall

The Hunchback of Notre Dame ****
ᴉᴉ   US   1939   117m   bw
RKO (Pandro S. Berman)
📼 ▤ ◉ ◕

This superb remake is one of the best examples of Hollywood expertise at work: art direction, set construction, costumes, camera, lighting and above all direction brilliantly support an irresistible story and bravura acting.
w Sonya Levien, Bruno Frank *d* William Dieterle *ph* Joseph H. August *m* Alfred Newman *ad* Van Nest Polglase

☆ Charles Laughton, Cedric Hardwicke, Maureen O'Hara, Edmond O'Brien, Thomas Mitchell, Harry Davenport, Walter Hampden, Alan Marshal, George Zucco, Katherine Alexander, Fritz Leiber, Rod la Rocque

'A super thriller-chiller. Will roll up healthy grosses at the ticket windows.' – *Variety*
'Has seldom been bettered as an evocation of medieval life.' – *John Baxter, 1968*
'It exceeds in sheer magnificence any similar film in history. Sets are vast and rich in detail, crowds are immense, and camera uses of both are versatile, varied and veracious.' – *Motion Picture Herald*
† Other versions: Esmeralda (1906, French); Notre Dame de Paris (1911, French); *The Darling of Paris* (1917, US, with Theda Bara); and see above and below

♪ Alfred Newman

The Hunchback of Notre Dame
France/Italy   1956   107m   Eastmancolor   Cinemascope
Paris Films/Panitalia (Robert and Raymond Hakim)
original title: *Notre Dame de Paris*

Crude international rehash with nothing to commend it, though the script before dubbing may have been interesting.
w Jacques Prévert, Jean Aurenche *d* Jean Delannoy *ph* Michel Kelber *m* Georges Auric

☆ Anthony Quinn, Gina Lollobrigida, Jean Danet, Alain Cuny, Robert Hirsch

The Hunchback of Notre Dame **
ᴉᴉ   US   1996   91m   Technicolor
Buena Vista/Walt Disney (Don Hahn)
📼 ▤ ◉

The deformed bellringer of Notre Dame saves a gypsy girl from the machinations of his master.
An unlikely subject for animation, and one that, despite moments of brilliance, proves intractable to Disney's soft-centred musical way with classics. Young children are likely to be bored or confused, for the tone is uncertain, and the emotional and sexual subtext too adult for the treatment it receives.
w Tab Murphy, Irene Mecchi, Bob Tzudiker, Noni White, Jonathan Roberts *novel* Notre Dame de Paris by Victor Hugo *d* Gary Trousdale, Kirk Wise *m* Alan Menken *m/ly* Alan Menken, Stephen Schwartz *ad* David Goetz *ed* Ellen Keneshea

☆ Featuring the voices of: Tom Hulce, Tony Jay, Paul Kandel, Kevin Kline, Demi Moore, Heidi Mollenhauer, Jason Alexander, David Ogden Stiers, Mary Wickes, Jane Withers

'A mild disappointment; not a disaster but a definite falling off from the studio's series of recent triumphs.' – *Adam Mars-Jones, Independent*
'Beautiful and transporting – the best of Disney's "serious" animated features in the multiplex era.' – *Owen Gleiberman, Entertainment Weekly*
† It was among the box-office successes of 1996, grossing some $284m around the world.

♪ Alan Menken, Stephen Schwartz

The Hundred Pound Window
GB   1943   84m   bw
Warner (Max Milder)

A racecourse clerk becomes involved with gamblers who bribe him to rig the totalizator, but he finally exposes them.
Routine programmer notable only for giving a leading role to an old character actor.
w Abem Finkel, Brock Williams, Rodney Ackland *d* Brian Desmond Hurst *ph* Otto Heller *m* Hans May

☆ Frederick Leister, Mary Clare, Anne Crawford, Richard Attenborough, David Farrar, Niall MacGinnis, David Hutcheson

Hundred Rifles: see *100 Rifles*

A Hungarian Fairy Tale
Hungary   1986   97m   bw
Mafilm/Objektiv
▤

original title: *Hol Volt, Hol Nem Volt ...*
After his mother is killed, a 10-year-old boy runs away to search for his father, not realizing that the person named on his birth certificate is a bureaucratic fiction.
An intermittently successful surreal road movie, using Mozart's Magic Flute as a counterpart to the on-screen events; its portrait of officialdom run mad does not travel well.
w Gyula Gazdag, Miklós Györffy *d* Gyula Gazdag *ph* Elemér Ragályi *m* Mozart *md* Mártha István

☆ Eszter Csákányi, Mária Varga, Hušák František, Dávid Vermes, Péter Trokán, Szilvia Tóth

'The Hunger is a mood, a look, an ambience created by Tony Scott. It is the lighting of Stephen Goldblatt, it is the production design of Brian Morris, it is the clothes created by Milena Canonero.'

The Hunger
US   1983   99m   Metrocolor   Panavision
MGM-UA/Richard Shepherd
📼 ▤ ◉ ◕

A couple of ageless vampires are desperate for blood.
Absurd attempt to update Dracula with lashings of sex, rock music and flashy photography. An ordeal.
w Ivan Davis, Michael Thomas *novel* Whitley Strieber *d* Tony Scott *ph* Stephen Goldblatt, Tom Mangravite *m* Michael Rubini, Denny Jaeger *pd* Brian Morris

☆ Catherine Deneuve, Susan Sarandon, David Bowie, Cliff de Young

'One of the most incoherent and foolish pictures of recent months.' – *Observer*

Hungry for Love: see *Adua e le Compagne*

Hungry Wives: see *Season of the Witch*

'Deadly. Silent. Stolen.'
The Hunt for Red October **
US   1990   137m   Technicolor   Panavision
Paramount/Mace Neufeld/Jerry Sherlock
📼 ▤ ◉ ◕

The Soviet commander of a top-secret submarine attempts to defect to the West in his vessel.
An intermittently suspenseful thriller, stronger on hardware than human interest.
w Larry Ferguson, Donald Stewart *novel* Tom Clancy *d* John McTiernan *ph* Jan de Bont *m* Basil Poledouris *pd* Terence Marsh *ad* Dianne Wager *ed* Dennis Virkler, John Wright *sp* Industrial Light & Magic

☆ Sean Connery, Alec Baldwin, Scott Glenn, Sam Neill, James Earl Jones, Joss Ackland, Richard Jordan, Peter Firth, Tim Curry

'A terrific adventure yarn, excitingly filmed.' – *Variety*
♪ best sound effects editing
♪ best film editing; best sound

Hunted *
GB   1952   84m   bw
GFD/Independent Artists (Julian Wintle)
📼

US title: *The Stranger In Between*
A runaway boy joins forces with a runaway murderer, and the latter sacrifices himself for the boy's safety.
Predictable pattern melodrama, nicely made and acted.
w Jack Whittingham *d* Charles Crichton *ph* Eric Cross *m* Hubert Clifford

☆ Dirk Bogarde, Jon Whiteley, Kay Walsh, Elizabeth Sellars, Frederick Piper, Geoffrey Keen, Julian Somers

The Hunted
US   1995   110m   DeLuxe
Universal/Bregman/Bauer/Davis (John Davis, Gary W. Goldstein)
📼 ▤ ◉

In Tokyo, a New York businessman witnesses a murder by a ninja assassin and goes on the run from the killer.
Risible action thriller, full of casual slaughter, and lacking the high-energy choreography of the genre that might have made it watchable.
wd J. F. Lawton *ph* Jack Conroy *m* Motofumi Yamaguchi *pd* Phil Dagort *ed* Robert A. Ferretti, Eric Strand

☆ Christopher Lambert, John Lone, Joan Chen, Yoshio Harada, Yoko Shimada, Mari Natsuki, Tak Kubota

'This grisly yet often laughable actioner most closely resembles the low-budget martial arts movies that used to air, badly dubbed, on independent TV stations.' – *Brian Lowry, Variety*

Hunted Men *
US   1938   67m   bw
Paramount

A killer on the run moves into a private home and is outwitted by the head of the house.
Competent second feature which sticks in the memory.
w Horace McCoy, William R. Lipman *d* Louis King *ph* Victor Milner

☆ Lloyd Nolan, Lynne Overman, Mary Carlisle, J. Carrol Naish, Anthony Quinn, Dorothy Peterson

The Hunter
US   1980   117m   Metrocolor
Paramount/Rastar/Mort Engelberg
▤ ◕

Episodes in the violent career of an urban bounty hunter.
The action scenes salvage a mysteriously banal screenplay full of continuity lapses and unexplained characters.
w Ted Leighton, Peter Hyams *book* Christopher Keane, and the life of Ralph Thorson *d* Buzz Kulik *ph* Fred J. Koenekamp *m* Michel Legrand

☆ Steve McQueen, Eli Wallach, Kathryn Harrold, LeVar Burton, Ben Johnson

'The final impression is of an extended TV pilot for yet another police-boosting serial with more action than sense.' – *Sunday Times*

The Hunters
US   1958   108m   DeLuxe   Cinemascope
TCF (Dick Powell)
▤

A fearless American pilot is sent to Korea on a special mission.
Standard war thriller, good to look at when airborne but pretty boring on the ground; propaganda element very strong.
w Wendell Mayes *novel* James Salter *d* Dick Powell *ph* Charles G. Clarke, Tom Tutwiler *m* Paul Sawtell

☆ Robert Mitchum, Robert Wagner, Richard Egan, May Britt

Hunting
Australia   1992   97m   colour
Boulevard

A married secretary becomes involved with a ruthless media tycoon.
A mix of business thriller and domestic drama that manages to be both dull and pretentious.
wd Frank Howson *ph* David Connell, Dan Burstall *m* John French, David Herzog *pd* Jon Dowding *ed* Philip Reid

☆ John Savage, Kerry Armstrong, Jeffrey Thomas, Rebecca Rigg, Rhys McConnochie, Guy Pearce

The Hunting Party
US   1971   108m   DeLuxe
UA/Brighton/Levy-Gardner-Levy

A sadistic Texas baron sets out to shoot one by one the outlaws who have kidnapped his wife.
Crude, brutish and repellent melodrama: the epitome of permissiveness, replete with gore, rape and sadism.
w William Norton, Gilbert Alexander, Lou Morheim *d* Don Medford *ph* Cecilio Paniagua *m* Riz Ortolani

☆ Gene Hackman, Candice Bergen, Oliver Reed

Huozhe: see *To Live*

Las Hurdes: see *Land Without Bread*

Hurlyburly *
US   1998   122m   colour
Fine Line/Storm (Anthony Drazan, Richard Gladstein, David Hamburger)
🎧

Two Hollywood casting agents and an unemployed actor dissect their relationships with women and each other.
Acerbic, conversational drama of unlovely people who are living on the edge; the performances manage to engage one's attention through its longueurs.
w David Rabe *play* David Rabe *d* Anthony Drazan *ph* Gu Changwei *m* David Baerwald, Steve Lindsey *pd* Michael Haller *ed* Dylan Tichenor

☆ Sean Penn, Kevin Spacey, Robin Wright Penn, Chazz Palminteri, Garry Shandling, Anna Paquin, Meg Ryan

'Two long hours with three self-absorbed misogynists and the articulate women who allow these guys to treat them like dirt is not most people's idea of a good time.' – *David Rooney, Variety*

Hurricane
US   1979   120m   Technicolor   Todd-AO 70
Dino de Laurentiis/Famous Films (Lorenzo Semple Jnr)

A remake of the 1937 film, lacking the style, the innocence, and even the technical splendour.
w Lorenzo Semple Jnr *d* Jan Troell *ph* Sven Nykvist *m* Nino Rota *pd* Danilo Donati

☆ Jason Robards, Mia Farrow, Trevor Howard, Max von Sydow, Dayton Ka'ne, Timothy Bottoms, James Keach

Hurricane
US   1997   88m   Technicolor
First Independent/UA (Galt Niederhoffer, Gill Holland, Morgan J. Freeman)
GB title: *Hurricane Streets*

The relationship between a 15-year-old petty criminal and his girlfriend is hampered by cops and her father.
Gritty drama of a familiar kind, in which teenage love is seen as redeeming criminality and manslaughter.
wd Morgan J. Freeman *ph* Enrique Chediak *m* Theodore Shapiro *pd* Petra Barchi *ed* Sabine Hoffman

☆ Brendan Sexton III, Shawn Elliott, José Zuñiga, David Roland Frank, Carlo Alban, Antoine McLean, Mtume Gant, Lynn Cohen, Edie Falco

'It zooms along with the terrific soundtrack and some very affecting sequences.' – *Marianne Gray, Film Review*

'Through miles of raging ocean he defied man's law!'
The Hurricane **
US   1937   110m   bw
Samuel Goldwyn (Merritt Hulburd)
▤ ◕

The simple life on a South Pacific island is disrupted, not only by a vindictive governor but by a typhoon.
Tolerable island melodrama with a spectacular climax and a generally good cast.
w Dudley Nichols, Oliver H. P. Garrett *novel* Charles Nordhoff, James Norman Hall *d* John Ford *ph* Bert Glennon *m* Alfred Newman

☆ Dorothy Lamour, Jon Hall, C. Aubrey Smith, Mary Astor, Raymond Massey, Thomas Mitchell, John Carradine, Jerome Cowan

'A big money picture ... a production masterpiece.' – *Variety*
'There's a hurricane all right. It's magnificent ... Few people will bother to remember what the rest of the film is about. It goes with the wind.' – *C. A. Lejeune*

ᴉᴉ film suitable for family viewing   📼 VHS video-cassette for the British PAL system   ▤ VHS video-cassette for the British PAL system in wide screen-format   ◌ Video cassette in a computer-colourised version   ▬ American NTSC video-cassette   ◕ Laser disc

† Remade in 1979.

⚜ Alfred Newman; Thomas Mitchell

'His Greatest Fight Was For Justice.'

The Hurricane **
US 1999 125m DeLuxe
Buena Vista/Beacon/Azoff/Rudy Langlais (Armyan Bernstein, John Ketcham, Norman Jewison)
◎ ⌒

After reading his autobiography, a youth campaigns for the release of a former middleweight boxer who spent 19 years in prison for murders he did not commit.

Washington's performance helps lift this often plodding biopic out of the ordinary, but its clumsy construction diminishes its impact.

w Armyan Bernstein, Dan Gordon *book The Sixteenth Round* by Rubin 'Hurricane' Carter *book Lazarus and the Hurricane* by Sam Chaiton and Terry Swinton d Norman Jewison ph Roger Deakins m Christopher Young pd Philip Rosenberg ed Stephen Rivkin

☆ Denzel Washington, Vicellous Reon Shannon, Deborah Kara Unger, Liev Schreiber, John Hannah, Dan Hedaya, Debbi Morgan, Clancy Brown, David Paymer, Harris Yulin, Rod Steiger, Garland Witt

'So intriguingly plotted and captivatingly acted that it's easy to overlook its dramatic flaws and overall soft gaze.' – *Emanuel Levy, Variety*

⚜ Denzel Washington

Hurricane Island
US 1951 71m Supercinecolor
Sam Katzman/Columbia

Spaniards colonizing Florida are beset by evil spirits.

Saturday matinee hokum in poor colour.

w David Matthews d Lew Landers ph Lester White

☆ Jon Hall, Edgar Barrier, Marie Windsor, Marc Lawrence

Hurricane Smith
US 1952 90m Technicolor
Paramount/Nat Holt

An adventurer charters a boat to find a South Sea treasure but the boat owner turns the tables on him.

Standard thick ear with plenty of action.

w Frank Gruber d Jerry Hopper ph Ray Rennahan m Paul Sawtell

☆ John Ireland, Yvonne de Carlo, James Craig, Forrest Tucker

Hurricane Streets: see *Hurricane*

'Will the south overcome the bigotry of the hate-laden white aristocrats?'

Hurry Sundown
US 1967 146m Technicolor Panavision
Paramount/Sigma (Otto Preminger)

Post-war racial problems in Georgia farmland, with degenerate whites and noble blacks.

Incredibly cliché-ridden epic melodrama with action and sex asides, from a rock bottom bestseller. It long outstays its welcome even for unintentional hilarity.

w Thomas C. Ryan, Horton Foote *novel* K. B. Gilden d Otto Preminger ph Loyal Griggs, Milton Krasner m Hugo Montenegro

☆ Jane Fonda, Michael Caine, Rex Ingram, Diahann Carroll, Burgess Meredith, Jim Phillip Law, Robert Hooks, Faye Dunaway, Beah Richards, George Kennedy, Madeleine Sherwood

'Critic Wilfrid Sheed wrote recently that no film is ever so bad that you can't find some virtue in it. He must not have seen *Hurry Sundown*.' – *Rex Reed*

'To criticize it would be like tripping a dwarf.' – *Wilfrid Sheed*

'A pantomime version of Greek tragedy.' – *MFB*

'Preminger's taste is atrocious. His idea of erotic symbolism is Jane Fonda caressing Michael Caine's saxophone.' – *Cue*

Hurry Up, or I'll Be 30 *
US 1973 88m colour
Avco Embassy (Joseph Jacoby)
⊞

A failure attempts to find success and love before he reaches the beginning of middle age.

Gentle and sometimes perceptive comedy of manners.

w Joseph Jacoby, David Wiltse d Joseph Jacoby ph Burleigh Wartes m Stephen Lawrence ed Stan Warnow

☆ John Lefkowitz, Linda de Coff, Ronald Anton, Maureen Byrnes, Danny DeVito, David Kirk, Frank Quinn

'A comedy about love, death, and freedom!'

Husbands *
US 1970 154m DeLuxe
Columbia/Faces Music Inc (Al Ruban)

Three married men, shocked by the death of their friend, impulsively get drunk, fly to London and set out on a weekend of dissipation.

Irritatingly rough hewn and insanely overlong, this half-improvised tragi-comedy forces three good actors to overplay embarrassingly; but its best moments are memorable.

wd John Cassavetes ph Victor Kemper m none

☆ Peter Falk, John Cassavetes, Ben Gazzara

Husbands and Wives ***
US 1992 108m DuArt
Columbia TriStar/TriStar (Jack Rollins, Charles H. Joffe)
⊞ ⊞

After their best friends announce that they are splitting up, a writer and his wife decide to separate and he becomes infatuated with a young student.

One of Allen's best films, a clever and insightful examination of the insecurities and often self-destructive behaviour of couples, though the nervy camera-work irritates.

wd Woody Allen ph Carlo Di Palma pd Santo Loquasto ed Susan E. Morse

☆ Woody Allen, Judy Davis, Mia Farrow, Juliette Lewis, Liam Neeson, Blythe Danner, Sydney Pollack, Lysette Anthony

'The thing that moviegoers will realize decades hence is that *Husbands and Wives* is a damn fine film.' – *Richard Corliss, Time*

'Rich in characterisation, waspishly witty and profound in its observations about the frailty and fallibilities of modern marriage.' – *Ian Johnstone, Sunday Times*

⚜ Judy Davis; Woody Allen (as writer)

🏆 original screenplay

Husband's Holiday
US 1931 70m bw
Paramount

A wife takes a passive attitude to her husband's affair.

Tepid sophisticated comedy which doesn't register.

w Ernest Pascal *play The Marriage Bed* by Ernest Pascal d Robert Milton

☆ Clive Brook, Vivienne Osborne, Charles Ruggles, Juliette Compton, Charles Winninger, Elizabeth Patterson

'Mild drawing-room problem play made even milder by repressed acting.' – *Variety*

Hush
US 1998 95m Technicolor
TriStar (Douglas Wick)
⊞ ⊞ ⊛ ⊙ ⊙

A jealous mother tries to wreck her son's marriage.

Dire, risible domestic melodrama, with a hysterical performance from Lange and a bland one from Paltrow.

w Jonathan Darby, Jane Rusconi d Jonathan Darby ph Andrew Dunn m Christopher Young pd Thomas A. Walsh, Michael Johnston ed Dan Rae, Lynzee Klingman, Robert Leighton

☆ Jessica Lange, Gwyneth Paltrow, Johnathon Schaech, Nina Foch, Debi Mazar, Richard Lineback, Kiaulani Lee, David Thornton, Hal Holbrook

'A tawdry, artistically vacant exercise in class snobbery and crude, objectionable sexism.' – *Sight and Sound*

† The movie was released direct to video in Britain.

'It starts with the most shocking scene of all time – and that's only the beginning!'

Hush Hush Sweet Charlotte *
US 1964 133m bw
TCF/Associates and Aldrich
⊞ ⊞ ⊛

A Southern belle lives 37 years in a lonely mansion tormented by nightmarish memories of her fiancé's murder. Suddenly, after a series of apparent hauntings and other strange events, she finds she didn't do it.

Padded but generally enjoyable replay of elements from Whatever Happened to Baby Jane, with a large helping of Les Diaboliques. The stars help more than the director.

w Henry Farrell, Lukas Heller d Robert Aldrich ph Joseph Biroc m Frank de Vol ad William Glasgow

☆ Bette Davis, Olivia de Havilland, Joseph Cotten, Cecil Kellaway, Victor Buono, William Campbell, Mary Astor, Agnes Moorehead

'The blood is on the cleaver, the madwoman is on the loose, the headless corpse is on the prowl and the Guignol is about as grand as it can get.' – *Judith Crist*

'Aldrich only just manages to keep this side of being disgusting and that side of being ridiculous.' – *Films and Filming*

⚜ Joseph Biroc; Frank de Vol; Agnes Moorehead; title song (m Frank de Vol, ly Mack David)

Hush Money
US 1931 68m bw
Fox

A girl serves a jail term, but afterwards gets involved with a racketeer.

Underworld comedy-drama which paid its way.

w Dudley Nichols, Courteney Terrett d Sidney Lanfield

☆ Joan Bennett, Owen Moore, Hardie Albright, Myrna Loy, C. Henry Gordon, George Raft

'A light programmer for fair grosses.' – *Variety*

Le Hussard sur le Toit: see *The Horseman on the Roof*

Hussy
GB 1979 94m Eastmancolor
Boyd/Watchgrove (Jeremy Watt)
⊞ ⊞

A high-class prostitute becomes involved with gangsters but eventually finds a new life for herself and her offspring.

Tedious exploitation melodrama, shot like a ninety-minute commercial.

wd Matthew Chapman ph Keith Goddard pd Hazel Peizer ed Bill Blunden

☆ Helen Mirren, John Shea, Daniel Chasin, Jenny Runacre, Murray Salem, Patti Boulaye, Sandy Ratcliff

Hustle
US 1975 118m Eastmancolor
Paramount/RoBurt (Robert Aldrich)
⊞

A police lieutenant lives with a call girl and is drawn into her corrupt life.

Doleful crime melodrama with both eyes in the gutter.

w Steve Shagan d Robert Aldrich ph Joseph Biroc m Frank de Vol

☆ Burt Reynolds, Catherine Deneuve, Ben Johnson, Paul Winfield, Eileen Brennan, Eddie Albert, Ernest Borgnine, Catherine Bach, Jack Carter

'A fine companion piece to *Kiss Me Deadly* in its vision of a journey to the end of the night in quest of a myth.' – *Tim Milne*

'Even with such a meandering script as this, one expects more than the paltry fare Aldrich offers.' – *Paul Coleman*

The Hustler ****
US 1961 135m bw Cinemascope
TCF/Robert Rossen
⊞ ⊞ ⊛

A pool room con man comes to grief when he falls in love.

Downbeat melodrama with brilliantly handled and atmospheric pool table scenes; the love interest is redundant.

w Robert Rossen, Sidney Carroll *novel* Walter Tevis d Robert Rossen ph Eugene Schufftan m Kenyon Hopkins

☆ Paul Newman, Jackie Gleason, George C. Scott, Piper Laurie, Myron McCormick, Murray Hamilton, Michael Constantine

'There is an overall impression of intense violence, and the air of spiritual decadence has rarely been conveyed so vividly.' – *David Robinson*

'The supreme classic of that great American genre, the low-life movie.' – *Observer*

⚜ Eugene Schufftan

⚜ best picture; script; Robert Rossen (as director); Paul Newman; Jackie Gleason; George C. Scott; Piper Laurie

🏆 best picture; Paul Newman

'See it with someone you've paid for.'

Hustler White
US 1996 79m Monaco Film Lab
ICA/Hustler White (Jürgen Brüning, Bruce LaBruce)

A writer goes in search of a hustler who can introduce him to homosexual life in Los Angeles.

A film intended to shock in its camply defiant depiction of unusual and painful sexual practices; in this, it succeeds.

wd Bruce LaBruce, Rick Castro ph James Carman m UFO or Die pd Bruce LaBruce, Rick Castro ed Rider Siphron

☆ Tony Ward, Bruce LaBruce, Alex Austin, Kevin Kramer, Ron Athey, Glen Meadmore

'A grossly prurient show. It doesn't possess the remotest artistic merit; nor the slightest concern for suffering humanity in its heart, mind or loins.' – *Alexander Walker*

Hyde Park Corner
GB 1935 84m bw
Grosvenor (Harcourt Templeman)

Events of 1780 at Hyde Park Corner seem to happen again in modern times.

Half-hearted reincarnation romance with good moments.

w D. B. Wyndham-Lewis *play* Walter Hackett d Sinclair Hill ph Cyril Bristow ad Aubrey Hammond

☆ Gordon Harker, Binnie Hale, Gibb McLaughlin, Harry Tate, Eric Portman, Donald Wolfit

Hyenes
Senegal/France/Germany 1992 95m colour
ADR/Thelma/Maag Daan/MK2 (Pierre-Alain Meier, Alain Rozanes)
aka: Hyenas

Returning to her poverty-stricken home town, a rich old woman offers a fortune to the people if they will kill the man who wronged her 30 years before.

A naïve and melodramatic version of a familiar story.

wd Djibril Diop Mambéty *play The Visit* by Friedrich Dürrenmatt ph Matthias Kälin m Wasis Diop ed Loredana Cristelli

☆ Mansour Diouf, Ami Diakhate, Mamadou Mahouredia Gueye, Mbaba Diop de Rufisque, Abdoulaye Yama Diop, Calgou Fall, Djibril Diop Mambéty

The Hypnotic Eye
US 1960 79m bw
Allied Artists

A mad killer hypnotizes pretty girls into defacing themselves.

Unattractive thriller including much mumbo-jumbo about hypnotism.

w Gitta and William Read Woodfield d George Blair ph Arch Dalzell m Marlin Skiles

☆ Jacques Bergerac, Allison Hayes, Merry Anders, Marcia Henderson

The Hypnotist: see *London After Midnight*

Hysteria
GB 1965 85m bw
MGM/Hammer (Jimmy Sangster)

An American suffering from amnesia is discharged from a London clinic and walks into a murder plot.

Complicated and rather unsympathetic Hammer twister.

w Jimmy Sangster d Freddie Francis ph John Wilcox m Don Banks pd Edward Carrick ed James Needs

☆ Robert Webber, Lelia Goldoni, Anthony Newlands, Jennifer Jayne, Maurice Denham, Peter Woodthorpe

I Accuse *

GB 1957 99m bw Cinemascope
MGM (Sam Zimbalist)

In 1894 Paris, Alfred Dreyfus is tried for treason and later defended by Emile Zola.

A well tried historical incident is stolidly retold and unsuitably wide-screened; the star cast tends to flounder for lack of assistance.

w Gore Vidal d José Ferrer ph Frederick A. Young m William Alwyn ad Elliot Scott

☆ José Ferrer, *Anton Walbrook*, Emlyn Williams, Viveca Lindfors, David Farrar, Leo Genn, Herbert Lom, Harry Andrews, Felix Aylmer, George Coulouris, Donald Wolfit

I Aim at the Stars

US 1960 107m bw
Columbia/Morningside/Fama (Charles H. Schneer)

The story of German rocket expert Wernher von Braun and his later work on American space vehicles.

Shaky biopic of a controversial scientist who changed sides.

w Jay Dratler d J. Lee-Thompson ph Wilkie Cooper m Laurie Johnson

☆ Curt Jurgens, Herbert Lom, James Daly, Gia Scala, Victoria Shaw, Adrian Hoven, Karel Stepanek

'Mannered panning shots and crafty cutting abound, leading to a stylistic St Vitus' Dance.' – *John Gillett*

'The biggest double exposure since Adam and Eve!'
I Am a Camera

GB 1955 99m bw
Romulus (Jack Clayton)

A young English writer observes life in Berlin in the early thirties, and has a platonic relationship with an amoral and reckless young English girl.

A rather flat and flabby treatment of the stories by Christopher Isherwood and the play by John Van Druten, all better known these days in the form of Cabaret. *Disappointingly unstylish.*

w John Collier d Henry Cornelius ph Guy Green m Malcolm Arnold

☆ Julie Harris, Laurence Harvey, Shelley Winters, Ron Randell, Anton Diffring

'A truly shocking and disgraceful mess.' – *Christopher Isherwood*

'Six sticks of dynamite that blasted his way to freedom ... and awoke America's conscience!'
I Am a Fugitive from a Chain Gang **

US 1932 90m bw
Warner (Hal B. Wallis)

An innocent man is convicted and after brutal treatment on the chain gang becomes a vicious criminal on the run.

Horrifying story in the semi-documentary manner; a milestone in Hollywood history and still a fairly compelling piece of shock entertainment.

w Howard J. Green, Brown Holmes book Robert E. Burns d Mervyn Le Roy ph Sol Polito m Bernhard Kaun

☆ *Paul Muni*, Glenda Farrell, Helen Vinson, Preston Foster, Allen Jenkins, Edward J. Macnamara, Berton Churchill, Edward Ellis

'A picture with guts ... everything about it is technically 100% ... shy on romantic angles, but should get nice money all over.' – *Variety*
'To be enthusiastically commended for its courage, artistic sincerity, dramatic vigour, high entertainment concept and social message.' – *Wilton A. Barrett*
'I quarrel with the production not because it is savage and horrible, but because each step in an inevitable tragedy is taken clumsily, and because each character responsible for the hero's doom is

shown more as a caricature than as a person.' – *Pare Lorentz*

§ best picture; Paul Muni

I Am a Thief

US 1934 64m bw
Warner (Henry Blanke)

Robbery and murder on the Orient Express.

Involved programmer which becomes as tiresome as its library footage.

w Ralph Block, Doris Malloy d Robert Florey

☆ Mary Astor, Ricardo Cortez, Dudley Digges, Robert Barrat, Irving Pichel

'Should be able to top on a double bill but will have a tough time singling.' – *Variety*

I Am Curious – Yellow *

Sweden 1967 116m bw
Sandrew Film

original title: *Jag är nyfiken – gul*

A drama student playing the role of a sociologist questions Swedish citizens on their attitudes to such matters as class, education, military service and non-violence while also discovering her own sexuality.

An important semi-documentary film of the 60s, influenced in its casual style by the French New Wave, and launching an all-out attack on bourgeois attitudes and morality. Its brief but uninhibited scenes of sex caused controversy at the time of its release and led to it becoming the centrepoint of debates on censorship.

wd Vilgot Sjöman ph Peter Wester

☆ Lena Nyman, Börje Ahlstedt, Peter Lindgren, Chris Wahlström, Marie Göranzon, Vilgot Sjöman

'Interesting in its shimmering, multifarious approach to life in Sweden today, in its frankness about sex, and in the considerable step ahead it marks in Vilgot Sjöman's artistic development.' – *John Simon*
'Tame by today's standards and tediously long.' – *Sight and Sound (1994)*

† The film was seized by US Customs and banned following a trial, but the verdict was overturned by the Court of Appeals. Much of the footage shot was used in a less interesting companion film, *I Am Curious – Blue.*

I Am Not Afraid

US 1939 59m bw
Warner (Bryan Foy)
GB title: *The Man Who Dared*

An old man testifies against political terrorists.

Tepid remake of Star Witness.

w Lee Katz story Lucien Hubbard d Crane Wilbur

☆ Charley Grapewin, Jane Bryan, Henry O'Neill, Elizabeth Risdon

'Filler for the duals.' – *Variety*

I Am Suzanne *

US 1933 99m bw
Fox (Jesse L. Lasky)

A dancer in love with a puppeteer comes under the influence of gangsters.

Curious but vaguely endearing mixture of music and mayhem, with the puppets used as symbolic furtherers of the plot.

w Edwin Justus Mayer, Rowland V. Lee d Rowland V. Lee

☆ Lilian Harvey, Gene Raymond, Leslie Banks, Georgia Caine, Halliwell Hobbes

'Not a wow, but rates fairly well.' – *Variety*

I Am the Cheese *

US 1983 95m TVC Color
Almi (David Lange)

With the aid of a therapist, a teenage boy recovers the truth about the death of his parents.

Slight and sometimes confusing psychological drama.

w David Lange, Robert Jiras novel Robert Cormier d Robert Jiras ph David Quaid m Jonathan Tunick ed Nicholas Smith

☆ Robert Macnaughton, Hope Lange, Don Murray, Robert Wagner, Cynthia Nixon, Sudie Bond, Robert Cormier

† The film was remade in 1992 as *Lapse of Memory* (qv).

I Am the Law *

US 1938 83m bw
Columbia (Everett Riskin)

A law professor is asked by a civic leader to become a special prosecutor cleaning up rackets.

Adequate star potboiler, quite enjoyable.

w Jo Swerling d Alexander Hall ph Henry Freulich md Morris Stoloff

☆ Edward G. Robinson, Otto Kruger, John Beal, Barbara O'Neil, Wendy Barrie, Arthur Loft, Marc Lawrence

'A slam-bang, rip-roaring meller that has all the elements of previous films inspired by District Attorney Thomas E. Dewey's career.' – *Variety*
'The liveliest melodrama in town.' – *New York Times*

I Became a Criminal: see *They Made Me a Fugitive*

I Believe in You *

GB 1952 95m bw
Ealing (Michael Relph)

Interwoven stories of probation officers.

Watchable and reasonable but not very compelling.

w Michael Relph, Basil Dearden, Jack Whittingham, Nicholas Phipps d Basil Dearden ph Gordon Dines m Ernest Irving

☆ Celia Johnson, Cecil Parker, Godfrey Tearle, Harry Fowler, George Relph, Joan Collins, Laurence Harvey, Ernest Jay, Ursula Howells, Sidney James, Katie Johnson, Ada Reeve, Brenda de Banzie

I Believed in You

US 1934 69m bw
Fox

A wife is driven to leave her radical agitator husband.

Initially interesting but unsatisfactory romantic melodrama.

w William Conselman d Irving Cummings

☆ Rosemary Ames, Victor Jory, John Boles, Gertrude Michael, George Meeker

'Some idea, but lacking punch in plot and direction.' – *Variety*

'Most Motorcycles Run on Petrol. This One Runs on Blood!'
I Bought a Vampire Motorcycle

GB 1989 105m colour
Hobo/Dirk Productions (Mycal Miller, John Wolskel)

A biker acquires a motorbike possessed by an evil spirit.

Low-budget tongue-in-cheek horror, full of ancient music-hall jokes.

w Mycal Miller d Dirk Campbell ph Tom Ingle m Dean Friedman pd Jose Furtado ed Mycal Miller sp Image Animation

☆ Neil Morrissey, Amanda Noar, Michael Elphick, Anthony Daniels, Andrew Powell, George Rossi, Midge Taylor, Daniel Peacock, Burt Kwouk

'An exuberant tribute to British comedy culture.' – *Screen International*

'The most spinechilling cry that can freeze the blood!'
I Bury the Living

US 1957 77m bw
UA/Maxim

The honorary chairman of a cemetery seems to have the power to mark people for death.

Unusual enough to be encouraging, sloppy enough to disappoint even mystery lovers.

w Louis Garfinkle d Albert Band ph Frederick Gately

☆ Richard Boone, Theodore Bikel, Herbert Anderson, Peggy Maurer

I Call First: see *Who's That Knocking at My Door*

I Can Get It for You Wholesale *

US 1951 89m bw
TCF (Sol C. Siegel)
GB title: *This Is My Affair*
US TV title: *Only the Best*

An ambitious young mannequin starts her own dressmaking firm and sets her sights high.

Watchable comedy-drama which quickly sheds the edge of satire which might have made it the dressmaker's All About Eve.

w Abraham Polonsky novel Jerome Weidman d Michael Gordon ph Milton Krasner m Sol Kaplan md Lionel Newman

☆ Susan Hayward, Dan Dailey, George Sanders, Sam Jaffe, Randy Stuart, Marvin Kaplan, Harry von Zell

'There is nothing remarkable about the film, except perhaps the carefree abandon with which pearl necklaces are broken, and the curious sidelight that is cast on the ethics of cutters and salesmen. It hadn't occurred to me before that the male partners of a modest costume house would go into voluntary bankruptcy sooner than let their dress designer live in sin, but I haven't moved much in wholesale circles of the garment trade.' – *C. A. Lejeune*

I Changed My Sex: see *Glen or Glenda*

I Cheated the Law

US 1948 71m bw
TCF (Sam Baerwitz)

An attorney wins a murder case but finds he has been tricked into providing an alibi.

Meandering crime story which fails to hold the attention.

w Richard G. Hubler story Sam Baerwitz d Edward L. Cahn ph Jackson A. Rose md Edward J. Kay

☆ Tom Conway, Steve Brodie, Robert Osterloh, Barbara Billingsley, Russell Hicks

I Come in Peace: see *Dark Angel*

'Crushed lips don't talk!'
I Confess **

US 1953 94m bw
Warner/Alfred Hitchcock

A priest hears the confession of a murderer and cannot divulge it to the police even though he is himself suspected.

Hitchcock is always worth watching, and although this old chestnut gives him very restricted scope he imbues the story with a strong feeling for its setting (Quebec) and an overpowering sense of doom.

w George Tabori, William Archibald play Paul Anthelme d Alfred Hitchcock ph Robert Burks m Dimitri Tiomkin

☆ Montgomery Clift, Anne Baxter, Brian Aherne, Karl Malden, Dolly Haas, O. E. Hasse

'Whatever its shortcomings, it has the professional concentration of effect, the narrative control, of a story teller who can still

---

| 🏃 film suitable for family viewing | 📼 VHS video-cassette for the British PAL system | 📼 VHS video-cassette for the British PAL system in wide screen-format | ⟳ Video cassette in a computer-colourised version | ▬ American NTSC video-cassette | ⌕ Laser disc |

I Could Go on Singing *
GB 1963 99m Eastmancolor Panavision
UA/Barbican (Lawrence Turman)

An American singing star in Britain looks up an old lover and tries to take over their illegitimate son, but the call of the footlights proves stronger.
The star enjoys her last specially-tailored role; a banal, old-fashioned agreeable one-woman show.
w Mayo Simon d Ronald Neame ph Arthur Ibbetson m Mort Lindsey
☆ Judy Garland, Dirk Bogarde, Aline MacMahon, Jack Klugman
'Merely standard fare in an age without standards.' – *John Simon*

I Cover the Waterfront *
US 1933 75m bw
Reliance (Edward Small)

A reporter uses a girl's friendship to expose her father's smuggling activities.
In its time a tough, even daring melodrama, this plot has now become the stuff of every other TV series episode.
w Wells Root, Jack Jevne, Max Miller d James Cruze ph Ray June m Alfred Newman
☆ Claudette Colbert, Ben Lyon, Ernest Torrence, Hobart Cavanaugh
'Combination of title, picturesque background and three good performances should offset inferior story for favourable business.' – *Variety*
'A bit raw and a bit sentimental and a bit routine, the film does let life in through the cracks.' – *Graham Greene*
† Credited with being the origin of the phrase, 'Not tonight, Josephine!'

'When You Go Undercover Remember One Thing. Who You Are.'
i.d.
GB/Germany 1995 107m colour
Polygram/BBC/Sales Company/Parallax/Metropolis (Sally Hibbin)

An ambitious young policeman, who goes undercover to expose the leaders of a gang of football hooligans, discovers that he enjoys violence.
A frenetic and gritty foray into topicality that avoids exploitation but not melodrama and overstatement.
w Vincent O'Connell story James Bannon d Philip Davis ph Thomas Mauch m Will Gregory pd Max Gottlieb ed Inge Behrens
☆ Reece Dinsdale, Richard Graham, Claire Skinner, Sean Pertwee, Saskia Reeves, Warren Clarke
'A raw-steak drama that packs a wallop when it's on form but suffers an intermittent i.d. crisis of its own in the script department when it comes to delivering the psychological goods.' – *Derek Elley, Variety*

I Didn't Do It
GB 1945 97m bw
Columbia (Ben Henry, Marcel Varnel)

Murder in a theatrical boarding house, with suspicion pointing at Our George.
One of the star's last vehicles: not too bad at all, but without the sweet smell of success.
w Howard Irving Young, Stephen Black, Norman Lee, Peter Fraser, Michael Vaughan d Marcel Varnel ph Roy Fogwell
☆ George Formby, Billy Caryll, Hilda Mundy, Gaston Palmer, Jack Daly, Carl Jaffe, Marjorie Browne, Wally Patch

I Died a Thousand Times
US 1955 109m Warnercolor Cinemascope
Warner (Willis Goldbeck)

An ex-convict plans a big hotel robbery, but things go wrong within his gang.
Overlong, heavygoing, tedious gangster melodrama with too much risk.
w W. R. Burnett d Stuart Heisler ph Ted McCord m David Buttolph
☆ Jack Palance, Shelley Winters, Lori Nelson, Lon Chaney Jnr, Lee Marvin, Gonzales Gonzales, Earl Holliman, Perry Lopez
'This remake of *High Sierra* is scarcely more inspired than its title.' – *MFB*

'It is an insult to the intelligence to pull this old mythological hero out of the archives and set him on a mountaintop again.' – *New York Times*

The I Don't Care Girl *
US 1953 78m Technicolor
TCF (George Jessel)

The life of musical entertainer Eva Tanguay, at her height during World War I, as told by three men in her life.
Breezy, conventional backstage musical biopic.
w Walter Bullock d Lloyd Bacon ph Arthur Arling md Lionel Newman ch Jack Cole, Seymour Felix
☆ Mitzi Gaynor, David Wayne, Oscar Levant, George Jessel, Warren Stevens

I Don't Kiss: see *J'Embrasse Pas*

'It's Evil...It's Horrific...It's Conceived By The Devil'
I Don't Want to Be Born
GB 1975 94m Eastmancolor
Rank/Unicapital (Norma Corney)

US title: *The Devil within Her*
An ex-stripper gives birth to a monstrous baby which goes on a murderous rampage.
Sick horror stuff with a high death rate and no notable credits.
w Stanley Price d Peter Sasdy ph Ken Talbot m Ron Grainer
☆ Joan Collins, Ralph Bates, Donald Pleasence, Eileen Atkins, George Claydon

I Don't Want to Talk about It: see *We Don't Want to Talk about It*

I Dood It!
US 1943 102m bw
MGM (Jack Cummings)

GB title: *By Hook or by Crook*
A tailor falls for a Hollywood star.
Boring star comedy with interpolated musical numbers.
w Sig Herzig, Fred Saidy d Vincente Minnelli ph Ray June md George Stoll
☆ Red Skelton, Eleanor Powell, John Hodiak, Lena Horne, Jimmy Dorsey and his Orchestra, Hazel Scott, Richard Ainley

I Dream of Jeannie
US 1952 90m Trucolor
Republic

The loves and financial problems of songwriter Stephen Foster.
Low-key musical biopic covering exactly the same ground as Swanee River.
w Alan Le May d Allan Dwan ph Reggie Lanning
☆ Ray Middleton, Bill Shirley, Muriel Lawrence, Rex Allen

I Dream Too Much
US 1935 95m bw
RKO (Pandro S. Berman)

A French girl singer marries an American composer.
Forgettable vehicle for an operatic star.
w Edmund North, James Gow d John Cromwell ph David Abel m/ly Jerome Kern, Dorothy Fields md Max Steiner
☆ Lily Pons, Henry Fonda, Eric Blore, Osgood Perkins, Lucien Littlefield, Lucille Ball, Esther Dale, Mischa Auer, Paul Porcasi
'It will be a winner at the box office without breaking any records.' – *Variety*

I Escaped from Devil's Island
US 1973 81m DeLuxe
UA (Roger Corman, Gene Corman)

In 1918, a black convict makes his plans for escape.
Rough, brutish melodrama which plainly aimed to beat Papillon to the box-office.
w Richard L. Adams d William Witney ph Rosalio Solano m Les Baxter
☆ Jim Brown, Christopher George, Rick Ely, James Luisi, Richard Rust
'Exploitation's own *Papillon*, mercifully free from big brother's pretentiousness.' – *Sight and Sound*

I Escaped from the Gestapo
US 1943 74m bw
Monogram/King Brothers

An expert counterfeiter is sprung from jail by American Nazis, but he turns the tables on them.
Mediocre second feature dramatics; the propaganda is incidental.
w Henry Blankfort, Wallace Sullivan d Harold Young
☆ Dean Jagger, John Carradine, Sidney Blackmer, Mary Brian

I Even Knew Happy Gypsies: see *Happy Gypsies*

I Found Stella Parish
US 1935 85m bw
Warner (Harry Joe Brown)

An actress tries to keep her naughty past from her child, but a blackmailer strikes.
One for the ladies, who flocked to it in its day.
w Casey Robinson d Mervyn Le Roy
☆ Kay Francis, Paul Lukas, Ian Hunter, Sybil Jason, Jessie Ralph, Barton MacLane
'Will receive widespread support at the box office all the way from the best runs down to the subsequents, in the big keys and in the smallest towns.' – *Variety*

I Have a New Master: see *L'Ecole Buissonière*

I Hired a Contract Killer
Finland/Sweden 1990 79m Metrocolor
Electric/Contemporary/Villealfa/Swedish Film Institute (Aki Kaurismäki)

An unhappy man hires someone to kill him, and then decides he wants to live.
Lacklustre comedy.
wd Aki Kaurismäki ph Timo Salminen pd John Ebden ed Aki Kaurismäki
☆ Jean-Pierre Léaud, Margi Clarke, Kenneth Colley, Trevor Bowen, Imogen Clare, Angela Walsh, Cyril Epstein, Nicky Tesco

I, Jane Doe
US 1948 85m bw
Republic

GB title: *Diary of a Bride*
A French girl comes to America in search of the flyer she married during the war. When she finds he was already married, she shoots him.
Melodrama for women, culminating in an unconvincing trial scene.
w Lawrence Kimble d John H. Auer
☆ Ruth Hussey, John Carroll, Vera Ralston, Gene Lockhart, John Howard

I Killed Rasputin
France/Italy 1967 100m Eastmancolor
Franscope
Copernic/CGC (Raymond Danon)

The evil monk of the Russian court is killed by Prince Yusopov.
Dull version of a much told story. One of the big international films that never seem to get shown anywhere.
w Alain Decaux, Claude Desailly, Robert Hossein d Robert Hossein ph Henri Persin m André Hossein
☆ Gert Frobe, Peter McEnery, Robert Hossein, Geraldine Chaplin, Ira Furstenberg, Patrick Balkany
'A tedious illustrated history lesson which actually manages to obscure the motivation behind the murder.' – *MFB*
† The script was authorized by Prince Yusopov.

I Killed the Count
GB 1939 89m bw
Grafton (Isadore Goldschmidt)

US title: *Who is Guilty?*
Four people confess to the murder of a philanderer.
Inept version of a West End success.
w Alec Coppel, Lawrence Huntington play Alec Coppel d Fred Zelnik ph Bryan Langley ed Sam Simmonds
☆ Syd Walker, Ben Lyon, Terence de Marney, Barbara Blair, Antoinette Cellier, Kathleen Harrison, Athole Stewart, Leslie Perrins, Ronald Shiner

I Know What You Did Last Summer
US 1997 101m Technicolor Panavision
Entertainment/Mandalay (Neal H. Moritz, Erik Feig, Stokely Chaffin)

A fisherman begins to murder a group of young friends, who concealed their involvement in the death of a stranger in a hit-and-run accident.
A knowing but predictable variation on the usual slasher movie; it merely reshuffles the clichés of the genre.
w Kevin Williamson novel Lois Duncan d Jim Gillespie ph Denis Crossan m John Debney pd Gary Wissner ed Steve Mirkovich
☆ Jennifer Love Hewitt, Sarah Michelle Gellar, Ryan Phillippe, Freddie Prinze Jnr, Muse Watson, Anne Heche, Bridgette Wilson, Johnny Galecki
'A polished genre piece with superior fright elements.' – *Variety*
† The film cost $17m and took more than $70m at the US box-office.

I Know Where I'm Going **
GB 1945 91m bw
GFD/The Archers (Michael Powell, Emeric Pressburger)

A determined girl travels to the Hebrides to marry a wealthy old man, but is stranded on Mull and marries a young naval officer instead.
A strange assembling of attractive but disparate elements: romance, comedy, bleak scenery, a trained hawk and a dangerous whirlpool. At the time it seemed to represent the Elizabethan age of the British cinema, and remains entertaining for its parts though a bit of a puzzle as a whole.
wd Michael Powell, Emeric Pressburger ph Erwin Hillier
☆ Wendy Hiller, Roger Livesey, Pamela Brown, Nancy Price, Finlay Currie, John Laurie, George Carney, Walter Hudd
'Continuously fresh and interesting, intelligently written and played, and full of beautiful photography.' – *Richard Mallett, Punch*
'The sensitive photography and the intelligent if not very imaginative use of sound do more than enough to make eloquent the influence of place on people; and the whole thing is undertaken with taste and modesty.' – *James Agee*

I Led Two Lives: see *Glen or Glenda*

I Like It Like That *
US 1994 105m Technicolor
Columbia TriStar/Think Again (Ann Carli, Lane Janger)

In the Bronx, a feckless husband and his wife begin affairs and separate, though their intention is to make each other jealous.
Stolid romance of raucous life on and off the New York streets, well observed though not straying far from movie conventions in its depiction of working-class existence.
wd Darnell Martin ph Alexander Gruszynski m Sergio George pd Scott Chambliss ed Peter C. Frank
☆ Lauren Velz, Jon Seda, Desiree Casado, Tomas Melly, Griffin Dunne, Rita Moreno, Lisa Vidal
'From its wittily choreographed opening shot onwards, the film crackles with unforced comedy and invention. Its freshness is all the more surprising when you consider that the movie is largely built from clichés.' – *Kevin Jackson, Independent*
† Darnell Martin is the first black woman to write and direct a movie for a major Hollywood studio.

I Like Money: see *Mr Topaze*

I Like Your Nerve
US 1931 70m bw
First National

A bookworm goes to Central America and becomes a romantic adventurer.
Junior aspiring to Senior's seven league boots; he doesn't quite make it, and that's the script's fault.
w Houston Branch story Roland Pertwee d William McGann
☆ Douglas Fairbanks Jnr, Loretta Young, Claud Allister, Henry Kolker, Edmund Breon, Boris Karloff
'Mediocre, unimpressive and implausible story ... strictly an off-day booking.' – *Variety*

I Live for Love

US   1935   83m   bw
Warner (Bryan Foy)
GB title: *I Live For You*
A socialite has show business leanings.
Minor musical.
w Jerry Wald, Julius Epstein, Robert Andrews
ph George Barnes md Leo F. Forbstein
d/ch Busby Berkeley
☆ Dolores del Rio, Everett Marshall, Allen Jenkins, Eddie Conrad, Guy Kibbee, Berton Churchill

I Live for You: see *I Live for Love*

I Live in Fear *

Japan   1955   113m   bw
Toho (S. Motoki)
original title: *Ikimono No Kiroku*
A family attempts to have its father, a wealthy industrialist, declared of unsound mind because he wants them all to move to Brazil to escape the danger of radiation and the atom bomb.
Although the main theme has lost its topicality, the drama of the dynamics of family relationships still holds the interest, as does Mifune's uncharacteristic performance as an old man.
w Shinobu Hashimoto, Hideo Oguni, Akira Kurosawa d Akira Kurosawa ph Asakazu Nakai m Fumio Hayasaka
☆ Toshiro Mifune, Takashi Shimura, Minoru Chiaki, Masao Shimizu, Eiko Miyoshi, Haruko Togo, Yutaka Sada, Norkiro Sengoku

I Live in Grosvenor Square

GB   1945   113m   bw
ABP (Herbert Wilcox)
US title: *A Yank in London*
A duke's daughter falls in love with an American air force sergeant.
Sloppily-made topical romance which was hot box-office at the time and started the producer's 'London' romances: Piccadilly Incident, Spring in Park Lane, Maytime in Mayfair, etc.
w Nicholas Phipps, William D. Bayles, Maurice Cowan d Herbert Wilcox ph Max Greene m Anthony Collins
☆ Anna Neagle, *Dean Jagger*, Rex Harrison, Robert Morley, Jane Darwell, Nancy Price, Irene Vanbrugh, Edward Rigby, Walter Hudd

I Live My Life

US   1935   85m   bw
MGM (Bernard H. Hyman)
A bored society girl falls for a working-class archaeologist.
Standard star romance.
w Joseph L. Mankiewicz story *Claustrophobia* by A. Carter Goodloe d W. S. Van Dyke II ph George Folsey m Dimitri Tiomkin
☆ Joan Crawford, Brian Aherne, Frank Morgan, Aline MacMahon, Eric Blore, Jessie Ralph, Arthur Treacher, Hedda Hopper, Etienne Girardot, Ed Brophy
'An amusing romance is backgrounded by clothes, cocktails and butlers.' – *Variety*

I Lived with You

GB   1933   100m   bw
Twickenham (Julius Hagen)
A Cockney family find that their lodger is an exiled Russian prince.
Overlong whimsy from a successful West End play.
w G. A. Cooper, H. Fowler Mear play Ivor Novello d Maurice Elvey ph Sydney Blyth m W. L. Trytel ad James Carter ed Jack Harris
☆ Ivor Novello, Ursula Jeans, Ida Lupino, Minnie Rayner, Eliot Makeham, Jack Hawkins

I Love a Man in Uniform *

Canada   1993   97m   colour
Metro Tartan/Alliance/Miracle (Paul Brown)
An actor who plays the part of a policeman in a television series carries the role over into real life.
A creepy drama, in which reality and illusion become increasingly blurred and sanity declines into madness.
wd David Wellington ph David Franco m Ron Sures and the Tragically Hip pd John Dondertman ed Susan Shipton
☆ Tom McCamus, Brigitte Bako, Kevin Tighe, David Hemblen, Alex Karzis, Graham McPherson

'A hugely impressive and highly compelling first feature.' – *Empire*

I Love a Mystery *

US   1945   68m   bw
Columbia
An eastern secret society offers a businessman a large sum for his head when he dies, as he resembles their founder whose embalmed head is deteriorating.
Start of a short series of mysteries from a radio series; the production was never up to the ingenious plots.
w Charles O'Neal d Henry Levin ph Burnett Guffey m Mario Castelnuovo-Tedesco
☆ George Macready, Jim Bannon, Nina Foch

'She kissed the boys goodbye – until Sonny said hello!'

I Love a Soldier

US   1944   106m   bw
Paramount (Mark Sandrich)
A San Francisco girl thinks hard before embarking on a wartime marriage.
Glossy, insubstantial sudser chiefly memorable for casting its leading lady as a welder.
w Allan Scott d Mark Sandrich ph Charles Lang m Robert Emmett Dolan
☆ Paulette Goddard, Sonny Tufts, Beulah Bondi, Walter Sande, Mary Treen, Ann Doran, Barry Fitzgerald

I Love Melvin *

US   1953   77m   Technicolor
MGM (George Wells)
A photographer's assistant falls for a high-born chorus girl.
Zippy little musical with all concerned working hard with thin material.
w George Wells d Don Weis ph Harold Rosson m/ly Josef Myrow, Mack Gordon md George Stoll ch Robert Alton
☆ Donald O'Connor, Debbie Reynolds, Una Merkel, Allyn Joslyn

I Love My Wife

US   1970   95m   Technicolor
Universal (Robert Kaufman)
The affairs of a successful doctor with a guilt complex about sex.
Frantic, fashionable comedy drama with wildly erratic treatment and performances.
w Robert Kaufman d Mel Stuart ph Vilis Lapenieks m Lalo Schifrin
☆ Elliott Gould, Brenda Vaccaro, Angel Tompkins
'A leer-laden, anti-feminist tract disguised as a comedy.' – *Judith Crist*

I Love Trouble

US   1947   93m   bw
Columbia/S. Sylvan Simon
A private eye tries to trace the background of a politician's wife.
Standard urban mystery with loose ends, a few notches below Raymond Chandler.
w Roy Huggins novel *The Double Take* by Roy Huggins d S. Sylvan Simon
☆ Franchot Tone, Janet Blair, Janis Carter, Adele Jergens, Glenda Farrell, Steve Geray, Tom Powers

I Love Trouble

US   1994   123m   Technicolor
Buena Vista/Touchstone/Caravan (Nancy Meyers)
A hard-drinking veteran journalist is scooped on an investigative story by a glamorous new reporter but marries her anyway.
A romantic comedy that misses out on the romance and the wit.
w Nancy Meyers, Charles Shyer d Charles Shyer ph John Lindley m David Newman pd Dean Tavoularis ed Paul Hirsch, Walter Murch, Adam Bernardi
☆ Julia Roberts, Nick Nolte, Saul Rubinek, Robert Loggia, James Rebhorn, Olympia Dukakis, Marsha Mason, Charles Martin Smith, Kelly Rutherford
'Stands as yet further proof of how hard it is to make a soufflé, as well as to successfully create the pure pleasure of the old movies today's filmmakers so revere.' – *Todd McCarthy, Variety*
'The most run-of-the-mill newspaper picture of 50 years ago was brisker, funnier, more exciting

(and an hour shorter) than Charles Shyer's feeble offering.' – *Philip French, Observer*

I Love You Again *

US   1940   99m   bw
MGM (Lawrence Weingarten)
A much married man gets amnesia and turns into a gay Lothario.
Sprightly romantic comedy with all concerned letting rip until the pace slows.
w Charles Lederer, George Oppenheimer, Harry Kurnitz d W. S. Van Dyke II ph Oliver T. Marsh m Franz Waxman
☆ William Powell, Myrna Loy, Frank McHugh, Edmund Lowe, Donald Douglas, Nella Walker, Pierre Watkin

I Love You, Alice B. Toklas *

US   1968   93m   Technicolor
Warner Seven Arts/Paul Mazursky, Larry Tucker
An asthmatic Los Angeles lawyer escapes his bullying fiancée by joining the flower people.
Quite amusing satirical farce about the dangers of marijuana, Gertrude Stein and Jewish mothers, thrown together with no great sense of style but achieving hilarious moments among the longueurs.
w Paul Mazursky, Larry Tucker d Hy Averback ph Philip Lathrop m Elmer Bernstein pd Pato Guzman
☆ Peter Sellers, Jo Van Fleet, Joyce Van Patten, Leigh Taylor-Young, David Arkin, Herb Edelman

I Love You No More: see *Je T'Aime Moi Non Plus*

I Love You to Death

US   1990   97m   Technicolor
Columbia TriStar/Chestnut Hill (Jeffrey Lurie, Ron Moler)
Discovering her husband's philandering, a wife decides to have him killed.
Black comedy that runs out of jokes.
w John Kostmayer d Lawrence Kasdan ph Owen Roizman m James Horner pd Lilly Kilvert ed Anne V. Coates
☆ Kevin Kline, Tracey Ullman, Joan Plowright, River Phoenix, William Hurt, Keanu Reeves, James Gammon, Jack Kehler, Victoria Jackson
'Over-the-top farce.' – *David Robinson, The Times*
'A stillborn attempt at black comedy that wastes considerable acting talent.' – *Variety*

'Lips of thunder on lips of fire!'

I Loved a Woman *

US   1933   90m   bw
Warner (Henry Blanke)
The career of a Chicago meat packer is hampered by his social-climbing wife.
Potboiling star melodrama which still holds some interest.
w Charles Kenyon, Sidney Sutherland d Alfred E. Green ph James Van Trees
☆ Edward G. Robinson, Kay Francis, Genevieve Tobin, J. Farrell MacDonald, Henry Kolker, Robert Barrat
'E.G.R. out of his class; may cut biz.' – *Variety*

I Loved You Wednesday

US   1933   77m   bw
Fox
A man vies with a married friend for a lady's favour.
Mildly amusing comedy of the second rank.
w Philip Klein, Horace Jackson play Molly Ricardel, William Dubois d Henry King, William Cameron Menzies
☆ Warner Baxter, Elissa Landi, Victor Jory, Miriam Jordan, Laura Hope Crews
'A romantic comedy-drama of first-rate possibilities, beautifully made and abundantly provided with class.' – *Variety*

I, Madman *

US   1989   89m   colour
Sarlui/Diamant (Rafael Eisenman)
A bookshop assistant finds that the trashy novel she is reading about a mad, murderous doctor is coming true.
Above average horror, sillier than most in its premise, but performed and directed with some style.

w David Chaskin d Tibor Takacs ph Bryan England m Michael Hoenig ed Marcus Manton sp Randall William Cook
☆ Jenny Wright, Clayton Rohner, Randall William Cook, Steven Memel, Stephanie Hodge, Michelle Jordan

I Married a Communist: see *The Woman on Pier 13*

I Married a Dead Man

France   1983   110m   colour
Sara/TF1 (Alain Sarde)
original title: *J'ai épousé Une Ombre*
aka: *I Married a Shadow*
Following a train crash, an abandoned pregnant woman assumes the identity of a wealthy mother-to-be.
Moderately effective remake of No Man of Her Own, which was made in 1950.
w Patrick Laurent, Robin Davis novel William Irish d Robin Davis ph Bernard Zitzermann m Philippe Sarde ad Ivan Maussion ed Marie Castro Vazquez
☆ Nathalie Baye, Francis Huster, Richard Bohringer, Madeleine Robinson, Guy Trejan, Victoria Abril

I Married a Doctor

US   1936   87m   bw
Warner (Harry Joe Brown)
An idealistic city girl marries a small-town doctor.
Solidly carpentered version of Main Street.
w Casey Robinson, Harriet Ford, Harvey O'Higgins novel Sinclair Lewis d Archie Mayo
☆ Josephine Hutchinson, Pat O'Brien, Ross Alexander, Guy Kibbee, Louise Fazenda
† *Main Street* was filmed under its own title in 1923, with Florence Vidor.

I Married a Monster from Outer Space *

US   1958   78m   bw
Paramount/Gene Fowler Jnr
A young man is taken over by alien invaders but his wife helps to destroy them and bring him back to normal.
Decent, plodding, reasonably effective low-budget science fiction on a well-trampled theme; its minor virtues have been effaced by its silly title.
w Louis Vittes d Gene Fowler Jnr ph Haskell Boggs sp John P. Fulton
☆ Tom Tryon, Gloria Talbott, Robert Ivers
'Carries imaginative plottage which makes it strong fare.' – *Variety*
'Its underlying messages about society and, more specifically, women, are important ones that are particularly relevant today.' – *Cinefantastique, 1974*

I Married a Nazi: see *The Man I Married*

I Married a Shadow: see *I Married a Dead Man*

'She knows all about love potions ... and lovely motions!'

I Married a Witch ***

US   1942   82m   bw
UA/Cinema Guild/René Clair
A Salem witch and her sorcerer father come back to haunt the descendant of the Puritan who had them burned.
Delightful romantic comedy fantasy which shows all concerned at the top of their form. Hollywood moonshine, impeccably distilled.
w Robert Pirosh, Marc Connelly novel *The Passionate Witch* by Thorne Smith d René Clair ph Ted Tetzlaff m Roy Webb
☆ Fredric March, Veronica Lake, Cecil Kellaway, Robert Benchley, Susan Hayward, Elizabeth Patterson, Robert Warwick
'A delightful sense of oddity and enchantment.' – *New York World Telegram*
♫ Roy Webb

I Married a Woman

US   1956   85m   bw (colour sequence)
RKOscope
RKO
A nervous young advertising executive neglects his wife, who determines to make him jealous.

Simple-minded comedy tailored to unsympathetic stars.
w Goodman Ace d Hal Kanter ph Lucien Ballard m Cyril Mockridge
☆ George Gobel, Diana Dors, Adolphe Menjou, Jessie Royce Landis, Nita Talbot

'It brings laughter and song to the screen as this pair from paradise is joyously reunited!'

I Married an Angel

US 1942 84m bw
MGM (Hunt Stromberg)

An attractive angel lures a playboy from his earthly girlfriends.
Silly musical fantasy which spelled the end of a great musical star partnership.
w Anita Loos *play* Vaszary Janos d W. S. Van Dyke ph Ray June m/ly Richard Rodgers, Lorenz Hart
☆ Jeanette MacDonald, Nelson Eddy, Edward Everett Horton, Binnie Barnes, Reginald Owen, Douglass Dumbrille
'As bland as operetta but without its energy.' – *New Yorker, 1978*

I Met a Murderer *

GB 1939 78m bw
Grand National/Gamma (Roy Kellino, Pamela Kellino, James Mason)

A murderer on the run meets a girl novelist who is touring in her motor caravan.
Semi-professional location melodrama which won commendation at the time but now seems very faded.
w Pamela Kellino, James Mason d Roy Kellino ph Roy Kellino m Eric Ansell ed Fergus McDonnell
☆ James Mason, Pamela Kellino, Sylvia Coleridge, William Devlin, Peter Coke
'Graceful, gallant, resourceful ... better and more enjoyable than most studio pictures.' – *James Agee*
'That it has a number of defects does not mean that it is not worthy of serious consideration.' – *Basil Wright*

I Met Him in Paris *

US 1937 86m bw
Paramount (Wesley Ruggles)

A fashion designer spends five years' savings on a fling in Paris and finds herself pursued to Switzerland by two philanderers.
Not very witty but likeable romantic comedy with polished performers near their best.
w Claude Binyon d Wesley Ruggles ph Leo Tover m John Leopold md Boris Morros
☆ Claudette Colbert, Melvyn Douglas, Robert Young, Lee Bowman, Mona Barrie
'A money picture ... laughs are piled on laughs.' – *Variety*
'At least half the footage is a perfect scream, and if you miss it you are an old sobersides, and who cares.' – *Otis Ferguson*

I Met My Love Again

US 1937 77m bw
Walter Wanger
📺

A small-town girl marries a drunken writer, but on his death returns to her first love, a biology professor.
Mildly pleasing, rather dated romantic drama with good local colour.
w David Hertz *novel* Summer Lightning by Aileen Corliss d Joshua Logan, Arthur Ripley ph Hal Mohr m Heinz Roemheld
☆ Henry Fonda, Joan Bennett, Alan Marshal, Dorothy Stickney, Dame May Whitty, Alan Baxter, Louise Platt, Tim Holt, Florence Lake
'Sentimentally as sticky as a gum drop, this sugar-coated romance will have to find its favour with the femmes.' – *Variety*

I, Mobster

US 1958 80m bw Cinemascope
Edward L. Alperson (Roger Corman, Gene Corman)
📺

A slum teenager becomes a top gangster.
Routine gangland thriller.
w Steve Fisher *novel* Joseph Hilton Smith d Roger Corman ph Floyd Crosby m Gerald Fried ad Daniel Haller ed William B. Murphy
☆ Steve Cochran, Lita Milan, Robert Strauss, Celia Lovsky, Grant Withers

I, Monster *

GB 1971 75m Eastmancolor
Amicus (Milton Subotsky)

A straight remake of *Dr Jekyll and Mr Hyde*, holding closely to the original novel but mysteriously using different names.
Interesting minor work.
w Milton Subotsky d Stephen Weeks ph Moray Grant m Carl Davis ad Tony Curtis
☆ Christopher Lee, Peter Cushing, Richard Hurndall, George Merritt, Mike Raven

I Never Promised You a Rose Garden

US 1977 96m colour
New World/Imorh/Fadsin (Roger Corman)
📺

A suicidal teenage girl is treated in a psychiatric hospital.
Careful, thoughtful case history which can't help, after so many TV movies of the kind, seeming rather too simple for a theatrical feature, as well as too heavy-going despite the upbeat ending.
w Gavin Lambert, Lewis John Carlino *novel* Hannah Green d Anthony Page ph Bruce Logan m Paul Chihara pd Toby Rafelson
☆ Kathleen Quinlan, Bibi Andersson, Sylvia Sidney, Ben Piazza, Lorraine Gary, Reni Santoni, Signe Hasso
⋏ best adapted screenplay

I Never Sang for My Father *

US 1969 92m Technicolor
Columbia/Jamel (Gilbert Cates)
📺

When his mother dies, a middle-aged widower is saddled with his cantankerous father, who tries to prevent him from remarrying.
Literal transcription of a Eugene O'Neillish play, a fascinating if depressing character study.
w Robert Anderson *play* Robert Anderson d Gilbert Cates ph Morris Hartzband, George Stoetzel m Al Gorgoni, Barry Mann
☆ Melvyn Douglas, Gene Hackman, Dorothy Stickney, Estelle Parsons
⋏ Robert Anderson; Melvyn Douglas; Gene Hackman

I Only Want You to Love Me *

West Germany 1976 104m colour
Bavaria Atelier (Peter Märthesheimer)
original title: *Ich Will Doch Nur, Das Ihr Mich Liebt*

A man denied parental affection, and discovering the lack of love between his mother and father, finds that he is unable to cope with the pressures of his own marriage.
Affecting small-scale domestic drama, probing the cause of violence, originally made for German television.
wd Rainer Werner Fassbinder *book* Life Sentence (Lebenslänglich) by Klaus Antes, Christiane Ehrhardt ph Michael Ballhaus m Peer Raben ed Liesgret Schmitt-Klink
☆ Vitus Zeplichal, Elke Aberle, Alexander Allerson, Ernie Mangold, Johanna Hofer, Wolfgang Hess

I Ought to Be in Pictures *

US 1982 107m DeLuxe
TCF (Herbert Ross, Neil Simon)

A young actress hitch-hikes to Hollywood to break into pictures and also to see her estranged scriptwriter father.
Fairly agreeable comedy-drama in the Neil Simon manner, with the studio background an extra plus.
w Neil Simon *play* Neil Simon d Herbert Ross ph David M. Walsh m Marvin Hamlisch pd Albert Brenner
☆ Walter Matthau, Ann-Margret, Dinah Manoff, Lance Guest, Lewis Smith

I Passed for White

US 1960 92m bw
Allied Artists (Fred M. Wilcox)

A light-skinned Negress comes to New York but fails to achieve happiness by pretending to be white.
Earnest, rather dreary social drama which doesn't get anywhere.
d Fred M. Wilcox m George J. Folsey m Johnny Williams
☆ Sonya Wilde, James Franciscus, Pat Michon, Elizabeth Council

I Promise to Pay

US 1937 68m bw
Columbia

An office worker finds himself at the wrong end of the loan shark racket.
Competent programmer from the headlines.
w Mary McCall Jnr, Lionel Houser d D Ross Lederman
☆ Chester Morris, Leo Carrillo, Helen Mack, Thomas Mitchell, Thurston Hall
'Just average ... if placed on a dual bill, it'll be found more than enough to float its end.' – *Variety*

I.Q.

US 1994 95m DeLuxe
UIP/Sandollar (Carol Baum, Fred Schepisi)
📀 📺 🎧

Albert Einstein encourages a garage mechanic to court his niece by pretending to be a physicist.
A downright peculiar romantic comedy that gains very little from its introduction of renowned scientists into a mundane situation comedy; what it really needed was for Einstein and his cronies to be played by the Three Stooges.
w Andy Breckman, Michael Leeson d Fred Schepisi ph Ian Baker m Jerry Goldsmith pd Stuart Wurtzel ed Jill Bilcock
☆ Tim Robbins, Meg Ryan, Walter Matthau, Gene Saks, Lou Jacobi, Stephen Fry, Joseph Maher, Frank Whaley, Tony Shalhoub, Charles Durning, Keene Curtis
'Disappointingly bland Capraesque comedy.' – *Philip French, Observer*

'The sweetest movie anyone would ever wish to see!'

I Remember Mama **

US 1948 134m bw
RKO (Harriet Parsons)
📺

A novelist remembers some of the adventures of growing up with her Norwegian-American family.
Overlong, but well-upholstered nostalgia: warm-hearted, sentimental, nicely detailed, richly acted but just a little boring in spots.
w De Witt Bodeen *play* John Van Druten *book* Mama's Bank Account by Kathryn Forbes d George Stevens ph Nicholas Musuraca m Roy Webb
☆ Irene Dunne, Barbara Bel Geddes, Oscar Homolka, Edgar Bergen, Philip Dorn, Ellen Corby, Florence Bates, Cedric Hardwicke, Barbara O'Neil, Rudy Vallee
⋏ Nicholas Musuraca; Irene Dunne; Barbara Bel Geddes; Oscar Homolka; Ellen Corby

I Saw What You Did

US 1965 82m bw
Universal/William Castle

A murderer thinks that two playful teenagers have witnessed his deed, and sets out to kill them too.
Predictable and long-winded suspenser, very short of inventive detail.
w William McGivern *novel* Ursula Curtiss d William Castle ph Joseph Biroc m Van Alexander
☆ John Ireland, Joan Crawford, Leif Erickson

I See a Dark Stranger **

GB 1945 112m bw
GFD/Individual (Frank Launder, Sidney Gilliat)
📀
US title: *The Adventuress*

An Irish colleen who hates the English comes to England to spy for the Germans but falls in love with a young English officer.
Slipshod plotting does not quite destroy the jolly atmosphere of this comedy-thriller which has the cheek to take an IRA member as its heroine. Good fun, very well staged.
w Frank Launder, Sidney Gilliat, Wolfgang Wilhelm d Frank Launder ph Wilkie Cooper m William Alwyn
☆ Deborah Kerr, Trevor Howard, Raymond Huntley, Norman Shelley, Michael Howard, Brenda Bruce, Liam Redmond, Brefni O'Rorke
'It is the cinematic equivalent of Irish blarney which inspires most of this picture.' – *MFB*
'There is some intelligence, grace and fun here, but essentially this seems to me a supercilious drama, as if it had been made by bright young men who had decided to package and toss a bone to the groundlings.' – *James Agee*

I See Ice

GB 1938 81m bw
ATP

The property man in an ice ballet company is a keen amateur photographer who accidentally snaps crooks at work.
Fair star comedy with good production.
w Anthony Kimmins, Austin Melford d Anthony Kimmins ph Ronald Neame, Gordon Dines ad Wilfred Shingleton
☆ George Formby, Kay Walsh, Betty Stockfeld, Cyril Ritchard, Garry Marsh

I Sell Anything

US 1935 70m bw
First National

An auctioneer rises in the business.
Mildly interesting comedy-drama with character progress but not much plot.
w Brown Holmes, Sidney Sutherland d Robert Florey
☆ Pat O'Brien, Ann Dvorak, Claire Dodd, Roscoe Karns, Hobart Cavanaugh
'Nicely made and played, but all in one key.' – *Variety*

I Sent a Letter to My Love **

France 1981 102m colour
Cineproductions (Lise Fauyolles, Giorgio Silvagni)
📺
original title: *Chère Inconnue*

A crippled brother unknowingly carries on a love affair by letter with his sister.
Gentle tale of two lonely people finding an unexpected release from each other.
w Moshe Mizrahi, Gérard Brach *novel* Bernice Rubens d Moshe Mizrahi ph Ghislain Cloquet m Philippe Sarde ad Bernard Evein ed Françoise Bonnot
☆ Simone Signoret, Jean Rochefort, Delphine Seyrig, Genevieve Fontanel, Dominique Labourier
'Insensitive direction and unconvincing performances ruin an interesting dramatic idea.' – *Variety*
'This muted, smouldering French film first teases and eventually clutches our emotions.' – *Judith Crist, Saturday Review*

I Shall Return: see *An American Guerilla in the Philippines*

'You only get one shot at fame.'

I Shot Andy Warhol *

GB 1996 106m Technicolor
Electric/Playhouse/Samuel Goldwyn/BBC Arena (Tom Kalin, Christine Vachon)
📀 📺 🎧 🎧

Frustrated by her failure to make an impact on the world, the lesbian founder of SCUM (the Society for Cutting Up Men) attempts to kill Andy Warhol.
Intriguing biopic, of interest not so much for its concentration on the inadequacies of its central character as for its recreation of New York's louche artistic community of the late 60s.
w Mary Harron, Daniel Minahan d Mary Harron ph Ellen Kuras m John Cale pd Therese Deprez ed Keith Reamer
☆ Lili Taylor, Jared Harris, Lothaire Bluteau, Martha Plimpton, Stephen Dorff, Anna Thompson, Peter Friedman, Tahnee Welch
'An exemplary and dynamic work that goes about as far as a narrative film can on both analyzing a complex personality and portraying a cultural scene.' – *Todd McCarthy, Variety*

I Shot Jesse James *

US 1948 81m bw
Lippert/Screen Guild (Carl K. Hittleman)
📺

The story of Bob Ford, who gunned down the famous outlaw.
Doubtfully historical but quite lively Western melodrama.
wd Samuel Fuller *story* Homer Croy ph Ernest Miller m Albert Glasser ad Frank Hotaling ed Paul Landres
☆ Preston Foster, John Ireland, Barbara Britton, Reed Hadley, J. Edward Bromberg, Victor Kilian, Tom Tyler

I Stand Alone: see *Seul contre Tous*

I Stand Condemned: see *Moscow Nights*

I Start Counting

GB 1969 105m DeLuxe
UA/Triumvirate (David Greene)

A young girl thinks her foster-brother may be the sex murderer known to be rampant in the locality. But after a great many red herrings, of course, he is not.

Strained psychological suspenser with good moments between the longueurs.

w Richard Harris *novel* Audrey Erskine Lindop
d David Greene ph Alex Thomson m Basil Kirchin pd Brian Eatwell

☆ Jenny Agutter, Bryan Marshall, Clare Sutcliffe, Simon Ward, Lana Morris, Billy Russell, Fay Compton, Lally Bowers

I Still Know What You Did Last Summer

US 1998 101m CFI color Panavision
Columbia/Mandalay (Neal H. Moritz, Erik Feig, Stokely Chaffin, William S. Beasley)

Four teenagers are stalked by a hook-handed killer.

A sequel to a successful, self-referential horror movie that settles for more old-fashioned shocks; the gore flows, but predictability sets in early.

w Trey Callaway d Danny Cannon ph Vernon Layton m John Frizzell pd Doug Kraner ed Peck Prior

☆ Jennifer Love Hewitt, Freddie Prinze Jnr, Brandy, Mekhi Phifer, Muse Watson, Matthew Settl, Bill Cobbs, Jeffrey Combs, Jennifer Esposito, John Hawkes

'An empty, farcical blood bath that's virtually shock-free except for one preposterous plot twist.' – *Stephen Holden, New York Times*

I Stole a Million

US 1939 89m bw
Universal (Burt Kelly)

A cab driver cheated by a finance company becomes a criminal to support his family.

Ho-hum star melodrama.

w Nathanael West *story* Lester Cole d Frank Tuttle ph Milton Krasner

☆ George Raft, Claire Trevor, Dick Foran, Henry Armetta, Victor Jory, Joe Sawyer, Stanley Ridges
'Crime drama neatly packaged ... topper for key duals at normal b.o.' – *Variety*

I Take This Woman

US 1931 74m bw
Paramount (Hector Turnbull)

A reckless society girl falls for a cowhand and agrees to live in his ramshackle house.

Patchy romantic comedy-drama of little remaining interest.

w Vincent Lawrence *novel* Lost Ecstasy by Mary Roberts Rinehart d Marion Gering, Slavko Vorkapich ph Victor Milner

☆ Gary Cooper, Carole Lombard, Helen Ware, Lester Vail, Charles Trowbridge, Clara Blandick

I Take This Woman

US 1939 97m bw
MGM (Louis B. Mayer)

A doctor marries a beautiful European and decides too late that he does not love her.

Thin comedy-drama which Louis B. Mayer unaccountably took it into his head to produce personally. The results had to be re-shot so much and so often that Hollywood dubbed the film I Re-Take This Woman. It offers little in the way of entertainment.

w James Kevin McGuinness *story* Charles MacArthur d W. S. Van Dyke ph Harold Rosson m Bronislau Kaper

☆ Spencer Tracy, Hedy Lamarr, Verree Teasdale, Kent Taylor, Laraine Day, Mona Barrie, Jack Carson, Paul Cavanagh, Marjorie Main

I Thank a Fool

GB 1962 100m Metrocolor Cinemascope
MGM (Anatole de Grunwald)

A woman found guilty of the murder of her lover is offered a fresh start in the home of the prosecutor's family ... but another nightmare situation builds up.

Jane Eyre melodrama of the loonier type, with good actors struggling through a wild but unrewarding script.

w Karl Tunberg *novel* Audrey Erskine Lindop d Robert Stevens ph Harry Waxman m Ron Goodwin

☆ Peter Finch, Susan Hayward, Diane Cilento, Cyril Cusack, Kieron Moore, Athene Seyler

I Thank You

GB 1941 81m bw
Gainsborough

Actors seeking a backer become servants to a titled ex-star.

Acceptable comedy vehicle.

w Howard Irving Young, Val Guest, Marriott Edgar d Marcel Varnel

☆ Arthur Askey, Richard Murdoch, Lily Morris, Moore Marriott, Graham Moffatt, Kathleen Harrison

I the Jury

US 1953 87m bw 3-D
Parklane (Victor Saville)

Private eye Mike Hammer avenges the murder of his friend.

Charmless toughie, roughly made and devoid of plot or character interest.

wd Harry Essex *novel* Mickey Spillane ph John Alton m Franz Waxman

☆ Biff Elliott, Peggie Castle, Preston Foster, Elisha Cook Jnr, John Qualen

I the Jury

US 1982 109m colour
American Cinema/Larco/Solofilm (Robert Solo)

An amoral private eye avenges the murder of his Vietnam buddy.

Hard, brutal thriller more in line than the previous version with the tone of the novel.

w Larry Cohen d Richard T. Heffron ph Andrew Laszlo m Bill Conti pd Robert Gundlach

☆ Armand Assante, Barbara Carrera, Laurene Landon, Alan King, Geoffrey Lewis, Paul Sorvino
'The repellent formula as usual, with the gun and the penis as interchangeable instruments of quick-fire tough-guy virility.' – *Sunday Times*

I, the Worst of All **

Argentina 1990 105m colour
Electric/Assai Communications/Screening 22/GEA (Lita Stantic)

original title: Yo, la peor de todas

In Mexico in the 17th century, the Church forces Sister Juana, a nun who is also a gifted poet and playwright, to forswear literature and the intellectual life.

An austere and moving account, based on fact and with an appeal wider than feminism, of a talent overwhelmed by religious and masculine prejudice and oppression.

w Maria Luisa Bemberg, Antonio Larreta *book* Sor Juana: Her Life and Her World (Sor Juana Ines de la Cruz o Las Trampas de la Fe) by Octavio Paz d Maria Luisa Bemberg ph Felix Monti m Luis Maria Serra pd Voytek ed Juan Carlos Macias

☆ Assumpta Serna, Dominique Sanda, Hector Alterio, Lautaro Murua, Alberto Segado, Franklin Caicedo, Graciela Araujo, Hugo Soto, Gerardo Romano

I Think I Do

US 1997 92m colour
Danger Filmworks/House of Pain/Robert Miller (Lane Janger)

When a group of old friends, all having doubts about their relationships, get together to celebrate a marriage, a gay TV writer discovers that his college room-mate, who once rejected his advances, now welcomes them.

Glossy sexual comedy that resembles an overstretched sitcom.

wd Brian Sloan ph Milton Kam pd Debbie Devilla ed François Keraudren

☆ Alexis Arquette, Christian Maelen, Maddie Corman, Guillermo Diaz, Lauren Velez, Jamie Harrold, Marianne Hagan, Tuc Watkins
'Just isn't funny enough or capable of providing enough food for thought about modern relationships.' – *Cosmo Landesman, Sunday Times*

I Wake Up Screaming **

US 1941 79m bw
TCF (Milton Sperling)

GB and alternative title: Hot Spot

A model is murdered and her sister joins forces with the chief suspect to find the real killer.

Moody thriller with plenty going for it including one memorable performance.

w Dwight Taylor *novel* Steve Fisher d H. Bruce Humberstone ph Edward Cronjager m Cyril Mockridge

☆ Betty Grable, Victor Mature, Carole Landis, Laird Cregar, William Gargan, Alan Mowbray, Allyn Joslyn, Elisha Cook Jnr

† Remade as Vicki (qv).

I Walk Alone *

US 1947 98m bw
Paramount (Hal B. Wallis)

An ex-smuggler comes out seeking vengeance after fourteen years in prison.

Dreary gangster drama unworthy of its stars.

w Charles Schnee *play* Beggars Are Coming to Town by Theodore Reeves d Byron Haskin ph Leo Tover m Victor Young

☆ Burt Lancaster, Kirk Douglas, Lizabeth Scott, Wendell Corey, Kristine Miller, George Rigaud, Marc Lawrence, Mike Mazurki
'The picture deserves, like four out of five other movies, to walk alone, tinkle a little bell, and cry Unclean, unclean.' – *James Agee*

I Walk the Line *

US 1970 97m Eastmancolor Panavision
Columbia/Frankenheimer/Lewis/Halcyon/Atticus (Harold D. Cohen)

A Tennessee sheriff protects moonshiners for the favours of their daughter; when an investigator arrives, bloodshed results.

Competent but uninteresting hothouse melodrama in which only the plot twists compel attention.

w Alvin Sargent *novel* An Exile by Madison Jones d John Frankenheimer ph David M. Walsh md Robert Johnson

☆ Gregory Peck, Tuesday Weld, Estelle Parsons, Ralph Meeker

'She's Alive ... Yet Dead! She's Dead ... Yet Alive!'

I Walked with a Zombie *

US 1943 68m bw
RKO (Val Lewton)

A nurse is retained by a Caribbean planter to care for his voodoo-sick wife.

Mild horror from the famous Lewton package; some style, but generally thin stuff, the plot having been mirthfully borrowed from Jane Eyre.

w Curt Siodmak, Ardel Wray d Jacques Tourneur ph J. Roy Hunt m Roy Webb

☆ Frances Dee, James Ellison, Tom Conway, Christine Gordon, Edith Barrett, James Bell, Sir Lancelot

I Wanna Hold Your Hand

US 1978 104m Technicolor
Universal/Steven Spielberg (Tamara Asseyev, Alex Rose)

A day in 1964 finds assorted New Jersey teenagers eagerly awaiting the Beatles' appearance on the Ed Sullivan Show.

Modest period comedy utilizing fresh young talent.

w Robert Zemeckis, Bob Gale d Robert Zemeckis ph Donald M. Morgan m The Beatles, Meredith Willson

☆ Nancy Allen, Bobby diCicco, Marc McClure, Susan Kendall Newman

I Want a Divorce

US 1940 74m bw
Paramount

A young law student marries rashly, but is prevented from doing anything about it by examples of the unhappiness brought by divorce.

Peculiar comedy-drama which never seems to make up its mind to any particular course.

w Frank Butler *story* Adela Rogers St Johns d Ralph Murphy ph Ted Tetzlaff m Victor Young

☆ Dick Powell, Joan Blondell, Frank Fay, Gloria Dickson, Jessie Ralph, Conrad Nagel, Harry Davenport, Sidney Blackmer, Louise Beavers

I Want to Live! *

US 1958 120m bw
UA/Walter Wanger

A vagrant prostitute is executed in the gas chamber despite growing doubt as to her guilt.

Sober, harrowing treatment of the Barbara Graham case, uneasily adapted to provide a star role amid the tirade against capital punishment.

w Nelson Gidding, Don Mankiewicz d Robert Wise ph Lionel Lindon m John Mandel ed William Hornbeck

☆ Susan Hayward, Simon Oakland, Virginia Vincent, Theodore Bikel, Wesley Lau, Philip Coolidge
'An inconclusive amalgam of variously unexplored themes.' – *Peter John Dyer*

Susan Hayward
Nelson Gidding, Don Mankiewicz; Robert Wise; Lionel Lindon; editing

I Want What I Want

GB 1971 105m Eastmancolor
Marayan (Raymond Stross)

Roy has a sex change operation and becomes Wendy.

Although based on an actual trans-sexual experience, this film confuses more than it informs, and provokes unintentional mirth when its glamorous star is playing a boy.

w Gillian Freeman *novel* Geoff Brown d John Dexter ph Gerry Turpin m Johnny Harris

☆ Anne Heywood, Paul Rogers, Harry Andrews, Jill Bennett

I Want You

US 1951 101m bw
Samuel Goldwyn

A family reacts to the Korean war.

Glossy small-town flagwaver; no Best Years of Our Lives.

w Irwin Shaw *stories* Edward Newhouse d Mark Robson ph Harry Stradling m Leigh Harline ad Richard Day ed Daniel Mandell

☆ Dorothy McGuire, Dana Andrews, Farley Granger, Peggy Dow, Robert Keith, Ray Collins, Mildred Dunnock, Martin Milner, Jim Backus
'A recruiting picture which seems to accept a third world war almost as a present reality.' – *Penelope Houston*
'Below the entertaining surface it has very little of value to offer.' – *Richard Mallett, Punch*

I Want You

GB 1998 87m Rank Colour 'Scope
Polygram/Revolution (Andrew Eaton)

A mute, voyeuristic youth observes the reunion of a hairdresser and her violent former lover, who has been released from prison after nine years.

An odd, disjointed, dingy drama of voyeurism, obsessive love and violent secrets that never comes to life.

w Eoin McNamee d Michael Winterbottom ph Slawomir Idziak m Adrian Johnston, Rare pd Mark Tildesley ed Trevor Waite

☆ Rachel Weisz, Alessandro Nivola, Labina Mitevska, Luka Petrusic, Graham Crowden, Ben Daniels, Carmen Ejogo, Geraldine O'Rawe
'An inhibiting ... that succeeds more as a stylistic exercise than as an involving, fully realized drama.' – *Derek Elley, Variety*

I Wanted to See Angels *

Russia 1992 83m colour/bw
Screen Angel/12A Studio (Carolyn Cavallero)

original title: Ya Hatiella Ooveedit Angelov

After travelling to Moscow to menace a former associate, the 20-year-old bodyguard of a provincial gangster neglects his task when he becomes involved with a young prostitute.

A bleak, grainy, low-budget look at disaffected youth, interesting less for its desultory narrative than for what it shows of present-day Moscow, which is here a harsh environment of casual cruelty and crime, punk rock and bikers on ancient machines, obsessed with American culture.

w Sergei Bodrov, Carolyn Cavallero d Sergei Bodrov ph Alosha Radionov m Mongol Shoodan ad Valeri Kostrin ed Olga Grinspoon

☆ Alexei Baranov, Natasha Ginko, Lea Akeojakova, Evgeni Livovarov
'Feels like a late 1960s Yank disillusioned teen biker pic.' – *Variety*

'Blonde bomber – she flew them into the ground!'

I Wanted Wings *

US 1941 131m bw
Paramount (Arthur Hornblow Jnr)

The fortunes of three recruits to the American Air Force.

Cheerful, overlong recruiting poster with concessions to melodrama.

---

w Richard Maibaum, Beirne Lay Jnr, Sig Herzig
d Mitchell Leisen ph Leo Tover, Elmer Dyer
m Victor Young
☆ Ray Milland, William Holden, Brian Donlevy, Wayne Morris, Veronica Lake, Constance Moore, Harry Davenport, Phil Brown
'Far more a potboiler than a drama.' – Howard Barnes, New York Herald Tribune

'All the life and death moments a man can know!'
I Was a Communist for the FBI
US 1951 83m bw
Warner (Bryan Foy)
Matt Cvetic, a Pittsburgh steel worker, is actually an FBI agent working undercover to trap communists.
Crude and shoddy Red-baiting melodrama, a kind of updating of Confessions of a Nazi Spy but using a sadly deteriorated technique.
w Crane Wilbur, Matt Cvetic d Gordon Douglas ph Edwin DuPar m Max Steiner
☆ Frank Lovejoy, Dorothy Hart, Phil Carey, James Millican, Richard Webb, Paul Picerni, Konstantin Shayne
'It seems that this is a subject which Hollywood is incapable of tackling even at its customary level of journalistic efficiency.' – Penelope Houston
⅄ documentary feature

I Was a Fireman: see Fires Were Started

I Was a Male War Bride **
US 1949 105m bw
TCF (Sol C. Siegel)
⊡ ⊞
GB title: You Can't Sleep Here
A WAC in Europe marries a French officer and can't get him home.
High-spirited farce against realistic backgrounds of war-torn Europe, which scarcely accord with Cary Grant's pretending to be a Frenchman (and later a Frenchwoman). Funny, though.
w Charles Lederer, Hagar Wilde, Leonard Spigelgass d Howard Hawks ph Norbert Brodine, Osmond Borradaile m Cyril Mockridge md Lionel Newman
☆ Cary Grant, Ann Sheridan, Marion Marshall, Randy Stuart
'It is excellent light entertainment but it is not likely to appeal to the prudish and some discretion should be exercised in booking it.' – CEA Film Report

I Was a Prisoner on Devil's Island
US 1941 71m bw
Columbia (Wallace MacDonald)
A young American seaman is involved in a brawl in which his captain dies; result, three years on Devil's Island.
Hokey but boring melodrama with production values at low level.
w Karl Brown d Lew Landers
☆ Donald Woods, Sally Eilers, Edward Ciannelli, Victor Kilian, Charles Halton

I Was a Spy **
GB 1933 89m bw
Gaumont (Michael Balcon)
⊞
In Belgium 1914, a nurse is trained as a spy.
Good standard war espionage melodrama.
w W. P. Lipscomb, Ian Hay book Marthe McKenna d Victor Saville ph Charles Van Enger md Louis Levy ad Alfred Junge ed Frederick Y. Smith
☆ Madeleine Carroll, Conrad Veidt, Herbert Marshall, Gerald du Maurier, Edmund Gwenn, Donald Calthrop, Nigel Bruce, Anthony Bushell, Martita Hunt

'Body of a boy! Mind of a monster! Soul of an unearthly thing!'
I Was a Teenage Frankenstein
US 1957 72m colour/bw
American International (Herman Cohen)
⊡ ⊞
GB title: Teenage Frankenstein
Professor Frankenstein fashions a creature from selected morsels of old corpses, and kills a teenager to give it a more handsome head.
It seemed gruesome enough at the time, but by 1980 standards this is tame, cheap stuff, only notable for its occasional bravura.
w Kenneth Langtry d Herbert L. Strock ph Lothrop Worth m Paul Dunlap

☆ Whit Bissell, Phyllis Coates, Gary Conway, Robert Burton
PROFESSOR TO MONSTER: 'Answer me! I know you have a civil tongue in your head, because I sewed it in there!'
† In-joke: when the professor crates up the monster to send it to London, the address is 113 Wardour Street, which was Hammer House.

'The most amazing motion picture of our time!'
I Was a Teenage Werewolf
US 1957 76m bw
AIP/Sunset (Herman Cohen)
⊡ ⊞
A scientist experiments on an aggressive student and turns him into a werewolf.
Hilarious farrago with a title which achieved a splendour of its own.
w Ralph Thornton d Gene Fowler Jnr ph Joseph LaShelle m Paul Dunlap
☆ Michael Landon, Whit Bissell, Yvonne Lime

I Was an Adventuress *
US 1940 81m bw
TCF (Darryl F. Zanuck)
A ballerina works as decoy for a pair of confidence tricksters.
Pleasing comedy drama with striking cast.
w Karl Tunberg, Don Ettlinger, John O'Hare d Gregory Ratoff ph Leon Shamroy, Edward Cronjager md David Buttolph
☆ Vera Zorina, Erich von Stroheim, Peter Lorre, Richard Greene, Sig Rumann, Fritz Feld, Cora Witherspoon

I Was an American Spy
US 1951 84m bw
Allied Artists (David Diamond)
Stranded in Manila after occupation, an American girl assumes Italian identity and charms Japanese officers.
Fairly gripping co-feature, remotely based on fact.
w Sam Rocca, from articles in Reader's Digest d Lesley Selander ph Harry Neumann m Edward J. Kay
☆ Ann Dvorak, Gene Evans, Douglas Kennedy, Richard Loo, Philip Ahn

I Was Happy Here *
GB 1965 91m bw
Partisan (Roy Millichip)
US title: Time Lost and Time Remembered
A girl leaves her husband in London and returns to the little Irish port of her childhood.
Nicely made, over-mannered study in nostalgia and lost illusions.
w Edna O'Brien, Desmond Davis d Desmond Davis ph Manny Wynn m John Addison
☆ Sarah Miles, Cyril Cusack, Julian Glover, Sean Caffrey, Marie Kean

I Was Monty's Double **
GB 1958 100m bw
Film Traders/Maxwell Setton
⊡
US title: Hell, Heaven and Hoboken
To distract the Nazis in Africa, an actor is hired to pose as General Montgomery.
An amusing and intriguing first hour gives way to spy chases, but the overall provides solid entertainment.
w Bryan Forbes book M. E. Clifton-James d John Guillermin ph Basil Emmott m John Addison
☆ John Mills, Cecil Parker, M. E. Clifton-James, Patrick Allen, Leslie Phillips, Michael Hordern, Marius Goring

'Silva Is Alone In New York ... But Not For Long...'
I Was on Mars *
Germany/Switzerland/US 1991 87m Eastmancolor
Metro Tartan/Luna/Fama/Balthazar/Good Machine (Gudrun Ruzickova-Steiner)
⊡
A young Polish woman, alone and reduced to penury in New York, follows a con man who has stolen all her savings.
An entertainingly eccentric and baleful account, made on a small budget, of an innocent abroad, with the city seen in close-up as a threatening, decaying slum populated by hustlers of one kind or another.
w Dani Levy, Maria Schrader d Dani Levy ph Carl-F. Koschnick m Niki Reiser pd Dan Ouellette ed Susann Lahaye
☆ Maria Schrader, Dani Levy, Mario Giacalone, Antonia Rey

'There's no denying Levi's eye for comic detail, and the film abounds in resonant little scenes.' – Sight and Sound

'Dis-organised Crime.'
I Went Down *
GB/Ireland/Spain 1997 107m colour
Buena Vista/BBC/Irish Film Board/Treasure (Robert Walpole)
⊡ ⌒
Two small-time crooks are given the task of finding the man who robbed the local gang boss.
A dark, comic road movie about outsiders moving with no great sense of purpose through a succession of dingy landscapes.
w Conor McPherson d Paddy Breathnach ph Cian de Buitlear m Dario Marianelli pd Zoe Macleod ed Emer Reynolds
☆ Brendan Gleeson, Peter McDonald, Peter Caffrey, Tony Doyle, Antoine Byrne, David Wilmot
'The film sustains its momentum, and its bad-taste scabrous humour, with likable aplomb.' – Philip Kemp, Sight and Sound

I Will ... I Will ... for Now
US 1975 108m Technicolor
Brut (C. O. Erickson)
⊞
Divorcees with sex problems eventually get together again.
Witless soft-core farrago of coy jokes, as clumsy and unappealing as its title.
w Norman Panama, Albert E. Lewin d Norman Panama ph John A. Alonzo m John Cameron pd Fernando Carrere
☆ Elliott Gould, Diane Keaton, Paul Sorvino, Victoria Principal, Warren Berlinger, Candy Clark, Robert Alda

I Wonder Who's Kissing Her Now *
US 1947 104m Technicolor
TCF (George Jessel)
The career of 1890s songwriter Joseph E. Howard.
Routine biopic, quite pleasantly handled.
w Lewis R. Foster d Lloyd Bacon ph Ernest Palmer md Alfred Newman ch Hermes Pan ad Richard Day, Boris Leven
☆ Mark Stevens, June Haver, Martha Stewart, Reginald Gardiner, Lenore Aubert, William Frawley, Gene Nelson

Ice Castles
US 1978 109m Metrocolor
Columbia/International Cinemedia Center (John Kemeny)
⊡ ⊞ ⌒
Nick and Lexie meet and fall in love at the ice rink. He goes into professional ice hockey; she becomes an Olympic champion but an accident leaves her blind.
Slick, empty, three-handkerchief wallow in the modern manner; well made but instantly forgettable.
w Donald Wrye, Gary L. Baim d Donald Wrye ph Bill Butler m Marvin Hamlisch pd Joel Schiller
☆ Robby Benson, Lynn-Holly Johnson, Colleen Dewhurst, Tom Skerritt, Jennifer Warren, David Huffman
⅄ song 'Through the Eyes of Love' (mMarvin Hamlisch, lyCarole Bayer Sager)

Ice Cold in Alex **
GB 1958 132m bw
ABP (W. A. Whittaker)
⊡
US title: Desert Attack
In 1942 Libya, the commander of a motor ambulance gets his vehicle and passengers to safety despite the hazards of minefields and a German spy.
Engrossing desert adventure with plenty of suspense sequences borrowed from The Wages of Fear; long, but very well presented.
w T. J. Morrison, Christopher Landon d J. Lee-Thompson ph Gilbert Taylor m Leighton Lucas
☆ John Mills, Sylvia Sims, Anthony Quayle, Harry Andrews

'Sparkling with Gaiety, Romance, Stars, Musical Thrills!'
Ice Follies of 1939
US 1939 82m bw (Technicolor sequence)
MGM (Harry Rapf)
⊛
A Hollywood star goes east to help her old ice-skating friends put on a show.
Tepid musical entertainment.

The downright peculiar sight of these particular stars on ice is backed by good turns and practically no story.
w Florence Ryerson, Edgar Allan Woolf d Reinhold Schunzel ph Joseph Ruttenberg, Oliver T. Marsh m Franz Waxman
☆ Joan Crawford, James Stewart, Lew Ayres, Lewis Stone, Lionel Stander, Bess Ehrhardt, Charles D. Brown, the International Ice Follies

Ice Palace
US 1960 143m Warnercolor
Warner (Henry Blanke)
After World War I, two men set up a fishery business in Alaska, and their subsequent lives are tied up with the political development of the state.
Tedious saga from a bestseller, with entertaining incidents but no real grip.
w Harry Kleiner novel Edna Ferber d Vincent Sherman ph Joseph Biroc m Max Steiner ad Malcolm Bert
☆ Richard Burton, Robert Ryan, Martha Hyer, Carolyn Jones, Jim Backus, Ray Danton, Diane McBain, Karl Swenson

The Ice Pirates
US 1984 94m Metrocolor
MGM-UA (John Foreman)
⊞ ⊛
On a distant planet in the future, water has become precious, and the evil Templars have cornered it.
Extraordinarily talkative and unpersuasive space opera: pretentious hokum.
w Stewart Raffill, Stanford Sherman d Stewart Raffill ph Matthew F. Leonetti m Bruce Broughton ad David M. Haber, Ronald Kent Foreman ed Tom Walls
☆ Robert Urich, Mary Crosby, Michael D. Roberts, Anjelica Huston, Ron Perlman, John Carradine

Ice Station Zebra
US 1968 148m Metrocolor Super Panavision
MGM/Filmways (James C. Pratt)
⊡ ⊞ ⊛
Russian and American agents speed towards the North Pole to recover a lost capsule containing vital military information.
Talky and unconvincingly staged spy adventure with a disappointing lack of action and a great many cold war platitudes.
w Douglas Heyes, Harry Julian Fink novel Alistair MacLean d John Sturges ph Daniel L. Fapp m Michel Legrand
☆ Rock Hudson, Patrick McGoohan, Ernest Borgnine, Jim Brown, Tony Bill, Lloyd Nolan, Gerald S. O'Loughlin, Alf Kjellin
'It's terrible in such a familiar way that at some level it's pleasant. We learn to settle for so little, we moviegoers.' – Pauline Kael
⅄ Daniel L. Fapp; special effects (Hal Miller, J. McMillan Johnson)

'It was 1973, and the climate was changing.'
The Ice Storm **
US 1997 113m DeLuxe
Fox Searchlight/Good Machine (Ted Hope, James Schamus, Ang Lee)
⊡ ⊞ ⊛ ⊚ ⊚ ⌒
In the 70s, a community of discontented middle-class families try to escape from their problems through sex: the adults with affairs and wife-swapping, the children with losing their virginity.
A cool and clever dissection of troubled people in confusing times, though its puritan connection between illicit sex and death seems forced.
w James Schamus novel Rick Moody d Ang Lee ph Frederick Elmes m Mychael Danna pd Mark Friedberg ed Tim Squyres
☆ Kevin Kline, Joan Allen, Henry Czerny, Adam Hann-Byrd, Tobey Maguire, Christina Ricci, Jamey Sheridan, Elijah Wood, Sigourney Weaver
'Smug connect-the-dots evisceration of the American dream.' – Joe Queenan
'Pointed, witty and beautifully directed.' – Geoff Brown, The Times
⍟ Sigourney Weaver

Ice-Capades
US 1941 88m bw
Republic
A newsreel cameraman fakes an ice show in Central Park.
Tepid musical entertainment.

w Jack Townley and others *d* Joseph Santley *md* Cy Feuer

☆ James Ellison, Phil Silvers, Jerry Colonna, Dorothy Lewis, Barbara Jo Allen, Alan Mowbray

♫ Cy Feuer

Ice-Capades Revue
US   1942   79m   bw
Republic (Robert North)
A New England farm girl inherits a bankrupt ice show.
Thin excuse for an ice revue, which is tolerable.
w Bradford Ropes, Gertrude Purcell *d* Bernard Vorhaus
☆ Ellen Drew, Richard Denning, Jerry Colonna, Barbara Jo Allen, Harold Huber, Vera Hruba, Joe Jackson Jnr

Iceland
US   1942   79m   bw
TCF (William LeBaron)
GB title: *Katina*
A marine in Reykjavik falls for a local belle.
Superficial musical with a stage farce plot and unreal musical numbers.
w Robert Ellis, Helen Logan *d* Bruce Humberstone *ph* Arthur Miller *m/ly* Mack Gordon, Harry Warren *md* Emil Newman
☆ Sonja Henie, John Payne, Jack Oakie, Felix Bressart, Osa Massen

Iceman
US   1984   99m   Technicolor
Universal (Patrick Palmer, Norman Jewison)
▣ ▦ ♫
An oil-drilling team in the Arctic discovers the perfectly preserved body of a Neanderthal man, who having been returned to civilization wakes up and creates havoc.
All civilization's fault, of course: initial suspense gives way to boredom when morals are preached.
w Chip Proser, John Drimmer *d* Fred Schepisi *ph* Ian Baker *m* Bruce Smeaton *ad* Leon Ericksen, Josan Russo *ed* Billy Weber
☆ Timothy Hutton, Lindsay Crouse, John Lone, Josef Sommer, Danny Glover

The Iceman Cometh
Hong Kong   1989   120m   colour
Golden Harvest
▣
aka: *Time Warriors*
The chief swordsman of a medieval Imperial Guard and his evil adversary, who has stolen a statue with occult powers, are trapped in ice and revived to continue their fight in modern-day Hong Kong.
Action-packed martial arts melodrama with a comic edge: it begins well, but its length is likely to deter all but addicts of the genre.
d Clarence Fok
☆ Yuen Biao, Yuen Wah, Maggie Cheung, Wong Jing
'Superb … whether you're a fantasy fan, or you like some good old modern day kung fu fighting or both, then this film is a serious recommendation.' – *Rick Baker, Eastern Heroes*

Ich Will Doch Nur, Das Ihr Mich Liebt:
see *I Only Want You to Love Me*

Ichabod and Mr Toad **
👫 US   1949   68m   Technicolor
Walt Disney
aka: *The Adventures of Ichabod and Mr Toad*
Cartoon versions of stories by Washington Irving and Kenneth Grahame.
An uncomfortable double bill; the story of Ichabod, though well narrated by Bing Crosby, is macabre without being very interesting; The Wind in the Willows, however, is charmingly pictured, and Mr Toad is splendidly voiced by Eric Blore.
d Jack Kinney, Clyde Geronimi, James Algar *supervisor* Ben Sharpsteen

The Icicle Thief **
Italy   1989   85m   colour
Metro/Bambù/Reitalia (Ernesto Di Sarro)
▣ ▦ ♫
original title: *Ladri Di Saponette*
Watching the television screening of his new film, a director enters the movie when he discovers his characters are changing their lines and leaving the action to appear in commercials.

Witty parody of neo-realistic cinema (the title recalls de Sica's classic Bicycle Thieves), commercialism and TV's treatment of films.
w Maurizio Nichetti, Mauro Monti *d* Maurizio Nichetti *ph* Maria Battistoni *m* Manuel de Sica *pd* Ada Legori *ed* Rita Rossi, Anna Missoni
☆ Maurizio Nichetti, Caterina Sylos Labini, Federico Rizzo, Renato Scarpa, Heidi Komarex, Carlina Torta, Massimi Sacilotto, Claudio G. Fava
'An unqualified treat … This sophisticated satire on the undifferentiated tap-flow of television is also a passionate declaration of love for the movies.' – *David Robinson, The Times*

I'd Climb the Highest Mountain *
US   1951   88m   Technicolor
TCF (Lamar Trotti)
A Methodist preacher and his wife face the problems of life in a remote part of North Georgia.
Pleasant, rambling, adequately serious and old-fashioned family entertainment, well presented in Hollywood's medium style.
w Lamar Trotti *novel* Corra Harris *d* Henry King *ph* Edward Cronjager *m* Sol Kaplan *md* Lionel Newman
☆ Susan Hayward, William Lundigan, Rory Calhoun, Barbara Bates, Gene Lockhart, Lynn Bari, Ruth Donnelly, Alexander Knox

I'd Rather Be Rich *
US   1964   96m   Eastmancolor
U-I/Ross Hunter
To comfort her dying grandfather, an heiress introduces an eligible stranger as her fiancé … but the old man recovers and begins matchmaking.
Reasonably zesty remake of It Started with Eve, kept afloat by Chevalier's performance.
w Oscar Brodney, Leo Townsend, Norman Krasna *d* Jack Smight *ph* Russell Metty *m* Percy Faith
☆ *Maurice Chevalier*, Sandra Dee, Robert Goulet, Andy Williams, Gene Raymond, Hermione Gingold, Charles Ruggles

An Ideal Husband *
GB   1947   96m   Technicolor
British Lion/London Films (Alexander Korda)
In the 1890s, the career of a London diplomat is threatened by the reappearance of an old flame.
A slight, stiff play is swamped by the cast, the decor, and very garish colour, but there are moments of enjoyment along the way.
w Lajos Biro *play* Oscar Wilde *d* Alexander Korda *ph* Georges Périnal *m* Arthur Benjamin *ad* Vincent Korda, Cecil Beaton
☆ Paulette Goddard, Hugh Williams, Michael Wilding, Diana Wynyard, C. Aubrey Smith, Constance Collier, Glynis Johns, Christine Norden
'The composing and cutting of this fine raw material is seldom above medium grade.' – *James Agee*

'He just doesn't know it yet.'

An Ideal Husband *
GB/USA   1999   98m   colour
Pathé/Icon/Arts Council/Fragile/Miramax (Barnaby Thompson, Uri Fruchtmann, Bruce Davey)
▣ ▦ ▦
An MP is saved from public disgrace at the hands of a scheming woman by his wife and his best friend.
Wilde's play has not gained from being opened up, though Everett's performance and Wilde's words keep the brittle comedy alive.
wd Oliver Parker *play* Oscar Wilde *ph* David Johnson *m* Charlie Mole *pd* Michael Howells *ed* Guy Bensley
☆ Cate Blanchett, Minnie Driver, Rupert Everett, Julianne Moore, Jeremy Northam, John Wood, Lindsay Duncan, Peter Vaughan, Jeroen Krabbé, Ben Pullen, Nickolas Grace
'It's on the film's determined stylishness that it loses the original's lightness of touch and somewhat downplays sparkling repartee in favour of a forced emotional element.' – *Angie Errigo, Empire*

Identification of a Woman
Italy   1982   130m   Technicolor   Technovision
Artificial Eye/Iter Film/Gaumont (Giorgio Nocella, Antonio Macri)
▣
original title: *Identificazione di una Donna*
A film director searches for an ideal woman to spark off his new film.

A quest that the audience will tire of long before the end.
w Michelangelo Antonioni, Gérard Brach, Tonino Guerra *d* Michelangelo Antonioni *ph* Carlo di Palma *ad* Andrea Crisanti *ed* Michelangelo Antonioni
☆ Tomas Milian, Daniela Silverio, Christine Boisson, Sandra Monteleoni, Giampaolo Saccarola, Alessandro Ruspoli, Giada Gerini, Sergio Tardioli

Idiot Box
Australia   1996   83m   Atlab   Panavision
Central Park/AFFC (Glenys Rowe)
▦ ♫
In a Sydney suburb two dim-witted, boozy, unemployed layabouts decide to rob a bank, and choose one under surveillance by the police, who are expecting a raid from professionals.
A slice of low-life among deadbeats that some found funny, though the company of its loud, foul-mouthed incompetents soon palls.
wd David Caesar *ph* Joseph Pickering *pd* Kerith Holmes *ed* Mark Perry
☆ Ben Mendelsohn, Jeremy Sims, John Polson, Graeme Blundell, Deborah Kennedy, Robyn Loau, Stephen Rae
'A wild ride, a fast, corrosive comedy.' – *Variety*

'Take a long ride on the short bus.'

The Idiots
Denmark   1998   115m   colour
Zentropa/DRTV/DBC/Liberator/La Sept/ZDF/Arte/Argus/VPRO (Vibeke Windelov)
▣
original title: *Idioterne*
In Copenhagen, friends form a commune in which they seek their 'inner idiot' by playing at being mentally and physically retarded.
A talented director pushes his art in the wrong direction: this is a scrappily filmed satire on family life, both conventional and communal, where the cult leader is far more parasitical and controlling than his abused suburban counterparts.
wd Lars von Trier *ph* Lars von Trier *ed* Molly Malene Stensgaard
☆ Bodil Jorgensen, Jens Albinus, Louise Hassing, Troels Lyby, Nikolaj Lie Kaas, Henrik Prip, Luis Mesonero, Louise Mieritz, Knud Romer Jorgensen, Trine Michelsen, Anne-Grethe Bjarup Riis
'Although some will find the jerky, shot-on-the-run style off-putting, this is real cinema: original, affecting, shattering.' – *Kim Newman, Empire*
'Weird and wonderful … I cannot decide whether this film is courageous, offensive or plain idiotic.' – *Nigel Cliff, The Times*

Idiot's Delight *
US   1939   105m   bw
MGM (Hunt Stromberg)
▦
At the outbreak of World War II, in a hotel on the Swiss border, a hoofer with an all-girl troupe meets an old flame masquerading as a Russian countess.
Interesting but quite unsuccessful film version of a highly artificial play which had been carried off superbly by the Lunts but was now somewhat less well cast, though it did represent an early Hollywood challenge to Hitler. The flagwaving in fact made it more than a little boring.
w Robert E. Sherwood *play* Robert E. Sherwood *d* Clarence Brown *ph* William Daniels *m* Herbert Stothart
☆ Clark Gable, Norma Shearer, Edward Arnold, Charles Coburn, Burgess Meredith, Joseph Schildkraut, Laura Hope Crews, Skeets Gallagher, Pat Paterson, Fritz Feld
'Exceptionally entertaining comedy, a b.o. sock.' – *Variety*
'The fun and excitement are still there, however filtered it may be.' – *Film Daily*
'The mood of the whole thing is forced and cheap – the coming world war staged by Maurice Chevalier.' – *Otis Ferguson*
'Exactly the same pseudo-qualities as The Petrified Forest: a moral pretentiousness, a kind of cellophane intellectuality.' – *Graham Greene*

The Idle Class *
👫 US   1922   30m   bw   silent
First National/Charles Chaplin
▦
A tramp dreams of the rich life and is mistaken for the husband of a lady.

Rather slight later Chaplin without the full-blooded farcical elements which made him so popular around 1917.
wd Charles Chaplin *ph* Rollie Totheroh
☆ Charles Chaplin, Edna Purviance, Mack Swain

The Idol
GB   1966   111m   bw
Embassy (Leonard Lightstone)
▦
A divorced woman falls in love with her son's friend.
Stupefyingly boring generation-gap sex drama.
w Millard Lampell *d* Daniel Petrie *ph* Ken Higgins *m* Johnny Dankworth
☆ Jennifer Jones, Michael Parks, John Leyton, Jennifer Hilary, Guy Doleman, Natasha Pyne
'Doesn't even qualify for worst picture of the year, missing the perfection and purity of that category by the sheer ineptness of script, direction, and performance.' – *Judith Crist*

Idol of Paris
GB   1948   105m   bw
Premier (R. J. Minney)
In old Paris, a ragman's daughter becomes queen of the demi-mondaines.
Unintentionally hilarious copy of the Gainsborough period romances which had been so popular; much criticized because the leading ladies fight a duel with whips, but that's the least of its faults.
w Norman Lee, Stafford Dickens, Henry Ostrer *novel* Paiva Queen of Love by Alfred Shirkauer *d* Leslie Arliss *ph* Jack Cox *m* Mischa Spoliansky
☆ Beryl Baxter, Christine Norden, Michael Rennie, Margaretta Scott, Keneth Kent, Henry Oscar, Miles Malleson, Andrew Osborn, Andrew Cruickshank

The Idolmaker
US   1980   119m   Technicolor
United Artists/Gene Kirkwood, Howard W. Koch
▦ ▦
A songwriter accurately sums up his own limited talent and turns agent and starmaker.
Sharp but padded look behind the scenes of the pop industry; in the end of interest only to initiates.
w Edward Di Lorenzo *d* Taylor Hackford *ph* Adam Holender *m* Jeff Barry
☆ Ray Sharkey, Tovah Feldshuh, Peter Gallagher, Paul Land

Idols in the Dust: see *Saturday's Hero*

If... ****
GB   1968   111m   Eastmancolor
Paramount/Memorial (Lindsay Anderson, Michael Medwin)
▦ ▦
Discontent at a boys' public school breaks out into rebellion.
Allegorical treatment of school life with much fashionable emphasis on obscure narrative, clever cutting, variety of pace, even an unaccountable changing from colour to monochrome and vice versa. It catches perfectly a mood of rebellion and dissatisfaction with the status quo.
w David Sherwin *d* Lindsay Anderson *ph* Miroslav Ondricek *m* Marc Wilkinson *ad* Jocelyn Herbert
☆ Malcolm McDowell, David Wood, Richard Warwick, Robert Swann, Christine Noonan, Peter Jeffrey, Arthur Lowe, Anthony Nicholls
'The school … is the perfect metaphor for the established system all but a few of us continue to accept.' – *David Wilson*
'It's something like the Writing on the Wall.' – *Lindsay Anderson*
'Combines a cold and queasy view of youth with a romantic view of violence.' – *New Yorker*

If a Man Answers
US   1962   102m   Technicolor
Universal/Ross Hunter
A wife decides to make her husband jealous.
Derivative second-team matrimonial comedy, all dressed up but with nowhere to go.
w Richard Morris *novel* Winifred Wolfe *d* Henry Levin *ph* Russell Metty *m* Hans Salter
☆ Sandra Dee, Bobby Darin, Micheline Presle, John Lund, Cesar Romero, Stefanie Powers

---

If Ever I See You Again

US 1978 105m colour
Columbia (Joe Brooks)

A songwriter attempts to win back the love of an old girlfriend.

Almost a one-man band of a movie that plays too long on one note and is better never seen at all.

w Joe Brooks, Martin Davidson d Joe Brooks ph Adam Holender m Joe Brooks ed Rich Shaine

☆ Joe Brooks, Shelley Hack, Jimmy Breslin, Jerry Keller, George Plimpton, Michael Decker

If I Had a Million **

US 1932 88m bw
Paramount (Benjamin Glazer, Louis D. Lighton)

Various people each receive a million dollars from an eccentric who wants to test their reactions.

Interesting, dated multi-part comedy drama remembered chiefly for the brief sequence in which Laughton blows a raspberry to his boss and Fields chases road hogs. As an entertainment it's patchy, lacking an overall style.

w Claude Binyon, Whitney Bolton, Malcolm Stuart Boylan, John Bright, Sidney Buchman, Lester Cole, Isabel Dawn, Boyce DeGaw, Walter de Leon, Oliver H. P. Garrett, Harvey Gates, Grover Jones, Ernst Lubitsch, Lawton Mackaill, Joseph L. Mankiewicz, William Slavens McNutt, Seton I. Miller, Tiffany Thayer *story* Robert D. Andrews d Ernst Lubitsch, Norman Taurog, Stephen Roberts, Norman Z. McLeod, James Cruze, William A. Seiter, H. Bruce Humberstone

☆ W. C. Fields, *Charles Laughton*, May Robson, Richard Bennett, Alison Skipworth, Gary Cooper, Wynne Gibson, George Raft, Jack Oakie, Frances Dee, Charles Ruggles, Mary Boland, Roscoe Karns, Gene Raymond, Lucien Littlefield

'Not uninteresting, but spotty in retrospect ... the cinematic porridge is naturally replete with a diversity of seasonings.' – *Variety*

'It develops an obvious idea in an obvious way.' – *Time*

If I Had My Way *

US 1940 82m bw
Universal (David Butler)

Two vaudevillians help an orphan girl and open a new night-club.

Quite likeable and very typical star vehicle of its period.

w William Conselman, James V. Kern d David Butler ph George Robinson m Frank Skinner

☆ Bing Crosby, Charles Winninger, Gloria Jean, El Brendel, Allyn Joslyn, Donald Woods, Eddie Leonard, Claire Dodd, Blanche Ring

If I Were Free

US 1933 65m bw
RKO

A man and woman, each unhappily married, try to get together.

Rather soppy drama which fails to develop.

w Dwight Taylor *play* Behold We Live *by* John Van Druten d Elliott Nugent

☆ Irene Dunne, Clive Brook, Nils Asther, Henry Stephenson, Laura Hope Crews

'Thin in texture, it never reaches a pace that really counts.' – *Variety*

'His love-making was as dangerous as his swordplay!'

If I Were King *

US 1938 101m bw
Paramount (Frank Lloyd)

The 14th-century poet and rascal François Villon matches wits with Louis XI and leads an uprising of the people.

A story which we have grown used to seeing with music as The Vagabond King is here well presented but somehow rings hollow, with insufficient derring-do; it is the wrong kind of swashbuckling for its star, who is for once outacted by Rathbone in an unusual wily characterization.

w Preston Sturges d Frank Lloyd ph Theodor Sparkuhl m Richard Hageman ad Hans Dreier, John Goodman

☆ Ronald Colman, *Basil Rathbone*, Frances Dee, Ellen Drew, C. V. France, Heather Thatcher, Henry Wilcoxon, Sidney Toler

'Healthy box office that will hit extended runs right down the line.' – *Variety*

'A well mounted and splendid production that carries along at a fascinating pace.' – *Daily Variety*

☋ Richard Hageman; Basil Rathbone; art direction

If I'm Lucky

US 1945 79m bw
TCF (Brian Foy)

A singer runs for state governor and exposes corruption.

Lacklustre remake of Thanks a Million, *with decidedly dispirited elements.*

w Snag Werris, Robert Ellis, Helen Logan, George Bricker d Lewis Seiler ph Glen MacWilliams m/ly Edgar de Lange, Joseph Myrow md Emil Newman

☆ Vivian Blaine, Perry Como, Carmen Miranda, Harry James, Phil Silvers, Edgar Buchanan, Reed Hadley

If It's Tuesday, This Must Be Belgium *

US 1969 98m DeLuxe
UA/Wolper (Stan Margulies)

A group of American tourists have various adventures during a lightning tour of Europe.

Amusing comedy which does pretty well by a good idea.

w David Shaw d Mel Stuart ph Vilis Lapenieks m Walter Scharf

☆ Suzanne Pleshette, Ian McShane, Mildred Natwick, Murray Hamilton, Michael Constantine, Sandy Baron, Norman Fell, Peggy Cass, Marty Ingels, Pamela Britton, Luke Halpin, Aubrey Morris

If Looks Could Kill: see Teen Agent

If Lucy Fell

US 1996 94m Technicolor
Sony/TriStar/Motion Picture Corp (Brad Krevoy, Steve Stabler, Brad Jenkel)

Two flatmates make a pact to jump from Brooklyn Bridge if they fail to find the perfect mate before they reach 30.

Dim and charmless attempt at a romantic comedy.

wd Eric Schaeffer ph Ron Fortunato m Amanda Kravat, Charles Pettis pd Ginger Tougas ed Sue Graef

☆ Sarah Jessica Parker, Eric Schaeffer, Ben Stiller, Elle Macpherson, James Rebhorn, Dominic Luchese, Robert John Burke

'The sparks fly with some memorable verbal sparring and screen chemistry between the principals.' – *Leonard Klady, Variety*

'If men and women were emotionally, physically, biologically, astrologically, hormonally, psychologically, orgasmically the same ... life would be easy.'

If Only

GB/France/Spain/Canada/Luxembourg 1998 95m colour
Pathé/HandMade/Paragon/Mandarin/Wild Rose/Parallel (Juan Gordon)

An actor, who lost the woman he loved when he told her of an affair, gets a chance to relive his life without repeating the mistake.

Curious little comedy about having to live with one's mistakes, which has a certain slight charm.

w Rafa Russo d Maria Ripoll ph Javier Salmones m Luis Mendo, Bernardo Fuster, Angel Illarramendi pd Grant Hicks ed Nacho Ruiz-Capillas

☆ Penelope Cruz, Douglas Henshall, Lena Headey, Gustavo Salmeron, Mark Strong, Eusebio Lazaro, Charlotte Coleman, Neil Stuke, Elizabeth McGovern

'Well-crafted and enjoyable.' – *Empire*

If This Be Sin: see That Dangerous Age

If Winter Comes

US 1948 97m bw
MGM (Victor Saville)

A sentimental idealist, unhappily married, finds himself at the mercy of village gossip when he takes in a pregnant girl.

Artificial romantic nonsense, unconvincingly staged and modernized from a very dated bestseller.

w Marguerite Roberts, Arthur Wimperis *novel* A. S. M. Hutchinson d Victor Saville ph George Folsey m Herbert Stothart

☆ Walter Pidgeon, Deborah Kerr, Janet Leigh, Angela Lansbury, Binnie Barnes, Dame May Whitty, Reginald Owen

If You Could Only Cook

US 1935 72m bw
Columbia

A young millionaire meets a poor girl and they get jobs as cook and butler.

Whimsical comedy-romance; thin but moderately beguiling.

w F. Hugh Herbert, Gertrude Purcell, Howard J. Green d William A. Seiter ph John Stumar ad Stephen Goosson ed Gene Havlick

☆ Jean Arthur, Herbert Marshall, Leo Carrillo, Lionel Stander, Frieda Inescort

'Plenty of chuckles ... offers particularly strong promise for the nabes.' – *Variety*

† This was the film which enabled Frank Capra to get out of his Columbia contract, because they accidentally promoted it in Europe as being directed by him.

If You Feel Like Singing: see Summer Stock

If You Knew Susie *

US 1948 90m bw
RKO (Eddie Cantor)

A vaudeville couple retire to his ancestral home in New England.

Mild family comedy capitalizing on the team established in Show Business.

w Warren Wilson, Oscar Brodney d Gordon Douglas ph Frank Redman

☆ *Eddie Cantor, Joan Davis*, Allyn Joslyn, Bobby Driscoll, Charles Dingle

If You Live Shoot!: see Django, Kill!

Il Bidone **

Italy/France 1955 109m bw
Titanus/SGC
aka: *The Swindlers*

A group of petty swindlers fails to move into the higher criminal bracket.

Sharply observed but rather sentimental melodrama with tragic pretensions.

w Federico Fellini, Ennio Flaiano, Tullio Pinelli d Federico Fellini ph Otello Martelli m Nino Rota

☆ Broderick Crawford, Richard Basehart, Franco Fabrizi, Giulietta Masina

Ikimono No Kiroku: see I Live in Fear

Ikiru **

Japan 1952 143m bw
Toho
aka: *Living*
aka: *Doomed*

A clerk learns that he is dying and spends his last months creating a children's playground.

A moving and beautifully made personal drama which also gives an interesting background of modern Japan.

w Hideo Oguni, Shinobu Hashimoto, Akira Kurosawa d Akira Kurosawa ph Asaishi Nakai m Fumio Hayasaka

☆ Takashi Shimura, Nobuo Kaneko, Kyoko Seki

Il était une fois un pays: see Underground (1995)

Il Faut Vivre Dangereusement

France 1975 100m colour
Fox/ORFT (Nelly Kaplan)
aka: *You've Got to Live Dangerously*

A private eye, hired to investigate a young woman, uncovers a plot to find a fabulous diamond.

Baroque thriller with more corpses than Hamlet, but one that fails to sustain interest, despite its recourse to naked flesh at every possible opportunity.

w Nelly Kaplan d Claude Makovsky m Claude Bolling ad Jacques Dugied ed Jocelyne Triquet

☆ Claude Brasseur, Annie Girardot

Il mio nome è Nessuno: see My Name Is Nobody

L'Ile au trésor: see Treasure Island

'Somewhere between L.A. and N.Y. Jake found the true meaning of Christmas.'

I'll Be Home for Christmas

US 1998 85m Technicolor
Buena Vista/Walt Disney/Mandeville (David Hoberman, Tracey Trench)

A spoilt, selfish student, abandoned in the Californian desert with no money, has 48 hours in which to get to New York so that he can get his Christmas present of a sports car.

Sentimental family comedy that runs along totally predictable lines; it is as bland as supermarket turkey.

w Tom Nursall, Harris Goldberg *story* Michael Allin d Arlene Sanford ph Hiro Narita m John Debney pd Cynthia Charette ed Anita Brandt-Burgoyne

☆ Jonathan Taylor Thomas, Jessica Biel, Adam LaVorgna, Sean O'Bryan, Gary Cole, Eve Gordon, Lauren Maltby, Andrew Lauer, Leslie Boone

'Both living a secret – each afraid to tell!'

I'll Be Seeing You **

US 1944 85m bw
David O. Selznick (Dore Schary)

A lady convict at home on parole for Christmas meets and falls for a shell-shocked soldier.

Schmaltzy, middle-American romantic drama with some nicely handled moments and plenty of talent on hand. In the Hollywood mainstream.

w Marion Parsonnet *novel* Charles Martin d William Dieterle ph Tony Gaudio m Daniele Amfitheatrof

☆ Ginger Rogers, Joseph Cotten, Shirley Temple, Spring Byington, Tom Tully, Chill Wills

'A sentimental, improbable picture, but unexpectedly rewarding in detail.' – *Richard Mallett, Punch*

I'll Be Your Sweetheart

GB 1945 104m bw
Gainsborough (Louis Levy)

In 1900, songwriters fight with copyright pirates.

Studio-bound musical romance without the necessary resonance.

w Val Guest, Val Valentine d Val Guest ph Phil Grindrod md Louis Levy

☆ Margaret Lockwood, Michael Rennie, Vic Oliver, Peter Graves, Moore Marriott, Frederick Burtwell, Maudie Edwards, Garry Marsh

I'll Be Yours

US 1947 90m bw
Universal (Felix Jackson)

A small-town girl tries to make good in the big city.

Slackly handled remake of The Good Fairy. A doubtful 'A' production which did nothing for its star's ailing career.

w Preston Sturges (adapted anonymously from his previous screenplay based on the Molnar original) d William A. Seiter ph Hal Mohr m Frank Skinner

☆ Deanna Durbin, Tom Drake, William Bendix, Adolphe Menjou, Walter Catlett, Franklin Pangborn

I'll Cry Tomorrow *

US 1955 119m bw
MGM (Lawrence Weingarten)

Lillian Roth, a Broadway/Hollywood star of the early thirties, becomes an alcoholic.

Fictionalized biopic, pretty well done of the True Confessions kind.

w Helen Deutsch, Jay Richard Kennedy *book* Lillian Roth, Gerold Frank d Daniel Mann ph Arthur E. Arling m Alex North ad Cedric Gibbons, Randall Duell

☆ *Susan Hayward*, Richard Conte, Eddie Albert, Jo Van Fleet, Don Taylor, Ray Danton, Margo

'By emphasizing physical degradation in almost every frame, the film makes her less an object of acutely personal concern than a street casualty seen remotely from the top of a bar.' – *Alexander Walker*

☋ Arthur E. Arling; Susan Hayward; art direction

I'll Do Anything

US   1994   115m   Technicolor
Columbia/Gracie (James L. Brooks, Polly Platt)

An out-of-work actor with a small daughter to support falls for a Hollywood executive while working as a chauffeur for an overbearing producer.
Moderate romantic comedy, more likely to interest those who work in Hollywood than a wider audience.
wd James L. Brooks ph Michael Ballhaus m Hans Zimmer pd Stephen J. Lineweaver ed Richard Marks
☆ Nick Nolte, Albert Brooks, Julie Kavner, Whittni Wright, Joely Richardson, Tracey Ullman, Joely Fisher, Jeb Brown
'Given its origins the movie is better than one might have anticipated yet has to be viewed as a disappointment relative to Brooks' earlier features.' – *Variety*
† The film was originally intended as a musical. Eleven of the 12 songs were cut after some of the audience walked out at previews, and new footage was added.

I'll Get By

US   1950   86m   Technicolor
TCF (William Perlberg)
Two songwriters meet success, then join the marines and are reunited with their former girlfriends.
Fair standard musical, a modernization of Tin Pan Alley.
w Mary Loos, Richard Sale d Richard Sale ph Charles G. Clarke md Lionel Newman
☆ June Haver, Gloria de Haven, William Lundigan, Dennis Day, Harry James, Thelma Ritter
♫ Lionel Newman

I'll Get You for This

GB   1950   83m   bw
Romulus
US title: *Lucky Nick Cain*
An American gambler in Italy goes after the gangsters who framed him.
Second-grade star thick ear.
w George Callahan, William Rose novel *High Stakes* by James Hadley Chase d Joseph M. Newman ph Otto Heller m Walter Goehr
☆ George Raft, Coleen Gray, Charles Goldner, Walter Rilla, Greta Gynt, Enzo Staiola

I'll Give a Million *

US   1938   70m   bw
TCF (Darryl F. Zanuck)
A millionaire becomes a tramp and disappears, letting it be known that he will give a fortune for genuine acts of kindness. Tramps are then royally entertained all over town.
Amusing Depression comedy with satirical touches.
w Boris Ingster, Milton Sperling d Walter Lang ph Lucien Andriot md Louis Silvers
☆ Warner Baxter, Peter Lorre, Marjorie Weaver, Jean Hersholt, John Carradine, J. Edward Bromberg, Lynn Bari, Fritz Feld, Sig Rumann
'Not worth that much … the plot sags at the halfway mark and the wind-up is disappointing.' – *Variety*

Ill Met by Moonlight

GB   1956   104m   bw   Vistavision
Rank/Vega (Michael Powell, Emeric Pressburger)
US title: *Night Ambush*
In Crete during the German occupation, British agents work with partisans to capture a German general.
Disappointingly dreary war adventure with too many night locations, too little suspense and characterization, and photography which seems to be deliberately unattractive.
wd Michael Powell, Emeric Pressburger book W. Stanley Moss ph Christopher Challis m Mikis Theodorakis
☆ Dirk Bogarde, Marius Goring, David Oxley, Cyril Cusack, John Cairney, Laurence Payne, Wolfe Morris, Michael Gough

I'll Never Forget Whatshisname *

GB   1967   96m   Technicolor
Universal/Scimitar (Michael Winner)
An advertising executive gives up power and money for integrity on a small literary magazine, but is won back by a mogul.
Vivid yet muddled tragi-comedy of the sixties, with splashes of sex and violence in trendy settings, a hero one really doesn't believe in, and a title which seems to have no meaning whatsoever.
w Peter Draper d Michael Winner ph Otto Heller m Francis Lai
☆ Oliver Reed, Orson Welles, Carol White, Harry Andrews, Michael Hordern, Wendy Craig, Marianne Faithfull

I'll Never Forget You: see *The House in the Square*

I'll See You in My Dreams *

US   1952   112m   bw
Warner (Louis F. Edelman)
The domestic and professional life of songwriter Gus Kahn.
Quiet-toned, well made, quite forgettable musical.
w Melville Shavelson, Jack Rose d Michael Curtiz ph Ted McCord md Ray Heindorf ch Le Roy Prinz
☆ Doris Day, Danny Thomas, Frank Lovejoy, Patrice Wymore, James Gleason

I'll Take Romance

US   1937   85m   bw
Columbia (Everett Riskin)
When an opera singer refuses to fulfil a South American contract, her impresario kidnaps her.
Moderate star vehicle.
w George Oppenheimer, Jane Murfin d Edward H. Griffith ph Lucien Andriot m/ly various
☆ Grace Moore, Melvyn Douglas, Helen Westley, Stuart Erwin, Margaret Hamilton, Walter Kingsford, Esther Muir

I'll Take Sweden

US   1965   96m   Technicolor
UA/Edward Small
A widowed oil company executive accepts a Stockholm posting to remove his teenage daughter from an unsuitable attachment.
Feeble comedy which unwisely attempts to be with it, but is bogged down by amateurish handling and witwise is sadly without it.
w Nat Perrin, Bob Fisher, Arthur Marx d Frederick de Cordova ph Daniel L. Fapp m Jimmy Haskell
☆ Bob Hope, Tuesday Weld, Frankie Avalon, Dina Merrill, Jeremy Slate, John Qualen, Walter Sande

I'll Tell the World

US   1945   76m   bw
Universal
A small-town sports announcer starts a lonely hearts programme.
Amiable second feature, a reworking of the star's earlier Advice to the Lovelorn.
w Henry Blankfort d Leslie Goodwins
☆ Lee Tracy, Brenda Joyce, Raymond Walburn, June Preisser, Thomas Gomez
'Feasible b.o., but not a strong drafter where the Tracy name can't help.' – *Variety*

Illegal *

US   1955   88m   bw
Warner (Frank P. Rosenberg)
A disillusioned District Attorney becomes a racketeer's lawyer but finally denounces him at the cost of his own life.
Competent remake of The Mouthpiece (*qv*), a good star melodrama.
w W. R. Burnett, James R. Webb story Frank J. Collins d Lewis Allen ph Peverell Marley m Max Steiner
☆ Edward G. Robinson, Nina Foch, Albert Dekker, Hugh Marlowe, Jayne Mansfield, Howard St John, Ellen Corby
'Hard-hitting stuff in the old gangster tradition.' – *MFB*

Illegal Entry

US   1949   84m   bw
Universal-International
Undercover agents investigate a smuggling racket.
Routine, quite entertaining alleged exposé.
w Joel Malone d Frederick de Cordova ph William H. Daniels
☆ Howard Duff, George Brent, Marta Toren, Tom Tully, Paul Stewart, Gar Moore

Illegal Traffic

US   1938   67m   bw
Paramount
The FBI tracks down an organization devoted to smuggling criminals away from danger.
Smart second feature based on J. Edgar Hoover's Persons in Hiding.
w Robert Yost, Lewis Foster, Stuart Anthony d Louis King
☆ J. Carrol Naish, Mary Carlisle, Robert Preston
'Good racketeer film … should do better than average business.' – *Variety*

Illegally Yours

US   1988   102m   Technicolor
UA/Crescent Moon/DEG (Peter Bogdanovich)
A juror sets out to prove the innocence of a woman he has loved from afar, who is accused of murder and blackmail.
Screwed-up attempt at a screwball comedy, painful to watch.
w M. A. Stewart, Max Dickens d Peter Bogdanovich ph Dante Spinotti m Phil Marshall pd Jane Musky ed Richard Fields, Ronald Krehel
☆ Rob Lowe, Colleen Camp, Kenneth Mars, Harry Carey Jnr, Kim Myers, Marshall Colt

Illicit

US   1931   81m   bw
Warner
A disillusioned wife walks out on her husband and seeks solace elsewhere.
Undistinguished weepie, which later became Ex-Lady.
w Harvey Thew d Archie Mayo
☆ Barbara Stanwyck, Ricardo Cortez, Joan Blondell, Charles Butterworth
'Lacks a wallop and action.' – *Variety*

'Don't dare stare …'
The Illustrated Man *

US   1969   103m   Technicolor   Panavision
Warner/SKM (Howard B. Kreitsek, Ted Mann)
A strange wanderer tells weird stories based on the tattooed pictures which cover him from tip to toe.
Oddball compendium based rather insecurely on Ray Bradbury stories; in this form they don't amount to much but the presentation is assured.
w Howard B. Kreitsek d Jack Smight ph Philip Lathrop m Jerry Goldsmith ad Joel Schiller
☆ Rod Steiger, Claire Bloom, Robert Drivas, Don Dubbins, Jason Evers
'A curiously passionless affair – efficient enough, meaty enough, but without poetry, without charm, without beauty.' – *Philip Strick*
'A pretentious comic strip of maudlin and muddled fantasies.' – *Judith Crist*

Illustrious Corpses *

Italy/France   1975   120m   Technicolor
PEA/UA (Alberto Grimaldi)
original title: *Cadaveri Eccellenti*
A right-wing conspiracy to arouse feelings against dissidents is found to be behind the murders of public figures.
Elegant police melodrama on an unlikely political thesis.
w Francesco Rosi, Tonino Guerra, Lino Jannuzzi novel *Il Contesto* by Leonardo Sciascia d Francesco Rosi ph Pasqualino de Santis m Piero Piccioni
☆ Lino Ventura, Alain Cuny, Paolo Bonacelli, Marcel Bozzuffi, Max von Sydow, Fernando Rey, Charles Vanel, Tina Aumont
'Like watching layer after layer peeled off some diseased flower until the poisoned root is reached.' – *Michael Billington, Illustrated London News*

I'm All Right Jack ***

GB   1959   104m   bw
British Lion/Charter (Roy Boulting)
A world-innocent graduate takes a job in industry; by starting at the bottom he provokes a national strike.
Satirical farce which manages to hit most of its widespread targets and finds corruption in high, low and middle places. A not inaccurate picture of aspects of British life in the fifties, and a presage of the satire boom to come with Beyond the Fringe *and* That Was The Week That Was.
w Frank Harvey, John Boulting novel *Private Life* by Alan Hackney d John Boulting ph Max Greene m Ken Hare

☆ Ian Carmichael, Peter Sellers, Irene Handl, Richard Attenborough, Terry-Thomas, Dennis Price, Margaret Rutherford, Liz Fraser, John Le Mesurier, Sam Kydd
✏ Peter Sellers; screenplay

I'm Dancing as Fast as I Can

US   1982   106m   Movielab
Paramount/Edgar J. Scherick/Scott Rudin
A documentary film-maker is rehabilitated after dependence on drugs.
Unabsorbing case history more suitable as a TV movie except that the acting for TV would not have been so far over the top.
w David Rabe book Barbara Gordon d Jack Hofsiss ph Jan de Bont m Stanley Silverman
☆ Jill Clayburgh, Nicol Williamson, Dianne Wiest, Joe Pesci, Geraldine Page, James Sutorius, Richard Masur, Kathleen Widdoes

I'm from Missouri

US   1939   77m   bw
Paramount
The wife of a Missouri farmer and mule breeder has social aspirations.
Rural comedy patterned after the Will Rogers successes.
w John C. Moffitt, Duke Atterbury d Theodore Reed
☆ Bob Burns, Gladys George, Gene Lockhart, Judith Barrett, William Henry, Patricia Morison, E. E. Clive, Melville Cooper
'Moderate grosser for family trade.' – *Variety*

I'm Gonna Git You, Sucka

US   1988   89m   DeLuxe
UIP/United Artists/Ivory Way/Raymond Katz/Front Films (Peter McCarthy, Carl Craig)
Black heroes are recruited to overthrow a white gangster.
Good-natured parody of black action movies such as Shaft.
wd Keenen Ivory Wayans ph Tom Richmond m David Michael Frank pd Melba Farquhar, Catherine Hardwicke ed Michael R. Miller
☆ Keenen Ivory Wayans, Bernie Casey, Antonio Fargas, Steve James, Isaac Hayes, Jim Brown, Ja'Net DuBois, Dawn Lewis, John Vernon, Clu Gulager

Im Innern des Wals: see *In the Belly of the Whale*

Im Lauf der Zeit: see *Kings of the Road*

'Just a sensitive gal who climbed the ladder of success … wrong by wrong! A story about a gal who lost her reputation – and never missed it!'
I'm No Angel ***

US   1933   88m   bw
Paramount (William Le Baron)
A carnival dancer gets off a murder charge, moves into society and sues a man for breach of promise.
The star's most successful vehicle, credited with saving the fortunes of Paramount, remains a highly diverting side show with almost a laugh a minute. Released before the Legion of Decency was formed, it also contains some of Mae's fruitiest lines.
w Mae West d Wesley Ruggles ph Leo Tover m/ly Harvey Brooks, Gladys Dubois
☆ Mae West, Edward Arnold, Cary Grant, Gregory Ratoff, Ralf Harolde, Kent Taylor, Gertrude Michael
'The most freewheeling of all Mae's screen vehicles, and the most satisfying of the lot.' – *James Robert Parish*
'A quality of balance and proportion which only the finest films attain.' – *Views and Reviews*

I'm Not Rappaport

US   1996   135m   DuArt
Gramercy/Greenstreet (John Penotti, John Starke)
Two 80-year-olds are determined not to go gentle into that good night.
Capable, sweetly comic performances from Matthau and Davis add a little humanity to what is a contrived and often implausible narrative.
wd Herb Gardner play Herb Gardner ph Adam Holender m Gerry Mulligan pd Mark Friedberg ed Wendey Stanzler, Emily Paine

☆ Walter Matthau, Ossie Davis, Amy Irving, Martha Plimpton, Craig T. Nelson, Boyd Gaines
'An uncomfortable mix of slap-shtick and social commentary, with the passage of time having dulled the story's sense of humor.' – *Leonard Klady, Variety*

Images

Eire   1972   101m   Technicolor   Panavision
Lions Gate/Hemdale (Tommy Thompson)
A semi-hysterical woman is confronted by the images of her former lovers.
Pretentious psycho-drama which might have made a good half-hour.
wd Robert Altman ph Vilmos Zsigmond m John Williams
☆ Susannah York, René Auberjonois, Marcel Bozzuffi
ß John Williams

'When a father doesn't live up to his dreams … a daughter has to stand up for hers.'

Imaginary Crimes *

US   1994   105m   colour
Warner/Morgan Creek (James G. Robinson)
◉ 🎬
A con man, forever dreaming of riches around the corner, struggles to bring up his two daughters after their mother dies.
Nostalgic reminiscence, seen from the viewpoint of a teenager and embryonic writer, in which love conquers all.
w Kristine Johnson, Davia Nelson book Sheila Ballantyne d Anthony Drazan ph John J. Campbell m Stephen Endelman pd Joseph T. Garrity ed Elizabeth Kling
☆ Harvey Keitel, Fairuza Balk, Kelly Lynch, Vincent D'Onofrio, Diane Baker, Chris Penn, Amber Benson, Seymour Cassel, Annette O'Toole
'The script has stretches of pure corn and the plot mechanics get in the way of genuine feeling. The movie tries hard, but it's far too slight to click on the big screen.' – *Kim Newman, Empire*

Imaginary Sweetheart: see *Professional Sweetheart*

An Imaginary Tale

France   1990   100m   colour
Mayfair/C. M. Luca/Télescène/National Film Board of Canada (Claudio Luca, Robin Spry)
French title: *Une histoire inventée*
In Montreal, a jazz trumpeter falls in love with an actress, to the annoyance of her actor-lover.
Performances of Shakespeare's Othello form a background to this tale of jealousy, treated as comic rather than tragic.
w André Forcier, Jacques Marcotte d André Forcier ph George Dufaux m Serge Fiore ad Réal Ouellette ed François Gill
☆ Jean Lapointe, Louise Marleau, Charlotte Laurier, Marc Messier, Jean-François Pichette, France Castel, Tony Nardi
'Too hermetic to be much more than a light diversion.' – *Sight and Sound*

Imitation General

US   1958   88m   bw
MGM (William Hawks)
France 1944: when a general is killed, a sergeant takes his place to preserve morale.
Odd, rather unpalatable war comedy-drama.
w William Bowers d George Marshall ph George Folsey
☆ Glenn Ford, Red Buttons, Taina Elg, Dean Jones, Kent Smith

Imitation of Life **

US   1934   109m   bw
Universal (John M. Stahl)
A woman becomes rich through the pancake recipe of her black servant, but the latter has a tragic life because her daughter passes for white.
Monumentally efficient tearjerker, generally well done.
w William Hurlbut novel Fannie Hurst d John Stahl ph Merritt Gerstad m Heinz Roemheld
☆ *Claudette Colbert*, Warren William, *Louise Beavers*, Ned Sparks, Rochelle Hudson, Fredi Washington, Alan Hale, Henry Armetta
'Grim and harsh stuff … its reception in the south cannot be judged or guessed by a northerner.' – *Variety*
'Classic, compulsively watchable rags-to-riches-and-heartbreak weeper.' – *New Yorker, 1977*
ß best picture

Imitation of Life *

US   1959   124m   Eastmancolor
U-I (Ross Hunter)
🔲
Glossy remake of the above with its heroine now an actress; stunningly produced but dully acted, making its racially sensitive plot seem insincere.
w Eleanore Griffin, Allan Scott d Douglas Sirk ph Russell Metty m Frank Skinner
☆ Lana Turner, Juanita Moore, John Gavin, Susan Kohner, Dan O'Herlihy, Sandra Dee, Robert Alda
ß Juanita Moore; Susan Kohner

Immaculate Conception *

GB   1991   120m   Metrocolor
Feature/Dehlavi Films/Film on Four (Jamil Dehlavi)
🔳
In Pakistan, a childless American woman is told that she will conceive if she returns to a shrine with her English husband, although she suspects him of having an affair with an Indian friend.
Tangled tale of adultery amid a clash of cultures, rendered exotic by its setting of a fertility cult administered by priestly eunuchs.
wd Jamil Dehlavi ph Nic Knowland m Richard Harvey ad Mike Porter ed Chris Barnes
☆ James Wilby, Melissa Leo, Shabana Azmi, Zia Mohyeddin, James Cossins, Shreeram Lagoo, Ronny Jhutti, Tim Choate

Immediate Family

US   1989   95m   DeLuxe
Columbia (Sarah Pillsbury, Midge Sanford)
◉ 🔲 🎬
A rich but childless couple arrange to adopt the newborn baby of a poor, unmarried teenager.
Well-meaning, predictable problem movie that fails to involve an audience.
w Barbara Benedek d Jonathan Kaplan ph John W. Lindley m Brad Fiedel ed Jane Kurson
☆ Glenn Close, James Woods, Mary Stuart Masterson, Kevin Dillon, Linda Darlow, Jane Greer, Jessica James

The Immigrant **

🎬🎬 US   1917   20m   bw   silent
Mutual
A penniless immigrant befriends a girl on the boat and later helps her in a café.
One of the most inventive early Chaplins, with touches of sentiment and social comment which for once only strengthen and do not antagonize.
wd Charles Chaplin ph William C. Foster, Rollie Totheroh
☆ Charles Chaplin, Edna Purviance, Albert Austin, Henry Bergman, Eric Campbell
'In its roughness and apparent simplicity it is as much a jewel as a story by O. Henry.' – *Photoplay*

Immoral Tales

France   1974   103m   Eastmancolor
Argos (Anatole Dauman)
Four bawdy stories, ranging from 1498 to 1970.
The usual sex portmanteau with a little more strength in the detail and interest in human behaviour than usual.
wd Walerian Borowczyk ph Bernard Daillencourt, Guy Durban, Michel Zolat, Noel Véry m Maurice Le Roux
☆ Lise Danvers, Charlotte Alexandra, Paloma Picasso, Florence Bellamy
'You come out having learned something about the waywardness of life and love and having been taken on a mystery tour into the present, the past, and the enigmatic strangeness of womanhood.' – *Michael Billington, Illustrated London News*

Immortal Battalion: see *The Way Ahead*

'The genius behind the music. The madness behind the man. The untold love story of Ludwig Van Beethoven.'

Immortal Beloved

GB/US   1994   120m   colour   Panavision
Entertainment/Majestic/Icon (Bruce Davey)
◉ 🔲 🎬 ♫ 🎧
Beethoven's secretary seeks to discover the identity of the mysterious woman that the unmarried Beethoven loved.
A narrative told in flashbacks to the women who played a part in Beethoven's life; the result is a standard and not particularly convincing portrait of the artist as a tortured genius.

wd Bernard Rose ph Peter Suschitzky m Beethoven md Sir Georg Solti pd Jiri Hlupy ed Dan Rae
☆ Gary Oldman, Jeroen Krabbe, Johanna Ter Steege, Isabella Rossellini, Marco Hofschneider, Valeria Golino, Matthew North, Miriam Margolyes
'Less than compelling due to the fragmentary telling of the story, off-putting nature of the main character and the failure of the filmmakers to make their investigation seem of any particular consequence.' – *Todd McCarthy, Variety*
'The whole thing is just this side of ludicrous.' – *Derek Malcolm, Guardian*

Immortal Sergeant *

US   1943   90m   bw
TCF (Lamar Trotti)
In the North African campaign, a battle-toughened sergeant is killed after inspiring the raw recruits under his command.
'Inspirational' war adventure, quite neatly done but a shade embarrassed by its own poetic leanings.
w Lamar Trotti novel John Brophy d John Stahl ph Arthur Miller m David Buttolph
☆ Henry Fonda, Thomas Mitchell, Maureen O'Hara, Allyn Joslyn, Reginald Gardiner, Melville Cooper, Bramwell Fletcher, Morton Lowry
'By the time the first soldier has bit the sand, the film identifies itself: it is none other than Hollywood's old friend the Foreign Legion of Beau Geste vintage, jerked from the shelf and clothed in a new uniform.' – *Time*

The Immortal Story

France   1968   60m   Eastmancolor
Albina/ORTF (Micheline Rozan)
🔲
In 19th-century Macao, a rich merchant tries to make an old seaman's story come true.
Muddled and stiltedly told fable which would have excited no attention if it had not been associated with the elusive Mr Welles.
wd Orson Welles story Isak Dinesen ph Willy Kurant m Erik Satie
☆ Orson Welles, Jeanne Moreau, Roger Coggio, Norman Eshley

Impact

US   1949   111m   bw
(UA)
🔲
A woman and her lover plan the murder of her rich industrialist husband, but things go wrong and the husband survives under another name…
Curiously elongated but watchable melodrama, with the impression of a second team doing its best.
w Dorothy Reid d Arthur Lubin ph Ernest Laszlo
☆ Brian Donlevy, Ella Raines, Charles Coburn, Helen Walker, Anna May Wong

Impact

GB   1963   61m   bw
Butcher's (John I. Phillips)
An investigative reporter is framed by a crooked night-club owner.
Efficient, unmemorable second feature.
w Conrad Phillips, Peter Maxwell d Peter Maxwell ph Gerald Moss m Johnny Gregory ad Harry White ed David Hawkins
☆ Conrad Phillips, George Pastell, Ballard Berkeley, Linda Marlowe, Richard Klee, Anita West

The Impatient Maiden

US   1932   78m   bw
Universal
A romantic maidservant learns the difference between life and fantasy.
Solidly made comedy-drama which doesn't seem to have inspired its director.
w Richard Schayer, Winifred Dunn novel The Impatient Virgin by Donald Henderson Clarke d James Whale
☆ Mae Clarke, Lew Ayres, Una Merkel, John Halliday, Andy Devine, Berton Churchill
'Trashy stuff … aims at smartness and sophistication, and achieves but crudity.' – *Variety*

The Impatient Years

US   1944   91m   bw
Columbia (Virginia Van Upp)
A soldier finds difficulty in adjusting to his civilian matrimonial state.
Thin star comedy.
w Virginia Van Upp d Irving Cummings ph Hal Mohr m Marlin Skiles
☆ Jean Arthur, Lee Bowman, Charles Coburn, Edgar Buchanan, Harry Davenport, Grant Mitchell, Jane Darwell

The Imperfect Lady: see *The Perfect Gentleman (1935)*

'Scandal seeks her out – even on her wedding night!'

The Imperfect Lady

US   1946   97m   bw
Paramount (Karl Tunberg)
GB title: *Mrs Loring's Secret*
In 1890s London, an MP marries a lady with a past.
Dusty melodrama, adequately produced.
w Karl Tunberg story Ladislas Fodor d Lewis Allen ph John F. Seitz m Victor Young
☆ Ray Milland, Teresa Wright, Cedric Hardwicke, Virginia Field, Anthony Quinn, Reginald Owen, Melville Cooper, George Zucco, Rhys Williams, Charles Coleman, Miles Mander, Edmund Breon, Frederick Worlock
'To be avoided at any cost.' – *Graham Greene*

The Impersonator *

GB   1961   64m   bw
Bryanston/Herald (Anthony Perry)
Americans at a British air base are suspected when a murderous prowler strikes.
Well made second-feature thriller with effective locations, suspense sequences and village atmosphere.
wd Alfred Shaughnessy ph John Coquillon m de Wolfe
☆ John Crawford, Jane Griffiths, Patricia Burke, John Salew

The Importance of Being Earnest **

GB   1952   95m   Technicolor
Rank/Javelin/Two Cities (Teddy Baird)
🔲
Two wealthy and eligible bachelors of the 1890s have problems with their marriage prospects.
Disappointingly stagey rendering (when compared, say, with Occupe-toi d'Amélie) of Britain's most wondrously witty lighter-than-air comedy of manners. As a record of a theatrical performance, however, it is valuable.
w Anthony Asquith play Oscar Wilde d Anthony Asquith ph Desmond Dickinson m Benjamin Frankel ad Carmen Dillon
☆ Michael Redgrave, Michael Denison, Edith Evans, Margaret Rutherford, Joan Greenwood, Miles Malleson, Dorothy Tutin, Walter Hudd
'A more positive decision on style should have been taken. A film of this kind must be either an adaptation or a piece of filmed theatre. This one, being partially both, is not wholly either.' – *Gavin Lambert*

The Impossible Lover: see *Huddle*

Impossible Object: see *Story of a Love Story*

The Impossible Years

US   1968   98m   Metrocolor   Panavision
MGM/Marten (Lawrence Weingarten)
A university psychiatrist has trouble controlling his nubile 17-year-old daughter.
Wacky farce which veers between the tasteless and the ludicrous, and is never more than momentarily entertaining.
w George Wells play Bob Fisher, Arthur Marx d Michael Gordon ph William H. Daniels m Don Costa
☆ David Niven, Lola Albright, Chad Everett, Ozzie Nelson, Cristina Ferrare, Don Beddoe
'A comedy of the generation gap which didn't bridge it but fell right into it.' – *Gerald Garrett*

'A musical, magical, cross-dressing, mistaken identity, cream puff-eating, hidden bomb kind of comedy!'

The Imposters *
US   1998   101m   Technicolor
TCF/Fox Searchlight/First Cold Press (Beth Alexander, Stanley Tucci)
♀
In the 30s, two out-of-work actors pretend to be stewards after they become inadvertent stowaways on an Atlantic liner.
An energetic farce of false identities and elaborate plots, which is enjoyable for as long as it lasts, though it hardly amounts to a successful revival of screwball comedy.
wd Stanley Tucci ph Ken Kelsch m Gary DeMichele pd Andrew Jackness ed Suzy Elmiger
☆ Oliver Platt, Stanley Tucci, Teagle F. Bougere, Elizabeth Bracco, Steve Buscemi, Billy Connolly, Allan Corduner, Hope Davis, Dana Ivey, Alfred Molina, Isabella Rossellini, Campbell Scott
  'More than a dozen of New York's finest actors ham it up with such unrestrained glee ... that it hardly matters if this swirl of cotton candy disappears even before it touches the tip of your tongue.' – *Stephen Holden, New York Times*
† Woody Allen appears uncredited.

The Impostor
US   1944   92m   bw
Universal
TV title: *Strange Confession*
A French convict escapes during a Nazi bombing raid, and in the guise of a dead man fights bravely for France.
Propagandist melodrama, more stiffly made than its talent would suggest.
wd Julien Duvivier
☆ Jean Gabin, Ellen Drew, Richard Whorf, Allyn Joslyn, Peter Van Eyck, Ralph Morgan

Impromptu *
GB   1989   107m   colour
Rank/Sovereign/Governor/Les Films Ariane (Stuart Oken, Daniel A. Sherkow)
▦ ▦ ♀
George Sand chases after Chopin to a country house-party and succeeds in seducing him later in Paris.
Lively re-telling of a well-known romance, but the modern, slangy dialogue makes it seem like a fancy-dress party, and it runs out of energy halfway through.
w Sarah Kernochan d James Lapine ph Bruno de Keyzer md Chris Walker ad Gérard Daoudal ed Michael Ellis
☆ Judy Davis, Hugh Grant, Mandy Patinkin, Bernadette Peters, Julian Sands, Ralph Brown, Georges Corraface, Anton Rodgers, Emma Thompson, Anna Massey
  'Not wholly successful, this is nevertheless a surprisingly perky addition to the mainly dreary catalogue of films about the loves of deadweight famous names from the past.' – *Kim Newman, MFB*

Improper Channels
Canada   1979   91m   colour
▦ ▦
A father runs into administrative trouble when he takes his injured daughter to hospital.
Salutary but not very commanding tale for our times, with a leading performance that suffers from overfamiliarity.
w Morrie Rubinsky, Ian Sutherland, Adam Arkin d Eric Till ph Anthony Richmond m Maribeth Solomon, Micky Erbe
☆ Alan Arkin, Mariette Hartley, Monica Parker, Harry Ditson

Improper Conduct
US   1994   95m   colour
Everest (Victor Bhalla/Jag Mundhra)
▦ ▦
A woman decides to expose the sleazy married marketing man whose sexual harassment led to the death of her sister.
Uninteresting thriller, which exemplifies its theme of exploitation by including many scenes of voyeuristic and gratuitous sexual activity.
w Carl Austin story Jag Mundhra d Jag Mundhra ph James Michaels m Alan Dermarderosian pd Brian McCabe ed Wayne Schmidt, David Schulman
☆ Steven Bauer, Tahnee Welch, John Laughlin, Nia Peeples, Lee Anne Beaman, Stuart Whitman

An Impudent Girl **
France   1985   97m   colour
Artificial Eye/Oliane/A2/Telema/Monthyon (Marie-Laure Reyre)
▦
original title: *L'Effrontée*
An awkward 13-year-old girl begins to grow up.
Charming film of adolescent trauma, owing much to Carson McCuller's The Member of the Wedding and superior to the US movie version.
w Claude Miller, Luc Beraud, Bernard Stora, Annie Miller d Claude Miller ph Dominique Chapuis m Alain Jomy pd Jean-Pierre Kohut Svelko ed Albert Jurgenson
☆ Charlotte Gainsbourg, Bernadette Lafont, Jean-Claude Brialy, Raoul Billerey, Clothilde Baudon, Jean-Philippe Ecoffey

Impulse
US   1984   99m   DeLuxe
Tim Zinnemann/ABC Motion Pictures
▦ ▦ ▦
After an earthquake, a small farming community is menaced by a mysterious subterranean substance which makes people self-destructive.
Modest, mildly humorous sci-fi which has its fun without explaining anything at all.
w Bart Davis, Don Carlos Dunaway d Graham Baker
☆ Tim Matheson, Meg Tilly, Hume Cronyn, John Karlen, Amy Stryker

Impulse
US   1990   108m   Technicolor
Warner (Albert S. Ruddy, André Morgan)
▦ ▦ ▦
An undercover cop keeps quiet about the murder of a missing witness.
Implausible thriller.
w John de Marco, Leigh Chapman d Sondra Locke ph Dean Semler m Michel Colombier pd William A. Elliott ed John W. Wheeler
☆ Theresa Russell, Jeff Fahey, George Dzundza, Alan Rosenberg, Nicholas Mele, Eli Danker, Charles McCaughan, Lynne Thigpen, Shawn Elliott

In a Lonely Place *
US   1950   93m   bw
Columbia/Santana (Robert Lord)
An embittered Hollywood scriptwriter escapes a murder charge but loses his girlfriend through his violent temperament.
Curious character melodrama which intrigues without satisfying.
w Andrew Solt novel Dorothy B. Hughes d Nicholas Ray ph Burnett Guffey m George Antheil
☆ Humphrey Bogart, Gloria Grahame, Frank Lovejoy, Carl Benton Reid, Art Smith, Jeff Donnell
  'It remains better than average, but lacks the penetration which would make it really interesting.' – *Gavin Lambert*

In a Year with 13 Moons
West Germany   1978   124m   colour
Tango/Project/Filmverlag der Autoren
▦
original title: *In einem Jahr mit 13 Monden*
Ordeals of a man who undergoes a sex change.
Unattractive case history with expressionist decoration.
wd Rainer Werner Fassbinder ph Rainer Werner Fassbinder m Peter Raben
☆ Volker Spengler, Ingrid Caven, Gottfried John, Elisabeth Trissenaar, Eva Mattes

'An Out-and-Out Comedy.'
In & Out *
US   1997   90m   DeLuxe
Paramount/Spelling Films (Scott Rudin)
▦ ▦ ▦
Just before his wedding, a small-town teacher is 'outed' as a homosexual during a speech by a former pupil, now a Hollywood star, as he accepts an Oscar.
Brisk, mildly amusing comedy that is careful not to offend.
w Paul Rudnick d Frank Oz ph Rob Hahn m Mark Shaiman pd Ken Adam ed Dan Hanley, John Jympson
☆ Kevin Kline, Joan Cusack, Matt Dillon, Debbie Reynolds, Wilford Brimley, Bob Newhart, Tom Selleck

'A screwball comedy that is always genial and often hilarious.' – *Stephen Amidon, Sunday Times*
† The inspiration for the comedy was a speech made by Tom Hanks when accepting an Oscar for *Philadelphia*.
†† Glenn Close, Whoopi Goldberg and Jay Leno appear as themselves.
♀ Joan Cusack

In Bed with Madonna: see *Truth or Dare*

In Caliente
US   1935   85m   bw
Warner
In a Mexican horse racing resort, a dancer falls for the magazine editor who criticized her act.
Very slim storyline fails to make this a major musical despite attractive numbers including 'The Lady in Red'.
w Jerry Wald, Julius Epstein d Lloyd Bacon ph Sol Polito, George Barnes m/ly various ch Busby Berkeley
☆ Dolores del Rio, Pat O'Brien, Edward Everett Horton, Leo Carrillo, Glenda Farrell, Judy Canova, Phil Regan, Wini Shaw, Herman Bing

In Celebration
GB   1974   131m   Eastmancolor
Ely Landau/Cinevision
Three sons travel north for their miner father's fortieth wedding anniversary.
Sharply observant but fairly predictable dramatics, plainly filmed.
w David Storey play David Storey d Lindsay Anderson ph Dick Bush m Christopher Gunning
☆ Alan Bates, James Bolam, Brian Cox, Constance Chapman, Bill Owen

In Cold Blood ***
US   1967   134m   bw   Panavision
Columbia/Richard Brooks
▦ ▦
An account of a real life crime in which an entire family was brutally murdered by wandering gunmen.
Unnecessarily complicated as narrative, and uncompromisingly brutal in treatment, this well-meaning film is hard to take in many ways.
wd Richard Brooks book Truman Capote ph Conrad Hall m Quincy Jones
☆ Robert Blake, Scott Wilson, John Forsythe, Paul Stewart, Gerald S. O'Loughlin, Jeff Corey
  'It marks a slight step up for its director, best remembered for reducing *Lord Jim* to pablum and *The Brothers Karamazov* to pulp.' – *John Simon*
† It was remade as an 180m TV mini-series in 1990, directed by Jonathan Kaplan and starring Anthony Edwards and Eric Roberts.
♀ Richard Brooks (as writer); Richard Brooks (as director); Conrad Hall; Quincy Jones

In Country
US   1989   115m   DuArt
Warner (Norman Jewison, Richard Roth)
▦ ▦ ▦
A young girl attempts to discover more about her father, a soldier who died in Vietnam.
Mundane account of a child coming to terms with her life.
w Frank Pierson, Cynthia Cidre novel Bobbie Ann Mason d Norman Jewison ph Russell Boyd m James Horner pd Jackson DeGovia ed Antony Gibbs, Lou Lombardo
☆ Bruce Willis, Emily Lloyd, Joan Allen, Kevin Anderson, Richard Hamilton, Judith Ivey, Peggy Rea, John Terry, Dan Jenkins

In Custody
GB   1993   120m   Technicolor
Merchant Ivory/Channel 4 (Walid Chowhan)
A teacher, sent to interview the greatest living poet of the dying Urdu language, finds that his hero is a broken-down drunk.
A stately, uninvolving examination of an urgent topic, that of tradition losing out to commerce and debased culture.
w Anita Desai, Shahrukh Husain novel Anita Desai d Ismail Merchant ph Larry Pizer m Zakir Hussain, Ustad Sultan Khan pd Suresh Sawant ed Roberto Silvi
☆ Shashi Kapoor, Om Puri, Shabana Azmi, Sushma Seth, Neena Gupta, Prayag Raj, Tinnu Anand
  'As for Merchant, perhaps he should stick to producing.' – *Robin Brooks, Empire*

'What started as a dream, ended as a nightmare.'
In Dreams
US   1999   99m   Technicolor   'Scope
DreamWorks (Stephen Woolley)
♀
A mother finds that she can communicate in dreams with the serial killer who murdered her young daughter.
Unattractive psychological thriller that begins on a note of hysteria and remains on that high-pitched level throughout.
w Bruce Robinson, Neil Jordan novel *Doll's Eyes* by Bari Wood d Neil Jordan ph Darius Khondji m Elliot Goldenthal pd Nigel Phelps ed Tony Lawson
☆ Annette Bening, Aidan Quinn, Robert Downey Jnr, Paul Guilfoyle, Dennis Boutsikaris, Stephen Rea, Prudence Wright Holmes, Katie Sagona
  'A silly and unpleasant psycho-chiller.' – *Peter Bradshaw, Guardian*

In Enemy Country
US   1968   107m   Techniscope
Universal (Harry Keller)
In 1939 Paris, the French secret service evolves an elaborate four-year undercover plan.
Standard, overlong espionage melodrama with no surprises.
w Edward Anhalt story Sy Bartlett d Harry Keller ph Loyal Griggs m William Lava
☆ Tony Franciosa, Anjanette Comer, Guy Stockwell, Paul Hubschmid, Tom Bell, Harry Townes, Michael Constantine, John Marley

'To Some, Losing Control Is ... Everything.'
In Excess
Italy   1991   94m   Fotocinema
Metrofilm/PAC (Galliano Juso)
▦
An English screenwriter grows increasingly jealous of his wife after she insists on spending her weekends with a sadistic lover.
Glossy, sterile, would-be erotic thriller that fails to satisfy on any level.
w Sergio Bazzini novel Alberto Moravia d Mauro Bolognini ph Giuseppi Lanci m Ennio Morricone pd Claudio Cinini ed Sergio Montanari
☆ Julian Sands, Joanna Pacula, Tcheky Karyo, Lara Wendel, Mario Di Stefano
  'A pretentious Euro-production which shifts between haunting lyricism and self-indulgence.' – *Sight and Sound*
  'Humourless tosh.' – *Empire*

In Gay Madrid
US   1930   78m   bw
MGM
A Spanish blade is torn between two women.
Feeble star vehicle, presumably aimed at the Spanish market.
w Bess Meredyth, Edwin Justus Mayer, Salisbury Field novel Alejandro Perez Lugin d Robert Z. Leonard
☆ Ramon Novarro, Dorothy Jordan, Lottice Howell, Claude King, Eugenie Besserer
  'Unreal story, poor acting, ditto direction and general lack of popular appeal.' – *Variety*

In God We Trust
US   1980   97m   Technicolor
Universal
A monk leaves his monastery to raise some ready cash.
Dismal and tasteless attempt at religious satire.
w Marty Feldman, Chris Allen d Marty Feldman ph Charles Correll m John Morris
☆ Marty Feldman, Peter Boyle, Louise Lasser, Richard Pryor, Wilfrid Hyde-White
  'A rare achievement – a comedy with no laughs. Its energy is prodigious. But only rarely is it matched by invention.' – *Variety*

In Harm's Way *
US   1965   167m   bw   Panavision
Paramount/Sigma (Otto Preminger)
▦ ▦ ▦
The American navy retaliates after Pearl Harbor.
Odd mix of all-star action, spectacle (mostly models) and personal romances, with a few interesting scenes; shorn of colour it seems rather half-hearted.
w Wendell Mayes novel James Bassett d Otto Preminger ph Loyal Griggs m Jerry Goldsmith titles Saul Bass

---

☆ John Wayne, Kirk Douglas, Patricia Neal, Tom Tryon, Paula Prentiss, Brandon de Wilde, Stanley Holloway, Burgess Meredith, Henry Fonda, Dana Andrews, Franchot Tone, Jill Haworth, George Kennedy, Hugh O'Brian, Carroll O'Connor and also Patrick O'Neal, Slim Pickens, Bruce Cabot, Larry Hagman, James Mitchum

'Lacks even a touch of the touch.' – *Stanley Kauffmann*

♫ Loyal Griggs

♔ Patricia Neal

In Like Flint

US   1967   107m   DeLuxe   Cinemascope

TCF (Saul David)

▦ ⊘ ♫

Top agent Derek Flint unmasks a subversive female spy ring which has kidnapped the President.

This sequel to Our Man Flint (qv) is silly rather than funny, a spy spoof which becomes irritatingly hard to take.

w Hal Fimberg   d Gordon Douglas   ph William Daniels   m Jerry Goldsmith

☆ James Coburn, Lee J. Cobb, Jean Hale, Andrew Duggan, Anna Lee

'It gently founders in yards of flat dialogue, lavishly uninteresting sets, fuzzy colour processing, and a supporting cast in which all the girls look alarmingly mass produced.' – *MFB*

In Love and War

US   1958   111m   Eastmancolor Cinemascope

TCF (Jerry Wald)

Three men from different backgrounds join the US Marines and see service in the Pacific.

Self-conscious propaganda concoction of bare routine interest.

w Edward Anhalt   *novel* Anton Myrer   d Philip Dunne   ph Leo Tover   m Hugo Friedhofer

☆ Jeffrey Hunter, Robert Wagner, Bradford Dillman, Dana Wynter, Hope Lange, Sheree North, France Nuyen

'In war they found each other ... In each other they found love...'

In Love and War *

US   1996   115m   Rank Colour   Panavision

Entertainment/New Line/Dimitri Villard

▦ ▤ ⊘ ♫

In Italy during the First World War, the 18-year-old Ernest Hemingway falls in love with a 26-year-old nurse.

Oddly stilted account of an experience that seems to have had a lasting effect on Hemingway; it's just a story of a sentimental interlude between a boy and a woman.

w Allan Scott, Clancy Sigal, Anna Hamilton Phelan   *book* Hemingway in Love and War by Henry S. Villard, James Nagel   d Richard Attenborough   ph Roger Pratt   m George Fenton   pd Stuart Craig   ed Lesley Walker

☆ Sandra Bullock, Chris O'Donnell, Mackenzie Astin, Ingrid Lacey, Emilio Bonucci, Margot Steinberg, Colin Stinton, Ian Kelly

'Doesn't get under the skin of its protagonists, leaving the viewer unmoved and passably interested at best.' – *Todd McCarthy, Variety*

In Name Only *

US   1939   94m   bw

RKO (Pandro S. Berman)

▦ ▤

A rich man falls in love but his wife refuses a divorce.

The stars seem unhappy in this sombre matrimonial drama, but of its kind it's surprisingly well made.

w Richard Sherman   *novel* Memory of Love by Bessie Brewer   d John Cromwell   ph J. Roy Hunt   m Roy Webb

☆ Cary Grant, Carole Lombard, Kay Francis, Charles Coburn, Helen Vinson

'Sock romantic drama ... will get maximum playing time and the best dating the country offers.' – *Variety*

'Shot with a refined taste for interior decoration ... it is oversweetened with the material for tears.' – *Graham Greene*

'The talking picture reaches perfection!'

In Old Arizona **

US   1929   95m   bw

Fox

Adventures of the Cisco Kid.

Primitive sound Western, a sensation in its day but now of purely historical interest.

w Tom Barry   *stories* O. Henry   d Raoul Walsh, Irving Cummings   ph Arthur Edeson

☆ Warner Baxter, Edmund Lowe, Dorothy Burgess, J. Farrell MacDonald

† See also *The Cisco Kid*.

♟ Warner Baxter

♟ best picture; Tom Barry; Irving Cummings; Arthur Edeson

In Old California

US   1942   89m   bw

Republic

▤ ⊘

A Boston pharmacist heads west towards gold rush California.

Moderate star Western with parsimonious budget.

w Gertrude Purcell, Frances Hyland   d William McGann

☆ John Wayne, Binnie Barnes, Albert Dekker, Helen Parrish, Patsy Kelly, Edgar Kennedy, Dick Purcell, Charles Halton

In Old Chicago ***

US   1937   115m   bw

TCF (Kenneth MacGowan)

▤

Events leading up to the great Chicago fire include a torrid romance between a gambler and a café singer.

Spectacular melodrama which with its two-million-dollar budget was a deliberate attempt to outdo San Francisco, and only failed because the cast was less interesting. A splendid studio super-production.

w Lamar Trotti, Sonya Levien   *novel* We the O'Learys by Niven Busch   d Henry King   ph Peverell Marley   md Louis Silvers   ad William Darling   ed Barbara McLean   sp H. Bruce Humberstone, Daniel B. Clark, Fred Sersen, Louis J. Witte, Ralph Hammeras

☆ Tyrone Power, Alice Faye, Don Ameche, *Alice Brady*, Andy Devine, Brian Donlevy, Phyllis Brooks, Tom Brown, Sidney Blackmer, Berton Churchill, Paul Hurst, Rondo Hatton, Eddie Collins

'Sock spectacle film ... an elaborate and liberally budgeted entertainment.' – *Variety*

♟ Alice Brady

♟ best picture; Niven Busch (original story); Louis Silvers

In Old Kentucky

US   1935   85m   bw

TCF (Edward Butcher)

A family feud is settled by a horse race.

Warm-hearted, old-fashioned stuff, and the star's last film.

w Sam Hellman, Gladys Lehman   *play* Charles T. Dazey   d George Marshall

☆ Will Rogers, Bill Robinson, Dorothy Wilson, Russell Hardie

In Old Mexico

US   1938   62m   bw

Paramount (Harry Sherman)

Hopalong Cassidy rides out in search of the outlaw who shot the son of a friend and is now trying to kill him.

Slow-moving Western, strictly for fans of our hero.

w Harrison Jacobs   d Edward D. Venturini   ph Russell Harlan   m Gregory Stone   ad Lewis J. Rachmil   ed Robert Warwick

☆ William Boyd, George Hayes, Russell Hayden, Paul Sutton, Allan Garcia, Jane Clayton, Glenn Strange

In Old Montana

US   1942   61m   bw

Equity (C. C. Burr)

In Montana in the 1880s, an army officer goes undercover to prevent a range war between cattlemen and sheep-herders.

Despite its theme, which is treated in a threadbare manner, the emphasis here is on songs and comedy, neither done with much style.

w Jackson Parks, Raymond K. Johnson, Homer King Gordon, Barney Hutchinson   d Raymond K. Johnson   ph Marcel Picard, Harvey Gould   ad Ben Berk   ed Charles Henkel

☆ Fred Scott, Jean Carmen, John Merton, Harry Harvey, Walter McGrail, Wheeler Oakman, Frank LaRue, Allen Cavan, Jane Keckley

† There is a continuity error early in the film, in which John Merton as the villain unbuttons his

shirt, removes his gunbelt and then unbuttons his shirt again.

In Old Oklahoma: see *War of the Wildcats*

In Our Time *

US   1944   110m   bw

Warner (Jerry Wald)

English girl marries Polish count and helps defy the Nazis.

Ambitious, would-be meaningful melodrama that doesn't quite come off.

w Ellis St Joseph, Howard Koch   d Vincent Sherman   ph Carl Guthrie   m Franz Waxman

☆ Ida Lupino, Paul Henreid, Nancy Coleman, Nazimova, Mary Boland, Victor Francen, Michael Chekhov

'The story starts a good many hares but prudently refrains from following them.' – *Richard Mallett, Punch*

In Person

US   1935   85m   bw

RKO (Pandro S. Berman)

▤ ⊘

A glamorous but exhausted film star tries to escape her public by fleeing incognito to the country.

Mild star comedy.

w Allan Scott   *novel* Samuel Hopkins Adams   d William A. Seiter   ph Edward Cronjager   m Roy Webb   *songs* Oscar Levant, Dorothy Fields

☆ Ginger Rogers, George Brent, Alan Mowbray, Grant Mitchell, Samuel S. Hinds, Spencer Charters

'Inept starring debut for Ginger Rogers ... a very weak affair.' – *Variety*

In Praise of Older Women

Canada   1978   108m   colour

Warner/Canadian Film Development/Famous Players & TSM Investments (Robert Lantos, Claude Héroux)

▤

A young Hungarian has affairs with older women in his homeland and, following the revolution, in Canada.

Episodic movie that soon becomes numbingly repetitious.

w Paul Gottlieb   *novel* Stephen Vizinczey   d George Kaczender   ph Miklos Lente   m Tibor Polgar   ad Wolf Kroeger   ed George Kaczender, Peter Wintonick

☆ Tom Berenger, Karen Black, Susan Strasberg, Helen Shaver, Marilyn Lightstone, Alexandra Stewart

In Rosie's Room: see *Rosie the Riveter*

In Search of Gregory

GB   1969   90m   Technicolor

Universal/Vic Films/Vera Films (Joe Janni, Daniele Senatore)

A girl attends her father's wedding to meet a mysterious guest named Gregory, whom she never quite contacts.

Irritatingly pretentious Pinterish puzzle-drama with apparently no hidden depths except the urge to be clever.

w Tonino Guerra, Lucile Laks   d Peter Wood   ph Otto Heller, Giorgio Tonti   m Ron Grainer

☆ Julie Christie, Michael Sarrazin, John Hurt, Adolfo Celi, Roland Culver, Tony Selby

'Moments in a vacuum: however lively the surface, the centre remains depressingly inert.' – *MFB*

'A thousand thrills ... and Hayley Mills'

In Search of the Castaways ***

⋔   GB   1961   100m   Technicolor

Walt Disney (Hugh Attwooll)

▤ ⊘

With the aid of an eccentric professor, three children seek their lost explorer father in some geographically fantastic regions of South America.

Engaging Victorian fantasy which starts realistically but builds up to sequences in the manner of The Wizard of Oz and concludes in Treasure Island vein. Jaunty juvenile fare.

w Lowell S. Hawley   *novel* Captain Grant's Children by Jules Verne   d Robert Stevenson   ph Paul Beeson   m William Alwyn   ad Michael Stringer

☆ Maurice Chevalier, Hayley Mills, George Sanders, Wilfrid Hyde-White, *Wilfrid Brambell*

In Society *

⋔   US   1944   74m   bw

Universal (Edmund Hartmann)

Two incompetent plumbers ruin a mansion.

One of the better A & C romps, with little padding between the comedy highlights, though the trimmings are fearsomely dated.

w John Grant, Hal Fimberg, Edmund L. Hartmann   d Jean Yarbrough   ph Jerome Ash   m Edgar Fairchild

☆ Bud Abbott, Lou Costello, Kirby Grant, Ann Gillis, Arthur Treacher, Steve Geray, George Dolenz, Marion Hutton

In the Belly of the Whale *

West Germany   1985   96m   colour

DNS Film/Haro Senft/NDR

original title: *Im Innern des Wals*

Fleeing from her violent father, an adolescent girl goes in search of the mother she has not seen for ten years.

Teenage angst is set against adult violence and unhappy love affairs.

w Michael Junker, Doris Dörrie   d Doris Dörrie   ph Alex Block   m Claus Bantzer   ad Jörg Neuman   ed Raimund Barthelmes

☆ Janna Marangosoff, Eisi Gulp, Peter Saltmann, Silvia Reize

'The drama. The passion. The intrigue. And rehearsals haven't even started.'

In the Bleak Midwinter *

GB   1995   98m   bw

Rank/Midwinter (David Barron)

▦

An out-of-work actor gathers together a motley crew of unemployed thespians to put on a production of *Hamlet* in a village church.

A sentimental comedy with amusing moments, although the script is too manipulative to achieve the required tear-jerking, and some of the performances shade into caricature.

wd Kenneth Branagh   ph Roger Lanser   m Jimmy Yuill   pd Tim Harvey   ed Neil Farrell

☆ Michael Maloney, Richard Briers, Mark Hadfield, Julia Sawalha, Nick Farrell, Gerard Horan, John Sessions, Celia Imrie, Hetta Charnley, Joan Collins, Jennifer Saunders

'Is only likely to end up as the answer to a riddle in a Christmas cracker: "What's broad and thin and weak and tired?"' – *Adam Mars-Jones, Independent*

'Both shrewdly written and well played.' – *Derek Malcolm, Guardian*

In the Company of Men **

US   1997   97m   colour

Alliance/Stephen Pevner/Atlantis/Fair and Square (Mark Archer, Stephen Pevner)

▦ ▤ ⊘ ⊘

Two corporate workers, unhappy at being ditched by their girlfriends, decide to get their revenge by dating and dumping on the first vulnerable woman they meet.

Effective but very manipulative piece of social drama, too diagrammatic to be dramatically convincing, but providing some biting dialogue and controversial subject-matter.

wd Neil LaBute   ph Tony Hettinger   m Ken Williams, Karel Roessing   pd Julia Henkel   ed Joel Plotch

☆ Aaron Eckhart, Stacy Edwards, Matt Malloy, Mark Rector, Jason Dixie, Emily Cline

'A serious, brainy and highly entertaining film – the best kind of popular cinema.' – *Richard Williams, Guardian*

'Passes itself off as an exposé of cynicism and manipulation but the movie itself is more cynical and manipulative than its subject. Like so many "issue" films, it's a talking point, not a movie.' – *Mark Steyn, Spectator*

In the Cool of the Day

GB   1962   91m   Metrocolor   Panavision

MGM (John Houseman)

The frail wife of a New York publisher dies in Greece after an affair with her colleague.

Travelogue with romantic asides; a pretty glum business.

w Meade Roberts   *novel* Susan Ertz   d Robert Stevens   ph Peter Newbrook   m Francis Chagrin   ad Ken Adam

☆ Jane Fonda, Peter Finch, Arthur Hill, Angela Lansbury, Constance Cummings

---

⊚ Digital Video Disc Region 2   ⊚ Digital Video Disc Region 1   ♫ Soundtrack released on compact disc   ☆ Cast in approximate order of importance   † Points of interest   ♫ Notable songs   ♟ Academy Award   ♟ Academy Award nomination   ♔ BAFTA

In the Doghouse

GB 1961 93m bw
Rank (Hugh Stewart)
Misadventures of a newly qualified vet.
Easy-going farce with animal interest and a great many familiar faces.
w Michael Pertwee *novel* It's a Vet's Life by Alex Duncan *d* Darcy Conyers *ph* Alan Hume *m* Philip Green
☆ Leslie Phillips, Peggy Cummins, Hattie Jacques, James Booth, Dick Bentley, Colin Gordon, Joan Heal, Fenella Fielding, Esma Cannon, Richard Goolden, Joan Hickson, Vida Hope, Harry Locke, Kynaston Reeves

In the Folds of the Flesh (dubbed)

Italy/Spain 1970 90m Eastmancolor
MGB/Talia (Sergio Bergonzelli)

original title: *Nelle Pieghe della Carne*
A murder tips a family into madness.
Absurd and bloody thriller which, with its incestuous trio of vulture-keeping homicidal maniacs, tilted camera angles and optical effects, fails to live up to its Freudian pretentiousness.
w Fabio de Agostini, Sergio Bergonzelli *d* Sergio Bergonzelli *ph* Jesus Villa Rojo *ad* Eduardo Torre de la Fuente *ed* Donatella Baglivo
☆ Eleonora Rossi Drago, Pier Angeli (Anna Maria Pierangeli), Fernando Sancho, Alfredo Majo, Emilio Gutierrez Caba, Maria Rosa Sclauzero

'Anywhere but Paris it would have been a scandal!'
In the French Style *

US/France 1962 105m bw
Columbia/Casanna/Orsay (Robert Parrish, Irwin Shaw)
An American girl in Paris has affairs with a young boy and with a divorced newspaperman.
Smooth, episodic, romantic character study, well made but with no perceptible dramatic point.
w Irwin Shaw *d* Robert Parrish *ph* Michel Kelber *m* Josef Kosma
☆ Jean Seberg, Stanley Baker, Philippe Fouquet

In the Good Old Summertime *

US 1949 102m Technicolor
MGM (Joe Pasternak)

In a Chicago music store in 1906, a salesgirl corresponds through a dating service with a man who turns out to be the manager she detests.
Cheerful remake of The Shop around the Corner (qv), with agreeable music, garish colour and not much style.
w Albert Hackett, Frances Goodrich, Ivan Tors *play* Miklos Laszlo *d* Robert Z. Leonard *ph* Harry Stradling *md* George Stoll *ch* Robert Alton *ad* Randell Duell *ed* Adrienne Fazan
☆ Judy Garland, Van Johnson, S. Z. Sakall, Spring Byington, Clinton Sundberg, Buster Keaton, Lillian Bronson

In the Heat of the Night ****

US 1967 109m DeLuxe
UA/Mirisch (Walter Mirisch)

In a small Southern town, the bigoted and bombastic sheriff on a murder hunt grudgingly accepts the help of a black detective.
A tense and exciting thriller that also explores racism through the explosive clash of two contrasting personalities.
w Stirling Silliphant *d* Norman Jewison *ph* Haskell Wexler *m* Quincy Jones *ad* Paul Groesse *ed* Hal Ashby
☆ Sidney Poitier, Rod Steiger, Warren Oates, Quentin Dean, William Schallert
'A very nice film and a very good film and yes, I think it's good to see a black man and a white man working together … but it's not going to take the tension out of New York City; it's not going to stop the riots in Chicago.' – Rod Steiger
† Poitier subsequently starred in a couple of very inferior sequels, They Call Me Mister Tibbs and The Organization (both qv).
♦ best picture; Stirling Silliphant; Rod Steiger; Hal Ashby; sound
♦ Norman Jewison; sound effects (James A. Richard)
♦ Rod Steiger

In the Line of Fire *

US 1993 129m Technicolor Panavision
Columbia (Jeff Apple)

A secret service agent, who is haunted by his failure to save President Kennedy, is taunted by a ruthless killer who announces he intends to assassinate the current US President.
An enjoyable thriller that provides Eastwood the opportunity to develop an unstereotypical character, but which also lets Malkovich go over the top as a carpet-chewing baddie, and lacks suspense.
w Jeff Maguire *d* Wolfgang Petersen *ph* John Bailey *m* Ennio Morricone *pd* Lilly Kilvert *ed* Anne V. Coates
☆ Clint Eastwood, John Malkovich, Rene Russo, Dylan McDermott, Gary Cole, Fred Dalton Thompson, John Mahoney, Greg Alan-Williams
'Meat-and-potatoes genre-picture entertainment: nothing fancy, nothing unusual.' – Terrence Rafferty, New Yorker
'The story is from recycled thrillersville, but it's snappy and appealing in its fast, tense treatment.' – Angie Errigo, Empire
♦ John Malkovich; Jeff Maguire; Anne V. Coates

In the Meantime, Darling

US 1944 72m bw
TCF (Otto Preminger)
A wealthy bride lives in an overcrowded boarding house to be near her husband's army camp.
Unassuming wartime soaper of very little interest.
w Arthur Kober, Michael Uris *d* Otto Preminger *ph* Joe MacDonald *m* David Buttolph *md* Emil Newman
☆ Jeanne Crain, Frank Latimore, Mary Nash, Eugene Pallette, Stanley Prager, Gale Robbins, Jane Randolph

In the Mood: see The Woo Woo Kid

In the Mouth of Madness

US 1995 95m Film House colour
New Line (Sandy King)

An insurance agent investigates the disappearance of a best-selling horror author, whose latest book is making its readers lose their sanity, and finds himself living in the author's fictional world.
An intriguing notion is abandoned after a while for a more conventional horror movie in the H. P. Lovecraft mould of monstrous beings striving to recapture the world.
w Michael de Luca *d* John Carpenter *ph* Gary B. Kibbe *m* Jim Lang *pd* Jeff Steven Ginn *ed* Edward A. Warschilka
sp Industrial Light and Magic
☆ Sam Neill, Julie Carmen, Jürgen Prochnow, Charlton Heston, David Warner, John Glover, Bernie Casey, Peter Jason, Frances Bay
'The plotline is so incoherent that in the end you don't much care what happens to whom and why.' – Derek Malcolm, Guardian

In the Name of the Father **

Eire/GB 1993 133m Technicolor
Universal/Hell's Kitchen/Gabriel Byrne (Jim Sheridan)

Four young Irish friends are framed by the police for planting an IRA bomb that blows up a Guildford pub.
A true story, filled with a righteous indignation and deftly told, but debasing its own authenticity with its final, hollow court-room scene which is not only completely invented and inaccurate in its portrayal of British procedure, but is played like the climax from a Perry Mason movie; it is at its best when exploring the relationship between father and son.
w Terry George, Jim Sheridan *d* Jim Sheridan *ph* Peter Biziou *m* Trevor Jones *pd* Caroline Amies *ed* Gerry Hambling
☆ Daniel Day-Lewis, Pete Postlethwaite, Emma Thompson, John Lynch, Mark Sheppard, Beatie Edney, Marie Jones, Britta Smith, Corin Redgrave
'Solid and well-crafted, with moments of great power.' – Adam Mars-Jones, Independent
'Unashamed Irish myth-making. But considering the sensitivity of the issues involved, it is a bit odd that Sheridan has taken quite such liberties with the truth. This is, after all, a film about a man who spent 14 years in prison because people made up stories about him.' – Martin Bright, Sight and Sound

♦ Daniel Day-Lewis; Pete Postlethwaite; Emma Thompson; Jim Sheridan (as director); Terry George, Jim Sheridan; Gerry Hambling

In the Navy *

US 1941 86m bw
Universal (Alex Gottlieb)

Two incompetents and a singing heart-throb are naval recruits.
A basically feeble follow-up to Buck Privates which outgrossed its predecessor and now stands as an interesting pointer to how mass entertainment has changed since 1941.
w John Grant, Arthur T. Horman *d* Arthur Lubin *ph* Joseph Valentine *m/ly* Gene de Paul, Don Raye
☆ Bud Abbott, Lou Costello, Dick Powell, The Andrews Sisters, Claire Dodd, Dick Foran, Shemp Howard

In the Realm of Passion: see Ai No Borei

In the Shadow of the Wind

French/Canadian 1987 107m colour
Cinevideo/Les Film Ariane/TFI Films (Justine Héroux)
original title: *Les Fous de Bassan*
A middle-aged artist recalls an earlier time when he disrupted the life of a small, puritanical fishing community.
Slow-moving movie that tries for, and misses, a tragic dimension.
w Sheldon Chad, Marcel Beaulieu, Yves Simoneau *novel* Anne Hébert *d* Yves Simoneau *ph* Alain Dostie *m* Richard Grégoire *ad* Michel Proulx *ed* Joele Van Effenterre
☆ Steve Banner, Charlotte Valandrey, Laure Marsac, Angèle Coutu, Paul Hébert, Marie Tifo, Bernard-Pierre Donnadieu, Lothaire Bluteau, Jean-Louis Millette

In the Soup

GB 1936 72m bw
Twickenham (Julius Hagen)
A solicitor and his wife are forced to pose as their own servants.
Undernourished star comedy.
w H. Fowler Mear *play* Ralph Lumley *d* Henry Edwards *ph* Sydney Blythe, William Luff *md* W. L. Trytel *ad* James Carter *ed* Jack Harris, Michael Chorlton
☆ Ralph Lynn, Judy Gunn, Morton Selten, Nelson Keys, Bertha Belmore

In the Soup **

US/Japan/Germany/France 1992 93m bw
Will Alliance/Pandora/Why Not/Odessa/Alta/Mikado (Jim Stark, Hank Blumenthal)

A con man and an independent film director trying to raise the money to finance his screenplay as a front for his schemes.
An amusing off-beat comedy about the education of an innocent.
w Alexandre Rockwell, Tim Kissell *d* Alexandre Rockwell *ph* Phil Parmer *m* Mader *pd* Mark Friedberg *ed* Dana Congdon
☆ Steve Buscemi, Seymour Cassel, Jennifer Beals, Pat Moya, Will Patton, Jim Jarmusch, Carol Kane
'Winning performances and gentle, self-deprecating humor put this across as an audience pleaser for the specialized film crowd.' – Variety
† Although the cinema release was in black and white, the film was issued on video in a colour print.

In the White City *

Portugal/Switzerland 1983 108m colour
Contemporary/Metro filme/Filmograph/WDR/Channel 4 (Paulo Branco, Alain Tanner, Antonio Vaz da Silver)
original title: *Dans La Ville Blanche*
Jumping ship in Lisbon, a married sailor falls in love with a local girl and sends home movies of the city to his wife.
A study in masculine alienation, dependent on its images to carry its message of disintegration and illusory freedom.
wd Alain Tanner *ph* Acacio de Almeida *m* Jean-Luc Barbier *ad* Maria Jose Branco *ed* Laurent Uhler
☆ Bruno Ganz, Teresa Madruga, Julia Vonderlinn, José Carvalho, Victor Costa, Francisco Baiao, José Wallenstein, Lidia Franco

In the Woods: see Rashomon

'No one is as good as Bette when she's bad!'
In This Our Life **

US 1942 101m bw
Warner (David Lewis)

A neurotic girl steals her sister's husband, leaves him in the lurch, dominates her hapless family and is killed while on the run from the police.
Splendid star melodrama with good supporting acting and background detail. /
w Howard Koch *novel* Ellen Glasgow *d* John Huston *ph* Ernest Haller *m* Max Steiner
☆ Bette Davis, Charles Coburn, Olivia de Havilland, Frank Craven, George Brent, Dennis Morgan, Billie Burke, Hattie McDaniel, Lee Patrick, Walter Huston (uncredited)

In Which We Serve ****

GB 1942 114m bw
Rank/Two Cities (Noël Coward)

Survivors from a torpedoed destroyer recall their life at sea and on leave.
Dated but splendid flagwaver; an archetypal British war film of almost limitless propaganda value.
w Noël Coward, David Lean *d* Noël Coward *ph* Ronald Neame *m* Noël Coward
☆ Noël Coward, Bernard Miles, John Mills, Richard Attenborough, Celia Johnson, Kay Walsh, Joyce Carey, Michael Wilding, Penelope Dudley Ward, Kathleen Harrison, Philip Friend, George Carney, Geoffrey Hibbert, James Donald
COMMANDER (NOËL COWARD): 'The Torrin has been in one scrap after another, but even when we've had men killed, the majority survived and brought the old ship back. Now she lies in 1500 fathoms and with her more than half our shipmates. If they had to die, what a grand way to go! And now they lie all together with the ship we loved, and they're in very good company. We've lost her, but they're still with her. There may be less than half the Torrin left, but I feel that we'll all take up the battle with even stronger heart. Each of us knows twice as much about fighting, and each of us has twice as good a reason to fight. You will all be sent to replace men who've been killed in other ships, and the next time you're in action, remember the Torrin! I should like to add that there isn't one of you that I wouldn't be proud and honoured to serve with again.'
'One of the screen's proudest achievements at any time and in any country.' – Newsweek
'Never at any time has there been a reconstruction of human experience which could touch the savage grandeur and compassion of this production.' – Howard Barnes, New York Herald Tribune
† The story and the Coward character were based on the experiences of Louis Mountbatten, whose ship, HMS Kelly, was sunk under him.
♦ Special Award to Noël Coward
♦ best picture; Noël Coward (as writer)

Inadmissible Evidence **

GB 1968 96m bw
Paramount/Woodfall (Ronald Kinnoch)
A frustrated 40-year-old solicitor is on the verge of a nervous breakdown.
Interesting and surprisingly successful transcription of a difficult play which was virtually an anti-humanity soliloquy.
w John Osborne *play* John Osborne *d* Anthony Page *ph* Kenneth Hodges *m* Dudley Moore *ad* Seamus Flannery
☆ Nicol Williamson, Eleanor Fazan, Jill Bennett, Peter Sallis, Eileen Atkins, Isabel Dean
'A play that was conceived as an increasingly bad dream has been made into a grittily detailed, naturalistic film.' – Stanley Kauffmann

'She was the biggest sucker of them all!'
Incendiary Blonde *

US 1945 112m Technicolor
Paramount (Joseph Sistrom)
The life of twenties night-club queen Texas Guinan.
Laundered biopic with guns, girls and gangsters as well as songs.
w Claude Binyon, Frank Butler *d* George Marshall *ph* Ray Rennahan *m* Robert Emmett Dolan
☆ Betty Hutton, Arturo de Cordova, Charles Ruggles, Albert Dekker, Barry Fitzgerald, Mary

Philips, Bill Goodwin, Eduardo Ciannelli, Maurice Rocco

'It runs its noisy but high-minded course through steamy emotion, painful misunderstanding and dramatic self-sacrifice, winding up in the snow among the blood of dead gangsters. Have we ever seen gangsters in Technicolor before?' – *Richard Mallett, Punch*
'A brassy synthesis of colour, song and dance, spattered with laughs.' – *Daily Herald*
♪ Robert Emmett Dolan

L'incendio di Roma: see *Fire over Rome*

Incense for the Damned

GB 1970 87m Eastmancolor
Grand National/Lucinda/Titan (Graham Harris)
aka: *Bloodsuckers*
An Oxford academic holidays in Greece and becomes a vampire.
A moderately successful attempt to create a modern-day vampire story, substituting sexual perversion for the usual occult approach.
w Julian More *novel* Doctors Wear Scarlet by Simon Raven d Michael Burrowes (Robert Hartford-Davis) ph Desmond Dickinson m Bobby Richards pd George Provis
☆ Patrick Macnee, Peter Cushing, Alex Davion, Johnny Sekka, Madeline Hinde, Patrick Mower, Imogen Hassall, Edward Woodward, William Mervyn, David Lodge
'Well enough constructed to amount to a richly subversive exercise in the genre.' – *David Pirie, MFB*
† The film was cut by four minutes for its British release and disowned by its director, who did not regard it as finished. It was given a trade show in 1972 but did not receive a London showing until 1976.

Inchon

US 1981 140m colour
One Way Productions (Mitsuharu Ishii)
♀
General MacArthur is affected by divine guidance during a major battle of the Korean war.
A very curious enterprise apparently financed by the Moonies. The religious angle sits oddly with the war scenes, and the result is an unsatisfactory film.
w Robin Moore, Laird Koenig d Terence Young ph Bruce Surtees m Jerry Goldsmith
☆ Laurence Olivier, Jacqueline Bisset, David Janssen, Ben Gazzara, Toshiro Mifune, Richard Roundtree, Gabriele Ferzetti, Rex Reed
'A near total loss as well as a laugh.' – *Bruce Williamson, Playboy*
'The worst movie ever made, a turkey the size of Godzilla.' – *Jack Kroll, Newsweek*
'Quite possibly the worst movie ever made … stupefyingly incompetent.' – *Peter Rainer, Los Angeles Herald Examiner*
'As military spectacles go, one of the sorriest in military history.' – *Richard Schickel, Time*

Incident at Owl Creek *

France 1961 27m bw
Marcel Ichac/Films de Centaure/Paul de Roubaix
original title: *La Rivière du Hibou*
US title: *An Occurrence At Owl Creek*
During the American Civil War a man is about to be hanged, and imagines how he might escape.
Intriguing but somewhat overpraised short with a rather obvious solution.
wd Robert Enrico *story* Ambrose Bierce ph Jean Boffety m Henri Lanoë
☆ Roger Jacquet, Anne Cornaly, Anker Larsen
'A powerful and remarkable film.' – *MFB*
♠ best short film

Incident at Phantom Hill

US 1966 88m Technicolor
Universal
Two men face desperate odds to reach one million dollars in gold.
Full-blooded Western programmer with useful performances.
w Frank Nugent d Earl Bellamy ph William Margulies m Hans J. Salter
☆ Robert Fuller, Dan Duryea, Jocelyn Lane, Claude Akins, Noah Beery Jnr

'Harry Donovan Is A Master In The Art Of Deception … Trapped In A Life So Perfect Even The Truth Can't Save Him.'
Incognito
US 1997 106m Technicolor
Warner/Morgan Creek (James G. Robinson)
☷ ☰ ♀
An art forger is offered a fortune to fake a Rembrandt for crooked dealers.
Ridiculous thriller, the cinematic equivalent of painting by numbers.
w Jordan Katz d John Badham ph Denis Crossan m John Ottman pd Jamie Leonard ed Frank Morriss
☆ Jason Patric, Irène Jacob, Thomas Lockyer, Ian Richardson, Simon Chandler, Rod Steiger, Pip Torrens, Ian Holm
'Starts badly and gets even worse, giving it a special kind of entertainment value.' – *George Perry*

Les Inconnus dans la Maison *

France 1941 94m bw
Continental
An embittered ex-barrister saves his teenage daughter from a murder charge.
Unlikely melodrama remade as Stranger in the House; this version has more compelling writing and acting.
w Henri-Georges Clouzot *novel* Georges Simenon d Henri Decoin ph Jules Kruger m Roland Manuel
☆ Raimu, Juliette Fabre, Jacques Baumer, Jean Tissier

The Incredible Journey **

♠♠ US 1963 80m Technicolor
Walt Disney (James Algar)
☰
Two dogs and a cat, separated from their owners, escape and travel 250 miles home.
A novelty attraction which keeps going purely on its animal interest, which is considerable.
w James Algar *book* Sheila Burnford d Fletcher Markle ph Kenneth Peach, Jack Couffer, Lloyd Beebe m Oliver Wallace

The Incredible Melting Man

US 1977 84m Movielab
AIP/Quartet (Max J. Rosenberg)
☷
The survivor of a space flight is rushed to hospital with radiation burns and an infection which causes his flesh to melt.
Unpleasant and nonsensical horror film with a few unintentional laughs and a plot borrowed from The Quatermass Experiment.
wd William Sachs ph Willy Curtis m Arlon Ober
☆ Alex Rebar, Burr DeBenning, Myron Healey, Michael Alldredge

The Incredible Mr Limpet

♠♠ US 1964 102m Technicolor
Warner (John C. Rose)
☰
A meek but patriotic clerk is turned down by the navy and turns into a fish. In this form he becomes a radar assistant to a warship.
Sentimental sub-Disney goo, part animated.
w Jameson Brewer, John C. Rose *novel* Theodore Pratt d Arthur Lubin ph Harold Stine m Frank Perkins
☆ Don Knotts, Andrew Duggan, Larry Keating, Jack Weston

The Incredible Sarah *

GB 1976 105m Technicolor Panavision
Readers Digest (Helen M. Strauss)
☰ ♀
The career of French actress Sarah Bernhardt up to the age of thirty-five.
Mildly pleasing old-fashioned biopic with remarkably unreliable detail and a regrettably bland approach to its fascinating subject.
w Ruth Wolff d Richard Fleischer ph Christopher Challis m Elmer Bernstein pd Elliot Scott
☆ Glenda Jackson, Daniel Massey, Yvonne Mitchell, Douglas Wilmer, David Langton, Simon Williams, John Castle, Edward Judd, Peter Sallis
'An incredibly old-fashioned movie full of the most unforgettable moments you have ever tried to forget.' – *Andrew Sarris, Village Voice*

'A job lot of obligatory Hollywood platitudes strung together with all the skill of Captain Hook trying to thread a needle.' – *Benny Green, Punch*
'In the stupefying tradition of *Song of Norway*.' – *Pauline Kael*

'So incredible you'll talk about it for years to come!'
The Incredible Shrinking Man *
US 1957 81m bw
U-I (Albert Zugsmith)
☷ ♀
After being caught in a radioactive mist, a man shrinks inexorably to micro-size.
Horrifyingly inevitable sci-fi with imaginative touches gracing a cheap production.
w Richard Matheson d Jack Arnold ph Ellis W. Carter m Hans Salter sp Clifford Stine, Roswell A. Hoffman, Everett H. Bronssard
☆ Grant Williams, Randy Stuart, April Kent, Paul Langton
'It opens up new vistas of cosmic terror.' – *Peter John Dyer*
'One hails a science fiction film which is both inventive and humane.' – *Sunday Times*
'Simple, ingenious, effective.' – *The Times*

The Incredible Shrinking Woman

US 1981 88m Technicolor
Universal/Lija (Hank Moonjean)
☷ ♀
A housewife finds herself shrinking after using a new perfume…
Hamfisted spoof on The Incredible Shrinking Man, with flat jokes and rather poor trick photography.
w Jane Wagner d Joel Schumacher ph Bruce Logan m Suzanne Ciani
☆ Lily Tomlin, Charles Grodin, Ned Beatty, Henry Gibson, Elizabeth Wilson
'Leaden satire on consumerism … even the special effects are barely passable.' – *Time Out, 1984*

The Incredible Torture Show: see *Bloodsucking Freaks*

The Incredible Two-Headed Transplant

US 1970 88m DeLuxe
Mutual General/Trident/American International (John Lawrence)
☷
A mad doctor grafts an extra head onto a homicidal maniac.
Full-blooded nonsense on a low budget; utterly repellent to some, but done with sufficient verve to be a minor cult title to others.
w James Gordon White, John Lawrence d Anthony M. Lanza ph John Steely, Glen Gano, Paul Hipp m John Barber
☆ Bruce Dern, Pat Priest, Casey Kasem, Berry Kroeger

The Incredibly Strange Creatures who Stopped Living and Became Mixed-up Zombies

US 1963 82m colour
Morgan Steckler Productions
☷ ☰
A gypsy fortune-teller keeps monsters of her own making at the back of her tent.
Murder and mayhem at the carnival: cheap exploitation item which for long was thought to be a fragment of someone's imagination, but turns out really to exist.
w Gene Pollock, Robert Silliphant d Cash Flagg (Ray Dennis Steckler) ph Joseph V. Mascelli m Libby Quinn
☆ Cash Flagg, Carolyn Brandt, Brett O'Hara

The Incredibly True Adventure of 2 Girls in Love

US 1995 94m colour
Feature/Smash (Dolly Hall)
☷ ☰
Two lesbian high-school students face rejection from friends and family when they fall in love.
Apart from the fact that its protagonists are of the same sex, this is otherwise a predictable movie of teenage angst and rebellion.
wd Maria Maggenti m Tami Reiker m Terry Dame pd Ginger Tougas ed Susan Graef
☆ Laurel Holloman, Maggie Moore, Kate Stafford, Sabrina Artel, Toby Poser, Nelson Rodriguez
'A pacy, sweet and candid treat.' – *Empire*

'The Dreams. The Nightmares. The Desires. The Fears. The Mystery. The Revelation. The Warning.'
Incubus
Canada 1981 92m colour
Guardian Trust Company
☷ ♀
Women are raped by a rampant demon.
Utterly distasteful horror film.
w George Franklin *novel* Ray Russell d John Hough
☆ John Cassavetes, Kerrie Keane, Helen Hughes, Erin Flannery, John Ireland

'A husband. A wife. A billionaire. A proposal.'
Indecent Proposal
US 1993 117m DeLuxe
Paramount (Sherry Lansing)
☷ ☰ ♀ ♀
In Las Vegas, after her husband has lost the last of his money in a desperate gamble, a wealthy man offers a woman a million dollars to spend a night with him.
Glutinous problem drama of transcendent silliness; perhaps the dilemma would have seemed more interesting if the millionaire had been less personable than Redford, although it would still have remained a ridiculous enterprise.
w Amy Holden Jones *novel* Jack Engelhard d Adrian Lyne ph Howard Atherton m John Barry pd Mel Bourne ed Joe Hutshing
☆ Robert Redford, Demi Moore, Woody Harrelson, Seymour Cassel, Oliver Platt, Billy Bob Thornton, Rip Taylor, Billy Connolly
'One of those high-concept pictures with a big windup and weak delivery.' – *Variety*
'Unredeemingly awful.' – *Philip French, Observer*

'Prepare for Impact!'
Independence Day *
US 1996 145m DeLuxe Super 35
TCF/Centropolis (Dean Devlin)
☷ ☰ ☰ ♀ ♀
A plucky pilot and a computer expert defeat an alien invasion of hundreds of vastly destructive spaceships.
Enjoyably silly, jingoistic nonsense that found an appreciative audience for its sensational effects of blowing up the White House and most of the world; it sticks closely to the plot of The War of the Worlds, offering a technological version of a biological virus to knock out the aliens.
w Dean Devlin, Roland Emmerich d Roland Emmerich ph Karl Walter Lindenlaub m David Arnold pd Oliver Scholl, Patrick Tatopolous ed David Brenner sp Volker Engel, Douglas Smith, Pacific Ocean Post Digital
☆ Will Smith, Bill Pullman, Jeff Goldblum, Mary McDonnell, Judd Hirsch, Margaret Colin, Randy Quaid, Robert Loggia, James Rebhorn, Harvey Fierstein, Adam Baldwin, Brent Spiner, Vivica A. Fox, Harry Connick Jnr
'Lavish in scale, cornball to a T and a wonderfully enthusiastic blend of fifties sci-fi and seventies disaster movies.' – *Derek Malcolm, Guardian*
'Apotheosis of the video zap games that kids play; but fun for folk with popcorn appetites.' – *Alexander Walker*
'The first futuristic disaster movie that's as cute as a button.' – *Lisa Schwarzbaum, Entertainment Weekly*
† The biggest box-office success of 1996, it grossed around $746m around the world, and $306m in the US.
♠ visual effects (Volker Engel, Douglas Smith, Clay Pinney, Joseph Viskocil)
♪ sound

'300,000 volts of horror!'
Indestructible Man
US 1956 70m bw
Allied Artists
The dead body of a vicious killer is given new life by a mad doctor.
Low-budget horror mayhem with no style at all.
w Vy Russell, Sue Bradford d Jack Pollexfen
☆ Lon Chaney Jnr, Robert Shayne, Casey Adams, Marian Carr

The Indian Fighter

US 1955 88m Technicolor Cinemascope
UA/Bryna (William Schorr)
An Indian fighter protects a wagon train from the Sioux.

Simple-minded Western with touches of philosophy and not much drive.

w Frank Davis, Ben Hecht d André de Toth ph Wilfrid M. Cline m Franz Waxman
☆ Kirk Douglas, Elsa Martinelli, Walter Abel, Walter Matthau, Diana Douglas, Eduard Franz, Lon Chaney Jnr, Alan Hale Jnr, Elisha Cook Jnr

The Indian in the Cupboard

↟↟ US 1995 96m DeLuxe
Columbia/Scholastic (Kathleen Kennedy, Frank Marshall, Jane Startz)
☷

A nine-year-old boy's toy Indian comes alive when put inside a magic cupboard.
A pleasant but unremarkable fairy story that makes limited use of its interesting central concept.
w Melissa Mathison novel Lynne Reid Banks d Frank Oz ph Russell Carpenter m Randy Edelman pd Leslie McDonald ed Ian Crafford sp Industrial Light and Magic
☆ Hal Scardino, Litefoot, Lindsay Crouse, Richard Jenkins, Rishi Bhat, David Keith, Steve Coogan
'Never comes to life as a movie. Earnest and well-intentioned, the promising concept feels stretched to feature length and should play best only with younger kids.' – *Variety*

The Indian Runner

US 1991 126m DeLuxe
Columbia TriStar/Mount Film Group/Mico/NHK Enterprises (Don Philips)
☷ ▦ ◕

A small-town cop has a stormy relationship with his criminally inclined brother.
Glum and talky drama drawn out to an inordinate length, long after it has exhausted any interest.
wd Sean Penn ph Anthony B. Richmond m Jack Nitzsche pd Michael Haller ed Jay Cassidy, Phil Linson song 'Highway Patrolman' by Bruce Springsteen
☆ David Morse, Viggo Mortensen, Valeria Golino, Patricia Arquette, Charles Bronson, Sandy Dennis, Dennis Hopper, Jordan Rhodes
'More than two hours' worth of predictable characters and plot developments visible at a distance of some miles.' – *Kim Newman, Empire*

Indian Scout

US 1949 70m bw
Edward Small
Episodes in the life of Davy Crockett.
Minor Western which hit the spot with small-town audiences, and in the late fifties, after the success of the Disney film, was reissued as Davy Crockett, Indian Scout.
w Richard Schayer d Ford Beebe ph John Mescall m Paul Sawtell
☆ George Montgomery, Ellen Drew, Philip Reed, Noah Beery Jnr

Indian Summer: see *The Judge Steps Out (1947)*

Indian Summer: see *Alive and Kicking (1996)*

Indian Summer

US 1993 97m Technicolor
Touchstone/Outlaw (Jeffrey Silver, Robert Newmyer)
☷ ▦ ◕
aka: *Alive and Kicking*
Friends meet up for one last week at summer camp after a gap of 20 years.
Nostalgic, sentimental drama that suggests problems can be solved by reverting to childhood behaviour, but it does have moments of charm.
wd Mike Binder ph Tom Sigel m Miles Goodman pd Craig Stearns ed Adam Weiss
☆ Alan Arkin, Matt Craven, Diane Lane, Bill Paxton, Elizabeth Perkins, Kevin Pollak, Sam Raimi, Vincent Spano, Julie Warner, Kimberly Williams

'The Man With The Hat Is Back. And This Time He's Bringing His Dad.'
Indiana Jones and the Last Crusade **

↟↟ US 1989 127m DeLuxe
UIP/Paramount/Lucasfilm (Robert Watts)
☷ ▦ ◕ 🎧
aka: *Alive and Kicking*
Indiana Jones goes in search of his father who disappeared while looking for the Holy Grail.
The formula as before, which still works thanks to some splendid set-pieces and the genial interplay between Ford and Connery.

w Jeffrey Boam story George Lucas, Menno Meyjes d Steven Spielberg ph Douglas Slocombe m John Williams pd Elliot Scott ed Michael Kahn
☆ Harrison Ford, Sean Connery, Denholm Elliott, Alison Doody, John Rhys-Davies, Julian Glover, River Phoenix, Michael Byrne, Kevork Malikyan, Robert Eddison, Richard Young, Alexei Sayle
🏅 sound
🏅 John Williams; sound effects editing

'The hero is back!'
Indiana Jones and the Temple of Doom **

↟↟ US 1984 118m Rank Colour/DeLuxe
Panavision
Paramount/Lucasfilm (Robert Watts)
☷ ▦ ◕ 🎧

A prequel to Raiders of the Lost Ark: Jones in 1935 finds the sacred Sankara stone.
Slow-starting adventure romp with much ingenuity and too much brutality and horror. In the US it caused the creation of a new censor certificate: PG(13).
w Willard Huyck, Gloria Katz story George Lucas d Steven Spielberg ph Douglas Slocombe, Allen Daviau m John Williams pd Elliot Scott
☆ Harrison Ford, Kate Capshaw, Ke Huy Quan, Philip Stone
'One of the most sheerly pleasurable physical comedies ever made.' – *Pauline Kael, New Yorker*
'A thin, arch, graceless affair.' – *Observer*
'A two-hour series of none too carefully linked chase sequences … sitting on the edge of your seat gives you a sore bum but also a numb brain.' – *Guardian*
🏅 music; visual effects

Indianapolis Speedway

US 1939 82m bw
Warner
A racetrack driver wants his kid brother to continue in college, but he has the racing fever.
Editor's-bench mélange of The Crowd Roars (1932) and Here Comes the Navy; this doesn't star Cagney.
w Sig Herzig, Wally Klein d Lloyd Bacon
☆ Pat O'Brien, Ann Sheridan, John Payne, Gale Page, Frank McHugh, Regis Toomey
'It contains just about every cliché such type melodrama can have.' – *Variety*
† Frank McHugh played the same role in the 1932 version.

Indio Black, Sai che ti Dico: Sei un Gran Figlio di…: see *The Bounty Hunters*

'Through one indiscretion … a woman with a future became a woman with a past!'
Indiscreet

US 1931 92m bw
Art Cinema Corporation (Joseph M. Schenck)
A socialite endangers her own romance when she tries to protect her younger sister.
Embarrassing and slow-moving farce which helped to kill its star's career.
d Leo McCarey w Ray June, Gregg Toland m Alfred Newman w/songs Brown, de Sylva and Henderson
☆ Gloria Swanson, Ben Lyon, Monroe Owsley, Barbara Kent, Arthur Lake, Maude Eburne, Henry Kolker

'How dare he make love to me – and not be a married man!'
Indiscreet **

GB 1958 100m Technicolor
Grandon (Stanley Donen)
☷ ▦

An American diplomat in London falls in love with an actress but protects himself by saying he is married.
Affairs among the ultra rich, amusing when played by these stars but with imperfect production values which the alarmingly thin plot allows one too much time to consider.
w Norman Krasna play Kind Sir by Norman Krasna d Stanley Donen ph Frederick A. Young m Richard Bennett, Ken Jones
☆ Cary Grant, Ingrid Bergman, Phyllis Calvert, Cecil Parker, David Kossoff, Megs Jenkins
'One is often on the point of being bored, but one never is, quite.' – *Richard Roud*
'A film to which you would not hesitate to take your jeweller, your architect, your home decorator, your dressmaker and your domestic staff.' – *Alexander Walker*

Indiscretion: see *Christmas in Connecticut (1945)*

Indiscretion: see *Indiscretion of an American Wife (1954)*

Indiscretion of an American Wife *

Italy/US 1954 75m bw
David O. Selznick (Vittorio de Sica)
☷
aka: *Terminus Station*
aka: *Indiscretion*
An American woman and an Italian professor say goodbye in Rome's terminal station.
Strained attempt to re-do Brief Encounter against the busy background of a great railway station; moments of interest, but artificiality prevails, and the plot never gets up enough steam.
w Cesare Zavattini, Truman Capote, etc d Vittorio de Sica ph G. R. Aldo m Aldo Cicognini
☆ Jennifer Jones, Montgomery Clift, Gino Cervi, Richard Beymer

Indochine **

France 1992 158m colour
Paradis/La Générale d'Images/BAC/Orly/Ciné Cinq (Eric Heumann)
☷ ▦ ◕ ⊘ 🎧

In the unsettled Indochina of the 1930s, the adopted Indochinese daughter of the female head of a rubber plantation runs away to be with the French naval officer loved by her and her mother.
A glossy romantic drama dominated by Deneuve's performance.
w Erik Orsenna, Louis Gardeal, Catherine Cohen, Régis Wargnier d Régis Wargnier ph François Catonne m Patrick Doyle ed Genevieve Winding
☆ Catherine Deneuve, Vincent Perez, Linh Dan Pham, Jean Yanne, Dominique Blanc, Henri Marteau, Mai Chau
'A riveting romantic saga.' – *Variety*
'It has the breadth and intelligence of the David Lean epics from whose plots it borrows so freely … And in Deneuve the movie has a star of epic glamour and gravity. Her presence is like some handsome monument to the French spirit miraculously preserved on the streets of Vietnam.' – *Richard Corliss, Time*
🏅 foreign language film
🏅 Catherine Deneuve

Inferno **

US 1953 83m Technicolor 3-D
TCF (William Bloom)
When a millionaire breaks his leg in the desert, his wife and her lover leave him to die; but he contrives to catch up with them.
An outdoor melodrama which made better use of 3-D than any other film, suggesting the lone handicapped figure in the vast spaces; but the lovers are dull and the fire climax perfunctory.
w Francis Cockrell d Roy Baker ph Lucien Ballard m Paul Sawtell
☆ Robert Ryan, William Lundigan, Rhonda Fleming
'Its chief merit is a strong and simple story.' – *C. A. Lejeune*

Inferno

Italy 1980 107m Technicolor
TCF (Claudio Argento)
☷ ▦ 🎧
A New York apartment house is occupied by satanists who murder those who learn their secret.
Absurdly overplotted and mainly incomprehensible shocker with some small pretensions to style.
wd Dario Argento ph Romano Albani m Keith Emerson ad Giuseppe Bassan sp Mario Bava, Germano Natali, Pino Leone
☆ Leigh McCloskey, Irene Miracle, Eleonora Giorgi, Daria Nicolodi, Alida Valli

Infinity

US 1996 119m DeLuxe
First Look (Joel Soisson, Michael Leahy, Patricia Broderick, Matthew Broderick)
☷ ▦ ◕ 🎧
A Nobel Prize-winning scientist looks back on his early life and his marriage to a woman dying of tuberculosis.
A slight but charming biopic that concentrates on the private life of a brilliant man, Richard Feynman, and his doomed romance with Arline Greenbaum.

w Patricia Broderick memoirs Richard Feynman d Matthew Broderick ph Toyomichi Kurita m Bruce Broughton pd Bernt Capra ed Elena Maganini, Bill Johnson, Amy Young
☆ Matthew Broderick, Patricia Arquette, Peter Riegert, Dori Brenner, Peter Michael Goetz, Zeljko Ivanek, James LeGros, Jeffrey Force
'A static, old-fashioned film that only intermittently involves the viewer.' – *Emanuel Levy, Variety*

The Informer ***

US 1935 91m bw
RKO (Cliff Reid)
An IRA leader is betrayed by a simple-minded hanger-on who wants money to emigrate; he is hounded by fellow rebels and his own conscience.
A tedious plot is turned into brilliant cinema by full-blooded acting and a highly stylized yet brilliantly effective mise en scène which never attempts reality.
w Dudley Nichols novel Liam O'Flaherty d John Ford ph Joseph H. August m Max Steiner ad Van Nest Polglase ed George Hively
☆ Victor McLaglen, Heather Angel, Margot Grahame, Una O'Connor, Wallace Ford, Preston Foster, J. M. Kerrigan, Joe Sawyer, Donald Meek
'A tough subject, a sure critic's picture, but dubious box office.' – *Variety*
'As impressive as Scarface, or anything in the whole powerful literature redolent of fog and grime and dreariness which the Germans gave to the Americans.' – *Bardèche and Brasillach*
'Among the best five pictures since the coming of sound.' – *Baltimore Sun*
† An early British sound version was made in 1929 by Arthur Robison for BIP, with Lars Hansen and Lya de Putti. Dudley Nichols became the first person to refuse to accept an Oscar, due to a quarrel between the Academy and some industry organizations.
🏅 Dudley Nichols; John Ford; Max Steiner; Victor McLaglen
🏅 best picture; editing

The Informers

GB 1963 104m bw
Rank (William MacQuitty)
US title: *Underworld Informers*
A police informer is murdered and his brother takes revenge.
Basic police melodrama, with clumsy script and jaded direction.
w Alun Falconer novel Death of a Snout by Douglas Warner d Ken Annakin ph Reg Wyer m Clifton Parker
☆ Nigel Patrick, Colin Blakely, Derren Nesbitt

L'Ingénue Libertine

France 1950 88m bw
Codo-Cinéma (Jean Velter)
A romantic girl lives in an imaginary world of affairs, but can't bring herself to consummate her marriage.
Minor period sex comedy which has the distinction of being Britain's first 'X' film, though the naughtiness is more implied than stated.
w P. Laroche novel Colette d Jacqueline Audry ph Grignon m Vincent Scotto
☆ Daniele Delorme, Frank Villard, Jean Tissier

Inherit the Wind **

US 1960 127m bw
UA/Lomitas (Stanley Kramer)
☷ ▦ ◕
A fictionalized account of the 1925 Scopes 'monkey trial', when a schoolmaster was accused of teaching the theory of evolution.
Splendid theatrics with fine performances, marred by boring subplots but enhanced by a realistic portrait of a sweltering Southern town.
w Nathan E. Douglas, Harold Jacob Smith play Jerome Lawrence, Robert E. Lee d Stanley Kramer ph Ernest Laszlo m Ernest Gold ed Frederic Knudtson
☆ Spencer Tracy, Fredric March, Florence Eldridge, Gene Kelly, Dick York, Donna Anderson, Harry Morgan, Elliott Reid, Claude Akins
🏅 script; Ernest Laszlo; Spencer Tracy; editing

The Inheritance: see *Uncle Silas (1947)*

The Inheritance

Italy 1976 121m Eastmancolor
Flag Productions (Gianni Hecht Lucari)

🔲 ⊘

original title: *L'Eredità Ferramonti*

In Rome of the 1880s, a wealthy father disinherits his children but succumbs to the wiles of his daughter-in-law.

Sumptuous period soap opera, for which Sanda won a best actress award at the Cannes Film Festival.

w Ugo Pirro, Sergio Bazzini *novel* Gaetano Carlo Chelli *d* Mauro Bolognini *ph* Ennio Guarnieri *m* Ennio Morricone *ad* Luigi Scaccianoce *ed* Nino Baragli

☆ Anthony Quinn, Fabio Testi, Dominique Sanda, Luigi Proietti, Adriana Asti, Paolo Bonacelli, Rosella Rusconi, Harold Bromley

The In-Laws

US 1979 103m Technicolor
Warner (Alan Arkin)

🔳 ⊚↗

A timorous dentist and a CIA spy, whose children are to marry, find themselves unwillingly linked together in gunplay in a South American republic.
Two charismatic actors can't fail to get some laughs, but the extended script makes it a bumpy ride.

w Andrew Bergman *d* Arthur Hiller *ph* David M. Walsh *m* John Morris *pd* Pato Guzman

☆ Peter Falk, Alan Arkin, Richard Libertini, Penny Peyser, Nancy Dussault

'It seems incapable either of adhering to the conventions of a comedy-thriller plot or of mustering sufficient invention to abandon plot altogether for a farcical free-for-all.' – *Tim Pulleine, MFB*

Inn for Trouble

GB 1960 90m bw
Film Locations/Eros

A suburban couple become country publicans.
Amiable extension of a popular TV series, The Larkins.

w Fred Robinson *d* C. M. Pennington-Richards *ph* Eric Cross *m* Philip Green

☆ Peggy Mount, David Kossoff, Leslie Phillips, Glyn Owen, Charles Hawtrey, A. E. Matthews, Yvonne Monlaur, Irene Handl

The Inn of the Sixth Happiness ★★

GB 1958 158m DeLuxe Cinemascope
TCF (Mark Robson)

🔲

An English servant girl becomes a missionary and spends many arduous years in China.
Romanticized biopic of Gladys Aylward, with lots of children, a happy ending, and everyone sensationally miscast. Somehow it all works, even North Wales standing in for China.

w Isobel Lennart *book* The Small Woman *by* Alan Burgess *d* Mark Robson *ph* Frederick A. Young *m* Malcolm Arnold *ed* Ernest Walter

☆ Ingrid Bergman, Curt Jurgens, Robert Donat, Athene Seyler, Ronald Squire, Richard Wattis, Moultrie Kelsall

⅄ Mark Robson

The Inner Circle

Italy 1991 137m Technicolor
Columbia TriStar/Numero Uno (Claudio Bonivento)

🔲 🔳 ⊚↗ ⊘

Italian title: *Il Proiezionista*

A cinema projectionist goes to work for Stalin, an act that has a devastating effect on his marriage.
A movie that attempts to explain the appeal to the Russian people of Stalin, but achieves only a trivialization of history.

w Andrei Konchalovsky, Anatoli Usov *d* Andrei Konchalovsky *ph* Ennio Guarnieri *m* Eduard Artemyev *pd* Ezio Frigerio *ed* Henry Richardson

☆ Tom Hulce, Lolita Davidovich, Bob Hoskins, Alexandre Zbruev, Feodor Chaliapin Jnr, Bess Meyer, Maria Baranova, Irina Kuptchenko

'A dramatically messy, momentarily compelling look at Stalin's tyranny.' – *Variety*

'The umpteenth film to turn truth-based political tragedy into dial-a-cliché melodrama. Overacted by almost everyone in sight and scripted for stark risibility ... it comes to life only when raiding history direct.' – *Nigel Andrews, Financial Times*

Inner Sanctum

The title was taken from a radio show featuring mystery stories with a last minute twist. The films

were introduced rather oddly by a misshapen head in a crystal ball on the empty table of a boardroom. The head belonged to David Hoffman, and he introduced each film: 'This ... is the inner sanctum...' (The original reference was presumably to the innermost working of the human mind.) The films, made for Universal, all starred Lon Chaney Jnr (who alternated as hero and villain); they were among the most boring and badly made second feature thrillers of the forties.

1943 Calling Dr Death
1944 Weird Woman, Dead Man's Eyes
1945 Strange Confession (remake of The Man Who Reclaimed His Head), The Frozen Ghost
1946 Pillow of Death

Innerspace *

👫 US 1987 120m Technicolor
Warner/Amblin/Steven Spielberg/Guber-Peters (Michael Finnell)

🔲 🔳 ⊚↗ ⊘

A miniaturized air force flyer is injected into the body of a grocery clerk.
Derivative comedy with clever twists; very tolerable of its kind, but no Back to the Future.

w Jeffrey Boam, Chip Proser *d* Joe Dante *ph* Andrew Laszlo *m* Jerry Goldsmith *pd* James H. Spencer

☆ Dennis Quaid, Martin Short, Meg Ryan, Kevin McCarthy, Fiona Lewis

🏆 special visual effects (Dennis Muren)

Innocence is Bliss: see *Miss Grant Takes Richmond*

Innocence Unprotected *

Yugoslavia 1968 78m Eastmancolor/bw
Avala

🔲

original title: *Nevinosti Bez Zastite*

Interviews with the actor-writer-director of, and those who worked on, Innocence Unprotected, the first Serbian talkie made in 1942, which was confiscated during the Nazi occupation, together with excerpts from the film and from contemporary newsreels.

A fascinating collage from Makavejev, providing a documentary frame to scenes from a primitive story of true love triumphant, in style more like a silent than a talking picture, and glorifying the death-defying acrobatics of its strong-man hero and director, filmed hanging from an aeroplane by a rope held in his teeth; both the new film and the old have a simple charm.

wd Dusan Makavejev *ph* Branko Perak, Stevan Miskovic *m* Vojislav Dostic *ed* Alexsander Popovic

☆ Dragoljub Aleksic, Ana Milosavljevic, Vera Jovanovic, Bratoljub Gligorijevic, Ivan Zivkovic, Pera Milosavljevic

The Innocent ***

Italy 1976 125m colour Technovision
Rizzoli (Giovanni Bertolucci)

🔲

original title: *Innocente*
aka: *The Intruder*

In Rome in the 1890s, a Sicilian aristocrat who keeps his wife informed of his own affair takes a terrible revenge when he discovers she also has a lover.

An elegant account of decadence and sexual politics, one that subverts the intentions of the novel on which it is based.

w Suso Cecchi D'Amico, Luchino Visconti, Enrico Medioli *novel* Gabriele d'Annunzio *d* Luchino Visconti *ph* Pasqualino de Santis *m* Chopin, Liszt, Mozart, Gluck *ad* Mario Garbuglia *ed* Ruggero Mastroianni

☆ Giancarlo Giannini, Laura Antonelli, Jennifer O'Neill, Rina Morelli, Didier Haudepin, Massimo Girotti, Marie Dubois

'An outstanding example of what Hemingway would have called grace under pressure.' – *Sight and Sound*

'The protagonist is meant to be an atheist hero, a brave anarch who pays the price for his amorality. But he comes out only a sordid, spoiled sensualist swine, with no kind of depth, so this story has no involvement for the viewer.' – *Stanley Kauffmann*

† Visconti had wanted Alain Delon and Romy Schneider for the two leads. He directed the film from a wheelchair and died just before its release.

'A passion beyond love. A crime beyond murder.'

The Innocent *

GB/Germany 1993 107m Eastmancolor
Island Lakeheart/Sievernich/Defa (Norma Heyman, Chris Sievernich, Wieland Schulz-Keil)

🔲 🔳 ⊘

As the Berlin Wall comes down, a bungling English engineer returns to Germany and recalls his time there during the Cold War of the 50s, when he was assigned to the CIA, fell in love with a local woman and became involved in murder.
Uninvolving drama for the most part, though it improves as it continues, intertwining horror and humour as a naïve man finds himself in a situation beyond his control or understanding.

w Ian McEwan *novel* Ian McEwan *d* John Schlesinger *ph* Dietrich Lohmann *m* Gerald Gouriet *pd* Luciana Arrighi *ed* Richard Marden

☆ Anthony Hopkins, Isabella Rossellini, Campbell Scott, Hart Bochner, Ronald Nitschke, Jeremy Sinden, James Grant, Richard Durden

'An interesting idea and characters are otherwise wasted on a thudding succession of obvious moments which topple over into bathos.' – *Kim Newman, Empire*

† Anthony Hopkins composed and performed the soundtrack piano étude.

'For generations, the Mafia preyed on the innocent. Tonight, someone's feasting on them.'

Innocent Blood

US 1992 113m Technicolor
Warner (Lee Rich, Leslie Belzberg)

🔲 🔳 ⊘

aka: *A French Vampire in America*

A female vampire regrets turning a Mafia hoodlum into a vampire.
Haphazard and anaemic vampire movie with comic elements which never really works on any level.

w Michael Wolk *d* John Landis *ph* Mac Ahlberg *m* Ira Newborn *pd* Richard Sawyer *ed* Dale Beldin *sp* Steve Johnson, Syd Dutton, Bill Taylor

☆ Anne Parillaud, Robert Loggia, Anthony LaPaglia, Don Rickles, Elaine Kagan, David Proval, Chazz Palminteri

'Teens and genre fans should eat up John Landis' latest mix of horror and camp comedy.' – *Variety*

'A gloomy, almost oppressive film.' – *Geoff Brown, The Times*

† Directors who make brief appearances in the movie include Dario Argento, Frank Oz, Sam Raimi, Michael Ritchie and Tom Savini.

Innocent Bystanders *

GB 1972 110m Eastmancolor
Sagittarius (George H. Brown)

The British secret service sends three agents to trace a Russian traitor.
Confused and violent espionage thriller; rather a waste of good production.

w James Mitchell *d* Peter Collinson *ph* Brian Probyn *m* John Keating

☆ Stanley Baker, Geraldine Chaplin, Dana Andrews, Donald Pleasence

Innocent Lies

GB/France 1995 88m colour
Polygram/Red Umbrella/Septieme (Simon Perry, Philippe Guez)

🔲

In France in 1938, an English policeman tries to clear up the mystery of the apparent suicide of his mentor and finds himself involved with an odd and incestuous English upper-middle-class family.
The credits include an acknowledgement to 'the inspiration provided by Agatha Christie for the making of this film, which does not purport to be a faithful adaptation of any of her work', but this stew of overheated sex and underdeveloped narrative bears little resemblance to the deadly gentility of her world. It is a thriller that contains no red herrings, only dead ends and lots of loose threads.

w Kerry Crabbe, Patrick Dewolf *d* Patrick Dewolf *ph* Patrick Blossier *m* Alexandre Desplat *pd* Bernd Lepel *ed* Chris Wimble, Joelle Hache

☆ Stephen Dorff, Gabrielle Anwar, Adrian Dunbar, Sophie Aubry, Joanna Lumley, Melvil Poupaud, Bernard Haller, Alexis Denisof

'It's a disgrace that, in its present form, this script was allowed to see the light of day.' – *Sheila Johnston, Independent*

'Fails on every count.' – *Sight and Sound*

An Innocent Man

US 1989 113m Technicolor
Warner/Touchstone/Silver Screen Partners IV (Ted Field, Robert W. Cort)

🔲 🔳 ⊘

Framed by crooked cops, an engineer learns lessons of survival in prison, which he applies to seeking vengeance on his release.
Undistinguished melodrama.

w Larry Brothers *d* Peter Yates *ph* William A. Fraker *m* Howard Shore *pd* Stuart Wurtzel *ed* Stephen A. Rotter, William S. Scharf

☆ Tom Selleck, F. Murray Abraham, Laila Robins, David Rasche, Richard Young, Badja Djola, Todd Graff, M. C. Gainey

Innocent Moves: see *Searching for Bobby Fischer*

Innocent Sinners ★★

GB 1957 95m bw
Rank (Hugh Stewart)

A 13-year-old London girl builds a garden in the rubble of a bombed church, and gets into trouble with the police.
Likeable, slightly unfinished, mildly astringent little human drama full of well-observed character sketches.

w Neil Paterson *novel* An Episode of Sparrows *by* Rumer Godden *d* Philip Leacock *ph* Harry Waxman *m* Philip Green

☆ Flora Robson, Catherine Lacey, David Kossoff, Barbara Mullen, June Archer

The Innocent Sleep

GB 1995 110m colour
Starlight/Timedial (Scott Michell, Matthew Vaughn)

🔲 ⊘

A tramp witnesses a murder in which a senior policeman was one of the killers.
Moderately gripping low-voltage thriller of corruption and cover-up.

w Ray Villis *d* Scott Michell *ph* Alan Dunlop *m* Mark Ayres *pd* Eve Mavrakis *ed* Derek Trigg

☆ Rupert Graves, Annabella Sciorra, Michael Gambon, Franco Nero, Graham Crowden, Oliver Cotton

† The film is loosely based on a real-life event: the death of Italian banker Roberto Calvi, who was found hanged under London's Blackfriars Bridge in the 80s.

The Innocents ★★

GB 1961 99m bw Cinemascope
TCF/Achilles (Jack Clayton)

In Victorian times, a spinster governess in a lonely house finds her young charges possessed by evil demons of servants now dead.
Elaborate revamping of Henry James's, The Turn of the Screw, the ghosts being now (possibly) the figments of a frustrated woman's imagination. The frissons would have worked better on a normal-shaped screen, but the decor, lighting and general handling are exceptional.

w William Archibald, Truman Capote *d* Jack Clayton *ph* Freddie Francis *m* Georges Auric *ad* Wilfrid Shingleton

☆ Deborah Kerr, Megs Jenkins, Pamela Franklin, Martin Stephens, Michael Redgrave, Peter Wyngarde

Les Innocents aux Mains Sales: see *Innocents with Dirty Hands*

Innocents in Paris

GB 1953 102m bw
Romulus (Anatole de Grunwald)

British tourists spend a weekend in the gay city.
Strained compendium of anecdotes which misses an easy target.

w Anatole de Grunwald *d* Gordon Parry *ph* Gordon Lang *m* Josef Kosma

☆ Alastair Sim, Margaret Rutherford, Jimmy Edwards, Claire Bloom, Laurence Harvey, Ronald Shiner

Innocents of Paris

US 1929 69m bw
Paramount/Jesse L. Lasky

A Parisian junk dealer saves a boy's life and falls for his aunt.
Heavygoing and dated musical comedy which introduced Chevalier to world audiences.

w Ethel Doherty, Ernest Vajda *play* Flea Market *by* Charles Andrews *d* Richard Wallace *ph* Charles Lang *m/ly* Leo Robin, Richard A. Whiting

☆ Maurice Chevalier, Sylvia Beecher, Russell Simpson, George Fawcett

Innocents with Dirty Hands ***

France/West Germany/Italy   1975   125m
Eastmancolor

Fox-Rank/Films la Boétie/Terra/Juppiter (André Génovès)

original title: Les Innocents aux Mains Sales

An unhappy wife and her new young lover decide to kill her alcoholic husband, but he is aware of their plan.

An enjoyable, teasing thriller that keeps its audience, as well as its characters, guessing as one double-cross quickly follows upon another.

wd Claude Chabrol *novel* The Damned Innocents by Richard Neely *ph* Jean Rabier *m* Pierre Jansen *ad* Guy Littaye *ed* Jacques Gaillard

☆ Romy Schneider, Rod Steiger, Paolo Giusti, Jean Rochefort, François Maistre, Pierre Santini, François Perrot

'One of cinema's most enjoyable charades.' – *Richard Combs, MFB*

Inquest *

GB   1939   60m   bw

Charter (John Boulting)

A coroner has his suspicions as to who murdered the deceased.

Modest courtroom suspenser which marked the Boultings' first attempt (the second was Suspect) to raise the standard of second features.

w Francis Miller *play* Michael Barringer *d* Roy Boulting *ph* D. P. Cooper *ad* John Maxted *ed* Roy Boulting

☆ Elizabeth Allan, Herbert Lomas, Hay Petrie, Barbara Everest, Olive Sloane

The Inquisitor **

France   1981   90m   Eastmancolor

Gala/Ariane/TF1 (Georges Dancigers, Alexandre Mnouchkine)

original title: Garde à Vu

On New Year's Eve, a police inspector questions a rich lawyer suspected of killing a child.

Excellently acted, engrossing contest of wits.

w Claude Miller, Jean Herman, Michel Audiard *novel* Brainwash by John Wainwright *d* Claude Miller *ph* Bruno Nuytten *m* Georges Delerue *ad* Eric Moulard *ed* Albert Jurgenson

☆ Lino Ventura, Michel Serrault, Guy Marchand, Romy Schneider, Didier Agostini. Patrick Depeyrat, Pierre Maguelon, Serge Malik

Inseminoid

GB   1980   92m   colour

Brent Walker/Jupiter (Richard Gordon, David Speechley)

US title: Horror Planet

On a far-off planet a scientist is raped by an alien and gives birth to monsters.

Cheap and nasty rip-off of Alien that is full of disgusting effects and violent deaths but lacks any suspense.

w Nick Maley, Gloria Maley *d* Norman J. Warren *ph* John Metcalfe *m* John Scott *pd* Hayden Pearce

☆ Robin Clarke, Jennifer Ashley, Stephanie Beacham, Judy Geeson, Victoria Tennant, Steven Grives, Barry Houghton

† Six minutes were cut from the film on its US release.

'A degenerate film with dignity!'

Inserts

GB   1975   117m   DeLuxe

UA/Film and General (Davina Belling, Clive Parsons)

In 1930 Hollywood, a fading silent queen and a has-been director take to drugs.

Curious, interesting semi-porno melodrama with Pinterish asides and an inaccurate but stimulating feel of the film city at its height.

wd John Byrum *ph* Denys Coop *md* Jessica Harper

☆ Richard Dreyfuss, Jessica Harper, Veronica Cartwright, Bob Hoskins, Stephen Davies

'The ludicrous plot and the painfully obvious symbolism make it tempting to interpret *Inserts* as a comedy. Yet to assume that a bad movie about the making of a bad movie is somehow good by virtue of its badness is to be guilty of a

kind of mimetic fallacy.' – *Robert Asahina, New Leader*

'This is the story of Daisy Clover ... Love at 15. Married at 16. Divorced at 17.'

Inside Daisy Clover *

US   1965   128m   Technicolor   Panavision

Warner/Pakula-Mulligan (Alan J. Pakula)

Tribulations of an adolescent movie star in thirties Hollywood.

Amusing, rather hysterical variant on A Star Is Born; agreeably wacky in spots, glum in others. Would have benefited from the greater permissiveness possible a few years later.

w Gavin Lambert *novel* Gavin Lambert *d* Robert Mulligan *ph* Charles Lang Jnr *m* André Previn *ch* Herbert Ross *ad* Robert Clatworthy

☆ Natalie Wood, Robert Redford, Ruth Gordon, Christopher Plummer, Roddy MacDowall

'The movie is short on characters, detail, activity, dialogue, even music; it's as if it's so determined to be stylish and sophisticated that rather than risk vulgarity or banality, it eliminates almost everything.' – *Pauline Kael, 1968*

Å Ruth Gordon

Inside Detroit

US   1955   82m   bw

Columbia (Sam Katzman)

A racketeer comes out of prison and tries to regain control of the car workers' union.

Tedious support, like a grossly extended Crime Does Not Pay. .

w Robert E. Kent, James B. Gordon *d* Fred F. Sears *ph* Henry Freulich *md* Mischa Bakaleinikoff

☆ Pat O'Brien, Dennis O'Keefe, Tina Carver, Mark Damon

Inside Moves

US   1980   113m   colour

Goodmark (Mark M. Tanz, R. W. Goodwin)

A failed suicide makes friends in Max's bar with other handicapped people.

Curious tragi-comedy which generally settles for sentimentality but provides a few funny moments along the way.

w Valerie Curtin, Barry Levinson *novel* Todd Walton *d* Richard Donner *ph* Laszlo Kovacs *m* John Barry

☆ John Savage, David Morse, Diana Scarwid, Amy Wright, Tony Burton, Harold Russell

'A dismal contribution in the Year of the Disabled Person.' – *John Pym, MFB*

'If you imagine The Iceman Cometh rewritten by William Saroyan as a tribute to Frank Capra, that's about it.' – *Sunday Times*

Å Diana Scarwid (supporting actress)

Inside Out *

GB/West Germany   1975   97m   Technicolor

Warner/Kettledrum (Judd Bernard)

TV title: The Golden Heist

aka: Hitler's Gold

A German ex-commandant of a POW camp enlists the aid of Americans in a daring plan to kidnap a Nazi war criminal from East Germany and find buried Nazi loot.

Entertaining but very silly actioner with too many changes of mood, though some sequences please.

w Judd Bernard, Stephen Schneck *d* Peter Duffell *ph* John Coquillon *m* Konrad Elfers

☆ Telly Savalas, James Mason, Robert Culp, Aldo Ray, Gunter Meisner, Adrian Hoven, Charles Korvin, Richard Warner

Inside Straight

US   1951   89m   bw

MGM (Richard Goldstone)

The life of a 19th-century tycoon is revealed in flashbacks during a poker game.

Solid melodrama which doesn't quite have the required spark.

w Guy Trosper *d* Gerald Mayer *ph* Ray June *m* Lennie Hayton

☆ David Brian, Arlene Dahl, Barry Sullivan, Mercedes McCambridge, Paula Raymond, Claude Jarman Jnr, Lon Chaney Jnr, John Hoyt

Inside the Walls of Folsom Prison

US   1951   87m   bw

Bryan Foy/Warner

A prison riot results in the death of the governor; when a replacement with more humane ideas is appointed, this does not stop violence from breaking out again.

Old-fashioned prison movie on highly predictable lines.

wd Crane Wilbur

☆ Steve Cochran, David Brian, Phil Carey, Ted de Corsia, Scott Forbes

'Ordinary Men Of Uncommon Courage Risk All To Speak Out... And Change Everything.'

'Two Angry Men Driven To Tell The Truth...Whatever The Cost'

The Insider ***

US   1999   158m   Technicolor   Super 35

Buena Vista/Touchstone/Forward Pass (Michael Mann, Pieter Jan Brugge)

A TV producer persuades a former tobacco company scientist to expose the official denials that cigarettes are injurious to health, only to discover that his investigation will not be broadcast.

A true-life, devastating exposé of the way corporations and the media respond to unwelcome facts, and a gripping drama of an ordinary, principled man caught up in events beyond his control; if the film has a fault, it is that it is too long.

w Eric Roth, Michael Mann *Vanity Fair article* The Man Who Knew Too Much by Marie Brenner *d* Michael Mann *ph* Dante Spinotti *pd* Brian Morris *ed* William Goldenberg, Paul Rubell, David Rosenbloom

☆ Al Pacino, Russell Crowe, Christopher Plummer, Diane Venora, Philip Baker Hall, Lindsay Crouse, Debi Mazar, Stephen Tobolowsky, Colm Feore, Bruce McGill, Gina Gershon, Michael Gambon, Rip Torn, Michael Moore, Wings Hauser

'An edge-of-your-sear, gut-churning thriller.' – *Newsweek*

'A brilliant nail-biter of a true-story conspiracy.' – *Adam Smith, Empire*

Å picture; Russell Crowe; Michael Mann; script (Eric Roth, Michael Mann); Dante Spinotti; William Goldenberg, Paul Rubell, David Rosenbloom; sound (Andy Nelson, Doug Hemphill, Lee Orloff)

Insignificance

GB   1985   108m   colour

Zenith/Recorded Picture Company (Jeremy Thomas)

On a hot night in 1953, a professor, an actress, a senator and a ballplayer meet in a New York hotel room.

Presumably meaningful but very boring talk piece in which the audience is supposed to recognize not merely well-known figures but a cross-section of America at the time.

w Terry Johnson *play* Terry Johnson *d* Nicolas Roeg *ph* Peter Hannan *m* Stanley Myers

☆ Gary Busey, Tony Curtis, Theresa Russell, Michael Emil

Insomnia **

Norway   1997   99m   colour

Norsk Film/Nordic Screen (Petter J. Borgli, Tomas Backstrom, Tom Remlov)

On the trail of a killer, a Swedish-born cop, working in Norway, accidentally shoots his partner and covers up his guilt.

Deft psychological thriller of a man on the edge, set in a time of continual sunlight.

w Nikolaj Frobenius, Erik Skjoldbjaerg *d* Erik Skjoldbjaerg *ph* Erling Thurmann-Andersen *m* Geir Jenssen *pd* Eli Bo *ed* Hakon Overas

☆ Stellan Skarsgard, Sverre Anker Ousdal, Bjorn Floberg, Gisken Armand, Maria Bonnevie

'Offers a complex and emotionally compelling tale that doesn't settle for mere quirkiness or the de rigueur cop-thriller gore currently in vogue.' – *Steven Gaydos, Variety*

Inspecteur Lavardin

France   1986   100m   colour

Artificial Eye/MK2/Antenne 2/Suisse Romande TV (Marin Karmitz)

A detective investigates the murder of a respected writer.

Sequel to Cop Au Vin, featuring an unorthodox cop, but less effective this time around.

w Claude Chabrol, Dominique Roulet *d* Claude Chabrol *ph* Jean Rabier *m* Matthieu Chabrol *ed* Monique Fardoulis, Angela Braga-Marmet

☆ Jean Poiret, Jean-Claude Brialy, Bernadette Lafont, Jean-Luc Bideau, Jacques Dacqmine, Hermine Clair

The Inspector *

GB   1961   111m   DeLuxe   Cinemascope

TCF (Mark Robson)

US title: Lisa

In 1946 a Dutch policeman rescues a Jewish girl from an ex-Nazi and helps smuggle her to Palestine.

Peripatetic melodrama with surface suspense and subdued thoughts of ideology and race. Moments of interest, but generally dully developed and acted.

w Nelson Gidding *novel* Jan de Hartog *d* Philip Dunne *ph* Arthur Ibbetson *m* Malcolm Arnold

☆ Stephen Boyd, Dolores Hart, Leo McKern, Hugh Griffith, Donald Pleasence, Harry Andrews, Robert Stephens, Marius Goring

'A sluggish mélange of melodrama, romance, mystery and what the inactive might call action.' – *Judith Crist*

An Inspector Calls **

GB   1954   79m   bw

British Lion/Watergate (A. D. Peters)

In 1912 a prosperous Yorkshire family is visited by a mysterious inspector who proves that each of them was partly responsible for the death of a young girl.

Tactful, enjoyable record of a celebrated play in its author's most typical manner.

w Desmond Davis *play* J. B. Priestley *d* Guy Hamilton *ph* Ted Scaife *m* Francis Chagrin *ad* Joseph Bato

☆ Alastair Sim, Jane Wenham, Arthur Young, Olga Lindo, Brian Worth, Eileen Moore, Bryan Forbes

Inspector Clouseau

ÅÅ GB   1968   105m   Eastmancolor
Panavision

UA/Mirisch (Lewis J. Rachmil)

An incompetent French policeman is brought to London to investigate the aftermath of the Great Train Robbery.

Tiresome charade with all the jokes well telegraphed, and a background of swinging London.

w Tom and Frank Waldman *d* Bud Yorkin *ph* Arthur Ibbetson *m* Ken Thorne

☆ Alan Arkin, Delia Boccardo, Frank Finlay, Patrick Cargill, Beryl Reid, Barry Foster

Inspector Gadget

US   1999   78m   Technicolor

Buena Vista/Walt Disney/Caravan (Jordan Kerner, Roger Birnbaum, Andy Heyward)

A half-human, half-robotic cop, equipped with mechanical devices for every occasion, battles against his evil twin.

Lavish, gimmick-laden extravaganza resembling a live-action cartoon, but, lacking a convincing narrative, the knockabout action soon palls.

w Kerry Ehrin, Zak Penn, Dana Olsen *characters created by* Andy Heyward, Jean Chalopin, Bruno Bianchi *d* David Kellogg *m* Adam Greenberg *m* John Debney *pd* Michael White, Leslie Dilley *ed* Thom Noble, Adam Cody

☆ Matthew Broderick, Rupert Everett, Joely Fisher, Michelle Trachtenberg, Andy Dick, Cheri Oteri, Michael G. Hagerty, Dabney Coleman, D.L. Hughley, Rene Auberjonois, Frances Bay, Don Adams

'Demonstrates how a movie with little more on its mind than tickling the eyeballs of 7-year-olds can feature spiffy, jack-in-the-box special effects and still end up a dud.' – *Owen Gleiberman, Entertainment Weekly*

The Inspector General **

US   1949   101m   Technicolor

Warner (Jerry Wald)

aka: Happy Times

An assistant elixir salesman with a travelling fair is mistaken by villagers for the dreaded inspector general.

Well wrought but basically boring version of a basically boring classic farce full of rhubarbing Old Russians. Nice production and hilarious moments do not quite atone for the dull stretches.

ÅÅ film suitable for family viewing   ▥ VHS video-cassette for the British PAL system   ▥ VHS video-cassette for the British PAL system in wide screen-format   ⟳ Video cassette in a computer-colourised version   ▤ American NTSC video-cassette   Ⓐ Laser disc

w Philip Rapp, Harry Kurnitz *play* Nikolai Gogol *d* Henry Koster *ph* Elwood Bredell *m* John Green *ad* Robert Haas *songs* Sylvia Fine
☆ Danny Kaye, Walter Slezak, Barbara Bates, Elsa Lanchester, Gene Lockhart, Alan Hale, Benny Baker, Walter Catlett

Inspector Hornleigh *
GB   1938   87m   bw
TCF (Robert T. Kane)
The Chancellor of the Exchequer's bag is stolen.
First of three police comedy-dramas based on a character created for the radio series Monday Night at Eight by Hans Priwin. Not bad, but the thinnest of the trio.
w Bryan Wallace, Gerald Elliott, Richard Llewellyn *d* Eugene Forde *ph* Derrick Williams, Phil Tannura *md* Bretton Byrd
☆ Gordon Harker, Alastair Sim, Miki Hood, Hugh Williams, Steve Geray, Wally Patch, Edward Underdown, Gibb McLaughlin, Ronald Adam
'The opening shots – the murder in the squalid lodging and the stamp auction with the rows of poker faces and the elaborately mute bids – are not only good cinema, they are good English cinema, as national as a shot, say, from a Feyder, a de Mille or a Pommer.' – *Graham Greene*
'Interest is well sustained from the exciting opening shots to the crescendo at the close.' – *MFB*

Inspector Hornleigh Goes to It *
GB   1940   87m   bw
TCF (Edward Black)
US title: *Mail Train*
Hornleigh and Bingham track down a fifth columnist.
Zestful comedy thriller climaxing on an express train: good fun for addicts of the genre.
w Val Guest, J. O. C. Orton, Frank Launder *d* Walter Forde *ph* John Cox *md* Louis Levy
☆ Gordon Harker, Alastair Sim, Phyllis Calvert, Edward Chapman, Charles Oliver, Raymond Huntley, Percy Walsh, David Horne, Peter Gawthorne

Inspector Hornleigh on Holiday *
GB   1939   87m   bw
TCF (Edward Black)
The inspector and his sergeant solve the death of a fellow boarder at a seaside hotel.
Lively Hitchcockian comedy-thriller romp with an excellent script and plenty of variety of location.
w Frank Launder, Sidney Gilliat, J. O. C. Orton *d* Walter Forde *ph* John Cox *md* Louis Levy
☆ Gordon Harker, Alastair Sim, Linden Travers, Wally Patch, Edward Chapman, Philip Leaver, Kynaston Reeves

Inspiration
US   1930   74m   bw
MGM
A French artists' model renounces her lover in case she harms his career.
Inane romantic melodrama.
w Gene Markey *d* Clarence Brown *ph* William Daniels
☆ Greta Garbo, Robert Montgomery, Lewis Stone, Marjorie Rambeau, Beryl Mercer, John Miljan
'As an adult problem it holds and never offends … box office certainly, and a cinch for women.' – *Variety*
'Camille without the cough.' – *Motion Picture*

'He Gave Up What He Believed In, For The Ones He Loved.'
Instinct
US   1999   124m   Technicolor   Panavision
Buena Vista/Touchstone/Spyglass (Michael Taylor, Barbara Boyle)
A psychiatrist evaluates the mental condition of an anthropologist, who has lived in isolation with apes for several years and is accused of killing members of the search party that came looking for him.
Ludicrous psycho-melodrama that sets out to show that human society is corrupt in contrast to the natural world; all it demonstrates is how easily actors, given an unsatisfactory script, can compensate with hammy performances.
w Gerald DiPego *novel* Ishmael by Daniel Quinn *d* Jon Turteltaub *ph* Philippe Rousselot *m* Danny

Elfman *pd* Garreth Stover *ed* Richard Francis-Bruce
☆ Anthony Hopkins, Cuba Gooding Jnr, Donald Sutherland, Maura Tierney, George Dzundza, John Ashton, John Aylward, Thomas Q. Morris, Doug Spinuzza, Paul Bates
'Awkward, sluggish, finally ludicrous mix of suspense, character drama and inspirational fodder is half-baked on all counts.' – *Dennis Harvey, Variety*
'A mess of sanctimonious eco-drivel.' – *Neil Norman, London Evening Standard*

Institute Benjamenta *
GB   1995   105m   bw
ICA/British Screen/Channel 4/Image/Pandora (Keith Griffiths, Janine Marmot)
A new arrival at a school for servants becomes the favourite of its owners.
Dense, slow, visually interesting movie, the first to use actors by makers of disturbing, surrealist animated films; there's not much animation in this feature, and the audience is left to tease out its meaning.
w The Brothers Quay, Alan Passes *novel* Jakob von Gunten by Robert Walser *d* The Brothers Quay *ph* Nic Knowland *m* Lech Jankowski *pd* Jennifer Kernke *ed* Larry Sider
☆ Mark Rylance, Alice Krige, Gottfried John, Daniel Smith, Joseph Alessi
'Powerful food for unrest, and the first half hour is certainly one of the most extraordinary stretches of cinema this year.' – *Jonathan Romney, Guardian*
'Meticulously conjures a visually interesting netherworld that commands attention until alienation and indifference to the film's rarefied pursuits take over.' – *David Rooney, Variety*
'Tedium and repetition have never been so thrillingly filmed before.' – *Sight and Sound*

The Intelligence Men
GB   1965   104m   Eastmancolor
Rank/Hugh Stewart
US title: *Spylarks*
Two incompetent spies blunder through a series of adventures.
Inept and rather embarrassing big-screen debut for two excellent television comedians.
w S. C. Green, R. M. Hills *d* Robert Asher *ph* Jack Asher *m* Phillip Green
☆ Eric Morecambe, Ernie Wise, William Franklyn, April Olrich, Richard Vernon, David Lodge, Warren Mitchell, Francis Matthews

Intent to Kill *
GB   1958   89m   bw   Cinemascope
TCF/Zonic (Adrian Worker)
In a Montreal hospital, attempts are made on the life of a South American dictator recovering from a brain operation.
Solidly entertaining suspenser.
w Jimmy Sangster *d* Jack Cardiff *ph* Desmond Dickinson *m* Kenneth V. Jones
☆ Richard Todd, Betsy Drake, Herbert Lom, Warren Stevens, Alexander Knox

Interceptor
US   1992   92m   colour
Trimark (Oliver G. Hess, Kevin M. Kallberg)
A pilot is the only man who can foil a terrorist attempt to steal two experimental Stealth fighters while they are being transported by air.
Run-of-the-mill action movie with the usual indestructible hero.
w John Brancato, Michael Ferris *d* Michael Cohn *ph* Lee Redmond *m* Rick Marvin *pd* Gary T. New *ed* Glenn A. Morgan *visual effects* Richard Kerrigan
☆ Andrew Divoff, Elizabeth Morehead, Jurgen Prochnow, J. Kenneth Campbell, Jon Cedar, John Prosky, Rick Marzan, Daniel Namath

Interference
US   1929   75m   bw
Paramount
To prevent his wife from being blackmailed, a dying man commits murder and turns himself in.
Dreary drama with the distinction of being Paramount's first talking picture.
w Ernest Pascal, Hope Loring *play* Roland Pertwee, Harold Dearden *d* Lothar Mendes, Roy Pomeroy

☆ William Powell, Evelyn Brent, Clive Brook, Doris Kenyon

Interiors *
US   1978   95m   Technicolor
UA/Jack Rollins-Charles H. Joffe
Everybody in a well-heeled American family has problems.
Curious attempt by Woody Allen to make his own version of the Bergmanesque psycho-dramas he usually satirizes. Apparently this is the real Woody, and the comedian was a mask. Oh, well.
wd Woody Allen *ph* Gordon Willis *m* none
☆ Kristin Griffith, Mary Beth Hurt, Richard Jordan, Diane Keaton, E. G. Marshall, Geraldine Page, Maureen Stapleton, Sam Waterston
'As dull as toothache and as predictable as a metronome.' – *Barry Took, Punch*
& script; direction; Geraldine Page; Maureen Stapleton
🏆 Geraldine Page

Interlude
US   1957   89m   Technicolor   Cinemascope
U-I (Ross Hunter)
An American girl in Munich falls in love with an orchestral conductor but leaves him because of his insane wife.
Dull remake of When Tomorrow Comes (qv), with poor script and performances.
w Daniel Fuchs, Franklin Coen *d* Douglas Sirk *ph* R. F. Schoengarth *m* Frank Skinner
☆ Rossano Brazzi, June Allyson, Françoise Rosay, Marianne Cook, Keith Andes, Jane Wyatt
'Contains every cliché known to romantic fiction.' – *MFB*

Interlude *
GB   1968   113m   Technicolor
Columbia/Domino (David Deutsch, Jack Hanbury)
A girl reporter falls for a celebrated orchestral conductor; they have an affair but he finally goes back to his wife.
Intermezzo remade for the swinging London set, quite agreeable in parts because of the acting but generally rather soggy.
w Lee Langley, Hugh Leonard *d* Kevin Billington *ph* Gerry Fisher *m* Georges Delerue *pd* Tony Woollard
☆ Oskar Werner, Barbara Ferris, Virginia Maskell, John Cleese, Donald Sutherland, Nora Swinburne, Alan Webb
'If you laughed at Brief Encounter you will roar over this one.' – *Wilfrid Sheed*
'It's got all the schmaltz and none of the style of the tearjerkers of yesteryear.' – *Judith Crist, 1973*

'Wild longings … fierce desires he could not name … for an interlude of stolen love! To one woman he gave his memories – to another he gave his dreams!'
Intermezzo ***
US   1939   69m   bw
David O. Selznick
GB title: *Escape to Happiness*
A renowned, married violinist has an affair with his musical protégée.
Archetypal cinema love story, Hollywoodized from a Swedish original but quite perfect in its brief, sentimental way.
w George O'Neil *original scenario* Gosta Stevens, Gustav Molander *d* Gregory Ratoff *ph* Gregg Toland *m* Lou Forbes *ad* Lyle Wheeler *ed* Hal C. Kern, Francis D. Lyon
☆ Leslie Howard, Ingrid Bergman, John Halliday, Edna Best, Cecil Kellaway
† William Wyler is said to have assisted in the direction.
& Lou Forbes

'Trust me … I'm a cop.'
Internal Affairs
US   1990   115m   Technicolor   Panavision
UIP/Paramount (Frank Mancuso Jnr)
A duel to the death develops between an honest and a corrupt cop.
Unconvincing melodrama in which loud voices substitute for passion and feeling.
w Henry Bean *d* Mike Figgis *ph* John A. Alonso *m* Mike Figgis, Anthony Marinelli, Brian Banks *pd* Waldemar Kalinowski *ed* Robert Estrin

☆ Richard Gere, Andy Garcia, Nancy Travis, Laurie Metcalf, Richard Bradford, William Baldwin, Michael Beach
'Where Internal Affairs really succeeds is in its cracking narrative drive, moody atmospherics, and excellent performances, even in the smallest roles.' – *MFB*

'Stars of stage, screen, radio and boudoir throw a party for your entertainment!'
International House *
US   1933   73m   bw
Paramount
A weird variety of travellers are quarantined in a Shanghai hotel where a local doctor has perfected television.
Madcap farce which succeeds in hits and misses.
w Francis Martin, Walter de Leon, Lou Heifetz, Neil Brant *d* Edward Sutherland *ph* Ernest Haller *m/ly* Ralph Rainger, Leo Robin
☆ W. C. Fields, George Burns, Gracie Allen, Peggy Hopkins Joyce, Stuart Erwin, Sari Maritza, Bela Lugosi, Edmund Breese, Lumsden Hare, Rose Marie, Rudy Vallee, Sterling Holloway, Cab Calloway and his band, Colonel Stoopnagle and Budd
'Cast includes enough names to offset the effects of an otherwise second-rate picture.' – *Variety*
'Constructed along the lines of a mammoth vaudeville show, the motivating story often is sidetracked entirely to permit a lot of unrelated hokum comedy.' – *Motion Picture Herald*

'A thousand thrills as two men battle across a continent!'
International Lady *
US   1941   102m   bw
Edward Small
An FBI man falls for the lady Axis agent he is chasing.
Cliché-ridden melodrama partially saved by light comedy touches.
w Howard Estabrook *d* Tim Whelan *ph* Hal Mohr *m* Lucien Moraweck
☆ George Brent, Basil Rathbone, Ilona Massey, Gene Lockhart, George Zucco, Francis Pierlot, Martin Kosleck, Marjorie Gateson

International Settlement
US   1938   75m   bw
TCF (Darryl F. Zanuck)
An adventurer becomes involved in Shanghai gun-running during the war between China and Japan.
Brisk action romance with good technical credits.
w Lou Breslow, John Patrick *d* Eugene Forde *ph* Lucien Andriot *md* Samuel Kaylin
☆ George Sanders, Dolores del Rio, June Lang, Dick Baldwin, Ruth Terry, John Carradine, Keye Luke, Harold Huber, Pedro de Cordoba
'Strong supporting picture for double bills.' – *Variety*

International Squadron *
US   1941   87m   bw
Warner (Edmund Grainger)
A playboy becomes a fighting air ace.
Standard war story, quite well done; remake of Ceiling Zero (qv).
w Barry Trivers, Kenneth Gamet *story* Frank Wead *d* Lothar Mendes *ph* James Van Trees, Ted McCord *ed* Frank McGee
☆ Ronald Reagan, James Stephenson, Julie Bishop, Cliff Edwards, Reginald Denny, Olympe Bradna, William Lundigan, John Ridgely

International Velvet
GB   1978   125m   Metrocolor
MGM (Bryan Forbes)
A hostile orphan becomes an international horsewoman.
Disappointing attempt to produce a sequel to 1944's National Velvet; none of it coheres, one is not clear to whom it is intended to appeal, and some of the dialogue is fearsome.
wd Bryan Forbes *ph* Tony Imi *m* Francis Lai *pd* Keith Wilson
☆ Nanette Newman, Tatum O'Neal, Anthony Hopkins, Christopher Plummer, Peter Barkworth, Dinsdale Landen

The Internecine Project *
GB   1974   89m   Eastmancolor
Maclean and Co/Lion International/Hemisphere
(Barry Levinson, Andrew Donally)
📺

A Harvard professor arranges the mutual extermination of four people who could spoil a politician's presidential chances.
Coldly murderous romp with plenty of style.
w Barry Levinson, Jonathan Lynn *novel* Mort W. Elkind d Ken Hughes ph Geoffrey Unsworth m Roy Budd pd Geoffrey Drake ed John Shirley
☆ James Coburn, Lee Grant, Harry Andrews, Ian Hendry, Michael Jayston, Keenan Wynn

'He risked his life to save a rat – and what did he get for it?'

Internes Can't Take Money *
US   1937   75m   bw
Paramount (Benjamin Glazer)
GB title: *You Can't Take Money*
A hospital doctor persuades a gangster friend to help a woman find her missing child.
Quite interesting minor melodrama, first of the Dr Kildare series which was subsequently recast and restyled by MGM.
w Rian James, Theodore Reed *story* Max Brand d Alfred Santell ph Theodor Sparkuhl m Gregory Stone
☆ Joel McCrea, Barbara Stanwyck, Lloyd Nolan, Stanley Ridges, Lee Bowman, Irving Bacon
'Satisfactory melodrama with a tear ... better than average standing at the box office.' – *Variety*

Interno d'un Convento: see *Behind Convent Walls*

'Their nights are as fast and frantic as their days! Don't miss the wildest party ever filmed!'
The Interns *
US   1962   130m   bw
Columbia/Interns Co./Robert Cohn
📺 ⌕

In an American hospital, newly qualified doctors have personal and career problems.
Birth, abortion, sudden death, drugs and women's lib all figure in this melodramatic compendium which succeeds well enough on its own level and spawned a sequel (The New Interns) and an unsuccessful TV series.
w Walter Newman, David Swift *novel* Richard Frede d David Swift ph Russell Metty m Leith Stevens
☆ Cliff Robertson, Michael Callan, James MacArthur, Nick Adams, Suzy Parker, Buddy Ebsen, Telly Savalas

Interpol
GB   1957   92m   bw   Cinemascope
Columbia/Warwick (Irving Allen, Albert R. Broccoli)
US title: *Pickup Alley*
The US Anti-Narcotics Squad trails across Europe the insane and ruthless leader of a drug ring.
Drearily routine thick ear electrified by one performance but not helped by wide screen.
w John Paxton d John Gilling ph Ted Moore m Richard Bennett
☆ Victor Mature, Anita Ekberg, *Trevor Howard*, Bonar Colleano, Marne Maitland, Eric Pohlmann, Alec Mango, Peter Illing, Sydney Tafler

Interrogation **
Poland   1982   120m   colour
Gala/Zespol Filmowy 'X' (Tadeusz Drewno)
original title: *Przesluchanie*
In the 1950s, a fun-loving singer is arrested, questioned and tortured by the secret police.
Harrowing, but uplifting in its depiction of an unquenchable human spirit. The film was banned by the authorities, its director moving to work in North America, and not released until 1990.
wd Ryszard Bugajski ph Jacek Petrycki pd Janusz Sosnowski ed Katarzyna Maciejko
☆ Krystyna Janda, Adam Ferency, Janusz Gajos, Agnieszka Holland, Anna Romantowska, Bozena Dykiel, Olgierda Lukaszewicza, Tomasz Dedek

The Interrupted Journey
GB   1949   80m   bw
Valiant (Anthony Havelock-Allan)
📺

An author leaves his wife for another woman, changes his mind on the journey, pulls the communication cord and causes a train crash. Or does he?
Minor melodrama with expressionist tendencies and a dream explanation. Interesting for its parts rather than its whole.
w Michael Pertwee d Daniel Birt ph Erwin Hillier
☆ Richard Todd, Valerie Hobson, Christine Norden, Tom Walls, Ralph Truman, Vida Hope

Interrupted Melody
US   1955   106m   Eastmancolor
Cinemascope
MGM (Jack Cummings)
The story of Marjorie Lawrence, an Australian opera singer who fell victim to polio.
Standard biopic which jells less well than some.
w William Ludwig, Sonya Levien d Curtis Bernhardt ph Joe Ruttenberg, Paul Vogel *music supervisor* Saul Chaplin
☆ Eleanor Parker, Glenn Ford, Roger Moore, Cecil Kellaway, Stephen Bekassy
† Eleanor Parker's singing was dubbed by Eileen Farrell.
🎬 script
🎬 Eleanor Parker

'Make every move as if it were your last.'
Intersection
US   1994   98m   DeLuxe
Paramount (Bud Yorkin, Mark Rydell)
📺 ⌕ ◉
An architect's love-life goes awry after a car crash.
Dim and glossy melodrama about the meaning of life; if you value every moment, then don't waste time watching it.
w David Rayfiel, Marshall Brickman *novel* Paul Guimard d Mark Rydell ph Vilmos Zsigmond m James Newton Howard pd Harold Michelson ed Mark Warner
☆ Richard Gere, Sharon Stone, Lolita Davidovich, Martin Landau, David Selby, Jenny Morrison
'A misguided attempt to retool a French art film as a Hollywood big-star vehicle.' – *Variety*
† It is a remake of *Les Choses de la Vie* (qv), directed in 1969 by Claude Sautet and starring Michel Piccoli and Romy Schneider.

Interview with a Serial Killer: see *White Angel*

'Drink From Me And Live Forever.'
Interview with the Vampire: The Vampire Chronicles **
US   1994   122m   Technicolor
Warner/Geffen (Stephen Woolley, David Geffen)
📺 📺 ⌕ ◉ ◉ ◉
A vampire reminisces about his life over the past 200 years and his enduring relationship with an older vampire, who initiated him and whom he later tries to kill, and the young girl vampire they both created.
A brooding period piece on horror themes and the price paid for immortality, with a homoerotic subtext, but lacking the necessary emotional depth and narrative credibility as it skips through the centuries; what lingers in the mind are some of the more spectacular set-pieces.
w Anne Rice *novel* Anne Rice d Neil Jordan ph Philippe Rousselot m Elliot Goldenthal pd Dante Ferretti ed Mick Audsley sp make-up: Stan Winston
☆ Tom Cruise, Brad Pitt, Antonio Banderas, Christian Slater, Stephen Rea, Kirsten Dunst, Virgina McCollam, John McConnell, Mike Seelig, Roger Lloyd Pack
'An anaemic experience. It doesn't frighten; still less, shock. For fear, it substitutes disgust. It's such a dishonest, hypocritical film. Largely an exercise in sado-masochism, it uses the traditional trappings of vampire legend as licence for its own fixation on an array of modern perversions it would be hard to get permission to show if they were performed in modern dress and contemporary times.' – *Alexander Walker, London Evening Standard*
'It seems that Neil Jordan is better at capturing the eternal ennui of the vampire condition than the cheap thrills which are the lifeblood of the genre.' – *Adam Mars-Jones, Independent*
'Best thought of as a lycanthropic *The Odd Couple*.' – *Joe Queenan*
🎬 Dante Ferretti; Elliot Goldenthal
🎬 Philippe Rousselot; Dante Ferretti

Intervista *
Italy   1987   105m   Eastmancolor
Aljosha/RAI Uno/Cinecittà (Ibrahim Moussa)
📺 📺 ⌕
Part autobiographical reminiscence, part celebration of the fiftieth anniversary of Cinecittà, part interview by Japanese television.
Fascinating, though also self-indulgent, trip through Fellini's past.
w Federico Fellini, Gianfranco Angelucci d Federico Fellini ph Tonino Delli Colli m Nicola Piovani ad Danilo Donati, Paul Mazursky, Leon Capetanos ed Nino Baragli
☆ Federico Fellini, Marcello Mastroianni, Anita Ekberg, Sergio Rubini, Lara Wendel, Paola Liguori, Nadai Ottaviani, Tonino Delli Colli, Danilo Donati

Intimacy *
US   1965   87m   bw
Goldstone (David Heilwell)
A businessman in need of a government contract tries to compromise the official concerned.
Unusual minor melodrama, interesting but not quite successful.
w Eva Wolas d Victor Stoloff ph Ted Saizis m Geordie Hormel
☆ Barry Sullivan, Nancy Malone, Jack Ging, Joan Blackman, Jackie Shannon

Intimate Relations: see *Les Parents Terribles* (1948)

'In the Spring of 1956, in a quaint little town, a crime took place that shocked a nation ... This is the true story.'
Intimate Relations *
GB/Canada   1995   99m   DeLuxe
TCF/Intimate Relations/Chandlertown/Handmade/Boxer/Paragon (Angela Hart, Lisa Hope, Jon Slan)
📺
In the mid-50s, a young sailor finds lodgings in a northern town and is seduced by his sex-starved middle-aged landlady and her pubescent daughter.
A blackly comic take on a true-life murder, in which a lower-middle-class gentility masks rapacious emotions; in its not-always-successful stylized approach, it edges towards the territory that Joe Orton marked out as his own.
wd Philip Goodhew ph Andrés Garretón m Lawrence Shragge pd Caroline Greville-Morris ed Pia di Ciaula
☆ Julie Walters, Rupert Graves, Matthew Walker, Laura Sadler, Holly Aird, Les Dennis, Elizabeth McKechnie
'A razor-sharp condemnation not of the historical 50s but of the mythic 50s so mistily invoked by John Major in his calls for a return to "decency" and "family values".' – *Claire Monk, Sight and Sound*

The Intimate Stranger *
GB   1956   95m   bw
Anglo-Guild (Alec Snowden)
US title: *Finger of Guilt*
An American film producer in England is plagued by a strange girl who claims to have been his mistress.
Acceptable mystery thriller which holds the interest and has good detail.
w Peter Howard *novel* Pay the Piper by Peter Howard d Joseph Walton (Joseph Losey) ph Gerald Gibbs m Trevor Duncan
☆ Richard Basehart, Mary Murphy, Mervyn Johns, Constance Cummings, Roger Livesey, Faith Brook

Intimate with a Stranger
GB   1994   94m   colour
Independent International (Roderick Mangin-Turner)
A former academic turned gigolo decides, after servicing a succession of women, that life would be better with his former girlfriend.
A series of vapid sexual encounters combined with a little psycho-babble make for a depressing movie, a throwback to the sexploitation cycle of the 70s but more pretentious and even less interesting.
w Mel Woods, Roderick Mangin-Turner d Mel Roberts ph Nicholas Tebbet m Ledsam & Pugh pd Graeme Story ed Brian Smedley-Ashton
☆ Roderick Mangin-Turner, Daphne Nayer, Amy Tolsky, Lorelei King, Ellenor Wilkinson, Janis Lee, Darcey Ferrer

'Jaw-droppingly, eye-bogglingly awful.' – *Sheila Johnston, Independent*

Into the Blue
GB   1950   83m   bw
Imperadio
US title: *Man in the Dinghy*
A cheerful stowaway on a yacht helps the owners catch smugglers.
Emaciated comedy which never gets going.
w Pamela Wilcox Bower, Donald Taylor, Nicholas Phipps d Herbert Wilcox ph Max Greene m Mischa Spoliansky
☆ Michael Wilding, Odile Versois, Jack Hulbert, Constance Cummings, Edward Rigby

Into the Night *
US   1985   115m   Technicolor
Universal/George Folsey Jnr, Ron Koslow
📺 ⌕
A harassed husband becomes even more so when one night at the airport he meets a dizzy girl with six smuggled emeralds.
A kind of nocturnal road film into which for some reason the director has crammed a number of his colleagues. None of it really works, even as an in-joke.
w Ron Koslow d John Landis ph Robert Paynter m Ira Newborn pd John Lloyd
☆ Jeff Goldblum, Michelle Pfeiffer, Richard Farnsworth, Irene Papas, Paul Mazursky, Roger Vadim, David Bowie

Into the Sun
US   1991   100m   Foto-Kem
Trimark (Kevin M. Kallberg, Oliver G. Hess)
📺 📺 ⌕
A top pilot is assigned to demonstrate his skills for the benefit of a Hollywood star of action movies.
Pleasant but unmemorable movie that becomes ridiculous towards the end.
w John Brancato, Michael Ferris d Fritz Kiersch ph Steve Grass m Randy Miller pd Gary T. New ed Barry Zetlin
☆ Anthony Michael Hall, Michael Paré, Deborah Maria Moore, Terry Kiser, Brian Haley, Michael St Gerard, Linden Ashby

'Where myth and magic walk the earth.'
Into the West *
🎬 Eire   1992   102m   Technicolor
Entertainment/Little Bird/Parallel/Majestic/Miramax/Film Four/Newcomm (Jonathan Cavendish, Tim Palmer)
📺 📺 ⌕ ◉
A father, a former traveller, hunts for his two sons who have run away from their Dublin home with a magical white horse, Tir na nOg.
An odd, likeable film, despite its not always successful mythic overtones, and one that should have an appeal to the young.
w Jim Sheridan, David Keating *story* Michael Pearce d Mike Newell ph Tom Sigel m Patrick Doyle pd Jamie Leonard ed Peter Boyle
☆ Gabriel Byrne, Ellen Barkin, Ciarán Fitzgerald, Ruaidhri Conroy, David Kelly, Johnny Murphy, Colm Meaney, John Kavanagh, Brendan Gleeson, Jim Norton
'Its heady mix of Irish myth and gritty realism will effortlessly capture the imaginations of all ages.' – *Empire*

Intolerance ***
US   1916   115m   bw   silent
D. W. Griffith
📺 📺 ⌕ ◉
Four stories – including Belshazzar's feast and the massacre of St Bartholomew – of intolerance through the ages are intercut and linked by the image of a mother and her baby: 'out of the cradle, endlessly rocking'.
A massive enterprise of which audiences at the time and after were quite intolerant. Hard to take in parts, it rises to a fine climax as all the stories come to a head, including a modern one with a race between a car and train, and has been called 'the only film fugue'. At the time, by far the most expensive film ever made.
wd D. W. Griffith ph Billy Bitzer, Karl Brown
☆ Mae Marsh, Lillian Gish, Constance Talmadge, Robert Harron, Elmo Lincoln, Eugene Pallette
'A mad, brilliant, silly extravaganza. Perhaps the greatest movie ever made. In it one can see the source of most of the major traditions of the screen: the methods of Eisenstein and von Stroheim, the Germans and the Scandinavians, and, when it's bad, de Mille.' – *New Yorker, 1980*

👪 film suitable for family viewing   📺 VHS video-cassette for the British PAL system   📺 VHS video-cassette for the British PAL system in wide screen-format   🖒 Video cassette in a computer-colourised version   ▬ American NTSC video-cassette   ⌕ Laser disc

Intrigue

US   1947   90m   bw
UA/Star (Sam Bischoff)

In Shanghai after the war, a civilian pilot becomes unwittingly involved in drug smuggling.

Tedious and flashy pot-boiler.

w Barry Trivers, George Slavin d Edwin L. Marin
ph Lucien Andriot m Louis Forbes
☆ George Raft, June Havoc, Tom Tully, Helena Carter

Intrigue in Paris: see *Miss V from Moscow*

The Intruder: see *The Innocent (1976)*

The Intruder *

GB   1953   84m   bw
British Lion/Ivan Foxwell

An ex-army officer surprises a burglar and recognizes his old comrade who has been ill-served by society.

Watchable but rather mechanical compendium drama in which a series of cameos supposedly sum up the problems of life in post-war Britain.

w Robin Maugham, John Hunter novel Line on Ginger by Robin Maugham d Guy Hamilton
ph Ted Scaife m Francis Chagrin
☆ Jack Hawkins, Michael Medwin, Hugh Williams, George Cole, Dennis Price, Dora Bryan

The Intruder *

US   1961   84m   bw
Filmgroup (Roger Corman)
🖥

GB title: *The Stranger*

A mild-mannered stranger arrives in a Southern town and stirs up racist trouble.

Cheaply-made social melodrama with many effective moments.

w Charles Beaumont novel Charles Beaumont
d Roger Corman ph Taylor Byars m Herman Stein
☆ William Shatner, Frank Maxwell, Beverly Lunsford, Robert Emhardt, Jeanne Cooper, Leo Gordon, Charles Beaumont

Intruder in the Dust ***

US   1949   87m   bw
MGM (Clarence Brown)
🖥

In a Southern town, a boy and an old lady solve a mystery and prevent a black man from being lynched.

Excellent character drama which also offers vivid local colour, a murder puzzle and social comment. A semi-classic.

w Ben Maddow novel William Faulkner
d Clarence Brown ph Robert Surtees m Adolph Deutsch
☆ Juano Hernandez, Elizabeth Patterson, David Brian, Claude Jarman Jnr, Porter Hall, Will Geer

'It is surely the years of range and experience which have given him a control of the medium so calm, sure and – apparently – easy that he can make a complex story seem simple and straightforward.' – *Pauline Kael*

'A really good movie that is also and incidentally the first honestly worked out "racial" film I have seen.' – *Richard Winnington*

'An example of gripping film craftsmanship.' – *News of the World*

The Invaders: see *49th Parallel*

'From out of space – came hordes of green monsters!'

Invaders from Mars

🎬 US   1953   82m   Cinecolor
Edward L. Alperson
🖥

Martian invaders use hypnotized humans as saboteurs.

Poverty Row sci-fi partly redeemed by its erratic but talented designer who provides flashes of visual imagination.

w Richard Blake ph John Seitz m Raoul Kraushaar d/pd William Cameron Menzies
☆ Helena Carter, Arthur Franz, Leif Erickson, Hillary Brooke

Invaders from Mars

🎬 US   1986   100m   TVC Color
Panavision
Cannon (Menahem Golan, Yoram Globus)
🖥 🎧 @~ @

A boy one night sees a space ship land in his back yard.

Astonishingly witless remake of a show that was a cheap second feature in 1953.

w Dan O'Bannon, Don Jakoby d Tobe Hooper
ph Daniel Pearl m Christopher Young
☆ Karen Black, Hunter Carson, Timothy Bottoms, Louise Fletcher, Bud Cort

Invasion *

GB   1966   82m   bw
AA/Merton Park (Jack Greenwood)
🖥

An English village is beset one night by invaders from outer space.

Understated, effective little suspenser, well done in all departments.

w Roger Marshall d Alan Bridges ph James Wilson m Bernard Ebbinghouse
☆ Edward Judd, Valerie Gearon, Lyndon Brook, Yoko Tani, Tsai Chin, Barrie Ingham, Arthur Sharp

'A modest but highly intelligent science fiction thriller.' – *Financial Times*

Invasion of Planet X: see *Invasion of the Astro-Monsters*

Invasion of the Astro-Monsters

🎬 Japan   1967   90m   colour
Toho/Henry G. Saperstein Enterprises (Tomoyuki Tanaka)
🖥 @

aka: *Monster Zero*

aka: *Invasion of Planet X; Godzilla vs Monster Zero*

Aliens program three monsters, Godzilla, Rodan and Ghidrah, to attack the Earth.

Dull monster movie, its only novelty being its American leading man.

w Shinichi Sekizawa d Inoshiro Honda
ph Hajime Koizumi m Akira Ifukube ad Takeo Kita ed Rhyohei Fujii sp Eiji Tsuburaya
☆ Nick Adams, Akira Takarada, Kumi Mizuno, Keiki Sawai, Jun Tazaki, Yoshio Tsuchiya, Akira Kubo

'The world as they knew it was slipping away from them. Time was running out for the human race. And there was nothing to hold on to – except each other!'

Invasion of the Body Snatchers ****

US   1955   80m   bw   Superscope
Allied Artists/Walter Wanger
🖥 🎧 @~ @

A small American town is imperceptibly taken over by an alien force.

Persuasive, thoroughly satisfying, low-budget science fiction, put across with subtlety and intelligence in every department.

w Daniel Mainwaring novel Jack Finney d Don Siegel ph Ellsworth Fredericks m Carmen Dragon
☆ Kevin McCarthy, Dana Wynter, Larry Gates, King Donovan, Carolyn Jones, Virginia Christine, Sam Peckinpah

Invasion of the Body Snatchers *

US   1978   115m   Technicolor
UA/Robert H. Solo
🖥 🎧 @~ @

Failing to get officials to listen to the fact that the population is being replaced by aliens, a San Francisco public health inspector imitates the emotionless pod people in order to infiltrate their organisation.

Flashy updating of the 1956 classic, mistakenly set in a big city and confusingly unravelled, with nobody for the audience to empathize with. Its nicest effect is to have Kevin McCarthy appear in a cameo.

w W. D. Richter d Philip Kaufman ph Michael Chapman m Denny Zeitlin pd Charles Rosen
☆ Donald Sutherland, Brooke Adams, Leonard Nimoy, Veronica Cartwright, Jeff Goldblum, Art Hindle, Lelia Goldoni, Kevin McCarthy, Don Siegel
† The film was remade in 1993 as *Body Snatchers*.

Invasion of the Saucermen

🎬 US   1957   90m   bw
AIP/Malibu (James H. Nicholson, Robert J. Gurney Jnr)
🖥

Little green aliens who land on Earth in a flying saucer are defeated by teenagers.

Science fiction with comic overtones, though done with so little finesse that it is difficult to know what is intentionally funny and what is accidentally so.

w Robert J. Gurney Jnr, Al Martin story Paul Fairman d Edward L. Cahn fred West
m Ronald Stein ad Don Ament ed Ronald Sinclair
☆ Steve Terrell, Gloria Castillo, Frank Gorshin

Invasion Quartet

GB   1961   87m   bw
MGM (Ronald Kinnoch)

An ill-assorted foursome of officers and a boffin take on the dangerous mission of silencing a Nazi gun trained on Dover.

A plot which could have been handled any way is played unsatisfactorily for farce, and all concerned are understandably uneasy.

w Jack Trevor Story, John Briley story Norman Collins d Jay Lewis ph Geoffrey Faithfull, Gerald Moss m Ron Goodwin
☆ Bill Travers, Spike Milligan, Grégoire Aslan, John Le Mesurier, Thorley Walters, Maurice Denham, Millicent Martin, Cyril Luckham

'America wasn't ready – but he was!'

Invasion USA

US   1952   70m   bw
Columbia (Albert Zugsmith)

A hypnotist in a New York bar gives a group of people a foretaste of what might happen to them under atomic attack.

Ludicrous, dangerous, hilarious low-budget exploitationer composed mainly of rubber rocks and old newsreels.

w Robert Smith d Alfred E. Green ph John L. Russell m Albert Glasser
☆ Dan O'Herlihy, Gerald Mohr, Peggie Castle

Invasion USA

US   1985   107m   TVC Color
Cannon (Menahem Golan, Yoram Globus)
🖥 🎧 @~

Ruthless foreign mercenaries invade the southern US.

Brainless farrago of violence which goes out of its way to be unpleasant but ends up being rather funny.

w James Bruner, Chuck Norris d Joseph Zito
ph Joao Fernandes m Jay Chattaway
☆ Chuck Norris, Richard Lynch, Melissa Prophet, Alexander Zale

'Love, beauty, happiness. If you don't have it … invent it.'

Inventing the Abbots *

US   1997   110m   DeLuxe
TCF/Imagine (Ron Howard, Brian Grazier, Janet Meyers)
🖥 🎧 @

A man remembers events in the 50s, when his working-class family became involved with the family of a wealthy neighbour.

A nostalgic, small-town soap opera, in which three brothers woo two sisters, which investigates the power of myths to warp reality.

w Ken Hixon story Sue Miller d Pat O'Connor
ph Kenneth MacMillan m Michael Kamen
pd Gary Frutkoff ed Ray Lovejoy
☆ Joaquin Phoenix, Billy Crudup, Liv Tyler, Will Patton, Kathy Baker, Jennifer Connelly, Joanna Going, Barbara Williams

'An emotionally powerful but extremely old-fashioned coming-of-age saga.' – *Variety*

Investigation of a Citizen above Suspicion *

Italy   1970   115m   Technicolor
Vera (Daniele Senatore)
🎧

A successful police inspector kills his mistress and, paranoically considering himself above suspicion, plants clues leading to himself and even confesses the crime.

Fairly engrossing character study with political undertones; cinematically quite striking, too.

w Ugo Pirro, Elio Petri d Elio Petri ph Luigi Kuveiller m Ennio Morricone
☆ Gian Maria Volonte, Florinda Bolkan, Salvo Randone, Gianni Santuccio

☀ best foreign film
👓 script

An Investigation of Murder: see *The Laughing Policeman*

The Investigator

France/Italy/Spain/West Germany   1967   98m
Technicolor   Techniscope
Warner/Waterview/Criterion/Franca/CCM (Nat Waschsberger)

original title: *Le Vicomte Règle Ses Comptes*

US title: *The Viscount*

An investigator chases across Europe to expose a gang of drug dealers.

Dull and dreary thriller that should have done better by its cast.

w Clark Reynolds, Georges Farrel novel Bonne Mesure by Jean Bruce d Maurice Cloche
ph Henri Raichi m Georges Garvarentz ad Jean Douarinou ed Raymond Leboursier
☆ Kerwin Matthews, Edmond O'Brien, Jean Yanne, Fernando Rey, Jane Fleming (Silvia Sorrente), Yvette Lebon

'Irredeemable gangster melodrama.' – *Clive Hirshhorn*

† Folco Lulli replaced Edmond O'Brien in the foreign-language versions of the film.

Invisible Adversaries

Austria   1977   109m   colour
Valie Export

original title: *Unsichtbare Gegner*

A female photographer becomes convinced that aliens are taking over people's bodies and robbing them of their humanity.

Bizarre images of alienation – a man urinating on a woman's head, a fish head gasping after it has been severed from its body, a baby in a fridge – reinforce an attack on conformity. But Invasion of the Body Snatchers it isn't.

w Peter Weibel d Valie Export ph Wolfgang Simon
☆ Susanne Widl, Peter Weibel, Dr Josef Plavek, Monica Helfer-Friedrich, Helke Sander, Dominick Dusek, Herbert Schmid, Edward Neversal

Invisible Agent *

US   1942   84m   bw
Universal (George Waggner)

Nazi and Japanese spies seek the secret of invisibility from its inventor.

Lively fantasy thriller with a cast more distinguished than it deserves.

w Curt Siodmak d Edwin L. Marin m Hans Salter sp John P. Fulton
☆ Cedric Hardwicke, Peter Lorre, Ilona Massey, Jon Hall, Albert Basserman, J. Edward Bromberg, John Litel

Invisible Boy

🎬 US   1957   89m   bw
MGM/Pan (Nicholas Nayfack)

A scientist allows his 10-year-old son to repair a robot, which comes under the control of an alien force.

Minor sci-fi utilizing the robot from Forbidden Planet.

w Cyril Hume d Herman Hoffman ph Harold Wellman m Les Baxter
☆ Richard Eyer, Philip Abbott, Harold J. Stone, Diane Brewster

The Invisible Ghost

US   1941   66m   bw
Monogram/Banner (Sam Katzman)
🖥

Maddened by the death of his wife, a doctor develops murderous tendencies.

Dire and chaotic horror that makes no sense at all.

w Helen Martin, Al Martin d Joseph H. Lewis
ph Marcel le Picard ed Robert Golden
☆ Bela Lugosi, Polly Ann Young, John Maguire, Betty Compson, Clarence Muse, Terry Walker, Ernie Adams

'Creaky but enjoyable.' – *Sight and Sound*

'Even the moon is frightened of me – frightened to death!'

The Invisible Man ****

US   1933   71m   bw

Universal (Carl Laemmle Jnr)

A scientist discovers a means of making himself invisible, but in the process becomes a megalomaniac.

Superb blend of eccentric character comedy, melodrama and trick photography in a Hollywood English setting; remarkably faithful to the spirit of the book. It made a star of Claude Rains in his first film, even though he is seen for only a couple of seconds.

w R. C. Sherriff, Philip Wylie *novel* H. G. Wells d James Whale ph Arthur Edeson m W. Frank Harling sp John P. Fulton

☆ Claude Rains, Gloria Stuart, William Harrigan, Henry Travers, E. E. Clive, Una O'Connor, Forrester Harvey, Dudley Digges, Holmes Herbert

GRIFFIN (CLAUDE RAINS): 'We'll start with a few murders. Big men, little men – just to show we make no distinction.'

'Well made and full of intentional and unintentional laughs. Should do well.' – *Variety* 'Taken either as a technical exercise or as a sometimes profoundly moving retelling of the Frankenstein fable, it is one of the most rewarding of recent films.' – *William Troy*

† Sequels, successively less interesting, were (all qv) *The Invisible Man Returns* (1940), *Invisible Woman* (1941), *Invisible Agent* (1942), *The Invisible Man's Revenge* (1944), *Abbott and Costello Meet the Invisible Man* (1951) and *Memoirs of an Invisible Man* (1992). A TV series with an anonymous hero was made by ATV in 1955; a Universal one with David McCallum followed in 1975, and was restructured as *The Gemini Man* in 1976. Boris Karloff had been first choice for the role, but he turned it down.

The Invisible Man Returns

US   1940   81m   bw

Universal (Ken Goldsmith)

A man convicted of killing his brother uses the secret of invisibility to find the real culprit.

Second in the series takes itself too seriously: a slow starter which works its way to a strong climax.

w Curt Siodmak, Lester Cole, Cedric Belfrage d Joe May ph Milton Krasner m Hans Salter, Frank Skinner sp John P. Fulton

☆ Vincent Price, Cedric Hardwicke, John Sutton, Nan Grey, Cecil Kellaway, Alan Napier, Forrester Harvey

'Though the film has its bright moments, and some weird ones too, the first freshness is gone. Even the effects seem repetitive.' – *Pauline Kael, 70s*

The Invisible Man's Revenge

US   1944   77m   bw

Universal (Ford Beebe)

A psychopathic killer on the run takes refuge with a doctor who has discovered the secret of invisibility.

Curious reversion to the original story in that the invisible man is now again the villain; but otherwise there's no flavour at all to this horror comic set in a phoney England.

w Bertram Millhauser d Ford Beebe m Hans Salter sp John P. Fulton

☆ Jon Hall, Leon Errol, John Carradine, Alan Curtis, Evelyn Ankers, Gale Sondergaard, Halliwell Hobbes

The Invisible Menace

US   1938   55m   bw

Warner

Murder at an army base brings strange revelations of the past.

Standard mystery in which the star seems misplaced.

w Crane Wilbur *play* Ralph S. Zink d John Farrow ph L. William O'Connell ed Harold McLernan

☆ Boris Karloff, Regis Toomey, Marie Wilson, Henry Kolker

'Undistinguished mystery meller, for bottom-lining the duals.' – *Variety*

† It was remade in 1943 as *Murder at the Waterfront*.

'Destruction To All He Touched Or Looked Upon!'

The Invisible Ray *

US   1935   79m   bw

Universal (Edmund Grainger)

A scientist discovers a superpowerful element which makes him homicidal.

Slow-moving science fiction with a touch of horror, and the pattern for its star's many later roles as a sympathetic man who turns into a monster. Interesting rather than stimulating.

w John Colton *story* Howard Higgin, Douglas Hodges d Lambert Hillyer ph George Robinson m Franz Waxman sp John P. Fulton

☆ Boris Karloff, Bela Lugosi, Frances Drake, Frank Lawton, Walter Kingsford, Beulah Bondi, Violet Kemble Cooper, Nydia Westman

'An easy number to sell, it should do pretty good business.' – *Variety*

Invisible Stripes

US   1939   82m   bw

Warner (Hal B. Wallis)

An ex-con finds it difficult to go straight.

By 1940 Warner must have been able to make rip-offs of Angels with Dirty Faces in their sleep, and this one, despite its cast, suggests that they did.

w Warren Duff *book* Warden Lewis E. Lawes d Lloyd Bacon ph Ernest Haller m Heinz Roemheld

☆ George Raft, Humphrey Bogart, William Holden, Flora Robson, Jane Bryan, Paul Kelly, Lee Patrick, Henry O'Neill, Moroni Olsen

'It's a familiar cinematic yarn but strengthened by a zippy pace, excellent performances and direction.' – *Variety*

The Invisible Woman

US   1941   72m   bw

Universal (Burt Kelly)

A mad scientist turns a model invisible.

Screwball comedy with a deteriorating star at his hammiest: generally very laboured, but with some funny moments.

w Robert Lees, Fred Rinaldo, Gertrude Purcell d A. Edward Sutherland ph Elwood Bredell md Charles Previn

☆ John Barrymore, Charles Ruggles, Virginia Bruce, John Howard, Oscar Homolka, Donald MacBride, Edward Brophy, Shemp Howard, Margaret Hamilton, Maria Montez

Invitation

US   1952   81m   bw

MGM (Lawrence Weingarten)

When a millionaire's daughter believes she is dying, revelations ensue about her beloved husband's original intentions.

Competently idiotic weepie with a happy ending.

w Paul Osborn *story* Jerome Weidman d Gottfried Reinhardt ph Ray June m Bronislau Kaper

☆ Dorothy McGuire, Van Johnson, Ruth Roman, Louis Calhern, Ray Collins, Michael Chekhov

'The dialogue is stagey and the treatment indeterminate, with overmuch reliance on the dubious emotional reinforcement of loud background music.' – *Penelope Houston*

L'Invitation ***

Switzerland/France   1973   100m   colour

Groupe 5/Television Suisse/Citel Films/Planfilm

Following his mother's death, a middle-aged bachelor buys a home in the country and invites his office colleagues to a garden party.

Delightful comedy of manners that won a Special Jury Prize at the Cannes Film Festival.

w Claude Goretta, Michel Viala d Claude Goretta ph Jean Zeller m Patrick Moraz ad Yanko Hodjis ed Joelle Van Effenterre

☆ Jean-Luc Bideau, Jean Champion, Corinne Coderey, Pierre Collet, Neige Dolsky, Jacques Rispal, Michel Robin, Rosine Rochette, François Simon, Cecile Vassort

Invitation to a Gunfighter *

US   1964   92m   DeLuxe

UA/Stanley Kramer (Richard Wilson)

A small-town tyrant hires a smooth gunfighter to keep down the farmers he has cheated.

Predictable, rather self-satisfied little Western with a studio look. Smart script and performances.

w Elizabeth and Richard Wilson d Richard Wilson ph Joseph MacDonald m David Raksin

☆ Yul Brynner, George Segal, Janice Rule, Pat Hingle

Invitation to Happiness

US   1939   95m   bw

Paramount (Wesley Ruggles)

A society girl marries a prizefighter.

Routine star romantic drama.

w Claude Binyon d Wesley Ruggles ph Leo Tover m Frederick Hollander

☆ Irene Dunne, Fred MacMurray, Charles Ruggles, Billy Cook, William Collier Snr, Marion Martin

'Heartthrob drama, geared for good biz.' – *Variety*

Invitation to the Dance **

GB   1954   92m   Technicolor

MGM (Arthur Freed)

Three stories in dance and mime.

Unsuccessful ballet film which closed its star's great period and virtually ended the heyday of the Hollywood musical. The simple fact emerged that European ballet styles were not Kelly's forte; yet there was much to enjoy in Circus, Ring around the Rosy and The Magic Lamp.

ph Frederick A. Young m Jacques Ibert, André Previn, Rimsky-Korsakov ad Alfred Junge wd/ch Gene Kelly

☆ Gene Kelly, Igor Youskevitch, Tommy Rall, Belita, Tamara Toumanova

Invitation to the Wedding

GB   1985   90m   colour   widescreen

Chancery Lane (Joseph Brooks)

An aristocratic wedding causes trouble when the bride's uncle, the bishop, marries her to the wrong man at rehearsal.

A situation which could have been mildly amusing in the Quiet Wedding vein is botched by an unfunny script and wildly eccentric casting, including Gielgud as an American evangelist.

w William Fairchild d Joseph Brooks ph Freddie Young m Joseph Brooks

☆ Ralph Richardson, John Gielgud, Paul Nicholas, Elizabeth Shepherd, Ronald Lacey, John Standing, Susan Brooks

IP5

France   1992   119m   colour

Artificial Eye/Cargo/Gaumont (Jean-Jacques Beineix)

A black rap performer and a graffiti artist steal a car on a trip across France and discover an old man on the back seat.

A road movie that covers a lot of ground without getting anywhere; it attempts romance but achieves whimsy.

w Jean-Jacques Beineix, Jacques Forgeas d Jean-Jacques Beineix ph Jean-François Robin m Gabriel Yared ad Dan Weil ed Joëlle Hache

☆ Yves Montand, Olivier Martinez, Sekkou Sall, Géraldine Pailhas, Colette Renard, Sotigui Kouyate

'Beineix specialises in a grandiloquent glossiness that masquerades as art.' – *Nigel Andrews, Financial Times*

'A dismal French road movie.' – *Philip French, Observer*

† It was Yves Montand's last film.

The Ipcress File **

GB   1965   109m   Techniscope

Rank/Steven/Lowndes (Harry Saltzman)

An intelligence man traces a missing scientist and finds that one of his own superiors is a spy.

The attempt to present a low-key James Bond (glasses, good at cookery, supermarket shopper) is frustrated by flashy direction and a confused plot. It did herald a new genre though the whole ambiance is now sadly dated, like an old copy of The Sunday Times Colour Supplement.

w Bill Canaway, James Doran *novel* Len Deighton d Sidney J. Furie ph Otto Heller m John Barry ad Ken Adam

☆ Michael Caine, Nigel Green, Guy Doleman, Sue Lloyd, Gordon Jackson

'The deglamorized espionage story, but with plenty of tingle and zest, both in plot and camerawork.' – *Judith Crist*

† Two sequels appeared starring 'Harry Palmer' (never named in the books): *Funeral in Berlin* and *Billion Dollar Brain* (both qv).

♔ best British film; Ken Adam; Otto Heller

Irene

US   1940   101m   bw (colour sequence)

RKO/Imperator (Herbert Wilcox)

A New York Irish shopgirl moves into society.

Fairly dim picturization of the old musical: the cast does its best.

w Alice Duer Miller *play* James H. Montgomery d Herbert Wilcox ph Russell Metty m/ly Harry Tierney, Joseph McCarthy md Anthony Collins

☆ Anna Neagle, Ray Milland, Roland Young, Alan Marshal, May Robson, Billie Burke, Arthur Treacher, Marsha Hunt, Isabel Jewell, Ethel Griffies

'This pre-camp version tries to be innocuously charming, and the effort is all too evident.' – *New Yorker, 1976*

† Previously filmed in 1926 with Colleen Moore.

♫ Anthony Collins

Irish Eyes Are Smiling **

US   1944   90m   Technicolor

TCF (Damon Runyon)

The life and times of an 1890s songwriter, Ernest R. Ball.

Standard musical biopic, handsomely mounted.

w Earl Baldwin, John Tucker Battle d Gregory Ratoff ph Harry Jackson md Alfred Newman, Charles Henderson

☆ Dick Haymes, June Haver, Monty Woolley, Anthony Quinn, Beverly Whitney, Maxie Rosenbloom, Veda Ann Borg, Clarence Kolb

♫ Alfred Newman, Charles Henderson

The Irish in Us

US   1935   84m   bw

Warner (Samuel Bischoff)

Adventures of three New York brothers.

Routine, good-natured star action frolic.

w Earl Baldwin d Lloyd Bacon ph George Barnes md Leo F. Forbstein

☆ James Cagney, Pat O'Brien, Olivia de Havilland, Mary Gordon, Frank McHugh, Allen Jenkins, J. Farrell MacDonald, Thomas Jackson

'A hokey laugh ensemble that will be oke.' – *Variety*

The Irishman *

Australia   1978   110m   Gevacolor

Forest Home/SAFC (Anthony Buckley)

In the 20s, a heavy-drinking, horse-loving Irish teamster finds it hard to come to terms with the arrival of motor-driven transport and the demands of his family.

Family drama acted out against spacious landscapes, good to look at but too predictable and with a score that emphasizes its sentimental aspects.

wd Donald Crombie *novel* Elizabeth O'Conner ph Peter James m Charles Marawood pd Owen Williams ed Tim Wellburn

☆ Michael Craig, Robyn Nevin, Simon Burke, Gerard Kennedy, Lou Brown, Tony Barry, Bryan Brown, John Bluthal

'A story of bloodshed, passion, desire and death ... everything in fact that makes life worth living!'

Irma La Douce *

US   1963   146m   Technicolor   Panavision

UA/Phalanx/Mirisch/Edward L. Alperson (Billy Wilder)

A Paris policeman falls for a prostitute and becomes her pimp.

A saucy yarn originally presented inventively as a small-scale stage musical becomes a tasteless yawn on the big screen, especially when presented at such length and without the songs. Minor compensations abound but are insufficient.

w Billy Wilder, I. A. L. Diamond d Billy Wilder ph Joseph LaShelle m Marguerite Monnot md André Previn ad Alexander Trauner

☆ Shirley MacLaine, Jack Lemmon, Lou Jacobi, Herschel Bernardi, Joan Shawlee, Bruce Yarnell

♟ André Previn

♫ Joseph LaShelle; Shirley MacLaine

Irma Vep *
France 1996 98m colour
ICA/Dacia (Georges Benayoun)
🎦 📺 ⊘

A Hong Kong actress goes to Paris to star as a mysterious thief in a disastrous television remake of Louis Feuillade's silent French film *Les Vampires*.
Enjoyable mix of nostalgia for cinema's past and a celebration of the trials and triumphs of high-energy, low-budget film-making.
wd Olivier Assayas ph Eric Gautier ad François-Renaud Labarthe ed Luc Barnier
☆ Maggie Cheung, Jean-Pierre Leaud, Nathalie Richard, Antoine Basler, Nathalie Boutefeu, Bulle Ogier, Lou Castel, Arsinee Khanjian
  'An inventive, often hilarious depiction of low-budget arthouse filmmaking.' – *Neon*
† The film was itself made in four weeks on a tiny budget.

Iron & Silk *
US 1990 92m DuArt
Sun/Tokyo Broadcasting (Shirley Sun)
🎦 📺 @. ⌂

A Chinese-speaking American graduate with a love of kung fu goes to China in the 80s to teach English and study martial arts.
Based on a true story, a film of great charm and good humour, as the representative of one culture tries to understand and appreciate another.
w Mark Salzman, Shirley Sun book Mark Salzman d Shirley Sun ph James Hayman m Michael Gibbs pd Calvin Tsao ed Geraldine Peroni, James V. Kwei
☆ Mark Salzman, Pan Qingfu, Jeanette Lin Tsui, Vivian Wu, Sun Xudong

The Iron Curtain
US 1948 87m bw
TCF (Sol C. Siegel)
A Russian official in Ottawa becomes disillusioned and reveals to the US authorities details of a spy ring.
Cold war biopic of Igor Gouzenko; not badly done in the semi-documentary mould.
w Milton Krims d William Wellman ph Charles G. Clarke md Alfred Newman, using Russian themes
☆ Dana Andrews, Gene Tierney, Berry Kroeger, Edna Best

The Iron Duke *
GB 1934 88m bw
Gaumont (Michael Balcon)
After Waterloo, the Duke of Wellington defeats a French scheme to discredit him.
A popular historical star vehicle of its time and a good example of British pre-war production in the Korda mould.
w Bess Meredyth story H. M. Harwood d Victor Saville ph Curt Courant md Louis Levy ad Alfred Junge ed Ian Dalrymple
☆ George Arliss, Gladys Cooper, Emlyn Williams, Ellaline Terriss, A. E. Matthews, Edmund Willard, Felix Aylmer

Iron Eagle
US 1986 119m Metrocolor
Tri-Star (Ron Samuels, Joe Wizan)
🎦 📺 @. ⌂
A young man rescues his hostage father from a Middle Eastern country.
Increasingly suspenseful adventure drama which suited America's mood.
w Kevin Elders, Sidney J. Furie d Sidney J. Furie ph Adam Greenberg m Basil Poledouris pd Robb Wilson King ed George Grenville
☆ Louis Gossett Jnr, Jason Gedrick, David Suchet, Tim Thomerson, Larry B. Scott
  'Theaters may have to stay open from high noon to red dawn to handle the crowd.' – *Variety*

Iron Eagle II
Canada 1988 100m Bellevue-Pathé
Guild/Alliance Entertainment/Harkot Productions (Jacob Kotzky, Sharon Harel, John Kemeny)
🎦 📺 @. ⌂
American and Russian pilots co-operate to destroy a nuclear missile base in the Middle East.
Silly fantasy, made occasionally bearable by its airborne sequences.
w Kevin Elders, Sidney J. Furie d Sidney J. Furie ph Alain Dostie m Amin Bhatia ad Ariel Roshko ed Rit Wallis

☆ Louis Gossett Jnr, Mark Humphrey, Stuart Margolin, Alan Scarfe, Sharon H. Brandon, Maury Chaykin, Colm Feore, Clark Johnson, Jason Blicker
† There was a further sequel, *Aces: Iron Eagle III* (qv).

Iron Eagle IV
Canada 1995 95m colour
Norstar (Peter Simpson)
📺
Delinquent teenagers training to be pilots uncover a high-level conspiracy involving toxic chemicals.
An action film aimed at an audience that can identify with its young heroes; they will also need to enjoy bad films.
w Michael Stokes d Sidney J. Furie ph Curtis Petersen m Paul Zaza ad Michael Parks ed Jeff Warren
☆ Louis Gossett Jnr, Al Waxman, Jason Cadieux, Joanne Vanicola
  'Never manages to get off the runway.' – *Variety*

The Iron Giant ***
👫 US 1999 86m Technicolor
Warner (Allison Abbate, Des McAnuff)
In 1957, a young boy tries to protect an iron giant from government officials who are convinced that it is an alien weapon and plan to destroy it.
Set at a time of Cold War and nuclear paranoia and the beginnings of space exploration, this is an engaging, well-animated fable of pacifism and self-realisation that should find a ready audience among adults as well as children.
w Tim McCanlies book *The Iron Man* by Ted Hughes d Brad Bird ph Mark Dinicola m Michael Kamen pd Mark Whiting ed Darren T. Holmes
☆ Featuring voices of: Jennifer Aniston, Eli Marienthal, Harry Connick Jnr, Vin Diesel, Christopher McDonald, James Gammon, Cloris Leachman, John Mahoney, M. Emmet Walsh
  'An unalloyed success that works on several levels.' – *Variety*
  'A modern classic.' – *Film Review*
† Despite critical plaudits, the movie did poorly at the box-office.

The Iron Glove
US 1954 77m Technicolor
Columbia (Sam Katzman)
A staunch supporter of the Old Pretender meets friends and enemies in London at the court of George I.
Stilted costume piece, unsuitably cast and flatly written.
w Jesse L. Lasky Jnr, De Vallon Scott, Douglas Heyes d William Castle ph Henry Freulich md Mischa Bakaleinikoff
☆ Robert Stack, Ursula Thiess, Richard Stapley, Alan Hale Jnr

The Iron Hand: see *Fist of Fury*

The Iron Horse *
US 1924 119m bw silent
Fox
A man seeking to avenge his father's murder works on the first transcontinental railroad.
Archetypal Western, very slow to start but with an authentic cast of thousands.
w Charles Kenyon, John Russell d John Ford ph George Schneiderman
☆ George O'Brien, Madge Bellamy, Cyril Chadwick, Fred Kohler
  'At last a film has come from America which trusts the railroad, and sees magic in it, and power; which honours the railroad and holds it mightier than man; which loves the railroad and is content to follow it into the heart of romance.' – C. A. *Lejeune*

The Iron Maiden
GB 1962 98m Eastmancolor
Anglo Amalgamated/GHW (Peter Rogers)
US title: *The Swinging Maiden*
An aircraft designer gets into trouble because of his affection for traction engines.
Feeble attempt to duplicate the success of Genevieve, this time starring a steamroller. Very English.
w Vivian Cox, Leslie Bricusse d Gerald Thomas ph Alan Hume m Eric Rogers

☆ Michael Craig, Alan Hale Jnr, Jeff Donnell, Cecil Parker, Noel Purcell, Roland Culver, the Duke of Bedford, Anne Helm

The Iron Major
US 1943 85m bw
RKO
📺
The life of Frank Cavanaugh, football coach and hero of World War I.
Sub-standard biopic.
w Aben Kandel, Warren Duff d Ray Enright
☆ Pat O'Brien, Ruth Warrick, Robert Ryan, Leon Ames
  'A respectful, rather dull picture ... all the talk is in words of less than one syllable.' – *James Agee*

Iron Man
US 1951 81m bw
Universal-International
A coal miner is persuaded to become a prizefighter, but success changes his character.
A somewhat changed version of the 1931 film; no better.
w George Zuckerman, Borden Chase d Joseph Pevney
☆ Jeff Chandler, Evelyn Keyes, Stephen McNally, Joyce Holden, Rock Hudson, Jim Backus, James Arness

The Iron Man
US 1931 73m bw
Universal (Carl Laemmle Jnr)
A prizefighter is spurred on by his money-hungry wife.
Competent, routine, ringside melodrama.
w Francis Edwards Faragoh novel W. R. Burnett d Tod Browning ph Percy Hilburn
☆ Lew Ayres, Jean Harlow, Robert Armstrong, John Miljan, Eddie Dillon, Ned Sparks
† Remade in 1937 as *Some Blondes Are Dangerous* and in 1951 under the original title.

The Iron Mask *
US 1929 87m bw talking sequences, sound and music score
UA/Douglas Fairbanks
📺 @.
The true prince of France is kidnapped and imprisoned, but the villains reckon without D'Artagnan and the three musketeers.
Spirited star rendition of Dumas, the last big silent costume drama of the twenties.
w Elton Thomas (Douglas Fairbanks) novel *Ten Years After* by Alexandre Dumas d Allan Dwan ph Henry Sharp m Hugo Riesenfeld pd Maurice Leloir
☆ Douglas Fairbanks, Nigel de Brulier, Belle Bennett, Marguerite de la Motte

'...a labyrinth of deception.'
Iron Maze
US/Japan 1991 102m CFI color
First Independent/Trans-Tokyo/J & M Entertainment (Ilona Herzberg, Hidenori Ueki)
🎦 📺 @.
A police-chief in a Pennsylvania steel town investigates the attempted murder of a Japanese businessman, who wants to build an amusement park on the site of the mill; the chief suspects are the man's American wife and her lover.
Based on the same story that Kurosawa used as an inspiration for Rashomon, which was first filmed in Hollywood as The Outrage, this seems little more than a muddled protest at the Japanese takeover of US businesses (and, perhaps, of Hollywood studios).
w Tim Metcalfe story *In A Grove* by Ryunosuke Akutagawa d Hiroaki Yoshida ph Morio Saequsa m Stanley Myers pd Toby Corbett, Toro Ueno ed Bonnie Koehler
☆ Jeff Fahey, Bridget Fonda, Hiroaki Murakami, J. T. Walsh, Gabriel Damon, John Randolph, Peter Allas, Carmen Filpi
  'A mess from beginning to end, presenting three cardboard characters and a flashback-infested narrative which rivals *Passage to Marseille* and *Millennium* as one of the most inelegant ever committed to film.' – *Empire*

The Iron Mistress
US 1952 107m Technicolor
Warner (Henry Blanke)
The life of Westerner Jim Bowie and his famous knife.

Stolid actioner with uninspired script and performances.
w James R. Webb novel Paul I. Wellman d Gordon Douglas ph John Seitz m Max Steiner
☆ Alan Ladd, Virginia Mayo, Joseph Calleia, Phyllis Kirk, Alf Kjellin, Douglas Dick, Tony Caruso, George Voskovec

The Iron Petticoat
GB 1956 96m Technicolor Vistavision
Remus/Harry Saltzman (Betty E. Box)
🎦
An American air force officer persuades a Russian lady flyer of the advantages of the western way of life.
Feeble imitation of Ninotchka with a saucy star team which simply doesn't jell.
w Ben Hecht d Ralph Thomas ph Ernest Steward m Benjamin Frankel
☆ Bob Hope, Katharine Hepburn, James Robertson Justice, Robert Helpmann, David Kossoff, Alan Gifford, Paul Carpenter, Noelle Middleton
  'They seem amazed to find themselves in a comedy that has no humour, and they go through the motions grimly, like children at dancing school, hoping it will all be over soon.' – *William K. Zinsser*

The Iron Road: see *Buckskin Frontier*

The Iron Triangle
US 1988 91m colour
Medusa/Eurobrothers/International Video Entertainment (Angela P. Schapiro, Tony Scotti)
🎦 📺 @.
An American officer is captured by two Vietcong, one idealistic, the other murderous.
War film more concerned with humanity than action, and effective enough in its small way.
w Eric Weston, John Bushelman, Lawrence Hilbrand book based on the diary of an unknown Vietcong soldier d Eric Weston ph Irv Goodnoff m Michael Lloyd, John D'Anrea, Nick Strimple pd Errol Kelly ed Roy Watts
☆ Beau Bridges, Haing S. Ngor, Liem Whatley, Johnny Hallyday, Jim Ishida, Ping Wu, Jack Ong, Sophie Trang

Iron Will
👫 US 1994 109m Technicolor
Buena Vista/Disney (Patrick Palmer, Robert Schwartz)
🎦 📺 @.
In 1917, a youth enters a 500-mile dog-sled race and becomes an American hero.
Predictable, soft-centred drama of success against the odds.
w John Michael Hayes, Djordje Milicevic, Jeff Arch d Charles Haid ph William Wages m Joel McNeely pd Stephen Storer ed Andrew Doerfer
☆ Mackenzie Astin, Kevin Spacey, August Schellenberg, David Ogden Stiers, Brian Cox, George Gerdes, John Terry, Penelope Windust

Ironweed
US 1987 143m Technicolor
Taft Entertainment/Keith Barish/Home Box Office
🎦 📺 @.
An alcoholic down-and-out returns to his home town, where he is haunted by his violent past. Although forgiven by his family, he takes to the road again.
Relentlessly gloomy and ploddingly faithful re-creation of a Pulitzer prizewinner.
w William Kennedy novel William Kennedy d Hector Babenco ph Lauro Escorel m John Morris pd Jeannine C. Oppewall
☆ Jack Nicholson, Meryl Streep, Carroll Baker, Michael O'Keefe, Diane Venora, Tom Waits
👤 Jack Nicholson; Meryl Streep

Irreconcilable Differences
US 1984 113m Technicolor
Lantana/Warner
📺 @.
Nine-year-old Casey interferes in her parents' planned divorce.
An ancient wheeze for a romantic comedy, here decked out with modern trimmings but no better intrinsically than it was in the thirties.
w Nancy Meyers, Charles Shyer d Charles Shyer
☆ Ryan O'Neal, Shelley Long, Drew Barrymore, Sam Wanamaker, Allen Garfield, Sharon Stone

Irresistible Force

US   1993   74m   colour
CBS/Davis (Michael Lake)

A suspended cop and his female partner combat a heavily armed group of white supremacists who take over a shopping mall.

Efficient, though ultimately silly, time-wasting action movie, designed mainly to display the high-kicking martial art skills of Rothrock.

w Carleton Eastlake d Kevin Hooks ph Kevan 'Loosey' Lind m David Michael Frank pd David R. Copping ed Andy Blumenthal

☆ Stacy Keach, Cynthia Rothrock, Christopher Neame, Kathleen Garrett, Michael Bacall, Nicholas Hammond, Paul Winfield

Is Everybody Happy?

US   1929   80m   bw
Warner

The life of a clarinettist who rises from poverty. Or, *The Ted Lewis Story*, a primitive musical.

w Joseph Jackson, James A. Starr d Archie Mayo
☆ Ted Lewis, Alice Day, Ann Pennington, Lawrence Grant

Is Everybody Happy?

US   1943   73m   bw
Columbia

A virtual remake of the above, with the star fourteen years older.

Low-budget filler with a few good numbers.

w Monte Brice d Charles Barton ph L. William O'Connell md Morris Stoloff
☆ Ted Lewis, Larry Parks, Michael Duane, Nan Wynn

Is Paris Burning?

France/US   1965   165m   bw   Panavision
(colour sequence)
Paramount/Transcontinental/Marianne (Paul Graetz)

A multi-storied account of the 1944 liberation of Paris.

Muddled, scribbled, tedious and confusing attempt at a thinking man's all-star war epic.

w Francis Ford Coppola, Gore Vidal book *Paris, brûle-t-il?* by Larry Collins and Dominique Lapierre d René Clément ph Marcel Grignon m Maurice Jarre

☆ Leslie Caron, Gert Frobe, Charles Boyer, Yves Montand, Orson Welles, Alain Delon, Jean-Pierre Cassel, Jean-Paul Belmondo, Kirk Douglas, Glenn Ford, Claude Dauphin, Daniel Gélin, Anthony Perkins, Simone Signoret, Robert Stack and also George Chakiris

'An incoherent, ponderous and shallow tribute to one of the great experiences of our time, an insult to those with intimate knowledge of or experience with the liberation of Paris, an embarrassment for those interested in spectacular moviemaking.' – *Judith Crist*

♫ Marcel Grignon

Isaac Littlefeathers

Canada   1985   90m   colour
Lauron/Allarcom/King Motion Picture (Barry Pearson, William Johnson)

A hot-headed Indian boy, abandoned by his mother and his white father and adopted by a Jewish grocer, fights the prejudice he meets with violence.

A well-made drama about racial intolerance, with some nice touches but an over-reliance on cliché.

w Les Rose, Barry Pearson, John Katz d Les Rose ph Ed Higginson m Paul Zaza ad Richard Hudolin ed Mairin Wilkinson

☆ Lou Jacobi, William Korbut, Scott Hylands, Tom Heaton, Lynda Mason Green, Lorraine Behnan, George Clutesi, Vincent Gale, Robert Astle

Isadora *

GB   1968   138m   Eastmancolor
Universal (Robert and Raymond Hakim)

US title: *The Loves of Isadora*

Eccentric character dancer Isadora Duncan reflects on her crowded and unconventional life.

Ambitious and expensive but finally unsatisfactory biopic of a controversial figure of the twenties.

w Melvyn Bragg, Clive Exton d Karel Reisz ph Larry Pizer m Maurice Jarre pd Jocelyn Herbert ad Michael Seymour, Ralph Brinton

☆ Vanessa Redgrave, Jason Robards Jnr, James Fox, Ivan Tchenko, John Fraser, Bessie Love

'A brave attempt at a daunting task.' – *Tom Milne*

♫ Vanessa Redgrave

Ishtar

♔♔   US   1987   107m   Technicolor
Columbia/Delphi V (Warren Beatty)

Two untalented songwriters get involved with Middle Eastern turmoil.

Bitty rehash of old jokes and situations, vaguely resembling a Hope-Crosby Road picture of long ago, but far less funny despite costing 50 million dollars.

wd Elaine May ph Vittorio Storaro pd Paul Sylbert

☆ Dustin Hoffman, Warren Beatty, Isabelle Adjani, Charles Grodin, Jack Weston, Tess Harper

'One can't help but wonder whether the camel was the only blind creature who had something to do with this picture.' – *Daily Variety*

The Island *

Japan   1961   92m   bw
Kindai Eiga Kyokai (Kaneto Shindo)

original title: *Hadaka no Shima*

The quiet tenor of life for the only family inhabiting a tiny island is eventually broken by illness and death.

Slow, controlled, beautiful film in which not a single word of dialogue is spoken. The artificiality of this concept eventually diminishes its stature.

wd Kaneto Shindo ph Kiyoshi Kuroda m Hikaru Hayashi

☆ Nobuko Otowa, Taiji Tonoyama, Shinji Tanaka, Masanori Horimoto

'A visual poem which mirrors tedium without ever inducing it.' – *MFB*

'For 300 years a terrifying secret has been kept from the outside world!'
The Island

US   1980   114m   Technicolor
Universal (Richard Zanuck, David Brown)

A journalist is in fear of his life on a Caribbean island inhabited by the bloodthirsty descendants of 17th-century buccaneers.

Ridiculous shocker from the Jaws people; stupidly plotted and gruesome in detail.

w Peter Benchley novel Peter Benchley d Michael Ritchie ph Henri Decaë m Ennio Morricone

☆ Michael Caine, David Warner, Angela Punch McGregor, Frank Middlemass, Dudley Sutton, Colin Jeavons

'Suspense gives way to gut-level sadism aimed at the lowest common audience denominator.' – *Variety*

The Island at the Top of the World **

♔♔   US   1974   93m   Technicolor
Walt Disney (Winston Hibler)

In 1907, a rich Englishman commissions an airship to take him to a mythical arctic Shangri-La in search of his lost son.

Generally brisk and effective adventure fantasy whose trick effects are sufficiently splendid to redeem a sag in the middle and an overplus of Viking chatter which has to be laboriously translated.

w John Whedon novel *The Lost Ones* by Ian Cameron d Robert Stevenson ph Frank Phillips m Maurice Jarre pd Peter Ellenshaw sp Art Cruickshank, Danny Lee

☆ Donald Sinden, David Hartman, Jacques Marin, Mako

Island Escape: see *No Man Is an Island*

Island in the Sky *

US   1953   109m   bw
Wayne-Fellows (Robert Fellows)

A transport plane makes a forced landing north of Greenland, and the crew must survive till help comes.

Well-made outdoor suspenser shot in the California Sierras.

w Ernest K. Gann novel Ernest K. Gann d William Wellman m Archie Stout m Hugo Friedhofer md Emil Newman

☆ John Wayne, Lloyd Nolan, Walter Abel, Allyn Joslyn, Andy Devine, James Arness

Island in the Sun *

GB   1957   119m   Technicolor   Cinemascope
TCF (Darryl F. Zanuck)

Sexual and racial problems erupt on a West Indian island.

Portmanteau romantic melodrama which generally misfires, especially in an attempt to parallel Crime and Punishment; but the cast is interesting.

w Alfred Hayes novel Alec Waugh d Robert Rossen ph Frederick A. Young m Malcolm Arnold

☆ James Mason, Joan Fontaine, Harry Belafonte, John Williams, Dorothy Dandridge, Joan Collins, Michael Rennie, Patricia Owens, Stephen Boyd, Basil Sydney, Diana Wynyard, Ronald Squire, John Justin

Island of Crime (dubbed)

Italy   1968   85m   Eastmancolor   Scope
Golden Era/Clesi (Silvio Clementelli)
original title: *Sequestro di Persona*

When a rich young man is kidnapped and killed in Sardinia, his friend decides to seek revenge.

A confusing story of murder and ransom demands, treated as an everyday happening, but never fully explained; it is a film that does not travel well.

w Ugo Pirro, Gianfranco Mingozzi d Gianfranco Mingozzi ph Ugo Piccone m Riz Ortolani ad Sergio Canevari ed Ruggero Mastroianni

☆ Franco Nero, Charlotte Rampling, Frank Wolff, Ennio Balbo, Pier Luigi Aprè, Steffen Zacharias

† The Italian version ran for 95m.

Island of Desire: see *Saturday Island*

The Island of Dr Moreau *

US   1977   98m   Movielab
AIP/Cinema 77 (Skip Steloff, John Temple-Smith)

In 1911, shipwrecked sailors land on a Pacific island where a mad doctor experiments with animal mutations.

A sprightly version of an old story; unfortunately it lacks any sense of the sinister, and the star is no match for Charles Laughton in Island of Lost Souls.

w John Herman Shaner, Al Ramrus story H. G. Wells d Don Taylor ph Gerry Fisher m Laurence Rosenthal

☆ Burt Lancaster, Michael York, Nigel Davenport, Barbara Carrera, Richard Basehart, Nick Cravat

'Cursed with lush colour photography instead of black and white atmospherics, and Lancaster's stolid mania instead of Laughton's manic zeal.' – *Sight and Sound*

The Island of Dr Moreau

US   1996   95m   DeLuxe   Panavision
Entertainment/New Line (Edward R. Pressman)

On a South Pacific island, genetically altered animals with human characteristics revolt against the mad scientist who created them.

Incoherent horror, notable for one of Brando's more eccentric performances, mercifully brief.

w Richard Stanley, Ron Hutchinson d John Frankenheimer ph William A. Fraker m Gary Chang pd Graham (Grace) Walker ed Paul Rubell

☆ Marlon Brando, Val Kilmer, David Thewlis, Fairuza Balk, Ron Perlman, Marco Hofschneider, Temuera Morrison, William Hootkins, Mark Dacascos, Nelson de la Rosa

'Astonishing four-fifths dreadful, one-fifth remarkable film.' – *Kim Newman, Sight and Sound*

† Director Richard Stanley was sacked after three days, though he returned incognito to play the part of a Dog-Man; David Thewlis replaced the originally cast Rob Morrow, and Walon Green worked uncredited on the script. The film cost $50m to make and grossed around $28m in the US.

Island of Lost Men

US   1939   64m   bw
Paramount

An Oriental girl seeks her lost father in waterfront dives and finds him on a prison island.

Adequate action programmer.

w William R. Lipman, Horace McCoy d Kurt Neumann

☆ Anna May Wong, Broderick Crawford, Anthony Quinn, J. Carrol Naish

† A remake of *White Woman.*

'Out of the dark fantastic madness of his science he created her – the panther woman – throbbing to the hot flush of new-found love!'
Island of Lost Souls *

US   1932   74m   bw
Paramount

On a remote South Sea island, mad Dr Moreau transforms animals into humans by vivisection.

Unchilling but interesting thriller with a rolling-eyed star performance.

w Waldemar Young, Philip Wylie story *The Island of Dr Moreau* by H. G. Wells d Erle C. Kenton ph Karl Struss

☆ Charles Laughton, Bela Lugosi, Richard Arlen, Kathleen Burke, Leila Hyams

Island of Lost Women

US   1958   72m   bw
Jaguar/Warner

A newspaperman lands on a remote island where a scientist has retired from the world with his daughters.

Unexciting hokum with more talk than action.

w Ray Buffum d Frank Tuttle
☆ Jeff Richards, Venetia Stevenson, John Smith, Alan Napier

Island of Love

US   1963   101m   Technicolor   Panavision
Warner/Belgrave (Morton da Costa)

A gangster finances a film providing his girlfriend stars, but when it flops he chases the producers to a Greek island.

Dismally unfunny comedy wasting a talented cast.

w David R. Schwartz d Morton da Costa ph Harry Stradling m George Duning

☆ Robert Preston, Tony Randall, Walter Matthau, Giorgia Moll

Island of Terror

GB   1966   89m   Eastmancolor
Planet (Tom Blakeley)

On an Irish island, a scientist makes monsters who thrive on bone.

Horror hokum, moderately done.

w Edward Andrew Mann, Alan Ramsen d Terence Fisher ph Reg Wyer m Malcolm Lockyer sp John St John Earl

☆ Peter Cushing, Edward Judd, Carole Gray, Eddie Byrne, Sam Kydd, Niall MacGinnis

Island of the Blue Dolphins

♔♔   US   1964   93m   Eastmancolor
U-I/Robert B. Radnitz

Two orphaned children grow up alone on a Californian island, protected by wild dogs.

Pleasant if unconvincing family film based on a true story.

w Ted Sherdeman, Jane Klove novel Scott O'Dell d James B. Clark ph Leo Tover m Paul Sawtell

☆ Celia Kaye, Larry Domasin, George Kennedy

Island of The Living Dead: see *Zombie Flesh Eaters*

Island of the Lost

♔♔   US   1968   92m   colour
Ivan Tors

An anthropologist sets sail for an uncharted island and is shipwrecked on it.

Good-looking but singularly plotless action adventure.

w Richard Carlson, Ivan Tors d John Florea, Ricou Browning (underwater scenes)

☆ Richard Greene, Luke Halpin, Mark Hulswit

Island Rescue: see *Appointment with Venus*

Islands in the Stream

US   1977   105m   Metrocolor   Panavision
Paramount (Peter Bart, Max Palevsky)

On a Bahamian island in 1940, an expatriate American artist welcomes his three sons and reflects on the futility of life.

Shapeless semi-autobiographical fragments culminating unpersuasively in an action climax of heroic self-sacrifice. A film on which no expense has been spared and which doesn't work at all.

w Denne Bart Petitclerc novel Ernest Hemingway d Franklin Schaffner ph Fred J. Koenekamp m Jerry Goldsmith

---

☆ George C. Scott, David Hemmings, Gilbert Roland, Susan Tyrrell, Richard Evans, Claire Bloom, Hart Bochner, Julius Harris
  'It is all too awful for words.' – Benny Green, Punch
⅋ photography

Isle of Forgotten Sins
US   1943   82m   bw
PRC (Peter R. Van Duinen)
In the South Seas, villains congregate in search of sunken treasure.
Patchy tropical melodrama with a cast more interesting than the script.
w Raymond L. Schrock story Edgar G. Ulmer d Edgar G. Ulmer
☆ John Carradine, Gale Sondergaard, Sidney Toler, Frank Fenton, Rita Quigley, Veda Ann Borg

Isle of Fury
US   1936   60m   bw
Warner
A fugitive from justice finds temporary peace on a South Sea island.
Limp remake of The Narrow Corner (qv); its star later pretended he hadn't made it.
w Robert Andrews, William Jacobs novel The Narrow Corner by W. Somerset Maugham d Frank McDonald
☆ Humphrey Bogart, Margaret Lindsay, Donald Woods

Isle of Missing Men
US   1942   67m   bw
Monogram
Convicts on a prison island try to make a break.
The very poor man's Papillon.
w Richard Oswald, Robert Chapin d Richard Oswald
☆ Gilbert Roland, Helen Gilbert, John Howard

Isle of Sinners: see Dieu a Besoin des Hommes

Isle of the Dead **
US   1945   72m   bw
RKO (Val Lewton)
▣ ▦ @~
On a Balkan island in 1912 a group of people shelter from the plague and fear that one of their number is a vampire.
Glum, ghoulish melodrama with some neatly handled shocks; quite different from any other horror film.
w Ardel Wray, Josef Mischel d Mark Robson ph Jack Mackenzie m Leigh Harline
☆ Boris Karloff, Ellen Drew, Helene Thimig, Marc Cramer, Katherine Emery, Alan Napier, Jason Robards

Isn't It Romantic *
US   1948   87m   bw
Paramount (Daniel Dare)
Romance hits the household of an ex-Civil War colonel in Indiana.
Pleasant but forgettable period semi-musical.
w Theodore Strauss, Josef Mischel, Richard Breen d Norman Z. McLeod ph Lionel Lindon m Joseph J. Lilley
☆ Veronica Lake, Mona Freeman, Mary Hatcher, Roland Culver, Billy de Wolfe, Patric Knowles, Richard Webb, Kathryn Givney, Pearl Bailey

Isn't Life Wonderful? *
US   1924   99m   bw   silent
UA/David Wark Griffith
The life of a family in post-war Germany.
An unpopular subject, and a grey-looking film, but the director shows a lot of his strength in it.
wd D. W. Griffith story Geoffrey Moss ph Hendrik Sartov, Hal Sintzenich
☆ Carol Dempster, Neil Hamilton, Helen Lowell, Frank Puglia, Marcia Harris, Lupino Lane

Isn't Life Wonderful? *
GB   1952   83m   Technicolor
ABP (Warwick Ward)
In 1902, drunken Uncle Willie runs a bicycle shop and manages to reconcile a lovers' quarrel.
Engaging, well-cast family comedy.
w Brock Williams novel Uncle Willie and the Bicycle Shop by Brock Williams d Harold French ph Erwin Hillier m Philip Green ad Terence Verity

☆ Donald Wolfit, Eileen Herlie, Cecil Parker, Eleanor Summerfield, Robert Urquhart, Cecil Trouncer

Istanbul
US   1956   84m   Technicolor   Cinemascope
U-I (Albert J. Cohen)
@~
Various adventurers and an amnesiac girl seek stolen diamonds in Istanbul.
Dim remake of a flat-footed piece of thick ear called Singapore.
w Seton I. Miller, Barbara Gray, Richard Alan Simmons d Joseph Pevney ph William Daniels m Joseph Gershenson
☆ Errol Flynn, Cornell Borchers, John Bentley, Torin Thatcher, Leif Erickson, Martin Benson, Vladimir Sokoloff, Werner Klemperer, Nat King Cole, Peggy Knudsen

Istoria Asi Klyachinoi, kotoraya lyubila, da nie vshla zamuzh: see Asya's Happiness

It *
US   1927   72m   bw   silent
Famous Players-Lasky/Paramount (B. P. Schulberg)
▣ ▦ @~
A shopgirl tries to live by the tenets of Elinor Glyn's book, and finally marries her boss.
In its day a fast and funny spoof, and the years have not dealt too unkindly with it.
w Hope Loring, Louis D. Lighton d Clarence Badger m H. Kinley Martin adaptation Elinor Glyn
☆ Clara Bow, Antonio Moreno, William Austin, Jacqueline Gadsdon, Gary Cooper, Elinor Glyn

It Ain't Hay
US   1943   79m   bw
Universal (Alex Gottlieb)
GB title: Money for Jam
When a racehorse dies, a New York cabbie and his friend try to find a new one for the impecunious owners.
Formula Abbott and Costello with a small injection of sentiment and Runyonese. Not their best by a mile.
w Allen Boretz, John Grant story Princess O'Hara by Damon Runyon d Erle C. Kenton ph Charles von Enger m/ly Harry Revel, Paul Francis Webster
☆ Bud Abbott, Lou Costello, Grace McDonald, Cecil Kellaway, Patsy O'Connor, Eugene Pallette, Shemp Howard, Eddie Quillan

It All Came True *
US   1940   97m   bw
Warner (Mark Hellinger)
A gangster hides out in a boarding house and puts it back on its feet.
Competent New York fairy story full of sweetness and light.
w Michael Fessier, Lawrence Kimble story Better Than Life by Louis Bromfield d Lewis Seiler ph Ernest Haller m Heinz Roemheld
☆ Humphrey Bogart, Ann Sheridan, Jeffrey Lynn, ZaSu Pitts, Una O'Connor, Jessie Busley, John Litel, Grant Mitchell, Felix Bressart

It All Starts Today **
France   1999   118m   colour
Artificial Eye/Alain Sarde/Little Bear/TFI
▣
original title: Ca Commence Aujourd'hui
In a deprived area, where unemployment is rife, an idealistic infant teacher tries to cope with inadequate aid from the local authorities and his own complicated private life.
Partly based on the experiences of his daughter's then-boyfriend (later her husband), Tavernier's film is suffused with a righteous anger, though he sweetens the pill with rather more glamour than one would expect.
w Dominique Sampiero, Tiffany Tavernier, Bertrand Tavernier d Bertrand Tavernier ph Alain Choquart m Louis Sclavis ad Thierry Francois ed Sophie Brunet
☆ Philippe Torreton, Maria Pitarresi, Nadia Kaci, Véronique Ataly, Nathalie Bécue, Emmanuelle Bercot, Françoise Bette, Christine Citti
  'Every piece of grittiness in the film is undone by a corresponding bit of slickness.' – Adam Mars-Jones, Times

It Always Rains on Sunday ***
GB   1947   92m   bw
Ealing (Henry Cornelius)
An escaped convict takes refuge in his married mistress's house in East London.
Influential slumland melodrama, now dated – the stuff of every other television play – but at the time electrifyingly vivid and very well done.
w Angus MacPhail, Robert Hamer, Henry Cornelius novel Arthur La Bern d Robert Hamer ph Douglas Slocombe m Georges Auric
☆ Googie Withers, John McCallum, Jack Warner, Edward Chapman, Susan Shaw, Sydney Tafler
  'Let me pay it the simplest of compliments and say that it has the persuasiveness of an exciting story professionally told.' – Sunday Times

It Came from beneath the Sea
US   1955   80m   bw
Columbia/Sam Katzman (Charles Schneer)
▣ ▦ @~
A giant octopus half destroys San Francisco.
Tepid monster movie; special effects only fair.
w George Worthing Yates, Hal Smith d Robert Gordon ph Henry Freulich md Mischa Bakaleinikoff ad Paul Palmentola ed Jerome Thoms sp Ray Harryhausen
☆ Kenneth Tobey, Faith Domergue, Donald Curtis, Ian Keith

It Came from Outer Space **
US   1953   80m   bw   3-D
U-I (William Alland)
▦
A young astronomer sees a space ship land in the Arizona desert and tracks down the occupants who can adopt human appearance at will.
Quite bright science fiction, the first to use this theme of borrowing bodies and the first to utilize the Western desert locations. 3-D adds a shock moment or two.
w Harry Essex story Ray Bradbury d Jack Arnold ph Clifford Stine m Herman Stein md Joseph Gershenson
☆ Richard Carlson, Barbara Rush, Charles Drake, Kathleen Hughes
  'A solid piece of eerie entertainment, replete with wild screams and bug-eyed monsters guaranteed to send scared customers out of this world.' – Hollywood Reporter
  'Desert was Arnold's favourite location, and he used it consistently to create a sense of strangeness and menace otherwise much restricted by his budgets.' – Time Out, 1982

It Can't Be Winter, We Haven't Had Summer Yet
Canada   1980   84m   colour
La Maison de Quatre (Louise Carré)
original title: ça Peut Pas être l'Hiver, On n'a Même Pas Eu d'été
A middle-aged woman, much to the apprehension of her children, enjoys a new lease of life after her husband's death.
Too pat and comfortable to be plausible, though it has some charm, apart from a dire excursion into a pop video halfway through.
wd Louise Carré ph Robert Vanherweghem m Marc O'Farrell ed André Théberge
☆ Charlotte Boisjoli, Jacques Galipeau, Céline Lomez, Serge Bélair, Mireille Thibault, Daniel Matte, Marie-Eve Doré, Martin Neufeld

It Comes Up Love
US   1942   64m   bw
Ken Goldsmith/Universal
GB title: A Date With an Angel
A businessman tries to bring up two motherless daughters.
A slim plotline serves as an excuse for a brief but snappy 'B' musical.
w Dorothy Bennett, Charles Kenyon d Charles Lamont
☆ Gloria Jean, Donald O'Connor, Ian Hunter, Frieda Inescort, Louise Allbritton, Charles Coleman

It Conquered the World
US   1956   68m   bw
AIP
▣ ▦
Something from another planet is sheltered by a well-meaning scientist who discovers too late that its intentions are evil.
Tolerable horror comic on a risibly low budget.

w Lou Rusoff d Roger Corman ph Frederick E. West m Ronald Stein
☆ Peter Graves, Beverly Garland, Lee Van Cleef, Sally Fraser, Charles B. Griffith

It Could Happen to You
US   1939   73m   bw
TCF
After a stag party, an advertising man finds a body in his car.
Neat second-feature mystery.
w Allen Rivkin, Lou Breslow d Alfred Werker
☆ Stuart Erwin, Gloria Stuart, Raymond Walburn, Douglas Fowley

'A Cop. A Waitress. A Lottery Ticket.'
'Life is full of surprises.'
It Could Happen to You
US   1994   101m   Technicolor
Columbia
TriStar/Adelson/Baumgarten/Lobell/Bergman (Mike Lobell)
▣ ▦ ⊚ ⊚
A married cop makes good on his offer to a waitress of half the proceeds of a lottery ticket instead of a tip, even when he wins four million dollars.
A comedy of mild charm, but too calculating to be convincing in its belief that love conquers all.
w Jane Anderson d Andrew Bergman ph Caleb Deschanel m Carter Burwell pd Bill Groom ed Barry Malkin
☆ Nicolas Cage, Bridget Fonda, Wendell Pierce, Rosie Perez, Isaac Hayes, Seymour Cassel, Victor Rojas, Red Buttons
  'A lame romantic comedy that is too calculating in its cornball sentimentality to tug effectively on the heartstrings.' – Colin Brown, Screen International
  'It's good escapist fun for those who enjoy the anodine.' – Marianne Gray, Film Review

It Grows on Trees
US   1952   84m   bw
U-I (Leonard Goldstein)
A housewife finds a money tree in her backyard.
Protracted fantasy comedy.
w Leonard Praskins, Barney Slater d Arthur Lubin ph Maury Gertsman m Frank Skinner
☆ Irene Dunne, Dean Jagger, Joan Evans, Richard Crenna, Edith Meiser, Dee Pollock
† It was Irene Dunne's last film.

It Had to Be You
US   1947   98m   bw
Columbia/Don Hartman
A dizzy dame runs out on three prospective husbands and is pursued by an Indian.
Weak sex farce without the courage of its lack of convictions.
w Norman Panama, Melvin Frank d Don Hartman, Rudolph Maté ph Rudolph Maté m Heinz Roemheld md Morris Stoloff
☆ Ginger Rogers, Cornel Wilde, Percy Waram, Spring Byington, Thurston Hall, Ron Randell

It Had to Happen
US   1936   80m   bw
TCF/Raymond Griffith
An Italian immigrant becomes the political boss of New York City.
Unconvincing melodrama with star appeal.
w Howard Ellis Smith, Kathryn Scola, Rupert Hughes d Roy del Ruth ph Peverell Marley md Arthur Lange
☆ George Raft, Rosalind Russell, Leo Carrillo, Arline Judge, Alan Dinehart, Andrew Tombes
  'Incredible story precludes its b.o. chances.' – Variety

It Happened at the Inn: see Goupí Mains Rouges

It Happened at the World's Fair
US   1962   104m   Metrocolor   Panavision
MGM/Ted Richmond
▦
At the Seattle World's Fair, two crop-dusting pilots have romantic intrigues.
Routine star vehicle.
w Si Rose, Seaman Jacobs d Norman Taurog ph Joseph Ruttenberg m Leith Stevens
☆ Elvis Presley, Gary Lockwood, Joan O'Brien, Yvonne Craig, Ginny Tiu

---

⊚ Digital Video Disc Region 2   ⊚ Digital Video Disc Region 1   ♫ Soundtrack released on compact disc   ☆ Cast in approximate order of importance   † Points of interest   ♫ Notable songs   ▮ Academy Award   ⅋ Academy Award nomination   ▯ BAFTA

It Happened Here **
GB 1963 99m bw
UA/Kevin Brownlow, Andrew Mollo

What might have happened if the Germans had invaded England in 1940.
A remarkable semi-professional reconstruction which took seven years to film and is totally convincing in detail, but unfortunately rather confused and padded as drama.
wd Kevin Brownlow, Andrew Mollo ph Peter Suschitzky m Jack Beaver
☆ Sebastian Shaw, Pauline Murray, Fiona Leland, Honor Fehrson
'For a grain of artistic truth, we can forgive even the grainy photography and wavering sound with which part of it is afflicted.' – *John Simon*

It Happened in Athens
US 1961 100m DeLuxe Cinemascope
TCF (James S. Elliott)
At the first revival of the Olympic Games in 1896 a publicity-seeking actress announces that she will marry whoever wins the Marathon.
Witless extravagant romp, well mounted but adding up to zero.
w Laszlo Vadnay d Andrew Marton ph Curt Courant m Manos Hadjidakis
☆ Jayne Mansfield, Trax Colton, Bob Mathias

It Happened in Brooklyn *
US 1947 103m bw
MGM (Jack Cummings)
Young New Yorkers with musical talents find their way to fame.
Well-handled routine musical of its time.
w Isobel Lennart d Richard Whorf ph Robert Planck m Johnny Green songs Jule Styne, Sammy Cahn
☆ Frank Sinatra, Jimmy Durante, Kathryn Grayson, Peter Lawford, Gloria Grahame
'Aside from Sinatra and Durante the show amounts to practically nothing, but there is a general kindliness about it which I enjoyed.' – *James Agee*

It Happened in Hollywood
US 1937 67m bw
Columbia
A silent cowboy star is washed up when talkies come in.
Indifferent studio story.
w Ethel Hill, Harvey Ferguson, Sam Fuller, Myles Connolly d Harry Lachman
☆ Richard Dix, Fay Wray, Victor Kilian, Franklin Pangborn, Charles Arnt, Granville Bates
'It will have difficulty fitting in … won't particularly satisfy 'em in the duals.' *Variety*

It Happened on Fifth Avenue *
US 1947 115m bw
Allied Artists (Roy del Ruth)
A child of divorce finds amiable squatters in her millionaire father's house.
Curious, overlong, cheerful Capraesque comedy with the mildest of social pretensions.
w Everett Freeman, Frederick Stephani, Herbert Clyde Lewis d Roy del Ruth ph Henry Sharp
☆ Gale Storm, Ann Harding, Victor Moore, Charles Ruggles, Don Defore
ဦ original story

'Together For The First Time!'
It Happened One Night ***
US 1934 105m bw
Columbia (Frank Capra)

A runaway heiress falls in love with the reporter who is chasing her across America.
Highly successful and influential romantic comedy, the first to use buses and motels as background and still come up sparkling; it remains superlative in patches, but overall has a faded, dated air.
w Robert Riskin story Night Bus by Samuel Hopkins Adams d Frank Capra ph Joseph Walker md Louis Silvers ad Stephen Goosson ed Gene Havlick
☆ Clark Gable, Claudette Colbert, Walter Connolly, Roscoe Karns, Alan Hale, Ward Bond, Jameson Thomas, Arthur Hoyt
'A laughing hit that will mean important coin.' – *Variety*

'It will be a long day before we see so little made into so much.' – *Otis Ferguson*
'Something to revive your faith in a medium which could belong among the great arts.' – *Robert Forsythe*
'We may look askance at Capra's sententious notions about the miserable rich and the happy poor, but there's no doubting the chord he struck in depression audiences.' – *Time Out, 1980*
'It made audiences happy in a way that only a few films in each era do. In the mid-30s, the Colbert and Gable of this film became Americans' idealized view of themselves – breezy, likeable, sexy, gallant, and maybe just a little harebrained. It was the *Annie Hall* of its day – before the invention of anxiety.' – *Pauline Kael, 70s*
'One of the most entertaining films that has ever been offered to the public.' – *Observer*
† Remade 1956 (badly) as *You Can't Run Away From It*.
†† Robert Montgomery was the first choice for the Gable role, but he refused it because he had been on a bus in *Fugitive Lovers*. The Colbert role was first offered to Myrna Loy, Margaret Sullavan and Constance Bennett. Colbert was lured by a 40,000-dollar fee.
††† Steven Spielberg paid $607,500 at a 1996 auction for Clark Gable's Oscar, which he then presented to the Academy of Motion Picture Arts and Sciences.
🏆 best picture; Robert Riskin; Frank Capra; Clark Gable; Claudette Colbert

It Happened One Summer: see State Fair (1945)

It Happened One Sunday
GB 1943 99m bw
ABPC
In Liverpool, a Canadian seaman falls for an Irish maid.
Overlong romantic comedy with nowhere to go.
w Victor Skutezky, Frederic Gotfurt, Stephen Black d Karel Lamac
☆ Robert Beatty, Barbara White, Marjorie Rhodes, Ernest Butcher, Judy Kelly, Irene Vanbrugh

'A warm, wonderful movie that's stacked with joy for the whole family!'
It Happened to Jane
US 1959 98m Technicolor Cinemascope
Columbia/Arwin (Richard Quine)
A lady lobster dealer becomes involved in a battle with the railroad whose inefficiency affects her business.
Witless, wholesome farce which promises more than it delivers.
w Norman Katkov d Richard Quine ph Charles Lawton Jnr m Joseph Duning
☆ Doris Day, Jack Lemmon, Ernie Kovacs, Steve Forrest
'Up to a point, this is a funny comedy. The point is reached about three-quarters of the way through when the film abruptly changes form and loses momentum.' – *Variety*

It Happened Tomorrow ***
US 1944 84m bw
UA/Arnold Pressburger

A reporter meets an old man with the power to show him tomorrow's newspaper headlines, so that he always gets scoops – including his own death…
Engaging fantasy, flawlessly made and quietly very entertaining.
w Dudley Nichols, René Clair d René Clair ph Archie Stout m Robert Stolz
☆ Dick Powell, Linda Darnell, Jack Oakie, John Philliber, Edgar Kennedy, Ed Brophy, George Cleveland, Sig Rumann
'Students of cinematic style will find many shrewdly polished bits to admire and enjoy.' – *James Agee*
'Diverting escapist entertainment for all audiences.' – *Variety*
ဦ Robert Stolz

It Happens Every Spring
US 1949 80m bw
TCF (William Perlberg)
A chemistry teacher discovers a formula that makes baseballs repellent to wood.
Smartly produced but rather desperate fantasy comedy.

w Valentine Davies d Lloyd Bacon ph Joe MacDonald m Leigh Harline
☆ Ray Milland, Jean Peters, Paul Douglas, Ed Begley, Ted de Corsia, Ray Collins, Jessie Royce Landis, Alan Hale Jnr
ဦ original story (Shirley W. Smith, Valentine Davies)

It Happens Every Thursday *
US 1953 80m bw
U-I (Anton Leader)
The new owner of a small-town newspaper becomes unpopular through his attempts to boost the circulation.
Pleasant comedy with amusing scenes.
w Dane Lussier d Joseph Pevney ph Russell Metty m Joseph Gershenson
☆ Loretta Young, John Forsythe, Jimmy Conlin, Frank McHugh, Edgar Buchanan, Jane Darwell

It Hurts Only When I Laugh: see Only When I Laugh

It Lives Again
US 1978 91m colour
Warner/Larco (Larry Cohen)

aka: *It's Alive II*
Three mutant killer babies are protected by a scientist from a cop determined to kill them.
A sequel to It's Alive that is less effective because the babies are too visible for too much of the time.
wd Larry Cohen ph Fenton Hamilton m Bernard Herrmann ed Curt Burch, Louis Friedman, Carol O'Blath
☆ Frederic Forrest, Kathleen Lloyd, John P. Ryan, John Marley, Andrew Duggan, Eddie Constantine, James Dixon
† It was followed by *It's Alive III* (qv).

It Pays to Advertise
US 1931 66m bw
Paramount
A mild youth is turned by his girl into a business success.
Fair film version of a popular stage comedy.
w Arthur Kober play Walter Hackett d Frank Tuttle
☆ Norman Foster, Carole Lombard, Skeets Gallagher, Eugene Pallette, Louise Brooks, Lucien Littlefield
'Good enough programme material.' – *Variety*

It Rains on Our Love *
Sweden 1946 95m bw
Sveriges Folkbiografer (Lorens Marmstedt)
original title: *Det Regnar Pa Var Kärlek*
aka: *Man with an Umbrella*
A pregnant girl meets an ex-prisoner while waiting for a train and they decide to live together.
A mainly light-hearted movie about two irresponsible people making the best of the worst that life has to offer.
w Ingmar Bergman, Herbert Grevenius play Oscar Braathen d Ingmar Bergman ph Göran Strindberg, Hilding Bladh m Erland von Koch ad P. A. Lundgren ed Tage Holmberg
☆ Barbro Kollberg, Birger Malmsten, Gösta Cederlund, Ludde Gentzel, Douglas Hage, Hjördis Pettersson, Benkt-Ake Benktsson, Sture Ericson

It Should Happen to You **
US 1954 80m bw
Columbia (Fred Kohlmar)

A slightly daffy New York model with an urge to be famous rents a huge billboard and puts her name on it.
Likeable comedy which starts brightly and slowly falls apart, disappointing considering the credentials of the talents involved and the satiric possibilities of the plot.
w Ruth Gordon, Garson Kanin d George Cukor ph Charles Lang m Frederick Hollander
☆ Judy Holliday, Jack Lemmon, Peter Lawford, Michael O'Shea
'One of the funniest films to come out of Hollywood.' – *Life*

It Shouldn't Happen to a Dog
US 1946 70m bw
TCF (William Girard)
A lady detective, her dog and a reporter solve a murder case more by good luck than good management.
Acceptable comedy support.

w Eugene Ling, Frank Gabrielson story Edwin Lanham d Herbert I. Leeds ph Glen MacWilliams m David Buttolph
☆ Allyn Joslyn, Carole Landis, Margo Woode, Henry Morgan, Reed Hadley, John Alexander

It Shouldn't Happen to a Vet
GB 1976 93m Technicolor
EMI/Talent Associates/Readers Digest
US title: *All Things Bright and Beautiful*
Adventures of a Yorkshire vet just before World War II.
Competent sequel to All Creatures Great and Small (qv).
w Alan Plater books James Herriot d Eric Till ph Arthur Ibbetson m Laurie Johnson
☆ John Alderton, Colin Blakely, Lisa Harrow, Bill Maynard, Richard Pearson, Raymond Francis, John Barrett, Paul Shelley

It Started in Naples *
US 1960 100m Technicolor Vistavision
Paramount/Capri (Jack Rose)

A Philadelphia lawyer goes to Naples to settle his dead brother's affairs, and falls for his nephew's aunt.
Nicely made, formula romantic comedy which started life as a vehicle for Gracie Fields.
w Melville Shavelson, Jack Rose, Suso Cecchi d'Amico d Melville Shavelson ph Robert Surtees m Alessandro Cicognini ad Hal Pereira, Roland Anderson
☆ Clark Gable, Sophia Loren, Vittorio de Sica, Marietto, Paulo Carlini
ဦ art direction

It Started in Paradise
GB 1952 94m Technicolor
GFD/British Film Makers (Leslie Parkyn, Sergei Nolbandov)
The career of an ambitious dress designer.
Stilted and garishly coloured but often amusing backstage melodrama of the fashion world: a Hollywood-style star vehicle which seems faintly surprising as a British product.
w Marghanita Laski d Compton Bennett ph Jack Cardiff m Malcolm Arnold ad Edward Carrick
☆ Jane Hylton, Ian Hunter, Terence Morgan, Muriel Pavlow, Brian Worth, Martita Hunt, Ronald Squire, Harold Lang, Joyce Barbour, Kay Kendall

It Started with a Kiss
US 1959 104m Metrocolor Cinemascope
MGM/Arcola (Aaron Rosenberg)

An army sergeant posted to Spain is embarrassed when his wife follows him.
Flabby comedy with the emphasis on sex and pratfalls.
w Charles Lederer d George Marshall ph Robert Bronner m Jeff Alexander
☆ Glenn Ford, Debbie Reynolds, Fred Clark, Edgar Buchanan, Eva Gabor

It Started with Eve **
US 1941 93m bw
Universal (Joe Pasternak)

A dying millionaire wants to see his grandson engaged, so a waitress obliges for an hour … but the old man recovers.
Charming comedy which was probably the star's best film; remade as I'd Rather be Rich (qv).
w Norman Krasna, Leo Townsend d Henry Koster ph Rudolph Maté md Charles Previn, Hans Salter
☆ Deanna Durbin, Charles Laughton, Robert Cummings, Margaret Tallichet, Guy Kibbee, Walter Catlett, Catherine Doucet
'The perfect 8 to 80 picture.' – *Variety*
ဦ Charles Previn, Hans Salter

It Takes Two
US 1988 79m colour
United Artists (Robert Lawrence)

Three days before his wedding, a gullible 20-year-old Texan goes to the big city to buy a car and is taken for a ride.
A broad comedy that confuses energy and wit, leaving its audience tired rather than amused.
w Richard Christian Matheson, Thomas Szollosi d David Beaird ph Peter Deming m Carter Burwell pd Richard Hoover ed David Garfield

---

☆ George Newbern, Leslie Hope, Kimberly Foster, Barry Corbin, Anthony Geary, Frances Lee McCain

It Takes Two

†† US 1995 98m DeLuxe
Entertainment/Rysher/Dualstar (James Orr, Jim Cruickshank)

A 10-year-old orphan switches places with a rich girl who resembles her.
A modern, not very interesting, variation on The Prince and the Pauper, *which may keep those who can identify with its twee heroines moderately quiet on a rainy afternoon.*
w Deborah Dean Davis d Andy Tennant ph Kenneth D. Zunder m Sherman Foote, Ray Foote pd Ed Pisoni ed Roger Bondelli
☆ Kirstie Alley, Steve Guttenberg, Mary-Kate Olsen, Ashley Olsen, Philip Bosco, Jane Sibbett, Michelle Grisom, Desmond Roberts
'A predictable but not entirely charmless film, assembled from all the hoary clichés known to "B"-grade Hollywood.' – *Andy Richards, Sight and Sound*

It! The Terror from Beyond Space

US 1958 69m bw
Vogue/United Artists

A space ship returning from Mars is invaded by a worm-like monster.
Laughable but lively precursor of Alien; *rather more fun on the whole.*
w Jerome Bixby d Edward L. Cahn ph Kenneth Peach m Paul Sawtell, Bert Shefter ad William Glasgow
☆ Marshall Thompson, Shawn Smith, Kim Spaulding, Ann Doran, Dabbs Greer

The Italian Job **

GB 1969 100m Eastmancolor Panavision
Paramount/Oakhurst (Michael Deeley)

Crooks stage a traffic jam in Turin in order to pull off a bullion robbery.
Lively caper comedy which provides a good measure of entertainment.
w Troy Kennedy Martin d Peter Collinson ph Douglas Slocombe, Norman Warwick m Quincy Jones
☆ Michael Caine, Noël Coward, Benny Hill, Raf Vallone, Tony Beckley, Rossano Brazzi, Maggie Blye, Irene Handl, John Le Mesurier, Fred Emney

An Italian Straw Hat ***

France 1927 74m bw silent
Albatross
original title: *Un Chapeau de Paille d'Italie*
The hero is prevented from getting to a wedding when his horse chews up a lady's straw hat and her escort demands that it be replaced.
Lively but gentle comedy of errors, a stage farce expanded for the screen and filled with visual gags. A very influential and still amusing piece.
wd René Clair play Eugène Labiche ph Maurice Desfassiaux, Nicolas Roudakoff ad Lazare Meerson
☆ Albert Préjean, Olga Tschekowa, Marise Maia, Alice Tissot
'The very springtime of screen comedy.' – *Tatler*
'One of the funniest films ever made.' – *Tribune, 1945*
'Still one of the funniest films in the world.' – *Sunday Times, 1948*

ItalianAmerican

US 1974 45m colour/bw
National Communications Foundation (Saul Rubin, Elaine Attias)

Martin Scorsese's affectionate portrait of his parents, as they talk about their upbringing, and their enjoyment of food, showing holiday snaps mainly of people at dinner.
A sophisticated home movie, rooting a family in their environment. The credits include the recipe for Mrs Scorsese's meatball sauce.
wd Martin Scorsese ph Alex Hirshfeld
☆ Catherine and Charles Scorsese
† It was released on video with three other shorts under the title 4 x Scorsese.

It's a 2'6" above the Ground World

GB 1972 96m Eastmancolor
British Lion/Welbeck/Betty E. Box-Ralph Thomas
aka: *The Love Ban*
A Roman Catholic couple go on the pill.
Smutty, not very funny sex comedy.
w Kevin Laffan play Kevin Laffan d Ralph Thomas ph Tony Imi m Stanley Myers
☆ Nanette Newman, Hywel Bennett, Russell Lewis, Simon Henderson, Milo O'Shea
'Offering cheap thrills and easy laughs on the side by filling the screen with capering nudes.' – *Clyde Jeavons*

It's a Big Country

US 1952 89m bw
MGM (Robert Sisk)
Seven stories show the diversity of the US and the glory of being one of its citizens.
Stultifying flagwaver memorable chiefly as a waste of good actors.
w William Ludwig, Helen Deutsch, George Wells, Allen Rivkin, Dorothy Kingsley, Isobel Lennart d Richard Thorpe, Don Weis, John Sturges, Don Hartman, William Wellman, Charles Vidor, Clarence Brown ph John Alton, Ray June, William Mellor, Joseph Ruttenberg m Bronislau Kaper, Rudolph G. Kopp, David Raksin, David Rose
☆ Ethel Barrymore, Keefe Brasselle, Nancy Davis, Van Johnson, Gene Kelly, Janet Leigh, Marjorie Main, Fredric March, George Murphy, William Powell, S. Z. Sakall, Lewis Stone, James Whitmore

It's a Boy

GB 1933 80m bw
Gainsborough (Michael Balcon)
A blackmailer claims to be a bridegroom's long-lost illegitimate son.
Heavy-footed version of a popular stage farce.
w John Paddy Carstairs, L. H. Gordon play Franz Arnold, Ernst Bach, Austin Melford d Tim Whelan ph Mutz Greenbaum ad Vetchinsky ed Harold M. Young
☆ Leslie Henson, Edward Everett Horton, Heather Thatcher, Alfred Drayton, Albert Burdon, Robertson Hare, Wendy Barrie

It's a Date *

US 1940 100m bw
Universal/Joe Pasternak

The daughter of a Broadway musical heroine has stage ambitions of her own, and chases an older man who is more interested in her mother.
Fairly pleasant but unduly elongated star comedy.
w Norman Krasna d William Seiter ph Joe Valentine m Charles Previn
☆ Deanna Durbin, Walter Pidgeon, Kay Francis, Eugene Pallette, Henry Stephenson, Cecilia Loftus, Samuel S. Hinds, S. Z. Sakall
'A natural which will roll grosses of upper bracket proportions.' – *Variety*

It's a Dog's Life: see The Bar Sinister

It's a Gift **

US 1934 73m bw
Paramount (William Le Baron)

A general store proprietor buys an orange ranch by mail and transports his family to California.
Roughly assembled comedy of disasters which happens to show the star more or less at his best, though the expected climax is lacking.
w Jack Cunningham story W. C. Fields, J. P. McEvoy d Norman Z. McLeod ph Henry Sharp
☆ W. C. Fields, Kathleen Howard, Jean Rouverol, Julian Madison, Tommy Bupp, Baby LeRoy
'An enormously amusing succession of rough and ready gags.' – *Literary Digest*

It's a Grand Life

GB 1953 102m bw
Mancunian/John E. Blakeley
A nitwit army private plays Cupid.
Senseless and under-rehearsed farce which has interest for fans of the usually drunken star.
w H. F. Maltby, Frank Randle d John E. Blakeley ph Ernest Palmer ad Alec Gray ed Dorothy Stimson
☆ Frank Randle, Diana Dors, Dan Young, Michael Brennan, Jennifer Jayne, John Blythe
† The film opens with the disclaimer: 'This film has been produced with the sole intention of

providing Burlesque Comedy Entertainment, and is not meant in any way to be derogatory to any of the Services.'

It's a Great Day!

GB 1956 71m bw
Butchers/Grove (Victor Lyndon)

A jobbing builder is suspected of theft and, with his family, prevented from attending a royal event.
Film version of The Grove Family, *Britain's first TV soap opera, a mix of comedy and domestic drama; it is well enough done, but more of sociological interest than anything else.*
w Michael and Roland Pertwee d John Warrington ph Cedric Williams m Eric Spear ad Norman Arnold ed Joseph Sterling
☆ Ruth Dunning, Edward Evans, Peter Bryant, Nancy Roberts, Sheila Sweet, Margaret Downs, Christopher Beeny, Vera Day, Sidney James, Victor Maddern

It's a Great Feeling *

US 1949 85m Technicolor
Warner (Alex Gottlieb)

No one will direct a Jack Carson movie, so he has to do it himself.
Amiable studio farce with plenty of guest appearances.
w Jack Rose, Mel Shavelson d David Butler ph Wilfred M. Cline m Ray Heindorf songs Jule Styne, Sammy Cahn
☆ Jack Carson, Doris Day, Dennis Morgan, Bill Goodwin, Gary Cooper, Joan Crawford, Errol Flynn, Sydney Greenstreet, Danny Kaye, Patricia Neal, Edward G. Robinson, Jane Wyman, Eleanor Parker, Ronald Reagan
♫ title song

It's a Mad Mad Mad Mad World **

†† US 1963 192m Technicolor Ultra Panavision 70
UA/Stanley Kramer

An assortment of people including a frustrated cop are overcome by greed when they hear of buried loot.
Three hours of frantic chasing and violent slapstick is too much even when done on this scale and with this cast, but one must observe that scene for scene it is extremely well done and most of the players are in unusually good form though they all outstay their welcome and are upstaged by the stunt men.
w William and Tania Rose d Stanley Kramer ph Ernest Laszlo m Ernest Gold stunts Carey Loftin titles Saul Bass
☆ Spencer Tracy, Jimmy Durante, Milton Berle, Sid Caesar, Ethel Merman, Buddy Hackett, Mickey Rooney, Dick Shawn, Phil Silvers, Terry-Thomas, Jonathan Winters, Edie Adams, Dorothy Provine, Eddie Anderson, Jim Backus and also William Demarest, Peter Falk, Paul Ford, Leo Gorcey, Ben Blue, Edward Everett Horton, Buster Keaton, Joe E. Brown, Carl Reiner, the Three Stooges, ZaSu Pitts, Sterling Holloway, Jack Benny, Jerry Lewis
'To watch on a Cinerama screen in full colour a small army of actors inflict mayhem on each other with cars, planes, explosives and other devices for more than three hours with stereophonic sound effects is simply too much for the human eye and ear to respond to, let alone the funny bone.' – *Dwight MacDonald*
⅋ Ernest Laszlo; Ernest Gold; title song (mErnest Gold, lyMack David)

It's a Pleasure

US 1945 90m Technicolor
International/RKO
The career of an ice-skating couple is interrupted when he takes to drink.
Unimpressive vehicle from the star's waning years: the numbers are good but the rest very soggy.
w Lynn Starling, Elliot Paul d William A. Seiter
☆ Sonja Henie, Michael O'Shea, Marie McDonald

It's a Small World

US 1935 72m bw
Fox
A man and woman fall in love after being stranded by a car crash in a small Louisiana town.
Mildly amusing comedy.
w Sam Hellman, Gladys Lehman d Irving Cummings
☆ Spencer Tracy, Wendy Barrie, Raymond Walburn, Virginia Sale, Irving Bacon

'Very weak entertainment, strictly for double bills.' – *Variety*

It's a Wise Child

US 1931 73m bw
Cosmopolitan/MGM
When a girl is thought to be pregnant, her family hunts the father.
Tasteless comedy with too few laughs.
w Laurence E. Johnson play Laurence E. Johnson d Robert Z. Leonard
☆ Marion Davies, Sidney Blackmer, James Gleason, Polly Moran, Marie Prevost, Lester Vail
'No subject matter here for family audiences … it must prove embarrassing to young unmarried couples attending the theatre together.' – *Variety*

It's a Wonderful Life ****

†† US 1946 129m bw
RKO/Liberty Films (Frank Capra)

A man is prevented from committing suicide by an elderly angel, who takes him back through his life to show him what good he has done.
Superbly assembled small-town comedy drama in a fantasy framework; arguably Capra's best and most typical work.
w Frances Goodrich, Albert Hackett, Frank Capra d Frank Capra play Philip Van Doren Stern m Dimitri Tiomkin ed William Hornbeck
☆ James Stewart, Henry Travers, Donna Reed, Lionel Barrymore, Thomas Mitchell, Beulah Bondi, Frank Faylen, Ward Bond, Gloria Grahame, H. B. Warner, Frank Albertson, Samuel S. Hinds, Mary Treen
CLARENCE (HENRY TRAVERS): 'Every time you hear a bell ring, it means that some angel's just got his wings.'
'One of the most efficient sentimental pieces since A Christmas Carol.' – *James Agee*
'The most brilliantly made motion picture of the 1940s, so assured, so dazzling in its use of screen narrative.' – *Charles Higham*
'In its own icky, bittersweet way, it's terribly effective.' – *New Yorker, 1977*
'At its best all this seems to me insipid, and at its worst an embarrassment to both flesh and spirit.' – *Richard Winnington, News Chronicle*
⅋ best picture; Frank Capra; James Stewart; editing

It's a Wonderful World *

US 1939 86m bw
MGM (Frank Davis)
Kidnapped by a suspected murderer, a girl helps him track down the real criminal.
Madcap comedy mystery which now seems much fresher and funnier than it did at the time. A highlight of the crazy comedy cycle.
w Ben Hecht, Herman J. Mankiewicz d W. S. Van Dyke II ph Oliver Marsh m Edward Ward
☆ Claudette Colbert, James Stewart, Guy Kibbee, Nat Pendleton, Frances Drake, Edgar Kennedy, Ernest Truex, Richard Carle, Sidney Blackmer, Andy Clyde, Cliff Clark, Hans Conried
'It's right down the alley for general audiences.' – *Variety*
'One of the few genuinely comic pictures in a dog's age.' – *Otis Ferguson*

It's a Wonderful World

GB 1956 90m Technicolor Spectascope
Renown/George Minter
Two songwriters struggle to compose a hit song, until one discovers a way to be successful: by recording an old tune backwards.
Dull and uninspired musical, making fun of modern styles, but only offering in its stead some extremely dreary examples of 50s pop.
wd Val Guest ph Wilkie Cooper md Robert Farnon ad Elven Webb ed John Pomeroy
☆ Terence Morgan, George Cole, Kathleen Harrison, Mylene Nicole (aka Mylene Demongeot), James Hayter, Richard Wattis, Reginald Beckwith, Maurice Kaufmann, Harold Lang, Ted Heath and His Music

'Save your screams till you see its face!'

It's Alive

US 1974 91m Technicolor
Warner/Larco (Larry Cohen)

A new-born baby turns out to be a vicious monster.
Exploitation horror flick in the worst of taste, with a good central performance.

---

wd Larry Cohen *ph* Fenton Hamilton *m* Bernard Herrmann *ed* Peter Honess

☆ John Ryan, Sharon Farrell, Andrew Duggan, Guy Stockwell, James Dixon, Michael Ansara
    'The best horror movie ever.' – *Quentin Crisp, Christopher Street*

† It was followed by *It Lives Again* and *It's Alive III: Island of The Alive* (qv).

It's Alive II: see *It Lives Again*

It's Alive III: Island of the Alive

US   1988   91m   Technicolor
Warner/Larco (Paul Stader)
📼

A mutant baby, whose father has gone to court to protect his right to live, swiftly grows to adulthood on a remote island with others of his kind and then heads back to America with his own child.
Wild, undisciplined horror film full of satirical thrusts at everything from attitudes to AIDS to media exploitation.
wd Larry Cohen *ph* Daniel Pearl *m* Laurie Johnson, Bernard Herrmann *ad* George Stoll *ed* David Kern *sp* Steve Neill, Rick Baker, William Hedge

☆ Michael Moriarty, Karen Black, Laurene Landon, James Dixon, Neal Israel, Art Lund, Ann Dane, Macdonald Carey, Gerrit Graham
    'This is from the Cohen home-movie stable and non-aficionados should beware: production values and special effects are as hokey as ever.' – *Anne Billson, Shock Xpress*

† The film was shot in four weeks in Hawaii and Los Angeles.

It's All Happening

GB   1963   101m   Eastmancolor
British Lion/Magna/KNP (Norman Williams)
US title: The Dream Maker

A talent scout for a recording agency helps to save an orphanage and makes himself a star in the process.
Unassuming, jolly little comedy with music; a better title would have made it more memorable.
w Leigh Vance *d* Don Sharp *ph* Ken Hodges *m* Philip Green

☆ Tommy Steele, Angela Douglas, Michael Medwin, Bernard Bresslaw, Walter Hudd, Jean Harvey, Richard Goolden

It's All Yours

US   1937   80m   bw
Columbia
A millionaire leaves a fortune to his favourite secretary, hoping that it will make his nephew take notice of her.
Unpersuasive romantic comedy with slightly crazy touches.
w Mary C. McCall Jnr *d* Elliott Nugent

☆ Madeleine Carroll, Francis Lederer, Mischa Auer, Grace Bradley
    'Of the whimsy, gay school currently in vogue … too light to figure importantly at solo b.o.' – *Variety*

It's Always Fair Weather **

US   1955   101m   Eastmancolor
Cinemascope
MGM (Arthur Freed)
📼 ▤ ⍟ ∩

In 1945 three army veterans vow to meet ten years on, but they find each other dull failures until they go on a wild spree.
Rather dejected New Yorkish comedy with musical sequences; some of it works very well, but the colour is crude and the wide screen doesn't help.
d Gene Kelly, Stanley Donen *ph* Robert Bronner *md* André Previn *w/m/ly* Betty Comden, Adolph Green

☆ Gene Kelly, Dan Dailey, Michael Kidd, Dolores Gray, Cyd Charisse

† Michael Kidd's vocals were dubbed by Jud Conlin.

⌕ Betty Comden, Adolph Green (as writers); André Previn

It's Great to Be Young *

👪 GB   1956   93m   Technicolor
AB-Pathé/Marble Arch (Victor Skutezky)
A popular teacher falls foul of the new headmaster who tries to disband the school orchestra.
Very acceptable but totally forgettable star comedy.
w Ted Willis *d* Cyril Frankel *ph* Gilbert Taylor *m* Ray Martin, Lester Powell, John Addison

☆ John Mills, Cecil Parker, Jeremy Spenser, Dorothy Bromiley, John Salew, Derek Blomfield, Eleanor Summerfield, Bryan Forbes

It's Hard to Be Good

GB   1948   93m   bw
GFD/Two Cities (Jeffrey Dell)
A demobbed war hero determines to spread peace and goodwill, but comes one cropper after another.
Well intended but somehow unprofessional comedy which irritates more than it amuses.
wd Jeffrey Dell *ph* Laurie Friedman *m* Antony Hopkins

☆ Jimmy Hanley, Anne Crawford, Raymond Huntley

It's Hot in Hell: see *A Monkey in Winter*

It's in the Air *

GB   1938   86m   bw
ATP (Basil Dean)
US title: George Takes the Air
Adventures of an accident-prone RAF recruit.
Amiable star comedy with good situations and songs.
wd Anthony Kimmins *ph* Gordon Dines, Ronald Neame

☆ George Formby, Garry Marsh, Polly Ward, Julien Mitchell, Jack Hobbs, Hal Gordon

It's in the Bag: see *L'Affaire est dans le Sac (1932)*

It's in the Bag **

US   1945   87m   bw
(UA)
GB title: The Fifth Chair
The owner of a flea circus seeks a legacy hidden in one of five chairs which have been sold to a variety of people.
Patchily amusing, star-studded comedy which was also filmed as Keep Your Seats Please and The Twelve Chairs. Full enjoyment requires some knowledge of American radio characters.
w Jay Dratler, Alma Reville *d* Richard Wallace *ph* Russell Metty *m* Werner Heymann

☆ Fred Allen, Binnie Barnes, Jack Benny, Robert Benchley, Don Ameche, Victor Moore, Rudy Vallee, William Bendix, Jerry Colonna
    'An untidy piece that doesn't make the most of itself but is full of fun.' – *Richard Mallett, Punch*

It's Love Again *

GB   1936   83m   bw
Gaumont (Michael Balcon)
📼
A chorus girl poses as a socialite who has hit the headlines without ever existing.
Delightfully dated comedy musical.
w Lesser Samuels, Marion Dix, Austin Melford *d* Victor Saville *ph* Glen MacWilliams *m* Louis Levy, Bretton Byrd *md* Louis Levy *ad* Alfred Junge *ed* A. L. Barnes *songs* Harry Woods, Sam Coslow

☆ Jessie Matthews, Robert Young, Sonnie Hale, Ernest Milton, Robb Wilton, Sara Allgood, Athene Seyler, Cyril Raymond
    'Mr Saville has directed it with speed, efficiency and a real sense of the absurd.' – *Graham Greene*

'The tops in topsy-turvy romance!'
It's Love I'm After *

US   1937   90m   bw
Warner (Harry Joe Brown)
A beloved stage star couple fight like cat and dog behind the scenes.
Amusing romantic farce which has worn rather less well than might have been expected but does present two stars at their peak.
w Casey Robinson *d* Archie Mayo *ph* James Van Trees *m* Heinz Roemheld

☆ Bette Davis, Leslie Howard, Olivia de Havilland, Patric Knowles, Eric Blore, George Barbier, Spring Byington, Bonita Granville, E. E. Clive
    'Smash comedy hit. Arrange extra playing time for this one.' – *Variety*
    'One of the most delightful and diverting comedies the madcap cinema has yet turned out.' – *New York World Telegram*
    'Proceeds like a somewhat deranged *Taming of the Shrew* … [BD and LH] are surrounded by that set of millionaires, valets and heiresses that were at one time as much of a convention in American comedy as the fops of Restoration theatre.' – *American Film Institute*

It's Magic: see *Romance on the High Seas*

It's My Party

US   1996   110m   DeLuxe
UA/Opala (Joel Thurm, Randal Kleiser)
📼 ▤ ⍟
A handsome Los Angeles architect, who discovers that he is HIV-positive and facing imminent death, decides to end his life with a two-day party.
A sentimental comedy with the most prolonged death-bed scene since the departure of Little Nell; those who can identify with its protagonist will enjoy it most.
wd Randal Kleiser *ph* Bernd Heinl *m* Basil Poledouris *pd* Clark Hunter *ed* Ila von Hasperg

☆ Eric Roberts, Gregory Harrison, Margaret Cho, Bruce Davison, Lee Grant, Devon Gummersall, Marlee Matlin, Roddy McDowall, Olivia Newton-John, Bronson Pinchot, George Segal, Dennis Christopher, Sally Kellerman
    'Not since Tom Sawyer attended his own funeral has there been such an orgy of weepy self-congratulation.' – *Stephen Farber, Movieline*

It's My Turn

US   1980   90m   Metrocolor
Columbia/Rastar/Martin Elfand
▤
A lady mathematics professor decides to seize her chances when she falls for the son of her father's new wife.
Unattractive and rather uninteresting comedy-drama with strong overtones of women's lib.
w Eleanor Bergstein *d* Claudia Weill *ph* Bill Butler *m* Patrick Williams

☆ Jill Clayburgh, Michael Douglas, Charles Grodin, Beverly Garland, Steven Hill

It's Never Too Late

GB   1956   95m   Eastmancolor
Park Lane/ABP
A mother considered dull by her family starts a new career as a scriptwriter.
Acceptable but quite unexciting matinée comedy.
w Edward Dryhurst *play* Felicity Douglas *d* Michael McCarthy

☆ Phyllis Calvert, Guy Rolfe, Susan Stephen, Patrick Barr, Delphi Lawrence, Sarah Lawson, Peter Hammond

It's Never Too Late to Mend

GB   1937   67m   bw
George King
An evil squire schemes for the hand of the farmer's beautiful daughter.
Archetypal melodrama of the 'Fie, Sir Jasper' school, mainly interesting in this version for the antics of its heavy-breathing star.
w H. F. Maltby *play* Charles Reade, Arthur Shirley *d* David MacDonald *ph* Hone Glendinning

☆ Tod Slaughter, Marjorie Taylor, Jack Livesey, Lawrence Hanray

It's Not Cricket

GB   1949   77m   bw
GFD/Gainsborough (Betty Box)
Bowler-hatted officers catch a Nazi spy.
Over-spoofed comedy which barely allows the stars a real chance.
w Gerard Bryant, Lyn Lockwood, Bernard MacNab *d* Alfred Roome, Roy Rich *ph* Gordon Lang *m* Arthur Wilkinson

☆ Basil Radford, Naunton Wayne, Maurice Denham, Susan Shaw, Nigel Buchanan, Diana Dors

It's Not Just You Murray! *

US   1964   16m   bw
New York University
📼
A crook describes how he made it to the top.
An exuberant short, revealing Scorsese's interest in American low-life and European film directors, expressed here in a light-hearted style with an ironic voice-over that rarely matches the truth of what is shown on-screen.
w Martin Scorsese, Mardik Martin *d* Martin Scorsese *ph* Richard H. Coll *m* Richard H. Coll *ed* Eli F. Bleich

☆ Ira Rubin, Sam DeFazio, Andrea Martin, Catherine Scorsese

† It was released on video with three other shorts under the title *4 x Scorsese*.

It's Not the Size that Counts: see *Percy's Progress*

It's Only Money: see *Double Dynamite* (1951)

It's Only Money

US   1962   84m   bw
Paramount/York/Jerry Lewis Productions (Paul Jones)
A TV repair mechanic hampers his detective friend in a search for a missing heir, which turns out to be himself.
Patchy mystery spoof with the star in rather better form than usual, and a memorable scene in which he is chased by an army of lawnmowers.
w John Fenton Murray *d* Frank Tashlin *ph* W. Wallace Kelley *m* Walter Scharf

☆ Jerry Lewis, Zachary Scott, Joan O'Brien, Jesse White, Jack Weston

It's That Man Again **

GB   1942   84m   bw
GFD/Gainsborough (Edward Black)
The Mayor of Foaming-at-the-Mouth puts on a show to save a bombed theatre.
Smart, fast-moving comedy which no longer seems particularly funny in itself but is an invaluable record of the characters and wisecracks of a radio show which proved a prime morale booster during World War II.
w Howard Irving Young, Ted Kavanagh *d* Walter Forde *ph* Basil Emmott *m* Hans May *ad* W. Murton *ed* R. E. Dearing

☆ Tommy Handley, Jack Train, Greta Gynt, Dino Galvani, Dorothy Summers, Horace Percival, Sidney Keith, Clarence Wright

It's Tough to be Famous

US   1932   81m   bw
First National
A young naval hero finds that fame destroys his private life.
Unco-ordinated comedy-drama.
w Robert Lord, Mary McCall Jnr *d* Alfred E. Green

☆ Douglas Fairbanks Jnr, Mary Brian, Walter Catlett, J. Carrol Naish
    'Lightweight feature possessing sufficient entertainment value to give theatres a moderate week.' – *Variety*

Ivan Groznyi: see *Ivan the Terrible*

Ivan the Terrible **

USSR   1942   100m   bw   some Agfacolor in part two
Mosfilm
📼 ▤ ⍟ ⍟ ∩
original title: Ivan Groznyi
The life of a 16th-century tsar.
A heavy-going film overflowing with grim, gloomy and superbly composed images: the plot is by the way, and part two (released in 1946 and also known as The Boyars' Plot) is not up to the standard of part one, in which the coronation sequence alone is a masterpiece of cinema.
ph Edouard Tissé (exteriors), Andrei Moskvin (interiors) *m* Sergei Prokofiev *ad* Isaac Shpinel, L. Naumova *wd/ed* Sergei Eisenstein

☆ Nikolai Cherkassov, Ludmilla Tselikovskaya, Serafima Birman
    'A visual opera, with all of opera's proper disregard of prose-level reality … an extraordinarily bold experiment, fascinating and beautiful to look at.' – *James Agee*

Ivanhoe *

👪 GB   1952   106m   Technicolor
MGM (Pandro S. Berman)
📼 ▤ ⍟ ∩
Derring-do among the knights of medieval England.
Tolerable, big-budget spectacular based on Sir Walter Scott's novel.
w Noel Langley, Aeneas Mackenzie *d* Richard Thorpe *ph* F. A. Young *m* Miklos Rozsa

☆ Robert Taylor, Joan Fontaine, Elizabeth Taylor, Emlyn Williams, George Sanders, Robert Douglas, Finlay Currie, Felix Aylmer, Francis de Wolff, Guy Rolfe, Norman Wooland, Basil Sydney

⌕ best picture; F. A. Young; Miklos Rozsa

Ivanovo Detstvo: see *Ivan's Childhood*

👪 film suitable for family viewing   📼 VHS video-cassette for the British PAL system   📼 VHS video-cassette for the British PAL system in wide screen-format   ⟳ Video cassette in a computer-colourised version   ▤ American NTSC video-cassette   ⍟ Laser disc

Ivan's Childhood ***

USSR 1962 95m bw
Mosfilm (G. Kuznetsov)
▨ ⌕

original title: *Ivanovo Detstvo*
A vengeful 12-year-old escapes from a concentration camp and joins the partisans after his family is killed by the Nazis.
Probably Tarkovsky's most accessible film, a tragic tale beautifully told.
w Vladimir Bogomolov, Mikhail Papava
novel Vladimir Bogomolov d Andrei Tarkovsky
ph Vadim Yusov m Vyacheslav Ovchinnikov
ad Evgeni Cherniaev ed G. Natanson
☆ Kolya Burlyaev, Irma Takovskaya, Valentin Zubkov, E. Zharikov, S. Krylov, Nikolai Grinko, L. Malyavina, Andrey Mikhalkov Konchalovsky
'The film is not disfigured by the unnaturally cheery or the conventionally hysterical. With one blow it annuls a whole cinémathèque of the war films of all lands.' – *Ivor Montagu, Sight and Sound*
† It won the Golden Lion for best film at the Venice Film Festival in 1962.

I've Always Loved You

US 1946 116m Technicolor
Republic
▨ ⌕

GB title: *Concerto*
A brilliant pianist becomes jealous of his girl pupil, despite his love for her.
High-flown romantic tosh with music, an unusual departure for this studio; most notable for Arthur Rubinstein on the sound track.
w Borden Chase d Frank Borzage ph Tony Gaudio m Walter Scharf
☆ Philip Dorn, Catherine McLeod, Felix Bressart, Maria Ouspenskaya, William Carter

I've Got Your Number

US 1934 68m bw
Warner
Telephone service engineers help prove a girl innocent of burglary.
Cheerful, fast-moving programmer typical of its studio at the time.
w Warren Duff, Sidney Sutherland d Ray Enright
☆ Joan Blondell, Pat O'Brien, Allen Jenkins, Glenda Farrell, Eugene Pallette

I've Gotta Horse

GB 1965 92m Technicolor Techniscope
Warner/Windmill (Larry Parnes, Kenneth Hume)
aka: *Wonderful Day*
An animal-loving pop singer becomes a racehorse owner.
A failed attempt to turn an English rocker into a family entertainer; the songs are trite and the script triter.
w Ronald Wolfe, Ronald Chesney story Kenneth Hume, Larry Parnes d Kenneth Hume ph Ernest Steward m/ly David Heneker, John Taylor
md Michael Leander ch Ross Taylor ad Scott McGregor ed Ernest Hosler
☆ Billy Fury, Michael Medwin, Amanda Barrie, Bill Fraser, Jon Pertwee, Fred Emney, Leslie Dwyer, Peter Gilmore, Marjorie Rhodes, The Bachelors

I've Heard the Mermaids Singing *

Canada 1987 84m colour
Contemporary/Electric/Ontario Arts Council/Canada Council/National Film Board/Ontario Film Development Corp/Telefilm Canada (Patricia Rozema)
▨ ⌕

An untalented woman falls in love with the owner of the art gallery where she works.
Gentle, quirky and enjoyable romance.
wd Patricia Rozema ph Douglas Koch m Mark Korven ad Valanne Ridgeway ed Patricia Rozema
☆ Sheila McCarthy, Ann-Marie MacDonald, John Evans, Brenda Kamino, Richard Monette

I've Lived Before

US 1956 82m bw
U-I (Howard Christie)
After a plane crash, the pilot recovers but believes himself to be another airman who died in 1918.
Dullish, talky drama which wastes its interesting reincarnation theme.
w Norman Jolley, William Talman d Richard Bartlett ph Maury Gertsman m Herman Stein
☆ Jock Mahoney, Leigh Snowden, Ann Harding, John McIntire, Raymond Bailey, Jerry Paris

Ivory Hunter: see *Where No Vultures Fly*

Ivy *

US 1947 99m bw
Universal (William Cameron Menzies)
In Edwardian society England, a lady poisoner gets her come-uppance.
Curiously ineffective period thriller in which the star is the elegant but artificial production design: the script is deadly dull.
w Charles Bennett novel Mrs Belloc Lowndes
d Sam Wood ph Russell Metty m Daniele Amfitheatrof pd William Cameron Menzies
☆ Joan Fontaine, Herbert Marshall, Patric Knowles, Richard Ney, Cedric Hardwicke, Lucile Watson, Sara Allgood, Henry Stephenson, Rosalind Ivan, Lillian Fontaine, Una O'Connor, Isobel Elsom, Alan Napier, Paul Cavanagh, Gavin Muir and also Norma Varden
'The real star is whoever was responsible for the dressing, setting, lighting and shooting, and that, I infer from past performance, is the producer, William Cameron Menzies.' – *James Agee*

J

J. R.: see *Who's That Knocking at My Door*

J. W. Coop *
US 1971 112m Eastmancolor
Columbia/Robertson and Associates (Cliff Robertson)
After ten years in prison, a rodeo rider returns to his home town.
Well-made but rather inconsequential drama with attractive locations.
w Cliff Robertson, Gary Cartwright, Bud Shrake d Cliff Robertson ph Frank Stanley m Don Randi, Louie Shelton
☆ Cliff Robertson, Cristina Ferrare, Geraldine Page, R. G. Armstrong

Jabberwocky
🏫 GB 1977 101m Technicolor
Umbrella (John Goldstone, Sandy Lieberson)
▣ ◎
A medieval cooper's apprentice is mistaken for a prince and slays the dragon which is terrorizing the neighbourhood.
An intellectual Carry On film, with very little more taste and a great deal more unpleasant imagery. Despite much re-editing, the laughs are very intermittent.
w Charles Alverson, Terry Gilliam d Terry Gilliam ph Terry Bedford m De Wolfe pd Roy Smith
☆ Michael Palin, Max Wall, Deborah Fallender, Warren Mitchell, John Le Mesurier, Harry H. Corbett, Rodney Bewes, Bernard Bresslaw
'The constant emphasis on blood, excrement, dismemberment and filth ultimately becomes rather wearing.' – *Michael Billington, Illustrated London News*

J'Accuse *
France 1939 95m bw
Forrester-Parant
▣
A scientist intends his invention to end war; when it is put to a contrary purpose, he calls the war dead to rise from their graves and accuse humanity.
Stern, well acted, but (as it proved) ineffective propaganda.
wd Abel Gance
☆ Victor Francen, Jean Max, Renée Devillers

Jack
US 1996 113m Technicolor
Buena Vista/Hollywood/American Zoetrope/Great Oaks (Ricardo Mestres, Fred Fuchs, Francis Ford Coppola)
▣ ▣ ◎ ⊚ ⊚ ◠
A 10-year-old boy, who has a rare condition that means he has the body of a 40-year-old, goes to school for the first time.
An unbelievably bad, totally risible movie played all out for sentimentality; it represents a regrettable infantile regression by its director and star.
w James DeMonaco, Gary Nadeau d Francis Ford Coppola ph John Toll m Michael Kamen pd Dean Tavoularis ed Barry Malkin
☆ Robin Williams, Diane Lane, Jennifer Lopez, Brian Kerwin, Fran Drescher, Bill Cosby, Michael McKean
'It's hard to shake the feeling that Coppola has become a hack in an artist's body.' – *Owen Gleiberman, Entertainment Weekly*

Jack Ahoy!
GB 1934 82m bw
Gaumont (Michael Balcon)
An accident-prone naval rating routs bandits and wins the girl.
Tailor-made star comedy with skilful moments.
w Jack Hulbert, Leslie Arliss, Gerard Fairlie, Austin Melford story Sidney Gilliat, J. O. C. Orton d Walter Forde ph Bernard Knowles m Bretton Byrd ed Ralph Kemplen

☆ Jack Hulbert, Nancy O'Neil, Alfred Drayton, Tamara Desni
'Mr Hulbert is equal to all his occasions ... his abounding energy and high spirits are never monotonous or wearisome.' – *E. V. Lucas, Punch*

'Sometimes ... It's The Little Things In Life That Bring People Together'
Jack & Sarah
GB/France 1995 110m colour
Polygram/British Screen/Canal/Granada TV/Mainstream (Pippa Cross, Simon Channing-Williams, Janette Day)
▣ ▣ ◠
A lawyer whose wife dies in childbirth tries to cope with bringing up his baby daughter.
Moderately entertaining, though unmemorable, comedy with romantic overtones, small in scope and ambition.
wd Tim Sullivan ph Jean Yves Escoffier m Simon Boswell pd Christopher J. Bradshaw ed Lesley Walker
☆ Richard E. Grant, Samantha Mathis, Judi Dench, Ian McKellen, Eileen Atkins, Cherie Lunghi, Imogen Stubbs, David Swift, Kate Hardie
'Good for an easy laugh and a warm glow, but it lacks the sharpness and dexterity of the best British comedies.' – *Geoff Brown, The Times*

Jack and the Beanstalk
🏫 US 1952 78m Supercinecolor
Warner/Alex Gottlieb
▣ ▣
A babysitter dreams the story he is reading aloud.
Rather feeble star comedy aimed entirely at the kiddie set, and with none of the familiar routines. The 'bookends', as is customary, are in black and white.
w Nat Curtis d Jean Yarbrough ph George Robinson m Heinz Roemheld
☆ Bud Abbott, Lou Costello, Buddy Baer, Dorothy Ford, William Farnum

Jack Be Nimble
New Zealand 1992 95m colour
Metro Tartan/Essential/New Zealand Film Commission (Jonathan Dowling, Kelly Rogers)
▣ ▣
An unhappy youth, separated from his psychic sister, invents a machine to hypnotize and kill his cruel, adopted parents, but their spirits seek revenge.
Ghoulish and disturbing horror, offering nothing in the way of comfort.
wd Garth Maxwell ph Donald Duncan m Chris Neal pd Grant Major ed John Gilbert sp Kevin Chisnall
☆ Alexis Arquette, Sarah Smuts-Kennedy, Bruno Lawrence, Tony Barry, Elizabeth Hawthorne, Brenda Simmons, Gilbert Goldie
'This deeply weird melodrama ... at once affecting, funny and horrifying.' – *Kim Newman, Empire*

'Miracles Can Happen.'
Jack Frost
🏫 US 1998 101m Technicolor
Warner (Irving Azoff, Mark Canton)
◠
A dead rock singer comes back to life as a snowman built by his 12-year-old son.
Gruesomely sentimental tale of male bonding.
w Mark Steven Johnson, Steve Bloom, Jonathan Roberts, Jeff Cesario d Troy Miller ph Laszlo Kovacs m Trevor Rabin pd Mayne Berke ed Lawrence Jordan
☆ Michael Keaton, Kelly Preston, Mark Addy, Joseph Cross, Andy Lawrence, Eli Marienthal, Will Rothhaar
'Any adults in the audience will find themselves fighting for breath beneath the film's avalanche-weight of sentiment. Pure slush.' – *Tom Shone, Sunday Times*

Jack London
US 1943 93m bw
Samuel Bronston/United Artists
Jack London seeks various kinds of adventure, writes a book about the Klondike, and warns the world of the Japanese menace.
Occasionally bright but generally faltering biopic, obviously made on the cheap.
w Ernest Pascal d Alfred Santell
☆ Michael O'Shea, Susan Hayward, Osa Massen, Harry Davenport, Virginia Mayo, Jonathan Hale
♫ Frederick E. Rich (music)

Jack McCall Desperado
US 1952 75m Technicolor
Columbia (Sam Katzman)
A Union officer is forced into outlawry but redeems himself.
Tolerable minor Western.
w John O'Dea d Sidney Salkow ph Henry Freulich
☆ George Montgomery, Angela Stevens, Douglas Kennedy, James Seay, Jay Silverheels

Jack of All Trades *
GB 1936 76m bw
Gainsborough (Michael Balcon)
A cheerful con man talks his way into a top job in an international firm.
Odd amalgam of star comedy, musical numbers of the Astaire/Rogers type, shafts of satire from the original play, and finally some flat-footed farce. Certainly worth a look.
w Jack Hulbert, Austin Melford, J. O. C. Orton play Youth at the Helm by Hubert Griffith, Paul Vulpuis d Jack Hulbert, Robert Stevenson ph Charles Van Enger md Louis Levy ad Vetchinsky ed T. R. Fisher
☆ Jack Hulbert, Gina Malo, Robertson Hare, Athole Stewart, Felix Aylmer, H. F. Maltby
'The film degenerates into nothing but the jutting jaw and the permanent grin, the same memory one takes away from all Mr Hulbert's films.' – *Graham Greene*

Jack of Diamonds
US/West Germany 1967 105m Metrocolor
MGM/Harris/Bavaria Atelier
A retired jewel thief introduces a brilliant pupil into society.
Repetitive and rather glum comedy-drama which perks up occasionally.
w Jack de Witt, Sandy Howard d Don Taylor ph Ernst Wild m Peter Thomas
☆ George Hamilton, Joseph Cotten, Marie Laforet, Maurice Evans, Wolfgang Preiss, Lilli Palmer, Carroll Baker, Zsa Zsa Gabor

Jack Slade
US 1953 90m bw
Allied Artists
GB title: *Slade*
A Western gunman becomes a psychopathic killer.
Cliché-ridden but rather brutish Western, thought sensationally violent at the time.
w Warren Douglas d Harold Schuster ph William Sickner m Paul Dunlap
☆ Mark Stevens, Dorothy Malone, Barton MacLane, John Litel, Paul Langton, Harry Shannon

'A Father. Two Sons. A Love Story.'
'Every Family Needs A Hero.'
Jack the Bear
🏫 US 1993 99m DeLuxe
TCF/American Filmworks/Lucky Dog (Bruce Gilbert)
▣ ▣ ◎
In the 1970s, following the death of his wife, an actor begins to drink heavily as he tries to cope with his two young sons and unbalanced neighbour.

Family drama that veers towards melodrama without becoming very interesting.
w Steven Zaillian novel Dan McCall d Marshall Herskovitz ph Fred Murphy m James Horner pd Lilly Kilvert ed Steven Rosenblum
☆ Danny DeVito, Robert J. Steinmiller Jnr, Miko Hughes, Gary Sinise, Art LaFleur, Stefan Gierasch, Erica Yohn, Andrea Marcovicci
'Its effect is that of a TV series that has been telescoped and packed, with each of its rather glib resolutions, into an hour and a half. Despite a surfeit of material, nothing is thorny enough to sustain and the result is a long haul.' – *Amanda Lipman, Sight and Sound*

Jack the Giant Killer **
🏫 US 1961 94m Technicolor
Zenith/Edward Small (Robert E. Kent)
▣ ◎
Demon Pendragon kidnaps the princess of Cornwall but she is rescued by a farmer's son.
Very creditable fairy tale, with the right style and atmosphere assisted by vigorous acting, good pace and excellent trick effects. Unfortunately it turned out rather scary for a child audience and so fell between two stools.
w Orville Hampton, Nathan Juran d Nathan Juran ph David S. Horsley m Paul Sawtell, Bert Shefter ad Fernando Carere, Frank McCoy sp Howard Anderson
☆ Kerwin Mathews, Judi Meredith, Torin Thatcher, Don Beddoe, Walter Burke, Barry Kelley

'He baffled the great Scotland Yard, the celebrated Arthur Conan Doyle, and Robert Louis Stevenson!'
Jack the Ripper
GB 1958 84m bw
Mid Century (Baker and Berman)
▣
In Victorian London the Ripper murders are finally attributed to a demented surgeon.
Flat and rather flabby treatment of a cause célèbre, saved by a reasonably convincing period look.
w Jimmy Sangster m Stanley Black d/ph Robert S. Baker, Monty Berman
☆ Ewen Solon, Lee Patterson, Eddie Byrne, Betty McDowall, John Le Mesurier

The Jackal
US 1997 124m DeLuxe Panavision
Universal/Mutual/Alphaville (James Jacks, Sean Daniel, Michael Caton-Jones, Kevin Jarre)
▣ ▣ ◎ ⊚
In revenge for his brother's death at the hands of the FBI, a Russian gangster hires a top assassin, a master of disguise, to kill a leading American.
Dull thriller, in which an audience is expected to care that someone appears to be planning to shoot the head of the FBI, while he is hunted by an IRA killer, a Basque terrorist and a former KGB agent.
w Chuck Pfarrer screenplay The Day of the Jackal by Kenneth Ross d Michael Caton-Jones ph Karl Walter Lindenlaub m Carter Burwell pd Michael White ed Jim Clark
☆ Bruce Willis, Richard Gere, Sidney Poitier, Diane Venora, Tess Harper, J. K. Simmons, Mathilda May, Stephen Spinella
'An involving high-tech thriller that occasionally hits peaks of pulsating excitement.' – *Variety*
'Such a banal and redundant blockbuster, one senses there was no reason to make it, other than the desire to cash in on the stars' names.' – *David Ise, Sight and Sound*

Jackass Mail
US 1942 80m bw
MGM (John Considine Jnr)
A horse thief marries the proprietress of a gambling saloon in the hope of hijacking her mail line, but she reforms him.

🏫 film suitable for family viewing   ▣ VHS video-cassette for the British PAL system   ▣ VHS video-cassette for the British PAL system in wide screen-format   ⊡ Video cassette in a computer-colourised version   ▤ American NTSC video-cassette   ◠ Laser disc

Boisterously conceived but anaemically scripted Western comedy with the stars in full throttle.
w Lawrence Hazard d Norman Z. McLeod ph Clyde de Vinna m David Snell, Earl Brent ☆ Wallace Beery, Marjorie Main, J. Carrol Naish, Darryl Hickman, William Haade, Hobart Cavanaugh

'This time at least they are repeating their variation on the Min-and-Bill routine among companions whose resemblance to burlesque is as unabashed as their own.' – Bosley Crowther, New York Times

Jackboot Mutiny

Germany 1955 77m bw
Arca-Ariston
original title: Es Geschah am 20 Juli
An account of the army officers' plot to assassinate Hitler.
Documentary-like treatment without much attempt at characterization. An important historical document nevertheless.
w W. P. Zibaso, Gustav Machaty d G. W. Pabst ph Kurt Hasse m Johannes Weissenbach ☆ Bernhard Wicki, Karl Ludwig Diehl, Carl Wery

Jackie Brown **

US 1997 155m CFI color
Buena Vista/Miramax/A Band Apart (Lawrence Bender)
▣ ▤ @~ ◎ ◉ ∩
An air stewardess outsmarts a ruthless gun-runner and the FBI.
An absorbing, if overlong, thriller, successfully combining intrigue and character development to create a satisfying mix that updates the style of the blaxploitation movies of the 70s.
wd Quentin Tarantino novel Rum Punch by Elmore Leonard ph Guillermo Navarro pd David Wasco ed Sally Menke
☆ Pam Grier, Samuel L. Jackson, Robert Forster, Bridget Fonda, Michael Keaton, Robert de Niro, Michael Bowen, Chris Tucker

'Offers an abundance of pleasures, especially in the realm of characterization and atmosphere.' – Variety

'Jackie Chan Fights For The World In His Biggest Action Film Ever!'

Jackie Chan's First Strike (dubbed) *

Hong Kong/US 1996 84m DeLuxe 'Scope
Entertainment/Paragon/New Line/Golden Harvest (Barbie Tung)
▣ ▤ @~ ◉
original title: Jingcha Gushi 4 Zhi Jiandan Renwu
A Hong Kong policeman becomes involved with arms dealers in Russia and Australia.
A typical Jackie Chan action film, not to be taken seriously but to be enjoyed for the panache and daring of its stunts, which are many and spectacular.
w Stanley Tong, Nick Tramontane, Greg Mellott, Elliot Tong, Doris Wang d Stanley Tong ph Jingle Ma m J. Peter Robinson pd Oliver Wong ed Peter Cheung, Chi Wai Yau
☆ Jackie Chan, Chen Chun Wu, Jackson Lou, Bill Tung, Jouri Petrov, Grishajeva Nonna

'Just one death-defying deed after another. But it's a sight more entertaining than films that cost a fortune and deliver only confusion.' – Alexander Walker, London Evening Standard

Jacknife

US 1988 103m Technicolor
Vestron/Kings Road Entertainment (Robert Schaffel, Carol Baum)
▣ ▤ @~
A Vietnam veteran begins a relationship with the sister of an old army friend.
Well-acted but only occasionally interesting.
w Stephen Metcalfe play Strange Snow by Stephen Metcalfe d David Jones ph Brian West pd Edward Pisoni ed John Bloom
☆ Robert DeNiro, Ed Harris, Kathy Baker, Charles Dutton, Elizabeth Franz, Tom Isbell, Loudon Wainwright III, Sloane Shelton, Ivan Brogger

The Jackpot **

US 1950 85m bw
TCF (Samuel G. Engel)
A suburban husband finds that life becomes complicated when winning the jackpot on a radio quiz makes him a celebrity.
Modest, skilful comedy in Hollywood's best manner.

w Phoebe and Henry Ephron d Walter Lang ph Joseph LaShelle m/l Lionel Newman
☆ James Stewart, Barbara Hale, James Gleason, Fred Clark, Alan Mowbray, Patricia Medina, Natalie Wood, Tommy Rettig, Robert Gist, Lyle Talbot

Jack's the Boy *

GB 1932 91m bw
Gainsborough (Michael Balcon)
▣
US title: Night and Day
The police commissioner's son proves his worth in rounding up a smash-and-grab gang.
Dated but lively farce which established its star as a British box-office attraction of the 30s.
w W. P. Lipscomb story Jack Hulbert, Douglas Furber d Walter Forde ph Leslie Rowson m/l/y Vivian Ellis, Douglas Furber md Louis Levy ad Vetchinsky ed Ian Dalrymple, John Goldman
☆ Jack Hulbert, Cicely Courtneidge, Francis Lister, Winifred Shotter, Peter Gawthorne, Ben Field

'A riotously funny, good, clean, honest British picture.' – Sydney Carroll, Sunday Times
† The film in which Hulbert sang 'The Flies Crawled Up the Window'.

Jack's Wife: see Season of the Witch

Jackson County Jail

US 1976 84m Metrocolor
UA/New World (Roger Corman)
▤
A lady driver is hijacked, attacked, disbelieved by the local police, thrown into jail and raped by the jailer, whom she brains with a stool.
An exploitation piece with social pretensions which it in no way justifies: it is however quite competently entertaining in its mindlessly violent way.
w Donald Stewart d Michael Miller ph Bruce Logan m Loren Newkirk
☆ Yvette Mimieux, Tommy Lee Jones, Robert Carradine, Frederic Cook, Severn Darden, Howard Hessman

Jacob's Ladder

US 1990 113m Technicolor
Tri-Star/Carolco (Alan Marshall)
▣ ▤ @~ ◎ ◉
A Vietnam veteran is unwittingly the subject of secret experiments with chemical weapons.
Exceedingly silly on every level, particularly in its supernatural dabblings.
w Bruce Joel Rubin d Adrian Lyne ph Jeffrey L. Kimball m Maurice Jarre pd Brian Morris ed Tom Rolf
☆ Tim Robbins, Elizabeth Pena, Danny Aiello, Matt Craven, Pruitt Taylor Vince, Jason Alexander, Patricia Kalember

'Dull, unimaginative and pretentious.' – Variety

Jacqueline *

GB 1956 93m bw
Rank (George H. Brown)
A Belfast shipyard worker cannot stand heights, takes to drink, and is helped by his small daughter.
Convincing, well-made, realistically set domestic comedy-drama.
w Patrick Kirwan, Liam O'Flaherty d Roy Baker ph Geoffrey Unsworth m Cedric Thorpe Davie
☆ John Gregson, Kathleen Ryan, Jacqueline Ryan, Noel Purcell, Cyril Cusack, Marie Kean, Liam Redmond, Maureen Delany

Jacqueline Susann's Once Is Not Enough: see Once Is Not Enough

Jacquot de Nantes **

France 1991 119m bw/colour
Cine-Tamaris/Canal/La Sept/La Sofiarp (Agnes Varda, Perrine Baudin)
▣
Biopic of the early years of the life of director Jacques Demy, combined with clips from his films and interviews with him, based on his own memoirs.
A labour of love from Demy's wife that is both moving as a tribute and fascinating in its exploration of a youthful obsession.
wd Agnes Varda ph Patrick Blossier, Agnes Godard, Georges Strouve m Joanna Bruzdowicz pd Robert Nardone, Olivier Radot ed Marie-Jo Audiard

☆ Philippe Maron, Edouard Joubeaud, Laurent Monnier, Brigitte de Villepoix, Daniel Dublet, Guillaume Navaud

'A delightful, if overlong, depiction of the formative years of a youngster determined to make films when he grows up.' – Variety

Jacula: see Female Vampire

'Some Fantasies Go Too Far.'

Jade

US 1995 95m DeLuxe
UIP/Paramount (Robert Evans, Craig Baumgarten, Gary Adelson)
▣ ▤ @~ ◉
In San Francisco, an assistant DA investigates the axe murder of a millionaire and discovers evidence that links it with a former girlfriend, now married to a successful lawyer, and the Governor of California.
A bungled attempt at an erotic thriller, in which the murder makes less sense the more we are told about it; the narrative is just an excuse for a little sleaze, including irrelevant scenes of sexual activity.
w Joe Eszterhas d William Friedkin ph Andrzej Bartkowiak m James Horner pd Alex Tavoularis ed Augie Hess
☆ David Caruso, Linda Fiorentino, Chazz Palminteri, Michael Biehn, Richard Crenna, Donna Murphy, Ken King

'Writer Joe Eszterhas's follow-up to his Showgirls fiasco is every bit as hopeless, and this time he takes some good actors down with him.' – Bruce Diones, New Yorker
'For sheer nastiness, allied to a lush, well-decorated camera style, William Friedkin's Jade ... takes some beating.' – Derek Malcolm, Guardian

Jag är nyfiken – gul: see I Am Curious – Yellow

Jagged Edge **

US 1985 108m Metrocolor
Columbia/Martin Ransohoff
▣ ▤ @~
A lady lawyer defends a newspaper publisher who may or may not be guilty of murder.
Well-crafted courtroom mystery with fashionable violence and a few unexpected twists.
w Joe Eszterhas d Richard Marquand ph Matthew F. Leonetti m John Barry pd Gene Callahan ed Sean Barton, Conrad Buff
☆ Jeff Bridges, Glenn Close, Peter Coyote, Robert Loggia, Leigh Taylor-Young, John Dehner
↓ Robert Loggia (supporting actor)

Jaguar Lives

US 1979 90m Eastmancolor
Jaguar (Sandy Howard)
▤
Exploits of an international secret agent with skill in the martial arts.
Flashy, violent, James Bond rip-off, years behind its time.
w Yabo Yablonsky d Ernest Pintoff ph John Cabrera m Robert Ragland
☆ Joe Lewis, Christopher Lee, Donald Pleasence, Capucine, Barbara Bach, Joseph Wiseman, Woody Strode, John Huston

J'ai épousé une Ombre: see I Married a Dead Man

Jailbirds: see Pardon Us

Jailhouse Rock *

US 1957 96m bw Cinemascope
MGM (Pandro S. Berman)
▣ ▤ @~ ◉
An ex-convict becomes a pop star.
Reasonably competent star vehicle, sourer in tone than most.
w Guy Trosper story Ned Young d Richard Thorpe ph Robert Bronner md Jeff Alexander
☆ Elvis Presley, Judy Tyler, Mickey Shaughnessy, Vaughn Taylor, Dean Jones

Jakarta

Indonesia/US 1988 95m colour Panavision
Medusa/Parkit Films/Troma
An ex-CIA agent is taken to Indonesia to put an end to a local big-time drug dealer.
Inconsequential thriller.

w Charles Kaufman, Ralph Soll d Charles Kaufman ph Robert Chappell, Kasiyo Hadiwijoyo m Jay Chattaway pd Susan Kaufman ed Michael Spence, Norman Benny
☆ Christopher Noth, Sue Francis Pai, Franz Tumbuan, Ronald Hunter, Zoraya Perucha, David Sharp, David Gale

Jake Speed

US 1986 100m Technicolor
Crawford/Lane/Foster/Balcor
▤ ◉
A famous hero tracks down an American girl abducted in Paris.
Adventure hokum with spoof elements which don't come off.
w Wayne Crawford, Andrew Lane d Andrew Lane ph Bryan Loftus m Mark Snow pd Norman Baron
☆ Wayne Crawford, John Hurt, Dennis Christopher, Karen Kopins, Leon Ames

'When all hope was lost, he invented it.'

Jakob the Liar *

US 1999 114m DeLuxe
Columbia/Blue Wolf/Kasso (Marsha Garces Williams, Steven Haft)
▣ ◉
In Nazi-occupied Poland, a Jewish café owner keeps hope in the ghetto high by pretending to own a radio and relaying news of a Russian advance.
Doggedly earnest drama with an ironic undertone, probably too restrained in its treatment to have a wide appeal.
w Peter Kassovitz, Didier Decoin book Jurek Becker d Peter Kassovitz ph Elemer Ragalyi m Edward Shearmur pd Luciana Arrighi ed Claire Simpson
☆ Robin Williams, Alan Arkin, Bob Balaban, Hannah Taylor Gordon, Michael Jeter, Armin Mueller-Stahl, Liev Schreiber, Nina Siemaszko, Mathieu Kassovitz, Justus von Dohnanyi, Mark Margolis, Gregg Bello

'A bitterly whimsical slice of mordant Yiddish-style humor that plays more like an Eastern European fable than a piece of emotional Hollywood pandering.' – Todd McCarthy, Variety
'A dreadful, enervated mess.' – Glenn Kenny, Premiere
† The film failed at the US box-office, grossing around $5m.

Jalna

US 1935 75m bw
RKO
Episodes in the life of the Whiteoaks family.
Flat adaptation of a Canadian bestseller.
w Anthony Veiller, Garrett Fort, Larry Bachmann novel Mazo de la Roche d John Cromwell
☆ Kay Johnson, Ian Hunter, C. Aubrey Smith, Jessie Ralph, Nigel Bruce, David Manners, Peggy Wood, Halliwell Hobbes

'Nice production of a not very good adaptation.' – Variety

Jalsaghar: see The Music Room

Jamaica Inn *

GB 1939 107m bw
Mayflower (Erich Pommer)
▤
In old Cornwall, an orphan girl becomes involved with smugglers.
Stagey, stilted adventure story which never loses its studio feel or takes fire as a Hitchcock picture. The cast keeps it interesting.
w Sidney Gilliat, Joan Harrison, J. B. Priestley novel Daphne du Maurier d Alfred Hitchcock ph Harry Stradling, Bernard Knowles m Eric Fenby ad Tom Morahan ed Robert Hamer
☆ Charles Laughton, Maureen O'Hara, Leslie Banks, Robert Newton, Emlyn Williams, Wylie Watson, Marie Ney, Morland Graham

'Should get good but not outstanding b.o. Superb direction, excellent casting, expressive playing and fine production offset an uneven screenplay.' – Variety
'I was irresistibly reminded of an all-star charity matinee.' – Graham Greene

---

Jamaica Run

US 1953 92m Technicolor
Paramount/Pine-Thomas

A search for documents, which may apportion a great house to another branch of the family, leads to murder.

Plot-bound romantic mystery in period, with elements of a Caribbean Rebecca. Watchable medium-budget hokum.

wd Lewis R. Foster *novel* Max Murray *ph* Lionel Lindon *m* Lucien Cailliet

☆ Ray Milland, Arlene Dahl, Wendell Corey, Patric Knowles

James and the Giant Peach **

†† US 1996 79m Technicolor
Guild/Disney/Allied Filmmakers (Denise di Novi, Tim Burton)

⊞ ▤ ◎~ ⊙ ⊘ ⌂

An unhappy boy goes on a magical journey inside a giant peach, accompanied by six friendly insects.

Witty stop-motion animated feature, softer-centred than Dahl's original, but still ripe with delights.

w Karey Kirkpatrick, Jonathan Roberts, Steve Bloom *novel* Roald Dahl *d* Henry Selick *ph* Pete Kozachik, Hiro Narita *m* Randy Newman *pd* Harley Jessup *ed* Stan Webb

☆ Paul Terry, Joanna Lumley, Miriam Margolyes, Pete Postlethwaite and also the voices of: Simon Callow, Richard Dreyfuss, Jane Leeves, Susan Sarandon, David Thewlis

'Can be recommended to almost anyone. It's a peach.' – *Tom Shone, Sunday Times*

♫ Randy Newman

The James Brothers: see *The True Story of Jesse James*

The James Gang

GB 1997 99m colour
Polygram/Paragon/HandMade/BBC/Revolution (Andrew Eaton)

⊞

After her home is burned down by a loan shark, a Scottish woman and her four children head for London to be reunited with her feckless husband; the family then drives round England committing a series of petty robberies.

An unhappy mix of gritty social realism and stylized comedy; its disparate elements never come together and the result, despite some effective acting, is a dispiriting road movie.

w Stuart Hepburn *story* Andrew Eaton, Paul Lee *d* Mike Barker *ph* Benjamin Seresin *m* Bernard Butler *pd* Alice Normington *ed* Guy Bensley

☆ John Hannah, Helen McCrory, Jason Flemyng, Toni Collette, Darren Brownlie, David Brownlie, Lauren McMurray, Lauren McCracken

'As with so many recent, mediocre British films, it's the quality of the performances which partly redeems *The James Gang*.' – *Leslie Felperin, Sight and Sound*

'A Film Where Women Eat Men And Men Eat Ham.'

Jamón Jamón *

Spain 1992 91m colour
Metro Tartan/Lolafilms/Ovideo/Sogepaq (Andrés Vicente Gómez)

⊞ ▤ ⌂

A wealthy mother decides she wants a local stud for herself after hiring him to seduce her son's girlfriend.

Broad and enjoyable comedy of sex and male virility, not to be taken seriously despite its downbeat, partner-swapping finale.

w Cuca Canals, Bigas Luna, Quim Monzó *d* Bigas Luna *ph* José Luis Alcaine *m* Nicola Piovani *pd* Chu Uroz, Noemi Campano *ad* Julio Esteban *ed* Teresa Font

☆ Stefania Sandrelli, Anna Galiena, Juan Diego, Penélope Cruz, Javier Bardem, Jordi Molla

'Racy and surreal farce.' – *Empire*
'His storytelling wanders too arbitrarily between slapstick eroticism and an exaggerated neo-realism to achieve any clarity of focus.' – *Philip Strick, Sight and Sound*

Jana-Aranya: see *The Middle Man*

Jane and the Lost City

GB 1988 92m colour
Blue Dolphin/Marcel-Robertson (Harry Robertson)

A girl with a penchant for stripping becomes a British agent during the Second World War.

Based on a once-famous Daily Mirror strip cartoon, a tatty, low-budget romp of no perceptible interest, other than to students of the decline of British cinema.

w Mervyn Haisman *story* Mervyn Haisman, Terry Marcel, Harry Robertson *d* Terry Marcel *ph* Paul Beeson *m* Harry Robertson *pd* Michael Pickwoad *ed* Alan Jones

☆ Sam Jones, Maud Adams, Jasper Carrott, Kirsten Hughes, Graham Stark, Robin Bailey, Ian Roberts, Elsa O'Toole

Jane Eyre

US 1934 62m bw
Monogram

A Poverty Row transcription of the Charlotte Brontë novel: see below.

w Adele Comandini *d* Christy Cabanne

☆ Virginia Bruce, Colin Clive, Beryl Mercer, Jameson Thomas, Aileen Pringle

'The cast appear to have considered their tasks with considerable melancholy.' – *Variety*

'A love story every woman would die a thousand deaths to live!'

Jane Eyre ***

†† US 1943 96m bw
TCF (William Goetz)

⊞ ▤ ◎~ ⌂

In Victorian times, a harshly treated orphan girl becomes governess in a mysterious Yorkshire mansion with a brooding master.

Sharply paced, reasonably faithful and superbly staged Hollywood version of Charlotte Brontë's archetypal romantic novel which stimulated so many imitations, including Rebecca.

w Aldous Huxley, Robert Stevenson, John Houseman *d* Robert Stevenson *ph* George Barnes *m* Bernard Herrmann *ad* Wiard B. Ihnen, James Basevi *sp* Fred Sersen

☆ Joan Fontaine, Orson Welles, Margaret O'Brien, Henry Daniell, John Sutton, Agnes Moorehead, Elizabeth Taylor, Peggy Ann Garner, Sara Allgood, Aubrey Mather, Hillary Brooke, Edith Barrett, Ethel Griffies, Barbara Everest, John Abbott

'A careful and tame production, a sadly vanilla-flavoured Joan Fontaine, and Orson Welles treating himself to broad operatic sculpturings of body, cloak and diction, his eyes glinting in the Rembrandt gloom, at every chance, like side orders of jelly.' – *James Agee*
'The essentials are still there; and the non-essentials, such as the gloom, the shadows, the ground mist, the rain and the storms, have been expanded and redoubled and magnified to fill up the gaps.' – *Richard Mallett, Punch*

Jane Eyre

GB 1970 110m Eastmancolor
British Lion/Omnibus/Sagittarius (Frederick H. Brogger)

A Victorian governess discovers that the master she comes to love hides a secret in his attic.

A generally lacklustre version of a classic story, enlivened by Scott's performance.

w Jack Pulman *novel* Charlotte Brontë *d* Delbert Mann *ph* Paul Beeson *m* John Williams *ad* Alex Vetchinsky *ed* Peter Boita

☆ George C. Scott, Susannah York, Ian Bannen, Jack Hawkins, Nyree Dawn Porter, Rachel Kempson, Kenneth Griffith, Peter Copley, Michele Dotrice, Clive Morton, Constance Cummings

'A pleasant if unispired reminder of Charlotte's most successful novel.' – *David Pirie, MFB*

Jane Eyre

US 1996 112m colour
Miramax/Rochester (Dyson Lovell)

⊞

In the 1820s, a governess falls in love with her secretive employer, who keeps a mystery hidden in the attic.

Glum and emotionally stolid version that fails to evoke the necessary romance.

w Hugh Whitemore, Franco Zeffirelli *novel* Charlotte Brontë *d* Franco Zeffirelli *ph* David Watkin *m* Alessio Vlad, Claudio Capponi *pd* Roger Hall *ed* Richard Marden

☆ William Hurt, Charlotte Gainsbourg, Joan Plowright, Anna Paquin, Geraldine Chaplin, Billie Whitelaw, Maria Schneider, Fiona Shaw, Elle Macpherson, John Wood, Amanda Root

'Zeffirelli's approach to period drama – faithful, four-square and flat as a miniseries – itself feels like something of a period piece.' – *Tom Shone, Sunday Times*

Janice Meredith

US 1924 153m bw silent
Metro-Goldwyn/Cosmopolitan

GB title: *The Beautiful Rebel*

Vicissitudes of the coquettish daughter of a New Jersey family through the War of Independence.

Marathon melodrama not unlike Gone with the Wind in subject matter, but of no general interest.

w Lillie Hayward *novel* Paul Leicester Ford *d* E. Mason Hopper *ph* Ira H. Morgan, George Barnes *m* Deems Taylor *ad* Joseph Urban

☆ Marion Davies, Harrison Ford, Macklyn Arbuckle, Joseph Kilgour, George Nash, Tyrone Power Snr, May Vokes, W. C. Fields, Olin Howland

Janie

†† US 1944 106m bw
Warner (Brock Pemberton)

The teenage daughter of a middle-class American household gets into innocent scrapes with the army.

Deafening tomboy farce.

w Agnes Christine Johnston, Charles Hoffman *play* Josephine Bentham, Herschel V. Williams Jnr *d* Michael Curtiz *ph* Carl Guthrie *m/ly* Lee David, Sammy Cahn, Jule Styne *ed* Owen Marks

☆ Joyce Reynolds, Robert Hutton, Ann Harding, Edward Arnold, Robert Benchley, Claire Foley, Hattie McDaniel

† *Janie Gets Married*, made the following year and running 89m, had almost identical credits except that Joan Leslie replaced Joyce Reynolds and Dorothy Malone joined the cast.

♫ Owen Marks

The Janitor: see *Eye Witness (1981)*

The January Man

US 1989 97m DeLuxe
UIP/MGM (Norman Jewison, Ezra Swerdlow)

▤ ◎~

A disgraced policeman tracks down a serial killer.

Ludicrously implausible thriller.

w John Patrick Shanley *d* Pat O'Connor *ph* Jerzy Zielinksi *m* Marvin Hamlisch *pd* Philip Rosenberg *ed* Lou Lombardo

☆ Kevin Kline, Susan Sarandon, Mary Elizabeth Mastrantonio, Harvey Keitel, Danny Aiello, Rod Steiger, Alan Rickman, Faye Grant, Ken Welsh

Japanese War Bride *

US 1952 94m bw
TCF/Bernhard (Joseph Bernhard)

An officer wounded in Korea marries his Japanese nurse and takes her home to California.

Predictable domestic drama very similar to the British Frieda, marginally interesting for sociological reasons.

w Catherine Turney *d* King Vidor *ph* Lionel Lindon *m* Arthur Lange *md* Emil Newman

☆ Shirley Yamaguchi, Don Taylor, Cameron Mitchell, Marie Windsor, James Bell, Louise Lorimer

Jarrapellejos **

Spain 1987 108m colour
Penelope/Television Española (Jose G. Blanco Sola, Jose Joaquin Aguirre)

In the early 1900s, a corrupt landowner in a small town covers up the rape and murder of a mother and daughter.

Devastating exposé of social and sexual hypocrisy, shot in a stately fashion.

w Antonio Gimenez Rico, Manuel Gutierrez Aragon *novel* Felipe Trigo *d* Antonio Gimenez Rico *ph* Jose Luis Alcaine *m* Carmelo A. Bernaola *ad* Rafael Palmero *ed* Miguel Gonzalez Sinde

☆ Antonio Ferrandis, Juan Diego, Lydia Bosch, Amparo Larrañaga, Joaquin Hinojosa, Miguel A. Rellan, Aitana Sanchez-Gijon, Carlos Tristancho, Florinda Chico, Jose Coronado

Jason and the Argonauts ***

†† GB 1963 104m Technicolor
Columbia/Charles H. Schneer

⊞ ▤ ◎~ ⊙ ⌂

With help and hindrance from the gods, Jason voyages in search of the Golden Fleece and meets all kinds of monsters.

Rambling semi-classic mythological fantasy which keeps its tongue firmly in its cheek and provides a framework for some splendid stop-frame animation.

w Jan Read, Beverley Cross *d* Don Chaffey *ph* Wilkie Cooper *m* Bernard Herrmann *sp* Ray Harryhausen

☆ Todd Armstrong, Honor Blackman, Niall MacGinnis, Andrew Faulds, Nancy Kovack

Jason Goes to Hell: The Final Friday

US 1993 88m DeLuxe
New Line (Sean S. Cunningham)

Jason attempts to kill his relatives so that he can live forever.

The series ends, but does not even manage a whimper on the way out; it simply fades away into witless, boring nonsense. The most frightening moment comes at the end, with the hint that he and Freddy, hero of the Nightmare on Elm Street series, may be teamed in a new movie.

w Dean Lorey, Jay Huguely *d* Adam Marcus *ph* William Dill *m* Harry Manfredini *pd* W. Brooke Wheeler *ed* David Handman

☆ Jon D. LeMay, Kari Keegan, Kane Hodder, Steve Williams, Steven Culp, Erin Gray, Rusty Schwimmer

'Jason goes to hell and not a moment too soon.' – *Variety*

† The film was the ninth and last film in the *Friday the 13th* series (qv).

Jason's Lyric *

US 1994 119m colour
Polygram/Propaganda (Doug McHenry, George Jackson)

⊞ ▤ ◎~ ⊙ ⌂

In Houston, a hard-working television salesman is drawn into the world of crime by his love for his crooked brother and for the sister of a local gangster.

Grim drama of characters trapped by circumstance and the ghetto, but one that recycles old themes without adding much to them.

w Bobby Smith Jnr *d* Doug McHenry *ph* Francis Kenny *m* Afrika, Matt Noble *pd* Simon Dobbin *ed* Andrew Mondshein

☆ Allen Payne, Jada Pinkett, Bokeem Woodbine, Anthony 'Treach' Criss, Lisa Carson, Forest Whitaker, Suzanne Douglas

'The soundtrack CD may find an audience, but no one should relish the film itself, a horrid collison between *West Side Story*, *East of Eden* and a pile of junk.' – *Geoff Brown, The Times*
'A tough film, well shot and directed but paying strict attention, above all, to the performances. Even though made with music that's obviously sellable in record form, it never resorts to out and out cliché.' – *Derek Malcolm, Guardian*

Jassy

GB 1947 102m Technicolor
GFD/Gainsborough (Sydney Box)

A gypsy servant girl falls in love with her master but is accused of murder.

Period romantic melodrama of the Man in Grey school; poor of its kind despite high production values.

w Dorothy and Campbell Christie, Geoffrey Kerr *novel* Norah Lofts *d* Bernard Knowles *ph* Jack Asher

☆ Margaret Lockwood, Patricia Roc, Dennis Price, Basil Sydney, Dermot Walsh, Nora Swinburne, Linden Travers, Ernest Thesiger, Cathleen Nesbitt, John Laurie, Jean Cadell, Clive Morton

'As a piece of unabashed romantic hokum, I found it more and more diverting as the plot thickened.' – *Evening Standard*

Java Head *

GB 1934 85m bw
ATP (Basil Dean)

In 1850 Bristol, a shipbuilder forsakes his Manchu wife for an English girl.

Rather obvious period melodrama with full-blooded acting.

w Martin Brown, Gordon Wellesley *novel* Joseph Hergesheimer *d* J. Walter Ruben *ph* Robert Martin *md* Ernest Irving *ad* Edward Carrick *ed* Thorold Dickinson, David Lean

☆ Anna May Wong, John Loder, Ralph Richardson, Elizabeth Allan, Edmund Gwenn, Herbert Lomas, George Curzon, Roy Emerton

---

Jaws **

👪 US 1975 125m Technicolor
Panavision
Universal/Zanuck-Brown (William S. Gilmore Jnr)

📼 📼 ▤ ⊚ 🎧

A man-eating shark causes havoc off the Long Island coast.

In the exploitation-hungry seventies this film took more money than any other. In itself, despite genuinely suspenseful and frightening sequences, it is a slackly narrated and sometimes flatly handled thriller with an over-abundance of dialogue and, when it finally appears, a pretty unconvincing monster.

w Peter Benchley, Carl Gottlieb *novel* Peter Benchley d Steven Spielberg ph Bill Butler m John Williams ad Joseph Alves Jnr ed Verna Fields

☆ Robert Shaw, Roy Scheider, Richard Dreyfuss, Lorraine Gary, Murray Hamilton, Carl Gottlieb

'A mind-numbing repast for sense-sated gluttons. Shark stew for the stupefied.' – *William S. Pechter*
'The opening sequences have few parallels in modern cinema; like the shower scene in *Psycho* they will haunt a whole generation.' – *Les Keyser, Hollywood in the Seventies*

🏆 John Williams; Verna Fields; sound
👥 best picture
👑 John Williams

Jaws 2

👪 US 1978 117m Technicolor
Panavision
Universal/Richard Zanuck, David Brown (Joe Alves)

📼 📼 ▤ ⊚ 🎧

Another man-eating shark menaces teenagers in the Long Island resort of Amity.

Repetitive and feeble sequel aimed directly at the popcorn market.

w Carl Gottlieb, Howard Sackler, Dorothy Tristan d Jeannot Szwarc ph Michael Butler, David Butler, Michael McGowan m John Williams

☆ Roy Scheider, Lorraine Gary, Murray Hamilton, Joseph Mascolo, Collin Wilcox

'A manipulation of the audience, in the best sense of the term' – *Jeannot Szwarc, director*

'The third dimension is terror!'

Jaws 3-D

US 1983 99m Technicolor ArriVision 3-D
Alan Landsburg/Universal (Rupert Hitzig)

📼 ▤ ⊚

A man-eating shark turns up in a Florida theme park.

Noisy additional chapter to this string of shocks.

w Richard Matheson, Carl Gottlieb *story* Guerdon Trueblood d Joe Alves ph James A. Contner m Alan Parker pd Woods Macintosh ed Randy Roberts, Corky Ehlers

☆ Dennis Quaid, Bess Armstrong, Simon MacCorkindale, Louis Gossett Jnr, John Putch, Lea Thompson

Jaws: The Revenge

US 1987 100m colour
UIP/Universal (Joseph Sargent)

📼 ▤ ⊚ 🎧

Superfluous fourth story in the Jaws series, almost indistinguishable from the others once you accept that the sharks are after Brody's widow.

w Michael de Guzman, Joseph Sargent ph John McPherson m Michael Small pd John Lloyd ed Michael Brown

☆ Lorraine Gary, Lance Guest, Mario Van Peebles, Karen Young, Michael Caine

The Jayhawkers

US 1959 110m Technicolor Vistavision
Paramount/Panama and Frank

▤

Before the Civil War, a farmer defeats a militant posse of private raiders.

Unconvincing but rather unusual Western, flat patches alternating with striking ones.

w Melvin Frank, Joseph Petracca, Frank Fenton, A. I. Bezzerides d Melvin Frank ph Loyal Griggs m Jerome Moross

☆ Fess Parker, Jeff Chandler, Nicole Maurey, Henry Silva, Herbert Rudley

Jazz Comedy *

USSR 1934 93m bw
Mosfilm

original title: *Vesolye Rebyata*

A shepherd is frequently mistaken for a famous conductor.

Peripatetic comedy with many sight gags and western slapstick: Russian comedy being still a rare thing, it seems something of a revelation.

w Grigori Alexandrov, Nikolai Erdman, V. Mass d Grigori Alexandrov ph Vladimir Nilsen m Isaac Dunayevsky

☆ Lubov Orlova, Leonid Utyosov, Maria Strelkova

'The best thing that has happened to the cinema since René Clair made *The Italian Straw Hat* ... a picture of almost ecstatic happiness.' – *Graham Greene*

Jazz on a Summer's Day ***

US 1959 85m DeLuxe
Galaxy/Raven (Allan Green)

📼 ▤

Exemplary documentary about the Newport Jazz Festival, incorporating many excellent performances from the musicians involved.

Made by a famous fashion photographer, this is visually as interesting as it is musically. With its witty juxtaposition of images and sound, it remains probably the best documentary of its kind so far.

w Arnold Pearl, Albert D'Annibale d Bert Stern ph Bert Stern, Courtney Hafela, Ray Phealan md George Avakian ed Aram Avakian

☆ Louis Armstrong, Mahalia Jackson, Gerry Mulligan, Dinah Washington, Chico Hamilton, Anita O'Day, George Shearing, Chuck Berry, Jack Teagarden, Thelonius Monk, Big Maybelle, Sonny Stitt

'New songs and old favourites sung by Mr Jolson during the action of the story on the Vitaphone!'

The Jazz Singer ****

US 1927 89m bw
Warner

📼 ▤ ⊚ 🎧

A cantor's son makes it big in show business.

Archetypal Jewish weepie which became of absorbing interest as the first talkie film (songs and a few fragments of speech) and in its way, surprisingly, is not half bad.

w Alfred A. Cohn *play* Samson Raphaelson d Alan Crosland ph Hal Mohr md Louis Silvers

☆ Al Jolson, May McAvoy, Warner Oland, Eugenie Besserer, Otto Lederer

'A beautiful period piece, extravagantly sentimental ... yet entirely compelling in its own conviction.' – *NFT, 1969*
'*The Jazz Singer* definitely establishes the fact that talking pictures are imminent. Everyone in Hollywood can rise up and declare that they are not, and it will not alter the fact. If I were an actor with a squeaky voice I would worry.' – *Welford Beaton, The Film Spectator*

🏆 Special Award to Warner for producing 'the pioneer outstanding talking picture'
👥 Alfred A. Cohn

The Jazz Singer

US 1953 107m Technicolor
Warner (Louis F. Edelman)

Ill-considered, schmaltzy remake of the above.

w Frank Davis, Leonard Stern, Lewis Meltzer d Michael Curtiz ph Carl Guthrie m Max Steiner md Ray Heindorf

☆ Danny Thomas, Peggy Lee, Mildred Dunnock, Eduard Franz

👥 Ray Heindorf; Max Steiner

The Jazz Singer

US 1980 115m DeLuxe
EMI/Jerry Leider

📼 ▤ ⊚ 🎧

Oddly-timed reprise of the above, with doting mum replaced by patient wife.

A good basis for a best-selling album, otherwise a pointless enterprise.

w Herbert Baker, Stephen H. Foreman d Richard Fleischer ph Isidore Mankofsky m Leonard Rosenman pd Harry Horner

☆ Neil Diamond, Laurence Olivier, Lucie Arnaz, Catlin Adams, Sully Boyar

'What is jazz to Neil Diamond and what is Neil Diamond to jazz? Old title has nothing to do

with music on display here and would seem meaningless to modern audiences.' – *Variety*

Jazzboat

GB 1959 96m bw Cinemascope
Warwick/Columbia

A jazz musician pretends to be a crook and leads the police to an important gang.

Flimsy comedy with a background of pop acts. Very dated.

w Ken Hughes, John Antrobus d Ken Hughes ph Ted Moore m Kenneth Jones ch Lionel Blair

☆ Anthony Newley, Anne Aubrey, David Lodge, Lionel Jeffries, Bernie Winters, James Booth, Al Mulock, Joyce Blair, Leo McKern, Ted Heath and his Music

Je T'Aime, Je T'Aime **

France 1967 94m Eastmancolor
TCF/Parc/Fox Europa (Mag Bodard)

During experiments with a time-machine, a suicidal man relives the experience of an unhappy love affair that led him to attempt to take his own life.

A fascinating, if sometimes confusing, speculation on the nature of time and the fact that there are no second chances in life.

w Jacques Sternberg d Alain Resnais ph Jean Boffety m Krzysztof Penderecki, Jean-Claude Pelletier, Jean Dandeny ad Jacques Dugied, Auguste Pace ed Albert Jurgenson, Colette Leloup

☆ Claude Rich, Olga Georges-Picot, Anouk Ferjac, Annie Fargue, Bernard Fresson, Yvette Etievant

'A work that deserves to be studied and discussed: to see it is essential.' – *Gordon Gow, Films and Filming*

Je T'Aime Moi Non Plus

France 1975 90m Eastmancolor
President/Renn (Jacques-Eric Strauss)

📼

aka: *I Love You No More*

A gay truck driver begins an affair with a boyish girl which proves difficult to consummate and also upsets his jealous Italian boyfriend.

Rambling, inconsequential, intermittently entertaining tale that gives the impression that the actors made it up as they went along.

wd Serge Gainsbourg ph Willy Kurant m Serge Gainsbourg ad Theo Meurisse ed Kenout Peltier

☆ Jane Birkin, Joe Dallesandro, Hugues Quester, Rene Kolldehoff, Gérard Depardieu, Michel Blanc

Je Vous Aime

France 1981 105m Eastmancolor
Renn Productions/FR3 (Pierre Grunstein)

A woman changes husbands as if they were dresses.

Shallow depiction of an incurable romantic, or obsessive promiscuity, depending on your viewpoint. From either, it makes for a dull movie.

w Claude Berri, Michel Grisolia d Claude Berri ph Etienne Becker m Serge Gainsbourg ad Pierre Guffroy ed Arlette Langmann

☆ Catherine Deneuve, Jean-Louis Trintignant, Gérard Depardieu, Serge Gainsbourg, Alain Souchon, Christian Marquand

Jealousy

US 1929 66m bw
Paramount

A young artist is jealous of his wife's older friend, and kills him.

Turgid adaptation of a two-character play; interesting only for its cast, though the star died before it was released.

w Garrett Fort, John D. Williams *play* Louis Verneuil d Jean de Limur

☆ Jeanne Eagels, Fredric March, Halliwell Hobbes, Henry Daniell

Jealousy

US 1934 66m bw
Columbia

A boxer is knocked out and dreams that his jealousy has landed him in the electric chair.

Disagreeable melodrama not saved by its tricks.

w Kubec Glasmon, Joseph Moncure March d Roy William Neill

☆ Nancy Carroll, George Murphy, Donald Cook, Raymond Walburn

Jealousy *

US 1945 70m bw
Republic

A failed writer, jealous of his wife's friendship with another man, is found murdered.

Curious but interesting melodrama with much talent breaking through.

w Arnold Phillips, Gustav Machaty, Dalton Trumbo d Gustav Machaty m Hanns Eisler

☆ Nils Asther, John Loder, Jane Randolph, Karen Morley

'It is a sympathetic film, and in spite of its overall failure, contains enough sincerity and enough artistry to make most of the other films mentioned here look sick.' – *James Agee*

Jealousy Italian Style *

Italy/Spain 1970 106m Technicolor
Panavision
Dean/Jupiter Generale/Midega (Pio Angeletti, Adriano de Micheli)

original title: *Dramma della Gelosia – Tutti i Particolari in Cronaca*
aka: *A Drama of Jealousy; The Pizza Triangle*

Two friends – a married bricklayer and a pizza cook – fall in love with the same woman, who cannot choose between them, resulting in disaster for all three.

Mildly amusing, if over-loud and vociferous, comedy that takes swipes at, among other targets, male–female relationships, modern Italian design, politics, and Fellini's liking for grotesques.

w Furio Scarpelli, Agenore Incrocci, Ettore Scola d Ettore Scola ph Carlo Di Palma m Armando Trovaioli ad Luciano Ricceri ed Alberto Gallitti

☆ Marcello Mastroianni, Giancarlo Giannini, Monica Vitti, Manolo Zarzo, Marisa Merlini, Hercules Cortes

† Mastroianni's performance won him the Best Actor award at the Cannes Film Festival in 1970.

Jean de Florette **

France 1986 121m Eastmancolor
Technovision
Renn/Films A2/RAI2/DD

📼 ▤ ⊚ 🎧 ⊚

Elemental story of feuding over water supplies in rural France in the 20s.

Stunning performances and detailed depiction of Provençal farming life made it a wild success in France, repeated to a remarkable extent abroad.

w Claude Berri, Gérard Brach *novel* Marcel Pagnol d Claude Berri ph Bruno Nuytten m Jean-Claude Petit pd Bernard Vezat

☆ Yves Montand, Gérard Depardieu, Daniel Auteuil, Elisabeth Depardieu

† The saga continued in *Manon des Sources* (qv), from Pagnol's sequel *L'eau de collines*.

👑 best picture; adapted screenplay; cinematography; Daniel Auteuil

Jeanne Eagels *

US 1957 114m bw
Columbia (George Sidney)

A sideshow dancer becomes a Broadway star of the twenties but dies of drugs.

Well-upholstered but basically too conventional showbiz biopic.

w Daniel Fuchs, Sonya Levien, John Fante d George Sidney ph Robert Planck m George Duning

☆ Kim Novak, Jeff Chandler, Agnes Moorehead, Charles Drake, Larry Gates, Virginia Grey

Jeanne la Pucelle: Part I, Les Batailles; Part II, Les Prisons **

France 1994 117m colour
Artificial Eye/Mayfair/La Sept/France 3/Pierre Grise

The story of the life and death at the stake of Joan of Arc. Part I deals with Joan persuading the French court that she has been sent by God to drive the English from France. Part II concentrates on the political machinations that followed her successes, her trial and death.

Absorbing, exhaustively detailed drama that follows Joan in close-up, ignoring opportunities for spectacle; its length, though, remains a problem.

w Christine Laurent, Pascal Bonitzer d Jacques Rivette ph William Lubtchansky m Jordi Savall pd Mau de Chauvigny ed Nicole Lubtchansky

☆ Sandrine Bonnaire, André Marcon, Jean-Louis Richard, Marcel Bozonnet, Didier Sauvegrain, Patrick Le Mauff, Jean-Pierre Lorit, Jean-Pierre Becker, Mathieu Busson

---

'An original, prowling and restless film with an outstanding central performance.' – *Empire*
'Is certainly a sumptuous costume drama, but it's also as cold and as dry as any history lesson.' – *Film Review*
† The original running time for the film's French release was Part I 160m, Part II 176m.

Jeanne's House **
France   1987   94m   colour
MDG/FR3 (Marie-Dominique Girodet)
original title: *La Maison de Jeanne*
A restaurateur, driven to the point of breakdown by her passive husband, demanding mother and noisy children, falls in love with her new landlord.
Witty movie of domestic conflict that comes to a surprising conclusion.
w Magali Clement ph Pierre Novion
m Raymond Alessandrini ad Bruno Bruneau
ed Amina Mazani
☆ Christine Boisson, Benoit Regent, Jean-Pierre Bisson, Marie Trintignant, Michelle Goddet, Maxime Leroux, Pascale Audret, Jacques Richard

Jeannie *
🏃🏃 GB 1941 101m bw
GFD/Tansa (Marcel Hellman)
US title: *Girl in Distress*
A Scots girl comes into money and takes a European holiday.
Mildly astringent, generally amusing comedy which overcomes shaky production. Remade as Let's Be Happy in 1952.
w Anatole de Grunwald, Roland Pertwee play Aimée Stuart d Harold French ph Bernard Knowles m Mischa Spoliansky
☆ Barbara Mullen, Michael Redgrave, Albert Lieven, Wilfrid Lawson, Kay Hammond, Edward Chapman, Googie Withers, Gus MacNaughton
'One of the easiest, sweetest of light comedies.' – *James Agee*
'As enchanting a bit of rue and nonsense as we've succumbed to in many a month.' – *New York Times*

Jeder für sich und Gott gegen alle: see
The Enigma of Kaspar Hauser

Jefferson in Paris
US 1995 139m colour
Buena Vista/Merchant Ivory (Ismail Merchant)
📼 ▇ ◑
In the 1780s, Thomas Jefferson becomes the US Ambassador to France, where he courts a married artist and fathers a child on a young, black slave in his household.
Glossily presented period drama that is all show and no substance.
w Ruth Prawer Jhabvala d James Ivory ph Pierre Lhomme m Richard Robbins pd Guy-Claude Françoise ed Andrew Marcus, Isabel Lorente
☆ Nick Nolte, Greta Scacchi, Jean-Pierre Aumont, Thandie Newton, Simon Callow, Seth Gilliam, James Earl Jones, Michel Lonsdale, Nancy Marchand, Gwyneth Paltrow
'A dreary, tedious, condescending film that, given its sexual subplot, is quite amazingly passionless.' – *Joe Queenan*
'The high-minded look of the film, combined with Jhabvala's uncharacteristically muddled handling of the story, makes for a distinctly queasy experience.' – *Adam Mars-Jones, Independent*
'Two-and-a-half hours of beautifully costumed inconsequence.' – *Tom Shone, Sunday Times*

Jeffrey *
US 1995 94m Technicolor
Film Four/Workin' Man/The Booking Office (Mark Balsam, Mitchell Maxwell, Victoria Maxwell)
📼 ▇ ◑
A gay actor decides to give up sex and then meets the man of his dreams.
A slight and bitchy comedy of the strains and confusions that the arrival of AIDS has brought to matters of love and sex.
w Paul Rudnick play Paul Rudnick
d Christopher Ashley ph Jeffrey Tufano
m Stephen Endelman pd Michael Johnston
ed Cara Silverman
☆ Steven Weber, Patrick Stewart, Bryan Batt, Sigourney Weaver, Nathan Lane, Olympia Dukakis
'Quite successfully walks the tightrope between utter sincerity and queenly silliness.' – *Derek Malcolm, Guardian*

J'Embrasse Pas *
France 1991 115m colour
President/BAC/Salome/Ciné Cinq/Canal Plus (Maurice Benart, Jacques Eric-Strauss, Jean Labadie)
📼
aka: *I Don't Kiss*
An ill-educated but ambitious youth from the country comes to Paris, finds success as a male prostitute and falls for a whore.
Dour moral tale of disillusioned youth that comes to no satisfactory conclusion.
w Jacques Nolot, André Téchiné, Michel Grisolia d André Téchiné ph Thierry Arbogast m Philippe Sarde ed Claudine Merlin, Edith Vassard
☆ Philippe Noiret, Emmanuelle Béart, Manuel Blanc, Hélène Vincent, Yvan Desni

Jennie: see *Portrait of Jennie*

'The drama of all women who meet the demands of love!'

Jennie Gerhardt
US 1933 85m bw
Paramount (B. P. Schulberg)
An unmarried mother is hard done by but gets the man she loves in the end.
Archetypal weepie, adequately put across.
w Josephine Lovett, Joseph M. March, S. K. Lauren, Frank Partos novel Theodore Dreiser d Marion Gering ph Leon Shamroy
☆ Sylvia Sidney, Donald Cook, Mary Astor, Edward Arnold, H. B. Warner, Theodore von Eltz
'Doesn't look to become a general b.o. favourite because it is a story without action.' – *Variety*

Jennifer
US 1953 73m bw
AA (Berman Swartz)
The lady housekeeper of a California mansion broods on the mysterious disappearance of her predecessor.
Slight, quietly effective suspenser with a letdown ending.
w Virginia Myers d Joel Newton ph James Wong Howe m Ernest Gold
☆ Ida Lupino, Howard Duff, Robert Nichols, Mary Shipp

'On the trail of a serial killer, Detective John Berlin has no clues and no suspects. And no alibi.'

Jennifer Eight
US 1992 120m DeLuxe
Paramount (Gary Lucchesi, David Wimbury)
📼 ▇ ◑ ◑ 🎧
A burnt-out cop, moving to a new small-town job, faces local derision when he decides a murder has been committed by a serial killer who targets blind women.
A drawn-out, predictable thriller that becomes more ridiculous the longer it lasts; and it lasts a long time.
wd Bruce Robinson ph Conrad L. Hall
m Christopher Young pd Richard Macdonald ed Conrad Buff
☆ Andy Garcia, Uma Thurman, John Malkovich, Lance Henriksen, Kathy Baker, Kevin Conway, Graham Beckel
'Although initially menacing, Robinson's addition to the serial killer genre falls back on clichés.' – *Sight and Sound*
'A sombre character-oriented suspense mystery, this is notable both for its stunningly atmospheric cinematography and the dark psychological undercurrents lurking beneath the surface.' – *Empire*
† The film was released direct to video in Britain.

Jenny Lind: see *A Lady's Morals*

Jeopardy
US 1952 69m bw
MGM (Sol Baer Fielding)
A man on a camping holiday falls off a jetty and gets stuck in the timbers while the water rises; his wife frantically seeks help from an escaped convict.
Panic melodrama enjoyable for its clichés.
w Mel Dinelli d John Sturges ph Victor Milner m Dimitri Tiomkin
☆ Barbara Stanwyck, Barry Sullivan, Ralph Meeker

'Some say he's dead ... some say he never will be!'

Jeremiah Johnson **
🏃🏃 US 1972 107m Technicolor Panavision
Warner (Joe Wizan)
📼 ▇ ◑ ◑ ◑
In the 1850s an ex-soldier becomes a mountain trapper.
Splendidly made if rather desultorily plotted adventure story with the feel of raw reality.
w John Milius, Edward Anhalt d Sydney Pollack ph Duke Callaghan m John Rubinstein, Tim McIntire
☆ Robert Redford, Will Geer, Allyn McLerie

Jeremy
US 1973 90m DeLuxe
UA/Kenasset (George Pappas)
A music student falls in love with a ballet dancer.
Sentimental love story with nothing positive to commend it, chiefly interesting because for commercial release it was blown up from 16mm.
wd Arthur Barron ph Paul Goldsmith m Lee Holdridge
☆ Robby Benson, Glynnis O'Connor, Len Bari, Leonardo Cimino

Jericho
GB 1937 77m bw
Buckingham (Walter Futter, Max Schach)
US title: *Dark Sands*
A court-martialled officer pursues a murderous deserter across Africa.
Lively star vehicle of its day.
w James Marion, George Barraud, Peter Ruric, Robert N. Lee d Thornton Freeland ph John W. Boyle
☆ Paul Robeson, Henry Wilcoxon, Wallace Ford, John Laurie, James Carew
'Can't fail to interest audiences throughout the world.' – *Variety*

The Jerk
US 1979 94m Technicolor
Universal/Aspen (Peter MacGregor-Scott)
📼 ▇ ◑ ◑
An innocent white man brought up by black sharecroppers goes out into the world and first makes, then loses a fortune.
Hit-or-miss star vehicle with flashes of satire and fallen aspirations to be a modern Candide.
w Steve Martin, Carl Gottlieb, Michael Elias d Carl Reiner ph Victor J. Kemper m Jack Elliott
☆ Steve Martin, Bernadette Peters, Catlin Adams, Bill Macy, Maurice Evans
'Goofy, dumb, innocent, loud, uncoordinated, bashful and quite dirty.' – *Variety*

Jerry and Tom *
US 1998 106m DeLuxe
Miramax/Lions Gate (Elinor Reid, Vivienne Leebosh, Michael Paseornek, Saul Rubinek)
📼 ▇
A hitman and his young apprentice have differing approaches to their job.
Deft, skilful, slow-burning, conversational thriller that breathes new vitality into over-familiar material.
w Rick Cleveland d Saul Rubinek ph Paul Sarossy m David Buchbinder pd David Hackl ed Sloane Klevin
☆ Joe Mantegna, Sam Rockwell, Maury Chaykin, Ted Danson, Charles Durning, William H. Macy, Peter Riegert
'Very well acted and beautifully directed.' – *Variety*

'Everybody loved him ... Everybody disappeared.'
'The rest of his life begins now...'

Jerry Maguire *
US 1996 139m Technicolor
Columbia TriStar/Gracie (James L. Brooks, Laurence Mark, Richard Sakai, Cameron Crowe)
📼 ▇ ◑ ◑ 🎧
A successful sports agent turns idealistic and loses his job but finds love and fulfilment.
An enjoyable movie that works best in its more intimate moments; its wider theme, of one man's redemption through learning to care for others, is vitiated by its feel-good ending, when the difference between agent-as-shark and agent-as-good-guy is obliterated.
wd Cameron Crowe ph Janusz Kaminski
m Nancy Wilson pd Stephen Lineweaver ed Joe Hutshing

☆ Tom Cruise, Cuba Gooding Jnr, Renee Zellweger, Kelly Preston, Jerry O'Connell, Jay Mohr, Regina King
'If this is the best Hollywood can offer, you wonder what all the talent is doing.' – *Derek Malcolm, Guardian*
🏆 Cuba Gooding Jnr
⚆ best picture; Tom Cruise; Cameron Crowe (as writer); Joe Hutshing

Jersey Girl
US 1992 95m Technicolor
Entertainment/Electric/Interscope
📼 ▇
A New Jersey teacher crashes her Volkswagen into a Mercedes belonging to the kind of person that she needs to improve her life: a successful and handsome man from Manhattan.
Amiable comedy of class differences with true love winning out in the end, to no one's surprise.
w Gina Wendkos d David Burton Morris ph Ron Fortunato m Misha Segal pd Lester Cohen ed Norman Hollyn
☆ Jami Gertz, Dylan McDermott, Molly Price, Aida Turturro, Star Jasper, Sheryl Lee, Joseph Bologna, Joseph Mazzello, Philip Casnoff
'Pic has the potential to warm the hearts of ancillary viewers, especially young women.' – *Variety*

The Jerusalem File
US/Israel 1971 96m Metrocolor
MGM/Sparta (Ram Ben Efraim)
American archaeologists in Jerusalem become involved in Arab/Israeli espionage.
Muddled mixture of action and politics.
w Troy Kennedy Martin d John Flynn ph Raoul Coutard m John Scott
☆ Bruce Davison, Nicol Williamson, Donald Pleasence, Ian Hendry

Jesse James **
US 1939 106m Technicolor
TCF (Nunnally Johnson)
📼 ▇ ◑
After the Civil War, two brothers take to train robbing when railroad employees harass their family.
The life of an outlaw turns into family entertainment when Hollywood bathes it in sentiment, soft colour, family background and warm humour. It works dangerously well, and the action sequences are splendid.
w Nunnally Johnson d Henry King ph George Barnes md Louis Silvers ad William Darling, George Dudley
☆ Tyrone Power, Henry Fonda, Nancy Kelly, Jane Darwell, Randolph Scott, Henry Hull, Slim Summerville, Brian Donlevy, J. Edward Bromberg, John Carradine, Donald Meek
'Sock outdoors meller, vigorous and intensely dramatic in its unfolding ... box office smacko.' – *Variety*
'An authentic American panorama.' – *New York Times*
† Sequel 1940: *The Return of Frank James*. Remake 1957: *The True Story of Jesse James*.

Jesse James Meets Frankenstein's Daughter
US 1965 82m Pathécolor
Avco Embassy/Circle/Embassy (Carroll Case)
▇
Baron Frankenstein's granddaughter moves to a Mexican village where she sets up in the family business and falls in love with Jesse James.
Low-budget nonsense, played and directed with little sense of style or purpose.
w Carl K. Hittleman d William Beaudine ph Lothrop Worth m Raoul Kraushaar ad Paul Sylos, Harry Reif ed Roy Livingston
☆ John Lupton, Estelita, Cal Bolder, Narda Onyx, Steven Geray, Raymond Barnes
'With script and direction proving equally frail, the film is only prevented from becoming the camper's delight promised by the title by the fact that the cast plod through it all with gravity hardly befitting the occasion.' – *Tom Milne, MFB*
† The same director was also responsible for *Billy the Kid vs Dracula* (qv).

🏃🏃 film suitable for family viewing   📼 VHS video-cassette for the British PAL system   ▇ VHS video-cassette for the British PAL system in wide screen-format   ✪ Video cassette in a computer-colourised version   ▇ American NTSC video-cassette   ◑ Laser disc

Jessica

France/Italy/US 1962 105m Technicolor
Panavision
UA/Ariane/Dear Film (Jean Negulesco)

📀

The attractive midwife in a Sicilian village causes the women to go on a sex strike.
Synthetic rustic naughtiness showing several influences imperfectly assimilated.
w Edith Sommer *novel The Midwife of Pont Clery* by Flora Sundstrom d Jean Negulesco ph Piero Portalupi m Mario Nascimbene
☆ Angie Dickinson, Maurice Chevalier, Noel Noel, Gabriele Ferzetti, Sylva Koscina, Agnes Moorehead, Marcel Dalio

Jesus Christ Superstar *

👫 US 1973 107m Technicolor Todd-AO 35
Universal (Norman Jewison, Robert Stigwood)

📀 📀 📼 📀 ⊙ ♫

Young tourists in Israel re-enact episodes of the life of Christ.
Location-set fantasia based on the phenomenally successful rock opera; some of it works, but the original concept was a theatrical one.
w Melvyn Bragg, Norman Jewison d Norman Jewison ph Douglas Slocombe m/ly Andrew Lloyd Webber, Tim Rice md André Previn
☆ Ted Neeley, Carl Anderson, Yvonne Elliman, Barry Dennen
'One of the true fiascos of modern cinema.' – Paul D. Zimmerman
♪ André Previn

Jesus of Montreal ***

Canada/France 1989 120m colour
Max Films/Gérard Mital Productions/NFB Canada (Roger Frappier, Pierre Gendron)

📀 📼 📀

original title: Jésus de Montréal

An actor, chosen to play Christ in a religious play, finds himself in conflict with the church authorities.
A modern morality, surprisingly effective despite sometimes forced parallels between the actor's experiences and those of Jesus, and fuelled by a passionate irony.
wd Denys Arcand ph Guy Dufaux m Yves Laferrière, François Dompierre, Jean-Marie Benoît ad François Seguin ed Isabelle Dedieu
☆ Lothaire Bluteau, Catherine Wilkening, Johanne-Marie Tremblay, Rémy Girard, Robert Lepage, Gilles Pelletier, Yves Jacques
'Arcand is a master of tone, a sympathetic director of actors, and an unsanctimonious moralist, who locates his fable within a well-observed society.' – Philip French, Observer
♪ best foreign film

Jet Men of the Air: see *Air Cadet*

Jet over the Atlantic

US 1958 95m bw
Warner/Inter Continental (Benedict Bogeaus)

📼

A noble British passenger on a plane from Madrid to New York has planted a gas bomb in the luggage compartment.
Mechanical airborne suspenser with the usual assortment of unconvincing types making unconvincing gestures.
w Irving H. Cooper d Byron Haskin ph George Stahl m Lou Forbes
☆ Guy Madison, Virginia Mayo, George Raft, George Macready, Ilona Massey, Anna Lee, Margaret Lindsay, Venetia Stevenson, Mary Anderson, Brett Halsey, Frederic Worlock

Jet Pilot

US 1957 112m Technicolor
Howard Hughes (Jules Furthman)

📀 📼 📀

A Russian lady spy falls for an American pilot.
Lamentably dull and stupid romantic actioner of which all concerned should be thoroughly ashamed, especially as it took seven years to complete and is not even technically competent.
w Jules Furthman d Josef von Sternberg (and others) ph Winton C. Hoch m Bronislau Kaper
☆ John Wayne, Janet Leigh, Jay C. Flippen, Paul Fix, Richard Rober, Roland Winters, Ivan Triesault, Hans Conried

'One of the most childish, tedious and futile cold war spy dramas yet concocted by a Hollywood screenwriter.' – John Gillett

Jet Storm *

GB 1959 99m bw
British Lion/Britannia/Pendennis (Steven Pallos)

An airliner in flight from London to New York is discovered to have a bomb on board.
All-star slice-of-life suspenser with competently handled dialogue and situations.
w Cy Endfield, Sigmund Miller d Cy Endfield ph Jack Hildyard m Thomas Rajna
☆ Richard Attenborough, George Rose, Hermione Baddeley, Mai Zetterling, Diane Cilento, Stanley Baker, Harry Secombe, Virginia Maskell, Elizabeth Sellars, Sybil Thorndike, Bernard Braden, Cec Linder, David Kossoff

Jetsons: The Movie

👫 US 1990 83m CFI color
UIP/Universal/Hanna-Berbera/Wang/Cuckoo's Nest Studios (Bruce David Johnson)

📼 📀 ♫

The Jetson family solve the problem of alien saboteurs who object to their asteroid being the site of a mining factory.
Poorly animated situation comedy that would be better suited to television and best suited to the nearest garbage disposal unit.
w Dennis Marks, Carl Sautter d William Hanna, Joseph Barbera ph Daniel Bunn m John Debney
☆ Featuring the voices of George O'Hanlon, Mel Blanc, Penny Singleton, Tiffany, Patric Zimmerman, Don Messick, Jean Vanderpyl
'This exercise in high-tech tedium might prove more bewildering than charming to its pre-teen audience.' – MFB

Jeu de Massacre *

France 1967 94m colour
Coficitel/A. J. Films/Films Modernes/Francinor (René Thevenet)

📀

US title: *The Killing Game*
aka: *Comic Strip Hero*

An impoverished comic-book writer and his artist wife become involved with a wealthy young fantasist.
Witty games-playing on the themes of illusion and reality.
wd Alain Jessua ph Jacques Robin m Jacques Loussier ad Claire Forestier ed Nicole Marko
☆ Claudine Auger, Jean-Pierre Cassel, Michel Duchaussoy, Eleonore Hirt, Guy Saint-Jean, Anna Gaylor, Nancy Holloway

La Jeune Fille Assassinée: see *Charlotte*

Le Jeune Werther *

France 1992 90m colour
Home Made Movies/Canal/Alain Sarde

📀

aka: *Young Werther*

Young teenagers try to discover why one of their friends killed himself.
An updated version of, and commentary on, Goethe's tale of impossibly romantic love, rather too doom-laden to be entirely convincing as a portrait of modern-day young.
wd Jacques Doillon ph Christophe Pollock m Philippe Sarde ed Nicole Lubtchansky
☆ Ismaël Jolé-Ménébhi, Thomas Brémond, Simon Clavière, Pierre Mézerette, Faye Anastasia, Miren Capello, Sunny Lebrati, Mirabelle Rousseau, Jessica Tharaud
'The writer-director does ask a lot of his audience to maintain interest in a feature film almost entirely devoted to 13-year-old talk sessions.' – Variety

Jeux Interdits ***

France 1952 84m bw
Robert Dorfmann (Paul Joly)

♫

aka: *Forbidden Games*
aka: *The Secret Game*

In 1940, the little daughter of refugee parents sees her parents killed, and takes refuge with a peasant family, the small son of which helps her bury her dead puppy. They make a game of building a cemetery, which leads to a village feud…
Poignant anti-war tract which seemed a masterpiece at the time and is full of marvellous moments, but no longer holds up as a whole.

w Jean Aurenche, Pierre Bost *novel* François Boyer d René Clément ph Robert Julliard m Narciso Yepes
☆ Brigitte Fossey, Georges Poujouly, Amédée, Laurence Badie, Jacques Marin, Suzanne Courtal, Lucien Hubert
'A truly imposing achievement of blending several seemingly unrelated elements into a totally meaningful whole.' – John Simon, 1967
👤 best foreign film
♪ François Boyer (original story)
💮 best picture

Les Jeux Sont Faits *

France 1947 91m bw
Films Gibe

Falling in love in Purgatory, two murdered people get a second chance to return to earth, but spend their time quarrelling.
Somewhat despondent romantic fantasy with morsels of wit.
w Jean-Paul Sartre d Jean Delannoy ph Christian Matras m Georges Auric
☆ Micheline Presle, Marcel Pagliero, Marguerite Moreno, Charles Dullin

Jew Suss **

GB 1934 109m bw
Gaumont (Michael Balcon)

US title: *Power*

In old Württemberg, a Jew gains power to help his people, then finds he is Gentile.
Interesting, heavy-handed historical satire on the pointlessness of race distinctions, made partly in answer to Nazi oppression in Germany.
w Dorothy Farnum, A. R. Rawlinson *novel* Lion Feuchtwanger d Lothar Mendes ph Bernard Knowles, Roy Kellino md Louis Levy ad Alfred Junge ed Otto Ludwig
☆ Conrad Veidt, Benita Hume, Frank Vosper, Cedric Hardwicke, Gerald du Maurier, Pamela Ostrer
'Powerful as an artistic film achievement … but may have to struggle for commercial contentment.' – Variety

Jew Suss *

Germany 1940 85m bw
Terra

Celebrated travesty of the above, in which the Jew is wholly evil and rapes Aryan girls.
w Ludwig Metzger, Veit Harlan, Eberhard Wolfgang Möller d Veit Harlan ph Bruno Mondi m Wolfgang Zeller
☆ Ferdinand Marian, Werner Krauss, Heinrich George, Kristina Söderbaum
'The epitome of anti-semitic propaganda … the most notorious film of the Third Reich and one which brought disgrace on almost everyone connected with it.' – Georges Sadoul
'Highly recommended for its artistic value and, to serve the politics of the State, recommended for young people.' – Josef Goebbels

'When the going gets tough, the tough get going!'

Jewel of the Nile *

👫 US 1985 104m Technicolor
TCF/Michael Douglas

📀 📼 📀

A lady novelist gets into trouble when she accepts an invitation from a Middle Eastern potentate.
Moderate sequel to Romancing the Stone; plenty of action, but dull spots in between.
w Mark Rosenthal, Lawrence Konner d Lewis Teague ph Jan DeBont m Jack Nitzsche pd Richard Dawking, Terry Knight
☆ Michael Douglas, Kathleen Turner, Danny DeVito, Spiros Focas
'Mass destruction, endless gunfire and a fiery finish … the only box office question is whether the film comes late in the cycle for Saturday matinee revivals.' – Variety

Jewel Robbery *

US 1932 68m bw
Warner

A jewel thief and a millionaire's wife fall in love in Vienna.
Good sparkling fun in the shadow of Trouble in Paradise (qv).
w Erwin Gelsey *story* Ladislaus Fodor d William Dieterle ph Robert Kurrle md Leo B. Forbstein ad Robert Haas ed Ralph Dawson

☆ William Powell, Kay Francis, Hardie Albright, André Luguet, Henry Kolker, Spencer Charters, Alan Mowbray, Helen Vinson, Lee Kohlmar

'The Greatest Actress Of The Screen … In The Greatest Romance Of The South!'

Jezebel ***

US 1938 104m bw
Warner (Henry Blanke)

📀 📼 📀

Before the Civil War, a Southern belle stirs up trouble among the menfolk by her wilfulness and spite, but atones when a plague strikes.
Superb star melodrama, tossed to her in compensation for losing Gone with the Wind, and dealt with in high style by all concerned.
w Clements Ripley, Abem Finkel, John Huston *play* Owen Davis Snr d William Wyler ph Ernest Haller m Max Steiner
☆ Bette Davis, Henry Fonda, George Brent, Margaret Lindsay, Fay Bainter, Richard Cromwell, Donald Crisp, Henry O'Neill, John Litel, Spring Byington, Eddie Anderson, Gordon Oliver, Irving Pichel
'Good femme film, assured of okay results.' – Variety
'Its excellences come from many sources – good plotting and writing, a director and photographer who know how to make the thing flow along with dramatic pictorial effect, and a cast that makes its story a record of living people.' – James Shelley Hamilton, National Board of Review
'Without the zing Davis gave it, it would have looked very mossy indeed.' – Pauline Kael, 1968
👤 Bette Davis; Fay Bainter
♪ best picture; Ernest Haller; Max Steiner

The Jezebels: see *Switchblade Sisters*

'He's a District Attorney. He will risk his life, the lives of his family, everything he holds dear for the one thing he holds sacred … the truth.'

JFK **

US 1991 189m DuArt Panavision
Warner/Le Studio Canal/Regency Enterprises/Alcor (A. Kitman Ho, Oliver Stone)

📀 📼 📀 📀 ⊙ ♫

New Orleans DA Jim Garrison investigates the assassination of President Kennedy and uncovers what amounts to a *coup d'état* to kill him because he wanted to pull out of Vietnam.
Bad history and a bullying, though engrossing, movie, mixing fact and dubious speculation indiscriminately.
w Oliver Stone, Zachary Sklar *book* On the Trail of the Assassins by Jim Garrison; Crossfire: The Plot That Killed Kennedy by Jim Marrs d Oliver Stone ph Robert Richardson m John Williams pd Victor Kempster ed Joe Hutshing, Pietro Scalia
☆ Kevin Costner, Sissy Spacek, Joe Pesci, Tommy Lee Jones, Gary Oldman, Jay O. Sanders, Michael Rooker, Laurie Metcalf, Gary Grubbs, John Candy, Jack Lemmon, Walter Matthau, Ed Asner, Donald Sutherland, Kevin Bacon and also Brian Doyle-Murray, Sally Kirkland, Jim Garrison
'A rebuke to official history and a challenge to continue investigating the crime of the century, Oliver Stone's JFK is electric muckraking filmmaking.' – Variety
'The first thing to be said about JFK is that it is a great movie, and the next is that it is one of the worst great movies ever made. It is great in spite of itself, and such greatness owes more to the moxie of the director than to his special talents.' – Norman Mailer, Vanity Fair
'Courageous, gripping, reckless … the culmination or apotheosis of the paranoid political thriller.' – Philip French, Observer
'Shortchanges the audience and at the end plays like a bait-and-switch scam.' – Vincent Canby, New York Times
👤 Robert Richardson; editing
♪ film; Oliver Stone; Tommy Lee Jones; Oliver Stone, Zachary Sklar (screenplay adaptation); John Williams; sound

Jigokumon: see *Gate of Hell*

Jigsaw

US 1949 72m bw
UA/Tower (The Danzigers)
◼

An assistant District Attorney uncovers a mob stirring up racial hatred.
Undistinguished piece of do-goodery, curiously decorated by guest stars doing bit parts as a gesture of goodwill.
w Fletcher Markle, Vincent McConnor
d Fletcher Markle ph Don Malkames m Robert Stringer
☆ Franchot Tone, Jean Wallace, Myron McCormick, Marc Lawrence, Marlene Dietrich, Henry Fonda, John Garfield, Marsha Hunt, Leonard Lyons, Burgess Meredith

Jigsaw **

GB 1962 107m bw Cinemascope
British Lion/Britannia/Figaro (Val Guest)
Brighton policemen track down the murderer of a woman found in a lonely house on the beach.
Absorbing and entertaining little murder mystery which sustains its considerable length with interesting detail and plays as fair as can be with the audience. Excellent unassuming entertainment.
wd Val Guest play Sleep Long My Love by Hilary Waugh ph Arthur Grant m none
☆ Jack Warner, Ronald Lewis, Michael Goodliffe, Yolande Donlan, John Barron

The Jigsaw Man

GB 1985 98m colour
J & M
◼ ◕~

A British traitor in Moscow is given a new face and sent back home, where he becomes a double agent.
Somewhat elementary cold war chicanery with an abundance of talk before a routine action finish. Production was interrupted by financial crises, and the final result is patchy to say the least.
w Jo Eisinger d Terence Young ph Freddie Francis m John Cameron
☆ Michael Caine, Laurence Olivier, Robert Powell, Susan George, Michael Medwin, Vladek Sheybal

Jim Buck

US 1977 86m colour
Wildfire (James Rokos, Andrzej Krakowski)
◼
aka: *Portrait of a Hitman*
An artistic hitman discovers that the person he has been hired to shoot is an old friend who once saved his life.
An incoherent and never-less-than-silly thriller, directed without style and acted with little conviction.
w Yabo Yablonsky d Allan A. Buckhantz ph Charles Correll pd Elayne Ceder ed Michael Ripps
☆ Jack Palance, Bo Svenson, Richard Roundtree, Ann Turkel, Rod Steiger, Herb Jeffries, Richard Ahn

Jim Thorpe, All-American

U3 1951 103m bw
Warner (Everett Freeman)
◼ ◕~
GB title: *Man of Bronze*
A Red Indian becomes a star footballer, but later succumbs to drink.
Adequate sporting biopic.
w Douglas Morrow, Everett Freeman d Michael Curtiz ph Ernest Haller m Max Steiner
☆ Burt Lancaster, Charles Bickford, Steve Cochran, Phyllis Thaxter, Dick Wesson

Jimmy Hollywood

US 1994 113m DeLuxe
Paramount/Baltimore Pictures (Mark Johnson, Barry Levinson)
◙ ◼ ◕~ ◠
An obsessive would-be actor becomes a celebrity when he turns vigilante after his car radio is stolen.
Drama of the low life and underside of Hollywood which lacks bite; nor does it work as a character study.
wd Barry Levinson ph Peter Sova m Robbie Robertson pd Linda DeScenna ed Jay Rabinowitz
☆ Joe Pesci, Christian Slater, Victoria Abril, Jason Beghe, John Cothran Jnr
'Oddball attempt to mix offbeat comedy with social commentary and fringe-level character study. However well intentioned, the contrary elements just don't mesh.' – *Variety*

'Creeps out to please the completists and mildly irritate anyone else who happens to rent it.' – *Kim Newman, Empire*
† Harrison Ford plays a cameo role, and Barry Levinson also appears, in the film's final joke. It was released direct to video in Britain.

Jimmy Reardon

US 1988 92m colour
Island/Enterprise/Fox (Russell Schwartz)
◙ ◼ ◕~
original title: *A Night in the Life of Jimmy Reardon*
A romantic youth finds he has a rival for the girl he loves.
Teenage angst, deftly done but lacking a wider perspective.
wd William Richert novel Aren't You Ever Gonna Kiss Me Goodbye by William Richert ph John J. Connor m Bill Conti pd Norman Newberry ed Suzanne Fenn
☆ River Phoenix, Ann Magnuson, Meredith Salenger, Matthew Perry, Ione Skye, Jane Hallaren, Paul Koslo, Jason Court

Jimmy the Gent *

US 1934 67m bw
Warner (Robert Lord)
A racketeer supplies heirs for unclaimed estates.
Adequate star crime comedy.
w Bertram Millhauser d Michael Curtiz ph Ira Morgan md Leo F. Forbstein
☆ James Cagney, Bette Davis, Alice White, Allen Jenkins, Arthur Hohl, Mayo Methot, Alan Dinehart, Hobart Cavanaugh, Ralf Harolde, Philip Reed, Joe Sawyer
'Fast and flip, rough and rowdy.' – *New York American*

Jimmy the Kid

US 1982 85m CFI color
Zephyr (Ronald Jacobs)
◙
An incompetent bunch of crooks kidnap a young boy, the precocious son of wealthy parents, who decides he does not want to go home.
An unendearing comedy that relies on contrived slapstick and features some charmless performances, especially from its teenage star.
w Sam Bobrick novel Donald E. Westlake d Gary Nelson ph Dennis Dalzell m John Cameron ad Bill Ross ed Richard C. Meyer
☆ Gary Coleman, Paul Le Mat, Ruth Gordon, Dee Wallace, Cleavon Little, Avery Schreiber, Pat Morita, Fay Hauser, Walter Olkewicz, Don Adams

Jingcha Gushi: see *Police Story*

Jingcha Gushi 4 Zhi Jiandan Renwu: see *Jackie Chan's First Strike*

Jingle All the Way

US 1996 88m DeLuxe
TCF (Chris Columbus, Mark Radcliffe, Michael Barnathan)
◙ ◼ ◕~ ◌
On Christmas Eve, a salesman searches frantically for the special toy, sold out in all the shops, that his son wants.
Tedious action comedy with heavy-handed slapstick; it's undiluted humbug.
w Randy Kornfield d Brian Levant ph Victor J. Kemper m David Newman pd Leslie McDonald ed Kent Beyda, Wilton Henderson, Adam Weiss
☆ Arnold Schwarzenegger, Sinbad, Phil Hartman, Rita Wilson, Robert Conrad, Martin Mull, Jake Lloyd, James Belushi, Harvey Korman
'This ghastly, paper-thin piece of Yuletide rubble from the Home Alone stable is rather like that Christmas pudding you forgot to eat last year, which now lies on a kitchen shelf, soft in the centre with a hard-as-nails exterior.' – *Derek Malcolm, Guardian*

Jinxed!

US 1982 103m Technicolor
MGM-UA/Herb Jaffe
◼
A frustrated blackjack dealer seduces the girl of a frequent winner.
Unfunny gambling comedy which never begins to cohere.
w Bert Blessing, David Newman d Don Siegel ph Vilmos Zsigmond m Bruce Roberts, Miles Goodman

☆ Bette Midler, Ken Wahl, Rip Torn, Val Avery, Jack Elam, Benson Fong, Jacqueline Scott
'Jinxed stinks.' – *Don Siegel*

Jit *

Zimbabwe 1990 92m bw
ICA/FilmAfrica/Makuvisi (Rory Kilalea)
A youth takes various jobs in order to raise the money he needs to buy the bride he wants.
Lively low-budget comedy, the first feature film to be made in Zimbabwe, with an engaging soundtrack of local popular music.
wd Michael Raeburn ph João Costa m Oliver Mtukudzi pd Lindie Pankiv ed Justin Krish
☆ Dominic Makuvachuma, Sibongile Nene, Farai Sevenzo, Winnie Ndemera, Oliver Mtukudzi, Lawrence Simbarashe

Jitsuroku Abe Sada: see *A Woman Called Abé Sada*

Jitterbugs *

♠♠ US 1943 75m bw
TCF (Sol M. Wurtzel)
Laurel and Hardy help a night-club singer to fight off gangsters.
The last Laurel and Hardy film to contain any good scenes, and almost the only one of their TCF films that did.
w Scott Darling d Mal St Clair ph Lucien Andriot m/ly Charles Newman, Lew Pollack md Emil Newman ed James Bashevi, Chester Gore
☆ Stan Laurel, Oliver Hardy, Vivian Blaine, Bob Bailey, Douglas Fowley, Noel Madison, Lee Patrick

Jivaro

US 1953 91m Technicolor 3D
Paramount/William H. Pine, William C. Thomas
GB title: *Lost Treasure of the Amazon*
A mixed party of Americans follows a drunken treasure seeker into the jungle.
Elementary treasure hunt adventure, hampered by studio foliage, bad script and half-hearted acting.
w Winston Miller story David Duncan d Edward Ludwig ph Lionel Lindon m Gregory Stone
☆ Fernando Lamas, Rhonda Fleming, Brian Keith, Lon Chaney Jnr, Marvin Miller, Richard Denning

Joan Medford Is Missing: see *House of Horrors*

Joan of Arc

US 1948 145m Technicolor
RKO/Sierra/Walter Wanger
◼ ◕~
The last campaign of the Maid of Orleans.
Strictly from Dullsville; one studio set-piece follows another, and a group of talented people clearly thought that prestige would sell itself without the hard work that goes into more commercial productions.
w Maxwell Anderson, Andrew Solt play Joan of Lorraine by Maxwell Anderson d Victor Fleming ph Joe Valentine m Hugo Friedhofer md Emil Newman ad Richard Day ed Frank Sullivan
☆ Ingrid Bergman, José Ferrer, George Coulouris, Francis L. Sullivan, Gene Lockhart, Ward Bond, John Ireland, Hurd Hatfield, Cecil Kellaway, George Zucco, J. Carrol Naish
'A bad film with one or two good things. It is childishly oversimplified, its battles papier mâché, its heroine far too worldly, its spiritual content that of a chromo art calendar.' – *Herman G. Weinberg*
⚊ Joe Valentine; Walter Wanger (Special Award for 'adding to the moral stature' of the industry by his production)
⚊ Hugo Friedhofer; Ingrid Bergman; José Ferrer; art direction; editing

Joan of Ozark

US 1942 82m bw
Republic
GB title: *The Queen of Spies*
A hillbilly sharpshooter becomes a national spy heroine.
Scatty comedy of moderate liveliness.
w Robert Harari, Eve Greene and Jack Townley d Joseph Santley
☆ Judy Canova, Joe E. Brown, Eddie Foy Jnr, Jerome Cowan, Alexander Granach

Joan of Paris

US 1942 95m bw
RKO (David Hempstead)
◼
A French resistance leader sacrifices herself so that Allied pilots can escape.
Well-made propaganda adventure dignified by excellent cast.
w Charles Bennett, Ellis St Joseph story Jacques Thery, Georges Kessel d Robert Stevenson ph Russell Metty m Roy Webb
☆ Michele Morgan, Paul Henreid, Thomas Mitchell, Laird Cregar, May Robson, Alexander Granach, Alan Ladd
⚊ Roy Webb

Joan the Woman **

US 1916 125m bw silent
Cardinal
◙
The story of Joan of Arc.
An epic spectacle typical of its director.
w Jeanie Macpherson d Cecil B. DeMille
☆ Geraldine Farrar, Raymond Hatton, Wallace Reid, Hobart Bosworth, Theodore Roberts

Joanna

GB 1968 122m DeLuxe Panavision
TCF/Laughlin (Michael S. Laughlin)
◠
A girl art student comes to London and quickly finds the road to ruin.
Antediluvian rubbish tarted up with swinging London settings.
wd Michael Sarne ph Walter Lassally m Rod McKuen
☆ Genevieve Waite, Christian Doermer, Calvin Lockhart, Donald Sutherland
'An unnecessarily protracted punishing of a very dead quadruped.' – *MFB*

The Job **

Italy 1961 90m bw
24 Horses Films (Alberto Soffientini)
original title: *Il Posto*
A teenage boy gets his first job, and progresses from office boy to clerk when a senior man dies.
Appealingly observant social comedy, very simple and extremely effective.
wd Ermanno Olmi ph Lamberto Caimi
☆ Sandro Panzeri, Loredana Detto
'Rueful and funny and honest … the players have been encouraged not so much to act as to behave. Olmi stalks them like a naturalist, and the result is a small, unique and perfect achievement in film-making.' – *Penelope Houston, MFB*

Jób Lázadása: see *The Revolt of Job*

Jobman *

South Africa 1990 97m Technicolor
Blue Rock/Three's Company (Christopher Coy)
In the 60s, the persecuted, deaf-mute son of a preacher is forced to fight to protect himself, his wife and child from attack by those who resent his strivings for an independent life.
A tense drama of persecution and retribution, much like a Western in style – and one that can be taken as a political allegory of the dispossessed, who are left with no voice in their country's concerns and no recourse to any means other than violence.
w Darrell Roodt, Greg Latter story Achmat Dangor, Darrell Roodt ph Paul Witte m Joel Goldsmith pd Dave Barkham ed Shelley Wells
☆ Kevin Smith, Tertius Meintjes, Lynn Gaines, Marcel Van Heerden, Goliath Edwards, Josephine Liedeman, Bill Curry
'A simple, poetic tale with a powerful central image that hints at underlying social and political themes but fails to really activate them.' – *Variety*

Jock of the Bushveld

South Africa 1988 90m colour
Toron (Duncan MacNeillie)
The adventures of an ambitious Irishman and his hunting dog, which was once the runt of the litter, in South Africa in the 1880s.
Based on a true story, of the early life of a prominent South African politician and author, an episodic adventure that never quite holds the attention; it is colourful but bland.

♠♠ film suitable for family viewing   ◙ VHS video-cassette for the British PAL system   ◙ VHS video-cassette for the British PAL system in wide screen-format   ◌ Video cassette in a computer-colourised version   ◼ American NTSC video-cassette   ◕~ Laser disc

w John Cundill book Sir Percy Fitzpatrick
d Gray Hofmeyr ph Mike Buckley m Kenneth Hutchinson ad John Gerber ed Valma Muir
☆ Jonathan Rands, Gordon Mulholland, Jocelyn Broderick, Wilson Dunster, Olivier Ngwenya

Joe *
US 1970 107m DeLuxe
Cannon (David Gil)
📀 📹

A construction worker in a bar meets a businessman who has just killed his daughter's drug addicted lover; they become buddies in their hatred of hippies.
Highly successful in America as a backlash against permissiveness, this rough-hewn opportunistic melodrama is vivid enough but moves in fits and starts.
w Norman Wexler m Bobby Scott d/ph John G. Avildsen
☆ Peter Boyle, Dennis Patrick, Audrey Caire, Susan Sarandon
'A bad film disfigured by brute strokes of tendentiousness.' – *Penelope Gilliatt*
& Norman Wexler

Joe Butterfly
US 1957 90m Technicolor Cinemascope
U-I (Aaron Rosenberg)
Shortly after World War II, American occupying troops are conned by a Japanese interpreter.
Dull comedy intent on healing old wounds.
w Sy Gomberg, Jack Sher, Marion Hargrove d Jesse Hibbs ph Irving Glassberg m Joseph Gershenson
☆ Burgess Meredith, Audie Murphy, George Nader, Keenan Wynn, Fred Clark, John Agar, Charles McGraw

Joe Dakota
US 1957 90m Technicolor Cinemascope
U-I (Howard Christie)
A stranger appears in a Western town in search of his Indian friend, who turns out to have been murdered by the townspeople so that they can share the profits from his oil well.
Feeble rip-off of Bad Day at Black Rock.
w William Talman, Norman Jolley d Richard Bartlett ph George Robinson m Hans Salter md Joseph Gershenson
☆ Jock Mahoney, Luana Patten, Charles McGraw, Barbara Lawrence, Claude Akins, Lee Van Cleef

Joe Hill: see *The Ballad of Joe Hill*

Joe Kidd
US 1972 87m Technicolor Panavision
Universal/Malpaso (Sidney Beckerman)
📀 📹 📹 ◎
A disreputable bounty hunter tracks down the leader of a tribe of Mexican bandits.
Rough-and-tumble star Western with untenable moral attitudes.
w Elmore Leonard d John Sturges ph Bruce Surtees m Lalo Schifrin
☆ Clint Eastwood, Robert Duvall, John Saxon, Don Stroud, James Wainwright

Joe Macbeth
GB 1955 90m bw
Film Locations/Frankovich (George Maynard)
A gangster is urged by his wife to rub out his boss.
Almost too bad to be funny, this effort to update Shakespeare has actors behaving as though they were stuck in treacle, and its gimmick quality is quickly dissipated by an indifferent production.
w Philip Yordan d Ken Hughes ph Basil Emmott m Trevor Duncan
☆ Paul Douglas, Ruth Roman, Grégoire Aslan, Bonar Colleano, Sidney James

Joe Palooka, Champ
US 1946 72m bw
Monogram (Hal E. Chester)
A boxing promoter grooms a young dope for the ring.
Modest series opener with plenty to be modest about.
w Cy Endfield, Albert de Pina d Reginald Le Borg
☆ Leon Errol, Joe Kirkwood, Elyse Knox, Eduardo Ciannelli, Joe Sawyer, Elisha Cook Jnr

Joe Smith American *
US 1942 63m bw
MGM (Jack Chertok)
GB title: *Highway to Freedom*
An aircraft factory worker with special knowledge is kidnapped by Nazis but leads the FBI to his captors.
Watchable propaganda thriller credited with easing Americans into a war mood.
w Allen Rivkin story Paul Gallico d Richard Thorpe ph Charles Lawton Jnr m Daniele Amfitheatrof
☆ Robert Young, Marsha Hunt, Darryl Hickman, Harvey Stephens, Jonathan Hale, Noel Madison, Joseph Anthony
'Not a high-powered movie, it is a first rate die for the new propaganda models which Hollywood is readying for mass production.' – *Time*

Joe versus the Volcano
US 1990 102m Technicolor Panavision
Warner/Amblin Entertainment (Teri Schwartz)
📀 📹 📹
Told that he has only a few months to live, a man agrees to jump into a volcano to prevent an eruption and save an island for an entrepreneur.
Weak whimsy, directed without flair.
wd John Patrick Shanley ph Stephen Goldblatt m Georges Delerue pd Bo Welch ed Richard Halsey
☆ Tom Hanks, Meg Ryan, Lloyd Bridges, Robert Stack, Abe Vigoda, Dan Hedaya, Barry McGovern, Amanda Plummer, Ossie Davis, Jayne Haynes

'Sex. Bugs. Rock 'n' Roll.'
Joe's Apartment
US 1996 80m colour
Warner/Geffen/MTV (Diana Phillips, Bonni Lee)
📀 📹 ◎
A youth having problems with his girlfriend and his evil landlord shares his apartment with hundreds of singing and dancing cockroaches.
A one-joke movie, stretched well beyond breaking point.
wd John Payson ph Peter Deming m Carter Burwell pd Carol Spier ed Peter Frank
☆ Jerry O'Connell, Megan Ward, Jim Turner, Jim Sterling, Sandra Denton, Robert Vaughn, Don Ho and also the voices of: Reginald Hudlin, Bill West
† It is based on a short film of the same name, made by Payson for MTV.

Joey Boy
GB 1965 91m colour
British Lion/Launder-Gilliatt
In 1941, a group of petty crooks join the army.
Abysmal service comedy, incredibly cheap and tatty and the nadir of several of the talents involved.
wd Frank Launder ph Arthur Lavis m Philip Green
☆ Harry H. Corbett, Stanley Baxter, Bill Fraser, Reg Varney, Percy Herbert, Lance Percival
'As visually shoddy as it is unfunny ... the final shot (Corbett pulling a lavatory chain) is all too crudely apt.' – *MFB*

Johann Mouse ***
👥 US 1952 8m Technicolor
MGM (Fred Quimby)
Strauss's mouse dances to his master's music; the cat, to lure him out, learns to play the piano.
Splendid Tom and Jerry cartoon from the great period of this neglected art.
♣ best cartoon

John and Julie
👥 GB 1955 82m Eastmancolor
Group Three (Herbert Mason)
Two children run away to see the coronation.
Genial little family comedy full of stock comic characters.
wd William Fairchild ph Arthur Grant m Philip Green
☆ Colin Gibson, Leslie Dudley, Peter Sellers, Moira Lister, Wilfrid Hyde-White, Sidney James, Andrew Cruickshank

John and Mary *
US 1969 92m DeLuxe Panavision
TCF/Debrod (Ben Kadish)
Two New Yorkers have a one-night affair and cannot decide whether to continue.
Slight, disappointing sex comedy vehicle for two stars who were very hot at the time.
w John Mortimer novel Mervyn Jones d Peter Yates ph Gayne Rescher m Quincy Jones pd John Robert Lloyd
☆ Dustin Hoffman, Mia Farrow, Michael Tolan, Sunny Griffin, Tyne Daly
'The emphasis is not on action but on acting, which although skilful and subtly nuanced does not in this case amount to the same thing as character.' – *Jan Dawson*
'Despite all the "now" sets and surfaces, it's like an old comedy of the thirties – minus the comedy.' – *Judith Crist*
🎬 Dustin Hoffman

John Carpenter's Escape from LA: see *Escape from LA*

'Prepare For The Dawn.'
John Carpenter's Vampires *
US 1998 104m Foto-Kem Panavision
Largo/Film Office/Storm King (Sandy King)
📀 📹 📹
aka: *Vampires*
A vampire killer and his gang of mercenaries are hired by the Vatican to destroy a 600-year-old vampire terrorizing the American Southwest.
Entertaining low-budget horror-cum-western that works up to a satisfying climax.
w John Carpenter, Don Jacoby, Dan Mazur novel *Vampire$* by John Steakley d John Carpenter ph Gary B. Kibbe m John Carpenter pd Thomas A. Walsh ed Edward A. Warschilka sp Darrell D. Pritchett; make-up fx: KNB EFX
☆ James Woods, Daniel Baldwin, Sheryl Lee, Thomas Ian Griffith, Tim Guinee, Maximilian Schell, Cary-Hiroyuki Tagawa
'Taps into an appealing mix of anti-clerical sentiment, unsentimental rebel codes and gung-ho gouging and splattering. Unlike garlic, Carpenter's humor-leavened handling of evil doesn't leave a bad taste in the mouth.' – *Lisa Nesselson, Variety*

John Goldfarb, Please Come Home
US 1965 96m DeLuxe Cinemascope
TCF/Steve Parker/J. Lee-Thompson
An American spy pilot crashlands near the palace of a Middle Eastern potentate at the same time as a girl reporter arrives for an interview.
Would-be satire on the cold war, anti-feminism, American football, American/Arab relations, etc. None of it works for a minute, and the actors' desperation can be plainly seen.
w William Peter Blatty d J. Lee-Thompson ph Leon Shamroy m Johnny Williams
☆ Shirley MacLaine, Richard Crenna, Peter Ustinov, Fred Clark, Wilfrid Hyde-White, Jim Backus

'They were totally unqualified to try the case of a lifetime ... but every underdog has his day.'
John Grisham's The Rainmaker **
Germany/US 1997 136m DeLuxe Panavision
UIP/Constellation/American Zoetrope (Michael Douglas, Steven Reuther, Fred Fuchs)
📀 📹 📹 ◎
With the aid of a sleazy para-legal, an idealistic young lawyer sues a big insurance company, which refuses to pay benefits to a man dying of leukaemia.
A well-made, satisfying account of a David versus Goliath contest that makes effective use of all the suspenseful tricks of courtroom dramas.
wd Francis Ford Coppola novel John Grisham ph John Toll m Elmer Bernstein pd Howard Cummings ed Barry Malkin, Melissa Kent
☆ Matt Damon, Claire Danes, Jon Voight, Mary Kay Place, Mickey Rourke, Danny de Vito, Dean Stockwell, Teresa Wright, Virginia Madsen, Roy Scheider
'One of the few films that say something important about life and work in the US today. This is a populist movie made by a master.' – *Alexander Walker, London Evening Standard*

John Loves Mary
US 1948 87m bw
Warner (Jerry Wald)
A GI returns home to get married, but unfortunately, to help a friend, he has already entered into a marriage of convenience.
Moderately amusing comedy with an excess of complications.
w Phoebe and Henry Ephron play Norman Krasna d David Butler ph Peverell Marley m David Buttolph
☆ Ronald Reagan, Patricia Neal, Jack Carson, Virginia Field

John Meade's Woman
US 1937 82m bw
Paramount
A timber industrialist marries a farm girl.
Solemn star drama.
w Vincent Lawrence, Herman J. Mankiewicz d Richard Wallace
☆ Edward Arnold, Francine Larrimore, Gail Patrick, George Bancroft
'One more picture with a message. Edward Arnold's pictures are beginning to look alike.' – *Variety*

John Paul Jones
US 1959 126m Technirama
Warner/Samuel Bronston
At the time of the American revolution a young Scotsman rises to great heights in the American navy.
Fragmented biopic with a succession of guest stars which turn it into a charade almost as silly as The Story of Mankind. On that level it is not unentertaining.
wd John Farrow ph Michel Kelber m Max Steiner
☆ Robert Stack, Charles Coburn, Bette Davis, Marisa Pavan, Jean-Pierre Aumont, Peter Cushing, Bruce Cabot, Macdonald Carey

John Woo's Once a Thief
US 1995 96m colour
Alliance/WCG/NDG
📀 📹
GB video title: *John Woo's Violent Tradition*
After double-crossing his boss, an American member of a Hong Kong criminal gang goes to work in Vancouver on a covert police operation against his former associates.
Mindless, violent thriller, although tame by Woo's standards, since it was made as a pilot for a TV series; its central characters are unattractive and the narrative unoriginal.
w Glenn Davis, William Laurin d John Woo ph Bill Wong m Amin Bhatia pd Douglas Higgins ed David Wu
☆ Sandrine Holt, Ivan Sergei, Nicholas Lea, Robert Ito, Michael Wong, Alan Scarfe, Jennifer Dale
'Tailor-made for stupid American audiences.' – *Total Cinema*
† The film is an American variation on Woo's Once a Thief (qv), made in Hong Kong in 1991.

Johnny Allegro *
US 1949 81m bw
Columbia (Irving Starr)
GB title: *Hounded*
A private eye eliminates a counterfeiter and marries his wife.
Cheeky variation on the plot of Gilda, with Macready repeating his role; later stages borrow from The Most Dangerous Game. All mildly diverting.
w Karen de Wolf, Guy Endore, James Edward Grant d Ted Tetzlaff ph Joseph Biroc m George Duning
☆ George Raft, George Macready, Nina Foch, Will Geer, Ivan Triesault
'Without any particular distinction, but certainly not boring.' – *Richard Mallett, Punch*

Johnny Angel *
US 1945 79m bw
RKO (William L. Pereira)
📹
A seaman solves the mystery of his father's ship, found empty and adrift in the Gulf of Mexico.
Very watchable mystery with plenty of plot twists and efficient presentation.
w Steve Fisher d Edwin L. Marin ph Harry J. Wild m Leigh Harline
☆ George Raft, Claire Trevor, Signe Hasso, Lowell Gilmore, Hoagy Carmichael, Marvin Miller

Johnny Apollo
US 1940 93m bw
TCF (Harry Joe Brown)
📹
A well-heeled young man turns crook.
Moderate crime melo, impeccably turned out.

w Philip Dunne, Rowland Brown *d* Henry Hathaway *ph* Arthur Miller *m* Cyril Mockridge *md* Alfred Newman

☆ Tyrone Power, Dorothy Lamour, Edward Arnold, Lloyd Nolan, Charles Grapewin, Lionel Atwill, Marc Lawrence, Jonathan Hale

'There was temptation in her helpless silence – and then torment!'

Johnny Belinda **
US 1948 103m bw
Warner (Jerry Wald)
▦

In a remote fishing community, a deaf mute girl is raped and the sympathetic local doctor is suspected of being the father of her baby.
Melodrama of the old school which in 1948 seemed oddly to mark a new permissiveness and made a big star of Jane Wyman; the production and locations were also persuasive.
w Irmgard von Cube, Allen Vincent *play* Elmer Harris *d* Jean Negulesco *ph* Ted McCord *m* Max Steiner *md* Leo F. Forbstein *ad* Robert Haas
☆ Jane Wyman, Lew Ayres, Charles Bickford, Agnes Moorehead, Stephen McNally, Jan Sterling, Rosalind Ivan, Mabel Paige
'Hollywood has tried something dangerously different here, and succeeded in making a powerful and sensitive job of it.' – *Observer*
'An atmosphere in which the hokey, tearjerking elements are used for more than mere pathos – an example of technique over subject matter.' – *Pauline Kael, 70s*
♟ Jane Wyman
♟ best picture; script; Jean Negulesco; Ted McCord; Max Steiner; Lew Ayres; Charles Bickford; Agnes Moorehead; art direction

Johnny Come Lately *
US 1943 97m bw
Cagney Productions (William Cagney)
▦ ▦ ☾
GB title: *Johnny Vagabond*
A travelling newspaperman is jailed for vagrancy in a small town and stays to expose corrupt politicians.
A turn-of-the-century folksy drama seemed an odd choice for a Cagney independent production, and it was not very persuasively made, but the star produced moments of his old charisma.
w John Van Druten *novel* McLeod's Folly by Louis Bromfield *d* William K. Howard *ph* Theodor Sparkuhl *m* Leigh Harline
☆ James Cagney, Grace George, Marjorie Main, Marjorie Lord, Hattie McDaniel, Edward McNamara, Bill Henry, Robert Barrat, George Cleveland, Margaret Hamilton, Lucien Littlefield, Irving Bacon
'The kind of business that might result if Jimmy Cagney, the immortal Hollywood movie star, had returned to play the lead in the annual production of his old high school's Masque and Film Club.' – *John T. McManus*
'The film does show a fatal commercial uncleanness and, I half suspect, radical loss or atrophy of cinematic judgment. But ... there is a general ambience of hope and pleasure about the production which, regrettably, loses its glow.' – *James Agee*
♟ Leigh Harline

Johnny Comes Flying Home
US 1946 65m bw
Aubrey Schenck/TCF
Three discharged flyers build an air freight company.
The Best Years of Our Lives it isn't, not on this budget, but it clumsily expresses some of the same concerns.
w Jack Andrews, George Bricker *d* Ben Stoloff
☆ Richard Crane, Faye Marlowe, Martha Stewart, Roy Roberts, Henry Morgan

Johnny Concho
US 1956 84m bw
UA/Kent (Frank Sinatra)
A coward runs Cripple Creek because he has a gunfighter brother, but when the latter is shot another gunman takes over.
Unexpected small-scale Western, pleasantly made but no High Noon.
w David P. Harmon, Don McGuire *d* Don McGuire *ph* William Mellor *m* Nelson Riddle
☆ Frank Sinatra, William Conrad, Phyllis Kirk, Wallace Ford, John Qualen

Johnny Cool *
US 1963 101m bw
UA/Chrislaw (William Asher)
☾
A Sicilian bandit is sent to the US on a mission of vengeance.
Chilling gangster thriller, the callousness of which is apparently meant to be counterpointed by the humorous cameo appearances of several well-known faces. This does not work.
w Joseph Landon *novel* John McPartland *d* William Asher *ph* Sam Leavitt *m* Billy May
☆ Henry Silva, Elizabeth Montgomery, Jim Backus, Marc Lawrence, John McGiver, Sammy Davis Jnr, Mort Sahl, Telly Savalas, Joseph Calleia, Robert Armstrong, Douglass Dumbrille, Elisha Cook Jnr

'Organized crime has never been so disorganized!'

Johnny Dangerously
US 1984 90m DeLuxe
TCF/Edgewood (Michael Hertzberg)
▦ ▦
A boy takes up crime to pay for an operation for his ailing mother.
1930s gangster send-up which fails to register, and is filled with unnecessary excesses.
w Norman Steinberg, Bernie Kukoff, Harry Colomby, Jeff Harris *d* Amy Heckerling *ph* David M. Walsh *m* John Morris *pd* Joseph R. Jennings *ed* Pembroke J. Herring
☆ Michael Keaton, Joe Piscopo, Marilu Henner, Maureen Stapleton, Peter Boyle, Griffin Dunne, Richard Dmitri, Glynnis O'Connor, Dom DeLuise, Ray Walston
'The material given all of them just gets worse and worse.' – *Variety*

Johnny Dark
US 1954 85m Technicolor
U-I (William Alland)
A motor company produces a new sports car designed by an employee, who drives it in a race.
Competent, unremarkable action melodrama tailor-made for its star.
w Franklin Coen *d* George Sherman *ph* Carl Guthrie *m* Hans Salter
☆ Tony Curtis, Piper Laurie, Don Taylor, Paul Kelly, Ilka Chase, Sidney Blackmer

Johnny Doesn't Live Here Any More
US 1944 77m bw
Monogram (Maurice and Frank King)
A girl using her army boyfriend's Washington flat finds that he has loaned keys to several friends.
Tepid farce which presumably amused at the time.
w Philip Yordan, John H. Kafka *d* Joe May
☆ Simone Simon, James Ellison, William Terry, Minna Gombell, Chick Chandler, Alan Dinehart, Robert Mitchum

Johnny Doughboy
US 1943 64m bw
Republic
A teenage girl star runs away, falls for a middle-aged playwright, and joins an acting troupe called The Hollywood Victory Caravan.
Curious attempt to make a child star grow up, with a supporting cast laced with others of her ilk.
w Lawrence Kimble *d* John H. Auer *m* Walter Scharf
☆ Jane Withers, Henry Wilcoxon, William Demarest, Ruth Donnelly; and Bobby Breen, Baby Sandy, Butch and Buddy, Spanky McFarland, etc
♟ Walter Scharf

'The flaming drama of a high-born beauty who blindly loved the most icy-hearted big shot gangland ever knew!'

Johnny Eager *
US 1942 107m bw
MGM (John W. Considine)
A gangster makes a play for a society girl.
Well-made, rather unattractive gangster melodrama.
w John Lee Mahin, James Edward Grant *d* Mervyn Le Roy *ph* Harold Rosson *m* Bronislau Kaper
☆ Robert Taylor, Van Heflin, Lana Turner, Edward Arnold, Robert Sterling, Patricia Dane, Glenda Farrell, Henry O'Neill
♟ Van Heflin

Johnny Frenchman
GB 1945 111m bw
Ealing (S. C. Balcon)
Rivalry between the fishermen of Cornwall and Brittany prevents the course of true love from running smooth.
Rhubarbing extras and studio sets make this an unreal and disappointing Ealing melodrama, and all the actors look helpless.
w T. E. B. Clarke *d* Charles Frend *ph* Roy Kellino *m* Clifton Parker
☆ Françoise Rosay, Tom Walls, Patricia Roc, Paul Dupuis, Ralph Michael, Frederick Piper, Arthur Hambling

Johnny Got His Gun
US 1971 111m colour
World Entertainments Ltd (Bruce Campbell)
▦ ☾
In 1918 a soldier is so badly wounded as to lose arms, legs, eyes, ears, mouth and nose, and begs his doctors to kill him.
A horrifying and fascinating premise turns out to have nowhere to go, at least not in this talky treatment which the author has nurtured too long.
wd Dalton Trumbo *ph* Jules Brenner *m* Jerry Fielding
☆ Timothy Bottoms, Jason Robards Jnr, Marsha Hunt, Donald Sutherland, Kathy Fields, Diane Varsi

Johnny Guitar *
US 1953 110m Trucolor
Republic (Nicholas Ray)
▦ ▦ ☾ ☾
In old Arizona, the proprietress of a gambling saloon stakes a claim to valuable land and incurs the enmity of a lady banker.
Weird Freudian Western notable for a running catfight between its lady protagonists; the title character is decidedly secondary. Not exactly a good movie, but memorable because it's almost always over the top.
w Philip Yordan *novel* Roy Chanslor *d* Nicholas Ray *ph* Harry Stradling *m* Victor Young
☆ Joan Crawford, Mercedes McCambridge, Sterling Hayden, Ernest Borgnine, Ward Bond, John Carradine, Scott Brady
'A very rum western, with cockeyed feminist attitudes.' – *New Yorker, 1975*

Johnny Handsome
US 1989 94m Technicolor
Guild/Carolco Pictures/Guber-Peters (Charles Roven)
▦ ☾ ☾
A deformed petty criminal undergoes surgery to give him a new appearance.
A thriller of betrayal and double-cross that never fully engages the attention.
w Ken Friedman *novel* The Three Worlds of Johnny Handsome by John Godey *d* Walter Hill *ph* Matthew F. Leonetti *m* Ry Cooder *pd* Gene Rudolf *ed* Freeman Davies, Carmel Davies, Donn Aron
☆ Mickey Rourke, Ellen Barkin, Elizabeth McGovern, Morgan Freeman, Forest Whitaker, Lance Henriksen, Scott Wilson, David Schramm, Yvonne Bryceland
'A taut, violent, moody thriller.' – *Philip French, Observer*
'A faintly risible mess, torn between a dozen stools and never managing to settle squarely on any of them.' – *Tom Milné, MFB*

Johnny Holiday
US 1949 92m bw
United Artists (R. W. Alcorn)
A reform school boy becomes a goodie through devotion to his sergeant.
Sentimental mush.
w Jack Andrews, Willis Goldbeck, Frederick Stephani *d* Willis Goldbeck *ph* Hal Mohr *m* Franz Waxman
☆ William Bendix, Stanley Clements, Allen Martin Jnr, Herbert Newcomb, Hoagy Carmichael

Johnny in the Clouds: see The Way to the Stars

'Meet the ultimate hard drive.'

Johnny Mnemonic
Canada 1995 98m Film House colour
TCF/Alliance (Don Carmody)
▦ ▦ ☾ ☾
In the future, ruthless killers hunt down a courier who will die unless he can quickly transfer important information implanted in a microchip in his brain.
A cyberpunk thriller that, like every other movie that has attempted to cash in on virtual reality, crashes and leaves only confusion behind.
w William Gibson *story* William Gibson *d* Robert Longo *ph* François Protat *m* Brad Fiedel *pd* Nilo Rodis Jamero *ed* Ronald Sanders *sp* Sony Pictures Imageworks, Fantasy II, CORE Digital Pictures
☆ Keanu Reeves, Dolph Lundgren, Takeshi Kitano, Ice T, Dina Meyer, Denis Akiyama, Henry Rollins, Barbara Sukowa, Udo Kier
'High-tech trash, film as video-game.' – *Variety*
'Colossally inept badaptation.' – *Premiere*

Johnny Nobody
GB 1960 88m bw Warwickscope
Columbia/Viceroy (Irving Allen, Albert Broccoli)
A drunken Irish author challenges God to strike him dead for blasphemy. When an amnesiac shoots him, a nationwide religious controversy begins, but the deed is found to have a mercenary motive.
A mysterious rigmarole which irritates more than it entertains.
w Patrick Kirwan *story* The Trial of Johnny Nobody by Albert Z. Carr *d* Nigel Patrick *ph* Ted Moore *m* Ron Goodwin
☆ Nigel Patrick, Aldo Ray, Yvonne Mitchell, William Bendix, Cyril Cusack, Niall MacGinnis, Bernie Winters, Noel Purcell, Jimmy O'Dea
'The more one thinks of it, the more one is amazed that anyone should have thought a plot and players as uniformly unlikely as these could have worked out satisfactorily.' – *Peter John Dyer, MFB*

Johnny O'Clock
US 1946 95m bw
Columbia
A gambler appears to be involved in the death of a crooked policeman, but a girl helps to clear him.
Tawdry material made palatable by surface slickness.
wd Robert Rossen *ph* Burnett Guffey
☆ Dick Powell, Ellen Drew, Lee J. Cobb, Evelyn Keyes

Johnny One-Eye
US 1950 80m bw
United Artists (Benedict Bogeaus)
Two gangsters out to get each other are led together by a small girl and a dog.
Unpalatable mixture of violence and sentiment.
w Richard E. Landau *story* Damon Runyon *d* Robert Florey
☆ Pat O'Brien, Wayne Morris, Dolores Moran, Gayle Reed

Johnny Rocco
US 1958 83m bw
Allied Artists
The small son of a gangster is affected by his father's notoriety.
Awful sentimental melodrama with tear-stained ending; for connoisseurs of cliché.
w James O'Hanlon, Samuel F. Roeca *d* Paul Landres *ph* William Margulies *m* Edward J. Kay
☆ Richard Eyer, Stephen McNally, Coleen Gray, Russ Conway

Johnny Stecchino **
Italy 1991 102m Technicolor
Tiger/Pentafilm (Mario and Vittorio Cecchi Gori)
▦ ☾
The wife of a Sicilian gangster whom many people want dead discovers that a naive bus driver is her husband's double.
Relaxed comedy of mistaken identity that makes fun of the Mafia and displays Benigni's gifts as a sweet-natured clown.
w Vincenzo Cerami, Roberto Benigni *d* Roberto Benigni *ph* Giuseppe Lanci *m* Evan Lurie *pd* Paolo Biagetti *ed* Nino Baragli
☆ Roberto Benigni, Nicoletta Braschi, Paolo Bonacelli, Franco Volpi, Ivano Marescotti, Turi Scalia, Loredana Romito
† The film broke all box-office records in Italy.

'Their bullets talked where law stopped!'

Johnny Stool Pigeon
US 1949 75m bw
U-I (Aaron Rosenberg)
A detective releases a convict on condition that he leads him to a drug smuggling gang.

Competent low budget addition to the documentary police cycle.
w Robert L. Richards d William Castle
ph Maury Gertsman m Milton Schwarzwald
☆ Howard Duff, Shelley Winters, Dan Duryea, Gar Moore, Tony Curtis, John McIntire, Barry Kelley, Leif Erickson

'A Smooth Comedy...'
Johnny Suede *
US/Switzerland/France 1991 97m Fujicolour
Artificial Eye/Vega/Balthazar/Starr/Arena (Yoram Mandel, Ruth Waldburger)
📼 ▤ ◎〰
After a pair of suede shoes drops on top of a phone booth he's using, an ineffectual young man with an exaggerated quiff puts them on and tries to become a rock star.
Stylish exploration of pop style, although a certain tedium sets in before the end.
wd Tom DiCillo ph Joe DeSalvo m Jim Farmer, Link Wray pd Patricia Woodbridge ed Geraldine Peroni
☆ Brad Pitt, Catherine Keener, Calvin Levels, Alison Moir, Nick Cave, Peter McRobbie, Ashley Gardner, Dennis Parlato, Ron Vawter, Tina Louise
'There are moments of quirky charm and humor in this odd, stylized fable.' – *Stephen Farber, Movieline*

Johnny Tiger
US 1966 102m colour
Nova Hook (John Hugh)
▤
A repressed schoolteacher learns to trust his feelings after working on an Indian reservation and encouraging a wild young half-breed Seminole to study.
Formulaic confrontational drama of minimal interest.
w Paul Crabtree, John Hugh d Paul Wendkos ph Charles Straumer m John Green ed Harry Coswick
☆ Robert Taylor, Geraldine Brooks, Chad Everett, Brenda Scott, Marc Lawrence

Johnny Tremain
👫 US 1957 81m Technicolor
Walt Disney
▤
In 1773 Boston an apprentice silversmith joins the Sons of Liberty and helps start the War of Independence.
Schoolbook history with little vitality.
w Tom Blackburn novel Esther Forbes d Robert Stevenson ph Charles P. Boyle m George Bruns
☆ Hal Stalmaster, Luana Patten, Jeff York, Sebastian Cabot, Richard Beymer, Walter Sande

Johnny Trouble
US 1956 88m bw
Clarion (John H. Auer)
An elderly widow becomes involved with a boys' college and thinks she has found her lost grandson.
Sentimental, whimsical star vehicle.
w Charles O'Neal, David Lord d John H. Auer ph Peverell Marley m Frank de Vol
☆ Ethel Barrymore, Stuart Whitman, Cecil Kellaway, Carolyn Jones, Jesse White

Johnny Vagabond: see *Johnny Come Lately*

Johns
US 1995 96m CFI color
Metrodome/Bandeira (Beau Flynn, Stefan Simchowitz)
📼 ▤ ◎ ◎〰
A male prostitute's attempt to help a fellow hustler pay off his debts goes wrong.
A downbeat chronicle of sex and violence, inadequate and unsatisfactory despite some earnest performances.
wd Scott Silver m Tom Richmond m Charles Brown, Danny Caron pd Amy Beth Silver ed Dorian Harris
☆ David Arquette, Lukas Haas, Wilson Cruz, Keith David, Christopher Gartin, Elliott Gould, Terrence Dashon Howard, Richard Timothy Jones
'Works well as an MTV-style day in the life of LA rent boys, but its heart (which is in the right place) isn't quite substantial enough to support the emotional resonance the film needs.' – *Peter Griffiths, Film Review*

The Johnstown Flood *
US 1926 70m bw silent
Fox
A construction worker is warned by his girlfriend of an approaching flood, in which she dies.
Curious melodrama with mild spectacle.
w Edfrid Bingham, Robert Lord d Irving Cummings
☆ George O'Brien, Janet Gaynor, Paul Panzer, George Harris

The Joke **
Czechoslovakia 1968 78m bw
Studio Barrandov (Milos Stejskal)
original title: *Zert*
Fifteen years after being severely punished for making a joke about Trotsky, a man takes revenge on one of his judges and discovers that his action rebounds upon him.
Deft and deadly ironic political fable of the Stalinist era, with its seamless mix of past despair and present regret.
w Milan Kundera, Jaromil Jires novel Milan Kundera d Jaromil Jires ph Jan Curik m Zdenek Pololanik ad Leos Karen
☆ Josef Somr, Jana Ditetova, Ludek Munzar, Jaroslava Obermaierova
† The film was banned by the Czech authorities in the 70s.

The Joker Is Wild *
US 1957 126m bw Vistavision
Paramount/Charles Vidor
Joe E. Lewis, a twenties night-club singer, loses his voice after an attack by gangsters, and becomes a comedian.
Reasonably lively showbiz biopic in jaundiced vein; good atmosphere but far too long.
w Oscar Saul book Art Cohn d Charles Vidor ph Daniel L. Fapp m Walter Scharf
☆ Frank Sinatra, Mitzi Gaynor, Eddie Albert, Jeanne Crain, Beverly Garland, Jackie Coogan, Ted de Corsia
🎵 song 'All the Way' (mJimmy Van Heusen, lySammy Cahn)

The Jokers **
GB 1967 94m Technicolor
Universal/Adastra/Gildor/Scimitar (Maurice Foster, Ben Arbeid)
Two young brothers in London society plan to create a sensation by borrowing (and replacing) the crown jewels.
Bright suspense comedy which sums up the swinging London era pretty well and is generally amusing though it finally lacks aplomb.
w Dick Clement, Ian La Frenais d Michael Winner ph Ken Hodges m Johnny Pearson
☆ Michael Crawford, Oliver Reed, Harry Andrews, James Donald, Daniel Massey, Michael Hordern, Gabriella Licudi, Frank Finlay, Warren Mitchell, Rachel Kempson, Peter Graves

A Jolly Bad Fellow *
GB 1964 95m bw
British Lion/Pax/Tower/Michael Balcon (Donald Taylor)
US title: *They All Died Laughing*
A brash chemistry don tries a new poison on his enemies.
Interesting but finally irritating comedy of murders with a punnish rather than a donnish script and only moments of genuine sub-Ealing hilarity.
w Robert Hamer, Donald Taylor novel *Don Among the Dead Men* by C. E. Vulliamy d Don Chaffey ph Gerald Gibbs m John Barry
☆ Leo McKern, Janet Munro, Maxine Audley, Duncan Macrae, Dennis Price, Miles Malleson, Leonard Rossiter

Jolson Sings Again **
US 1949 96m Technicolor
Columbia (Sidney Buchman)
📼 ▤ ◎〰
Al Jolson's later career and second marriage to a nurse he met while entertaining troops in World War II.
Breezy, routine, rather empty sequel to the following.
w Sidney Buchman d Henry Levin ph William Snyder md Morris Stoloff, George Duning
☆ Larry Parks, Barbara Hale, William Demarest, Ludwig Donath, Bill Goodwin, Tamara Shayne, Myron McCormick
'Just relax and enjoy yourself.' – *Daily Express*

'I love it now – every last sentimental showbiz cliché, every oversung song.' – *Daily Telegraph, 1969*
👤 Sidney Buchman; William Snyder; Morris Stoloff, George Duning

The Jolson Story ****
👫 US 1946 129m Technicolor
Columbia (Sidney Skolsky)
▤ ◎〰
Asa Yoelson, son of a cantor, becomes Al Jolson, the great entertainer of the twenties; but showbiz success brings marital difficulties.
Whitewashed biopic in impeccable Hollywood style, with everything working shamelessly right, a new star in the leading role, perfect if unambitious production values, and a deluge of the best songs ever written.
w Stephen Longstreet d Alfred E. Green, Joseph H. Lewis ph Joseph Walker md Morris Stoloff ed William Lyon
☆ Larry Parks, William Demarest, Evelyn Keyes, Ludwig Donath, Tamara Shayne, Bill Goodwin, Scotty Beckett, John Alexander
'I have nothing in the world against this picture except that at least half of it seemed to me enormously tiresome.' – *James Agee*
† 3rd biggest moneyspinner of 1946, after *The Best Years of Our Lives* and *Duel in the Sun*.
†† Jolson dubbed Larry Parks's singing of his songs.
🏆 Morris Stoloff
👤 Joseph Walker; Larry Parks; William Demarest; William Lyon

'Everyone's book is now everyone's motion picture!'
Jonathan Livingston Seagull
👫 US 1973 114m DeLuxe Panavision
Paramount/JLS Partnership/Hall Bartlett
📼 ▤ ◎
The life of a seagull who aims to fly faster than any of his peers and eventually arrives in a perfect world.
Weird 'family' fantasy based on a phenomenally successful book which clearly could not translate easily to the screen. The bird photography is much more successful than the mysticism.
w Richard Bach novel Richard Bach d Hall Bartlett ph Boris Leven m Neil Diamond, Lee Holdridge
'A parable couched in the form of a nature film of overpowering beauty and strength in which, perhaps to our horror, we are forced to recognize ourselves in a seagull obsessed with the heights.' – *Michael Korda*
'It may be that the creature best qualified to review it is another seagull.' – *Benny Green, Punch*
'If one must spend two hours following the adventures of a bird, far better that the hero be Donald Duck.' – *Jay Cocks, Time*
'The sort of garbage that only a seagull could love.' – *Judith Crist*
👤 Jack Couffer

The Jones Family
Less human, more farcical than the Hardy films (qv), this series was TCF's second feature answer to MGM's money-makers, and pleased a lot of people at the time. Pop was Jed Prouty, Mom was Spring Byington, Grandma was Florence Roberts, and the youngsters included Kenneth Howell, George Ernest, Billy Mahan, June Carlson and June Lang. The first script was from a play by Katharine Cavanaugh, and the principal director was Frank Strayer.
1936 Every Saturday Night, Educating Father, Back to Nature
1937 Off to the Races, Borrowing Trouble, Hot Water
1938 Love on a Budget, Trip to Paris, Safety in Numbers, Down on the Farm
1939 Everybody's Baby, Quick Millions, The Jones Family in Hollywood, Too Busy to Work
1940 On Their Own
† An earlier series with different actors was abandoned after two episodes: *Young as You Feel* (1931), *Business and Pleasure* (1932).

'The epic love story in which everybody has a great role and a big part.'
Joseph Andrews
GB 1976 104m Eastmancolor
UA/Woodfall (Neil Hartley)
Adventures of a naïve 18th-century footman.
Woebegone attempt to restage Tom Jones.

w Allan Scott, Chris Bryant d Tony Richardson ph David Watkin m John Addison pd Michael Annals
☆ Peter Firth, Ann-Margret, Michael Hordern, Beryl Reid, Jim Dale, Peter Bull, John Gielgud, Hugh Griffith, Timothy West, Wendy Craig, Peggy Ashcroft, James Villiers, Karen Dotrice, Ronald Pickup
'Even the incidental pleasures cannot offset the sense of *déjà vu* which pervades this musty enterprise.' – *John Pym, MFB*

Joseph Conrad's The Secret Agent: see *The Secret Agent*

Josephine and Men
GB 1955 98m Eastmancolor
Charter (John and Roy Boulting)
The three romances of a determined young woman.
Alarmingly thin, old-fashioned romantic comedy with all resolved in a country cottage. Nothing quite works, especially the colour.
w Nigel Balchin, Roy Boulting, Frank Harvey d Roy Boulting ph Gilbert Taylor m John Addison
☆ Glynis Johns, Jack Buchanan, Donald Sinden, Peter Finch, Heather Thatcher, Ronald Squire

Josette
US 1938 73m bw
TCF (Gene Markey)
A New Orleans coquette teases two men.
Very minor musical, well enough presented but adding up to almost nothing.
w James Edward Grant d Allan Dwan ph John Mescall m/ly Harry Revel, Mack Gordon
☆ Simone Simon, Don Ameche, Robert Young, Joan Davis, Bert Lahr, Paul Hurst, William Collier Snr, Lynn Bari, William Demarest
'Rollicking farce with music ... a corking good entertainment.' – *Variety*

'Why run away from home when you can drive?'
Josh and S.A.M.
👫 US 1993 98m Technicolor
Rank/Castle Rock/New Line/City Lights (Martin Brest)
📼 ▤ ◎〰 ◎
Two young brothers, unhappy at home with their father, run away.
An odd, sentimental drama of adolescent fantasy, which mainly shows how a 12-year-old can become a success by the use of deft lies and deceit.
w Frank Deese d Billy Weber ph Don Burgess m Thomas Newman pd Marcia Hinds-Johnson ed Chris Lebenzon
☆ Jacob Tierney, Noah Fleiss, Martha Plimpton, Stephen Tobolowsky, Chris Penn, Joan Allen, Maury Chaykin, Udo Kier
'A marvellous example of how uninspired and lacking in vision most American movie-making has become. Competent and reasonably entertaining, it's ultimately forgettable.' – *Nigel Robinson, Film Review*

'The hunted has become the hunter. And there will be no mercy.'
Joshua Tree
US 1993 94m Foto-Kem
Vision International (Illana Diamant, Andy Armstrong)
📼 ▤
A trucker escapes from prison, takes a female cop as hostage and goes to seek revenge on those who killed his partner and framed him for murder.
An action film with a familiar plot but also possessing a slight sense of irony, with a little bow along the way to Bogart and a violent confrontation with Chinese crooks straight out of a Hong Kong movie.
w Steven Pressfield d Vic Armstrong ph Dan Turrett m Joel Goldsmith pd John J. Moore ed Paul Morton
☆ Dolph Lundgren, George Segal, Kristian Alfonso, Geoffrey Lewis, Bert Remsen, Michelle Phillips
'Serviceable action-suspense pic.' – *Sight and Sound*

Jour de Fête ***
👫 France 1948 87m bw
Francinex (Fred Orain)
📼 ▤ ◎〰
A village postman sees a film about the efficiency of the American postal service and decides to smarten himself up.

First, and some say best, of Tati's comedy vehicles: two-thirds superb local colour, one-third hilarious slapstick.

w Jacques Tati, Henri Marquet d *Jacques Tati* ph Jacques Mercanton m Jean Yatove
☆ Jacques Tati, Guy Decomble, Paul Fankeur, Santa Relli

'You could watch it with a bout of toothache and it would make you laugh.' – *Daily Express*

'It is not progressive; it won't be a landmark in the history of the cinema; but it gives me more pleasure than any film for the last five years.' – *Dilys Powell*

† A reissue version had colour items hand-painted in each frame, and proved quite effective.

†† A restored version in colour, made by Tati on experimental Thomsoncolour film but never printed at the time due to technical problems, was released in 1994 as part of France's celebration of the centenary of cinema. It has also been released on video-cassette.

Le Jour Se Lève ***
France   1939   95m   bw
Sigma
🔲

aka: Daybreak

A murderer is besieged by police in his attic room, remembers his past through the night, and shoots himself.

A model of French poetic realism, and a much-praised film which was almost destroyed when it was bought for an American remake (The Long Night).

w Jacques Viot, Jacques Prévert d *Marcel Carné* ph Curt Courant, Philippe Agostini, André Bac m Maurice Jaubert ad Alexander Trauner
☆ Jean Gabin, Jules Berry, Arletty, Jacqueline Laurent

'The man walks about his room, moves a few things, lies on his bed, looks out of the window, chain-smokes … and one is genuinely interested in him all the time (remembering afterwards that there exist directors who contrive to be boring even when they use fifteen characters in a motor car chase crackling with revolver shots).' – *Richard Mallett, Punch*

Le Journal de Lady M: see *The Diary of Lady M*

Journal d'un Curé de Campagne: see *The Diary of a Country Priest*

Le Journal d'une Femme de Chambre: see *The Diary of a Chambermaid*

Journal of a Crime
US   1934   65m   bw
Warner
A woman shoots her husband's mistress and gets amnesia before she can confess.

Melodramatic farrago which entertains by its very excesses.

w F. Hugh Herbert, Charles Kenyon *play* Jacques Deval d William Keighley
☆ Ruth Chatterton, Adolphe Menjou, Claire Dodd, Douglass Dumbrille, George Barbier

'High in sympathetic interest and force.' – *Variety*

Une Journée Bien Remplie: see *A Full Day's Work*

The Journey
US   1959   125m   Technicolor
MGM/Alby (Anatole Litvak)
During the 1956 Hungarian uprising, a busload of international passengers is detained overnight by a Russian major.

Pretentious, predictable and dull multi-melodrama peopled by uninteresting characters; different handling might have made a Casablanca of it.

w George Tabori d Anatole Litvak ph Jack Hildyard m Georges Auric
☆ Yul Brynner, Deborah Kerr, Jason Robards Jnr, Anouk Aimée, Robert Morley, E. G. Marshall, Anne Jackson, David Kossoff, Kurt Kasznar, Gerard Oury

'Ten minutes of this and we know where we are: we are back in the 1930s with Alfred Hitchcock and that glamorous band of international characters trapped in Mitteleuropa.' – *Steven Marcus*

Journey Back to Oz *
👫   US   1974   90m   colour
Norm Prescott and Lou Scheimer/Filmation
📼

Dorothy makes a return journey over the rainbow to fight the wicked witch's sister.

Competent cartoon version of Frank Baum themes from The Wizard of Oz.

d Hal Sutherland
☆ Featuring the voices of Liza Minnelli, Milton Berle, Ethel Merman, Margaret Hamilton, Mickey Rooney, Paul Ford

† Made in 1964, but not released for a decade.

Journey Beneath the Desert
Italy/France   1961   195m   Eastmancolor
CCM/Fidès
📼

original title: Antinea, l'Amante della Città Sepolta
After a forced landing in the Sahara Desert, three engineers discover underground the lost continent of Atlantis, ruled over by a despotic queen.

Leisurely adventure of a familiar kind, the fourth version of the story, which was first filmed in 1921 as L'Atlantide (qv). Here the actors seem unable to compete with the set design.

w André Tabet, Ugo Liberatore, Remigio Del Grosso, Amedeo Nazzari *novel* L'Atlantide by Pierre Benoit d Edgar G. Ulmer, Giuseppe Masini ph Enzo Serafin m Carlo Rustichelli pd Piero Filippone ed Renato Cinquini
☆ Haya Harareet, Jean-Louis Trintignant, James Westmoreland, Amedeo Nazzari, Georges Riviere, Giulia Rubini, Gian Maria Volonte

† The uncredited Frank Borzage also directed some sequences.

Journey for Margaret *
US   1942   81m   bw
MGM (B. P. Fineman)
📼

An American correspondent brings home an orphan from the London blitz.

Efficient tearful propaganda which coincidentally made a star of little Margaret O'Brien.

w David Hertz, William Ludwig *book* William L. White d W. S. Van Dyke ph Ray June m Franz Waxman
☆ Robert Young, Laraine Day, Margaret O'Brien, Billy Severn, Fay Bainter, Signe Hasso, Nigel Bruce, Halliwell Hobbes

Journey into Autumn *
Sweden   1954   86m   bw
Sandrews (Rune Waldekrantz)
📼

original title: Kvinnodrom
Two business women visiting Gothenburg have difficult relationships to settle.

Moody, impressionist sex drama which succeeds by fits and starts.

wd Ingmar Bergman ph Hilding Bladh
☆ Eva Dahlbeck, Harriet Andersson, Gunnar Bjornstrand, Ulf Palme, Inga Landgre, Naima Wifstrand

'Scenes of austere anti-romanticism and painful irony.' – *Peter John Dyer, MFB*

Journey into Fear ***
US   1942   71m   bw
RKO (Orson Welles)
📼

A munitions expert finds himself in danger from assassins in Istanbul, and has to be smuggled home.

Highly enjoyable impressionist melodrama supervised by Orson Welles and full of his touches and excesses.

w Joseph Cotten, Orson Welles *novel* Eric Ambler d Norman Foster (and Orson Welles) ph Karl Struss m Roy Webb md Constantin Bakaleinikoff
☆ Joseph Cotten, Dolores del Rio, Jack Moss, Orson Welles, Ruth Warrick, Agnes Moorehead

'Brilliant atmosphere, the nightmare of pursuit, eccentric encounters on the way, and when the shock comes it leaps at eye and ear.' – *William Whitebait*

† A 1976 remake, much heralded, was for obscure legal reasons hardly seen. Directed by Daniel Mann for New World, it starred Zero Mostel, Shelley Winters, Stanley Holloway, Vincent Price, Donald Pleasence, Sam Waterston, Joseph Wiseman, Scott Marlowe and Yvette Mimieux.

Journey into Light
US   1951   87m   bw
TCF/Joseph Bernhard
A minister loses his faith, becomes a derelict, and is reformed by a blind girl.

An old-fashioned tract in pictures. Has to be seen to be believed, but quite nicely made.

w Stephanie Nordli, Irving Shulman d Stuart Heisler m Paul Dunlap
☆ Sterling Hayden, Viveca Lindfors, Thomas Mitchell, H. B. Warner, Ludwig Donath, Jane Darwell, Charles Evans

'Slow, inept, and often extremely embarrassing.' – *MFB*

The Journey of August King
US   1995   92m   Technicolor
Miramax (Nick Wechsler, Sam Waterston)
📼

In 1815, a farmer protects a runaway slave girl, who has escaped from a rich and ruthless landowner.

Slow-moving drama that never sparks into life, despite the good intentions of those involved.

w John Ehle *novel* John Ehle d John Duigan ph Slawomir Idziak m Stephen Endelman pd Patricia Norris ed Humphrey Dixon
☆ Jason Patric, Thandie Newton, Larry Drake, Sam Waterston, Nesbitt Blaisdell, John Doman

'A strongly crafted, if unexcitingly simple drama of moral courage.' – *Variety*

† Directors George Roy Hill and Robert Mulligan earlier tried to set up productions of Ehle's novel, which was published in 1971.

Journey of Honor: see *Shogun Warrior*

Journey of Hope *
Switzerland   1990   110m   colour
Mainline/Catpics/Condor/SRG/RTSI/Film Four (Alfi Sinniger, Peter Fueter)
📼   💿

original title: Reise der Hoffnung
A Turkish father and mother and their young son, part of a group of illegal immigrants abandoned by their guide, try to make their way across a mountain pass into Switzerland.

Moving, almost documentary account of refugees seeking a better life.

w Xavier Koller, Feride Çiçekoğlu, Heike Hubert d Xavier Koller ph Elemer Ragalyi ad Luigi Pelizzo, Kathrin Brunner ed Galip Iyitanir
☆ Necmettin Çobanoğlu, Nur Srer, Emin Sivas, Erdinç Akbas, Yaman Okay, Yasar Gner, Hseyin Mete, Yaman Tarcan
🏆 best foreign film

The Journey of Natty Gann
👫   US   1985   105m   colour
Walt Disney (Michael Lobell)
📼   💿

During the Chicago depression, a girl follows her father west and hitch-hikes across America.

A kind of human Lassie Come Home: doggedly watchable but not inspiring, especially since it was shot in Canada.

w Jeanne Rosenberg d Jeremy Kagan ph Richard Bush m James Horner
☆ Meredith Salenger, John Cusack, Ray Wise, Scatman Crothers

'Cut to an hour, it would make a fine Disney telepic.' – *Variety*
🏆 costumes (Albert Wolsky)

Journey to Italy: see *Voyage to Italy*

Journey to Shiloh
US   1967   101m   Techniscope
Universal
Seven young Texans leave home to fight in the Civil War.

Episodic Western which failed in its ambition to reach epic stature.

w Gene Coon *novel* Fields of Honour by Will Henry d William Hale ph Enzo A. Martinelli m David Gates
☆ James Caan, Michael Sarrazin, Brenda Scott, Paul Petersen, Don Stroud, Michael Burns, Michael Vincent, Harrison Ford, John Doucette, Noah Beery Jnr

Journey to the Beginning of the World *
Portugal/France   1997   95m   colour
Artificial Eye/Madragoa/Gemini (Paulo Branco)
An elderly film director goes on a journey into his past in the company of three actors.

Elegiac celebration of, and farewell to, the forces and places that form an individual; it was Mastroianni's last film.

wd Manoel de Oliveira ph Renato Berta m Emmanuel Nunes pd Maria José Branco ed Valérie Loiseleux
☆ Marcello Mastroianni, Jean-Yves Gautier, Leonor Silveira, Diogo Dória, Isabel de Castro, Cecile Sanz de Alba

'The star takes it like a sweet swansong that makes his performance feel like an unforced tribute to his own long career. An unusually touching obituary.' – *Alexander Walker, London Evening Standard*

'A more stupefyingly uncinematic film has probably never been made.' – *Gaby Wood, Guardian*

Journey to the Center of the Earth ***
👫   US   1959   132m   DeLuxe
Cinemascope
TCF (Charles Brackett)
📼   🔲   🎧   💿

An Edinburgh professor and assorted colleagues follow an explorer's trail down an extinct Icelandic volcano to the Earth's centre.

Enjoyable hokum which gets more and more fantastic but only occasionally misses its footing; it ends splendidly with the team being catapulted out of Stromboli on a tide of lava.

w Walter Reisch, Charles Brackett *novel* Jules Verne d Henry Levin ph Leo Tover m Bernard Herrmann ad Lyle R. Wheeler, Franz Bachelin, Herman A. Blumenthal
☆ James Mason, Arlene Dahl, Pat Boone, Peter Ronson, Diane Baker, Thayer David

'The attraction of a Jules Verne fantasy … is in the endearing contrast between the wildest adventures and the staidest Victorian propriety on the part of those undergoing them … There is about the whole film a good-natured enjoyment of its own excesses.' – *Penelope Houston*
& art direction

'Caught in a fantastic time trap.'

Journey to the Center of Time
👫   US   1967   82m   colour
Ember/Flamingo/Borealis-Dorad (Ray Dorn, David L. Hewitt)
Scientists inadvertently send themselves to the year 5000 AD, at a time of a war with aliens, and then travel to 1,000,000 BC where they are attacked by monsters.

Low-budget, unexciting sci-fi, with the prehistoric world represented by one medium-sized lizard, dry ice and coloured lights.

w David Prentiss d David L. Hewitt ph Robert Caramico pd Edward D. Engoron ed Bill Welburn sp Modern Film Effects
☆ Scott Brady, Gigi Perreau, Anthony Eisley, Abraham Sofaer, Poupee Gamin

Journey to the Far Side of the Sun *
GB   1969   99m   DeLuxe   Cinemascope
Universal/Century 21 Productions (Gerry Anderson)
📼   💿

aka: Doppelgänger
An astronaut on a mission to a hitherto undetected planet discovers it to be an exact duplicate of Earth, and his own double returns in his place.

Intriguing, impeccably produced, but rather dull science fiction.

w Gerry and Sylvia Anderson, Donald James d John Parrish ph John Read m Barry Gray sp Harry Oakes models Derek Meddings
☆ Ian Hendry, Roy Thinnes, Patrick Wymark, Lynn Loring, Herbert Lom, George Sewell, Ed Bishop

Journey to the South (dubbed)
Argentina/Yugoslavia   1988   90m   colour
Art Film 80/Smart Egg/CFS (Jorge Estrada Mora, Aleksandar Stojanović)
📼

original title: El Camino del Sur
In the 1920s, a young Yugoslavian girl thinks she is marrying a wealthy European who lives in Buenos

Aires, but discovers instead that she has been sold to work in a brothel.

Episodic treatment of the once-flourishing white slave trade in East European women, a colourful but unconvincing melodrama.

w Juan Bautista Stagnaro, Elida Cecconi *story* Beda Docampo Feijoo *d* Juan Bautista Stagnaro *m* Karpo A. Godina *m* Zoran Simjanović *ad* Nikola Lazarevski, Santijago Eider *ed* Enrique Muzio, Snezana Ivanović

☆ Mirjana Joković, Adrian Ghio, Zarko Lausević, Mira Furlan, Osvaldo Santoro

Journey Together *

GB 1944 95m bw
RAF Film Unit (John Boulting)
🖭

Trainee pilots receive instruction in England and America before going on their first bombing mission.

Modest wartime semi-documentary, pleasingly done.

w Terence Rattigan *d* John Boulting *ph* Harry Waxman *m* Gordon Jacob *pd* John Howell

☆ Richard Attenborough, Jack Watling, David Tomlinson, Edward G. Robinson, Hugh Wakefield, Sebastian Shaw, Ronald Adam, Bessie Love

'It has a natural dignity as well as a natural fun.' – *Listener*

'One of the most realistic and brilliant films of the war in the air.' – *News Chronicle*

Journey's End *

GB/US 1930 120m bw
Gainsborough/Welsh-Pearson/Tiffany-Stahl (George Pearson)

France 1917: personal tensions mount as men die in the trenches.

Primitive early sound version (made in Hollywood because of better equipment) of a justly celebrated play first performed a year earlier. Cinematically uninteresting, with acting generally over the top, but it kept Whale and Clive in Hollywood where they shortly collaborated on Frankenstein.

w Joseph Moncure March, Gareth Gundrey *play* R. C. Sherriff *d* James Whale *ph* Benjamin Kline *m* none *ad* Harvey Libbert *ed* Claude Berkeley

☆ Colin Clive, Ian MacLaren, David Manners, Billy Bevan, Anthony Bushell, Robert Adair

'No crystal gazing required to forecast a big measure of success.' – *Variety*

'It has been transferred to the screen with the greatest possible tact and discretion.' – *James Agate*

'Hollywood has produced its first sex-appeal-less film. Mr George Pearson is to be congratulated on his restraint.' – *Punch*

'Almost painfully English … I cannot believe that the strangulated emotions which resulted can have meant much to audiences outside the English-speaking world.' – *Basil Wright, 1972*

† It was the first Anglo-American co-production.

Jours Tranquilles à Clichy: see *Quiet Days in Clichy*

Joy House

France 1964 98m bw Franscope
MGM (Jacques Bar)
🖭

aka: *The Love Cage*

The husband of a wealthy American woman in France tries to kill her boyfriend.

Weird hothouse drama, an unsuccessful attempt to combine French and American styles.

w René Clément, Pascal Jardin, Charles Williams *novel* Day Keene *d* René Clément *ph* Henri Decae *m* Lalo Schifrin *ad* Jean Andre *ed* Fedora Zincone

☆ Jane Fonda, Alain Delon, Lola Albright

Joy in the Morning

US 1965 103m Metrocolor
MGM (Henry T. Weinstein)

Early episodes in the marriage of a poor teenage student.

Glutinous romantic drama, quite well made.

w Sally Benson, Alfred Hayes, Norman Lessing *novel* Betty Smith *d* Alex Segal *ph* Ellsworth Fredricks *m* Bernard Herrmann

☆ Richard Chamberlain, Yvette Mimieux, Arthur Kennedy, Oscar Homolka, Joan Tetzel, Sidney Blackmer

---

'Between every mother and daughter there is a story that must be told.'

The Joy Luck Club

US 1993 139m Technicolor
Buena Vista/Hollywood Pictures (Wayne Wang, Amy Tan, Ronald Bass, Patrick Markey)
🖭 ▤ ◎ ∩

The relationships of four Chinese-American daughters with their Chinese mothers are recalled.

A long, slick, mostly sentimental wallow in the past that fails to throw much light on the present or the future; it lacks the sense of culture clash and quirky humour evident in the director's earlier, low-budget films.

w Amy Tan, Ronald Bass *novel* Amy Tan *d* Wayne Wang *ph* Amir Mokri *m* Rachel Portman *pd* Donald Graham Burt *ed* Maysie Hoy

☆ Kieu Chinh, Tsai Chin, France Nuyen, Lisa Lu, Ming-Na Wen, Tamlyn Tomita, Lauren Tom, Victor Wong

'Beautifully made and acted and emotionally moving into the bargain.' – *Variety*

'Delivers neither subtlety nor heart-warming ebullience. Everything is shoe-horned into the fake conflicts and resolutions of soap opera … If you go to this film with a date whom you want to impress with your sensitivity, bring onions.' – *Adam Mars-Jones, Independent*

Joy of Living *

US 1938 90m bw
RKO (Felix Young)
🖭 ◎

A practical-minded Broadway songstress succumbs to the charms of an aristocratic freewheeler.

Zany romantic comedy, not quite zippy enough to make one forget its irritating archness, but socio-historically very interesting, in the mould of You Can't Take It with You.

w Gene Towne, Allan Scott, Graham Baker *story* Dorothy Fields, Herbert Fields *d* Tay Garnett *ph* Joseph Walker *m/ly* Jerome Kern, Dorothy Fields *md* Frank Tours

☆ Irene Dunne, Douglas Fairbanks Jnr, Alice Brady, Guy Kibbee, Lucille Ball, Eric Blore, Jean Dixon, Warren Hymer, Billy Gilbert

'Fair farce … bereft of sufficient novelty or comedy plot to sustain itself through an hour and a half of gags.' – *Variety*

Joyless Street *

Germany 1925 139m bw silent
Sofar Film
🖭 ◎

original title: *Die Freudlose Gasse*

Problems of the inhabitants of a street in Vienna after World War I.

Realistic but studio-set melodrama which brought its director and Greta Garbo to international fame. In itself the film begins by stimulating and ends by boring.

w Willy Haas *novel* Hugo Bettauer *d* G. W. Pabst *ph* Guido Seeber, Curt Oertel, Robert Lach

☆ Asta Nielsen, Werner Krauss, Greta Garbo, Valeska Gert, Agnes Esterhazy

'Moments of searing pain, of mental anguish, of sheer unblemished beauty.' – *Paul Rotha, The Film Till Now*

Joyriders

GB 1988 96m Technicolor
Pathé/Granada/British Screen/Little Bird/Film Four (Emma Hayter)

A battered wife runs away with a petty criminal.

Road movie that, for all its squalor, never comes near to reality.

w Andy Smith *story* Aisling Walsh, Andy Smith *d* Aisling Walsh *ph* Gabriel Beristain *pd* Leigh Malone *ed* Thomas Schwalm

☆ Patricia Kerrigan, Andrew Connolly, Billie Whitelaw, David Kelly, John Kavanagh, Deirdre Donoghue, Tracy Peacock, Rolf Saxon, Otto Jarman

Ju Dou **

Japan/China 1990 94m Eastmancolor
ICA/Tokuma Shoten/China Film/X'ian Film Studio (Shigeru Mori, Hiroyuki Kato, Zhao Hangao)
🖭 ▤

An impotent old man succeeds in revenging himself on his adulterous wife and her lover, his nephew, through their son.

A tragic folk-tale, colourfully told.

w Liu Heng *story* Fuxi Fuxi by Liu Heng *d* Zhang Yimou, Yang Fengliang *ph* Gu Changwei, Yang

---

Lun *m* Zhao Jiping *ad* Cao Jiuping, Xia Rujin *ed* Du Yuan

☆ Li Wei, Gong Li, Li Baotian, Zhang Yi, Zheng Jian

'A film where the images do the talking, and almost everything they have to say is deeply cautionary.' – *MFB*

† The film was banned in China.

⚖ best foreign film

'See it now! Remember it always!'
'A story so momentous it required six Academy Award stars and a cast of 1,186 players!'

Juarez **

US 1939 132m bw
Warner (Hal. B. Wallis, Henry Blanke)

A revolutionary leader causes the downfall of Emperor Maximilian of Mexico.

Spectacular historical drama with many fine moments which do not quite coalesce into a dramatic whole, chiefly owing to the lack of a single viewpoint.

w John Huston, Wolfgang Reinhardt, Aeneas Mackenzie *d* William Dieterle *ph* Tony Gaudio *m* Erich Wolfgang Korngold

☆ Brian Aherne, Bette Davis, Paul Muni, Claude Rains, John Garfield, Donald Crisp, Gale Sondergaard, Joseph Calleia, Gilbert Roland, Henry O'Neill, Pedro de Cordoba, Montagu Love, Harry Davenport

'With such potent box office values, its success at theatres seems assured.' – *Variety*

'A million dollars' worth of ballroom sets, regimentals, gauze shots and whiskers.' – *Otis Ferguson*

'Dramatically by far the most effective of Warners' biographical films of the thirties.' – *Graham Greene*

'Muni's big-star solemn righteousness is like a dose of medicine.' – *New Yorker, 1977*

† Based vaguely on two novels: *The Phantom Crown* by Bertita Harding, and *Maximilian and Carlotta* by Franz Werfel.

†† According to Brian Aherne the film was to have been called *The Phantom Crown*, but Muni's contract enabled him to insist that the name of his character should appear in the title.

⚖ Brian Aherne

'Remember his name … You'll remember his story!'

Jubal

US 1956 101m Technicolor Cinemascope
Columbia (William Fadiman)
🖭 ◎

A rancher's wife causes trouble when she falls in love with a wandering cowhand.

Solid sex Western, moderately interestingly done.

w Russell S. Hughes, Delmer Daves *novel* Jubal Troop by Paul Wellman *d* Delmer Daves *ph* Charles Lawton *m* David Raksin

☆ Glenn Ford, Ernest Borgnine, Felicia Farr, Rod Steiger, Valerie French, Charles Bronson, Noah Beery Jnr

Jubilee *

GB 1978 104m colour
Whaley-Malin/Megalovision
🖭

Queen Elizabeth I is transported by her astrologer into the latter part of the 20th century, and is appalled by what she sees.

Outrageous dissection of modern urban life, full of black jokes: it has the right attitudes but is not free of a determination to shock at all costs.

w Derek Jarman and others *d* Derek Jarman *ph* Peter Middleton *m* Brian Eno

☆ Jenny Runacre, Little Nell, Toyah Willcox, Jordan, Hermine Demoriane

'One of the most intelligent and interesting films to be made in Britain in a long time.' – *Scott Meek, MFB*

Jubilee Trail *

US 1954 103m Trucolor
Republic (Joseph Kane)

Jealousy and murder by covered wagon en route from New Orleans to the California gold fields.

Bumpy adventure melodrama, generally quite entertaining.

w Bruce Manning *novel* Gwen Bristow *d* Joseph Kane *ph* Jack Marta *m* Victor Young

☆ Vera Hruba Ralston, Forrest Tucker, Joan Leslie, Pat O'Brien, John Russell, Ray Middleton

---

Judas Was a Woman: see *La Bête Humaine*

'A time without pity. A society without mercy. A love without equal.'

Jude *

GB 1996 123m Technicolor Panavision
PolyGram/BBC Films/Revolution (Andrew Eaton)
🖭 ▤ ◎ ∩

After his wife leaves him, a rural labourer decides to revive his dream of becoming a teacher and moves to a university town, where he falls in love with his cousin.

An unhappy adaptation, with some jarringly anachronistic dialogue, which only occasionally gets to grips with Hardy's tragic story.

w Hossein Amini *novel* Thomas Hardy *d* Michael Winterbottom *ph* Eduardo Serra *m* Adrian Johnston *pd* Joseph Bennett *ed* Trevor Waite

☆ Christopher Eccleston, Kate Winslet, Liam Cunningham, Rachel Griffiths, June Whitfield, Ross Colvin Turnbull, James Daley

'A little triumph.' – *Adam Mars-Jones*

'An ambitious, sensitive, but ultimately uninvolving effort.' – *Geoff Andrew, Time Out*

Judex **

France 1916 125m bw silent
Gaumont

A Robin Hood type crimefighter destroys the empire of an evil banker.

Stylishly enjoyable serial from the maker of Les Vampires and Fantômas.

w Arthur Bernade, Louis Feuillade *d* Louis Feuillade

☆ René Creste, Musidora, Yvette Andreyor, Louis Leubas

† Another *Judex* serial was made in 1917, and in 1933 came a feature version directed by Maurice Champreux, with René Ferte. In 1963 Georges Franju directed another feature remake with Channing Pollock, and this was extremely well received.

The Judge and the Assassin **

France 1976 125m colour Panavision
Arrow/Lira (André Hoss)
🖭 ▤ ◎

original title: *Le Juge et L'Assassin*

In the 1890s, at a time of unrest, unemployment and poverty, a judge expends his energies in persuading a former sergeant, disappointed in love, to confess to raping and killing children as he tramped across France.

Gripping examination of the mind of a mass murderer and a passionate indictment of a society that uses justice as a means of oppression.

w Jean Aurenche, Bertrand Tavernier, Pierre Bost *d* Bertrand Tavernier *ph* Pierre William Glenn *m* Philippe Sarde *ad* Antoine Roman *ed* Armand Psenny

☆ Philippe Noiret, Michel Galabru, Isabelle Huppert, Jean-Claude Brialy, Renée Faure, Cecile Vassort, Yves Robert .

'In The Future, One Man Is The Law.'

Judge Dredd

US 1995 96m Technicolor Panavision
Guild/Cinergi (Charles M. Lippincott, Beau E. L. Marks)
🖭 ▢ ▤ ◎ ⊚ ∩

In Mega City One in AD 2139, Judge Dredd is exiled after being framed for a murder committed by his evil clone.

John Wagner and Carlos Ezquerra's comic-book creation of a shoot-first-ask-questions-later cop who is also judge and jury finds the ideal actor in Sylvester Stallone, but the film strands him without a decent script in which he can flex his muscles.

w William Wisher, Steven E. De Souza *d* Danny Cannon *ph* Adrian Biddle *m* Alan Silvestri *pd* Nigel Phelps *ed* Alex Mackie, Harry Keramidas

☆ Sylvester Stallone, Armand Assante, Diane Lane, Rob Schneider, Joan Chen, Jürgen Prochnow, Max von Sydow, Joanna Miles, Balthazar Getty, Maurice Roeves, Ian Dury

'What's worrying is that so much time and energy can be spent on such a crashingly stale chunk of genre hardware.' – *Jonathan Romney*

'With its routine story-line and unsurprising visuals, you feel as if you have already seen Judge Dredd before it is even 10 minutes old.' – *Stephen Amidon, Sunday Times*

'Thunderous, unoriginal futuristic hardware show for teenage boys.' – *Variety*

'Continuously beautiful and interesting from beginning to end ... With its first-rate rumbling sound effects, its lavish, old-fashioned score and its exquisite palette of muted browns and pale blues, *Judge Dredd* offers a sophisticated aesthetic experience.' – *Camille Paglia, TLS*

† The film took around $34m at the US box-office and another $78m elsewhere during 1995.

'Enough laughs to make your head spin!'
Judge Priest *
US   1934   79m   bw
Fox (Sol M. Wurtzel)
▦

A political judge sees fair play through a criminal case.
Mainly effective star vehicle.
w Dudley Nichols, Lamar Trotti *stories* Irvin S. Cobb *d* John Ford *ph* George Schneiderman *m* Samuel Kaylin
☆ Will Rogers, Tom Brown, Anita Louise, Henry B. Walthall, David Landau, Rochelle Hudson
'A great part for Will Rogers and a box office bet.' – *Variety*

The Judge Steps Out *
US   1947   91m   bw
RKO
▦
GB title: *Indian Summer*
A middle-aged judge leaves his wife and sets off on an aimless journey in the course of which he falls in love with a café proprietress.
A pleasing human story, simply told in a manner which at the time seemed more French than American.
w Boris Ingster, Alexander Knox *d* Boris Ingster *ph* Robert de Grasse *m* Constantin Bakaleinikoff
☆ Alexander Knox, Ann Sothern, George Tobias, Sharyn Moffett

A Judgement in Stone: see *La Cérémonie*

'The things you'll see and the things you'll feel are the things that will be part of you as long as you live!'
Judgment at Nuremberg **
US   1961   190m   bw
UA/Roxlom (Stanley Kramer)
▦ ▤ ◉ ✿

A fictionalized version of the 1948 trial of the Nazi leaders for crimes against humanity.
Interminable, heavy-going dramatic documentary expanded from a succinct TV play into a courtroom marathon with philosophical asides. All good stuff, but too much of it.
w Abby Mann *play* Abby Mann *d* Stanley Kramer *ph* Ernest Laszlo *m* Ernest Gold *pd* Rudolph Sternad
☆ Spencer Tracy, Marlene Dietrich, Burt Lancaster, Richard Widmark, Maximilian Schell, Judy Garland, Montgomery Clift, William Shatner, Edward Binns, Werner Klemperer, Torben Meyer, Alan Baxter, Ray Teal
'Some believe that by tackling such themes Kramer earns at least partial remission from criticism. How much? 20 per cent off for effort?' – *Stanley Kauffmann*
† Burt Lancaster replaced Laurence Olivier, who was originally cast.
👤 Abby Mann; Maximilian Schell
👥 best picture; Stanley Kramer; Ernest Laszlo; Spencer Tracy; Judy Garland; Montgomery Clift

Judgment Deferred
GB   1951   88m   bw
Group Three (John Baxter)
A collection of Dorset eccentrics brings to book the head of a dope smuggling ring who has framed one of their associates.
An unusual story can't compensate for stagey handling in this first disappointing production of a company set up by the National Film Finance Corporation to make low budget films with top talent.
w Geoffrey Orme, Barbara Emary, Walter Meade *d* John Baxter *ph* Arthur Grant *m* Kennedy Russell
☆ Hugh Sinclair, Helen Shingler, Abraham Sofaer, Leslie Dwyer, Joan Collins, Harry Locke, Elwyn Brook Jones, Bransby Williams, Maire O'Neill, Harry Welchman
† This was an expanded remake of *Doss House*.

Judgment in Berlin
US   1988   96m   Eastmancolor
Hobo/Bibo TV/January Enterprises/Sheen-Greenblatt (Joshua Sinclair, Ingrid Windisch)
▦ ▤ ◉

An East German is tried by an American court in Berlin after hijacking a Polish airliner.
Despite being based on an actual incident, this courtroom drama lacks conviction.
w Joshua Sinclair, Leo Penn *book* Herbert J. Stern *d* Leo Penn *ph* Gabor Pogany *ad* Jan Schlubach, Peter Alteneder *ed* Teddy Darvas
☆ Martin Sheen, Sam Wanamaker, Max Gail, Juergen Heinrich, Heinz Hoenig, Carl Lumbly, Max Volkert Martens, Christine Rose, Sean Penn

Judgment Night
US   1993   110m   colour
Universal/Largo/JVC (Gene Levy)
▦ ▤ ◉ ✿

Four friends are pursued by killers after they get lost in a city slum and witness a gangland murder.
Violent and implausible chase thriller that requires only that its protagonists behave with great stupidity.
w Lewis Colick *d* Stephen Hopkins *ph* Peter Levy *m* Alan Silvestri *pd* Joseph Nemec III *ed* Timothy Wellburn
☆ Emilio Estevez, Cuba Gooding Jnr, Denis Leary, Stephen Dorff, Jeremy Piven, Peter Greene, Erik Schrody, Michael Wiseman
'Exceedingly well directed, cleverly filmed and edited, tension-filled affair. It is also a wholly preposterous, muddled, paranoid view of the inner-city nightmare.' – *Leonard Klady, Variety*

Judith
US   1965   109m   Technicolor   Panavision
Paramount/Cumulus/Command (Kurt Unger)
🎧

In 1947 Israel, loyalists rescue the wife of an escaped war criminal and ask her to identify him, but she takes her own revenge.
Glowering kibbutz adventures, well enough made but adding up to neither one thing nor the other, and rather confusing to non-Jews.
w John Michael Hayes *story* Lawrence Durrell *d* Daniel Mann *ph* John Wilcox *m* Sol Kaplan *pd* Wilfrid Shingleton
☆ Sophia Loren, Peter Finch, Jack Hawkins, Hans Verner, André Morell
'Tasteless and pretentious ... Here is tragedy and glory being used as window dressing for some cheap little undercover-agent episodes and fleshly exploitation.' – *Judith Crist*

Judith of Bethulia
US   1913   42m   bw   silent
Biograph (D. W. Griffith)
◉

A widow in a city attacked by the Assyrians courts their leader and beheads him.
Semi-biblical melodrama in Griffith's most Victorian style.
w Frank Woods *d* D. W. Griffith *ph* Billy Bitzer
☆ Blanche Sweet, Henry B. Walthall, Lillian Gish, Dorothy Gish, Lionel Barrymore, Mae Marsh, Robert Harron

Juggernaut
GB   1937   64m   bw
Ambassador (Julius Hagen)
A scientist lacking funds for his experiments agrees to commit murder.
Tedious melodrama which wastes Karloff's time.
w Cyril Campion, H. Fowler Mear, H. Fraenkel *d* Henry Edwards *ph* Sidney Blythe
☆ Boris Karloff, Mona Goya, Joan Wyndham, Arthur Margetson, Anthony Ireland, Morton Selten
'It gets into motion slowly and reaches the meat of the plot after numerous distractions.' – *Variety*

Juggernaut **
GB   1974   110m   DeLuxe   Panavision
United Artists/David E. Picker (Richard Alan Simmons)
▦ ▤

A transatlantic liner is threatened by a mad bomber.
Elaborate suspense spectacular, most of which works pretty well.
w Richard Alan Simmons *d* Richard Lester *ph* Gerry Fisher *m* Ken Thorne *pd* Terence Marsh

☆ Richard Harris, David Hemmings, Omar Sharif, Anthony Hopkins, Ian Holm, Shirley Knight, Roy Kinnear, Cyril Cusack, Freddie Jones
'However unoriginal its basic ingredients, it hardly ever slackens its pace or diverts attention from its central premise.' – *Jonathan Rosenbaum*
'Jaunty, cynical slapstick.' – *New Yorker*

The Juggler
US   1953   88m   bw
Columbia/Stanley Kramer
A Jewish refugee in Palestine has a horror of being imprisoned, and runs away from a transit camp with a small wandering boy.
Well-meaning cheapie, a curiously aimless topical drama which fails to make any of its several points.
w Michael Blankfort *novel* Michael Blankfort *d* Edward Dmytryk *ph* Roy Hunt *m* Georges Antheil
☆ Kirk Douglas, Milly Vitale, Paul Stewart, Joey Walsh

'Power. Respect.'
Juice **
US   1992   91m   Technicolor
Electric/Paramount/Island World (David Heyman, Neal H. Moritz, Peter Frankfurt)
▦ ▤ ◉ ✿

Four young friends from Harlem find their relationship alters after they rob a store and kill its owner.
Gripping tale of inner-city despair and the dead end offered by violence.
w Gerard Brown, Ernest R. Dickerson *d* Ernest R. Dickerson *ph* Larry Banks *m* Hank Shocklee & The Bomb Squad *pd* Lester Cohen *ed* Sam Pollard, Brunilda Torres
☆ Omar Epps, Tupac Shakur, Jermaine Hopkins, Khalil Kain, Cindy Herron, Vincent Laresca, Samuel L. Jackson, George O. Gore, Grace Garland, Queen Latifah
'A vivid slice of everyday fun and mortal danger in young Harlem.' – *Joe Brown, Washington Post*
'Demonstrates the black community's untapped talent waiting for opportunities on both sides of the camera, but it also reflects the confined realm within which the filmmakers and performers are forced to operate.' – *Variety*

Jujiro: see *Crossroads*

Juke Girl
US   1942   90m   bw
Warner (Jack Saper, Jerry Wald)
Fruit workers in Florida get involved in murder.
Hokum melodrama with all concerned treading water.
w A. I. Bezzerides *novel* Theodore Pratt *d* Curtis Bernhardt *ph* Bert Glennon *m* Adolph Deutsch
☆ Ann Sheridan, Ronald Reagan, Richard Whorf, Gene Lockhart, Faye Emerson, George Tobias, Alan Hale, Howard da Silva, Donald McBride, Fuzzy Knight, Willie Best

Jules et Jim ****
France   1962   105m   bw   Franscope
Films du Carrosse/SEDIF (Marcel Berbert)
▦ ▤ ◉ 🎧

Before World War I, in Paris, a girl alternates between a French and a German student, and after the war they meet again to form a constantly shifting triangle.
Charming, quintessentially French period romance, technically interesting, emotionally up-lifting, and acted and directed with verve and feeling.
w François Truffaut, Jean Gruault *novel* Henri-Pierre Roche *d* François Truffaut *ph* Raoul Coutard *m* Georges Delerue
☆ Oskar Werner, Jeanne Moreau, Henri Serre
'The sense is of a director intoxicated with the pleasure of making films.' – *Penelope Houston, MFB*

Jules Verne's Rocket to the Moon
👫 US   1967   95m   colour   Panavision
AIP (Harry Alan Towers)
▤
aka: *Those Fantastic Flying Fools*
aka: *Blast-Off*
Escaping from his creditors to England, Phineas T. Barnum finances a trip to the moon in an attempt to recoup his fortunes.
Farcical Victoriana that owes little to Jules Verne and more to the Carry On films, though it leans more to

genteel slapstick than genial vulgarity. Some skilled character actors provide moments of amusement.
w Dave Freeman *story* Peter Welbeck (Harry Alan Towers), 'inspired by the writings of Jules Verne' *d* Don Sharp *ph* Reg Wyer *m* Patrick John Scott *ad* Frank White *ed* Ann Chegwidden
☆ Burl Ives, Troy Donahue, Gert Frobe, Hermione Gingold, Lionel Jeffries, Dennis Price, Terry-Thomas, Daliah Lavi, Stratford Johns, Graham Stark, Jimmy Clitheroe
† Jules Verne's novel was filmed more seriously, but no more successfully, in 1958 as *From the Earth to the Moon* (qv).

Jules Verne's Sea Devils (dubbed)
Spain   1981   87m   Eastmancolor   Dinavision
Almena/Cinevision (Alfredo Casado)
original title: *Los Diablos del Mar*
A group of youthful immigrants, on their way to Australia, escape from pirates only to be shipwrecked in Africa, where they fall foul of slave traders.
Vapid, politically incorrect action movie, particularly unconvincing in scenes involving attacks by wild animals and in its heavy-handed moments of comedy.
w Joaquin Grau, Juan Piquer *story* Fifteen years old Captain by Jules Verne *d* J. Piquer Simon *ph* Juan Marine *m* Alfonso Agullo, Carlos Villa *pd* Gumer Andres *ed* Antonio Gimeno
☆ Ian Sera, Frank Brana, Patty Shepard, Flavia Zarzo, Gaby Gimenez, Aldo Sambrell

'A story of turmoil, of courage, of love!'
Julia ***
US   1977   117m   Technicolor
TCF (Richard Roth)
▦ ◉

Lillian Hellman reflects on the fortunes of her friend Julia, filled with enthusiasm for European causes and finally killed by the Nazis.
Thoughtful, elegant patchwork of thirties memories, a vehicle for actors and a subtle, self-effacing director.
w Alvin Sargent *book* Pentimento by Lillian Hellman *d* Fred Zinnemann *ph* Douglas Slocombe *m* Georges Delerue *pd* Carmen Dillon, Gene Callahan, Willy Holt *ed* Walter Murch
☆ Jane Fonda, Vanessa Redgrave, Jason Robards Jnr, Maximilian Schell, Hal Holbrook, Meryl Streep, Rosemary Murphy, Cathleen Nesbitt, Maurice Denham
'After a while it becomes apparent that Zinnemann and Sargent are trafficking in too many quotations and flashbacks because they can't find the core of the material.' – *Pauline Kael*
👤 script; Vanessa Redgrave; Jason Robards Jnr
👥 best picture; Fred Zinnemann; Douglas Slocombe; Georges Delerue; Jane Fonda; Maximilian Schell
🏆 best picture; Alvin Sargent; Douglas Slocombe; Jane Fonda

'An erotic comedy about life on the line.'
Julia Has Two Lovers
US   1990   85m   colour
Oneira (Bashar Shbib)
▦

A woman, who has ambivalent feelings about her current lover, begins a romance with a man who dials her number by mistake.
Low-budget romance that fails to ring bells.
w Daphna Kastner, Bashar Shbib *d* Bashar Shbib *ph* Stephen Reizes *m* Emilio Kauderer *ed* Dan Foegelle, Bashar Shbib
☆ Daphna Kastner, David Duchovny, David Charles, Tim Ray

Julia Misbehaves
US   1948   99m   bw
MGM (Everett Riskin)
▦

An actress returns to her stuffy husband when her daughter is about to marry.
Desperate attempt to find a vehicle for a fading star team.
w William Ludwig, Arthur Wimperis, Harry Ruskin *novel* The Nutmeg Tree by Margery Sharp *d* Jack Conway *ph* Joseph Ruttenberg *m* Adolph Deutsch
☆ Greer Garson, Walter Pidgeon, Elizabeth Taylor, Peter Lawford, Cesar Romero, Lucile Watson, Nigel Bruce, Mary Boland, Reginald Owen, Ian Wolfe, Edmund Breon, Fritz Feld, Aubrey Mather, Henry Stephenson

---

Julian Po
US 1997 78m Technicolor
Entertainment/Fine Line/Cypress/Mindel/Shaw
(Joseph Pierson, Jon Glascoe)
■ 🖭
Small townspeople make a hero out of stranger who claims that he has come to their town to kill himself.
Bland mystery of a movie that never quite explains itself.
wd Alan Wade *novella* La Mort de Monsieur Golouga by Branimir Scepanovic *ph* Bernd Heinl *m* Patrick Williams *pd* Stephen McCabe *ed* Jeffrey Wolf
☆ Christian Slater, Robin Tunney, Michael Parks, Cherry Jones, Frankie R. Faison, Harve Presnell, Allison Janney
'A dull, faintly puzzling nullity of a movie.' – *Peter Bradshaw, Guardian*

Julie *
US 1956 97m bw
MGM/Arwin (Marty Melcher)
A concert pianist plans to murder his wife.
Wildly improbable but entertaining suspenser in which the lady finally has to assume control of an airplane.
wd Andrew Stone *ph* Fred Jackman Jnr *m* Leith Stevens
☆ Doris Day, Louis Jourdan, Barry Sullivan, Frank Lovejoy, John Gallaudet
'Some of the dialogue reaches a fine pitch of banality.' – *MFB*
⬧ Andrew Stone (as writer); title song (*m*Leith Stevens, *ly*Tom Adair)

'You've got to risk it all to get your first hit.'
Julie and the Cadillacs
GB 1997 107m colour
Capricorn/Parker Mead (John Dean, Sean O'Mahony)
In the mid 60s, a girl singer and her band move from Liverpool to London in search of stardom.
Bland 'B' movie of British pop that arrived 30 years too late to find an audience.
w John Dean *d* Bryan Izzard *ph* Les Young *m/ly* John Dean *pd* Jeremy Bear *ed* James Thomas
☆ Toyah Willcox, Victor Spinetti, Peter Polycarpou, Thora Hird, James Grout, Mike Berry, Tina Russell, Ben Richards, Billy Boyd, David Habbin, Chris O'Neill, Matt Rayner
'Starry-eyed, amateurish and endearingly bouncy.' – *Philip Kemp, Sight and Sound*

Juliet of the Spirits *
Italy/France 1965 145m Technicolor
Federiz/Francoriz (Clemente Fracassi)
⬤ 🖭 🖭
original title: *Giulietta degli Spiriti*
A bored middle-aged woman finds she can conjure up spirits who lead her into a life of sensual gratification.
A fascinating patchwork of autobiographical flashbacks, the distaff side of Eight and a Half.
w Federico Fellini, Tullio Pinnelli, Brunello Rondi, Ennio Flaiano *d* Federico Fellini *ph* Gianni di Venanzo *m* Nino Rota
☆ Giulietta Masina, Mario Pisu, Sandra Milo, Valentina Cortese, Sylva Koscina
'A kaleidoscope of fantasy, a series of cerebral inventions, of which only a few are artistically justified … an extravagant illusion, a huge confidence trick, with little new to say and an often pedantic way of saying it.' – *David Wilson, MFB*

'Greater than Ivanhoe!'
'Thrill to ruthless men and their goddess-like women in a sin-swept age!'
'Thrill to traitors and heroes, killings and conspiracies, passions and violence in Rome's most exciting age!'
Julius Caesar **
US 1953 121m bw
MGM (John Houseman)
⬤ 🖭 🖭
Cassius and Brutus lead the conspirators who murder Caesar, but are themselves routed by Mark Antony.
Straightforward, rather leaden presentation of Shakespeare's play, lit by effective moments in the acting, but the sudden change from talk to battle is not smoothed over.
wd Joseph L. Mankiewicz *ph* Joseph Ruttenberg *m* Miklos Rozsa *ad* Cedric Gibbons, Edward Carfagno

☆ John Gielgud, James Mason, Marlon Brando, Greer Garson, Deborah Kerr, Louis Calhern, Edmond O'Brien, George Macready, Michael Pate, John Hoyt, Alan Napier
⬧ art direction
⬧ best picture; Joseph Ruttenberg; Miklos Rozsa; Marlon Brando
⬧ John Gielgud; Marlon Brando

Julius Caesar
GB 1969 116m Technicolor Panavision
Commonwealth United (Peter Snell)
■ 🖭
Elementary production with a surprising number of faults and very few merits.
w Robert Furnival *d* Stuart Burge *ph* Ken Higgins *m* Michael Lewis *pd* Julia Trevelyan Oman
☆ Richard Johnson, Jason Robards Jnr, John Gielgud, Charlton Heston, Robert Vaughn, Richard Chamberlain, Diana Rigg, Jill Bennett, Christopher Lee, Alan Browning, Andrew Crawford
'Ugly, ill-spoken, ham-fisted.' – *Sight and Sound*

Jumanji *
US 1995 104m Technicolor
Columbia TriStar/Interscope/Teitler (Scott Kroopf, William Teitler)
⬤ ■ 🖭 🖭
Two children play a mysterious board game that releases after 25 years a child, now grown to be a man, who was trapped within it, together with an invasion of jungle animals.
Unsuccessful, convoluted fantasy that surprises only with its special effects of wild animals rampaging through a house and the streets of an American town.
w Jonathan Hensleigh, Greg Taylor, Jim Strain *book* Chris Van Allsburg *d* Joe Johnston *ph* Thomas Ackerman *m* James Horner *pd* James Bissell *ed* Robert Dalva *sp* Industrial Light and Magic
☆ Robin Williams, Bonnie Hunt, Kirsten Dunst, Bradley Pierce, Bebe Neuwirth, Jonathan Hyde, David Alan Grier, Patricia Clarkson, Adam Hann-Byrd
'The filmmakers re-create safari beasts with wizardly finesse but can't think of anything to do with them but zap you. The plot is cardboard Spielberg.' – *Entertainment Weekly*

Jumbo *
US 1962 124m Metrocolor Panavision
MGM (Joe Pasternak, Martin Melcher)
⬤ 🖭
aka: *Billy Rose's Jumbo*
In 1910, the daughter of the owner of a shaky circus prevents a take-over bid.
Hoary circus story with music. General effect disappointing: the elephant steals the show.
w Sidney Sheldon *play* Ben Hecht, Charles MacArthur *d* Charles Walters *ph* William H. Daniels *m/ly* Richard Rodgers, Lorenz Hart *md* George Stoll *ch* Busby Berkeley
☆ Doris Day, Jimmy Durante, Stephen Boyd, Martha Raye, Dean Jagger
† Stephen Boyd's singing was dubbed by James Joyce.
⬧ George Stoll

Jump for Glory
GB 1937 89m bw
Criterion (Douglas Fairbanks Jnr, Marcel Hellman)
US title: *When Thief Meets Thief*
Adventures of a cat burglar who accidentally kills his ex-partner.
Curious star comedy drama with pleasing scenes.
w John Meehan Jnr, Harold French *novel* Gordon MacDonnell *d* Raoul Walsh *ph* Cedric Williams
☆ Douglas Fairbanks Jnr, Valerie Hobson, Alan Hale, Edward Rigby, Barbara Everest, Jack Melford, Anthony Ireland
'Starts off at a commendable pace but doesn't carry through.' – *Variety*

Jump into Hell
US 1955 93m bw
Warner (David Weisbart)
Paratroops relieve a fort in Indo-China.
Mediocre semi-documentary war heroics.
w Irving Wallace *d* David Butler *ph* Peverell Marley *m* David Buttolph

☆ Jacques Sernas, Kurt Kasznar, Arnold Moss, Peter Van Eyck, Pat Blake

'Living in Hell and Loving It!'
Jump the Gun *
GB/South Africa 1996 124m Metrocolor
Film Four/Parallax/Xencat (Indra de Lanerolle)
Johannesburg is the destination of an oil-rig worker looking for fun and a singer hoping for work.
Slight but engaging movie of a city undergoing change, seen from the perspective of the streets.
wd Les Blair *ph* Seamus McGarvey *m* Joe Nina *pd* David Barkham *ed* Oral Norrie Ottey
☆ Baby Cele, Lionel Newton, Thulani Nyembe, Rapulana Seiphemo, Danny Keogh, Joe Nina
'Despite unevenness and not much dramatic structure, the partly improvised screenplay works well.' – *Derek Malcolm, Guardian*

Jumpin' Jack Flash
US 1986 100m DeLuxe
TCF (Lawrence Gordon-Joel Silver)
⬤ ■ 🖭
A black office worker finds herself plunged into espionage.
Tiresome, dirty-talking, would-be wild and woolly comedy which fails to establish itself.
w David H. Franzoni, J. W. Melville, Patricia Irving, Christopher Thompson *d* Penny Marshall *ph* Matthew F. Leonetti *m* Thomas Newman *pd* Robert Boyle *ed* Mark Goldblatt
☆ Whoopi Goldberg, Stephen Collins, John Wood, Carol Kane, Annie Potts, Roscoe Lee Browne

Jumping for Joy
GB 1955 88m bw
Rank/Raymond Stross
⬤
A track attendant acquires a winning greyhound and exposes a group of crooks.
Totally predictable star comedy which needs livening up.
w Jack Davies, Henry E. Blyth *d* John Paddy Carstairs *ph* Jack Cox *m* Larry Adler
☆ Frankie Howerd, Stanley Holloway, A. E. Matthews, Tony Wright, Alfie Bass, Joan Hickson, Lionel Jeffries

Jumping Jacks *
US 1952 96m bw
Paramount/Hal B. Wallis
⬤ 🖭
Two cabaret comedians join the paratroops.
Standard star farce, one of Martin and Lewis's best.
w Robert Lees, Fred Rinaldo, Herbert Baker *d* Norman Taurog *ph* Daniel L. Fapp *m* Joseph J. Lilley
☆ Dean Martin, Jerry Lewis, Mona Freeman, Robert Strauss, Don Defore

June Bride
US 1948 97m bw
Warner (Henry Blanke)
■
Two bickering reporters are sent to cover a small-town wedding.
Sloppily structured romantic farce in which nothing ever comes together.
w Ranald MacDougall *play* Feature for June by Eileen Tighe, Graeme Lorimer *d* Bretaigne Windust *ph* Ted McCord *m* David Buttolph
☆ Bette Davis, Robert Montgomery, Fay Bainter, Tom Tully, Betty Lynn, Barbara Bates, Jerome Cowan, Mary Wickes, Debbie Reynolds

June Night
Sweden 1940 90m bw
AB Svensk Filmindustri
■ 🖭
original title: *Juninatten*
Recovering from being shot by her lover, a shop assistant moves to Stockholm but cannot escape her past.
A complex examination of the power of passion and the public fascination with scandal, even though its resolution is bungled.
w Ragnar Hyltén-Cavallius *story* Tora Nordstrom-Bonnier *d* Per Lindberg *ph* Åke Dahlquist *m* Jules Sylvain, Gunnar Johansson
☆ Ingrid Bergman, Marianne Löfgren, Lill-Tollie Zellman, Marianne Aminoff, Olof Widgren, Gunnar Sjöberg

Jungfrukällan: see *The Virgin Spring*

Jungle 2 Jungle *
🏃 US 1997 105m colour
Buena Vista/Walt Disney/TF1 (Brian Reilly)
⬤ ■
A New York businessman brings back to the city his 13-year-old son, who has lived all his life in the Amazon jungle.
Mildly entertaining comedy of a father–son relationship in two differing cultures, so that each has a turn at getting things wrong.
w Bruce A. Evans, Raynold Gideon *d* John Pasquin *ph* Tony Pierce-Roberts *m* Michael Convertino *pd* Stuart Wurtzel *ed* Michael A. Stevenson *film* Un Indien dans la ville by Hervé Palud, Thierry Lhermitte, Igor Aptekman, Philippe Bruneau de la Salle
☆ Tim Allen, Martin Short, JoBeth Williams, Lolita Davidovich, Sam Huntington, David Ogden Stiers, Bob Dishy
'A warm-hearted family outing.' – *Variety*

Jungle Book *
🏃 US 1967 78m Technicolor
Walt Disney
⬤ ■ 🖭
Cartoon version relying less on action than on songs and voices; patchily successful but no classic.
d Wolfgang Reitherman *m/ly* Richard and Robert Sherman, Terry Gilkyson
☆ Featuring the voices of George Sanders, Phil Harris, Louis Prima, Sebastian Cabot, Sterling Holloway
⬧ song 'The Bare Necessities' (*m/ly* Terry Gilkyson)

'More thrilling than the deeds of man … more beautiful than the love of woman … more wonderful than the dreams of children!'
The Jungle Book *
🏃 US 1942 109m Technicolor
Alexander Korda
⬤ ■ 🖭 ⬤ 🎧
aka: *Rudyard Kipling's Jungle Book*
Growing up with animals in an Indian forest, a boy forestalls the getaway of three thieves.
High-budgeted but rather boring live action version with stiff-jointed model animals.
w Laurence Stallings *stories* Rudyard Kipling *d* Zoltan Korda, André de Toth *ph* Lee Garmes, W. Howard Greene *m* Miklos Rozsa *ad* Vincent Korda
☆ Sabu, Joseph Calleia, John Qualen, Frank Puglia, Rosemary de Camp
⬧ cinematography; Miklos Rozsa; Vincent Korda

Jungle Captive
US 1945 63m bw
Universal
A mad doctor steals the body of Paula the ape woman and restores it to life.
Arrant rubbish, a sequel to Captive Wild Woman *and* Jungle Woman.
w M. Coates Webster, Dwight V. Babcock *d* Harold Young
☆ Otto Kruger, Phil Brown, Rondo Hatton, Jerome Cowan, Amelita Ward

Jungle Fever **
US 1991 132m DuArt
UIP/Universal/Forty Acres and A Mule Filmworks (Spike Lee)
⬤ ■ 🖭 ⬤ 🎧
A black architect leaves his wife and child to live with his Italian-American secretary.
Sharply observed drama of racism and prejudice that raises more questions than it attempts to answer.
wd Spike Lee *ph* Ernest Dickerson *m* Terence Blanchard, Stevie Wonder *pd* Wynn Thomas *ed* Sam Pollard, Brunilda Torres
☆ Wesley Snipes, Annabella Sciorra, Spike Lee, Ossie Davis, Ruby Dee, Samuel L. Jackson, Lonette McKee, John Turturro, Frank Vincent, Anthony Quinn, Tim Robbins, Brad Dourif
'An inspired and very welcome return to form.' – *Empire*

Jungle Fighters: see *The Long and the Short and the Tall*

Jungle Jim
When Johnny Weissmuller began to show his middle-age spread, Columbia put him in a jacket and more or less redid his Tarzan thing in a series

of second features which appeared to be shot in producer Sam Katzman's back garden and gradually indulged in wilder and wilder plots. None of them has more than curiosity value.
1948 Jungle Jim
1949 The Lost Tribe
1950 Captive Girl, Mark of the Gorilla, Pygmy Island
1951 Fury of the Congo, Jungle Manhunt
1952 Jungle Jim in the Forbidden Land, Voodoo Tiger
1953 Savage Mutiny, Valley of the Headhunters, Killer Ape
1954 Jungle Maneaters, Cannibal Attack
1955 Jungle Moon Men, Devil Goddess
w main scriptwriters were Carroll Young, Dwight Babcock, Sam Newman d main directors William Berke, Lee Sholem, Spencer G. Bennet

'Men staked their lives for just one look at the thrilling beauty of this tiger woman!'
The Jungle Princess *
US 1936 84m bw
Paramount (E. Lloyd Sheldon)
A British hunter is injured on a tropical island and rescued by a native girl and her animal retinue.
Dorothy Lamour's first film role cast her as the female Tarzan she was to play (in a sarong, of course) a dozen times again. This is strictly a programmer, but after its success it was all done again, rather better, as Her Jungle Love.
w Cyril Hume, Gerald Geraghty, Gouverneur Morris d William Thiele ph Harry Fischbeck md Boris Morros
☆ Dorothy Lamour, Ray Milland, Akim Tamiroff, Lynne Overman, Molly Lamont, Hugh Buckler
  'Fairly palatable entertainment most of the way.' – Variety
  'Poor Mr Lynne Overman is expected to lend humorous relief to a film already richly comic.' – Graham Greene
† On this trip the tiger was Liamu and the chimp Bogo.

Jungle Woman
US 1944 54m bw
Universal
A mad doctor restores an ape to life. It turns into a beautiful woman.
Middle section of a talentless trio of which the first is Captive Wild Woman and the third Jungle Captive.
w Bernard Schubert, Henry Sucher, Edward Dein d Reginald LeBorg
☆ J. Carrol Naish, Acquanetta, Evelyn Ankers, Milburn Stone, Richard Davis, Lois Collier

'Nothing is inconceivable.'
Junior
US 1994 109m Eastmancolor
UIP/Northern Lights (Ivan Reitman)
A scientist tests a fertility drug on a male colleague, with the result that he becomes pregnant.
A less amusing reunion of the team that produced Twins, a still-born, surprisingly old-fashioned comedy with its belief that the essence of femininity resides in being helpless and hopeless, nagging and clinging; the old jokes are not always the best.
w Kevin Wade, Chris Conrad d Ivan Reitman ph Adam Greenberg m James Newton Howard pd Stephen Lineweaver ed Sheldon Kahn, Wendy Greene Bricmont
☆ Arnold Schwarzenegger, Danny DeVito, Emma Thompson, Frank Langella, Judy Collins, Pamela Reed, Aida Turturro, James Eckhouse
  'What separates this straightforward chuckler from the pack is its shrewd reliance on character rather than plot, and that human dimension proves surprisingly poignant.' – Leonard Klady
♫ song 'Look What Love Has Done'

Junior Army
US 1943 70m bw
Columbia (Colbert Clark)
An English boy goes to an American military academy.
Routine propaganda item which might almost have been titled David Copperfield Meets the Dead End Kids.
w Albert Bein, Paul Gangelin d Lew Landers
☆ Freddie Bartholomew, Billy Halop, Huntz Hall, Bobby Jordan, Don Beddoe, Peter Lawford, Boyd Davis

Junior Bonner *
US 1972 105m Movielab Todd-AO 35
ABC/Booth-Gardner/Joe Wizan/Solar
An ageing rodeo star returns to his home town and finds his family in trouble.
Well-made, rather downcast and not very interesting drama, remarkably gentle from this director.
w Jeb Rosebrook d Sam Peckinpah ph Lucien Ballard m Jerry Fielding
☆ Steve McQueen, Ida Lupino, Robert Preston, Joe Don Baker, Ben Johnson

Junior Miss *
US 1945 94m bw
TCF (William Perlberg)
A teenager causes trouble by meddling in the lives of her family.
Amusing family comedy from a hit play.
w George Seaton play Jerome Chodorov, Joseph Fields stories Sally Benson d George Seaton ph Charles Clarke m David Buttolph
☆ Peggy Ann Garner, Allyn Joslyn, Faye Marlowe, Mona Freeman, Michael Dunne, John Alexander

'A black comedy about love, money, cold canned spaghetti, karaoke, involuntary good deeds and the joy of being comatose.'
Junk Mail *
Norway 1997 79m colour
MovieMakers/Norsk Film/Atlas (Dag Nordahl, Peter Boe)
original title: Budbringeren
An inquisitive postman becomes involved in the complicated life of a young woman.
An edgy and glumly enjoyable semi-thriller, about a hapless individual out of his depth.
w Pal Sletaune, Jonny Halberg d Pal Sletaune ph Kjell Vassdal m Joachim Holbek pd Karl Juliusson ed Pal Gengenbach
☆ Robert Skjaerstad, Andrine Saether, Per Egil Aske, Eli Anne Linnestad
  'An offbeat, blackly humorous love story with a grotesque edge.' – Derek Elley, Variety

Juno and the Paycock
GB 1930 85m bw
British International (John Maxwell)
US title: The Shame of Mary Boyle
During the Irish troubles of the early twenties, tragedy comes to a poor Dublin family.
A plainly done film version of a modern classic whose changes of mood would not in any case have worked well on the screen.
w Alfred Hitchcock, Alma Reville play Sean O'Casey d Alfred Hitchcock ph Jack Cox ad Norman Arnold ed émile de Ruelle
☆ Sara Allgood, Edward Chapman, Maire O'Neill, Sidney Morgan, John Longden
  'A film which completely justifies the talkies.' – James Agate
  'Just a photograph of a stage play.' – Alfred Hitchcock

Jupiter's Darling *
US 1954 96m Eastmancolor
Cinemascope
MGM (George Wells)
Advancing on Rome, Hannibal falls in love with the dictator's fiancée.
A splendid example of the higher lunacy, with coloured elephants decorating an MGM musical about the fall of the Roman Empire. Small elements can be salvaged, and the gall is enough to be divided into three parts.
w Dorothy Kingsley play The Road to Rome by Robert E. Sherwood d George Sidney ph Paul C. Vogel, Charles Rosher m David Rose m/ly Burton Lane, Harold Adamson ch Hermes Pan ad Cedric Gibbons, Uric McCleary
☆ Esther Williams, Howard Keel, George Sanders, Marge and Gower Champion, Richard Haydn, William Demarest
  'If it had been my first picture, there wouldn't have been a second.' – Esther Williams

'An adventure 65 million years in the making.'
Jurassic Park **
US 1993 127m colour
UIP/Universal/Amblin (Kathleen Kennedy, Gerald R. Molen)
Genetically re-created from blood taken from ancient mosquitoes, dinosaurs run amok in a theme park.
The dinosaurs are amazing: living, breathing, believable creatures, which is more than you can say for the actors in this otherwise cardboard creation, hung up on toilet jokes and often seeming no more than an elongated commercial for all the merchandise associated with the movie, which includes a long, shameless pan along shelves of the toys and books available. The film was distributed with a warning that it might upset sensitive children. Sensitive adults are likely to be disappointed, too.
w Michael Crichton, David Koepp novel Michael Crichton d Steven Spielberg ph Dean Cundey m John Williams pd Rick Carter ed Michael Kahn sp Dennis Muren, Stan Winston, Phil Tippett, Pamela Easley
☆ Sam Neill, Laura Dern, Jeff Goldblum, Richard Attenborough, Bob Peck, Martin Ferrero, B. D. Wong, Joseph Mazello, Ariana Richards, Samuel L. Jackson
  'Doesn't have the imagination – or the courage – to take us any place we haven't been a thousand times before. It's just a creature feature on amphetamines.' – Terrence Rafferty, New Yorker
  'The dinosaurs are wonderful, but they aren't on the set enough of the time (yes, I know how much more they cost than human actors). Unfortunately, the plot line for the human actors reduces to pap and romantic drivel of the worst kind, the very antithesis of the book's grappling with serious themes.' – Stephen Jay Gould
† Among the many inconsistencies in the narrative, Sam Neill warns that the Tyrannosaurus Rex reacts to movement when he can have no knowledge or experience of this fact.
🏆 sound; sound effects editing; visual effects

'There Is No Defence.'
The Juror
US 1996 118m Technicolor
Columbia (Irwin Winkler, Rob Cowan)
A sculptor, intimidated by a gangster to free a killer when serving on a jury, finds herself caught between the Mob and the law.
Routine woman-in-jeopardy movie that does not even maintain a sense of suspense.
w Ted Tally book George Dawes Green d Brian Gibson ph Jamie Anderson m James Newton Howard pd Jan Roelfs ed Robert Reitano
☆ Demi Moore, Alec Baldwin, Joseph Gordon-Levitt, Anne Heche, James Gandolfini, Lindsay Crouse, Tony Lo Bianco
  'Has only a transitory impact – once seen, soon forgotten – though it does have its moments of inevitable chill.' – Tom Hutchinson, Film Review

Jury Duty
US 1995 86m Technicolor
TriStar/Triumph/Weasel (Yoran Ben-Ami, Peter M. Lenkov)
A layabout member of a jury attempts to prolong the trial of a serial killer so that he can continue to enjoy being sequestered in a luxury hotel.
Ineffably terrible comedy, a celebration of stupidity and tasteless plans.
w Neil Tolkin, Barbara Williams, Samantha Adams d John Fortenberry ph Avi Karpick m David Kitay pd Deborah Raymond ed Stephen Semel
☆ Pauly Shore, Tia Carrere, Stanley Tucci, Brian Doyle-Murray, Abe Vigoda, Charles Napier, Richard Edson, Shelley Winters, Andrew Dice Clay (uncredited)
  'Not only has the distinction of being one of the worst major studio releases of recent memory, it's also one of the most morally dubious.' – Brian Lowry, Variety

Jury's Evidence
GB 1935 71m bw
British Lion (Herbert Smith)
The jury in a murder trial disagrees.
Courtroom drama with an unsatisfactory finish.

w Ian Dalrymple play Jack de Leon, Jack Celestin d Ralph Ince ph George Stretton
☆ Hartley Power, Margaret Lockwood, Nora Swinburne, Sebastian Shaw

The Jury's Secret
US 1937 64m bw
Universal
The guilty man in a murder case is on the jury.
Slow-moving courtroom drama with an unsatisfactory twist.
w Lester Cole, Newman Levy d Edward Sloman
☆ Kent Taylor, Fay Wray, Jane Darwell, Nan Grey, Larry Blake, Fritz Leiber
  'Doomed for no honours such as b.o.' – Variety

Just a Gigolo
US 1931 71m bw
MGM
A young lord masquerades as a gigolo to avoid being the prey of gold diggers.
Slackly handled comedy which doesn't come off.
w Hans Kraly, Richard Schayer, Claudine West d Jack Conway
☆ William Haines, Irene Purcell, C. Aubrey Smith, Lillian Bond
  'Too much talk, too little action.' – Variety

Just a Gigolo
West Germany 1978 147m colour
Leguan (Rolf Thiele)
A young Prussian veteran of World War 1 intends to succeed, but stumbles through the Berlin underworld and is accidentally shot in a street skirmish.
An international misadventure whose English version is not only interminable and badly dubbed but extremely clumsily made.
w Ennio de Concini, Joshua Sinclair d David Hemmings ph Charly Steinberger m Gunther Fischer pd Peter Rothe
☆ David Bowie, Sydne Rome, Kim Novak, Marlene Dietrich, David Hemmings, Maria Schell, Curt Jurgens, Erika Pluhar
  'It often goes for laughs it hasn't a hope of getting; sometimes it aspires to tragic dignity and looks truly inept. It would be kinder to yourself and to everybody involved to overlook it.' – Time Out

Just Across the Street
US 1952 78m bw
Universal-International/Leonard Goldstein
Complications arise when a plumber's secretary pretends to be rich.
Silly and pointless comedy which provides its talent with nothing to do.
w Roswell Rogers, Joel Malone d Joseph Pevney ph Maury Gertsman ed Virgil Vogel
☆ Ann Sheridan, John Lund, Robert Keith, Cecil Kellaway, Harvey Lembeck, Natalie Schafer, Alan Mowbray

'If you think you know her, think again.'
Just Another Girl on the I.R.T.
US 1992 97m colour
Metro Tartan/Miramax/Truth 24 F.P.S. (Erwin Wilson)
A 17-year-old rebellious black Brooklyn girl with aspirations to be a doctor becomes pregnant by a boy she meets at a party.
A sympathetic portrait of a teenager refusing to come to terms with reality, brightly performed but hampered by a script that sticks to the obvious and settles for an easy resolution.
wd Leslie Harris ph Richard Connors m Eric Sadler, Willie Bruno II pd Michael O'Dell Green ed Jack Haigis
☆ Ariyan A. Johnson, Kevin Thigpen, Ebony Jerido, Jerard Washington, Chequita Jackson
  'A crude but disturbing exposé of teenage ignorance and denial about the facts of life on the streets and in the bedroom.' – Variety
  'The movie's only strong point is its sharp and zappy cast. But hazy vision finally saps even their energy – just as the pasted-on happy ending mocks their efforts to keep things real.' – Cynthia Rose, Sight and Sound

---

🏫 film suitable for family viewing 　　📺 VHS video-cassette for the British PAL system 　　📺 VHS video-cassette for the British PAL system in wide screen-format 　　💱 Video cassette in a computer-colourised version 　　▬ American NTSC video-cassette 　　◉ Laser disc

Just Around the Corner

👥 US 1938 70m bw
TCF (David Hempstead)
📺

A little girl helps her dad to get on in business.
Tedious Little Miss Fixit tale from the period when Shirley's star was sliding.
w Ethel Hill, J. P. McEvoy, Darrell Ware d Irving Cummings ph Arthur Miller md Louis Silvers
☆ Shirley Temple, Charles Farrell, Bert Lahr, Joan Davis, Amanda Duff, Bill Robinson, Franklin Pangborn, Cora Witherspoon

'Top flight for general all-round entertainment.' – *Variety*

Just Before Dawn

US 1980 90m Movielab
Oakland

Visitors to a mountain area are terrorized by a cleaver-wielding killer.
Teenage shocker with just a little more style than most.
w Mark Arywitz, Gregg Irving d Jeff Lieberman
☆ George Kennedy, Mike Kellin, Chris Lemmon, Gregg Henry, Deborah Benson

Just Between Friends

US 1986 120m DeLuxe
Orion/MTM (Edward Teets, Allan Burns)
📺

A middle-aged woman finds little excitement in her household, and fancies a lesbian relationship; but her husband dies and she finds herself pregnant.
Ho-hum melodrama of our time.
wd Allan Burns ph Jordan Cronenweth m Patrick Williams pd Sydney Z. Litwack
☆ Mary Tyler Moore, Ted Danson, Christine Lahti, Sam Waterston, Salome Jens

'The main difference between this and a TV movie is that this doesn't have commercials.' – *Variety*

'Buried deep in the Florida Everglades is a secret that can save an innocent man or let a killer kill again.'

Just Cause

US 1995 colour
Warner/Fountainbridge (Lee Rich, Arne Glimcher, Steve Perry)
📀 🎧 🎧

A Harvard law professor goes to Florida to prove that a black youth awaiting execution for murder is innocent, accompanied by the detective who he claims beat him into confessing to the crime.
Lacklustre thriller that becomes increasingly silly and derivative the longer it lasts, so that it exhausts patience and credibility long before the end.
w Jeb Stuart, Peter Stone novel John Katzenbach d Arne Glimcher ph Lajos Koltai m James Newton Howard pd Patrizia von Brandenstein ed William Anderson
☆ Sean Connery, Laurence Fishburne, Kate Capshaw, Blair Underwood, Ruby Dee, Ed Harris, Christopher Murray, Daniel J. Travanti, Ned Beatty, Scarlett Johansson

'We watch a passable investigative thriller spiral into an absurd, ineffectual melodrama.' – *Geoff Brown, The Times*

Just for You

US 1952 104m Technicolor
Paramount (Pat Duggan)

A successful songwriter finds that his troublesome teenage son is in love with his own fiancée.
Tiresomely scripted, pleasantly played romantic comedy with music.
w Robert Carson novel Famous by Stephen Vincent Benet d Elliott Nugent ph George Barnes m Hugo Friedhofer m/ly Harry Warren, Leo Robin md Emil Newman
☆ Bing Crosby, Jane Wyman, Bob Arthur, Ethel Barrymore, Natalie Wood, Cora Witherspoon, Regis Toomey
♫ song 'Zing a Little Zong'

Just Heroes

Hong Kong 1989 96m colour
Magnum (Tsui Hark)
📼

When a gang leader is assassinated, a power struggle begins among surviving members to succeed him and discover the identity of his killer.
A movie that grows misty-eyed and sentimental about ruthless killers; admirers of John Woo may enjoy the final shoot-out, with its jokey references to A Better Tomorrow (a film that all the best gangsters have evidently seen).
w Nieh Kuang, Tommy Hau d John Woo, Wu Ma ph Chu Wai Ki, Yee Tung Lung m Romeo Diaz, James Wong ad Ringo Cheung, Andy Lee ed Choi Hung
☆ John Chiang, Danny Lee, Chan Kwon Tai, Kelly Chu, Cally Kwong, Wu Ma, Ti Lung, Chiu Lui

Just Imagine

US 1930 102m bw
Fox

A man who dies in 1930 is revived in 1980 and can't get used to the pace of life.
Famous oddity which doesn't live up to its reputation and can now be seen as hampered by poor sets, script and acting. Futuristic sets are few but choice.
d David Butler ph Ernest Palmer m Hugo Friedhofer md Arthur Kay ch Seymour Felix ad Stephen Goosson, Ralph Hammeras w/songs De Sylva, Brown, Henderson
☆ El Brendel, Maureen O'Sullivan, John Garrick, Frank Albertson, Marjorie White, Hobart Bosworth, Mischa Auer, Wilfred Lucas

'Needs to be sold in advance on its novelty angle … it seems essential that something be done to make them say "Go down and take a look at that crazy picture".' – *Variety*
⚒ art direction

Just Like a Woman

GB 1966 89m Eastmancolor
Dormar (Bob Kellett)

A TV director's wife leaves him and gets ideas above her station.
Curious comedy which aims at sophistication but starts flagging in the first five minutes. Familiar performers just about keep it afloat.
wd Bob Fuest ph Billy Williams m Ken Napper
☆ Wendy Craig, Francis Matthews, John Wood, Dennis Price, Miriam Karlin, Peter Jones, Clive Dunn, Ray Barrett

'She stole his heart. He stole her clothes.'

Just Like a Woman

GB 1992 106m Eastmancolor
Rank/Zenith/LWT/British Screen (Nick Evans)
📀 🎧

An American living in London moves into lodgings after his wife throws him out, and reveals to his landlady that he is a transvestite.
Tedious comedy of minimal interest, even to cross-dressers.
w Nick Evans novel Geraldine, for the Love of a Transvestite by Monica Jay d Christopher Monger ph Alan Hume m Michael Storey pd John Box ed Nicolas Gaster
☆ Julie Walters, Adrian Pasdar, Paul Freeman, Susan Wooldridge, Gordon Kennedy, Ian Redford, Shelley Thompson

'The film remains poky, parochial, and its message is clear – no sex, please, we're British.' – *Geoff Brown, The Times*
'A tepid comedy of Anglo-Saxon inhibition.' – *Philip French, Observer*

Just My Luck

GB 1957 86m bw
Rank (Hugh Stewart)

A jeweller's assistant becomes involved in horse racing.
Flat star vehicle.
w Alfred Shaughnessy d John Paddy Carstairs

ph Jack Cox m Philip Green
☆ Norman Wisdom, Jill Dixon, Leslie Phillips, Margaret Rutherford, Delphi Lawrence

Just Off Broadway

US 1942 66m bw
TCF/Sol M. Wurtzel

Michael Shayne investigates a court case on which he is sitting as a juror.
Standard second feature mystery, reasonably well made.
w Arnaud D'Usseau d Herbert I. Leeds
☆ Lloyd Nolan, Marjorie Weaver, Phil Silvers, Janis Carter, Richard Derr, Chester Clute

Just Tell Me What You Want

US 1980 112m Technicolor
Warner/Jay Presson Allen, Sidney Lumet
📺

A powerful tycoon starts to weave plots when one of his harem wants to go independent.
Thoroughly silly melodrama with a few incidental humours.
w Jay Presson Allen novel Jay Presson Allen d Sidney Lumet ph Oswald Morris m Charles Strouse pd Tony Walton
☆ Ali MacGraw, Alan King, Myrna Loy, Keenan Wynn, Tony Roberts, Dina Merrill, Peter Weller

'Jay Presson Allen has adapted her trashy novel into a trashy picture … Myrna Loy looks as if she's constantly amazed at the kinds of films getting made these days, and she's absolutely right.' – *Variety*

'In love, you can't accept anything at face value.'

Just the Ticket

US 1998 115m DeLuxe
Entertainment/CineSon (Gary Lucchesi, Andy Garcia)
🎧

In order to impress his girlfriend, a tout tries to corner the market in tickets for the Pope's Mass at Yankee Stadium.
Gritty romantic comedy with no spark between its stars, and not much comedy either.
wd Richard Wenk ph Ellen Kuras m Rick Marotta pd Franckie Diago ed Christopher Cibelli
☆ Andy Garcia, Andie MacDowell, Richard Bradford, Laura Harris, Andre Blake, Elizabeth Ashley, Patrick Breen, Fred Asparagus, Louis Mustillo, Ron Leibman, Chris Lemmon, Don Novello, Abe Vigoda, Irene Worth

'Even though his performance is passable, the only real romance on show in this vanity vehicle is Garcia's love affair with himself.' – *Total Film*

Just the Way You Are

US 1984 95m Metrocolor
MGM-UA (Leo L. Fuchs)
📺

A young fluteplayer tries to carve a career for herself while overcoming a physical disability.
Odd little comedy-drama with little plot beyond the central character's crippled leg; not likely to make much headway.
w Allan Burns d Edouard Molinaro ph Claude Lecomte m Vladimir Cosmar ad François de Lamotte ed Claudio Ventura, Georges Klotz
☆ Kristy McNichol, Michael Ontkean, Kaki Hunter, André Dussolier, Robert Carradine

Just William

👥 GB 1939 94m bw
Associated British (Walter C. Mycroft)

William, hunting for bomb-carrying spies, foils a con man and helps his father in his campaign to become a local councillor.
The first and best of the William series, with a good cast and a genuine feeling for children's fantasy and anarchy.
w Graham Cutts, Doreen Montgomery, Ireland Wood novel Richmal Crompton d Graham Cutts ph Walter Harvey ad Cedric Dawe ed E. B. Jarvis

☆ Fred Emney, Basil Radford, Iris Hoey, Amy Veness, Dicky Lupino, Roddy McDowall, Norman Robinson, Peter Miles, Jenny Laird, David Tree

Just William's Luck

👥 GB 1947 85m bw
Alliance (James Carter)

William tries to marry off his brother so that he can inherit his bicycle, and succeeds in foiling a gang of smugglers.
Limp comedy that fails to translate to the screen the verbal exuberance and mayhem of the novels.
wd Val Guest novel Richmal Crompton ph Bert Mason m Robert Farnon ad Harry Moore ed Anne Barker
☆ William Graham, Leslie Bradley, Garry Marsh, Jane Walsh, Hugh Cross, Kathleen Stuart, Muriel Aked, Joan Hickson, A. E. Matthews
† It was followed by a sequel, *William at the Circus* (qv).

Just You and Me, Kid

US 1979 93m Metrocolor
Columbia/Irving Fein-Jerome M. Zeitman

An elderly comedian reluctantly takes care of a naked teenager on the run from a dope pusher.
Virtually a one-set comedy which quickly tires the eye and ear; not a good idea despite the veteran star.
w Oliver Hailey, Leonard Stern d Leonard Stern ph David Walsh m Jack Elliott
☆ George Burns, Brooke Shields, Burl Ives, Lorraine Gary, John Schuck, Keye Luke, Leon Ames, Ray Bolger, Carl Ballantine

Justice Est Faite *

France 1950 105m bw
Silver Films

The personal lives of jurors in a mercy killing case affect their verdict.
Absorbing courtroom drama with a message.
w Charles Spaak, André Cayatte d André Cayatte ph Jean Bourgoin m Raymond Legrand
☆ Valentine Tessier, Claude Nollier, Jacques Castelot, Michel Auclair

Justice for Sale: see *Night Court*

Justine

US 1969 116m DeLuxe Panavision
TCF/Pandro S. Berman
📺 🎧

In Alexandria in the thirties, the beautiful wife of a wealthy banker influences the lives of all who meet her.
Disastrous condensed version of a very unusual set of novels whose atmosphere has not translated at all well. The result is like a bad rehearsal for a film, which is not surprising in view of the number of producers variously involved. The author feared 'a sort of Peyton Place with camels', and got it.
w Lawrence B. Marcus novels The Alexandria Quartet by Lawrence Durrell d George Cukor ph Leon Shamroy m Jerry Goldsmith
☆ Anouk Aimée, Michael York, Dirk Bogarde, Anna Karina, John Vernon, George Baker, Philippe Noiret, Robert Forster, Jack Albertson, Michael Dunn, Barry Morse, Cliff Gorman, Severn Darden

'Could well stand as a model of what can happen when Hollywood gets to grips with a celebrated literary property.' – *David Wilson*
'Despite leaden forays into homosexuality, transvestitism, incest, and child prostitution, it remains as naively old-fashioned in its emotional and intellectual vocabulary as in its actual verbiage and cinematic technique.' – *John Simon*
† The film is said to have been eight years in preparation. Joseph Strick was fired as director when the cast and crew returned to Los Angeles after shooting exteriors in Tunisia. Cukor, reported Michael York, 'made his disapproval of some of his inherited cast quite unambiguous. At the mention of our leading lady his face would flush.'

K

K2
US 1991 111m Technicolor
Entertainment/TransPacific/Majestic (Jonathan Taplin, Marilyn Weiner, Tim Van Rellim)
⬚ ▤ ⚬~ ∩

Two friends join an ill-assorted expedition to climb the Himalayan mountain K2.
A tame buddy-buddy movie that has nowhere to go but down.
w Patrick Myers, Scott Roberts *play* Patrick Myers d Franc Roddam ph Gabriel Beristain m Chaz Jankel pd Andrew Sanders ed Sean Barton
☆ Michael Biehn, Matt Craven, Raymond J. Barry, Hiroshi Fujioka, Luca Bercovici, Patricia Charbonneau, Julia Nickson-Soul, Jamal Shah
'Begins as mindlessly as it means to – and does – go on.' – *Sight and Sound*
'On this evidence, climbing K2 can't be any harder than sitting through it.' – *Kim Newman, Empire*

K-9
US 1988 102m DeLuxe
UIP/Universal (Lawrence Gordon, Charles Gordon)
⬚ ▤ ⚬~

A narcotics cop teams up with an Alsatian.
A not-so-shaggy dog story with a couple of laughs.
w Steven Siegel, Scott Myers d Rod Daniel ph Dean Semler m Miles Goodman pd George Costello ed Lois Freeman-Fox
☆ James Belushi, Mel Harris, Kevin Tighe, Ed O'Neill, Jerry Lee, James Handy, Daniel Davis, Cotter Smith, John Snyder, Pruitt Taylor Vince

K9000
US 1989 90m colour
Fries Entertainment (J. Rickley Dunn)

A cop teams up with a cybernetic dog to bust a crime syndicate.
Witless compendium of action picture clichés.
w Steven E. de Souza, Michael Part d Kim Manners ph Frank Raymond m Jan Hammer pd Elliott Gilbert ed J. P. Farrell
☆ Chris Mulkey, Catherine Oxenberg, Dennis Haysbert, Dana Gladstone, Jerry Houser, Judson Scott, Anne Haney, Thom McFadden

Kàdisbellan: see *The Slingshot*

Kafka *
US/France 1991 98m bw/colour
Guild/Renn/Baltimore/Pricel (Stuart Cornfeld, Harry Benn)
⬚ ▤ ⚬~ ∩

A timid insurance clerk finds himself drawn into an anarchist plot when he investigates the disappearance of a friend.
An intriguing attempt to create a paranoid fiction combining elements of Kafka's life and his stories; it is stylish though not entirely successful, closer to the basics of a horror movie than to its author's works.
w Lem Dobbs d Steven Soderbergh ph Walt Lloyd m Cliff Martinez pd Gavin Bocquet ed Steven Soderbergh
☆ Jeremy Irons, Theresa Russell, Joel Grey, Ian Holm, Jeroen Krabbé, Armin Mueller-Stahl, Alec Guinness, Brian Glover, Robert Flemyng
'Soderbergh's film has few surprises because he sticks too matter-of-factly to Kafka basics, where others have spun out their own distinctive take.' – *Nick James, Sight and Sound*
'Soderbergh's most entertaining, least pretentious film to date, this is weirdly recommended.' – *Kim Newman, Empire*

Kagemusha ***
Japan 1980 179m Eastmancolor
TCF/Toho (Akira Kurosawa)
⬚ ▤ ⚬~
aka: *The Double*
aka: *Shadow Warrior*

On the death of a clan chief his place is taken by the lookalike hired to overlook battlefields while the chief is really busy elsewhere.
Fascinating Japanese epic centring on stately ritual and court intrigue, with the occasional battle for spectacular action; one of the director's most impressive works.
w Akira Kurosawa, Masato Ide d Akira Kurosawa ph Kazuo Miyagawa, Asakazu Nakai m Shinichiro Ikebe ad Yoshiro Muraki
☆ Tatsuya Nakadai, Tsutomu Yamazaki, Kenichi Hagiwara, Kota Yui, Hideo Murata, Takayuki Shiho, Shuhei Sugimori, Noboru Shimizu
🏅 best foreign film; art direction
🎬 direction; costume design

Kakushi Toride No San-Akunin: see *The Hidden Fortress*

El Kalaa *
Algeria 1988 98m Eastmancolor
Metro/Le Centre Algérien de l'Art et l'Industrie Cinématographique (Tahar Harhoura)
aka: *The Citadel*

A merchant runs into opposition when he decides to take a fourth wife.
Successful on the level of a village soap opera.
wd Mohamed Chouikh ph Allel Yahyaoui ad Zerrouki Boukhari, Ahmed Kobbi ed Yamina Chouikh
☆ Khaled Barkat, Djillali Ain Tedelles, Fettouma Ousliha, Fatima Belhadj, Momo

'The switched-on thriller!!!'
Kaleidoscope *
GB 1966 103m Technicolor
Warner/Winkast (Elliott Kastner)
reissue title: *The Bank Breaker*

An American playboy breaks into a playing card factory and marks the designs so that he can win in every European casino.
Would-be swinging comedy-thriller which in fact is entertaining only when it stops trying to dazzle.
w Robert and Jane Howard-Carrington d Jack Smight ph Christopher Challis m Stanley Myers ad Maurice Carter
☆ Warren Beatty, Susannah York, Clive Revill, Eric Porter, Murray Melvin
'A "groovie movie" it certainly is, with a battery of fashionable camera tricks, kaleidoscopic dissolves, and virtually every scene introduced from behind an irrelevant piece of furniture.' – *David Wilson*

'Fear Never Travels Alone.'
Kalifornia
US 1993 118m DeLuxe Cinemascope
Rank/Propaganda/Polygram/Viacom (Tim Clawson)
⬚ ▤
aka: *They Loved Life*

A couple driving across America to write about and photograph sites of murders unwittingly have as travelling companions a killer and his girlfriend.
An unlovely road movie, simultaneously violent and smug – and too knowing for its own good.
w Tim Metcalfe d Dominic Sena ph Bojan Bazelli m Carter Burwell pd Michael White ed Martin Hunter
☆ Brad Pitt, Juliette Lewis, David Duchovny, Michelle Forbes, Sierra Pecheur, Gregory Mars Martin
'An extremely handsome production imbued with a chilling surrealistic sensibility.' – *Variety*
'Looks a treat, tells what ought to be a fascinating story but ends up wallowing in its own pretensions.' – *Derek Malcolm, Guardian*

'Submit to love and feel the pain of too much tenderness.'
Kama Sutra
India/GB/Japan/Germany 1996 114m Technicolor
Film Four/Rasa/NDF/Pony Canyon/Pandora/Mirabai (Mira Nair, Lydia Dean Pilcher)
⬚ ▤ ⚬~

In 16th-century India, a servant girl seeks sexual freedom after she is cast out of the court for seducing the king just before his marriage to her childhood friend.
Exotic settings and beautiful women fail to enliven a dull movie, peopled by cardboard characters mouthing romantic clichés.
w Helena Kriel, Mira Nair d Mira Nair ph Declan Quinn m Mark Friedberg ed Kristina Boden
☆ Naveen Andrews, Sarita Choudhury, Ramon Tikaram, Rekha, Indira Varma, Pearl Padamsee, Arundhati Rao
'Reactionary soft-core erotica that could be sold as "Emmanuelle Goes to Bollywood".' – *Philip French, Observer*

Kameradschaft *
Germany 1931 92m bw
Nerofilm
aka: *Comradeship*

On the Franco-German border French miners are imprisoned below ground and Germans burrow to free them.
Salutary message film with good dramatic pointing.
w Laszlo Vajda, Karl Otten, Peter Martin Lampel d G. W. Pabst ph Fritz Arno Wagner, Robert Baberski
☆ Ernst Busch, Alexander Granach, Fritz Kampers, Gustav Puttjer

Kamikaze
France 1986 89m Eastmancolor
Cinemascope
Blue Dolphin/Les Films du Loup/ARP/Gaumont (Luc Besson)

An electronics engineer develops a deadly weapon that can kill anyone appearing live on television.
Weak thriller that fails to make anything of its silly central concept.
w Luc Besson, Didier Grousset d Didier Grousset ph Jean-François Robin m Eric Serra ed Olivier Mauffroy
☆ Richard Bohringer, Michel Galabru, Dominique Lavanant, Riton Leibman, Kim Massée, Harry Cleven, Romane Bohringer, Etienne Chicot, Philippe Girard
'When the action stops and the talking starts, the amiable triviality of the whole exercise becomes tediously apparent.' – *Philip Strick, MFB*

Kanal *
Poland 1956 97m bw
Film Polski (Stanislaw Adler)
⬚ ▤
aka: *They Loved Life*

In 1944, an anti-Nazi resistance group is trapped in a sewer.
A suffocatingly unpleasant film to watch; its message and technical excellence are undoubted.
w Jerzy Stawinski *novel* Kloakerne by Jerzy Stawinski d Andrzej Wajda ph Jerzy Lipman m Jan Krenz
☆ Teresa Izewska, Tadeusz Janczar, Emil Kariewicz, Wienczylaw Glinski

Kanchenjungha **
India 1962 102m colour
NCA Productions

During an afternoon on holiday in Darjeeling, a domineering father tries to arrange his daughter's marriage to an older, eligible bachelor.

Leisurely examination of attitudes to love and marriage and of the relationship between the sexes. It was Ray's first film in colour.
wd Satyajit Ray ph Subrata Mitra m Satyajit Ray ad Bansi Chandragupta ed Dulal Dutta
☆ Chhabi Biswas, Anil Chatterjee, Karuna Banerjee, Anubha Gupta, Subrata Sen, Sibani Singh, Alaknanda Roy, Arun Mukherjee, N. Viswanathan
'Under the primitive working circumstances, the story about love and ambition and the collision of cultures was perhaps too complex, but the setting and the beautiful women help to compensate for the awkwardness and naiveté.' – *Pauline Kael*

Kangaroo
US 1952 84m Technicolor
TCF (Robert Bassler)

In old Australia, a con man pretends to be a rancher's long-lost heir, then complicates things by falling in love with the rancher's daughter.
Standard romantic action hokum.
w Harry Kleiner d Lewis Milestone ph Charles G. Clarke m Sol Kaplan
☆ Maureen O'Hara, Peter Lawford, Finlay Currie, Richard Boone, Chips Rafferty, Charles Tingwell

Kangaroo *
Australia 1987 110m colour Panavision
Ross Dimsey
⬚ ▤

After the First World War, an English writer and his German-born wife decide to settle in Australia, where they become involved with the leader of a secret fascist organization, who plans to become the country's dictator.
Effective treatment of Lawrence's semi-autobiographical novel, attacking what he saw as England's cultural decline, with Friels's performance based firmly upon the personality of its author.
w Evan Jones *novel* D. H. Lawrence d Tim Burstall ph Dan Burstall m Nathan Waks pd Tracy Watt ed Edward McQueen-Mason
☆ Colin Friels, Judy Davis, Hugh Keays-Byrne, John Walton, Julie Nihill, Peter Hehir, Peter Cummins
† The film was made in 1985 and not released for two years.

'I'll make this town keep the peace – if I have to blow it to pieces!'
The Kansan
US 1943 79m bw
UA (Harry Sherman)
▤

A wandering marksman stops off to become marshal of a frontier town.
Solid routine Western with good performances.
w Harold Shumate *book* Frank Gruber d George Archainbaud m Gerard Carbonara
☆ Richard Dix, Albert Dekker, Jane Wyatt, Eugene Pallette, Victor Jory, Robert Armstrong, Clem Bevans, Hobart Cavanaugh, Willie Best
♫ Gerard Carbonara

Kansas
US 1988 106m colour
Cannon/Trans World Entertainment (George Litto)
⬚ ▤

A drifter falls foul of a crook and in love with a farmer's daughter.
Well-photographed wide open spaces that are empty of interest.
w Spencer Eastman d David Stevens ph David Eggby m Pino Donaggio pd Matthew Jacobs ed Robert Barrere
☆ Andrew McCarthy, Matt Dillon, Leslie Hope, Brent Jennings, Kyra Sedgwick, Harry Northup, Arlen Dean Snyder

---

⚧ film suitable for family viewing ⬚ VHS video-cassette for the British PAL system ▤ VHS video-cassette for the British PAL system in wide screen-format ✿ Video cassette in a computer-colourised version ▤ American NTSC video-cassette ⚬~ Laser disc

Kansas City *

US 1996 115m CFI color
Electric/Sandcastle 5/CiBy 2000 (Robert Altman)
▢▢ ▦ ◷. ◯

The wife of a petty thief, who is being held captive by a powerful gangster, kidnaps a politician's drug-addicted wife in a bid to get her husband released.
Muddled story of power and corruption in Kansas City of the 30s, though admirers of the blues-tinged jazz of the period will appreciate the wonderful music on display.
w Robert Altman, Frank Barhydt d Robert Altman ph Oliver Stapleton m John Cale pd Stephen Altman ed Geraldine Peroni
☆ Jennifer Jason Leigh, Miranda Richardson, Harry Belafonte, Michael Murphy, Dermot Mulroney, Steve Buscemi
'The film-making seems almost careless, and often perfunctory, as if Altman's memories – a mixture of fond nostalgia and his usual acerbic irony – aren't quite clear enough for the deal in hand.' – *Derek Malcolm, Guardian*

Kansas City Bomber

US 1972 99m Metrocolor
MGM/Levy-Gardner-Laven/Raquel Welch (Marty Elfand)
A roller skating star finds time between affairs to beat her rival in a big match.
Vulgar melodrama with good action scenes.
w Thomas Rickman, Calvin Clements d Jerrold Freedman ph Fred Koenekamp m Don Ellis
☆ Raquel Welch, Kevin McCarthy, Norman Alden, Jeanne Cooper

Kansas City Confidential

US 1952 98m bw
United Artists/Edward Small
▦

GB title: *The Secret Four*
An ex-detective plans a perfect crime, and recruits three confederates who all remain unknown to each other by wearing masks.
Moderately lively if violent thriller which gets less inventive as it goes along but satisfies the action buffs.
w George Bruce, Harry Essex d Phil Karlson ph George Diskant m Paul Sawtell
☆ Preston Foster, John Payne, Coleen Gray, Lee Van Cleef, Neville Brand, Jack Elam, Dona Drake

Kansas City Princess

US 1934 64m bw
Warner (Lou Edelman)
Gold diggers go to Paris.
Light farce comedy, somewhat lacking in punch.
w Sy Bartlett, Manuel Seff d William Keighley
☆ Joan Blondell, Glenda Farrell, Hugh Herbert, Robert Armstrong, Osgood Perkins, Hobart Cavanaugh
'Just a comedy, good for better than moderate biz.' – *Variety*

Kansas Raiders

US 1951 80m Technicolor
Universal-International
During the Civil War, Jesse James joins Quantrill's Raiders.
Fast-moving, fairly violent Western only remotely based on fact.
w Robert L. Richards d Ray Enright ph Irving Glassberg m Joseph Gershenson
☆ Audie Murphy, Brian Donlevy, Marguerite Chapman, Scott Brady, Tony Curtis, Richard Arlen, James Best, Richard Long

Kaos **

Italy 1984 188m Eastmancolor
RAI-TV/Filmtre (Giuliano de Negri)
◯
Five stories by Pirandello are combined in settings near his birthplace.
Generally fascinating mixture of tales which range from comedy to horror, styled by master film-makers.
wd Paolo and Vittorio Taviani ph Giuseppe Lanci m Nicola Piovani ed Roberto Perignani
☆ Margarita Lozano, Claudio Bigagli, Enrica Maria Modugno, Ciccio Ingrassia, Franco Franchi, Biagio Barone, Omero Antonutti

Kapo

Italy/France 1960 115m bw
Vides/Zebra/Francinex
A French Jewess survives the horrors of a Nazi concentration camp and becomes camp guard.

Curious exploitation piece which turns tragedy into melodrama, and doesn't even do that with much flair.
w Franco Solinas, Gillo Pontecorvo d Gillo Pontecorvo ph Goffredo Bellisario, Alexander Sekulovic m Carlo Rustichelli
☆ Susan Strasberg, Laurent Terzieff, Emmanuelle Riva
⚜ best foreign film

Karakter: see *Character*

The Karate Kid *

🏃🏃 US 1984 127m Metrocolor
Columbia/Delphi II (Jerry Weintraub)
▢▢ ▦ ◷. ◯
A teenage boy, new to California, joins a karate club and defeats the local bullies.
A kind of amateur Rocky, not bad in its way, but its huge commercial success in the US remains mystifying.
w Robert Mark Kamen d John G. Avildsen ph James Crabe m Bill Conti pd William J. Cassidy ed Bud Smith, Walt Mulconery
☆ Ralph Macchio, Noriyuki 'Pat' Morita, Elisabeth Shue, Martin Kove, Randee Heller, William Zabka
⚜ Pat Morita (supporting actor)

Karate Kid III

🏃🏃 US 1989 112m DeLuxe
Columbia TriStar (Jerry Weintraub)
▢▢ ▦ ◷. ◯
The karate kid defeats villains who attempt to humiliate him.
Even less interesting than Part II.
w Robert Mark Kamen d John G. Avildsen ph Stephen Yaconelli m Bill Conti pd William F. Matthews ed John Carter, John G. Avildsen
☆ Ralph Macchio, Noriyuki 'Pat' Morita, Robyn Lively, Thomas Ian Griffith, Martin L. Kove, Sean Kanan, Jonathan Avildsen
'Young love, meanwhile, has rarely been shown so boringly on screen.' – *MFB*

The Karate Kid Part II

🏃🏃 US 1986 113m DeLuxe
Columbia/Delphi II (Jerry Weintraub)
▢▢ ▦ ◷.
Daniel's teacher heads back to Okinawa where his father is gravely ill.
Tedious attempt to spin out a surprise hit; no surprises this time.
w Robert Mark Kamen d John G. Avildsen ph James Crabe m Bill Conti pd William J. Cassidy ed David Garfield, Jane Kurson, John G. Avildsen
☆ Pat Morita, Ralph Macchio, Nobu McCarthy, Danny Kamekona
⚜ song 'Glory of Love'

The Karate Killers

US 1967 90m Metrocolor
MGM/Arena (Boris Ingster)
The men from U.N.C.L.E. foil enemy agents who steal a formula for making gold out of sea water.
Comic-strip spy spoof, featuring two incompetent agents who are forever being knocked out by the opposition, even when it's no stronger than geisha girls; a starry cast is given very little to do.
w Norman Hudis story Boris Ingster d Barry Shear ph Fred Koenekamp m Richard Shores ad George W. Davis
☆ Robert Vaughn, David McCallum, Joan Crawford, Curt Jurgens, Telly Savalas, Herbert Lom, Terry Thomas, Leo G. Carroll, Kim Darby, Diane McBain
† The film was edited from episodes of the television series *The Man from U.N.C.L.E.*

Käre John: see *Dear John*

Kaspar Hauser

Germany 1993 139m colour
Arrow/Multimedia
München/WDR/ORF/SVT/ARTE/Telepool/LFA (Andreas Meyer)
◯
original title: *Verbrechen am Seelenleben eines Menschens*
The heir to the throne of Baden becomes a pawn in a European power struggle; he is imprisoned for years, set free when he is unable to talk, but is still unable to escape his enemies.
A complex political drama that overwhelms the human interest of its story; it pales in comparison with Werner Herzog's The Enigma of Kaspar Hauser (qv).

wd Peter Sehr ph Gernot Roll m Nikos Mamangakis ad O. Jochen Schmidt, Karel Vacek ed Heidi Handorf, Susanne Hartmann
☆ André Eisermann, Udo Samel, Jeremy Clyde, Katharina Thalbach, Cécile Paoli, Hansa Czypionka, Dieter Mann
'It ends up as *Dynasty* in funny wigs, although much cruder, submerging the fascinating story at its core with coarse couplings and obscure plot points.' – *Tom Shone, Sunday Times*
† It was originally shown in a version that ran for 182m.

Kate Plus Ten

GB 1938 81m bw
Wainwright (Richard Wainwright)
A police inspector falls for the attractive female leader of a bullion gang.
Curious comedy thriller with insufficient of either commodity.
w Jack Hulbert, Jeffrey Dell novel Edgar Wallace d Reginald Denham ph Roy Kellino m Allan Gray ad D. L. W. Daniels ed E. M. Hunter
☆ Jack Hulbert, Genevieve Tobin, Noel Madison, Francis L. Sullivan, Arthur Wontner, Frank Cellier, Googie Withers, Peter Haddon, Felix Aylmer, Leo Genn, Edward Lexy

Kathleen

US 1941 88m bw MGM (George Haight)
A neglected daughter finds a new wife for her widowed father.
One of the reasons for Shirley Temple's early retirement.
w Mary McCall Jnr story Kay Van Riper d Harold S. Bucquet ph Sidney Wagner m Franz Waxman
☆ Shirley Temple, Herbert Marshall, Laraine Day, Gail Patrick, Felix Bressart, Nella Walker, Lloyd Corrigan

Kathy O

US 1958 99m Eastmancolor Cinemascope
U-I (Sy Gomberg)
A temperamental child star befriends a lonely columnist.
Overlong Hollywood comedy drama with amusing moments.
w Jack Sher, Sy Gomberg d Jack Sher ph Arthur E. Arling m Frank Skinner m/ly Charles Tobias, Ray Joseph
☆ Patty McCormack, Dan Duryea, Jan Sterling, Sam Levene

Katia Ismailova *

France/Russia 1994 94m colour
Films du Rivage/Studio TTL/Lumière/CNC/Gorki Studios (Marc Ruscart, Igor Tolstunov)
original title: *Podmoskovnye vechera*
A woman who acts as secretary to her husband's mother, a romantic novelist, begins an affair with a carpenter during a stay at her mother-in-law's rural retreat.
An updated version of Nikolai Leskov's story of passion, murder and class conflict, with the passion downplayed; it has a certain fascination, though.
w Alla Krinitsyna, François Gérif, Cécile Vargaftig novella Maria Sheptunova, Stanislav Govorukhin d Valerii Todorovsky ph Sergei Koslov m Leonid Dessiatnikov ad Aleksandr Osipov ed Hélène Gargarin, Alla Streinikova
☆ Ingeborga Dapkunaite, Vladmir Mashkov, Alisa Freindlikh, Aleksandr Feklistov, Yuri Kuznetsov
'Slyly sustained noir atmosphere puts across the classic murder-without-remorse narrative.' – *Variety*
† Leskov's story *Katarina Ismailova* was also the basis for Shostakovich's opera *Lady Macbeth of the Mtsensk District*, which was filmed in 1966 by Mikhail Shapiro, starring Galina Vishnevskaya.

Katie Did It

US 1951 81m bw
Universal-International (Leonard Goldstein)
A small town is shocked when young Katie comes back having posed in scanty attire for a commercial artist.
Feeble comedy which totters to a lame conclusion.
w Jack Henley d Frederick de Cordova ph Russell Metty m Frank Skinner
☆ Ann Blyth, Mark Stevens, Cecil Kellaway, Elizabeth Patterson, Jesse White, Harold Vermilyea, Craig Stevens

Katie's Passion: see *Keetje Tippel*

Katina: see *Iceland*

Katinka *

Denmark/Sweden 1988 96m colour
Nordisk Film/AB Svensk Filmindustri (Bo Christensen)
The wife of a village station master and a new farm foreman fall in love.
Intense domestic tragedy, in the manner of Ingmar Bergman.
w Klaus Rifberg novel Ved Vejen by Herman Bang d Max von Sydow ph Sven Nykvist m Georg Riedel ed Janus Billeskov Jansen
☆ Tammi Øst, Ole Ernest, Kurt Ravn

Kavkazskii Plennik: see *Prisoner of the Mountains*

Kazaam

US 1996 93m Technicolor
Buena Vista/Touchstone/Interscope/PolyGram (Scott Kroopf, Paul M. Glaser, Bob Engelman)
▢▢ ▦ ◷.
An unhappy boy, searching for his father, a petty criminal, finds a genie who grants him three wishes.
Grim fantasy of minimal interest, other than to watch an attempt to turn a sporting baseball hero into a film star.
w Christian Ford, Roger Soffer story Paul Michael Glaser d Paul Michael Glaser ph Charles Minsky m Christopher Tyng pd Donald Burt ed Michael E. Polokow
☆ Shaquille O'Neal, Francis Capra, Ally Walker, James Acheson, Marshall Manesh, Fawn Reed, John Costelloe, JoAnne Hart
'Too gritty, violent and downbeat for tykes, it's also a bit juvenile and fairy tale-like for teens and older auds.' – *Godfrey Cheshire, Variety*

The Keep

US 1983 93m Metrocolor Scope
Paramount (Gene Kirkwood, Howard W. Koch Jnr)
▦ ◷.
German troops in 1941 occupy a castle in the Carpathian Alps, and discover that it contains an evil force.
Extraordinary combination of war and fantasy fiction, not entirely dissimilar from Castle Keep which had a similar exposition.
wd Michael Mann novel F. Paul Wilson ph Alex Thomson m Tangerine Dream
☆ Scott Glenn, Alberta Watson, Jurgen Prochnow, Robert Prosky, Gabriel Byrne, Ian McKellen

Keep an Eye on Amelia: see *Occupe-Toi d'Amélie*

Keep 'Em Flying

🏃🏃 US 1941 86m bw
Universal (Glenn Tryon)
▦
Two incompetents in the Army Air Corps get mixed up with identical twin girls.
A big moneymaker of its day, this comedy now seems especially resistible.
w True Boardman, Nat Perrin, John Grant d Arthur Lubin ph Joseph Valentine m Frank Skinner
☆ Bud Abbott, Lou Costello, Martha Raye, Carol Bruce, William Gargan, Dick Foran, Charles Lang
⚜ song 'Pig Foot Pete' (mGene de Paul, lyDon Raye)

Keep Fit *

GB 1937 82m bw
ATP (Basil Dean)
A barber mistaken for an athlete finally excels at sport and also catches a thief.
Good star vehicle with snappy songs and fast comedy scenes.
w Anthony Kimmins, Austin Melford d Anthony Kimmins ph Ronald Neame, Gordon Dines m/ly Harry Gifford, Fred E. Cliffe ad Wilfred Shingleton ed Ernest Aldridge
☆ George Formby, Kay Walsh, Guy Middleton, Gus McNaughton, Edmund Breon, George Benson, C. Denier Warren, Hal Gordon, Hal Walters, Leo Franklyn

Keep It Up Downstairs

GB 1976 94m Technicolor
EMI/Pyramid (Hazel Adair)
A bed-hopping aristocratic family are faced with losing their ancestral home.

Dire sex farce that apes but fails to emulate the low style of the Carry On movies.
w Hazel Adair d Robert Young ph Alan Pudney m Michael Nyman ad Jacqueline Charrott-Lodwige ed Mike Campbell

☆ Diana Dors, Jack Wild, William Rushton, Aimi MacDonald, Françoise Pascal, Neil Hallett, Julian Orchard

'The cast, required to bare breasts and buttocks at regular intervals, is able to make no headway against the inane script and consistently mistimed direction.' – *Verina Glaessner, MFB*

Keep Smiling *
GB 1938 91m bw
TCF (Robert T. Kane)
US title: *Smiling Along*
Problems of a touring concert party.
Pretty good star vehicle, though with unfortunate signs of an attempt to glamorize Our Gracie.
w Val Valentine, Rodney Ackland story Sandor Farago, Alexander G. Kemedi d Monty Banks ph Max Greene md Bretton Byrd ad Oscar Werndorff ed James B. Clark
☆ Gracie Fields, Roger Livesey, Mary Maguire, Peter Coke, Jack Donohue, Tommy Fields, Eddie Gray, Edward Rigby, Hay Petrie

Keep Smiling
US 1938 77m bw
TCF (John Stone)
The niece of a Hollywood director finds him on the skids.
More than usually substantial star comedy-drama.
w Frances Hyland, Albert Ray story Frank Fenton, Lynn Root d Herbert I. Leeds ph Edward Cronjager md Samuel Kaylin
☆ Jane Withers, Henry Wilcoxon, Gloria Stuart, Helen Westley, Jed Prouty, Pedro de Cordoba, Douglas Fowley

'A kids' picture with an adult punch.' – *Variety*

Keep the Aspidistra Flying
GB 1997 100m Rank Colour
First Independent/Overseas/Arts Council/Bonaparte/UBA/Sentinel (Peter Shaw)
US title: *A Merry War*
A copywriter gives up his job to become a poet, but, after he makes his girlfriend pregnant, embraces the middle-class, suburban life.
A misguided, glossy production that emasculates all the passion and vitality of the original.
w Alan Plater novel George Orwell d Robert Bierman ph Giles Nuttgens m Mike Batt pd Sarah Greenwood ed Bill Wright
☆ Richard E. Grant, Helena Bonham Carter, Julian Wadham, Jim Carter, Harriet Walter, Lesley Vickerage, Liz Smith, Barbara Leigh Hunt, Bill Wallis

'Drains the novel of its class anger and turns it into a celebration of the joys of capitalism.' – *Richard Williams, Guardian*
'A betrayal of art.' – *Alexander Walker*

Keep Your Powder Dry
US 1945 93m bw
MGM (George Haight)
Three girls from different backgrounds join the WACS.
Totally uninteresting and unconvincing female flagwaver.
w Mary C. McCall Jnr, George Bruce d Edward Buzzell ph Ray June m David Snell
☆ Lana Turner, Laraine Day, Susan Peters, Agnes Moorehead, Bill Johnson, Natalie Schafer, June Lockhart, Lee Patrick

Keep Your Seats Please *
GB 1936 82m bw
ATP (Basil Dean)
A prospective heir seeks a fortune hidden in one of six chairs.
Good star comedy on a theme later reworked in It's in the Bag (qv) and The Twelve Chairs (qv).
w Tom Geraghty, Ian Hay, Anthony Kimmins play Twelve Chairs by Elie Ilf, Eugene Petrov d Monty Banks ph John W. Boyle m/ly Harry Parr-Davies, Harry Gifford, Fred E. Cliffe ad R. Holmes Paul ed Jack Kitchin
☆ George Formby, Florence Desmond, Alastair Sim, Gus McNaughton, Harry Tate

Keeper of the Bees
US 1935 76m bw
Monogram (Trem Carr)
A country boy makes good.
Victorian-style fable for rural audiences.
w Adele Buffington novel Gene Stratton Porter d Christy Cabanne
☆ Neil Hamilton, Betty Furness, Emma Dunn, Edith Fellows, Hobart Bosworth

'For discriminating patronage, a washout … a calico narrative for the crossroads.' – *Variety*

Keeper of the Flame *
US 1942 100m bw
MGM (Victor Saville)
A reporter befriends the widow of a politician and forces her to disclose her husband's guilty secret.
Well-acted but over-solemn melodrama which badly needs a sting in the tail.
w Donald Ogden Stewart novel I. A. R. Wylie d George Cukor ph William Daniels m Bronislau Kaper
☆ Spencer Tracy, Katharine Hepburn, Richard Whorf, Margaret Wycherly, Donald Meek, Stephen McNally, Audrey Christie, Frank Craven

'An expensive testimonial to Hollywood's inability to face a significant theme.' – *Time*
'Unorthodox and on the whole absorbing drama. Ominous portents and overtones take the place of physical action.' – *Christian Science Monitor*
'A gothic wet blanket of a movie.' – *Pauline Kael, 70s*

Keepers of Youth
GB 1931 70m bw
BIP (John Maxwell)
A young schoolmaster finds his fresh ideas make him unpopular, especially when he is found in a compromising position with the assistant matron.
Old-fashioned drama with a few lively scenes.
w Frank Launder, Thomas Bentley, Walter Mycroft play Arnold Ridley d Thomas Bentley ph James Wilson, Bert Ford
☆ Garry Marsh, Ann Todd, Robin Irvine, John Turnbull, O. B. Clarence, Mary Clare

Keeping Company
US 1940 80m bw
MGM
A young man announces his engagement but has trouble when his ex-girlfriend returns to town.
Amiable family comedy which was announced to be the first of a series, but stayed lonely.
w James Hill, Harry Ruskin, Adrian Scott d S. Sylvan Simon
☆ Frank Morgan, Irene Rich, John Shelton, Ann Rutherford, Virginia Weidler, Dan Dailey, Gene Lockhart, Virginia Grey

Keetje Tippel
Netherlands 1975 104m Technicolor
Rob Houwer Film
aka: *Katie's Passion*
aka: *A Girl Called Katy Tippel; Cathy Tippel; Hot Sweat*
In the 1880s, a young woman moves with her poverty-stricken family from the country to Amsterdam, where she rises from reluctant prostitution to a life in high society.
Pleasant period piece, although too episodic to give much insight into its central character, despite a fine performance from van de Ven.
w Gerard Soeteman book Neel Doff d Paul Verhoeven ph Jan de Bont m Rogier van Otterloo ad Roland de Groot, Dik Schillemans ed Jane Sperr
☆ Monique van de Ven, Rutger Hauer, Andrea Domburg, Hannah de Leeuwe, Peter Faber, Eddy Brugman, Fons Rademakers
† The film is based on the autobiography of Katy Neel Doff. It was released on video in Britain in a dubbed version under the title *Katie's Passion*.

Kelly and Me
US 1956 86m Technicolor Cinemascope
U-I (Robert Arthur)
The ups and downs of a song and dance man and the dog who shares his act.
Mild vaudeville saga with totally predictable twists.
w Everett Freeman d Robert Z. Leonard ph Maury Gertsman m Joseph Gershenson
☆ Van Johnson, Piper Laurie, Martha Hyer, Onslow Stevens

Kelly the Second
US 1936 71m bw
MGM
A determined lady trains a dimwitted prizefighter.
Easy-going farce from a studio which knew how to make them; but this wasn't one of the best.
w Jack Jevne, Gordon Douglas d Hal Roach
☆ Patsy Kelly, Guinn Williams, Charley Chase, Pert Kelton, Harold Huber

Kelly's Heroes
US/Yugoslavia 1970 143m Metrocolor Panavision
MGM/The Warriors/Avala (Irving Leonard)
During World War II, an American platoon abducts a German general and accidentally discovers the whereabouts of a fortune in gold.
Crude slam-bang actioner for the obvious market.
w Troy Kennedy Martin d Brian G. Hutton ph Gabriel Figueroa m Lalo Schifrin second unit Andrew Marton
☆ Clint Eastwood, Telly Savalas, Don Rickles, Donald Sutherland, Carroll O'Connor, Stuart Margolin, Dick Davalos

'Over two hours of consistently devastating explosions, pyrotechnics and demolition.' – *MFB*
'Made for no possible reason other than a chance to use the Yugoslav army at cut rates.' – *Judith Crist, 1973*

The Kennel Murder Case **
US 1933 73m bw
Warner (Robert Presnell)

Philo Vance proves that an apparent suicide is really murder.
Complex murder mystery, very smartly handled and often cited as a classic of the genre; later remade as Calling Philo Vance.
w Robert N. Lee, Peter Milner novel S. S. Van Dine d Michael Curtiz ph William Reese
☆ William Powell, Mary Astor, Eugene Pallette, Ralph Morgan, Helen Vinson, Jack La Rue, Paul Cavanagh, Robert Barrat

'Entertaining all the way.' – *Variety*
'Players are cast so inevitably to type that the film is like a demonstration of the principles of running a stock company.' – *New Yorker, 1978*
'Stylistically a little gem.' – *Clive Hirschhorn*
† See also *Philo Vance*.

The Kentuckian
US 1955 104m Technicolor Cinemascope
UA/Hecht-Lancaster (Howard Hecht)
A Kentucky backwoodsman takes his small son to settle in Texas.
Ambling mid-Western with moments of interest.
w A. B. Guthrie Jnr novel The Gabriel Horn by Felix Holt d Burt Lancaster ph Ernest Laszlo m Bernard Herrmann
☆ Burt Lancaster, Dianne Foster, Diana Lynn, Walter Matthau, John McIntire, Una Merkel, John Carradine

Kentucky *
US 1938 95m Technicolor
TCF (Gene Markey)
Horse-breeding rivalry prevents the smooth running of true love.
Harmless family entertainment, more professionally handled than its innumerable later imitations. Remade as April Love.
w Lamar Trotti novel The Look of Eagles by John Taintor Foote d David Butler ph Ernest Palmer md Louis Silvers
☆ Loretta Young, Richard Greene, Walter Brennan, Douglass Dumbrille, Karen Morley, Moroni Olsen, Russell Hicks

'An outstanding effort, geared for top money.' – *Variety*
🏆 Walter Brennan

The Kentucky Fried Movie
US 1977 90m colour
Alpha/Kentucky Fried Theatre (Robert K. Weiss)

Comedy sketches from the University of Wisconsin parodying television programmes and commercials.
The writers later gave us Airplane. Enough said?
w David and Jerry Zucker, Jim Abrahams d John Landis ph Stephen M. Katz ad Rick Harvel ed George Folsey Jnr

☆ Marilyn Joi, Saul Kahan, Marcy Goldman, Joe Medalis

Kentucky Kernels
US 1934 74m bw
RKO
GB title: *Triple Trouble*
An orphan left with two musicians proves to be the heir to a fortune, but the way to it is through feuding hillbilly country.
Fairly funny Wheeler and Woolsey comedy, in other words one of their better efforts.
w Bert Kalmar, Harry Ruby and Fred Guiol d George Stevens
☆ Bert Wheeler, Robert Woolsey, Mary Carlisle, Spanky McFarland, Noah Beery, Willie Best

'It's Fun O'Clock, Mountain Time! And How The Fun Keeps Mountin' Up!'

Kentucky Moonshine *
US 1938 87m bw
TCF (Darryl F. Zanuck)
In the hope of a radio contract, the Ritz Brothers masquerade as hillbillies and find themselves in the middle of a feud.
One of the trio's best solo vehicles.
w Art Arthur, M. M. Musselman d David Butler ph Robert Planck m/ly Lew Pollack, Sidney Mitchell md Louis Silvers
☆ The Ritz Brothers, Tony Martin, Marjorie Weaver, Slim Summerville, John Carradine, Wally Vernon, Berton Churchill, Eddie Collins

'It's crazy and it's wild, but it's funny and grand entertainment.' – *Variety*

Keoma (dubbed) *
Italy 1976 101m Eastmancolor
Uranos (Manolo Bolognini)
aka: *Keoma – Violent Breed*
aka: *The Violent Breed*
A half-breed Indian returns to his home to save the town from a ruthless landowner who is letting the people die from a plague.
Melodramatic spaghetti Western with metaphysical overtones, including a Mother Courage-like figure wandering through desolate landscapes; with its themes of revenge and family feuds, it plays like a Greek tragedy and is stylishly done, apart from the abysmal musical accompaniment, featuring Nero singing like an out-of-tune Lee Marvin.
w Mino Roli, Nico Ducci, Luigi Montefiori, Enzo G. Castellari d Enzo G. Castellari ph Aiace Parolin m Guido and Maurizio de Angelis ad Carlo Simi ed Gianfranco Amicucci
☆ Franco Nero, William Berger, Woody Strode, Olga Karlatos, Orso Maria Guerrini, Gabriella Giacobbe, Antonio Marsina, John Loffredo

La Kermesse Héroïque **
France 1935 115m bw
Tobis
aka: *Carnival in Flanders*
When Spaniards invade a Flemish town in 1616, the men make themselves scarce and the women find other ways of conquering.
Sprightly though overlong comedy which seemed risqué at the time and therefore enjoyed international success.
w Charles Spaak, Jacques Feyder novel Charles Spaak d Jacques Feyder ph Harry Stradling m Louis Beydts ad Lazare Meerson
☆ Françoise Rosay, Louis Jouvet, Jean Murat, Alfred Adam, André Alerme

'A mixture of gay absurdity and shrewd comment, selecting its own pitch and holding it – comedy, you might say, self-contained.' – *Otis Ferguson*
'Everything fits perfectly into the pattern of cultured and sophisticated entertainment. Nowhere is there a false touch.' – *The Times, 1952*

The Kerosene Seller's Wife
USSR 1989 104m colour
Circle Film Unit
A former surgeon, reduced to selling kerosene in the street, is betrayed by his bureaucratic twin brother while his wife begins an affair with a young musician.
A bleak, disjointed, absurdist comedy of life among the dispossessed.

🏋 film suitable for family viewing 📼 VHS video-cassette for the British PAL system 📼 VHS video-cassette for the British PAL system in wide screen-format ⭥ Video cassette in a computer-colourised version ▤ American NTSC video-cassette ⌕ Laser disc *wd* Alexander Kaidanovsky *ph* Alexei Rodionov *m* Bach, Beethoven, Mozart, Schubert *ad* Teador Tezhik, Viktor Zenkov

☆ Anna Myasoedova, Alexander Baluev, Vitautas Paukshte

Kes ****

GB 1969 109m Technicolor
UA/Woodfall (Tony Garnett)

In a northern industrial town, a boy learns about life from the fate of his pet bird.
Realistic family drama that is one of the key British films of its period.
w Barry Hines, Ken Loach, Tony Garnett *novel A Kestrel for a Knave* by Barry Hines *d* Ken Loach *ph* Chris Menges *m* John Cameron
☆ David Bradley, Lynne Perrie, Colin Welland, Freddie Fletcher, Brian Glover
'There emerges a most discouraging picture of life in the industrial north ... infinitely sad in its total implications, it is also immensely funny in much of its detail.' – *Brenda Davies*
'Particularly to be admired is the way in which the dialogue has been kept flowing, as if it were always spontaneous, something proceeding from the moment.' – *Dilys Powell*
🎭 Colin Welland; David Bradley

The Kettles

The rustic couple evolved from characters in *The Egg and I* (qv); Marjorie Main and Percy Kilbride went on to play them in a cheap but very popular series for Universal, variously scripted and directed.
1949 Ma and Pa Kettle
1950 Ma and Pa Kettle Go to Town
1951 Ma and Pa Kettle Back on the Farm
1952 Ma and Pa Kettle at the Fair
1953 Ma and Pa Kettle on Vacation
1954 Ma and Pa Kettle at Home
1955 Ma and Pa Kettle at Waikiki
1956 The Kettles in the Ozarks (Arthur Hunnicutt instead of Kilbride)
1957 The Kettles on Old Macdonald's Farm (Parker Fennelly instead of Kilbride)

'All They Want To Do Is...Do It!!!'
Kevin & Perry Go Large

GB/US 2000 83m DeLuxe
Icon/Tiger Aspect/Fragile (Peter Bennett-Jones, Jolyon Symonds, Harry Enfield)
🎧

Two teenage boys go to Ibiza in the hope of losing their virginity.
Coarse and smutty comedy, using characters familiar from TV comedy sketches, where they did not so quickly wear out their welcome.
w Harry Enfield, David Cummings *d* Ed Bye *ph* Alan Almond *pd* Tom Brown *ed* Mark Wyborn
☆ Harry Enfield, Kathy Burke, Rhys Ifans, Laura Fraser, James Fleet, Louisa Rix, Tabitha Waddy, Paul Whitehouse, Ken Cranham, Patsy Byrne
'Just one overlong middle-aged sneer at teen life.' – *Cosmo Landesman, Sunday Times*
'As a British answer to the wave of American gross-out comedies, it falls woefully short.' – *Andrew Pulver, Guardian*
'Connoisseurs of bodily fluids on screen will doubtless appreciate how the makeover sequence climaxes with a multiple zit-squeezing money-shot.' – *Mark Sinker, Sight and Sound*

The Key *

US 1934 71m bw
Warner
In Ireland in the twenties, a British army captain falls for the wife of an intelligence officer.
Heroics among the black and tans; interesting but dated drama.
w Laird Doyle *play* R. Gore-Brown, J. L. Hardy *d* Michael Curtiz *ph* Ernest Haller
☆ William Powell, Edna Best, Colin Clive, Hobart Cavanaugh, Halliwell Hobbes, Henry O'Neill, Arthur Treacher, Donald Crisp

'The door opened into a haven from hell ... and the girl came with the key!'
The Key *

GB 1958 134m bw Cinemascope
Columbia/Open Road (Carl Foreman)

World War II tugboat skippers, about to embark on dangerous missions, pass on the key to an apartment and a girl to go with it.

Rather foolish symbolic melodrama which never makes its purpose clear but along the way provides fragments of love story, chunks of the supernatural and dollops of war action, rather languidly assembled with great technical competence but little real feeling. The talent occasionally shows through.
w Carl Foreman *novel Stella* by Jan de Hartog *d* Carol Reed *ph* Oswald Morris *m* Malcolm Arnold
☆ William Holden, Sophia Loren, *Trevor Howard*, Oscar Homolka, Kieron Moore
🎭 Trevor Howard

The Key

Italy 1984 116m Technicolor
Enterprise/San Francisco Film (Giovanni Bertolucci)

As Mussolini begins his rise to power, an art professor keeps a diary concerning his frustration over his wife's prudery; in turn she begins a diary of her affair with her daughter's boyfriend.
Atrocious soft-core porn that takes in transvestism, necrophilia and urolagnia and includes Finlay dressed in bra, panties, suspenders and stockings having a heart attack while making love. Avoid.
wd Tinto Brass *novel Kagi* by Junichiro Tanizaki *ph* Silvano Ippoliti *m* Ennio Morricone *ad* Paolo Biagetti *ed* Tinto Brass
☆ Frank Finlay, Stefania Sandrelli, Franco Branciaroli, Barbara Cupisti, Armando Marra, Maria Grazia Bon, Gino Cavalieri
'Where there's muck, there's brass; and where there's cinematic muck, there's Tinto Brass.' – *Virgin Film Yearbook*

'A storm of fear and fury in the sizzling Florida keys!'
Key Largo ***

US 1948 101m bw
Warner (Jerry Wald)

A returning war veteran fights gangsters on the Florida keys.
Moody melodrama on similar lines to To Have and Have Not: it sums up the post-war mood of despair, allows several good acting performances, and builds up to a pretty good action climax.
w Richard Brooks, John Huston *play* Maxwell Anderson *d* John Huston *ph* Karl Freund *m* Max Steiner
☆ Humphrey Bogart, Lauren Bacall, *Claire Trevor*, Edward G. Robinson, Lionel Barrymore, Thomas Gomez, Marc Lawrence
'It's a confidently directed, handsomely shot movie, and the cast go at it as if the nonsense about gangsters and human dignity were high drama.' – *New Yorker, 1977*
'A completely empty, synthetic work.' – *Gavin Lambert*
🏆 Claire Trevor

Key to the City

US 1950 101m bw
MGM (Z. Wayne Griffin)
At a San Francisco convention, two mayors get involved in several escapades and fall in love.
Routine romantic comedy.
w Robert Riley Crutcher *d* George Sidney *ph* Harold Rosson *m* Bronislau Kaper
☆ Clark Gable, Loretta Young, Frank Morgan, James Gleason, Marilyn Maxwell, Raymond Burr, Lewis Stone, Raymond Walburn, Pamela Britton
'A comedy made to measure ... the script concerns itself with wringing every possible laugh from a number of stock situations.' – *Variety*

'Don't come if you're afraid to see what's on the other side of...'
The Keyhole *

US 1933 70m bw
Warner (Hal Wallis)
A divorce investigator falls for the wife he is commissioned to frame.
Unsavoury little drama, unusual enough to be interesting.
w Robert Presnell *novel Adventures* by Alice Duer Miller *d* Michael Curtiz
☆ Kay Francis, George Brent, Glenda Farrell, Allen Jenkins, Monroe Owsley

The Keys of the Kingdom *

US 1944 137m bw
TCF (Joseph L. Mankiewicz)
🏆 🎬 🎧
The life of a 19th-century Scottish priest in China.

Studio-made missionary melodrama, a big hit for its new star but otherwise an undistinguished piece of work with a shuffling pace and not much by way of climax.
w Joseph L. Mankiewicz, Nunnally Johnson *novel* A. J. Cronin *d* John M. Stahl *ph* Arthur Miller *m* Alfred Newman *ad* James Basevi, William Darling
☆ Gregory Peck, Thomas Mitchell, Vincent Price, Rose Stradner, Roddy McDowall, Edmund Gwenn, Cedric Hardwicke, Peggy Ann Garner, James Gleason, Anne Revere
'Long, earnest, long, worthy, interesting and long.' – *Richard Mallett, Punch*
🏆 Arthur Miller; Alfred Newman; Gregory Peck; art direction

Keys to Tulsa

US 1997 113m CFI color
Polygram/ITC/Peyton/Empire (Leslie Greif, Harley Peyton)

The prodigal son of a wealthy family falls among blackmailers and murderers.
Barnstorming, scenery-chewing performances help stave off apathy for a while, but this thriller runs short of excitement long before its end.
w Harley Peyton *novel* Brian Fair Berkey *d* Leslie Greif *ph* Robert Fraisse *m* Stephen Endelman *pd* Derek R. Hill *ed* Eric L. Beason, Louis F. Cioffi, Michael R. Miller
☆ Eric Stoltz, Cameron Diaz, Randy Graff, Mary Tyler Moore, James Coburn, Deborah Kara Unger, Michael Rooker, Peter Strauss, James Spader
'A wonderfully written and performed comic crime meller.' – *Variety*

'Where the Nile divides, their mighty conflict begins!'
Khartoum *

GB 1966 134m Technicolor Ultra Panavision
UA/Julian Blaustein
🎬 🎬
The last years of General Gordon.
Dullish history book stuff which fails to explain Gordon the man but occasionally enjoys some billowing action.
w Robert Ardrey *d* Basil Dearden *ph* Edward Scaife, Harry Waxman *m* Frank Cordell
☆ Charlton Heston, Laurence Olivier, Ralph Richardson, Richard Johnson, Hugh Williams, Alexander Knox, Johnny Sekka, Nigel Green, Michael Hordern
'Academic accuracy and spectacular battles are unhappy partners.' – *MFB*
'Beautifully photographed, lavishly mounted, intelligently acted, but ultimately dull.' – *Sight and Sound*
🏆 Robert Ardrey

Kick!

US 1978 90m Movielab
Sean S. Cunningham Films (Sean S. Cunningham, Stephen Miner)
A soccer team of orphans decide to bet on themselves with stolen money to win a championship game so that they can pay off their coach's gambling debts.
A dull and clumsy comedy that offers the messages that theft is good and obsessive gambling is endearing, though few will stay awake long enough to discover them.
w Victor Miller *story* Stephen Miner *d* Sean S. Cunningham *ph* Barry Abrams *m* Harry Manfredini *ad* Virginia Field *ed* Stephen Miner
☆ Jim Baker, Malachy McCourt, Chet Doherty, Sel Skolnick

Kickboxer

US 1989 103m Technicolor
Entertainment/Kings Road Entertainment (Mark DiSalle)
🎬 🎬
After his brother is crippled in a fight, an American kickboxer seeks revenge.
Standard martial arts adventure.
w Glenn Bruce *story* Mark DiSalle, Jean Claude Van Damme *d* Mark DiSalle, David Worth *ph* Jon Kranhouse *m* Paul Hertzog *pd* Shay Austin *ed* Wayne Wahrman
☆ Jean Claude Van Damme, Dennis Alexio, Dennis Chan, Tong Po (Michel Qissi), Haskell Anderson, Rochelle Ashana, Steve Lee, Richard Foo, Ricky Lui

Kickboxer II: The Road Back

US 1990 89m colour
Entertainment/Kings Road (Tom Karnowksi)
🎬 🎬
A retired kickboxer is forced back into the ring to defeat a Thai gangster's champion.
Direly inept sequel.
w David S. Goyer *d* Albert Pyun *ph* Mark Emery Moore *m* Tony Riparetti, James Saad *ad* Nicholas T. Prevost *ed* Alan E. Baumgarten
☆ Sasha Mitchell, Peter Boyle, Dennis Chan, Cary-Hiroyuki Tagawa, John Diehl, Michel Qissi, Heather McComb, Vince Murducco, Matthias Hues
'Has all the faults of many Stateside chop-socky carbons: slow pacing, fortune-cookie philosophy and fight sequences shot from all the wrong angles.' – *Variety*

Kickboxer III: The Art of War

US 1992 92m DeLuxe
Vision International (Michael Pariser)
🎬
In Rio de Janeiro, an American kick-boxer takes revenge on a fight promoter who is also a white slaver.
Only a slight variation here on the single plot that seems to serve for every martial arts movie, and there is no variation at all on the usual high-kicking and predictable action.
w Dennis Pratt *d* Rick King *ph* Edgar Moura *m* Harry Manfredini *pd* Clovis Bueno *ed* Dan Lowenthal
☆ Sasha Mitchell, Dennis Chan, Richard Comar, Noah Verduzco, Milton Goncalves, Alethea Miranda, Miguel Orniga
'A routine martial arts pic that benefits from attractive Brazilian location photography.' – *Variety*

Kicking and Screaming *

US 1995 96m Foto-Kem
Trimark/Sandollar/Joel Castleberg
🎬 🎬 🎬
Newly graduated students find that they cannot tear themselves away from their university campus.
Slick and witty comedy of young men and women postponing adult life for as long as they can.
wd Noah Baumbach *story* Noah Baumbach, Oliver Berkman *d* Steven Bernstein *m* Phil Marshall *pd* Dan Whifler *ed* J. Kathleen Gibson
☆ Josh Hamilton, Olivia D'Abo, Chris Eigeman, Parker Posey, Jason Wiles, Cara Buono, Carlos Jacott, Elliott Gould, Eric Stoltz
'Mildly amusing and occasionally exasperating – a self-analysis of the self-analysis of a self-analytical generation.' – *Variety*

Kicking the Moon Around

GB 1938 78m bw
Vogue (Howard Welsch)
US title: *The Playboy*
aka: *Millionaire Merry Go Round*
A millionaire goes into show business to establish a career for his singing protégée.
Mild, frothy comedy, dated but quite fluent.
w Angus MacPhail, Roland Pertwee, Michael Hogan, Harry Fowler Mear *story* Tom Geraghty *d* Walter Forde *ph* Francis Carver *ad* John Bryan *ed* Derek Twist
☆ Ambrose and his Orchestra, Evelyn Dall, Hal Thompson, Florence Desmond, Harry Richman, C. Denier Warren, Max Bacon

Kid

US 1990 91m Alpha Cine
Entertainment/Tapestry Films (Robert L. Levy, Peter Abrams, Nathan Zahavi)
🎬 🎬
A teenager returns to his home town for revenge on the locals who killed his parents.
Dull, morally confused modern Western.
w Leslie Bohem *d* John Mark Robinson *ph* Robert Yeoman *m* Tim Truman *pd* Sharon Seymour *ed* Nathan Zahavi
☆ C. Thomas Howell, Sarah Trigger, Brian Austin Green, R. Lee Ermey, Dale Dye, Michael Bowen, Damon Bowen, Lenore Kasdorf
'Ludicrously recasts a barely stubbled youth in the role of the outsider-avenger.' – *MFB*

'6 Reels of Joy.'

The Kid ***
US   1921   52m   bw   silent
First National/Charles Chaplin

A tramp brings up an abandoned baby, and later loses him to his mother; but there is a happy ending.

Sentimental comedy set in the slums. The comedy is very sparingly laid on, but the effect of the whole is much less painful than the synopsis would suggest, the production is comparatively smooth, the child actor is sensational, and the film contains much of the quintessential Chaplin.

wd Charles Chaplin *ph* Rollie Totheroh
☆ Charles Chaplin, Jackie Coogan, Edna Purviance

Kid Auto Races at Venice
US   1914   6m   bw   silent
Keystone/Mack Sennett

This much-mentioned film is no more than a few candid camera shots of a children's car race on the California beach. It so happened that the young Charles Chaplin was called upon to liven up proceedings by causing a nuisance, and hastily conceived his tramp costume to do so. His fragments of comedy, primitive though they now seem, made him a star.

wd Henry Lehrman *ph* Frank D. Williams

Kid Blue
US   1973   100m   DeLuxe   Panavision
TCF/Marvin Schwarz Productions

In 1902 Texas a young outlaw tries to go straight.
Deliberately myth-deflating Western with agreeably rich detail.

w Edwin Shrake *d* James Frawley *ph* Billy Williams *m* Tim McIntire, John Rubinstein *pd* Joel Schiller
☆ Dennis Hopper, Warren Oates, Peter Boyle, Ben Johnson, Lee Purcell, Janice Rule, Clifton James

The Kid Brother ****
US   1927   83m   bw   silent
Paramount/Lloyd (Harold Lloyd)

The youngest son in the family proves that he is more than the household drudge.
Lively, slapstick comedy with the star at his best.

w John Grey, Tom Crizer, Ted Wilde *d* Ted Wilde, J. A. Howe, Lewis Milestone *ph* Walter Lundin, Henry N. Kohler *ad* Liell K. Vedder *ed* Allen McNeil
☆ Harold Lloyd, Jobyna Ralston, Walter James, Leo Willis, Olin Francis, Constantine Romanoff
'As gaggy a gag picture as he has ever done.' – Variety

The Kid Comes Back
US   1937   61m   bw
Warner (Bryan Foy)

A tenderfoot from Texas is trained by an ex-champion prizefighter.
Not really a sequel to Kid Galahad, but a second feature in its wake; as such, fair.

w George Bricker, E. J. Flanagan *d* B. Reeves Eason
☆ Wayne Morris, Barton MacLane, June Travis, Maxie Rosenbloom
'Brisk, fast, strong dualler.' – Variety

A Kid for Two Farthings *
GB   1955   96m   Eastmancolor
London Films (Carol Reed)

Among the colourful characters of London's Petticoat Lane market moves a boy whose pet goat seems to have the magical power of a unicorn.
Whimsical character comedy-drama made with some style but too insubstantial and unconvincing to be affectionately remembered.

w Wolf Mankowitz *d* Carol Reed *ph* Ted Scaife *m* Benjamin Frankel
☆ Celia Johnson, Diana Dors, David Kossoff, Brenda de Banzie, Sydney Tafler, Primo Carnera, Joe Robinson, Jonathan Ashmore

The Kid from Brooklyn
US   1946   114m   Technicolor
Samuel Goldwyn

A timid milkman becomes a prizefighter.
Yawn-provoking comedy, a remake of Harold Lloyd's The Milky Way; the first indication that Danny Kaye could be a bore.

---

w Grover Jones, Frank Butler, Richard Connell *d* Norman Z. McLeod *ph* Gregg Toland *m/ly* Jule Styne, Sammy Cahn *md* Carmen Dragon
☆ Danny Kaye, Virginia Mayo, Vera-Ellen, Steve Cochran, Eve Arden, Walter Abel, Lionel Stander, Fay Bainter, Clarence Kolb
† Lionel Stander played the same role in *The Milky Way.*

The Kid from Kokomo
US   1939   92m   bw
Warner (Sam Bischoff)

A farm boy's fight manager decides that for publicity purposes he must acquire a family.
Yet another follow-up to Kid Galahad, this time on the farcical side. Not bad, but too long.

w Jerry Wald, Richard Macaulay, Dalton Trumbo *d* Lewis Seiler
☆ Pat O'Brien, Wayne Morris, Joan Blondell, May Robson, Jane Wyman, Stanley Fields, Maxie Rosenbloom, Sidney Toler, Ed Brophy
'Full of laughs, and a very probable money-getter.' – Variety

The Kid from Left Field
US   1953   80m   bw
TCF (Leonard Goldstein)

A big league basketball player is reduced to selling peanuts at the games, but passes on advice through his small son, who is appointed team manager.
Half-hearted whimsy for addicts.

w Jack Sher *d* Harmon Jones *ph* Harry Jackson *m* Lionel Newman
☆ Dan Dailey, Billy Chapin, Anne Bancroft, Lloyd Bridges, Ray Collins, Richard Egan

The Kid from Spain **
US   1932   90m   bw
Samuel Goldwyn

A simpleton is mistaken for a celebrated bullfighter.
Charmingly dated star musical which, though primitive in some respects, is a splendid reminder of its period.

w William Anthony McGuire, Bert Kalmar, Harry Ruby *d* Leo McCarey *ph* Gregg Toland *m/ly* Bert Kalmar, Harry Ruby *ch* Busby Berkeley
☆ Eddie Cantor, Lyda Roberti, Robert Young, Ruth Hall, John Miljan, Noah Beery, J. Carrol Naish, Stanley Fields, Betty Grable, Paulette Goddard
'A corking comedy … it'll get a lot of money.' – Variety

The Kid from Texas
US   1950   85m   Technicolor
Universal-International
GB title: *Texas Kid, Outlaw*

The last rampage of Billy the Kid.
Surprisingly violent Western for its time; otherwise unremarkable.

w Robert Hardy Andrews, Karl Kamb *d* Kurt Neumann
☆ Audie Murphy, Gale Storm, Albert Dekker, Shepperd Strudwick, Will Geer, William Talman

Kid Galahad *
US   1937   101m   bw
Warner (Samuel Bischoff)

TV title: *Battling Bellhop*

A bellhop is groomed as a prizefighter, and his trainer grows jealous.
Good standard prizefight melodrama, remade as The Wagons Roll at Night and later as Kid Galahad with Elvis Presley (see below).

w Seton I. Miller *novel* Francis Wallace *d* Michael Curtiz *ph* Tony Gaudio *m* Heinz Roemheld, Max Steiner
☆ Edward G. Robinson, Bette Davis, Wayne Morris, Jane Bryan, Humphrey Bogart, Harry Carey
'Good prizefight picture with action, melodrama and names. Unusual in that women will like it.' – Variety

Kid Galahad
US   1962   96m   DeLuxe   Panavision
UA/Mirisch (David Weisbart)

Tolerable light-hearted musical remake of the above.
w William Fay *d* Phil Karlson *ph* Burnett Guffey *m* Jeff Alexander
☆ Elvis Presley, Lola Albright, Gig Young, Joan Blackman, Charles Bronson, Ned Glass, David Lewis, Robert Emhardt

---

Kid Glove Killer *
US   1942   73m   bw
MGM (Jack Chertok)

A police laboratory scientist tracks down the murderer of the mayor and finds his best friend is the culprit.
Professional police suspenser of the kind now tackled by television.

w John Higgins, Allen Rivkin *d* Fred Zinnemann *ph* Paul C. Vogel *m* David Snell
☆ Van Heflin, Lee Bowman, Marsha Hunt, Samuel S. Hinds, Eddie Quillan

A Kid in King Arthur's Court
US   1995   89m
Buena Vista/Trimark/Tapestry (Robert L. Levy, Peter Abrams, J. P. Guerin)

During an earthquake, a teenager is transported back to the sixth century and helps an aged King Arthur defeat his enemies.
A youthful twist to Mark Twain's fantasy does nothing to persuade an audience that it was worth doing.

w Michael Part, Robert L. Levy *d* Michael Gottlieb *ph* Elemer Ragalyi *m* J. A. C. Redford *pd* Laszlo Gardonyi *ed* Michael Ripps, Anita Brandt-Burgoyne
☆ Thomas Ian Nicholas, Joss Ackland, Art Malik, Paloma Baeza, Kate Winslet, Ron Moody, Daniel Craig, David Tysall
'Run-of-the-mill.' – Variety

Kid Millions *
US   1934   90m   bw (Technicolor sequence)
Samuel Goldwyn

An East Side kid inherits a fortune and has the time of his life.
Dated star musical with moments which still please.

w Arthur Sheekman, Nat Perrin, Nunnally Johnson *d* Roy del Ruth *ph* Ray June *m/ly* Walter Donaldson and Gus Kahn, Burton Lane and Harold Adamson, Irving Berlin *md* Alfred Newman *ad* Richard Day *ed* Stuart Heisler
☆ Eddie Cantor, Ethel Merman, Ann Sothern, George Murphy, Warren Hymer
'Goldwyn-Cantor girl-and-gag socko.' – Variety

Kid Nightingale
US   1939   56m   bw
Warner

A waiter is promoted into a prizefighter, and sings as he knocks out each opponent.
Self-spoofing comedy with some laughs.

w Charles Belden, Raymond Schrock, Lee Katz *d* George Amy
☆ John Payne, Jane Wyman, Walter Catlett, Ed Brophy, Charles D. Brown
'It's so absolutely silly it's almost good.' – Variety

'One man had been like any other to Nora. Then she met the kid.'

Kid Rodelo
US/Spain   1966   91m   bw
Trident/Fenix/Paramount

An outlaw fresh from prison races his former partners for the hidden loot.
Dull Western.

w Jack Natteford *story* Louis L'Amour *d* Richard Carlson
☆ Don Murray, Janet Leigh, Richard Carlson, Broderick Crawford, Jose Nieto

Kidco
US   1984   105m   colour
TCF (Frank Yablans, David Niven Jnr)

A boy who thinks up a series of money-making schemes in the hope of getting rich while young finds himself in trouble with the law.
Mildly amusing comedy, said to be based on a true story, but one without a natural audience: its concerns are too old for kids, and too silly for adults.

w Bennett Tramer *d* Ronald F. Maxwell *ph* Paul Lohmann *m* Michael Small *pd* Fred Price *ed* David E. McKenna
☆ Scott Schwartz, Clifton James, Charles Hallahan, Maggie Blye, Basil Hoffman, Phil Rubenstein, Cinnamon Idles, Tristine Skyler, Elizabeth Gorcey

Kidnapped: see *Miss Fane's Baby Is Stolen (1933)*

'Strangely they met … gallantly they risked their lives for each other … a valiant three against a nation's vengeful might!'

Kidnapped *
US   1938   93m   bw
TCF (Kenneth MacGowan)

During the Jacobite rebellion a young boy is sold by his wicked uncle as a slave, and is helped by an outlaw.
Much altered version of a classic adventure story, exciting enough in its own right, and well made in the thirties tradition.

w Sonya Levien, Richard Sherman, Walter Ferris *novel* Robert Louis Stevenson *d* Alfred L. Werker *ph* Bert Glennon *m* Arthur Lange
☆ Warner Baxter, Freddie Bartholomew, Arleen Whelan, John Carradine, C. Aubrey Smith, Nigel Bruce, Reginald Owen
'Strange modifications have been wrought … ambitious effort which misses top rating.' – Variety

Kidnapped *
GB   1959   95m   Technicolor
Walt Disney (Hugh Attwooll)

A remake fairly faithful to the book, which results in a few *longueurs*; but in general the action is spirited.

wd Robert Stevenson *ph* Paul Beeson *m* Cedric Thorpe Davie
☆ Peter Finch, James MacArthur, Bernard Lee, John Laurie, Finlay Currie, Niall MacGinnis, Peter O'Toole, Miles Malleson, Oliver Johnston, Duncan Macrae, Andrew Cruickshank

Kidnapped *
GB   1971   107m   Movielab   Panavision
Omnibus (Frederick H. Brogger)

Remake incorporating sections of *Catriona*. Not particularly exciting, but the acting helps.

w Jack Pulman *d* Delbert Mann *ph* Paul Beeson *m* Roy Budd
☆ Michael Caine, Lawrence Douglas, Trevor Howard, Jack Hawkins, Donald Pleasence, Gordon Jackson, Freddie Jones, Jack Watson

The Kidnappers *
GB   1953   95m   bw
Rank/Nolbandov-Parkyn
US title: *The Little Kidnappers*

In a Nova Scotian village at the turn of the century a stern old man denies his young grandchildren a pet, so they borrow a baby and hide it in the woods.
Fairly pleasing and popular whimsy for family audiences.

w Neil Paterson *d* Philip Leacock *ph* Eric Cross *m* Bruce Montgomery
☆ Duncan Macrae, Vincent Winter, Jon Whiteley, Theodore Bikel, Jean Anderson

The Kidnapping of the President *
Canada   1980   113m   DeLuxe
Sefel (George Mendeluk, John Ryan)

Third-world terrorists devise a plot to bring America to its knees by kidnapping the president.
Spirited political thriller which suffers chiefly from overlength.

w Richard Murphy *novel* Charles Templeton *d* George Mendeluk *ph* Mike Malloy *m* Paul J. Zaza
☆ Hal Holbrook, William Shatner, Van Johnson, Ava Gardner, Miguel Fernandez, Cindy Girling, Elizabeth Shepherd

Kids **
US   1995   90m   colour
Electric/Shining Excalibur/Independent/The Guys Upstairs (Cary Woods)

A day in the life of a group of teenagers, involved in their favourite pastimes of skateboarding, drugs and sex; one boy seeks out virgins for sex, while one of the girls he has deflowered discovers that she is HIV-positive.
A gritty, documentary-style drama of street life among the middle-class young, one that caused much controversy on its release; it has a feel of truth about it, together with a desire to shock and indulge in fantasies. In a few years' time, it may seem no more than a

---

skilful variation on the themes of 50s youth exploitation movies like High School Confidential.
w Harmony Korine d Larry Clark ph Eric Edwards m Lou Barlow, John Davis pd Kevin Thompson ed Christopher Tellefsen
☆ Lee Fitzpatrick, Sarah Henderson, Justin Pierce, Jonathan S. Kim, Adriane Brown, Sajam Bhagat, Billy Valdes

'Personally, this film has left flash-frames and memory triggers in my mind that won't quite shift, and there has to be something said for any work of art that's that powerful.' – Leslie Felperin, Sight and Sound
'That the end product is an experience can hardly be denied. Whether it is an experience that anyone would wish to endure on a Saturday night, though, is another question altogether.' – Clark Collis, Empire
† The version shown in Britain was cut by one minute. The film was banned from its cinemas in Britain by Warner Bros Theatres.

Kids in the Hall: Brain Candy
US 1996 89m DeLuxe
Starlight/Paramount/Lake Shore (Lorne Michaels)
📀 Ⓡ
A pharmaceutical company markets a new drug that makes everyone happy, ignoring its side effects.
Ineffectual satire, performed with more enthusiasm than skill.
w Norm Hiscock, Bruce McCullough, Kevin McDonald, Mark McKinney, Scott Thompson d Kelly Makin ph David A. Makin m Craig Northey pd Gregory P. Keen ed Christopher Cooper
☆ David Foley, Bruce McCulloch, Kevin McDonald, Mark McKinney, Scott Thompson, Kathryn Greenwood, Amy Smith
'Both screenplay and jokes leave a lot to be desired.' – Derek Malcolm, Guardian

The Kid's Last Fight: see The Life of Jimmy Dolan

Kids Return *
Japan 1996 107m Fujicolour
ICA/Office Kitano (Masayuki Mori, Yasushi Tsuge, Takio Yoshida)
Two young friends meet up after a long absence and recall their delinquent past, when both failed in their ambitions: one to become a successful boxer, the other a gangster.
A meandering portrait of two losers, observed with a compassionate detachment.
wd Takeshi Kitano ph Katsumi Yanagishima m Joe Hisaishi md Yukio Yamashita pd Norishiro Isoda ed Takeshi Kitano, Yoshinori Ota
☆ Masanobu Ando, Ken Kaneko, Leo Morimoto, Hatsuo Yamaya, Mitsuko Oka, Ryo Ishibashi, Susumu Terajima
'It goes further and deeper than earlier Kitano films, which means that it is the most interesting Japanese film in some time.' – Tony Rayns, Sight and Sound
'Ultimately it's just plain depressing and somewhat pointless.' – Nick Briggs, Film Review

Kika
Spain 1993 114m colour
Electric Pictures/El Deseo/Ciby 2000 (Esther Garcia)
📀 📀 Ⓡ 🎧
The overlapping lives of a psychologist turned reporter, who videotapes sexual scandals and murders for a TV show, and a beautician, who lives with a depressed photographer mourning his mother's suicide, after she is raped by a pornographic movie star on the run from the police.
A chic and glossy look at voyeurism, a sort of Spanish Peeping Tom that is also partly a satire on television's habit of serving up 'reality' as entertainment, but is mainly a recycling of the themes of Almodóvar's previous movies. The director's shock tactics are beginning to lose their impact, especially when combined with an ill-constructed narrative.
wd Pedro Almodóvar ph Alfredo Mayo ad Javier Fernandez, Alain Bainée ed José Salcedo
☆ Veronica Forqué, Peter Coyote, Victoria Abril, Alex Casanova, Charo Lopez, Rossy de Palma, Santiago Lajusticia, Anabel Alonso, Bibi Andersen, Manuel Bandera
'What use is style when the content is all over the place, and a genuine attempt to say

something that matters simply gets lost in the making.' – Philippa Bloom, Empire

Kiki
US 1931 96m bw
UA/Mary Pickford (Joseph M. Schenck)
A tomboyish chorus girl sets her cap at her divorced producer.
Long unseen star musical.
w Sam Taylor play David Belasco d Sam Taylor ph Karl Struss m Alfred Newman
☆ Mary Pickford, Reginald Denny, Joseph Cawthorn, Margaret Livingston
'Too long and too light … what was to have been a cocktail has turned out to have been a soda.' – Variety

Kikuchi
Japan 1990 68m colour
ICA/Vortex Japan (Shuichi Ohi)
A laundry worker, who leads an aimless life, becomes obsessed with a check-out girl at a supermarket.
Quirky small film, with little in the way of action or dialogue.
wd Kenchi Iwamoto ph Hideo Fukuda pd Takashi Iwai ed Keiichi Okada
☆ Jiro Yoshimura, Yasuhiro Oka, Misa Kukuma, Papa Akiyama, Mama Akiyama, Masaya Yasumura

Kill
France/Spain/Italy/West Germany 1971 102m
Eastmancolor
Procinex-Barnabe/Este/ICAR/Dieter Geissler (Alexander Salkind)
aka: Kill, Kill, Kill
The International Narcotics Bureau's best agent goes to Pakistan to catch the boss of a worldwide drugs syndicate, whose dealers are being killed by a vigilante.
Risible and amateurish thriller, occasionally almost engagingly silly – as when blues pianist Memphis Slim performs in a room occupied by naked, manacled women, dismembered mannequins and a worried man wearing a monocle, or when the dead bounce on trampolines – but more often merely very, very bad. An unshaven Boyd postures in brown leather, Mason frowns, and Seberg's vacuous role is the worst in a career notable for poor performances.
wd Romain Gary m Edmond Richard m Berto Pisano, Jacques Chaumont ad Enrique Alarcon ed Roger Dwyre
☆ James Mason, Jean Seberg, Stephen Boyd, Curt Jurgens, Daniel Emilfork, Mauro Parenti, Carlos Montoya, Henri Garcin

Kill and Pray (dubbed) *
Italy/W. Germany 1967 102m colour
Castor/Mancor Chretien/Luce/Tefi (Carlo Lizzani)
📀
original title: Requiescant
The adopted son of a preacher discovers that he is the sole survivor of a massacre, instigated by an American in order to steal land promised to the Mexican peasants.
Stylish Marxist spaghetti Western, though the politics are subsumed in the usual ingredients of plangent music, over-the-top confrontations, bizarre happenings and multiple deaths. Pasolini pops up unexpectedly as a revolutionary priest.
w Andrew Baxter, Denis Greene, Edward Williams story Arnold Elias, Frank Mills d Carlo Lizzani ph Alexander Clark m Roger Higgins ad Geoffrey Bailey ed Frank Rubien
☆ Lou Castel, Mark Damon, Pier Paolo Pasolini, Barbara Frey, Rossana Krisman, Mary Ellen Maxwell

Kill Her Gently
GB 1958 75m bw
Fortress/Columbia
A madman hires two convicts to murder his wife.
Very mild and unmemorable thriller.
w Paul Erickson d Charles Saunders ph Walter Harvey m Edwin Astley
☆ Griffith Jones, Maureen Connell, Marc Lawrence, George Mikell

Kill Me Again
US 1989 96m DeLuxe
Palace/Propaganda Films/ITC (David W. Warfield, Sigurjon Sighvatsson, Steve Golin)
📀
On the run from her boyfriend, whom she robbed, a woman pays a private eye to fake her death.

Not very successful attempt to recreate the style of 1940s film noir.
w John R. Dahl, David W. Warfield d John R. Dahl ph Jacques Steyn m William Olvis pd Michelle Minch ed Frank Jiminez, Jonathan Shaw, Eric Beason
☆ Val Kilmer, Joanne Whalley-Kilmer, Michael Madsen, Jonathan Gries, Pat Mulligan, Nick Dimitri

Kill Me Tomorrow
GB 1957 80m bw
Delta
A down-and-out reporter confesses to murder in order to obtain cash for his son's operation.
Tepid melodrama without much chemistry.
w Robert Falconer, Manning O'Brine d Terence Fisher ph Geoffrey Faithfull m Temple Abady
☆ Pat O'Brien, Lois Maxwell, George Coulouris, Wensley Pithey, Tommy Steele, Freddie Mills

Kill or Cure
GB 1962 88m bw
MGM (George H. Brown)
A series of murders at a nature clinic are solved by a bumbling private detective.
Flatfooted and unprofessional murder farce whose only pace is slow.
w David Pursall, Jack Seddon d George Pollock ph Geoffrey Faithfull m Ron Goodwin
☆ Terry-Thomas, Eric Sykes, Dennis Price, Lionel Jeffries, Moira Redmond, David Lodge, Ronnie Barker

Kill the Umpire
US 1950 78m bw
Columbia
An over-age baseball player can't get the game out of his mind, and returns as an argumentative umpire.
Minor comedy of presumed pleasure to sports addicts.
w Frank Tashlin d Lloyd Bacon
☆ William Bendix, Una Merkel, Ray Collins, Gloria Henry, William Frawley

Killer: see Bulletproof Heart (1995)

Killer!: see Que la Bête Meure

The Killer *
Hong Kong 1989 111m colour
Palace/Film Workshop/Golden Princess/Magnum (Tsui Hark)
📀 🎧 Ⓡ ◉
original title: Diexue Shuang Xiong
A hired killer is double-crossed by his employer.
Excessively violent imitation of Hollywood gangster movies.
wd John Woo ph Wong Wing-Hang, Peter Pao m Lowell Lowe ad Luk Man-Wah ed Fan Kung-Ming
☆ Chow Yun-Fat, Danny Lee, Sally Yeh, Chu Kong, Kenneth Tsang, Lam Chung, Shing Fui-On
'In its serenely overstated way, it is as resonant and emotive as the "classics" it refers to.' – Tony Rayns, MFB

Killer: a Journal of Murder *
US 1995 92m Technicolor
First Independent/Spelling/Ixtlan (Janet Yang, Mark Levinson)
📀 🎧 Ⓡ ◉
In the 20s, a prisoner is befriended by a guard who persuades him to write the story of his life; it turns out to be a confession to 21 murders, and he soon increases the number by beating to death a brutal guard.
A portrait of a self-destructive, cold-blooded killer, based on a true story, but turned into familiar Hollywood fare, notable only for Woods' chilling performance in the title role.
wd Tim Metcalfe book Thomas E. Gaddis, James O. Long ph Ken Kelsch m Graeme Revell pd Sherman Williams ed Richard Gentner
☆ James Woods, Robert Sean Leonard, Ellen Greene, Cara Buono, Robert John Burke, Richard Riehle, Harold Gould

Killer Calibre 32 (dubbed)
Italy 1967 95m Eastmancolor
Explorer '58 (Turan Turchetto)
A gunman, who hires himself out to kill criminals at $1000 a time, eliminates a ruthless gang of bank robbers.

Unexceptional, slow-moving spaghetti western that packs in most of the clichés of the genre.
w Enzo Gicca d Al Bradley (Alfonso Brescia) ph Bob Roberts ad Lambert Walker ed Edwin Zimmerman
☆ Peter Lee Lawrence, Sherill Morgan, Agnès Spaak, Cole Kitosch, Lucy Slade, Andrew Bosich, Mirko Ellis, Max Dean, John Barth

The Killer Elite
US 1975 120m DeLuxe Panavision
UA/Exeter-Persky Bright (Martin Baum, Arthur Lewis)
📀 Ⓡ ◉
A private crime fighting organization handles cases which the CIA prefers not to.
Smooth, fashionable violence which seems to proclaim the end of a cycle.
w Marc Norman, Stirling Silliphant novel Monkey in the Middle by Robert Rostand d Sam Peckinpah ph Philip Lathrop m Jerry Fielding
☆ James Caan, Robert Duvall, Arthur Hill, Gig Young, Mako, Bo Hopkins, Burt Young, Tom Clancy
'Merely a commercial chore.' – Tom Milne
'A mysterious, elliptical, visually triumphant film about personal survival in a world of mean-minded machination.' – Michael Billington, Illustrated London News

Killer Fish
France/Brazil 1978 101m colour
Victoria/Filmar do Brasil/Fawcett-Majors (Alex Ponti)
📀
The leader of a burglary gang hides their haul in a dammed reservoir which he stocks with piranha fish.
Heavy-going underwater shocker, with no fun while the fish are off-screen.
w Michael Rogers d Antonio Margheriti
☆ Lee Majors, Karen Black, Margaux Hemingway, Marisa Berenson, James Franciscus
'A slapdash actioner which casts its rod in water so overfished of late that it's amazing there's still anything down there biting.' – Variety

Killer Force: see The Diamond Mercenaries

Killer Grizzly: see Grizzly

The Killer Inside Me
US 1976 99m Metrocolor Panavision
Devi (Michael W. Leighton)
📀
A well-respected small-town deputy sheriff in Montana, seriously disturbed by memories of his violent childhood, finds that his life is out of control.
Unimpressive and implausible psychological study of a man's disintegration, lacking the sleazy authenticity of the novel.
w Edward Mann, Robert Chamblee novel Jim Thompson d Burt Kennedy ph William A. Fraker m Tim McIntire, John Rubinstein ed Danford B. Greene, Aaron Stell
☆ Stacy Keach, Susan Tyrrell, Tisha Sterling, Keenan Wynn, John Carradine, Don Stroud, Charles McGraw, John Dehner, Pepe Serna, Royal Dano, Julie Adams

The Killer Is Loose
US 1956 73m bw
Crown/United Artists
A bank robber swears revenge on a policeman who accidentally killed his wife.
Star potboiler, just about tolerable.
w Harold Medford d Budd Boetticher ph Lucien Ballard m Lionel Newman
☆ Joseph Cotten, Wendell Corey, Rhonda Fleming, Alan Hale Jnr, Michael Pate

The Killer Is on the Phone
Italy 1972 102m Eastmancolor Cinescope
Cathay/Difnei (Vittorio Bartattolo, Aldo Scavarda)
original title: Assassino … è al telefono
An unstable actress is stalked by a killer.
A dull and unimaginative thriller.
w Alberto di Martino, Vincenzo Mannino, Adriano Bolzoni, Renato Izzo d Alberto de Martino ph Aristide Massaccesi m Stelvio Cipriani ad Antonio Visone ed Otello Colangeli
☆ Anne Heywood, Telly Savalas, Rossella Falk
† The film was cut to 83m for its British release.

◉ Digital Video Disc Region 2   ◉ Digital Video Disc Region 1   🎧 Soundtrack released on compact disc   ☆ Cast in approximate order of importance   † Points of interest   🎵 Notable songs   🏆 Academy Award   🎖 Academy Award nomination   🏅 BAFTA

Killer McCoy

US   1947   104m   bw
MGM (Sam Zimbalist)
A prizefighter becomes involved in a murder.
Grade A production applied to a grade B script.
w Frederick Hazlitt Brennan, Thomas Lennon, George Bruce, George Oppenheimer d Roy Rowland ph Joseph Ruttenberg m David Snell
☆ Mickey Rooney, Ann Blyth, Brian Donlevy, James Dunn, Tom Tully, Sam Levene, James Bell, Gloria Holden

Killer Meets Killer: see *Each Dawn I Die*

'From the secret archives of the Vatican.'

Killer Nun

Italy   1978   90m   colour
Cinesud (Enzo Gallo)

original title: *Suor Omicidi*
In a lunatic asylum, a nun kills the male patients while framing another nun for the murders.
An over-the-top melodramatic horror, given matching histrionics by the cast.
w Giulio Berruti, Alberto Tarallo d Giulio Berruti ph Tonino Maccoppi
☆ Anita Ekberg, Alida Valli, Massimo Serato, Lou Castel, Joe Dallesandro, Laura Nucci
   'This hits all the proper lurid notes. But like many Italian exploitation movies, it's torn between sleaze and artiness.' – *Empire*

Killer of Killers: see *The Mechanic*

Killer on a Horse: see *Welcome to Hard Times*

The Killer That Stalked New York

US   1950   75m   bw
Columbia (Robert Cohn)
GB title: *Frightened City*
New York is on the alert for a girl smallpox carrier.
Absurdly-titled minor thriller, quite competent but wholly unsurprising.
w Harry Essex d Earl McEvoy ph Joseph Biroc m Hans Salter
☆ Charles Korvin, Evelyn Keyes, William Bishop, Dorothy Malone, Lola Albright, Barry Kelley, Carl Benton Reid, Ludwig Donath

Killer Tongue

GB/Spain   1996   99m   colour   'Scope
Entertainment/Lolafilms/Sogatel/Spice Factory/Noel Gay (Christopher Figg, Andrés Vicente Gómez)

A Martian meteor transforms a bank robber, waiting for her boyfriend, into a creature with a killer tongue, and her pet poodles become drag queens.
Direly stupid comic horror, nasty and tasteless and displaying neither wit nor imagination.
wd Alberto Sciamma ph Denis Crossan m Fangoria pd José Luis del Barco, Cath Pater Lancuski ed Jeremy Gibbs
☆ Melinda Clarke, Jason Dar, Mapi Galán, Mabel Karr, Robert Englund, Alicia Borrachero, Doug Bradley
   'Just trash.' – *Sight and Sound*
   'Never sharp or funny enough to engage even passing interest.' – *Alan Jones, Empire*

The Killers ***

US   1946   105m   bw
U-I (Mark Hellinger)
TV title: *A Man Alone*
In a small sleazy town a gangster waits for two assassins to kill him, and we later find out why.
Elaborate tale of cross and double-cross, stunningly executed.
w Anthony Veiller story Ernest Hemingway d Robert Siodmak ph Elwood Bredell m Miklos Rozsa ed Arthur Hilton
☆ Burt Lancaster, Edmond O'Brien, Ava Gardner, Albert Dekker, Sam Levene, John Miljan, Virginia Christine, Vince Barnett, Charles D. Brown, Donald MacBride, Phil Brown, Charles McGraw, William Conrad
   'About one tenth Hemingway's, the rest is Universal-International's.' – *Richard Winnington*
   'Seldom does a melodrama maintain the high tension that distinguishes this one.' – *Variety*
   'There is nothing unique or even valuable about the picture, but energy combined with attention to form and detail doesn't turn up every day; neither does good entertainment.' – *James Agee*

† John Huston contributed to the script but is not credited.
ß Anthony Veiller; Robert Siodmak; Miklos Rozsa; Arthur Hilton

The Killers ***

US   1964   95m   Pathécolor
U-I (Don Siegel)

Zesty, brutal remake intended for TV, but released theatrically because of its violence.
w Gene L. Coon story Ernest Hemingway d Don Siegel ph Richard L. Rawlings m Johnny Williams ad Frank Arrigo, George Chan ed Richard Belding
☆ John Cassavetes, *Lee Marvin*, Clu Gulager, Angie Dickinson, Ronald Reagan, Claude Akins
† This was Ronald Reagan's last feature film and the first in which he played a bad guy.
ʊ Lee Marvin

'Her soft mouth was the road to sin-smeared violence!'

Killer's Kiss

US   1955   64m   bw
UA/Stanley Kubrick

A prizefighter rescues a girl from her gangster lover, and is marked for death.
Tedious low-budget indie which first brought its director into notice.
m Gerald Fried wd/ph Stanley Kubrick
☆ Frank Silvera, Irene Kane, Jamie Smith

The Killers of Kilimanjaro

GB   1959   91m   Technicolor   Cinemascope
Columbia/Warwick (John R. Sloan)
US title: *Adamson of Africa*
A railroad engineer helps a girl find her lost father and fiancé.
Old-fashioned safari adventure full of action and animals.
w Richard Maibaum, Cyril Hume d Richard Thorpe ph Ted Moore m William Alwyn
☆ Robert Taylor, Anne Aubrey, Grégoire Aslan, Anthony Newley

The Killing **

US   1956   83m   bw
UA/Harris-Kubrick (J. B. Harris)

An ex-convict recruits helpers to steal two million dollars from a racetrack.
Incisive, entertaining, downbeat caper movie clearly influenced by The Asphalt Jungle and Rififi.
wd Stanley Kubrick novel *Clean Break* by Lionel White ph Lucien Ballard m Gerald Fried
☆ Sterling Hayden, Marie Windsor, Jay C. Flippen, Elisha Cook Jnr, Coleen Gray, Vince Edwards, Ted de Corsia, Joe Sawyer, Tim Carey
   'The visual authority constantly dominates a flawed script.' – *Arlene Croce*
   'The camera watches the whole shoddy show with the keen eye of a terrier stalking a pack of rats.' – *Time*

The Killing Game: see *Jeu de Massacre*

'It was a war unlike any other war ... Against an enemy unlike any other enemy.'

The Killing Box *

US   1992   92m   colour
Motion Picture Corporation/Fred Kuehnert (Brad Krevoy, Steve Stabler)

In the 1860s, a Confederate regiment wiped out in a massacre in Tennessee becomes possessed by inhuman forces from Africa, brought to America by slavers, and forms an army of vampiric zombies.
Quirky, atmospheric horror movie with overtones of voodoo and Lovecraft; it can be taken as an allegory of racism or some other plague, or enjoyed as an intelligent essay in creepiness, although its lack of gore may disappoint fans of the more visceral horrors.
w Matt Greenberg d George Hickenlooper ph Kent Wakeford m Cory Lerios, John D'Andrea pd Mick Strawn ed Monte Hellman sp make-up effects: KNB EFX Group
☆ Corbin Bernsen, Adrian Pasdar, Ray Wise, Cynda Williams, Roger Wilson, Alexis Arquette, Martin Sheen, Josh Evans, Billy Bob Thornton, Jefferson Mays
   'An eerie blend of bleak war movie and mainstream horror ... an outstanding debut.' – *Sight and Sound*

† Hickenlooper has said that the available version was cut by the producers. He also appears in a small role as an artist.

Killing Cars (dubbed)

West Germany   1985   94m   colour
Sentana (Mario Krebs)
The designer of a car that runs without petrol finds himself enmeshed in an international conspiracy to bury his invention.
Heavy-handed ecological thriller, more interested in slick surfaces and fashionable posturing than in its ostensible message.
wd Michael Verhoeven ph Jacques Steyn ad Norbert Scherer ed Fred Srp
☆ Jurgen Prochnow, Senta Berger, Agnes Soral, Daniel Gélin, Bernhard Wicki, William Conrad

Killing Dad

GB   1989   93m   Technicolor   Panavision
Palace/Scottish TV Film Enterprises/British Screen/Applecross (Iain Smith)

When a down-at-heel father tries to return to the family he abandoned more than twenty years before, his ineffectual son decides to kill him.
Limp, forced and unfunny attempt at a black comedy.
wd Michael Austin novel *Berg* by Anna Quinn d Michael Austin ph Gabriel Beristain m Chaz Jankel, David Storrs pd Adrienne Atkinson ed Edward Marner, Derek Trigg
☆ Denholm Elliott, Julie Walters, Richard E. Grant, Anna Massey, Laura del Sol
   'Signally fails to amuse.' – *MFB*

The Killing Fields ***

GB   1984   141m   colour
Goldcrest/Enigma (David Puttnam)

An American journalist is engulfed in the horror of Cambodia, and his native adviser disappears and is thought to be dead.
Brilliantly filmed, but probably too strong for a commercial audience to stomach, this true adventure tosses one onto the horror of modern war and leaves one reeling despite its comparatively happy ending.
w Bruce Robinson, from the article 'The Death and Life of Dith Pran' by Sidney Schanberg d Roland Joffe ph Chris Menges m Mike Oldfield pd Roy Walker ed Jim Clark
☆ Sam Waterston, Haing S. Ngor, John Malkovich, Julian Sands, Craig T. Nelson
🏆 Haing S. Ngor (supporting actor); photography; editing
ß best picture; Sam Waterston; adapted screenplay; Roland Joffe
ʊ best picture; adapted screenplay; Haing S. Ngor (supporting actor)

The Killing Game: see *Jeu de Massacre*

Killing Machine

Spain   1984   96m   colour
Golden Sun/Esme (Carlos Vasallo)

A Spanish lorry driver and explosives expert, on his final journey to Germany, takes revenge on the French gangsters who burned his truck and killed his pregnant wife.
Uninvolving and violent thriller which, despite its transcontinental setting, lacks much sense of place or purpose; the conflict of accents and styles of acting does not aid enjoyment.
wd J. Antony Loma ph Alexander Ulloa m Guido and Maurizio de Angelis ed Nicholas Wentworth
☆ Jorge Rivero, Margaux Hemingway, Lee Van Cleef, Willie Aames, Hugo Stiglitz, Ana Obregon, Richard Jaeckel

The Killing of a Chinese Bookie

US   1976   113m   colour
John Cassavetes

A Los Angeles night-club owner is prevailed upon by gangsters to pay off his debt by eliminating a troublesome Chinese.
Another unendurable slab of Cassavetes pretentiousness; why he went on trying, in the face of twenty years of public indifference, is beyond imagining.
wd John Cassavetes
☆ Ben Gazzara, Timothy Carey, Seymour Cassel, Morgan Woodward

The Killing of Angel Street

Australia   1981   100m   colour
Forest Home Films (Anthony Buckley)

Residents fight to save old terraced houses from demolition.
Rather routine light drama, like an Ealing comedy without laughs.
w Michael Craig, Cecil Holmes, Evan Jones d Donald Crombie ph Peter James m Brian May
☆ Elizabeth Alexander, John Hargreaves, Reg Lye, David Downer

The Killing of Sister George *

US   1969   138m   Metrocolor
Associates and Aldrich/Palomar

An ageing lesbian actress is fired from a TV serial and her life collapses around her.
Heavily handled film version of an amusing and moving play; everything is clumsily spelt out, including the love scenes, and the actresses are forced to repeat themselves.
w Lukas Heller play Frank Marcus d Robert Aldrich ph Joseph Biroc m Gerald Fried
☆ Beryl Reid, Susannah York, Coral Browne, Ronald Fraser, Patricia Medina, Hugh Paddick, Cyril Delevanti
   'The play was second-rate, but with its nice blend of the homely and the chilling, the absurdist and the perverse, it had the quality of a Kraft-Ebbing comic book. Aldrich and Heller have turned this material into a crawling tearjerker, the lines spoken at a speed adjusted to non-English or non-language-speaking audiences.' – *John Simon*
   'A clumpingly archaic piece of film-making.' – *New Yorker, 1982*

The Killing Time

US   1987   95m   Foto-Kem
New World/Tapestry (Peter Abrams, Robert L. Levy)

Corruption thrives in a small Californian town, where the sheriff agrees to help his former lover kill her husband, a ruthless businessman, and a murderer has assumed the identity of his new deputy.
Unconvincing thriller with stereotyped characters and a basic plot that has been recycled too often; there's no tension in the tale.
w Don Bohlinger, James Nathan, Bruce Franklin Singer ph Paul H. Goldsmith m Paul Chihara pd Bernt Amadeus Capra ed Lorenzo Destefano
☆ Beau Bridges, Kiefer Sutherland, Joe Don Baker, Wayne Rogers, Camelia Kath, Janet Carroll, Michael Madsen

Killing Zoe *

US   1993   96m   CFI color
Rank/Davis (Samuel Hadida)

An American joins a Parisian gang planning a bank raid on Bastille Day.
Violent, blood-soaked thriller, filmed in a consciously arty manner and borrowing moments from other films on similar themes; there is talent on show, but not a great deal of originality.
wd Roger Avary ph Tom Richmond m Tomandandy pd David Wasco ed Kathryn Himoff
☆ Eric Stoltz, Julie Delpy, Jean-Hugues Anglade, Gary Kemp, Bruce Ramsay, Tai Thai, Kario Salem
   'Has not much in its head and less in its heart.' – *Jonathan Romney, Guardian*

The Kill-Off *

US   1989   97m   Technicolor
Palace/Filmworld International (Lydia Dean Pilcher)

Three men set out to kill a vindictive, bed-ridden town gossip.
Low-life thriller that manages an authentic sleaziness.
wd Maggie Greenwald novel Jim Thompson d Maggie Greenwald ph Declan Quinn m Evan Lurie pd Pamela Woodbridge ed James Y. Kwei
☆ Loretta Gross, Andrew Lee Barrett, Jackson Sims, Steve Monroe, Cath Haase, William Russell, Jorjan Fox, Sean O'Sullivan, Ellen Kelly

Kilroy Was Here

US   1947   68m   bw
Monogram (Sid Luft)
A hellraiser of the Pacific war goes to college.

ϮϮ film suitable for family viewing   VHS video-cassette for the British PAL system   VHS video-cassette for the British PAL system in wide screen-format   ♡ Video cassette in a computer-colourised version   American NTSC video-cassette   Laser disc

Mild comedy reuniting two former child stars, but without any other ideas.

w Dick Irving Hyland d Phil Karlson ph William Sickner

☆ Jackie Cooper, Jackie Coogan, Wanda McKay, Frank Jenks

Kim *
👥👥 US 1950 112m Technicolor
MGM (Leon Gordon)
📀 🟰

The orphaned son of a British soldier in India has adventures with his horseman friend who belongs to the British secret service.

Colourful Boys' Own Paper high jinks, quite lively but never convincing.

w Leon Gordon, Helen Deutsch, Richard Schayer novel Rudyard Kipling d Victor Saville ph William Skall m André Previn

☆ Errol Flynn, Dean Stockwell, Paul Lukas, Robert Douglas, Thomas Gomez, Cecil Kellaway, Arnold Moss, Reginald Owen

'Ornate, lavish, but curiously lacking in genuine atmosphere, vitality or period sense.' – Penelope Houston

Kind Hearts and Coronets ***
GB 1949 106m bw
Ealing (Michael Relph)
📀 🟰 📀

An impecunious heir eliminates eight D'Ascoynes who stand between him and the family fortune.

Witty, genteel black comedy well set in the stately Edwardian era and quite deserving of its reputation for wit and style; yet the effect is curiously muffled and several opportunities are missed.

w Robert Hamer, John Dighton novel Israel Rank by Roy Horniman d Robert Hamer ph Douglas Slocombe md Ernest Irving ad William Kellner ed Peter Tanner

☆ Dennis Price, Alec Guinnessn, Valerie Hobson, Joan Greenwood, Miles Malleson, Arthur Lowe, Audrey Fields, John Penrose, Hugh Griffith, Clive Morton

'A brilliant misfire for the reason that its plentiful wit is literary and practically never pictorial.' – Richard Winnington

'Enlivened with cynicism, loaded with dramatic irony and shot through with a suspicion of social satire.' – Daily Telegraph

'The film in general lacks a visual style equal to its script … All the same, Kind Hearts and Coronets is a very funny film and it gets away with a great deal. With so much, in fact, that its makers deserve salutation as pioneers in the little-explored territory of adult British cinema.' – Lindsay Anderson

'A film which can be seen and seen again with undiminished pleasure.' – Basil Wright, 1972

Kind Lady *
US 1935 76m bw
MGM/Lucien Hubbard
aka: House of Menace

A confidence trickster insinuates himself and his criminal friends into the house of an invalid lady.

Unusual but unconvincing melodrama with overwrought leading performances.

w Bernard Schubert play Edward Chodorov story Hugh Walpole d George B. Seitz ph George Folsey m Edward Ward

☆ Basil Rathbone, Aline MacMahon, Mary Carlisle, Frank Albertson, Dudley Digges, Doris Lloyd

'Leisurely pace cramps effectiveness.' – Variety

Kind Lady *
US 1951 78m bw
MGM (Armand Deutsch)

Edwardian-set remake of the above, rather more subtly acted but failing to extract all possible frissons.

w Jerry Davis, Edward Chodorov, Charles Bennett d John Sturges ph Joseph Ruttenberg m David Raksin

☆ Maurice Evans, Ethel Barrymore, Angela Lansbury, Keenan Wynn, Betsy Blair, John Williams

'A curiously tame melodrama whose shocks, when they do come, are muffled and ineffectual.' – Penelope Houston

'Get even... or go under?'
A Kind of Hush
GB 1998 95m Technicolor
Metrodome/First Film/British Screen (Roger Randall-Cutler)

A gang of rent boys, sexually abused as children, take their revenge by beating up and robbing customers and attempting to blackmail a pimp.

Unlovely revenge drama, in which being abused in the past is shown as excusing abusive behaviour in the present; despite the efforts of a likable cast, it fails to make a convincing case for vengeance.

wd Brian Stirner novel Getting Even by Richard Johnson ph Jack Petrycki m Arvo Part pd Mark Stevenson ed David Martin

☆ Harley Smith, Marcella Plunkett, Nathan Constance, Ben Roberts, Paul Williams, Peter Saunders, Mike Fibbens, Roy Hudd

'One big, bland, liberal platitude performed by second-rate actors from a shallow, self-satisfied screenplay.' – Cosmo Landesman, Sunday Times

A Kind of Loving ****
GB 1962 112m bw
Anglo-Amalgamated/Waterhall/Vic Films (Joe Janni)
📀 🟰

A young north country draughtsman is forced into marriage, has to live with his dragon-like mother in law, and finally sorts out a relationship with his unhappy wife.

Blunt melodrama with strong kinship to Saturday Night and Sunday Morning, strikingly directed and photographed amid urban grime and suburban conformity.

w Keith Waterhouse, Willis Hall novel Stan Barstow d John Schlesinger ph Denys Coop m Ron Grainer

☆ Alan Bates, June Ritchie, Thora Hird, Bert Palmer, Gwen Nelson

'You will be shocked by this highly moral film only if you are shocked by life.' – Evening News

Kindergarten Cop
US 1990 110m colour
Universal (Ivan Reitman, Brian Grazer)
📀 🟰 📀 🎧

A cop, attempting to catch a drug dealer, works undercover as a teacher.

Muscle-bound would-be comedy, with an undercurrent of brutality and objectionable morality.

w Murray Salem, Herschel Weingrod, Timothy Harris d Ivan Reitman ph Michael Chapman m Randy Edelman pd Bruno Rubeo ed Sheldon Kahn, Wendy Bricmont

☆ Arnold Schwarzenegger, Penelope Ann Miller, Pamela Reed, Linda Hunt, Richard Tyson, Carroll Baker, Joseph Cousins, Christian Cousins

The Kindred
US 1987 97m Technicolor
Norkat/F-M Entertainment (Jeffrey Obrow)
🟰 📀

Young scientists fall foul of a genetically engineered monster.

Unoriginal and uninteresting.

w Jeffrey Obrow, Stephen Carpenter, John Penney, Earl Ghaffari, Joseph Stefano d Jeffrey Obrow, Stephen Carpenter ph Stephen Carpenter m David Newman pd Chris Hopkins ed John Penney, Earl Ghaffari

☆ David Allen Brooks, Rod Steiger, Amanda Pays, Talia Balsam, Kim Hunter, Timothy Gibbs, Peter Frechette, Julia Montgomery

King and Country *
GB 1964 86m bw
BHE (Norman Priggen, Joseph Losey)
📀

In the trenches during World War I, a private is court-martialled and shot for desertion.

Neat cinematic treatment of a very downbeat play.

w Evan Jones play Hamp by John Wilson d Joseph Losey ph Denys Coop m Larry Adler pd Richard Macdonald

☆ Tom Courtenay, Dirk Bogarde, Leo McKern, Barry Foster, James Villiers, Peter Copley

The King and Four Queens
US 1956 86m DeLuxe Cinemascope
UA/Russ/Field/Gabco (David Hempstead)
🟰

A cowboy braves the wrath of a lady sharpshooter to gain gold and the hand of one of her four daughters.

Tawdry sex Western sporadically enlivened by good-humoured playing.

w Margaret Fitts, Richard Alan Simmons d Raoul Walsh ph Lucien Ballard m Alex North

☆ Clark Gable, Eleanor Parker, Jo Van Fleet, Jean Willes, Barbara Nichols, Sara Shane, Roy Roberts

'A superficially cynical exercise in the rival attractions of sex and money.' – MFB

The King and I *
👥👥 US 1956 133m Eastmancolor
Cinemascope 55
TCF (Charles Brackett)
📀 🟰 📀 📀 🎧

Musical remake of Anna and the King of Siam (qv), from the highly successful stage production.

The film is opulent in lush detail but quite lacking in style.

w Ernest Lehman book/ly Oscar Hammerstein II d Walter Lang ph Leon Shamroy m Richard Rodgers md Alfred Newman, Ken Darby ad Lyle Wheeler, John DeCuir

☆ Deborah Kerr, Yul Brynner, Rita Moreno, Martin Benson, Alan Mowbray, Geoffrey Toone, Terry Saunders

'Gaiety has something of a struggle to survive.' – Penelope Houston

† Deborah Kerr's singing was dubbed by Marni Nixon, and Rita Moreno's by Leona Gordon.

🎗 Yul Brynner; Alfred Newman, Ken Darby; art direction

🎗 best picture; Walter Lang; Leon Shamroy; Deborah Kerr

The King and I
👥👥 US 1999 87m colour 'Scope
Warner/Morgan Creek/Rankin/Bass/Nest (James G. Robinson, Arthur Rankin, Peter Bakalian)
🎧

An English governess helps foil a palace coup against the King of Siam.

An animated, cut-down version of the Broadway musical, now aimed at a youthful audience, with only a handful of the original 20 songs surviving; it may suffice for a wet afternoon.

w Peter Bakalian, Jacqueline Feather, David Seidler; Brian Nissen (additional dialogue) musical Richard Rodgers, Oscar Hammerstein II adaptor Arthur Rankin d Richard Rich md William Kidd ed James D. Koford

☆ Featuring the voices of: Miranda Richardson (sung by Christiane Noll), Martin Vidnovic, Ian Richardson, Darrell Hammond, Allen D. Hong (sung by David Burnham), Armi Arabe (sung by Tracy Venner Warren), Adam Wylie, Sean Smith

'Broadway musical purists will shudder in horror, but parents will be whistling a happy tune that there's at least one acceptable pic out there for their kids.' – Robert Koehler, Variety

🎵 I Whistle a Happy Tune; Hello Young Lovers; Shall I Tell You What I Think of You?; The March of the Siamese Children; Getting to Know You; A Puzzlement; I Have Dreamed; Shall We Dance?

The King and the Chorus Girl
US 1937 94m bw
Warner (Mervyn Le Roy)
GB title: Romance Is Sacred

A European prince on the spree falls for a New York chorine.

Reasonably lively romantic comedy.

w Norman Krasna, Groucho Marx story Grand Passion by Norman Krasna, Groucho Marx d Mervyn Le Roy ph Tony Gaudio m Werner Heymann

☆ Joan Blondell, Fernand Gravet, Edward Everett Horton, Jane Wyman, Alan Mowbray, Mary Nash, Kenny Baker

'Sure word of mouth and a shoo-in for dough.' – Variety

King Arthur Was a Gentleman
GB 1942 99m bw
GFD/Gainsborough (Edward Black)

A soldier becomes a hero when he believes he has King Arthur's sword.

Not-too-successful attempt to turn a music hall comedian into a figure of Chaplinesque pathos.

w Val Guest, Marriott Edgar d Marcel Varnel ph Arthur Crabtree

☆ Arthur Askey, Evelyn Dall, Anne Shelton, Max Bacon, Jack Train, Peter Graves, Vera Frances, Ronald Shiner, Brefni O'Rorke

'Don't Mess With Mother Nature!'
King Cobra
US 1998 105m CFI
Trimark/Hill & Brand (David Hillenbrand, Scott Hillenbrand)
📀 🟰 📀

After a scientific experiment goes wrong, a giant snake, which is a cross between a cobra and a rattlesnake, threatens a small town.

This might have been called Fangs so closely does it stick to the narrative format of Jaws, with a monster on the loose, a mayor who ignores warnings, and an expert who is brought in for a battle to the death; it is competently done.

wd David Hillenbrand, Scott Hillenbrand ph Philip D. Schwartz m David Berrel pd Jack Cloud ed Guy W. Cearley sp CBFX: Charles Chiodo, Stephen Chiodo, Edward Chiodo

☆ Pat Morita, Scott Brandon, Kasey Fallo, Joseph Ruskin, Courtney Gains, Eric Lawson, Arell Blanton, Jerry Kernion, Michael Leopard, Erik Estrada, Hoyt Axton

'The resultant hokum even manages to make 1997's Anaconda look like a genre triumph. And if that isn't a telling indictment, nothing is.' – Empire

King Creole
US 1958 116m bw Vistavision
Paramount/Hal B. Wallis
📀 🟰 📀 📀

A failed graduate becomes a singer in a New Orleans night-club, and gets involved with gangsters.

Disagreeable crook melodrama turned into a musical star vehicle.

w Herbert Baker, Michael V. Gazzo novel A Stone for Danny Fisher by Harold Robbins d Michael Curtiz ph Russell Harlan m Walter Scharf

☆ Elvis Presley, Carolyn Jones, Dean Jagger, Walter Matthau, Dolores Hart, Paul Stewart

King David
GB/US 1985 114m Rank Colour
Panavision
Paramount/Martin Elfand
📀 🟰 📀

The biblical story of David's involvements with Saul, Goliath and Bathsheba.

Astonishingly tedious, confused and inept retelling of familiar tales, especially so for an audience which needs to be lured back to them.

w Andrew Birkin, James Costigan d Bruce Beresford ph Donald McAlpine m Carl Davis pd Ken Adam ed William Anderson

☆ Richard Gere, Edward Woodward, Denis Quilley, Jack Klaff, Cherie Lunghi, Alice Krige, Hurd Hatfield, John Castle, Niall Buggy

King for a Night
US 1933 78m bw
Universal

A minister's son becomes a boxer and goes to the electric chair for a murder committed by his sister.

Glum and incredible moral saga.

w W. A. McGuire and others d Kurt Neumann

☆ Chester Morris, Helen Twelvetrees, Grant Mitchell, Alice White, John Miljan, George E. Stone

A King in New York *
GB 1957 109m bw
Attica (Charles Chaplin)
🟰 📀

A penniless European king finds himself at odds with the American way of life.

Feeble Chaplin comedy from his anti-American period; tedious dialogue and poor physical production allow only momentary flashes of the satire intended.

ph Georges Périnal wd/m Charles Chaplin

☆ Charles Chaplin, Michael Chaplin, Oliver Johnston, Dawn Addams, Jerry Desmonde, Harry Green, Maxine Audley, Sid James

'Unhappily he is a sadder and an older man; the real punch is gone. His dethroned king is an ironically apt image.' – Marvin Felheim

'Maybe the worst film ever made by a celebrated film artist.' – New Yorker, 1977

'It shows how the coming of sound was a curse to Chaplin; how its freedoms dissipated his strengths; how his attempts to exploit it intellectually and ideologically played to his weaknesses; how, in short, he was much more grievously hurt by history in art than by history in politics.' – Stanley Kauffmann

---

'An overblown, self-piteous excursion into autobiography.' – *Time Out*, 1984

King Kong ****

↟↟ US 1933 100m bw
RKO (Merian C. Cooper)
▣ ▦ ◕ ⌓

A film producer on safari brings back a giant ape which terrorizes New York.
The greatest monster movie of all, a miracle of trick work and suspense, with some of the most memorable moments in film history.
w James Creelman, Ruth Rose *story* Edgar Wallace d Merian C. Cooper, Ernest Schoedsack ph Edward Linden, Vernon Walker, L. O. Taylor m Max Steiner *sound effects* Murray Spivak *chief technician* Willis J. O'Brien
☆ Robert Armstrong, Fay Wray, Bruce Cabot, Frank Reicher

CARL DENHAM (ROBERT ARMSTRONG): 'It wasn't the airplanes. It was beauty killed the beast.'
'If properly handled, should gather good grosses in a walk ... and may open up a new medium for scaring babies via the screen.' – *Variety*
'Just amusing nonsense punctuated by such reflections as why, if the natives wanted to keep the monster on the other side of the wall, they should have built a door big enough to let him through.' – *James Agate*

'The most exciting motion picture event of all time!'

King Kong

↟↟ US 1976 135m Metrocolor
Panavision
Dino de Laurentiis
▣ ▦ ◕ ⌓

Semi-spoof remake with added sexual overtones; though launched on a massive wave of publicity, it lacks both the charm and the technical resources of its predecessor.
w Lorenzo Semple Jnr d John Guillermin ph Richard H. Kline m John Barry pd Dale Hennesy, Mario Chiari
☆ Jeff Bridges, Charles Grodin, Jessica Lange, John Randolph, René Auberjonois, Julius Harris, Ed Lauter

'The one and original lovable monster is lost amid all the hydraulic manipulations in what now emerges as the story of a dumb blonde who falls for a huge plastic finger.' – *Judith Crist, Saturday Review*
'Even with colour, the settings of Kong II are no match for the rich black-and-white chiaroscuro of Kong I, with its echoes of artists like Gustave Doré and Max Ernst and its sensitivity to the emotional values of tone and texture.' – *Jack Kroll, Newsweek*
† *King Kong Lives* (L) crept out minimally in 1986.
▲ visual effects (Carlo Rambaldi, Glen Robinson, Frank Van Der Veer)
⌓ Richard H. Kline

King Lear *

GB/Denmark 1970 137m bw
Columbia/Filmways-Laterna (Michael Birkett)
▣ ▦

Tragedy ensues when an old king prematurely divides his kingdom between his daughters.
Miserably photographed in freezing Jutland, this is a deliberately downbeat version which despite its varied points of interest is extremely hard to sit through.
wd Peter Brook *play* William Shakespeare ph Henning Kristiansen m none pd Georges Wakhevitch
☆ Paul Scofield, Irene Worth, Alan Webb, Tom Fleming, Susan Engel, Cyril Cusack, Patrick Magee, Jack MacGowran

King Lear

US 1987 90m colour
Cannon (Menahem Globus, Yoram Golan)
▦

A culture expert travelling in France thinks of a mad old man and his daughter as subjects for a film.
Sheer nonsense doodled by the director with someone else's money.
wd Jean-Luc Godard *play* William Shakespeare ph Sophie Maintigneux ed Jean-Luc Godard
☆ Burgess Meredith, Peter Sellars, Molly Ringwald, Jean-Luc Godard, Norman Mailer, Kate Mailer, Woody Allen

King of Alcatraz *

US 1938 56m bw
Paramount (William C. Thomas)
Convicts escape on a freighter, but one needs surgery.
Pacy programmer with a stalwart cast.
w Irving Reis d Robert Florey ph Harry Fischbeck md Boris Morros
☆ Gail Patrick, J. Carrol Naish, Lloyd Nolan, Harry Carey, Robert Preston, Anthony Quinn, Dennis Morgan, Porter Hall

'Good gangster actioner ... will please those liking crime cinematics.' – *Variety*

King of Burlesque *

US 1935 88m bw
TCF (Kenneth MacGowan)
▦

A vaudeville impresario overcomes his troubles.
Well-written musical with plenty of variety talent.
w James Seymour, Gene Markey, Harry Tugend d Sidney Lanfield ph Peverell Marley m/ly various ch Sammy Lee
☆ Warner Baxter, Alice Faye, Jack Oakie, Mona Barrie, Arline Judge, Dixie Dunbar, Gregory Ratoff, Herbert Mundin, Fats Waller, Kenny Baker

'Big-time musical, with production, material and cast making up for story shortcomings.' – *Variety*
† It was remade as *Hello Frisco Hello*.
♫ 'I've Got My Fingers Crossed'; 'Lovely Lady'; 'Spreadin' Rhythm Around'; 'Whose Big Baby Are You?'; 'I'm Shooting High'; 'I Love to Ride the Horses'
⌕ Sammy Lee

King of Chinatown

US 1939 56m bw
Paramount (Stuart Walker)
A top racketeer is double-crossed by his henchman.
Smartly paced underworld melodrama.
w Lillie Hayward, Irving Reis, Herbert Biberman d Nick Grinde
☆ Anna May Wong, Akim Tamiroff, Sidney Toler, J. Carrol Naish, Philip Ahn, Anthony Quinn

'Good support for key duals.' – *Variety*

King of Comedy ****

US 1983 109m Technicolor
TCF/Embassy International (Arnon Milchan)
▦ ◕

Obsessed with becoming a chat show host, an aspiring comedian kidnaps his idol and ransoms him for a spot in the show.
Amusing, underplayed farce with a tragic lining: a very convincing picture of the media today.
w Paul D. Zimmerman d Martin Scorsese ph Fred Shuler m various md Robbie Robertson pd Boris Leven
☆ Robert DeNiro, Jerry Lewis, Diahnne Abbott, Sandra Bernhard

'This is a very frightening film, and in retrospect nothing about it seems funny at all.' – *Variety*
'Unquestionably one of the films of the year.' – *Guardian*
'A most eerie and memorable picture.' – *Spectator*
✇ best original screenplay

King of Gamblers

US 1937 79m bw
Paramount
aka: *Czar of the Slot Machines*
A ruthless gangster loves a singer who loves a reporter who is out to expose him.
A muddled script mars this pacy lower-birth item.
w Doris Anderson d Robert Florey ph Harry Fischbeck m Boris Morros
☆ Akim Tamiroff, Claire Trevor, Lloyd Nolan, Buster Crabbe, Porter Hall

'Well enough done to rate okay in the smaller spots solo.' – *Variety*

King of Hearts

France/Italy 1966 110m Eastmancolor
UA/Fildebroc/Montoro (Philippe de Broca)
▣

original title: *Le Roi de Coeur*
In World War I, a Scottish soldier finds a war-torn town occupied only by lunatics who have escaped from the asylum and who want to make him their king.

Heavy-handed whimsy which never catches fire despite the talents involved.
w Daniel Boulanger d Philippe de Broca ph Pierre Lhomme m Georges Delerue
☆ Alan Bates, Geneviève Bujold, Jean-Claude Brialy, Françoise Christophe, Pierre Brasseur, Micheline Presle, Adolfo Celi, Julien Guiomar

King of Jazz ***

US 1930 101m Technicolor
Universal (Carl Laemmle Jnr)
▦

Musical revue.
Stylish, spectacular, revelatory early musical: a treasure trove.
w Harry Ruskin, Charles MacArthur ph Hal Mohr, Ray Rennahan, Jerome Ash ad Herman Rose *devised/d* John Murray Anderson
☆ Paul Whiteman and his orchestra, John Boles, Bing Crosby (with the Rhythm Boys), Laura La Plante, Glenn Tryon, Slim Summerville, Walter Brennan

'A box office picture anywhere for one week.' – *Variety*
♫ 'Happy Feet'; 'A Bench in the Park'; 'My Bridal Veil'; 'Song of the Dawn'; 'I Like to Do Things for You'; 'Music Has Charms'; 'My Lover'; 'It Happened in Monterey'; 'Ragamuffin Romeo'; 'So the Bluebirds and the Blackbirds Got Together'
⌕ Herman Rose

'Under a master director and the reverent genius of great players, the story of Christ has taken human form and greater understanding!'
'Dramatic magnificence, spectacular splendour, riotous joy, tigerish rage, undying love, terrifying tempests, appalling earthquakes!'

King of Kings **

US 1927 155m bw silent
Pathé/Cecil B. de Mille
▦ ▦

The life of Jesus, seen more or less from the viewpoint of Mary Magdalene.
A patchy but frequently moving and pictorially effective work, ranging from the sublime (the first view of Jesus as a blind man regains his sight) to the ridiculous ('Harness my zebras, gift of the Nubian king!' says the Queen of Sheba in a sub-title).
w Jeanie Macpherson d Cecil B. de Mille ph J. Peverell Marley ed Anne Bauchens, Harold McLernon
☆ H. B. Warner, Jacqueline Logan, Joseph Schildkraut, Ernest Torrence, Victor Varconi, Dorothy Cumming, Rudolph Schildkraut, Alan Brooks

'The most impressive of all motion pictures.' – *Mordaunt Hall, New York Times*
'A picture which will tend to standardize the world's conception of the New Testament ... de Mille has one of the best business minds in pictures and making King of Kings was the most brilliant stroke of his successful business career.' – *Welford Beaton, The Film Spectator*

'A story of the Christ! The glory of his spoken words!'

King of Kings *

↟↟ US 1961 161m Super Technirama
MGM/Samuel Bronston
▣ ◕ ◕

The life of Jesus Christ.
Known in the trade as I Was a Teenage Jesus, this good-looking but rather tedious film is neither vulgar nor very interesting; a solemn, decent, bible-in-pictures pageant.
w Philip Yordan d Nicholas Ray ph Franz Planer, Manuel Berenger m Miklos Rozsa ad Georges Wakhevitch
☆ Jeffrey Hunter, Robert Ryan, Siobhan McKenna, Frank Thring, Hurd Hatfield, Rip Torn, Harry Guardino, Viveca Lindfors, Rita Gam

'I have decided to confer on King of Kings both my 1961 Scripture Prizes: (1) Dullest; (2) Most Undenominational.' – *Dilys Powell*
† Nicholas Ray's reaction to film critics who attacked the film was, 'They are not hip enough with the times of Christ.'

The King of Marvin Gardens *

US 1972 104m Eastmancolor
Columbia/BBS (Bob Rafelson)
▦ ◕

The host of a late night radio talk show gets embroiled in his brother's schemes.
Thoughtful tragi-comedy overweighted by talk, but with good performances.

w Jacob Brackman d Bob Rafelson ph Laszlo Kovacs
☆ Jack Nicholson, Bruce Dern, Ellen Burstyn, Julia Anne Robinson

'Indecipherable dark nonsense about brothers and goals and the American dream. An unqualified disaster.' – *New Yorker*
'Glum news from the people who made Five Easy Pieces, which had a lot of good work in it along with some pretentious flab. In their new picture the flab has taken over.' – *Stanley Kauffmann*

King of New York

US 1990 103m colour
Rank/Reteitalia/Scena/Caminito (Mary Kane)
▣ ▦ ◕ ◕

Released from prison, a New York gangster takes over the city's drug trafficking by murdering his rivals.
Excessively violent and sadistic fantasy, with a mannered leading performance.
w Nicholas St John d Abel Ferrara ph Bojan Bazelli m Joe Delia pd Alex Tavoularis ed Anthony Redman
☆ Christopher Walken, David Caruso, Larry Fishburne, Victor Argo, Wesley Snipes, Janet Julian, Joey Chin, Giancarlo Esposito

'Executed with the mix of splatter and gallows humour that Ferrara has made his own.' – *Sight and Sound*
'A nihilistic exercise in designer pessimism stating that the American system is corrupt from top to bottom.' – *Philip French, Observer*

King of Paris

GB 1935 75m bw
British and Dominions (Herbert Wilcox)
The story of a French stage impresario, supposedly based on Sacha Guitry.
Interesting try for a minority audience.
w W. P. Lipscomb, John Drinkwater, Paul Gangelin *play* La Voie Lactée by Alfred Savoir, John van Druten d Jack Raymond ph Freddie Young ad L. P. Williams
☆ Cedric Hardwicke, Marie Glory, Ralph Richardson, Phyllis Monkman

'Nothing much to be desired in this picture, excepting a story.' – *Variety*

King of the Children *

China 1988 107m colour
ICA/Xi'an Film Studio (Wu Tianming)
A youth, first sent from the city to work on a farm during the Cultural Revolution, is transferred to teach at a remote school where he uses unconventional methods which soon cause trouble.
Pleasant film with much of interest, though its deeper implications are likely to be understood only by a Chinese audience.
w Chen Kaige, Wan Zhi *story* Haizi Wang by Ah Cheng d Chen Kaige ph Gu Changwei m Qu Xiaosong ad Chen Shaohua ed Liu Miaomiao
☆ Xie Yuan, Yank Xuewen, Chen Shaohua, Zhang Camimei, Xu Guoqing

King of the Damned *

GB 1935 76m bw
Gaumont (Michael Balcon)
On a tropical island convict settlement, harsh treatment leads to mutiny.
A downright peculiar project for a British studio at this time, but technically very competent for those who like this kind of thing.
w Charles Bennett, Sidney Gilliat, Noel Langley *play* John Chancellor d Walter Forde ph Bernard Knowles md Louis Levy ad Oscar Werndorff ed C. Randell
☆ Conrad Veidt, Helen Vinson, Noah Beery, Cecil Ramage, Edmund Willard, Raymond Lovell, Allan Jeayes, Percy Parsons

'Goes so far overboard on gloom that it defeats its own end.' – *Variety*

King of the Gypsies

US 1978 112m Technicolor
Paramount/Dino de Laurentiis (Anna Gross)
▦

A gypsy leader is denied the hand in marriage of the daughter of a rival, so he kidnaps her.
Ethnic melodrama which despite its vigorous insistence on tradition – or perhaps because of it – plays like a mad musical without any songs.

↟↟ film suitable for family viewing   **▣** VHS video-cassette for the British PAL system   **▦** VHS video-cassette for the British PAL system in wide screen-format   **↻** Video cassette in a computer-colourised version   **▦** American NTSC video-cassette   **◕** Laser disc

w Frank Pierson *novel* Peter Maas *d* Frank Pierson *ph* Sven Nykvist, Edward Lachman *m* David Grisman *pd* Gene Callahan
☆ Sterling Hayden, Brooke Shields, Shelley Winters, Susan Sarandon, Judd Hirsch, Eric Roberts

King of the Hill *

🏃🏃 US 1993 102m DeLuxe Panavision
Wildwood/Bona Fide/Gramercy (Albert Berger, Barbara Maltby, Ron Yerxa)
📀 ▦ ◉〜 ⌒

A 10-year-old boy grows up in St Louis during the Depression of the 30s.
A gentle, sometimes touching drama of an observant boy trying to make the best of life, but steeped in a somewhat rosy nostalgia.
wd Steven Soderbergh *book* A. E. Hotchner *ph* Elliot Davis *m* Cliff Martinez *pd* Gary Frutkoff *ed* Steven Soderbergh
☆ Jesse Bradford, Jeroen Krabbé, Lisa Eichhorn, Karen Allen, Spalding Gray, Elizabeth McGovern, Joseph Krest, Cameron Boyd
'This densely detailed, superbly acted evocation of a resourceful boy's life during the depths of the Depression animates another time and place, while quietly underlining the parallels to contemporary problems.' – *Variety*

'Body of a Greek god! Strength of a Hercules!'
King of the Jungle

🏃🏃 US 1933 73m bw
Paramount

A small boy grows up with lions; he is captured with them and sold to an American circus.
Sub-Tarzan hokum which cheered up the kids.
w Philip Wylie, Fred Niblo Jnr, C. T. Stoneham *d* H. Bruce Humberstone, Max Marcin
☆ Buster Crabbe, Frances Dee, Douglass Dumbrille, Robert Adair, Robert Barrat
'Minus any help from the marquee it will have to attract on merit alone, and on merit it rates fair business.' – *Variety*

King of the Khyber Rifles

🏃🏃 US 1953 100m Technicolor
Cinemascope
TCF (Samuel Bischoff, David Diamond)
⌒

In 1857 a British garrison in India is threatened by the forces of Kuuram Khan but saved by a half-caste officer.
Standard North-West Frontier adventure, old-fashioned and rather dull.
w Ivan Goff, Ben Roberts *d* Henry King *ph* Leon Shamroy *m* Bernard Herrmann *ad* Lyle Wheeler
☆ Tyrone Power, Terry Moore, Michael Rennie, Guy Rolfe, John Justin

King of the Roaring Twenties

US 1961 106m bw
Warner/AA/Bischoff-Diamond
▦

GB title: *The Big Bankroll*
A gambler, Arnold Rothstein, becomes powerful among twenties gangsters.
Routine crime drama, shoddily made.
w Jo Swerling *book* The Big Bankroll by Leo Katcher *d* Joseph M. Newman *ph* Carl Guthrie *m* Franz Waxman
☆ David Janssen, Dianne Foster, Mickey Rooney, Mickey Shaughnessy, Diana Dors, Dan O'Herlihy, Jack Carson, Keenan Wynn, William Demarest, Joseph Schildkraut, Regis Toomey, Murvyn Vye
'Superficial, shopworn biography of an infamous bookie.' – *MFB*

King of the Turf

US 1939 88m bw
Edward Small
A gambler out of luck befriends a small boy who turns out to be his own son.
Hard to take even at the time, this sentimental tariddiddle does not bear later scrutiny.
wd George Bruce
☆ Adolphe Menjou, Dolores Costello, Walter Abel, Roger Daniel
'Dandy racetrack yarn ... it has a refreshing appeal and the dialogue is excellent.' – *Variety*

King of the Underworld

US 1938 69m bw
Warner (Bryan Foy)
When her husband is killed by gangsters, a doctor takes her own steps to round them up.

Sex-change remake of Dr Socrates; certainly no better.
w George Bricker, Vincent Sherman *d* Lewis Seiler
☆ Kay Francis, Humphrey Bogart, James Stephenson, John Eldredge
'It will have trouble even in the duals.' – *Variety*

King of the Wind

🏃🏃 US 1989 102m Technicolor
Enterprise/Davis Panzer/HTV International (Michael Guest, Paul Sarony, Peter S. Davis, William Panzer)
📀 ▦ ◉〜 ⌒

Adventures in France and England of a young Arab groom and his horse.
Lamely told and a waste of everyone's time.
w Phil Frey *novel* Marguerite Henry *d* Peter Duffell *ph* Brian Morgan *m* John Scott *pd* Ken Sharp *ed* Lyndon Matthews
☆ Frank Finlay, Jenny Agutter, Nigel Hawthorne, Navin Chowdhry, Ralph Bates, Neil Dickson, Barry Foster, Jill Gascoine, Joan Hickson, Anthony Quayle, Ian Richardson, Norman Rodway, Peter Vaughan, Richard Harris, Glenda Jackson

King, Queen, Knave *

US/West Germany 1972 92m Eastmancolor
Wolper/Maran (Lutz Hengst)
▦

The wife of a Munich bookseller falls for his adolescent nephew.
Amusing, capriciously directed sex comedy.
w David Shaw, David Seltzer *novel* Vladimir Nabokov *d* Jerzy Skolimowski *ph* Charly Steinberger *m* Stanley Myers
☆ Gina Lollobrigida, David Niven, John Moulder-Brown, Mario Adorf, Carl Fox-Duering

King Ralph

🏃🏃 US 1991 97m Eastmancolor
UIP/Universal/Mirage/Ibro (Jack Brodsky)
📀 ▦ ◉〜 ⌒

A Las Vegas entertainer becomes King of England when the Royal Family is electrocuted.
Witless farce, set in an England that even P.G. Wodehouse would have found quaintly old hat.
wd David S. Ward *novel* Headlong by Emlyn Williams *ph* Kenneth MacMillan *m* James Newton Howard *pd* Simon Holland *ed* John Jympson
☆ John Goodman, Peter O'Toole, John Hurt, Camille Coduri, Richard Griffiths, Leslie Phillips, James Villiers, Joely Richardson, Niall O'Brian, Julian Glover, Judy Parfitt
'As the man who wouldn't be King if he could help it, Goodman redeems what might have been just another high-concept comedy for the party of humanity.' – *Richard Schickel, Time*

'Even Hell had to have a monarch!'
King Rat **

US 1965 134m bw
Columbia/Coleytown (James Woolf)
▦ ⌒

In Singapore's Changi Gaol during World War II an American corporal lives more comfortably than the other prisoners by shabby dealings with the camp guards.
Overlong but generally gripping character melodrama – 'not a story of escape but a story of survival'.
wd Bryan Forbes *novel* James Clavell *ph* Burnett Guffey *m* John Barry
☆ George Segal, Tom Courtenay, John Mills, James Fox, Denholm Elliott, Todd Armstrong, Patrick O'Neal, James Donald, Alan Webb, Leonard Rossiter, Geoffrey Bayldon
♟ Burnett Guffey

King Richard and the Crusaders

🏃🏃 US 1954 113m Warnercolor
Cinemascope
Warner (Henry Blanke)
▦ ⌒

During the Crusades, the dreaded Saladin arrives in England in disguise and falls in love with Lady Edith...
Crudely confected comic strip version of Sir Walter Scott's The Talisman, ineptly written and cast, with poor production values.
w John Twist *d* David Butler *ph* Peverell Marley *m* Max Steiner
☆ Rex Harrison, Virginia Mayo, George Sanders, Laurence Harvey, Robert Douglas
LADY EDITH (VIRGINIA MAYO): 'Fight, fight, fight! That's all you think of, Dick Plantagenet!'

'Do not adjust your set – the sound you hear is Sir Walter Scott turning in his grave.' – *Sunday Express*
'It shows why the Crusades never really amounted to much.' – *Time*

King Solomon of Broadway

US 1935 72m bw
Universal
A night-club owner gambles away money he has borrowed from the mob.
Stale underworld melodrama.
w Harry Clork, Doris Malloy *d* Alan Crosland
☆ Edmund Lowe, Dorothy Page, Pinky Tomlin, Louise Henry, Charles Grapewin
'Won't go very far; mostly for doubles.' – *Variety*

King Solomon's Mines *

🏃🏃 GB 1937 80m bw
Gainsborough (Geoffrey Barkas)
Explorers in Africa persuade an exiled chief to help them find a diamond mine.
Rather somnolent though well-cast version of a favourite adventure novel, with a splendid final reel.
w Michael Hogan, A. R. Rawlinson, Roland Pertwee, Ralph Spence, Charles Bennett *novel* H. Rider Haggard *d* Robert Stevenson *ph* Glen MacWilliams *m* Mischa Spoliansky
☆ Cedric Hardwicke, Paul Robeson, Roland Young, John Loder, Anna Lee, Sydney Fairbrother, Robert Adams
'If the pop houses can accept its half-throttle speed, they'll get all the thrills and entertainment they want.' – *Variety*
'They kept the eye of the camera open for every form of wild and savage life and crammed it all into the picture, so one gets the impression that Allan Quartermain is delivering a lecture with illustrations rather than taking part in an adventure.' – *Richard Mallett, Punch*

King Solomon's Mines *

🏃🏃 US 1950 102m Technicolor
MGM (Sam Zimbalist)
▦ ◉〜

A remake which is largely travelogue with the merest trimmings of story.
w Helen Deutsch *d* Compton Bennett *ph* Robert Surtees *ed* Ralph E. Winters, Conrad A. Nervig
☆ Stewart Granger, Deborah Kerr, Richard Carlson, Hugo Haas, Lowell Gilmore
† Andrew Marton directed the second unit sequences.
♣ Robert Surtees; editing
♟ best picture

King Solomon's Mines

🏃🏃 US 1985 100m colour Cinemascope
Cannon
📀 ▦ ⌒

Quartermain is hired by a girl who wants to find her kidnapped father.
Adaptation in the vein of Indiana Jones and then some: the leading characters are almost boiled in a pot. Enjoyment depends on your sense of humour.
w Gene Quintano, James R. Silke *d* J. Lee-Thompson *ph* Alex Phillips *m* Jerry Goldsmith
☆ Richard Chamberlain, Sharon Stone, Herbert Lom, John Rhys-Davies, Ken Gampu
'The cinema's equivalent to junk food.' – *Sunday Mail*

The King Steps Out *

US 1936 85m bw
Columbia (William Perlberg)
▦

Emperor Franz Josef falls in love with the sister of the princess to whom he is betrothed.
Rather heavy-handed romance with music, not in its director's best style but showing flashes of his decorative talent.
w Sidney Buchman *operetta* Cissy by Herbert and Ernst Marischka *d* Josef von Sternberg *ph* Lucien Ballard *m/ly* Fritz Kreisler, Dorothy Fields *ad* Stephen Goosson
☆ Grace Moore, Franchot Tone, Walter Connolly, Raymond Walburn, Herman Bing, Victor Jory, Elizabeth Risdon, Nana Bryant, Frieda Inescort, Thurston Hall
'Josef von Sternberg asked that it not be included in retrospectives of his work, but he really did make the damned thing.' – *New Yorker, 1977*

The Kingdom **

Denmark 1994 279m colour
ICA/Zentropa/Denmark Radio TV/Swedish TV/WDR/Arte (Ole Reim)
▦

original title: *Riget*

Ghosts stalk a large Copenhagen hospital, staffed by unbalanced doctors and nurses.
Bizarre drama, originally made for television, that resembles a patient's worst nightmares, where one doctor abandons his charges to practise voodoo and another is impregnated by the ghost of a malignant murderer; it is the obverse of your average soap opera and compulsive viewing.
w Tómas Gislason, Lars von Trier, Nils Vorsel *d* Lars von Trier *ph* Eric Kress *m* Joachim Holbek *ad* Jett Lehmann *ed* Jacob Thuesen, Molly Marlene Stensgaard
☆ Ernst Hugo Järegard, Kirsten Rolffes, Ghita Norby, Soren Pilmark, Udo Kier, Otto Brandenburg, Jens Okking, Holger Juul Hansen
'Meld of black-comedy soap and Z-grade horror flick that looks like an instant cult item among auds willing to go the stretch.' – *Variety*

Kingdom of the Spiders

US 1977 95m colour
Arachnid/Dimension (Henry Fownes)
In an Arizona valley the death rate soars when tarantulas begin preying in groups on humans instead of singly on each other.
The spiders is coming, as Hitch might have remarked, and not even giant-size. Standard shudders, efficiently presented.
w Richard Robinson, Alan Caillou *d* John Cardos *ph* John Morrill, John Wheeler *md* Igo Kantor
☆ William Shatner, Tiffany Bolling, Woody Strode, David MacLean

'From the idiots what brung you *Dumb and Dumber*.'
Kingpin

US 1996 113m DeLuxe
Entertainment/Rysher/Motion Picture Corp (Brad Krevoy, Steve Stabler, Bradley Thomas)
📀 ▦ ◉〜 ⌒

A sleazy tenpin bowling champion is matched against one of his former victims, a one-armed alcoholic.
Dismal, rotten comedy, peopled by grotesques and driven by disgust.
w Barry Fanaro, Mort Nathan *d* Peter Farrelly, Bobby Farrelly *ph* Mark Irwin *m* Freedy Johnston *pd* Sidney J. Bartholomew Jnr *ed* Christopher Greenbury
☆ Woody Harrelson, Randy Quaid, Vanessa Angel, Bill Murray, Chris Elliott, William Jordan, Richard Tyson
'Another unsubtle, ugly farce featuring people to whom even the dimmest audience can feel intellectually superior.' – *George Perry*

Kings and Desperate Men

Canada 1983 118m colour
Alexis Kanner
A radio talk show host is held hostage by a group of unpredictable, idealistic terrorists.
Indulgently scripted, directed and acted, and dreary to watch.
w Edmund Ward, Alexis Kanner *d* Alexis Kanner *ph* Henry Lucas, Paul Van der Linden *m* Michel Robidoux, Pierre F. Brault *ad* Will McCrow *ed* Henry Lucas
☆ Patrick McGoohan, Alexis Kanner, Andrea Marcovicci, Margaret Trudeau

Kings Go Forth

US 1958 109m bw
UA/Ross-Eton (Frank Ross)
⌒

August 1944: two American soldiers fall out over a black French woman who is torn between them.
Heavy-going war melodrama, well enough done for those who can take it.
w Merle Miller *novel* Joe David Brown *d* Delmer Daves *ph* Daniel Fapp *m* Elmer Bernstein
☆ Frank Sinatra, Tony Curtis, Natalie Wood, Leora Dana, Karl Swenson

---

Kings of the Road

Germany   1975   176m   bw
Wim Wenders Productions
📼 🎞

original title: *Im Lauf der Zeit*
Two men on a bus talk of their past lives, their problems, their hopes and their fears.
Impossibly tedious two-hander which doubtless says something about life for those with the patience to sit it out.
wd Wim Wenders ph Robby Müller, Martin Schäfer m Axel Linstädt ed Peter Pryzgodda
☆ Rüdiger Vogler, Hanns Zischler, Lisa Kreuzer

Kings of the Sun

US   1963   108m   DeLuxe   Panavision
UA/Mirisch (Lewis J. Rachmil)
A Mayan tribe emigrates from Mexico to Texas and makes peace with the local Indian chief.
Ponderous dark age epic replete with human sacrifice, high-mindedness and solemn pauses. The actors and sets carry it as far as it will go.
w Elliott Arnold, James R. Webb d J.Lee-Thompson ph Joe MacDonald m Elmer Bernstein ad Alfred Ybarra
☆ Yul Brynner, George Chakiris, Shirley Anne Field, Richard Basehart, Brad Dexter, Barry Morse

'The king's ships ... the king's gold ... the king's girls ... were the treasure!'

The King's Pirate

👪 US   1967   100m   Technicolor
Universal (Robert Arthur)
An American in the 18th-century British navy infiltrates a pirate stronghold in Madagascar.
Tatty remake of Against All Flags, rising to a few minor heights of swashbuckling.
w Paul Wayne d Don Weis ph Clifford Stine m Ralph Ferraro
☆ Doug McClure, Jill St John, Guy Stockwell, Kurt Kasznar, Torin Thatcher, Richard Deacon, Sean McClory

King's Rhapsody

GB   1955   93m   Eastmancolor   Cinemascope
Everest (Herbert Wilcox)
An exiled Ruritanian king leaves his mistress to return home to a political marriage.
Love versus duty in a ludicrously inept film of Ivor Novello's highly theatrical musical drama, cheaply made and killed stone dead by casting and wide screen.
w Pamela Bower, Christopher Hassall, A. P. Herbert d Herbert Wilcox ph Max Greene
☆ Errol Flynn, Anna Neagle, Patrice Wymore, Martita Hunt, Finlay Currie

'Out of the hushed strangeness of these lives, and out of the shadows that hid their shame, filmdom has fashioned a drama most unusual, most touching and most wonderful!'
'The town they talk of in whispers!'

Kings Row ****

US   1942   127m   bw
Warner (Hal B. Wallis)
📼 🎞 ⊗ 🎧

In a small American town during the early years of the century, three children grow up into a world of cruelty and madness.
Superb Hollywood melodrama, a Peyton Place with great visual strength, haunting music and a wholly absorbing if incredible plot.
w Casey Robinson novel Henry Bellamann d Sam Wood ph James Wong Howe m Erich Wolfgang Korngold pd William Cameron Menzies
☆ Ann Sheridan, Robert Cummings, Ronald Reagan, Claude Rains, Betty Field, Charles Coburn, Nancy Coleman, Maria Ouspenskaya, Harry Davenport, Judith Anderson, Karen Verne
  DRAKE (RONALD REAGAN): 'Where's the rest of me?'
  'Half masterpiece and half junk.' – James Agate
  'Tranquilly accepting many varieties of psychopathic behaviour as the simple facts of life, this film has its own kind of sentimental glow, yet the melodramatic incidents are surprisingly compelling.' – New Yorker, 1982
  'One of the great melodramas, a veritable Mount Rushmore of physical and emotional cripples.' – Time Out, 1981
† The film was made in 1941, but its release was delayed for a year because the studio thought it too downbeat. It was not a great box-office success.
⅄ best picture; Sam Wood; James Wong Howe

A King's Story *

GB   1965   102m   Technicolor
Le Vien Films (Jack Le Vien)
Interviews with the Duke and Duchess of Windsor are interspersed with newsreels of the abdication crisis.
Earnest popular documentary with many points in its favour, including a resounding commentary by Orson Welles.
w Glyn Jones d Harry Booth m Ivor Slaney
⅄ best documentary

The King's Thief

👪 US   1955   79m   Eastmancolor   Cinemascope
MGM (Edwin H. Knopf)
🎧

The Duke of Brampton plots treason against Charles II but a highwayman robs him of an incriminating notebook.
Dismal swashbuckler with neither zest nor style, just a cast of unhappy-looking actors.
w Christopher Knopf story Robert Hardy Andrews d Robert Z. Leonard ph Robert Planck m Miklos Rozsa
☆ David Niven, Edmund Purdom, Ann Blyth, George Sanders, Roger Moore

The King's Vacation

US   1933   62m   bw
Warner
A king abdicates to seek the simple life.
Pleasing fable with a few theatrical ironies.
w Ernest Pascal, Maude T. Howell d John Adolfi
☆ George Arliss, Florence Arliss, Dick Powell, Marjorie Gateson, Dudley Digges

The King's Whore *

France/GB/Austria/Italy   1990   138m   colour
ASC/FR3/Cinema e Cinema/Umbrella (Maurice Benart, Wieland Schullz-Keil, Paolo Zaccaria)
📼 🎞 ⊗ 🎧

The beautiful wife of a courtier is forced to become a king's mistress.
Sumptuously romantic drama, conceived on a grand scale, but ultimately failing to live up to it.
w Daniel Vigne, Frederic Raphael, Axel Corti, Derek Marlowe novel Jeanne, Putain du Roi by Jacques Tournier d Axel Corti ph Gernot Roll m Gabriel Yared pd Francesco Frigeri ed Joelle Van Effenterre
☆ Timothy Dalton, Valeria Golino, Stephane Freiss, Robin Renucci, Feodor Chaliapin, Eleanor David, Margaret Tyzack, Paul Crauchet
  'The 17th century melodrama is less magnificent than it first appears, as it proves to be built around the small and inflexible obsessions of less-than-heroic characters.' – Variety
  'A movie that makes one glad to have missed the 17th century.' – Derek Malcolm, Guardian

Kini and Adams *

France   1997   93m   colour   'Scope
Noe/Les Films de la Plaine/Polar/Framework (Cedomir Kola, Sophie Salbot, Frédérique Dumas)
Two impoverished farmers, who dream of starting a new life in the city, fall out when one of them gets a better job than the other.
Ambitious, but not always successful, drama of male rivalry, where the landscapes come near to overwhelming the characters.
w Idrissa Ouedraogo, Olivier Lorelle, Santiago Amigorena d Idrissa Ouedraogo ph Jean-Paul Meurisse m Wally Badarou ad Heather Cameron ed Monica Coleman
☆ Vusi Kunene, David Mohloki, Nthati Moshesh, John Kani, Netsayi Chigwendere, Fidelis Cheza

Kinjite: Forbidden Subjects

US   1989   97m   TVC Color
Cannon/Golan Globus (Pancho Kohner)
📼 🎞 ⊗

A cop goes after a pimp specializing in child prostitutes.
Depressingly violent and nasty thriller, little more than a rerun of the star's Death Wish vigilante series.
w Harold Nebenzal d J. Lee-Thompson ph Gideon Porath ed Peter Lee-Thompson, Mary E. Jochem
☆ Charles Bronson, Perry Lopez, Juan Fernandez, Peggy Lipton, James Pax, Sy Richardson, Marion Kodama Yue, Bill McKinney

Kipps ***

👪 GB   1941   112m   bw
TCF (Edward Black)
US title: *The Remarkable Mr Kipps*
In 1906, a draper's assistant comes into money and tries to crash society.
Charming, unassuming film of a well-loved novel, later musicalized as Half a Sixpence.
w Sidney Gilliat novel H. G. Wells d Carol Reed ph Arthur Crabtree m Charles Williams
☆ Michael Redgrave, Phyllis Calvert, Diana Wynyard, Arthur Riscoe, Max Adrian, Helen Haye, Michael Wilding, Lloyd Pearson, Edward Rigby, Hermione Baddeley, Frank Pettingell, Beatrice Varley, Kathleen Harrison, Felix Aylmer
  'It has the old fashioned charm of wax roses under a glass bell.' – New York Times

Kisenga, Man of Africa: see Men of Two Worlds

Kismet

US   1930   90m   bw   65mm Vitascope
Warner
An Oriental magician overcomes a wicked vizier.
Rather tame filming of a spectacular which belongs on the stage.
w Howard Estabrook play Edward Knoblock d John Francis Dillon ph John Seitz
☆ Otis Skinner, Loretta Young, David Manners, Mary Duncan, Sidney Blackmer, Ford Sterling, Edmund Breese, Montagu Love

Kismet *

US   1944   100m   Technicolor
MGM (Everett Riskin)
TV title: *Oriental Dream*
Hollow and humourless but striking-looking remake of the above.
w John Meehan d William Dieterle ph Charles Rosher m Herbert Stothart ad Cedric Gibbons, Daniel B. Cathcart
☆ Ronald Colman, Marlene Dietrich, James Craig, Edward Arnold, Hugh Herbert, Joy Ann Page, Florence Bates, Harry Davenport, Hobart Cavanaugh, Robert Warwick
  'Enormous sets and crowding players are handled with such a clarity of line and colour that their gorgeousness never becomes untidy.' – MFB
  ⅄ Charles Rosher; Herbert Stothart; art direction

Kismet

👪 US   1955   113m   Eastmancolor   Cinemascope
MGM (Arthur Freed)
📼 🎞 ⊗ 🎧

Unlucky musical remake from the stage show with Borodin music.
w Charles Lederer, Luther Davis musical play Charles Lederer, Luther Davis d Vincente Minnelli ph Joseph Ruttenberg ch Jack Cole ad Cedric Gibbons, Preston Ames
☆ Howard Keel, Ann Blyth, Dolores Gray, Vic Damone, Monty Woolley, Sebastian Cabot, Jay C. Flippen, Mike Mazurki, Jack Elam
  'The whole thing was done with too heavy a hand.' – Howard Keel

The Kiss *

US   1929   64m   bw   silent
MGM (Albert Lewin)
📼 🎞

A woman is accused of the murder of her jealous husband.
A wisp of a melodrama, enlivened by its star; otherwise only notable as MGM's last silent picture.
w Hans Kraly d Jacques Feyder ph William Daniels
☆ Greta Garbo, Lew Ayres, Conrad Nagel, Holmes Herbert, Anders Randolf

The Kiss

US   1988   98m   colour
Columbia TriStar/Trilogy Entertainment/Astral Film Enterprises (Pen Densham, John Watson)
📼 🎞 ⊗

A glamorous model is possessed by a demonic snake-like creature.
Unimaginative horror movie.
w Stephen Volk, Tom Ropelewski d Pen Densham ph François Protat m J. Peter Robinson pd Roy Forge Smith ed Stan Cole sp Chris Walas

☆ Pamela Collyer, Peter Dvorsky, Joanna Pacula, Meredith Salenger, Mimi Kuzyk, Nicholas Kilbertus, Sabrina Boudot, Shawn Levy, Jan Rubes, Celine Lomez

'Women were putty in his hands!'

Kiss and Make Up

US   1934   80m   bw
Paramount (B. P. Schulberg)
A Parisian beauty specialist forsakes a rich client for his loyal secretary.
Forgettable romantic comedy.
w Harlan Thompson, George Marion Jnr play Stephen Bekeffi d Harlan Thompson ph Leon Shamroy
☆ Cary Grant, Genevieve Tobin, Helen Mack, Edward Everett Horton, Lucien Littlefield, Mona Maris
  'More gags than romance ... a nice picture lacking sufficient strength to wow, but should do all right.' – Variety

Kiss and Tell *

US   1945   92m   bw
Columbia (Sol C. Siegel)
To protect another girl, an irrepressible teenager pretends to be pregnant.
Good-humoured farcical comedy which at the time was thought pretty shocking, especially with the infant darling of the thirties in the lead.
w F. Hugh Herbert play F. Hugh Herbert d Richard Wallace ph Charles Lawton m Werner Heymann
☆ Shirley Temple, Robert Benchley, Walter Abel, Jerome Courtland, Katherine Alexander, Porter Hall, Tom Tully
  'All brilliantly characteristic of the worst anyone could think of American life.' – James Agee

A Kiss before Dying *

US   1956   94m   DeLuxe   Cinemascope
UA/Crown (Robert Jacks)
A college boy kills women who get in his way.
Reasonably absorbing exercise in psychopathology which would have been more effective on a smaller screen.
w Lawrence Roman novel Ira Levin d Gerd Oswald ph Lucien Ballard m Lionel Newman
☆ Jeffrey Hunter, Joanne Woodward, Robert Wagner, Virginia Leith, Mary Astor, George Macready

A Kiss before Dying *

US   1991   93m   Eastmancolor
UIP/Universal/Initial (Robert Lawrence)
📼 🎞 ⊗ 🎧

A woman discovers that the man she married is a multiple murderer.
Moderately effective thriller, though it offers a considerable simplification of the novel on which it is based.
wd James Dearden novel Ira Levin ph Mike Southon m Howard Shore pd Jim Clay ed Michael Bradsell
☆ Matt Dillon, Sean Young, Max von Sydow, Jim Fyfe, Ben Browder, Diane Ladd, James Bonfanti
  'As exciting as watching someone go bald.' – Anthony Lane, Independent on Sunday

The Kiss before the Mirror

US   1933   66m   bw
Universal
A lawyer defends a man who killed his wife from jealousy, then finds that the same thing is happening to him.
Stilted drama which was thought stylish at the time but is now a disappointment from this director; miscast, too.
w William Anthony McGuire play Lazslo Fodor d James Whale
☆ Frank Morgan, Nancy Carroll, Gloria Stuart, Paul Lukas, Charles Grapewin
  'Direction and adaptation lift this one into passable entertainment.' – Variety
† It was remade in 1938 as Wives Under Suspicion.

A Kiss for Corliss

US   1949   88m   bw
UA/Strand/James Nasser (Colin Miller)
📼
aka: *Almost a Bride*
A teenager develops a crush on a middle-aged roué.

Dismal sequel to Kiss and Tell *in the shadow of* The Bachelor *and the* Bobby Soxer.
w Howard Dimsdale d Robert Wallace
ph Robert de Grasse m Werner Heymann
☆ David Niven, Shirley Temple, Tom Tully, Darryl Hickman, Virginia Welles

'A disastrous teenage potboiler.' – *David Niven*

'I sometimes think that David Niven/Should not take all the parts he's given;/While of the art of Shirley Temple/I, for the moment, have had ample.' – *C. A. Lejeune*

A Kiss in the Dark
US 1949 87m bw
Warner (Harry Kurnitz)
A concert pianist finds romance in a boarding house peopled with zany characters.
Paper-thin romantic comedy.
w Harry Kurnitz d Delmer Daves ph Robert Burks m Max Steiner
☆ David Niven, Jane Wyman, Broderick Crawford, Maria Ouspenskaya, Victor Moore, Wayne Morris, Joseph Buloff, Curt Bois

Kiss Me Again **
US 1925 77m bw silent
Warner
A bored wife is tempted to stray, but doesn't.
Excellent silent comedy from an old boulevard farce, remade to less effect in the forties as That Uncertain Feeling.
w Hans Kraly *play* Divorçons *by* Victorien Sardou, Emile de Najac d Ernst Lubitsch ph Charles von Enger
☆ Marie Prévost, Monte Blue, John Roche, Willard Louis, Clara Bow

'Another sex masterpiece from the Attila of Hollywood … Continental high comedy done in the central European manner with Germanic harshness and irony of attack.' – *Ted Shane, New Yorker*

'Perhaps the most exquisite light screen comedy ever made on the subject of l'amour.' – *Herman G. Weinberg*

Kiss Me Again
US 1931 74m Technicolor
Warner
GB title: *Toast of the Legion*
A French lieutenant and a cabaret singer chase each other half across the world.
Modest musical from Victor Herbert's Mademoiselle Modiste; *popular at the time as a vehicle for two-colour Technicolor.*
w Julien Josephson, Paul Perez d William A. Seiter
☆ Walter Pidgeon, Bernice Claire, Frank McHugh, Edward Everett Horton

'Doubtful as strong b.o. but clean, deserving, and may get a break.' – *Variety*

'I don't care what you do to me, Mike – just do it fast!'

Kiss Me Deadly ***
US 1955 105m bw
UA/Parklane (Robert Aldrich)
▭ ▭ ⌖
By helping a girl who is nevertheless murdered, Mike Hammer prevents crooks from stealing a case of radio-active material.
Exuberant and harsh thriller set in an unlovely world and shot with brutal close-ups and unusual camera angles that create a disquieting effect. It is as unremittingly tough as its thuggish hero.
w A. I. Bezzerides *novel* Mickey Spillane d Robert Aldrich ph Ernest Laszlo m Frank de Vol
☆ Ralph Meeker, Albert Dekker, Cloris Leachman, Paul Stewart, Juano Hernandez, Wesley Addy, Maxene Cooper

'This meeting of "art" and pulp literature is, to say the least, curious.' – *MFB*

Kiss Me Goodbye
US 1982 101m DeLuxe
TCF/Boardwalk/Burt Sugarman/Keith Barish (Robert Mulligan)
▭
A widow planning to marry again is harassed by the ghost of her first husband.
It worked in Blithe Spirit, *but this is on a different level, a toned-down rendering of the heavy-breathing Brazilian farce* Donna Flor and Her Two Husbands, *and it doesn't work on any level.*

w Charlie Peters d Robert Mulligan ph Donald Peterman m Ralph Burns pd Philip M. Jefferies ed Sheldon Kahn
☆ James Caan, Sally Field, Jeff Bridges, Paul Dooley, Claire Trevor, Mildred Natwick, William Prince

Kiss Me Guido
US/GB 1997 86m colour
Paramount/Capitol/Kardana/Swinsky/Redeemable (Ira Deutchman, Christine Vachon)
▭ ▭
A hopeful heterosexual actor leaves home for a flat-share and discovers that his fellow-tenant is gay.
Feeble sitcom with few laughs and nothing else to recommend it, whatever your sexual predilections.
wd Tony Vitale d Claudia Raschke pd Jeffrey Rathaus ed Alexander Hall
☆ Nick Scotti, Anthony Barrile, Anthony DeSando, Craig Chester, Dominick Lombardozzi, Molly Price, Christopher Lawford

'A bright, snappy culture-clash farce.' – *Variety*

Kiss Me Kate **
↟↟ US 1953 111m Anscocolor 3-D
MGM (Jack Cummings)
▭ ▭ ⌂
The married leading players of a musical version of *The Taming of the Shrew* lead an equally tempestuous life backstage.
Brisk, bright screen version of the Broadway musical hit.
w Dorothy Kingsley *play* Samuel and Bella Spewack d George Sidney ph Charles Rosher m/ly Cole Porter md André Previn, Saul Chaplin ch Hermes Pan
☆ Howard Keel, Kathryn Grayson, Ann Miller, Keenan Wynn, Bobby Van, Tommy Rall, James Whitmore, Bob Fosse, Kurt Kasznar
♫ André Previn, Saul Chaplin

Kiss Me Stupid *
US 1964 124m bw Panavision
UA/Mirisch/Phalanx/ (Billy Wilder)
▭ ▭ ⌖
A womanizing pop singer stops overnight in a small California desert town and shows interest in an unsuccessful songwriter in order to get at his wife.
Draggy, tasteless, surprisingly unamusing smoking room story, with the actors behaving as though driven against their will (apart from Dean Martin, ideally cast as the idol who gets a headache if he doesn't have sex every night). Some good wisecracks, but it should have been much faster and funnier.
w Billy Wilder, I. A. L. Diamond *play* L'oro della fantasia *by* Anna Bonacci d Billy Wilder ph Joseph LaShelle m André Previn m/ly George and Ira Gershwin pd Alexander Trauner
☆ Dean Martin, Kim Novak, Ray Walston, Cliff Osmond

'A work of ferocious tastelessness … Swiftian in its relentless disgust.' – *Peter Barnes*

'You know what I do to squealers? I let them have it in the belly. So they can roll around for a long time thinking it over!'

Kiss of Death **
US 1947 98m bw
TCF (Fred Kohlmar)
A captured thief informs on his own gang, and a psychopathic killer is sent to extract vengeance.
Gloomy, well-made semi-location thriller which descends into heavy melodrama. Remade as The Fiend Who Walked the West.
w Ben Hecht, Charles Lederer d Henry Hathaway ph Norbert Brodine m David Buttolph
☆ Victor Mature, Richard Widmark, Brian Donlevy, Coleen Gray, Karl Malden, Taylor Holmes

'A tense, terrifying crime melodrama with an unusually authentic seamy atmosphere.' – *New Yorker, 1980*

'Economy of narration enhances the compactness and tautness of the whole and achieves that rarity, a picture minus unnecessary footage.' – *National Board of Review*

'It illustrates a new and vigorous trend in US moviemaking. One of the best things that is happening in Hollywood is the tendency to move out of the studio – to base fictional pictures on fact, and to shoot them not in painted studio sets but in actual places.' – *James Agee*

♫ original story (E. Lipsky); Richard Widmark

'Whatever doesn't kill you … makes you stronger.'

Kiss of Death *
US 1995 101m DeLuxe
TCF (Barbet Schroeder, Susan Hoffman)
A former car thief finds himself locked in a battle of survival with a vicious criminal.
A heavily rewritten remake of the above, which was intended to launch Caruso, from TV's NYPD Blue, *as a film star, but his performance seemed wan when confronted by the scenery-chewing Cage as a quirky psychopath, unbalancing the narrative and reducing interest in the story's outcome.*
w Richard Price *story* Eleazar Lipsky d Barbet Schroeder ph Luciano Tovoli m Trevor Jones pd Mel Bourne ed Lee Percy
☆ David Caruso, Nicolas Cage, Samuel L. Jackson, Helen Hunt, Kathryn Erbe, Stanley Tucci, Michael Rapaport, Ving Rhames, Philip Baker Hall, Anthony Head

'Far too loud and silly, but quite entertaining should you wish to suspend your disbelief.' – *Derek Malcolm, Guardian*

Kiss of Evil: see *Kiss of the Vampire*

Kiss of Fire
US 1955 86m Technicolor
Universal-International (Samuel Marx)
An ex-soldier escorts an exiled princess on a dangerous journey through Mexico.
Slightly unusual but rather clumsy swashbuckler of no especial merit.
w Franklin Coen, Richard Collins *novel* The Rose and the Flame *by* Jonreed Lauritzen d Joseph M. Newman m Carl Guthrie m Hans Salter md Joseph Gershenson
☆ Jack Palance, Barbara Rush, Martha Hyer

Kiss of the Spider Woman **
US/Brazil 1985 119m MGM Color
HB/Sugarloaf (David Weisman)
▭ ▭ ⌖
Fantasies of two prisoners in a South American jail.
One of those lucky flukes, an opening up of a fringe novel about the relationship between a flagrant homosexual and a political prisoner; the former entertains the latter with accounts of his favourite pulp movies. Not for Aunt Edna.
w Leonard Schrader *novel* Manuel Puig d Hector Babenco ph Rodolfo Sanchez m John Neschling pd Clovis Bueno
☆ William Hurt, Raul Julia, Sonia Braga
🏆 William Hurt
🏆 best picture; direction; adapted screenplay
👤 William Hurt

Kiss of the Tarantula
US 1976 84m Eastmancolor
New Realm/Manson (Daniel B. Cady)
▭
GB title: *Shudder*
A young girl kills those she does not like with her pet spiders.
Excessively dim horror movie without thrills or shudders.
w Warren Hamilton Jnr *story* Daniel B. Cady d Chris Munger ph Henning Schellerup m Phillan Bishop ed Warren Hamilton Jnr
☆ Suzanne Ling, Eric Mason, Herman Wallner, Patricia Landon, Beverly Eddins, Jay Scott Neal, Rebecca Eddins, Rita French

'The spiders are good for one or two mild sensations as they crawl lovingly over their initial victims, but even they are gradually overcome by the appalling banality of the script and the general lethargy of the direction.' – *Tom Milne*

Kiss of the Vampire *
GB 1964 88m Eastmancolor
Rank/Hammer (Anthony Hinds)
US title: *Kiss of Evil*
In 1910 a Bavarian disciple of Dracula lures a British honeymoon couple.
This unsubtle variation on Dracula is handled in lively fashion, with a splendid climax in which assorted white-robed vampires are destroyed by bats.
w John Elder (Anthony Hinds) d Don Sharp ph Alan Hume m James Bernard pd Bernard Robinson ed James Needs

☆ Noel Willman, Clifford Evans, Edward de Souza, Jennifer Daniel, Isobel Black

PROF. ZIMMER (NOEL WILLMAN): 'You must not expect your Queensberry rules here, Mr Harcourt.'

Kiss or Kill **
Australia 1997 95m Atlab
AFFC/Bill Bennett
▭ ▭
Two edgy petty thieves go on the run with a video of child pornography, chased by a murderous famous footballer who features on the tape, and the police.
A tense road movie that resembles an Australian variation on Badlands, *with an amoral young couple on the run across wide-open spaces; it adds a few original twists of its own to the familiar genre, and dispenses with a musical soundtrack.*
wd Bill Bennett ph Malcolm McCulloch pd Andrew Plumer ed Henry Dangar
☆ Frances O'Connor, Matt Day, Chris Haywood, Barry Otto, Max Cullen, Andrew S. Gilbert, Barry Langrishe

'Solid scripting, intelligent thesping and a bold sense of humor.' – *David Stratton, Variety*

'They won't stop us – nobody can stop us!'

Kiss the Blood Off My Hands
US 1948 80m bw
Universal/Hecht-Norma (Harold Hecht)
GB title: *Blood on My Hands*
A nurse helps a seaman on the run for murder.
Risible romantic melodrama in never-was London docks setting, with Newton large as life and twice as villainous.
w Leonardo Bercovici *novel* Gerald Butler d Norman Foster ph Russell Metty m Miklos Rozsa
☆ Joan Fontaine, Burt Lancaster, Robert Newton, Lewis Russell, Aminta Dyne

Kiss the Boys Goodbye *
US 1941 85m bw
Paramount (Paul Jones)
A Broadway producer falls for one of his chorines.
Moderately smart musical entertainment of its time.
w Harry Tugend, Dwight Taylor *play* Clare Boothe d Victor Schertzinger ph Ted Tetzlaff m/ly Victor Schertzinger, Frank Loesser
☆ Don Ameche, Mary Martin, Oscar Levant, Rochester, Raymond Walburn, Connee Boswell, Virginia Dale, Barbara Jo Allen, Elizabeth Patterson

Kiss the Bride Goodbye
GB 1944 89m bw
Butcher
A runaway couple are unwittingly abetted by her uncle.
Unsubtle family farce.
w Jack Whittingham d Paul Stein
☆ Patricia Medina, Jimmy Hanley, Frederick Leister, Marie Lohr, Claud Allister, Ellen Pollock, Wylie Watson

'There's only one way Det. Alex Cross can get close to a deadly collector … with the help of the only woman who got away.'

Kiss the Girls
US 1997 120m DeLuxe Panavision
Paramount/Rysher (David Brown, Joe Wizan)
▭ ▭ ⌖ ◉ ⌂
A forensic psychologist goes on the track of a psychopath who is kidnapping and killing women.
Unpleasant thriller which expects its audience to get its pleasures from watching women being stalked and threatened.
w David Klass *novel* James Patterson d Gary Fleder ph Aaron Schneider m Mark Isham pd Nelson Coates ed William Steinkamp, Harvey Rosenstock
☆ Morgan Freeman, Ashley Judd, Cary Elwes, Tony Goldwyn, Jay O. Sanders, Bill Nunn, Brian Cox

'Devotes itself to exploiting every fear and phobia about men to which women are prey. It's a flagrantly dangerous picture … a grossly indecent product.' – *Alexander Walker, London Evening Standard*

Kiss the Girls and Make Them Die

Italy 1966 106m Technicolor
Dino de Laurentiis
original title: Si Tutte le Donne del Mondo...
A rich industrialist has a plan to sterilize the whole male population of the world and restock it with his own mistresses, whom he keeps in suspended animation.
Patchy James Bond spoof.
w Jack Pulman, Dino Maiuri d Henry Levin, Dino Maiuri ph Aldo Tonti m Mario Nascimbene
☆ Michael Connors, Dorothy Provine, Raf Vallone, Terry-Thomas

Kiss Them for Me

US 1957 105m Eastmancolor
Cinemascope
TCF (Jerry Wald)
Three navy pilots spend a weekend's unofficial leave in San Francisco, and get into various kinds of trouble.
Based on a novel which also served as source for the musical Hit the Deck, this very heavy-footed comedy with serious asides is most unsuitably cast and generally ill-timed and unattractive.
w Julius Epstein novel Shore Leave by Frederic Wakeman d Stanley Donen ph Milton Krasner m Lionel Newman
☆ Cary Grant, Jayne Mansfield, Suzy Parker, Ray Walston, Larry Blyden, Leif Erickson, Werner Klemperer

Kiss Tomorrow Goodbye

US 1950 102m bw
Cagney Productions (William Cagney)
A violent criminal breaks jail and plans several daring robberies.
Surprisingly brutal star melodrama which failed to repeat the success of White Heat.
w Harry Brown novel Horace McCoy d Gordon Douglas ph Peverell Marley m Carmen Dragon
☆ James Cagney, Barbara Payton, Ward Bond, Luther Adler, Helena Carter, Steve Brodie, Rhys Williams, Barton MacLane, Frank Reicher, John Litel
'The mixture as before without an ingredient changed.' – Otis Guernsey Jnr

Kissed *

Canada 1996 78m colour
Metro/Tartan/Boneyard (Dean English, Lynne Stopkewich)
A young woman working in a funeral home makes love to the more attractive male corpses.
A dreamy evocation of the taboo subject of necrophilia which borders on the lifeless.
w Angus Fraser, Lynne Stopkewich story Barbara Gowdy d Lynne Stopkewich ph Gregory Middleton m Don MacDonald pd Eric McNab ed John Pozer, Peter Roeck, Lynne Stopkewich
☆ Molly Parker, Peter Outerbridge, Jay Brazeau, Natasha Morley, Jessie Winter Mudie, James Timmons
'This gently humorous film manages to present its disturbing psychology with understanding.' – George Perry, Sunday Times
'It's far too insultingly simplistic and naive on both the psychological and narrative levels to be taken that seriously.' – Alan Jones, Film Review

Kisses for Breakfast

US 1941 81m bw
Warner
A man just married loses his memory and marries again.
Poorly developed farce comedy with stars who can't help.
w Kenneth Gamet play Seymour Hicks d Lewis Seiler
☆ Dennis Morgan, Jane Wyatt, Shirley Ross, Lee Patrick, Jerome Cowan, Una O'Connor, Barnett Parker, Cornel Wilde

Kisses for My President

US 1964 113m bw
Warner/Pearlayne (Curtis Bernhardt)
America's first woman president causes problems for her husband.
Solidly-carpentered comedy with too few ideas for its length.
w Claude Binyon, Robert G. Kane d Curtis Bernhardt ph Robert Surtees m Bronislau Kaper

☆ Polly Bergen, Fred MacMurray, Arlene Dahl, Eli Wallach, Edward Andrews

Kissin' Cousins

US 1963 96m Metrocolor Panavision
MGM/Four Leaf (Sam Katzman)
The USAF wants to build a missile base on Smokey Mountain, and their PR man discovers that one of the hillbillies is his double.
A feeble production in every sense, even below its star's usual standard.
w Gerald Drayson Adams, Gene Nelson d Gene Nelson ph Ellis W. Carter md Fred Karger
☆ Elvis Presley, Arthur O'Connell, Glenda Farrell, Jack Albertson

Kissing a Fool

US 1998 94m DeLuxe
Universal/Largo/RL (Tag Mendillo, Andrew Form, Rick Lashbrook)
A sportswriter asks his best friend to attempt to seduce his girlfriend, in order to test her fidelity.
Contrived comedy that needs a lightness of touch, rather than the clumping treatment it gets here.
w James Frey, Doug Ellin d Doug Ellin ph Thomas Del Ruth m Joseph Vitarelli pd Charles Breen ed David Finfer
☆ David Schwimmer, Jason Lee, Mili Avital, Bonnie Hunt, Vanessa Angel, Kari Wuhrer, Frank Medrano, Bitty Schram
'Tries too hard to shake things up just a little, but falls between rather too many stools.' – Bob McCabe, Empire

The Kissing Bandit

US 1948 102m Technicolor
MGM (Joe Pasternak)
In old California, a young businessman finds he is expected to keep up his bandit father's criminal and romantic reputation.
Silly, witless musical which never settles into gear; mocked by its star as Benny mocked The Horn Blows at Midnight.
w Isobel Lennart, John Briard Harding d Laslo Benedek ph Robert Surtees m Georgie Stoll m/ly Nacio Herb Brown, Earl Brent, Edward Heyman
☆ Frank Sinatra, Kathryn Grayson, J. Carrol Naish, Mildred Natwick, Mikhail Rasumny, Billy Gilbert, Clinton Sundberg
'Was Kissing Bandit the nadir of my career? Hell, it was the nadir of anybody's career.' – Frank Sinatra

Kit Carson

US 1940 95m bw
Edward Small
Adventures of the pioneer Indian scout.
Thinly scripted Western imaginings with a sturdy but not alluring cast.
w George Bruce d George B. Seitz
☆ Jon Hall, Lynn Bari, Dana Andrews, Harold Huber, Ward Bond, Renie Riano, Raymond Hatton

Kitchen

Hong Kong/Japan 1997 112m colour
Alliance/Golden Harvest Crown/Amuse (Yim-Ho, Akira Morishige)
original title: Wo Ai Chufang
Homeless after her grandmother's death, a grieving woman goes to live with a hairdresser and his transsexual father.
A strange, muted tale of love and loss among eccentric misfits, filmed in an expressionist style among dated artefacts; definitely an acquired taste.
wd Yim Ho novel Banana Yoshimoto ph Poon Hang-Sang m Otomo Yoshihide, Uchihashi Kazuhisa ad James Leung, Jason Mok ed Poon Hung-Yiu
☆ Jordan Chan, Yasuko Tomita, Law Kar-Ying, Karen Mok, Lau Siu-Ming, Lo Koon Lan

The Kitchen Toto *

GB 1987 95m colour
Cannon/Skreba/British Screen/Film Four (Ann Skinner)
1950: in Kenya, a police officer agrees to take in the son of a black priest murdered by the Mau Mau.

Rather lumpy but well-meaning drama with a tragic ending.
wd Harry Hook ph Roger Deakins m John Keane pd Jamie Leonard ed Tom Priestley
☆ Bob Peck, Phyllis Logan, Edwin Mahinda, Robert Urquhart

Kitten with a Whip

US 1964 83m bw
Universal
A girl escaped from reform school takes refuge with a politician whose wife is away.
Over-the-top melodrama thought bannable at the time.
wd Douglas Heyes book Wade Miller
☆ Ann-Margret, John Forsythe, Patricia Barry, Ann Doran, Audrey Dalton

Kitty

GB 1928 90m bw silent
BIP/Burlington (Victor Saville)
A shopgirl loves a paralysed amnesiac, but his mother interferes.
Uninteresting romantic melodrama, notable only as Britain's first sound film: a few dialogue sequences were quickly added (in New York).
w Violet Powell, Benn W. Levy novel Warwick Deeping d Victor Saville ph Karl Puth
☆ John Stuart, Estelle Brody, Dorothy Cumming, Marie Ault, Olaf Hytten

'She had all London on a MARRY-go-round!'

Kitty ***

US 1945 103m bw
Paramount (Karl Tunberg)
In 18th-century London, an aristocrat makes a duchess of a guttersnipe.
Well-detailed period Pygmalion which works much better than one would expect.
w Darrell Ware, Karl Tunberg novel Rosamund Marshall d Mitchell Leisen ph Daniel L. Fapp m Victor Young ad Hans Dreier, Walter Tyler
☆ Paulette Goddard, Ray Milland, Cecil Kellaway, Constance Collier, Reginald Owen, Patric Knowles, Dennis Hoey, Sara Allgood, Eric Blore, Gordon Richards, Michael Dyne
'Enough sex, wit and urbane cynicism to make one forget a footling ending.' – Peter John Dyer, MFB
'It is excellently cast, delightfully acted, and the rather sordid story is told with subtlety and skill.' – Picture Show
'The most glamorous study of unrelieved sordidness that the screen has presented.' – Motion Picture Herald
🏆 art direction

'The most daring novel ever written by a man about a woman!'

Kitty Foyle **

US 1940 108m bw
RKO (Harry E. Edgington, David Hempstead)
A white-collar girl has a troubled love life.
Solid entertainment of its time, especially aimed at ambitious young ladies.
w Dalton Trumbo, Donald Ogden Stewart novel Christopher Morley d Sam Wood ph Robert de Grasse m Roy Webb
☆ Ginger Rogers, Dennis Morgan, James Craig, Eduardo Ciannelli, Ernest Cossart, Gladys Cooper, Mary Treen
👤 Ginger Rogers
🏆 best picture; Dalton Trumbo; Sam Wood

The Klansman

US 1974 112m Technicolor
Paramount/Atlanta (William Alexander)
An Alabama sheriff confronts the Ku Klux Klan.
Violent melodrama, all noise, brutality and bad acting.
w Millard Kaufman, Samuel Fuller novel William Bradford Huie d Terence Young ph Lloyd Ahern, Aldo Tonti m Stax Organization
☆ Lee Marvin, Richard Burton, Cameron Mitchell, O. J. Simpson, Lola Falana, David Huddleston, Luciana Paluzzi, Linda Evans
'There's not a shred of quality, dignity, relevance or impact in this yahoo-oriented bunk.' – Variety

'Mae goes north and Alaska goes west!'

Klondike Annie

US 1936 83m bw
Paramount (William Le Baron)
A torch singer on the run disguises herself as a missionary and revivifies a Klondike mission.
Laundered Mae West vehicle, from her fading period but not too bad.
w Mae West, Marion Morgan, George B. Dowell d Raoul Walsh ph George Clemens
☆ Mae West, Victor McLaglen, Philip Reed, Helen Jerome Eddy, Harry Beresford, Harold Huber, Esther Howard
'I found the whole film fun, more fun than any other of Miss West's since the superb period piece, She Done Him Wrong.' – Graham Greene

Klute ***

US 1971 114m Technicolor Panavision
Warner (Alan J. Pakula)
A policeman leaves the force to investigate the disappearance of a research scientist, and takes up with a call girl who is involved.
Excellent adult thriller with attention to detail and emphasis on character.
w Andy K. Lewis, Dave Lewis d Alan J. Pakula ph Gordon Willis m Michael Small
☆ Jane Fonda, Donald Sutherland, Charles Cioffi, Roy Scheider, Rita Gam
👤 Jane Fonda
🏆 Andy K. Lewis, Dave Lewis

The Knack ****

GB 1965 84m bw
UA/Woodfall (Oscar Lewenstein)
A sex-starved young teacher lets one room of his house to a successful womanizer, another to an innocent girl from the north.
An excuse for an anarchic series of visual gags, a kaleidoscope of swinging London in which anything goes. Brilliantly done in the style of A Hard Day's Night.
w Charles Wood play Ann Jellicoe d Richard Lester ph David Watkin m John Barry
☆ Michael Crawford, Ray Brooks, Rita Tushingham, Donal Donnelly
'The whole film has the anarchic quality modish today and at all times appealing to a new generation understandably bent on overturning the ideas which have hardened in the minds of their elders.' – Dilys Powell
'The running jokes and gags never come off.' – Pauline Kael

Knave of Hearts *

GB 1954 103m bw
Transcontinental (Paul Graetz)
aka: Monsieur Ripois et Son Nemesis
US title: Lover Boy
A born philanderer confesses all his affairs to his wife.
Well-observed though strangely flat and disappointing sex comedy, something of a pioneer in its time and therefore perhaps too diffident in its approach.
w René Clément, Hugh Mills d René Clément ph Oswald Morris m Roman Vlad
☆ Gérard Philipe, Margaret Johnston, Joan Greenwood, Natasha Parry, Valerie Hobson

Knickerbocker Holiday *

US 1944 84m bw
UA/PCA/Harry Joe Brown
In old New Amsterdam, a one-legged tyrant finally sees the light.
Artificial musical from a famous Broadway original, staged in 1938, with engaging moments including Charles Coburn singing 'September Song'.
w David Boehm, Harry Goldman, Rowland Leigh, Thomas Lennon novel Father Knickerbocker's History of New York by Washington Irving d Harry Joe Brown ph Phil Tannura m Werner Heymann m/ly Kurt Weill, Maxwell Anderson
☆ Charles Coburn, Nelson Eddy, Constance Dowling, Ernest Cossart, Shelley Winters, Otto Kruger
🏆 Werner Heymann, Kurt Weill

Knife in the Water *

Poland   1962   94m   bw
ZRF Kamera (Stanislaw Zylewicz)
📀 📀 ⊛ 🎧

original title: *Noz w Wodzie*
A young couple ask a hitchhiker to spend a weekend on their yacht, and regret it.
Detached little melodrama in which the sex and violence hover beneath the surface. All very watchable, but in a minor key.
w Jerzy Skolimowski, Roman Polanski, Jakub Goldberg d Roman Polanski ph Jerzy Lipman m Krzystof Komeda
☆ Leon Niemczyk, Jolanta Umecka, Zygmunt Malanowicz
'Has all the virtues of an intensely psychological, sardonically probing modern novel.' – *John Simon*
⚜ best foreign film

Knight Moves

US/Germany   1992   116m   Eastmancolor
Columbia TriStar/Knight Moves/Cine Vox (Ziad El Khoury, Jean-Luc Defait)
📀 📀 ⊛ 🎧

A chess champion is suspected of being a serial killer.
Lacklustre thriller with little suspense or sense of reality.
w Brad Mirman d Carl Schenkel ph Dietrich Lohmann md Anne Dudley pd Graeme Murray ed Norbert Herzner
☆ Christopher Lambert, Diane Lane, Tom Skerritt, Daniel Baldwin, Ferdinand Mayne, Katherine Isobel, Charles Bailey-Gates, Arthur Strauss
'Mannered, heavy-handed and rather ridiculous.' – *Philip French, Observer*

Knight of the Plains

US   1938   57m   bw
Equity/Spectrum/Stan Laurel (Jed Buell)
A cowboy defeats a confidence trickster who tries to cheat settlers out of their land.
Amiable Western, starring one of the many singing cowboys of the time; although it sticks to all the conventions – bearded comic sidekick, a hero who puts away his gun to fight the villain with his fists – it has more sprightly narrative than most of its kind.
w Fred Myton d Sam Newfield ph Mack Stengler md Lew Porter ed Robert Jahns
☆ Fred Scott, Al St John, Marion Weldon, John Merton, Richard Kramer, Frank La Rue, Lafe McKee

Knight without Armour **

GB   1937   107m   bw
London Films (Alexander Korda)
📀 📀

During the Russian Revolution of 1917, a widowed countess is helped to safety by a British translator.
Underrated romantic adventure with big production values and some splendid moments.
w Lajos Biro, Arthur Wimperis, Frances Marion novel James Hilton d Jacques Feyder ph Harry Stradling, Bernard Browne, Jack Cardiff m Miklos Rozsa md Muir Mathieson ad Lazare Meerson ed William Hornbeck, Francis Lyon
☆ Robert Donat, Marlene Dietrich, Irene Vanbrugh, Herbert Lomas, Austin Trevor, Basil Gill, David Tree, John Clements, Lawrence Hanray
'Another feather in the cap of Alexander Korda for his series of artistic film productions. There is relatively little to find fault with and much to praise.' – *Variety*
'A first-class thriller, beautifully directed, with spare and convincing dialogue and a nearly watertight scenario.' – *Graham Greene*

Knightriders

US   1981   155m   colour
United (Richard P. Rubinstein)
📀 ⊛

A group of wandering hippies, led by a man obsessed with notions of chivalry, re-enact medieval tournaments on motor-bikes.
A glum and wordy movie, revealing little point or purpose
wd George A. Romero ph Michael Gornick m Donald Rubinstein pd Cletus Anderson ed George A. Romero, Pasquale Buba
☆ Ed Harris, Gary Lahti, Tom Savini, Amy Ingersoll, Patricia Tallman, Christine Forrest

Knights and Emeralds

👫👫   GB   1986   94m   colour
Warner/Goldcrest/Enigma (Susan Richards, Raymond Day)
A young white drummer joins a rival black band for the national marching bands championship.
Dull teen drama of racial relationships, accompanied by a great deal of uninteresting music.
wd Ian Emes ph Richard Greatrex m Colin Towns ad Deborah Gillingham ed John Victor-Smith
☆ Christopher Wild, Beverley Hills, Warren Mitchell, Bill Leadbitter, Rachel Davies

Knights of the Round Table *

👫👫   GB   1953   115m   Eastmancolor   Cinemascope
MGM (Pandro S. Berman)
📀 ⊛

Lancelot, banished from King Arthur's court for loving Guinevere, returns to defeat the evil Modred.
Disappointingly flat, pageant-like adaptation of the legends, with a few lively strands insufficiently firmly drawn together.
w Talbot Jennings, Jan Lustig, Noel Langley d Richard Thorpe ph Frederick A. Young, Stephen Dade m Miklos Rozsa ad Alfred Junge, Hans Peters
☆ Robert Taylor, Mel Ferrer, Ava Gardner, Anne Crawford, Stanley Baker, Felix Aylmer, Robert Urquhart, Niall MacGinnis
⚜ art direction

Knights of the Teutonic Order *

Poland   1960   180m   Eastmancolor   Dyaliscope
Studio Unit (Zygmunt Krol)
original title: *Krzyzacy*
Teutonic knights pillage Poland on the pretext of converting the inhabitants to Christianity; when they kill a noblewoman, her daughter swears revenge.
Medieval epic differing little from those of Hollywood, but splendid to look at.
w Jerzy Stefan Stawinski, Aleksander Ford novel Henryk Sienkiewicz d Aleksander Ford ph Mieczyslaw Jahoda m Kazimierz Serocki
☆ Urszula Modrzynska, Grazyna Staniszewska, Andrzej Szalawski

Knock Off

US   1998   91m   DeLuxe
Knock/MDP/Film Workshop/Val D'Oro (Nansun Shi)
📀 📀

In Hong Kong, a former forger of designer clothes and his partner, a CIA agent, foil the activities of violent smugglers.
Hectic action movie with a confusing plot and frantic fights, which is to say the mixture as usual for its star.
w Steven E. de Souza d Tsui Hark m Arthur Wong m Ron Mael, Russell Mael pd James Leung, Bill Lui ed Mak Chi Sin
☆ Jean-Claude Van Damme, Rob Schneider, Lela Rochon, Paul Sorvino, Michael Fitzgerald Wong, Carmen Lee, Glen Chin, Jeff Joseph Wolfe, Wyman Wong
'Much of the movie simply consists of the gung-ho heroes doing the standard acrobatic butt-kicking that passes for action in the undemanding Far East market.' – *Alexander Walker*

Knock on Any Door *

US   1949   100m   bw
Columbia/Santana (Robert Lord)
📀 ⊛

A defence lawyer pleads with the jury for the life of a slum boy on a murder charge.
Smartly-made but empty melodrama making facile social points.
w Daniel Taradash, John Monks Jnr novel Willard Motley d Nicholas Ray ph Burnett Guffey m George Antheil
☆ Humphrey Bogart, John Derek, George Macready, Allene Roberts

Knock on Wood **

US   1954   103m   Technicolor
Paramount (Norman Panama, Melvin Frank)
Stolen plans are hidden inside the dummy of an unsuspecting ventriloquist.
Excellent star comedy with good script and production (but some strange ideas of London's geography).
wd Norman Panama, Melvin Frank ph Daniel Fapp m Leith Stevens m/ly Sylvia Fine ch Michael Kidd
☆ Danny Kaye, Mai Zetterling, David Burns, Torin Thatcher, Leon Askin, Abner Biberman, Steve Geray
⚜ Norman Panama, Melvin Frank (script)

Knockout: see *Knute Rockne, All American*

Knocks at My Door **

Venezuela/Cuba/Argentina (Liz Mago)   1993   106m   Agfacolor
Foncine/CONAC/ASP/ICAIC/Channel 4 (Alejandro Saderman)
original title: *Golpes a Mi Puerta*
Two nuns face execution for sheltering a young radical being hunted by a military death-squad.
Gripping and timely drama of courage and obduracy, political expediency and state brutality.
w Juan Carlos Gene, Alejandro Saderman play Juan Carlos Gene d Alejandro Saderman ph Jonny Semeco, Adriano Moreno m Julio D'Escrivan ad Marietta Perroni ed Claudia Uribe
☆ Verónica Oddó, Elba Escobar, Juan Carlos Gené, José Antonio Rodriguez, Ana Castell, Mirta Ibarra, Frank Spano

Knute Rockne, All American

US   1940   98m   bw
Warner (Robert Fellows)
📀

GB title: *Knockout*
aka: *A Modern Hero*
The career of a famous Notre Dame football coach.
Standard sporting biopic.
w Robert Buckner d Lloyd Bacon ph Tony Gaudio m Ferde Grofé
☆ Pat O'Brien, Ronald Reagan, Gale Page, Donald Crisp, Albert Basserman, John Qualen, John Sheffield

Koenigsmark

France   1935   114m   bw
Roger Richebé/Capitol
A princess falls for a commoner.
Rather elementary royal romance in a Ruritanian background, filmed simultaneously in French and English by the same principals.
novel Pierre Benoit d Maurice Tourneur ph Victor Armenise m Jacques Ibert
☆ Elissa Landi, Pierre Fresnay, John Lodge

Kokaku Kidotai: see *Ghost in the Shell*

Kokoda Crescent

Australia   1988   83m   colour
Phillip Emanuel
When a youth dies from an overdose of heroin, his grandfather decides to take action against the drug dealer involved.
Ponderous tale of old soldiers finding a new campaign to fight.
w Patrick Cook d Ted Robinson ph Dan Burstall m Peter Best pd Leslie Binns ed Robert Gibson
☆ Warren Mitchell, Ruth Cracknell, Bill Kerr, Madge Ryan, Martin Vaughan, Steve Jacobs, Penne Hackforth-Jones

Koks I Kulissen: see *Ladies on the Rocks*

Kolobos

US   1999   83m   FotoKem
Armitage (Nne Ebong, Dana Altman)
📀 📀

Five young people answer an advert to appear in an experimental film and find themselves trapped in an old dark house with doors and windows sealed.
Cheap and nasty horror movie, low on imagination and high on gruesome effects; it finally leaves its audience as much in the dark as its characters.
w Nne Ebong, Daniel Liatowitsch, David Todd Ocvirk d Daniel Liatowitsch, David Todd Ocvirk ph Yoram Astrakhan m William Kidd pd Preston Fisher ed Brian Olson
☆ Amy Weber, Donny Terranova, Nichole Pelerine, John Fairlie, Promise LaMarco, Ilia Volok, Linnea Quigley
'Wholly baffling horror farrago.' – *Sight and Sound*

Kolya ***

Czech Republic/France/GB   1996   105m   colour
Buena Vista/Portobello/Ceska Televize/Biograf Jan Sverák
📀 📀 ⊛ 🎧

In Prague, a penniless musician marries for cash a Russian woman who needs Czech papers and finds that the transaction leaves him with her five-year-old son.
Charming, tough-minded drama of people trying to get by within a system that leaves them little room for manoeuvre.
w Zdenek Sverák idea Pavel Taussig d Jan Sverák ph Vladimir Smutny m Ondrej Soukup ed Alois Visárek
☆ Zdenek Sverák, Andrei Chalimon, Libuse Safránková, Ondrej Vetchy, Stella Závorková, Ladislav Smoljak, Irina Livanova
'Balances heart-warming sentiment with gentle humor and observations that strike universal chords.' – *David Rooney, Variety*
⚜ foreign film

Komissar **

USSR   1967   108m   colour   Cinemascope
Artificial Eye/Gorky Studios (V. Levin, L. Prilutzkaya)
aka: *The Commissar*
During the Civil War of the 1920s, a pregnant soldier of the Red Army moves in with a poor Jewish family to have her child.
First publicly shown twenty years after it was made, the film's events indict anti-Semitism and foreshadow the later treatment of the Jews within the context of a simple domestic story.
wd Alexander Askoldov novel In the Town of Berdichev by Vasily Grossman ph Valery Ginsburg m Alfred Schnittke ad Sergei Serebrennikov ed V. Isayeva, N. Loginova, S. Lyashinskaya
☆ Nonna Mordyukova, Rolan Bykov, Raisa Niedashkovskaya, Vasily Shukshin

Komitas

West Germany   1988   106m   colour
ICA/Margarita Woskanjan Filmproduction/WDR/SFB/Channel 4
Visually striking meditation on an Armenian monk and composer traumatized into silence by the Turkish massacre of his countrymen in 1915.
Limited in its appeal.
wd Don Askarjan ph Jorgos Arvanitis, Martin Gressmann, Eberhard Geik m Komitas and others ad Jurgen Kiebach, Michael Poladian ed Rene Perraudin, Marion Regentrop
☆ Samvel Ovasapain, Margarita Woskanjan, Onig Saadetian, Yeghishe Mougikian

Koneko Monogatari: see *The Adventures of Milo and Otis*

Konga

GB   1960   90m   Eastmancolor   Spectamation
Anglo Amalgamated/Merton Studios (Nat Cohen, Stuart Levy)
📀

A scientist's experiments on a chimpanzee turn it into a monstrous killer ape.
Ridiculous mad-scientist movie, with some over-the-top acting in an attempt to distract attention from the risible script.
w Aben Kandel, Herman Cohen d John Lemont ph Desmond Dickinson m Gerard Schurmann md Muir Mathieson ad Wilfred Arnold ed Jack Slade
☆ Michael Gough, Margo Johns, Jess Conrad, Claire Gordon, Jack Watson, Austin Trevor, George Pastell, Leonard Sachs

Kongbufenzi: see *The Terrorizer*

Kongo

US   1932   86m   bw
MGM
An embittered African recluse takes revenge on the daughter of his former enemy.
No-holds-barred melodrama which never really exerts the right grip; a remake of the Lon Chaney silent West of Zanzibar.
w Leon Gordon play Chester de Vonde, Kilbourn Gordon d William Cowen ph Harold Rosson
☆ Walter Huston, Lupe Velez, Virginia Bruce, Conrad Nagel, C. Henry Gordon
'Horror and tropical stuff combined ... chiefly for the daily grinds.' – *Variety*

Der Kongress Tanzt: see *Congress Dances*

Kontrakt: see *The Contract*

Konyets Sankt-Peterburga: see *The End of St Petersburg*

Kopek and Broom: see *Find the Lady*

Korczak
Poland/Germany/France/GB   1990   118m
colour
Artificial Eye/Filmstudio 'Perspektywa'/Regina Ziegler Filmproduktion/Erato Films/BBC Films/Telmar Film International (Regina Ziegler, Janusz Morgenstern, Daniel Tocsan du Plantier)
📼
The director of a Polish orphanage attempts to protect his charges from the Nazis.
Despite, or perhaps because of, being based on reality, the film fails to engage satisfactorily with its subject matter.
w Agnieszka Holland   d Andrzej Wajda
ph Robby Müller   m Wojciech Kilar   pd Allan Starski   ed Ewa Smal
☆ Wojtek Pszoniak, Ewa Dalkowska, Piotr Kozlowski, Marzena Trybala, Wojciech Klata, Adam Siemion, Karolina Czernicka, Agnieszka Kruk

Korkalen: see *Thy Soul Shall Bear Witness*

Koroshi No Rakuin: see *Branded to Kill*

Korotkie Vstrechi: see *Short Encounters*

Koshikei: see *Death by Hanging*

Kotch *
US   1971   114m   Metrocolor
ABC/Kotch Company (Richard Carter)
📼
An eccentric 72-year-old widower is at odds with his family and helps a pregnant babysitter.
Variously amusing, moving and sentimental, this generally likeable film about a crotchety grandpa is sustained by its star performance.
w John Paxton   novel Katherine Topkins   d Jack Lemmon   ph Richard H. Kline   m Marvin Hamlisch
☆ Walter Matthau, Deborah Winters, Felicia Farr, Charles Aidman
   'A nice, sentimental, Life-Can-Be-Beautiful comedy of the second order.' – *Judith Crist*
♪ Walter Matthau; song 'Life Is What You Make It' (mMarvin Hamlisch, lyJohnny Mercer)

Koyaanisqatsi *
US   1983   86m   DeLuxe
Island Alive/Blue Dolphin/Institute for Regional Education (Godfrey Reggio)
📼 💿
A panoramic view of contemporary America without commentary or narrative, using time-lapse photography. The title is an Indian word meaning 'a state of life that calls for another way of living'.
A rather pointless, very beautiful, and finally rather boring experience.
w Ron Fricke, Godfrey Reggio, Michael Hoenig, Alton Walpole   d Godfrey Reggio   ph Ron Fricke
m Philip Glass   ed Anton Walpole, Ron Fricke
   'Arrogant bombast, provoking no response except "wow".' – *Sight & Sound*
† It was followed by *Powaqqatsi* (qv), which gave a similar treatment to the Third World.

Krakatoa, East of Java
US   1968   136m   Technicolor   Cinerama
ABC/Cinerama (Lester A. Sansom)
⊚
In 1883 the SS *Batavia Queen* leaves Singapore and is engulfed by the Krakatoa eruption.
Mindless spectacular, technically quite impressive but with no dramatic interest whatsoever. (Krakatoa is actually west of Java.)
w Clifford Newton Gould, Bernard Gordon
d Bernard Kowalski   ph Manuel Berenguer
m Frank de Vol   pd/sp Eugene Lourié
☆ Maximilian Schell, Diane Baker, Brian Keith, Rossano Brazzi, Barbara Werle, John Leyton, Sal Mineo, J. D. Cannon, Marc Lawrence
   'Apparently designed to disprove the old adage, "they don't make them like that any more". At a conservative count it includes such sure-fire cinematic ingredients as hidden treasure, deep-

sea divers with shattered lungs and claustrophobia, mutiny and fire on board ship, nuns, convicts, a lost orphan boy, girl divers and even a little striptease, climaxing in the biggest explosion and the greatest tidal wave known to history.' – *MFB*
♫ special visual effects

'There are three sides to this love story!'
Kramer versus Kramer ***
US   1979   105m   Technicolor
Columbia/Stanley Jaffe (Richard C. Fischoff)
📼 📼 💿 🎧
A divorced advertising executive gets temporary custody of his seven-year-old son.
New-fashioned tearjerker, as slick as a colour supplement and camp to the emotion-starved masses.
wd Robert Benton   novel Avery Corman   ph Nestor Almendros   md Erma E. Levin   pd Paul Sylbert
ed Jerry Greenberg
☆ Dustin Hoffman, Justin Henry, Meryl Streep, Jane Alexander, Howard Duff
   'Pastel colours, a cute kid and a good script made this one of the most undeserved successes of the year: wall-to-wall sentiment.' – *Time Out*
🏆 best picture; Robert Benton (as director); Dustin Hoffman; Meryl Streep; screenplay adapted from another medium
♫ Justin Henry; Jane Alexander; Nestor Almendros; editing

'When people are afraid of you ... You can do everything. Remember that.'
The Krays **
GB   1990   119m   colour
Rank/Parkfield (Dominic Anciano, Ray Burdis)
📼 📼 💿 🎧 ⊚
Twins, who grow up in a mother-dominated household, become feared and fearsome East End thugs.
Made with the cooperation of its real-life protagonists, it stays within a gangster milieu and comes close to glamorizing them both.
w Philip Ridley   d Peter Medak   ph Alex Thomson   m Michael Kamen   pd Michael Pickwoad   ed Martin Walsh
☆ Billie Whitelaw, Gary Kemp, Martin Kemp, Susan Fleetwood, Charlotte Cornwell, Jimmy Jewel, Avis Bunnage, Kate Hardie, Alfred Lynch, Tom Bell, Steven Berkoff
   'The direction does not flinch, as do most other British crime-class-nostalgia movies, from graphic violence.' – *MFB*
   'The movie comes over like a collaboration between Joan Littlewood's Theatre Workshop, an ungifted follower of Sigmund Freud and the postcard artist Donald McGill.' – *Philip French, Observer*

Kreitzerova Sonata
USSR   1987   135m   colour
Cannon/Mosfilm (Maria Zakharova)
aka: *The Kreutzer Sonata*
A jealous husband tells a fellow traveller how he came to kill his wife.
Restlessly faithful to the book, but failing to engage its audience.
w Mikhail Schweitzer   novel Leo Tolstoy
d Mikhail Schweitzer, Sofia Milkina   ph Mikhail Agraovich   m Sofia Gubaidulina   pd Igor Lemeshev, Vladimir Fabrikov   ed Lyudmila Feiginova
☆ Oleg Yankovsky, Aleksandr Trofimov, Irina Seleznyova, Dmitri Pokrovsky

'If you miss the first five minutes you miss one suicide, two executions, one seduction and the key to the plot!'
The Kremlin Letter
US   1970   122m   DeLuxe   Panavision
TCF (Carter de Haven, Sam Wiesenthal)
An American intelligence team is sent undercover to Moscow to retrieve an arms treaty mistakenly signed.
Tediously violent cold war mystifier: a few good performances do not make it worth unravelling.
w John Huston, Gladys Hill   novel Noel Behn
d John Huston   ph Ted Scaife   m Robert Drasnin
pd Ted Haworth
☆ Richard Boone, Orson Welles, Bibi Andersson, Max von Sydow, Patrick O'Neal, Ronald Radd, George Sanders, Dean Jagger, Nigel Green, Barbara Parkins, Lila Kedrova, Michael MacLiammoir, Sandor Eles, Niall MacGinnis, John Huston

'One of those all-star international spy sagas that trick out an indecipherably tortuous plot with a series of vignettes in which the pleasures of star-spotting are expected to compensate for any narrative longueurs.' – *Nigel Andrews*

Krippendorf's Tribe
US   1998   94m   Technicolor
Buena Vista/Touchstone/Mora-Brezner-Steinberg-Tenenbaum/Dreyfuss-James (Larry Brezner)
📼 🎧
A widowed anthropologist, who has spent his research grant on his children, invents a lost New Guinea tribe, faking film of them in his back yard.
Energetic comedy, though lacking in wit or humour; its sexual jokes are likely to alienate a family audience, for which it was presumably intended.
w Charlie Peters   book Frank Parkin   d Todd Holland   ph Dean Cundey   m Bruce Broughton
pd Scott Chambliss   ed Jon Poll
☆ Richard Dreyfuss, Jenna Elfman, Natasha Lyonne, Gregory Smith, Carl Michael Lindner, Stephen Root, Elaine Stritch, Tom Poston, David Ogden Stiers, Lily Tomlin, Zakes Mokae
   'Frenetic, formulaic and instantly forgettable.' – *Joe Leydon, Variety*
† The film was released direct to video in Britain.

Krótki Film o Milości: see *A Short Film about Love*

Krótki Film o Zabijaniu: see *A Short Film about Killing*

Krull
🏕 GB   1983   121m   Metrocolor
Columbia/Ted Mann-Ron Silverman
📼 📼 💿 🎧
Prince Colwyn's bride-to-be is abducted by the Beast of the Black Fortress.
Old-fashioned derring-do taking place on a somewhat unattractive planet; nevertheless fairly lively in its action and trick effects.
w Stanford Sherman   d Peter Yates   ph Peter Suschitzky   m James Horner   pd Stephen Grimes
☆ Ken Marshall, Lysette Anthony, Freddie Jones, Francesca Annis, Alun Armstrong, David Battley, Bernard Bresslaw, John Welsh, Tony Church, Bernard Archard
   'Nearly everything in it has been done before, in some cases rather better, but rarely quite so likeably.' – *Nick Roddick, MFB*
   'Not really thrilling enough to be a blockbuster and not light enough to be anything else.' – *Sight and Sound*

Krzyzacy: see *Knights of the Teutonic Order*

'When you have attitude, who needs experience?'
Kuffs
US   1992   101m   Technicolor
Universal/EvansGideon (Raynold Gideon)
📼 📼 💿 🎧
A high-school dropout inherits his murdered brother's private police business and sets out to avenge his death.
Messily coarse comedy not helped by the star's direct addresses to the camera.
w Bruce A. Evans, Raynold Gideon   d Bruce A. Evans   ph Thomas Del Ruth   m Harold Faltermeyer   pd Victoria Paul, Armin Ganz
ed Stephen Semel
☆ Christian Slater, Tony Goldwyn, Milla Jovovich, Bruce Boxleitner, Troy Evans, George de la Pena, Leon Rippy
   'Film veers from ultra-violence to slapstick comedy in an arbitrary and irritating fashion. Hokey camera angles and flashy dissolves fail to pump up the action.' – *Variety*
   'The film comes to resemble the bastard child of *Miami Vice* and an especially bad movie-of-the-week.' – *New York Times*

Kühle Wampe ***
Germany   1932   73m   bw
Prometheus/Praesens (George Hoellering)
aka: *Whither Germany?*
During the Depression in Berlin, a working-class family is forced to move to a shantytown on the outskirts of the city.
A powerful attack on capitalist brutality and working-class apathy, which also suggested that the hope of the future lay with the revolutionary young, an optimism that was sadly misplaced. It is the only film in which

Brecht was in control, working with a collective of like-minded collaborators.
w Bertold Brecht, Ernst Ottwald   d Slaten Dodow
ph Günther Krampf   m Hanns Eisler, Josef Schmidt
☆ Hertha Thiele, Ernst Busch, Martha Wolter, Adolf Fischer, Lili Schönborn, Max Sablotzki, Alfred Schaefer
† German authorities banned the film on its release as offending 'against the vital interests of the state' and as being 'a summons to violence and subversion'. Brecht, by lying, persuaded the censor to release it with a few minor cuts. He later wrote, 'Leaving the building we did not conceal our high opinion of the censor. He had penetrated the essence of our artistic intentions with far greater sagacity than our most benevolent critics.'

'Courage conquers all.'
Kull the Conqueror
US   1997   95m   DeLuxe   Panavision
Universal (Raffaella de Laurentiis)
📼 📼 💿 🎧
The ancient evil spirit is summoned up to prevent a lowly born barbarian inheriting the throne of Valusia.
Routine sword-and-sorcery stuff that lacks any panache or visual magic.
w Charles Edward Pogue   characters created by Robert E. Howard   d John Nicolella
ph Rodney Charters   m Joel Goldsmith
pd Benjamin Fernandez   ed Dallas Puett   sp Kit West; Richard Malzahn; make-up fx: Gianetto de Rossi
☆ Kevin Sorbo, Tia Carrere, Thomas Ian Griffith, Litefoot, Karina Lombard, Roy Brocksmith, Harvey Fierstein, Edward Tudor-Pole, Douglas Henshall
   'No more than a well-crafted, diverting romp.' – *Variety*

Kumonosu-Jo: see *Throne of Blood*

Kundun *
US   1997   134m   Technicolor   'Scope
Buena Vista/Touchstone (Barbara de Fina)
📼 📼 💿 🎧
Biopic of the Dalai Lama, from his discovery as a baby to his exile from Tibet after the Chinese invasion of his country.
A visually splendid, but intellectually flabby, hagiography: by concentrating on a child's-eye view of events, its makers deliberately evade any attempt to provide a political or social context for what is shown.
w Melissa Mathison   d Martin Scorsese   ph Roger Deakins   m Philip Glass   pd Dante Ferretti
ed Thelma Schoonmaker
☆ Tenzin Thuthob Tsarong, Sonam Phunstok, Gyatso Lukhang, Robert Lin, Tencho Gyalpo, Tsewang Migyur Khangsa
   'One from the heart, a majestic spectacle of images and sounds. But pic is bogged down by a routine screenplay.' – *Variety*
♫ Dante Ferretti (art direction; costume design)

Kung Fu Street Fighter (dubbed)
Japan   1974   74m   Eastmancolor
Actionscope
Eural/Toei-Kyoto Eiga/Titan (Norimichi Matsudaira)
original title: *Gekitotsu! Satsujinken*
A Japanese hitman offers his services to protect an oil heiress, who is threatened by Chinese businessmen with Mafia connections.
An unsavoury martial arts movie with a thuggish hero, whose behaviour is excused because his father was killed by a Chinese firing squad.
w Koji Yakada, Motohiro Torii   d Shigehiro Ozawa   ph Kenji Horikoshi   m Tony Tsushima
ad Takatoshi Suzuki   ed Kozo Horiike
☆ Sonny Chiba, Gerald Yamada, Doris Nakajima, Tony Cetera, Tatsuro Endo, Masashi Ishibashi
   'The plentiful fight scenes are choreographed and stage-managed with unusual vigour, rising to operatic delirium for the climax.' – *Tony Rayns, MFB*
† It was followed by a sequel, *Blood of the Dragon* (qv).

Kuroi Ame: see *Black Rain*

'Beware the haunted women who lurk in the bamboo forest as black cats craving the blood of men!'

Kuroneko **
Japan 1968 99m bw
Toho/Indai Eiga/Nihon Eiga Shinsha
📀
aka: *Black Cat*
Raped and murdered by a wandering gang of soldiers, a woman and her daughter-in-law return as vengeful spirits, haunting a city gate and killing the samurai they meet.
A bleak and impassively elegant fable of the casual slaughters of war and the suffering of women.
wd Kaneto Shindo *ph* Kiyomi Kuroda *m* Hikaru Hayashi *ed* Hisao Enoki
☆ Kichiemon Nakamura, Nobuko Otowa, Kei Sato, Rokko Toura, Kiwako Taichi, Taiji Tonoyama, Takao Kanze

'The Film Courtney Doesn't Want You To See!'

Kurt and Courtney
GB 1998 100m colour
Downtown/Strength (Nick Broomfield)
A documentary on rock singer Kurt Cobain's suicide, in which various interested parties advance their own paranoid theories, claiming he was murdered.

Courtney Love, Cobain's widow, refused to participate in the movie or to allow his music to be played, which is here treated as an assault on civil liberties rather than the good sense it was.
d Nick Broomfield *ph* Joan Churchill *ed* Mark Atkins
'Seems a labour of hate, full of feeble excuses and sluggish charisma. It's just another way of saying "the dog ate my homework".' – *Gaby Wood, Guardian*

Kvinnodrom: see *Journey into Autumn*

Kvinnors Väntan: see *Waiting Women*

Kwaidan ****
Japan 1964 164m Eastmancolor
Tohoscope
Ninjin Club/Bungei
📀 🎞 🔉
Four elegant ghost stories by Laadio Hearn.
A literally haunting film that is among the most beautiful ever made, with its succession of exotic, perfectly composed images and strange narratives.
w Yoko Mizuki *d* Masaki Kobayashi *ph* Yoshio Miyajima *m* Toru Takemitsu *ad* Shigemasa Toda
☆ Rentaro Mikuni, Ganjiro Nakamura, Katsuo Nakamura
☖ best foreign film

L

L.627 **

France 1992 146m colour
Artificial Eye/Little Bear (Alain Sarde)
📼 ▦

A dedicated Paris cop joins a newly established team set up to deal with drug dealers.
A documentary-style film of police at work that inevitably reveals the grim underside of urban life, and problems that defy solution.
w Michel Alexandre d Bertrand Tavernier ph Alain Choquart m Philippe Sarde pd Guy-Claude François ed Ariane Boeglin
☆ Didier Bezace, Charlotte Kady, Philippe Torreton, Nils Tavernier, Jean-Paul Comart, Jean-Roger Milo, Lara Guirao, Cécile Garcia-Fogel, Claude Brosset
'With extraordinary documentary realism, the director has produced one of his best and most challenging films.' – *Variety*
† The title refers to the legislation against the possession and use of narcotics.

'Something Funny Is Happening in L.A.'
L.A. Story *

US 1991 95m Technicolor
Guild/Rastar (Daniel Melnick, Michael Rachmil)
📼 ▦ 🔲 ⊚ 🎧

A TV weather forecaster in Los Angeles falls for a visiting English journalist.
A pleasant romantic comedy, though the love affair is mainly with Los Angeles itself.
w Steve Martin d Mick Jackson ph Andrew Dunn m Peter Melnick pd Lawrence Miller ed Richard A. Harris
☆ Steve Martin, Victoria Tennant, Richard E. Grant, Marilu Henner, Sarah Jessica Parker, Susan Forristal, Kevin Pollak, Patrick Stewart
'A light-headed joyride for an audience.' – *Pauline Kael, New Yorker*

L.A. Takedown *

US 1989 95m CFI color
Ajar/WIN (Patrick Markey)
📼 ▦

A dedicated cop with marital problems pits his wits against a highly professional and ruthless gang.
Slick, melodramatic thriller, made for TV, which its director remade as the big-budget Heat, starring Robert DeNiro and Al Pacino; this version is less strenuous and emphatic, and plays down the male bonding between its two protagonists.
wd Michael Mann ph Ron Garcia m Tim Truman pd Dean Taucher ed Dov Hoenig
☆ Scott Plank, Michael Rooker, Ely Pouget, Vincent Guastaferro, Richard Chaves, Victor Rivers, Laura Harrington, Daniel Baldwin, Juan Fernandez
'A brisk little thriller, enjoyable in its own right, but fascinating as a trial run for the real thing.' – *Sight and Sound*

La Bamba *

US 1987 108m colour
New Visions/Columbia (Taylor Hackford, Bill Borden)
📼 ▦ 🔲 ⊚ 🎧

The brief life of 1950s rock-and-roller Ritchie Valens, who at 17 was killed in the Buddy Holly plane crash.
Palatable biopic, for those who can stand this kind of music.
wd Luis Valdez ph Adam Greenberg m Carlos Santana, Miles Goodman pd Vince Cresciman ed Sheldon Kahn, Don Brochu
☆ Lou Diamond Phillips, Esai Morales, Rosana de Soto, Elizabeth Pena, Danielle von Zerneck, Marshall Crenshaw

La Bohème *

US 1926 75m bw silent
MGM

Mimi starves to death in a Paris garret.

Overacted straight version of the opera, with two passionate star performances.
w Harry Behn, Ray Doyle, after Murger d King Vidor
☆ Lillian Gish, John Gilbert, Renee Adoree, Edward Everett Horton

'Everything Is Suspect ... Everyone Is For Sale ... And Nothing Is What It Seems.'
LA Confidential ****

US 1997 136m Technicolor Panavision
Warner/Regency (Arnon Milchan, Curtis Hanson, Michael Nathanson)
📼 ▦ 🔲 ⊚ ⊚ 🎧

In Los Angeles in the early 50s, an incorruptible cop learns that you cannot always play by the rules.
Exemplary, excellently acted thriller of creeping corruption, full of surprises; only the coda disappoints.
w Brian Helgeland, Curtis Hanson novel James Ellroy d Curtis Hanson ph Dante Spinotti m Jerry Goldsmith pd Jeannine Oppewall ed Peter Honess
☆ Kevin Spacey, Russell Crowe, Guy Pearce, James Cromwell, David Strathairn, Kim Basinger, Danny DeVito, Graham Beckel
'It's not quite the full-strength java Ellroy writes, but it's about as hard as a 1990s studio picture can be.' – *Kim Newman, Empire*
'An irresistible treat with enough narrative twists and memorable characters for a half-dozen films.' – *Variety*
† It grossed around $38m in the US, and another $30m elsewhere.
🏆 Kim Basinger; Curtis Hanson, Brian Helgeland
🏅 best picture; Curtis Hanson (as director); Dante Spinotti; Jerry Goldsmith; Jeannine Oppewall; Peter Honess; sound
▽ Peter Honess

La Conga Nights

US 1940 59m bw
Universal

An elderly music moron helps to found a night-club.
Flimsy excuse for a musical, with the star playing himself, four sisters and his mother.
w Jay Dratler, Harry Clork, Paul Smith d Lew Landers
☆ Hugh Herbert, Dennis O'Keefe, Constance Moore, Eddie Quillan

La Passione

GB 1996 109m colour
Warner/Fugitive (Chris Rea)

A working-class boy makes a fortune with a secret family formula and becomes a racing driver, but does not find happiness.
A movie of quite startling banality, little more than an elongated music video.
w Chris Rea d John B. Hobbs ph Roger Bonnici m Chris Rea pd Garry Freeman ed Paul Endacott
☆ Shirley Bassey, Sean Gallagher, Thomas Orange, Paul Shane, Jan Ravens, Carmen Silvera, Keith Barron
'The style is strained and vacuous.' – *George Perry, Sunday Times*

LA Without a Map

GB/France/Finland/Luxembourg 1998 107m
DeLuxe Technovision
United Media/Dan/Euro American/Marianna (Julie Baines, Sarah Daniel, Pierre Assouline)

An English aspiring writer falls for an American actress and follows her to Los Angeles.
Dreary, ambling narrative of uninteresting people passing the time in a futile manner.
w Mika Kaurismaki, Richard Rayner novel Richard Rayner d Mika Kaurismaki ph Michel Amathieu m Sebastien Cortella pd Caroline Hanania ed Ewa J. Lind
☆ David Tennant, Vinessa Shaw, Julie Delpy, Vincent Gallo, Cameron Bancroft, Joe

Dallesandro, Anouk Aimée, Saskia Reeves, Margi Clarke, Monte Hellman
'A pointless, directionless film.' – *Guardian*
'Dire.' – *Alexander Walker*

Laberinto de Pasiones: see *Labyrinth of Passion*

Laburnum Grove **

GB 1936 73m bw
ATP (Basil Dean)

A suburban father reveals he is a forger.
Agreeable worm-turns comedy melodrama, much copied since.
w Gordon Wellesley, Anthony Kimmins play J. B. Priestley d Carol Reed ph John W. Boyle
☆ Cedric Hardwicke, Edmund Gwenn, Victoria Hopper, Ethel Coleridge, Katie Johnson, Francis James
'Here at last is an English film one can unreservedly praise.' – *Graham Greene*

Labyrinth

👪 US 1986 101m colour
Tri-Star/Eric Rattray, George Lucas
📼 ▦ 🔲

A young girl embarks on a fantasy adventure to save her stepbrother from the clutches of the Goblin King.
Bizarre but tedious attempt to create a new Alice in Wonderland, with the inventor of the Muppets in charge. Unfortunately his creatures become less attractive with each attempt, and the script is emaciated.
w Terry Jones, from script by Dennis Less and Jim Henson d Jim Henson ph Alex Thomson m Trevor Jones pd Elliot Scott conceptual designer Brian Froud
☆ David Bowie, Jennifer Connelly, Toby Froud, Shelley Thompson
'A crashing bore ... no real charm or texture to capture the imagination.' – *Variety*

Labyrinth of Passion

Spain 1982 100m colour
Metro/Alphaville/Ha Sido Producida (Andrés Santana)
📼 ▦ 🔲

original title: *Laberinto de Pasiones*
The sexual adventures of a nymphomaniac and the gay son of an emperor.
The Spanish equivalent of an Andy Warhol movie: a delirious farrago of sex and psychobabble intended to shock and amuse.
wd Pedro Almodóvar ph Angel L. Fernandez pd Pedro Almodóvar ed José Salcedo
☆ Cecilia Roth, Imanol Arias, Helga Liné, Marta Fernandez-Muro, Angel Alcazar, Antonio Banderas, Agustin Almodóvar
'The quintessential Spanish cult movie.' – *Sight and Sound*

The Lacemaker

France/Switzerland/West Germany 1977 107m Eastmancolor
Action/FR3/Citel/Janus (Yves Gasser)
📼 🔲

original title: *La Dentellière*
An 18-year-old girl becomes ill and withdrawn when her first affair breaks up.
Careful social character study, witty and observant but in memory insufficiently differentiated from numerous exploitation pieces with similar plots.
w Pascal Lainé, Claude Goretta novel Pascal Lainé d Claude Goretta ph Jean Boffety m Pierre Jansen ad Serge Etter, Claude Chevant ed Joelle van Henterre, Nelly Meunier, Martine Charasson
☆ Isabelle Huppert, Yves Beneyton, Florence Giorgetti, Anne-Marie Düringer
▽ Isabelle Huppert

Lacombe, Lucien ****

France 1974 141m Eastmancolor
Rank/NEF/UPF/Vides/Hallelujah Films (Louis Malle)
📼

A boy is rejected for the French resistance and joins the Gestapo instead.
Tragic fable, a mite overlong, which caused its creator to migrate to America because of criticism received in France.
w Louis Malle, Patrick Modiano d Louis Malle ph Tonino Delli Colli m Django Reinhardt
☆ Pierre Blaise, Aurore Clement, Holger Lowenadler, Thérèse Gieshe
'Malle's film is a long, close look at the banality of evil; it is – not incidentally – one of the least banal movies ever made.' – *Pauline Kael, New Yorker*
🏆 best foreign film
▽ best film

The Lad

GB 1935 74m bw
Univeral (Julius Hagen)

A good-natured con man discovers that the inhabitants of a stately home have all got secrets to hide.
Old-fashioned, stagey but neatly plotted and quite watchable comedy thriller.
w Gerard Fairlie play Edgar Wallace d Henry Edwards ph Sydney Blythe md William L. Trytel ad James A. Carter ed Lister Laurance
☆ Gordon Harker, Betty Stockfeld, Jane Carr, Gerald Barry, Michael Shepley, Geraldine Fitzgerald, Sebastian Shaw, Barbara Everest

Ladder of Swords *

GB 1988 98m
Hobo/Film Four International/British Screen/Arden (Jennifer Howarth)
📼

A circus performer is investigated by a policeman convinced that he has murdered his wife.
Well acted but rarely believable with its contrivances of a convenient death and a dim cop.
w Neil Clarke story Norman Hull, Neil Clarke d Norman Hull ph Thaddeus O'Sullivan m Stanley Myers pd Caroline Hanania ed Scott Thomas
☆ Martin Shaw, Eleanor David, Juliet Stevenson, Bob Peck, Simon Molloy, Pearce Quigley, Anthony Benson, Graham Rigby
'The whole enterprise is marked by a nimble, self-confident energy.' – *MFB*

Laddie

US 1935 70m bw
RKO (Pandro S. Berman)

A young farmer loves the squire's daughter, but the squire says no.
Rather dim old-fashioned rural romance.
w Ray Harris, Dorothy Yost play Gene Stratton Porter novel Gene Stratton Porter d George Stevens
☆ John Beal, Gloria Stuart, Virginia Weidler, Charlotte Henry, Donald Crisp
† Remade in 1940 by Cliff Reid for RKO, with Tim Holt, Virginia Gilmore.

Ladies Courageous

US 1944 88m bw
Universal (Walter Wanger)

Girls ferry war planes from base for the USAF.
Absolutely predictable propaganda potboiler.
w Norman Reilly Raine, Doris Gilbert d John Rawlins ph Hal Mohr m Dimitri Tiomkin
☆ Loretta Young, Geraldine Fitzgerald, Diana Barrymore, Evelyn Ankers, Anne Gwynne, Philip Terry, David Bruce, Lois Collier, Samuel S. Hinds
'Needs exploitation hype to catch nominal biz ... wandering continuity fails to generate much punch.' – *Variety*

Ladies' Day

US 1943 62m bw
Bert Gilroy/RKO

A baseball pitcher loses his touch when he falls in love, so has to be kept away from his latest girl.
Mildly wacky comedy with a fairly nimble touch.
w Charles E. Roberts, Dane Lussier *play* Robert Considine, Edward C. Lilley and Bertrand Robinson *d* Leslie Goodwins
☆ Lupe Velez, Eddie Albert, Patsy Kelly, Max Baer, Jerome Cowan, Iris Adrian

Ladies in Love *

US 1936 97m bw
TCF (B. G. de Sylva)

Man-hunting girls in Budapest form a joint plan.
Amusing romantic nonsense.
w Melville Baker *play* Ladislaus Bus-Fekete *d* Edward H. Griffith *ph* Hal Mohr *md* Louis Silvers
☆ Janet Gaynor, Loretta Young, Constance Bennett, Simone Simon, Don Ameche, Paul Lukas, Tyrone Power, Alan Mowbray, Wilfrid Lawson, J. Edward Bromberg, Virginia Field

Ladies in Retirement **

US 1941 92m bw
Columbia (Lester Cowan)

A housekeeper murders her employer for the sake of her two mentally disturbed sisters.
Splendidly effective Grand Guignol, from a well-written play but filmically quite interesting. Remade with lots of gore as The Mad Room *(qv).*
w Reginald Denham, Edward Percy, Garrett Fort *play* Reginald Denham, Edward Percy *d* Charles Vidor *ph* George Barnes *m* Ernst Toch, Morris Stoloff *ad* Lionel Banks
☆ Ida Lupino, Louis Hayward, Isobel Elsom, Edith Barrett, Elsa Lanchester, Emma Dunn
'General excellence of script, direction, acting and mounting ... but too strong to catch general audience reaction on favourable plane.' – *Variety*
♟ Ernst Toch, Morris Stoloff; Lionel Banks

Ladies Love Brutes

US 1930 83m bw
Paramount

A gangster tries to improve himself to marry a socialite.
Uneasy comedy-drama with good moments.
w Waldemar Young, Herman J. Mankiewicz *play* Pardon My Glove *by* Zoë Akins *d* Rowland V. Lee *ph* Harry Fischbeck
☆ George Bancroft, Mary Astor, Fredric March, Margaret Quimby, Stanley Fields

Ladies Love Danger

US 1935 69m bw
Fox

A playwright and amateur sleuth solves a series of murders.
Light, bright whodunnit.
w Samson Raphaelson *story* Ilya Zorn *d* H. Bruce Humberstone
☆ Gilbert Roland, Mona Barrie, Donald Cook, Adrienne Ames, Hardie Albright, Herbert Mundin
'Stronger marquee strength would have sent it into ace spots. As is, looks best for secondaries.' – *Variety*

Ladies' Man *

US 1931 70m bw
Paramount

A man of the world preys successfully on rich women until one grows jealous when her daughter falls for him.
Vivid, hard melodrama showing the blacker side of early thirties high society living.
w Herman J. Mankiewicz *d* Lothar Mendes *ph* Victor Milner
☆ William Powell, Kay Francis, Carole Lombard, Gilbert Emery, Olive Tell

'He's a hit with the misses, they go for his kisses!'

Ladies' Man

US 1947 90m bw
Paramount

A poor farmer strikes oil, becomes a millionaire, and finds himself a prize for the ladies.
Below-par comedy which wastes an agreeable cast.
w Edmund Beloin, Jack Rose and Lewis Meltzer *d* William D. Russell
☆ Eddie Bracken, Cass Daley, Virginia Welles, Spike Jones and his City Slickers

The Ladies Man

US 1961 106m Technicolor
Paramount/York (Jerry Lewis)
▣ ⊙
The adventures of an accident-prone houseboy at a Hollywood hotel for aspiring actresses.
Hit-or-miss collection of comic scraps which might have benefited from being put together on a less grandiose scale.
w Jerry Lewis, Bill Richmond *d* Jerry Lewis *ph* W. Wallace Kelley *m* Walter Scharf *ad* Hal Pereira, Ross Bellar *ed* Stanley Johnson
☆ Jerry Lewis, Helen Traubel, Jack Kruschen, Doodles Weaver, Gloria Jean, Kathleen Freeman, Hope Holiday, Pat Stanley, George Raft, Harry James and his band
'Regression into infantilism cannot be carried much further than this.' – MFB

Ladies Must Live: see *The Home Towners*

Ladies of Leisure

US 1930 98m bw
Columbia

A gold digger gets an attack of conscience and gives up her rich fiancé.
Only fitfully interesting early Capra, with little sparkle in any department.
w Jo Swerling *play* Ladies of the Evening *by* Milton Herbert Gropper *d* Frank Capra *ph* Joseph Walker
☆ Barbara Stanwyck, Lowell Sherman, Ralph Graves, Marie Prevost
† The film was also released in a silent version for cinemas which had not yet been equipped for sound.

Ladies of the Big House

US 1931 77m bw
Paramount

A married couple are framed on a murder charge and sent to prison.
Melodramatic nonsense in the wake of The Big House.
w Louis Weitzenkorn *d* Marion Gering *ph* David Abel
☆ Sylvia Sidney, Gene Raymond, Wynne Gibson, Rockcliffe Fellowes, Earle Foxe
'Powerful in heart appeal and should do very well.' – *Variety*

Ladies of the Chorus

US 1948 61m bw
Columbia
▣
A Broadway burlesque queen falls for a socialite.
Threadbare backstage support, notable only for the first leading performance of Marilyn Monroe.
w Harry Sauber and Joseph Carole *d* Phil Karlson *ph* Frank Redman *md* Mischa Bakaleinikoff
☆ Adele Jergens, Rand Brooks, Marilyn Monroe

Ladies of the Jury

US 1932 64m bw
RKO

A lady changes the minds of a murder jury to 'not guilty'.
Light-hearted early variation on Twelve Angry Men.
play Frederick Ballard *d* Lowell Sherman
☆ Edna May Oliver, Ken Murray, Roscoe Ates, Kitty Kelly, Guinn Williams, Cora Witherspoon
'A highly satisfying B house release.' – *Variety*

Ladies of the Park: see *Les Dames du Bois de Boulogne*

Ladies on the Rocks *

Denmark 1983 110m colour
Artificial Eye/Komme Films/Danish Film Institute
original title: *Koks I Kulissen*
Two women take their cabaret act on the road.
Small but well-observed film, with good performances.
w Christian Braad Thomsen, Helle Ryslinge, Annemarie Helger *d* Christian Braad Thomsen *ph* Dirk Bruel *m* Helle Ryslinge, Pernille Grumme, Annemarie Helger *ed* Grete Moldrup
☆ Helle Ryslinge, Annemarie Helger, Flemming Quist Moller, Hans Henrick Clemmensen, Gyda Hansen, Aksel Erhardsen

Ladies Should Listen

US 1934 63m bw
Paramount (Douglas MacLean)
A knowledgeable switchboard operator helps a financier with his problems.

Moderately beguiling, instantly forgettable romantic frou-frou.
w Claude Binyon, Frank Butler, Guy Bolton *d* Frank Tuttle *ph* Harry Sharp
☆ Cary Grant, Frances Drake, Edward Everett Horton, Rosita Moreno, George Barbier, Nydia Westman, Charles Ray
'Synthetic farce that strains too hard for laughs.' – *Variety*

Ladies They Talk About *

US 1933 69m bw
Warner
▣
Trouble in a women's prison.
Entertaining comedy-melodrama which had some brushes with the Hays Office because of its frankly man-hungry characters.
w Sidney Sutherland, Brown Holmes *play* Women in Prison *by* Dorothy Mackaye, Carlton Miles *d* Howard Bretherton, William Keighley *ph* John Seitz
☆ Barbara Stanwyck, Lyle Talbot, Preston Foster, Dorothy Burgess, Lillian Roth, Maude Eburne, Ruth Donnelly, Harold Huber
'Will get average business if sold to the hilt.' – *Variety*

Ladies Who Do

GB 1963 85m bw
British Lion/Bryanston/Fanfare (George H. Brown)
▣▣
Charladies form a successful company from tips they salvage from wastepaper baskets.
Mild farce sustained by familiar actors.
w Michael Pertwee *d* C. M. Pennington-Richards *ph* Geoffrey Faithfull *m* Ron Goodwin
☆ Peggy Mount, Miriam Karlin, Robert Morley, Harry H. Corbett, Dandy Nichols

Ladri di Biciclette: see *Bicycle Thieves*

Ladri di Saponette: see *The Icicle Thief*

Il Ladro di Bambini: see *The Stolen Children*

The Lady and the Bandit

US 1951 78m bw
Columbia (Harry Joe Brown)
GB title: *Dick Turpin's Ride*
A highwayman sacrifices his own life to avenge his father and protect his wife.
Fairly pathetic example of historical whitewashing to provide minor excitements.
w Robert Libbott, Frank Burt *story* Duncan Renaldo from the poem by Alfred Noyes *d* Ralph Murphy *ph* Henry Freulich, Harry Waxman *m* George Duning
☆ Louis Hayward, Patricia Medina, Suzanne Dalbert, Tom Tully, John Williams, Alan Mowbray

The Lady and the Doctor: see *The Lady and the Monster*

The Lady and the Mob

US 1939 65m bw
Columbia (Fred Kohlmar)
A lady bank owner menaced by gangsters forms her own mob.
Weak comedy.
w Richard Maibaum, Gertrude Purcell *d* Ben Stoloff *ph* John Stumar
☆ Fay Bainter, Ida Lupino, Lee Bowman, Henry Armetta, Warren Hymer, Harold Huber
'Neat, entertaining farce; rates exploitation.' – *Variety*

The Lady and the Monster

US 1944 86m bw
Republic (George Sherman)
aka: *Tiger Man*
GB title: *The Lady and the Doctor*
A scientist keeps alive the brain of a mortally injured financier, and it comes to dominate him.
Fair, over-padded version of a much filmed thriller (see also Donovan's Brain, Vengeance).
w Dane Lussier, Frederick Kohner *novel* Donovan's Brain *by* Curt Siodmak *d* George Sherman *ph* John Alton *m* Walter Scharf
☆ Erich von Stroheim, Richard Arlen, Vera Hruba Ralston, Mary Nash, Sidney Blackmer, Helen Vinson

The Lady and the Outlaw: see *Billy Two Hats*

Lady and the Tramp **

🏠🏠 US 1955 76m Technicolor
Cinemascope
Walt Disney (Erdmann Penner)
▣ ⊙
A pedigree spaniel falls foul of two Siamese cats and has a romantic adventure with a mongrel who helps her.
Pleasant cartoon feature in Disney's cutest and most anthropomorphic vein.
d Hamilton Luske, Clyde Geronimi, Wilfred Jackson *m* Oliver Wallace *m/ly* Peggy Lee, Sonny Burke
☆ Featuring the voices of Peggy Lee, Barbara Luddy, Bill Thompson, Bill Baucon, Stan Freberg

Lady Be Good

US 1941 111m bw
MGM (Arthur Freed)
▣ ⊙
Married songwriters produce a musical.
Thin musical with good talent and tunes; very little connection with the 1924 musical show.
w Jack McGowan, Kay Van Riper, John McClain *d* Norman Z. McLeod *ph* George J. Folsey, Oliver T. Marsh *md* George Stoll *songs* various
☆ Eleanor Powell, Robert Young, Ann Sothern, Red Skelton, Dan Dailey, Virginia O'Brien, Reginald Owen, John Carroll, Lionel Barrymore, Jimmy Dorsey and his Orchestra
'A molasses-paced picture that extravagantly wastes talent and time ... poor direction, unimaginative story-telling and slipshod photography.' – *Variety*
♫ Songs include: 'Hang on to Me'; 'Fascinating Rhythm'; 'Lady Be Good'; 'You'll Never Know'; 'Your Words and My Music'.
♪ song 'The Last Time I Saw Paris' (*m*Jerome Kern, *ly*Oscar Hammerstein II)

Lady By Choice *

US 1934 78m bw
Columbia
A publicity-mad dancer adopts an old rummy as a Mother's Day stunt.
Amusing sentimental comedy in the wake of Lady for A Day.
w Jo Swerling, Dwight Taylor *d* David Burton *ph* Ted Tetzlaff
☆ Carole Lombard, May Robson, Walter Connolly, Roger Pryor, Arthur Hohl, Raymond Walburn, James Burke, Henry Kolker
'Can very well stand on its own outside the deluxers if properly sold.' – *Variety*

Lady Caroline Lamb *

GB 1972 123m Eastmancolor Panavision
EMI/GEC/Pulsar/Video Cinematographica (Fernando Ghia)
▣▣ ▣ 𝄞
In 1805, impulsive Lady Caroline Ponsonby marries William Lamb, later Lord Melbourne, and then disgraces him by her wildness.
Pale, disappointing historical fiction with good spots but no reverence for fact; slackly written and handled, and not helped by the wide screen.
wd Robert Bolt *ph* Oswald Morris *m* Richard Rodney Bennett *ad* Carmen Dillon
☆ Sarah Miles, Jon Finch, Richard Chamberlain, Margaret Leighton, John Mills, Ralph Richardson, Laurence Olivier

Lady Chatterley's Lover

France 1955 101m bw
Regie du Film/Orsay Film (Gilbert Cohen-Séat)
The wife of a crippled and impotent mine-owner has an affair with a coarse gamekeeper and enjoys it.
Hilariously po-faced transcription of a notorious novel, of no cinematic interest whatever.
w Gaston Bonheur, Philippe de Rothschild, Marc Allégret *novel* D. H. Lawrence *d* Marc Allégret *ph* Georges Périnal *m* Joseph Kosma
☆ Danielle Darrieux, Leo Genn, Erno Crisa

'The classic of erotic literature!'

Lady Chatterley's Lover

GB/France 1981 104m colour
Cannon/Producteurs Associés
▣▣ ▣
A 'period' remake, lovingly photographed but with some risible soft porn episodes and no great interest in the acting.

---

w Christopher Wicking, Just Jaeckin d Just
Jaeckin ph Robert Fraisse m Stanley Myers,
Richard Harvey pd Anton Furst ed Eunice
Mountjoy
☆ Sylvia Kristel, Nicholas Clay, Shane Briant,
Ann Mitchell, Elizabeth Spriggs

The Lady Consents

US   1936   76m   bw
RKO (Edward Kaufman)
When a doctor's wife sees that he is in love with
another woman, she makes it easy for him to get a
divorce; but he finally comes back to her.
Unbelievable matinée drama for star fans.
w P. J. Wolfson, Anthony Veiller *play* The
Indestructible Mrs Talbot *by* P. J. Wolfson
d Stephen Roberts ph J. Roy Hunt m Roy Webb
☆ Ann Harding, Herbert Marshall, Margaret
Lindsay, Walter Abel, Edward Ellis, Hobart
Cavanaugh, Ilka Chase
   'Pretty fair entertainment; good woman's
   picture.' – Variety

The Lady Cop: see La Femme-flic

'Eve Sure Knows Her Apples!'
The Lady Eve ***

US   1941   97m   bw
Paramount (Paul Jones)
A lady cardsharper and her father are outsmarted
on a transatlantic liner by a millionaire simpleton;
she plans an elaborate revenge.
*Hectic romantic farce, the first to show its director's
penchant for mixing up sexual innuendo, funny men
and pratfalls. There are moments when the pace drops,
but in general it's scintillating entertainment, especially
after viewing its weak remake* The Birds and the Bees
(qv).
wd Preston Sturges *play* Monckton Hoffe
ph Victor Milner m Leo Shuken, Charles
Bradshaw ad Hans Dreier, Ernst Fegte ed Stuart
Gilmore
☆ Barbara Stanwyck, Henry Fonda, Charles Coburn,
Eugène Pallette, William Demarest, Eric Blore,
Melville Cooper, Martha O'Driscoll, Janet
Beecher, Robert Greig, Luis Alberni, Jimmy
Conlin
   'The whole theme, with all its variations of keys,
   is played to one end, to get laughs, and at several
   different levels it gets them.' – National Board of
   Review
   'Preston Sturges, they tell me, is known in
   Hollywood as "the streamlined Lubitsch". This
   needn't put you off, because if he goes on
   producing films as lively as this one he will one
   day come to be known as Preston Sturges.' –
   William Whitebait
   'This time Preston Sturges has wrapped you up
   another package that is neither very big nor very
   flashy, but the best fun in months.' – Otis
   Ferguson
   'A mixture of visual and verbal slapstick, of high
   artifice and pratfalls … it represents the dizzy
   high point of Sturges' writing.' – New Yorker,
   1977
   'The brightest sort of nonsense, on which
   Preston Sturges' signature is written large. The
   result has a sustained comic flavour and an
   individual treatment that are rarely found in
   Hollywood's antic concoctions.' – New York
   Herald Tribune
   'A more charming or distinguished gem of
   nonsense has not occurred since It Happened
   One Night.' – New York Times
   ஃ Monckton Hoffe (original story)

Lady for a Day ***

👥 US   1933   95m   bw
Columbia (Frank Capra)
Gangsters help an old apple seller to pose as a rich
woman when her daughter visits.
*Splendid sentimental comedy full of cinematic resource;
the best translation of Runyon to the screen.*
w Robert Riskin *story* Madame La Gimp *by* Damon
Runyon d Frank Capra ph Joseph Walker
☆ May Robson, Warren William, Guy Kibbee,
Glenda Farrell, Ned Sparks, Jean Parker, Walter
Connolly, Nat Pendleton
   'Exceptionally adroit direction and scenario …
   sell it with plenty of adjectives as it will please
   everybody.' – Variety
   ஃ best picture; Robert Riskin; Frank Capra; May
   Robson

Lady for a Night

US   1942   87m   bw
Republic (Albert J. Cohen)
The lady owner of a gambling boat determines to
break into society.
Moderate period comedy with a belated murder plot.
w Isabel Dawn, Boyce DeGaw d Leigh Jason
ph Norbert Brodine m David Buttolph
☆ Joan Blondell, John Wayne, Ray Middleton,
Philip Merivale, Blanche Yurka, Edith Barrett,
Leonid Kinskey, Montagu Love

The Lady from Cheyenne

US   1941   87m   bw
Universal (Frank Lloyd)
In 1860 Wyoming, a schoolmistress fights for
women's rights.
Mild Western star romance.
w Kathryn Scola, Warren Duff d Frank Lloyd
ph Milton Krasner m Frank Skinner
☆ Loretta Young, Robert Preston, Gladys George,
Edward Arnold, Frank Craven, Jessie Ralph,
Spencer Charters, Alan Bridge

Lady from Lisbon

GB   1942   75m   bw
Shaftesbury/British National
A millionaire spies for the Nazis in return for the
promise of art treasures.
Modest potboiling comedy-melodrama.
w Michael Barringer d Leslie Hiscott
☆ Jane Carr, Francis L. Sullivan, Martita Hunt,
Charles Victor, Antony Holles

Lady from Louisiana

US   1941   84m   bw
Republic (Bernard Vorhaus)
In old Mississippi, a lottery-owner's daughter falls
in love with a lawyer employed to make her
father's business illegal.
*Curious pot-boiler containing everything but the
kitchen stove, including murder and a raging storm.*
w Vera Caspary, Guy Endore, Michael Hogan
d Bernard Vorhaus ph Jack Marta m Cy Feuer
☆ John Wayne, Ona Munson, Ray Middleton,
Henry Stephenson, Helen Westley, Dorothy
Dandridge, Jack Pennick

The Lady from Nowhere

US   1936   60m   bw
Columbia
A manicurist tries to lose her identity after
witnessing a gangland killing.
*A silly plot robs this second feature of the interest it
might otherwise deserve.*
w Fred Niblo Jnr, Ben G. Kohn, Arthur Strawn,
Joseph Krumgold d Gordon Wiles
☆ Mary Astor, Charles Quigley, Thurston Hall,
Victor Kilian, Spencer Charters
   'Mild entertainment.' – Variety

The Lady from Shanghai **

US   1948   87m   bw
Columbia (Richard Wilson, William Castle)
A seaman becomes involved in the maritime
wanderings of a crippled lawyer and his homicidal
frustrated wife.
*Absurd, unintelligible, plainly much cut and
rearranged, this thriller was obviously left too much in
Welles's hands and then just as unfairly taken out of
them; but whole sequences of sheer brilliance remain,
notably the final shoot-out in the hall of mirrors.*
wd Orson Welles *novel* If I Die Before I Wake *by*
Sherwood King ph Charles Lawton Jnr m Heinz
Roemheld
☆ Orson Welles, Rita Hayworth, Everett Sloane,
Glenn Anders, Ted de Corsia, Erskine Sanford, Gus
Schilling
   'The slurred social conscience of the hero leads
   him to some murky philosophizing, all of which
   with many individualities of diction clog the
   issue and the sound track. Sub-titles, I fear,
   would have helped.' – Richard Winnington

The Lady from Texas

US   1951   78m   Technicolor
Universal-International (Leonard Goldstein)
A Civil War widow is thought to be committable.
Mild comedy of insanity, a pale shadow of Harvey
whose star it borrows.
w Gerald Drayson Adams and Connie Lee
Bennett d Joseph Pevney

☆ Josephine Hull, Mona Freeman, Howard Duff,
Gene Lockhart, Craig Stevens, Ed Begley

The Lady from the Shanghai Cinema

Spain   1988   117m   colour
Metro/Star/Raiz/Embrafilme/Chroma (Assunção
Hernandes)
original title: A dama do cine Shanghai
After becoming obsessed with the wife of a lawyer
who may also be a criminal, a cinema-going estate
agent contemplates murder.
*Murky pastiche of film noir that deliberately confuses
fantasy and reality; the central character might have
been spared a great deal of misery if he had been better
acquainted with Welles's* The Lady from Shanghai.
wd Guilherme Del Almeida Prado ph Cláudio
Portioli, José Roberto Eliezer m Hermelino Neder
pd Hector Gomez
☆ Maite Proença, Antonio Fagundes, José
Lewgoy, Jorge Doria, José Mayer, Miguel Falabella,
Paulo Villaca

'The relentless drama of a woman driven to the
depths of emotion by a craving beyond control!'
The Lady Gambles

US   1949   99m   bw
U-I (Michael Kraike)
A happy woman destroys her marriage when she
becomes addicted to gambling.
Boring, overwrought, underplotted fiction for women.
w Roy Huggins *story* Lewis Meltzer, Oscar Saul
d Michael Gordon ph Russell Metty m Frank
Skinner
☆ Barbara Stanwyck, Robert Preston, Stephen
McNally, Edith Barrett, John Hoyt
   'A kind of Lost Weekend of the gaming tables.' –
   Ella Smith

Lady Godiva

US   1955   89m   Technicolor
U-I (Robert Arthur)
GB title: Lady Godiva of Coventry
Lord Leofric tames a Saxon shrew but she suspects
his motives and rides naked through the streets of
Coventry to prove the loyalty of the Saxons.
*Comic strip historical legend, reliably turned out for
midwestern family audiences.*
w Oscar Brodney, Harry Ruskin d Arthur Lubin
ph Carl Guthrie m Hans Salter
☆ George Nader, Maureen O'Hara, Victor
McLaglen, Eduard Franz, Torin Thatcher

Lady Godiva of Coventry: see Lady Godiva

Lady Godiva Rides Again

GB   1951   90m   bw
British Lion/London Films/Sidney Gilliat, Frank
Launder
A waitress wins a local beauty contest and becomes
a charm school starlet and later a stripteaser.
Disappointing satirical comedy with good credentials.
w Frank Launder, Val Valentine d Frank Launder
ph Wilkie Cooper m William Alwyn
☆ Pauline Stroud, Stanley Holloway, Diana Dors,
Alastair Sim, George Cole, Dennis Price, John
McCallum, Bernadette O'Farrell, Kay Kendall,
Dora Bryan

Lady Hamilton: see That Hamilton Woman

The Lady Has Plans

US   1942   77m   bw
Paramount (Fred Kohlmar)
A lady reporter in Lisbon is mistaken for a Nazi
spy.
*Competent fluff which veers between comedy and
melodrama.*
w Harry Tugend d Sidney Lanfield ph Charles
Lang m Leo Shuken, Leigh Harline
☆ Paulette Goddard, Ray Milland, Albert Dekker,
Roland Young, Margaret Hayes, Cecil Kellaway,
Addison Richards, Edward Norris

Lady Ice

US   1973   92m   Technicolor   Panavision
Tomorrow Entertainment (Harrison Starr)
An insurance investigator steals a diamond and
goes into partnership with a gangster's daughter.
Unamusing Miami-based thriller.
w Alan Trustman, Harold Clemins d Tom Gries
ph Lucien Ballard m Perry Botkin Jnr
☆ Donald Sutherland, Jennifer O'Neil, Robert
Duvall, Patrick Magee

'Because of its frank nature, we urge you – do not
see it alone!'
Lady in a Cage

US   1964   97m   bw
American Entertainments Corp. (Luther Davis)
A rich widow is trapped by roving marauders in her
private elevator.
Unpleasant and boring suspenser with nasty details.
w Luther Davis d Walter Grauman ph Lee
Garmes m Paul Glass pd Rudolf Sternad
☆ Olivia de Havilland, James Caan, Ann
Sothern, Jeff Corey
   'The film parades its pretensions on a note of
   high-pitched hysteria.' – MFB

Lady in a Jam

US   1942   78m   bw
Universal (Gregory La Cava)
A scatterbrained socialite loses her money and
inherits an Arizona farm.
A very thin vehicle for a star who deserved better.
w Eugene Thackrey, Frank Cockrell, Otho
Lovering d Gregory La Cava ph Hal Mohr
m Frank Skinner
☆ Irene Dunne, Patric Knowles, Ralph Bellamy,
Eugene Pallette, Robert Homans, Samuel S. Hinds

Lady in Cement

US   1968   93m   DeLuxe   Panavision
TCF/Arcola/Millfield (Aaron Rosenberg)
A Florida private eye on his morning swim finds a
dead blonde.
*Routine private eye stuff with fashionable sex and
violence added.*
w Marvin H. Albert, Jack Guss d Gordon
Douglas ph Joseph Biroc m Hugo Montenegro
☆ Frank Sinatra, Raquel Welch, Richard Conte,
Martin Gabel, Lainie Kazan, Pat Henry, Steve
Peck
   'While Tony Rome seemed to herald a return to
   the forties thriller, Lady in Cement marks
   nothing more exciting than a return to Tony
   Rome.' – MFB

Lady in Distress: see A Window in London

The Lady in Question *

US   1940   81m   bw
Columbia
A Parisian shopkeeper on a jury is responsible for
getting a girl acquitted of a murder charge, but
begins to worry when his son falls in love with her.
*Stagey but quite satisfying Hollywood remake of the
French drama Gribouille, with Raimu and Michele
Morgan.*
w Lewis Meltzer *story* Marcel Achard d Charles
Vidor ph Lucien Andriot m Lucien Moraweck
☆ Brian Aherne, Rita Hayworth, Glenn Ford,
Irene Rich, George Coulouris, Lloyd Corrigan,
Evelyn Keyes, Edward Norris, Curt Bois, Frank
Reicher

The Lady in Red

US   1979   93m   Metrocolor
New World
The story of Dillinger's mistress.
*Okay but uninspired gangster drama from a fresh
angle.*
w John Sayles d Lewis Teague
☆ Pamela Sue Martin, Robert Conrad, Louise
Fletcher, Robert Hogan, Rod Gist

The Lady in the Car with Glasses and a Gun

France/US   1969   105m   Eastmancolor
Panavision
Lira Film/Columbia (Anatole Litvak)
An English secretary in Paris decides to drive to
the coast but has various adventures which make
her believe she is either mad or amnesiac.
*Muddled, tedious suspenser with a totally implausible
'explanation'.*
w Richard Harris, Eleanor Perry *novel* Sebastien
Japrisot d Anatole Litvak ph Claude Renoir
m Michel Legrand
☆ Samantha Eggar, Oliver Reed, John McEnery,
Stéphane Audran

👥 film suitable for
   family viewing

📼 VHS video-cassette for
   the British PAL system

📼 VHS video-cassette for the British
   PAL system in wide screen-format

💱 Video cassette in a computer-
   colourised version

◼ American NTSC video-cassette

🔘 Laser disc

'The minx in mink with a yen for men!'

Lady in the Dark **
US 1944 100m Technicolor
Paramount (Richard Blumenthal)

The editress of a fashion magazine is torn between three men, has worrying dreams, and takes herself to a psychoanalyst.

Lush, stylish and frequently amusing version of a Broadway musical, lacking most of the songs; despite its faults, an excellent example of studio spectacle and a very typical forties romantic comedy.

w Frances Goodrich, Albert Hackett *play* Moss Hart d Mitchell Leisen *ph* Ray Rennahan *m* Kurt Weill *md* Robert Emmett Dolan *ad* Hans Dreier, Raoul Pene du Bois *sp* Gordon Jennings *ly* Ira Gershwin

☆ Ginger Rogers, Warner Baxter, Ray Milland, Jon Hall, Mischa Auer, Mary Philips, Barry Sullivan
† The film was completed in 1942 but held up because of overstock.
†† Paramount chief Buddy de Sylva is credited with ruining the film by cutting the theme song, 'My Ship', which is the key to the psychoanalysis.
♫ Ray Rennahan; Robert Emmett Dolan; art direction

Lady in the Iron Mask
US 1952 78m Natural Color
Wanger-Frenke/TCF

Princess Anne's twin sister is kept in an iron mask to prevent dispute about the succession.

Naïve twist on a well-worn legend; production values below par.

w Jack Pollexfen, Aubrey Wisberg d Ralph Murphy *ph* Ernest Laszlo *m* Dimitri Tiomkin
☆ Louis Hayward, Patricia Medina, Alan Hale Jnr, Judd Holdren, Steve Brodie, John Sutton

The Lady in the Lake *
US 1946 103m bw
MGM (George Haight)
📀

A private eye is assigned to find a missing wife…

Complex private eye yarn which makes the original Chandler dialogue sound childish by over-reliance on the subjective camera method: we see the hero's face only when he looks in a mirror. An experiment that failed because it was not really understood.

w Steve Fisher *novel* Raymond Chandler d Robert Montgomery *ph* Paul C. Vogel *m* David Snell

☆ Robert Montgomery, Audrey Totter, Lloyd Nolan, Tom Tully, Leon Ames

Lady in the Morgue *
US 1938 70m bw
Universal
GB title: *The Case of the Missing Blonde*

A private eye investigates a suicide and uncovers three murders.

Smart 'B' feature frequently cited as a model of its kind.

w Eric Taylor and Robertson White *novel* Jonathan Latimer d Otis Garrett
☆ Preston Foster, Frank Jenks, Patricia Ellis, Thomas Jackson
† A previous film with the same characters and actors was *The Westland Case*, directed by Christy Cabanne in 1937.

Lady in White *
US 1988 113m DeLuxe
Virgin/New Sky Productions/Samuel Goldwyn Company (Andrew G. La Marca, Frank LaLoggia)
📀 ☆ 🎧

After seeing the ghost of a murdered girl, a young boy discovers the identity of her killer.

Modest, but rewarding, movie in its depiction of childhood traumas.

wd Frank LaLoggia *ph* Russell Carpenter *m* Frank LaLoggia *pd* Richard K. Hummel *ed* Steve Mann

☆ Lukas Haas, Len Cariou, Alex Rocco, Katherine Helmond, Jason Presson, Renata Vanni, Angelo Bertolini, Joelle Jacobi, Jared Rushton
'A ghost movie with an overcomplicated plot, but it has a poetic feeling that makes up for much of the clutter.' – *Pauline Kael, New Yorker*

The Lady Is a Square
GB 1958 99m bw
ABP/Wilcox-Neagle

An impoverished socialite widow tries to keep her husband's symphony orchestra going and is helped by a pop singer.

Strained attempt to carry on the Spring in Park Lane tradition, with a few inspirations from Joe Pasternak and One Hundred Men and a Girl. Earnest performances, obvious jokes.

w Harold Purcell, Pamela Bower, Nicholas Phipps d Herbert Wilcox *ph* Gordon Dines *md* Wally Stott

☆ Anna Neagle, Frankie Vaughan, Anthony Newley, Janette Scott, Wilfrid Hyde-White

The Lady Is Willing
GB 1933 74m bw
Columbia British

An ex-officer becomes a detective and takes his revenge on the financier who ruined him.

Interesting comedy-melodrama with strong cast.

w Guy Bolton *play* Louis Verneuil d Gilbert Miller

☆ Leslie Howard, Cedric Hardwicke, Binnie Barnes, Nigel Playfair, Nigel Bruce

The Lady Is Willing
US 1942 91m bw
Columbia (Mitchell Leisen)

A musical comedy star adopts a baby and falls in love with its pediatrician.

Dull mixture of light drama and heavy comedy, with all concerned ill at ease.

w James Edward Grant, Albert McCleery d Mitchell Leisen *ph* Ted Tetzlaff *m* W. Franke Harling

☆ Marlene Dietrich, Fred MacMurray, Aline MacMahon, Stanley Ridges, Arline Judge, Marietta Canty

Lady Jane
GB 1986 142m Technicolor
Paramount/Peter Snell
📀 📀 ☆

After the death in 1553 of Edward VI, a faction pushes into power his second cousin Lady Jane Grey.

The puzzle is why this dreary and overlong historical piece was made in an unsympathetic age; and why such an unsuitable leading lady was cast.

w David Edgar, Chris Bryant d Trevor Nunn *ph* Douglas Slocombe *m* Stephen Oliver *pd* Allan Cameron *ed* Anna V. Coates

☆ Helena Bonham Carter, Cary Elwes, John Wood, Michael Hordern, Jill Bennett, Jane Lapotaire, Sara Kestelman, Joss Ackland, Patrick Stewart, Richard Vernon
† The story was previously told in 1936 as *Tudor Rose*.

Lady Killer ***
US 1933 76m bw
Warner (Henry Blanke)
📀 ☆

A cinema usher turns to crime, flees to Hollywood, and becomes a movie star.

Hectic slam-bang action comedy with melodramatic moments. Great fun.

w Ben Markson *novel* The Finger Man by Rosalind Keating Shaffer d Roy del Ruth *ph* Tony Gaudio *md* Leo F. Forbstein

☆ James Cagney, Mae Clarke, Leslie Fenton, Margaret Lindsay, Henry O'Neill, Willard Robertson, Raymond Hatton, Russell Hopton
'An all-time high in roughneck character work even for this rough-and-tumble star.' – *Variety*
'A kind of résumé of everything he has done to date in the movies.' – *New York Evening Post*
'Sprightly, more or less daring, thoroughly entertaining.' – *New York World Telegram*

The Lady Killers: see The Ladykillers

Lady L
France/Italy/US 1965 124m Eastmancolor
Panavision
Concordia/Champion/MGM (Carlo Ponti)

An 80-year-old lady recalls her romantic life from her youth as a Paris laundress.

Unhappy, lumbering, styleless attempt to recapture several old forms, indifferently though expensively made and acted.

wd Peter Ustinov *novel* Romain Gary *ph* Henri Alekan *m* Jean Françaix *ad* Jean D'Eaubonne, Auguste Capelier

☆ Sophia Loren, David Niven, Paul Newman, Peter Ustinov, Claude Dauphin, Philippe Noiret, Michel Piccoli, Marcel Dalio, Cecil Parker, Eugène Deckers

Lady, Let's Dance
US 1944 86m bw
Scott R. Dunlap/Monogram

An entertainment director for a California resort needs a new star.

Thin musical with production values ambitious for its source.

w Peter Milne and Paul Gerard Smith d Frank Woodruff

☆ Belita, James Ellison, Frick and Frack, Walter Catlett, Lucien Littlefield
♫ Edward Kay (music); song 'Silver Shadows and Golden Dreams' (m Lew Pollack, ly Charles Newman)

The Lady Lies
US 1929 75m bw
Paramount

A wealthy widowed attorney courts a working-class girl and offends his children.

Dated melodrama in primitive talkie technique.

w John Meehan, Garrett Fort d Hobart Henley
☆ Walter Huston, Claudette Colbert, Charles Ruggles, Tom Brown

Lady Luck
US 1946 97m bw
RKO (Warren Duff)

The daughter of a long line of ill-fated gamblers marries one and tries to reform him, but the reverse happens.

Tedious comedy drama.

w Lynn Root, Frank Fenton d Edwin L. Marin *ph* Lucien Andriot *m* Leigh Harline
☆ Robert Young, Barbara Hale, Frank Morgan, James Gleason, Don Rice, Harry Davenport, Lloyd Corrigan

Lady of Burlesque *
US 1943 91m bw
Hunt Stromberg
📀

GB title: *Striptease Lady*

A burlesque dancer solves a number of backstage murders.

Agreeable murder mystery with strong injections of comedy.

w James Gunn *novel* The G-String Murders by Gypsy Rose Lee d William A. Wellman *ph* Robert de Grasse *m* Arthur Lange

☆ Barbara Stanwyck, Michael O'Shea, J. Edward Bromberg, Iris Adrian, Gloria Dickson, Charles Dingle
♫ Arthur Lange

Lady of Deceit: see Born to Kill

Lady of Scandal
US 1930 67m bw
MGM

The son of a noble house wants to marry an actress, but the family is nasty to her.

Dated melodrama with sophisticated comedy asides.

w Hans Kraly *play* The High Road by Frederick Lonsdale d Sidney Franklin

☆ Ruth Chatterton, Basil Rathbone, Ralph Forbes, Nance O'Neil, Frederick Kerr, Herbert Bunston
'Should register well in any but the lowest grind.' – *Variety*

Lady of Secrets
US 1936 73m bw
B. P. Schulberg/Columbia

A rich girl's father prevents her marriage without knowing that she is pregnant.

Complicated and very boring mother-love yarn with the faint perfume of a bygone age.

w Joseph Anthony, Zoe Akins, Katherine Brush d Marion Gering

☆ Ruth Chatterton, Otto Kruger, Lionel Atwill, Lloyd Nolan, Marian Marsh, Elizabeth Risdon
'Chatterton, back to the screen after a long absence, is still having trouble with her offspring. This time she is also having trouble with the play, the direction, and the photography.' – *Variety*

Lady of the Boulevards: see Nana

The Lady of the Camelias (dubbed)
France/Italy/Germany (Margaret Menegoz, Monolo Bolognini) 1981 121m Technicolor
Gaumont/Films du Losange/FR3/Opera/Tele-München
📀

original title: *La Dame aux Camélias*

As Alexandre Dumas rehearses his play *La Dame aux Camélias*, he recalls the tragic life of Alphonsine Plessis, the courtesan who was the model for its central character.

Uninspired and ponderous period drama, lacking in any sign of passion; what little life it might have had has been flattened by the dubbing.

w Enrico Medioli, Jean Aurenche, Vladimir Pozner d Mauro Bolognini *ph* Ennio Guarnieri *m* Ennio Morricone *ad* Mario Garbuglia *ed* Nino Baragli

☆ Isabelle Huppert, Gian Maria Volonte, Bruno Ganz, Fabrizio Bentivoglio, Fernando Rey, Clio Goldsmith, Mario Maranzana, Carla Fracci

Lady of the Night (dubbed)
Italy 1986 100m Telecolor
San Francisco/Metrofilm (Giovanni Bertolucci)
📀

original title: *La Signora della Notte*

After three years of marriage, a wife decides she wants to have sex with strangers.

Risible and sleazy sexploitation movie, full of violence towards women.

w Galliano Juso, Piero Schivazappa d Piero Schivazappa *ph* Giuseppe Ruzzolini *m* Guido and Maurizio de Angelis *ad* Bruno Amalfitano *ed* Daniele Alabiso

☆ Serena Grandi, Fabio Sartor, Francesca Topi, Alberto di Stasio, Emanuela Taschini, Stanko Molnar

Lady of the Tropics
US 1939 92m bw
MGM (Sam Zimbalist)

An American playboy in Saigon marries a half-caste girl but her former admirer prevents her from getting a passport.

Interminable romantic melodrama with stars apparently straight from the taxidermist.

w Ben Hecht d Jack Conway *ph* George Folsey *m* Franz Waxman

☆ Robert Taylor, Hedy Lamarr, Joseph Schildkraut, Gloria Franklin, Ernest Cossart
'Mediocre and stagey romance, but stars should pull it through.' – *Variety*

Lady on a Train *
US 1945 84m bw
Universal (Felix Jackson)

A girl arriving in New York by train sees a murder committed and can't make anyone believe her.

Cheerful mystery which starts in the right spirit but does not progress too satisfactorily.

w Edmund Beloin, Robert O'Brien *novel* Leslie Charteris d Charles David *ph* Elwood Bredell *m* Miklos Rozsa

☆ Deanna Durbin, Ralph Bellamy, David Bruce, Edward Everett Horton, George Coulouris, Allen Jenkins, Dan Duryea, Patricia Morison

The Lady Pays Off
US 1951 80m bw
Universal-International (Albert J. Cohen)

A gambling schoolteacher agrees to pay off her debts by tutoring the casino owner's daughter.

Flat and unprofitable romantic comedy-drama.

w Frank Gill Jnr, Albert J. Cohen d Douglas Sirk *ph* William H. Daniels *m* Frank Skinner

☆ Linda Darnell, Stephen McNally, Gigi Perreau, Virginia Field, Ann Codee
'The sort of thing that people who shun the cinema imagine all films to be.' – *C. A. Lejeune*

Lady Possessed
US 1952 86m bw
Republic/Portland (James Mason)

An unbalanced woman imagines she is destined to take the place of a pianist's dead wife.

Weary melodramatic nonsense dating from Hollywood's first obsession with psychiatry.

w Pamela Kellino, James Mason *novel* Del Palma by Pamela Kellino d William Spier, Roy Kellino *ph* Karl Struss *m* Nathan Scott

☆ James Mason, June Havoc, Stephen Dunne, Fay Compton, Pamela Kellino, Steven Geray

The Lady Says No

US   1951   83m   bw
UA/Stillman (Frank Ross, John Stillman Jnr)

A magazine photographer tames a female chauvinist author.
Very silly comedy with neither wit nor style.
w Robert Russell d Frank Ross ph James Wong Howe m Emil Newman
☆ Joan Caulfield, David Niven, James Robertson Justice, Lenore Lonergan, Henry Jones

Lady Scarface

US   1941   69m   bw
RKO (Cliff Reid)
A police lieutenant captures a dangerous female gangster.
Weird gangster second feature with too many domestic comedy asides; notable only for the appearance in it of its dignified lead, fresh from Rebecca.
w Arnaud D'Usseau, Richard Collins d Frank Woodruff ph Nicholas Musuraca
☆ Judith Anderson, Dennis O'Keefe, Frances Neal, Mildred Coles, Eric Blore, Marc Lawrence

Lady Sings the Blues *

US   1972   144m   Eastmancolor   Panavision
Paramount/Motown/Weston/Furie (Jay Weston, James S. White)

The disastrous private life of jazz singer Billie Holiday.
Old-fashioned showbiz biopic with new-fashioned drugs, sex and squalor.
w Terence McCloy, Chris Clark, Suzanne de Passe d Sidney J. Furie ph John Alonzo m Michel Legrand md Gil Askey
☆ Diana Ross, Billy Dee Williams, Richard Pryor, James Callahan, Sid Melton
♫ script; Gil Askey; Diana Ross

A Lady Surrenders: see Love Story (1944)

A Lady Surrenders

US   1930   95m   bw
Universal
A misunderstanding turns an innocent husband into a bigamist after his wife has supposedly divorced him.
Totally effete romantic drama with no comedy relief.
w Gladys Lehman novel Sincerity by John Erskine d John Stahl
☆ Conrad Nagel, Genevieve Tobin, Basil Rathbone, Rose Hobart, Carmel Myers
'It fails from all angles: too stilted, slow, talky and punchless.' – Variety

A Lady Takes a Chance

US   1943   86m   bw
RKO (Frank Ross)

aka: The Cowboy and the Girl
A New York office girl on holiday in Oregon falls for a rodeo rider.
Slender star action romance.
w Robert Ardrey d William A. Seiter ph Frank Redman m Roy Webb
☆ Jean Arthur, John Wayne, Charles Winninger, Phil Silvers, Mary Field, Don Costello, John Philliber, Grady Sutton, Hans Conried

The Lady Takes a Flyer

US   1958   95m   Eastmancolor   Cinemascope
Universal-International (William Alland)
A pilot's wife finds that life at home is not easy, especially with a baby.
Heavy comedy or light drama; on either count a bore.
w Danny Arnold d Jack Arnold
☆ Lana Turner, Jeff Chandler, Richard Denning, Chuck Connors, Andra Martin

The Lady Takes a Sailor *

US   1949   99m   bw
Warner
A girl devoted to telling the truth insists on proving her story of a mysterious submarine which saved her after a sailing accident.
Curious romantic farce with echoes of the old slapstick tradition.
w Everett Freeman d Michael Curtiz ph Ted McCord m Max Steiner
☆ Jane Wyman, Dennis Morgan, Eve Arden, Allyn Joslyn, Robert Douglas, William Frawley

A Lady to Love

US   1930   92m   bw
MGM
An ageing grape grower spots an attractive waitress, sends her a marriage proposal by mail, but encloses a photo of his handsome foreman.
Rather primitive but well-acted version of a subject later filmed more fluently under the title of the original play.
w Sidney Howard play They Knew What They Wanted by Sidney Howard d Victor Seastrom ph Merritt B. Gerstad
☆ Edward G. Robinson, Vilma Banky, Robert Ames, Richard Carle
'A hit as a talker: well directed, acted and treated.' – Variety

Lady Tubbs

US   1935   69m   bw
Universal
An ex-cook crashes society and shows up the pretenders.
Mildly agreeable sentimental farce.
w Barry Trivers novel Homer Croy d Alan Crosland
☆ Alice Brady, Douglass Montgomery, Anita Louise, Alan Mowbray, Minor Watson, Russell Hicks, Hedda Hopper
'Solid laugh fare for the nabes.' – Variety

'Spies! Playing the game of love – and sudden death!'

The Lady Vanishes ****

† GB   1938   97m   bw
Gaumont British/Gainsborough (Edward Black)

En route back to England by train from Switzerland, an old lady disappears and two young people investigate.
The disappearing lady trick brilliantly refurbished by Hitchcock and his screenwriters, who even get away with a horrid model shot at the beginning. Superb, suspenseful, brilliantly funny, meticulously detailed entertainment.
w Sidney Gilliat, Frank Launder novel The Wheel Spins by Ethel Lina White d Alfred Hitchcock ph Jack Cox md Louis Levy
☆ Margaret Lockwood, Michael Redgrave, Dame May Whitty, Paul Lukas, Basil Radford, Naunton Wayne, Catherine Lacey, Cecil Parker, Linden Travers, Googie Withers, Mary Clare, Philip Leaver
'If it were not so brilliant a melodrama, we should class it as a brilliant comedy.' – Frank S. Nugent
'No one can study the deceptive effortlessness with which one thing leads to another without learning where the true beauty of this medium is to be mined.' – Otis Ferguson
'Directed with such skill and velocity that it has come to represent the very quintessence of screen suspense.' – Pauline Kael, 70s
† Hitchcock was actually second choice as director. The production was ready to roll as Lost Lady, directed by Roy William Neill, with Charters and Caldicott already in place, when Neill became unavailable and Hitch stepped in.

The Lady Vanishes

† GB   1979   97m   Eastmancolor   Panavision
Rank/Hammer (Michael Carreras, Tom Sachs)

A remake of the above in which everything goes wrong: wrong shape, wrong actors, wrong style (or lack of it).
Reasonable adherence to the original script can't save it.
w George Axelrod d Anthony Page ph Douglas Slocombe m Richard Hartley pd Wilfred Shingleton
☆ Cybill Shepherd, Elliott Gould, Angela Lansbury, Herbert Lom, Arthur Lowe, Ian Carmichael, Gerald Harper, Jenny Runacre, Jean Anderson

The Lady Wants Mink

US   1953   92m   Trucolor
Republic (Herbert J. Yates)
A wife causes domestic upsets when she decides to start a mink farm in order to get the fur coat that she has always wanted.
A by-the-numbers comedy which comes to the predictable conclusions that the rural life is better than an urban existence and that money can't buy happiness; it fails to convince or even amuse.

w Dane Lussier, Richard Alan Simmons story Leonard Neubauer, Lou Schor d William A. Seiter ph Reggie Lanning m Stanley Wilson ad Martin Obzina ed Fred Allen
☆ Dennis O'Keefe, Ruth Hussey, Eve Arden, William Demarest, Gene Lockhart, Hope Emerson, Hillary Brooke, Tommy Rettig

Lady Windermere's Fan: see The Fan (1949)

Lady Windermere's Fan *

US   1925   80m   bw   silent
Warner
The mysterious Mrs Erlynne almost causes a scandal in London society.
Oscar Wilde's play transposed to the twenties, with the Lubitsch touch daringly displacing Wildean epigrams. Still more amusing than the sound remake, The Fan.
w Julien Josephson d Ernst Lubitsch ph Charles Van Enger
☆ Ronald Colman, May McAvoy, Irene Rich, Bert Lytell, Edward Martindel
'Lubitsch's best silent film, full of incisive details, discreet touches, nuances of gestures, where behaviour betrays the character and discloses the sentiment of the personages.' – Georges Sadoul

The Lady with a Lamp *

† GB   1951   110m   bw
British Lion/Imperadio (Herbert Wilcox)
The life of Florence Nightingale and her work in reforming the nursing service in 19th-century England.
Solid biopic, not quite in accord with history.
w Warren Chetham Strode play Reginald Berkeley d Herbert Wilcox ph Max Greene m Anthony Collins ad William C. Andrews
☆ Anna Neagle, Michael Wilding, Gladys Young, Felix Aylmer, Julian D'Albie, Arthur Young, Edwin Styles, Barbara Couper, Cecil Trouncer, Rosalie Crutchley
'A slow, sedate, refined chronicle … Herbert Wilcox is a good deal more at ease with the balls and dinners, than with anything that happens later.' – Penelope Houston
'It may please fans of Anna Neagle and Michael Wilding, but not fans of Florence Nightingale.' – Richard Mallett, Punch

Lady with a Past *

US   1932   80m   bw
RKO (Charles R. Rogers)
GB title: Reputation
A wealthy but shy girl almost accidentally finds herself with a reputation as a scarlet woman, and the men flock around her.
Moderately enjoyable star comedy drama.
w Horace Jackson novel Harriet Henry d Edward H. Griffith ph Hal Mohr m Max Steiner
☆ Constance Bennett, Ben Lyon, David Manners, Astrid Allwyn, Merna Kennedy, Blanche Frederici, Nella Walker
'Light and satisfying material for the women.' – Variety

The Lady with Red Boots (dubbed) *

France/Spain   1974   98m   colour
UGC/CFDC (Claude Jaeger, Daniel Carrillo)
original title: La Femme aux Bottes Rouges
A poor and glamorous avant-garde novelist is attracted to a married publisher, and attracts in turn the attentions of a mysterious financier.
Enjoyably quirky study in obsession, with surrealist overtones.
w Pierre Jean Maintigneux, Jean-Claude Carrière, Clem Wood, Juan Buñuel d Juan Buñuel ph Leopold Villasenor ad Adolfe Cofino ed Genevieve Vaury, Maryse Siclier
☆ Catherine Deneuve, Fernando Rey, Adalberto Maria Merli, Jacques Weber, Jose Sacristan, Emma Cohen, Laura Betti

Lady with Red Hair *

US   1940   78m   bw
Warner (Edmund Grainger)
The life of actress Mrs Leslie Carter and her association with impresario David Belasco.
Mildly interesting but unsatisfying biopic of a lady scarcely remembered.
w Charles Kenyon, Milton Krims, N. Brewster Morse, Norbert Faulkner d Curtis Bernhardt ph Arthur Edeson m Heinz Roemheld
☆ Miriam Hopkins, Claude Rains, Richard Ainley, John Litel, Laura Hope Crews, Helen

Westley, Mona Barrie, Victor Jory, Cecil Kellaway, Fritz Leiber, Halliwell Hobbes

The Lady with the Little Dog *

USSR   1959   90m   bw
Lenfilm
original title: Dama s Sobachkoi
In Yalta at the turn of the century, an unhappily married woman and a married man start an affair which lasts secretly over the years.
Modestly pleasing, subtly acted anecdote.
wd Josef Heifits story Anton Chekhov ph Andrei Moskvin m Jiri Sternwald ed D. Meschiev
☆ Iya Savvina, Alexei Batalov, Ala Chostakova

A Lady without Passport *

US   1950   84m   bw
MGM (Samuel Marx)
A secret service undercover man tracks down aliens being smuggled into the US, and falls in love with one of them.
Routine material, very well handled.
w Howard Dimsdale story Lawrence Taylor d Joseph H. Lewis ph Paul C. Vogel m David Raksin
☆ Hedy Lamarr, John Hodiak, James Craig, George Macready, Steve Geray

Ladybird Ladybird **

GB   1994   101m   colour
UIP/Parallax/Film Four (Sally Hibbin)

An unmarried mother whose four children have been taken into care also loses her next two to the social services, despite a stable relationship with a Paraguayan refugee.
A fierce and passionate attack on official attitudes to the unconforming, based on a true story – although the facts, or the interpretation of them here, have been questioned since the film's release. It gains from its powerful performance by Crissy Rock.
w Rona Munro d Ken Loach ph Barry Ackroyd m George Fenton, Mauricio Venegas pd Martin Johnson ed Jonathan Morris
☆ Crissy Rock, Vladimir Vega, Sandie Lavelle, Mauricio Venegas, Ray Winstone, Clare Perkins, Luke Brown, Lilly Farrell, Jason Strachey

'A Comedy With Balls.'

Ladybugs

US   1992   90m   DeLuxe
Warner/Morgan Creek (Albert S. Ruddy, Andre E. Morgan)

A salesman takes over managership of a women's soccer team and has his son join it in drag.
Dismayingly stupid comedy that is embarrassing to watch.
w Curtis Burch d Sidney J. Furie m Richard Gibbs pd Robb Wilson King ed John W. Wheeler, Timothy N. Board
☆ Rodney Dangerfield, Jackée, Jonathan Brandis, Ilene Graff, Vinessa Shaw, Tom Parks
'This picture doesn't deserve any respect. Sexist, homophobic and woefully unfunny to boot, Rodney Dangerfield's latest starring effort is a waste of comic talent.' – Variety
'This week's candidate for the worst film in history.' – Geoff Brown, The Times

'Cursed for eternity! No force in heaven will release them … no power on earth can save them!'

Ladyhawke

† US   1985   124m   Technicolor
Warner/Richard Donner, Lauren Schuler

Medieval boy and girl lovers have been changed respectively into a wolf and a hawk, never simultaneously to resume their true forms.
Unpersuasive legend, dolefully told at excessive length.
w Edward Khmara, Michael Thomas, Tom Mankiewicz d Richard Donner ph Vittorio Storaro m Andrew Powell pd Wolf Kroeger ed Stuart Baird
☆ Matthew Broderick, Rutger Hauer, Michelle Pfeiffer, Leo McKern, John Wood

The Ladykillers ***

† GB   1955   97m   Technicolor
Ealing (Michael Balcon)

An old lady takes in a sinister lodger, who with his four friends commits a robbery. When she finds out, they plot to kill her, but are hoist with their own petards.

---

† film suitable for family viewing   VHS video-cassette for the British PAL system   VHS video-cassette for the British PAL system in wide screen-format   ✪ Video cassette in a computer-colourised version   American NTSC video-cassette   Laser disc

Witty black comedy, shot in muted colours, which approaches the grotesque without damaging its acerbic humour or sense of fantasy; it is one of the few films where death is both shocking and funny.

w William Rose d Alexander Mackendrick ph Otto Heller m Tristram Cary ad Jim Morahan ed Jack Harris

☆ Alec Guinness, *Katie Johnson*, Peter Sellers, Cecil Parker, Herbert Lom, Danny Green, Jack Warner, Frankie Howerd, Kenneth Connor

'To be frivolous about frivolous matters, that's merely boring. To be frivolous about something that's in some way deadly serious, that's true comedy.' – *Alexander Mackendrick*

'The acting is triumphant ... Artistically, I suspect, *The Ladykillers* needs a shade more of the macabre; it would be a better film if it were blacker. But I am beginning to find that I can see a joke better in twilight than midnight.' – *Dilys Powell*

'This sinister black comedy of murder accelerates until it becomes a grotesque fantasy of murder. The actors seem to be having a boisterous good time getting themselves knocked off.' – *Pauline Kael*

'One of the neatest blends of the mirthful and macabre I can remember.' – *Fred Majdalany, Time and Tide*

'Undoubtedly the most stylish, inventive and funniest British comedy of the year.' – *Alan Brien, London Evening Standard*

† The role of Professor Marcus, played by Alec Guinness, was originally intended for Alistair Sim. It has been claimed, though Guinness has denied it, that his toothy appearance was based on the critic Kenneth Tynan who worked for Ealing as a script editor.

♕ William Rose
♛ Katie Johnson; William Rose

The Lady's from Kentucky
US   1939   75m   bw
Jeff Lazarus/Paramount
A crooked bookie is reformed by a lady horse breeder.
Yawnworthy drama with an unattractive hero.
w Malcolm Stuart Boylan d Alexander Hall
☆ George Raft, Ellen Drew, Hugh Herbert, ZaSu Pitts, Louise Beavers, Forrester Harvey
'It starts with promise, stumbles in the middle section, and drags itself across the line for the finish.' – *Variety*

A Lady's Morals
US   1930   86m   bw
MGM
GB title: *Jenny Lind*
aka: *The Soul Kiss*
The 'Swedish nightingale' learns that love is more important than a singing career.
Cliché-strewn romance with music.
w Hans Kraly, Claudine West, John Meehan, Arthur Richman d Sidney Franklin m Herbert Stothart
☆ Grace Moore, Reginald Denny, Wallace Beery, Jobyna Howland
'Class production of money potentialities.' – *Variety*
† Wallace Beery played P. T. Barnum, a role he was to repeat four years later in *The Mighty Barnum.*

A Lady's Profession
US   1933   65m   bw
Paramount
A British nobleman comes to America to retrieve his lost fortune, and starts a speakeasy.
Rather silly farce which generally disappoints.
w Walter de Leon, Malcolm Stuart Boylan d Norman McLeod
☆ Alison Skipworth, Roland Young, Sari Maritza, Kent Taylor, Roscoe Karns
'Slow. Some bright spots, but too widely spaced.' – *Variety*

Lafayette
France/Italy   1961   158m   Super Technirama 70
Copernic/Cosmos (Maurice Jacquin)
French officers help America in the revolutionary war of 1776.
Nerveless international epic, interesting only for its star cameos.
w Jean-Bernard Luc, Suzanne Arduini, Jacques Sigurd, François Ponthier, Jean Dréville, Maurice Jacquin d Jean Dréville ph Claude Renoir, Roger Hubert m Steve Laurent, Pierre Duclos

☆ Michel Le Royer, Jack Hawkins, Orson Welles, Howard St John, Vittorio de Sica, Edmund Purdom, Jacques Castelot, Folco Lulli
'It looks, sounds and smells like nothing so much as the same old indigestible, ill-dubbed, co-produced continental spectaculars which have already turned the stomach in a whole range of lesser screen ratios.' – *MFB*

Lafayette Escadrille
US   1957   93m   bw
Warner (William Wellman)
GB title: *Hell Bent for Glory*
Early in World War I, a young American joins the French air force.
The director's valedictory film, on a subject close to his heart, is a curiously disappointing, flat and disjointed affair, partly salvaged by a good period feel.
w A. S. Fleischman d William A. Wellman ph William Clothier m Leonard Rosenman
☆ Tab Hunter, Etchika Choreau, David Janssen, Clint Eastwood, Will Hutchins, Paul Fix

The Lair of the White Worm
GB   1988   93m   Technicolor
Vestron (Ken Russell)
◉ ▤ ⊚ ◎
A female vampire attempts to make human sacrifices to an ancient snake god.
Grotesque horror done without finesse or subtlety.
wd Ken Russell novel Bram Stoker ph Dick Bush m Stanislas Syrewicz ed Peter Davies sp Geoff Portass
☆ Amanda Donohoe, Hugh Grant, Catherine Oxenberg, Peter Capaldi, Sammi Davis, Stratford Johns, Paul Brooke, Imogen Claire, Christopher Gable
'He proves incapable of handling straight suspense, horror, or supernatural sequences.' – *MFB*
'How on earth can you take seriously the vision of Catherine Oxenberg, dressed in Marks & Spencer's underwear, being sacrificed to a fake, phallic worm two hundred feet long?' – *Ken Russell*

Lake Consequence
US   1992   90m   colour
Rank/10dB/Zalman King (Avram Butch Kaplan)
◉ ▤ ⊚
A housewife who was gang-raped by a rock band wants more of the same.
Glossy, cliché-ridden would-be erotica for the easily pleased.
w Zalman King, Melanie Finn, Henry Cobbold story MacGregor Douglas d Rafael Eisenman ph Harris Savides m George S. Clinton pd Dominic Watkins ed James Gavin Bedford, Curtis Edge
☆ Billy Zane, Joan Severance, May Karasun, Whip Hubley, Courtland Mead, Dan Reed, Christi Allen
'Slickly shot, but over dramatised (some of the editing is positively epileptic) at the expense of any remotely believable dialogue or acting, this, given its pedigree, is high on sauce but low on just about everything else.' – *Empire*

'You'll never know what bit you.'

Lake Placid
US   1999   82m   Technicolor   Panavision
TCF/Fox 2000/Phoenix/Rocking Chair (David E. Kelley, Michael Pressman)
▤ ◎ ◉
A New York expert investigates reports of giant crocodiles inhabiting a lake in northern Maine.
A cheapjack horror movie that puts the emphasis on jokes, but a few good one-liners are not enough to enliven so much predictability.
w David E. Kelley d Steve Miner ph Daryn Okada m John Ottman pd John Willett ed Marshall Harvey, Paul Hirsch sp Stan Winston
☆ Bill Pullman, Bridget Fonda, Oliver Platt, Brendan Gleeson, Betty White, David Lewis, Tim Dixon, Natassia Malthe, Mariska Hargitay, Meredith Salenger
'A B-movie dud.' – *Entertainment Weekly*

Lake Placid Serenade
US   1944   85m   bw
Republic (Harry Grey)
A Czech girl skater is sent to America to represent her country.

Simple-minded entertainment overloaded with musical numbers.
w Dick Irving Hyland, Doris Gilbert book Frederick Kohner d Steve Sekely
☆ Vera Hruba Ralston, Robert Livingston, Eugene Pallette, Vera Vague, Walter Catlett, Lloyd Corrigan, William Frawley

'She gave her innocence, her passion, her body. The one thing she couldn't give was her love.'

L'Amant *
GB/France   1992   115m   colour
Guild/A2/Burrill/Giai Phong Film (Claude Berri, Timothy Burrill)
◉ ▤ ⊚ ◎
aka: *The Lover*
A 15-year-old French girl in Vietnam begins an obsessive affair with a wealthy Chinese man.
Lushly romantic drama that exerts a certain charm.
w Gérard Brach, Jean-Jacques Annaud novel Marguerite Duras d Jean-Jacques Annaud ph Robert Fraisse m Gabriel Yared ad Thanh At Hoang ed Noëlle Boisson
☆ Jane March, Tony Leung, Frédérique Meininger, Arnaud Giovaninetti, Melvil Poupaud, Lisa Faulkner, Jeanne Moreau
'Lacks the distinctive voice and ambiance of the book, but the abundant sex – soft-core and tasteful – and the splendid sets make up for the film's banal style.' – *Variety*
'Duras's subtle portrait of festering colonialism is brought to the screen with some resource by Annaud ... But neither Leung nor March, given a difficult role in her first film and certainly looking more fetching than she sounds, can provide a truly holding centre.' – *Derek Malcolm, Guardian*
'Touching, clear-eyed, utterly unsentimental, produced lavishly but with such discipline that the exotic locale never gets in the way of the minutely detailed drama at the center.' – *Vincent Canby, New York Times*
♛ Robert Fraisse

Lamb
GB   1986   110m   Eastmancolor
Cannon/Flickers/Limehouse/Channel 4 (Neil Zeiger)
◉
A young priest at a harsh Irish reform school absconds with a 14-year-old pupil, an act with tragic consequences for them both.
Rather wearisome transcription of religious thesis into makeshift drama: disturbing but not satisfying.
w Bernard MacLaverty novel Bernard MacLaverty d Colin Gregg ph Mike Garfath m Van Morrison pd Austen Spriggs ad Peter Delfgou
☆ Liam Neeson, Hugh O'Conor, Harry Towb, Frances Tomelty, Ian Bannen

Lambada
US   1990   98m   Alpha Cine   Panavision
Warner/Cannon/Film and Television Company (Peter Shepherd)
◉ ▤ ⊚
A teacher spends his nights as a lambada dancer so that he can give lessons to a gang of dropouts.
Dismal attempt to cash in on a short-lived American dance craze.
w Joel Silberg, Sheldon Renan d Joel Silberg ph Roberto D'Ettore Piazzoli m Greg DeBelles pd Bill Cornfield ed Marcus Manton
☆ J. Eddie Peck, Melora Hardin, Shabba-Doo, Ricky Paul Goldin, Basil Hoffman, Dennis Burkley, Keene Curtis

Lambada: Forbidden Dance
US   1990   97m   Foto-Kem
Columbia/21st Century (Richard L. Albert, Marc S. Fischer)
◉ ▤ ⊚
aka: *The Forbidden Dance*
aka: *Lambada: Baile Prohibido*
A Brazilian princess travels to Los Angeles to try to save her rain-forest from being destroyed by American developers – and becomes a lambada dancer so she can make a public appeal on television.
Risibly clumsy attempt to exploit both a short-lived dance craze and ecological concern; after watching Laura Herring dance, you will understand why it should be forbidden.
w Roy Langsdon, John Platt story Joseph Goldman d Greydon Clark ph R. Michael Stringer m Vladimir Horunzhy ed Robert Edwards, Earl Watson

☆ Laura Herring, Jeff James, Richard Lynch, Sid Haig, Kid Creole and the Coconuts, Barbra Brighton

The Lambeth Walk
GB   1939   84m   bw
CAPAD/Pinebrook (Anthony Havelock-Allan)
A Cockney bloke inherits a dukedom.
Mild screen version of a popular musical play and a song which became a nationwide hit.
w Clifford Grey, John Paddy Carstairs, Robert Edmunds play Me and My Girl by Louis Rose, Douglas Furber, Noel Gay d Albert de Courville ph Francis Carver
☆ Lupino Lane, Sally Gray, Seymour Hicks, Enid Stamp Taylor, Wilfrid Hyde-White, Charles Heslop, Norah Howard

Lamerica ***
Italy/France   1994   125m   colour
Cinemascope
CGG Tiger/Arena (Mario and Vittorio Cecchi Gori)
◎
Two Italian con men come unstuck when they go to Albania to get rich quick.
Powerful and bleak drama of appalling poverty and despair, and of the humanity that somehow survives in the direst situations.
w Gianni Amelio, Andrea Porporati, Alessandro Sermoneta d Gianni Amelio ph Luca Bigazzi m Franco Piersanti ad Giuseppe M. Gaudino ed Simona Paggi
☆ Enrico Lo Verso, Michele Placido, Carmelo di Mazzarelli, Piro Milkani
'Its evangelical sincerity and the sweeping emotion of its finale could win the director new admirers abroad.' – *Variety*
† The film won a Felix as European film of the year in 1994.

The Lamp Still Burns
GB   1943   90m   bw
GFD/Two Cities (Leslie Howard)
Adventures of wartime probationary nurses.
Understated wartime morale-builder, no longer very interesting.
w Elizabeth Baron, Roland Pertwee novel One Pair of Feet by Monica Dickens d Maurice Elvey ph Robert Krasker
☆ Rosamund John, Stewart Granger, Godfrey Tearle, Sophie Stewart, John Laurie, Margaret Vyner, Cathleen Nesbitt, Joyce Grenfell

Lan Fengzheng: see *The Blue Kite*

Lancashire Luck
GB   1937   74m   bw
Paramount British
A poor girl's life is changed when her father wins the pools.
Modest comedy which started its star's career.
w A. R. Rawlinson story Ronald Gow d Henry Cass
☆ Wendy Hiller, George Carney, Muriel George, Nigel Stock, George Galleon

Lancelot and Guinevere *
GB   1962   117m   Eastmancolor
Panavision
Emblem (Cornel Wilde)
US title: *Sword of Lancelot*
Sir Lancelot covets the wife of his beloved King Arthur, but after Arthur's death she takes the veil.
Decently made, rather tame transcription of the legends, with all concerned doing quite creditably but not brilliantly.
w Richard Schayer, Jefferson Pascal d Cornel Wilde ph Harry Waxman m Ron Goodwin
☆ Cornel Wilde, Jean Wallace, Brian Aherne, George Baker, John Barrie

Lancelot du Lac ***
France/Italy   1974   85m   Eastmancolor
Mara/Laser/ORTF/Gerico Sound (Jean Yanne, Jean-Pierre Rassam)
◉ ▤
aka: *Le Graal*
aka: *The Grail*
The high ideals of chivalry wither as Lancelot, with the few remaining Knights of the Round Table, returns disillusioned from the failed quest to find the Holy Grail and resumes his love affair with Guinevere, wife of King Arthur.

Austerely impressive drama of the loss of faith, conjuring up a medieval world with great economy of means.

w *Robert Bresson* ph *Pasqualino de Santis* m *Philippe Sarde* ad *Pierre Charbonnier* ed *Germaine Lamy*

☆ Luc Simon, Laura Duke Condominas, Humbert Balsan, Vladimir Antolek-Oresek, Patrick Bernard, Arthur de Montalembert

'Like so much of Bresson's work this is not so much a movie more a religious experience, but you don't have to be religious to enjoy it.' – *Tom Hutchinson, Film Review*

Lancer Spy *
US 1937 80m bw
TCF
A German spy is captured and his English double is sent back to replace him.
World War I yarn on the lines of The Great Impersonation *(qv). Excellent production and a good beginning and end, but a slow middle.*
w *Philip Dunne* novel *Marthe McKenna* d *Gregory Ratoff* ph *Barney McGill* m *Arthur Lange*
☆ George Sanders, Dolores del Rio, Peter Lorre, Joseph Schildkraut, Virginia Field, Sig Rumann, Fritz Feld
'Sometimes exciting, always absorbing, and played with serious intensity.' – *Variety*

'A Story from the Spanish Civil War'

Land and Freedom ***
GB/Germany/Spain 1995 110m colour
Artificial Eye/Parallax/Messidor/Road Movies (Rebecca O'Brien)
🔲 ⊛
An unemployed Liverpudlian Communist goes to fight in the Spanish Civil War on the side of the socialist POUM, but comes to discover that the activities of the Stalinist Republican forces and Communists in suppressing other left-wing groups will give victory to the Fascists.
An engrossing and passionate Orwellian account of the Spanish Civil War, as experienced on an individual level, which is framed by a death in present-day Liverpool in an attempt to point up the contemporary relevance of its story of a revolution betrayed.
w *Jim Allen* d *Ken Loach* m *Barry Ackroyd* m *George Fenton* pd *Martin Johnson* ed *Jonathan Morris*
☆ Ian Hart, Rosana Pastor, Iciar Bollain, Tom Gilroy, Marc Martinez, Frederic Pierrot, Suzanne Maddock
'Direct, passionate and formidably informed by political conviction.' – *Derek Malcolm, Guardian*
'Ken Loach's real triumph is to get the viewer rooting for characters in a conflict that, for most, is as remote as the Trojan War.' – *John Hopewell, Variety*

The Land before Time
👫 US 1988 69m Technicolor
UIP/Universal/Amblin (Don Bluth, Gary Goldman, John Pomeroy)
🔲 ⊛ 🎧
An orphaned dinosaur sets out with friends to find the way to a valley of plenty.
Over-cute, immensely sentimental animated feature.
w *Stu Krieger* story *Judy Freudberg, Tony Geiss* d *Don Bluth* ph *Jim Mann* m *James Horner*
☆ Featuring Voices of Gabriel Damon, Helen Shaver, Bill Erwin, Candice Houston, Pat Hingle, Burke Barnes, Judith Barsi, Will Ryan

Land of Desire: see *A Ship to India*

Land of Fury: see *The Seekers*

Land of Liberty *
US 1939 137m bw
Motion Picture Producers and Distributors of America
A compilation of footage from American historical films, amounting hopefully to a history of America as seen by Hollywood.
A pretty impressive job of selection and editing, compiled for the New York World's Fair.
w *Jeannie Macpherson, Jesse Lasky Jnr* ed *Cecil B. de Mille and others*

'Her treachery stained every stone of the pyramid!'
'20,000 workers and technicians! 1,600 camels! 104 specially built barges! 9,753 players in one scene alone!'

Land of the Pharaohs *
US 1955 105m Warnercolor Cinemascope
Warner/Continental (Howard Hawks)
🔲 ⊛ 🎧
Pharaoh is obsessed with life after death and builds a great pyramid for himself and his treasures … but his wife is ambitious…
Unexpected, interesting excursion into Ancient Egypt, distended by Cinemascope; basically a macabre melodrama with a final spectacular twist. The engineering details would make a fascinating documentary.
w *William Faulkner, Harry Kurnitz, H. Jack Bloom* d *Howard Hawks* ph *Lee Garmes, Russell Harlan* m *Dimitri Tiomkin* ad *Alexander Trauner*
☆ Jack Hawkins, Joan Collins, Alexis Minotis, James Robertson Justice, Sydney Chaplin

Land Raiders
US 1969 100m Technicolor
Columbia (Charles H. Schneer)
🔲
Two brothers quarrel when one attempts to exterminate neighbouring Apaches so that he can take over their lands.
Routine Western of jealousy and greed, not helped by the miscasting of its two protagonists.
w *Ken Pettus* d *Nathan H. Duran* ph *Wilkie Cooper* m *Bruno Nicolai* ad *Jose Alguero* ed *Archie Ludski*
☆ Telly Savalas, George Maharis, Arlene Dahl, Janet Landgard, Phil Brown, Paul Picerni, George Colouris, Guy Rolfe, Jocelyn Lane

The Land that Time Forgot *
👫 GB 1974 91m Technicolor
Amicus (John Dark)
🔲 ⊛
In 1916, survivors from a torpedoed supply ship find themselves on a legendary island full of prehistoric monsters.
Lively old-fashioned adventure fantasy with good technical credits.
w *James Cawthorne, Michael Moorcock* novel *Edgar Rice Burroughs* d *Kevin Connor* ph *Alan Hume* m *Douglas Gamley* pd *Maurice Carter* sp *Derek Meddings, Roger Dicken*
☆ Doug McClure, John McEnery, Susan Penhaligon, Keith Barron, Anthony Ainley

The Land Unknown *
👫 US 1957 78m bw Cinemascope
U-I (William Alland)
A plane is forced down into a strange Antarctic valley where dinosaurs still roam.
Efficient adventure fantasy on King Kong lines but without any of that film's panache.
w *Laszlo Gorog* d *Virgil Vogel* ph *Ellis Carter* m *Hans Salter* m *Roswell Hoffman, Fred Knoth, Orien Ernest, Jack Kevan*
☆ Jock Mahoney, Shawn Smith, William Reynolds, Henry Brandon

Land without Bread *
Spain 1932 27m bw
Ramon Acin
aka: *Las Hurdes*
A famous documentary showing the poorest region of northern Spain, notable for some stunningly unpleasant images impeccably staged.
ph *Eli Lotar* wd/ed *Luis Buñuel*
'An honest and hideous picture.' – *Graham Greene*

Land without Music *
GB 1936 80m bw
Capitol Films (Max Schach)
US title: *Forbidden Music*
The ruler of a Ruritanian country bans music because her subjects are too busy singing to make money. A revolutionary singer however wins the duchess's hand and reverses her decision.
Artless but attractively played operetta with the star in excellent form.
w *Marion Dix, L. Du Garde Peach* story *Fritz Koselka, Armin Robinson* d *Walter Forde* ph *John Boyle* m *Oscar Straus*
☆ Richard Tauber, Jimmy Durante, Diana Napier, June Clyde, Derrick de Marney, Esme Percy, George Hayes, Edward Rigby

Landfall
GB 1949 88m bw
ABPC (Victor Skuzetzky)
A test pilot mistakenly believes that he accidentally sank a British submarine.
Second-rate transcription of a popular novel.
w *Talbot Jennings, Gilbert Gunn, Anne Burnaby* novel *Nevil Shute* d *Ken Annakin* ph *Wilkie Cooper*
☆ Michael Denison, Patricia Plunkett, Kathleen Harrison, David Tomlinson, Joan Dowling, Maurice Denham, A. E. Matthews, Margaretta Scott, Sebastian Shaw, Laurence Harvey

The Landgirls *
GB/France 1997 111m colour Panavision
Film Four/InterMedia/Greenpoint/West Eleven (Simon Relph)
🔲 ⊗
During the Second World War, three young women go to work as labourers on an isolated Dorset farm, and are attracted to the farmer's son.
Pleasant nostalgic wallow, which eschews class conflicts for gentler romance.
w *David Leland, Keith Dewhurst* novel *Angela Huth* d *David Leland* ph *Henry Braham* m *Brian Lock* pd *Caroline Amies* ed *Nick Moore*
☆ Catherine McCormack, Rachel Weisz, Anna Friel, Steven Mackintosh, Tom Georgeson, Maureen O'Brien, Lucy Akhurst
'The period is created in such loving detail that the film risks looking like a museum piece, complete with old planes, Hovis ad-like farm workers in breeches and braces, and even fun-loving GIs.' – *Geoffrey Macnab, Sight and Sound*

The Landlord *
US 1970 110m DeLuxe
United Artists/Mirisch/Carter (Norman Jewison)
A tycoon's son buys a tenement in Brooklyn's black ghetto, and conscience diverts him into improving the lot of his tenants.
Overlong satirical comedy, good on detail but short on structure.
w *Bill Gunn* novel *Kristin Hunter* d *Hal Ashby* ph *Gordon Willis* m *Al Kooper* pd *Robert Boyle*
☆ Beau Bridges, Lee Grant, Pearl Bailey, Diana Sands
'Bad taste from start to finish … not an avenue of offensiveness to any race is left unexplored.' – *Judith Crist*
⧗ Lee Grant

Landru
France/Italy 1962 115m Eastmancolor
Rome-Paris/CC Champion (Carlo Ponti, Georges de Beauregard)
aka: *Bluebeard*
The true story of a furniture dealer who murdered women for financial gain, also treated by Chaplin in *Monsieur Verdoux*.
A curious artificial style has been adopted, making a tragi-comedy look like a farce which isn't very funny, and falls on very stony ground indeed despite the all star cast.
w *Françoise Sagan* d *Claude Chabrol* ph *Jean Rabier* m *Pierre Jansen*
☆ Charles Denner, Michèle Morgan, Danielle Darrieux, Hildegarde Knef, Stéphane Audran, Catherine Rouvel

Landscape in a Mist *
Greece/France/Italy 1988 125m colour
Artificial Eye/Paradis Films/ET-1/Basicinematografica/Channel 4 (Theo Angelopoulos)
🎧
original title: *Topio Stin Omichli*
Two children, an eleven-year-old girl and her five-year-old brother, travel through Greece in an attempt to reach Germany and the father they have never known.
Lyrical, but slow-moving account of a child's discovery of the world that would have been as meaningful at half its length.
w *Theo Angelopoulos, Tonino Guerra, Thanassis Valtinos* d *Theo Angelopoulos* ph *Giorgos Arvanitis* m *Eleni Karaindrou* ad *Mikes Karapiperis* ed *Yannis Tsitsovanos*
☆ Michalis Zeke, Tania Palaiologou, Stratis Tzortzoglou

Lapse of Memory
Canada/France 1992 90m colour
Rank/Max/Gérard Mital/FR3/SGGC/Jean-Bernard Fetoux
🔲
aka: *Mémoire Tranquée*
With the help of a psychiatrist, a teenage boy attempts to relive the shocking events that caused him to lose his memory.
Dull thriller, done with plodding flashbacks, which fails to come to a satisfactory conclusion.
w *Patrick Dewolf, Philippe Le Guay, John Frizzell* novel *I Am the Cheese by Robert Cormier* d *Patrick Dewolf* ph *Alexandre Desplat* pd *François Seguin* ed *Fabienne Alvarez-Giro*
☆ John Hurt, Marthe Keller, Matthew Mackay, Kathleen Robertson, Marion Peterson
'Fine direction, acting and editing should add up to a strong commercial potential.' – *Variety*
† The novel was first filmed in 1983 as *I Am the Cheese* (qv).

Larceny
US 1948 89m bw
Universal (Aaron Rosenberg)
A con man fleeces a war widow into paying for a memorial to her husband, but falls in love with her.
Drearily predictable melodrama.
w *Herbert F. Margolis, Louis Markein, William Bowers* novel *The Velvet Fleece by Lois Ely, John Fleming* d *George Sherman* ph *Irving Glassberg* m *Leith Stevens*
☆ Joan Caulfield, John Payne, Dan Duryea, Shelley Winters, Dorothy Hart, Richard Rober, Dan O'Herlihy

Larceny, Inc
US 1942 95m bw
Warner (Jack Saper, Jerry Wald)
An ex-convict tries to rob a bank but finds that honesty pays best.
Tepid comedy-drama from the period when Warner were taming their gangster image.
w *Everett Freeman, Edwin Gilbert* play *The Night before Christmas by Laura and S. J. Perelman* d *Lloyd Bacon* ph *Tony Gaudio*
☆ Edward G. Robinson, Jane Wyman, Broderick Crawford, Anthony Quinn, Jack Carson, Edward Brophy, Harry Davenport, John Qualen, Barbara Jo Allen, Jackie Gleason, Grant Mitchell, Andrew Tombes

Larceny Lane: see *Blonde Crazy*

Larger than Life
1996 93m DeLuxe
MGM/UA/Trilogy/RCS/Majestic/Trilogy (Richard B. Lewis, John Watson, Pen Densham)
🔲 🎧
A motivational speaker takes an elephant, left to him by his father, a circus clown, on a journey across America.
Bland comedy, from which its star seems to be distancing himself as fast as he can; in that, he has my sympathy.
w *Roy Blount Jnr* story *Pen Densham, Garry Williams* d *Howard Franklin* ph *Elliot Davis* m *Miles Goodman* pd *Marcia Hinds-Johnson* ed *Sidney Levin*
☆ Bill Murray, Janeane Garofalo, Matthew McConaughey, Keith David, Pat Hingle, Jeremy Piven, Lois Smith, Harve Presnell, Linda Fiorentino
'An enjoyably daft comedy with high production values and a watertight script that combines a feelgood message concerning personal growth with all the slapstick one would expect from an elephant road movie.' – *Liese Spencer, Sight and Sound*

Larks on a String **
Czechoslovakia 1969 94m colour
Barrandov Filmstudio (Karel Kochman)
original title: *Skrivanci Na Niti*
Intellectuals and the displaced middle class prove resistant to change when they are punished by being forced to work on an industrial scrapheap.
Witty, blackly humorous satire on the Communist re-education of the bourgeoisie, marked by humanity, well-aimed barbs – a trade union executive gets out of his chauffeur-driven car and puts on a cloth cap before addressing the workers – and a scathing contempt for ideologically blinkered bureaucrats.

👫 film suitable for family viewing   🔲 VHS video-cassette for the British PAL system   🔲 VHS video-cassette for the British PAL system in wide screen-format   ⧗ Video cassette in a computer-colourised version   🖥 American NTSC video-cassette   ⊛ Laser disc

w Bohumil Hrabal, Jiri Menzel d Jiri Menzel
ph Jaromir Sofr m Jiri Sust ed Josef Lojik
☆ Rudolf Hrusinsky, Vlastimil Brodsky, Vaclav Neckar, Jitka Zelenohorska, Jaroslav Satoransky, Vladmir Smeral, Ferdinand Kruta
'A courageous, bittersweet comedy of considerable charm and invention.' – *Variety*
† The film was banned for 21 years and not seen publicly until the 1990 Berlin Film Festival, where it shared the Golden Bear award as best film.

The Las Vegas Story
US 1952 88m bw
RKO (Robert Sparks)
When an investment broker and his new wife stop at Las Vegas, her shady past begins to emerge.
So-so programmer with some eccentric talents in average form, capped by a desert helicopter chase.
w Earl Felton, Harry Essex d Robert Stevenson ph Harry J. Wild m Leigh Harline md Constantin Bakaleinikoff
☆ Jane Russell, Victor Mature, Vincent Price, Hoagy Carmichael, Colleen Miller, Brad Dexter, Jay C. Flippen

The Laser Man
Hong Kong 1988 90m colour
Peter Wang Films/Hong Kong Film Workshop (Peter Wang)
An out-of-work laser scientist is hired by a mysterious corporation to develop a deadly weapon.
Quirky thriller – the Chinese hero has a Jewish mother – but lacking anything other than its deliberate eccentricity.
wd Peter Wang ph Ernest Dickerson m Mason Daring pd Lester Cohen ed Graham Weinbren
☆ Marc Hayashi, Maryann Urbano, Joan Copeland, Tony Ka-Fei Leung, Neva Small, David Chan, Sally Yeh, Peter Wang

The Lash
US 1930 76m bw
First National
Adventures of a Spanish-Californian Robin Hood.
Or, The Mark of Zorro in all but name: a stalwart early talkie.
w Bradley King story Adios by Lanier and Virginia Bartlett d Frank Lloyd
☆ Richard Barthelmess, Mary Astor, James Rennie, Marian Nixon
'A good action talker in the western romantic strain.' – *Variety*
† Filmed in VitaScope (65mm).

Lashou Shentan: see *Hard Boiled*

Lasky Jedne Plavovlasky: see *Loves of a Blonde*

Lassie
The official Lassie series, made by MGM, was as follows:
1943 Lassie Come Home (qv)
1945 Son of Lassie d S. Sylvan Simon with Peter Lawford, Donald Crisp, Nigel Bruce
1946 Courage of Lassie d Fred M. Wilcox with Elizabeth Taylor, Frank Morgan, Tom Drake
1948 The Hills of Home (GB: Master of Lassie) d Fred M. Wilcox with Edmund Gwenn, Donald Crisp, Tom Drake
1949 The Sun Comes Up d Richard Thorpe with Jeanette MacDonald, Lloyd Nolan
1949 Challenge to Lassie d Richard Thorpe with Edmund Gwenn, Donald Crisp
1951 The Painted Hills d Harold F. Kress with Paul Kelly, Bruce Cowling
† Later 'Lassie' features were taken from episodes of the long-running TV series.

Lassie
🏃🏃 US 1994 92m DeLuxe
Paramount/Broadway Pictures (Lorne Michaels)
▨ ▤ ◎ ∩
A city boy is captivated by a sheepdog when he moves with his family to the country.
Glossy updating of the old story, but the magic has worn rather thin by now.
w Matthew Jacobs, Gary Ross, Elizabeth Anderson d Daniel Petrie ph Kenneth MacMillan m Basil Poledouris pd Paul Peters ed Steve Mirkovich
☆ Helen Slater, Thomas Guiry, Jon Tenney, Frederic Forrest, Richard Farnsworth, Brittany Boyd, Michelle Williams

'A hollow, post-yuppie update ... Everything in the movie smacks of trend-surfing.' – *Michael Sragow, New Yorker*

Lassie Come Home *
🏃🏃 US 1943 88m Technicolor
MGM (Samuel Marx)
▤
A poor family is forced to sell its beloved dog, but she makes a remarkable journey to return to them.
First of the Lassie films and certainly the best: an old-fashioned heartwarmer.
w Hugo Butler novel Eric Knight d Fred M. Wilcox ph Leonard Smith m Daniele Amfitheatrof
☆ Roddy McDowall, Elizabeth Taylor, Donald Crisp, Edmund Gwenn, Dame May Whitty, Nigel Bruce, Elsa Lanchester, J. Pat O'Malley
'The late Eric Knight wrote this immortal essay in Doggery-Woggery. MGM finished it off.' – *Richard Winnington*
⊗ Leonard Smith

Lassiter
US 1984 100m Technicolor
Pan Pacific/Golden Harvest (Albert S. Ruddy)
▨ ▤
An American detective in pre-war London is forced by Scotland Yard to steal papers from the German Embassy.
Flat to the point of stultification, this marks yet another failure to make a big screen star out of Tom Selleck.
w David Taylor d Roger Young ph Gil Taylor m Ken Thorne pd Peter Mullins ed Benjamin Weissman, Richard Hiscott
☆ Tom Selleck, Jane Seymour, Lauren Hutton, Bob Hoskins, Joe Regalbuto, Ed Lauter, Warren Clarke

Last Action Hero
🏃🏃 US 1993 131m Technicolor
Panavision
Columbia TriStar/Columbia (Steve Roth, John McTiernan)
▨ ◎ ◎ ◎ ∩
A magic ticket enables a boy to enter the world of an action movie, but it also allows the villain to escape into the real world, where he is followed by the boy and the film's muscular hero.
A film that tries to have it both ways, simultaneously mocking and celebrating the conventions of action movies, which leaves audiences, as well as the actors and director, in a state of bewildered confusion.
w Shane Black, David Arnott story Zack Penn, Adam Leff d John McTiernan ph Dean Semler m Michael Kamen pd Eugenio Zanetti ed John Wright
☆ Arnold Schwarzenegger, F. Murray Abraham, Art Carney, Charles Dance, Frank McRae, Tom Noonan, Robert Prosky, Anthony Quinn, Mercedes Ruehl, Ian McKellen, Joan Plowright, Tina Turner
'A joyless, soulless machine of a movie.' – *Variety*
'A perfect example of cinematic self-hatred.' – *Sight and Sound*
† The film's production costs were reportedly $100 million. It took around $28 million at the US box-office, though better results elsewhere meant that its final loss was reckoned to be some $20 million, although some estimates put it much higher.

The Last Adventurers
GB 1937 77m bw
Conway (H. Fraser Passmore)
Adventures on board a fishing trawler.
Acceptable low-budget outdoor drama.
w Denison Clift d Roy Kellino ph Eric Cross m Eric Ansell ad W. R. Brinton ed David Lean
☆ Niall MacGinnis, Linden Travers, Roy Emerton, Kay Walsh, Peter Gawthorne, Katie Johnson

The Last American Hero *
US 1973 95m DeLuxe Panavision
TCF/Wizan/Rojo (John Cutts, William Roberts)
▤
The adventures of an illicit whisky distiller with a passion for fast cars.
Observant, amusing hillbilly comedy drama based on the early life of racing driver Junior Johnson.
w William Roberts d Lamont Johnson ph George Silano m Charles Fox
☆ Jeff Bridges, Valerie Perrine, Geraldine Fitzgerald, Ned Beatty, Art Lund, Gary Busey

'A pop saga phrased with rough vernacular authenticity.' – *Bruce Williamson, Playboy*
† Reissue title: Hard Driver.

The Last Angry Man *
US 1959 100m bw
Columbia (Fred Kohlmar)
▤
An old doctor in a Brooklyn slum is made the subject of a TV documentary.
Self-confidently sentimental wallow which just about works.
w Gerald Green novel Gerald Green d Daniel Mann ph James Wong Howe m George Duning ad Carl Anderson
☆ Paul Muni, David Wayne, Betsy Palmer, Luther Adler, Dan Tobin, Robert F. Simon
⊗ Paul Muni; art direction

The Last Battle
France 1983 92m bw Cinemascope
ICA/Les Films du Loup (Luc Besson)
original title: Le Dernier Combat
A samurai swordsman runs amok in a world destroyed by nuclear war.
Chic, virtually silent film that borrows from dozens of other works on the same theme.
wd Luc Besson ph Carlo Varini m Eric Serra ed Sophie Schmit
☆ Pierre Jolivet, Jean Bouise, Fritz Wepper, Jean Reno, Maurice Lamy, Pierre Carrive, Jean-Michel Castanie, Michel Doset

The Last Blitzkrieg
US 1959 84m bw
Columbia/Sam Katzman
During the Battle of the Bulge a German leads a squad of American saboteurs.
Weakly pacifist, technically incompetent war adventure.
w Lou Morheim d Arthur Dreifuss ph Ted Scaife m Hugo de Groot
☆ Van Johnson, Kerwin Mathews, Dick York, Larry Storch

'They're two fallen heroes up against the gambling syndicate in pro sports. Everyone had counted them out. But they're about to get back into the game.'

The Last Boy Scout
US 1991 105m Technicolor Panavision
Warner/Geffen/Silver (Joel Silver, Michael Levy)
▨ ▤ ◎ ∩
A too-honest secret agent turned private eye is hired by a former football player to protect his girlfriend, a stripper.
Standard buddy-buddy action movie with high-budget special effects and non-stop violence.
w Shane Black story Shane Black, Greg Hicks d Tony Scott ph Ward Russell m Michael Kamen pd Brian Morris ed Mark Goldblatt, Mark Helfrich
☆ Bruce Willis, Damon Wayans, Chelsea Field, Noble Willingham, Taylor Negron, Danielle Harris, Halle Berry, Bruce McGill
'Entertaining if mindless shoot-'em-up ... the Boy Scouts' "Be Prepared" motto could be taken as a warning to check one's brain at the door.' – *Variety*
'To give it a negative review would be dishonest. To be positive is to seem to approve its sickness.' – *Roger Ebert*
† Shane Black was reportedly paid $1.75 million for his screenplay.

The Last Bridge
Austria/Yugoslavia 1953 95m bw
Cosmopol/UFUS (Carl Szokoll)
During World War II, a German nurse in Yugoslavia is captured by partisans and turns to their point of view.
Message melodrama, very ably put together with a bleakly tragic climax; but nothing at all new.
w Helmut Kautner, Norbert Kunze d Helmut Kautner ph Elio Carniel m Carl de Groof
☆ Maria Schell, Bernhard Wicki, Barbara Rütting, Carl Möhner

The Last Broadcast *
US 1998 86m colour
Metrodome/FFM (Stefan Avalos, Lance Weiler)
▨ ▤
An amateur film-maker investigates the 'Jersey Devil' murder of 1996, in which cable TV presenters died while presenting a live show from a

remote forest where they were attempting a contact with the supernatural.
Clever, inventive low-budget horror that predates The Blair Witch Project(qv), with which it has some similarities.
wd Stefan Avalos, Lance Weiler ph Lance Weiler m A.D. Roso, Stefan Avalos ed Stefan Avalos
☆ David Beard, Jim Seward, Stefan Avalos, Lance Weiler, Rein Clabbers, Michele Pulaski, Tom Brunt, Mark Rublee, A.D. Roso, Dale Worstall
'All dull film... Don't expect to be scared or shocked. Or in any way entertained.' – *Rupert Laight, Film Review*

The Last Chance *
Switzerland 1945 105m bw
Praesens Film
In 1943 an Englishman and an American escape from a fascist camp in northern Italy and with the help of refugees cross the mountains into Switzerland.
Earnest propaganda piece which struck the spot at the time: cinematically rather plodding, but with some exciting scenes.
w Richard Schweitzer d Leopold Lindtberg ph Emil Berna m Robert Blum
☆ E. G. Morrison, Ray Reagan, John Hoy, Luisa Rossi

The Last Command **
US 1928 100m bw silent
Paramount
An exiled Russian general goes berserk when given a role in a movie which virtually involves playing himself.
Fascinating ironic comedy tailored for an international star who was not to survive the talkies.
w John F. Goodrich story Lajos Biro d Josef von Sternberg ph Bert Glennon ad Hans Dreier
☆ Emil Jannings, William Powell, Evelyn Brent, Nicholas Soussanin
🎬 Emil Jannings
⊗ best picture; Lajos Biro

The Last Command *
US 1955 110m Trucolor
Republic (Frank Lloyd)
▤
Jim Bowie returns to Texas in the 1830s and dies at the Alamo alongside other famous men.
Reasonably interesting Western on a subject which has often figured but seldom worked.
w Warren Duff d Frank Lloyd ph Jack Marta m Max Steiner
☆ Ernest Borgnine, Sterling Hayden, Anna Maria Alberghetti, Arthur Hunnicutt, Richard Carlson, J. Carrol Naish

'Sometimes justice is a crime.'

Last Dance
US 1996 103m Technicolor
Buena Vista/Touchstone (Steven Haft)
▨ ▤ ◎ ∩
An idealistic lawyer fights to have a death sentence on a murderess commuted to life imprisonment, after she has spent 12 years on Death Row.
Earnest, old-fashioned melodrama, aimed at the tear ducts of the susceptible.
w Ron Koslow d Bruce Beresford ph Peter James m Mark Isham pd John Stoddart ed John Bloom
☆ Sharon Stone, Rob Morrow, Randy Quaid, Peter Gallagher, Jack Thompson, Don Harvey, Jayne Brook, Pamela Tyson, Skeet Ulrich
'That most joyless of beasts: melodrama without the guts, a weepie with its plumbing pulled out.' – *Tom Shone, Sunday Times*

Last Days of Chez Nous *
Australia 1992 96m Eastmancolor
Metro/Jan Chapman/Australian Film Finance Corp.
▨ ▤ ∩
In Sydney, while a wife is away on holiday, her sister has an affair with her French husband and her daughter goes to bed with the lodger.
A slight but perceptive domestic drama.
w Helen Garner d Gillian Armstrong ph Geoffrey Simpson m Paul Grabowsky pd Janet Patterson ed Nicholas Beauman
☆ Lisa Harrow, Bruno Ganz, Kerry Fox, Miranda Otto, Kiri Paramore, Bill Hunter
'Beautifully acted and crafted.' – *Variety*
'Poignantly observed and dry-humoured account of emotional blundering and bruising.' – *Lizzie Franke, Sight and Sound*

'History is made at night.'

The Last Days of Disco *
US 1998 113m Technicolor
Warner/Castle Rock/Westerly (Whit Stillman)

A loquacious group of friends congregate in a New York night-club that is under investigation by the police.

A smart comedy of sexual manners in an incongruous setting.

w/d Whit Stillman ph John Thomas m Mark Suozzo ch John Carrafa pd Ginger Tougas ed Andrew Hafitz, Jay Pires

☆ Chloe Sevigny, Kate Beckinsale, Chris Eigeman, Matt Keeslar, Mackenzie Astin, Matthew Ross, Tara Subkoff, Burr Steers, David Thornton, Jaid Barrymore, Michael Weatherly, Robert Sean Leonard, Jennifer Beals

'Is as interesting to watch for its serious disjuncture between style and content as for its cute cast and fabulous soundtrack.' – *Todd McCarthy, Variety*

The Last Days of Dolwyn *
GB 1949 95m bw
London/BLPA (Anatole de Grunwald)

US title: *Woman of Dolwyn*

A Welsh valley is flooded to make a reservoir and a village has to be evacuated.

Interesting but rather stagey drama based on an actual 19th-century event, with personal melodrama added.

w/d Emlyn Williams ph Otto Heller m John Greenwood

☆ Edith Evans, Emlyn Williams, Richard Burton, Hugh Griffith, Barbara Couper, Allan Aynesworth

'The conventionally picturesque Welsh flavour and mounting probabilities apart, the treatment is stiff and episodic.' – *MFB*

The Last Days of Man on Earth: see *The Final Programme*

'Pompeii ... drunk with wealth and power ... rotten with pagan pleasures ... doomed to fiery death from the skies!'

The Last Days of Pompeii *
🏃 US 1935 96m bw
RKO (Merian C. Cooper)

In ancient Pompeii, various personal dramas are submerged in the eruption of Vesuvius.

Starchy melodrama capped by a reel of spectacular disaster.

w Ruth Rose, Boris Ingster *novel* Lord Lytton d Merian C. Cooper, Ernest Schoedsack ph Eddie Linden Jnr, J. Roy Hunt m Roy Webb sp Vernon Walker, Harry Redmond

☆ Preston Foster, Basil Rathbone, Alan Hale, Dorothy Wilson

'Well-done spectacle minus romance and cast names. Should do all right generally.' – *Variety*

The Last Detail **
US 1973 104m Metrocolor
Columbia/Acrobat/Persky-Bright (Gerald Ayres)

Two hardened naval petty officers escort a young recruit, sentenced for thieving, from Virginia to a New Hampshire jail, and give him a wild last night.

Foul-mouthed weekend odyssey, with a few well-observed moments for non-prudes. Technically the epitome of Hollywood's most irritating seventies fashion, with fuzzy sound recording, dim against-the-light photography, and a general determination to show up the ugliness of everything around us.

w Robert Towne *novel* Darryl Ponicsan d Hal Ashby ph Michael Chapman m Johnny Mandel

☆ Jack Nicholson, Otis Young, Randy Quaid, Clifton James, Carol Kane

'Visually it is relentlessly lower-depths gloomy, and the material, though often very funny, is programmed to wrench your heart.' – *New Yorker*

☒ Robert Towne; Jack Nicholson; Randy Quaid
🏆 Jack Nicholson; Robert Towne

The Last Dinosaur
🏃 US 1977 100m colour
Rankin-Bass Productions

An oil-drilling team discovers a *tyrannosaurus rex* while probing the polar oil-cap.

Inept monster saga with poorish special effects from a Japanese team.

---

w William Overgard d Alex Grasshoff, Tom Kotani ph Shoshi Ueda m Maury Laws
☆ Richard Boone, Joan Van Ark, Steven Keats

The Last Dragon
US 1985 109m colour
TriStar/Motown (Rupert Hitzig)

aka: *Berry Gordy's The Last Dragon*

A martial arts expert returns to Harlem and saves a video disc jockey from gangsters and the neighbourhood from a self-styled shogun and his high-kicking gang.

A camp mix of kung-fu and music, directed in a broad and unsubtle manner and aimed at a young and undiscriminating audience; it is more an extended rock video than a conventional movie.

w Louis Venosta d Michael Schultz ph James A. Contner m Misha Segal, Willie Hutch, Norman Whitfield pd Peter Larkin ed Christopher Holmes

☆ Taimak, Vanity, Julius J. Carry III, Chris Murney, Leo O'Brien, Faith Prince, Glen Eaton, Mike Starr, Jim Moody

'He thinks someone is trying to kill him. He's dead right!'

Last Embrace
US 1979 101m Technicolor
UA (Michael Taylor, Dan Wigutow)

An investigator survives a number of attacks on his life, though his wife is killed in the first of them.

Hitchcockian mystery without the master's zest or humour, though it leads to a pretty exciting climax at Niagara Falls.

w David Shaber *novel* The 13th Man by Murray Teigh Bloom d Jonathan Demme ph Tak Fujimoto m Miklos Rozsa

☆ Roy Scheider, Janet Margolin, Sam Levene, John Glover, Charles Napier, Christopher Walken, Jacqueline Brookes

'A case study of late seventies movie-making which does everything in its power to avoid taking risks.' – *John Pym, MFB*

The Last Emperor **
Italy/Hong Kong/GB 1987 160m Technicolor Technovision
Columbia/Yanco Films/Tao Films/Recorded Picture Company/Screenframe/AAA Soprofilm (Jeremy Thomas)

The life of China's last imperial ruler, from ascending the throne as a puppet-like 3-year-old, to serene old age as a gardener in Mao's People's Republic.

A lavish spectacle which caught the imagination of audiences, though many found the compression of 60 years of Chinese politics baffling.

w Mark Peploe, Bernardo Bertolucci d Bernardo Bertolucci ph Vittorio Storaro m Ryuichi Sakamoto, David Byrne, Cong Su pd Ferdinando Scarfiotti ad Bruno Cesari ed Gabriella Cristiani

☆ John Lone, Joan Chen, Peter O'Toole, Ying Ruocheng

† A director's cut, a version running for 219m, was released in December 1998, and is also available

Reviewing it for the *New York Times*, director-writer Oliver Stone called it 'a masterpiece – a fully shaped historical epic'.

🏆 best picture; best director; best adapted screenplay; best cinematography; best original score; best film editing; best art direction; best costume design; best sound
🎬 best picture

The Last Escape
GB 1970 90m DeLuxe
Oakmont/UA

An American officer in Munich tries to rescue a German scientist from the Nazis.

Standard World War II actioner.

w Herman Hoffman d Walter Grauman ph Gernot Roll ad Rolf Zehetbauer

☆ Stuart Whitman, John Collin, Martin Jarvis, Pinkas Braun

Last Exit to Brooklyn ***
West Germany 1989 98m colour
Guild/Neue Constantin Film Produktion/Bavaria Film/Allied Filmmakers (Bernd Eichinger)

Striking workers and their families and a prostitute lead thwarted lives in Brooklyn in the early 1950s.

True to the spirit of Selby's grim, but compassionate, low-life novel, with some brilliant ensemble acting.

w Desmond Nakano *novel* Hubert Selby Jnr d Uli Edel ph Stefan Czapsky m Mark Knopfler pd David Chapman ad Mark Haak ed Peter Przygodda

☆ Stephen Lang, Jennifer Jason Leigh, Burt Young, Peter Dobson, Christopher Murney, Jerry Orbach, Alexis Arquette

'Edel surprisingly has managed to capture exactly the horrified yet tender tone of Selby's book.' – *MFB*

The Last Flight ***
US 1931 80m bw
Warner

In 1919, four veteran American flyers stay on in Paris in the hope of calming their shattered physical and emotional states.

Fascinatingly offhand study on post-war cynicism and the faint hope of a better world, beautifully written and directed in a manner more effective than The Sun Also Rises.

w John Monk Saunders *novel* Single Lady by John Monk Saunders d William Dieterle ph Sid Hickox

☆ Richard Barthelmess, Helen Chandler, David Manners, John Mack Brown, Elliott Nugent, Walter Byron

'If the crowd can understand that girl character in this picture the film is an undoubted grosser.' – *Variety*

'A narrative as tight and spare as a Racine tragedy ... unique in Hollywood of that time in its persistent, calculated understatement.' – *Tom Milne, 1975*

† In magazine form the story was known as 'Nikki and her War Birds'.

The Last Flight of Noah's Ark
🏃 US 1980 98m Technicolor
Walt Disney

An impecunious pilot reluctantly flies an orphanage worker and a cargo of animals across the Pacific, only to be stranded with them on a desert island.

It must have sounded like a good idea, but if it was to work at all it needed much sharper handling.

w Steven W. Carabatsos, Sandy Glass, George Arthur Bloom *story* The Gremlin's Castle by Ernest K. Gann d Charles Jarrott ph Charles F. Wheeler m Maurice Jarre

☆ Elliott Gould, Geneviève Bujold, Ricky Schroder, Tammy Lauren, Vincent Gardenia

The Last Frontier: see *Savage Wilderness (1956)*

The Last Gangster: see *Roger Touhy, Gangster (1944)*

'The big fellow is out of Alcatraz – ready to show them no mercy!'

The Last Gangster *
US 1937 81m bw
MGM (J. J. Cohn)

A gangster is released from Alcatraz and plans vengeance on his wife for deserting him.

Clean-cut star melodrama which suddenly turns sentimental.

w John Lee Mahin d Edward Ludwig ph William Daniels m Edward Ward *montage* Slavko Vorkapich

☆ Edward G. Robinson, Rose Stradner, James Stewart, Lionel Stander, Douglas Scott, John Carradine, Sidney Blackmer, Edward Brophy

'May indeed be the last gangster movie ... a good film which will blossom at the b.o.' – *Variety*

'A lot of water has flowed under the bridge since Little Caesar, but Mr Robinson has breasted the tides to make his impersonation of a 1937 thug as persuasive as was his portrait of a killer in that earlier classic of rats and rackets.' – *Frank Nugent*

The Last Gentleman
US 1934 80m bw
Fox

The career of a New England millionaire.

Pleasing star family drama.

w Leonard Praskins d Sidney Lanfield

☆ George Arliss, Edna May Oliver, Ralph Morgan, Janet Beecher, Charlotte Henry

'A prolonged monologue ... mediocre film which must depend on the star's rep.' – *Variety*

The Last Grenade
GB 1969 93m Eastmancolor Panavision
Cinerama/Dimitri de Grunwald/Josef Shaftel

An army mercenary is betrayed by an ex-friend in the Congo and pursues him to Hong Kong.

Violent action melodrama with few redeeming qualities.

w Kenneth Ware *novel* The Ordeal of Major Grigsby by John Sherlock d Gordon Flemyng ph Alan Hume m Johnny Dankworth

☆ Stanley Baker, Alex Cord, Honor Blackman, Richard Attenborough, Rafer Johnson, Andrew Keir, Ray Brooks, Julian Glover, John Thaw

The Last Hard Men
US 1976 97m DeLuxe Panavision
TCF/Belasco-Seltzer-Thatcher

A train robber breaks jail and sets out to revenge himself on the now-retired lawman who committed him.

Tough action adventure without much sense except to paint the end of the golden days of the west.

w Guerdon Trueblood *novel* Gun Down by Brian Garfield d Andrew V. McLaglen ph Duke Callaghan m Jerry Goldsmith

☆ Charlton Heston, James Coburn, Barbara Hershey, Christopher Mitchum, Michael Parks, Jorge Rivero, Thalmus Rasulala

'Script and direction seem equally tired.' – *Sight and Sound*

'The action proceeds slackly from one setpiece shoot-up to the next, barely providing the voltage for the two leads to expand their stereotyped roles into displays of star power.' – *Richard Combs, MFB*

The Last Harvest *
Argentina 1992 91m colour
Arenas/Jorge Estrada Mora (Julio Lencina, Ricardo Freixa)

original title: *La Ultima Siembra*

On an Argentinian ranch, conflict grows between an Indian miner turned maize farmer and the American-educated son of the landowner who wants to replace the cattle with a tobacco plantation.

Leisurely examination of a clash between races, classes and entrenched attitudes, coming heavily down on the side of conservatism.

w/d Miguel Pereira *novel* Los Humildes by Miguel Angel Pereira ph Pablo Esteban Courtalón m Ariel Petrocelli, Tukuta Gordillo Isamara ad Mirta Spagarino ed Miguel Perez

☆ Patricio Contreras, Leonor Manso, Mario Pasik, Alberto Benegas, Gonzalo Morales, Antonio Paleari

Last Holiday *
GB 1950 88m bw
ABPC/Watergate (Stephen Mitchell, A. D. Peters, J. B. Priestley)

A man with a short time to live has a thoroughly enjoyable and useful final fling.

Slight, amusing and moving comedy drama spoiled by an unnecessary double twist.

w J. B. Priestley d Henry Cass ph Ray Elton m Francis Chagrin

☆ Alec Guinness, Kay Walsh, Beatrice Campbell, Grégoire Aslan, Bernard Lee, Wilfrid Hyde-White, Helen Cherry, Sidney James, Muriel George

'To Avoid Fainting Keep Repeating, It's Only A Movie ... Only A Movie ... Only A Movie ... Only A Movie.'

Last House on the Left
US 1972 91m colour
Hallmark (Sean S. Cunningham)

Parents seek revenge after their daughter is raped and killed by a gang of escaped convicts.

Low-budget shocker, updating and debasing Ingmar Bergman's Virgin Spring.

w/d Wes Craven ph Victor Hurwitz m Steve Chapin, David Hess ed Wes Craven

☆ David Hess, Lucy Grantham, Sandra Cassel, Marc Sheffler, Jeramie Rain, Fred Lincoln

Last House on the Left Part II: see *A Bay of Blood*

The Last Hunt *
US 1956 103m Eastmancolor Cinemascope
MGM (Dore Schary)

Buffalo hunters fall out with each other.

Terse, brutish outdoor Western with something to say about old Western myths and a famous ending in which the bad guy freezes to death while waiting to gun down the hero.

wd Richard Brooks *ph* Russell Harlan *m* Daniele Amfitheatrof

☆ Stewart Granger, Robert Taylor, Debra Paget, Lloyd Nolan, Russ Tamblyn, Constance Ford

The Last Hurrah **
US   1958   125m   bw
Columbia (John Ford)
▦   ◎⌣

The political boss of a New England town fights his last campaign.

Enjoyable if disjointed melodrama, an old man's film crammed with cameo performances from familiar faces: important as one of Hollywood's great sentimental reunions.

w Frank Nugent *novel* Edwin O'Connor *d* John Ford *ph* Charles Lawton Jnr

☆ Spencer Tracy, Jeffrey Hunter, Dianne Foster, Pat O'Brien, Basil Rathbone, Edward Brophy, Donald Crisp, James Gleason, John Carradine, Ricardo Cortez, Wallace Ford, Frank McHugh, Frank Albertson, Anna Lee, Jane Darwell and also Willis Bouchey, Basil Ruysdael

† A TV version was subsequently made with Carroll O'Connor.

Last Images of the Shipwreck
Argentina/Spain   1989   129m   colour
Palace/Cinequanon/TVE (Hugo Lauria)
▦

original title: *Ultimas Imagenes del Naufragio*

A would-be writer befriends a prostitute and her crooked brother in order to gather material for a novel.

Playing rather unsuccessful games with illusion and reality, this odd movie soon loses its way.

wd Eliseo Subiela *h* Alberto Basail *m* Pedro Aznar *pd* Abel Facello *ed* Mercela Saenz

☆ Lorenzo Quinteros, Noemi Frenkel, Hugo Soto, Pablo Brichta, Sara Benitez, Andres Tiengo, Alicia Aller, Alfredo Stuart

The Last Island
Netherlands   1990   109m   colour
First Floor (Laurens Geels, Dick Maas)

Four men and two women, the only survivors of an air crash on an uninhabited island who also believe that they are the last people left alive in the world, find that their lives are dominated by an increasingly unbalanced military and religious bigot.

A feminist retelling of a familiar scenario, watchable, but too schematic to be entirely successful.

wd Marleen Gorris *ph* Marc Felperlaan *m* Boudewijn Tarenskeen *ad* Harry Ammerlaan *ed* Hans van Dongen

☆ Paul Freeman, Shelagh McLeod, Patricia Hayes, Kenneth Colley, Mark Hembrow, Marc Berman, Ian Tracey

The Last Journey *
GB   1935   66m   bw
Twickenham (Julius Hagen)
▦

The driver of an express train, driven mad with jealousy, goes berserk.

Workmanlike little train suspenser with an exciting climax.

w John Soutar, H. Fowler Mear *story* J. Jefferson Farjeon *d* Bernard Vorhaus *ph* Percival Strong, Billy Luff *ad* James Carter

☆ Godfrey Tearle, Hugh Williams, Julien Mitchell, Judy Gunn, Nelson Keys, Frank Pettingell, Olga Lindo, Sydney Fairbrother

The Last Laugh ***
Germany   1924   73m   bw   silent
UFA
▦   ◎⌣

original title: *Der Letzte Mann*

The old doorman of a luxury hotel is given the job of lavatory attendant but comes into a fortune and gets his revenge.

Ironic anecdote made important by its virtual abandonment of dialogue and whole-hearted adoption of the camera eye technique which gives some thrilling dramatic effects.

w Carl Mayer *d* F. W. Murnau *ph* Karl Freund
☆ Emil Jannings, Max Hiller, Maly Delschaft, Hans Unterkirchen

'A marvellous picture – marvellous in its simplicity, its economy of effect, its expressiveness, and its dramatic power.' – *Life*

† A German remake of 1955 had Hans Albers in the lead and was of no interest.

Last Man Standing *
US   1996   101m   CFI color   Panavision
New Line (Walter Hill, Arthur Sarkissian)
▦   ▦   ▦   ◎⌣   ◎   ◎   ◎   ⌒

In the 30s, a gunman on the run finds himself in a small Texas town ruled by two rival gangs of bootleggers.

A Hollywood Western influenced by other schools of film-making. The wit and charm of Kurosawa's original, Yojimbo, has been replaced by a raw energy and gunfights in the style of John Woo; but its glum, conscienceless protagonist lacks the style of Toshiro Mifune or even Clint Eastwood in the spaghetti Western version, A Fistful of Dollars.

wd Walter Hill *story* Ryuzo Kikushima, Akira Kurosawa *ph* Lloyd Ahern *m* Ry Cooder *pd* Gary Wissner *ed* Freeman Davies

☆ Bruce Willis, Christopher Walken, Bruce Dern, Alexandra Powers, David Patrick Kelly, William Sanderson, Karina Lombard, Ned Eisenberg, Michael Imperioli

'Goes wholly down the comic book route Hill marked out as early as The Warriors, offering wham-bang style but nothing else.' – *Kim Newman, Sight and Sound*

† The film cost $57m to make, including $16m to Bruce Willis, and took $18m at the US box-office.
†† Elmer Bernstein's original score, which was rejected by Hill, has also been released on CD.

The Last Man to Hang?
GB   1956   75m   bw
ACT Films/Columbia

Sir Roderick Strood is on trial for the murder of his neurotic wife.

Reasonably interesting co-feature based on Gerald Bullett's The Jury; the title refers to the no-hanging bill then passing through Parliament.

w Gerald Bullett and others *d* Terence Fisher
☆ Tom Conway, Elizabeth Sellars, Eunice Gayson, Freda Jackson, Hugh Latimer, Anthony Newley, Margaretta Scott

The Last Married Couple in America
US   1979   102m   Technicolor
Universal/Cates Brothers (John Shaner)
▦

A Los Angeles couple resist the efforts of their friends to involve them in the swinging life.

Tolerable sex comedy of modern mores, a shade too long delayed after Bob and Carol and Ted and Alice.

w John Herman Shaner *d* Gilbert Cates *ph* Ralph Woolsey *m* Charles Fox *pd* Gene Callahan

☆ Natalie Wood, George Segal, Richard Benjamin, Arlene Golonka, Alan Arbus, Marilyn Sokol, Dom DeLuise, Valerie Harper

The Last Metro ****
France   1980   131m   Fujicolour
Les Films du Carrosse/Andrea/SEDIF/TF1/SFP (Jean-José Richer)
▦   ▦   ▦   ◎⌣

original title: *Le Dernier Métro*

In occupied Paris, the Jewish manager of a theatre hides in the cellar of the building.

Tightly enclosed symbolic melodrama of oppression and release that concentrates on individual lives caught up in a moment of mass madness and seeking refuge in their dedication to their art.

w François Truffaut, Suzanne Schiffman *d* François Truffaut *ph* Nestor Almendros *m* Georges Delerue *ad* Jean-Pierre Kohut Svelko *ed* Martine Barraque

☆ Catherine Deneuve, Gérard Depardieu, Jean Poiret, Heinz Bennent
⅋ best foreign film

The Last Mile *
US   1932   84m   bw
World Wide (E. W. Hammons)
▦

Tensions mount in jail as the execution of Killer Mears approaches.

Strident melodrama which works up quite a head of hysteria.

w Seton I. Miller *play* John Wexley *d* Sam Bischoff *ph* Arthur Edeson

☆ Preston Foster, Howard Phillips, George E. Stone, Noel Madison

'Subject's lure is confined to the morbid-minded sensation seeker … without feminine interest.' – *Variety*

The Last Mile
US   1959   81m   bw
UA/Vanguard (Milton Subotsky)

Even more hysterical remake, retaining the original period.

A cheerless, though literally electrifying, entertainment.

w Milton Subotsky, Seton I. Miller *d* Howard W. Koch *ph* Joseph Brun *m* Van Alexander

☆ Mickey Rooney, Clifford David, Frank Conroy, Frank Overton, Leon Janney

The Last Movie
US   1971   108m   Technicolor
Universal
▦

Moviemakers go to Peru to film a Western.

Muddled and pretentious melodrama following the success of Easy Rider.

w Stewart Stern *d* Dennis Hopper *m* Kris Kristofferson

☆ Dennis Hopper, Julie Adams, Peter Fonda, Kris Kristofferson, Rod Cameron, Daniel Ades, Michael Anderson Jnr, Sam Fuller

Last Night *
Canada   1998   94m   colour
Rhombus/CBC/La Seot Arte/Haut Et Court (Niv Fichman, Daniel Iron)
▦   ▦   ◎   ⌒

With the world ending at midnight, a man who decides to spend his last hours alone finds himself trying instead to help a stranded woman get home to her husband.

Genial comedy of the death of the world, which ends not with an apocalypse but a few hapless, genteel gestures of regret.

wd Don McKellar *ph* Douglas Koch *m* Alexina Louie, Alex Pauk *pd* John Dondertman *ed* Reginald Harkema

☆ Don McKellar, Sandrah Oh, Callum Keith Rennie, Sarah Polley, Trent McMullen, David Cronenberg, Robin Gammell, Roberta Maxwell, Tracy Wright, Michael McMurtry, Geneviève Bujold

'Bittersweet pic is funny, heart-wrenching and life-affirming. The modestly produced first feature has offbeat appeal.' – *Leonard Klady, Variety*

The Last of England
GB   1987   87m   bw/colour
Blue Dolphin/Anglo International/British Screen/Channel 4/ZDF-Tartan Films (James Mackay, Don Boyd)
◎⌣   ⌒

Impressionistic mix of home movies and images of urban disintegration.

Too personal to communicate much, even to a sympathetic audience.

d Derek Jarman *ph* Derek Jarman, Christopher Hughes, Cerith Wyn Evans, Richard Heslop *m* Simon Turner, Andy Gill, Mayo Thompson, Albert Oehlen, Barry Adamson, El Tito *pd* Christopher Hobbs *ed* Peter Cartwright, Angus Cook, Sally Yeadon, John Maybury

☆ Spring, John Phillips, Gay Gaynor, Gerrard McArthur, Matthew Hawkins, Tilda Swinton, Spencer Leigh

The Last of His Tribe
US   1992   90m   CFI color
HBO Pictures/River City (John Levoff, Robert Lovenheim)
▦   ▦

In the early 1900s a Californian anthropologist forms a friendship with Ishi, the last surviving Yahi Indian who still lives in the traditional way.

Well-meaning but dull re-telling of a fascinating true story.

w Stephen Harrigan *d* Harry Hook *ph* Martin Fuhrer *m* John E. Keane *pd* Michael Baugh *ed* Bill Yahraus

☆ Jon Voight, Graham Greene, David Ogden Stiers, Jack Blessing, Anne Archer

† The film was made for cable television in the States and released direct to video in Britain.

The Last of Mrs Cheyney
US   1929   94m   bw
MGM

A confidence woman in British high society falls in love.

Old theatrical warhorse, much filmed but never very satisfactorily. (See below.)

w Hans Kraly, Claudine West *play* Frederick Lonsdale *d* Sidney Franklin *ph* William Daniels

☆ Norma Shearer, Basil Rathbone, George Barraud, Hedda Hopper, Maude Turner Gordon, Herbert Bunston
⅋ Hans Kraly

The Last of Mrs Cheyney
US   1937   98m   bw
MGM (Lawrence Weingarten)

Adequate, unexciting remake.

w Leon Gordon, Samson Raphaelson, Monckton Hoffe *d* Richard Boleslawski *ph* George Folsey *m* William Axt

☆ Joan Crawford, Robert Montgomery, William Powell, Frank Morgan, Jessie Ralph, Nigel Bruce, Benita Hume, Melville Cooper, Sara Haden

'Good film fodder, although not particularly socko.' – *Variety*

† A further remake was The Law and the Lady (qv).

'Any number can play; any number can die!'

The Last of Sheila *
US   1973   123m   Technicolor
Warner (Herbert Ross)
▦

A Hollywood star is killed by a hit-and-run driver; a year later her husband invites six friends to his yacht, and murders begin.

Confused, in-jokey showbiz whodunnit with flashes of interest.

w Stephen Sondheim, Anthony Perkins *d* Herbert Ross *ph* Gerry Turpin *m* Billy Goldenberg *ad* Ken Adam

☆ Richard Benjamin, Dyan Cannon, James Coburn, James Mason, Joan Hackett, Ian MacShane, Raquel Welch

'The most teasing riddles for an audience are likely to be the real identities of the personalities being satirized.' – *MFB*

Last of the Bad Men
US   1957   79m   DeLuxe   Cinemascope
Allied Artists (Vincent M. Fennelly)

In the 1870s, a Chicago detective poses as a wanted man in order to infiltrate a gang of outlaws in Colorado.

A mediocre Western in which much of the narrative consists of a portentous voice-over in the documentary style of Dragnet, turning it into more of an illustrated lecture than a movie.

w Daniel B. Ullman, David Chantler *d* Paul Landres *ph* Ellsworth Fredricks *m* Paul Sawtell *ad* David Milton *ed* William Austin

☆ George Montgomery, James Best, Douglas Kennedy, Keith Larsen, Robert Foulk, Willis Bouchey, Michael Ansara

The Last of the Buccaneers
US   1950   79m   Technicolor
Columbia (Sam Katzman)

The story of Jean Lafitte, French privateer in the war of 1812.

Cheerful low-budget swashbuckler.

w Robert E. Kent *d* Lew Landers *ph* Vincent Farrar *m* Mischa Bakaleinikoff

☆ Paul Henreid, Jack Oakie, Karin Booth, Edgar Barrier, Mary Anderson, John Dehner

The Last of the Comanches *
US   1953   85m   Technicolor
Columbia (Buddy Adler)
▦

GB title: *The Sabre and the Arrow*

Survivors of an Indian raid take refuge in an abandoned mission until help arrives.

Competent Western remake of Sahara (which was a remake of The Lost Patrol).

w Kenneth Gamet *d* André de Toth *ph* Charles Lawton Jnr *m* George Duning

☆ Broderick Crawford, Barbara Hale, Lloyd Bridges, Martin Milner

'A Secret Lost In Time For Over 130 Years Is About To Be Discovered.'

Last of the Dogmen
US   1995   117m   DeLuxe
Guild/Last of the Dogmen/Carolco/Savoy (Joel B. Michaels)

A bounty hunter, searching for escaped convicts, discovers instead a group of Cheyenne still following their old way of life in an isolated part of Montana.
Confused tale that aims for some spiritual meaning but misses, ending queasily as a celebration of noble savages.
wd Tab Murphy ph Karl Walter Lindenlaub m David Arnold pd Trevor Williams ed Richard Halsey
☆ Tom Berenger, Barbara Hershey, Kurtwood Smith, Steve Reevis, Andrew Miller, Gregory Scott Cummins, Mark Boone Jnr
'Thick with implausibilities and sentimental twaddle, and even the breathtaking scenery of the Rockies cannot excuse it.' – George Perry

Last of the Fast Guns
US   1959   82m   Eastmancolor   Cinemascope
Universal-International
Rival gunfighters form a friendship but fall out over their mission.
Mildly unusual Western programmer.
w David P. Harmon d George Sherman ph Alex Phillips ad Alexander Golitzen
☆ Gilbert Roland, Jock Mahoney, Linda Cristal, Eduard Franz, Lorne Greene, Carl Benton Reid

The Last of the Finest: see Blue Heat

'When School Ends ... And Life Begins.'
Last of the High Kings
Ireland/GB/Denmark   1996   104m   colour
First Independent/Parallel/Northolme/Nordisk (Tim Palmer)

In the mid-70s, an Irish teenager enjoys an event-filled summer holiday in which he discovers sex.
Pleasant but very predictable family drama of the dawning of maturity, offering nothing that hasn't been seen many times before.
w David Keating, Gabriel Byrne novel Ferdia Mac Anna d David Keating ph Bernd Heinl m Michael Convertino pd Frank Conway ed Ray Lovejoy
☆ Catherine O'Hara, Jared Leto, Christina Ricci, Gabriel Byrne, Stephen Rea, Colm Meaney
'Ambles along with a twinkle in its eye for most of the time.' – Variety

The Last of the Mohicans
US   1936   91m   bw
Edward Small

Incidents during colonial America's French-Indian war.
Vigorous if rough-and-ready Western, later remade (poorly) as Last of the Redmen and as a Canadian TV series.
w Philip Dunne, John Balderston, Paul Perez, Daniel Moore novel James Fenimore Cooper d George B. Seitz ph Robert Planck m Roy Webb
☆ Randolph Scott, Binnie Barnes, Bruce Cabot, Henry Wilcoxon, Heather Angel, Hugh Buckler

The Last of the Mohicans *
US   1992   122m   colour   Scope
Warner/Morgan Creek (Michael Mann, Hunt Lowry)

The white, adopted son of an Indian rescues a British officer's two daughters from hostile Indians and falls in love with one of them.
An ambitious but flawed epic adventure: the characterization is as shallow as the photography, the action is repetitious, the narrative lacks suspense and the romance is unconvincing, with Cooper's self-reliant woodsman here tamed into domesticity.
w Michael Mann, Christopher Crowe novel James Fenimore Cooper screenplay Philip Dunne d Michael Mann ph Dante Spinotti m Trevor Jones, Randy Edelman pd Wolf Kroeger ed Dov Hoenig, Arthur Schmidt
☆ Daniel Day-Lewis, Madeleine Stowe, Russell Means, Eric Schweig, Jodhi May, Steven Waddington, Wes Studi, Maurice Roeves, Patrice Chereau

'Whether it was because we were young or the movies were young or the world was at least youngish, old-fashioned Hollywood history was exhilarating. In retrospect there is something alarming about its simplicities and the enthusiasm we brought to it. It is the great virtue of this grandly scaled yet deliriously energetic movie that it reanimates that long-ago feeling without patronizing it – and without making us think we will wake up some day once again embarrassed by it.' – Richard Schickel, Time
'Michael Mann has been aiming all along at two very different targets, trying to turn an adventure story into a responsible account of Native American life, while also making it lovey-dovey enough for the market place.' – Adam Mars-Jones, Independent
§ sound
℣ Dante Spinotti

Last of the Red Hot Lovers *
US   1972   98m   Technicolor
Paramount (Howard W. Koch)

A middle-aged fish restaurateur feels the need for an extra-marital spree.
Modest, plainly-filmed sex comedy from a reliable stable.
w Neil Simon play Neil Simon d Gene Saks ph Victor J. Kemper m Neal Hefti
☆ Alan Arkin, Paula Prentiss, Sally Kellerman, Renée Taylor

Last of the Redmen
US   1947   78m   Vitacolor
Sam Katzman/Columbia
GB title: Last of the Redskins
British soldiers escort a general's children through Indian country.
Tinpot rendition of The Last of the Mohicans.
w Herbert Dalmas, George H. Plympton d George Sherman
☆ Jon Hall, Michael O'Shea, Evelyn Ankers, Julie Bishop, Buster Crabbe

Last of the Secret Agents
US   1966   90m   Technicolor
Paramount
Two odd job men are recruited as spies.
Pratfall comedy featuring a briefly existing comedy double act.
w Mel Tolkin d Norman Abbott
☆ Marty Allen, Steve Rossi, John Williams, Nancy Sinatra, Lou Jacobi, Theo Marcuse, Sig Rumann

'Open war between a handful of English and swarming tribesmen! Hidden war between fellow-officers who love the same woman!'
The Last Outpost *
US   1935   75m   bw
Paramount (E. Lloyd Sheldon)
A British officer is captured by the Kurds and freed by an adventurer whose wife he covets.
Patchy, unusual adventure story with good moments.
w Philip MacDonald story F. Britten Austin d Charles Barton, Louis Gasnier ph Theodor Sparkuhl
☆ Cary Grant, Claude Rains, Gertrude Michael, Kathleen Burke, Colin Tapley, Akim Tamiroff, Billy Bevan, Jameson Thomas
'Loosely-woven melodramatic mélange.' – Variety
'Half of it is remarkably good and half of it quite abysmally bad. One can even put one's finger on the joins.' – Graham Greene

The Last Outpost
US   1951   89m   Technicolor
Paramount/Pine-Thomas
A Civil War colonel finds his brother fighting on the other side.
Routine historical action romance.
w Geoffrey Homes, G. Worthing Yates, Winston Miller d Lewis R. Foster ph Loyal Griggs m Lucien Cailliet
☆ Ronald Reagan, Bruce Bennett, Rhonda Fleming, Noah Beery Jnr

The Last Page
GB   1952   84m   bw
Exclusive/Hammer-Lippert
US title: Manbait
A bookseller is framed for the death of a blackmailer.

Curious English mystery with American stars.
w Frederick Knott play James Hadley Chase d Terence Fisher ph Walter J. Harvey md Frank Spencer
☆ George Brent, Marguerite Chapman, Diana Dors, Raymond Huntley, Peter Reynolds, Eleanor Summerfield

The Last Parade
US   1931   82m   bw
Columbia
A detective and a racketeer are buddies in the war, but not afterwards.
Predictable character melodrama with no remaining interest.
w Dorothy Howell, Casey Robinson d Erle C. Kenton
☆ Jack Holt, Constance Cummings, Tom Moore, Gaylord Pendleton
'In for money, but not that strong for a holdover.' – Variety

The Last Picture Show ****
US   1971   118m   bw
Columbia/LPS/BBS (Stephen J. Friedman)

Teenage affairs in a small Texas town in 1951, ending with the hero's embarkation for Korea and the closing of the tatty cinema.
Penetrating nostalgia with over-emphasis on sex; the detail is the attraction.
w Larry McMurtry, Peter Bogdanovich d Peter Bogdanovich ph Robert Surtees m original recordings pd Polly Platt
☆ Timothy Bottoms, Jeff Bridges, Cybill Shepherd, Ben Johnson, Cloris Leachman, Ellen Burstyn
'The most important work by a young American director since Citizen Kane.' – Paul D. Zimmerman
'So many things in it are so good that I wish I liked it more.' – Stanley Kauffmann
'Colour always had a tendency to prettify, and I didn't want that. I didn't want it to be a nostalgic piece.' – Peter Bogdanovich
† Texasville (qv), a sequel featuring many of the same actors, was filmed by Bogdanovich in 1990.
♪ Ben Johnson; Cloris Leachman
§ best picture; script; Peter Bogdanovich (as director); Robert Surtees; Jeff Bridges; Ellen Burstyn
℣ script; Ben Johnson; Cloris Leachman

The Last Posse
US   1953   73m   bw
Columbia
Members of a thief-catching posse fall out on the way and return in disgrace.
Stumbling little Western, a poor return to the star after All the King's Men.
w Seymour and Connie Lee Bennett, Kenneth Gamet d Alfred Werker
☆ Broderick Crawford, John Derek, Wanda Hendrix, Charles Bickford

'A different kind of love story!'
The Last Remake of Beau Geste
US   1977   85m   Technicolor
Universal (William S. Gilmore Jnr)

The Geste brothers find themselves in the Foreign Legion after the theft of the Blue Water sapphire.
Woebegone spoof of a romantic original, with most of the jokes totally irrelevant to the purpose and seldom at all funny.
w Marty Feldman, Chris J. Allen d Marty Feldman ph Gerry Fisher m John Morris
☆ Marty Feldman, Michael York, Ann-Margret, Peter Ustinov, Trevor Howard, James Earl Jones, Henry Gibson, Terry-Thomas, Roy Kinnear, Spike Milligan, Hugh Griffith, Irene Handl
'A ragbag of a film which looks like nothing so much as a Monty Python extravaganza in which inspiration has run dry and the comic timing gone sadly awry.' – Tom Milne, MFB

Last Rites
US   1988   103m   DeLuxe
MGM (Donald P. Bellisario, Patrick McCormick)
A Catholic priest falls in love with a woman whom his gangster father wishes to kill.
Turgid thriller, slow-paced and uninteresting despite its hints of incest and emphasis on sex.

wd Donald P. Bellisario ph David Watkin m Bruce Broughton ed Pembroke J. Herring
☆ Tom Berenger, Daphne Zuniga, Chick Vennera, Anne Twomey, Paul Dooley, Dane Clark, Vassili Lambrinos

The Last Run *
US   1971   92m   Metrocolor   Panavision
MGM (Carter de Haven)
An ex-Chicago gangster retired to a Portuguese fishing village undertakes one last fatal job.
Well-made, rather uninteresting downbeat melodrama.
w Alan Sharp d Richard Fleischer ph Sven Nykvist m Jerry Goldsmith
☆ George C. Scott, Tony Musante, Trish Van Devere

The Last Safari
GB   1967   110m   Technicolor
Paramount (Henry Hathaway)

A disillusioned white hunter takes on one last safari.
Dullsville adventure story with good animal photography redeeming some of the clichés.
w John Gay novel Gilligan's Last Elephant by Gerald Hanley d Henry Hathaway ph Ted Moore m Johnny Dankworth
☆ Stewart Granger, Kaz Garas, Gabriella Licudi, Johnny Sekka, Liam Redmond, Eugene Deckers

The Last Seduction ***
US   1994   110m   CFI color
ITC (Jonathan Shestack)

A tough, manipulative New York woman leaves her husband, taking with her a million dollars he made on a drug deal.
Virtuoso revamping of the film noir genre, with a clever, tightly written, witty script, taut direction and a splendidly tart performance from Fiorentino.
w Steve Barancik d John Dahl ph Jeffrey Jur m Joseph Vitarelli pd Linda Pearl ed Eric L. Beason
☆ Linda Fiorentino, Peter Berg, J. T. Walsh, Bill Nunn, Bill Pullman
'Funny, sexy and so intricately plotted that you are never quite sure what is going to happen next.' – Derek Malcolm, Guardian
'Erotically ravenous, exceptionally witty, and impressively knowledgeable about all the dirty deals and low maneuvers that keep a corrupt world going.' – David Denby, New York

The Last Shot You Hear
GB   1970   90m   bw
Lippert-TCF (Jack Parsons)
Lovers plot murder, but the scheme backfires.
Unassuming mystery programmer from a West End success.
w Tim Shields play The Sound of Murder by William Fairchild d Gordon Hessler
☆ Hugh Marlowe, Zena Walker, Patricia Haines, William Dysart, Thorley Walters

The Last Stage *
Poland   1947   110m   bw
Film Polski
original title: Ostatni Etap
Women suffer but one is finally rescued from the Nazi concentration camp at Auschwitz.
A dour, obsessive, horrifying record of human inhumanity, set in the actual camp and made by two former inmates.
w Wanda Jakubowska, Gerda Schneider d Wanda Jakubowska ph Borys Monastyrski m R. Palester
☆ Huguette Faget, W. Bartowna, T. Gorecka

The Last Starfighter *
US   1984   101m   Technicolor
Panavision
Lorimar/Universal (Gary Adelson, Edward O. Denault)

A teenage whiz at video games is abducted by the survivors of a distant planet who need his skills if they are to outwit their enemies.
A surprisingly pleasant variation on the Star Wars boom, with sharp and witty performances from two reliable character actors and some elegant gadgetry to offset the teenage mooning.
w Jonathan Betuel d Nick Castle ph King Baggot m Craig Safan pd Ron Cobb ed C. Timothy O'Meara

---

film suitable for family viewing   VHS video-cassette for the British PAL system   VHS video-cassette for the British PAL system in wide screen-format   Video cassette in a computer-colourised version   American NTSC video-cassette   Laser disc

☆ Lance Guest, *Robert Preston, Dan O'Herlihy*, Catherine Mary Stewart, Barbara Bosson, Norman Snow

Last Summer *

US 1969 97m Eastmancolor
Alsid/Francis (Alfred Crown, Sidney Beckerman)

📀

Well-to-do teenagers have sexual adventures on a summer seaside holiday.
Striking off-beat melodrama with vividly sketched characters.
w *Eleanor Perry* novel *Evan Hunter* d *Frank Perry*
ph Gerald Hirschfeld m John Simon
☆ Barbara Hershey, Richard Thomas, Bruce Davison, Cathy Burns, Ernesto Gonzales, Ralph Waite
🎧 Cathy Burns

Last Summer in the Hamptons

US 1995 105m Technicolor
Revere/Rainbow/Jagtoria (Judith Wolinsky)
Family, friends and hangers-on gather for a final weekend at the home of an ageing Hollywood actress.
A tame comedy of theatrical chit-chat and tantrums, in which self-absorbed people fail to communicate with an audience.
w Henry Jaglom, Victoria Foyt d Henry Jaglom
ph Hanania Baer ad Bruce Postman, Jeff Monte
ed Henry Jaglom
☆ Victoria Foyt, Viveca Lindfors, Jon Robin Baitz, Savannah Boucher, Roscoe Lee Browne, André Gregory, Roddy McDowall, Martha Plimpton
  'One has the uneasy feeling that Jaglom actually admires this pretentious, narcissistic circle of pseuds, which, of course, nullifies its satiric thrust.' – *George Perry*

The Last Sunset

US 1961 112m Eastmancolor
U-I (Brynaprod) (Eugene Frenke, Edward Lewis)
A killer and his hunter learn a lot about each other before the final showdown.
Slow psycho-Western with pretensions to tragedy.
w Dalton Trumbo novel *Showdown at Crazy Horse* by Howard Rigsby d Robert Aldrich ph Ernest Laszlo m Ernest Gold
☆ Rock Hudson, Kirk Douglas, Dorothy Malone, Carol Lynley, Joseph Cotten, Regis Toomey, Neville Brand

The Last Supper *

Cuba 1976 125m colour
Cuban Film Institute (Santiago Llapin, Camilo Vives)
original title: *La Ultima Cena*
In 18th-century Cuba, an aristocratic plantation owner attempts to get on better terms with his slaves.
Intermittently powerful, if overlong, political drama on the corruption of power and the acquiesence of the Church in the requirements of the State.
w Tomás Gonzalez, Maria Eugenia Haya, T. G. Alea d T. G. Alea ph Mario García Joya m Leo Brouwer ad Carlos Arditi ed Nelson Rodriguez
☆ Nelson Villagra, Silvano Rey, Luis Alberto García, José Antonio Rodriguez, Mario Balmaseda
  'A laborious historical analogy, clumsy in the making and in implication, ineffectual esthetically and, for that matter, politically.' – *Stanley Kauffmann*

'Eat ... drink ... and be buried...'
The Last Supper

US 1996 100m CFI color
Electric/Vault (Matt Cooper, Larry Weinberg)

📀 📼 🎞️

A group of graduate students, who share a house, invite illiberal people to dinner and poison them.
A slight black comedy that skirts around the matter of the end justifying the means, but which fails to develop its theme in an interesting way.
w Dan Rosen d Stacy Title ph Paul Cameron m Mark Mothersbaugh pd Linda Burton ed Luis Colina
☆ Annabeth Gish, Cameron Diaz, Jonathan Penner, Courtney B. Vance, Ron Eldard, Jason Alexander, Nora Dunn, Charles Durning, Bryn Erin, Mark Harmon, Bill Paxton, Ron Perlman
  'It may be too clever for immediate cultdom – it would make a great stage play, which means there's just little showy film business – but it's one of those films you'll remember.' – *Kim Newman, Empire*

Last Tango in Paris *

France/Italy/US 1972 129m Technicolor
Les Artistes Associés/PEA/UA (Alberto Grimaldi)

📼 📀

A middle-aged man and a young French girl have a doomed love affair.
Pretentious sex melodrama mainly notable for being banned.
w Bernardo Bertolucci, Franco Arcalli
d Bernardo Bertolucci ph Vittorio Storaro
m Gato Barbieri ad Ferdinando Scarfiotti
ed Franco Arcalli, Roberto Perpignani
☆ Marlon Brando, Maria Schneider, Jean-Pierre Léaud, Massimo Girotti, Veronica Lazare, Maria Michi, Gitt Magrini
  'An intense meditation on the realization of mortality.' – *Sight and Sound*
🎧 Bernardo Bertolucci (as director); Marlon Brando

The Last Temptation of Christ *

US/Canada 1988 163m Technicolor
Universal/Cineplex Odeon (Harry Ufland)

📼 📀 🎞️ 🎵 🎧

On the cross, Jesus dreams of escaping his destiny and living the life of an ordinary man.
Beautifully shot and strikingly acted, but wordy and too long; pre-release notoriety muffled consideration of the film's intentions.
w Paul Schrader novel Nikos Kazantzakis
d Martin Scorsese ph Michael Ballhaus m Peter Gabriel pd John Beard ed Thelma Schoonmaker
☆ Willem Dafoe, Harvey Keitel, Barbara Hershey, Harry Dean Stanton, David Bowie, Verna Bloom, Andre Gregory, Juliette Caton, Roberts Blossom, Irvin Kershner
  'A film of challenging ideas and not salacious provocations.' – *Variety*
🎧 Martin Scorsese

The Last Thrill: see Female Vampire

The Last Time I Committed Suicide

US 1997 92m colour/bw
Feature Film/Kushner-Locke/Tapestry (Edward Bates, Louise Rosner)
Beat writer Neal Cassady loses his girlfriend and his chance of employment.
Meandering tale of minimal interest, totally dependent on an audience's knowledge that Cassady was said to be the inspiration behind Jack Kerouac's novel On the Road.
wd Stephen Kay letter Neal Cassady ph Bobby Bukowski m Amy Ancona ed Dorian Harris
☆ Thomas Jane, Keanu Reeves, Adrien Brody, Joe Doe, Claire Forlani, Marg Helgenberger, Gretchen Mol, Tom Bower (uncredited)
  'If, halfway through you feel you can't take any more, it's not because it's immoral or chauvinist, it's because it's boring.' – *Gaby Wood, Guardian*

The Last Time I Saw Archie

US 1961 98m bw
UA/Mark VII/Manzanita/Talbot (Jack Webb)
Adventures of a con man amid overage civilian pilots at an army/air force base.
Patchy service comedy.
w William Bowers d Jack Webb ph Joe MacDonald m Frank Comstock
☆ Jack Webb, Robert Mitchum, Martha Hyer, France Nuyen, Louis Nye, Jimmy Lydon, Richard Arlen, Don Knotts, Robert Strauss, Joe Flynn

The Last Time I Saw Paris

US 1954 116m Technicolor
MGM (Jack Cummings)

📼 📀 🎞️

A writer recalls his romance with a wealthy American girl in Paris.
Dull romantic drama which very deadeningly and predictably updates F. Scott Fitzgerald's Babylon Revisited.
w Julius J. and Philip G. Epstein, Richard Brooks
d Richard Brooks ph Joseph Ruttenberg
m Conrad Salinger
☆ Elizabeth Taylor, Van Johnson, Walter Pidgeon, Donna Reed, Eva Gabor

Last Train (dubbed)

France/Italy 1973 100m Eastmancolor/bw
Panavision
Lira/Capitolina (Raymond Danon)
original title: *Le Train*
In 1941, on a train fleeing from the Germans, a Frenchman becomes separated from his pregnant wife and young daughter and begins an affair with a German Jewish refugee.
Somewhat glum romance, set against a background of war and casual death, with a downbeat ending.
w Pascal Jardin, Pierre Granier-Deferre
novel Georges Simenon d Pierre Granier-Deferre
ph Walter Wottitz m Philippe Sarde ad Jacques Saulnier ed Jean Ravel
☆ Jean-Louis Trintignant, Romy Schneider, Maurice Biraud, Regine, Serge Marquand, Anne Wiazemsky, Nike Arrighi

Last Train from Bombay

US 1952 72m bw
Sam Katzman/Columbia
A diplomat in Bombay is falsely accused of the murder of an old friend.
Stilted melodrama culminating in a hectic train ride.
w Robert Yale Libbott d Fred F. Sears
☆ Jon Hall, Christine Larson, Lisa Ferraday, Douglas Kennedy

Last Train from Gun Hill *

US 1959 98m Technicolor Vistavision
(Paramount)

📼 📼

A marshal tracks down the man who raped and murdered his wife; it turns out to be the son of an old friend.
Good suspense and action Western culminating in a High Noon situation.
w James Poe story Les Crutchfield d John Sturges
ph Charles Lang Jnr m Dimitri Tiomkin
☆ Kirk Douglas, Anthony Quinn, Earl Holliman, Carolyn Jones, Brian Hutton

'Flaming love drama set against the background of Spain's Civil War!'
The Last Train from Madrid

US 1937 85m bw
Paramount (George M. Arthur)
A variety of people escape the fighting in the Spanish Civil War.
Tawdry topical melodrama with cliché characters and situations.
w Louis Stevens, Robert Wyler d James Hogan
ph Harry Fischbeck md Boris Morros
☆ Dorothy Lamour, Lew Ayres, Gilbert Roland, Karen Morley, Lionel Atwill, Helen Mack, Robert Cummings, Olympe Bradna, Anthony Quinn, Lee Bowman, George Lloyd
  'It is probably the worst film of the decade and should have been the funniest.' – *Graham Greene*
  'Simply a topical and different background for a glib little fiction.' – *Frank S. Nugent*

The Last Tycoon

US 1976 124m Technicolor
Paramount/Academy/Sam Spiegel

📼 🎞️

The production head of a Hollywood studio in the thirties has his troubles complicated when he falls in love with a girl who reminds him of his dead wife.
Astonishingly inept and boring big budget all-star melodrama which doesn't even begin promisingly (the scenes from supposed thirties films are woefully inaccurate in style); it then bogs down in interminable dialogue scenes, leaving its famous cast all at sea.
w Harold Pinter novel F. Scott Fitzgerald d Elia Kazan ph Victor Kemper m Maurice Jarre
pd Eugene F. Callahan
☆ Robert DeNiro, Robert Mitchum, Tony Curtis, Jeanne Moreau, Jack Nicholson, Ingrid Boulting, Donald Pleasence, Ray Milland, Dana Andrews, John Carradine
  'So enervated it's like a vampire movie after the vampires have left.' – *New Yorker*
  'That the result is incoherent is no surprise; that it is so hollow and visually graceless adds a kind of wonder to the disappointment.' – *Sight and Sound*
  'The breathless reverence that informs the movie kills it stone dead.' – *Michael Billington, Illustrated London News*
  'It seems to me that Kazan and Pinter have failed disastrously, but then perhaps the task is impossible anyway.' – *Benny Green, Punch*

The Last Valley

GB 1970 128m Eastmancolor Todd-AO
ABC/Season/Seamaster (James Clavell)

🎞️ 🎧

In 1641 during the Thirty Years War a scholar tries to defend a remote and prosperous Swiss valley against a horde of mercenaries.
Big-scale historical action picture crammed with pillage, torture, rape, death at the stake, throat cutting and general carnage; reasonably literate for all that, and convincingly set.
wd James Clavell novel J. B. Pick ph Norman Warwick m John Barry ad Peter Mullins
☆ Michael Caine, Omar Sharif, Florinda Bolkan, Nigel Davenport, Per Oscarsson, Arthur O'Connell, Brian Blessed

The Last Voyage *

US 1960 91m Metrocolor
MGM/Andrew and Virginia Stone

A boiler room explosion causes an old passenger liner to sink.
Spectacular if dramatically deficient actioner for which a genuine liner (awaiting scrapping) was sunk.
wd Andrew L. Stone ph Hal Mohr m Rudy Schrager
☆ Robert Stack, Dorothy Malone, Edmond O'Brien, George Sanders, Woody Strode, Jack Kruschen
  'A prolonged nerve stretcher.' – *MFB*

'They pitted the fire of their youth against the flame of the frontier – when America was moving west!'
The Last Wagon

US 1956 99m Eastmancolor Cinemascope
TCF (William B. Hawks)
A half-breed wanted for murder joins an 1875 wagon train.
Heavy-going big-scale Western.
w James Edward Grant, Delmer Daves, Gwen Bagni d Delmer Daves ph Wilfrid Cline
m Lionel Newman
☆ Richard Widmark, Felicia Farr, Tommy Rettig, Susan Kohner, Ray Stricklyn, Nick Adams, Carl Benton Reid

The Last Waltz ***

US 1978 115m DeLuxe
UA/Martin Scorsese, Jonathan Taplin (Robbie Robertson)

🎞️ 🎵 🎧

Documentary featuring the last concert of the rock group The Band at the Winterland, San Francisco, on Thanksgiving Day, 1976, after 16 years on the road.
Perhaps the best movie so far of a rock concert, one that also features many of the most influential performers of the era, together with some brief but revealing interviews with the band members.
d Martin Scorsese ph Michael Chapman, Laszlo Kovacs, Vilmos Zsigmond, David Myers, Bobby Byrne, Michael Watkins, Hiro Narita pd Boris Leven ed Yeu-Bun Yee, Jan Roblee
☆ Robbie Robertson, Rick Danko, Richard Manuel, Levon Helm, Garth Hudson, Eric Clapton, Neil Diamond, Bob Dylan, Joni Mitchell, Neil Young, Emmylou Harris, Ringo Starr, Paul Butterfield, Dr John, Van Morrison and also Ronnie Hawkins, The Staples, Muddy Waters, Ron Wood

The Last Warning *

US 1929 88m bw
Universal
Murder backstage.
Shot as a silent film, with sound hurriedly added, this remains a stylish comedy-thriller with all the familiar ingredients of the whodunnit.
w Alfred A. Cohn d Paul Leni ph Hal Mohr
☆ Laura La Plante, Montagu Love, Roy D'Arcy, John Boles, Mack Swain, Slim Summerville, Margaret Livingston
† Remade in 1938 as *The House of Fear*, a William Gargan second feature.

The Last Warning

US 1938 62m bw
Universal (Irving Starr)
A private eye mystery.
Better-than-average second feature.
w Edmund L. Hartmann novel *The Dead Don't Care* by Jonathan Latimer d Albert S. Rogell
☆ Preston Foster, Joyce Compton, Frank Jenks

The Last Warrior: see *Flap*

The Last Wave *
Australia 1977 106m Atlab
(UA)
🎞
During a spell of freak weather, a lawyer has recurrent dreams which give him the key to an Aborigine prophecy about the world being destroyed by flood…
Curious supernatural drama successfully played as a mystery, with excellent atmosphere and special effects.
w Peter Weir, Tony Morphett, Petru Popescu d Peter Weir ph Russell Boyd m Charles Wain pd Goran Warff
☆ Richard Chamberlain, Olivia Hamnet, Frederick Parslow
'A Hitchcockian sense of minatory dislocation.' – *Tim Pulleine, MFB*

The Last Winter
Canada 1989 103m colour
Telefilm Canada/CIDO/Rode/John Aaron/NFBC (Jack Clements, Ken Rodeck)
A young boy is upset to discover that his father is planning to move the family from their farm to work in the city.
Pleasant, nostalgic, forgettable drama of childhood, with too little action and too much talk to interest the young.
wd Aaron Kim Johnston ph Ian Elkin m Victor Davies pd Perri Gorrara ed Lara Mazur
☆ Gerard Parkes, David Ferry, Wanda Cannon, Marsha Moreau, Nathaniel Moreau, Katie Murray, Joshua Murray

The Last Word
US 1979 105m colour
Variety International Pictures
An Irish inventor by wily stratagems prevents the demolition of the apartment block he occupies.
Oddly old-fashioned comedy drama of little obvious appeal.
w Michael Varhol, Greg Smith, Kit Carson d Roy Boulting
☆ Richard Harris, Karen Black, Martin Landau, Biff McGuire, Dennis Christopher

Last Year at Marienbad *
France/Italy 1961 94m bw Dyaliscope
Terra/Tamara/Cormoran/Precitel/Como/Argos/Cinetel/Silver/Cineriz (Raymond Froment)
🎞 🎞
original title: *L'Année Dernière à Marienbad*
In a vast old-fashioned hotel, a man meets a woman who may or may not have had an affair with him the previous year in Marienbad – or was it Frederiksbad?
A dreamy, elegant film which presents a puzzle with no solution. It has its attractions for film buffs and cryptogram addicts, but is not for anyone who simply wants to be told a story.
w Alain Robbe-Grillet d Alain Resnais ph Sacha Vierny m Francis Seyrig ad Jacques Saulnier
☆ Delphine Seyrig, Giorgio Albertazzi, Sacha Pitoeff
'Elaborate, ponderous and meaningless.' – *Newsweek*
'Clearly the film's creators know exactly what they want to do and have done it with complete success. Whether one responds to the result is entirely a matter of temperament.' – *John Russell Taylor, MFB*
⅛ Alain Robbe-Grillet

The Last Yellow
GB/Germany 1999 94m colour
Capitol/Scala/Hollywood Partners/Arts Council/BBC (Jolyon Symonds)
🎞
A dim-witted youth pays £500 to an overweight fantasist to go to London to kill the thug who left his brother brain-damaged.
Low-key, small-scale drama of two losers unable to deal with life's little difficulties; it looks misplaced on the big screen.
w Paul Tucker play Paul Tucker d Julian Farino ph David Odd m Adrian Johnston pd John Paul Kelly ed Pia di Ciaula
☆ Mark Addy, Charlie Creed-Miles, Samantha Morton, Kenneth Cranham, Alan Atherall
'Well-made, but unremarkable and depressingly unappealing at times.' – *Nick Briggs, Film Review*

Late August, Early September
France 1999 111m colour
Artificial Eye/Dacia/Cinéa (Georges Benayoun, Philippe Carcassonne)
🎞
original title: *Fin Août, Début Septembre*
A dying writer influences the lives of a close-knit group of friends.
Restless drama of changing partners and emotional crises that is so intensely focused as to exclude spectators.
wd Olivier Assayas ph Denis Lenoir pd François-Renaud Labarthe ed Luc Barnier
☆ Mathieu Amalric, Virginie Ledoyen, François Cluzet, Jeanne Balibar, Alex Descas, Arsinée Khanjian, Nathalie Richard, Mia Hanson-Love
'I understand Assayas's wish is to lower daily reality to the point of ordinariness. I think he's lowered it to the point of dullness.' – *Alexander Walker, London Evening Standard*

The Late Edwina Black *
GB 1951 78m bw
IFD/Elvey-Gartside (Ernest Gartside)
🔍
US title: *Obsessed*
When a schoolteacher's wife is found dead, the police have three suspects.
Adequately suspenseful Victorian thriller from a successful play.
w Charles Frank, David Evans play William Dinner, William Morum d Maurice Elvey ph Stephen Dade m Allan Gray
☆ Geraldine Fitzgerald, David Farrar, Roland Culver, Jean Cadell, Mary Merrall, Harcourt Williams, Charles Heslop, Ronald Adam
'Tomorrow wasn't just another day.'

Late for Dinner
US 1991 93m DeLuxe
First Independent/New Line/Castle Rock (Dan Lupovitz, W. D. Richter)
🎞 🎞 🔍
After being unwittingly frozen for 19 years, a man and his retarded brother-in-law wake up to discover that the world has moved on to 1991.
Rip van Winkle without a twinkle.
w Mark Andrus d W. D. Richter ph Peter Sova m David Mansfield pd Lilly Kilvert ed Richard Chew, Robert Leighton
☆ Brian Wimmer, Peter Berg, Marcia Gay Harden, Peter Gallagher, Colleen Flynn, Kyle Secor, Michael Beach

The Late George Apley *
US 1946 96m bw
TCF (Fred Kohlmar)
The uneventful family life of a Boston blueblood.
Pleasant but tame family comedy-drama, solidly carpentered.
w Philip Dunne novel John P. Marquand d Joseph L. Mankiewicz ph Joseph LaShelle m Cyril Mockridge
☆ Ronald Colman, Edna Best, Vanessa Brown, Richard Haydn, Peggy Cummins, Charles Russell

The Late Show *
US 1977 93m Metrocolor
Warner (Robert Altman)
🎞 🔍
An ageing private eye in Los Angeles finds that his ex-partner's death and a lost cat have a complex connection.
A more-or-less engaging spoof of, or perhaps a valediction to, the private eye genre, with engaging scenes marred by poor colour and occasional excesses of violent action.
wd Robert Benton ph Chuck Rosher m Ken Wannberg ed Lou Lombardo, Peter Appleton
☆ Art Carney, Lily Tomlin, Bill Macy, Ruth Nelson, Howard Duff, Joanna Cassidy, Eugene Roche
'On its own terms, it's perfectly executed. The squalid settings stink of decay; the spare pacing captures the tough style of Hammett prose; and the stylized use of blood puts some sting into murder.' – *Frank Rich, New York Post*
⅛ Robert Benton (for script)

Latin Lovers
US 1953 104m Technicolor
MGM (Joe Pasternak)
An heiress on holiday in Brazil looks for a man who will love her for herself alone.

Barren romantic drama, flatfooted and drawn out.
w Isobel Lennart d Mervyn Le Roy ph Joseph Ruttenberg m George Stoll
☆ Lana Turner, Ricardo Montalban, John Lund, Louis Calhern, Jean Hagen

Latin Quarter *
GB 1945 80m bw
British National (Louis H. Jackson, Derrick de Marney)
US title: *Frenzy*
In 1890s Paris a mad sculptor murders his fiancée and hides her inside his latest exhibit.
Artificial-looking but melodramatically effective thriller with a chilling climax and a detailed Degas-period background.
wd Vernon Sewell play L'Angoisse by Pierre Mills, Charles Vylars ph Gunther Krampf
☆ Derrick de Marney, Joan Greenwood, Beresford Egan, Frederick Valk, Lily Kann, Martin Miller

Laugh and Get Rich
US 1931 72m bw
RKO (William Le Baron)
A man invests his wife's money in a tyre with a whistling valve.
Inconsequential comedy with ancient jokes.
w Ralph Spence, Gregory La Cava d Gregory La Cava ph Jack MacKenzie ad Max Ree
☆ Hugh Herbert, Edna May Oliver, Dorothy Lee, Robert Emmett Keane
'Entertainment for the willing.' – *Variety*

Laugh with Max Linder *
👫 France 1963 88m bw
Films Max Linder
original title: *En Compagnie de Max Linder*
Excerpts from three of the dapper comedian's most famous American comedies: *Be My Wife* (1921), *The Three Must-Get-Theres* (1922), *Seven Years' Bad Luck* (1923).
A compilation which must serve as a consensus of this almost forgotten comedian's work. The gag with a broken mirror in particular was borrowed by innumerable other comedians, notably the Marx Brothers in Duck Soup. Audiences new to Linder's work will find him not especially sympathetic but capable of many felicities. He wrote, produced and directed all three films.
compiler Maud Max Linder

Laugh Your Blues Away
US 1943 65m bw
Jack Fier/Columbia
Jobless actors pose as guests at a society party.
Feeble filler.
w Harry Sauber d Charles Barton
☆ Jinx Falkenburg, Bert Gordon, Isobel Elsom, Douglass Drake
† Bert Gordon was best known as the 'Mad Russian' on Eddie Cantor's radio show.

Laughing Anne
GB 1953 90m Technicolor
Republic/Wilcox-Neagle
French Anne and her boxing lover are characters of the Javanese waterfront; he kills her after she has fallen for a sea captain.
Cheap and turgid adaptation of a Joseph Conrad story; the author would not recognize it. Studio settings put the lid on hilariously bad work all round.
w Pamela Bower d Herbert Wilcox ph Max Greene m Anthony Collins
☆ Margaret Lockwood, Forrest Tucker, Ronald Shiner, Wendell Corey, Robert Harris

Laughing at Trouble
US 1937 60m bw
Max Golden/TCF
A small town newspaper editress untangles personal problems.
Acceptable second feature which almost became a series.
w Robert Ellis and Helen Logan d Frank R. Strayer
☆ Jane Darwell, Sara Haden, Lois Wilson, Margaret Hamilton, Allan Lane, John Carradine

Laughing Boy
US 1934 80m bw
MGM
A young Navajo brave marries an outcast maiden.
Misguided and absurd melodrama for unsuitable stars.
w John Colton and John Lee Mahin novel Oliver La Farge d W. S. Van Dyke

☆ Ramon Novarro, Lupe Velez, Chief Thunderbird, William Davidson
'Touchy theme and plot … below par as entertainment.' – *Variety*

Laughing Gravy *
👫 US 1931 20m bw
Hal Roach
🎞 ♻
Stan and Ollie retrieve their dog when the landlord throws it out into the snow.
One of the most endearing comedies of these stars, and one of the simplest.
w H. M. Walker d James W. Horne ph Art Lloyd ed Richard Currier
☆ Stan Laurel, Oliver Hardy, Charlie Hall, Harry Bernard

The Laughing Lady
GB 1946 93m Technicolor
Louis H. Jackson/British National
During the French revolution, an artist under sentence is required to steal an English lady's pearls.
Heavy-going operetta with the sense that all concerned have bitten off more than they can chew.
w Jack Whittingham play Ingram d'Abbes d Paul Stein
☆ Anne Ziegler, Webster Booth, Peter Graves, Felix Aylmer, Francis L. Sullivan, Paul Dupuis, Ralph Truman, Chili Bouchier
'Eight people know who the killer is – and they're all dead!'

The Laughing Policeman *
US 1973 112m DeLuxe
TCF (Stuart Rosenberg)
🎞
GB title: *An Investigation of Murder*
A mad machine-gunner eludes the San Francisco police.
Downbeat, semi-documentary police thriller with pretensions. Too complex by half, with an overplus of characterization, but the location work is excellent.
w Thomas Rickman novel Maj Sjowall, Per Wahloo d Stuart Rosenberg ph David Walsh m Charles Fox
☆ Walter Matthau, Bruce Dern, Lou Gossett, Albert Paulsen, Anthony Zerbe

Laughing Sinners
US 1931 71m bw
MGM
A girl with a past joins the Salvation Army.
Glum romance which however started an effective star combination.
w Bess Meredyth and Martin Flavin d Harry Beaumont
☆ Joan Crawford, Clark Gable, Neil Hamilton, Marjorie Rambeau, Guy Kibbee

Laughter *
US 1930 99m bw
Paramount (Herman J. Mankiewicz)
An ex-Follies girl marries a millionaire but later goes on a spree with the composer she once loved.
Sharply observed, before its time romantic comedy reminiscent now of the later Philadelphia Story in its attitudes to wealth and love. A precursor of the smart crazy comedies of the mid-thirties.
w Donald Ogden Stewart d Harry d'Abbadie d'Arrast ph George Folsey
☆ Fredric March, Nancy Carroll, Frank Morgan, Glenn Anders, Diane Ellis
'One of the best talking pictures I have ever seen.' – *James Agate*
'A talkie with so fast a pace that it crowds the comprehension of half the customers … marked at intervals by superb dialogue and the quick hand of a smart director.' – *Pare Lorentz*
'A lovely sophisticated comedy.' – *New Yorker, 1977*
⅛ original story (Donald Ogden Stewart, Harry d'Abbadie d'Arrast, Douglas Doty)

Laughter in Paradise *
GB 1951 93m bw
Transocean (Mario Zampi)
An eccentric leaves in his will a fortune for each of his relations providing they will perform certain embarrassing or criminal acts.
A funny idea gets half-hearted treatment, but the good bits are hilarious.

---

w Michael Pertwee, Jack Davies d Mario Zampi ph William McLeod m Stanley Black

☆ Alastair Sim, Joyce Grenfell, Hugh Griffith, Fay Compton, John Laurie, George Cole, Guy Middleton, Ronald Adam, Leslie Dwyer, A. E. Matthews, Beatrice Campbell

† Remade 1972 as Some Will, Some Won't.

Laughter in the Dark *
GB/France 1969 104m DeLuxe
UA/Woodfall/Winkast/Marceau (Neil Hartley)

A wealthy art dealer is taken in by an ambitious usherette and her lover, and after being blinded in a car accident tries to kill them.

Unsatisfactory adaptation of a novel with a very specialized appeal: conventional swinging London and Riviera settings only confuse the spectator. Moments do work, though.

w Edward Bond novel Vladimir Nabokov d Tony Richardson ph Dick Bush m Raymond Leppard ad Julia Trevelyan Oman

☆ Nicol Williamson, Anna Karina, Jean-Claude Drouot, Peter Bowles, Sian Phillips

'It fails to create the slightest interest in its trio of repulsive characters.' – Philip Strick

Laughterhouse *
🛉🛉 GB 1984 93m colour
Greenpoint/Film Four International (Ann Scott)
aka: Singleton's Pluck

A Norfolk farmer decides to walk his fattened geese to market.

An attempt to revive the tradition of Ealing comedy lands up somewhere on the wrong side of Group Three. Not enough plot, almost no jokes, and the geese are almost the only pleasant creatures.

w Brian Glover d Richard Eyre ph Clive Tickner m Dominic Muldowney

☆ Ian Holm, Penelope Wilton, Bill Owen, Richard Hope, Stephen Moore, Rosemary Martin

Laura ***
US 1944 85m bw
TCF (Otto Preminger)
📀 📼 📀~ 🎧

A beautiful girl is murdered ... or is she? A cynical detective investigates.

A quiet, streamlined little murder mystery that brought a new adult approach to the genre and heralded the mature film noir of the later forties. A small cast responds perfectly to a classically spare script, and in Clifton Webb a new star is born.

w Jay Dratler, Samuel Hoffenstein, Betty Reinhardt novel Vera Caspary d Otto Preminger ph Joseph LaShelle m David Raksin ad Lyle Wheeler, Leland Fuller

☆ Dana Andrews, Clifton Webb, Gene Tierney, Judith Anderson, Vincent Price, Dorothy Adams, James Flavin

WALDO LYDECKER (CLIFTON WEBB): 'It's lavish, but I call it home.'

WALDO: 'I shall never forget the weekend Laura died. A silver sun burned through the sky like a huge magnifying glass. It was the hottest Sunday in my recollection. I felt as if I were the only human being left in New York ... I had just begun Laura's story when one of those detectives came to see me. I had him wait.'

WALDO: 'In my case, self-absorption is completely justified. I have never discovered any other subject quite so worthy of my attention.'

'Everybody's favourite chic murder mystery.' – New Yorker, 1977

† Rouben Mamoulian directed some scenes before handing over to Preminger.

🏆 Joseph LaShelle
👤 script; Otto Preminger; Clifton Webb; art direction

Laurel and Hardy in Toyland: see Babes in Toyland (1934)

The Laurel and Hardy Murder Case *
🛉🛉 US 1930 30m bw
Hal Roach

Heirs to a fortune are menaced by a mad murderer.
Empty spoof on The Cat and the Canary which affords little scope.

w H. M. Walker d James Parrott ph George Stevens, Walter Lundin

☆ Stan Laurel, Oliver Hardy, Fred Kelsey, Del Henderson, Dorothy Granger, Frank Austin, Tiny Sandford

Laurel and Hardy's Laughing Twenties **
🛉🛉 US 1965 90m bw
MGM/Robert Youngson
📀 📼 📀~

Excerpts from lesser comedians of the period – Max Davidson, Charlie Chase – are interspersed with highlights from Laurel and Hardy's silent two-reelers.

A hilarious and craftsmanlike compilation, perhaps a little too long for its own good.

m Skeets Alquist w/ed Robert Youngson commentator Jay Jackson

† Films extracted include Putting Pants on Philip, From Soup to Nuts, Wrong Again, The Finishing Touch, Liberty, Double Whoopee, Leave 'Em Laughing, You're Darn Tooting and the custard pie climax from The Battle of the Century.

Laurin (dubbed)
Germany 1985 80m colour
Salinas/TS-Film/Dialog/Südwestfunk (Bernhardt Stampfer, Andreas Bareiss)
📀

In a small village, a young girl outwits a child murderer.

Confused attempt at a spooky narrative; its length and the great many loose ends suggest it has been heavily cut. All that remains is a little queasy atmosphere.

w Robert Sigl, Adam Rozgonyi d Robert Sigl ph Nyika Jancso m Jacques Zwart, Hans Jansen ed Teri Losonci

☆ Dora Szinetar, Brigitte Karner, Karoly Eperjes, Hedi Temessy

The Lavender Hill Mob ****
🛉🛉 GB 1951 78m bw
Ealing (Michael Truman)
📀 📼 📀~

A timid bank clerk conceives and executes a bullion robbery.

Superbly characterized and inventively detailed comedy, one of the best ever made at Ealing or in Britain.

w T.E.B. Clarke d Charles Crichton ph Douglas Slocombe m Georges Auric ad William Kellner ed Seth Holt

☆ Alec Guinness, Stanley Holloway, Sidney James, Alfie Bass, Marjorie Fielding, Edie Martin, John Gregson, Gibb McLaughlin, Sydney Tafler, Audrey Hepburn

'Amusing situations and dialogue are well paced and sustained throughout: the climax is delightful.' – MFB

'An outrageous comedy, of course, but the observations of detail and character are so true, the sense of a familiar place so sharp, that few will resent the gusto with which the outrage is perpetrated.' – C. A. Lejeune

🏆 T. E. B. Clarke
👤 Alec Guinness
🏆 best British film

The Law: see Where the Hot Wind Blows

Law and Disorder: see Spies of the Air (1939)

Law and Disorder
GB 1940 73m bw
K. C. Alexander/British Consolidated

A solicitor's partner unmasks saboteurs.
Light topical comedy thriller, capably performed.

w Roger MacDonald d David MacDonald

☆ Barry K. Barnes, Diana Churchill, Alastair Sim, Edward Chapman, Austin Trevor, Leo Genn

Law and Disorder *
GB 1958 76m bw
British Lion/Hotspur (Paul Soskin)

Crooks rally round a confederate about to be arrested, to prevent his son from learning of his father's real career.

Amusing, well-pointed caper on sub-Ealing lines.

w T. E. B. Clarke novel Smuggler's Circuit by Denys Roberts d Charles Crichton ph Ted Scaife m Humphrey Searle

☆ Michael Redgrave, Robert Morley, Joan Hickson, Lionel Jeffries, Ronald Squire, Elizabeth Sellars

Law and Disorder *
US 1974 102m Technicolor Panavision
Memorial/Leroy Street/Ugo Fadsin (William Richert)
📀 📼

New York suburbanites aghast at escalating violence form themselves into a vigilante patrol.
Bewilderingly uneven comedy drama which starts as satirical comedy and ends with one of the heroes dead and the other moralizing. Sporadically interesting, and certainly topical.

w Ivan Passer, William Richert, Kenneth Harris Fishman d Ivan Passer ph Arthur J. Ornitz m Andy Badale

☆ Ernest Borgnine, Carroll O'Connor, Karen Black, Ann Wedgeworth, Leslie Ackerman, David Spielberg

The Law and Jake Wade *
US 1958 86m Metrocolor Cinemascope
MGM (William Hawks)

A marshal helps an old outlaw friend to escape from jail, and lives to regret it.
Good standard Western, enjoyable throughout but with no outstanding merits.

w William Bowers d John Sturges ph Robert Surtees

☆ Robert Taylor, Richard Widmark, Patricia Owens, Robert Middleton, Henry Silva

Law and Order *
US 1932 80m bw
Universal

A cowboy becomes marshal and cleans up Tombstone.
Drily effective fictionalization of Wyatt Earp's exploits, with a good star performance.

w John Huston novel Saint Johnson by W. R. Burnett d Edward L. Cahn

☆ Walter Huston, Harry Carey, Raymond Hatton, Russell Simpson, Russell Hopton

Law and Order
US 1953 80m Technicolor
Universal-International

Curious belated sequel to the above with Johnson moving on to tame Cottonwood; actual presentation rather dull.

w John and Gwen Bagni and D. D. Beauchamp d Nathan Juran

☆ Ronald Reagan, Dorothy Malone, Preston Foster, Alex Nicol, Russell Johnson

The Law and the Lady
US 1951 104m bw
MGM (Edwin H. Knopf)

A couple of confidence tricksters inveigle themselves into the house of a vulgar millionairess, but one of them has an attack of conscience.
Dreary remake of The Last of Mrs Cheyney (qv) with the locale altered, the plot simplified, and the level of wit diluted.

w Leonard Spigelgass, Karl Tunberg d Edwin H. Knopf ph George Folsey m Carmen Dragon

☆ Greer Garson, Michael Wilding, Fernando Lamas, Marjorie Main, Hayden Rorke, Margalo Gillmore, Ralph Dumke

Law of Desire *
Spain 1987 101m colour
Other Cinema/El Deseo/Laurenfilm (Ester Garcia)
📀 📼 📀~
original title: La Ley del Deseo

A glamorous homosexual film director is pursued by a male would-be lover while sharing his apartment with his former brother, who has undergone a sex change, and her transvestite lover's daughter.
Delirious, stylish mix of sex and passion, though many may regard it as too camp and overdone.

wd Pedro Almodovar ph Angel Luis Fernandez pd Javier Fernandez ed Jose Salcedo

☆ Eusebio Poncela, Carmen Maura, Antonio Banderas, Miguel Molina, Manuela Velasco, Bibi Andersen, Fernando Guillen

'Almodovar's tone is not like anyone else's; the film has the exaggerated plot of an absurdist Hollywood romance ... The film is festive. It doesn't disguise its narcissism; it turns it into bright-coloured tragi-comedy.' – Pauline Kael, New Yorker

The Law of the Lawless
US 1963 87m Techniscope
Paramount/A. C. Lyles

A judge arrives in a small Western town to conduct the murder trial of a former friend.
Jaded Western of interest only for the producer's custom of packing the bit roles with former stars.

w Steve Fisher d William F. Claxton ph Lester Shorr

☆ Dale Robertson, Yvonne de Carlo, William Bendix, Bruce Cabot, Barton MacLane, John Agar, Richard Arlen, Kent Taylor, Lon Chaney Jnr

Law of the Tropics
US 1941 76m bw
Warner (Ben Stoloff)

A café singer on the run from a murder charge marries a South American rubber plantation owner.
Hackneyed melodrama born from a mating of Oil for the Lamps of China and Tropic Zone.

w Charles Grayson d Ray Enright ph Sid Hickox m Howard Jackson

☆ Constance Bennett, Jeffrey Lynn, Regis Toomey, Mona Maris, Frank Puglia, Thomas Jackson, Craig Stevens

The Law Versus Billy the Kid
'Out of the most exciting pages of frontier history!'
US 1954 73m Technicolor
Sam Katzman/Columbia

Billy the Kid is driven into crime to avenge a friend.
Technicolor seems wasted on this two-bit Western which can't even manage to tell a clear story.

w John T. Williams d William Castle

☆ Scott Brady, Betta St John, James Griffith, Alan Hale Jnr, Paul Cavanagh

The Lawless
US 1949 83m bw
Paramount/Pine-Thomas
GB title: The Dividing Line

The editor of a California small-town newspaper defends a Spanish boy who is being victimized by the racist element.
Well-meaning 'realistic' melodrama, unfortunately among the dullest of the socially conscious movies of this period.

w Geoffrey Homes d Joseph Losey ph Roy Hunt m Mahlon Merrick

☆ Macdonald Carey, Gail Russell, John Sands, John Hoyt, Lee Patrick, Lalo Rios

The Lawless Breed
US 1952 83m Technicolor
U-I (William Alland)

The adventures and repentance of badman John Wesley Hardin.
Standard Western programmer with the star in an unlikely role.

w Bernard Gordon d Raoul Walsh ph Irving Glassberg m Joseph Gershenson

☆ Rock Hudson, Julie Adams, John McIntire, Dennis Weaver, Hugh O'Brian

The Lawless Frontier
US 1934 53m bw
Lone Star/Malvern
📀 📼 📀

A cowboy comes to the rescue when a ruthless renegade takes a fancy to a gold prospector's granddaughter.
Rudimentary Western with stilted, melodramatic acting and not much action other than a couple of examples of Canutt's stunt riding.

wd Robert North Bradbury ph Archie Stout ad E. R. Hickson ed Charles Hunt

☆ John Wayne, Sheila Terry, Jack Rockwell, George Hayes, Buffalo Bill Jnr, Yakima Canutt, Earl Dwire

A Lawless Street
US 1955 78m Technicolor
Columbia (Harry Joe Brown)

A marshal marries a dance hall entertainer, and loses interest in his job when she leaves him.
Enjoyable minor Western.

w Kenneth Gamet novel Marshal of Medicine Bend by Brad Ward d Joseph H. Lewis ph Ray Rennahan m Paul Sawtell

☆ Randolph Scott, Angela Lansbury, Warner Anderson, Jean Parker, Wallace Ford, John Emery, James Bell, Ruth Donnelly, Michael Pate, Jeanette Nolan, Don Megowan

Lawman *
US   1970   99m   Technicolor
UA/Scimitar (Michael Winner)
📺 ▣
When a marshal tracks down drunken cowboys who have killed an old man, the townsfolk's resistance leads to a bloodbath.
Terse, violent Western with a good cast.
w Gerald Wilson d Michael Winner ph Bob Paynter m Jerry Fielding
☆ Burt Lancaster, Robert Ryan, Lee J. Cobb, Sheree North, Robert Duvall, Joseph Wiseman, John McGiver, Albert Salmi, J. D. Cannon

Lawn Dogs **
GB   1997   101m   Rank Colour
Carlton/Rank/Toledo (Duncan Kenworthy)
📺 ▣ 🎧
A young girl, whose parents live in a secure community behind protected gates, forms a friendship with the tough youth who cuts the grass.
A fable, both charming and dark, of the dangers of civilizing the environment.
w Naomi Wallace d John Duigan ph Elliot Davis pd John Myhre ed Humphrey Dixon
☆ Sam Rockwell, Christopher McDonald, Kathleen Quinlan, Bruce McGill, Mischa Barton, David Barry Gray
  'A true and compelling portrait of a so-called "secure community" which proves instead to be imprisoned by its own paranoia. A gem.' – Mark Steyn, Spectator

'God Made Him Simple. Science Made Him A God.'
The Lawnmower Man *
GB/US   1992   108m   DeLuxe
First Independent/Allied Vision/Lane Pringle/Fuji Eight (Gimel Everett)
📺 ▣ 🎧 🎧
aka: Stephen King's The Lawnmower Man
A doctor experiments with drugs and computer technology to improve the mind of his retarded gardener, with startling and unforeseen results.
Some impressive special effects, simulating 'virtual reality' – a computer-created world – enliven an otherwise drab and predictable science fiction movie.
w Brett Leonard, Gimel Everett story Stephen King d Brett Leonard ph Russell Carpenter m Dan Wyman pd Alex McDowell ed Alan Baumgarten sp Angel Studios, Xaos Inc.
☆ Jeff Fahey, Pierce Brosnan, Jenny Wright, Geoffrey Lewis, Mark Bringleson, Jeremy Slate, Dean Norris
  'It all works surprisingly well, with interesting and well-integrated visual effects, some nice humour and a few genuinely visionary effects.' – Kim Newman, Empire
† Stephen King was granted an injunction forbidding the film's producers from using his name in connection with the film.
†† A director's cut of the film was also released on video with a running time of 142m.

Lawnmower Man 2: Beyond Cyberspace
US   1995   92m   colour
First Independent/Allied Entertainments/Fuji Eight (Edward Simons, Keith Fox)
📺 ▣ 🎧 🎧
A legless former imbecile attempts to create the city of the future in cyberspace, where he can control the world.
An incoherent and incompetent fantasy aimed at the young.
wd Farhad Mann ph Ward Russell m Robert Folk pd Ernest Roth ed Peter Berger, Joel Goodman sp Cinesite
☆ Patrick Bergin, Matt Frewer, Austin O'Brien, Ely Pouget, Camille Cooper, Kevin Conway, Patrick La Breque, Crystal Celeste Grant
  'Stumbles from one unconnected moment to the next unexciting one.' – Alan Jones, Film Review

Lawrence of Arabia ****
GB   1962   221m   Technicolor   Super Panavision 70
Columbia/Horizon (Sam Spiegel)
📺 ▣ 🎧 🎧
An adventurer's life with the Arabs, told in flashbacks after his accidental death in the thirties.
Sprawling epic which manages after four hours to give no insight whatever into the complexities of character of this mysterious historic figure, but is often spectacularly beautiful and exciting along the way.

w Robert Bolt d David Lean ph Frederick A. Young m Maurice Jarre pd John Box ad John Stoll
☆ Peter O'Toole, Omar Sharif, Arthur Kennedy, Jack Hawkins, Donald Wolfit, Claude Rains, Anthony Quayle, Alec Guinness, Anthony Quinn, José Ferrer, Michel Ray, Zia Mohyeddin
  'Grandeur of conception is not up to grandeur of setting.' – Penelope Houston
  'Lean has managed to market epics as serious entertainment rather than as the spectacles they are.' – Time Out, 1980
† Albert Finney turned down the role before O'Toole was offered it.
†† Michael Wilson also worked on the script, but was uncredited.
🎬 best picture; David Lean; Frederick A. Young; Maurice Jarre
👥 Robert Bolt; Peter O'Toole; Omar Sharif
🏆 best picture; best British picture; Robert Bolt; Peter O'Toole

Laws of Gravity *
🧍🧍 US   1992   98m   colour
Oasis/The Shooting Gallery (Bob Gosse, Larry Meistrich)
In Brooklyn, friendship between two young, petty crooks is strained when they become involved with a gangster who is trying to sell guns.
Down-beat drama of losers, effectively filmed and acted in a documentary style although it does cover familiar territory.
wd Nick Gomez ph Jean de Segonzac m Douglas Cuomo pd Monica Bretherton ed Tom McArdle
☆ Peter Greene, Edie Falco, Adam Trese, Arabella Field, Paul Schulze, Saul Stein, James McCauley
  'Reasonably acted with some funny, protracted conversations.' – Empire

The Lawyer *
US   1970   120m   Technicolor
Paramount (Brad Dexter)
An ambitious young Italian-American defence lawyer takes on a murder case.
Smartly scripted, perfectly ordinary courtroom drama in a well-detailed Western setting. The star subsequently played the same character in a TV series, Petrocelli.
w Sidney J. Furie, Harold Buchman d Sidney J. Furie ph Ralph Woolsey m Malcolm Dodds
☆ Barry Newman, Harold Gould, Diana Muldaur, Robert Colbert, Kathleen Crowley, Booth Colman

Lawyer Man
US   1932   68m   bw
Warner
An honest lawyer becomes corrupted by success.
Smart, cynical melodrama, dated but sufficiently fast-paced to remain interesting.
w Rian James, James Seymour novel Max Trell d William Dieterle ph Robert Kurrle
☆ William Powell, Joan Blondell, Helen Vinson, Alan Dinehart, Allen Jenkins, David Landau, Claire Dodd
  'Good picture in the lawyer cycle.' – Variety

Laxdale Hall
GB   1952   77m   bw
Group Three (Alfred Shaughnessy)
US title: Scotch on the Rocks
MPs are sent to investigate a tiny Hebridean island which refuses to pay road tax.
Thin rehash of Whisky Galore put together without the Ealing style. Minor compensations can be found.
w John Eldridge, Alfred Shaughnessy d John Eldridge ph Arthur Grant m Frank Spencer
☆ Raymond Huntley, Ronald Squire, Sebastian Shaw, Fulton Mackay, Kathleen Ryan, Kynaston Reeves
  'Constantly amusing in its quiet and wry fashion.' – Cinema

Lazy Bones: see Hallelujah I'm a Bum

Lazy River
US   1934   75m   bw
MGM
Ex-convicts go to work in a shrimp cannery and defeat a Chinese smuggler.
Curious comedy drama which defeats all participants.
w Lucien Hubbard story Ruby by Lea David Freeman d George B. Seitz
☆ Jean Parker, Robert Young, Ted Healy, C. Henry Gordon, Nat Pendleton

Le Mans *
US   1971   108m   DeLuxe   Panavision
Solar/Cinema Center (Jack N. Reddish)
A sullen American enters for the 24-hour race.
Almost no plot and little documentary examination; what's left is a multitude of racing shots with Steve McQueen at the wheel. For some this may be enough.
w Harry Kleiner d Lee H. Katzin ph Robert B. Hauser, René Gruissart Jnr m Michel Legrand
☆ Steve McQueen, Siegfried Rauch, Elga Anderson, Ronald Leigh-Hunt

Leadbelly *
US   1976   126m   Eastmancolor
CIC/Brownstone/David Paradine (Marc Merson)
Biopic of the tough folk and blues singer and guitarist Huddie Ledbetter, concentrating on his earlier years and his times in chain gangs.
Pleasing, if stolid, account of a fascinating performer who sang his way out of prison.
w Ernest Kinoy d Gordon Parks ph Bruce Surtees m Fred Karlin m/ly Huddie Ledbetter pd Robert Boyle ed Harry Howard
☆ Roger E. Mosley, Paul Benjamin, Madge Sinclair, Alan Manson, Albert P. Hall, Art Evans, James E. Brodhead, John Henry Faulk
  'Little more than the traditional biopic molasses.' – MFB
† Leadbelly's songs are sung by HiTide Harris.

'Indecent. Immoral. Irresistible. It's the role he was born to play.'
The Leading Man
GB   1996   99m   Metrocolor
Guild/J&M (Bertil Ohlsson, Paul Raphael)
📺 ▣ 🎧
An English playwright permits his star, a Hollywood actor, to seduce his wife so that he can continue his affair with his play's leading actress.
Drab domestic drama of cultural differences, treated like a soap opera.
w Virginia Duigan d John Duigan ph Jean-François Robin m Edward Shearmur pd Caroline Hanania ed Humphrey Dixon
☆ Jon Bon Jovi, Lambert Wilson, Anna Galiena, Thandie Newton, Barry Humphries, David Warner, Patricia Hodge, Diana Quick, Harriet Walter
  'It's all predictable, artificial and long past its sell-by date.' – Alexander Walker, London Evening Standard

League of Frightened Men
US   1937   71m   bw
Columbia
Nero Wolfe solves another murder case from his armchair.
Fair detective story, but a negation of film.
w Eugene Solow, Guy Endore novel Rex Stout d Alfred E. Green
☆ Walter Connolly, Lionel Stander, Eduardo Ciannelli, Irene Hervey, Victor Kilian, Nana Bryant
  'Hardly any audience likes to watch a character who just sits and thinks.' – Variety

The League of Gentlemen ***
GB   1960   112m   bw
Rank/Allied Film Makers (Michael Relph)
📺 ▣
An ex-army officer recruits high-class misfits with guilty secrets to help him in a bank robbery.
Delightfully handled comedy adventure, from the days (alas) when crime did not pay; a lighter ending would have made it a classic.
w Bryan Forbes novel John Boland d Basil Dearden ph Arthur Ibbetson m Philip Green
☆ Jack Hawkins, Richard Attenborough, Roger Livesey, Nigel Patrick, Bryan Forbes, Kieron Moore, Terence Alexander, Norman Bird, Robert Coote, Melissa Stribling, Nanette Newman, Gerald Harper, Patrick Wymark, David Lodge, Doris Hare and also Lydia Sherwood

'Once in a lifetime you get a chance to do something different.'
A League of Their Own *
US   1992   128m   Technicolor
Columbia/Parkway
📺 ▣ 🎧 🎧
During the Second World War, women are recruited to play in an all-female baseball league.
A comedy that trundles along in a predictable fashion, settling for sentimentality rather than humour.

w Lowell Ganz, Babaloo Mandel story Kim Wilson, Kelly Candaele d Penny Marshall ph Miroslav Ondricek m Hans Zimmer pd Bill Groom ed George Bowers
☆ Tom Hanks, Geena Davis, Madonna, Lori Petty, Jon Lovitz, David Strathairn, Garry Marshall, Bill Pullman, Megan Cavanagh, Tracy Reiner, Rosie O'Donnell, Ann Cusack
  'This movie aims for the tear ducts and the funny bone as ruthlessly as the summer's big action-fantasy hits go after the viscera. It unfolds in field-of-dreams land – complete with cornstalks.' – Michael Sragow, New Yorker
  'Awash in sentimentality and manic energy but only occasionally bubbling over with high humor.' – Variety

Lean on Me
US   1989   108m   Technicolor
Warner (Norman Twain)
📺 ▣ 🎧 🎧
A stern teacher tames the pupils at New Jersey's toughest school.
Given its subject matter, a surprisingly soft-centred drama, based on a true story.
w Michael Schiffer, Douglas Seelig d John G. Avildsen ph Victor Hammer m Bill Conti pd Doug Kraner ed John Carter, John G. Avildsen
☆ Morgan Freeman, Beverly Todd, Robert Guillaume, Alan North, Lynne Thigpen, Robin Bartlett, Ethan Phillips

Leap of Faith
US   1992   108m   colour
Paramount (Michael Manheim, David V. Picker)
📺 ▣ 🎧
A fraudulent preacher works a miracle.
Unsatisfactory drama that begins as an exposé of cheapjack evangelists and their tricks and ends as something even more exploitative and crass.
w Janus Cercone d Richard Pearce ph Matthew F. Leonetti m Cliff Eidelman pd Patrizia von Brandenstein ed Don Zimmerman, Mark Warner, John F. Burnett
☆ Steve Martin, Debra Winger, Lolita Davidovich, Liam Neeson, Lukas Haas, Meat Loaf
  'One finds oneself just thanking God the movie's ended.' – Film Review

The Learning Tree *
US   1969   107m   Technicolor   Panavision
Warner
A black youth comes to maturity in Kansas, as he experiences the good and the bad in the society around him.
Despite its semi-autobiographical nature, the prevailing tone is nostalgic and almost elegiac; the past, despite its racism, is recollected with affection.
wd Gordon Parks novel Gordon Parks ph Burnett Guffey m Gordon Parks ad Ed Engoron ed George R. Rohrs
☆ Kyle Johnson, Alex Clarke, Estelle Evans, Dana Elcar, Mira Waters, Joel Fluellen, Malcolm Atterbury, James Rushing

Lease of Life *
GB   1954   94m   Eastmancolor
Ealing (Jack Rix)
A poor clergyman is given a year to live, and puts it to good use.
Somewhat depressing but well-acted drama with excellent village atmosphere.
w Eric Ambler d Charles Frend ph Douglas Slocombe m Alan Rawsthorne
☆ Robert Donat, Kay Walsh, Adrienne Corri, Denholm Elliott

The Leather Boys *
GB   1963   108m   bw   Cinemascope
British Lion/Garrick (Raymond Stross)
📺 ▣
Two working-class teenagers marry for sex; she becomes a drudge and he develops a relationship with a homosexual motorcyclist.
Sharply-observed slice of low life which now seems quite dated, the central figures no longer being of the 'heroic' interest given them at the time. Technically the film is tediously and fashionably flashy.
w Gillian Freeman novel Elliot George d Sidney J. Furie ph Gerald Gibbs m Bill McGuffie
☆ Rita Tushingham, Dudley Sutton, Colin Campbell, Gladys Henson

---

The Leather Saint

US 1955 86m bw Vistavision
Paramount (Norman Retchin)

To provide his parish hospital with medical equipment, a Catholic priest becomes a commercial prizefighter.

Unlikely piece of religiosity, not too badly done.

w Norman Retchin, Alvin Ganzer d Alvin Ganzer ph Haskell Boggs md Irvin Talbot
☆ Paul Douglas, John Derek, Cesar Romero, Ernest Truex, Jody Lawrance

Leathernecking

US 1930 80m bw (colour sequence)
RKO (Louis Sarecky)

GB title: *Present Arms*

A Honolulu socialite falls for a marine, but grows cool when she discovers that he is a private and not an officer as he pretended.

Curiously cast, spasmodically funny non-musical version of a Rodgers and Hart Broadway hit.

w Alfred Jackson, Jane Murfin *play Present Arms* by Herbert Fields, Rodgers and Hart d Edward Cline ph J. Roy Hunt m Oscar Levant
☆ Irene Dunne, Ken Murray, Eddie Foy Jnr, Louise Fazenda, Ned Sparks, Lilyan Tashman
'Weak medley of horseplay and romantic musical, and both poor.' – *Variety*

Leave All Fair *

New Zealand 1984 88m colour
Pacific Films (John O'Shea)

At the end of his life, John Middleton Murry recalls his relationship with his first wife, the writer Katherine Mansfield.

Intelligent and ambivalent drama, leaving open the question of whether Murry was the betrayer or saviour of his wife's reputation.

w Stanley Harper, Maurice Pons, Jean Betts, John Reid d John Reid ph Bernard Lutic m Stephen McCurdy ad Joe Bleakley ed Ian John
☆ John Gielgud, Jane Birkin, Feodor Atkine, Simon Ward

Leave 'Em Laughing *

🎭🎭 US 1928 20m bw silent
Hal Roach

Stan has toothache, visits the dentist, and accidentally causes all concerned to inhale an overdose of laughing gas.

The earlier sequences are only mildly funny, but the laughing finale is irresistible.

w Hal Roach, Reed Heustis d Clyde Bruckman ph George Stevens ed Richard Currier supervisor Leo McCarey
☆ Stan Laurel, Oliver Hardy, Edgar Kennedy, Charlie Hall

'The sum total of all human emotion!'

Leave Her to Heaven

US 1946 111m Technicolor
TCF (William A. Bacher)

📺

A selfish, jealous woman causes unhappiness for those around her, even in her suicide.

No-holds-barred melodrama of the old school; what seemed lush production at the time now looks tatty.

w Jo Swerling *novel* Ben Ames Williams d John M. Stahl ph Leon Shamroy m Alfred Newman ad Lyle Wheeler, Maurice Ransford
☆ Gene Tierney, Cornel Wilde, Jeanne Crain, Vincent Price, Mary Philips, Ray Collins, Gene Lockhart, Reed Hadley, Chill Wills
'The story's central idea might be plausible enough in a dramatically lighted black and white picture … but in the rich glare of Technicolor, all its rental library characteristics are doubly glaring.' – *James Agee*
♣ Leon Shamroy
🎗 Gene Tierney; art direction

'The Beav is back.'

Leave It to Beaver

🎭🎭 US 1997 88m DeLuxe
Universal (Robert Simmonds)

📀 📺

Two young brothers in an all-American family overcome the problems in their lives.

Those never exposed to the nostalgic TV sitcom of minor domestic happenings are likely to find this deadening entertainment; those who were may come to the same conclusion.

w Brian Levant and Lon Diamond *TV serial* Bob Mosher and Joe Connelly d Andy Cadiff

---

ph Thomas Del Ruth m Randy Edelman pd Perry Andelin Blake
☆ Christopher McDonald, Janine Turner, Cameron Finley, Erik von Detten, Adam Zolotin, Barbara Billingsley, Ken Osmond, Erika Christensen
'Mildly subversive touches are separated by long stretches of unremarkable tedium.' – *Variety*
† Barbara Billingsley and Ken Osmond both appeared in the original TV sitcom, which ran from 1957 to 1963.

The Leavenworth Case

US 1935 66m bw
Republic

Police investigate the murder of a wealthy man.

Sluggish transcription of what claims to be the first American detective story.

w Albert DeMond, Sidney Sutherland *novel* Anna Katherine Green
☆ Donald Cook, Jean Rouverol, Norman Foster, Erin O'Brien-Moore, Maude Eburne, Warren Hymer
'Just another detective meller.' – *Variety*

Leaves from Satan's Book *

Denmark 1919 80m bw silent
Nordisk

Episodes from the activities of Satan through the ages: with Christ, the Inquisition, the French Revolution, and the Russian Revolution.

Vaguely propagandist short-story compilation with effective moments.

w Edgar Hoyer, Carl Dreyer *novel The Sorrows of Satan* by Marie Corelli d Carl Dreyer ph George Schneevoigt

Leaving Las Vegas **

US 1995 112m Foto-Kem
Entertainment/Initial (Lila Cazes, Annie Stewart)

📀 📺 📀 🎧 ♫

An alcoholic writer goes to Las Vegas to drink himself to death and meets a prostitute who invites him to live with her.

A tragic drama that leaves unexplained the self-destructive motives of its protagonists; at times Cage's performance recalls James Stewart's in Harvey, and Shue's kindly tart amid the Vegas glitz seems as much an alcoholic's fantasy as a large white rabbit. The movie's emotional force is undercut by the maudlin ballads that swell on the soundtrack at climactic moments.

wd Mike Figgis *novel* John O'Brien ph Declan Quinn m Mike Figgis pd Waldemar Kalinowski ed John Smith
☆ *Nicolas Cage*, Elisabeth Shue, Julian Sands, Richard Lewis, Valeria Golino, Graham Beckel, Laurie Metcalf, Lou Rawls, Carey Lowell
'Although the movie is terribly, crushingly sad, its honesty is invigorating: it names its poison and downs it, neat.' – *Terrence Rafferty, New Yorker*
'Jazzy, soulfully florid fairy tale – as affecting and sublimely irresponsible as its doomed protagonist.' – *J. Hoberman, Premiere*
† Author John O'Brien committed suicide just before the film went into production.
♣ Nicolas Cage
🎗 Elisabeth Shue; Mike Figgis (as director and as writer)

Leaving Lenin **

GB 1993 93m colour
Feature/Gaucho/SC4 (Pauline Williams)

📀

original title: *Gadael Lenin*

On a school trip to St Petersburg, the three teachers in charge become separated from the sixth-formers they are accompanying.

A slight but enjoyable Welsh comedy about the pains and pleasures of adolescence.

w Endaf Emlyn, Sion Eirian d Endaf Emlyn ph Ray Orton m John Hardy ad Vera Zelenkskaya ed Chris Lawrence
☆ Sharon Morgan, Ifan Huw Dafydd, Wyn Bowen Harris, Steffan Trevor, Ivan Shvedov, Catrin Mai, Richard Harrington, Shelley Rees
'The joy of this captivating comedy is that in spite of the ludicrousness of its situations, it is totally credible.' – *James Cameron-Wilson, Film Review*

Leaving Normal

Canada/US 1992 110m colour
Universal (Lindsay Doran)

📀 📺 📀

An abrasive cocktail waitress and a young wife running from her second husband leave the small Western town of Normal and head for Alaska and freedom, which does not entirely live up to their expectations.

Loud and unsubtle road movie of female bonding, with a little male–female bonding on the side.

w Edward Solomon d Edward Zwick ph Ralf Bode m W. G. Snuffy Walden pd Patricia Morris ed Victor DuBois
☆ Christine Lahti, Meg Tilly, Lenny von Dohlen, Maury Chaykin, Patrika Darbo, Eve Gordon, James Eckhouse, Brett Cullen, James Gammon
'Not for all tastes … has a serious undertone in its depiction of losers who keep struggling to assert themselves in an unfeeling and male-dominated world.' – *Variety*
† Cher and Demi Moore were originally cast in the leading roles.

Lebenszeichen: see *Signs of Life*

La Lectrice **

France 1988 98m colour
Curzon Films/Elefilm/AAA/TSF/Ciné 5/Sofimage (Rosalinde Deville)

📺 📀

A beautiful young woman, hired to read books out loud to people who are disabled in some way, has unexpected effects on her customers.

Witty games-playing comedy.

w Michel Deville, Rosalinde Deville *novel* Raymond Jean d Michel Deville ph Dominique Le Rigoleur m Beethoven pd Thierry Leproust ed Raymonde Guyot
☆ Miou-Miou, Régis Royer, Christian Ruché, Maria Cesars, Patrick Chesnais, Marianne Denicourt, Pierre Dux
'A frothy conceit, a true jeu d'esprit, but when it has said all that it has to say, albeit with panache, it has said nothing.' – *MFB*

'You can count the truly daring concepts in the making of motion pictures on the fingers of your right hand. Now add…'

The Left Hand of God

US 1955 87m DeLuxe Cinemascope
TCF (Buddy Adler)

📺

China, 1947: a Catholic priest newly arrived in a small village proves to be an American flyer on the run from a warlord; but he contrives to work a small 'miracle'.

Hollywood religiosity at its most contrived, put together without distinction; the players have a wary look.

w Alfred Hayes *novel* William E. Barrett d Edward Dmytryk ph Franz Planer m Victor Young
☆ Humphrey Bogart, Gene Tierney, Lee J. Cobb, E. G. Marshall, Agnes Moorehead

The Left Handed Gun *

US 1958 102m bw
Warner/Harold (Fred Coe)

📀 📺 📀

Billy the Kid sets out to shoot four men who have killed his friend.

'Method'-oriented Western, efficiently made but somewhat downcast.

w Leslie Stevens, *TV play* Gore Vidal d Arthur Penn m Peverell Marley m Alexander Courage
☆ Paul Newman, John Dehner, Lita Milan, Hurd Hatfield

Left Luggage

Netherlands/Belgium/USA 1997 100m colour
Downtown/Shooting Star/Flying Dutchman (Ate de Jong, Hans Pos, David Schram)

📀

In Antwerp, a philosophy student becomes the nanny of a four-year-old boy, whose parents are Hassidic Jews.

A study in contrasts, between modern attitudes and non-materialistic traditional ones, that is unfortunately overwhelmed by its sentimentality.

w Edwin de Vries *novel The Shovel and the Loom* by Carl Friedman d Jeroen Krabbé ph Walther Vanden Ende m Henny Vrienten ad Hemmo Sportal ed Edgar Burcksen

---

☆ Isabella Rossellini, Maximilian Schell, Laura Fraser, Jeroen Krabbé, Marianne Saegebrecht, David Bradley, Adam Monty, Chaim Topol
'It's a pity that a film which otherwise has a great deal going for it ultimately winds up as ghettoised as the community it portrays.' – *Caroline Westbrook, Empire*

'Top of the poll for laughs!'

Left Right and Centre *

GB 1959 95m bw
Vale/Launder and Gilliat

A TV personality becomes Tory candidate at a by-election.

Scrappy political comedy with the saving grace of a large number of comic talents.

w Sidney Gilliat, Val Valentine d Sidney Gilliat ph Gerald Gibbs m Humphrey Searle
☆ Ian Carmichael, Alastair Sim, Patricia Bredin, Richard Wattis, Eric Barker, Gordon Harker, George Benson, Frederick Leister

The Legacy

GB 1978 102m colour
Columbia/Pethurst/Turman-Foster (David Foster)

An American designer goes to stay with her employer and finds herself in the middle of an occult murder plot.

Cliché-ridden screamer which will please the easily pleased.

w Jimmy Sangster, Patrick Tilley, Paul Wheeler d Richard Marquand ph Dick Bush, Alan Hume m Michael J. Lewis pd Disley Jones ed Anne Coates
☆ Katharine Ross, Sam Elliott, Roger Daltrey, John Standing, Ian Hogg, Margaret Tyzack, Charles Gray, Lee Montague, Hildegard Neil

'Like father, like son…'

Legacy of Rage (dubbed)

Hong Kong 1987 82m colour
Imperial (John Sham, Linda Kuk)

📀

After six years in jail for a crime he did not commit, a former waiter teams up with a cell-mate to seek revenge on the gangster who framed him.

Standard martial arts adventure, notable only for Brandon Lee's debut.

wd Ronny Yu
☆ Brandon Lee, Onno Boelee (Bolo Yeung), Michael Wong, Regina Kent, Tanya George
'Offers too few thrills to satisfy hard-core action fans.' – *Film Review*

Legal Eagles

US 1986 114m Technicolor Panavision
Universal/Northern Lights (Ivan Reitman)

📀 📺 📀 📀

An assistant DA becomes involved for the defence in an arson case.

Sophisticated but messy comedy with odd unrelated asides, reminiscent of the TV series Moonlighting but with top production values.

w Jim Cash, Jack Epps Jnr d Ivan Reitman ph Laszlo Kovacs m Elmer Bernstein
☆ Robert Redford, Debra Winger, Daryl Hannah, Brian Dennehy, Terence Stamp, Steven Hill

Legend *

🎭🎭 GB 1985 94m Fujicolour Panavision
(TCF/Universal) Legend Productions (Arnon Milchan)

📀 📺 📀 🎧

Young peasant Jack takes his sweetheart on a quest to see the last surviving unicorns, but Satan uses them as pawns in his own game.

Elegant fairy tale for the few grown-ups who have use for such a thing. More to look at than to listen to.

w William Hjortsberg d Ridley Scott ph Alex Thomson m Jerry Goldsmith pd Assheton Gorton ed Terry Rawlings
☆ Tim Curry, Mia Sara, Tom Cruise, David Bennent
'The dying gasp of the sword and sorcery cycle.' – *Philip French, Observer*
'The enchanted forests constantly threaten to sell us something – most frequently soft toilet paper.' – *Ibid.*
🎗 make-up (Rob Bottin, Peter Robb-King)

'An Epic Story Of A Man Who Could Do Anything... Except Be Ordinary.'

The Legend of 1900 *
Italy   1998   125m   Cinecittà colour
Technovision
Fine Line/Medusa/Sciarlo
original title: *La Leggenda Del Pianista Sull'Oceano*
US title: *The Legend of the Pianist on the Ocean*
An abandoned child, named 1900 after the year of his birth, spends his entire life as a virtuoso pianist aboard the trans-Atlantic liner on which he was born.
Lavish, good-looking but curious fable that suggests significance without ever revealing it.
wd Giuseppe Tornatore *monologue Novecento* by Alessandro Baricco *ph* Lajos Koltai *m* Ennio Morricone *pd* Francesco Frigeri *ed* Massimo Quaglia *cos* Maurizio Millenotti
☆ Tim Roth, Pruitt Taylor Vince, Melanie Thierry, Bill Nunn, Peter Vaughan, Niall O'Brien, Alberto Vasquez, Clarence Williams III, Gabrielle Lavia
   'A darn good yarn told in classic style, but invigorated by inventiveness and imagination. Truly magnificent.' – *Nick Briggs, Film Review*
† The film ran for 170m when first shown at the Cannes Film Festival.

The Legend of Billie Jean
US   1985   96m   Metrocolor
Tri-Star/Rob Cohen (Jon Peters, Peter Guber)
⬛
While protecting her brother, a girl becomes an outlaw by accident.
Unattractive and even distasteful farrago which is presumably intended to teach kids, so far as the law is concerned, how to eat their cake and have it.
w Mark Rosenthal, Lawrence Konner *d* Matthew Robbins *ph* Jeffrey L. Kimball *m* Craig Safan *pd* Ted Haworth *ed* Cynthia Scheider
☆ Helen Slater, Keith Gordon, Christian Slater, Richard Bradford, Peter Coyote
   'The germ of an idea, but hardly a reason for a film.' – *Variety*

The Legend of Fong Sai Yuk: see *Fong Sai Yuk*

The Legend of Fong Sai Yuk II: see *Fong Sai Yuk II*

'For the sake of your sanity, pray it isn't true!'
The Legend of Hell House *
GB   1973   94m   DeLuxe
TCF/Academy (Albert Fennell, Norman T. Herman)
⬛   ⊘
Four people arrive at a haunted house in which several psychic investigators have been killed.
Harrowing thriller, a less solemn but more frightening version of The Haunting.
w Richard Matheson *novel* Richard Matheson *d* John Hough *ph* Alan Hume *m* Brian Hodgson, Delia Derbyshire
☆ Pamela Franklin, Roddy McDowall, Clive Revill, Gayle Hunnicutt, Roland Culver, Peter Bowles, Michael Gough
   'One of the most absorbing, goose-fleshing and mind-pleasing ghost breaker yarns on film.' – *Judith Crist, 1977*

The Legend of Lobo *
👥 US   1962   67m   Technicolor
Walt Disney (James Algar)
⬛   ⊘
The life of a forest wolf.
Anthropomorphic entertainment in which a dreaded animal becomes something of a hero and finally saves his mate from bounty hunters. Impeccably contrived, like a live-action Bambi.
w Dwight Hauser, James Algar *story* Ernest Thompson Seton *d* James Algar *ph* Jack Couffer, Lloyd Beebe *m* Oliver Wallace

The Legend of Lylah Clare *
US   1968   130m   Metrocolor   Panavision
MGM/Robert Aldrich
A mad director brings an unknown actress to Hollywood because of her resemblance to a former star, his creation, who had died mysteriously.
Unintentionally risible melodrama with echoes of Svengali and Sunset Boulevard; not to the public's taste, or anyone else's, in the late sixties.
w Hugo Butler, Jean Rouverol *TV play* Robert Thom, Edward de Blasio *d* Robert Aldrich *ph* Joseph Biroc *m* Frank de Vol

☆ Peter Finch, Kim Novak, Ernest Borgnine, Coral Browne, Milton Seltzer, Rossella Falk, Gabriele Tinti, Valentina Cortesa, George Kennedy

Legend of the Demon Womb
Japan   1990   84m   colour
Toshio Maeda/West Cape
original title: *Urotsukidoji II*
Demons and man-beasts fight to prevent the son of a mad Nazi from gaining ultimate power by killing the boy who is destined to be the over-fiend, the god of gods.
Extremely gruesome animated fantasy, concentrating on graphic sex, from masturbation, fellatio and lesbianism to rape, and much violence, including decapitations, multiple murders and human sacrifice.
w Noboru Aikawa *story* Toshio Maeda *d* Hideki Takayama *ph* Hideo Okazaki *m* Masamichi Amano *ad* Hitoshi Nagao *ed* Shigeru Nishiyama
☆ Featuring the voices of Christopher Courage, Rebel Joy, Danny Bush, Lucy Morales, Rose Palmer
† A sequel to the equally gruesome *Legend of the Overfiend* (qv). It was followed by the video releases of *Urotsukidoji III: Episode 1* and *Urotsukidoji III: Episode 2*, which both continue the mixture as before with an unintelligible narrative, an impenetrable mythology, a comic-book style of animation, and much sex and violence.

Legend of the Holy Drinker **
Italy   1988   128m   colour
Artificial Eye/Aura Film/Cecchi Gori Group/Tiger Cinematografica/RAI Uno (Roberto Cicutto, Vincenzo de Leo)
⬛
original title: *La Leggenda del Santo Bevitore*
An alcoholic tramp is repeatedly frustrated in his attempts to repay money to the shrine of a saint.
An odd fable, beautifully presented.
w Tullio Kezich, Ermanno Olmi *novel Die Legende des Heiligen Trinkers* by Joseph Roth *d* Ermanno Olmi *ph* Dante Spinotti *m* Stravinsky *pd* Gianni Quaranta *ed* Ermanno Olmi
☆ Rutger Hauer, Anthony Quayle, Sandrine Dumas, Dominique Pinon, Sophie Segalen, Jean Maurice Chanet, Cecile Paoli, Joseph de Medina

'The film where you hiss the villain and cheer the hero!'
The Legend of the Lone Ranger
👥 US   1981   98m   Technicolor
Panavision
ITC/Jack Wrather (Walter Coblenz)
A much-betrayed young Texan, almost killed in an ambush, is nursed back to health by an Indian and becomes a masked avenger.
Extremely ill-constructed and moody Western, apparently photographed through brown Windsor soup, which doesn't slip into the right gear until twenty minutes before the end.
w Ivan Goff, Ben Roberts, Michael Kane, William Roberts *d* William A. Fraker *ph* Laszlo Kovacs *m* John Barry
☆ Klinton Spilsbury, Michael Horse, Christopher Lloyd, Matt Clark
   'Wallows in endless sentiment before switching to what may possibly have been intended as parody.' – *Sight and Sound*
   'Tedious hokum … the kind of film that closes cinemas.' – *Sunday Times*

Legend of the Lost
👥 US   1957   107m   Technirama
UA/Batjac/Robert Haggiag/Dear (Henry Hathaway)
Two adventurers and a slave girl seek a lost city in the Sahara.
Tediously vague and underplotted desert adventure with a few attractive moments.
w Robert Presnell Jnr, Ben Hecht *d* Henry Hathaway *ph* Jack Cardiff *m* A. F. Lavagnino
☆ John Wayne, Sophia Loren, Rossano Brazzi

Legend of the Overfiend (dubbed)
Japan   1989   96m   colour
West Cape Corp (Yasuhito Yamaki)
⬛
original title: *Urotsukidoji*
Creatures from two parallel universes battle to become supreme rulers of the Earth.
Revolting and thoroughly nasty animated feature, full of rape, masturbation, mutilation and grotesque mutations, with heads exploding and eyeballs popping.

What narrative there is amid the sex and violence makes little sense.
w Noboru Aikawa *story* Toshio Maeda *d* Hideki Takayama *m* Masamichi Amano *ad* Shigemi Ikeda *ed* Shigeru Nishiyma
☆ Featuring the voices of Christopher Courage, Rebel Joy, Danny Bush, Lucy Morales, Rose Palmer
   'Formula heroics, facile science fiction futurism, slavering monsters and tediously repetitive violence – the animated fantasies of the Manga school have everything to satisfy the adolescent mind.' – *Sight and Sound*

The Legend of the Pianist on the Ocean: see *The Legend of 1900*

The Legend of the Seven Golden Vampires
GB/Hong Kong   1974   89m   Eastmancolor
Panavision
Hammer-Shaw (Don Houghton, Vee King Shaw)
⬛
US title: *The Seven Brothers Meet Dracula*
In 1904 Chungking, Professor Van Helsing finds his old enemy Dracula behind a Chinese vampire cult.
Hectic, outlandish mix of Hammer horror and Kung Fu; plenty of gusto but not much sense.
w Don Houghton *d* Roy Ward Baker *ph* John Wilcox, Roy Ford *m* James Bernard
☆ Peter Cushing, David Chiang, Julie Ege, Robin Stewart, John Forbes Robertson

Legend of the Suram Fortress *
USSR   1984   87m   colour
Poseidon/Georgianfilm Studio (X. Gogiladze, M. Simxaev)
⬛
original title: *Legenda Suramskoi Kreposti*
A youth lets himself be immured in the walls of a fortress to stop it from crumbling.
Colourful re-enactment of a folk tale, though not up to the director's best work.
w Vazha Gigashvili *book* D. Tchonghadze *d* Sergo Paradjanov, Dodo Abashidze *ph* Sergo Sixarulidze *m* Dzhansugh K'axidze *ad* Alexandr Dzhanishiev *ed* K'ora Ts'ereteli
☆ Venerik'o Andzhaparidze, Dodo Abashidze, Sopik'o Ch'iaureli, Duduxana Ts'erodze, Tamar Tsitsishuili

Legend of the Werewolf
GB   1974   90m   Eastmancolor
Tyburn (Kevin Francis)
⬛
In the 1860s, a boy brought up by wolves changes into one at the full moon.
Cheap and cheerful horror movie, much in the Hammer style, bright but unsubtle.
w Anthony Hinds *d* Freddie Francis *ph* John Wilcox *m* Harry Robinson *ad* Jack Shampan *ed* Henry Richardson
☆ Peter Cushing, David Rintoul, Ron Moody, Hugh Griffith, Roy Castle, Stefan Gryff, Lynn Dalby, Renée Houston, Marjorie Yates

The Legend of Tom Dooley
US   1959   77m   bw
Columbia/Shpetner
At the end of the Civil War, Confederate youths take the law into their own hands and attack Unionists.
Youthful rebellion in historical mould, decently but rather dully delivered, based on a folk ballad.
w Stan Shpetner *d* Ted Post *ph* Gilbert Warrenton *m* Ronald Stein
☆ Michael Landon, Richard Rust, Jo Morrow

'The men of the Ludlow family. A woman's grace brought them together. Then her passion tore them apart.'
Legends of the Fall
US   1994   134m   Technicolor
TriStar/Bedford Falls/Pangaea (Edward Zwick, Bill Wittliff)
⬛   ⬛   ⬛   ⊙   ⊙   ⊙   ⊙
An army officer retires to a ranch with his three sons: one is killed in the First World War, the surviving two fall in love with the same woman; one goes on to become a successful politician, and the other a bootlegger and outcast.
Period family saga, reminiscent of East of Eden, with Brad Pitt glowering as a latter-day James Dean; enjoyable as a soap opera but its aspirations to be something more come to nothing.

w Susan Shilliday, Bill Wittliff *novel* Jim Harrison *d* Edward Zwick *ph* John Toll *m* James Horner *pd* Lilly Kilvert *ed* Steven Rosenblum
☆ Anthony Hopkins, Brad Pitt, Aidan Quinn, Henry Thomas, Julia Ormond, Karina Lombard, Gordon Tootoosis, Tantoo Cardinal, Paul Desmond
   'A silly melodrama trying to be an epic.' – *Time*
   'A visceral, thoughtful and emotionally exhausting saga.' – *Variety*
🎬 John Toll
🎬 Lilly Kilvert

La Leggenda Del Pianista Sull'Oceano: see *The Legend of 1900*

The Lemon Drop Kid *
US   1951   91m   bw
Paramount (Robert A. Welch)
⬛   ⊘
A gangster forces a bookie to find the money which he has lost on a horse through the bookie's incompetence.
Amusing Bob Hope/Runyon vehicle despite heavy sentiment about an old folks' home. The Santa Claus sequences are memorable.
w Edmund Hartmann, Frank Tashlin, Robert O'Brien *story* Damon Runyon *d* Sidney Lanfield *ph* Daniel L. Fapp *m* Victor Young
☆ Bob Hope, Marilyn Maxwell, Lloyd Nolan, Jane Darwell, Andrea King, Fred Clark, Jay C. Flippen, William Frawley, Harry Bellaver
† The previous 1934 version starred Lee Tracy, Helen Mack and William Frawley; ran 60m; and was directed by Marshall Neilan for Paramount

The Lemon Sisters
US   1990   93m   Technicolor
Miramax/Lightyear (Joe Kelly)
⬛   ⬛   ⊘
In Atlantic City, three childhood friends with dreams of becoming stars grow up to face the realities of life and love.
Drearily witless comedy, in which most of the narrative thrust is confined to a voice-over; the inert direction only emphasizes that this is a bland movie about the dull lives of people of limited talent.
w Jeremy Pikser *d* Joyce Chopra *ph* Bobby Byrne *m* Dick Hyman *pd* Patrizia von Brandenstein *ed* Joe Weintraub, Michael R. Miller
☆ Diane Keaton, Carol Kane, Kathryn Grody, Elliott Gould, Ruben Blades, Estelle Parsons, Richard Libertini, Aidan Quinn

Lena's Holiday
US   1991   97m   colour
Crown International/Marimark (Marilyn Jacobs Tenser)
⬛   ⊘
A young East German girl goes on holiday to Los Angeles.
Mildly agreeable comedy of a culture clash.
w Deborah Tilton, Ronald Keusch *d* Michael Keusch *ph* Louis DiCesare *m* Steve Schiff *pd* Milo *ed* Bill Swenson
☆ Chris Lemmon, Nick Mancuso, Michael Sarrazin, Felicity Waterman, Pat Morita, Bill Dana, Liz Torres, Susan Anton

Lenin in October *
USSR   1937   111m   bw
Mosfilm
original title: *Lenin v Octiabrye*
The activities of Lenin during the revolution.
Stalwart propaganda piece, of solid but not outstanding cinematic interest.
w Alexei Kapler *d* Mikhail Romm *ph* Boris Volchok *m* Anatoli Alexandrov
☆ Boris Shchukin
   'We have reached the end of the Communist film. It is to be all "Heroes and Hero-Worship" now: the old films are to be remade for the new leaders: no more anonymous mothers will run in the van of the workers against the Winter Palace. The USSR is to produce Fascist films from now on.' – *Graham Greene*
† The success of this film provoked *Lenin in 1918*, made in the following year (132m) by the same talents, with Cherkassov as Gorky. Many other Russian films on Lenin have followed.

Lenin v Octiabrye: see *Lenin in October*

'Somewhere in the tundra lived the worst rock'n'roll band in the world…'

Leningrad Cowboys Go America ★★
Finland/Sweden 1989 78m
Artificial Eye/Villealfa/Swedish Film Institute/Finnish Film Foundation (Aki Kaurismäki, Klas Olofsson, Katinka Farago)
▣ ▦ ◎

An inept rock band travels through America in search of fame and fortune, which prove elusive.
Engagingly ramshackle comedy, with keen observation of the underside of the American dream
wd Aki Kaurismäki story Sakke Järvenpää, Aki Kaurismäki, Mato Valtonen ph Timo Salminen m Mauri Sumén ed Raija Talvio
☆ Matti Pellonpää, Kari Väänänen, Sakke Jarvenpää, Hiekki Keskinen, Pimme Oinonen, Silu Seppälä, Mauri Sumén, Mato Valtonen, Pekka Virtanen, Jim Jarmusch

Lenny ★★★
US 1974 111m bw
UA (Marvin Worth)
▣ ▦ ◎ ⌒

The career of obscene comedian Lenny Bruce and his struggles with the law.
Old-fashioned rags-to-riches-to-rags story, rampant with the new permissiveness. Filmically extremely clever, emotionally hollow.
w Julian Barry play Julian Barry d Bob Fosse ph Bruce Surtees md Ralph Burns pd Joel Schiller
☆ Dustin Hoffman, Valerie Perrine, Jan Miner, Stanley Beck, Gary Morton
'For audiences who want to believe that Lenny Bruce was a saintly gadfly who was martyred for having lived before his time.' – *New Yorker*
⅋ best picture; Julian Barry; Bob Fosse; Bruce Surtees; Dustin Hoffman; Valerie Perrine
Ⓥ Valerie Perrine

Leo the Last
GB 1969 104m DeLuxe
UA/Char/Wink/Boor (Irwin Winkler, Robert Chartoff)
An alienated aristocrat brings his retinue to a London slum and has an effect on most of the inhabitants.
Infuriating symbolic fantasy; only the writer-director (presumably) has any idea what it is about.
w William Stair, John Boorman d John Boorman ph Peter Suschitsky m Fred Myrow pd Tony Woollard
☆ Marcello Mastroianni, Billie Whitelaw, Calvin Lockhart, Glenna Forster Jones, Graham Crowden, Gwen Ffrangcon Davies, David de Keyser, Vladek Sheybal, Kenneth J. Warren
'One must be grateful for the bold, high-spirited experiments and surprises … They are never boring.' – *Dilys Powell*

'The Classic Novel. The Timeless Love Story.'
Leo Tolstoy's Anna Karenina
Warner/Icon (Bruce Davey) 1997 108m
Technicolor Panavision
Warner/Icon (Bruce Davey)
▣ ◎

In Russia, a married woman begins a doomed affair with a gallant and infatuated cavalry officer.
A clumsy, by-the-numbers treatment, often opulent to look at, well enough acted, but lacking in any depth or feeling.
wd Bernard Rose novel Leo Tolstoy ph Daryn Okada m Tchaikovsky et al md Sir Georg Solti pd John Myhre ed Victor Du Bois
☆ Sophie Marceau, Sean Bean, Alfred Molina, Mia Kirshner, James Fox, Fiona Shaw, Danny Huston, Phyllida Law, David Scofield, Saskia Wickham, Jennifer Hall
'This passionless Classics Illustrated-style rendition possesses no distinction to attract an audience.' – *Todd McCarthy, Variety*

'Léolo's fantasy is of Bianca and Sicily. His reality is Murder and Madness.'
Léolo ★
Canada/France 1992 103m colour
Alliance/Verseau/Flach/Canal (Lyse Lafontaine, Aimée Danis)
▣ ▦ ◎

In a poor part of Montreal, a dreamy small boy, growing up at odds with his mainly demented family, retreats from reality.
A dark tragi-comic account of the flowering and the failure of an imagination.

wd Jean-Claude Lauzon ph Guy Dufaux ad François Séguin m Michel Arcand
☆ Ginette Reno, Pierre Bourgault, Maxime Collin, Giuditta Del Vecchio, Julien Guiomar
'A semi-autobiographical phantasmagoria about growing up in a 1960s East-Montreal French-Canadian tenement populated by Fellini-esque grotesques.' – *Philip French, Observer*

'He Moves Without Sound, Kills Without Emotion, Disappears Without Trace.'
'If you want the job done right, hire a professional.'
Leon ★★
France 1994 110m Technicolor
Buena Vista/Gaumont/Dauphin (Luc Besson)
▣ ▦ ◎ ⌒
US title: *The Professional*
A hitman makes the mistake of befriending a 12-year-old girl whose family is murdered by a crooked policeman and his thugs.
Tense and involving thriller, dealing in heightened fantasy rather than reality, about a killer with a weakness.
wd Luc Besson ph Thierry Arbogast m Eric Serra pd Dan Weil ed Sylvie Landra
☆ Jean Reno, Gary Oldman, Natalie Portman, Danny Aiello, Peter Appel, Michael Badalucco, Ellen Greene, Elizabeth Regen
'The most satisfactory blend of brilliance and not quite original thought. It's a well-orchestrated thriller that never treats itself too seriously, skates on fairly thin ice but comes out smelling mainly of roses.' – *Derek Malcolm, Guardian*
'A naïve fairy tale splattered with blood. Mix of cynicism and sentiment will ring hollow to cine-literate sophisticates but may play well to the gallery.' – *Lisa Nesselson, Variety*

Léon Morin, Priest ★
France/Italy 1961 117m bw
Rome – Paris Films (Georges de Beauregard)
During the German occupation of France a young widow finds herself falling in love with the young priest who is converting her to religion.
An intellectual romance, sharp and witty for the most part, with vivid wartime backgrounds.
wd Jean-Pierre Melville novel Béatrix Beck ph Henri Decaë m Martial Solal, Albert Raisner
☆ Jean-Paul Belmondo, Emmanuele Riva, Irène Tunc, Marielle Gozzi

Leon the Pig Farmer
GB 1992 104m colour
Electric/Leon the Pig Farmer Production (Gary Sinyor, Vadim Jean)
▣ ▦
A Jewish estate agent discovers that his real father is a Yorkshire pig farmer.
Laboured low-budget comedy of racial stereotypes.
w Gary Sinyor, Michael Norman d Vadim Jean, Gary Sinyor ph Gordon Hickie m John Murphy pd Simon Hicks ed Ewa Lind
☆ Mark Frankel, Gina Bellman, Janet Suzman, Brian Glover, Connie Booth, Maryam D'Abo
'Overall, flashes of inspiration are outweighed by laboured skits that fall somewhat flat, but this is a worthy and promising effort.' – *Empire*
'The comedy has wit and pace. It has originality that Mel Brooks might envy.' – *Alexander Walker, London Evening Standard*
† The film was made on a budget of £160,000. It won the International Critics' Prize at the Venice Film Festival and an award for best first film at the Edinburgh Film Festival.

The Leopard ★★★★
US/Italy 1963 205m Technirama
TCF/Titanus/SNPC/GPC (Goffredo Lombardo)
⌒
original title: *Il Gattopardo*
The family life of an Italian nobleman at the time of Garibaldi.
Elaborate, complex family saga, painted like an old master with great care and attention to detail, but with not much chance outside Italy of delivering its original dramatic force. Visconti had asked for Lancaster, so TCF picked up the international release but couldn't make head or tail of it commercially; they even ruined its high quality by releasing a dubbed, shortened version in Cinemascope and DeLuxe colour of poor standard.
wd Luchino Visconti novel Giuseppe de Lampedusa ph Giuseppe Rotunno m Nino Rota ad Mario Garbuglia

☆ Burt Lancaster, Claudia Cardinale, Alain Delon, Paolo Stoppa, Serge Reggiani, Leslie French

Leopard in the Snow
GB/Canada 1977 94m Technicolor
Seastone/Leopard in the Snow (W. Laurence Heisey)
▦
A girl caught in a Cumberland blizzard is rescued by a mysterious stranger with a pet leopard. He turns out to be a disfigured racing driver, and she falls in love with him.
A deliberate cross between Jane Eyre and a shopgirl's romance, adequately produced for its intended audience.
w Anne Mather, Jill Hyem novel Anne Mather d Gerry O'Hara ph Alfie Hicks m Kenneth V. Jones
☆ Keir Dullea, Susan Penhaligon, Jeremy Kemp, Kenneth More, Billie Whitelaw

The Leopard Man ★★
US 1943 59m bw
RKO (Val Lewton)
▦ ▣
Murders in a Mexican border town are attributed to an escaped leopard.
Effective minor piece in the Lewton horror gallery; poor plot countered by highly effective suspense sequences.
w Ardel Wray, Edward Dein novel Black Alibi by Cornell Woolrich d Jacques Tourneur ph Robert de Grasse m Roy Webb
☆ Dennis O'Keefe, Jean Brooks, Margo, James Bell, Isabel Jewell
'It's all confusion, too much for an audience to follow.' – *Variety*

Lepa Sela Lepo Gore: see *Pretty Village Pretty Flame*

Lepke
US 1974 110m DeLuxe Panavision
Warner/AmeriEuro Pictures (Menahem Golan)
▣ ▦
After World War I a small-time crook becomes head of Murder Incorporated.
Violent but totally uninteresting gangster melodrama; fidelity to fact is not enough.
w Wesley Lau, Tamar Hoffs d Menahem Golan ph Andrew Davis m Ken Wannberg pd Jack Degovia
☆ Tony Curtis, Anjanette Comer, Michael Callan, Warren Berlinger, Milton Berle, Gianni Russo
'A kosher version of The Godfather.' – *Verina Glaessner*

Leprechaun
US 1992 92m CFI color
Trimark (Jeffrey B. Mallian)
▣ ▦ ◎ ⌒
A leprechaun terrorizes a household while searching for gold that was stolen from him.
Lugubrious, trivial horror with some nasty moments of violence.
wd Mark Jones ph Levie Isaacs m Kevin Kiner pd Naomi Slodki ed Christopher Roth
☆ Warwick Davis, Jennifer Aniston, Mark Holton, Ken Olandt, Robert Gorman, John Sanderford
'A dull, unscary horror movie whose sole selling point is some extraneous gore footage.' – *Variety*

'The Gold, the Bride and the Ugly…'
Leprechaun 2
US 1994 85m CFI color
Trimark (Donald Borchers)
▣ ▦ ◎ ⌒
GB title: *One Wedding and Lots of Funerals*
A leprechaun returns after a thousand years to claim as his bride a girl who sneezes three times.
A sequel that bears little resemblance to the original in its narrative, apart from the accumulation of dead bodies to the accompaniment of jokey violence.
w Turi Meyer, Al Septien d Rodman Flender m Jonathan Elias pd Anthony Tremblay ed Christopher Roth, Richard Gentner
☆ Warwick Davis, Charlie Heath, Sandy Baron, Shevonne Durkin, Adam Biesk, James Lancaster
'This malevolent little horror item is a nasty bit of business that revels in chicanery and gore.' – *Leonard Klady, Variety*

Les Bicyclettes de Belsize ★
GB 1969 29m Eastmancolor
Delmore/Ullustria (Jacques de Lane Lea)
The way to true love for a Hampstead shop owner is found through his bicycle.
Mildly attractive whimsy, obviously patterned after Les Parapluies de Cherbourg but not quite hitting the spot.
w Michael Newling d Douglas Hickox ph Wolfgang Suschitzky m/ly Les Reed, Barry Mason
☆ Anthony May, Judy Huxtable

Les Girls: see *Girls*

Les Misérables: see *Misérables*

Les Patterson Saves the World
Australia 1987 90m
Recorded Releasing/Humpstead (Sue Milliken)
▦
A coarse and slobbish Australian diplomat foils a dastardly plot to unleash a deadly virus.
Gross and tasteless comedy, without wit or style.
w Barry Humphries, Diane Milstead d George Miller ph David Connell m Tim Finn pd Graham 'Grace' Walker ed Tim Wellburn
☆ Barry Humphries, Pamela Stephenson, Thaao Penghlis, Andrew Clarke, Henri Szeps, Hugh Keays-Byrne

Lesbian Vampires: see *Vampyros Lesbos*

Less than Zero
US 1987 98m DeLuxe
TCF (Jon Avnet, Jordan Kerner)
▣ ▦ ◎ ⌒
A group of the rich young and upwardly mobile in Los Angeles become hooked on a meaningless round of drugs, parties and sex.
Limp attempt to film a best-selling novel of the blank generation, concentrating not so much on the despair and self-pity of the participants as on their enviable life-style.
w Harley Peyton novel Bret Easton Ellis d Marek Kanievska ph Edward Lachman m Thomas Newman pd Barbara Ling ed Peter E. Berger, Michael Tronick
☆ Andrew McCarthy, Jami Gertz, Robert Downey Jnr, James Spader, Tony Bill, Nicholas Pryor, Donna Mitchell

A Lesson in Love
Sweden 1954 95m bw
Svensk Filmindustri (Allan Ekelund)
original title: *En Lektion I Kärlek*
A gynaecologist and his wife grow bored and turn to other partners, but are reconciled.
Slight comedy, surprisingly unsubtle for its creator, but passable.
wd Ingmar Bergman ph Martin Bodin, Bengt Nordwal m Dag Wirén ad P. A. Lundgren ed Oscar Rosander
☆ Gunnar Björnstrand, Eva Dahlbeck, Harriet Andersson, Yvonne Lombard, Ake Grönberg

Lest We Forget: see *Hangmen Also Die*

Let 'Em Have It ★
US 1935 90m bw
Edward Small
GB title: *False Faces*
The FBI go after criminals on a terror spree.
Lively cops and robbers with some starkly effective moments.
w Joseph Moncure March, Elmer Harris d Sam Wood ph J. Peverell Marley, Robert Planck
☆ Richard Arlen, Virginia Bruce, Alice Brady, Bruce Cabot, Harvey Stephens, Eric Linden, Joyce Compton, J. Farrell MacDonald

Let Freedom Ring
US 1939 100m sepia
MGM (Harry Rapf)
A Westerner returns to his home town and clears it of corruption.
Elementary Hollywood actioner with curious credits, climaxed by Eddy singing The Star Spangled Banner.
w Ben Hecht d Jack Conway ph Sidney Wagner m Arthur Lange
☆ Nelson Eddy, Victor McLaglen, Virginia Bruce, Lionel Barrymore, H. B. Warner, Raymond Walburn, Edward Arnold, Guy Kibbee, Charles Butterworth, Billy Bevan

'Big box office … lusty patriotic meller. Cinch for exploitation.' – *Variety*

Let George Do It **

GB 1940 82m bw

Ealing (Basil Dearden)

A ukelele player accidentally goes to Bergen instead of Blackpool and is mistaken for a spy.
Generally thought to be the best George Formby vehicle, with plenty of pace, good situations and catchy tunes.

w John Dighton, Austin Melford, Angus MacPhail, Basil Dearden d Marcel Varnel ph Gordon Dines, Ronald Neame

☆ George Formby, Phyllis Calvert, Garry Marsh, Romney Brent, Bernard Lee, Coral Browne, Torin Thatcher, Hal Gordon

'The shocking true story of an unbelievable miscarriage of justice.'

Let Him Have It **

GB 1991 115m colour

First Independent/Vivid/Le Studio Canal Plus/British Screen (Luc Roeg, Robert Warr)

Derek Bentley, an 18-year-old with a low IQ, is hanged for a murder committed by another.
Affecting drama that keeps its focus on its central character.

w Neal Purvis, Robert Wade d Peter Medak ph Oliver Stapleton m Michael Kamen pd Michael Pickwoad ed Ray Lovejoy

☆ Christopher Eccleston, Paul Reynolds, Tom Bell, Eileen Atkins, Clare Holman, Michael Elphick, Mark McGann, Tom Courtenay, Michael Gough

'A powerful mix of social conscience and solid entertainment.' – *Variety*

'The straightforward, chronological narrative of this often moving naturalistic drama is both its major emotional strength and its chief dramatic weakness.' – *Nigel Floyd, Sight and Sound*

'Woolly liberal armchair bollocks. And I was crap in it.' – *Christopher Eccleston*

Let It Ride

US 1989 86m Technicolor

Paramount (David Giler)

A compulsive and unsuccessful gambler comes good at the race-track.
A comedy that limps along for most of its length.

w Ernest Morton (Nancy Dowd) book Good Vibes by Jay Cronley d Joe Pytka ph Curtis J. Wehr m Giorgio Moroder pd Wolf Kroeger ed Dede Allen

☆ Richard Dreyfuss, David Johansen, Teri Garr, Allen Garfield, Jennifer Tilly, Michelle Phillips, Mary Woronov, Robbie Coltrane

Let No Man Write My Epitaph

US 1960 106m bw

Columbia/Boris D. Kaplan

A slum boy wants to become a concert pianist but falls in with gangsters.
Squalid, predictable melodrama without many redeeming features.

w Robert Presnell Jnr novel Willard Motley d Philip Leacock ph Burnett Guffey m George Duning

☆ James Darren, Shelley Winters, Burl Ives, Jean Seberg, Jeanne Cooper, Ricardo Montalban, Ella Fitzgerald

Let the People Sing *

GB 1942 105m bw

British National (John Baxter)

An out-of-work comedian persuades a drunken nobleman to join a protest against the closing of a village hall.
A development of The Good Companions which compares quite nicely with the Capra films from across the water: naïve but entertaining, with good star performances.

w John Baxter, Barbara K. Emery, Geoffrey Orme novel J. B. Priestley d John Baxter ph James Wilson

☆ Alastair Sim, Fred Emney, Edward Rigby, Patricia Roc, Oliver Wakefield, Marian Spencer, Olive Sloane, Gus McNaughton, Charles Hawtrey

Let Them Live

US 1937 71m bw

Universal

A young man matches wits with a crooked town boss.
Tepid second-feature drama.

w Bruce Manning, Lionel Houser d Harold Young

☆ John Howard, Nan Grey, Edward Ellis, Judith Barrett

'Better than many of its kind … should please in nabes.' – *Variety*

Let Us Be Gay

US 1930 79m bw

MGM

Divorcees meet again, many years later, in Paris.
Predictable star romance, now very dated, like its title.

w Frances Marion play Rachel Crothers d Robert Z. Leonard

☆ Norma Shearer, Rod La Rocque, Marie Dressler, Sally Eilers, Raymond Hackett, Hedda Hopper

'Strong on all counts, romance, comedy, human sympathy and gorgeous clothes against a glamorous setting.' – *Variety*

Let Us Live

US 1937 67m bw

Columbia

An innocent taxi driver is convicted of murder.
Intense little melodrama which served its purpose.

w Joseph F. Dineen, Anthony Veiller and Allen Rivkin d John Brahm

☆ Maureen O'Sullivan, Henry Fonda, Ralph Bellamy

'Heavy dramatic preachment with limited appeal.' – *Variety*

Lethal Tender

Canada 1996 93m colour

Le Monde (Julian Grant)

A Chicago cop is the only one who can save the city's water supply when gangsters take over the filtration plant as part of an elaborate multi-million dollar robbery.
A standard action movie that gains a little from its unusual setting, though otherwise it sticks to the usual genre conventions, with otherwise ruthless killers suddenly becoming squeamish when they have a chance to shoot the hero.

w Tony Johnston d John Bradshaw ph Gerald R. Goozee m Lou Natale pd John Gillespie ed Paul Day

☆ Jeff Fahey, Kim Coates, Carrie-Ann Moss, Gary Busey, Denis Akiyama, David Mucci, David Fraser, Martin Roach

Lethal Weapon *

US 1987 110m Technicolor

Warner/ Richard Donner, Joel Silver

A slightly unhinged cop uncovers a drug smuggling operation.
Extremely violent policier which caters to the Rambo crowd but has enough pizazz to recommend it to most classes.

w Shane Black d Richard Donner ph Stephen Goldblatt m Michael Kamen, Eric Clapton

☆ Mel Gibson, Danny Glover, Gary Busey, Mitchell Ryan, Tom Atkins, Darlene Love

'Style masquerading as content.' – *Daily Variety*

Lethal Weapon 2

US 1989 111m colour Panavision

Warner/Silver Pictures (Richard Donner, Joel Silver)

Two cops hunt down drug smugglers protected by diplomatic immunity.
Slick action film with South Africans as the villains, fast-paced enough for the many implausibilities of plot and character to flash by.

w Jeffrey Boam story Shane Black, Warren Murphy d Richard Donner ph Stephen Goldblatt m Michael Kamen, Eric Clapton, David Sanborn pd J. Michael Riva ed Stuart Baird

☆ Mel Gibson, Danny Glover, Joe Pesci, Joss Ackland, Derrick O'Connor, Patsy Kensit

'The magic is back again.'

Lethal Weapon 3

US 1992 118m Technicolor Panavision

Warner/Silver Pictures (Richard Donner, Joel Silver)

Two detectives expose a former cop who is running an arms racket.
A succession of violent set pieces substitutes for narrative and character in this increasingly cynical series.

w Jeffrey Boam, Robert Mark Kamen d Richard Donner ph Jan de Bont m Michael Kamen, Eric Clapton, David Sanborn pd James Spencer ed Robert Brown, Battle Davis

☆ Mel Gibson, Danny Glover, Joe Pesci, Rene Russo, Stuart Wilson, Steve Kahan, Darlene Love, Traci Wolfe

'A pic that's really more about moments – comic or thrilling – than any sort of cohesive whole.' – *Variety*

'It celebrates a luxurious kind of destruction and disorder that can only appear mindless amid today's realities.' – *Vincent Canby, New York Times*

'The action you expect, the faces you love.'

Lethal Weapon 4

US 1998 127m Technicolor Panavision

Warner/Silver/Doshudo (Joel Silver, Richard Donner)

Two LA cops tangle with Chinese gangsters smuggling illegal immigrants into the country.
When even the publicity tag stresses the predictability of what's on offer, then it's no surprise to discover that the usual fare is on offer: noisy explosions, noisy dialogue, and effusive male bonding.

w Channing Gibson story Jonathan Lemkin, Alfred Gough, Miles Millar d Richard Donner ph Andrzej Bartkowiak m Michael Kamen, Eric Clapton, David Sanborn ch martial arts: Cory Yuen, Huen Chiu Ku, Chi Wah Ling pd J. Michael Riva ed Frank J. Urioste, Dallas Puett

☆ Mel Gibson, Danny Glover, Joe Pesci, Rene Russo, Chris Rock, Jet Li, Steve Kahan, Kim Chan, Darlene Love, Traci Wolfe, Eddy Ko, Steven Lam, Richard Libertini

'Hollywood cinema that justifies big bucks and bigger bangs.' – *Richard Williams, Guardian*

'I almost fell asleep during one explosion, only to be rudely awoken by the din of comic business going on in the foreground. Hard to believe, I know, but then you haven't heard the noise levels that the director, Richard Donner, appears to believe are essential to great comedy – levels equalled only by the shrill creak of contrivance as he cranks up each comic situation.' – *Tom Shone, Sunday Times*

Let's Be Famous

GB 1939 83m bw

Ealing (Michael Balcon)

A stage-struck Irish lad and Lancashire lass have various adventures in London.
Easy-going comedy introducing radio personalities of the day.

w Roger MacDougall, Allan MacKinnon d Walter Forde ph Ronald Neame, Gordon Dines md Ernest Irving

☆ Jimmy O'Dea, Betty Driver, Sonnie Hale, Patrick Barr, Basil Radford, Milton Rosmer, Garry Marsh

Let's Be Happy

GB 1957 107m Technicolor Cinemascope

ABP/ Marcel Hellman

Footling musical remake of *Jeannie* (qv).

w Diana Morgan d Henry Levin ph Erwin Hillier m Nicholas Brodszky md Louis Levy songs Nicholas Brodszky, Paul Francis Webster

☆ Vera-Ellen, Tony Martin, Robert Flemyng, Zena Marshall, Guy Middleton, Katherine Kath, Jean Cadell, Gordon Jackson

'Success still eludes the Anglo-American musical.' – *MFB*

Let's Dance

US 1950 112m Technicolor

Paramount (Robert Fellows)

Show business partners reunite after five years of private life.
Tediously plotted musical with a couple of good numbers.

w Allan Scott story Maurice Zolotow d Norman Z. McLeod ph George Barnes m Robert Emmett Dolan songs Frank Loesser

☆ Fred Astaire, Betty Hutton, Roland Young, Ruth Warrick, Lucile Watson, Barton MacLane, Shepperd Strudwick, Melville Cooper, Harold Huber, George Zucco

Let's Do It Again

US 1953 95m Technicolor

Columbia (Oscar Saul)

A songwriter and his wife plan a divorce but call it off in the nick of time.
Tame musical remake of The Awful Truth (qv), pleasant enough but lacking style and punch.

w Mary Loos, Richard Sale d Alexander Hall ph Charles Lawton Jnr m George Duning md Morris Stoloff songs Lester Lee, Ned Washington

☆ Jane Wyman, Ray Milland, Aldo Ray, Leon Ames

Let's Do It Again

US 1975 113m Technicolor

Warner/First Artists/Verdon (Melville Tucker, Pembroke J. Herring)

Three Atlanta workers conceive a zany plan to raise money for their church by hypnotizing a boxer into winning a big fight.
Lively but overlong farce reassembling the black talents of Uptown Saturday Night.

w Richard Wesley d Sidney Poitier ph Donald M. Morgan m Curtis Mayfield

☆ Sidney Poitier, Bill Cosby, Calvin Lockhart, John Amos, Denise Nicholas, Ossie Davis, Jimmy Walker

Let's Face It

US 1943 76m bw

Paramount (Fred Kohlmar)

A smart-alec soldier has a plot involving a ladies' health camp, but finds himself up to his neck in spies.
Tepid star comedy which unaccountably ditches almost all the numbers from the musical on which it was based.

w Harry Tugend play Cradle Snatchers by Norma Mitchell, Russell Medcraft musical play Dorothy and Herbert Fields, Cole Porter d Sidney Lanfield ph Lionel Lindon songs Cole Porter

☆ Bob Hope, Betty Hutton, Eve Arden, Phyllis Povah, Dona Drake, ZaSu Pitts, Marjorie Weaver, Raymond Walburn, Joe Sawyer

Let's Fall in Love

US 1933 67m bw

Columbia

A film director passes off a circus attendant as a glamorous foreign star.
Lightweight comedy with music which did okay.

w Herbert Fields d David Burton

☆ Edmund Lowe, Ann Sothern, Miriam Jordan, Gregory Ratoff

'No chorus, no legs, no undressing for a change … moderately geared for moderate income.' – *Variety*

Let's Get Lost *

US 1988 120m bw

Mainline/Little Bear (Bruce Weber)

Documentary on the life of jazz trumpeter and drug addict Chet Baker.
Fascinating series of interviews with friends, associates and lovers, interspersed with film from Baker's earlier life and some modern-day performances.

w Susan Stribling d Bruce Weber ph Jeff Preiss m Chet Baker ad Sam Shahid, Donald Sterzin, Rise Daniels ed Angelo Corrao

Let's Get Married

US 1937 68m bw

Columbia

A politician's daughter falls for the weather bureau chief.
Aimless romantic comedy which gets by on its performers.

w Ethel Hill story A. H. Z. Carr d Alfred E. Green

☆ Ida Lupino, Walter Connolly, Ralph Bellamy, Reginald Denny, Raymond Walburn

'Mediocre dualler.' – *Variety*

ᛏᛏ film suitable for family viewing   ▨ VHS video-cassette for the British PAL system   ▨ VHS video-cassette for the British PAL system in wide screen-format   ✿ Video cassette in a computer-colourised version   ▤ American NTSC video-cassette   ◔ Laser disc

Let's Go Native

US 1930 75m bw
Paramount

Various people are shipwrecked on a South Sea island.
Easy-going farce comedy with music.
w George Marion Jnr, Percy Heath d Leo MacCarey
☆ Jack Oakie, Jeanette MacDonald, Skeets Gallagher, James Hall, Kay Francis
'Hokum laughs with songs and dances.' – *Variety*

Let's Go Places

US 1930 70m bw
Fox

A young tenor goes to Hollywood, is mistaken for someone more famous and becomes a star.
Lightweight comedy with mildly interesting studio scenes.
w William K. Wells d Frank Strayer
☆ Joseph Wagstaff, Lola Lane, Sharon Lynn, Ilka Chase, Walter Catlett, Dixie Lee
'Plenty of music, no drawing names. Rates moderate for the big houses.' – *Variety*

Let's Hope It's a Girl *

Italy/France 1985 119m colour
Artificial Eye/Clemi Cinematografica/Producteurs Associes/Soprofilms/A2 (Raimondo Castelli, Bruno Ridolfi)

original title: *Speriamo Che Sia Femmina*
A countess strives, with the help of other women of the household, to keep running the family farm.
Gently amusing, rambling comedy.
w Leo Benvenuti, Tullio Pinelli, Suso Cecchi D'Amico, Piero de Bernardi, Mario Monicelli
d Mario Monicelli ph Camillo Bazzoni m Nicola Piovani ad Enrico Fiorentini ed Ruggero Mastroianni
☆ Liv Ullmann, Catherine Deneuve, Philippe Noiret, Bernard Blier, Giuliana de Sio, Stefania Sandrelli, Athina Cenci, Lucrezia Lante Della Rovere

Let's Kill Uncle

US 1966 92m colour
Universal/William Castle

A boy is threatened by his wicked uncle, and retaliates.
Mildly intriguing black comedy, leadenly handled.
w Mark Rodgers novel Rohan O'Grady
d William Castle ph Harold Lipstein m Herman Stein
☆ Nigel Green, Mary Badham, Pat Cardi, Robert Pickering

Let's Live a Little

US 1948 85m bw
Eagle-Lion/United California Productions

An advertising agent falls for his lady psychiatrist, and after many vicissitudes they and their former partners make it to the altar.
Mild comedy which just about bubbles along despite a rather uncomfortable cast.
w Albert J. Cohen, Jack Harvey d Richard Wallace ph Ernest Laszlo m Werner Heymann
☆ Hedy Lamarr, Robert Cummings, Anna Sten, Robert Shayne, Mary Treen

Let's Live Tonight

US 1935 75m bw
Columbia

Two millionaire brothers in Monte Carlo love the same girl.
Flimsy romantic comedy which gets by on its music.
w Gene Markey, Bradley King d Victor Schertzinger
☆ Lilian Harvey, Tullio Carminati, Hugh Williams, Janet Beecher, Tala Birell, Luis Alberni
'A parrot gets most of the laughs, which tips off the script.' – *Variety*

Let's Make a Night of It

GB 1937 92m bw
Associated British

In Nice, a husband and wife own rival night-clubs.
Slim musical with rather too many interpolated turns.
w Hugh Brooke radio play *The Silver Spoon* by Henrik Ege d Graham Cutts ph Otto Kanturek
m/ly Jimmie Kennedy, Michael Carr
☆ Buddy Rogers, June Clyde, Claire Luce, Fred Emney, Iris Hoey, Steve Geray, Syd Walker, Afrique, Oliver Wakefield, Brian Michie, Joe Loss and his Band, Sidney Lipton and his Band
'Definitely no appeal for the US.' – *Variety*

Let's Make It Legal

US 1951 77m bw
TCF

An attractive grandmother divorces her gambler husband and takes up with an old boyfriend.
Unremarkable but competent star comedy.
w F. Hugh Herbert, I. A. L. Diamond d Richard Sale ph Lucien Ballard m Cyril Mockridge
☆ Claudette Colbert, Zachary Scott, Macdonald Carey, Barbara Bates, Robert Wagner, Marilyn Monroe

Let's Make Love *

US 1960 118m DeLuxe Cinemascope
TCF (Jerry Wald)

A multi-millionaire, learning that he is to be burlesqued in a Broadway show, joins the cast as an actor.
Complex, moderately sophisticated, occasionally funny musical inspired by On The Avenue (qv); lively characterizations but poor numbers.
w Norman Krasna d George Cukor ph Daniel L. Fapp md Lionel Newman, Earl H. Hagen ch Jack Cole songs Sammy Cahn, Jimmy Van Heusen
☆ Yves Montand, Marilyn Monroe, Tony Randall, Wilfrid Hyde-White, Frankie Vaughan, David Burns, and guests Bing Crosby, Gene Kelly, Milton Berle
♪ Lionel Newman, Earl H. Hagen

Let's Make Music

US 1940 85m bw
RKO (Howard Benedict)

An old maid of a teacher writes a school song that unexpectedly becomes a novelty hit.
Slight but pleasant time-filler that includes a performance of Crosby's hit 'Big Noise from Winnetka'. Its only surprise is that it was written by the acerbic novelist Nathanael West during his time as an ill-paid Hollywood hack.
w Nathanael West; special dialogue for Bob Crosby by Helen Phillips, Bernard Dougall
d Leslie Goodwins ph Jack Mackenzie ad Van Nest Polglase ed Desmond Marquette
☆ Bob Crosby, Jean Rogers, Elisabeth Risdon, Joseph Buloff, Joyce Compton, Bob Crosby's Orchestra featuring The Bobcats

Let's Make Up: see *Lilacs in the Spring*

Let's Scare Jessica to Death

US 1971 89m colour
Paramount/Jessica Co (Charles B. Moss Jnr)

Back home after a nervous breakdown, our heroine is troubled by voices and visions, not to mention an ambulant corpse and a vampire or two.
Competent screamie.
w Norman Jonas, Ralph Rose d John Hancock
ph Bob Baldwin m Orville Stoeber
☆ Zohra Lampert, Barton Heyman, Kevin O'Connor

Let's Spend the Night Together

US 1982 94m Technicolor
Embassy (Ronald L. Schwary)

A concert film shot on the Rolling Stones' tour of America in 1981, including performances from the Sun Devil Stadium in Tempe, Arizona and the Brendan Byrne Arena in Rutherford, New Jersey.
Fan material, providing nothing of backstage interest, and performances, in the large and impersonal arenas favoured by rock stars, which seem strictly by rote despite their energy.
d Hal Ashby ph Caleb Deschanel, Gerald Feil m/ly Mick Jagger, Keith Richards and others ed Lisa Day, Sonya Sones, Lorinda Hollingshead
♪ Songs performed include 'All Down the Line', 'Beast of Burden', 'Black Limousine', 'Brown Sugar', 'Hang Fire', 'Honky Tonk Woman', 'Jumpin' Jack Flash', 'Let It Bleed', 'Let's Spend the Night Together', 'Satisfaction', 'Under My Thumb' and 'You Can't Always Get What You Want'.

Let's Try Again

US 1934 64m bw
RKO

GB title: *The Marriage Symphony*
A doctor and his wife drift apart, then get back together again.
Formula high-life drama without much conviction.
w Worthington Miner, Allan Scott play Vincent Lawrence d Worthington Miner

☆ Diana Wynyard, Clive Brook, Irene Hervey, Helen Vinson
'Talky, tedious and far from original: where the cast doesn't mean anything the picture will have plenty of worries.' – *Variety*

The Letter *

US 1929 61m bw
Paramount

Early talkie version of a solid piece of theatre.
See below.
play W. Somerset Maugham story W. Somerset Maugham d Jean de Limur
☆ Jeanne Eagels, O. P. Heggie, Reginald Owen, Herbert Marshall, Irene Browne
♟ Jeanne Eagels

'With all my heart, I still love the man I killed!'

The Letter ****

US 1940 95m bw
Warner (Robert Lord)

A rubber plantation owner's wife kills a man in what seems to have been self-defence; but a letter from her proves it to have been a crime of passion, and becomes an instrument of blackmail.
Excellent performances and presentation make this the closest approximation on film to reading a Maugham story of the Far East, though censorship forced the addition of an infuriating moral ending.
w Howard Koch story W. Somerset Maugham d William Wyler ph Tony Gaudio m Max Steiner ed Warren Low
☆ Bette Davis, Herbert Marshall, James Stephenson, Sen Yung, Frieda Inescort, Gale Sondergaard, Bruce Lester, Tetsu Komai
'The writing is taut and spare throughout … the unravelling of Maugham's story is masterly and the presentation visual and cinematic … the audience at the trade show did not move a finger.' – *James Agate*
† Herbert Marshall played the lover in the first version and the husband in the second.
♟ best picture; William Wyler; Tony Gaudio; Max Steiner; Bette Davis; James Stephenson; Warren Low

A Letter for Evie

US 1945 88m bw
William H. Wright/MGM

A girl starts confusion when she writes a letter to an unknown soldier; a wimp writes back but sends his he-man buddy's photograph.
Predictable comedy with longueurs.
w De Vallon Scott, Alan Friedman d Jules Dassin
☆ Marsha Hunt, John Carroll, Hume Cronyn, Spring Byington, Pamela Britton, Norman Lloyd

'The story that will live … as long as there is love!'

Letter from an Unknown Woman ***

US 1948 89m bw
Universal/Rampart (John Houseman)

A woman wastes her life in unrequited love for a rakish pianist.
Superior 'woman's picture' which gave its director his best chance in America to recreate his beloved Vienna of long ago. Hollywood production magic at its best.
w Howard Koch novel Stefan Zweig d Max Ophuls ph Franz Planer m Daniele Amfitheatrof ad Alexander Golitzen
☆ Joan Fontaine, Louis Jourdan, Mady Christians, Art Smith, Marcel Journet
'A film full of snow, sleigh bells, lights gleaming in ornamental gardens and trysts at night.' – *Charles Higham, 1972*
'It is fascinating to watch the sure deft means by which Ophuls sidetracks seemingly inevitable clichés and holds on to a shadowy, tender mood, half buried in the past. Here is a fragile filmic charm that is not often or easily accomplished.' – *Richard Winnington*
'Film narrative of a most skilled order.' – *William Whitebait*
'Probably the toniest "woman's picture" ever made.' – *Pauline Kael, 70s*

Letter of Introduction *

US 1938 100m bw
Universal (John M. Stahl)

A young actress is encouraged by an ageing star whom she does not know is her father.
Commercial melodrama with luxury trimmings, all very neatly packaged.

w Sheridan Gibney, Leonard Spigelgass d John M. Stahl ph Karl Freund m Charles Previn
☆ Adolphe Menjou, Andrea Leeds, Edgar Bergen and Charlie McCarthy, George Murphy, Eve Arden, Rita Johnson, Ernest Cossart, Ann Sheridan
'Headed for big business everywhere.' – *Variety*

A Letter to Brezhnev **

GB 1985 95m colour
Yeardream/Film Four International/Palace Productions (Janet Goddard)

Two girls from Liverpool spend a busy night with Russian sailors; when one of them receives no subsequent letters, she writes to Brezhnev and is invited to Moscow.
Vivid it is, but also raucous and seedy until true love enters as a redeeming factor. The critics loved it, thinking it about unemployment and urban decline; it certainly paints a low picture of Liverpool.
w Frank Clarke d Chris Bernard ph Bruce McGowan m Alan Gill ed Lesley Walker
☆ Alfred Molina, Peter Firth, Margi Clarke, Tracy Lea, Alexandra Pigg
'Fast-moving, funny, entertaining and poignant … in short how to make a British film.' – *Jill Forbes, MFB*

'A peek into the other woman's male!'

A Letter to Three Wives **

US 1949 102m bw
TCF (Sol C. Siegel)

Three wives on a picnic receive word from a friend that she has run off with one of their husbands.
Amusing short-story compendium which seemed more revelatory at the time than it does now, and paved the way for its writer-director's heyday.
wd Joseph L. Mankiewicz novel John Klempner
ph Arthur Miller m Alfred Newman
☆ Jeanne Crain, Ann Sothern, Linda Darnell, Jeffrey Lynn, Kirk Douglas, Paul Douglas, Barbara Lawrence, Connie Gilchrist, Florence Bates, Hobart Cavanaugh, and the voice of Celeste Holm
'A mere shadow of those acid Hollywood comedies of the thirties … over-written and under-directed … but it has a supply of ironies and makes a certain alkaline comment on present-day American customs and manners.' – *Richard Winnington*
'Replete with sharp dialogue. He aims barbed darts at the country's favourite institutions, and makes them score with telling effect.' – *Variety*
♟ Joseph L. Mankiewicz (as writer); Joseph L. Mankiewicz (as director)
♟ best picture

Letters from a Dead Man *

USSR 1986 87m colour/bw
Artificial Eye/Lenfilm/Sovexportfilm

original title: *Pisma Myortvovo Cheloveka*
After a nuclear holocaust, a scientist composes letters to his missing son while trying to rescue young survivors thrown out of the central shelter.
Grim and powerful for the most part, although not always easy to watch.
w Konstantin Lopushansky, Vyacheslav Rybakov, Boris Strugatsky d Konstantin Lopushansky
ph Nikolai Pokoptsev m Alexander Zhurbin, Faure ad Yelema Amshinskaya, Viktor Ivanov
☆ Rolan Bykov, I. Ryklin, V. Mikailov, A. Sabinin, V. Lobanov, N. Gryakalova, V. Mayorova, V. Dvorzhetski

Letty Lynton

US 1932 84m bw
MGM

When one lover is murdered, Letty turns to another to prove her innocent.
Bad girl drama which established the star's box-office appeal.
w John Meehan and Wanda Tuchock d Clarence Brown
☆ Joan Crawford, Robert Montgomery, Nils Asther, May Robson, Lewis Stone
'Big grosses are written all over this one.' – *Variety*

Letyat Zhuravli: see *The Cranes are Flying*

Der Letzte Mann: see *The Last Laugh*

Leviathan

US/Italy 1989 98m Technicolor
Fox/Gordon Company/Filmauro (Luigi de Laurentiis,
Aurelio de Laurentiis)

Deep sea miners are the victims of a monstrous
genetic experiment gone wrong.
*An underwater variation on Alien, lacking originality
and suspense.*
w David Peoples, Jeb Stuart d George P.
Cosmatos ph Alex Thomson m Jerry Goldsmith
pd Ron Cobb ed Roberto Silvi, John F. Burnett
sp Perpetual Motion Pictures, Stan Winston
Studios
☆ Peter Weller, Richard Crenna, Amanda Pays,
Daniel Stern, Ernie Hudson, Michael Carmine,
Meg Foster, Lisa Eilbacher, Hector Elizondo
  'Given the familiarity of it all, Leviathan is at
  least an enjoyable rip-off.' – MFB

Les Lèvres Rouges: see *Daughters of Darkness*

Lewis & Clark & George

US 1997 84m CFI color
Davis/Dark Matter (J. Todd Harris, Dan Gunther)

Two escaped convicts team up with a cigar-
smoking woman to search for a gold mine.
*A tongue-in-cheek, offbeat cowboy road movie, a tale
of double- and triple-cross, which rounds up the usual
situations and violently recycles them.*
wd Rod McCall ph Michael Mayers m Ben
Vaughn pd John Huke ed Ed Marx
☆ Rose McGowan, Salvator Xuereb, Dan
Gunther, Art LaFleur, James Brolin, Paul Bartel
  'This self-consciously quirky offering is
  unashamed of regurgitating most of the genre's
  clichés.' – Independent

La Ley del Deseo: see *Law of Desire*

Les Liaisons Dangereuses *

France 1959 106m bw
Films Marceau

Valmont and his wife compare notes on each
other's affairs.
Showy modernization of a notorious minor classic.
w Roger Vailland, Roger Vadim, Claude Brulé
novel Choderlos de Laclos d Roger Vadim
ph Marcel Grignon m Jack Murray, Thelonius
Monk
☆ Gérard Philipe, Jeanne Moreau, Annette
Vadim, Jeanne Valerie, Simone Renant, Jean-Louis
Trintignant
  'A woman's picture par excellence.' – John
  Russell Taylor, MFB

Lianlian Feng Chen: see *Dust in the Wind*

Lianna

US 1983 112m DuArt
Winwood

A wife and mother becomes a lesbian.
*That's all there is, folks, not much in the way of plot,
and barely enough for a TV movie; but some good
observation and acting come through.*
ph Austin de Besche m Mason Daring
wd/ed John Sayles
☆ Linda Griffiths, Jane Hallaren, Jon de Vries, Jo
Henderson

'You come looking, you might not like what you
find.'

Liar *

US 1997 102m Foto-Kem 'Scope
First Independent/MDP (Peter Glatzer)

aka: Deceiver
A wealthy alcoholic playboy investigates the cops
who questioned him over the murder of a
prostitute.
*Tricksy, over-elaborate thriller, intent on confusing its
audience; but its makers show promise of better things
to come.*
wd Jonas and Joshua Pate ph Bill Butler m Harry
Gregson-Williams pd John Kretschmer ed Dan
Lebental
☆ Tim Roth, Chris Penn, Michael Rooker, Renee
Zellweger, Ellen Burstyn, Rosanna Arquette
  'Flashy exercise in style and obfuscation.' –
  Variety

'Trust Me.'

Liar, Liar

US 1997 87m DeLuxe
Universal/Imagine (Brian Grazer)

A young boy's wish becomes true – and his father,
an unscrupulous lawyer, is forced to tell the truth
for 24 hours.
*A comedy that merges Carrey's now familiar frenetic
mugging with some gruesome sentimentality; soft-
centred slapstick is not a pretty sight.*
w Paul Guay, Stephen Mazur d Tom Shadyac
ph Russell Boyd m John Debney pd Linda de
Scenna ed Don Zimmerman
☆ Jim Carrey, Maura Tierney, Jennifer Tilly,
Swoosie Kurtz, Amanda Donohoe, Cary Elwes
  'Isn't designed to win Carrey any converts, but is
  shrewdly calculated to include enough lightly
  lewd humor to keep adults amused while the kids
  enjoy the slapstick shenanigans.' – Todd
  McCarthy, Variety
† A similar notion was used in the Bob Hope
comedy Nothing but the Truth (qv).

Libel *

GB 1959 100m bw
MGM/Comet (Anatole de Grunwald)

An ex-POW baronet is accused of being an
impostor.
*Old-fashioned courtroom spellbinder, quite adequately
done though occasionally creaky.*
w Anatole de Grunwald, Karl Tunberg
play Edward Wooll d Anthony Asquith
ph Robert Krasker m Benjamin Frankel ad Paul
Sheriff
☆ Dirk Bogarde, Olivia de Havilland, Paul
Massie, Wilfrid Hyde-White, Robert Morley,
Anthony Dawson, Richard Wattis, Martin Miller,
Millicent Martin

Libeled Lady **

US 1936 98m bw
MGM (Lawrence Weingarten)

An heiress sues a newspaper, and the editor hires a
friend to compromise her.
*Lively four-star romantic comedy which sums up its era
as well as any.*
w Maurine Watkins, Howard Emmett Rogers,
George Oppenheimer d Jack Conway ph Norbert
Brodine m William Axt
☆ Jean Harlow, Myrna Loy, Spencer Tracy, William
Powell, Walter Connolly, Charley Grapewin, Cora
Witherspoon, E. E. Clive, Charles Trowbridge
  'Handsomely mounted and produced, lavishly
  costumed, cleverly written and artfully directed,
  Libeled Lady is entirely worthy of the noble
  comedians who head its cast.' – Bland Johaneson,
  New York Daily Mirror
† Remade as Easy to Wed (qv); central situation
borrowed for Man's Favorite Sport (qv).
ⵣ best picture

'All she wanted was her black man's money and her
white man's love!'

The Liberation of L. B. Jones *

US 1970 102m Technicolor
Columbia/Liberation Co (Ronald Lubin)

Racial murder is the result when a black
undertaker wants a divorce in a small Tennessee
town.
*Violent, pointless but well-made melodrama which
really does not take matters much further than
Intruder in the Dust.*
w Stirling Silliphant, Jesse Hill Ford, from Ford's
novel d William Wyler ph Robert Surtees
m Elmer Bernstein
☆ Lee J. Cobb, Anthony Zerbe, Roscoe Lee
Browne, Lola Falana, Lee Majors, Barbara Hershey,
Yaphet Kotto, Arch Johnson, Chill Wills
  'With its genuinely ferocious climax it adds up to
  probably the most powerful, if not the most
  sophisticated, race-war film the commercial
  studios have yet produced.' – Nigel Andrews

Liberty **

US 1929 20m bw silent
Hal Roach

Two convicts escape and have adventures high on
a construction site.
*Amusing gags are succeeded by breathtaking thrills in
the Harold Lloyd style.*

w Leo McCarey, H. M. Walker d Leo McCarey
ph George Stevens ed Richard Currier, William
Terhune
☆ Stan Laurel, Oliver Hardy, James Finlayson,
Jean Harlow, Tom Kennedy
† Lloyd French and James Horne also directed
some sequences.

Licence to Kill *

US 1989 133m Technicolor Panavision
UIP/United Artists/Danjaq (Albert R. Broccoli, Michael
G. Wilson)

James Bond goes after a drug dealer who has
injured his best friend.
*The mixture is much as usual, though the action is
more violent and Bond has become more of a free
agent.*
w Michael G. Wilson, Richard Maibaum d John
Glen ph Alec Mills m Michael Kamen pd Peter
Lamont ed John Grover
☆ Timothy Dalton, Carey Lowell, Robert Davi,
Talisa Soto, Anthony Zerbe, Frank McRae, Everett
McGill, Wayne Newton, Benicio del Toro

License to Drive

US 1988 88m DeLuxe
TCF/Davis/Licht/Mueller

A 16-year-old, unable to tell his friends that he has
failed his driving test, borrows his grandfather's car
for a date with the girlfriend of his dreams.
*Heavy-handed and tiresome teenage farce; it works on
a mechanical level, managing to maintain an
accelerating momentum of incident, but rarely
produces even a smile.*
w Neil Tolkin d Greg Beeman ph Bruce Surtees
m Jay Ferguson pd Lawrence G. Paull ed Wendy
Greene Bricmont
☆ Corey Haim, Corey Feldman, Carol Kane,
Richard Masur, Heather Graham, Michael
Manasseri, Harvey Miller, M. A. Nickles, Nina
Siemaszko

Licensed to Kill

GB 1965 97m Eastmancolor
Alistair Films (Estelle E. Richmond)
US title: The Second Best Secret Agent in the Whole
Wide World

The Foreign Office calls in agent Charles Vine to
protect a top international scientist.
*Cheap copy of James Bond which wins no laurels but
produces a few efficient routine thrills.*
w Howard Griffiths, Lindsay Shonteff d Lindsay
Shonteff ph Terry Maher m Bertram Chappell
☆ Tom Adams, Veronica Hurst, Karel Stepanek,
Felix Felton, Peter Bull

The Lie: see *Mensonge*

Eine Liebe in Deutschland: see *A Love in
Germany*

Liebelei *

Austria 1932 85m bw
Fred Lissa

A young army officer falls in love; but he is killed
in a duel and his girl commits suicide.
*Semi-classic romantic novelette, like a warm-up for
Letter from an Unknown Woman.*
w Hans Wilhelm, Kurt Alexander story Arthur
Schnitzler d Max Ophuls ph Franz Planer
m Theo Macheber
☆ Magda Schneider, Wolfgang Liebeneiner, Luise
Ullrich, Willy Eichberger, Gustaf Gruendgens,
Paul Hoerbiger
† A revised French version played as Une Histoire
d'Amour. The story had previously been shot under
the same title in Germany in 1927; and in the
sixties Romy Schneider and Alain Delon appeared
in a French remake called Christine.

Liebestraum

US 1991 113m DuArt
UIP/MGM/Initial (Eric Fellner)

An architectural writer, returning home to visit his
dying mother, unwittingly uncovers her violent
past which has repercussions in the present.
*Involved thriller that leaves a lot of questions
unanswered.*
wd Mike Figgis ph Juan Ruiz Anchia m Mike
Figgis pd Waldemar Kalinowski ed Martin
Hunter

☆ Kevin Anderson, Pamela Gidley, Bill Pullman,
Kim Novak, Graham Beckel, Zach Grenier,
Thomas Kopache
  'Seldom has the gulf between artistic intentions
  and end result yawned so protractedly.' – Empire
† A central scene, set in a brothel and lasting
eleven minutes, was cut from the film before its
release in America.

Lien-lien feng-ch'en: see *Dust in the Wind*

Les Liens du Sang: see *Blood Relatives*

Lies My Father Told Me

Canada 1975 102m colour
Columbia/Pentimento/Pentacle (Anthony Bedrich,
Harry Gulkin)

Adventures of a poor Jewish boy and his
grandfather in Montreal in the twenties.
*Effectively if rather dishonestly sentimental, this is the
kind of family picture for which critics are always
clamouring but which few people in the seventies would
pay to see.*
w Ted Allan book Ted Allan d Jan Kadar
ph Paul Van der Linden m Sol Kaplan
☆ Yossi Yadin, Len Birman, Marilyn Lightstone,
Jeffrey Lynas
  'Sentiment by numbers … a lovable child
  awakening to discovery of the world; a lovable,
  whimsical old grandfather; a lovable, ne'er-do-
  well father; a lovable, long-suffering mother; a
  lovable, broken-down horse; lovable neighbours;
  a lovable whore across the way. It all strives so
  hard to be lovable that you want to scream.' –
  David Robinson, The Times
† A British low-budget film was made from the
same material in 1960, changing the venue to
Ireland and the race to Irish.
ⵣ Ted Allan

The Lieutenant Wore Skirts

US 1955 99m Eastmancolor Cinemascope
TCF (Buddy Adler)

When a TV writer joins the service, his wife enlists
to be near him; but he is rejected on medical
grounds.
*Raucous, tasteless farce which tries far too hard to raise
laughs.*
w Albert Beich, Frank Tashlin d Frank Tashlin
ph Leo Tover m Cyril Mockridge
☆ Tom Ewell, Sheree North, Rita Moreno, Rick
Jason, Les Tremayne

'Share It With Someone You Love.'

Life *

US 1999 109m DeLuxe
Universal/Imagine (Brian Grazer, Eddie Murphy)

A conman and a bank clerk, both framed for
murder, spend a lifetime together in prison.
*Amiable prison variation on The Odd Couple, which
gets by on the interplay between its two stars, though
reality never intrudes.*
w Robert Ramsey, Matthew Stone d Ted Demme
ph Geoffrey Simpson m Wyclef Jean pd Dan
Bishop ed Jeffrey Wolf sp make-up fx: Rick Baker
cos Lucy Corrigan
☆ Eddie Murphy, Martin Lawrence, Obba
Babatunde, Ned Beatty, Bernie Mac, Miguel A.
Nunez Jnr, Clarence Williams III, Bokeem
Woodbine, Michael 'Bear' Taliferro, Barry Shabaka
Henley, R. Lee Ermey, Nick Cassavetes, Noah
Emmerich, Rick James
  'Careens from decade to decade, and from
  relative dramatic realism to frequent hilarity, in
  often-winning fashion.' – Todd McCarthy, Variety
  'It's unfunny, it lacks excitement, tension or
  even a sense of oppression, and it never involves
  us for a moment with its characters.' – Philip
  Kemp, Sight and Sound
ⵣ make-up (Rick Baker)

Life After Dark: see *Girls in the Night*

The Life and Death of a Hollywood
Extra *

US 1927 11m bw silent
(Robert Florey and Slavko Vorkapich)

A nonentity arrives in Hollywood and dreams of
becoming a star.
*Avant-garde short, still interesting if less revolutionary
than it seemed at the time.*

---

wd Robert Florey and Slavko Vorkapich · **ph** Slavko Vorkapich and Gregg Toland · **ad/ed** Slavko Vorkapich

☆ Jules Raucort, Georges Voya

The Life and Death of Colonel Blimp ***

GB 1943 163m Technicolor
GFD/Archers (Michael Powell, Emeric Pressburger)
🔲 🟦 ⊛
US title: *Colonel Blimp*
A British soldier survives three wars and falls in love with three women.
Not the Blimp of the cartoon strip, but a sympathetic figure in a warm, consistently interesting if idiosyncratic love story against a background of war. The Archers as usual provide a sympathetic German lead (friend of the hero); quite a coup in wartime.
wd Michael Powell, Emeric Pressburger **ph** Georges Perinal **m** Allan Gray **ad** Alfred Junge
☆ Roger Livesey, Anton Walbrook, Deborah Kerr, Roland Culver, James McKechnie, Albert Lieven, Arthur Wontner, A. E. Matthews, David Hutcheson, Ursula Jeans, John Laurie, Harry Welchman
'There is nothing brilliant about the picture, but it is perceptive, witty and sweet-tempered.' – *James Agee*
'No one else has so well captured English romanticism banked down beneath emotional reticence.' – *Time Out, 1985*

The Life and Extraordinary Adventures of Private Ivan Chonkin *

GB/France/Italy/Czechoslovakia/Russia 1994
111m colour
Portbello/MK2/Canal/La Sept/CNC/Channel 4/Fandango/Domenico Procacci/Studio 89/Studio Trite (Eric Abraham)
An army private, sent to an isolated village to guard a plane crash, begins an affair with the local postmistress and attracts the attention of the secret police.
Interesting, slightly ramshackle comedy, championing simple virtues in the face of repressive bureaucracy.
w Zdenek Sverák, Vladimir Voinovich *novel* Vladimir Voinovich **d** Jiri Menzel **ph** Jaromir Sofr **m** Jiri Sust **pd** Milan Bycek **ed** Jiri Brozek, Elisabeth Guido
☆ Gennadiy Nazarov, Zoya Buryak, Vladimir Ilyin, Valeriy Dubrovin, Alexei Zharkov, Zinovil Gerdt
† Vladimir Voinovich turned his original film script, written in the mid-60s, into a novel which was banned in the Soviet Union and published in Paris; it led to his exile in 1980, after he lost his citizenship, which was not restored to him until 1990.

Life and Nothing But **

France 1989 134m colour Panavision
Artificial Eye/Hachette Première et Cie/AB Films/Little Bear/A2 (René Cleitman)
🔲 🟦 ⊛ ♫
original title: *La Vie Et Rien D'Autre*
Two women, one searching for her missing husband, the other for her lover among the patients at a military hospital, discover that they are looking for the same man.
Complex and affecting movie of love and disillusion, of individual tragedy and national pride, set at the end of the First World War.
w Jean Cosmos, Bertrand Tavernier **d** Bertrand Tavernier **ph** Bruno de Keyzer **m** Oswald d'Andrea **pd** Guy-Claude François **ed** Armand Psenny
☆ Philippe Noiret, Sabine Azéma, Pascale Vignal, Maurice Barrier, François Perrot, Jean-Pol Dubois, Daniel Russo, Michel Duchaussoy, Arlette Gilbert
🎬 best foreign picture

'I want peace – and I don't care who I kill to get it!'
The Life and Times of Judge Roy Bean *

US 1972 124m Technicolor Panavision
National General/First Artists (John Foreman)
🔲 ⊛
A fantasia on the famous outlaw judge of the old west.
Sporadically entertaining but schematically messy mixture of burlesqued folklore and violent action, not in the same league as Butch Cassidy.
w John Milius **d** John Huston **ph** Richard Moore **m** Maurice Jarre
☆ Paul Newman, Ava Gardner, Jacqueline Bisset, Tab Hunter, Stacy Keach, Roddy McDowall, Anthony Perkins, John Huston

♫ song 'Marmalade, Molasses and Honey' (**m**Maurice Jarre, **ly**A. and M. Bergman)

Life at the Top *

GB 1965 117m bw
Columbia/Romulus (James Woolf)
Ten years after marrying into money, Joe Lampton is dissatisfied, and he and his wife both have affairs.
Rough-talking but basically predictable and old-fashioned sequel to Room at the Top, a bit compromised by having to reflect the sixties London scene; the early Yorkshire sequences are the best.
w Mordecai Richler **d** Ted Kotcheff **ph** Oswald Morris **m** Richard Addinsell
☆ Laurence Harvey, Jean Simmons, Honor Blackman, Michael Craig, Donald Wolfit, Margaret Johnston, Allan Cuthbertson, Ambrosine Philpotts, Robert Morley, Nigel Davenport, George A. Cooper
'Another thoroughly mean-spirited film of a kind which has been taking root in the British cinema.' – *Tom Milne*
† The character of Joe Lampton was later used in a long-running TV series called *Man at the Top*, which sprouted a film of its own under that title.

Life Begins

US 1932 72m bw
Warner (Ray Griffith)
GB title: *Dream of Life*
A night in a maternity hospital.
Multi-melodrama later remade as A Child Is Born. Passable.
w Earl Baldwin *play* Mary McDougal Axelson **d** James Flood **ph** James Van Trees
☆ Loretta Young, Eric Linden, Aline MacMahon, Preston Foster, Glenda Farrell, Frank McHugh, Clara Blandick, Elizabeth Patterson, Gilbert Roland
'Splendid women's picture promising at least solid matinée business.' – *Variety*

Life Begins at 40

US 1935 85m bw
TCF (Sol M. Wurtzel)
A small-town editor, whose paper is repossessed by the bank manager, starts a rival publication and investigates the conviction for robbery of a bank clerk.
Mildly entertaining rustic humour, aimed at giving Rogers the opportunity to spout his cracker-barrel philosophy.
w Lamar Trotti, Robert Quillen *book* Walter B. Pitkin **d** George Marshall **ph** Harry Jackson **md** Samuel Kaylin **ad** Duncan Cramer, Albert Hogsett
☆ Will Rogers, Richard Cromwell, George Barbier, Rochelle Hudson, Jane Darwell, Slim Summerville, Sterling Holloway

Life Begins at Eight-Thirty *

US 1942 85m bw
TCF (Nunnally Johnson)
GB title: *The Light of Heart*
A distinguished actor is reduced through drink to being a street corner Santa Claus.
Diluted and sentimentalized version of an agreeable play.
w Nunnally Johnson *play* The Light of Heart by Emlyn Williams **d** Irving Pichel **ph** Edward Cronjager **m** Alfred Newman
☆ Monty Woolley, Ida Lupino, Cornel Wilde, Sara Allgood, Melville Cooper, J. Edward Bromberg

Life Begins in College *

US 1937 80m bw
TCF
GB title: *The Joy Parade*
Three zanies save the honour of the college football team.
Another of the myriad college football stories of the thirties, but this time enlivened by comedians in the leads.
w Karl Tunberg, Don Ettlinger **d** William A. Seiter
☆ The Ritz Brothers, Joan Davis, Tony Martin, Gloria Stuart, Fred Stone, Nat Pendleton
'The Ritzes soar to stardom; a box office touchdown.' – *Variety*

Life Dances On: see *Un Carnet de Bal*

Life for Ruth *

GB 1962 91m bw
Rank/Allied Film Makers (Michael Relph, Basil Dearden)
US title: *Condemned to Life*
A little girl dies because her parents' religion forbids blood transfusions.
Dramatized from the headlines, this little case history is small beer as film-making, and not exactly entertainment, but absorbing as a comment on human behaviour.
w Janet Green, John McCormick **d** Basil Dearden **ph** Otto Heller **m** William Alwyn **md** Muir Mathieson
☆ Michael Craig, Patrick McGoohan, Janet Munro, Paul Rogers, Megs Jenkins, Frank Finlay, Maureen Pryor

Life in Danger

GB 1959 63m bw
Butchers/Parroch (Jack Parsons)
Angry villagers hunt for a murderer who has escaped from a nearby mental hospital.
Competent thriller with a twist in its tail.
w Malcolm Hulke, Eric Paice **d** Terry Bishop **ph** Peter Hennessy **m** William Davies **ad** Peter Proud **ed** John Trumper
☆ Derren Nesbitt, Julie Hopkins, Howard Marion Crawford, Victor Brooks, Jack Allen, Christopher Witty, Carmel McSharry, Bruce Seton

Life in Emergency Ward 10

GB 1958 84m bw
Eros Films (Ted Lloyd)
A new consultant at the hospital causes controversy by introducing an experimental modification to heart surgery techniques and becoming involved with a colleague's wife.
A spin-off from a popular TV series, though still looking as if it were made for the small screen and scripted as a series of anecdotal episodes that mix comedy and sentimentality in predictable ways.
w Tessa Diamond, Hazel Adair **d** Robert Day **ph** Geoffrey Faithfull **m** Philip Green **ad** George Beech **ed** Lito Carruthers
☆ Michael Craig, Wilfrid Hyde-White, Dorothy Alison, Glyn Owen, Charles Tingwell, Frederick Bartman, Rosemary Miller, Joan Sims

A Life in the Balance *

US 1954 75m bw
TCF/Panoramic (Leonard Goldstein)
A Mexican widower springs into action when his young son is kidnapped by a murderer.
Taut little melodrama taking place during one night in Mexico City; made with vigour on a low budget.
w Robert Presnell Jnr, Leo Townsend *d* Harry Horner **ph** J. Gomez Urquiza **m** Raul Lavista
☆ Ricardo Montalban, Anne Bancroft, Lee Marvin

Life Is a Bed of Roses *

France 1983 111m Eastmancolor
Philippe Dusart/Soprofilms/Films A2/Fideline/Ariane/Filmedis/Ministry of Culture (Philippe Dusart)
original title: *La Vie est un Roman*
A count opens a temple of happiness and starts to re-educate his friends.
Dense fantasy which never really explains itself but provides pleasant moments along the way.
w Jean Gruault **d** Alain Resnais **ph** Bruno Nuytten **m** M. Philippe-Gerard
☆ Vittorio Gassman, Ruggero Raimondi, Geraldine Chaplin, Fanny Ardant, Pierre Arditi

Life Is a Circus

🎬🎬 GB 1958 84m bw
Vale Film (M. Smedley Aston)
An odd-job man in a rundown circus finds Aladdin's lamp.
Feeble comedy by the Crazy Gang in a state of geriatric disrepair, simply going through the motions, which is an understandable reaction given the script. Chesney Allen makes a brief appearance to sing 'Underneath the Arches' with his old partner, Bud Flanagan.
wd Val Guest **ph** Arthur Graham **m** Philip Green **ad** Tony Masters **ed** Bill Lenny
☆ Bud Flanagan, Jimmy Nervo, Teddy Knox, Cahrlie Naughton, Jimmy Gold, Monsewer Eddie Gray, Shirley Eaton, Michael Holliday, Joseph Tomelty, Lionel Jeffries

Life Is a Long Quiet River: see *La Vie Est un Long Fleuve Tranquille*

'The unforgettable film that proves love, family and imagination conquer all.'
Life Is Beautiful ***

Italy 1997 122m colour
Buena Vista/Melampo (Elda Ferri, Gianluigi Braschi)
🔲 🟦 ⊛
original title: *La Vita è Bella*
During the Second World War, a Jewish bookshop owner, sent with his family to a concentration camp, protects his young son by pretending that they are in a holiday camp.
A bold and brave film, and one well worth seeing, despite some rather contrived slapstick in the early sequences; yet, in the end, clowning does not merely seem an inappropriate response to the realities of a concentration camp, but the wrong response.
w Vincenzo Cerami, Roberto Benigni **d** Roberto Benigni **ph** Tonino Delli Colli **m** Nicola Piovani **pd** Danilo Donati **ed** Simona Paggi
☆ Roberto Benigni, Nicoletta Braschi, Giustino Durano, Sergio Bustric, Marisa Paredes, Horst Buchholz, Lydia Alfonsi, Giuliana Lojodice, Giorgio Cantarini
'Sluggish, uneven and lacking in rhythm, it nonetheless has enough pathos and winning humor to ensure national success.' – *David Rooney, Variety*
'What he has made is not, in fact, a comedy about the Holocaust – a project that would have required a sinewy nerve and a black spluttering wit. He has made an allegory about comedy's redemptive power – a softer, more fogbound beast.' – *Tom Shone, Sunday Times*
'One of the most unconvincing and self-congratulatory movies ever made.' – *David Denby, New Yorker*
† The film took in excess of $40m at the US box-office, more than any other foreign-language film, and also grossed more than $152m around the world.
†† Benigni's concentration-camp number, 7397, was chosen as a tribute to Charlie Chaplin, who wore the same number in *The Great Dictator*.
🎬 foreign-language film; Roberto Benigni (actor); Nicola Piovani
🎬 best picture; Roberto Benigni (director); Vincenzo Cerami, Roberto Benigni (script); Simona Paggi
🎬 Roberto Benigni (actor)

Life Is Cheap ... But Toilet Paper Is Expensive *

US 1990 88m colour
ICA/Forever Profit Investments/Far East Stars (Winnie Fredriksz)
🟦 ⊛
Travelling from San Francisco to Hong Kong to deliver a gift to a local gangster, an Asian-American is plunged into a society he fails to understand and circumstances that lead to his humiliation.
Inventive, low-budget thriller of cultural bewilderment, mixed in with documentary-style monologues from the locals.
w Spencer Nakasako *story* Amir Mokri, Spencer Nakasako, Wayne Wang **d** Wayne Wang **ph** Amir Mokri **m** Mark Adler **ad** Colette Koo **ed** Chris Sanderson, Sandy Nervig
☆ Chan Kim Wan, Spencer Nakasako, Victor Wong, Cheng Kwan Min, Cora Miao, Lam Chung
'Audaciously stylish and visually mesmerizing ... Wayne Wang's take on the conundrum of Chinese identity has all the narrative logic of a tilted pinball machine.' – *Variety*

Life Is Sweet

GB 1990 103m Metrocolor
Palace/Thin Man/Film Four International/British Screen (Simon Channing-Williams)
🔲 🟦 ⊛
An unexceptional couple and their grown-up children survive minor disasters.
Mildly amusing suburban comedy, though the actors' attitude to their characters ranges from condescension to caricature.
wd Mike Leigh **ph** Dick Pope **m** Rachel Portman **pd** Alison Chitty **ed** Jon Gregory
☆ Alison Steadman, Jim Broadbent, Claire Skinner, Jane Horrocks, Stephen Rea, Timothy Spall

A Life Less Ordinary *
GB   1997   103m   Rank Colour
Polygram/Figment (Andrew Macdonald)
👪 ▦ ⌕ ⓦ ⊚ 🎧

Two angels are given the task of making a wealthy, spoilt young woman and a janitor fall in love.
A surreal romantic comedy where fantasy and reality fail to cohere into a satisfactory whole.
w John Hodge d Danny Boyle ph Brian Tufano m David Arnold pd Kave Quinn ed Masahiro Hirakubo
☆ Ewan McGregor, Cameron Diaz, Holly Hunter, Delroy Lindo, Ian Holm, Ian McNeice, Stanley Tucci, Dan Hedaya, Maury Chaykin
'A pleasant enough ride in parts, but has too many half-realised ideas in the script to satisfy at any emotional level.' – Derek Elley, *Variety*
† The film cost $12m and took $4.3m at the US box-office.

The Life of Adolf Hitler *
West Germany   1961   102m   bw
Real Film
A documentary culled from newsreel material; somehow less arresting than one would have hoped, though undoubtedly worthy.
w Helga Koppel d Paul Rotha ed Paul Rotha

The Life of Brian: see Monty Python's Life of Brian

'He plucked from the gutter a faded rose and made an immortal masterpiece!'
The Life of Emile Zola ***
US   1937   116m   bw
Warner (Henry Blanke)
▦ ⌕ ⓦ

The French writer intervenes in the case of Alfred Dreyfus, condemned unjustly to Devil's Island.
The box-office success of this solidly-carpentered piece of Hollywood history was compounded in equal parts of star power and the sheer novelty of having such a thing turn up at the local Odeon.
w Norman Reilly Raine story Heinz Herald and Geza Herczeg d William Dieterle ph Tony Gaudio m Max Steiner ad Anton Grot
☆ Paul Muni, Joseph Schildkraut, Gale Sondergaard, Gloria Holden, Donald Crisp, Erin O'Brien Moore, John Litel, Henry O'Neill, Morris Carnovsky, Ralph Morgan, Louis Calhern, Robert Barrat, Vladimir Sokoloff, Harry Davenport, Robert Warwick and also Walter Kingsford
'Destined to box office approval of the most substantial character. It is finely made and merits high rating as cinema art and significant recognition as major showmanship.' – *Variety*
'Along with Louis Pasteur, it ought to start a new category – the Warner crusading films, costume division.' – *Otis Ferguson*
'A grave story told with great dignity and superbly played and produced.' – *Pare Lorentz*
'One of the fine ones which begin as a film and end as an experience.' – *John Grierson*
'Rich, dignified, honest and strong, it is at once the finest historical film ever made and the greatest screen biography.' – *New York Times*
🏆 best picture; script; Joseph Schildkraut
⚐ original story; William Dieterle; Max Steiner; Paul Muni; Anton Grot

A Life of Her Own
US   1950   108m   bw
MGM (Voldemar Vetluguin)
An innocent girl from Kansas becomes one of New York's top models.
Road to ruin, American style, from the pages of a women's magazine.
w Isobel Lennart d George Cukor ph George Folsey m Bronislau Kaper
☆ Lana Turner, Ray Milland, Tom Ewell, Louis Calhern, Ann Dvorak, Barry Sullivan, Jean Hagen
'This story belongs to the realms of soap opera – extremely artificial, highly moral in tone, and deliberately concocted to combine luxurious settings with an elementary assault on the audience's emotions.' – *MFB*

The Life of Jimmy Dolan
US   1933   85m   bw
Warner (Hal B. Wallis)
GB title: *The Kid's Last Fight*
An amiable wanderer is mistaken for a prize fighter wanted for murder.

Modest character romance, later remade as They Made Me a Criminal.
w David Boehm, Erwin Gelsey play Bertram Millhauser, Beulah Marie Dix d Archie Mayo ph Arthur Edeson
☆ Douglas Fairbanks Jnr, Loretta Young, Aline MacMahon, Guy Kibbee, Lyle Talbot, Fifi D'Orsay, Harold Huber, George Meeker

The Life of Oharu ***
Japan   1952   110m   bw
Shin Toho
👪 ▦

original title: *Saikaku Ichidai Onna*
In the 1680s the daughter of a samurai recalls her descent to prostitution through her love for a servant.
Superbly photographed and acted tragedy of a woman trapped by a remorseless fate.
w Yoshikata Yoda, Kenji Mizoguchi novel Saikaku Ihara d Kenji Mizoguchi ph Yoshima Kono, Yoshimi Hirano m Ichiro Saito
☆ Kinuyo Tanaka, Hisako Yamane, Toshiro Mifune, Yuriko Hamada

The Life of Riley
US   1948   87m   bw
Universal-International (Irving Brecher)
The trials of a family man in a low-paid job.
Adequate transcription from a radio series.
wd Irving Brecher ph William H. Daniels m Frank Skinner
☆ William Bendix, James Gleason, Rosemary de Camp, Bill Goodwin, Beulah Bondi, Richard Long

Life of the Party
US   1930   78m   Technicolor
Warner
Two gold-digging shop girls operate from a modiste's.
Half-hearted vulgar comedy, rather oddly given colour status.
w Arthur Caesar story Melville Crossman (Darryl F. Zanuck) d Roy del Ruth
☆ Winnie Lightner, Irene Delroy, Charles Butterworth, Jack Whiting
'Spotty for laughs and business.' – *Variety*

Life of the Party
US   1937   86m   bw
RKO
A girl tries to evade suitors arranged by her mother.
Very thin comedy with several second-bracket names; not at all memorable.
w Bert Kalmar, Harry Ruby, Viola Brothers Shore d William A. Seiter ph J. Roy Hunt md Roy Webb
☆ Joe Penner, Harriet Hilliard, Gene Raymond, Parkyakarkus, Victor Moore, Helen Broderick, Billy Gilbert, Ann Miller
'Should prove fairish entertainment and do fairly at the b.o.' – *Variety*

The Life of Vergie Winters
US   1934   82m   bw
RKO (Pandro S. Berman)
A rising politician marries for position but keeps watch over his mistress and their child.
Archetypal soap opera, a cross between Stella Dallas and Back Street.
w Jane Murfin novel Louis Bromfield d Alfred Santell ph Lucien Andriot m Max Steiner
☆ Ann Harding, John Boles, Helen Vinson, Frank Albertson, Lon Chaney Jnr, Sara Haden, Ben Alexander, Donald Crisp

Life on a String **
GB/Germany/China   1991   120m   Eastmancolor
Serene/Pandora/Beijing Film Studio/Herald Ace/Film Four/Berlin Filmforderung (Don Ranvaud)
▦

original title: *Bian Zhou Bian Chang*
Accompanied by a blind youth, an elderly blind musician wanders the countryside waiting for a cure for his affliction which will come when he has broken a thousand strings while playing his three-stringed guitar.
Beautiful to look at, full of spectacular and striking images, this sedately-paced movie remains obscure at the end.
wd Chen Kaige story Shi Tiesheng ph Gu Changwei m Qu Xiaosong pd Shao Ruigang ed Pei Xiaonan
☆ Li Zhongyuan, Huang Lei, Xu Qing, Ma Ling, Zhang Zhengyuan

'A rich film experience, but its length and lack of conventional narrative will be factors to overcome in getting the film across to arthouse audiences.' – *Variety*

Life Returns
US   1938   62m   bw
Scienart
A fictional story leads up to the actual experiment performed in 1934 by Dr Robert E. Cornish when he brought a dead dog back to life.
Weird mélange of fact and fiction; despite the achievement, the presentation never catches fire. The film was banned in Britain.
w Arthur Horman, John F. Goodrich d Eugene Frenke
☆ Onslow Stevens, George Breakston, Valerie Hobson, Lois Wilson
'A picture much longer to the audience than its accredited running time would indicate.' – *Variety*

Life Stinks
US   1991   95m   DeLuxe
TCF/Brooks Films/Le Studio Canal Plus (Mel Brooks)
A rich property developer takes a bet that he can survive on his own on the streets of a slum for thirty days.
Crass, tasteless comedy in which the jokes are poor.
w Mel Brooks, Rudy de Luca, Steve Haberman story Mel Brooks, Ron Clark, Rudy de Luca, Steve Haberman d Mel Brooks ph Steven Poster m John Morris pd Peter Larkin ed David Rawlins
☆ Mel Brooks, Lesley Ann Warren, Jeffrey Tambor, Stuart Pankin, Howard Morris, Rudy de Luca, Teddy Wilson, Billy Barty
'Antic comedy has more laughs than the filmmaker's last couple of efforts, and presents an amiably sympathetic, if unreliable, look at the homeless.' – *Variety*

Life Upside Down *
France   1964   92m   bw
A.J. Films
original title: *La Vie à l'Envers*
A pleasant, ordinary young man discovers the joy of being absolutely alone, and begins to detach himself from his surroundings, ending up in a barren flat and a private hospital ward.
Engaging semi-comic case history which generates much sympathy for its eccentric hero.
wd Alain Jessua ph Jacques Robin m Jacques Loussier
☆ Charles Denner, Anna Gaylor, Guy Saint-Jean, Nicole Gueden
'The tone is civilized, quiet, infinitely peaceful and often brilliantly funny.' – *Brenda Davies*, MFB
'Amusing or disturbing depending on whether it is viewed from the outside or the inside, but perceptive and artistic whichever way one views it.' – *John Simon*

'Take your cookie to see the picture that takes the cake for laughs!'
Life with Father *
👪 US   1947   118m   Technicolor
Warner (Robert Buckner)
▦ ⌕

Turn-of-the-century anecdotes of an irascible well-to-do paterfamilias who won't be baptized.
Well-upholstered screen version of a long-running play; oddly tedious considering the talent involved.
w Donald Ogden Stewart play Howard Lindsay, Russel Crouse d Michael Curtiz ph Peverell Marley, William V. Skall m Max Steiner ad Robert Haas
☆ William Powell, Irene Dunne, Edmund Gwenn, ZaSu Pitts, Elizabeth Taylor, Martin Milner, Jimmy Lydon, Emma Dunn, Moroni Olsen, Elizabeth Risdon
'Everybody seems to be trying too hard ... the director is totally out of his element in this careful, deadly version.' – *New Yorker, 1978*
† Censorship of the day absurdly clipped Father's famous last line: 'I'm going to be baptized, damn it!'
⚐ Peverell Marley, William V. Skall; Max Steiner; William Powell; Robert Haas

Life with Mikey
👪 US   1993   91m   Technicolor
Buena Vista/Touchstone (Scott Rudin, Teri Schwartz)
▦ ⌕ 🎧

GB title: *Give Me a Break*
A former child star turned agent discovers a new talent when a 10-year-old girl tries to steal his wallet.
Pleasant, undemanding, unmemorable comedy.
w Marc Lawrence d James Lapine ph Rob Hahn m Alan Menken pd Adrianne Lobel ed Robert Leighton
☆ Michael J. Fox, Christina Vidal, Nathan Lane, Cyndi Lauper, David Huddleston, David Krumholtz
'Screams "cute" from every pore but should play well with kids and won't insult the intelligence of adults.' – *Variety*
† It was released direct to video in Britain.

'Doggie's got a bone ... Whose bone?'
Life with the Cannibals
US   1996   95m   Foto-Kem
Dorian (Harry Bromley-Davenport)
▦

A wimp finds a new life, living next to the neighbourhood serial killer.
A weak and witless black comedy; all that can be said in its favour is that, considering its theme of multiple murder, it downplays any depiction of violence.
w Daryl Haney d Harry Bromley-Davenport ph Marco Cappetta, Ricardo Gale, Hector Rivera m Mark Hart pd Kate Perotti, Yvette Taylor ed Van Rieben
☆ Kieran Mulroney, Juliet Landau, Mason Adams, Bette Ford, Daryl Haney, Wings Hauser

Life with the Lyons
GB   1954   81m   bw
Exclusive/Hammer (Robert Dunbar)
The Lyon family have problems with their landlord when they move into a fashionable house by London's Marble Arch.
An extended low-budget situation comedy, based on a popular radio series, given rather more skilled playing than it deserves.
w Val Guest, Robert Dunbar d Val Guest ph Walter Harvey m Arthur Wilkinson ad Wilfred Arnold ed Douglas Myers
☆ Ben Lyon, Bebe Daniels Lyon, Richard Lyon, Barbara Lyon, Horace Percival, Molly Weir, Hugh Morton, Arthur Hill, Doris Rogers, Gwen Lewis, Belinda Lee

Lifeboat **
US   1944   96m   bw
TCF (Kenneth MacGowan)
👪 ▦ ⌕

Survivors from a torpedoed passenger ship include the U-Boat commander responsible.
Propaganda gimmick melodrama interesting for the casting and for Hitchcock's response to the challenge of filming in one cramped set.
w Jo Swerling story John Steinbeck d Alfred Hitchcock ph Glen MacWilliams m Hugo Friedhofer
☆ Tallulah Bankhead, Walter Slezak, Henry Hull, John Hodiak, Canada Lee, William Bendix, Mary Anderson, Heather Angel, Hume Cronyn
'The initial idea – a derelict boat and its passengers as microcosm – is itself so artificial that ... it sets the whole pride and brain too sharply to work on a tour de force for its own sake.' – *James Agee*
⚐ John Steinbeck; Alfred Hitchcock; Glen MacWilliams

Lifeforce
US   1985   101m   Eastmancolor
Cannon (Menahem Golan, Yoram Globus)
▦ ⌕ ⓦ 🎧

An Anglo-American space expedition investigating Halley's Comet discovers that it hides a two-mile-high alien spaceship containing the bodies of giant, bat-like creatures and three humanoids in suspended animation.
Extraordinarily bizarre mix of science fiction and vampire movie, more likely to provoke derision than any other emotion.
w Dan O'Bannon, Don Jakoby novel Space Vampires by Colin Wilson d Tobe Hooper ph Alan Hume m Henry Mancini, Michael Kamen, James Guthrie pd John Graysmark ed John Grover sp John Dykstra, Nick Maley, John Gant

☆ Steve Railsback, Peter Firth, Frank Finlay, Patrick Stewart, Michael Gothard, Nicholas Ball, Mathilda May, Aubrey Morris

Lifeguard

US 1976 96m CFI color
Paramount (Ron Silverman)
A beach guard at 30 reviews his life and his future.
Odd but not unlikeable little personal drama which barely got released.
w Ron Koslow d Daniel Petrie ph Ralph Woolsey md Dale Menten
☆ Sam Elliott, Anne Archer, Stephen Young, Parker Stevenson, Kathleen Quinlan

Lifespan

US/Netherlands 1975 85m Eastmancolor
Respectable/Whitepal (Alexander Whitelaw)
An American expert on ageing discovers that a Dutch colleague who killed himself was conducting successful experiments in prolonging life.
Mundane drama that promises more than it finally delivers; it strains for significance without achieving it.
w Alexander Whitelaw, Judith Roscoe, Alva Ruben d Alexander Whitelaw ph Eddie van der Enden m Terry Riley ad Dick Schillemans ed Guust Verschuuren, Jann Dopp, Hetty Konig
☆ Hiram Keller, Tina Aumont, Klaus Kinski, Fons Rademakers, Eric Schneider, Frans Mulders

The Lift

Netherlands 1983 99m Eastmancolor
Warner/Sigma Films (Matthijs Van Heijningen)
An office block elevator seems to assume deadly powers. After a murderous car, a murderous lift.
Slick but rather empty semi-horror.
wd Dick Maas ph Marc Felperlaan m Dick Maas ad Harry Ammerlaan ed Hans Van Dongen
☆ Huub Stapel, Willeke Van Ammelrooy, Josine Van Dalsum

Lift to the Scaffold *

France 1957 89m bw
Nouvelles Editions de Films (Jean Thuillier)
original title: *Ascenseur pour l'Echafaud*
US title: *Frantic*
An executive murders his employer but is trapped in the building all night; meanwhile his car is stolen and he is arrested for a murder committed by the thief.
Complex, watchable suspenser with pretensions.
w Roger Nimier, Louis Malle novel Noel Calef d Louis Malle ph Henri Decaë m Miles Davis
☆ Maurice Ronet, Jeanne Moreau, Georges Poujouly, Yori Bertin, Lino Ventura
'Cold, clever and rather elegant.' – *Penelope Houston, MFB*

The Light across the Street

France 1955 99m bw
EGC/Fernand Rivers (Jacques Gauthier)
original title: *La Lumière d'en Face*
A lorry driver, injured in an accident, becomes insanely jealous of his young wife.
Low-life melodrama tailored for the sultry attractions of its new star.
w Louis Cahavance, René Masson, René Lefèvre d Georges Lacombe ph Louis Page m Norbert Glanzberg
☆ Brigitte Bardot, Raymond Pellégrin, Roger Pigaut, Claude Romain

The Light at the Edge of the World

↟↟ US/Spain/Liechtenstein 1971 120m
Eastmancolor Panavision
Bryna/Jet/Triumfilm (Kirk Douglas, Ilya Salkind)
A lighthouse keeper near Cape Horn resists a band of wreckers.
Pretentious, disaster-prone version of a simple adventure story; one wonders not so much what went wrong as whether anything went right in this international venture.
w Tom Rowe novel Jules Verne d Kevin Billington ph Henri Decaë m Piero Piccioni
☆ Kirk Douglas, Yul Brynner, Samantha Eggar, Jean-Claude Drouot, Fernando Rey, Renato Salvatori

The Light Fantastic: see Love Is Better Than Ever

The Light in the Forest

↟↟ US 1958 92m Technicolor
Walt Disney
Kidnapped by Indians as an infant, a teenager is returned to his parents but finds the white man's ways disturbing.
Modest frontier drama with a moral.
w Lawrence Edward Watkin novel Conrad Richter d Herschel Daugherty ph Ellsworth Fredericks m Paul Smith
☆ James MacArthur, Carol Lynley, Jessica Tandy, Wendell Corey, Fess Parker, Joanne Dru, Joseph Calleia

The Light in the Piazza

GB 1962 101m Metrocolor Cinemascope
MGM (Arthur Freed)
An American matron in Florence tries to marry off her mentally retarded daughter to a wealthy Italian.
Puzzling romantic drama in which one is never quite sure why the characters behave as they do; in the end all one appreciates is the tour of northern Italy.
w Julius J. Epstein novel Elizabeth Spencer d Guy Green ph Otto Heller m Mario Nascimbene
☆ Olivia de Havilland, Yvette Mimieux, George Hamilton, Rossano Brazzi, Barry Sullivan

Light of Day

US 1987 107m Astrocolor
Taft/Keith Barish/Tri-Star
A Cleveland family is upset by illness and rock'n'roll.
Drab musical wallow which seems to have little point.
wd Paul Schrader ph John Bailey m Thomas Newman pd Jeannine Claudia Oppewall ed Jacqueline Cambas
☆ Michael J. Fox, Joan Jett, Gena Rowlands, Michael McKean

The Light of Heart: see Life Begins at Eight-Thirty

Light Sleeper *

US 1991 103m DuArt
Guild/Grain of Sand (Linda Reisman)
A drug delivery man and former addict contemplates his future as his employer decides to give up the business and go straight.
An intelligent and occasionally gripping thriller.
wd Paul Schrader ph Ed Lachman m Michael Been pd Richard Hornung ed Kristina Boden
☆ Willem Dafoe, Susan Sarandon, Mary Beth Hurt, Dana Delany, David Clennon, Victor Garber, Jane Adams, Paul Jabara
'Contemplative and violent by turns, this quasi-thriller about a long-time drug dealer leaving the business has a great deal to recommend it but could have been significantly better had Schrader done some fresh plotting and not relied on his standby gunplay to resolve issues.' – *Variety*

'Laugh, you little fool, laugh ... for I'm giving you something you never had before – a soul ... on canvas!'

The Light that Failed *

US 1939 97m bw
Paramount (William A. Wellman)
A London artist is going blind as the result of a war wound, and must finish the portrait of the little Cockney whom he loves.
Nicely-made but rather boring star romance; no surprises in plot or performance.
w Robert Carson story Rudyard Kipling d William Wellman ph Theodor Sparkuhl m Victor Young
☆ Ronald Colman, Walter Huston, Ida Lupino, Dudley Digges, Muriel Angelus, Fay Helm
'Production fine for moderate b.o. Will catch attention of the carriage trade, the literati crowd and the critics.' – *Variety*
† Previously filmed in 1916 and 1923.

The Light Touch: see Touch and Go (1955)

The Light Touch

US 1951 107m bw
MGM (Pandro S. Berman)
An elegant art thief tries to doublecross the gangster who employs him.

Elongated and witless romantic charade on European locations.
wd Richard Brooks story Jed Harris, Tom Reed ph Robert Surtees m Miklos Rozsa
☆ Stewart Granger, George Sanders, Pier Angeli, Kurt Kasznar, Larry Keating, Rhys Williams, Norman Lloyd, Mike Mazurki
'A comedy thriller which moves far too slowly for its imperfections to be overlooked.' – *Penelope Houston, MFB*

Light Up the Sky

GB 1960 90m bw
British Lion/Bryanston (Lewis Gilbert)
Life on a searchlight battery during World War II.
Wartime comedy-drama with accent on the laughs but adding dollops of tragedy and sentiment. A very patchy entertainment.
w Vernon Harris play *Touch It Light* by Robert Storey d Lewis Gilbert ph John Wilcox m Douglas Gamley
☆ Ian Carmichael, Tommy Steele, Benny Hill, Sydney Tafler, Victor Maddern, Harry Locke, Johnny Briggs, Dick Emery

The Lighthorsemen *

Australia 1988 110m colour
Medusa/RKO (Simon Wincer, Ian Jones)
Comrades take part in the cavalry charge on the fortified city of Beersheba in the First World War.
Intermittently exciting re-creation of a historic event, at its best in the battle scenes.
w Ian Jones d Simon Wincer ph Dean Semler m Mario Millo pd Bernard Hides ed Adrian Carr
☆ Jon Blake, Peter Phelps, Tony Bonner, Bill Kerr, John Walton, Gary Sweet, Tim McKenzie, Sigrid Thornton, Anthony Andrews

Lightnin' *

US 1930 94m bw
Fox
A country fellow is wiser than he seems, and in between settling other folks' lives right, persuades his own wife not to divorce him.
Archetypal Will Rogers star part which he played on the stage; now his first big talkie hit.
play Frank Bacon, Winchell Smith d Henry King
☆ Will Rogers, Louise Dresser, Joel McCrea, Sharon Lynn, J. M. Kerrigan
'A production of the highest quality in all its phases.' – *Variety*

Lightning Jack

Australia 1994 93m colour
Buena Vista/Lightning Ridge/Village Roadshow (Paul Hogan, Greg Coote, Simon Wincer)
The adventures of a bungling, near-sighted outlaw and his mute companion.
A spoof Western a few bullets short of a six-shooter, with its few tired jokes milked relentlessly for laughs.
w Paul Hogan d Simon Wincer ph David Eggby m Bruce Rowland pd Bernard Hides ed O. Nicholas Brown
☆ Paul Hogan, Cuba Gooding Jnr, Beverly D'Angelo, Pat Hingle, Kamala Dawson, Roger Daltrey, L. Q. Jones, Richard Riehle, Frank McRae
'A good natured, if laconic, oater that rides along nicely.' – *Variety*

Lightning over Water

West Germany/Sweden 1980 91m Movielab
Road Movies/Viking Film (Renée Gunde-Lach, Pierre Cottrell, Chris Sievernich)
aka: *Nick's Movie*
A record of the last months of Nicholas Ray's life, when he was hoping to revive his career while visibly dying from cancer.
Unique and uneasy, something for film buffs to chew over.
wd Nicholas Ray, Wim Wenders m Ronee Blakley ed Wim Wenders, Peter Przygodda

Lightning Strikes Twice

US 1951 91m bw
Warner (Henry Blanke)
A woman decides to clear her lover of suspicion of murder, but later has her own doubts.
Silly melodrama with no credibility, little suspense, and too much talk.
w Lenore Coffee novel Margaret Echard d King Vidor ph Sid Hickox m Max Steiner

☆ Richard Todd, Ruth Roman, Mercedes McCambridge, Zachary Scott, Darryl Hickman, Frank Conroy, Kathryn Givney

Lights of New York ***

US 1928 57m bw
Warner
A chorus girl becomes involved with gangsters.
The first '100 per cent all-talking' film, dramatically primitive but historically important.
w F. Hugh Herbert, Murray Roth d Bryan Foy ph E. B. DuPar
☆ Helene Costello, Cullen Landis, Wheeler Oakman, Eugene Pallette, Tom Dugan, Gladys Brockwell, Mary Carr
'100 per cent crude.' – *Variety*

Lights of Old Broadway

US 1925 80m bw silent
MGM
Twin orphan girls find very different routes to happiness.
One of the star's most popular vehicles.
w Carey Wilson d Monta Bell
☆ Marion Davies, Conrad Nagel, George K. Arthur, Julia Swayne Gordon

Lights of Variety *

Italy 1950 94m bw
Film Capitolium (Alberto Lattuada)
original title: *Luci del Varieta*
A stage-struck young girl forsakes the manager of the troupe in which she found stardom for the bright lights of the city.
Tragi-comical backstage story in which the bits of detail are more entertaining than the plot.
w Federico Fellini d Alberto Lattuada ph Otello Martelli m Felice Lattuada
☆ Peppino de Filippo, Carla del Poggio, Giulietta Masina, John Kitzmiller, Folco Lulli
'Told with the humor and compassion, the subtlety and sensitivity, and marked by the satiric eye, the keenness of insight, the appreciation of human frailty, that are Fellini's strong points.' – *Judith Crist*

Lights Out: see Bright Victory

The Lightship

US 1985 89m colour
Rank/CBS (Moritz Borman, Bill Benenson)
A lightship is taken over by a gang of psychopathic crooks on the run.
Echoes of Key Largo abound in this dreary suspense melodrama which aspires to more meaning than is evident.
w William Mai, David Taylor novel Siegfried Lenz d Jerzy Skolimowski m Stanley Myers ad Holger Gross ed Barry Vince, Scott Hancock
☆ Robert Duvall, Klaus Maria Brandauer, Tom Bower, Robert Constanzo

Like Father Like Son

US 1987 98m Technicolor
Grazer-Valdes/Tri-Star
A surgeon and his son find themselves in each other's bodies.
Role-reversal comedy at the beginning of a trend; in itself a bore.
w Lorne Cameron, Steven L. Bloom d Rod Daniel ph Jack N. Green m Miles Goodman pd Dennis Gassner ed Lois Freeman-Fox
☆ Dudley Moore, Kirk Cameron, Sean Astin, Patrick O'Neal, Margaret Colin

Like Grains of Sand *

Japan 1995 129m Fujicolour
ICA/Toho/Pia/YES (Yoshishige Shimatani, Kazuo Hayashi, Kiyomi Kanazawa, Yuuka Nakazawa)
original title: *Nagisa no Sindbad*
A teenage boy discovers that he is gay.
Sensitive and provocative account of the emotional confusions and self-imposed repressions of a growing sexual awareness.
wd Ryosuke Hashiguchi ph Shogo Ueno m Kazuya Takahashi ed Miho Yoneda
☆ Yoshinori Okada, Kota Kusano, Ayumi Hamazaki, Koji Yamaguchi, Kumi Takada, Shizuka Isami

'Very probably the best film ever made about problems faced by a gay kid in his teens ... It gets inside adolescent emotions and insecurities with piercing accuracy.' – *Tony Rayns, Sight and Sound*

'A Delicious Love Story.'

Like Water for Chocolate **

Mexico 1991 114m colour
Electric/Cinevista/NCCA/NTDF/Alfonso Arau

original title: *Como agua para chocolate*
In Mexico in the early 1900s, forced to stay at home to look after her mother and to see the man she loves marry her sister, the youngest of three daughters puts all her emotions into her cooking.
Part soap opera, part delightful fable and wholly enjoyable, this is a sweet, rich but not indigestible romantic drama.
w Laura Esquivel *novel* Laura Esquivel d Alfonso Arau *ph* Emmanuel Lubezki, Steve Bernstein m Leo Brower *pd* Marco Antonio Arteaga, Mauricio de Aguinaci, Denise Pizzini *ed* Carlos Bolado, Francisco Chiu
☆ Marco Leonardi, Lumi Cavazos, Regina Torne, Mario Ivan Martinez, Ada Carrasco, Yareli Arizmendi, Claudette Maille, Pilar Aranda
'This classic love story bridging generations is so compelling and splendidly expressed in the script that the frustrated filmgoer can only shake his head at the incompetent handling.' – *Variety*
'The film acts as a kind of palliative for the middle-class audiences with which it has been so successful. Despite all the changes brought about in Mexican society by the Revolution and its aftermath, they can still feel comfortable with those things that have remained the same: the servants in their kitchens.' – *John Kraniauskas, Sight and Sound*
† The title refers to the heroine's temper, kept just below boiling point – like water for chocolate.

The Likely Lads *

GB 1976 90m bw
EMI (Aida Young)

Two Geordie friends, with wife and mistress, go on a touring holiday.
Valuable as a record of an excellent and long-running TV series, this big-screen version finds most of the humour regrettably broadened.
w Dick Clement, Ian La Frenais d Michael Tuchner *ph* Tony Imi m Mike Hugg
☆ Rodney Bewes, James Bolam, Brigit Forsyth, Mary Tamm, Sheila Fearn, Zena Walker

A Likely Story

US 1947 88m bw
RKO (Richard H. Berger)
A man thinks he has only a short time to live, and in trying to do his best for a girlfriend gets mixed up with gangsters.
Even a star cast could not have made much of this zany comedy script.
w Bess Taffel d H. C. Potter *ph* Roy Hunt m Leigh Harline *md* Constantin Bakaleinikoff
☆ Barbara Hale, Bill Williams, Lanny Rees, Sam Levene, Dan Tobin, Nestor Paiva

Li'l Abner *

⋔⋔ US 1959 113m Technicolor
Vistavision
Paramount/Panama-Frank (Norman Panama)

The hillbilly town of Dogpatch, tagged the most useless community in America, fights being used as a test site for A-bombs.
Set-bound, intrinsically American, but bright and cheerful film of a stage show about Al Capp's famous comic strip characters.
wd Norman Panama, Melvin Frank *from the musical show* (ly Johnny Mercer, words Gene de Paul) *ph* Daniel L. Fapp m Gene de Paul *md* Joseph Lilley, Nelson Riddle *ch* Dee Dee Wood, Michael Kidd
☆ Peter Palmer, Leslie Parrish, Billie Hayes, Howard St John, Stubby Kaye, Stella Stevens, Julie Newmar, Robert Strauss
'As joyous, screwy, dancin' and jokin' a musical show as Hollywood has sent us for a long time.' – *Sunday Dispatch*
♫ Joseph Lilley, Nelson Riddle

The Lilac Domino

GB 1937 79m bw
Grafton-Capitol-Cecil
A Hungarian count is attracted at the gambling tables by a masked girl.
Surprisingly undercast version of a popular operetta.
w Basil Mason, Neil Gow, R. Hutter and Derek Neame *play* Rudolf Bernauer, E. Gatti and B. Jenbach d Fred Zelnik
☆ June Knight, Michael Bartlett, Athene Seyler, Richard Dolman, S. Z. Sakall, Fred Emney, Jane Carr

Lilac Time *

US 1928 90m bw silent with sound effects
First National
GB title: *Love Never Dies*
A French girl promises to wait for an American flyer, but his stern father tells her he is dead.
Popular war romance which retains moments of interest.
w Carey Wilson *play* Jane Cowl, Jane Murfin *ph* Sid Hickox m Nathaniel Shilkret *d/p* George Fitzmaurice
☆ Colleen Moore, Gary Cooper, Eugenie Besserer, Burr McIntosh, Arthur Lake

Lilacs in the Spring

GB 1954 94m Trucolor
Republic/Everest (Herbert Wilcox)
US title: *Let's Make Up*
During the London blitz a young actress is knocked unconscious and dreams of herself as Nell Gwyn, Queen Victoria and her own mother before waking up to deal with her personal problems.
Good-humoured theatrical charade deadened by poorish production and colour, strengthened by the star's game run-through of her staple characters. How Mr Flynn came to be involved is anybody's guess.
w Miles Malleson (uncredited) *play* The Glorious Days by Harold Purcell d Herbert Wilcox *ph* Max Greene m Robert Farnon
☆ Anna Neagle, Errol Flynn, Peter Graves, David Farrar, Kathleen Harrison

Lili *

US 1953 81m Technicolor
MGM (Edwin H. Knopf)

A 16-year-old orphan girl joins a carnival and falls in love with the magician.
Romantic whimsy dependent entirely on treatment, which is sometimes heavy-handed. Charm, ballet and puppets are provided, but a little cheerful song and dance would not have been amiss.
w Helen Deutsch *novel* Paul Gallico *ph* Robert Planck m Bronislau Kaper *ad* Cedric Gibbons, Paul Groesse *d/ch* Charles Walters
☆ Leslie Caron, Jean-Pierre Aumont, Mel Ferrer, Kurt Kasznar
'A lovely and beguiling little film, touched with the magic of romance.' – *Bosley Crowther*
♪ Bronislau Kaper
♧ Helen Deutsch; Charles Walters; Robert Planck; Leslie Caron; art direction
⚏ Leslie Caron

Lili Marleen *

West Germany 1980 116m colour
Roxy/CIP/Rialto/Bayerische Rundfunk (Luggi Waldleitner)

A German girl singer becomes famous and notorious during World War II by her rendition of an old song.
Curious mixture of melodrama and satire which doesn't really work but is always lively to watch.
w Manfred Purzer, Joshua Sinclair, Rainer Werner Fassbinder *novel* The Sky Has Many Colours by Lale Andersen d Rainer Werner Fassbinder *ph* Xaver Schwarzenberger m Peer Raben *ed* Juliane Lorenz, Rainer Werner Fassbinder
☆ Hanna Schygulla, Giancarlo Giannini, Mel Ferrer, Karl Heinz

Lilies *

Canada 1996 95m colour
Alliance/Triptych (Anna Stratton, Arnie Gelbart, Robin Cass)

In Quebec, a bishop who visits a prison to hear an inmate's confession is taken hostage and forced to watch a play about his homosexual past.
Complex drama on the theme of obsessive love and betrayal; its setting provides a reason for its extreme theatricality, with female roles played by men in drag.
w Michel Marc Bouchard *play* Les Feluettes ou La Répétition d'un Drame Romantique by Michel Marc Bouchard d John Greyson *ph* Daniel John m Myschael Danna *pd* Sandra Kybartas *ed* Andre Corriveau
☆ Brent Carver, Marcel Sabourin, Albert Pallascio, Jason Cadieux, Danny Gilmore, Matthew Ferguson, Alexander Chapman, Ian D. Clark
'Aesthetically and conceptually very impressive, but it is less than the sum of its parts, its intelligence not sufficiently balanced and buttressed by the careful observation of character.' – *Rob White, Sight and Sound*

Lilies of the Field

US 1930 60m bw
First National
A chorus girl has been robbed of her child by framed divorce court evidence.
Backstage melodrama with music, very dated now but with interesting credits.
w John Goodrich *play* William Hurlbut d Alexander Korda *ph* Lee Garmes
☆ Corinne Griffith, Ralph Forbes, John Loder, Patsy Paige, Freeman Wood, Virginia Bruce
'Big revue sequences in backstage locale. Better than average programmer.' – *Variety*
† It was a remake of a 1924 film directed by John Francis Dillon and starring Corinne Griffith.

Lilies of the Field *

US 1963 94m bw
UA/Rainbow/Ralph Nelson

An itinerant black workman in New Mexico helps a group of German nuns to build a chapel.
Liberal, sentimental, under-dramatized little comedy with everyone coming to understand each other's point of view, so that the audience feels improved if not especially entertained.
w James Poe *novel* William E. Barrett d Ralph Nelson *ph* Ernest Haller m Jerry Goldsmith
☆ Sidney Poitier, Lilia Skala, Lisa Mann
⚏ Sidney Poitier
♧ best picture; James Poe; Ernest Haller; Lilia Skala

Liliom *

US 1930 94m bw
Fox
A Budapest carnival man is killed in a fight but later comes back from heaven to see how his family is doing.
Ingeniously-staged fantasy, very dated but a lot more interesting than its musical remake Carousel (qv).
w S. N. Behrman *play* Ferenc Molnar d Frank Borzage *ph* Chester Lyons m Richard Fall
☆ Charles Farrell, Rose Hobart, Estelle Taylor, Lee Tracy, Walter Abel, Guinn Williams, H. B. Warner, Dawn O'Day (Anne Shirley)
'Beyond the depth of Farrell's dramatic ability ... shapes up as passable for a week-stand in the keys.' – *Variety*

'Before Eve there was Evil ... and her name was Lilith!'

Lilith *

US 1964 126m bw
Columbia/Centaur (Robert Rossen)

A trainee therapist at an asylum falls in love with a patient.
Strange, wistful, poetic and rather soporific character melodrama.
wd Robert Rossen *novel* J. R. Salamanca *ph* Eugene Schufftan m Kenyon Hopkins *pd* Richard Sylbert
☆ Warren Beatty, Jean Seberg, Peter Fonda, Kim Hunter, Anne Meacham, James Patterson, Jessica Walter, Gene Hackman
'A remarkable attempt to dig a little deeper in an almost untilled field, and to throw some light on the relationship between madness and the creative imagination.' – *Tom Milne*

Lillian Russell *

US 1940 130m bw
TCF (Gene Markey)
The life and loves of the famous 1890s entertainer.
Flabby and inaccurate biopic, worth seeing for its highlights but flatly and incompetently written.
w William Anthony McGuire d Irving Cummings, Leon Shamroy *md* Alfred Newman *ad* Richard Day, Joseph C. Wright
☆ Alice Faye, Don Ameche, Edward Arnold, Warren William, Henry Fonda, Leo Carrillo, Helen Westley, Dorothy Peterson, Ernest Truex, Nigel Bruce, Claud Allister, Lynn Bari, Weber and Fields, Eddie Foy Jnr, Una O'Connor
♧ art direction

Lillies

Canada 1996 92m colour
Dangerous to Know/Alliance/Triptych/Galafilm (Anna Stratton, Robert Cass, Arnie Gelbart)
In Quebec in the 50s, prisoners hold a bishop hostage while they act out scenes from his adolescence, involving his voyeuristic relationship with two boys.
A melodramatic work, about homophobia and its effects, which may well work on stage, with sensational happenings of scandal, arson and murder, its play within a play, and female roles played by actors; opened out for the cinema, it seems overblown and otiose.
w Michel Marc Bouchard, Linda Gaboriau *play* Michel Marc Bouchard d John Greyson *ph* Daniel Jobin m Myschael Danna *pd* Sandra Kybartas *ed* André Corriveau
☆ Brent Carver, Marcel Sabourin, Matthew Ferguson, Danny Gilmore, Alexander Chapman, Gary Farmer, Robert Lalonde, Rémy Girard
'A film for those who aren't easily offended by homosexuality and love a great story told with passion. One of the most intriguing, beautiful, delightful and strange films I've ever seen.' – *Terry Richards, Film Review*

Lilly Turner

US 1933 65m bw
Warner
A girl unwittingly marries a bigamist, then a drunk who will give her baby a name.
Turgid mother-love saga.
w Gene Markey, Kathryn Scola *play* Philip Dunning, George Abbott d William A. Wellman
☆ Ruth Chatterton, George Brent, Frank McHugh, Ruth Donnelly, Guy Kibbee, Robert Barrat
'Spotty returns most probable.' – *Variety*

Lily in Love

US/Hungary 1985 103m colour
Robert Halmi

Denied the lead in a film scripted by his wife, an actor disguises himself as an Italian in order to get the part.
A weak comedy, done with some style.
w Frank Cucci d Karoly Makk *ph* John Lindley m Szaboks Fenyes *ad* Tamas Vayer *ed* Norman Gay
☆ Christopher Plummer, Maggie Smith, Elke Sommer, Adolph Green

Limbo *

US 1972 111m Technicolor
Universal (Linda Gottlieb)
aka: *Chained to Yesterday*
Women wait for their husbands to return from Vietnam.
Worthy but dramatically uninteresting multi-storied semi-propaganda piece with an untried cast.
w Joan Silver, James Bridges d Mark Robson *ph* Charles Wheeler m Anita Kerr
☆ Kate Jackson, Katherine Justice, Stuart Margolin, Hazel Medina, Kathleen Nolan

'A condition of unknowable outcome.'

Limbo

US/Germany 1999 127m CFI
Columbia TriStar/Global/Screen Gems (Maggie Renzi)

Fleeing from murderous drug dealers, a former fisherman, a nightclub singer and her teenage daughter are stranded on a remote, uninhabited island.
This odd, broken-backed story begins as a portrait of life in a small Alaskan community, with a tentative romance on the side, and then changes into a survival story. The ending is calculated to infuriate all who make it through the rest of the movie.
wd John Sayles *ph* Haskell Wexler *pd* Gemma Jackson *ed* John Sayles
☆ Mary Elizabeth Mastrantonio, David Strathairn, Vanessa Martinez, Kris Kristofferson,

Casey Siemaszko, Kathryn Grody, Rita Taggart, Leo Burmester, Michael Laskin

'A thinly realized survival tale that falls flat dramatically and cinematically.' – *Todd McCarthy, Variety*

'Romantic ruler of London's half-world!'
Limehouse Blues *
US 1934 65m bw
Paramount
aka: *East End Chant*
In London's shady quarter, an oriental roustabout tries to leave his jealous mistress for a girl with a shady past.
Artificial, atmospheric melodrama set in a never-never Limehouse redolent of Broken Blossoms. Interesting for its very excesses.
w Arthur Phillips, Cyril Hume, Grover Jones d Alexander Hall ph Harry Fischbeck
☆ George Raft, Anna May Wong, Jean Parker, Kent Taylor, Billy Bevan
'Weak and slow-moving ... won't satisfy the average fan.' – *Variety*

Limelight
GB 1935 80m bw
GFD/Herbert Wilcox
US title: *Backstage*
A chorus girl helps a street singer to become a star.
Highly predictable backstage musical drama which made a nine days wonder of 'The Street Singer'.
w Laura Whetter d Herbert Wilcox ph Henry Harris
☆ Anna Neagle, Arthur Tracy, Jane Winton, Ellis Jeffreys, Muriel George
'A syrupy concatenation to win all British hearts.' – *James Agate*

Limelight ***
♟♟ US 1952 144m bw
Charles Chaplin
A broken-down music hall comedian is stimulated by a young ballerina to a final hour of triumph.
Sentimental drama in a highly theatrical London East End setting. In other hands it would be very hokey, but Chaplin's best qualities, as well as his worst, are in evidence, and in a way the film sums up his own career.
wd Charles Chaplin ph Karl Struss m Charles Chaplin, Raymond Rasch, Larry Russell ad Eugene Lourié photographic consultant Rollie Totheroh
☆ Charles Chaplin, Claire Bloom, Buster Keaton, Sydney Chaplin, Nigel Bruce, Norman Lloyd
'From the first reel it is clear that he now wants to talk, that he loves to talk ... where a development in the story line might easily be conveyed by a small visual effect, he prefers to make a speech about it ... it is a disturbing rejection of the nature of the medium itself.' – *Walter Kerr*
'Surely the richest hunk of self-gratification since Huck and Tom attended their own funeral.' – *New Yorker, 1982*
'His exhortations about life, courage, consciousness and "truth" are set in a self-pitying, self-glorifying story.' – *Pauline Kael, 70s*
♟ Charles Chaplin, Raymond Rasch, Larry Russell
♙ Claire Bloom (best newcomer)

'Tell Them I'm Coming.'
The Limey *
US 1999 90m CFI
Artisan (John Hardy, Scott Kramer)
After he leaves prison, an English criminal goes to Los Angeles to discover how his daughter died.
A revenge thriller told in an elliptical manner that does not quite conceal the familiarity and predictability of its story.
w Lem Dobbs d Steven Soderbergh ph Ed Lachman m Cliff Martinez pd Gary Frutkoff ed Sarah Flack
☆ Terence Stamp, Peter Fonda, Lesley Ann Warren, Luis Guzman, Barry Newman, Joe Dallesandro, Nicky Katt, Amelia Heinle, Melissa George
'A contemplative, character-driven drama that underplays the familiar crime genre and underworld milieu in favor of a more resonant story about family and intergenerational issues.' – *Emanuel Levy, Variety*
† The scenes showing Stamp as a young man are taken from Ken Loach's *Poor Cow* (qv), made in 1967.

Limit Up
US 1989 88m colour
Medusa/Management Company Entertainment
(Jonathan D. Krane)
A woman sells her soul to an apparent demon in exchange for a successful career on the stock exchange.
A dull fantasy, dimly directed.
w Richard Martini, Luana Anders d Richard Martini ph Peter Lyons Collister m John Tesh pd R. Clifford Searcy ed Sonny Baskin
☆ Nancy Allen, Dean Stockwell, Brad Hall, Danitra Vance, Ray Charles, Rance Howard, Sandra Bogan

The Limping Man
GB 1953 74m bw
Banner/Eros (Donald Ginsberg)
An American leaving his plane at Heathrow sees another passenger shot by a limping man.
Initially intriguing thriller which gives up the ghost and tacks on a dream ending.
w Reginald Long, Alistair MacLean d Charles de Lautour ph Jonah Jones m Arthur Wilkinson
☆ Lloyd Bridges, Moira Lister, Helene Cordet, Bruce Beeby, Alan Wheatley, Leslie Phillips

Linda *
GB 1960 61m bw
Independent Artists
A teenage girl falls for a member of a street gang.
Nicely atmospheric low-life romance; no real content but plenty of raw style.
w Bill MacIlwraith d Don Sharp ph Michael Reed m Garry Hughes
☆ Carol White, Alan Rothwell, Cavan Malone, Lois Dane, Edward Cast

The Lineup *
US 1958 86m bw
Columbia (Frank Cooper)
San Francisco police trap a gunman who is also a drug contact.
Energetic, polished movie version of a popular TV series, San Francisco Beat.
w Stirling Silliphant d Don Siegel ph Hal Mohr m Mischa Bakaleinikoff
☆ Warner Anderson, Robert Keith, Eli Wallach

'He wants to be tied down. She wants to be tied up. It's not what you think.'
The Linguini Incident
US 1992 98m CFI color
Rank/Isolar (Arnold Orgolini)
A waitress who wants to be an escape artist and a barman seeking a wife set out to rob an antique shop of a ring that once belonged to Houdini.
No escape from boredom in this trivial and lacklustre comedy.
w Richard Shepard, Tamar Brott d Richard Shepard ph Robert Yeoman m Thomas Newman pd Marcia Hinds-Johnson ed Sonya Polonsky
☆ Rosanna Arquette, David Bowie, Eszter Balint, André Gregory, Buck Henry, Viveca Lindfors, Marlee Matlin
'Energetic actors can't overcome the uninspired, poverty-row production values.' – *Variety*

Link
GB 1986 103m Technicolor
Cannon/EMI (Richard Franklin)
A scientist in a lonely house educates chimpanzees, but one proves malevolent.
Not much plot for a long film, and no suspense either.
w Everett DeRoche d Richard Franklin ph Mike Malloy m Jerry Goldsmith
☆ Terence Stamp, Elisabeth Shue, Steven Pinner, Richard Garnett
'What is missing from Link is a reason to see it.' – *Variety*

The Lion
♟♟ GB 1962 96m DeLuxe Cinemascope
TCF (Samuel G. Engel)
An American lawyer goes to Africa to visit his ex-wife and their child.
Unabsorbing marital drama with child and animal interest.
w Irene and Louis Kamp novel Joseph Kessel d Jack Cardiff ph Ted Scaife m Malcolm Arnold

☆ William Holden, Trevor Howard, Capucine, Pamela Franklin
'The main fault must be attributed to the spiritless direction of Jack Cardiff, whose recent change of métier has resulted in the industry losing a great lighting cameraman.' – *John Gillett*

The Lion Has Wings *
GB 1939 76m bw
London Films (Alexander Korda)
A documentary drama tracing the steps leading up to the outbreak of war.
Once-inspiring propaganda piece, now regrettably hilarious. Valuable social history, though.
w Adrian Brunel, E. V. H. Emmett m Michael Powell, Brian Desmond Hurst, Adrian Brunel ph Harry Stradling m Richard Addinsell
☆ Merle Oberon, Ralph Richardson, June Duprez, Robert Douglas, Anthony Bushell, Derrick de Marney, Brian Worth, Austin Trevor
'As a statement of war aims, one feels, this leaves the world beyond Roedean still expectant.' – *Graham Greene*

The Lion in Winter *
GB 1968 134m Eastmancolor Panavision
Avco Embassy/Haworth (Martin Poll)
Henry II and Eleanor of Aquitaine celebrate Christmas together and have a family row.
An acting feast for two principals and assorted supports, a talking marathon in which not all the talk is good, a smart comedy with sudden lapses into melodrama; stimulating in parts but all rather tiresome by the end, especially as there is not much medieval splendour.
w James Goldman play James Goldman d Anthony Harvey ph Douglas Slocombe m John Barry
☆ Katharine Hepburn, Peter O'Toole, Jane Merrow, John Castle, Anthony Hopkins, Nigel Terry, Timothy Dalton
'He is not writing a factual movie about the Plantagenets but an interpretation in which he combines their language and ours.' – *Philip T. Hartung*
♟ James Goldman; John Barry; Katharine Hepburn
♙ best picture; Anthony Harvey; Peter O'Toole
♛ John Barry

A Lion Is in the Streets *
US 1953 88m Technicolor
Warner/Cagney Productions (William Cagney)
An itinerant confidence trickster becomes a defender of the people, is nominated for governor, and becomes corrupt.
Busy melodrama which came a bit soon after All the King's Men.
w Luther Davis novel Adria Locke Langley d Raoul Walsh ph Harry Stradling m Franz Waxman pd Wiard Ihnen
☆ James Cagney, Barbara Hale, Anne Francis, Warner Anderson, John McIntire, Jeanne Cagney, Lon Chaney Jnr, Frank McHugh, Larry Keating, Onslow Stevens, James Millican, Sara Haden
'A headlong and dynamic drama which offers Mr Cagney one of his most colourful and meaningful roles.' – *Bosley Crowther*

The Lion King ***
♟♟ US 1994 88m Technicolor
Buena Vista/Walt Disney (Don Hahn)
A lion cub, exiled by his evil uncle, grows up enjoying the easy life, but is persuaded that he must fight to restore himself to his rightful place as king.
An entertaining animated drama with some stunning moments, but a somewhat preachy tone; it isn't as much fun as the recent Disney features, although it found great favour with the public.
w Irene Mecchi, Jonathan Roberts, Linda Woolverton d Roger Allers, Rob Minkoff m Hans Zimmer, Lebo M m/ly Elton John, Tim Rice pd Chris Sanders
☆ Featuring the voices of Matthew Broderick, Rowan Atkinson, Niketa Calame, Jim Cummings, Whoopi Goldberg, Jeremy Irons, Robert Guillaume, James Earl Jones, Cheech Marin, Jonathan Taylor Thomas
'Bambi, but with carnivores ... The animation, computer-assisted in some of the more elaborate

sequences, is sometimes impressive, but rarely impressive enough to overcome a certain impersonality – a stubborn mechanical coldness.' – *Terrence Rafferty, New Yorker*
'Its true glories are in storytelling, voicemanship and scenic splendour – virtues that would be familiar by now from earlier Disney cartoons if they weren't, each time, so wonderfully fresh.' – *Time*
† The film was the biggest earner of 1994 in the US, taking $298.9m at the box-office. Its plot reportedly resembles that of *Jungle Taitei* (aka *Jungle Emperor*), a Japanese animated series made in the 60s.
♟ Hans Zimmer; song 'Can You Feel the Love Tonight' (mElton John, lyTim Rice)
♛ songs 'Circle of Life', 'Hakuna Matata'

Lion of the Desert
US 1980 163m Eastmancolor Panavision
Falcon International (Moustapha Akkad)
In 1929 an Italian general in Libya withstands the attacks of rebel leader Omar Mukhtar.
Whitewashed account of the activities of a patriarchal partisan who was hanged in 1931. Of interest primarily to Arab zealots.
w H. A. L. Craig d Moustapha Akkad ph Jack Hildyard m Maurice Jarre pd Mario Garbuglia, Syd Cain
☆ Anthony Quinn, Oliver Reed, Irene Papas, Raf Vallone, Rod Steiger, John Gielgud, Andrew Keir

Lionheart: see AWOL (1990)

Lionheart
♟♟ US 1987 104m colour
Orion (Stanley O'Toole, Talia Shire)
On his way to join King Richard the Lionheart's crusade, a young knight rescues a band of children from a slave trader.
Aimed at a family audience, it lacks excitement and pace and is best treated as a soporific.
w Menno Meyjes, Richard Outten d Franklin J. Schaffner ph Alec Mills m Jerry Goldsmith pd Gil Parrondo ed David Bretherton, Richard Haines
☆ Eric Stoltz, Gabriel Byrne, Nicola Cowper, Dexter Fletcher, Deborah Barrymore, Nicholas Clay, Bruce Purchase, Neil Dickson, Chris Pitt
'High on heart-warming ideals, but low in every other department.' – *Empire*

The Lion's Den: see La Boca del Lobo

'Rape was only the beginning!'
Lipstick
US 1976 90m Technicolor
Paramount/Dino de Laurentiis (Freddie Fields)
A girl is raped but gets nowhere in court until her sister lures the man to rape her too.
Franker but not very interesting extension of a fifties co-feature, with all the developments well telegraphed.
w David Rayfiel d Lamont Johnson ph Bill Butler m Michel Polnareff
☆ Margaux Hemingway, Perry King, Anne Bancroft, Chris Sarandon, Mariel Hemingway, Robin Gammell
'One of Lipstick's points is that voyeurism encourages senseless crime, but it unfortunately ignores its own lesson.' – *Marsha McCreadie, Films in Review*

Liquid Sky
US 1982 118m TVC Color
Z Films (Slava Tsukerman)
Aliens in a flying saucer land on the roof of a New York skyscraper in search of a heroin-like drug, which they obtain by killing people during orgasm.
A film with an undeserved cult reputation, presumably because it is set among punks and junkies; otherwise it is tediously plotted and poorly written and acted, dealing with unattractive characters in an unpleasant environment.
w Slava Tsukerman, Anne Carlisle, Nina V. Kerova d Slava Tsukerman ph Yuri Neyman m Slava Tsukerman, Brenda L. Hutchinson, Clive Smith pd Marina Levikova-Neyman ed Sharyn Leslie Ross
☆ Anne Carlisle, Paula E. Sheppard, Bob Brady, Susan Doukas, Elaine C. Grove, Stanley Knap, Jack Adalist, Otto von Wernherr

---

'By turns self-consciously bizarre and beautiful.' – *Sight and Sound*

The Liquidator *

GB 1965 104m Metrocolor Panavision
MGM/Leslie Elliott (Jon Pennington)

An ex-war hero is recruited by the secret service as an eliminator of security risks.

Fairly lively James Bond spoof which is never quite as funny as it imagines.

w Peter Yeldham *novel* John Gardner d Jack Cardiff ph Ted Scaife m Lalo Schifrin

☆ Rod Taylor, Trevor Howard, *David Tomlinson*, Jill St John, Wilfrid Hyde-White, Derek Nimmo, Eric Sykes, Akim Tamiroff

Lisa: see *The Inspector*

Lisa and the Devil

Italy 1974 93m Technicolor
Leone International (Alfred Leone)

☒☒   ⊜   ⊘

original title: *Il Diavolo e il Morto*

A tourist stranded in a small town takes refuge in an old, dark villa.

Baroque thriller that constantly teeters on the edge of absurdity before finally falling.

w Mario Bava, Alfred Leone d Mario Bava
ph Cecilio Paniagua m Carlo Savina ad Nedo Azzini ed Carlo Reali

☆ Telly Savalas, Elke Sommer, Sylva Koscina, Alessio Orano, Alida Valli, Gabriele Tinti, Kathy Leone

'Not quite in the first rank of the director's work, it's still a bizarre gem.' – *Empire*

Lisbon

US 1956 90m Trucolor Naturama
Republic (Ray Milland)

☒☒

An international crook negotiates an Iron Curtain prisoner's release, but the man's wife has other ideas.

Glossy international intriguer with smart performances.

w John Tucker Battle d Ray Milland ph Jack Marta m Nelson Riddle

☆ Ray Milland, *Claude Rains*, Maureen O'Hara, Yvonne Furneaux, Francis Lederer, Percy Marmont, Edward Chapman

The Lisbon Story

GB 1946 103m bw
British National

Spies in 1940 Lisbon rescue a French atom scientist.

Flat filming of a musical show which kept Britons humming 'Pedro the Fisherman' throughout World War II.

w Jack Whittingham *play* Harold Purcell, Harry Parr-Davies d Paul Stein ph Ernest Palmer m/ly Harold Purcell, Harry Parr-Davies

☆ Patricia Burke, David Farrar, Walter Rilla, Richard Tauber, Austin Trevor, Harry Welchman

The List of Adrian Messenger **

US 1963 98m bw
U-I/Joel (Edward Lewis)

☒☒

An intelligence officer traps a mass murderer with a penchant for disguise.

Old-fashioned mystery thriller, as though Holmes and Watson were combating a modern Moriarty (and a rough-hewn production). The whole thing is camped up like an end-of-term treat, and as a further gimmick four guest stars allegedly appear under heavy disguise in cameo parts.

w Anthony Veiller *novel* Philip MacDonald d John Huston ph Joe MacDonald m Jerry Goldsmith

☆ George C. Scott, Kirk Douglas, Clive Brook, Dana Wynter, Jacques Roux, Walter Tony Huston, Herbert Marshall, Bernard Archard, Gladys Cooper; and Frank Mitchum, Frank Sinatra, Burt Lancaster, Tony Curtis

'A leisurely, underplayed thriller with some good performances and a gimmick which turns it into a guessing contest.' – *L.A. Times*

Listen

US 1996 101m Eastmancolor Panavision
Orion/Greg H. Sims/Devin/Rampage (Diane Patrick-O'Connor)

A San Francisco advertising executive overhears some telephone conversations and realizes that a serial killer lives in the same apartment block as her.

Convoluted and derivative thriller that requires more attention than it deserves to follow the improbabilities of its narrative.

w Jonas Quastel, Michael Bafaro d Gavin Wilding ph Brian Pearson m David Davidson pd Cathy Robertson ed Melinda Seabrook

☆ Brooke Langton, Gordon Currie, Sarah Buxton, Joel Wyner, Evan Taylor, Andy Romano, Jeff Burnett

'A stylish, and extremely empty-headed, film.' – *Variety*

Listen Darling

US 1938 70m bw
MGM (Jack Cummings)

☒☒   ⊜⊾

Children try to find their widowed mother a new husband.

Slight domestic comedy chiefly notable for its young talent.

w Elaine Ryan, Anne Morrison Chapin *story* Katherine Brush d Edwin L. Marin ph Charles Lawton Jnr m George Axt md George Stoll

☆ Mary Astor, Judy Garland, Freddie Bartholomew, Walter Pidgeon, Alan Hale, Scotty Beckett, Charley Grapewin, Barnett Parker, Gene Lockhart

'Inauspicious start for the Garland- Bartholomew team … mediocre story hurts.' – *Variety*

Listen to Britain ****

GB 1941 20m bw
Ministry of Information (Crown Film Unit)

Images of Britain at war.

A brilliant compilation of almost poetic sights and sounds which distil the essence of a year.

ph H. E. Fowle d/ed Humphrey Jennings

Listen to Me

US 1989 110m CFI color
Columbia TriStar/Weintraub Entertainment/Martin Bregman (Markay Powell)

☒☒   ⊜⊾

Two students fall in love while being members of their college debating team.

Of limited interest, unless you happen to be a member of a debating team, and even then it is unlikely to hold your attention for long.

wd Douglas Day Stewart ph Fred J. Koenekamp m David Foster pd Gregory Pickrell ed Anne V. Coates

☆ Kirk Cameron, Jami Gertz, Roy Scheider, Amanda Peterson, Tim Quill, George Wyner, Anthony Zerbe, Christopher Atkins

Listen Up: The Lives of Quincy Jones

US 1990 115m Technicolor
Warner/Cort (Courtney Sale Ross)

☒☒   ⊜⊾

Documentary on the life of the influential record producer, arranger and composer who began as a big-band trumpeter.

Distractingly edited, as if intended for an audience with a very short attention span, and mainly given over to performances and uninformative interviews with those with whom Jones has worked, from jazz musicians such as Lionel Hampton, Miles Davis and Ella Fitzgerald to rock singer Michael Jackson and rapper Big Daddy Kane.

d Ellen Weissbrod ph Stephen Kazmierski m Quincy Jones ed Milton Moses

Lisztomania

GB 1975 104m colour Panavision
Warner/VPS/Goodtimes (Roy Baird, David Puttnam)

The life of Liszt seen in terms of a modern pop performer.

The most excessive and obscene of all this director's controversial works, incapable of criticism on normal terms except that it seems unusually poor in production values.

wd Ken Russell ph Peter Suschitzky md John Forsyth

☆ Roger Daltrey, Sara Kestelman, Paul Nicholas, Fiona Lewis, John Justin, Ringo Starr

'ample dialogue: 'Piss off, Brahms!''

'Ken Russell's first completely unmitigated catastrophe in several years … a welter of arbitrary gags, manic self-references and frantic exploitation-movie clichés.' – *Tony Rayns*

'Oscar Wilde once said "Each man kills the thing he loves", and the remark perfectly suits Ken Russell's film treatments of classical composers … he has bludgeoned into pulp some of the finest music civilization has produced.' – *Patrick Snyder*

'This gaudy compendium of camp, second-hand Freud and third-rate pastiche is like a bad song without end.' – *Sight and Sound*

Liten Ida: see *Little Ida*

Little Accident

US 1930 82m bw
Universal

A man is about to marry again when he finds that his first wife is having his baby.

Stretched-out comedy which fumbles its way along.

w Gladys Lehman *play* Floyd Dell, Thomas Mitchell d William James Craft

☆ Douglas Fairbanks Jnr, Anita Page, Sally Blane, ZaSu Pitts, Joan Marsh, Roscoe Karns, Slim Summerville

'If anybody thinks 82 minutes is the proper time for this film, they should be made to sit through it twice.' – *Variety*

Little Accident

US 1939 65m bw
Universal

A baby is passed from hand to hand after her father abandons her.

Simple-minded comedy bearing little relation to the above; it's now a vehicle for the baby.

w Paul Yawitz, Eve Greene d Charles Lamont

☆ Baby Sandy, Hugh Herbert, Richard Carlson, Florence Rice, Ernest Truex, Fritz Feld, Edgar Kennedy

'Elemental comedy for supporting attraction in nabes.' – *Variety*

Little Annie Rooney *

US 1925 99m bw silent
United Artists/Mary Pickford

☒☒

A 12-year-old tomboy in a New York slum rounds up the killer of her policeman father.

Sentimental melodrama, unless you happen to be a 32-year-old star who liked playing kids. Of minor historical interest.

w Hope Loring, Louis D. Lighton d William Beaudine ph Charles Rosher, Hal Mohr m Joseph Plunkett

☆ Mary Pickford, William Haines, Walter James, Gordon Griffith

The Little Ark

🏃🏃   US 1971 86m DeLuxe Panavision
Cinema Center/Robert B. Radnitz

Two war orphans and their pets, trapped in a flood, sail to safety in a houseboat.

Well-meaning, somewhat allegorical family film, too desultory to maintain interest and rather too frightening for children.

w Joanna Crawford *novel* Jan de Hartog d James B. Clark ph Austin Dempster, Denys Coop m Fred Karlin

☆ Theodore Bikel, Philip Frame, Genevieve Ambas

♬ song 'Come Follow Follow Me' (mFred Karlin, lyMarsha Karlin)

Little Big Horn *

US 1951 86m bw
Lippert (Carl K. Hittleman)

☒☒

GB title: *The Fighting Seventh*

A cavalry squad sets out to warn Custer about Little Big Horn, but all the men are massacred before Custer arrives.

Dour, impressive low-budget Western.

wd Charles Marquis Warren ph Ernest Miller m Paul Dunlap

☆ Lloyd Bridges, John Ireland, Marie Windsor, Reed Hadley, Hugh O'Brian, Wally Cassell, King Donovan

Little Big League

🏃🏃   US 1994 119m Technicolor
Rank/Castle Rock/Lobell/Bergman

☒☒   ⊜⊾

A 12-year-old boy is left a baseball team by his grandfather and decides to take over as manager.

Amiable but uninvolving entertainment for sports-struck kids.

w Gregory K. Pincus, Adam Scheinman d Andrew Scheinman ph Donald E. Thorin m Stanley Clarke pd Jeffrey Howard ed Michael Jablow

☆ Luke Edwards, Timothy Busfield, John Ashton, Ashley Crow, Kevin Dunn, Jason Robards, Billy L. Sullivan

'Has its heart in the right place but never makes it out of the infield in terms of laughs or excitement.' – *Variety*

'The Cavalry Against The Indians And Dustin Hoffman Is On Both Sides!'

Little Big Man *

US 1970 147m Technicolor Panavision
Stockbridge/Hiller/Cinema Center (Stuart Millar)

☒☒   ☒☒   ⊜⊾

An aged veteran of the old west recounts his life story – with elaborations.

A number of episodes varying from stark tragedy to satirical farce are framed for no good reason by the star in heavy disguise; the intention is hard to guess but there are goodies along the way.

w Calder Willingham *novel* Thomas Berger d Arthur Penn ph Harry Stradling m John Hammond pd Dean Tavoularis

☆ Dustin Hoffman, Martin Balsam, Faye Dunaway, *Chief Dan George*, Richard Mulligan, Jeff Corey

'A hip epic, with an amiable first hour. Then the massacres and messages take over.' – *New Yorker*, 1976

'A tangy and, I think, unique film with American verve, about some of the things American verve has done.' – *Stanley Kauffmann*

& Chief Dan George

Little Big Shot

US 1935 80m bw
Warner

A gangster's child is orphaned and cared for by two con men.

Reasonably lively vehicle for a new child star who didn't last.

w Jerry Wald, Julius J. Epstein, Robert Andrews d Michael Curtiz

☆ Sybil Jason, Glenda Farrell, Robert Armstrong, Edward Everett Horton, Jack La Rue, J. Carrol Naish, Edgar Kennedy

'Should pave the way handily for young Miss Jason's future.' – *Variety*

A Little Bit of Heaven

🏃🏃   US 1940 87m bw
Universal (Joe Pasternak)

A 12-year-old girl becomes a singing sensation but runs into family opposition.

Predictable vehicle for a young star being built up as a stop-gap Deanna Durbin.

w Daniel Taradash, Gertrude Purcell, Harold Goldman *story* Grover Jones d Andrew Marton ph John Seitz m Charles Previn

☆ Gloria Jean, Robert Stack, Hugh Herbert, C. Aubrey Smith, Stuart Erwin, Nan Grey, Eugene Pallette, Billy Gilbert, Butch and Buddy

Little Boy Lost

US 1953 95m bw
Paramount (William Perlberg)

An American returns to Paris after the war to find his wife dead and his small son missing.

Rather dull tearjerker.

wd George Seaton *novel* Marghanita Laski ph George Barnes m Victor Young

☆ Bing Crosby, Claude Dauphin, Christian Fourcade, Gabrielle Dorziat, Nicole Maurey

Little Buddha *

🏃🏃   France/UK 1993 123m Technicolor Technovision
Buena Vista/Ciby 2000/Recorded Picture (Jeremy Thomas)

☒☒   ☒☒   ⊜⊾   🎧

A lama, who leaves his monastery in Bhutan to find the reincarnation of his own teacher, discovers three candidates, including a young American boy.

Two themes – a childlike retelling of the story of how Siddharta becomes the Buddha and the drama of an American family's immersion in an unfamiliar culture – exist uneasily together, despite their symmetry. There is a naïvety in both; the photography – predominantly a cool blue in its American settings, glowing golden in its eastern scenes – and composition provide a constant visual fascination.

🏃🏃 film suitable for family viewing   ☒☒ VHS video-cassette for the British PAL system   ☒☒ VHS video-cassette for the British PAL system in wide screen-format   ⊘ Video cassette in a computer-colourised version   ▬ American NTSC video-cassette   ⊜⊾ Laser disc w Rudy Wurlitzer, Mark Peploe *story* Bernardo Bertolucci d Bernardo Bertolucci *ph* Vittorio Storaro m Ryuichi Sakamoto *pd* James Acheson *ed* Pietro Scalia

☆ Keanu Reeves, Ying Ruocheng, Chris Isaak, Bridget Fonda, Alex Wiesendorf, Raju Lal, Greishma Makar Singh

'After 30 years of making passionately skeptical movies, Bertolucci has made a film of the most sophisticated simplicity. His triumph is to make you see the Buddhist world through his eyes. It shines like innocence reincarnated.' – *Richard Corliss, Time*

'Long, solemn and humourless, this isn't going to win many converts to the cinema, let alone Buddhism.' – *Kim Newman, Empire*

Little Caesar ****
US 1931 77m bw
Warner
📼 🎞 🎥

The rise and fall of a vicious gangster.
Its central character clearly modelled on Al Capone, this also has historical interest as vanguard of a spate of noisy gangster films. The star was forever identified with his role, and the film, though technically dated, moves fast enough to maintain interest over sixty years later.

w Francis Faragoh, Robert N. Lee *novel* W. R. Burnett d *Mervyn Le Roy ph* Tony Gaudio m Erno Rapee

☆ *Edward G. Robinson*, Douglas Fairbanks Jnr, Glenda Farrell, William Collier Jnr, Ralph Ince, George E. Stone, Thomas Jackson, Stanley Fields, Sidney Blackmer

'It has irony and grim humour and a real sense of excitement and its significance does not get in the way of the melodrama.' – *Richard Dana Skinner*

'One of the best gangster talkers yet turned out ... a swell picture.' – *Variety*
🏆 Francis Faragoh, Robert N. Lee

The Little Colonel **
👪 US 1935 80m bw (colour sequence)
Fox (B. G. de Sylva)
🎞

In a Southern household after the Civil War, a little girl ends a family feud, plays Cupid to her sister, routs a few villains and mollifies her cantankerous grandfather.
First-class Temple vehicle, the first to boast an expensive production.

w William Conselman *novel* Annie Fellows Johnston d David Butler *ph* Arthur Miller *md* Arthur Lange

☆ *Shirley Temple*, Lionel Barrymore, Evelyn Venable, John Lodge, Bill Robinson, Hattie McDaniel, Sidney Blackmer

The Little Damozel
GB 1933 73m bw
British and Dominions
A gambler marries a young singer for a bribe, but falls in love with her.
Lavender-tinted romance with music; notable as its star's first major role.

w Donovan Pedelty *play* Monckton Hoffe d Herbert Wilcox m Ray Noble, Noël Coward
☆ Anna Neagle, James Rennie, Benita Hume, Athole Stewart, Alfred Drayton

Little Darlings
US 1980 92m Metrocolor
Paramount/Stephen J. Friedman
📼 🎞 🎥

Teenage girls at a summer camp take bets on who will lose her virginity first.
Crass and tasteless comedy with only prurient appeal.
w Kimi Peck, Dalene Young d Ronald F. Maxwell *ph* Fred Batka m Charles Fox *pd* William Hiney *ed* Pembroke J. Herring
☆ Tatum O'Neal, Kristy McNichol, Krista Errickson, Armand Assante

Little Dorrit **
👪 GB 1987 357m Technicolor
Sands/Cannon (John Brabourne)
📼 🎞 🎥

Faithful adaptation of classic novel.
Lovingly made by a large team, economically and authentically re-creating Dickens's London, with a starry cast giving their all. Adored by audiences who could take the length.

wd Christine Edzard *novel* Charles Dickens *ph* Bruno de Keyzer m Giuseppe Verdi
☆ Derek Jacobi, Joan Greenwood, Max Wall, *Alec Guinness*, Cyril Cusack, Sarah Pickering, Eleanor Bron, Robert Morley
† Part 1 is 176m, Part 2 runs to 181m.
🏆 Alec Guinness; best adapted screenplay

The Little Drummer Girl *
US 1984 130m Technicolor
Warner/Pan Arts (Robert L. Crawford)
📼 🎞

An American actress in Britain is persuaded by Israeli agents to lose her Arab sympathies and spy for them.
Tediously protracted and unexciting version of a novel which was generally agreed to have been based on Vanessa Redgrave. Interesting for its quality look and surface style only: the intricate plotting of the Le Carré manner is surely no longer fashionable.

w Loring Mandel *novel* John Le Carré d George Roy Hill *ph* Wolfgang Treu m Dave Grusin *pd* Henry Bumstead *ed* William Reynolds
☆ Diane Keaton, Yorgo Voyagis, Klaus Kinski, Sami Frey, Michael Cristofer, David Suchet, Eli Danker, Thorley Walters, Anna Massey
† Author Le Carré appears in a small role under his real name of David Cornwell.

Little Egypt
US 1951 81m Technicolor
Universal-International (Jack Gross)
GB title: *Chicago Masquerade*
An American girl poses as an Egyptian princess at the Chicago World's Fair.
Sluggish turn-of-the-century romantic melodrama based on a factual swindle involving a phoney Nile reclamation project.
w Oscar Brodney, Doris Gilbert d Frederick de Cordova *ph* Russell Metty *md* Joseph Gershenson
☆ Rhonda Fleming, Mark Stevens, Nancy Guild, Charles Drake, Tom D'Andrea, Minor Watson, Steve Geray

Little Fauss and Big Halsy
US 1970 99m Movielab Panavision
Paramount/Alfran/Furie (Albert S. Ruddy)
Two motor cycle track racers team up and have violent adventures round the country.
Rather pointless capers in the wake of Easy Rider, neither interesting nor well done.
w Charles Eastman d Sidney J. Furie *ph* Ralph Woolsey m Johnny Cash, Bob Dylan, Carl Perkins
☆ Robert Redford, Michael J. Pollard, *Noah Beery Jnr*, Lauren Hutton
'A sort of *Batman and Robin* on wheels.' – *Rex Reed*

The Little Foxes ***
US 1941 116m bw
Samuel Goldwyn
📼 🇺🇸 🎥

A family of schemers in post-Civil War days will stop at nothing to outwit each other.
Superb film of a brilliant play; excellent to look at and listen to, with a compelling narrative line and memorable characters.

w Lillian Hellman *play* Lillian Hellman d William Wyler m Gregg Toland m Meredith Willson *ad* Stephen Goosson *ed* Daniel Mandell
☆ Bette Davis, Herbert Marshall, Teresa Wright, Richard Carlson, Charles Dingle, Dan Duryea, Carl Benton Reid, Patricia Collinge, Jessica Grayson, Russell Hicks

HORACE GIDDENS (HERBERT MARSHALL): 'Maybe it's easy for the dying to be honest. I'm sick of you, sick of this house, sick of my unhappy life with you. I'm sick of your brothers and their dirty tricks to make a dime. There must be better ways of getting rich than building sweatshops and pounding the bones of the town to make dividends for you to spend. You'll wreck the town, you and your brothers. You'll wreck the country, you and your kind, if they let you. But not me, I'll die my own way, and I'll do it without making the world any worse. I leave that to you.'

'One of the really beautiful jobs in the whole range of movie making.' – *Otis Ferguson*
'No one knows better than Wyler when to shift the camera's point of view, when to cut, or how to relate the characters in one shot to those in the next ... you never have to wonder where you are in a Wyler picture.' – *Arthur Knight*

The Little Hut
US 1957 90m Eastmancolor
MGM/Herbson SA (F. Hugh Herbert, Mark Robson)
A man, his wife and her lover are shipwrecked on a desert island.
Sophisticated French farce which falls resoundingly flat in this bowdlerized Hollywood version in bilious colour,

🏆 best picture; Lillian Hellman; William Wyler; Meredith Willson; Bette Davis; Teresa Wright; Patricia Collinge; Stephen Goosson; Daniel Mandell

Little Friend
GB 1934 85m bw
Gaumont
A girl is driven to attempt suicide by her parents' proposed divorce.
Fairly well written but rather stilted domestic drama which maintained a small reputation.
w Margaret Kennedy, Christopher Isherwood, Berthold Viertel *novel* Ernst Lothar d Berthold Viertel
☆ Nova Pilbeam, Matheson Lang, Lydia Sherwood, Arthur Margetson, Allan Aynesworth, Jean Cadell, Jimmy Hanley

'From homicide to house parties – from dames to debutantes!'
Little Giant
US 1946 91m bw
Universal (Joseph Gershenson)
GB title: *On the Carpet*
Misadventures of a vacuum cleaner salesman.
Curious, unsatisfactory Abbott and Costello comedy in which the boys play separate characters instead of working as a team. They should have waited for a better script before experimenting.
w Paul Jarrico, Richard Collins, Walter de Leon d William A. Seiter *ph* Charles van Enger m Edgar Fairchild
☆ Bud Abbott, Lou Costello, Brenda Joyce, George Cleveland, Elena Verdugo

The Little Giant
US 1933 74m bw
Warner
📼 🎥

At the end of Prohibition, a beer baron moves to California and tries to break into society.
Disappointingly unfunny gangster comedy which never really gets going.
w Robert Lord, Wilson Mizner d Roy del Ruth *ph* Sid Hickox m Leo F. Forbstein
☆ Edward G. Robinson, Mary Astor, Helen Vinson, Kenneth Thomson, Russell Hopton, Donald Dillaway
'It makes Robinson a comedy character surrounded by semi-travesty and the fans are likely to resent it.' – *Variety*

Little Giants *
👪 US 1994 105m colour
Warner/Amblin (Arne L. Schmidt)
📼 🎞 🎥 🎧

When his sporting hero of a brother rejects his daughter as not good enough to play in a junior football team, a wimp decides to create his own team featuring her and other rejects.
Amiable and amusing sporting comedy, despite its predictability.
w James Ferguson, Robert Shallcross, Tommy Swerdlow, James Haggin, Michael Goldberg d Duwayne Dunham *ph* Janusz Kaminski m John Debney *pd* Bill Kenney *ed* Donn Cambern
☆ Rick Moranis, Ed O'Neill, John Madden, Shawna Waldron, Mary Ellen Trainor, Matthew McCurley, Susanna Thompson, Brian Haley

The Little Girl Who Lives Down the Lane
US/Canada/France 1976 94m colour
Zev Braun/ICL/Filmedis-Filmel (Zev Braun)
🎞 🎥

A 13-year-old girl, when her father dies, is discovered to be keeping her mother's corpse in the cellar, and doesn't stop at more murders to keep her secret.
Tasteless piece of grand guignol, badly directed and over-acted.
w Laird Koenig *novel* Laird Koenig d Nicolas Gessner *ph* Rene Verzier m Christian Gaubert
☆ Jodie Foster, Alexis Smith, Martin Sheen, Scott Jacoby
† Originally intended as a TV movie.

The Little Hut
US 1957 90m Eastmancolor
MGM/Herbson SA (F. Hugh Herbert, Mark Robson)
A man, his wife and her lover are shipwrecked on a desert island.
Sophisticated French farce which falls resoundingly flat in this bowdlerized Hollywood version in bilious colour,

fatally compromising itself at the beginning with a 'realistic' London prologue.
w F. Hugh Herbert *play* André Roussin and Nancy Mitford d Mark Robson *ph* Frederick A. Young m Robert Farnon *ad* Elliot Scott *ed* Ernest Walter
☆ Stewart Granger, David Niven, Ava Gardner, Walter Chiari, Finlay Currie, Jean Cadell

Little Ida **
Norway 1981 79m Eastmancolor
Minema/Norsk Film/Svenska Filminstituten (Harald Ohrvik, Sven Johansen)
original title: *Liten Ida*
A seven-year-old girl is ostracized because of her mother's relationship with a Nazi soldier.
Unsentimental, excellently acted account of childhood suffering.
w Marit Paulsen, Laila Mikkelsen *novel* Marit Paulsen d Laila Mikkelsen *ph* Hans Welin, Kjell Vassdal m Eyvind Solas *ad* Anders Barreus *ed* Peter Falck
☆ Sunniva Lindekleiv, Howard Halvorsen, Lise Fjeldstad, Arne Lindtner Ness, Ellen Westerfjell, Roennaug Alten

Little Johnny Jones
US 1929 73m bw
First National
An American jockey wins the Derby.
Mild comedy with music from the old George M. Cohan play.
w Adelaide Heilbron and Eddie Buzzell d Mervyn Le Roy
☆ Eddie Buzzell, Alice Day, Edna Murphy, Robert Edeson
'Familiar formula but done nicely.' – *Variety*

The Little Kidnappers: see *The Kidnappers*

Little Lord Fauntleroy *
👪 US 1921 11m bw silent
United Artists/Mary Pickford
An American boy who lives with his widowed mother discovers he is heir to an English dukedom.
Over-upholstered sentimental extravaganza tailored for a star in her twenties playing both young Cedric and his mother, a curious double. One can now only wonder at the immense appeal this film had in its own time; but that is not to diminish the vitality of its star.
w Bernard McConville *novel* Frances Hodgson Burnett d Jack Pickford, Alfred E. Green *ph* Charles Rosher m Louis F. Gottschalk
☆ Mary Pickford, Claude Gillingwater, Kate Price, James A. Marcus, Emmett King

Little Lord Fauntleroy *
👪 US 1936 98m bw
David O. Selznick
🎞

A sound remake which did surprisingly well at the box-office and is still very watchable.
w Richard Schayer, Hugh Walpole, David O. Selznick d John Cromwell *ph* Charles Rosher m Max Steiner
☆ *Freddie Bartholomew, C. Aubrey Smith*, Mickey Rooney, Dolores Costello, Jessie Ralph, Guy Kibbee
† A TV movie version appeared in 1980, with Ricky Schroder and Alec Guinness.

Little Man Tate *
US 1991 99m DeLuxe
Columbia TriStar/Orion (Scott Rudin, Peggy Rajski)
📼 🎞 🎥 🎧

A battle develops over the future of a precociously bright child between his working-class mother and a teacher of gifted children.
A drama of family tensions that might have worked better on television.
w Scott Frank d Jodie Foster *ph* Mike Southon m Mark Isham *pd* Jon Hutman *ed* Lynzee Klingman
☆ Jodie Foster, Dianne Wiest, Adam Hann-Byrd, Harry Connick Jnr, David Pierce, Debi Mazar, P. J. Ochian
'A nice little film, but what audience it is meant to appeal to is, frankly, something of a mystery.' – *Angie Errigo, Empire*

Little Man, What Now? *
US 1934 95m bw
Universal
Problems of Germany in the grip of unemployment.

One of the studio's several 'sequels' to *All Quiet on the Western Front*, *poignant at the time but now very dated.*

w William Anthony McGuire *novel* Hans Fallada d Frank Borzage *ph* Norbert Brodine
☆ Margaret Sullavan, Douglass Montgomery, Alan Hale, Muriel Kirkland, Alan Mowbray, Mae Marsh

'Human, homely and romantic ... should get ample b.o. attention.' – *Variety*

Little Men

US   1935   77m   bw
Mascot

Joe and her professor run a school for boys.
Slapdash sequel to Little Women; not an ambitious production.

w Gertrude Orr *novel* Louisa M. Alcott d Phil Rosen
☆ Ralph Morgan, Erin O'Brien-Moore, Junior Durkin, Cora Sue Collins, Frankie Darro, Dickie Moore

'Goes overboard on pathos ... tears flow over the most insignificant matters.' – *Variety*
† A remake emerged from RKO in 1940, but was ill received. Running 84 minutes, it starred Kay Francis, Jack Oakie, James Lydon, and Ann Gillis, not to mention Elsie the cow. Mark Kelly and Arthur Caesar wrote it, Norman Z. McLeod directed; for Graham Towne and Gene Baker.

The Little Mermaid **

🏫   US   1989   83m
Warner/Walt Disney/Silver Screen Partners IV (Howard Ashman, John Musker)
🔲 ▬ ◎ ◯

A mermaid falls in love with a prince and longs to be human.
A return to Disney's classic manner, with some excellent animation, though sentimentality is rampant.
wd John Musker, Ron Clements *story* Hans Christian Andersen m Alan Menken
m/ly Howard Ashman, Alan Menken
☆ Featuring Voices of Rene Auberjonois, Christopher Daniel Barnes, Jodi Benson, Pat Carroll, Paddi Edwards, Buddy Hackett, Jason Marin, Kenneth Mars, Edie McClurg, Will Ryan, Ben Wright, Samuel E. Wright
🏆 best original score; best song 'Under the Sea' (m/lAlan Menken; Howard Ashman)
Ⓖ song 'Kiss the Girl' (m/lAlan Menken; Howard Ashman)

The Little Minister

US   1934   110m   bw
RKO (Pandro S. Berman)
▬ ◎

In 1840 Scotland, the gypsy girl with whom the new pastor falls unsuitably in love is really the local earl's wayward ward.
Tedious film version of a cloyingly whimsical play.
w Jane Murfin, Sarah Y. Mason, Victor Heerman *play* J. M. Barrie d Richard Wallace *ph* Henry Gerrard m Max Steiner
☆ *Katharine Hepburn*, John Beal, Alan Hale, Donald Crisp, Lumsden Hare, Andy Clyde, Beryl Mercer, Dorothy Stickney, Frank Conroy, Reginald Denny

'Fine production of an old favourite.' – *Variety*
'Although dear Babbie's elfin whimsies are likely to cause teeth-gnashing among unsympathetic moderns, Miss Hepburn plays the part with likeable sprightliness and charm.' – *André Sennwald, New York Times*

Little Miss Broadway

🏫   US   1938   70m   bw
TCF (David Hempstead)
▬

A small girl is adopted by the owner of a hotel for vaudeville artistes.
One of the child star's more casual vehicles, but quite pleasing.
w Harry Tugend, Jack Yellen d Irving Cummings *ph* Arthur Miller *md* Louis Silvers
☆ Shirley Temple, George Murphy, Jimmy Durante, Edna May Oliver, Phyllis Brooks, George Barbier, Edward Ellis, Jane Darwell, El Brendel, Donald Meek, Claude Gillingwater, Russell Hicks

'It can't be old age, but it does look like weariness.' – *New York Times*
'Shirley's better than her new vehicle, which in turn is better than her last one.' – *Variety*

Little Miss Marker **

🏫   US   1934   80m   bw
Paramount (B. P. Schulberg)
🔲

GB title: *The Girl in Pawn*

A cynical racetrack gambler is forced to adopt a little girl, who not only softens him but saves him from his enemies.
The twin appeals of Temple (a new hot property) and Runyon made this a big hit of its time.
w William R. Lipman, Sam Hellman, Gladys Lehman *story* Damon Runyon d Alexander Hall *ph* Alfred Gilks *songs* Leo Robin, Ralph Rainger
☆ *Shirley Temple, Adolphe Menjou*, Dorothy Dell, Charles Bickford, Lynne Overman, Frank McGlynn Snr, Willie Best

'A good response to that element which claims there is nothing good in pictures. Clean, funny, with thrills and heart appeal all nicely blended.' – *Variety*
'No one can deny that the infant was a trouper: she delivers her lines with a killer instinct.' – *Pauline Kael, 70s*
† Remade as *Sorrowful Jones* (qv).

Little Miss Marker

🏫   US   1980   103m   Technicolor
Universal (Jennings Lang)
▬

Mainly glutinous remake of the above, with acerbic asides from the star.
wd Walter Bernstein *ph* Philip Lathrop m Henry Mancini
☆ Walter Matthau, Julie Andrews, Tony Curtis, Bob Newhart, Sara Stimson, Lee Grant, Brian Dennehy

Little Mr Jim

US   1946   92m   bw
Orville O. Dull/MGM

The plight of a youngster when mother dies and father takes to drink.
Unabashed tearjerker with a fairly resistible child star.
w George Bruce *novel* Army Brat by Tommy Wadelton d Fred Zinnemann
☆ Jackie 'Butch' Jenkins, James Craig, Frances Gifford, Luana Patten, Spring Byington

Little Murders

US   1971   108m   DeLuxe
TCF/Brodsky-Gould (Jack Brodsky)
▬

A young photographer rises above all the urban horror of New York life, but when his wife is killed by a sniper he takes to violence.
This adaptation of an ultrablack comedy would have worked better as a comic strip, for its characters are satirical puppets, and when played by human beings the whole thing seems violently silly.
w Jules Feiffer *play* Jules Feiffer d Alan Arkin *ph* Gordon Willis m Fred Kaz
☆ Elliott Gould, Marcia Rodd, Elizabeth Wilson, Vincent Gardenia, Alan Arkin

Little Nellie Kelly *

US   1940   100m   bw
MGM (Arthur Freed)

The daughter of a New York Irish cop patches up a family feud.
Sentimental nostalgic vehicle for young Judy Garland, who plays both wife and daughter and sings plenty of standard melodies.
w Jack McGowan *play* George M. Cohan d Norman Taurog *ph* Ray June *songs* George M. Cohan, Roger Edens, Nacio Herb Brown, Arthur Freed
☆ Judy Garland, George Murphy, Charles Winninger, Douglas McPhail, Arthur Shields, Forrester Harvey

A Little Night Music *

Austria/West Germany   1977   125m
Eastmancolor
Sascha Film/S & T (Elliott Kastner)
🔲 ▬ ◎

In Vienna at the turn of the century, a middle-aged lawyer, frustrated by the virginity of his young wife, turns to an old actress flame.
Fumbled version of a rather splendid Broadway musical based on Ingmar Bergman's Smiles of a Summer Night. The locale is changed, several of the songs are cut, and the leads are miscast.
w Hugh Wheeler *play* Hugh Wheeler d Harold Prince *ph* Arthur Ibbetson *m/ly* Stephen Sondheim

☆ Elizabeth Taylor, Diana Rigg, Len Cariou, Lesley-Anne Down, Hermione Gingold, Christopher Guard, Laurence Guittard
Ⓙ Jonathan Tunick (music adaptation)

Little Nikita

US   1988   98m   DeLuxe
Columbia (Harry Gittes)
🔲 ▬ ◎

aka: *The Sleepers*

An all-American boy discovers from an FBI agent that his parents are not the average couple they seem, but Soviet spies.
Ineptly plotted thriller that piles on complexity at the cost of credibility; the acting is better than the script or direction deserve.
w John Hill, Bo Goldman *story* Tom Musca, Terry Schwartz d Richard Benjamin *ph* Laszlo Kovacs m Marvin Hamlisch, Joe Curiale *pd* Gene Callahan *ed* Jacqueline Cambas
☆ Sidney Poitier, River Phoenix, Richard Jenkins, Caroline Kava, Richard Bradford, Loretta Devine, Richard Lynch, Lucy Deakins

'Between good and evil and heaven and hell is...'
Little Odessa *

US   1994   98m   Foto-Kem
First Independent/New Line (Paul Webster)
🔲 ▬ ◎

An exiled, edgy, hired killer returns to his Russian-Jewish community in Brighton Beach on an assignment and to see his family: heavy-handed father, dying mother and mixed-up younger brother.
Downbeat tale of melancholy lives, in which death and violence loom large; it compels almost as much as it repels.
wd James Gray *ph* Tom Richmond *pd* Kevin Thompson *ed* Dorian Harris
☆ Tim Roth, Edward Furlong, Moira Kelly, Vanessa Redgrave, Paul Guilfoyle, Natasha Andreichenko, Maximilian Schell

'A sparse, unforgiving work – part Oedipal drama, part thriller, bound together by a dense web of threat.' – *Tom Shone, Sunday Times*

Little Old New York

US   1940   100m   bw
TCF (Raymond Griffith)

The story of Robert Fulton and his invention of the steamboat.
Romantic hokum with a veneer of fact; good production.
w Harry Tugend *play* Rida Johnson Young d Henry King *ph* Leon Shamroy m Alfred Newman
☆ Alice Faye, Richard Greene, Fred MacMurray, Henry Stephenson, Brenda Joyce, Andy Devine, Fritz Feld, Ward Bond

Little Orphan Annie

US   1932   60m   bw
RKO

A girl orphan charms a millionaire.
Ineffective early version of the comic strip used many years later (equally ineffectively) as the basis for Annie.
w Wanda Tuchock, Tom McNamara d John Robertson *ph* Jack MacKenzie *ad* Carroll Clark
☆ Mitzi Green, Edgar Kennedy, May Robson, Buster Phelps

The Little Prince

🏫   US   1974   89m   Technicolor
Paramount/Stanley Donen
▬ ◎

A small boy leaves the asteroid he rules to learn of life on Earth.
A whimsical bestseller turns into an arch musical which falls over itself early on and never recovers; in any case it fatally lacks the common touch, though it has pleasing moments.
w Alan Jay Lerner *novel* Antoine de St-Exupery d Stanley Donen *ph* Christopher Challis *m/ly* Frederick Loewe, Alan Jay Lerner *pd* John Barry
☆ Richard Kiley, Steven Warner, *Bob Fosse*, Gene Wilder, Joss Ackland, Clive Revill, Victor Spinetti, Graham Crowden

'Handsome production cannot obscure limited artistic achievement.' – *Variety*
† Kiley replaced Frank Sinatra, who backed out.
Ⓖ title song; musical adaptation (Angela Morley, Douglas Gamley)

A Little Princess **

🏫   US   1995   97m   Technicolor
Warner/Baltimore (Mark Johnson)
🔲 ▬ ◎ ◯

An English girl is sent by her father to an exclusive New York boarding school; when he is killed in the First World War, she is reduced to working as a servant.
A charming, highly coloured version of a familiar tale, done with a touch of magic.
w Richard LaGravenese, Elizabeth Chandler *novel* Frances Hodgson Burnett d Alfonso Cuaron *ph* Emmanuel Lubezki m Patrick Doyle *pd* Bo Welch *ed* Steven Weisberg
☆ Eleanor Bron, Liam Cunningham, Liesel Matthews, Rusty Schwimmer, Arthur Malet, Vanessa Lee Chester, Errol Sitahal, Heather DeLoach, Taylor Fry

'An exquisite, perfectly played serious fantasy that movingly stresses the importance of magic and the imagination in the scheme of things. A classic the moment it hits the screen, this should delight audiences of all persuasions.' – *Todd McCarthy, Variety*
Ⓖ Emmanuel Lubezki; Bo Welch

The Little Princess **

🏫   US   1939   93m   Technicolor
TCF (Gene Markey)
◎ ◯ ◎

In Victorian London a little girl is left at a harsh school when her father goes abroad.
One of the child star's plushest vehicles, a charming early colour film complete with dream sequence and happy ending.
w Ethel Hill, Walter Ferris *novel* Frances Hodgson Burnett d Walter Lang *ph* Arthur Miller, William Skall *md* Louis Silvers
☆ Shirley Temple, Richard Greene, Anita Louise, Ian Hunter, Cesar Romero, Arthur Treacher, Mary Nash, Sybil Jason, Miles Mander, Marcia Mae Jones, Beryl Mercer, E. E. Clive

Little Rascals

🏫   US   1994   82m   DeLuxe
UIP/Amblin (Michael King, Bill Oakes)
🔲 ▬ ◎

It takes the loss of their clubhouse and go-cart for members of the He-Man Woman Haters Club to discover that girls are not so bad after all.
Redundant, cloying and long-winded revival of a series of shorts starring small kids that belonged to the early, more innocent era of cinema by a director once noted for her sharpness in dealing with today's youth; this, in contrast, is soft and fuzzy and has nothing to offer other than precociousness.
w Paul Guay, Stephen Mazur, Penelope Spheeris, Robert Wolterstorff, Mike Scott d Penelope Spheeris *ph* Richard Bowen m William Ross *pd* Larry Fulton *ed* Ross Albert
☆ Travis Tedford, Bug Hall, Brittany Ashton Holmes, Kevin Jamal Woods, Zachary Mabry, Ross Elliot Bagley, Sam Saletta, Mel Brooks, Whoopi Goldberg, Daryl Hannah, Reba McEntire

'A brainless exercise in exploitation that boasts the worst ensemble acting I have ever seen.' – *James Cameron-Wilson, Film Review*

Little Red Monkey

GB   1954   74m   bw
Anglo Amalgamated/Merton Park (Alec C. Snowden)

Police and an American secret service agent protect a defecting missile expert from an assassin who has already murdered four scientists.
Based on a television serial, a soft-paced spy thriller that provides only a modicum of entertainment.
w James Eastwood, Ken Hughes *story* Eric Maschwitz d Ken Hughes *ph* Joseph Ambor m Trevor Duncan, Jack Jordan *ad* George Haslam *ed* Geoffrey Muller, Inman Hunter
☆ Richard Conte, Rona Anderson, Russell Napier, Colin Gordon, Arnold Marlé, Sylva Langova, Noel Johnson, Donald Bisset

A Little Romance

US   1979   108m   Technicolor
Warner/Orion (Patrick Kelley)
▬ ◎ ◯

A French teenager elopes with an American girl, encouraged by a garrulous old pickpocket.
Treacly juvenile romance enriched by in-jokes and an enjoyably over-the-top star performance.

---

w Allan Burns *novel* Patrick Cauvin *d* George Roy Hill *ph* Pierre William Glenn *m* Georges Delerue *pd* Henry Bumstead
☆ *Laurence Olivier*, Diane Lane, Thelonious Bernard, Arthur Hill, Sally Kellerman, Broderick Crawford, David Dukes
🏆 Georges Delerue
⚲ Allan Burns

A Little Sex
US 1982 94m Technicolor
Universal/MTM (Robert de Laurentiis, Bruce Paltrow)
A young husband has a wandering eye.
Very thin comedy drama more suitable for TV if it were a little less outspoken.
w Robert de Laurentiis *d* Bruce Paltrow *ph* Ralf D. Bode *m* Georges Delerue
☆ Tim Matheson, Kate Capshaw, Edward Herrmann, John Glover

Little Shop of Horrors **
US 1960 70m bw
Santa Clara (Roger Corman)
📼
A dim flower-shop assistant nurtures a man-eating plant.
A Corman quickie, allegedly shot in two days, that is a lively, if occasionally ramshackle, comic delight with a notable cameo from Nicholson as a masochist.
w Charles B. Griffith *d* Roger Corman *ph* Arch Dalzell *m* Fred Katz *ad* Daniel Haller *ed* Marshall Neilan Jnr
☆ Jonathan Haze, Jack Nicholson, Jackie Joseph, Mel Welles, Myrtle Vail, Dick Miller, Leola Wendorff
'One big sick joke, but it's essentially harmless and good-natured.' – *Variety*

Little Shop of Horrors *
🏠 US 1986 88m Technicolor
Warner (David Geffen)
📼 🏴 ⚲ ♫
Workers in a flower shop are menaced by a plant with sinister intent.
Transcript of the off-Broadway musical curiously inspired by a 1960 Roger Corman horror flick which few people saw. A strange item with occasional effective moments.
w Howard Ashman *play* Howard Ashman *d* Frank Oz *ph* Robert Paynter *m* Alan Menken *pd* Roy Walker *ed* John Jympson, Derek Trigg, Bob Gavin
☆ Rick Moranis, Ellen Greene, Vincent Gardenia, Steve Martin
'The best movie ever made about a man-eating plant.' – *People*
♫ song 'Mean Green Mother from Outer Space'

Little Tokyo USA
US 1942 64m bw
Bryan Foy/TCF
A cop ferrets out Japanese espionage agents in Los Angeles.
Tolerable wartime second feature.
w George Bricker *d* Otto Brower
☆ Preston Foster, Brenda Joyce, June Duprez, Harold Huber, Don Douglas, George E. Stone, Abner Biberman

Little Tough Guy
US 1938 83m bw
Universal
📼
A New York slum boy gets involved with a gang and is sent to reform school.
A development of the Dead End Kids, with attitudes not yet crystallized, the overall tone being heavy.
w Gilson Brown, Brenda Weisberg *d* Harold Young
☆ Billy Halop, Helen Parrish, Marjorie Main, Huntz Hall, Gabriel Dell, Bernard Punsley, Jackie Searl, Hally Chester
'One of the best melodramas in recent years – very nearly as good as *Dead End*, and with the same cast of boys.' – *Graham Greene*

Little Tough Guys in Society
US 1938 75m bw
Universal
A society matron invites slum boys to her mansion as a corrective for her stuffy son.
The cast makes it plain that the Dead End Kids/Little Tough Guys are now headed for comedy, the reason being that their 'serious' films were thought to set a bad example.

w Edward Eliscu, Mortimer Offner *d* Erle C. Kenton
☆ Mary Boland, Mischa Auer, Edward Everett Horton, Helen Parrish, Jackie Searl, Frankie Thomas, Billy Benedict, Hally Chester, David Gorcey

Little Vera *
USSR 1988 134m colour
Mainline/Gorky Studios (Yuri Prober)
original title: Malenkaya Vera
A young woman in a grim Russian town leads a disaffected life.
With its drunken father, promiscuous daughter and nagging mother, it will bring a sense of déjà vu to anyone familiar with the British kitchen sink dramas of the 1960s.
w Mariya Khmelik *d* Vasili Pichul *ph* Yefim Reznikov *m* Vladimir Matetski *ad* Vladimir Pasternak *ed* Yelena Zabolotskaya
☆ Natalya Negoda, Ludmilla Zaitseva, Andrei Sokolov, Yuri Nazarov, Alexander Alexeyev-Negreba, Alexandra Tabakova

'Finding Your Own Voice Can Be Magic.'
Little Voice *
GB 1998 96m DeLuxe
Miramax/Scala (Elizabeth Karlsen)
📼 🏴 ⚲ ♫
A sleazy agent spots star potential in an almost mute young woman who can impersonate singers such as Judy Garland and Marlene Dietrich.
About six plots are squeezed together here – including an unlikely romance, and a daughter's queasy worship of her dead father – to the benefit of none; where the film comes to life is in the scenes between Horrocks and Caine, and the finale in a tawdry club. But to enjoy that, you also have to endure the grotesqueries of Brenda Blethyn's screeching performance.
wd Mark Herman *play The Rise and Fall of Little Voice* by Jim Cartwright *ph* Andy Collins *m* John Altman *pd* Don Taylor *ed* Michael Ellis
☆ Jane Horrocks, Michael Caine, Ewan McGregor, Jim Broadbent, Brenda Blethyn, Annette Badland, Philip Jackson
'There's a full-bloodedness about the film which bludgeons you into admiration. It slaps you on the back, kicks you in the gut, dares you not to laugh and cry and leaves your subconscious reeling.' – *Andy Medhurst, Sight and Sound*
⚲ Brenda Blethyn

'They leap from the book and live!'
Little Women ***
🏠 US 1933 115m bw
RKO (David O. Selznick, Merian C. Cooper, Kenneth MacGowan)
📼 🏴 ⚲
The growing up of four sisters in pre-Civil War America.
Charming 'big picture' of its day, with excellent production and performances.
w Sarah Y. Mason, Victor Heerman *novel* Louisa May Alcott *d* George Cukor *ph* Henry Gerrard *m* Max Steiner
☆ Katharine Hepburn, Paul Lukas, Joan Bennett, Frances Dee, Jean Parker, Spring Byington, Edna May Oliver, Douglass Montgomery, Henry Stephenson, Samuel S. Hinds, John Lodge, Nydia Westman
'If to put a book on the screen with all the effectiveness that sympathy and good taste and careful artifice can devise is to make a fine motion picture, then *Little Women* is a fine picture.' – *James Shelley Hamilton*
'One of the most satisfactory pictures I have ever seen.' – *E. V. Lucas, Punch*
'A reminder that emotions and vitality and truth can be evoked from lavender and lace as well as from machine guns and precision dances.' – *Thornton Delehanty, New York Post*
⚲ script
⚲ best picture; George Cukor

Little Women *
🏠 US 1949 122m Technicolor
MGM (Mervyn Le Roy)
📼 🏴
Syrupy Christmas-card remake, notably lacking the light touch.
w Andrew Solt, Sarah Y. Mason, Victor Heerman *d* Mervyn Le Roy *ph* Robert Planck, Charles Schoenbaum *m* Adolph Deutsch (after Max Steiner) *ad* Cedric Gibbons, Paul Groesse

☆ June Allyson, Elizabeth Taylor, Peter Lawford, Margaret O'Brien, Janet Leigh, Mary Astor
'It will raise a smile and draw a tear from the sentimental.' – *MFB*
🏆 art direction
⚲ cinematography

Little Women **
🏠 US 1994 118m colour
Columbia TriStar/Di Novi Pictures
📼 🏴 ⚲ ⓓ ⓓ ♫
Four girls grow to womanhood in 19th-century New England.
A pleasing remake with a decidedly feminist tone that occasionally lapses into oversweetness.
w Robin Swicord *novel* Louisa May Alcott *d* Gillian Armstrong *ph* Geoffrey Simpson *m* Thomas Newman *pd* Jan Roelfs *ed* Nicholas Beauman
☆ Winona Ryder, Gabriel Byrne, Trini Alvarado, Samantha Mathis, Kirsten Dunst, Claire Danes, Susan Sarandon, Eric Stoltz, John Neville, Mary Wickes
'The kind of film which, even when overlaid by the emotional goo of an often too insistent score, succeeds in preventing nausea by its sensible attention to the detail of Alcott's story.' – *Derek Malcolm, Guardian*
⚲ Winona Ryder; costume design; Thomas Newman

The Little World of Don Camillo *
France/Italy 1952 106m bw
Rizzoli-Amato-Francinex (Giuseppe Amato)
📼
In a small Italian village the parish priest and the communist mayor are in a constant state of amiable feud.
Slightly lethargic character comedy with a mild message for its times, popular enough to warrant several sequels.
w Julien Duvivier, René Barjaval *novel* Giovanni Guareschi *d* Julien Duvivier *ph* Nicolas Hayer *m* Alessandro Cicognini
☆ Fernandel, Gino Cervi, Sylvie, Manara, Vera Talqui, Franco Interlenghi
'Cute and cosy.' – *MFB*

The Littlest Rebel *
🏠 US 1935 70m bw
TCF (B. G. de Sylva)
📼
A small Southern girl persuades President Lincoln to release her father.
Charming, archetypal early Temple vehicle, very well produced.
w Edwin Burke *play* Edward Peple *d* David Butler *ph* John Seitz *m* Cyril Mockridge
☆ Shirley Temple, John Boles, Jack Holt, Karen Morley, Bill Robinson, Guinn Williams, Willie Best, Frank McGlynn Snr
'Shirley Temple as the public likes her ... which means money.' – *Variety*

Live a Little, Steal a Lot
US 1974 102m CFI color
American International (Dominick Galate)
aka: Murph the Surf
Jewel thieves go from success to success, but the police finally force them to strike a bargain and return the gems.
Elaborate but rather unattractive caper story based on the exploits of two real criminals.
w E. Arthur Kean *story* Allan Dale Kuhn *d* Marvin Chomsky *ph* Michel Hugo *m* Philip Lambro
☆ Robert Conrad, Don Stroud, Donna Mills, Robyn Miller, Luther Adler, Paul Stewart

Live and Let Die *
GB 1973 121m Eastmancolor
UA/Eon (Harry Saltzman)
📼 🏴 ⚲ ♫
James Bond chases a black master criminal and becomes involved in West Indian Voodoo.
Standard tongue-in-cheek spy adventure with a new lightweight star and an air of déjà vu. Professional standards high.
w Tom Mankiewicz *novel* Ian Fleming *d* Guy Hamilton *ph* Ted Moore *m* George Martin *titles* Maurice Binder
☆ Roger Moore, Yaphet Kotto, Jane Seymour, Clifton James, David Hedison, Bernard Lee, Lois Maxwell

'Plot lines have descended further to the level of the old Saturday afternoon serial, and the treatment is more than ever like a cartoon.' – *Variety*
'A Bond movie is not made. It is packaged. Like an Almond Joy. So much coconut to this much chocolate and a dash of raisins.' – *Joseph Gelmis*
⚲ title song (m/ly Paul and Linda McCartney)

Live Flesh **
France/Spain 1997 100m colour 'Scope
El Deseo/CiBy 2000/France 3 (Agustín Almodóvar)
📼 🏴 ⚲
original title: Carne Trémula
In Madrid, the lives and loves of two policemen, their wives and an ex-convict, the son of a prostitute, intertwine.
Colourful, intricate, entertaining drama of love and loss, revenge and passion, moving from a time of repression to freedom.
w Pedro Almodóvar, Ray Loriga, Jorge Guerricaechevarria *novel* Ruth Rendell *d* Pedro Almodóvar *ph* Affonso Beato *m* Alberto Iglesias *ad* Antxon Gómez *ed* José Salcedo
☆ Javier Bardem, Francesca Neri, Liberto Rabal, Angela Molina, José Sancho, Penelope Cruz, Pilar Bardem
'Discerning viewers internationally should be impressed and entertained by the mature flow of the twisty narrative, in which earned emotion takes precedence over shock value.' – *Lisa Nesselson, Variety*

Live for Life
France/Italy 1967 130m Eastmancolor
UA/Ariane/Vides
♫
original title: Vivre pour Vivre
A news reporter forsakes his wife for a fashion model.
Interminable and unoriginal romantic drama against Sunday supplement backgrounds.
w Pierre Uytterhoeven, Claude Lelouch *m* Francis Lai *d/ph* Claude Lelouch
☆ Yves Montand, Candice Bergen, Annie Girardot, Irene Tunc
'The overall effect is of *Gone with the Wind* remade by Jacopetti.' – *New Yorker*
⚲ best foreign film

The Live Ghost
🏠 US 1934 20m bw
Hal Roach
Two reluctant sailors think they have murdered one of their mates.
Somewhat unyielding material for Stan and Ollie, but still funnier than any of their rivals at the time.
w H. M. Walker *d* Charles Rogers
☆ Laurel and Hardy, Walter Long, Arthur Housman

Live, Love and Learn
US 1937 78m bw
MGM (Harry Rapf)
A bohemian painter is tamed by marriage.
Tiresome romantic trifle.
w Charles Brackett, Cyril Hume, Richard Maibaum *d* George Fitzmaurice *ph* Ray June *m* Edward Ward
☆ Robert Montgomery, Rosalind Russell, Robert Benchley, Helen Vinson, Mickey Rooney, Monty Woolley, E. E. Clive, Maude Eburne
'Mildly entertaining mixture of slapstick and drama around the theme of art vs material success.' – *Variety*

Live Now, Pay Later
GB 1962 104m bw
(Regal) Woodlands/Jay Lewis (Jack Hanbury)
A credit store salesman is himself heavily in debt, and his private life is in ruins; but even after a chapter of unexpected and tragic events he remains irrepressibly optimistic.
A satirical farce melodrama which lets fly in too many directions at once and has a cumulatively cheerless effect despite funny moments.
w Jack Trevor Story *d* Jay Lewis *ph* Jack Hildyard *m* Ron Grainer
☆ Ian Hendry, John Gregson, June Ritchie, Geoffrey Keen, Liz Fraser

---

ⓓ Digital Video Disc Region 2   ⓓ Digital Video Disc Region 1   ♫ Soundtrack released on compact disc   ☆ Cast in approximate order of importance   † Points of interest   ♫ Notable songs   🏆 Academy Award   ⚲ Academy Award nomination   🅑 BAFTA

Live Nude Girls

US   1995   92m   colour
Republic (Cara Tapper, Steve White, Barry Bernardi)

Six women gather for the female equivalent of a stag party, and consider their various relationships.
Unenlightening drama of small talk about tiny events by an uninteresting ensemble.
wd Julianna Lavin ph Christopher Taylor m Anton Sanko pd Jerry Fleming ed Kathryn Himoff
☆ Dana Delany, Kim Cattrall, Cynthia Stevenson, Laila Robins, Lora Zane, Olivia D'Abo, Glenn Quinn, Tim Choate, Jeremy Jordan

Live Today for Tomorrow: see *An Act of Murder* (1964)

'1750 to 1! Always outnumbered! Never outfought!'
Lives of a Bengal Lancer **

👪   US   1934   119m   bw
Paramount (Louis D. Lighton)

Adventures on the North-West Frontier.
British army heroics are here taken rather solemnly, but the film is efficient and fondly remembered.
w Waldemar Young, John L. Balderston, Achmed Abdullah, Grover Jones, William Slavens McNutt book Francis Yeats-Brown d Henry Hathaway ph Charles Lang m Milan Roder ad Hans Dreier, Roland Anderson ed Ellsworth Hoagland
☆ Gary Cooper, Franchot Tone, Richard Cromwell, Sir Guy Standing, C. Aubrey Smith, Monte Blue, Kathleen Burke, Colin Tapley, Douglass Dumbrille, Akim Tamiroff, Noble Johnson
'The best army picture ever made.' – *Daily Telegraph*
⊗ best picture; script; Henry Hathaway; art direction; editing

Living: see *Ikiru*

The Living Corpse *

Germany/USSR   1928   108m   bw   silent
Prometheus/Mezhrabpomfilm
original title: *Zhivoi Trup*
An unhappy husband, whose wife loves another, tries all manner of means to give her a divorce. Refused by both church and state, he kills himself.
Heavy-going dramatic tract, photographed and directed with stirring style.
w B. Gusman, Anatoly Marienhof play Leo Tolstoy d Fedor Ozep ph Anatoly Golovnya
☆ Vsevolod Pudovkin, Maria Jacobini, V. Garden, Gustav Diessl
'One of the really few achievements of the Russian industry: a picture so gripping that it will hold any audience.' – *Variety*

The Living Daylights **

👪   GB   1987   130m   Technicolor
Panavision
MGM-UA/Eon (Albert R. Broccoli, Michael G. Wilson)

James Bond helps the Soviets chase a KGB defector with sinister intent.
25th-anniversary Bond heroics with more adult style than usual, and all technical aspects up to par.
w Richard Maibaum, Michael G. Wilson d John Glen ph Alec Mills m John Barry pd Peter Lamont
☆ Timothy Dalton, Maryam d'Abo, Jeroen Krabbe, Joe Don Baker, John Rhys-Davies, Art Malik, Robert Brown

The Living Dead at the Manchester Morgue (dubbed) *

Spain/Italy   1974   93m   Eastmancolor
Miracle/Star/Flaminia (Edmundo Amati)

original title: *Fin de Semana para los Muertos*
aka: *Don't Open the Window*
The dead are brought back to life as flesh-eating zombies by insects infected by an experimental crop-dusting machine.
An effectively creepy variation on The Night of the Living Dead, filmed in England.
w Sandro Continenza, Marcello Coscia d Jorge Grau ph Francisco Sempere m Giuliano Sorgini pd Carlo Leva ed Vincenzo Tomassi sp Giannetto de Rossi, Luciano Bird
☆ Ray Lovelock, Christine Galbo, Arthur Kennedy, Aldo Massasso, Giorgio Trestini, Roberto Posse

'A director with a genuine talent for the macabre mood and unsettling detail.' – *Verina Glaessner*

The Living Dead Girl *

France   1982   98m   colour
ABC/Aleriaz/Du Yaka/Sam Selsky

original title: *La Morte Vivante*
Toxic waste, released by an earthquake, revives the corpse of a young woman who needs blood to survive.
Spooky movie with some original touches, including a reluctant zombie, but containing rather too much gore for most tastes.
w Jean Rollin, Jacques Ralf d Jean Rollin ph Max Monteillet m Philippe d'Aram ed Janette Kronegger sp Benoit Lestang
☆ Marina Pierro, Françoise Blanchard, Mike Marshall, Carina Barone, Fanny Magieri, Patricia Besnard-Rousseau, Veronique Pinson
'This has a weird feel achieved by combining pastoral visions of an idyllic French countryside with oddly-staged tableaux of blood sacrifice and monstrous innocence. Very violent but not really scary.' – *Empire*
† The British video release runs for 86m.

The Living Desert ***

👪   US   1953   72m   Technicolor
Walt Disney (James Algar)

A light-hearted documentary showing the animals and insects which live in American desert areas.
The aim is entertainment and Disney is not above faking, e.g. the famous sequence in which scorpions appear to do a square dance, but on its level the thing is brilliantly done.
w James Algar, Winston Hibler, Ted Sears d James Algar ph N. Paul Kenworthy Jnr, Robert H. Grandall m Paul Smith special processes Ub Iwerks
'The film has the same cosy anthropomorphism as a Disney cartoon and its facetious commentary and vulgar music score are typical of others in the series.' – *Georges Sadoul*
† The other 'True Life Adventures' were: *Seal Island* 49 (2 reels), *Beaver Valley* 50 (2 reels), *Nature's Half Acre* 51 (2 reels), *Water Birds* 52 (2 reels), *Bear Country* 53, *Prowlers of the Everglades* 53, *The Vanishing Prairie* 54, *The African Lion* 55, *Secrets of Life* 56, *White Wilderness* 58, *Jungle Cat* 60.
⚱ Documentary

'A gleeful journey of sex and violence.'
The Living End *

US   1992   84m   colour
Mainline/Strand Releasing/Desperate Pictures (Marcus Hu, Jon Gerrans)

Two HIV-positive homosexuals – one a drifter, the other a film critic – head for San Francisco, indulging in casual sex and slaughter along the way.
A movie that its director has defined as 'irresponsible', although deliberately unpleasant and self-pitying would seem a more accurate description.
wd Gregg Araki ph Gregg Araki m Cole Coonce ed Gregg Araki
☆ Mike Dytri, Craig Gilmore, Mark Finch, Mary Woronov, Johanna Went, Darcy Marta, Paul Bartel
'Mark this down as the first, worst film of a director who may improve when he empties his system of gay special pleading and camp melodramatics.' – *Nigel Andrews, Financial Times*

Living Free *

👪   GB   1972   92m   colour
Columbia/Open Road/High Road (Paul Radin)

On the death of Elsa the lioness, George and Joy Adamson capture her three cubs and transfer them for their own safety to Serengeti.
Sloppy sequel to Born Free, depending very heavily on the appeal of the cubs.
w Millard Kaufman d Jack Couffer ph Wolfgang Suschitzky m Sol Kaplan
☆ Susan Hampshire, Nigel Davenport, Geoffrey Keen

'Amazing adventures beneath the curse of the jaguar god!'
The Living Idol

Mexico/US   1956   100m   Eastmancolor
Cinemascope
MGM (Albert Lewin)

A Mexican girl becomes possessed by the spirit of the jaguar to whom local maidens were once sacrificed.
Pretentious but rather enjoyable highbrow hokum of the heady kind expected from this producer.
wd Albert Lewin ph Jack Hildyard m Rodolpho Halffter
☆ James Robertson Justice, Steve Forrest, Liliane Montevecchi

Living in a Big Way

US   1947   103m   bw
MGM (Pandro S. Berman)

A demobbed GI finds he can't get on with his rich selfish wife and opens up a charity home for the families of war casualties.
Odd mixture of comedy, drama and a few songs and dances, not forgetting a message or two. It mostly falls flat on its face.
w Gregory La Cava, Irving Ravetch d Gregory La Cava ph Harold Rosson m Lennie Hayton
☆ Gene Kelly, Marie McDonald, Charles Winninger, Phyllis Thaxter, Spring Byington, Clinton Sundberg

'Meet The Film Crew From Hell! In The Looniest Movie About The Movies'
'Warning. This Film Contains Explicit Scenes of Sex, Violence And People Being Perfectly Horrid To One Another.'
'This Is No Place For Luvvies'
Living in Oblivion **

US   1995   90m   colour/bw
Entertainment/JDI/Lemon Sky (Michael Griffiths, Marcus Viscidi)

A low-budget film-maker has nightmares about his current project, while dealing with an egomaniacal leading man, a temperamental cinematographer and a dwarf who objects to appearing in dream sequences.
Energetic and entertaining joke at the expense of wannabe film-makers, skewering pretentiousness while demonstrating that what happens behind the camera can be more interesting than what takes place in front of it; James LeGros provides a nice turn as an impossibly vain star – any resemblance between him and Brad Pitt, who appeared in the director's Johnny Suede (qv), is presumably coincidental.
wd Tom DeCillo ph Frank Prinzi m Jim Farmer pd Thérèse DePrez ed Camilla Toniolo
☆ Steve Buscemi, Catherine Keener, Dermot Mulroney, Danielle von Zerneck, James LeGros, Peter Dinklage
'It has a sharp, fresh feel to it: a joke that'll please not only insiders, but any movie lover.' – *Alexander Walker*

Living It Up *

US   1954   95m   Technicolor
Paramount/Hal B. Wallis (Paul Jones)

A suspected victim of radium poisoning is played up by the press into a national hero.
Remake of Nothing Sacred with Lewis as Carole Lombard; deserves a mark for cheek.
w Jack Rose, Mel Shavelson d Norman Taurog ph Daniel Fapp m Walter Scharf
☆ Dean Martin, Jerry Lewis, Janet Leigh, Edward Arnold, Fred Clark, Sheree North, Sig Rumann

Living on Velvet *

US   1935   77m   bw
Warner (Edward Chodorov)

A happy-go-lucky aviator changes his life style when he narrowly escapes death in a crash.
Reasonably dramatic 'serious' drama of its period.
w Jerry Wald, Julius Epstein d Frank Borzage ph Sid Hickox md Leo F. Forbstein
☆ George Brent, Kay Francis, Warren William, Helen Lowell, Henry O'Neill, Samuel S. Hinds, Russell Hicks, Edgar Kennedy
'Three good names but doubtful of pulling above ordinary business.' – *Variety*

Living Out Loud

US   1998   93m   Technicolor   Panavision
Entertainment/New Line/Jersey (Danny de Vito, Michael Shamberg, Stacey Sher)

An abandoned wife makes a friend of her building's lift operator, whose wife has thrown him out.
Romantic drama about an odd couple's failure to get together, mainly because the script raises issues only to avoid working them out.
wd Richard LaGravenese ph John Bailey m George Fenton pd Nelson Coates ed Jon Gregory, Lynzee Klingman
☆ Holly Hunter, Danny de Vito, Queen Latifah, Martin Donovan, Richard Schiff, Elias Koteas
'A talky, introspective character study laced with flights of musical fantasy.' – *Janet Maslin, New York Times*
'A movie that looks as if it wants to have its cake and eat it, preferably from a highly gilded plate.' – *Derek Malcolm, Guardian*

Lizzie

US   1957   81m   bw
MGM/Bryna (Jerry Bresler)

Murder and rape turn a girl into a triple personality.
Preposterous cash-in on The Three Faces of Eve, too silly to be even funny.
w Mel Dinelli novel *The Bird's Nest* by Shirley Jackson d Hugo Haas ph Paul Ivano m Leith Stevens
☆ Eleanor Parker, Richard Boone, Joan Blondell, Hugo Haas
'Ruddy peculiar.' – *MFB*

Ljubavni Slucaj: see *The Switchboard Operator*

The Llano Kid

US   1939   70m   bw
Paramount

A bandit is persuaded to impersonate the long-lost son of a wealthy Mexican family.
Uninteresting minor Western, indifferently directed.
w Wanda Tuchock story *Double-Dyed Deceiver* by O. Henry d Edward D. Venturini ph Russell Harlan m Victor Young ad Lewis J. Rachmil ed Sherman A. Rose
☆ Tito Guizar, Gale Sondergaard, Alan Mowbray, Jane Clayton, Emma Dunn, Minor Watson, Glenn Strange
† It was a remake of *The Texan* (qv).

'The Love Story Which Changed The Story Of An Empire!'
'The Picture The World Is Waiting For!'
Lloyd's of London **

US   1936   115m   bw
TCF (Kenneth MacGowan)

A young messenger boy in the 18th century grows up to found a great insurance company.
Thoroughly well mounted, if unconvincing and slightly boring, historical charade in which the Prince of Wales, Lord Nelson, Dr Johnson and other personages make guest appearances. An archetypal prestige film of its time which also turned out to be box-office.
w Ernest Pascal, Walter Ferris book Curtis Kenyon d Henry King ph Bert Glennon md Louis Silvers ad William S. Darling
☆ Tyrone Power, Madeleine Carroll, George Sanders, Freddie Bartholomew, C. Aubrey Smith, Guy Standing, Virginia Field, Montagu Love, Gavin Muir, Miles Mander, Una O'Connor, E. E. Clive
'Fictional history with fine production but weak from marquee standpoint ... basically it's the story of the beginning and rise of an insurance company, and how can average audiences be asked to get excited about that?' – *Variety*
'The name of England is so freely on the characters' lips that we recognize at once an American picture. These people live, make love, bear children all from the most patriotic motives, and it's all rather like London in coronation week.' – *Graham Greene*
⊗ art direction

Lo Chiamavano Trinità: see *They Call Me Trinity*

Loaded
GB/New Zealand 1994 96m colour
Blue Dolphin/NFTC/British Screen/NZFC (David Hazlett, Caroline Hewitt, Bridget Ikin, John Maynard)
⬚ ⬚

A group of schoolfriends, who travel to the country to make a horror video, panic when, after taking drugs, one of them is killed in a motorcycle accident.
Ambitious but muddled and disjointed movie of adolescent longings and power games; its point gets lost among its video voyeurisms.
wd Anna Campion ph Alan Almond m Simon Fisher Turner pd Alistair Kay ed John Gilbert
☆ Oliver Milburn, Catherine McCormack, Thandie Newton, Dearbhla Molloy, Danny Cunningham, Nick Patrick
'Talky and embarrassingly pretentious bore about 20-something angst.' – *Film Review*
† The film was shown at the 1994 Venice Film Festival as *Bloody Weekend* and given a release two years later.

Loan Shark *
US 1952 79m bw
Lippert

A detective goes undercover as a tyre worker in order to undermine a loan shark operation.
Competent co-feature with technical aspects in good shape.
w Martin Rackin, Eugene Ling d Seymour Friedman ph Joseph Biroc
☆ George Raft, Dorothy Hart, Paul Stewart, Helen Westcott, John Hoyt

Local Hero **
👫 GB 1983 111m colour
Enigma/Goldcrest (David Puttnam)
⬚ ⬚ ⬚ ♫

A young American executive meets various difficulties when he is sent to a Scottish coastal village to arrange for the building of a new refinery.
Reminiscent of various Ealing comedies, especially Whisky Galore and The Maggie, this ambitious comedy is really not funny enough for its great length.
wd Bill Forsyth ph Chris Menges m Mark Knopfler
☆ Burt Lancaster, Peter Riegert, *Denis Lawson*, Peter Capaldi, Fulton Mackay, Jenny Seagrove
'Little in the way of obvious commercial hooks … dominated by a constantly surprising sense of whimsicality.' – *Variety*
🎬 direction

Le Locataire: see The Tenant

Loch Ness
👫 GB 1995 101m Metrocolor
Polygram/Working Title/Stephen Ujlaki (Tim Bevan)
⬚ ⬚

An American scientist goes to Scotland to debunk the myth of the Loch Ness monster.
A romantic comedy that tries to get by on charm, and cannot quite manage it.
w John Fusco d John Henderson ph Clive Tickner m Trevor Jones pd Sophie Becher ed Jon Gregory
☆ Ted Danson, Joely Richardson, Ian Holm, Harris Yulin, James Frain, Keith Allen, Nick Brimble, Kirsty Graham, John Savident, Richard Vernon
'At its best a pleasant enough movie that more subdued, narcoleptic children might well enjoy. At its worst, it's really rather dull.' – *Bob McCabe, Empire*

'A Disgrace To Criminals Everywhere.'
Lock, Stock and Two Smoking Barrels **
GB 1998 95m colour
Polygram/Steve Tisch/SKA Films (Matthew Vaughan)
⬚ ⬚ ⬚ ⑨ ♫

Four friends who lose everything in a rigged poker game resort to robbery in order to pay their debts.
Clever, stylish, intricately plotted black farce, enjoyable if you can surrender to its gleeful delight in murder and mayhem.
wd Guy Ritchie ph Tim Maurice-Jones m David A. Hughes, John Murphy pd Iain Andrews, Eve Mavrakis ed Niven Howie
☆ Jason Flemyng, Dexter Fletcher, Nick Moran, Jason Statham, Steven Mackintosh, Vinnie Jones, Sting, Lenny McLean, P. H. Moriarty, Steve Sweeney, Frank Harper, Stephen Marcus, Peter McNicholl

'The film has a pounding, free energy, and the swift slang of the script gives it a lightness of touch amid the threats and the bloodbaths.' – *Gaby Wood, Guardian*
† It was also released on video in 'The director's cut', which adds an extra 10 minutes of footage.
🏆 audience award

Lock Up
US 1989 109m Technicolor
Guild/White Eagle/Carolco/Gordon Company (Lawrence Gordon, Charles Gordon)
⬚ ⬚ ⑨ ⑨

A tough prison warden tries to break the spirit of a tougher prisoner.
Nasty and sadistic, with no redeeming qualities.
w Richard Smith, Jeb Stuart, Henry Rosenbaum d John Flynn ph Donald E. Thorin m Bill Conti pd Bill Kenney ed Michael N. Knue, Donald Brochu
☆ Sylvester Stallone, Donald Sutherland, John Amos, Sonny Landham, Tom Sizemore, Frank McRae, Darlanne Fluegel, William Allen Young

'The restoration comedy about what cannot be restored!'
Lock Up Your Daughters
GB 1969 103m Technicolor
Columbia/Domino (David Deutsch)

In 18th-century London an aristocratic rake and various lower orders are all in search of female companionship and get their wires crossed.
Noisy, vulgar, ill-acted version (without music) of a successful musical based on two old theatrical warhorses.
w Keith Waterhouse, Willis Hall play *Rape upon Rape* by Henry Fielding and *The Relapse* by John Vanbrugh d Peter Coe ph Peter Suschitzky m Ron Grainer pd Tony Woollard
☆ Christopher Plummer, Roy Kinnear, Georgia Brown, Susannah York, Glynis Johns, Ian Bannen, Tom Bell, Elaine Taylor, Jim Dale, Kathleen Harrison, Roy Dotrice, Vanessa Howard, Fenella Fielding, Peter Bayliss, *Richard Wordsworth* and also Peter Bull, Fred Emney
'Subtlety is neither required nor displayed.' – *Jack Ibberson*

Lock Your Doors: see The Ape Man

The Locked Door
US 1929 70m bw
United Artists

Husband and wife try to save each other by assuming guilt for a murder.
Rather static filmed play.
w C. Gardner Sullivan play *The Sign on the Door* by Channing Pollock d George Fitzmaurice
☆ Barbara Stanwyck, Rod la Rocque, William Boyd, Betty Bronson, ZaSu Pitts, Mack Swain

The Locket
US 1946 85m bw
RKO (Bert Granet)
⑨

A femme fatale is bent on destroying men, and eventually we discover why.
Dark, confusing melodrama very typical of the immediate post-war years; it has little to say but says it dourly, even achieving flashbacks within flashbacks within flashbacks.
w Sheridan Gibney d John Brahm ph Nicholas Musuraca m Roy Webb
☆ Laraine Day, Robert Mitchum, Brian Aherne, Gene Raymond, Ricardo Cortez

The Lodger ***
GB 1926 84m bw silent
Gainsborough (Michael Balcon)

Subtitle: *A Story of the London Fog*
US title: *The Case of Jonathan Drew*
A modern version of the novel about a stranger who is (in this case) wrongly thought to be Jack the Ripper.
The first true Hitchcock film, full of his familiar dramatic visual touches. Oddly enough it was followed by three years during which he seemed to forget them.
w Eliot Stannard, Alfred Hitchcock novel Mrs Belloc Lowndes d Alfred Hitchcock ph Baron Ventimiglia ed Ivor Montagu
☆ Ivor Novello, June, Marie Ault, Arthur Chesney, Malcolm Keen

'It was the first time I exercised my style … you might almost say it was my first picture.' – *Alfred Hitchcock, 1966*

The Lodger *
GB 1932 85m bw
Twickenham (Julius Hagen)
US title: *The Phantom Fiend*
The upstairs lodger is suspected of being Jack the Ripper…
Modernized version of a story already tackled by Hitchcock as a silent and to be done again in costume in 1944. Not bad, for a minor British film of the time.
w Ivor Novello, Miles Mander, Paul Rotha, H. Fowler Mear, novel Mrs Belloc Lowndes d Maurice Elvey ph Stanley Blythe, Basil Emmott
☆ Ivor Novello, Elizabeth Allan, A. W. Baskcomb, Jack Hawkins, Barbara Everest, Peter Gawthorne, Kynaston Reeves
'They can make pictures in England … the only point for discussion is why they do not make them oftener.' – *Variety*

The Lodger *
US 1944 84m bw
TCF (Robert Bassler)
1880s version of the above in which the lodger is Jack the Ripper.
Nicely mounted apart from some anachronisms, but a little dull.
w Barre Lyndon d John Brahm ph Lucien Ballard m Hugo Friedhofer
☆ Laird Cregar, Merle Oberon, George Sanders, Cedric Hardwicke, Sara Allgood, Aubrey Mather, Queenie Leonard, Helena Pickard, Lumsden Hare, Frederick Worlock

'The only thing you can't have in this perfect world of total pleasure is your 30th birthday … Logan is 29.'
Logan's Run *
US 1976 118m Metrocolor Todd-AO
MGM (Saul David)
⬚ ⬚ ⑨ ⑨ ♫

In the future, people try to escape from a society which dooms everyone to death at thirty.
Interesting and quite exciting fantasy melodrama which mercifully moves instead of preaching.
w David Zelag Goodman novel William F. Nolan d Michael Anderson ph Ernest Laszlo m Jerry Goldsmith pd Dale Hennesy
☆ Michael York, Richard Jordan, Jenny Agutter, Roscoe Lee Browne, Farrah Fawcett-Majors, Peter Ustinov, Michael Anderson Jnr
'A science fiction film made by people who don't understand science fiction for the amusement of people who don't care one way or the other.' – *S. Frank, L. A. Panorama*
'It puts the future back two thousand years.' – *Benny Green, Punch*
Ⓐ Ernest Laszlo

La Loi: see Where the Hot Wind Blows

Lola: see Twinky (1969)

Lola *
France/Italy 1960 91m bw Franscope
Rome-Paris/Euro-International
⬚ ⬚

A cabaret dancer in Nantes chooses between three men.
A slight romance which was much admired for its decoration and visual style, which reminded many of Max Ophuls.
wd Jacques Demy ph Raoul Coutard m Michel Legrand
☆ Anouk Aimée, Jacques Harden, Marc Michel, Elina Labourdette
'Like an adolescent's dream of romance, formed from old movies.' – *Pauline Kael, 70s*

Lola *
West Germany 1982 113m colour
Rialto-Trio (Horst Wendlandt)
♫

A cabaret singer leads a double life.
Blue Angel country is the setting for this over-predictable fable from a director whose films always have interest.
w Peter Marthesheimer, Pea Froelich, Rainer Werner Fassbinder d Rainer Werner Fassbinder ph Xaver Schwarzenberger m Peer Raben ed Juliane Lorenz, Rainer Werner Fassbinder

☆ Barbara Sukowa, Mario Adorf, Armin Mueller-Stahl, Matthias Fuchs

Lola + Bilidikid *
Germany 1998 95m colour
Millivres/Zero/WDR/Arte (Martin Hagemann)
aka: *Lola and Billy the Kid*
In Berlin, a teenaged Turkish youth acknowledges his own homosexuality after discovering that his brother, who has been thrown out of home, has become a transvestite dancer.
A melodramatic tale of homophobia, revenge, and repression within gay culture and in the wider world, lightened by a camp sense of humour.
wd E. Kutlug Ataman ph Chris Squires m Arpad Bondy ad Mona Kino ed Ewa J. Lind
☆ Gandi Mukli, Baki Davrak, Erdal Yildiz, Inge Keller, Michael Gerber, Hasan Ali Mete
'By no means a cosy family film, but it is well worth watching.' – *Nick Briggs, Film Review*
† The director received death threats after the film was shown in Turkey.

Lola Montes *
France/Germany 1955 140m Eastmancolor Cinemascope
Gamma/Florida/Oska

The life of the famous courtesan and her romance with the King of Bavaria, told in diverting fragments by a circus ringmaster.
An elaborate, expensive and trickily presented historical charade which confused the public and bankrupted its production company; but the various shorter versions released didn't help.
w Max Ophuls, Annette Wademant, Franz Geiger novel Cécil Saint-Laurent d Max Ophuls ph Christian Matras m Georges Auric ad Jean d'Aubonne, Willy Schatz
☆ Martine Carol, Anton Walbrook, Peter Ustinov, Ivan Desny, Oskar Werner, Will Quadflieg
'If you want to know what form can really do for content, rush along.' – *Derek Malcolm, Guardian*

Lola Rennt: see Run Lola Run

Lolita **
GB 1962 152m bw
MGM/Seven Arts/AA/Anya/Transworld (James B. Harris)
⬚

A middle-aged lecturer falls for a 14-year-old girl and marries her mother to be near her.
Fitfully amusing but slightly plotted and very lengthy screen version of a sensational novel in which the heroine is only twelve, which makes a difference. The flashback introduction and various comic asides are pretentious and alienating.
w Vladimir Nabokov novel Vladimir Nabokov d Stanley Kubrick ph Oswald Morris m Nelson Riddle
☆ James Mason, Shelley Winters, Sue Lyon, Peter Sellers
'The director's heart is apparently elsewhere. Consequently, we face the problem without the passion, the badness without the beauty, the agony without the ecstasy.' – *Andrew Sarris*
'A diluted Blue Angel with a teenage temptress instead of a tart.' – *Stanley Kauffmann*
'So clumsily structured that you begin to wonder whether what was shot and then cut out, whether the beginning was intended to be the end; and it is edited in so dilatory a fashion that after the first hour, almost every scene seems to go on too long.' – *Pauline Kael*
† Before Mason was cast, Noël Coward and Laurence Olivier were sought for the role of Humbert Humbert.
Ⓐ Vladimir Nabokov

Lolita *
US/France 1997 137m colour
Pathé (Mario Kassar, Joel B. Michaels)
⬚ ⬚ ⑨

A college lecturer loves and loses a 12-year-old girl.
An unexpectedly bland remake, though it is, in outline, faithful to Nabokov's original; it fails in its depiction of the forbidden, lacking any sense of obsessional passion.
w Stephen Schiff novel Vladimir Nabokov d Adrian Lyne ph Howard Atherton m Ennio Morricone pd Jon Hutman ed Julie Monroe, David Bremner, F. Paul Benz

☆ Jeremy Irons, Melanie Griffith, Frank Langella, Dominique Swain, Suzanne Shepherd, Keith Reddin, Erin J. Dean

'Almost everything about the film testifies to Lyne's empty craftsmanship … The truly shocking thing about his *Lolita* is its banality.' – *Richard Williams, Guardian*

'The crunch is, does this transgressive movie portray a sympathetic paedophile? The answer has to be yes.' – *Alexander Walker, London Evening Standard*

'Quite innocuous, and Lyne's finest film, for what it's worth.' – *Geoff Andrew, Time Out*

† The film failed to find a distributor in the United States; after some controversy, it was released uncut in Britain.

The Lolly Madonna War: see *Lolly Madonna XXX*

Lolly Madonna XXX
US   1973   105m   Metrocolor
MGM (Rodney Carr-Smith)
GB title: *The Lolly Madonna War*
Tennessee hillbilly farmers fight over a meadow.
Violent feudin' melodrama, technically accomplished but of limited interest to non hillbillies.
w Rodney Carr-Smith, Sue Grafton *novel* Sue Grafton d Richard C. Sarafian ph Philip Lathrop m Fred Myrow
☆ Rod Steiger, Robert Ryan, Scott Wilson, Jeff Bridges, Season Hubley

London **
GB   1994   85m   colour
BFI/Channel 4 (Keith Griffiths)
A traveller reluctantly returns to London at the urgent summons of a friend and former lover, a part-time teacher, and they explore the city, contrasting its present with its past and its missed potentialities.
An intriguing and original semi-documentary that is a voice-over narration by a sceptical, fictional observer together with an all-too-accurate portrait of a decaying and embattled place, with its freedoms restricted by the government's deliberate neglect and its dismantling of local power.
wd Patrick Keiller ph Patrick Keiller ed Larry Sider
☆ Paul Scofield

London after Midnight *
US   1927   75m   bw   silent
MGM (Tod Browning)
GB title: *The Hypnotist*
A creepy house murder is solved by hypnotism, and a grinning monster proves to be a red herring.
Famous star thriller of which lamentably no prints survive; remade as Mark of the Vampire.
w Tod Browning, Waldemar Young d Tod Browning ph Merritt Gerstad
☆ Lon Chaney, Marceline Day, Conrad Nagel, Henry B. Walthall, Polly Moran

London Belongs to Me **
GB   1948   112m   bw
GFD/Individual (Frank Launder, Sidney Gilliat)
US title: *Dulcimer Street*
A young boy is arrested on a murder charge and his boarding-house friends rally to his defence.
Unconvincing but highly entertaining sub-Dickensian comedy-drama with a rousing finish and an abundance of character roles.
w Sidney Gilliat, J. B. Williams *novel* Norman Collins d Sidney Gilliat ph Wilkie Cooper m Benjamin Frankel
☆ Alastair Sim, Stephen Murray, Richard Attenborough, Fay Compton, Wylie Watson, Susan Shaw, Ivy St Helier, Joyce Carey, Andrew Crawford, Eleanor Summerfield, Hugh Griffith, Gladys Henson

'Memorable for its character-drawing and for the excellence of its writing and acting.' – *Dilys Powell*

The London Blackout Murders
US   1942   58m   bw
Republic
GB title: *Secret Motive*
A mild tobacconist murders people who are sabotaging the war effort.
Curious, set-bound little melodrama with an interesting lead performance.

w Curt Siodmak d George Sherman
☆ John Abbott, Mary McLeod, Lloyd Corrigan, Lester Matthews, Anita Bolster, Billy Bevan, Frederick Worlock

London by Night *
US   1937   70m   bw
MGM
Apparent murders are really part of a blackmail scheme.
Reasonably intriguing mystery with good cast and atmosphere.
w George Oppenheimer *play* The Umbrella Man by Will Scott d William Thiele
☆ George Murphy, Rita Johnson, Leo G. Carroll, George Zucco, Virginia Field, Montagu Love, Eddie Quillan, Leonard Mudie

'Quality is there, but drawing power isn't.' – *Variety*

London Can Take It ****
GB   1940   9m   bw
The Ministry of Information
Quentin Reynolds, an American war correspondent, shows Americans what the London blitz was like.
Historically significant short, credited with inclining Americans towards participation. In its own right, a brilliant job of editing and presentation.
w Quentin Reynolds d Harry Watt ph Jonah Jones, H. E. Fowle

London Kills Me
GB   1991   107m   colour
Rank/Working Title/Polygram/Film Four (Tim Bevan)
A drug pusher, down on his luck, is told that he can have a job as a waiter providing he acquires a good pair of shoes.
Aimless drama of young drug addicts and hangers-on that goes nowhere slowly.
wd Hanif Kureishi ph Ed Lachman m Mark Springer, Sarah Sarhandi pd Stuart Walker ed Jon Gregory
☆ Justin Chadwick, Steven Mackintosh, Emer McCourt, Roshan Seth, Fiona Shaw, Brad Dourif, Tony Haygarth, Alun Armstrong

'The motivation is often obscure, the action is sometimes lacking in simple credibility, which is not to be blamed on the performers, and ultimately Kureishi fails to make his people interesting either as individuals or as social types. Nevertheless, he has attempted to take us into an unfamiliar subculture without making us feel that we are slumming.' – *Philip French, Observer*

'An amazing, hypnotizing, mind-bending shambles … Photographed like a home video that has been savaged by the cat, the film is earnestly ugly and passionately shapeless.' – *Nigel Andrews, Financial Times*

London Melody
GB   1937   75m   bw
GFD/Herbert Wilcox
US title: *Girls in the Street*
A diplomat falls for a dancer.
Light but rather humourless musical drama.
w Florence Tranter, Monckton Hoffe d Herbert Wilcox ph F. A. Young
☆ Anna Neagle, Tullio Carminati, Robert Douglas, Horace Hodges

'Excellent compilation of bromidial mush, beautifully produced and directed, which should satisfy.' – *Variety*

The London Nobody Knows *
GB   1967   53m   Eastmancolor
Norcon/British Lion
James Mason wanders round the capital's by-ways in search of relics from former ages.
Unhurried but generally delightful documentary.
w Geoffrey Fletcher *book* Geoffrey Fletcher d Norman Cohen

London Town *
GB   1946   126m   Technicolor
GFD/Wesley Ruggles
US title: *My Heart Goes Crazy*
An understudy finally achieves stardom thanks to his daughter's schemes.
Disastrous and expensive attempt to make a major British musical without a single new idea. Tasteless,

tawdry and sluggish, but it does record for posterity four of the star's sketches.
w Elliot Paul, Siegfried Herzig, Val Guest d Wesley Ruggles ph Erwin Hillier
☆ Sid Field, Greta Gynt, Kay Kendall, Tessie O'Shea, Claude Hulbert, Sonnie Hale, Mary Clare, Petula Clark, Jerry Desmonde

'I can't see the point of importing an American director and giving him all the time and money in the world to play with when we can make bad musicals on our own, and quicker.' – *Richard Winnington*

The Lone Hand
US   1953   80m   Technicolor
Universal-International
A quiet Western farmer is really a Pinkerton detective.
Slightly unusual Western in which the happy ending is not however in doubt.
w Joseph Hoffman d George Sherman ph Maury Gertsman md Joseph Gershenson
☆ Joel McCrea, Barbara Hale, Alex Nicol, Charles Drake, James Arness

The Lone Ranger
This high-minded Western character, with his black mask, his horse Silver and his Indian friend Tonto, originated (complete with 'William Tell' overture) as a 1933 radio serial in which he was played by George Seaton.

In 1938 he came to film via a Republic serial with a sequel in 1939 (see below). In 1949 Clayton Moore brought him to TV in innumerable half-hour adventures. These eventually encouraged two feature versions; see below. Also, *The Legend of the Lone Ranger* (qv).

The Lone Ranger
🎬 US   1956   85m   Warnercolor
Jack Wrather
The masked do-gooder foils a ranchers' plot to destroy an Indian reservation.
Tolerably watchable adventures.
w Herb Meadow d Stuart Heisler ph Edwin DuPar m David Buttolph
☆ Clayton Moore, Jay Silverheels, Lyle Bettger, Bonita Granville, Perry Lopez

The Lone Ranger and the Lost City of Gold
🎬 US   1958   81m   colour
Jack Wrather
The masked rider solves murders which have been committed for a mysterious medallion.
Lively Western for kids.
w Robert Schaefer and Eric Freiwald d Lesley Selander ph Kenneth Peach m Les Baxter
☆ Clayton Moore, Jay Silverheels, Douglas Kennedy, Charles Watts

The Lone Rider Ambushed
US   1941   67m   bw
Equity/PRC (Sigmund Neufeld)
A cowboy impersonates an outlaw in order to recover stolen bank money.
The best of the Lone Rider series, mainly owing to the gimmick of having Houston play the villain as well as the hero.
w Oliver Drake d Sam Newfield ph Jack Greenhalgh m Johnny Lang, Lew Porter ad Vin Taylor ed Holbrook N. Todd
☆ George Houston, Al St John, Maxine Leslie, Frank Hagney, Jack Ingham, Hal Price, Ted Adams, George Chesebro

The Lone Rider Fights Back
US   1941   64m   bw
Equity/PRC (Sigmund Neufeld)
A wandering cowboy helps a rancher's niece solve the murder of her uncle.
Standard second-feature Western, with songs, fist- and gunfights and a little comedy between the action.
w Joseph O'Donnell d Sam Newfield ph Jack Greenhalgh m Johnny Lange, Lew Porter ad Vin Taylor ed Holbrook N. Todd
☆ George Houston, Al St John, Dorothy Short, Dennis Moore, Frank Hagney, Charles King, Frank Ellis

The Lone Rider in Ghost Town
US   1941   64m   bw
PRC (Sigmund Neufeld)
A wandering cowboy rescues a mine engineer who has been kidnapped and hidden in a deserted town.
A mix of comedy, songs and a little action following the usual pattern of the Lone Rider series, in which our hero is suspected to be the bad guy, but proves his innocence by beating a confession out of the villains.
w Joe O'Donnell d Sam Newfield ph Jack Greenhalgh m Johnny Lange, Lew Porter ed Holbrook N. Todd
☆ George Houston, Al St John, Alaine Brandes, Budd Buster, Frank Hagney, Alden Chase, Reed Howes

Lone Star
US   1952   90m   bw
MGM (Z. Wayne Griffin)
Andrew Jackson enlists the aid of a Texas adventurer to persuade Sam Houston to change his mind about an agreement with Mexico.
Slow-moving semi-Western, hard to follow for non-Americans. Production values quite high.
w Borden Chase, Howard Estabrook d Vincent Sherman ph Harold Rosson m David Buttolph
☆ Clark Gable, Ava Gardner, Lionel Barrymore, Broderick Crawford, Ed Begley, Beulah Bondi, James Burke, William Farnum, Lowell Gilmore, Moroni Olsen, Russell Simpson, William Conrad

'John Sayles invites you to return to the scene of the crime.'

Lone Star **
US   1996   135m   colour
Rank/Castle Rock/Turner/Rio Dulce (R. Paul Miller, Maggie Renzi)
In a Texan border town a sheriff investigates the murder of one of his predecessors, who vanished in the mid-50s.
Engrossing, wide-ranging tale of the way in which the past and the present impinge upon the lives of a small community.
wd John Sayles ph Stuart Dryburgh m Mason Daring pd Dan Bishop ed John Sayles
☆ Chris Cooper, Elizabeth Peña, Kris Kristofferson, Matthew McConaughey, Jesse Borrego, Ron Canada, Frances McDormand, Joe Morton

'Never quites lives up, in its storytelling, to its incidental observations.' – *Adam Mars-Jones, Independent*
& John Sayles (as writer)

The Lone Wolf
The jewel thief turned sleuth was created by Louis Joseph Vance and turned up in several silent films. During the talkie period several actors played Michael Lanyard; the role of his valet passed from Raymond Walburn to Eric Blore to Alan Mowbray. All the films were made for Columbia, but only the first was anything like a main feature.
1935 The Lone Wolf Returns d Roy William Neill with Melvyn Douglas
1938 The Lone Wolf in Paris d Albert S. Rogell with Francis Lederer
1939 The Lone Wolf Spy Hunt d Peter Godfrey with Warren William
1940 The Lone Wolf Strikes (qv)
1941 The Lone Wolf Meets a Lady (qv), The Lone Wolf Takes a Chance (qv), The Lone Wolf Keeps a Date (qv)
1941 Secrets of the Lone Wolf d Edward Dmytryk; WW
1943 One Dangerous Night (qv)
1943 Passport to Suez (qv)
1946 The Notorious Lone Wolf d D. Ross Lederman; with Gerald Mohr
1947 The Lone Wolf in London d Leslie Goodwins; GM
1947 The Lone Wolf in Mexico d D. Ross Lederman, GM
1949 The Lone Wolf and His Lady d John Hoffman; Ron Randell

The Lone Wolf Keeps a Date
US   1941   65m   bw
Columbia
The Lone Wolf saves his stamp collection from villains and foils a kidnap plot.
Dull thriller, hampered by an overcomplex plot and rather too much broad comedy to be at all effective.

🎬 film suitable for family viewing   📺 VHS video-cassette for the British PAL system   📺 VHS video-cassette for the British PAL system in wide screen-format   💿 Video cassette in a computer-colourised version   📺 American NTSC video-cassette   💿 Laser disc *w* Earl Felton, Sidney Salkow *novel* Louis Joseph Vance *d* Sidney Salkow *ph* Barney McGill *md* M. W. Stoloff *ad* Lionel Banks *ed* Richard Fantl

☆ Warren William, Frances Robinson, Bruce Bennett, Eric Blore, Thurston Hall, Jed Prouty, Fred Kelsey, Don Beddoe

Lone Wolf McQuade

US   1983   107m   DeLuxe
1818/Top Kick/Orion (Yoram Ben-Ami, Steve Carver)
📀 📼 📼 🎧

A tough Texas Ranger takes on horse rustlers and hijackers.
Adults-only action rubbish, disarmingly competently made.
w B. J. Nelson *d* Steve Carver *ph* Roger Shearman *m* Francesco de Masi *pd* Norm Baron *ed* Anthony Redman
☆ Chuck Norris, David Carradine, Barbara Carrera, Leon Isaac Kennedy
'A winningly ludicrous mish-mash of mayhem-movie rudiments and action-man reputations.' – *Paul Taylor, MFB*

The Lone Wolf Meets a Lady

US   1941   71m   bw
Columbia
The Lone Wolf offers to help a bride when, on the eve of her society marriage, her ex-husband helps a thief steal her wedding present, a priceless diamond necklace.
Routine programmer, enlivened by the occasional line of smart dialogue.
w John Larkin, Wolfe Kaufman *story* Louis Joseph Vance *d* Sidney Salkow *ph* Henry Freulich *ad* M. W. Stoloff *ad* Lionel Banks *ed* Al Clark
☆ Warren William, Eric Blore, Jean Muir, Victor Jory, Roger Pryor, Warren Hull, Thurston Hall, Georgia Caine

The Lone Wolf Strikes

US   1940   57m   bw
Columbia (Fred Kohlmar)
The Lone Wolf impersonates a fence in order to recover a heiress's priceless pearl necklace and solve the murder of a friend.
One of the best of the series: a brisk and enjoyable thriller, with comic relief cut to the minimum.
w Harry Segall, Albert Duffy *story* Dalton Trumbo *d* Sidney Salkow *ph* Henry Freulich *md* M. W. Stoloff *ad* Lionel Banks *ed* Al Clark
☆ Warren William, Eric Blore, Joan Perry, Alan Baxter, Montagu Love, Robert Wilcox, Astrid Allwyn, Don Beddoe, Fred A. Kelsey

The Lone Wolf Takes a Chance

US   1941   76m   bw
Columbia
Michael Lanyard, the Lone Wolf, bets a police inspector that he can stay out of trouble for 24 hours, and finds himself accused of murder and searching for a kidnapped inventor a few minutes later.
Watchable 'B' feature comedy-thriller that keeps the action and fun moving fast.
w Earl Fenton, Sidney Salkow *novel* Louis Joseph Vance *d* Sidney Salkow *ph* John Stumar *md* M. W. Stoloff *ad* Lionel Banks *ed* Viola Lawrence
☆ Warren William, Eric Blore, June Storey, Henry Wilcoxon, Don Beddoe, Thurston Hall, Lloyd Bridges

The Loneliness of the Long Distance Runner ***

GB   1962   104m   bw
British Lion/Bryanston/Woodfall (Tony Richardson)
📀 📼 🎧

The only thing a Borstal boy does well is run, and as he trains he thinks back to his depressing life.
Rather pale study of a social outcast; interesting scenes do not quite form a compelling whole.
w Alan Sillitoe *story* Alan Sillitoe *d* Tony Richardson *ph* Walter Lassally *m* John Addison
☆ Tom Courtenay, Michael Redgrave, James Bolam, Avis Bunnage, Alec McCowen, Joe Robinson, Julia Foster
🎖 Tom Courtenay

'In The Tradition Of The Great Ones!'

Lonely Are the Brave *

US   1962   107m   bw   Panavision
U-I/Joel (Edward Lewis)
📼 📼 🎧

The last of the cowboy rebels is no match for pursuit by jeep and helicopter.
A strange, sad, rather moving fable, with very good performances and action scenes, but a shade too unrelenting in its downbeat tone to become a popular classic.
w Dalton Trumbo *novel* Brave Cowboy by Edward Abbey *d* David Miller *ph* Philip Lathrop *m* Jerry Goldsmith
☆ Kirk Douglas, Walter Matthau, Gena Rowlands, Michael Kane, Carroll O'Connor, Karl Swenson, George Kennedy, Bill Raisch
'Above all a portrait to remember and cherish, alive, doomed, tragic, by Kirk Douglas.' – *Dilys Powell*

The Lonely Guy

US   1984   90m   Technicolor
Universal (Arthur Hiller)
📼 📼 📼 🎧

After being thrown out by his girlfriend, a writer discovers a secret society of single men.
Glossy but heavy-handed comedy, attempting satire but not succeeding in its aim.
w Ed Weinberger, Stan Daniels, Neil Simon *book* The Lonely Guy's Book of Life by Bruce J. Friedman *d* Arthur Hiller *ph* Victor J. Kemper *m* Jerry Goldsmith *pd* James D. Vance *ed* William Reynolds
☆ Steve Martin, Charles Grodin, Judith Ivey, Steve Lawrence, Robyn Douglass, Merv Griffin, Dr Joyce Brothers
'Generally likeable, but it makes you feel as though you were watching television.' – *Pauline Kael, New Yorker*

Lonely Hearts *

Australia   1981   95m   Eastmancolor
Adams Packer Films (John B. Murray)
📼 📼 🎧

When his mother dies, a 50-year-old attempts to go on a belated romantic spree.
Unexpectedly amusing comedy reminiscent of a New Yorker cartoon.
w Paul Cox, John Clarke *d* Paul Cox *ph* Yuri Sokol *m* Norman Kaye
☆ Wendy Hughes, *Norman Kaye*, John Finlayson, Julia Blake, Jonathan Hardy

Lonely in America *

US   1990   96m   DuArt
Arista/Apple (Tirlok Malik, Phil Katzman)
📼

A young Indian arrives in New York to work for his uncle, and decides to strike out on his own.
Engaging comedy of an innocent abroad, with an eye for the foibles of both nationalities.
w Satyajit Joy Palit, Barry Alexander Brown, Nicholas Spencer *story* Tirlok Malik *d* Barry Alexander Brown *ph* Phil Katzman *m* Gregory Arnold *ad* Eduardo Capilla *ed* Tula Goenka
☆ Ranjit Chowdhry, Adelaide Miller, Robert Kessler, Melissa Christopher, David Toney, Franke Hughes, Anila Singh, R. Ganesh, Tirlok Malik

The Lonely Lady

US   1982   92m   Technicolor
KGA Industries/Harold Robbins International
📼 🎧

A girl graduate in Los Angeles suffers various setbacks and assaults on her way to being a film star.
Risible concoction designed to show off the non-talents of a non-star in a film financed by her husband.
w John Kershaw, Shawn Randall *novel* Harold Robbins *d* Peter Sasdy *ph* Brian West *m* Charles Calello
☆ Pia Zadora, Lloyd Bochner, Bibi Besch, Joseph Cali, Anthony Holland, Jared Martin

The Lonely Man

US   1957   87m   bw   Vistavision
Paramount (Pat Duggan)
An outlaw hopes to regain social recognition and contacts the son who abhors him.
Dullish psycho Western.
w Harry Essex, Robert Smith *d* Henry Levin *ph* Lionel Lindon *m* Van Cleave

☆ Jack Palance, Anthony Perkins, Elaine Aiken, Neville Brand, Lee Van Cleef, Elisha Cook Jnr, Robert Middleton

The Lonely Passion of Judith Hearne **

GB   1987   116m   Fujicolour
HandMade (George Harrison, Denis O'Brien)
📼 📼

A middle-aged piano teacher's hopeless life in Dublin boarding houses.
Inevitably gloomy tale, intelligently crafted and with wonderfully detailed performances.
w Peter Nelson *novel* Brian Moore *d* Jack Clayton *ph* Peter Hannan *m* Georges Delerue *pd* Michael Pickwoad
☆ Maggie Smith, Bob Hoskins, Wendy Hiller, Marie Kean, Prunella Scales
🎖 Maggie Smith

The Lonely Woman: see Voyage to Italy

Lonelyhearts *

US   1958   103m   bw
UA/Dore Schary
📼

A young journalist finds himself engrossed, appalled and sickened by his work on the agony column.
Episodic, occasionally interesting but generally too vaguely liberal; an intellectual reshaping of a despairing novel. The producer as usual is well meaning but doesn't quite make it.
w Dore Schary *novel* Nathanael West *d* Vincent J. Donehue *ph* John Alton *m* Conrad Salinger
☆ Montgomery Clift, Robert Ryan, Myrna Loy, Dolores Hart, Maureen Stapleton
🎗 Maureen Stapleton

Lonesome *

US   1928   69m   bw   silent
Universal (Carl Laemmle Jnr)
Young lovers lose each other at Luna Park but later discover that they are neighbours.
Amiable exploration of the life of city workers, comparable with The Crowd but showing a lighter touch.
w Edward T. Lowe *d* Paul Fejos *ph* Gilbert Warrenton
☆ Glenn Tryon, Barbara Kent
† Had sound effects and some talking sequences.

Lonesome Cowboys

US   1968   105m   colour
Andy Warhol Films
📼

aka: *Andy Warhol's Lonesome Cowboys*
A gang of outlaws rides into town, where the only inhabitants are a wealthy woman, her male nurse and a transvestite sheriff.
A sort of improvised and inspired home movie, a gay Western made by city lovers who regard wide-open spaces and horses with great suspicion.
wd Paul Morrissey
☆ Viva, Taylor Mead, Tom Hompertz, Louis Waldron, Joe Dallesandro, Eric Emerson

The Long Absence: see Une Aussi Longue Absence

Long Ago Tomorrow: see The Raging Moon

The Long and the Short and the Tall *

GB   1960   105m   bw
ABP/Michael Balcon
📼

US title: *Jungle Fighters*
In Malaya during World War II a Japanese scout is captured by a British patrol.
Stark war melodrama with the emphasis on character. Vivid at the time, it now seems very routine.
w Wolf Mankowitz *play* Willis Hall *d* Leslie Norman *ph* Erwin Hillier *m* Stanley Black
☆ Laurence Harvey, Richard Todd, David McCallum, Richard Harris, Ronald Fraser, John Meillon, John Rees, Kenji Takaki

The Long Arm **

GB   1956   96m   bw
Ealing (Tom Morahan)
📼

US title: *The Third Key*
A Scotland Yard superintendent solves a series of robberies.
Good straightforward police thriller with careful detail.

w Janet Green, Robert Barr *d* Charles Frend *ph* Gordon Dines *m* Gerbrand Schurmann
☆ Jack Hawkins, Dorothy Alison, John Stratton, Michael Brooke, Geoffrey Keen, Sydney Tafler, Meredith Edwards, Ralph Truman, Ursula Howells
'A generally efficient example of popular British film-making.' – *MFB*

The Long Dark Hall

GB   1951   86m   bw
British Lion/Five Oceans (Anthony Bushell)
A chorus girl is murdered and her married lover is accused.
Miserable mystery with a trick ending, most inappropriately cast.
w Nunnally Johnson, W. E. C. Fairchild *d* Anthony Bushell, Reginald Beck *ph* Wilkie Cooper *m* Benjamin Frankel
☆ Rex Harrison, Lilli Palmer, Raymond Huntley, Denis O'Dea, Anthony Bushell, Henry Longhurst, Patricia Wayne, Meriel Forbes, Brenda de Banzie, Anthony Dawson

The Long Day Closes ***

GB   1992   85m   colour
Mayfair/Palace/Film Four/BFI (Olivia Stewart)
📼 📼 🎧

A man remembers growing up in working-class Liverpool of the mid-1950s as a solitary, movie-obsessed 11-year-old.
Remarkable, atmospheric, understated, nostalgic movie, dealing with emotional repression and the release offered by the cinema.
wd Terence Davies *ph* Michael Coulter *md* Robert Lockhart *pd* Christopher Hobbs *ed* William Diver
☆ Marjorie Yates, Leigh McCormack, Anthony Watson, Nicholas Lamont, Ayse Owens, Tina Malone, Jimmy Wilde, Robin Polley
'A technically elaborate, dryly witty mood piece.' – *Variety*
'A warm and oddly moving experience.' – *Empire*
'Davies' best film yet testifies to the vigour and flexibility of cinematic realisms.' – *Raymond Durgnat, Sight and Sound*

The Long Day's Dying

GB   1968   95m   Techniscope
Paramount/Junction Films (Harry Fine)
Three British paratroopers in Europe are cut off from their unit and die pointlessly.
Violent, irritating anti-war film which resurrects all the clichés and makes itself unpleasant into the bargain.
w Charles Wood *novel* Alan White *d* Peter Collinson *ph* Brian Probyn *m* Malcolm Lockyer *pd* Disley Jones
☆ David Hemmings, Tom Bell, Tony Beckley, Alan Dobie
'It is typical of all that is wrong with the film that it should end on a frozen frame of a soldier in the act of dying while heavily ironic patriotic music swells on the sound track.' – *David Wilson*

Long Day's Journey into Night **

US   1962   174m   bw
Ely Landau
Connecticut 1912: days in the life of an ageing actor, his drug addicted wife and their sons, one of whom is an alcoholic and the other Eugene O'Neill.
Heavy going, nicely handled, superbly acted version of a play which can be a player's triumph and certainly is here; but it still has more effect in the theatre.
w Eugene O'Neill *d* Sidney Lumet *ph* Boris Kaufman *m* André Previn *pd* Richard Sylbert
☆ Ralph Richardson, Katharine Hepburn, Jason Robards Jnr, Dean Stockwell
'Letting his players have their head, lighted miraculously so that every flicker of emotion is preserved, and pursuing them with Kaufman's unobtrusive camera, Lumet illuminates the play, line by line, and gives it all the impact of a live performance.' – *Brenda Davies*
'A very great play has been not translated to the screen but reverently put behind glass.' – *John Simon*
🎗 Katharine Hepburn

The Long Duel

GB   1967   115m   Technicolor   Panavision
Rank (Ken Annakin)
On the North-West Frontier in the twenties, British officers disagree about handling the natives, and one of them forms a strong regard for the native leader.

⊚ Digital Video Disc Region 2   ⊚ Digital Video Disc Region 1   🎧 Soundtrack released on compact disc   ☆ Cast in approximate order of importance   † Points of interest   🎵 Notable songs   🎖 Academy Award   🎗 Academy Award nomination   🏆 BAFTA

Unconvincing cut-price Indian adventure with little cohesion and less entertainment value.

w Peter Yeldham d Ken Annakin ph Jack Hildyard m Patrick John Scott

☆ Trevor Howard, Yul Brynner, Harry Andrews, Charlotte Rampling, Virginia North, Andrew Keir, Laurence Naismith, Maurice Denham

'The dialogue seems to have been written by a computer fed a programme of execrable films on the same theme.' – MFB

The Long Good Friday *

GB 1980 105m colour
Black Lion/Calendar (Barry Hanson)
A gangland boss faces violent reprisals from the competition.
Heavily melodramatic stylish updating of Scarface in a London East End setting. A critical success despite vicious detail and IRA plot involvement.

w Barrie Keefe d John Mackenzie ph Phil Meheux m Francis Monkman

☆ Bob Hoskins, Helen Mirren, Dave King, Bryan Marshall, Eddie Constantine, Stephen Davis

'Nothing says goodbye like a bullet!'
The Long Goodbye

US 1973 111m Technicolor Panavision
UA/Lions Gate (Jerry Bick)
Philip Marlowe helps an eccentric friend who is suspected of murdering his wife.
Ugly, boring travesty of a well-respected detective novel, the apparent intention being to reverse the author's attitudes completely and to substitute dullness and incomprehensibility.

w Leigh Brackett novel Raymond Chandler d Robert Altman ph Vilmos Zsigmond m John T. Williams

☆ Elliott Gould, Nina Van Pallandt, Sterling Hayden, Mark Rydell, Henry Gibson

'Altman's fragmentation bomb blows up itself rather than the myths he has said he wants to lay to rest.' – Sight and Sound
'The trouble is that this Marlowe is an untidy, unshaven, semi-literate dimwit slob who could not locate a missing skyscraper and who would be refused service at a hot dog stand.' – Charles Champlin
'A spit in the eye to a great writer.' – Michael Billington, Illustrated London News

The Long Gray Line *

US 1955 138m Technicolor Cinemascope
Columbia (Robert Arthur)
The career of an athletics trainer at West Point.
Dim biopic, the kind of true life yarn that Americans like, produced in the cheerful, sentimental, sparring way that John Ford likes.

w Edward Hope book Bringing Up the Brass by Marty Maher d John Ford ph Charles Lawton Jnr m George Duning md Morris Stoloff

☆ Tyrone Power, Maureen O'Hara, Donald Crisp, Ward Bond, Robert Francis, Betsy Palmer, Phil Carey, Harry Carey Jnr, Patrick Wayne, Sean McClory

'Its celebration of the codes and ideals of West Point vexatiously combines sentimental cosiness and a kind of religious awe.' – Gavin Lambert

The Long Hot Summer *

US 1958 118m Eastmancolor
Cinemascope
TCF (Jerry Wald)
Conflict arises between a Mississippi town boss and a tenant farmer.
Busy Peyton Place-style family brawling saga with sex on the side, flabby as narrative but compulsive as character study.

w Irving Ravetch, Harriet Frank stories William Faulkner d Martin Ritt ph Joseph LaShelle m Alex North

☆ Orson Welles, Paul Newman, Joanne Woodward, Tony Franciosa, Lee Remick, Angela Lansbury

Long John Silver

Australia 1953 106m Eastmancolor
Cinemascope
TI Pictures (Joseph Kaufman)
Back from Treasure Island, Silver and Hawkins plan a return visit with fresh clues to the treasure.

Cheaply produced, bitsy-piecy adventure fragments with no one to restrain the star from eye-rolling.

w Martin Rackin d Byron Haskin ph Carl Guthrie m David Buttolph

☆ Robert Newton, Connie Gilchrist, Kit Taylor, Rod Taylor

The Long Kiss Goodnight

US 1996 120m CFI color
Entertainment/New Line/Forge/Steve Tisch (Renny Harlin, Stephanie Austin, Shane Black)
With the help of a private eye, an amnesiac teacher discovers that she was once a CIA assassin and so puts her life at risk.
Daft, fast-paced thriller with the usual paranoia about government double-dealing, with only its extreme silliness to differentiate it from others of its genre.

w Shane Black d Renny Harlin ph Guillermo Navarro m Alan Silvestri pd Howard Cummings ed William Goldenberg

☆ Geena Davis, Samuel L. Jackson, Patrick Malahide, Craig Bierko, Brian Cox, David Morse, G. D. Spradlin

'A superbly entertaining action movie, perhaps the best of this year's many shoot-'em-ups.' – Sight and Sound

† The film cost around $70m, including $4m to its screenwriter, with another $25m being spent on marketing. It took some $33.8m at the US box-office.

†† Samuel L. Jackson's character originally died at the end of the film, which upset preview audiences. As a result, the ending was reshot so that he lived.

Long Live Life **

France 1984 Eastmancolor
UGC/Les Films 13/Top No. 1 (Eugene Bellin)
Police and scientists investigate after a businessman and an actress are both unable to account for a three-day absence from their homes.
Tricksy whodunnit in the shadow of the nuclear holocaust, mixing dreams and reality and with several twists in its tale.

wd Claude Lelouch ph Bernard Lutic m Didier Barbelivien pd Jacques Bufnoir ed Hugues Darmois, Pauline Leroy

☆ Charlotte Rampling, Michel Piccoli, Jean-Louis Trintignant, Evelyne Bouix, Charles Aznavour, Laurent Malet, Tanya Lopert, Anouk Aimee

Long Live the Lady! **

Italy 1987 106m colour
Artificial Eye/Rai Channel 1 Cinemaundici (Giampietro Bonamigo)
original title: Lunga Vita Alla Signora!
Six catering students go to a hotel converted from a mysterious castle to help prepare a grand banquet presided over by a spectral old lady.
Innocence and inexperience meet sophistication and tradition in a witty, deliberately ambiguous film.

wd Ermanno Olmi ph Maurizio Zaccaro, Ermanno Olmi m George Philip Telemann ed Giulia Ciniselli, Ermanno Olmi

☆ Marco Esposito, Simona Brandalise, Stefania Busarello, Simone Dalla Rosa, Lorenzo Paolini, Tarcisio Tosi, Marisa Abbate

The Long Long Trailer *

US 1954 96m Anscocolor
MGM (Pandro S. Berman)
A construction engineer and his bride buy a trailer for their honeymoon, and wish they hadn't.
Disaster comedy with long bright periods and the inevitable saggy bits.

w Frances Goodrich, Albert Hackett novel Clinton Twiss d Vincente Minnelli ph Robert Surtees m Adolph Deutsch

☆ Lucille Ball, Desi Arnaz, Marjorie Main, Keenan Wynn, Moroni Olsen

Long Lost Father

US 1934 63m bw
RKO
A restaurant owner saves his daughter from a theft charge.
Competent minor star drama.

w Dwight Taylor novel G. B. Stern d Ernest B. Schoedsack ph Nicholas Musuraca m Max Steiner

☆ John Barrymore, Helen Chandler, Donald Cook, Alan Mowbray, Claude King

'A mild piece with an unbelievable story ... British background and dialogue, mostly dull.' – Variety

The Long Memory

GB 1952 96m
Rank/Europa (Hugh Stewart)
An ex-con, framed for a murder he did not commit, plots revenge but instead uncovers a fresh crime.
Slow and dreary melodrama set largely on a barge, never rising to anything like excitement.

w Robert Hamer, Frank Harvey novel Winston Clewes d Robert Hamer ph Harry Waxman m William Alwyn

☆ John Mills, John McCallum, Elizabeth Sellars, Geoffrey Keen

'Love that promised the world – and paid off in bullets!'
The Long Night *

US 1947 97m bw
(RKO)
A young man shoots the seducer of his sweetheart and barricades himself in a room against the police.
Good-looking but empty remake of Le Jour se Lève.

w John Wexley story Jacques Viot d Anatole Litvak ph Sol Polito m Dimitri Tiomkin

☆ Henry Fonda, Barbara Bel Geddes, Vincent Price, Ann Dvorak, Queenie Smith

'This film faithfully reproduces the letter while altering the spirit of the original almost beyond recognition.' – MFB
'It would be interesting to see it on a double bill with its French original. Both films clearly rate themselves as tragedies; they are merely intelligent trash. But the old one is much more discreet with its self-pity and much more sharply edged.' – James Agee

'A classic of the bashful age!'
Long Pants *

US 1927 58m bw silent
First National/Harry Langdon
A country bumpkin has trouble in the city.
Far from the best Langdon comedy, but funny in flashes.

w Arthur Ripley d Frank Capra ph Elgin Lessley

☆ Harry Langdon, Gladys Brockwell, Alan Roscoe, Alma Bennett

The Long Ride Home: see A Time for Killing

'All the world loves an outlaw. For some damn reason they remember 'em!'
The Long Riders

US 1980 99m colour
UA/Huka (Tim Zinnemann)
The story of Western outlaw brothers named Younger, Miller and James.
Well-worn territory with new-fangled violent detail. Not much of an attraction despite the gimmick of having the various anti-heroes played by real brothers.

w Bill Bryden, Steven Phillip Smith, Stacy Keach, James Keach d Walter Hill ph Ric Waite m Ry Cooder pd Jack T. Collis

☆ Stacy Keach, James Keach, David Carradine, Keith Carradine, Robert Carradine, Dennis Quaid, Randy Quaid

'A satisfying, intelligently worked-out retelling of the classic movie-Western folk romance about the James brothers.' – New Yorker

The Long Ships

GB/Yugoslavia 1963 126m Technirama
Columbia/Warwick/Avila (Irving Allen)
A Viking adventurer and a Moorish prince fall out over a golden bell.
Stilted medieval epic with some visual compensations but more chat than action.

w Berkely Mather, Beverley Cross novel Frans T. Bengtsson d Jack Cardiff ph Christopher Challis m Dusan Radic

☆ Richard Widmark, Sidney Poitier, Russ Tamblyn, Rosanna Schiaffino, Oscar Homolka, Colin Blakely

'To say it was disastrous is a compliment.' – Sidney Poitier

The Long, the Short and the Tall: see The Long and the Short and the Tall

'The love of woman in their eyes – the salt of the sea in their blood!'
The Long Voyage Home **

US 1940 104m bw
Walter Wanger
Merchant seamen on shore leave get drunk, philosophize and have adventures.
Stagey-looking but dramatically interesting amalgam of four one-act plays by Eugene O'Neill, with talent abounding.

w Dudley Nichols d John Ford ph Gregg Toland m Richard Hageman ed Sherman Todd

☆ John Wayne, Thomas Mitchell, Ian Hunter, Ward Bond, Barry Fitzgerald, Wilfrid Lawson, Mildred Natwick, John Qualen, Arthur Shields, Joe Sawyer

'One of the finest of all movies that deal with life at sea.' – Pauline Kael, 70s

↧ best picture; Dudley Nichols; Gregg Toland; Richard Hageman; Sherman Todd

The Long Wait

US 1954 93m bw
UA/Parklane (Lesser Samuels)
An amnesia victim returns home to solve a murder in which he was involved.
Flatulent version of a Mickey Spillane novel, overplotted and inadequately motivated.

w Alan Green, Lesser Samuels d Victor Saville ph Franz Planer m Mario Castelnuovo Tedesco

☆ Anthony Quinn, Charles Coburn, Gene Evans, Peggie Castle, Dolores Donlan

Long Weekend

Australia 1977 100m colour Panavision
Dugong Films (Colin Eggleston)
Wild life appears to gang up on a couple with marital problems who go for a camping trip to an isolated beach.
Didactic thriller, too predictable to hold anyone's interest for long.

w Everett de Roche d Colin Eggleston ph Vincent Monton m Michael Carlos pd Larry Eastwood ed Brian Kavanagh

☆ John Hargreaves, Briony Behets

The Longest Day **

US 1962 169m bw Cinemascope
TCF (Darryl F. Zanuck, Elmo Williams)
A multi-faceted account of the landings in Normandy in June 1944.
Extraordinarily noisy war spectacular, enjoyable as a violent entertainment once one has caught all the threads, but emotionally unaffecting because every part is played by a star.

w Cornelius Ryan, Romain Gary, James Jones, David Pursall, Jack Seddon book Cornelius Ryan d Andrew Marton, Ken Annakin, Bernhard Wicki ph Henri Persin, Walter Wottitz, Pierre Levent, Jean Bourgoin m Maurice Jarre, Paul Anka

☆ John Wayne, Robert Mitchum, Henry Fonda, Robert Ryan, Rod Steiger, Robert Wagner, Paul Anka, Fabian, Tommy Sands, Richard Beymer, Mel Ferrer, Jeffrey Hunter, Sal Mineo, Roddy McDowall, Stuart Whitman and also Steve Forrest, Eddie Albert, Edmond O'Brien, Red Buttons, Tom Tryon, Alexander Knox, Ray Danton, Ron Randell, Richard Burton, Donald Houston, Kenneth More, Peter Lawford, Richard Todd, Leo Genn, John Gregson, Sean Connery, Michael Medwin, Leslie Phillips, Irina Demich, Bourvil, Jean-Louis Barrault, Christian Marquand, Arletty, Curt Jurgens, Paul Hartmann, Gert Frobe, Wolfgang Preiss, Peter Van Eyck, Christopher Lee, Eugene Deckers, Richard Wattis

✕ photography
↧ best picture

The Longest Yard

US 1974 122m Technicolor
Paramount/Long Road (Albert S. Ruddy)
GB title: The Mean Machine
Imprisoned for drunkenness and car theft, a football star is blackmailed into training a prison football team of hulking misfits.
Violent, meandering comedy-drama with murderous jokes but no narrative grip.

w Tracy Keenan Wynn d Robert Aldrich ph Joseph Biroc m Frank de Vol

☆ Burt Reynolds, Eddie Albert, Ed Lauter, Michael Conrad, Jim Hampton

The Longshot

US 1986 89m DeLuxe

Orion/Longshot (Lang Elliott)

Four disgruntled punters borrow money from a local gangster to bet on a horse that a con man has told them is a certain winner.

An also-ran of a comedy, inconsequential and witless.

w Tim Conway d Paul Bartel ph Robby Muller m Charles Fox ad Joseph M. Altadonna ed Adam Toomayan

☆ Tim Conway, Harvey Korman, Jack Weston, Ted Wass, Stella Stevens, Jonathan Winters, Anne Meara, George DiCenzo, Jorge Cervera

Longtime Companion *

US 1990 99m colour

Palace/Companion Productions/American Playhouse (Stan Wlodkowski)

A group of homosexuals, watching their lovers and friends dying of AIDS, decide to become actively involved in fighting the disease.

While tracing its characters' lives from the beginning to the end of the 1980s, the film avoids easy emotion and sentimentality, though it stays with the somewhat sexless affluent middle-classes who are able to articulate their concerns.

w Craig Lucas d Norman Rene ph Tony Jannelli m Greg DeBelles pd Andrew Jackness ed Katherine Wenning

☆ Stephen Caffrey, Patrick Cassidy, Brian Cousins, Bruce Davison, John Dossett, Mark Lamos, Dermot Mulroney, Mary-Louise Parker

& Bruce Davison

Look Back in Anger *

GB 1959 99m bw

ABP/Woodfall (Gordon L. T. Scott)

A bad-tempered young man with a grudge against life and the government runs a market stall, lives in a squalid flat, and has an affair with his wife's best friend.

Well-made version of a play whose sheer dreariness was theatrically stimulating but in terms of film realism becomes only depressing and stupid despite competence all round. It also set shoddy standards for its many less proficient imitators.

w Nigel Kneale play John Osborne d Tony Richardson ph Oswald Morris m Chris Barber

☆ Richard Burton, Mary Ure, Claire Bloom, Edith Evans, Gary Raymond, Glen Byam Shaw, Phyllis Neilson-Terry, Donald Pleasence, George Devine

Look Before You Love

GB 1948 96m bw

Burnham/Rank

Romance in Rio for a girl of the embassy staff.

Abysmal romantic comedy with little of either commodity in evidence.

w Reginald Long d Harold Huth

☆ Margaret Lockwood, Griffith Jones, Norman Wooland, Phyllis Stanley, Michael Medwin, Maurice Denham

'The sunshine story of Broadway's glory girl!'

Look for the Silver Lining *

US 1949 106m Technicolor

Warner (William Jacobs)

The life story of twenties stage star Marilyn Miller.

Harmless musical biopic with a sense of humour.

w Phoebe and Henry Ephron, Marian Spitzer story Bert Kalmar, Harry Ruby d David Butler ph Peverell Marley md Ray Heindorf

☆ June Haver, Ray Bolger, Charles Ruggles, Gordon MacRae, Rosemary de Camp, S. Z. Sakall, Walter Catlett

& Ray Heindorf

Look in Any Window

US 1961 87m bw

Allied Artists

A rich but psychotic youth despises his friends and relations and is arrested as a peeping tom.

Psychiatric case history which also wags a social finger. Not particularly convincing.

w Laurence E. Mascott d William Alland ph W. Wallace Kelley m Richard Shores

☆ Paul Anka, Ruth Roman, Alex Nicol, Gigi Perreau, George Dolenz, Jack Cassidy

Look Up and Laugh *

GB 1935 82m bw

ATP (Basil Dean)

Market stallholders defy a big chain store.

Good star comedy with music.

w Gordon Wellesley story J. B. Priestley d Basil Dean ph Robert G. Martin md Ernest Irving

☆ Gracie Fields, Douglas Wakefield, Harry Tate, Alfred Drayton, Morris Harvey, Vivien Leigh, Robb Wilton

Look Who's Laughing

US 1941 75m bw

RKO (Allan Dwan)

See also: *Here We Go Again*

Fibber McGee and Molly act as unexpected hosts to Edgar Bergen and Charlie McCarthy.

Exploitation of radio sitcoms, acceptable at the time. With Lucille Ball.

w James V. Kern and others d Allan Dwan ph Frank Redman m Roy Webb

Look Who's Talking

US 1989 96m Technicolor

Columbia TriStar (Jonathan D. Krane)

A baby comments on the growing relationship between his unmarried mother and a taxi driver.

Indifferent comedy that enjoyed a great success through the novelty of adult speech and attitudes issuing from the mouth of a baby.

wd Amy Heckerling ph Thomas Del Ruth m David Kitay ad Reuben Freed, Graeme Murray ed Debra Chiate

☆ John Travolta, Kirstie Alley, Olympia Dukakis, George Segal, Abe Vigoda, Bruce Willis, Twink Caplan, Joy Boushel, Don S. Davis

'Carelessly put together, ugly to look at and mawkish and stupid in turn.' – *Derek Malcolm, Guardian*

Look Who's Talking Now

US 1993 97m colour

Columbia TriStar (Jonathan D. Krane)

A mongrel and a spoilt poodle comment on family tribulations when they are not snapping insults at each other.

Direly unamusing sequel in a series that ran out of momentum halfway through the first film; the dogs get the best lines, but even they should complain to their agents.

w Tom Ropelewski, Leslie Dixon d Tom Ropelewski ph Oliver Stapleton m William Ross pd Michael Bolton ed Michael A. Stevenson, Harry Hitner

☆ John Travolta, Kirstie Alley, Lysette Anthony, Olympia Dukakis, David Gallagher, Tabitha Lupien, George Segal and also the voices of Danny DeVito, Diane Keaton

'There is clearly still a collection of folk in Tinseltown insisting that a third instalment of an enjoyable one-joke movie made with no imagination, irony or flair is a really good idea ... it isn't.' – *Philip Thomas, Empire*

Look Who's Talking Too

US 1990 81m Technicolor

Columbia TriStar (Jonathan D. Krane)

Small babies comment on the disagreements between a husband and wife.

All that this sad comedy has to recommend it is the novelty of adult voices issuing from the mouths of babes, a joke that quickly outstays its welcome.

w Amy Heckerling, Neal Israel d Amy Heckerling ph Thomas Del Ruth m David Kitay pd Reuben Freed ed Debra Chiate

☆ John Travolta, Kirstie Alley, Olympia Dukakis, Elias Koteas, Twink Caplan and also the voices of Bruce Willis, Roseanne Barr, Damon Wayans, Mel Brooks

'Whenever Heckerling runs out of inspiration, which is every couple of minutes, she slaps an old rock 'n' roll record on the turntable and transforms the film into a music-video.' – *Philip French, Observer*

Looker

US 1981 94m colour

Warner/The Ladd Company (Howard Jeffrey)

A plastic surgeon investigates the murders of beautiful models who were his clients.

Unconvincing, paranoid science-fiction thriller about advertising.

wd Michael Crichton ph Paul Lohmann m Barry DeVorzon pd Dean Edward Mitzner ed Carl Kress

☆ Albert Finney, James Coburn, Susan Dey, Leigh Taylor-Young, Dorian Harewood, Tim Rossovich

Lookin' to Get Out

US 1982 105m colour

Lorimar/North Star/Voight-Schaffel (Robert Schaffel)

A couple of inveterate gamblers take on the Las Vegas establishment.

Fairly pleasant, mindless, quite forgettable comedy.

w Al Schwartz, Jon Voight d Hal Ashby ph Haskell Wexler m Johnny Mandel pd Robert Boyle

☆ Jon Voight, Ann-Margret, Burt Young, Bert Remsen, Jude Farese, Richard Bradford

Looking for Love

US 1964 83m Metrocolor Panavision

Joe Pasternak/MGM

A talented girl can't decide between show business and marriage.

Limp, would-be-cute romantic nonsense with poor musical numbers.

w Ruth Brooks Flippen d Don Weis ph Milton Krasner m George Stoll

☆ Connie Francis, Jim Hutton, Susan Oliver, Joby Baker, Barbara Nichols, Jay C. Flippen, Jesse White, Charles Lane

Looking for Mr Goodbar

US 1977 136m Metrocolor Panavision

Paramount (Freddie Fields)

A teacher of deaf children leads a sordid secret night life.

Exploitative and very boring sex melodrama which doesn't even make one believe in its central character.

wd Richard Brooks novel Judith Rossner ph William A. Fraker m Artie Kane ad Edward Carfagno

☆ Diane Keaton, Tuesday Weld, William Atherton, Richard Kiley

'Brooks has laid a windy jeremiad about permissive sex on top of fractured film syntax.' – *Judith Crist*

& William A. Fraker; Tuesday Weld

'A four hundred year old work-in-progress.'

Looking for Richard **

US 1996 109m DuArt

TCF (Michael Hadge, Al Pacino)

Al Pacino investigates the problems of playing Shakespeare's Richard III with American actors, rehearses the play and films parts of it in costume.

Fascinating glimpse into an actor's preparation for a classic role, done without pretentiousness.

w Al Pacino, Frederic Kimball play *Richard III* by William Shakespeare d Al Pacino ph Robert Leacock, John Kedrem, John Kranhouse, Steve Confer m Howard Shore ad Kevin Ritter ed Pasquale Buba, William A. Anderson, Ned Bastille, Andre Betz

☆ Al Pacino, Penelope Allen, Harris Yulin, Alec Baldwin, Kevin Spacey, Estelle Parsons, Winona Ryder, Aidan Quinn

'This is not just a film about Shakespeare's *Richard III* – it is also a lucid and compelling adaptation of the play.' – *Geoffrey Macnab, Sight and Sound*

Looking for Trouble

US 1934 77m bw

UA/Darryl F. Zanuck

Two telephone engineers brawl over a girl.

Early star vehicle, quite watchable.

w Leonard Praskins, Elmer Harris story J. R. Bren d William Wellman

☆ Spencer Tracy, Jack Oakie, Constance Cummings, Morgan Conway, Arline Judge

'Too much of a plug for the phone company ... plus an overpacked plot and certain dialogue failings.' – *Variety*

Looking Forward

US 1933 76m bw

MGM

A shop owner finds he must sell his property and fire valued staff.

Depression fable from Dodie Smith's play Service, adequately mounted.

w Bess Meredyth, H. M. Harwood d Clarence Brown

☆ Lewis Stone, Lionel Barrymore, Benita Hume, Elizabeth Allan, Phillips Holmes, Colin Clive

The Looking Glass War

GB 1969 107m Technicolor Panavision

Columbia/M. J. Frankovich (John Box)

The British secret service sends a young Pole into East Germany to find a top secret film.

Jaundiced spy story which aims for irony and tragedy but becomes merely verbose and irritating.

wd Frank R. Pierson novel John Le Carré ph Austin Dempster m Wally Stott

☆ Christopher Jones, Pia Degermark, Ralph Richardson, Anthony Hopkins, Paul Rogers, Susan George, Ray McAnally, Robert Urquhart, Maxine Audley, Anna Massey

'There are a lot of incidental pleasures, but in the final analysis they only add up to half a film.' – *Nigel Andrews*

Looking on the Bright Side *

GB 1931 81m bw

ATP (Basil Dean)

A songwriter gets ideas above his station but eventually returns to the manicurist who loves him.

Dated but lively musical which helped confirm Gracie's stardom.

w Basil Dean, Archie Pitt, Brock Williams d Basil Dean, Graham Cutts ph Robert G. Martin md Carroll Gibbons

☆ Gracie Fields, Richard Dolman, Julian Rose, Wyn Richmond

Loophole

GB 1980 105m colour

Brent Walker (Julian Holloway, David Korda)

A safecracker plans to rob the vault of a London bank.

Dim caper yarn which can't make its mind up how serious it means to be. As it stands, it is all very old hat and has a cop-out finish.

w Jonathan Hales novel Robert Pollock d John Quested ph Michael Reed m Lalo Schifrin

☆ Albert Finney, Martin Sheen, Susannah York, Colin Blakely, Jonathan Pryce, Robert Morley, Alfred Lynch

Loose Ankles

US 1930 66m bw

First National

A girl's inheritance will be cancelled if she is involved in scandal. Rival claimants try to ensure that she is.

Thin, amiable comedy based on a Broadway success.

w Gene Towne play Sam Janney d Ted Wilde

☆ Loretta Young, Douglas Fairbanks Jnr, Louise Fazenda, Otis Harlan, Mary Pollard, Inez Courtney

'Will bring a chuckle to the most hard-boiled metropolite.' – *Variety*

Loose Cannons

US 1990 94m colour Panavision

TriStar (Aaron Spelling, Alan Griesman)

Two misfit cops track down a gang of killers who are attempting to recover a pornographic movie of Hitler and friends, which is to be used to discredit a German politician.

Poor, coarse-toned comedy thriller, one of the worst movies of the decade; the jokes are based on madness and violence, and Aykroyd's lunatic turns are embarrassing.

w Richard Christian Matheson, Richard Matheson, Bob Clark d Bob Clark ph Reginald H. Morris m Paul Zaza pd Harry Pottle ed Stan Cole

☆ Dan Aykroyd, Gene Hackman, Dom DeLuise, Ronny Cox, Nancy Travis, Paul Koslo, Dick O'Neill, Robert Prosky

Loose Connections *
GB   1983   96m   colour
Umbrella/Greenpoint (Simon Perry)
Adventures on a drive to Munich.
Thin, easy-going road comedy. Pleasant enough, but no Genevieve.
w Maggie Brooks d Richard Eyre ph Clive Tickner m Dominic Muldowney
☆ Lindsay Duncan, Stephen Rea, Carole Harrison, Frances Low

Loot *
GB   1970   101m   Eastmancolor
Performing Arts Ltd (Arthur Lewis)
▣ ▤
A crook hides his mother's body and uses the coffin to carry the proceeds of a robbery.
Breakneck black farce which still can't move quite fast enough to cover up its bad taste, though well done by all concerned.
w Ray Galton, Alan Simpson play Joe Orton d Silvio Narizzano ph Austin Dempster m Keith Mansfield, Richard Willing-Denton ad Anthony Pratt
☆ Richard Attenborough, Lee Remick, Hywel Bennett, Milo O'Shea, Dick Emery

The Looters
US   1955   87m   bw
Universal
A plane crashes on Pike's Peak, and rescuers fall out about whether to loot the wreckage.
Competent co-feature of its period and style.
w Richard Alan Simmons d Abner Biberman
☆ Rory Calhoun, Ray Danton, Thomas Gomez, Julie Adams, Frank Faylen, Rod Williams

Lord Camber's Ladies
GB   1932   80m   bw
BIP
A nobleman tries to murder his way out of a romantic tangle.
Rather dull suspenser notable only for its stagey cast and the fact that Alfred Hitchcock produced it.
w Benn W. Levy from Edwin Greenwood and Gilbert Wakefield novel The Case of Lady Camber by Horace Annesley Vachell d Benn W. Levy
☆ Gerald du Maurier, Gertrude Lawrence, Benita Hume, Nigel Bruce, Clare Greet, A. Bromley Davenport

Lord Edgware Dies
GB   1934   81m   bw
Real Art
Hercule Poirot proves that an elderly nobleman was not killed by his young wife.
Modest whodunnit: the intended series did not catch on.
w H. Fowler Mear novel Agatha Christie d Henry Edwards
☆ Austin Trevor, Jane Carr, Richard Cooper, John Turnbull, Michael Shepley

Lord Jeff
🏃 US   1938   78m   bw
MGM (Frank Davis)
GB title: The Boy from Barnardo's
A well-brought-up boy gets into trouble and is sent under supervision to a naval school.
Adequate family film with absolutely no surprises.
w James K. McGuinness story Bradford Ropes, Val Burton, Endré Bohem d Sam Wood ph John Seitz m Edward Ward
☆ Freddie Bartholomew, Mickey Rooney, Charles Coburn, Herbert Mundin, Terry Kilburn, Gale Sondergaard, Peter Lawford

Lord Jim *
GB   1964   154m   Technicolor   Super Panavision
Columbia/Keep (René Dupont)
▤
Adventures of a sailor who prowls the Far East looking for truth; he helps enslaved natives, is raped by a tribal chief, and finally sacrifices his life.
Lush and very boring farrago of miscellaneous incident, with a central character about whose fate no one can care. However, an expensive production must have its points of interest, and the belated introduction of a gentleman villain gives a little edge.
wd Richard Brooks novel Joseph Conrad ph Frederick A. Young m Bronislau Kaper pd Geoffrey Drake

☆ Peter O'Toole, James Mason, Eli Wallach, Paul Lukas, Jack Hawkins, Daliah Lavi, Curt Jurgens, Akim Tamiroff

Lord Love a Duck *
US   1966   105m   bw
UA/Charleston (George Axelrod)
A senior Los Angeles student practises hypnotism on his girlfriend.
Rather sloppy satire on American culture and fancies, dressed up as crazy comedy; occasional laughs.
w Larry H. Johnson, George Axelrod novel Al Hine d George Axelrod ph Daniel Fapp m Neal Hefti
☆ Roddy McDowall, Tuesday Weld, Lola Albright, Ruth Gordon, Harvey Korman, Max Showalter
'The ne plus ultra of cinematic bad taste, blending in equal and unsurpassable measure vulgarity, pretentiousness, inept imitation (usually posing as parody), stupidity and such a proliferation of stomach-turning jokes as would take your average smut pedlar a lifetime to assemble.' – John Simon

Lord of the Flies
🏃🏃 GB   1963   91m   bw
Allen-Hodgon Productions/Two Arts (Lewis M. Allen)
▤
After a plane crash, a party of English schoolboys are stranded on an uncharted tropical island and gradually turn savage.
Semi-professional production of a semi-poetic novel which worked well on the printed page but on screen seems crude and unconvincing.
wd Peter Brook novel William Golding ph Tom Hollyman, Gerald Feil m Raymond Leppard
☆ James Aubrey, Tom Chapin, Hugh Edwards, Roger Elwin, Tom Gaman

'A Classic Story of Conflict and Survival'
Lord of the Flies
🏃🏃 US   1990   90m   DeLuxe   Panavision
Columbia/Castle Rock/Nelson/Jack's Camp/Signal Hill (Ross Milloy)
▣ ▤ ▨ 🎧
Boys from a US military school, survivors of an air crash on an uninhabited tropical island, revert to savagery.
Dull remake, with crude melodrama substituting for the subtle social disintegration of the original.
w Sara Schiff novel William Golding d Harry Hook ph Martin Fuhrer m Philippe Sarde pd Jamie Leonard ed Harry Hook
☆ Balthazar Getty, Chris Furrh, Danuel Pipoly, Badgett Dale, Edward Taft, Andrew Taft, Bob Peck, Bill Schoppert, Michael Greene
'Individual performances mostly never rise above the semi-amateur level.' – Variety
'A Technicolor travel brochure in which a pack of already uncivilized kids act rough and talk dirty like children temporarily freed from the vigilance of their parents.' – Alexander Walker, London Evening Standard

Lord of the Rings *
🏃🏃 GB   1978   133m   DeLuxe
UA/Fantasy (Saul Zaentz)
▤ 🎧
In Middle Earth the Dark Lord loses a powerful ring, and a Hobbit tries to prevent him from getting it back.
Disappointingly stolid, overlong and confused cartoon version of a modern classic which may well deserve all those adjectives. Parts of it are charming, and the method of making cartoons from film of actors photographed in the ordinary way is certainly ingenious though it denies the cartoon characters their own full richness.
w Chris Conkling, Peter S. Beagle books J. R. R. Tolkien d Ralph Bakshi ph Timothy Galfas m Leonard Rosenman
☆ Featuring the voices of Christopher Guard, John Hurt, William Squire, Michael Scholes

The Lords of Discipline
US   1982   103m   Eastmancolor
Paramount (Herb Jaffe, Gabriel Katzka)
▣ ▤
Murky goings-on at the Carolina Military Institute.
Strictly for those interested in army cadets being unpleasant to each other.
w Thomas Pope, Lloyd Fonvielle novel Pat Conroy d Franc Roddam ph Brian Tufano

m Howard Blake pd John Graysmark ed Michael Ellis
☆ David Keith, Robert Prosky, G. D. Spradlin, Barbara Babcock, Michael Biehn, Rick Rossovich

The Lords of Flatbush *
US   1974   86m   Technicolor
Columbia (Stephen F. Verona)
▣ ▤
Adventures of Brooklyn street gangs.
Not quite the violent movie one might think, and interesting for its cast as well as some thoughtful passages.
w Stephen F. Verona, Martin Davidson, Gayle Glecker, Sylvester Stallone d Stephen F. Verona, Martin Davidson
☆ Perry King, Henry Winkler, Sylvester Stallone, Paul Mace, Susan Blakely, Maria Smith

Lorenzo's Oil **
US   1992   135m   Technicolor
UIP/Universal/Kennedy Miller (Doug Mitchell, George Miller)
▣ ▤ ▨ 🎧
After they are told their young son has a fatal disease, his parents defy medical opinion to find a cure.
An inspiring true story of faith and determination, but acted and directed as an all-out emotional assault that some will find wearying before the end.
w George Miller, Nick Enright d George Miller ph John Seale pd Kristi Zea ed Richard Francis-Bruce, Marcus D'Arcy, Lee Smith
☆ Nick Nolte, Susan Sarandon, Peter Ustinov, Kathleen Wilhoite, Gerry Bamman, Margo Martindale, James Rebhorn, Ann Hearn, Maduka Steady, Zack O'Malley Greenburg
'As gruelling a medical case study as any audience would ever want to sit through … A one-of-a-kind film that will devastate some viewers and prove too overbearing and clinical for others, it is as obsessive and relentless as its leading characters.' – Variety
† Medical research released in 1993 claimed that the oil produced 'no detectable clinical improvement' in sufferers from the brain disease.
⌛ Susan Sarandon; George Miller (as writer), Nick Enright

Lorna Doone **
🏃 GB   1934   90m   bw
ATP (Basil Dean)
In 1625 on Exmoor, a farmer comes to love an outlaw's daughter who proves to be in reality a kidnapped heiress.
Simple, straightforward, effective version of the famous romance, with refreshing use of exteriors.
w Dorothy Farnum, Miles Malleson, Gordon Wellesley novel R. D. Blackmore d Basil Dean ph Robert Martin
☆ Victoria Hopper, John Loder, Margaret Lockwood, Roy Emerton, Edward Rigby, Mary Clare, Roger Livesey, George Curzon, D. A. Clarke-Smith, Lawrence Hanray, Amy Veness, Eliot Makeham
'It has polish, but it lacks drama and grip.' – Variety

Lorna Doone
🏃 US   1951   89m   Technicolor
Columbia (Edward Small)
Grotesque remake which treats the story like a cheap Western.
w Jesse L. Lasky Jnr, Richard Schayer d Phil Karlson ph Charles Van Enger m George Duning
☆ Barbara Hale, Richard Greene, Anne Howard, William Bishop, Carl Benton Reid, Ron Randell, Sean McClory, Onslow Stevens, Lester Matthews, John Dehner

Los Amantes del Circulo Polar: see Lovers of the Arctic Circle

Loser Takes All
GB   1956   88m   Eastmancolor   Cinemascope
British Lion/John Stafford
An accountant and his wife are invited to Monte Carlo but the high life estranges them.
Tedious taradiddle from an unexpected quarter; not a success by any standard.
w Graham Greene novel Graham Greene d Ken Annakin ph Georges Périnal m Alessandro Cicognini

☆ Glynis Johns, Rossano Brazzi, James Morley, Joyce Carey, A. E. Matthews, Tony Britton, Felix Aylmer, Albert Lieven, Geoffrey Keen

Loser Takes All
GB   1990   87m   Technicolor
Miramax/British Screen/Ideal Communications/BBC/Flamingo (Christine Oestreicher, Graham Easton)
▤   ▨
aka: Strike It Rich
A poor accountant discovers that his gift for winning at roulette causes problems on his honeymoon.
Slick, glossy and dull drama, with none of the needed sense of romance and irony.
wd James Scott novel Graham Greene ph Robert Paynter m Cliff Eidelman, Shirley Walker pd Christopher Hobbs
☆ Robert Lindsay, Molly Ringwald, John Gielgud, Michel Blanc, Frances de la Tour, Vladek Sheybal, Marius Goring, Max Wall, Margi Clarke, Simon de la Brosse

Losing Isaiah
US   1995   106m   DeLuxe
Paramount (Howard W. Koch Jnr, Naomi Foner)
▣
A black single mother, a former drug addict, goes to the law to get back the baby she abandoned, which has been adopted by a white, middle-class couple.
A contrived drama, concentrating on racism, in which the characters are little more than cardboard cut-outs, representing a particular viewpoint; it rarely convinces.
w Naomi Foner novel Seth Margolis d Stephen Gyllenhaal ph Andrzej Bartkowiak m Mark Isham pd Jeannine C. Oppewall ed Harvey Rosenstock
☆ Jessica Lange, Halle Berry, David Straithairn, Cuba Gooding Jnr, Samuel L. Jackson, Daisy Egan, Marc John Jefferies
'Audiences will assuredly get worked up by this grimly serious, issue-oriented drama.' – Variety
† It was released direct to video in Britain.

Loss of Innocence: see The Greengage Summer

The Loss of Sexual Innocence *
GB/US   1998   106m   colour
Columbia TriStar/Summit/Newmarket/Red Mullet (Mike Figgis, Annie Stewart)
A film director's childhood in Africa, his adolescence and his experiences filming in Tunisia are contrasted with the story of Adam and Eve and their expulsion from paradise.
A very personal film that does not always connect with a wider audience, though it has its moments; the links between the episodic events and the clumsily handled Bible story are tenuous at best.
wd Mike Figgis ph Benoit Delhomme m Mike Figgis pd Giorgio Desideri ed Matthew Wood
☆ Julian Sands, Saffron Burrows, Stefano Dionisi, Jonathan Rhys Meyers, Kelly Macdonald, Femi Ogumbanjo, Hanne Klintoe, Johanna Torrel, George Moktar, John Cowey, Bernard Hill, Rossy de Palma
'Visually exquisite, intensely personal meditation on the story of Adam and Eve.' – Stephen Holden, New York Times

Lost *
GB   1955   89m   Technicolor
Rank (Vivian A. Cox)
US title: Tears for Simon
The police go on the trail of a stolen child.
Mildly effective semi-documentary police story, with good use of locations.
w Janet Green d Guy Green ph Harry Waxman m Benjamin Frankel
☆ David Farrar, David Knight, Julia Arnall, Anthony Oliver, Thora Hird, Eleanor Summerfield, Marjorie Rhodes, Joan Sims

Lost and Found
US   1979   105m   Technicolor   Panavision
Columbia/Gordon (Melvin Frank)
▣ ▤
A widowed American professor meets an English divorcee on a skiing holiday, but after marriage they prove to be incompatible.

🏃🏃 film suitable for family viewing   ▣ VHS video-cassette for the British PAL system   ▤ VHS video-cassette for the British PAL system in wide screen-format   ⛶ Video cassette in a computer-colourised version   ▨ American NTSC video-cassette   🎧 Laser disc

Unattractive romantic comedy-drama which despite capable stars degenerates into a series of wounding slanging matches.

w Melvin Frank, Jack Rose d Melvin Frank
ph Douglas Slocombe m John Cameron
pd Trevor Williams

☆ Glenda Jackson, George Segal, Maureen Stapleton, Paul Sorvino, John Cunningham, Hollis McLaren

Lost Angel *
US 1943 91m bw
MGM (Robert Sisk)
A lost little girl is adopted by a reporter.
Good star vehicle for the sentimentally-inclined, with solid production and casting back-up.

w Isobel Lennart d Roy Rowland ph Robert Surtees m Daniele Amfitheatrof

☆ Margaret O'Brien, James Craig, Marsha Hunt, Philip Merivale, Henry O'Neill, Donald Meek, Keenan Wynn

'A beautiful opportunity for true satire is offered and, I regret to say, thrown away. For our little Gulliver is rapidly decivilized by all the familiar bromidic palliatives: love, crooning, fairies and night clubs.' – Richard Winnington

Lost Angels: see The Road Home

Lost Boundaries *
US 1949 105m bw
Film Classics (Louis de Rochemont)
In a New Hampshire town in the forties, a beloved doctor and his wife are found to have negro blood.
Well-meaning but dramatically ineffective racial drama which meanders along allowing an occasional burst of genuine feeling to come through.

w Virginia Shaler, Eugene Ling d Alfred Werker ph William J. Miller m Louis Applebaum

☆ Mel Ferrer, Beatrice Pearson, Richard Hylton, Susan Douglas, Canada Lee, Grace Coppin

'It cannot be said to betray its subject, but is, rather, unequal to it.' – Gavin Lambert

The Lost Boys
US 1987 92m Technicolor Panavision
Warner (Harvey Bernhard)
Vampiric bikers corrupt innocent teenagers.
Wild nonsense which affronts all classes by its sheer excesses.

w Janice Fischer, James Jeremias, Jeffrey Boam d Joel Schumacher ph Michael Chapman m Thomas Newman pd Bo Welch ed Robert Brown

☆ Jason Patric, Corey Haim, Dianne Wiest, Barnard Hughes, Kiefer Sutherland

'Wherever their feet touched ground, a new adventure was born!'
Lost Command
US 1966 128m Technicolor Panavision
Columbia/Red Lion (Mark Robson)
Adventures of a French paratroop regiment in Indo-China and Algeria.
Anti-war war adventure; noisy but scarcely inspired.

w Nelson Gidding novel The Centurions by Jean Larteguy d Mark Robson ph Robert Surtees m Franz Waxman

☆ Anthony Quinn, Alain Delon, George Segal, Michèle Morgan, Maurice Ronet, Claudia Cardinale, Grégoire Aslan, Jean Servais

The Lost Continent *
GB 1968 98m Technicolor
Hammer (Michael Carreras)
The captain of a tramp steamer illegally carries dynamite, and he and his passengers are stranded in a weird Sargasso Sea colony run by the Spanish Inquisition.
Hilariously imaginative hokum with splendid art direction and some of the grottiest monsters on film; but memorable moments do not quite add up to a classic of the genre.

w Michael Nash novel Uncharted Seas by Dennis Wheatley d Michael Carreras ph Paul Beeson m Gerard Schurmann ad Arthur Lawson sp Robert A. Mattey, Cliff Richardson

☆ Eric Porter, Hildegarde Neff, Suzanna Leigh, Tony Beckley, Nigel Stock, Neil McCallum, James Hanley, James Cossins, Victor Maddern

'One of the most ludicrously enjoyable bad films since Salome Where She Danced.' – MFB

Lost Highway *
US 1996 134m CFI color
Polygram/CiBy 2000/Asymmetrical (Deepak Nayar, Tom Sternberg, Mary Sweeney)
The character of a man found guilty of murdering his wife melds with that of a garage mechanic involved with a gangster's girlfriend.
An exploration of four characters in search of each other that leaves them, and the audience, too often stranded in limbo.

w David Lynch, Barry Gifford d David Lynch ph Peter Deming m Angelo Badalamenti pd Patricia Norris ed Mary Sweeney

☆ Bill Pullman, Patricia Arquette, Balthazar Getty, Robert Blake, Natasha Gregson Wagner, Richard Pryor, Gary Busey, Jack Nance, Henry Rollins

'The most radical, dreamlike and complicated movie David Lynch has made.' – Derek Malcolm, Guardian
'Asserts an all American, suburban-Puritan belief in the idiosyncratic eyewitness and the visionary, the truth of an individual viewpoint and even of messianic derangement, while all the while conveying almost wearily that such subjectivity as idealised elsewhere has entered terminal decline.' – Marina Warner, Sight and Sound

Lost Honeymoon
US 1947 70m bw
Eagle-Lion
An amnesiac GI fails to remember either his wife or his young family.
Artificial comedy which the actors can't carry off.

w Joseph Fields d Leigh Jason

☆ Franchot Tone, Ann Richards, Tom Conway

Lost Horizon ****
US 1937 130m bw
Columbia (Frank Capra)
Escaping from a Chinese revolution, four people are kidnapped by plane and taken to an idyllic civilization in a Tibetan valley, where the weather is always kind and men are not only gentle to each other but live to a very advanced age.
Much re-cut romantic adventure which leaves out some of the emphasis of a favourite Utopian novel but stands up pretty well on its own, at least as a supreme example of Hollywood moonshine, with perfect casting, direction and music. If the design has a touch of Ziegfeld, that's Hollywood.

w Robert Riskin novel James Hilton d Frank Capra ph Joseph Walker m Dimitri Tiomkin ad Stephen Goosson

☆ Ronald Colman, H. B. Warner, Thomas Mitchell, Edward Everett Horton, Sam Jaffe, Isabel Jewell, Jane Wyatt, Margo, John Howard

'One of the most impressive of all thirties films, a splendid fantasy which, physically and emotionally, lets out all the stops.' – John Baxter, 1968
'One is reminded of a British critic's comment on Mary of Scotland, "the inaccuracies must have involved tremendous research".' – Robert Stebbins
'The best film I've seen for ages, but will somebody please tell me how they got the grand piano along a footpath on which only one person can walk at a time with rope and pickaxe and with a sheer drop of three thousand feet or so?' – James Agate
'If the long dull ethical sequences had been cut to the bone there would have been plenty of room for the real story: the shock of western crudity and injustice on a man returned from a more gentle and beautiful way of life.' – Graham Greene

† A 1943 reissue trimmed down the negative still further, to 109 minutes; but in 1979 the American Film Institute restored a print of the original length.

♪ Stephen Goosson

♫ best picture; Dimitri Tiomkin; H. B. Warner

'The adventure that will live forever has been transformed into spectacular musical drama!'
'Come to Shangri-La and a new world of love!'
Lost Horizon *
US 1973 143m Technicolor
Panavision
Columbia/Ross Hunter
Torpid remake with a good opening followed by slabs of philosophizing dialogue and an unbroken series of tedious songs.

w Larry Kramer d Charles Jarrott ph Robert Surtees m Burt Bacharach ad Preston Ames songs Burt Bacharach, Hal David

☆ Peter Finch, Liv Ullmann, Sally Kellerman, Bobby Van, George Kennedy, Michael York, Olivia Hussey, James Shigeta, John Gielgud, Charles Boyer

'It will never play again outside of Shangri-La.' – Les Keyser, Hollywood in the Seventies
'Only Ross Hunter would remake a 1937 movie into a 1932 one.' – Judith Crist
'It can't even be enjoyed as camp.' – Newsweek
'The narrative has no energy, and the pauses for the pedagogic songs are so awkward that you feel the director's wheelchair needs oiling.' – Pauline Kael

The Lost Hours
GB 1952 72m bw
Tempean (Robert S. Baker, Monty Berman)
US title: The Big Frame
A pilot wakes up in a strange hotel, discovers he is the chief suspect for the murder of a former member of his squadron, and begins his own investigation.
Risible thriller, a compendium of old-time clichés that suggest the style of a serial rather than that of a feature film.

w John Gilling, Steve Fisher story Robert S. Baker, Carl Nystrom d David MacDonald ph Monty Berman m William Hill-Bowen md Eric Robinson ad Andrew Mazzie ed Reginald Beck

☆ Mark Stevens, Jean Kent, John Bentley, Dianne Foster, Garry Marsh, Bryan Coleman, Jack Lambert, Leslie Perrins, John Horsley, Duncan Lamont, Sam Kydd, Thora Hird

The Lost Illusion: see The Fallen Idol

Lost in a Harem **
US 1944 89m bw
MGM (George Haight)
Two travelling entertainers in the Middle East get mixed up with a conniving sultan, who hypnotizes them.
Lively, well-staged romp which shows the comedians at their best and uses astute borrowings from burlesque, pantomime, and Hollywood traditions of fantasy and running jokes.

w Harry Ruskin, John Grant, Harry Crane d Charles Reisner m Lester White m David Snell

☆ Bud Abbott, Lou Costello, Douglass Dumbrille, Marilyn Maxwell, John Conte, Jimmy Dorsey and his Orchestra

Lost in Alaska: see Abbott and Costello Lost in Alaska

Lost in America *
US 1985 91m Technicolor Panavision
Warner/Geffen Company (Marty Katz)
A successful couple drop out of their expensive life-style to discover that poverty has its disadvantages.
Witty demolition of yuppie attitudes to the simple life.

w Albert Brooks, Monica Johnson d Albert Brooks ph Eric Saarinen m Arthur B. Rubinstein pd Richard Sawyer ed David Finfer

☆ Albert Brooks, Julie Hagerty, Michael Greene, Garry K. Marshall, Maggie Roswell, Tom Tarpey

Lost in Siberia
GB/USSR 1992 108m Eastmancolor
Winstone/Spectator/Mosfilm
aka: Zateriannyi v Sibiri
In the late 40s an English archaeologist working on the border between Persia and Russia is accused of being a spy and sent to Siberia.
One of an unsuccessful series of co-productions with the West; this has the effect of diminishing the Russian

experience of the gulags in favour of a thriller-like movie, but it has its moments.

w James Brabazon, Alexander Mitta, Valery Fried, Yuri Korotkov d Alexander Mitta ph Vladimir Shevtsik m Leonid Desyatnikov ad Valery Yurkevitch, Vatali Klimenkov ed Anthony Sloman, Nadezhda Veselovskaya

☆ Anthony Andrews, Yelena Mayorova, Vladimir Ilyin, Ira Mikhalyova, Yevgeni Mironov, Alexei Zharkov, Valentin Gaft, Alexander Bureyev

Lost in Space
US 1998 131m colour Panavision
New Line/Prelude/Irwin Allen (Mark W. Koch, Stephen Hopkins, Akiva Goldsman, Carla Fry)
In 2058, a family journey to another planet is sabotaged and they become lost.
Yet another doomed attempt to transfer a creaking 60s TV series to the big screen; its makers might have found a better script than the tired specimen on offer.

w Akiva Goldsman d Stephen Hopkins ph Peter Levy m Bruce Broughton pd Norman Garwood ed Ray Lovejoy

☆ William Hurt, Mimi Rogers, Heather Graham, Lacey Chabert, Jack Johnson, Gary Oldman, Matt LeBlanc, Jared Harris, Mark Goddard, Lennie James, Marta Kristen, June Lockhart, Edward Fox, Dick Tufeld

'Plays more towards the serious with hi-tech gloomier sets and lighting and an examination of the disintegration of the family. At its core, however, the movie is stupid.' – James E. Brooks, Film Review

† June Lockhart played Maureen Robinson, Mark Goddard was pilot Don West, and Dick Tufeld was the robot's voice in the TV series, which ran from 1965 to 1968.

Lost in the Stars *
US 1974 114m colour
American Express/Cinevision/Ely Landua
A country priest goes to Johannesburg in search of his son, and discovers him in prison, awaiting trial for murder.
Effective treatment of a bestselling book, though it does incline towards over-earnestness.

w Alfred Hayes novel Cry the Beloved Country by Alan Paton d Daniel Mann ph Robert Hauser m/ly Kurt Weill, Maxwell Anderson md Alex North pd Jack Martin Smith ed Walter Hannemann

☆ Brock Peters, Melba Moore, Raymond St Jacques, Clifton Davis, Paul Rogers, Paula Kelly, John Williams

Lost in Time: see Waxwork II: Lost in Time

Lost in Yonkers *
US 1993 114m colour
Columbia TriStar/Rastar (Ray Stark)
aka: Neil Simon's Lost in Yonkers
In the early 40s, two youths go to stay with their formidable grandmother and her handicapped daughter.
Often charming version of a nostalgic Simon play, crisply acted but rather bland.

w Neil Simon d Martha Coolidge ph Johnny E. Jensen m Elmer Bernstein pd David Chapman ed Steven Cohen

☆ Richard Dreyfuss, Mercedes Ruehl, Irene Worth, Mike Damus, Brad Stoll, Robert Guy Miranda, Jack Laufer

'You laugh a little, you cry a little, you admire the skill with which everything is put together.' – Caren Myers, Sight and Sound

A Lost Lady
US 1934 71m bw
Warner
A girl falls in love with a much older man.
Empty-headed and over-familiar romantic melodrama.

w Gene Markey, Kathryn Scola novel Willa Cather d Alfred E. Green

☆ Barbara Stanwyck, Frank Morgan, Ricardo Cortez, Lyle Talbot, Philip Reed, Hobart Cavanaugh, Henry Kolker

'Lightweight in story and interesting only as a femme style display.' – Variety

'He crowded a lifetime into 37 suspenseful hours!'

The Lost Man

US 1969 113m Technicolor Panavision

Universal (Ernest B. Wehmeyer)

After a robbery, a crook is pursued by the police and goes into hiding.

Odd Man Out made over as a vehicle for polemics about civil rights for blacks: too shiny, too long, too talky to have any grip.

wd Robert Alan Aurthur ph Jerry Finnerman

m Quincy Jones

☆ Sidney Poitier, Joanna Shimkus, Al Freeman Jnr, Michael Tolan, Leon Bibb, Richard Dysart, David Steinberg, Paul Winfield

'In a strange house of hate – they loved where love had never dared to live before!'

The Lost Moment *

US 1947 89m bw

Universal/Walter Wanger (Martin Gabel)

■. @.

An American publisher goes to Venice to recover love letters written by a famous poet to a lady now aged 105.

Slightly absurd but memorable period drama with a guilty secret eventually coming to light, all put across with apparently deliberate artificiality.

w Leonardo Bercovici novel The Aspern Papers by Henry James d Martin Gabel ph Hal Mohr

m Daniele Amfitheatrof

☆ Robert Cummings, Susan Hayward, Agnes Moorehead, Joan Lorring, Eduardo Ciannelli

'A compelling piece, highly stylized and very personal, with a beautifully photographed studio recreation of Venice.' – *NFT, 1973*

'Boiling passions in the burning sands!'

The Lost Patrol *

US 1934 74m bw

RKO (Cliff Reid)

■   @.

A small British army group is lost in the Mesopotamian desert under Arab attack.

Much-copied adventure story of a small patrol under attack (compare Sahara, Bataan and The Last of the Comanches for a start). The original now seems pretty starchy but retains moments of power.

w Dudley Nichols story Patrol by Philip MacDonald d John Ford ph Harold Wenstrom

m Max Steiner

☆ Victor McLaglen, Boris Karloff, Wallace Ford, Reginald Denny, J. M. Kerrigan, Billy Bevan, Alan Hale

'Although the running time is long, there's nothing draggy about it.' – *Variety*

† A silent British version was released in 1929, written and directed by Walter Summers for British Instructional, with Cyril McLaglen, Sam Wilkinson and Terence Collier.

♫ Max Steiner

The Lost People

GB 1949 89m bw

GFD/Gainsborough (Gordon Wellesley)

Displaced persons gather for comfort in a disused German theatre.

Once again a very flat film has been unsuitably made from an effective piece of theatre, with all possible types present and all views represented. Not on.

w Bridget Boland play Cockpit by Bridget Boland

d Bernard Knowles ph Jack Asher m John Greenwood

☆ Richard Attenborough, Mai Zetterling, Siobhan McKenna, Dennis Price, Maxwell Reed, William Hartnell, Gerard Heinz, Harcourt Williams, Marcel Poncin

'Innocence Isn't Lost. It's Taken...'

The Lost Son *

GB/France 1999 102m colour

UIP/Film Consortium/Le Studio Canal+/Scala/Ima Films (Finola Dwyer)

(🞰)   ⊙

A French private eye, working in London, is hired to find a drug-addicted photographer, the son of a wealthy couple, and finds himself investigating an international paedophile ring.

Tense, violent thriller that leaves too much unexplained in the motivation of its protagonist and has a final revelation that will surprise no-one.

w Eric and Margaret Leclerc, Mark Mills d Chris Menges ph Barry Ackroyd m Goran Bregovic

pd John Beard ed Pamela Power, Luc Barnier

☆ Daniel Auteuil, Nastassja Kinski, Katrin Cartlidge, Ciaran Hinds, Marianne Denicourt, Bruce Greenwood, Billie Whitelaw, Cyril Shaps

'Has all the makings of a powerful thriller. But the drama never really clicks into gear, and the thrills are fleeting.' – *Derek Elley, Variety*

'Shot at only by cameras – yet falling in flames!'

The Lost Squadron *

US 1932 79m bw

RKO (David O. Selznick)

■   @.

World War I pilots find work stunting for a movie studio.

Unusual comedy-drama with several points of interest.

w Herman J. Mankiewicz, Wallace Smith

d George Archainbaud ph Leo Tover, Edward Cronjager m Max Steiner

☆ Richard Dix, Mary Astor, Erich von Stroheim, Joel McCrea, Dorothy Jordan, Hugh Herbert, Robert Armstrong

'A pretty good show … whether it will get back what it cost is something else again.' – *Variety*

Lost Treasure of the Amazon: see *Jivaro*

'From the best-seller that was talked about in whispers!'

'The picture that dares to bare a man's soul!'

The Lost Weekend ****

US 1945 101m bw

Paramount (Charles Brackett)

■   @.   🎧

Two days in the life of a young dipsomaniac writer.

Startlingly original on its release, this stark little drama keeps its power, especially in the scenes on New York streets and in a dipso ward. It could scarcely have been more effectively filmed.

w Charles Brackett, Billy Wilder novel Charles Jackson d Billy Wilder ph John F. Seitz m Miklos Rozsa ed Doane Harrison

☆ Ray Milland, Jane Wyman, Philip Terry, Howard da Silva, Frank Faylen

DON BIRNAM (RAY MILLAND): 'It shrinks my liver, doesn't it, Nat? It pickles my kidneys, yeah. But what does it do to my mind? It tosses the sandbags overboard so the balloon can soar. Suddenly I'm above the ordinary. I'm competent, supremely competent. I'm walking a tightrope over Niagara Falls. I'm one of the great ones. I'm Michelangelo, moulding the beard of Moses. I'm Van Gogh, painting pure sunlight. I'm Horowitz, playing the Emperor Concerto. I'm John Barrymore before the movies got him by the throat. I'm Jesse James and his two brothers – all three of 'em. I'm W. Shakespeare. And out there it's not Third Avenue any longer – it's the Nile, Nat, the Nile – and down it moves the barge of Cleopatra.'

'A reminder of what celluloid is capable of achieving when used by a good director.' – *Spectator*

'I undershtand that liquor interesh; innerish; intereshtsh are rather worried about thish film. Thatsh tough.' – *James Agee*

'Most to be admired are its impressions of bare dreadful truth: the real crowds in the real streets as the hero-victim lugs his typewriter to the pawnshop, the trains screaming overhead, the awful night as he makes his escape from the alcoholics' ward.' – *Dilys Powell*

'A distinguished film, rich in cinematic ingenuity.' – *The Times*

🏆 best picture; script; Billy Wilder (as director); Ray Milland

♫ John F. Seitz; Miklos Rozsa; editing

'Sir Arthur Conan Doyle's Stupendous Story of Adventure and Romance.'

The Lost World **

US 1925 60m bw

First National

(🞰)   ■   @.   ◐

The irascible Professor Challenger leads an expedition to prove his claim that prehistoric creatures are still living on a remote plateau in South America.

A sensational film of its time, complete with dinosaurs, an apeman, a volcanic eruption, a forest fire and a brontosaurus running wild in the streets of London, destroying Tower Bridge. It still retains a naïve charm, as well as providing a narrative that has served as a prototype for dozens of similar films since.

novel Arthur Conan Doyle d Harry O. Hoyt

ph Arthur Edeson sp Willis O'Brien, Ralph Hammeras, Fred Jackman

☆ Wallace Beery, Lewis Stone, Bessie Love, Lloyd Hughes, Alma Bennett, Arthur Hoyt, Margaret McWade, Bull Montana

'This has precious few touches to visual imagination to complement its wonderful monsters and stirring romance.' – *Empire*

'In the middle of the twentieth century you fall off the brink of time!'

The Lost World *

🏅 US 1960 98m DeLuxe Cinemascope

TCF/Saratoga (Irwin Allen)

Professor Challenger is financed by a newspaper to confirm the report of prehistoric life on a South African plateau.

Pitiful attempt to continue the success of Journey to the Center of the Earth, with the story idiotically modernized, unconvincing monsters, a script which inserts conventional romance and villainy, and fatal miscasting of the central part.

w Irwin Allen, Charles Bennett novel Sir Arthur Conan Doyle d Irwin Allen ph Winton C. Hoch

m Bert Shefter, Paul Sawtell

☆ Claude Rains, Michael Rennie, David Hedison, Richard Haydn, Fernando Lamas, Jill St. John, Ray Stricklyn

'Resembles nothing so much as a ride on a rundown fairground Ghost Train.' – *MFB*

The Lost World: Jurassic Park *

US 1997 134m DeLuxe

Universal/Amblin (Gerald R. Molen, Colin Wilson)

■.   ■   @.   🎧

A team of experts goes to investigate how an island used as a breeding ground for the recreated dinosaurs of Jurassic Park has become a self-supporting eco-system.

The special effects are to be wondered at, as is the fact that the script is cloned from the oldest and most familiar elements of monster movies; this is a dinosaur about dinosaurs.

w David Koepp novel Michael Crichton

d Steven Spielberg ph Janusz Kaminski m John Williams pd Rick Carter ed Michael Kahn

sp Dennis Muren, Stan Winston, Randal M. Dutra, Michael Lantieri

☆ Jeff Goldblum, Julianne Moore, Pete Postlethwaite, Vince Vaughn, Vanessa Lee Chester, Arliss Howard, Richard Attenborough, Peter Stormare, Harvey Jason, Richard Schiff

'The dinosaur creations are even better than those in the first film. But underneath the technical virtuosity is a standard chase film.' – *Variety*

'This feels like the kind of sequel a master hands over to an apprentice, and you sense that although much effort was lavished on the special effects, Spielberg's interest in the story was perfunctory.' – *Roger Ebert, Chicago Sun Times*

† The film had the biggest worldwide gross of 1997, of more than $611m.

♫ visual effects

The Lottery Bride

US 1930 85m bw

Arthur Hammerstein/United Artists

■

A girl goes on the run when she finds herself first prize in a lottery.

Dismal operetta from the period when silent techniques were still giving way to sound.

w Horace Jackson, Howard Emmett Rogers

story Herbert Stothart d Paul Stein

☆ Jeanette MacDonald, Joe E. Brown, John Garrick, ZaSu Pitts

'One of the worst of the really very bad features released since sound.' – *Variety*

Lottery Lover

US 1935 80m bw

Fox

A shy sailor wins a lottery prize, an introduction to a Folies Bergère star, but falls in love with the public relations girl organizing the stunt.

Faded romantic comedy of little surviving interest.

w Sig Herzig d William Thiele

☆ Lew Ayres, Reginald Denny, Pat Paterson, Sterling Holloway

The Loudest Whisper: see *The Children's Hour*

Louisa *

US 1950 90m bw

Universal-International

A much-married man finds that both his daughter and his mother have boyfriend trouble.

Friendly generation gap comedy with practised talent.

w Stanley Roberts d Alexander Hall ph Maury Gertsman m Frank Skinner

☆ Ronald Reagan, Spring Byington, Charles Coburn, Ruth Hussey, Edmund Gwenn, Piper Laurie, Scotty Beckett

Louise *

France 1939 99m bw

European Film Distributors

A seamstress is rescued from a life of shame.

Ill-advised venture into film opera for an American star.

w Steve Passeur opera Gustave Charpentier

d Abel Gance

☆ Grace Moore, Georges Thill, André Pernet

'Tedious and unconvincing.' – *Variety*

'Visually and dramatically it is one of the funniest films to be seen in London. It is all bacchanalia among the blossoms and situations whose grotesqueness is deliciously enhanced by the personality of the distinguished singer. Oh, the tiptoeings of Miss Moore, the sedate coquetry, the little trills and carollings, and the great stony teeth.' – *Graham Greene*

Louisiana

US 1947 82m bw

Lindsley Parsons/Monogram

A poor singing farmer becomes governor.

Musical biopic of only historical interest.

w Jack de Witt d Phil Karlson

☆ Jimmie Davis, Margaret Lindsay, John Gallaudet, Freddie Stewart

Louisiana Purchase *

US 1941 98m Technicolor

Paramount (Harold Wilson)

Efforts are made to compromise a politician.

Quite lively transcription of a Broadway musical success with elements of political satire including a climactic filibuster scene.

w Jerome Chodorov, Joseph Fields play Morrie Ryskind d Irving Cummings ph Harry Hallenberger, Ray Rennahan ad Raoul Pene du Bois songs Irving Berlin

☆ Bob Hope, Vera Zorina, Victor Moore, Irene Bordoni, Dona Drake, Raymond Walburn, Maxie Rosenbloom, Frank Albertson, Donald MacBride, Andrew Tombes

♫ Harry Hallenberger, Ray Rennahan; Raoul Pene du Bois

Louisiana Story *

🏅 US 1948 77m bw

Standard Oil Company (Robert Flaherty)

■

In the Louisiana bayous a young native boy watches as oil drillers make a strike.

Quite beautiful but over-extended semi-documentary.

w Robert and Frances Flaherty d Robert Flaherty

ph Richard Leacock m Virgil Thomson ed Helen Van Dongen

☆ Joseph Boudreaux, Lionel Leblanc, Frank Hardy

'The film will be remembered, not for its content, but for the sustained beauty of photography and music, harmonised in shots recalling the delicacy of Chinese landscape painting.' – *Campbell Dixon*

♫ original story

Loulou

France 1980 105m Eastmancolor

Gaumont/Action Films

(🞰)

A smart young business woman sets up an uneasy menage with a working-class layabout.

Curious but not particularly interesting character study, watchable mainly for its detail.

w Arlette Langmann d Maurice Pialat ph Pierre-William Glenn, Jacques Loiseleux md Philippe Sarde

☆ Isabelle Huppert, Gérard Depardieu, Guy Marchand, Humbert Balsan

The Lovable Cheat

US 1949 79m bw

Film Classics/Skyline (Edward Lewis, Richard Oswald)

📀

A bankrupt merchant tries to keep the bailiffs at bay by hurriedly finding a rich husband for his daughter.

A stolid, stagey treatment that lacks cinematic flair and humour.

w Edward Lewis, Richard Oswald *play Mercadet Le Faiseur* by Honoré de Balzac d Richard Oswald ph Paul Wano m Karl Hajos ad Boris Leven ed Douglas Bagier

☆ Charlie Ruggles, Peggy Ann Garner, Buster Keaton, Curt Bois, Richard Ney, Alan Mowbray, Iris Adrian, Fritz Feld, Ludwig Donath

'Caught in the swirl of passions and sacrifice!'

Love *

US 1927 82m bw silent

MGM (Edmund Goulding)

📀

Anna Karenina leaves her husband and child for Count Vronsky.

Marginally interesting first shot at a famous subject by a star who came back to it in 1935.

w Frances Marion, Lorna Moon *novel* Leo Tolstoy d Edmund Goulding ph William Daniels m Ernst Luz ad Cedric Gibbons, Alexander Toluboff

☆ Greta Garbo, John Gilbert, Brandon Hurst, Philippe de Lacy, George Fawcett, Emily Fitzroy

† An alternative happy ending was provided for exhibitors who wanted it.

Love Affair

US 1932 68m bw

Columbia

An heiress falls for a flying instructor.

Mild romantic comedy drama.

w Jo Swerling *story* Ursula Parrott d Thornton Freeland ph Ted Tetzlaff

☆ Dorothy Mackaill, Humphrey Bogart, Jack Kennedy, Astrid Allwyn, Halliwell Hobbes, Barbara Leonard

'A neighbourhood operation, that's about its worth.' – *Variety*

Love Affair ***

US 1939 89m bw

RKO (Leo McCarey)

📀 📀

On a transatlantic crossing, a European man of the world meets a New York girl, but their romance is flawed by misunderstanding and physical accident.

The essence of Hollywood romance, and one of the most fondly remembered films of the thirties, perhaps because of the easy comedy sense of the first half.

w Delmer Daves, Donald Ogden Stewart *story* Mildred Cram, Leo McCarey d Leo McCarey ph Rudolph Maté m Roy Webb ad Van Nest Polglase, Al Herman

☆ Charles Boyer, Irene Dunne, Maria Ouspenskaya, Lee Bowman, Astrid Allwyn, Maurice Moscovich

'Production is of grade A quality … its b.o. chances look good.' – *Variety*

'Those excited over the mastery of form already achieved in pictures, will like to follow this demonstration of the qualities of technique and imagination the films must always have and keep on recruiting to their service … Clichés of situation and attitude are lifted almost beyond recognition by a morning freshness of eye for each small thing around.' – *Otis Ferguson*

'McCarey brought off one of the most difficult things you can attempt with film. He created a mood, rather than a story; he kept it alive by expert interpolations; he provided comedy when he needed comedy and poignancy when he needed substance; and he did it with the minimum of effort.' – *Pare Lorentz*

† Remade as *An Affair to Remember* (qv).

🏆 best picture; original story; Irene Dunne; Maria Ouspenskaya; art direction; song 'Wishing' (*m/ly* Buddy de Sylva)

Love Affair

US 1994 108m Technicolor

Warner/Mulholland (Warren Beatty)

📀 📀 🎧

A couple find that the course of true love does not run smooth and similar clichés.

An inexplicable remake of a sentimental weepie, predicated on the fact that its stars are married to one another, which is hardly reason enough to disinter

something done with much more style a generation ago; an affair to forget.

w Robert Towne, Warren Beatty *story* Mildred Cram, Leo McCarey *screenplay Delmer Daves, Donald Ogden Stewart* d Glenn Gordon Caron m Ennio Morricone pd Fernando Scarfiotti ed Robert C. Jones

☆ Warren Beatty, Annette Bening, Katharine Hepburn, Garry Shandling, Pierce Brosnan, Kate Capshaw, Chloe Webb

'Not a disaster, but it's not good either; its kitsch derives from old "woman's film" formulas but put together without the conviction or the moral urgency that once made such stuff irresistible.' – *David Denby, New York*

'Marks the nadir of Hollywood's obsession with re-makes to date.' – *Denis Seguin, Screen International*

† The film was first made by Leo McCarey in 1939 starring Charles Boyer and Irene Dunne and remade as *An Affair to Remember* in 1957, again directed by Leo McCarey and starring Cary Grant and Deborah Kerr.

Love Affair, or the Case of the Missing Switchboard Operator: see *The Switchboard Operator*

Love among the Millionaires

US 1930 70m bw

Paramount

A waitress falls for the son of a railroad president.

Ho-hum star vehicle without much get-up-and-go.

w Grover Jones, William Conselman, Joseph L. Mankiewicz d Frank Tuttle

☆ Clara Bow, Stanley Smith, Mitzi Green, Skeets Gallagher, Stuart Erwin

'It will call for a lot of faith from the Clara Bow admirers to accept her in this kind of a part, the sweet wishy-washy thing, after the bum publicity she's been getting.' – *Variety*

Love and a 45 *

US 1994 101m colour

Trimark (Darin Scott)

📀 📀 🎧

A petty crook, who shoots his psychotic partner for killing a checkout girl during a robbery, takes to the road with his girl pursued by the law and assorted low-life.

Slick, enjoyably trashy exploitation movie that updates a familiar theme.

wd C. M. Talkington ph Tom Richmond m Tom Verlaine pd Deborah Pastor ed Bob Ducsay

☆ Gil Bellows, Renee Zellweger, Rory Cochrane, Jeffrey Combs, Jace Alexander, Jack Nance, Michael Bowen, Peter Fonda

'The fact that *Love and a 45* is so unapologetically irresponsible (the lingering tattoo torture scene is lip-smackingly sadistic) only makes it more endearing.' – *Sight and Sound*

Love and Bullets

US 1978 103m Metrocolor

ITC (Pancho Kohner)

A gangster's mistress is brought back from Switzerland by a revengeful Phoenix cop.

Downbeat bang-bang with a high death rate and a glum finale; generally low-grade stuff.

w Wendell Mayes, John Melson d Stuart Rosenberg ph Fred Koenekamp m Lalo Schifrin pd John DeCuir

☆ Charles Bronson, Jill Ireland, Rod Steiger, Henry Silva, Strother Martin, Bradford Dillman, Michael V. Gazzo

'A relatively dismaying example of the Lew Grade entertainment formula: as locations, production values and clichéd set-pieces proliferate, scripts increasingly look like shaggy dog stories desperately in search of a point, and actors are left to do their own thing as characters disintegrate.' – *Richard Combs, MFB*

'Love and bullets my eye: embarrassment and tedium would be more like it.' – *Time Out*

Love and Death *

US 1975 85m DeLuxe Panavision

UA/Jack Rollins, Charles H. Joffe

📀 📀 🎧

In 1812 Russia, a man condemned reviews the follies of his life.

Personalized comedy fantasia inspired by War and Peace, Ingmar Bergman and S. J. Perelman. Basically only for star fans.

wd Woody Allen ph Ghislain Cloquet m Prokofiev

☆ Woody Allen, Diane Keaton, Georges Adel, Despo, Frank Adu

'I have a feeling that one of these days Allen will get it most dreadfully together and make a film which is more than a string of funny one-liners and set-pieces. He hasn't quite done it here.' – *Benny Green, Punch*

Love and Death on Long Island **

GB/Canada 1996 93m Technicolor

Guild/Skyline/Imagex/British Screen/Telefilm Canada/Arts Council/NSFDC (Steve Clark-Hall, Christopher Zimmer)

📀 📀

A reclusive, intellectual British novelist becomes obsessed with a good-looking American actor, who appears in trashy movies, and goes to America to try to seduce him.

Engaging, witty, slender movie that extracts much amusement from a clash between two cultures and vastly differing sensibilities.

wd Richard Kwietniowski *novel* Gilbert Adair ph Oliver Curtis m The Insects, Richard Grassby-Lewis pd David McHenry ed Susan Shipton

☆ John Hurt, Jason Priestley, Fiona Loewi, Sheila Hancock, Maury Chaykin, Gawn Grainger, Elizabeth Quinn

'Bittersweet blend of *Death in Venice* and *Porky's*.' – *David Parkinson, Empire*

Ⓥ Richard Kwietniowski (best newcomer)

Love and Hisses *

US 1937 84m bw

TCF (Kenneth MacGowan)

A gossip columnist and a bandleader continue their feud.

Moderate sequel to Wake Up and Live (qv); it got by.

w Art Arthur, Curtis Kenyon d Sidney Lanfield ph Robert Planck m Louis Silvers

☆ Walter Winchell, Ben Bernie and his orchestra, Joan Davis, Bert Lahr, Simone Simon, Ruth Terry

Love and Human Remains *

Canada 1993 100m colour

Rank/Max/Atlantis (Roger Frappier)

📀 📀 📀

A gay actor turned waiter searches for sex while his flatmate, a female book reviewer, looks for love among people with hang-ups of their own.

A modern romance in a world of AIDS and serial killers, often witty and sceptical but also increasingly unbelievable and hysterical.

w Brad Fraser *play Unidentified Human Remains and the Nature of Love* by Brad Fraser d Denys Arcand ph Paul Sarossy m John McCarthy pd François Seguin ed Alain Baril

☆ Thomas Gibson, Ruth Marshall, Cameron Bancroft, Mia Kirshner, Joanne Vannicola, Matthew Ferguson, Rick Roberts

'A bawdy and spirited comedy about a group of mostly 30ish urbanites trying to get a grip on their sexuality and place in the world.' – *Todd McCarthy, Variety*

'The more it progresses, the more it falls into banality and melodrama.' – *Derek Malcolm, Guardian*

Love and Learn

US 1947 83m bw

Warner

Two impoverished songwriters are secretly helped by a rich girl.

Tame comedy with few laughs.

w Eugene Conrad, Francis Swann and I. A. L. Diamond d Frederick de Cordova

☆ Jack Carson, Robert Hutton, Martha Vickers, Janis Paige, Otto Kruger

† Martha Vickers' singing was dubbed by Trudy Erwin.

Love and Money

US 1980 95m Metrocolor

Lorimar

A banker kidnaps a financier's wife, and finds himself in dead trouble.

Incoherent light melodrama which barely got released.

wd James Toback ph Fred Schuler ad Lee Fischer

☆ Ray Sharkey, Ornella Muti, Klaus Kinski, Armand Assante, King Vidor, William Prince

'The trouble with love is, you never know where it's going to strike next.'

Love and Other Catastrophes **

Australia 1996 79m Cinevex

TCF/Screwball Five/AFC (Stavros Andonis Efthymiou)

In Melbourne, five university students cope with the problems of life, learning and love.

High-spirited, episodic account of the young enjoying the little dramas of everyday experience, which skates on the surface of life without putting a foot wrong.

w Yael Bergman, Emma-Kate Crogan, Helen Bandis d Emma-Kate Crogan ph Justin Brickle m Oleh Witer ad Lisa Collins ed Ken Sallows

☆ Matt Day, Frances O'Connor, Alice Garner, Radha Mitchell, Matthew Dyktynski, Kim Gyngell, Suzi Dougherty, Suzanne Dowling, Torquil Neilson

'A sharp, short, excellent little movie that comes in looking suspiciously like an Andy Warhol home movie and grows into a truly rewarding, original and spontaneous piece of entertainment.' – *Marianne Gray, Film Review*

Love and Pain and the Whole Damn Thing

US 1972 113m Eastmancolor

Columbia/Gus (Alan J. Pakula)

An asthmatic young American on holiday in Spain has an affair with an older woman suffering from an incurable disease.

Dreary doomed romance studiously treated as tourist comedy.

w Alvin Sargent d Alan J. Pakula ph Geoffrey Unsworth m Michael Small

☆ Maggie Smith, Timothy Bottoms

Love and Sacrifice: see *America*

Love at First Bite *

US 1979 96m colour

Simon (Joel Freeman)

📀 📀 📀

Count Dracula flees from the communists and settles in New York.

Energetic spoof, with jokes on the sexy side; good work all round.

w Robert Kaufman d Stan Dragoti ph Edward Rosson m Charles Bernstein pd Serge Krizman

☆ George Hamilton, Susan St James, Richard Benjamin, Dick Shawn, Arte Johnson

'Love is so hard to find you have to hire a detective'

Love at Large

US 1990 97m DeLuxe

Rank/Orion (David Blocker)

📀 📀 🎧

A private eye checks on the wrong man, while a female detective is hired by his girlfriend to check on him.

Enjoyably light-hearted treatment of an intricate plot of double-cross and double lives.

wd Alan Rudolph ph Elliot Davis m Mark Isham pd Stephen Legler ed Lisa Churgin

☆ Tom Berenger, Elizabeth Perkins, Anne Archer, Kate Capshaw, Annette O'Toole, Ted Levine, Ann Magnuson, Kevin J. O'Connor, Ruby Dee, Barry Miller, Neil Young

The Love Ban: see *It's a 2' 6" Above the Ground World*

Love before Breakfast

US 1936 90m bw

Universal

Two Park Avenue beaux vie for a socialite.

Thinly plotted but quite amusing romantic comedy.

w Herbert Fields *novel Spinster Dinner* by Faith Baldwin d Walter Lang ph Ted Tetzlaff md Franz Waxman

☆ Carole Lombard, Preston Foster, Cesar Romero, Janet Beecher, Bert Roach

A Love Bewitched

Spain 1985 98m colour

Emilian Piedra

original title: *El Amor Brujo*

The future marriage of two children is arranged by their gypsy fathers with tragic results.

A dance drama likely to appeal only to aficionados of the genre.

w Carlos Saura, Antonio Gades d Carlos Saura ph Teo Escamilla m Manuel de Falla pd Gerardo Vera ed Pedro Del Rey

---

☆ Antonio Gades, Cristina Hoyos, Laura Del Sol, Juan Antonio Jiminez, Emma Penella, La Polaca, Gomez de Jerez

The Love Bug **
👫 US 1968 107m Technicolor
Walt Disney (Bill Walsh)
📼 ▬ ◎ ⬡ ⬡

An unsuccessful racing driver finds that his small private Volkswagen has a mind of its own.
Amusing, pacy period fantasy in the best Disney style.
w Bill Walsh, Don da Gradi d Robert Stevenson ph Edward Colman m George Bruns sp Eustace Lycett
☆ David Tomlinson, Dean Jones, Michele Lee, Buddy Hackett, Joe Flynn, Benson Fong, Joe E. Ross

The Love Cage: see Joy House

'He promised to love, honor and protect. She promised to love, cheat and steal.'
Love, Cheat & Steal
US 1994 96m Foto-Kem
ITC/Showtime Network/MPCA (Brad Kevoy, Steve Stabler)
📼 ▬

A killer escapes from prison and forces his former wife to help him to rob her new husband's bank.
Formula thriller of betrayal and double-cross that early promises more than it ultimately delivers.
wd William Curran ph Kent Wakeford pd Jane Ann Stewart ed Carole Kravetz
☆ John Lithgow, Eric Roberts, Madchen Amick, Donald Moffat, Richard Edson, Dan O'Herlihy, David Ackroyd
'A desperate wannabe film noir that lacks the form's crucial elements of suapenseful ambience and steamy sexuality.' – Emanuel Levy, Variety

The Love Child
GB 1987 101m colour
BFI/Frontroom Pro/Channel 4/VPRO TV (Angela Topping)
An orphaned South London youth falls in love with an artist living in a squat.
Weak whimsy of working-class life.
w Gordon Hann d Robert Smith ph Thaddeus O'Sullivan m Colin Gibson, Kenny Craddock pd Caroline Hanania ed John Davies
☆ Sheila Hancock, Peter Capaldi, Percy Herbert, Lesley Sharp, Alexei Sayle, Arthur Hewlett, Cleo Sylvestre, Stephen Lind

Love Crazy *
US 1941 100m bw
MGM (Pandro S. Berman)
When his wife threatens to divorce him, a businessman hatches all manner of crazy schemes, including disguising himself as his own sister.
Zany romantic comedy, over-stretched but with a fair share of hilarity.
w William Ludwig, Charles Lederer, David Hertz d Jack Conway ph Ray June m David Snell
☆ William Powell, Myrna Loy, Gail Patrick, Jack Carson, Florence Bates, Sidney Blackmer, Vladimir Sokoloff, Donald MacBride, Sig Rumann, Sara Haden, Elisha Cook Jnr, Kathleen Lockhart

Love Crimes
US 1991 90m DeLuxe
Rank/Sovereign/Miramax (Lizzie Borden, Rudy Langlais)
📼

An assistant DA goes undercover so that she can trap a photographer who is raping the women who pose for him.
Confused thriller that seems uncertain as to what kind of film it wants to be; it finally settles for mediocrity.
w Allan Moyle, Laurie Frank d Lizzie Borden ph Jack N. Green m Graeme Revell, Roger Mason pd Armin Ganz ed Nicholas C. Smith, Mike Jackson
☆ Sean Young, Patrick Bergin, Arnetia Walker, James Read, Ron Orbach, Fern Dorsey, Tina Hightower, Donna Biscoe

A Love Divided *
Ireland 1999 100m colour
RTE/BBC/IFB/Parallel (Alan Moloney, Tim Palmer, Gerry Gregg)
In Ireland in the 1950s, a Protestant woman marries a Catholic farmer; but she leaves him when

the local priest insists that their daughters must be educated at the village Catholic school.
Based on a true story, an effective narrative of a domestic disagreement that escalates into a bigoted religious controversy that destroys a community.
w Stuart Hepburn screenplay Deirdre Dowling, Gerry Gregg d Sydney Macartney ph Cedric Culliton m Fiachra Trench pd Alan Farquharson ed Ray Roantree
☆ Liam Cunningham, Orla Brady, Tony Doyle, Peter Caffrey, John Kavanagh, Brian McGrath, Jim Norton, Ali White
† In 1998, the Catholic church formally apologised for its role in the affair.

Love etc.
France 1996 104m colour Panavision
Pathé/Aliceléo/France3/Canal+ (Patrick Godeau)
📼

Two friends, one shy, the other flamboyant, compete for the love of the same woman.
Slight, playful treatment of a triangular romance.
w Marion Vernoux, Dodine Herry novel Talking It Over by Julian Barnes d Marion Vernoux ph Eric Gautier m Alexandre Desplat pd François Emmanuelli ed Jennifer Auge
☆ Charlotte Gainsbourg, Yvan Attal, Charles Berling, Thibault de Montalembert, Elodie Navarre, Marie Adam

Love Eternal *
France 1943 111m bw
André Paulvé
📼

original title: L'Eternel Retour
The love story of Tristan and Isolde.
This modernized version had a Teutonic look and was respected rather than admired.
w Jean Cocteau d Jean Delannoy ph Roger Hubert m Georges Auric ad Wakhevitch
☆ Jean Marais, Madeleine Sologne, Jean Murat, Yvonne de Bray
'There it is, the whole dolorous bag of tricks, the island, the love potion, the scarf on the mast, the dark tower, the aching rejection of life, valid according to its intentions, often superbly beautiful in its execution, but rotted.' – Richard Winnington

Love Field
US 1992 104m DeLuxe
Orion (Sarah Pillsbury, Midge Sanford)
📼 ▬ ◎

A hairdresser in Dallas who identifies with Jacqueline Kennedy goes to attend President Kennedy's funeral and is attracted to a black man she meets on the way.
Intensely American movie that is too parochial to be rewarding.
w Don Roos d Jonathan Kaplan ph Ralf Bode m Jerry Goldsmith pd Mark Freeborn ed Jane Kurson
☆ Michelle Pfeiffer, Dennis Haysbert, Stephanie McFadden, Brian Kerwin, Louise Latham, Peggy Rea, Beth Grant
⅄ Michelle Pfeiffer

Love from a Stranger *
GB 1936 90m bw
Trafalgar (Max Schach)
▬

A young woman realizes she may have married a maniac.
Stalwart suspenser from a popular novel and play.
w Frances Marion play Frank Vosper story Philomel Cottage by Agatha Christie d Rowland V. Lee ph Philip Tannura m Benjamin Britten
☆ Ann Harding, Basil Rathbone, Binnie Hale, Bruce Seton, Jean Cadell, Bryan Powley, Joan Hickson, Donald Calthrop
'Gorgeously photographed and splendidly cut … takes first rank with the long list of gruesome films produced in recent years.' – Variety

Love from a Stranger
US 1947 81m bw
Eagle Lion (James J. Geller)
▬

GB title: A Stranger Walked In
Stilted period remake.
w Philip MacDonald d Richard Whorf ph Tony Gaudio m Hans Salter
☆ Sylvia Sidney, John Hodiak, Ann Richards, John Howard, Isobel Elsom, Frederick Worlock

The Love God?
US 1969 103m Techniscope
Universal (Edward J. Montagne)
A meek ornithologist is thought to be the brains behind a girlie magazine, and becomes a national sex symbol.
Dispiriting and very talkative star farce which would have been long at half the time.
wd Nat Hiken ph William Margulies m Vic Mizzy
☆ Don Knotts, Edmond O'Brien, Anne Francis, James Gregory, Maureen Arthur
'Strictly for admirers of Don Knotts. Can there really be many?' – MFB

The Love Goddesses **
US 1965 87m bw
Paramount/Walter Reade/Sterling
▬ ◎

A light-hearted account of female sexuality on the Hollywood screen.
Sharp-eyed compilation film which is worth a dozen books on the subject.
w Saul J. Turell, Graeme Ferguson m Percy Faith narrator Carl King
'A compilation of shrapnel from old sex-bomb movies, full of deliciously improbable moments.' – Newsweek
† Clips include Blonde Venus, Morocco, True Heart Susie, Cleopatra (1934), Intolerance, The Cheat, The Sheik, Blood and Sand, The Sorrows of Satan, The Love of Sunya, Diary of a Lost Girl, Ecstasy, L'Atlantide, Peter the Tramp, Cabin in the Cotton, Platinum Blonde, Gold Diggers of 1933, No Man of Her Own, Professional Sweetheart, Love Me Tonight, I'm No Angel, Baby Face, They Won't Forget, College Swing, Her Jungle Love, Gilda, A Place in the Sun, Some Like it Hot.

Love Happy *
👫 US 1949 85m bw
Lester Cowan/Mary Pickford
📼 ▬ ◎

A group of impoverished actors accidentally gets possession of the Romanov diamonds.
The last dismaying Marx Brothers film, with Harpo taking the limelight and Groucho loping in for a couple of brief, tired appearances. A roof chase works, but Harpo tries too hard for sentiment, and the production looks shoddy.
w Ben Hecht, Frank Tashlin, Mac Benoff d David Miller ph William Mellor m Ann Ronell
☆ Groucho Marx, Harpo Marx, Chico Marx, Eric Blore, Ilona Massey, Marilyn Monroe, Vera-Ellen

Love Has Many Faces
US 1964 104m Eastmancolor
Columbia/Jerry Bresler
▬

A rich woman marries a beach boy and has an affair with another, who is murdered.
Hilarious but unentertaining sex melodrama built around an overage star.
w Marguerite Roberts d Alexander Singer ph Joseph Ruttenberg m David Raksin
☆ Lana Turner, Cliff Robertson, Hugh O'Brian, Stefanie Powers, Ruth Roman, Virginia Grey
'For connoisseurs of perfectly awful movies.' – Judith Crist

Love Hate: see L'Albatross

'Till Death Us Do Part.'
Love, Honour and Obey
GB 1999 98m DeLuxe
UIP/BBC/Fugitive (Dominic Anciano, Ray Burdis)
⍥

Trouble erupts when a North London gangster admits a new member to his gang.
Dreary would-be thriller, in which actors who ought to know better play at being criminals.
wd Dominic Anciano, Ray Burdis ph John Ward pd Nick Burnell ed Rachel Meyrick
☆ Sadie Frost, Jonny Lee Miller, Jude Law, Ray Winstone, Kathy Burke, Sean Pertwee, Denise Van Outen, Rhys Ifans, Dominic Anciano, Ray Burdis
'Another strong contender for the worst Britflick of the year.' – Sight and Sound
'What's more unforgivable than the raggedness and puerility is the pervasive smugness.' – Angie Errigo, Empire
† The same writer-directors, together with many of the same cast, made the equally dire The Final Cut (v).

'A big comedy about life's little heartaches'
Love Hurts
US 1990 115m CFI color
Vestron/Love Hurts Production (Bud Yorkin, Doro Bachrach)
📼 ▬ ⍥

Returning home for his sister's wedding, a philanderer puts his past behind him.
A botched attempt, with unsympathetic characters, to return to comic style of Capra.
w Ron Nyswaner d Bud Yorkin ph Adam Greenberg m Frank DeCaro pd Armin Ganz ed John C. Horger
☆ Jeff Daniels, Judith Ivey, John Mahoney, Cynthia Sikes, Amy Wright, Cloris Leachman, Mary Griffin, Thomas Allen

Love in a Goldfish Bowl
US 1961 88m Technicolor Panavision
Paramount/Jurow-Shepherd
On holiday in Honolulu, two teenagers get into mischief.
Tiresome youth-oriented family comedy with pleasant backgrounds.
wd Jack Sher ph Loyal Griggs m Jimmy Haskell
☆ Tommy Sands, Fabian, Jan Sterling, Toby Michaels, Edward Andrews, John McGiver

Love in Black and White *
France 1920 23m bw
Saturnfilm
📼

The cast of a travelling show fall in love with a sleeping beauty.
One of the director's lesser efforts, with a less coherent story than usual and less inspired stop-motion animation; the characters include a Charlie Chaplin doll.
wd Ladislaw Starewicz story René Buzelin m Roger White
† The film has been released on video with the feature-length The Tale of the Fox (qv) and four other shorts under the title Ladislaw Starewicz: Selected Films.

Love in Bloom
US 1934 76m bw
Paramount
A carnival owner's daughter marries a songwriter.
Lame little romance broken up by crosstalk from Burns and Allen; an ill-considered entertainment.
w J. P. McEvoy, Keene Thompson d Elliott Nugent
☆ George Burns, Gracie Allen, Dixie Lee, Joe Morrison
'Radio pair may save their latest celluloid effort, but it won't help their future on the screen.' – Variety
⅄ song 'She Loves Me Not' (mRalph Rainger, lyLeo Robin)

Love in Exile
GB 1936 78m bw
Capitol
A Ruritanian king is induced to abdicate but fights back.
Airy comedy with little general appeal.
w Herman Mankiewicz, Roger Burford, Ernest Betts novel His Majesty's Pajamas by Gene Markey d Alfred L. Werker
☆ Clive Brook, Helen Vinson, Mary Carlisle, Will Fyffe, Ronald Squire, Tamara Desni, Henry Oscar

A Love in Germany *
West Germany/France 1983 107m colour
Artificial Eye/CCC Filmkunst/Gaumont/TFL/Stand'Art (Arthur Brauner)
▬

original title: Eine Liebe in Deutschland
A German woman and a Jewish prisoner-of-war fall in love during the Second World War.
Powerful drama, though it lacks a tragic dimension.
w Boleslaw Michalek, Agnieszka Holland novel Rolf Hochhuth d Andrzej Wajda ph Igor Luther m Michel Legrand ad Allan Starski, Gotz Heymann, Jurgen Henze ed Halina Prugar-Ketling
☆ Hanna Schygulla, Marie-Christine Barrault, Armin Mueller-Stahl, Elisabeth Trissenaar, Daniel Olbrychski, Piotr Lysak

Love in Las Vegas: see Viva Las Vegas

Love in the Afternoon: see L'Amour, L'Après-midi

👫 film suitable for family viewing   📼 VHS video-cassette for the British PAL system   ▬ VHS video-cassette for the British PAL system in wide screen-format   ⟳ Video cassette in a computer-colourised version   ▬ American NTSC video-cassette   ◎ Laser disc

Love in the Afternoon
US   1957   126m   bw
AA (Billy Wilder)
🖳

The daughter of a private detective warns an American philanderer in Paris that an enraged husband is en route to shoot him.
Tired and dreary romantic sex comedy, miscast and far too long. With the talent around, there are of course a few compensations.
w Billy Wilder, I. A. L. Diamond *novel* Ariane by Claude Anet d Billy Wilder ph William Mellor m Franz Waxman ad Alexander Trauner
☆ Gary Cooper, Audrey Hepburn, Maurice Chevalier, John McGiver

Love in the Strangest Way **
France   1994   107m   colour
Gala/Fildebroc/TF1/Capac/Ice (Michelle de Broca)
🖳

original title: Elles n'oublient pas
A woman takes her revenge on the married businessman who picked her up for a one-night stand.
Icy, gripping drama that follows a familiar pattern – the plot resembles that of Fatal Attraction *– but spins some original and unexpected variations.*
wd Christopher Frank m Bertrand Chatry m Jean-Marie Senia ad Dominique Andre ed Catherine Dubeau
☆ Thierry L'hermitte, Maruschka Detmers, Nadia Fares
'Those who like French films, even when not sufficiently French, may well enjoy the thought of a swine slowly but surely twisting on the spit of fate.' – *Derek Malcolm, Guardian*
† Christopher Frank died before the film was edited.

Love Is a Ball
US   1962   112m   Technicolor   Panavision
UA/Oxford/Gold Medal (Martin H. Poll)
GB title: *All This and Money Too*
A Riviera matchmaker recruits instructors to train his star pupil, but one of them walks away with the lady.
Forgettable comedy in which more effort goes into the glamorous background than the script.
w David Swift, Tom and Frank Waldman *novel* The Grand Duke and Mr Pimm by Lindsay Hardy d David Swift ph Edmond Séchan m Michel Legrand
☆ Glenn Ford, Charles Boyer, Hope Lange, Ricardo Montalban, Telly Savalas, Ruth McDevitt, Ulla Jacobsson

Love Is a Headache
US   1938   73m   bw
MGM
An actress on hard times gets a break through freak publicity.
Wholly artificial comedy, hammed up to little avail.
w Marion Parsonnet, Harry Ruskin, William Lipman, Lou Heifetz, Herbert Klein d Richard Thorpe
☆ Franchot Tone, Gladys George, Mickey Rooney, Ralph Morgan, Jessie Ralph, Ted Healy, Barnett Parker, Frank Jenks, Virginia Weidler, Fay Holden
'Dialogue is pungent, but fails to cover up slap-happy situations.' – *Variety*

'A love that defied five thousand years of tradition!'
Love Is a Many Splendored Thing *
US   1955   102m   DeLuxe   Cinemascope
TCF (Buddy Adler)
🖳 🖳 🖳 🎧

During the Korean War, a Eurasian lady doctor in Hong Kong falls in love with a war correspondent.
Self-admittedly sentimental soaper with a tragic ending; the theme tune kept it popular for years.
w John Patrick *novel* Han Suyin d Henry King ph Leon Shamroy m Alfred Newman ad Lyle Wheeler, George W. Davis
☆ Jennifer Jones, William Holden, Torin Thatcher, Isobel Elsom, Murray Matheson, Virginia Gregg, Richard Loo
🎵 Alfred Newman; title song (mSammy Fain, lyPaul Francis Webster)
🏆 best picture; Leon Shamroy; Jennifer Jones; art direction

Love Is a Racket
US   1932   72m   bw
Warner
GB title: *Such Things Happen*
A newspaperman covers up for a girl suspected of murder, but she lets him down.
Jaundiced comedy-drama of Broadway night life; quite effective.
w Courteney Terrett d William Wellman
☆ Douglas Fairbanks Jnr, Frances Dee, Ann Dvorak, Lee Tracy, Lyle Talbot, Warren Hymer

Love Is Better Than Ever
US   1951   81m   bw
MGM (William H. Wright)
🖳
GB title: *The Light Fantastic*
A small-town girl falls for a New York theatrical agent.
Only moderate production values are brought to bear on this wispy plot which shows no signs of development.
w Ruth Brooks Flippen d Stanley Donen ph Harold Rosson md Lennie Hayton
☆ Larry Parks, Elizabeth Taylor, Josephine Hutchinson, Tom Tully, Ann Doran

Love Is My Profession: see En Cas de Malheur

Love Is News *
US   1937   78m   bw
TCF (Earl Carroll, Harold Wilson)
An heiress marries a scoop-hunting reporter just to show him how embarrassing publicity can be.
Silly romantic comedy with plenty of laughs.
w Harry Tugend, Jack Yellen d Tay Garnett ph Ernest Palmer
☆ Tyrone Power, Loretta Young, Don Ameche, Slim Summerville, Dudley Digges, Walter Catlett, Jane Darwell, Stepin Fetchit, George Sanders, Frank Conroy, Elisha Cook Jnr
'Fast-moving comedy and good star names. Surefire.' – *Variety*
† Remade as *Sweet Rosie O'Grady* and *That Wonderful Urge*.

'Study for a portrait of Francis Bacon.'
Love Is the Devil **
GB   1998   91m   colour
Artificial Eye/BBC/BFI/Première Heure/Uplink/Arts Council/Partners in Crime (Chiara Menage)
🖳
A homosexual artist begins a doomed love affair with a petty crook he discovers trying to burgle his home.
A wittily artificial biopic of Francis Bacon, which, in the absence of any of Bacon's paintings, contrives to imitate their style; it is blessed with a brilliant performance from Jacobi as the self-absorbed artist.
wd John Maybury ph John Mathieson m Ryuichi Sakamoto pd Alan Macdonald ed Daniel Goddard
☆ Derek Jacobi, Daniel Craig, Tilda Swinton, Anne Lambton, Adrian Scarborough, Karl Johnson, Annabel Brooks, Richard Newbold
'Unconventional, audacious and uncompromising in every sense.' – *David Rooney, Variety*

Love Jones *
US   1997   108m   DeLuxe
Entertainment/New Line (Nick Wechsler, Jeremiah Samuels)
🖳 🎧
A poet who performs in a night-club becomes involved in an on-and-off affair with a photographer who has given up on love.
A small-scale romantic drama among the arty that has charm and wit, though a little too much gloss and contrivance for its own good.
wd Theodore Witcher ph Ernest Holzman m Darryl Jones pd Roger Fortune ed Maysie Hoy
☆ Larenz Tate, Nia Long, Isaiah Washington, Lisa Nicole Carson, Khalili Kain, Leonard Roberts, Bernadette L. Clarke
'A sexy and appealing love story set in the flavorsome world of black bohemians in contemporary Chicago.' – *Variety*

Love Lessons **
Sweden/Denmark   1995   128m   colour
Gala/Per Holst Film
🖳
original title: Lust och Fägring Stor
aka: *All Things Fair*
In Sweden in the early 40s, a sexually curious 15-year-old boy begins an affair with his teacher, who is married to an alcoholic salesman.
Sprightly domestic drama of inexperience and maturity, hope and despair, affectionately acted and directed.
wd Bo Widerberg ph Morten Bruus m Mahler, Beethoven et al pd Palle Arestrup ed Bo Widerberg
☆ Johan Widerberg, Marika Lagercrantz, Tomas von Brömssen, Karin Huldt, Björn Kjellman
'A highly likeable film … has a constant sense of sexuality and sensuality.' – *Gunnar Rehlin, Variety*

The Love Letter
US   1999   87m   Technicolor
DreamWorks (Sarah Pillsbury, Midge Sanford, Kate Capshaw)
🖳 🖳 ⊚
In a small, seaside town several people imagine that an unsigned love letter is addressed to them.
Amiable, and forgettable, small-scale romantic comedy that springs no surprises.
w Maria Maggenti *novel* Cathleen Schine d Peter Ho-Sun Chan ph Tami Reiker m Luis Bacalov pd Andrew Jackness ed Jacqueline Cambas
☆ Kate Capshaw, Blythe Danner, Ellen DeGeneres, Geraldine McEwan, Julianne Nicholson, Tom Everett Scott, Tom Selleck, Gloria Stuart, Bill Buell, Alice Drummond
'It's a flimsy excuse for a movie and therefore no surprise that the end result is as charmless and cloying as it is.' – *James Cameron-Wilson, Film Review*

'Blood on her hands … love in her heart!'
Love Letters *
US   1945   101m   bw
Paramount (Hal B. Wallis)
A girl who has lost her memory through war shock is threatened by more physical danger.
Oddly unexciting romantic melodrama directed and designed in heavy but satisfying style. Typical post-war depressive fare.
w Ayn Rand *novel* Pity My Simplicity by Chris Massie d William Dieterle ph Lee Garmes m Victor Young ad Hans Dreier, Roland Anderson
☆ Jennifer Jones, Joseph Cotten, Ann Richards, Gladys Cooper, Anita Louise, Cecil Kellaway, Robert Sully, Byron Barr, Reginald Denny, Lumsden Hare
🎵 Jennifer Jones; title song (mVictor Young, lyEdward Heyman); Victor Young; art direction

Love Letters *
US   1983   89m   DeLuxe
Roger Corman/Millennium
🖳 🖳 ⊚
Affected by her mother's old letters revealing an unconsummated love, a twenty-two-year-old girl begins an affair with an older man.
Low-budget drama which might have worked better as a television play; but it has its memorable aspects.
wd Amy Jones ph Alec Hirschfeld m Ralph Jones
☆ Jamie Lee Curtis, James Keach, Matt Clark, Bonnie Bartlett, Bud Cort, Amy Madigan

Love Letters of a Star
US   1936   66m   bw
Universal
A blackmailed rich girl takes poison.
Complicated but efficient murder mystery.
w Lewis R. Foster, Milton Carruth, James Mulhauser *novel* The Case of the Constant God by Rufus King d Lewis R. Foster, Milton Carruth
☆ Henry Hunter, Polly Rowles, C. Henry Gordon, Walter Coy, Hobart Cavanaugh, Mary Alice Rice
'Good family entertainment … ought to do all right.' – *Variety*

Love, Life and Laughter *
GB   1934   83m   bw
ATP (Basil Dean)
A film actress catches the eye of a Ruritanian prince.
Lively star vehicle ranging from sentiment to slapstick.
w Robert Edmunds d Maurice Elvey

☆ Gracie Fields, John Loder, Norah Howard, Allan Aynesworth, Esme Percy, Robb Wilton, Fred Duprez, Horace Kenney, Veronica Brady

The Love Lottery
GB   1953   83m   Technicolor
Ealing (Monja Danischewsky)
A British film star is persuaded to offer himself as first prize in a lottery.
Satirical farce which doesn't come off, mainly owing to paucity of comedy ideas.
w Harry Kurnitz d Charles Crichton ph Douglas Slocombe m Benjamin Frankel pd Tom Morahan
☆ David Niven, Herbert Lom, Peggy Cummins, Anne Vernon, Charles Victor, Gordon Jackson, Felix Aylmer, Hugh McDermott

The Love Machine
US   1971   110m   Eastmancolor
Columbia/Mike Frankovich
Megalomaniac TV reporter progresses to network programme controller but is finally undone by his vivid sex life.
Stodgy, silly melodrama from a bestseller whose inspiration was well known in TV circles.
w Samuel Taylor *novel* Jacqueline Susann d Jack Haley Jnr ph Charles Lang Jnr m Artie Butler
☆ John Phillip Law, Dyan Cannon, Robert Ryan, Jackie Cooper, David Hemmings, Shecky Greene

The Love Match *
GB   1955   85m   bw
British Lion/Beaconsfield (Maclean Rogers)
A North Country train driver's enthusiasm for his local football team lands him in trouble at home and work.
A regional farce, full of stock characters and situations, but given some individuality by the likeable performances of its cast.
w Geoffrey Orme *play* Glenn Melvyn d David Paltenghi ph Arthur Grant m Wilfred Burns ad Bernard Robinson ed J. M. Sterling
☆ Arthur Askey, Thora Hird, Glenn Melvyn, Robb Wilton, Shirley Eaton, Edward Chapman, William Franklyn, Patricia Hayes, Maurice Kaufmann

Love Me Darling
Denmark   1971   88m   Eastmancolor
Cinecenta/Gabriel Axel
original title: Med Kaerlig Hilsen
Two lovers journey through time, enjoying themselves from the Garden of Eden onwards.
A series of farcical sketches on the subject of sex, without any evidence of humour or eroticism.
wd Gabriel Axel m Rolf Rinne m B. Fabricius Bjerre ad Erik Bjoric ed Anders Refn
☆ Buster Larsen, Birte Tove, Christian Sarvig, Lone Helmer
'Completely lacking in style or originality, the film also fails to titillate, since its actors project about as much sex-appeal as damp cardboard.' – *Carol Howard, MFB*

Love Me Forever
US   1935   92m   bw
Columbia
GB title: *On Wings of Song*
A down and out singer makes good.
Fair star vehicle.
w Jo Swerling, Sidney Buchman d Victor Schertzinger md Joe Walker md Louis Silvers
☆ Grace Moore, Leo Carrillo, Robert Allen, Spring Byington, Michael Bartlett, Thurston Hall, Douglas Dumbrille, Luis Alberni
'Gangsters and grand opera are tough to mix, but … should be all right in major towns.' – *Variety*

Love Me or Leave Me **
US   1955   122m   Eastmancolor
Cinemascope
MGM (Joe Pasternak)
🖳 ⊚
Twenties singer Ruth Etting is befriended by a racketeer who pushes her to the top but drives her to drink and despair in the process.
Agreeably bitter showbiz biopic which gives the impression of being not too far from the truth.
w Daniel Fuchs, Isobel Lennart d Charles Vidor ph Arthur E. Arling md Percy Faith, George Stoll ad Cedric Gibbons, Urie McCleary

☆ *Doris Day, James Cagney, Cameron Mitchell, Robert Keith, Tom Tully, Harry Bellaver, Richard Gaines*

🎭 original story (Daniel Fuchs)

🎵 script; Percy Faith, George Stoll; James Cagney; song 'I'll Never Stop Loving You' (*m*Nicholas Brodzsky, *ly*Sammy Cahn)

Love Me Tender
US   1956   95m   bw   Cinemascope
TCF (David Weisbart)
📼

Three brothers fall out over loot they have brought home from the Civil War.

Odd Western designed (perhaps after shooting began) as Presley's introductory vehicle; he sings four songs before getting shot, and reappears in ghostly form at the end.

w Robert Buckner *d* Robert D. Webb *ph* Leo Tover *m* Lionel Newman

☆ Richard Egan, Debra Paget, Elvis Presley, Robert Middleton, William Campbell, Neville Brand, Mildred Dunnock, Bruce Bennett, James Drury, Ken Clark, Barry Coe

'I understand that this performance is tame compared with the one Mr Presley can put up when not handicapped by a motion picture. My concern is with a moving picture made nonsense of by him.' – *C. A. Lejeune*

Love Me Tonight ****
US   1932   104m   bw
Paramount (Rouben Mamoulian)

A Parisian tailor accidentally moves into the aristocracy.

The most fluently cinematic comedy musical ever made, with sounds and words, lyrics and music, deftly blended into a compulsively and consistently laughable mosaic of sophisticated nonsense; one better than the best of Lubitsch and Clair.

w Samuel Hoffenstein, Waldemar Young, George Marion Jnr *play* Tailor in the Château by Leopold Marchand and Paul Armont *d* Rouben Mamoulian *ph* Victor Milner *songs* Rodgers and Hart

☆ *Maurice Chevalier, Jeanette MacDonald, Charles Butterworth, Charles Ruggles, Myrna Loy, C. Aubrey Smith, Elizabeth Patterson, Ethel Griffies, Blanche Frederici, Robert Greig*

'A musical frolic, whimsical in its aim and delicately carried out in its pattern.' – *Variety*
'Gay, charming, witty, it is everything that the Lubitsch musicals should have been but never were.' – *John Baxter, 1968*
'With the aid of a pleasant story, a good musician, a talented cast and about a million dollars, he has done what someone in Hollywood should have done long ago – he has illustrated a musical score.' – *Pare Lorentz*
'It has that infectious spontaneity which distinguishes the American musical at its best.' – *Peter Cowie, 1970*
'A rich amalgam of filmic invention, witty decoration and wonderful songs.' – *NFT, 1974*
'What a picture! First you have Chevalier, and last you have Chevalier!' – *Photoplay*

Love, Mother **
Hungary   1987   102m   colour
Mafilm/Objektiv
original title: *Csok, Anyu*

A small boy plays truant from school and, using a home-made periscope and binoculars, spies on the life of his preoccupied parents and their neighbours, discovering more than it is good for him to know.

A charming and quirky comedy of the little mishaps, misbehaviours and pressures of everyday life which gradually moves into darker territory, analysing a family that is falling apart.

w Istvan Kardos *d* Janos Rozsa *ph* Elemer Ragalyi *m* Janos Brody

☆ Dorottya Udvaros, Robert Koltai, Sandor Gaspar, Kati Lajtai, Simon G. Gevai, Peter Andorai

Love Nest
US   1951   84m   bw
TCF

A writer and his wife invest in an apartment building but find their tenants time-consuming.

Fairly lively comedy with varied talent.

w I. A. L. Diamond *novel* Scott Corbett *d* Joseph Newman *ph* Lloyd Ahern *m* Cyril Mockridge

☆ William Lundigan, June Haver, Frank Fay, Marilyn Monroe, Jack Paar, Leatrice Joy

The Love Nest
US   1923   22m   bw   silent
Buster Keaton Productions

Buster dreams of a solitary voyage in a small boat. Long lost but ultimately disappointing Keaton short.

wd Buster Keaton, Eddie Cline

☆ Buster Keaton, Joe Roberts, Virginia Fox

Love Never Dies: see Lilac Time

The Love of Jeanne Ney *
Germany   1927   98m   bw   silent
UFA

In the Crimea during the Russian Revolution, a political observer is accidentally killed by his daughter's lover.

Inconsistently-styled contemporary melodrama. The abiding interest is in the detailed treatment rather than the story or acting.

w Ladislas Vajda, Rudolf Leonhardt, Ilya Ehrenberg *d* G. W. Pabst *ph* Fritz Arno Wagner, Walter Robert Lach

☆ Edith Jehane, Uno Henning, Fritz Rasp, Brigitte Helm

The Love of Sunya
US   1927   80m   bw   silent
Swanson Producing Corporation

A yogi recognizes two young lovers as people he wronged in a previous existence, and warns them of impending disaster.

Star tosh of its period, unthinkable now as a screen attraction.

w Earle Brown *play* The Eyes of Youth by Max Marcin, Charles Guernon *d* Albert Parker *ph* Robert Martin *ad* Hugo Ballin

☆ Gloria Swanson, John Boles, Anders Randolf, Hugh Miller, Flobelle Fairbanks, Raymond Hackett

† Previously filmed as *Eyes of Youth* with Clara Kimball Young.

Love on the Dole ***
GB   1941   100m   bw
British National (John Baxter)
📼

Life among unemployed cotton workers in industrial Lancashire between the wars.

Vividly characterized, old-fashioned social melodrama, well made on a low budget; a rare problem picture for Britain at this time.

w Walter Greenwood, Barbara K. Emery, Rollo Gamble *novel* Walter Greenwood *d* John Baxter *ph* James Wilson *m* Richard Addinsell

☆ *Deborah Kerr, Clifford Evans, George Carney, Joyce Howard, Frank Cellier, Geoffrey Hibbert, Mary Merrall, Maire O'Neill, Marjorie Rhodes, A. Bromley Davenport, Marie Ault, Iris Vandeleur, Kenneth Griffith*

'Kissing and kidding their way from Mayfair to the Mediterranean in a transcontinental caravan of jollity!'

Love on the Run *
US   1936   81m   bw
MGM (Joseph L. Mankiewicz)
📼   💿

Rival newspapermen help an heiress to escape an unwanted wedding and in the process uncover a ring of spies.

Harebrained star farce, smoothly assembled and still fairly funny.

w John Lee Mahin, Manuel Seff, Gladys Hurlbut *d* W. S. Van Dyke *ph* Oliver T. Marsh *m* Franz Waxman

☆ Clark Gable, Joan Crawford, Franchot Tone, Reginald Owen, Mona Barrie, Ivan Lebedeff, William Demarest

'Should collect its share at the gate through the sheer momentum of the Gable-Crawford combo.' – *Variety*
'A slightly daffy cinematic item of absolutely no importance.' – *New York Times*

Love on the Run *
France   1979   95m   Eastmancolor
Les Films du Carrosse (François Truffaut)
📼   💿

Antoine Doinel, separated from his family, is still having girl trouble.

Amorous adventure of the character first glimpsed in Les Quatre Cent Coups *and presumably based on the director; fair sophisticated fun for those who appreciate the joke.*

w François Truffaut, Marie-France Pisier, Jean Aurel, Suzanne Schiffman *d* François Truffaut *ph* Nestor Almendros *m* Georges Delerue *pd* Jean-Pierre Kohut Svelko *ed* Martine Barraqué

☆ Jean-Pierre Léaud, Marie-France Pisier, Claude Jade, Rosy Varte

Love on Wheels
GB   1932   87m   bw
Gainsborough

A department store assistant becomes publicity-conscious.

Zippy little comedy of its day.

w Victor Saville, Angus MacPhail, Robert Stevenson and Douglas Furber *d* Victor Saville

☆ Jack Hulbert, Edmund Gwenn, Leonora Corbett, Gordon Harker, Percy Parsons, Roland Culver, Miles Malleson

The Love Parade **
US   1929   112m   bw
Paramount (Ernst Lubitsch)

The prince of Sylvania marries.

Primitive sound operetta set among the idle European rich, with clear but faded instances of the Lubitsch touch.

w Ernest Vajda, Guy Bolton *play* The Prince Consort by Leon Xanrof and Jules Chancel *d* Ernst Lubitsch *ph* Victor Milner *ad* Hans Dreier *songs* Victor Schertzinger, Clifford Grey

☆ Maurice Chevalier, Jeanette MacDonald, Lupino Lane, Lillian Roth, Edgar Norton, Lionel Belmore, Eugene Pallette

'The first truly cinematic screen musical in America.' – *Theodore Huff*

🎵 best picture; Ernst Lubitsch; Victor Milner; Maurice Chevalier; Hans Dreier

'Imagine if sex appeal came in a bottle.'
'If you've got it – you get it!'

Love Potion No. 9
US   1992   97m   CFI color
TCF (Dale Launer)
📼   💿   💿

Unattractive scientists discover a chemical that makes the user irresistible to the opposite sex.

Occasionally amusing teen comedy, but one that fails to develop its central idea to any effect.

wd Dale Launer *ph* William Wages *m* Jed Leiber *pd* Linda Pearl *ed* Suzanne Petit

☆ Tate Donovan, Sandra Bullock, Mary Mara, Dale Midkiff, Hillary Bailey Smith, Dylan Baker, Anne Bancroft

'A light-hearted one-joke romantic comedy that tries too hard to be cute.' – *Variety*

Love, Soldiers and Women
France/Italy   1953   96m   bw
Franco-London/Continental
original title: *Destinées*
US title: *Daughters of Destiny*

Three stories of women in war: Joan of Arc, Lysistrata, and a modern American war widow visiting her husband's grave.

Uninteresting patchwork with Lysistrata predictably stealing the show.

Jeanne
w Jean Aurenche, Pierre Bost *d* Jean Delannoy with Michèle Morgan
Elizabeth
w Sergio Amedei *d* Marcel Pagliero with Claudette Colbert, Eleanora Rossi Drago
Lysistrata
w Jean Ferry, Henri Jeanson, Carlo Rim *play* Aristophanes *d* Christian-Jaque with Martine Carol, Raf Vallone, Paolo Stoppa

Love Story: see Une Histoire d'Amour (1951)

Love Story
GB   1944   112m   bw
GFD/Gainsborough (Harold Huth)
US title: *A Lady Surrenders*

In Cornwall during World War II, a half-blind airman falls for a pianist with a weak heart.

Novelettish love story which became popular because of its Cornish Rhapsody.

w Leslie Arliss, Doreen Montgomery, Rodney Ackland *novel* J. W. Drawbell *d* Leslie Arliss *ph* Bernard Knowles *m* Hubert Bath

☆ Margaret Lockwood, Stewart Granger, Patricia Roc, Tom Walls, Reginald Purdell, Moira Lister

'A splendid, noble and fatuous piece.' – *C. A. Lejeune*
'In psychology and dialogue this is straight out of Mabel's Weekly.' – *Richard Winnington*

Love Story *
US   1970   100m   Movielab
Paramount (David Golden)
📼   📼   💿   🎧

Two students marry; she dies.

A barrage of ripe old Hollywood clichés spiced with new-fangled bad language. In the circumstances, well enough made, and certainly astonishingly popular.

w Erich Segal *novelette* Erich Segal *d* Arthur Hiller *ph* Dick Kratina *m* Bach, Mozart, Handel *md* Francis Lai

☆ Ali MacGraw, Ryan O'Neal, Ray Milland, John Marley

'Camille with bullshit.' – *Alexander Walker*

🎭 Francis Lai

🎵 best picture; Erich Segal; Arthur Hiller; Ali MacGraw; Ryan O'Neal; John Marley

Love Streams
US   1984   141m   Metrocolor
Cannon (Menahem Golan, Yoram Globus)
📼

A distraught woman whose marriage has gone sour moves in with her philandering brother.

Elongated study of two life styles, not so shapeless as most Cassavetes films, but not exactly dramatic or endearing either.

w Ted Allan, John Cassavetes *play* Ted Allan *d* John Cassavetes *ph* Al Ruban *m* Bo Harwood *ad* Phedon Papamichael *ed* George C. Villasenor

☆ Gena Rowlands, John Cassavetes, Diahnne Abbott, Seymour Cassel, Margaret Abbott

The Love Test
GB   1935   63m   bw
Fox British (Leslie L. Landau)

Research scientists plot to prevent a woman from taking over as head of the laboratory by selecting one of their number to seduce her.

Competent, if unoriginal, comedy with an occasional directorial touch that lifts it out of the very ordinary.

w Selwyn Jepson *story* Jack Celestin *d* Michael Powell *ph* Arthur Crabtree

☆ Judy Gunn, Louis Hayward, David Hutcheson, Googie Withers, Morris Harvey, Aubrey Dexter, Gilbert Davis, Bernard Miles

'A light, bright romantic comedy.' – *Variety*

Love That Brute
US   1950   85m   bw
TCF (Fred Kohlmar)

A ruthless Chicago gangleader is actually a softy, leaving his supposedly rubbed-out enemies in a comfortable cellar; a young governess persuades him to reform.

Rickety, dully-scripted gangster farce.

w Darrell Ware, John Lee Mahin, Karl Tunberg *d* Alexander Hall *ph* Lloyd Ahern *m* Cyril Mockridge

☆ Paul Douglas, Jean Peters, Cesar Romero, Joan Davis, Arthur Treacher

Love Thy Neighbour *
US   1940   81m   bw
Paramount

Two radio comics fall out.

Curious mixture of fact and fiction, basing its plot on the publicity feud between Benny and Allen, who appear 'in character' as themselves.

w William Morrow, Edmund Beloin, Ernest Pagano, Z. Myers *pd* Mark Sandrich

☆ Jack Benny, Fred Allen, Mary Martin, Eddie Anderson, Verree Teasdale, Virginia Dale, Richard Denning

Love Thy Neighbour
GB   1973   85m   Technicolor
EMI/Hammer (Roy Skeggs)
📼

A prejudiced white worker has coloured neighbours.

Elongated screen version of the popular TV series in which the West Indians smile through all the insults and come out top in the end. It might have been worse, but not much.

w Vince Powell, Harry Driver *d* John Robins *ph* Moray Grant *m* Albert Elms

---

👫 film suitable for family viewing   📼 VHS video-cassette for the British PAL system   📼 VHS video-cassette for the British PAL system in wide screen-format   ⬘ Video cassette in a computer-colourised version   ▬ American NTSC video-cassette   💿 Laser disc

☆ Jack Smethurst, Kate Williams, Rudolph Walker, Nina Baden-Semper, Bill Fraser, Charles Hyatt, Keith Marsh, Patricia Hayes, Arthur English

Love Time

US 1934 72m bw
Fox
Franz Schubert falls for a duke's daughter.
Curious, off-putting costumer with music.
w William Conselman, Henry Johnson d James Tinling
☆ Pat Paterson, Nils Asther, Herbert Mundin, Harry Green, Henry B. Walthall, Lucien Littlefield
'Thin story, and slim chances.' – *Variety*

Love under Fire

US 1937 75m bw
TCF (Nunnally Johnson)
A detective catches up with a lady jewel thief in Madrid during the Spanish Civil War.
Adequately entertaining but rather tasteless adventure comedy.
w Gene Fowler, Allen Rivkin, Ernest Pascal *play* Walter Hackett d George Marshall ph Ernest Palmer m Arthur Lange
☆ Loretta Young, Don Ameche, Frances Drake, Walter Catlett, John Carradine, Borrah Minevitch and his Rascals, Sig Rumann, Harold Huber, E. E. Clive, Katherine de Mille
'Melodrama with music cooked up for the duals.' – *Variety*

Love! Valour! Compassion! *

US 1997 110m DeLuxe
Entertainment/New Line/Fine Line (Doug Chapin, Barry Krost)
Eight homosexual friends and lovers get together for three weekend house parties.
Witty, occasionally poignant, account of shifting relationships in the shadow of AIDS.
w Terrence McNally *play* Terrence McNally d Joe Mantello ph Alik Sakharov m Harold Wheeler pd François Séguin ed Colleen Sharp
☆ Jason Alexander, Randy Becker, Stephen Bogardus, John Glover, John Benjamin Hickey, Justin Kirk, Stephen Spinella
'A perceptive, often hilarious look at life in the AIDS era.' – *Variety*

'There is a moment ... a long moment ... when everything is risked with the proper stranger!'
Love with the Proper Stranger **

US 1964 100m bw
Paramount/Boardwalk (Alan J. Pakula)
📀 ᷓ
A musician tries to help his pregnant shopgirl friend get an abortion, but they decide to get married instead.
Oddly likeable comedy drama set on New York's Italian East Side, with an excellent location sense.
w Arnold Schulman d Robert Mulligan ph Milton Krasner m Elmer Bernstein
☆ Steve McQueen, Natalie Wood, Tom Bosley, Edie Adams, Herschel Bernardi
⅃ Arnold Schulman; Milton Krasner; Natalie Wood

'In her heart she embraced it. In her soul she feared it.'
Loved

US 1996 103m DeLuxe
Downtown/Crosslight/MDP/Clyde Is Hungry/Palisades (Philippe Caland, Sean Penn)
📀 📀
A woman testifies against her former boyfriend, a serial abuser of women.
Enigmatic exploration of obsessive female–male relationships, which never quite clarifies the issues, despite a strong central performance.
wd Erin Dignam ph Reynaldo Villalobos m David Baerwald pd Barry Robison ed Gillian Hutchings, David Rogow, Ann Trulove
☆ William Hurt, Robin Wright Penn, Amy Madigan, Lucinda Jenny, Joanna Cassidy, Paul Dooley, Anthony Lucero, Jennifer Rubin, Sean Penn
'Deserves kudos for eschewing standard entertainment values.' – *Ken Eisner, Variety*

The Loved One *

US 1965 118m bw
MGM/Filmways (Neil Hartley)
📀 ᷓ
A young English poet in California gets a job at a very select burial ground.
A pointed satire on the American way of death has been allowed to get out of hand, with writer and actors alike laying it on too thick; but there are pleasantly waspish moments in a movie advertised as 'the motion picture with something to offend everybody'.
w Terry Southern, Christopher Isherwood *novel* Evelyn Waugh d Tony Richardson ph Haskell Wexler m John Addison pd Rouben Ter-Arutunian
☆ Robert Morse, John Gielgud, Rod Steiger, Liberace, Anjanette Comer, Jonathan Winters, Dana Andrews, Milton Berle, James Coburn, Tab Hunter, Margaret Leighton, Roddy McDowall, Robert Morley, Lionel Stander
'Even a chaotic satire like this is cleansing, and it's embarrassing to pan even a bad movie that comes out against God, mother and country.' – *Pauline Kael, 1968*
'A spineless farrago of collegiate gags.' – *Stanley Kauffmann*
'A sinking ship that makes it to port because everyone on board is too giddy to panic.' – *New Yorker, 1978*

'The Meanest ... Roughest ... Toughest ... Gang Ever To Hit The Screen! Muscles Clad In Black Leather ... Incest ... And Murder!'
'Sworn To Fun ... Loyal To None!!!'
The Loveless

US 1983 83m colour
Mainline/Pioneer Films (Grafton Nunes, A. Kitman Ho)
In the 1950s, a gang of bikers cause problems in a small Southern town.
Arty (the settings are reminiscent of the paintings of Edward Hopper), derivative and inconsequential drama.
wd Kathryn Bigelow, Monty Montgomery ph Doyle Smith m Robert Gordon pd Lilly Kivert ed Nancy Kantner
☆ Willem Dafoe, Robert Gordon, Marin Kanter, J. Don Ferguson, Tina L'Hotsky

Lovely to Look At: see *Thin Ice (1937)*

Lovely to Look At *

US 1952 102m Technicolor
MGM (Jack Cummings)
📀 📀 ᷓ
Three Broadway producers inherit a Paris fashion house.
Lavish but dullish remake of Roberta (qv), in itself no great shakes as a storyline; again the fashions and the numbers are the thing.
w George Wells, Harry Ruby d Mervyn Le Roy ph George J. Folsey m Jerome Kern ad Cedric Gibbons, Gabriel Scognamillo
☆ Howard Keel, Kathryn Grayson, Ann Miller, Red Skelton, Marge and Gower Champion, Zsa Zsa Gabor, Kurt Kasznar
⅃ 'Lovely to Look At'; 'I'll Be Hard to Handle'; 'Yesterdays'; 'The Most Exciting Night'; 'You're Devastating'; 'I Won't Dance'; 'Smoke Gets in Your Eyes'; 'The Touch of Your Hand'.

A Lovely Way to Die

US 1968 98m Techniscope
Universal (Richard Lewis)
GB title: *A Lovely Way to Go*
An ex-cop becomes bodyguard to a suspected murderess, but proves her innocent.
Offbeat mélange of caper comedy, black farce, private eye detection, courtroom drama, spectacular action and routine thick ear. Doesn't work.
w A. J. Russell d David Lowell Rich ph Morris Hartzband m Kenyon Hopkins
☆ Kirk Douglas, Sylva Koscina, Eli Wallach, Martyn Green, Kenneth Haigh, Sharon Farrell
'The net result is rather as though Philip Marlowe had met Doris Day on his not very inspiring way to the forum.' – *MFB*

A Lovely Way to Go: see *A Lovely Way to Die*

The Lover: see *L'Amant*

A Lover and His Lass *

Sweden 1975 90m Eastmancolor
SF/SFI (Bengt Forslund, Olle Hellbom, Olle Nordemar)
original title: *En Kille Och En Tjej*
aka: *Boy Meets Girl*
The amorous adventures of a hypochrondriac unemployed journalist.
Pleasant comedy about the slow maturing of a young drifter.
w Lasse Hallström, Lasse Brännström d Lasse Hallström ph Eddie Akberg, Lasse Ulander m Berndt Egerbladh ad Stig Limer ed Lasse Hallström
☆ Lasse Brännström, Mariann Rudberg, Christer 'Bonzo' Jonsson, Börje Ahlstedt, Roland Hedlund, Chatarina Larsson, Anna Godenus, Gun Jönsson

Lover Boy: see *Knave of Hearts*

Lover Come Back

US 1946 90m bw
Universal (Howard Benedict)
When a war correspondent returns, his wife discovers that he hasn't been so lonely overseas as he might have been.
Very tolerable star comedy which at the time seemed quite fresh.
w Michael Fessier, Ernest Pagano d William A. Seiter ph Joseph Valentine m Hans J. Salter
☆ George Brent, Lucille Ball, Vera Zorina, Charles Winninger, Carl Esmond, Raymond Walburn, Franklin Pangborn, Louise Beavers
'Should chalk up good grosses in most situations.' – *Variety*

Lover Come Back **

US 1961 107m Eastmancolor
U-I/Seven Pictures/Nob Hill/Arwin (Stanley Shapiro, Marty Melcher)
📹 📀
Rival executives find themselves advertising a non-existent product.
Fairly sharp advertising satire disguised as a romantic comedy; the most entertaining of the Day-Hudson charmers.
w Stanley Shapiro, Paul Henning d Delbert Mann ph Arthur E. Arling m Frank de Vol
☆ Doris Day, Rock Hudson, Tony Randall, Jack Oakie, Edie Adams
⅃ Stanley Shapiro, Paul Henning

Loverboy

US 1989 99m Technicolor
Columbia TriStar/Crescent Film Enterprises (Gary Foster, Willie Hunt)
📹 📀
A pizza delivery boy pays his way through college by becoming a lover to his female customers.
Feeble comedy with little wit or sense.
w Robin Schiff, Tom Ropelewski, Leslie Dixon d Joan Micklin Silver ph John Davis m Michel Colombier pd Dan Leigh ed Rick Shaine
☆ Patrick Dempsey, Kate Jackson, Kirstie Alley, Carrie Fisher, Robert Ginty, Nancy Valen, Charles Hunter Walsh, Barbara Carrera
'The material often suggests a crude and juvenile variation on The Graduate.' – *MFB*

'This landlady has more than just rent on her mind.'
Lovers *

Spain 1991 103m colour
Mainline/TVE/Pedro Costa
📹 📀 ᷓ
original title: *Amantes*
In the 1950s, a young Spanish man finds himself torn between his virginal fiancée and the sexy, sophisticated widow with whom he lodges.
Overheated and old-fashioned drama that becomes increasingly melodramatic as it continues.
w Carlos Perez, Alvaro Del Amo, Vicente Aranda d Vicente Aranda ph José Luis Alcaine m José Nieto ad Josep Rosell ed Teresa Font
☆ Victoria Abril, Jorge Sanz, Maribel Verdu, Enrique Cerro, Mabel Escano, José Cerro, Gabriel Latorre
'A nicely photographed, well-dressed, at times distinctly tedious love triangle thriller.' – *Empire*

The Lovers

GB 1972 89m Eastmancolor
British Lion/Gildor (Maurice Foster)
A Manchester bank clerk with a prim girlfriend finds it difficult to lose his virginity.
Well-written but rather arch comedy which seemed much funnier and fresher as a TV series.
w Jack Rosenthal d Herbert Wise ph Bob Huke m Carl Davis
☆ Richard Beckinsale, Paula Wilcox, Joan Scott, Susan Littler, John Comer, Stella Moray, Nikolas Simmonds

Lovers and Other Strangers ***

US 1970 104m Metrocolor
ABC/David Susskind
📹
After living together for eighteen months, Susan and Mike decide to get married, and find their parents have sex problems of their own.
Wise, witty and well-acted sex farce, with many actors making the most of ample chances under firm directorial control.
w Renée Taylor, Joseph Bologna, David Zelag Goodman d Cy Howard ph Andrew Laszlo m Fred Karlin
☆ Gig Young, Anne Jackson, Richard Castellano, Bonnie Bedelia, Michael Brandon, Beatrice Arthur, Robert Dishy, Harry Guardino, Diane Keaton, Cloris Leachman, Anne Meara, Marian Hailey
'An extremely engaging comedy.' – *Gillian Hartnoll*
♪ song 'For All We Know' (mFred Karlin, lyRobb Wilson, Arthur James)
⅃ script, Richard Castellano

Lovers Courageous

US 1932 78m bw
MGM
An unsuccessful playwright covets the admiral's daughter.
Heavily-titled comedy with good performances of the period.
w Frederick Lonsdale d Robert Z. Leonard
☆ Robert Montgomery, Madge Evans, Roland Young, Frederick Kerr, Reginald Owen, Halliwell Hobbes, Alan Mowbray

Lovers Like Us: see *Call Him Savage*

Lovers Must Learn: see *Rome Adventure*

The Lovers of Lisbon *

France 1954 112m bw
EGC/Hoche/Fides (Jacques Gauthier)
original title: *Les Amants du Tage*
A man who has killed his unfaithful wife is acquitted of murder, gets a job as a taxi driver in Lisbon, and falls for a rich Englishwoman who has killed her husband and is being pursued by a police inspector.
Pretentious tosh with a few compensations.
w Marcel Rivet *novel* Joseph Kessel d Henri Verneuil ph Roger Hubert m Lucien Legrand
☆ Daniel Gélin, Françoise Arnoul, Trevor Howard, Ginette Leclerc, Marcel Dalio

Lovers of Montparnasse *

France 1958 110m bw
Franco London Films (Ralph Baum)
original title: *Les Amants de Montparnasse*
US title: *Modigliani of Montparnasse*
Alcoholic and ill, Modigliani pursues his art and the young woman who inspires him to paint.
Moderate biopic, though with an unconvincing performance from Philipe.
w Jacques Becker, Max Ophuls, Henri Jeanson *novel* Les Montparnos by Michel Georges Michel d Jacques Becker ph Christian Matras m Paul Misraki pd J. A. d'Eaubonne ed Marguerite Renoir
☆ Gérard Philipe, Lilli Palmer, Léa Padovani, Lino Ventura, Anouk Aimée

'Destiny cannot be denied.'
Lovers of the Arctic Circle ***

Spain/France 1998 108m colour
Metro Tartan/Alicia/Bailando en la Luna/Sogetel (Fernando Bovaira, Enrique Lopez Lavinge)
📹
original title: *Los Amantes del Circulo Polar*
The lives of a man and a woman interlock from their first meeting in childhood, but their later attempts to meet one another are frustrated.

The Lovers: see *Les Amants (1958)*

A unusual, lyrical movie about predestination, and the way one life links unexpectedly with another; it is also a charmingly romantic tale of loves lost and won.
d Julio Medem ph Gonzalo F. Berridi m Alberto Iglesias pd Satur Udarreta, Karmele Soler, Estibaliz Markiegi, Itziar Arrieta ed Ivan Aledo
☆ Najwa Nimri, Fele Martinez, Nancho Nova, Maru Valdivieslo, Peru Medem, Sara Valiente, Victor Hugo Oliveira, Kristel Diaz, Pep Munné
'It never loses the air of a dispassionate exercise, arranged by its creator according to an oppressively rigid pattern of his own.' – Edward Porter, Sunday Times

The Lovers of Toledo

Italy/France/Spain   1952   82m   bw
EGE/Lux/Athenea (Raymond Eger)
In 1825 a cruel police chief releases a political prisoner in return for the hand in marriage of his mistress.
Curiously unpersuasive period melodrama with good credits but too many international cooks.
w Claude Vermorel story Le Coffre et le Revenant by Stendhal d Henri Decoin ph Michel Kelber m Jean-Jacques Grunenwald
☆ Pedro Armendariz, Alida Valli, Gérard Landry, Françoise Arnoul

The Lovers of Verona: see Les Amants de Vérone

Lovers on the Pont-Neuf: see Les Amants du Pont-Neuf

Love's Labours Lost *

GB/France/US   2000   94m   colour   Super 35
Pathé/Intermedia/Shakespeare/Arts Council/Canal+/Miramax (David Barron, Kenneth Branagh)
In 1939, the King of Navarre goes on a celibate retreat into the woods with three friends; then the Princess of France arrives with three female companions.
Lively attempt to revive the Hollywood musical, though why the 30s melodies were hung upon the bare bones of Shakespeare's comedy is hard to understand; the result is a lightweight romantic romp with songs that have been better sung elsewhere.
wd Kenneth Branagh play William Shakespeare ph Alex Thomson m Patrick Doyle m/ly Irving Berlin, George Gershwin, Jerome Kern, Cole Porter ch Stuart Hopps pd Tim Harvey ed Neil Farrell, Dan Farrell cos Anna Buruma
☆ Alessandro Nivola, Alicia Silverstone, Natascha McElhone, Kenneth Branagh, Carmen Ejogo, Matthew Lillard, Adrian Lester, Emily Mortimer, Richard Briers, Geraldine McEwan, Stefania Rocca, Jimmy Yuill, Timothy Spall, Anthony O'Donnell
'The result is not a classic, but it is fun: short, sharp and fast-paced.' – Derek Malcolm, Screen International
♫ I'd Rather Charleston; I Get a Kick Out of You; I Won't Dance; No Strings; Cheek to Cheek; The Way You Look Tonight; I've Got a Crush on You; Let's Face the Music and Dance; There's No Business Like Show Business; They Can't Take That Away From Me

Loves of a Blonde *

Czechoslovakia   1965   82m   bw
Barrandov Studios
original title: Lasky Jedne Plavovlasky
aka: A Blonde in Love
A factory girl falls for a visiting musician but meets suspicion from his family when she pursues him.
Mild anecdote with excellent humorous detail which endeared it to international critics.
w Milos Forman, Jaroslav Papousek, Ivan Passer d Milos Forman ph Miroslav Ondricek m Evzen Illin
☆ Hanna Brejchova, Vladimir Pucholt
'It depends on an instinctive sense of timing and a consistent vision of life and people.' – Georges Sadoul
冠 best foreign film

The Loves of a Dictator: see The Dictator

The Loves of Carmen

US   1948   99m   Technicolor
Columbia (Charles Vidor)
In 1820s Seville, a dragoon corporal is enslaved by a gypsy, kills her husband and becomes an outlaw.
Unrewarding version of the original much-filmed story, with both stars plainly wishing they were elsewhere.
w Helen Deutsch novel Prosper Mérimée d Charles Vidor ph William Snyder m Mario Castelnuovo-Tedesco
☆ Rita Hayworth, Glenn Ford, Victor Jory, Ron Randell, Luther Adler, Arnold Moss, Margaret Wycherly, Bernard Nedell
冠 William Snyder

The Loves of Count Iorga, Vampire: see Count Yorga Vampire

The Loves of Edgar Allan Poe

US   1942   67m   bw
TCF (Bryan Foy)
The famous writer marries his childhood sweetheart but becomes an alcoholic.
A curiosity which fails to bring out the bizarre truth and emerges as a stilted charade.
w Samuel Hoffenstein, Tom Reed d Harry Lachman ph Lucien Andriot m Emil Newman
☆ John Shepperd, Linda Darnell, Virginia Gilmore, Jane Darwell, Frank Conroy, Henry Morgan

The Loves of Isadora: see Isadora

The Loves of Joanna Godden

GB   1947   89m   bw
Ealing (Sidney Cole)
On Romney Marsh at the turn of the century, a woman farmer has three suitors.
Dullish 'woman's picture'.
w H. E. Bates, Angus Macphail novel Sheila Kaye-Smith d Charles Frend ph Douglas Slocombe m Ralph Vaughan Williams
☆ Googie Withers, John McCallum, Jean Kent, Derek Bond, Chips Rafferty, Henry Mollison, Sonia Holm, Edward Rigby, Josephine Stuart
'Made with sincerity, and its outdoor backgrounds abound in freshness and beauty, but I felt that it faltered because the script writers and the director permitted themselves to become so obsessed by the landscape and local colour that they regarded the plot as somewhat of a hindrance to their documentary explorations.' – Ewart Hodgson, News of the World
† Robert Hamer directed some scenes.

The Loves of Salammbo: see Salambo

Lovesick

US   1983   96m   Technicolor
Warner/Ladd (Charles Okun)
A New York psychiatrist in love with a patient is guided by the ghost of Sigmund Freud.
Depressing comedy with a non-star and supporting players who must have been embarrassed.
wd Marshall Brickman ph Gerry Fisher m Philippe Sarde pd Philip Rosenberg
☆ Dudley Moore, Elizabeth McGovern, Alec Guinness, John Huston, Larry Rivers, Gene Saks, Renee Taylor, Alan King
'Flat, lamebrained and indigestible.' – Geoff Brown, MFB

Lovin' Molly *

US   1973   98m   Movielab
Stephen Friedman (David Golden)
In Texas between 1925 and 1945, two men friends and an accommodating lady have a shifting relationship.
Odd little drama compendium, with fragments told by each in turn; too slight in structure and substance for complete success, but interesting most of the way.
w Stephen Friedman novel Leaving Cheyenne by Larry McMurtry d Sidney Lumet ph Edward Brown m Fred Hellerman
☆ Blythe Danner, Anthony Perkins, Beau Bridges, Edward Binns, Susan Sarandon

Loving **

US   1970   90m   Eastmancolor
Columbia/Brooks Ltd (Don Devlin)
A commercial artist reaches crisis point with both his wife and his mistress.

Smart New Yorkish sex comedy, typical of many but better than most.
w Don Devlin novel Brooks Wilson Ltd by J. M. Ryan d Irvin Kershner ph Gordon Willis m Bernardo Segall pd Walter Scott Herndon
☆ George Segal, Eva Marie Saint, Sterling Hayden, Keenan Wynn, Nancie Phillips, Janis Young, David Doyle

Loving Couples *

Sweden   1964   118m   bw
Sandrew (Rune Waldekranz)
original title: älskande Par
Three expectant mothers think back over their sex lives.
Superbly made, rather hollow diatribe against sex, presented as a series of intricate flashbacks. Along the way, there is much to enjoy, but the result is not really a film of importance.
w Mai Zetterling, David Hughes novel Froknarna von Pahlen by Agnes von Krusenstjerna d Mai Zetterling ph Sven Nykvist m Rodger Wallis
☆ Harriet Andersson, Gunnel Lindblom, Anita Bjork, Gunnar Bjornstrand, Eva Dahlbeck, Frank Sundstrom, Inga Landgre
'…that air of packaged neurosis so peculiar to the Swedish cinema.' – Tom Milne, MFB

Loving Couples

US   1980   98m   Metrocolor
Time Life (Renee Valente)
Man-and-wife doctors decide to liven up their lives by having affairs.
Embarrassingly with-it romantic charade.
w Martin Donovan d Jack Smight ph Philip Lathrop m Fred Karlin
☆ Shirley MacLaine, James Coburn, Susan Sarandon, Stephen Collins, Sally Kellerman

Loving in the Rain

France/Italy/West Germany   1973   90m
Eastmancolor
Lira Films/Terra Film (Raymond Danon)
original title: Un Amour de Pluie
A mother and her teenage daughter both experience a holiday love affair.
An inconsequential romance involving inconsequential people.
w Jean-Claude Brialy, Yves Simon d Jean-Claude Brialy ph Andreas Winding m Francis Lai ed Eva Zorn
☆ Romy Schneider, Nino Castelnuovo, Mehdi, Benedicte Bucher, Suzanne Flon

Loving You

US   1957   101m   Technicolor
Vistavision
Paramount/Hal B. Wallis
A press agent signs a young hillbilly singer to give zest to her husband's band.
Empty-headed, glossy star vehicle.
w Herbert Baker, Hal Kanter d Hal Kanter ph Charles Lang Jnr m Walter Scharf
☆ Elvis Presley, Lizabeth Scott, Wendell Corey, Dolores Hart, James Gleason

A Low Down Dirty Shame

US   1994   100m   Technicolor
Buena Vista/Hollywood (Joe Roth, Roger Birnbaum)
A private eye investigates the South American drug dealer who cost him his job as a Los Angeles cop.
An action comedy that fails on both counts, unless you find men with guns inherently amusing.
wd Keenen Ivory Wayans ph Matthew F. Leonetti m Marcus Miller pd Robb Wilson King ed John F. Link
☆ Keenen Ivory Wayans, Charles S. Dutton, Jada Pinkett, Salli Richardson, Andrew Divoff, Corwin Hawkins, Gary Cervantes, Gregory Sierra
'A predictable and sluggishly paced plot with obligatory car chases and shoot-outs.' – Lizzie Francke

The Lower Depths: see Les Bas-fonds (1936)

The Lower Depths **

Japan   1957   124m   bw
Toho
original title: Donzoko
An elderly pilgrim moves into a hovel and changes the lives of the derelicts who live there.
Effectively unsentimental, claustrophobic version of life at the bottom, although it betrays its theatrical origins, with more talk than action.
w Akira Kurosawa, Hideo Oguni play Maxim Gorky d Akira Kurosawa ph Ichio Yamazaki m Masaru Sato
☆ Isuzu Yamada, Toshiro Mifune, Bokuzen Hidari, Kyoko Kagawa, Akemi Nigishi, Nijiko Kiyokawa
'Lesser Kurosawa, but still high-quality cinema.' – Empire

Loyalties

GB   1934   74m   bw
Associated British
A vengeful Jew turns the tables when his wallet is stolen at a society party.
Badly made film version of a significant play.
w W. P. Lipscomb play John Galsworthy d Basil Dean ph Robert Martin ed Thorold Dickenson
☆ Basil Rathbone, Miles Mander, Heather Thatcher, Joan Wyndham, Philip Strange

The L-Shaped Room *

GB   1962   142m   bw
British Lion/Romulus (James Woolf, Richard Attenborough)
A girl intending to have an abortion takes a room in a London suburban house which is none too clean but full of characters.
Watchable, mildly sensational low-life melodrama of the pre-swinging London era when well-to-dos thought it amusing to live in garrets. Hellishly overlong but enjoyable in patches because of the professionalism with which it is made.
w Bryan Forbes novel Lynne Reid Banks d Bryan Forbes ph Douglas Slocombe m Brahms, John Barry
☆ Leslie Caron, Tom Bell, Brock Peters, Cicely Courtneidge, Bernard Lee, Avis Bunnage, Patricia Phoenix, Emlyn Williams
'It would be hard to imagine a more unlikely, or commercially more sure-fire group of lodgers living under a single roof than this pregnant French girl, maladjusted negro, lesbian actress, couple of prostitutes, and unpublished writer who finally commits it all to paper – shades of I Am a Camera as well as A Taste of Honey.' – MFB
冠 Leslie Caron
Ⓥ Leslie Caron

Lt Robin Crusoe USN

US   1966   114m   Technicolor
Walt Disney (Bill Walsh, Ron Miller)
A navy pilot parachutes on to a Pacific island and gets involved in the local women's lib movement.
Slow-paced family comedy with very few laughs.
w Bill Walsh, Don da Gradi d Byron Paul ph William Snyder m Bob Brunner
☆ Dick Van Dyke, Nancy Kwan, Akim Tamiroff

Lucas

US   1986   100m   DeLuxe
TCF (David Nicksay)
A studious 14-year-old boy tries for the football team after falling for a new 16-year-old girl at school.
Pleasant little movie about the problems of growing up, though it steers clear of reality and tries too hard to be charming.
wd David Seltzer ph Reynaldo Villalobos m Dave Grusin ad James Murakami ed Priscilla Nedd
☆ Corey Haim, Kerri Green, Charlie Sheen, Courtney Thorne-Smith, Winona Ryder, Guy Boyd

Luci del Varieta: see Lights of Variety

Lucie Aubrac **

France   1997   116m   colour   Technovision
Pathé/Renn/TF1/DA/Pricel (Patrick Bordier)
A French woman is determined to liberate from prison her husband, a leading member of the

Resistance, who has been sentenced to death by the Gestapo.
An emotional romance set against wartime privations and tribulations, all the more moving because it is based on a true story.
wd Claude Berri *book* Outwitting the Gestapo by Lucie Aubrac *ph* Vincenzo Marano *m* Philippe Sarde *ad* Olivier Radot *ed* Hervé de Luze
☆ Carole Bouquet, Daniel Auteuil, Patrice Chéreau, Eric Boucher, Jean-Roger Milo, Heino Ferch
'Tethered by a detached tone and directorial restraint, ultimately rendering a potential heartwrenching yarn decidedly lacklustre.' – *Ian Freer, Empire*
† Juliette Binoche was replaced in the title role after several weeks' shooting.

The Luck of Ginger Coffey *
Canada/US   1964   100m   bw
Crawley/Roth-Kershner (Leon Roth)
An Irish layabout in Canada finds it difficult to keep a job or protect his family.
Mildly interesting character study with good background detail of Montreal.
w Brian Moore *novel* Brian Moore *d* Irvin Kershner *ph* Manny Wynn *m* Bernardo Segall
☆ Robert Shaw, Mary Ure, Liam Redmond

The Luck of the Irish *
US   1948   99m   bw
TCF (Fred Kohlmar)
A New York newsman's love life is complicated by a helpful leprechaun he meets in Ireland.
Hollywood moonshine, second class: the will and the players are there, but the script is not funny enough.
w Philip Dunne *novel* There Was a Little Man by Constance and Guy Jones *d* Henry Koster *ph* Joseph LaShelle *m* Cyril Mockridge
☆ Tyrone Power, *Cecil Kellaway*, Anne Baxter, Lee J. Cobb, James Todd, Jayne Meadows, J. M. Kerrigan, Phil Brown
⅋ Cecil Kellaway

The Luckiest Girl in the World
US   1936   75m   bw
Charles R. Rogers/Universal
A rich girl bets her father that she can live in New York for a month on 150 dollars.
Lighthearted comedy with farcical trimmings.
w Herbert Fields, Henry Myers, Anne Jordan *d* Eddie Buzzell
☆ Jane Wyatt, Louis Hayward, Eugene Pallette, Nat Pendleton, Catherine Doucet, Philip Reed
'Speed and gags offset story absurdity.' – *Variety*

Lucky Boy
US   1929   97m   bw   part silent
Tiffany-Stahl
A young Jewish boy makes it big on Broadway.
Simple-minded fable inspired by The Jazz Singer (which Jessel is said to have turned down).
w George Jessel *d* Norman Taurog, Charles C. Wilson
☆ George Jessel, Rosa Rosanova, William K. Strauss, Margaret Quimby

Lucky Devils
US   1933   63m   bw
David O. Selznick/RKO
Hollywood stuntmen rescue an actress from a suicide attempt.
Tolerable action special with interesting sidelights.
w Agnes Christine Johnston, Ben Markson *story* Casey Robinson, Bob Rose *d* Ralph Ince *ph* J. Roy Hunt
☆ William Boyd, Dorothy Wilson, William Gargan, Robert Rose, Roscoe Ates, Bruce Cabot

Lucky Jim **
GB   1957   95m   bw
British Lion/Charter (Roy Boulting)
⊞ ⊙
At a provincial university, an accident-prone junior lecturer has a disastrous weekend with his girlfriend and his professor.
Quite funny in its own right, this is a vulgarization of a famous comic novel which got its effects more subtly, with more sense of place, time and character.
w Jeffrey Dell, Patrick Campbell *novel* Kingsley Amis *d* John Boulting *ph* Max Greene *m* John Addison
☆ Ian Carmichael, Hugh Griffith, Terry-Thomas, Sharon Acker, Jean Anderson, Maureen Connell,

Clive Morton, John Welsh, Reginald Beckwith, Kenneth Griffith
'An almost endless ripple of comfortable laughter.' – *News Chronicle*

'When he smiles, it's not because he likes you – it's because he likes what he's going to do to you!'
Lucky Jordan
US   1942   83m   bw
Paramount (Fred Kohlmar)
A con man is drafted and overcomes Nazi agents.
Forgettable star cheapie.
w Darrell Ware, Karl Tunberg *d* Frank Tuttle *ph* John F. Seitz *m* Adolph Deutsch
☆ *Alan Ladd*, Helen Walker, Sheldon Leonard, Marie McDonald, Mabel Paige, Lloyd Corrigan, Dave Willock, Miles Mander
'It's still cops and robbers, no matter how you slice it … Mr Ware and Mr Tunberg are not above dragging in mother love as the reason the gangster changes from a selfish killer to a patriot.' – *Joseph Pihodna, New York Herald Tribune*

Lucky Lady
US   1975   118m   DeLuxe
TCF/Gruskoff/Venture (Michael Gruskoff)
A cabaret girl in 1930 Tijuana joins two adventurers in smuggling liquor into the US by boat.
Whatever can be done wrong with such a story has been done, including irritatingly washed out photography, kinky sex, and sudden switches from farce to gore. None of it holds the interest for a single moment.
w Willard Huyck, Gloria Katz *d* Stanley Donen *ph* Geoffrey Unsworth *m* Ralph Burns *pd* John Barry
☆ Liza Minnelli, Gene Hackman, Burt Reynolds, Michael Hordern, Geoffrey Lewis, Robby Benson
'A manic mess that tries to be all things to all people and ends up offering nothing to anyone.' – *Frank Rich*
'It sports its calculations on its sleeve like rhinestones.' – *Sight and Sound*
'They're all rumrunners in the early 30s, and they're meant to be adorable. This is a big expensive movie for people who don't mind being treated like hicks: the audience is expected to shudder with delight every time it hears an obscenity or sees a big movie star grin.' – *Pauline Kael, New Yorker*

Lucky Mascot: see The Brass Monkey

Lucky Me *
US   1954   100m   Warnercolor   Cinemascope
Warner (Henry Blanke)
⊞ ⊙
Theatrical entertainers stranded in Florida get a lucky break.
Watchable, forgettable musical.
w James O'Hanlon, Robert O'Brien, Irving Elinson *d* Jack Donohue *ph* Wilfrid M. Cline *md* Ray Heindorf
☆ Doris Day, Robert Cummings, Phil Silvers, Eddie Foy Jnr, Nancy Walker, Martha Hyer, Bill Goodwin, Marcel Dalio
'The first Cinemascope musical … pleasant, light-hearted, frothy entertainment.' – *MFB*

Lucky Nick Cain: see I'll Get You for This

Lucky Night
US   1939   90m   bw
MGM (Louis D. Lighton)
An heiress goes out into the world to make a life for herself, and falls for a man she finds on a park bench.
Tedious pattern romance which did neither of its stars any good.
w Vincent Lawrence, Grover Jones *d* Norman Taurog *ph* Ray June *m* Franz Waxman
☆ Myrna Loy, Robert Taylor, Joseph Allen, Henry O'Neill, Douglas Fowley, Marjorie Main, Charles Lane, Bernard Nedell
'Light romantic comedy, okay for box office … but certain sections might object to so much liquor-imbibing.' – *Variety*

Lucky Partners *
US   1940   101m   bw
RKO (George Haight)
▬
Two strangers share a sweepstake ticket and fall in love.
A very thin comedy kept afloat by its stars.
w Allan Scott, John Van Druten *story* Bonne Chance by Sacha Guitry *d* Lewis Milestone *ph* Robert de Grasse *m* Dimitri Tiomkin
☆ *Ronald Colman*, Ginger Rogers, Jack Carson, Spring Byington, Cecilia Loftus, Harry Davenport

The Lucky Star *
Canada   1980   110m   colour
Tele Metropole International/Claude Leger
During World War II a Dutch Jewish boy studies wild west films and captures a German colonel.
Unusual and likeable family adventure story with an unnecessary downbeat ending.
w Max Fischer, Jack Rosenthal *d* Max Fischer *ph* Frank Tidy *m* Art Philipps
☆ Rod Steiger, Louise Fletcher, Brett Marx, Lou Jacobi, Helen Hughes

The Lucky Stiff
US   1949   101m   bw
Amusement Enterprises/UA
A cabaret singer sentenced to death for murder is secretly reprieved but comes back as a 'ghost' to scare the real culprit into confession.
Weird comedy-melodrama which seems to embarrass all concerned.
wd Lewis R. Foster *novel* Craig Rice *ph* Ernest Laszlo
☆ Dorothy Lamour, Brian Donlevy, Claire Trevor, Irene Hervey

The Lucky Texan
US   1933   56m   bw
Monogram/Lone Star (Paul Malvern)
▬
Two crooked assayers try to cheat an old man out of his ranch and gold mine, but the son of his former partner saves the day.
Brisk programmer, with some novel stunts, including Wayne almost walking on water, 'Gabby' Hayes beginning to perfect the comic role of a whiskery and garrulous sidekick which he was to play for the next 18 years, and an unusual final chase involving horses, an automobile and a railcar.
wd Robert N. Bradbury *ph* Archie Stout *ed* Carl Pierson
☆ John Wayne, Barbara Sheldon, Lloyd Whitlock, George Hayes, Yakima Canutt, Ed Parker, Gordon Demaine, Earl Dwire

Lucretia Borgia
France/Italy   1952   105m   Technicolor
Ariane/Filmsonor/Rizzoli
Cesare Borgia uses his beautiful sister as a political pawn.
Well-mounted but rather boring period barnstormer.
w Cécil Saint-Laurent, Jacques Sigurd, Christian-Jaque *d* Christian-Jaque *ph* Christian Matras *m* Maurice Thiriet
·☆ Martine Carol, Pedro Armendariz, Massimo Serato, Valentine Tessier

Lucy Gallant *
US   1955   104m   Technicolor   Vistavision
Paramount/Pine-Thomas
The success story of a dressmaker who comes to run a group of fashion shops but neglects her love life.
Efficient, smartly-handled woman's picture.
w John Lee Mahin, Winston Miller *novel* The Life of Lucy Gallant by Margaret Cousins *d* Robert Parrish *ph* Lionel Lindon *m* Van Cleave
☆ Jane Wyman, Charlton Heston, Claire Trevor, Thelma Ritter, William Demarest, Wallace Ford, Tom Helmore, Mary Field

Ludwig *
Italy/France/West Germany   1972   186m   Technicolor   Panavision
Mega/Cinetel/Dieter Gessler/Divina (Robert Gordon Edwards)
The 19th-century King of Bavaria becomes involved in scandal and goes mad.
A stylish but historically questionable and highly coloured view of events; it drags its heels long before history did.

w Luchino Visconti, Enrico Medioli *d* Luchino Visconti *ph* Armando Nannuzzi *md* Franco Nannino
☆ Helmut Berger, Romy Schneider, Trevor Howard, Silvana Mangano, Helmut Griem, Nora Ricci, Gert Frobe, John Moulder Brown

The Lullaby: see The Sin of Madelon Claudet

'Happiness is busting out all over!'
Lullaby of Broadway *
US   1951   92m   Technicolor
Warner (William Jacobs)
⊞ ⊙
The daughter of a faded Broadway star becomes the new toast of the town.
Reasonably lively musical with solid production values but little style or wit.
w Earl Baldwin *d* David Butler *ph* Wilfrid Cline *md* Ray Heindorf
☆ Doris Day, Billy de Wolfe, Gene Nelson, Gladys George, Florence Bates, S. Z. Sakall

Lulu: see Pandora's Box

Lulu Belle
US   1948   87m   bw
Benedict Bogeaus/Columbia
A selfish singer has a bad effect on one man after another.
Dreary melodrama with a miscast star.
w Everett Freeman *play* Charles MacArthur, Edward Sheldon *d* Leslie Fenton
☆ Dorothy Lamour, George Montgomery, Otto Kruger, Albert Dekker, Glenda Farrell

La Lumière d'en Face: see The Light Across the Street

Lumière d'Eté *
France   1943   112m   bw
Discina (André Paulvé)
The idle and decadent rich in a mountain hotel are affected in various ways by workmen in the valley below.
Unusual and generally interesting character melodrama.
w Jacques Prévert, Pierre Laroche *d* Jean Grémillon *ph* Louis Page *m* Roland Manuel
☆ Madeleine Renaud, Pierre Brasseur, Madeleine Robinson, Paul Bernard, Jane Marken, Georges Marchal

La Luna
Italy   1979   142m   Eastmancolor
TCF/Fiction Cinematografica (Giovanni Bertolucci)
A singer has an incestuous relationship with her teenage son.
Interminable catalogue of events few people wanted to experience; the kindest description would be 'pretentious claptrap'.
w Giuseppe and Bernardo Bertolucci, Clare Peploe *d* Bernardo Bertolucci *ph* Vittorio Storaro *m* operatic excerpts
☆ Jill Clayburgh, Matthew Barry, Laura Betti, Renato Salvatori, Fred Gwynne

Luna de Miel: see Honeymoon

'A seriously wicked comedy hot from Jamaica'
The Lunatic
US   1992   93m   CFI color
Island (Paul Heller, John Pringle)
⊞ ♫
A German photographer visiting Jamaica falls for a local butcher and a boy who talks to the trees.
Whimsical fable that passes an idle hour or so.
w Anthony C. Winkler *novel* Anthony C. Winkler *d* Lol Creme *ph* Richard Greatrex *m* Wally Badarou *ad* Giorgio Ferrarri *ed* Michael Connell
☆ Julie T. Wallace, Paul Campbell, Reggie Carter, Carl Bradshaw, Winston Stona, Linda Gambrill, Rosemary Murray, Lloyd Reckord
'An annoyingly cute fable.' – *Variety*

Lunch Hour
GB   1962   64m   bw
Eyeline (John Mortimer, Harold Orton)
An executive's affair with a young woman at work goes wrong when he hires a hotel room for a lunchtime meeting.
Amusing little anecdote about thwarted love.
w John Mortimer *d* James Hill *ph* Wolfgang Suschitzky *m* James Hill *ad* Jack Stevens *ed* Ted Hooker

☆ Shirley Anne Field, Robert Stephens, Kay Walsh, Michael Robbins, Nigel Davenport

Lunch on the Grass **
France   1959   91m   Eastmancolor
Compagnie Jean Renoir
original title: *Déjeuner sur l'Herbe*
An international scientist hears the pipes of Pan, embarks on a country idyll and impregnates a housemaid whom he later marries.
Charming if overlong frolic with ideas, a harking back to earlier Renoir themes such as in Boudu Sauvé des Eaux.
wd Jean Renoir *ph* Georges Leclerc *m* Joseph Kosma
☆ Paul Meurisse, Catherine Rouvel, Fernand Sardou, Ingrid Nordine
'A warm, loving, garrulous, undisciplined film.' – *Penelope Houston, MFB*

La Lune dans le Caniveau: see *The Moon in the Gutter*

Lunes de fiel: see *Bitter Moon*

Lunga Vita All Signora!: see *Long Live the Lady*

Lure of the Wilderness
US   1952   92m   Technicolor
TCF (Robert L. Jacks)
A man falsely accused of murder hides for eight years in Georgia's Okefenokee swamp.
Remake of Swamp Water, *with Walter Brennan playing the same part. The plot works fairly well still, but colour doesn't suit the scenery.*
w Louis Lantz *story* Vereen Bell *d* Jean Negulesco *ph* Edward Cronjager *m* Franz Waxman
☆ Jeffrey Hunter, Jean Peters, Walter Brennan, Constance Smith, Jack Elam

Lured *
US   1947   102m   bw
(UA) Hunt Stromberg (James Nasser)
▣
GB title: *Personal Column*
An American dancer stranded in London helps Scotland Yard catch a killer.
Minor murder mystery with a pleasing cast.
w Leo Rosten, *from the French film* Pièges *d* Douglas Sirk *ph* William Daniels *m* Michel Michelet *pd* Nicolai Remisoff
☆ Lucille Ball, George Sanders, Charles Coburn, Boris Karloff, Cedric Hardwicke, Alan Mowbray, George Zucco, Joseph Calleia, Robert Coote, Alan Napier

'Devils In Female Bodies Whose Embrace Is The Kiss Of Death For Man Or Woman!'
Lust for a Vampire
GB   1970   95m   Technicolor
Hammer (Harry Fine, Michael Style)
☾
In 1830 an English writer discerns that a pupil in

an exclusive mid-European girls' school is a reincarnated vampire.
Dull Hammer horror, with the emphasis on lesbianism and nudity.
w Tudor Gates *novel* Carmilla *by* J. Sheridan Le Fanu *d* Jimmy Sangster *ph* David Muir *m* Harry Robinson
☆ Ralph Bates, Michael Johnson, Barbara Jefford, Suzanna Leigh, Yutte Stensgaard, Mike Raven, Helen Christie
'An embarrassment.' – *Jimmy Sangster*

Lust for Evil: see *Plein Soleil*

Lust for Gold
US   1949   90m   bw
Columbia (S. Sylvan Simon)
▤
A young man goes to Arizona to search for a lost gold mine discovered by his grandfather.
Moderate Western drama consisting largely of flashbacks.
w Ted Sherdeman, Richard English *novel* Thunder God's Gold *by* Barry Storm *d* S. Sylvan Simon *ph* Archie Stout *m* George Duning
☆ Ida Lupino, Glenn Ford, Gig Young, William Prince, Edgar Buchanan, Will Geer, Paul Ford

Lust for Life **
US   1956   122m   Metrocolor   Cinemascope
MGM (John Houseman)
▤ ▣ ☾ ☍
The life of Vincent Van Gogh.
Fairly absorbing, not inaccurate, but somehow uninspiring biopic, probably marred by poor colour and wide screen; despite good work all round, it simply doesn't fall into a classic category.
w Norman Corwin *book* Irving Stone *d* Vincente Minnelli *ph* Freddie Young, Russell Harlan *m* Miklos Rozsa *ad* Cedric Gibbons, Hans Peters, Preston Ames *ed* Adrienne Fazan *cos* Walter Plunkett
☆ Kirk Douglas, Anthony Quinn, James Donald, Pamela Brown, Everett Sloane, Niall MacGinnis, Noel Purcell, Henry Daniell, Lionel Jeffries, Madge Kennedy, Jill Bennett, Laurence Naismith
'Two hours of quite shattering and exciting entertainment.' – *Alan Dent, Illustrated London News*
† Anthony Quinn was on the screen for a total of eight minutes in his Oscar-winning role.
♟ Anthony Quinn
♟ Norman Corwin; Kirk Douglas; art direction

Lust in the Dust
US   1984   87m   CFI color
Fox Run (Allan Glaser, Tab Hunter)
▣ ▤
In the old west, a strong silent man and a drag queen beat the baddies to the gold.
Fitfully funny spoof for adults.
w Philip Taylor *d* Paul Bartel *ph* Paul Lohmann *m* Peter Matz *ed* Alan Toomayan
☆ Tab Hunter, Divine, Lainie Kazan, Geoffrey Lewis, Henry Silva, Cesar Romero, Woody Strode

Lust in the Sun (dubbed)
France/Spain   1971   84m   Eastmancolor
Golden Era/Kerfrance/IMF
original title: *Dans la Poussiére du Soleil*
A son, who is regarded by many as a coward, revenges his father's death by killing his uncle.
Enjoyably bizarre updating of Hamlet *to a cowboy setting, with Polonius becoming the town's sheriff, and faithful enough to the original to include the 'play within the play'.*
wd Richard Balducci *play* Hamlet *by* William Shakespeare *ph* Tadusu G. Suzuki *m* Francis Lai *pd* Santiago Ontanon *ed* Liliane Fattori
☆ Maria Schell, Bob Cunningham, Daniel Beretta, Karin Meier, Pépé Calvo, Colin Drake
'The inherent silliness of the conception … quickly converts the film into a variety skit.' – *MFB*

Lust och Fägring Stor: see *Love Lessons*

The Lusty Men *
US   1952   113m   bw
RKO/Wald-Krasna (Jerry Wald)
▤ ▣
Tensions lead to the death of one of a pair of rider friends on a rodeo tour.
Standard melodrama with semi-documentary detail and star performances.
w Horace McCoy, David Dortort *d* Nicholas Ray *ph* Lee Garmes *m* Roy Webb
☆ Robert Mitchum, Arthur Kennedy, Susan Hayward, Arthur Hunnicutt

Luther *
GB   1973   112m   Eastmancolor
American Express/Ely Landau/Cinevision
▤
In 1525, the teachings of Luther culminate in the Peasants' Revolt.
Hard-to-watch filming by the American Film Theatre of a singularly theatrical play, and not a very good one at that. Some good acting.
w Edward Anhalt *play* John Osborne *d* Guy Green *ph* Freddie Young *m* John Addison *pd* Peter Mullins
☆ Stacy Keach, Patrick Magee, Hugh Griffith, Robert Stephens, Alan Badel, Julian Glover, Judi Dench, Leonard Rossiter, Maurice Denham

Luv
US   1967   95m   Technicolor   Panavision
Columbia/Jalem (Martin Manulis)
▤ ☾
When a man prevents an old friend from jumping off the Brooklyn Bridge and brings him home, a sexual square dance develops.
A modern comedy that should have stayed in the theatre.
w Elliott Baker *play* Murray Schisgal *d* Clive Donner *ph* Ernest Laszlo *m* Gerry Mulligan
☆ Jack Lemmon, Peter Falk, Elaine May, Nina Wayne, Eddie Mayehoff, Paul Hartman, Severn Darden

'A light but incisive comedy about the patterns and language of love in a Freud-ridden society has become an inept and lethally unamusing film farce.' – *MFB*

Luxury Liner
US   1933   72m   bw
Paramount
Stories of various passengers on a liner bound from New York to Bremerhaven.
Interesting minor multi-drama, like a rough sketch for Ship of Fools *(qv).*
w Gene Markey, Kathryn Scola *novel* Gina Kaus *d* Lothar Mendes *ph* Victor Milner
☆ George Brent, Zita Johann, Vivienne Osborne, Alice White, Verree Teasdale, C. Aubrey Smith, Frank Morgan, Henry Wadsworth, Billy Bevan
'Not even the frank hook-up with Grand Hotel will help this entry much … a loose and thin catch-as-catch-can affair.' – *Variety*

Luxury Liner
US   1948   98m   Technicolor
MGM (Joe Pasternak)
▤ ☾
The captain of a liner has trouble with his teenage daughter.
Minor shipboard musical with pleasing talents applied.
w Gladys Lehman, Richard Connell *d* Richard Whorf *ph* Ernest Laszlo *md* George Stoll
☆ George Brent, Jane Powell, Lauritz Melchior, Frances Gifford, Marina Koshetz, Xavier Cugat, Richard Derr, Connie Gilchrist

'The girl who thought she knew all about love!'
Lydia *
US   1941   104m   bw
Alexander Korda (Lee Garmes)
An ageing lady recalls her former beaux.
Pleasing remake of Carnet du Bal, *with excellent production values.*
w Ben Hecht, Samuel Hoffenstein *story* Julien Duvivier, Laszlo Bus-Fekete *d* Julien Duvivier *ph* Lee Garmes *m* Miklos Rozsa *pd* Vincent Korda
☆ Merle Oberon, Joseph Cotten, Alan Marshal, Edna May Oliver, Hans Yaray, George Reeves, John Halliday, Sara Allgood
♟ Miklos Rozsa

Lydia Bailey
US   1952   89m   Technicolor
TCF (Jules Schermer)
In 1802 a Boston lawyer visits Haiti to obtain the signature of a wayward heiress, and becomes involved in the negro fight against the French.
Standard adventure romance with plenty of excitements.
w Michael Blankfort, Philip Dunne *novel* Kenneth Roberts *d* Jean Negulesco *ph* Harry Jackson *m* Hugo Friedhofer
☆ Dale Robertson, Anne Francis, Charles Korvin, William Marshall, Adeline de Walt Reynolds

---

M ***
Germany 1931 118m bw
Nero Film (Seymour Nebenzal)

A psychopathic murderer of children evades the police but is caught by the city's criminals who find his activities getting them a bad name.
An unmistakable classic whose oddities are hardly worth criticizing, this is part social melodrama and part satire, but entirely unforgettable, with most of its sequences brilliantly staged.
w Thea von Harbou, Paul Falkenberg, Adolf Jansen, Karl Vash d Fritz Lang ph Fritz Arno Wagner m Adolf Jansen ad Karl Vollbrecht, Emil Hasler
☆ Peter Lorre, Otto Wernicke, Gustav Gründgens
'Visual excitement, pace, brilliance of surface and feeling for detail.' – *New Yorker, 1977*
† Of Lang's later work, *Fury* comes closest to the feeling and style of M.

M *
US 1951 82m bw
Columbia (Seymour Nebenzal)

Faithful but fated remake; without the heavy expressionist techniques, the story seems merely silly and the atmosphere is all wrong.
w Norman Reilly Raine, Leo Katcher d Joseph Losey ph Ernest Laszlo m Michel Michelet pd John Hubley ed Edward Mann
☆ David Wayne, Howard Da Silva, Luther Adler, Martin Gabel, Glenn Anders, Karen Morley, Norman Lloyd, Walter Burke
'I consciously repeated only one shot ... essentially Lang's villain was my hero.' – *Joseph Losey*

M*A*S*H ****
US 1970 116m DeLuxe Panavision
TCF/Aspen (Ingo Preminger, Leon Ericksen)

Surgeons at a mobile hospital in Korea spend what spare time they have chasing women and bucking authority.
Savage comedy of man's rebellion in the face of death, alternating sex farce with gory operation scenes; hailed as the great anti-everything film, and certainly very funny for those who can take it. It led to a television series which for once did not disgrace its original.
w Ring Lardner Jnr novel Richard Hooker d Robert Altman ph Harold E. Stine m Johnny Mandel
☆ Donald Sutherland, Elliott Gould, Tom Skerritt, Sally Kellerman, Robert Duvall, Jo Ann Pflug, René Auberjonois, Gary Burghoff
'Bloody funny. A hyper-acute wiretap on mankind's death wish.' – *Joseph Morgenstern*
'The laughter is blood-soaked and the comedy cloaks a bitter and terrible truth.' – *Judith Crist*
'A foul-mouthed, raucous, anti-establishment comedy, combining gallows humour, sexual slapstick and outrageous satire.' – *Les Keyser, Hollywood in the Seventies*
🏆 Ring Lardner Jnr
🏅 best picture; Robert Altman; Sally Kellerman

M. Butterfly
US 1993 101m colour
Warner/Geffen (Gabriella Martinelli)

A French diplomat begins an affair with a Chinese performer in the Beijing Opera, unaware that he is being deceived.
Based on an actual scandal, which became a successful play, this is an unsuccessful movie, one that never convinces as to the truth or likelihood of its central relationship.
w David Henry Hwang play David Henry Hwang d David Cronenberg ph Peter Suschitzky m Howard Shore pd Carol Spier ed Ronald Sanders

☆ Jeremy Irons, John Lone, Barbara Sukowa, Ian Richardson, Shizuko Hoshi, Annabel Leventon, Vernon Dobtcheff, Richard McMillan
'Gets all dressed up in fancy threads but goes nowhere, due to a lack of chemistry and heat on the part of the two leads.' – *Todd McCarthy, Variety*
'The end result, while not entirely unrewarding, is another step away from the singular vision Cronenberg once expressed even in his marginal work.' – *Kim Newman, Empire*

Ma and Pa Kettle *
US 1949 75m bw
U-I (Leonard Goldstein)

Pa Kettle wins a house in a contest and is accused of cheating.
First of a series of low-budget comedies which, based on characters from The Egg and I (qv), had astonishing commercial success in America. The standard varied from adequate to painful.
w Herbert Margolis, Louis Morheim, Al Lewis d Charles Lamont ph Maury Gertsman m Milton Schwarzwald
☆ Marjorie Main, Percy Kilbride, Richard Long, Meg Randall
'Not exactly Noël Coward.' – *Leonard Maltin*
† For others in the series, see under *The Kettles*.

Ma Nuit Chez Maud *
France 1969 110m bw
Films du Losange (Pierre Cottreill)

aka: *My Night at Maud's*
A Catholic clerk in a small town falls in love with an elegant divorcee but can't bring himself to court her openly and marries someone else.
Subdued, literate talk-piece which finally exhausts rather than stimulates.
wd Eric Rohmer ph Nestor Almendros ad Nicole Rachline ed Cécile Decugis
☆ Jean-Louis Trintignant, Françoise Fabian, Marie-Christine Barrault
🏅 best foreign film; Eric Rohmer (as writer)

Ma Saison Préférée **
France 1993 127m colour Panavision
Arrow/TF1/DA/Alain Sarde

aka: *My Favourite Season*
An estranged brother and his married sister meet for some uneasy reunions as their mother becomes ill and increasingly frail.
Emotionally true, devastatingly accurate portrait of the subterranean tensions, guilt and anguish that exist within a conventional middle-class family, told in four chapters, each corresponding to a season.
w André Téchiné, Pascal Bonitzer d André Téchiné ph Thierry Arbogast m Philippe Sarde pd Carlos Conti ed Martine Giordano
☆ Catherine Deneuve, Daniel Auteuil, Marthe Villalonga, Jean-Pierre Bouvier, Chiara Mastroianni, Carmen Chaplin, Anthony Prada, Ingrid Caven
'A dull exposition of the glacial shifts in the emotional alignments within a dysfunctional middle-class family.' – *Variety*

Ma Vie en Rose **
France/Belgium/Switzerland/GB 1997 89m colour
Buena Vista/Haut et Court/WFE/Freeway/CAB/La Sept/RTBF/TF1 (Carole Scotta)

To the surprise of his parents and the horror of their neighbours, a seven-year-old boy insists that he is really a girl.
A strange but compelling movie about gender and identity, with a remarkable performance from its young protagonist.

w Chris Vander Stappen, Alain Berliner d Alain Berliner ph Yves Cape m Dominique Dalcan pd Véronique Melery ed Sandrine Deegan
☆ Michèle Laroque, Jean-Philippe Ecoffey, Hélène Vincent, Georges du Fresne, Daniel Hanssens, Laurence Bibot
'A generous and at times gorgeous instance of cinema's true powers and promise.' – *Sight and Sound*

Ma Vie Sexuelle **
France 1996 180m colour
BAC/Why Not/La Sept/France2/Canal+

original title: *Comment je me suis disputé ... ('ma vie sexuelle')*
An unhappy 29-year-old academic with an unsatisfactory 10-year relationship and a desire for his best friend's girlfriend begins an affair with the girlfriend of a friend.
Complex and talkative disquisition on love, responsibility and the pleasures and pains of adultery; its tone is intellectual but not solemn: one character has a religious revelation while a girl dances in her underwear, while another says, 'I think I'm incredibly depressed,' as the woman he wants takes off her clothes.
w Arnaud Desplechin, Emmanuel Bourdieu d Arnaud Desplechin ph Eric Gautier m Krishna Lévy pd Antoine Platteau ed François Gédigier
☆ Mathieu Amalric, Emmanuelle Devos, Emmanuel Salinger, Marianne Denicourt, Thibault de Montalembert, Chiara Mastroianni
'Has its moments, but there are too few of them to justify the running time.' – *Empire*

Maborosi *
Japan 1995 109m colour
ICA/TV Man Union (Naoe Gozu)

A wife, who has continued to mourn the death of her husband, a suicide, remarries a widower.
Austerely moving account of a twilight existence, of people trapped within a bleakly implacable landscape.
w Yoshihisa Ogita story Teru Miyamoto d Hirokazu Koreeda ph Masao Nakabori m Cheng Ming-Chang ad Kyoko Heya ed Tomoya Oshima
☆ Makiko Esumi, Takeshi Naito, Tadanobu Asano, Goki Kashiyama, Naomi Watanabe
'A powerful insight into the disabling force of grief.' – *George Perry*

'Every success has its story. And its price.'

Mac *
US 1992 118m Technicolor
Entertainment/Macfilm (Nancy Tenenbaum, Brenda Goodman)

A construction worker, irritated by the sloppy standards of his foreman, decides to start his own business, working to the best of his ability; his two brothers join him but then leave.
A drama of obsession and integrity, with splendid ensemble acting and a gritty reality.
w John Turturro, Brandon Cole d John Turturro ph Ron Fortunato m Richard Termini, Vin Tese pd Robert Standefer ed Michael Berenbaum
☆ John Turturro, Katherine Borowitz, Michael Badalucco, Carl Capotorto, Ellen Barkin, John Amos, Dennis Farina
'Obviously made as a labour of love. But it is a bit of a labour to sit through.' – *Alexander Walker, London Evening Standard*
'A film of old-fashioned virtues – sincerity, worthiness, and probity – used in an unpatronising way.' – *Philip French*

Mac and Me
US 1988 99m
Guild/R. J. Louis

A family of aliens is inadvertently dumped in California.
A cardboard confection, copying much of the plot of E.T., that is little more than a dull and extended commercial for fast foods.
w Steven Feke, Stewart Raffill d Stewart Raffill ph Nick McLean m Alan Silvestri pd W. Stewart Campbell ed Tom Walls
☆ Christine Ebersole, Jonathan Ward, Tina Caspary, Lauren Stanley, Jade Calegory, Vinnie Torrente, Martin West

'See it with someone who can carry you home!'
'So terrifying we have to insure your life!'

Macabre
US 1958 73m bw
AA (William Castle)

When a small-town doctor's daughter is kidnapped, he fears she may have been buried alive in the cemetery.
Genuine but unsuccessful attempt to film a horror comic; incredibly stodgy writing, acting and direction put the lid on it.
w Robb White d William Castle ph Carl Guthrie m Les Baxter
☆ William Prince, Jim Backus, Jacqueline Scott, Philip Tonge, Ellen Corby
'A ghoulish but totally ineffective horror piece, set mainly in undertakers' offices and an atmosphere of graveyards and swirling fog.' – *MFB*
† When first released, admission carried insurance against death by fright. Some said it should have been death by boredom.

'Keep A Cool Head!'

Macabre (dubbed)
Italy 1980 90m Telecolor
Medusa/AMA (Gianni Minervini, Antonio Avati)

original title: *Macabro*
A blind man becomes curious about his neighbour, a demented woman who, unknown to him, takes to bed every night the head of her dead lover, which she keeps in the refrigerator during the day.
Gruesome, though stylish, horror movie, which marked the debut of director Lamberto Bava.
w Lamberto Bava, Pupi Avati, Antonio Avati, Roberto Gandus d Lamberto Bava ph Francesco delli Colli m Ubaldo Continiello ad Katia Dottori ed Piera Gabutti sp Tonino Corridori, Angelo Mattei
☆ Bernice Stegers, Stanko Molnar, Roberto Posse, Veronica Zinny, Ferdinando Orlandi

Macao
US 1952 81m bw
RKO (Alex Gottlieb)

A wandering American in the Far East helps a detective catch a gangster.
A few flashy decorative touches show the director's hand, otherwise this is routine, murky thick ear.
w Bernard C. Schoenfeld, Stanley Rubin d Josef von Sternberg (and Nicholas Ray) ph Harry J. Wild m Anthony Collins
☆ Robert Mitchum, Jane Russell, William Bendix, Gloria Grahame, Thomas Gomez

Macaroni (dubbed) *
Italy 1985 104m Eastmancolor
Massfilm/Filmauro (Luigi and Aurelio de Laurentiis, Franco Committeri)

An American engineer returns to Naples, where he fought 40 years earlier in the Second World War, and begins to relive a past he never had.

Gentle, nostalgic, bitter-sweet comedy of middle-aged frustrations, helped by the charm of the leading performances.

w Ruggero Maccari, Furio Scarpelli, Ettore Scola d Ettore Scola ph Claudio Ragona m Armando Trovaioli pd Luciano Ricceri ed Carla Simoncelli

☆ Jack Lemmon, Marcello Mastroianni, Daria Nicolodi, Isa Danieli, Maria Luisa Santella, Fabio Tenore, Patrizia Sacchi, Bruno Esposito

'A star vehicle, but it seems awfully out of date and joyless.' – Vincent Canby, New York Times

MacArthur the Rebel General *
US 1977 130m Technicolor
Universal/Richard D. Zanuck, David Brown (Frank McCarthy)
🔲

The exploits of General MacArthur during the Pacific wars and his strained relationships with two presidents.
Sober, earnest political biography with war sequences; very well done but somehow unsympathetic.
w Hal Barwood, Matthew Robbins d Joseph Sargent ph Mario Tosi m Jerry Goldsmith pd John J. Lloyd ed George Nicholson sp Albert Whitlock
☆ Gregory Peck, Dan O'Herlihy, Ed Flanders, Ward Costello, Marj Dusay, Ivan Bonar

'A biopic that begins when its subject is sixty lacks roots – and in this case revelation.' – Judith Crist

'Taking on the drug lords is impossible. Taking on a country is insane.'
McBain
US 1991 102m TVC Color
Shapiro Glickenhaus (J. Boyce Harman Jnr)
🔲 🔲 ⊙~

A former soldier agrees to help the sister of a friend overthrow the corrupt government in Colombia.
Predictable and interminable, lacking any sense of reality.
wd James Glickenhaus ph Robert M. Baldwin Jnr m Christopher Franke pd Charles C. Bennett ed Jeffrey Wolf
☆ Christopher Walken, Maria Conchita Alonso, Michael Ironside, Steve James, Jay Patterson, T. G. Waites, Victor Argo, Hechter Ubarry, Russell Dennis Baker, Chick Vennera

'A silly action film geared mainly to overseas audiences.' – Variety

Macbeth *
US 1948 89m bw
Republic/Mercury (Orson Welles)
🔲 ⊙ ⊙~

A famous – or infamous – attempt to film Shakespeare in twenty-one days in papier mâché settings running with damp; further hampered by the use of a form of unintelligible bastard Scots.
A few striking moments at the beginning remain; the rest should be silence.
w Orson Welles play William Shakespeare d Orson Welles ph John L. Russell m Jacques Ibert ed Fred Ritter ed Louis Lindsay
☆ Orson Welles, Jeanette Nolan, Dan O'Herlihy, Roddy McDowall, Edgar Barrier, Erskine Sanford

Macbeth
GB 1972 140m Technicolor Todd-AO 35
Playboy/Caliban (Andrew Braunsberg)
🔲 🔲 ⊙~

A sharpened and brutalized version; the blood swamps most of the cleverness and most of the poetry.
w Roman Polanski, Kenneth Tynan play William Shakespeare d Roman Polanski ph Gilbert Taylor m the Third Ear Band pd Wilfrid Shingleton ed Alastair MacIntyre
☆ Jon Finch, Francesca Annis, Martin Shaw, Nicholas Selby, John Stride, Stephan Chase, Paul Shelley, Terence Bayler, Keith Chegwin

Macbeth
Scotland 1997 129m colour
CJP/Cromwell/Lamancha/Grampian (Shona Donaldson)
In Scotland in the 11th century, Macbeth pays the price for murdering the king and seizing the throne.
Low-budget approach to Shakespeare's Scottish play, emphasizing the fact that it comes from north of the border, and by far the least interesting version so far.
w Bob Carruthers, Jeremy Freeston play William Shakespeare d Jeremy Freeston ph Dave Miller

m Richard Cherns ed Owen Parker, Chris Gormlie
☆ Jason Connery, Helen Baxendale, Graham McTavish, Kenny Bryans, Kern Falconer, Hildegard Neil, Chris Gormlie, John Corvin, Brian Blessed

'What do we get? A cross between a 1970s schools programme and a Scottish Tourist Board video. This is indeed a tragic Macbeth.' – Giala Murray, Empire
† Brian Blessed was credited as artistic adviser and for 'special direction of witches scenes'.

McCabe and Mrs Miller
US 1971 120m Technicolor Panavision
Warner (David Foster, Mitchell Brower)
🔲 🔲 ⊙ ⊙~

At the turn of the century a gambling gunfighter comes to a northwest mining town and uses his money to set up lavish brothels.
Obscurely scripted, muddy-coloured and harshly recorded Western melodrama whose squalid 'realism' comes as close to fantasy as does The Wizard of Oz.
w Robert Altman, Brian McKay novel McCabe by Edmund Naughton d Robert Altman ph Vilmos Zsigmond pd Leon Ericksen
☆ Warren Beatty, Julie Christie, René Auberjonois, Shelley Duvall, John Schuck

'A fleeting, diaphanous vision of what frontier life might have been.' – Pauline Kael
'Altman directed M*A*S*H, which wandered and was often funny; then Brewster McCloud, which wandered and was not funny; now this, which wanders and is repulsive. The thesis seems to be that if you take a corny story, fuzz up the exposition, vitiate the action, use a childishly ironic ending, and put in lots of profanity and nudity, you have Marched On with Time.' – Stanley Kauffmann
§ Julie Christie

The McConnell Story
US 1955 107m Warnercolor Cinemascope
Warner (Henry Blanke)
🔲 ⊙~
GB title: Tiger in the Sky
The career and accidental death of a jet ace of the Korean war.
Crude, obvious and saccharine biopic.
w Ted Sherdeman, Sam Rolfe d Gordon Douglas ph John Seitz, Ted McCord m Max Steiner
☆ Alan Ladd, June Allyson, James Whitmore, Frank Faylen, Willis Bouchey

MacDonald of the Canadian Mounties:
see Pony Soldier

McFadden's Flats
US 1935 65m bw
Paramount
The quarrel between a bricklayer and a barber affects their children.
Modest working-class comedy from a well-worn play.
w Arthur Caesar, Edward Kaufman, Casey Robinson, Andy Rice play Gus Hill d Ralph Murphy
☆ Walter C. Kelly, Andy Clyde, Richard Cromwell, Jane Darwell, Betty Furness, George Barbier

'Better-than-average family picture.' – Variety

McGuire Go Home: see The High Bright Sun

McHale's Navy
US 1997 108m DeLuxe
Universal/Bubble Factory (Sid, Bill and Jon Sheinberg)
🔲 🔲

On a Caribbean island, an ex-naval officer, who uses his ill-gotten money to finance good causes, finds his schemes thwarted when a tough new commander tightens up discipline on the naval base.
A misfiring comedy, ridiculous for all the wrong reasons, which suddenly veers into frenetic action, and finally sinks with all hands lost.
w Peter Crabbe d Bryan Spicer ph Buzz Feitshans m Dennis McCarthy pd Gene Rudolf ed Russel Denove
☆ Tom Arnold, Tim Curry, Dean Stockwell, David Alan Grier, Debra Messing, Ernest Borgnine, Tommy Chong, Bruce Campbell

'A ham-fisted, fitfully amusing lark that quickly runs aground.' – Variety
† The film is based on the TV sitcom, a waterlogged copy of Phil Silver's Sgt Bilko, that

ran from 1962 to 1966 and starred Ernest Borgnine as McHale, the role played by Tom Arnold in the film.

The Machine (dubbed) *
France/Germany 1994 96m colour
Hachette Première/DD/Prima/M6/France 2/Studio Babelsberg (Patrick Bordier)
🔲 🔲 ⊙ ⊙~
original title: La Machine
A brain specialist working with the criminally insane builds a machine to enable him to get inside the mind of a serial killer; but the experiment goes wrong, and the two switch bodies.
A deft psychological thriller, a variation on Frankenstein, which creates an atmosphere of unease that is maintained until its horrific climax.
wd François Dupeyron novel La Machine by René Belletto ph Dietrich Lohmann m Michel Portal pd Carlos Conti ed Noelle Boisson
☆ Gérard Depardieu, Nathalie Baye, Didier Bourdon, Natalia Woerner, Erwan Baynaud

'A cleverly choreographed roller-coaster ride of identity and appearances – with a stomach-churning dip yet to come.' – Lisa Nesselson, Variety
† There is an error in the video release. After an opening sequence, a caption reads 'eighteen months later'; it should read 'eighteen months earlier'.

'Even the Mafia calls him Mister!'
Machine Gun McCain
Italy 1970 94m Techniscope
Euroatlantica/Columbia
⊙
The Mafia springs a hardened criminal from jail and puts him to use.
Dull but violent Las Vegas-set mobster story with some echoes of Bonnie and Clyde.
w Giuliano Montaldo, Mino Roli d Giuliano Montaldo m Ennio Morricone
☆ John Cassavetes, Peter Falk, Britt Ekland, Gabriele Ferzetti

Macho Callahan
US 1970 100m Movielab Panavision
Avco/Felicidad (Bernard Kowalski, Martin C. Schute)
A vengeful cowboy annihilates all who stand in his way.
Squalid Mexican-made Western with unremitting emphasis on violence.
w Clifford Newton Gould d Bernard Kowalski ph Gerry Fisher m Pat Williams
☆ David Janssen, Lee J. Cobb, David Carradine, James Booth, Jean Seberg

MacKenna's Gold *
US 1969 136m Technicolor Super Panavision
Columbia/Highroad (Carl Foreman, Dimitri Tiomkin)
🔲 🔲 ⊙~
A dying Indian entrusts a sheriff with a map of the legendary Valley of Gold, and when the news breaks the map is in demand.
Curious serial-like Western melodrama packed with stars and pretensions above its station. On a lower level, it is quite enjoyable.
w Carl Foreman novel Will Henry d J. Lee-Thompson ph Joseph MacDonald, Harold Wellman m Quincy Jones pd Geoffrey Drake
☆ Gregory Peck, Omar Sharif, Telly Savalas, Camilla Sparv, Keenan Wynn, Julie Newmar, Ted Cassidy, Eduardo Ciannelli, Eli Wallach, Edward G. Robinson, Raymond Massey, Burgess Meredith, Anthony Quayle, Lee J. Cobb

'Preposterous hotch-potch of every cliché known to the gold lust book.' – MFB
'Twelve-year-olds of all ages might tolerate it.' – Judith Crist
'A western of truly stunning absurdity, a thriving example of the old Hollywood maxim about how to succeed by failing big.' – Vincent Canby

The McKenzie Break *
GB 1970 106m DeLuxe
UA/Levy-Gardner-Laven
During World War II, German prisoners at a Scottish camp stage an escape.
Effective little action suspenser.
w William Norton d Lamont Johnson ph Michael Reed m Riz Ortolani
☆ Brian Keith, Helmut Griem, Ian Hendry, Jack Watson, Patrick O'Connell, Horst Janson

'Only Mackintosh can save them now – and Mackintosh is dead!'
The Mackintosh Man *
GB 1973 99m Technicolor
Warner/Newman-Foreman/John Huston
🔲

A government agent is sent to prison to contact a criminal gang.
Convoluted but entertaining spy thriller with good performances and action sequences.
w Walter Hill novel The Freedom Trap by Desmond Bagley d John Huston ph Oswald Morris m Maurice Jarre
☆ Paul Newman, James Mason, Dominique Sanda, Nigel Patrick, Harry Andrews, Michael Hordern, Ian Bannen, Peter Vaughan, Roland Culver, Percy Herbert, Robert Lang, Leo Genn

McLintock *
US 1963 127m Technicolor Panavision
UA/Batjac (Michael Wayne)
🔲 ⊙ ⊙~
A cattle baron can control a whole town but not his termagant wife.
Sub-Ford Western farce borrowed from The Taming of the Shrew, with much fist-fighting and mud-splattering, and rather too much chat in between.
w James Edward Grant d Andrew V. McLaglen ph William H. Clothier m Frank de Vol
☆ John Wayne, Maureen O'Hara, Yvonne de Carlo, Patrick Wayne, Stefanie Powers, Chill Wills, Bruce Cabot, Jack Kruschen

The McMasters
US 1969 90m Technicolor
JayJen (Dimitri de Grunwald)

A black man returning home from the Civil War gets unexpected help from a tough landowner.
Racial Western with black, white and red points of view, all very violently expressed.
w Harold Jacob Smith d Alf Kjellin ph Lester Shorr m Coleridge-Taylor Parkinson
☆ Brock Peters, Burl Ives, David Carradine, Nancy Kwan, Jack Palance, Dane Clark, John Carradine, L. Q. Jones, R. G. Armstrong

The Macomber Affair *
US 1946 89m bw
(UA) Benedict Bogeaus (Casey Robinson)
The wife of a bullying big game hunter falls for their guide.
Safari melodrama with a plot which has become a cliché but seemed fresh enough at the time. Goodish writing and acting.
w Casey Robinson story The Short Happy Life of Francis Macomber by Ernest Hemingway d Zoltan Korda ph Karl Struss m Miklos Rozsa
☆ Gregory Peck, Joan Bennett, Robert Preston, Reginald Denny, Carl Harbord, Jean Gillie

'The best movie job on Hemingway to date.' – James Agee
'It has survived the hazardous crossing from brilliant short story to film with practically no casualties.' – Daily Mail

Macon County Line
US 1973 89m Eastmancolor
Sam Arkoff/Max Baer
🔲
In mid-fifties Louisiana, a couple of hell-raisers are harassed by a local sheriff, and much bloodshed results.
Shapeless melodrama more or less in the wake of Easy Rider; an unattractive film which unaccountably had great box-office success.
w Max Baer, Richard Compton d Richard Compton ph Daniel Lacambre m Stu Phillips
☆ Alan Vint, Cheryl Waters, Geoffrey Lewis, Joan Blackman, Jesse Vint, Max Baer

'He's a busted cop, his gun is unlicensed, his methods unlawful, his story incredible!'
McQ
US 1974 111m Technicolor Panavision
Warner/Batjac/Levy-Gardner
🔲 🔲 ⊙~
A Seattle police detective goes after the gangster who killed his friend.
Rambling, violent thriller with good sequences but no cohesion.
w Lawrence Roman d John Sturges ph Harry Stradling Jnr m Elmer Bernstein

☆ John Wayne, Eddie Albert, Diana Muldaur, Colleen Dewhurst, Clu Gulager, David Huddleston, Julie Adams

Macu, the Policeman's Wife

Venezuela 1987 102m colour
Macu Films/Cinearte (Olegario Barrera)
original title: *Macu*

The young wife of a policeman suspects her husband of having murdered her lover and his friends.
Slice-of-life drama that was a big hit in its own country, but does not travel well.
w Solveig Hoogesteijn, Milagros Rodriguez d Solveig Hoogesteijn ph Andrés Agusti m Victor Cuica ed José Alcalde
☆ Maria Luisa Mosquera, Daniel Alvarado, Frank Hernández, Tito Aponte, Ana Castell, Carmen Palma, Iván Feo

McVicar

GB 1980 112m Eastmancolor
The Who Films/Brent-Walker (Bill Curbishley, Roy Baird, Roger Daltrey)
▭ ▬

The true story of the escapes from prison of a violent criminal who was subsequently reformed and rehabilitated.
Some smart sequences don't prevent this from being an exploitation item.
w John McVicar and Tom Clegg d Tom Clegg ph Vernon Layton m Jeff Wayne ad Fred Carter ed Peter Boyle
☆ Roger Daltrey, Adam Faith, Cheryl Campbell, Billy Murray, Georgina Hale, Steven Berkoff

Mad about Men

GB 1954 90m Technicolor
GFD/Group Films (Betty Box)
By mutual agreement, a sports mistress and a mermaid change places for a while.
Laborious rehash of Miranda with familiar jokes.
w Peter Blackmore d Ralph Thomas ph Ernest Steward m Benjamin Frankel
☆ Glynis Johns, Donald Sinden, Anne Crawford, Margaret Rutherford, Dora Bryan, Nicholas Phipps, Irene Handl

Mad about Music *

⭢ US 1938 98m bw
Universal (Joe Pasternak)
A girl at a Swiss school adopts a personable visitor as her father.
Pleasing star vehicle with charm and humour; badly remade as Toy Tiger (qv).
w Bruce Manning, Felix Jackson d Norman Taurog ph Joseph Valentine m Frank Skinner, Charles Previn m/ly Harold Adamson, Jimmy McHugh
☆ *Deanna Durbin*, Herbert Marshall, Gail Patrick, Arthur Treacher, Helen Parrish, Marcia Mae Jones, William Frawley
'Another Durbin smash ... will mop up at the b.o.' – *Variety*
♫ original story (Marcella Burke, Frederick Kohner); Joseph Valentine; Frank Skinner, Charles Previn

The Mad Adventures of 'Rabbi' Jacob:

see *Les Aventures de Rabbi Jacob*

The Mad Bomber *

US 1972 91m Movielab
Scotia-Barber/College (Bert I. Gordon)
▬

A detective tries to track down a bomber who is killing people by dynamiting buildings in Los Angeles in order to punish society.
Low-budget thriller, effective in a harsh and unpolished way.
wd Bert I. Gordon *story* Marc Behm m Michel Mention ed Gene Ruggiero
☆ Vince Edwards, Chuck Connors, Neville Brand, Christina Hart, Faith Quabius
'An attempt not to be sneezed at.' – *Tom Milne, MFB*
† The film was cut to 87m for its British release.

'A Desperate Man. An Ambitious Reporter. A Situation Gone Mad.'

Mad City **

US 1997 114m Technicolor
Warner/Punch (Arnold and Anne Kopelson)
▭ ▬ ⊘ ⌒

To aid his slipping career, a reporter attempts to manipulate the accidental shooting of a museum security guard into an attention-grabbing television event.
Deft satire on the live television media circus that accompanies modern-day crime and terrorism; in part, it was suggested by the Waco siege in 1993, and is also an updating of Billy Wilder's Ace in the Hole (qv).
w Tom Matthews d Costa-Gavras ph Patrick Blossier m Thomas Newman pd Catherine Hardwicke ed Françoise Bonnot
☆ John Travolta, Dustin Hoffman, Mia Kirshner, Alan Alda, Robert Prosky, Blythe Danner, William Atherton, Ted Levine
'Despite its easy social conscience, the movie is often hilarious and zeroes in on an essential, heartless truth about journalism.' – *David Tse, Sight and Sound*
† The film did poorly at the US box-office, taking around $10.4m.

'They don't take no bull.'

Mad Cows

GB 1999 90m Technicolor
Entertainment/Capitol/Newmarket/Flashlight (Frank Mannion, Aaron Simpson)
Jailed for shoplifting, an Australian woman breaks out of prison in order to get even with the uncaring, aristocratic father of her child and to stop the baby being adopted.
A failed farce that tempts its cast into overacting whenever possible, which is made worse by the clichéd directorial style, full of meaningless flourishes.
w Sara Sugarman, Sasha Hails *novel* Kathy Lette d Sara Sugarman ph Pierre Aim m Mark Thomas pd Joseph Nemec III ed John Jympson
☆ Anna Friel, Joanna Lumley, Anna Massey, Greg Wise, Phyllida Law, John Standing, Nicholas Woodeson, Prunella Scales, Jodie Kidd, Sophie Dahl
'So astonishingly bad it made me break out in a thin film of cold sweat.' – *Peter Bradshaw, Guardian*
'A third-rate Carry On farce that will only make you weep and wonder: how did they ever get the money to make a film as bad as this?' – *Cosmo Landesman, Sunday Times*

'She knew the ecstasy and terror of loving him!'

The Mad Doctor

US 1941 90m bw
Paramount (George Arthur)
GB title: *A Date with Destiny*
A doctor marries wealthy women and then murders them.
Naïve melodrama of little interest except as a vehicle for its star.
w Howard J. Green d Tim Whelan ph Ted Tetzlaff m Victor Young
☆ Basil Rathbone, Ellen Drew, John Howard, Barbara Jo Allen, Ralph Morgan, Martin Kosleck

The Mad Doctor of Blood Island

Philippines/USA 1969 86m colour
Westland/Hemisphere (Eddie Romero)
▬
aka: *Tomb of the Living Dead*
Visitors to a Pacific island discover that a scientist searching for the secret of eternal life has created a vegetable monster.
Dreary horror that receives the inept treatment it deserves from all those concerned in its making.
w Reuben Candy d Gerardo de Leon, Eddie Romero ph Justo Paulino m Tito Arevalo
☆ John Ashley, Angelique Pettyjohn, Ronald Remy, Alicia Alonso
'The script is trite, the dramatic structure slack and the violence unconvincing.' – *Paul Joannides, MFB*

The Mad Doctor of Market Street

US 1942 61m bw
Universal
Shipwrecked people on a tropical island find that one of their number is a dangerous paranoiac.
Dull and misleadingly titled second-feature melodrama.
w Al Martin d Joseph H. Lewis
☆ Lionel Atwill, Nat Pendleton, Una Merkel, Claire Dodd

Mad Dog and Glory

US 1992 97m Technicolor
UIP/Universal (Barbara DeFina, Martin Scorsese)
▭ ▬ ⓠ ⌒

A timid and conventional Chicago cop is embarrassed when a gangster he inadvertently helps gives him a present of a beautiful woman for a week.
A movie that promises much but fails to deliver, quickly dwindling into something inconsequential, though it occasionally amuses; the problem lies in the passivity of its two central characters, including a female role that is totally inert.
w Richard Price d John McNaughton ph Robby Müller m Elmer Bernstein pd David Chapman ed Craig McKay, Elena Maganini
☆ Robert DeNiro, Uma Thurman, Bill Murray, David Caruso, Mike Starr, Tom Towles, Kathy Baker
'A pleasurably offbeat picture that manages the rare trick of being both charming and edgy.' – *Variety*
'Price's macho fantasy smells way past its dwell-by date.' – *Ian Penman, Sight and Sound*

Mad Dog Coll

US 1961 87m bw
Columbia-Warner/Thalia (Edward Schreiber)
Biopic about a violent gangster of the 1930s.
Predictable low-budget exploitation movie, offering new insights into the times and the vicious mobsters it bred.
w Edward Schreiber *story* Leo Lieberman d Burt Balaban ph Gayne Reschner m Stu Phillips ad Richard Sylbert ed Ralph Rosenblum
☆ John Davis Chandler, Neil Nephew, Brooke Hayward, Jerry Orbach, Telly Savalas, Vincent Gardenia, Gene Hackman

Mad Dog Time: see *Trigger Happy*

Mad Dogs and Englishmen

GB 1995 97m Technicolor
Entertainment/Movie Screen/Moor Street (Peter Watson-Wood, Nigel Thomas)
▭
An aristocratic drug addict is targeted by a corrupt cop who wants her dead.
Dim, daft thriller that becomes ever-more risible as it continues.
w Tim Sewell d Henry Cole ph John Peters m Barrie Guard pd Tony Stringer ed Lionel Selwyn, Simon Hilton
☆ Elizabeth Hurley, C. Thomas Howell, Joss Ackland, Claire Bloom, Frederick Treves, Andrew Connolly, Jeremy Brett, Louise Delamere
'Baffling to the point of boredom, this British thriller is as gripping as KY Jelly.' – *Empire*

The Mad Game

US 1933 73m bw
Fox
A gangster turns stool pigeon to round up kidnappers.
Fairly lively crime melodrama.
w William Conselman, Henry Johnson d Irving Cummings
☆ Spencer Tracy, Claire Trevor, Ralph Morgan, J. Carrol Naish, John Miljan
'Enough romance and action to satisfy.' – *Variety*

'Adults Only! Censor's orders!'

The Mad Genius

US 1931 81m bw
Warner
A crippled puppeteer adopts a boy and makes him into a great dancer.
Curious variation on Trilby, filmed as Svengali the previous year with much the same cast. Not a great success: the script is dreadful.
w J. Grubb Alexander, Harvey Thew *play* The Idol by Martin Brown d Michael Curtiz ph Barney McGill ad Anton Grot
☆ John Barrymore, Marian Marsh, Donald Cook, Luis Alberni, Carmel Myers, Charles Butterworth, Boris Karloff, Frankie Darro
'Magnificent acting, but not the sort of thing that will panic the fans.' – *Variety*
† Many of the sets in this production had ceilings, ten years before the idea was supposed to have been invented for Citizen Kane.

The Mad Ghoul

US 1943 65m bw
Universal (Ben Pivar)
▭ ⓠ
A mad scientist needs fresh hearts to keep alive the victims of his experiments with a poison vapour.
Stagey, tasteless horror melodrama.
w Brenda Weisberg, Paul Gangelin *story* Hans Kraly d James Hogan ph Milton Krasner md Hans Salter
☆ George Zucco, David Bruce, Evelyn Ankers, Turhan Bey, Robert Armstrong, Charles McGraw, Milburn Stone

Mad Holiday

US 1936 72m bw
MGM
A rebellious film actor goes on a cruise and gets involved in a murder.
Spotty mystery comedy in which the elements don't really jell.
w Florence Ryerson, Edgar Allan Woolf *story* Murder in a Chinese Theatre by Joseph Santley d George B. Seitz
☆ Edmund Lowe, Elissa Landi, Edmund Gwenn, ZaSu Pitts, Ted Healy, Edgar Kennedy
'Very draggy ... largely a bore.' – *Variety*

Mad Little Island: see *Rockets Galore*

Mad Love **

US 1935 83m bw
MGM (John Considine Jnr)
GB title: *The Hands of Orlac*
A pianist loses his hands in an accident; a mad surgeon, in love with the pianist's wife, grafts on the hands of a murderer.
Absurd Grand Guignol done with great style which somehow does not communicate itself in viewer interest, only in cold admiration.
w Guy Endore, P. J. Wolfson, John Balderston *novel* The Hands of Orlac by Maurice Renard d Karl Freund ph Chester Lyons, Gregg Toland m Dmitri Tiomkin
☆ Colin Clive, Peter Lorre, Frances Drake, Ted Healy, Edward Brophy, Isabel Jewell, Sara Haden
'The results in screen potency are disappointing ... will probably do fair biz.' – *Variety*
'Mr Lorre cuts deeply into the darkness of the morbid brain.' – *New York Times*

Mad Love

US 1995 95m Technicolor
Buena Vista (David Manson)
▭ ▬ ⓠ
An inhibited youth runs off with a lively girl whose behaviour soon becomes unbalanced.
A road movie about a manic depressive that is only occasionally interesting; neither of its main characters attains any individuality.
w Paula Milne d Antonia Bird ph Fred Tammes m Andy Roberts pd David Brisbin ed Jeff Freeman
☆ Chris O'Donnell, Drew Barrymore, Matthew Lillard, Richard Chaim, Robert Nadir, Joan Allen, Jude Ciccolella, Amy Sakasitz
'There's a half-decent road movie desperate to break free, but it gets stuck in a mire of fatuous slush.' – *Empire*

The Mad Magician

US 1954 72m bw
Columbia (Bryan Foy)
A magician's star-struck inventor murders his employer and several others who stand between him and the big time.
Hokey horror flick set in the eighties and originally shown in 3-D.
w Crane Wilbur d John Brahm ph Bert Glennon m Emil Newman
☆ Vincent Price, Mary Murphy, Eva Gabor, John Emery, Patrick O'Neal

The Mad Martindales

US 1942 55m bw
Walter Morosco/TCF
In 1900 San Francisco, an eccentric family gets out of debt.
The star's last film for a major studio is a filler of unrelieved tedium.
w Francis Edward Faragoh d Alfred Werker
☆ Jane Withers, Alan Mowbray, Marjorie Weaver, Jimmy Lydon, Byron Barr, George Reeves

---

Mad Masquerade: see *Washington Masquerade*

Mad Max *

Australia 1979 100m Eastmancolor Todd-AO 35

Warner/Mad Max Pty (Byron Kennedy)

In the future, motor cycle gangs combat the police.

Violent extravaganza with no real merit save its enthusiasm for destruction of both bikes and bodies.

w James McCausland, George Miller d George Miller ph David Eggby m Brian May ad Jon Dowding ed Tony Paterson, Cliff Hayes

☆ Mel Gibson, Joanne Samuel, Hugh Keays-Byrne, Steve Bisley

'Ruthless ... Savage ... Spectacular'

Mad Max 2 *

Australia 1981 96m colour Panavision

Warner/Kennedy Miller Entertainment (Byron Kennedy)

US title: *The Road Warrior*

A shortage of petrol causes all-out war between police and bikers.

Not much more than a retread of the above, but a more expensive, spectacular and violent one.

w Terry Hayes, George Miller, Brian Hannant d George Miller ph Dean Semler m Brian May ad Graham Walker ed David Stiven, Tim Wellburn, Michael Chirgwin

☆ Mel Gibson, Bruce Spence, Vernon Wells, Emil Minty

'Essentially just another display of vehicles smashing into each other.' – *David McGillivray, MFB*

Mad Max Beyond Thunderdome

Australia 1985 106m colour Panavision

Warner/Kennedy Miller (George Miller)

A drifter arrives in a desert town ruled by a ruthless woman.

More violent futuristic rubbish in similar vein to its predecessors.

w Terry Hayes, George Miller d George Miller and George Ogilvie ph Dean Semler m Maurice Jarre pd Graham Walker ed Richard Francis-Bruce

☆ Mel Gibson, Tina Turner, Angelo Rossitto, Helen Buday

The Mad Miss Manton *

US 1938 80m bw

RKO (Pandro S. Berman)

A zany socialite involves her friends in a murder mystery.

Mildly funny comedy thriller without too much of either, but a good example of the style of thirties craziness at its zenith.

w Philip G. Epstein d Leigh Jason ph Nicholas Musuraca m Roy Webb

☆ Barbara Stanwyck, Henry Fonda, Sam Levene, Frances Mercer, Stanley Ridges, Whitney Bourne, Hattie McDaniel, Miles Mander

'Something ground out by people in a desperate mood.' – *Pauline Kael, 70s*

The Mad Monkey

Spain 1990 108m Eastmancolor Panavision

Hobo/Iberoamericana Films/Emmanuel Schlumberger (Andres Vincente Gomez)

original title: *El Mono Loco*

A screenwriter becomes involved with a young, incestuous brother and sister.

Ridiculous farrago of sex and drugs, devoid of sense and sensuality.

w Fernando Trueba, Manolo Matji novel *The Dream of the Mad Monkey* by Christopher Frank d Fernando Trueba ph Jose Luis Alcaine m Antoine Duhamel ad Pierre-Louis Thevenet ed Carmen Frias

☆ Jeff Goldblum, Miranda Richardson, Anemone, Dexter Fletcher, Daniel Ceccaldi, Liza Walker, Jerome Natali, Arielle Dombasle, Micaela Sebastian

The Mad Monster

US 1942 77m bw

Sigmund Neufeld/PRC

A mad scientist injects wolf blood into a man, who goes around at night killing people.

Inept and uncontrolled shocker, the kind of thing that gives horror films a bad name.

w Fred Myton d Sam Newfield

☆ George Zucco, Johnny Downs, Glenn Strange, Anne Nagel

Mad Monster Party

👫 US 1967 94m Eastmancolor Animagic

Embassy/Videocraft (Arthur Rankin Jnr)

Baron von Frankenstein invites Dracula, the Mummy, the Werewolf, the Hunchback of Notre Dame and other monsters to a party to celebrate his new invention.

A children's film that uses stop-motion animated figures, it is harmless but trivial entertainment.

w Len Korobkin, Harvey Kurtzman story Arthur Rankin Jnr d Jules Bass m Maury Laws m/ly Maury Laws, Jules Bass sp character design: Jack Davis

☆ Featuring the voices of Boris Karloff, Phyllis Diller, Alan Swift, Gale Garnett

The Mad Parade

US 1931 62m bw

Liberty/Paramount

A story told by women about the effect of the war on their sex.

Not really strong enough to be taken seriously, this was played as a novelty.

w Henry McCarthy and Frank R. Conkin story Gertrude Orr and Doris Malloy d William Beaudine

☆ Evelyn Brent, Irene Rich, Louise Fazenda, Lilyan Tashman, Marceline Day

'Chances for disappointing business greater than the opposite.' – *Variety*

The Mad Room

US 1969 92m Berkeley-Pathé

Columbia/Norman Mauer

A companion kills her wealthy employer so that her mentally retarded brother and sister will have a home.

Tasteless remake of Ladies in Retirement, in the brutalized vein which audiences are supposed to want. In modern dress and sharp locations, it succeeds only in being nauseating.

w Bernard Girard, A. Z. Martin d Bernard Girard ph Harry Stradling Jnr m Dave Grusin

☆ Stella Stevens, Shelley Winters, Skip Ward, Carol Cole, Severn Darden

Mad Wednesday *

US 1947 79m bw

Howard Hughes

aka: *The Sin of Harold Diddlebock*

A middle-aged book-keeper is sacked and goes on the town.

Woolly and unattractive farce which proved something of a disaster for all the talents concerned but historically is of considerable interest. It begins with an excerpt from The Freshman and continues to comic adventures with a lion.

ph Robert Pittack m Werner Richard Heymann wd/pd Preston Sturges (re-edited by others)

☆ Harold Lloyd, Jimmy Conlin, Raymond Walburn, Franklin Pangborn, Al Bridge, Margaret Hamilton, Edgar Kennedy

† It has been released on video in Sturges' original 90m version, which was later cut to 79m by Howard Hughes.

Madagascar Skin

GB 1995 93m colour

BFI/Channel 4/Dan (Julie Baines)

A shy young homosexual, whose face bears a large birthmark in the shape of Madagascar, forms an uneasy relationship with a burly older man, whom he finds on a lonely beach buried up to his neck in sand.

A thin, almost arid tale of an unlikely love, well acted, but directed with a greater interest in visual compositions than in people.

wd Chris Newby ph Oliver Curtis pd Paul Cross ed Chris Newby, Annabel Ware

☆ Bernard Hill, John Hannah, Mark Anthony, Mark Petit, Danny Earl

'An eccentric and unselfconscious comedy which will surprise as much as it satisfies.' – *Empire*

Madam Satan *

US 1930 105m bw

MGM (C. B. de Mille)

When her husband strays, a socialite disguises herself as a mysterious *femme fatale* and wins him back.

Abysmal comedy in which both director and principals appear frozen until the closing reels present a crazy, spectacular party on a dirigible which crashes but allows a happy ending.

w Jeanie Macpherson, Gladys Unger, Elsie Janis d C. B. de Mille ph Harold Rosson m Herbert Stothart m/ly Clifford Grey, Herbert Stothart, Elsie Janis, Jack King ad Cedric Gibbons, Mitchell Leisen ed Anne Bauchens

☆ Kay Johnson, Reginald Denny, Lillian Roth, Roland Young

'A strange conglomeration of unreal incidents that are sometimes set forth with no little technical skill.' – *Mordaunt Hall, New York Times*

Madame: see *Madame Sans-Gêne (1962)*

Madame Bovary *

France 1933 120m bw

NSF (Robert Aron)

The bored wife of a provincial doctor seeks excitement and finds only disappointment and death.

A flawed version of Flaubert's novel, not helped by having had an hour cut from it before its original release, so that it has lost some of its characterization and continuity; the stylized acting by a cast drawn largely from the theatre, in contrast to the reality of the settings, adds to a feeling of dislocation.

wd Jean Renoir novel Gustave Flaubert ph Jean Bachelet m Darius Milhaud ad Robert Bys ed Marguerite Renoir

☆ Max Dearly, Valentine Tessier, Pierre Renoir, Daniel Lecourtois, Fernand Fabre

'Whatever it is that French women have – Madame Bovary had more of it!'

Madame Bovary

US 1949 114m bw

MGM (Pandro S. Berman)

A passionate girl marries a dull husband, takes a lover, and commits suicide.

Dull, emasculated version of a classic.

w Robert Ardrey novel Gustave Flaubert d Vincente Minnelli ph Robert Planck m Miklos Rozsa ad Cedric Gibbons, Jack Martin Smith

☆ Jennifer Jones, Van Heflin, James Mason, Louis Jourdan, Christopher Kent, Gene Lockhart, Gladys Cooper, John Abbott, George Zucco

'If you hadn't read the book, you wouldn't guess what it was about from this film.' – *Pauline Kael, 70s*

† Previously filmed in 1932 as *Unholy Love*.

& art direction

Madame Bovary

France 1991 120m colour

Arrow/MK2/CED/FR3 (Marin Karmitz)

A bored housewife with social pretensions, married to a doctor, indulges in self-destructive behaviour.

A reasonably faithful, but lifeless, adaptation, which seems as stultifying as the middle-class existence it portrays.

novel Gustave Flaubert d Claude Chabrol ph Jean Rabier m Matthieu Chabrol ad Michèle Abbé ed Monique Fardoulis

☆ Isabelle Huppert, Jean-François Balmer, Christophe Malavoy, Jean Yanne, Lucas Belvaux, Christiane Minazzoli

'Respectful, luxurious and eminently forgettable.' – *Sight and Sound*

'One of the world's magnificent romances of great, unselfish love!'

Madame Butterfly

US 1932 88m bw

Paramount (B. P. Schulberg)

A Japanese geisha commits hara kiri when an American lieutenant passes her up for a western girl.

Drearily modernized version of the opera without its music; an odd idea to say the least.

w Josephine Lovett, Joseph M. March story John Luther Long play David Belasco d Marion Gering ph David Abel md W. Franke Harling

☆ Sylvia Sidney, Cary Grant, Charlie Ruggles, Sandor Kallay, Irving Pichel, Helen Jerome Eddy

'The long-drawn tragedy might be bearable if it were expressed in music or poetry, without any such embellishment it is apt to be painfully pathetic.' – *The Times*

'Travels slow and makes for only fair entertainment.' – *Variety*

Madame Butterfly **

France/Japan/Germany/GB 1995 134m colour 'Scope

Blue Dolphin/Erato/Idéale/France3/Imalyre/VTCOM/Sony Classical (Daniel Toscan du Plantier, Pierre-Olivier Bardet)

In Japan in the early 1900s, an American naval officer casually marries and abandons a Japanese girl.

An effective and authentic-looking staging of the opera, acted and sung with conviction.

wd Frédéric Mitterrand opera Giacomo Puccini libretto Giuseppe Giacosa, Luigi Illica ph Philippe Welt md James Conlon ad Michel Glotz, Daniel Zalay, Michèle Abbe-Vannier, Taïeb Jellouli ed Luc Barnier

☆ Ying Huang, Richard Troxell, Ning Liang, Richard Cowan, Jing Ma Fan, Christopheren Nomura, Constance Hauman

'Mr and Mrs Miniver together again!'

Madame Curie *

US 1943 124m bw

MGM (Sidney Franklin)

The life and marriage of the woman who discovered radium.

Dignified and rather dull biopic which well exemplifies MGM's best production style of the forties.

w Paul Osborn, Paul H. Rameau book Eve Curie d Mervyn Le Roy ph Joseph Ruttenberg m Herbert Stothart ad Cedric Gibbons, Paul Groesse

☆ Greer Garson, Walter Pidgeon, Henry Travers, Albert Basserman, Robert Walker, C. Aubrey Smith, Dame May Whitty, Victor Francen, Elsa Basserman, Reginald Owen, Van Johnson

'It achieves a notable triumph in making the discovery of a new element seem almost as glamorous as an encounter with Hedy Lamarr.' – *C. A. Lejeune*

& best picture; Joseph Ruttenberg; Herbert Stothart; Greer Garson; Walter Pidgeon; art direction

Madame De *

France/Italy 1953 102m bw

Franco-London/Indus/Rizzoli

US title: *The Earrings of Madame de*

Tragic misunderstandings arise when a society wife sells her earrings and tells her husband she has lost them.

Elegant, rather heavy-handed but superbly glossy extension of a fashionable novelette.

w Marcel Achard, Max Ophuls, Annette Wademant novel Louise de Vilmorin d Max Ophuls ph Christian Matras m Oscar Straus, Georges Van Parys ad Jean d'Eaubonne

☆ Charles Boyer, Danielle Darrieux, Vittorio de Sica, Lea di Lea, Jean Debucourt

Madame Dubarry **

Germany 1919 85m bw silent

Union-UFA

US title: *Passion*

The life and times of the glamorous courtesan of Louis XV.

Milestone silent film which introduced to the cinemas of America and Britain not only the subtleties of the European cinema but the more adaptable subtleties of a

---

key director, here dealing rather heavy-handedly with material which he should later have re-used.
w Fred Orbing, Hans Kraly d Ernst Lubitsch
ph Theodor Sparkuhl
☆ Pola Negri, Emil Jannings, Harry Liedtke, Reinhöld Schünzel

Madame Dubarry
US 1934 77m bw
Warner
The life of the legendary courtesan at Versailles.
Utterly unpersuasive but sometimes decorative historical charade.
w Edward Chodorov d William Dieterle
☆ Dolores del Rio, Reginald Owen, Victor Jory, Anita Louise, Osgood Perkins, Verree Teasdale
'A lavish but not particularly distinguished production.' – *Variety*

Madame Pimpernel: see *Paris Underground*

Madame Racketeer
US 1932 68m bw
Paramount
Tactics of a middle-aged lady larcenist.
Light crime comedy drama, not bad but overlookable.
w Malcolm Stuart Boylan, Harvey Gates
d Alexander Hall, Harry Wagstaff Gribble
☆ Alison Skipworth, Richard Bennett, Evalyn Knapp, George Raft, Robert McWade
'The subtle high comedy that flows so gently through the script is likely to pass over the hats of the peasantry.' – *Variety*

Madame Rosa
France 1977 120m Eastmancolor
Lira Films
📧
original title: La Vie Devant Soi
An elderly Jewish prostitute runs an unofficial nursery school and cares especially for a fourteen-year-old Arab.
Splendidly acted but basically dreary fable twisted from a novel which took the child's point of view.
wd Moshe Mizrahi *novel* Emile Ajar ph Nestor Almendros m Philippe Sarde
☆ Simone Signoret, Claude Dauphin, Samy Ben Youb
🎗 best foreign film

Madame Sans-Gêne
US 1925 110m bw silent
Paramount
During the French Revolution, Napoleon plays Cupid to a laundry-maid and her lover.
The story formed the basis of one of Gloria Swanson's last successes; but it was made in France and did not have the zip of her Hollywood productions.
w Forrest Halsey d Léonce Perret
☆ Charles de Roche, Emile Drain, Gloria Swanson

Madame Sans-Gêne
France/Italy/Spain 1962 100m Technirama
TCF/Cine Alliance/Gesi/Champion/Agata (Maleno Malenotti)
GB and US title: *Madame*
Historical romp based on an old theatrical warhorse.
Pretty stilted in this version; especially when dubbed.
w Henri Jeanson and others *play* Victorien Sardou d Christian-Jaque ph Roberto Gerardi
m Francesco Lavagnino
☆ Sophia Loren, Robert Hossein, Julien Bertheau, Marina Berti

Madame Sousatzka
GB 1988 122m Eastmancolor
Curzon/Sousatzka Productions (Robin Dalton)
📧 📧 ⊙ 📀
A piano teacher is reluctant to let go of her star pupil.
A parade of eccentrics is mixed with a little domestic drama, but it all remains inert and uninteresting.
w Ruth Prawer Jhabvala, John Schlesinger
novel Bernice Rubens d John Schlesinger ph Nat Crosby m Gerald Gouriet pd Luciana Arrighi
ed Peter Honess
☆ Shirley MacLaine, Peggy Ashcroft, Twiggy, Shabana Azmi, Leigh Lawson, Geoffrey Bayldon, Lee Montague, Robert Rietty, Navin Chowdhry
'No amount of technical finesse, or polite musical trappings, can make the film seem other than an unswallowable, old-fashioned, overlong slab of confectionery.' – *Geoff Brown, MFB*

Madame Spy
US 1934 70m bw
Universal
Russian and Austrian spies are married to each other.
Absurd melodrama which never gets a grip.
w William Hurlbut from a German film, *Under False Flags* d Karl Freund
☆ Fay Wray, Nils Asther, Edward Arnold, John Miljan, David Torrence
'Story too hopeless to mean money anywhere.' – *Variety*

Madame Spy
US 1942 63m bw
Universal
A glamorous Nazi spy turns out to be an American secret agent.
Elementary espionage stuff without much in the way of plot development.
w Lynn Riggs and Clarence Upson Young d Roy William Neill
☆ Constance Bennett, Don Porter, John Litel, Edward Brophy, John Eldredge

Madame X *
US 1929 95m bw
MGM
⊙
TV title: *Absinthe*
After an accidental death, a wealthy woman disappears and goes down in the world; at a subsequent murder trial she is defended by her unrecognizing son.
Two silent versions (with Dorothy Donnelly and Pauline Frederick) had been made of this old theatrical warhorse; two sound versions followed this one. The thing defies criticism.
w Willard Mack *play* Alexandre Bisson d Lionel Barrymore
☆ Ruth Chatterton, Raymond Hackett, Mitchell Lewis, Sidney Toler, Carroll Nye, Lewis Stone, Richard Carle
'Works like this confound the reformers, elevate the name of pictures, and tell the world that there is an art in film making.' – *Variety*
🎗 Lionel Barrymore; Ruth Chatterton

Madame X *
US 1937 72m bw
MGM (James K. McGuinness)
Competent remake with an excellent cast.
w John Meehan d Sam Wood ph John B. Seitz
m David Snell ad Cedric Gibbons ed Frank Hull
☆ Gladys George, John Beal, Warren William, Reginald Owen, Lynne Carver, Henry Daniell, Emma Dunn, Ruth Hussey, George Zucco, William Henry
'An upper bracketer when played with a strong companion.' – *Variety*
'A fine old play, dated and outmoded. Audiences will leave the theatre expecting to find the coachman with horse and buggy.' – *Variety*

'One man drove her to it – one man tempted her – one man degraded her – one man defended her!'
Madame X
US 1965 100m Technicolor
Universal/Ross Hunter/Eltee
📧
An elaborately dressed remake which suffered from a wooden lead; the more expensive the production, the more obvious the holes in the plot and the psychology.
w Jean Holloway d David Lowell Rich
ph Russell Metty m Frank Skinner
☆ Lana Turner, John Forsythe, Ricardo Montalban, Constance Bennett, Burgess Meredith, Keir Dullea, Virginia Grey, Warren Stevens
'One is free to enjoy a luxurious wallow in emotions that are all the more enjoyable for having no connection whatever with reality.' – *Brenda Davies*

The Madcap Adventures of Mr Toad: see *Ichabod and Mr Toad*

Das Mädchen Rosemarie: see *The Girl Rosemarie*

Made for Each Other *
US 1938 90m bw
David O. Selznick
📧 ⊙
Problems of a lawyer and his new wife culminate in the near-death of their infant son.
Smooth star tearjerker.
w Jo Swerling d John Cromwell ph Leon Shamroy m Hugo Friedhofer, David Buttolph
pd William Cameron Menzies *theme* Oscar Levant
☆ Carole Lombard, James Stewart, Charles Coburn, Lucile Watson, Harry Davenport, Eddie Quillan, Esther Dale, Louise Beavers
'Made to order for strong box office.' – *Variety*

Made for Each Other *
US 1971 107m DeLuxe
TCF/Wylde Films (Roy Townshend)
Romance between two New Yorkers with inferiority complexes.
Elongated cabaret sketch, a Brooklynesque comedy of flashy brilliance but limited general interest.
w Renée Taylor, Joe Bologna d Robert B. Bean
ph William Storz
☆ Renée Taylor, Joe Bologna

'At the sperm-bank, she asked for a tall, intelligent, black man. One out of three ain't bad.'
Made in America
US 1993 110m Technicolor
Warner/Stonebridge/Kalola/Regency/Canal (Arnon Milchan, Michael Douglas, Rick Bieber)
📧 📧 ⊙ 📀
A black teenager, born by artificial insemination, discovers that her father is a white car-salesman with a crass manner.
An occasionally amusing comedy, owing more to the performances than the script, which skirts all the racial issues it raises to settle for a comforting situation comedy.
w Holly Goldberg Sloan *story* Marcia Brandwynne, Nadine Schiff d Richard Benjamin
ph Ralf Bode m Mark Isham pd Evelyn Sakash
ed Jacqueline Cambas
☆ Whoopi Goldberg, Ted Danson, Will Smith, Nia Long, Paul Rodriguez, Jennifer Tilly, Peggy Rea, Clyde Kusatsu
'It's a likeable effort, good enough for a sultry summer evening at the multiplex when the film you came to see is sold out.' – *Sight and Sound*

Made in Heaven
GB 1952 81m Technicolor
Rank/Fanfare
Married couples compete for the Dunmow Flitch.
Easy-going family comedy which aims to be liked.
w William Douglas Home d John Paddy Carstairs
ph Geoffrey Unsworth m Ronald Hanmer
☆ David Tomlinson, Petula Clark, Sonja Ziemann, A. E. Matthews, Charles Victor, Sophie Stewart, Richard Wattis, Athene Seyler

Made in Heaven
US 1987 103m colour
Rudolph-Blocker/Lorimar (Raynold Gideon, Bruce A. Evans, David Blocker)
📧
A boy is sent back from heaven to find his lost love.
Droopy fantasy on the lines of Here Comes Mr Jordan but without the wit.
w Bruce A. Evans, Raynold Gideon d Alan Rudolph ph Jan Kiesser m Mark Isham pd Paul Peters ed Tom Walls
☆ Timothy Hutton, Kelly McGillis, Maureen Stapleton, Don Murray, Marj Dusay, Debra Winger

Made in Hong Kong *
Hong Kong 1997 109m colour
ICA/Shu Kei's Creative Workshop/Nicetop/Team Work (Andy Lau, Doris Yang)
original title: *Xianggang Zhizao*
A gangster's debt collector believes he is haunted by the spirit of a dead schoolgirl, as he tries to raise money for a kidney transplant for the teenager he loves.
Nihilistic thriller of rootless young people on the edge; it de-glamorises violence and crime and doesn't leave its audience feeling good about life.
wd Fruit Chan ph O Sing-pui, Lam Wah-chuen
m Lam Wah-chuen ad Ma Ka-kwan ed Tin Sam-fat cos Tin Muk

☆ Sam Lee Chan-Sam, Wenbers Li Tung-Chuen, Neiky Yim, Amy Tam, Chan Tat-Yee, Doris Chow, Chang Sang
'A portrait of angry youth that's as hypnotic as it's often maddeningly kinetic.' – *Derek Elley, Variety*
† The film was made for $80,000, using non-professional actors, and utilising the short-ends of film stock from movies that Chan had worked on over the years as an assistant director.

Made on Broadway
US 1933 65m bw
MGM
GB title: *The Girl I Made*
A public relations man deals with the mayor's dirty linen.
Flat and unconvincing political comedy drama.
w Gene Markey *book Public Relations* by Courteney Terrett d Harry Beaumont
☆ Robert Montgomery, Sally Eilers, Madge Evans, Eugene Pallette, C. Henry Gordon, Jean Parker

Madeleine *
GB 1949 114m bw
GFD/David Lean/Cineguild (Stanley Haynes)
📧
In Victorian Glasgow a well-to-do young woman is accused of murdering her lover, but the verdict is 'not proven'.
Dramatically dead because of its ambiguous ending, this lavish and good-looking treatment of a cause célèbre was a mistake for all concerned, but its incidental pleasures are considerable.
w Nicholas Phipps, Stanley Haynes d David Lean
ph Guy Green m William Alwyn pd John Bryan
cos Margaret Furse
☆ Ann Todd, Leslie Banks, Elizabeth Sellars, Ivor Barnard, Ivan Desny, Norman Wooland, Edward Chapman, Barbara Everest, André Morell, Barry Jones, Jean Cadell, John Laurie, Eugene Deckers

'In an old house in Paris that was covered in vines, lived twelve little girls in two straight lines.'
Madeline *
👥👥 US 1998 90m Technicolor
Sony Pictures/TriStar Pictures/Jaffilms/Pancho Kohner/Saul Cooper
📧 📧 ⊙ 📀
In Paris, a girl rescues the son of an ambassador and ensures that the orphanage in which she lives is not shut down.
Energetic children's film of resourceful and plucky girls; adults may find it a little trying before the end.
w Mark Levin, Jennifer Flackett *book* Ludwig Bemelmans d Daisy von Scherler Mayer
ph Pierre Aim m Michel Legrand pd Hugo Luczyy-Wyhowski ed Jeffrey Wolf
☆ Frances McDormand, Nigel Hawthorne, Hatty Jones, Stéphane Audran, Ben Daniels, Arturo Venegas, Katia Caballero, Chantal Neuwirth, Kristian de la Osa
'Witless and dramatically inept.' – *Cosmo Landesman, Sunday Times*

Mademoiselle Docteur *
GB 1937 84m bw
Grafton/Trafalgar (Max Schach)
A German lady spy falls for a British agent.
War melodrama vaguely based on fact and later remade as Fräulein Doktor.
w Jacques Natanson, Marcel Achard, Ernest Betts
d Edmond Greville ph Otto Heller
☆ Dita Parlo, John Loder, Erich von Stroheim, Claire Luce, Gyles Isham, Clifford Evans, John Abbott
'Even a thriller cannot thrill unless the characters are established in our imaginations, and the packed plot of this film allows them no chance.' – *Graham Greene*

Mademoiselle Fifi *
US 1944 69m bw
RKO (Val Lewton)
⊙
During the Franco-Prussian war a stagecoach is held up because a prostitute, despite the urging of her fellow passengers, refuses to sleep with a Prussian officer. When she gives in, they shun her, and she kills him.
Interesting low budget version of a story which inspired many films.
w Josef Mischel, Peter Ruric *stories* Boule de Suif/Mademoiselle Fifi by Guy de Maupassant

---

d Robert Wise *ph* Harry Wild *m* Werner Heymann

☆ Simone Simon, Kurt Kreuger, John Emery, Alan Napier, Jason Robards Sr, Norma Varden, Helen Freeman, Fay Helm

'There is a gallant, fervent quality about the whole picture, faults and all, which gives it a peculiar kind of life and likeableness, and which signifies that there is one group of men working in Hollywood who have neither lost nor taken care to conceal the purity of their hope and intention.' – *James Agee*

Mademoiselle France: see Reunion in France

Madhouse *
GB 1974 92m Eastmancolor
AIP/Amicus (Milton Subotsky)

A reluctant horror actor makes a comeback and finds himself involved in a series of grisly murders.
In-jokey horror piece with clips from old AIP chillers; quite likeable.
w Greg Morrison *novel* Devilday by Angus Hall *d* Jim Clark *ph* Ray Parslow *m* Douglas Gamley
☆ Vincent Price, Peter Cushing, Robert Quarry, Adrienne Corri, Natasha Pyne, Linda Hayden, Barry Dennen

Madhouse
US 1990 90m colour
Rank/Orion/A Boy of the Year (Leslie Dixon)

Unwanted friends and neighbours move in as house guests of a young couple.
Remarkably unfunny domestic comedy, directed with a heavy hand.
wd Tom Ropelewski *ph* Denis Lewiston *m* David Newman *pd* Dan Leigh *ed* Michael Jablow
☆ John Larroquette, Kirstie Alley, Alison LaPlaca, John Diehl, Jessica Lundy, Bradley Gregg, Dennis Miller, Robert Ginty, Wayne Tippit

Madigan *
US 1968 100m Techniscope
Universal (Frank P. Rosenberg)

A Brooklyn police detective brings in a dangerous escaped criminal at the cost of his own life.
Lively, well-characterized police thriller with excellent locations.
w Henri Simoun, Abraham Polonsky *novel* The Commissioner by Richard Dougherty *d* Don Siegel *ph* Russell Metty *m* Don Costa
☆ Richard Widmark, Henry Fonda, Michael Dunn, Inger Stevens, Harry Guardino, James Whitmore, Susan Clark, Steve Ihnat, Don Stroud, Sheree North, Warren Stevens, Raymond St Jacques
† The character was later resurrected for a TV series also starring Richard Widmark.

Madison Avenue
US 1961 94m bw Cinemascope
TCF (Bruce Humberstone)

An advertising executive plans to revenge himself on his treacherous boss.
Predictable melodrama with an adequate plot but dismal acting and presentation.
w Norman Corwin *novel* The Build-Up Boys by Jeremy Kirk *d* Bruce Humberstone *ph* Charles G. Clarke *m* Harry Sukman
☆ Dana Andrews, Jeanne Crain, Eleanor Parker, Eddie Albert, Howard St John, Henry Daniell, Kathleen Freeman
'Simply nowhere near grand enough.' – *MFB*

'His Majesty was all powerful and all knowing. But he wasn't quite all there.'
'First he lost America. Now he's losing his mind.'
The Madness of King George ***
GB 1994 107m Technicolor
Rank/Samuel Goldwyn/Channel 4/Close Call (Stephen Evans, David Parfitt)

In the 1780s, King George III's behaviour becomes more and more eccentric and unbalanced until he is diagnosed as mad and comes close to losing his power.
Entertaining drama of the eccentricities of royalty, speculating that the King's problem may have been caused by the illness porphyria, and which also obliquely questions the point of the monarchy. Directed with a sense of pace and an excellent eye for the inequalities of society, even within palaces, it gains immeasurably by the superb performance of

Hawthorne in the title role, honed by his having played it so often on stage.
w Alan Bennett *play* The Madness of George III by Alan Bennett *d* Nicholas Hytner *ph* Andrew Dunn *m* George Fenton, Handel *pd* Ken Adam *ed* Tariq Anwar
☆ Nigel Hawthorne, Helen Mirren, Ian Holm, Amanda Donohoe, Rupert Graves, Rupert Everett, Jim Carter, Geoffrey Palmer, John Wood, Jeremy Child, Cyril Shaps
'Essentially it is Hawthorne's triumph and no one else's, since he provides the holding centre without which the rest might have seemed an ephemeral romp, uncertain as to whether to comment on its own times or ours and drifting towards parody in both instances.' – *Derek Malcolm, Guardian*
† The title of the play, The Madness of George III, was not used in case audiences thought it was the third film in a series (just as audiences are said to have come out of Henry V regretting that they had missed the first four films).
🏆 Ken Adam
🏆 Nigel Hawthorne; Helen Mirren; Alan Bennett
🏆 best British picture; Nigel Hawthorne

Madness of the Heart
GB 1949 105m bw
GFD/Two Cities (Richard Wainwright)

A blind girl marries a French aristocrat and has to cope with a jealous neighbour.
Heavily disguised version of the Rebecca theme, with a happy ending after many alarums and excursions, most of them irrelevant. As film-making, very thin.
wd Charles Bennett *novel* Flora Sandstrom *ph* Desmond Dickinson *m* Allan Gray
☆ Margaret Lockwood, Paul Dupuis, Kathleen Byron, Maxwell Reed

Madonna of the Seven Moons
GB 1944 110m bw
GFD/Gainsborough (R. J. Minney)

Affected by childhood rape, a demure lady has a second life as a daring gypsy.
Novelettish balderdash killed stone dead by stilted presentation; but highly successful in its day.
w Roland Pertwee, Brock Williams *novel* Margery Lawrence *d* Arthur Crabtree *ph* Jack Cox
☆ Phyllis Calvert, Stewart Granger, Patricia Roc, Peter Glenville, John Stuart, Jean Kent, Nancy Price, Peter Murray Hill, Reginald Tate
'One of the most diverting British films of the forties.' – *Richard Roud*
'The purplest production English cinema has yet achieved.' – *Time and Tide*

The Madonna's Secret
US 1946 79m bw
Stephen Auer/Republic

Women attracted to a Parisian painter are all found dead.
Slow-moving mystery which manages to remain suspenseful.
w Bradbury Foote, William Thiele *d* William Thiele
☆ Francis Lederer, Gail Patrick, Ann Rutherford, Edward Ashley, Linda Stirling, John Litel

'Killing Is As Easy As Stealing Candy From A Baby'
La Madre Muerta
Spain 1993 107m colour
Metro Tartan/Gasteizko Zinema (Juanma Bajo Ulloa)

A petty crook kidnaps a mentally retarded woman whom he recognizes as the witness to his murder of her mother a decade earlier, but is unable to bring himself to kill her.
An oddly disturbing drama, of casual deaths and murky happenings suffused with a melodramatic religiosity; no doubt its director will go on to better films.
w Juanma Bajo Ulloa, Eduardo Bajo Ulloa *d* Juanma Bajo Ulloa *ph* Javier Aguirresarobe *m* Bingen Mendizabal *ad* Satur Idaretta *ed* Pablo Blanco
☆ Karra Elejalde, Lio, Ana Alvarez, Silvia Marsó
'As a dark thriller it is remarkably unpleasant.' – *George Perry*

Madron
US/Israel 1970 93m colour
Four Star Excelsior/GBC/Edric/Isracine/Zev Braun (Emanuel Henigman, Eric Weaver)

A nun, the only survivor of a massacre, attempts to escape the attentions of Apache warriors with the aid of a passing gunfighter.
A downbeat Western that concentrates on the contrasting characters of its two protagonists, but which fails to make the clash of personalities interesting. It was mostly filmed in the Negev Desert, which accounts for the uninteresting scenery.
w Edward Chappell, Leo McMahon *d* Jerry Hopper *ph* Marcel Grignon, Adam Greenberg *m* Riz Ortolani *ad* Robert Ramsey *ed* Renzo Lucidi
☆ Richard Boone, Leslie Caron, Gabi Amrani

The Madwoman of Chaillot *
GB 1969 142m Technicolor
Warner/Commonwealth United (Ely Landau)

An eccentric Parisian lady has equally eccentric friends, but her real life is in the past.
A highly theatrical whimsy which somewhat lacks humour, this should never have been considered as a film, certainly not as an all-star extravaganza; but it was, and it falls flat on its face in the first reel of tedious conversation.
w Edward Anhalt *play* Jean Giraudoux *d* Bryan Forbes *ph* Claude Renoir, Burnett Guffey *m* Michael J. Lewis *pd* Ray Simm
☆ Katharine Hepburn, Yul Brynner, Danny Kaye, Edith Evans, Charles Boyer, Claude Dauphin, John Gavin, Paul Henreid, Nanette Newman, Oscar Homolka, Margaret Leighton, Giulietta Masina, Richard Chamberlain, Donald Pleasence, Fernand Gravet
'One finds oneself too often longing for the drop of the curtain.' – *Brenda Davies*
'The intentions are honourable – defeat is inevitable.' – *Rex Reed*
'One of Giraudoux's less good and most fragile plays has been rewritten, bloated with inept contemporary references, drawn out to gigantic proportions of humourless vacuity, and peopled with a barrelful of nonacting stars.' – *John Simon*
'The remnants of Giraudoux' slight, whimsical play can still be perceived in Edward Anhalt's vile modernization, and a lot of famous actors can be recognized even in the performances they give here.' – *Pauline Kael, New Yorker*

Maedchen in Uniform *
Germany 1931 90m bw
Deutsche Film-Gemeinschaft

aka: *Girls in Uniform*
A girl at a strict boarding school falls in love with one of the teachers and commits suicide.
Famous early stab at lesbianism, remade in 1958 with Romy Schneider and Lilli Palmer. Interesting for content, not style.
w F. D. Andam, Christa Winsloe *play* Gestern und Heute by Christa Winsloe *d* Leontine Sagan *ph* Reimar Kuntze *m* Hansen Milde-Meissner
☆ Dorothea Wieck, Ellen Schwannecke, Hertha Thiele, Emilie Lunde
'At once a strident warning against the consequences of Hitler's regime and the first truly radical lesbian film.' – *Time Out, 1981*

Il Maestro
Belgium/France 1989 92m Fujicolour
Man's Films/Flach Film/RTBF/BTR (Marion Hänsel, François Lepetit)
aka: *The Maestro*
Returning to Italy to conduct Madame Butterfly, a Jewish conductor reveals a wartime betrayal that brings on a breakdown.
Small-scale, overstretched drama.
wd Marion Hänsel *story* La Giacca Verde by Mario Soldati *ph* Acacio de Almeida *m* Frederick Devreese *ad* Ernita Frigato, Antonello Geleng
☆ Malcolm McDowell, Charles Aznavour, Andréa Ferréol, Francis Lemaire

El Maestro de Esgrima: see The Fencing Master

Il Maestro di Don Giovanni: see Crossed Swords

Maestro – Ma Non Troppo
French 1985 90m colour
Antenne 2

A provincial orchestral conductor is kidnapped to prevent him from performing at a concert for world peace.
Farcical attempt at political satire.
w Christian Watton, Serge Korber *d* Serge Korber *ph* André Dumaître, Bernard Dumont *m* Greco Casadesus *ed* Claude Dufour
☆ Alain Doutey, Sophie Barjac, Claude Villers, Joelle Guillaud, Jean Gaven, Jacques Spiesser, Jess Hahn, Clément Harari

Mafia!
US 1998 84m Technicolor
Buena Vista/Touchstone/Tapestry (Bill Badalato)

aka: *Jane Austen's Mafia*
Two brothers vie with one another to take over the leadership of a Mafia family from their ageing father.
A tired send-up of The Godfather trilogy and similar gangster movies; a few jokes might have helped.
w Jim Abrahams, Greg Norberg, Michael McManus *d* Jim Abrahams *ph* Steve Bridges *m* Gianni Frizzelli *pd* William Elliott *ed* Terry Stokes
☆ Jay Mohr, Billy Burke, Christina Applegate, Pamela Gidley, Olympia Dukakis, Lloyd Bridges, Jason Fuchs, Joe Viterelli, Tony Lo Bianco
'Has far more fart jokes than laughs.' – *Rob Mackie, Guardian*

The Maggie **
GB 1953 93m bw
Ealing (Michael Truman)
US title: *High and Dry*
An American businessman is tricked into sending his private cargo to a Scottish island on an old puffer in need of repair.
Mildly amusing comedy about the wily Scots; not the studio at its best, but pretty fair.
w William Rose *d* Alexander Mackendrick *ph* Gordon Dines *m* John Addison
☆ Paul Douglas, Alex Mackenzie, James Copeland, Abe Barker, Dorothy Alison, Hubert Gregg, Geoffrey Keen, Andrew Keir, Tommy Kearins

Magic
US 1978 107m Technicolor
TCF/Joseph E. Levine

A ventriloquist obsessed by his dummy is impelled to murder.
Pretentious and occasionally unpleasant version of an oft-told tale.
w William Goldman *novel* William Goldman *d* Richard Attenborough *ph* Victor J. Kemper *m* Jerry Goldsmith *pd* Terence Marsh
☆ Anthony Hopkins, Ann-Margret, Burgess Meredith, Ed Lauter, E. J. Andre, David Ogden Stiers
'The gloomily withdrawn Hopkins has no vulgarity in his soul – nothing that suggests any connection with the world of entertainment – and the picture grinds along.' – *New Yorker*

The Magic Bow
GB 1946 106m bw
GFD/Gainsborough (R. J. Minney)
Episodes in the life of the violin virtuoso Paganini.
Poor costumer, dramatically and historically unpersuasive.
w Norman Ginsburg, Roland Pertwee *novel* Manuel Komroff *d* Bernard Knowles *ph* Jack Cox *m* Paganini, Beethoven, Tartini, Phil Green, Henry Geehl *md* Louis Levy *ad* Andrew Mazzei *ed* Alfred Roome *violin solos* Yehudi Menuhin
☆ Stewart Granger, Jean Kent, Phyllis Calvert, Dennis Price, Cecil Parker, Felix Aylmer, Frank Cellier, Marie Lohr, Henry Edwards

The Magic Box *
GB 1951 118m Technicolor
Festival Films (Ronald Neame)

The life of William Friese-Greene, a British cinema pioneer who died in poverty.
A joint British film industry venture to celebrate the Festival of Britain, this rather downbeat and uneventful story takes on the nature of a pageant or a series of charades, with well-known people appearing to no good purpose. But it means well.

---

w Eric Ambler d John Boulting ph Jack Cardiff
m William Alwyn pd John Bryan
☆ Robert Donat, Margaret Johnson, Maria Schell,
John Howard Davies, Renée Asherson, Richard
Attenborough, Robert Beatty, Michael Denison,
Leo Genn, Marius Goring, Joyce Grenfell,
Robertson Hare, Kathleen Harrison, Jack Hulbert,
Stanley Holloway and also Glynis Johns, Mervyn
Johns, Barry Jones, Miles Malleson, Muir
Mathieson, A. E. Matthews, John McCallum,
Bernard Miles, Laurence Olivier, Cecil Parker, Eric
Portman, Dennis Price, Michael Redgrave,
Margaret Rutherford, Ronald Shiner, Sybil
Thorndike, David Tomlinson, Cecil Trouncer,
Peter Ustinov, Kay Walsh, Emlyn Williams,
Harcourt Williams, Googie Withers
  'An honest and often a very moving film.' –
  Daily Express
  'Patriotic, sentimental, overlong and faintly
  embarrassing.' – Time Out, 1984

The Magic Carpet
†† US 1951 84m Supercinecolor
Sam Katzman/Columbia
The caliph's son returns as the Scarlet Falcon to
rout the usurper.
Hopeless kid's matinée rubbish, not even performed
with verve.
w David Matthews d Lew Landers ph Ellis
Carter ad Paul Palmentola
☆ Lucille Ball, Raymond Burr, John Agar, Patricia
Medina, George Tobias

The Magic Christian
GB 1969 95m Technicolor
Commonwealth United/Grand Films (Dennis O'Dell)
⊞ ⊞ ⊛
An eccentric millionaire spends his wealth
deflating those who pursue money or power.
A series of variably funny but always unpleasant
sketches, climaxing with citizens delving for spoils in a
vat of blood and manure. In its aim to be satirical, very
typical of its time.
w Terry Southern, Joseph McGrath, Peter Sellers
novel Terry Southern d Joseph McGrath
ph Geoffrey Unsworth m Ken Thorne
pd Assheton Gorton
☆ Peter Sellers, Ringo Starr, Richard
Attenborough, Laurence Harvey, Christopher Lee,
Spike Milligan, Yul Brynner, Roman Polanski,
Raquel Welch, Wilfrid Hyde-White, Fred Emney,
John Le Mesurier, Dennis Price, Patrick Cargill,
John Cleese and also Graham Chapman

The Magic Face
US 1951 90m bw
Columbia (Mort Briskin, Robert Smith)
A brilliant German impersonator kills Hitler, takes
his place, and leads Germany deliberately into
defeat.
Hilariously unlikely anecdote 'as told to William
Shirer', performed with vigour but handicapped by a
shoddy production.
w Mort Briskin, Robert Smith d Frank Tuttle
ph Tony Braun m Herschel Burke Gilbert
☆ Luther Adler, Patricia Knight, Ilka Windish,
William L. Shirer
  'If Shirer believed this story, then he must be the
  only person in the world to do so.' – Gavin
  Lambert

Magic Fire
US 1954 94m Trucolor
Republic (William Dieterle)
The life and loves of Richard Wagner.
Remarkably boring biopic with much music but little
story or characterization. Ugly colour minimizes
German locations.
w Bertita Harding, E. A. Dupont, David Chantler
d William Dieterle ph Ernest Haller md Erich
Wolfgang Korngold
☆ Alan Badel, Yvonne de Carlo, Peter Cushing,
Frederick Valk, Carlos Thompson, Valentina
Cortesa

Magic Night: see Goodnight Vienna

The Magic of Lassie
†† US 1978 99m colour
Lassie Productions (Bonita Granville Wrather, William
Beaudine Jnr)
A collie dog is sold but makes its way back home.
Downright peculiar revamp of Lassie Come Home
with music and an ageing all-star cast.

w Jean Holloway, Richard M. Sherman, Robert B.
Sherman d Don Chaffey m Irwin Kostal
songs Richard and Robert Sherman
☆ James Stewart, Alice Faye, Mickey Rooney,
Pernell Roberts, Stephanie Zimbalist, Gene Evans
♫ song 'When You're Loved'

The Magic Sword
†† US 1962 80m Eastmancolor
UA/Bert I. Gordon
⊞
The son of a well-meaning witch rescues a princess
from the clutches of an evil sorcerer.
Shaky medieval fantasy on too low a budget.
w Bernard Schoenfeld d Bert I. Gordon ph Paul
Vogel m Richard Markowitz sp Milt Rice
☆ Basil Rathbone, Estelle Winwood, Gary
Lockwood, Anne Helm

The Magic Sword: Quest for Camelot:
see Quest for Camelot

'The guy with the dynamite heart meets the girl with
the firecracker eyes!'
Magic Town
US 1947 103m bw
Robert Riskin Productions
⊞ ⊛
An opinion pollster discovers a small town which
exactly mirrors the views of the USA at large.
A bright Capraesque idea is extraordinarily dully
scripted, the production looks dim, and all concerned
are operating one degree under.
w Robert Riskin d William A. Wellman
ph Joseph Biroc m Roy Webb
☆ James Stewart, Jane Wyman, Kent Smith, Regis
Toomey, Donald Meek, Ned Sparks, Wallace Ford

The Magic Toyshop *
GB 1986 107m colour
Granada (Steve Morrison)
Three children are left in the care of their uncle, a
puppet-maker.
Weird, sometimes grotesque fantasy focusing on an
adolescent girl's sexual awakening.
w Angela Carter novel Angela Carter d David
Wheatley ph Ken Morgan m Bill Connor
pd Stephen Fineren ed Anthony Ham
☆ Tom Bell, Caroline Milmoe, Kilian McKenna

The Magician: see The Face (1958)

The Magician *
US 1926 80m bw silent
MGM
A dabbler in the occult comes to grief when he
tries to influence a young girl.
A melodrama with interesting credits; unfortunately no
prints remain.
novel Somerset Maugham d Rex Ingram
☆ Paul Wegener, Ivan Petrovich, Alice Terry

The Magician of Lublin
West Germany/Israel 1979 114m colour
Geria-Golan-Globus (Harry N. Blum)
In 1901 an itinerant magician with an active sex
life dreams of being able really to fly.
Curious muddled fable with apparent correspondences
to the Christ story, like Bergman's The Face. In the
end it does not confidently address itself to any
audience, despite clever moments.
w Irving S. White, Menahem Golan novel Isaac
Bashevis Singer d Menahem Golan ph David
Gurfinkel m Maurice Jarre pd Jürgen Kiebach
☆ Alan Arkin, Louise Fletcher, Valerie Perrine,
Shelley Winters, Lou Jacobi, Warren Berlinger
  'California Polish accents grapple with hamfisted
  direction and a script of surpassing banality.' –
  Sight and Sound

The Magnet
†† GB 1950 79m bw
Ealing (Sidney Cole)
⊞
A small boy steals a magnet and accidentally
becomes a hero.
Very mild Ealing comedy, not really up to snuff.
w T. E. B. Clarke d Charles Frend ph Lionel
Banes m William Alwyn
☆ Stephen Murray, Kay Walsh, William Fox,
Meredith Edwards, Gladys Henson, Thora Hird,
Wylie Watson

The Magnetic Monster *
US 1953 75m bw
UA/Ivan Tors
A new radio-active element causes 'implosions' of
increasing size by drawing energy from the area
around it.
Well-told low-budget sci-fi with the audience kept
abreast of all developments; the undersea lab scenes are
borrowed from an old German film, Gold.
w Curt Siodmak, Ivan Tors d Curt Siodmak
ph Charles Van Enger m Blaine Sanford
pd George Van Marter
☆ Richard Carlson, King Donovan, Jean Byron,
Byron Foulger
  'A crackling mixture of science and fiction.' –
  Time

'Real life screened more daringly than it's ever been
before!'
The Magnificent Ambersons ****
US 1942 88m bw
RKO/Mercury (Orson Welles)
⊞⊞ ⊞ ⊛ ♫
A proud family loses its wealth and its control of
the neighbourhood, and its youngest male member
gets his come-uppance.
Fascinating period drama told in brilliant cinematic
snippets; owing to studio interference the last reels are
weak, but the whole is a treat for connoisseurs, and a
delight in its fast-moving control of cinematic narrative.
wd Orson Welles novel Booth Tarkington
ph Stanley Cortez m Bernard Herrmann ad Mark-
Lee Kirk ed Robert Wise, Mark Robson
☆ Joseph Cotten, Dolores Costello, Agnes
Moorehead, Tim Holt, Anne Baxter, Ray Collins,
Richard Bennett, Erskine Sanford, Donald Dillaway
  NARRATOR (WELLES): 'And now Major
  Amberson was engaged in the profoundest
  thinking of his life, and he realized that everything
  which had worried him or delighted him during his
  lifetime – all his buying and building and trading
  and banking – that it was all a trifle and a waste
  beside what concerned him now, for the Major
  knew now that he had to plan how to enter an
  unknown country where he was not even sure of
  being recognized as an Amberson.'
  NARRATOR: 'Something had happened. A thing
  which years ago had been the eagerest hope of
  many, many good citizens of the town. And now it
  had come at last: George Amberson Minafer had
  got his come-uppance. He got it three times filled
  and running over. But those who had so longed for
  it were not there to see it, and they never knew it.
  Those who were still living had forgotten all about
  it and all about him.'
  'Rich in ideas that many will want to copy,
  combined in the service of a story that few will
  care to imitate.' – C. A. Lejeune
  'Nearly every scene is played with a casual
  perfection which could only come from endless
  painstaking planning and rehearsals, and from a
  wonderful sense of timing.' – Basil Wright, 1972
  'Even in this truncated form it's amazing and
  memorable.' – Pauline Kael, 70s
  † Previously filmed in 1925 as Pampered Youth.
  †† The credits are all at the end and all spoken,
  ending with: 'I wrote and directed the picture. My
  name is Orson Welles.'
  ⚹ best picture; Stanley Cortez; Agnes Moorehead

The Magnificent Brute
US 1936 77m bw
Universal
A blast furnace boss becomes involved with stolen
money.
Star character drama; very predictable.
w Owen Francis, Lewis R. Foster, Bertram
Millhauser d John G. Blystone ad Albert S.
Agostino, Jack Otterson
☆ Victor McLaglen, Binnie Barnes, Billy Burrud,
William Hall, Jean Dixon
⚹ art direction

'The whisper of every woman – the toast of every
man!'
Magnificent Doll
US 1946 95m bw
Universal/Hallmark (Jack H. Skirball, Bruce Manning)
Dolly Madison, wife of the President, finds that
traitor Aaron Burr is a memory from her own past.
Uneasy historical semi-fiction, badly cast and rather
boring, yet with some sense of period style.
w Irving Stone d Frank Borzage ph Joseph
Valentine m Hans Salter

☆ Ginger Rogers, David Niven, Burgess Meredith,
Stephen McNally, Peggy Wood, Robert Barrat
  'No duller case has ever been made out for
  liberty.' – Daily Mail
  'Some day the moviemakers will discover that
  they can make history wonderfully believable
  and exciting by just sticking roughly to the
  facts.' – The Times

The Magnificent Dope
US 1942 83m bw
TCF (William Perlberg)
⊞
As a publicity stunt a success school brings the
nation's most complete failure to New York, and he
outsmarts them all.
Dim sub-Capra comedy.
w George Seaton d Walter Lang ph Peverell
Marley m David Raksin and others md Emil
Newman
☆ Henry Fonda, Lynn Bari, Don Ameche, Edward
Everett Horton, George Barbier, Frank Orth,
Hobart Cavanaugh

The Magnificent Fraud
US 1939 78m bw
Paramount
The president of a Latin American republic is
murdered, and an impersonator takes his place.
Sharply played dramatic hokum.
w Gilbert Gabriel and Walter Ferris d Robert
Florey
☆ Akim Tamiroff, Lloyd Nolan, Patricia Morison,
Mary Boland
  'Dull drama; no marquee names; filler fodder for
  duals.' – Variety

The Magnificent Matador
US 1955 94m Eastmancolor Cinemascope
Edward L. Alperson
⊞
GB title: The Brave and the Beautiful
A matador trains his illegitimate son to follow in
his footsteps but has a premonition of his death in
the ring.
Dreary bullfighting drama with romantic interludes.
w Charles Lang d Budd Boetticher ph Lucien
Ballard m Raoul Kraushaar
☆ Anthony Quinn, Maureen O'Hara, Manuel
Rojas, Richard Denning, Thomas Gomez, Lola
Albright

Magnificent Obsession **
US 1935 112m bw
Universal (John M. Stahl)
The playboy who is half-responsible for the death
of a woman's husband and for her own blindness
becomes a surgeon and cures her.
Absurd soaper which was phenomenally popular and is
certainly well done.
w George O'Neil, Sarah Y. Mason, Victor
Heerman novel Lloyd C. Douglas d John M. Stahl
ph John Mescall m Franz Waxman
☆ Irene Dunne, Robert Taylor, Ralph Morgan,
Sara Haden, Charles Butterworth, Betty Furness,
Arthur Hoyt, Gilbert Emery, Arthur Treacher
  'Capital romance, a cinch for the femme trade.' –
  Variety

Magnificent Obsession **
US 1954 108m Technicolor
Universal (Ross Hunter)
⊞
Glossy remake which sent Ross Hunter to the
commercial heights as a remaker of thirties
weepies.
This one worked best.
w Robert Blees d Douglas Sirk ph Russell Metty
m Frank Skinner
☆ Jane Wyman, Rock Hudson, Agnes Moorehead,
Barbara Rush, Otto Kruger, Gregg Palmer, Paul
Cavanagh, Sara Shane
⚹ Jane Wyman

The Magnificent Rebel
US 1960 94m Technicolor
Walt Disney (Peter V. Herald)
Episodes in the life of the young Beethoven.
Solid Disney biopic, shot in Vienna with good period
detail.
w Joanne Court d Georg Tressler ph Göran
Strindberg m Frederick Stark
☆ Karl Boehm, Ernst Nadhering, Ivan Desny,
Gabriele Porks

'They were seven – and they fought like seven hundred!'

The Magnificent Seven **

US   1960   138m   DeLuxe   Panavision
UA/Mirisch-Alpha (John Sturges)
▦▤ ▦ ▨ ⚫

A Mexican village hires seven American gunmen for protection against bandits.
Popular Western based on the Japanese Seven Samurai; good action scenes, but the rest is verbose and often pretentious.
w William Roberts d John Sturges ph Charles Lang Jnr m Elmer Bernstein
☆ Yul Brynner, Steve McQueen, Robert Vaughn, James Coburn, Charles Bronson, Horst Buchholz, Eli Wallach, Brad Dexter, Vladimir Sokoloff, Rosenda Monteros
♫ Elmer Bernstein

The Magnificent Seven Deadly Sins

GB   1971   107m   colour
Tigon (Graham Stark)
▦▤

Compendium of comedy sketches, a very variable ragbag of old jokes.
w Bob Larbey, John Esmonde, Dave Freeman, Barry Cryer, Graham Chapman, Graham Stark, Marty Feldman, Alan Simpson, Ray Galton, Spike Milligan d Graham Stark ph Harvey Harrison Jnr m Roy Budd
☆ Bruce Forsyth, Joan Sims, Roy Hudd, Harry Secombe, Leslie Phillips, Julie Ege, Harry H. Corbett, Ian Carmichael, Alfie Bass, Spike Milligan, Ronald Fraser

The Magnificent Seven Ride

US   1972   100m   DeLuxe
UA/Mirisch (William A. Calihan)
▦▤

Tired finale to a patchy series (*Return of the Seven, Guns of the Magnificent Seven*) in which the original leader returns to save a Mexican village once again from bandits.
Very modest.
w Arthur Rowe d George McCowan ph Fred Koenekamp m Elmer Bernstein
☆ Lee Van Cleef, Stefanie Powers, Mariette Hartley, Pedro Armendariz Jnr, Luke Askew

The Magnificent Showman: see Circus World

The Magnificent Two

GB   1967   100m   Eastmancolor
Rank (Hugh Stewart)

One of two incompetent travelling salesmen in a Latin American banana republic is persuaded to pose as a dead rebel leader.
More or less a Bob Hope vehicle, adapted for the less realistic Morecambe and Wise with unhappy results: too few sight gags and a curious emphasis on violence. The third and last of their attempts to find film vehicles.
w S. C. Green, R. M. Hills, Michael Pertwee, Peter Blackmore d Cliff Owen ph Ernest Steward m Ron Goodwin
☆ Eric Morecambe, Ernie Wise, Margit Saad, Cecil Parker, Virgilio Teixeira, Isobel Black, Martin Benson

The Magnificent Yankee *

US   1950   88m   bw
MGM (Armand Deutsch)
GB title: *The Man with Thirty Sons*
Episodes in the later life of Judge Oliver Wendell Holmes.
Vaguely well-meaning biopic without much dramatic sense.
w Emmet Lavery play Emmet Lavery d John Sturges ph Joseph Ruttenberg m David Raksin
☆ Louis Calhern, Ann Harding, Eduard Franz, Philip Ober, Richard Anderson, Edith Evanson
♫ Louis Calhern

'Things fall down. People look up. And when it rains, it pours.'

Magnolia **

US   1999   188m   DeLuxe   Panavision
New Line/Ghoulardi (Joanne Sellar)
▦▤ ▤ ▨

In Los Angeles, the lives of various dysfunctional people coincidentally intertwine and interact.
A sprawling, episodic drama which examines unhappy people: a dying father, suffused with guilt, his hysterical wife, an estranged, misogynistic son, an unloved cop, a bullying father and his clever, timid son, a dying games

---

show host and his estranged daughter. It is a clever, intense film about relationships and the need for love, but ultimately seems so contrived and manipulative that much of its emotional power is dissipated.
wd Paul Thomas Anderson ph Robert Elswit m John Brion m/ly Aimee Mann pd William Arnold, Mark Bridges ed Dylan Tichenor
☆ Jason Robards, Julianne Moore, Tom Cruise, Philip Seymour Hoffman, John C. Reilly, Melora Walters, Philip Baker Hall, Melinda Dillon, Emmanuel Johnson
'May be self-regarding and pretentious, but there are some fiendishly clever moments.' – *James Christopher, Times*
'A remarkably inventive and audacious film that almost overcomes its flaws.' – *Emanuel Levy, Variety*
♫ Tom Cruise; Paul Thomas Anderson; song 'Save Me' (m/l Aimee Mann)

Magnum Force

US   1973   124m   Technicolor   Panavision
Warner/Malpaso (Robert Daley)
▦▤ ▤ ▨ ⚫

Inspector Harry Callahan has to track down the cops who are slaughtering gangsters in cold blood.
Toned-down sequel to Dirty Harry; the violence is still there but the hero no longer commits it.
w John Milius, Michael Cimino d Ted Post ph Frank Stanley m Lalo Schifrin
☆ Clint Eastwood, Hal Holbrook, Mitch Ryan, Felton Perry, David Soul
'A ragbag of western mythology and head-on thuggery.' – *Sight and Sound*

The Magus

GB   1968   116m   DeLuxe   Panavision
TCF/Blazer (John Kohn, Jud Kinberg)
An English schoolmaster on a Greek island is influenced by the local magician.
Fashionable philosophical nonsense, an elaborate mystery with no solution; the kind of film that all concerned begin to wish they had never thought of, especially as the presentation has nothing like the panache required, so that not even the critics liked it.
w John Fowles novel John Fowles d Guy Green ph Billy Williams m Johnny Dankworth pd Don Ashton
☆ Michael Caine, Anthony Quinn, Candice Bergen, Anna Karina, Paul Stassino, Julian Glover, George Pastell
'Faintly ludicrous some of the time and painfully unexciting all of the time.' – *MFB*
'This may not be the most misguided movie ever made, but it's in there pitching.' – *Rex Reed*
'There's enough incoherence pretending to be enigma, sex play and chat about existentialism and self-discovery to make teenagers think they're having an experience; for grown-ups it's an ordeal.' – *Judith Crist*
'It has much of the fascination of a Chinese puzzle, but it would have been infinitely more enthralling if it hadn't been quite so flatly acted and directed.' – *Michael Billington, Illustrated London News*
'Probably the only movie in which one will ever see a copy of Empson's Seven Types of Ambiguity.' – *Pauline Kael, New Yorker*

The Mahabharata *

France   1989   171m   colour
Virgin/Les Productions du 3ème Etage (Michel Propper)
⚞
A boy listens to the story of a great war between competing tribes.
The vast Indian epic poem of 100,000 couplets in this condensed cinematic form results in a complex incident-crammed narrative, in which the significance of specific events can be hard to comprehend.
w Peter Brook, Jean-Claude Carrière, Marie-Hélène Estienne play Jean Claude Carrière d Peter Brook ph William Lubtchansky m Toshi Tsuchitori, Djamchid Chemirani, Kudsi Erguner, Kim Menzer, Mahmoud Tabrizi-Zadeh pd Chloe Oboloensky ed Nicholas Gaster
☆ Urs Biher, Ryszard Cieslak, Georges Corraface, Mamadou Dioumé, Miriam Goldschmidt, Jeffrey Kissoon, Sotigui Kouyate, Tuncel Kurtiz, Robert Langdon Lloyd

Mahanagar: see *The Big City (1963)*

Mahler *

GB   1974   115m   Technicolor
Goodtimes Enterprises (Roy Baird)
▦▤ ▨
Fantasia on the life and times of the Jewish composer.
Fairly successful Ken Russell musical biopic on the lines of his early BBC specials.
wd Ken Russell ph Dick Bush ad Ian Whittaker ed Michael Bradsell
☆ Robert Powell, Georgina Hale, Richard Morant, Lee Montague, Rosalie Crutchley, Benny Lee, David Collings
'A piece of movie making that sets my pulses racing.' – *Michael Billington, Illustrated London News*
'Whether the title of the opus happens to be Strauss or Tchaikovsky or Elgar or Brubeck, the real title is always Russell.' – *Benny Green, Punch*
🎭 Georgina Hale

Mahogany

US   1975   109m   colour   Panavision
Paramount/Nikor (Rob Cohen, Jack Ballard)
▤ ▨ ⚫
The love life of a model and fashion designer.
Virtually a Joan Crawford vehicle redesigned for a black heroine who creates her own clothes. Fairly hilarious.
w John Byrum d Berry Gordy ph David Watkin m Michael Masser ly Gerry Goffin
☆ Diana Ross, Billy Dee Williams, Anthony Perkins, Jean-Pierre Aumont, Nina Foch, Beah Richards, Marisa Mell
'The level of silliness rises steadily.' – *Geoff Brown*
'Movies as frantically bad as Mahogany can be enjoyed on at least one level; the spectacle of a lot of people making fools of themselves.' – *Time*
'What Mahogany does so fascinatingly and sometimes hilariously is to pilfer certain stock clichés of 50's Hollywood and adapt them to a black milieu.' – *Molly Haskell*
♫ song 'Do You Know Where You're Going To?' (mMichael Masser, lyGerry Goffin)

'Love so glorious it was denounced as sin!'

Maid of Salem *

US   1937   86m   bw
Paramount (Frank Lloyd)
In 1692 Salem, a young girl is accused of witchcraft but saved by her lover.
Remarkably solemn period melodrama, unfortunately betrayed by amiable but miscast leads.
w Bradley King, Walter Ferris, Durward Grinstead d Frank Lloyd ph Leo Tover m Victor Young
☆ Claudette Colbert, Fred MacMurray, Harvey Stephens, Gale Sondergaard, Louise Dresser, Edward Ellis, Beulah Bondi, Bonita Granville
'Weak and slow saga of witchcraft: stars the only hope.' – *Variety*
'Once the panic of witchcraft starts you are carried along on a vicious crescendo of madness and terror.' – *Stage*

Maid to Order

👪 US   1987   96m   DeLuxe
Vista/New Century (Herb Jaffe, Mort Engelberg)
▦▤ ▤ ▨
A spoiled rich girl takes work as a maid but finds she has a fairy godmother.
Weird semi-fantasy which wasn't wanted in the 80s, Cinderella being out of fashion.
wd Amy Jones (co-writers Perry and Randy Howze) ph Shelly Johnson m Georges Delerue pd Jeffrey Townsend ed Sidney Wolinski
☆ Ally Sheedy, Michael Ontkean, Beverly D'Angelo, Valerie Perrine, Dick Shawn, Tom Skerritt

Maiden Voyage: see *Bridal Suite*

The Maids

GB   1974   95m   Technicolor
Ely Landau/Cinevision
▤
Two Paris maids evolve a sado-masochistic ritual involving the death of their employer, but never go through with it.
Unbalanced and dreary film version of an essentially theatrical play.
w Robert Enders, Christopher Miles play Jean Genet d Christopher Miles ph Douglas Slocombe m Laurie Johnson

---

☆ Glenda Jackson, Susannah York, Vivien Merchant, Mark Burns
'In view of the huge technical, stylistic and even metaphysical difficulties, I think it succeeds very well.' – *Stanley Kauffmann*

Maid's Night Out

US   1938   65m   bw
RKO
A wealthy girl falls for the milkman, who is really a rich man who thinks she's the maid.
Skittish second-feature comedy which helped to build a new star.
w Bert Granet d Ben Holmes
☆ Joan Fontaine, Allan Lane, Billy Gilbert, Cecil Kellaway, Hedda Hopper

Maigret Sets a Trap *

France/Italy   1957   119m   bw
Intermondia/J. P. Guibert/Jolly Film
Maigret sets a policewoman as decoy for a knife murderer…
Probably the best Maigret film, with excellent Parisian atmosphere and excellent acting.
w Michel Audiard novel Georges Simenon d Jean Delannoy ph Louis Page m Paul Misraki ad René Renoux
☆ Jean Gabin, Annie Girardot, Jean Desailly, Olivier Hussenot, Alfred Adam, Lino Ventura
'It is puzzling, it is intermittently exciting, it is not offensive to a modest intelligence, not at any rate a modest intelligence used to crime stories.' – *Dilys Powell*

Mail Order Bride

US   1963   83m   Metrocolor   Panavision
MGM (Richard E. Lyons)
GB title: *West of Montana*
An old Westerner tries to find a bride for a wild young man in his charge.
Mild Western comedy drama; quite tolerable.
wd Burt Kennedy ph Paul C. Vogel m George Bassman
☆ Buddy Ebsen, Lois Nettleton, Keir Dullea, Warren Oates, Marie Windsor

Mail Train: see *Inspector Hornleigh Goes To It*

The Main Attraction

GB   1962   90m   Metrocolor
Seven Arts (John Patrick)
A wandering singer causes emotional problems backstage at a circus.
Limp melodrama with the star miscast as a fatal charmer.
w John Patrick d Daniel Petrie ph Geoffrey Unsworth m Andrew Adorian
☆ Pat Boone, Mai Zetterling, Nancy Kwan, Yvonne Mitchell, John Le Mesurier

The Main Event

US   1979   112m   Technicolor
Warner/First Artists/Barwood (Jon Peters, Barbra Streisand)
▦▤ ▤ ▨ ⚫ ▨ ♫
A lady entrepreneur takes on a prizefighter.
Thin and very patchy comedy for confirmed addicts of its star.
w Gail Parent, Andrew Smith d Howard Zieff ph Mario Tosi m Michael Melvoin pd Charles Rosen
☆ Barbra Streisand, Ryan O'Neal, Paul Sand, Whitman Mayo, James Gregory

Main Street: see *I Married a Doctor*

Main Street After Dark

US   1944   57m   bw
MGM/Jerry Bresler
The police launch an assault on con men and petty thieves preying on returning ex-servicemen.
Watchable crime filler.
w Karl Kamb, John C. Higgins d Edward L. Cahn
☆ Edward Arnold, Selena Royle, Tom Trout, Audrey Totter, Dan Duryea, Hume Cronyn

Main Street to Broadway *

US   1953   102m   bw
Lester Cowan Productions
▤
After several reverses a young playwright sees his work through to a Broadway opening night; it fails, but he has learned several lessons.

Curious, flat attempt to show the public how Broadway works, with big stars playing themselves in cameo roles.
w Samson Raphaelson d Tay Garnett ph James Wong Howe

☆ Tom Morton, Mary Murphy, Ethel Barrymore, Lionel Barrymore, Shirley Booth, Rex Harrison, Lilli Palmer, Helen Hayes, Henry Fonda, Tallulah Bankhead, Mary Martin, Louis Calhern, John Van Druten, Cornel Wilde, Joshua Logan and also Agnes Moorehead, Gertrude Berg

Les Mains Sales

France 1951 103m bw
Fernand Rivers
aka: Dirty Hands
A young communist intellectual, required to kill a traitor, finds he can do so only when he suspects the man of making love to his wife.
Verbose and dull version of a play which had some international success as Crime Passionel.
wd Fernand Rivers play Jean-Paul Sartre ph Jean Bachelet

☆ Pierre Brasseur, Daniel Gélin, Claude Nollier

Maisie

US 1939 74m bw
MGM (J. Walter Ruben)
Adventures of a Brooklyn showgirl.
Acceptable programmer which led to a series, all quite watchable and absolutely forgettable.
The succeeding titles, mostly written by Mary McCall and directed by Marin or Harry Beaumont or Roy del Ruth, were:
1940 Congo Maisie (with John Carroll; a remake of Red Dust), Gold Rush Maisie (with Lee Bowman), Maisie Was a Lady (with Lew Ayres, Maureen O'Sullivan)
1941 Ringside Maisie (qv) (with George Murphy; GB title Cash and Carry)
1942 Maisie Gets Her Man (with Red Skelton; GB title She Got Her Man)
1943 Swing Shift Maisie (with James Craig; GB title The Girl in Overalls)
1944 Maisie Goes to Reno (qv) (with John Hodiak; GB title You Can't Do That to Me)
1946 Up Goes Maisie (with George Murphy; GB title Up She Goes)
1947 Undercover Maisie (with Barry Nelson; GB title Undercover Girl)
w Mary McCall Jnr novel Dark Dame by Wilson Collison d Edwin L. Marin ph Leonard Smith
☆ Ann Sothern, Robert Young, Ian Hunter, Ruth Hussey, Anthony Allan (John Hubbard), Cliff Edwards

Maisie Goes to Reno

US 1944 90m bw
MGM (George Haight)
GB title: You Can't Do That to Me
Maisie saves a rich wife from divorcing her soldier-husband.
Pleasant light-hearted programmer with a few comic moments.
w Mary C. McCall Jnr story Harry Ruby, James O'Hanlon d Harry Beaumont ph Robert Planck m David Snell ad Cedric Gibbons, Howard Campbell ed Frank E. Hull
☆ Ann Sothern, John Hodiak, Tom Drake, Marta Linden, Paul Cavanagh, Ava Gardner, Donald Meek

La Maison de Jeanne: see Jeanne's House

Le Maître de Musique: see The Music Teacher

Maitresse *

France 1976 112m Eastmancolor
Films du Losange/Jean Pierre Rassam (Pierre Andrieux)
📺
A young man, newly arrived in Paris, begins an affair with a woman who earns her living as a dominatrix, but he becomes concerned about the difference between her relationship with him and her sado-masochistic professional life.
Love is seen as akin to a Venus fly-trap, a painful and devouring business, in this elegant, icy romantic drama that, with its emphasis on bizarre, masochistic activities, is not for the squeamish. It forces audiences to acknowledge that the behaviour on show is merely an extreme form of everyday relationships and games-playing.
w Barbet Schroeder, Paul Voujargol d Barbet Schroeder ph Nestor Almendros m Carlos

D'Alessio ad Roberto Plate ed Denise de Casabianca cos Karl Lagerfeld
☆ Gérard Depardieu, Bulle Ogier, André Rouver, Nathalie Keryan, Roland Bertin, Tony Taffin, Holger Lowenadler

'Is she a kid – or is she kidding?'
The Major and the Minor **

US 1942 100m bw
Paramount (Arthur Hornblow Jnr)
A girl poses as a child in order to travel half fare on a train, and is helped by an officer who falls for her.
Moderately smart comedy showing the writer-director's emergent style. Remade as You're Never Too Young (qv).
w Charles Brackett, Billy Wilder d Billy Wilder ph Leo Tover m Robert Emmett Dolan
☆ Ginger Rogers, Ray Milland, Rita Johnson, Robert Benchley, Diana Lynn, Edward Fielding, Frankie Thomas, Charles Smith
OSBORNE (ROBERT BENCHLEY): 'Why don't you get out of that wet coat and into a dry martini?'
'The script seems to have been concocted after the title.' – New Yorker, 1977

Major Barbara ***

GB 1941 121m bw
Gabriel Pascal
📺
The daughter of an armaments millionaire joins the Salvation Army but resigns when it accepts her father's donation.
Stagey but compulsive version of a play in which the author takes typical side swipes at anything and everything within reach, allowing for some gorgeous acting (and overacting) by an impeccable cast.
w Anatole de Grunwald, Gabriel Pascal play Bernard Shaw d Gabriel Pascal, Harold French, David Lean ph Ronald Neame m William Walton ad Vincent Korda, John Bryan ed Charles Frend cos Cecil Beaton
☆ Wendy Hiller, Rex Harrison, Robert Morley, Robert Newton, Marie Lohr, Emlyn Williams, Sybil Thorndike, Deborah Kerr, David Tree, Felix Aylmer, Penelope Dudley Ward, Walter Hudd, Marie Ault, Donald Calthrop
'Shaw's ebullience provides an unslackening fount of energy … his all-star cast of characters are outspoken as no one else is in films except the Marx Brothers.' – William Whitebait
'To call it a manifest triumph would be an arrant stinginess with words.' – New York Times

Major Dundee *

US 1964 134m Eastmancolor Panavision
Columbia (Jerry Bresler)
📺 ⊚ ♫
A small group of men from a US cavalry post sets out to annihilate marauding Indians.
Large-scale, rough-and-ready Western which rambles along in humourless vein but rises to some spectacular bloodthirsty climaxes.
w Harry Julian Fink, Oscar Saul, Sam Peckinpah d Sam Peckinpah ph Sam Leavitt m Daniele Amfitheatrof
☆ Charlton Heston, Richard Harris, Jim Hutton, James Coburn, Michael Anderson Jnr, Warren Oates, Senta Berger, Slim Pickens

Major League

US 1989 106m Technicolor
Braveworld/Fox (Mark Rosenberg)
📀 📺 ⊚ ♫
A hopeless baseball team turn winners when they learn their owner wants them to lose.
Broad and often tasteless comedy, too predictable to be funny.
wd David S. Ward ph Reynaldo Villalobos m James Newton Howard pd Jeffrey Howard ed Dennis M. Hill, Tony Lombardo
☆ Tom Berenger, Charlie Sheen, Corbin Bernsen, Margaret Whitton, James Gammon, Rene Russo, Wesley Snipes, Charles Cyphers

Major League II

US 1994 104m Technicolor
Warner/Morgan Creek (James G. Robinson, David S. Ward)
📀 📺 ⊚ ♫
A baseball team reverts to its losing ways before the players pull themselves together and begin winning.
A smudged copy of the original, recycling the same narrative and failing to produce a moment of wit or originality.

w R. J. Stewart, Tom S. Parker, Jim Jennewein d David S. Ward ph Victor Hammer m Michel Colombier pd Stephen Hendrickson ed Paul Seydor, Donn Cambern
☆ Charlie Sheen, Tom Berenger, Corbin Bernsen, Dennis Haysbert, Eric Bruskotter, Omar Epps, David Keith, Randy Quaid
'A singularly unfunny, dramatically tepid follow-up.' – Variety

Major Payne

US 1995 97m DeLuxe
Universal/Wife 'n' Kids (Eric L. Gold, Michael Rachmil)
📀 📺 ⊚ ♫
A tough military martinet is put in charge of a school cadet troop.
Soft-centred drama about a hard man learning that killing isn't everything in life, but the comedy is strictly by the numbers.
w Dean Lorey, Damon Wayans, Gary Rosen d Nick Castle ph Richard Bowen m Craig Safan pd Peter Larkin ed Patrick Kennedy
☆ Damon Wayans, Karyn Parsons, Bill Hickey, Michael Ironside, Albert Hall, Steven Martini, Andrew Harrison Leeds, Joda Blare-Hershman, Damien Wayans
'It's what is sometimes called a "warmedy", a cuddly comedy in which a crotchety hero sees the light by rubbing shoulders with humanity.' – Leonard Klady, Variety
† It is a remake of The Private War of Major Benson (qv).

A Majority of One

US 1961 156m Technicolor
Warner (Mervyn Le Roy)
A Jewish widow has a shipboard romance with a Japanese businessman.
Interminable stage-bound comedy-drama, boringly assembled and fatally compromised by the casting of stars who are neither Jewish nor Japanese.
w Leonard Spigelgass play Leonard Spigelgass d Mervyn Le Roy ph Harry Stradling m Max Steiner
☆ Rosalind Russell, Alec Guinness, Ray Danton, Madlyn Rhue
♟ Harry Stradling

Make a Wish

👫 US 1937 75m bw
(RKO)
📺
A composer discovers a boy singer at a summer camp.
Acceptable family entertainment.
w Gertrude Berg, Bernard Schubert, Earle Snell d Kurt Neumann m John Mescall m Hugo Riesenfeld songs Oscar Straus
☆ Basil Rathbone, Bobby Breen, Marion Claire, Leon Errol, Henry Armetta, Ralph Forbes, Donald Meek
♟ Hugo Riesenfeld

Make Haste to Live

US 1954 89m bw
Republic (William A. Seiter)
A lady newspaper owner is embarrassed, to say the least, by the reappearance of her murderer husband, long thought dead.
Competent but rather dull programmer.
w Warren Duff novel The Gordons d William A. Seiter ph John L. Russell m Elmer Bernstein
☆ Dorothy McGuire, Stephen McNally, Mary Murphy, Edgar Buchanan, John Howard

Make Me a Star

US 1932 80m bw
Paramount (Lloyd Sheldon)
A grocery clerk goes to Hollywood and becomes a film star.
Modest remake of a silent success; see also Merton of the Movies.
w Sam Mintz, Walter de Leon, Arthur Kober novel Merton of the Movies by Harry Leon Wilson d William Beaudine ph Allen Siegler
☆ Stuart Erwin, Joan Blondell, ZaSu Pitts, Ben Turpin, Florence Roberts, Tallulah Bankhead, Clive Brook, Gary Cooper, Maurice Chevalier, Claudette Colbert, Fredric March, Jack Oakie, Charlie Ruggles, Sylvia Sidney
'Packed with laughs which offsets the longish running time.' – Variety

Make Me an Offer *

GB 1954 88m Eastmancolor
Group Three (W. P. Lipscomb)
📺
An antique dealer has an ambition to own a famous vase.
Mildly pleasant Jewish comedy with interesting sidelights on the antique business.
w W. P. Lipscomb novel Wolf Mankowitz d Cyril Frankel ph Denny Densham m John Addison
☆ Peter Finch, Adrienne Corri, Meier Tzelniker, Rosalie Crutchley, Finlay Currie, Ernest Thesiger, Wilfrid Lawson, Alfie Bass

Make Mine a Million

GB 1959 82m bw
British Lion/Elstree Independent/Jack Hylton (John Baxter)
A TV make-up man strikes it rich by showing advertisements on non-commercial television.
Amiable, low-key comedy, relying heavily on the personality of its star.
w Peter Blackmore, Arthur Askey, Talbot Rothwell story Jack Francis d Lance Comfort ph Arthur Grant m Stanley Black ad Dennis Wreford ed Peter Pitt
☆ Arthur Askey, Sidney James, Dermot Walsh, Olga Lindo, Clive Morton, Sally Barnes, Leigh Madison, Bernard Cribbins, Gillian Lynee, The Penge Formation Dancers

Make Mine Mink **

GB 1960 101m bw
Rank (Hugh Stewart)
📺
Members of a high-class boarding establishment steal furs to give the proceeds to charity.
Enjoyable comedy, expertly performed.
w Michael Pertwee, Peter Blackmore play Breath of Spring by Peter Coke d Robert Asher ph Reginald Wyer m Philip Green ad Carmen Dillon ed Roger Cherrill
☆ Terry-Thomas, Athene Seyler, Hattie Jacques, Billie Whitelaw, Raymond Huntley, Irene Handl, Kenneth Williams, Noel Purcell, Sydney Tafler
† The film was reissued with 21m cut.

Make Mine Music **

👫 US 1946 74m Technicolor
Walt Disney (Joe Grant)
A programme of cartoon shorts: Johnny Fedora, All the Cats Join in, Without You, Two Silhouettes, Casey at the Bat, The Martins and the Coys, Blue Bayou, After You've Gone, Willie the Singing Whale, Peter and the Wolf
An insubstantial banquet, sometimes arty and sometimes chocolate boxy, which occasionally rises to the expected heights.
w various d various
'There is enough genuine charm and imagination and humour to make up perhaps one good average Disney short.' – James Agee

Make Way for a Lady

US 1936 63m bw
Zion Myers/RKO
A girl determines to find a mate for her widowed father.
Rather irritating comedy of embarrassment.
w Gertrude Purcell novel Daddy and I by Elizabeth Jordan d David Burton
☆ Herbert Marshall, Anne Shirley, Gertrude Michael, Margot Grahame, Clara Blandick, Taylor Holmes, Willie Best
'It lacks suspense, surprise, and plausibility.' – Variety

'Grandpa moves in! Daughter moves out! And the riot starts!'
Make Way for Tomorrow **

US 1937 94m bw
Paramount (Leo McCarey)
An elderly couple are in financial difficulty and have to be parted because their children will not help.
Sentimental drama which had a devastating effect at the time but now seems oversimplified and exaggerated.
w Vina Delmar novel The Years Are So Long by Josephine Lawrence d Leo McCarey ph William C. Mellor m George Antheil
☆ Victor Moore, Beulah Bondi, Thomas Mitchell, Fay Bainter, Porter Hall, Barbara Read, Maurice Moscovich, Elizabeth Risdon, Gene Lockhart

---

◎ Digital Video Disc Region 2   ◎ Digital Video Disc Region 1   ♫ Soundtrack released on compact disc   ☆ Cast in approximate order of importance   † Points of interest   ♫ Notable songs   ♟ Academy Award   ♟ Academy Award nomination   🏆 BAFTA

'Needs special exploitation: even so, business is apt to be spotty where played solo.' – *Variety*
'The most brilliantly directed and acted film of the year.' – *John Grierson*
'A sense of misery and inhumanity is left vibrating in the nerves.' – *Graham Greene*

Make Your Own Bed
US　1944　82m　bw
Warner
A detective and his girlfriend pretend to be servants in order to protect an inventor from Nazis.
Mirthless pratfall farce.
w Francis Swann, Edmund Joseph　d Peter Godfrey
✫ Jack Carson, Jane Wyman, Irene Manning, Ricardo Cortez, Alan Hale, George Tobias

The Maker *
US　1997　98m　colour　Panavision
Midsummer/New Image (Andrew Lazar, Demitri Samaha)
◧ ▦
A suburban high-school youth becomes involved in criminal activities when his elder brother returns home after ten years away.
An enjoyable thriller that centres on the confusions and mixed loyalties of teenage life, avoiding both sentimentality and melodrama.
w Rand Ravich　d Tim Hunter　ph Hubert Taczanowski　m Paul Buckmaster　pd Jane Ann Stewart　ed Scott Chestnut
✫ Matthew Modine, Jonathan Rhys Myers, Mary-Louise Parker, Michael Madsen, Fairuza Balk, Jesse Borrego
'Satisfies as both a clever suspenser and fairly believable drama.' – *Dennis Harvey, Variety*
† The film was released direct to video in Britain.

Making It: see *Les Valseuses*

Making Love
US　1982　111m　DeLuxe
TCF/IndieProd (Allen Adler, Danny Melnick)
A young married doctor declares that he is gay and moves in with a friend.
Would-be daring melodrama whose producers quickly found that nobody was interested.
w Barry Sandler　story A. Scott Berg　d Arthur Hiller　ph David M. Walsh　m Leonard Rosenman　pd James D. Vance　ed William H. Reynolds
✫ Michael Ontkean, Kate Jackson, Harry Hamlin, Wendy Hiller, Arthur Hill, Nancy Olson

Making Mr Right
US　1987　98m　colour
Rank/Orion (Mike Wise, Joel Tuber)
▦　◕　◠
An android falls in love with a public relations consultant.
Slight comedy that soon runs out of anywhere to go.
w Floyd Byars, Laurie Frank　d Susan Seidelman　ph Edward Lachman　m Chaz Jankel　pd Barbara Ling　ed Andrew Mondshein
✫ Ann Magnuson, John Malkovich, Glenne Headly, Ben Masters, Laurie Metcalf, Polly Bergen, Harsh Nayyar, Hart Bochner

Making Up *
Germany　1993　55m　colour
Electric Pictures/Vela-X/Bayerischer Rundfunk (Ewa Karlström)
original title: *Abgeschminkt!*
Two single women fall in and out of love with unsuitable men.
A film-school graduation project that was a hit in its home country, this is an enjoyable comedy, mocking the over-enthusiastic pursuit of the opposite sex.
w Benjamin Taylor, Katja von Garnier, Hannes Jaenicke　d Katja von Garnier　ph Torsten Breuer　m Peter Wenke, Tillmann Höhn　ad Irene Edenhofer, Nikolai Ritter　ed Katja von Garnier
✫ Katja Riemann, Nina Kronjäger, Gedeon Burkhard, Max Tidof, Daniela Lunkewitz, Peter Sattmann, Jochen Nickel
'An above-average single-woman's date comedy.' – *Variety*

Mala Noche *
US　1988　78m　bw
The Other Cinema/Northern Film/Respectable (Gus Van Sant)
A homosexual store worker falls for a heterosexual illegal Mexican immigrant.

Interesting first feature, a study in obsession, shot on a minimal budget.
wd Gus Van Sant　story Walt Curtis　ph John Campbell　m Creighton Lindsay
✫ Tim Streeter, Doug Cooeyate, Ray Monge, Nyla McCarthy
'Reminds you how exciting independent film-making can be … has a sure feel for the more awkward corners of sexual exchange which we might prefer to forget.' – *Judith Williamson, New Statesman*

Malachi's Cove
⍟⍟　GB　1973　75m　Technicolor
Penrith/Impact Quadrant Films (Andrew Sinclair, Kent Walwin)
aka: *The Seaweed Children*
In 1880 Cornwall, a 14-year-old girl lives by selling seaweed.
Slimly-plotted film for the family, pleasant without being very interesting.
wd Henry Herbert　story Anthony Trollope　ph Walter Lassally　m Brian Gascoigne
✫ Donald Pleasence, Dai Bradley, Veronica Quilligan, Arthur English, David Howe

Malaga: see *Moment of Danger* (1962)

Malaga
GB　1954　84m　Technicolor
M. J. Frankovich/Film Locations
US title: *Fire Over Africa*
An American woman agent catches drug smugglers in Tangier.
Routine international thick ear.
w Robert Westerby　d Richard Sale　ph Christopher Challis　m Benjamin Frankel
✫ Maureen O'Hara, Macdonald Carey, Binnie Barnes, Guy Middleton, Leonard Sachs

Malarek
Canada　1989　100m　colour
Telescene (Jamie Brown, Robin Spry)
▦
In Montreal in the early 70s, an aggressive would-be journalist, investigating the cover-up of a killing, exposes widespread abuse at a juvenile detention centre.
A true story is forced into a familiar thriller format, but given some life by the intensity of Koteas's performance.
w Avrum Jacobson　autobiography *Hey Malarek* by Victor Malarek　d Roger Cardinal　ph Karol Ike　m Alexandre Stanké　ad Claude Paré　ed Yves Langlois
✫ Elias Koteas, Kerrie Keane, Al Waxman, Michael Sarrazin, Daniel Pilon, Kahil Karn

Malaya *
US　1949　95m　bw
MGM (Edwin H. Knopf)
GB title: *East of the Rising Sun*
An adventurer attempts to smuggle rubber out of Japanese-occupied Malaya.
Dour action melodrama, unworthy of its considerable cast but watchable.
w Frank Fenton　d Richard Thorpe　ph George Folsey　m Bronislau Kaper
✫ Spencer Tracy, James Stewart, Sydney Greenstreet, John Hodiak, Valentina Cortesa, Lionel Barrymore, Gilbert Roland

Malcolm
Australia　1986　86m　colour
Enterprise/Cascade (David Parker, Nadia Tass)
◧　▦　◠
A retarded but mechanically talented youth lives alone in a Melbourne suburb and takes in a petty criminal and his girlfriend.
Initially interesting but mishandled character study which never settles into a comfortable groove.
w David Parker　d Nadia Tass　ph David Parker　m Simon Jeffes　ad Ken Sallows
✫ Colin Friels, John Hargreaves, Lindy Davies, Chris Haywood, Charles Tingwell

Malcolm X **
US　1992　201m　DuArt
Warner/Largo/Forty Acres and a Mule (Marvin Worth, Spike Lee)
◧　▦　◠　◠
Biopic of the turbulent life and violent death of the black revolutionary leader.

Despite Washington's powerful performance in the title role, an overlong and somewhat subdued treatment that seems anxious not to offend.
w Arnold Perl, Spike Lee　book *The Autobiography of Malcolm X* as told to Alex Haley　d Spike Lee　ph Ernest Dickerson　m Terence Blanchard　pd Wynn Thomas　ed Barry Alexander Brown
✫ Denzel Washington, Angela Bassett, Albert Hall, Al Freeman Jnr, Delroy Lindo, Spike Lee, Theresa Randle, Kate Vernon, Lonette McKee, Tommy Hollis
'A disappointingly sluggish and conventional film.' – *Variety*
'Always watchable even if one can't call it memorable.' – *Derek Malcolm, Guardian*
♟ Denzel Washington; Ruth Carter (costume design)

The Male Animal *
US　1942　101m　bw
Warner (Wolfgang Reinhardt)
A dry college professor emancipates himself when his wife becomes attracted to a football star.
Stagebound but amusing college comedy with pleasant humour and good performances. Remade as She's Working Her Way through College (qv).
w Julius J. and Philip G. Epstein, Stephen Morehouse Avery　play James Thurber and Elliott Nugent　d Elliott Nugent　ph Arthur Edeson　m Heinz Roemheld
✫ Henry Fonda, Olivia de Havilland, Jack Carson, Joan Leslie, Eugene Pallette, Don Defore, Herbert Anderson, Hattie McDaniel

Malenkaya Vera: see *Little Vera*

'Deception. Betrayal. Murder. Some Things You Never See Coming.'

Malice
US　1993　107m　Technicolor
Rank/Castle Rock/New Line (Rachel Pfeffer, Charles Mulvehill, Harold Becker)
◧　▦　◠　◠
An academic finds that he is the victim of a confidence trick.
Elaborate, involved, over-heated thriller that makes little sense and provides less enjoyment.
w Aaron Sorkin, Scott Frank, Jonas McCord　d Harold Becker　ph Gordon Willis　m Jerry Goldsmith　pd Philip Harrison　ed David Bretherton
✫ Alec Baldwin, Nicole Kidman, Bill Pullman, Bebe Neuwirth, George C. Scott, Anne Bancroft, Peter Gallagher, Josef Sommer, Tobin Bell
'A virtual scrapbook of elements borrowed from other suspense pics, but no less enjoyable for being so familiar.' – *Variety*
'One of the most shameless pieces of unadultered trash.' – *Alexander Walker, London Evening Standard*

Mallrats
US　1995　108m　DeLuxe
Gramercy/Alphaville/View Askew (James Jacks, Sean Daniel, Scott Mosier)
▦
A group of teenagers hang out in a shopping mall.
The laid-back, inconsequential humour of Smith's first film, Clerks, wears thin here in a similar, but much more conventional, outing.
wd Kevin Smith　ph David Klein　m Ira Newborn　pd Dina Lipton　ed Paul Dixon
✫ Shannen Doherty, Jeremy London, Jason Lee, Claire Forlani, Michael Rooker, Priscilla Barnes, Ben Affleck, Joey Lauren Adams, Renee Humphrey, Jason Mewes, Kevin Smith
'While admittedly ragged and ribald, it's a picture with an innate charm and honesty that should win over audiences.' – *Leonard Klady, Variety*

Malone
US　1987　92m　DeLuxe
Orion (Leo L. Fuchs)
◧　▦　◠
A disillusioned CIA hit man is not allowed to go 'straight'.
Moody but not unwatchable thriller largely set in Oregon.
w Christopher Frank　novel *Shotgun* by William Wingate　d Harley Cokliss　ph Gerald Hirschfeld　m David Newman　pd Graeme Murray　ed Todd Ramsay

✫ Burt Reynolds, Cliff Robertson, Kenneth McMillan, Cynthia Gibb, Scott Wilson, Lauren Hutton

Malou *
West Germany　1980　93m　colour
Regina Ziegler
A teacher goes on a journey to discover more about her dead mother and, ultimately, herself.
This simple story of a woman trying to come to terms with the past and the present is sometimes too didactic, but often rewarding.
wd Jeanine Meerapfel　ph Michael Ballhaus　m Peer Raben　ad Rainer Schaper　ed Dagmar Hirtz
✫ Ingrid Caven, Grischa Huber, Helmut Griem, Ivan Desny, Marie Colbin, Peter Chatel, Margarita Calahorra

The Malta Story
GB　1953　103m　bw
GFD/British Film Makers (Peter de Sarigny)
▦
An English flyer is involved in the defence of Malta during World War II.
Glib propaganda piece which is not very excitingly written and characterized, and fails to convince on any but the most elementary level.
w William Fairchild, Nigel Balchin　d Brian Desmond Hurst　ph Robert Krasker　m William Alwyn
✫ Alec Guinness, Anthony Steel, Muriel Pavlow, Jack Hawkins, Flora Robson, Renée Asherson, Ralph Truman, Reginald Tate, Hugh Burden

The Maltese Bippy
US　1969　92m　Metrocolor　Panavision
MGM
A skin flick star thinks he is turning into a werewolf.
Failed attempt to construct a crazy comedy for the stars of Laugh-In; even the spooky house sequences don't go.
w Everett Freeman, Ray Singer　d Norman Panama
✫ Dan Rowan, Dick Martin, Carol Lynley, Julie Newmar, Mildred Natwick, Fritz Weaver, Robert Reed

The Maltese Falcon **
US　1931　80m　bw
Warner
▦
TV title: *Dangerous Female*
After the death of his partner, private eye Sam Spade is dragged into a quest for a priceless statuette.
Excellent crime melodrama with smart pace and performances. Remade as Satan Met a Lady (1936); and see below.
w Maude Fulton, Lucien Hubbard, Brown Holmes　novel *Dashiell Hammett*　d Roy del Ruth　ph William Rees
✫ Ricardo Cortez, Bebe Daniels, Dudley Digges, Dwight Frye, Robert Elliott, Thelma Todd, Oscar Apfel
'Any type of audience will enjoy it.' – *Variety*
'The best mystery thriller of the year.' – *New York Times*
'A nice blend of humour, intelligence and suspense.' – *Clive Hirschhorn, 1979*

'A guy without a conscience! A dame without a heart!'
'He's as fast on the draw as he is in the drawing room!'

The Maltese Falcon ****
US　1941　101m　bw
Warner (Henry Blanke)
◧　▦　◠
A private eye is hired to find a black sculpture of a bird.
A remake which shows the difference between excellence and brilliance; here every nuance is subtly stressed, and the cast is perfection.
wd John Huston　ph Arthur Edeson　m Adolph Deutsch
✫ Humphrey Bogart, Mary Astor, Sydney Greenstreet, Elisha Cook Jnr, Barton MacLane, Lee Patrick, *Peter Lorre*, Gladys George, *Ward Bond*, Jerome Cowan
GUTMAN (SYDNEY GREENSTREET): 'I distrust a close-mouthed man. He generally picks the wrong time to talk and says the wrong things. Talking's something you can't do judiciously, unless you keep

in practice. Now, sir, we'll talk if you like. I'll tell you right out. I'm a man who likes talking to a man who likes to talk.'

SPADE (HUMPHREY BOGART) TO CAIRO (PETER LORRE): 'When you're slapped, you'll take it and like it!'

SPADE TO BRIGID (MARY ASTOR): 'Don't be too sure I'm as crooked as I'm supposed to be.'

GUTMAN: 'I distrust a man who says when. If he's got to be careful not to drink too much, it's because he's not to be trusted when he does.'

'The first crime melodrama with finish, speed and bang to come along in what seems like ages.' – *Otis Ferguson*

'A work of entertainment that is yet so skilfully constructed that after many years and many viewings, it has the same brittle explosiveness – and some of the same surprise – that it had in 1941.' – *Pauline Kael, 1968*

'The trick which Mr Huston has pulled is a combination of American ruggedness with the suavity of the English crime school – a blend of mind and muscle – plus a slight touch of pathos.' – *Bosley Crowther, New York Times*

'Admirable photography of the sort in which black and white gives full value to every detail, every flicker of panic.' – *Francis Wyndham*

♟ best picture; John Huston (as writer); Sydney Greenstreet

Mama Loves Papa *
US   1933   70m   bw
Paramount
A middle-class wife decides to do some social climbing.
Slight but amusing comedy which put together a useful team.
w Arthur Kober, Nunnally Johnson, Douglas MacLean, Keene Thompson d Norman Z. McLeod
☆ Charles Ruggles, Mary Boland, Lilyan Tashman, George Barbier, Morgan Wallace
'Exceptionally funny comedy … a cinch builder.' – *Variety*
† A second film under this title was a Leon Errol vehicle of 1945.

La Maman et la Putain: see *The Mother and the Whore*

Mamba
US   1930   76m   Technicolor
Tiffany
Germans in East Africa go to the bad during World War I.
Absurd melodrama climaxing with a Zulu uprising.
w Tom Miranda, Winifred Dunn story F. Schumann-Heink and John Reinhardt d Al Rogell
☆ Jean Hersholt, Eleanor Boardman, Ralph Forbes, Josef Swickard
'It has its lowlights and highlights; in between it's not a bad programmer.' – *Variety*

Mamba
Italy   1988   81m   colour
Medusa/Eidoscope/Reteitalia (Mario Orfini)
aka: *Fair Game*
A woman is locked in a room with a deadly snake by her murderous ex-boyfriend.
Modest, moderately suspenseful thriller that just manages to eke out its length.
w Lidia Ravera, Mario Orfini d Mario Orfini ph Dante Spinotti m Giorgio Moroder pd Ferdinando Scarfiotti ed Claudio Cutry
☆ Trudie Styler, Gregg Henry, Bill Moseley

Mambo
Italy/USA   1954   92m   bw
Paramount/Ponti/De Laurentiis
A Venetian shopgirl loves a worthless gambler, is romanced by a haemophiliac count, and joins a dance troupe.
Patchy melodrama with plenty going on but no grip.
w Guido Piovene, Ivo Perelli, Ennio de Concini, Robert Rossen d Robert Rossen ph Harold Rosson m Nino Rota, Francesco Lavagnino ch Katherine Dunham sets Andrei Andrejew
☆ Silvana Mangano, Michael Rennie, Shelley Winters, Vittorio Gassman, Eduardo Ciannelli, Mary Clare, Katherine Dunham and her troupe

The Mambo Kings *
US   1992   104m   DeLuxe
Warner/Canal/Regency/Alcor (Arnon Milchan, Arne Glimcher)
In the 1950s, a Cuban trumpeter and his brother, a singer, leave home to seek their fortunes in New York.
Energetic but dull version of a best-selling novel.
w Cynthia Cidre novel *The Mambo Kings Play Songs of Love* by Oscar Hijuelos d Arne Glimcher ph Michael Ballhaus m Robert Kraft, Carlos Franzetti pd Stuart Wurtzel ed Claire Simpson
☆ Armand Assante, Antonio Banderas, Cathy Moriarty, Maruschka Detmers, Pablo Calogero, Scott Cohen, Mario Grillo, Desi Arnaz Jnr, Roscoe Lee Browne, Tito Puente
'An ambitious, old-fashioned Hollywood film … is bound to win converts to the intoxicating rhythms of Latino music.' – *Variety*
♫ Song: 'Beautiful Maria of My Soul' (mRobert Kraft, lyArne Glimcher)

'She'll coax the blues right out of your heart'
Mame *
US   1974   131m   Technicolor   Panavision
Warner/ABC (Robert Fryer, James Cresson)
In 1928, a 10-year-old boy goes to live with his eccentric, sophisticated aunt.
Old-fashioned and rather bad film of a much overrated Broadway musical, inept in most departments but with occasional show-stopping moments.
w Paul Zindel play Jerome Lawrence, Robert E. Lee book Patrick Dennis d Gene Saks ph Philip Lathrop m/ly Jerry Herman pd Robert F. Boyle
☆ Lucille Ball, Beatrice Arthur, Robert Preston, Bruce Davison, Jane Connell, Joyce Van Patten, John McGiver
'It makes one realize afresh the parlous state of the Hollywood musical, fighting to survive against misplaced superstars and elephantine budgets matched with minuscule imagination.' – *Geoff Brown*
'The cast seem to have been handpicked for their tone-deafness, and Lucille Ball's close-ups are shot blatantly out of focus.' – *Sight and Sound*
'So terrible it isn't boring; you can get fixated staring at it and wondering what Lucille Ball thought she was doing.' – *New Yorker, 1977*

Mamma Roma *
Italy   1962   114m   bw
Arco/Cineriz (Alfredo Bini)
A pimp tries to blackmail a former prostitute into resuming her old profession by threatening to tell her teenage son about her past.
Ravishing photography is allied with over-emphatic moralizing in a film sympathetic to the deprivations of an underclass and overawed by the presence of Magnani among its otherwise non-professional cast.
wd Pier Paolo Pasolini ph Tonino delli Colli m Antonio Vivaldi md Carlo Rustichelli ad Flavio Mogherini ed Nino Baragli
☆ Anna Magnani, Franco Citti, Ettore Garofolo, Silvana Corsini, Luisa Loiano, Paolo Volponi, Luciano Gonini

Mammy *
↟↟ US   1930   84m   bw
Warner (Walter Morosco)
Murder backstage at a minstrel show.
One of the star's better musicals.
w L. G. Rigby, Joseph Jackson d Michael Curtiz ph Barney McGill m Irving Berlin
☆ Al Jolson, Lowell Sherman, Hobart Bosworth, Louise Dresser, Lee Moran
'Looks like money … a lively picture playing fast.' – *Variety*

Mam'selle Striptease: see *Plucking the Daisy*

A Man, a Woman and a Bank
Canada   1979   101m   CFI color
Bennett/McNichol
A civil engineer and a computer expert devise a foolproof way of robbing a bank.
We have been here before, except that these days the criminals are allowed to get away with it. Ho-hum.

w Raynold Gideon, Bruce A. Evans and Stuart Margolin d Noel Black ph Jack Cardiff m Bill Conti
☆ Donald Sutherland, Brooke Adams, Paul Mazursky

Man about the House
GB   1974   90m   colour
EMI/Hammer (Roy Skeggs)
Two young women, their male flatmate and their landlords combine forces to prevent the terrace from being razed for redevelopment.
Mild and rather exhausting sex comedy from the TV series, as relentlessly single-minded as a 'Carry On'.
w Johnnie Mortimer, Brian Cooke d John Robins ph Jimmy Allen m Christopher Gunning
☆ Richard O'Sullivan, Paula Wilcox, Sally Thomsett, Yootha Joyce, Brian Murphy, Peter Cellier, Patrick Newell, Spike Milligan, Arthur Lowe

A Man about the House
GB   1947   95m   bw
British Lion (Edward Black)
Two English ladies inherit an Italian villa and fall under the spell of the handsome handyman, who marries one of them and proceeds slowly to poison her.
Now clearly dull, at the time this seemed a fairly enterprising rehash of Gaslight, Kind Lady and Rebecca.
w J. B. Williams, Leslie Arliss play John Perry novel Francis Brett Young d Leslie Arliss ph Georges Perinal m Nicholas Brodsky
☆ Margaret Johnston, Dulcie Gray, Kieron Moore, Felix Aylmer, Lilian Braithwaite

Man about Town
US   1932   75m   bw
Fox
A society gambler is really a secret service man.
Flabby melodrama which practically dislocates the long arm of coincidence.
w Leon Gordon novel Denison Clift d John Francis Dillon
☆ Warner Baxter, Karen Morley, Conway Tearle, Lawrence Grant, Leni Stengel, Alan Mowbray, Lillian Bond, Halliwell Hobbes
'Plenty of hodge-podge, and doubtful b.o. Will need strong support almost everywhere.' – *Variety*

Man about Town *
US   1939   85m   bw
Paramount (Arthur Hornblow Jnr)
A Broadway producer in London makes his girlfriend jealous.
Fairly amusing comedy-musical programmer.
w Morrie Ryskind d Mark Sandrich ph Ted Tetzlaff md Victor Young
☆ Jack Benny, Dorothy Lamour, Edward Arnold, Binnie Barnes, Phil Harris, Eddie Anderson, Monty Woolley, Isabel Jeans, Betty Grable, E. E. Clive
'Good comedy, rates okay biz.' – *Variety*

Man Afraid
US   1957   84m   bw   Cinemascope
Universal-International
A priest is forced to kill a hoodlum in self-defence, and is then threatened by the dead man's psychopathic father.
Heavy-going melodrama not helped at all by the very wide screen.
w Herb Meadow d Harry Keller ph Russell Metty m Henry Mancini
☆ George Nader, Phyllis Thaxter, Harold J. Stone, Tim Hovey, Eduard Franz

Man Alive
US   1945   70m   bw
RKO
A husband thought to be dead comes back as a 'ghost' and frightens away his wife's new suitor.
Curious and rather tasteless comedy.
w Edwin Harvey Blum d Ray Enright
☆ Pat O'Brien, Ellen Drew, Adolphe Menjou, Rudy Vallee, Jack Norton

A Man Alone: see *The Killers (1946)*

A Man Alone *
US   1955   96m   Trucolor
Republic
A wandering gunman is framed by other badmen.
Solemn, slow-moving but generally interesting Western, the star's first attempt at direction.
w John Tucker Battle d Ray Milland ph Lionel Lindon m Victor Young
☆ Ray Milland, Mary Murphy, Ward Bond, Raymond Burr, Arthur Space, Lee Van Cleef, Alan Hale Jnr

A Man and a Woman **
France   1966   102m   Eastmancolor
Les Films 13
original title: *Un Homme et une Femme*
A racing driver and a script girl, both of whose spouses are dead, meet while visiting their children, and an affair leads to marriage.
Slight romantic drama so tricked out with smart images that it looks like a series of expensive commercials. A great box-office success, but its director never again succeeded in this vein which he made his own.
w Claude Lelouch, Pierre Uytterhoeven d Claude Lelouch ph Jean Columb, Patrice Pouget m Francis Lai
☆ Anouk Aimée, Jean-Louis Trintignant
'When in doubt, Lelouch's motto seems to be, use a colour filter or insert lyrical shots of dogs and horses; when in real doubt, use both.' – *Tom Milne, MFB*
'A slick item with all the Hollywood ingredients.' – *John Simon*
♟ best foreign film; Claude Lelouch, Pierre Uytterhoeven
♟ Claude Lelouch (as director); Anouk Aimée
♛ Anouk Aimée

A Man and a Woman: Twenty Years Later
France   1986   120m   Eastmancolor
Films 13/Warner
original title: *Un Homme Et Une Femme: Vingt Ans Déjà*
Slightly macabre attempt to extend the appeal with the same actors, the same technique, and even shots from Lelouch's other movies.
A bit of a wallow.
w Claude Lelouch, Pierre Uytterhoeven, Monique Lange, Jérôme Tonnerre d Claude Lelouch ph Jean-Yves Le Mener m Francis Lai
☆ Anouk Aimée, Jean-Louis Trintignant, Evelyne Bouix, Marie-Sophie Pochat

Man and His Mate: see *One Million BC*

The Man at the Gate
GB   1941   48m   bw
GHW
The war takes its toll of Cornish fishermen.
Modest family drama which strives to be inspirational via a speech made by King George VI.
w Lydia Hayward and Harold Simpson story Manning Haynes poem Louise Haskin d Norman Walker ph Eric Cross m Albert Cazabon
☆ Wilfrid Lawson, Mary Jerrold, Kathleen O'Regan
† The film has been released on video together with *Turn of the Tide*.

Man at the Top *
GB   1973   87m   Technicolor
Hammer/Dufton (Peter Charlesworth)
A pharmaceutical executive finds that his firm is marketing an unsafe drug.
Further adventures of the belligerent hero of Room at the Top (qv), this time following a popular television series. All very fashionable and predictable.
w Hugh Whitemore d Mike Vardy ph Bryan Probyn m Roy Budd
☆ Kenneth Haigh, Nanette Newman, Harry Andrews, John Quentin, Charlie Williams

The Man Behind the Gun
US   1952   82m   Technicolor
Warner
A cavalry officer is sent to quell a rebellion and helps to found Los Angeles.
Cheerful Western programmer.

◉ Digital Video Disc Region 2   ◉ Digital Video Disc Region 1   ♫ Soundtrack released on compact disc   ☆ Cast in approximate order of importance   † Points of interest   ♫ Notable songs   ♟ Academy Award   ♛ Academy Award nomination   ♛ BAFTA

w John Twist d Felix Feist ph Bert Glennon
m David Buttolph
☆ Randolph Scott, Patrice Wymore, Dick
Wesson, Phil Carey

The Man Behind the Mask

GB   1936   79m   bw
Joe Rock
A mad scientist kidnaps a nobleman's daughter.
Serial-like hokum with interesting credits.
w Ian Hay, Syd Courtenay, Jack Byrd and Stanley
Haynes d Michael Powell
☆ Hugh Williams, Maurice Schwartz, Jane Baxter,
Donald Calthrop, Henry Oscar

A Man Betrayed

US   1941   82m   bw
Armand Schaefer/Republic
📼 🟰
GB title: *Citadel of Crime*
A hick lawyer in the big city smashes corruption.
*Somewhat inconsequential melodrama which fails to
come through with the powerful entertainment it
promises.*
w Isabel Dawn d John H. Auer
☆ John Wayne, Frances Dee, Edward Ellis,
Wallace Ford, Ward Bond, Harold Huber,
Alexander Granach, Barnett Parker

The Man Between *

GB   1953   101m   bw
British Lion/London Films (Carol Reed)
📼
Ivo Kern operates successfully as a West Berlin
racketeer; love causes a softening of his attitudes
and leads to his death.
Imitation Third Man *with an uninteresting mystery
and a solemn ending. Good acting and production can't
save it.*
w Harry Kurnitz d Carol Reed ph Desmond
Dickinson m John Addison ad Andrei Andreiev
☆ James Mason, Hildegarde Neff, Claire Bloom,
Geoffrey Toone, Ernst Schroeder
'Reed's love of photogenic corruption, his
technical finesse, and his feeling for atmospheric
intrigue almost make something really good out
of a synthetic script.' – *Variety*
'A cold-hearted film about people with cold
feet.' – *Daily Express*

Man Bites Dog **

Belgium   1992   96m   bw
Metro/Les Artistes Anonymes (Rémy Belvaux, André
Bonzel, Benoît Poelvoorde)
📼 🟰 🎧
original title: *C'est arrivé près de chez vous*
A documentary film crew begins by recording the
activities of a motiveless serial killer and ends by
helping him with his murders.
*A black comedy that makes some effective points about
the relationship between cinema (or TV) and
exploitation and voyeurism but which becomes ever
harder to watch or enjoy, with its scenes of gang rape
and murder. A remarkable, if sometimes repellent, first
feature, nevertheless.*
w Rémy Belvaux, André Bonzel, Benoît
Poelvoorde, Vincent Tavier d Rémy Belvaux,
André Bonzel, Benoît Poelvoorde ph André
Bonzel m Jean-Marc Chenut ed Rémy Belvaux,
Eric Dardill
☆ Benoît Poelvoorde, Jacqueline Poelvoorde-
Pappaert, Nelly Pappaert, Jenny Drye, Malou
Madou, Willy Vandenbroeck
'To encounter Man Bites Dog is to submit to a
torrent of hilariously cruel humour, enacted
without fuss or rancour, and inconceivably
authentic.' – *Philip Strick, Sight and Sound*
'Offbeat, darkly hilarious … Violent yet
trenchant, potential sleeper should attract a cult
following and will look just right on video.' –
Variety
'Carefully shaped to draw us in and repel us, to
make us laugh and wipe the smiles off our faces.
The most horrendous scenes are calculated to
force us into asking how we can bear to watch
such things.' – *Philip French, Observer*

A Man Called Gannon

US   1969   105m   Technicolor
Universal
A wandering cowboy helps a widow rancher in her
fight against encroaching cattlemen.
Adequate remake of Man Without a Star, *which
somehow had much more stature.*

w Gene Kearney, D. D. Beauchamp and Borden
Chase d James Goldstone
☆ Tony Franciosa, Michael Sarrazin, Judi West,
Susan Oliver, John Anderson

A Man Called Horse *

US   1970   114m   Technicolor   Panavision
Cinema Center/Sanford Howard
📼 🟰 🎧
In 1825 an English aristocrat is captured by
Indians, lives with them and eventually becomes
their leader.
*Harrowing account of tribal life and customs, with
much bloodshed and torture and most of the dialogue in
Indian. Occasionally impressive but not exactly
entertaining.*
w Jack de Witt story Dorothy M. Johnson
d Elliot Silverstein ph Robert Hauser m Leonard
Rosenman
☆ Richard Harris, Judith Anderson, Jean Gascon,
Manu Tupou
† Sequels 1976: *The Return of a Man Called Horse.*
1984: *Triumphs of a Man Called Horse.*

The Man Called Noon

GB/Spain/Italy   1973   95m   Technicolor
Frontier/Montana/Finarco (Euan Lloyd)
🎧
A Western gunslinger loses his memory.
Childish Western melodrama in the violent manner.
w Scot Finch novel Louis L'Amour d Peter
Collinson ph John Cabrera m Luis Bacalov
☆ Richard Crenna, Stephen Boyd, Rosanna
Schiaffino, Farley Granger

A Man Called Peter *

US   1955   119m   DeLuxe   Cinemascope
TCF (Samuel G. Engel)
🟰
The life of Peter Marshall, a Scottish clergyman
who became chaplain to the US Senate.
Careful but rather dreary biopic.
w Eleanore Griffin book Catherine Marshall
d Henry Koster ph Harold Lipstein m Alfred
Newman
☆ Richard Todd, Jean Peters, Marjorie Rambeau,
Jill Esmond, Les Tremayne, Robert Burton
🧑 Harold Lipstein

A Man Called Sledge

Italy   1970   92m   Techniscope
Dino de Laurentiis (Carl Olsen)
🟰
A bandit tries in vain to mastermind a bank
robbery.
*Curious change of pace for a genial star. A spaghetti
Western without style but with plenty of violence, the
result doesn't linger in the memory.*
w Vic Morrow, Frank Kowalski d Vic Morrow
ph Luigi Kuveiller
☆ James Garner, Dennis Weaver, Claude Akins,
John Marley

A Man Called Sullivan: see *The Great John L.*

A Man Could Get Killed *

US   1966   98m   Technicolor   Panavision
Universal/Cherokee (Ernest Wehmeyer)
An American businessman in Lisbon is mistaken
for a secret agent.
*Minor thrill comedy with a confused plot and a willing
cast.*
w T. E. B. Clarke, Richard Breen novel *Diamonds
Are Danger* by David Walker d Ronald Neame,
Cliff Owen ph Gabor Pogany m Bert Kaempfert
☆ James Garner, Melina Mercouri, Sandra Dee,
Tony Franciosa, Robert Coote, Roland Culver,
Cecil Parker, Grégoire Aslan, Dulcie Gray, Martin
Benson, Niall MacGinnis

A Man for All Seasons ****

GB   1966   120m   Technicolor
Columbia/Highland (Fred Zinnemann)
📼 🟰 🎞 🎞
Sir Thomas More opposes Henry VIII's divorce,
and events lead inexorably to his execution.
*Irreproachable film version of a play which has had its
narrative tricks removed but stands up remarkably
well. Acting, direction, sets, locations and costumes all
have precisely the right touch.*
w Robert Bolt play Robert Bolt d Fred Zinnemann
ph Ted Moore m Georges Delerue pd John Box
☆ Paul Scofield, Wendy Hiller, Susannah York,
Robert Shaw, Orson Welles, Leo McKern, Nigel

Davenport, John Hurt, Corin Redgrave, Cyril
Luckham, Jack Gwillim
'Mr Zinnemann has crystallized the essence of
this drama in such pictorial terms as to render
even its abstractions vibrant.' – *New York Times*
'A beautiful and satisfying film, the ultimate
demonstration, perhaps, of how a fine stage play
can be transcended and, with integrity and
inspiration, turned into a great motion picture.'
– *Judith Crist*
† Reports indicate that Charlton Heston badly
wanted the role of Sir Thomas More.
👤 best picture; Robert Bolt; Fred Zinnemann; Ted
Moore; Paul Scofield
🧑 Wendy Hiller; Robert Shaw
🎬 best picture; best British film; Ted Moore; John
Box; Paul Scofield

'If you've read the book, forget it!'
Man Friday

GB   1975   115m   Eastmancolor   Panavision
Avco-Embassy/ITC/ABC/Keep Films (Jules Buck)
🟰
The story of Robinson Crusoe told so that Friday
appears the more intelligent.
*A pointless and not very entertaining exercise which
wears out its welcome very early.*
w Adrian Mitchell d Jack Gold ph Alex Phillips
m Carl Davis
☆ Peter O'Toole, Richard Roundtree
'Liberal intentions trail sadly through every
sequence and cause absurd fluctuations of tone,
since no one seems to have decided whether
laborious slapstick, heavy portentousness or
method acting is the best vehicle for the
message.' – *Jill Forbes*

The Man from Bitter Ridge

US   1955   80m   Technicolor
Universal-International
A special agent goes undercover to nail stagecoach
bandits, but himself comes under suspicion.
Adequate Western programmer.
w Lawrence Roman d Jack Arnold
☆ Lex Barker, Mara Corday, Stephen McNally,
Trevor Bardette, John Dehner

The Man from Blankley's

US   1930   67m   bw
Warner
A drunken aristocrat goes to the wrong party and
teaches those present, and himself, a thing or two.
Amusing star trifle, previously filmed as a silent.
w Harvey Thew, Joseph Jackson story F. Anstey
d Alfred E. Green ph James Van Trees
☆ John Barrymore, Loretta Young, William
Austin, Albert Gran, Emily Fitzroy
'Dickens comedy, in the Sennett vein, with the
Barrymore finesse.' – *Variety*

The Man from Colorado

US   1948   99m   Technicolor
Columbia (Jules Schermer)
🟰
A maladjusted Civil War veteran becomes a
Western judge and rules by the gun.
Slightly unusual, watchable star Western.
w Robert D. Andrews, Ben Maddow story Borden
Chase d Henry Levin ph William Snyder
m George Duning
☆ Glenn Ford, William Holden, Ellen Drew, Ray
Collins, Edgar Buchanan, Jerome Courtland, James
Millican, Jim Bannon
'No more humour than a lawyer's shingle, but it
has suspense and some exciting shots of fist
fights and burning houses.' – *Time*

The Man from Dakota *

US   1940   75m   bw
MGM
GB title: *Arouse and Beware*
A Yankee soldier is taken prisoner by the South
and becomes a spy.
Good period action piece.
w Laurence Stallings novel Mackinlay Kantor
d Leslie Fenton
☆ Wallace Beery, Dolores Del Rio, John Howard,
Donald Meek, H. B. Warner, Victor Varconi

Man from Del Rio

US   1956   82m   bw
UA/Robert L. Jacks
A Mexican hobo becomes sheriff and forces the
local badman to leave town.
Modest, efficient, rather brutal little Western.

w Richard Carr d Harry Horner ph Stanley
Cortez m Fred Steiner
☆ Anthony Quinn, Katy Jurado, Peter Whitney,
Douglas Fowley

The Man from Down Under

US   1943   103m   bw
MGM
A veteran of World War I smuggles two orphans
back into Australia.
*Appallingly indulgent sentimental star vehicle, a
mistake for all concerned.*
w Wells Root, Thomas Seller d Robert Z.
Leonard
☆ Charles Laughton, Binnie Barnes, Donna Reed,
Richard Carlson, Horace McNally, Arthur Shields

'He came a thousand miles to kill someone he'd
never seen!'
The Man from Laramie **

US   1955   104m   Technicolor   Cinemascope
Columbia (William Goetz)
📼 🟰 🎥
A wandering cowman seeks revenge on those who
killed his brother.
*Grade-A Western with new-fangled touches of
brutality touching off the wide screen spectacle.*
w Philip Yordan, Frank Burt d Anthony Mann
ph Charles Lang Jnr m George Duning
md Morris Stoloff ad Cary Odell ed William
Lyon
☆ James Stewart, Arthur Kennedy, Donald Crisp,
Cathy O'Donnell, Alex Nicol, Aline MacMahon,
Wallace Ford, Jack Elam

The Man from Majorca *

Sweden   1984   105m   colour
Cannon/Drakfilm (Göran Lindström)
original title: *Mannen Fròn Mallorca*
Two policemen are thwarted in their attempt to
uncover a political and sexual scandal.
A taut thriller that maintains its suspense until the end.
wd Bo Widerberg novel *Grisfesten* by G. W.
Persson ph Thomas Wahlberg m Björn Jason
Lindh ad Jan öquist ed Bo Widerberg
☆ Sven Wollter, Tomas von Brömssen, Hakan
Serner, Ernst Günther, Thomas Hellberg, Ingvar
Hirdvall, Niels Jensen

The Man from Monterey

US   1933   57m   bw
Warner (Leon Schlesinger)
📼 🟰
A US Army captain helps Mexican landowners
prevent their lands from being taken over by
unscrupulous speculators and saves the girl from
marrying a villain.
*A standard quickie that was Wayne's last Western for
Warner, as he went on to better movies and paydays.*
w Lesley Mason d Mack V. Wright
☆ John Wayne, Ruth Hall, Nina Quartero, Lillian
Leighton, Luis Alberni, Francis Ford, Donald Reed

The Man from Morocco

GB   1944   116m   bw
ABP (Warwick Ward)
Members of the international brigade are captured
and later sent by Vichy to build a Sahara railway
for the Germans; one escapes to London with vital
information.
*Stilted, meandering and extremely unconvincing
melodrama with a star ill at ease.*
w Warwick Ward, Edward Dryhurst, Marguerite
Steen story Rudolph Cartier d Max Greene
ph Basil Emmott
☆ Anton Walbrook, Margaretta Scott, Mary
Morris, Reginald Tate, Peter Sinclair, David Horne

The Man from Nevada: see *The Nevadan*

The Man from Planet X

US   1951   70m   bw
Sherrill Corwin/United Artists (Aubrey Wisberg and
Jack Pollexfen)
On a remote Scottish island a spacecraft deposits a
strange creature with a large head and mesmeric
powers.
*Early, minor, moderately pleasing fragment in the
Close Encounters cycle.*
w Aubrey Wisberg, Jack Pollexfen d Edgar G.
Ulmer ph John Russell m Charles Koff
☆ Margaret Field, Raymond Bond, William
Schallert

🔼🔼 film suitable for
family viewing
📼 VHS video-cassette for
the British PAL system
📼 VHS video-cassette for the British
PAL system in wide screen-format
🔄 Video cassette in a computer-
colourised version
🟰 American NTSC video-cassette
🎥 Laser disc

The Man from Snowy River

Australia 1982 104m Eastmancolor
Panavision
Cambridge Films/Michael Edgley International (Geoff
Burrowes)

In 1888, an orphan boy grows up with an obsession
about wild horses.
*Essentially no more than an Audie-Murphy-style
Western given full down-under treatment. An
Australian smash, a programmer elsewhere.*
w John Dixon, Fred Cullen poem A. B. Paterson
d George Miller ph Keith Wagstaff m Bruce
Rowland
☆ Kirk Douglas, Jack Thompson, Sigrid
Thornton, Tom Burlinson, Terence Donovan,
Lorraine Bayly

The Man from Snowy River Part II: see
Return to Snowy River

Man from Tangier

GB 1957 66m bw
Butcher's (W. G. Chalmers)
A pilot becomes mixed up with rival gangs trying
to get their hands on a forger's valuable plates.
*Dull, cramped thriller with little action and much talk
in small rooms.*
w P. Manning O'Brine d Lance Comfort
ph Geoffrey Faithfull md Wilfred Burns ad John
Stoll ed Peter Mayhew
☆ Robert Hutton, Lisa Gastoni, Martin Benson,
Leonard Sachs, Derek Sydney, Robert Raglan,
Harold Berens, Michael Balfour

The Man from the Alamo *

US 1953 79m Technicolor
U-I (Aaron Rosenberg)

A survivor of the Alamo is thought to be a deserter
but proves his story and exposes a villain.
Satisfying Western programmer.
w Steve Fisher, D. D. Beauchamp d Budd
Boetticher ph Russell Metty m Frank Skinner
☆ Glenn Ford, Victor Jory, Julia Adams, Hugh
O'Brian

The Man from the Diners' Club *

US 1963 96m bw
Columbia/Dena/Ampersand (Bill Bloom)
A clerk accidentally lets a credit card go to a
notorious gangster, and makes desperate efforts to
retrieve it.
*Minor star comedy with funny moments surviving a
slapdash script.*
w Bill Blatty d Frank Tashlin ph Hal Mohr
m Stu Philips
☆ Danny Kaye, Telly Savalas, Martha Hyer, Cara
Williams, Everett Sloane, George Kennedy

The Man from the Folies Bergère: see
Folies Bergère

The Man from Tokyo: see *Tokyo Drifter*

The Man from U.N.C.L.E

This long-running one-hour TV series (1964–68)
began as a spoof of James Bond, which was itself a
spoof.
*Not much more serious or convincing than Batman,
they caused a lot of people to suspend their disbelief.*
☆ Robert Vaughn, David McCallum, Leo G.
Carroll
† Several feature films were made up from various
episodes, and did well in cinemas in some
countries. They were: To Trap a Spy, The Spy with
My Face, The Karate Killers, The Spy in the Green
Hat, One of Our Spies Is Missing, The Helicopter
Spies, How to Steal the World, and One Spy Too
Many.

The Man from Utah

US 1934 55m bw
Lone Star (Paul Malvern)

At the urging of a US Marshal, a cowboy goes
undercover to expose a gang organizing a crooked
rodeo.
*Dull Western, with some moderately interesting rodeo
footage. It opens, uncharacteristically, with Wayne as
a guitar-toting cowboy on a white horse, singing a love
song in an unpleasing baritone.*
w Lindsley Parsons d Robert Bradbury ph Archie
Stout m William Barber ed Carl Pierson

☆ John Wayne, Polly Ann Young, Anita
Compillo, Edward Peil, George Hayes, Yakima
Canutt, George Cleveland

A Man from Wyoming

US 1930 70m bw
Paramount
A slow-speaking engineer joins the army, serves
overseas and marries an ambulance driver.
*Uncertain star vehicle which helped to mould his screen
character.*
w John Weaver and Albert Shelby Le Vino
d Rowland V. Lee
☆ Gary Cooper, June Collyer, Regis Toomey, E. H.
Calvert, Morgan Farley
'Bad enough to be good entertainment if taken
as farce.' – *New York Evening Post*.

'Her body ached for the man she loved!'

The Man from Yesterday

US 1932 71m bw
Paramount
A man is reported missing in World War I, but
years later his wife and her new fiancé find him in
Switzerland, dying of gas poisoning.
Enoch Arden rides again, and very boringly.
w Oliver H. P. Garrett d Berthold Viertel
ph Karl Struss
☆ Claudette Colbert, Clive Brook, Charles Boyer,
Andy Devine, Alan Mowbray, Christian Rub
'Rather too late in the day to expect war scenes,
and when the war peters out, there is only
scenery and conversation.' – *Variety*

Man Hunt

US 1932 65m bw
Warner
A cub reporter hunts a bank robber.
Standard support action fare of its time.
w Roy Chanslor, Earl Felton d William Clemens
☆ William Gargan, Ricardo Cortez, Marguerite
Chapman, Chic Sale, Maude Eburne
'Script never lives up to the title's promise.' –
Variety

Man Hunt **

US 1941 98m bw
TCF (Kenneth MacGowan)
A big game hunter misses a shot at Hitler and is
chased back to England by the Gestapo.
*Despite hilariously inaccurate English backgrounds, this
is perhaps its director's most vivid Hollywood thriller,
though watered down in tone from the original novel.*
w Dudley Nichols novel Rogue Male by Geoffrey
Household d Fritz Lang ph Arthur Miller
m Alfred Newman
☆ Walter Pidgeon, Joan Bennett, George Sanders,
John Carradine, Roddy McDowall, Ludwig Stossel,
Heather Thatcher, Frederick Worlock
'A tense and intriguing thriller that is both
propaganda and exciting entertainment.' – *Paul
M. Jensen, 1969*
'In its manipulation of these dark and intent
forces on a checkerboard, it manages to take
your breath away.' – *Otis Ferguson*
† Remade for TV in 1976 as *Rogue Male*.

The Man I Killed: see *Broken Lullaby*

The Man I Love

US 1947 76m bw
Warner (Arnold Albert)
A night-club singer is involved with a mobster.
Dreary little melodrama which never really gets going.
w Catherine Turney d Raoul Walsh ph Sid
Hickox m Max Steiner
☆ Ida Lupino, Robert Alda, Andrea King, Martha
Vickers, Bruce Bennett, Alan Hale, Dolores
Moran, John Ridgely

The Man I Married *

US 1940 79m bw
TCF (Raymond Griffith)
aka: *I Married a Nazi*
When an American couple take a European
vacation, the wife is horrified to find her husband,
who is of German parentage, agreeing with the
Nazis.
*Naïve but striking melodrama exploring attitudes of its
time.*
w Oliver H. P. Garrett novel Swastika by Oscar
Shisgall d Irving Pichel ph Peverell Marley
m David Buttolph

☆ Joan Bennett, Francis Lederer, Lloyd Nolan,
Anna Sten, Otto Kruger, Maria Ouspenskaya,
Ludwig Stossel, Johnny Russell

Man in a Cocked Hat: see *Carlton-Browne of
the FO*

The Man in Grey **

GB 1943 116m bw
GFD/Gainsborough (Edward Black)

In Regency times, an aristocratic girl's love for her
less fortunate friend is repaid by jealousy, treachery
and murder.
*Rather dully performed flashback costume melodrama
which caught the public imagination in the middle of a
dreary world war, especially as its evil leading
characters were played by stars who rapidly went right
to the top. The several imitations which followed,
including The Wicked Lady, Jassy and Hungry Hill,
became known as the Gainsborough school.*
w Margaret Kennedy, Leslie Arliss, Doreen
Montgomery novel Lady Eleanor Smith d Leslie
Arliss ph Arthur Crabtree m Cedric Mallabey
ad Walter Murton
☆ James Mason, Margaret Lockwood, Phyllis
Calvert, Stewart Granger, Helen Haye, Nora
Swinburne, Raymond Lovell, Martita Hunt
'There was not a moment when I would not
gladly have dived for my hat.' – *James Agate*
'All the time-tested materials: gypsy fortune-
teller; scowling, black-browed villain; gushy
diary kept by a doe-eyed girl who munches
candied violets; fire-breathing adventuress who
dotes on discord and low-cut gowns...' – *Time*

'Even the one girl who loved enough to ask no
questions – had to face the fearful truth!'

The Man in Half Moon Street

US 1944 91m bw
Paramount (Walter MacEwen)
A mysteriously handsome young scientist is
actually a 90-year-old who has discovered a surgical
method of preserving youth.
*Boring screen version of a play which was conceived in
an almost romantic vein; Hollywood has taken it too
literally.*
w Charles Kenyon play Barre Lyndon d Ralph
Murphy ph Henry Sharp m Miklos Rozsa
☆ Nils Asther, Helen Walker, Brandon Hurst,
Reinhold Schunzel
† Remade in straight horror vein as *The Man Who
Could Cheat Death* (qv).

The Man in Her Life

Philippines 1998 103m colour
Star Pacific/Reyna (Armida Siguion-Reyna)
original title: *Ang Lalaki Sa Buhay Ni Selya*
A homosexual headmaster, scandalising the locals
over his relationship with a married man, decides
to marry the school's new teacher, who has left
home to find her lover, a travelling salesman.
*Amiable, but long-winded domestic drama that never
fully engages with its subject matter.*
w Bibeth Orteza d Carlos Siguion-Reyna ph Yam
Laranas m Ryan Cayabyab pd Joey Luna
ed Manet A. Dayrit
☆ Ricky Davao, Gardo Versoza, Rosanna Roces,
Alan Paule, Eva Darren, Renato del Prado, Crispin
Pineda

Man in Love *

France/Italy 1987 110m colour
Virgin/Fox/Camera One/Alexandra Films/JMS (Michel
Seydoux, Diane Kurys)

original title: *Un Homme Amoureux*
A married American film star falls in love with an
actress while making a movie in Italy.
*Overlong romantic melodrama that generates little
heat.*
w Diane Kurys, Olivier Schatzky d Diane Kurys
ph Bernard Zitzermann m Georges Delerue
ad Dean Tavoularis ed Joelle Van Effenterre
☆ Peter Coyote, Greta Scacchi, Peter Riegert,
Claudia Cardinale, John Berry, Vincent Lindon,
Jamie Lee Curtis

The Man in Possession: see *Personal Property
(1937)*

The Man in Possession

US 1931 81m bw
MGM
A lady falls in love with the bailiff's man in
temporary charge of her establishment.
*Light comedy subsequently remade as Personal
Property; quite tolerable.*
w Sarah Y. Mason play H. M. Harwood d Sam
Wood
☆ Robert Montgomery, Irene Purcell, Charlotte
Greenwood, C. Aubrey Smith, Beryl Mercer,
Reginald Owen, Alan Mowbray
'Should have no trouble where the censors don't
interfere ... where it gets by with the dirt, the
dirt should get it over.' – *Variety*

The Man in the Attic

US 1953 82m bw
TCF (Robert L. Jacks)
Remake of the much-remade *The Lodger*, this time
with parsimonious production values and no style.
w Robert Presnell Jnr, Barre Lyndon d Hugo
Fregonese ph Leo Tover md Lionel Newman
☆ Jack Palance, Constance Smith, Byron Palmer,
Frances Bavier, Rhys Williams

The Man in the Back Seat *

GB 1961 57m bw
Independent Artists (Julian Wintle, Leslie Parkyn)
Two robbers fail to separate a bookie from the
locked bag chained to his wrist, at first taking him
with them they finally kill him and are apparently
haunted by him.
*Taut, downbeat little crime thriller which won a few
critical plaudits.*
w Malcolm Hulke, Eric Paice d Vernon Sewell
ph Reg Wyer m Stanley Black
☆ Derren Nesbitt, Keith Faulkner, Carol White,
Harry Locke

'Death at the carnival – as a killer takes over the
switchback!'

Man in the Dark *

US 1953 70m bw 3-D
Columbia (Wallace Macdonald)
A convict submits to a brain operation which will
remove his criminal tendencies. Unfortunately it
also removes his memory, and on his release he is
bewildered when gangsters expect him to know
where the loot is hidden.
*Silly low-budgeter which is only notable as the 3-D film
which most exploited the short-lived medium. Apart
from a roller coaster ride, objects hurled at the audience
include scissors, spiders, knives, forceps, fists and
falling bodies.*
w George Bricker, Jack Leonard d Lew Landers
ph Floyd Crosby md Ross de Maggio
☆ Edmond O'Brien, Audrey Totter, Ted de Corsia,
Horace MacMahon

The Man in the Gray Flannel Suit *

US 1956 152m Eastmancolor
Cinemascope
TCF (Darryl F. Zanuck)

A young New York executive is offered a
demanding job but decides that his first loyalty is
to his wife and children.
*An amusingly accurate novel of Madison Avenue
mores becomes a marathon emotional melodrama in
which the mordant bits quickly give way to domestic
problems and a guilt complex about a wartime affair,
shown in lengthy flashback. It's all too much.*
wd Nunnally Johnson novel Sloan Wilson
ph Charles G. Clarke m Bernard Herrmann
☆ Gregory Peck, Fredric March, Jennifer Jones,
Ann Harding, Arthur O'Connell, Henry Daniell,
Marisa Pavan, Lee J. Cobb, Keenan Wynn, Gene
Lockhart, Gigi Perreau, Connie Gilchrist, Joseph
Sweeney

'Free Him!'
'Is he my wooer, my loved one? Or is he the tyrant
who bleeds my people? Is he ardent lover – or cold-
blooded killer? Let me look upon his face! Let me
touch him!'

The Man in the Iron Mask **

US 1939 110m bw
Edward Small

King Louis XIV keeps his twin brother prisoner.
*Exhilarating swashbuckler based on a classic novel,
with a complex plot, good acting and the three
musketeers in full cry.*

◉ Digital Video Disc Region 2   ◉ Digital Video Disc Region 1   ♫ Soundtrack released on compact disc   ☆ Cast in approximate order of importance   † Points of interest   ♫ Notable songs   🏆 Academy Award   🏆 Academy Award nomination   🏆 BAFTA

w George Bruce novel Alexandre Dumas d James Whale ph Robert Planck m Lucien Moraweck, Lud Gluskin ad John DuCasse Schulze ed Grant Whytock
☆ Louis Hayward, Warren William, Alan Hale, Bert Roach, Miles Mander, Joan Bennett, Joseph Schildkraut, Walter Kingsford, Marion Martin, Montagu Love, Albert Dekker
'Substantial entertainment for general appeal and satisfaction.' – Variety
'A sort of combination of The Prisoner of Zenda and The Three Musketeers, with a few wild west chases thrown in … not unentertaining.' – Richard Mallett, Punch
† Remade 1976 as a TV movie with Richard Chamberlain, and 1978 as The Fifth Musketeer (qv).
♫ Lucien Moraweck, Lud Gluskin

The Man in the Iron Mask *
US 1998 132m DeLuxe
MGM/UA (Randall Wallace, Russell Smith)
When King Louis XIV rules badly and connives in the death of Athos's son, the former musketeers decide to replace him with his imprisoned twin brother.
A stolid version that limits the swashbuckling, and provides little else to excite, with its motley international quartet of musketeers and a twin performance from DiCaprio that fails to convince.
wd Randall Wallace novel Alexandre Dumas ph Peter Suschitzky m Nick Glennie-Smith pd Anthony Pratt ed William Hoy
☆ Leonardo DiCaprio, Jeremy Irons, John Malkovich, Gérard Depardieu, Gabriel Byrne, Anne Parillaud, Judith Godrèche, Edward Atterton, Peter Sarsgaard
'An unusually sober and serious-minded telling of Alexandre Dumas' classic tale, this handsome costumer is routinely made and comes up rather short in boisterous excitement.' – Todd McCarthy, Variety
† MGM discovered that the audience the movie attracted was 'directly related to the appeal of Leonardo DiCaprio', being 55 per cent female, and 46 per cent under-25.

The Man in the Middle *
GB 1964 94m bw Cinemascope
TCF/Pennebaker/Belmont (Walter Seltzer)
In India during World War II, an American lieutenant is indicted for murder and the defence counsel is instructed to lose the case.
Courtroom melodrama with unusual angles; quite intriguing, though the wide screen doesn't help.
w Keith Waterhouse, Willis Hall novel The Winston Affair by Howard Fast d Guy Hamilton ph Wilkie Cooper m John Barry
☆ Robert Mitchum, Trevor Howard, Keenan Wynn, Barry Sullivan, France Nuyen, Alexander Knox
'For once Mitchum seems to have an excuse for keeping his eyes at half mast.' – Judith Crist

The Man in the Mirror
GB 1936 82m bw
JH Productions (Julius Hagen)
A timid man's reflection steps out of the mirror and organizes him.
Modest comedy with a pleasing star.
w F. McGrew Willis, Hugh Mills novel William Garrett d Maurice Elvey ph Curt Courant
☆ Edward Everett Horton, Geneviève Tobin, Garry Marsh, Ursula Jeans, Alastair Sim, Aubrey Mather, Felix Aylmer
'High speed sequences of comic incident put over in fine style.' – Cinema

Man in the Moon
GB 1960 99m bw
Allied Film Makers/Excalibur (Michael Relph)
A man who earns his living as Mr Normal, a human guinea pig for scientific research, is chosen as the first astronaut.
Dated comedy which rather dismayingly turns from mild satire to outright farce and fantasy.
w Michael Relph, Bryan Forbes d Basil Dearden ph Harry Waxman m Philip Green
☆ Kenneth More, Shirley Anne Field, Michael Hordern, John Phillips, John Glyn-Jones, Charles Gray, Norman Bird

The Man in the Moon *
US 1991 99m Eastmancolor
UIP/MGM/Pathé (Mark Rydell)
In the 1950s, a 14-year-old girl falls in love with a 17-year-old boy, but he prefers her sister.
Weepy period account of growing-up, handled with skill.
w Jenny Wingfield d Robert Mulligan ph Freddie Francis m James Newton Howard pd Gene Callahan ed Trudy Ship
☆ Sam Waterston, Tess Harper, Gail Strickland, Reese Witherspoon, Jason London, Emily Warfield
'A disappointing return by Mulligan to the well-ploughed cliché.' – Philip Strick, Sight and Sound
'One of the most delicate and heart-warming movies of the year.' – Roger Ebert

The Man in the Net
US 1958 96m bw
UA/Mirisch-Jaguar (Walter Mirisch)
When a painter is accused of murdering his wife, he goes into hiding and is helped by children.
Extremely tedious and inept mystery, doubly disappointing in view of the credits.
w Reginald Rose novel Patrick Quentin d Michael Curtiz ph John Seitz m Hans Salter
☆ Alan Ladd, Carolyn Jones, Diane Brewster, John Lupton, Charles McGraw, Tom Helmore, John Alexander

The Man in the Road
GB 1957 83m bw
Gibraltar
An amnesiac scientist is deceived by communists.
Mildly diverting spy caper with a good cast.
w Guy Morgan novel He Was Found in the Road by Anthony Armstrong d Lance Comfort ph Stan Pavey m Bruce Campbell
☆ Derek Farr, Ella Raines, Donald Wolfit, Lisa Daniely, Karel Stepanek, Cyril Cusack

Man in the Saddle
US 1951 87m Technicolor
Harry Joe Brown/Columbia
GB title: The Outcast
A small rancher is victimized by his wealthy neighbour.
Fairly lively Western which develops into a series of gunfights.
w Kenneth Gamet d André de Toth ph Charles Lawton Jnr m George Duning
☆ Randolph Scott, Alexander Knox, Joan Leslie, Ellen Drew, Richard Rober

Man in the Shadow *
US 1957 80m bw Cinemascope
U-I (Albert Zugsmith)
GB title: Pay the Devil
The sheriff of a small western town investigates a murder against the wishes of a powerful local rancher.
Mini-social drama in which the honest man wins out at last … and who would expect anything different. A brooding melodrama which delivers less than it promises.
w Gene L. Coon d Jack Arnold ph Arthur E. Arling m Hans Salter
☆ Jeff Chandler, Orson Welles, Colleen Miller, John Larch, Joe Schneider, Leo Gordon

The Man in the Sky *
GB 1956 87m bw
Ealing (Seth Holt)
US title: Decision against Time
A test pilot refuses to bale out when an engine catches fire; his plight is interwoven with scenes of his family, friends and associates.
Thin suspense drama with some effective moments but too many irrelevant asides.
w William Rose, John Eldridge d Charles Crichton m Douglas Slocombe m Gerbrand Schurmann
☆ Jack Hawkins, Elizabeth Sellars, Walter Fitzgerald, Eddie Byrne, John Stratton, Victor Maddern, Lionel Jeffries, Donald Pleasence

The Man in the Trunk
US 1942 70m bw
TCF
The ghost of a murder victim helps a young attorney to nail the culprit.
Slightly uneasy spook comedy with a good star performance.

w John Larkin d Malcolm St Clair
☆ Raymond Walburn, Lynne Roberts, George Holmes, J. Carrol Naish, Dorothy Peterson

The Man in the White Suit ****
GB 1951 81m bw
Ealing (Sidney Cole)
A scientist produces a fabric that never gets dirty and never wears out. Unions and management are equally aghast.
Brilliant satirical comedy played as farce and put together with meticulous cinematic counterpoint, so that every moment counts and all concerned give of their very best.
w Roger MacDougall, John Dighton, Alexander Mackendrick d Alexander Mackendrick ph Douglas Slocombe m Benjamin Frankel
☆ Alec Guinness, Joan Greenwood, Cecil Parker, Vida Hope, Ernest Thesiger, Michael Gough, Howard Marion Crawford, Miles Malleson, George Benson, Edie Martin
'The combination of an ingenious idea, a bright, funny and imaginative script, skilful playing and perceptive brisk direction has resulted once more in a really satisfying Ealing comedy.' – Richard Mallett, Punch
♫ script

Man in the Wilderness *
US 1971 105m Technicolor Panavision
Warner/Wilderness (Sanford Howard)
In 1820 in the Canadian northwest, a fur trapper is mauled by a grizzly and left for dead, but he learns to survive and sets out for revenge.
Endurance melodrama modelled after A Man Called Horse; a bit stretched and only for the hardened, but taking an agreeably unromantic view of nature.
w Jack de Witt d Richard Sarafian ph Gerry Fisher m Johnny Harris
☆ Richard Harris, John Huston, John Bindon, Prunella Ransome, Henry Wilcoxon, Ben Carruthers

The Man Inside
GB 1958 97m bw Cinemascope
Columbia/Warwick (Harold Huth)
A jeweller's book-keeper steals a priceless diamond and is trailed by various factions half across Europe.
Fairly modest and unenterprising British thriller which hadn't much hope of the world market it was aiming at.
w John Gilling, David Shaw novel M. E. Chaber d John Gilling ph Ted Moore m Richard Bennett
☆ Nigel Patrick, Jack Palance, Anita Ekberg, Anthony Newley, Bonar Colleano, Sid James, Donald Pleasence

A Man is Ten Feet Tall: see Edge of the City

A Man Like Eva *
West Germany 1983 89m colour
Blue Dolphin/Cinevista/Schier-Straub/Trio/Impuls/Maran (Horst Schier, Laurens Straub)
original title: Ein Mann Wie Eva
While making a film, its director marries the female star and seduces the male star.
Based on the messy, manipulative life of bisexual film director Rainer Werner Fassbinder, it has one of his leading ladies, Eva Mattes, in the role of the male director, surprising casting that works well and adds an extra spice to an already over-heated narrative.
w Radu Gabrea, Laurens Straub d Radu Gabrea ph Horst Schier m Verdi ad Herbert Buchenberger ed Dragos-Emmanuel Witowski
☆ Eva Mattes, Lisa Kreuzer, Werner Stocker, Charles Regnier, Carola Regnier, Charly Muhamed Huber, Albert Kitzl

Man Made Monster *
US 1940 57m bw
Universal (Jack Bernard)
GB title: The Electric Man
A scientist experiments with a man who is impervious to electric shock, and turns him into a walking robot.
A smart little semi-horror originally planned for Karloff and Lugosi.
w Joseph West d George Waggner ph Elwood Bredell m Hans Salter md Charles Previn sp John P. Fulton

☆ Lon Chaney Jnr, Lionel Atwill, Anne Nagel, Frank Albertson, Samuel S. Hinds
'Who were the women who twisted his life and love – gutting the flame of his incredible genius?'

Man of a Thousand Faces **
US 1957 122m bw Cinemascope
U-I (Robert Arthur)
The rise to fame of silent screen character actor Lon Chaney.
Moderately commendable biopic with a strong sense of period Hollywood, an excellent star performance, but too much sudsy emoting about deaf mute parents and an ungrateful wife.
w R. Wright Campbell, Ivan Goff, Ben Roberts d Joseph Pevney ph Russell Metty m Frank Skinner ad Alexander Golitzen ed Ted J. Kent sp Clifford Stine
☆ James Cagney, Dorothy Malone, Robert Evans, Roger Smith, Marjorie Rambeau, Jane Greer, Jim Backus
'The script and conception are so maudlin and degrading that Cagney's high dedication becomes somewhat oppressive.' – Pauline Kael, 70s
♫ script

Man of Affairs: see His Lordship (1936)

Man of Affairs
GB 1937 70m bw
Gaumont British
When the foreign secretary is kidnapped, his twin brother impersonates him.
Lighthearted star vehicle which satisfied.
w Maude Howell d L. Du Garde Peach play The Nelson Touch by Neil Grant d Herbert Mason
☆ George Arliss, Romilly Lunge, Rene Ray, Jessie Winter, Allan Jeayes
'Business possibilities only moderate.' – Variety

Man of Aran **
GB 1934 75m bw
Gainsborough (Michael Balcon)
The primitive life of crofting and fishing folk in the west of Ireland.
A lowering documentary very typical of its maker: highly impressive scene for scene, but tedious as a whole; still, highly remarkable that it was made at all for the commercial cinema.
w Robert and Frances Flaherty d Robert Flaherty m John Greenwood
☆ Colman King, Maggie Dirane
'In so far as it is a rendering of the efforts of the Atlantic to overwhelm and demolish a wall of rock, it is magnificent; but the human note is inadequate and unnecessary.' – E. V. Lucas, Punch
'However real, it would have made better truth if it had been handled with more of the art of fiction.' – Otis Ferguson
'Six thousand feet of such fine and purposeful pictorial composition have seldom been seen on the screen.' – Observer

Man of Bronze: see Jimmy Thorpe, All American

Man of Conquest
US 1939 99m bw
Republic (Sol C. Siegel)
The life of Western hero Sam Houston, who became president of Texas.
Competent action/domestic biopic.
w Wells Root, E. E. Paramore Jnr d George Nicholls Jnr ph Joseph H. August m Victor Young ad John Victor Mackay
☆ Richard Dix, Joan Fontaine, Gail Patrick, Edward Ellis, Victor Jory, Robert Barrat, George Hayes, Ralph Morgan, Robert Armstrong, C. Henry Gordon, Janet Beecher
'A grown-up hoss opera, based on authentic and colorful history, with fairly believable characters, ample action and reasonable suspense.' – Variety
♫ Victor Young; art direction

Man of Evil: see Fanny by Gaslight

Man of Flowers *

Australia   1983   91m   Fujicolour
Flowers International (Jane Ballantyne, Paul Cox)

A model's relationship with her lover, a blackmailing, cocaine-snorting artist, and her admirer, a wealthy, repressed, middle-aged aesthete, leads to violence.
A study of sexual hang-ups that teeters on the edge of black farce.
w Paul Cox, Bob Ellis d Paul Cox ph Yuro Sokol ad Asher Bilu ed Tim Lewis
☆ Norman Kaye, Alyson Best, Chris Haywood, Sarah Walker, Werner Herzog

Man of Iron

US   1935   62m   bw
Warner

A steel works foreman rises to the boardroom, but doesn't like it.
Rather obvious moral tale without much excitement.
w William Wister Haines, Dawn Powell d William McGann
☆ Barton MacLane, Mary Astor, John Eldredge, Dorothy Peterson, Joseph Crehan
'Unimportant programme material.' – Variety

Man of Iron *

Poland   1981   152m   colour/bw
PRF/Filmowy X
original title: Czlowiek Z Zelaza
The events of 1980 in Poland are seen through the eyes of a strike leader.
A stirring companion piece to Man of Marble; *hard tack for the entertainment seeker but as honest a piece of history as one is likely to get from a so-called fiction film.*
w Aleksander Scibor-Rylski d Andrzej Wajda ph Edward Klosinski m Andrzej Korzynski
☆ Jerzy Radziwilowicz, Krystyna Janda, Marian Opania
⚐ best foreign film

Man of La Mancha *

⚏⚏ US   1972   132m   DeLuxe
UA/PEA (Arthur Hiller)

Arrested by the Inquisition and thrown into prison, Miguel de Cervantes relates the story of Don Quixote.
Unimaginative but generally good-looking attempt to recreate on the screen an essentially theatrical experience.
w Dale Wasserman play Dale Wasserman d Arthur Hiller ph Goffredo Rotunno m Mitch Leigh md Laurence Rosenthal ad Luciano Damiani ly Joe Darion
☆ Peter O'Toole, Sophia Loren, James Coco, Harry Andrews, John Castle, Brian Blessed
'Needful of all the imagination the spectator can muster.' – Variety
⚐ Laurence Rosenthal

Man of Marble *

Poland   1978   165m   colour
PRF/Zespol X (Andrzej Wajda)

original title: Czlowiek Z Marmur
Young film makers gather material on a political hero of the fifties.
An extended drama on the style of Citizen Kane but with much more relevance to contemporary history. A key film to students of Poland, but too specialized for general entertainment.
w Aleksander Scibor-Rylski d Andrzej Wajda ph Edward Klosinski m Andrzej Korzynski
☆ Jerzy Radziwilowicz, Krystyna Janda, Michael Tarkowski, Tadeusz Lomnicki

The Man of My Life: see L'Homme de Ma Vie

A Man of No Importance

GB/Ireland   1994   99m   Eastmancolor
Clarence/Majestic/BBC/Little Bird (Jonathan Cavendish)

In Dublin in the early 60s, a middle-aged bus conductor, who is staging an amateur performance of Oscar Wilde's *Salome*, realizes that it is time to come out of the closet and admit that he is homosexual and in love with his driver.
A pointless and virtually witless exercise that resembles a timidly gay reworking of a third-rate Ealing comedy;
it is heavy-handed whimsy weighed down by some broad acting.
w Barry Devlin d Suri Krishnamma ph Ashley Rowe m Julian Nott pd Jamie Leonard ed David Freeman
☆ Albert Finney, Brenda Fricker, Michael Gambon, Tara Fitzgerald, Rufus Sewell, Patrick Malahide, Anna Manahan
'Faced with all the fuss as quietly bad, as lazy in its pathos (even the title is sentimental), it's hard to know whether to crush it with rock or to run circles round it sniggering.' – Adam Mars-Jones, Independent

Man of the East (dubbed)

Italy/France   1972   125m   Technicolor
Techniscope
UA/PEA/Artistes Associés (Alberto Grimaldi)
original title: ...E Poi Lo Chiamarono Il Magnifico
An English fop is taught how to fight and shoot by three outlaws.
Over-long comedy Western, in which the jokes are few and far between.
w Enzo Barboni d E. B. Clutcher (Enzo Barboni) ph Aldo Giordani m Guido de Angelis, Maurizio de Angelis ad Enzo Bulgarelli ed Eugenio Alabiso
☆ Terence Hill (Mario Girotti), Yanti Somer, Gregory Walcott, Harry Carey, Dominici Barto, Riccardo Pizzuti
'A predictable plot ... is strung out to almost interminable length by the director's own script which never misses an opportunity to employ five sequences where one would do.' – David Pirie, MFB

Man of the Hour: see Colonel Effingham's Raid

The Man of the House

US   1995   96m   Technicolor
Buena Vista/Walt Disney/Forever Girls (Bonnie Bruckheimer, Marty Katz)

A young boy attempts to sabotage his mother's romance with the lawyer who comes to live with them.
A dim and uninteresting account of male bonding in the woods; it is impossible to imagine at what audience it is aimed.
w James Orr, Jim Cruickshank story David Peckinpah, Richard Jefferies d James Orr ph Jamie Anderson m Mark Mancina pd Lawrence G. Paull ed Harry Keramidas
☆ Chevy Chase, Farrah Fawcett, Jonathan Taylor Thomas, George Wendt, David Shiner, Art LaFleur, Richard Portnow
'A dreadful film, with absolutely no redeeming features whatsoever – except that it does eventually end.' – Derek Malcolm, Guardian
'Jaw-droppingly awful.' – Independent

Man of the Moment

GB   1935   82m   bw
Warner

An engaged young man saves a girl from suicide and falls in love with her.
Minor romantic comedy of predictable development.
w Roland Pertwee, Guy Bolton, A. R. Rawlinson play Yves Mirande d Monty Banks ph Basil Emmott ad Peter Proud
☆ Douglas Fairbanks Jnr, Laura La Plante, Claude Hulbert, Margaret Lockwood, Donald Calthrop, Monty Banks

Man of the Moment

GB   1955   88m   bw
Rank (Hugh Stewart)
A Whitehall filing clerk has to pretend to be a high-level diplomat at an international conference in Geneva.
Slapstick comedy of the obvious kind, but one of the better showcases for Norman Wisdom's sentimental 'little man' act.
w Vernon Sylvaine, John Paddy Carstairs story Maurice Cowan d John Paddy Carstairs ph Jack Cox m Philip Green ad Cedric Dawe ed John Shirley
☆ Norman Wisdom, Lana Morris, Belinda Lee, Jerry Desmonde, Karel Stephanek, Garry Marsh, Inia te Wiata

Man of the People

US   1937   80m   bw
Lucien Hubbard/MGM
An Italian immigrant works for a law degree but is forced in with crooks.

Political power play without much zest despite good acting.
w Frank Dolan d Edwin L. Marin
☆ Joseph Calleia, Thomas Mitchell, Florence Rice, Ted Healy, Catherine Doucet
'Patently primed for duals, where it can hold its own.' – Variety

Man of the West

US   1958   100m   DeLuxe   Cinemascope
UA/Ashton (Walter M. Mirisch)

In 1874 Arizona, a reformed gunman is cajoled by his old buddies to help them rob a bank.
Talkative, set-bound, cliché-ridden star Western with minor compensations.
w Reginald Rose novel Will C. Brown d Anthony Mann ph Ernest Haller m Leigh Harline
☆ Gary Cooper, Lee J. Cobb, Julie London, Arthur O'Connell, Jack Lord, John Dehner, Royal Dano, Robert Wilke

Man of the World

US   1931   71m   bw
Paramount
A gentleman racketeer operates on American playboys in Paris.
Predictable but smooth star vehicle.
w Herman J. Mankiewicz d Richard Wallace
☆ William Powell, Carole Lombard, Wynne Gibson, Guy Kibbee, Lawrence Gray
'Anything better than moderate for gross must come through the star's personal pull.' – Variety

'He was the centrefold that revealed everything ... but the truth.'

Man of the Year

US   1995   87m   bw/colour
Artisan (Matt Keener)

Dirk Shafer, voted *Playgirl* magazine's Man of the Year in 1992, strives to conceal the fact that he is gay.
A light-hearted documentary that plays around with the form, also parodying straighter factual films.
wd Dirk Shafer ph Stephen Timberlake m Peitor Angell pd Michael Mueller ed Barry Silver, Ken Solomon
☆ Dirk Shafer, Vivian Paxton, Deidra Shafer, Michael Ornstein, Claudette Sutherland, Cal Bartlett, Beth Broderick

Man of Two Worlds

US   1934   92m   bw
RKO
An Eskimo is temporarily civilized, but returns to the Arctic wild.
Uneventful and somewhat chilly drama which fails to convince.
w Howard J. Green, Ainsworth Morgan novel Ainsworth Morgan d J. Walter Ruben
☆ Francis Lederer, Elissa Landi, Henry Stephenson, J. Farrell MacDonald, Walter Byron

Man on a String

US   1960   92m   bw
Columbia/Louis de Rochemont
GB title: Confessions of a Counterspy
A Russian-born Hollywood producer is asked by the Russians to work as a spy but becomes a double agent.
Slightly unbelievable biopic about Boris Morros, rather childlike in its simplicity and not too entertaining either.
w John Kafka, Virginia Shaler book Ten Years a Counterspy by Boris Morros d André de Toth ph Charles Lawton Jnr and others m George Duning
☆ Ernest Borgnine, Kerwin Mathews, Colleen Dewhurst, Alexander Scourby, Glenn Corbett, Vladimir Sokoloff

Man on a Swing

US   1975   108m   Technicolor
Paramount (Howard B. Jaffe)
Investigations into a murder are helped by a would-be medium.
Overlong and confused psycho-mystery with one stand-out performance.
w David Zelag Goodman d Frank Perry ph Adam Holender m Lalo Schifrin
☆ Cliff Robertson, Joel Grey, Dorothy Tristan, Peter Masterson
'Runs out of interest long before it runs out of film.' – Variety

---

Man on a Tightrope *

US   1953   105m   bw
TCF (Robert L. Jacks)
A Czech circus owner has trouble with the communist authorities and tries to escape.
Adventure story with cold war pretensions which virtually kill it.
w Robert Sherwood d Elia Kazan ph Georg Krause m Franz Waxman
☆ Fredric March, Cameron Mitchell, Adolphe Menjou, Gloria Grahame, Terry Moore, Richard Boone, John Dehner, Dorothea Wieck

The Man on America's Conscience: see Tennessee Johnson

Man on Fire

US   1957   95m   bw
MGM (Sol C. Siegel)
When his wife divorces him, a middle-aged man refuses to hand over their son.
Low-key personal drama of very moderate interest and modest budget.
wd Ranald MacDougall ph Joseph Ruttenberg m David Raksin
☆ Bing Crosby, Inger Stevens, Mary Fickett, E. G. Marshall

Man on Fire

France/Italy   1987   92m   Eastmancolor
Rank/Sept/FR3/Cima (Arnon Milchan)

An ex-CIA agent, working as a bodyguard in Italy, takes revenge on the gang who kidnapped a young girl he was protecting.
Uninteresting action movie, with a great deal of dull talk and hysterical acting interspersed by moments of violence that become ever more ludicrous. One of the many low points comes when Joe Pesci sings Johnny B. Goode.
w Eli Chouraqui, Sergio Donati novel A. J. Quinnell d Eli Chouraqui ph Gerry Fisher m John Scott ad Giantito Burchiellaro ed Noelle Boisson
☆ Scott Glenn, Brooke Adams, Danny Aiello, Joe Pesci, Jonathan Pryce, Paul Shenar, Laura Morante, Alessandro Haber, Franco Trevisi, Jade Malle
† The film was cut by 30 seconds for its British video release.

A Man on the Beach

GB   1956   29m   Eastmancolor
Exclusive/Hammer (Anthony Hinds)
A man on the run is cared for and handed over to the police by a blind recluse.
Modest featurette which scarcely justifies its credits.
w Jimmy Sangster story Victor Canning d Joseph Losey ph Wilkie Cooper m John Hotchkis
☆ Donald Wolfit, Michael Medwin, Michael Ripper

The Man on the Eiffel Tower *

US   1949   82m   Anscocolor
A & T (Irving Allen)

A crazy killer defies Inspector Maigret to discover his identity.
Early independent production, an unsatisfactory crime melodrama with international talent and Paris locations. Some quirky acting carries it through.
w Harry Brown novel A Battle of Nerves by Georges Simenon d Burgess Meredith ph Stanley Cortez m Michel Michelet
☆ Charles Laughton, Burgess Meredith, Franchot Tone, Robert Hutton, Jean Wallace, Patricia Roc, Wilfrid Hyde-White, Belita
† Some scenes were directed by Charles Laughton and some by Franchot Tone.

The Man on the Flying Trapeze *

US   1935   65m   bw
Paramount (William Le Baron)
GB title: The Memory Expert
Adventures of an oppressed family man who is useful to his boss because of his prodigious memory.
Plotless rigmarole of shapeless comedy sketches, for star fans.
w Ray Harris, Sam Hardy, Jack Cunningham, Bobby Vernon story Charles Bogle (W. C. Fields) d Clyde Bruckman ph Al Gilks
☆ W. C. Fields, Kathleen Howard, Mary Brian, Grady Sutton, Vera Lewis, Lucien Littlefield, Oscar Apfel

---

'A series of gags unrelated to the title. Under average.' – *Variety*

Man on the Moon *

US 1999 119m DeLuxe Panavision
Universal/Mutual/Jersey/Cinehaus (Danny DeVito, Michael Shamberg, Stacey Sher)

Biopic of stand-up, self-destructive comic Andy Kaufman, who enjoyed success on the TV sitcom *Taxi*, but then pushed at the bounds of comedy until his early death from cancer.
An intriguing story of an unusual and uncomfortable talent, with a good performance from Carrey; those who were never exposed to Kaufman's comedy are likely to need more convincing that he is worth this elaborate treatment.
w Scott Alexander, Larry Karaszewski d Milos Forman ph Anastas Michos m R.E.M.
pd Patrizia von Brandenstein ed Christopher Tellefsen, Lynzee Klingman cos Jeffrey Kurland
☆ Jim Carrey, Danny DeVito, Courtney Love, Paul Giamatti, Vincent Schiavelli, Peter Bonerz, Jerry Lawler, Gerry Becker, Leslie Lyles
'All the audience is left with is the impression of a thoroughly obnoxious man you'd never want to meet in real life, a hopeless neurotic of little discernible talent other than for making the lives of those around him miserable.' – *Todd McCarthy, Variety*

The Man on the Roof *

Sweden 1976 109m Eastmancolor
Svensk Filmindustri (Per Berglund)
original title: *Mannen pöå Taket*
A brutal policeman is murdered, and a rooftop sniper turns out to be the culprit.
Alternately vivid and lumbering police thriller with a regrettable tendency to moralize.
wd Bo Widerberg novel *The Abominable Man* by Max Sjöwall, Max Wahlöös ph Odd Geir Saether, Per Kallberg, others m Björn Lindh
☆ Carl-Gustaf Lindstedt, Gunnel Wadner, Hakan Serner, Sven Wollter

Man on the Run

GB 1949 82m bw
ABPC
A deserter becomes innocently involved in a jewel robbery.
Competent crime programmer.
wd Lawrence Huntington
☆ Derek Farr, Joan Hopkins, Edward Chapman, Laurence Harvey, John Stuart

Man Proof

US 1937 74m bw
MGM (Louis D. Lighton)
In trying to win back her man a woman discovers she really loves someone else.
Modest romantic comedy which leaves its stars at sea.
w Vincent Lawrence, Waldemar Young, George Oppenheimer novel *The Four Marys* by Fanny Heaslip Lea d Richard Thorpe ph Karl Freund m Franz Waxman
☆ Myrna Loy, Franchot Tone, Walter Pidgeon, Rosalind Russell, Nana Bryant, Ruth Hussey
'A smartly produced, well-directed and excellently acted society comedy drama.' – *Variety*

The Man They Could Not Hang

US 1939 65m bw
Columbia
A scientist working on a mechanical heart causes the death of a volunteer student. He is executed, but his assistant restores him to life and he determines to murder those who convicted him.
Predictable horror hokum which set Karloff on his mad doctor cycle.
w Karl Brown story Leslie T. White, George W. Sayre d Nick Grinde ph Benjamin Kline md Morris Stoloff
☆ Boris Karloff, Lorna Gray, Robert Wilcox, Roger Pryor, Don Beddoe, Byron Foulger

A Man to Remember *

US 1938 80m bw
RKO (Robert Sisk)
At a small-town doctor's funeral, his life is remembered by mourners.
Modestly effective family film.

w Dalton Trumbo novel *Failure* by Katharine Haviland-Taylor d Garson Kanin ph J. Roy Hunt m Roy Webb
☆ Edward Ellis, Anne Shirley, Lee Bowman, William Henry, Granville Bates
'No sock for the marquee but a fine, well-made little picture.' – *Variety*

A Man to Respect

Italy/West Germany 1972 108m Technicolor Techniscope
Eagle/Verona Cinematografica/Paramount-Orion (Marina Cicogna)
aka: *Un Uomo da Rispettare*
On his release from jail, a safebreaker trains a young acrobat in his skills so that they can commit a double robbery.
An ingeniously plotted thriller that indulges in over-statement.
w Mino Roli story Franco Bucceri, Roberto Leoni d Michele Lupo ph Tonino Delli Colli m Ennio Morricone ad Francesco Bronzi ed Tony Zila
☆ Kirk Douglas, Giuliano Gemma, Florinda Bolkan
'A small triumph of dehumanised style.' – *Richard Combs, MFB*

'She Put Her Life In His Hands. Unfortunately, His Hands Have A Life Of Their Own.'

Man Trouble

US 1992 100m DeLuxe
First Independent/Penta/American Filmworks/Budding Grove (Bruce Gilbert, Carole Eastman)
A dog-trainer becomes involved with an opera singer when she decides she needs a guard dog to protect her home.
An unlikely romance is at the centre of an even unlikelier narrative – and even if you swallow the implausibilities, the result is still sickly.
w Carole Eastman d Bob Rafelson ph Stephen H. Burum m Georges Delerue pd Mel Bourne ed William Steinkamp
☆ Jack Nicholson, Ellen Barkin, Harry Dean Stanton, Beverly D'Angelo, Michael McKean, Saul Rubinek, Viveka Davis
'An insultingly trivial star vehicle.' – *Variety*
'Unredeemedly awful.' – *Philip French, Observer*

The Man Upstairs *

GB 1958 88m bw
British Lion/ACT (Robert Dunbar)
A mild-mannered lodger becomes violent, injures a policeman, and barricades himself in his room.
Character melodrama reminiscent of both Fourteen Hours and Le Jour se Lève, but not so interesting as either.
w Alun Falconer d Don Chaffey ph Gerald Gibbs
☆ Richard Attenborough, Bernard Lee, Donald Houston, Dorothy Alison, Maureen Connell, Kenneth Griffith, Virginia Maskell, Patricia Jessel

Man Wanted

US 1932 60m bw
Warner
A business woman takes on a male secretary.
Yawnworthy comedy drama with no surprises.
w Robert Lord d William Dieterle
☆ Kay Francis, David Manners, Andy Devine, Una Merkel, Kenneth Thomson
'Threadbare plot weakens this for the big theatres and makes it extremely light and familiar entertainment for the others.' – *Variety*

The Man Who Broke the Bank at Monte Carlo *

US 1935 67m bw
Twentieth Century (Nunnally Johnson)
A Russian émigré becomes a taxi driver, wins a fortune at roulette, loses it all again, and returns happily to his cab.
Very mild, unconvincing and not very entertaining malarkey which rested squarely on its star, who carried it with aplomb.
w Nunnally Johnson d Stephen Roberts ph Ernest Palmer md Oliver Bradley
☆ Ronald Colman, Joan Bennett, Colin Clive, Nigel Bruce, Montagu Love, Frank Reicher, Ferdinand Gottschalk
'Nice production though lacks dash … Colman at times seems to be playing under wraps. Should do fairly well.' – *Variety*

The Man Who Changed His Mind

GB 1936 66m bw
Gainsborough
US title: *The Man Who Lived Again*
A scientist dabbles in brain transplants.
Mild British-style horror piece; not a success.

The Man Who Came Back: see *Swamp Water (1941)*

'The richest roles of romance and redemption they ever played!'

The Man Who Came Back

US 1930 74m bw
Fox
A reckless young man is reformed when he finds his erstwhile sweetheart now a drug addict in Hong Kong.
Earnest melodrama which not surprisingly damaged the talkie success of a celebrated screen team, and must now seem risible in the extreme.
w Edwin J. Burke play Jules Eckert Goodman story and novel John Fleming Wilson d Raoul Walsh ph Arthur Edeson pd Joseph Urban
☆ Janet Gaynor, Charles Farrell, Kenneth MacKenna, William Holden, Mary Forbes, Peter Gawthorne
'Gripping old melodrama of drugs and degradation tamed down and made into a cheerful sentimental piece. Co-star names make it a strong bid.' – *Variety*
'Sophisticates will give it one big horse laugh.' – *Photoplay*

The Man Who Came to Dinner ***

US 1941 112m bw
Warner (Jack Saper, Jerry Wald)
An acid-tongued radio celebrity breaks his hip while on a lecture tour, and terrorizes the inhabitants of the suburban home where he must stay for several weeks.
Delightfully malicious caricature of Alexander Woollcott which, though virtually confined to one set, moves so fast that one barely notices the lack of cinematic variety, and certainly provides more than a laugh a minute, especially for those old enough to understand all the references.
w Julius J. and Philip G. Epstein play George S. Kaufman, Moss Hart d William Keighley ph Tony Gaudio m Frederick Hollander
☆ Monty Woolley, Bette Davis, Ann Sheridan, Jimmy Durante, Reginald Gardiner, Richard Travis, Billie Burke, Grant Mitchell, Ruth Vivian, Mary Wickes, George Barbier, Elisabeth Fraser
WHITESIDE (MONTY WOOLLEY) TO HIS NURSE, WHO WON'T LET HIM EAT CHOCOLATES: 'I had an aunt who ate a box of chocolates every day of her life. She lived to be a hundred and two, and when she had been dead three days, she looked healthier than you do now!'
NURSE (MARY WICKES): 'I am not only walking out on this case, Mr Whiteside, I am leaving the nursing profession. I became a nurse because all my life, ever since I was a little girl, I was filled with the idea of serving a suffering humanity. After one month with you, Mr Whiteside, I am going to work in a munitions factory. From now on, anything I can do to help exterminate the human race will fill me with the greatest of pleasure. If Florence Nightingale had ever nursed YOU, Mr Whiteside, she would have married Jack the Ripper instead of founding the Red Cross!'
WHITESIDE (INTRODUCING HIS SECRETARY): 'This ageing debutante, Mr Jefferson, I retain in my employ only because she is the sole support of her two-headed brother.'
BANJO (JIMMY DURANTE): 'Did you ever get the feeling that you wanted to stay, and still get the feeling that you wanted to go?'
BEVERLY CARLTON (REGINALD GARDINER IMPERSONATING NOËL COWARD): 'Don't tell me how you are, Sherry, I want none of the tiresome details. I've very little time, and so the conversation will be entirely about me, and I shall love it. Shall I tell you how I glittered through the South Seas like a silver scimitar, or would you rather hear how I finished a three-act play with one hand and made love to a maharaja's daughter with the other?'
† The inspiration for the play came after Alexander Woollcott had stayed with Moss Hart and, on leaving, had written in Hart's guest book, 'This is to certify that I had one of the most unpleasant times I ever spent.'

The Man Who Changed His Mind

GB 1936 66m bw
Gainsborough
US title: *The Man Who Lived Again*
A scientist dabbles in brain transplants.
Mild British-style horror piece; not a success.

w John L. Balderston, L. DuGarde Peach and Sidney Gilliat d Robert Stevenson
☆ Boris Karloff, Anna Lee, Donald Calthrop, John Loder, Frank Cellier, Cecil Parker
'A spine-freezer of routine construction. The accents are very limey and the way laboratory is pronounced may have American schoolchildren wondering.' – *Variety*

The Man Who Changed His Name

GB 1934 80m bw
Universal/Twickenham (Julius Hagen)
A wife begins to suspect that her husband is trying to murder her and her former lover.
Tepid comedy thriller that betrays its stage origins and is not helped by being somnambulistically acted and directed.
w H. Fowler Mear, Edgar Wallace play Edgar Wallace d Henry Edwards ph Sydney Blythe md W. L. Trytel ad James A. Carter ed Jack Harris, Michael C. Chorlton
☆ Lyn Harding, Betty Stockfeld, Leslie Perrins, Ben Welden, Aubrey Mather, Stanley Vine

The Man Who Cheated Himself

US 1950 81m bw
TCF (Jack M. Warner)
A woman shoots her husband and her homicide detective lover covers up for her.
Efficient crime melodrama.
w Seton I. Miller, Philip MacDonald d Felix Feist ph Russell Harlan m Louis Forbes
☆ Lee J. Cobb, Jane Wyatt, John Dall, Terry Frost

The Man Who Could Cheat Death

GB 1959 83m Technicolor
Paramount/Hammer (Anthony Nelson-Keys)
A surgeon looks 35 but is really 104, having had a series of gland operations performed on himself.
Vulgar, gory, gruesomely coloured Hammer version of a rather attractive play, previously filmed under its original title The Man in Half Moon Street (qv). The shocks are routine, and entertainment value is minimal.
w Jimmy Sangster play Barrie Lyndon d Terence Fisher ph Jack Asher m Richard Rodney Bennett
☆ Anton Diffring, Hazel Court, Christopher Lee, Arnold Marle, Delphi Lawrence, Francis de Wolff

The Man Who Could Work Miracles ***

GB 1936 82m bw
London (Alexander Korda)
A city clerk discovers he has the power to work miracles (given him by sportive gods) and nearly causes the end of the Earth.
Slow-moving but rather pleasing variation on a simple theme.
w Lajos Biro story H. G. Wells d Lothar Mendes ph Harold Rosson m Mischa Spoliansky
☆ Roland Young, Ralph Richardson, Ernest Thesiger, Edward Chapman, Joan Gardner, Sophie Stewart, Robert Cochran, George Zucco, Lawrence Hanray, George Sanders
'Supposedly a comedy. A weakling: little draw power on this side.' – *Variety*
'Sometimes fake poetry, sometimes unsuccessful comedy, sometimes farce, sometimes sociological discussion, without a spark of creative talent or a trace of film ability.' – *Graham Greene*

The Man Who Couldn't Get Enough: see *Confessions of a Sex Maniac*

The Man Who Cried Wolf

US 1937 67m bw
Universal
An actor continually confesses to crimes he didn't commit in the hope that when he does commit one he won't be believed.
An attractive idea rather poorly handled.
w Charles Grayson, Sy Bartlett d Lewis R. Foster
☆ Lewis Stone, Tom Brown, Barbara Read, Marjorie Main, Forrester Harvey
'Will get by as the number two feature on dual bills.' – *Variety*

The Man Who Dared

US 1933 72m bw
Fox
The life of a local politician, based on Mayor Cermak of Chicago.
Episodic but not unpleasant biopic; it adds up to very little, though.

---

w Dudley Nichols, Lamar Trotti d Hamilton McFadden

☆ Preston Foster, Zita Johann, Joan Marsh, Irene Biller, Leon Waycoff

'The most flattering account ever written of any man's life … but as a commercial talker it's not likely to get very far. Even in Chicago they didn't care for it.' – *Variety*

The Man Who Fell to Earth *

GB 1976 138m colour Panavision
British Lion (Michael Deeley, Barry Spikings)

A visitor from another planet tries to colonize Earth, but his powers are destroyed and he ends an alcoholic cripple.

A weird piece of intellectual science fiction made weirder by longueurs of all varieties: obscure narrative, voyeuristic sex, pop music and metaphysics. Not an easy film or a likeable one, despite its great technical skill.

w Paul Mayersberg novel Walter Tevis d Nicolas Roeg ph Anthony Richmond md John Phillips

☆ David Bowie, Rip Torn, Candy Clark, Buck Henry

'Once you have pierced through its glittering veneer, you find only another glittering veneer underneath.' – *Michael Billington, Illustrated London News*

'There is a punch line, but it takes forever, and great expectations slump away.' – *Charles Champlin, L.A. News*

'You feel finally that all that has been achieved has been to impose an aura of mystery and enigma where essentially there is none; to turn a simple tale into the sort of accumulation of sensations that has become fashionable.' – *David Robinson, The Times*

The Man Who Finally Died

GB 1962 100m bw Cinemascope
British Lion/Magna/White Cross (Norman Williams)
A German-born Englishman returns to Bavaria for news of his father, and becomes involved in a spy plot.
Busy adaptation of a TV serial with a convoluted plot which might have been more pacily developed and better explained.

w Lewis Greifer, Louis Marks d Quentin Lawrence m Stephen Dade m Philip Green

☆ Stanley Baker, Peter Cushing, Mai Zetterling, Eric Portman, Niall MacGinnis, Nigel Green, Barbara Everest, Harold Scott

The Man Who Found Himself

US 1937 67m bw
RKO (Cliff Reid)
A nurse helps a downcast doctor face his problems and renew his enthusiasm for life.
Simple-minded programmer.

w J. Robert Bren, Edmund Hartmann, G. V. Atwater d Lew Landers ph Roy Hunt

☆ John Beal, Joan Fontaine, Philip Huston, Jane Walsh, George Irving

'No names in this hokey B session … flapdoodle with a capital F.' – *Variety*

The Man Who Had His Hair Cut Short *

Belgium 1966 94m bw
Belgian Cultural Ministry
A frustrated law clerk has an aberration after attending an autopsy and meeting again an old love.
Pessimistic case history with unpleasant details often brilliantly recorded.

w Anna de Pagter, André Delvaux d André Delvaux ph Ghislain Cloquet m Freddy Devreese

☆ Seene Rouffaer, Beata Tyszkiewicz, Hector Camerlynck

The Man Who Had Power over Women

GB 1970 89m Eastmancolor
Avco/Kettledrum
A successful public relations man comes to hate himself, his job and what it has done to his marriage.
Fashionable wallow in guilt and luxury, not very convincingly done.

w Allan Scott, Chris Bryant novel Gordon Williams d John Krish ph Gerry Turpin m · Johnny Mandel

☆ Rod Taylor, Carol White, James Booth, Penelope Horner, James Korvin, Alexandra Stewart, Keith Barron

The Man Who Haunted Himself

GB 1970 94m Technicolor
ABP/Excalibur (Michael Relph)

After recovering from a road accident, a staid businessman finds that he has an evil doppelganger who steals his wife and his job.
Mildly effective if inexplicable story idea which served more suitably as a Hitchcock TV half hour and here, despite adequate production, outstays its welcome.

w Basil Dearden, Michael Relph story The Case of Mr Pelham by Anthony Armstrong d Basil Dearden ph Tony Spratling m Michael Lewis

☆ Roger Moore, Hildegarde Neil, Olga-Georges Picot, Anton Rodgers, Freddie Jones, Thorley Walters, John Carson, John Welsh

The Man Who Knew Too Little *

US 1997 94m Technicolor
Warner/Regency/Taurus (Arnon Milchan, Michael Nathanson, Mark Tarlov)

A holidaying American is mistaken for a hired killer.
Pleasant, undistinguished comedy that pokes fun at the sort of identity mix-up that Hitchcock used to better effect.

w Robert Farrar, Howard Franklin novel Watch That Man by Robert Farrar d Jon Amiel ph Robert Stevens m Chris Young pd Jim Clay ed Pamela Power, Paul Karasick

☆ Bill Murray, Peter Gallagher, Joanne Whalley, Alfred Molina, Richard Wilson, Geraldine James, John Standing, Anna Chancellor, Nicholas Woodeson

'Scores a reasonable number of laughs, but its ultimate impact is pretty mild.' – *Variety*

The Man Who Knew Too Much ***

GB 1934 84m bw
GFD/Gaumont British (Ivor Montagu)

A child is kidnapped by spies to ensure her father's silence, but he springs into action.
Splendid early Hitchcock film which after a faded start moves into memorable sequences involving a dentist, an East End mission and the Albert Hall. All very stagey by today's standards, but much more fun than the expensive remake.

w A. R. Rawlinson, Charles Bennett, D. B. Wyndham Lewis, Edwin Greenwood, Emlyn Williams d Alfred Hitchcock ph Curt Courant m Arthur Benjamin

☆ Leslie Banks, Edna Best, Peter Lorre, Nova Pilbeam, Frank Vosper, Hugh Wakefield, Pierre Fresnay

'A natural and easy production that runs smoothly and has the hallmark of sincerity.' – *Variety*

'The film's mainstay is its refined sense of the incongruous.' – *Peter John Dyer, 1964*

'A single clash of cymbals that will rock the lives of an American family!'

The Man Who Knew Too Much *

US 1956 120m Technicolor Vistavision
(Paramount)

Flaccid remake of the above, twice as long and half as entertaining, though it does improve after a very slow start.

w John Michael Hayes, Angus MacPhail d Alfred Hitchcock ph Robert Burks m Bernard Herrmann

☆ James Stewart, Doris Day, Bernard Miles, Brenda de Banzie, Daniel Gelin, Ralph Truman, Mogens Wieth, Alan Mowbray, Hillary Brooke

'The balance between character and incident in the earlier film makes a far better thriller.' – *Observer*

'The remake is heavy and oppressive, the suspense often risible, and the moments of comic relief fall flat.' – *Sunday Times*

'Let's say the first version is the work of a talented amateur and the second was made by a professional.' – *Alfred Hitchcock*

♪ song 'Que Sera Sera' (m/ly Jay Livingston, Ray Evans)

The Man Who Lived Again: see *The Man Who Changed His Mind*

The Man Who Lived Twice

US 1936 73m bw
Columbia (Ben Pivar)
An eminent doctor is unaware that he was formerly a criminal who was cured by a brain operation that also removed his memory; but his past begins to catch up with him.
Daft melodrama, acted with far more intensity than it deserves; there's a little pleasure to be gained from watching Bellamy play a disfigured murderer on the run before reverting to his more familiar blandness.

w Tom Van Dycke, Arthur Strawn, Fred Niblo Jnr d Harry Lachman ph James Van Trees ed Byron Robinson

☆ Ralph Bellamy, Marian Marsh, Thurston Hall, Isabel Jewell, Nana Bryant, Ward Bond, Henry Kolker, Willard Robertson

† It was remade in 1953 as *Man in the Dark* (qv).

The Man Who Lost Himself

US 1941 71m bw
Universal
A man back from the tropics finds himself playing the part of a lookalike millionaire.
Pleasantly nimble farce; not original but agreeable to watch.

w Eddie Moran novel H. DeVere Stacpoole d Edward Ludwig

☆ Brian Aherne, Kay Francis, S. Z. Sakall, Henry Stephenson, Nils Asther, Sig Rumann

The Man Who Loved Cat Dancing

US 1973 114m Metrocolor Panavision
MGM (Martin Poll, Eleanor Perry)

A runaway wife is kidnapped by train thieves and comes to love one of them.
Outdoor variation on No Orchids for Miss Blandish, remarkably lacking in any kind of entertainment value.

w Eleanor Perry novel Marilyn Durham d Richard Sarafian ph Harry Stradling Jnr m John Williams

☆ Sarah Miles, Burt Reynolds, Lee J. Cobb, Jack Warden, George Hamilton, Bo Hopkins, Robert Donner, Jay Silverheels

'Any number of things have gone wrong with this peculiarly dreary western.' – *Tom Milne*

'Sarah Miles undergoes more perils than Pauline.' – *Variety*

The Man Who Loved Redheads

GB 1954 90m Eastmancolor
British Lion/London Films (Josef Somlo)
Throughout his career, a diplomat seeks women who resemble the redhead with whom in youth he had had an idyllic affair.
West End theatrical moonshine, poorly filmed in ugly colour but saved by the cast.

w Terence Rattigan play Who Is Sylvia? by Terence Rattigan d Harold French ph Georges Périnal m Benjamin Frankel

☆ John Justin, Moira Shearer, Roland Culver, Gladys Cooper, Denholm Elliott, Harry Andrews, Patricia Cutts, Moyra Fraser, Joan Benham, Jeremy Spenser

'Deciding which woman in the world he loved most is driving him out of his mind!'

The Man Who Loved Women

France 1977 119m Eastmancolor
Les Films du Carrosse/PAA (Marcel Bebert)

A man spends his life in pursuit of women and dies in the chase.
Sour comedy which doesn't quite come off.

w François Truffaut, Michel Fermaud, Suzanne Schiffman d François Truffaut ph Nestor Almendros m Maurice Jaubert

☆ Charles Denner, Brigitte Fossey, Leslie Caron, Nelly Borgeaud, Nathalie Baye

'Doesn't just miss: it has virtually nothing.' – *Stanley Kauffmann*

The Man Who Loved Women

US 1983 110m Metrocolor
Columbia/Delphi/Blake Edwards (Blake Edwards, Tony Adams)

An American remake of the above, with even less success.

w Blake Edwards, Milton Wexler, Geoffrey Edwards d Blake Edwards ph Haskell Wexler m Henry Mancini

☆ Burt Reynolds, Julie Andrews, Kim Basinger, Marilu Henner, Cynthia Sikes, Jennifer Edwards

'The strangest story in the annals of naval espionage!'

The Man Who Never Was **

GB 1955 102m DeLuxe Cinemascope
Sumar/André Hakim

In 1943, the British secret service confuses the Germans by dropping a dead man into the sea with false documents.
Mainly enjoyable true life war story marred by an emotional romantic sub-plot with a double twist but helped by an equally fictitious spy hunt which cheers up the last half hour.

w Nigel Balchin book Ewen Montagu d Ronald Neame ph Oswald Morris m Alan Rawsthorne

☆ Clifton Webb, Robert Flemyng, Gloria Grahame, Stephen Boyd, Laurence Naismith, Josephine Griffin

🎬 Nigel Balchin

The Man Who Played God *

US 1932 81m bw
Warner
GB title: *The Silent Voice*
A musician goes deaf but finds satisfaction in helping a young student.
Stagey but effective star vehicle which Arliss also played as a silent film. Remade as Sincerely Yours (qv).

w Julien Josephson, Maude Howell play The Silent Voice by Jules Eckert Goodman d John G. Adolfi ph James Van Trees

☆ George Arliss, Violet Heming, Ivan Simpson, Bette Davis, Louise Closser Hale, Donald Cook, Ray Milland

'Will need all the Arliss name strength to pull average returns.' – *Variety*

The Man Who Reclaimed His Head *

US 1934 81m bw
Universal (Henry Henigson)
A writer who feels he has been betrayed and his brain sapped by his publisher takes a gruesome revenge.
Oddball period melodrama tailored rather unsuccessfully for a new star. Remade as Strange Confession (see Inner Sanctum).

w Jean Bart, Samuel Ornitz play Jean Bart d Edward Ludwig ph Merritt Gerstad m Heinz Roemheld

☆ Claude Rains, Joan Bennett, Lionel Atwill, Juanita Quigley, Henry O'Neill, Lawrence Grant

'Interesting screen diversion … Far from a smash, but good enough to keep to the average level or above.' – *Variety*

The Man Who Shot Liberty Valance ***

US 1962 122m bw
Paramount/John Ford (Willis Goldbeck)

A tenderfoot becomes a hero for shooting a bad man, but the shot was really fired by his friend and protector.
Clumsy, obvious Western with the director over-indulging himself but providing some good scenes in comedy vein.

w James Warner Bellah, Willis Goldbeck d John Ford m William H. Clothier m Cyril Mockridge

☆ James Stewart, John Wayne, Vera Miles, Lee Marvin, Edmond O'Brien, Andy Devine, Jeanette Nolan, John Qualen, Ken Murray, Woody Strode, Lee Van Cleef, Strother Martin, John Carradine

FAMOUS LINE: 'When truth becomes legend, print the legend.'

'Like Queen Victoria, John Wayne has become lovable because he stayed in the saddle into a new era.' – *Judith Crist*

'A heavy-spirited piece of nostalgia.' – *Pauline Kael, 1975*

'A film whose fascination lies less in what it is itself than in what it reveals about the art of its maker.' – *William S. Pechter*

The Man Who Talked Too Much

US 1940 75m bw
Warner (Edmund Grainger)
A smart defence attorney gets the goods on a gangster and decides to turn him in.
Below-par remake of The Mouthpiece (qv), later filmed again as Illegal (qv).

w Walter de Leon, Tom Reed play The Mouthpiece by Frank J. Collins d Vincent Sherman ph Sid Hickox

☆ George Brent, Brenda Marshall, Richard Barthelmess, Virginia Bruce, William Lundigan,

John Litel, George Tobias, Henry Armetta, Alan Baxter

'Human or inhuman, no woman is safe!'

The Man Who Turned to Stone

US   1957   71m   bw
Clover/Columbia
▤

A girls' reformatory is taken over by a group of zombie scientists born in the 18th century.
Cheap horror item with a few choice moments for connoisseurs of the absurd.
w Raymond T. Marcus d Leslie Kardos
ph Benjamin Kline
☆ Victor Jory, Ann Doran, Charlotte Austin, William Hudson, Paul Cavanagh

The Man Who Understood Women

US   1959   105m   Eastmancolor
Cinemascope
TCF (Nunnally Johnson)
An arrogant, exhibitionist film producer finally alienates his long-suffering wife.
Something of an aberration, with good scenes submerged in an unholy mixture of sharp comedy and sentimental melodrama.
wd Nunnally Johnson *novel* Colours of the Day by Romain Gary ph Milton Krasner m Robert Emmett Dolan
☆ Henry Fonda, Leslie Caron, Myron McCormick, Cesare Danova, Marcel Dalio, Conrad Nagel, Harry Ellerbe
  'A pretentious extravaganza on a romantic theme.' – *MFB*

The Man Who Watched Trains Go By

GB   1952   80m   Technicolor
Raymond Stross
▤
aka: *Paris Express*
A clerk steals money in order to fulfil his wish of world travel, and this leads to murder.
Miscast minor Simenon, not exactly badly made but with no spark of excitement or suspense.
wd Harold French *novel* Georges Simenon
ph Otto Heller m Benjamin Frankel
☆ Claude Rains, Marius Goring, Marta Toren, Anouk Aimée, Herbert Lom, Ferdy Mayne

The Man Who Would Be King *

US   1975   129m   colour   Panavision
Columbia/Allied Artists/Persky-Bright/Devon (John Foreman)
▣   ▤   ◉.   ⊚   ∩

In India in the 1880s, two adventurers find themselves accepted as kings by a remote tribe, but greed betrays them.
After an ingratiating start this ambitious fable becomes more predictable, and comedy gives way to unpleasantness. Despite its sporadic high quality, one does not remember it with enthusiasm.
w John Huston, Gladys Hill *story* Rudyard Kipling d John Huston ph Oswald Morris
m Maurice Jarre pd Alexander Trauner
ed Russell Lloyd
☆ Sean Connery, Michael Caine, Christopher Plummer, Saeed Jaffrey, Jack May, Shakira Caine
  'Huston has now made a good picture – not up to the standard of his early best but with sweep and guts and with nicely overblown cinematic eloquence.' – *Stanley Kauffmann*
& John Huston, Gladys Hill (script); Alexander Trauner

The Man Who Wouldn't Talk

US   1940   72m   bw
Sol M. Wurtzel/TCF
A man on trial for murder has such a mysterious background that he may even be the victim.
Efficient remake of Paul Muni's The Valiant.
w Robert Ellis, Helen Logan, Lester Ziffren and Edward Ettinger d David Burton
☆ Lloyd Nolan, Jean Rogers, Richard Clarke, Eric Blore, Mae Marsh

The Man Who Wouldn't Talk

GB   1957   97m   bw
British Lion/Everest (Herbert Wilcox)
A lady QC gets an acquittal for a man who can't defend himself on a murder charge because of loyalty to a scientist on the run.
Efficient courtroom melodrama based on a somewhat incredible and even uninteresting situation.

w Edgar Lustgarten *story* Stanley Jackson
d Herbert Wilcox ph Gordon Dines m Stanley Black
☆ Anna Neagle, Anthony Quayle, Zsa Zsa Gabor, Katherine Kath, Dora Bryan, Patrick Allen

The Man with a Cloak *

US   1951   81m   bw
MGM (Stephen Ames)
In 1848 New York, a mysterious stranger (who turns out to be Edgar Allan Poe) helps a young French girl to keep her inheritance.
Curious domestic melodrama set on MGM's choicest sets; its playful literary allusion causes it to fall between suspense thriller and character drama, but the acting keeps one watching.
w Frank Fenton *story* John Dickson Carr
d Fletcher Markle ph George Folsey m David Raksin
☆ Joseph Cotten, Barbara Stanwyck, Leslie Caron, Louis Calhern, Joe de Santis, Jim Backus, Margaret Wycherly

The Man with a Hundred Faces: see
Crackerjack

Man with a Million: see *The Million Pound Note*

The Man with an Umbrella: see *It Rains on Our Love*

The Man with Bogart's Face

US   1980   106m   CFI color
TCF/Melvin Simon (Andrew J. Fenady)
▤
An unremarkable private eye gets lots of assignments because he looks like Humphrey Bogart.
Amiably nostalgic romp, not too spoofy to be enjoyable for its own sake, but notably underproduced.
w Andrew J. Fenady *novel* Andrew J. Fenady
d Robert Day ph Richard C. Glouner m George Duning
☆ Robert Sacchi, Misty Rowe, Michelle Phillips, Franco Nero, Olivia Hussey, Victor Buono, Herbert Lom, George Raft, Yvonne de Carlo, Jay Robinson, Mike Mazurki, Henry Wilcoxon, Victor Sen Yung

The Man with My Face

US   1951   77m   bw
UA/Edward F. Gardner
A successful young man finds a double in his place at both home and office, and himself branded as an impostor.
Intriguing yarn which deserved a better production.
w Samuel W. Taylor, Edward J. Montagne, T. J. McGowan and Vincent Bogart *novel* Samuel W. Taylor d Edward J. Montagne
☆ Barry Nelson, Lynn Ainley, John Harvey, Carole Mathews, Jack Warden

The Man with Nine Lives *

US   1940   73m   bw
Columbia
GB title: *Behind the Door*
A scientist believes he can cure cancer by freezing, but accidentally locks himself and his patients in an underground ice chamber for seven years, and goes berserk when thawed out.
Interesting, rather prophetic science fiction thriller which rather lacks the style required to put it over.
w Karl Brown *story* Harold Shumate d Nick Grinde ph Benjamin Kline
☆ Boris Karloff, Byron Foulger, Roger Pryor, Jo Ann Sayers

The Man with One Red Shoe

US   1985   93m   colour
TCF (Victor Drai)
▣   ▤
A violinist wearing odd shoes is mistaken for a spy and becomes a pawn in a battle being waged by rival factions for control of the CIA.
Farcical comedy that rarely achieves the right tempo or timing for its occasional jokes.
w Robert Klane d Stan Dragoti ph Richard H. Kline m Thomas Newman pd Dean E. Mitzner
ed Bud Molin, O. Nicholas Brown
☆ Tom Hanks, Dabney Coleman, Lori Singer, Charles Durning, Jim Belushi, Carrie Fisher, Ed Herrmann, Irving Metzman, Tom Noonan, David Ogden Stiers

† It was a remake of the French film *Le Grand Blond avec une Chaussure Noire* (qv), written by Francis Veber and Yves Robert.

The Man with the Deadly Lens: see *Wrong Is Right*

The Man with the Golden Arm *

US   1956   119m   bw
Otto Preminger
▣   ▤   ◉.   ∩
A Chicago poker dealer finally kicks the drug habit.
Sensational on its first release, with its cold turkey scenes, this now seems a muddled impressionist melodrama with echoes of the silent German cinema and much over-acting and miscasting all round. But Sinatra is good; and it is different...
w Walter Newman, Lewis Meltzer *novel* Nelson Algren d Otto Preminger ph Sam Leavitt
m Elmer Bernstein pd Joe Wright titles Saul Bass
☆ Frank Sinatra, Kim Novak, Eleanor Parker, Darren McGavin, Arnold Stang, Robert Strauss, John Conte, Doro Merande, George E. Stone
  'Nothing very surprising or exciting ... a pretty plain and unimaginative look-see at a lower depths character.' – *Bosley Crowther*
  'A very inferior film ... the script is inexcusably clumsy, the sets are unbelievable and the casting is ridiculous.' – *Diana Willing, Films in Review*
  'It has the same running time as Citizen Kane but it seems a whole lot longer.' – *Robert James*
& Elmer Bernstein; Frank Sinatra; art direction

The Man with the Golden Gun *

👫   GB   1974   125m   Eastmancolor
UA/Eon (Harry Saltzman, Albert R. Broccoli)
▣   ▤   ◉.   ⊚   ∩
James Bond goes to the Far East to liquidate a professional assassin named Scaramanga.
Thin and obvious Bond extravaganza with conventional expensive excitements.
w Richard Maibaum, Tom Mankiewicz *novel* Ian Fleming d Guy Hamilton ph Ted Moore, Oswald Morris m John Barry pd Peter Murton
☆ Roger Moore, Christopher Lee, Britt Ekland, Maud Adams, Hervé Villechaize, Clifton James, Richard Loo, Marc Lawrence
  'The script lacks satiric insolence and the picture grinds on humourlessly.' – *New Yorker*

The Man with the Green Carnation: see *The Trials of Oscar Wilde*

Man with the Gun *

US   1955   83m   bw
UA/Samuel Goldwyn Jnr
aka: *Deadly Peacemaker*
A gunfighter is hired to clean up a town overrun by hired guns.
A well-made Western, tough, grim and suspenseful.
w N. B. Stone Jnr, Richard Wilson d Richard Wilson ph Lee Garmes m Alex North
ad Hilyard Brown ed Gene Milford
☆ Robert Mitchum, Jan Sterling, Karen Sharpe, Henry Hull, Emile Meyer, John Lupton, Barbara Lawrence, Ted DeCorsia, Leo Gordon, James Westerfield

The Man with the Movie Camera **

USSR   1928   60m   bw   silent
VUFKU
▣   ⊚
original title: *Chelovek sKinoapparatom*
A 'camera eye' documentary without any plot, showing, through a succession of street and interior scenes, all the tricks of which the instrument is capable; it takes a bow at the end.
Unique documentary which was understandably a sensation when it first appeared but now often seems merely quaint.
ph Mikhail Kaufman wd/ed Dziga Vertov

The Man with Thirty Sons: see *The Magnificent Yankee*

The Man with Two Brains

US   1983   93m   colour
Warner/Aspen (David V. Picker, William E. McEuen)
▤   ◉.   ⊚
A surgeon, trapped in a frustrating marriage, falls in love with a brain in a jar.
Offbeat, broad comedy that is never as funny as it promises to be.

w Carl Reiner, Steve Martin, George Gipe d Carl Reiner ph Michael Chapman m Joel Goldsmith
ad Polly Platt ed Bud Molin
☆ Steve Martin, Kathleen Turner, David Warner, Paul Benedict, Richard Brestoff, James Cromwell, Sissy Spacek
  'Indefensible by any known standard of comedy form – or formlessness. It's not much of anything, but it moves along enjoyably.' – *Pauline Kael, New Yorker*

The Man with Two Faces *

US   1934   72m   bw
Warner
An actor takes revenge on a scoundrel who had preyed on his sister.
Pleasing melodrama hinging on disguise; the Hays Office surprisingly allowed the hero to get away with it.
w Tom Reed, Niven Busch *play* The Dark Tower by George S. Kaufman, Alexander Woollcott
d Archie Mayo ph Tony Gaudio
☆ Edward G. Robinson, Mary Astor, Ricardo Cortez, Louis Calhern, Mae Clarke, John Eldredge
  'Fair fodder, but undistinguished in the main, and in spots very confusing.' – *Variety*

The Man with X-Ray Eyes: see *X–The Man with X-Ray Eyes*

The Man Within *

GB   1947   88m   Technicolor
GFD/Production Film Service (Muriel and Sydney Box)
US title: *The Smugglers*
An orphan boy discovers that his mysterious new guardian is a smuggler.
Unconvincing period yarn which has managed to drain every vestige of subtlety from the novel, but at least looks good.
w Muriel and Sydney Box *novel* Graham Greene
d Bernard Knowles ph Geoffrey Unsworth
m Clifton Parker
☆ Michael Redgrave, Richard Attenborough, Jean Kent, Joan Greenwood
  'With more style this might have been rather good. Outside of life more private than I am normally party to I can't recall hearing so many men so often say, to other men, I hate him! or I hate you!' – *James Agee*

The Man without a Body

GB   1957   80m   bw
Eros/Filmplays (Guido Coen)
A tycoon with a brain tumour steals the head of Nostradamus and has it kept alive to replace his own.
Hilarious horror comic, inept in every department.
w William Grote d W. Lee Wilder, Charles Saunders ph Brendan J. Stafford m Albert Elms
☆ George Coulouris, Robert Hutton, Nadja Regin, Julia Arnall

The Man without a Face

US   1993   115m   Technicolor
Entertainment/Icon (Bruce Davey)
▣   ▤   ◉.   ∩
A boy remembers how he was helped to enter a military academy by a disfigured former teacher who had become an outcast in the community.
A well-meaning but rather dull movie that makes heavy weather of a not very affecting drama.
w Malcolm MacRury *novel* Isabelle Holland
d Mel Gibson ph Donald M. McAlpine m James Horner pd Barbara Dunphy ed Tony Gibbs
☆ Mel Gibson, Margaret Whitton, Fay Masterson, Gaby Hoffman, Geoffrey Lewis, Richard Masur, Nick Stahl, Viva
  'The overall effect is sincere, sentimental and slightly uneasy.' – *Philip French, Observer*
  'A contrived story, overloaded with pop psychology, that would never reach the big screen unless a major star insisted. As director, Mel Gibson proves no visual stylist.' – *Geoff Brown, The Times*

Man without a Star *

US   1955   89m   Technicolor
U-I (Aaron Rosenberg)
A wandering cowboy helps settlers to put up barbed wire against an owner of vast cattle herds.
Conventional but entertaining star Western.
w Borden Chase, D. D. Beauchamp *novel* Dee Linford d King Vidor ph Russell Metty m Hans Salter

---

☆ Kirk Douglas, Jeanne Crain, Claire Trevor, William Campbell, Jay C. Flippen, Mara Corday, Richard Boone

† Remade for TV as *A Man Called Gannon*.

Man, Woman and Child

US 1982 100m DeLuxe
Gaylord
🎧

A married professor discovers that he has a son by his only infidelity.

Angst among the well-to-do, from the author of Love Story.

w Erich Segal, David Zelag Goodman *novel* Erich Segal d Dick Richards *ph* Richard H. Kline m George Delerue

☆ Martin Sheen, Blythe Danner, Craig T. Nelson, David Hemmings, Nathalie Nell

Man, Woman and Sin

US 1927 85m bw silent
MGM

A reporter has an affair with his boss's mistress.

Glossy romantic drama marking the first screen appearance of a sensational stage star; her effect on screen was more muted.

w Alice Duer Miller d Monta Bell

☆ Jeanne Eagels, John Gilbert, Marc McDermott

Manbait: see *The Last Page*

The Manchurian Candidate ****

US 1962 126m bw
UA/MC (Howard W. Koch)
⬚⬚ ▦ ◉ 🎧

A Korean war 'hero' comes back a brainwashed zombie triggered to kill a liberal politician, his control being his own monstrously ambitious mother.

Insanely plotted but brilliantly handled spy thriller, a mixture of Hitchcock, Welles and All the King's Men.

w George Axelrod *novel* Richard Condon d John Frankenheimer *ph* Lionel Lindon m David Amram *pd* Richard Sylbert

☆ Frank Sinatra, Laurence Harvey, Janet Leigh, James Gregory, Angela Lansbury, Henry Silva, John McGiver

'The unAmerican film of the year.' – *Penelope Houston*

'An intelligent, funny, superbly written, beautifully played, and brilliantly directed study of the all-embracing fantasy in everyday social, emotional and political existence.' – *Philip Strick, 1973*

'Although it's a thriller, it may be the most sophisticated political satire ever to come out of Hollywood.' – *Pauline Kael, 70s*

⅛ Angela Lansbury

Mandalay

US 1934 65m bw
Warner

A lady of the tropics murders her lover and pushes his body through a porthole.

Steamy melodrama which the masses found absorbing.

w Austin Parker, Charles Kenyon d Michael Curtiz

☆ Kay Francis, Ricardo Cortez, Lyle Talbot, Ruth Donnelly, Shirley Temple, Warner Oland, Lucien Littlefield, Reginald Owen

Mandela *

US 1995 123m colour
Nubian/Island/Clinica Estetico (Jonathan Demme, Edward Saxon, Jo Menell)

A factual biography of Nelson Mandela from childhood to becoming leader of the ANC, imprisonment for more than 20 years, his triumphant release and his election as the first democratic president of South Africa.

A less-than-satisfactory documentary, despite the fact that it includes an interview with Mandela himself and interesting archive footage.

d Jo Menell, Angus Gibson *ph* Dewald Aukema, Peter Tischhauser m Cedric Gradus Samson, Hugh Masekela *ed* Andy Keir, Mona Davis

☆ Patrick Shai

Mandela *

US 1996 123m colour
Nubian Tales/Island/Clinica Estetico (Jonathan Demme, Edward Saxon, Jo Menell)
⬚⬚

Documentary on the life of Nelson Mandela, from childhood through his involvement with the ANC, imprisonment for more than two decades and final triumph as president of a democratic South Africa.

Great subject, but a dull documentary, perhaps circumscribed by including a long interview with Mandela himself, which is often used as a commentary on the images; his need not to inflame those who opposed him for so long leads to blandness.

d Jo Menell, Angus Gibson *ph* Dewald Aukema, Peter Tischhauser m Cedric Gradus Samson, Hugh Masekela *ed* Andy Keir

'Very much the authorised biography … The film-makers should still have tried harder to humanise him and the great struggle he led by opening up the complexities rather than closing down into pat clichés.' – *Kevin Macdonald, Sight and Sound*

⅛ documentary

Manden I Manen: see *The Dark Side of the Moon*

Mandingo

US 1975 126m Technicolor
Dino de Laurentiis (Peter Herald)
▦ ◉

On a slave-breeding plantation in 1840 Louisiana, passions ride high.

Like Gone with the Wind with all the characters on heat, this exuberant and unpleasant melodrama goes several points over the top from start to finish but proved to have wide appeal for the groundlings, in the Tobacco Road tradition of a wallow in other people's depravities.

w Norman Wexler *play* Jack Kirkland *novel* Kyle Onstott d Richard Fleischer *ph* Richard H. Kline m Maurice Jarre *pd* Boris Leven

☆ James Mason, Susan George, Perry King, Richard Ward, Brenda Sykes, Ken Norton

Mandrake the Magician

US 1939 bw
Columbia

A world-famous magician trails an underworld leader called The Wasp.

Rather stylish serial exploits with the added effect of illusions.

d Sam Nelson, Norman Denning

☆ Warren Hull, Doris Weston, Al Kikume, Rex Downing, Don Beddoe

† Serial in 12 episodes.

'She'll find a home in every heart! She'll reach the heart of every home!'

Mandy ***

🏠 GB 1952 93m bw
Ealing (Leslie Norman)
⬚⬚ ▦

US title: *The Crash of Silence*

A little girl, born deaf, is sent to a special school.

Carefully wrought and very sympathetic little semi-documentary film in which all the adults underplay in concession to a new child star who alas did not last long at the top.

w Nigel Balchin, Jack Whittingham *novel* This Day Is Ours by Hilda Lewis d Alexander Mackendrick *ph* Douglas Slocombe m William Alwyn

☆ Jack Hawkins, Terence Morgan, Phyllis Calvert, Mandy Miller, Godfrey Tearle, Dorothy Alison

'An extremely touching film, in spite of occasional obviousness in a plot never dull, and in spite of its subject never saccharine.' – *Dilys Powell*

Maneater of Kumaon

US 1948 78m bw
Monty Shaff-Frank Rosenberg/Universal

A doctor in the Himalayas helps track down a man-eating tiger.

Slightly unusual adventure story based on a currently popular book.

w Jeanne Bartlett and Lewis Meltzer *book* Jim Corbett d Byron Haskin

☆ Sabu, Wendell Corey, Joanne Page, Morris Carnovsky

Manèges *

France 1950 90m bw
Films Modernes-Discina (Emil Natan)
GB title: *The Wanton*

A scheming girl marries the middle-aged owner of a riding school and, with her greedy mother, milks him of his money.

A neat little melodrama with flashbacks so arranged that the girl, paralysed in an accident, seems for the first half to have an angelic character.

w Jacques Sigurd d Yves Allégret *ph* Jean Bourgoin

☆ Simone Signoret, Bernard Blier, Frank Villard, Jane Marken

The Mangler

US 1995 106m Technicolor
Guild/Distant Horizon/Allied/Anant Singh
▦ ◉

After human blood falls on an industrial steam-iron at a laundry, it turns into a killer machine.

Ludicrous and stupid horror movie, full of gore but sadly lacking in any sense or the ability to scare.

w Tobe Hooper, Stephen Brooks, Peter Welbeck (Harry Alan Towers) *story* Stephen King d Tobe Hooper *ph* Amnon Salomon m Barrington Pheloung *pd* David Barkham *ed* David Heitner

☆ Robert Englund, Ted Levine, Daniel Matmor, Jeremy Crutchley, Vanessa Pike, Demetre Phillips, Lisa Morris

'Lackluster story and thesping should guarantee the would-be frightfest a short spin and quick fade at the box office.' – *Variety*

Manhandled

US 1949 97m bw
Paramount/Pine-Thomas

The secretary of a bogus psychiatrist becomes involved in a murder and finds herself in danger from all comers.

Modest, overlong suspenser with adequate production values.

w Lewis R. Foster, Whitman Chambers *novel* The Man Who Stole a Dream by L. S. Goldsmith d Lewis R. Foster *m* Ernest Laszlo m David Chudnow

☆ Dorothy Lamour, Dan Duryea, Sterling Hayden, Irene Hervey, Harold Vermilyea, Philip Reed, Alan Napier, Art Smith, Irving Bacon

Manhattan ****

US 1979 96m bw Panavision
UA/Jack Rollins/Charles H. Joffe
⬚⬚ ▦ ◉ 🎧

Episodes in the sex life of a TV comedy writer with an obsession about New York.

As close to a summation of Woody Allen's views and oeuvre as anybody needs; some smart jabs about the lives we lead are sometimes bogged down in earnestness and half-comic despair.

w Woody Allen, Marshall Brickman d Woody Allen *ph* Gordon Willis *md* Tom Pierson

☆ Woody Allen, Diane Keaton, Meryl Streep, Mariel Hemingway, Michael Murphy

'Given that the identity of his films has increasingly been determined by his compulsion to talk about the things he finds important, but also by his fear of having them come out as anything but a joke, it is not surprising that he has scarcely been able to decide on a form for his "art": from the anything-for-a-laugh skittering of his early films, to the broad parodies and pastiches of his middle period, to the recent confessional/psychoanalytical mode.' – *Richard Combs, MFB*

'A masterpiece that has become a film for the ages by not seeking to be a film of the moment.' – *Andrew Sarris*

⅛ script; Mariel Hemingway

🏆 best picture

Manhattan Heartbeat

US 1940 71m bw
Sol M. Wurtzel/TCF

A husband is reluctant to assume the responsibilities of fatherhood.

Oddly-titled support, a remake of Bad Girl; no great shakes from any angle.

w Harold Buchman, Clark Andrews, Jack Jungmeyer Jnr, Edith Skouras d David Burton

☆ Robert Sterling, Virginia Gilmore, Joan Davis, Edmund MacDonald, Don Beddoe

Manhattan Madness: see *Adventure in Manhattan*

Manhattan Melodrama **

US 1934 93m bw
MGM (David O. Selznick)
▦ ◉

Two slum boys grow up friends, one as district attorney and one as a gangster.

Archetypal American situation drama (cf Angels with Dirty Faces, Cry of the City, etc), with the bad guy inevitably indulging in self-sacrifice at the end. An all-star cast makes it palatable in this case, though the film is inevitably dated.

w Oliver H. P. Garrett, Joseph L. Mankiewicz *story* Arthur Caesar d W. S. Van Dyke *ph* James Wong Howe m William Axt

☆ William Powell, Clark Gable, Myrna Loy, Leo Carrillo, Nat Pendleton, George Sidney, Isabel Jewell, Thomas E. Jackson

'Action meller of the big town … replete with punchy, popularly-appealing ingredients.' – *Variety*

† *Manhattan Melodrama* gained some irrelevant fame as the movie John Dillinger was watching before he was cornered and shot.

⅏ Arthur Caesar

Manhattan Merry-go-round *

US 1937 82m bw
Republic
▦

A sound recording studio is taken over by a band of racketeers.

Sufficient comedy plot to sustain a revue of historical interest.

w Harry Sauber, Frank Hummert d Charles F. Reisner *ad* Victor MacKay

☆ Phil Regan, Leo Carrillo, Ann Dvorak, Tamara Geva, James Gleason, Ted Lewis and his Orchestra, Cab Calloway and his Orchestra, the Kay Thompson Ensemble, Louis Prima and his Band, Gene Autry, Joe Di Maggio

'So much talent and novelty has been compressed within the limits of the film that customers dare not sneeze for fear of missing something … for the territorial distributors and independent theatres it is something to get excited about.' – *Variety*

⅛ Victor MacKay

Manhattan Murder Mystery *

US 1993 105m Technicolor
TriStar (Robert Greenhut)
⬚⬚ ▦ ◉ 🎧

A husband becomes concerned when his wife decides that the woman who lives next door has been murdered.

Amiable comedy whodunnit that jogs along nicely without arriving anywhere that is particularly interesting.

w Woody Allen, Marshall Brickman d Woody Allen *ph* Carlo Di Palma *pd* Santo Loquasto *ed* Susan E. Morse

☆ Woody Allen, Alan Alda, Anjelica Huston, Diane Keaton, Jerry Adler, Joy Behar, Ron Rifkin, Lynn Cohen, Melanie Norris

'Light, insubstantial and utterly devoid of the heavier themes Allen has grappled with in most of his recent outings, this confection keeps the chuckles coming and is mainstream enough in sensibility to be a modest success.' – *Variety*

'God, it's good to get a film which gives you only fun to worry about.' – *Alexander Walker*

Manhattan Parade

US 1931 77m Technicolor
Warner

Behind the scenes as a theatrical costumier tries to get into the revue business.

Aimless backstage comedy with turns.

w Robert Lord and Houston Branch *play* Sam Shipman and Lloyd Bacon

☆ Smith and Dale, Winnie Lightner, Charles Butterworth, Walter Miller, Luis Alberni

'A few laughs dot the scenery, and they're all this musical possesses in value.' – *Variety*

The Manhattan Project

US   1986   117m   Technicolor
Cannon/Gladden (Jennifer Ogden, Marshall Brickman)
🔲 ▤ 🔍
aka: *Deadly Game*

A clever student steals plutonium from a weapons laboratory and builds his own nuclear bomb; when the authorities track him down, he threatens to explode it.

Efficiently made but very silly thriller, a piece of teenage wish fulfilment.

w Marshall Brickman, Thomas Baum d Marshall Brickman ph Billy Williams m Philippe Sarde pd Philip Rosenberg ed Nina Feinberg

☆ John Lithgow, Christopher Collet, Cynthia Nixon, Jill Eikenberry, John Mahoney, Robert Sean Leonard

Manhunt: see *From Hell to Texas*

Manhunter **

US   1986   120m   Technicolor   Panavision
Recorded Releasing/Red Dragon/De Laurentiis Entertainment (Richard Roth)
🔲 🔲 ▤ ⚹ 🔍 🔘

An FBI agent with an ability to think like a killer tracks down a serial murderer.

Slick and glossy thriller, enjoyable enough if you can accept its premise.

novel *Red Dragon* by Thomas Harris ph Dante Spinotti m Michael Rubini, The Reds pd Mel Bourne ed Dov Hoenig wd/p Michael Mann

☆ William L. Petersen, Kim Greist, Joan Allen, Brian Cox, Dennis Farina, Stephen Lang, Tom Noonan, David Seaman, Benjamin Hendrickson

Le Mani sulla Città: see *Hands over the City*

Maniac

GB   1963   86m   bw   Hammerscope
Columbia/Hammer (Jimmy Sangster)
▤ 🔘

Murders by oxyacetylene torch in the Camargue, with the wrong lunatic going to the asylum.

Hammer's mark two plot, the shuddery murder mystery in which someone is not quite what he seems; feebly done in this case, with a fatally slow start.

w Jimmy Sangster m Michael Carreras ph Wilkie Cooper

☆ Kerwin Mathews, Donald Houston, Nadia Gray, Justine Lord

Maniac Cop

US   1988   85m   colour
Medusa/Shapiro Glickenhaus Entertainment (Larry Cohen)
🔲 ▤ 🔘

A former cop turns killer in New York.

Excessively violent thriller that is too implausible to be enjoyable.

w Larry Cohen d William Lustig ph Vincent J. Rabe m Jay Chataway ad Jonathan Hodges, Ann Cudworth ed David Kern

☆ Tom Atkins, Bruce Campbell, Laurene Landon, Richard Roundtree, William Smith, Robert Z'Dar, Sheree North

Maniac Cop 2

US   1990   88m   Foto-Kem   Panavision
Medusa/Movie House Sale/Fadd Enterprises (David Hodgins, Frank D'Alessio)
🔲 ▤ 🔘

A murderous and deranged former policeman teams up with a mass murderer to terrorize New York.

Limply directed sequel that offers nothing new, but just increases the body count.

w Larry Cohen d William Lustig ph James Lemmo m Jay Chattaway pd Gene Abel, Charles Logola ed David Kern

☆ Robert Davi, Claudia Christian, Michael Lerner, Bruce Campbell, Laurene Landon, Robert Z'Dar, Clarence Williams III, Leo Rossi

'The Wrong Arm Of The Law Is Back.'
Maniac Cop 3: Badge of Silence

US   1992   81m   Foto-Kem
Neo/First Look (Larry Cohen)
🔲 ▤

Resurrected by occult methods, a dead cop acts as a vigilante to protect the reputation of a policewoman, shot during a hold-up and accused of killing an innocent hostage.

An action adventure rather than a horror movie, with the maniac cop remaining a shadowy figure; it avoids predictability, has an inventive car chase and manages a moderate amount of suspense.

w Larry Cohen d William Lustig ph Jacques Haitkin m Joel Goldsmith pd Clark Hunter ed David Kern, Michael Eliot

☆ Robert Davi, Caitlin Dulany, Gretchen Becker, Paul Gleason, Jackie Earle Haley, Julius Harris, Grand Bush, Doug Savant, Robert Z'Dar

'A promising exploitation sequel, laced with Cohen's dark humour, which collapses in its final act into a series of dull stunts.' – *Sight and Sound*

Maniacs on Wheels: see *Once a Jolly Swagman*

Manifesto

US   1988   94m   colour
Cannon/Menahem Golan, Yoram Globus
▤ 🎧

In an Eastern European village in the 1920s, a lecherous secret policeman waylays revolutionaries before a visit by a king.

Sex-obsessed black comedy that muffs its climaxes.

wd Dusan Makavejev story *For a Night of Love* by Emile Zola ph Tomislav Pinter m Nicola Piovani pd Velijo Despotovic ed Tony Lawson

☆ Alfred Molina, Camilla Soeberg, Simon Callow, Lindsay Duncan, Eric Stoltz, Rade Serbedzija, Chris Haywood, Linda Marlowe, Ronald Lacey

Manila Calling

US   1942   82m   bw
TCF/Sol M. Wurtzel

Americans in the Philippines try to install a short-wave radio transmitter before the Japs take over.

Acceptable thick ear with professional trimmings.

w John Larkin d Herbert I. Leeds

☆ Lloyd Nolan, Carole Landis, Cornel Wilde, James Gleason, Martin Kosleck, Ralph Byrd

Manipulation *

GB   1991   5m   colour
Tandem
🔲

A cartoon character tries to assert his independence from the artist who drew him.

A clever, if somewhat sterile, exercise in animation.

d Daniel Greaves ed Rod Howick

👤 animated short

The Manitou

US   1978   104m   CFI color
Herman Weist/Melvin Simon (William Girdler)
🔲 ▤ 🔘

A fake spiritualist finds his girlfriend is possessed by the demon of a 400-year-old Indian.

Boring retread of The Exorcist.

w William Girdler, Jon Cedar, Tom Pope novel Graham Masterton d William Girdler ph Michel Hugo m Lalo Schifrin

☆ Tony Curtis, Susan Strasberg, Michael Ansara, Stella Stevens, Jon Cedar, Ann Sothern, Burgess Meredith, Paul Mantee

Mannen pò Taket: see *The Man on the Roof*

Mannequin

US   1937   95m   bw
MGM (Joseph L. Mankiewicz)
▤ 🔘

The wife of a small-time crook gets a modelling job and falls for a shipping magnate.

Competent star melodrama about a working girl's harassments.

w Lawrence Hazard d Frank Borzage ph George Folsey m Edward Ward

☆ Joan Crawford, Spencer Tracy, Alan Curtis, Ralph Morgan, Mary Philips, Elizabeth Risdon, Leo Gorcey

'A star vehicle in which the star is so solemnly noble that you want to strangle her.' – *New Yorker*

♫ song 'Always and Always' (mEdward Ward, lyChet Forrest, Bob Wright)

Mannequin

👫 US   1987   89m   DuArt
TCF/Gladden (Art Levinson)
🔲 ▤ 🔘

A window dresser falls in love with a mannequin who changes into a real live girl.

Feeble and never less than idiotic fantasy.

w Edward Rugoff, Michael Gottlieb d Michael Gottlieb ph Tim Suhrstedt m Sylvester Levay pd Josan Russo ed Richard Halsey, Frank Jiminez

☆ Andrew McCarthy, Kim Cattrall, Estelle Getty, James Spader, G. W. Bailey, Carole Davis, Stephen Vinovich, Christopher Maher, Meshach Taylor

♫ song 'Nothing's Gonna Stop Us Now' (Albert Hammond, Diane Warren)

Mannequin Two: On the Move

Rank/Gladden (Edward Rugoff)
🔲 ▤ 🔘

A window dresser discovers that a mannequin holds the imprisoned spirit of a bewitched peasant girl.

Even less enjoyable than the original, if that's possible.

w Edward Rugoff, David Isaacs, Ken Levine, Betty Israel d Stewart Raffill ph Larry Pizer m David McHugh ad Norman B. Dodge Jnr ed Joan Chapman

☆ Kristy Swanson, William Ragsdale, Meshach Taylor, Terry Kizer, Stuart Pankin, Cynthia Harris, Andrew Hill Newman

'If this stiff ever shows any life, it will be a wonder indeed.' – *Variety*
'A messy rehash of clichés and tired jokes.' – *Empire*

Männer...: see *Men...*

Mano dello Straniero: see *The Stranger's Hand*

Manon *

France   1949   96m   bw
Alcina (P. E. Decharme)

After the liberation, a girl who has been a collaborator becomes involved in the black market, passes from man to man, and ends up being shot by Arabs in the Sahara desert.

Oddball modernized version of Manon Lescaut, with post-war pessimism and the glamour of sin going hand in hand. Worth comparing with Gilda.

w H. G. Clouzot, J. Ferry novel L'Abbé Prévost d H. G. Clouzot ph Armand Thirard m Paul Misraki

☆ Michel Auclair, Cécile Aubry, Serge Reggiani, Gabrielle Dorziat

'A clever idea, handled cleverly, but without depth of feeling.' – *Penelope Houston*
'Though I have been going to the pictures since I wore rompers, I do not recall a more horrible film.' – *Leonard Mosley*

Manon des Sources

France   1952   190m   bw
Films Marcel Pagnol

A Provençal girl who lives in the hills with her goats is thought to be a witch, and takes her revenge on the populace by stopping the water supply.

Insanely long idyll of the countryside with the writer-director unintentionally caricaturing himself.

wd Marcel Pagnol m Willy m Raymond Legrand
☆ Jacqueline Pagnol, Raymond Péllégrin, Henri Vibert

'Something of an endurance test for all but the most enthusiastic Pagnol admirers.' – *John Gillett, MFB*

† Pagnol later expanded the story into two novels which were the basis for a two-part film, *Jean de Florette* (qv) and *Manon des Sources* (1986) (qv).

Manon des Sources ***

France   1986   114m   colour
Renn Productions/A2/RAI 2/DD Productions (Roland Thenot)
🔲 🔲 ▤ 🔘 🎧

A young girl avenges the wrong done to her father by a farmer and his nephew.

Absorbing drama of rural life, impeccably performed and directed.

w Claude Berri, Gérard Brach novel Marcel Pagnol d Claude Berri ph Bruno Nuytten m Jean-Claude Petit pd Bernard Vizat ed Geneviève Louveau, Hervé de Luze

☆ Yves Montand, Daniel Auteuil, Emmanuelle Béart, Hippolyte Girardot, Margarita Lozano, Gabriel Bacquier

Manpower *

US   1941   103m   bw
Warner (Mark Hellinger)

Power linesmen fall out over a night-club hostess.

Yet another variation on Tiger Shark, with vivid fisticuff and storm sequences supporting the star performers.

w Richard Macaulay, Jerry Wald d Raoul Walsh ph Ernest Haller m Adolph Deutsch

☆ Edward G. Robinson, George Raft, Marlene Dietrich, Alan Hale, Frank McHugh, Eve Arden, Barton MacLane, Walter Catlett, Joyce Compton, Ward Bond

'The pace and cutting are those of the best gangster films ... the climax outdoes anything the Lyceum may have known.' – *William Whitebait*

Man's Best Friend

US   1993   87m   DeLuxe
Guild/New Line/Roven-Cavello (Bob Engelman)
🔲 ▤ 🔘

A reporter releases from an experimental laboratory a genetically altered dog that combines size and intelligence with the ability of a chameleon and the instincts of a killer.

A moderately entertaining, but gory, thriller that at least provides a welcome antidote to the Beethoven series.

wd John Lafia ph Mark Irwin m Joel Goldsmith pd Jaymes Hinkle ed Michael N. Knue sp Kevin Yagher

☆ Ally Sheedy, Lance Henriksen, Robert Constanzo, Frederic Lehne, John Cassini, J. D. Daniels, William Sanderson

'Combines increasingly gory black-comic bits ... with a plethora of gimmicks. The mixture is far from boring, but it coarsens the comedy about the hidden life of dogs.' – *Michael Sragow, New Yorker*
'How we all laughed at this movie's awful lines and clichéd plot contrivances, down to the closing, sequel-bound litter of pyscho puppies.' – *Sheila Johnston, Independent*

Man's Castle *

US   1933   70m   bw
Columbia (Frank Borzage)

Romance blooms among the unemployed who live in a shanty town on the banks of the East River.

Depression moonshine which at the time was taken for realism; sociologically very interesting but very faded as entertainment.

w Jo Swerling play Lawrence Hazard d Frank Borzage ph Joseph August m W. Franke Harling

☆ Spencer Tracy, Loretta Young, Glenda Farrell, Walter Connolly, Arthur Hohl, Marjorie Rambeau, Dickie Moore

'A picture that goes contrary to normal entertainment appetites and tastes, its possibilities of going places look slender at best.' – *Variety*
'Heavily sentimental yet magically romantic.' – *New Yorker, 1977*

Man's Favourite Sport? *

US   1963   120m   Technicolor
Universal/Gibraltar/Laurel (Howard Hawks)
▤

A star salesman of fishing tackle finds his bluff called when he has to enter a fishing competition.

Over-extended romantic farce drawn by the director from memories of older and better films, such as Libeled Lady and his own Bringing Up Baby.

w John Fenton Murray d Howard Hawks ph Russell Harlan m Henry Mancini

☆ Rock Hudson, Paula Prentiss, Maria Perschy, Charlene Holt, John McGiver, Roscoe Karns

'Hawks' deadpan documentation of a physical gag is as effective as ever, but the overall pace of his direction is curiously contemplative, as though he was savoring all his past jokes for the last time.' – *Andrew Sarris*

Man's Hope: see *Espoir*

'Discover The Year's Most Passionate Film!'
'Jane Austen's Wicked Comedy.'
Mansfield Park *

GB/US   1999   112m   DeLuxe
Buena Vista/Miramax HAL/BBC (Sarah Curtis)
🎧

A poor young girl goes to live with her wealthy relations and falls in love with her cousin.

Fanny Price, Austin's timid, neurasthenic heroine is here transformed into a forceful writer (based on Rozema's view of Jane Austen herself); other alterations include shifting the action back in time to make points about the slave trade. More seriously, other changes mean that Fanny is no longer the moral centre of the action, so that the point of the novel is lost.

wd Patricia Rozema *novel, letters and early journals* Jane Austen ph Michael Coulter m Lesley Barber pd Christopher Hobbs ed Martin Walsh cos Andrea Galer
☆ Embeth Davidtz, Jonny Lee Miller, Alessandro Nivola, Frances O'Connor, Harold Pinter, Lindsay Duncan, Sheila Gish, James Purefoy, Hugh Bonneville, Justine Waddell, Victoria Hamilton, Sophia Myles, Hilton McRae, Hannah Taylor Gordon, Charles Edwards

'Rozema can't seem to hold a single tone for more than a few minutes, and she has too many other axes to grind besides just getting the story up on the screen.' – *Derek Elley, Variety*
'Seldom has a film played quite so fast and loose with an enduring literary work in the dubious cause of seeming "accessible" and "relevant".' – *Angie Errigo, Empire*

Manslaughter *
US 1922 80m bw silent
Paramount/Famous Players (Cecil B. de Mille)
An idle rich girl accidentally kills a man while driving, and is sent to prison, but falls for the district attorney who convicted her.
De Mille was here testing out his Ten Commandments format, with a long flashback during the DA's speech to the idle rich of ancient Rome. It worked like a charm at the box-office.
w Jeanie Macpherson *novel* Alice Duer Miller d Cecil B. de Mille ph Alvin Wyckoff
☆ Leatrice Joy, Thomas Meighan, Lois Wilson, John Miltern
† A 1930 sound remake for Paramount was directed by George Abbott, who also tried in vain to modernize the screenplay (by omitting the flashback). Claudette Colbert and Fredric March starred.

Mantrap
US 1961 93m bw Panavision
Paramount/Tiger (Edmond O'Brien, Stanley Frazen)
An honest man is lured by an old Marine friend into a hi-jack attempt which leads to the death of his wife.
Rather uninteresting melodrama, played and directed for more than it's worth.
w Ed Waters *novel Taint of the Tiger* by John D. Macdonald d Edmond O'Brien ph Loyal Griggs m Leith Stevens
☆ Jeffrey Hunter, David Janssen, Stella Stevens, Hugh Sanders

The Mantrap
US 1943 57m bw
Republic (George Sherman)
A retired Scotland Yard man helps the DA's office in a murder case.
Entertaining second feature with a geriatric hero; alas, the clues don't play quite fair.
w Curt Siodmak d George Sherman
☆ Henry Stephenson, Lloyd Corrigan, Joseph Allen Jnr, Dorothy Lovett

Manuela *
GB 1957 95m bw
British Lion/Ivan Foxwell
US title: *Stowaway Girl*
In a South American port, the engineer of a tramp steamer smuggles aboard a half caste girl, but it is the disillusioned captain who falls in love with her.
Downbeat seafaring melodrama, fine for those seeking a mood piece.
w William Woods *novel* William Woods d Guy Hamilton ph Otto Heller m William Alwyn
☆ Trevor Howard, Elsa Martinelli, Pedro Armendariz, Donald Pleasence

The Manxman
GB 1929 90m bw silent
British International (John Maxwell)
A fisherman thought drowned comes back to find that his girl is expecting his best friend's baby.
Stern romantic melodrama of virtually no interest despite its director.
w Eliot Stannard *novel* Hall Caine d Alfred Hitchcock ph Jack Cox
☆ Carl Brisson, Malcolm Keen, Anny Ondra, Randle Ayrton, Clare Greet
† Previously filmed in 1916 with Henry Ainley and Elizabeth Risdon.

Many Happy Returns
US 1934 62m bw
Paramount
A scatty girl jinxes her father's department store and a Hollywood studio.
Silly comedy with stops for vaudeville.
w J. P. McEvoy, Claude Binyon, Keene Thompson, Ray Harris *story* Lady Mary Cameron(!)
d Norman Z. McLeod
☆ George Burns, Gracie Allen, Guy Lombardo and his Band, Veloz and Yolanda, Ray Milland, George Barbier, Joan Marsh, Franklin Pangborn, William Demarest, Larry Adler
'Often very funny, at other moments it lags.' – *Variety*

Many Rivers to Cross *
US 1955 94m Eastmancolor Cinemascope
MGM (Jack Cummings)
A trapper bound for Canada is helped by a sharp-shooting girl, and in return he saves her from marauding Indians.
Simple-minded, cheerful, quite refreshing Western compounded of equal parts comedy and action.
w Harry Brown, Guy Trosper d Roy Rowland ph John Seitz m Cyril Mockridge
☆ Robert Taylor, Eleanor Parker, Victor McLaglen, Josephine Hutchinson, Jeff Richards, Russ Tamblyn, James Arness, Alan Hale Jnr

'From a Kingdom of Ice to a Land of Fire ... A Love That Knows No Boundaries.'

Map of the Human Heart *
GB/Australia 1992 109m colour
Rank/Working Title/Map/Sunrise/Polygram/AFFC/Vincent Ward
An elderly Eskimo recalls to a surveyor the events of his life: how he helped map his remote part of the Arctic as a boy, was sent to Canada to cure his tuberculosis, served in the RAF and loved and lost a girl he met in hospital and later in England.
An ambitious, sprawling and flawed film that attempts to take in too much, in time and emotion – with a 'feelgood' ending that seems out of place with the tragic story that has gone before.
w Louis Nowra *story* Vincent Ward d Vincent Ward ph Eduardo Serra m Gabriel Yared pd John Beard ed John Scott, Frans Vandenburg
☆ Patrick Bergin, Anne Parillaud, Jason Scott Lee, John Cusack, Jeanne Moreau
'What we learn about the human heart remains a matter of guesswork, but as a map the film certainly offers some eye-catching perspectives.' – *Philip Strick, Sight and Sound*
'A true one-off, this is a poignant, thoughtfully drawn map of love, death and life.' – *Angie Errigo, Empire*
† The film was cut from 126m after it was shown at the Cannes Film Festival, and had an extra day's shooting in London to add scenes with Lee and Parillaud. The ending was also recut to give it a more upbeat feeling.

Mapantsula *
South Africa 1988 104m Agfacolor
Electric/One Look Productions/David Hannay Productions/Haverbeam (Max Montoccchio)
A petty criminal in Soweto stands firm against police oppression.
Lively look at the underside of life in a black township, but lacking in depth.
w Oliver Schmitz, Thomas Mogotlane d Oliver Schmitz ph Rod Stewart m The Ouens ad Robin Hofmeyr ed Mike Baard
☆ Thomas Mogotlane, Thembi Mtshali, Peter Sephuma, Marcel Van Heerden, Eugene Majola, Dolly Rathebe, Darlington Michaels

Mara Maru
US 1952 98m bw
Warner (David Weisbart)
A Manila salvage expert locates a sunken treasure and defeats crooks who are also in pursuit of it.
Lethargic but pleasant-looking star vehicle with a plot borrowed from The Maltese Falcon.
w N. Richard Nash, Philip Yordan, Sidney Harmon, Hollister Noble d Gordon Douglas ph Robert Burks m Max Steiner
☆ Errol Flynn, Ruth Roman, Raymond Burr, Paul Picerni, Richard Webb

Maracaibo
US 1958 88m Technicolor Vistavision
Paramount/Theodora (Cornel Wilde)
A Texan oil fire expert finds himself unexpectedly busy when on holiday in Venezuela.
Meandering action melodrama with too much local colour.
w Ted Sherdeman *novel* Stirling Silliphant d Cornel Wilde ph Ellsworth Fredericks m Laurindo Almeida
☆ Cornel Wilde, Jean Wallace, Abbe Lane, Francis Lederer, Joe E. Ross, Michael Landon

The Marat/Sade *
GB 1966 116m DeLuxe
UA/Marat Sade (Michael Birkett)
aka: *The Persecution and Assassination of Jean-Paul Marat as performed by the inmates of the Asylum of Charenton under the direction of the Marquis de Sade*
The title tells all, except that at the end the inmates go berserk.
Fairly plain filming of an Old Vic succès d'estime which it became fashionable to announce that one had seen and understood. The film makes no effort to attract the unbeliever.
w Adrian Mitchell *play* Peter Weiss d Peter Brook ph David Watkin m Richard Peaslee
☆ Glenda Jackson, Patrick Magee, Ian Richardson, Michael Williams, Robert Lloyd, Clifford Rose, Freddie Jones
'I loathed and detested doing the play. I couldn't wait for it to end. Then we all did the film and it was a shattering experience. People twitching, slobber running down their chins, everyone screaming from nerves and exhaustion.' – *Glenda Jackson*

Marathon Man ***
US 1976 126m Metrocolor
Paramount (Robert Evans, Sidney Beckerman)
A vicious Nazi returns from Uruguay to New York in search of diamonds which had been kept for him by his now-dead brother, and is outwitted by the young brother of an American agent he has killed.
Complex mystery thriller which seems to have things to mutter about freedom and McCarthyism and Nazism, but finally settles down to being a simple shocker with a nick-of-time climax. The presentation is dazzling.
w William Goldman *novel* William Goldman d John Schlesinger ph Conrad Hall m Michael Small pd Richard MacDonald
☆ Dustin Hoffman, Laurence Olivier, Roy Scheider, William Devane, Marthe Keller, Fritz Weaver, Marc Lawrence
'A film of such rich texture and density in its construction, so fascinatingly complex in its unfolding, so engrossing in its personalities, and so powerful in its performance and pace that the seduction of the senses has physical force.' – *Judith Crist, Saturday Review*
'Fashionably violent ... distinctly self-conscious ... conventionally moralistic ... and absolutely devoid of resonance.' – *Tom Milne, MFB*
'If at the film's end, you have followed the series of double and triple crosses, braved the torture scenes, and still don't know what it was about, you're bound to have company.' – *Paul Coleman, Film Information*
'A Jewish revenge fantasy.' – *Pauline Kael*
'He has made a most elegant, bizarre, rococo melodrama out of material which, when you think about it, makes hardly any sense at all.' – *Vincent Canby, New York Times*
Ŋ Laurence Olivier

The Marauders
US 1955 81m Eastmancolor
MGM (Arthur M. Loew Jnr)
A rancher hires gunmen to drive away squatters, but the gunmen kill him and take over.
Slightly sinister Western with a plot probably worth trying again.
w Jack Leonard, Earl Fenton *novel* Alan Marcus d Gerald Mayer ph Harold Marzorati m Paul Sawtell
☆ Dan Duryea, Jeff Richards, Keenan Wynn, Jarma Lewis, Harry Shannon

March of the Wooden Soldiers: see *Babes in Toyland*

March or Die
GB 1977 107m Technicolor
ITC/Associated General (Dick Richards, Jerry Bruckheimer)
In 1918, tensions rise at a Foreign Legion outpost threatened by Arabs.
Incredibly old-hat romantic melodrama of the kind that was being spoofed forty years ago. The considerable talent involved seems unfortunately under instruction to take it seriously.
w David Zelag Goodman d Dick Richards ph John Alcott m Maurice Jarre
☆ Gene Hackman, Terence Hill (Mario Girotti), Catherine Deneuve, Max von Sydow, Ian Holm, Marcel Bozzuffi
† The writer and director more successfully revived a different set of clichés in *Farewell My Lovely*.

Marching Along: see *Stars and Stripes Forever*

Marco the Magnificent: see *The Fabulous Adventures of Marco Polo*

Mardi Gras
US 1958 107m DeLuxe Cinemascope
TCF (Jerry Wald)
In New Orleans at holiday time, a film star falls for a cadet.
Mindless musical using up available talent.
w Winston Miller, Hal Kanter d Edmund Goulding ph Wilfrid M. Cline md Lionel Newman
☆ Pat Boone, Christine Carere, Sheree North, Tommy Sands, Gary Crosby, Fred Clark, Richard Sargent, Barrie Chase
Ŋ Lionel Newman

Mare Nostrum *
US 1925 110m bw silent
MGM
A Spanish captain loves a German spy.
Tragic romantic melodrama, a major attraction of its time.
w Willis Goldbeck *novel* Vicente Blasco Ibanez d Rex Ingram ph John Seitz
☆ Antonio Moreno, Alice Terry

Margaret's Museum **
Canada/GB 1995 100m colour
Ranfilm/Imagex/Télé-Action/Skyline (Mort Ransen, Christopher Zimmer, Claudio Luca, Steve Clark-Hall)
In the late 40s, in a small Novia Scotia town, a woman is driven to madness by the deaths of the men in her life, who had no option but to work as miners.
Compelling drama of female suffering that comes to an unexpected climax, and owes much to the equally unexpected performance of Bonham Carter as a working-class wife.
w Gerald Wexler, Mort Ransen *novel The Glace Bay Miner's Museum* by Sheldon Currie d Mort Ransen ph Vic Sarin m Milan Kymlicka pd William Fleming, David McHenry ed Rita Roy
☆ Helena Bonham Carter, Kate Nelligan, Clive Russell, Craig Olejnik, Andrea Morris, Peter Boretski, Kenneth Welsh
'A moving, funny pic that's actually quite uplifting for most of the time.' – *Brendan Kelly, Variety*
† Ransen spent most of the 90s trying to get backing for the film. In Canada's 1995 Genie awards it won plaudits for best writing, score, actress (Bonham Carter), supporting actress (Nelligan) and supporting actor (Welsh).

La Marge
France 1976 90m Eastmancolor
Paris Film/Robert and Raymond Hakim
aka: *The Margin*
aka: *The Streetwalker*
After receiving a letter telling him that his wife has committed suicide after his son was drowned, a husband working in Paris spends several days with a prostitute.
Trite tale of the wages of sin, filmed without much enthusiasm from the participants, despite a great deal of nudity and sexual activity.
wd Walerian Borowczyk *novel* André Pieyre de Mandiargues ph Bernard Daillencourt ed Louisette Hautecoeur

☆ Sylvia Kristel, Joe Dallesandro, André Falcon, Mireille Audibert, Denis Manuel

'Borowczyk is at his least impressive with this story.' – *Sight and Sound*

'His masterpiece.' – *Movie Collector*

† A dubbed version running for 80m has also been released on video.

'The girl of the moment in the picture of America's hey! hey! day!'

Margie ***

US   1946   94m   Technicolor

TCF (Walter Morosco)

A married woman reminisces about her college days, when she married the French teacher despite her tendency to lose her bloomers at the most embarrassing moments.

Wholly pleasing nostalgia, very smartly and brightly handled.

w F. Hugh Herbert *stories* Ruth McKinney, Richard Bransten d Henry King ph Charles Clarke md Alfred Newman

☆ Jeanne Crain, Glenn Langan, Alan Young, Lynn Bari, Barbara Lawrence, Conrad Janis, Esther Dale

'Direction, script and settings skilfully interpret the fashions and crazes of the twenties.' – *MFB*

The Margin: see *La Marge*

Margin for Error *

US   1943   74m   bw

TCF (Ralph Dietrich)

Just before World War II, the Nazi consul in New York is murdered in his own office.

Mildly intriguing whodunnit with the case solved by a Jewish cop.

w Lillie Hayward *play* Clare Boothe Luce d Otto Preminger ph Edward Cronjager m Leigh Harline

☆ Milton Berle, Joan Bennett, Otto Preminger, Carl Esmond, Howard Freeman, Poldy Dur, Hans von Twardowski

Le Marginal: see *The Outsider* (1983)

Marguerite de la Nuit *

France/Italy   1955   126m   Technicolor

SNEG/Gaumont Actualités/Cino del Duca (Léon Carré)

An octogenarian signs a pact with the devil in return for his lost youth; but when he has it he causes the death of the woman he loves.

Expensive, sporadically interesting, but unpersuasive updating of Faust.

w Ghislaine Autant-Lara, Gabriel Arout d Claude Autant-Lara ph Jacques Natteau m René Cloërc

☆ Michèle Morgan, Yves Montand, Jean-François Calvé, Massimo Girotti

Le Mari de la coiffeuse: see *The Hairdresser's Husband*

Maria Chapdelaine *

France   1934   73m   bw

Société Nouvelle

In a hard Quebec winter Maria loses her mother and her lover, but resists temptation by a man from the city.

Artistically telling drama, later flatly remade as The Naked Heart.

novel Louis Hémon d Julien Duvivier

☆ Madeleine Renaud, Jean Gabin, Suzanne Despres, Jean-Pierre Aumont

'A fine achievement, it gives the feeling of a sort of epic poem.' – *Variety*

Maria Marten, or The Murder in the Red Barn

GB   1935   67m   bw

George King

A wicked Victorian squire kills his pregnant mistress and is haunted.

Stilted melodrama, ripely played, from a real-life case. (The villain's scalp is still exhibited in a museum at Bury St Edmunds.)

w Randall Faye d Milton Rosmer ph George Stretton md Lionel Claff ad D. W. Daniels ed Charles Saunders

☆ Tod Slaughter, Sophie Stewart, Eric Portman, Clare Greet, D. J. Williams

† Several versions had been made in silent days.

El Mariachi: see *under E*

Maria's Lovers

US   1984   103m   colour

Cannon/Golan-Globus (Bosko Djordjevic, Lawrence Taylor-Mortorff)

A soldier returns from a Japanese prisoner-of-war camp to marry the girl of his dreams and discovers that he is impotent with her.

Turgid domestic drama, taken at a funereal pace and with acting that is unable to make the lugubrious script convincing; it is rather as if Tennessee Williams had been rewritten by William Faulkner.

w Gerard Brach, Andrei Konchalovsky, Paul Zindel, Marjorie David d Andrei Konchalovsky ph Juan Ruiz-Anchia m Gary S. Remal pd Jeannine Oppewall ed Humphrey Dixon

☆ Nastassja Kinski, John Savage, Robert Mitchum, Keith Carradine, Anita Morris, Bud Cort, Karen Young, Tracy (credited as Tracey) Nelson, John Goodman, Vincent Spano

Marie

US   1985   112m   Technicolor   Dunton vision

Dino de Laurentiis (Frank Capra Jnr)

A battered wife leaves her husband and becomes chairman of the Tennessee parole board.

An edifying biopic to which the only answer is, so what?

w John Briley *book* Peter Maas d Roger Donaldson ph Chris Menges m Francis Lai

☆ Sissy Spacek, Jeff Daniels, Morgan Freeman, Fred Thompson

'Blessed are the pure in heart but also deadly dull.' – *Time Out*

'A highly accomplished piece of work. It moves, it looks professional, and it's well acted.' – *Pauline Kael, New Yorker*

† Fred Thompson, who was the real-life Marie Ragghianti's lawyer, plays himself in the film. He then became a movie actor under the name Fred Dalton Thompson, appearing in *The Hunt for Red October* and *Die Hard 2* among other films.

Marie Antoinette *

US   1938   160m   bw

MGM (Hunt Stromberg)

The last days of the French court before the revolution.

Too slow by half, and so glamorized and fictionalized as to lack all interest, this long delayed production stands only as an example of MGM's expensive prestige movies of the thirties.

w Claudine West, Donald Ogden Stewart, Ernest Vajda d W. S. Van Dyke ph William Daniels m Herbert Stothart ad Cedric Gibbons montage Slavko Vorkapich

☆ Norma Shearer, Tyrone Power, John Barrymore, Robert Morley, Gladys George, Anita Louise, Joseph Schildkraut, Henry Stephenson, Reginald Gardiner, Peter Bull, Albert Dekker, Cora Witherspoon, Barnett Parker, Joseph Calleia, Henry Kolker and also George Zucco, Henry Daniell, Harry Davenport, Barry Fitzgerald, Mae Busch, Robert Barrat

'Produced on a scale of incomparable splendour and extravagance, it approaches real greatness as cinematic historical literature.' – *Variety*

'A resplendent bore.' – *New Yorker, 1977*

♫ Herbert Stothart; Norma Shearer; Robert Morley

Marie Baie des Anges: see *Angel Sharks*

La Marie du Port

France   1949   95m   bw

Sacha Gordine

A Cherbourg restaurateur takes his mistress home for her father's funeral, and falls in love with her younger sister.

Slight romantic drama, well enough put over but not very memorable except for its slightly cynical mood.

w Louis Chavance, Marcel Carné *novel* Georges Simenon d Marcel Carné ph Henri Alekan m Joseph Kosma

☆ Jean Gabin, Blanchette Brunoy, Nicole Courcel, Claude Romain, Louis Seigner, Jeanne Marken, Carette

La Mariée Est Trop Belle: see *The Bride Is Much Too Beautiful*

Marie Galante

US   1934   90m   bw

Fox

A French girl stranded in the Canal Zone becomes involved in international intrigue.

Slightly unusual spy romance.

w Reginald Berkeley *novel* Jacques Deval d Henry King

☆ Spencer Tracy, Ketti Gallian, Ned Sparks, Helen Morgan, Sig Rumann, Leslie Fenton, Stepin Fetchit

'Production and handling should carry it to moderate grosses.' – *Variety*

Marie Octobre

France   1958   102m   bw

Orex/SF/Abbey/Doxa (Lucien Viard)

US title: *Secret Meeting*

At a reunion dinner of a wartime resistance group, a traitor is exposed and killed.

Stultifying one-set talkfest employing Hitchcock's long-discarded ten-minute take.

w Julien Duvivier, Jacques Robert *novel* Jacques Robert d Julien Duvivier ph Robert Le Fèbvre m Jean Yatove ad Georges Wakhevitch

☆ Danielle Darrieux, Serge Reggiani, Bernard Blier, Paul Meurisse, Noel Roquevert, Lino Ventura, Paul Guers, Paul Frankeur

Marie Walewska: see *Conquest*

La Mariée Etait en Noir: see *The Bride Wore Black*

Mariés de L'An Deux: see *The Scoundrel* (1971)

Marine Raiders

US   1944   90m   bw

RKO (Robert Fellows)

The marines do battle in Guadalcanal.

Standard romantic flagwaver.

w Warren Duff d Harold Schuster ph Nick Musuraca m Roy Webb

☆ Pat O'Brien, Robert Ryan, Ruth Hussey, Frank McHugh, Barton MacLane

The Marines Fly High

US   1940   68m   bw

RKO

Two leathernecks combat a mysterious South American villain.

Formula action fare, intended as a Flagg and Quirt adventure but made with a second team.

w Jerry Cady, A. J. Bolton d George Nicholls Jnr, Ben Stoloff

☆ Richard Dix, Chester Morris, Lucille Ball, John Eldredge, Steffi Duna

'Up to their necks in fights and loving!'

Marines Let's Go

US   1961   103m   DeLuxe   Cinemascope

TCF (Raoul Walsh)

Marines fighting in Korea are granted leave in Japan.

Brawling tragi-farce with predictable characters, a long way after What Price Glory.

w John Twist *story* Raoul Walsh d Raoul Walsh ph Lucien Ballard m Irving Gertz

☆ Tom Tryon, David Hedison, Tom Reese, Linda Hutchins, William Tyler

'A typically noisy, insensitive and maudlin tribute to the American Marines.' – *MFB*

Marius **

France   1931   125m   bw

Marcel Pagnol/Paramount

The son of a Marseilles waterfront café owner gives up his sweetheart to go to sea.

Celebrated character drama which succeeds through the realism and vitality of its people and their dialogue.

w Marcel Pagnol *play* Marcel Pagnol d Alexander Korda ph Ted Pahle m Francis Grammon

☆ Raimu, Pierre Fresnay, Charpin, Orane Demazis

† Two sequels with the same players and from the same pen made this a famous trilogy: *Fanny* (qv) and *César* (qv).

†† *Port of Seven Seas* (MGM 1938) was a hammy and stagey Hollywood compression of the trilogy. See also *Fanny* (1960), a dull version of the stage musical, with the songs removed.

Marius et Jeanette *

France   1997   102m   colour

Porter Frith/La Sept/Agat (Gilles Sandoz, Robert Guédiguian)

A security guard finds it difficult to cope with his new relationship with a single mother with two young children.

A soft-centred romance about a couple experiencing hard times; the craft of its director and the performances of the cast compensate for its old-fashioned tone.

w Jean-Louis Milesi, Robert Guédiguian d Robert Guédiguian ph Bernard Cavalié ed Bernard Sasia

☆ Ariane Ascaride, Gérard Meylan, Pascale Roberts, Jacques Boudet, Frédérique Bonnal, Jean-Pierre Darroussin

'A rough-cut gem.' – *Empire*

Marjorie Morningstar

US   1958   123m   Warnercolor

(Warner) United States Pictures (Milton Sperling)

A New York Jewish girl has great ambitions for herself but ends up a suburban housewife.

Stodgy 'woman's picture' with all talents somewhat uneasy in their assignments, mainly because the Jewish quality is imperfectly conveyed.

w Everett Freeman *novel* Herman Wouk d Irving Rapper ph Harry Stradling m Max Steiner

☆ Natalie Wood, Gene Kelly, Claire Trevor, Everett Sloane, Ed Wynn, Martin Milner, Carolyn Jones, George Tobias, Jesse White, Martin Balsam

† The first film in which perfume was credited.

♫ song 'A Very Precious Love' (mSammy Fain, lyFrancis Webster)

'Lock me up! Please lock me up!'

The Mark *

GB   1961   127m   bw   Cinemascope

TCF/Raymond Stross/Sidney Buchman

A sexual psychopath finds on emerging from prison that his past still haunts him despite the help of his psychiatrist.

Worthy but evasive social drama which outstays its welcome but provides good performances.

w Sidney Buchman, Stanley Mann d Guy Green ph Douglas Slocombe m Richard Rodney Bennett

☆ Stuart Whitman, Maria Schell, Rod Steiger, Brenda de Banzie, Maurice Denham, Donald Wolfit, Paul Rogers, Donald Houston

'There is seriousness and care, but neither boldness nor passion ... no hint of the truly sordid is allowed to seep through.' – *MFB*

♫ Stuart Whitman

The Mark of Cain

GB   1947   88m   bw

GFD/Two Cities (W. P. Lipscomb)

The attractive housekeeper of a Manchester businessman is blamed when his brother accidentally poisons him.

Turgid period melodrama in which few opportunities are offered and none taken.

w Francis Crowdy, Christianna Brand, W. P. Lipscomb *novel* Airing in a Closed Carriage by Joseph Shearing d Brian Desmond Hurst ph Erwin Hillier m Bernard Stevens

☆ Sally Gray, Eric Portman, Patrick Holt, Dermot Walsh, Denis O'Dea, Edward Lexy, Miles Malleson

'Positively The Most Horrifying Film Ever Made.'

'Likely to upset your stomach.'

Mark of the Devil (dubbed)

West Germany   1969   97m   colour

Atlas/Hi-Fi Stereo 70 (Adrian Hoven)

original title: *Hexen geschändet und zu Tode gequält*

aka: *Austria 1700*

A bloodthirsty and lecherous witch-finder's activities are usurped by an even more sadistic aristocrat, acting in the name of the Church.

A nasty, garish horror that lingers over scenes of torture and brutality. The movie claims to be based on cases 'taken from authentic documents', but the result is the same old exploitative rubbish as usual.

w Sergio Casstner (Michael Armstrong), Percy Parker (Adrian Hoven) d Michael Armstrong ph Ernst W. Kulinke m Michael Holm ad Max Mellin ed Siegrun Jager

☆ Herbert Lom, Olivera Vuco, Udo Kier, Reggie Nalder, Herbert Fux, Michael Maien, Ingeborg Schoener, Johannes Buzalski, Gaby Fuchs

---

† The film was refused a certificate and never shown in British cinemas. It was released on video in the 1980s and quickly withdrawn before being given a British video release in 1993 with an 18 certificate. When it first opened in America, audiences were supplied with sick-bags as they went in.

The Mark of the Hawk

US 1958 84m Technicolor Superscope
Universal-International

An educated African fights for the emergence of his people by peaceful means.
Well-intentioned but muddled topical drama.
w H. Kenn Carmichael d Michael Audley
☆ Sidney Poitier, Juano Hernandez, Eartha Kitt, John McIntire, Marne Maitland, Patrick Allen

Mark of the Phoenix

GB 1959 65m bw
Butchers (W. G. Chalmers)

An American jewel thief becomes accidentally involved in a plan to smuggle into Russia a cigarette case made of a secret alloy.
Dull second feature; it is typical that its brief moments of action should take place in the dark.
w Norman Hudis story Desmond Cory d Maclean Rogers ph Geoffrey Faithfull md Wilfred Burns ad John Stoll ed Harry Booth
☆ Julia Arnall, Sheldon Lawrence, Anton Diffring, Eric Pohlmann, George Margo, Michael Peake, Martin Miller, Bernard Rebel, Roger Delgado

Mark of the Renegade

US 1951 81m Technicolor
Jack Gross/Universal-International

In 1824, a Mexican agent in California pretends to be a rotter in order to unmask villains.
Shakily constructed action piece which quickly wears out its welcome.
w Louis Solomon and Robert Hardy Andrews story Johnston McCulley d Hugo Fregonese
☆ Ricardo Montalban, Gilbert Roland, Cyd Charisse, J. Carrol Naish, Andrea King, George Tobias, Antonio Moreno

Mark of the Vampire *

US 1935 61m bw
MGM (E. J. Mannix)

A policeman tries to solve an old murder in an eerie house by hiring vaudeville performers to pose as vampires.
Semi-spoof horror which is flawed by lack of pace and a patchy script, but contains splendid visual moments. A remake of the Lon Chaney silent, London After Midnight.
w Guy Endore, Bernard Schubert d Tod Browning ph James Wong Howe
☆ Lionel Barrymore, Jean Hersholt, Elizabeth Allan, Bela Lugosi, Carol Borland, Lionel Atwill, Henry Wadsworth, Donald Meek, Jessie Ralph, Ivan Simpson, Holmes Herbert
'Deftly combines murder mystery, chiller and novelty elements for pretty good entertainment results.' – *Variety*
'Even the adults in the audience may feel a bit skittery at the sight of two or three vampires, a bevy of bats, a drove of rodents, a herd of spiders and a cluster of cobwebs, not forgetting the swarm of fog.' – *New York Times*

The Mark of Zorro *

US 1920 90m bw silent
Douglas Fairbanks

A Mexican Robin Hood carves his initial wherever he turns up to harass the Spanish invaders.
A little faded now, but this swashbuckler opened up a whole new career for its star; the 1940 version clearly has more style.
novel *The Curse of Capistrano* by Johnston McCulley d Fred Niblo ph William McGann m William Perry
☆ Douglas Fairbanks, Marguerite de la Motte, Noah Beery

The Mark of Zorro ***

⇧ US 1940 94m bw
TCF (Raymond Griffith)

After being educated in Spain, Diego de Vega returns to California and finds the country

---

enslaved and his father half-corrupted by tyrants. Disguising himself as a masked bandit, he leads the country to expel the usurpers.
Splendid adventure stuff for boys of all ages, an amalgam of The Scarlet Pimpernel *and* Robin Hood *to which in this version the director adds an overwhelming pictorial sense which makes it stand out as the finest of all.*
w John Taintor Foote, Garrett Fort, Bess Meredyth d Rouben Mamoulian ph Arthur Miller m Alfred Newman ad Richard Day, Joseph C. Wright
☆ Tyrone Power, Basil Rathbone, J. Edward Bromberg, Linda Darnell, Eugene Pallette, Montagu Love, Janet Beecher, Robert Lowery
♪ Alfred Newman

The Mark of Zorro (dubbed)

Italy/France/Spain 1963 90m Eastmancolor
Dyaliscope
CCM/Fidès/Benito Perojo (Harry Joe Brown)
original title: *Il Segno di Zorro*
US title: *Duel at the Rio Grande*

Returning from Spain to his Mexican home, an aristocrat discovers that his father has been killed and his lands confiscated by the governor on a false charge of treason.
Cut-rate swashbuckler with little of the necessary panache about it.
w Guido Malatesta, Casey Robinson d Nathan Juran ph Adalberto Albertini m Gregorio Garcia Segura ad Enrique Alarçon ed Alberto Gallitti, Antonio Boccianti
☆ Sean Flynn, Danielle de Metz, Armando Calvo, Mario Petri, Gaby André, Mino Doro, Folco Lulli, Alfredo Rizzo
† Nathan Juran directed the US dubbed version; the Italian version was directed by Mario Caiano

Marked for Death

US 1990 93m DeLuxe
TCF/Steamroller (Michael Grais, Mark Victor, Steven Seagal)

A former agent takes action against a Jamaican drug dealer and his gang.
Familiar scenario offering the usual mix of grunts and orchestrated violence.
w Michael Grais, Mark Victor d Dwight H. Little ph Ric Waite m James Newton Howard pd Robb Wilson King ed O. Nicholas Brown
☆ Steven Seagal, Basil Wallace, Keith David, Tom Wright, Joanna Pacula, Elizabeth Gracen, Bette Ford, Danielle Harris

Marked Woman *

US 1937 96m bw
Warner (Lou Edelman)

A night-club girl is persuaded to testify against an underworld boss.
A twist on the usual run of gangster melodramas, performed with the star's accustomed intensity and presented with the studio's usual panache.
w Robert Rossen, Abem Finkel d Lloyd Bacon ph George Barnes m Heinz Roemheld md Leo F. Forbstein
☆ Bette Davis, Humphrey Bogart, Jane Bryan, Eduardo Ciannelli, Isabel Jewell, Allen Jenkins, Mayo Methot, Lola Lane, Henry O'Neill
'Spotty shape depending on feminine reaction … there is nothing that is light, and very little that is funny.' – *Variety*
† Remade as *Lady Gangster.*
†† Humphrey Bogart's character was based on Thomas E. Dewey, and Eduardo Ciannelli's on Lucky Luciano.

Marlowe *

US 1969 95m Metrocolor
MGM (Gabriel Katzka, Sidney Beckerman)

Private eye Philip Marlowe is hired by a nervous girl to find her missing brother.
The authentic Chandler atmosphere is caught by this busy thriller, but there seems to be a deliberate attempt to make a confusing plot even more obscure, so that the end result is more tiresome than amusing.
w Stirling Silliphant novel *The Little Sister* by Raymond Chandler d Paul Bogart ph William H. Daniels m Peter Matz ad George W. Davis, Addison Hehr ed Gene Ruggiero
☆ James Garner, Rita Moreno, Sharon Farrell, Bruce Lee, Gayle Hunnicutt, Carroll O'Connor, William Daniels, Jackie Coogan, H. M. Wynant, Kenneth Tobey

---

'One does wonder whether the simple squalor of the Bogart-Chandler era can ever be recaptured by an increasingly meretricious Hollywood.' – *MFB*

Marnie *

US 1964 130m Technicolor
Universal/Geoffrey Stanley Inc (Alfred Hitchcock)

A rich man marries a kleptomaniac and cures her, but a nightmare in her past makes her still sexually frigid.
Psychodrama with background crime and suspense, lethargically handled by the old master, who alone knows what he saw in it in the first place, as this heroine does not even have fire under her ice. The production is curiously artificial in many ways, from dummy horses to backcloths to back projection.
w Jay Presson Allen novel Winston Graham d Alfred Hitchcock ph Robert Burks m Bernard Herrmann pd Robert Boyle
☆ Tippi Hedren, Sean Connery, Martin Gabel, Diane Baker, Louise Latham

Maroc 7

GB 1967 91m Eastmancolor Panavision
Rank/Cyclone

The lady editor of a top fashion magazine doubles as a jewel thief and becomes involved in Moroccan intrigue.
Complex sub-Bond tale of cross and double cross; hardly worth following, really.
w David Osborn d Gerry O'Hara ph Ken Talbot m Kenneth Jones
☆ Gene Barry, Elsa Martinelli, Cyd Charisse, Leslie Phillips, Denholm Elliott, Alexandra Stewart, Eric Barker, Angela Douglas

Marooned *

US 1969 134m Technicolor Panavision 70
Columbia/Frankovich-Sturges (Frank Capra Jnr)

Three astronauts are stranded in space, and a rescue mission gets under way.
Very heavy-going space suspenser with all possible technical accomplishment but little life of its own.
w Mayo Simon novel Martin Caidin d John Sturges ph Daniel Fapp pd Lyle R. Wheeler
☆ Gregory Peck, Richard Crenna, David Janssen, James Franciscus, Gene Hackman, Lee Grant, Nancy Kovack, Mariette Hartley, Scott Brady
'In something like the plight of Ironman One, Sturges' work seems on the point of slowing to a standstill as it drifts further into projects of ever-increasing, self-effacing size and anonymous technical dexterity.' – *Richard Combs*
'It has all the zip, zest and zing of a moon walk, and I suspect a computer fed a dictionary could come up with better dialogue.' – *Judith Crist, 1973*
'A space epic with a horse-and-buggy script.' – *Pauline Kael*
⚱ special visual effects (Robbie Robertson)
♪ Daniel Fapp

'The Marquis de Sade at his most bestial.'
Marquis

Belgium/France 1989 83m colour
ICA/Y. C. Aligator/Constellation/Tchin Tchin

Imprisoned in the Bastille in the 1780s, Marquis, an aristocratic spaniel, who passes the time by writing pornography and talking to his chatty penis, Colin, is accused of raping another prisoner, a cow impregnated by the king.
Bizarre, erotic fantasy about the Marquis de Sade by an iconoclastic French cartoonist in which all the characters are played by actors wearing animal masks. Its point remains obscure, though there are a few good jokes, as well as some unpleasant moments, along the way.
w Roland Topor, Henri Xhonneux d Henri Xhonneux ph Etienne Fauduet m Reinhardt Wagner ad Roland Topor ed Chantal Hymans
☆ Philippe Bizot, Bien de Moor, Gabrielle Van Damme, Olivier Duchaveau, Bernard Cogneux, Pierre Decuypere

---

Marquise

France/Italy/Switzerland/Spain 1997 117m colour
Downtown/Stephan/France 3/AMLF/3 Emme/Multivideo (Nicola Venditti)

In 17th-century France, a dancer beds the playwright Molière to become an actress, and then begins an affair with his rival, Jean Racine.
Lurid melodrama of theatrical life and tragedy that never comes to life.
w Jean-François Josselin, Vera Belmont, Marcel Beaulieu, Gérard Mordillat d Vera Belmont ph Jean-Marie Dreujou m Jordi Savall, Marin Marais, Jean-Baptiste Lully ad Gianni Quaranta ed Martine Giordano, Babak Karimi
☆ Sophie Marceau, Bernard Giraudeau, Lambert Wilson, Patrick Timsit, Thierry Lhermitte, Anémone, Remo Girone, Romina Mondello, Estelle Skornik
'A muddled, decidedly soapified, not unintelligent yarn.' – *Empire*
'My worst movie.' – *Sophie Marceau*

The Marquise of O *

West Germany/France 1976 107m
Eastmancolor
Janus/Films du Losange

At the end of the 18th century, during the Russian invasion of an Italian town, a noblewoman finds herself pregnant…
Careful novella with many ambiguities, more concerned with what might have happened than with what did. Interesting but exasperating.
wd Eric Rohmer story Heinrich von Kleist ph Nestor Almendros m Roger Delmotte
☆ Edith Clever, Bruno Ganz, Peter Luhr, Edda Seippel
'Some may find it slow, sentimental, naïve and old-fashioned; others leisurely, beautiful, controlled and illuminating. I found it both, often at the same time.' – *Alan Brien, Sunday Times*
'A bold, funny story becomes a formal, tame film, like a historical work recreated for educational TV.' – *New Yorker, 1980*

The Marriage Circle **

US 1924 78m bw silent
Warner

A bachelor on the loose becomes amorously involved in two marriages.
Feather-light comedy of manners which began a whole new American school, heavily influenced by various European masters.
w Paul Bern play *Only a Dream* by Lothar Schmidt d Ernst Lubitsch ph Charles Van Enger
☆ Monte Blue, Florence Vidor, Marie Prevost, Adolphe Menjou, Creighton Hale
'A vanished world of roses, kisses and embraces, of whispers and sighs, of a woman's shadowed arm encased in georgette beckoning across a moonlit garden … and hand-kissing all over the place.' – *Herman G. Weinberg*
'At once perfect cinematography and perfect conventional drama.' – *Iris Barry, The Spectator*
'So slim a plot, so hackneyed if you will, is told with gaiety and a wit that lift it into the very first rank of screen comedy.' – *National Board of Review*
† Remade as *One Hour with You,* also by Lubitsch.

'It's the most hilarious proposition a wife ever had!'
The Marriage Go Round

US 1961 98m DeLuxe Cinemascope
TCF (Leslie Stevens)

A Swedish girl suggests to a married American professor that she borrow his body for mating purposes, believing they would produce the perfect child.
Silly, unfunny sex comedy.
w Leslie Stevens play Leslie Stevens d Walter Lang ph Leo Tover m Dominic Frontière
☆ James Mason, Susan Hayward, Julie Newmar, Robert Paige, June Clayworth
'As tedious as it is tasteless.' – *Evening Standard*
'It offers James Mason, an actor who couldn't crack a joke if it was a lichee nut, and Susan Hayward, a bargain basement Bette Davis whose lightest touch as a comedienne would stun a horse.' – *Time*

Marriage Is a Private Affair

US   1944   116m   bw

MGM (Pandro S. Berman)

A spoilt rich girl becomes a petulant wife.

Abysmally slow, uninvolving and poorly acted star fodder.

w David Hertz, Lenore Coffee *novel* Judith Kelly
d Robert Z. Leonard *ph* Ray June *m* Bronislau
Kaper

☆ Lana Turner, James Craig, John Hodiak,
Frances Gifford, Keenan Wynn, Natalie Schafer,
Hugh Marlowe, Paul Cavanagh

The Marriage of a Young Stockbroker ★★

US   1971   95m   DeLuxe

TCF/Lawrence Turman

A stockbroker who finds his life and his marriage
dull tries voyeurism and extramarital sex.

*Sardonic adult comedy of the battle between the sexes,
pretty lively from start to finish.*

w Lorenzo Semple Jnr *novel* Charles Webb
d Lawrence Turman *ph* Laszlo Kovacs *m* Fred
Karlin

☆ Richard Benjamin, Joanna Shimkus, Elizabeth
Ashley, Adam West, Patricia Barry

The Marriage of Corbal

GB   1936   93m   bw

Capitol

US title: *Prisoner of Corbal*

Before the French revolution, an aristocratic lady
tries to escape disaster by the right marriage.

Stilted adventure story with too much talk.

w S. Fullman *novel The Nuptials of Corbal* by
Rafael Sabatini *d* Karl Grune

☆ Nils Asther, Hugh Sinclair, Hazel Terry, Noah
Beery, Davy Burnaby

The Marriage of Maria Braun ★

West Germany   1978   119m   Fujicolour

Albatros/Trio/WDR/FdA (Michael Fengler)

original title: *Die Ehe der Maria Braun*

Vicissitudes of a post-war bride who is eventually
blown up in a gas explosion.

*A mixture of solemnity and irony which keeps its basic
points well concealed but, despite a sometimes flagging
pace, more or less consistently entertains the eye.*

w Peter Märthesheimer, Pea Fröhlich *d* Rainer
Werner Fassbinder *ph* Michael Ballhaus *m* Peer
Raben

☆ Hanna Schygulla, Klaus Löwitsch, Ivan Desny,
Gottfried John

Marriage on the Rocks

US   1965   109m   Technicolor   Panavision

Warner/A-C/Sinatra (William H. Daniels)

An ad man and his wife decide to go to Mexico for
a divorce but once there change their minds; she
ends up accidentally married to his best friend.

*All this talent retreats fearfully from a witless, tasteless
script and slow handling. A dismal comedy.*

w Cy Howard *d* Jack Donohue *ph* William H.
Daniels *m* Nelson Riddle

☆ Frank Sinatra, Dean Martin, Deborah Kerr,
Cesar Romero, Hermione Baddeley, Tony Bill,
Nancy Sinatra, John McGiver

'A long, coarse, and nearly always unfunny
comedy, hammered together for no apparent
reason except to make money.' – *New Yorker*

The Marriage Playground

US   1929   70m   bw

Paramount

Children of divorced rich parents wander round
Europe in a group.

*Slightly unusual drama of its day; sound technique very
thin.*

w J. Walter Ruben, Doris Anderson *novel The
Children* by Edith Wharton *d* Lothar Mendes
ph Victor Milner

☆ Fredric March, Kay Francis, Mary Brian, Lilyan
Tashman, Huntley Gordon, Anita Louise

Married Before Breakfast

US   1937   70m   bw

MGM

An impecunious inventor has a razorless shaving
cream.

Scatty comedy which seldom amuses.

w George Oppenheimer, Everett Freeman, Harry
Ruskin *d* Edwin L. Marin

☆ Robert Young, Florence Rice, June Clayworth,
Barnett Parker, Warren Hymer

'It has practically nothing in its favour.' – *Variety*

Married but Single: see *This Thing Called Love*

Married to It

US   1993   112m   DeLuxe

Orion (Thomas Baer)

Three ill-assorted couples, who meet through a
school function, become friends while suffering
marital problems.

*A somewhat lifeless domestic comedy that never
escapes the restraints of its over-schematic screenplay;
it fails to animate its stock characters.*

w Janet Kovalcik *d* Arthur Hiller *ph* Victor
Kemper *m* Henry Mancini *pd* Robert Gundlach
ed Robert C. Jones

☆ Beau Bridges, Stockard Channing, Robert Sean
Leonard, Mary Stuart Masterson, Cybill Shepherd,
Ron Silver

† The film was made in 1991 and not released for
two years.

Married to the Mob ★★

US   1988   103m   DuArt

Rank/Orion/Mysterious Arts (Kenneth Utt, Edward
Saxon)

The wife of a murdered gangster tries to live an
honest life after her husband's death.

Effervescent comedy-thriller that bubbles merrily along.

w Barry Strugatz, Mark R. Burns *d* Jonathan
Demme *ph* Tak Fujimoto *m* David Byrne
pd Kristi Zea *ed* Craig McKay

☆ Michelle Pfeiffer, Matthew Modine, Dean
Stockwell, Mercedes Ruehl, Alec Baldwin, Trey
Wilson, Joan Cusack

'A smart, genial entertainment that gives us
plenty to look at and listen to.' – *Terrence
Rafferty, New Yorker*

໖ Dean Stockwell

A Married Woman ★

France   1964   98m   bw

Anouchka/Orsay (Philippe Dusart)

original title: *Une Femme Mariée*

A pilot's wife has an actor lover.

*Fragments of character observation, in various
cinematic techniques, build up into an intense personal
study if not a plot.*

wd Jean-Luc Godard *ph* Raoul Coutard *m* Claude
Nougaro

☆ Macha Meril, Bernard Noel, Roger Leenhardt

'A minefield of paradoxes … the essence of
cinema 1965.' – *Peter John Dyer, MFB*

Marry Me

GB   1949   97m   bw

GFD/Gainsborough (Betty Box)

Four stories of a marriage bureau.

*A styleless portmanteau of anecdotes put over by a
clear second team.*

w Lewis Gilbert, Denis Waldock *d* Terence Fisher
ph Ray Elton *m* Clifton Parker

☆ Derek Bond, Susan Shaw, Patrick Holt, Carol
Marsh, David Tomlinson, Zena Marshall, Guy
Middleton, Nora Swinburne, Jean Cadell, Mary
Jerrold

Marry Me Again

US   1953   73m   bw

RKO (Alex Gottlieb)

A man returns from war to find that his fiancée has
inherited a million dollars.

Zany comedy with tilts at psychiatry: not too bad.

wd Frank Tashlin *ph* Robert de Grasse *m* Raoul
Kraushaar

☆ Robert Cummings, Marie Wilson, Ray Walker,
Mary Costa, Jess Barker

Marry the Girl

US   1937   66m   bw

Warner

A crazy family owns a newspaper syndicate.

Fashionable comedy which goes far too far.

w Sig Herzig, Pat C. Flick, Tom Reed
novel Edward Hope *d* William McGann

☆ Mary Boland, Frank McHugh, Hugh Herbert,
Mischa Auer, Carol Hughes, Allen Jenkins, Alan
Mowbray, Hugh O'Connell

'Pic will probably get by on duals in the nabes
and should be a panic with juve audiences. But it
will probably lay an egg in first runs.' – *Variety*

The Marrying Kind ★

US   1952   93m   bw

Columbia (Bert Granet)

A couple seeking divorce tell their troubles to a
judge, and change their minds.

*Smart, New Yorkish, tragi-comic star vehicle which
works pretty well.*

w Ruth Gordon, Garson Kanin *d* George Cukor
ph Joseph Walker *m* Hugo Friedhofer

☆ Judy Holliday, Aldo Ray, Madge Kennedy,
Mickey Shaughnessy

The Marrying Man

US   1991   116m   Technicolor

Warner/Hollywood Pictures/Silver Screen Partners
IV/Odyssey (David Permut)

GB title: *Too Hot To Handle*

A playboy, forced to marry a gangster's girlfriend,
finds himself repeating the experience several
times.

*A misfiring romantic comedy, both involved and
uninvolving.*

w Neil Simon *d* Jerry Rees *ph* Donald E. Thorin
m David Newman *pd* William F. Matthews
ed Michael Jablow

☆ Kim Basinger, Alec Baldwin, Elisabeth Shue,
Armand Assante, Paul Reiser, Fisher Stevens,
Peter Dobson, Steve Hytner

'A still-born romantic comedy of staggering
ineptitude. Industry bad-mouthing of the stars
during production was just a preview of the
terrible picture.' – *Variety*

'A comedy that bounces skittishly down a lane
that memory has not travelled in a while. Maybe
it's silly. But it does awaken a nostalgic fondness
for an era when celebrity dreaming was goofier,
giddier and less consequential than it is now.' –
Richard Schickel, Time

'Nice Planet. We'll Take It!'

Mars Attacks! ★

US   1996   103m   Technicolor   Panavision

Warner (Tim Burton, Larry Franco)

Martians conquer the world, until they are
defeated by being subjected to the singing of Slim
Whitman.

*The film begins brilliantly, with a stampede of flaming
cows, but is then content to recycle, at great expense,
the style of 50s sci-fi films while its cast parody their
more serious roles; despite its occasional antic charm, it
is not as enjoyable as it ought to be.*

w Jonathan Gems *d* Tim Burton *ph* Peter
Suschitzky *m* Danny Elfman *pd* Wynn Thomas
ed Chris Lebenzon

☆ Jack Nicholson, Glenn Close, Annette Bening,
Michael J. Fox, Pierce Brosnan, Sarah Jessica
Parker, Martin Short, Lisa Marie, Rod Steiger,
Danny DeVito, Lukas Haas, Natalie Portman, Jim
Brown, Pam Grier, Joe Don Baker and also Tom
Jones, Jerzy Skolimowsky, Barbet Schroeder

'A cult sci-fi comedy miscast as an elaborate all-
star studio extravaganza. Continually inventive,
parodistic sendup of alien invasion movies that
owes its style to genre classics of the '50s, the
technically brilliant picture possesses a quirky,
somewhat facetious insider tone.' – *Todd
McCarthy, Variety*

La Marseillaise ★

France   1938   145m   bw

Films La Marseillaise (André Zwoboda)

The story of the French revolution of 1789.

*A rather disconnected epic which, despite a few
splendid scenes, never moved its audiences to
enthusiasm.*

wd Jean Renoir *ph* Jean Bourgoin and others
md Joseph Kosma

☆ Pierre Renoir, Lise Delemare, Louis Jouvet,
Léon Larive, Georges Spanelly, Elisa Ruis, William
Aguet

'France's super-super film production is a near
flopperoo.' – *Variety*

The Marseille Contract

GB/France   1974   89m   Eastmancolor

Warner/AIP/Kettledrum/PECF (Judd Bernard)

US title: *The Destructors*

An American narcotics agent in Paris hires an
assassin to dispose of a drug smuggler.

*Routine action melodrama with a jokey atmosphere not
sustained by a downbeat script.*

w Judd Bernard *d* Robert Parrish *ph* Douglas
Slocombe *m* Roy Budd

☆ Michael Caine, Anthony Quinn, James Mason,
Alexandra Stewart, Marcel Bozzuffi, Maurice
Ronet

Marseilles trilogy: see *Marius; Fanny; César*

Marshmallow Moon: see *Aaron Slick from
Punkin Crick*

Martha & Ethel ★★

US   1993   colour/bw

Columbia TriStar/Canobie (Jyll Johnstone)

A documentary on the lives of two nannies and
the families they influence: Martha, 87, German-
born and a disciplinarian, who worked for the same
family for 30 years, bringing up five children; and
Ethel, 88, from southern Carolina and easy-going,
who was nanny to six children and still lives with
her employer.

*A fascinating glimpse into the lives of two ordinary but
exceptional working women, including interviews with
them and the children they raised through changing
times.*

d Jyll Johnstone *ph* Joseph Friedman *ed* Toby
Shimin

'As light as a breeze, and there's a lot of bright,
natural humour emanating from her subjects, but
she raises dark questions.' – *Independent*

'Two's Company. Three's A Crowd. Four's A
Catastrophe.'

Martha Meet Frank, Daniel & Laurence

GB   1998   90m   colour

Film Four/Channel 4/Banshee (Grainne Marmion)

Three friends in London fall in love with the same
young American woman.

*A romantic comedy heavy with charm, but lacking in
substance.*

w Peter Morgan *d* Nick Hamm *ph* David
Johnson *m* Edward Shearmur *pd* Max Gottlieb
ed Michael Bradsell

☆ Monica Potter, Rufus Sewell, Tom Hollander,
Joseph Fiennes, Ray Winstone

'Minuscule romantic comedy … looks skimpy
and feels plodding.' – *Alexander Walker*

Martha, Ruth & Edie

Canada   1988   90m   Film House colour

Sunrise (Deepa Mehta Saltzman)

Three women tell each other of the most
significant event in their lives.

*Portmanteau movie of female bonding, which is no more
rewarding than the more usual tales of the male variety.*

w Anna Sandor, Janet Maclean, Barbara O'Kelly
story How I Met My Husband by Alice Munro, *The
California Aunts* by Cynthia Flood, *Guilt* by Betty
Lambert *d* Norma Bailey, Daniele J. Suissa, Deepa
Mehta Saltzman *ph* Doug Koch *m* Alexina
Louie, Alex Pauk *ad* Tom Doherty *ed* Lara Mazur

☆ Jennifer Dale, Margaret Langrick, Andrea
Martin, Tom Butler, Jeff Christensen, Page
Fletcher, Lois Maxwell

Martin

US   1978   95m   colour

Laurel (Richard Rubinstein)

A disturbed youth may be a vampire or just a boy
with sexual hangups and an appetite for blood.

*Gory thriller with a sense of irony, making fun of the
superstitions surrounding vampires yet utilizing them
for its shocking climax.*

wd George A. Romero *ph* Michael Gornick
m Donald Rubinstein

☆ John Amplas, Lincoln Maazel, Christine
Forrest, Elyane Nadeau, Tom Savini, Sarah
Venable, Fran Middleton, Al Lavistsky

Martin Luther ★

US/Germany   1953   114m   bw

Louis de Rochemont/Lutheran Church Productions
(Lothar Wolff)

The career and doubts of Martin Luther.

*Frequently vivid, occasionally boring, small-scale
account of the first Protestant.*

w Allan Sloane, Lothar Wolff, others *d* Irving
Pichel *ph* Joseph C. Brun *m* Mark Lothar
ad Fritz Maurischat, Paul Markwitz

☆ Niall MacGinnis, John Ruddock, Pierre Lefèvre,
Guy Verney, David Horne, Philip Leaver, Irving
Pichel, Alexander Gauge

໖ Joseph C. Brun; art direction

Martin Roumagnac

France 1946 99m bw

Alcina (Marc Le Pelletier)

The trial, with flashbacks, of a small-town businessman who has murdered his mistress.

Wholly unabsorbing and ordinary story of a crime passionnel, totally wasting its stars.

wd Georges Lacombe ph Roger Hubert m Marcel Mirouze

☆ Jean Gabin, Marlene Dietrich, Margo Lion, Marcel Hérrand

Martin's Day

Canada 1985 98m Medallion

World Film Services/MGM-UA (Richard F. Dalton, Roy Krost)

📼

An escaped convict and the young boy he kidnaps become friends.

Predictable melodrama which gets nowhere.

w Allan Scott, Chris Bryant d Alan Gibson ph Frank Watts m Wilfred Josephs pd Trevor Williams ed David de Wilde

☆ Richard Harris, Lindsay Wagner, James Coburn, Justin Henry, Karen Black, John Ireland

Marty **

US 1955 91m bw

UA/Hecht-Hill-Lancaster (Harold Hecht)

📀 📼

A 34-year-old Bronx butcher fears he will never get a girl because he is unattractive, but at a Saturday night dance he meets a girl with similar fears. Unfortunately she is not Italian…

The first of the filmed teleplays which in the mid-fifties seemed like a breath of spring to Hollywood (they were cheap) and also brought in a new wave of talent. This is one of the best, its new naturalistic dialogue falling happily on the ear; but it has been so frequently imitated since that its revolutionary appearance is hard to imagine.

w Paddy Chayefsky play Paddy Chayefsky d Delbert Mann ph Joseph LaShelle m Roy Webb ad Edward S. Howarth, Walter Simonds

☆ Ernest Borgnine, Betsy Blair, Esther Minciotti, Joe Mantell, Karen Steele, Jerry Paris

'Something rare in the American cinema today: a subtle, ironic and compassionate study of ordinary human relationships.' – *Gavin Lambert*

† The original 1953 television version was also directed by Delbert Mann and starred Rod Steiger.

🏆 best picture; Paddy Chayefsky; Delbert Mann; Ernest Borgnine

🏅 Joseph LaShelle; Betsy Blair; Joe Mantell; art direction

🏆 Ernest Borgnine; Betsy Blair

Marusa no onna: see *A Taxing Woman*

'A story about the years that keep us apart … And the moments that bring us together.'

Marvin's Room *

US 1996 98m DeLuxe

Buena Vista/Miramax (Scott Rudin, Jane Rosenthal, Robert de Niro)

📼 📀 🎧

A woman who cares for her dying father and eccentric aunt discovers that she is terminally ill, and turns for help to her estranged sister, who has family troubles of her own.

A movie that betrays its theatrical origins, and which gives its cast the opportunity for acting with the stops full out, of which they take full advantage.

w Scott McPherson play Scott McPherson d Jerry Zaks ph Piotr Sobocinski m Rachel Portman pd David Gropman ed Jim Clark

☆ Meryl Streep, Leonardo DiCaprio, Diane Keaton, Robert de Niro, Hume Cronyn, Gwen Verdon, Hal Scardino, Dan Hedaya

'A film of many small but glorious moments.' – *Emanuel Levy, Variety*

'This seems a particularly nasty view of old age by a man who knew he'd never be around to experience it.' – *Mark Steyn, Spectator*

† Scott McPherson died of AIDS in 1992, aged 33.

🏅 Diane Keaton

The Marx Brothers at the Circus: see *At the Circus*

Mary Burns Fugitive *

US 1935 84m bw

Paramount (Walter Wanger)

The innocent girlfriend of a gangster is convicted through circumstantial evidence, escapes from prison and finds true love.

Competent meshing of well-tried thirties elements, a good typical wish-fulfilment melodrama of its time.

w Gene Towne, Graham Baker, Louis Stevens d William K. Howard ph Leon Shamroy

☆ Sylvia Sidney, Melvyn Douglas, Alan Baxter, Pert Kelton, Wallace Ford, Brian Donlevy, Esther Dale

'As a piece of synthetic studio slickness it has enough on the ball to qualify.' – *Variety*

Mary Forever: see *Mery per sempre*

Mary Jane's Pa

US 1935 70m bw

Warner

GB title: *Wanderlust*

A husband goes wandering for ten years. On his return, his wife has magnified what he left into a newspaper empire.

Adequate stagey comedy, well acted.

w Tom Reed, Peter Milne play Edith Ellis Furness novel Norman Way d William Keighley

☆ Aline MacMahon, Guy Kibbee, Tom Brown, Robert McWade, Minor Watson, Nan Grey

'Okay for secondary bills.' – *Variety*

Mary Magdalene: see *The Sword and the Cross*

Mary Mary

US 1963 126m Technicolor

Warner (Mervyn Le Roy)

A publisher falls in love again with his ex-wife but finds she is being pursued by a film star.

Feeble film version of a lighter-than-air Broadway success, with the actors paralysed behind the footlights and the camera asleep in the stalls.

w Richard L. Breen play Jean Kerr d Mervyn Le Roy ph Harry Stradling m Frank Perkins

☆ Debbie Reynolds, Barry Nelson, Michael Rennie, Diane McBain

Mary of Scotland *

US 1936 123m bw

RKO (Pandro S. Berman)

📼 📀

Mary Stuart refuses to give up her claim to the English throne, and is eventually executed.

Sombre historical charade with splendid sets and atmosphere but suffering from script and performances that don't quite make it despite effort all round.

w Dudley Nichols play Maxwell Anderson d John Ford ph Joseph H. August m Nathaniel Shilkret ad Van Nest Polglase, Carroll Clark

☆ Katharine Hepburn, Fredric March, Donald Crisp, Florence Eldridge, Douglas Walton, John Carradine, Robert Barrat, Monte Blue, Moroni Olsen, Frieda Inescort, Alan Mowbray

'An unpromising and stagey play is fleshed out into a rich and confident exercise in filmcraft.' – *John Baxter, 1968*

'Events are walked through as though they were rooms in a museum, and closing time at three.' – *Otis Ferguson*

Mary Poppins *

👨‍👩‍👧 US 1964 139m Technicolor

Walt Disney (Bill Walsh)

📼 📀 🎧

In Edwardian London a magical nanny teaches two slightly naughty children to make life enjoyable for themselves and others.

Sporadically a very pleasant and effective entertainment for children of all ages, with plenty of brightness and charm including magic tricks, the mixing of live with cartoon adventures, and just plain fun. It suffers, however, from a wandering narrative in the second half (when Miss Poppins scarcely appears) and from Mr Van Dyke's really lamentable attempt at Cockney.

w Bill Walsh, Don da Gradi novel P. L. Travers d Robert Stevenson ph Edward Colman m/ly Richard M. and Robert B. Sherman md Irwin Kostal pd Tony Walton ad Carroll Clark, William H. Tuntke ed Cotton Warburton sp Eustace Lycett, Peter Ellenshaw, Robert A. Mattey

☆ Julie Andrews, David Tomlinson, Glynis Johns, Dick Van Dyke, Reginald Owen, Ed Wynn, Matthew Garber, Karen Dotrice, Hermione

Baddeley, Elsa Lanchester, Arthur Treacher, Jane Darwell

'A charming, imaginative and technically superb movie musical, sparkling with originality, melody and magical performances.' – *Judith Crist*

🏅 Richard M. and Robert B. Sherman; Julie Andrews; song 'Chim Chim Cheree'; special visual effects; editing

🏆 best picture; script; Robert Stevenson; Edward Colman; Irwin Kostal; art direction

🎭 Julie Andrews

'They used every passion in their incredible duel, and every man in their savage games of intrigue!'

Mary Queen of Scots

👨‍👩‍👧 GB 1971 128m Technicolor

Panavision

Universal/Hal B. Wallis

The story of Mary Stuart's opposition to Elizabeth I, her imprisonment and execution.

Schoolbook history in which none of the characters comes to life; dramatic movement is almost entirely lacking despite the liberties taken with fact.

w John Hale d Charles Jarrott ph Christopher Challis m John Barry

☆ Vanessa Redgrave, Glenda Jackson, Trevor Howard, Patrick McGoohan, Nigel Davenport

'Without a better script, Hercules couldn't lift this story off the ground.' – *Pauline Kael, New Yorker*

🏆 John Barry; Vanessa Redgrave

'Evil is irresistible.'

Mary Reilly

US 1996 109m Technicolor

TriStar (Ned Tanen, Nancy Graham Tanen, Norma Heyman)

📼 📀 🎧

The new chambermaid in the household of Dr Jekyll is attracted by the doctor's lecherous assistant, Mr Hyde.

A handsome but dull attempt to turn Stevenson's tale of a split personality into a Jane Eyre-like romantic drama, but neither of the two leads is convincing and there is little sign of any attraction between them.

w Christopher Hampton novel Valerie Martin d Stephen Frears ph Philippe Rousselot m George Fenton pd Stuart Craig ed Lesley Walker

☆ Julia Roberts, John Malkovich, George Cole, Michael Gambon, Glenn Close, Kathy Staff, Michael Sheen, Ciaran Hinds

'Has plenty of production polish but little of the dramatic force and erotic spark needed.' – *Variety*

† The film, which cost $47m to make, flopped at the box-office.

Mary Shelley's Frankenstein *

US 1994 123m Technicolor

Columbia TriStar/American Zoetrope/Japan Satellite/IndieProd (Francis Ford Coppola, James V. Hart, John Veitch)

📼 📀 📀 🎞 🎞 🎧

A scientist tells a sea captain how he gave life to a creature, which, when he refused to create a mate for it, took revenge on his family.

A bold and brash attempt to be true to the original novel, but which, like its monster, gets lost in the Arctic wastes and then confuses the narrative by focusing the attention on its over-production; it fails to dislodge the original film from folk memory.

w Steph Lady, Frank Darabont novel Mary Shelley d Kenneth Branagh ph Roger Pratt m Patrick Doyle pd Tim Harvey ed Andrew Marcus

☆ Robert DeNiro, Kenneth Branagh, Tom Hulce, Helena Bonham Carter, Aidan Quinn, Ian Holm, Richard Briers, John Cleese, Robert Hardy, Cherie Lunghi, Celia Imrie

'A highly paced costume drama that propels us along the trajectory of Frankenstein's ambition with a speed reminiscent of Indiana Jones.' – *Oscar Moore, Screen International*

'Much of Frankenstein is spectacular and hyperbolic, but in a good way. Kenneth Branagh has made a very fleshy and visceral movie, though not a horror movie in the normal sense.' – *David Denby, New York*

'A gargoyle short of the Gothic horror that made the original unforgettable.' – *Ingrid Pitt*

'More a case of Mary Shelley's Frankie Goes to Hollywood.' – *Adam Mars-Jones, Independent*

🏆 make-up

Mary Stevens M.D.

US 1933 71m bw

Warner

A lady doctor decides to have a baby before getting married.

Saucy drama which engrossed audiences in its day.

w Rian James novel Virginia Kellogg d Lloyd Bacon

☆ Kay Francis, Lyle Talbot, Glenda Farrell, Thelma Todd, Una O'Connor, Hobart Cavanaugh, Harold Huber

'Exceptionally good adult entertainment, with a pronounced feminine appeal.' – *Variety*

Maryland

US 1940 92m Technicolor

TCF (Gene Markey)

After her husband is killed in a fox-hunting accident, his wife tries to keep their son away from horses.

Over-lavish treatment of a trite story; money has been spent on everything except the script.

w Ethel Hill, Jack Andrews d Henry King md Alfred Newman

☆ Walter Brennan, Fay Bainter, Brenda Joyce, John Payne, Charles Ruggles, Hattie McDaniel, Marjorie Weaver, Sidney Blackmer, Ben Carter

Masala *

Canada 1991 106m colour

Metro/Divani/Telefilm Canada/Ontario Film Development/Ontario Arts Council (Srinivas Krishna, Camelia Freiberg)

The Hindu god Krishna grants a miracle to a Sikh family living in Toronto.

An irreverent small-scale movie that provides pleasure.

wd Srinivas Krishna ph Paul Sarossy m The West India Company, Leslie Winston pd Tamara Deverell ed Michael Munn

☆ Srinivas Krishna, Sakina Jaffrey, Zohra Segal, Saeed Jaffrey, Heri Johal, Madhuri Bhatia, Ronica Sajnani, Les Porter

'A highly entertaining work.' – *Sight and Sound*

La Maschera *

Italy 1988 90m Eastmancolor

RAIDVE/Istituto Luce/Best International (Lilia Smecchia, Ettore Rosboch)

aka: *The Mask*

In the 18th century a young actress rejects the advances of a dissolute aristocrat and then falls in love with a mysterious masked stranger.

Lugubrious romance, concentrating on glossy surfaces.

w Adriano Apra, Fiorella Infascelli, Enzo Ungari, Ennio de Concini d Fiorella Infascelli ph Acacio de Almeida m Luis Bacalov ad Antonello Geleng ed Francisco Malvestito

☆ Helena Bonham Carter, Michael Maloney, Feodor Chaliapin Jnr, Roberto Herlitzka, Michele de Marchi, Alberto Cracco

La Maschera del Demonio: see *Mask of Satan*

The Mascot *

France 1916 20m bw

H. Rose/Gelma

📼

The adventures of a toy dog, who goes to hell and back.

A mix of live action and stop-motion animation, amusing and macabre, by an early master of the craft.

wd Ladislaw Starewicz

† The film has been released on video with the feature-length *The Tale of the Fox* (qv) and four other shorts under the title *Ladislaw Starewicz: Selected Films.*

Masculin Féminin *

France/Sweden 1966 110m bw

Gala/Anouchka/Argos/Svensk/Sandrews (Philippe Dussart)

📼 📀

A young, romantic revolutionary imagines that he is in love with a would-be singer.

An exploration of pop culture and politics, in a sequence of episodes intercut with arbitrary happenings, and as much concerned with form as content, moving cinema away from straightforward narrative to something more abstract and less interesting.

wd Jean-Luc Godard story La Femme de Paul by Guy de Maupassant ph Willy Kurant m Francis Lai ed Agnès Guillemot

☆ Jean-Pierre Léaud, Chantal Goya, Catherine-Isabelle Duport, Marlène Jobert, Michel Debord,

Birger-Malmsten, Eva Britt Strandberg, Brigitte Bardot, Françoise Hardy

'Godard's exercise in self-indulgence.' – *John Simon*

'That rare movie achievement: a work of grace and beauty in a contemporary setting.' – *Pauline Kael*

'By this defiantly unrealistic system of narrative, Godard manages to present us with all the problems facing his hero and facing boys of his generation.' – *Richard Roud*

'Mainly it seems to be a movie happening, in which Mr Godard can play whimsical and sometimes comical stunts, not leading to any clear conclusion as to the stability of youth. He himself, as a motion-picture maker, seems to have little more concentration-span than his saucy, good-looking youngsters, who evidently have none at all.' – *Bosley Crowther*

† For its American release, it was cut to 103m.

Mask **
US   1985   120m   Technicolor
Universal/Martin Starger
▣ ▤ ▩ ◗

A boy of 16 has a rare and disfiguring bone disease, but his mother fights for his rights.
More of a character study than a movie, this also has the problem of being emotionally hard to take; but one ends up respecting it.
w Anna Hamilton Phelan, from her true story of Rocky Dennis d Peter Bogdanovich ph Laszlo Kovacs m Dennis Ricotta ed Barbara Ford
☆ Cher, Sam Elliott, Eric Stoltz, Estelle Getty
'Anyone looking for a good uplifting cry should be well satisfied.' – *Variety*

The Mask: see *La Maschera (1988)*

'From Zero To Hero.'
The Mask **
🏚 US   1994   101m   Foto-Kem
Entertainment/New Line/Dark Horse (Bob Engelman)
▣ ▣ ▤ ◗ ◉ ◉ ∩

A wimpish bank clerk in a constant state of humiliation finds a mask that transforms him into a green-faced comic-book hero capable of humiliating everyone.
Antic, amusing comedy that finds a perfect setting for the exaggerated style of Jim Carrey: cartoon-style humour, borrowing heavily from Chuck Jones and Tex Avery. The jokes are often familiar, but never seen before in a real-life setting thanks to the spectacular digital special effects.
w Mike Werb story Michael Fallon, Mark Verheiden based on characters appearing in Dark Horse Comics d Charles Russell ph John R. Leonetti m Randy Edelman pd Craig Stearns ed Arthur Coburn sp make-up: Greg Cannom; visual effects: Ken Ralston, Scott Squires, Steve 'Spaz' Williams, Industrial Light and Magic
☆ Jim Carrey, Peter Riegert, Cameron Diaz, Peter Greene, Amy Yasbeck, Richard Jeni, Orestes Matacena, Tim Bagley, Nancy Fish, Johnny Williams
'The story is predictable and has little imagination outside its technical prowess – some extraordinary special effects.' – *Derek Malcolm, Guardian*
'As dull-witted and straitjacketed by cliché as it is visually hellzapoppin, the film may be a watershed moment in the cultural current that looks to loot the baby-boomer memory banks for recyclable cinematic ideas.' – *Michael Atkinson, Sight and Sound*
§ visual effects

The Mask of Dijon
US   1946   73m   bw
PRC
A conjuror becomes obsessed by hypnotism and takes to murder to prove his superiority.
Heavy-going thriller with little discernible point.
w Arthur St Claire and Griffin Jay d Lew Landers
☆ Erich von Stroheim, Jeanne Bates, William Wright

The Mask of Dimitrios **
US   1944   99m   bw
Warner (Henry Blanke)
A timid Dutch novelist is drawn into a Middle-Eastern mystery with money at the centre of it.
Generally successful international intriguer, moodily shot in evocative sets, and remarkable for its time in

that the story is not distorted to fit romantic stars: character actors bear the entire burden.
w Frank Gruber novel Eric Ambler d Jean Negulesco ph Arthur Edeson m Adolph Deutsch
☆ Peter Lorre, Sydney Greenstreet, Zachary Scott, Faye Emerson, Victor Francen, Steven Geray, Florence Bates, Eduardo Ciannelli, Kurt Katch, John Abbott, Monte Blue
'The picture has more mood than excitement.' – *Pauline Kael, 70s*

The Mask of Fu Manchu **
US   1932   70m   bw
MGM
Nayland Smith and his party are caught and threatened with torture by the yellow terror.
Highly satisfactory episode in the nefarious adventures of the master criminal, fast moving, humorous and very good to look at.
w John Willard, Edgar Woolf, Irene Kuhn stories Sax Rohmer d Charles Brabin, Charles Vidor ph Tony Gaudio
☆ Boris Karloff, Edgar Woolf, Lewis Stone, Karen Morley, Charles Starrett, Jean Hersholt, Lawrence Grant
'The diabolical stuff is piled on so thick at the finish, audiences are liable to laugh where they oughtn't.' – *Variety*
'A tolerable, campy entertainment.' – *Pauline Kael, 70s*

Mask of Satan *
Italy   1960   84m   bw
Galatea/Jolly (Massimo de Rita)
▣
original title: *La Maschera del Demonio*
aka: *Black Sunday; Revenge of the Vampire*
A princess who was executed for witchcraft by her brother returns 200 years later to wreak vengeance on his descendants.
A stylish, though gruesome, horror movie.
w Mario Bava, Ennio de Concini, Marcello Coscia, Mario Serandrei d Mario Bava ph Mario Bava, Ubaldo Terzano sp Mario Bava
☆ Barbara Steele, John Richardson, Ivo Garrani, Andrea Cecchi, Arturo Dominici, Enrico Olivieri, Clara Bindi
'The greatest gothic horror movie ever made in Italy.' – *Empire*

Mask of the Avenger
US   1951   83m   Technicolor
Columbia (Hunt Stromberg)
During the Austro-Italian War, a count's son avenges his father's death and exposes a traitor.
Very moderate swashbuckler on the lines of The Mark of Zorro.
w Jesse Lasky Jnr d Phil Karlson ph Charles Lawton Jnr m George Duning
☆ John Derek, Anthony Quinn, Jody Lawrance, Arnold Moss, Eugene Iglesias

The Mask of Zorro **
🏚 US   1998   136m   CH color   Panavision
Columbia TriStar/Amblin/Zorro (Doug Claybourne, David Foster)
▣ ▤ ◗ ◉ ◉
An ageing Zorro trains a young man to take his place and prevent the man who killed his wife and kidnapped his daughter from ruling over California.
An enjoyable, high-spirited return to the style of an old-fashioned swashbuckler, with added sex appeal.
w John Eskow, Ted Elliott, Terry Rossio d Martin Campbell ph Phil Meheux m James Horner pd Cecilia Montiel ed Thom Noble
☆ Antonio Banderas, Anthony Hopkins, Catherine Zeta-Jones, Stuart Wilson, Matt Letscher, Maury Chaykin, Tony Amendola, Pedro Armendariz, L. Q. Jones
'You haven't seen anything like this since the good old Indiana Jones days.' – *Alan Jones, Film Review*
§ sound; sound effects editing

Maskerade *
Austria   1935   87m   bw
Tobis/Sascha
An inveterate ladies' man finds himself trapped.
Charming romantic comedy.
w Walter Reisch d Willi Forst ph Franz Planer
☆ Anton Walbrook, Paula Wessely, Olga Tscheshowa
'Not a real masterpiece like *Liebelei*, but it has the same b.o. elements.' – *Variety*

The Masque of the Red Death **
GB   1964   89m   Pathécolor   'Scope
AIP/Alta Vista (George Willoughby)
▤ ▩
A medieval Italian prince practises devil worship while the plague rages outside, but when he holds a ball, death is an uninvited guest.
Languorous, overstretched, often visually striking horror piece with some extremely effective touches among its longueurs.
w Charles Beaumont, R. Wright Campbell story Edgar Allan Poe d Roger Corman ph Nicolas Roeg m David Lee ad Robert Jones cos Laura Nightingale
☆ Vincent Price, Hazel Court, Jane Asher, Patrick Magee, John Westbrook

Masquerade *
GB   1965   101m   Eastmancolor
UA/Novus (Michael Relph)
To avert friction between Arab states the young heir to one of them is abducted by a British secret service agent; but one of the plotters has other fish to fry.
Quite a lively spy romp with a spectacular action climax, but the plot is simply too complicated.
w Michael Relph, William Goldman novel Castle Minerva by Victor Canning d Basil Dearden ph Otto Heller m Philip Green pd Don Ashton
☆ Cliff Robertson, Jack Hawkins, Charles Gray, Bill Fraser, Marisa Mell, Michel Piccoli, John Le Mesurier

Masquerade
US   1988   91m   colour
UIP/MGM (Michael I. Levy)
▤ ▩
A gigolo marries a wealthy woman with the intention of murdering her for her money.
Dull thriller that fails to maintain interest.
w Dick Wolf d Bob Swaim ph David Watkin m John Barry pd John Kasarda ed Scott Conrad
☆ Rob Lowe, Meg Tilly, Kim Cattrall, Doug Savant, John Glover, Dana Delany, Erik Holland, Brian Davies, Barton Heyman
'A tranquil, sophisticated thriller.' – *Pauline Kael, New Yorker*

'A gay and gorgeous whirl of romance, adventure and rhythm … in the billion-dollar pan-American postwar playground!'
Masquerade in Mexico
US   1945   96m   bw
Paramount (Karl Tunberg)
A stranded showgirl is hired by a Mexican banker to entice a gigolo away from his wife.
Talent-starved remake of Midnight (qv), which seems second-hand even if you don't know why.
w Karl Tunberg d Mitchell Leisen ph Lionel Lindon m Victor Young
☆ Dorothy Lamour, Arturo de Cordova, Patric Knowles, Ann Dvorak, George Rigaud, Natalie Schafer, Mikhail Rasumny, Billy Daniels

The Masquerader *
US   1933   75m   bw
Samuel Goldwyn
A drug-addicted politician is replaced by his lookalike cousin.
Pleasing dual role star vehicle with good production and support. Very much of its period.
w Howard Estabrook, Moss Hart play John Hunter Booth novel Katherine Cecil Thurston d Richard Wallace ph Gregg Toland m Alfred Newman
☆ Ronald Colman, Elissa Landi, Halliwell Hobbes, Juliette Compton, David Torrence
'A fine production with too much story handicap … Colman's best is not enough.' – *Variety*
'The first amusing and believable tale of English politics and society … made of all places in Hollywood.' – *Newsweek*

Masques *
France   1987   100m   colour
Cannon/MK2 Productions/A2 (Marin Karmitz)
A thriller writer inveigles his way into the home of a TV game-show host to solve the mysterious disappearance of his sister.
Glossy, well-made thriller that promises more than it delivers, but is enjoyable for Noiret's performance as a hypocritically hearty television celebrity.

w Odile Barski, Claude Chabrol d Claude Chabrol ph Jean Rabier m Matthieu Chabrol ad Françoise Benoit-Fresco ed Monique Fardoulis
☆ Philippe Noiret, Robin Renucci, Bernadette Lafont, Monique Chaumette, Anne Brochet, Roger Dumas, Pierre-François Dumeniaud

Mass Appeal *
US   1984   100m   Technicolor
Universal/Turman-Foster
▤ ▩
An idealistic student matches wits with a compromising priest.
Amusing, opened-out version of a two-character play: good for minority audiences.
w Bill C. David play Bill C. David d Glenn Jordan ph Don Peterman m Bill Conti pd Philip Jefferies
☆ Jack Lemmon, Zeljko Ivanek, Charles Durning, Louise Latham
'Saved from damnation by the originality of its central theme and by the excellence of its acting.' – *Quentin Crisp*

Massacre Hill: see *Eureka Stockade*

Massacre in Rome
Italy   1973   103m   Technicolor
Compagnia Cinematografica Champion (Carlo Ponti)
▤ ∩
In 1944, after partisans blow up a detachment of SS troops in a Rome street, a German colonel makes an ineffectual attempt to resist an order to shoot 330 Italians in retaliation.
Moderately effective drama, based on a true story.
w Robert Katz, George Pan Cosmatos book Death in Rome by Robert Katz d George Pan Cosmatos ph Marcello Gatti m Ennio Morricone pd Morton Haack ed Françoise Bonnot, Roberto Silvi
☆ Richard Burton, Marcello Mastroianni, Leo McKern, John Steiner, Anthony Steel, Robert Harris, Peter Vaughan, Delia Boccardo

The Master Gunfighter
US   1975   120m   Metrocolor   Panavision
Avondale/Warner
In gold rush California, a mysterious avenger rights a variety of wrongs.
Pretentious Western which failed to advance the career of its somewhat over-confident creator.
w Harold Lapland d Tom Laughlin ph Jack Marta m Lalo Schifrin pd Albert Brenner
☆ Tom Laughlin, Ron O'Neal, Lincoln Kilpatrick, Barbara Carrera
† From a Japanese film Goyokin written by Kei Tasaka and Hideo Gosha

The Master of Ballantrae
🏚 GB   1953   89m   Technicolor
Warner
▣ ▤ ▩
Two brothers toss to decide which shall join Bonnie Prince Charlie's 1745 rebellion.
Half-hearted version of a classic adventure novel.
w Herb Meadow novel R. L. Stevenson d William Keighley ph Jack Cardiff m William Alwyn
☆ Errol Flynn, Anthony Steel, Roger Livesey, Beatrice Campbell, Felix Aylmer, Mervyn Johns, Jacques Berthier, Yvonne Furneaux, Ralph Truman
'All that can be salvaged from this rather unforgivable Anglo-American junket are some pleasant exteriors.' – *Gavin Lambert*

Master of Bankdam *
GB   1947   105m   bw
GFD/Holbein (Nat Bronsten, Walter Forde, Edward Dryhurst)
19th-century chronicles of a mill-owning Yorkshire family.
Archetypal 'trouble at t'mill' saga with moderate production, good acting and undeniably compulsive story.
w Edward Dryhurst, Moie Charles novel The Crowthers of Bankdam by Thomas Armstrong d Walter Forde ph Basil Emmott
☆ Tom Walls, Anne Crawford, Dennis Price, Stephen Murray, Linden Travers, Jimmy Hanley, Nancy Price, David Tomlinson, Herbert Lomas

Master of Lassie: see *The Hills of Home*

🏚 film suitable for family viewing   ▣ VHS video-cassette for the British PAL system   ▤ VHS video-cassette for the British PAL system in wide screen-format   ↻ Video cassette in a computer-colourised version   ▩ American NTSC video-cassette   ◗ Laser disc

Master of the House *

Denmark 1925 107m bw
Palladium
📀 ▦

original title: *Du Skal Aere Din Hustru*
A husband is cured of his domestic tyranny.
Enjoyable account of a man's comeuppance at the hands of his old nanny, one that is also perceptive about relationships.
w Carl Theodor Dreyer, Sven Rindom *play* Tyraennens Fald *by* Sven Rindom *d* Carl Theodor Dreyer *ph* George Schnéevoigt *ad* Carl Theodor Dreyer
☆ Johannes Meyer, Astrid Holm, Karin Nellemose, Clara Schonfeld, Mathilde Nielsen, Johannes Nielsen, Petrine Sonne

Master of the Islands: see *The Hawaiians*

Master of the World

👪👪 US 1961 104m Magnacolor
AIP/Alta Vista (James H. Nicholson, Anthony Carras)
▦

In 1848 a mad inventor takes to the air in his magnificent flying machine in the hope of persuading men to stop war.
Aerial version of Twenty Thousand Leagues under the Sea, with cheap sets and much use of stock footage; some scenes however have a certain vigour.
w Richard Matheson *novel* Jules Verne *d* William Witney *ph* Gil Warrenton *m* Les Baxter
☆ Vincent Price, Charles Bronson, Henry Hull, Mary Webster, David Frankham

The Master Plan

GB 1954 78m bw
Gibraltar
An American agent, concealing the fact that he suffers from blackouts, is sent to investigate information leakages in England.
Quite lively second feature spylarks.
wd Hugh Raker (i.e. Cy Endfield) *ph* Jonah Jones
☆ Wayne Morris, Tilda Thamar, Norman Wooland, Mary Mackenzie, Arnold Bell

The Master Race

US 1944 96m bw
Edward Golden
▦
German generals realize that the war is lost, and plan counter-measures.
Timely propaganda melodrama warning against premature rejoicing, from the producer of Hitler's Children.
wd Herbert J. Biberman.
☆ George Coulouris, Osa Massen, Stanley Ridges, Nancy Gates, Carl Esmond, Morris Carnovsky, Lloyd Bridges

Master Spy

GB 1963 74m bw
Grand National/Eternal (Maurice J. Wilson)
A defecting Russian scientist goes to work on a top-secret project.
Dull melodrama of espionage that, despite its short length, seems interminable.
w Maurice J. Wilson, Montgomery Tully *story* They Also Serve *by* Gerald Anstruther, Paul White *d* Montgomery Tully *ph* Geoffrey Faithfull *m* Ken Thorne *md* Philip Martell *ad* Harry White *ed* Eric Boyd-Perkins
☆ Stephen Murray, June Thorburn, Alan Wheatley, John Carson, John Bown, Ernest Clark, Jack Watson, Peter Gilmore, Derek Francis, Ellen Pollock

The Masters

Italy 1975 100m Technospes
Campagnia Cinematografica Champion (Carlo Ponti)
original title: *Gente di rispetto*
A new and naïve schoolteacher in a small Sicilian town becomes involved in corrupt local politics after a man who insulted her is murdered by the Mafia.
Glossy thriller that fails to carry any conviction.
w Leo Benevenuti, Piero de Bernardi, Luigi Zampa *story* Giuseppe Fava *d* Luigi Zampa *ph* Ennio Guarnieri *m* Ennio Morricone *ad* Luigi Scaccianoce *ed* Franco Fraticelli
☆ James Mason, Jennifer O'Neill, Franco Nero, Orazio Orlando, Claudio Gora, Franco Fabrizi, Aldo Giuffré

Masters of Menace

US 1990 84m colour
Cinetel/Hertzberg-Hanson-Insana
📀 ▦

A motorcycle gang violates its three-year probation in order to bury one of its members in Las Vegas.
Coarse and aimless send-up of biker movies, which at least ends appropriately, with a vat of manure.
w Tino Insana *d* Daniel Raskov *ph* Edward J. Pei *m* Hawk Wolinski *ed* Stephen Myers
☆ David Rasche, Catherine Bach, Lance Kinsey, Teri Copley, Ray Baker, David L. Lander
'Original humor was obviously not required.' – *Variety*
† Dan Aykroyd, Jim Belushi, John Candy and George Wendt appear in cameo roles.

Masters of the Universe

👪👪 US 1987 106m Metrocolor
Edward R. Pressman/Cannon
📀 ▦ 🎧

He-Man defends the planet Eternia from the evil Skeletor.
Live action version of the TV cartoons of the toys of the comic strip. Pretty weak stuff, even for five-year-olds.
w David Odell *d* Gary Goddard *ph* Hanania Baer *m* Bill Conti *pd* William Stout *ed* Anne V. Coates
☆ Dolph Lundgren, Frank Langella, Meg Foster, Billy Barty

Masterson of Kansas

US 1955 73m Technicolor
Columbia (Sam Katzman)
The sheriff of Dodge City prevents an Indian uprising by saving an innocent man from the gallows.
Unhistorical two-bit Western.
w Douglas Heyes *d* William Castle *ph* Henry Freulich *md* Mischa Bakaleinikoff
☆ George Montgomery, Nancy Gates, James Griffith, Jean Willes

Mat: see *Mother*

Mat i syn: see *Mother and Son*

'Men worshipped her like a goddess, only to be betrayed by a kiss!'

Mata Hari **

US 1931 92m bw
MGM
▦ 📷
The career of the famous lady spy of World War I.
Elaborate melodrama, pictorially satisfying and generally more entertaining than might be supposed, with both star and supporting cast in rich thespian form.
w Benjamin Glazer, Leo Birinsky, Doris Anderson, Gilbert Emery *d* George Fitzmaurice *ph* William Daniels
☆ Greta Garbo, Ramon Novarro, Lionel Barrymore, Lewis Stone, C. Henry Gordon, Karen Morley, Blanche Frederici
'Picture's strength is all in the players; an important grosser on that account.' – *Variety*

Mata Hari

US 1985 108m Eastmancolor
Rony Yacov/Cannon
The career of the famous lady spy of World War I.
Absurd melodrama which in places seems to be spoofing itself.
w Joel Ziskin *d* Curtis Harrington
☆ Sylvia Kristel, Christopher Cazenove, Oliver Tobias, Gaye Brown, William Fox

Mata Hari, Agent H21 *

France/Italy 1964 99m bw
Filmel/Les Films du Carrosse/Simar/Fida Cinematografica (Eugene Lepicier)
A rather unnecessary revamp of the same story, with interesting details but not much resonance.
w Jean-Louis Richard, François Truffaut *d* Jean-Louis Richard *m* Michel Kelber *m* Georges Delerue *ad* Claude Pignot
☆ Jeanne Moreau, Jean-Louis Trintignant, Claude Rich, Frank Villard
'All that we are left with is a generous dollop of period charm, and the fascinating spontaneity of an actress.' – *Peter John Dyer, MFB*

Matador *

Spain 1988 106m colour
Iberoamericana de TV/Televisión Española (Andrés Vicente Gómez)
📀 ▦ 📷
A lame, death-obsessed matador is smitten by a sex- and death-obsessed woman, the defending lawyer of a psychic, guilt-obsessed, would-be bullfighter who has confessed to a series of murders he did not commit.
An intense though unerotic treatment of decadent passions; it is comparatively restrained by its director's usual standards, avoiding camp, though it manages to encompass scenes of attempted rape, violent death, and masturbation to images of mutilation.
w Jesus Ferrero, Pedro Almodóvar *d* Pedro Almodóvar *ph* Angel Luis Fernández *m* Bernardo Bonezzi *ad* Roman Arango, José Morales, José Rosell *ed* Pepe Salcedo
☆ Assumpta Serna, Antonio Banderas, Bibi Andersen, Nacho Martinez, Eva Cobo, Julieta Serrano, Chus Lampreave, Carmen Maura, Eusebio Poncela
'Chips away at the surface elegance of the bourgeoisie to expose its private vices.' – *Sight and Sound*
'A piece of voluptuous tom-foolery.' – *Pauline Kael, New Yorker*

The Match

GB/US/Ireland 1999 96m Technicolor
Polygram/Propaganda/Irish Dreamtime (Allan Scott, Guymon Casady)
📀
A pub football team, which has lost its annual match against a neighbouring inn for 99 years, gets ready to compete in the 100th game, with the loser agreeing to shut down his business.
Thoroughly predictable Scottish comedy about a group of losers discovering a winning community spirit; it might have worked had it been funny, or even amusing.
wd Mick Davis *ph* Witold Stok *m* Harry Gregson-Williams *ed* John Frankish *ed* Kate Williams
☆ Max Beesley, Isla Blair, James Cosmo, Laura Fraser, Richard E. Grant, David Hayman, Ian Holm, Neil Morrissey, Bill Paterson, Iain Robertson, Tom Sizemore, Pierce Brosnan, Alan Shearer
'Truly dire.' – *Guardian*

The Match Factory Girl **

Finland/Sweden 1990 70m Eastmancolor
Electric Pictures/Swedish Film Institute/ Viillealfa/Aki Kaurismäki
📀 ▦

original title: *Tulitikkutehtaan Tytto*
A downtrodden factory girl takes her revenge on those who have taken her for granted.
Quietly savage comedy, filmed in a minimalist style.
wd Aki Kaurismäki *ph* Timo Salminen *pd* Risto Karhula *ed* Aki Kaurismäki
☆ Kati Outinen, Elina Salo, Esko Nikkari, Vesa Vierikko, Reijo Taipale, Silu Seppälä

The Match King

US 1932 80m bw
Warner
A world-famous match manufacturer gets into spectacular money difficulties.
Thinly veiled biopic of Ivar Kreuger; not at all bad.
w Houston Branch and Sidney Sutherland *d* Howard Bretherton
☆ Warren William, Lili Damita, Glenda Farrell, Harold Huber
'Good entertainment, uncommonly well acted ... in Swedish-populated sections should be top moneymaker.' – *Variety*

The Matchmaker *

US 1958 101m bw Vistavision
Paramount (Don Hartman)
▦ 📷 🎧
In New York at the turn of the century, a rich merchant decides to marry again but the matchmaker he consults has her own eye on him.
Cold and lifeless version of an amusing play which also served as the basis for the musical Hello Dolly (qv).
w John Michael Hayes *play* Thornton Wilder *d* Joseph Anthony *ph* Charles Lang *m* Adolph Deutsch
☆ Shirley Booth, Paul Ford, Anthony Perkins, Shirley MacLaine, Wallace Ford, Robert Morse, Perry Wilson

DOLLY LEVI (SHIRLEY BOOTH) TO THE AUDIENCE:
'Life's never quite interesting enough, somehow. You people who come to the movies know that.'
'Long static dialogue exchanges are further extended by frequent confidences expressed directly to the audience ... but in spite of the general lack of pace, lightness and dimension there is still a great deal to enjoy.' – *Peter John Dyer*

La Maternelle *

France 1932 89m bw
Photosonor
A maid in a nursery school becomes devoted to the children and in particular to one who causes trouble when her friend decides to marry.
A touching drama of its day which now seems rather primitive.
w Jean Benoit-Lévy *d* Jean Benoit-Lévy, Marie Epstein *ph* Georges Asselin *m* Edouard Flament
☆ Madeleine Renaud, Paulette Elambert, Alice Tissot, Mady Berry
'By any standard the finest foreign-language talker shown in the US in a couple of years.' – *Variety*

Matewan **

US 1987 133m DuArt
Enterprise/Cinecom Entertainment/Film Gallery/Red Dog (Peggy Rajski, Maggie Renzi)
📀 ▦
Striking miners battle against brutal owners determined to break the strike.
Engaging hard-edged political drama.
wd John Sayles *ph* Haskell Wexler *pd* Nora Chavooshian *ed* Sonya Polonsky
☆ Chris Cooper, Mary McDonnell, Will Oldham, David Strathairn, Ken Jenkins, Kevin Tighe, Gordon Clapp, James Earl Jones, Bob Gunton, Jace Alexander
🎬 Haskell Wexler

Matilda

👪👪 US 1978 105m Movielab
AIP/Albert S. Ruddy
A down-at-heel theatrical agent finds success with a boxing kangaroo.
Damon Runyon meets Walt Disney in an old-fashioned family audience picture for which there may no longer be an audience.
w Albert S. Ruddy, Timothy Galfas *novel* Paul Gallico *d* Daniel Mann *ph* Jack Woolf *m* Jerrold Immel *pd* Boris Leven
☆ Elliott Gould, Robert Mitchum, Harry Guardino, Clive Revill, Karen Carlson, Lionel Stander, Art Metrano, Roy Clark

'Lawrence Woolsey presents the end of civilisation as we know it. Make that ... Proudly Presents'

Matinee *

US 1993 99m DeLuxe
Guild/Universal
📀 ▦ 📷 📀 🎧
At the time of the Cuban missile crisis, a B-movie-maker arrives at a US naval base to stage the premiere of his new horror film about a half-man, half-ant, incorporating the cinema-seat-shaking Rumblerama.
An enjoyable celebration of the nuclear-inspired, gimmicky horror movies of the 50s, brilliantly parodied; but it is hampered by a teen romance, presented without appropriate irony, which might have been lifted from any drive-in movie of the period.
w Charlie Haas *story* Jerico *d* Joe Dante *ph* John Hora *m* Jerry Goldsmith *pd* Steven Legler *ed* Marshall Harvey
☆ John Goodman, Cathy Moriarty, Simon Fenton, Omri Katz, Lisa Jakub, Kellie Martin, Jesse Lee, Dick Miller, John Sayles
'Even when the film gets bogged down in romantic drivel, there are enough clever in-jokes and well-remembered period details to keep buffs happy.' – *Variety*
† The character played by Goodman is based on the showman-producer-director William Castle.

The Mating Game

US 1958 96m Metrocolor Cinemascope
MGM (Philip Barry Jnr)
An income-tax inspector becomes involved in the affairs of an unorthodox farming family.
Dismally unfunny adaptation for Americans of a very English novel; everyone works hard to no avail.

---

w William Roberts *novel* The Darling Buds of May by H. E. Bates d George Marshall ph Robert Bronner m Jeff Alexander

☆ Debbie Reynolds, Tony Randall, Paul Douglas, Fred Clark, Una Merkel, Philip Ober, Charles Lane, Philip Coolidge

'Every joke is driven past the point of exhaustion.' – MFB

† H. E. Bates's novel was the basis for a successful television series, *The Darling Buds of May* (1991–93), starring David Jason and Pam Ferris.

The Mating of Millie

US 1948 87m bw
Columbia

A self-confident young woman wants to adopt a small boy and tries to propel a bus driver into a marriage of convenience.

Amiable if protracted romantic comedy with dashes of sentiment and an obvious outcome.

w Louella MacFarlane, St Clair McKelway
d Henry Levin

☆ Glenn Ford, Evelyn Keyes, Willard Parker, Jimmy Hunt, Ron Randell

The Mating Season

US 1950 101m bw
Paramount (Charles Brackett)

A factory draughtsman marries an ambassador's daughter; his mother loses her job and comes incognito to work for them as a cook.

Uninteresting mechanical domestic comedy in which the young bride are dull and the older ones overplay.

w Walter Reisch, Charles Brackett, Richard Breen d Mitchell Leisen ph Charles Lang m Joseph J. Lilley

☆ Gene Tierney, John Lund, Miriam Hopkins, Thelma Ritter, Jan Sterling

⚧ Thelma Ritter

Matka Joanna od Aniolow: see *The Devil and the Nun*

'Believe the unbelievable.'

The Matrix ***

US/Australia 1999 136m Technicolor
Panavision
Warner/Village Roadshow/Groucho II (Joel Silver)

An insignificant worker turns out to be the promised leader who fights against the Matrix, an artificial intelligence that controls the world and consumes its inhabitants.

Spectacular special effects, slick design and the speed and vitality of the narrative overcome its deficiencies, particularly its derivative plot that draws on so many science-fiction clichés and conventions.

wd Andy Wachowski, Larry Wachowski ph Bill Pope m Don Davis pd Owen Paterson ed Zach Staenberg sp Geoffrey Darrow; Bob McCarron; Makeup Effects Group Studio

☆ Keanu Reeves, Laurence Fishburne, Carrie-Anne Moss, Hugo Weaving, Gloria Foster, Joe Pantoliano, Marcus Chong, Paul Goddard, Robert Taylor, Julian Arahanga, Matt Doran, Belinda McClory, Anthony Ray Parker

'Eye-popping but incoherent extravaganza of morphing and superhuman martial arts. Ultra-cool visuals that truly deliver something new to the sci-fi action lexicon will make this time-jumping thriller a must-see among genre fans, especially guys in their teens and 20s.' – Todd McCarthy, Variety

'A dazzlingly nifty slice of sci-fi cool.' – Empire

† Yuen Woo-Ping was responsible for the kung fu choreography.

†† The film cost $60m to make and grossed $475m at cinemas around the world.

💿 Zach Staenberg; sound (John Reitz, Gregg Rudloff, David Campbell, David Lee); sound effects editing (Dane A. Davis); visual effects (John Gaeta, Janek Sirrs, Steve Courtley, Jon Thum)

Ⓥ special visual effects; sound

A Matter of Choice

GB 1963 79m bw
Bryanston/Holmwood (George Maynard)

Two young men-about-town become accidentally involved with the police and inadvertently expose a wife's adultery.

A dull melodrama, involving uninteresting people, with a narrative that depends on an escalation of unlikely coincidences.

w Paul Ryder *story* Vernon Sewell, Derren Nesbitt d Vernon Sewell ph Arthur Lavis m Robert Sharples ad Scott MacGregor ed Lee Doig

☆ Anthony Steel, Jeanne Moody, Ballard Berkeley, Malcolm Gerard, Michael Davis, Richard Bebb, Penny Morrell

A Matter of Dignity *

Greece 1957 104m bw
Finos (Anis Nohra)

original title: *To Teleftteo Psemma*

The daughter of a bankrupt family reluctantly agrees to marry a millionaire, and the family's false values lead to tragedy.

Rather offbeat melodrama with the director in good form.

wd Michael Cacoyannis ph Walter Lassally m Manos Hadjidakis

☆ Ellie Lambetti, Georges Pappas, Athena Michaelidou

A Matter of Innocence: see *Pretty Polly*

A Matter of Life and Death ****

GB 1946 104m Technicolor
GFD/Archers (Michael Powell, Emeric Pressburger)

US title: *Stairway to Heaven*

A pilot with brain damage after bailing out is torn between this world and the next, but an operation puts things to rights.

Outrageous fantasy which seemed more in keeping after the huge death toll of a world war, and in any case learned the Hollywood lesson of eating its cake and still having it, the supernatural elements being capable of explanation. A mammoth technical job in the heavenly sequences, it deserves full marks for its sheer arrogance, wit, style and film flair.

wd Michael Powell, Emeric Pressburger ph Jack Cardiff m Allan Gray pd Hein Heckroth

☆ David Niven, Roger Livesey, Kim Hunter, Marius Goring, Raymond Massey, Abraham Sofaer

'Powell and Pressburger seem to have reached their heaven at last … an illimitable Wembley stadium, surrounded by tinkly music and mists, from which all men of insight, if they were ever careless enough to get there, would quickly blaspheme their way out.' – Richard Winnington

'A dazzling mesh of visionary satire, postwar politics and the mystical side of English romanticism.' – Tony Rayns, Time Out, 1979

'Beautifully written, beautifully acted, beautifully executed … you would think such formidable merits would add up to quite a film – and darned if they don't.' – Time Out

'This film, whether or not you find its philosophy half-baked, is downright good cinema, doing things that couldn't be done in any other medium' – Tribune

'It compelled attention and created emotion.' – Basil Wright, 1972

A Matter of Resistance: see *La Vie de Château*

'Some women are born to have a glorious affair with life … !'

A Matter of Time

US/Italy 1976 97m Technicolor
(AIP)

An Italian country chambermaid is taught about life by a faded countess.

Interminable even in its abbreviated form, this woebegone fantasy is a tribute to his miscast daughter by a director who never had much sense of plot to begin with. It has to be seen to be believed.

w John Gay *novel* The Film of Memory by Maurice Druon d Vincente Minnelli ph Geoffrey Unsworth m Nino Oliviero

☆ Liza Minnelli, Ingrid Bergman, Charles Boyer, Tina Aumont, Gabriele Ferzetti, Spiros Andros

'So hackneyed, inept and stupid as to be almost amusing.' – John Simon, New York

'So spectacularly crazy that if Minnelli could only persuade Mel Brooks to put his name on it, A Matter of Time might yet be the comedy sleeper of the year.' – Frank Rich, New York Post

A Matter of Who

GB 1961 92m bw
MGM/Foray (Walter Shenson, Milton Holmes)

The World Health Organization tracks down a smallpox outbreak.

Curious blend of semi-documentary with suspense and comedy; not really a starter.

w Milton Holmes d Don Chaffey ph Erwin Hillier m Edwin Astley

☆ Terry-Thomas, Sonja Ziemann, Alex Nicol, Guy Deghy, Richard Briers, Clive Morton, Geoffrey Keen, Martin Benson, Honor Blackman, Carol White

Les Maudits

France 1947 103m bw
Speva/Discina

UK title: *The Damned*

A U-boat with an assorted human cargo escapes the allied blockade as the war ends.

Striking but aimless melodrama which plays like an early Ship of Fools.

w J. Companeez, V. Alexandrov d René Clément ph Henri Alekan m Yves Baudrier

☆ Dalio, Henri Vidal, Michel Auclair, Florence Marly, Paul Bernard

Maurice *

GB 1987 140m Technicolor
Cinecom/Merchant Ivory (Ismail Merchant)

The life of a Cambridge homosexual.

Hothouse study of E. M. Forster's posthumously published and semi-autobiographical novel. An acquired taste, but many scenes have general appeal.

w Kit Hesketh-Harvey, James Ivory d James Ivory ph Pierre Lhomme m Richard Robbins pd Brian Ackland-Snow ed Katherine Wenning

☆ James Wilby, Hugh Grant, Rupert Graves, Denholm Elliott, Simon Callow, Billie Whitelaw, Ben Kingsley, Judy Parfitt

⚧ costume design (Jenny Beavan, John Bright)

Mauvais Sang: see *The Night Is Young*

'In Their Hands, A Deck Of Cards Was The Only Thing More Dangerous Than A Gun.'

Maverick *

US 1994 127m Technicolor Panavision
Warner/Icon (Bruce Davey, Richard Donner)

A gambler raises the money to take part in a poker championship, where his opponents include a woman who tried to rob him.

Based on the TV series that starred James Garner, this is a relaxed and rambling romp, a jokey tale of double-cross in a Western setting which would have been far better with its last half-hour excised.

w William Goldman d Richard Donner ph Vilmos Zsigmond m Randy Newman pd Tom Sanders

★ Mel Gibson, Jodie Foster, James Garner, Graham Greene, James Coburn, Alfred Molina

'Good solid fun.' – Empire

† Danny Glover appears uncredited in a Lethal Weapon in-joke.

⚧ costume design

The Maverick Queen

US 1955 90m Trucolor Naturama
Republic

A lady rustler falls for a Pinkerton detective sent to arrest her.

Tedious Western in bilious colour.

w Kenneth Gamet, De Vallon Scott *novel* Zane Grey d Joe Kane ph Jack Marta m Victor Young

☆ Barbara Stanwyck, Barry Sullivan, Scott Brady, Mary Murphy, Wallace Ford, Jim Davis

Max Dugan Returns **

US 1983 98m colour
TCF (Herbert Ross, Neil Simon)

A hard-up widow with a 15-year-old son is visited by her dying father who abandoned her when she was a child.

Slight, sentimental but gently amusing comedy.

w Neil Simon d Herbert Ross ph David M. Walsh m David Shire ad Albert Brenner ed Richard Marks

☆ Marsha Mason, Jason Robards, Donald Sutherland, Matthew Broderick

'A consistently happy comedic fable.' – Variety

Max Mon Amour

France/US 1986 97m colour
Electric/Greenwich Film/A2 (Serge Silberman)

The wife of a British diplomat in Paris falls in love with a chimpanzee.

Odd tale that strives for, but fails to achieve, an air of unease.

w Nagisa Oshima, Jean-Claude Carrière d Nagisa Oshima ph Raoul Coutard m Michel Portal pd Pierre Guffroy ed Hélène Plemiannikov

☆ Charlotte Rampling, Anthony Higgins, Bernard-Pierre Donnadieu, Victoria Abril, Anne-Marie Besse, Nicole Clafan, Pierre Etaix, Bernard Haller, Sabine Haudepin

Maxie

US 1985 98m DeLuxe
Orion/Aurora/Elsboy/Carter De Haven

The ghost of a twenties starlet revisits her old apartment and takes over the body of the wife of the tenant.

Heavenly comedy which would have been funnier in the forties.

w Patricia Resnick *novel* Marion's Wall by Jack Finney d Paul Aaron ph Fred Schuler m Georges Delerue pd John Lloyd ed Lynzee Klingman

☆ Glenn Close, Mandy Patinkin, Ruth Gordon, Barnard Hughes, Valerie Curtin

Maximum Overdrive

US 1986 97m Technicolor
Dino de Laurentiis (Martha Schumacher)

In a corner of North Carolina, all mechanical devices go haywire, and trucks menace a group of humans caught in a filling station.

Idiotic premise for sensational action sequences, which are well staged but go on too long.

wd Stephen King ph Armando Nannuzzi m AC/DC pd Giorgio Postiglione ed Evan Lottman

☆ Emilio Estevez, Pat Hingle, Laura Harrington, Yeardley Smith, John Short, Ellen McElduff, J.C. Quinn

Maximum Risk

US 1996 100m DeLuxe Panavision
Columbia (Moshe Diamant)

A French cop takes revenge on the gangsters who killed his twin brother by assuming his identity.

Standard action-film clichés are well orchestrated in this predictable fast-paced nonsense.

w Larry Ferguson d Ringo Lam ph Alexander Gruszynski m Robert Folk pd Steven Spence ed Bill Pankow

☆ Jean-Claude Van Damme, Natasha Henstridge, Zach Grenier, Jean-Hugues Anglade, Paul Ben-Victor, Stéphane Audran

'A visceral delight that refuses to be deterred by niceties of plot or character consistency and prefers sweat to emotion.' – Leonard Klady, Variety

Maya

🚹 US 1966 91m Technicolor
Panavision
MGM/King Brothers (Mary P. Murray, Herman King)

A teenage American boy arrives in India to visit his disillusioned father, who finally comes to understand him only after he has run away.

Good-looking but otherwise uninteresting animal drama which served as the pilot for a TV series.

w John Fante d John Berry ph Gunter Senftleben m Riz Ortolani

☆ Clint Walker, Jay North, I. S. Johar, Sajid Khan

Maybe Baby

US 1988 98m colour
Columbia/Tri-Star (Jerry Belson, Walter Coblenz)

US title: *For Keeps*

Two teenagers, who marry when pregnancy looms, face up to adult responsibilities.

Tiresome and sentimental account of young motherhood.

w Tim Kazurinsky, Denise DeClue d John G. Avildsen ph James Crabe m Bill Conti pd William J. Cassidy ed John G. Avildsen

☆ Molly Ringwald, Randall Batinkoff, Kenneth Mars, Miriam Flynn, Conchata Ferrell, Sharon Brown

---

🚹 film suitable for family viewing   📼 VHS video-cassette for the British PAL system   📼 VHS video-cassette for the British PAL system in wide screen-format   ↻ Video cassette in a computer-colourised version   ▬ American NTSC video-cassette   ⓐ Laser disc

Maybe, Maybe Not: see *The Most Desired Man*

Mayerling **
France   1935   90m   bw
Seymour Nebenzahl/Nero Film
🎬

In 1889, imperial lovers are found dead in a country house.
Classic French version of a somewhat chilly subject.
w Joseph Kessel, V. Cube *novel* Claude Anet d Anatole Litvak
☆ Charles Boyer, Danielle Darrieux, Marthe Regnier, Yolande Laffon, Suzy Prim
'As good a picture as Hollywood could produce, plus some local touches that are inaccessible to Hollywood.' – *Variety*

Mayerling
France/GB   1968   141m   Eastmancolor
Panavision
Corona/Winchester (Robert Dorfmann)
📀

In 1889 the heir to the Habsburg Empire is forced into a suicide pact with his mistress.
Tedious dramatization of historical events which in 1935 had made a delicate French film but in these hands seems an endless and boring manipulation of doubtful events into turgid romance.
wd Terence Young *novel* Claude Anet ph Henri Alekan m Francis Lai pd Georges Wakhevitch
☆ Omar Sharif, Catherine Deneuve, James Mason, Ava Gardner, James Robertson Justice, Genevieve Page, Ivan Desny, Maurice Teynac

The Mayor of 44th Street
US   1942   86m   bw
RKO (Cliff Reid)
Dance bands are threatened by hooligans demanding protection money.
Boring melodrama with music.
w Lewis R. Foster d Alfred E. Green ph Robert de Grasse *songs* Mort Greene, Harry Revel
☆ George Murphy, Anne Shirley, Richard Barthelmess, William Gargan, Joan Merrill, Millard Mitchell, Mary Wickes, Freddy Martin and band
♫ song 'There's a Breeze on Lake Louise'

The Mayor of Hell *
US   1933   90m   bw
Warner
A racketeer becomes superintendent of a reform school, and it changes his life.
Moderate star vehicle with a plot that did yeoman service thereafter in Dead End Kids films.
w Edward Chodorov d Archie Mayo ph Barney McGill m Leo F. Forbstein
☆ James Cagney, Madge Evans, Allen Jenkins, Dudley Digges, Frankie Darro
'Has the outline of a junior Big House. Offers exploitation easily.' – *Variety*
'Propaganda for nothing: like most of what comes out of Hollywood, it is entertaining trash.' – *Time*
† Remade in 1938 as *Crime School* with Humphrey Bogart, 1939 as *Hell's Kitchen* with Ronald Reagan.

Maytime **
US   1937   132m   bw (sepia sequence)
MGM (Hunt Stromberg)
🎬 ♫

An opera star falls in love with a penniless singer but her jealous impresario shoots him.
Lush romantic musical which turns gradually from melodrama and ends in a ghostly reunion for the lovers. If that's what you like, it could scarcely be better done.
w Noel Langley *operetta* Rida Johnson Young d Robert Z. Leonard m Oliver T. Marsh m Sigmund Romberg md Herbert Stothart
☆ Jeanette MacDonald, Nelson Eddy, John Barrymore, Herman Bing, Lynne Carver, Rafaela Ottiano, Paul Porcasi, Sig Rumann
'Click operetta ... cinch for the foreign market also.' – *Variety*
'Enjoyable for more than camp reasons ... the atmosphere of thwarted passion is compelling.' – *Pauline Kael, 70s*
† Shooting had begun in colour with Frank Morgan in Bing's part and Paul Lukas in Barrymore's; this footage, directed by Edmund Goulding, was abandoned on Irving Thalberg's death.
♫ Herbert Stothart

Maytime in Mayfair
GB   1949   95m   Technicolor
British Lion/Imperadio (Herbert Wilcox)
🎬

A playboy inherits a dress salon and falls for the lady manager.
Witless comedy fit to set one's teeth on edge, with over-acting and poor musical numbers. Not in the same street as its predecessor Spring in Park Lane.
w Nicholas Phipps d Herbert Wilcox ph Max Greene md Robert Farnon
☆ Anna Neagle, Michael Wilding, Nicholas Phipps, Peter Graves, Tom Walls
'Painstakingly refined.' – *MFB*

The Maze
US   1953   81m   bw   3-D
Allied Artists (Richard Heermance)
The heir to a title also inherits a family curse and turns into a giant frog.
Rather splendidly idiotic horror film which raises plenty of laughs but no frissons.
w Dan Ullman *story* Maurice Sandoz d William Cameron Menzies ph Harry Neumann m Marlin Skiles
☆ Richard Carlson, Veronica Hurst, Katherine Emery, Michael Pate, Lillian Bond, Hillary Brooke, Owen McGiveney

Me and Him
US   1988   90m   colour
Columbia/Egmont/Neue Constantin (Bernd Eichinger)
📀 🎬

A New Yorker's penis begins to talk back to him.
A comedy about male chauvinism that fails to raise a smile.
w Warren D. Leight, Michael Junker, Doris Dörrie *novel* Io e Lui by Alberto Moravia d Doris Dörrie ph Helge Weindler m Raimund Barthelmes
☆ Griffin Dunne, Ellen Greene, Steven Marcus, Craig T. Nelson, Kelly Bishop, Carey Lowell, Kara Glover, Kim Flowers

Me and Marlborough *
GB   1935   84m   bw
GFD/Gainsborough (Michael Balcon)
In Marlborough's army, a woman takes the place of her soldier husband to prove his innocence of spying.
Curious period service farce, not quite a success but an interesting attempt at something different.
w Ian Hay, Marjorie Gaffney *story* W. P. Lipscomb, Reginald Pound d Victor Saville ph Charles Van Enger
☆ Cicely Courtneidge, Tom Walls, Barry McKay, Alfred Drayton
'In most cases the comedy is totally uncalled for and destroys the period atmosphere.' – *Variety*

Me and My Gal *
US   1932   79m   bw
Fox
GB title: *Pier 13*
A cop on the beat romances a hashslinger and catches a crook.
Pleasant little programmer, very evocative of its period.
w Arthur Kober d Raoul Walsh ph Arthur Miller
☆ Spencer Tracy, Joan Bennett, George Walsh, Marion Burns, J. Farrell MacDonald, Noel Madison, Henry B. Walthall
'Lacking in nearly everything that makes box office.' – *Variety*
† Remade in 1949 as *Pier 13*.

Me and My Pal *
🎬 US   1933   20m   bw
Hal Roach
Ollie becomes engrossed in a jigsaw puzzle and forgets to get married.
Oddball star comedy which nearly comes off but simply doesn't provide enough jokes.
w Stan Laurel, Charles Rogers, Lloyd French ph Art Lloyd ed Bert Jordan
☆ Stan Laurel, Oliver Hardy, James Finlayson, Eddie Dunn

Me and the Colonel
US   1958   110m   bw
Columbia/Court-Goetz (William Goetz)
In 1940 an anti-semitic Polish colonel is obliged to flee from France in the company of a Jewish refugee.
Rather obvious war comedy with predictable but not very entertaining situations, sentiment, action and
pathos. *The stars cope well enough but the picture never picks up steam.*
w S. N. Behrman, George Froeschel *play* Franz Werfel d Peter Glenville ph Burnett Guffey m George Duning
☆ Danny Kaye, Curt Jurgens, Nicole Maurey, Françoise Rosay, Akim Tamiroff, Martita Hunt, Alexander Scourby, Liliane Montevecchi, Ludwig Stossel

Me, Natalie *
US   1969   111m   DeLuxe
Cinema Center (Stanley Shapiro)
An unattractive 18-year-old girl moves into Greenwich Village and learns to accept herself as she is.
Basically very predictable but rather well done character study with excellent detail.
w A. Martin Zweiback d Fred Coe ph Arthur J. Ornitz m Henry Mancini
☆ Patty Duke, James Farentino, Martin Balsam, Elsa Lanchester, Salome Jens, Nancy Marchand, Al Pacino

Mean Guns
US   1996   96m   Foto-Kem
Polygram/Filmwerks (Gary Schmoeller, Tom Karnowski)
📀 🎬
A group of hitmen are gathered together in an unopened prison and told that the last three alive at the end of six hours can claim $10 million hidden in the building.
Explosive action movie, essentially men with guns running around shooting at one another.
w Andrew Witham d Albert Pyun ph George Mooradian m Tony Riparetti ed Ken Morrisey
☆ Christopher Lambert, Ice-T, Michael Halsey, Deborah Van Valkenburgh, Tina Cotè, Yuji Okomoto, Thom Matthews
'Make no mistake, this is one of the worst films you will ever see.' – *Ben Mitchell, Guardian*

The Mean Machine: see *The Longest Yard*

The Mean Season
US   1985   103m   DeLuxe   Panavision
Orion/Turman-Foster
🎬 🎧
A Miami police reporter becomes the personal spokesman for a murderous psychopath.
Tolerable murder thriller with asides on politics and the media.
w Leon Piedmont *novel* In the Heat of the Summer by John Katzenbach d Phillip Borsos ph Frank Tidy m Lalo Schifrin pd Philip Jefferies
☆ Kurt Russell, Mariel Hemingway, Richard Jordan, Richard Masur, Richard Bradford, Joe Pantoliano

Mean Streets ****
US   1973   110m   Technicolor
Taplin-Perry-Scorsese (Jonathan T. Taplin)
📀 🎬 🎧 🎵
Four young Italian-Americans use Tony's Bar as a base for drinking, brawling and hustling.
Relentlessly sordid melodrama with a good eye for realistic detail. The first film in which Scorsese announced himself as a major talent and discovered the subject matter that has served him so well.
w Martin Scorsese, Mardik Martin d Martin Scorsese m Kent Wakeford ed Sid Levin
☆ Harvey Keitel, Robert DeNiro, David Proval, Amy Robinson, Richard Romanus
'Lacks a sense of story and structure ... unless a film-maker respects the needs of his audience, he can't complain if that audience fails to show up.' – *Variety*
'A thicker-textured rot than we have ever had in an American movie, and a deeper sense of evil.' – *New Yorker*
'Extraordinarily rich and distinguished on many levels.' – *Joseph Gelmis*

The Meanest Man in the World
US   1943   57m   bw
TCF (William Perlberg)
🎵
An easy-going small-town lawyer finds that business picks up when he becomes tough and mean.
Very minor star comedy with a muddled opening followed by strictly rationed laughs.
w George Seaton, Allan House *play* George M. Cohan d Sidney Lanfield ph Peverell Marley
m Cyril J. Mockridge ad Richard Day, Albert Hogsett ed Robert Bischoff
☆ Jack Benny, Priscilla Lane, Rochester, Edmund Gwenn, Anne Revere

The Meaning of Life: see *Monty Python's The Meaning of Life*

Meatballs
Canada   1979   92m   Sonolab Color
Paramount (Dan Goldberg)
🎬 🎧 🎵
Adventures at an ineptly run summer camp.
Adolescent fun and games for easily pleased teens.
w Len Blum, Dan Goldberg, Harold Ramis, Janis Allen d Ivan Reitman ph Don Wilder m Elmer Bernstein ad David Charles ed Debra Karen
☆ Bill Murray, Harvey Atkin, Russ Banham, Ron Barry, Jack Blum, Kate Lynch, Matt Craven, Kristine DeBell, Cindy Girling
'A smooth—running narrative that makes the camp hijinks part of an overall human mosaic... without the usual grossness and cynicism of many contempo comedy pix.' – *Variety*

Meatballs 4
US   1992   87m   colour
Moviestore (Donald P. Borchers)
🎬
A water skier tries to prevent a lakeside summer camp being taken over by a ruthless developer.
Tired comedy with a predictable plot, occasionally enlivened by the action on water skis.
wd Bob Logan ph Vance Burberry m Steve Hunter pd Deborah Raymond ed Peter H. Verity
☆ Corey Feldman, Jack Nance, Sarah Douglas, Bojesse Christopher, Johnny Cocktails, J. Trevor Edmond, Paige French, John Mendoza

'Rudy struck out two summers in a row... this will be his year to score!'

Meatballs III: Summer Job
Canada   1987   94m   Sonolab color
(John Dunning, Don Carmody)
🎬 🎧
A wimp loses his virginity at summer camp with the aid of the ghost of a pornographic filmstar.
Tedious, frequently distasteful, run-through, slapstick comedy; underlying all the antics is an adolescent fear of sex, or possibly its makers' fear of adolescent sex.
w Michael Paseorner, Bradley Kesden *story* Carl Workman d George Mendeluk ph Peter Benison m Paul Zaza pd Charles Dunlop ed Debra Karen
☆ Sally Kellerman, Al Waxman, Patrick Dempsey, Shannon Tweed, Maury Chaykin, Isabelle Mejias, Ronnie Hawkins, George Suza

Meatballs Part II
Canada   1984   87m   Movielab color
TriStar (Stephen Poe, Tony Bishop)
🎬 🎧
The future of a summer camp depends upon the outcome of a boxing match.
Raucous lowbrow comedy, a series of slapstick jokes and parodies.
w Bruce Singer *story* Martin Kitrosser, Carol Watson d Donald M. Morgan m Ken Harrison pd James William Newport ed George Berndt
☆ Archie Hahn, John Mengatti, Tammy Taylor, Kim Richards, Ralph Seymour, Richard Mulligan, Hamilton Camp, John Larroquette, Paul Reubens

'The Mechanic must be dead sure ... or dead!'

The Mechanic
US   1972   100m   Technicolor
UA/Chartoff/Winkler/Carlino
🎬 🎧
reissue title: *Killer of Killers*
A professional assassin under contract to the Mafia makes his missions look like accidents.
Violent thriller with a few pretensions, but too flashily made to be taken seriously.
w Lewis John Carlino d Michael Winner ph Richard Kline, Robert Paynter m Jerry Fielding
☆ Charles Bronson, Jan-Michael Vincent, Keenan Wynn, Jill Ireland
'A hymn to technological violence, efficiently and convincingly made.' – *George Melly, Observer*

Med Kaerlig Hilsen: see *Love Me Darling*

A Medal for Benny *

US   1945   77m   bw
Paramount (Paul Jones)

An old rustic is the centre of small town celebrations in honour of his dead war hero son.

Satirical-sentimental location drama, effective but not memorable.

w Frank Butler *original story* John Steinbeck, Jack Wagner d Irving Pichel ph Lionel Lindon m Victor Young

☆ Dorothy Lamour, Arturo de Cordova, J. Carrol Naish, Mikhail Rasumny, Charles Dingle, Frank McHugh, Grant Mitchell

ஃ original story; J. Carrol Naish

Medal for the General

GB   1944   99m   bw
British National

An old general takes in evacuees and finds a new interest in life.

Uneventful character drama which seemed mildly pleasing at the time.

w Elizabeth Baron *novel* James Ronald d Maurice Elvey ph James Wilson

☆ Godfrey Tearle, Jeanne de Casalis, Morland Graham, Mabel Constanduros, John Laurie, Petula Clark

Medals: see Seven Days Leave (1929)

Medea *

Italy/France/West Germany   1970   118m
Eastmancolor
San Marco/Number One/Janus (Franco Rossellini, Marina Cicogna)

Jason brings back as his wife the high priestess of the Golden Fleece, but her adjustment is to say the least uncomfortable.

In modern terms the case history of a psychopath, this weird production plays like an opera without music, and seems to have been designed as a vehicle for its charismatic star.

wd Pier Paolo Pasolini *play* Euripides ph Ennio Guarnieri

☆ Maria Callas, Giuseppe Gentile, Laurent Terzieff, Massimo Girotti

'He turned his back on civilization. Only to discover he had the power to save it.'

Medicine Man

US   1992   105m   Technicolor   Panavision
Guild/Cinergi (Andrew G. Vajna, Donna Dubrow)

A scientist, who has discovered a cure for cancer while working in the South American rain forest, is upset to find that his new research assistant is a woman.

Unpalatable mix of ecology and romance, with a long-delayed outcome that is predictable from the opening minutes.

w Tom Schulman, Sally Robinson d John McTiernan ph Donald McAlpine m Jerry Goldsmith

☆ Sean Connery, Lorraine Bracco, José Wilker, Rodolfo de Alexandre, Angelo Barra Moreira

'This jumbo-budget two-character piece suffers from a very weak script and a lethal job of miscasting.' – Variety

† Tom Schulman was reportedly paid $3 million for his script, with another $1 million being spent on rewrites. And still they got it wrong.

'A film dedicated to all those who are running away.'

Mediterraneo *

Italy   1991   90m   Technicolor
Mayfair/Penta/AMA/Berlusconi (Gianni Minervini)

During the Second World War, eight Italian soldiers find themselves forgotten and stranded on an idyllic Aegean island.

Based on a true story, this is a pleasant, bitter-sweet, nostalgic comedy that prefers the past to the present.

w Vincenzo Monteleone d Gabriele Salvatores ph Italo Pettricione m Giancarlo Bigazzi, Marco Falagiani ad Thalia Istikopoulos ed Nino Baragali

☆ Diego Abatantuono, Claudio Bigagli, Giuseppe Cederna, Claudio Bisio, Gigio Alberti, Ugo Conti, Memo Dini, Vasco Mirondola, Vanna Barba

'An ironic, gently amusing charmer, even though its anti-war elements jostle clumsily with its not entirely persuasive case for running away

from real life's disappointments.' – Angie Errigo, Empire

ஃ best foreign film

The Medium *

Italy   1951   80m   bw
Transfilm (Walter Lowendahl)

A fake medium feels a genuine manifestation, shoots at it and kills her assistant, but is still not sure whether he was responsible.

A filmic but not entirely satisfactory treatment of a modest but popular modern opera.

ph Enzo Serafin wd/m Gian-Carlo Menotti, his opera co-d Alexander Hammid

☆ Marie Powers, Anna Maria Alberghetti, Leo Coleman

ஃ Gian-Carlo Menotti (for music)

Medium Cool **

US   1969   111m   Technicolor
Paramount/H & J Pictures (Tully Friedman)

A TV news cameraman is made apathetic by the events around him.

Stimulating if overlong comment on the quality of life in the sixties, immaculately made and with a rather effective though obvious twist ending.

wd Haskell Wexler ph Haskell Wexler m Mike Bloomfield ad Leon Ericksen

☆ Robert Forster, Verna Bloom, Peter Bonerz, Marianna Hill, Sid McCoy

'A deeply moving questioning of America's violence and voyeurism.' – Jan Dawson
'I can't think of any film that tells one more about the texture of American life today.' – Michael Billington, Illustrated London News

'By the time he was eleven he had killed nine people!'

The Medusa Touch *

GB/France   1978   109m   Technicolor
ITC/Bulldog/Citeca (Arnon Milchan, Elliott Kastner)

A novelist is haunted by the belief that he can cause disaster.

And he does, very predictably, while any intellectual excitement in the script is rapidly replaced by mere mayhem. Different, but not exciting.

w John Briley *novel* Peter Van Greenway d Jack Gold ph Arthur Ibbetson m Michael J. Lewis sp Doug Ferris

☆ Richard Burton, Lee Remick, Lino Ventura, Harry Andrews, Alan Badel, Jeremy Brett, Michael Hordern, Gordon Jackson

Meet Danny Wilson *

US   1951   83m   bw
U-I (Leonard Goldstein)

An overbearing crooner gets to the top with the help of gangsters.

Fairly abrasive star vehicle, almost amounting to self-parody.

w Don McGuire d Joseph Pevney ph Maury Gertsman md Joseph Gershenson

☆ Frank Sinatra, Shelley Winters, Alex Nicol, Raymond Burr

Meet Dr Christian

US   1939   68m   bw
William Stephens/RKO

A dedicated small-town doctor has no concern for financial reward.

Adequate pot-boiler based on a radio character, and following Hersholt's popularity as Dr Dafoe.

w Ian McLellan Hunter, Harvey Gates, Ring Lardner Jnr d Bernard Vorhaus ph Robert Pittack

☆ Jean Hersholt, Dorothy Lovett, Robert Baldwin, Enid Bennett, Paul Harvey, Marcia Mae Jones

'First of a series … profitable programme material for the family trade.' – Variety

'Sooner or later everyone does.'

Meet Joe Black *

US   1998   180m   DeLuxe
Universal/City Light (Martin Brest)

Death, in the form of a handsome young man, comes calling for a media tycoon and is attracted to the man's daughter.

A movie more than half in love with Brad Pitt; the camera swoons around him endlessly, while little of interest goes on elsewhere.

w Ron Osborn, Jeff Reno, Kevin Wade, Bo Goldman *play* Death Takes a Holiday by Alberto

Casella, adapted by Walter Ferris
screenplay Maxwell Anderson, Gladys Lehman
d Martin Brest ph Emmanuel Lubezki m Thomas Newman pd Dante Ferretti ed Joe Hutshing, Michael Tronick sp Industrial Light & Magic

☆ Brad Pitt, Anthony Hopkins, Claire Forlani, Jake Weber, Marcia Gay Harden, Jeffrey Tambor, David S. Howard, Lois Kelly-Miller

† The film was a box-office flop, costing around $100m to make and market, and grossing around $43.25m at the US box-office.

Meet John Doe ***

US   1941   123m   bw
Liberty Films (Frank Capra)

A tramp is hired to embody the common man in a phony political drive, and almost commits suicide.

Vividly staged but over-sentimental Capra extravaganza with high spots outnumbering low.

w Robert Riskin d Frank Capra ph George Barnes m Dimitri Tiomkin

☆ Gary Cooper, Barbara Stanwyck, Edward Arnold, Walter Brennan, James Gleason, Spring Byington, Gene Lockhart, Rod la Rocque, Irving Bacon, Regis Toomey, Ann Doran, Warren Hymer, Andrew Tombes

'Capra is as skilled as ever in keeping things moving along briskly and dramatically.' – National Board of Review
'The meanings were so distorted that the original authors sued … It starts out in the confident Capra manner, but with a darker tone; by the end, you feel puzzled and cheated.' – Pauline Kael, 70s

ஃ original story (Richard Connell, Robert Presnell)

Meet Me after the Show *

US   1951   88m   Technicolor
TCF (George Jessel)

A musical star thinks she has discovered an affair between her husband and his glamorous backer.

Surprisingly bright routine musical.

w Mary Loos, Richard Sale d Richard Sale ph Arthur E. Arling md Lionel Newman songs Jule Styne, Leo Robin

☆ Betty Grable, Macdonald Carey, Rory Calhoun, Eddie Albert, Irene Ryan

Meet Me at Dawn

GB   1946   99m   bw
Excelsior/Marcel Hellman
US title: The Gay Duellist

A professional duellist is commissioned to provoke a duel with a senator, but unwittingly hires the senator's daughter to play the injured party.

A totally laborious and artificial period comedy which never seems even to aspire to the style required.

w Lesley Storm, James Seymour, Maurice Cowan story Le Tueur by Anatole Litvak, Marcel Achard d Thornton Freeland ph Gunther Krampf m Mischa Spoliansky

☆ Hazel Court, William Eythe, Stanley Holloway, Margaret Rutherford, Basil Sydney, Irene Browne

Meet Me at the Fair

US   1952   87m   Technicolor
U-I (Albert J. Cohen)

In 1900, an orphan joins a travelling medicine show.

Mildly pleasing open-air comedy drama.

w Irving Wallace *novel* The Great Companions by Gene Markey d Douglas Sirk ph Maury Gertsman md Joseph Gershenson

☆ Diana Lynn, Dan Dailey, Hugh O'Brian, Chet Allen, Rhys Williams

Meet Me in Las Vegas

US   1956   112m   Eastmancolor
Cinemascope
MGM (Joe Pasternak)

GB title: Viva Las Vegas!

A gambler's luck changes when he grabs the hand of a passing ballerina.

Listless song-and-dance extravaganza which wastes a great deal of talent.

w Isobel Lennart d Roy Rowland ph Robert Bronner m Georgie Stoll, Johnny Green ch Eugène Loring, Hermes Pan ly Sammy Cahn

☆ Dan Dailey, Cyd Charisse, Agnes Moorehead, Lili Darvas, Paul Henreid, Oscar Karlweis, Lena Horne, Jerry Colonna, Frankie Laine

'A large-scale musical of almost stupefying banality.' – MFB

ஃ Georgie Stoll, Johnny Green

Meet Me in St Louis ***

US   1944   113m   Technicolor
MGM (Arthur Freed)

Scenes in the life of an affectionate family at the turn of the century.

Patchy but generally highly agreeable musical nostalgia with an effective sense of the passing years and seasons.

w Irving Brecher, Fred Finklehoffe *novel* Sally Benson d Vincente Minnelli ph George Folsey md Georgie Stoll

☆ Judy Garland, Margaret O'Brien, Tom Drake, Leon Ames, Mary Astor, Lucille Bremer, June Lockhart, Harry Davenport, Marjorie Main, Joan Carroll, Hugh Marlowe, Robert Sully, Chill Wills

'A family group framed in velvet and tinsel … it has everything a romantic musical should have.' – Dilys Powell, 1955
'A charming picture. There is much more in it than meets the ear.' – C. A. Lejeune

ஃ script; George Folsey; Georgie Stoll; song 'The Trolley Song' (m/ly Ralph Blane, Hugh Martin)

Meet Me on Broadway

US   1946   77m   bw
Columbia (Burt Kelly)

A young musical director determines to hit Broadway.

Mild revue with a skimpy plot.

w George Bricker, Jack Henley d Leigh Jason m/ly Allen Roberts, Doris Fisher

☆ Marjorie Reynolds, Fred Brady, Jinx Falkenburg, Spring Byington, Gene Lockhart, Allen Jenkins

Meet Me Tonight

GB   1952   85m   Technicolor
British Film Makers/Anthony Havelock Allan

Three short Noël Coward plays: Red Peppers, Fumed Oak, Ways and Means.

Regrettably bald treatment of three playlets which have not lasted well. A thoroughly artificial evening.

w Noël Coward d Anthony Pelissier ph Desmond Dickinson m/ly Noël Coward

☆ Ted Ray, Kay Walsh, Stanley Holloway, Betty Ann Davies, Nigel Patrick, Valerie Hobson

Meet Mr Callaghan

GB   1954   88m   bw
Pinnacle

A private detective unmasks a rich man's killer.

Routine thick ear on American lines; moderately popular at the time, it spawned no sequels.

w Brock Williams *play* Gerald Verner (based on novel *The Urgent Hangman* by Peter Cheyney) d Charles Saunders ph Harry Waxman m Eric Spear

☆ Derrick de Marney, Harriet Johns, Peter Neil, Adrienne Corri, Delphi Lawrence, Belinda Lee

Meet Mr Lucifer *

GB   1953   81m   bw
Ealing (Monja Danischewsky)

The Demon King in a tatty provincial pantomime dreams he is the devil preventing people from wasting time watching television.

Clean and occasionally amusing piece of topical satire on tellymania; but the prologue is funnier than the sketches.

w Monja Danischewsky *play* Beggar My Neighbour by Arnold Ridley d Anthony Pelissier ph Desmond Dickinson m Eric Rogers

☆ Stanley Holloway, Peggy Cummins, Jack Watling, Barbara Murray, Joseph Tomelty, Gordon Jackson, Jean Cadell, Kay Kendall, Ian Carmichael, Gilbert Harding, Charles Victor, Humphrey Lestocq

Meet Mr Penny

GB   1938   70m   bw
British National

A meek clerk leads a revolt against a speculator who wants to build on allotments.

Early Ealing-style social comedy based on a radio character; of no abiding interest.

w Victor Kendall, Doreen Montgomery, from the character created by Maurice Moisiewicz d David MacDonald

☆ Richard Goolden, Vic Oliver, Fabia Drake, Kay Walsh, Patrick Barr, Hermione Gingold, Wilfrid Hyde-White

Meet Nero Wolfe *
US   1936   73m   bw
Columbia

A corpulent stay-at-home sleuth solves a disappearance and a murder.
The film début of an engaging crime character, who oddly never made it to a series.
w Howard J. Green, Bruce Manning, Joseph Anthony *play* Fer de Lance *by* Rex Stout d Herbert Biberman ph Henry Freulich
☆ Edward Arnold, Lionel Stander, Joan Perry, Rita Hayworth, Victor Jory, Nana Bryant, Walter Kingsford, John Qualen

Meet Simon Cherry
GB   1949   67m   bw
Hammer/Exclusive (Anthony Hinds)

A clergyman on holiday proves that a rich recluse was not murdered.
Elementary programme filler from a radio series.
w Gale Pedrick, A. R. Rawlinson, Godfrey Grayson *radio series* Meet the Rev *by* Gale Pedrick d Godfrey Grayson ph Cedric Williams m Frank Spencer
☆ Hugh Moxey, Zena Marshall, John Bailey, Anthony Forwood, Ernest Butcher, Courtney Hope

'The human race is about to be destroyed by people who wouldn't hurt a fly'
Meet the Applegates
US   1990   82m   DuArt
Castle Premier/New World (Denise Di Novi)
▣ ▥ ⌂
US title: *The Applegates*

Giant insects, whose habitat in the Brazilian rain forests has been destroyed, disguise themselves as humans and go to America to wreck a nuclear power plant.
Ineffectual slapstick satire aimed at suburban life-styles.
w Redbeard Simmons, Michael Lehmann d Michael Lehmann m Mitchell Dubin m David Newman pd John Hutman ad Kara Lindstrom, Adam Lustig ed Norman Hollyn
☆ Ed Begley Jnr, Stockard Channing, Dabney Coleman, Bobby Jacoby, Cami Cooper, Glenn Shadix, Susan Barnes, Adam Biesk
   'This wayward movie has a great deal of charm.' – *MFB*

Meet the Baron
US   1933   79m   bw
MGM

A nincompoop is fêted as the real Baron Münchhausen.
An incoherent script provides an opportunity for several comics to do their stuff.
w Herman J. Mankiewicz, Norman Krasna, Allen Rivkin, P. J. Wolfson, Arthur Kober, William K. Wells d Walter Lang
☆ Jack Pearl, Jimmy Durante, ZaSu Pitts, Ted Healy and his Stooges, Edna May Oliver, Henry Kolker
   'Not so forte in the material division, but saved by its capable crew of comics.' – *Variety*

Meet the Feebles
New Zealand   1989   97m   colour
Arrow/Wingnut (Jim Booth, Peter Jackson)
▣ ▥ ⌂

A troupe of puppets indulge in sex, drugs, violence and general vulgarity.
A semi-pornographic horror with Muppet-like creatures that is determined to offend.
w Danny Mulheron, Frances Walsh, Stephen Sinclair, Peter Jackson d Peter Jackson ph Murray Milne m Peter Dasent pd Mike Kane ed Jamie Selkirk sp Steve Ingram
☆ Danny Mulheron and also the voices of: Donna Akersten, Stuart Devenie, Mark Hadlow, Ross Jolly, Brian Sergent, Peter Vere Jones, Mark Wright
   'No excuse for spurting bodily secretions – blood, pus, vomit, or whatever – is passed up.' – *Sight and Sound*

Meet the Mayor
US   1938   63m   bw
Frank Fay/Times

A veteran small-town elevator operator becomes involved in politics.
Curious semi-comedy in which the star uses up most of his old vaudeville routines.

w Walter DeLeon, Charles Belden, Frank Fay d Ralph Ceder
☆ Frank Fay, Ruth Hall, Hale Hamilton, George Meeker, Berton Churchill, Franklin Pangborn
   'Flimsy meller for secondary duallers.' – *Variety*

Meet the Missus
US   1937   65m   bw
Albert Lewis/RKO

A worm turns when his wife constantly involves him in newspaper contests.
Very slight farce for the rurals.
w Jack Townley, Bert Granet, Joel Sayre *story* Lady Average *by* Jack Goodman, Albert Rice d Joseph Santley
☆ Victor Moore, Helen Broderick, Anne Shirley, Alan Bruce, Willie Best
   'Destined for the lower half of duals.' – *Variety*

Meet the Navy
GB   1946   85m   bw (Technicolor sequence)
British National

The story of a revue featuring amateurs from the allied navies.
Patchy but generally good-natured wartime entertainment.
w Lester Cooper, James Seymour d Alfred Travers
☆ Lionel Murton, John Pratt, Oscar Naske, Alan Lund

Meet the People
US   1944   100m   bw
MGM (E. Y. Harburg)

A Broadway musical star proves she isn't snooty by taking a job in a shipyard.
Thin propaganda musical which wastes a fair amount of talent.
w S. M. Herzig, Fred Saidy *play* Louis Lantz, Sol and Ben Barzman d Charles Reisner ph Robert Surtees *songs* various
☆ Lucille Ball, Dick Powell, Virginia O'Brien, Bert Lahr, Rags Ragland, June Allyson, Steve Geray, Phil Regan, Spike Jones and his City Slickers, Vaughn Monroe and his Orchestra

Meet the Stewarts
US   1942   74m   bw
Columbia

Newlyweds have trouble when he's poor and she's used to rich living.
Modest marital comedy with young talent.
w Elizabeth Dunn, Karen de Wolf d Alfred E. Green
☆ William Holden, Frances Dee, Grant Mitchell

Meet Wally Sparks
US   1997   104m   CFI color
Trimark/Largo (Leslie Greif)
▤ ◉

Injured in an accident, the failing host of a scurrilous TV chat show takes over the governor's residence as a broadcasting studio.
A dim-witted variation on The Man Who Came to Dinner *that long overstays its welcome.*
w Rodney Dangerfield, Harry Basil d Peter Baldwin ph Richard Kline m Michel Colombier pd Bryan Jones ed Raul Davalos
☆ Rodney Dangerfield, Debi Mazar, Cindy Williams, Burt Reynolds, David Ogden Stiers, Alan Rachins
   'A broad comedy of the kitchen sink school.' – *Variety*
† There are uncredited cameos by Tim Allen, Tony Danza, Jay Leno and Roseanne.

Meet Whiplash Willie: see *The Fortune Cookie*

'Love. Lust. Betrayal. Chaos. And the overture hasn't even begun.'
Meeting Venus *
GB   1990   120m   colour
Warner/Enigma/BSB/County NatWest (David Puttnam)
▣ ▤ ◉ ⌂

A married Hungarian conductor, having problems over a performance of *Tannhäuser* to an international audience, has an affair with the principal singer.
Bold attempt at a European film, but one that works only fitfully.
w Istvan Szabo, Michael Hirst d Istvan Szabo ph Lajos Koltai m Richard Wagner md Marek Janowski pd Attila Kovacs ed Jim Clark

☆ Glenn Close, Niels Arestrup, Moscu Alcallay, Macha Meril, Johanna Ter Steege, Maite Nahyr, Victor Poletti, Marian Labuda
   'A comedy with something to say, and the audacity to mix its laughs with a decent seriousness of purpose.' – *Derek Malcolm, Guardian*

Mein Kampf *
Sweden   1961   118m   bw
Tôre Sjöberg/Minerva International
▤ ⌂
original title: *Den Blodiga Tiden*

A newsreel compilation tracing the rise and fall of Nazi Germany.
A simple but highly effective and reliable selection of actualities leaves conclusions to the viewer, letting the events speak for themselves. A powerful documentary.
wd Erwin Leiser ed Erwin Leiser

Melancholia
GB   1989   87m   colour
BFI/Lichtblik Filmproduktion/Channel 4/Norddeutscher Rundfunk/Film Fons Hamburg/Hamburger Filmbüro (Colin MacCabe, Helga Bahr)
▣ ⌂

A German art critic, a former radical, is asked to take part in a political assassination in London.
Downbeat thriller built around an enigmatic protagonist.
w Andi Engel, Lewis Rodia d Andi Engel ph Denis Crossan m Simon Fisher Turner pd Jock Scott ed Christopher Roth
☆ Jeroen Krabbé, Susannah York, Ulrich Wildgruber, Jane Gurnett, Kate Hardie, Saul Reichlin, John Sparkes

Melba
GB   1953   113m   Technicolor
Horizon (Sam Spiegel)
▣

The life of the internationally famous Australian opera singer of Victorian days.
Moderately interesting recreation of a woman and an era, though dramatically rather stodgy.
w Harry Kurnitz d Lewis Milestone ph Ted Scaife md Muir Mathieson ad Andrei Andreiev
☆ Patrice Munsel, Robert Morley, Alec Clunes, Martita Hunt, Sybil Thorndike, John McCallum

O Melissokomos: see *The Beekeeper*

Mélo **
France   1986   112m   colour
Artificial Eye/MK2/Films A2/CNC (Marin Karmitz)

A wife, tormented by her affair with another man, kills herself.
Deliberately theatrical treatment of a once-potent play of the 1920s that gives its principals a chance to revel in their roles.
wd Alain Resnais *play* Henry Bernstein ph Charlie Van Damme m Philippe Gérard pd Jacques Saulnier ad Albert Jurgenson, Jean-Pierre Besnard
☆ Sabine Azéma, Fanny Ardant, Pierre Aditi, André Dussollier, Jacques Dacqmine
† The same play was filmed as *Dreaming Lips* in 1936.

Melody
🎵🎵 GB   1971   106m   Eastmancolor
Hemdale/Sagittarius/Goodtimes (David Puttnam)
▤
aka: *S.W.A.L.K.*

Calf love at school causes jealousy between two boys.
Tough-sentimental teenage comedy-drama of little interest to adults.
w Alan Parker d Waris Hussein ph Peter Suschitzky m Richard Hewson
☆ Jack Wild, Mark Lester, Tracy Hyde

Melody Cruise
US   1933   74m   bw
Merian C. Cooper/RKO

A lady killer gets his come-uppance on board ship, but wins the girl he really wants.
Very messy mixture of comedy, romance and music.
w Mark Sandrich, Ben Holmes d Mark Sandrich
☆ Phil Harris, Charles Ruggles, Greta Nissen, Helen Mack, Chick Chandler

'Ought to be a moderate grosser … the meat just isn't there for the principals, and they seem to feel it in their work.' – *Variety*

Melody for Two
US   1937   60m   bw
Warner

A singing bandleader argues with his team and picks up with an all-girl crew.
Simple-minded peg for a few songs; rather a yawn.
w George Bricker, Luci Ward, Joseph K. Watson d Louis King
☆ James Melton, Patricia Ellis, Wini Shaw, Marie Wilson, Fred Keating, Dick Purcell
   'Okay twin-bill fodder.' – *Variety*

Melody in Spring
US   1934   75m   bw
Paramount (Douglas MacLean)

An ambitious radio singer follows the sponsor's daughter on a European holiday.
Mild vehicle for a tenor who didn't sustain.
w Benn W. Levy d Norman Z. McLeod
☆ Lanny Ross, Charles Ruggles, Mary Boland, Ann Sothern, George Meeker, Herman Bing
   'Farfetched, somewhat boresome, and generally airy.' – *Variety*

Melody Inn: see *Riding High*

The Melody Lingers On
US   1935   65m   bw
Edward Small

During World War I, an Italian soldier is killed after fathering an illegitimate baby, which grows up with no knowledge of mother, who watches from afar.
Old-fashioned tearjerker with musical background.
w Ralph Spence, Philip Dunne *novel* Lowell Brentano d David Burton
☆ Josephine Hutchinson, George Houston, John Halliday, Mona Barrie, Helen Westley, Laura Hope Crews
   'Will probably wind up topping the duals.' – *Variety*

Melody of Life: see *Symphony of Six Million*

Melody of Youth: see *They Shall Have Music*

Melody Time *
🎭 US   1948   75m   Technicolor
Walt Disney (Ben Sharpsteen)

An unlinked variety show of cartoon segments.
A mainly mediocre selection with the usual moments of high style: Once upon a Wintertime, Bumble Boogie, Johnny Appleseed, Little Toot, Trees, Blame it on the Samba, Pecos Bill.
wd various.
   'There seems to be an obvious connection between the Disney artists' increasing insipidity and their increasing talent for fright, but I will leave it to accredited sado-masochists to make the discovery.' – *James Agee*

Melvin and Howard **
US   1980   95m   Technicolor
Universal (Terry Nelson)
▤

The life of a factory worker is changed when a man he picks up in the Nevada desert claims to be Howard Hughes.
Eccentric comedy which has been compared to the work of Preston Sturges, but has an agreeable style of its own.
w Bo Goldman d Jonathan Demme ph Tak Fujimoto m Bruce Langhorne
☆ Paul Le Mat, Jason Robards Jnr, Mary Steenburgen, Elizabeth Cheshire, Michael J. Pollard, Gloria Grahame
   'An almost flawless act of sympathetic imagination … it's what might have happened if Jean Renoir had directed a comedy script by Preston Sturges.' – *New Yorker*
♟ Bo Goldman; Mary Steenburgen
♟ Jason Robards Jnr (supporting actor)

The Member of the Wedding *
US   1952   91m   bw
Columbia/Stanley Kramer
▤

A 12-year-old girl learns something about life when her sister gets married and a young boy dies.

Boringly contained in a kitchen set, this filmed play has interesting characters but is really not good enough for the talent involved.

w Edna and Edward Anhalt *play and novel* Carson McCullers *d* Fred Zinnemann *ph* Hal Mohr *m* Alex North

☆ Julie Harris, Ethel Waters, Brandon de Wilde, Arthur Franz, Nancy Gates, James Edwards

♫ Julie Harris

Memed My Hawk

GB   1984   110m   colour
Fuad Kavur/Peter Ustinov Productions

In 1923 Turkey, an inept tyrant chases one of his young villagers, who flees to the rebels.
Weird but not wonderful mix of comedy and melodrama in an unfamiliar and unattractive setting.
wd Peter Ustinov *novel* Yashar Kemal *ph* Freddie Francis *m* Manos Hadjidakis *ad* Veljko Despotovic *ed* Peter Honess

☆ Peter Ustinov, Herbert Lom, Denis Quilley, Michael Elphick, Simon Dutton

Mémoire Tranquée: see *Lapse of Memory*

Memoirs of a Survivor

GB   1981   115m   Technicolor
EMI/Memorial (Michael Medwin, Penny Clark)

In the future, a single woman finds that urban civilization has decayed, and after many horrors finds refuge in an old Victorian house.
Unappetizing mixture of 1984 and Alice in Wonderland, too despairing and plotless to find many takers.
w Kerry Crabbe, David Gladwell *novel* Doris Lessing *d* David Gladwell *ph* Walter Lassally *m* Mike Thorn *pd* Keith Wilson *ed* William Shapter

☆ Julie Christie, Christopher Guard, Debbie Hutchings, Leonie Mellinger, Nigel Hawthorne, Pat Keen

'A film of wild ambition, sadly and hopelessly bungled.' – *Geoff Brown, MFB*

'Women want him for his wit. The C.I.A. wants him for his body. All Nick wants is his molecules back.'
'An adventure like you've never seen.'

Memoirs of an Invisible Man *

US   1992   99m   Technicolor   Panavision
Warner/Le Studio Canal Plus/Regency Enterprises/Alcor (Bruce Bodner, Dan Kolsrud)

A CIA agent pursues a stock analyst who has turned invisible after an accident.
Clever special effects fail to compensate for the lacklustre script and uninspired performances.
w Robert Collector, Dana Olsen, William Goldman *novel* H. F. Saint *d* John Carpenter *ph* William A. Fraker *m* Shirley Walker *pd* Lawrence G. Paull *ad* Marion Rothman *sp* Industrial Light and Magic

☆ Chevy Chase, Daryl Hannah, Sam Neill, Michael McKean, Stephen Tobolowsky, Jim Norton

'Where's the wit? It fades into invisibility while you're watching it.' – *Los Angeles Times*

Memories of Me

👫 US   1988   105m   colour
MGM/Odyssey (Alan King, Billy Crystal, Michael Hertzberg)

After he suffers a heart attack, a surgeon attempts a reconciliation with his father, an unsuccessful actor working as a Hollywood extra.
Slick, wisecracking mix of comedy and drama in which everyone communicates in one-liners. It is sometimes funny, but more often creakingly sentimental in the manner of soap opera and sitcoms, with nothing to offer in the way of insight except another joke.
w Eric Roth, Billy Crystal *d* Henry Winkler *ph* Andrew Dintenfass *m* Georges Delerue *pd* William J. Cassidy *ed* Peter E. Berger

☆ Billy Crystal, Alan King, JoBeth Williams, Janet Carroll, David Ackroyd, Phil Fondacaro

The Memory Expert: see *The Man on the Flying Trapeze*

Memphis Belle **

GB   1990   106m   colour
Warner/Enigma (David Puttnam, Catherine Wyler)

In the Second World War, the crew of an American B-17 bomber fly their final mission over Germany.
Sentimental drama that is a throwback to war films of an earlier era.
w Monte Merrick *d* Michael Caton-Jones *ph* David Watkin *m* George Fenton *pd* Stuart Craig *ed* Jim Clark

☆ Matthew Modine, Eric Stoltz, Tate Donovan, D. B. Sweeney, Billy Zane, Sean Astin, Harry Connick Jnr, Reed Edward Diamond, Courtney Gains, Neil Giuntoli

'Another chapter in David Puttnam's peculiar cinema of history lessons without cinematic depth or sound dramatic portfolio.' – *Richard Combs, MFB*

The Memphis Belle *

US/GB   1944   43m   Technicolor
War Activities Commission

The last mission over Germany of a Flying Fortress.
Impressive on-the-spot documentary which provided a lot of library footage for later movies.
d William Wyler

Men... **

West Germany   1985   99m   colour
Artificial Eye/Olga Film/ZDF (Harald Kugler)

original title: *Männer...*

A bourgeois husband turns his wife's lover, a hippy artist, into a carbon copy of himself
Light-hearted indictment of men as overgrown children
wd Doris Dörrie *ph* Helge Weindler *m* Claus Bantzer *ed* Raimund Barthelmes, Jeanette Magerl

☆ Heiner Lauterbach, Uwe Ochsenknecht, Ulrike Kriener, Janna Marangosoff

'Dörrie's deadpan giddiness is likeable enough. The picture is insignificant, though – a piece of fluff without the wit that you might hope for.' – *Pauline Kael, New Yorker*

'A completely new experience between men and women!'
'I was afraid I was gonna die ... now I'm afraid I'm gonna live!'

The Men ***

US   1950   85m   bw
Stanley Kramer

reissue title: *Battle Stripe*

Paraplegic war veterans are prepared for civilian life; the fiancée of one of them helps overcome his problems.
Vivid semi-documentary melodrama, at the time rather shocking in its no-holds-barred treatment of sexual problems.
w Carl Foreman *d* Fred Zinnemann *ph* Robert de Grasse *m* Dimitri Tiomkin

☆ Marlon Brando, Teresa Wright, Everett Sloane, Jack Webb, Howard St John

'Don't be misled into feeling that to see this film is merely a duty; it is, simply, an experience worth having.' – *Richard Mallett, Punch*
'As a bold, brave motion picture, The Men is to be applauded; but it would be a mistake to imagine that noble intentions and the courage to speak in hitherto unmentionable medical jargon necessarily make great films.' – *Margaret Hinxman*

♫ Carl Foreman

Men Against the Sky

US   1940   73m   bw
Howard Benedict/RKO

A stunt pilot advises on a new plane design instrumental to the war effort.
Routine heroics mixed with romance.
w Nathanael West *d* Leslie Goodwins

☆ Richard Dix, Kent Taylor, Edmund Lowe, Wendy Barrie, Grant Withers

Men Are Not Gods

GB   1936   92m   bw
UA/London (Alexander Korda)

An actor playing Othello nearly strangles his wife.
Tepid melodramatic attempt at a theme later used in A Double Life.

w Walter Reisch, G. B. Stern, Iris Wright *d* Walter Reisch *ph* Charles Rosher *m* Geoffrey Toye *ad* Vincent Korda *ed* Henry Cornelius

☆ Miriam Hopkins, Sebastian Shaw, Rex Harrison, Gertrude Lawrence, A. E. Matthews, Val Gielgud, Laura Smithson

'A nearer approximation to box office quality than some recent London productions.' – *Variety*

Men Are Such Fools

US   1938   69m   bw
Warner

The worm turns when his wife threatens to leave him for a singing career.
Mediocre is the word for this threadbare drama.
w Norman Reilly Raine, Horace Jackson *d* Busby Berkeley

☆ Wayne Morris, Humphrey Bogart, Priscilla Lane, Hugh Herbert, Penny Singleton

Men at Work

US   1990   98m   DeLuxe
Entertainment/Epic Productions/Euphoria Films/Sarlui/Diamant (Cassian Elwes)

Two garbage men find a corpse and set out to discover its killer.
Clumsily directed, witless rubbish.
wd Emilio Estevez *ph* Tim Suhrstedt *m* Stewart Copeland, Greg DeBelles *pd* Dins Danielsen *ed* Craig Bassett

☆ Charlie Sheen, Emilio Estevez, Leslie Hope, Keith David, Dean Cameron, John Getz, Hawk Wolinski, John Lavachielli, Geoffrey Blake

'This still manages to be an ordeal thanks to its endless procession of excrement jokes, kindergarten-level sex-jokes, contrived and pointless wandering around, and collection of arbitrary and oft-forgotten MacGuffins.' – *Kim Newman, MFB*

Men Behind Bars: see *Duffy of San Quentin*

Men Don't Leave

US   1990   115m   CFI color
Warner (Jon Avnet)

Following the death of her husband in an accident, a widow with two sons strives to keep the family together.
Just about rises above the level of an average soap opera.
w Barbara Benedek, Paul Brickman *d* Paul Brickman *ph* Bruce Surtees *m* Thomas Newman *pd* Barbara Ling *ed* Richard Chew

☆ Jessica Lange, Arliss Howard, Joan Cusack, Kathy Bates, Tom Mason, Chris O'Donnell, Charlie Korsmo, Belita Moreno, Jim Haynie, Cory Carrier, Shannon Moffett

'Protecting The Earth From The Scum Of The Universe.'

Men in Black **

US   1997   90m   Technicolor
Columbia/Amblin (Walter F. Parkes, Laurie MacDonald)

A cop is recruited to be the partner of a government agent whose task it is to track down illegal aliens.
Quick-witted science fiction with a couple of engaging, contrasting performances from its leads, and some excellent special effects, though a little more originality in its Earth-in-peril scenario would have been welcome.
w Ed Solomon *comic* Lowell Cunningham *d* Barry Sonnenfeld *ph* Don Peterman *m* Danny Elfman *pd* Bo Welch *ed* Jim Miller *sp* Industrial Light and Magic; make-up: Rick Baker, David LeRoy Anderson

☆ Tommy Lee Jones, Will Smith, Linda Fiorentino, Vincent D'Onofrio, Rip Torn, Tony Shalhoub, Siobhan Fallon

'Undemanding popular entertainment with a modicum of irony to back it up. It never becomes camp. But it never becomes truly sophisticated either.' – *Derek Malcolm, Guardian*
† The film cost $90m and grossed $250m in the US and another $313m around the world.

👤 make-up
♫ Bo Welch; Danny Elfman

Men in Her Diary

US   1945   73m   bw
Universal

A jealous woman tries to hire an unattractive girl as her husband's secretary.
Very mild lower-berth comedy.
w F. Hugh Herbert and Elwood Ullman *story* Kerry Shaw *d* Charles Barton

☆ Peggy Ryan, Jon Hall, Louise Allbritton, William Terry, Virginia Grey, Ernest Truex, Alan Mowbray, Eric Blore, Sig Rumann

The Men in Her Life

US   1941   90m   bw
Columbia (Gregory Ratoff)

A former circus rider becomes a ballerina.
Well-worn rags-to-riches romance of little interest.
w Frederick Kohner, Michael Wilson, Paul Trivers *novel* Ballerina by Lady Eleanor Smith *d* Gregory Ratoff *ph* Harry Stradling, Arthur Miller *md* David Raksin

☆ Loretta Young, Conrad Veidt, Dean Jagger, Eugenie Leontovich, Shepperd Strudwick, Otto Kruger, Paul Baratoff

Men in War

US   1957   104m   bw
Security (Sidney Harmon)

Korea 1950: an infantry platoon is cut off from HQ and tries to take an enemy-occupied hill.
Stereotyped small-scale war heroics; the film makes its points but fails to entertain.
w Philip Yordan *novel* Day without End by Van van Praag *d* Anthony Mann *ph* Ernest Haller *m* Elmer Bernstein

☆ Robert Ryan, Robert Keith, Aldo Ray, Vic Morrow, James Edwards, Sen Yung

Men in White *

US   1934   80m   bw
MGM (Monta Bell)

An ambitious intern is in love with an attractive socialite who resents his devotion to duty.
Popular but obvious star drama.
w Waldemar Young *play* Sidney Kingsley *d* Richard Boleslawski *ph* George Folsey

☆ Clark Gable, Myrna Loy, Jean Hersholt, Elizabeth Allan, Otto Kruger, C. Henry Gordon, Wallace Ford

'Belongs in the strictly adult class of pictures ... show spells money from plenty of angles.' – *Variety*

Men Must Fight

US   1933   73m   bw
MGM

War comes to New York in 1940.
A forgotten pacifist tract which trod the same paths as did H. G. Wells; of historical interest only apart from a spectacular air raid climax.
w S. K. Lauren, Reginald Lawrence, C. Gardner Sullivan *d* Edgar Selwyn

☆ Robert Young, Diana Wynyard, May Robson, Phillips Holmes, Lewis Stone

Men o' War *

👫 US   1929   20m   bw
Hal Roach

Two sailors and two girls have adventures in a park.
Simple-minded early talkie star comedy featuring their famous soda fountain routine.
w H. M. Walker *d* Lewis R. Foster *ph* George Stevens, Jack Roach *ed* Richard Currier

☆ Stan Laurel, Oliver Hardy, James Finlayson, Anne Cornwall, Gloria Greer

Men of Boys' Town

US   1941   106m   bw
MGM (John W. Considine Jnr)

Further adventures of Father Flanagan.
Mushy sequel to Boys' Town (qv).
w James Kevin McGuinness *d* Norman Taurog *ph* Harold Rosson *m* Herbert Stothart

☆ Spencer Tracy, Mickey Rooney, Bobs Watson, Larry Nunn, Lee J. Cobb, Mary Nash, Henry O'Neill, Darryl Hickman, Anne Revere

---

Men of Means

Canada 1999 80m colour
Libra/Producers Network (Daniel D'Or, G. Philip Jackson)

In New York, a loan shark for the mob begins to develop a conscience and decides it is time to find another line of work.
Thuggish chase-thriller, of unpleasant people being nasty to one another; there are many better ways of passing the time.
w Shane Perez d George Mendeluk ph Ludek Bogner m Donald Quan pd Thomas Carnegie ed John Whitcher
☆ Michael Paré, Kaela Dobkin, Raymond Serra, Austin Pendleton, Mark Hutchinson, Tony Cucci, Ron Holgate, Tie Domi

Men of Respect

US 1990 113m colour
Central City/Arthur Goldblatt (Ephraim Horowitz)

Told by a fortune-teller that he will become the next Mafia Godfather, a gangster is urged by his wife to make sure the prediction comes true.
Shakespeare's Macbeth is the inspiration for this odd little thriller, with the plot sticking close to the original and some of the dialogue being repeated virtually word for word. But guilt over a murder seems an unlikely emotion for a hitman to feel.
wd William Reilly ph Bobby Bukowski m Misha Segal ad William Barclay ed Elizabeth Kling
☆ Jim Turturro, Katherine Borowitz, Dennis Farina, Peter Boyle, Rod Steiger
'One has the feeling of watching an end-of-the-term show at Yale Drama School.' – *Philip French, Observer*
† An earlier thriller, *Joe Macbeth* (qv), also borrowed its plot from Shakespeare's play.

Men of Sherwood Forest

GB 1954 77m Eastmancolor
Hammer (Michael Carreras)
Robin Hood frees King Richard from bondage.
Fairly lively adventure romp on a low level.
w Allan MacKinnon d Val Guest ph Jimmy Harvey m Doreen Corwithen
☆ Don Taylor, Reginald Beckwith, Eileen Moore, David King-Wood, Patrick Holt, John Van Eyssen

Men of Texas

US 1942 81m bw
Universal (George Waggner)
At the end of the American Civil War, a Chicago journalist and a photographer are sent to Texas to find Sam Houston and discover an outlaw gang pretending to be patriots.
Flag-waving minor Western, quite lively when not overearnest.
w Harold Shumate, Richard Brooks d Ray Enright ph Milton Krasner md Edward Ward ad Jack Otterson ed Clarence Kolster
☆ Robert Stack, Broderick Crawford, Jackie Cooper, Anne Gwynne, Ralph Bellamy, Jane Darwell, Leo Carillo, John Litel

Men of the Fighting Lady

US 1954 80m Anscocolor
MGM (Henry Berman)
Adventures of an aircraft carrier during the Korean War.
Tepid war actioner with a few effective semi-documentary sequences of naval tactics.
w Art Cohn d Andrew Marton ph George Folsey m Miklos Rozsa
☆ Van Johnson, Walter Pidgeon, Louis Calhern, Dewey Martin, Keenan Wynn, Frank Lovejoy, Robert Horton

Men of the Sea: see Midshipman Easy

Men of Tomorrow

GB 1932 88m bw
Paramount/London Films (Alexander Korda)
Oxford students have more than academic work on their minds.
Dim comedy-drama with an interesting cast.
w Arthur Wimperis, Anthony Gibbs play *Young Apollo* by Anthony Gibbs d Leontine Sagan, Zoltan Korda ph Bernard Browne ad Vincent Korda ed Leontine Sagan
☆ Maurice Braddell, Joan Gardner, Emlyn Williams, Merle Oberon, Robert Donat

Men of Two Worlds

GB 1946 109m Technicolor
GFD/Two Cities (John Sutro)

US title: *Witch Doctor*
aka: *Kisenga, Man of Africa*
In Tanganyika, an educated native helps white men to counter the force of witch doctors and persuade tribes to leave an infected area.
Earnest but totally unpersuasive semi-documentary shot in unconvincing sets and garish colour.
w Thorold Dickinson, Joyce Cary, E. Arnot Robertson, Herbert Victor d Thorold Dickinson ph Geoffrey Unsworth, Desmond Dickinson m Arthur Bliss
☆ Eric Portman, Phyllis Calvert, Robert Adams, Orlando Martins, Arnold Marle, Cathleen Nesbitt, David Horne, Cyril Raymond

Men of War

US 1994 99m DeLuxe
MDP/Pomerance/Grandview Avenue (Arthur Goldblatt, Andrew Pfeffer)

A Swedish mercenary has a change of heart after hiring a gang of thugs to persuade some islanders in the South China Sea to part with their mining rights.
An action film that tries for a little originality and even wit in dealing with matters of morality versus expediency, but settles in the end for the usual over-the-top psychopathic villain and a gloating emphasis on violence.
w John Sayles, Ethan Reiff, Cyrus Voris story Stan Rogow d Perry Lang ph Ronn Schmidt m Gerald Gouriet pd Steve Spence, Jim Newport ed Jeffrey Reiner
☆ Dolph Lundgren, Charlotte Lewis, B. D. Wong, Anthony John Denison, Tim Guinee, Don Harvey, Trevor Goddard, Kevin Tighe
'Shot from an intelligent, witty, cliché-overturning script and featuring lashings of gritty violence, this is an action gem.' – *Film Review*

Men of Yesterday

GB 1936 82m bw
UK Films
Old army rivalries die down at a reunion.
Dated but interesting drama with interpolated variety talent.
w Gerald Elliott, Jack Francis d John Baxter
☆ Stewart Rome, Sam Livesey, Hay Petrie, Cecil Parker, George Robey, Ella Shields, Will Fyffe, Dick Henderson

Men on Her Mind: see The Girl from Tenth Avenue

Men with Guns *

US 1997 126m Technicolor
Lexington Road/Clear Blue Sky/IFC/Anarchists' Convention (R. Paul Miller, Maggie Renzi)
An ageing doctor goes to visit some former students, now working in poor villages, and discovers that they have been killed by those in authority.
A Spanish-language film from an American director, though not obviously set in any particular country; its narrative, about a man whose eyes are opened to the atrocities he has deliberately ignored, is a simple one, but told with feeling.
wd John Sayles ph Slawomir Idziak m Mason Daring pd Felipe Fernandez Del Paso ed John Sayles
☆ Federico Luppi, Damian Delgado, Dan Rivera, Tania Cruz, Damian Alcazar, Mandy Patinkin, Kathryn Grody, Iguandili Lopez, Nandi Luna Ramirez, Rafael de Quevedo, Roberto Sosa
'An absorbing, thoughtful and thoroughly rewarding watch.' – *Ian Freer, Empire*

'Dreamers Who Dare To Make Their Dreams Come True...'
Men with Wings

US 1938 106m Technicolor
Paramount (William Wellman)
Civil aviation pioneers fall out over a girl.
Disappointing epic from the maker of Wings, with highly predictable story line, modest acting and ho-hum spectacle.
w Robert Carson d William Wellman ph W. Howard Greene m W. Franke Harling, Gerard Carbonara
☆ Fred MacMurray, Ray Milland, Louise Campbell, Andy Devine, Lynne Overman, Porter Hall, Walter Abel, Virginia Weidler, Donald O'Connor
'To all women who love and admire the fearless heroes of the air, and who, with brave hearts, encourage them, hope, and pray for them.' – *director's dedication*
'Lavish air spectacle in Technicolor that means big business ... it will triumph through rain, sleet or snow.' – *Variety*

'Give the rats a taste of their own medicine!'
Men without Names

US 1935 67m bw
Paramount
Bank robbers are cornered in a small town and picked off by the FBI.
Routine crime feature, less exciting than it sounds.
w Marguerite Roberts, Kubec Glasmon, Dale Van Every d Ralph Murphy
☆ Fred MacMurray, Madge Evans, Lynne Overman, David Holt, John Wray, Dean Jagger
'Another of the new gangster films, and too flimsy. Grooved for the pops.' – *Variety*

Men without Women

US 1930 77m bw
Fox
Men in a submarine are trapped on the ocean bed.
Early talkie action drama noted more for its credits than its accomplishment.
w Dudley Nichols d John Ford ph Joseph H. August
☆ Kenneth MacKenna, Frank Albertson, Paul Page, Pat Somerset, Stuart Erwin, Warren Hymer, John Wayne
'Stunning, realistic picture that will make talk.' – *Variety*

Men Women: A User's Manual **

France 1996 122m colour 'Scope
Gala/UFD/Films 13/TF1/Canal+ (Claude Lelouch)

original title: *Hommes Femmes: Mode d'emploi*
An actor-turned-cop and an adulterous and successful businessman are among those who experience the trials of love, chance and betrayal.
Subtitled 'an inhuman comedy', this is an engrossing account about the loss of love and the search for it; despite the title, its perspective is a masculine one.
w Claude Lelouch, Rene Bonnell, Jean-Philippe Chatrier d Claude Lelouch ph Claude Lelouch, Philippe Pavans de Ceccatty m Francis Lai pd Jacques Bufnoir
☆ Fabrice Luchini, Bernard Tapie, Alessandra Martines, Pierre Arditi, Carlone Cellier, Ticky Holgado, Ophélie Winter, Anouk Aimée, Patrick Husson, Salome
'The intricate and suspense-laced narrative is a satisfying puzzle full of funny touches, just-missed opportunities and a few short cuts in social Darwinism.' – *Lisa Nesselson, Variety*
† Bernard Tapie, a controversial French businessman, had not acted before being cast in one of the leading roles, as a controversial businessman.

Menace

US 1934 58m bw
Paramount
Murders follow the suicide of a mining engineer.
Compact little dark house thriller with good stagey performances.
w Chandler Sprague, Anthony Veiller story Philip MacDonald d Ralph Murphy
☆ Gertrude Michael, Paul Cavanagh, Henrietta Crosman, John Lodge, Ray Milland, Berton Churchill, Halliwell Hobbes
'A pat specimen of the mystery film, expertly manipulated.' – *Variety*

The Menace

US 1932 64m bw
Columbia
A convict escapes, gets a new face through plastic surgery, and plans his revenge.
Muddled melodrama.
w Dorothy Howell, Charles Logue, Roy Chanslor novel *Feathered Serpent* by Edgar Wallace d Roy William Neill
☆ Walter Byron, H. B. Warner, Bette Davis, Natalie Moorhead, William Davidson, Halliwell Hobbes
'A halting and frequently clumsy development leads to a weak climax.' – *Variety*

'This is the truth. This is what's real.'
Menace II Society *

US 1993 97m Foto-Kem
First Independent/New Line (Darin Scott)

In the Watts district of Los Angeles, young blacks become involved in robbery and murder.
A harsh and violent movie that sticks close to the expectations of gangster films while claiming to be dealing with reality; its young directors show promise.
w Tyger Williams, Allen Hughes, Albert Hughes d Allen Hughes, Albert Hughes ph Lisa Rinzler m QD III pd Penny Barrett ed Christopher Koefoed
☆ Tyrin Turner, Jada Pinkett, Larenz Tate, Arnold Johnson, MC Eiht, Marilyn Coleman, Vonte Sweet, Clifton Powell, Samuel L. Jackson
'The clichés of racial stereotyping lie piled as high as the bodies ... It's a dreadfully inflammatory film to bring to our society. Hollywood is exporting too many of America's menaces.' – *Alexander Walker, London Evening Standard*
'A grim, nihilistic trip to the inner city ... Fierce, violent and searing in its observation, the film makes all previous excursions seem like a walk in the park.' – *Variety*

Menilmontant *

France 1924 50m bw silent
Dimitri Kirsanov (for his own company)
Respected but fairly impenetrable piece of avant-garde which appears to be about two sisters haunted by memories of the murder of their parents, for which they may or may not have been responsible.
wd *Dimitri Kirsanov* ed Dimitri Kirsanov
'A flurry of hand-held camera shots, incisive montages and elliptical progressions.' – *Geoff Brown, MFB, 1981*

The Men's Club

US 1986 100m colour
Atlantic Releasing/Howard Gottfried

Friends nearing forty get together and bemoan their lot.
Curious, talky, rather dreary piece which gets almost nowhere.
w Leonard Michaels novel Leonard Michaels d Peter Medak ph John Fleckenstein m Lee Holdridge pd Ken Davis ed Cynthia Scheider, David Dresser, Bill Butler
☆ Roy Scheider, Frank Langella, Harvey Keitel, Treat Williams, Richard Jordan, David Dukes, Craig Wasson, Stockard Channing, Jennifer Jason Leigh
'A club few will want to join ... a distasteful piece of work that displays the worst in men.' – *Variety*

Menschen am Sonntag: see People on Sunday

Mensonge *

France 1993 89m colour
Gala/Cuel Lavalette/France-3/Alain Sarde

aka: *The Lie*
A faithful wife discovers that she is both pregnant and HIV positive.
Interesting, though too easily resolved, exploration of relationships and the effect of AIDS on those innocently involved.
w Denis Saada, François Margolin d François Margolin ph Caroline Champetier pd Julie Sfez, Arnaud de Moleron ed Martine Giordano
☆ Nathalie Baye, Didier Sandre, Hélène Lapiower, Marc Citti, Dominique Besnehard, Christophe Bourseiller, Louis Ducreux, Adrien Beau
'Rather than flagging the disease as a metaphor of sanctification-through-degradation, it rolls it into a disease-of-the-week movie and uses it as a trigger for tears, lots of talk, pat ironies and soapy symbolism. And on that level, it's actually quite accomplished.' – *Steve Beard, Empire*

Mephisto ****

Hungary 1981 144m Eastmancolor
Mafilm/Manfred Durniok

In Germany in the twenties, an actor committed to the idea of a workers' theatre becomes a puppet of the Nazis.

Chilling and fiercely compelling melodrama of moral corruption, with a bravura performance from Brandauer as a man who willingly sells his soul.
w Peter Dobai, Istvan Szabo *novel* Klaus Mann d Istvan Szabo *ph* Lajos Koltai *m* Zdenko Tamassy

☆ Klaus Maria Brandauer, Ildikó Bánsági, Krystyna Janda

🏆 best foreign film

The Mephisto Waltz *
US 1971 109m DeLuxe
TCF/QM Productions
▣ ◖
A satanic concert pianist on the point of death wills his soul into the body of a journalist.
Complex diabolical mumbo-jumbo with plenty of style.
w Ben Maddow *novel* Fred Mustard Stewart d Paul Wendkos *ph* William H. Spencer *m* Jerry Goldsmith

☆ Alan Alda, Jacqueline Bisset, Curt Jurgens, Barbara Parkins

Le Mépris: see *Contempt*

La Mer Cruelle
Kuwait 1983 107m bw
Sakr Films (Abbas Redha, Hassan Redha)
original title: Bas Ya Bahar
aka: Sea of Silence
In Kuwait before the discovery of oil, a youth becomes a pearl diver against his father's wishes.
Competent, but slow-moving and of interest mainly for its documentary content.
w Rahman Saleh d Khalid Al Siddiq *ph* Tanfig Al Amir *m* Abu Tariq *ed* Hassanof

☆ Saad Al Faraj, Mohammed Al Mansour, Hayat Al Fahd

The Mercenaries
GB 1968 100m Metrocolor Panavision
MGM/George Englund
US title: Dark of the Sun
In the Belgian Congo in 1960 a mercenary officer is ordered to bring back a fortune in diamonds by armoured train.
Basically an old-fashioned thriller about the hazards of a journey beset by brutish villains and damsels in distress, this unpleasant film is notable for the amount of sadistic action it crams into its running time.
w Quentin Werty, Adrian Spies *novel* Dark of the Sun by Wilbur Smith d Jack Cardiff *ph* Edward Scaife *m* Jacques Loussier *ed* Ernest Walter

☆ Rod Taylor, Yvette Mimieux, Kenneth More, Jim Brown, Peter Carsten, André Morell, Guy Deghy, Calvin Lockhart, Alan Gifford

'The violence done to the human body is matched by violence done to the intelligence by a stock adventure story given a gloss of topicality and social insult.' – *Judith Crist*

The Mercenary
Italy/Spain 1968 103m Technicolor
Techniscope
United Artists/PEA/Delphos/Profilms 21 (Alberto Grimaldi)
▣
aka: A Professional Gun
In revolutionary Mexico, a European gunfighter hires himself out to a group of rebellious peasants and turns them into a rampaging army.
Violent, action-packed spaghetti Western in which all the protagonists are motivated by greed and a pleasure in killing.
w Luciano Vincenzoni, Sergio Spina, Adriano Bolzoni, Sergio Corbucci *story* Franco Solinas, Giorgio Arlorio d Sergio Corbucci *ph* Alejandro Ulloa *m* Ennio Morricone, Bruno Nicolai *ad* Luis Vazquez *ed* Eugenio Alabiso

☆ Franco Nero, Tony Musante, Jack Palance, Giovanna Ralli, Franco Giacobini, Eduardo Fajardo, Franco Bessel, Alvaro de Luna

† A sequel, *Companeros* (qv), followed in 1970.

Merci La Vie **
France 1991 119m Eastmancolor/bw
Cine Valse/Film par Film/Orly/DD/SEDIF/A2 (Barnard Marescot)
▣
A bored teenager befriends a girl with a venereal disease, who has been persuaded by a doctor to infect as many men as she can in order to provide him with patients.
Inventive, playful film which mixes the present day and the Nazi occupation of France, switching between

reality, day-dreams and movies in which the girls appear – though the final effect may be more exhausting than invigorating.
wd Bertrand Blier *ph* Philippe Rousselot *pd* Theobald Meurisse *ed* Claudine Merlin

☆ Charlotte Gainsbourg, Anouk Grinberg, Gérard Depardieu, Michael Blanc, Jean Carmet, Catherine Jacob, Annie Girardot, Jean-Louis Trintignant, Thierry Frémont

'A bold, often exciting, sometimes frustrating but always challenging pic.' – *Variety*
'The art-house equivalent of a Hollywood rollercoaster where sensation is all and decorous values – logic, good taste, some ultimate meaning – get trampled in the rush to amaze.' – *Geoff Brown, The Times*

Mercury Rising
US 1998 112m DeLuxe Panavision
Universal/Imagine (Brian Grazer, Karen Kehela)
▣ ▣ ◉ ◉ ◖
A maverick agent protects an autistic child whose gift for mathematics makes him a security risk.
A by-the-numbers action flick, through which Willis glowers ferociously.
w Lawrence Konner, Mark Rosenthal *novel* Simple Simon by Ryne Douglas Peardon d Harold Becker *ph* Michael Seresin *m* John Barry *pd* Patrizia von Brandenstein *ed* Peter Honess *sp* Industrial Light & Magic

☆ Bruce Willis, Alec Baldwin, Miko Hughes, Chi McBride, Kim Dickens, Robert Stanton, Bodhi Pine Elfman, Carrie Preston, L. L. Ginter, John Carroll Lynch, Peter Stormare

'A real pot-boiler.' – *Guardian*

Merely Mary Ann
US 1931 74m bw
Fox
The maid of all work falls for the gentleman lodger.
Cinderella stuff redesigned for two popular stars, but of no lasting appeal.
w Jules Furthman *story* Israel Zangwill d Henry King

☆ Janet Gaynor, Charles Farrell, Beryl Mercer, J. M. Kerrigan, G. P. Huntley Jnr

'Bound to pull after a summer of gang violence, mystery shockers, and much sex urge study.' – *Variety*

Mermaids
US 1990 110m colour
Rank/Orion (Lauren Lloyd, Wallis Nichita, Patrick Palmer)
▣ ▣ ◔ ◖
A daughter, torn between becoming a nun and her feelings for a handsome boy, resolves her difficulties with her flirtatious mother.
A romantic comedy uncertain whether it is trying for laughs or tears; it attempts, unsuccessfully, to settle for both.
w June Roberts *novel* Patty Dann d Richard Benjamin *ph* Howard Atherton *m* Jack Nitzsche *pd* Stuart Wurtzel *ed* Jacqueline Cambas

☆ Cher, Bob Hoskins, Winona Ryder, Michael Schoeffling, Christina Ricci, Caroline McWilliams, Jan Miner, Betsey Townsend

'It wavers between arch comedy and hollow melodrama, each desperately over-pitched.' – *Sight and Sound*

† Lasse Halstrom was replaced by Frank Oz as director before filming began. Two weeks after filming started, Richard Benjamin replaced Frank Oz. Winona Ryder's role as Cher's daughter was to have been played by Emily Lloyd until Cher objected that Lloyd did not look like her.

Merrill's Marauders *
US 1962 98m Technicolor Cinemascope
Warner/US Pictures (Milton Sperling)
▣ ▣ ◖
Adventures of a crack US army unit in 1942 Burma.
Physically exhausting war adventure with emphasis on hand-to-hand fighting and much bloodshed.
w Samuel Fuller, Milton Sperling *novel* Charlton Ogburn Jnr d Samuel Fuller *ph* William Clothier *m* Howard Jackson *ed* Folmar Blangsted

☆ Jeff Chandler, Ty Hardin, Andrew Duggan, Peter Brown, Will Hutchins, Claude Akins

Merrily We Go to Hell
US 1932 78m bw
Paramount
GB title: Merrily We Go to –
A socialite marries a dipsomaniac journalist.
Glum problem drama.
w Edwin Justus Mayer *novel* I Jerry Take Thee Joan by Cleo Lucas d Dorothy Arzner *ph* David Abel

☆ Sylvia Sidney, Fredric March, Adrianne Allen, Richard Gallagher, Florence Burton, Esther Howard, Kent Taylor

Merrily We Live *
US 1938 90m bw
Hal Roach
A zany family hires a chauffeur who is actually a famous writer posing as a tramp.
Quite likeable compound of My Man Godfrey and You Can't Take It with You.
w Eddie Moran, Jack Jevne d Norman Z. McLeod *ph* Norbert Brodine *md* Marvin Hatley *ad* Charles D. Hall

☆ Constance Bennett, Brian Aherne, Billie Burke, Alan Mowbray, Patsy Kelly, Ann Dvorak, Tom Brown, Bonita Granville, Marjorie Rambeau, Clarence Kolb

'In the high cost bracket and rates top billing when dualled, with a chance it is strong enough to carry first runs as a single.' – *Variety*
⚲ Norbert Brodine; Billie Burke; title song (mPhil Craig, lyArthur Quenzer); Charles D. Hall

Merry Andrew
👫 US 1958 103m Metrocolor
Cinemascope
MGM/Sol C. Siegel
A stuffy teacher in search of an ancient statue joins a travelling circus.
Deliberately charming star comedy which plumps too firmly for whimsy and, despite its professionalism, provokes barely a smile, let alone a laugh.
w Isobel Lennart, I. A. L. Diamond *story* Paul Gallico *ph* Robert Surtees *m* Saul Chaplin *d/ch* Michael Kidd *ly* Johnny Mercer

☆ Danny Kaye, Pier Angeli, Baccaloni, Noel Purcell, Robert Coote, Patricia Cutts, Rex Evans, Walter Kingsford, Tommy Rall, Rhys Williams

Merry Christmas, Mr Lawrence *
GB 1982 124m Eastmancolor
Recorded Picture/Cineventure/Oshima (Jeremy Thomas)
▣ ▣ ◖
In a Japanese prisoner-of-war camp in Java in 1942, an English captive strikes up a strange relationship with the commandant.
Uncomfortably titled and unavoidably downbeat character drama with some unpleasant moments; despite good work all round it seems to head straight for every cliché perpetuated by The Bridge on the River Kwai.
w Nagisa Oshima, Paul Mayersberg *novel* The Seed and the Sower by Laurens van der Post d Nagisa Oshima *ph* Toichiro Narushima *m* Ryuichi Sakamoto

☆ David Bowie, Tom Conti, Ryuichi Sakamoto, Takeshi, Jack Thompson, Johnny Okura, Alistair Browning

'It always seems like a cocktail of saleable ingredients rather than genuine cinema.' – *Sunday Times*
🎬 Ryuichi Sakamoto

Merry Comes to Town
GB 1937 79m bw
Embassy/Sound City
US title: Merry Comes to Stay
A professor's family is disappointed when a relative visiting from America turns out to be as poor as they are.
Thin, predictable comedy with the visitor finally hailed as a saviour.
w Evadne Price d George King

☆ ZaSu Pitts, Guy Newall, Betty Ann Davies, Muriel George, Basil Langton

'A pleasant comedy which will improve with cutting.' – *Variety*

The Merry Frinks
US 1934 68m bw
First National
GB title: Happy Family
A sportswriter down on his luck has a crazy family.
And didn't everybody in the mid-thirties? But this one is crazy without being very funny.

w Gene Markey, Kathryn Scola d Alfred E. Green

☆ Aline MacMahon, Guy Kibbee, Allen Jenkins, Hugh Herbert, Frankie Darro

'The most disagreeable family group since Three Cornered Moon. Poor comedy and lacks names.' – *Variety*

'A King's Ransom To Make America Laugh!'
Merry Go Round of 1938
US 1937 87m bw
Universal
Four vaudevillians adopt a small girl, and later head for Hollywood.
Sentimental farce with zany moments and an encouraging cast.
w Monte Brice, A. Dorian Otvos d Irving Cummings

☆ Jimmy Savo, Bert Lahr, Mischa Auer, Billy House, Alice Brady, Louise Fazenda

'First rate filmusical packed with laughs.' – *Variety*

The Merry Monahans
US 1944 90m bw
Universal (Michael Fessier, Ernest Pagano)
Adventures of a family of vaudeville performers.
Acceptable backstage comedy drama with good atmosphere.
w Michael Fessier, Ernest Pagano d Charles Lamont *ph* Charles Van Enger *m* Hans Salter

☆ Donald O'Connor, Jack Oakie, Rosemary de Camp, Peggy Ryan, Ann Blyth, Isabel Jewell, John Miljan
⚲ Hans Salter

A Merry War: see *Keep the Aspidistra Flying*

The Merry Widow *
US 1925 111m bw silent
MGM (Irving Thalberg)
A bankrupt king orders a nobleman to woo a wealthy American widow.
An operetta without music (or dialogue) is usually a poor thing, but the director added a few unpredictable touches.
w Erich von Stroheim, Benjamin Glazer *operetta* Victor Leon, Leo Stein d Erich von Stroheim *ph* Oliver Marsh, Ben Reynolds, William Daniels *m* William Axt, D. Mendoza

☆ Mae Murray, John Gilbert, Roy D'Arcy, Tully Marshall

† The story goes that when reproved by Thalberg for wasting film stock on, for instance, endless shots of a wardrobe full of shoes, von Stroheim remarked: 'The character has a foot fetish.' 'And you,' said Thalberg, 'have a footage fetish!'

'Surrender to the happy seduction of Ernst Lubitsch's most glorious picture holiday!'
The Merry Widow **
US 1934 99m bw
MGM
▣ ◔
Patchy, but sometimes sparkling version.
w Samson Raphaelson, Ernest Vajda d Ernst Lubitsch *ph* Oliver T. Marsh *m* Franz Lehar *ad* Cedric Gibbons, Frederic Hope

☆ Maurice Chevalier, Jeanette MacDonald, Edward Everett Horton, Una Merkel, George Barbier, Donald Meek, Sterling Holloway, Shirley Ross

'Fine all-around job and an entertainment natural.' – *Variety*
'It is Lubitsch; it is also Hollywood; it is the cream of the American bourgeois film. It is a charlotte russe.' – *Peter Ellis, New Masses*

🏆 art direction

The Merry Widow
US 1952 105m Technicolor
MGM (Joe Pasternak)
Chill, empty remake.
w Sonya Levien, William Ludwig d Curtis Bernhardt *ph* Robert Surtees

☆ Fernando Lamas, Lana Turner, Richard Haydn, Una Merkel, Thomas Gomez, John Abbott

'Nothing has been omitted (except the spirit of the original).' – *MFB*

† Lana Turner's singing was dubbed by Trudy Erwin.

The Merry Wives of Reno *

US 1934 61m bw
Warner

Three couples go to a Reno hotel to get a divorce.

Amusing but scrappy comedy in the vein of the successful Convention City.

w Robert Lord d H. Bruce Humberstone
☆ Margaret Lindsay, Donald Woods, Guy Kibbee, Glenda Farrell, Ruth Donnelly, Hugh Herbert, Frank McHugh, Roscoe Ates, Hobart Cavanaugh
'Stylized farce with excellent cast and considerable humour.' – *Variety*

Merton of the Movies *

US 1947 82m bw
MGM

An innocent young man in Hollywood becomes a star.

The plot and characterizations of this old chestnut are resistible, but the Hollywood background is well managed and convincing.

w George Wells, Lou Breslow *novel* Harry Leon Wilson d Robert Alton ph Paul C. Vogel m David Snell
☆ Red Skelton, Virginia O'Brien, Alan Mowbray, Gloria Grahame, Leon Ames
† There were previous versions in 1924 and (as *Make Me a Star*) in 1932.

Mery per sempre

Italy 1988 106m Telecolor
BFI/Numero Uno (Claudio Bonivento)
aka: *Forever Mary*
aka: *Mary Forever*

In Sicily, a new liberal teacher at a reform school tries to win over the tough and suspicious pupils.

Downbeat documentary-style movie that substitutes earnestness for art.

w Sandro Petraglia, Stefano Rulli *novel* Aurelio Grimaldi d Marco Risi ph Mauro Marchetti m Giancarlo Bigazzi ad Massimo Spano ed Claudio Di Mauro
☆ Michele Placido, Claudio Amendola, Francesco Benigno, Alessandro Di Sanzo

Mes Petites Amoureuses

France 1975 123m Eastmancolor
Gala/Elite (Pierre Cottrell)

A sex-obsessed schoolboy finds life full of frustrations when he goes to live with his mother and her Spanish lover.

A long-winded exploration of adolescence, which offers no fresh insights.

wd Jean Eustache ph Nestor Almendros ed Françoise Belleville, Alberto Yacelini, Vincent Cottrell
☆ Martin Loeb, Ingrid Caven, Jacqueline Dufranne, Dionys Mascolo, Henri Martinez, Pierre Edelman, Maurice Pialat

Mesa of Lost Women

US 1952 70m bw
Wade Williams Productions/Howco (G. William Perkins, Melvin Gordon)

A scientist experiments in the Mexican desert to combine the qualities of beautiful women and spiders.

Bizarre B-movie, ineptly directed, with portentous voice-over, a score played by piano and guitar, and two mad scientists, one of them one-eyed, as well as scantily clad female assistants and dwarfs, operating from a laboratory carved into a mountainside. It also has what may be the least erotic would-be seductive dance on film.

w Herbert Tevos d Herbert Tevos, Ron Ormond ph Karl Struss, Gil Warrenton m Hoyt S. Curtin ed W. Donn Hayes, Hugh Winn, Ray H. Lockert
☆ Jackie Coogan, Allan Nixon, Richard Travis, Mary Hill, Robert Knapp, Tandra Quinn
'A really barmy B-movie that has to be seen to be disbelieved.' – *The Dark Side*

The Message: see Mohammed, Messenger of God

Message in a Bottle

US 1999 132m Technicolor Panavision
Warner/Bel-Air/Tig (Denise Di Novi, Jim Wilson, Kevin Costner)

A female reporter finds a love letter in a bottle on a beach and traces the man who sent it.

Soporific and soft-centred romantic drama that is yet another nail in the coffin of Costner's career.

w Gerald DiPego *novel* Nicholas Sparks d Luis Mandoki ph Caleb Deschanel m Gabriel Yared pd Jeffrey Beecroft ed Steven Weisberg
☆ Kevin Costner, Robin Wright Penn, John Savage, Illeana Douglas, Robbie Coltrane, Paul Newman, Jesse James, Bethel Leslie, Tom Aldredge, Viveka Davis
'A prettily torpid film with the warm glow of a hazelnut coffee commercial.' – *Janet Maslin, New York Times*
'Dreary, lachrymose and incredibly poky tear-jerker.' – *Todd McCarthy, Variety*

A Message to Garcia *

US 1936 86m bw
TCF (Raymond Griffith)

During the Spanish-American war a Cuban girl helps an American agent get through to the rebel leader with a diplomatic message.

Agreeable embroidery of a historical incident: good production values and entertaining star performances.

w W. P. Lipscomb, Gene Fowler *book* Andrew S. Rowan d George Marshall ph Rudolph Maté md Louis Silvers ad William Darling
☆ Wallace Beery, Barbara Stanwyck, John Boles, Alan Hale, Herbert Mundin, Mona Barrie

The Messenger: The Story Of Joan Of Arc *

France 1999 158m colour Technovision
Columbia/Gaumont (Patrice Ledoux)

GB title: *Joan of Arc*

In the 15th century, a young girl, traumatised by the rape and murder of her sister by English soldiers, hears voices telling her to rid France of invaders and put the Dauphin on the throne.

Besson's action-film approach really needed Arnold Schwarzenegger in the title role to make it credible; here he concentrates on the spectacle and lets his cast do what they will, which is overact.

w Andrew Birkin, Luc Besson d Luc Besson ph Thierry Arbogast m Eric Serra pd Hugues Tissandier ed Sylvie Landra
☆ Milla Jovovich, John Malkovich, Dustin Hoffman, Faye Dunaway, Pascal Greggory, Vincent Cassel, Tcheky Karyo, Richard Ridings, Desmond Harrington
'Both visually spectacular and staggeringly awful: a sense-pummeling, mind-numbing feast of bad ideas and laughable performances.' – *Michael Wilmington, Chicago Tribune*
'The lack of a plausible leading lady is enough to sink what is otherwise an eye-catching, although heavily '90s-style, telling of one of history's most frequently filmed stories.' – *Todd McCarthy, Variety*

'It's five miles wide ... It's coming at 30,000 mph ... and there's no place on Earth to hide!'

Meteor

US 1979 107m Movielab Panavision
Palladium (Sandy Howard, Gabriel Katzka)

A huge meteor, preceded by dangerous fragments, heads relentlessly towards Earth…

Talkative disaster movie with occasional moments of interest.

w Stanley Mann, Edmund H. North d Ronald Neame ph Paul Lohmann m Laurence Rosenthal *visual effects* Margo Anderson, William Cruse
☆ Sean Connery, Natalie Wood, Karl Malden, Brian Keith, Martin Landau, Trevor Howard, Henry Fonda, Joseph Campanella
'There are moments that make Godzilla look like a masterpiece.' – *Boxoffice*

The Meteor Man

US 1993 99m DeLuxe
MGM/Tinsel Townsend (Loretha C. Jones)

A schoolteacher hit by a meteor acquires super-human powers and begins to clean up his gang-ridden neighbourhood.

Mild morality tale for our times, pleasant enough, but it lacks impact.

wd Robert Townsend ph John A. Alonzo m Cliff Eidelman pd Toby Corbett ed Adam Bernardi sp Industrial Light and Magic
☆ Robert Townsend, Marla Gibbs, Eddie Griffin, Robert Guillaume, James Earl Jones, Bill Cosby, Frank Gorshin

'A cute skit expanded out of all proportion for the big screen.' – *Variety*
'Townsend's good nature will win most audiences over.' – *Adam Mars-Jones*

'Life Is A Negotiation.'

Metro

US 1997 117m Technicolor
Buena Vista/Touchstone/Caravan (Roger Birnbaum)

In San Francisco, a police hostage negotiator becomes involved in a battle of wits with a murderous jewel thief.

Murphy returns to familiar ground, as a smart, wise-cracking cop, but the style has worn thin through overuse; cast and director go through their predictable motions in an efficient but uninspired manner.

w Randy Feldman d Thomas Carter ph Fred Murphy m Steve Porcaro pd William Elliott ed Peter E. Berger
☆ Eddie Murphy, Michael Rapaport, Michael Wincott, Carmen Ejogo, Denis Arndt, Art Evans, Donal Logue, Paul Ben-Victor, Kim Miyori
'This formulaic ordeal – a notably sadistic exercise involving lots of beating, shooting, and stabbing.' – *Lisa Schwarzbaum, Entertainment Weekly*

Metroland

GB/Germany 1997 105m colour
Pandora/Blue Horizon/Mact/Filmania/BBC/Sogepaq (Andrew Bendel)

When an old friend from his bachelor days in Paris comes calling, a young advertising executive begins to have doubts about his settled life with a wife and young daughter.

Slight drama about the pull between a bourgeois and a bohemian existence; but there's something wrong when the only felt emotion comes in a vignette from John Wood as a teetotal commuter retiring after 42 years in the same firm with a farewell gift of a whisky decanter.

w Adrian Hodges *novel* Julian Barnes d Philip Saville ph Jean-François Robin m Mark Knopfler pd Don Taylor ed Greg Miller
☆ Christian Bale, Lee Ross, Emily Watson, Elsa Zylberstein, Rufus, Jonathan Aris, Ifan Meredith, Amanda Ryan, John Wood
'The film alternately whines and whimpers its way to a soporific end.' – *Demetrios Matheou, Sight and Sound*

Metropolis ***

Germany 1926 120m bw silent
UFA (Erich Pommer)

In the year 2000, the workers in a modernistic city live underground and unrest is quelled by the persuasion of a saintly girl, Maria; but a mad inventor creates an evil Maria to incite them to revolt.

Always somewhat overlong, and certainly heavy-going in places, this futuristic fantasy not only has many brilliant sequences which created genuine excitement and terror, but it inspired a great many Hollywood clichés to come, notably the Frankenstein theme. The BBC's version of the seventies, with an electronic music sound track, is the most satisfactory.

w Thea von Harbou d Fritz Lang ph Karl Freund, Günther Rittau ad Otto Hunte, Erich Kettelhut, Karl Volbrecht sp Eugene Schüfftan
☆ Brigitte Helm, Alfred Abel, Gustav Fröhlich, Rudolf Klein-Rogge, Fritz Rasp
'It goes too far and always gets away with it.' – *New Yorker, 1978*
'A wonderful, stupefying folly.' – *New Yorker, 1982*
† In 1984 Giorgio Moroder put out his own new version, with tinted sequences and a re-edited running time of 83 minutes. It was received with a mixture of distaste, respect and caution. The latest version on video is 139m long.

Metropolitan *

US 1935 79m bw
TCF (Darryl F. Zanuck)

A capricious prima donna walks out of the Metropolitan Opera and forms her own company.

Earnest and well-made melodrama with song; it earned critical plaudits but was a disappointment at the box-office.

w Bess Meredyth, George Marion Jnr d Richard Boleslawski ph Rudolph Maté md Alfred Newman

☆ Lawrence Tibbett, Alice Brady, Virginia Bruce, Cesar Romero, Thurston Hall, Luis Alberni
'Tibbett and exploitation should carry so-so operatic story into fair money.' – *Variety*

Metropolitan ***

US 1989 98m DuArt
Mainline/Westerly Film-Video/Allagash Films (Whit Stillman)

A left-wing student becomes a member of a group of rich young people intent on having a good time.

A conversation piece with wit and style to recommend it.

wd Whit Stillman ph John Thomas m Mark Suozzo, Tom Judson ed Christopher Tellefsen
☆ Carolyn Farina, Edward Clements, Christopher Eigeman, Taylor Nichols, Allison Rutledge-Parisi, Dylan Hundley, Isabel Gillies, Bryan Leder, Will Kempe
'A cast of attractive young newcomers plays out this ironic, arch, gently mocking and refreshingly original comedy with confident style.' – *David Robinson, The Times*
⅋ best original screenplay

Meurtres *

France 1950 91m bw
Cité Film/Fides

A doctor's wife suffering from an incurable illness begs him to give her an overdose of morphia; he does so and proposes to give himself up for murder; his family, afraid of scandal, try to have him certified.

A distinct change of pace for a star comedian, and not an unsuccessful one, though the satire is rather crudely handled.

w Charles Plisnier, Maurice Barry d Richard Pottier ph André Germain m Raymond Legrand
☆ Fernandel, Raymond Souplex, Jacques Varennes, Jeanne Moreau

Mexican Hayride

US 1948 77m bw
Universal (Robert Arthur)

Various swindlers come together at a Mexican bullfight.

A Cole Porter Broadway musical without the music makes an odd sort of vehicle for Abbott and Costello, but they inject a few good vaudeville gags.

w Oscar Brodney, John Grant *play* Herbert and Dorothy Fields d Charles Barton ph Charles Van Enger
☆ Bud Abbott, Lou Costello, Virginia Grey, John Hubbard, Pedro de Cordoba, Fritz Feld, Luba Malina

Mexican Manhunt

US 1953 73m bw
Lindsley Parsons/AA

A detective helps solve an old crime.

Routine support which coasts along on the strength of its star.

w George Bricker d Rex Bailey ph William Sickner md Edward Kay
☆ George Brent, Hillary Brooke, Morris Ankrum, Karen Sharpe, Marjorie Lord

Mexican Spitfire

A series of second feature comedies nominally about a young businessman and his temperamental Mexican wife (Donald Woods and Lupe Velez), whose interest shifted firmly to the young man's accident-prone uncle Matt and his aristocratic boss Lord Epping, both of whom were played by the rubber-legged Ziegfeld comic Leon Errol at something near the top of his form. The plots made little sense, but the hectic situations provoked hearty roars of laughter. The films were all made by RKO, and all directed by Leslie Goodwins.

1939 The Girl from Mexico, Mexican Spitfire
1940 Mexican Spitfire Out West
1941 Mexican Spitfire's Baby, Mexican Spitfire at Sea
1942 Mexican Spitfire Sees a Ghost, Mexican Spitfire's Elephant
1943 Mexican Spitfire's Blessed Event

Mexicana

US 1945 83m bw
Republic (Alfred Santell)

The Frank Sinatra of Mexico is beset by bobbysoxers.

Thin excuse for a moderate musical.
w Frank Gill Jnr d Alfred Santell
☆ Tito Guizar, Constance Moore, Leo Carrillo, Howard Freeman, Steve Geray, Estelita Rodriguez

MGM's Big Parade of Comedy: see *The Big Parade of Comedy*

Mi Familia: see *My Family*

Mi Vida Loca: see *My Crazy Life*

Mia Eoniotita Ke Mia Mera: see *Eternity and a Day*

**Miami Blues ** **
US   1990   97m
Rank/Orion/Tristes Tropiques (Jonathan Demme, Gary Goetzman)
▣ ▤ ◎~ ◉
A dogged policeman follows the trail of a murderous criminal who pretends to be an undercover cop.
Slick thriller with an undercurrent of lugubrious black humour.
wd George Armitage *novel* Charles Willeford ph Tak Fujimoto m Gary Chang pd Maher Ahmad ed Craig McKay, Bill Johnson
☆ Fred Ward, Jennifer Jason Leigh, Alec Baldwin, Cecilia Perez-Cervera, Georgie Cranford, Edward Saxon, Jose Perez, Obba Babatunde

'America's playground becomes gang war battleground!'
Miami Exposé
US   1956   74m   bw
Columbia (Sam Katzman)
An undercover policeman cracks down on a vice operation.
Routine thick ear with more suspense than sense.
w James B. Gordon d Fred F. Sears ph Benjamin Kline md Mischa Bakaleinikoff
☆ Lee J. Cobb, Patricia Medina, Edward Arnold

'Love is great. Marriage is a completely different affair.'
**Miami Rhapsody ** **
US   1995   95m   Technicolor
Buena Vista/Hollywood/Cantaloupe (Barry Jossen, David Frankel)
▣ ▤ ◎~ ◉
A woman contemplating marriage observes the marital errors being committed by her siblings and friends.
Deft and observant comedy of relationships, smartly done and neatly worked out; the style is close to Woody Allen's, but lusher.
wd David Frankel ph Jack Wallner m Mark Isham pd J. Mark Harrington ed Steven Weisberg
☆ Sarah Jessica Parker, Gil Bellows, Antonio Banderas, Mia Farrow, Paul Mazursky, Kevin Pollak, Barbara Garrick, Naomi Campbell
'No more than superior American sitcom, and the film's wit goes no further than its immaculately tasteful interiors. But it was fun while it lasted, and, anyway, maybe it was never meant to be a long-term-commitment kind of thing.' – *Tom Shone, Sunday Times*
'An upscale Saturday date movie: not great but polished, amusing and above all competent – a quality which, these days, gives it a head start on most other comers.' – *Sheila Johnston, Independent*

The Miami Story
US   1954   75m   bw
Columbia (Sam Katzman)
The syndicate is cracked by a reformed gangster.
Routine gangster alarms and excursions, like an extended Crime Does Not Pay.
w Robert E. Kent d Fred F. Sears ph Henry Freulich m Mischa Bakaleinikoff
☆ Barry Sullivan, Luther Adler, John Baer, Adele Jergens, Beverly Garland

'He's an angel ... Not a saint.'
Michael
US   1996   105m   Technicolor
Rank/Castle Rock/Turner/Alphaville (Sean Daniel, Nora Ephron, James Jacks)
▣ ▤ ◎~ ◉
Tabloid reporters discover an angel, who turns out to be a charming, beer-swilling, womanizing slob.
Hellish attempt at a romantic comedy, in which unpleasant characters behave badly and fall in love.

w Nora Ephron, Delia Ephron, Peter Dexter, Jim Quinlan d Nora Ephron ph John Lindley m Randy Newman pd Dan Davis ed Geraldine Peroni
☆ John Travolta, Andie MacDowell, William Hurt, Bob Hoskins, Robert Pastorelli, Jean Stapleton, Teri Garr
'At once underwritten and overwritten. Rowdy, slapdash and unevenly directed, the movie is basically a collection of episodes tied together with a flimsy string.' – *Emanuel Levy, Variety*

Michael and Mary
GB   1931   85m   bw
Gaumont
A husband thought dead for many years returns to disturb his wife's second marriage.
Acceptable comedy from a popular stage play; it headed its stars towards Hollywood.
w Angus MacPhail, Robert Stevenson, Lajos Biro *play* A. A. Milne d Victor Saville
☆ Herbert Marshall, Edna Best, Elizabeth Allan, Frank Lawton, D. A. Clarke-Smith

'An Epic Tale Of Passion And Destiny.'
**Michael Collins ** *
US   1996   132m   Technicolor
Warner/Geffen (Stephen Woolley)
▣ ▤ ◎~ ◉
Following the failure of the 1916 rising against the British, Michael Collins becomes a leading figure in the Irish Republican Army and, after negotiating the Anglo-Irish treaty, is repudiated by his former colleagues and assassinated.
Effective and dramatic political drama that simplifies the facts and has at its centre a glaring gap – Collins's negotiations with the British – into which the narrative unfortunately collapses.
wd Neil Jordan ph Chris Menges m Elliot Goldenthal pd Antony Pratt ed J. Patrick Duffner, Tony Lawson
☆ Liam Neeson, Aidan Quinn, Stephen Rea, Alan Rickman, Julia Roberts, Ian Hart, Richard Ingram, John Kenny
'Large-scale and comfortably epic in proportion, but, given that any film-maker has to make the best of his fictional way home without regarding facts as absolutely sacred, has a clear sense of history, or at least interprets it with intelligence.' – *Derek Malcolm, Guardian*
'A serious historical drama drained of serious history.' – *Ken Tucker, Entertainment Weekly*
† It won the Golden Lion for best film and Liam Neeson won the award for best actor at the 1996 Venice Film Festival.
♫ Chris Menges; Elliot Goldenthal

Michael Shayne
The private eye created by Brett Halliday was featured in several second features starring Lloyd Nolan, mostly Eugene Forde for Fox. They were adequate time-passers without too much sparkle.
1940 Michael Shayne Private Detective
1941 Dressed to Kill, Just Off Broadway, The Man Who Wouldn't Die
1942 Time to Kill (a version of Chandler's The High Window), Blue White and Perfect

Michael Strogoff: see *The Soldier and the Lady*

The Michigan Kid
US   1947   70m   Cinecolor
Universal
▤
Several people hunt for treasure stolen from a stagecoach.
Lower-berth Western.
w Roy Chanslor *novel* Rex Beach d Ray Taylor
☆ Jon Hall, Victor McLaglen, Rita Johnson, Andy Devine, Byron Foulger, Milburn Stone

'A Romantic Comedy You Can't Refuse.'
**Mickey Blue Eyes ** *
US   1999   103m   Technicolor
Universal/Castle Rock/Simian (Elizabeth Hurley, Charles Mulvehill)
▣ ▤ ◎~ ◉
A very English auctioneer in New York becomes involved with the Mafia when he falls in love with a teacher, whose father is a mobster.
Intermittently amusing comedy of a clash between two cultures, though the mechanical contrivances of farce take over from the intended romantic comedy, and Grant's act as a floppy-haired bumbler is wearing a little thin.

w Adam Scheinman, Robert Kuhn d Kelly Makin ph Donald E. Thorin m Basil Poledouris pd Gregory Keen ed David Freeman cos Ellen Mirojnick
☆ Hugh Grant, James Caan, James Tripplehorn, Burt Young, James Fox, Joe Viterelli, Gerry Becker, Maddie Corman, Tony Darrow, Paul Lazar
'An engaging, often very funny fish-out-of-water story.' – *Lael Loewenstein, Variety*
'A promising set-up; but all it develops into are knots of insane plot no one would waste time unpicking.' – *Alexander Walker, London Evening Standard*

Mickey One *
US   1965   93m   bw
Columbia/Florin/Tatira (Arthur Penn, Harrison Starr)
A night-club entertainer runs away after an orgy to find some meaning in his life.
Obscure symbolic melodrama whose flashes of talent and interest needed firmer control.
w Alan Surgal d Arthur Penn ph Ghislain Cloquet m Eddie Sauter pd George Jenkins ed Aram Avakian
☆ Warren Beatty, Hurd Hatfield, Alexandra Stewart, Franchot Tone, Teddy Hart, Jeff Corey
'Arresting at first, it becomes more and more bogged down by its own pretensions, until one's main interest is simply in seeing it through.' – *MFB*

Mickey's Christmas Carol *
♔♔ US   1983   26m   Technicolor
Disney
▣ ▤ ◎~
A cartoon version of Dickens with the parts played by familiar Disney characters; and a supreme re-establishment of the old Disney production values.
d Burney Mattinson
'For anyone over 35, this little jewel of a film is truly the Ghost of Christmas Past.' – *Gilbert Adair, MFB*
♫ animated film

Micki and Maude *
US   1984   118m   Metrocolor   Panavision
Columbia/Delphi III/B.E.E. (Tony Adams)
▤ ◎~
A TV show host accidentally gets his wife and his mistress pregnant at the same time.
Wild and overlong farce with some undeniably funnier scenes than have been noted in the participants' work for some years.
w Jonathan Reynolds d Blake Edwards ph Harry Stradling Jnr m Lee Holdridge pd Rodger Maus ed Ralph E. Winters
☆ Dudley Moore, Amy Irving, Ann Reinking, Richard Mulligan, George Gaynes, Wallace Shawn, John Pleshette

**Microcosmos ** **
France/Switzerland/Italy   1996   75m   colour
Guild/Galatée/France 2/Bac/Delta/JMH/Urania (Jacques Perrin, Christophe Barratier, Yvette Mallet)
▣ ▤ ◎~ ◉
A day in the (mainly) insect life of a French meadow.
Intriguing, marvellously photographed documentary evocation of the often-ignored world beneath our feet; there is no commentary, so there is no explanation for the strange behaviour we witness, which detracts from the impact, as does the knowledge that some of the film was shot under studio conditions.
d Claude Nuridsany, Marie Pérennou ph Claude Nuridsany, Marie Pérennou, Hugues Ryffel, Thierry Machado m Bruno Coulais ed Marie-Josèphe Yoyotte, Florence Ricard sp Ex Machina; Jean-Pierre Maricourt
'What's on screen is no longer primary material but something staged to illustrate observations made elsewhere ... Alarm bells should ring when we're told that in some cases the real sounds "ring false in relation to the images", and have been faked. What sort of nature film is so willing to improve upon nature?' – *Adam Mars-Jones, Independent*

Midas Run
US   1969   104m   Technicolor
Raymond Stross/MPI (Leon Chooluck)
GB title: *A Run on Gold*
An ageing secret service chief plans to hi-jack a bullion shipment.

Incompetently handled caper story with interest unwisely shifted for romantic purposes to the plotter's recruits.
w James D. Buchanan, Ronald Austin, Berne Giler d Alf Kjellin ph Ken Higgins m Elmer Bernstein
☆ Fred Astaire, Richard Crenna, Anne Heywood, Ralph Richardson, Roddy McDowall, Adolfo Celi, Maurice Denham, Cesar Romero

Middle Age Crazy
Canada   1980   91m   DeLuxe
Barber International/Sid & Marty Krofft/Robert Cooper & Ronald Cohen
A 40-year-old husband begins to feel his age.
Mildly satirical sex comedy, all too easily forgotten among the rest.
w Carl Kleinschmitt d John Trent ph Reginald Morris m Matthew McCauley ad Jill Scott ed John Kelly
☆ Bruce Dern, Ann-Margret, Graham Jarvis, Eric Christmas

**The Middle Man ** **
India   1975   131m   bw
Connoisseur/Indus (Subir Guha)
original title: *Jana-Aranya*
Unable to find a job in overcrowded Calcutta, a young graduate has no option but to set up as a small 'middle man', buying goods cheaply and selling them at a profit, and slips into acting as a pimp for his customers.
Satirical, cutting portrait of the moral corruption of an innocent, which produces some fine ensemble acting from its cast.
wd Satyajit Ray *novel* Shankar ph Soumendu Roy m Satyajit Ray ad Ashoke Bose ed Dulal Dutt
☆ Pradip Mukherji, Satya Bannerji, Dipankar Dey, Lily Chakravarti, Aparna Sen, Goutam Chakravarti, Sudeshna Das, Utpal Dutt
'Nothing can detract from the film's overall success and its penetrating charm.' – *MFB*

Middle of Nowhere: see *The Webster Boy*

**Middle of the Night ** **
US   1959   118m   bw
Columbia (George Justin)
An elderly garment manufacturer falls in love with a young girl.
Serious and moving examination of a human predicament, shot against beautifully observed New York backgrounds.
w Paddy Chayefsky, from his TV play d Delbert Mann ph Joseph Brun m George Bassman
☆ Fredric March, Kim Novak, Glenda Farrell, Jan Norris, Lee Grant
'A work of greater cogency than his New York play script and of deeper maturity than his Marty.' – *Time*
'The best of the TV transformations into film.' – *Stanley Kauffmann*

The Middle Watch *
GB   1930   112m   bw
BIP
Female guests on board ship have to be hidden from the captain.
Naval froth in primitive talkie form; absurdly long but popular.
w Norman Walker, Frank Launder *play* Ian Hay, Stephen King-Hall d Norman Walker
☆ Owen Nares, Jacqueline Logan, Jack Raine, Dodo Watts, Reginald Purdell
† In 1939 ABPC made a smoother version with Jack Buchanan, Greta Gynt, David Hutcheson, Kay Walsh, Fred Emney and Reginald Purdell (in the same role); directed by Thomas Bentley. Another version followed in 1958, titled *Girls at Sea* (qv).

Middleton's Changeling *
GB   1997   96m   Rank Colour   Cinemascope
UIP/High Time (Marcus Thompson)
An aristocrat's daughter hires a hitman to murder the man her father wants her to marry, and finds herself drawn into sexual intrigue and further killings.
One of those Jacobean plays that still furnishes the basic plots for many films noirs and revenge movies is here updated and cut about to provide some rough-and-ready entertainment.

♔♔ film suitable for family viewing   ▣ VHS video-cassette for the British PAL system   ▤ VHS video-cassette for the British PAL system in wide screen-format   ☼ Video cassette in a computer-colourised version   ▤ American NTSC video-cassette   ◎~ Laser disc wd Marcus Thompson *play* Thomas Middleton, William Rowley *ph* Richard K. J. Butland *pd* Rob Swinburn *ed* Marcus Thompson

☆ Ian Dury, Amanda Ray-King, Colm O Maonlai, Billy Connolly, Campbell Morrison, Moya Brady, Richard Mayes, Leo Wringer, Julia Tarnoky, James Maker, Vivian Stanshall

'In modern-day Alicante, characters wander around in Jacobean finery and baseball boots, alighting from horses to get into limousines. These Jarmanesque anachronisms misfire, not helped by the worst mismatch possible – blank verse does not sit well in the mouths of an inexperienced cast.' – *Edward Porter, Sunday Times*

† The original play was performed in the early 1620s and borrowed its plot from another work of the period, John Reynold's *God's Revenge against Murther*, adding a comic subplot that was probably the work of William Rowley, an actor noted for his roles as a fat clown.

†† The film took seven years to make, during which time Fernando Rey died before his scenes were filmed, and Vivian Stanshall before he could be voiced.

Midnight
US 1934 80m bw
Universal/All Star (Chester Erskine)
aka: Call It Murder

A jury foreman in a murder trial tips the scales in favour of guilty, but is haunted when his own daughter kills her lover.

Tepid family melodrama, very stagebound.

wd Chester Erskine *play* Paul and Claire Sifton *ph* William Steiner

☆ Sidney Fox, O. P. Heggie, Henry Hull, Humphrey Bogart, Margaret Wycherly, Lynne Overman, Richard Whorf, Cora Witherspoon

'It's pretty strong stuff and will hold audiences once they're in ... but it's not a good adaptation and is badly dialogued.' – *Variety*

Midnight ***
US 1939 95m bw
Paramount (Arthur Hornblow Jnr)

A girl stranded in Paris is hired by an aristocrat to seduce the gigolo paying unwelcome attention to his wife.

Sparkling sophisticated comedy which barely flags until a slightly disappointing ending; all the talents involved are in excellent form.

w Billy Wilder, Charles Brackett *story* Edwin Justus Mayer, Franz Schultz *d* Mitchell Leisen *ph* Charles Lang *m* Frederick Hollander

☆ *Claudette Colbert*, Don Ameche, John Barrymore, Francis Lederer, Mary Astor, Elaine Barrie, Hedda Hopper, Rex O'Malley

'Leisen's masterpiece, one of the best comedies of the thirties.' – *John Baxter, 1968*
'One of the authentic delights of the thirties.' – *New Yorker, 1976*
'It has the elements of an American *La Règle du Jeu*.' – *John Gillett*
'Just about the best light comedy ever caught by the camera.' – *Motion Picture Daily*

Midnight
US 1989 86m colour
SVS/Kuys Entertainment/Gomillion (Norman Thaddeus Vane, Gloria J. Morrison)
◼ ◉

The hostess of a horror movie show on TV is targeted by a murderer.

Occasionally amusing spoof of horror films, though too stately to create any tension on its own account.

wd Norman Thaddeus Vane *ph* David Golia *m* Michael Weatherwax *ad* Mark Simon *ed* Sam Adelman

☆ Lynn Redgrave, Tony Curtis, Steve Parrish, Rita Gam, Gustav Vintas, Karen Witter, Frank Gorshin

Midnight at Madame Tussauds
GB 1936 74m bw
Premier

For a bet, an explorer spends the night in a waxworks Chamber of Horrors.

Tepid thriller, done in a stilted manner.

w Kim Peacock *story* James S. Edwards, Roger MacDougall *d* George Pearson *ph* Jimmy Berger *ad* Donald Russell *ed* E. D. G. Pilkington

☆ James Carew, Charles Oliver, Lucille Lisle, Kim Peacock, Patrick Barr, Billy Hartnell, Lydia Sherwood, Bernard Miles

'At the frontlines of life, near the end of innocence, came the beginning of manhood.'
A Midnight Clear **
US 1992 107m CFI color
Sovereign/Beacon/A&M (Dale Pollock, Bill Borden)
◉

In the Ardennes Forest in 1944, a reconnaissance patrol composed of young and reluctant American soldiers goes disastrously wrong.

Effectively low-key, quietly ironic tale of the idiocies of war.

wd Keith Gordon *novel* William Wharton *ph* Tom Richmond *m* Mark Isham *pd* David Nichols *ed* Don Brochu

☆ Peter Berg, Kevin Dillon, Arye Gross, Ethan Hawke, Gary Sinise, Frank Whaley, John C. McGinley

'An extremely well-crafted and entirely absorbing movie.' – *Philip Thomas, Empire*

Midnight Club
US 1933 65m bw
Paramount

An American detective in London nabs a jewel gang.

Very tolerable smart-set crime melodrama.

w Seton I. Miller, Leslie Charteris *story* E. Phillips Oppenheim *d* Alexander Hall

☆ Clive Brook, George Raft, Helen Vinson, Alison Skipworth, Sir Guy Standing, Alan Mowbray

'Its London manners and locale lend it a polish which should renew interest in this school of celluloid melodramatics.' – *Variety*

'To tell you the truth, I ain't a real cowboy. But I'm one helluva stud!'
Midnight Cowboy ****
US 1969 113m DeLuxe
UA/Jerome Hellman
◼ ◉ ◉ ◉ ◉ ◔

A slightly dim-witted Texan comes to New York to offer his services as a stud for rich ladies, but spends a hard winter helping a tubercular con man.

Life in the New York gutter, brilliantly if not too accurately observed by a master showman with no heart.

w Waldo Salt *novel* James Leo Herlihy *d* John Schlesinger *ph* Adam Holender *md* John Barry *pd* John Robert Lloyd

☆ *Jon Voight, Dustin Hoffman*, Brenda Vaccaro, Sylvia Miles, John McGiver

'If only Schlesinger's directorial self-discipline had matched his luminous sense of scene and his extraordinary skill in handling actors, this would have been a far more considerable film.' – *Arthur Schlesinger Jnr (no relation)*
'A great deal besides cleverness, a great deal of good feeling and perception and purposeful dexterity.' – *Stanley Kauffmann*

🏆 best picture; Waldo Salt; John Schlesinger
🏅 Dustin Hoffman; Jon Voight; Sylvia Miles
🏅 best picture; Waldo Salt; John Schlesinger; Dustin Hoffman; Jon Voight

Midnight Crossing
US 1987 104m Technicolor
Vestron/Team Effort/Limelite Studios (Mathew Hayden)
◼ ◉

An insurance agent returns to a small Caribbean island to retrieve stolen treasure.

Glossily empty, often hysterical thriller that never rises above the ordinary.

w Roger Holzberg, Doug Weiser *d* Roger Holzberg *ph* Henry Vargas *m* Paul Buckmaster, Al Gorgoni *pd* José Duarte *ed* Earl Watson

☆ Faye Dunaway, Daniel J. Travanti, Kim Cattrall, Ned Beatty, John Laughlin

Midnight Dancers *
Philippines 1994 100m colour
Tangent
◼ ◉

original title: Sibak

Returning home to Manila, a poor youth joins his two brothers who work as 'macho dancers' in a homosexual night-club.

A gaudy exposé of Manila's gay sub-culture and the moral and social deprivations behind the thriving business of male prostitution; but one that is also concerned with the affirmations of love and desire.

w Ricardo Lee *d* Mel Chionglo *ph* George Tutanes *m* Nonong Buencamino *pd* Edgar Martin Littaua *ed* Jess Navarro

☆ Alex del Rosario, Lawrence David, Gandong Cervantes, Richard Cassity, Luis Cortes, John Mendoza, Danny Ramos, Leonard Manalansan, Perla Bautista

† The film was banned in the Philippines.

Midnight Episode
GB 1950 78m bw
Columbia/Triangle (Thomas Lageard)

An old busker stumbles over a dead body and a lot of money.

Tame British version of Raimu's French success Monsieur La Souris, saved only by its star performance.

w Rita Barisse, Reeve Taylor, Paul Vincent Carroll, David Evans, William Templeton *d* Gordon Parry *ph* Hone Glendinning

☆ Stanley Holloway, Natasha Parry, Leslie Dwyer, Reginald Tate, Meredith Edwards, Wilfrid Hyde-White, Joy Shelton

Midnight Express **
GB 1978 121m Eastmancolor
Columbia/Casablanca (Alan Marshall, David Puttnam)
◼ ◼ ◉ ◉ ◉ ◔

Tribulations of an American student arrested in Turkey for carrying hashish.

Misleadingly-titled wallow in prison atrocities, extremely well made but certainly not entertaining and with little discernible point.

w Oliver Stone *memoirs* Billy Hayes *d* Alan Parker *ph* Michael Seresin *m* Giorgio Moroder

☆ Brad Davis, Randy Quaid, John Hurt, Irene Miracle, Bo Hopkins

'One of the ugliest sado-masochistic trips, with heavy homosexual overtones, that our thoroughly nasty movie age has yet produced.' – *Richard Schickel, Time*
'The film details all [the horrors] so relentlessly on one screaming note that it is rather like being hit in the gut until you no longer feel a thing.' – *Derek Malcolm, Guardian*
'Muted squalor with a disco beat in the background, all packaged as social protest.' – *New Yorker, 1982*

🎼 script; music
🏅 best picture; Alan Parker; John Hurt
🏆 Alan Parker; John Hurt

Midnight Fear
US 1990 90m colour
Danyves/Crain

An alcoholic sheriff, investigating the murder of a woman skinned alive, suspects a deaf-mute who has escaped from an institution for the criminally insane.

Dreary psychological thriller, peopled by familiar and dull stereotypes.

w Chuck Hughes, Bill Crain, Craig Wasson *d* Bill Crain *ph* Michael Crain *m* Steve Edwards *pd* Pat Tagliaferro *ed* Brian Crain

☆ Craig Wasson, David Carradine, Page Fletcher, Mark Carlton, August West, Evan Richards

Midnight in Saint Petersburg
GB/Canada/Russia 1995 86m colour
Quebec 3099-3081/Lenfilm/Harry Palmer (Edward Simons, Kent Walwin, Alexander Goloutva, John Dunning, André Link)
◼ ◼

In Russia, a British private investigator goes in search of some missing plutonium and a kidnapped ballet dancer.

Slack and uninteresting thriller, a sequel of sorts to Bullet to Beijing (qv), and even worse than that flat film.

w Peter Welbeck (Harry Alan Towers) *novel* Len Deighton *d* Doug Jackson *ph* Peter Benison *m* Rick Wakeman *pd* Chris Tulloch *ed* Vidal Beique

☆ Michael Caine, Jason Connery, Michael Gambon, Michael Sarrazin, Tanya Jackson, Serge Houde, Anatoly Davidov

'Welcome To Savannah, Georgia. A City Of Hot Nights And Cold Blooded Murder.'
Midnight in the Garden of Good and Evil *
US 1997 155m Technicolor
Warner/Malpaso/Silver (Clint Eastwood, Arnold Stiefel)
◼ ◼ ◉ ◉ ◉ ◔

In Savannah, Georgia, a journalist investigates the shooting by a rich bachelor of his young male lover and his subsequent trial for murder.

Overlong retelling of a true story in an exotic setting; the leisurely style allows room for the characters to flower, but at the expense of the narrative tension.

w John Lee Hancock *book* John Berendt *d* Clint Eastwood *ph* Jack N. Green *m* Lennie Niehaus *pd* Henry Bumstead *ed* Joel Cox

☆ Kevin Spacey, John Cusack, Jack Thompson, The Lady Chablis, Alison Eastwood, Irma P. Hall, Paul Hipp, Jude Law, Dorothy Loudon, Anne Haney, Kim Hunter, Geoffrey Lewis

Midnight Lace *
US 1960 108m Eastmancolor
Universal (Ross Hunter, Martin Melcher)

The wife of a rich Londoner is terrorized by threatening phone calls and voices in the fog.

Thoroughly silly rehash of Gaslight and The Boy Who Cried Wolf; its glamorous accoutrements can't fight a lack of humour or predictable plot development.

w Ivan Goff, Ben Roberts *play* Matilda Shouted Fire *by* Janet Green *d* David Miller *ph* Russell Metty *m* Frank Skinner

☆ Doris Day, Rex Harrison, John Gavin, Myrna Loy, Roddy McDowall, Herbert Marshall, Natasha Parry, John Williams, Anthony Dawson, Hermione Baddeley, Richard Ney, Rhys Williams, Doris Lloyd

Midnight Madonna
US 1937 56m bw
Paramount

There is a legal fight for custody of a child who has inherited a fortune.

Efficient programmer built around a new child actress, Kitty Clancy, who didn't take.

w Doris Malloy, Gladys Lehman *d* James Flood

☆ Warren William, Mady Correll, Edward Ellis, Robert Baldwin, Jonathan Hale

'It will be found fairly entertaining by the family trade.' – *Variety*

The Midnight Man
US 1974 117m Technicolor
Universal/Norlan (Roland Kibbee, Burt Lancaster)

An ex-cop, paroled after killing his wife's lover, takes a job as security guard and runs into a murder case.

Muddled mystery with pretentious characterization and bouts of violence.

wd Roland Kibbee, Burt Lancaster *novel* The Midnight Lady and the Mourning Man by David Anthony *ph* Jack Priestley *m* Dave Grusin

☆ Burt Lancaster, Susan Clark, Cameron Mitchell, Morgan Woodward, Harris Yulin, Robert Quarry, Joan Lorring, Lawrence Dobkin, Ed Lauter

'A thriller that has the impenetrability of Chandler but none of the flavour.' – *Tom Milne*
'Efficient enough but lifeless, and burdened with portentous sentiments about solitude, violence and the nature of the beast.' – *Sight and Sound*

Midnight Mary
US 1933 76m bw
MGM

A gangster's moll on trial for her life thinks back to her past.

Intolerable now, but a hit of its year despite star miscasting.

w Gene Markey and Anita Loos *d* William Wellman

☆ Loretta Young, Ricardo Cortez, Franchot Tone, Una Merkel, Andy Devine, Harold Huber

Midnight Melody: see *Murder in the Music Hall*

Midnight Patrol *
🏃 US 1933 20m bw
Hal Roach
◼

Incompetent policemen arrest their own chief as a burglar.

Good standard star slapstick.

w uncredited *d* Lloyd French

☆ Laurel and Hardy, Charlie Hall, Walter Plinge

◎ Digital Video Disc Region 2   ◉ Digital Video Disc Region 1   ◔ Soundtrack released on compact disc   ☆ Cast in approximate order of importance   † Points of interest   🎵 Notable songs   🏆 Academy Award   🏅 Academy Award nomination   🏵 BAFTA

Midnight Run **

US   1988   126m   colour
UIP/Universal (Martin Brest)

A bounty hunter tries to bring in an embezzler, despite attempts by rivals, gangsters and the FBI to stop him.

Fast-paced action comedy, full of quick-fire wit and graced by some excellent performances.

w George Gallo d Martin Brest ph Donald Thorin m Danny Elfman pd Angelo Graham ed Billy Weber, Chris Lebenzon, Michael Tronick ☆ Robert DeNiro, Charles Grodin, Yaphet Kotto, John Ashton, Dennis Farina, Joe Pantoliano

Midnight Sting: see Diggstown

Midnight Taxi

US   1936   73m   bw
TCF

A G-man becomes a taxi driver to rout a gang of counterfeiters.

Competent, predictable crime programmer.

w Lou Breslow, John Patrick d Eugene Forde ☆ Brian Donlevy, Frances Drake, Alan Dinehart, Sig Rumann, Gilbert Roland, Harold Huber, Lon Chaney Jnr

The Midshipmaid

GB   1932   84m   bw
Gaumont
US title: *Midshipmaid Gob*

A naval commander loves the daughter of a politician out to effect navy cuts.

Very modest comedy with music, a key step in the star's success story.

w Ian Hay, Stephen King-Hall play Ian Hay, Stephen King-Hall d Albert de Courville m Noel Gay ☆ Jessie Matthews, Frederick Kerr, Basil Sydney, Nigel Bruce, Claud Allister, John Mills, George Zucco

Midshipman Easy

👪   GB   1935   77m   bw
ATP (Basil Dean, Thorold Dickinson)
US title: *Men of the Sea*

In 1790, young naval officers rescue a girl from Spanish bandits.

Stilted adventure story with interesting credits.

w Anthony Kimmins novel Frederick Marryat d Carol Reed ph John W. Boyle ☆ Hughie Green, Margaret Lockwood, Harry Tate, Robert Adams, Roger Livesey, Lewis Casson

'It is simply and dramatically cut, it contains the best fight I can remember on the screen, and I can imagine no child too sophisticated to be excited and amused.' – *Graham Greene*

A Midsummer Night's Dream: see William Shakespeare's A Midsummer Night's Dream

'Three centuries in the making!'

A Midsummer Night's Dream ***

👪   US   1935   133m   bw
Warner (Max Reinhardt)

Two pairs of lovers sort out their problems with fairy help at midnight in the woods of Athens.

Shakespeare's play is treated with remarkable respect in this super-glamorous Hollywood adaptation based on the Broadway production by Max Reinhardt. Much of it comes off, and visually it's a treat.

w Charles Kenyon, Mary McCall Jnr play William Shakespeare d Max Reinhardt, William Dieterle ph Hal Mohr, Fred Jackman, Byron Haskin, H. F. Koenekamp m Mendelssohn md Erich Wolfgang Korngold ch Bronislawa Nijinska ad Anton Grot ed Ralph Dawson ☆ James Cagney, Dick Powell, Jean Muir, Ross Alexander, Olivia de Havilland, Joe E. Brown, Hugh Herbert, Arthur Treacher, Frank McHugh, Otis Harlan, Dewey Robinson, Victor Jory, Verree Teasdale, Mickey Rooney, Anita Louise and also Grant Mitchell, Ian Hunter, Hobart Cavanaugh

'General b.o. chances could be improved by judicious pruning and appreciative selling … a fine prestige picture not only for Warners but for the industry as a whole.' – *Variety*
'You must see it if you want to be in a position to argue about the future of the film!' – *Picturegoer*
'The publicity push behind the film is tremendous – it is going to be a success or

everyone at Warner Brothers is going to get fired.' – *Robert Forsythe*
'Its assurance as a work of film technique is undoubted.' – *John Baxter, 1968*
'Its worst contradiction lies in the way Warners first ordered up a whole batch of foreign and high-sounding names to handle music, dances, general production – and then turned around and handed them empty vessels for actors.' – *Otis Ferguson*
🎥 photography; editing
🏆 best picture

A Midsummer Night's Dream *

GB   1996   105m   colour
Film Four/Edenwood/Arts Council/Capitol (Paul Arnott)

In Athens, a boy dreams a dream of lovers whose romances go wrong before they come right.

Originally staged by the Royal Shakespeare Company, this transfers unhappily to the screen as something of a nightmare, messy rather than magical, and too often ill-spoken.

wd Adrian Noble play William Shakespeare ph Ian Wilson m Howard Blake pd Anthony Ward ed Paul Hodgson, Peter Hollywood ☆ Lindsay Duncan, Alex Jennings, Desmond Barrit, Barry Lynch, Monica Dolan, Daniel Evans, Kevin Doyle, Emily Raymond, Alfred Burke, Osheen Jones

'It's so busy whipping up a stylistic storm that it lays low Shakespeare's true topic – love.' – *Matt Wolf, Variety*

A Midsummer Night's Sex Comedy *

US   1982   88m   Technicolor
Warner/Orion/Rollins-Joffe (Robert Greenhut)

Around the turn of the century, a Wall Street broker expects various weekend guests at his country retreat.

Subdued, melancholy and rather uninventive Woody Allen variation on Smiles of a Summer Night.

wd Woody Allen ph Gordon Willis m from Mendelssohn pd Mel Bourne ed Susan E. Morse ☆ Woody Allen, Mia Farrow, José Ferrer, Julie Hagerty, Tony Roberts, Mary Steenburgen

Midway *

US   1976   131m   Technicolor   Panavision   Sensurround
Universal/Mirisch Corporation (Walter Mirisch)
GB title: *The Battle of Midway*

The tide turns for the Americans when the Japanese attack the Pacific island of Midway in 1942.

Noisy flagwaver with confused strategy and too many stars in small parts.

w Donald S. Sanford d Jack Smight ph Harry Stradling Jnr m John Williams ☆ Charlton Heston, Henry Fonda, Robert Mitchum, Glenn Ford, Edward Albert, James Coburn, Hal Holbrook, Toshiro Mifune, Robert Wagner, Robert Webber, Ed Nelson, James Shigeta, Monte Markham, Christopher George, Glenn Corbett

'We are over-informed about the movements of every ship and plane, under-informed about how the battle was finally won, and positively swamped with tedious human interest.' – *Sight and Sound*

Mifune **

Denmark/Sweden   1999   101m   colour
Alliance/Nimbus/Zentropa/DRTV/STV (Brigitte Hald, Morten Kaufmann)
original title: *Mifunes Sidste Sang*

After marrying his boss's daughter, a thrusting young businessman is forced by his father's death to return to the family farm and find a housekeeper to look after his mentally handicapped brother.

Enjoyable, though too often predictable, drama of a tart with a heart of gold redeeming a selfish yuppie.

w Soren Kragh-Jacobsen, Anders Thomas Jensen d Soren Kragh-Jacobsen ph Anthony Dod Mantle m Thor Backhausen, Karl Bille, Christian Sievert ed Valdis Oskarasdottir ☆ Anders W. Berthelsen, Iben Hjejle, Jesper Asholt, Emil Tarding, Anders Hove, Sofie Grabol, Paprika Steen, Mette Bratlann

'Well-constructed mixture of romance, sex and humor should be a crowd-pleaser in most territories.' – *David Stratton, Variety*

Mifunes Sidste Sang: see Mifune

'The quest for friendship is the noblest cause of all.'
'Courage comes in all sizes.'

The Mighty *

US   1998   100m   DeLuxe
Miramax/Scholastic (Jane Startz, Simon Fields)

A small, physically handicapped but bright and brave boy forms a symbiotic friendship with a hulking near-illiterate youth.

Quirky movie about the attraction of opposites that thankfully avoids sentimentality.

w Charles Leavitt novel Freak the Mighty by Rodman Philbrick d Peter Chelsom ph John de Borman m Trevor Jones pd Caroline Hanania ed Martin Walsh ☆ Sharon Stone, Gena Rowlands, Harry Dean Stanton, Kieran Culkin, Elden Hanson, Gillian Anderson, James Gandolfini, Joe Perrino, Meat Loaf, Jenifer Lewis

'While the pic's core appeal is decidedly to young viewers, the material hits an emotional chord for all ages.' – *Leonard Klady, Variety*

Mighty Aphrodite **

US   1995   95m   Technicolor
Miramax/Seetland/Jean Doumanian (Robert Greenhut)

A sports writer tries to rescue the mother of his adopted son from a life as a prostitute.

Witty comedy of love and marriage, not up to Allen's best, but highly enjoyable for all that.

wd Woody Allen ph Carlo DiPalma pd Santo Loquasto ed Susan E. Morse ☆ Woody Allen, Helena Bonham Carter, Mira Sorvino, Michael Rapaport, F. Murray Abraham, Claire Bloom, Olympia Dukakis, David Ogden Stiers, Jack Warden, Peter Weller, Dan Moran

'The suspicion lingers that Woody Allen deserves a good spanking, and not from a prostitute with a heart of gold. But, listen: humor and sentiment can triumph over stern morality any day. Once the picture gets going, it reminds us that Allen is also an artist with an acute feel for movie romance. So scruples be damned. This time, Mighty makes all righty.' – *Richard Corliss, Time*
🏆 Mira Sorvino
🎥 Woody Allen (as writer)

The Mighty Barnum *

US   1934   87m   bw
Twentieth Century (Darryl F. Zanuck)

A fictionalized biopic of the great showman of the 1890s.

Lively without being very memorable.

w Gene Fowler, Bess Meredyth play Gene Fowler, Bess Meredyth d Walter Lang ph Peverell Marley m Alfred Newman ☆ Wallace Beery, Virginia Bruce, Adolphe Menjou, Janet Beecher, Rochelle Hudson

The Mighty Ducks

👪   US   1992   101m   Technicolor   Panavision
Buena Vista/Walt Disney (Jordan Kerner, Jon Avnet)
GB title: *Champions*
video title: *The Mighty Ducks Are Champions*

A lawyer doing community service for drunk driving turns a group of drop-out kids into a winning hockey team.

Simple-minded and sentimental movie hymning the joys of team spirit.

w Steven Brill d Stephen Herek ph Thomas Del Ruth m David Newman pd Randy Ser ed Larry Bock, John F. Link ☆ Emilio Estevez, Joss Ackland, Lane Smith, Heidi King, Josef Sommer, Joshua Jackson

'A formulaic pic meant for children but actually focusing on a yuppie's struggle for redemption. Mildly entertaining but unexciting.' – *Variety*
† A sequel, D2: The Mighty Ducks (qv), followed in 1994.

'The ten most terrific thrills ever pictured!'

Mighty Joe Young *

👪   US   1949   94m   bw
RKO (Merian C. Cooper)

A little girl brings back from Africa a pet gorilla which grows to enormous size and causes a city to panic.

Rather tired comic-sentimental follow-up to King Kong, with a tedious plot and variable animation but a few endearing highlights.

w Ruth Rose d Ernest Schoedsack ph J. Roy Hunt m Roy Webb sp Willis O'Brien, Ray Harryhausen ☆ Terry Moore, Ben Johnson, Robert Armstrong, Frank McHugh, Douglas Fowley

Mighty Joe Young *

👪   US   1998   114m   colour   Panavision
Buena Vista/Walt Disney/RKO (Ted Hartley, Tom Jacobson)
GB title: *Mighty Joe*

Fearing for the safety of a giant gorilla she has known since both were young, a woman takes him from Africa to live in LA.

An ecologically sound remake with splendid special effects, though it is no more successful than the original version as a successor to King Kong.

w Mark Rosenthal, Lawrence Konner screenplay Ruth Rose story Merian C. Cooper d Ron Underwood ph Don Peterman, Oliver Wood m James Horner pd Michael Corenblith ed Paul Hirsch sp creature designer: Rick Baker; Dreamquest Images; Industrial Light & Magic ☆ Charlize Theron, Bill Paxton, Rade Sherbedgia, Peter Firth, David Paymer, Regina King, Robert Wisdom, Naveen Andrews, Lawrence Pressman, Linda Purl, Mika Boorem, John Alexander

'Makes the most of modern technology, adding color, computer graphics and impressive animatronics to a rather predictable storyline.' – *Lael Loewenstein, Variety*
🎥 visual effects

The Mighty McGurk

US   1946   83m   bw
Nat Perrin/MGM

In the Bowery in the 1890s, a bragging ex-fighter takes in a small boy.

Sentimental melodrama which unspools like a joint remake of The Champ and The Bowery.

w William R. Lipman, Grant Garrett, Harry Clork d John Waters ☆ Wallace Beery, Dean Stockwell, Edward Arnold, Aline MacMahon, Cameron Mitchell, Aubrey Mather

Mighty Morphin Power Rangers: The Movie

👪   US   1995   95m   DeLuxe
TCF/Saban/Toei (Haim Saban, Shuki Levy, Suzanne Todd)

Six teenagers who can transform themselves into Power Rangers, martial arts experts on the side of good, combat the evil Ivan Ooze.

Criticism is redundant faced with the movie version of a vapid though aggressive fantasy that was briefly many children's favourite television viewing. The TV original showed the joins between its tacky fights and special effects, filmed in Japan, and the remainder, made in America. The movie is considerably slicker, but as depressing in the low quality of its imagination.

w Arne Olsen, John Kamps d Bryan Spicer ph Paul Murphy m Graeme Revell pd Craig Stearns ed Wayne Wahrman ☆ Karan Ashley, Johnny Yong Bosch, Steve Cardenas, Jason David Frank, Amy Jo Johnson, David Yost, Paul Schrier, Jason Narvy, Paul Freeman

'A curious hybrid of tepid California teen drama and "chop socky" karate serial. Watching it provides the strange sensation of channel-surfing without having to touch the remote.' – *Stephen Amidon, Sunday Times*

The Mighty Quinn

US   1989   98m   colour
UIP/MGM/Star partners II/A & M Films (Sandy Lieberson, Marion Hunt, Ed Elbert)

On a Caribbean island, the police chief investigates the murder of an American.

Routine thriller offering little in the way of suspense or excitement.

w Hampton Fancher novel Finding Maubee by A. H. Z. Carr d Carl Schenkel ph Jacques Steyn m Anne Dudley pd Roger Murray-Leach ed John Jympson ☆ Denzel Washington, James Fox, Mimi Rogers, M. Emmet Walsh, Sheryl Lee Ralph, Art Evans, Esther Rolle, Norman Beaton, Alex Colon

---

'A spy thriller, a buddy movie, a musical, a comedy, and a picture that is wise about human nature. And yet with all of those qualities, it never seems to strain. This is a graceful, almost charmed, entertainment.' – *Roger Ebert*

Mighty Ursus: see *Ursus*

The Mighty Warrior: see *The Vengeance of Ursus*

Mignon Has Left **
Italy/France   1988   90m   Eastmancolor
Metro/Ellepi Film/Chrysalide Film/RAI/RAITRE (Leo Pescarolo, Guido de Laurentiis)
original title: *Mignon è Partita*
Adolescent traumas come to a head in a Rome household when their French cousin comes to stay.
A slight but charming study of children in the transition to adulthood, much admired by Continental audiences.
w Francesca Archibugi, Gloria Malatesta, Claudia Sbarigia   d Francesca Archibugi   ph Luigi Verga   m Roberto Gatto, Battista Lena   ad Massimo Spano   ed Alfredo Muschietti
☆ Stefania Sandrelli, Jean-Pierre Duriez, Leonardo Ruta, Celine Beauvallet, Francesca Antonelli, Lorenzo de Pasqua, Eleonora Sambiagio, Daniele Zaccaria

The Mikado *
GB   1939   91m   Technicolor
GFD/G and S (Geoffrey Toye, Joseph Somlo)
⊚
In Japan, a timid official is appointed Lord High Executioner and finds that his first intended victim is the Emperor's son, travelling incognito.
Agreeable film version of the classic Gilbert and Sullivan comic opera, with some of the D'Oyly Carte Company's most celebrated members in excellent form.
w Geoffrey Toye   opera W. S. Gilbert   d Victor Schertzinger   ph Bernard Knowles   m Arthur Sullivan
☆ Martyn Green, John Barclay, Sydney Granville, Kenny Baker, Jean Colin, Constance Willis
'An odd film that pulls this way and that way and never quite gets anywhere. On the credit side must be put down the colour and the music.' – *C. A. Lejeune*
† The 1966 version by British Home Entertainment featured a later D'Oyly Carte company including John Reed but suffered from a frozen camera and flat lighting, so that little of the original vivacity and charm came over

Mike's Murder
US   1984   97m   Technicolor
Warner/Ladd Company/Skyeway
⊟⊟
A bank teller decides to investigate the killing of the man she loved, an unstable, bisexual drug-dealer and tennis coach.
A turn-off: a combination of an unlikely narrative, a mediocre script, sleazy characters and indifferent performances.
wd James Bridges   ph Reynaldo Villalobos   m John Barry, Joe Jackson   pd Peter Jamison   ed Jeff Gourson, Dede Allen
☆ Debra Winger, Mark Keyloun, Darrell Larson, Brooke Alderson, Paul Winfield, Daniel Shor

Mikey and Nicky
US   1976   118m   colour
Paramount (Michael Hausman)
⊟
Two crooks are old friends, but one has been hired to kill the other…
Intolerable improvisatory sentimental melodrama. Who on earth shells out the money for pictures like this?
wd Elaine May   ph Victor Kemper   m John Strauss
☆ Peter Falk, John Cassavetes, Ned Beatty, Sanford Meisner, Rose Arrick, Joyce Van Patten
'An impenetrable, ugly and almost unendurable mess.' – *Frank Rich, New York Post*
'A pretext for Falk and Cassavetes to indulge in one of those long, lugubrious Actors' Studio exercises that wore out its welcome with the last frame of *Husbands* and the first frame of *The Killing of a Chinese Bookie*.' – *Molly Haskell, Village Voice*

The Milagro Beanfield War
US   1988   118m   MGM Color
Universal (Robert Redford)
⊟⊟ ⊠ ⊙
Impoverished farmers in New Mexico defy developers who try to take over their land.
Serious issues treated with quirky humour and visual lyricism.
w David Ward, John Nichols   book John Nichols   d Robert Redford   ph Robbie Greenberg   m Dave Grusin   ad Joe Aubel
☆ Ruben Blades, Richard Bradford, Sonia Braga, Julie Carmen, James Gammon, John Heard, M. Emmet Walsh
'A very peculiar mixture of warmed-over movie conventions.' – *MFB*
🎵 Dave Grusin

'The kind of woman most men want … and shouldn't have!'

Mildred Pierce **
US   1945   113m   bw
Warner (Jerry Wald)
⊟⊟
A dowdy housewife breaks with her husband, becomes the owner (through hard work) of a restaurant chain, and survives a murder case before true love comes her way.
A woman's picture par excellence, glossily and moodily photographed, with a star suffering in luxury on behalf of the most ungrateful daughter of all time.
w Ranald MacDougall, Catherine Turney   novel James M. Cain   d Michael Curtiz   ph Ernest Haller   m Max Steiner   ad Anton Grot
☆ Joan Crawford, Jack Carson, Zachary Scott, Eve Arden, Ann Blyth, Bruce Bennett, George Tobias, Lee Patrick, Moroni Olsen
'Constant, lambent, virulent attention to money and its effects, and more authentic suggestions of sex than one hopes to see in American films.' – *James Agee*
🎵 Joan Crawford
⧓ best picture; script; Ernest Haller; Eve Arden; Ann Blyth

Miles from Home *
US   1988   108m   DeLuxe
Fox/Braveworld/Cinemcom/J & M Entertainment (Frederick Zollo, Paul Kurta)
⊟⊟ ⊠
Facing hard times, two brothers burn down their farm and take to the road.
Unconventional road movie with some interesting moments.
w Chris Gerolmo   d Gary Sinise   ph Elliot Davis   m Robert Folk   pd David Gropman   ed Jane Schwartz Jaffe
☆ Richard Gere, Kevin Anderson, Brian Dennehy, Jason Campbell, Austin Bamgarner, Larry Poling, Terry Kinney, Penelope Ann Miller, Helen Hunt, John Malkovich

Military Policeman: see *Off Limits*

Milk and Honey
Canada   1988   95m   colour
Zenith/JA Film (Peter O'Brian)
In an attempt to improve her life, a Jamaican woman leaves her home and young son to work in Canada as a nanny.
Moderate domestic drama, given a little fillip by the novelty of its subject matter.
w Glen Salzman, Trevor Rhone   d Rebecca Yates, Glen Salzman   ph Guy Dufaux   m Mickey Erbe, Maribeth Solomon   ad François Seguin   ed Bruce Nyznik
☆ Josette Simon, Lyman Ward, Djanet Sears, Fiona Reid, Leonie Forbes, Richard Mills

Milk Money
US   1994   109m   DeLuxe
UIP (Kathleen Kennedy, Frank Marshall)
⊟⊟ ⊠ ⊙
A big-city tart with a heart of gold returns to their homes three 12-year-old boys who paid to see her strip and falls for the father of one of them.
Uninteresting would-be romantic comedy, which fails on both counts.
w John Mattson   d Richard Benjamin   ph David Watkin   m Michael Convertino   pd Paul Sylbert   ed Jacqueline Cambas
☆ Melanie Griffith, Ed Harris, Michael Patrick Carter, Malcolm McDowell, Anne Heche, Casey Siemaszko, Philip Bosco, Brian Casey

'Could curdle your stomach and the execution of the idea is just plain rancid … obvious, loud, mean-spirited and has its mind in the gutter.' – *Variety*

The Milkman
US   1950   87m   bw
Universal-International (Ted Richmond)
Two milkmen tangle with gangsters.
Odd little comedy which gets the benefit of the doubt more by bringing its stars together than by giving them anything to do.
w Albert Beich, James O'Hanlon, Martin Ragaway, Leonard Stern   d Charles Barton   ph Clifford Stine   m Milton Rosen
☆ Donald O'Connor, Jimmy Durante, Joyce Holden, Piper Laurie, William Conrad, Paul Harvey, Henry O'Neill

The Milky Way *
🎢 US   1936   88m   bw
Paramount/Harold Lloyd (Edward Sheldon)
⊟⊟ ⊠
A milkman becomes a prizefighter and overcomes a gang of crooks.
Modest Harold Lloyd comedy towards the end of his career; remade as The Kid from Brooklyn (qv).
w Grover Jones, Frank Butler, Richard Connell   play Lynn Root, Harry Clork   d Leo McCarey   ph Alfred Gilks
☆ Harold Lloyd, Adolphe Menjou, Verree Teasdale, Helen Mack, William Gargan, George Barbier, Lionel Stander
'The work of many hands, all laid on expertly.' – *Otis Ferguson*
'One is more amazed than ever at the good fortune of this youngish man whose chief talent is not to act at all, to do nothing, to serve as a blank wall for other people to scrawl their ideas on.' – *Graham Greene*

The Milky Way *
France/Italy   1968   102m   Eastmancolor
Greenwich/Medusa (Serge Silberman)
⊟⊟ ⊠
original title: *La Voie Lactée*
Two tramps set off on pilgrimage from Paris to a Spanish shrine, and have various surprising encounters.
A picaresque examination of Catholic doctrine, full of surface interest but requiring special knowledge for full appreciation.
w Luis Buñuel, Jean-Claude Carrière   d Luis Buñuel   ph Christian Matras   m Luis Buñuel
☆ Laurent Terzieff, Paul Frankeur, Delphine Seyrig, Edith Scon
'A mere trifle wrapped in a triple cloak of befuddling obscurantism.' – *John Simon*

The Mill on the Floss
GB   1937   94m   bw
Morgan/National Provincial
⊟
A Victorian mill owner and the lord of the manor start a family feud which ends in tragedy.
Romeo and Juliet in crinolines; a stilted and unpersuasive film of the book.
w John Drinkwater, Garnett Weston, Austin Melford, Tim Whelan   novel George Eliot   d Tim Whelan
☆ Geraldine Fitzgerald, Frank Lawton, James Mason, Victoria Hopper, Fay Compton, Griffith Jones, Mary Clare, Athene Seyler, Felix Aylmer
'A series of stiff little sequences, decorously posed.' – *New York Times*

Millennium
US   1989   105m   DeLuxe
Rank/First Millennium Partnership/Gladden Entertainment (Douglas Leiterman, Robert Vince)
⊟⊟ ⊠ ⊙
The investigator of a mid-air collision of two planes discovers that people from the future are involved.
Implausible time travel story that never holds together or keeps an audience's interest.
w John Varley   story Air Raid by John Varley   d Michael Anderson   ph Rene Ohashi   pd Gene Rudolf   ed Ron Wisman
☆ Kris Kristofferson, Cheryl Ladd, Daniel J. Travanti, Robert Joy, Lloyd Bochner, Brent Carver, David McIlwraith, Maury Chaykin, Al Waxman

Miller's Crossing **
US   1990   115m   DuArt
Fox/Circle Films/Ted an Pedas/Ben Barenholtz/Bill Durkin (Ethan Coen)
⊟⊟ ⊠ ⊙ ⊙
The duplicitous aide to a corrupt and powerful politician is caught in the crossfire between two rival gangsters.
Sombre, solidly made thriller, directed with a macabre skill.
w Joel Coen, Ethan Coen   d Joel Coen   ph Barry Sonnenfeld   m Carter Burwell   pd Dennis Gassner   ed Michael Miller
☆ Gabriel Byrne, Marcia Gay Harden, John Turturro, Jon Polito, J. E. Freeman, Albert Finney, Mike Starr, Al Mancini, Richard Woods

Le Million ****
France   1931   89m   bw
Tobis (Frank Clifford)
⊟⊟
An artist and an ingratiating crook search Paris for a lost lottery ticket.
With its delicate touch, perfect sense of comedy timing and infectious use of recitative and song, this is superb screen entertainment using most of the medium's resources.
wd René Clair   musical comedy Georges Berr, M. Guillemaud   ph Georges Périnal   m Georges Van Parys, Armand Bernard, Philippe Parès   ad Lazare Meerson
☆ Annabella, René Lefèvre, Paul Olivier, Louis Allibert, Vanda Gréville, Raymond Cordy
'A good musical farce that ought to do well everywhere … it has speed, laughs, splendid photography and a good cast.' – *Variety*
'René Clair at his exquisite best; no one else has ever been able to make a comedy move with such delicate inevitability.' – *New Yorker, 1978*
'I wanted an atmosphere of foolishness … we put gauze between the actors and the sets, which created an illusion of unreality.' – *René Clair*
† The style of this film was developed and expanded in Hollywood by Lubitsch in *One Hour with You* and by Mamoulian in *Love Me Tonight*

Million Dollar Baby
US   1941   100m   bw
Warner (Hal B. Wallis, David Lewis)
A girl inherits a fortune and a lot of problems.
Very predictable but sometimes sprightly comedy with a hard-working cast.
w Richard Macaulay, Jerry Wald   story Miss Wheelwright Discovers America by Leonard Spigelgass   d Curtis Bernhardt   ph Charles Rosher   m Max Steiner
☆ Priscilla Lane, Jeffrey Lynn, Ronald Reagan, May Robson, Lee Patrick, Helen Westley, George Barbier, John Qualen, Walter Catlett, Nan Wynn

Million Dollar Duck
🎢 US   1971   92m   Technicolor
Walt Disney (Bill Anderson)
A duck lays eggs with solid gold yolks, which provoke interest from gangsters as well as the government.
Minor Disney fantasy borrowed without permission from Mr Drake's Duck (qv).
w Roswell Rogers   d Vincent McEveety   ph William Snyder   m Buddy Baker
☆ Dean Jones, Sandy Duncan, Joe Flynn, Tony Roberts

The Million Dollar Hotel *
Germany/US   1999   122m   colour
Panavision
Icon/Road MoviesKintop (Deepak Nayar, Bono, Nicholas Klein, Bruce Davey, Wim Wenders)
⊙
An FBI agent investigates the death of the son of a media tycoon, who fell off the roof of a seedy Los Angeles hotel inhabited by social misfits.
An intermittently engaging look at the trashier side of American culture, though you need more than a collection of freaks and eccentrics to make an interesting movie.
w Nicholas Klein   idea Bono   d Wim Wenders   ph Phedon Papamichael   m Jon Hassell, Bono, Daniel Lanois, Brian Eno   pd Robbie Freed   ed Tatiana S. Riegel
☆ Jeremy Davies, Milla Jovovich, Mel Gibson, Jimmy Smits, Peter Stormare, Amanda Plummer, Gloria Stuart, Tom Bower, Donal Logue, Bud Cort,

---

⊚ Digital Video Disc Region 2   ⊟⊟ Digital Video Disc Region 1   ⊙ Soundtrack released on compact disc   ☆ Cast in approximate order of importance   † Points of interest   🎵 Notable songs   🎵 Academy Award   ⧓ Academy Award nomination   Ⓑ BAFTA

Julian Sands, Harris Yulin, Richard Edson, Charlayne Woodard, Tim Roth
'Profoundly irritating' – *Times*
'Ultimately, the superb craftsmanship and cultish aura can't compensate for an underdeveloped and not very interesting story, especially when none of the characters is the least bit sympathetic or engaging.' – *David Stratton, Variety*

'Roaring laughs in a story built of goofer dust and frog fur!'

Million Dollar Legs *
US   1932   64m   bw
Paramount
A mythical sport-ridden country decides to enter the Olympic Games.
The good gags in this film are weighted down by plodding treatment, and the general effect is more doleful than funny.
w Harry Myers, Nick Barrows, Joseph L. Mankiewicz d Edward Cline ph Arthur Todd
☆ W. C. Fields, Jack Oakie, Andy Clyde, Lyda Roberti, Ben Turpin, Hugh Herbert, Billy Gilbert, George Barbier, Susan Fleming
'One of the silliest and funniest pictures ever made.' – *New Yorker, 1977*

Million Dollar Legs
US   1939   59m   bw
Paramount
College students back a favourite horse.
Very modest collegiate comedy.
w Lewis Foster, Richard English d Nick Grinde ph Harry Fischbeck
☆ Betty Grable, John Hartley, Donald O'Connor, Jackie Coogan, Buster Crabbe, Thurston Hall

Million Dollar Mermaid *
US   1952   115m   Technicolor
MGM (Arthur Hornblow Jnr)
GB title: *The One Piece Bathing Suit*
The story of Australian swimmer Annette Kellerman.
Inaccurate biopic with a raison d'être in its spectacular aquashow scenes, but nothing at all new in its script.
w Everett Freeman d Mervyn Le Roy ph George J. Folsey md Adolph Deutsch ch Busby Berkeley
☆ Esther Williams, Victor Mature, Walter Pidgeon, David Brian, Jesse White, Maria Tallchief, Howard Freeman
♫ George J. Folsey

Million Dollar Mystery: see Money Mania

Million Dollar Ransom
US   1934   67m   bw
Universal
A racketeer consolidates his family affairs before being bumped off by his gang.
Slightly odd underworld melodrama, interesting but not very satisfying.
w William R. Lipman, Ben Ryan story Damon Runyon d Murray Roth
☆ Edward Arnold, Phillips Holmes, Mary Carlisle, Wini Shaw, Andy Devine
'Lacks names but offers fair possibilities.' – *Variety*

The Million Pound Note *
GB   1953   91m   Technicolor
GFD/Group Films (John Bryan)
US title: *Man with a Million*
A man is given a million pounds in the form of a single banknote and finds it difficult to spend.
Fairly pleasing period comedy which wears its one joke pretty thin but is nicely decorated and acted.
w Jill Craigie story Mark Twain d Ronald Neame ph Geoffrey Unsworth m William Alwyn ed Clive Donner
☆ Gregory Peck, Jane Griffiths, Ronald Squire, Joyce Grenfell, A. E. Matthews, Reginald Beckwith, Hartley Power, Wilfrid Hyde-White

The Millionaire *
US   1931   80m   bw
Warner
A bored millionaire retires and secretly buys a garage.
Fairly deft star comedy which well satisfied Depression audiences.
w Julien Josephson and Booth Tarkington story Earl Derr Biggers d John Adolfi

☆ George Arliss, Florence Arliss, Evalyn Knapp, David Manners, Noah Beery, J. Farrell MacDonald, James Cagney
'Should bring Arliss within mental reach of all theatres … Should enjoy a substantial career.' – *Variety*
† Remade in 1947 as *That Way with Women* (qv)

A Millionaire for Christy
US   1951   91m   bw
TCF (Bert Friedlob)
A lawyer's secretary is sent to Los Angeles to inform an heir of his good fortune, and decides to marry him.
Modest romantic comedy with plenty to be modest about.
w Ken Englund d George Marshall ph Harry Stradling m Victor Young
☆ Eleanor Parker, Fred MacMurray, Richard Carlson, Douglass Dumbrille

Millionaire Merry Go Round: see Kicking the Moon Around

'From naughty, notorious George Bernard Shaw, the sultry story of the beautiful babe in the Balmain gowns who pants for romance … !'

The Millionairess *
GB   1960   90m   DeLuxe   Cinemascope
TCF/Dimitri de Grunwald (Pierre Rouve)
The richest woman in the world falls for a poor Indian doctor.
Messy travesty of a Shavian comedy that was never more than a star vehicle to begin with. Hardly any of it works despite the star cast, who are mostly miscast.
w Wolf Mankowitz play Bernard Shaw d Anthony Asquith ph Jack Hildyard m Georges Van Parys
☆ Sophia Loren, Peter Sellers, Alastair Sim, Vittorio de Sica, Dennis Price, Gary Raymond, Alfie Bass, Miriam Karlin, Noel Purcell
'The result, lacking any sort of dramatic cohesion or continuity and seemingly planned less as a film than as a series of haphazard effects, is merely tiring.' – *Peter John Dyer*

Millions
GB   1936   70m   bw
Herbert Wilcox
A struggling composer is really the son of a millionaire.
Fairly lively comedy of rival self-made men.
w Michael Barringer d Leslie Hiscott ph Freddie Young
☆ Gordon Harker, Frank Pettingell, Richard Hearne, Jane Carr

Millions in the Air
US   1935   72m   bw
Harold Hurley/Paramount
Complications of a radio amateur contest.
Scrappy comedy with more historical interest than entertainment value.
w Sig Herzig, Jane Storm d Ray McCarey
☆ Willie Howard, John Howard, Robert Cummings, Inez Courtney, Benny Baker, Dave Chasen, Wendy Barrie, Samuel S. Hinds
'Without a substantial monicker in the cast, it hasn't much to offer at the box office.' – *Variety*

Millions like Us **
GB   1943   103m   bw
GFD/Gainsborough (Edward Black)
The tribulations of a family in wartime, especially of the meek daughter who goes into war work and marries an airman, who is killed.
Fragmentary but reasonably accurate picture of the Home Front during World War II; a little more humour would not have been out of place, but as propaganda it proved an effective weapon.
wd Frank Launder, Sidney Gilliat ph Jack Cox md Louis Levy ad John Bryan ed Alfred Roome
☆ Patricia Roc, Gordon Jackson, Moore Marriott, Eric Portman, Anne Crawford, Basil Radford, Naunton Wayne, Joy Shelton, Megs Jenkins
'There is an unsentimental warmheartedness which I hope we shall cling to and extend in filmed representations of the British scene.' – *Richard Winnington*
† The only picture Launder and Gilliat directed side by side on the floor.

Mills of the Gods
US   1934   66m   bw
Columbia
An elderly businesswoman, unimpressed by her family, turns her business over to a committee of executives.
Interesting plot which would have justified better production.
w Garrett Fort, John S. Kirkland, Melville Baker d Roy William Neill
☆ May Robson, Fay Wray, Victor Jory, Raymond Walburn, Mayo Methot
'Stilted story with some good trouping. A double-upper.' – *Variety*

Milou in May ***
France/Italy   1989   108m   colour
Gala/Nouvelles Editions de Films/TF1/Ellepi Film (Jean-Yves Asselin)
Following the death of his mother, a 60-year-old man invites his relatives to the funeral.
Gentle, well-observed study of family relationships.
w Louis Malle, Jean-Claude Carrière d Louis Malle ph Renato Berta m Stéphane Grappelli ed Emmanuelle Castro
☆ Michel Piccoli, Miou-Miou, Michel Duchaussoy, Dominique Blanc, Harriet Walter, Bruno Carette, François Berléand, Martine Gautier, Paulette Dubost
'A film of Chekhovian generosity that never strays into sentimentality or cynicism.' – *Philip French, Observer*

Mimi
GB   1935   94m   bw
BIP
In a Paris garret, a poor girl dies after encouraging a playwright.
La Bohème without the music; not a good idea.
w Clifford Grey, Paul Merzbach, Jack Davies, Denis Waldock novel La Vie Bohème by Henri Murger d Paul Stein
☆ Douglas Fairbanks Jnr, Gertrude Lawrence, Diana Napier, Harold Warrender, Carol Goodner, Richard Bird

Mimic *
US   1997   105m   DeLuxe
Buena Vista/Dimension (Bob Weinstein, B. J. Rack, Ole Bornedal)
Mutant killer bugs, created to rid New York of a plague, evolve into creatures that resemble human beings.
Effective and atmospheric horror movie, with much of the action taking place in subway tunnels; its visual style creates unease without resorting to shock effects.
w Matthew Robbins, Guillermo Del Toro, Matthew Greenberg, John Sayles story Donald A. Wolheim d Guillermo Del Toro ph Dan Laustsen m Marco Beltrami pd Carol Spier ed Patrick Lussier sp creature design Rob Bottin, Tyruben Ellingson
☆ Mira Sorvino, Jeremy Northam, Josh Brolin, Giancarlo Giannini, Charles S. Dutton, Alexander Goodwin, Alix Koromzay, F. Murray Abraham
'A murkily good job in scary subterranean suspense of the *Alien* kind, with sound effects prompting worse apocalyptic imaginings than the actual sight of the VW-sized bugs.' – *Alexander Walker, London Evening Standard*

'A cyclone of human emotion roars across the screen!'

Min and Bill **
US   1930   69m   bw
MGM
A boozy old waterfront character and his wife try to keep her daughter from being placed in care.
Well-remembered and much-loved character comedy which led to the even more successful Tugboat Annie with the same team.
w Frances Marion, Marion Jackson play Dark Star by Lorna Moon d George Hill ph Harold Wenstrom
☆ Marie Dressler, Wallace Beery, Dorothy Jordan, Marjorie Rambeau, Donald Dillaway, Russell Hopton
'Comedy-drama of distinction. All ingredients for all theatres, from keys down.' – *Variety*
♟ Marie Dressler

Mina Tannenbaum **
France   1993   128m   colour
Mayfair/IMA/UGC/Christian Bourgois/La Sept/SFPC/L'Etang/Belbo/RTBF (Georges Benayoun)
Friends and relatives remember the life of a gifted Jewish artist, a misfit as a young girl, who kills herself after the relationships in her life go awry.
Assured exploration of the lives of two women growing up over 25 years, with men relegated to walk-on parts although the women also become marginalized; it starts light-heartedly and becomes much darker, while some of the narrative devices distance the audience, with the dead commenting on the action, and the women seen with 'ghosts' of how they might have been.
wd Martine Dugowson ph Dominique Chapuis m Peter Chase ad Philippe Chiffre ed Martine Barraqué, Dominique Gallieni
☆ Romane Bohringer, Elsa Zylberstein, Hugues Quester, Nils Tavernier, Stéphane Slima, Chantal Krief, Florence Thomassin, Eric Defosse, Jean-Philippe Ecoffey
'An unusual, sometimes uneven mix of comedy and melodrama. Yet it is a film of immense charm and humour which works surprisingly well.' – *Ginette Vincendeau, Sight and Sound*

Minbo No Onna **
Japan   1992   126m   colour
Itami Films (Yasushi Tamaoki)
aka: *Anti-Extortion Woman*
aka: *The Gangster's Moll*
A female lawyer is hired to prevent yakuza from ruining a high-class hotel and blackmailing its manager.
Engaging, though sometimes broad, satire that changes tone into a more straightforward drama halfway through, mocking Japanese gangsters and exposing their methods of extortion and intimidation.
wd Juzo Itami ph Yonezo Maeda m Toshiyuki Honda pd Shuji Nakamura ed Akira Suzuki
☆ Nobuko Miyamoto, Yasuo Daichi, Takehiro Murata, Shiro Ito, Akira Nakao, Akira Takarada, Hideji Otaki, Norburo Mitani, Hosei Komatsu
† Japan's yakuza were not amused by the film: six days after its release Itami was hospitalized after being cut around the face and neck by gangsters. In a related incident in Tokyo, a man slashed a cinema screen during the showing of another of Itami's films.

The Mind Benders *
GB   1963   113m   bw
Anglo-Amalgamated/Novus (Michael Relph)
A scientist undergoes an experiment aimed at depriving him of all sensation. It works too well; he becomes a sadist; and his colleagues can't reverse the process.
Matter-of-factly played hocus-pocus with spy asides; quite gripping while it's on, but in no way memorable.
w James Kennaway d Basil Dearden ph Denys Coop m Georges Auric
☆ Dirk Bogarde, John Clements, Mary Ure, Michael Bryant

The Mind of Mr Reeder *
GB   1939   75m   bw
Jack Raymond
An elderly government employee unmasks a forger and murderer.
Entertaining crime comedy-drama which never quite realizes its potential.
w Bryan Edgar Wallace, Marjorie Gaffney, Michael Hogan novel Edgar Wallace d Jack Raymond
☆ Will Fyffe, Kay Walsh, George Curzon, Chili Bouchier, John Warwick

The Mind of Mr Soames
GB   1970   98m   Technicolor
Columbia/Amicus (Teresa Bolland)
A man who has lived in a coma for thirty years is cured but faces the world as a new-born infant.
Ill-advised attempt at science fiction with meaning; its earnestness becomes a bore.
w John Hale, Edward Simpson novel Charles Eric Maine d Alan Cooke ph Billy Williams m Michael Dress
☆ Terence Stamp, Robert Vaughn, Nigel Davenport, Donal Donnelly, Christian Roberts, Vickery Turner, Scott Forbes

---

The Mind Reader *
US 1933 69m bw
Warner
A phoney mind reader tries to go straight for his wife's sake, and ends up in jail.
Reasonably mordant satirical drama with good performances.
w Wilson Mizner, Robert Lord *play* Vivian Cosby d Roy del Ruth
☆ *Warren William*, Constance Cummings, Allen Jenkins, Donald Dillaway, Mayo Methot, Clarence Muse
'Star performance plus laugh dialogue enough to send this into okay programmer class.' – *Variety*

Mind Your Own Business
US 1937 75m bw
Paramount/Emmanuel Cohen
Boy scouts help to capture gangsters.
Slightly rocky comedy which finally comes across as unsatisfactory.
w Dore Schary *story* John Francis Larkin d Norman Z. McLeod
☆ Charles Ruggles, Alice Brady, Lyle Talbot, Benny Baker, Jack La Rue, William Demarest, Frankie Darro
'It will have a tough time standing alone.' – *Variety*

Mine Own Executioner ***
GB 1947 108m bw
London Films (Anthony Kimmins, Jack Kitchin)
A lay psychiatrist undertakes the care of a mentally disturbed war veteran, but fails to prevent him from murdering his wife.
When this film first appeared it seemed like the first adult drama featuring sophisticated people to emerge from a British studio. Time and television have blunted its impact, but it remains a well told suspense melodrama with memorable characters.
w Nigel Balchin *novel* Nigel Balchin d Anthony Kimmins ph Wilkie Cooper m Benjamin Frankel ad William C. Andrews ed Richard Best
☆ Burgess Meredith, Kieron Moore, Dulcie Gray, Barbara White, Christine Norden
'The first psychoanalytical film that a grown-up can sit through without squirming.' – *Richard Winnington*
'One feels invigorated by having seen and understood other people's lives.' – *Daily Worker*

'His secret meant death to one man if he didn't talk ... to countless thousands if he did!'
Ministry of Fear **
US 1944 85m bw
Paramount (Seton I. Miller)
During World War II in England, a man just out of a mental hospital wins a cake at a village fair and finds himself caught up in bewildering intrigues.
Little to do with the novel, but a watchable, well-detailed little thriller on Hitchcock lines, once you forgive the usual phoney Hollywood England.
w Seton I. Miller *novel* Graham Greene d Fritz Lang ph Henry Sharp m Victor Young ad Hans Dreier, Hal Pereira ed Archie Marshek
☆ Ray Milland, Marjorie Reynolds, Carl Esmond, Hillary Brooke, Dan Duryea, Percy Waram, Alan Napier, Erskine Sanford
'A crisp and efficiently made thriller with no pretension to intellectual content.' – *Paul Jensen*

The Miniver Story
GB 1950 104m bw
MGM (Sidney Franklin)
Mrs Miniver faces the tribulations of post-war Britain.
Glum sequel to Mrs Miniver, with the dauntless heroine finally succumbing to a glossy but fatal disease. Well enough made, but very hard to take.
w Ronald Millar, George Froeschel d H. C. Potter ph Joseph Ruttenberg m Miklos Rozsa
☆ Greer Garson, Walter Pidgeon, Cathy O'Donnell, John Hodiak, Leo Genn, Reginald Owen, Henry Wilcoxon, William Fox, Anthony Bushell

Minnie and Moskowitz *
US 1971 115m Technicolor
Universal (Al Rubin)
Two lonely Los Angeles misfits have a bumpy courtship.

Enjoyably aimless character comedy.
wd John Cassavetes ph Arthur J. Ornitz m Bob Harwood ed Robert Heffernan, Frederic Knudtson
☆ Gena Rowlands, Seymour Cassel, Val Avery, Tom Carey

Minstrel Man *
US 1944 70m bw
PRC
A minstrel star seeks his long-lost daughter.
Interesting sidelights on old-time minstrel shows in a production somewhat less tatty than is usual from this company.
w Irwin Franklin, Pierre Gendron d Joseph H. Lewis m Leo Erdody, Ferde Grofe
☆ Benny Fields, Gladys George, Roscoe Karns
♫ song, 'Remember Me to Carolina' (mHarry Revel, lyPaul Webster); music

A Minute to Pray, a Second to Die: see Dead or Alive

The Miracle
Italy 1948 40m bw
Tania Film (Roberto Rossellini)
A simple-minded peasant woman is seduced by a shepherd but believes her baby has been immaculately conceived.
Curious, rather unsatisfactory parable originally intended as part of a two-item tribute to the power of a star actress. (The other section, Cocteau's The Human Voice, was withdrawn for copyright reasons.)
w Tullio Pinelli, Roberto Rossellini, Federico Fellini d Roberto Rossellini ph Aldo Tonti m Renzo Rossellini
☆ Anna Magnani, Federico Fellini
'Acting on a plane scarcely known to the cinema.' – *Sunday Times*

'The mightiest story of fame and the flesh known to our time!'
The Miracle
US 1959 121m Technirama
Warner (Henry Blanke)
In Spain during the Peninsular War, a nun breaks her vows in order to follow a British soldier, and a statue of the Virgin Mary steps down to take her place.
And that's only the beginning in this very tall tale, full of heavy breathing, violent action and religiosity, from the old Max Reinhardt pageant. Quite incredible, and sloppily done.
w Frank Butler *play* Karl Vollmoeller d Irving Rapper ph Ernest Haller m Elmer Bernstein
☆ Carroll Baker, Roger Moore, Walter Slezak, Vittorio Gassman, Katina Paxinou, Dennis King, Isobel Elsom, Torin Thatcher

The Miracle
GB 1990 97m colour
Palace/Promenade/British Screen/Film Four (Stephen Woolley, Redmond Morris)
An actress becomes the focus of the romantic attentions of an adolescent saxophonist.
Desultory tale of incipient incest with a few striking moments.
wd Neil Jordan ph Philippe Rousselot m Anne Dudley ed Gemma Jackson ad Joke Van Wijk
☆ Beverly D'Angelo, Donal McCann, Niall Byrne, Lorraine Pilkington, J. G. Devlin, Cathleen Delany, Tom Hickey, Shane Connaughton
'Insubstantial fare, with predictable situations and plotting.' – *Variety*

A Miracle Can Happen: see On Our Merry Way

Miracle in Milan **
Italy 1951 101m bw
PDS/ENIC (Vittorio de Sica)
A foundling goes to live with the poor on the outskirts of Milan, and his erstwhile guardian returns from heaven to help them repel capitalists and fly away on broomsticks to a better land.
An unlikely fable which manages to avoid all the obvious pitfalls and sends one out of the cinema in a warm glow.
w Cesare Zavattini, Vittorio de Sica *novel* Toto il Buono by Cesare Zavattini d Vittorio de Sica ph G. R. Aldo m Alessandro Cicognini
☆ Francesco Golisano, Brunella Bovo, Emma Gramatica, Paolo Stoppa

Miracle in Soho
GB 1957 93m Eastmancolor
Rank (Emeric Pressburger)
A Soho roadworker falls for a barmaid.
Rudimentary romantic whimsy in an unconvincing street set, with characters either too voluble or just plain dull.
w Emeric Pressburger d Julian Amyes ph Christopher Challis m Brian Easdale
☆ John Gregson, Belinda Lee, Cyril Cusack

'A street corner pick-up that worked a miracle of love! A picture of very special greatness!'
Miracle in the Rain **
US 1955 107m bw
Warner (Frank P. Rosenberg)
A plain New York girl falls for a soldier; when he is killed in action, he keeps their appointment on the church steps as a ghost.
Archetypal Hollywood schmaltz, half acute observation of amusing types, half sentimental whimsy, with a final supernatural touch of eating your cake and having it.
w Ben Hecht *novel* Ben Hecht d Rudolph Maté ph Russell Metty m Franz Waxman
☆ Jane Wyman, Van Johnson, Fred Clark, Eileen Heckart, William Gargan

The Miracle Maker
♔ GB/Russia 1999 91m Technicolor
Icon/S4C/British Screen/Christmas (Naomi Jones, Renat Zinnurov)
Jesus leaves home to do God's work, performs miracles, is crucified and rises from the dead.
Reverential treatment of the Gospel story, told using animated clay figures.
w Murray Watts d Stanislav Sokolov, Derek Hayes ph Alexander Vikhanski m Anne Dudley ad Helena Livanova ed William Oswald, John Richards
☆ Featuring voices of: Ralph Fiennes, Michael Bryant, Julie Christie, Rebecca Callard, James Frain, Richard E. Grant, Ian Holm, William Hurt, Anton Lesser, Daniel Massey, Tim McInnerny, Alfred Molina, Bob Peck, Miranda Richardson, Anthony Sher, David Thewlis, Ken Stott
'Even as one admires the aesthetics and good intentions of this piece, the film falls flat since it's hard to feel in any way emotionally connected.' – *James Cameron-Wilson, Film Review*

The Miracle Man
US 1932 85m bw
Paramount
A gang of crooks is reformed by a faith healer they have exploited.
Adequate remake of the silent Lon Chaney vehicle; no sparks this time.
w Waldemar Young, Samuel Hoffenstein *play* Frank L. Packard, George M. Cohan d Norman Z. McLeod ph David Abel m W. Franke Harling
☆ Sylvia Sidney, Chester Morris, Irving Pichel, John Wray, Robert Coogan, Hobart Bosworth, Boris Karloff, Ned Sparks, Virginia Bruce

'50 minutes and counting...'
Miracle Mile *
US 1989 88m CFI color
Hemdale (John Daly, Derek Gibson)
A town panics as it learns that a nuclear strike is on the way.
Suspense and black humour are maintained to the final moments in an engagingly odd little movie.
wd Steve DeJarnatt ph Theo Van de Sande m Tangerine Dream ed Christopher Horner ed Stephen Semel, Kathie Weaver
☆ Anthony Edwards, Mare Winningham, John Agar, Lou Hancock, Mykel T. Williamson, Kelly Jo Minter, Kurt Fuller, Denise Crosby

The Miracle of Fatima: see The Miracle of Our Lady of Fatima

The Miracle of Morgan's Creek ***
US 1943 99m bw
Paramount (Preston Sturges)
Chaos results when a stuttering hayseed tries to help a girl accidentally pregnant by a soldier she met hazily at a dance.
Weird and wonderful one-man assault on the Hays Office and sundry other American institutions such as motherhood and politics; an indescribable, tasteless,

roaringly funny mêlée, as unexpected at the time as it was effective, like a kick in the pants to all other film comedies.
wd Preston Sturges ph John Seitz m Leo Shuken, Charles Bradshaw
☆ Betty Hutton, Eddie Bracken, William Demarest, Diana Lynn, Porter Hall, Akim Tamiroff, Brian Donlevy, Alan Bridge
OFFICER KOCKENLOCKER (WILLIAM DEMAREST): 'Daughters. They're a mess no matter how you look at 'em. A headache till they get married – if they get married – and after that they get worse ... Either they leave their husbands and come back with four kids and move into your guest room or the husband loses his job and the whole caboodle comes back. Or else they're so homely that you can't get rid of them at all and they sit around like Spanish moss and shame you into an early grave.'
EMILY KOCKENLOCKER (DIANA LYNN): 'If you don't mind my mentioning it, father, I think you have a mind like a swamp.'
'Like taking a nun on a roller coaster.' – *James Agee*
'This film moves in a fantastic and irreverent whirl of slapstick, nonsense, farce, sentiment, satire, romance, melodrama – is there any ingredient of dramatic entertainment except maybe tragedy and grand opera that hasn't been tossed into it?' – *National Board of Review*
'Bad taste, or no bad taste, I thoroughly enjoyed it.' – *Richard Mallett, Punch*
♝ Preston Sturges (as writer)

The Miracle of Our Lady of Fatima
US 1952 102m Warnercolor
Warner (Bryan Foy)
GB title: *The Miracle of Fatima*
An account of the 1917 appearance of the Virgin Mary to three Portuguese peasant children.
Poorly staged religious film which manages to be less pro-Catholic than anti-communist, and was clearly seen by Jack L. Warner as a means of atoning for Mission to Moscow. A real cold war piece.
w Crane Wilbur, James O'Hanlon d John Brahm ph Edwin DuPar m Max Steiner ad Edward Carrere
☆ Gilbert Roland, Frank Silvera, Angela Clarke, Jay Novello
♝ Max Steiner

The Miracle of the Bells
US 1948 120m bw
Jesse L. Lasky
The death of a glamorous film star causes a small-town miracle and a nationwide publicity stunt.
One hopes that this oddity was intended as a satire; as a straight entertainment it's more than a little icky, and good production values scarcely help.
w Ben Hecht *novel* Russell Janney d Irving Pichel ph Robert de Grasse m Leigh Harline
☆ Fred MacMurray, Alida Valli, Frank Sinatra, Lee J. Cobb
'An offensive exhibition of vulgar insensitivity.' – *MFB*
'I hereby declare myself the founding father of the Society for the Prevention of Cruelty to God.' – *James Agee*

The Miracle of the White Stallions *
US 1963 118m Technicolor
Walt Disney (Peter V. Herald)
GB title: *The Flight of the White Stallions*
During World War II the Nazis occupy Vienna and the owner of the Spanish Riding School guides his stallions to safety.
Adequate family adventure fare with a dull hero but interesting backgrounds.
w A. J. Carothers d Arthur Hiller ph Gunther Anders m Paul Smith
☆ Robert Taylor, Lilli Palmer, Eddie Albert, Curt Jurgens

Miracle on 34th Street ***
US 1947 94m bw
TCF (William Perlberg)
GB title: *The Big Heart*
A department store Santa Claus claims to be the real thing.
Mainly charming comedy fantasy which quickly became an American classic but does suffer from a few dull romantic stretches.

wd George Seaton *story* Valentine Davies *ph* Charles Clarke, Lloyd Ahern *m* Cyril Mockridge

☆ Edmund Gwenn, Maureen O'Hara, John Payne, Natalie Wood, Gene Lockhart, Porter Hall, William Frawley, Jerome Cowan, Thelma Ritter
'Altogether wholesome, stimulating and enjoyable.' – *Motion Picture Herald*
♟ George Seaton (as writer); Valentine Davies; Edmund Gwenn
♙ best picture

'Discover the Miracle.'
Miracle on 34th Street *
🏃🏃 US   1994   114m   DeLuxe
TCF (John Hughes)
📼 🖥 📺 ◎〜
A department store Santa Claus promises a child that he will provide her with a house, a father and a brother for Christmas.
A rather tired remake of the original which makes little attempt to engage with present-day realities, but gains from Attenborough's cuddly performance as Kriss Kringle.
w George Seaton, John Hughes *d* Les Mayfield *ph* Julio Macat *m* Bruce Broughton *pd* Doug Kraner *ed* Raja Gosnell
☆ Richard Attenborough, Elizabeth Perkins, Dylan McDermott, Mara Wilson, Robert Prosky, J. T. Walsh, James Remar, William Windom
'Glaringly predictable, and although some may succumb to its old-fashioned charm and naïvely simple message, others will find its look and feel too cloying.' – *Patricia Dobson, Screen International*

Miracle on Main Street *
US   1940   76m   bw
RKO/Jack Skirball
A cabaret dancer finds an abandoned baby but her plans are thwarted by the return of her husband.
Odd, interesting but flatly handled melodrama.
w Sam Ornitz, Boris Ingster *story* Felix Jackson *d* Steve Sekely *ph* Charles Van Enger *m* Walter Jurmann, Hans Salter
☆ Walter Abel, Margo, William Collier, Jane Darwell, Lyle Talbot, Wynne Gibson

'Never give away what you can sell!'
The Miracle Woman *
US   1931   90m   bw
Columbia (Harry Cohn)
📺
A lady evangelist turns confidence trickster.
Mild satirical drama inspired by the career of Aimée Semple Macpherson.
w Jo Swerling *play* Bless You Sister by Robert Riskin, John Meehan *d* Frank Capra *ph* Joseph Walker
☆ Barbara Stanwyck, Sam Hardy, David Manners, Beryl Mercer, Russell Hopton
'Splendid programme leader, a big and strong film opening up numerous channels of publicity' – *Variety*
'Such a beauty, well staged and handsomely lighted.' – *New Yorker, 1977*

The Miracle Worker *
US   1962   106m   bw
UA/Playfilms (Fred Coe)
📼 🖥 ◎〜
The childhood of Helen Keller, taught by Annie Sullivan after being left blind, deaf and dumb in an illness.
A moving real-life story is given hysterical treatment and the good scenes have a hard task winning through; in any case a documentary might have been more persuasive.
w William Gibson *play* William Gibson *d* Arthur Penn *ph* Ernest Caparros *m* Laurence Rosenthal *ad* George Jenkins
☆ Anne Bancroft, Patty Duke, Victor Jory, Inga Swenson, Andrew Prine, Beah Richards
♟ Anne Bancroft; Patty Duke
♙ William Gibson; Arthur Penn
🎖 Anne Bancroft

Miracles
US   1985   87m   Technicolor   Super Technicolor
Orion/Steve Roth, Bernard Williams
📺 ◎〜
A chase begins when bank robbers kidnap an innocent couple.
Exhausting action comedy with no real finesse.

wd Jim Kouf *ph* John Alcott *m* Peter Bernstein *pd* Terence Marsh
☆ Tom Conti, Teri Garr, Paul Rodriguez, Christopher Lloyd

Miracles for Sale
US   1939   71m   bw
MGM
An illusionist catches a murderer.
What could have been a smart mystery piece is sabotaged by stilted writing and direction, a muddled narrative style, and illusions which are patently faked by the camera.
w James Edward Grant, Marion Parsonnet, Harry Ruskin *novel* Death in a Top Hat by Clayton Rawson *d* Tod Browning *ph* Charles Lawton
☆ Robert Young, Florence Rice, Henry Hull, Frank Craven, Lee Bowman, William Demarest
'Unexciting whodunit ... the plot stumbles over itself most of the time.' – *Variety*

Mirage **
US   1965   109m   bw
U-I (Harry Keller)
📺
During a New York power blackout, an executive falls to his death from a skyscraper and a cost accountant loses his memory.
Striking puzzler, rather slowly developed but generally effective and with a strong sense of place and timing.
w Peter Stone *novel* Walter Ericson *d* Edward Dmytryk *ph* Joe MacDonald *m* Quincy Jones
☆ Gregory Peck, Diane Baker, Walter Abel, Walter Matthau, Leif Erickson, Kevin McCarthy
'Worthy of Hitchcock at his vintage best.' – *Daily Express*

Miranda *
GB   1947   80m   bw
GFD/Gainsborough/Sydney Box (Betty Box)
A doctor on holiday in Cornwall catches a mermaid and takes her to London disguised as an invalid.
Simple-minded comedy which scores a few easy laughs on obvious targets.
w Peter Blackmore *play* Peter Blackmore *d* Ken Annakin *ph* Ray Elton *m* Temple Abady
☆ Glynis Johns, Griffith Jones, Googie Withers, Margaret Rutherford, David Tomlinson, Sonia Holm, John McCallum
† Sequel 1949, *Mad about Men*.

Miranda (dubbed)
Italy   1985   90m   colour
San Francisco (Giovanni Bertolucci)
📼
A woman keeps an inn and also manages to service a string of lovers.
From the opening shot of a woman's pubic hair and a man's bare bottom, we are in the tiresome world of Tinto Brass, a director who concentrates on voyeuristic, soft-focus scenes of sexual activity and displays no interest in style or narrative.
w Carla Cipriani, Tinto Brass *d* Tinto Brass *ph* Silvano Ippoliti *m* Riz Ortolani *ad* Paolo Biagetti *ed* Tinto Brass
☆ Serena Grandi, Andrea Occhipinti, Franco Interlenghi, Andy J. Forest, Franco Branciaroli

Mirror **
USSR   1974   106m   bw/colour
Artificial Eye/Mosfilm Unit 4 (E. Waisberg)
📼 🖥
original title: Zerkalo
An artist considers his relationships with his parents and with his wife and young son.
Intensely personal meditation, with the director's father reading his own poems and his mother playing the narrator's mother, which may baffle audiences, despite its assurance and visual beauty.
w Andrei Tarkovsky, Aleksandr Misharin *d* Andrei Tarkovsky *ph* Georgy Rerberg *m* Eduard Artemyev *ad* Nikolai Dvigubsky *ed* L. Feiginova
☆ Innokenti Smoktunovsky, Margarita Terekhova, L. Tarkovskaya, Philip Yankovsky, Ignat Daniltsev, Anatoli Solonitsin
'Tarkovsky's autobiographical essay in the interaction of private and collective memories, via a multi-layered structure of flashbacks, dream sequences and newsreel footage, is chillingly impressive even at its most hermetic.' – *Sight and Sound*
† Tarkovsky said of the film, 'We wanted to make a simple film which would signify only what was

shown'. It was given a very restricted release in the USSR.

The Mirror
West Germany/Turkey   1984   94m   colour
Von Vietinghoff Filmproduction/ZDF/Channel 4 (Joachim von Vietinghoff)
original title: Der Spiegel Ayna
A Turkish peasant reacts violently on discovering that the son of the local landowner is in love with his wife.
Ponderously told folk tale, full of stolid symbolism.
wd Erden Kiral *novel* The White Ox by Osman Sahin *ph* Kenan Ormanler *m* Brymor Jones
☆ Nur Surer, Suavi Eren, Hikmet Celik

'Mirror, mirror, on the wall, who's the killer among them all?'
The Mirror Crack'd
GB   1980   105m   Technicolor
EMI/John Brabourne, Richard Goodwin
📼 🖥 ◎〜
Murders result from the making of an all-star film in an English village.
After adventures on the Orient Express and the Nile, this follow-up in the Agatha Christie stakes seems woefully restricted with stilted dialogue and playing.
w Jonathan Hales, Barry Sandler *novel* Agatha Christie *d* Guy Hamilton *ph* Christopher Challis *m* John Cameron *pd* Michael Stringer
☆ Angela Lansbury, Geraldine Chaplin, Elizabeth Taylor, Rock Hudson, Tony Curtis, Edward Fox, Kim Novak, Marella Oppenheim, Charles Gray

'A story about just how wrong two people can be before they can be right...'
The Mirror Has Two Faces
US   1996   126m   Technicolor
Columbia TriStar/Phoenix/Arnon Milchan/Barwood (Barbra Streisand, Arnon Milchan)
📼 🖥 ◎ ◎ ◎ ◎ 🎧
A dowdy academic marries a professor more interested in companionship than sex, until she reinvents herself as a desirable woman.
Creaky, frequently risible romantic hokum about the need to be adored, somewhat undermined by the fact that Streisand looks better before, rather than after, her transformation into a sex goddess.
w Richard LaGravenese *d* Barbra Streisand *ph* Dante Spinotti, Andrzej Bartkowiak *m* Marvin Hamlisch, Barbra Streisand *pd* Tom John *ed* Jeff Werner
☆ Barbra Streisand, Jeff Bridges, Pierce Brosnan, George Segal, Mimi Rogers, Brenda Vaccaro, Lauren Bacall, Austin Pendleton, Elle Macpherson
'A vanity production of the first order. A staggeringly obsessive expression of the importance of appearances, good looks and being adored, Barbra Streisand's third directorial outing is also, incidentally, a very old-fashioned wish-fulfillment romantic comedy that has been directed and performed in the broadest possible manner.' – *Todd McCarthy, Variety*
'I have never seen so many shots of a star staring into a mirror. Streisand seems to be in the unique position of being her own co-star for most of the movie. This has to be a cinema first: a romantic comedy for one.' – *Tom Shone, Sunday Times*
† It is based on the French film *Le Miroir à Deux Faces*, written by André Cayatte and Gerard Oury, directed by Cayatte in 1958 and starring Michele Morgan.
♙ Lauren Bacall; song 'I Finally Found Someone' (*m/ly* Barbra Steisand, Marvin Hamlisch, Bryan Adams, Robert 'Mutt' Lange)

'In her book, there's a fine line between fantasy and reality – and she's walking it!'
The Misadventures of Margaret
GB/France   1998   93m   DeLuxe
Feature/Mandarin/TF1/Lunatics and Lovers (Ian Benson)
📼 🖥
A married American writer becomes excessively flirtatious as the result of researching a novel set in 18th-century France.
An odd comedy of sexual exploration that never quite manages the sophistication it needs.
wd Brian Skeet *novel* Rameau's Niece by Cathleen Schine *ph* Romain Winding *m* James Shearman *pd* Martin Childs *ed* Clare Douglas
☆ Parker Posey, Jeremy Northam, Craig Chester, Elizabeth McGovern, Brooke Shields, Corbin Bernsen, Justine Waddell, Patrick Bruel

'Coarse in the current female-laddish fashion, but not badly performed. And it's often verbally funny.' – *Philip French, Observer*

Mischief *
US   1985   93m   DeLuxe
Jere Henshaw-Michael Nolin/TCF
📼 🖥 ◎〜
Teenage anxieties in smalltown America in 1956
Clearly not for export, but a smooth piece of its kind.
w Noel Black *d* Mel Damski *ph* Donald E. Thorin *pd* Paul Peters *ed* Nick Brown
☆ Doug McKeon, Catherine Mary Stewart, Kelly Preston, Chris Nash

Les Misérables ****
🏃🏃 US   1935   109m   bw
Twentieth Century (Darryl F. Zanuck)
📺 ◎〜
Unjustly convicted and sentenced to years in the galleys, Jean Valjean emerges to build up his life again but is hounded by a cruel and relentless police officer.
Solid, telling, intelligent version of a much-filmed classic novel; in adaptation and performance it is hard to see how this film could be bettered.
w W. P. Lipscomb *novel* Victor Hugo *d* Richard Boleslawski *ph* Gregg Toland *m* Alfred Newman *ed* Barbara McLean
☆ Fredric March, Charles Laughton, Cedric Hardwicke, Rochelle Hudson, Frances Drake, John Beal, Jessie Ralph, Florence Eldridge
'Brilliant filmization, sure fire for heavy money.' – *Variety*
'Unbelievably thrilling in all the departments of its manufacture ... a memorable experience in the cinema.' – *New York Times*
'A superlative effort, a thrilling, powerful, poignant picture.' – *New York Evening Post*
'Deserving of rank among the cinema's finest achievements.' – *New York World Telegram*
† Other versions of the story: 1909, 1913 (French); 1917 (William Farnum); 1923 (French: Gabriel Gabrio); 1929 as *The Bishop's Candlesticks* (Walter Huston); 1934 (French: Harry Baur); 1946 (Italian: Gino Cervi); 1952 (see below); 1956 (French: Jean Gabin; see below); 1978 (British: Richard Jordan)
♙ best picture; Gregg Toland; editing

Les Misérables **
🏃🏃 US   1952   106m   bw
TCF (Fred Kohlmar)
📺
Solemn remake, well done but lacking the spark of inspiration.
w Richard Murphy *d* Lewis Milestone *ph* Joseph LaShelle *m* Alex North
☆ Michael Rennie, Robert Newton, Edmund Gwenn, Debra Paget, Cameron Mitchell, Sylvia Sidney, Elsa Lanchester, James Robertson Justice, Joseph Wiseman, Rhys Williams

Les Misérables ***
France   1995   177m   colour
Warner/Films 13/TF1/Canal (Claude Lelouch)
📼 🖥
A former boxing champion who helps a Jewish couple during the Nazi occupation of France finds that his life begins to resemble that of Jean Valjean, the hero of Victor Hugo's novel.
An engrossing, intriguing, emotionally satisfying drama that both echoes and dramatizes Hugo's epic, revealing the timelessness of the story and the changes that time and circumstance might have made to its characters.
wd Claude Lelouch *novel* Victor Hugo *ph* Claude Lelouch, Philippe Pavans de Ceccatty *m* Francis Lai, Didier Barbelivien, Philippe Servain, Erik Berchot, Michel Legrand *ad* Jacques Bufnoir *ed* Hélène de Luze
☆ Jean-Paul Belmondo, Michel Boujenah, Alessandra Martines, Annie Girardot, Philippe Leotard, Clementine Celarie, Rufus, Ticky Holgado
'Hugely ambitious in both theme and scope and brimming with sheer delight in the medium.' – *Derek Elley, Variety*
'A righteous, passionate and witty soap opera.' – *Sarah Kerr, New Yorker*

Les Misérables *

US   1998   134m   Technicolor   Panavision

Entertainment/Mandalay (Sarah Radclyffe, James Gorman)

A former convict who makes good is hounded by a ruthless policeman.

Dour version of the classic novel, one that takes itself too seriously, repressing the romantic sweep of its narrative.

w Rafael Yglesias *novel* Victor Hugo d Bille August ph Jörgen Persson m Basil Poledouris pd Anna Asp ed Janus Billeskov-Jansen

☆ Liam Neeson, Geoffrey Rush, Uma Thurman, Claire Danes, Hans Matheson, Reine Brynolfsson, Peter Vaughan

'An impressive, brooding monolith of a film … Unfortunately, it really isn't much fun, a cardinal sin in this sort of epic spectacle.' – *Andrew O'Hehir, Sight and Sound*

Les Misérables de Victor Hugo *

France/Italy   1958   210m   Technicolor   Technirama

Pathé/P.A.C./Serena (Paul Cadeac)

Jean Valjean escapes from prison and makes a new life for himself, but his old one catches up with him.

Stolid version of Hugo's classic, gaining what distinction it has from Gabin's performance.

w René Barjavel, Jean-Paul Le Chanois d Jean-Paul Le Chanois ph Jacques Natteau m Georges Van Parys ad Serge Pimenoff, Karl Schneider ed Emma Le Chanois

☆ Jean Gabin, Bernard Blier, Danièle Delorme, Serge Reggiani, Bourvil, Gianni Esposito, Martine Havet, Béatrice Altariba, Elfriede Florin, Jimmy Urbain, Jean Murat, Lucien Baroux, Silvia Monfort

† The film is sometimes shown in two parts. The best French version is that of Raymond Bernard, who made a three-part adaptation of the novel in 1933 starring Harry Baur under the titles *Tempête sous un Crane* (120m), *Les Thénardiers* (90m), and *Liberté, Liberté Chérie* (95m). He later cut it to a two-part film: *Jean Valjean* (109m) and *Cosette* (100m).

'Paul Sheldon used to write for a living. Now he's writing to stay alive.'

Misery **

US   1990   107m   CFI color

Medusa/Castle Rock/Nelson (Andrew Scheinman, Rob Reiner)

A disturbed fan kidnaps an injured novelist and forces him to write a novel featuring her favourite heroine.

Impeccably directed, tense thriller.

w William Goldman *novel* Stephen King d Rob Reiner ph Barry Sonnenfeld m Marc Shaiman pd Norman Garwood ed Robert Leighton

☆ James Caan, Kathy Bates, Richard Farnsworth, Frances Sternhagen, Lauren Bacall, Graham Jarvis, Jerry Potter

'This astonishing film is a taut, darkly comic thriller and a post-modernist examination of the relationship between writer and reader, detached producer and vulnerable consumer, artist and critic.' – *Philip French, Observer*

🎭 Kathy Bates

The Misfits *

US   1961   124m   bw

United Artists/Seven Arts (Frank E. Taylor)

Cowboys gather in the Nevada desert to rope wild mustangs, and a divorcee becomes involved with one of them.

Ill-fated melodrama whose stars both died shortly afterwards; a solemn, unattractive, pretentious film which seldom stops wallowing in self-pity.

w Arthur Miller d John Huston ph Russell Metty m Alex North

☆ Clark Gable, Marilyn Monroe, Montgomery Clift, Eli Wallach, Thelma Ritter, James Barton, Estelle Winwood, Kevin McCarthy

'The theme with its implications of an essentially male savagery suits Mr Huston, and he has drawn extraordinary qualities from all his chief players.' – *Dilys Powell*

Mishima *

US   1985   120m   Technicolor   Panavision

Coppola-Lucas/Warner

Fragments of autobiography by the self-destructing Japanese writer.

A complete switch-off for all but the initiated, this indulgent, delicate, violent kaleidoscope is half a work of art and half an utter waste of other people's money.

w Paul and Leonard Schrader d Paul Schrader ph John Bailey m Philip Glass

☆ Ken Ogata, Kanji Sawada, Yasosuke Bando

The Misleading Lady

US   1932   75m   bw

Paramount

A social butterfly aspires to be an actress.

Ho-hum romantic comedy, quite unmemorable.

w Adelaide Heilbron, Caroline Francke *play* Charles W. Goddard, Paul Dickey d Stuart Walker

☆ Claudette Colbert, Edmund Lowe, Stuart Erwin, Robert Strange, George Meeker

'Lightweight stuff of conventional pattern.' – *Variety*

Misplaced

US   1989   95m   colour

Subway (Lisa Zwerling)

In the early 80s, a Polish woman and her teenage son leave the political unrest of Poland to settle in Washington with family that she has not seen for more than 30 years.

Earnestly effective low-key drama of the problems of assimilation into a different culture, on a personal and a public level.

w Louis Yansen, Thomas DeWolfe d Louis Yansen ph Igor Sunara m Michael Urbaniak pd Beth Kuhn ed Michael Berenbaum

☆ John Cameron Mitchell, Viveca Lindfors, Elzbieta Czyzewska, Drew Snyder, Deirdre O'Connell, John Christopher Jones, Debralee Scott

Miss Amerigua

Paraguay/Sweden   1994   93m   colour

FilmTeknik/Latino (Luis R. Vera)

A man returns home from Nicaragua to revenge the death of his father, which he witnessed as a boy, only to discover that the city is in the grip of a beauty competition.

Ham-fisted, if amiable and meandering, political farce.

w Luis R. Vera, Andrés Colmán d Luis R. Vera ph Mårten Nilsson m Jan Tolf ad Carlos dos Santos ed Lisskulla Moltke-Hoff

☆ Sonia Marchewka, Raquel Baeza, Ayesa Frutos, Jesús Perez, Hector Silva, Jorge Baez, Jorge Ramos

'Mild political satire with touches of magical realism that paints an agreeably sketchy portrait of a fictional South American town.' – *Ken Eisner, Variety*

† It was the first feature to be made in Paraguay for 30 years.

Miss Annie Rooney

US   1942   86m   bw

Edward Small

Poor Irish girl loves rich boy.

A totally routine offering for a teenage star; no wonder she didn't make it.

w George Bruce d Edwin L. Marin ph Lester White md Edward Paul

☆ Shirley Temple, William Gargan, Guy Kibbee, Dickie Moore, Peggy Ryan, Gloria Holden, Jonathan Hale, Mary Field

Miss Fane's Baby Is Stolen

US   1933   67m   bw

Paramount

GB title: *Kidnapped*

A film star's baby is kidnapped.

Fairly straightforward crime yarn with comic asides.

w Adela Rogers St Johns, Rupert Hughes d Alexander Hall

☆ Dorothea Wieck, Alice Brady, Baby LeRoy, William Frawley, George Barbier, Alan Hale, Jack La Rue

'Box office as well as entertainment … the first picture of its kind since the Lindbergh kidnapping.' – *Variety*

Miss Firecracker *

US   1989   103m   DuArt

Rank/Firecracker Company/Corsair (Fred Berner)

An orphaned girl enters her home-town beauty contest.

Unconvincing in its portrayal of a young woman discovering her individuality.

w Beth Hanley *play* The Miss Firecracker Contest by Beth Hanley d Thomas Schlamme ph Arthur Albert m David Mansfield, Homer Denison pd Maher Ahmad ed Peter C. Frank

☆ Holly Hunter, Mary Steenburgen, Tim Robbins, Alfre Woodard, Scott Glenn, Veanne Cox, Ann Wedgeworth, Trey Wilson, Amy Wright, Kathleen Chalfant

Miss Grant Takes Richmond *

US   1949   87m   bw

Columbia (S. Sylvan Simon)

GB title: *Innocence Is Bliss*

A dumb secretary helps defeat crooks and improve the local housing situation.

Mildly amusing star comedy.

w Nat Perrin, Devery Freeman, Frank Tashlin d Lloyd Bacon ph Charles Lawton Jnr m Heinz Roemheld md Morris Stoloff

☆ Lucille Ball, William Holden, Janis Carter, James Gleason, Gloria Henry, Frank McHugh, George Cleveland

'One of the more delightful comedies of the season.' – *Lawrence J. Quirk*

Miss Julie *

Sweden   1950   87m   bw

Sandrew (Rune Waldekranz)

In a lonely house, the count's daughter kills herself after being seduced by a valet.

Intense melodramatic fragment, just a little long for comfort.

wd Alf Sjöberg *play* August Strindberg ph Göran Strindberg m Dag Wirén

☆ Anita Björk, Ulf Palme, Anders Henrikson

'The outstanding achievement of the Swedish cinema in recent years.' – *Gavin Lambert, Sight and Sound*

Miss London Ltd

GB   1943   99m   bw

GFD/Gainsborough (Edward Black)

An escort agency is formed to assist soldiers on leave.

Flagwaving light entertainment with popular performers of the time.

w Val Guest, Marriott Edgar d Val Guest ph Basil Emmott md Louis Levy *songs* Manning Sherwin (m), Val Guest (ly)

☆ Arthur Askey, Anne Shelton, Evelyn Dall, Richard Hearne, Max Bacon, Jack Train, Peter Graves, Jean Kent

Miss Marple

Agatha Christie's inquisitive spinster detective was brought to the screen by director George Pollock and star Margaret Rutherford in four increasingly disappointing films for MGM.

1962 Murder She Said (qv)
1963 Murder at the Gallop
1964 Murder Most Foul, Murder Ahoy
See also *The Mirror Crack'd*.

Miss Mary

Argentina   1986   110m   Eastmancolor

New World/GEA (Lita Stantic)

During the period between the two world wars, an English governess gets too close an attachment to the young son of the household.

An attempt to chart the social changes in Argentina, culminating in Perón's takeover, through the upheavals in one dysfunctional family; but the focus is too diffused, and there is little cohesion between its succession of effective individual episodes.

w Maria Luisa Bemberg, Jorge Goldenberg d Maria Luisa Bemberg ph Miguel Rodriguez ed Luisa Cesar d'Angiolillo

☆ Julie Christie, Nacha Guevara, Eduardo Pavlovsky, Luisina Brando, Gerardo Romano, Iris Marga, Guillermo Battaglia

Miss Pacific Fleet

US   1935   76m   bw

Warner

Two stranded show girls enter a popularity contest to win the fare back home.

A comedy with little to laugh at.

w Lucille Newmark, Peter Milne, Patsy Flick d Ray Enright

☆ Glenda Farrell, Joan Blondell, Hugh Herbert, Allen Jenkins, Warren Hull, Guinn Williams

'Maybe OK for double feature bills, but that's the best it can hope for.' – *Variety*

Miss Pilgrim's Progress

GB   1949   87m   bw

Daniel M. Angel

An American working girl in Britain helps to save a village from development.

Wholly artificial and unendearing comedy.

wd Val Guest ph Bert Mason m Phillip Martell

☆ Yolande Donlan, Michael Rennie, Garry Marsh, Emrys Jones, Reginald Beckwith, Helena Pickard, Jon Pertwee

Miss Pinkerton *

US   1932   66m   bw

Warner

A private nurse helps a police detective to solve a murder case.

Pleasing little mystery comedy.

w Lillian Hayward, Niven Busch *story* Mary Roberts Rinehart d Lloyd Bacon ph Barney McGill

☆ Joan Blondell, George Brent, Mae Madison, John Wray, Ruth Hall, C. Henry Gordon, Elizabeth Patterson

'Formula mystery story … picture is outdated and has nothing to draw.' – *Variety*

† Remade as *The Nurse's Secret* (1946).

Miss Robin Hood

GB   1952   78m   bw

Group 3

A lady author pits her wits against crooks and saves an old lady's fortune.

Disappointing star comedy with no build-up.

w Val Valentine, Patrick Campbell, Geoffrey Orme d John Guillermin ph Arthur Grant m Temple Abady

☆ Margaret Rutherford, Richard Hearne, Michael Medwin, Peter Jones, James Robertson Justice, Sidney James, Dora Bryan

Miss Sadie Thompson *

US   1953   91m   Technicolor   3-D

Columbia (Lewis J. Rachmil)

Vigorous semi-musical remake of *Rain* (qv); a good star vehicle, but not otherwise notable.

w Harry Kleiner d Curtis Bernhardt ph Charles Lawton md George Duning

☆ Rita Hayworth, José Ferrer, Aldo Ray, Russell Collins, Harry Bellaver

♫ song 'Blue Pacific Blues' (mLester Lee, lyNed Washington)

'A story for lovers … past, present and perfect!'

Miss Susie Slagle's

US   1946   88m   bw

Paramount (John Houseman)

Romances of nursing students in 1910 Baltimore.

Modest melodramatic potboiler.

w Anne Froelick, Hugo Butler *novel* Augusta Tucker d John Berry ph Charles Lang Jnr m Daniele Amfitheatrof

☆ Veronica Lake, Joan Caulfield, Sonny Tufts, Lillian Gish, Ray Collins, Billy de Wolfe, Bill Edwards, Roman Bohnen, Morris Carnovsky, Lloyd Bridges

Miss Tatlock's Millions *

US   1948   101m   bw

Paramount (Charles Brackett)

A stunt man impersonates the idiot heir to a fortune.

Tasteless but quite funny comedy with a cast of eccentrics indulging in enjoyable fooling.

w Charles Brackett, Richard L. Breen d Richard Haydn ph Charles Lang Jnr m Victor Young

☆ John Lund, Wanda Hendrix, Monty Woolley, Barry Fitzgerald, Robert Stack, Ilka Chase, Dorothy Stickney

Miss V from Moscow
US   1942   70m   bw
PRC
A Russian spy impersonates a German spy in Paris.
Hilariously inept propaganda piece; since the Cold War it has been retitled Intrigue in Paris.
w Arthur St Claire and Sherman Lowe   d Albert Herman
☆ Lola Lane, Noel Madison, Howard Banks

'Loyalty Without Question. Friendship Without Equal.'

Mrs Brown ***
GB   1997   103m   colour
Miramax/Ecosse (Sarah Curtis)
🔲 ▤ ◑ 🔒 ◎ ◎ ∩
Faithful Scottish servant John Brown lifts Queen Victoria out of her funereal gloom, arousing the jealousy of her household staff.
Absorbing, deftly directed, excellently acted drama that, while concentrating on personal relationships, raises still-vital questions about the point and purpose of the monarchy.
w Jeremy Brock   d John Madden   ph Richard Greatrex   m Stephen Warbeck   pd Martin Childs   ed Robin Sales
☆ Judi Dench, Billy Connolly, Geoffrey Palmer, Anthony Sher, Gerald Butler, Richard Pasco, David Westhead
'Possesses resonances that are rich, complex and instructive.' – *Richard Williams, Guardian*
† Executive producer Douglas Rae conceived the film in the 60s and originally planned to cast Sean Connery in the role of John Brown, but the film was then abandoned when he learned that the Royal Family was not happy with the project.
⚲ Judi Dench; make-up
⊙ Judi Dench; Deidre Clancy (costumes)

Mrs Brown, You've Got a Lovely Daughter
GB   1968   95m   Metrocolor   Panavision
MGM/Allen Klein
▤
A young singer inherits a prize greyhound.
Inoffensive comedy musical with a swinging London background.
w Thaddeus Vane   d Saul Swimmer   ph Jack Hildyard   m/ly Graham Couldman, Geoff Stephens, Kenny Young
☆ Peter Noone and Herman's Hermits, Stanley Holloway, Mona Washbourne, Lance Percival, Marjorie Rhodes

Mrs Dalloway **
GB/US/Netherlands   1997   97m   Rank Colour
Artificial Eye/First Look (Stephen Bayly, Lisa Katselas Paré)
🔲 ▤ ◑ ∩
In the 20s, a society hostess looks back on her life and thinks of what might have been.
Gripping, pensive examination of the possibilities and missed opportunities of life.
w Eileen Atkins   novel Virginia Woolf   d Marleen Gorris   ph Sue Gibson   m Ilona Sekacz   pd David Richens   ed Michiel Reichwein
☆ Vanessa Redgrave, Natascha McElhone, Rupert Graves, Michael Kitchen, John Standing, Alan Cox, Lena Headey, Margaret Tyzack, Sarah Badel, Phyllis Calvert
'A highly romantic, deeply melancholy drama, the film offers psychological and existential insights about the inevitable effects – and price – of life choices.' – *Emanuel Levy, Variety*

'She makes dinner. She does windows. She reads bedtime stories. She's a blessing ... in disguise.'
Mrs Doubtfire *
👫 US   1993   125m   DeLuxe   Panavision
TCF/Blue Wolf (Marcia Garces Williams, Robin Williams, Mark Radcliffe)
🔲 ▤ ◑ ∩
An unemployed actor, allowed only weekly visits to his two children, disguises himself as a nanny so that he can spend more time with them.
If you can accept Williams as an Englishwoman – he looks like a truck driver in drag and sounds like Miss Jean Brodie long past her prime – there is occasional slapstick amusement to be found in this over-long and sickly sweet comedy.
w Randi Mayem Singer, Leslie Dixon   novel *Alias Madam Doubtfire* by Anne Fine   d Chris Columbus   ph Donald McAlpine   m Howard Shore   pd Angelo Graham   ed Raja Gosnell   sp Greg Cannom

☆ Robin Williams, Sally Field, Pierce Brosnan, Harvey Fierstein, Polly Holiday, Lisa Jakub, Matthew Lawrence, Mara Wilson, Robert Prosky
'Lessons are learned, loved ones are hugged, and personal growth is achieved – as usual, at the expense of the comedy. Some, apparently, including Williams, like it warm and cuddly, too. Nobody's perfect.' – *Terrence Rafferty, New Yorker*
'A really wholesome movie about a man in a bra; it's like watching a John Waters movie rewritten by John Hughes.' – *Libby Gelman-Waxner, Premiere*
'This Robin Williams-in-drag vehicle provides the comic with a slick surface for doing his shtick, within a story possessing broad family appeal.' – *Variety*
† The film was a success in America, taking more than $200m at the box-office.
⚲ make-up

Mrs Fitzherbert
GB   1947   99m   bw
British National (Louis H. Jackson)
The Prince Regent secretly marries a Catholic widow.
Stilted, ill-cast historical charade.
wd Montagu Tully   novel Winifred Carter   ph James Wilson   m Hans May
☆ Peter Graves, Joyce Howard, Leslie Banks, Margaretta Scott

Mrs Gibbons' Boys
GB   1962   82m   bw   Byronscope
Byron/British Lion
A widow plans to marry respectably for the sake of her three convict sons.
Unattractive farce with clodhopping characters and too much slapstick.
w Peter Blackmore, Max Varnel   play Joseph Stein, Will Glickman   d Max Varnel
☆ Kathleen Harrison, Lionel Jeffries, Diana Dors, John Le Mesurier, Frederick Bartman, David Lodge, Dick Emery, Eric Pohlmann, Milo O'Shea

Mrs Loring's Secret: see *The Imperfect Lady*

Mrs Mike
US   1949   99m   bw
Nassour/Huntingdon Hartford (Edward Gross)
A Mountie takes his new wife to live in the frozen northwest.
Predictable sentimental drama, well enough done to keep interest, but only just.
w Lewis Levitt, De Witt Bodeen   d Louis King   ph Joseph Biroc   m Max Steiner
☆ Dick Powell, Evelyn Keyes, J. M. Kerrigan, Angela Clarke

Mrs Miniver **
US   1942   134m   bw
MGM (Sidney Franklin)
🔲 ▤ ◑ ∩
An English housewife survives World War II.
This is the rose-strewn English village, Hollywood variety, but when released it proved a beacon of morale despite its false sentiment, absurd rural types and melodramatic situations. It is therefore beyond criticism, except that some of the people involved should have known better.
w Arthur Wimperis, George Froeschel, James Hilton, Claudine West   novel Jan Struther   d William Wyler   ph Joseph Ruttenberg   m Herbert Stothart   ed Harold F. Kress
☆ Greer Garson, Walter Pidgeon, Teresa Wright, Richard Ney, Dame May Whitty, Henry Travers, Reginald Owen, Henry Wilcoxon, Helmut Dantine, Rhys Williams, Aubrey Mather
VICAR (HENRY WILCOXON) PREACHING FINAL SERMON IN BOMBED CHURCH: 'This is not only a war of soldiers in uniforms. It is a war of the people – of all the people – and it must be fought not only on the battlefield but in the cities and in the villages, in the factories and on the farms, in the home and in the heart of every man, woman and child who loves freedom. Well, we have buried our dead, but we shall not forget them. Instead, they will inspire us with an unbreakable determination to free ourselves and those who come after us from the tyranny and terror that threaten to strike us down. This is the people's war. It is our war. We are the fighters. Fight it, then. Fight it with all that is in us. And may God defend the right.'

'That almost impossible feat, a war picture that photographs the inner meaning, instead of the outward realism of World War II.' – *Time*
⚑ best picture; script; William Wyler; Joseph Ruttenberg; Greer Garson; Teresa Wright
⚲ Walter Pidgeon; Dame May Whitty; Henry Travers; Harold F. Kress

Mrs O'Malley and Mr Malone *
US   1950   69m   bw
MGM (William H. Wright)
On a train to New York, a radio contest winner and a lawyer help solve a murder.
Lively second feature farce.
w William Bowers   d Norman Taurog   ph Ray June   m Adolph Deutsch
☆ Marjorie Main, James Whitmore, Ann Dvorak, Fred Clark, Dorothy Malone, Phyllis Kirk

'A Woman Ahead Of Her Time. A Movie That Can't Be Missed.'
'New York in the 1920's. The only place to be was the Algonquin, and the only person to know was Dorothy Parker.'
Mrs Parker and the Vicious Circle
US   1994   124m   colour
Artificial Eye/Miramax/Fine Line (Robert Altman)
🔲 ▤ ∩
Dorothy Parker, a successful Hollywood screenwriter, recalls her earlier days and love affairs with wits and writers in New York and her regard for Robert Benchley.
A disappointing biopic of a complex, unhappy and talented writer. Jennifer Jason Leigh's mannered performance and drawled monotone may be true to the externals of Dorothy Parker but render her witticisms in such an unintelligible way that it is surprising that anyone was able to record them.
w Alan Rudolph, Randy Sue Coburn   d Alan Rudolph   ph Jan Kiesser   m Mark Isham   pd François Séguin   ed Suzy Elmiger
☆ Jennifer Jason Leigh, Matthew Broderick, Campbell Scott, Peter Gallagher, Jennifer Beals, Andrew McCarthy, Wallace Shawn, Martha Plimpton, Sam Robards, Lili Taylor, James LeGros
'Buys into the self-pity, morbidity and pathos of Dorothy Parker's writing and life, rather than her robustness, comic verve and bracing good sense; it also seems to buy into the modern therapised view that wounding wit is the first resort of the wounded.' – *Kevin Jackson, Independent*

Mrs Parkington
US   1944   124m   bw
MGM (Leon Gordon)
▤
A lady's maid marries a miner who becomes wealthy, and pushes her way into society.
Thoroughly unconvincing three-generation drama, with a bewigged and powdered star giving the boot to her conniving relations. It has production values and nothing else.
w Robert Thoeren, Polly James   novel Louis Bromfield   d Tay Garnett   ph Joseph Ruttenberg   m Bronislau Kaper
☆ Greer Garson, Walter Pidgeon, Edward Arnold, Agnes Moorehead, Cecil Kellaway, Gladys Cooper, Frances Rafferty, Tom Drake, Peter Lawford, Dan Duryea, Hugh Marlowe, Selena Royle
† The heroine is shown having a romance with Edward VII when Prince of Wales; special scenes were shot for the European version substituting Cecil Kellaway, who played Edward, by Hugo Haas who played a European king of indeterminate origin.
⚲ Greer Garson; Agnes Moorehead

Mrs Pollifax – Spy
US   1970   110m   DeLuxe
UA/Mellor (Frederick Brisson)
A respectable American matron offers her services to the CIA and sees active service in Albania.
Incredible comedy-dramatic vehicle for a star who won't give up. An obvious failure from the word go.
w C. A. McKnight   novel Dorothy Gilman   d Leslie Martinson   ph Joseph Biroc   m Lalo Schifrin
☆ Rosalind Russell, Darren McGavin
† C. A. McKnight was Rosalind Russell.

Mrs Pym of Scotland Yard
GB   1939   65m   bw
Hurley/Grand National
A lady detective exposes a fake spiritualist.

A would-be series character bites the dust through plot malnutrition.
w Fred Elles, Peggy Barwell, Nigel Morland   novel Nigel Morland   d Fred Elles
☆ Mary Clare, Edward Lexy, Nigel Patrick, Anthony Ireland, Irene Handl

Mrs Soffel
US   1984   110m   Metrocolor
MGM-UA/Edgar Scherick/Scott Rudin
🔲 ▤ ◑
In 1901 Pittsburgh, a warder's wife falls for a prisoner and helps him escape.
A basis in truth does not prevent this from being both glum and dull from beginning to end, and pretentious treatment doesn't help.
w Ron Nyswaner   d Gillian Armstrong   ph Russell Boyd   m Mark Isham   pd Luciana Arrighi   ed Nicholas Beauman
☆ Diane Keaton, Mel Gibson, Matthew Modine, Edward Herrmann

Mrs Wiggs of the Cabbage Patch *
US   1934   80m   bw
Paramount (Douglas MacLean)
Adventures of a poor family who live on the wrong side of the tracks in a broken down old shack.
A Depression fantasy of respectability and optimism, almost incredible to see now, although it plumbed the same never-never milieu as did Chaplin. Moments of comedy still please, but one does long for Mr Fields's delayed entry.
w William Slavens McNutt, Jane Storm   novel Alice Hegan Rice   d Norman Taurog   ph Charles Lang
☆ Pauline Lord, ZaSu Pitts, W. C. Fields, Evelyn Venable, Kent Taylor, Charles Middleton, Donald Meek, Edith Fellows, Virginia Weidler, George Breakston
'A nasty all's-right-with-the-world burlesque of poverty, with emotions to tug at such heartstrings as are worn dangling from the mouth.' – *Otis Ferguson*

Mrs Wiggs of the Cabbage Patch
US   1942   80m   bw
Paramount
Curiously quick remake, almost word for word, but without the moments of inspiration.
w Doris Anderson, Jane Storm, William Slavens McNutt   d Ralph Murphy   ph Leo Tover
☆ Fay Bainter, Hugh Herbert, Vera Vague, Barbara Britton, Carl Switzer, Moroni Olsen, Billy Lee

Mrs Winterbourne
US   1996   104m   Technicolor
TriStar/A&M (Dale Pollock, Ross Canter, Oren Koules)
🔲 ▤ ◑
A poor, pregnant woman is mistaken for the widow of a millionaire and taken in by his family.
A thriller is here turned into a family comedy for no good reason.
w Phoef Sutton, Lisa-Maria Radano   story I Married a Dead Man by Cornell Woolrich   d Richard Benjamin   ph Alex Nepomniaschy   m Patrick Doyle   pd Evelyn Sakash   ed Jacqueline Cambas, William Fletcher
☆ Shirley MacLaine, Ricki Lake, Brendan Fraser, Miguel Sandoval, Loren Dean, Paula Prentiss
'A sappy, old-fashioned and predictable vehicle ... that delivers requisite warmth but few laughs.' – *Brian Lowry, Variety*
† It is a remake of No Man of Her Own (qv), directed in 1950 by Mitchell Leisen and starring Barbara Stanwyck.

Missiles from Hell: see *The Battle of the V1*

Missing *
US   1982   122m   Technicolor
Universal/Polygram/Peter Guber, Jon Peters (Edward and Mildred Lewis)
▤ ◑
An American seeks his young son who has disappeared in Chile.
A further link in the chain of political thrillers from this director; well-wrought and compulsive but finally disappointing in its mixture of fact and fiction.
w Costa-Gavras, Donald Stewart   book Thomas Hauser   d Costa-Gavras   ph Ricardo Aronovich   m Vangelis   pd Peter Jamison   ed Françoise Bonnot
☆ Jack Lemmon, Sissy Spacek, Melanie Mayron, John Shea, Charles Cioffi, Richard Bradford

---

👫 film suitable for family viewing   🔲 VHS video-cassette for the British PAL system   ▤ VHS video-cassette for the British PAL system in wide screen-format   ⟳ Video cassette in a computer-colourised version   ▤ American NTSC video cassette   ◑ Laser disc

'Provocation and entertainment prove to be uneasy allies.' – *Tom Milne, MFB*

👤 screenplay (adaptation)
🏆 Jack Lemmon; best picture; Sissy Spacek
🏆 screenplay

The Missing Corpse
US 1945 54m bw
PRC/Leon Fromkess
A publisher tries to hide a corpse he is suspected of murdering.
Adequate filler for indulgent audiences.
w Ray Schrock d Albert Herman
☆ J. Edward Bromberg, Ben Welden, Frank Jenks, Isabel Randolph

Missing in Action
US 1984 101m Metrocolor
Cannon (Menahem Golan, Yoram Globus)
An American colonel, having been taken prisoner and escaped, returns to Vietnam to find other 'missing' men.
Naïve, violent, jingoistic romp which caused quite a lot of box-office business around the world.
w James Bruner d Joseph Zito ph Joao Fernandes m Jay Chattaway ad Ladi Wilheim, Toto Castillo ed Joel Goodman
☆ Chuck Norris, M. Emmet Walsh, Lenore Kasdorf, James Hong

Missing in Action 2 – The Beginning
US 1985 95m TVC Color
Cannon (Menahem Golan, Yoram Globus)
A prequel to the above, showing the colonel's first escape.
More cheaply made, it runs like a series of offcuts, with emphasis on unpleasant violence.
w Arthur Silver, Larry Levinson, Steve Bing d Lance Hool ph Jorge Stahl Jnr m Brian May pd Michael Baugh ed Mark Conte, Marcus Nanton
☆ Chuck Norris, Soon Teck-Oh, Cosie Costa, Steven Williams

The Missing Juror
US 1944 71m bw
Columbia
Members of a murder jury are killed off one by one.
Minor puzzle piece from the I Love a Mystery series.
w Charles O'Neal d Budd Boetticher
☆ Jim Bannon, Janis Carter, George Macready

Missing Link
US 1988 92m colour
Universal
A million years in the past, a solitary man-ape, the rest of his kind having been killed by humans, wanders across the African continent.
Quirky film with no dialogue, notable for some arresting wildlife photography – of nature red in tooth and claw – though it does not convince with its creation of a missing link between ape and humans, a hairy, harmless dimwit who walks into trees.
wd David and Carolyn Hughes sp make-up: Rick Baker
☆ Peter Elliott, Michael Gambon

Missing Pieces
US 1991 92m colour
Rank/Aaron Russo Entertainment
An out-of-work writer and an unemployed musician are pursued by crooks as they try to solve a riddle that will net them a fortune.
A chase comedy that rounds up the usual clichés and then recycles them.
wd Leonard Stern ph Peter Stein m Marvin Hamlisch pd Michael Z. Hanan ed Evan Lottman
☆ Eric Idle, Robert Wuhl, Lauren Hutton, Bob Gunton, Richard Belzer, Bernie Kopell, Kim Lankford, Don Gibb

The Missing Rembrandt
GB 1932 82m bw
Twickenham
Sherlock Holmes saves a lady's honour and nails a blackmailer.
Not the best of this particular series, but Wontner is a Holmes to relish.
w Cyril Twyford, H. Fowler Mear story Charles Augustus Milverton by Arthur Conan Doyle d Leslie Hiscott ph Basil Emmott
☆ Arthur Wontner, Ian Fleming, Jane Welsh, Miles Mander, Francis L. Sullivan

Missing Ten Days: see Ten Days in Paris

The Mission **
GB 1986 128m Rank Colour JDC wide screen
Goldcrest/Kingsmere/Enigma/Fernando Ghia (David Puttnam)
In mid-18th-century South America, Jesuit priests fall foul of avaricious colonialists.
Sincere to the point of boredom, this 22-million-dollar would-be epic is short on plot development, long on superb photography of remote actualities.
w Robert Bolt d Roland Joffe ph Chris Menges m Ennio Morricone pd Stuart Craig, Norman Dorme ed Jim Clark
☆ Robert DeNiro, Jeremy Irons, Ray McAnally, Liam Neeson, Aidan Quinn, Ronald Pickup, Cherie Lunghi
👤 Chris Menges
🏆 best picture; Roland Joffe; Ennio Morricone; Jim Clark; art direction (Stuart Craig); sound (Jack Stephens); costumes (Enrico Sabbatini)
🏆 Ray McAnally; Ennio Morricone

'Expect the impossible.'
Mission: Impossible *
US 1996 110m DeLuxe Panavision
Paramount (Tom Cruise, Paula Wagner)
A secret agent sets out to discover who double-crossed him and killed his colleagues.
A movie very much in the James Bond style, with added paranoia; the gimmick-laden narrative makes little sense, but the set-piece stunts are spectacularly over-the-top.
w David Koepp, Robert Towne, Steven Zaillian d Brian de Palma ph Stephen H. Burum m Danny Elfman pd Norman Reynolds ed Paul Hirsch sp visual: John Knoll; make-up: Rob Bottin
☆ Tom Cruise, Jon Voight, Emmanuelle Beart, Henry Czerny, Jean Reno, Ving Rhames, Kristin Scott-Thomas, Vanessa Redgrave
'A headache with a great soundtrack and some lustrous set pieces.' – *Tom Shone, Sunday Times*
† The film is based on the TV series created by Bruce Geller, which ran from 1967 to 1973 and from 1988 to 1990. The theme music, which was written by Lalo Schifrin and also features in the movie, was a hit in 1968.
†† It was among the box-office successes of 1996, grossing more than $452m around the world.

Mission in Morocco
US/Spain 1959 79m bw
Republic/John Mather/Hispamer (Sergio Newman)
An oil-man goes to Morocco to investigate the murder of his partner and the whereabouts of a missing microfilm.
Sub-standard action adventure, with acting to match.
w Brian Clemens story Guy Elmes, Ken Annakin d Anthony Squire ph Cecilio Paniagua m Guenther Kauer ad Tadeo Villalba ed Max Benedict
☆ Lex Barker, Juli Reding, Fernando Rey, Silvia Morgan, Alfredo Mayo

'For centuries we've been looking for the origin of life on earth. We've been looking on the wrong planet.'
Mission to Mars
US 2000 112m Technicolor Panavision
Buena Vista/Touchstone (Tom Jacobson)
A rescue party goes to Mars to find the sole survivor of the first manned expedition to the planet, who has discovered evidence that it was once inhabited.
Grandiose attempt at science-fiction with a spiritual message; it never achieves lift-off.
w Jim Thomas, John Thomas, Graham Yost d Brian De Palmer ph Stephen H. Burum m Ennio Morricone pd Ed Verreaux ed Paul Hirsch sp Industrial Light & Magic; Dream Quest Images; CIS Hollywood
☆ Gary Sinise, Tim Robbins, Don Cheadle, Connie Nielsen, Jerry O'Connell, Kim Delaney,

Elise Neal, Peter Outerbridge, Jill Teed, Kavan Smith
'Dull and eventually ludicrous while trying to be moving and profound.' – *Todd McCarthy, Variety*
'It's been a long time since such a grandiloquent souffle of majesty and silliness refused to rise on the big screen.' – *Elvis Mitchell, New York Times*

Mission to Moscow **
US 1943 112m bw
Warner (Robert Buckner)
The Russian career of US Ambassador Joseph E. Davies.
Stodgy but fascinating wartime propaganda piece viewing the Russians as warm-hearted allies; in the later days of the McCarthy witch hunt, Jack L. Warner regretted he had ever allowed it to be made.
w Howard Koch book Joseph E. Davies d Michael Curtiz ph Bert Glennon m Max Steiner ad Carl Weyl
☆ Walter Huston, Ann Harding, Oscar Homolka, George Tobias, Gene Lockhart, Eleanor Parker, Richard Travis, Helmut Dantine, Victor Francen, Henry Daniell, Barbara Everest, Dudley Field Malone, Roman Bohnen, Maria Palmer, Moroni Olsen and also Minor Watson
'A mishmash: of Stalinism with New Dealism with Hollywoodism with opportunism with shaky enthusiasm with mesmerism with onanism, all mosaicked into a remarkable portrait of what the makers of the film think the Soviet Union is like – a great glad two-million-dollar bowl of canned borscht, eminently approvable by the Institute of Good Housekeeping.' – *James Agee*
🏆 Carl Weyl

The Missionary *
GB 1983 86m colour Panavision
HandMade Films (Michael Palin)
In 1906, a clergyman returns from darkest Africa and sets up a Mission to Fallen Women in the East End of London.
Sporadically amusing comedy of a reformer being tempted; the decoration is funnier than the central theme.
w Michael Palin d Richard Loncraine ph Peter Hannan m Mike Moran ad Norman Garwood
☆ Michael Palin, Maggie Smith, Michael Hordern, Trevor Howard, Denholm Elliott, Graham Crowden, Phoebe Nicholls, Roland Culver
'It leaves one with a half-frozen smile, in anticipation of a comic fulfilment which never quite happens.' – *Nick Roddick, MFB*
'A deliciously straight-faced acceptance of the palpably absurd.' – *Daily Mail*

Mississippi *
US 1935 75m bw
Paramount (Arthur Hornblow Jnr)
A showboat singer has a cloud on his reputation.
Mild period musical with occasional stops for comedy.
w Herbert Fields, Claude Binyon story Booth Tarkington d A. Edward Sutherland ph Charles Lang m/ly Rodgers and Hart
☆ Bing Crosby, W. C. Fields, Joan Bennett, Gail Patrick, Claude Gillingwater, John Miljan, Queenie Smith
'A dull film, rambling and hokey.' – *Variety*

Mississippi Burning **
US 1988 127m DeLuxe
Rank/Orion (Frederick Zollo, Robert F. Colesberry)
In Mississippi in the mid-1960s, FBI agents investigate the murder of three civil rights workers.
Melodramatic and sensational account of racism in action that caused controversy on its release because of its concentration on white activists; but it has a power that sweeps its audience along with it.
w Chris Gerolmo d Alan Parker ph Peter Biziou m Trevor Jones pd Philip Harrison, Geoffrey Kirkland ed Gerry Hambling
☆ Gene Hackman, Willem Dafoe, Frances McDormand, Brad Dourif, R. Lee Ermey, Gailard Sartain, Stephen Tobolowsky, Michael Rooker, Pruitt Taylor Vince
👤 Peter Biziou
🏆 best picture; Alan Parker; Gene Hackman; Frances McDormand; Gerry Hambling; best sound
🏆 Peter Biziou

Mississippi Gambler
US 1953 98m Technicolor
U-I (Ted Richmond)
A showboat gambler has trouble with a bad loser, but finally marries his sister.
Picturesque star melodrama with period settings and not much meat in the story.
w Seton I. Miller d Rudolph Maté ph Irving Glassberg m Frank Skinner
☆ Tyrone Power, Piper Laurie, John McIntire, Julia Adams, Dennis Weaver

'Romeo And Juliet Had It Easy.'
Mississippi Masala *
US 1991 colour
SCS/Odyssey/Cinecom/Film Four/Mirabai/Movieworks/Black River (Michael Nozick, Mira Nair)
A young Asian woman living in Mississippi falls in love with a black American, to the distress of both their families.
Uninvolving treatment of romance and racism.
w Sooni Taraporevala d Mira Nair ph Ed Lachman m L. Subramaniam pd Mitch Epstein ed Roberto Silvi
☆ Denzel Washington, Roshan Seth, Sarita Choudhury, Charles S. Dutton, Joe Seneca, Sharmila Tagore, Ranjit Chowdhry
'A film about racial issues which manages to avoid hatred and this leaves a joyously hopeful, if occasionally naive, aftertaste.' – *Empire*

The Mississippi Mermaid *
France/Italy 1969 123m Eastmancolor Dyaliscope
Films du Carrosse/PAA/Delphos (Marcel Berbert)
original title: *La Sirène du Mississipi*
After a courtship by mail, a factory owner on a remote African island finds that the girl who arrives by steamer does not fit his preconceptions…
Oddly obsessive romantic murder mystery: the hero continues to love the girl who tries to kill him, and at the end they are still together. Interesting when it is not uncomfortable.
wd François Truffaut novel Waltz into Darkness by William Irish ph Denys Clerval m Antoine Duhamel ad Claude Pignot ed Agnès Guillemot
☆ Jean-Paul Belmondo, Catherine Deneuve, Michel Bouquet, Nelly Borgeaud, Marcel Berbert

'One Steals. One Kills. One Dies.'
The Missouri Breaks
US 1976 126m DeLuxe
UA/Elliott Kastner/Robert B. Sherman
Montana ranchers and rustlers fight over land and livestock, and a hired killer shoots it out with a horse thief.
Savage, dislikeable Western with both stars over the top.
w Thomas McGuane d Arthur Penn ph Michael Butler m John Williams
☆ Marlon Brando, Jack Nicholson, Randy Quaid, Kathleen Lloyd, Frederic Forrest, Harry Dean Stanton
'It is typical of the film's richness and ambiguity that the title has about five possible punning meanings.' – *Michael Billington, Illustrated London News*
'Although listed as the director, Mr Penn finds himself perched on Brando's knee and manipulated as shamelessly as Edgar Bergen used to waggle Charlie McCarthy.' – *Benny Green, Punch*
'Nothing more than the self-conscious cleverness of some merry prankster with a blanket of scorn for all who don't share his flippancy.' – *William S. Pechter*
'A pair of million dollar babies in a five and ten cent flick.' – *Charles Champlin, Los Angeles Times*
'A picture of which it might be said they shouldn't make 'em like that any more … a picture that explains very little, including why anyone thought it a work that demanded to be made.' – *Robert Hatch, Nation*

Mister 880 **
US 1950 90m bw
TCF (Julian Blaustein)
An elderly counterfeiter perplexes the US Secret Service.

Whimsical star comedy which moves along cheerfully enough to be a good example of the Hollywood programmer at its prime.
w Robert Riskin *d* Edmund Goulding *ph* Joseph LaShelle *m* Sol Kaplan
☆ Edmund Gwenn, Burt Lancaster, Dorothy McGuire, Millard Mitchell
⑧ Edmund Gwenn

Mr Ace

US   1946   84m   bw
Benedict Bogeaus
▦ ℗
A rich, spoiled congresswoman is backed by a gangster but gets religion.
Odd star drama, perfunctorily made.
w Fred Finklehoffe *d* Edwin L. Marin *ph* Karl Struss *m* Heinz Roemheld
☆ Sylvia Sidney, George Raft, Stanley Ridges, Sara Haden, Jerome Cowan

Mr and Mrs North

US   1941   68m   bw
Irving Asher/MGM
Mr and Mrs find a corpse in their closet.
Reasonably lively transcription of a Broadway success.
w S. K. Lauren *play* Owen Davis *d* Robert B. Sinclair
☆ Gracie Allen, William Post Jnr, Paul Kelly, Rose Hobart, Virginia Grey, Tom Conway, Felix Bressart, Porter Hall, Millard Mitchell, Keye Luke, Jerome Cowan

Mr and Mrs Smith *

US   1941   95m   bw
RKO (Harry E. Edington)
▦▦ ℗
A much-married couple discover that their marriage wasn't legal.
Smartish matrimonial comedy, surprisingly but not obviously by the master of suspense.
w Norman Krasna *d* Alfred Hitchcock *ph* Harry Stradling *m* Edward Ward
☆ Carole Lombard, Robert Montgomery, Gene Raymond, Jack Carson, Philip Merivale, Lucile Watson, William Tracy
    'I doubt that your interest or amusement will last as long as the picture.' – *Otis Ferguson*

Mr Arkadin: see *Confidential Report*

Mr Ashton Was Indiscreet: see *The Senator Was Indiscreet*

Mr Baseball

US/Japan   1992   109m   DeLuxe   Panavision
Buena Vista/Walt Disney/Universal/Outlaw/Pacific Artists/Dentsu (Fred Schepisi, Doug Claybourne, Robert Newmyer)
▦▦ ▬ ℗ ⑤
A failing American baseball player is traded to a Japanese team.
Unhappy comedy of a culture clash, unlikely to be of interest to anyone except the keenest and most undemanding fan of the sport.
w Gary Ross, Kevin Wade, Monte Merrick *story* Theo Pelletier, John Junkerman *d* Fred Schepisi *ph* Ian Baker *m* Jerry Goldsmith *pd* Ted Haworth *ed* Peter Honess
☆ Tom Selleck, Ken Takakura, Aya Takanashi, Dennis Haysbert, Toshi Shioya, Kohsuke Toyohara
    'A strikeout is a strikeout. Universal's $40 million-plus exercise in cross-cultural comedy will land in a b.o. league of its own – in the cellar.' – *Variety*

Mr Belvedere Goes to College *

US   1949   88m   bw
TCF (Samuel G. Engel)
A self-styled genius goes back to school and helps a college widow.
Flat follow up to Sitting Pretty (qv), with only a few laughs.
w Richard Sale, Mary Loos, Mary McCall Jnr *d* Elliott Nugent *ph* Lloyd Ahern *m* Alfred Newman
☆ Clifton Webb, Shirley Temple, Alan Young, Tom Drake, Jessie Royce Landis, Kathleen Hughes, Taylor Holmes

Mr Belvedere Rings the Bell *

US   1951   87m   bw
TCF (André Hakim)
Imperturbable Mr Belvedere enters an old folk's home under false pretences to test his theories of ageing.
A not unagreeable star vehicle for those who can stand the sentiment.
w Ranald MacDougall *play* The Silver Whistle *by* Robert E. McEnroe *d* Henry Koster *ph* Joseph LaShelle *m* Cyril Mockridge
☆ Clifton Webb, Joanne Dru, Hugh Marlowe, Zero Mostel, Doro Merande

Mr Big

US   1943   73m   bw
Ken Goldsmith/Universal
Drama school students concoct a musical show.
Tolerable minor showcase for a new young star.
w Jack Pollexfen, Dorothy Bennett *d* Charles Lamont
☆ Donald O'Connor, Gloria Jean, Peggy Ryan, Robert Paige, Elyse Knox, Samuel S. Hinds, Florence Bates

Mr Billion *

US   1977   93m   DeLuxe
TCF/Pantheon (Gabriel Katzka, Steve Bach, Ken Friedman)
▦▦
An Italian garage mechanic becomes heir to a vast estate, providing he can get to San Francisco in time for the signing ceremony and outwit the villains trying to stop him.
Moderately engaging old-fashioned comedy-adventure.
w Ken Friedman, Jonathan Kaplan *d* Jonathan Kaplan *ph* Matthew F. Leonetti *m* Dave Grusin
☆ Terence Hill (Mario Girotti), Valerie Perrine, Jackie Gleason, Slim Pickens, William Redfield, Chill Wills

Mr Blandings Builds His Dream House ***

US   1948   84m   bw
RKO (Norman Panama, Melvin Frank)
▦▦ ℗
A New York advertising man longs to live in the Connecticut countryside, but finds the way to rural satisfaction is hard.
It hasn't the lightness and brightness of the book, but this is a fun film for the middle-aged who like to watch three agreeable stars doing their thing.
w Norman Panama, Melvin Frank *novel* Eric Hodgins *d* H. C. Potter *ph* James Wong Howe *m* Leigh Harline *md* Constantin Bakaleinikoff *ad* Albert S. D'Agostino, Carroll Clark *ed* Harry Marker
☆ Cary Grant, Myrna Loy, Melvyn Douglas, Reginald Denny, Louise Beavers, Ian Wolfe, Harry Shannon, Nestor Paiva, Jason Robards, Lex Barker
    'A bulls-eye for middle-class middlebrows.' – *James Agee*
    'I loved it. That was really a pleasure to make,' – *H. C. Potter, 1973*

Mister Buddwing

US   1966   99m   bw
MGM/DDD/Cherokee (Douglas Laurence, Delbert Mann)
GB title: *Woman without a Face*
An amnesiac wakes up in Central Park and goes in search of his identity.
Rather muddled melodrama in which the characters are so dull that by the time the flashbacks fall into place we scarcely care.
w Dale Wasserman *novel* Buddwing *by* Evan Hunter *d* Delbert Mann *ph* Ellsworth Fredericks *m* Kenyon Hopkins
☆ James Garner, Jean Simmons, Angela Lansbury, Suzanne Pleshette, Katharine Ross, George Voskovec, Jack Gilford, Joe Mantell, Raymond St Jacques
    'Its distinction is its pretension, its banality and its complete success in making all the authentic New York backgrounds look like the studio's cheaper backdrops.' – *Judith Crist*

Mr Bug Goes to Town *

†† US   1941   78m   Technicolor
Max Fleischer
▬ ℗
aka: *Hoppity Goes to Town*
An urban community of insects is in danger from developers.

A cartoon feature which failed to make its mark despite clever detail; perhaps because insects make poor heroes, or because there simply wasn't enough plot.
d Dave Fleischer *m* Leigh Harline

Mr Chedworth Steps Out

Australia   1939   92m   bw
Cinesound
In a period of redundancy a clerk has to take a job as a caretaker, but discovers a cache of counterfeit money.
Mild comedy-drama.
w Frank Harvey *d* Ken G. Hall
☆ Cecil Kellaway, Jean Hatton, James Raglan, Rita Pauncefort, Peter Finch

Mister Cinderella

US   1936   75m   bw
Hal Roach/MGM
A meek-and-mild youth aspires to crash high society.
Milk-and-water comedy with insufficient get-up-and-go.
w Arthur Vernon Jones, Richard Flournoy, Jack Jevne *d* Edward Sedgwick
☆ Jack Haley, Betty Furness, Arthur Treacher, Raymond Walburn, Rosina Lawrence, Monroe Owsley
    'Too crammed with slaptrap hokum to stand alone.' – *Variety*

Mister Cory

US   1957   92m   Eastmancolor   Cinemascope
U-I (Robert Arthur)
A small-time gangster leaves the Chicago slums to seek fame and fortune among the country-club set.
Modest star comedy drama.
wd Blake Edwards *ph* Russell Metty *m* Joseph Gershenson
☆ Tony Curtis, Martha Hyer, Charles Bickford, Kathryn Grant

Mr Deeds Goes to Town ***

US   1936   118m   bw
Columbia (Frank Capra)
▦▦ ▬ ℗
A small-town poet inherits a vast fortune and sets New York on its heels by his honesty.
What once was fresh and charming now seems rather laboured in spots, and the production is parsimonious indeed, but the courtroom scene still works, and the good intentions conquer all.
w Robert Riskin *story* Opera Hat *by* Clarence Budington Kelland *d* Frank Capra *ph* Joseph Walker *m* Adolph Deutsch *md* Howard Jackson
☆ Gary Cooper, Jean Arthur, Raymond Walburn, Lionel Stander, Walter Catlett, George Bancroft, Douglass Dumbrille, H. B. Warner, Ruth Donnelly, Margaret Seddon, Margaret McWade
    'I have an uneasy feeling he's on his way out. He's started to make pictures about themes instead of people.' – *Alistair Cooke*
    'Everywhere the picture goes, from the endearing to the absurd, the accompanying business is carried through with perfect zip and relish.' – *Otis Ferguson*
    'A comedy quite unmatched on the screen.' – *Graham Greene*
    'The film culminates in a courtroom sequence that introduced the word "pixilated" to just about every American home, and set people to examining each other's casual scribbles or sketches – their "doodles".' – *Pauline Kael, 70s*
⑤ Frank Capra
⑧ best picture; Robert Riskin; Gary Cooper

Mr Denning Drives North

GB   1951   93m   bw
London Films (Anthony Kimmins, Stephen Mitchell)
A wealthy man accidentally kills a criminal in love with his daughter; he hides the body, which then disappears.
Initially suspenseful but finally disappointing melodrama which seems to lack a twist or two.
w Alec Coppel *d* Anthony Kimmins *ph* John Wilcox *m* Benjamin Frankel
☆ John Mills, Phyllis Calvert, Sam Wanamaker, Freda Jackson

Mr Destiny

US   1990   105m   colour
Buena Vista/Touchstone/Silver Screen Partners IV (James Orr, Jim Cruikshank)
▦▦ ℗
A 35-year-old failure is given the chance to re-live his life as a success.
Dim comedy with the dimmer moral that everyone gets the life they deserve.
w James Orr, Jim Cruickshank *d* James Orr *ph* Alex Thomson *m* David Newman *pd* Michael Seymour *ed* Michael R. Miller
☆ James Belushi, Linda Hamilton, Michael Caine, Jon Lovitz, Hart Bochner, Bill McCutcheon, René Russo
    'A heavy-handed by-the-numbers fantasy.' – *Variety*

Mr District Attorney

US   1941   69m   bw
Leonard Fields/Republic
A lady reporter helps a young assistant DA to ferret out crooks.
Dim movie version of a radio series.
w Karl Brown, Malcolm Stuart Boylan *d* William Morgan
☆ Dennis O'Keefe, Florence Rice, Peter Lorre, Stanley Ridges, Minor Watson

Mr Dodd Takes the Air

US   1937   78m   bw
Warner (Mervyn Le Roy)
A country cousin becomes a hit as a crooner.
Modest comedy for small towns.
w William Wister Haines, Elaine Ryan *story* Clarence Budington Kelland *d* Alfred E. Green *ph* Arthur Edeson *md* Adolph Deutsch *songs* Al Dubin, Harry Warren
☆ Kenny Baker, Jane Wyman, Alice Brady, Gertrude Michael, Frank McHugh, Luis Alberni, Henry O'Neill, Harry Davenport
⑧ Al Dubin and Harry Warren for 'Remember Me'

Mr Drake's Duck **

†† GB   1950   85m   bw
Daniel M. Angel/Douglas Fairbanks
A duck lays a uranium egg, and a gentleman farmer finds himself at the centre of international military disagreement.
Brisk and amusing minor comedy deploying British comic types to good purpose.
wd Val Guest *radio play* Ian Messiter *ph* Jack Cox *m* Philip Martell
☆ Douglas Fairbanks Jnr, Yolande Donlan, Wilfrid Hyde-White, A. E. Matthews, Jon Pertwee, Reginald Beckwith, Howard Marion-Crawford, Peter Butterworth, Tom Gill
    'One of the funniest films I have ever seen.' – *News of the World*

Mr Dynamite

US   1935   75m   bw
Universal
An unconventional private detective outsmarts the police.
Amusing, wisecracking crime caper.
w Doris Malloy, Harry Clork *story* Dashiell Hammett *d* Alan Crosland
☆ Edmund Lowe, Jean Dixon, Esther Ralston, Victor Varconi, Minor Watson, Robert Gleckler
    'Nice entertainment.' – *Variety*

Mr Emmanuel *

GB   1944   97m   bw
Two Cities (William Sistrom)
In 1936 an elderly Jew visits Germany in search of the mother of an orphan boy.
Simply made but quite effective and unusual story giving Aylmer his only star part.
w Gordon Wellesley, Norman Ginsburg *novel* Louis Golding *d* Harold French *ph* Otto Heller
☆ Felix Aylmer, Greta Gynt, Walter Rilla, Peter Mullins, Ursula Jeans, Elspeth March, Meier Tzelniker

Mr Forbush and the Penguins *

†† GB   1971   101m   Technicolor
EMI/PGI/Henry Trettin
A biologist is sent to the Antarctic to study penguins, and gets a new understanding of life.
Rather broken-backed animal film with a moral; pleasant enough, its two halves don't fit together.

---

w Anthony Shaffer *novel* Graham Billey *d* Roy Boulting *ph* Harry Waxman, Ted Scaife *m* John Addison

☆ John Hurt, Hayley Mills, Tony Britton, Thorley Walters, Judy Campbell, Joss Ackland, Sally Geeson, Cyril Luckham

Mister Frost

France/UK 1990 104m colour
Blue Dolphin/AAA/Hugo Films/Overseas Multi Media (Xavier Gelin)
▣ ▤ ℚ
The devil incarnate tempts a hospital doctor.
Nonsensical and incomprehensible, a lurid mess from start to finish.
w Philippe Setbon, Brad Lynch *d* Philippe Setbon *ph* Dominique Brenguier *m* Steve Levine *ad* Max Berto *ed* Ray Lovejoy
☆ Jeff Goldblum, Alan Bates, Kathy Baker, Roland Giraud, Jean-Pierre Cassel, Daniel Gelin, François Negret, Maxime Leroux, Boris Bergman
'Staggeringly bad.' – *Philip French, Observer*

Mr Griggs Returns: see *The Cockeyed Miracle*

Mr Hobbs Takes a Vacation *

US 1962 116m DeLuxe Cinemascope
TCF (Jerry Wald)
A city dweller takes a seaside house for a family holiday, but it turns out to be a crumbling ruin.
Overlong, sloppy comedy which devotes too much time to teenage romance but manages occasional smiles.
w Nunnally Johnson *novel* Edward Streeter *d* Henry Koster *ph* W. C. Mellor *m* Henry Mancini
☆ James Stewart, Maureen O'Hara, Fabian, John Saxon, Marie Wilson, Reginald Gardiner, John McGiver

Mr Hobo: see *The Guvnor*

Mr Holland's Opus *

👪 US 1995 143m Technicolor Panavision
Polygram/Interscope/Charlie Mopic (Ted Field, Michael Nolin, Robert W. Cort)
▣ ▤ ℚ ♫
An ambitious composer takes a temporary job as a teacher and discovers that his true vocation is to inspire others with a love of music.
A relentlessly corny and sentimental drama that pulls out all the emotional stops as it plays slight variations on the themes of It's a Wonderful Life *and* Goodbye Mr Chips. *Its tone is populist: classical music is regarded as much less fun than jazz or rock.*
w Patrick Sheane Duncan *d* Stephen Herek *ph* Oliver Wood *m* Michael Kamen *pd* David Nichols *ed* Trudy Ship
☆ Richard Dreyfuss, Glenne Headly, Jay Thomas, Olympia Dukakis, W. H. Macy, Alicia Witt, Jean Louisa Kelly, Anthony Natale
'Older audiences will be moved by the story, but the crucial variable is to what extent younger viewers will embrace this schmaltzy, Capraesque saga that's not only set mainly in the past but also feels as if it were made back when.' – *Emanuel Levy, Variety*
ჯ Richard Dreyfuss

Mr Imperium

US 1951 87m Technicolor
MGM (Edwin H. Knopf)
GB title: *You Belong to My Heart*
An exiled king in Hollywood meets a famous film star with whom he once had a romance.
Minor romantic drama with songs.
w Edwin Knopf, Don Hartman *d* Don Hartman *ph* George J. Folsey *m* Bronislau Kaper *songs* Harold Arlen (m), Dorothy Fields (ly)
☆ Lana Turner, Ezio Pinza, Marjorie Main, Barry Sullivan, Cedric Hardwicke, Debbie Reynolds

'He's a proper Englishman in his heart. But Africa is in his soul'
Mr Johnson **

US 1990 101m Eastmancolor Panavision
TCF/Avenue Pictures (Michael Fitzgerald)
▣ ▤ ℚ
In West Africa in the 1920s a naïve and feckless clerk, who attempts to be more English than the English, destroys himself by seeking the easy way out of his problems.
Deftly acted and directed tragi-comedy of human fallibility and colonial attitudes.

w William Boyd *novel* Joyce Cary *d* Bruce Beresford *m* Georges Delerue *pd* Herbert Pinter *ed* Humphrey Dixon
☆ Pierce Brosnan, Edward Woodward, Maynard Eziashi, Beatie Edney, Denis Quilley, Bella Enahoro, Kwabena Manso, Nick Reding, Femi Fatoba
'Suffers the same fate as its title character, never coming close to being as important as it desperately wants to be.' – *Variety*
'A very generous, thoughtful and affecting movie.' – *Philip French, Observer*

Mr Jones

US 1993 114m Technicolor
Columbia TriStar/Rastar (Alan Greisman, Debra Greenfield)
▣ ▤ ℚ ◎
A manic depressive begins an affair with the psychiatrist who treats him for his condition.
An unsatisfactory movie that was cut by the studio over the director's objections; the result is less a psychological drama than a standard Hollywood romance with a slightly different twist that gives Richard Gere the chance to display energy and charm.
w Eric Roth, Michael Cristofer *d* Mike Figgis *ph* Juan Ruiz Anchia *m* Maurice Jarre *pd* Waldemar Kalinowski *ed* Tom Rolf
☆ Richard Gere, Lena Olin, Anne Bancroft, Bruce Altman, Delroy Lindo, Tom Irwin, Lauren Tom
'Inoffensive rainy afternoon fodder, this is one Jones most cinemagoers would be wise not to keep up with.' – *Film Review*

Mister Kingstreet's War

US 1970 92m colour
H.R.S. Films (Thys Heyns)
▤
aka: *Heroes Die Hard*
In Central Africa in 1939, an American game warden and his wife try to prevent the Italian and British armies from ruining his reserve, which contains the only water-holes in the area.
Clichéd drama – the baddie wears a black eye-patch – that makes no perceptible point and takes little advantage of the local flora and fauna.
w Percival Rubens, George Harding *d* Percival Rubens *ph* Grenville Middleton *m* Harry Sukman *ad* Roy Taylor *ed* John Bushelman
☆ John Saxon, Tippi Hedren, Rossano Brazzi, Brian O'Shaughnessy, Kerry Jordan, Joseph Sekatski

Mr Klein *

France/Italy 1976 123m Eastmancolor
Lira/Adel/Nova/Mondial Te-Fi (Raymond Danon, Alain Delon)
▣ ▤ ♫
In 1942 Paris, a prosperous antique dealer is mistaken for a mysterious Jew of the same name, and despite the danger gradually assumes his identity.
Complex Kafkaesque character study: occasionally arresting but generally rather glum.
w Franco Solinas *d* Joseph Losey *ph* Gerry Fisher *m* Egisto Macchi, Pierre Porte
☆ Alain Delon, Jeanne Moreau, Suzanne Flon, Michael Lonsdale, Louis Seigner, Juliet Berto

Mr Lord Says No: see *The Happy Family*

Mr Love

GB 1986 91m colour
Warner/Goldcrest/Enigma (Susan Richards, Robin Douet)
A mild-mannered cinema projectionist develops an erroneous reputation as a Don Juan.
Ineffective character comedy with too few laughs and a minimum of accurate observation.
w Kenneth Eastaugh *d* Roy Battersby *ph* Clive Tickner *m* Willy Russell
☆ Barry Jackson, Maurice Denham, Margaret Tyzack, Linda Marlowe, Cristina Collier
'It renders would-be regional fantasy into something merely parochial.' – *Tim Pulleine, MFB*

Mr Lucky *

US 1943 98m bw
RKO (David Hempstead)
▣ ▤
During World War II a gambling ship owner goes straight and instigates Bundles for Britain.

Unconvincing mixture of comedy and drama with the actors looking somewhat bewildered.
w Milton Holmes, Adrian Scott *d* H. C. Potter *ph* George Barnes *m* Roy Webb
☆ Cary Grant, Laraine Day, Charles Bickford, Gladys Cooper, Alan Carney, Henry Stephenson, Paul Stewart, Walter Kingsford
'If it weren't for Cary Grant's persuasive personality the whole thing would melt away to nothing at all.' – *Philip G. Hartung*
† Remade 1950 as *Gambling House*.

Mr Magoo

👪 US 1997 87m colour
Buena Vista/Walt Disney (Ben Myron)
▣ ▤ ℚ ◎
A myopic millionaire stumbles into trouble.
Tedious live-action version of the briefly witty UPA cartoons of the early 50s, with some misfiring slapstick and ponderous jokes.
w Pat Proft, Tom Sherohman *d* Stanley Tong *ph* Jingle Ma *m* Michael Tavera *pd* John Willett *ed* Stuart Pappe, David Rawlins, Michael R. Miller
☆ Leslie Nielsen, Kelly Lynch, Matt Keeslar, Nick Chinlund, Stephen Tobolowsky, Ernie Hudson, Jennifer Garner, Malcolm McDowell, Miguel Ferrer
'Unlikely to engage the younger audience for whom it is so obviously intended. When even the outtakes you see over the end titles don't raise a single titter, you know you're in trouble.' – *Bob McCabe, Empire*
† The National Federation of the Blind asked Disney to halt production because the character was insulting to the visually impaired. The credits include the announcement: 'Nothing in *Mr Magoo* should be interpreted as an accurate portrayal of blindness or poor eyesight.'

Mr Majestyk *

US 1974 103m DeLuxe
UA/Mirisch (Walter Mirisch)
A Colorado melon grower crosses swords with the local Mafia.
Violent but unexpectedly enjoyable action melodrama.
w Elmore Leonard *d* Richard Fleischer *ph* Richard Kline *m* Charles Bernstein
☆ Charles Bronson, Al Lettieri, Linda Cristal, Lee Purcell, Paul Keslo
'What I liked best about this trash is that Bronson begins each action sequence like Nureyev beginning a difficult solo.' – *Stanley Kauffmann*

Mr Mom

👪 US 1983 91m Metrocolor
Fox/Sherwood (Lynn Loring)
▣ ▤ ℚ ◎
GB title: *Mr Mum*
Dad loses his executive job and stays home to mind the kids while his wife works.
Obvious farce with too much messy slapstick and no real development.
w John Hughes *d* Stan Dragoti *ph* Victor J. Kemper *m* Lee Holdridge *pd* Alfred Sweeney *ed* Patrick Kennedy
☆ Michael Keaton, Teri Garr, Frederick Koehler, Martin Mull, Ann Jillian
'The jokes almost sink without trace in a hazy domestic setting straight from the hoariest sitcom.' – *Geoff Brown, MFB*

Mister Moses *

GB 1965 103m Technicolor Panavision
UA/Frank Ross/Talbot
A quack doctor is the only person who can persuade an African tribe to move before their land is flooded, and he leads them to their promised land.
Adventure spectacle with naïve biblical parallels; quite agreeable.
w Charles Beaumont, Monja Danischewsky *novel* Max Catto *d* Ronald Neame *ph* Oswald Morris *m* John Barry
☆ Robert Mitchum, Carroll Baker, Ian Bannen, Alexander Knox, Reginald Beckwith, Raymond St Jacques

Mr Moto

The Japanese detective created by John P. Marquand and played by Peter Lorre figured in several above-average second features of the late thirties, but the outbreak of war caused him to vanish.

The casts were interesting, the TCF production excellent, and the director usually Norman Foster. The 1965 attempt to revive the character with Henry Silva was painfully boring.
1937 Think Fast Mr Moto (with Virginia Field, Sig Rumann), Thank You Mr Moto (with Pauline Frederick, Sidney Blackmer)
1938 Mr Moto's Gamble (qv) (with Keye Luke, Lynn Bari), Mr Moto Takes a Chance (qv) (with Rochelle Hudson, J. Edward Bromberg), Mysterious Mr Moto (qv) (with Henry Wilcoxon, Erik Rhodes)
1939 Mr Moto's Last Warning (qv) (with Ricardo Cortez, George Sanders, Robert Coote, John Carradine), Mr Moto in Danger Island (qv) (with Jean Hersholt, Warren Hymer), Mr Moto Takes a Vacation (with Joseph Schildkraut, Lionel Atwill)
1965 The Return of Mr Moto

Mr Moto in Danger Island

US 1939 64m bw
TCF
Mr Moto investigates diamond smuggling in Puerto Rico with the aid of a dim-witted wrestler.
Moderately entertaining fast-paced programmer.
w Peter Milne *novel* John W. Vandercook *story* John Reinhardt, George Bricker *d* Herbert I. Leeds *ph* Lucien Andriot *md* Samuel Kaylin *ad* Richard Day, Chester Gore *ed* Harry Reynolds
☆ Peter Lorre, Jean Hersholt, Amanda Duff, Warren Hymer, Richard Lane, Leon Ames, Douglas Dumbrille
† Rewritten to feature Moto, the film was a remake of *Murder in Trinidad* (qv), which was made in 1934 by Seton I. Miller, starring Nigel Bruce. It was the last of the Moto series to be made, though it was released before *Mr Moto Takes a Vacation*.

Mr Moto Takes a Chance

US 1938 63m bw
TCF
Mr Moto thwarts two rebellions and helps save the life of a spy and two naïve American film-makers.
Enjoyable, though silly, jungle adventure set in Indonesia.
w Lou Breslow, John Patrick *story* Willis Cooper, Norman Foster *d* Norman Foster *ph* Virgil Miller *md* Samuel Kaylin *ad* Albert Hogsett *ed* Nick DeMaggio
☆ Peter Lorre, Rochelle Hudson, Robert Kent, Edward Bromberg, Chick Chandler, George Regis, Fredrik Vogeding

Mr Moto's Gamble

US 1938 71m bw
TCF
Mr Moto investigates the murder of a boxer in the ring.
An enjoyable, if silly, B feature; it is a more conventional mystery than most of the Moto series, owing to its origins as a movie intended to feature Charlie Chan.
w Charles Belden, Jerry Cady *d* James Tinling *ph* Lucien Andriot *ad* Bernard Herzbrun, Haldane Douglas *ed* Nick DeMaggio
☆ Peter Lorre, Keye Luke, Dick Baldwin, Lynn Bari, Douglas Fowley, Jayne Regan, Harold Huber, Maxie Rosenbloom, Ward Bond, Lon Chaney Jnr
† The script was originally intended as a Charlie Chan mystery, but was changed following the death of the star of that series, Warner Oland. It explains the appearance here of Key Luke as Chan's Number One son.

Mr Moto's Last Warning

US 1939 71m bw
TCF
▤
Mr Moto outwits agents and double agents who gather in Port Said to scupper the French fleet in the Suez Canal.
Pleasant thriller with some heavy-handed comedy but displaying a notable collection of suave villains.
w Philip MacDonald, Norman Foster *d* Norman Foster *ph* Virgil Miller *md* Samuel Kaylin *pd* Bernard Herzbrun, Lewis Creber *ed* Norman Colbert
☆ Peter Lorre, Ricardo Cortez, Virginia Field, John Carradine, George Sanders, Joan Carol, Robert Coote, Leyland Hodgson

Mr & Mrs Bridge **
US   1990   124m   Technicolor
Palace/Cineplex Odeon/Merchant Ivory/Robert Halmi (Ismail Merchant)
An inhibited lawyer snuffs out his wife's individuality during a long and apparently happy marriage.
Intriguing portrait of two self-limiting lives, made more effective by being played by a real-life husband and wife.
w Ruth Prawer Jhabvala *novels* Evan S. Connell d James Ivory ph Tony Pierce-Roberts m Richard Robbins pd David Gropman ed Humphrey Dixon
☆ Paul Newman, Joanne Woodward, Robert Sean Leonard, Margaret Walsh, Kyra Sedgwick, Blythe Danner, Simon Callow, Saundra McClain
'Brilliantly written and acted, and immensely watchable.' – *MFB*
⚐ Joanne Woodward

Mr Muggs Rides Again
US   1945   63m   bw
Monogram/Pathé/Banner (Sam Katzman, Jack Dietz)
Framed by his crooked employer and suspended, a jockey rights wrongs and rides a winner.
Familiar East Side Kids material, mixing gangsters and guns, romance and gags in which the cast go through their usual routines with a notable lack of interest and enthusiasm.
w Harvey H. Gates d Wallace Fox ph Ira Morgan md Edward Kay ad David Milton ed William Austin
☆ Leo Gorcey, Huntz Hall, Billy Benedict, Nancy Brinkman, Bernard Thomas, George Meeker, Minerva Urecal, Johnny Duncan, Milton Kibbee

Mr Mum: see *Mr Mom*

Mr Music *
US   1950   113m   bw
Paramount (Robert L. Welch)
A college girl is employed to keep an idle middle-aged songwriter's nose to the grindstone.
Bland musical remake of Accent on Youth *(qv); pleasant performances, moments of comedy, guest stars.*
w Arthur Sheekman *play* Samson Raphaelson d Richard Haydn ph George Barnes ad Hans Dreier, Earl Hedrick *songs* Johnny Burke, James Van Heusen
☆ Bing Crosby, Nancy Olson, Charles Coburn, Ruth Hussey, Marge and Gower Champion, Peggy Lee, Groucho Marx

Mr Nanny
🏃 US   1992   84m   colour
Entertainment (Bob Engelman)
A child-hating wrestler acts as a bodyguard to the two small and mischievous children of an inventor.
Wearying comedy that might amuse the very young, in which Hulk Hogan can be seen trying, and failing, to find a suitable role for himself in the movies.
w Edward Rugoff, Michael Gottlieb d Michael Gottlieb ph Peter Stein m David Johansen, Brian Koonin pd Don de Fina ed Earl Ghaffari, Michael Ripps
☆ Terry 'Hulk' Hogan, Sherman Hemsley, Austin Pendleton, Robert Gorman, Madeline Zima, Raymond O'Connor, David Johansen
'A banal exercise in low-budget comedy.' – *Sight and Sound*

'Fight First ... Apologise Later.'
Mr Nice Guy *
Hong Kong   1997   113m   Cineart
Panavision
New Line/Raymond Chow/Golden Harvest (Chua Lam)
A television chef goes to the aid of an investigative reporter threatened by a gangster.
An entertaining mix of comedy and martial arts, undemanding to watch and with some enjoyable stunts.
w Edward Tang, Fibe Ma d Samo Hung ph Raymond Lam m J. Peter Robinson pd Horace Ma ed Peter Cheung
☆ Jackie Chan, Richard Norton, Gabrielle Fitzpatrick, Miki Lee, Karen McLymont, Vince Poletto, Barry Otto, Samo Hung
'Chock-a-block with stunts and gags ... definitely ranks as one of his most entertaining outings. Properly promoted and positioned, the

film could prove to be his most popular outside Asia.' – *Leonard Klady, Variety*

Mr North *
US   1988   93m   Metrocolor
Columbia TriStar/Heritage Entertainment/Showcase Productions (Steven Haft, Skip Steloff)
In the wealthy society of Newport in the 1920s, a young man angers the local doctor by gaining a reputation as a miracle healer.
Gentle, amusing fable, peopled by some engaging eccentrics.
w Janet Roach, John Huston, James Costigan *novel* Theophilus North *by* Thornton Wilder d Danny Huston ph Robin Vidgeon m David McHugh pd Eugene Lee ed Roberto Silvi
☆ Anthony Edwards, Robert Mitchum, Lauren Bacall, Harry Dean Stanton, Anjelica Huston, Mary Stuart Masterson, Virginia Madsen, Tammy Grimes, David Warner

Mr Peabody and the Mermaid
US   1948   89m   bw
U-I (Nunnally Johnson)
A middle-aged husband imagines an affair with a mermaid.
Bone-headed quick-cash-in on Miranda *(qv); it never begins to work.*
w Nunnally Johnson *novel* Guy and Constance Jones d Irving Pichel ph Russell Metty m Robert Emmett Dolan
☆ William Powell, Ann Blyth, Irene Hervey, Andrea King, Clinton Sundberg

Mr Perrin and Mr Traill *
GB   1948   92m   bw
GFD/Two Cities (Alexander Galperson)
A handsome young master at a boys' school incurs the jealousy of an embittered colleague.
Flat, over-acted but mildly watchable picturization of a well-known story.
w L. A. G. Strong *novel* Hugh Walpole d Lawrence Huntington ph Erwin Hillier m Alan Gray
☆ Marius Goring, David Farrar, Greta Gynt, Edward Chapman, Raymond Huntley, Mary Jerrold, Finlay Currie, Ralph Truman

Mr Potts Goes to Moscow: see *Top Secret*

Mister Quilp
🏃 GB   1975   119m   Technicolor
Panavision
Reader's Digest (Helen M. Straus)
aka: *The Old Curiosity Shop*
In 1840 London, an antique-shop owner is in debt to a hunchback moneylender who has designs on his business.
The novel, with its villainous lead, is a curious choice for musicalizing, and in this treatment falls desperately flat, with no sparkle of imagination visible anywhere.
w Louis Kamp, Irene Kamp *novel* The Old Curiosity Shop *by* Charles Dickens d Michael Tuchner ph Christopher Challis m Anthony Newley md Elmer Bernstein ch Gillian Lynne pd Elliot Gould
☆ Anthony Newley, Michael Hordern, David Hemmings, Sarah-Jane Varley, David Warner, Paul Rogers, Jill Bennett
'Another soggy piece of family entertainment from Reader's Digest, who produced the toothless screen musicals of Tom Sawyer and Huckleberry Finn.' – *Philip French*
'Dickens shorn of sentiment, melodrama or love ... Mr Newley's Quilp, a galvanized Quasimodo on a permanent high, is something of a strain to watch.' – *Michael Billington, Illustrated London News*

'A wickedly comic tale of cold drinks, Barbies, a seige [sic], & a shot dog!'
'An unbelievable true story.'
Mr Reliable (A True Story) *
Australia   1996   113m   Cinevex
Polygram/AFFC/Hayes McElroy/Specific (Jim McElroy, Terry Hayes, Michael Hamlyn)
Police mistakenly believe that a convict is holding his girlfriend and her child hostage and besiege his house.
A ramshackle, misfiring comedy, apparently based on an actual incident in 1968, but with little sense of reality in evidence.

w Don Catchlove, Terry Hayes d Nadia Tass ph David Parker m Philip Judd pd Jon Dowding ed Peter Carrodus
☆ Colin Friels, Jacqueline McKenzie, Paul Sonkkila, Frank Gallacher, Lisa Hensley, Aaron Blabey, Geoff Morrell, Neil Fitzpatrick
'You should enjoy this charming, riotous comedy as a satire on the Australian condition.' – *Film Review*

Mr Ricco
US   1975   98m   colour   Panavision
MGM (Douglas Netter)
A defence counsel risks his life to prove his black client innocent.
Complex urban action thriller with a tired, ageing hero and impenetrable plot.
w Robert Hoban d Paul Bogart ph Frank Stanley m Chico Hamilton
☆ Dean Martin, Eugene Roche, Thalmus Rasulala, Denise Nicholas, Cindy Williams, Geraldine Brooks, Frank Puglia

Mister Roberts **
US   1955   123m   Warnercolor   Cinemascope
Warner/Leland Hayward
Life aboard a World War II cargo ship yearning for action.
A mixture of comedy and sentimentality which has become an American minor classic as a play; this film version is a shambling affair but gets most of the effects over.
w Frank Nugent, Joshua Logan *play* Thomas Heggen and Joshua Logan *novel* Thomas Heggen d John Ford, Mervyn Le Roy ph Winton Hoch m Franz Waxman
☆ Henry Fonda, James Cagney, William Powell, Jack Lemmon, Betsy Palmer, Ward Bond, Phil Carey, Ken Curtis, Harry Carey Jnr
'Probably the most eagerly awaited movie of the year. It is also one of the best.' – *Newsweek*
⚑ Jack Lemmon
⚐ best picture

Mr Robinson Crusoe
US   1932   76m   bw
Douglas Fairbanks
A playboy takes a bet that he could live alone on a desert island ... but a girl turns up.
Mild adventure comedy with the star in subdued form.
w Douglas Fairbanks d Edward Sutherland ph Max Dupont m Alfred Newman
☆ Douglas Fairbanks, William Farnum, Earle Browne, Maria Alba

'A man so evil – his face could stop a heart!'
Mr Sardonicus
US   1961   90m   bw
Columbia/William Castle
A surgeon is lured to an ex-girlfriend's remote home to cure her sadistic husband's crippled face.
Flatly handled, boring semi-horror.
w Robb White d William Castle ph Burnett Guffey m Von Dexter
☆ Ronald Lewis, Guy Rolfe, Audrey Dalton, Oscar Homolka

'It's lonely at the middle.'
Mr Saturday Night *
US   1992   119m   colour
Columbia/Castle Rock/New Line (Billy Crystal)
In his dotage, a successful comedian looks back over his long career.
Intermittently amusing comedy, not helped by over-generous dollops of sentimentality.
w Billy Crystal, Lowell Ganz, Babaloo Mandel d Billy Crystal ph Don Peterman m Marc Shaiman pd Albert Brenner ed Kent Beyda
☆ Billy Crystal, David Paymer, Julie Warner, Helen Hunt, Ron Silver
'What's so special about this movie is that the funny parts are so funny, with gags coming too fast and too good to be assimilated on first hearing. At such moments, the main reaction is exhausted gratitude. It's as if you hired a painter to do your bathroom and he gave you the Sistine Chapel at no extra cost.' – *Richard Corliss, Time*
⚐ David Paymer

Mr Scoutmaster
🏃 US   1953   87m   bw
TCF
A TV personality wants to understand children and is persuaded to take over a scout troop.
A star vehicle which starts promisingly enough in the Sitting Pretty *vein but quickly falls headlong into an abyss of sentimentality.*
w Leonard Praskins, Barney Slater d Henry Levin ph Joseph LaShelle m Cyril Mockridge md Lionel Newman
☆ Clifton Webb, Edmund Gwenn, George Winslow, Frances Dee, Veda Ann Borg

Mr Skeffington ***
US   1944   127m   bw
Warner (Julius J. and Philip G. Epstein)
A selfish beauty finally turns to her discarded dull husband; when he is blind, he doesn't mind her faded looks.
Long, patchily made, but thoroughly enjoyable star melodrama.
w Julius J. and Philip G. Epstein *novel* Elizabeth von Arnim d Vincent Sherman ph Ernest Haller m Franz Waxman
☆ Bette Davis, Claude Rains, Walter Abel, Richard Waring, George Coulouris, John Alexander, Jerome Cowan
'An endless woman's page dissertation on What To Do When Beauty Fades.' – *James Agee*
'To call the film a good one would be to exaggerate; but entertaining and interesting, I insist, it is.' – *Richard Mallett, Punch*
⚐ Bette Davis; Claude Rains

Mr Skitch
🏃 US   1933   70m   bw
Fox
A Missouri family heads for California.
Very passable star family entertainment.
w Anne Cameron *novel* Green Dice *by* Anne Cameron d James Cruze
☆ Will Rogers, ZaSu Pitts, Florence Desmond, Rochelle Hudson
'Enough laughs to please in general.' – *Variety*

'Stirring – in the seeing! Precious – in the remembering'
Mr Smith Goes to Washington ****
US   1939   130m   bw
Columbia (Frank Capra)
Washington's youngest senator exposes corruption in high places, almost at the cost of his own career.
Archetypal high-flying Capra vehicle, with the little man coming out top as he seldom does in life. Supreme gloss hides the corn, helter-skelter direction keeps one watching, and all concerned give memorable performances. A cinema classic.
w Sidney Buchman *story* Lewis R. Foster d Frank Capra ph Joseph Walker m Dimitri Tiomkin ad Lionel Banks *montage* Slavko Vorkapich
☆ James Stewart, Claude Rains, Jean Arthur, Thomas Mitchell, Edward Arnold, Guy Kibbee, Eugene Pallette, Beulah Bondi, Harry Carey, H. B. Warner, Astrid Allwyn, Ruth Donnelly, Charles Lane, Porter Hall
SMITH (JAMES STEWART): 'I wouldn't give you two cents for all your fancy rules if, behind them, they didn't have a little bit of plain, ordinary kindness – and a little looking out for the other fella, too.'
'Timely and absorbing drama presented in best Capra craftsmanship.' – *Variety*
'More fun, even, than the Senate itself ... not merely a brilliant jest, but a stirring and even inspiring testament to liberty and freedom.' – *Frank S. Nugent, New York Times*
'It says all the things about America that have been crying out to be said again – and says them beautifully.' – *Los Angeles Times*
'The great American picture.' – *Billboard*
'I feel that to show this film in foreign countries will do inestimable harm to American prestige all over the world.' – *Joseph P. Kennedy, then American ambassador to Great Britain*
'A totally compelling piece of movie-making, upholding the virtues of traditional American ideals.' – *NFT, 1973*
'Very good, beautifully done and extremely entertaining; long, but worth the time it takes.' – *Richard Mallett, Punch*
'More of the heartfelt than is good for the stomach.' – *New Yorker, 1977*

♟ Lewis R. Foster
♞ best picture; Sidney Buchman; Frank Capra;
Dimitri Tiomkin; James Stewart; Claude Rains;
Harry Carey; Lionel Banks

Mr Soft Touch

↑↑ US 1949 93m bw
Columbia
GB title: *House of Settlement*
A gangster is reformed at Christmas by a social
worker.
*Dewy-eyed romance with Damon Runyonish asides;
only for soft touches.*
w Orin Jannings d Henry Levin, Gordon Douglas
ph Joseph Walker m Heinz Roemheld
☆ Glenn Ford, Evelyn Keyes, John Ireland,
Beulah Bondi, Percy Kilbride, Roman Bohnen

Mister Ten Per Cent

GB 1967 84m Technicolor
ABPC (W. A. Whittaker)
🟐
An impresario stages a play, expecting it to flop in
order to provide a tax loss, and finds himself with a
hit on his hands.
*A comedy vehicle for its diminutive, slapstick star, but
too ramshackle to carry him very far.*
w Norman Hudis, Charlie Drake *story* Mira
Avrech d Peter Graham Scott ph Gerald Gibbs
m Ron Goodwin ch Gillian Lynne ad Terence
Knight ed Jack Harris
☆ Charlie Drake, Derek Nimmo, John Le
Mesurier, Wanda Ventham, Anthony Nicholls,
Noel Dyson, Ronald Radd, John Laurie, George
Baker, Una Stubbs

Mr Topaze

GB 1961 84m Eastmancolor Cinemascope
TCF/Dimitri de Grunwald (Pierre Rouve)
US title: *I Like Money*
An honest ex-schoolmaster becomes prosperous
when he joins some shady businessmen.
*Predictable, sluggish character comedy, with a good
actor unable to make it as a star. Or as a director.*
w Pierre Rouve *play* Topaze by Marcel Pagnol
d Peter Sellers ph John Wilcox m Georges Van
Parys
☆ Peter Sellers, Herbert Lom, Leo McKern, Nadia
Gray, Martita Hunt, John Neville, Billie Whitelaw,
Michael Gough, Joan Sims, John Le Mesurier,
Michael Sellers
'A film of minor pleasures and major
inadequacies.' – *Penelope Houston, MFB*
† See also *Topaze* (1933).

Mr Universe

US 1951 79m bw
Laurel/Eagle Lion
Con men promote a new wrestler.
Fair low-class comedy with some laughs.
w Earle Kramer d Joseph Lerner ph Gerald
Hirschfeld m Dimitri Tiomkin
☆ Bert Lahr, Jack Carson, Vincent Edwards, Janis
Paige, Robert Alda

Mister V: see *Pimpernel Smith*

Mr Winkle Goes to War

US 1944 80m bw
Columbia (Jack Moss)
GB title: *Arms and the Woman*
A middle-aged bank clerk joins the army and
becomes a hero.
Agreeable, forgettable propaganda comedy-drama.
w Waldo Salt, George Corey, Louis Solomon
novel Theodore Pratt d Alfred E. Green
ph Joseph Walker m Carmen Dragon, Paul
Sawtell
☆ Edward G. Robinson, Ruth Warrick, Ted
Donaldson, Bob Haymes, Richard Lane, Robert
Armstrong, Walter Baldwin

'Sometimes the wrong person is the only right
person for you.'

Mr Wonderful

US 1992 97m Technicolor
Buena Vista/Samuel Goldwyn (Marianne Moloney)
🟐 ♪ ◉
A divorced couple decide to get together again.
*A romantic comedy about star-crossed lovers becoming
uncrossed that lacks force or passion.*
wd Anthony Minghella from original screenplay
by Amy Schor, Vicki Polon ph Geoffrey Simpson

m Michael Gore pd Doug Kraner ed John
Tintori
☆ Matt Dillon, Annabella Sciorra, Mary-Louise
Parker, William Hurt, Vincent D'Onofrio, David
Barry Gray, Dan Hedaya
'Makes a good shot at the difficult assignment of
making romantic comedy for a modern
audience.' – *Adam Mars-Jones, Independent*

Mr Wong

A cheeseparing set of second features from
Monogram, based on stories by Hugh Wiley.
*Boris Karloff was unsuitably cast as a Chinese
detective, and in the last film he was replaced by Keye
Luke. The films were directed by William Nigh.*
1938 Mr Wong Detective
1939 The Mystery of Mr Wong, Mr Wong in
Chinatown
1940 The Fatal Hour, Doomed to Die (GB title:
The Mystery of the Wentworth Castle)
1941 Phantom of Chinatown

Mr Wrong *

New Zealand 1985 89m colour
NZFC/Barclays (Robin Laing, Gaylene Preston)
📻
aka: *Dark of the Night*
A young woman moves to the big city and
discovers that the car she buys to make weekend
visits to her parents appears to be haunted by a
woman who was murdered by a hitch-hiker.
*An intriguing psychological thriller, though occasionally
it makes heavy weather of marrying its ghost story with
a feminist account of a woman trying to survive among
predatory men.*
w Gaylene Preston, Geoff Murphy, Graeme Tetley
story Elizabeth Jane Howard d Gaylene Preston
ph Thom Burstyn m Jonathan Crayford ad Mike
Becroft ed Simon Reece
☆ Heather Bolton, David Letch, Perry Piercy,
Suzanne Lee, Margaret Umbers, Danny Mulheron,
Gary Stalker, Kate Harcourt

Mr Wu *

US 1927 80m bw silent
MGM
A Chinese villain kills his daughter when she
wants to marry an Englishman.
*Turgid outmoded melodrama from a stage success:
purely a star vehicle.*
w Lorna Moon *play* Maurice Vernon, Harold
Owen d William Nigh ph John Arnold
☆ Lon Chaney, Louise Dresser, Anna May Wong,
Ralph Forbes, Renee Adoree, Holmes Herbert

Il Mistero di Oberwald: see *The Oberwald Mystery*

'Everybody's trying to get their girlfriend into the
movies...'

Mistress *

US 1992 110m CFI color
Tribeca (Meir Teper, Robert DeNiro)
🟐 📻 ◉ ♪
A writer-director discovers that all those
approached to finance his movie have girlfriends
who want a leading part in it, providing he changes
the script to suit them.
*Enjoyable satire on the dangers of integrity among
minor players in a movie-making industry.*
w Barry Primus, Jonathan L. Lawton d Barry
Primus ph Sven Kirsten m Galt MacDermot
pd Phil Peters ed Steve Weisberg
☆ Robert Wuhl, Martin Landau, Robert DeNiro,
Jace Alexander, Laurie Metcalf, Danny Aiello,
Christopher Walken, Eli Wallach, Tuesday Weld,
Sheryl Lee Ralph, Ernest Borgnine
'Can't seem to decide if it's supposed to be a
comedy about Hollywood small-timers trying to
get an indie pic off the ground, or a somber
drama in which greed and lust overwhelm art.' –
Variety

Mix Me a Person

GB 1961 116m bw
Wessex (Sergei Nolbandov)
A barrister's psychiatrist wife takes on one of his
failures, a client condemned to death for murder.
*Once it gets started, a routine suspense thriller with the
wrong man convicted and an espresso bar background.
Not a very good one, though.*
w Ian Dalrymple *novel* Jack Trevor Story
d Leslie Norman ph Ted Moore md Muir
Mathieson *songs* Johnny Worth

☆ Anne Baxter, Donald Sinden, Adam Faith,
Walter Brown, Glyn Houston

Mixed Company

US 1974 109m DeLuxe
UA/Cornell (Melville Shavelson)
A basketball coach and his wife adopt several
children of different races.
*Room for One More and then some, but not very
interesting.*
w Melville Shavelson, Mort Lachman d Melville
Shavelson ph Stan Lazan m Fred Karlin pd Stan
Jolley
☆ Barbara Harris, Joseph Bologna, Lisa Gerritsen,
Ariane Heller

Mixed Nuts

US 1995 97m Technicolor
TriStar (Paul Junger Witt, Tony Thomas, Joseph
Hartwick)
🟐 📻 ◉
The staff of a telephone help-line face eviction
from their office as they are overwhelmed by
eccentrics needing aid.
*Absolutely abysmal comedy, in which all hands sink
without trace, leaving not a joke behind.*
w Nora Ephron, Delia Ephron, *from the film* Le Père
Noël est une ordure d Nora Ephron ph Sven
Nykvist m George Fenton pd Bill Groom
ed Robert Reitano
☆ Steve Martin, Madeline Kahn, Robert Klein,
Anthony LaPaglia, Juliette Lewis, Rob Reiner,
Adam Sandler, Rita Wilson, Garry Shandling
'It's a total misfire with no commercial vital signs
registering on-screen.' – *Variety*

M'liss

US 1936 66m bw
RKO
A drunkard's daughter washes dishes in a Western
saloon.
*Laundered and fairly inept family version of a roistering
tale.*
w Dorothy Yost *story* Bret Harte d George
Nicholls Jnr
☆ Anne Shirley, Guy Kibbee, John Beal, Douglass
Dumbrille, Moroni Olsen, Arthur Hoyt

Mo' Better Blues *

US 1990 127m DeLuxe
UIP/40 Acres and a Mule Filmworks/Spike Lee
🟐 📻 ◉ ♪
A jazz trumpeter redeems himself as a person, but
loses out as a musician.
*An unfocused narrative, caused by trying to say too
much about too many things, results in an
unsatisfactory film, though it has its moments.*
wd Spike Lee ph Ernest Dickerson m Bill Lee
pd Wynn Thomas ed Sam Pollard
☆ Denzel Washington, Spike Lee, Wesley Snipes,
Joie Lee, Cynda Williams, Giancarlo Esposito,
Robin Harris, Bill Nunn
'he film's movement is fitful and arbitrary – all
mood swings and unpersuasive melodrama.' –
Richard Schickel, Time

Mo' Money

US 1992 90m colour
Columbia TriStar/Columbia/A Wife N'Kids (Michael
Rachmil)
🟐 📻 ◉ ♪
After trying and failing to go straight, a hustler and
his brother make money with a stolen credit card
but also expose a big-time crook.
*A vehicle of dubious morality, with some street-wise
comedy, expertly delivered, from its star.*
w Damon Wayans d Peter Macdonald ph Don
Burgess m Jay Gruska pd William Arnold
ed Hubert C. de La Bouillerie
☆ Damon Wayans, Stacey Dash, Joe Santos, John
Diehl, Harry J. Lennix, Marlon Wayans, Mark
Beltzman
'The comedy is, in truth, pretty feeble – rancid
without the redeeming virtue of wit.' – *Sheila
Johnston, Independent*
'If this is grown-up cinema, give me Peter
Rabbit.' – *Geoff Brown, The Times*

The Mob *

US 1951 87m bw
Columbia (Jerry Bresler)
GB title: *Remember That Face*
A policeman works undercover to catch a dockside
racketeer.

*Tough, lively thriller with effectively sustained mystery
and a serial-like finale.*
w William Bowers d Robert Parrish ph Joseph
Walker m George Duning
☆ Broderick Crawford, Richard Kiley, Ernest
Borgnine, Neville Brand, Charles Bronson

Mob Town

US 1941 61m bw
Universal
A policeman tries to rehabilitate the young brother
of an executed gangster.
*Another spin-off from the Dead End Kids, quite
unremarkable.*
w Brenda Weisberg d William Nigh
☆ Dick Foran, Anne Gwynne, Billy Halop, Huntz
Hall, Bernard Punsley, Gabriel Dell, Samuel S.
Hinds

Mobsters

US 1991 104m DeLuxe
Universal (Steve Roth)
🟐 📻 ◉ ♪
GB title: *Mobsters – The Evil Empire*
Four youths grow up to become gangsters Lucky
Luciano, Meyer Lansky, Bugsy Siegel and Frank
Costello.
*Bungled attempt, full of gratuitous violence, to create
an adolescent Godfather.*
w Michael Mahern, Nicholas Kazan d Michael
Karbelnikoff ph Lajos Koltai m Michael Small
pd Richard Sylbert ed Scott Smith, Joe
D'Augustine
☆ Christian Slater, Patrick Dempsey, Richard
Grieco, Costas Mandylor, F. Murray Abraham, Lara
Flynn Boyle, Michael Gambon, Christopher Penn,
Anthony Quinn
'Armed with teen appeal thanks to its leads, this
hollow pic may mow down strong boxoffice early
but will start hemorrhaging quickly as mixed-to-
poor word-of-mouth cuts off its legs.' – *Variety*

'America's greatest actor – as you like him!'

Moby Dick *

US 1930 75m bw
Warner
Captain Ahab returns minus a leg from fighting
the white whale, and finds that his fiancée is too
shocked to love him.
*Mangled remake of a fine novel filmed in silent form as
The Sea Beast.*
w J. Grubb Alexander *novel* Herman Melville
d Lloyd Bacon ph Robert Kurrie
☆ John Barrymore, Joan Bennett, Lloyd Hughes,
May Boley, Walter Long
'Money picture, guaranteed by its action and by
Barrymore.' – *Variety*

'In All The World – In All The Seas – In All Adventure
There Is No Might Like The Might of Moby Dick.'

Moby Dick **

GB 1956 116m Technicolor
Warner/Moulin (John Huston)
🟐 📻 ◉ ♪
A whaling skipper is determined to harpoon the
white whale which robbed him of a leg.
*Pretentious period adventure, rather too slowly
developed, but full of interesting detail which almost
outweighs the central miscasting.*
w Ray Bradbury, John Huston *novel* Herman
Melville d John Huston ph Oswald Morris
m Philip Sainton
☆ Gregory Peck, Richard Basehart, Friedrich
Ledebur, Leo Genn, Orson Welles, James
Robertson Justice, Harry Andrews, Bernard Miles,
Noel Purcell, Edric Connor, Joseph Tomelty,
Mervyn Johns
'Interesting more often than exciting.' – *Variety*

Mockery

US 1927 75m bw silent
MGM
A noble peasant saves a countess from the Russian
revolution.
*Overly serious vehicle for a star more at ease in
melodrama.*
wd Benjamin Christensen ph Merritt B. Gerstad
☆ Lon Chaney, Barbara Bedford, Ricardo Cortez,
Emily Fitzroy, Mack Swain

Ⓢ Digital Video Disc
Region 2
Ⓢ Digital Video Disc
Region 1
♩ Soundtrack released
on compact disc
☆ Cast in approximate
order of importance
† Points of interest
♪ Notable songs
♟ Academy Award
♞ Academy Award nomination
W BAFTA

'Sexy. Cool. Mod.'
The Mod Squad
US   1999   94m   DeLuxe
MGM (Ben Myron, Alan Riche, Tony Ludwig)
⌒

After infiltrating the counter-culture, three young hippie undercover agents discover that LA cops are involved with drug pushers.
Trivial movie version of an uninteresting TV series that recalls some of the worst of the 'swinging' films of the 60s.
w Stephen Kay, Scott Silver, Kate Lanier *characters created by* Buddy Ruskin d Scott Silver ph Ellen Kuras m B. C. Smith pd Patrick Sherman ed Dorian Harris
☆ Claire Danes, Giovanni Ribisi, Omar Epps, Dennis Farina, Josh Brolin, Steve Harris, Richard Jenkins, Larry Brandenburg, Lionel Mark Smith, Sam McMurray, Michael Lerner
    'Foul word of mouth will spread quickly to send this exercise in pipsqueak crime-fighting back to its vid roots in short order.' – Todd McCarthy, *Variety*
† The TV series ran from 1968 to 1973 and starred Michael Cole, Clarence Williams III and Peggy Lipton as the three agents. It was based on the experiences of its creator, Bud Ruskin, a former cop who had been a member of an undercover narcotics squad.

The Model and the Marriage Broker
US   1951   103m   bw
TCF (Charles Brackett)
A broker conceals her profession from a friend but gets the friend fixed up.
Moderate, unsurprising comedy somewhat overweighted by talent which can't express itself.
w Charles Brackett, Walter Reisch, Richard Breen d George Cukor ph Milton Krasner m Cyril Mockridge
☆ Thelma Ritter, Jeanne Crain, Scott Brady, Zero Mostel, Michael O'Shea, Nancy Kulp

The Model Murder Case: see *The Girl in the Headlines*

Model Wife
US   1941   78m   bw
Universal
Young marrieds must pretend to be single in order to keep their jobs.
Tedious comedy.
w Charles Kaufman, Horace Jackson, Grant Garrett d Leigh Jason
☆ Joan Blondell, Dick Powell, Charles Ruggles, Lee Bowman, Lucile Watson

A Modern Hero: see *Knute Rockne, All American (1940)*

A Modern Hero *
US   1934   70m   bw
Warner
A young circus rider becomes an automobile tycoon but overreaches himself.
Unconvincing moral tale, performed and presented with nice touches.
w Gene Markey, Kathryn Scola *novel* Louis Bromfield d G. W. Pabst
☆ Richard Barthelmess, Jean Muir, Marjorie Rambeau, Verree Teasdale, Florence Eldridge
    'Essentially weak on plot and characterization.' – *Variety*

Modern Love
US   1990   109m   CFI color   Panavision
Skouras/SVS/Lyric (Robby Benson)
▦   ▤
A man and a woman meet, marry, have a child and keep on smiling most of the time.
A story that is about as modern as Adam and Eve; it is given a resolutely old-fashioned comic treatment that quickly becomes tedious.
wd Robby Benson ph Christopher G. Tufty m Don Peake pd Carl E. Copeland ed Gib Jaffe
☆ Robby Benson, Karla DeVito, Rue McClanahan, Burt Reynolds, Frankie Valli, Kaye Ballard, Cliff Bemis, Louise Lasser, Lyric Benson

The Modern Miracle: see *The Story of Alexander Graham Bell*

Modern Romance *
US   1981   93m   Metrocolor
Columbia (Andrew Scheinman, Martin Shafer)
▦   ▤   ⌬
A film editor leaves his girlfriend, then tries to get her back and becomes jealous of her every move.
Clever study of a neurotic in love, with some good jokes about the film business along the way.
w Albert Brooks, Monica Johnson d Albert Brooks ph Eric Saarinen m Lance Rubin pd Edward Richardson ed David Finfer
☆ Albert Brooks, Kathryn Harrold, Bruno Kirby, James L. Brooks, Meadowlark Lemon, George Kennedy, Jane Hallaren, Bob Einstein, Albert Henderson

'You'll never laugh as long and as loud again as long as you live! The laughs come so fast and so furious you'll wish it would end before you collapse!'
Modern Times ***
✿ US   1936   87m   bw
Charles Chaplin
▦   ▤   ⌬   ⌖
An assembly-line worker goes berserk but can't get another job.
Silent star comedy produced in the middle of the sound period; flashes of genius alternate with sentimental sequences and jokes without punch.
wd Charles Chaplin ph Rollie Totheroh, Ira Morgan m Charles Chaplin
☆ Charles Chaplin, Paulette Goddard, Henry Bergman, Chester Conklin, Tiny Sandford
    'A natural for the world market ... box office with a capital B.' – *Variety*
    'A feature picture made out of several one- and two-reel shorts, proposed titles being *The Shop, The Jailbird, The Singing Waiter*.' – *Otis Ferguson*

El Moderno Barba Azul: see *Boom in the Moon*

The Moderns **
US   1988   126m   colour
Rank/Alive Films/Nelson (Carolyn Pfeiffer, David Blocker)
▦   ▤   ⌬   ⌒
In Paris in the 1920s a struggling American expatriate artist agrees to fake some modern masterpieces.
Witty recreation of the past and an enjoyable dissection of the aspirations of the second-rate.
w Alan Rudolph, Jon Bradshaw d Alan Rudolph ph Toyomichoi Kurita m Mark Isham pd Steven Legler ed Debra T. Smith, Scott Brock
☆ Keith Carradine, Linda Fiorentino, Geneviève Bujold, Geraldine Chaplin, Wallace Shawn, John Lone, Kevin O'Connor, Elsa Raven, Ali Giron
    'Beautifully shot and impeccably acted all the way down the cast list, weaving an astonishingly complex path through the "seems" and "is" of countless varieties of relationship, *The Moderns* is undoubtedly Rudolph's best film to date.' – *Tom Milne, MFB*

Modesty Blaise
GB   1966   119m   Technicolor
TCF/Modesty Blaise Ltd (Joseph Janni)
Female arch-agent Modesty Blaise defends a shipload of diamonds against a sadistic master criminal.
Comic-strip adventures made by people with no sense of humour; Fu Manchu was much more fun.
w Evan Jones *comic strip* Peter O'Donnell, Jim Holdaway d Joseph Losey ph Jack Hildyard m Johnny Dankworth
☆ Monica Vitti, Dirk Bogarde, Terence Stamp, Harry Andrews, Michael Craig, Scilla Gabel, Clive Revill, Rossella Falk, Joe Melia
    'Demonstrated that Joseph Losey is completely without a sense of humour when dealing with comedy.' – *Judith Crist*

Modigliani of Montparnasse: see *The Lovers of Montparnasse*

'Flaming love found in the savage heart of the jungle!'
Mogambo *
GB   1953   116m   Technicolor
MGM (Sam Zimbalist)
▤   ⌬
The headquarters of a Kenyan white hunter is invaded by an American showgirl and a British

archaeologist and his wife, and they all go off on a gorilla hunt.
Amiable, flabby remake of Red Dust, with direction scarcely in evidence and the gorillas out-acting a genial cast.
w John Lee Mahin d John Ford ph Robert Surtees, F. A. Young m A. N. Watkins
☆ Clark Gable, Ava Gardner, Grace Kelly, Donald Sinden, Laurence Naismith, Philip Stainton
† The story was also made as *Congo Maisie* in 1940.
⧗ Ava Gardner; Grace Kelly

La Moglie del Prete: see *The Priest's Wife*

Mohammed, Messenger of God
Lebanon   1976   182m   Eastmancolor
Panavision
Filmco International (Moustapha Akkad)
▦   ▤
aka: The Message
The life of the seventh-century religious leader.
Predictably reverential and exceedingly tedious religious epic, rather like a lesser de Mille item and fatally handicapped by the decision never to show Mohammed at all.
w H. A. L. Craig (with Arab advice) d Moustapha Akkad ph Jack Hildyard m Maurice Jarre pd Tambi Larsen, Maurice Fowler
☆ Anthony Quinn, Irene Papas, Michael Ansara, Johnny Sekka, Michael Forest, André Morell
    'For well over three hours this film stumbles, staggers, lurches and bumbles ahead, without any true rhythm, construction, vision, or even bare minimum of craft.' – *John Simon, New York*
⧗ Maurice Jarre

Mohawk
US   1956   79m   Pathécolor
National Pictures (Edward L. Alperson)
▤   ⌖
An artist falls in love with the daughter of an Iriquois chief who is provoked into waging war on the settlers.
Amiable Western, with a modicum of originality in its narrative, though the implausibility of its romance is increased by the unconvincing performances of the actors playing the Indians.
w Maurice Geraghty, Milton Krims d Kurt Neumann ph Karl Struss m Edward L. Alperson Jnr md Raoul Kraushaar pd Ernst Fegté ed William B. Murphy
☆ Scott Brady, Rita Gam, Neville Brand, Allison Hayes, Lori Nelson, John Hoyt, Rhys Williams, Mae Clarke, Tommy Cook, Vera Vague, Ted de Corsia, John Hudson

Moi Drug Ivan Lapshin: see *My Friend Ivan Lapshin*

Le Moine: see *The Monk (1972)*

Mojo
GB   1997   93m   Technicolor
Portobello/BBC/British Screen/Mojo (Paul Cowan)
In Soho of the 50s, a club-owner and a gangster battle over who controls a new rock singer.
Lurid melodrama which was a stage success, but transfers uneasily to the screen; it has its moments, particularly in a confrontation between Hart and Pinter, but they are few and far between.
wd Jez Butterworth *play* Jez Butterworth ph Bruno de Keyser m Murray Gold pd Hugo Luczyc-Wyhowski ed Richard Milward
☆ Ian Hart, Ewen Bremner, Aiden Gillen, Martin Gwynn Jones, Hans Matheson, Andy Serkis, Ricky Tomlinson, Harold Pinter
    'There's talent and substance to distract in a picture that never quite gels into an effective whole.' – *Darren Bignell, Empire*

'Horror crawls from the depths of the earth!'
The Mole People
US   1956   78m   bw
Universal-International
▤
Archaeologists fall down a shaft and find themselves in a subterranean civilization where mole people are ruled by albinos.
Thoroughly boring nonsense which would insult a Saturday matinée.
w Laszlo Gorog d Virgil Vogel ph Ellis Carter

☆ John Agar, Cynthia Patrick, Hugh Beaumont, Alan Napier

'The remarkable story of one woman's unbreakable spirit.'
Moll Flanders
US   1996   123m   DeLuxe   'Scope
TCF/Spelling (John Watson, Richard B. Lewis, Pen Densham)
▦   ▤   ⌬   ⌒
In 18th-century London, a poor woman becomes a prostitute and wife before escaping to a better life in the New World.
A very free adaptation of Defoe's novel, substituting a less interesting narrative, in which the bawdiness of the original is replaced by a tedious gentility.
wd Pen Densham *based on the character from the novel by* Daniel Defoe ph David Tattersall m Mark Mancina pd Caroline Hanania ed Neil Travis, James R. Symons
☆ Robin Wright, Morgan Freeman, Stockard Channing, John Lynch, Brenda Fricker, Geraldine James, Aisling Corcoran, Jim Sheridan, Jeremy Brett, Harry Towb
    'Comprehensively dire.' – *Independent*

Molly
✿ Australia   1983   82m   colour
NSW Film Corp./Greater Union/M&L (Hilary Linstead)
⌖
A little girl, with the help of some circus children, looks after a singing dog when its owner is taken ill.
Amusing, although slow-moving, family film that will appeal most to soft-hearted sub-teens.
w Phillip Roope, Mark Thomas, Hilary Linstead, Ned Lander d Ned Lander ph Vincent Monton md Graeme Isaac ad Robert Dein ed Stewart Young
☆ Claudia Karvan, Garry McDonald, Reg Lye, Melissa Jaffer, Ruth Cracknell

Molly and Me
US   1945   76m   bw
TCF
A cantankerous old man is tamed by his new housekeeper.
Sentimental little star vehicle.
w Leonard Praskins d Lewis Seiler ph Charles G. Clarke m Cyril Mockridge
☆ Gracie Fields, Monty Woolley, Reginald Gardiner, Roddy McDowall, Natalie Schafer, Edith Barrett
† This followed the more successful teaming of the stars in *Holy Matrimony*.

The Molly Maguires
US   1970   123m   Technicolor   Panavision
Paramount/Tamm (Martin Ritt, Walter Bernstein)
▤   ⌖
In the Pennsylvania coalmining district in the 1870s, an undercover detective exposes the leaders of a secret company.
Sober-sided and slow-moving account of actual events which also formed the basis for Conan Doyle's rather more entertaining The Valley of Fear. Expensive, nicely photographed, but unpersuasive and empty.
w Walter Bernstein d Martin Ritt ph James Wong Howe m Henry Mancini
☆ Richard Harris, Sean Connery, Samantha Eggar, Frank Finlay, Anthony Zerbe, Bethel Leslie, Art Lund
    'The film's vague sense of grievance and harrowing circumstances hangs in the air like the smoky pall cast up by the anthracite workings.' – *Richard Combs*
    'A cold, dry and rather perfunctory film.' – *Arthur Schlesinger Jnr*

Mom and Dad Save the World
✿ US   1992   88m   Foto-Kem
Warner/HBO/Cinema Plus/Douglas (Michael Phillips)
▦   ▤   ⌬   ⌒
A Californian couple are transported to an alien planet ruled by a mad dictator who has imprisoned the king.
A dim comedy for easily pleased children.
w Chris Matheson, Ed Solomon d Greg Beeman ph Jacques Haitkin m Jerry Goldsmith pd Craig Stearns ed W. O. Garret sp Alterian Studios; Perpetual Motion Pictures
☆ Teri Garr, Jeffrey Jones, Jon Lovitz, Thalmus Rasulala, Wallace Shawn, Eric Idle, Dwier Brown, Kathy Ireland

---

✿ film suitable for family viewing   ▦ VHS video-cassette for the British PAL system   ▤ VHS video-cassette for the British PAL system in wide screen-format   ⌬ Video cassette in a computer-colourised version   ▬ American NTSC video-cassette   ⌒ Laser disc

'With garish color, goofy-looking creatures in rubbery costumes and sets parodying old Flash Gordon serials, pic flaunts its modest budget with engaging candor.' – *Variety*

Moment by Moment

US   1979   105m   Technicolor   Panavision
Universal (Robert Stigwood)

A bored Beverly Hills wife has an affair with a young drifter.

Tedious proof that even the biggest new stars of the seventies can't carry a no-good picture.

wd Jane Wagner   ph Philip Lathrop   m Lee Holdridge   pd Harry Horner

☆ John Travolta, Lily Tomlin, Andra Akers, Bert Kramer, Debra Feuer

'Little more than an animated snapshot of its leading man, baring body and soul to various effect … truly terrible.' – *Gilbert Adair, MFB*

Un Moment d'Egarement: see *A Summer Affair*

Moment of Danger

GB   1960   87m   bw
ABPC/Douglas Fairbanks Jnr

US title: *Malaga*

Thieves fall out and pursue each other to Malaga.

Falling between the stools of thriller and character drama, this is a poor effort in either category.

w David Osborn, Donald Ogden Stewart *novel* Donald MacKenzie   d Laslo Benedek   ph Desmond Dickinson   m Matyas Seiber

☆ Trevor Howard, Dorothy Dandridge, Edmund Purdom, Michael Hordern, Paul Stassino

Moment to Moment

US   1966   108m   Technicolor
Universal (Mervyn Le Roy)

A housewife finds herself with a body on her hands.

Incredibly old-fashioned romantic/melodramatic malarkey set on the French Riviera but scarcely moving a step out of Hollywood. Lush settings made it marketable to women.

w John Lee Mahin, Alec Coppel   d Mervyn Le Roy   ph Harry Stradling   m Henry Mancini

☆ Jean Seberg, Honor Blackman, Sean Garrison, Arthur Hill, Grégoire Aslan

Mommie Dearest

US   1981   129m   Metrocolor
Paramount/Frank Yablans

An account of the private life of Joan Crawford, from the biography by her adopted daughter Christina, who claimed spectacular ill-treatment.

On the screen it all seemed too silly for words, and nobody cared anyway.

w Frank Yablans, Frank Perry, Tracy Hotchner, Robert Getchell   d Frank Perry   ph Paul Lohmann   m Henry Mancini   pd Bill Malley

☆ Faye Dunaway, Diana Scarwid, Steve Forrest, Howard da Silva

'The only thing that is not transparent about this film is why it was ever made.' – *Jo Imeson, MFB*

Mon Homme

France   1996   99m   colour
Artificial Eye/BAC/Alain Sarde

A contented prostitute takes in a tramp, who becomes her pimp; when he is imprisoned and she discovers he has been unfaithful, she becomes a housewife.

An oddly broken-backed and unsatisfactory movie, though it begins well as a brisk comedy of sexual needs before shifting into sentimentality and pointlessness.

wd Bertrand Blier   ph Pierre Lhomme   m Barry White et al   pd Willy Holt, Georges Glon   ed Claudine Merlin

☆ Anouk Grinberg, Gérard Lanvin, Valéria Bruni-Tedeschi, Olivier Martinez, Dominique Valadié, Jacques François, Michel Galabru, Robert Hirsch, Bernard Fresson, Aurore Clément, Jean-Pierre Léaud, Sabine Azéma

'Since pic isn't sure what it's about (except flying in the face of conventional morality), this stylish, keenly acted item runs out of both steam and substance before its less than satisying conclusion.' – *Lisa Nesselson, Variety*

Mon Oncle *

France   1956   116m   Eastmancolor
Specta/Gray/Alterdel-Centaure (Louis Dolivet)

An image An image An image

A small boy has less affection for his parents than for his vague, clumsy uncle.

Tiresomely long star vehicle, with Tati harping on his theory of detachment, i.e. keeping his comic character on the fringes of the action. It really doesn't work in a film of this length, and the jokes are thin.

w Jacques Tati, Jacques Lagrange   d Jacques Tati   ph Jean Bourgoin   m Alain Romains, Franck Barcellini

☆ Jacques Tati, Jean-Pierre Zola, Adrienne Servatie, Alain Becourt, Yvonne Arnaud

'Deft, elusive, full of heart.' – *Brenda Davies, MFB*

'Cinema humour at its brilliant best.' – *Daily Worker*

♟ best foreign film

Mon Oncle Américain: see *My American Uncle*

Mon Oncle Benjamin: see *Uncle Benjamin*

Mon Père, Ce Héros

France   1991   104m   colour
Gala/Film Par Film/DD/Orly/TF1/Paravision/Canal (Jean-Louis Livi)

An image

A teenage girl on holiday tells a boy she fancies that her father is a spy and her lover.

A dull and sentimental comedy that sanitizes incest.

wd Gérard Lauzier   ph Patrick Blossier   m François Bernheim   ad Christian Marti   ed Georges Klotz

☆ Gérard Depardieu, Marie Gillain, Patrick Mille, Catherine Jacob, Charlotte de Turckheim, Jean-François Rangasamy, Koomaren Chetty

'This syrupy teen romance would be all but unwatchable were it not for the presence of Depardieu.' – *Empire*

† The film was remade in America in 1994 as *My Father, the Hero*, again starring Gèrard Depardieu.

Mona Lisa **

GB   1986   104m   Technicolor
HandMade/Palace (Stephen Woolley, Patrick Cassavetti)

An image An image An image

An ex-convict becomes chauffeur for a prostitute and becomes involved in the kinkier areas of the vice trade.

Only this actor could make a hit of this unsavoury yarn, with its highlights of sex and violence. But he did.

w Neil Jordan, David Leland   d Neil Jordan   ph Roger Pratt   m Michael Kamen   pd Jamie Leonard   ed Lesley Walker

☆ Bob Hoskins, Cathy Tyson, Michael Caine, Robbie Coltrane, Clarke Peters, Sammi Davis

'A film to see again, with the certainty that each viewing will add something new.' – *MFB*

🎭 Bob Hoskins

Monache di Sant'Arcangelo: see *The Nun and the Devil*

Un Monde sans Pitié: see *A World without Pity*

Mondo Cane *

Italy   1961   105m   Technicolor
Cineriz

An image An image

aka: *A Dog's Life*

A documentary of thirty sequences of violently eccentric human behaviour, including cannibalism, pig killing, a dog meal restaurant, etc.

Emetic exploitation piece, quite glibly assembled. Its huge commercial success made one worry for the world.

wd Gualtiero Jacopetti   ph Antonio Climati, Benito Frattari

♪ song 'More' (mRiz Ortolani, Nino Oliviero, lyNorman Newell)

Money and the Woman

US   1940   80m   bw
First National/Warner

A bank executive falls for the wife of a thieving teller.

Muddled drama which never gets its storyline straight.

w Robert Presnell   *story* James M. Cain   d William K. Howard

☆ Jeffrey Lynn, Brenda Marshall, John Litel, Lee Patrick, Henry O'Neill, Roger Pryor, Henry Kolker

Money for Jam: see *It Ain't Hay*

Money from Home

US   1954   100m   Technicolor   3-D
Paramount/Hal Wallis

A racing tipster and an assistant veterinary surgeon find themselves in charge of a horse.

A comedy with two strokes against it: the stars, and that never-never gangster land which was already a terrible cliché in the early fifties.

w Hal Kanter   *story* Damon Runyon   d George Marshall   ph Daniel L. Fapp   m Leigh Harline

☆ Dean Martin, Jerry Lewis, Marjie Millar, Pat Crowley, Richard Haydn, Robert Strauss, Gerald Mohr, Sheldon Leonard

Money Mania

US   1987   95m   Technicolor
De Laurentiis (Stephen F. Kesten)

An image An image

aka: *Million Dollar Mystery*

A dying man tells a group of people at a wayside diner that he has hidden four million dollars in four hiding places.

A vigorous reworking of It's a Mad Mad Mad Mad World, even broader and cruder than the original.

w Tim Metcalfe, Miguel Tejada-Flores, Rudy de Luca   d Richard Fleischer   ph Jack Cardiff   m Al Gorgoni   pd Jack G. Taylor Jnr   ed John W. Wheeler

☆ Jamie Alcroft, Royce D. Applegate, Penny Baker, Eddie Deezen, Mack Dryden, Douglas Emerson, Tawny Ferée, H. B. Haggerty, Rich Hall, Tom Bosley

Money Movers

Australia   1978   90m   colour
South Australian Film Corp (Matt Carroll)

A supervisor of a security firm plans a $20-million robbery.

An engaging, though occasionally violent, tale of crooked cops and double-crossing robbers.

wd Bruce Beresford   *novel The Money Movers* by Devon Minchin   ph Don McAlpine   ed William Anderson, Jeanine Chialvo

☆ Terence Donovan, Tony Bonner, Ed Dévereaux, Charles 'Bud' Tingwell, Candy Raymond, Jeanie Drynan, Bryan Brown, Lucky Grills

The Money Pit

US   1986   91m   DuArt
Universal/Steven Spielberg (Frank Marshall, Kathleen Kennedy, Art Levinson)

An image An image An image

New Yorkers take on an old suburban house, and find it was no bargain.

Witless semi-remake of Mr Blandings Builds His Dream House, with screams instead of subtlety and no real humour at all.

w David Giler   d Richard Benjamin   ph Gordon Willis   m Michel Colombier   pd Patrizia von Brandenstein   ed Jacqueline Cambas

☆ Tom Hanks, Shelley Long, Alexander Godunov, Maureen Stapleton, Joe Mantegna, Philip Bosco, Josh Mostel

'It begins unpromisingly and slides irrevocably downward from there.' – *Variety*

Money Talks

US   1997   96m   DeLuxe
Entertainment/New Line (Walter Coblenz, Tracy Kramer)

An image An image

A campaigning journalist shields an escaped convict in return for an exclusive story.

Indifferent thriller that seems a pale imitation of the Eddie Murphy–Nick Nolte pairing in 48 Hrs.

w Joel Cohen, Alec Sokolow   d Brett Ratner   ph Russell Carpenter, Robert Primes   m Lalo Schifrin   pd Robb Wilson King   ed Mark Helfrich

☆ Chris Tucker, Charlie Sheen, Heather Locklear, Gerard Ismaël, Damian Chapa, Elise Neal, Michael Wright, Veronica Cartwright, Paul Sorvino

'Chemistry between the mismatched stars is imperceptible. A new low point in Sheen's career slide.' – *Sight and Sound*

Money Train

US   1995   110m   Technicolor
Columbia/Peters Entertainment (Jon Peters, Neil Canton)

An image An image An image An image An image

Two New York cops who are foster brothers decide to rob a train carrying the money collected from the subway system each day.

A tired action movie, loud and unsubtle with performances to match.

w Doug Richardson, David Loughery   d Joseph Ruben   ph John W. Lindley   m Mark Mancina   pd Bill Groom   ed George Bowers, Bill Pankow

☆ Wesley Snipes, Woody Harrelson, Jennifer Lopez, Robert Blake, Chris Cooper, Joe Grifasi

'Bounces along with a lame script and inconsistent pace.' – *Variety*

'A big, noisy headache of a movie.' – *Entertainment Weekly*

The Money Trap

US   1966   92m   bw   Panavision
MGM (Max E. Youngstein, David Karr)

A hard-up policeman turns to crime.

A cheap thriller decorated with waning stars; competent at the lowest level.

w Walter Bernstein   *novel* Lionel White   d Burt Kennedy   ph Paul C. Vogel   m Hal Schaefer

☆ Glenn Ford, Rita Hayworth, Elke Sommer, Ricardo Montalban, Joseph Cotten, Tom Reese, James Mitchum

Money, Women and Guns

US   1959   80m   Eastmancolor   Cinemascope
Universal-International

A murdered prospector scrawls a will before dying; a detective investigates the beneficiaries.

What could have been an effective Western whodunnit is jinxed by erratic writing and direction.

w Montgomery Pittman   d Richard H. Bartlett   ph Philip Lathrop   ad Alexander Golitzen

☆ Jock Mahoney, Kim Hunter, Tim Hovey, Gene Evans, William Campbell, Lon Chaney Jnr, Tom Drake, James Gleason

Mongkok Kamun: see *As Tears Go By*

The Monk (dubbed)

France/Italy/West Germany   1972   90m   Eastmancolor
Rank/Maya/Comacico/Peri/Tritone/Studio Films (Henry Lange)

original title: *Le Moine*

An abbot, seduced by a woman disguised as a monk, sinks into a life of debauchery and escapes punishment by selling his soul to the devil.

Ineptly directed, poorly dubbed version of the classic Gothic novel which makes one regret that Buñuel did not direct as well as writing the script.

w Luis Buñuel, Jean-Claude Carrière   *novel* M. G. Lewis   d Ado Kyrou   ph Sacha Vierny   m Piero Piccione   ad Max Douy   ed Eric Pluet

☆ Franco Nero, Nathalie Delon, Nicol Williamson, Nadja Tiller, Elizabeth Wiener, Denis Manuel

'A near disaster … Kyrou's treatment, in fact, reduces the whole thing to the level of a kinky charade.' – *MFB*

The Monk

GB/Spain   1990   106m   colour
Arrow/Celtic/Mediterraneo Cine-TV (Muir Sutherland, Paco Lara)

An image

A priest is corrupted by a woman who enters his monastery disguised as a boy.

Highly coloured version of a Gothic classic, although it adds a touch of morality and repentance missing from the original.

wd Paco Lara   *novel* M. G. Lewis   ph Angel Luis Fernandez   m Anton Garcia Abril   pd Gumersindo Andres   ed José Luis Matesanz   sp Alberto Nombela

☆ Paul McGann, Sophie Ward, Isla Blair, Freda Dowie, Aitana Sanchez-Gijon, Laura Davenport, Suzanne Bertish, Mark Elstob

Monk Dawson

GB   1997   107m   colour
De Warrenne (Tom Waller)

An outspoken monk leaves the priesthood to become a tabloid journalist, and then has second thoughts.

Glossy melodrama of the tug between spiritual and fleshy needs, but one that carries no great conviction.

w James Magrane *novel* Piers Paul Read *d* Tom Waller *ph* Teoh Gay Hian *m* Mark Jensen *pd* Harold Chapman *ed* Tom Waller
☆ John Michie, Ben Taylor, Paula Hamilton, Martin Kemp, Rupert Vansittart, Frances Tomelty, Rhona Mitra
   'A rewarding low-budget British independent that really deserves to find an audience.' – *Mark Wyman, Sight and Sound*

'The 1931 nut crop is ready!'
Monkey Business ***
♦♦ US 1931 81m bw
Paramount (Herman J. Mankiewicz)
🔲 ▤ ⊚ ⊚
Four ship's stowaways crash a society party and catch a few crooks.
The shipboard part of this extravaganza is one of the best stretches of Marxian lunacy, but after the Chevalier impersonations it runs out of steam. Who's grumbling?
w S. J. Perelman, Will B. Johnstone, Arthur Sheekman *d* Norman Z. McLeod. *ph* Arthur L. Todd
☆ Groucho Marx, Chico Marx, Harpo Marx, Zeppo Marx, Thelma Todd, Rockcliffe Fellowes, Ruth Hall, Harry Woods
   'Surefire for laughs despite working along familiar lines … picture has started off by doing sweeping business all over, and no reason why it shouldn't continue to tickle wherever it plays.' – *Variety*

Monkey Business *
US 1952 97m bw
TCF (Sol C. Siegel)
original title: Darling I Am Growing Younger
A chimpanzee in a research lab accidentally concocts an elixir of youth.
Remarkably laboured comedy by and with top people; it can't fail to have funny moments, but they are few and far between.
w Ben Hecht, Charles Lederer, I.A.L. Diamond *d* Howard Hawks *ph* Milton Krasner *m* Leigh Harline
☆ Cary Grant, Ginger Rogers, *Charles Coburn, Marilyn Monroe,* Hugh Marlowe
   CHARLES COBURN TO MARILYN MONROE (PLAYING HIS SECRETARY): 'Find someone to type this.'

Monkey Grip
Australia 1983 102m Eastmancolor
Mainline/Pavilion/Cinecom (Patricia Lovell)
A single mother begins an affair with a drug-addict.
Sprawling, downbeat story of suburban desolation and shiftless lives in Melbourne.
w Ken Cameron, Helen Graham *novel* Helen Graham *d* Ken Cameron *ph* David Gribble *m* Bruce Smeaton *pd* Clark Munro *ed* David Huggett
☆ Noni Hazelhurst, Colin Friels, Alice Garner, Harold Hopkins, Candy Raymond, Michael Caton, Tim Burns, Christina Amphlett

A Monkey in Winter *
France 1962 103m bw Totalvision
CIPRA/Cité (Jacques Bar)
aka: *Une Singe en Hiver*
aka: *It's Hot in Hell*
In a small Normandy resort, a hotel owner and a literary guest get drunk together and plan great fantasies, but finally return to their responsibilities.
Amiable, meandering star character comedy.
w François Boyer *novel* Antoine Blondin *d* Henri Verneuil *ph* Louis Page *m* Michel Magne
☆ Jean Gabin, Jean-Paul Belmondo, Suzanne Flon, Noël Roquevert, Paul Frankeur, Gabrielle Dorziat

Monkey on My Back
US 1957 93m bw
UA/Imperial/Edward Small
A Guadalcanal hero is given morphine to relieve malaria and becomes addicted.
Dreary case history sold as exploitation.
w Crane Wilbur, Anthony Veiller, Peter Dudley, from the experiences of Barney Ross *d* André de Toth *ph* Maury Gertsman *m* Paul Sawtell, Bert Shefter
☆ Cameron Mitchell, Dianne Foster, Jack Albertson, Paul Richards

Monkey Shines *
US 1988 109m DeLuxe
Rank/Orion (Charles Evans)
🔲 ▤
A student, paralysed in an accident, forms a deadly symbiotic relationship with a monkey trained to help him.
Deft psychological thriller, spoilt by its ending, which was forced on its director.
wd George A. Romero *novel* Michael Stewart *ph* James A. Contner *m* David Shire *pd* Cletus Anderson *ed* Pasquale Buba
☆ Jason Beghe, John Pankow, Kate McNeil, Joyce Van Patten, Christine Forrest

'He's Cute. He's Cuddly. He's A Klepto.'
Monkey Trouble
♦♦ US 1994 95m Technicolor
Entertainment/New Line/Percy Main/Effe/Victor (Mimi Polk, Heidi Rufus Isaacs)
🔲 ▤ ⊚
A small girl adopts a light-fingered monkey and cures him of his thieving ways, to the annoyance of his owner, an organ grinder in league with gangsters.
Amiable comedy for children, provided you don't mind its reliance for laughs on a domesticated performing monkey in waistcoat and fez.
w Franco Amurri, Stu Krieger *d* Franco Amurri *ph* Luciano Tovoli *m* Mark Mancina *pd* Les Dilley *ed* Ray Lovejoy, Chris Peppe
☆ Harvey Keitel, Thora Birch, Mimi Rogers, Christopher McDonald, Kevin Scannell, Finster
   'A touching children's adventure that belongs among the great animal movies.' – *Variety*

Monkeys Go Home
♦♦ US 1966 101m Technicolor
Walt Disney (Ron Miller)
▤
An American inherits a French olive farm and trains chimpanzees to harvest the crop.
Footling comedy with not much of an idea, let alone a plot.
w Maurice Tombragel *novel The Monkeys* by G. K. Wilkinson *d* Andrew V. McLaglen *ph* William Snyder *m* Robert F. Brunner
☆ Maurice Chevalier, Dean Jones, Yvette Mimieux, Bernard Woringer, Jules Munshin, Alan Carney
   'Innocuous, extrovertly cheerful and good-humoured – and very dull.' – *MFB*

El Mono Loco: see *The Mad Monkey*

The Monolith Monsters
US 1957 77m bw
Ul (Howard Christie)
A meteorite lands in the desert and causes rocks to rise and expand, becoming toppling pillars which threaten a local community.
Dully-written science fiction with moderate special effects.
w Norman Jolley, Robert M. Fresco *d* John Sherwood *ph* Ellis Carter *md* Joseph Gershenson
☆ Lola Albright, Grant Williams, Les Tremayne, Phil Harvey

Monsieur Beaucaire *
US 1946 93m bw
Paramount (Paul Jones)
King Louis XV's bumbling barber impersonates a court dandy.
What seemed a lively period burlesque has faded somewhat with age, but it still has its moments. Any relation between this and the silent Valentino film is quite accidental.
w Melvin Frank, Norman Panama *d* George Marshall *ph* Lionel Lindon *md* Robert Emmett Dolan
☆ Bob Hope, Joan Caulfield, Patric Knowles, Marjorie Reynolds, Cecil Kellaway, Joseph Schildkraut, Reginald Owen, Constance Collier, Hillary Brooke, Douglass Dumbrille, Mary Nash
   'Whether you yawn or rather wearily laugh depends chiefly on your chance state of mind.' – *James Agee*

Monsieur Hire **
France 1989 82m colour Panavision
Palace/Cinea/Hachette Premiere/FR3
🔲 ▤
A middle-aged voyeur, disliked by his neighbours and suspected by the police of murder, becomes involved with a young girl on whom he spies.
Meticulously stylish study of sexual obsession.
w Patrice Leconte, Patrick Dewolf *novel Les Fiançailles de M. Hire* by Georges Simenon *d* Patrice Leconte *ph* Denis Lenoir *m* Michael Nyman *pd* Ivan Mausson *ed* Joelle Hache
☆ Michel Blanc, Sandrine Bonnaire, André Wilms, Luc Thuillier
   'Brilliantly conceived, admirably acted, and staged with stunning confidence.' – *Tom Milne, MFB*
   'A classic psychological thriller made with all the subtlety, elegance and skill which have placed the French at the head of the field in this genre.' – *Daily Telegraph*

Monsieur Hulot's Holiday ****
♦♦ France 1953 91m bw
Cady/Discina (Fred Orain)
🔲 ▤
original title: Les Vacances de Monsieur Hulot
An accident-prone bachelor arrives at a seaside resort and unwittingly causes havoc for himself and everyone else.
Despite lame endings to some of the jokes, this is a film to set the whole world laughing, Hulot himself being an unforgettable character and some of the timing magnificent. One feels that it could very nearly happen.
w Jacques Tati, Henri Marquet *d* Jacques Tati *ph* Jacques Mercanton, Jean Mouselle *m* Alain Romans
☆ Jacques Tati, Nathalie Pascaud, Michèle Rolla, Valentine Camax
   'The casual, amateurish air of his films clearly adds to their appeal: it also appears to explain their defects.' – *Penelope Houston, MFB*
   'It had me laughing out loud with more enjoyment than any other comedy film this year.' – *Daily Express*
⊗ script

Monsieur Ripois et Son Némésis: see *Knave of Hearts*

Monsieur Verdoux **
US 1947 125m bw
Charles Chaplin
🔲 ▤
A bank cashier marries and murders rich women to support his real wife.
Interesting but unsatisfactory redrafting of the Landru case; the star is more dapper than funny, the moral is unconvincing, and the slapstick sequences too often raise yawns.
wd Charles Chaplin *ph* Rollie Totheroh *m* Charles Chaplin
☆ Charles Chaplin, Martha Raye, Isobel Elsom
   'The cleverest and most brilliant film I have yet made.' – *Charles Chaplin*
   'The result is pure Chaplin; and his genius alone has perfected the astonishing central portrait, among the few which, owing nothing to stage or fiction, belong entirely to the cinema.' – *Dilys Powell*
   'Even today it will seem a failure to anyone who has taken half a dozen lessons in film technique.' – *Andrew Sarris, 1970*
⊗ Charles Chaplin (as writer)

Monsieur Vincent *
France 1947 113m bw
EDIC/UGC
The life of 17th-century St Vincent de Paul, who gave up all worldly goods to devote his life to the poor.
Earnest, realistic Catholic biopic.
w Jean-Bernard Luc, Jean Anouilh *d* Maurice Cloche *ph* Claude Renoir *m* J. J. Grunenwald
☆ Pierre Fresnay, Aimé Clairiond, Jean Debucourt, Lise Delemare
   'In the sum of things writers and director, players, composer and technicians, have laboured together to make a film with a humanity which makes one forget the narrow criteria of cinema.' – *Dilys Powell*
⊗ best foreign film

Monsignor
US 1982 121m DeLuxe
TCF/Frank Yablans (Kurt Neumann)
▤
An Irish cardinal supports the Vatican by doubtful financial means.
A largely boring roman à clef, with a sluggish story and uninspired performances.
w Abraham Polonsky, Wendell Mayes *novel* Jack Alain Leger *d* Frank Perry *ph* Billy Williams *m* John Williams *pd* John DeCuir
☆ Christopher Reeve, Geneviève Bujold, Fernando Rey, Jason Miller, Joe Cortese, Adolfo Celi, Leonardo Cimino
   'Irrevocably grounded in a hash of breast-beating and pious platitudes.' – *Sight and Sound*

Monster: see *Humanoids of the Deep (1980)*

The Monster: see *I Don't Want to Be Born (1975)*

The Monster
US 1925 70m bw silent
MGM
▤
A scientist abducts passing motorists and uses them in his experiments at bringing the dead back to life.
Typical star grotesquerie without much flair.
w Willard Mack, Albert Kenyon *play* Crane Wilbur *d* Roland West
☆ Lon Chaney, Gertrude Olmstead, Hallam Cooley, Walter James

The Monster and the Girl
US 1940 64m bw
Paramount (Jack Moss)
🔲 ▤
A man is wrongfully executed and his brain is implanted in a gorilla, which goes on the rampage.
Curiously ineffectual considering its plot and cast, this little horror thriller seems to have been the first to use this particular situation, which became very well worn later.
w Stuart Anthony *d* Stuart Heisler *ph* Victor Milner *m* Sigmund Krumgold
☆ Paul Lukas, Ellen Drew, Joseph Calleia, George Zucco, Robert Paige, Rod Cameron, Phillip Terry, Onslow Stevens, Gerald Mohr
   'The ape steals the picture.' – *Variety*

Monster City
Japan 1991 78m colour
Asahi Sonorama/Video Art/Japan Home Video/Hideyuki Kikuchi (Kenji Kurata, Makoto Sedani)
🔲
A boy and a girl set out to save the world from being taken over by demons.
Dull sequel to Wicked City, with little to recommend it even to fans of anime.
w Kaoru Okamura *d* Yoshiaki Kawajiri *ph* Kinichi Ishikawa *md* Motoichi Umeda *ad* Yuji Ikeda *ed* Nobuyuki Ogata
☆ Featuring the voices of Teresa Gallagher, Brad Lovelle, Alan Sherman, George Little, Bob Sessions, Gareth Armstrong
   'Style, wit and an eerie twisted beauty are a refreshing change from the usual "rape 'n' pillage" supernatural fare.' – *Manga Mania*

The Monster Club
GB 1980 97m colour
ITC/Chips (Milton Subotsky)
▤ ⊚
A vampire introduces his victim to a club for ghouls and witches, who tell their stories.
A spoofy but not very entertaining variation on a too-familiar formula.
w Edward and Valerie Abraham *stories* R. Chetwynd-Hayes *d* Roy Ward Baker *ph* Peter Jessop *md* Graham Walker
☆ Vincent Price, John Carradine, Anthony Steel, Simon Ward, James Laurenson, Geoffrey Bayldon, Donald Pleasence, Richard Johnson, Britt Ekland, Anthony Valentine, Stuart Whitman, Patrick Magee

Monster from Green Hell
US 1956 71m bw/colour
Grosse-Krasne (Al Zimbalist)
🔲 ▤
Wasps sent into space and exposed to cosmic radiation in an experiment return to Earth as huge killer mutants with tiny wings.

Silly low-budget science fiction, with risible monsters, which has an underlying theme of the fear of a nuclear holocaust.
w Louis Vittes, Endre Bohem d Kenneth G. Crane ph Ray Flin m Albert Glasser pd Ernst Fegte ed Kenneth G. Crane sp Jack Rabin, Louis DeWitt
☆ Jim Davis, Robert E. Griffin, Barbara Turner, Joel Fluellen, Eduardo Ciannelli, Vladimir Sokoloff

Monster in a Box *
GB   1991   88m   Eastmancolor
ICA/Jon Blair Film Co.
A monologue by actor Spalding Gray about his 'monster' of an autobiographical novel.
Engaging encounter with a master of the casual anecdote.
w Spalding Gray play Spalding Gray d Nick Broomfield ph Michael Coulter m Laurie Anderson ed Graham Hutchings
☆ Spalding Gray

The Monster Maker
US   1944   64m   bw
Sigmund Neufeld/PRC
A doctor frustrated in love turns his girlfriend's father into a monster by injecting him with acromegaly, a distorting disease.
Ludicrous tinpot shocker.
w Pierre Gendron, Martin Mooney, Lawrence Williams d Sam Newfield
☆ Ralph Morgan, J. Carrol Naish, Tala Birell, Wanda McKay, Glenn Strange

'Horror that waited 100 million years becomes a terrifying reality!'
Monster on the Campus
US   1958   76m   bw
Joseph Gershenson/Universal
A college professor studies a prehistoric fossilized fish, which turns everything that touches it into monsters.
Silly horror stuff with little to take the attention.
w David Duncan d Jack Arnold ph Russell Metty md Joseph Gershenson
☆ Arthur Franz, Whit Bissell, Joanna Moore

The Monster Squad *
†† Canada   1987   81m   Metrocolor
Panavision
Keith Barish/Taft/Tri-Star
Dracula, Frankenstein's monster, the Wolf Man, the Gill Man and the Mummy take refuge in a small American town.
Mildly amusing spoof for the teenage audience.
w Shane Black, Fred Dekker d Fred Dekker
☆ Stephen Macht, Duncan Regehr, Andre Gower, Robby Kiger, Tom Noonan

'Crawling Up From The Depths … To Terrify And Torture!'
'A New Kind Of Terror To Numb The Nerves!'
The Monster that Challenged the World
†† US   1957   83m   bw
Levy-Gardner-Laven/United Artists
A giant caterpillar lays eggs in California's Salton Sea: one hatches…
Overlong shocker for kids.
w Pat Fielder d Arnold Laven ph Lester White m Heinz Roemheld
☆ Tim Holt, Audrey Dalton, Hans Conried, Harlan Warde

The Monster Walks
US   1932   57m   bw
Like/Action
A supposed paralytic plans the death of his rich niece.
Spooky house murder mystery, too hammy by half.
w Robert Ellis d Frank Strayer
☆ Sheldon Lewis, Mischa Auer, Martha Mattox, Vera Reynolds, Willie Best
'Not badly done, but lacking utterly in novelty.' – *Variety*

Monster Zero: see Invasion of the Astro-Monsters

Monsters from an Unknown Planet
(dubbed)
†† Japan   1975   80m   colour
Miracle/Toho (Tomoyuki Tanaka)
original title: *Mekagojira No Gyakushu*
aka: *The Escape of Mechagodzilla; Terror of Mechagodzilla*
Godzilla is outclassed when aliens reanimate Mechagodzilla and loose Titanosaurus on Tokyo with the help of a renegade scientist and his cyborg daughter.
The usual nonsense from one of the later Godzilla movies, with the monsters inactive for much of the time.
w Yukiko Takayama d Inoshiro Honda
☆ Katsuhiko Sasaki, Tomoko Ai, Akihiko Mirata, Tadao Nakamaru, Katsumasu Uchida

Montana
US   1950   76m   Technicolor
Warner (William Jacobs)
An Australian sheepman fights the cattle barons of Montana.
Modest Western from the star's declining years at Warner.
w James R. Webb, Borden Chase, Charles O'Neal story Ernest Haycox d Ray Enright ph Karl Freund m David Buttolph
☆ Errol Flynn, Alexis Smith, S. Z. Sakall, Douglas Kennedy, James Brown, Ian MacDonald

Montana Belle
US   1952   82m   Trucolor
RKO (Howard Welsch)
The Daltons rescue Belle Starr and insist that she works with them on a dangerous raid.
Warmed-over Western melodramatics, quite unmemorable.
w Horace McCoy, Norman S. Hall d Allan Dwan ph Jack Marta m Nathan Scott
☆ Jane Russell, George Brent, Scott Brady, Forrest Tucker, Andy Devine, Jack Lambert, John Litel, Ray Teal
† The film was completed in 1948, but held over.

Montana Moon
US   1930   88m   bw
MGM
A wealthy rancher's spoiled daughter is about to leave for New York when she falls for a handsome cowboy.
A long string of nothings with bursts of song; incompetent early talkie.
w Sylvia Thalberg, Frank Butler d Malcolm St Clair
☆ Joan Crawford, Johnny Mack Brown, Ricardo Cortez, Lloyd Ingraham, Cliff Edwards

Monte Carlo *
US   1930   94m   bw
Paramount (Ernst Lubitsch)
A count passes himself off as a hairdresser to win a gambling lady.
Faded but charming romantic comedy with music, the first to show its director's sound style in full throttle, notably in the final 'Beyond the Blue Horizon' sequence.
w Ernest Vajda play *The Blue Coast* by Hans Muller novel *Monsieur Beaucaire* by Booth Tarkington d Ernst Lubitsch ph Victor Milner m W. Franke Harling ad Hans Dreier songs Leo Robin, Richard Whiting
☆ Jack Buchanan, Jeanette MacDonald, ZaSu Pitts, Tyler Brooke, Claud Allister, Lionel Belmore
'Nothing extra beyond usual par programmer.' – *Variety*
'Very stylish and sly, not to be missed.' – *New Yorker, 1978*

Monte Carlo or Bust: see Those Daring Young Men in Their Jaunty Jalopies

The Monte Carlo Story
Italy/US   1956   101m   Technirama
Tatanus (Marcello Girosi)
A gambler looks for a rich wife, and finds instead a glamorous woman as penniless as himself: they become confidence tricksters but suffer a change of heart.
Lubitsch might have made something of it, but this is a flavourless pudding of a film and the stars can do nothing with it.

wd Samuel Taylor story Marcello Girosi, Dino Risi ph Giuseppe Rotunno m Renzo Rossellini
☆ Marlene Dietrich, Vittorio de Sica, Arthur O'Connell, Mischa Auer, Natalie Trundy, Jane Rose, Renato Rascel

'He's a cowboy. She's a woman. He's the best at what he does. And so is she.'
Monte Walsh *
US   1970   108m   Technicolor
Cinema Center (Hal Landers, Bobby Roberts)
Two ageing cowboys find life increasingly hard and hopeless; an old acquaintance kills one and is shot by the other.
'Realistic' Western developed in leisurely style with the emphasis on character and on the real drudgery of frontier life.
w David Z. Goodman, Lukas Heller novel Jack Schaefer d William A. Fraker ph David M. Walsh m John Barry
☆ Lee Marvin, Jack Palance, Jeanne Moreau, Mitch Ryan, Jim Davis
'As boring a western as ever involved a bronco-busting scene that alone cost almost half a million dollars.' – *Judith Crist*

Montenegro
Sweden/GB   1981   96m   Eastmancolor
Viking/Europa/Smart Egg (Bo Jonsson)
A housewife driven mad by boredom takes a lover and murders him.
Another case history in which the creator finds more symbolic meaning than the audience is likely to see. On the surface, a mildly entertaining piece of near-pornography.
wd Dusan Makavejev ph Tomislav Pinter m Kornell Kovach
☆ Susan Anspach, Erland Josephson, Bora Todorovic, Per Oscarsson

'A charming, wealthy English gentleman. Two beautiful women. If it only takes a moment to fall in love, imagine what can happen in…'
A Month by the Lake
US/GB   1994   91m   Telecolor
Buena Vista/Miramax/Anuline (Robert Fox)
Holidaying in a villa on Lake Como in the mid-30s, a middle-aged English spinster tries to attract the attentions of an English major.
Moody, languid, reticent romance, pretty to look at but without much substance.
w Trevor Bentham novella H. E. Bates d John Irvin ph Pasqualino de Santis m Nicola Piovani pd Gianni Giovagnoni ed Peter Tanner
☆ Vanessa Redgrave, James Fox, Uma Thurman, Alida Valli, Alessandro Gassman, Carlo Cartier, Natalia Bizzi, Paolo Lombardi
'This isn't exactly a vacation to remember.' – *Sight and Sound*

A Month in the Country *
GB   1987   96m   colour
Euston Films (Kenith Trodd)
In the English countryside, two men recover from the horrors of World War I.
Traditional British teledrama with much going for it despite a final lack of direction.
w Simon Gray novel J. L. Carr d Pat O'Connor ph Kenneth MacMillan m Howard Blake pd Leo Austin ed John Victor
☆ Colin Firth, Kenneth Branagh, Natasha Richardson, Patrick Malahide, Tony Haygarth, Richard Vernon

'Makes *Ben-Hur* look like an epic!'
Monty Python and the Holy Grail ***
GB   1975   90m   Technicolor
EMI/Python (Monty) Pictures/Michael White (Mark Forstater)
King Arthur and his knights seek the Holy Grail.
Hellzapoppin-like series of linked sketches on a medieval theme; some slow bits, but often uproariously funny and with a remarkable visual sense of the Middle Ages.
w Graham Chapman, John Cleese, Terry Gilliam, Eric Idle, Michael Palin d Terry Gilliam, Terry Jones ph Terry Bedford m Neil Innes pd Roy Smith ed John Hackney
☆ Graham Chapman, John Cleese, Terry Gilliam, Eric Idle, Michael Palin

'The team's visual buffooneries and verbal rigmaroles are piled on top of each other with no attention to judicious timing or structure, and a form which began as a jaunty assault on the well-made revue sketch and an ingenious misuse of television's fragmented style of presentation, threatens to become as unyielding and unfruitful as the conventions it originally attacked.' – *Geoff Brown*

Monty Python's Life of Brian **
GB   1979   93m   Eastmancolor
Hand Made Films (John Goldstone)
A contemporary of Jesus is mistaken for him and crucified.
Controversial middle-eastern romp which left its creators battered but extremely wealthy. In the face of such an onslaught of bad taste, criticism seems irrelevant.
w John Cleese, Graham Chapman, Eric Idle, Michael Palin, Terry Gilliam, Terry Jones d Terry Jones ph Peter Biziou m Geoffrey Burgon ad Roger Christian ed Julian Doyle
☆ Graham Chapman, John Cleese, Terry Gilliam, Eric Idle, Michael Palin, Terry Jones, Kenneth Colley, Gwen Taylor, Carol Cleveland

Monty Python's The Meaning of Life
GB   1983   90m   Technicolor
Universal/Celandine/The Monty Python Partnership (John Goldstone)
A series of sketches in questionable taste.
Subjects include organ transplants, sex, death and the results of overeating.
w Graham Chapman, John Cleese, Terry Gilliam, Eric Idle, Michael Palin, Terry Jones d Terry Jones ph Peter Hannam m various pd Harry Lange ed Julian Doyle animation Terry Gilliam
☆ Graham Chapman, John Cleese, Eric Idle, Terry Jones, Michael Palin, Terry Gilliam, Carol Cleveland

Moon 44
West Germany   1989   99m   colour
Medusa/Centropolis Filmproduktion (Dean Heyde, Roland Emmerich)
In the future, an undercover agent is sent to a far-away planet to unearth a saboteur.
Science fiction melodrama that borrows from most other recent films in the genre to little effect.
w Dean Heyde, Oliver Eberle story Roland Emmerich, Dean Heyde, Oliver Eberle, P. J. Mitchell d Roland Emmerich ph Karl Walter Undenlaub m Joel Goldsmith pd Oliver Scholl ed Tony Wigand
☆ Michael Pare, Lisa Eichhorn, Malcolm McDowell, Dean Devlin, Brian Thompson, Stephen Geoffreys, Leon Rippy, Jochen Nickel, Mechmed Yilmez

The Moon and Sixpence ***
US   1943   85m   bw (colour sequence)
Albert Lewin/David L. Loew (Stanley Kramer)
A stockbroker leaves his wife and family, spends some selfish years painting in Paris and finally dies of leprosy on a South Sea island.
Pleasantly literary adaptation of an elegant novel based on the life of Gauguin; a little stodgy in presentation now, but much of it still pleases.
w Albert Lewin novel W. Somerset Maugham d Albert Lewin ph John Seitz m Dimitri Tiomkin ad Gordon Willis ed Richard L. Van Enger
☆ George Sanders, Herbert Marshall, Steve Geray, Doris Dudley, Elena Verdugo, Florence Bates, Heather Thatcher, Eric Blore, Albert Basserman
'An admirable film until the end, when it lapses into Technicolor and techni-pathos.' – *James Agate*
♫ Dimitri Tiomkin

The Moon in the Gutter
French/Italian   1983   130m   Eastmancolor
Panavision
Palace/Gaumont/TFI Films/SFPC/Opera Film Produzione (Lise Fayolle)
original title: *La Lune dans le Caniveau*
A stevedore, haunting the docks to find the man who raped his sister, becomes involved with a rich woman.

Relentlessly fashionable, now dated, low-life mystery that gets nowhere slowly.
w Jean-Jacques Beineix, Olivier Mergault *novel* David Goodis d Jean-Jacques Beineix ph Philippe Rousselot m Gabriel Yared ad Hilton McConnico ed Monique Prim, Yves Deschamps
☆ Gérard Depardieu, Nastassia Kinski, Victoria Abril, Beatrice Reading, Gabriel Monnet, Dominique Pinon, Milena Vukotic, Vittorio Mezzogiorno

The Moon Is Blue *
US   1953   99m   bw
Otto Preminger
▦ ◎~

A spry young girl balances the attractions of a middle-aged lover against her young one.
Paper-thin comedy partly set on top of the Empire State Building (and thereafter in a dowdy set); mildly amusing in spots, it gained notoriety, and a Production Code ban, by its use of such naughty words as 'virgin' and 'mistress'.
w F. Hugh Herbert *play* F. Hugh Herbert d Otto Preminger ph Ernest Laszlo m Herschel Burke Gilbert ed Otto Ludwig
☆ Maggie McNamara, David Niven, William Holden, Tom Tully, Dawn Addams
PATTY (MAGGIE MCNAMARA): 'Men are usually bored with virgins. I'm so glad you're not ... Have you a mistress?'
DONALD: 'Don't you think it's better for a girl to be preoccupied with sex than occupied with it?'
'It adds nothing to the art of cinema and certainly does not deserve the attention it will get for flouting the Production Code.' – *Philip T. Hartung*
† The film was made simultaneously in German, as *Die Jungfrau auf dem Dach*, with Hardy Kruger, Johanna Matz and Johannes Heesters.
♫ Maggie McNamara; title song (mHerschel Burke Gilbert, lySylvia Fine); editing

The Moon Is Down **
US   1943   90m   bw
TCF (Nunnally Johnson)
A Norwegian village resists the Nazis.
Sombre, talkative, intelligent little drama, the best of the resistance films, shot on the set of How Green Was My Valley (with snow covering).
w Nunnally Johnson *novel* John Steinbeck d Irving Pichel ph Arthur Miller m Alfred Newman ad James Basevi, Maurice Ransford ed Louis Loeffler
☆ Henry Travers, Cedric Hardwicke, Lee J. Cobb, Dorris Bowdon, Margaret Wycherly, Peter Van Eyck, John Banner
'This may well be a true picture of Norway and its people. But it fails to strike fire, to generate passion. It leaves one feeling rather proud but also sad.' – *Bosley Crowther*

'Jungle love tease! It's hot!'
Moon over Burma
US   1940   76m   bw
Paramount
Jungle lumbermen fight over a stranded American entertainer.
Routine adventure romance climaxing in a forest fire.
w Frank Wead, W. P. Lipscomb, Harry Clork d Louis King ph William Mellor m Victor Young
☆ Dorothy Lamour, Robert Preston, Preston Foster, Doris Nolan, Albert Basserman, Frederick Worlock, Addison Richards

Moon over Miami *
US   1941   92m   Technicolor
TCF (Harry Joe Brown)
▦
Two sisters seek rich husbands in Florida.
Musical remake of Three Blind Mice, which was suspiciously similar to Golddiggers of Broadway, The Greeks Had a Word for Them, etc., and the later How to Marry a Millionaire and Three Little Girls in Blue. In short, a Hollywood standard, not too badly done.
w Vincent Lawrence, Brown Holmes d Walter Lang ph Peverell Marley, Leon Shamroy md Alfred Newman *songs* Leo Robin, Ralph Rainger
☆ Don Ameche, Betty Grable, Carole Landis, Robert Cummings, Charlotte Greenwood, Jack Haley, Cobina Wright Jnr, Robert Greig

Moon over Parador
US   1988   104m   DeLuxe
UIP/Universal (Paul Mazursky)
▦ ▦ ◎~ ◖
An actor is kidnapped and forced to impersonate the president of a Caribbean country.
Occasionally amusing, but the joke is too thin to bear much watching.
w Leon Capetanos, Paul Mazursky *story* Charles G. Booth d Paul Mazursky ph Donald McAlpine m Maurice Jarre pd Pato Guzman ed Stuart Pappe
☆ Richard Dreyfuss, Raul Julia, Sonia Braga, Jonathan Winters, Fernando Rey, Sammy Davis Jnr, Michael Greene, Polly Holliday, Milton Goncalves, Charo, Marianne Sagebrecht

Moon Pilot **
⊀ US   1961   98m   Technicolor
Walt Disney (Ron Miller)
A reluctant astronaut falls in love with a girl from outer space, who finally accompanies him on his mission.
Engaging science-fiction spoof with good performances.
w Maurice Tombragel *serial* Robert Buckner d James Neilson ph William Snyder m Peter Smith sp Eustace Lycett
☆ Edmond O'Brien, Tom Tryon, Brian Keith

The Moon Spinners *
⊀ GB   1964   119m   Technicolor
Walt Disney (Bill Anderson)
A young girl holidaying in Crete becomes involved with jewel thieves.
Teenage adventure against attractive locations; quite agreeable but overlong.
w Michael Dyne *novel* Mary Stewart d James Neilson ph Paul Beeson m Ron Grainer
☆ Hayley Mills, Peter McEnery, Eli Wallach, Joan Greenwood, John Le Mesurier, Pola Negri

Moon Warriors
Hong Kong   1992   83m   colour
Team Work (Andy Lau)
▦ ◎
An exiled prince, escaping from his usurping brother's army, finds refuge with a fisherman and his friendly killer whale.
Epic romance with spectacular, acrobatic sword fights, and good to look at despite its often trite narrative.
w Ching Siu Tung d Samo Hung
☆ Andy Lau, Maggie Cheung, Anita Mui, Kenny Bee
'Delirious feudal martial arts adventure which boasts expensive production values, well-composed widescreen images and flawless choreography ... highly enjoyable.' – *Sight and Sound*

'The number one space western!'
Moon Zero Two
GB   1969   100m   Technicolor
Hammer (Michael Carreras)
▦
In 2021, the moon is being colonized and crooks are trying to get control of an asteroid.
A self-acknowledged 'space western' which has a few bright ideas but suffers from a childish script.
w Michael Carreras *story* Gavin Lyall, Frank Hardman, Martin Davidson d Roy Ward Baker ph Paul Beeson m Don Ellis
☆ James Olson, Catherina von Schell, Warren Mitchell, Ori Levy, Adrienne Corri, Dudley Foster, Bernard Bresslaw, Neil McCallum
'It's all just about bad enough to fill older audiences with nostalgia for the inspired innocence of Flash Gordon, or even the good old days of Abbott and Costello in outer space.' – *MFB*

Moonfleet *
⊀ US   1955   87m   Eastmancolor
Cinemascope
MGM (John Houseman)
▦ ▦ ◖
In Dorset in 1770 an orphan boy finds that his elegant guardian leads a gang of smugglers.
Period gothic melodrama which nearly, but not quite, comes off; the script simply doesn't build to the right climax, and too many characters come to nothing. But there are splendid moments.

w Margaret Fitts, Jan Lustig *novel* J. Meade Falkner d Fritz Lang ph Robert Planck m Miklos Rozsa
☆ Stewart Granger, Jon Whiteley, George Sanders, Joan Greenwood, Viveca Lindfors, Liliane Montevecchi, Melville Cooper, Sean McClory, John Hoyt, Alan Napier

'A film as funny, complicated and real ... as life itself.'
Moonlight and Valentino
US   1995   104m   Technicolor
Polygram/Working Title (Alison Owen, Eric Fellner, Tim Bevan)
▦ ▦
Her friend, a sister and her divorced stepmother help a young academic cope with the unexpected death of her husband.
Talky drama of female bonding and dealing with grief that has some, but not enough, effective moments.
w Ellen Simon *play* Ellen Simon d David Anspaugh ph Julio Macat m Howard Shore pd Robb Wilson King ed David Rosenbloom
☆ Elizabeth Perkins, Gwyneth Paltrow, Jon Bon Jovi, Kathleen Turner, Whoopi Goldberg, Jeremy Sisto, Josef Sommer
'"Gently dreary" would be the best chosen words for this film which is so slow at times it is almost stationary.' – *Marianne Gray, Film Review*

Moonlight in Havana
US   1942   63m   bw
Bernard W. Burton/Universal
A baseball catcher goes to Havana for spring training.
Another in the long line of lightweight musical supports from this studio.
w Oscar Brodney d Anthony Mann
☆ Allan Jones, Jane Frazee, Marjorie Lord, William Frawley, the Jiving Jacks and Jills

Moonlight Sonata *
GB   1937   90m   bw
Pall Mall (Lothar Mendes)
▦
Stranded victims of a plane crash are affected by the art of a famous pianist.
Curious, slight, unexpected play-on-film designed to showcase the talent of Paderewski.
w Edward Knoblock, E. M. Delafield d Lothar Mendes ph Jan Stallich
☆ Ignace Paderewski, Eric Portman, Marie Tempest, Charles Farrell, Barbara Greene, Binkie Stuart
'Should make good with class audiences.' – *Variety*
'Dame Marie is a sparking line-tosser who keeps the script alive when Paderewski (then 77) is not putting it to music.' – *New York Times*

The Moonlighter
US   1953   77m   bw   3-D
Warner (Joseph Bernhard)
A cattle rustler moves towards reforming.
Ho-hum Western which offers its stars little to work with and was not even very exciting in 3-D.
w Niven Busch d Roy Rowland ph Bert Glennon m Heinz Roemheld
☆ Fred MacMurray, Barbara Stanwyck, Ward Bond, William Ching, John Dierkes, Morris Ankrum

Moonlighting ***
GB   1982   97m   colour
Michael White/Channel 4 (Mark Shivas, Jerzy Skolimowski)
▦ ▦ ◎~
In 1981 four Polish building workers arrive in London to renovate a house for their boss and make a quick profit. The scheme is somewhat upset by the news of martial law at home…
Very interesting and well-acted anecdote, virtually constructed out of the headlines.
wd Jerzy Skolimowski ph Tony Pierce Roberts m Stanley Myers pd Tony Woollard ed Barrie Vince
☆ Jeremy Irons, Eugene Lipinski, Jiri Stanislaw, Eugeniusz Haczkiewicz

Moonraker
GB   1979   126m   Technicolor   Panavision
UA/Eon (Albert R. Broccoli)
▦ ▦ ◎~ ◖
James Bond investigates the disappearance of a space shuttle during a test flight.

Adventures in Venice, Rio and the upper Amazon; all very repetitive and no longer more than faintly amusing.
w Christopher Wood *novel* Ian Fleming d Lewis Gilbert ph Jean Tournier m John Barry pd Ken Adam
☆ Roger Moore, Lois Chiles, Michael Lonsdale, Richard Kiel, Geoffrey Keen, Lois Maxwell, Bernard Lee
'Conspicuously expensive production values but an unmistakably cut price plot.' – *Sight and Sound*

The Moonraker *
GB   1957   82m   Technicolor
ABPC (Hamilton Inglis)
During the English Civil War, a noble highwayman smuggles the king's son into France.
Likeable swashbuckler which confines its second half to suspense at an inn, a who-is-it rather than a whodunnit. Good fun.
w Robert Hall, Wilfred Eades, Alistair Bell *play* Arthur Watkyn d David MacDonald ph Max Greene m Laurie Johnson
☆ George Baker, Sylvia Syms, Marius Goring, Peter Arne, Richard Leech, Clive Morton, Paul Whitsun-Jones, Gary Raymond, John Le Mesurier, Patrick Troughton, Michael Anderson Jnr

Moonrise *
US   1948   90m   bw
Republic/Frank Borzage Productions (Charles F. Haas)
▦ ◎~
A murderer's son is driven into violence by memories and fears of his childhood.
Broody melodrama set against a remote village and swamp background; not a very interesting story, but memorable detail.
w Charles Haas d Frank Borzage ph John L. Russell m William Lava ed Harry Keller
☆ Gail Russell, Dane Clark, Ethel Barrymore, Allyn Joslyn, Rex Ingram
'The story is told with a unity of mood, sombre and poignant, set by some impressionistic opening passages and sustained by the slow yet firmly compressed style and the strong, low-toned images.' – *Gavin Lambert*

'If the world is sane – then they're completely mad!'
The Moon's Our Home *
US   1936   80m   bw
Paramount (Walter Wanger)
▦
A headstrong actress marries an adventurer on impulse, and they both try to work it out.
Light, bright romantic comedy with the zany tinge then in fashion.
w Isabel Dawn, Boyce DeGaw *novel* Faith Baldwin d William A. Seiter ph Joseph Valentine m Gerard Carbonara
☆ Margaret Sullavan, Henry Fonda, Beulah Bondi, Charles Butterworth, Margaret Hamilton, Dorothy Stickney, Lucien Littlefield
'It isn't, of course, as good as all that; nothing is as good as all that in the cinema, but the great commercial wheels don't grind here quite so effortlessly; a little satire, a little imagination, a little feeling for human inconsistency, has got into the works.' – *Graham Greene, The Spectator*

The Moonshine War
US   1970   100m   Metrocolor   Panavision
MGM/Filmways (James C. Pratt, Leonard Blair)
In Kentucky just before the repeal of prohibition, a corruptible revenue agent regrets bringing in a sadistic crook to help confiscate illegal whisky.
Downright peculiar hillbilly melodrama, neither straight nor satirical; interesting only in fits and starts.
w Elmore Leonard *novel* Elmore Leonard d Richard Quine ph Richard H. Kline m Fred Karger
☆ Patrick McGoohan, Richard Widmark, Alan Alda, Melodie Johnson, Will Geer
'Patrick McGoohan walked over to me the only day I was on the set and said, "What's it like to hear your lines all fucked up?"{?is0p1.5Y'} – *Elmore Leonard*

The Moonspinners: see *The Moon Spinners*

Moonstruck *
US 1987 102m Technicolor
Patrick Palmer/Norman Jewison
📺 🎬 🎬 💿 🎧

Young widow falls for the estranged brother of her husband-to-be.
Noisy, sometimes heavy-handed romantic comedy of Italian-American manners.
w John Patrick Shanley d Norman Jewison ph David Watkin m Dick Hyman pd Philip Rosenberg
☆ Cher, Nicolas Cage, Vincent Gardenia, Olympia Dukakis, Danny Aiello
👤 Cher; John Patrick Shanley; Olympia Dukakis
👥 best picture; Norman Jewison; Vincent Gardenia

Moontide *
US 1942 94m bw
TCF (Mark Hellinger)
A seaman cares for an unhappy waif.
A Hollywood attempt at romantic melodrama in the French manner. It looks good, and the cast is fine, but everything is just a bit too glum.
w John O'Hara novel Willard Robertson d Archie Mayo ph Charles G. Clarke m Cyril Mockridge, David Buttolph
☆ Jean Gabin, Ida Lupino, Claude Rains, Thomas Mitchell, Jerome Cowan, Sen Yung, Tully Marshall, Helene Reynolds
👥 Charles G. Clarke

Moonwalker
👫 US 1988 93m
Warner/Ultimate Productions
📺 🎬
Episodic look at the life and performances of Michael Jackson, culminating in a fantasy in which he stops a gangster turning children into junkies.
Strictly for fans.
w David Newman story Michael Jackson d Colin Chilvers, Jerry Kramer ph John Hora, Tom Ackerman, Bob Collins, Fred Elmes, Crescenzo Notarile m Bruce Broughton pd Michael Ploog ed David E. Blewitt, Mitchell Sinoway, Dale Beldin
☆ Michael Jackson, Joe Pesci, Sean Lennon, Kellie Parker, Brandon Adams

The Morals of Marcus
GB 1936 75m bw
Real Art (W. J. Locke)
A girl escapes from a Middle Eastern harem by stowing away with a British aristocrat.
Feeble 'naughty' comedy, killed by lack of wit and pace.
w Guy Bolton, Miles Mander play W. J. Locke d Miles Mander ph John W. Boyle
☆ Lupe Velez, Ian Hunter, Adrianne Allen, Noel Madison, J. H. Roberts, H. F. Maltby
'Acceptable feature for general consumption.' – *Variety*

Die Mörder Sind Unter Uns: see The Murderers Are Among Us

More American Graffiti
US 1979 111m Technicolor
Universal/Lucasfilm (Howard Kazanjian)
📺 🎬
In 1964, American small-town teenagers quarrel over drugs and drag racing.
Tedious sequel to a movie which was more than enough.
wd B. W. L. Norton ph Caleb Deschanel m various
☆ Candy Clark, Bo Hopkins, Ron Howard, Paul Le Mat, Mackenzie Phillips, Richard Bradford
'What once was a crate of dynamite has been cosmetically giftwrapped à la Happy Days.' – *Cynthia Rose, MFB*

More Dead Than Alive
US 1968 99m DeLuxe
United Artists/Aubrey Schenck
Revenge erupts some years after a violent jail break.
Eccentric and pretentious Western with a complex story which might have intrigued if handled better.
w George Schenck d Robert Sparr ph Jack Marquette m Philip Springer
☆ Clint Walker, Vincent Price, Anne Francis, Paul Hampton, Mike Henry, Craig Littler

More than a Secretary
US 1936 80m bw
Columbia
A dowdy secretary loses her glasses and wins her boss.
That old story, and the treatment isn't anything to get excited about either.
w Dale Van Every, Lynn Starling d Alfred E. Green
☆ Jean Arthur, George Brent, Lionel Stander, Ruth Donnelly, Reginald Denny, Dorothea Kent, Charles Halton
'Fair b.o. possibilities, but the story doesn't belong on the same block as the production afforded to it.' – *Variety*

The More the Merrier ***
US 1943 104m bw
Columbia (George Stevens)
📺 🎬
In crowded Washington during World War II, a girl allows two men to share her apartment and falls in love with the younger one.
Thoroughly amusing romantic comedy with bright lines and situations; remade less effectively as Walk Don't Run (qv).
w Robert Russell, Frank Ross, Richard Flournoy, Lewis R. Foster d George Stevens ph Ted Tetzlaff m Leigh Harline md Morris Stoloff
☆ Jean Arthur, Joel McCrea, Charles Coburn, Richard Gaines, Bruce Bennett
'The gayest comedy that has come from Hollywood in a long time. It has no more substance than a watermelon, but is equally delectable.' – *Howard Barnes*
'Farce, like melodrama, offers very special chances for accurate observation, but here accuracy is avoided ten times to one in favour of the easy burlesque or the easier idealization which drops the bottom out of farce. Every good moment frazzles or drowns.' – *James Agee*
† Garson Kanin has claimed to have written virtually all the script.
👤 Charles Coburn
👥 best picture; script; original story (Frank Ross, Robert Russell); George Stevens; Jean Arthur

The More Things Change...
Australia 1985 95m Eastmancolor
Panvision
Syme International/NSWFC (Jill Robb)
A successful journalist tries to cope with the strains of a demanding job and marriage when her husband decides to move to the country to become self-sufficient.
Small-scale, routine drama of a marriage in trouble; nothing out of the ordinary.
w Moya Wood d Robyn Nevin ph Dan Burstall m Peter Best pd Josephine Ford ed Jill Bilcock
☆ Judy Morris, Barry Otto, Victoria Longley, Peter Carroll, Louise Le Nay, Lewis Fitz-Gerald, Owen Johnson

Morgan – A Suitable Case for Treatment ***
GB 1966 97m bw
British Lion/Quintra (Leon Clore)
📺 🎬
US title: Morgan!
A young woman determines to leave her talented but half-mad artist husband, who has a fixation on gorillas and behaves in a generally uncivilized manner.
Archetypal sixties marital fantasy, an extension of Look Back in Anger in the mood of swinging London. As tiresome as it is funny – but it is funny.
w David Mercer play David Mercer d Karel Reisz ph Larry Pizer, Gerry Turpin m Johnny Dankworth
☆ Vanessa Redgrave, David Warner, Robert Stephens, Irene Handl, Newton Blick, Nan Munro
'Poor Morgan: victim of a satire that doesn't bite, lost in a technical confusion of means and ends, and emerging like an identikit photograph, all bits and pieces and no recognizable face.' – *Penelope Houston*
'The first underground movie made above ground.' – *John Simon*
'I think Morgan is so appealing to college students because it shares their self-view: they accept this mess of cute infantilism and obsessions and aberrations without expecting the writer and director to resolve it and without themselves feeling a necessity to sort it out.' – *Pauline Kael*
👥 Vanessa Redgrave
🎬 David Mercer

Morituri: The Saboteur: see The Saboteur, Code Name Morituri

The Morning After
US 1986 103m DeLuxe
TCF/Lorimar/American Filmworks (Bruce Gilbert)
📺 🎬 🎬
A drunken actress wakes up one morning next to a man with a dagger in his heart.
A mystery which starts as intriguing but is insufficiently developed and peters out into a series of casual encounters between unattractive people.
w James Hicks d Sidney Lumet ph Andrzej Bartkowiak m Paul Chihara pd Albert Brenner ed Joel Goodman
☆ Jane Fonda, Jeff Bridges, Raul Julia, Diane Salinger
👥 Jane Fonda

Morning Departure *
GB 1950 102m bw
Rank/Jay Lewis (Leslie Parkyn)
US title: Operation Disaster
Twelve men are caught in a trapped submarine, and only eight can escape.
Archetypal stiff-upper-lip service tragedy, which moves from briskness to a slow funereal ending.
w William Fairchild play Kenneth Woollard d Roy Baker ph Desmond Dickinson
☆ John Mills, Richard Attenborough, Nigel Patrick, Lana Morris, Peter Hammond, Helen Cherry, James Hayter, Andrew Crawford, George Cole, Michael Brennan, Wylie Watson, Bernard Lee, Kenneth More

Morning Glory **
US 1933 74m bw
RKO (Pandro S. Berman)
🎬
A young actress comes to New York determined to succeed.
Marvellously evocative theatrical drama which provided a strong star part for a fresh young actress and surrounded her with accomplished thespians. Remade to much less effect as Stage Struck (qv).
w Howard J. Green play Zoe Akins d Lowell Sherman ph Bert Glennon m Max Steiner
☆ Katharine Hepburn, Douglas Fairbanks Jnr, Adolphe Menjou, Mary Duncan, C. Aubrey Smith, Don Alvarado
'Star vastly superior to this sometimes misdirected arty story.' – *Variety*
👤 Katharine Hepburn

Morning Glory
US 1993 95m Foto-Kem
Overseas/Dove Audio (Michael Viner)
🎬
In 1941, a former convict, who answers an advert for a husband by a pregnant widow with three children, is accused of murder when the town's good-time girl is killed.
Dull and predictable small-town soap opera, given a plodding treatment.
w Charles Jarrott, Deborah Raffin novel Lavyrle Spencer d Steven Hilliard Stern ph Laszlo George m Jonathan Elias ad David Hiscox ed Richard Benwick
☆ Christopher Reeve, Deborah Raffin, Lloyd Bochner, Nina Foch, Helen Shaver, J. T. Walsh

Morning of the Earth
Australia 1972 80m colour
Woolloomooloo/AFD (David Elfick)
📺
Documentary film that tries to communicate the pleasure and adrenalin rush of surfing big waves in Australia and Hawaii.
Surfers are likely to enjoy this the most; the images of sand, sea and surfers have a charm, though after a while one wave begins to look much like another.
d Albert Falzon ph Albert Falzon m G. Wayne Thomas, Brian Cadd, Taman Shud et al ed Grant Shanks
☆ Nat Young, Chris Brock, Stephen Cooney, David Treloar, Mark Warren, Rusty Miller, Michael Peterson, Terry Fitzgerald, Ted Spencer, Reno Abelliro, Jerry Lopez

'Revealing the amazing things a woman will do for love!'

Morocco ***
US 1930 97m bw
Paramount (Louis D. Lighton)
📺 🎬
A cabaret singer arrives in Morocco and continues her wicked career by enslaving all the men in sight; but true love reaches her at last.
The star's first American film reveals her quintessence, and although wildly dated in subject matter remains a perversely enjoyable entertainment.
w Jules Furthman novel Amy Jolly by Benno Vigny d Josef von Sternberg ph Lee Garmes m Karl Hajos ad Hans Dreier
☆ Marlene Dietrich, Gary Cooper, Adolphe Menjou, Ullrich Haupt, Juliette Compton, Francis McDonald
'Lightweight story with good direction ... needs plenty of exploitation to do over average.' – *Variety*
'A definite step forward in the art of motion pictures.' – *National Board of Review*
'A cinematic pattern, brilliant, profuse, subtle, and at almost every turn inventive.' – *Wilton A. Barrett*
'Enchantingly silly, full of soulful grand passions, drifting cigarette smoke, and perhaps a few too many pictorial shots of the Foreign Legion marching this way and that.' – *New Yorker, 1979*
👥 Josef von Sternberg; Lee Garmes; Marlene Dietrich; Hans Dreier

Morons from Outer Space
👫 GB 1985 91m colour
Thorn EMI (Barry Hanson)
📺
Dopey space travellers arrive on Earth.
Spoofy comedy which, apart from staging a spectacular motorway landing and mocking various popular film genres, never decides where to go.
w Griff Rhys Jones, Mel Smith d Michael Hodges ph Phil Meheux m Peter Brewis
☆ Mel Smith, Griff Rhys Jones, Paul Bown, Joanne Pearce, Jimmy Nail, Dinsdale Landen, James B. Sikking
'It remains stuck on the launch pad.' – *Variety*

Morris West's The Naked Country: see The Naked Country

Mortal Kombat
US 1995 101m colour
First Independent/New Line/Threshold (Lawrence Kasanoff)
📺 📺 🎬 🎬 💿 🎧
Good guys with muscles battle evil in an attempt to save the world from the denizens of another universe.
On its level, of mindless, violent entertainment, this can be counted something of a success: it is the first film based on a video game to reproduce some of the visceral excitement of the original.
w Kevin Droney d Paul Anderson ph John R. Leonetti m George S. Clinton pd Jonathan Carlson ed Martin Hunter
☆ Christopher Lambert, Robin Shou, Cary-Hiroyuki Tagawa, Bridgette Wilson, Talisa Soto, Chris Casamassa, Linden Ashby
'It is well-served by a cast clearly well-versed in dopey grinning. All the actors have to do is talk, fight a bit, and vaguely resemble their digitised counterparts. Tough gig.' – *Guardian*

Mortal Kombat 2: Annihilation
US 1997 94m Foto-Kem
Entertainment/New Line/Threshold/Lawrence Kasanoff
📺 🎬 🎬 💿 💿
Martial artists who triumphed over evil are attacked by a wicked emperor who wants to create hell on Earth.
There is a problem in converting the mindless mayhem of video games to the mindless mayhem of action films: the latter require an engaging narrative to replace the interactive charms of the former, something this mess fails to achieve.
w Brent V. Friedman, Bryce Zabel d John R. Leonetti ph Matthew F. Leonetti m George S. Clinton pd Charles Wood ed Peck Prior sp Chuck Comisky, Alison Savitch
☆ Robin Shou, Talisa Soto, James Remar, Sandra Hess, Lynn Red Williams, Brian Thompson, Reiner Schoene

'Consists largely of choppily edited fight scenes (usually involving somersaults and back flips) combined with various computer graphic effects.' – *Variety*

Mortal Passions
US   1990   98m   Foto-Kem
Gibraltar (Gwen Field)
☒ ▤

A lying wife, attempting to manipulate her lover into killing her weak husband, finds herself unexpectedly involved in murder.
A feeble, vacuous attempt at a thriller in the tradition of film noir, with dull characters, uninteresting dialogue and no suspense.
w Alan Moscowitz d Andrew Lane ph Christian Sebaldt m Parmer Fuller pd Robert Sissman ed Kimberly Ray
☆ Zach Galligan, Krista Errickson, Michael Bowen, Luca Bercovici, Sheila Kelley, Cassandra Gava, David Warner

'The love story of today with the popular stars of The Shop Around the Corner!'

The Mortal Storm **
US   1940   100m   bw
MGM (Sidney Franklin)
A German family in the thirties is split by Nazism.
Solid anti-Nazi melodrama typical of the period before America entered the war; good performances outweigh unconvincing studio sets.
w Claudine West, George Froeschel, Anderson Ellis novel Phyllis Bottome d Frank Borzage ph William Daniels m Edward Kane
☆ Margaret Sullavan, Robert Young, James Stewart, Frank Morgan, Robert Stack, Bonita Granville, Irene Rich, Maria Ouspenskaya
† The film caused Goebbels to ban the showing of MGM pictures in all German territories.

'Murder is a secret that should never be shared.'
Mortal Thoughts *
US   1991   103m   DeLuxe
Columbia TriStar/New Visions/Polar/Rufglen (John Fiedler, Mark Tarlov)
☒ ▤ ⚲ ◎

Two women, who are best friends, are questioned about the murder of the husband of one of them.
Entertaining thriller which sustains its mystery to the end.
w William Reilly, Claude Kerven d Alan Rudolph ph Elliot Davis m Mark Isham pd Howard Cummings ed Tom Walls
☆ Demi Moore, Glenne Headly, Bruce Willis, John Pankow, Harvey Keitel, Billie Neal, Frank Vincent
'A bravely downbeat movie.' – *Empire*

Morte a Venezia: see *Death in Venice*

La Morte Vivante: see *The Living Dead Girl*

Mortifero: see *The Stranger (1987)*

Moscow Distrusts Tears *
USSR   1979   148m   Sovcolor
Mosfilm (V. Kuchinsky)
original title: *Moskva Slezam Ne Verit*
US title: *Moscow Does Not Believe In Tears*
In Moscow in 1958, three working girls have love affairs. Twenty years later they compare notes.
Odd portmanteau drama, most interesting for its picture of life in Russia.
w Valentin Chernykh d Vladimir Menshov ph Igor Slabnevich m Sergei Nikitin
☆ Vera Alentova, Alexei Batalov, Irina Muravera, Alexander Fatiushin, Raisa Ryazanova, Boris Smorchkov
♟ best foreign film

Moscow Nights
GB   1936   75m   bw
London Films/Capitol Films (Alexis Granowsky, Max Schach)
▤
US title: *I Stand Condemned*
A Russian girl sacrifices her virtue to save her lover from execution.
Cardboard melodrama of pre-revolutionary Moscow; not by any means a classic.
w Erich Seipmann novel Pierre Benoît d Anthony Asquith ph Phil Tannura md Muir Mathieson ad Vincent Korda ed Francis Lyon

☆ Laurence Olivier, Penelope Dudley Ward, Harry Baur, Robert Cochran, Morton Selten, Athene Seyler
'Completely bogus … The direction is puerile.' – *Graham Greene, The Spectator*
† This was based directly on a 1934 French film, *Nuits Moscovites*, with Annabella, Pierre-Richard Willm, and Harry Baur.

Moscow on the Hudson *
US   1984   117m   Metrocolor
Columbia/Delphi (Paul Mazursky)
☒ ▤ ⚲
A Soviet circus artiste defects in New York but has second thoughts.
Not so much a political comedy as an immigrant one, with the Big Apple shown at its worst. As such, occasionally funny in a desperate way, but overlong.
w Paul Mazursky, Leon Capetanos d Paul Mazursky ph Donald McAlpine m David McHugh pd Pato Guzman
☆ Robin Williams, Maria Conchita Alonso, Cleavant Derricks, Alejandro Rey, Savely Kramarov

The Mosquito Coast *
US   1986   117m   Technicolor
Saul Zaentz/Jerome Hellman
☒ ▤ ⚲ ◎ ⌂
A frustrated visionary packs up and moves his family to a remote Caribbean island, where he fails to notice the seeds of downfall.
An antidote to Robinson Crusoe which is often wryly amusing, but the leading character is too hysterical and his fall too complete to make good drama.
w Paul Schrader novel Paul Theroux d Peter Weir ph John Seale m Maurice Jarre pd John Stoddart ed Thom Noble
☆ Harrison Ford, Helen Mirren, River Phoenix, Jadrien Steele, André Gregory
'In the end there is barely a thread of hope to take home, other than some strikingly beautiful and sad images of a man grasping for something just beyond his reach.' – *Variety*

Mosquito Squadron
GB   1968   90m   DeLuxe
Lewis J. Rachmil/UA
In 1944, the RAF tries out bouncing bombs in a French offensive.
Very minor and belated war heroics for double-billing.
w Donald Sanford, Joyce Perry d Boris Sagal ph Paul Beeson m Frank Cordell
☆ David McCallum, Suzanne Neve, David Buck, Dinsdale Landen, Charles Gray

Moss Rose
US   1947   82m   bw
TCF (Gene Markey)
A Victorian chorus girl suspects her aristocratic admirer of being a murderer.
Absurd, stilted mystery melodrama with a better-looking production than it deserves.
w Jules Furthman, Tom Reed d Gregory Ratoff ph Joe MacDonald m David Buttolph
☆ Peggy Cummins, Victor Mature, Ethel Barrymore, Vincent Price

The Most Dangerous Game ***
US   1932   63m   bw
(RKO)
▤
GB title: *The Hounds of Zaroff*
A mad hunter lures guests on to his island so that he can hunt them down like animals.
Dated but splendidly shivery melodrama with moments of horror and mystery and a splendidly photographed chase sequence. Much imitated in curious ways, and not only by direct remakes such as A Game of Death and Run for the Sun (qv).
w James Creelman story Richard Connell d Ernest B. Schoedsack, Irving Pichel ph Henry Gerrard m Max Steiner
☆ Leslie Banks, Joel McCrea, Fay Wray, Robert Armstrong, Noble Johnson
'Futile stab at horror film classification, ineffective as entertainment and minus cast names to compensate.' – *Variety*

The Most Dangerous Man in the World
GB   1969   99m   DeLuxe   Panavision
TCF/APJAC (Mort Abrahams)
US title: *The Chairman*
A top scientist is sent by western intelligence on a mission into Red China, with a transmitter and a detonator implanted in his skull.
Wild Boys' Own Paper adventure which regrettably slows down in the middle for political philosophizing.
w Ben Maddow novel The Chairman by Jay Richard Kennedy d J. Lee-Thompson ph Ted Moore m Jerry Goldsmith
☆ Gregory Peck, Anne Heywood, Arthur Hill, Conrad Yama, Francisca Tu, Keye Luke, Alan Dobie, Ori Levy

The Most Desired Man
Germany   1994   94m   colour
Gala/Neue Constantin/Olga (Bernd Eichinger)
original title: *Der Bewegte Mann*
After he is thrown out of their flat by his girlfriend, a handsome philanderer moves in with two homosexual men, who both fall for him.
Perhaps something has been lost in the translation, but this highly regarded (in Germany) comedy has little wit and not much humour.
wd Sönke Wortmann comics Der Bewegte Mann, Pretty Baby by Ralf König ph Gernot Roll m Torsten Breuer pd Monika Bauert ed Ueli Christen
☆ Til Schweiger, Katja Riemann, Joachim Krol, Rufus Beck, Armin Rohde, Nico van der Knapp, Antonia Lang
'Capped by endearing performances all round, this is a very funny movie which should ring recognition bells with under-35s of every romantic persuasion.' – *Empire*
'Ends up being a drab miscalculation.' – *Sight and Sound*
† It is the highest-grossing German film so far released in Germany.

The Most Precious Thing
US   1934   67m   bw
Columbia
A college boy marries a waitress; his mother eases the girl out but keeps the baby.
Unconvincing domestic drama, rather drab.
w Ethel Hill, Dore Schary story Travis Ingham d Lambert Hillyer
☆ Anita Louise, Mary Forbes, Jane Darwell, Ben Alexander, John Wray, Ward Bond
'Not enough strength for the more important spots.' – *Variety*

Most Wanted
US   1997   99m   DeLuxe
New Line/Ivory Way (Eric L. Gold)
☒ ▤ ⚲ ◎
A former marine, working as an undercover agent, becomes the chief suspect when the President's wife is murdered.
Formulaic conspiracy-and-chase thriller; its only interest lies in another over-the-top performance from Voight as a crazed general.
w Keenen Ivory Wayans d David Glenn Hogan ph Marc Reshovsky m Paul Bruckmaster pd Jean-Philippe Carp ed Michael J. Duthie
☆ Keenen Ivory Wayans, Jon Voight, Jill Hennessy, Paul Sorvino, Eric Roberts, Robert Culp, Wolfgang Bodison, Simon Baker Denny
'Plays like a made-for-video B movie that somehow won the lottery and got a theatrical release.' – *Joe Leydon, Variety*

'It takes all kinds of critters to make Farmer Vincent's fritters!'
Motel Hell
US   1980   106m   Technicolor
United Artists/Camp Hill (Herb Jaffe)
☒ ⚲
Benign motel owners are famous for their spiced meat, which is in fact made from their human guests.
Horror comic intended to amuse, but too repulsive to do so.
w Robert Jaffe, Steven-Charles Jaffe d Kevin Connor ph Thomas Del Ruth m Lance Rubin
☆ Rory Calhoun, Paul Linke, Nancy Parsons, Nina Axelrod, Wolfman Jack

Mother ***
USSR   1926   90m   bw   silent
Mezhrabpom-Russ
☒ ▤
original title: *Mat*
A mother incriminates her strike-breaking son, but realizes her error.
Propagandist social melodrama which is also brilliantly conceived and edited, with sequences matching those of Eisenstein.
w N. Zarkhi, V. I. Pudovkin novel Maxim Gorky d V. I. Pudovkin ph A. Golovnia
☆ Vera Baranovskaya, Nikolai Batalov
† Other versions appeared in 1920 and ([KW]d[/KW]Mark Donskoi) 1955

Mother and Son ***
Russia/Germany   1997   71m   colour
Zero/O-Film/Severnij Fond/Lenfilm
☒
original title: *Mat i syn*
In a large house near the sea, a son tends his dying mother.
A gently lyrical film about love and the immanence of death, and the beauty of the natural world. It has little dialogue, the actors are not professional, and it has no action in the conventional sense; yet it maintains a hushed, hypnotic hold.
w Yuri Arabov d Alexandr Sokurov ph Alexei Yodorov m Mikhail Ivanovich Glinka, Otmar Nussio ad Vera Zelinskaya ed Leda Semyonova
☆ Gudrun Geyer, Alexei Ananishov
'Its majestic, affective power makes most of cinema seem trivial, raucous, faked.' – *Julian Graffy, Sight and Sound*

The Mother and the Whore **
France   1973   219m   bw
Gala/Films du Losange/Elite/Cine Qua Non/Simar/V.M. (Pierre Cottrell)
original title: *La Maman et la Putain*
A charming but idle man, who lives with his older mistress, dates a young nurse who moves in with them.
A long, sometimes desultory, but often engrossing debate on love, fidelity, sex, marriage and the comedy of human affairs.
wd Jean Eustache ph Pierre Lhomme, Jacques Renard, Michel Cenet m Mozart, Offenbach and others ed Jean Eustache, Denise de Casabianca
☆ Jean-Pierre Léaud, Françoise Lebrun, Bernadette Lafont, Isabelle Weingarten, Jacques Renard, Jean Eustache
'What is extraordinary is that Eustache mesmerises us into caring about each emotional quaver, creating suspense from seemingly inert surfaces, a tension between elusive sensibility and indisputable presence.' – *Jan Dawson, MFB*

Mother Carey's Chickens
RKO (Pandro S. Berman)
US   1938   82m   bw
The tribulations of a small-town family in the 1890s.
Modest domestic drama, not totally unpleasing.
w S. K. Lauren, Gertrude Purcell novel Kate Douglas Wiggin d Rowland V. Lee ph Roy Hunt m Frank Tours
☆ Anne Shirley, Ruby Keeler, Fay Bainter, James Ellison, Walter Brennan, Donnie Dunagan, Frank Albertson, Alma Kruger, Jackie Moran, Virginia Weidler, Margaret Hamilton
† Remade 1963 as *Summer Magic*.

Mother Didn't Tell Me
US   1950   88m   bw
TCF (Fred Kohlmar)
A working girl marries a doctor and their off duty hours don't coincide.
Thin comedy.
wd Claude Binyon novel The Doctor Wears Three Faces by Mary Bard ph Joseph LaShelle m Cyril Mockridge
☆ Dorothy McGuire, William Lundigan, June Havoc, Gary Merrill, Jessie Royce Landis

Mother Is a Freshman
US   1948   80m   Technicolor
TCF
GB title: *Mother Knows Best*
A mother goes to college and falls for the teacher with whom her daughter is infatuated.

Thin romantic comedy lacking the piquancy at which it aims.

w Mary Loos, Richard Sale d Lloyd Bacon ph Arthur Arling m Alfred Newman

☆ Loretta Young, Van Johnson, Rudy Vallee, Barbara Lawrence, Betty Lynn, Robert Arthur

Mother Joan of the Angels: see *The Devil and the Nun*

Mother, Jugs and Speed

US 1976 98m DeLuxe Panavision
TCF (Joseph R. Barbera)

Comic and tragic events in the lives of Los Angeles drivers of private commercial ambulances.
Black comedy of incidents ranging from farcical to sentimental, sometimes funny but basically unacceptable in either vein.

w Tom Mankiewicz d Peter Yates ph Ralph Woolsey m various md Joel Sill

☆ Bill Cosby, Raquel Welch, Harvey Keitel, Allen Garfield, Bruce Davison, Larry Hagman
'The writer has found a way to get into the underbelly of a city, to survey the twilight territory where tragedy and comedy trip over each other and make an unsightly mess.' – *Time*

Mother Knows Best: see *Mother Is A Freshman*

'The lure of gold can make a man do anything!'

Mother Lode

US 1982 101m colour
Agamemnon/Martin Shafter, Andrew Scheinman (Fraser Clarke Heston, Andrew Snell)

A villainous miner stops at nothing to protect his goldfield.
More-or-less old-fashioned Western with a change of pace for the star. No world beater, but not bad.

w Fraser Clarke Heston, Peter Snell d Charlton Heston ph Richard Leiterman m Ken Wannberg pd Douglas Higgins

☆ Charlton Heston, Nick Mancuso, Kim Basinger, John Marley

'Howard W. Campbell, Jr. Is The Most Patriotic American In The Third Reich.'

Mother Night **

US 1996 110m bw/Foto-Kem
Fine Line/Whyaduck (Keith Gordon, Robert B. Weide)

While awaiting trial for war crimes, a German-born American recalls his career as an Allied agent and a Nazi sympathizer.
An engrossing attempt to film a complex novel concerned with moral relativities, although, despite its intelligence, it doesn't quite capture the original's ironic humour.

w Robert B. Weide novel Kurt Vonnegut d Keith Gordon ph Tom Richmond m Michael Convertino pd François Seguin ed Jay Rabinowitz

☆ Nick Nolte, Sheryl Lee, Alan Arkin, John Goodman, Kirsten Dunst, Arye Gross, Frankie Faison, David Strathairn, Bernard Behrens, Henry Gibson
'A movie that offers no easy rewards, this is still a deeply satisfying experience.' – *Bob McCabe, Empire*

Mother Riley Meets the Vampire

GB 1952 74m bw
Renown (John Gilling)
US title: *My Son the Vampire*
An old washerwoman accidentally catches a robot-wielding crook called The Vampire.
Childish farce notable for Lucan's last appearance in his dame role, and Lugosi's last substantial appearance of any kind – two pros at the end of their tether.

w Val Valentine d John Gilling ph Stan Pavey m Linda Southworth

☆ Arthur Lucan, Bela Lugosi, Dora Bryan, Richard Wattis
'Stupid, humourless and repulsive.' – *MFB*

Mother, Sir!: see *Navy Wife*

Mother Wore Tights *

US 1947 109m Technicolor
TCF (Lamar Trotti)
Recollections of a vaudeville team and their growing family.

Well-mounted, reasonably charming family musical, one of the best of the many TCF examples of this genre.

w Lamar Trotti book Miriam Young d Walter Lang ph Harry Jackson md Alfred Newman, Charles Henderson

☆ Betty Grable, Dan Dailey, Mona Freeman, Connie Marshall, Vanessa Brown, Robert Arthur, Sara Allgood, William Frawley, Ruth Nelson

🏆 Alfred Newman, Charles Henderson

⚖ Harry Jackson; song 'You Do' (m Josef Myrow, ly Mack Gordon)

Mother's Boys

US 1994 95m colour
Miramax/CBS (Jack E. Freedman, Wayne S. Williams, Patricia Herskovic)

A mother who left her husband and three sons decides she wants to return, despite the fact that no one wants her back.
Uninteresting attempt at a psychological thriller-cum-chiller, with an unconvincing script that steers clear of any suspense or emotional involvement.

w Barry Schneider, Richard Hawley novel Bernard Taylor d Yves Simoneau ph Elliot Davis m George S. Clinton ad David Bomba ed Michael Ornstein

☆ Jamie Lee Curtis, Peter Gallagher, Joanne Whalley-Kilmer, Vanessa Redgrave, Luke Edwards, Joss Ackland, Colin Ward, Joey Zimmerman
'A film that has an uninteresting beginning, an exploitative middle that actually cheats by genre standards, and a ludicrous climax that is borderline laughable.' – *Emanuel Levy, Variety*

La Motocyclette: see *Girl on a Motorcycle*

Motorcycle Gang

US 1957 78m bw
AIP/Golden State (Alex Gordon)

A bad boy returns from prison to antagonize the local law-abiding motorcycle club.
Low-budget, low-grade drive-in movie, though its dialogue, written in what purports to be the latest teenage slang ('You're not hip to this new lingo. Miger? Mad tiger') has acquired a period curiosity.

w Lou Rusoff d Edward L. Cahn ph Frederick E. West m Albert Glasser ad Don Ament ed Richard C. Meyer

☆ Anne Neyland, Steve Terrell, John Ashley, Carl Switzer, Raymond Hatton, Wayne Taylor, Hal Bogart, Edmund Cobb

Mouchette *

France 1966 90m bw
Argos/Parc (Anatole Dauman)

An unloved 14-year-old schoolgirl contemplates her unhappy life with her alcoholic father and dying mother.
Grim, austere, unsparing examination of the misery of an outsider.

wd Robert Bresson novel Nouvelle Histoire de Mouchette by Georges Bernanos ph Ghislain Cloquet m Jean Wiener, Monteverdi ad Pierre Guffroy ed Raymond Lamy

☆ Nadine Nortier, Jean-Claude Guilbert, Marie Cardinal, Paul Hébert, Jean Vimenet, Marie Susini

Moulin Rouge

US 1934 69m bw
Twentieth Century (Darryl F. Zanuck)
The wife of a songwriter impersonates her own sister in order to revitalize her marriage and her stage career.
Predictable minor star vehicle, quite competently done.

w Nunnally Johnson, Henry Lehrman play Lyon de Bri d Sidney Lanfield ph Charles Rosher md Alfred Newman songs Harry Warren, Al Dubin

☆ Constance Bennett, Franchot Tone, Tullio Carminati, Helen Westley, Andrew Tombes, Hobart Cavanaugh

Moulin Rouge **

GB 1952 119m Technicolor
Romulus (John Clayton)

Fictional biopic of Toulouse Lautrec.
The dramatic emphasis is on the love affairs of the dwarfish artist, but the film's real interest is in its evocation of 19th-century Montmartre, and especially in the first twenty-minute can-can sequence. Nothing

later can stand up to the exhilaration of this, and the film slowly slides into boredom.

w John Huston, Anthony Veiller novel Pierre La Mure d John Huston ph Oswald Morris m Georges Auric ad Paul Sheriff ed Ralph Kemplen

☆ José Ferrer, Zsa Zsa Gabor, Katherine Kath, Colette Marchand, Suzanne Flon

🏆 art direction

⚖ best picture; John Huston (as director); José Ferrer; Colette Marchand; editing

The Mountain *

US 1956 105m Technicolor Vistavision
Paramount (Edward Dmytryk)

After an airplane crash the wreck is difficult to reach. A young man sets off alone to loot it, and his elder brother follows to stop him.
An indeterminate production in which one believes neither the setting, the plot nor the characters, especially not with Vistavision making everything sharply unreal and the brothers seeming two generations apart.

w Ranald MacDougall novel Henri Troyat d Edward Dmytryk ph Franz Planer m Daniele Amfitheatrof

☆ Spencer Tracy, Robert Wagner, Claire Trevor, William Demarest, E. G. Marshall
'A terrible picture. It goes on forever and it's bad.' – *Claire Trevor*

The Mountain Eagle

GB 1926 72m bw silent
Gainsborough/Emelka (Michael Balcon)
US title: *Fear o' God*
A young schoolmistress resists the attentions of a businessman, escapes to the mountains, and marries a recluse.
Unremarkable romantic drama; one of the lost Hitchcock films.

w Eliot Stannard d Alfred Hitchcock ph Baron Ventimiglia

☆ Nita Naldi, Bernard Goetzke, Malcolm Keen

Mountain Justice

US 1937 82m bw
Warner
A frightened hillbilly girl kills her brutal father and is protected by a lawyer.
Involved backwoods melodrama, not really worth the trouble.

w Norman Reilly Raine, Luci Ward d Michael Curtiz

☆ Josephine Hutchinson, George Brent, Robert Barrat, Guy Kibbee, Mona Barrie, Margaret Hamilton, Robert McWade
'Too much plot, but okay for duals.' – *Variety*

The Mountain Men

US 1980 102m Metrocolor Panavision
Columbia (Martin Ransohoff)

Two 19th-century trappers have adventures with Indians.
Rumbustious, foul-mouthed and lethargic Western of the primitive kind; no possible interest.

w Fraser Clarke Heston d Richard Lang ph Michel Hugo m Michel Legrand

☆ Charlton Heston, Brian Keith, Victoria Racimo, Stephen Macht, John Glover
'It plays like a Sunn Classic four-waller uncomfortably spiced up with violence and profanity.' – *Variety*

'It's The Snappiest Ole Swing Music, An' It's Echoin' Thru The Land.'

Mountain Music

US 1937 76m bw
Paramount
A hillbilly runs from a marriage and loses his memory.
Tiresome comedy with music.

w J. C. Moffitt, Duke Atterbury, Russel Crouse, Charles Lederer story Mackinlay Kantor d Robert Florey

☆ Martha Raye, Bob Burns, John Howard, George Hayes, Rufe Davis, Fuzzy Knight
'Burns and Raye have trouble topping a cast. Mild and minor.' – *Variety*

The Mountain Road

US 1960 102m bw
Columbia/William Goetz

In 1944 China, an American officer helps peasants against the Japanese.
Confused and rather dreary war adventure with pretensions.

w Alfred Hayes novel Theodore White d Daniel Mann ph Burnett Guffey m Jerome Moross md Morris Stoloff

☆ James Stewart, Lisa Lu, Glenn Corbett, Henry Morgan, Frank Silvera, James Best, Mike Kellin, Frank Maxwell, Alan Baxter

Mountains of the Moon **

US 1989 136m Technicolor
Guild/Carolco/IndieProd (Daniel Melnick)

Explorers Richard Burton and John Hanning Speke go in search of the source of the Nile.
Exuberant and engrossing epic that catches the mood of the times.

w William Harrison, Bob Rafelson story Burton and Speke by William Harrison d Bob Rafelson ph Dick Pope m Michael Small pd Norman Reynolds ed Thom Noble

☆ Patrick Bergin, Iain Glen, Richard E. Grant, Fiona Shaw, John Savident, James Villiers, Adrian Rawlins, Peter Vaughan, Delroy Lindo, Bernard Hill
'Somehow it conveys, as few movies ever have, the miserable realities that underlay the 19th century's heroic age of exploration.' – *Richard Schickel, Time*
'Worth seeing principally because it is a real film, by a director who understands the true nature of cinema as a visual medium.' – *Derek Malcolm, Guardian*

'Mother and daughter! Rivals in love!'

Mourning Becomes Electra *

US 1947 170m bw
RKO/Theatre Guild (Dudley Nichols)

Murder, doom and guilt affect a New England family at the end of the Civil War.
A mark for trying is all. This is a clearly fated attempt to film the unfilmable, a long and lugubrious updating of Sophocles with more than its share of risible moments.

wd Dudley Nichols play Eugene O'Neill ph George Barnes m Richard Hagemann ad Albert D'Agostino

☆ Michael Redgrave, Rosalind Russell, Katina Paxinou, Kirk Douglas, Raymond Massey, Nancy Coleman, Leo Genn
'A star cast fumbles with helpless and sometimes touching ineptitude.' – *Gavin Lambert*
'Within its own terms of mistaken reverence, a good, straight, deliberately unimaginative production.' – *James Agee*
'It is apparent from their accents that they have only recently become a family.' – *Pauline Kael, 70s*

⚖ Michael Redgrave; Rosalind Russell

'The squeak shall inherit the earth'

Mouse Hunt **

US 1997 97m Technicolor
DreamWorks (Alan Riche, Tony Ludwig, Bruce Cohen)

Two antagonistic brothers attempt to get rid of a mouse that inhabits the derelict mansion they inherit.
Slick slapstick comedy with a dark, Gothic tone that only lightens at the very end. There's an occasional nod to Laurel and Hardy, but the edgy humour owes much more to Tom and Jerry.

w Adam Rifkin d Gore Verbinski ph Phedon Papamichael m Alan Silvestri pd Linda DeScenna ed Craig Wood sp Stan Winston

☆ Nathan Lane, Lee Evans, Vicki Lewis, Maury Chaykin, Eric Christmas, Michael Jeter, Christopher Walken, Debra Christofferson, Camilla Soeberg, William Hickey
'This often screamingly funny comedy about a resilient rodent has enough across-the-board appeal to click with audiences of all ages.' – *Joe Leydon, Variety*

† The picture is dedicated to William Hickey, who died soon after his filming was completed.

The Mouse on the Moon

GB 1963 85m Eastmancolor
UA/Walter Shenson

The tiny duchy of Grand Fenwick discovers that its home-made wine makes excellent rocket fuel.
Piddling sequel to The Mouse that Roared, suffering from a hesitant script, too few jokes, and overacting.
w Michael Pertwee *novel* Leonard Wibberley
d Richard Lester *ph* Wilkie Cooper *m* Ron Grainer
☆ Margaret Rutherford, Ron Moody, Bernard Cribbins, David Kossoff, Terry-Thomas, Michael Crawford

The Mouse that Roared **

GB 1959 85m Technicolor
Columbia/Open Road (Carl Foreman)

The tiny duchy of Grand Fenwick is bankrupt, and its minister decides to declare war on the United States, be defeated, and receive Marshall Aid.
Lively comedy which sounds rather better than it plays, but has bright moments.
w Roger Macdougall, Stanley Mann *novel* Leonard Wibberley *d* Jack Arnold *ph* John Wilcox *m* Edwin Astley *ad* Geoffrey Drake *ed* Raymond Poulton
☆ Peter Sellers, Jean Seberg, David Kossoff, William Hartnell, Leo McKern, Macdonald Parke, Harold Kasket, Timothy Bateson
'The kind of irrepressible topical satire whose artistic flaws become increasingly apparent but whose merits outlast them.' – *Peter John Dyer*

Mouth to Mouth

Australia 1978 94m colour
Vega (Jon Sainken)

Two sisters, who squat in a deserted warehouse and live by petty theft and occasional prostitution, form a casual relationship with two young men looking for work.
A dull slice of Melbourne low-life, peopled by no-hopers looking for something to rebel against.
wd John Duigan *ph* Tom Cowan *m* Roy Ritchie *ad* Tracy Watt *ed* Tony Paterson
☆ Kim Krejus, Sonia Peat, Ian Gilmour, Sergio Frazzetto, Walter Pym, Michael Carman

The Mouthpiece **

US 1932 90m bw
Warner (Lucien Hubbard)

A prosecuting counsel successfully turns to defence but becomes corrupt.
A hard-hitting and entertaining melodrama allegedly based on the career of William Fallon, a New York lawyer.
w Joseph Jackson, Earl Baldwin *d* James Flood, Elliott Nugent *ph* Barney McGill
☆ Warren William, Sidney Fox, Aline MacMahon, John Wray, Ralph Ince, Guy Kibbee
'First-grade melodrama, a bet for all grades of houses.' – *Variety*

Le Mouton a Cinq Pattes: see The Sheep Has Five Legs

Move

US 1970 88m DeLuxe Panavision
TCF

A frustrated playwright writes pornography to make money; he moves to a larger apartment but his mind is full of fantasies.
None of which are of much interest to the paying customers, the movie being drenched with self-pity.
w Joel Lieber, Stanley Hart *novel* Joel Lieber
d Stuart Rosenberg
☆ Elliott Gould, Paula Prentiss, Genevieve Waite, John Larch, Joe Silver

Move Over Darling **

US 1963 103m DeLuxe Cinemascope
TCF/Arcola/Arwin (Aaron Rosenberg, Marty Melcher)

A wife who has spent five years shipwrecked on a desert island returns to find that her husband has just remarried.
Thin but fitfully amusing remake of My Favorite Wife; sheer professionalism gets it by.
w Hal Kanter, Jack Sher *d* Michael Gordon *ph* Daniel L. Fapp *m* Lionel Newman
☆ Doris Day, James Garner, Polly Bergen, Thelma Ritter, Chuck Connors, Fred Clark

Movers and Shakers

US 1985 79m Metrocolor
MGM-UA/BHC (Charles Grodin, William Asher)

A Hollywood writer tries to cope with a difficult project while having personal problems with his wife.
Mishmash of unrealized anecdotes with pauses for studio in-jokes. Despite the talent, it could never have worked, not even under the previously announced title Dreamers.
w Charles Grodin *d* William Asher *ph* Robbie Greenberg *m* Ken and Mitzie Welch
☆ Walter Matthau, Charles Grodin, Vincent Gardenia, Tyne Daly, Bill Macy, Gilda Radner, Steve Martin, Nita Talbot
'Only occasionally amusing: faces a bleak box-office future.' – *Variety*

Movie Crazy **

US 1932 82m bw
Harold Lloyd

A filmstruck young man is mistakenly invited to Hollywood for a film test.
The silent comedian is not quite at his best in this early sound comedy, but it contains his last really superb sequences and its picture of Hollywood is both amusing and nostalgic.
w Harold Lloyd and others *d* Clyde Bruckman
ph Walter Lundin
☆ Harold Lloyd, Constance Cummings
'A corking comedy, replete with wow belly laughs. Sure-fire.' – *Variety*

Movie Movie **

US 1978 106m bw/colour
ITC (Stanley Donen)

A pastiche of a thirties double bill, including a boxing yarn (*Dynamite Hands*) and a Busby-Berkeley style girlie show (*Baxter's Beauties of 1933*).
Unfortunately there weren't enough paying customers to appreciate the spoofs, which are pretty patchy anyway; but golden moments stay in the mind.
w Larry Gelbart, Sheldon Keller *d* Stanley Donen *ph* Chuck Rosher Jnr, Bruce Surtees *m* Ralph Burns *ch* Michael Kidd
☆ George C. Scott, Trish Van Devere, Red Buttons, Eli Wallach, Michael Kidd, Barbara Harris, Barry Bostwick, Art Carney, Jocelyn Brando
'Camp, which has to do with a switch of vision from one era to another, cannot be created, and where it is, as this and previous attempts testify, it is immediately swallowed in its own idiocy.' – *Richard Combs, MFB*

Movietone Follies of 1930

US 1930 70m bw
Fox

A rich boy courts a chorus girl, and her friends give a show on his estate.
Thin, fumbling drama which doesn't remember to become a musical till it's halfway through, and even then has little spark.
w William K. Wells *d* Ben Stoloff *ph* William O'Connell *md* Arthur Kay
☆ El Brendel, Marjorie White, William Collier Jnr, Miriam Seegar, Frank Richardson

Moving

US 1988 89m Technicolor
Warner (Stuart Cornfeld)

A traffic engineer runs into all kinds of trouble when he decides to move his family from New Jersey to Idaho.
Disappointingly predictable comedy, making all the obvious jokes in a leaden way.
w Andy Breckman *d* Alan Metter *ph* Donald McAlpine *m* Howard Shore *pd* David L. Snyder *ed* Alan Balsam
☆ Richard Pryor, Beverly Todd, Randy Quaid, Dave Thomas, Dana Carvey, Stacey Dash, Gordon Jump, Morris Day

The Moving Target: see Harper

Moving Violation *

US 1976 91m DeLuxe
TCF/Roger Corman

Small-town teenagers are pursued by the sheriff because they saw him commit a murder.
Old hat suspenser with a smart new line in thrills.
w David R. Osterhout, William Norton *d* Charles S. Dubin *ph* Charles Correll *m* Don Leake
☆ Stephen McHattie, Kay Lenz, Eddie Albert, Lonny Chapman, Will Geer
'Probably the most hair-raising pursuit sequences in the history of film.' – *Cleveland Amory*

Moving Violations

US 1985 90m DeLuxe
Ufland-Roth-IPI-James G. Robinson/TCF

Misadventures of trainee traffic school cops.
Wasn't Police Academy bad enough?
w Neal Israel, Pat Proft *d* Neal Israel
☆ John Murray, Jennifer Tilly, James Keach, Brian Backer

'A Romantic Comedy For Anyone Who's Ever Been In Love.'

Much Ado about Nothing **

GB 1993 111m Technicolor
Samuel Goldwyn/Renaissance (Stephen Evans, David Parfitt, Kenneth Branagh)

A man and a woman who have sworn never to marry are tricked into falling in love with each other.
A lively version of Shakespeare's witty romantic comedy, but suffering from some miscasting, plodding direction and rather too much forced jollity to be entirely successful.
wd Kenneth Branagh *play* William Shakespeare *ph* Roger Lanser *m* Patrick Doyle *pd* Tim Harvey *ed* Andrew Marcus
☆ Kenneth Branagh, Richard Briers, Michael Keaton, Denzel Washington, Robert Sean Leonard, Keanu Reeves, Emma Thompson, Kate Beckinsale, Brian Blessed, Patrick Doyle, Imelda Staunton, Phyllida Law, Ben Elton
'This isn't the best Shakespeare on film ... but it may be the best movie Shakespeare.' – *Richard Corliss, Time*
'Triumphantly romantic, comic and emotionally alive.' – *Vincent Canby, New York Times*
'One of the few movies of recent years that could leave audiences weeping for joy.' – *David Denby, New York*

Much Too Shy

GB 1942 92m bw
Columbia (Ben Henry)

A gormless handyman gets into trouble when the portraits of his lady clients are sold to an advertising agency with nude bodies added to them.
A slightly vulgar and talkative farce which restricts the star.
w Ronald Frankau *d* Marcel Varnel *ph* Arthur Crabtree
☆ George Formby, Kathleen Harrison, Hylda Bayley, Eileen Bennett, Joss Ambler, Jimmy Clitheroe

Muddy River *

Japan 1981 105m bw
Unifilm/Contemporary/Kimura Productions (Motoyasu Kimura)
original title: *Doro No Kawa*

Two nine-year-old boys become friends and try to make sense of the adult world around them.
A small and charming story, sharply observed and photographed.
w Takaki Shigemori *novel* Teru Miyamoto *d* Kohei Oguri *ph* Shohei Ando *m* Kuroudo Mori *ad* Akira Naito *ed* Nobuo Ogawa
☆ Nobutaka Asahara, Takahiro Tamura, Yumiko Fujita, Masako Yagi, Minoru Sakurai, Makiko Shibata, Mariko Kaga
⊕ best foreign film

Der Müde Tod: see Destiny

The Mudlark **

GB 1950 98m bw
TCF (Nunnally Johnson)

A scruffy boy from the docks breaks into Windsor Castle to see Queen Victoria and ends her fifteen years of seclusion.
A pleasant whimsical legend which could have done without the romantic interest, but which despite an air of unreality provides warm-hearted, well upholstered entertainment for family audiences.
w Nunnally Johnson *novel* Theodore Bonnet
d Jean Negulesco *ph* Georges Périnal *m* William Alwyn *ad* C. P. Norman
☆ Alec Guinness, Irene Dunne, Andrew Ray, Anthony Steel, Constance Smith, Finlay Currie, Edward Rigby

La Muerte de un Burocrata: see Death of a Bureaucrat

Muerte de un Ciclista: see Death of a Cyclist

Mug Town

US 1942 60m bw
Universal

The Little Tough Guys get mixed up with hi-jackers.
A failing entry in this series: the ageing teenagers shortly decided to play for laughs.
w Brenda Weisberg, Harold Tarshis, Harry Sucher and Lewis Amster *d* Ray Taylor
☆ Billy Halop, Huntz Hall, Bernard Punsley, Gabriel Dell, Grace McDonald, Edward Norris, Jed Prouty

Mùi Du Du Xanh: see The Scent of the Green Papaya

Mujeres al Borde de un Ataque de Nervios: see Women on the Verge of a Nervous Breakdown

Mulan *

US 1998 88m Technicolor
Buena Vista/Walt Disney (Pam Coats)

A Chinese girl disguises herself as a warrior and rescues the Emperor from the barbarian hordes threatening the country.
An animated film that will no doubt be enjoyed by its target audience; for adults it offers less, despite its attractive style, incorporating something of a Chinese approach to art within the familiar Disney manner.
w Rita Hsiao, Christopher Sanders, Philip Lazebnik, Raymond Singer, Eugenia Bostwick-Singer *story* Robert D. San Souci *d* Barry Cook, Tony Bancroft *m* Jerry Goldsmith *m/ly* Matthew Wilder, David Zippel *pd* Hans Bacher *ed* Michael Kelly
☆ Featuring the voices of: Ming-Na Wen (singing: Lea Salonga), Eddie Murphy, B. D. Wong (singing: Donny Osmond), Harvey Fierstein, Jerry S. Tondo, Gedde Watanabe (singing: Matthew Wilder), James Hong, Miguel Ferrer, Soon-Tek Oh, Freda Foh Shen, Pat Morita, June Foray (singing: Marni Nixon), George Takei, Miriam Margolyes, James Shigeta, Frank Welker
'Quite likely the first animated cross-dressing action musical.' – *Todd McCarthy, Variety*
'Kids are going to love this movie.' – *Observer*
♫ Jerry Goldsmith, Matthew Wilder, David Zippel

Mule Train

US 1950 60m bw
Columbia/Gene Autry (Armand Schaefer)

Gene Autry prevents unscrupulous businessmen and a crooked sheriff from taking over a supply of cement needed for a new dam.
Amiable, unmemorable Western.
w Gerald Geraghty *story* Alan James *d* John English *ph* William Bradford *md* Mischa Bakaleinikoff *ad* Charles Clague *ed* Richard Fantl
☆ Gene Autry, Pat Buttram, Sheila Ryan, Robert Livingston, Frank Jaquet, Vince Barnett, Syd Saylor, Sandy Sanders

---

'A New Kind Of Law Enforcement.'

Mulholland Falls *

US 1996 107m DeLuxe
Polygram/MGM/Largo/Zanuck (Richard D. Zanuck, Lili Fini Zanuck)

In Los Angeles in the 50s, four detectives investigate the death of a woman who is linked with work at an atomic test site.

Period thriller that looks better than it plays; it never fully engages an audience's attention, and the ending is unsatisfactory.

w Pete Dexter, Floyd Mutrux d Lee Tamahori ph Haskell Wexler m Dave Grusin pd Richard Sylbert ed Sally Menke

☆ Nick Nolte, Melanie Griffith, Chazz Palminteri, Michael Madsen, Chris Penn, Treat Williams, Jennifer Connelly, Daniel Baldwin, Andrew McCarthy, John Malkovich, Bruce Dern, Ed Lauter

'It will pleasure everyone in love with the old Forties landscape of no-nonsense cynicism that Bogart and Stanwyck sculpted.' – *Alexander Walker*

'She's always known he's the one. She didn't know he was also the two, the three and the four...'

Multiplicity

US 1996 117m Technicolor Panavision
Columbia (Trevor Albert, Harold Ramis)

A workaholic runs into problems when he clones himself in order to spend more time with his wife and children.

A clever concept, which ought to have resulted in a much funnier comedy instead of this conventional farce, though Keaton does well in differentiating his various roles.

w Chris Miller, Mary Hale, Lowell Ganz, Babaloo Mandel d Harold Ramis ph Laszlo Kovacs m George Fenton pd Jackson DeGovia ed Pem Herring, Craig Herring

☆ Michael Keaton, Andie MacDowell, Harris Yulin, Richard Masur, Eugene Levy, Ann Cusack, John de Lancie, Brian Doyle-Murray

'Afterwards you can't help wishing you'd got someone else to watch it for you.' – *Tom Shone, Sunday Times*

'It comes to life!'
'A love story that lived for three thousand years!'

The Mummy **

US 1932 72m bw
Universal (Stanley Bergerman)

An Egyptian mummy comes back to life and covets a young girl.

Strange dreamlike horror film with only fleeting frissons but plenty of narrative interest despite the silliest of stories and some fairly stilted acting.

w John L. Balderston d Karl Freund ph Charles Stumar m Tchaikovsky ad Willy Pogany

☆ Boris Karloff, Zita Johann, David Manners, Arthur Byron, Edward Van Sloan

'Should show profit despite fairy tale theme.' – *Variety*

'It beggars description ... one of the most unusual talkies ever produced.' – *New York Times*

'Editing very much in the Germanic style, magnificent lighting and a superb performance from Karloff make this a fantasy almost without equal.' – *John Baxter, 1968*

† The star was billed simply as 'Karloff the uncanny'.

The Mummy *

GB 1959 88m Technicolor
Hammer (Michael Carreras)

A mummy brought back to England by archaeologists wakes up and goes on the rampage.

Typical Hammer vulgarization of a Hollywood legend; starts slowly and erratically, but picks up speed and resource in the last half hour.

w Jimmy Sangster d Terence Fisher ph Jack Asher m Frank Reizenstein

☆ Peter Cushing, Christopher Lee, Yvonne Furneaux, Eddie Byrne, Felix Aylmer, Raymond Huntley, John Stuart

† Hammer sequels, of little interest, were *Curse of the Mummy's Tomb* (1964), *The Mummy's Shroud* (1966) and *Blood from the Mummy's Tomb* (1971).

'The Legend Rises Again.'

The Mummy *

US 1999 124m DeLuxe Panavision
Universal/Alphaville (James Jacks, Sean Daniel)

An Egyptian priest, who was mummified alive more than two thousand years previously, is revived when his burial place is discovered by an American explorer.

A tongue-in-cheek Boy's Own adventure, which is played mostly for laughs and the occasional shock, and is notable only for its computer-generated special effects.

wd Stephen Sommers ph Adrian Biddle m Jerry Goldsmith pd Allan Cameron ed Bob Ducsay sp John Andrew Berton Jnr; Chris Corbould; Nick Dudman

☆ Brendan Fraser, Rachel Weisz, John Hannah, Arnold Vosloo, Kevin J. O'Connor, Jonathan Hyde, Oded Fehr, Erick Avari, Stephen Dunham, Corey Johnson, Tuc Watkins

'Universal's attempt to find gold by bringing to new life one of the mustier items in its vaults is pure hokum and scarcely of the first order.' – *Todd McCarthy, Variety*

† The film was a box-office success, taking $43.3m in its first three days at the US box-office, the ninth-best opening gross so far. It went on to gross more than $155m at the US box-office.

♫ sound (Leslie Shatz, Chris Carpenter, Rick Kline, Chris Munro)

Mummy's Boys

US 1936 68m bw
RKO (Lee Marcus)

Two ditch diggers in Egypt encounter some dirty work by a mad archaeologist.

Ho-hum comedy with tired old gags.

w Jack Townley, Philip G. Epstein, Charles Roberts d Fred Guiol ph Jack MacKenzie md Roy Webb

☆ Bert Wheeler, Robert Woolsey, Barbara Pepper, Moroni Olsen, Willie Best

'Poorly acted, raggedly written ... net result of the dialogue is about four snickers.' – *Variety*

'Egypt's ancient loves live again in evil!'

The Mummy's Curse

US 1945 62m bw
Universal (Oliver Drake)

Sequel to *The Mummy's Ghost* (qv), notable for many loose ends of narrative.

Last of the Universal mummy films (until Abbott and Costello met him).

w Bernard Schubert d Leslie Goodwins

☆ Peter Coe, Martin Kosleck, Kay Harding, Kurt Katch, Virginia Christine, Lon Chaney Jnr

'This film contains the most nauseous horror imaginable and is not for the squeamish.' – *MFB*

† See also *Abbott and Costello Meet the Mummy.*

'Nameless! Fleshless! Deathless!'

The Mummy's Ghost

US 1944 60m bw
Universal (Ben Pivar)

The slow but unstoppable Kharis is now on the trail of his long-lost princess.

A slight improvement on its predecessor, The Mummy's Tomb.

w Griffin Jay, Henry Sucher, Brenda Weisberg d Reginald LeBorg ph Virgil Miller md Paul Sawtell

☆ John Carradine, George Zucco, Ramsay Ames, Robert Lowery, Barton MacLane, Lon Chaney Jnr

'Tomb of a thousand terrors!'

The Mummy's Hand **

US 1940 67m bw
Universal (Ben Pivar)

The high priest of an evil sect revivifies an Egyptian mummy and uses it to kill off members of an archaeological expedition.

Semi-sequel to 1932's The Mummy, economically using the same flashback. It starts off in comedy vein, but the last half hour is among the most scary in horror film history.

w Griffin Jay, Maxwell Shane d Christy Cabanne ph Elwood Bredell

☆ Dick Foran, Wallace Ford, George Zucco, Cecil Kellaway, Peggy Moran, Tom Tyler, Eduardo Ciannelli

† Sequels, of decreasing merit, were *The Mummy's Tomb* (1942) (in which the heroes of *The Mummy's Hand* are killed off), *The Mummy's Ghost* (1944) and *The Mummy's Curse* (1944). See also *Abbott and Costello Meet the Mummy.*

'Buried alive for 3700 years! Brought back to live, love and kill!'
'Beware the beat of the cloth-wrapped feet!'

The Mummy's Shroud

GB 1966 84m Technicolor
Hammer (Anthony Nelson-Keys)

In the twenties, an exhumed mummy brought to the city museum is restored to life and slaughters those who disturbed his rest.

Uninventive rehash of every other mummy movie; too hackneyed to be saved even by a good cast and production values.

wd John Gilling ph Arthur Grant m Don Banks

☆ John Phillips, André Morell, David Buck, Elizabeth Sellars, Catherine Lacey, Maggie Kimberley, Michael Ripper, Tim Barrett, Roger Delgado, Dickie Owen

The Mummy's Tomb

US 1942 61m bw
Ben Pivar/Universal

The aged high priest sends a young disciple to America, where Kharis dutifully kills off those who violated his tomb.

Shoddily made sequel to The Mummy's Hand, with much re-used footage; astonishingly, it broke box-office records for its year, and provoked two more episodes.

w Griffin Jay, Henry Sucher d Harold Young

☆ Turhan Bey, George Zucco, Dick Foran, Wallace Ford, Elyse Knox, Lon Chaney Jnr

'Buried alive 3700 years!'

Mumsy, Nanny, Sonny and Girly

GB 1969 102m Eastmancolor
CIRO/Brigitte (Ronald J. Kahn)

aka: *Girly*

Two adolescents bring home lonely people as playthings for a homicidal family.

Revolting black comedy for masochists, representing the British cinema at its lowest ebb.

w Brian Comport play Maisie Mosco d Freddie Francis ph David Muir m Bernard Ebbinghouse

☆ Michael Bryant, Ursula Howells, Pat Heywood, Howard Trevor, Vanessa Howard

Münchausen **

Germany 1943 134m Agfacolor
UFA (Eberhard Schmidt)

aka: *The Adventures of Baron Münchausen*

In the 1940s Baron Münchausen tells stories of his fabulous ancestor who, it is soon clear, is himself, having been given immortality by a magician.

Lavish but somewhat stilted spectacle, produced on the orders of Nazi propagandist Joseph Goebbels to mark the studio's twenty-fifth anniversary. His influence is evident in the way that all other nationalities are shown as comic.

w Berthold Bürger (Erich Kästner) d Josef von Baky ph Werner Krien m Georg Haentzschel ad Emil Hasler, Otto Gulstorff

☆ Hans Albers, Wilhelm Bendow, Michael Bohnen, Marina von Ditmar, Hans Brausewetter, Brigitte Horney, Käthe Haack

† Kästner used a pseudonym because his writings had been banned since 1933. After the film was released, Hitler ordered that he should receive no further commissions.

Munkbrogreven: see *The Count of the Old Town*

'The Ultimate Muppet Trip.'

The Muppet Christmas Carol *

US 1992 86m colour
Buena Vista/Walt Disney/Jim Henson (Brian Henson, Martin G. Baker)

A Christmas-hating miser is reformed by the visitations of five ghosts.

Cheerful adaptation of the perennial story, in a version that should appeal to the young.

w Jerry Juhl story A Christmas Carol by Charles Dickens d Brian Henson ph John Fenner m Miles Goodman m/ly Paul Williams pd Val Strazovec ed Michael Jablow sp The Computer Film Company

☆ Michael Caine, Steven MacKintosh, Meredith Brown, Robin Weaver, Kermit the Frog, Miss Piggy, The Great Gonzo, Fozzie Bear

'The film sinks into a quagmire of sentimentality; the Muppets withdraw discreetly during Scrooge's ghostly visitations and the dominant flavour is more saccharine than humbug. Nice try, though.' – *Sheila Johnston, Independent*

'More entertainment than humanly possible!'

The Muppet Movie **

GB 1979 97m Eastmancolor
ITC (Jim Henson)

Kermit the Frog and friends travel across America to Hollywood and are offered a film contract by Lew Lord, the famous impresario.

Technically an adroit transfer of the celebrated puppets from their TV backstage milieu to a wider canvas; but the latter tends to dwarf them, the material is very variable, the guest stars look embarrassed and the show goes on too long.

w Jerry Juhl, Jack Burns d James Frawley ph Isidore Mankofsky m Paul Williams, Kenny Ascher pd Joel Schiller

☆ Charles Durning, Edgar Bergen, Bob Hope, Milton Berle, Mel Brooks, James Coburn, Dom DeLuise, Elliott Gould, Cloris Leachman, Telly Savalas, Orson Welles

♫ Paul Williams, Kenny Ascher; song 'The Rainbow Connection'

Muppet Treasure Island

US 1996 99m Technicolor
Buena Vista/Walt Disney/Jim Henson (Martin G. Baker, Brian Henson)

The adventures of an orphan who is given a map to buried pirate treasure and sets sail to find it.

A rollicking, unmemorable musical treatment of an oft-told tale which has some difficulty accommodating the story to its Muppet characters: Miss Piggy appears as Benjamina Gunn, Fozzie Bear is Squire Trelawney and Kermit becomes Captain Smollett.

w Jerry Juhl, Kirk R. Thatcher, James V. Hart novel Robert Louis Stevenson d Brian Henson ph John Fenner m Hans Zimmer m/ly Barry Mann, Cynthia Weil pd Val Strazovec ed Michael Jablow

☆ Tim Curry, Kevin Bishop, Steve Whitmire, Frank Oz, Billy Connolly, David Goelz, Jennifer Saunders

'A breezily entertaining yet old-fashioned brew.' – *Empire*

'The Ultimate Muppet Trip.'

Muppets from Space

GB/US 1999 88m DeLuxe
Columbia/Jim Henson Pictures (Brian Henson, Martin G. Baker)

Gonzo discovers he is an alien and that his relatives are coming to take him home.

Lacklustre movie with few jokes and unexciting action that concentrates on one of the least charismatic of Henson's creations.

w Jerry Juhl, Joseph Mazzarino, Ken Kaufman d Tim Hill ph Alan Caso m Jamshied Sharifi ch Toni Basil pd Stephen Marsh ed Michael A. Stevenson, Richard Pearson

☆ Jeffrey Tambor, F. Murray Abraham, Rob Schneider, Josh Charles, Ray Liotta, David Arquette, Andie MacDowell, Kathy Griffin, Pat Hingle, Hollywood Hogan and also voices of: Dave Goelz, Steve Whitmire, Bill Barretta, Jerry Nelson, Brian Henson, Kevin Clash, Frank Oz

'Ploddingly whimsical caper.' – *Entertainment Weekly*

'The movie peaks very early, and never quite regains its early momentum until the end. But even in its slackest moments you've been put in such a good mood you can let them get away with the occasional lapse.' – *Lee Binding, Film Review*

The Muppets Take Manhattan *

US 1984 94m Technicolor
Tri-Star (David Lazer)

The Muppets' varsity show is promised a New York opening.

Probably the best of the Muppet features, but by the time of its arrival the early brilliance had been forgotten and even Miss Piggy had worn out her welcome.

---

w Frank Oz, Tom Patchett, Jay Tarses *d* Frank Oz *ph* Bob Paynter *m* Ralph Burns

☆ Dabney Coleman, Art Carney, James Coco, Joan Rivers, Gregory Hines, Linda Lavin

♫ Jeffrey Moss (music)

Le Mur: see *The Wall*

La Mura de Malapaga: see *Au delà des Grilles*

Murder **

GB   1930   92m   bw
British International (John Maxwell)

A girl is convicted of murder, but one of the jurors sets out to prove her innocent.
Interesting early Hitchcock, a rare whodunnit for him.
w Alma Reville *novel* Enter Sir John by Clemence Dane, Helen Simpson *d* Alfred Hitchcock *ph* Jack Cox

☆ *Herbert Marshall*, Norah Baring, Phyllis Konstam, Edward Chapman, Miles Mander, Esmé Percy, Donald Calthrop

'If Hitchcock produced in Hollywood and was wise enough to keep his films to six or seven reels, he might be a rave anywhere.' – *Variety*

Murder Ahoy

GB   1964   74m   bw
MGM (Lawrence P. Bachmann)

Miss Marple investigates murders on a naval cadet training ship.
Weakest of the Marple mysteries: all chat and no interest.
w David Pursall, Jack Seddon *d* George Pollock *ph* Desmond Dickinson *m* Ron Goodwin

☆ Margaret Rutherford, Lionel Jeffries, Stringer Davis, Charles Tingwell, William Mervyn, Joan Benham, Nicholas Parsons, Miles Malleson, Henry Oscar, Derek Nimmo, Francis Matthews, Gerald Cross

Murder among Friends

US   1941   61m   bw
Ralph Dietrich-Walter Morosco/TCF
Subscribers to a 200,000-dollar insurance policy die one by one.
Pleasingly efficient supporting mystery.
w John Larkin *d* Ray McCarey

☆ John Hubbard, Marjorie Weaver, Cobina Wright Jnr, Mona Barrie, Douglass Dumbrille, Sidney Blackmer, Lucien Littlefield, Milton Parsons

'This address changes all the rules'
Murder at 1600

US   1997   107m   Technicolor   Panavision
Warner/Monarchy/Regency (Arnold Kopelson, Arnon Milchan)

A detective who investigates the murder of the mistress of the President's son in the White House discovers a conspiracy that threatens the nation.
Dull and unconvincing thriller, lacking both mystery and suspense.
w Wayne Beach, David Hodgin *d* Dwight Little *ph* Steven Bernstein *m* Christopher Young *pd* Nelson Coates *ed* Billy Weber, Leslie Jones

☆ Wesley Snipes, Diane Lane, Daniel Benzali, Dennis Miller, Alan Alda, Ronny Cox, Diane Baker, Tate Donovan, Mary Moore, Harris Yulin

'A trashy movie that's intermittently intriguing and enjoyable on its own terms.' – *Emanuel Levy, Variety*

Murder at Monte Carlo

GB   1934   70m   bw
Warner (Irving Asher)
A professor is murdered for his roulette system.
Modest second feature notable only as a springboard for the career of its star.
w John Hastings Turner, Michael Barringer *novel* Tom Van Dyke *d* Ralph Ince *ph* Basil Emmott

☆ Errol Flynn, Eve Gray, Paul Graetz, Molly Lamont, Ellis Irving

Murder at the Baskervilles: see *Silver Blaze*

'By the first lady of mystery – with the last word in detectives!'
Murder at the Gallop *

GB   1963   81m   bw
MGM (George H. Brown)

Miss Marple investigates when an old man is apparently frightened to death by a cat.
Probably the best of the Marples, with a good sense of place and lively performances.
w James P. Cavanagh *novel* After the Funeral by Agatha Christie *d* George Pollock *ph* Arthur Ibbetson *m* Ron Goodwin *ad* Frank White

☆ Margaret Rutherford, Flora Robson, Robert Morley, Stringer Davis, Charles Tingwell, Duncan Lamont, James Villiers, Robert Urquhart, Katya Douglas

Murder at the Vanities *

US   1934   95m   bw
Paramount (E. Lloyd Sheldon)

Murder backstage at the first night of Earl Carroll's Vanities.
Curious, stylish mixture of musical numbers, broad comedy and mystery. Dated, but fun.
w Carey Wilson, Joseph Gollomb, Sam Hellman *d* Mitchell Leisen *ph* Leo Tover *md* Rudolph Kopp *songs* Arthur Johnston, Sam Coslow

☆ Jack Oakie, Victor McLaglen, Carl Brisson, Kitty Carlisle, Dorothy Stickney, Gertrude Michael, Jessie Ralph, Gail Patrick

'Above average and for the masses … long but does not drag.' – *Variety*
'It can boast lavish staging, tuneful melodies, and a host of attractive girls.' – *New York Times*

Murder at the Windmill

GB   1949   70m   bw
Daniel Angel and Nat Cohen
US title: *Murder at the Burlesque*
At London's famous girlie show, a front row patron is murdered.
Rather rushed-looking whodunnit with interesting detail.
wd Val Guest *ph* Bert Mason *md* Phillip Martell

☆ Garry Marsh, Jack Livesey, Jon Pertwee, Diana Decker, Jimmy Edwards, Eliot Makeham

Murder by Contract *

US   1958   81m   bw
Columbia/Orbin (Leon Chooluck)
A professional killer makes a fatal mistake and is shot down by police.
Low-budgeter which seemed stark and original at the time, but television has familiarized its contents.
Moody, contrasty photography and restrained style give it a minor distinction.
w Ben Simcoe *d* Irving Lerner *ph* Lucien Ballard *m* Perry Botkin

☆ Vince Edwards, Philip Pine, Herschel Bernardi, Caprice Toriel

'Ice cold and completely unsentimental.' – *John Gillett*

'A bloody funny movie!'
Murder by Death *

US   1976   94m   Metrocolor
Columbia/Ray Stark

Several (fictional) detectives are invited to stay at the home of a wealthy recluse, and mystery and murder follow.
Sometimes thin but generally likeable spoof of a longstanding genre; the stars seize their opportunities avidly, and the film does not outstay its welcome.
w Neil Simon *d* Robert Moore *ph* David M. Walsh *m* Dave Grusin *pd* Stephen Grimes

☆ Peter Falk, Alec Guinness, Peter Sellers, Truman Capote, Estelle Winwood, Elsa Lanchester, Eileen Brennan, James Coco, David Niven, Maggie Smith, Nancy Walker

'Plenty of scene stealing actors but not many scenes worth stealing.' – *Michael Billington, Illustrated London News*
'Polished performances fail to compensate for a vacuous and frustratingly tortuous plot.' – *Sight and Sound*
'It seems to me that if you haven't watched the real Thin Man and the real Bogie in the real Maltese Falcon you won't see the joke; and if you have watched them, the joke is not good enough.' – *Dilys Powell, Sunday Times*

Murder by Decree

GB/Canada   1978   112m   Metrocolor
Avco/Decree Productions/Saucy Jack (René Dupont, Bob Clark)

Sherlock Holmes investigates the matter of Jack the Ripper and comes upon a Masonic conspiracy.
Interminably long and unpardonably muddled variation on this over-familiar theme, with halts for the performances of guest artists and no clear grip on narrative or character.
w John Hopkins *d* Bob Clark *ph* Reginald H. Morris *m* Carl Zittrer, Paul Zaza *pd* Harry Pottle

☆ Christopher Plummer, James Mason, Anthony Quayle, David Hemmings, Susan Clark, John Gielgud, Donald Sutherland, Frank Finlay, Geneviève Bujold

Murder by Illusion: see *F/X*

Murder by Television

US   1935   60m   bw
Edward M. Spitz/Imperial
The inventor of a television process is murdered.
Static whodunnit with the star as twin brothers. Only a curio.
w Joseph O'Donnell *d* Clifford Sanforth *ph* Arthur Reed *m* Oliver Wallace

☆ Bela Lugosi, June Collyer, Huntley Gordon, George Meeker

Murder by the Clock

US   1931   76m   bw
Paramount
Creepy goings on in an old house after the death of a dowager who has built herself a tomb from which she can escape if buried alive.
Tasteless chiller which had the distinction of being withdrawn from British circulation after public protests.
w Henry Myers, Rufus King, Charles Beahan *play* Charles Beahan *novel* Rufus King *d* Edward Sloman *ph* Karl Struss

☆ Lilyan Tashman, William 'Stage' Boyd, Regis Toomey, Irving Pichel, Blanche Frederici, Walter McGrail

'Lacking in punch as a strongie for first runs. Below that should do oke.' – *Variety*

Murder Can Be Deadly: see *The Painted Smile*

Murder Goes to College

US   1937   77m   bw
Paramount
A reporter on vacation helps solve a campus killing.
Reasonably lively comedy mystery which might have started a series, but didn't.
w Brian Marlow, Eddie Welch, Robert Wyler *novel* Kurt Steele *d* Charles Reisner

☆ Roscoe Karns, Lynne Overman, Marsha Hunt, Astrid Allwyn, Harvey Stephens, Larry Crabbe

'Dialogue crackles with humour … this whodunit will be welcome material on many programmes.' – *Variety*

'You'll die laughing!'
Murder He Says **

US   1945   91m   bw
Paramount (E. D. Leshin)
An insurance salesman stays with a homicidal family of hillbillies.
A curious black farce which seems to be compounded of Cold Comfort Farm and The Red Inn. Very funny, and ahead of its time.
w Lou Breslow *d* George Marshall *ph* Theodor Sparkuhl

☆ Fred MacMurray, Marjorie Main, Helen Walker, Peter Whitney, Jean Heather, Porter Hall, Mabel Paige

Murder in a Blue World (dubbed) *

Spain/France   1973   110m
Jose Frade (Angel Parrondo)

original title: *Una Gota De Sangre Para Morir Amando*
While the state attempts to cure criminals by electric shock treatment, and delinquents roam the streets, a serial killer targets young men.
A quirky, low-budget attack on social and sexual repression, one that acknowledges its debt to Kubrick's A Clockwork Orange.
w Eloy de la Iglesia, Jose Luis Garci, Antonio Fos, Antonio Artero, George Lebourg *d* Eloy de la Iglesia *ph* Francisco Fraile *m* George Garvarent

ad Eduardo Torre De La Fuente *ed* Jose Luis Matesanz

☆ Sue Lyon, Christopher Mitchum, Jean Sorel, Charlie Bravo, Ramon Pons, Alfredo Alba, Antionio Real, David Carpenter

† In an in-joke, during the film Sue Lyon reads Nabokov's *Lolita*, the role that began her screen career.

'What If The Perfect Crime Was All In Your Mind?'
Murder in Mind

US/GB   1996   85m   CFI color
Lakeshore/Evergreen/BBC/Alva/Storyteller (Vicki Slotnick, Jeremy Paige)

A psychiatrist who uses hypnotic techniques is called in by the police to examine a woman accused of murdering her wealthy husband.
Tricksy thriller that betrays its stage origins, relying entirely on narrative twists to maintain interest and distract attention from its implausibilities.
w Michael Cooney *play* Michael Cooney *d* Andrew Morahan *ph* John Aranson *m* Paul Buckmaster *pd* Ben Morahan *ed* Andrea MacArthur

☆ Nigel Hawthorne, Mary Louise Parker, Jimmy Smits, Gailard Sartain, Jason Scott Lee

Murder in Reverse

GB   1945   88m   bw
British National
After long imprisonment for a supposed murder, a convict comes out and hunts down the victim, who isn't really dead.
A reasonable crime entertainment of its day which seemed to introduce a new star; but it hasn't worn well.
wd Montgomery Tully *novel* Austin Small *ph* Ernest Palmer *m* Hans May

☆ William Hartnell, Jimmy Hanley, Chili Bouchier, John Slater, Dinah Sheridan, Wylie Watson

Murder in the Big House

US   1942   67m   bw
Warner
Two reporters uncover a murder ring in a prison.
Acceptable second feature which catapulted its star to fame – at another studio.
w Raymond Schrock *d* B. Reeves Eason

☆ Van Johnson, George Meeker, Faye Emerson, Frank Wilcox

† A previous 1936 version was called *Jailbreak* and starred Craig Reynolds. *Murder in the Big House* was reissued in 1945 as *Born for Trouble*.

Murder in the Blue Room

US   1944   61m   bw
Frank Gross/Universal
Volunteering to sleep in a room where a murder was committed, a guest is found dead.
Tepid remake of The Secret of the Blue Room.
w I. A. L. Diamond, Stanley Davis *d* Leslie Goodwins

☆ Anne Gwynne, Donald Cook, John Litel, Grace McDonald, June Preisser, Regis Toomey

Murder in the Cathedral

GB   1951   136m   bw
Film Traders/George Hoellering
The 12th-century struggle between Henry II and his archbishop culminates in the assassination of Becket in Canterbury Cathedral.
Plainly filmed, slightly amateur version of the celebrated verse play; scarcely a rewarding cinematic experience.
wd George Hoellering *play* T. S. Eliot *ph* David Kosky *m* Laszlo Lajtha *ad* Peter Pendrey

☆ Father John Grosner, Alexander Gauge, David Ward, George Woodbridge, Basil Burton, Paul Rogers, Niall MacGinnis, Mark Dignam, Leo McKern

'A curious ordeal for the audience … a no-man's-land between cinema and drama has been discovered, rather than any extension of either.' – *Gavin Lambert*

Murder in the Family

GB   1938   75m   bw
TCF
Who killed rich Aunt Octavia?
Mild whodunnit with interesting cast.
w David Evans *novel* James Ronald *d* Al Parker

☆ Barry Jones, Jessica Tandy, Evelyn Ankers, Donald Gray, David Markham, Glynis Johns, Roddy McDowall

'One Broke His Silence. The Other Broke The System'

Murder in the First *

US 1995 122m Foto-Kem
Guild/Canal/Wolper (Marc Frydman, Mark Wolper)
▨ ▧

In the early 40s, a young lawyer defends on a murder charge a prisoner who spent three years in solitary confinement in Alcatraz and exposes the brutalities of the system.
Effective and powerful courtroom drama, with some good performances; yet right and wrong are so clearly delineated from the opening scenes that there is no tension, apart from that supplied by the nervy camerawork.
w Dan Gordon d Marc Rocco ph Fred Murphy m Christopher Young pd Kirk M. Petruccelli ed Russell Livingstone
☆ Christian Slater, Kevin Bacon, Gary Oldman, Embeth Davidtz, Bill Macy, Stephen Tobolowsky, Brad Dourif, Mia Kirshner, Kyra Sedgwick
'From among the flotsam of prison movie clichés emerges a flawed but stirring piece of entertainment.' – *Empire*

Murder in the Fleet

US 1935 70m bw
MGM (Lucien Hubbard)
Sabotage on a navy cruiser turns out to be the work of a mad inventor.
Weak and confused mixture of melodrama and comedy.
wd Edward Sedgwick ph Milton Krasner
☆ Robert Taylor, Jean Parker, Jean Hersholt, Ted Healy, Una Merkel, Nat Pendleton, Raymond Hatton, Donald Cook, Mischa Auer

Murder in the Music Hall

US 1946 84m bw
Republic (Herman Millakowsky)
reissue title: *Midnight Melody*
A former criminal, now Broadway producer, is murdered on opening night.
Humdrum extravaganza built round its star, whose last skating appearance this was.
w Frances Hyland, Laszlo Gorog d John English ph John Alton md Walter Scharf
☆ Vera Hruba Ralston, William Marshall, Helen Walker, Nancy Kelly, William Gargan, Ann Rutherford, Julie Bishop, Jerome Cowan, Edward Norris, Paul Hurst, Jack La Rue

Murder in the Private Car *

US 1934 60m bw
Lucien Hubbard/MGM
GB title: *Murder on the Runaway Train*
Mysteries proliferate aboard a fast-moving train.
Adequate second feature which builds up to a remarkably well-staged climax in a runaway carriage.
w Ralph Spence, Edgar Allan Woolf, Al Boasberg, Harvey Thew d Harry Beaumont
☆ Russell Hardie, Charles Ruggles, Mary Carlisle, Una Merkel, Porter Hall
'About the swiftest 61 minutes of entertainment you are ever likely to see.' – *Picturegoer*

The Murder in Thornton Square: see *Gaslight* (1944)

Murder in Times Square

US 1943 72m bw
Columbia
An actor-playwright is suspected of four theatrical murders.
Standard detection work with some slight claim to sophistication.
w Stuart Palmer, Paul Gangelin d Lew Landers
☆ Edmund Lowe, Sidney Blackmer, Marguerite Chapman, John Litel

Murder in Trinidad

US 1934 74m bw
Fox
A quiet detective solves a murder in the tropics.
Modest whodunnit with Nigel Bruce for once playing the sleuth instead of Watson.
w Seton I. Miller novel John W. Vandercook d Louis King
☆ Nigel Bruce, Heather Angel, Victor Jory, Murray Kinnell, Douglas Walton, J. Carrol Naish

'Amusing, but not particularly intriguing.' – *Variety*

Murder Inc: see *The Enforcer*

Murder, Incorporated

US 1960 103m bw Cinemascope
TCF (Burt Balaban)
In the thirties, Anastasia and Lepke build up their crime syndicate which spreads terror through New York.
Tedious and poorly made gangster thriller, unforgivable faults considering the many admirable models it has to follow.
w Irv Tunick, Mel Barr d Burt Balaban, Stuart Rosenberg ph Gayne Rescher m Frank de Vol
☆ Stuart Whitman, May Britt, Henry Morgan, Peter Falk, David J. Stewart, Simon Oakland, Morey Amsterdam
ℚ Peter Falk

Murder Is News: see *The Delavine Affair*

The Murder Man *

US 1935 84m bw
MGM (Harry Rapf)
A reporter investigating a murder becomes one of the suspects.
Good low-key melodrama with an interesting cast.
w Tim Whelan, John C. Higgins d Tim Whelan ph Lester White m William Axt
☆ Spencer Tracy, Virginia Bruce, Lionel Atwill, James Stewart, Harvey Stephens, William Collier Snr
'It will please in the lesser houses.' – *Variety*

Murder Most Foul

GB 1964 91m bw
MGM/Lawrence P. Bachmann (Ben Arbeid)
Refusing to return a guilty verdict, juror Miss Marple makes her own murder investigation backstage at a third-rate repertory company.
Moderate Marple mystery which hasn't quite found the light touch it seeks.
w David Pursall, Jack Seddon novel *Mrs McGinty's Dead* by Agatha Christie d George Pollock ph Desmond Dickinson m Ron Goodwin ed Ernest Walter
☆ Margaret Rutherford, Ron Moody, Charles Tingwell, Andrew Cruickshank, Megs Jenkins, Ralph Michael, James Bolam, Stringer Davis, Francesca Annis, Dennis Price, Terry Scott

Murder My Sweet: see *Farewell My Lovely* (1944)

The Murder of Dr Harrigan

US 1935 67m bw
Warner
A hospital founder disappears while on his way to the operating room.
Formula murder mystery without much special interest.
w Peter Milne, Sy Bartlett novel *Mignon G. Eberhart* d Frank McDonald
☆ Kay Linaker, Ricardo Cortez, Mary Astor, John Eldredge, Joseph Crehan, Frank Reicher
'Will probably do no better than mildly.' – *Variety*

Murder on a Honeymoon

US 1935 74m bw
RKO (Kenneth Macgowan)
When a passenger dies on a holiday flight, a schoolmistress is convinced that it is murder.
Deft little comedy thriller that has acquired a period charm.
w Seton I. Miller, Robert Benchley story *Puzzle of the Pepper Tree* by Stuart Palmer d Lloyd Corrigan ph Nick Musuraca md Alberto Colombo ad Van Nest Polglase, Perry Ferguson ed William Morgan
☆ Edna May Oliver, James Gleason, Lola Lane, Chick Chandler, George Meeker, Dorothy Libaire, Morgan Wallace, Leo G. Carroll
† It was the third, and last, film in the Hildegarde Withers series starring Edna May Oliver, following on from *Penguin Pool Murder* and *Murder on the Blackboard* (qqv).

Murder on Diamond Row: see *The Squeaker*

Murder on Monday: see *Home at Seven*

Murder on the Blackboard

US 1934 72m bw
RKO (Kenneth Macgowan)
When the music teacher is murdered at her school, Hildegarde Withers helps the police with their enquiries.
Pleasant little mystery, with some enjoyable exchanges between Gleason's inspector and Oliver's tart-tongued teacher.
w Willis Goldbeck story Stuart Palmer d George Archainbaud ph Nick Musuraca md Max Steiner ad Van Nest Polglase, Albert D'Agostino ed Archie F. Marsheck
☆ Edna Mae Oliver, James Gleason, Bruce Cabot, Gertrude Michael, Regis Toomey, Tully Marshall, Fredrik Vogeding, Edgar Kennedy
† It was the second film in the Hildegarde Withers series. See also: *Penguin Pool Murder*, *Murder on a Honeymoon*.

Murder on the Orient Express **

GB 1974 131m Technicolor
EMI/GW Films (John Brabourne, Richard Goodwin)
▨ ▧ ◎ ♫ ⌂
In the early thirties, Hercule Poirot solves a murder on a snowbound train.
Reasonably elegant but disappointingly slackly-handled version of a classic mystery novel. Finney overacts and his all-star support is distracting, while as soon as the train chugs into its snowdrift the film stops moving too, without even a dramatic 'curtain'.
w Paul Dehn novel Agatha Christie d Sidney Lumet ph Geoffrey Unsworth m Richard Rodney Bennett pd Tony Walton
☆ Albert Finney, Ingrid Bergman, Lauren Bacall, Wendy Hiller, Sean Connery, Vanessa Redgrave, Michael York, Martin Balsam, Richard Widmark, Jacqueline Bisset, Jean-Pierre Cassel, Rachel Roberts, George Coulouris, John Gielgud, Anthony Perkins and also Colin Blakely, Jeremy Lloyd, Denis Quilley
'Audiences appear to be so hungry for this type of entertainment that maybe it hardly matters that it isn't very good.' – *Judith Crist*
♟ Ingrid Bergman
ℚ Paul Dehn; Geoffrey Unsworth; Richard Rodney Bennett; Albert Finney
♛ Richard Rodney Bennett; John Gielgud; Ingrid Bergman

Murder She Said *

GB 1961 87m bw
MGM (George H. Brown)
▨ ▧
An elderly spinster investigates after seeing a woman strangled in a passing train.
Frightfully British and disappointingly tame adaptation of an Agatha Christie character, with only the star (who is somewhat miscast) holding one's attention.
w David Pursall, Jack Seddon novel *4.50 from Paddington* by Agatha Christie d George Pollock ph Geoffrey Faithfull m Ron Goodwin ed Ernest Walter
☆ Margaret Rutherford, Charles Tingwell, Muriel Pavlow, Arthur Kennedy, James Robertson Justice, Thorley Walters, Gerald Cross, Conrad Phillips
† Thanks to Miss Rutherford's popularity, three increasingly poor sequels were made: *Murder at the Gallop* (qv) (1963), *Murder Most Foul* (qv) (1964), *Murder Ahoy* (qv) (1964).

Murder Will Out: see *The Voice of Merrill*

Murder without Crime

GB 1950 76m bw
ABPC
A blackmailer extracts money for a crime not yet committed.
Thin four-hander from a rather mysterious West End success.
wd J. Lee-Thompson play *Double Error* by J. Lee-Thompson ph William McLeod m Philip Green
☆ Dennis Price, Derek Farr, Joan Dowling, Patricia Plunkett

The Murderer Lives at 21: see *L'Assassin habite au 21*

The Murderers Are Among Us *

Germany 1947 87m bw
Defa
original title: *Die Mörder Sind Unter Uns*
In the ruins of Berlin several post-war characters indulge in gloomy self-examination.

Almost a caricature of what one would expect from a defeated people, this now-curious item has a certain power of its own.
wd Wolfgang Staudte ph Friedl Behn-Grund, Eugen Klagemann m Ernst Roters
☆ Hildegard Knef, Ernst Fischer, Arno Paulsen
'It is sombre, slow, intense, tragically moving and in common with the post-war Italian films as true as it can be to the surrounding reality. It would seem that only the impoverished and defeated can focus the camera lens on life.' – *Richard Winnington*

Murderer's Row

US 1966 108m Technicolor
Columbia/Meadway-Claude/Euan Lloyd
▨
Matt Helm tracks down an international villain who has kidnapped an inventor.
Witless and uninventive spy spoof which drags itself wearily along but never attempts an explanation of its own title.
w Herbert Baker novel Donald Hamilton d Henry Levin ph Sam Leavitt m Lalo Schifrin
☆ Dean Martin, Ann-Margret, Karl Malden, Camilla Sparv, James Gregory, Beverly Adams, Tom Reese

'The blood will run cold in your veins!'

Murders in the Rue Morgue *

US 1932 62m bw
Universal (Carl Laemmle Jnr)
▨ ▧
A series of grisly murders prove to be the work of a trained ape.
A distant relation of the original story, mildly interesting for its obvious Caligari influences, but not very good in any way.
w Tom Reed, Dale Van Every, John Huston story Edgar Allan Poe d Robert Florey ph Karl Freund
☆ Bela Lugosi, Sidney Fox, Leon Ames, Bert Roach, Brandon Hurst
'Synthetic studio rewrite … Poe wouldn't recognize his story.' – *Variety*

'Where sights of passion end in screams of terror!'

Murders in the Rue Morgue *

US 1971 86m Foto Film Color
AIP (Louis M. Heyward)
▨
Poe's story is being presented at a Grand Guignol theatre in Paris, and when murders happen within the company Inspector Vidocq comes to investigate.
Playfully plotted chiller which has more to do with The Phantom of the Opera than with Poe. A good time-waster for addicts.
w Charles Wicking, Henry Slesar d Gordon Hessler ph Manuel Berengier m Waldo de Los Rios
☆ Jason Robards Jnr, Herbert Lom, Lilli Palmer, Adolfo Celi, Michael Dunn, Christine Kaufmann

Murders in the Zoo

US 1933 64m bw
Paramount
A jealous zoologist finds interesting ways to murder any man who shows interest in his wife.
Modest time-passer with a rampant star.
w Philip Wylie, Seton I. Miller d Edward Sutherland ph Ernest Haller
☆ Lionel Atwill, Charles Ruggles, Kathleen Burke, John Lodge, Randolph Scott, Gail Patrick
'Has what it takes to chill and entertain.' – *Variety*

Muriel *

France/Italy 1963 116m Eastmancolor
Argos/Alpha/Eclair/Films de la Pléiade/Dear Films (Anatole Dauman)
▨
aka: *Muriel, ou le Temps d'un Retour*
A widow and her stepson are both misled by memories of past loves.
Elusive character drama which, though over-generous in length, fails to satisfy.
w Jean Cayrol d Alain Resnais ph Sacha Vierny m Hans Werner Henze
☆ Delphine Seyrig, Jean-Pierre Kérien, Nita Klein, Jean-Baptiste Thierrée
'One has to watch and listen with every nerve alert.' – *Tom Milne, MFB*

Muriel, ou le Temps d'un Retour: see
Muriel

'A Story of Love, Laughter and the Pursuit of
Matrimony.'

Muriel's Wedding *
Australia   1994   105m   colour
Buena Vista/CIBY 2000/AFFC (Lynda House, Jocelyn
Moorhouse)

A fat, unhappy 22-year-old, the butt of her
companions, robs her father and sets out to enjoy
herself and find a husband.
*Enjoyable, rumbustious soap opera, poking fun at
small-time political corruption and the small-town
desire for marriage at any cost, though it offers little
that is positive and the constant presence of Abba on
the soundtrack does little for its feel-good qualities.*
wd P. J. Hogan   m Martin McGrath   m Peter Best
pd Patrick Reardon   ed Jill Bilcock
☆ Toni Collette, Bill Hunter, Rachel Griffiths,
Jeanie Drynan, Gennie Nevinson, Matt Day,
Daniel Lapaine, Sophie Lee, Chris Haywood
  'The film would be more convincing in poking
  fun at the world of soap opera if it didn't reach
  for the instant dramas of illness and breakdown,
  cancer and kleptomania in such a soapy way.' –
  Adam Mars-Jones, Independent
  'Provides a nicely vicious portrait of Australian
  suburban life, with its young people aiming to be
  as much like their peers as possible and the older
  generation piously performing moral somersaults
  to justify their tepid respectability.' – *Derek
  Malcolm, Guardian*
† The film won the 1994 Australian Film Institute
awards for best film, best actress (Toni Collette),
best supporting actress (Rachel Griffiths), and
sound.

Murmur of the Heart: see *Le Souffle au Coeur*

Un Muro de Silencio: see *Black Flowers*

Murph the Surf: see *Live a Little, Steal a Lot*

Murphy's Law
US   1986   100m   TVC Color
Cannon (Pancho Kohner)

A tough LA cop with a drink problem is arrested
for his ex-wife's murder.
*Unattractively violent and foul-mouthed urban thriller
in the wake of Dirty Harry.*
w Gail Morgan Hickman   d J. Lee Thompson
ph Alex Phillips   m Marc Donahue, Valentine
McCallum
☆ Charles Bronson, Carrie Snodgress, Kathleen
Wilhoite, Robert F. Lyons, Richard Romanus

Murphy's Romance
US   1985   107m   Metrocolor   Panavision
Columbia/Martin Ritt-Fogwood (Laura Ziskin)

A divorcée determined to make a living as a horse
trainer in rural Arizona falls for the ageing local
chemist.
*Well-meaning but somewhat yawnworthy romantic
comedy-drama which might almost have strayed from
the days of the Hardy family.*
w Harriet Frank Jnr, Irving Ravetch   d Martin
Ritt   ph William A. Fraker   m Carole King
pd Joel Schiller
☆ Sally Field, James Garner, Brian Kerwin, Corey
Haim
  'Sweet and homey, but falls far short of
  compelling film-making.' – *Variety*
⚒ James Garner; photography

Murphy's War *
GB   1971   108m   Eastmancolor   Panavision
Hemdale/Yates Deeley (Michael Deeley)

A torpedoed British merchantman in Venezuela
devotes himself to bombing a U-boat from a home-
made plane.
*Modest adventure story with the star in better form
than the script.*
w Stirling Silliphant   novel Max Catto   d Peter
Yates   ph Douglas Slocombe   m John Barry
☆ Peter O'Toole, Sian Phillips, Philippe Noiret,
Horst Janson

Muscle Beach Party
US   1964   94m   Pathécolor   Panavision
AIP (James H. Nicholson, Robert Dillon)

A fickle, rich Italian widow falls for a teenage
surfer and plans to make him a star, to the
annoyance of his friends, whose beach has been
invaded by body-builders.
*Tiresome comedy of teenage bonding, one of the many
pumped out in the mid-60s and marked by banal plot,
dialogue and songs, though providing brief employment
for some ageing actors and comedians.*
w Robert Dillon   d William Asher   ph Harold
Wellman   m Les Baxter   m/ly Roger Christian,
Gary Usher, Brian Wilson, Guy Hemric, Jerry
Styner   ad Lucius Croxton   ed Eve Newman, Fred
Feitshans
☆ Frankie Avalon, Annette Funicello, Luciana
Paluzzi, John Ashley, Don Rickles, Peter Turgeon,
Jody McCrea, Dick Dale and the Del Tones, Candy
Johnson, Morey Amsterdam, Buddy Hackett, Little
Stevie Wonder, Peter Lorre
† It was a sequel to *Beach Party* and was followed
by *Bikini Beach* and *Pajama Party* (qqv).

'If You Want A Leg Up In Hollywood, It's Time You
Met...'

The Muse **
US   1999   96m   DeLuxe
Entertainment/October (Herb Nanas)

A Hollywood screenwriter in trouble meets a
woman claiming to be a daughter of Zeus, who
offers to inspire him providing that he indulges her
every whim.
*Sourly amusing take on what constitutes success and
failure in Hollywood, though slackly directed.*
w Albert Brooks, Monica Johnson   d Albert
Brooks   ph Thomas Ackerman   m Elton John
pd Dina Lipton   ed Peter Teschner
☆ Albert Brooks, Sharon Stone, Andie
MacDowell, Jeff Bridges, Mark Feuerstein, Steven
Wright, Bradley Whitford, Mario Opinato, Dakin
Matthews, Concetta Tomei
  'Brooks will always be funny; but, if anything, his
  own muse deserts him here, revealing a man
  with a cynical view of the town he works in.' –
  Bob McCabe, Empire
† Cybill Shepherd, Lorenzo Lamas, Jennifer
Tilly, Rob Reiner, James Cameron and Martin
Scorsese appear as themselves.

Mushrooms
Australia   1994   93m   colour
J.A.M./AFFC/Rosen-Harper

The ageing widows of two fences have problems
when a police sergeant becomes a lodger at the
same time as a violent criminal seeks refuge in
their house.
*Gruesome black comedy, done with a certain style, but
likely to be best enjoyed by cannibals.*
wd Alan Madden   ph Louis Irving   m Paul
Grabowsky   pd George Liddle   ed Henry Dangar
☆ Julia Blake, Simon Chilvers, Lynette Curran,
Brandon Burke, George Shevtsov, Boris Brkic

'As a lawyer all she wanted was the truth. As a
daughter all she wanted was his innocence. How well
do you really know your father?'

Music Box *
US   1989   126m   colour   Cinemascope
Guild/Carolco (Irwin Winkler)

A lawyer defends her father against charges that he
was a war criminal.
*An effectively melodramatic courtroom drama, but no
more than that, despite winning the Golden Bear at the
Berlin Film Festival in 1990.*
w Joe Eszterhas   d Costa-Gavras   ph Patrick
Blossier   m Philippe Sarde   pd Jeannine Claudia
Oppewall   ed Joelle Van Effenterre
☆ Jessica Lange, Armin Mueller-Stahl, Frederic
Forrest, Donald Moffat, Lukas Haas, Cheryl Lynn
Bruce, Mari Torocsik, J. S. Block, Sol Frieder
⚒ Jessica Lange

The Music Box ****
US   1932   30m   bw
Hal Roach

Two delivery men take a piano to a house at the
top of a flight of stairs.
*Quintessential Laurel and Hardy, involving almost all
their aspects including a slight song and dance. With
Billy Gilbert.*

w H. M. Walker   d James Parrott
⚒ best short

Music for Madame
US   1937   81m   bw
RKO (Jesse L. Lasky)

An opera singer goes to Hollywood and becomes
the dupe of jewel thieves.
*Tolerable star musical with rather stale comedy
elements.*
w Gertrude Purcell, Robert Harari   d John G.
Blystone
☆ Nino Martini, Joan Fontaine, Alan Mowbray,
Erik Rhodes, Alan Hale, Billy Gilbert, Grant
Mitchell, Lee Patrick
  'Seems that Nino just can't make the grade as a
  film star.' – *Variety*

Music for Millions *
US   1944   117m   bw
MGM (Joe Pasternak)

A small girl helps her pregnant sister who is a
member of José Iturbi's orchestra.
*Dewy-eyed wartime musical, full of popular classics,
sentimentality and child interest, all smoothly
packaged. As an example of what the public wanted in
1944, quite an eye-opener.*
w Myles Connolly   d Henry Koster   ph Robert
Surtees   md George Stoll
☆ Margaret O'Brien, June Allyson, José Iturbi,
Jimmy Durante, Marsha Hunt, Hugh Herbert,
Harry Davenport, Connie Gilchrist
⚒ Myles Connolly

Music Hath Charms *
GB   1935   70m   bw
BIP (Walter C. Mycroft)

A dance band's broadcast has various effects on
listeners.
Pleasing, modest portmanteau of sketches with music.
w L. du Garde Peach, Jack Davies Jnr   d Thomas
Bentley, Alexander Esway, Walter Summers,
Arthur Woods   ph Horace Wheddon, Jack Cox,
Bryan Langley, Otto Kanturek   ad Clarence Elder
ed J. Corbett
☆ Henry Hall and his Orchestra, Carol Goodner,
W. H. Berry, Arthur Margetson, Antoinette
Cellier, Billy Milton

Music in Darkness: see *Music Is My Future*

Music in Manhattan
US   1944   81m   bw
RKO

A Broadway actress is rumoured to be secretly
married to a war hero, much to the annoyance of
her fiancé.
*A minor musical that gets up a little comic steam until
the unmemorable songs cool it down.*
w Lawrence Kimble   story Maurice Tombragel,
Hal Smith, Jack Scholl   d John H. Auer
ph Russell Metty   m Leigh Harline   m/ly Herb
Magidson, Lew Pollack
☆ Anne Shirley, Dennis Day, Phillip Terry,
Raymond Walburn, Jane Darwell, Patti Brill, Nino
Menendez, Charlie Barnet, Jason Robards

Music in My Heart
US   1940   70m   bw
Columbia

An alien singer wins the lead in a Broadway
musical, which prevents him from being deported.
*Forgettable second feature which was its leading lady's
last stepping stone before stardom.*
w James Edward Grant   d Joseph Santley
☆ Rita Hayworth, Tony Martin, Edith Fellows,
Alan Mowbray, George Tobias, Eric Blore, André
Kostelanetz and his orchestra
⚒ song 'It's a Blue World' (m/ly Chet Forrest, Bob
Wright)

Music in the Air
US   1934   85m   bw
Fox (Erich Pommer)

An opera singer is torn between two men.
Heavy-going light entertainment.
w Howard Young, Billy Wilder   play Oscar
Hammerstein II, Jerome Kern   d Joe May
ph Ernest Palmer
☆ Gloria Swanson, John Boles, Douglass
Montgomery, June Lang, Al Shean, Reginald
Owen, Joseph Cawthorn, Hobart Bosworth
  'Mild operetta of class appeal, which limits its
  b.o. sturdiness.' – *Variety*

Music Is Magic
US   1935   67m   bw
TCF

By a series of unexpected events, a young girl
becomes a Hollywood star.
*Unpretentious and fairly snappy musical which still
provides moments to enjoy.*
w Edward Eliscu, Lou Breslow   d George Marshall
☆ Alice Faye, Bebe Daniels, Ray Walker, Frank
Mitchell, Jack Durant, Hattie McDaniel
  'One of those flighty affairs that will have
  trouble getting past the dual barricade.' – *Variety*

Music Is My Future *
Sweden   1948   85m   bw
Terrafilm (Lorens Marmstedt)
original title: *Musik i Mörker*
aka: *Music In Darkness, Night is My Future*

Blinded in an accident, a young pianist forms a
relationship with a poor girl.
*Saved from its persistent sentimentality by occasional
stringency, it survives as an early example of a
developing talent.*
w Dagmar Edquist   novel Dagmar Edquist
d Ingmar Bergman   ph Göran Strindberg
m Erland von Koch   ad P. A. Lundgren
ed Lennart Wallén
☆ Mai Zetterling, Birger Malmsten, Olaf
Winnerstrand, Naima Wifstrand, Bibi Skoglund,
Hilda Borgström, Douglas Hage, Gunnar
Björnstrand, Bengt Eklund
  'My fourth film became a modest success, thanks
  to Lorens Marmstedt's wisdom, thoughtfulness
  and patience … It was he who taught me how to
  make films.' – *Ingmar Bergman, The Magic
  Lantern*

'The story of a homosexual who married a
nymphomaniac!'

The Music Lovers *
GB   1970   123m   Eastmancolor   Panavision
UA/Rossfilms (Roy Baird)

Homosexual composer Tchaikovsky is impelled to
marry, loses his sponsor, drives his wife into an
asylum and dies of cholera.
*Absurd fantasia on the life of a great composer,
produced in a manner reminiscent of MGM's sillier
musicals; up to a point hysterically (and
unintentionally) funny, then rather sickening.*
w Melvyn Bragg   book Beloved Friend by C. D.
Bowen, Barbara von Meck   d Ken Russell
ph Douglas Slocombe   md André Previn
☆ Richard Chamberlain, Glenda Jackson,
Christopher Gable, Max Adrian, Isabella Telezynska,
Maureen Pryor, Andrew Faulds
  'Tchaikovsky has been made the excuse for a
  crude melodrama about sex.' – *Konstantin
  Bazarov*
  'Libellous not only to the composer but to his
  music.' – *Roger Ebert*

The Music Man ***
US   1962   151m   Technirama
Warner (Morton da Costa)

A confidence trickster persuades a small-town
council to start a boys' band, with himself as the
agent for all the expenses.
*Reasonably cinematic, thoroughly invigorating
transference to the screen of a hit Broadway musical.
Splendid period 'feel', standout performances, slight sag
in second half.*
w Marion Hargrove   book Meredith Willson
d Morton da Costa   ph Robert Burks   md Ray
Heindorf   ch Onna White   songs Meredith Willson
☆ Robert Preston, Shirley Jones, Buddy Hackett,
Hermione Gingold, Pert Kelton, Paul Ford
  'This is one of those triumphs that only a
  veteran performer can have; Preston's years of
  experience and his love of performing come
  together joyously.' – *Pauline Kael*
† Robert Preston, who originated the part on
Broadway, was only offered the film role after Cary
Grant had turned it down.
⚒ Ray Heindorf
⚒ best picture

ↂↂ film suitable for
family viewing   ▤ VHS video-cassette for
the British PAL system   ▥ VHS video-cassette for the British
PAL system in wide screen-format   ▢ Video cassette in a computer-
colourised version   ▦ American NTSC video-cassette   ⌕ Laser disc

The Music of Chance *

US   1993   97m   Foto-Kem
Feature film/I.R.S. Media/American Playhouse
(Frederick Zollo, Dylan Sellers)

Two millionaires force two poker players, who lose all their money in a game, to work off the debt by remaining on their estate and building a wall.
A good-looking, well-acted, minimalist, lightweight drama of men trapped by their own greed.
w Philip Haas, Belinda Haas *novel* Paul Auster d Philip Haas m Philip Johnston pd Hugo Luczyc-Wyhowski ed Belinda Haas
☆ James Spader, Mandy Patinkin, M. Emmet Walsh, Charles Durning, Joel Grey, Samantha Mathis, Christopher Penn
'A lean, convincing fable in the tradition of Kafka, Borges and Pinter.' – *Philip French, Observer*

'She gave them a gift they could never imagine. They gave the system a fight it would never forget.'

Music of the Heart *

US   1999   124m   DeLuxe
Miramax (Marianne Maddalena, Susan Kaplan, Allan Miller, Walter Scheuer)

Abandoned by her husband, a mother of two small children becomes a noted children's violin teacher; when her work is threatened by cuts in funding, she organises a charity concert at Carnegie Hall.
A heartening true life story re-told without much subtlety or finesse; Craven goes unashamedly for tears as he more usually does for shocks.
w Pamela Gray *documentary Small Wonders* by Allan and Lana Miller d Wes Craven ph Peter Deming m Mason Daring pd Bruce Miller ed Patrick Lussier
☆ Meryl Streep, Aidan Quinn, Angela Bassett, Cloris Leachman, Josh Pais, Jay O. Sanders, Charlie Hofheimer, Kieran Culkin, Michael Angarano, Henry Dinhofer
'A gloriously sentimental true-life drama in which Meryl Streep offers another indelible portrayal.' – *David Stratton, Variety*
† Isaac Stern, Itzhak Perlman, and Arnold Steinhardt appear as themselves.
♪ Meryl Streep; song 'Music of My Heart' (m/l Diane Warren)

The Music Room **

India   1958   100m   bw
Satyajit Ray Productions
original title: *Jalsaghar*
An elderly and reclusive aristocratic connoisseur of music stages a magnificent musical evening in his crumbling palace as a gesture of defiance to the modern world.
Elegant, small-scale work of a man destroying himself through his obsessive pride.
wd Satyajit Ray *story* Tarasankar Banerjee ph Subrata Mitra m Vilayat Khan ad Bansi Chandragupta ed Dulal Dutta
☆ Chhabi Biswas, Padman Devi, Pinaki Sen Gupta, Gangapada Bose
'A deeply felt, extremely tedious film. On the one hand its western derivations are patent (the Greek-revival mansion no more than the Chekhovian theme). On the other hand its chief indigenous element, the Indian music, is simply uncongenial and tiresome to our ears. No doubt these are excellent musical performances for those who understand them, but they make us start counting the bulbs in the theater chandelier.' – *Stanley Kauffmann*
'A great, flawed, maddening film – hard to take but probably impossible to forget. It's often crude and it's poorly constructed, but it's a great experience.' – *Pauline Kael*
† The film was hampered by casting an unmusical actor in the leading role.

The Music Teacher *

Belgium   1988   98m   Fujicolour
Mainline/RTBF/K2-One (Alexandre Pletser)
original title: *Le Maître de Musique*
Protégées of two rival singing teachers engage in a contest.
Resolutely old-fashioned drama, done with a certain style.
w Gérard Corbiau, André Corbiau *story* Luc Jabon, Gérard Corbiau d Gérard Corbiau

ph Walther Van Den Ende m Ronald Zollman ad Zouc Lanc ed Denise Vindevogel
☆ José Van Dam, Anne Roussel, Philippe Volter, Sylvie Fennec, Patrick Bauchau, Johan Leysen, Marc Schreiber
'Verbal and visual clichés provide the setting for a selection of popular operatic gems. Culture of this kind makes gun-reaching Goerings of us all.' – *Philip French, Observer*
♫ best foreign film

Musik I Mörker: see *Music Is My Future*

Muss 'em Up

US   1936   70m   bw
RKO/Pandro S. Berman
A cop with a Philo Vance complex routs out gangsters.
Competent crime programmer.
w Erwin Gelsey, James Edward Grant d Charles Vidor
☆ Preston Foster, Margaret Callahan, Alan Mowbray, Ralph Morgan, Guinn Williams, Maxie Rosenbloom
'Enough comedy and other values to make it fairly passable fare.' – *Variety*

Mustang Country

US   1976   79m   Technicolor
Universal (John Champion)
In 1925 Montana, a rancher comes out of retirement to help to round up a wild stallion.
Mild outdoor yarn for family audiences.
wd John Champion ph J. Barry Herron m Lee Holdridge
☆ Joel McCrea, Nika Mina, Robert Fuller, Patrick Wayne

The Mutations

GB   1974   92m   Eastmancolor
Columbia/Getty (Robert D. Weinbach)
A bio-chemist uses circus freaks in his experiments to find the perfect synthesis of plant and animal.
Tasteless horror film with little style of any kind.
w Robert D. Weinbach, Edward Mann d Jack Cardiff ph Paul Beeson m Basil Kirchin
☆ Donald Pleasence, Tom Baker, Brad Harris, Julie Ege, Michael Dunn, Scott Antony, Jill Haworth, Lisa Collings
'Bloody awful!' – *Julie Ege*

Mute Witness **

GB   1995   90m   colour
Columbia TriStar/Cobblestone (Alexander Buchman, Norbert Soentgen, Anthony Waller)
In a Moscow film studio, a mute make-up artist is locked in at night and witnesses the filming of a real-life murder.
Tense, darkly comic chase thriller that maintains an exciting level of suspense and plays some clever tricks along the way.
wd Anthony Waller ph Egon Werdin m Wilbert Hirsch pd Matthias Kammermeir ed Peter Adam
☆ Mary Sudina, Fay Ripley, Evan Richards, Oleg Jankowskij, Igor Volkow, Sergei Karlenkov, Alec Guinness
'A seductive piece of real filmmaking that should keep audiences hyperventilating to the last reel.' – *Variety*

Mutiny

US   1952   77m   Technicolor
King Brothers/United Artists
During the war of 1812, an American ship runs the English blockade to collect gold bullion from France.
Fairly lively swashbuckler.
w Philip Yordan, Sidney Harmon d Edward Dmytryk ph Ernest Laszlo m Dimitri Tiomkin
☆ Mark Stevens, Angela Lansbury, Patric Knowles, Gene Evans, Rhys Williams

Mutiny in the Big House

US   1939   83m   bw
Monogram
A chaplain is at the centre of a prison break, and tries to calm the mob.
Archetypal cellblock movie, and not the worst of them.
w Robert D. Andrews, Martin Mooney d William Nigh
☆ Charles Bickford, Barton MacLane

'Will edge toward the profit side of the ledger for the pop-pricers.' – *Variety*

The Mutiny of the Elsinore

GB   1937   79m   bw
Argyle British
A reporter on a sailing ship for a story finds himself in the middle of a mutiny.
Very studio-bound seafaring adventure.
w Walter Summers and Beaufoy Milton *novel* Jack London d Roy Lockwood ph Bryan Langley m Guy Jones
☆ Paul Lukas, Lyn Harding, Kathleen Kelly, Clifford Evans

'They'll take this town by storm … fighting, laughing, loving, breaking every law of the seven seas!'

Mutiny on the Bounty ***

US   1935   135m   bw
MGM (Irving Thalberg, Albert Lewin)
An 18th-century British naval vessel sets off for South America but during a mutiny the captain is cast adrift and the mutineers settle in the Pitcairn Islands.
A still-entertaining adventure film which seemed at the time like the pinnacle of Hollywood's achievement but can now be seen to be slackly told, with wholesale pre-release editing very evident. Individual scenes and performances are however refreshingly well-handled.
w Talbot Jennings, Jules Furthman, Carey Wilson *book* Charles Nordhoff, James Hall d Frank Lloyd ph Arthur Edeson m Herbert Stothart ed Margaret Booth
☆ Charles Laughton, Clark Gable, Franchot Tone, Movita, Dudley Digges, Henry Stephenson, Donald Crisp, Eddie Quillan, Francis Lister, Spring Byington, Ian Wolfe
BLIGH (CHARLES LAUGHTON): 'Casting me adrift 3,500 miles from a port of call! You're sending me to my doom, eh? Well, you're wrong, Christian. I'll take this boat, as she floats, to England if I must. I'll live to see you – all of you – hanging from the highest yardarm in the British fleet…'
'Nothing to stand in the way of a box office dynamite rating.' – *Variety*
'Incidents are made vivid in terms of the medium – the swish and pistol crack of the lash, the sweating lean bodies, the terrible labour, and the ominous judgment from the quarterdeck.' – *Otis Ferguson*
♣ best picture
♫ script; Frank Lloyd; Herbert Stothart; Charles Laughton; Clark Gable; Franchot Tone (whose role was originally to have been played by Robert Montgomery); Margaret Booth

Mutiny on the Bounty

US   1962   185m   Technicolor   Ultra Panavision 70
MGM/Arcola (Aaron Rosenberg)
Overlong and unattractive remake marred principally by Brando's English accent and various production follies, not to mention his overlong and bloody death scene.
The shipboard sadism still works pretty well, but after the landing in Tahiti boredom takes over.
w Charles Lederer d Lewis Milestone ph Robert Surtees m Bronislau Kaper
☆ Trevor Howard, Marlon Brando, Richard Harris, Hugh Griffith, Tarita, Richard Haydn, Percy Herbert, Duncan Lamont, Gordon Jackson, Chips Rafferty, Noel Purcell
♫ best picture; Robert Surtees; Bronislau Kaper; Song 'Follow Me' (mBronislau Kaper, lyPaul Francis Webster)

My Ain Folk ***

GB   1973   55m   bw
Connoisseur/BFI (Nick Nascht)
Following the death of his maternal grandmother, a boy is reluctantly taken in by his father's mother until he goes away to an orphanage.
Stark account of narrow and damaged lives, told with an intense sympathy.
wd Bill Douglas ph Gale Tattersall ed Peter West
☆ Stephen Archibald, Hughie Restorick, Jean Taylor Smith, Bernard McKenna, Mr Munro, Paul Kermack, Helena Gloag, Jessie Combe
'A very considerable work of art, more profound, more terrible and ultimately more inspiring than

My Childhood, all of whose virtues it shares.' – *Elizabeth Sussex, MFB*
† The second part of an autobiographical trilogy that began with *My Childhood* and was completed by *My Way Home* (qqv).

My American Cousin *

♟ Canada   1985   95m   Alpha Cine
Borderline/Okanagan/Peter O'Brian
In the summer of 1959, a 12-year-old girl falls for her blond Californian cousin when he arrives in his red Cadillac on a visit to her home in British Columbia.
Gently nostalgic film of family life and mild teenage rebellion, with a rock soundtrack.
wd Sandy Wilson ph Richard Leiterman ad Phil Schmidt ed Haida Paul
☆ Margaret Langrick, John Wildman, Richard Donat, Jane Mortifee, T. J. Scott, Camille Henderson, Darsi Bailey, Allison Hale, Samantha Jocelyn
† The film won Canadian Genie awards for best film, director, screenplay, editing, actress (Margaret Langrick), and actor (John Wildman).

My American Uncle ***

France   1980   126m   Eastmancolor
Andrea Films/TF1 (Philippe Dussart)
original title: *Mon Oncle Américain*
Professor Henri Laborit explains the lives of two men and a woman in terms of animal behaviour.
Fascinatingly assembled but basically pessimistic dissection of human life, in the director's most meticulous style. The American uncle is the piece of good luck which may be just around the corner (but probably isn't).
w Jean Gruault *books* Henri Laborit d Alain Resnais ph Sacha Vierny m Arié Dzierlatka
☆ Gérard Depardieu, Nicole Garcia, Roger Pierre, Henri Laborit
♫ screenplay

My Beautiful Laundrette *

GB   1985   97m   colour
Working Title/SAF/Channel 4 (Sarah Radclyffe, Tim Bevan)
A young south London Asian manages his uncle's launderette and falls for a white racist boy.
Made for TV, but fashionable enough to get critical acclaim and cinema distribution, this soft-centred anecdote was a bit of a puzzle to those neither Asian nor homosexual.
w Hanif Kureishi d Stephen Frears ph Oliver Stapleton m Ludus Tonalis
☆ Saeed Jaffrey, Roshan Seth, Daniel Day-Lewis, Gordon Warnecke, Shirley Anne Field, Rita Wolf
♫ best original screenplay

My Best Friend's Girl

France   1983   100m   Eastmancolor
Cannon/Renn Productions/Sara Films (Alain Sarde)
original title: *La Femme de Mon Pote*
A day worker asks his friend, a night worker, to look after his girlfriend.
Mildly amusing comedy.
w Bertrand Blier, Gérard Brach d Bertrand Blier ph Jean Penzer, Yves Agostini, Michel Coteret, Eric Vallée m J. J. Cale ed Claudine Merline, Sylvie Quester, Annick Menier, Jeanne Kef
☆ Coluche, Isabelle Huppert, Thierry Lhermitte, Farid Chopel, François Perrot, Daniel Colas, Frédérique Michot

'Julianne fell in love with her best friend the day he decided to marry someone else.'

My Best Friend's Wedding **

US   1997   105m   Technicolor   Panavision
Columbia TriStar/Predawn (Jerry Zucker, Ronald Bass)
When she discovers that her former lover is about to marry, a woman decides to break up the romance and win him back for herself.
Enjoyable, slightly tart comedy, with a star turn from Everett to compensate for the occasional predictability of the plot.
w Ronald Bass d P. J. Hogan ph Laszlo Kovacs m James Newton Howard pd Richard Sylbert ed Garth Craven
☆ Julia Roberts, Dermot Mulroney, Cameron Diaz, Rupert Everett, Philip Bosco, M. Emmet Walsh, Rachel Griffiths

'Straddling several genres, the film has an underlying veracity that should strike an emotional chord with audiences.' – *Leonard Klady, Variety*

† After preview audiences liked the character played by Rupert Everett, extra scenes involving him were shot, and a new ending added.

†† It was one of the most successful movies of the year, grossing more than $126m in the US, and another $129m elsewhere in the world.

🔈 James Newton Howard

My Best Girl *
US   1927   84m   bw   silent
Mary Pickford Corporation

A shopgirl falls for a co-worker, unaware that he is the son of the owner.
The star's last silent film is a charming comedy which tends to fade in the memory.
w Allen McNeil, Tim Whelan d Sam Taylor ph Charles Rosher m Gaylord Carter
☆ Mary Pickford, Charles 'Buddy' Rogers, Sunshine Hart, Lucien Littlefield, Hobart Bosworth
🔈 Charles Rosher

'Perhaps it is not for the living to know the truth about reincarnation!'
'If you give away the ending, may your blood run cold forever!'

My Blood Runs Cold
US   1965   108m   bw   Panavision
Warner (William Conrad)

A spoilt heiress meets a strange young man who claims she is the reincarnation of a long dead charmer; he turns out to be a madman who has come across an old diary.
Initially intriguing but eventually exhausting melodrama with a weak solution.
w John Mantley d William Conrad ph Sam Leavitt m George Duning
☆ Troy Donahue, Joey Heatherton, Barry Sullivan, Jeanette Nolan
'Not all that bad, but not worth missing *I Love Lucy* for either.' – *Leonard Maltin*

My Blue Heaven
US   1950   96m   Technicolor
TCF (Sol C. Siegel)

A pair of troupers want a family, by adoption if not otherwise.
Routine musical drenched in sentimentality.
w Lamar Trotti, Claude Binyon d Henry Koster ph Arthur E. Arling m Alfred Newman songs Harold Arlen (m), Ralph Blane (ly)
☆ Betty Grable, Dan Dailey, Mitzi Gaynor, David Wayne, Jane Wyatt, Una Merkel

My Blue Heaven
US   1990   95m   Technicolor
Warner (Herbert Ross, Anthea Sylbert)
🗜 📼 ⚭

Relocated in a small town, a gangster who has turned state's evidence decides not to go straight.
Dull comedy, broadly acted and directed.
w Nora Ephron d Herbert Ross ph John Bailey m Ira Newborn pd Charles Rosen ed Stephen A. Rotter, Robert Reitano
☆ Steve Martin, Rick Moranis, Joan Cusack, Melanie Mayron, William Irwin, Carol Kane, William Hickey, Deborah Rush, Daniel Stern, Jesse Bradford

My Bodyguard
US   1980   96m   CFI color
Market Street/Melvin Simon
📼

A 15-year-old Chicago boy has trouble at school.
Oddly stilted, uncommercial but quite watchable drama of adolescence. Not surprisingly, it failed to find an audience.
w Alan Ormsby d Tony Bill ph Michael D. Margulies m Dave Grusin pd Jackson de Govia
☆ Chris Makepeace, Adam Baldwin, Ruth Gordon, Matt Dillon, Martin Mull, John Houseman

My Boyfriend's Back
US   1993   84m   DeLuxe
Buena Vista/Touchstone (Sean S. Cunningham)

A high-school student, killed in a bungled robbery planned to impress a girl, returns as a zombie to demonstrate his undying love.
Ghoulish and unedifying horror.

w Dean Lorey d Bob Balaban ph Mac Ahlberg m Harry Manfredini pd Michael Hanan ed Michael Jablow
☆ Andrew Lowery, Traci Lind, Danny Zorn, Edward Herrmann, Mary Beth Hurt, Austin Pendleton, Cloris Leachman, Paxton Whitehead
'Lacking any redeeming quality, it's a matter of days before this tasteless pic is buried without trace in the sands of Hollywood.' – *Variety*

My Brilliant Career ***
Australia   1979   100m   Eastmancolor
NSW Film Corporation/Margaret Fink
📼

The daughter of an Australian bush farmer at the turn of the century dreams of the world beyond and writes a memoir.
Pleasing but very slow picture of a world gone by.
w Eleanor Witcombe novel Miles Franklin d Gillian Armstrong ph Don McAlpine m Nathan Waks
☆ Judy Davis, Sam Neill, Wendy Hughes, Robert Grubb, Max Cullen
🎦 Judy Davis

My Brother Jonathan
GB   1947   108m   bw
ABP (Warwick Ward)

The life of a small-town doctor who wanted to be a great surgeon.
Unobjectionable, unexciting novel-on-film with the typically British artificial studio look of the time.
w Leslie Landau, Adrian Arlington novel Francis Brett Young d Harold French ph Derick Williams m Hans May
☆ Michael Denison, Dulcie Gray, Ronald Howard, Stephen Murray

My Brother Talks to Horses
US   1946   93m   bw
MGM (Samuel Marx)

A boy who can talk to horses finds himself in demand by racetrack gamblers.
Well-mounted but uninspired whimsy with a fatal lack of pace.
w Morton Thompson novel Joe the Wounded Tennis Player by Morton Thompson d Fred Zinnemann ph Joseph Ruttenberg m Rudolph Kopp
☆ Butch Jenkins, Peter Lawford, Charlie Ruggles, Edward Arnold, Beverly Tyler, Spring Byington

My Brother's Keeper
GB   1948   91m   bw
GFD/Gainsborough (Anthony Darnborough)

Two convicts escape, handcuffed together; one is violent, the other innocent.
Pre-Defiant Ones social melodrama, quite well made but suffering from miscasting.
w Frank Harvey story Maurice Wiltshire d Alfred Roome, Roy Rich ph Gordon Lang m Clifton Parker
☆ Jack Warner, George Cole, Jane Hylton, David Tomlinson, Bill Owen, Raymond Lovell, Yvonne Owen, Beatrice Varley

My Buddy *
US   1944   67m   bw
Eddy White/Republic

A World War I veteran is forced into crime.
Not a new message, but a second feature with sincerity and conviction. A better title would have helped.
w Arnold Manoff, Prescott Chaplin d Steve Sekely
☆ Don Barry, Alexander Granach, Ruth Terry, Lynne Roberts, Emma Dunn, John Litel, George E. Stone

My Childhood ***
GB   1972   48m   bw
Connoisseur/BFI (Geoffrey Evans)
📼

An eight-year-old boy lives with his half-brother and ailing grandmother in dire poverty in a Scottish mining village.
Passionate, autobiographical account of a life of almost total bleakness observed with scrupulous honesty.
wd Bill Douglas ph Mick Campbell ed Brand Thumim
☆ Stephen Archibald, Hughie Restorick, Jean Taylor Smith, Karl Fieseler, Paul Kermack, Helena Gloag
'The story unfolds with pathos, tension and considerable humour.' – *MFB*

† The first part of an autobiographical trilogy that was followed by *My Ain Folk* and *My Way Home* (qqv).

My Cousin Rachel *
US   1952   98m   bw
TCF (Nunnally Johnson)

A Cornish gentleman dies in Italy after marrying a mysterious lady; when she comes to England she arouses the hostility, and love, of her husband's foster son.
Well-wrought but dramatically unsatisfactory Victorian melodrama from a bestseller; plenty of suspicion but no solution makes Rachel a dull girl.
w Nunnally Johnson novel Daphne du Maurier d Henry Koster ph Joseph LaShelle m Franz Waxman ad Lyle Wheeler, John DeCuir
☆ Olivia de Havilland, Richard Burton, John Sutton, Audrey Dalton, Ronald Squire
🔈 Joseph LaShelle; Richard Burton; art direction

My Cousin Vinny *
US   1992   119m   DeLuxe
TCF/Peter V. Miller Investment Corp. (Dale Launer, Paul Schiff)
🗜 📼 ⚭ 🎧

An inexperienced New York lawyer goes to Alabama to defend his cousin who is charged with murder.
Ramshackle comedy that raises an occasional smile and one or two laughs.
w Dale Launer d Jonathan Lynn ph Peter Deming m Randy Edelman pd Victoria Paul ed Tony Lombardo
☆ Joe Pesci, Ralph Macchio, Marisa Tomei, Mitchell Whitfield, Fred Gwynne, Lane Smith, Austin Pendleton, Bruce McGill, Maury Chaykin
'The bits and pieces never quite add up. Somewhere during this film's making I suspect that half the script was mysteriously lost down a street grating.' – *Nigel Andrews, Financial Times*
👥 Marisa Tomei

My Crasy Life
US   1992   98m   colour
BBC/FR3 (Daniel Marks, Cameron Allan)
American-Samoan members of a Californian street-gang talk about their violent lives.
Unilluminating mix of documentary and fiction about the inarticulate young being assimilated into a ghetto culture.
w Jean-Pierre Gorin, Howard Rodman d Jean-Pierre Gorin ph Babette Mangolte m Joyi Yuasa ed Brad Thumin
'An aggravatingly tedious docu-drama.' – *Variety*

'Lipstick and attitude – the girls from Echo Park are hard!'

My Crazy Life
US   1993   95m   DeLuxe
🗜 📼 ⚭
aka: *Mi Vida Loca*

In Los Angeles, Hispanic teenagers, members of a street gang, hang out, talk tough and try to make sense of their lives and the men they become involved with.
Voice-overs rob this account of much of its dramatic impact; the narrative interest is slight and the performances often amateurish despite their authenticity.
wd Allison Anders ph Rodrigo Garcia m John Taylor pd Jane Stewart ed Kathryn Himoff, Tracy Granger
☆ Angel Aviles, Seidy Lopez, Jacob Vargas, Mario Marron, Nelida Lopez, Jessie Borrego, Magali Alvarado
'Dramatically fuzzy and very flat visually and in performance.' – *Variety*

'She was everything the west was – young, fiery, exciting!'

My Darling Clementine ***
US   1946   97m   bw
TCF (Samuel G. Engel)
🗜 📼 ⚭

Wyatt Earp cleans up Tombstone and wipes out the Clanton gang at the OK corral.
Archetypal Western mood piece, full of nostalgia for times gone by and crackling with memorable scenes and characterizations.
w Samuel G. Engel, Winston Miller book Wyatt Earp, Frontier Marshal by Stuart N. Lake d John Ford ph Joe MacDonald m Cyril Mockridge

☆ Henry Fonda, Victor Mature, Walter Brennan, Linda Darnell, Cathy Downs, Tim Holt, Ward Bond, Alan Mowbray, John Ireland, Jane Darwell
'Every scene, every shot is the product of a keen and sensitive eye.' – *Bosley Crowther*
'Considerable care has gone to its period reconstruction, but the view is a poetic one.' – *Lindsay Anderson*

My Daughter Joy
GB   1950   81m   bw
London Films/Gregory Ratoff
US title: *Operation X*

In order to cement a new trade pact, an international financier plans to marry his daughter to the son of an African sultan.
Turgid melodrama swamping some good actors.
w Robert Thoeren, William Rose novel David Golder by Irene Neirowsky d Gregory Ratoff ph Georges Périnal m Raymond Gallois-Montbrun
☆ Edward G. Robinson, Peggy Cummins, Nora Swinburne, Richard Greene, Finlay Currie, Gregory Ratoff, Ronald Adam, Walter Rilla, James Robertson Justice, David Hutcheson

My Dear Miss Aldrich
US   1937   73m   bw
MGM

The glamorous new owner of a newspaper never agrees with its editor.
Skilful light comedy with good work all round.
w Herman Mankiewicz d George B. Seitz
☆ Maureen O'Sullivan, Walter Pidgeon, Edna May Oliver, Rita Johnson, Janet Beecher

My Dear Secretary
US   1948   96m   bw
Cardinal/UA

A secretary marries her boss and becomes jealous of his new secretary.
Slow-paced, frivolous romantic comedy.
wd Charles Martin
☆ Kirk Douglas, Laraine Day, Keenan Wynn, Rudy Vallee, Helen Walker, Florence Bates, Alan Mowbray

My Dinner with André *
US   1981   111m   Movielab
André Company/George W. George/Michael White
📼 ⚭ ⛑

Two men start a dinner table conversation which becomes a philosophical argument.
Curious two-hander which can please the right audience when it's in the mood; for selling tickets, forget it.
w Wallace Shawn, André Gregory d Louis Malle ph Jeri Sopanen m Allen Shawn
☆ Wallace Shawn, André Gregory, Jean Lenauer, Roy Butler
'A magical mystery tour of thoughts, dreams, fantasies and emotions.' – *Time Out*
'An adventure through a magically cracked looking glass.' – *San Francisco Chronicle*
'A dazzling cerebral comedy of ideas.' – *Los Angeles Times*

My Dream Is Yours
US   1949   101m   Technicolor
Warner (Michael Curtiz)
🗜 📼

A Hollywood talent scout discovers a new singer.
Competent, forgettable musical.
w Harry Kurnitz, Dane Lussier d Michael Curtiz ph Ernest Haller m Harry Warren ch Le Roy Prinz ly Ralph Blane
☆ Doris Day, Jack Carson, Lee Bowman, Adolphe Menjou, Eve Arden, S. Z. Sakall
† A remake of *Twenty Million Sweethearts*.

My English Grandfather **
USSR   1986   75m   colour/bw
Georgia Film Studios
aka: *Robinson Crusoe in Georgia*

A Russian composer dedicates his new symphony to his English grandfather, sent to Georgia to maintain the London–Delphi telephone line, who takes up residence in the three metres around a telephone post which remain British territory when the revolution comes.
Enjoyable and quirky drama, with ironic and comic overtones, which shuttles between the present, in colour, and the past, mainly in monochrome.

---

w Irakli Kvirikadze d Nana Djordjadze ph Levan Paatashvili m Enri Lolashvili ad Vakhtang Rurua
☆ Zhanri Lolashvili, Nineli Chankvetadze, Guram Pirtskhalava, Gudja Burduli, Rusudan Bolkvadze, Tiko Eliosidze

My Fair Lady ***

🏃 US 1964 175m Technicolor Super Panavision 70
CBS/Warner (Jack L. Warner)
▦ ⊚ ⊚ ⊙ ⌒

Musical version of *Pygmalion*, about a flower girl trained by an arrogant elocutionist to pass as a lady.
Careful, cold transcription of a stage success; cinematically quite uninventive when compared with Pygmalion *itself, but a pretty good entertainment.*
w Alan Jay Lerner play *Pygmalion* by Bernard Shaw d George Cukor ph Harry Stradling m Frederick Loewe md André Previn ch Hermes Pan ad Gene Allen ed William Ziegler cos Cecil Beaton
☆ Rex Harrison, Audrey Hepburn, Stanley Holloway, Wilfrid Hyde-White, Gladys Cooper, Jeremy Brett, Theodore Bikel, Isobel Elsom, Mona Washbourne, Walter Burke
'The property has been not so much adapted as elegantly embalmed.' – *Andrew Sarris*
† Audrey Hepburn's singing was dubbed by Marni Nixon. In the restored 30th-anniversary laser disc edition, Hepburn can be heard singing two songs – 'Wouldn't It Be Luvverly' and 'Show Me' – on alternate tracks on the disc.
🏆 best picture; George Cukor; Harry Stradling; Rex Harrison; André Previn (scoring of music); costumes; sound
⚜ Alan Jay Lerner; Stanley Holloway; Gladys Cooper; editing
Ⓣ best picture

My Family

US 1995 125m colour
Entertainment/New Line/Majestic/American Playhouse/American Zoetrope/Newcomm/Anna Thomas
▦ ⊙ ⊚
aka: *Mi Familia*
UK video title: *East L.A.*
The life of a Mexican family in California over three generations, from the 20s to the 80s.
A soft-centred domestic saga that never quite engages the heart or the mind.
w Gregory Nava, Anna Thomas d Gregory Nava ph Edward Lachman m Pepe Avila, Mark McKenzie pd Barry Robison ed Nancy Richardson
☆ Jimmy Smits, Esai Morales, Eduardo Lopez Rojas, Jenny Gago, Elpidia Carrillo, Lupe Ontiveros, Edward James Olmos, Scott Bakula
'More a superior television soap than a proper film.' – *Derek Malcolm, Guardian*
⚜ make-up

My Father Is Coming

Germany/US 1991 81m TVC Color
Out on a Limb/Hyane/Hyena (Monika Treut)
▦
A German would-be actress in New York auditions for a sex movie, makes friends with a transsexual and goes to bed with a Puerto Rican woman.
A movie without a redeeming feature, other than its short running time.
w Monika Treut, Bruce Benderson, Sarah Schulman d Monika Treut ph Elfi Mikesch m David Van Tieghem pd Robin Ford ed Steve Brown
☆ Alfred Edel, Shelley Kästner, Annie Sprinkle, Mery Lou Graulau, David Bronstein, Michael Massee
'A scrappy little film, ill-scripted, photographed and, in particular, directed, and the weird, but very likeable cast is the only reason to see it.' – *Sheila Johnston, Independent*
'Treut's film seems to condemn rather than celebrate the effects of implementing consumerist notions of choice within the field of sexuality.' – *Verina Glaessner, Sight and Sound*

My Father, the Hero

US 1994 90m Technicolor
Buena Vista/Touchstone/Cité (Jacques Bar, Jean-Louis Livi)
▦ ▦ ⊚
A young girl on holiday in the Caribbean pretends that her father is actually her lover.

Dull and corny comedy, with little appeal to any age group.
w Francis Veber, Charlie Peters d Steve Miner ph Daryn Okada m David Newman pd Christopher Nowak ed Marshall Harvey
☆ Gérard Depardieu, Katherine Heigl, Emma Thompson, Dalton James, Lauren Hutton, Faith Prince, Stephen Tobolowsky, Ann Hearn
'You don't have to be a black-polo-neck-wearing francophile to see that hardly a single remake of a French movie has been any good. Let us hope the flopping of this latest atrocity augurs the cessation of this insidious Hollywood habit.' – *Leslie Felperin Sharman, Sight and Sound*
† The film is a remake of *Mon Père, Ce Héros*, which also starred Gérard Depardieu.

My Father's Glory: see La Gloire de mon père

My Favorite Blonde ***

US 1942 78m bw
Paramount (Paul Jones)
A burlesque comic travelling by train helps a lady in distress and lives to regret it.
Smartly paced spy comedy thriller, one of its star's best vehicles.
w Don Hartman, Frank Butler, Melvin Frank, Norman Panama d Sidney Lanfield ph William Mellor m David Buttolph
☆ Bob Hope, Madeleine Carroll, Gale Sondergaard, George Zucco, Lionel Royce, Walter Kingsford, Victor Varconi

My Favorite Brunette *

US 1947 87m bw
Paramount/Hope Enterprises (Daniel Dare)
▦ ⊚ ⊚
A photographer gets mixed up with mobsters.
Pretty fair star vehicle which half-heartedly spoofs Farewell My Lovely.
w Edmund Beloin, Jack Rose d Elliott Nugent ph Lionel Lindon m Robert Emmett Dolan
☆ Bob Hope, Dorothy Lamour, Peter Lorre, Lon Chaney Jnr, John Hoyt, Charles Dingle, Reginald Denny

My Favorite Martian

🏃 US 1999 93m Technicolor
Buena Vista/Walt Disney (Robert Shapiro, Jerry Leider, Mark Toberoff)
▦
A TV producer rescues a stranded Martian, who has the ability to assume human form.
Yet another lumbering attempt to turn a forgotten sitcom into a movie, and yet more evidence that dead television comedy isn't worth reviving.
w Sherri Stoner, Deanna Oliver TV serial John L. Greene d Donald Petrie ph Thomas Ackerman m John Debney pd Sandy Veneziano ed Malcolm Campbell sp Phil Tippett, John T. Van Vliet; Alec Gillis, Tom Woodruff Jnr
☆ Christopher Lloyd, Jeff Daniels, Elizabeth Hurley, Daryl Hannah, Wallace Shawn, Christine Ebersole, Michael Lerner, Ray Walston
'The kind of leering, obnoxious picture that seizes you by the neck and gnaws at your skull like a giant, snot-nosed child.' – *New York Post*
† The TV series, starring Ray Walston and Bill Bixby, ran from 1963 to 1966.

My Favorite Spy

US 1942 86m bw
RKO
▦ ⊚
The bandleader Kay Kyser has to postpone his honeymoon when he is called up and set to spy-catching.
Fairly slick nonsense featuring a band popular at the time.
w Sig Herzig, William Bowers d Tay Garnett ph Robert de Grasse
☆ Kay Kyser, Ginny Simms, Ish Kabibble, Ellen Drew, Jane Wyman

My Favorite Spy *

US 1951 93m bw
Paramount (Paul Jones)
A burlesque comic is asked by the US government to pose as an international spy who happens to be his double.
Moderately funny star vehicle with more willing hands than good ideas. The chase finale however is worth waiting for.
w Edmund Hartmann, Jack Sher d Norman Z. McLeod ph Victor Milner m Victor Young

☆ Bob Hope, Hedy Lamarr, Francis L. Sullivan, Arnold Moss, Mike Mazurki, Luis Van Rooten

'The funniest, fastest honeymoon ever screened!'

My Favorite Wife ***

US 1940 88m bw
RKO (Leo McCarey)
▦ ⊚
A lady explorer returns after several shipwrecked years to find that her husband has married again.
A well-worn situation gets its brightest treatment in this light star vehicle.
w Sam and Bella Spewack, Leo McCarey d Garson Kanin ph Rudolph Maté m Roy Webb ad Van Nest Polglase ed Robert Wise
☆ Cary Grant, Irene Dunne, Randolph Scott, Gail Patrick, Ann Shoemaker, Donald MacBride
'One of those comedies with a glow on it.' – *Otis Ferguson*
† Other variations (qv): *Too Many Husbands, Our Wife, Three for the Show, Move Over Darling.*
⚜ story; Roy Webb; art direction

'I can't go on *live*! I'm a movie star, not an actor!'

My Favorite Year ***

US 1982 92m Metrocolor
MGM-UA/Brooksfilms/Michael Gruskoff
▦ ▦ ⊚
In 1954, a legendary Hollywood star noted for wine and women is unwisely invited to star in a television series.
A good-humoured and well-researched romp with a central character not too far removed from Errol Flynn.
w Norman Steinberg, Dennis Palumbo d Richard Benjamin ph Gerald Hirschfeld m Ralph Burns pd Charles Rosen ed Richard Chew
☆ Peter O'Toole, Mark Linn-Baker, Jessica Harper, Joseph Bologna, Bill Macy, Lainie Kazan, Lou Jacobi, Cameron Mitchell
'A field day for a wonderful bunch of actors.' – *Variety*
⚜ Peter O'Toole

My Fellow Americans

US 1996 101m
Warner/Peters/Storyline (Jon Peters)
▦ ⊚ ⊚ ⌒
Two ageing and antagonistic former presidents of the USA are forced to co-operate with one another when they find themselves targeted for assassination.
An uneasy mix of weak political satire and thriller, with the Odd Couple pairing of Lemmon as an uptight conservative and Garner as a libidinous liberal, swopping insults as they dodge bullets.
w E. Jack Kaplan, Richard Chapman, Peter Tolan d Peter Segal ph Julio Macat m William Ross pd James Bissell ed William Kerr
☆ Jack Lemmon, James Garner, Dan Aykroyd, John Heard, Sela Ward, Wilford Brimley, Everett McGill, Bradley Whitford, Lauren Bacall, James Rebhorn

My First 40 Years

Italy 1989 107m Technicolor
Columbia TriStar/CG Silver Film/Reteitalia (Mario Cecchi Gori, Vittorio Cecchi Gori)
A fashion designer recalls her numerous affairs on her fortieth birthday.
Charmless romantic drama, not helped by some inept dubbing.
w Enrico Vanzina, Carlo Vanzina *novel* I Miei Primi 40 Anni by Marina Ripa Di Meana d Carlo Vanzina ph Luigi Kuveiller m Umberto Smaila ad Mario Chiari ed Ruggero Mastroianni
☆ Carol Alt, Elliott Gould, Jean Rochefort, Pierre Cosso, Massimo Venturiello, Isabel Russinova, Paolo Quattrini, Riccardo Garrone, Capucine

My First Wife *

Australia 1984 98m colour
Artificial Eye/Dofine Productions/Film Victoria/Spectrafilm (Jane Ballantyne, Paul Cox)
▦
A composer is heart-stricken when his wife decides to leave him.
Passionate, emotionally painful study of relationships over two generations that comes to the somewhat pat conclusion that the family is everything.
w Paul Cox, Bob Ellis d Paul Cox ph Yuri Sokol m Gluck, Orff, Haydn and others pd Asher Bilu ed Tim Lewis

☆ John Hargreaves, Wendy Hughes, Lucy Angwin, David Cameron, Anna Jemison, Charles Tingwell, Betty Lucas, Robin Lovejoy

'I was a good girl – wasn't I?'

My Foolish Heart *

US 1949 98m bw
Samuel Goldwyn
A woman deceives her husband into thinking her forthcoming child is his.
A 'woman's picture' par excellence, and among the first to benefit from commercial plugging of a schmaltzy theme tune.
w Julius J. and Philip G. Epstein *story* J. D. Salinger d Mark Robson ph Lee Garmes m Victor Young
☆ Susan Hayward, Dana Andrews, Kent Smith, Robert Keith, Gigi Perreau, Lois Wheeler, Jessie Royce Landis
'Obviously designed to pull the plugs out of the tear glands and cause the ducts to overflow.' – *Bosley Crowther, New York Times*
'In its dry-eyed moments, this damp fable is brightened by some well-written patches of wryly amusing dialogue.' – *Time*
⚜ Susan Hayward; title song (mVictor Young, lyNed Washington)

My Forbidden Past

US 1951 81m bw
RKO (Polan Banks)
▦
A New Orleans beauty seeks vengeance when her cousin prevents her marriage.
Stuffy period melodrama with vigorous performances.
w Marion Parsonnet *novel* Polan Banks d Robert Stevenson ph Harry J. Wild m Frederick Hollander ad Albert S. D'Agostino
☆ Ava Gardner, Melvyn Douglas, Robert Mitchum, Janis Carter, Lucile Watson

My Friend Flicka *

🏃 US 1943 89m Technicolor
TCF (Ralph Dietrich)
▦
Adventures of a young boy and his pet colt.
Winsome boy-and-horse story, one of the most popular family films of the forties. Sequel 1945 with virtually the same cast: Thunderhead Son of Flicka.
w Lillie Hayward *novel* Mary O'Hara d Harold Schuster ph Dewey Wrigley m Alfred Newman
☆ Roddy McDowall, Preston Foster, Rita Johnson, James Bell, Jeff Corey

My Friend Irma *

US 1949 103m bw
Paramount/Hal B. Wallis
Dumb blonde Irma's con man boyfriend lends her apartment to two soda jerks.
Comic strip humour responsible for the screen début of Martin and Lewis. Sequel 1950: My Friend Irma Goes West.
w Cy Howard, Parke Levy *radio show* Cy Howard d George Marshall ph Leo Tover m Roy Webb
☆ Marie Wilson, John Lund, Diana Lynn, *Dean Martin, Jerry Lewis*, Don Defore, Hans Conried, Kathryn Givney

My Friend Irma Goes West

US 1950 90m bw
Paramount/Hal Wallis
Irma's friends Steve and Seymour are offered a Hollywood contract and have adventures on the train.
Witless farce of mild historical interest.
w Cy Howard, Parke Levy d Hal Walker ph Lee Garmes m Leigh Harline
☆ John Lund, Marie Wilson, Dean Martin, Jerry Lewis, Diana Lynn, Corinne Calvet, Lloyd Corrigan
'The general mental level can be judged from the fact that the performance of the chimpanzee seems the most natural thing in the film.' – *MFB*

My Friend Ivan Lapshin **

USSR 1986 99m bw/colour
Metro/Lenfilm
Memories of life in a provincial Russian town in the 1930s, where a harassed policeman pursues a criminal gang.
Made in 1982, but not shown for four years, this is a well-observed, well-directed and acted slice-of-Soviet-life.

w Eduard Volodarski d Alexei Gherman
ph Valeri Fedosov m Arkadi Gagulachvili
ad Yuri Pougatch ed L. Semionovi

☆ Andrei Boltnev, Nina Rousianova, Andrei
Mironov, Alexei Zharkov, Z. Adamovich, A.
Filippenko

'It takes a girl like Rita to play a gal like Sal!'
My Gal Sal *
US   1942   103m   Technicolor
TCF (Robert Bassler)
The career and romances of songwriter Paul
Dresser.
*Conventional 1890s musical biopic, more vigorous and
likeable than most.*
w Seton I. Miller, Darrell Ware, Karl Tunberg
book *My Brother Paul* by Theodore Dreiser
d Irving Cummings ph Ernest Palmer md Alfred
Newman ad Richard Day, Joseph Wright
☆ Rita Hayworth, Victor Mature, John Sutton,
Carole Landis, James Gleason, Phil Silvers, Walter
Catlett, Mona Maris, Frank Orth
† The title role was intended for Alice Faye, but
she was pregnant. Irene Dunne was too busy, Mae
West refused, and Betty Grable didn't test well.
†† Rita Hayworth's singing was dubbed by Nan
Wynn.
▣ Richard Day, Joseph Wright
▣ Alfred Newman

My Geisha
US   1962   120m   Technirama
Paramount/Steve Parker
▣
A director makes a film in Japan; his wife disguises
herself as a geisha and gets the leading role.
Silly, overstretched comedy with pretty locations.
w Norman Krasna d Jack Cardiff ph Shunichuro
Nakao m Franz Waxman
☆ Shirley Maclaine, Yves Montand, Robert
Cummings, Edward G. Robinson, Yoko Tani

My Giant
US   1998   103m   Technicolor
Columbia/Castle Rock/Face (Billy Crystal)
▣▣ ▣ ▣
An unsuccessful agent discovers a giant-sized
Romanian and takes him to America to make him
into a movie star.
*Strangely unappealing drama that veers between
mawkishness and acerbity and seems uncertain about
the point of its odd central relationship.*
w David Seltzer, Billy Crystal d Michael Lehman
ph Michael Coulter m Marc Shaiman pd Jackson
DeGovia ed Stephen Semel
☆ Billy Crystal, Kathleen Quinlan, Gheorghe
Muresan, Joanna Pacula, Zane Carney, Rider
Strong, Steven Seagal, Harold Gould, Doris
Roberts, Philip Sterling, Heather Thomas
'An uneven film with limited commercial
appeal.' – *Variety*

'Mac's back and he's not alone...'
My Girl
▣▣ US   1991   102m   Technicolor
Columbia TriStar/Imagine (Brian Grazer)
▣▣ ▣ ▣
In the 1970s, the 11-year-old daughter of an
undertaker comes to terms with her widowed
father's romance and the death of a friend.
*Slick, over-sentimental account of growing up, part of
Hollywood's early 90s cycle of films centred on
children. It provided the first screen kiss for Culkin.*
w Laurice Elehwany d Howard Zieff ph Paul
Elliott m James Newton Howard pd Joseph T.
Garrity ed Wendy Greene Bricmont
☆ Dan Aykroyd, Jamie Lee Curtis, Macaulay
Culkin, Anna Chlumsky, Richard Masur, Griffin
Dunne, Ann Nelson
'As pleasant as a warm summer day and as
ephemeral.' – *Variety*
'A hilarious mix of schmaltz, angst and shlock.
In other words a joy to watch. One asks
hopefully, it can't get worse, surely, can it? But it
does.' – *Alexander Walker, London Evening
Standard*

My Girl II
▣▣ US   1994   99m   colour
Columbia TriStar/Imagine (Brian Grazer)
▣▣ ▣ ▣
In the mid-70s, a young teenage girl travels to Los
Angeles to find out more about her mother, who
died giving birth to her.

*Enjoyable enough sentimental domestic drama,
although its appeal is likely to be limited to those of the
same gender and age group as its heroine.*
w Janet Kovalcik d Howard Zieff ph Paul Elliott
m Cliff Eidelman pd Charles Rosen ed Wendy
Greene Bricmont
☆ Dan Aykroyd, Jamie Lee Curtis, Anna
Chlumsky, Richard Masur, Austin O'Brien,
Christine Ebersole, Aubrey Morris, Gerrit Graham,
Keone Young
'Pleasant, painless and, as sequels go, genuinely
ambitious in its efforts to be a continuation
rather than just a retread.' – *Joe Leydon, Variety*

My Girl Tisa ***
US   1948   95m   bw
United States Pictures (Milton Sperling)
An immigrant girl in New York in the 1890s falls
for an aspiring politician, is threatened with
deportation but saved by the intervention of
Theodore Roosevelt.
*Charming period fairy tale with excellent background
detail and attractive performances.*
w Allen Boretz play Lucille S. Prumbs, Sara B.
Smith d Elliott Nugent ph Ernest Haller m Max
Steiner
☆ Lilli Palmer, Sam Wanamaker, Alan Hale, Stella
Adler, Akim Tamiroff

My Girlfriend's Boyfriend *
France   1987   102m   colour
Artificial Eye/AAA/Les Films Du Losange (Margaret
Menegoz)
▣▣
original title: *L'Ami de Mon Amie*
Two young couples find themselves attracted to
each other's partner.
*Charming conversation piece, the sixth in Rohmer's
series of Comedies and Proverbs.*
wd Eric Rohmer ph Bernard Lutic, Sabine
Lanceline m Jean-Louis Valero ed Luisa Garcia
☆ Emmanuelle Chaulet, Sophie Renoir, Anne-
Laure Meury, Eric Vieillard, François-Eric Gendron
'Fluff of a rarefied order. The movie is so rigorous
and elegant and extreme that it seems, finally, to
be about its own weightlessness – not so much a
thin romantic comedy as a comic meditation on
the thinness of romance.' – *Terrence Rafferty,
New Yorker*

My Gun Is Quick
US   1957   90m   bw
United Artists/Victor Saville
Mike Hammer investigates the murder of a bar girl
and is led to rival gangs of jewel thieves.
*Impenetrably plotted but quite violent brew of typical
Spillane ingredients.*
w Richard Collins, Richard Powell novel Mickey
Spillane d George A. White, Phil Victor
ph Harry Neumann m Marlin Skiles
☆ Robert Bray, Whitney Blake, Pat Donahue,
Pamela Duncan, Booth Colman

My Heart Belongs to Daddy
US   1942   78m   bw
Sol C. Siegel/Paramount
A cabby helps a pregnant widow to find shelter in
the home of a professor.
Unsparkling B romance with a totally unrelated title.
w F. Hugh Herbert d Robert Siodmak
☆ Richard Carlson, Martha O'Driscoll, Cecil
Kellaway, Frances Gifford, Florence Bates

My Heart Goes Crazy: see London Town

My Heart Is Calling
GB   1935   91m   bw
Cine-Allianz (Ivor Montagu, Arnold Pressburger)
An opera singer falls for a stowaway to Monte
Carlo.
Musical trifle with little to be said for or against it.
w Sidney Gilliat story Ernst Marischka
d Carmine Gallone ph Glen MacWilliams
m Robert Stolz
☆ Jan Kiepura, Marta Eggerth, Sonnie Hale,
Hugh Wakefield, Ernest Thesiger, Marie Lohr

My Hero: see A Southern Yankee

My Heroes Have Always Been Cowboys
US   1991   106m   DeLuxe
Samuel Goldwyn (Martin Poll, E. K. Gaylord II)
▣▣ ▣ ▣
A rodeo rider, returning home to look after his
ageing father, resumes his relationship with an old

girlfriend and decides to try for the big time once
more.
*Moderate but unoriginal drama of domestic wranglings,
with some enjoyable bull-riding footage at the climax.*
w Joel Don Humphreys d Stuart Rosenberg
ph Bernd Heinl m James Horner ed Dennis M.
Hill
☆ Scott Glenn, Kate Capshaw, Ben Johnson, Tess
Harper, Balthazar Getty, Gary Busey, Mickey
Rooney, Clarence Williams III, Dub Taylor, Clu
Gulager
'Pic casts its lot with the underdog in true
American fashion, but is bland and unexciting.'
– *Variety*

My Hustler *
US   1965   70m   bw
Vaughan/Factory Films (Andy Warhol)
Two men and two women compete for the sexual
attentions of a blond hustler.
*An apparently unedited two reels of film that, for all its
apparent casualness and spontaneity, maintains its
interest.*
w Chuck Wein d Andy Warhol ph Andy
Warhol
☆ Paul America, Ed Hood, Joseph Campbell,
John McDermott, Genevieve Charbon, Dorothy
Dean
'A complex and unified whole, in which the
form and the content relate in new and
surprising ways. The film is the clearest guide we
have to the innovations which are uniquely
Warhol's.' – *Tony Rayns, MFB*
'The downer, and it is a major one, is that these
shallow, one-dimensional people are worth
examining at all. They, and their situation, like
their existence, are not really worth a second
look, let alone seventy minutes of film.' – *Peter
Buckley, Films and Filming*

My Kingdom for a Cook
US   1943   81m   bw
P. J. Wolfson/Columbia
An English author on a US lecture tour steals his
hostess's cook.
*Curious comedy with the star seeming to play an
unsympathetic Alexander Woollcott type.*
w Harold Goldman, Andrew Solt, Joseph
Hoffman, Jack Henley d Richard Wallace
☆ Charles Coburn, Marguerite Chapman, Bill
Carter, Isobel Elsom, Ed Gargan

My Learned Friend ***
GB   1943   76m   bw
Ealing (Michael Balcon)
A shady lawyer is last on a mad ex-convict's
murder list of those who helped get him convicted.
*Madcap black farce, plot-packed and generally
hilarious; the star's last vehicle, but one of his best, with
superbly timed sequences during a pantomime and on
the face of Big Ben.*
w John Dighton, Angus MacPhail d Basil Dearden
Will Hay ph Wilkie Cooper m Ernest Irving
ad Michael Relph
☆ Will Hay, Claude Hulbert, Mervyn Johns, Ernest
Thesiger, Charles Victor, Lloyd Pearson, Maudie
Edwards, G. H. Mulcaster, Gibb McLaughlin

My Left Foot **
GB   1989   103m   Technicolor
Palace/Ferndale Films/Granada TV
International/Radio Telefis Eireann (Noel Pearson)
▣▣ ▣ ▣ ▣ ▣
Biopic of the Irish writer and painter Christy
Brown, crippled from birth by cerebral palsy.
*Pedestrian narrative, relying on cinematic clichés, but
enlivened by the intensity of Day-Lewis's performance
and some good ensemble acting.*
w Shane Connaughton, Jim Sheridan
book Christy Brown d Jim Sheridan ph Jack
Conroy m Elmer Bernstein pd Austen Spriggs
ed J. Patrick Duffner
☆ Daniel Day-Lewis, Ray McAnally, Brenda
Fricker, Ruth McCabe, Fiona Shaw, Eanna
MacLiam, Alison Whelan, Declan Croghan, Hugh
O'Conor, Cyril Cusack
▣ Daniel Day-Lewis; Brenda Fricker
▣ best picture; best director; best adapted
screenplay
▣ Daniel Day-Lewis; Ray McAnally (as
supporting actor)

My Life
US   1993   116m   Technicolor
Guild/Zucker Brothers (Jerry Zucker, Bruce Joel Rubin,
Hunt Lowry)
▣▣ ▣ ▣ ▣
A man dying of cancer decides to make a
videotape explaining himself to his unborn son.
*A film that is interesting as a social document, in
articulating American attitudes to life and its
championing of childish attitudes, but which is much
less successful as a movie, content to evoke easy tears.*
wd Bruce Joel Rubin ph Peter James m John
Barry pd Neil Spisak ed Richard Chew
☆ Michael Keaton, Nicole Kidman, Bradley
Whitford, Queen Latifah, Michael Constantine,
Rebecca Schull, Mark Lowenthal, Haing S. Ngor
'The sincere, often touching story tugs
shamelessly at the heart strings.' – *Variety*
'This bravely sentimental Hollywood film misses
the mark.' – *Derek Malcolm, Guardian*
'The sort of New Age film that believes in
everything and nothing at the same time, and
turns every emotion into a therapy-wallow.' –
Adam Mars-Jones, Independent

My Life and Times with Antonin
Artaud *
France   1993   90m   bw
Metro Tartan/Archipel 33/Laura/La Sept/France 2
(Denis Freyd)
▣
original title: *En compagnie d'Antonin Artaud*
In 1946, an unsuccessful poet becomes a friend of
Artaud, the writer and actor, on his release from
the asylum where he has been held for nine years.
*An understated biopic of the last two years of Artaud's
life, as witnessed by a young admirer; despite its
portrait of a driven, self-obsessed man only slightly
sane, it has both charm and wit.*
w Gérard Mordillat, Jérôme Prieur book Jacques
Prevel d Gérard Mordillat ph François Catonné
m Jean-Claude Petit ad Jean-Pierre Clech
ed Sophie Rouffio
☆ Sami Frey, Marc Barbé, Julie Jézéquel, Valérie
Jeannet, Clotilde de Bayser, Charlotte Valandrey
'Compulsively told, its (sometimes heavyweight)
intellectualizing never fails to engage both the
mind and the eye.' – *Nigel Robinson, Film Review*

My Life as a Dog **
Sweden   1985   101m   Fujicolour
Svensk Filmindustri/Film-Teknik
▣▣ ▣ ▣ ▣
12-year-old Ingemar learns to cope with his
mother's illness and death, and his own propensity
for getting into trouble, while staying with his aunt
and uncle in the country.
*By turns painful and funny, the film manages to
achieve genuine charm while steering clear of
sentimentality.*
w Lasse Hallström, Reidar Jonsson, Brasse
Brännström, Per Berglund novel Reidar Jonsson
d Lasse Hallström ph Jörgen Persson, Rolf
Lindström m Björn Isfält
☆ Anton Glanzelius, Manfred Serner, Anki
Lidén, Tomas von Bromssen, Melinda Kinnaman,
Ing-Marie Carlsson
▣ best director; best adapted screenplay

My Life with Caroline *
US   1941   81m   bw
RKO (Lewis Milestone)
An understanding husband thinks his high-spirited
wife may be having an affair.
*Very minor romantic comedy with an agreeable air but
no substance whatever.*
w John Van Druten, Arnold Belgard d Lewis
Milestone ph Victor Milner m Werner Heymann
☆ Ronald Colman, Anna Lee, Reginald Gardiner,
Charles Winninger, Gilbert Roland

My Little Chickadee *
US   1939   83m   bw
Universal (Lester Cowan)
▣ ▣
A shady lady and an incompetent cardsharp
unmask a villain in the old West.
*A clash of comedy personalities which is affectionately
remembered but in truth does not play very well apart
from the odd line.*
w Mae West, W. C. Fields d Edward Cline
ph Joseph Valentine m Frank Skinner
md Charles Previn
☆ Mae West, W. C. Fields, Joseph Calleia, Dick
Foran, Margaret Hamilton

'It obstinately refuses to gather momentum.' – *The Times*

'A classic among bad movies … the satire never really gets off the ground. But the ground is such an honest mixture of dirt, manure and corn that at times it is fairly aromatic.' – *Pauline Kael, 1968*

My Little Girl *
US 1986 117m colour
Hemdale (Ismail Merchant)
🖭 💿

A privileged teenager encounters problems when she goes to work at a centre for children in care.
Well-acted, moderately engaging drama of innocence and experience.
w Connie Kaiserman, Nan Mason d Connie Kaiserman ph Pierre Lhomme m Richard Robbins pd Dan Leigh ed Katherine Wenning
☆ James Earl Jones, Geraldine Page, Mary Stuart Masterson, Anne Meara, Pamela Payton Wright, Peter Michael Goetz, Peter Gallagher, Erika Alexander, Traci Lin

My Little Pony
🎠 US 1986 100m Technicolor
Sunbow/Hasbro
🖭

The inhabitants of Ponyland fear the wicked witch Hydia.
Immensely distended cartoon meant to plug a fashionable line of children's dolls.
w George Arthur Bloom d Michael Jones
† Animated in Japan.

My Love Came Back
US 1940 85m bw
Warner
🖭

A millionaire helps the career of a pretty young violinist.
Palatable comedy of its day, promptly forgotten.
w Robert Buckner, Ivan Goff, Earl Baldwin d Curtis Bernhardt
☆ Olivia de Havilland, Jeffrey Lynn, Charles Winninger, Eddie Albert, Spring Byington, S. Z. Sakall, Jane Wyman

'A Modern Girl Having A Modern Good Time.'
My Lucky Star *
US 1938 84m bw
TCF (Harry Joe Brown)
A shopgirl is innocently caught in a compromising situation with the owner's son.
Fluffy comedy, acceptable as a background for skating sequences.
w Harry Tugend, Jack Yellen story Karl Tunberg, Don Ettlinger, pd Roy del Ruth ph John Mescall md Louis Silvers songs Mack Gordon, Harry Revel
☆ Sonja Henie, Richard Greene, Joan Davis, Buddy Ebsen, Cesar Romero, Arthur Treacher, George Barbier, Louise Hovick, Billy Gilbert

'The characters act and talk like living people!'
My Man
US 1928 85m bw part talkie
Warner
A poor girl becomes a Broadway star.
Lachrymose and technically primitive début for the ebullient Fanny Brice.
w Joe Jackson story Robert Lord, Darryl F. Zanuck d Archie Mayo
☆ Fanny Brice, Guinn Williams, André de Segurola, Edna Murphy

My Man and I
US 1952 99m bw
MGM (Stephen Ames)
A Mexican farm labourer, proud of his American citizenship, is drawn into trouble.
Eccentric melodrama in which all the native Americans are whores, cheats or murderers; well enough made but not very interesting.
w John Fante, Jack Leonard d William Wellman ph William Mellor m David Buttolph
☆ Ricardo Montalban, Shelley Winters, Claire Trevor, Wendell Corey

My Man Godfrey ***
US 1936 90m bw
Universal (Gregory La Cava)
🖭 💿

A zany millionaire family invite a tramp to be their butler and find he is richer than they are.

Archetypal Depression concept which is also one of the best of the thirties crazy sophisticated comedies, though its pacing today seems somewhat unsure.
w Morrie Ryskind, Eric Hatch, Gregory La Cava d Gregory La Cava ph Ted Tetzlaff m Charles Previn
☆ Carole Lombard, William Powell, Alice Brady, Mischa Auer, Eugene Pallette, Gail Patrick, Alan Mowbray, Jean Dixon
§ script; Gregory La Cava (as director); Carole Lombard; William Powell; Alice Brady; Mischa Auer

'The butler did it! He made every lady in the house oh so very happy!'
My Man Godfrey
US 1957 92m Technicolor Cinemascope
U-I (Ross Hunter)
Tepid remake which without the period background, and in unsuitable wide screen, raises very few laughs.
w Everett Freeman, Peter Berneis, William Bowers d Henry Koster ph William Daniels m Frank Skinner
☆ June Allyson, David Niven, Jessie Royce Landis, Jay Robinson, Robert Keith, Martha Hyer, Eva Gabor

My Marriage
US 1936 68m bw
TCF
A girl finds that her marriage is not accepted by her high society in-laws.
Satisfactory woman's picture.
w Frances Hyland d George Archainbaud
☆ Claire Trevor, Kent Taylor, Pauline Frederick, Paul Kelly, Thomas Beck, Beryl Mercer
'Will get by with family audiences.' – *Variety*

My Mother My Daughter
US 1981 75m Eastmancolor
Golden Gate
A young feminist photographer, who has a stormy relationship with her mother, decides to leave San Francisco to live in Alaska.
Packaged tedium, a domestic non-drama that looks and sounds like a home movie made by people with no interest in movies and no ability as actors (Shelley Winters excepted, although her strident performance is one of the worst of her career).
wd Nadia Werba ph John Newby ed Mauro Bonanni
☆ Shelley Winters, Alice Werblowsky, Ann Ward, Joshua Stein, Mary Wynn, Sean Kilcoyne

My Mother's Castle: see Le Château de ma Mère

My Mother's Courage *
Germany/Austria/GB 1995 90m colour
Clarence/Sentana/Little Bird/Vega (Michael Verhoeven)
An author, celebrating his 80th birthday, explains that we are to see a film based on his novel about his mother's escape from a Nazi train taking her from Budapest to Auschwitz.
A small-scale sidelight on the horror of the concentration camps, effective and moving for its focus on a fortunate individual.
wd Michael Verhoeven novel George Tabori ph Michael Epp, Theo Bierkens m Julian Nott, Simon Verhoeven ed David Freeman
☆ Pauline Collins, Ulrich Tukur, Heirbert Sasse, Natalie Morse, Robert Giggenbach, Günther Bothur, Simon Verhoeven, George Tabori
'Achieves its aims with something of a twinkle in its eye. For that, it's rather remarkable, in its understated way.' – *Nick Kimberley, Sight and Sound*

My Name Is Joe ***
GB/Germany 1998 105m colour
Parallax/Road Movies (Rebecca O'Brien)
💿 🖭

In Glasgow, a reformed alcoholic ruins his developing relationship with a nurse when he agrees to carry drugs for a local gangster in order to help a friend stay out of trouble.
Grim, compassionate account of deprivation, and the desperation of poverty, in which only the energy of Mullan's performance offers any optimism for the future.
w Paul Laverty d Ken Loach ph Barry Ackroyd m George Fenton pd Martin Johnson ed Jonathan Morris

☆ Peter Mullan, Louise Goodall, David McKay, Annemarie Kennedy, David Hayman, Gary Lewis, Lorraine McIntosh
'Ken Loach works very near the top of his form, his angrily unblinkered vision of life at the rough end of modern Britain tempered with humanity, humour and a storyline that could almost come from a classic screwball romantic comedy.' – *Kim Newman, Empire*
† Peter Mullan won the best actor award at the Cannes Film Festival of 1998.
†† The film was subtitled for American audiences.

My Name Is Julia Ross **
US 1945 65m bw
Columbia
A girl is kidnapped and forced to impersonate an heiress.
A very good second feature which has been culted into a reputation beyond its worth, though it is undeniably slick and entertaining.
w Muriel Roy Bolton novel The Woman in Red by Anthony Gilbert d Joseph H. Lewis ph Burnett Guffey md Mischa Bakaleinikoff
☆ Nina Foch, Dame May Whitty, George Macready, Roland Varno, Doris Lloyd
'A superior, well-knit thriller.' – *Don Miller*
'A likeable, unpretentious, generally successful attempt to turn good trash into decently artful entertainment.' – *James Agee*

My Name Is Nobody *
Italy/France/West Germany 1973 116m
Technicolor Panavision
Gala/Rafran/Jacques Leitienne/Alcinter/Société Imp. Ex. Ci./Rialto (Claudio Mancini)
🖭 🎧
original title: *Il mio nome è Nessuno*
A young admirer persuades an ageing gunfighter to end his career in an explosive fashion.
This is less a conventional Western and more a comic horse opera, complete with a tombstone bearing the name of Sam Peckinpah and with Wagner's Ride of the Valkyrie, scored country and western style, accompanying the 150-strong Wild Bunch as they thunder by. Along the way it makes the occasional interesting comment about the reality and the mythology of the West.
w Ernesto Gastaldi story Fulvio Morsella, Ernesto Gastaldi, from an idea by Sergio Leone d Tonino Valerii pd Giuseppe Ruzzolini, Armando Nannuzzi m Ennio Morricone ad Gianni Polidori ed Nino Baragli
☆ Henry Fonda, Terence Hill (Mario Girotti), Jean Martin, Piero Lulli, Leo Gordon, Neil Summers, R. G. Armstrong, Steve Kanaly, Geoffrey Lewis
'Constitutes an explicit, thoroughgoing critique of Sam Peckinpah's work up to 1970, and if its own whimsical/elegiac tone is closer to the romantic comedy of Cable Hogue than to the romantic tragedies of Major Dundee and The Wild Bunch, then that signifies the warmth of its engagement with its subject rather than any reluctance to face up to Peckinpah's capacity for nihilism.' – *Tony Rayns, MFB*

My New Gun
US 1992 99m Foto-Kem
Feature/IRS (Michael Flynn)
💿 🖭 💿
A housewife finds that her life becomes full of danger after her husband buys her a gun and she lends it to her neighbour.
A one-joke suburban sitcom that misses most of its targets.
wd Stacy Cochran ph Ed Lachman m Pat Irwin pd Tony Corbett ed Camilla Toniolo
☆ James LeGros, Diane Lane, Stephen Collins, Tess Harper, Bruce Altman, Maddie Corman, Phillip Seymour, Bill Raymond
'Feeble farrago … flimsily inept.' – *Tom Hutchinson, Film Review*
'In a word? Dull.' – *Independent*

My Night with Maud: see Ma Nuit chez Maud

My Old Dutch
GB 1934 82m bw
Gainsborough
Ageing Cockney parents see their son die a hero.
Historically interesting sentimental wallow, built around a popular song; very primitive by most standards.

w Bryan Wallace, Marjorie Gaffney, Mary Murillo, Michael Hogan d Sinclair Hill ph Leslie Rowson
☆ Gordon Harker, Betty Balfour, Michael Hogan, Florrie Forde, Finlay Currie, Felix Aylmer
† A 1915 version had starred the original singer, Albert Chevalier, with Florence Turner and Henry Edwards.

My Old Man's a Fireman: see The Chief

My Outlaw Brother
US 1951 78m bw
Eagle Lion
🖭
A young man is shocked to find that his elder brother is a notorious bandit.
Glum little semi-Western, unpersuasively cast.
w Gene Fowler Jnr d Elliott Nugent
☆ Mickey Rooney, Robert Preston, Robert Stack, Wanda Hendrix

'Wherever, Whatever, Have a nice day.'
My Own Private Idaho *
US 1991 102m Alpha Cine
New Line (Laurie Parker)
💿 🖭 💿
A narcoleptic male prostitute makes friends with a slumming rich youth.
A variation on Shakespeare's Henry IV, complete with a seductive but dangerous Falstaffian figure, which becomes a distracting device, lessening the film's impact.
wd Gus Van Sant ph Eric Alan Edwards, John Campbell pd David Brisbin ed Curtiss Clayton
☆ River Phoenix, Keanu Reeves, James Russo, William Richert, Rodney Harvey, Michael Parker, Udo Kier
'One of those ambitious, over-reaching disappointments that is more interesting than some conservative successes.' – *Variety*
'It's a beautiful disaster, like a bomb test in the middle of nowhere.' – *New Yorker*

'Desperately loved by two men – father and son!'
My Own True Love
US 1948 84m bw
Paramount (Val Lewton)
A lonely man home from the war quarrels with his son over a girl twenty years younger than himself.
Minor romantic drama, competently but coldly presented.
w Arthur Kober novel Yolanda Foldes d Compton Bennett ph Charles Lang m Robert Emmett Dolan
☆ Phyllis Calvert, Melvyn Douglas, Philip Friend, Wanda Hendrix, Binnie Barnes

My Pal Gus
US 1952 84m bw
TCF (Stanley Rubin)
A business man has a five-year-old problem son and in sorting him out falls in love with his schoolteacher.
Unrewarding domestic drama with actors who look as though they would rather be somewhere else.
w Fay and Michael Kanin d Robert Parrish ph Leo Tover m Leigh Harline
☆ Richard Widmark, Joanne Dru, Audrey Totter, George Winslow, Joan Banks, Regis Toomey, Ludwig Donath

My Pal Trigger
🎠 US 1946 79m bw
Armand Schaefer/Republic
A cowboy tracks down the man who killed his horse's sire.
Folksy Western drama, a cut above the usual Rogers episode.
w Jack Townley, John K. Butler d Frank McDonald
☆ Roy Rogers, Dale Evans, Jack Holt, George 'Gabby' Hayes, Roy Barcroft

My Reputation
US 1946 96m bw
Warner (Henry Blanke)
A widow is talked about for dispensing too soon with her weeds.
Dim drama, hastily shot on familiar sets with a reach-me-down script.
w Catherine Turney novel Instruct My Sorrows by Clare Jaynes d Curtis Bernhardt ph James Wong Howe m Max Steiner

☆ Barbara Stanwyck, George Brent, Warner Anderson, Lucile Watson, John Ridgely, Eve Arden, Jerome Cowan, Esther Dale, Scotty Beckett

My Science Project
US   1985   91m   Technicolor
Touchstone/Silver Screen Partners
▤   ◕~

A high school student investigates an old UFO and finds an energy-absorbing machine which can materialize objects from the past and future.
Disney-style fare with teenage sex: the mixture may not be for many.
wd Jonathan R. Betuel ph David M. Walsh
m Peter Bernstein
☆ John Stockwell, Danielle von Zerneck, Fisher Stevens, Raphael Sbarge, Richard Masur, Dennis Hopper

My Sin
US   1931   79m   bw
Paramount
A drunken lawyer helps a woman who has shot her husband.
Turgid melodrama which failed to make a screen idol of its star.
w Owen Davis, Adelaide Heilbron
story Frederick Jackson d George Abbott
☆ Tallulah Bankhead, Fredric March, Harry Davenport, Scott Kolk, Ann Sutherland
'Fair returns will be top.' – *Variety*

My Sister Eileen *
US   1942   96m   bw
Columbia (Max Gordon)
▤   ◕~

Two Ohio girls come to New York and live with some zany friends in a Greenwich Village basement apartment.
Rather strained high jinks which were, not surprisingly, later musicalized.
w Ruth McKinney, Joseph Fields, Jerome Chodorov book Ruth McKinney d Alexander Hall ph Joseph Walker md Morris Stoloff
☆ Rosalind Russell, Janet Blair, Brian Aherne, Allyn Joslyn, George Tobias, Elizabeth Patterson, June Havoc
♟ Rosalind Russell

'Gayest Show Ever To Go Singing Across The CinemaScope Screen!'

My Sister Eileen *
US   1955   108m   Technicolor   Cinemascope
Columbia (Fred Kohlmar)
▤   ◕~

Musical version of the above, via a Broadway show.
Watchable but hardly stimulating.
w Blake Edwards, Richard Quine play Joseph Fields, Jerome Chodorov d Richard Quine ph Charles Lawton Jnr m George Duning md Morris Stoloff ch Bob Fosse songs Jule Styne, Leo Robin
☆ Betty Garrett, Janet Leigh, Jack Lemmon, Bob Fosse, Kurt Kasznar, Horace MacMahon, Dick York
'Even those well-acquainted with all of the material will find a freshness here that assures acceptance.' – *Variety*

My Six Convicts *
US   1952   104m   bw
Columbia/Stanley Kramer
A psychologist joins the staff of an American prison and gains the trust of six inmates.
Moderately interesting semi-documentary melodrama marred by a conventional prison break climax.
w Michael Blankfort book Donald Powell Wilson d Hugo Fregonese ph Guy Roe m Dmitri Tiomkin
☆ John Beal, Millard Mitchell, Gilbert Roland, Marshall Thompson, Regis Toomey

My Six Loves
US   1963   101m   Technicolor
Paramount/Gant Gaither
A musical comedy star goes to the country for a rest and with the help of the local minister adopts six scruffy children.
Icky sentimental comedy for the easily pleased.
w John Fante, Joseph Calvelli, William Wood d Gower Champion ph Arthur E. Arling m Walter Scharf songs Jimmy Van Heusen, Sammy Cahn
☆ Debbie Reynolds, David Janssen, Cliff Robertson, Eileen Heckart

---

'Enough to make you settle for cyclamates – or cyanide.' – *Judith Crist, 1973*

My Son Alone: see *American Empire*

My Son John
US   1952   122m   bw
Paramount/Rainbow (Leo McCarey)
An American Catholic family is horrified when its eldest son is revealed as a communist.
The lower depths of Hollywood's witch hunt cycle are marked by this Goldwynesque family saga, all sweetness and light, in which the commie son is treated as though he had rabies. Purely as entertainment the plot is pretty choppy and defeats all attempts at acting.
w Myles Connolly, Leo McCarey d Leo McCarey ph Harry Stradling m Robert Emmett Dolan
☆ Helen Hayes, Robert Walker, Dean Jagger, Van Heflin, Minor Watson, Frank McHugh, Richard Jaeckel
♟ Leo McCarey (original story)

'Their tangled loves wove a web of hate!'

My Son, My Son *
US   1940   117m   bw
Edward Small
A man who becomes rich spoils his son and lives to regret it.
Solid narrative from a bestseller.
w Lenore Coffee novel Howard Spring d Charles Vidor ph Harry Stradling m Edward Ward ad John DuCasse Schulze
☆ Brian Aherne, Madeleine Carroll, Louis Hayward, Laraine Day, Henry Hull
♟ art direction

My Son the Fanatic **
GB   1997   86m   Metrocolor
BBC/UGC/Arts Council/Zephyr (Chris Curling)
◉◉   ◉   ◎
A Pakistani taxi driver, who has embraced British ways, is horrified by his son's reversion to a fundamentalist religious outlook.
Engrossing domestic drama with a twist, as the young uphold traditional values; it makes some effective points about tolerance and bigotry and the clash between cultures and generations.
w Hanif Kureishi story Hanif Kureishi d Udayan Prasad ph Alan Almond m Stephen Warbeck pd Grenville Horner ed David Gamble
☆ Om Puri, Rachel Griffiths, Stellan Skarsgard, Akbar Kurtha, Gopi Desai, Harish Patel, Sarah Jane Potts
'An engagingly offbeat love story.' – *Variety*

My Son the Vampire: see *Mother Riley Meets the Vampire*

My Song for You
GB   1934   90m   bw
Gaumont-British
A grand opera tenor tries to help a young girl and falls for her.
The story is an excuse for the songs, and looks it.
w Austin Melford, Robert Edmunds, Richard Benson from a German original, Ein Lied für Dich, by Ernst Marischka, Irmgard von Cube d Maurice Elvey
☆ Jan Kiepura, Aileen Marson, Sonnie Hale, Emlyn Williams, Gina Malo

My Stepmother Is an Alien
US   1988   108m   Film House colour
Columbia TriStar/Weintraub Entertainment (Ronald Parker, Franklin R. Levy)
◉◉   ▤   ◕~   ◎   ◉
A scientist marries a beautiful woman from another planet.
Feeble comedy with little point and no taste.
w Jerico, Herschel Weingrod, Timothy Harris, Jonathan Reynolds d Richard Benjamin ph Richard H. Kline m Alan Silvestri pd Charles Rosen ed Jacqueline Cambas, Brian Chambers
☆ Dan Aykroyd, Kim Basinger, Jon Lovitz, Alyson Hannigan, Joseph Maher, Seth Green, Ann Prentiss, Wesley Mann, Tony Jay, Peter Bromilow

My Sweet Little Village **
Czechoslovakia   1985   100m   colour
Cannon/Barrandov Film Studio '85 (Jan Suster)
Life in a small village, where a mentally-retarded worker is forced to move to Prague.
Charming, good-hearted film of a small community where individuality flourishes.
w Zdenek Sverak d Jiri Menzel ph Jaromir Sofr m Jiri Sust pd Zbyner Hoch ed Jiri Brozeck

---

☆ Janos Ban, Marian Labuda, Rudolf Hrusinsky, Milena Dvorska, Ladislav Zupanic, Petr Cepek
♟ best foreign film

My Teenage Daughter
GB   1956   100m   bw
British Lion/Everest (Herbert Wilcox)
US title: *Teenage Bad Girl*
A widow's seventeen-year-old daughter meets an aggressive young man and ends up in court.
Predictable domestic drama, a tame British version of Rebel without a Cause.
w Felicity Douglas d Herbert Wilcox ph Max Greene
☆ Anna Neagle, Sylvia Syms, Kenneth Haigh, Norman Wooland, Wilfrid Hyde-White, Julia Lockwood, Helen Haye

My Tutor
US   1982   97m   DeLuxe
Crown
▤   ◕~   ◎
Two teenage boys try to lose their virginity.
As woeful as it sounds.
w Joe Roberts d George Bowers ph Mac Ahlberg m Webster Lewis
☆ Matt Lattanzi, Caren Kaye, Kevin McCarthy, Arlene Golonka, Crispin Slater

My Two Husbands: see *Too Many Husbands*

My Uncle Antoine
Canada   1971   110m   Eastmancolor
National Film Board of Canada
▤
In a Quebec village a young boy reluctantly helps his undertaker uncle to collect a coffin.
French-speaking comedy drama with a sour edge, as thoughts of death mar a family Christmas.
w Clément Perron d Claude Jutra ph Michel Brault m Jean Cousineau
☆ Jacques Gagnon, Lyne Champagne, Jean Duceppe, Olivette Thibault

My Way Home **
GB   1979   72m   bw
BFI (Judy Cottam, Richard Craven)
◉◉
Leaving a children's home to become a miner and then a tramp, a young man's miserable life changes for the better when he is called up for National Service and goes to Egypt.
The poverty of the lives depicted is mirrored by the directorial style – austere, spare, non-committal – to create a Calvinist masterpiece illumined by a little hope.
wd Bill Douglas ph Ray Orton ad Oliver Bouchier, Elsie Restorick ed Mick Audsley
☆ Stephen Archibald, Paul Kermack, Jessie Combe, William Carrol, Morag McNee, Lennox Milne, Gerald James
† The third of a trilogy of autobiographical films that began with *My Childhood* and *My Ain Folk* (qqv).

My Weakness *
US   1933   74m   bw
Fox
As part of a joke, a hotel slavey is disguised as a grand lady, and warms to the part.
Tolerable comedy with songs, using some ingenuity of presentation to ingratiate its German star with American audiences.
w B. G. de Sylva d David Butler
☆ Lilian Harvey, Lew Ayres, Charles Butterworth, Harry Langdon, Sid Silvers, Henry Travers
'A highly favourable début.' – *Variety*

My Wife's Best Friend
US   1952   87m   bw
TCF
A wife learns of her husband's infidelity, and imagines how Cleopatra, Joan of Arc and other historical figures might handle the situation.
A sharp little comedy rather similar to Unfaithfully Yours.
w Isobel Lennart d Richard Sale
☆ Anne Baxter, Macdonald Carey, Cecil Kellaway, Casey Adams, Catherine McLeod

---

My Wife's Family
GB   1931   80m   bw
BIP
A wife thinks her husband has an illegitimate child. Archetypal British farce.
This may be the best version; it was also made with Charlie Clapham in 1941 and with Ronald Shiner in 1956.
w Fred Duprez and Val Valentine play Fred Duprez, Hal Stephens and Harry B. Linton d Monty Banks
☆ Gene Gerrard, Muriel Angelus, Jimmy Godden, Amy Veness

My Wild Irish Rose
US   1947   101m   Technicolor
Warner (William Jacobs)
The ups and downs of Irish tenor Chauncey Olcott and his encounters with Lillian Russell.
Inoffensive but not very exciting period musical, rather lacking in humour.
w Peter Milne book Rita Ilcott d David Butler ph Arthur Edeson m Ray Heindorf, Max Steiner ch Le Roy Prinz
☆ Dennis Morgan, Arlene Dahl, Andrea King, Alan Hale, George Tobias
♟ Ray Heindorf, Max Steiner

My World Dies Screaming: see *Terror in the Haunted House*

'At last, the book that couldn't be written is now the motion picture that couldn't be made!'

Myra Breckinridge
US   1970   94m   DeLuxe   Panavision
TCF (Robert Fryer)
◉◉
After a sex-change operation a film critic goes to Hollywood to accomplish the deflation of the American male.
A sharply satirical novel has been turned into a sleazy and aimless picture which became a watershed of permissiveness; after international outcry it was shunned even by its own studio. A few good laughs do emerge from the morass, but even the old clips are misused.
w Mike Sarne, David Giler novel Gore Vidal d Mike Sarne ph Richard Moore m John Philips md Lionel Newman
☆ Mae West, Raquel Welch, John Huston, Rex Reed, Jim Backus, John Carradine, Andy Devine
'Whatever the novel may be like, it surely cannot be this sort of witless, lip-smacking, continuously inept cop-out.' – *John Simon*
'About as funny as a child molester.' – *Time*
'A disjointed patchwork of leers, vulgarity and general ineptness.' – *Cue*
'An incompetent attempt at exploitation by an industry that knew once, at the very least, how to make a dishonest buck.' – *Newsweek*
'I don't want subtlety. I want vulgarity.' – *Michael Sarne*

The Mysterious Doctor
US   1942   57m   bw
Warner
Nazis strike at an English village by staging a headless ghost.
Risible propaganda hokum which somehow earned an 'H' certificate.
w Richard Weil d Ben Stoloff
☆ John Loder, Eleanor Parker, Bruce Lester, Lester Matthews, Forrester Harvey

The Mysterious Dr Fu Manchu
US   1929   80m   bw
Paramount
After the Boxer rebellion an evil Chinese seeks the death of British officers.
First but not the worst of the yellow peril's sinister adventures; to be taken for what it is, however.
w Florence Ryerson, Lloyd Corrigan d Rowland V. Lee
☆ Warner Oland, Jean Arthur, Neil Hamilton, O. P. Heggie, William Austin

Mysterious Intruder
US   1946   62m   bw
Columbia
A private detective seeks a missing heiress.
Intriguing minor thriller, part of the Whistler series.
w Eric Taylor d William Castle
☆ Richard Dix, Barton MacLane, Nina Vale, Regis Toomey

Mysterious Invader: see *The Astounding She-Monster*

Mysterious Island *
★↟↟ GB 1961 101m Technicolor
Columbia/Ameran (Charles Schneer)
▣ ◉ ♫

Union officers escape by balloon and join shipwrecked English ladies on a strange island where they are menaced by prehistoric monsters and helped by Captain Nemo.
Rambling, lively juvenile adventure with good moments and excellent monsters.
w John Prebble, Dan Ullman, Crane Wilbur *novel* Jules Verne *d* Cy Endfield *ph* Wilkie Cooper *m* Bernard Herrmann *sp* Ray Harryhausen
☆ Joan Greenwood, Michael Craig, Herbert Lom, Michael Callan, Gary Merrill
† An early sound version was made by MGM in 1929, directed by Lucien Hubbard. Despite Technicolor and a cast which included Lionel Barrymore it was judged unsatisfactory, and concentrated less on stop-frame monsters than on the submarine elements ignored in the above but remade in *Captain Nemo and the Underwater City* (qv).

The Mysterious Lady
US 1928 84m bw silent
MGM
▣

A glamorous Russian spy has to save her lover from execution as a traitor.
Threadbare star melodrama.
w Bess Meredyth *d* Fred Niblo *ph* William Daniels
☆ Greta Garbo, Conrad Nagel, Gustav von Seyffertitz

Mysterious Mr Moto
US 1938 62m bw
TCF

Mr Moto goes to London to expose the leader of The League of Assassins, Continental criminals who work as contract killers.
One of the lesser episodes in the series; the problem is what one character calls 'local character': London has rarely looked so unconvincing.
w Philip MacDonald, Norman Foster *d* Norman Foster *ph* Virgil Miller *md* Samuel Kaylin *ad* Bernard Herzbrun, Lewis Creber *ed* Norman Colbert
☆ Peter Lorre, Mary Maguire, Henry Wilcoxon, Erik Rhodes, Harold Huber, Leon Ames, Forrester Harvey, Karen Sorrell

Mysterious Mr Wong
US 1935 60m bw
Monogram
▣ ◉

A mandarin in New York's Chinatown will stop at nothing to collect the twelve coins of Confucius.
Tolerable programme filler with old-fashioned thrills.
w Nina Howatt *story* Stephen Keeler *d* William Nigh
☆ Bela Lugosi, Wallace Ford, Arline Judge, Fred Warren
'Passably exciting.' – *Variety*

Mystery Broadcast
US 1943 63m bw
Republic

A radio crime writer tackles a real case.
Acceptable lower-case mystery.
w Dane Lussier *d* George Sherman
☆ Frank Albertson, Ruth Terry, Nils Asther, Wynne Gibson, Addison Richards

Mystery Date
US 1991 99m DeLuxe
Orion (Cathleen Summers)
▣ ▣ ◉

Out on a date with a new girlfriend, a shy youth is mistaken for a thief and a killer.
Dim, blackish 'teen comedy that tries hard to amuse and fails miserably.
w Parker Bennett, Terry Runté *d* Jonathan Wacks *ph* Oliver Wood *m* John DuPrez *pd* John Willett *ed* Tina Hirsch
☆ Ethan Hawke, Teri Polo, Brian McNamara, Fisher Stevens, Tony Rosato, Don Davis, James Hong, Victor Wong, B. D. Wong
'A reasonably entertaining pic but too lame to generate word-of-mouth.' – *Variety*

Mystery in Mexico
US 1948 65m bw
RKO

An insurance detective disappears in Mexico; another is sent to find him and uncovers a complex plot.
Fairly effective time-passer shot on location.
w Lawrence Kimble *d* Robert Wise *ph* Jack Draper *m* Paul Sawtell
☆ William Lundigan, Ricardo Cortez, Jacqueline White, Tony Barrett

Mystery Junction
GB 1951 67m bw
Merton Park

Passengers stranded in a snowbound railway station solve a mystery.
One of the better second features of its type.
wd Michael McCarthy
☆ Sydney Tafler, Barbara Murray, Pat Owens, Martin Benson

Mystery Liner
US 1934 62m bw
Monogram
▣

Several murders take place at sea on a passenger liner.
Reputedly above-average whodunnit.
w Wellyn Totman *novel* The Ghost of John Holling by Edgar Wallace *d* William Nigh
☆ Noah Beery, Astrid Allwyn, Cornelius Keefe, Gustav von Seyffertitz, Edwin Maxwell
'Too good for the lesser grinds: exceptional indie entertainment.' – *Variety*

'They're Not Your Classic Superheroes... They're The Other Guys.'
Mystery Men *
US 1999 120m DeLuxe
Universal/Dark House (Lawrence Gordon, Mike Richardson, Lloyd Levin)
▣ ▣

An odd group of incompetent would-be superheroes attempt to fight crime.
An often amusing send-up of superheroes, slickly made and with an excellent cast, though it would have been a much funnier film had it been half-an-hour shorter.
w Neil Cuthbert *comic book* Bob Burden *d* Kinka Usher *ph* Stephen H. Burum *m* Stephen Warbeck *pd* Kirk M. Petruccelli *ed* Conrad Buff
☆ Hank Azaria, Janeane Garofalo, William H. Macy, Kel Mitchell, Paul Reubens, Ben Stiller, Wes Studi, Greg Kinnear, Lena Olin, Geoffrey Rush, Tom Waits, Eddie Izzard, Claire Forlani, Ricky Jay, Louise Lasser
'A better action movie than the last *Batman* and funnier than most recent comedies.' – *Hot Dog*

The Mystery of Alexina
France 1985 90m colour
Electric Pictures/Les Cinéastes Associés/TF1
original title: Mystère Alexina

A convent-educated girl discovers that in reality she is masculine.
Although based on the diary of a 19th-century hermaphrodite, it fails to explore the subject in any depth, preferring a glossy romanticism instead.
w Jean Gruault, René Feret *d* René Feret *ph* Bernard Zitzermann *m* Anne-Marie Deschamps *ed* Ariane Boeglin
☆ Philippe Vuillemin, Valerie Stroh, Véronique Silver, Bernard Freyd, Marianne Basler, Pierre Vial

'A thing to bewitch your senses for days and days! Charming in the thrills! Gripping in the suspense!'
The Mystery of Edwin Drood *
US 1935 85m bw
Universal
▣

In a cathedral town, a drug-addicted choirmaster is his nephew's rival for the hand of Rosa Bud.
Fairly creditable attempt to deal with a famous unfinished novel. Slightly stilted, but good visuals and performances.
w John L. Balderston, Gladys Unger, Bradley King, Leopold Atlas *novel* Charles Dickens *d* Stuart Walker *ph* George Robinson *m* Edward Ward
☆ Claude Rains, Douglass Montgomery, Heather Angel, David Manners, E. E. Clive, Valerie Hobson

The Mystery of Edwin Drood
GB 1993 112m Metrocolor
Mayfair/First Standard Media (Keith Hayley)

An opium-addicted choirmaster becomes obsessed with the fiancée of his nephew and plots to marry her.
A low-budget thriller that fails to match Dickens's lurid imaginings and makes a poor job of completing the novel satisfactorily.
wd Timothy Forder *novel* Charles Dickens *ph* Martin McGrath *m* Kick Production *pd* Edward Thomas *ed* Sue Alhadeff
☆ Robert Powell, Nanette Newman, Gemma Craven, Jonathan Phillips, Rupert Rainsford, Michelle Evans, Rosemary Leach, Finty Williams, Ronald Fraser, Glyn Houston, Andrew Sachs, Freddie Jones, Barry Evans
'The only mystery about this Edwin Drood is why anyone bothered to make it.' – *Philip Kemp, Sight and Sound*

The Mystery of Kaspar Hauser: see *The Enigma of Kaspar Hauser*

The Mystery of Marie Roget
US 1942 61m bw
Universal (Paul Malvern)

A Parisian music hall star plots to kill her sister but herself disappears.
Ham-fisted, stilted mystery drama relying hardly at all on its original.
w Michel Jacoby *story* Edgar Allan Poe *d* Phil Rosen *ph* Elwood Bredell *m* Hans Salter
☆ Maria Montez, Patric Knowles, *Maria Ouspenskaya*, Lloyd Corrigan, John Litel, Edward Norris, Frank Reicher

The Mystery of Mr X *
US 1934 84m bw
MGM (Lawrence Weingarten)

In foggy London, a jewel thief protects himself by finding the murderer of several policemen.
Passable mystery, later remade as The Hour of Thirteen.
w Howard Emmett Rogers, Philip MacDonald, Monckton Hoffe *novel* X vs Rex by Philip MacDonald *d* Edgar Selwyn *ph* Oliver T. Marsh
☆ Robert Montgomery, Elizabeth Allan, Lewis Stone, Ralph Forbes, Henry Stephenson, Forrester Harvey
'One of the best-made mystery mellers yet.' – *Variety*

The Mystery of the 13th Guest
US 1943 60m bw
Lindsley Parsons/Monogram

A girl beneficiary under her uncle's will is menaced when she goes to visit.
Ham-fisted remake of The Thirteenth Guest, which was a mite too complex in the first place. This version makes no sense at all and is cheaply produced.
w Charles Marion, Tim Ryan *play* Armitage Trail *d* William Beaudine
☆ Helen Parrish, Dick Purcell, Tim Ryan, Frank Faylen

The Mystery of the Mary Celeste
GB 1935 80m bw
Hammer
▣

US title: Phantom Ship
A mad sailor kills his fellow crew members and jumps overboard.
Unpersuasive solution to an unsolved mystery in a production which sounds more interesting than it is.
wd Denison Clift
☆ Bela Lugosi, Shirley Grey, Arthur Margetson, Edmund Willard, Dennis Hoey
'Very strong stuff for those who like tragic entertainment.' – *Variety*

'Images of wax that throbbed with human passion. Almost woman! What did they lack?'
Mystery of the Wax Museum ***
US 1933 77m Technicolor
Warner (Henry Blanke)
▣ ▣ ◉

A sculptor disfigured in a fire builds a wax museum by covering live victims in wax.
Archetypal horror material is augmented by a sub-plot about drug-running and an authoritative example of the wisecracking reporter school of the early thirties. The film is also notable for its highly satisfactory use of two-colour Technicolor and for its splendid art direction. Remade 1953 as House of Wax (qv).
w Don Mullally, Carl Erickson *play* Charles S. Belden *d* Michael Curtiz *ph* Ray Rennahan *ad* Anton Grot
☆ Lionel Atwill, Fay Wray, Glenda Farrell, Frank McHugh, Gavin Gordon, Allen Vincent, Edwin Maxwell
ATWILL: 'I offer you immortality, my child. Think of it: in a thousand years you shall be as lovely as you are now!'
'Would have been certain of better gate support a year ago. Recognizing this, the Technicolor and hyper-weirdness were apparently mandatory studio precautions to offset the element of belated arrival.' – *Variety*
'Marvellously grisly chiller.' – *Judith Crist, 1977*
'Its most telling details are its horrific ones. The fire at the beginning, with lifelike figures melting into grisly ooze; night time in the city morgue, with a dead body suddenly popping up as a side effect of embalming fluid; chases through shadows as the ghoulish sculptor collects bodies for his exhibit; and the shock when Atwill's homemade wax face crumbles to the floor and exposes the hidden demon.' – *Tom Shales, The American Film Heritage, 1972*

The Mystery of the Wentworth Castle: see *Mr Wong*

The Mystery of the Yellow Room *
France 1931 96m bw
Osso

An attempt is made on the life of a scientist's daughter.
Complex mystery which has maintained some reputation.
wd Marcel L'Herbier *novel* Gaston Leroux *ph* L. H. Burel *m* Edouard Flament
☆ Hugette Ex-Duclos, Roland Toutain, Maxime Desjardins

Mystery Science Theater 3000: The Movie
US 1996 73m DeLuxe
Gramercy/Best Brains (Jim Mallon)
▣

A mad scientist forces an astronaut and his robots to watch an edited version of the 50s sci-fi movie *This Island Earth*.
A joke that anyone can play at home, since it consists of three characters, seen in silhouette at the bottom of the screen, making fun of an old movie; occasionally the remarks are amusing, but more often they are irritating.
w Michael J. Nelson, Trace Beaulieu, Jim Mallon, Kevin Murphy, Mary Jo Pehl, Paul Chaplin, Bridget Jones *d* Jim Mallon *ph* Jeff Stonehouse *m* Billy Barber *pd* Jef Maynard *ed* Bill Johnson
☆ Michael J. Nelson, Trace Beaulieu, Kevin Murphy, Jim Mallon, John Brady
'Infectiously funny while it's unspooling but instantly forgettable, goofy item will play best to teenagers in an altered state and looks unlikely to go beyond cult status.' – *Todd McCarthy, Variety*

Mystery Sea Raider
US 1940 76m bw
Paramount/Eugene J. Zukor

A ship is hijacked and converted into a German raider in the Caribbean.
Standard propaganda potboiler with little imagination.
w Edward E. Paramore Jnr *d* Edward Dmytryk
☆ Carole Landis, Henry Wilcoxon, Onslow Stevens, Kathleen Howard, Henry Victor

Mystery Street *
US 1950 93m bw
MGM (Frank E. Taylor)

Harvard medical scientists help solve a murder by examining the victim's bones.
Standard semi-documentary police thriller; well paced and quite entertaining.
w Sydney Boehm, Richard Brooks *d* John Sturges *ph* John Alton *m* Rudolph Kopp
☆ Ricardo Montalban, Sally Forrest, Elsa Lanchester, Bruce Bennett, Marshall Thompson, Jan Sterling
⚂ Leonard Spigelgass (original story)

Mystery Submarine

GB   1962   92m   bw
British Lion/Britannia/Bertram Ostrer
US title: *Decoy*

A Nazi submarine is captured and sent out again with a British crew.
Routine war adventure.
w Hugh Woodhouse, Bertram Ostrer, Jon Manchip White d C. M. Pennington-Richards ph Stan Pavey m Clifton Parker
☆ Edward Judd, James Robertson Justice, Laurence Payne, Albert Lieven

Mystery Train **

US   1989   110m   DuArt
Palace/JVC (Jim Stark)

📼 ▦ ◖◗ ⌀ ◠

Episodic film involving two Elvis Presley fans in Memphis, an Italian woman who sees Elvis's ghost and a Presley look-alike, all of whom converge on a seedy hotel for the night.
Rambling, leisurely film that contains a multitude of small pleasures.
wd Jim Jarmusch ph Robby Müller m John Lurie pd Dan Bishop ed Melody London
☆ Masatoshi Nagase, Youki Kudoh, Screamin' Jay Hawkins, Cinque Lee, Rufus Thomas, Nicoletta Braschi, Elizabeth Bracco, Joe Strummer, Rick Aviles, Steve Buscemi

Mystery Woman

US   1934   69m   bw
Fox

Recovery of a secret document will mean freedom for a soldier sent to Devil's Island.
Tolerable time-passer, with action mostly on a liner.
w Philip MacDonald, Dudley Nichols, E. E. Paramore Jnr d Eugene Forde
☆ Mona Barrie, Gilbert Roland, John Halliday, Rod La Rocque, Mischa Auer, Billy Bevan
'Entertainment of a just passable sort.' – *Variety*

Mystic Pizza

US   1988   104m   colour
Virgin/Samuel Goldwyn Company (Mark Levinson, Scott Rosenfelt)

📼 ▦ ◖◗

Three young women experience love and affairs for the first time.
Likely to appeal to a young female audience and offering little of interest to anyone else.
w Amy Jones, Perry Howze, Randy Howze, Alfred Uhry story Amy Jones d Donald Petrie ph Tim Suhrstedt m David McHugh pd David Chapman ed Marion Rothman, Don Brochu
☆ Vincent Phillip D'Onofrio, Annabeth Gish, William R. Moses, Julia Roberts, Adam Storke, Lili Taylor, Conchata Ferrell, Porscha Radcliffe

The Myth of Fingerprints

US   1997   90m   DuArt
Feature Film/Good Machine/Eureka (Mary Jane Skalski, Tim Perell, Bart Freundlich)

📼 ▦ ◎

Four children return home to their ageing parents for the Thanksgiving weekend.
A predictable slice of dysfunctional family life, with a distant, overbearing father and a forgiving mother.
wd Bart Freundlich ph Stephen Kazmierski m David Bridie, John Phillips pd Susan Bolles ed Kate Williams, Ken J. Sackheim
☆ Arija Bareikis, Blythe Danner, Hope Davis, Laurel Holloman, Brian Kerwin, James LeGros, Julianne Moore, Roy Scheider, Michael Vartan, Noah Wyle
'This is one angst-ridden family saga that needn't be a totally repellent experience.' – *Empire*

N

Nada ***
France/Italy 1974 134m Eastmancolor
Academy/Connoisseur/Veróna/Films La Boétie (André Génovès)

A tough policeman tracks down a group of anarchists who kidnap the American Ambassador in Paris.
Bleak and violent film, expertly made, in which it is difficult to tell the good guys from the bad.
w Jean-Patrick Manchette *novel* Jean-Patrick Manchette *d* Claude Chabrol *ph* Jean Rabier *m* Pierre Jansen *ad* Guy Littaye *ed* Jacques Gaillard
☆ Fabio Testi, Michel Duchaussoy, Maurice Garrel, Michel Aumont, Lou Castel, Didier Kaminka, Lyle Joyce, Viviane Romance
'Chabrol's most profoundly cynical film to date … he lays bare the cause-and-effect mechanism of terrorism.' – *Jan Dawson, MFB*

Nadine *
US 1987 88m Metrocolor
Columbia TriStar/ML Delphi (Arlene Donovan)

Husband and wife on the brink of divorce are drawn together by a suspicious killing.
Unresolvedly old-fashioned comedy which seems to need the Cary Grant touch.
wd Robert Benton *ph* Nestor Almendros *m* Howard Shore *pd* Paul Sylbert *ed* Sam O'Steen
☆ Jeff Bridges, Kim Basinger, Rip Torn, Gwen Verdon, Glenne Headly, Jerry Stiller

'Hurry, The Dead Travel Fast!'
Nadja
US 1995 100m bw
ICA/Kino Link (Mary Sweeney, Amy Hobby)

Dracula's daughter attempts to revive her father while beginning an affair with the wife of the nephew of vampire hunter Van Helsing.
Despite being executive-produced by David Lynch, this is more an exhumation than a revival of an increasingly tired genre: the narrative owes much to Dracula's Daughter, merely adding a lesbian twist, and its use of the toy camera Pixelvision to suggest a vampire's-eye view emphasizes that the project lacks any sharpness of style.
wd Michael Almereyda *ph* Jim Denault *m* Simon Fisher Turner *pd* Kurt Ossenfort *ed* David Leonard
☆ Suzy Amis, Elina Löwensohn, Galaxy Craze, Martin Donovan, Peter Fonda, Karl Geary, Jared Harris
'Almost completely devoid of urgency or warmth. A calculated attempt to evoke the zero degree existential dreadfulness of its immortal predators' lifestyles, the film is a pretty slow one to watch.' – *Kim Newman*

Nagana
US 1933 73m bw
Universal

Doctors in Africa try to cure sleeping sickness.
Dreary drama with cut-in animal footage.
w James Light, Dale Van Every, Don Ryan, Lester Cohen *d* Ernst L. Frank
☆ Tala Birell, Melvyn Douglas, M. Morita, Onslow Stevens

Nagisa no Sindbad: *see Like Grains of Sand*

Naked *
GB 1993 131m Metrocolor
First Independent/Thin Man/Film Four (Simon Channing-Williams)

Running away from Manchester, where he rapes a woman, an unemployed, compulsively talkative

misogynist comes to London and moves in with a former girlfriend.
A saga of an unlovely man out to destroy himself and others, which is bleak and despairing at its best, but more often is embittered overstatement and caricature.
wd Mike Leigh *ph* Dick Pope *m* Andrew Dickson *pd* Alison Chitty *ed* Jon Gregory
☆ David Thewlis, Lesley Sharp, Katrin Cartlidge, Greg Cruttwell, Claire Skinner, Peter Wight, Ewen Bremner, Susan Vidler
'It would be hard to imagine a film much sourer than *Naked*, but sourness is not a fault, merely a characteristic. Hollowness, now, self-indulgence, a sort of gloating emotional ugliness – those are faults.' – *Adam Mars-Jones, Independent*
'This is a neorealist monster movie, and the monster won't lie down and die – he just keeps coming.' – *Gavin Smith, Film Comment*
'A startling leap from the petty comic viciousness of Mike Leigh's domestic satires into darker, more complex philosophical territory.' – *Claire Monk, Sight and Sound*
† David Thewlis won the award for best actor, and Mike Leigh for best director, at the Cannes Film Festival in 1993.

Naked Alibi *
US 1954 85m bw
U-I (Ross Hunter)

The police track a homicidal baker to a Mexican border town.
Modest police thriller which sags after it crosses the border.
w Lawrence Roman *d* Jerry Hopper *ph* Russell Metty *m* Hans Salter
☆ Sterling Hayden, Gene Barry, Gloria Grahame, Marcia Henderson, Casey Adams, Chuck Connors

The Naked and the Dead *
US 1958 131m Technicolor RKOscope
RKO Teleradio/Gregjac (Paul Gregory)

Adventures of an army platoon in the Pacific war.
Shorn of the four letter words which made the novel notorious, this is a routine war film, neither very good nor very bad.
w Denis and Terry Sanders *novel* Norman Mailer *d* Raoul Walsh *ph* Joseph LaShelle *m* Bernard Herrmann
☆ Aldo Ray, Cliff Robertson, Raymond Massey, William Campbell, Richard Jaeckel, James Best, Joey Bishop, Robert Gist, Jerry Paris, L. Q. Jones
'One of the worst movies ever made.' – *Norman Mailer*

Naked as Nature Intended *
GB 1961 65m Eastmancolor
Compass/Markten (Harrison Marks)

Five women visit British tourist attractions before going to a Cornish naturist resort, where they briefly take off their clothes and romp in the sun.
Innocuous film that helped start the British sexploitation cycle of the 60s and 70s and made Pamela Green the best-known unclothed actress of her time.
wd Harrison Marks *ph* Roy Poynter
☆ Pamela Green, Jackie Salt, Petrina Forsyth, Stuart Samuels, Bridget Leonard, Angela Jones
† The film was originally going to be titled *Cornish Holiday*. It was at first banned by the British Board of Film Censors, but the makers submitted it to the London County Council and other local authorities who passed it for exhibition, forcing the BBFC to change its policy and certify such films.

The Naked City ****
US 1948 96m bw
Universal (Mark Hellinger)

New York police track down a killer.

Highly influential documentary thriller which, shot on location in New York's teeming streets, claimed to be giving an impression of city life; actually its real mission was to tell an ordinary murder tale with an impressive accumulation of detail and humour. The narrator's last words became a cliché: 'There are eight million stories in the naked city. This has been one of them.'
w Malvin Wald, Albert Maltz *d* Jules Dassin *ph* William Daniels *m* Frank Skinner, Miklos Rozsa *md* Milton Schwarzwald *ed* Paul Weatherwax
☆ Barry Fitzgerald, Don Taylor, Howard Duff, Dorothy Hart, Ted de Corsia, Adelaide Klein
♦ William Daniels; Paul Weatherwax
§ original story (Malvin Wald)

The Naked Country
Australia 1985 90m colour
Naked Country Productions (Ross Dimsey)

aka: *Morris West's The Naked Country*
In the outback, a rancher engaged in a bloody conflict with the aborigines over land they regard as sacred comes to understand their attitudes through his suffering.
An Australian variation on cowboys and Indians, average for the most part though managing a rousing climax reminiscent of Sam Peckinpah in its theme of redemption through violence.
w Tim Burstall, Ross Dimsey *novel* Morris West *d* Tim Burstall *ph* David Eggby *m* Bruce Smeaton *ad* Philip Warner *ed* Tony Paterson
☆ John Stanton, Rebecca Gilling, Ivar Kants, Tommy Lewis, Donald Blitner, John Stanton, Malcolm Cork, John Jarratt

The Naked Dawn
US 1956 82m Technicolor
Universal-International
A hired robber finds that his boss is not to be trusted.
Heavy-going Mexican Western.
w Nina and Herman Schneider *d* Edgar G. Ulmer *ph* Frederick Gately *m* Herschel Burke Gilbert
☆ Arthur Kennedy, Eugene Iglesias, Betta St John

Naked Earth
GB 1958 96m bw Cinemascope
TCF/Foray Films (Adrian Worker)
In 1895 a young Irish farmer goes to Africa to grow tobacco, but moves on to crocodile hunting.
Predictable and uninteresting epic of endurance; not very convincing either.
w Milton Holmes *d* Vincent Sherman *ph* Erwin Hillier
☆ Richard Todd, Juliette Greco, John Kitzmiller, Finlay Currie, Laurence Naismith, Christopher Rhodes, Orlando Martins

The Naked Edge *
GB 1961 100m bw
UA/Pennebaker/Baroda (Walter Seltzer, George Glass)

A successful executive is suspected by his wife of an old murder in which he testified against the man who was convicted.
Dreary thriller which piles up red herrings in shoals, then abandons them all for a razor-and-bathroom finale.
w Joseph Stefano *novel* First Train to Babylon by Max Ehrlich *d* Michael Anderson *ph* Erwin Hillier *m* William Alwyn
☆ Gary Cooper, Deborah Kerr, Peter Cushing, Eric Portman, Diane Cilento, Hermione Gingold, Michael Wilding, Ronald Howard

The Naked Face
US 1984 106m Metrocolor
Cannon (Rony Yacov)

A Chicago psychiatrist finds himself a potential victim of the Mafia.

Muddled and violent mystery with a rather boring solution.
wd Bryan Forbes *novel* Sidney Sheldon *ph* David Gurfinkel *m* Michael J. Lewis *pd* William Fosser
☆ Roger Moore, Rod Steiger, Elliott Gould, Anne Archer, David Hedison, Art Carney, Ron Parady

Naked Fury
GB 1959 60m bw
Butcher's/Coenda (Guido Coen)

A robbery goes wrong when a gang is forced to take the night watchman's daughter as well as their loot.
Unconvincing thriller in which most of the crooks act like gentlemen, which robs the drama of any suspense as well as credibility.
w Brock Williams *story* Guido Coen *d* Charles Saunders *ph* Jimmy W. Harvey *m* Edwin Astley *ad* Duncan Sutherland *ed* Peter Pitt
☆ Reed de Rouen, Kenneth Cope, Leigh Madison, Arthur Lovegrove, Alexander Field, Tommy Eytle, Ann Lynn, Marianne Brauns, Arthur Gross

Naked Gun 2½: The Smell of Fear *
US 1991 85m Technicolor
UIP/Paramount/Zucker/Abrahams/Zucker (Robert K. Weiss)

A clumsy police lieutenant investigates an attempt to kill a solar energy expert.
The mixture as before, although this time around the slapstick comedy is enlivened with fewer good jokes.
w David Zucker, Pat Proft *d* David Zucker *ph* Robert Stevens *m* Ira Newborn *pd* John J. Lloyd *ed* James Symons, Chris Greenbury
☆ Leslie Nielsen, Priscilla Presley, George Kennedy, O.J. Simpson, Robert Goulet, Richard Griffiths, Jacqueline Brookes, Anthony James, Lloyd Bochner
'At least two-and-a-half times less funny than its hilarious progenitor.' – *Variety*
'An appealing rag-bag of the ribald and the ridiculous, showing only the slightest signs of running out of steam.' – *Philip Strick, Sight and Sound*

Naked Gun 33⅓: The Final Insult *
US 1994 82m DeLuxe
Paramount (Robert K. Weiss, David Zucker)

Detective Frank Drebin retires from the force and is persuaded to return as an undercover cop.
With some new jokes this time around, and deft parodies, this is the funniest of the series so far.
w Pat Proft, David Zucker, Robert LoCash *d* Peter Segal *ph* Robert Stevens *m* Ira Newborn *pd* Lawrence G. Paull *ed* Jim Symons
☆ Leslie Nielsen, Priscilla Presley, George Kennedy, O. J. Simpson, Fred Ward, Kathleen Freeman, Anna Nicole Smith, Ellen Greene, Ed Williams
'Loaded with the usual barrage of irreverent, politically incorrect and virtually non-stop gags.' – *Variety*

The Naked Gun: From the Files of Police Squad *
US 1988 85m Technicolor
UIP/Paramount (Robert K. Weiss)

A bungling detective foils attempts to assassinate the Queen in Los Angeles.
A barrage of gags, some good, some dreadful, is harnessed to a limp narrative. Not as funny as it should be.
w Jerry Zucker, Jim Abrahams, David Zucker, Pat Proft *d* David Zucker *ph* Robert Stevens *m* Ira Newborn *pd* John J. Lloyd *ed* Michael Jablow
☆ Leslie Nielsen, Priscilla Presley, Ricardo Montalban, George Kennedy, O. J. Simpson, Susan

---

◎ Digital Video Disc Region 2   ◎ Digital Video Disc Region 1   ♫ Soundtrack released on compact disc   ☆ Cast in approximate order of importance   † Points of interest   ♫ Notable songs   ♦ Academy Award   § Academy Award nomination   ⚜ BAFTA

Beaubian, Nancy Marchand, Raye Birk, Jeannette Charles

'Quickly and efficiently establishes its pattern of wildly escalating absurdity within each scene, combined with a series of gags related to each character throughout the film.' – *Philip Strick, MFB*

The Naked Hills

US   1955   73m   Pathécolor
Allied Artists/La Salle (Josef Shaftel)

Starting in 1849, a young prospector spends his life looking for gold.
Curious, mildly interesting saga with an obsession instead of a plot.
wd Josef Shaftel ph Frederick Gately m Herschel Burke Gilbert
☆ David Wayne, Marcia Henderson, Keenan Wynn, James Barton, Jim Backus, Denver Pyle

Naked in New York *

US   1993   86m   colour
Fine Line/Pandora (Frederick Zollo)
📼 ■ ⊛ ⌒

A young hopeful playwright reflects on his upbringing in a fatherless home, his on-and-off relationship with his girlfriend and the way his life is taken over by others.
Pleasant low-key drama of the young attempting to come to terms with the compromises of life.
w Dan Algrant, John Warren d Dan Algrant ph Joey Forsyte m Angelo Badalamenti pd Kalina Ivanov ed Bill Pankow
☆ Eric Stoltz, Mary-Louise Parker, Ralph Macchio, Jill Clayburgh, Tony Curtis, Kathleen Turner, Timothy Dalton, Roscoe Lee Browne, Whoopi Goldberg, Eric Bogosian, Quentin Crisp
'A charming, creative, but slightly inconsistent look at the dreams and loves of the artsy twentysomethings.' – *Variety*
† Martin Scorsese became the film's executive producer after reading Algrant's semi-autobiographical script.

The Naked Jungle *

US   1954   95m   Technicolor
Paramount/George Pal (Frank Freeman Jnr)
■ ⊛

In 1901 a young woman is married by proxy to a South American cocoa planter, and when she arrives at his jungle home she has to conquer not only him but an army of soldier ants.
Mixture of Rebecca elements with a more unusual kind of thrill; all quite watchable, and the ant scenes very effective.
w Philip Yordan, Ranald MacDougall story *Leiningen Versus the Ants* by Carl Stephenson d Byron Haskin ph Ernest Laszlo m Daniele Amfitheatrof
☆ Charlton Heston, Eleanor Parker, William Conrad, Abraham Sofaer, John Dierkes, Douglas Fowley

The Naked Kiss *

US   1964   92m   bw
Allied Artists/F and F/AA (Samuel Fuller)
📼 ■ ⊛ ⊚

A prostitute tries to enter mainstream society.
Tough early work by a director who never compromised but seldom hit the public fancy.
wd Samuel Fuller ph Stanley Cortez m Paul Dunlap ad Eugene Lourie ed Jerome Thoms
☆ Constance Towers, Anthony Eisley, Michael Dante, Virginia Grey, Patsy Kelly, Betty Bronson

'Exterminate all rational thought.'

Naked Lunch *

Canada/GB   1991   115m   Film House colour
First Independent (Jeremy Thomas)
📼 ■ ⊛ ⌒

In the 1950s, a drug-addicted writer kills his wife while trying to emulate William Tell and flees to Interzone, an exotic place of paranoid fantasy.
Instead of the savagery and rampant homosexuality of the original, the film concerns the act of the book's creation, through the hallucinatory experiences of a writer, based on Burroughs, among the expatriate artistic community of Tangier. All that is carried over from the novel is the title and lack of narrative coherence.
wd David Cronenberg novel William S. Burroughs ph Peter Suschitzky m Howard Shore, Ornette Coleman (alto sax solos) pd Carol Spier

ed Ronald Sanders sp creature effects: Chris Walas Inc.
☆ Peter Weller, Judy Davis, Ian Holm, Julian Sands, Roy Scheider, Monique Mercure, Nicholas Campbell, Michael Zelniker, Robert A. Silverman, Joseph Scorsiani
'A fascinating, demanding, mordantly funny picture that echoes many of the book's chief concerns, but also stands as a distinctively personal creation in its own right.' – *Variety*
'It's impossible to make a movie out of *Naked Lunch*. A literal translation just wouldn't work. It would cost $400 million to make and would be banned in every country of the world.' – *David Cronenberg*

The Naked Maja

Italy/US   1959   112m   Technirama
MGM/Titanus (Goffredo Lombardo)
◌

Peasant Francisco Goya becomes a famous painter through the influence of the Duchess of Alba.
Boring and unconvincing biopic.
w Giorgio Prosperi, Norman Corwin, Albert Lewin, Oscar Saul d Henry Koster ph Giuseppe Rotunno m Francesco Lavagnino
☆ Anthony Franciosa, Ava Gardner, Amedeo Nazzari, Gino Cervi, Lea Padovani, Massimo Serrato
'This travesty of Goya's life, country and period adds up to nothing more entertaining than a perfunctory, heavy-handed pageant.' – *MFB*

The Naked Night: see Sawdust and Tinsel

The Naked Prey *

US   1966   94m   Technicolor   Panavision
Paramount/Theodora/Sven Persson (Cornel Wilde)
■ ⊛

In 1840, a white hunter becomes brutalized when a tribe hunts him down as though he were a lion.
Savage adventure story with bloodthirsty detail; unusual and certainly effective.
w Clint Johnston, Don Peters d Cornel Wilde ph H. A. R. Thomson md Andrew Tracy, from African folk music
☆ Cornel Wilde, Gert Van Den Berg, Ken Gampu
'Overtones pretentious, but it tries.' – *Sight and Sound*
⌂ script

The Naked Runner

GB   1967   104m   Techniscope
Warner/Artanis (Brad Dexter)
British intelligence conceive a plan to turn an innocent businessman into a spy killer.
Silly espionage thriller marred by its director's penchant for making a zany composition of every frame.
w Stanley Mann novel Francis Clifford d Sidney J. Furie ph Otto Heller m Harry Sukman
☆ Frank Sinatra, Peter Vaughan, Derren Nesbitt, Nadia Gray, Toby Robins, Cyril Luckham, Edward Fox, Inger Stratton
'It might be a good movie to read by if there were light in the theatre.' – *Pauline Kael*

The Naked Spur *

US   1952   91m   Technicolor
MGM (William H. Wright)
■

A bounty hunter has trouble getting his quarry back to base.
Standard big-studio Western shot in Colorado, with all characters motivated by greed.
w Sam Rolfe, Harold Jack Bloom d Anthony Mann ph William Mellor m Bronislau Kaper
☆ James Stewart, Robert Ryan, Janet Leigh, Millard Mitchell
⌂ script

The Naked Street

US   1955   83m   bw
Edward Small
A racketeer's daughter marries a worthless crook: her father saves him from the electric chair but he murders again.
Semi-documentary exposé melodrama about unpleasant people; reasonably proficient on its level.
w Maxwell Shane, Leo Katcher d Maxwell Shane ph Floyd Crosby m Ernest Gold md Emil Newman
☆ Anthony Quinn, Anne Bancroft, Farley Granger, Peter Graves

Naked Tango

US   1990   92m   DeLuxe
Blue Dolphin/Sugarloaf/Gotan/Towa/Praesens/Grupo Baires (David Weisman)
📼

In the 1920s a bored wife assumes the identity of a suicide, marries a dubious night-club owner in Buenos Aires, and falls in love with a tango-dancing gangster.
Luridly directed and acted, over-the-top romance that fails to convince, particularly in its attempt at a period setting.
wd Leonard Schrader story inspired by the work of Manuel Puig ph Juan Ruiz-Anchia m Thomas Newman pd Anthony Pratt ed Lee Percy, Debra McDermott
☆ Vincent D'Onofrio, Mathilda May, Esai Morales, Fernando Rey, Cipe Lincovsky, Josh Mostel, Patricio Bisso, Constance McCashin
'Too morbid and narrowly conceived to interest mainstream audiences.' – *Variety*

The Naked Truth *

GB   1957   92m   bw
Rank/Mario Zampi
📼

US title: *Your Past is Showing*
Celebrities band together to kill a blackmailer who threatens to expose unsavoury aspects of their lives.
Frenzied black farce, quite a lot of which comes off.
w Michael Pertwee d Mario Zampi ph Stan Pavey m Stanley Black
☆ Peter Sellers, Terry-Thomas, Peggy Mount, Dennis Price, Shirley Eaton, Georgina Cookson

Naked under Leather: see Girl on a Motorcycle

The Naked Vampire: see La Vampire Nue

Naked Warriors: see The Arena

Namayeh Nazdik: see Close-Up

'Even men of God can trade with the Devil'

The Name of the Rose *

US   1986   130m   colour
TCF/Bernd Eichinger/Bernd-Schaefers/Cristaldi/Ariane/ZDF
📼 ■ ⊛ ⌒

In the 14th century, an English monk's visit to an Italian abbey is soured by a series of murders.
Curious, remote, randomly developed and edited, this can never have been an obvious candidate for box-office success: yet it did pretty well.
w Andrew Birkin, Gerard Brach, Howard Franklin, Alain Godard novel Umberto Eco d Jean-Jacques Annaud ph Tonino Delli Colli m James Horner pd Dante Ferretti ed Jane Seitz
☆ Sean Connery, F. Murray Abraham, Christian Slater, Michael Lonsdale, Elya Baskin
'A plodding misfire ... sorrowfully mediocre.' – *Variety*
📼 Sean Connery

Namu the Killer Whale *

�* US   1966   88m   DeLuxe
United Artists (Lazlo Benedek)
A marine biologist traps a killer whale in a small cove so that he can study it, causing fear and suspicion among the local fishermen and villagers.
Pleasant movie of prejudice overcome by reason and example, aimed at a family audience and treating its animals with respect.
w Arthur Weiss d Laslo Benedek ph Lamar Boren m Samuel Matlovsky ad Eddie Imazu ed Erwin Dumbrille
☆ Robert Lansing, John Anderson, Richard Erdman, Lee Meriwether, Robin Mattson, Joe Higgins, Michael Shea

Nana *

US   1934   89m   bw
Samuel Goldwyn
📼

GB title: *Lady of the Boulevards*
The high life and subsequent degradation of a Parisian demi-mondaine in the 1890s.
Stylish yet stolid slice of le beau monde, intended to create a new star.
w Willard Mack, Harry Wagstaff Gribble novel Emile Zola d Dorothy Arzner ph Gregg Toland m Alfred Newman

☆ Anna Sten, Lionel Atwill, Phillips Holmes, Richard Bennett, Mae Clarke, Muriel Kirkland, Reginald Owen, Jessie Ralph
'The star's resources should be sufficient to offset some of the lesser script deficiencies.' – *Variety*

Nana

France/Italy   1955   100m
Cygno Films/FLF (Jacques Roitfeld)
A courtesan and actress comes to grief.
Glossily unconvincing version, with a performance in the title role in the style of Lucille Ball.
w Henri Jeanson, Albert Valentin d Christian-Jaque ph Christian Matras m Georges Van Parys ad Robert Gys ed Jacques Desagneaux
☆ Charles Boyer, Martine Carol, Walter Chiari, Marguerite Pierry, Paul Frankeur, Elisa Cegani, Dora Doll, Jacques Castlelot, Noel Roquevert

Nancy Drew

🏗
This series of second features starring Bonita Granville as a teenage small-town detective was moderately well received but quickly forgotten. The character was created in novels by Edward Stratemeyer and his daughter Harriet Evans; the films were all directed by William Clemens for Warner.
1938 Nancy Drew, Detective
1939 Nancy Drew, Reporter, Nancy Drew, Trouble Shooter, Nancy Drew and the Hidden Staircase

Nancy Goes to Rio

US   1950   99m   Technicolor
MGM (Joe Pasternak)
Two actresses, mother and daughter, are both after the same part.
Mild showboard musical.
w Sidney Sheldon d Robert Z. Leonard ph Ray June m George Stoll
☆ Jane Powell, Ann Sothern, Carmen Miranda, Barry Sullivan, Louis Calhern, Fortunio Bonanova, Hans Conried

Nancy Steele is Missing *

US   1937   85m   bw
TCF (Nunnally Johnson)
Crooks try to pass off a girl as the long lost heir to a fortune.
Slightly unusual, well cast melodrama.
w Gene Fowler, Hal Long novel C. F. Coe d George Marshall ph Barney McGill m David Buttolph
☆ Victor McLaglen, Peter Lorre, June Lang, Jane Darwell, John Carradine, Walter Connolly

The Nanny *

GB   1965   93m   bw
ABP/Hammer (Jimmy Sangster)
A 10-year-old boy hates his nanny, and with good reason, for she is a neurotic murderess.
Muted Hammer experiment in psycho- pathology, with too much equivocation before the dénouement; the star's role allows few fireworks, and the plot is rather unpleasant.
w Jimmy Sangster novel Evelyn Piper d Seth Holt ph Harry Waxman m Richard Rodney Bennett
☆ Bette Davis, Jill Bennett, William Dix, James Villiers, Wendy Craig, Pamela Franklin, Maurice Denham

Nanook of the North *

US   1921   57m   bw   silent
Revillon Frères
■ ⊚

The life of an Eskimo and his family.
Primitive but trail-blazing documentary, hard to sit through for modern audiences.
wd/ph/ed Robert Flaherty
'In a day of emotional and artistic deliquescence on the screen. a picture with the fresh strength and pictorial promise of Nanook of the North is in the nature of a revolution.' – *Frances Taylor Patterson*
† Nanook himself died of hunger on the ice shortly after the film was released.

Nanou

UK/France   1986   110m   Eastmancolor
Umbrella-Caulfield/Arion
A young English girl, travelling through France, has an affair with a political activist.
Unsatisfactory film of an unsatisfactory romance.

---

wd Conny Templeman *ph* Martin Fuhrer *m* John Keane *ph* Andrew Mollo *m* Tom Priestley
☆ Imogen Stubbs, Jean-Philippe Ecoffey, Daniel Day-Lewis, Lou Castel, Valentine Pelka, Anne-Marie Jabraud, Dominique Rousseau, Michel Robin, Roger Ibanez

Napló Gyermekeimnek: see *Diary for My Children*

Napoleon ****
France 1927 378m bw (some colour)
silent
WESTI/Société Générale de Films
▤ ⊘⊾
The early life of Napoleon.
A cinematic epic which, although brilliant in most particulars, owes its greatest interest to its narrative sweep, its flair for composition and its use of triptych screens which at the end combine to show one giant picture, the clear precursor of Cinerama. In 1934 Gance revised his film and added stereophonic sound.
ph various *m* Arthur Honegger *wd/ed* Abel Gance
☆ Albert Dieudonné, Antonin Artaud, Pierre Batcheff
† The 1934 version ran 140m and included three-dimensional sound.

Napoleon and Samantha
†↑ US 1972 91m Technicolor
Walt Disney (Winston Hibler)
▤
When his old guardian dies, a small boy and his girl friend run away with their pet lion.
Patchy, episodic action drama for older children, with a very sleepy lion.
w Stewart Raffill *d* Bernard McEveety
ph Monroe Askins *m* Buddy Baker
☆ Michael Douglas, Will Geer
♫ Buddy Baker

Nära Livet: see *So Close to Life*

Narayama Bushi-Ko: see *The Ballad of Narayama*

The Narrow Corner
US 1933 71m bw
Warner
On an eastern island, a man on the run for murder finds he can't escape his fate.
Mediocre adaptation of a Somerset Maugham novel in which very little happens; the added love interest doesn't help.
w Robert Presnell *d* Alfred E. Green
☆ Douglas Fairbanks Jnr, Ralph Bellamy, Dudley Digges, Arthur Hohl, Patricia Ellis
'Considerably better than fair.' – *Variety*
† Remade three years later as *Isle of Fury* (qv).

'They Want Her Dead. He Needs Her Alive.'
Narrow Margin
US 1990 97m Technicolor Panavision
Guild/Carolco (Jonathan A. Zimbert)
▨⊡ ▤ ⊘⊾ ⊘
A district attorney and a key witness in a trial take refuge on a train from pursuing gangsters.
Inferior remake of the 1952 film, with little sense of suspense.
w Earl Fenton Jnr *story* Martin Goldsmith, Jack Leonard *m* Bruce Broughton *pd* Joel Schiller *ad* Kim Mooney *ed* James Mitchell *d/ph* Peter Hyams
☆ Gene Hackman, Anne Archer, James B. Sikking, J. T. Walsh, M. Emmet Walsh, Susan Hogan, Nigel Bennett, J. A. Preston
† *Variety* reported that while the original film cost $230,000 to make, the remake was nearly a hundred times more expensive, at $21 million.

The Narrow Margin ***
US 1952 70m bw
RKO (Stanley Rubin)
⊘⊾
Police try to guard a prosecution witness on a train from Chicago to Los Angeles.
Tight little thriller which takes every advantage of its train setting. What the trade used to call a sleeper, it gave more satisfaction than many a top feature.
w Earl Fenton *d* Richard Fleischer *ph* George E. Diskant
☆ Charles McGraw, Marie Windsor, Jacqueline White, Queenie Leonard
'A taut, breathlessly fast and highly suspenseful "sleeper" par excellence.' – *Time Out, 1986*

♫ original story (Martin Goldsmith, Jack Leonard)

The Narrowing Circle
GB 1955 66m bw
Fortress Films/Eros
Murder on the staff of a magazine.
Very tolerable mystery which wastes no time and plays fair.
w Doreen Montgomery *novel* Julian Symons
d Charles Saunders *ph* Jonah Jones *m* Reg Owen
☆ Paul Carpenter, Hazel Court, Ferdy Mayne, Russell Napier, Trevor Reid

'The damnedest thing you ever saw!'
Nashville ***
US 1975 161m Metrocolor Panavision
Paramount/ABC (Robert Altman)
▤ ⊘⊾
A political campaign in Nashville organizes a mammoth pop concert to gain support.
Kaleidoscopic, fragmented, multi-storied musical melodrama, a mammoth movie which can be a bore or an inspiration according to taste. Certainly many exciting moments pass by, but the length is self-defeating.
w Joan Tewkesbury *d* Robert Altman *ph* Paul Lohmann *md* Richard Baskin
☆ Geraldine Chaplin, David Arkin, Barbara Baxley, Ned Beatty, Karen Black, Keith Carradine, Henry Gibson, Keenan Wynn, Lily Tomlin, Ronee Blakley
'A gigantic parody ... crammed with samples taken from every level of Nashville society, revealed in affectionate detail bordering on caricature in a manner that would surely delight Norman Rockwell.' – *Philip Strick*
'Wildly over-praised Altman, with all the defects we once looked on as marks of healthy ambitiousness: terrible construction, messy editing, leering jokes at its own characters, unending pomposity.' – *Time Out, 1980*
♪ song 'I'm Easy' (*m/ly* Keith Carradine)
♫ best picture; Robert Altman; Lily Tomlin; Ronee Blakley

The Nasty Girl ***
West Germany 1990 92m Eastmancolor
Mainline/Sentana/ZDF
▨⊡ ▤ ⊘⊾
original title: *Das Schreckliche Mädchen*
Despite local hostility, a girl researches into events in her home town during the Nazi regime.
A witty and exuberant social satire, using very effectively a documentary approach to the subject.
wd Michael Verhoeven *ph* Axel de Roche *m* Mike Hertung, Elmar Schloter, Billy Gorlt, Lydie Auvray *ad* Hubert Popp *ed* Barbara Hennings
☆ Lena Stolze, Monika Baumgartner, Michael Gahr, Fred Stillkrauth, Elisabeth Bertram, Robert Giggenbach, Karin Thaler, Hans-Reinhard Muller
♫ best foreign film
♉ best foreign film

Nasty Habits *
GB 1976 92m Technicolor
Brut/Bowden (Robert Enders)
▤
An abbess dies and the nuns vie for succession.
Satirical comedy rather obviously based on the Watergate scandals; initially amusing, but very tiresome by the end.
w Robert Enders *novel* The Abbess of Crewe by Muriel Spark *d* Michael Lindsay-Hogg
ph Douglas Slocombe *m* John Cameron
☆ Glenda Jackson, Melina Mercouri, Geraldine Page, Sandy Dennis, Anne Jackson, Anne Meara, Edith Evans, Susan Penhaligon, Rip Torn, Eli Wallach, Jerry Stiller
'The sort of material just about fit for a half-hour TV sketch.' – *Richard Combs, MFB*

The National Health *
GB 1973 97m Eastmancolor
Columbia (Ned Sherrin, Terry Glinwood)
▤
Life in the general men's ward of a large antiquated hospital.
Acerbic comedy from a National Theatre play which mixes tragedy and farce into a kind of Carry on Dying.
w Peter Nichols *play* Peter Nichols *d* Jack Gold
ph John Coquillon *m* Carl Davis *pd* Ray Simm
☆ Jim Dale, Lynn Redgrave, Eleanor Bron, Sheila Scott-Wilkinson, Donald Sinden, Colin Blakely, Clive Swift

National Lampoon Goes to the Movies: see *National Lampoon's Movie Madness*

National Lampoon's Animal House *
US 1978 109m Technicolor
Universal (Matty Simmons, Ivan Reitman)
▨⊡ ▤ ⊘⊾ ⊘ ⌒
On an American campus around 1962, scruffy newcomers challenge the elegant élite.
A ragbag of college gags, of interest only to those who have had the experience; but its success caused much imitation, especially in American television.
w Harold Ramis, Douglas Kenney, Chris Miller
d John Landis *ph* Charles Correll *m* Elmer Bernstein
☆ John Belushi, Tim Matheson, John Vernon, Donald Sutherland, Verna Bloom, Cesare Danova, Mary Louise Weller

National Lampoon's Christmas Vacation
†↑ US 1989 97m colour
Warner/Hughes Entertainment (John Hughes, Tom Jacobson)
▨⊡ ▤ ⊘⊾ ⊘
A father decides to give the family an old-fashioned Christmas at home.
Unsubtle comedy that always goes for the easy laugh.
w John Hughes *d* Jeremiah S. Chechik
ph Thomas Ackerman *m* Angelo Badalmenti
pd Stephen Marsh *ed* Jerry Greenberg
☆ Chevy Chase, Beverly D'Angelo, Randy Quaid, Diane Ladd, E. G. Marshall, Doris Roberts, Julia Louis-Dreyfus, Mae Questel, William Hickey

National Lampoon's Class Reunion
US 1982 85m Metrocolor
Fox/ABC Productions (Matty Simmons)
▤ ⊘⊾ ⊘
The class of '72 foregathers at Lizzie Borden High, where a murderer is lurking.
An entertainment in which the presentation is better than the material, which is a vague spoof of high school and horror films.
w John Hughes *d* Michael Miller *ph* Phil Lathrop *m* Peter Bernstein, Mark Goldenberg
pd Dean Edward Mitzner *ed* Richard C. Meyer, Ann Mills
☆ Gerrit Graham, Michael Lerner, Fred McCarren, Miriam Flynn, Stephen Furst

National Lampoon's European Vacation
†↑ US 1985 94m Technicolor
Warner (Matty Simmons)
▨⊡ ▤ ⊘⊾
An American family determines to see Europe.
Hopelessly unfunny and simple-minded comedy, lacking even the usual schoolboy smut.
w John Hughes, Robert Klane *d* Amy Heckerling
ph Bob Paynter *m* Charles Fox *pd* Bob Cartwright *ed* Paul Herring
☆ Chevy Chase, Beverly D'Angelo, Jason Lively, Dana Hill, Eric Idle

'See it before they make the sequel!'
National Lampoon's Loaded Weapon 1
US 1993 83m DeLuxe
Guild/New Line (Suzanne Todd, David Willis)
▨⊡ ▤ ⊘⊾ ⊘
Two cops investigate a cocaine-cookie smuggling ring.
A lacklustre parody of the Lethal Weapon movies; it not only has no style, it does not even have any jokes.
w Don Holley, Gene Quintano *d* Gene Quintano
ph Peter Dening *m* Robert Folk *pd* Jaymes Hinkle *ed* Christopher Greenbury
☆ Emilio Estevez, Samuel L. Jackson, Jon Lovitz, Tim Curry, Kathy Ireland, Frank McRae, William Shatner, James Doohan, F. Murray Abraham
'This would-be comedy is very short on laughs and virtually all are given away in its trailer.' – *Variety*

National Lampoon's Movie Madness
US 1981 89m Technicolor Panavision
UA (Matty Simmons)
▤
aka: *National Lampoon Goes to the Movies*
Three parodies of movie genres: an insurance salesman seeks personal growth; a stripper becomes First Lady in three days; a young cop learns how to be tough.
Cinema audiences were spared this inept and witless display, though it turns up on late-night TV to bore the unwary.

National Lampoon's Senior Trip
US 1995 91m colour
New Line/Alliance (Wendy Grean)
High-school seniors cause political mayhem when the US President invites them to Washington.
Dim and dumb comedy with jokes that rarely rise above the subjects of flatulence and vomit; sick-making it is.
w Roger Kumble, I. Marlene King *d* Kelly Makin
ph François Protat *m* Steve Bartek *pd* Gregory Keen *ed* Stephen Lawrence
☆ Matt Frewer, Valerie Mahaffey, Lawrence Dane, Tommy Chong, Jeremy Renner, Rob Moore
'A witless item.' – *Variety*

National Lampoon's Vacation
US 1983 98m Technicolor
Warner (Matty Simmons)
▨⊡ ▤ ⊘⊾ ⊘
An inventor drives his family on a holiday starting in Chicago and ending in California, but the journey is fraught with disaster.
Episodic, more or less straight black comedy, with detail more often boring or repellent than funny.
w John Hughes *d* Harold Ramis *ph* Victor J. Kemper *m* Ralph Burns *pd* Jack Collis *ed* Paul Herring
☆ Chevy Chase, Imogene Coca, Beverly D'Angelo, Randy Quaid, Eddie Bracken

National Velvet *
†↑ US 1945 125m Technicolor
MGM (Pandro S. Berman)
Children train a horse to win the Grand National.
A big bestseller from another era; its flavour of conception and production quickly became evident.
w Theodore Reeves, Helen Deutsch *novel* Enid Bagnold *d* Clarence Brown *ph* Leonard Smith
m Herbert Stothart *ed* Robert J. Kern
☆ Mickey Rooney, Elizabeth Taylor, *Anne Revere*, Donald Crisp, Angela Lansbury, Jackie Jenkins, Reginald Owen, Terry Kilburn, Norma Varden, Alec Craig, Arthur Shields, Dennis Hoey
† Sequel 1978: *International Velvet*.
♦ Anne Revere; Robert J. Kern
♫ Clarence Brown; Leonard Smith

Native Son
US 1986 112m colour
Cinecom/Diane Silver/American Playhouse/Cinetudes
A poor black teenager commits murder.
Heavy-going adaptation of a novel seen in some American quarters as a symbol of classic guilt.
w Richard Wesley *novel* Richard Wright
d Jerrold Freedman *ph* Thomas Burstyn *m* James Mtume
☆ Carroll Baker, Akousuwa Busia, Matt Dillon, Art Evans, Elizabeth McGovern, John McMartin, Geraldine Page
† A low-budget Argentine version had been filmed in 1950 by Pierre Chenal, with the author in the leading role

Nattevagten: see *Nightwatch*

Nattlek: see *Night Games*

Nattvardsgästerna: see *Winter Light*

The Natural *
US 1984 137m Technicolor
Tri-Star/Delphi II (Mark Johnson)
▨⊡ ▤ ⊘⊾ ⊘
The life of a baseball star who reaches the heights and can only fall.
Curious attempt to modernize the King Arthur legend, with a baseball bat substituting for Excalibur and hints of magic everywhere. A generally mystifying if occasionally an attractive experience.
w Roger Towne, Phil Dusenberry *novel* Bernard Malamud *d* Barry Levinson *ph* Caleb Deschanel
m Randy Newman
☆ Robert Redford, Robert Duvall, Glenn Close, Kim Basinger, Wilford Brimley, Barbara Hershey, Robert Prosky, Joe Don Baker, Robert Farnsworth

♫ Glenn Close (supporting actress); photography; music; art direction

'In The Media Circus Of Life, They Were The Main Attraction.'

Natural Born Killers *
US 1994 119m Technicolor
Warner/Regency/Alcor/JD/Ixtlan/New Regency (Jame Hamsher, Don Murphy, Clayton Townsend)
▦ ⚲ ⌒

A young couple become mass murderers and media favourites.

An over-the-top assault on an audience's sensibilities, making its points with a heavy hand and a brutally jokey style, utilizing every movie- and video-making style in its deadly assault through a dislocating barrage of images. The message of all this manipulation is that the media manipulate violence for their own sensationalist aims. As a technical exercise, it is dazzling; as a contribution to a moral debate, it is deadening.

w David Veloz, Richard Rutowski, Oliver Stone *story* Quentin Tarantino *ph* Robert Richardson *pd* Victor Kempster *ed* Hank Corwin, Brian Berdan

☆ Woody Harrelson, Juliette Lewis, Robert Downey Jnr, Tommy Lee Jones
  'Plunders every visual trick of avant-garde and mainstream cinema – morphing, back projection, slow motion, animation and pixilation on five kinds of film stock – and, for two delirious hours, pushes them in your face like a Cagney grapefruit. The actors go hyper-hyper, the camera is ever on the bias, the garish colors converge and collide into a vision of America in heat. The ride is fun, too, daredevil fun of the sort only Stone seems willing to provide in this timid-film era.' – *Richard Corliss, Time*
  'The oddest thing about this would-be satire is that, for all the gore and hysteria, the film doesn't feel particularly impassioned; it's a frivolous barrage.' – *Terrence Rafferty, New Yorker*
  'Oliver Stone would have a lot more chance of proving the proposition that violence is only exciting at second hand if he himself were able to show a prison riot without adding a pounding rock soundtrack. What makes him think he's a critic of an over-stimulated society when synthetic adrenalin is his stock-in-trade?' – *Adam Mars-Jones, Independent*
  'How is it possible that Stone has made a picture of such staggering awfulness and jaw-dropping amateurishness?' – *Henry Joyce, Movie Collector*
  'Isn't so much a cry against the dying of the light as the kind of movie that dims the light in the first place. We all make mistakes. But this time Stone has made a colossal blunder.' – *Derek Malcolm, Guardian*
  'It's like watching two weeks of television in two hours.' – *Oliver Stone*
† Quentin Tarantino objected when his original script was rewritten by Stone.
†† Although the video was given an '18' certificate in Britain, Warner Home Video withdrew its UK release indefinitely following mass killings in Scotland and Tasmania in 1996.

A Natural Born Salesman: see *Earthworm Tractors*

The Nature of the Beast: see *Hatchet Man (1994)*

The Nature of the Beast *
UK 1988 95m colour
Cannon/Film Four International/British Screen (Joanna Smith)

In a small industrial town, where unemployment is rife, a young boy and his friend stalk a mysterious beast that is killing animals.

An unsuccessful allegory of social disintegration that stays in the shadow of Kes.

w Janni Howker *novel* Janni Howker *d* Franco Rosso *ph* Nat Crosby *m* Stanley Myers, Hans Zimmer *pd* Jamie Leonard *ed* George Akers
☆ Lynton Dearden, Paul Simpson, Tony Melody, Freddie Fletcher, Dave Hill, Roberta Kerr, David Fleeshman

Naughty Arlette: see *The Romantic Age*

Naughty Blue Knickers: see *The Folies of Elodie*

Naughty but Nice
US 1939 90m bw
Warner (Sam Bischoff)

A professor of classical music accidentally writes a popular song.

Mildly amusing comedy musical with all the tunes adapted from the classics (cf That Night with You).

w Jerry Wald, Richard Macaulay *d* Ray Enright *ph* Arthur L. Todd *songs* Harry Warren, Johnny Mercer
☆ Dick Powell, Ann Sheridan, Ronald Reagan, Gale Page, ZaSu Pitts, Jerry Colonna

Naughty Marietta **
US 1935 106m bw
MGM (Hunt Stromberg)
▦ ⚲

A French princess goes to America and falls in love with an Indian scout.

Period operetta which set the seal of success on the MacDonald-Eddy team. In itself, dated but quite pleasing for those who like the genre.

w John Lee Mahin, Frances Goodrich, Albert Hackett *operetta* Rida Johnson Young *d* W. S. Van Dyke *ph* William Daniels *m* Victor Herbert *ad* Cedric Gibbons
☆ Jeanette MacDonald, Nelson Eddy, Frank Morgan, Elsa Lanchester, Douglass Dumbrille, Joseph Cawthorn, Cecilia Parker, Walter Kingsford
  'Slow-moving operetta which singing must sustain.' – *Variety*
  'When these two profiles come together to sing Ah Sweet Mystery of Life, it's beyond camp, it's in a realm of its own.' – *Judith Crist, 1977*
♫ best picture

The Naughty Nineties
US 1945 72m bw
Universal (Edward L. Hartmann, John Grant)
▦ ⚲

Two incompetents help an old showboat owner.

Dim star comedy apart from the team's rendition of their most famous routine, 'Who's On First'.

w Edmund L. Hartmann, John Grant, Edmund Joseph, Hal Fimberg *d* Jean Yarbrough *ph* George Robinson
☆ Bud Abbott, Lou Costello, Henry Travers, Alan Curtis, Rita Johnson, Joe Sawyer

The Navigator ***
🏃‍♂️ US 1924 63m bw silent
Metro-Goldwyn/Buster Keaton (Joseph M. Schenck)
▦ ▦ ⚲

A millionaire and his girl are the only people on a transatlantic liner marooned in mid-ocean.

A succession of hilarious sight gags: the star in top form.

w Jean Havez, Clyde Bruckman, J. A. Mitchell *d* Buster Keaton, Donald Crisp *ph* Elgin Lessley, Byron Houck
☆ Buster Keaton, Kathryn McGuire
  'Studded with hilarious moments and a hundred and one adroit gags.' – *Photoplay*

The Navigator: A Medieval Odyssey **
Australia 1988 91m colour/bw
Recorded Releasing/Arenafilm (John Maynard, Gary Hannam)
▦ ▦ ⚲

Medieval villagers, fearful of the Black Death, go on a pilgrimage through a mine and emerge in the modern world.

Oddly disturbing fable, imaginatively presented.

w Vincent Ward, Kely Lyons, Geoff Chapple *d* Vincent Ward *ph* Geoffrey Simpson *m* Davood A. Tabrizi *pd* Sally Campbell *ed* John Scott
☆ Bruce Lyons, Chris Haywood, Hamish McFarlane, Marshall Napier, Noel Appleby, Paul Livingstone, Sarah Pierse, Mark Wheatley, Tony Herbert

'It is not the victory that is important, it is how the game is played!'

Navy Blue and Gold
US 1937 93m bw
Sam Zimbalist/MGM

An unpopular naval cadet makes good.

Ingenuous flagwaver, like a wrap-up of umpteen others but with better production.

w George Bruce *d* Sam Wood
☆ Robert Young, James Stewart, Florence Rice, Billie Burke, Lionel Barrymore, Tom Brown, Samuel S. Hinds, Paul Kelly
  'Expertly made and sure box office.' – *Variety*

Navy Blues
US 1941 109m bw
Warner (Jerry Wald)

Naval ratings get into trouble in Honolulu.

Undernourished musical comedy with not too much of either commodity.

w Jerry Wald, Richard Macaulay, Arthur T. Horman *d* Lloyd Bacon *ph* Tony Gaudio *ch* Seymour Felix *songs* Arthur Schwartz, Johnny Mercer
☆ Ann Sheridan, Jack Oakie, Martha Raye, Jack Haley, Herbert Anderson, Jack Carson, Richard Lane, Jackie Gleason, Howard da Silva

The Navy Comes Through
US 1942 81m bw
RKO

The story of a merchant marine ship.

Propaganda potboiler with a reasonably efficient cast and production.

w Roy Chanslor, Aeneas Mackenzie *story* Borden Chase *d* A. Edward Sutherland *ph* Nick Musuraca *m* Roy Webb
☆ Pat O'Brien, George Murphy, Jane Wyatt, Jackie Cooper, Carl Esmond, Max Baer, Desi Arnaz, Ray Collins

Navy SEALS
US 1990 114m Technicolor
Rank/Orion (Brenda Feigen, Bernard Williams)
▦ ▦ ⚲ ⌒

Naval commandos attempt to kidnap an Arab terrorist and destroy a missile store in Lebanon.

Flaccid action picture, peopled by comic-strip stereotypes and full of nothing but sound and fury.

w Chuck Pfarrer, Gary Goldman *d* Lewis Teague *ph* John A. Alonzo *m* Sylvester Levay *pd* Guy J. Comtois, Veronica Hadfield *ed* Don Zimmerman
☆ Charlie Sheen, Michael Biehn, Joanne Whalley-Kilmer, Rick Rossovich, Cyril O'Reilly, Bill Paxton, Dennis Haysbert, Paul Sanchez
  'Quite what this balefully predictable action-adventure is trying to prove totally escapes me. Unless it is that there is nothing much these days that the American public won't take in the way of flag-waving juvenilia.' – *Derek Malcolm, Guardian*

The Navy Steps Out: see *A Girl, a Guy and a Gob*

The Navy versus The Night Monsters
US 1965 90m DeLuxe
Standard Club (George Edwards)
▦ ▦
aka: *Monsters of the Night*
aka: *Night Crawlers*

Botanical specimens taken from the Antarctic to a remote naval base include man-eating plants.

There is a certain silly pleasure to be derived from watching Mamie Van Doren being threatened by carnivorous vegetables, which hardly look a match for her, but The Day of the Triffids it isn't, despite some atmospheric photography.

wd Michael A. Hoey *novel* Monsters from the Earth's End by Murray Leinster *ph* Stanley Cortez *m* Gordon Zahler *ad* Paul Sylos *ed* George White
☆ Anthony Eisley, Mamie Van Doren, Walter Sande, Bobby Van, Billy Gray, Phillip Terry, Pamela Kellino

Navy Wife
US 1935 72m bw
Fox

A girl who marries a navy doctor is unhappy with the life.

Routine domestic drama with a propaganda angle.

w Sonya Levien *novel* Beauty's Daughter by Kathleen Norris *d* Allan Dwan
☆ Claire Trevor, Ralph Bellamy, Jane Darwell, Ben Lyon, Warren Hymer, Kathleen Burke
  'Problem play for the duals.' – *Variety*

Navy Wife
US 1956 83m bw
Allied Artists
GB title: *Mother, Sir!*

A commander's wife visits her husband in Japan and learns about Japanese attitudes.

Silly hands-across-the-sea comedy which takes a long time to get nowhere.

w Kay Lenard *d* Edward Bernds *ph* Wilfred Cline *m* Hans Salter

☆ Joan Bennett, Gary Merrill, Shirley Yagamuchi, Judy Nugent

Nazarin *
Mexico 1958 94m bw
Barbachano Ponce
▦ ⚲

A Catholic priest tries to take the teachings of Christ literally, but is drastically misunderstood.

A black atheistic satire pretty typical of its director, but not among his most enjoyable works.

w Julio Alejandro, Luis Buñuel *novel* Benito Perez Galdos *d* Luis Buñuel *ph* Gabriel Figueroa
☆ Francisco Rabal, Marga Lopez, Rita Macedo, Ignacio Lopez Tarso

Nazi Agent *
US 1942 84m bw
MGM (Irving Asher)

A German-American is forced by his Nazi twin to help a group of German spies.

Modest suspenser with a plot twist similar to The Great Impersonation and Dead Ringer.

w Paul Gangelin, John Meehan Jnr *d* Jules Dassin *ph* Harry Stradling *m* Lennie Hayton
☆ Conrad Veidt, Ann Ayars, Frank Reicher, Dorothy Tree, Martin Kosleck

Neak Sre: see *Rice People*

The Neanderthal Man
US 1953 75m bw
United Artists/Global

A scientist transforms a cat into a sabre-toothed tiger and himself into a neanderthal man; he is then eaten by the tiger.

By no means as amusing as it sounds.

w Aubrey Wisberg, Jack Pollexfen *d* E. A. Dupont *ph* Stanley Cortez
☆ Robert Shayne, Richard Crane, Doris Merrick, Joyce Terry

Near Dark
US 1987 94m colour
Entertainment/Scotti Brothers/International Video Entertainment (Steven-Charles Jaffe)
▦ ▦ ⚲ ⌒

A cowboy is seduced into joining a roving gang of vampires.

Fast moving, moderately successful attempt to bring the vampire movie screaming into the 20th century.

w Eric Red, Kathryn Bigelow *d* Kathryn Bigelow *ph* Adam Greenberg *m* Tangerine Dream *pd* Stephen Altman *ed* Howard Smith
☆ Adrian Pasdar, Jenny Wright, Lance Henriksen, Bill Paxton, Jenette Goldstein, Tim Thomerson, Joshua Miller
  'Projects a truly upsetting image of revulsion and horror, and its scenes of blood-letting – especially a long spectacular set piece featuring the killing of the clientele of a lowlife tavern – are not merely gross, but genuinely disturbing.' – *Henry Sheehan, L A Reader*

Near Misses: see *Near Mrs*

Near Mrs
US/France 1991 89m colour
Chrysalide/Canal+/Movie Group (Monique Annaud)
▦ ▦
aka: *Near Misses*

A bigamist runs into difficulties when he assumes the identity of a marine in order to have a dirty weekend with his mistress.

Frenetic but rarely amusing farce; its opening sequence of multiple murder kills the fun before the film has begun.

w Peter Baloff, David Wollert *d* Baz Taylor *ph* Yves Dahan *m* Didier Vasseur *ad* Nicolas Prier *ed* Michele Robert-Lauliac
☆ Judge Reinhold, Casey Siemaszko, Rebecca Pauly, Cecile Paoli, Kashia Figura, Muriel Combeau, Andrzej Jagora

The Near Room
GB 1995 90m colour
Metrodome/Inverclyde/Glasgow Film Fund/British Screen (Len Crooks)
▦

An investigative journalist, who is hired by his former wife to track down a missing teenager involved in prostitution and drugs, realizes that she is the illegitimate daughter he abandoned at birth.

A low-budget film noir, stylishly made but lacking conviction and often bordering on the incomprehensible.

w Robert Murphy d David Hayman ph Kevin Rowley m James Grant, Paul McGeechan pd Andy Harris ed Martin Sharpe

☆ Adrian Dunbar, David O'Hara, Julie Graham, David Hayman, Tom Watson, James Ellis, Robert Pugh, Emma Faulkner, Andy Serkis, Peter McDougall

'Aspires to delve into the dark side: to show madness, violence and exploitation. Instead, it is as ludicrous and as luridly enjoyable as an old B-movie.' – *Geoffrey Macnab, Sight and Sound*

Nearly a Nasty Accident
⋔⋔ GB 1961 91m bw
British Lion/Britannia/Marlow (Bertram Ostrer)
A mild-mannered aircraftman causes disaster wherever he goes.
Familiar faces just about save from disaster this underscripted comedy for indulgent audiences.
w Jack Davies, Hugh Woodruff *play* Touch Wood by David Stringer, David Carr d Don Chaffey ph Paul Beeson m Ken Jones
☆ Kenneth Connor, Jimmy Edwards, Shirley Eaton, Richard Wattis, Ronnie Stevens, Jon Pertwee, Eric Barker, Peter Jones, Jack Watling, Joyce Carey, Terry Scott

'Neath the Arizona Skies
US 1934 54m bw
Monogram/Lone Star (Paul Malvern)
A cowboy searches for the father of a young Indian girl, who is heiress to oil riches, and threatened by bandits.
One of the nine films that Wayne rolled out in the same year, and a standard production-line effort, with the usual fist- and gunfights, chases, and good triumphing over evil.
w Burl Tuttle d Harry Fraser ph Archie Stout ad E. R. Hickson ed Charles Hunt
☆ John Wayne, Sheila Terry, Shirley Jane Rickert, Jack Rockwell, Yakima Canutt, Weston Edwards, Buffalo Bill Jnr, George Hayes

'Three men and a woman face death beside a man they want to kill!'
The Nebraskan
US 1953 66m Technicolor 3D
Columbia
An army scout proves the innocence of an Indian supposed to have murdered a Sioux chief.
Two-bit Western which looked even worse in three dimensions.
w David Lang, Martin Berkeley d Fred F. Sears
☆ Phil Carey, Roberta Haynes, Wallace Ford, Richard Webb, Lee Van Cleef

Necessary Roughness
US 1991 104m Technicolor
UIP/Paramount (Mace Neufeld, Robert Rehme)
⬛ ▦ ⬚
After a college football team has been dismissed for corruption, a coach attempts to create a new squad from unathletic students.
Drear movie that is never less than predictable and never more than tedious.
w Rick Natkin, David Fuller d Stan Dragoti ph Peter Stein m Bill Conti pd Paul Peters ed John Wright, Steve Mirkovich, Wayne Wahrman
☆ Scott Bakula, Robert Loggia, Hector Elizondo, Harley Jane Kozak, Larry Miller, Sinbad, Fred Dalton Thompson
'All the expected clichés of the losers-make-a-comeback plot.' – *Variety*
'As phoney as the Astroturf on which most of it takes place.' – *Philip French, Observer*

Necromancy
US 1973 83m colour
Cinerama (Bert I. Gordon)
▦
Two young people become involved in small-town witchcraft.
Low-key, low-talent thriller overbalanced by its star.
wd Bert I. Gordon ph Winton C. Hoch m Fred Karger
☆ Orson Welles, Pamela Franklin, Michael Ontkean, Lee Purcell

'It'll Take You To Hell and Back...'
Necronomicon
US 1993 Foto-Kem
August/Davis Film/Brian Yuzna (Samuel Hadida, Brian Yuzna)
⬛ ▦
Horror writer H. P. Lovecraft discovers that a copy of the *Necronomicon*, containing the secrets of the universe, is in America and seeks it out to inspire his work.
Dull compendium of three stories of demonic possession, with cheesy special effects and little that will either thrill or terrify.
w Brent V. Friedman, Christophe Gans, Kazunori Ito, Brian Yuzna d Brian Yuzna, Christophe Gans, Shusuke Kaneko ph Gerry Lively, Russ Brandt m Joseph Lo Duca, Daniel Licht pd Antony Tremblay ed Christopher Roth sp Thomas C. Rainone, John Vulich, Magic Media, Screaming Mad George, Todd Masters, Bart Mixon's Monster Fixin's and others
☆ Jeffrey Combs, Bruce Payne, Belinda Bauer, David Warner, Signy Coleman, Don Calfa, Bess Meyer, Millie Perkins, Dennis Christopher, Maria Ford, Richard Lynch
'B horror movies are often fun but this is Pillocksville.' – *Derek Malcolm, Guardian*

Necronomicon – Geträumte Sünden: see
Succubus

Ned Kelly
GB 1970 103m Technicolor
UA/Woodfall (Neil Hartley)
▦ ⌓
The career of a 19th-century Australian outlaw.
Obstinately unlikeable action picture with some kind of message which never becomes clear amid all the cleverness.
w Tony Richardson, Ian Jones d Tony Richardson ph Gerry Fisher m Shel Silverstein pd Jocelyn Herbert
☆ Mick Jagger, Allen Bickford, Geoff Gilmour, Mark McManus

'The town of Castle Rock just made a deal with the Devil ... Now it's time to pay!'
Needful Things
US 1993 120m Technicolor
Rank/Castle Rock/New Line (Jack Cummins)
⬛ ▦ ⬚ ⌓ ◎
The owner of an antique shop creates havoc and murder by offering customers what they want in return for carrying out practical jokes on their neighbours.
A down-market version of Faust that provides some moments of black comedy in its depiction of small-town rivalries, but outstays its welcome.
w W. D. Richter *novel* Stephen King d Fraser C. Heston ph Tony Westman m Patrick Doyle pd Douglas Higgins ed Rob Kobrin sp make-up: Tibor Farkas
☆ Max von Sydow, Ed Harris, Bonnie Bedelia, Amanda Plummer, J. T. Walsh, Ray McKinnon, Duncan Fraser, Shane Meier, Valri Bromfield
'This darkly comic picture proves a sadistic, mean-spirited, overlong exercise that should have a devilish time sustaining any box-office fire.' – *Brian Lowry, Variety*

Nefertite, Queen of the Nile (dubbed)
Italy 1962 85m colour SuperCinemascope
Max (Ottavio Poggi)
original title: Nefertite – Regina del Nilo
aka: Queen of the Nile
A sculptor is condemned to death for falling in love with the high priest's daughter, who is intended as a bride for the new Pharaoh.
Uninteresting romantic drama that gains nothing from being set in ancient Egypt.
d Fernando Cerchio ph Massimi Dallamano ed Renato Cinquini
☆ Vincent Price, Edmund Purdom, Jeanne Crain, Amedeo Nazzari, Liana Orfei

Negatives *
GB 1968 98m Eastmancolor
Crispin/Kettledrum (Judd Bernard)
⬛
Three people indulge in sexual fantasies involving Dr Crippen and Baron von Richthofen.
Smoothly done but impenetrable psychological poppycock: what is fact and what is fancy, only the author knows.

w Peter Everett, Roger Lowry *novel* Peter Everett d Peter Medak ph Ken Hodges m Basil Kirchin
☆ Glenda Jackson, Peter McEnery, Diane Cilento, Maurice Denham, Stephen Lewis, Norman Rossington

'Justice At Any Price.'
The Negotiator
US 1998 138m Technicolor Panavision
Warner/Regency/Mandeville/Taurus (David Hoberman, Arnon Milchan)
⬛ ▦ ⬚ ⌓ ◎ ⌓
Realizing that he is being set up by his colleagues, a police hostage negotiator takes hostages of his own, and is besieged by corrupt cops who want him dead.
A noisy thriller that delivers big bangs and obtrusive acting.
w James DeMonaco, Kevin Fox d F. Gary Gray ph Russell Carpenter m Graeme Revell pd Holger Gross ed Christian Wagner
☆ Samuel L. Jackson, Kevin Spacey, David Morse, Ron Rifkin, John Spencer, J. T. Walsh, Regina Taylor, Siobahn Fallon, Paul Giamatti
'Doesn't stretch the Hollywood thriller much beyond its big, loud self-important traditions.' – *Anthony Quinn, Independent*

Neighbors *
US 1981 94m Technicolor
Columbia/Zanuck-Brown
▦ ⬚
A staid suburbanite is first irritated, then taken over by his splashy neighbours.
Hit-or-miss but generally quite funny comedy in a style familiar to viewers of American late night television.
w Larry Gelbart *novel* Thomas Berger d John G. Avildsen ph Gerald Hirschfeld m Bill Conti pd Peter Larkin ed Jan Kurson
☆ John Belushi, Dan Aykroyd, Kathryn Walker, Cathy Moriarty, Igors Gavon, Dru-Ann Chukron

Neither the Sea nor the Sand
GB 1972 94m Eastmancolor
LMG/Portland (Jack Smith, Peter Fetterman)
Holidaying in Jersey, a married woman begins a love-affair with a local man which survives his sudden death.
An attempt at a Gothic romance ruined by half-hearted acting and direction; all that remains is a dull zombie movie and an unpleasant exercise in necrophilia.
w Gordon Honeycombe, Rosemary Davies *novel* Gordon Honeycombe d Fred Burnley ph David Muir m Nachum Heiman ad Michael Bastow ed Norman Wanstall
☆ Susan Hampshire, Frank Finlay, Michael Petrovitch, Michael Craze, Jack Lambert, Betty Duncan, David Garth, Tony Booth
'To depict the macabre in the midst of the everyday requires a greater degree of artifice than is displayed here.' – *MFB*
'Hampshire and Petrovitch are no Heathcliff and Cathy, and the director's "realistic" style which stops short at the genuinely macabre makes a mockery of the story's metaphysical overtones.' – *Films and Filming*

Nel Segno di Roma: see Sign of the Gladiator

'An Extraordinary Motion Picture About the Power of Innocence.'
'Her heart. Her soul. Her language are a mystery ... A mystery called...'
Nell
US 1994 113m colour Panavision
Polygram/Egg Pictures/Lost Pond (Jodie Foster, Renée Missel)
⬛ ▦ ⬚
Two doctors study, and try to communicate with, a young woman, brought up in the wilderness and speaking a language only she and her speech-impaired mother, now dead, can understand.
This is little more than an ordinary romance between two opposites, spiced with a bizarre turn from Jodie Foster; it confuses innocence and ignorance.
w William Nicholson, Mark Handley *play* Idioglossia by Mark Handley d Michael Apted m Mark Isham pd Dante Spinotti ed Jim Clark
☆ Jodie Foster, Liam Neeson, Natasha Richardson, Richard Libertini, Nick Searcy, Robin Mullins, Jeremy Davies
'One of those films about the mentally challenged that is so anxious to be politically correct that it over-compensates every which way it can.' – *Derek Malcolm, Guardian*
⚇ Jodie Foster

Nell Gwyn **
GB 1934 85m bw
B and D (Herbert Wilcox)
The affair of Charles II and an orange seller.
Naïve, vivid account of a famous couple; physically cheap and rather faded, but the best film on the subject and one of the best covering this period.
w Miles Malleson d Herbert Wilcox ph F. A. Young
☆ Anna Neagle, Cedric Hardwicke, Jeanne de Casalis, Muriel George, Miles Malleson, Esmé Percy, Moore Marriott
'Slow costumer, also lacking marquee value.' – *Variety*

Nelly and M Arnaud **
France/Germany/Italy 1995 106m colour
Guild/TFI/Cecchi Gori/Prokino/Canal/Alain Sarde
⬛ ▦
A young wife leaves her husband to form an uneasy relationship with a wealthy elderly businessman for whom she works as a secretary.
A cool, immaculately acted, restrained drama of two people unable or unwilling to resolve their feelings for one another.
w Claude Sautet, Jacques Fieschi, Yves Ulmann d Claude Sautet ph Jean-François Robin m Philippe Sarde pd Carlos Conti ed Jacqueline Thiedot
☆ Emmanuelle Béart, Michel Serrault, Jean-Hugues Anglade, Claire Nadeau, Françoise Brion, Michèle Laroque, Michel Lonsdale
'Orchestrates the progress of the obsessional relationship with the precision that only a director fully in command of both his style and material can muster. As a quiet, intimate dissection of the emotions, it is hard to beat.' – *Derek Malcolm, Guardian*

The Nelson Affair: see Bequest to the Nation

The Nelson Touch: see Corvette K 225

'In The Future ... It Pays To Be More Than Human.'
Nemesis
US 1993 95m colour
Imperial (Ash R. Shah, Eric Karson, Tom Karnowski)
⬛ ▦ ⬚ ⌓ ◎
In Los Angeles in 2027, where most people speak with thick foreign accents, a cop shot to pieces is reassembled as an android for a special assignment and uncovers a plot to take over the world.
Derivative and violent action film, strictly for those whose idea of a good time is bimbos with big guns.
w Rebecca Charles d Albert Pyun ph George Mooradian m Michel Rubini pd E. Colleen Saro ed David Kern, Mark Conte sp Gene Warren Jnr, Fantasy II Film Effects
☆ Olivier Gruner, Tim Thomerson, Cary-Hiroyuki Tagawa, Merle Kennedy, Yuji Okumoto, Marjorie Monaghan, Brion James, Deborah Shelton
'Fails in almost every respect.' – *Variety*

The Neon Bible *
GB/US 1995 92m Metrocolor Cinemascope
Artificial Eye/Mayfair/Scala/Channel 4 (Elizabeth Karlsen, Olivia Stewart)
⬛ ▦ ◎
A boy grows up in Georgia in the 1940s, living with a harsh and unsuccessful father and his increasingly demented mother, with only his aunt, a singer, adding any colour to his narrow life.
A carefully composed account of a very limited and repressed existence, much in the style of Davies's earlier The Long Day Closes, but lacking its wider resonance.
wd Terence Davies *novel* John Kennedy Toole ph Mick Coulter pd Christopher Hobbs ed Charles Rees
☆ Gena Rowlands, Jacob Tierney, Diana Scarwid, Denis Leary, Leo Burmester, Frances Conroy, Peter McRobbie, Drake Bell
'Kitchen-sink drama that pulls its own plug.' – *Tom Shone, Sunday Times*

The Neptune Disaster: see The Neptune Factor

'Wherever you've been – this is where you've never been before!'

The Neptune Factor
Canada 1972 98m DeLuxe Panavision
TCF/Quadrant/Bellevue-Pathé (Sanford Howard)

later retitled: *The Neptune Disaster*

American oceanologists conduct an experiment in underwater living.
Wet 'actioner' in which very little happens except a few porthole views of magnified fish.
w Jack de Witt d Daniel Petrie ph Harry Makin m Lalo Schifrin
☆ Ben Gazzara, Walter Pidgeon, Yvette Mimieux, Ernest Borgnine, Chris Wiggins

Neptune's Daughter *
US 1949 93m Technicolor
MGM (Jack Cummings)

A lady bathing suit designer has a South American romance.
Generally thought one of the better aquatic musicals, and certainly very typical of them and its studio at this time.
w Dorothy Kingsley d Edward Buzzell ph Charles Rosher m George Stoll songs Frank Loesser
☆ Esther Williams, Red Skelton, Ricardo Montalban, Betty Garrett, Keenan Wynn, Xavier Cugat and his Orchestra, Mike Mazurki, Ted de Corsia, Mel Blanc
♫ song 'Baby, It's Cold Outside'

Neskolko Intervyu Po Lichnyam Voprosam: see *Several Interviews On Personal Problems*

The Net
GB 1953 86m bw
Rank/Two Cities (Anthony Darnborough)
US title: *Project M7*
Tension among boffins in an aviation research station leads to murder and the discovery of a spy.
Low-key suspenser, quite adequately presented.
w William Fairchild novel John Pudney d Anthony Asquith ph Desmond Dickinson m Benjamin Frankel
☆ Phyllis Calvert, Noel Willman, Herbert Lom, James Donald, Robert Beatty, Muriel Pavlow, Walter Fitzgerald, Maurice Denham

The Net
US 1995 112m Technicolor
Columbia (Irwin Winkler, Rob Cowan)

A reclusive software tester's life is threatened after she discovers a conspiracy that allows crooks to gain access to, and manipulate, top-secret data held on government computers.
A dully paranoid thriller that is a bad imitation of Hitchcock. Its plot is full of implausibilities and it is also computer illiterate, which doesn't help, though Sandra Bullock's performance does, even if it is not enough to save the film.
w John Brancato, Michael Ferris d Irwin Winkler ph Jack N. Green m Mark Isham pd Dennis Washington ed Richard Halsey
☆ Sandra Bullock, Jeremy Northam, Dennis Miller, Diane Baker, Wendy Gazelle, Ken Howard, Ray McKinnon
'This high-tech but modestly scaled meller adroitly alternates between anxiety provoked by powerful computers and old-fashioned peril posed by duplicitous men, dark alleys, speeding cars and deserted warehouses.' – Todd McCarthy, Variety
† The film was the basis of a US TV series, *The Net*, starring Brooke Langton.

'Television will never be the same!'
'Prepare yourself for a perfectly outrageous motion picture!'

Network ****
US 1976 121m Metrocolor Panavision
MGM/UA (Howard Gottfried, Fred Caruso)

A network news commentator begins to say what he thinks about the world and becomes a new messiah to the people and an embarrassment to his sponsors.
A deliberately melodramatic satire on media corruption, it is passionate and compulsively watchable in its attack on demagoguery and in its depiction of the dangerous madness exploited by the mass media. What once seemed overheated satire has come, with time, to

resemble accurate reporting. Its very existence in a commercial system is as remarkable as its box-office success.
w Paddy Chayefsky d Sidney Lumet ph Owen Roizman m Elliot Lawrence
☆ Peter Finch, William Holden, Faye Dunaway, Robert Duvall, Wesley Addy, Ned Beatty, Beatrice Straight, John Carpenter
HOWARD BEALE (PETER FINCH) ON LIVE TELEVISION: 'I don't know what to do about the depression and the inflation and the Russians and the crime in the streets. All I know is that first you've got to get mad. You've got to say: "I'm a human being, god damn it, my life has some value!" So I want you to get up now. I want all of you to get up out of your chairs. I want you to get up right now and go to the window, open it and stick your head out and yell "I'm mad as hell, and I'm not going to take this any more!"'
DITTO: 'Ladies and gentlemen, I would like at this moment to announce that I will be retiring from this programme in two weeks' time because of poor ratings. Since this show was the only thing I had going for me in my life, I have decided to kill myself. I'm going to blow my brains out right on this programme a week from today.'
MAX SCHUMACHER (WILLIAM HOLDEN): 'You're television incarnate, Diana, indifferent to suffering, insensitive to joy. All of life is reduced to the common rubble of banality. War, murder, death – all the same to you as bottles of beer, and the daily business of life is a corrupt comedy. You even shatter the sensations of time and space into split seconds and instant replays. You're madness, Diana.'
'The cast of this messianic farce take turns yelling at us souless masses.' – New Yorker
'Too much of this film has the hectoring stridency of tabloid headlines.' – Michael Billington, Illustrated London News
† The theme was taken up a year later in the shortlived TV series *W.E.B.*
♫ Paddy Chayefsky; Peter Finch; Faye Dunaway; Beatrice Straight
⟡ best picture; Sidney Lumet; Owen Roizman; William Holden; Ned Beatty
⟁ Peter Finch

Neutral Port
GB 1940 92m bw
Gainsborough
A merchant navy captain avenges the loss of his ship by sabotaging a German U-boat.
Unconvincing propaganda, rather stagily presented.
w J. B. Williams, T. J. Morrison d Marcel Varnel ph Jack Cox, Arthur Crabtree
☆ Will Fyffe, Phyllis Calvert, Leslie Banks, Yvonne Arnaud, Hugh McDermott, Frederick Valk

Nevada Smith *
US 1966 131m Eastmancolor Panavision
Avco/Solar (Joe Levine, Henry Hathaway)

A cowboy takes a long revenge on the outlaws who murdered his parents.
Violent, sour, occasionally lively but frequently boring Western melodrama on a well worn theme.
w John Michael Hayes, from the 'early life' of a character in The Carpetbaggers by Harold Robbins d Henry Hathaway ph Lucien Ballard m Alfred Newman
☆ Steve McQueen, Karl Malden, Brian Keith, Suzanne Pleshette, Arthur Kennedy, Janet Margolin, Howard da Silva, Raf Vallone, Pat Hingle

The Nevadan
US 1950 81m Cinecolor
Harry Joe Brown/Columbia
GB title: *The Man from Nevada*
A marshal recovers stolen gold.
Solid Western programmer, compromised by poor colour.
w George W. George, George F. Slavin d Gordon Douglas ph Charles Lawton Jnr m Arthur Morton
☆ Randolph Scott, Dorothy Malone, Forrest Tucker, Frank Faylen, George Macready

Never a Dull Moment
US 1943 60m bw
Universal
Three comedians prevent a night-club owner from carrying out a robbery.

The last thin vehicle for a famous comedy trio; even here they have their moments.
w Mel Ronson, Stanley Roberts d Edward Lilley
☆ The Ritz Brothers, Frances Langford, Mary Beth Hughes, George Zucco, Franklin Pangborn

Never a Dull Moment
US 1950 89m bw
RKO (Harriet Parsons)

A lady music critic marries a rodeo cowboy and finds life hard down on the ranch.
Very mild star programmer.
w Lou Breslow, Doris Anderson novel Who Could Ask for Anything More? by Kay Swift d George Marshall ph Joseph Walker m Frederick Hollander and Constantin Bakaleinikoff
☆ Irene Dunne, Fred MacMurray, William Demarest, Andy Devine, Gigi Perreau, Natalie Wood, Philip Ober, Jack Kirkwood

Never a Dull Moment
🏃 US 1967 100m Technicolor
Walt Disney (Ron Miller)

An unsuccessful actor is mistaken for a notorious gangster.
Slapstick romp with vigour but not much flair.
w A. J. Carothers novel John Godey d Jerry Paris ph William Snyder m Robert F. Brunner
☆ Dick Van Dyke, Edward G. Robinson, Dorothy Provine, Henry Silva, Joanna Moore, Tony Bill, Slim Pickens, Jack Elam

'Some Things Are Worth Waiting For.'
'The Class Geek Just Turned Chic.'

Never Been Kissed
US 1998 107m DeLuxe Panavision
TCF/Fox 2000/Flower/Bushwood (Sandy Isaac, Nancy Juvonen)

A journalist in her mid-20s pretends to be a high-school girl so that she can write a feature on modern teenagers.
Mildly amusing comedy of a clash between generations, in which the teens are cool and the adults are silly; teenagers are most likely to enjoy it.
w Abby Kohn, Marc Silverstein d Raja Gosnell ph Alex Nepomniaschy m David Newman pd Steven Jordan ed Debra Chiate, Marcelo Sansevieri
☆ Drew Barrymore, David Arquette, Michael Vartan, Leelee Sobieski, Jeremy Jordan, Molly Shannon, Garry Marshall, John C. Reilly, Sean Whalen
'If you like your cinema entertainment broad and drippy, then this is for you.' – James Cameron-Wilson, Film Review

'They thought he couldn't do the job: that's why they chose him!'

Never Cry Wolf
🏃 US 1983 105m Technicolor
Walt Disney

A scientist is dumped alone in the Arctic to collect evidence against wolves.
Weird fable whose comic asides diminish its serious intent, and whose leading characterization is so eccentric as to bewilder any audience.
w Curtis Hanson, Sam Hamm, Richard Kletter book Farley Mowat d Carroll Ballard
☆ Charles Martin Smith, Brian Dennehy, Samson Jorah
'There are sequences in this movie that make your jaw drop open out of genuine amazement. To put it simply, he shows you sights you've never seen before ... It's no mere environmentalist film, but a meditation on survival and the story of its hero's inner rebirth.' – David Ansen, Newsweek

Never Give a Sucker an Even Break *
US 1941 70m bw
Universal
GB title: *What a Man*
W. C. Fields dives off an aeroplane into the lap of a young woman who has never seen a man; she falls in love with him.
Stupefyingly inept in its scripting and pacing, this comedy is often irresistibly funny because of the anti-everything personality of its writer-star. No one else could have got away with it, or would have been likely to try.

w John T. Neville, Prescott Chaplin story Otis Criblecoblis (W. C. Fields) d Edward Cline ph Charles Van Enger m Frank Skinner
☆ W. C. Fields, Gloria Jean, Leon Errol, Butch and Buddy, Franklin Pangborn, Anne Nagel, Mona Barrie, Susan Miller, Margaret Dumont
'A beautifully timed exhibition of mock pomposity, puzzled ineffectualness, subtle understatement and true-blue nonchalance.' – James Agee

Never Give an Inch: see *Sometimes a Great Notion*

Never Let Go
GB 1960 91m bw
Rank/Julian Wintle-Leslie Parkin (Peter de Sarigny)

A travelling salesman has his car stolen and stands up to the sadistic gang boss responsible.
Brutishly unattractive thriller, apparently designed for the sole purpose of giving Peter Sellers a villainous part.
w Alun Falconer d John Guillermin ph Christopher Challis m John Barry
☆ Richard Todd, Peter Sellers, Elizabeth Sellars, Adam Faith, Carol White, Mervyn Johns, Noel Willman

Never Let Me Go
GB 1953 94m bw
MGM (Clarence Brown)
After World War II an American correspondent marries a Russian ballerina but is later deported by the authorities.
Ho-hum romantic melodrama, quite interestingly cast.
w Ronald Millar, George Froeschel novel Came the Dawn by Roger Bax d Delmer Daves ph Robert Krasker m Hans May
☆ Clark Gable, Gene Tierney, Richard Haydn, Belita, Bernard Miles, Kenneth More, Karel Stepanek, Theodore Bikel, Frederick Valk

Never Look Back
GB 1952 73m bw
Exclusive/Hammer (Michael Carreras)
A lady barrister finds she must defend an old boyfriend on a murder charge.
Plausible drama which never quite comes to the boil.
w John Hunter, Guy Morgan, Francis Searle d Francis Searle ph Reginald Wyer m Temple Abady
☆ Rosamund John, Hugh Sinclair, Guy Middleton, Henry Edwards, Terence Longdon

Never Love a Stranger
US 1958 93m bw
Harold Robbins/Allied Artists (Peter Gettlinger)

A Catholic boy who has become a gangster helps his Jewish friend who has become assistant district attorney to trap a vicious hoodlum.
The old Manhattan Melodrama theme is dusted off once again, this time to very little effect.
w Harold Robbins, Richard Day novel Harold Robbins d Robert Stevens ph Lee Garmes m Raymond Scott
☆ John Drew Barrymore, Steve McQueen, Robert Bray, Lita Milan, R. G. Armstrong, Salem Ludwig

Never on Sunday *
Greece 1959 97m bw
Lopert/Melinafilm (Jules Dassin)

original title: *Pote tin Kyriaki*
An American scholar in Greece is infatuated by a prostitute and sets about improving her.
Amiable if rather shoddy variation on Pygmalion: the star performance and the music carried it, along with its own naughtiness, to success.
wd Jules Dassin ph Jacques Natteau m Manos Hadjidakis
☆ Melina Mercouri, Jules Dassin, Georges Foundas, Titos Vandis, Despo Diamantidou
'It barely stands scrutiny, but it communicates cheerfulness, and this in itself is no mean achievement.' – Penelope Houston, MFB
♫ title song (Manos Hadjidakis)
⟡ direction; script; Melina Mercouri

Never Put It in Writing *
GB 1963 93m bw
MGM/Andrew Stone

A young executive tries to recover from the mail an indiscreet letter he has written to his boss.

Frantic hit-or-miss farcical comedy distinguished by Dublin locations and cast.
wd Andrew Stone ph Martin Curtis m Frank Cordell
☆ Pat Boone, Fidelma Murphy, Reginald Beckwith, John Le Mesurier, Colin Blakely, Milo O'Shea

Never Say Die *
US 1939 80m bw
Paramount (Paul Jones)
A millionaire hypochondriac is convinced he is dying.
Thin farce with Hope on the very brink of stardom; some bright moments.
w Don Hartman, Frank Butler, Preston Sturges
d Elliott Nugent ph Leo Tover md Boris Morros
☆ Martha Raye, Bob Hope, Andy Devine, Alan Mowbray, Gale Sondergaard, Sig Rumann, Ernest Cossart, Monty Woolley, Christian Rub
'Needs strong support for top dual spots.' – *Variety*
'The most enjoyable film for weeks … consistently absurd … no dignity, no passion, and a magnificent cast.' – *Graham Greene*

Never Say Goodbye
US 1946 97m bw
Warner (William Jacobs)
A seven-year-old girl draws her divorced parents back together.
Highly derivative romantic comedy mishmash which did its star's career no good at all.
w James V. Kern, I. A. L. Diamond, Lewis R. Foster, Ben and Norma Barzman d James V. Kern ph Arthur Edeson m Frederick Hollander
☆ Errol Flynn, Eleanor Parker, Lucile Watson, S. Z. Sakall, Donald Woods, Patti Brady, Forrest Tucker, Hattie McDaniel

Never Say Goodbye
US 1955 96m Technicolor
U-I (Albert J. Cohen)
In 1945 Berlin an American army doctor marries a pianist who is later trapped in the Russian zone; they meet years later in America.
Romantic drama aimed at a female audience, remade from This Love of Ours (qv).
w Charles Hoffman d Jerry Hopper ph Maury Gertsman m Frank Skinner
☆ Rock Hudson, George Sanders, Cornell Borchers, Ray Collins, David Janssen

Never Say Never Again *
♔♔ GB 1983 134m Technicolor Panavision
Warner/Woodcote/Taliafilm (Jack Schwartzman)
📀 ▦ 🎥 🎧
James Bond foils a world domination attempt by Blofeld.
Reasonably enjoyable mishmash of Bondery; the plot is technically a remake of Thunderball, not that it matters much until the end, when the underwater stuff becomes tiresome because one hardly knows who is under the masks.
w Lorenzo Semple Jnr d Irvin Kershner ph Douglas Slocombe m Michel Legrand pd Philip Harrison, Stephen Grimes
☆ Sean Connery, Klaus Maria Brandauer, Max von Sydow, Barbara Carrera, Kim Basinger, Bernie Casey, Alec McCowen, Edward Fox, Rowan Atkinson
'Q' (ALEC MCCOWEN): 'Good to see you again, Mr Bond. Let's get back to some gratuitous sex and violence, I say.'

Never So Few
US 1959 124m Metrocolor Cinemascope
MGM/Canterbury (Edmund Grainger)
▦ 🎥
Adventures of World War II Americans commanding Burmese guerrillas.
Jungle actioner with pauses for philosophizing; well enough made but not very interesting.
w Millard Kaufman novel Tom Chamales d John Sturges ph William H. Daniels m Hugo Friedhofer
☆ Frank Sinatra, Gina Lollobrigida, Peter Lawford, Steve McQueen, Paul Henreid, Richard Johnson, Brian Donlevy, Charles Bronson, Dean Jones

Never Steal Anything Small
US 1958 94m Eastmancolor Cinemascope
U-I (Aaron Rosenberg)
▦
The reformation of a corrupt but sympathetic dockers' union boss.
Curious semi-musical which doesn't come off at all despite excellent credentials.
wd Charles Lederer play The Devil's Hornpipe by Rouben Mamoulian, Maxwell Anderson ph Harold Lipstein m Allie Wrubel ch Hermes Pan ly Maxwell Anderson
☆ James Cagney, Shirley Jones, Roger Smith, Cara Williams, Nehemiah Persoff, Royal Dano, Anthony Caruso
'The closest thing to it, I'd say, is *The Threepenny Opera*. It's witty, and it has some good radical lyrics. Films must have some comment to make.' – *James Cagney*

Never Take No for an Answer *
♔♔ GB 1951 82m bw
Constellation (Anthony Havelock-Allan)
A small boy goes to Rome to get permission from the Pope to take his sick donkey to be blessed in the church.
Slight, easy-going whimsy with attractive sunlit locations.
w Paul and Pauline Gallico novel The Small Miracle by Paul Gallico d Maurice Cloche, Ralph Smart ph Otto Heller m Nino Rota
☆ Vittorio Manunta, Denis O'Dea, Guido Cellano, Nerio Bernardi
'The main pleasures of this slender film are visual ones.' – *MFB*
† Remade as a TV movie *The Small Miracle*.

Never Take Sweets from a Stranger
GB 1960 81m bw Megascope
Hammer/Columbia
In a Canadian town, a respected elderly man is accused of improper sexual advances to a child.
In the awful warning category, and rather predictable.
w John Hunter play The Pony Cart by Roger Garis d Cyril Frankel ph Freddie Francis m Elisabeth Lutyens
☆ Gwen Watford, Patrick Allen, Felix Aylmer, Niall MacGinnis, Bill Nagy, Janina Faye, Michael Gwynn

Never Talk to Strangers
Canada/US 1995 86m DeLuxe
Columbia TriStar/Never Talk to Strangers/Alliance (Andras Hamori, Jeffrey R. Neuman, Martin J. Wiley)
📀 ▦ 🎥
A criminal psychologist, who is examining a serial killer, begins to receive death threats.
Risible thriller, stuffed with clichés and given a fashionable gloss with talk of multiple personality disorders and repressed memory syndrome; it is one memory that most audiences will be anxious to suppress.
w Lewis Green, Jordan Rush d Peter Hall ph Elemér Ragályi m Pino Donaggio pd Linda del Rosario, Richard Paris ed Roberto Silvi
☆ Rebecca De Mornay, Antonio Banderas, Dennis Miller, Len Cariou, Harry Dean Stanton, Beau Starr, Tim Kelleher, Eugene Lipinski
'The plot is so silly and the screenplay so unconvincing that nothing could be done to save it.' – *Derek Malcolm, Guardian*

Never the Twain Shall Meet
US 1931 89m bw
MGM
A young lawyer goes native when he falls for a South Sea island girl.
Stilted misalliance melodrama, previously made in 1925 as a silent with Bert Lytell and Anita Stewart; its faded notions simply didn't survive sound.
w Ruth Cummings and Edwin Justus Mayer novel Peter B. Kyne d W. S. Van Dyke
☆ Leslie Howard, Conchita Montenegro, Karen Morley, C. Aubrey Smith

Never to Love: see *A Bill of Divorcement* (1940)

Never Too Late
US 1965 104m Technicolor Panavision
Warner/Lear-Yorkin (Norman Lear)
A well-to-do middle-aged housewife discovers she is pregnant.
Predictable, rather hysterical domestic comedy, flatly developed from a successful play which offered two star parts for old stagers.

w Sumner Arthur Long play Sumner Arthur Long d Bud Yorkin ph Philip Lathrop m David Rose
☆ Paul Ford, Maureen O'Sullivan, Connie Stevens, Jim Hutton, Lloyd Nolan, Henry Jones, Jane Wyatt

Never Too Young to Rock
GB 1975 99m Fujicolour
GTO (Greg Smith, Ron Inkpen)
After rock'n'roll is no longer shown on TV in the near future, one man gathers together leading groups to perform at a concert to get the ban overturned, hampered by his elderly driver.
An inept comedy by a director who believes punch-ups and chickens are automatically funny. It is an excuse for a succession of performances by various bubblegum and glam-rock groups, including Mud performing Tiger Feet, a No. 1 hit at the time, and the Glitter Band.
w Ron Inkpen, Dennis Abey d Dennis Abey ph Harvey Harrison ad Denis Gordon-Orr ed Ray Lovejoy
☆ Peter Denyer, Freddie Jones, Sheila Steafel, Joe Lynch, John Clive, Peter Noone, Sally James, Scott Fitzgerald, Mud, Bob Kerr's Whoopee Band, The Glitter Band, The Rubettes, Slick

Never Wave at a WAC
US 1952 87m bw
Independent Artists (Frederick Brisson)
▦
GB title: *The Private Wore Skirts*
A Washington hostess joins the WACs and finds she can't get beyond the rank of private.
Pattern comedy, unconvincing in all respects but with a smattering of funny moments. Flagwaving takes over towards the end.
w Ken Englund d Norman Z. McLeod ph William Daniels m Elmer Bernstein
☆ Rosalind Russell, Paul Douglas, Marie Wilson, William Ching, Leif Erickson, Arleen Whelan, Charles Dingle

'A boy who needs a friend finds a world that needs a hero in a land beyond imagination!'

The Neverending Story *
♔♔ West Germany 1984 94m Technicolor Technovision
Warner/Bavaria Studios/WDR/Neue Constantin Filmproduktion (Bernd Eichinger, Dieter Geissler)
📀 ▦ 🎥 🎧
A reluctant student reads a book instead: dealing with mystical monsters and make-believe, it takes him back into their world.
Slow-starting fantasy with agreeable enough creations but not a lot of humour despite its intended stimulus to the imagination.
wd Wolfgang Petersen novel Michael Ende ph Jost Vacano m Klaus Doldinger, Giorgio Moroder pd Rolf Zehetbauer ed Jane Seitz
☆ Barret Oliver, Gerald McRaney, Moses Gunn, Patricia Hayes

The Neverending Story II: The Next Chapter
♔♔ Germany 1990 89m Eastmancolor Panavision
Warner/Soriba & Dehle (Dieter Geissler)
📀 ▦ 🎥
A boy and his fantasy alter-ego search for an imprisoned empress in a fairy-tale land of dreams.
Sequel that does little to expand the imagination.
w Karin Howard novel Michael Ende d George Miller ph Dave Connell m Robert Folk pd Bob Laing, Götz Weidner ed Peter Hollywood, Chris Blunden sp creature effects Colin Arthur
☆ Jonathan Brandis, Kenny Morrison, Clarissa Burt, Alexandra Johnes, Martin Umbach, John Wesley Shiff, Helena Michell, Chris Burton, Thomas Hill

The Neverending Story III
♔♔ Germany 1994 95m Agfacolor
Warner/Cinevox/Babelsberg/Dieter Geissler
📀 ▦
School bullies corrupt the book of the Neverending Story, so that the kingdom of Fantasia begins to decay and some of its inhabitants escape into the real world.
Limp sequel that cuts down on the magic and sets most of the action in a dull, real world of shopping malls and school.
w Jeff Lieberman story Karin Howard d Peter Macdonald ph Robin Vidgeon m Peter Wolf pd Rolf Zehetbauer ed Michael Bradsell

☆ Jason James Richter, Melody Kay, Freddie Jones, Ryan Bollman, Jack Black, Tracey Ellis, Kevin McNulty, Carole Finn, Julie Cox
'A charmless, desperate reworking … aimed at a generation of moppets with one finger on the fast forward button.' – *Derek Elley, Variety*

The New Adventures of Don Juan: see *The Adventures of Don Juan*

The New Adventures of Get-Rich-Quick Wallingford
US 1931 76m bw
MGM
Exploits of an attractive go-getter.
Reliable comedy of its day.
w Charles MacArthur novel G. R. Chester d Sam Wood
☆ William Haines, Jimmy Durante, Leila Hyams, Guy Kibbee

The New Adventures of Pippi Longstocking
♔♔ US/Sweden 1988 100m DeLuxe
Columbia/Svensk Filmindustri (Gary Mehlman, Walter Moshay)
📀 ▦ 🎥
Pippi Longstocking causes havoc when she returns home alone from a sea voyage.
The classic children's stories were turned into some dreary Swedish movies; this American effort is no better, being tiresome, dull and witless, unsuited to any age of audience.
wd Ken Annakin novel Astrid Lindgren ph Roland 'Ozzie' Smith m Misha Segal pd Jack Senter ed Ken Zemke
☆ Tami Erin, Eileen Brennan, Dennis Dugan, Dianne Hull, George di Cenzo, John Schuck, Dick Van Patten

The New Age
US 1994 110m Technicolor
Warner/Regency/Alcor (Nick Wechsler, Keith Addis)
📀 ▦
A couple's upwardly mobile progress, founded on the belief that shopping is good, comes to an abrupt stop.
A bleak look at a vapid society, so distanced from the characters it dispassionately observes that they dwindle to the level of uninteresting insects.
wd Michael Tolkin ph John H. Campbell m Mark Mothersbaugh pd Robin Standefer ed Suzanne Fenn
☆ Peter Weller, Judy Davis, Patrick Bauchau, Corbin Bernsen, Jonathan Hadary, Patricia Heaton, Samuel L. Jackson, Adam West
'Suffers from the pretentiousness it is surely designed to expose.' – *Derek Malcolm, Guardian*

The New Babylon *
USSR 1929 80m bw silent
Sovkino
original title: *Novyi Vavilon*
The rise and fall of the 1871 French commune, seen through the eyes of a girl department store worker.
Propagandist socio-historical melodrama, most interesting now for its sub-Eisenstein technique.
wd Leonid Trauberg, Grigori Kozintsev ph Andrei Moskvin, Yevgeni Mikhailov m Dmitri Shostakovich ad Yevgeni Enei
☆ Yelena Kuzmina, Pyotr Sobelevsky, Sophie Magarill
'A slow decorative romantic picture.' – *Graham Greene*

The New Barbarians
Italy 1983 91m Telecolor
Entertainment/Deaf International (Fabrizi de Angelis)
original title: *I Nuovi Barbari*
In a post-holocaust future, two wandering warriors destroy a vicious gang of murdering homosexuals.
Mad Max, Italian-style, in an untalented low-budget rip-off.
w Tito Carpi, Enzo Girolami d Enzo G. Catellari ph Fausto Amicucci m Claudio Simonetti pd Antonio Visune ed Gianfranco Amicucci
☆ Fred Williamson, Timothy Brent, George Eastman, Anna Kanakis, Thomas Moore

---

◎ Digital Video Disc Region 2   ◎ Digital Video Disc Region 1   🎧 Soundtrack released on compact disc   ☆ Cast in approximate order of importance   † Points of interest   🎵 Notable songs   🏆 Academy Award   🏵 Academy Award nomination   🏆 BAFTA

The New Centurions *

US 1972 103m Eastmancolor Panavision
Columbia/Chartoff-Winkler

▦ ▣ ◕

GB title: *Precinct 45: Los Angeles Police*
An old cop teaches a new one.
'Realistic' crime prevention saga which spawned the TV series Police Story *and* Police Woman. *Well done within its limits.*
w Stirling Silliphant *novel* Joseph Wambaugh d Richard Fleischer *ph* Ralph Woolsey *m* Quincy Jones
☆ George C. Scott, Stacy Keach, Jane Alexander, Rosalind Cash, Scott Wilson

New Face in Hell: see P.J.

New Faces *

US 1954 99m Eastmancolor Cinemascope
Edward L. Alperson (Leonard Sillman)

▦

A revue goes on despite money problems.
Five minutes of plot, ninety-five minutes of revue from the Broadway stage; mostly quite amusing, and chiefly notable for introducing Eartha Kitt with all her standards.
w various d Harry Horner *ph* Lucien Ballard *m* Raoul Kraushaar *revue deviser* John Murray Anderson
☆ Eartha Kitt, Ronny Graham, Alice Ghostley, Robert Clary, Paul Lynde

New Faces of 1937

US 1937 105m bw
RKO

◕

Talent auditions for a Broadway show.
Shapeless agglomeration of variety acts with a wisp of story; the level of talent is not outstandingly high.
w Nat Perrin, P. G. Epstein, Irving Brecher, Harold Russell, Harry Clork, Howard J. Green *story* Shoestring *by* George Bradshaw d Leigh Jason
☆ Joe Penner, Milton Berle, Parkyakarkus, Harriet Hilliard, Jerome Cowan, Bert Gordon, Ann Miller, Richard Lane
'A hodgepodge of vaudeville, night club and radio talent, unskilfully blended and rather inanely promulgated.' – *Variety*

New Frontier

US 1939 57m bw
Republic (William Berke)

▦

aka: *Frontier Horizon*
aka: *Raiders of the Wasteland*
Cowboys come to the rescue of settlers who are losing their land to crooked dam builders.
A typical action-packed adventure for the Three Mesquiteers, which was also Wayne's last film in the series before he went on to better movies.
w Betty Burbridge, Luci Ward d George Sherman *ph* Reggie Lanning *m* William Lava
☆ John Wayne, Ray Corrigan, Raymond Hatton, Phylis Isley (Jennifer Jones), Eddy Waller, LeRoy Mason, Sammy McKim

The New Gulliver *

USSR 1933 85m bw

Gulliver's Travels is retold in puppet form, but the plot has become a satire against capitalism.
Interesting both as animation and as propaganda.
w A. Ptoushko, B. Roshal d Alexander Ptoushko, A. Vanitchkin
'The invention is often delightful (one wonders how such humour in detail can exist with so humourless a philosophy), and the marvellous ingenuity of the puppets is beyond praise.' – *Graham Greene, The Spectator*

The New Interns

US 1964 123m bw
Columbia (Robert Cohn)
Young doctors at a city hospital have trouble saving a rapist and his victim.
Unnecessary sequel to The Interns, *its 'realism' requiring large pinches of salt.*
w Wilton Schiller d John Rich *ph* Lucien Ballard *m* Earle Hagen
☆ George Segal, Telly Savalas, Michael Callan, Dean Jones, Inger Stevens, Stefanie Powers, Lee Patrick

New Jack City **

US 1991 100m Technicolor
Warner (Doug McHenry, George Jackson)

▦▦ ▣ ◕ ◔

Undercover cops go after a successful gangster dealing drugs in Harlem.
Fast-moving, street-wise thriller with an anti-drugs stance.
w Thomas Lee Wright, Barry Michael Cooper d Mario Van Peebles *ph* Francis Kenny *m* Michel Colombier *pd* Charles C. Bennett *ed* Steven Kemper, Kevin Stitt
☆ Wesley Snipes, Ice T, Allen Payne, Chris Rock, Mario Van Peebles, Michael Michele, Bill Nunn, Russell Wong, Bill Cobbs
'A provocative, pulsating update on gangster pics.' – *Variety*

New Jersey Drive

US 1995 95m Technicolor
Universal/Gramercy/40 Acres and a Mule Filmworks/Shooting Gallery (Larry Meistrich, Bob Gosse)

▦▦ ▣ ◕ ◔

Police engage in a war with young black joyriders and car thieves.
Gritty but unconvincing urban melodrama; its feeling for street life doesn't compensate for its reliance on stereotypical characters and situations.
wd Nick Gomez *ph* Adam Kimmel *m* Wendy Blackstone *pd* Lester Cohen *ed* Tracy Granger
☆ Sharron Corley, Gabriel Casseus, Saul Stein, Gwen McGee, Andre Moore, Donald Adeosun Faison, Conrad Meertin, Christine Baranski
'Lack of a discernible point of view on this out-of-control lawlessness and mayhem until the final minutes is a nagging problem throughout, leaving the viewer nowhere to put one's concerns or sympathies.' – *Todd McCarthy, Variety*

A New Kind of Love

US 1963 110m Technicolor
Paramount/Llenroc (Melville Shavelson)
An American dress designer in Paris is softened by a boorish newspaper columnist.
Very thin sex comedy, dressed to kill but with nowhere to go.
wd Melville Shavelson *ph* Daniel Fapp *m* Leith Stevens
☆ Paul Newman, Joanne Woodward, Maurice Chevalier, Thelma Ritter, George Tobias
♫ Leith Stevens

The New Land: see The Emigrants

A New Leaf *

US 1970 102m Movielab
Paramount/Aries/Elkins (Joe Manduke)

▦

A middle-aged playboy, close to bankruptcy, thinks of acquiring a wealthy wife.
Agreeably mordant comedy which sparkles in patches rather than as a whole.
wd Elaine May *story* The Green Heart *by* Jack Ritchie *ph* Gayne Rescher *m* John Mandel, Neal Hefti *pd* Richard Fried
☆ Walter Matthau, Elaine May, Jack Weston, George Rose, William Redfield, James Coco
'Unashamedly a thirties fairy tale in modern, but not fashionable, dress.' – *Jan Dawson*

A New Life

US 1988 104m Technicolor Panavision
Paramount (Martin Bregman)

▦ ▣

A middle-aged couple divorce and find new partners and problems.
Occasionally wry, but more often sentimental, romantic comedy.
wd Alan Alda *ph* Kelvin Pike *m* Joseph Turrin *pd* Barbara Dunphy *ed* William Reynolds
☆ Alan Alda, Ann-Margret, Hal Linden, Veronica Hamel, John Shea, Mary Kay Place

New Mexico

US 1952 78m Anscocolor
United Artists (Irving Allen)
A cavalry officer tries to make peace with the Indians, but when an Indian child is accidentally killed a savage war breaks out.
Standard Western, not badly made.
w Max Trell d Irving Reis *ph* William Snyder *m* Lucien Moraweck, Rene Garriguenc

☆ Lew Ayres, Marilyn Maxwell, Robert Hutton, Andy Devine, Raymond Burr, Jeff Corey

New Moon *

US 1940 105m bw
MGM (Robert Z. Leonard)

▦

Romance in old French Louisiana.
Stalwart adaptation of an operetta previously filmed in 1930 with Lawrence Tibbett and Grace Moore.
w Jacques Deval, Robert Arthur d Robert Z. Leonard *ph* William Daniels *m/ly* Sigmund Romberg, Oscar Hammerstein
☆ *Jeanette MacDonald, Nelson Eddy,* Mary Boland, George Zucco, H. B. Warner, Stanley Fields, Grant Mitchell

New Morals for Old

US 1932 77m bw
MGM
John Van Druten's play *After All,* about the generation gap in the London aristocracy, was here rather unwisely translated to the American middle class and emerged as a decided curiosity.
w Zelda Sears, Wanda Tuchock d Charles Brabin
☆ Robert Young, Myrna Loy, Jean Hersholt, Lewis Stone, Laura Hope Crews, Elizabeth Patterson
'A weak sister, swathed in gloom, muddled, and without names that will draw.' – *Variety*

New Orleans *

US 1947 89m bw
Jules Levey

◕

How jazz was born, according to the movies.
Routine low-budgeter enlivened by a splendid array of guest musicians.
w Elliot Paul, Dick Irving Hyland d Arthur Lubin *ph* Lucien Andriot *md* Nathaniel Finston
☆ Louis Armstrong and his All Stars, Arturo de Cordova, Dorothy Patrick, Richard Hageman, *Billie Holiday, Meade Lux Lewis, Woody Herman and his Orchestra*
† Richard Hageman's piano-playing was dubbed by Arthur Schutt.

New Wine

US 1941 89m bw
Gloria/UA
GB title: *The Great Awakening*
Franz Schubert seeks the patronage of Beethoven and sacrifices his love life to music.
Weirdly cast romantic drama, rather fumbling in all departments.
w Howard Estabrook, Nicholas Jory d Reinhold Schunzel
☆ Alan Curtis, Ilona Massey, Albert Basserman, Binnie Barnes, Sterling Holloway

New Year's Day *

US 1989 92m Technicolor
Contemporary/International Rainbow/Jagfilm (Judith Wolinsky)

▦

A writer moves back from Los Angeles to his New York apartment and becomes involved in the lives of three young women, his previous tenants, and their friends.
A conversation piece, in which a varied group sound off about their lives and loves in a manner ranging from the engaging to the uninteresting; worth a listen for the most part.
wd Henry Jaglom *ph* Joey Forsyte *ad* Barbara Flood *ed* Ruth Zucker Ward
☆ Maggie Jakobson, Gwen Welles, Henry Jaglom, David Duchovny, Milos Forman, Michael Emil, Donna Germain, Tracy Reiner, Harvey Miller, Irene Moore
'Warm, perceptive, wryly comic.' – *Philip French, Observer*

New York Confidential

US 1955 87m bw
Warner/Russel Rouse, Clarence Greene
The head of a crime syndicate is assassinated by his own hired killer.
Unexciting 'realistic' thriller with the gangsters presented as family and businessmen; seventeen years later The Godfather *did it rather better.*
w Clarence Greene, Russel Rouse d Russel Rouse *ph* Edward Fitzgerald *m* Joseph Mullendore *pd* Fernando Carrere
☆ Broderick Crawford, Richard Conte, Anne Bancroft, Marilyn Maxwell, Onslow Stevens, J.

Carrol Naish, Barry Kelley, Mike Mazurki, Celia Lovsky

The New York Hat *

US 1912 10m bw silent
D. W. Griffith
A small-town minister is gossiped about when he buys a hat for a young girl.
Influential early short story film with good local backgrounds.
w Anita Loos d D. W. Griffith *ph* Billy Bitzer
☆ Mary Pickford, Lionel Barrymore, Lillian Gish, Dorothy Gish, Robert Harron, Mack Sennett, Mae Marsh

New York, New York *

US 1977 153m Technicolor Panavision
UA/Chartoff-Winkler (Gene Kirkwood)

▦▦ ▦ ◕ ◔

In the late forties in New York, a single-minded saxophonist fails to do right by his girlfriend, who becomes a Hollywood star.
A clever recreation of the big band era, hampered by gross overlength, unattractive characters and a pessimistic plot.
w Earl Mac Rauch, Mardik Martin d Martin Scorsese *ph* Laszlo Kovacs *md* Ralph Burns *pd* Boris Leven
☆ Liza Minnelli, Robert DeNiro, Lionel Stander, Barry Primus
'A dazzling modern musical, this is one of the rare films which is actually constructed with as much passion as it depicts.' – *Judith Williamson*

New York Nights

US 1929 81m bw
UA/Talmadge
A musical comedy star has a husband who drinks, and she accepts help from a gangster.
The star's sound début was a hit-and-miss affair composed of familiar elements.
w Jules Furthman *play* Tin Pan Alley *by* Hugh Stanislaus Stange d Lewis Milestone
☆ Norma Talmadge, Gilbert Roland, John Wray, Lilyan Tashman, Roscoe Karns
'Good performance, fair picture.' – *Variety*

New York Stories **

US 1989 124m Technicolor
Warner/Touchstone (Robert Greenhut)

▦ ◕ ◔

Anthology of three stories: 'Life Lessons', dealing with a painter's attitude to life and art; 'Life Without Zoë', in which a 12-year-old girl brings her parents back together; and 'Oedipus Wrecks', in which a son is tyrannized by his mother materializing in the sky over New York.
Worth watching for Scorsese's sharp look at the art world and Allen's ultimate Jewish mother joke. Sandwiched between them is Coppola at his most disastrously winsome.
w Richard Price, Francis Coppola, Sofia Coppola, Woody Allen d Martin Scorsese, Francis Coppola, Woody Allen *ph* Nestor Almendros, Vittorio Storaro, Sven Nykvist *m* Carmine Coppola, Kid Creole and the Coconuts *pd* Kristi Zea, Dean Tavoularis, Santo Loquasto *ed* Thelma Schoonmaker, Barry Malkin, Susan E. Morse
☆ Nick Nolte, Patrick O'Neal, Rosanna Arquette, Heather McComb, Talia Shire, Gia Coppola, Giancarlo Giannini, Woody Allen, Marvin Chatinover, Mae Questel, Mia Farrow

New York Town

US 1941 94m bw
Paramount (Anthony Veiller)
A girl new to the Big Apple befriends a sidewalk photographer.
Flat romantic comedy, a soufflé which doesn't rise despite the talents involved.
w Lewis Seltzer (and, uncredited, Preston Sturges) d Charles Vidor (and Sturges) *ph* Charles Schoenbaum *m* Leo Shuken
☆ Fred MacMurray, Mary Martin, Robert Preston, Akim Tamiroff, Lynne Overman, Eric Blore, Cecil Kellaway, Fuzzy Knight

Newman's Law

US 1974 99m Technicolor
Universal (Richard Irving)
A cop uses unconventional methods to trap drug smugglers.
Very routine police actioner, just above TV movie level.

---

w Anthony Wilson d Richard Heffron ph Vilis
Lapenieks m Robert Prince
☆ George Peppard, Roger Robinson, Eugene
Roche, Gordon Pinsent, Abe Vigoda

The News Boys: see *Newsies*

News Is Made at Night
US 1939 72m bw
TCF
To boost circulation, a news editor pins a string of
murders on a well-known gangster, and soon
regrets it.
*Pacy crime comedy-drama, very acceptable as the
lower half of a double bill.*
w John Larkin d Alfred Werker
☆ Preston Foster, Lynn Bari, Eddie Collins,
Russell Gleason, George Barbier, Charles Halton
'Above average B; should do all right where
properly placed.' – *Variety*

Newsboys' Home
🏃 US 1939 73m bw
Universal
A girl inherits a newspaper which sponsors a home
for boys.
*Modest debut for the East Side Kids, a spin-off group
from the Dead End Kids.*
w Gordon Kahn d Harold Young
☆ Jackie Cooper, Edmund Lowe, Wendy Barrie,
Edward Norris, Samuel S. Hinds; and Elisha Cook
Jnr, Hally Chester, Harris Berger, David Gorcey,
Billy Benedict, Charles Duncan
'Another in the tough kid cycle. Will easily
handle its end of dual depots.' – *Variety*

Newsfront ***
Australia 1978 110m colour/bw
Palm Beach Productions (David Elfick)
In the fifties, rival news teams battle to get the best
shots for cinema newsreels.
Lively nostalgic feature with slick modern technique.
wd Phillip Noyce, from a concept by David Elfick
ph Vincent Monton pd Lissa Coote ed John
Scott
☆ Bill Hunter, Wendy Hughes, Gerard Kennedy,
Chris Haywood

Newsies
🏃 US 1992 121m Technicolor
Panavision
Warner/Walt Disney/Touchwood Pacific Partners I
(Michael Finnell)
In the 1890s news boys in New York call a strike
when a newspaper publisher charges them more for
his papers.
*Unsuccessful attempt to create a youthful musical – the
model seems to be Oliver! but it lacks any Dickensian
dimension despite its subplot of the exploitation of child
labour.*
w Bob Tzudiker, Noni White d Kenny Ortega
ph Andrew Laszlo m Alan Menken ch Kenny
Ortega, Peggy Holmes pd William Sandell
ed William Reynolds
☆ Christian Bale, Bill Pullman, Ann-Margret,
Robert Duvall, David Moscow, Ele Keats, Kevin
Tighe, Luke Edwards
'With many catchy if forgettable ditties littered
throughout, one is led to the inevitable
conclusion that nine-year-old girls will just love
it.' – *Angie Errigo, Empire*

The Newton Boys
US 1998 122m colour
TCF/Detour (Anne Walker-McBay)
In the 20s, four rural brothers become bank
robbers.
*Atmospheric but somewhat lethargic drama, set in a
period of change.*
w Richard Linklater, Claude Stanush, Clark Lee
Walker book Claude Stanush d Richard Linklater
ph Peter James m Edward D. Barnes
pd Catherine Hardwicke ed Sandra Adair
☆ Matthew McConaughey, Skeet Ulrich, Ethan
Hawke, Vincent D'Onofrio, Julianna Margulies,
Dwight Yoakam, Chloe Webb
'A story that's too diffuse and lacks a discernible
point of view that would make it dramatically
engaging.' – *Variety*
† The film was released direct to video in Britain.

'The suburbs make the hood look good.'

Next Friday
US 2000 98m DeLuxe
Entertainment/New Line/Cubevision (Ice Cube)
Hiding from a thug, a unemployed man leaves his
neighourhood to stay with his lottery-rich uncle in
the suburbs.
*Amiable enough romp, a sequel of sorts to Friday (qv),
which ambles along without getting anywhere very
interesting.*
w Ice Cube d Steve Carr ph Christopher J. Baffa
m Terence Blanchard pd Dina Lipton ed Elena
Maganini
☆ Ice Cube, Mike Epps, Justin Pierce, John
Witherspoon, Don "DC" Curry, Jacob Vargas, Lobo
Sebastian, Rolando Molina, Lisa Rodriguez
'There are a good few laughs but few surprises.' –
Joe Leydon, Variety

The Next Karate Kid
🏃 US 1994 104m Technicolor
Columbia (Jerry Weintraub)
An unhappy teenage girl, whose parents died in a
car crash, discovers that karate is a means of
gaining self-respect.
*This is another series running out of steam; the attempt
to revive it by changing the gender of its protagonist
yields small returns, since otherwise the story is as
before.*
w Mark Lee d Christopher Cain ph Laszlo
Kovacs m Bill Conti pd Walter P. Martishius
ed Ronald Roose
☆ Pat Morita, Hilary Swank, Michael Ironside,
Constance Towers, Christian Conrad, Arsenio
Trinidad, Michael Cavalieri
'Wholesome apprenticeship tale has its scattered
moments of humor and insight but lacks
sustained verve.' – *Variety*

The Next Man
US 1976 107m Technicolor
Artists Entertainment Complex (Martin Bregman)
A female assassin is hired to kill the Saudi Arabian
Minister of State at the United Nations.
*Fractured and uninteresting thriller in which all manner
of cinematic styles obscure the storyline but point up
the lack of narrative skill.*
w Mort Fine, Alan R. Trustman, David M. Wolf,
Michael Chapman d Richard C. Sarafian
ph Michael Chapman m Michael Kamen
pd Gene Callahan
☆ Sean Connery, Cornelia Sharpe, Albert
Paulsen, Adolfo Celi, Charles Cioffi
'The director takes forever to set up the film's
premise, and then he lingers over interminable
street festivals and lush scenery.' – *Dave
Pomeroy, Film Information*

Next of Kin
Australia 1982 86m Eastmancolor
Miracle/SIS Productions/Filmco (Robert Le Tet)
A young girl teacher inherits an old people's home,
and finds murder lurking.
*Slow-starting but finally over-the-top melodrama, with
elements borrowed from Psycho, Taste of Fear and a
score of other creepies.*
w Michael Heath, Tony Williams d Tony
Williams ph Gary Hansen m Klaus Schulze
ad Richard Francis, Nick Hepworth ed Max
Lemon
☆ Jackie Kerin, John Jarratt, Alex Scott, Gerda
Nicolson
'Genre awareness is one thing; a dreary sense of
déjà vu is another matter entirely.' – *Paul Taylor,
MFB*

Next of Kin
US 1989 108m Metrocolor
Warner/Lorimar (Les Alexander, Don Enright)
Two brothers, one a cop, the other a hillbilly, take
their revenge when another brother is killed by
gangsters.
Dreary action movie of no originality.
w Michael Jenning, Jeb Stuart d John Irvin
ph Steven Poster m Jack Nitzsche, Gary Chang,
Todd Hayen pd Jack T. Collis ed Peter Honess
☆ Patrick Swayze, Liam Neeson, Adam Baldwin,
Helen Hunt, Andreas Katsulas, Bill Paxton, Ben
Stiller, Michael J. Pollard, Ted Levine

The Next of Kin ***
GB 1942 102m bw
Ealing (S. C. Balcon)
Careless talk causes loss of life in a commando raid.
*A propaganda instructional film which was made so
entertainingly that it achieved commercial success and
remains an excellent example of how to make a bitter
pill palatable.*
w Thorold Dickinson, Basil Bartlett, Angus
Macphail, John Dighton d Thorold Dickinson
ph Ernest Palmer m William Walton
☆ Mervyn Johns, Nova Pilbeam, Stephen Murray,
Reginald Tate, Basil Radford, Naunton Wayne,
Geoffrey Hibbert, Philip Friend, Mary Clare, Basil
Sydney
'The detail everywhere is curious and surprising,
with something of the fascination of a Simenon
crime being unravelled.' – *William Whitebait*

The Next One
US 1984 105m colour
Allstar Productions (Constantine Vlachakis)
An American widow, living on a Greek island,
becomes involved with a mysterious stranger she
finds washed up on the beach.
*Glossy, dull fantasy about a man from the future with
a Christ complex, made in 1981.*
wd Nico Mastorakis ph Ari Stavrou m Stanley
Myers pd Paul Acciari ed George Rosenberg
☆ Keir Dullea, Adrienne Barbeau, Peter Hobbs,
Phaedon Georgitsis, Betty Arvanitis, Jeremy Licht

Next Stop Greenwich Village *
US 1975 111m Movielab
TCF (Paul Mazursky, Tony Ray)
In 1953 in a poor quarter of New York, a young Jew
tries to stretch his wings.
*A bumper bundle of Jewish clichés dressed up as
autobiography, and switching abruptly from comedy to
tragedy and back. Vivid, but not exactly entertaining.*
wd Paul Mazursky ph Arthur Ornitz m Bill
Conti
☆ Lenny Baker, Shelley Winters, Ellen Greene,
Lois Smith, Dori Brenner
'Some tartly comic observation, but the
fragmented structure keeps the mixture inert.' –
Sight and Sound

The Next Time I Marry
US 1938 64m bw
RKO
In order to become the richest girl in America, an
heiress must marry in haste.
Tedious comedy which falls apart halfway.
w John Twist, Helen Meinardi d Garson Kanin
ph Russell Metty md Roy Webb
☆ Lucille Ball, James Ellison, Lee Bowman,
Granville Bates, Mantan Moreland
'A very poor entry. The story is banal,
production values poor, direction sloppy and
most of the performances bad.' – *Variety*

Next Time We Live: see *Next Time We Love*

Next Time We Love
US 1936 87m bw
Universal (Paul Kohner)
GB title: *Next Time We Live*
The wife of a war correspondent has plenty of time
for romance.
*Romantic drama which badly needs an injection of
comedy.*
w Melville Baker stories Ursula Parrott d Edward
H. Griffith ph Joseph Valentine m Franz
Waxman
☆ Margaret Sullavan, Ray Milland, James
Stewart, Grant Mitchell, Robert McWade
'Draggy, complex tale … will have to be sold on
the star's past performances.' – *Variety*

Next to No Time
GB 1958 93m Eastmancolor
British Lion/Montpelier (Albert Fennell)
A meek-and-mild engineer crossing the Atlantic
gains confidence when told that anything is
possible during the hour 'lost' every day.
Whimsical comedy which never gains momentum.
wd Henry Cornelius story *The Enchanted Hour* by
Paul Gallico ph Freddie Francis m Georges Auric

☆ Kenneth More, Betsy Drake, Bessie Love, Harry
Green, Roland Culver, Reginald Beckwith, John
Welsh, John Laurie, Howard Marion-Crawford

The Next Voice You Hear *
US 1950 83m bw
MGM (Dore Schary)
God speaks to mankind on the radio, and the life
of Joe Smith American is changed.
*Soppy parable, the archetypal instance of Schary's reign
of do-goodery at MGM. (He wrote a book about it,
Case History of a Movie.) The idea is handled with
deadly reverence, and falls quite flat, while the
depiction of the inhabitants of American suburbia is
depressing.*
w Charles Schnee d William Wellman
ph William Mellor m David Raksin
☆ James Whitmore, Nancy Davis, Lillian
Bronson, Jeff Corey
'The sins of the American working man are
singularly uninteresting and their obliteration
seems scarcely to require the very voice of God.'
– *Henry Hart*

Ngati *
New Zealand 1987 90m colour
Pacific/NZFC (John O'Shea)
In the late 40s, a young Australian-born doctor
returns to the small New Zealand community
where his father lived and his mother, a Maori,
died.
*Austere and affecting study of the sometimes uneasy
relations between two cultures, and between modern
and traditional attitudes to life, filmed in a deliberately
spare manner.*
w Tama Poata d Barry Barclay ph Rory O'Shea
m Dalvanius ad Matthew Murphy ed Dell King
☆ Tuta Ngarimu Tamati, Iranui Haig, Tawai
Moana, Michael Tibble, Oliver Jones, Wi Kuki
Kaa, Ross Girven

Ni ju-seiki Shonen Dokuhon: see *Circus
Boys*

'A raging torrent of emotion that even nature can't
control!'

Niagara ***
US 1952 89m Technicolor
TCF (Charles Brackett)
While visiting Niagara Falls, a faithless wife is
plotting to murder her husband, but he turns the
tables.
*Excellent suspenser with breathtaking locations; in the
best Hitchcock class though slightly marred by the
emphasis on Monroe's wiggly walk (it was her first big
part).*
w Charles Brackett, Walter Reisch, Richard Breen
d Henry Hathaway ph Joe MacDonald m Sol
Kaplan
☆ Joseph Cotten, Jean Peters, Marilyn Monroe, Don
Wilson, Casey Adams
'The story is most imaginatively treated, the
production values are excellent.' – *CEA Film
Report*
'Seen from any angle, the Falls and Miss Monroe
leave little to be desired.' – *New York Times*
'A masterly example of fluid screen narrative.' –
Charles Higham
'It would have turned out a much better picture
if James Mason had played the husband as I
wanted. He has that intensity, that neurotic
edge. He was all set to do it, but his daughter
Portland said she was sick of seeing him die in
his pictures.' – *Henry Hathaway*
'This isn't a good movie but it's compellingly
tawdry and nasty … the only movie that
explored the mean, unsavoury potential of
Marilyn Monroe's cuddly, infantile perversity.' –
Pauline Kael, 70s

Niagara Falls
US 1941 43m bw
Hal Roach
Confusion reigns in a hotel overlooking the falls.
*Potted farce in the producer's season of 'shorties'; not
the worst, but far from brilliant.*
w Paul Gerard Smith, Hal Yates, Eugene Conrad
d Gordon Douglas
☆ ZaSu Pitts, Slim Summerville, Tom Brown,
Marjorie Woodworth, Chester Clute

Nice Girl? *

US   1941   95m   bw
Universal (Joe Pasternak)
A teenager finds herself in demand by two older men.
Amusing romantic trifle supposed to mark the growing up of Universal's great teenage star.
w Richard Connell, Gladys Lehman d William A. Seiter ph Joseph Valentine md Charles Previn
☆ Deanna Durbin, Franchot Tone, Robert Stack, Walter Brennan, Robert Benchley, Helen Broderick, Ann Gillis

A Nice Girl Like Me

GB   1969   91m   Eastmancolor
Anglo Embassy/Partisan (Roy Millichip)
A sheltered young lady sets out to see life but keeps getting pregnant.
Insufferable romantic whimsy, made to look like a marathon TV commercial but never so interesting.
w Anne Piper, Desmond Davis d Desmond Davis ph Gil Taylor, Manny Wynn m Pat Williams
☆ Barbara Ferris, Harry Andrews, Gladys Cooper, Joyce Carey, Bill Hinnant, James Villiers, Christopher Guinee, Fabia Drake
'High-toned woman's magazine nostalgia.' – *MFB*

Nice Girls Don't Explode

US   1987   bw
New World/Nice Girls (Douglas Curtis, John Wells)
An over-protective mother persuades her teenage daughter that she will cause fires whenever she becomes sexually excited.
Dim and exceedingly unfunny comedy, taken at a painfully slow pace.
w Paul Harris d Chuck Martinez ph Stephen Katz m Anthony Marinelli, Brian Banks
pd Sarina Rotstein ed Wende Phifer Mate
☆ Barbara Harris, Michelle Meyrink, William O'Leary, Wallace Shawn, James Nardini, Irwin Keyes, Belinda Wills

A Nice Little Bank That Should Be Robbed

US   1958   87m   bw   Cinemascope
TCF (Anthony Muto)
GB title: *How to Rob a Bank*
Two incompetent crooks rob a bank and buy a racehorse.
Feeble comedy, a sad waste of its stars.
w Sydney Boehm d Henry Levin ph Leo Tover m Lionel Newman
☆ Mickey Rooney, Tom Ewell, Mickey Shaughnessy, Dina Merrill

Nicholas and Alexandra *

GB   1971   189m   Eastmancolor   Panavision
Columbia/Horizon (Sam Spiegel)
The life of Tsar Nicholas II from 1904 to the execution of the family in 1918.
Inflated epic of occasional interest, mainly for its sets; generally heavy going.
w James Goldman book Robert K. Massie d Franklin Schaffner ph Frederick A. Young m Richard Rodney Bennett pd John Box ed Ernest Walter
☆ Michael Jayston, Janet Suzman, Laurence Olivier, Jack Hawkins, Tom Baker, Harry Andrews, Michael Redgrave, Alexander Knox
† Original preferred casting: Rex Harrison, Vanessa Redgrave
‡ art direction; costumes (Yvonne Blake, Antonio Castillo)
§ best picture; Frederick A. Young; Richard Rodney Bennett; Janet Suzman

Nicholas Nickleby **

♚♟ GB   1947   108m   bw
Ealing (John Croydon)
The adventures of a Victorian schoolmaster, deprived of his rightful fortune, who joins a band of travelling entertainers.
Quite tasteful and expert but too light-handed potted version of Dickens, which suffered by comparison with the David Lean versions.
w John Dighton novel Charles Dickens d Alberto Cavalcanti ph Gordon Dines m Lord Berners
☆ Derek Bond, Cedric Hardwicke, Alfred Drayton, Sybil Thorndike, Stanley Holloway, James Hayter,

Sally Ann Howes, Jill Balcon, Cyril Fletcher, Fay Compton
'Here's richness! Not all the novel, perhaps, but enough to make a film full of the Dickens spirit.' – *Star*

Nick Carter, Master Detective

US   1939   57m   bw
MGM (Lucien Hubbard)
Carter uncovers a spy ring in a plane factory.
Dull, devitalized version of the old dime novel adventures; generally characterless and unmemorable.
w Bertram Millhauser d Jacques Tourneur ph Charles Lawton Jnr m Edward Ward
☆ Walter Pidgeon, Rita Johnson, Henry Hull, Stanley Ridges, Donald Meek, Addison Richards, Milburn Stone, Martin Kosleck
'Just another screen sleuth.' – *Variety*

Nick of Time

US   1995   89m   DeLuxe
Paramount (John Badham)
A man is given 90 minutes to kill the Governor of California or his young daughter will die.
A thriller in which real time and the film's time are the same, but it still drags at times, failing to create the necessary suspense, owing mainly to the spiralling absurdity of its narrative.
w Patrick Sheane Duncan d John Badham ph Roy H. Wagner m Arthur B. Rubinstein pd Philip Harrison ed Frank Morriss, Kevin Stitt
☆ Johnny Depp, Christopher Walken, Courtney Chase, Charles S. Dutton, Roma Maffia, Marsha Mason, Peter Strauss, Gloria Reuben
'This OK but undistinguished thriller takes a simple Hitchcockian premise and milks things about as well as it can, given its confines, before a rather silly and abrupt conclusion.' – *Brian Lowry, Variety*

The Nickel Queen

Australia   1971   89m   colour
Fox/Rank/Woomera (Bob Austin, Lee Robinson)
A back country barmaid becomes a rich woman with a nickel share in the mineral boom; but she is swindled by con men.
Mild comedy-drama.
w Henry C. James, John McCallum, Joy Cavill d John McCallum ph John Williams m Sven Libaek
☆ Googie Withers, John McCallum, John Laws, Ed Devereaux

The Nickel Ride

US   1975   110m   DeLuxe
TCF
A wheeler dealer in downtown Los Angeles learns that he is marked for elimination.
Unpleasant and entirely uninteresting low-life crime melodrama.
w Eric Roth d Robert Mulligan
☆ Jason Miller, Linda Haynes, Victor French, John Hillerman, Bo Hopkins

Nickelodeon *

US/GB   1976   122m   Metrocolor
Columbia/EMI/Chartoff-Winkler (Frank Marshall)
In 1910, various characters come together to make movies, finally attending the 1915 opening in Hollywood of *The Birth of a Nation*.
What should have been a hugely entertaining chunk of comic nostalgia is killed stone dead by embarrassed acting, poor timing, and a general lack of funny ideas, despite having so much to borrow from.
w W. D. Richter, Peter Bogdanovich d Peter Bogdanovich ph Laszlo Kovacs md Richard Hazard
☆ Ryan O'Neal, Burt Reynolds, Tatum O'Neal, Brian Keith, Stella Stevens, John Ritter, Jane Hitchcock
'Ponderous slapstick and a pathetic parody of Harold Lloyd.' – *Sight and Sound*
'Another collection of scenes from other people's films.' – *Howard Kissel, Women's Wear Daily*
'The slightest familiarity with the early works of Hal Roach – not to mention D. W. Griffith, here pretentiously quoted – reveals how little Bogdanovich understands his vastly superior predecessors.' – *Robert Asahina, New Leader*
'The crudest, stupidest, unfunniest farce of this or any other year.' – *John Simon, New York*

Nick's Movie: see *Lightning Over Water*

Nicky and Gino

US   1988   109m   DeLuxe
Rank/Orion (Marvin Minoff, Mike Farrell)
aka: *Dominick and Eugene*
A hospital doctor tries to keep his brain-damaged twin brother out of trouble.
Sentimental drama of no particular distinction.
w Alvin Sargent, Corey Blechman story Danny Porfirio d Robert M. Young ph Curtis Clark m Trevor Jones pd Doug Kraner ed Arthur Coburn
☆ Tom Hulce, Ray Liotta, Jamie Lee Curtis, Todd Graff, Bill Cobbs, David Strathairn, Mimi Cecchini, Robert Levine

Nico: see *Above the Law*

The Niebelungen ***

Germany   1924   bw   silent
Decla-Bioscop (Erich Pommer)
Part 1: *Siegfried*, 115m approx (24 fps)
Part 2: *Kriemhild's Revenge*, 125m approx (24 fps)
Siegfried kills a dragon and marries a princess of Burgundy but the fierce queen Brunhilde arranges his death. His widow marries Attila the Hun and they massacre the Burgundians.
Stately, warlike legends are transformed into a slow, chilling, awe-inspiring sequence of films, the décor being of special interest. The films were conceived as a tribute to the German nation, and were among Hitler's favourites.
w Thea von Harbou d Fritz Lang ph Carl Hoffman, Günther Rittau ad Otto Hunte, Karl Vollbrecht, Erich Kettelhut
☆ Paul Richter, Marguerite Schön, Theodor Loos, Hannah Ralph, Rudolf Klein-Rogge

'They all loved him – a schoolteacher, a night club hostess, and a luscious society bud!'

Night after Night *

US   1932   76m   bw
Paramount
An ex-boxer seeking refinement buys a night-club and falls for a socialite.
Dim little drama which is remembered for introducing Mae West to the screen with her famous line, 'Goodness had nothing to do with it'.
w Vincent Laurence novel Single Night by Louis Bromfield d Archie Mayo ph Ernest Haller
☆ George Raft, Constance Cummings, Wynne Gibson, Mae West, Alison Skipworth, Roscoe Karns, Louis Calhern
'Mae West stole everything but the cameras. I never made another picture with her. I knew she had me licked.' – *George Raft*

Night Ambush: see *Ill Met by Moonlight*

Night and Day *

US   1946   132m   Technicolor
Warner (Arthur Schwarz)
The life of Cole Porter.
Or rather, a fictitious story about a composer who happens to be called Cole Porter. A careful but undistinguished musical with pleasant moments.
w Charles Hoffman, Leo Townsend, William Bowers d Michael Curtiz ph Peverell Marley, William V. Skall m/ly Cole Porter md Max Steiner, Ray Heindorf ch Le Roy Prinz
☆ Cary Grant, Alexis Smith, Monty Woolley, Mary Martin, Ginny Simms, Jane Wyman, Eve Arden, Victor Francen, Alan Hale, Dorothy Malone
§ Max Steiner, Ray Heindorf

Night and Day *

France   1991   100m   colour
Artificial Eye/Pierre Grise Productions (Martine Marignac, Maurice Tinchant)
original title: *Nuit et Jour*
A woman has simultaneous and passionate affairs with two men.
A celebration of guilt-free sex, rather than love, with men depicted as adjuncts to a strong woman.
wd Chantal Akerman ph Jean-Claude Neckelbrouck m Marc Herouet ad Michel Vandestein, Dominique Douret ed Francine Sandberg, Camille Bordes-Resnais
☆ Guillaine Londez, Thomas Langmann, François Negret, Nicole Colchat, Pierre Laroche

Night and Fog *

France   1955   31m   Eastmancolor
Argos/Como
original title: *Nuit et Brouillard*
An account of the concentration camp at Auschwitz, contrasted with the peaceful surroundings ten years after its disbandment.
An official film of great dignity.
ph Ghislain Cloquet, Sacha Vierny d/ed Alain Resnais

Night and the City

GB   1950   101m   bw
TCF (Samuel G. Engel)
A crooked wrestling promoter is tracked down by an underworld gang.
A fated attempt to extend the success of Naked City in a London setting; the surface is accomplished enough, but the plot and characters are just plain dull, especially as little is seen of the police.
w Jo Eisinger novel Gerald Kersh d Jules Dassin ph Max Greene m Benjamin Frankel
☆ Richard Widmark, Gene Tierney, Googie Withers, Hugh Marlowe, Herbert Lom
'Brilliantly photographed, it is an example of neo-expressionist techniques at their most potent.' – *Richard Roud, 1964*

'When you're down to your last dream, you either live it or lose it.'

Night and the City

US   1992   104m   colour
First Independent/Penta/Tribeca (Jane Rosenthal, Irwin Winkler)
A small-time lawyer talks himself into trouble when he sets up as a boxing promoter and has an affair with the wife of one of his backers.
Dully directed, the movie comes to life only spasmodically; for the most part, it just lies there, completely inert.
w Richard Price novel Gerald Kersh d Irwin Winkler ph Tak Fujimoto m James Newton Howard pd Peter Larkin ed David Brenner
☆ Robert DeNiro, Jessica Lange, Cliff Gorman, Jack Warden, Alan King, Eli Wallach, Barry Primus
'It resembles a cigarette lighter with a worn flint and a dry wick that never ignites, leaving everyone with bruised thumbs from vainly flicking the spiked wheel.' – *Philip French, Observer*
'A useless film.' – *Rupert Murdoch*
† A remake of Jules Dassin's 1950 film.

The Night Angel

US   1931   75m   bw
Paramount
A Prague lawyer falls for the daughter of the brothel keeper he has sent to prison, and after killing a jealous suitor is himself accused of murder.
Would-be Dietrichean high-style melodrama which did its stars no good at all and virtually ended Miss Carroll's career.
wd Edmund Goulding
☆ Fredric March, Nancy Carroll, Alan Hale, Alison Skipworth, Katherine Emmett
'Mild and frequently boring entertainment of the kind that can just about last a week in most of the de luxers.' – *Variety*

A Night at Earl Carroll's

US   1940   63m   bw
Paramount
When gangsters kidnap stars of Earl Carroll's night-club, the restaurant staff put on their own show.
Tinseltown time-passer which served a very small purpose.
w Lynn Starling d Kurt Neumann
☆ Ken Murray, J. Carrol Naish, Lilian Cornell, Blanche Stewart

A Night at the Opera ****

♚♟ US   1935   96m   bw
MGM (Irving Thalberg)
Three zanies first wreck, then help an opera company.
Certainly among the best of the Marxian extravaganzas, and the first to give them a big production to play with as well as musical interludes by

other than themselves for a change of pace. The mix plays beautifully.

w George S. Kaufman, Morrie Ryskind d Sam Wood ph Merritt Gerstad md Herbert Stothart ad Cedric Gibbons, Ben Carre ed William LeVanway

☆ Groucho Marx, Chico Marx, Harpo Marx, Margaret Dumont, Kitty Carlisle, Allan Jones, Walter Woolf King, Sig Rumann

'Corking comedy with the brothers at par and biz chances excellent … songs in a Marx picture are generally at a disadvantage because they're more or less interruptions, the customers awaiting the next laugh.' – Variety

† Zeppo Marx absented himself from here on.

'Score!'

A Night at the Roxbury
US 1998 81m DeLuxe
Paramount/SNL (Lorne Michaels, Amy Heckerling)
🔲 📼 ⊘ ⌂

Two brothers, desperate to be cool, manage against the odds to be allowed into an exclusive LA night-club.

Yet another comic spin-off from the US TV series Saturday Night Live; on the big screen, it is dumb, stupid and not at all funny.

w Steve Koren, Will Ferrell, Chris Kattan d John Fortenberry ph Francis Kenny m David Kitay pd Steven Jordan ed Jay Kamen

☆ Will Ferrell, Chris Kattan, Molly Shannon, Dan Hedaya, Richard Grieco, Loni Anderson, Elisa Donovan, Gigi Rice, Lochlyn Munro

'We have to survive on a diet of low calorie slapstick and quick-fix buffoonery. Even at just 82 minutes it can still seem like an hour-and-a-half too long.' – Trevor Lewis, Empire

Night Beat
GB 1948 91m bw
BLPA (Harold Huth)

Demobbed, a commando becomes a policeman and his friend becomes a crook.

Manhattan Melodrama, British style; no more than an adequate offering of its type.

w T. J. Morrison, Roland Pertwee, Guy Morgan d Harold Huth ph Vaclav Vich m Benjamin Frankel ed Grace Garland

☆ Anne Crawford, Maxwell Reed, Ronald Howard, Christine Norden, Hector Ross, Sidney James

Night Boat to Dublin
GB 1945 99m bw
ABP (Hamilton Inglis)

An MI5 man saves an atom scientist from kidnapping.

Generally watchable low key thriller with familiar British ingredients.

w Lawrence Huntington, Robert Hall d Lawrence Huntington ph Otto Heller

☆ Robert Newton, Raymond Lovell, Muriel Pavlow, Guy Middleton, Herbert Lom, Martin Miller, Marius Goring

Night Caller (dubbed)
France/Italy 1975 125m Eastmancolor
Columbia-Warner/Cerito/Mondial (Henri Verneuil)
original title: Peur sur la Ville

A moody inspector, obsessed with his personal vendetta against a crook, pays little attention to tracking down a serial killer who is murdering women.

Slight but enjoyable thriller, with some fancy stunts to enliven a familiar story.

w Henri Verneuil, Francis Veber d Henri Verneuil ph Jean Penzer m Ennio Morricone ad Jean André ed Pierre Gillette, Henri Lanoë

☆ Jean-Paul Belmondo, Charles Denner, Catherine Morin, Adalberto-Maria Merli, Lea Massari, Giovanni Cianfriglia, Rosy Varte, Henri-Jacques Huet

'A routine policier, which seems to have one eye on the American tough cop series.' – John Gillett, MFB

The Night Caller *
GB 1965 84m bw
New Art/Armitage
🔲 ⊘⌁ ⊘
US title: Blood Beast from Outer Space

An alien being arrives on Earth to abduct girls for genetic purposes.

Reasonably well made science fiction thriller.

w Jim O'Connolly novel Frank Crisp d John Gilling ph Stephen Dade m Johnny Gregory

☆ John Saxon, Maurice Denham, Patricia Haines, Alfred Burke, John Carson, Jack Watson, Warren Mitchell

Night Club Hostess: see Unmarried

Night Club Lady
US 1932 66m bw
Columbia

A police commissioner solves the murder of a night-club hostess.

Straightforward cops and killers melodrama with the star in his first non-romantic role.

w Robert Riskin novel Anthony Abbott d Irving Cummings

☆ Adolphe Menjou, Mayo Methot, Skeets Gallagher, Blanche Friderici, Nat Pendleton

Night Club Scandal
US 1937 74m bw
Paramount

A society doctor murders his wife and incriminates her lover.

Smooth second feature remake of Guilty as Hell, chiefly notable for its star's last controlled performance.

w Lillie Hayward play Riddle Me This by Daniel Rubin d Ralph Murphy ph Leo Tover

☆ John Barrymore, Lynne Overman, Charles Bickford, Elizabeth Patterson, Evelyn Brent, Louise Campbell, J. Carrol Naish

Night Court
US 1932 90m bw
MGM
GB title: Justice for Sale

A corrupt judge frames a girl on a prostitution charge.

Tough star melodrama.

w Mark Hellinger, Bayard Veiller, Charles Beehan, Lenore Coffee d W. S. Van Dyke

☆ Walter Huston, Lewis Stone, Anita Page, Phillips Holmes, Jean Hersholt

'Political frame-up of women is made the subject of a vigorous melodrama, though it comes after the New York scandal on the subject is largely forgotten.' – Variety

Night Crawlers: see The Navy versus The Night Monsters

Night Creatures: see Captain Clegg

Night Crossing
👫 US 1982 106m Technicolor
Walt Disney (Tom Leetch)
🔲 ⌂

East Germans escape to the west via air balloon.

Well-meaning melodrama which sadly lacks plot development and suspense, and is also rather miserable to look at.

w John McGreevey d Delbert Mann ph Tony Imi m Jerry Goldsmith

☆ John Hurt, Jane Alexander, Doug McKeon, Frank McKeon, Beau Bridges, Glynnis O'Connor, Ian Bannen

The Night Digger
GB 1971 100m colour
MGM

A frustrated spinster protects a handyman clearly guilty of murder, and runs away with him.

How this came to be made at all when the Finney version of Night Must Fall had recently flopped is a mystery; it had so little box-office appeal that it was barely released.

w Roald Dahl story Joy Cowley d Alastair Reid

☆ Patricia Neal, Nicholas Clay, Pamela Browne, Jean Anderson, Yootha Joyce, Peter Sallis, Graham Crowden

Night Eyes
US/India 1990 98m colour
Amritraj-Baldwin (Ashok Amritraj)
🔲 📼

A rock star hires a security guard to look after his estranged wife, hoping to catch her in an affair.

Cheap, unsubtle thriller of the sort that gives direct-to-video movies a bad name: the dialogue sounds as if it was bought by the yard, and the acting and direction are uninteresting.

w Tom Citrano, Andrew Stevens d Jag Mundhra ph James Mathers m Richard Glasser pd Brian McCabe ed David H. Lloyd

☆ Andrew Stevens, Tanya Roberts, Warwick Sims, Karen Elise Baldwin, Cooper Huckabee, Stephen Meadows, Chick Vennera

† It was followed by three sequels, none of which managed to be any more watchable.

'In a city of nine million people is there room for one honest man?'

Night Falls on Manhattan *
US 1997 114m DuArt
Paramount/Spelling (Thom Mount, Josh Kramer)
🔲 📼

Investigating the shooting of his father, a policeman, by a drug dealer, an honest cop-turned-lawyer uncovers high-level corruption.

Effective investigative drama on a somewhat familiar theme, but given urgency by the lead performances.

wd Sidney Lumet novel Tainted Evidence by Robert Daley ph David Watkin m Mark Isham pd Philip Rosenberg ed Sam O'Steen

☆ Andy Garcia, Richard Dreyfuss, Lena Olin, Ian Holm, James Gandolfini, Colm Feore, Ron Liebman

'Intelligent and reasonably compelling, this is solid fare.' – Empire

Night Fighters: see A Terrible Beauty

Night Flight *
US 1933 84m bw
MGM (David O. Selznick)

The president of a civil airline insists that dangerous night flights must continue as a mark of progress.

Spurious, unsatisfactory, multi-star air melodrama lacking both narrative flow and the common touch.

w Oliver H. P. Garrett stories Antoine de St Exupéry d Clarence Brown ph Oliver T. Marsh, Elmer Dyer, Charles Marshall

☆ John Barrymore, Helen Hayes, Lionel Barrymore, Clark Gable, Robert Montgomery, Myrna Loy, William Gargan, C. Henry Gordon

'Punch aviation film with a flock of potent marquee names.' – Variety

'It is in the sense it conveys of human beings caught in the swift machinery of modern living that Night Flight soars above other pictures of its kind.' – James Shelley Hamilton

Night Full of Rain: see The End of the World (in our usual bed in a night full of rain)

Night Games *
Sweden 1966 105m bw
Sandrews (Lena Malmsjö)
original title: Nattlek

A 35-year-old man is sexually inhibited by memories of his dead mother's passions and perversions.

Curious Freudian parable apparently intended as a comment on the state of Europe. Audiences found it merely peculiar.

wd Mai Zetterling novel Mai Zetterling ph Rune Ericson m Jan Johansson, George Riedel

☆ Ingrid Thulin, Keve Hjelm, Lena Brundin, Naima Wifstrand

'The best one can say is that it never lets up for a moment.' – David Wilson, MFB

Night Games
US 1980 100m Technicolor
Golden Harvest/Avco
🔲 ⌂

A neurotic Beverly Hills housewife is terrified of men.

Crazy mix of case history, eroticism and suspense with insufficient of any to satisfy fans.

w Anton Diether, Clarke Reynolds d Roger Vadim ph Denis Lewiston m John Barry

☆ Cindy Pickett, Joanna Cassidy, Barry Primus

Night Hair Child
GB 1971 89m Movielab
Leander/Harry Alan Towers (Graham Harris)

A 12-year-old boy makes sexual advances to his stepmother.

Corrupt voyeuristic weirdie which has to be seen to be believed.

w Trevor Preston d James Kelly ph Harry Waxman m Stelvio Cipriani

☆ Mark Lester, Britt Ekland, Hardy Kruger, Harry Andrews, Lilli Palmer

'Was his strange power a blessing or a curse? He was a refugee from love – because he could foretell that their marriage and their kisses would dissolve in a tragedy of tears!'

Night Has a Thousand Eyes
US 1948 80m bw
Paramount (André Boehm)

A vaudeville mentalist finds that he really does have the power to predict the future.

Predictable supernatural melodrama closely modelled on The Clairvoyant (qv); quite nicely made but simply not exciting.

w Barre Lyndon, Jonathan Latimer novel Cornell Woolrich d John Farrow ph John F. Seitz m Victor Young

☆ Edward G. Robinson, Gail Russell, John Lund, Virginia Bruce, William Demarest, Richard Webb, Jerome Cowan

'For those who like sweet hocus-pocus and Edward G. Robinson.' – Sunday Express

The Night Has Eyes *
GB 1942 79m bw
ABP (John Argyle)
📼
US title: Terror House

A young teacher disappears on the Yorkshire moors; her friend goes in search, and comes under the influence of a strange young man and his sinister housekeeper.

Stagey but effective little thriller, with oodles of fog and bog to help the suspense.

w Alan Kennington d Leslie Arliss ph Günther Krampf m Charles Williams

☆ James Mason, Joyce Howard, Wilfrid Lawson, Mary Clare, Tucker McGuire, John Fernald

'Some ingenuity and not a little style.' – The Times

The Night Holds Terror *
US 1955 86m bw
Columbia (Andrew Stone)

Three gunmen on the run kidnap a factory worker and hold him to ransom.

Effective, detailed, low-budget police melodrama; its plot may be over familiar now, but at the time it was refreshing and the whole film an intelligent exercise in suspense.

wd Andrew Stone ph Fred Jackman Jnr m Lucien Cailliet

☆ Jack Kelly, Hildy Parks, John Cassavetes, David Cross, Edward Marr, Jack Kruschen

A Night in Cairo: see The Barbarian

A Night in Casablanca **
👫 US 1946 85m bw
David L. Loew
🔲

Three zanies rout Nazi refugees in a North African hotel.

The last authentic Marxian extravaganza; it starts uncertainly, builds to a fine sustained frenzy, then peters out in some overstretched airplane acrobatics.

w Joseph Fields, Roland Kibbee, Frank Tashlin d Archie Mayo ph James Van Trees m Werner Janssen pd Duncan Cramer

☆ Groucho Marx, Chico Marx, Harpo Marx, Sig Rumann, Lisette Verea, Charles Drake, Lois Collier, Dan Seymour

KORNBLOW (GROUCHO MARX): 'I don't mind being killed, but I resent hearing it from a character whose head comes to a point.'

KORNBLOW: 'From now on the essence of this hotel will be speed. If a customer asks you for a three-minute egg, give it to him in two minutes. If he asks you for a two-minute egg, give it to him in one minute. If he asks you for a one-minute egg, give him the chicken and let him work it out for himself.'

BEATRICE (LISETTE VEREA): 'My name's Beatrice Ryner. I stop at the hotel.'
KORNBLOW: 'My name's Ronald Kornblow. I stop at nothing.'

'It is beside the main point to add that it isn't one of their best movies; for the worst they might ever make would be better worth seeing than most other things I can think of.' – James Agee

A Night in Havana: see The Big Boodle

'It's a swell night for kissing or killing – or both!'

A Night in New Orleans
US   1941   75m   bw
Paramount
A policeman goes after gamblers and finds one of them murdered.
Routine mystery, competently made.
w Jonathan Latimer d William C. Clemens
☆ Preston Foster, Albert Dekker, Patricia Morison, Charles Butterworth, Dooley Wilson

A Night in Paradise
US   1946   84m   Technicolor
(Universal)
Aesop falls in love at the court of King Croesus.
Deadly boring, unintentionally funny Arabian Nights farrago without the saving grace of action.
w Ernest Pascal, Emmet Lavery *novel Peacock's Feather* by George S. Hellman d Arthur Lubin ph Hal Mohr m Frank Skinner
☆ Merle Oberon, Turhan Bey, Thomas Gomez, Gale Sondergaard, Ray Collins, George Dolenz, John Litel, Ernest Truex, Jerome Cowan, Douglass Dumbrille

A Night in the Life of Jimmy Reardon:
see *Jimmy Reardon*

Night into Morning
US   1951   86m   bw
MGM (Edwin H. Knopf)
A college professor loses his wife and son in an accident; despair drives him to drink and attempted suicide.
Well-made and well-meaning melodrama whose virtual absence of plot makes it seem by the end merely maudlin.
w Karl Tunberg, Leonard Spigelgass d Fletcher Markle ph George Folsey m Carmen Dragon
☆ Ray Milland, Nancy Davis, John Hodiak, Lewis Stone, Jean Hagen, Rosemary de Camp
'Tediously uneventful, as sincere and futile as a note of condolence.' – *Time*

The Night Invader
GB   1943   81m   bw
Warner
A Britisher in an occupied country is helped to capture a Nazi count.
Propaganda potboiler for double billing.
w Brock Williams, Edward Dryhurst, Roland Pertwee *novel Rendezvous with Death* by John Bentley d Herbert Mason
☆ Anne Crawford, David Farrar, Carl Jaffe, Sybilla Binder, Marius Goring

The Night Is Ending: see *Paris After Dark*

Night Is My Future: see *Music Is My Future*

The Night Is Young
US   1934   82m   bw
MGM
A European archduke loves a ballerina.
High-class musical which failed despite an intriguing cast and a Romberg and Hammerstein score.
w Vicki Baum d Dudley Murphy
☆ Evelyn Laye, Ramon Novarro, Una Merkel, Edward Everett Horton, Rosalind Russell, Charles Butterworth, Herman Bing, Henry Stephenson, Donald Cook
'Disappointing entertainment … feeble in plot, with a cast struggling to carry assignments and failing to ignite any real romantic fire, film also seems to lack a single strong musical number.' – *Variety*

The Night Is Young
France   1986   119m   colour
Artificial Eye/Les Films Plain Chant/Soporfilms/FR3 (Philippe Diaz)
⬚
original title: *Mauvais Sang*
In the future, a gang of criminals sets out to steal an antidote to a disease which kills those who indulge in sex without love.
Chic, slight tale, influenced for the bad by Godard.
wd Leos Carax ph Jean-Yves Escoffier pd Michel Vandestien ed Nelly Quettier
☆ Michel Piccoli, Juliette Binoche, Denis Lavant, Hans Meyer, Julie Delpy, Carroll Brooks, Hugo Pratty

Night Key
US   1937   67m   bw
Universal (Robert Presnell)
An inventor's idea is stolen by his former partner, and he takes an appropriate revenge.
Low-key star melodrama: competent, but no great shakes.
w Tristram Tupper, John C. Moffitt d Lloyd Corrigan ph George Robinson m Louis Forbes make-up Jack Pierce
☆ Boris Karloff, Jean Rogers, Warren Hull, Samuel S. Hinds, Alan Baxter, Ward Bond, Edwin Maxwell
'Mildly entertaining dualler … one of those impossible gadget yarns with liberal injections of cops and robbers stuff.' – *Variety*

The Night Life of the Gods
US   1935   75m   bw
Universal
An inventor turns statues into people, and vice versa.
Fantasy comedy from a well-known comic novel; interesting despite low level of invention.
w Barry Trivers *novel* Thorne Smith d Lowell Sherman
☆ Alan Mowbray, Florine McKinney, Richard Carle, Peggy Shannon
'Universal has managed to keep in the fun and restrain it from getting too rough.' – *Variety*

A Night Like This
GB   1932   74m   bw
British and Dominions
An Irish policeman breaks up a crooked gambling club.
Minor Aldwych farce which hasn't worn well.
w Ben Travers *play* Ben Travers d Tom Walls ph Freddie Young
☆ Tom Walls, Ralph Lynn, Robertson Hare, Winifred Shotter, Mary Brough, Claude Hulbert

Night Mail *
GB   1936   24m   bw
GPO Film Unit (John Grierson)
A 'film poem' showing the journey of the mail train from London to Glasgow.
One of the best and most influential of British documentaries: despite a few absurdities, it remains a pleasure to watch.
wd Basil Wright, Harry Watt *poem* W. H. Auden ph J. Jones, H. E. Fowle m Benjamin Britten *sound arrangements* Alberto Cavalcanti
'The final sequences as the train drives at dawn through the northern moors, the sheep-dog racing the train and the rabbits scurrying to cover, set to the simple visual verses of Mr Auden, are extraordinarily exciting.' – *Graham Greene, The Spectator*

Night Mayor
US   1932   65m   bw
Columbia
The Mayor of New York pays too much attention to night life and not enough to his desk.
Thinly veiled account of the Jimmy Walker affair, released after Walker had been discredited. As entertainment, punchy, but in the end only fair.
w Gertrude Purcell, Sam Marx d Ben Stoloff
☆ Lee Tracy, Evalyn Knapp, Eugene Pallette, Warren Hymer, Donald Dillaway, Astrid Allwyn
'It is a safe general statement that the screen ought never to exploit a public character who is the center of debate.' – *Variety*

Night Monster
US   1942   73m   bw
Universal (Ford Beebe)
GB title: *House of Mystery*
Murders are committed in a spooky house by a cripple who produces synthetic legs by self-hypnotism.
Stilted, creaky would-be thriller with a good cast and an impertinent plot.
w Clarence Upson Young d Ford Beebe ph Charles Van Enger
☆ Ralph Morgan, Don Porter, Irene Hervey, Bela Lugosi, Lionel Atwill, Nils Asther, Leif Erickson, Frank Reicher

'Night, Mother
US   1986   96m   DeLuxe
Universal/Aaron Spelling, Alan Greisman
▤   ▣
A mother gets to grips with the problems of her suicidal daughter.
Rueful drama which pares down the nerve ends but was clearly not designed for box-office, and remains a play rather than a film.
w Marsha Norman *play* Marsha Norman d Tom Moore ph Stephen M. Katz m David Shire
☆ Anne Bancroft, Sissy Spacek, Ed Berke, Carol Robbins

'Maybe he would find the girl – maybe he would find himself!'

Night Moves *
US   1975   99m   Technicolor
Warner/Hiller/Layton (Robert M. Sherman)
▤   ▣
A private eye is engaged to find a runaway teenager.
Apparently a Chandlerish mystery, this is really a Pinterish audience-teaser with obsessions about communication and the meaning of life. A smart-ass entertainment for eager trendies.
w Alan Sharp d Arthur Penn ph Bruce Surtees m Michael Small pd George Jenkins
☆ Gene Hackman, Jennifer Warren, Edward Binns, Harris Yulin, Kenneth Mars
'Beneath the complicated unravelling of a mystery, an anti-mystery, with the hero's detection registering as an evasion of his own problems; beneath a densely charted intrigue of betrayals and cross purposes, a cryptic void…' – *Jonathan Rosenbaum*
'A suspenseless suspenser … there's very little rhyme or reason for the plot's progression.' – *Variety*
'Rich and dense enough to set up reverberations long after one has left the cinema.' – *Michael Billington, Illustrated London News*

Night Must Fall *
US   1937   117m   bw
MGM (Hunt Stromberg)
A bland young bellboy who is really a psychopathic murderer attaches himself to the household of a rich old lady.
Unconvincing but memorable Hollywood expansion of an effective British chiller.
w John Van Druten *play* Emlyn Williams d Richard Thorpe ph Ray June m Edward Ward
☆ Robert Montgomery, Rosalind Russell, May Whitty, Alan Marshal, Merle Tottenham, Kathleen Harrison, Matthew Boulton, E. E. Clive
'Too long and not box office … tedious, slow, and even dull in spots.' – *Variety*
'A pretty little murder play has made a long dim film.' – *Graham Greene*
'The most exhilarating shrouds of horror hang over it. It represents a provocative imagination, a skillful adapter, a sensitive director, a splendid acting job.' – *Bland Johaneson, New York Daily Mirror*
† Louis B. Mayer so disliked this film that at the New York première he ordered the distribution of leaflets disowning it on behalf of MGM.
⚉ Robert Montgomery; May Whitty

Night Must Fall
GB   1964   105m   bw
MGM (Albert Finney, Karel Reisz)
Dreary remake with a mannered star performance and the emphasis on axe murders. A mistake from beginning to end.
w Clive Exton d Karel Reisz ph Freddie Francis m Ron Grainer
☆ Albert Finney, Susan Hampshire, Mona Washbourne, Sheila Hancock, Michael Medwin, Joe Gladwin, Martin Wyldeck
'Not so much a thriller as a typically humourless example of that overworked genre known as psychological drama … [Finney] constantly recalls a ventriloquist's dummy.' – *MFB*

The Night My Number Came Up *
GB   1954   94m   bw
Ealing (Tom Morahan)
▤
A man dreams that his plane will crash, and the dream begins to come true.
Intriguing little melodrama which badly lacks a twist ending and foxes itself by a flashback construction

which leaves very little open to doubt. *Production generally good.*
w R. C. Sherriff d Leslie Norman ph Lionel Banes m Malcolm Arnold
☆ Michael Redgrave, Alexander Knox, Sheila Sim, Denholm Elliott, Ursula Jeans, George Rose, Nigel Stock, Michael Hordern, Ralph Truman, Victor Maddern, Bill Kerr, Alfie Bass
'A story which, in its delicately measured suspenses and reliefs, has been beautifully built.' – *Times Educational Supplement*
'The idea of destiny as predestiny is an old psychological trump, but it still takes tricks.' – *Time*
† The story was taken from a personal account by Sir Victor Goddard.

Night Nurse *
US   1931   72m   bw
Warner
▤   ▣
A nurse uncovers a plot by other members of the household against her patient's children.
Fast-moving melodrama with solid star performances; just what the public wanted in 1931.
w Oliver H. P. Garrett, Charles Kenyon *novel* Dora Macy d William Wellman ph Chick McGill md Leo Forbstein ad Max Parker ed Edward M. McDermott
☆ Barbara Stanwyck, Ben Lyon, Joan Blondell, Clark Gable, Charles Winninger, Vera Lewis, Blanche Frederici, Charlotte Merriam
'A conglomeration of exaggerations, often bordering on serial dramatics.' – *Hollywood Reporter*

Night of Counting the Years **
Egypt   1969   102m   colour
Egyptian Cinema General Organization
original title: *El Mumia*
Horrified to discover that his tribe has grown rich by robbing the tombs of the Pharaohs, a young leader faces the dilemma of what to do about it.
Engrossing, if rather stately, account of a moral choice against the magnificent background of Egypt's past. The film was sponsored by Italian director Roberto Rossellini.
wd Shadi Abdelsalam ph Abdel Aziz Fahmy m Mario Nascimbene
☆ Ahmed Marel, Zouzou El Hakim, Ahmad Hegazi, Nadia Loutfy, Gaby Karraz

Night of Dark Shadows
US   1971   97m   Metrocolor   Panavision
MGM (Dan Curtis)
▤
aka: *Curse of Dark Shadows*
After moving to his ancestral home, an artist begins to experience strange and violent visions of the past.
Tame tale of the supernatural that fails to hold one's interest.
w Sam Hall *story* Sam Hall, Dan Curtis d Dan Curtis ph Richard Shore m Robert Cobert pd Trevor Williams ed Charles Goldsmith
☆ David Selby, Grayson Hall, Lara Parker, John Karlen, Nancy Barrett, James Storm, Thayer David, Christopher Pennock, Diana Millay, Kate Jackson
† The film was an unsuccessful follow-up to Curtis's 1970 film *House of Dark Shadows* (qv).

The Night of January 16th
US   1941   79m   bw
Paramount
A secretary is arrested for her boss's murder; but is he really dead?
A stage thriller full of theatrical trickery becomes a very mundane film.
w Delmer Daves, Robert Pirosh, Eve Greene *play* Ayn Rand d William Clemens
☆ Robert Preston, Ellen Drew, Nils Asther, Margaret Hayes

The Night of June 13th
US   1932   76m   bw
Paramount
A suburban street is transformed when one of its residents goes on trial for murder.
Combination courtroom and slice-of-life drama which satisfied most audiences.
w Agnes Brand Leahy, Brian Marlow, William Slavens McNutt *story* Vera Caspary d Stephen Roberts

---

🏃 film suitable for family viewing   ▣ VHS video-cassette for the British PAL system   ▣ VHS video-cassette for the British PAL system in wide screen-format   ⬚ Video cassette in a computer-colourised version   ▤ American NTSC video-cassette   ▣ Laser disc

☆ Clive Brook, Lila Lee, Mary Boland, Adrianne Allen, Gene Raymond, Frances Dee, Charley Grapewin

'Absorbingly worked out with fascinating character study and a touch of satire.' – *Variety*

'What happens after they turn the lights out on Broadway?'

The Night of Nights

US 1939 86m bw
Paramount

A once-famous Broadway writer, now a drunk, tries to ensure his daughter's fame.
Curious downbeat melodrama without the courage of its convictions, or the actors to give the right bravura performances.
w Donald Ogden Stewart d Lewis Milestone
☆ Pat O'Brien, Olympe Bradna, Reginald Gardiner, Roland Young

'Backstage drama lightened by direction and cast performances. Nominal supporter for key duals.' – *Variety*

The Night of San Lorenzo **

Italy 1981 107m Agfacolor
UA/Premier/RAI/Ager Cinematografica (Giuliani G. de Negri)
🖭 🎧

original title: *La Notte Di San Lorenzo*
aka: *Night of the Shooting Stars*
In the Second World War a six-year-old girl watches events in her town as American forces advance to liberate it.
Touching, powerfully nostalgic study of a community in ferment.
wd Paolo Taviani, Vittorio Taviani ph Franco Di Giacomo m Nicola Piovani ad Gianni Sbarra ed Roberto Perpignani
☆ Omero Antonutti, Margarita Lozano, Claudio Bigagli, Massimo Bonetti, Norma Martelli, Enrica Maria Modugno, Sabina Vannucchi

Night of the Big Heat

GB 1967 94m Eastmancolor
Tom Blakeley/Planet
US title: *Island of the Burning Damned*
Invaders from outer space take over a remote Scottish island and make it unbearably hot so that they can survive.
Sloppily made and over-prolonged science fiction with far too much irrelevant talk.
w Ronald Liles novel John Lymington d Terence Fisher ph Reginald Wyer m Malcolm Lockyer
☆ Christopher Lee, Peter Cushing, Patrick Allen, Sarah Lawson, Jane Merrow, William Lucas, Kenneth Cope

Night of the Bloody Apes (dubbed)

Mexico 1970 82m Eastmancolor
Grand National/Unistar (Alfredo Salazar)
🖭 🖭

original title: *Horriplante Bestia Humana*
aka: *Gomar the Human Gorilla*
In an attempt to save his son's life, a doctor gives him the heart of a gorilla, causing him to change into a murderous ape.
Bizarre horror that may appeal to lovers of terrible movies; it borrows from every major film of the genre, from Jekyll and Hyde and Frankenstein to King Kong and The Murders of the Rue Morgue.
w René Cardona, René Cardona Jnr d René Cardona ph Raúl Martinez Solares m Antonio Diaz Conde ad Carlos Arjona ed Jorge Bustos sp Javier Torres Torija
☆ José Elias Moreno, Carlos López Moctezuma, Armando Silvestre, Norma Lazareno, Agustin Martinez Solares, Noelia Noel

'Patience is severely tried by the stately pace, the endless expressions of paternal devotion, and the script's risible attempts to offer medical explanations and justifications.' – *Tom Milne, MFB*

Night of the Comet

US 1984 98m colour
Atlantic/Thomas Coleman-Michael Rosenblatt
(Andrew Lane, Wayne Crawford)
🖭 🖭

In Los Angeles two sisters are the only survivors of a cosmic storm that kills the population or turns them into zombies.
Low-budget science-fiction thriller, done with humour and some imagination.

wd Thom Eberhardt ph Arthur Albert m David Richard Campbell pd John Muto ed Fred Stafford
☆ Robert Beltran, Catherine Mary Stewart, Kelli Maroney, Sharon Farrell, Mary Woronov, Geoffrey Lewis

Night of the Cyclone

US 1990 90m colour
Maroon (Edgar Bold)
🖭 🖭

aka: *Perfume of the Cyclone*
A maverick Chicago cop goes to a tropical island to find his spoilt 16-year-old daughter, who has not returned from a modelling assignment.
Glossy thriller that is both exotic and uninteresting, affected and very ordinary.
w Rick Brotherhood d David Irving ph James Robb m David Pollecutt pd Graeme Orwin ed Ettie Feldman
☆ Kris Kristofferson, Jeff Meek, Marisa Berenson, Winston Ntshona, Dick Reineke, Marcel van Heerden, Alla Korot

Night of the Demon ***

GB 1957 87m bw
Columbia/Sabre (Frank Bevis)
🖭 🖭

US title: *Curse of the Demon*
An occultist despatches his enemies by raising a giant medieval devil.
Despite dim work from the leads, this supernatural thriller is intelligently scripted and achieves several frightening and memorable sequences in the best Hitchcock manner.
w Charles Bennett, Hal E. Chester story *Casting the Runes* by M. R. James d Jacques Tourneur ph Ted Scaife m Clifton Parker ad Ken Adam
☆ Dana Andrews, Peggy Cummins, Niall MacGinnis, Athene Seyler, Brian Wilde, Maurice Denham, Ewan Roberts, Liam Redmond, Reginald Beckwith

Night of the Demons

US 1988 92m colour
Meridian/Paragon (Joe Augustyn, Jeff Geoffray, Walter S. Josten)
🖭 🖭 🖭

Teenagers release demonic spirits when they hold a Halloween party in a mortuary.
Direly predictable, cheaply produced horror flick with some gruesome make-up effects.
w Joe Augustyn d Kevin S. Tenney ph David Lewis m Dennis Michael Tenney ad Ken Aichele ed Daniel Duncan sp make-up: Steve Johnson
☆ Alvin Alexis, Alison Barron, Lance Fenton, William Gallo, Hal Havins, Mimi Kinkade, Linnea Quigley; Lance Fenton

'Angela's Back ... And She's Throwing Another Party ... Trick Or Treat, Sucker!'

Night of the Demons 2

US 1994 98m colour
Republic/Blue Rider (Walter Josten, Jeff Geoffray)
🖭 🖭 🖭

aka: *Night of the Demons: Angela's Revenge*
A girl invites fellow students to a creepy old house for Halloween night, causing the malevolent spirit of its former owner to wreak havoc and create zombie killers.
A more polished retread of the original, with the welcome addition of graveyard humour.
w Joe Augustyn, James Penzi d Brian Trenchard-Smith ph David Lewis m Jim Manzie pd Wendy Guidery ed Daniel Duncan sp prosthetic make-up: Steve Johnson
☆ Cristi Harris, Bobby Jacoby, Merle Kennedy, Amelia Kinkade, Rod McCary, Zoe Trilling, Jennifer Rhodes

'Rises above most slice-and-dice fare and may tantalize some more discriminating palettes in addition to the usual teen suspects.' – *Variety*

Night of the Doomed

Italy 1965 97m bw
Emmeci (Carlo Caiano)
🖭 🖭

original title: *Amanti d'Oltretomba*
GB title: *The Faceless Monster*; US title: *Nightmare Castle*
A sadistic scientist tries to drive his dead wife's stepsister, who has inherited her money, insane.
Lurid thriller that circles endlessly around Barbara Steele, running the gamut of emotions in two roles.

w Carlo Caiano, Fabio de Agostini d Allan Grunewald (Mario Caiano) ph Enzo Barboni m Ennio Morricone ad Massimo Tavazzi ed Renato Cinquini
☆ Barbara Steele, Paul Muller, Helga Liné, Laurence Clift, Rik Battaglia, Giuseppe Addobbati

The Night of the Eagle **

GB 1961 87m bw
Independent Artists (Albert Fennell)
US title: *Burn, Witch, Burn*
At a medical school, a jealous witch sets an evil force on her rival.
Pretty good supernatural thriller, let down by leading performances and sustained by character roles and solid production values in creepy sequences.
w Charles Beaumont, Richard Matheson, George Baxt novel *Conjure Wife* by Fritz Leiber Jnr d Sidney Hayers ph Reg Wyer m William Alwyn
☆ Margaret Johnston, Janet Blair, Peter Wyngarde, Anthony Nicholls, Reginald Beckwith, Kathleen Byron

The Night of the Following Day *

US 1969 100m Technicolor
Universal/Gina (Hubert Cornfield)
🖭 🖭

A young girl arriving in Paris to stay with her father is kidnapped and held to ransom by an eccentric gang.
Straightforward suspense thriller with delusions of grandeur; the second half bogs down in pretentious talk and the end suggests that the whole thing was a dream.
w Hubert Cornfield, Robert Phippeny novel *The Snatchers* by Lionel White d Hubert Cornfield ph Willy Kurant m Stanley Myers
☆ Marlon Brando, Richard Boone, Rita Moreno, Pamela Franklin, Jess Hahn

Night of the Garter

GB 1933 86m bw
British and Dominions (Herbert Wilcox)
A newly married man tries to retrieve an intimate gift from an old flame.
One of the best-remembered comedies of Sydney Howard.
w Austin Melford, Marjorie Gaffney play *Getting Gertie's Garter* by Avery Hopwood, Wilson Collison d Jack Raymond
☆ Sydney Howard, Winifred Shotter, Elsie Randolph, Austin Melford

The Night of the Generals **

GB 1967 148m Technicolor Panavision
Columbia/Horizon/Filmsonor (Sam Spiegel)
🖭 🖭 🎧

A German intelligence agent tracks down a psychopathic Nazi general who started killing prostitutes in Warsaw during World War II.
A curiously bumpy narrative which is neither mystery nor character study but does provide a few effective sequences and impressive performances. The big budget seems well spent.
w Joseph Kessel, Paul Dehn novel Hans Helmut Kirst d Anatole Litvak ph Henri Decaë m Maurice Jarre ad Alexander Trauner
☆ Peter O'Toole, Omar Sharif, Tom Courtenay, Donald Pleasence, Joanna Pettet, Philippe Noiret, Charles Gray, Coral Browne, John Gregson, Harry Andrews, Nigel Stock, Christopher Plummer, Juliette Greco

'The "who" is obvious from the first and the "dunnit" interminable.' – *Judith Crist, 1973*
'Lurid and vivid, if nothing else.' – *Robert Windeler*

Night of the Ghouls

US 1958 75m bw
Wade Williams (Edward D. Wood Jnr)
🖭 🖭

aka: *Revenge of the Dead*
Dr Acula, a fake medium, takes up residence in a haunted house where he manages to raise the dead.
Aficianados of the work of the totally inept Wood may enjoy this, since it has all the hallmarks of his movies: bad acting, irrelevant voice-over and hopeless direction, although it lacks the delirium of Plan 9 from Outer Space.
wd Edward D. Wood Jnr ph William C. Thompson md Gordon Zahler ad Kathleen O'Hara Everett
☆ Criswell, Kenne Duncan, 'Duke' Moore, Valda Hansen, Tor Johnson, John Carpenter, Paul Marco

The Night of the Grizzly

US 1966 102m Techniscope
Paramount (Burt Dunne)
🖭

A Wyoming ex-sheriff kills a marauding bear and earns the respect of his son.
Stout-hearted family film, rather sluggishly made.
w Warren Douglas d Joseph Pevney ph Harold Lipstein, Loyal Griggs m Leith Stevens
☆ Clint Walker, Martha Hyer, Keenan Wynn, Leo Gordon, Kevin Brodie, Nancy Kulp, Ellen Corby, Jack Elam, Ron Ely

'The scenes! The story! The stars! But above all – the suspense!'

The Night of the Hunter ***

US 1955 93m bw
UA/Paul Gregory
🖭 🖭 🎧 🎧

A psychopathic preacher goes on the trail of hidden money, the secret of which is held by two children.
Weird, manic fantasy in which evil finally comes to grief against the forces of sweetness and light (the children, an old lady, water, animals). Although the narrative does not flow smoothly there are splendidly imaginative moments, and no other film has ever quite achieved its texture.
w James Agee novel Davis Grubb d Charles Laughton ph Stanley Cortez m Walter Schumann
☆ Robert Mitchum, Shelley Winters, Lillian Gish, Don Beddoe, Evelyn Varden, Peter Graves, James Gleason

PREACHER (ROBERT MITCHUM): 'Lord, you sure knew what you was doing when you brung me to this very cell at this very time. A man with ten thousand dollars hid somewhere, and a widder in the makin'.'

'One of the most frightening movies ever made.' – *Pauline Kael, 1968*
'A genuinely sinister work, full of shocks and over-emphatic sound effects, camera angles and shadowy lighting.' – *NFT, 1973*
'One of the most daring, eloquent and personal films to have come from America in a long time.' – *Derek Prouse*

'One man ... three women ... one night!'

The Night of the Iguana ***

US 1964 125m bw
MGM/Seven Arts (Ray Stark)
🖭 🖭

A disbarred clergyman becomes a travel courier in Mexico and is sexually desired by a teenage nymphomaniac, a middle-aged hotel owner and a frustrated itinerant artist.
The author is most tolerable when poking fun at his own types, and this is a sharp, funny picture with a touch of poetry.
w Anthony Veiller play Tennessee Williams d John Huston ph Gabriel Figueroa m Benjamin Frankel ad Stephen Grimes
☆ Richard Burton, Deborah Kerr, Ava Gardner, Sue Lyon, Grayson Hall, Cyril Delevanti

'Whatever poetry it had seems to have leaked out.' – *New Yorker, 1982*
⅄ Gabriel Figueroa; Grayson Hall

Night of the Juggler

US 1980 100m Technicolor
Columbia
🖭 🖭

A New Yorker relentlessly pursues the kidnapper of his daughter.
Average chase thriller with good location staging of car crashes.
w Bill Norton Snr, Rick Natkin novel William P. McGivern d Robert Butler ph Victor J. Kemper m Art Kane
☆ James Brolin, Cliff Gorman, Richard Castellano, Abby Bluestone

Night of the Laughing Dead: see *The House in Nightmare Park*

'There's a herd of killer rabbits heading this way!'

Night of the Lepus

US 1972 88m Metrocolor
MGM (A. C. Lyles)

A serum meant to control a surplus of rabbits instead produces monster varieties four feet tall.
Tolerable sci-fi tailored to a very tired formula.
w Don Holiday, Gene R. Kearney novel *The Year of the Angry Rabbit* by Russell Braddon d William F. Claxton ph Ted Voigtlander m Jimmie Haskell

☆ Stuart Whitman, Rory Calhoun, Janet Leigh, Paul Fix, DeForest Kelley
'For insomniacs with lax standards.' – *Judith Crist*

Night of The Living Dead
US   1990   89m   TVC Color
Columbia/21st Century/George A. Romero/Menahem Golan (John A. Russo, Russ Steiner)

Cannibalistic corpses rise from their graves to terrorize people trapped in a farmhouse.
Remake lacking the relentless intensity of the original.
w George A. Romero d Tom Savini ph Frank Prinzi m Paul McCollough ad James Feng ed Tom Dubensky
☆ Tony Wood, Patricia Tallman, Tom Towles, McKee Anderson, William Butler, Katie Finnerman, Bill Mosley, Heather Mazur
'A crass bit of cinematic grave-robbing.' – *Variety*

The Night of The Living Dead ***
US   1968   98m   bw
Image Ten

Flesh-eating zombies, activated by radiation from a space rocket, ravage the countryside.
Gruesome horror comic with effective moments; the director was still doing the same schtick ten years later. One of the most influential, and most imitated, of modern horror movies.
w John A. Russo d/ph George A. Romero
☆ Judith O'Dea, Duane Jones, Karl Hardman, Keith Wayne
'The best film ever made in Pittsburgh.' – *Anon.*
'Casts serious aspersions on the integrity of its makers … the film industry as a whole and exhibs who book the pic, as well as raising doubts about the future of the regional cinema movement and the moral health of filmgoers who cheerfully opt for unrelieved sadism.' – *Variety*

The Night of the Party
GB   1934   60m   bw
Gaumont-British (Jerome Jackson)

A game of murder at a dinner party leads to a real one.
Solid supporting thriller with interesting credits.
w Ralph Smart play Roland Pertwee, John Hastings Turner d Michael Powell ph Glen MacWilliams ad Alfred Junge
☆ Leslie Banks, Jane Baxter, Viola Keats, Ian Hunter, Ernest Thesiger, Malcolm Keen
'Nothing original, but good entertainment.' – *Variety*

Night of the Prowler
GB   1962   60m   bw
Butcher's Film Distributors (John I. Phillips)
Partners in an engineering firm receive death threats.
Dim and implausible second feature thriller that is mediocre in every respect.
w Paul Erickson d Francis A. Searle ph Walter J. Harvey m Johnny Gregory ad George Provis ed Jim Connock
☆ Patrick Holt, Colette Wilde, Bill Nagy, Mitzi Rogers, John Horsley, Benny Lee

'Assigned to kill … There can be no escape.'
Night of the Running Man
US   1994   89m   CFI color
Trimark/American World (Mark L. Lester, Dana Dubovsky, George W. Perkins)

A Las Vegas taxi driver finds a suitcase containing a million stolen dollars in his cab and goes on the run with it, hunted by a ruthless hitman from the Mob.
Unpleasantly violent and sleazy chase thriller with a narrative that favours repetition over invention.
w Lee Wells novel Lee Wells d Mark L. Lester ph Mark Irwin m Christopher Franke pd Alfred Sole ed David Berlatsky
☆ Scott Glenn, Andrew McCarthy, Janet Gunn, Wayne Newton, John Glover, Peter Lacangelo, Matthew Laurance
'A run-of-the-mill thriller plucked from obscurity by its prolonged torture sequence which will have even hardened viewers squirming.' – *Sight and Sound*

Night of the Shooting Stars: see *The Night of San Lorenzo*

Night on Earth **
US   1992   129m   colour
Electric/Locus Solus/Victor/Victor Musical Industries/Pyramide/Canal/Pandora/Channel 4 (Jim Jarmusch)

Five individuals take simultaneous taxi rides in five cities: Los Angeles, New York, Paris, Rome and Helsinki.
Engaging series of shaggy dog stories, expertly told.
wd Jim Jarmusch ph Frederick Elmes m Tom Waits ed Jay Ribinowitz
☆ Winona Ryder, Gena Rowlands, Giancarlo Esposito, Armin Mueller-Stahl, Rosie Perez, Isaach de Bankolé, Béatrice Dalle, Roberto Benigni, Paolo Bonacelli, Matti Pellonpää
'For the most part, the movie induces in the viewer an eerie, suspended feeling that mimics the time-stands-still monotony of a long airplane journey. It tries for a chipper, lighthearted tone, but it gives the audience a gruelling flight – a red-eye to nowhere.' – *Terrence Rafferty, New Yorker*

Night on the Town
US   1987   99m   DeLuxe
Touchstone/Silver Screen Partners III/Debra Hill/Linda Obst

US title: *Adventures in Babysitting*
Babysitting young children, a girl takes them for a ride in her car and unwittingly becomes a target for gangsters.
A sequence of tepid chases aimed at an undemanding audience.
w David Simkins d Chris Columbus ph Ric Waite m Michael Kamen pd Todd Hallowell ad Gregory Keen ed Fredric Steinkamp
☆ Elisabeth Shue, Maia Brewton, Keith Coogan, Anthony Rapp, Calvin Levels

Night Owls *
🎔 US   1930   20m   bw
Hal Roach

A policeman wanting to record an arrest bribes two tramps to burgle a house.
The stars at their most hilariously incompetent, unable even to get through a doorway efficiently.
w Leo McCarey, H. M. Walker d James Parrott ph George Stevens ed Richard Currier
☆ Stan Laurel, Oliver Hardy, Edgar Kennedy, James Finlayson

Night Passage *
US   1957   90m   Technirama
U-I (Aaron Rosenberg)

A railroad worker entrusted with a payroll finds that the bandits trying to rob it are led by his own brother.
Obscurely titled and rather empty Western providing standard excitements.
w Borden Chase d James Neilson ph William Daniels m Dimitri Tiomkin
☆ James Stewart, Audie Murphy, Dan Duryea, Brandon de Wilde, Dianne Foster, Elaine Stewart

'You have never really seen Gregory Peck until you see him in CinemaScope!'
'We didn't say nice people, we said *night people*!'
Night People *
US   1954   93m   Technicolor   Cinemascope
TCF (Nunnally Johnson)

When a US corporal stationed in Berlin is kidnapped by the Russians, his influential father flies into action.
Curiously titled cold war suspenser which would have been more memorable if not in Cinemascope; the pace and talent are visible, but the wide screen and poor colour dissipate them.
wd Nunnally Johnson ph Charles G. Clarke m Cyril Mockridge
☆ Gregory Peck, Broderick Crawford, Anita Bjork, Walter Abel, Rita Gam, Buddy Ebsen, Jill Esmond, Peter Van Eyck
🎱 original story (Jed Harris, Tom Reed)

'Seven in the skies over China – and one of them a dangerous Axis spy!'
Night Plane from Chungking
US   1942   69m   bw
Paramount
Assorted international passengers are flown from Chungking to India, but one of their number is a

German spy who will kill to get his hands on vital information.
A lower-case 'who is it' based on Shanghai Express. Not bad according to its lights.
w Earl Felton, Theodore Reeves, Lester Cole d Ralph Murphy ph Theodor Sparkuhl m Gerard Carbonara
☆ Ellen Drew, Robert Preston, Otto Kruger, Steve Geray, Ernest Dorian, Tamara Geva, Sen Yung

'The most controversial film of our time!'
The Night Porter
Italy   1973   118m   Technicolor
Lotar Films (Robert Gordon Edwards, Esa de Simone)

The wife of an opera conductor recognizes a hotel porter as the sadistic SS commandant of a concentration camp in which she spent the war years; they now resume a sado-masochistic love affair.
A downright deplorable film, with no cinematic skill or grace to excuse it; the visuals are as loathsome as the sound is indecipherable, and the sheer pointlessness of it is insulting.
w Liliana Cavani, Italo Moscati d Liliana Cavani ph Alfio Contini m Daniele Paris
☆ Dirk Bogarde, Charlotte Rampling, Philippe Leroy, Gabriele Ferzetti, Isa Miranda
'Its claim to be saying something important is offensive, but the picture is too crudely trumped up to be a serious insult.' – *New Yorker*

Night Ride
GB   1937   70m   bw
Paramount
Unemployed lorry drivers start an independent co-operative.
Brisk action programmer.
w Ralph Bettinson d John Paddy Carstairs
☆ Julian Vedey, Wally Patch, Jimmy Hanley, Joan Ponsford

Night Shift
US   1982   106m   Technicolor
Warner/Ladd (Brian Grazer)

A weary financial analyst becomes a morgue attendant and finds himself involved with gangsters and pimps.
Unattractive comedy that outstays its welcome, which wasn't very enthusiastic in the first place.
w Lowell Ganz, Babaloo Mandel d Ron Howard ph James Crabe m Burt Bacharach pd Jack Collis
☆ Henry Winkler, Michael Keaton, Shelley Long, Gina Hecht

Night Song
US   1947   101m   bw
RKO (Harriet Parsons)
A wealthy socialite falls for a blind pianist and pretends to be blind also, and poor to boot.
Silly, pretentious soaper, moodily photographed.
w Frank Fenton, Irving Hyland, De Witt Bodeen d John Cromwell ph Lucien Ballard m Leith Stevens
☆ Dana Andrews, Merle Oberon, Hoagy Carmichael, Ethel Barrymore, Artur Rubinstein, Eugene Ormandy

Night Sun *
Italy/France/Germany   1990   113m
Eastmancolor
Artificial
Eye/Filmtre/Raiuno/Capoul/Interpool/Sara/Direkt (Giuliani G. de Negri)

original title: *Il sole anche di notte*
In 18th-century Italy, a nobleman, upset to discover that he is expected to marry the king's mistress, becomes a hermit credited with miraculous powers.
Austere fable of a search for salvation that is likely to tire most audiences before the end.
w Paolo and Vittorio Taviani, Tonino Guerra story Father Sergius by Leo Tolstoy d Paolo and Vittorio Taviani ph Giuseppe Lanci m Nicola Piovani ad Gianni Sbarra ed Roberto Perpignani
☆ Julian Sands, Charlotte Gainsbourg, Nastassja Kinski, Massimo Bonetti, Margarita Lozano, Patricia Millardet, Rudiger Vogler, Pamela Villoresi
'A hauntingly spiritual film which is never afraid to explore the unfashionable themes of longing, solitude and meditation.' – *Sight and Sound*

The Night the Lights Went Out in Georgia
US   1981   120m   Technicolor
Avco Embassy/Viacom (Elliot Geisinger, Howard Kuperman, Ronald Saland, Howard Smith)

A young girl tries to guide her rambunctious brother to success as a country and western singer.
A poorly constructed narrative ensures that the level of interest remains low.
w Bob Bonney d Ronald F. Maxwell ph Bill Butler m David Shire pd Gene Rudolf ed Anne Goursaud song Bobby Russell
☆ Kristy McNichol, Dennis Quaid, Don Stroud, Mark Hamill, Arlen Dean Snyder

The Night They Invented Striptease: see *The Night They Raided Minsky's*

The Night They Killed Rasputin
France/Italy   1960   95m   Eastmancolor
Faro/Explorer/Rialto
original title: *Les Nuits de Raspoutine*
In 1916, a prince leads a gang of aristocrats to kill Rasputin, a monk who exercises an evil power over the Russian court and the Tsarina.
This is bad history and not a very good film, with a great deal of posturing from its cast.
w Ugo Liberatore, André Tabet d Pierre Chenal ph Angelo Francesco Lavagnino ad Arrigo Equini ed Antonietta Zita
☆ Edmund Purdom, Gianna Maria Canale, Jany Clair, John Drew Barrymore, Ugo Sasso, Giulia Rubini

The Night They Raided Minsky's **
US   1968   99m   DeLuxe
UA/Tandem (Norman Lear)

GB title: *The Night They Invented Striptease*
Various human problems are posed and solved during a night at a burlesque theatre.
Marvellous kaleidoscopic ragbag of brilliant fragments which unfortunately don't cohere in the mind into a really memorable film, though it gives detailed pleasure on every viewing.
w Arnold Schulman, Sidney Michaels, Norman Lear book Rowland Barber d William Friedkin ph Andrew Laszlo m Charles Strouse ch Danny Daniels pd William Eckart, Jean Eckart narrator Rudy Vallee
☆ Jason Robards, Britt Ekland, Norman Wisdom, Forrest Tucker, Joseph Wiseman, Bert Lahr, Harry Andrews, Denholm Elliott, Elliott Gould, Jack Burns
'The Fanny Brice country stunningly brought to life – every face a snapshot of yesterday.' – *Alexander Walker*
'It's lightweight and disorganized; it's a shambles; yet a lot of it is charming, and it has a wonderful seedy chorus line – a row of pudgy girls with faces like slipped discs.' – *Pauline Kael, New Yorker*
'A brilliant pastiche of classic American burlesque on the lower east side in the twenties.' – *Time*
'An entire way of life is encapsulated' – *Morning Star*

Night Tide
US   1961   84m   bw
Virgo Films

A sailor falls in love with a fairground freak show girl who may be a real mermaid.
Cheaply made and very derivative romantic fantasy which seemed to hold a promise never fulfilled.
wd Curtis Harrington ph Vilis Lapenieks m David Raksin
☆ Dennis Hopper, Linda Lawson, Gavin Muir, Luana Anders

A Night to Remember *
US   1943   91m   bw
Columbia (Samuel Bischoff)

A Greenwich Village mystery-writing couple try to solve a murder.
Reasonably sparkling comedy whodunnit with a zany tinge.
w Richard Flournoy, Jack Henley d Richard Wallace ph Joseph Walker m Werner Heymann md Morris Stoloff

---

☆ Loretta Young, Brian Aherne, Jeff Donnell, William Wright, Sidney Toler, Gale Sondergaard, Donald MacBride, Lee Patrick, Blanche Yurka

'A first-rate gloom chaser.' – *Picture Show*

A Night to Remember ***
GB 1958 123m bw
Rank (William MacQuitty)
▦ ▦ ◎ ◎

The story of the 1912 sea disaster when the *Titanic* struck an iceberg.

A major film enterprise featuring hundreds of cameos, none discernibly more important than the other. On this account the film seems alternately stiff and flabby as narrative, but there is much to enjoy and admire along the way, though the sense of awe is dissipated by the final model shots.

w Eric Ambler book Walter Lord d Roy Baker ph Geoffrey Unsworth m William Alwyn

☆ Kenneth More, Honor Blackman, Michael Goodliffe, David McCallum, George Rose, Anthony Bushell, Ralph Michael, John Cairney, Kenneth Griffith, Frank Lawton, Michael Bryant

'A worthy, long-drawn-out documentary, with noticeably more honesty about human nature than most films, but little shape or style.' – *Kenneth Cavender*

Night Train: see *Night Train to Munich*

Night Train
GB 1999 92m colour
Alternative/Subotica (Tristan Lynch)

An ex-convict, still being hunted by a gangster, hides out in a Dublin boarding house, where he plays with a giant train set and forms a relationship with his landlady's daughter.

Tepid romance of two misfits who find that they fit together, which suddenly becomes a violent escapist drama for no good reason.

w Aodhan Madden d John Lynch ph Seamus Deasy m Adam Lynch pd Alan Farquaharson ed J. Patrick Duffner

☆ John Hurt, Brenda Blethyn, Pauline Flanagan, Rynagh O'Grady, Peter Caffrey, Paul Roe, Lorcan Cranitch, Cathy White

'Grey, parochial and unambitious.' – *Edward Porter, Sunday Times*

Night Train to Munich ***
GB 1940 93m bw
TCF (Edward Black)
▦ ◎
aka: *Gestapo*
aka: *Night Train*

A British agent poses as a Nazi in order to rescue a Czech inventor.

First-rate comedy suspenser obviously inspired by the success of The Lady Vanishes and providing much the same measure of thrills and laughs.

w Frank Launder, Sidney Gilliat novel Report on a Fugitive by Gordon Wellesley d Carol Reed ph Otto Kanturek m Charles Williams md Louis Levy

☆ Margaret Lockwood, Rex Harrison, Basil Radford, Naunton Wayne, Paul Henreid, Keneth Kent, Felix Aylmer, Roland Culver, Eliot Makeham, Raymond Huntley, Wyndham Goldie

'A very nice triumph of skill and maturity in films, and thus a pleasure to have.' – *Otis Ferguson*
♪ Gordon Wellesley

Night Train to Venice
Germany 1993 97m colour
Take Munich (Toni Hirtreiter)
▦

A journalist travelling to Venice to deliver an exposé of fascist groups falls in love with an actress he meets on the Orient Express; also on board is a gang of neo-Nazi thugs.

A senseless and incomprehensible thriller with occult overtones, one in which everyone behaves oddly, never making a normal response to any situation. Irrelevant dream sequences interrupt what action there is; it ends with the lines: 'Imagine you woke up one day and realized it was all a dream.' This is a nightmare.

w Leo Tichat, Toni Hirtreiter d Carlo U. Quinterio ph Armando Nannuzzi m Wolfgang Hammerschmid pd Heinz Eickmeyer ed Wicktor Grodecki

☆ Hugh Grant, Tahnee Welch, Malcolm McDowell, Evelyn Opela, Samy Langs, Rachel Rice, Kristina Soederbaum

'A work of such thoroughgoing ineptitude it makes even Ed Wood's movies look like they're touched by genius.' – *Film Review*
'Too deadingly awful to be enjoyably bad.' – *Variety*

Night unto Night *
US 1949 85m bw
Warner (Owen Crump)

An epileptic scientist falls for a girl hallucinated by the ghost of her dead husband.

Cheerless nuthouse melodrama, one of the well-meant aberrations which Hollywood studios used to produce as a sop to conscience.

w Kathryn Scola novel Philip Wylie d Don Siegel ph Peverell Marley m Franz Waxman

☆ Ronald Reagan, Viveca Lindfors, Rosemary de Camp, Broderick Crawford, Osa Massen, Craig Stevens, Erskine Sanford

'Locked in the cold asylum of the mind – a sane man stalks his prey!'

The Night Visitor
Sweden/US 1971 102m Eastmancolor
UMC/Hemisphere
▦

Imprisoned for an axe murder he didn't commit, a man escapes and takes revenge.

Overdone Grand Guignol which simply doesn't come off.

w Guy Elmes story Salem Came to Supper by Samuel Roecca d Laslo Benedek

☆ Max von Sydow, Trevor Howard, Liv Ullmann, Rupert Davies, Per Oscarsson, Andrew Keir

'Do you know that a dream can kill you?'

The Night Walker *
US 1965 86m bw
U-I/William Castle
▦

The widow of a tough executive, killed and disfigured in an explosion, is haunted in her dreams not only by him but by a mysterious lover who turns up in reality.

Stiff and unconvincing but still fairly frightening low-budget shocker with a plot twist or two.

w Robert Bloch d William Castle ph Harold Stine m Vic Mizzy

☆ Robert Taylor, Barbara Stanwyck, Lloyd Bochner, Rochelle Hudson, Judi Meredith, Hayden Rorke

Night Was Our Friend
GB 1951 61m bw
Monarch (Gordon Parry)

Returning home after being thought dead for two years, an unhinged explorer discovers that his wife is in love with another man.

Gloomy psychological drama that never quite comes to life.

w Michael Pertwee play Michael Pertwee d Michael Anderson ph Moray Grant

☆ Elizabeth Sellars, Michael Gough, Ronald Howard, Marie Ney, Edward Lexy, Nora Gordon, John Salew

Night Watch
GB 1973 98m Technicolor
Avco/Brut (David White)
▦

A widow recovering from a nervous breakdown keeps seeing bodies in the night. Her friends try to help, but things are not quite what they seem.

Predictable coiled-spring shocker which goes curiously flat despite a star cast and lashings of blood. Perhaps we have all been here once too often.

w Tony Williamson play Lucille Fletcher d Brian G. Hutton ph Billy Williams m John Cameron

☆ Elizabeth Taylor, Laurence Harvey, Billie Whitelaw, Robert Lang, Tony Britton, Bill Dean

'It has all the trappings of a Joan Crawford vehicle of the forties, with numerous elegant dresses for Miss Taylor, an appropriately unbecoming wardrobe for Miss Whitelaw, and a set which is an art director's dream.' – *Brenda Davies*
'Elizabeth Taylor's gowns are by Valentino, her jewellery is by Van Cleef and Arpels, even her kitchen is by Westinghouse. And she is still going out of her mind.' – *Alexander Walker*

The Night We Dropped a Clanger
GB 1959 86m bw
Rank/Sydney Box/Four Star
US title: *Make Mine a Double*

During World War II, a wing commander's double is accidentally sent to the front line in his place.

Feeble take-off on I Was Monty's Double; a few bright gags survive.

w John Chapman d Darcy Conyers ph Ernest Steward m Edwin Braden

☆ Brian Rix, Cecil Parker, William Hartnell, Leslie Phillips, Leo Franklyn, John Welsh, Liz Fraser

The Night We Got the Bird
GB 1960 82m bw
British Lion/Rix-Conyers

A husband is driven bonkers by a talking parrot which he believes to be the reincarnation of his predecessor.

Pretty awful farce with the sole virtue of a frantic pace.

w Ray Cooney, Tony Hilton, Darcy Conyers d Darcy Conyers ph S. D. Onions m Tommy Watt

☆ Brian Rix, Dora Bryan, Ronald Shiner, Leo Franklyn, Irene Handl, John Slater, Liz Fraser, Reginald Beckwith, Robertson Hare, John Le Mesurier, Terry Scott

The Night We Never Met
US 1993 99m DuArt
Guild/Miramax (Michael Peyser)
▦ ▦ ◎

Three young New Yorkers organize a time-share on a Greenwich Village apartment, but the days on which each uses the place become confused.

Brash and not very likeable farce that will mean little outside the city in which it is set.

wd Warren Leight ph John A. Thomas m Evan Lurie pd Lester Cohen ed Camilla Toniolo

☆ Matthew Broderick, Annabella Sciorra, Kevin Anderson, Jeanne Tripplehorn, Justine Bateman, Michael Mantell, Christine Baranski

'If you're in the mood to indulge in some light cultural snobbery, you'll enjoy this film ... a rickety structure with trendy interior design, an old-fashioned sex comedy for the nouveau hip.' – *Leslie Felperin Sharman, Sight and Sound*

Night without Sleep
US 1952 77m bw
TCF (Robert Bassler)

A man reconstructs his drunken actions the night before, and fears he has committed a murder.

Dreary melodrama, all frayed tempers, drunkenness and cigarette smoke.

w Frank Partos, Elick Moll d Roy Baker ph Lucien Ballard m Cyril Mockridge

☆ Gary Merrill, Linda Darnell, Hildegarde Neff, Hugh Beaumont, Mae Marsh

Night without Stars
GB 1951 86m bw
Hugh Stewart/GFD

A blind lawyer solves the death of a traitor.

Enervated romantic melodrama.

w Winston Graham novel Winston Graham d Anthony Pelissier ph Guy Green m William Alwyn

☆ David Farrar, Nadia Gray, Maurice Teynac, Gilles Queyant

Night World
US 1932 58m bw
Universal

Characters with an assortment of problems congregate in a night-club.

Tolerable slice-of-life drama with interesting cast.

w Richard Schayer story P.J. Wolfson and Allen Rivkin d Hobart Henley

☆ Lew Ayres, Boris Karloff, Mae Clarke, Russell Hopton, George Raft, Dorothy Revier, Bert Roach, Hedda Hopper

'Sum total is an impression that this was a two-reeler blown up into five.' – *Variety*

Night Zoo
Canada 1987 115m colour
Hendring/Oz Productions/National Film Board Of Canada (Roger Frappier, Pierre Gendron)
▦ ▦ ◎
original title: *Un Zoo la Nuit*

A drug dealer, out of prison on parole, is reconciled with his father and outwits his former bosses, who include a sadistic homosexual cop.

Lurid thriller which, inexplicably, was much honoured in its home country.

wd Jean-Claude Lauzon ph Guy Dufaux m Jean Corriveau ad Jean-Baptiste Tard ed Michel Arcand

☆ Roger Le Bel, Gilles Maheu, Lorne Brass, Germain Houde, Jerry Snell, Corrado Mastropasqua, Lynne Adams, Amulette Garneau, Anna-Maria Giannotti

Nightbreed
US 1990 102m Technicolor
Fox/Morgan Creek (Gariella Martinelli)
▦ ▦ ◎ ◎

A teenager discovers Midian, a world of shape-shifting monsters.

Novel horror movie, in which the monsters are nicer than the humans, but without much narrative drive.

wd Clive Barker novel Cabal by Clive Barker ph Robin Vidgeon pd Steve Hardie, Mark Haskins ed Richard Marden, Mark Goldblatt sp Image Animation

☆ Craig Sheffer, Anne Bobby, David Cronenberg, Charles Haid, Hugh Quarshie, Hugh Ross, Doug Bradley, Catherine Chevalier, Malcolm Sith, Bob Sessions, Oliver Parker

The Nightcomers *
GB 1971 96m Technicolor
Scimitar/Kastner-Kanter-Ladd (Michael Winner)
▦ ◎

How the ghost-ridden children in *The Turn of the Screw* became evil; they became involved in aberrant sexual activities between the gardener and the housekeeper, and finally murdered the former.

Despite its unexpected literariness this is unpleasant and unconvincing nonsense with a boring script punctuated by shock cuts and very little period feel.

w Michael Hastings d Michael Winner ph Robert Paynter m Jerry Fielding

☆ Stephanie Beacham, Marlon Brando, Thora Hird, Harry Andrews, Verna Harvey, Christopher Ellis

'It leaves the viewer cold – perhaps even repelled. How could anybody think this movie would be entertaining?' – *Pauline Kael, New Yorker*

Nightfall *
US 1956 78m bw
Columbia (Ted Richmond)

The police and two bank robbers chase an innocent artist who happens to know that the loot is hidden in a Wisconsin snowdrift.

Occasionally stylish but obscurely narrated suspenser.

w Stirling Silliphant novel David Goodis d Jacques Tourneur ph Burnett Guffey m George Duning

☆ Anne Bancroft, Aldo Ray, Brian Keith, James Gregory, Jocelyn Brando, Frank Albertson

Nighthawks
GB 1978 113m Eastmancolor
Cinegate/Nashburgh/Four Corner Films (Ron Peck, Paul Hallam)
▦

The life of an actively homosexual schoolteacher.

Painful low-life drama with many signs of its amateur status.

wd Ron Peck, Paul Hallam ph Joanna Davis, Patrick Duval, Sebastian Dewsbery, Ian Owles, Steve Shaw m David Graham Ellis ad Jan Sender ed Richard Taylor, Mary Pat Leece, Debra Daley, Tim Horrocks

☆ Ken Robertson and non-professionals

Nighthawks
US 1981 99m Technicolor
Universal/Herb Nanas (Martin Poll)
▦ ◎

New York cops track an international terrorist.

Kojak-style thriller with a rather glum attitude to its subject.

w David Shaber d Bruce Malmuth ph James A. Contner m Keith Emerson

☆ Sylvester Stallone, Billy Dee Williams, Rutger Hauer, Lindsay Wagner, Persis Khambatta, Nigel Davenport

Nighthawks 2: Strip Jack Naked

GB   1991   94m   bw/colour
BFI/Channel 4 (Ron Peck)

An autobiographical documentary on the background to the making of *Nighthawks*, including material cut from the original film.
An amateurish and boring film, on the level of a home movie, and a demonstration that earnestness can be trying.
w Ron Peck, Paul Hallam d Ron Peck ph Ron Peck, Christopher Hughes m Adrian James Carbutt ed Ron Peck, Adrian James Carbutt
☆ John Brown, John Daimon, Nick Bolton

Nightmare

US   1942   81m   bw
Universal (Dwight Taylor)

A gambler in wartime London helps a beautiful girl escape from Nazi spies.
Thin espionage thriller with a good sequence or two and a smooth villain.
w Dwight Taylor novel *Escape* by Philip MacDonald d Tim Whelan ph George Barnes m Frank Skinner
☆ Brian Donlevy, Diana Barrymore, Gavin Muir, Henry Daniell, Hans Conried, Arthur Shields

Nightmare *

US   1956   89m   bw
UA/Pine-Thomas/Shane (Maxwell Shane)

A young musician is hypnotized into committing a murder, and reconstructs his actions with the help of his policeman brother-in-law.
Lethargic remake of the ingenious Fear in the Night (qv). Watchable.
wd Maxwell Shane novel Cornell Woolrich ph Joseph Biroc m Herschel Burke Gilbert
☆ Edward G. Robinson, Kevin McCarthy, Virginia Christine, Connie Russell
'A chilling, highly suspenseful little item.' – *Motion Picture Herald*

'Three shocking murders … did she dream them? … or do them?'

Nightmare *

GB   1964   82m   bw   Hammerscope
U-I/Hammer (Jimmy Sangster)

18-year-old Janet still has nightmares after seeing her mad mother kill her father six years ago; brought home, even more frightening visions afflict her.
Genuinely scary Diabolique-type mystery with the usual Hammer borrowings put to good use.
w Jimmy Sangster d Freddie Francis ph John Wilcox m Don Banks
☆ Moira Redmond, David Knight, Brenda Bruce, John Welsh, Jennie Linden

Nightmare Alley **

US   1947   112m   bw
TCF (George Jessel)

A fairground barker becomes a successful confidence trickster dealing with the supernatural, but finally sinks to the depths.
Unusual road to ruin melodrama, a striking oddity from Hollywood at the time, and still quite interesting and well done.
w Jules Furthman novel William Lindsay Gresham d Edmund Goulding ph Lee Garmes m Cyril Mockridge
☆ Tyrone Power, Coleen Gray, Joan Blondell, Taylor Holmes, Helen Walker, Mike Mazurki, Ian Keith
'The picture goes just short of all that might have made it very interesting … even so, two or three sharply comic and cynical scenes make it worth seeing.' – *James Agee*

The Nightmare before Christmas ***

🏃🏃 US   1993   75m   Technicolor
Buena Vista/Touchstone (Tim Burton, Denise Di Novi)

aka: *Tim Burton's The Nightmare before Christmas*
Jack Skellington, Pumpkin King of Halloween Town, tries to take over Christmas as well.
Imaginative, superbly animated (using stop-motion techniques with figures) musical, although children may not warm to its quirky humour.
w Caroline Thompson, Michael McDowell story Tim Burton d Henry Selick m/ly Danny Elfman ed Stan Webb sp Pete Kozachik, Eric Leighton, Ariel Velasco Shaw, Gordon Baker

☆ Featuring the voices of Danny Elfman, Chris Sarandon, Catherine O'Hara, William Hickey, Glenn Shadix, Paul Reubens
'The dazzling techniques employed here create a striking look that has never been seen in such a sustained form before, making this a unique curio that will appeal to kids and film enthusiasts alike.' – *Variety*
'An animated fun-house for eeek freaks of all ages.' – *Peter Travers, Rolling Stone*
'It displays more inventiveness than some studios can manage in an entire year.' – *Kenneth Turan, Los Angeles Times*
§ visual effects

Nightmare Castle: see Night of the Doomed

Nightmare in the Sun *

US   1963   81m   DeLuxe
Afilmco (Marc Lawrence, John Derek)

A rich man kills his wife and blames a hitch-hiker who has had a brief affair with her.
Modest independent melodrama, quite interestingly made though not entirely effective.
w Ted Thomas d Marc Lawrence ph Stanley Cortez m Paul Glass
☆ John Derek, Ursula Andress, Arthur O'Connell, Aldo Ray

'See Freddy – before he sees you!'

A Nightmare on Elm Street

US   1984   91m   DeLuxe
New Line/Media/Smart Egg/Elm Street Venture/Robert Shaye

Suburban teenagers find their communal dreams becoming reality when they are menaced by a creepy figure with knives for fingernails.
Unpleasant semi-splatter movie which was well enough made to take a lot of money.
wd Wes Craven ph Jacques Haitkin m Charles Bernstein pd Greg Fonseca ed Rick Shaine sp Jim Doyle
☆ John Saxon, Ronee Blakley, Heather Langenkamp, Amanda Wyss, Nick Corri, Robert Englund, Johnny Depp, Charles Fleischer

A Nightmare on Elm Street Part Four: The Dream Master

US   1988   93m   Metrocolor
Palace/New Line Cinema/Heron Communications/Smart Egg Pictures (Robert Shaye, Rachel Talalay)

As Freddy goes on his usual killing spree, a teenager discovers that she can destroy him.
A mixture, as before, of spectacularly unpleasant special effects and grotesque humour, except that Freddy is now firmly established as the star.
w Brian Helgeland, Scott Pierce story Brian Helgeland, Jim Kotzwinkle d Renny Harlin ph Steven Fierberg m Craig Safan pd Mick Strawn, C. J. Strawn ed Michael N. Knue, Chuck Weiss, Jack Tucker, Charley Coleman
☆ Robert Englund, Rodney Eastman, Danny Hassel, Andras Jones, Tuesday Knight, Toy Newkirk, Ken Sagoes
'The fact remains that the child-killer of Elm Street has simply run out of things to do and say.' – *MFB*

A Nightmare on Elm Street Part Three: Dream Warriors

US   1987   96m   DeLuxe
Heron/Smart Egg/New Line/Robert Shaye

Freddy now invades the minds of teenagers under group hypnosis for nightmares.
Diminishing returns set in as this tedious bloodbath (all in the mind) gets under way.
w Wes Craven, Bruce Wagner d Chuck Russell ph Roy H. Wagner m Angelo Badalamenti, Don Dokken ad Mick Strawn, C. J. Strawn ed Terry Stokes
☆ Heather Langenkamp, Patricia Arquette, Larry Fishburne, Robert Englund, Priscilla Pointer, Craig Wasson

A Nightmare on Elm Street Part Two: Freddy's Revenge

US   1985   84m   DeLuxe
Heron/Smart Egg/New Line/Robert Shaye

Freddy comes back and tries to take over the mind and body of a young boy.
More horror nonsense in the same mould as the above.
w David Chaskin d Jack Sholder ph Jacques Haitkin m Christopher Young ed Bob Brady
☆ Mark Patton, Kim Myers, Hope Lange, Clu Gulager, Robert Englund
'Much as one loves watching unpleasant American teenagers ripped to death, the slasher formula has worn thin of late.' – *Time Out*

A Nightmare on Elm Street: The Dream Child

US   1989   89m   Metrocolor
Enterprise/New Line Cinema/Heron Communications/Smart Egg Pictures (Robert Shaye, Rupert Harvey)

Freddy attempts to possess a girl's unborn child.
The murderer of the young continues in an incoherent sequel with some clever special effects. It is time that Freddy was laid to rest.
w Leslie Bohem story John Skipp, Craig Spector, Leslie Bohem d Stephen Hopkins ph Peter Levy m Jay Ferguson pd C. J. Strawn ed Chuck Weiss, Brent Schoenfeld
☆ Robert Englund, Lisa Wilcox, Kelly Jo Minter, Danny Hassel, Erika Anderson, Nick Mele, Whitby Hertford, Joe Seely
'The scariest idea in the film, underlined by yet another open ending, is the possibility that this nightmare will never end, the non-existent story spinning out forever.' – *Kim Newman, MFB*
† The sequel was *Freddy's Dead: The Final Nightmare* (qv)

Nights of Cabiria: see Cabiria

The Nights of Lucretia Borgia

Italy/France   1959   92m   Eastmancolor Totalscope
Fidès/Musa Cinematografica (Carlo Caiano)
original title: *Le Notti di Lucrezia Borgia*
aka: *Nights of Temptation*
Lucretia Borgia falls in love with one of her brother's soldiers, who loves another.
Silly historical romp, occasionally enjoyable in the way that bad films can be.
w Sergio Grieco, Mario Caiano, Aldo Segri, Duncan Elliot, Barbara Sohmers play *Lucrece Borgia* by Victor Hugo d Sergio Grieco ph Massimo Dallamano m Alexandre Derevitsky ad Saverio D'Eugenio ed Enzo Alfonsi
☆ Belinda Lee, Michèle Mercier, Jacques Sernas, Arnoldo Foa, Franco Fabrizio, Marco Tulli

Nightwatch

Denmark   1994   105m   colour
Metro Tartan/Thura/DR TV/Danske Filminstitut (Michael Obel)

original title: *Nattevagten*
A law student who also works as a night watchman in a morgue is suspected of killing and scalping prostitutes.
Slow but suspenseful thriller that comes near to equating sex and death; it manages some jokes to lighten its pervading and chilling claustrophobia.
wd Ole Bornedal ph Dan Laustsen m Joachim Holbeck ad Soren Krag Sorensen ed Camilla Skousen
☆ Nicolai Coster Waldau, Sofie Grabol, Kim Bodnia, Ulf Pilgaard, Lotte Andersen, Rikke Louise Andersson, Stig Hoffmeyer
'The movie took Scandinavia by storm, which says something rather quaint about Scandinavia's desire to import the blueprint for the serial killer movie and make their own version with local ingredients. Like a Big Mac, it's a bit stale by the time it's re-exported.' – *Tom Shone, Sunday Times*

Nightwatch

US   1998   101m   colour
Miramax/Dimension (Michael Obel)

A student takes a job in a city morgue, and is suspected of being a serial killer.

Although it retains its original director, this American remake of a Danish thriller has lost the creepiness that made it memorable.
w Steven Soderbergh, Ole Bornedal d Ole Bornedal ph Dan Lausten m Joachim Holbeck pd Richard Hoover ed Sally Menke
☆ Ewan McGregor, Nick Nolte, Josh Brolin, Patricia Arquette, Alix Koromzay, John C. Reilly, Brad Dourif
'A laboured black comedy which is overacted, overwritten and far too conceited for its own good.' – *Sight and Sound*

Nightwing

Netherlands   1979   105m   Metrocolor
Columbia/Polyc/Martin Ransohoff

In Arizona, mysterious deaths turn out to be caused by plague-bearing vampire bats.
Tedious shocker in the vein of Them but with 'modern' unpleasantness of detail.
w Steve Shagan, Bud Shrake novel Martin Cruz Smith d Arthur Hiller ph Charles Rosher m Henry Mancini
☆ David Warner, Kathryn Harrold, Stephen Macht, Strother Martin, Nick Mancuso, Ben Piazza

'Genius. Madman. Animal. God.'

Nijinsky *

US   1980   125m   Metrocolor
Paramount/Hera (Harry Saltzman)

The rise and fall of a great dancer groomed for stardom in the Ballets Russes by the impresario Diaghilev.
Rather boringly scripted with the emphasis on homosexual love, this film finally survives through its electrifying personalities and its strong sense of period.
w Hugh Wheeler d Herbert Ross ph Douglas Slocombe md John Lanchbery pd John Blezard
☆ Alan Bates, George de la Pena, Leslie Browne, Alan Badel, Colin Blakely, Ronald Pickup, Ronald Lacey, Jeremy Irons, Anton Dolin, Janet Suzman, Sian Phillips, members of the London Festival Ballet
'The impression is left of a fascinating subject which proved too challenging for its makers, who settle eventually for what is uncomfortably near All About Eve with Bette Davis in a dinner jacket and Anne Baxter in a jock strap.' – *Alan Brien, Sunday Times*

Nikita *

France/Italy   1990   117m   Eastmancolor Technovision
Palace/Gaumont/Cecci/Tiger (Jérôme Chalou)

aka: *La Femme Nikita*
A young criminal turns assassin for the intelligence services.
Implausible, though stylish and very watchable, thriller.
wd Luc Besson ph Thierry Arbogast m Eric Serra pd Dan Weil ed Olivier Mauffroy
☆ Anne Parillaud, Jean-Hugues Anglade, Tcheky Karyo, Jeanne Moreau, Jean Reno, Roland Blanche, Marc Duret
'An absurd, shrill, ultraviolent but soft-centered urban thriller.' – *Variety*
† In 1997 the film was turned into a successful US TV series, *La Femme Nikita*, starring Peta Wilson.

Nikki, Wild Dog of the North *

🏃🏃 US   1961   74m   Technicolor
Walt Disney (Winston Hibler)

The life of a Canadian trapper's wolf dog.
Pleasing 'true life fiction' which didn't quite reach top feature status.
w Ralph Wright, Winston Hibler novel James Oliver Curwood d Jack Couffer m Oliver Wallace
☆ Emile Genest, Jean Coutu

Nil by Mouth ▲▲

GB   1997   128m   DuArt
TCF/SE8 (Luc Besson, Douglas Urbanski, Gary Oldman)

In South London, a violent alcoholic terrorizes his family.
A bleak and unsparing account of devastated life in the slums, where drinks and drugs provide a momentary escape and masculinity is measured by the size of the fist; this semi-autobiographical drama is given vitality by the conviction of its performances.

🏃🏃 film suitable for family viewing
📼 VHS video-cassette for the British PAL system
📼 VHS video-cassette for the British PAL system in wide screen-format
⟳ Video cassette in a computer-colourised version
▬ American NTSC video-cassette
💿 Laser disc

wd Gary Oldman *ph* Ron Fortunato *m* Eric Clapton *pd* Hugo Luczyc-Wyhowski *ed* Brad Fuller

☆ Ray Winstone, Kathy Burke, Charlie Creed-Miles, Laila Morse, Edna Doré, Chrissie Cotterill, Jon Morrison, Jamie Forman

'A film of hard, unyielding brilliance that, given the choice, I would quite happily unwatch.' – *Tom Shone, Sunday Times*

† Kathy Burke won the best actress award at the Cannes Film Festival in 1997, and Gary Oldman the best director award at the 1997 Edinburgh Film Festival.

🎬 best British film; Gary Oldman (as writer)

Nilouhe, Nuer: see *Daughter of the Nile*

9/30/55 *
US   1977   101m   colour
Columbia (Jerry Weintraub)
The death of James Dean on 30th September 1955 has a devastating effect on a teenager at an Arkansas college who identifies with him.
Effective story of adolescent feelings and frustrations.
wd James Bridges *ph* Gordon Willis *m* Leonard Rosenman *ad* Robert Luthardt *ed* Jeff Gourson
☆ Richard Thomas, Susan Tyrrell, Deborah Benson, Lisa Blount, Thomas Hulce, Dennis Quaid, Dennis Christopher
'This is the sort of low-budget, personal moviemaking that Hollywood is presumed to shy away from, and it would be a shame if it got overlooked.' – *David Ansen, Newsweek*
† Leonard Rosenman wrote the music for two films starring James Dean, *East of Eden* and *Rebel without a Cause*.

Nine and a Half Weeks *
US   1986   113m   colour
MGM/UA/PSO/Sidney Kimmel/Keith Barish/Jonesfilm/Galactic Films/Triple Ajaxx (Anthony Rufus Isaacs, Zalman King)
A Wall Street executive and an art gallery employee embark upon a passionate affair.
Crash course in hot sex for those who wish to major in such studies; of no other interest despite its aspirations to being some sort of art.
w Patricia Knop, Zalman King, Sarah Kernochan *novel* Elizabeth McNeill *d* Adrian Lyne *ph* Peter Biziou *m* Jack Nitzsche *pd* Ken Davis
☆ Mickey Rourke, Kim Basinger, Margaret Whitton, David Margulies, Christine Baranski
'The virtual absence of anything happening between them – like plausible attraction, amazing sex or, God forbid, good dialogue – leaves one great hole on the screen for two hours.' – *Variety*

Nine Days a Queen: see *Tudor Rose*

9 Deaths of the Ninja
US   1985   94m   colour
Crown International (Ashok Amritraj)
An anti-terrorist outfit rescues hostages captured by a mad German drug dealer.
Bungled attempt at a comic martial arts movie.
wd Emmett Alston *ph* Roy H. Wagner *m* Cecile Colayco *pd* Rodell Cruz *ed* Emmett Alston, Robert E. Waters
☆ Sho Kosugi, Brent Huff, Emilia Lesniak, Regina Richardson, Vijay Amritraj, Blackie Dammett

Nine Girls *
US   1944   78m   bw
Columbia (Burt Kelly)
College girls are murdered in a sorority house.
Cheapjack whodunnit with a cardboard look and feel.
w Karen de Wolf, Connie Lee *play* Wilfred H. Pettit *d* Leigh Jason *ph* James Van Trees *m* John Leopold
☆ Ann Harding, Evelyn Keyes, Jinx Falkenburg, Anita Louise, Leslie Brooks, Lynn Merrick, Jeff Donnell, Nina Foch, Marcia Mae Jones, William Demarest

Nine Hours to Rama *
GB   1962   125m   DeLuxe   Cinemascope
TCF/Red Lion (Mark Robson)
Events leading to the assassination of Mahatma Gandhi.
Fictionalized, sensationalized and very dull, this multi-character drama holds interest only for snatches of acting and location backgrounds.

w Nelson Gidding *novel* Stanley Wolpert *d* Mark Robson *ph* Arthur Ibbetson *m* Malcolm Arnold
☆ José Ferrer, Diane Baker, Robert Morley, J. S. Casshyap, Horst Buchholz, Harry Andrews
'The only interesting line in the movie is the thick brown one visible on the inside of every white collar.' – *John Simon*

976-Evil
US   1988   100m   colour
Medusa/Cinetel/Horrorscope (Lisa M. Hansen)
A teenager gains evil powers after summoning a demon by telephone.
Directed by the star of A Nightmare on Elm Street and its sequels, it resembles those films in its mixture of grotesque humour and gruesome special effects.
w Rhet Topham, Brian Helgeland *d* Robert Englund *ph* Paul Elliott *m* Thomas Chase, Steve Rucker *ad* David Brian Miller *ed* Stephen Myers
☆ Stephen Geoffreys, Patrick O'Bryan, Sandy Dennis, Jim Metzler, Maria Rubell, Robert Picardo, Lezlie Deane, J. J. Cohen, Paul Wilson

Nine Lives Are Not Enough
US   1941   63m   bw
Warner
A reporter solves a multi-murder in a boarding house.
Lively second feature which moves at a commendable pace.
w Fred Niblo Jnr *d* A. Edward Sutherland
☆ Ronald Reagan, Howard da Silva, James Gleason, Ed Brophy, Faye Emerson, Peter Whitney, Charles Drake

The Nine Lives of Fritz the Cat
US   1974   76m   DeLuxe
AIP/Two Gees (Steve Krantz)
Stoned on pot, a cat dreams of the lives he might have led.
An animated sequel of sorts to Fritz the Cat (qv), but done by other, cruder hands and lacking imagination and wit; it is far removed from Robert Crumb's original.
w Fred Halliday, Eric Monte, Robert Taylor *d* Robert Taylor *m* Tom Scott and the LA Express *ed* Marshall M. Borden
☆ Featuring the voices of Skip Hinnant, Reva Rose, Bob Holt, Fred Smoot, Robert Ridgely
'Boringly diffuse, completely negating any possible shock effect through the overwhelming quantity of obscenity and gutter language.' – *David Rider, MFB*

Nine Men *
GB   1943   68m   bw
Ealing
A sergeant and a handful of men in an old fort hold off the Italians in the Libyan desert.
Sharp semi-documentary of the war which paled against the mightier epics to follow.
wd Harry Watt *ph* Roy Kellino *m* John Greenwood
☆ Jack Lambert, Gordon Jackson, Frederick Piper, Grant Sutherland, Bill Blewett

'Ready or Not.'
Nine Months
US   1995   103m   DeLuxe   Panavision
TCF/1492 (Ann François, Chris Columbus, Mark Radcliffe, Michael Barnathan)
An English child psychologist working in San Francisco is horrified to discover that his girlfriend is pregnant.
A still-born comedy, bereft of wit or style, in which Hugh Grant acts embarrassed for most of the time, as well he might.
wd Chris Columbus *ph* Donald McAlpine *m* Hans Zimmer *pd* Angelo P. Graham *ed* Raja Gosnell
☆ Hugh Grant, Julianne Moore, Tom Arnold, Joan Cusack, Jeff Goldblum, Robin Williams
'A dim-witted romp that makes little use of its leading man – if Tinseltown is looking for the next Cary Grant, this isn't the vehicle.' – *Denis Seguin, Screen International*
'Truly dreadful.' – *Guardian*
† It is based on a French film, *Neuf Mois*, written and directed by Patrick Brauodé.

Nine to Five *
US   1980   110m   DeLuxe
TCF/IPC (Bruce Gilbert)
Three office women plot to get rid of their boss, and nearly make it.
Sporadically agreeable comedy somewhat reminiscent of Sturges's Unfaithfully Yours.
w Colin Higgins, Patricia Resnick *d* Colin Higgins *ph* Reynaldo Villalobos *m* Charles Fox *pd* Dean Mitzner
☆ Jane Fonda, Dolly Parton, Lily Tomlin, Dabney Coleman, Sterling Hayden, Elizabeth Wilson, Henry Jones
'An effective escapist feast with lotsa funny physical schtick.' – *Variety*
♫ title song (Dolly Parton)

19/19
GB   1984   99m   colour/bw
BFI/Channel 4 (Nita Amy)
Two former patients of Sigmund Freud meet in old age to recall their past treatment.
Interminable and unilluminating conversation piece, intercut with documentary footage and flashbacks that illustrate what has just been said.
w Hugh Brody, Michael Ignatieff *d* Hugh Brody *ph* Ivan Strasburg *m* Brian Gascoigne *ad* Caroline Amies *ed* David Gladwell
☆ Paul Scofield, Maria Schell, Frank Finlay, Diana Quick, Clare Higgins, Colin Firth

99 and 44/100 Per Cent Dead
US   1974   98m   DeLuxe   Panavision
TCF/Joe Wizan/Vashon
aka: *Call Harry Crown*
A losing gang boss hires a trouble shooter.
Violent gangster melodrama apparently intended as a black comedy; if so, as clumsy as its title.
w Robert Dillon *d* John Frankenheimer *ph* Ralph Woolsey *m* Henry Mancini
☆ Richard Harris, Edmond O'Brien, Bradford Dillman, Ann Turkel, Chuck Connors, Constance Ford
'Esthetically, commercially and morally, a quintessential fiasco.' – *Variety*
† The title in fact spoofs an ad familiar to Americans for a soap which was said to be '99 and 44/100 per cent pure'.

99 River Street *
US   1953   83m   bw
UA/Edward Small
A taxi driver becomes involved in a diamond robbery.
Adequate thick ear with quite good detection and action sequences.
w Robert Smith *d* Phil Karlson *ph* Franz Planer
☆ John Payne, Evelyn Keyes, Frank Faylen, Brad Dexter, Peggie Castle

92 in the Shade *
US   1975   88m   colour
United Artists (George Pappas)
A drifter who becomes a fishing guide in Florida's Key West finds himself in competition with the captain of another fishing boat.
For the most part, an engaging and atmospheric study of coolly observed eccentricity, though lacking any narrative thrust.
wd Thomas McGuane *novel* Thomas McGuane *ph* Michael C. Butler *m* Michael J. Lewis *ed* Ed Rothkowitz
☆ Peter Fonda, Warren Oates, Margot Kidder, Elizabeth Ashley, Burgess Meredith, Harry Dean Stanton, Sylvia Miles, William Hickey, Louise Latham
† The film was recut and re-released in 1981.

'He has the Power. He can stop the killings. He is the...'
Ninja Dragon (dubbed)
Hong Kong   1986   87m   colour
IFD Films and Arts (Joseph Lai, Betty Chan)
The daughter of a murdered gang-leader returns to take over his territory and precipitates a power struggle between rival gangsters on the streets of Shanghai.
Ludicrous thriller, with unconvincing martial arts interludes, notable for its high body-count and for having not one redeeming character in its large cast;

with its hooded avenger, wearing a great deal of eye-liner, and cackling black-hatted hoodlums, its overwrought style can best be described as high camp.
wd Godfrey Ho *story* Frank Hor, AAV Creative Unit *d* Joseph Lai *ph* Raymond Chang *m* Stephen Tsang *pd* Hiram Lai *ed* Nicky Au *sp* Simon Chu
☆ Richard Harrison, Bruce Stallion, Melvin Pitcher, Konrad Chang, Lily Lan, Freya Patrick

'The picture that kids the commissars!'
'Garbo laughs!'
'Don't pronounce it – see it!'
Ninotchka ***
US   1939   110m   bw
MGM (Ernst Lubitsch)
A Paris playboy falls for a communist emissary sent to sell some crown jewels.
Sparkling comedy on a theme which has been frequently explored; delicate pointing and hilarious character comedy sustain this version perfectly until the last half hour, when it certainly sags; but it remains a favourite Hollywood example of this genre.
w Charles Brackett, Billy Wilder, Walter Reisch *story* Melchior Lengyel *d* Ernst Lubitsch *ph* William Daniels *m* Werner Heymann
☆ Greta Garbo, Melvyn Douglas, Sig Rumann, Alexander Granach, Felix Bressart, Ina Claire, Bela Lugosi
PROLOGUE: THIS PICTURE TAKES PLACE IN PARIS IN THOSE WONDERFUL DAYS WHEN A SIREN WAS A BRUNETTE AND NOT AN ALARM – AND IF A FRENCHMAN TURNED OUT THE LIGHT IT WAS NOT ON ACCOUNT OF AN AIR RAID!
NINOTCHKA (GRETA GARBO): 'I must have a complete report of your negotiations and a detailed expense account.'
BULJANOFF (FELIX BRESSART): 'No, non, Ninotchka. Don't ask for it. There is an old Turkish proverb that says, if something smells bad, why put your nose in it?'
NINOTCHKA: 'And there is an old Russian saying, the cat who has cream on his whiskers had better find good excuses.'
NINOTCHKA: 'The last mass trials were a great success. There are going to be fewer but better Russians.'
'High calibre entertainment for adult audiences, and a top attraction for the key de-luxers.' – *Variety*
'The Lubitsch style, in which much was made of subtleties – glances, finger movements, raised eyebrows – has disappeared. Instead we have a hard, brightly lit, cynical comedy with the wisecrack completely in control.' – *John Baxter, 1968*
† William Powell and Robert Montgomery were formerly considered for the Melvyn Douglas role.
🎬 best picture; script; story; Greta Garbo

The Ninth Configuration
US   1980   105m   Metrocolor
ITC/Lorimar (William Peter Blatty)
A new psychiatrist in a compound of military misfits becomes the victim of a terror campaign.
Weirdly obscure would-be thriller which only mystifies and annoys.
wd William Peter Blatty *novel* Twinkle, Twinkle 'Killer' Kane *by* William Peter Blatty *ph* Gerry Fisher *m* Barry DeVorzon *pd* Bill Malley, J. Dennis Washington *ed* Peter Taylor
☆ Stacy Keach, Scott Wilson, Jason Miller, Ed Flanders, Neville Brand, Moses Gunn, Robert Loggia, Joe Spinell
'Quite astonishingly garbled, trailing yards of portentous religious allegory.' – *Observer*
'The pretensions are enough to raise the *Titanic* – and sink it again.' – *Guardian*
† Blatty released a longer version, running for 118m, in 1985.

'Leave the unknown alone.'
The Ninth Gate *
France/Spain   1999   127m   colour   'Scope
Artisan/R.P./OrlyTF1/Kino Vision/Origen/Bac/Canal+/Via Digital (Roman Polanski)
A wealthy New York collector hires a rare-book dealer to check the authenticity of a 17th century book said to have been co-authored by the devil.
An uncertain tone bedevils this tale of decadence and satanism among the very rich, veering as it does

between horror and satire; ultimately, it's nothing very much.
w Enrique Urbizu, John Brownjohn, Roman Polanski *novel El Club Dumas by Arturo Perez-Reverte* d Roman Polanski *ph* Darius Khondji *m* Wojciech Kilar *pd* Dean Tavoularis *ed* Herve de Luze *cos* Anthony Powell
☆ Johnny Depp, Frank Langella, Lena Olin, Emmanuelle Seigner, Barbara Jefford, Jack Taylor, Jose Lopez Rodero, James Russo
'About as scary as a sock-puppet re-enactment of *The Blair Witch Project* and not nearly as funny.'
– Elvis Mitchell, *New York Times*

The Ninth Guest
US   1934   65m   bw
Columbia
Eight people are trapped by a murderer in a penthouse suite.
Whodunnit which must have been seen by Agatha Christie before she wrote And Then There Were None. *This version however is flatly scripted and characterized, with no real interest in the (unlikely) outcome.*
w Garnett Weston *novel* Gwen Bristow *stage play* Owen Davis *d* Roy William Neill
☆ Donald Cook, Genevieve Tobin, Hardie Albright, Edward Ellis, Edwin Maxwell, Vince Barnett, Samuel S. Hinds
'It ought to get a neat return in most spots.' – *Variety*

Nirvana Street Murder
Australia   1990   75m   colour
AFC (Fiona Cochrane)
An abattoir worker tries to keep control of his own life, and that of his simple-minded, violent brother, who has hazy notions of right and wrong.
A short, grimly realistic working-class drama that quickly degenerates into unconvincing melodrama.
wd Aleksi Vellis *ph* Mark Lane *pd* Lisa Thompson *ed* Aleksi Vellis
☆ Mark Little, Ben Mendelsohn, Mary Coustas, Sheila Florance, Roberto Micale, Tamara Saulwick, Yiorgo, Russell Gilbert

The Nitwits
US   1935   81m   bw
RKO
☾.
Two cigar-stand assistants solve the murder of a music publisher.
Overlong crime comedy with a good finale.
w Fred Guiol, Al Boasberg, Stuart Palmer
d George Stevens
☆ Bert Wheeler, Robert Woolsey, Fred Keating, Betty Grable, Evelyn Brent
'Fair.' – *Variety*

Niu-Peng **
China/France   1989   100m   colour
Titane/Flach Film/La Sept (Jean-Luc Ormieres)
aka: *China, My Sorrow*
A 13-year-old boy is sent to Niu-Peng, a detention centre for 'the re-education of enemies of the people', for listening to love songs on his record-player.
Moving and compassionate account of a community of independent spirits surviving in the face of intransigence.
w Dai Sijie, Shan Yuan Zhu *d* Dai Sijie *ph* Jean-Michael Humeau *m* Chen Qi Gang *ad* Christian Marti *ed* Chantal Delattre
☆ Guo Liang Yi, Tien Quan Nghieu, Vuong Han Lai, Sam Chi-Vy, Truong Loi

Nixon ***
US   1995   192m   Technicolor
Entertainment/Illusion/Cinergi (Clayton Townsend, Oliver Stone, Andrew G. Vajna)
🔲 ▦ ☾. ⌖
As the Watergate cover-up begins to unravel, Richard Nixon recalls his past, from his Quaker childhood to his marriage and the triumphs of his political career.
A boldly conceived film on the corruption of power. It attempts to cast Nixon as the protagonist of a tragedy in a Shakespearean mould – like Macbeth, he clambers over the dead bodies of others to seize power and to retain it. While the film fails to show that Nixon had sufficient stature to qualify as a tragic hero, it does provide a fascinating portrait of a flawed and envious man, seeking support from dubious allies and brought down by his own failings. Hopkins is utterly convincing in the title role.

w Stephen J. Rivele, Christopher Wilkinson, Oliver Stone *d* Oliver Stone *ph* Robert Richardson *m* John Williams *pd* Victor Kempster *ed* Brian Berdan, Hank Corwin
☆ Anthony Hopkins, Joan Allen, Powers Boothe, Ed Harris, E. G. Marshall, David Paymer, David Hyde Pierce, Paul Sorvino, J. T. Walsh, James Woods, Mary Steenburgen
'Inescapably interesting due to the parade of recent history on view, but it finally emerges as an honorable, and rather too strenuous, failure.' – Todd McCarthy, *Variety*
'Achieves the dubious distinction of being a film about Nixon that is actually more paranoid than Nixon was.' – Tom Shone, *Sunday Times*
⚐ Anthony Hopkins, Joan Allen; John Williams; screenplay

Nô *
Canada   1998   85m   colour/bw
Alliance/In Extremis Images/Telefilm Canada/Sodec (Bruno Jobin)
🔲 ▦
In 1970, at a time of martial law in Quebec, a pregnant Canadian actress decides to return home to her lover, who has become involved with violent separatists.
An enjoyable, cleverly constructed movie that moves from stylized comedy to realistic drama, though its political concerns are too local to mean much in the wider world.
w Robert Lepage, Andre Morency *play* The Seven Branches of the River Ota *by* Robert Lepage
d Robert Lepage *ph* Pierre Mignot *m* Michel F. Cote, Bernard Falaise *pd* Fanfan Boudreau *ed* Aube Foglia
☆ Anne-Marie Cadieux, Alexis Martin, Marie Brassard, Richard Fréchette, Marie Gignac, Eric Bernier
'Witty, always intriguing and amusing, and maintains the director's reputation as an inventive cinematic stylist.' – Richard Falcon, *Sight and Sound*

No Big Deal
US   1984   86m   Movielab
Kandel/Film Gallery/Cinétudes (Gale Goldberg, Christine Jurzykowski)
🔲 ▦
A juvenile delinquent fails to make the grade.
Drear high-school drama of adolescent angst, indifferently acted and directed.
w Jeffrey Kindley *book* Would You Settle for Improbable? *by* P. J. Petersen *d* Robert Charlton *ph* Jeff Lion Weinstock *m* Lynn Ahrens *ad* Joshua Harrison *ed* Margot Francis
☆ Kevin Dillon, Christopher Gartin, Mary Joan Negro, Jane Krakowski, Stacy Lauren, Daniel Hess, Wayne Daniels, Tammy Grimes, Sylvia Miles

No Blade of Grass
GB   1970   97m   Metrocolor   Panavision
MGM (Cornel Wilde)
Industrial pollution sets a destructive virus ruining the crops of the world; anarchy spreads through Britain and one family takes refuge in the Lake District.
Apocalyptic sci-fi, moderately well done though so humourless as to be almost funny.
w Sean Forestal, Jefferson Pascal *novel* The Death of Grass *by* John Christopher *d* Cornel Wilde *ph* H. A. R. Thomson *m* Burnell Whibley
☆ Nigel Davenport, Jean Wallace, Patrick Holt, John Hamill

No Deposit, No Return
US   1976   112m   Technicolor
Walt Disney (Ron Miller)
▦
Airport confusion causes crooks to abduct (unwittingly) a millionaire's grandchildren; the millionaire gives chase.
Overlong and tedious action comedy which makes little sense.
w Arthur Alsberg, Don Nelson *d* Norman Tokar *ph* Frank Phillips *m* Buddy Baker
☆ David Niven, Darren McGavin, Don Knotts, Herschel Bernardi, Barbara Feldon, John Williams, Vic Tayback, Kim Richards
'Once again one is left wondering why there should be such an unbridgeable gulf between the brilliant professionalism and the sometimes innovative genius of the Disney animated films, and the dull artlessness of the majority of their live-action pictures.' – Philip French, *The Times*

'You can't throw so many young couples together and not expect explosions!'
No Down Payment **
US   1957   105m   bw   Cinemascope
TCF (Jerry Wald)
Tension among smart suburban couples in a Los Angeles housing development.
Lively domestic melodrama, very useful to sociologists as a mirror of its times.
w Philip Yordan *novel* John McPartland *d* Martin Ritt *ph* Joseph LaShelle *m* Leigh Harline
☆ Joanne Woodward, Tony Randall, Sheree North, Jeffrey Hunter, Cameron Mitchell, Patricia Owens, Barbara Rush, Pat Hingle

No End *
Poland   1984   107m   colour
Artificial Eye/Zespoly Filmowe (Ryszard Chutkowski)
original title: *Bez Konca*
The ghost of a radical lawyer watches over his wife and son and an elderly lawyer who has taken over his final case, defending the leader of a strike.
Intense domestic and political drama, set against a background of the imposition of martial law.
w Krzysztof Kieslowski, Krzysztof Piesiewicz *d* Krzysztof Kieslowski *ph* Jacek Petrycki *m* Zbigniew Preisner *ad* Allan Starski *ed* Krystyna Rutowska
☆ Grazyna Szapolowska, Maria Pakulnis, Aleksander Bardini, Jerzy Radziwilowicz, Artur Barcis, Michel Bajor, Marek Kondrat

No Escape
GB   1936   85m   bw
Pathé Welwyn
A man pretends to be dead as a hoax, and when he is found so, his accomplice is suspected.
Twisty thriller from a popular play.
w George Goodchild, Frank Witty *play* No Exit *by* George Goodchild, Frank Witty *d* Norman Lee
☆ Valerie Hobson, Leslie Perrins, Robert Cochran, Billy Milton, Henry Oscar
'Good programme picture for almost anywhere.' – *Variety*

'No Guards. No Walls.'
No Escape
US   1994   118m   Eastmancolor
Savoy/Allied Filmmakers/Pacific Western (Gale Anne Hurd)
🔲 ▦ ☾. ⌖ ⌂
In 2022, when prisons have been privatized, a vicious warden illegally dumps a convicted soldier on a remote island where gangs of criminals, some violent, one attempting to be civilized, strive for supremacy.
Slick action movie that follows conventional lines and, despite its future setting, most closely resembles ancient jungle escape stories; all it lacks is Tarzan.
w Michael Gaylin, Joel Gross *novel* The Penal Colony *by* Richard Herley *d* Martin Campbell *ph* Phil Meheux *m* Graeme Revell *pd* Allan Cameron *ed* Terry Rawlings
☆ Ray Liotta, Lance Henriksen, Stuart Wilson, Kevin Dillon, Kevin J. O'Connor, Don Henderson, Ian McNeice, Jack Shepherd, Michael Lerner, Ernie Hudson
'This offers muscular widescreen thrills, but is sorely lacking in any cranial tissue.' – *Jack Yeovil, Empire*

No Funny Business
GB   1933   75m   bw
John Stafford
Two professional co-respondents are sent to the Riviera; each mistakes the other as his client.
Stagey farce, notable for its unlikely star teaming and its hilariously dated style.
w Victor Hanbury, Frank Vosper, Dorothy Hope *d* John Stafford, Victor Hanbury *ph* Bryan Langley *songs* Noel Gay, Clifford Grey
☆ Gertrude Lawrence, Laurence Olivier, Jill Esmond, Edmund Breon, Gibb McLaughlin, Muriel Aked

No Greater Glory
US   1934   78m   bw
Columbia
Boys learn through their play that there is no greater glory than to die for one's country.
Glum parable which probably worked better in the original German.
w Jo Swerling *film script* The Paul Street Boys *by* Ferenc Molnar *d* Frank Borzage

☆ George Breakston, Jimmy Butler, Jackie Searl, Frankie Darro, Ralph Morgan, Christian Rub
'Not for the general trade, but a prospective hit in the arties.' – *Variety*

No Habra Mas Penas Ni Olvido: see *A Funny Dirty Little War*

No Hands on the Clock
US   1941   76m   bw
Pine-Thomas/Paramount
A private eye on honeymoon steps right into a kidnapping.
Rather flat time-passer with too many loose ends.
w Maxwell Shane *novel* Geoffrey Homes *d* Frank McDonald
☆ Chester Morris, Jean Parker, Rose Hobart, Dick Purcell, Astrid Allwyn, Rod Cameron

'Turn back, I tell you! Any minute may be too late!'
No Highway **
GB   1951   98m   bw
TCF (Louis D. Lighton)
US title: *No Highway in the Sky*
During a transatlantic flight, a boffin works out that the plane's tail is about to fall off from metal fatigue.
The central premise of this adaptation from a popular novel is fascinating, but the romantic asides are a distraction and the characters cardboard; the film still entertains through sheer professionalism.
w R. C. Sherriff, Oscar Millard, Alec Coppel *novel* Nevil Shute *d* Henry Koster *ph* Georges Périnal
☆ James Stewart, Marlene Dietrich, Glynis Johns, Jack Hawkins, Janette Scott, Elizabeth Allan, Kenneth More, Niall MacGinnis, Ronald Squire

No Highway in the Sky: see *No Highway*

No Kidding
👪 GB   1960   86m   bw
Peter Rogers/GHW/Anglo Amalgamated
US title: *Beware of Children*
An old house is turned into a holiday home for deprived rich children.
Strained comedy with agreeable cast.
w Norman Hudis, Robin Estridge *novel* Verity Anderson *d* Gerald Thomas *ph* Alan Hume *m* Bruce Montgomery
☆ Leslie Phillips, Geraldine McEwan, Julia Lockwood, Noel Purcell, Irene Handl, Joan Hickson, Cyril Raymond

No Leave, No Love
US   1946   118m   bw
MGM (Joe Pasternak)
Sailors on leave meet an English girl.
Witless, overlong musical extravaganza.
w Charles Martin, Leslie Karkos *d* Charles Martin *ph* Harold Rosson, Robert Surtees *md* Georgie Stoll
☆ Van Johnson, Pat Kirkwood, Keenan Wynn, Guy Lombardo and his Orchestra, Edward Arnold, Marie Wilson, Leon Ames

No Limit *
GB   1935   79m   bw
ATP (Basil Dean)
🔲
A motor mechanic enters for the TT Races.
Lively star comedy with Isle of Man locations.
w Tom Geraghty, Fred Thompson *story* Walter Greenwood *d* Monty Banks *ph* Bob Martin
☆ George Formby, Florence Desmond, Edward Rigby, Jack Hobbs, Peter Gawthorne, Alf Goddard

No Love for Johnnie *
GB   1960   111m   bw   Cinemascope
Rank/Five Star (Betty E. Box)
▦
The personal and political problems of a Labour MP.
Predictable but quite lively study of ambition and frustration, with good cameos; Cinemascope all but ruins its impact.
w Nicholas Phipps, Mordecai Richler *novel* Wilfred Fienburgh *d* Ralph Thomas *ph* Ernest Steward *m* Malcolm Arnold
☆ Peter Finch, Mary Peach, Stanley Holloway, Donald Pleasence, Billie Whitelaw, Hugh Burden, Rosalie Crutchley, Michael Goodliffe, Mervyn Johns, Geoffrey Keen, Paul Rogers, Dennis Price, Peter Barkworth, Fenella Fielding, Gladys Henson
⚐ Peter Finch

No Man Is an Island
US 1962 114m Eastmancolor
U-I/Gold Coast (John Monks Jnr, Richard Goldstone)
GB title: *Island Escape*
After the Japanese attack on Guam, a radioman finds refuge in a leper colony and sets up his own resistance unit.
Unexceptionable war adventure in the jungle.
wd John Monks Jnr, Richard Goldstone *ph* Carl Kayser *m* Restie Umali
☆ Jeffrey Hunter, Marshall Thompson, Barbara Perez, Ronald Remy
'Good clean fun for right-minded teenagers.' – *MFB*

'He was a hit and run lover ... personally, he preferred a cigarette to any dame!'
No Man of Her Own *
US 1933 98m bw
Paramount
A big-time gambler marries a local girl on a bet and tries to keep her innocent of his activities.
Star romantic comedy drama, quite professionally assembled and played.
w Maurine Watkins, Milton H. Gropper *d* Wesley Ruggles *ph* Leo Tover
☆ Clark Gable, Carole Lombard, Dorothy Mackaill, Grant Mitchell, George Barbier, Elizabeth Patterson, J. Farrell MacDonald
'Entertaining film with national appeal.' – *Variety*
'Just about everything that the ordinary picture fan looks for: drama, romance, comedy, strong build-ups, exciting climaxes, a fine line of human interest.' – *Film Daily*

No Man of Her Own *
US 1950 98m bw
Paramount (Richard Maibaum)
A pregnant wanderer is involved in a train crash and assumes the identity of the wife of a dead passenger.
Glossy star melodrama, very watchable.
w Catherine Turney, Sally Benson, Mitchell Leisen *novel* William Irish (Cornell Woolrich) *d* Mitchell Leisen *ph* Daniel L. Fapp *m* Hugo Friedhofer
☆ *Barbara Stanwyck*, John Lund, Lyle Bettger, *Jane Cowl*, Phyllis Thaxter, Henry O'Neill, Richard Denning

No Man's Land *
France/Switzerland 1985 110m colour
Filmograph/MK2 (Alain Tanner, Marin Karmitz)
A group of smugglers, each wanting a better way of life, operate on the borders of France and Switzerland.
Coolly detached account of people on the point of breakdown.
wd Alain Tanner *ph* Bernard Zitzermann *m* Terry Riley *pd* Alain Nicolet *ed* Laurent Uhler
☆ Jean-Philippe Ecoffey, Betty Berr, Marie-Luce Felber, Hugues Quester, Myriam Mézières

No Man's Land
1987 105m colour
Rank/Orion (Joseph Stern, Dick Wolf)
A young undercover cop falls in love with the sister of the car thief he is trying to bring to justice.
Moderate low-key thriller with lacklustre performances.
w Dick Wolf *d* Peter Werner *ph* Hiro Narita *m* Basil Poledouris *pd* Paul Peters *ed* Steve Cohen
☆ D. B. Sweeney, Charlie Sheen, Lara Harris, Randy Quaid, Bill Duke, R. D. Call, Arlen Dean Snyder, M. Emmet Walsh, Al Shannon

No Mercy
US 1986 105m Metrocolor
Tri-Star/Delphi IV (D. Constantine Conte)
Policemen pretend to be hit men in an attempt to infiltrate a murder-by-contract organization.
Fashionable violence, slick production, nothing new.
w Jim Carabatsos *d* Richard Pearce *ph* Michael Brault *m* Alan Silvestri *pd* Patrizia von Brandenstein *ed* Jerry Greenberg, Bill Yahraus
☆ Richard Gere, Kim Basinger, Jeroen Krabbe, George Dzundza, Gary Basaraba, William Atherton

No Mercy, No Future
West Germany 1981 100m colour
Mainline/Helma Sanders-Brahms
original title: *Die Berührte*
A suicidal schizophrenic wanders through Berlin looking for Christ and indulging in casual affairs.
Uncompromisingly downbeat study of madness that provides a succession of shocking images which become hard to bear.
wd Helma Sanders-Brahms *ph* Thomas Mauch *m* Manfred Opitz, Harald Grosskopf *ed* Ursula West, Hanni Lewerenz
☆ Elisabeth Stepanek, Hubertus von Weyrauch, Irmgard Mellinger, Nguyen Chi Canh

No Minor Vices
US 1948 96m bw
(MGM) Enterprise (Lewis Milestone)
A doctor brings home an artist friend who proceeds to wreck his household.
Interminable thin comedy which gives no clue as to what the talent involved thought it was doing.
w Arnold Manoff *d* Lewis Milestone *ph* George Barnes *m* Franz Waxman
☆ Dana Andrews, Lilli Palmer, Louis Jourdan, Jane Wyatt, Norman Lloyd

No More Ladies
US 1935 79m bw
MGM
A society girl thinks that by marrying a rake she can reform him.
Breezy sophisticated comedy which doesn't quite maintain its impetus.
w Donald Ogden Stewart, Horace Jackson *play* A. E. Thomas *d* Edward H. Griffith, George Cukor *ph* Oliver T. Marsh *m* Edward Ward
☆ Joan Crawford, Robert Montgomery, Franchot Tone, Charles Ruggles, Edna May Oliver, Gail Patrick, Reginald Denny, Arthur Treacher
'Sophistication plus in society setting and probably too much on the ultra side for sock appreciation. But okay.' – *Variety*

No More Women
US 1934 73m bw
Paramount
Deep-sea divers compete for jobs and a woman.
Flagg and Quirt in all but name, with action melodrama largely substituted for skirt-chasing.
w Delmer Daves, Lou Breslow *story* John M. Strong *d* Al Rogell
☆ Edmund Lowe, Victor McLaglen, Sally Blane, Minna Gombell, Harold Huber
'Quirt and Flagg under the Hays morality code, and they can't take it.' – *Variety*

No, My Darling Daughter
GB 1961 96m bw
Rank/Five Star/Betty E. Box-Ralph Thomas
Chaos ensues when a tycoon's daughter is thought to be eloping with an American boyfriend.
Clumsy comedy with moments of brightness provided by the actors.
w Frank Harvey *play* A Handful of Tansy by Harold Brooke, Kay Bannerman *d* Ralph Thomas *ph* Ernest Steward *m* Norrie Paramor
☆ Michael Redgrave, Michael Craig, Roger Livesey, Rad Fulton, Juliet Mills, Renee Houston, Joan Sims, Peter Butterworth

No Name on the Bullet
US 1958 77m Eastmancolor Cinemascope
Universal (Howard Christie, Jack Arnold)
A hired gunman books into the hotel of a small Western town, and everybody wonders who he is after.
Tolerable Western programmer with more emphasis than usual on characterization.
w Gene L. Coon *d* Jack Arnold *ph* Harold Lipstein *m* Herman Stein
☆ Audie Murphy, Charles Drake, Joan Evans, R. G. Armstrong, Willis Bouchey, Karl Swenson

No No Nanette
US 1930 90m bw with Technicolor sequences
Warner
A married bible publisher secretly helps three girls, who all visit him on the same day.
Early talkie version of the rather naïve musical hit, with a priceless moment or two among the dross.
w Howard Emmett Rogers *play* Otto Harbach, Frank Mandel *d* Clarence Badger
☆ Bernice Claire, Lucien Littlefield, Lilyan Tashman, Bert Roach, ZaSu Pitts

No No Nanette
US 1940 90m bw
RKO/Suffolk (Herbert Wilcox)
Slightly altered remake with too little attention to the musical numbers.
w Ken Englund *d* Herbert Wilcox *md* Anthony Collins
☆ Anna Neagle, Richard Carlson, Victor Mature, Helen Broderick, Roland Young, ZaSu Pitts, Eve Arden, Billy Gilbert
'It's overboard on inaction, with most of the dead wood up front.' – *Variety*

No Orchids for Miss Blandish
GB 1948 102m bw
Alliance/Tudor (A. R. Shipman, Oswald Mitchell)
An heiress is kidnapped by gangsters and falls for their psychopathic leader.
Hilariously awful gangster movie from a bestselling shocker. Everyone concerned is all at sea, and the result is one of the worst films ever made.
wd St John L. Clowes *novel* James Hadley Chase *ph* Gerald Gibbs
☆ Jack La Rue, Linden Travers, Hugh McDermott, Walter Crisham, Lily Molnar, Zoe Gail
'This must be the most sickening exhibition of brutality, perversion, sex and sadism ever to be shown on a cinema screen ... with pseudo-American accents the actors literally battle their way through a script laden with suggestive dialogue.' – *MFB*
'A most vicious display of sadism, brutality and suggestiveness.' – *Milton Shulman, Evening Standard*
'The morals are about level with those of a scavenger dog.' – *Daily Express*
'It has all the morals of an alley cat and all the sweetness of a sewer.' – *Observer*
'The worst film I have ever seen.' – *Sunday Express*
† Remade as *The Grissom Gang* (qv).

No Parking
GB 1938 72m bw
Herbert Wilcox
A car park attendant is mistaken for an American killer.
Modest, entertaining star comedy.
w Gerald Elliott *story* Carol Reed *d* Jack Raymond *ph* Francis Carver
☆ Gordon Harker, Leslie Perrins, Irene Ware, Cyril Smith

No Peace among the Olives
Italy 1950 99m bw
Lux (Domenico Davanzati)
A young shepherd goes home after the war and finds himself at war again – against a local racketeer.
A rather crude melodrama comparable with the American Thieves' Highway and other films noirs of the time.
w Giuseppe de Santis and others *d* Giuseppe de Santis *ph* Pietro Portalupi *m* Goffredo Petrassi
☆ Lucia Bose, Raf Vallone, Folco Lulli, Dante Maggio

No Place for Jennifer
GB 1949 90m bw
ABPC
Divorcing parents think again when their twelve-year-old daughter runs away.
Very predictable tearjerker which kept box offices busy in its day.
w J. Lee-Thompson *novel* No Difference to Me by Phyllis Hambledon *d* Henry Cass *ph* William McLeod *m* Allan Gray
☆ Leo Genn, Rosamund John, Janette Scott, Beatrice Campbell, Guy Middleton, Anthony Nicholls, Jean Cadell

No Problem! (dubbed) *
France 1975 100m Eastmancolor
Gaumont International 2000 (Alain Poiré)
original title: *Pas de Problème*
Enlisting the aid of a medical student in ridding her flat of a dead man, a young woman triggers a series of mishaps.
A hectic farce that, despite some unsympathetic dubbing, manages to raise a few smiles.
w Jean-Marie Poiré *d* Georges Lautner *ph* Maurice Fellous *m* Philippe Sarde *ed* Michelle David
☆ Miou-Miou, Bernard Menez, Jean Lefebvre, Anny Duperey, Henri Guybet, Renée Saint-Cyr, Patrick Dewaere (cameo)

No Questions Asked
US 1951 80m bw
MGM (Nicholas Nayfack)
A young lawyer undertakes shady business and finds himself framed for murder.
Well made second feature on conventional lines.
w Sidney Sheldon *d* Harold Kress *ph* Harold Lipstein *m* Leith Stevens
☆ Barry Sullivan, George Murphy, Arlene Dahl, Jean Hagen, William Reynolds, Mari Blanchard

No Regrets for Our Youth **
Japan 1946 110m bw
Toho (Keiji Matsuzaki)
original title: *Waga Seishun ni Kui Nashi*
The urbane widow of a left-wing journalist goes to live and work with his parents, who are peasants.
A moving account of the cost of individual survival, and of liberal ideals, at a time of repression and militarism in Japan.
w Eijiro Hisaita, Akira Kurosawa *d* Akira Kurosawa *ph* Asakazu Nakai *m* Tadashi Hattori
☆ Setsuko Hara, Susumu Fujita, Denjiro Okochi, Eiko Miyoshi, Kokuten Kodo, Haruko Sugimura

No Resting Place
GB 1951 77m bw
Colin Lesslie
A wandering Irish tinker accidentally kills a man and is hounded by a Civil Guard.
Interesting attempt at realistic location drama, suffering from a dejected plot and unsympathetic characters.
w Paul Rotha, Colin Lesslie, Michael Orrom *novel* Ian Niall *d* Paul Rotha *ph* Wolfgang Suschitzky *m* William Alwyn
☆ Michael Gough, Noel Purcell, Jack MacGowran

No Retreat, No Surrender
US 1986 90m Technicolor
Entertainment/New World/Seasonal/Balcor (Ng See Yuen)
An American kick-boxer, aided by the ghost of Bruce Lee, conquers a Russian champion who beat up his father.
Standard martial arts revenge movie, with Van Damme as the villain of the piece.
w Keith W. Strandberg *story* Ng See Yuen, Corey Yuen *d* Corey Yuen *ph* John Huneck, David Golia *m* Paul Gilreath *ed* Alan Poon, Mark Pierce, James Melkonian, Dane Davis
☆ Jean-Claude Van Damme, Kurt McKinney, J. W. Fails, Kathie Sileno, Kim Tai Chong, Kent Lipham

No Road Back
GB 1957 83m bw
Gibraltar/RKO (Steven Pallos)
A doctor discovers that his blind mother and fiancée are involved with a gang of violent thieves.
Agreeable time-waster, competently made but unexciting and notable mainly for one of Connery's early performances, as a Scottish crook with a speech impediment.
w Charles A. Leeds, Montgomery Tully *play* Falkland L. Cary, Philip Weathers *d* Montgomery Tully *ph* Lionel Banes *m* John Veale *md* Philip Martell *ad* John Stoll *ed* Jim Connock
☆ Skip Homeier, Paul Carpenter, Patricia Dainton, Norman Wooland, Margaret Rawlings, Eleanor Summerfield, Alfie Bass, Sean Connery

No Room at the Inn
GB 1948 82m bw
British National (Ivan Foxwell)
A monstrous woman half-starves evacuees and turns her house into a brothel.
Absurd melodrama from a play which was popular because it offered a full-blooded star performance. The film is less convincing but works pretty well on its level.
w Ivan Foxwell, Dylan Thomas *play* Joan Temple *d* Dan Birt *ph* James Wilson
☆ Freda Jackson, Joy Shelton, Hermione Baddeley, Joan Dowling, Harcourt Williams, Sydney Tafler, Frank Pettingell, Niall MacGinnis

No Room for the Groom *
US   1952   82m   bw
Universal-International (Ted Richmond)
An army veteran returns to his wife, who has moved in with her family without telling them of her marriage.
Amiable comedy which rises to a fair pitch of frenzy.
w Joseph Hoffman *story* Darwin H. Teilhet d Douglas Sirk *ph* Clifford Stine *m* Frank Skinner

☆ Tony Curtis, Piper Laurie, Don Defore, Spring Byington, Lee Aaker, Jack Kelly, Lillian Bronson

No Sad Songs for Me
US   1950   89m   bw
Columbia (Buddy Adler)
A young wife discovers she has only eight months to live, and spends it planning her husband's future.
Well-meant but rather icky melodrama featuring one of those beautiful illnesses that appear to have no physical effect.
w Howard Koch *novel* Ruth Southard d Rudolph Maté *ph* Joseph Walker *m* George Duning

☆ Margaret Sullavan, Wendell Corey, Viveca Lindfors, Natalie Wood, John McIntire

♫ George Duning

No Secrets
GB   1982   90m   colour
Fulsetcourt (Elizabeth Curran)
With the help of a female spy, an African emperor kidnaps two US astronauts and demands a huge ransom.
An unbelievably atrocious movie: a crude mix of dim-witted script, bad acting and heavy-handed, mistimed comedy.
w George Fowler, Peter Curran d Peter Curran *ph* David Mason *ed* Peter Curran

☆ Oliver Reed, Sylvaine Charlet, Peter Cushing, Keenan Wynn, Edwin Manda, Wilfrid Hyde-White, Hilary Pritchard, Melvyn Hayes

No Sex Please, We're British
GB   1973   91m   Technicolor
Columbia/BHP (John R. Sloan)
🎞
Confusion ensues when a wrongly addressed parcel of dirty postcards arrives at a bank.
Fairly lively farce with everything from mistaken identity to falling trousers.
w Anthony Marriott, Johnnie Mortimer, Brian Cooke *play* Anthony Marriott, Alistair Foot d Cliff Owen *ph* Ken Hodges *m* Eric Rogers

☆ Ronnie Corbett, Arthur Lowe, Beryl Reid, Ian Ogilvy, Susan Penhaligon, David Swift, Michael Bates

No Sleep Till Dawn: see Bombers B52

No Smoking
GB   1955   72m   bw
Tempean (Robert S. Baker, Monty Berman)
Tobacco companies take action when a simple-minded village chemist invents a no-smoking pill that works.
Dreary B-feature comedy with a ludicrous plot that failed to make an amiable radio comedian funny on the screen.
w Kenneth Hayles, Phil Park *play* George Moresby-White, Rex Rientis d Henry Cass *ph* Monty Berman *m* Ivor Slaney *md* Stanley Black *ad* Wilfred Arnold *ed* Jack Slade

☆ Reg Dixon, Belinda Lee, Lionel Jeffries, Ruth Trouncer, Alexander Gauge, Myrtle Rowe, Arthur Young, Hal Osmond, Tom Gill, Ronnie Stevens

No Surrender *
GB   1985   104m   colour
Dumbarton/NFFC/Lauron/Film Four International (Mamoun Hassan)
🎞 🎞
Irish factions collide in a Liverpool club.
Black comedy typical of the author of Boys from the Black Stuff.
w Alan Bleasdale d Peter Smith *ph* Mick Coulter *m* Daryl Runswick

☆ Michael Angelis, Avis Bunnage, James Ellis, Ray McAnally, Tom Georgeson, Bernard Hill, J. G. Devlin

'Monstrous and marvellous, it combines the disturbing, the disorienting and the downright daft.' – Paul Taylor, MFB

No Time for Comedy *
US   1940   93m   bw
Warner (Robert Lord)
A playwright is depressed by the times and has lost the knack of making people laugh.
Smooth film version of a thoughtful romantic comedy play.
w Julius J. and Philip G. Epstein *play* S. N. Behrman d William Keighley *ph* Ernest Haller *m* Heinz Roemheld

☆ James Stewart, Rosalind Russell, Charles Ruggles, Genevieve Tobin, Allyn Joslyn, Clarence Kolb, Louise Beavers

'Claudette loves the men with muscles!'
No Time for Love *
US   1943   83m   bw
Paramount (Mitchell Leisen)
A lady photographer falls for the foreman of a crew digging a tunnel under the Hudson.
Agreeable romantic slapstick farce.
w Claude Binyon d Mitchell Leisen *ph* Charles Lang Jnr *m* Victor Young *ad* Hans Dreier, Robert Usher

☆ Claudette Colbert, Fred MacMurray, Ilka Chase, Richard Haydn, June Havoc, Marjorie Gateson, Bill Goodwin

♫ art direction

No Time for Sergeants
👪👪   US   1958   111m   bw
Warner (Mervyn Le Roy)
🎞
Adventures of a hillbilly army conscript.
Heavy-handed adaptation of the stage success, a real piece of filmed theatre with not much sparkle to it.
w John Lee Mahin *play* Ira Levin *novel* Mac Hyman d Mervyn Le Roy *ph* Harold Rosson *m* Ray Heindorf

☆ Andy Griffith, William Fawcett, Murray Hamilton, Nick Adams, Myron McCormick, Bartlett Robinson

No Time for Tears
GB   1957   86m   Eastmancolor   Cinemascope
ABPC (W. A. Whittaker)
Problems of a children's hospital.
Totally predictable British tearjerker with a happy ending.
w Anne Burnaby d Cyril Frankel *ph* Gilbert Taylor *m* Francis Chagrin

☆ Anna Neagle, Anthony Quayle, Sylvia Syms, Flora Robson, George Baker, Alan White, Daphne Anderson, Michael Hordern, Joan Hickson, Sophie Stewart, Rosalie Crutchley

No Trace
GB   1950   70m   bw
Eros/Tempean (Robert S. Baker, Monty Berman)
An English crime novelist is invited by the police to help investigate a murder he has committed.
Ingenious minor thriller, not helped by being directed at a plodding pace.
wd John Gilling *story* Robert S. Baker, Carl Nystrom *ph* Monty Berman *m* John Lanchberry *md* Eric Robinson *ad* Walter Scott *ed* Gerald Landau

☆ Hugh Sinclair, Dinah Sheridan, John Laurie, Dora Bryan, Barry Morse, Beatrice Varley, Michael Brennan, Michael Ward

No Trees in the Street
GB   1958   96m   bw
ABP/Allegro (Frank Godwin)
Problems of a London slum family in the thirties.
Artificial and unconvincing attempt at a London Love on the Dole, dragged up and redigested in a later era when 'realism' was thought to be fashionable.
w Ted Willis *play* Ted Willis d J. Lee-Thompson *ph* Gilbert Taylor *m* Laurie Johnson

☆ Sylvia Syms, Herbert Lom, Joan Miller, Melvyn Hayes, Stanley Holloway, Liam Redmond, Ronald Howard, Carole Lesley, Lana Morris, Lily Kann

'Nothing remains but crude sensationalism and several moments of unconscious humour.' – MFB

No Way Home *
US   1996   93m   DuArt
Blue Dolphin/Back Alley/Orenda (Lisa Bruce, Robert Nickson)
🎞 🎞 🎞
A gentle, dim-witted man leaves jail after serving a six-year sentence for murder to live with his drug-dealing brother and new sister-in-law, who is a stripper.
Effective, low-key, foul-mouthed drama of sibling differences for the most part, until it resolves its narrative problems with a melodramatic climax.
wd Buddy Giovinazzo *ph* Claudia Raschke *m* Rick Giovinazzo *pd* Phyllis Cedar *ed* Stan Warnow

☆ Tim Roth, James Russo, Deborah Kara Unger, Joseph Ragno, Catherine Kellner, Saul Stein, Bernadette Penotti

'This feels like a down-market Martin Scorsese movie – which makes it engaging enough.' – Amanda Lipman, Sight and Sound

No Way Out *
US   1950   106m   bw
TCF (Darryl F. Zanuck)
A crook stirs up racial feeling against a black doctor in whose hands his brother has died.
Vivid, hard-hitting melodrama with a hospital background and a strong sociological flavour.
w Joseph L. Mankiewicz, Lesser Samuels d Joseph L. Mankiewicz *ph* Milton Krasner *m* Alfred Newman

☆ Richard Widmark, Sidney Poitier, Linda Darnell, Stephen McNally, Harry Bellaver, Stanley Ridges, Ossie Davis, Ruby Dee

'A production designed solely for purposes of agitation and propaganda, unworthy of literary or cinematic consideration.' – Henry Hart, Films in Review

♫ script

No Way Out *
US   1987   116m   Metrocolor
Orion/Neufeld/Ziskin/Garland (Laura Ziskin, Robert Garland)
🎞 🎞 🎞 🎞 🎞 🎞
A Pentagon officer is convinced his boss is guilty of murder, but the evidence points to himself.
Fast-paced remake of The Big Clock (qv) which does not efface the memory of the original.
w Robert Garland *novel* Kenneth Fearing d Roger Donaldson *ph* John Alcott *m* Maurice Jarre *pd* Dennis Washington

☆ Kevin Costner, Gene Hackman, Sean Young, Will Patton, Howard Duff, George Dzundza

No Way to Treat a Lady *
US   1968   108m   Technicolor
Paramount/Sol C. Siegel
🎞
A mass murderer of women who is also a master of disguise has a running battle with a police detective.
Curious mixture of star show-off piece, murder mystery, black farce, suspense melodrama and Jewish comedy. Bits of it come off very well, but it's a bumpy ride.
w John Gay *novel* William Goldman d Jack Smight *ph* Jack Priestley *m* Stanley Myers

☆ Rod Steiger, George Segal, Lee Remick, Eileen Heckart, Murray Hamilton, Michael Dunn

'The sweetest love story ever told! The epic drama of the age! Drama with a world sweep, colossal and sublime!'
Noah's Ark **
US   1929   135m   bw
Warner
The biblical story of Noah is paralleled, rather loosely, with a tragedy of World War I.
Naïve but fascinating Hollywood epic which in patches triumphantly overcomes the problems of the part-talkie period and is always fascinating to look at.
w Anthony Coldeway, Darryl F. Zanuck d Michael Curtiz *ph* Hal Mohr, Barney McGill *pd* Anton Grot

☆ Dolores Costello, Noah Beery, Louise Fazenda, Guinn Williams, Paul McAllister, Myrna Loy, George O'Brien

'The biggest and best edited picture of the industry ... mobs, Niagaras, train wrecks, war aplenty, crashes, deluges and everything that goes to give the picture fan a thrill.' – Variety

'Staggering ... the greatest thing the screen has done.' – The Film Spectator

† On première it was Warner's longest film, but the release version was cut by nearly half.

Nob Hill *
US   1945   95m   Technicolor
TCF (André Daven)
In the gay 1890s, a San Francisco saloon owner tries to step into society and win one of its most eligible young ladies.
Engaging period musical drama with all talents working well.
w Wanda Tuchock, Norman Reilly Raine d Henry Hathaway *ph* Edward Cronjager *m* David Buttolph *md* Emil Newman, Charles Henderson

☆ George Raft, Joan Bennett, Peggy Ann Garner, Vivian Blaine, Alan Reed, B. S. Pully, Edgar Barrier

Nobi: see Fires on the Plain

Nobody Lives Forever
US   1946   100m   bw
Warner (Robert Buckner)
A con man fleeces a rich widow, then falls in love with her.
Forgettable romantic melodrama.
w W. R. Burnett d Jean Negulesco *ph* Arthur. Edeson *m* Adolph Deutsch

☆ John Garfield, Geraldine Fitzgerald, Walter Brennan, Faye Emerson, George Coulouris, George Tobias

Nobody Runs Forever *
GB   1968   101m   Eastmancolor
Rank/Selmur (Betty E. Box)
US title: The High Commissioner
An Australian detective is sent to arrest the high commissioner in London on a charge of murdering his first wife.
Sub-Hitchcock thriller which comes to life in patches but has a plot and dialogue which obviously embarrass the actors.
w Wilfred Greatorex *novel* The High Commissioner by Jon Cleary d Ralph Thomas *ph* Ernest Steward *m* Georges Delerue

☆ Rod Taylor, Christopher Plummer, Lilli Palmer, Camilla Sparv, Daliah Lavi, Clive Revill, Lee Montague, Calvin Lockhart, Derren Nesbitt, Leo McKern, Franchot Tone

Nobody's Baby
US   1937   67m   bw
MGM (Hal Roach)
Girls at a training school for nurses find themselves looking after a baby.
Lightweight comedy filler.
w Harold Law, Hal Yates, Pat C. Flick d Gus Meins

☆ Lyda Roberti, Patsy Kelly, Lynne Overman, Robert Armstrong, Rosina Lawrence, Don Alvarado, Tom Dugan

'Agreeable enough number two feature for duals.' – Variety

Nobody's Fool
US   1986   107m   CFI color
Enterprise/Island (James C. Katz, Jon S. Denny)
🎞 🎞 🎞
A small-town girl with a mild past falls for a lighting technician with a visiting theatrical troupe.
Much ado about nothing; good observant touches don't stifle the yawns.
w Beth Henley d Evelyn Purcell *ph* Mikhail Suslov *m* James Newton Howard *pd* Jackson DeGovia *ed* Dennis Virkler

☆ Rosanna Arquette, Eric Roberts, Mare Winningham, Jim Youngs, Louise Fletcher, Gwen Welles

'In A Town Where Nothing Ever Happens ... Everything Is About To Happen To Sully.'
Nobody's Fool
US   1994   110m   colour
TCF/Paramount/Capella/Scott Rudin/Cinehaus (Scott Rudin, Arlene Donovan)
🎞 🎞 🎞 🎞
In a small town, a 60-year-old handyman, for whom life has rarely gone right, has one more chance to make good.
A story of understated charm that also observes sharp-edged and unsuccessful relationships with a beady eye.
wd Robert Benton *novel* Richard Russo *ph* John Bailey *m* Howard Shore *pd* David Gropman *ed* John Bloom

☆ Paul Newman, Jessica Tandy, Bruce Willis, Melanie Griffith, Dylan Walsh, Pruitt Taylor Vince, Gene Saks, Philip Bosco

'Shrewd, agreeable, ultimately dishonest.' – *Richard Schickel, Time*

'A nice film, funny and doleful at the same time, which says more than most about those small things which, taken together, make up most of our everyday lives.' – *Derek Malcolm, Guardian*

🏆 Paul Newman; Robert Benton (Screenplay)

Nobody's Perfect
US 1968 103m Techniscope
Universal (Howard Christie)

An ex-naval officer returns to Japan to make amends for stealing a buddha.
Flatfooted comedy adventure.
w John D. F. Black *novel* The Crows of Edwina Hill by Allan R. Bosworth d Alan Rafkin ph Robert H. Wyckoff m Irving Gertz
☆ Doug McClure, Nancy Kwan, Steve Carlson, James Whitmore, David Hartman, Gary Vinson, James Shigeta

Noce Blanche
France 1989 92m colour
Gala/Les films du Losange/La Sept/La Sorcière Rouge/Sofia/Investimage 2 (Margaret Menégoz)

A middle-aged teacher has a stormy affair with his seventeen-year-old pupil.
Cliché-ridden account of mid-life fantasies and adolescent problems, from drugs to prostitution, that offers little in the way of enlightenment.
wd Jean-Claude Brisseau ph Romain Winding ad Maria-Luisa Garcia ed Maria-Luisa Garcia
☆ Vanessa Paradis, Bruno Cremer, Ludmila Mikaël, François Negret, Jean Daste, Véronique Silver, Philippe Tuin

La Noche del Terror Ciego: see *Tombs of the Blind Dead*

Nocturne *
US 1946 87m bw
RKO (Joan Harrison)

A police detective investigates the death of a composer.
Amusingly self-mocking crime thriller, quite smoothly done in all departments.
w Jonathan Latimer d Edwin L. Marin ph Harry J. Wild m Leigh Harline
☆ George Raft, Lynn Bari, Virginia Huston, Joseph Pevney, Myrna Dell, Edward Ashley, Walter Sande, Mabel Paige

'As for the plot, I confess I could not follow it, nor did I care.' – *Paul Holt, Daily Express*

Noi Tre
Italy 1984 96m colour
Instituto Luce/Duea Film/RAI (Paolo Bacchi, Francesco Guerrieri)

aka: *The Three of Us*
On a summer visit to the estate of an Italian count, the young Mozart falls in love.
Pleasant but inconsequential pastoral idyll which treats the composer as an exceptionally innocent adolescent.
w Pupi Avati, Antonio Avati, Cesare Bornazzini d Pupi Avati ph Pasquale Rachini m Riz Ortolani pd Giancarlo Basili, Leonardo Scarpa ed Amedeo Salfa
☆ Lino Capolicchio, Gianni Cavina, Carlo Delle Piane, Ida Di Benedetto, Giulio Pizzirani

La Noia: see *The Empty Canvas*

Noir et Blanc
France 1986 80m bw
Electric/Les Films Du Volcan

A timid accountant forms a sado-masochistic relationship with a black masseur.
Claustrophobic study of sexual obsession which eschews sensationalism.
wd Claire Devers *story* Desire and the Black Masseur by Tennessee Williams ph Daniel Desbois, Christopher Doyle, Alain Lasfargues, Jean-Paul de Costa pd Claire Devers ed Fabienne Alvarez, Yves Sarda
☆ Francis Frappat, Jacques Martial, Joséphine Fresson, Marc Berman, Claire Rigollier

Noises Off
US 1992 104m Technicolor
Warner/Touchstone/Touchstone Pacific Partners 1/Amblin (Frank Marshall)

The American cast of a British sex comedy suffers a series of disasters, on-stage and off, during a pre-Broadway tour.
Brave though misguided attempt to transfer to the screen an intensely theatrical work, depending on live performance for its effect. It begins well but soon ceases to amuse.
w Marty Kaplan *play* Michael Frayn d Peter Bogdanovich ph Tim Suhrstedt m Phil Marshall pd Norman Newberry ed Lisa Day
☆ Carol Burnett, Michael Caine, Denholm Elliott, Julie Hagerty, Marilu Henner, Mark Linn-Baker, Christopher Reeve, John Ritter, Nicollette Sheridan

'Serves up plenty of laughs, and in many ways it stands as a model transfer of a play to the screen.' – *Variety*

'If I say that I laughed till I cried, I have a dreadful fear the words will be ripped out and stuck on the poster. But I did.' – *Nigel Andrews, Financial Times*

'On screen, Noises Off fails in the only way that films can fail – bit by bit. But utterly.' – *Adam Mars-Jones, Independent*

Nomads
US 1985 100m Eastmancolor
PSO/Elliott Kastner/Cinema 7 (George Pappas, Cassian Elwes)

An anthropologist settling in Los Angeles is haunted by vengeful spirits of remote tribes he had investigated.
Stylish nonsense, but nonsense none the less: it would have seemed more striking if it hadn't been five-hundredth in line.
wd John McTiernan ph Stephen Ramsey m Bill Conti pd Marcia Hinds
☆ Pierce Brosnan, Lesley-Anne Down, Anna Maria Monticelli, Adam Ant, Hector Mercado

Non Stop New York
GB 1937 71m bw
GFD/Gaumont (Michael Balcon)

In 1940, gangsters on a transatlantic airliner try to kill a key witness.
Slightly futuristic thriller of its time, now hilariously dated but quite entertaining as well as giving a rare picture of air travel in the thirties.
w Curt Siodmak, Roland Pertwee, J. O. C. Orton, Derek Twist *novel* Sky Steward by Ken Attiwill d Robert Stevenson ph Max Greene md Louis Levy
☆ John Loder, Anna Lee, Francis L. Sullivan, Frank Cellier, Desmond Tester, Athene Seyler, Jerry Verno

None but the Brave: see *For the Love of Mike (1960)*

None but the Brave
US 1965 105m Technicolor Panavision
Warner/Eiga/Toho/Artanis (Frank Sinatra)

During World War II a plane carrying US Marines to the Pacific front crashlands on an island held by Japanese.
Anti-war melodrama in which the action scenes are more memorable than the admirable sentiments.
w John Twist, Katsuya Susaki *story* Kikumaru Okuda d Frank Sinatra ph Harold Lipstein m Johnny Williams
☆ Frank Sinatra, Clint Walker, Tommy Sands, Tony Bill, Brad Dexter

'When is the world coming out of its midnight? When is the human race going to get off its knees?'
None but the Lonely Heart *
US 1944 113m bw
RKO (David Hempstead)

In the thirties, a Cockney drifter finds himself when he learns that his mother is dying.
Wildly astonishing moodpiece to come from Hollywood during World War II; its picture of East End low life is as rocky as its star performance, but it started Miss Barrymore on the west coast career which sustained her old age.

wd Clifford Odets *novel* Richard Llewellyn ph George Barnes m Hanns Eisler md Constantin Bakaleinikoff ed Roland Gross
☆ Cary Grant, Ethel Barrymore, June Duprez, Barry Fitzgerald, Jane Wyatt, George Coulouris, Dan Duryea, Konstantin Shayne, Morton Lowry, Helene Thimig

'A perplexing mixture of good and bad, authentic and phony.' – *Hermione Rich Isaacs, Theatre Arts*

🏆 Ethel Barrymore
🏆 Hanns Eisler; Cary Grant; Roland Gross

None Shall Escape *
US 1944 85m bw
Columbia (Sam Bischoff)

The career of a Nazi officer shown as flashbacks from his trial as a war criminal.
Taut topical melodrama reflecting the mood of the time.
w Lester Cole d André de Toth ph Lee Garmes m Ernst Toch
☆ Alexander Knox, Marsha Hunt, Henry Travers, Dorothy Morris, Richard Crane
🏆 original story (Alfred Neumann, Joseph Than)

De Noorderlingen: see *The Northerners*

Noose: see *Snitch (1998)*

Noose
GB 1948 98m bw
ABPC/Edward Dryhurst

A Soho black market gang is exposed.
Vivid though rather tatty film version of a West End play success.
w Richard Llewellyn *play* Richard Llewellyn d Edmond T. Greville ph Hone Glendinning m Charles Williams
☆ Nigel Patrick, Carole Landis, Derek Farr, Joseph Calleia, Stanley Holloway, Hay Petrie, John Slater

The Noose Hangs High
US 1948 77m bw
Eagle-Lion

Two window washers are hired by a crooked bookie who finds their incompetence hard to tolerate when they lose his winnings.
Thin star comedy filled with the team's cornier routines, not too cleverly revived.
w John Grant and Howard Harris d Charles Barton
☆ Bud Abbott, Lou Costello, Leon Errol, Joseph Calleia, Murray Leonard, Cathy Downs, Mike Mazurki, Fritz Feld
† A previous film of the same story was made in 1939 under the title For Love or Money, with June Lang, Robert Kent and Ed Brophy.

Nor the Moon By Night
GB 1958 92m Eastmancolor
Rank (John Stafford)
US title: *Elephant Gun*

An African game warden marries a longtime penfriend who finds that Africa presents unexpected problems.
Paperback romance with pleasant backgrounds.
w Guy Elmes *novel* Joy Packer d Ken Annakin ph Harry Waxman m James Bernard
☆ Belinda Lee, Michael Craig, Patrick McGoohan, Anna Gaylor, Eric Pohlmann
'Neither character nor incident nor theme has any coherence or interest.' – *MFB*

'A mouth like hers is just for kissing ... not for telling!'
Nora Prentiss *
US 1946 117m bw
Warner (William Jacobs)

A doctor falls for a café singer who ruins his life.
Standard star melodrama aimed at women, and appreciated by them.
w N. Richard Nash *story* Paul Webster, Jack Sobell d Vincent Sherman ph James Wong Howe m Franz Waxman
☆ Ann Sheridan, Kent Smith, Bruce Bennett, Robert Alda, Rosemary de Camp, John Ridgely, Wanda Hendrix

Norma Rae *
US 1979 114m DeLuxe Panavision
TCF (Tamara Asseyev, Alex Rose)

A Southern girl becomes an angry union organizer.

Well-intentioned and well-acted pamphlet of political enlightenment with an inevitably ambivalent attitude.
w Irving Ravetch, Harriet Frank Jnr d Martin Ritt ph John A. Alonzo m David Shire pd Walter Scott Herndon
☆ Sally Field, Beau Bridges, Ron Leibman, Pat Hingle, Barbara Baxley
🏆 Sally Field; song 'It Goes Like It Goes' (mDavid Shire, lyNorman Gimbel)
🏆 best picture; best script

Normal Life
US 1996 103m colour
First Independent/Spelling/Fine Line (Richard Maynard)

A Chicago cop marries an alcoholic, drug-addicted blonde, loses his job and turns bank robber.
Bleak, documentary-style narrative of a downward spiral into despair and death, based on a true story.
w Peg Haller, Bob Schneider d John McNaughton ph Jean DeSegonzac m Robert McNaughton pd Rick Paul ed Elena Maganini
☆ Luke Perry, Ashley Judd, Bruce Young, Jim True, Edmund Wyson, Michael Skewes, Dawn Maxey
'Hasn't quite been able to translate its diverse raw elements into fully formed drama.' – *Variety*

Norman, Is That You?
US 1976 92m Metrocolor
MGM (George Schlatter)

Adulterous parents find that their son is a homosexual.
Unattractive comedy roughly filmed and given a black ambience. Not worth buying a ticket.
w Ron Clark, Sam Bobrick *play* Ron Clark, Sam Bobrick d George Schlatter ph Gayne Rescher m William Goldstein
☆ Redd Foxx, Pearl Bailey, Dennis Dugan, Michael Warren, Tamara Dobson

The Norseman
US 1978 90m Movielab
AIP/Charles B. Pierce/Fawcett Majors

A Viking heads across the sea to America in search of his long lost father.
Low grade hokum for the easily pleased.
wd Charles B. Pierce ph Robert Bethard m Jaime Mendoza-Nava
☆ Lee Majors, Cornel Wilde, Mel Ferrer, Jack Elam, Chris Connelly

El Norte **
GB/US 1983 139m
Independent Productions/American Playhouse Theatre/Channel 4 (Anna Thomas)

Fleeing from a murderous army in Guatemala, a brother and sister travel north to try to make a new life in the United States.
Conceived on a grand scale and often moving, it is nevertheless too long to bear its fragile narrative.
w Gregory Nava, Anna Thomas d Gregory Nava ph James Glennon ed Betsy Blankett
☆ Zaide Silvia Gutierrez, David Villalpando, Ernesto Gomez Cruz, Alicia del Lago, Eraclio Zepeda
🏆 screenplay

'North's hopping mad with his parents and now he's off on a world wide adventure!'
North
US 1994 88m Technicolor
Rank/Columbia/Castle Rock (Rob Reiner, Alan Zweibel)

An 11-year-old boy, who decides to divorce his parents, sets out to find the ideal mother and father.
A disaster, unless you can derive pleasure from Bruce Willis dressed as a fluffy, bright pink bunny rabbit; it is neither amusing nor adventurous and fails to be interesting or enlightening as it drags its child hero from one grotesque encounter to another.
w Alan Zweibel, Andrew Scheinman *novel* Alan Zweibel d Rob Reiner ph Adam Greenberg m Marc Shaiman pd J. Michael Riva ed Robert Leighton
☆ Elijah Wood, Bruce Willis, Jon Lovitz, Matthew McCurley, Alan Arkin, Abe Vigoda, Richard Belzer, Kathy Bates, Jason Alexander, Dan Aykroyd, Kelly McGillis, Alexander Godunov

'The director, Rob Reiner, slips on a banana peel and crushes an entire cast in this fantasy.' – *Michael Sragow, New Yorker*

'Embarrassingly bad.' – *Guardian*

The North Avenue Irregulars

↟↟ US 1978 99m Technicolor
Disney

▤

GB title: *Hill's Angels*

A Presbyterian minister becomes an undercover agent for the FBI, helping to expose a crooked gambling syndicate.

Very heavy comedy which seems to find itself much funnier than the audience does.

w Don Tait *novel* the Rev. Albert Fay Hill d Bruce Bilson ph Leonard South m Robert F. Brunner

☆ Edward Herrmann, Barbara Harris, Susan Clark, Karen Valentine, Michael Constantine, Cloris Leachman, Patsy Kelly, Douglas Fowley, Alan Hale Jnr

North by Northwest ****

US 1959 136m Technicolor Vistavision
MGM (Alfred Hitchcock)

▤ ▤ ◔ ♁

A businessman is mistaken for a spy, and enemy agents then try to kill him because he knows too much.

Delightful chase comedy-thriller with a touch of sex, a kind of compendium of its director's best work, with memories of The 39 Steps, Saboteur and Foreign Correspondent among others.

w Ernest Lehman d Alfred Hitchcock ph Robert Burks m Bernard Herrmann ad William A. Horning, Robert Boyle, Merrill Pye ed George Tomasini

☆ Cary Grant, Eva Marie Saint, James Mason, Leo G. Carroll, Martin Landau, Jessie Royce Landis, Adam Williams

'It is only when you adopt the basic premise that Cary Grant could not possibly come to harm that the tongue in Hitchcock's cheek becomes plainly visible.' – *Hollis Alpert, Saturday Review*

'North by Northwest is never brutal. Mr Grant calls it a comedy; I would agree that it is consistently entertaining, its excitement pointed by but never interrupted by the jokes.' – *Dilys Powell*

'You get a lot of entertainment for your money. You get a couple of clever, sophisticated screen actors and an elegant actress with a fine-drawn, exciting face. You get one scene that will be talked about as long as people talk about films at all.' – *C. A. Lejeune*

⌕ Ernest Lehman; art direction; editing

North Dallas Forty

US 1979 118m Metrocolor
Paramount (Frank Yablans)

▤ ◔

The gruelling life of a professional football player, laced with drugs, sex and alcohol.

Well made but generally unattractive, the kind of movie for which one wouldn't expect to find an audience.

w Frank Yablans, Ted Kotcheff, Peter Gent *novel* Peter Gent d Ted Kotcheff ph Paul Lohmann m John Scott pd Alfred Sweeney

☆ Nick Nolte, Mac Davis, Charles Durning, Dayle Haddon, Bo Svenson

North Sea Hijack

GB 1979 100m Technicolor
Universal/Cinema Seven (Mo Rothman)

▤ ♁

US title: *ffoulkes*

A British oil rig in the North Sea is held for ransom.

Asinine Boys' Own Paper adventure story with the very minimum of thrills and a totally miscast hero.

w Jack Davis *novel* Esther, Ruth and Jennifer by Jack Davis d Andrew V. McLaglen ph Tony Imi m Michael J. Lewis pd Maurice Carter

☆ Roger Moore, Anthony Perkins, James Mason, Michael Parks, David Hedison, Jack Watson, George Baker, Faith Brook

North Star *

US 1943 105m bw
Samuel Goldwyn (William Cameron Menzies)

▤ ◔

aka: *Armored Attack*

A Russian village defends itself against the Nazi onslaught.

Highly artificial propaganda piece later disowned by its makers and retitled. Good acting can't make its mark when the Russian steppes become a never-never land.

w Lillian Hellman d Lewis Milestone ph James Wong Howe m Aaron Copland ad Perry Ferguson

☆ Anne Baxter, Farley Granger, Jane Withers, Dana Andrews, Walter Brennan, Erich von Stroheim, Dean Jagger, Ann Harding, Carl Benton Reid, Walter Huston

'Putting American villagers into Russian costumes and calling them by Russian names is never going to deceive this old bird.' – *James Agate*

'Its failure is the case history of every Hollywood film that steps out of its scope.' – *Richard Winnington*

'Something to be seen more in sorrow than in anger and more in the attitude of the diagnostician in any emotion at all.' – *James Agee*

⌕ Lillian Hellman; James Wong Howe; Aaron Copland; Perry Ferguson

North Star

GB/France/Norway/Italy 1996 88m colour
Warner/Regency/AFCL/M6/Federal (Anne François)

▤

In Alaska in the 1890s, a halfbreed trapper earns the enmity of a crooked businessman when he refuses to mine for gold on land that he considers sacred.

Broadly acted chase drama that lacks any impetus or dramatic interest.

w Sergio Donati, Lorenzo Donati, Paul Ohl *novel* Will Henry *story* Gilles Behat, Philippe Schwartz, Marc Pecas d Nils Gaup ph Bruno de Keyser m Bruce Rowland pd Ben Morahan ed Kant Pan, Michael A. Hoey

☆ James Caan, Christopher Lambert, Catherine McCormack, Burt Young

'Drearily uninspired.' – *Variety*

North to Alaska *

US 1960 122m DeLuxe Cinemascope
TCF (Henry Hathaway)

▤ ▤ ◔

In 1900, two successful gold prospectors have woman trouble.

Good-natured brawling adventure story which could do with cutting but is certainly the type of action movie they don't make 'em like any more.

w John Lee Mahin, Martin Rackin, Claude Binyon *play* Birthday Gift by Ladislas Fodor d Henry Hathaway ph Leon Shamroy m Lionel Newman

☆ John Wayne, Stewart Granger, Fabian, Capucine, Ernie Kovacs, Mickey Shaughnessy, Karl Swenson, Joe Sawyer, John Qualen

North to the Klondike

US 1941 60m bw
Universal

Gold hunters protect the rights of a girl who has made a strike.

Typical economy size programme filler with a studio look and a stalwart cast.

w Clarence Upson Young, Lew Sarecky, George Bricker, William Castle d Erle C. Kenton

☆ Broderick Crawford, Lon Chaney Jnr, Andy Devine, Evelyn Ankers, Keye Luke

Northern Pursuit *

US 1943 94m bw
Warner (Jack Chertok)

A Mountie tracks a stranded Nazi pilot through the Canadian wastes.

Rather unusual star actioner, not badly done.

w Frank Gruber, Alvah Bessie d Raoul Walsh ph Sid Hickox m Adolph Deutsch

☆ Errol Flynn, Helmut Dantine, Julie Bishop, John Ridgely, Gene Lockhart, Tom Tully, Bernard Nedell

The Northerners *

Holland 1993 105m colour
Mayfair/First Floor (Laurens Geels, Dick Maas)

▤

original title: *De Noorderlingen*

In the only occupied street on a half-built housing estate at the edge of nowhere, everyone is acting rather strangely.

A cool and bizarre comedy of frustrated lives and eccentric behaviour.

w Alex Van Warmerdam, Aat Ceelen d Alex Van Warmerdam, Aat Ceelen d Alex Van Warmerdam pd Rikke Jelier ed René Wiegmans

☆ Leonard Lucieer, Jack Wouterse, Rudolf Lucieer, Alex Van Warmerdam, Annet Malherbe, Loes Wouterson, Veerle Dobbelaere

'Witty and original comedy … Showcases a vision and style reminiscent of both Jacques Tati and Aki Kaurismäki.' – *Variety*

'Mean-spirited in its emphasis on the characters' physical indignity, this is a cold, unwelcoming movie whose studied weirdness soon becomes wearisome in the extreme.' – *Kim Newman*

Northwest Frontier ***

GB 1959 129m Eastmancolor
Cinemascope
Rank/Marcel Hellman

▤

US title: *Flame Over India*

In 1905 an English officer during a rebellion escorts a young Hindu prince on a dangerous train journey.

Thoroughly enjoyable Boys' Own Paper adventure story with excellent set-pieces and a spot-the-villain mystery.

w Robin Estridge d J. Lee-Thompson ph Geoffrey Unsworth m Mischa Spoliansky

☆ Kenneth More, Lauren Bacall, Herbert Lom, Ursula Jeans, Wilfrid Hyde-White, I. S. Johar, Eugene Deckers, Ian Hunter

'Northwest Frontier seems to have borrowed its eccentric engine from *The General*, its hazardous expedition from *Stagecoach* and its background of tribal violence from *The Drum*.' – *Penelope Houston*

'Ten stars! Two love stories! One thousand thrills!'

Northwest Mounted Police *

US 1940 125m Technicolor
Paramount (Cecil B. de Mille)

A Texas Ranger seeks a fugitive in Canada.

Typical big-scale action concoction by de Mille, but in this case none of it's very memorable and the detail is poor.

w Alan Le May, Jesse Lasky Jnr, C. Gardner Sullivan d Cecil B. de Mille ph Victor Milner, Howard Greene m Victor Young ad Hans Dreier, Roland Anderson ed Anne Bauchens

☆ Gary Cooper, Paulette Goddard, Madeleine Carroll, Preston Foster, Robert Preston, George Bancroft, Lynne Overman, Akim Tamiroff, Walter Hampden, Lon Chaney Jnr, Montagu Love, George E. Stone

'Two hours of colour, killing, kindness and magnificent country.' – *Otis Ferguson*

'A movie in the grand style. God's own biggest trees and mountains for prop and backdrop; staunch courage and lofty aims among the good people; cunning and treachery lurking within the sinister forces, the ominous note of doom finally stifled by the fortitude of noble men.' – *Time*

⌕ Anne Bauchens

⌕ Victor Milner, Howard Greene; Victor Young; art direction

Northwest Outpost

US 1947 91m bw
Republic (Allan Dwan)

GB title: *End of the Rainbow*

Adventures of California cavalrymen.

Milk-and-water adventures in a forgettable operetta.

w Elizabeth Meehan, Richard Sale d Allan Dwan ph Reggie Lanning m Rudolf Friml

☆ Nelson Eddy, Ilona Massey, Hugo Haas, Elsa Lanchester

'Half men, half demons, warriors such as the world has never known … they lived with death and danger for the women who hungered for their love!'

Northwest Passage (Part One, Rogers' Rangers) ***

US 1940 126m Technicolor
MGM (Hunt Stromberg)

▤ ▤ ◔

Colonial rangers fight it out with hostile Indians.

Part Two was never made, but no one seemed to mind that the characters in Part One never got round to seeking the titular sea route. The adventures depicted had the feel of historical actuality, and the star was well cast.

w Laurence Stallings, Talbot Jennings *novel* Kenneth Roberts d King Vidor ph Sidney Wagner, William V. Skall m Herbert Stothart

☆ Spencer Tracy, Robert Young, Ruth Hussey, Walter Brennan, Nat Pendleton, Robert Barrat, Lumsden Hare, Donald MacBride

⌕ Sidney Wagner, William V. Skall

Northwest Stampede

US 1948 79m Cinecolor
Eagle-Lion (Albert S. Rogell)

The female foreman of a horse ranch hires a new hand, not knowing that he is the son of its recently dead owner, come to claim his inheritance.

An easy-going outdoor drama, although it is a slightly uncomfortable mix of documentary-style footage of rodeo events and capturing and breaking wild horses, and a broadly comic battle of the sexes.

w Art Arthur, Lillie Hayward *Saturday Evening Post article* Wild Horse Roundup by Jean Muir d Albert S. Rogell ph John W. Boyle m Paul Sawtell md Irving Friedman ad Edward L. Ilou ed Philip Cahn

☆ Joan Leslie, James Craig, Jack Oakie, Chill Wills, Victor Kilian, Stanley Andrews, Ray Bennett, Lane Chandler

Norwood

US 1969 95m Technicolor
Paramount/Hal B. Wallis

A Vietnam veteran returns to his Texas home but feels restless and decides to become a radio singer.

A rather ordinary film about an innocent abroad, neither very funny nor very moving.

w Marguerite Roberts d Jack Haley Jnr ph Robert B. Hauser m Al de Lory

☆ Glen Campbell, Kim Darby, Joe Namath, Carol Lynley, Pat Hingle, Tisha Sterling, Dom DeLuise, Jack Haley, Cass Daley, Gil Lamb

Nosferatu ***

Germany 1921 72m bw
Prana

▤ ▤ ◔ ⊙ ⊚

Count Dracula goes to Bremen and is destroyed by sunlight.

An unofficial treatment of the Bram Stoker novel, with a terrifying count and several splendid moments. It took its director to Hollywood.

w Henrik Galeen d F. W. Murnau ph Fritz Arno Wagner ad Albin Grau

☆ Max Schreck, Gustav von Wangenheim, Greta Schröder, Alexander Granach

Nosferatu a Venezia: see *Vampires in Venice*

Nosferatu, Phantom der Nacht: see *Nosferatu the Vampyre*

Nosferatu the Vampyre *

West Germany/France 1979 107m
Eastmancolor
Gaumont/Werner Herzog Filmproduktion

▤ ⊙

original title: *Nosferatu, Phantom der Nacht*

Excruciatingly slow retread of the German silent film.

Despite the star's splendidly loathsome appearance, the overall is no improvement, and the colour in the English prints is quite dreadful.

wd Werner Herzog ph Jörg Schmidt-Reitwein m Popol Vuh

☆ Klaus Kinski, Isabelle Adjani, Bruno Ganz, Walter Ladengast

'Like a dream from which you keep waking with indigestion.' – *Guardian*

Nostalgia *

Italy 1983 126m Eastmancolor
Artificial Eye/Opera Film/Sovin Film/RAI (Francesco Casati)

▤

A Russian writer in Italy meets a social outcast who is expecting the end of the world.

Indescribably doomladen, occasionally beautiful, stylistically interesting and for the most part very boring parable of a kind unique to this director.

w Andrei Tarkovsky, Tonino Guerra d Andrei Tarkovsky ph Giuseppe Lanci ad Andrea Crisanti ed Erminia Marani, Amedeo Salfa

☆ Oleg Jankovsky, Erland Josephson, Domiziana Giordano

'There's Still Time To Understand His Words…'

Nostradamus
GB/Germany   1994   118m   DeLuxe
First Independent/Allied/Vereinigte (Edward Simons, Harald Reichebner)

In the early 16th century, a French scientist is persecuted for his visions of future catastrophic events.
Rambling bio-pic, with its visionary hero watching modern newsreels in a bowl of water, which fails to tell its audience anything it didn't know about the present and reveals the past as a time of hysterical sexually influenced power struggles; not even Hauer, as 'The Mystic Monk' in an illuminated hat, can save it.
w Knut Boeser, Brian Clark *story* Piers Ashworth, Roger Christian d Roger Christian ph Denis Crossan m Barrington Pheloung pd Peter J. Hampton ed Alan Strachan
☆ Tcheky Karyo, Amanda Plummer, Julia Ormond, Assumpta Serna, Rutger Hauer, F. Murray Abraham, Anthony Higgins, Diana Quick, Michael Gough, Maja Morgenstern
  'Crushingly dull.' – Sheila Johnston, Independent

Not as a Stranger **
US   1955   135m   bw
UA/Stanley Kramer

A medical student has professional and personal struggles.
Earnest filming of a bestseller, with all the actors too old for their parts.
w Edna and Edward Anhalt *novel* Morton Thompson d Stanley Kramer ph Franz Planer m George Antheil pd Rudolph Sternad
☆ Robert Mitchum, Olivia de Havilland, Broderick Crawford, Frank Sinatra, Gloria Grahame, Charles Bickford, Myron McCormick, Lon Chaney Jnr, Jesse White, Henry Morgan, Lee Marvin, Virginia Christine

Not Now, Comrade
GB   1977   90m   Technicolor
EMI/Not Now (Martin C. Chute)

A defecting Russian ballet dancer, and his girlfriend, a stripper, are offered refuge by the daughter of a top-ranking Ministry of Defence official, without the knowledge of her father.
Depressing, frenetic farce that worked on the stage but looks lost, cramped and merely silly on the screen.
w Ray Cooney *play* Chase Me, Comrade by Ray Cooney d Harold Snoad, Ray Cooney ph Jack Hildyard m Harry Robinson ad Edward Marshall ed Peter Thornton
☆ Leslie Phillips, Roy Kinnear, Windsor Davies, Don Estelle, Michele Dotrice, Ray Cooney, June Whitfield, Carol Hawkins, Lewis Fiander, Ian Lavender
  'Settles into the familiar round of harmless double entendres buried in the ramifications of a mistaken-identity plot played by the familiar troupers of British farce … mirthless.' – John Pym, MFB

Not Now, Darling
GB   1972   97m   Eastmancolor
LMG/Sedgemoor/Not Now Films

A furrier gets into a complicated situation when he arranges for his mistress to have a cheap mink coat.
Interminable film version (in Multivista, a shoot-and-edit equivalent to TV taping which gives a dingy look and can only work in a single set) of a West End farce which wasn't marvellous to begin with.
w John Chapman *play* Ray Cooney d Ray Cooney, David Croft ph Alan Hume m Cyril Ornadel
☆ Leslie Phillips, Ray Cooney, Moira Lister, Julie Ege, Joan Sims, Derren Nesbitt, Barbara Windsor, Jack Hulbert, Cicely Courtneidge, Bill Fraser

Not of This Earth **
US   1957   72m   bw
AA (Roger Corman)

An alien comes to Earth in human form in search of blood which may save his planet.
Modestly budgeted minor sci-fi; ruthless, original and competent.
w Charles Griffith, Mark Hanna d Roger Corman ph John Mescall m Ronald Stein
☆ Paul Birch, Beverly Garland, Morgan Jones

Not Quite Jerusalem
GB   1985   114m   colour
Rank/Acorn/Lewis Gilbert

An Israeli girl and an American volunteer fall in love on the kibbutz.
A curious misfire. Interest in the subject is cancelled out by unattractive, slangy or caricatured people and by a muddled approach suggesting that a fairer title might have been Carry on Terrorist.
w Paul Kember *play* Paul Kember d Lewis Gilbert ph Tony Imi m Rondo Veneziano
☆ Joanna Pacula, Sam Robards, Kevin McNally, Todd Graff, Selina Cadell

Not So Dumb
US   1929   80m   bw
MGM

A naïve girl throws a big party in the hope of advancing her boyfriend's career.
Popular comedy of its time.
w Wanda Tuchock, Edwin Justus Mayer *play* Dulcy by George S. Kaufman, Marc Connolly d King Vidor
☆ Marion Davies, Elliott Nugent, Raymond Hackett, Franklin Pangborn, Julia Faye
† Previously made as Dulcy by Warner in 1923, directed by Sidney Franklin, with Constance Talmadge.

Not Wanted on Voyage
GB   1957   82m   bw
Renown

A necklace is stolen on an ocean liner.
Feeble fun from an old play.
w Michael and Roland Pertwee and others *play* Evadne Price, Ken Attiwill d Maclean Rogers ph Arthur Grant m Tony Lowry
☆ Ronald Shiner, Brian Rix, Griffith Jones, Katie Boyle, Fabia Drake, Michael Brennan

Not with My Wife, You Don't!
US   1966   119m   Technicolor
Warner/Fernwood/Reynard (Norman Panama, Joel Freeman)

A Korean war veteran is furious when an old rival turns up in London and again makes eyes at his wife.
Extraordinarily flat star comedy of cross and double cross among friends.
w Norman Panama, Larry Gelbart, Peter Barnes d Norman Panama ph Charles Lang, Paul Beeson m Johnny Williams pd Edward Carrere ed Aaron Stell
☆ Tony Curtis, George C. Scott, Virna Lisi, Carroll O'Connor, Richard Eastham, Eddie Ryder, George Tyne
  'About as frothy as a tin of dehydrated milk.' – MFB
  'It has all the verve, subtlety and sophistication of its title.' – Judith Crist

Not without My Daughter
US   1991   114m   colour
UIP/MGM/Pathé (Harry J. and Mary Jane Ufland)

Accompanying her Iranian husband to his homeland for a holiday, an American-born wife discovers that she and her young daughter will not be permitted by him to return to America.
A plodding account of a true story, told with little imagination or flair.
w David W. Rintels *book* Betty Mahmoody, William Hoffer d Brian Gilbert ph Peter Hannan m Jerry Goldsmith pd Anthony Pratt ed Terry Rawlings
☆ Sally Field, Alfred Molina, Sheila Rosenthal, Roshan Seth, Sarah Badel, Soudabeh Farrokhnia
  'It is certainly as propaganda that the film is most successful, for its artlessness in all other respects will be noticeable even to those who may be convulsed by the central dilemma.' – Variety
  'Fits with eerie precision into the cycle of paranoid and xenophobic Hollywood films familiar from the Cold War era.' – Verina Glaessner, Sight and Sound

Notebook on Cities and Clothes *
Germany   1989   80m   colour
Road Movies

A documentary on the Japanese fashion designer Yohji Yamamoto and his relationship to, and with, Tokyo and Paris.
A quirky examination of the images we create of ourselves and the people we really are, or may be, in a world of quick change. Yamamoto is thoughtful but not particularly articulate about his work, other than when expressing his enjoyment of irresponsibility, which contrasts with Wenders's fussily pedantic style. The quality of the images is variable, owing to much of the material being shot with a video camera.
wd Wim Wenders ph Robby Müller, Muriel Edelstein, Uli Kidicke, Wim Wenders, Masatoshi Nakajima, Masashi Chikamori m Laurent Petitgand ed Dominique Auvray

Nothing Barred
GB   1961   83m   bw
British Lion (Brian Rix, Darcy Conyers)

A burglar helps a noble lord steal one of his own paintings.
Leaden-footed farce.
w John Chapman d Darcy Conyers ph Geoffrey Faithfull m Ken Jones
☆ Brian Rix, Leo Franklyn, Naunton Wayne, Charles Heslop, John Slater, Vera Pearce

Nothing but a Man *
US   1964   95m   bw
Roemer-Young/DuArt (Robert Young, Michael Roemer, Robert Rubin)

In a small Southern town, a black railroad worker, who decides to marry and settle down, runs into trouble with the locals when he asserts his independence.
One of the first movies to treat the subject of racial discrimination without condescension, it is effective and engaging for the most part with its documentary-style approach, even though Abbey Lincoln's wife is too good to be true.
w Michael Roemer, Robert Young d Michael Roemer ph Robert Young ed Luke Bennett
☆ Ivan Dixon, Abbey Lincoln, Julius Harris, Gloria Foster, Martin Priest, Leonard Parker, Yaphet Kotto, Stanley Greene
  'A fine film – a first one that sets a towering standard for its makers.' – Judith Crist

Nothing but the Best **
GB   1964   99m   Eastmancolor
Anglo Amalgamated/Domino (David Deutsch)

An ambitious clerk learns to fight his way to the top by cheek and one-upmanship.
Hard, skilful, rather unattractive comedy with interesting social comments on its time.
w Frederic Raphael d Clive Donner ph Nicolas Roeg m Ron Grainer ad Reece Pemberton
☆ Alan Bates, Denholm Elliott, Harry Andrews, Millicent Martin, Pauline Delany
  'It is a film with a smooth, smiling elegant fun, witty but never concentrating on wit to the detriment of tension; it makes a logical step-by-step progression towards a climax which is hilarious in a Stygian way without resort to the usual bangabout.' – Dilys Powell

'The nightmare has already killed five people. Now it's yours to live!'

Nothing but the Night *
GB   1972   90m   Eastmancolor
Rank/Charlemagne (Anthony Nelson Keys)

The trustees of an orphanage die off mysteriously, and it seems that the orphans themselves are responsible.
Convoluted murder mystery with horror elements and a twist hardly worth waiting for; earnest performances help.
w Brian Hayles *novel* John Blackburn d Peter Sasdy ph Ken Talbot m Malcolm Williamson
☆ Christopher Lee, Peter Cushing, Diana Dors, Georgia Brown, Keith Barron, John Robinson

Nothing but the Truth
US   1941   90m   bw
Paramount (Arthur Hornlow Jnr)

A stockbroker takes a bet that he can tell the absolute truth for twenty-four hours.
Rather unsurprising version of a stage comedy previously filmed as a silent. The style one might expect from the team which made The Cat and the Canary.
w Don Hartman, Ken Englund *play* James Montgomery *novel* Frederic S. Isham d Elliott Nugent ph Charles Lang
☆ Bob Hope, Paulette Goddard, Edward Arnold, Leif Erickson, Glenn Anders, Helen Vinson, Grant Mitchell, Willie Best

Nothing but Trouble
US   1944   70m   bw
MGM (B. F. Ziedman)

A chef and butler accidentally prevent a poison plot against a young king.
Feebly-devised star comedy, their last for a big studio.
w Russel Rouse, Ray Golden d Sam Taylor ph Charles Salerno Jnr m Nathaniel Shilkret ad Cedric Gibbons, Henry McAfee ed Conrad Nervig
☆ Stan Laurel, Oliver Hardy, Mary Boland, Henry O'Neill, David Leland

Nothing but Trouble
US   1991   94m   Technicolor
Warner/Applied Action (Robert K. Weiss)

A New York couple find themselves stranded in a village where a centenarian judge has absolute rule.
Exceedingly dismal comedy, in which a group of self-indulgent comedians, having been given a great deal of rope, proceed to hang themselves; it is not a pretty sight.
wd Dan Aykroyd *story* Peter Aykroyd ph Dean Cundey m Michael Kamen pd William Sandell ed Malcolm Campbell, James Symons
☆ Chevy Chase, Dan Aykroyd, John Candy, Demi Moore, Valri Bromfield, Taylor Negron, Bertila Damas, Raymond J. Barry, Brian Doyle-Murray, Peter Aykroyd
  'Astonishingly poor effort … one of the longest 94 minutes on record.' – Variety
  'Combines absolute failure as a comedy with a surprisingly interesting and disgusting vision of grotesque America.' – Kim Newman, Sight and Sound

Nothing in Common
US   1986   118m   Metrocolor
Tri-Star/Rastar (Alexandra Rose)

Problems of an eccentric family when mum decides to walk out after 36 years.
Edgy comedy which misfires in all directions.
w Rick Podell, Michael Preminger d Garry Marshall m John A. Alonzo m Patrick Leonard
☆ Jackie Gleason, Eva Marie Saint, Tom Hanks, Hector Elizondo, Barry Corbin, Bess Armstrong

Nothing Lasts Forever *
US   1984   82m   bw/Metrocolor
MGM/Broadway (Lorne Michaels)

The adventures of an innocent returning from abroad and seeking artistic fulfilment in a New York he hardly recognizes.
Engagingly bizarre comedy, part parody of 30s biopics, which eventually goes out of control as it takes our hero on a shopping trip to the Moon.
wd Tom Schiller ph Fred Schuler m Howard Shore pd Woods Mackintosh ed Kathleen Dougherty, Margot Francis
☆ Zach Galligan, Apollonia Van Ravenstein, Lauren Tom, Dan Aykroyd, Imogene Coca, Anita Ellis, Eddie Fisher, Sam Jaffe, Bill Murray, Paul Rogers, Mort Sahl

Nothing Personal
US   1980   97m   Movielab
AIP (David M. Perlmutter)

A professor and a lady lawyer try to stop seal hunting.
The subject is an unsuitable starting point for a thin and zany comedy which gets nowhere and stays there.
w Robert Kaufman d George Bloomfield ph Arthur Ibbetson, Laszlo George m Peter Mann
☆ Donald Sutherland, Suzanne Somers, Lawrence Dane, Roscoe Lee Browne

Nothing Personal
GB/Ireland   1995   85m   Metrocolor
Film Four/Irish Film Board/British Screen/Little Bird (Jonathan Cavendish, Tracey Seaward)

In Belfast in the mid-70s, armed conflict between republican and loyalist paramilitary groups claims innocent lives.
A well-made drama of the Irish troubles, showing faults on both sides, but one that is likely to leave a viewer

little wiser, other than with the conclusion that violence causes more problems than it solves.
w Daniel Mornin *novel* All Our Fault by Daniel Mornin d Thaddeus O'Sullivan *ph* Dick Pope m Philip Appleby *pd* Mark Geraghty *ed* Michael Parker
☆ Ian Hart, John Lynch, James Frain, Michael Gambon, Gary Lydon, Ruaidhri Conroy, Maria Doyle Kennedy, Jeni Courtney, Gerard McSorley
'A film to laud for the courage and sincerity of its aspirations rather than its modest, perhaps muffled achievement.' – Trevor Johnston, *Sight and Sound*

'Boy Makes Girl Make Fool Of New York.'
Nothing Sacred ***
US 1937 77m Technicolor
David O. Selznick
▦ ◎ ◍
A girl thought to be dying of a rare disease is built up by the press into a national heroine; but the diagnosis was wrong.
Hollywood's most bitter and hilarious satire, with crazy comedy elements and superb wisecracks; a historical monument of screen comedy, though its freshness at the time can't now be recaptured.
w Ben Hecht *story* Letter to the Editor by James H. Street d William Wellman *ph* W. Howard Greene m Oscar Levant
☆ Carole Lombard, Fredric March, Walter Connolly, Charles Winninger, Sig Rumann, Frank Fay, Maxie Rosenbloom, Margaret Hamilton, Hedda Hopper, Monty Woolley, Hattie McDaniel, Olin Howland, John Qualen
DOCTOR (CHARLES WINNINGER): 'I'll tell you briefly what I think of newspapermen. The hand of God, reaching down into the mire, couldn't elevate one of them to the depths of degradation.'
EDITOR (WALTER CONNOLLY): 'I am sitting here, Mr Cook, toying with the idea of cutting out your heart and stuffing it – like an olive!'
'Hit comedy … will be one of the big grossers of the year.' – *Variety*
'Because it does hold up a mirror, even though a distorting mirror, to a very real world of ballyhoo and cheap sensationalism, the pleasure to be obtained from it is something more than the usual mulish guffaw.' – *Spectator*
† Refashioned in 1953 as a stage musical, *Hazel Flagg*, with Jule Styne; this in turn became a Martin and Lewis comedy *Living It Up* (Jerry Lewis in the Carole Lombard part).

'Slick advertising guy who's lost it. Small-time thief who can't find it. When life sucks this bad, you may as well blow it all…'
Nothing to Lose
US 1997 98m Technicolor Panavision
Buena Vista/Touchstone (Martin Bregman, Dan Jinks, Michael Bregman)
▦ ◎ ◎ ◎ ◍
Believing that his wife is having an affair with his boss, an advertising executive goes on the rampage with the aid of a petty thief.
Tired and dim-witted action comedy in desperate search of an audience.
wd Steve Oedekerk *ph* Donald E. Thorin m Robert Folk *pd* Maria Caso *ed* Malcolm Campbell
☆ Tim Robbins, Martin Lawrence, John C. McGinley, Giancarlo Esposito, Michael McKean, Susan Barnes
'Sharper and funnier than you'd expect from a racist, formulaic comedy starring a high-minded director and an angry sitcom star.' – *Entertainment Weekly*

'Fateful Fascination! Electric Tension!'
'The screen's top romantic stars in a melodramatic masterpiece!'
Notorious ***
US 1946 101m bw
RKO (Alfred Hitchcock)
▦ ◎ ◍
In Rio, a notorious lady marries a Nazi renegade to help the US government but finds herself falling in love with her contact.
Superb romantic suspenser containing some of Hitchcock's best work.
w Ben Hecht d Alfred Hitchcock *ph* Ted Tetzlaff m Roy Webb
☆ Cary Grant, Ingrid Bergman, Claude Rains, Louis Calhern, Leopoldine Konstantin, Reinhold Schünzel

'Velvet smooth in dramatic action, sharp and sure in its characters, and heavily charged with the intensity of warm emotional appeal.' – Bosley Crowther
'The suspense is terrific.' – *New Yorker*, 1976
'A film in the supercharged American idiom which made *Casablanca* popular.' – Hermione Rich Isaacs, *Theatre Arts*
⧧ Ben Hecht; Claude Rains

Notorious Gentleman: see The Rake's Progress (1945)

A Notorious Gentleman
US 1935 73m bw
Universal
A man plans murder and incriminates the victim's fiancée.
Basically intriguing crime yarn spoiled by over-enthusiastic direction.
w Leopold Atlas, Robert Trasker d Edward Laemmle
☆ Charles Bickford, Helen Vinson, Sidney Blackmer, Onslow Stevens, Dudley Digges
'Too heavily handled for first consideration.' – *Variety*

The Notorious Landlady
US 1962 127m bw
Columbia/Kohlmar/Quine (Fred Kohlmar)
An American diplomat in London takes rooms with a murder suspect; after many mysterious happenings he helps to clear her.
Flatly whimsical goings on in comical old London, complete with fog and eccentrics. The actors all try hard but are deflated by the script.
w Larry Gelbart, Richard Quine d Richard Quine *ph* Arthur E. Arling m George Duning
☆ Kim Novak, Jack Lemmon, Fred Astaire, Lionel Jeffries, Estelle Winwood, Maxwell Reed
'A picture that is entertaining and exciting, often simultaneously, and that ends with a wildly funny chase.' – Edith Oliver, *New Yorker*

The Notorious Sophie Lang
US 1934 60m bw
Paramount
A lady jewel thief matches wits with a rival from abroad.
Frothy crime comedy which isn't quite smart enough to avoid boredom.
w Anthony Veiller d Ralph Murphy
☆ Gertrude Michael, Paul Cavanagh, Arthur Byron, Alison Skipworth, Leon Errol
'No marquee strength, but nice pace and some genuine amusement.' – *Variety*
† There was a sequel in 1937, *Sophie Goes West*, also starring Gertrude Michael, directed by Charles Reisner.

Notre Histoire: see Our Story

La Notte *
Italy/France 1960 121m bw
Nepi/Sofitedip/Silver
◍
A moderately successful novelist and his wife begin to question their marriage and their life.
Slow but engaging character drama set during one night in Milan.
w Michelangelo Antonioni, Ennio Flaiano, Antonio Guerra d Michelangelo Antonioni *ph* Gianni di Venanzo m Giorgio Gaslini
☆ Marcello Mastroianni, Jeanne Moreau, Monica Vitti, Bernhard Wicki
'A film of supreme, of ferocious elegance: a film belonging in its rejection of the traditional forms of narrative to the new worlds of fiction.' – Dilys Powell

La Notte di San Lorenzo: see The Night of San Lorenzo

Le Notti di Cabiria: see Cabiria

Notting Hill **
US/GB 1999 123m DeLuxe
Polygram/Working Title (Duncan Kenworthy)
▦ ◎ ◍
In a fashionable part of London, a diffident English bookseller becomes romantically involved with a famous American film star.
Slight but clever and often funny romantic comedy, making witty use of national stereotypes.

w Richard Curtis d Roger Michell *ph* Michael Coulter m Trevor Jones *pd* Stuart Craig *ed* Nick Moore
☆ Julia Roberts, Hugh Grant, Hugh Bonneville, Emma Chambers, James Dreyfus, Rhys Ifans, Tim McInnerny, Gina McKee, Richard McCabe, Alec Baldwin
'Solid, crowd-pleasing entertainment.' – *Empire*
⊞ audience award

Nous Sommes Tous les Assassins *
France 1952 108m bw
UGC
aka: *Are We All Murderers?*
An illiterate youth is taught to kill during the war; afterwards he kills again for money and is sent for execution.
A solemn sermon on capital punishment, and a powerful though rather glib one.
w André Cayatte, Charles Spaak d André Cayatte *ph* Jean Bourgoin
☆ Marcel Mouloudji, Raymond Pellégrin, Antoine Balpêtre, Claude Laydu

Les Nouveaux Messieurs *
France 1928 135m bw silent
Albatros/Séquence
A glamorous dancer forsakes a count for a rising trade union official.
Lengthy political satire which caused a few headlines when first released.
w Charles Spaak, Jacques Feyder *play* Robert de Flers, Francis de Grosset d Jacques Feyder *ph* Georges Périnal, Maurice Defassiaux *ad* Lazare Meerson
☆ Albert Préjean, Gaby Morlay, Henri Roussel

Novecento: see 1900

A Novel Affair: see The Passionate Stranger

Novembermond
West Germany 1984 106m colour
ICA/Ottokar Runze Film/Sun 7
A Jewish refugee fleeing from Nazi Germany has a lesbian love affair in Germany.
Slight, anecdotal film with little insight into the period.
wd Alexandra von Grote *ph* Bernard Zitzermann *ad* Helger Gross, Jean-Pierre Balzerolla *ed* Susan Lahaye
☆ Gabrile Osburg, Christine Millet, Danièle Delorme, Bruno Pradal, Stéphane Garcin, Louise Martini

The Novices (dubbed)
France/Italy 1970 95m Eastmancolor
Scotia-Barber/Les Films La Boétie/Rizzoli (André Génovès)
original title: *Les Novices*
After trying to become a prostitute in Paris, a nun decides that convent life is best.
Occasionally amusing comedy, sabotaged by its unsympathetic and out of sync dubbing.
wd Guy Casaril *ph* Claude Lecomte m François de Roubaix *ed* Nicole Gauduchon
☆ Brigitte Bardot, Annie Girardot, Lucien Barjon, Angelo Bardi, Jean Carmet, Jess Hahn
† The film was cut to 90m on its British release.

Novyi Vavilon: see The New Babylon

Now About These Women … *
Sweden 1964 80m Eastmancolor
Svensk Filmindustri
aka: *All These Women*
A critic comes to stay with a famous cellist whose biography he is writing, but his efforts are hampered by all the women in the house.
Virtually indescribable black farce comedy which doesn't really work, yet, as always with this director, is continually of interest.
w Erland Josephson, Ingmar Bergman d Ingmar Bergman *ph* Sven Nykvist m Erik Nordgren
☆ Jarl Kulle, Georg Funkquist, Eva Dahlbeck, Karen Kavli, Harriet Andersson, Bibi Andersson, Gertrud Fridh

Now and Forever *
US 1934 82m bw
Paramount (Louis D. Lighton)
A jewel thief and his mistress are taught a thing or two by his small daughter.
Odd mixture of comedy and drama which was box-office at the time but seems pretty dated after nearly fifty years, though technically very smooth.

w Vincent Lawrence, Sylvia Thalberg d Henry Hathaway *ph* Harry Fischbeck
☆ Gary Cooper, Carole Lombard, Shirley Temple, Guy Standing, Charlotte Granville, Gilbert Emery, Henry Kolker
'Cinch b.o. entertainment.' – *Variety*
'Expertly contrived to furnish first-rate entertainment.' – Thornton Delehanty, *New York Post*

Now and Forever
GB 1955 91m Technicolor
ABPC/Mario Zampi
A lonely schoolgirl plans an elopement and is chased across England by two sets of parents.
Teenage romance with elements of both farce and melodrama. It seemed to please at the time.
w R. F. Delderfield, Michael Pertwee *play* The Orchard Walls by R. F. Delderfield d Mario Zampi *ph* Erwin Hillier m Stanley Black
☆ Janette Scott, Vernon Gray, Kay Walsh, Jack Warner, Pamela Brown, Charles Victor, Wilfrid Lawson, Marjorie Rhodes, Sonia Dresdel, Ronald Squire, David Kossoff

'A summer when four friends made a promise to return anytime they needed each other. Twenty years later, that time has come.'
Now and Then
US 1995 96m DeLuxe
First Independent/New Line/Moving Pictures (Suzanne Todd, Demi Moore)
▦ ▦
A novelist, an actress and a doctor meet at the home of a pregnant friend and recall their childhood friendship.
Routine coming-of-age drama, given an overtly sentimental and nostalgic treatment.
w I. Marlene King d Lesli Linka Glatter *ph* Ueli Steiger m Cliff Eidelman *pd* Gershon Ginsburg *ed* Jacqueline Cambas
☆ Rosie O'Donnell, Christina Ricci, Melanie Griffith, Thora Birch, Demi Moore, Gaby Hoffmann, Rita Wilson, Ashleigh Aston Moore, Janeane Garofalo, Lolita Davidovich
'Semi-autobiographical screenplay is so predictable, audiences may grow impatient while waiting for the inevitable to occur.' – *Variety*

Now Barabbas…
GB 1949 87m bw
Warner/Anatole de Grunwald
aka: *Now Barabbas Was a Robber*
Stories of men in prison.
Thinly intercut dramas; from a stage success.
w Anatole de Grunwald *play* William Douglas Home d Gordon Parry *ph* Otto Heller
☆ Richard Greene, Cedric Hardwicke, William Hartnell, Kathleen Harrison, Leslie Dwyer, Richard Burton, Kenneth More, Ronald Howard, Stephen Murray, Beatrice Campbell, Betty Ann Davies, Alec Clunes

Now Barabbas Was a Robber: see Now Barabbas…

Now I'll Tell
US 1934 72m bw
Fox (Winfield Sheehan)
GB title: *When New York Sleeps*
The story of Arnold Rothstein, gambler-racketeer of the twenties, as told by his widow.
Competent crime/domestic programmer.
wd Edwin Burke *ph* Ernest Palmer m Hugo Friedhofer
☆ Spencer Tracy, Helen Twelvetrees, Hobart Cavanaugh, Alice Faye, G. P. Huntley Jnr, Shirley Temple, Leon Ames
'In spite of the breezy sequences with which it starts, it quickly gets improbable and goes from bad to maudlin.' – Otis Ferguson

Now Voyager ***
US 1942 117m bw
Warner (Hal B. Wallis)
▦ ▦ ◎ ◍
A dowdy frustrated spinster takes the psychiatric cure and embarks on a doomed love affair.
A basically soggy script still gets by, and how, through the romantic magic of its stars, who were all at their best; and suffering in mink went over very big in wartime.
w Casey Robinson *novel* Olive Higgins Prouty d Irving Rapper *ph* Sol Polito m Max Steiner *ad* Robert Haas *ed* Warren Low

---

☆ *Bette Davis, Claude Rains, Paul Henreid*, Gladys Cooper, John Loder, Bonita Granville, Ilka Chase, Lee Patrick, Charles Drake, Franklin Pangborn, Janis Wilson

CHARLOTTE (BETTE DAVIS): 'Oh, Jerry, don't let's ask for the moon. We have the stars!'

'If it were better, it might not work at all. This way, it's a crummy classic.' – *New Yorker*, 1977

♪ Max Steiner

♑ Bette Davis; Gladys Cooper

Now You See Him Now You Don't

👫 US 1972 88m Technicolor

Walt Disney

Two students discover an elixir of invisibility and help prevent a gangster from taking over the college.

Flat Disney frolic with fair trick effects.

w Joseph L. McEveety d Robert Butler ph Frank Phillips m Robert F. Brunner sp Eustace Lycett, Danny Lee

☆ Kurt Russell, Cesar Romero, Joe Flynn, Jim Backus, William Windom, Edward Andrews, Richard Bakalyan

Nowhere *

US/France 1997 82m colour

Pathé/Kill/Desperate/Blurco/Why Not (Andrea Sperling, Gregg Araki)

A group of friends indulge in a variety of sexual experiences.

Delirious send-up of high-school movies – one character turns into a giant cockroach – with alienated teenagers indulging in polymorphous perversities.

wd Gregg Araki ph Arturo Smith pd Patti Podesta ed Gregg Araki

☆ James Duval, Rachel True, Nathan Bexton, Chiara Mastroianni, Debi Mazar, Kathleen Robertson, Joshua Gibran Mayweather, Christina Applegate, Jordan Ladd, Ryan Phillippe, Heather Graham

'Without a doubt his most accessible, sensual and superficially entertaining movie to date.' – *Emanuel Levy, Variety*

'Its storm of sex and violence celebrates American pop culture with punning, postmodern artifice.' – *Liese Spencer, Sight and Sound*

Nowhere to Go

GB 1958 87m bw

Ealing (Eric Williams)

A thief escapes from prison but can get no help from the underworld and is accidentally shot after being sheltered by a socialite.

Glum character melodrama which fails to sustain interest despite the best intentions.

w Seth Holt, Ken Tynan book Donald MacKenzie d Seth Holt ph Paul Beeson m Dizzy Reece

☆ George Nader, Maggie Smith, Bernard Lee, Geoffrey Keen, Andree Melly, Bessie Love, Howard Marion Crawford

'When the law can't protect the innocent ... it takes an outlaw to deliver justice.'

Nowhere to Run

US 1992 94m Technicolor

Columbia (Craig Baumgarten, Gary Adelson)

An escaped prisoner helps a widow and her two young sons who are being threatened by an evil property developer.

Tedious action movie with a little added sentimentality, intended, but failing, to give its star a wider appeal.

w Joe Eszterhas, Leslie Bohem, Randy Feldman d Robert Harmon ph David Gribble m Mark Isham pd Dennis Washington ed Zach Staenberg, Mark Helfrich

☆ Jean-Claude Van Damme, Rosanna Arquette, Kieran Culkin, Ted Levine, Tiffany Taubman, Edward Blatchford, Anthony Starke, Joss Ackland

'A relentlessly corny and shamelessly derivative vehicle.' – *Variety*

Noz w Wodzie: see *Knife in the Water*

Nuclear Run: see *The Chain Reaction*

The Nude Bomb

US 1980 94m Technicolor

Universal/Time-Life Films (Jennings Lang)

📀 📀

aka: *The Return of Maxwell Smart*

An incompetent secret agent chases a missile launching villain.

Curious and unsatisfactory attempt to revive a twenty-year-old TV situation comedy minus half its personnel.

w Arne Sultan, Bill Dana, Leonard B. Stern d Clive Donner ph Harry L. Wolf m Lalo Schifrin pd William Tuntke ed Walter Hannemann

☆ Don Adams, Sylvia Kristel, Dana Elcar, Rhonda Fleming, Andrea Howard, Norman Lloyd

'Fans of the vidshow will derive much more enjoyment by crowding round their television sets with a bowl of popcorn watching *Get Smart* reruns.' – *Variety*

La Nuit Américaine: see *Day for Night*

La Nuit de Varennes *

France/Italy 1982 165m Eastmancolor Technovision

Electric/Contemporary/Gaumont-FR3/Opera Film (Renzo Rossellini)

📀

In the early days of the French Revolution, a mixed coachload of travellers, including Restif de la Bretonne, Tom Paine and Casanova, make their way to Varennes, where King Louis is held captive.

Moderately engaging historical tale that does not take itself, or the times, too seriously.

w Sergio Amidei, Ettore Scola d Ettore Scola ph Armando Nannuzzi m Armando Trovajoli pd Dante Ferretti ed Raimondo Crociani

☆ Jean-Louis Barrault, Marcello Mastroianni, Hanna Schygulla, Harvey Keitel, Jean-Claude Brialy, Daniel Gelin, Andrea Ferreol, Michael Vitold, Laura Betti

Nuit et Brouillard: see *Night and Fog*

Les Nuits de la Pleine Lune: see *Full Moon in Paris*

Les Nuits Fauves: see *Savage Nights*

Number One

US 1969 105m DeLuxe

Walter Seltzer

Age and injury overtake a quarterback, once regarded as the greatest.

Unconvincing sporting drama, which plods around its subject-matter without creating anything of even passing interest.

w David Moessinger d Tom Gries ph Michel Hugo m Dominic Frontiere ad Arthur Loel ed Richard Brockway

☆ Charlton Heston, Jessica Walter, Bruce Dern, John Randolph, Diana Muldaur, Al Hirt, Roy Jenson, Mike Henry, Bobby Troup, Richard Elkins, Ernie Barnes

Number One

GB 1984 106m Technicolor

Videoform (Mark Forstater, Raymond Day)

Adventures of a snooker hall hustler.

Unappetizingly foul-mouthed low-life saga.

w G. F. Newman d Les Blair ph Bahram Manocheri m David Mackay pd Martin Johnson ed Jon Gregory

☆ Bob Geldof, Mel Smith, Alison Steadman, P. H. Moriarty, Phil Daniels, Alfred Molina

Number One Fan

US 1994 93m CFI color

MCEG Sterling

📀 📀

A film star is seduced by an unbalanced female fan, who is determined to have him for herself.

Lurid and increasingly risible thriller, notable only for the number of children of successful stars that it features.

w Anthony Laurence Greene d Jane Simpson ph Sead Mutarevic m Robert J. Walsh pd Gary Randall ed Ivan Ladizinsky

☆ Chad McQueen, Catherine Mary Stewart, Rennee Ammann, Paul Bartel, Charles Matthau, Hoyt Axton, Dean Morris, Mary Woronow, Eric Da Re, Dick Miller

Number One with a Bullet

US 1987 101m colour

Cannon

📀

An LA detective is obsessed with busting a big drug dealer who is also a pillar of the community.

Ho-hum policier with routine violence.

w Gail Morgan Hickman and others d Jack Smight

☆ Robert Carradine, Billy Dee Williams, Valerie Bertinelli, Peter Graves, Doris Roberts

Number Seventeen *

GB 1932 63m bw

BIP (John Maxwell)

A girl jewel thief reforms and helps the police track down her former gang.

Minor Hitchcock thriller largely confined to a single interior until the final train chase, which despite obvious models remains exhilarating.

w Alfred Hitchcock, Alma Reville, Rodney Ackland play J. Jefferson Farjeon d Alfred Hitchcock ph Jack Cox

☆ Leon M. Lion, Anne Grey, John Stuart, Donald Calthrop, Barry Jones, Garry Marsh

'Only spasmodically good photography and usual slow tempo British direction. Wonder why they can't speed up a picture? Maybe it's the tea.' – *Variety*

† The same play had been filmed as a silent in 1928 by Geza Bolvary, with Guy Newall; it was shot in Germany.

The Nun and the Devil

Italy/France 1973 102m Technicolor

PAC/Splendida/Jacques Leitienne (Tonino Cervi)

📀

original title: *Monache di Sant'Arcangelo*

aka: *The Nuns of Saint Archangel*

At an Italian convent in the 1570s, one sister uses any means at her disposal to become Mother Superior.

Sex and death among the nuns turns out to be a dull affair.

wd Domenico Paolella story Stendhal ph Giuseppe Ruzzolini m Piero Piccioni ed Nino Baragli

☆ Anne Heywood, Ornella Muti, Duilio del Prete, Martine Brochard, Luc Merenda, Claudia Gravi

'Basically a sexploitation piece of exceeding dignity, it boasts a modestly attractive visual surface, with deft photography and neat compositions, and suffers from a debilitating lack of dramatic impetus.' – *Geoff Brown, MFB*

† The version released in Britain ran for 93m.

The Nun and the Sergeant

US 1962 74m bw

UA/Springfield

In Korea, a tough sergeant commanding a 'dirty dozen' mission is joined by a schoolgirl and a nun.

Minor war adventure, moderately well done but highly unconvincing.

w Don Cerveris d Franklin Adreon ph Paul Ivano m Jerry Fielding

☆ Anna Sten, Robert Webber, Leo Gordon, Hari Rhodes

The Nuns of Saint Archangel: see *The Nun and the Devil*

Nuns on the Run

👫 GB 1990 92m Technicolor

Palace/Handmade Films (Michael White)

📀 📀 📀

Two petty criminals disguise themselves as nuns to escape capture.

Broad, slapstick comedy that provides scant amusement, although it went down well in America.

wd Jonathan Lynn ph Michael Garfath m Hidden Faces pd Simon Holland ed David Martin

☆ Eric Idle, Robbie Coltrane, Camille Coduri, Janet Suzman, Doris Hare, Lila Kaye, Robert Patterson, Robert Morgan, Winston Dennis, Tom Hickey

'Filmed in Belgium, Italy, Africa ... and mostly in the conscience of a beautiful young girl!'

The Nun's Story ***

US 1959 151m Technicolor

Warner (Henry Blanke)

📀 📀 📀 🎧

A Belgian girl joins a strict order, endures hardship in the Congo, and finally returns to ordinary life.

The fascinating early sequences of convent routine are more interesting than the African adventures, but this is a careful, composed and impressive film with little Hollywood exaggeration.

w Robert Anderson book Kathryn C. Hulme d Fred Zinnemann ph Franz Planer m Franz Waxman ed Walter Thompson

☆ Audrey Hepburn, Peter Finch, Edith Evans, Peggy Ashcroft, Dean Jagger, Mildred Dunnock, Patricia Collinge, Beatrice Straight

'A major directorial achievement ... the best study of the religious life ever made in the American cinema.' – *Albert Johnson, Film Quarterly*

♑ best picture; Robert Anderson; Fred Zinnemann; Franz Planer; Franz Waxman; Audrey Hepburn; editing

♔ Audrey Hepburn

I Nuovi Barbari: see *The New Barbarians*

Nuovo Cinema Paradiso: see *Cinema Paradiso*

Nurse Edith Cavell

US 1939 98m bw

Imperator/RKO

The story of a British nurse executed as a spy during World War I; previously filmed in 1930 as *Dawn* with Sybil Thorndike.

This is a moderately touching but uninspired treatment.

w Michael Hogan novel *Dawn* by Reginald Berkeley d Herbert Wilcox m Anthony Collins

☆ Anna Neagle, George Sanders, May Robson, Edna May Oliver, Alan Marshal

'Excellently produced documentary film, but not for general audience appeal ... no light moments to relieve the tragic aspects.' – *Variety*

'Miss Neagle looked nice as Queen Victoria, she looks just as nice as Nurse Cavell: she moves rigidly on to the set, as if wheels were concealed under the stately skirt: she says her piece with flat dignity and trolleys out again – rather like a mechanical marvel from the World's Fair.' – *Graham Greene, The Spectator*

♑ Anthony Collins

Nurse on Wheels

GB 1963 86m bw

Anglo Amalgamated/GHW (Peter Rogers)

Adventures of a young District Nurse.

Part sentimental, part Carry On; watchable of its curious kind.

w Norman Hudis novel *Nurse Is a Neighbour* by Joanna Jones d Gerald Thomas ph Alan Hume m Eric Rogers

☆ Juliet Mills, Ronald Lewis, Joan Sims, Raymond Huntley, Athene Seyler

The Nursemaid Who Disappeared

GB 1939 86m bw

Warner

A domestic agency hides a gang of kidnappers.

Fairly pleasing mystery of the old school.

w Paul Gangelin and Connery Chappell novel Philip MacDonald d Arthur Woods

☆ Arthur Margetson, Peter Coke, Lesley Brook, Edward Chapman, Coral Browne, Martita Hunt

The Nurse's Secret

US 1941 56m bw

First National/Warner

A hired nurse solves her patient's murder.

Potboiling remake of Miss Pinkerton, rather better written than the original.

w Anthony Coldeway d Noel M. Smith

☆ Lee Patrick, Regis Toomey, Julie Bishop, Charles D. Waldron, Charles Trowbridge, Leonard Mudie

Nutcracker

GB 1982 101m Eastmancolor

Rank/Ezshaw (Panos Nicolaou)

A Russian ballerina defects in London but finds that she is being used for business/political purposes.

Weird, dated and utterly mediocre melodrama with pauses for sexual revels. Not a goer.

w Raymond Christodoulou *d* Anwar Kawadri
ph Peter Jessop *m* Simon Park
☆ Joan Collins, Carol White, Paul Nicholas,
Finola Hughes, William Franklyn, Murray Melvin

Nutcracker – The Motion Picture *
🏋 US   1986   85m   colour
Entertainment/Hyperion/Kushner/Locke
📼 ▬ 📀 ◎

A movie based on the Pacific Northwest Ballet
company's version of the classic ballet.
*The restless and moody direction does not always do
justice to the dancing, although it effectively conjures a
slightly sinister atmosphere.*
d Carroll Ballard *ph* Stephen M. Burum
m Tchaikovsky *pd* Maurice Sendak *ed* John
Nutt, Michael Silvers
☆ Hugh Bigney, Vanessa Sharp, Patricia Barker,
Wade Walthall

Nuts
US   1987   116m   Technicolor
Warner (Barbra Streisand)
📼 ▬ 📀

Classy prostitute kills a client; at her trial she battles
against attempts to find her mentally unstable.
Star vehicle, strictly for fans.
w Tom Topor and others *play* Tom Topor
d Martin Ritt *ph* Andrzej Bartkowiak *m* Barbra
Streisand *pd* Joel Schiller
☆ Barbra Streisand, Richard Dreyfuss, Maureen
Stapleton, Karl Malden, Eli Wallach

The Nutty Professor
🏋 US   1963   107m   Technicolor
Paramount/Jerry Lewis (Ernest D. Glucksman)
▬ 📀

An eccentric chemistry professor discovers an
elixir which turns him into a pop idol.

*Long dreary comedy which contains patches of its star
at somewhere near his best; but even Dr Jekyll and Mr
Hyde is funnier.*
w Jerry Lewis, Bill Richmond *d* Jerry Lewis
ph W. Wallace Kelley *m* Walter Scharf *ad* Hal
Pereira, Walter Tyler *ed* John Woodcock
☆ Jerry Lewis, Stella Stevens, Howard Morris,
Kathleen Freeman, Del Moore, Les Brown and His
Band of Renown

The Nutty Professor *
US   1996   95m   DeLuxe
UIP/Universal/Imagine (Brian Grazer, Russell
Simmons)
📼 ▬ 📀 ◎ ◎

A shy, fat chemistry professor discovers a
formula that turns him into a slim, brash man-
about-town.
*One of the few remakes that is an improvement on the
original, with Murphy demonstrating his abilities by
playing an entire family at dinner; the humour is
broad, but occasionally beguiling.*
w David Sheffield, Barry W. Blaustein, Tom
Shadyac, Steve Oedekerk *film* Jerry Lewis, Bill
Richmond *d* Tom Shadyac *ph* Julio Macat
m David Newman *pd* William Elliott *ed* Don
Zimmerman *sp* make
☆ Eddie Murphy, Jada Pinkett, James Coburn,
Larry Miller, Dave Chappelle, John Ales
'Combining the riotously funny and the sweetly
sentimental, the new outing is a welcome entry
in a season suffering from a paucity of comedy.' –
Variety
† It was among the box-office successes of 1996,
grossing around $254m around the world.
†† A sequel is planned.
👤 Rick Baker, David Leroy Anderson

🏋 film suitable for
family viewing   📼 VHS video-cassette for
the British PAL system   📼 VHS video-cassette for the British
PAL system in wide screen-format   ◎ Video cassette in a computer-
colourised version   ▬ American NTSC video-cassette   📀 Laser disc

O. C. and Stiggs

US 1987 109m Metrocolor
MGM (Robert Altman, Peter Newman)
Two teenagers spend their summer playing practical jokes, particularly on their obnoxious neighbour.
Tedious comedy with an air of desperate improvisation about it.
w Donald Cantrell, Ted Mann *story* Tod Carroll, Ted Mann *d* Robert Altman *ph* Pierre Mignot *m* King Sunny Ade and his African Beats *pd* Scott Bushnell *ed* Elizabeth Kling
☆ Daniel H. Jenkins, Neill Barry, Paul Dooley, Jane Curtin, Jon Cryer, Ray Walston, Louis Nye, Tina Louise, Dennis Hopper, Melvin Van Peebles

O Dragao da Maldade contra o Santo Guerreiro: see Antonio das Mortes

O.H.M.S.

GB 1936 86m bw
Gaumont (Geoffrey Barkas)
US title: *You're in the Army Now*
British forces fighting in China are joined by an American gangster on the run, who dies a hero.
Stiff-upper-lip adventure of no particular interest.
w Bryan Edgar Wallace, Austin Melford, A. R. Rawlinson *story* Lesser Samuels, Ralph Bettinson *d* Raoul Walsh *ph* Roy Kellino
☆ John Mills, Wallace Ford, Anna Lee, Frank Cellier, Grace Bradley, Frederick Leister
'As near 100% entertainment value as can reasonably be hoped for without the employment of a superstar, super-cast, super-director and super-production.' – *Variety*

O. Henry's Full House **

US 1952 117m bw
TCF (André Hakim)
GB title: *Full House*
John Steinbeck introduces five stories by O. Henry.
Modelled on the success of Quartet *(qv), this compendium was less successful because these turn-of-the-century tales of New York depend less on character than on the sting in the tail; but the cast and production were lavish.*
The Cop and the Anthem:
w Lamar Trotti *d* Henry Koster *ph* Lloyd Ahern with Charles Laughton, David Wayne, Marilyn Monroe
The Clarion Call:
w Richard Breen *d* Henry Hathaway *ph* Lucien Ballard with Dale Robertson, Richard Widmark
The Last Leaf:
w Ivan Goff, Ben Roberts *d* Jean Negulesco *ph* Joe MacDonald with Anne Baxter, Jean Peters, Gregory Ratoff
The Ransom of Red Chief:
w Nunnally Johnson *d* Howard Hawks *ph* Milton Krasner with Fred Allen, Oscar Levant
The Gift of the Magi:
w Walter Bullock *d* Henry King *ph* Joe MacDonald with Jeanne Crain, Farley Granger
m Alfred Newman

'Smile while you're makin' it/Laugh while you're takin' it/Even though you're fakin' it/Nobody's gonna know...'
O Lucky Man! ***

GB 1973 174m Eastmancolor
Warner/Memorial/Sam (Michael Medwin, Lindsay Anderson)
The odyssey of a trainee salesman who after a while as an international financier settles down to be a do-gooder.
Modern revue-style version of Candide/Decline and Fall; *very hit or miss in style and effect, and hellishly overlong, but with good things along the way.*
w David Sherwin *d* Lindsay Anderson
ph Miroslav Ondricek *m* Alan Price *pd* Jocelyn Herbert

☆ *Malcolm McDowell, Arthur Lowe, Ralph Richardson, Rachel Roberts, Helen Mirren, Mona Washbourne, Dandy Nichols*
'A sort of mod Pilgrim's Progress.' – *New Yorker*
🎵 Alan Price; Arthur Lowe

O Mary This London

GB 1994 90m colour
BBC (Helen Greaves)
Two Irish teenagers and their girlfriend come to London in search of adventure and an abortion.
A desultory, episodic road movie that manages to caricature the English and the Irish without creating any identity of its own.
w Shane Connaughton *d* Suri Krishnamma
ph Sean Van Hales *m* Stephen Warbeck *ed* Sue Wyatt
☆ Jason Barry, Oba Seagrave, Dylan Tighe, Ram John Holder, Lesley Manville, John Otway
'The writer of this dismal, overlong farrago did his research in three London hostels; which suggests that the young Irish people he talked to must enjoy playing up all the most damaging stereotypes of their nation.' – *Hugh Hebert, Guardian*
'An implausible production, full of cultural clichés and based on a plot which threw in a dollop of mindless violence whenever things began to pall. The fact that much of the dialogue sounded like a preliminary read-through by an amateur dramatic society might be taken as a clever way of symbolising the inarticulateness of the characters, but somehow I don't think it was that smart.' – *John Naughton, Observer*
† Seen first in BBC-TV's *Screen Two* series, it was shown in cinemas in the United States.

'He's deep in danger, deeper in love!'
O.S.S. *

US 1946 107m bw
Paramount (Richard Maibaum)
American spies are parachuted into France in 1943.
Espionage heroics with an unhappy ending and a slight documentary flavour. Not bad of its kind.
w Richard Maibaum *d* Irving Pichel *ph* Lionel Lindon *m* Daniele Amfitheatrof, Heinz Roemheld
☆ Alan Ladd, Geraldine Fitzgerald, Patric Knowles, John Hoyt, Don Beddoe

Oasis

France/Germany 1956 100m Eastmancolor
Cinemascope
TCF/Roxy/Criterion (Gerd Oswald, Luggi Waldleitner)
An ex-pilot gets involved with two attractive women who are smuggling gold across the Sahara.
Glum romantic adventure.
w Joseph and Georges Kessel *d* Yves Allégret
ph Roger Hubert *m* Paul Misraki
☆ Pierre Brasseur, Michèle Morgan, Cornell Borchers, Grégoire Aslan

Obchod na Korze: see The Shop on Main Street

Obecna Skola: see Elementary School

Oberst Redl: see Colonel Redl

The Oberwald Mystery

Italy 1980 129m colour
Artificial Eye/Polytel International/RAI (Sergio Benevenuti, Alessandro von Norman)
original title: *Il Mistero di Oberwald*
The queen of a Middle European country falls in love with an assassin who looks like her dead husband.
Shot on videotape and transferred to film, it is in unpleasing colour and takes an understated approach to a melodramatic work.
w Michelangelo Antonioni, Tonino Guerra
play L'Aigle A Deux Têtes by Jean Cocteau

d Michelangelo Antonioni *ph* Luciano Tovoli
m Strauss, Schoenberg, Brahms *ad* Mischa Scandella *ed* Michelangelo Antonioni, Francesco Grandoni
☆ Monica Vitti, Franco Branciaroli, Luigi Diberti, Elisabetta Pozzi, Amad Saha Alan, Paolo Bonacelli

Object of Beauty

US/GB 1991 103m colour
Samuel Goldwyn/Winston/Avenue/BBC (Jon S. Denny, Alex Gohar)
In a luxurious London hotel, a deaf-mute maid steals a Henry Moore bronze from the bedroom of an adulterous American couple.
Dull and muted romantic comedy with obnoxious protagonists.
wd Michael Lindsay-Hogg *ph* David Watkin
m Tom Bahler *pd* Derek Dodd *ed* Ruth Foster
☆ John Malkovich, Andie MacDowell, Lolita Davidovich, Rudi Davies, Joss Ackland, Bill Paterson, Ricci Harnett, Peter Riegert, Jack Shepherd
'A mildly diverting but empty picture.' – *Variety*

'Sometimes The Most Desirable Relationship Is The One You Can't Have.'
The Object of My Affection

US 1998 111m DuArt
TCF (Laurence Mark)
As they lose their existing boyfriends, a pregnant woman and a gay teacher develop a close relationship.
Another contemporary American take on relationships, which seems predicated on a dislike of sexual activities, insisting that a homosexual man is a woman's best friend.
w Wendy Wasserstein *novel* Stephen McCauley
d Nicholas Hytner *ph* Oliver Stapleton
m George Fenton *pd* Jane Musky *ed* Tariq Anwar
☆ Jennifer Aniston, Paul Rudd, Alan Alda, Nigel Hawthorne, John Pankow, Tim Daly, Allison Janney, Steve Zahn, Amo Gulinello, Bruce Altman, Kevin Carroll
'Tries to mix the messy realities of mismatched relationships with the structural neatness of a musical-comedy view of the world, with mild, occasionally diverting results.' – *Todd McCarthy, Variety*

Objective Burma! *

US 1945 142m bw
Warner (Jerry Wald)
Exploits of an American platoon in the Burma campaign.
Overlong but vivid war actioner which caused a diplomatic incident by failing to mention the British contribution.
w Ranald MacDougall, Lester Cole, Alvah Bessie
d Raoul Walsh *ph* James Wong Howe *m* Franz Waxman *ed* George Amy
☆ Errol Flynn, James Brown, William Prince, George Tobias, Henry Hull, Warner Anderson, John Alvin
'At the rate Errol Flynn and co. knock off the Japanese, it may make you wonder why the war need outlast next weekend.' – *Time*
'I am amazed that Warner Brothers ever made it, or having made it failed to think again and smother it.' – *Reynolds News*
† The film was not released in Britain until 1952, and then with an apologetic prologue.
𝄞 original story (Alvah Bessie); Franz Waxman; George Amy

The Obliging Young Lady

US 1941 80m bw
RKO
A secretary escorts a wealthy child out of town while her parents wrangle over custody.
Tedious comedy with interest occasionally provided by the supporting cast.
w Frank Ryan, Bert Granet *d* Richard Wallace
☆ Joan Carroll, Ruth Warrick, Edmond O'Brien, Eve Arden, Franklin Pangborn, Marjorie Gateson, John Miljan, George Cleveland, Luis Alberni, Charles Lane

The Oblong Box

GB 1969 95m Eastmancolor
AIP (Gordon Hessler)
One of two 19th-century brothers is mysteriously disfigured and buried alive; he recovers and runs amok.
Nastily effective horror film with a frail story but good background detail.
w Lawrence Huntington *d* Gordon Hessler
ph John Coquillon *m* Harry Robinson
☆ Vincent Price, Christopher Lee, Alastair Williamson, Hilary Dwyer, Peter Arne, Maxwell Shaw, Rupert Davies
'A pervasive aura of evil.' – *MFB*

Obsessed: see The Late Edwina Black (1951)

Obsessed

Canada 1989 100m colour
Telescene (Robin Spry, Jamie Brown)
A mother is determined to track down and bring to justice the hit-and-run driver who killed her skateboarding son.
A movie as relentlessly one-track as its title suggests; it is well enough done, but somewhat wearing, and less than believable, by the end.
w Douglas Bowie, Robin Spry *novel* Hit and Run by Tom Alderman *d* Robin Spry *ph* Ron Stannett *m* Jean-Alain Roussel *pd* Claude Paré *ed* Diann Ilnicki
☆ Kerrie Keane, Daniel Pilon, Saul Rubinek, Alan Thicke, Mireille Deyglun, Leif Anderson, Colleen Dewhurst

Obsession *

GB 1948 98m bw
GFD/Independent Sovereign (Nat Bronsten)
US title: *The Hidden Room*
A doctor decides to kill his wife's lover by imprisoning him in a lonely cellar while he accumulates enough acid to destroy all traces of his body.
Implausible, overstretched thriller, carefully enough done to be bearable.
w Alec Coppel *play* A Man About a Dog by Alec Coppel *d* Edward Dmytryk *ph* C. Pennington Richards *m* Nino Rota
☆ Robert Newton, Sally Gray, Phil Brown, Naunton Wayne

Obsession *

US 1976 98m Technicolor Panavision
Columbia (Robert S. Bremson)
A widower with guilt feelings meets the double of his dead wife and is drawn into a strange plot.
Hitchcockian adventure with a few unwise attempts at seriousness, à la Don't Look Now. Generally entertaining, skilled and quite rewarding.
w Paul Schrader *d* Brian de Palma *ph* Vilmos Zsigmond *m* Bernard Herrmann
☆ Cliff Robertson, Geneviève Bujold, John Lithgow, Sylvia Williams, Wanda Blackman, Patrick McNamara
'An unholy mess. Intended as an *hommage* to Hitchcock ... it attitudinizes [also] towards the

---

old-fashioned tearjerker and towards the sophisticated European film, with cultural references strewn like breadcrumbs along the way of Hansel and Gretel…' – *John Simon, New York*

'Merely a mannered cerebral exercise without any emotional underpinning or unconscious feeling of its own.' – *Andrew Sarris, Village Voice*

♫ Bernard Herrmann

O'Cangaceiro: see *The Bandit*

Occupe-Toi d'Amélie ***
France   1949   95m   bw
Lux (Louis Wipf)
aka: *Keep an Eye on Amelia*

A Parisian cocotte agrees to go through a mock marriage ceremony with her lover's best friend to fool his uncle: but the ceremony turns out to be real.
Hilarious and superbly stylized adaptation of a period boulevard farce: the play starts in a theatre, showing the audience, but gradually cinema technique takes over. Acting, timing and editing are all impeccable, and the production stands as a model of how such things should be done.
w Jean Aurenche, Pierre Bost *play* Georges Feydeau d Claude Autant-Lara ph André Bac m René Cloërc

☆ Danielle Darrieux, Jean Desailly, Bourvil, Carette, Grégoire Aslan

'Even those who do not respond to the artificialities of French vaudeville will admire the ingenuity and elegance of treatment.' – *Gavin Lambert, MFB*

'Most people, I think, could see it with considerable enjoyment even twice on the same evening.' – *Richard Mallett, Punch*

Ocean's Eleven *
US   1960   128m   Technicolor   Panavision
Warner/Dorchester (Lewis Milestone)
▦   ℚ

A gang of friends plan to rob a Las Vegas casino.
Self-indulgent and overlong caper comedy which marked Hollywood's entry into a subsequently much overworked field. In this case the plot stops all too frequently for guest spots and in-jokes.
w Harry Brown, Charles Lederer d Lewis Milestone ph William H. Daniels m Nelson Riddle

☆ Frank Sinatra, Peter Lawford, Sammy Davis Jnr, Richard Conte, Dean Martin, Angie Dickinson, Cesar Romero, Joey Bishop, Patrice Wymore, Akim Tamiroff, Henry Silva, Ilka Chase

October ****
USSR   1927   95m   bw   silent
Sovkino
▦   ▤   ℚ   ⊚

In 1917, the Kerensky regime is overthrown by the Bolsheviks.
A propaganda masterpiece whose images have all too often been mistaken and used for genuine newsreel. Cinematically, an undoubted masterpiece.
w Sergei M. Eisenstein, Grigory Alexandrov d Sergei M. Eisenstein ph Edouard Tissé, V. Popov

The October Man **
GB   1947   98m   bw
GFD/Two Cities (Eric Ambler)
▤

After an accident which causes a head injury and subsequent depression, a lonely man staying at a small hotel is suspected of a local murder.
Nice blend of character study, mystery and suspense, with excellent attention to suburban detail.
w Eric Ambler d Roy Baker ph Erwin Hillier

☆ John Mills, Joan Greenwood, Edward Chapman, Kay Walsh, Catherine Lacey, Joyce Carey, Adrianne Allen, Felix Aylmer

'This film of psychological suspense tells its complicated story with complete clarity, but it is mainly to be noted for its settings.' – *Basil Wright, 1972*

'A new type of thriller in which tension is heightened by the vivid realism of its setting and the complete credibility of its characters.' – *Reynolds News*

October Moth
GB   1959   54m   bw
Independent Artists
A mentally retarded farmhand goes berserk after causing a fatal car crash.

Unattractive and singularly pointless little melodrama which neither edifies nor entertains.
wd John Kruse ph Michael Reed m Humphrey Searle

☆ Lana Morris, Lee Patterson, Peter Dyneley, Robert Cawdron

'A boy who could see the future. A father stuck in the past. A dream that wouldn't die.'
October Sky
US   1999   107m   DeLuxe   Panavision
Universal Pictures (Charles Gordon, Larry Franco)
Inspired by the sight of Sputnik, a teenager in a coal-mining town decides to build his own rocket with a little help from his friends.
Based on the biography of a man who became a NASA engineer, this is a gently nostalgic flag-waver of small-town Americana in the 50s, amiable but forgettable.
w Lewis Colick *book* Rocket Boys by Homer H. Hickam Jnr d Joe Johnston ph Fred Murphy m Mark Isham pd Barry Robinson ed Robert Dalva

☆ Jake Gyllenhaal, Chris Cooper, Laura Dern, Chris Owen, William Lee Scott, Chad Lindberg, Natalie Canerday, Scott Miles, Randy Stripling, Chris Ellis

'A feelgood movie of some power.' – *Empire*

Octopussy
♙♙   GB   1983   131m   Technicolor
Panavision
Eon/Danjaq (Albert R. Broccoli)
▦   ▤   ℚ

James Bond takes on an evil Afghan prince and a glamorous woman who plan between them to plunder Tsarist treasures.
Bond at the end of his tether: such far-stretched adventures have become merely a tedious way of passing the time.
w George MacDonald Fraser, Richard Maibaum, Michael G. Wilson d John Glen ph Alan Hume m John Barry pd Peter Lamont

☆ Roger Moore, Maud Adams, Louis Jourdan, Kristina Wayborn, Kabir Bedi, Desmond Llewelyn, Lois Maxwell

'As the films drift further and further into self-parody, no one seems to notice and no one (at any rate in box office terms) seems to mind.' – *Nick Roddick, MFB*

The Odd Couple **
US   1968   105m   Technicolor   Panavision
Paramount (Howard W. Koch)
▤   ℚ

A fussy divorce-shocked newswriter moves in with his sloppy sportscaster friend, and they get on each other's nerves.
Straight filming of a funny play which sometimes seems lost on the wide screen, but the performances are fine.
w Neil Simon *play* Neil Simon d Gene Saks ph Robert B. Hauser m Neal Hefti

☆ Jack Lemmon, Walter Matthau, John Fiedler, Herb Edelman, David Sheiner, Larry Haines, Monica Evans, Carole Sheely, Iris Adrian

OSCAR (WALTER MATTHAU): 'I can't take it anymore, Felix. I'm crackin' up. Everything you do irritates me. And when you're not here, the things I know you're gonna do when you come in irritate me. You leave me little notes on my pillow. I told you 158 times I cannot stand little notes on my pillow. "We are all out of cornflakes, F.U." It took me three hours to figure out that F.U. was Felix Ungar. It's not your fault, Felix. It's a rotten combination, that's all.'

♫ Neil Simon

The Odd Couple II
US   1998   96m   DeLuxe   Panavision
UIP/Paramount (Neil Simon, Robert W. Cort, David Madden)
▦   ▤

The adventures of two fathers, whose children are marrying one another, on the road to Los Angeles.
Not content with the derivative Grumpy Men series, Lemmon and Matthau revive their earlier, grumpiest success; but it lacks any semblance of life.
w Neil Simon d Howard Deutch ph Jamie Anderson m Alan Silvestri pd Dan Bishop ed Seth Flaum

☆ Jack Lemmon, Walter Matthau, Christine Baranski, Barnard Hughes, Jonathan Silverman, Jean Smart, Lisa Waltz

'The film feels like an extended television episode.' – *Sight and Sound*

The Odd Job
GB   1978   86m   colour
Charisma/Steve O'Rourke (Mark Forstater, Graham Chapman)
▦

A husband, upset because his wife has left him, hires an odd-job man to kill him; then his wife returns…
Listless comedy that lacks the necessary invention or style to be funny.
w Bernard McKenna, Graham Chapman d Peter Medak ph Ken Hodges m Howard Blake ad Tony Curtis ed Barrie Vince

☆ Graham Chapman, David Jason, Simon Williams, Diana Quick, Edward Hardwicke, Bill Paterson, Michael Elphick, Joe Melia, Carolyn Seymour, Richard O'Brien

Odd Man Out ***
GB   1946   115m   bw
GFD/Two Cities (Carol Reed)
▦   ▤   ℚ   ⊚
US title: *Gang War*

An IRA gunman, wounded and on the run in Belfast, is helped and hindered by a variety of people.
Superbly crafted but rather empty dramatic charade, visually and emotionally memorable but with nothing whatever to say.
w F. L. Green, R. C. Sherriff *novel* F. L. Green d Carol Reed ph Robert Krasker m William Alwyn ad Roger Furse ed Fergus McDonnell

☆ James Mason, Robert Newton, Kathleen Ryan, F. J. McCormick, Cyril Cusack, Robert Beatty, Fay Compton, Dan O'Herlihy, Denis O'Dea, Maureen Delany, Joseph Tomelty, William Hartnell

'The story seems to ramify too much, to go on too long, and at its unluckiest to go arty. Yet detail by detail *Odd Man Out* is made with great skill and imaginativeness and with a depth of ardour that is very rare.' – *James Agee*

'Quite simply the most imaginative film yet produced in England, comparable with *Quai des Brumes* and *Le Jour se Lève*.' – *William Whitebait, New Statesman*

♫ Fergus McDonnell
♙ best British picture

Odds against Tomorrow *
US   1959   96m   bw
UA/Harbel (Robert Wise)
▤   ∩

Three crooks plan to rob a bank, but two of them cause the enterprise to fail because of their own racist hatreds.
Sour, glossy crime thriller with elementary social significance.
w John O. Killens, Nelson Gidding *novel* William P. McGivern d Robert Wise ph Joseph Brun m John Lewis

☆ Robert Ryan, Harry Belafonte, Ed Begley, Shelley Winters, Gloria Grahame, Will Kuluva, Kim Hamilton

'An efficient but unnecessarily portentous thriller.' – *Penelope Houston*

† The writer was actually Abraham Polonsky, who was blacklisted at the time.

Ode to Billy Joe *
US   1976   106m   CFI color
Columbia-Warner/Max Baer Productions (Max Baer, Roger Camras)
▤

In Mississippi in the early 1950s a 17-year-old youth, who is in love with a 15-year-old girl, is driven to kill himself.
Based on the hit song of the 1960s by Bobbie Gentry, a melodramatic account of the frustrations of growing up in a small town.
w Herman Raucher d Max Baer ph Michel Hugo m Michel Legrand ad Philip Jefferies ed Frank E. Morriss

☆ Robby Benson, Glynnis O'Connor, Joan Hotchkis, Sandy McPeak, James Best, Terence Goodman, Becky Brown

'The ultimate tribute earned by the film is that it retrospectively makes Bobbie Gentry's song sound still better – the distillation of a complex experience charted by the film rather than just an isolated epigram and postscript framing it.' – *Jonathan Rosenbaum, MFB*

'Unusually refreshing and moving' – *Films and Filming*

The Odessa File **
GB   1974   129m   Eastmancolor   Panavision
Columbia/Domino/Oceanic (John Woolf)
▦   ▤   ℚ

In 1963, a young German reporter tracks down a gang of neo-Nazis.
Elaborate but uninvolving suspenser with several excellent cliffhanging sequences and a let-down climax.
w Kenneth Ross, George Markstein *novel* Frederick Forsyth d Ronald Neame ph Oswald Morris m Andrew Lloyd Webber pd Rolf Zehetbauer

☆ Jon Voight, Maria Schell, Maximilian Schell, Mary Tamm, Derek Jacobi, Peter Jeffrey, Noel Willman

'As resistible a parcel of sedative entertainment as ever induced narcolepsy in a healthy man.' – *Benny Green, Punch*

Odette *
GB   1950   123m   bw
Herbert Wilcox
▦

A Frenchwoman with an English husband spies for the French resistance, is caught and tortured.
Deglamorized true life spy story with emotional moments let down by generally uninspired handling, also by the too well-known image of its star, who however gives a remarkable performance.
w Warren Chetham Strode *book* Jerrard Tickell d Herbert Wilcox ph Max Greene m Anthony Collins

☆ Anna Neagle, Trevor Howard, Peter Ustinov, Marius Goring

'As a work of art, pretty flat … though innumerable people will find it moving and impressive, they will have done the work themselves.' – *Richard Mallett, Punch*

Odongo
♙♙   GB   1956   85m   Technicolor
Cinemascope
Warwick/Columbia
A collector of animals for zoos runs into various kinds of trouble during an African safari.
Elementary jungle adventure centring on a small Sabu-like jungle boy. For the now extinct family audience.
wd John Gilling ph Ted Moore m George Melachrino

☆ Macdonald Carey, Rhonda Fleming, Juma, Eleanor Summerfield, Francis de Wolff, Earl Cameron

Oedipus Rex **
Italy/Morocco   1967   110m   Technicolor
Panoramica
Arco/Somafis
▦   ▤   ℚ
original title: *Edipo Re*

Oedipus, returning to his home of Thebes, suffers through unwittingly killing his father and marrying his mother.
Austerely involving adaptation of the Greek tragedy, sandwiched between scenes set in modern Italy.
wd Pier Paolo Pasolini *play* Sophocles ph Giuseppe Ruzzolini ad Luigi Scaccianoce ed Nino Baragli

☆ Franco Citti, Silvana Mangano, Carmelo Bene, Julian Beck, Pier Paolo Pasolini, Alida Valli, Ninetto Davoli

Of Freaks and Men **
Russia   1998   94m   sepia/bw
Metro Tartan/STV/Soiuzkino (Sergei Selyanov, Oleg Botogov)
original title: *Po Urodov i Liudei*

In St. Petersburg in the early 1900s, a pornographer and his assistant destroy two families by exposing them to their photographs of scenes of flagellation.
A genuinely original and very strange movie, tinted to look like old photographs and dealing with the corruption and liberation that photography and film brings in its wake.
d Alexei Balabanov ph Sergei Astakhov pd Vera Zelinskaya ed Marina Lipartia cos Nadya Vasilyeva

☆ Sergei Makovetskii, Dinara Drukarova, Lika Nevolina, Victor Sukhorukov, Alyesha De, Chingiz Tsydendabayev, Vadim Prokhorov, Alexandr Mezentsev, Darya Lesnikova, Igor Shibanov, Tatyana Polonskaya

'A film of pungent and distinctive flavour, maybe not to all tastes; but, for its originality

and style, it must be seen.' – *Peter Bradshaw,*
Guardian
'Thought-provoking, funny, disturbing, utterly
involving.' – *Steven Gaydos, Variety*

Of Human Bondage **
US · 1934 · 83m · bw
(RKO)
📼 ▦ 📀

A well-to-do Englishman is brought down by his
infatuation with a sluttish waitress.
This version of the famous novel brought Bette Davis
to prominence but is not otherwise any better than the
others.
w Lester Cohen *novel* W. Somerset Maugham
d John Cromwell *ph* Henry W. Gerrard *m* Max
Steiner *ad* Van Nest Polglase, Carroll Clark
ed William Morgan
☆ *Leslie Howard, Bette Davis*, Frances Dee,
Reginald Owen, Reginald Denny, Kay Johnson,
Alan Hale
'Stars and the novel rep will have to carry a
lethargic romance.' – *Variety*
'A totally obtuse concoction, serving only to
demonstrate how untalented an actress Bette
Davis was before she perfected those camp
mannerisms.' – *John Simon, 1967*

Of Human Bondage *
US · 1946 · 105m · bw
Warner (Henry Blanke)
A doctor suffers through his infatuation with a
common waitress.
Good-looking but thoroughly dull remake of
Maugham's novel.
w Catherine Turney *d* Edmund Goulding
ph Peverell Marley *m* Erich Wolfgang Korngold
☆ Paul Henreid, Eleanor Parker, Alexis Smith,
Edmund Gwenn, Patric Knowles, Janis Paige,
Henry Stephenson

Of Human Bondage
GB · 1964 · 99m · bw
MGM/Seven Arts (James Woolf)
▦
An upper-class doctor is brought low by his
relationship with a waitress.
Disastrous remake with both star roles miscast.
w Bryan Forbes *d* Henry Hathaway, Ken Hughes
ph Oswald Morris *m* Ron Goodwin *pd* John Box
☆ Laurence Harvey, Kim Novak, Nanette
Newman, Roger Livesey, Jack Hedley, Robert
Morley, Siobhan McKenna, Ronald Lacey

Of Human Hearts *
US · 1938 · 100m · bw
MGM (John Considine Jnr)
A 19th-century idyll of middle America and
especially of a preacher and his wayward son.
Curious all-American moral fable, splendidly made
and acted.
w Bradbury Foote *novel Benefits Forgot* by Honoré
Morrow *d* Clarence Brown *ph* Clyde de Vinna
m Herbert Stothart
☆ Walter Huston, James Stewart, Beulah Bondi,
Gene Reynolds, Charles Coburn, Guy Kibbee,
John Carradine, Gene Lockhart, Ann Rutherford
'Long on narrative and short on romance … the
box office reaction is likely to dampen the
enthusiasm of those who believe the film
possesses any wide public appeal.' – *Variety*
† The title was chosen via a radio contest, the
winner being a high-school student.
⚵ Beulah Bondi

Of Love and Desire
US · 1963 · 97m · DeLuxe
New World (Victor Stoloff)
An engineer in Mexico takes up with the boss's
nymphomaniac sister.
Unwise sensationalist vehicle for an ageing leading lady
who is past such carryings on.
w Laslo Gorag, Richard Rush *d* Richard Rush
ph Alex Phillips *m* Ronald Stein
☆ Merle Oberon, Steve Cochran, John Agar, Curt
Jurgens

'I'm decent, I tell ya! Nobody's got the right to call
me names!'
'The picture Hollywood said could never be made!'
Of Mice and Men ***
US · 1939 · 107m · bw
Hal Roach (Lewis Milestone)
▦ · ⊘

An itinerant worker looks after his mentally
retarded cousin, a giant who doesn't know his own
strength.
A strange and unexpected tragedy which has strength
and is very persuasively made but seems somehow
unnecessary.
w Eugene Solow *novel* John Steinbeck *d* Lewis
Milestone *ph* Norbert Brodine *m* Aaron Copland
☆ *Burgess Meredith*, Lon Chaney Jnr, Betty Field,
Charles Bickford, Roman Bohnen, Bob Steele,
Noah Beery Jnr
'The film is excellently acted by everyone …
there are, mercifully, no stars to intrude their
tedious flat personalities into this picture of life.
It is a picture which, for all its grief, is not
depressing; and if it should be said that this is no
time for adding to one's own melancholy, let me
reply that it is sometimes well not to lose from
sight the individual pity of the lives of men.' –
Dilys Powell
⚵ best picture; Aaron Copland

'We have a dream. Someday we'll have a little house
and a couple of acres. A place to call home.'
Of Mice and Men *
US · 1992 · 111m · DeLuxe
UIP/MGM (Russ Smith, Gary Sinise)
📼 ▦ 📀 🎧
While dreaming of better times, an itinerant farm
worker tries to keep his companion, a dim but well-
meaning giant, out of trouble.
Despite the good intentions of those involved, a
strangely unemotional and inert remake.
w Horton Foote *novel* John Steinbeck *d* Gary
Sinise *ph* Kenneth MacMillan *m* Mark Isham
pd David Gropman *ed* Robert L. Sinise
☆ John Malkovich, Gary Sinise, Ray Walston,
Casey Siemaszko, Sherilyn Fenn, John Terry
'Little more than a lacklustre ramble through an
old favourite.' – *Geoffrey Macnab, Sight and*
Sound

Ofelas: see *Pathfinder*

Off and Running
US · 1991 · 90m · colour
Rank/Aaron Russo Entertainment (Aaron Russo,
William C. Carraro)
An actress flees from the killer of her fiancé while
she tries to discover why he was murdered.
Misfiring romantic comedy with some violent action
thrown in for bad measure.
w Mitch Glazer *d* Edward Bianchi *ph* Andrzej
Bartkowiak *m* Mason Daring *ad* Norman E.
Weber *ed* Rick Shaine
☆ Cyndi Lauper, David Keith, Johnny Pinto,
David Thornton, Richard Belzer, José Perez, Anita
Morris, Hazen Gifford

Off Beat
US · 1986 · 92m · DeLuxe
Buena Vista/Touchstone/Ufland/Roth/Ladd
📼 ▦ 📀
An accident-prone librarian, persuaded by his
policeman friend to take his place at a charity
dance competition, falls in love with a female cop
and continues with his impersonation.
A pleasant, though undistinguished romantic comedy,
undermining macho posturings.
w Mark Medoff *story* Dezso Magyar *d* Michael
Dinner *ph* Carlo DiPalma *m* James Horner
pd Woods Mackintosh *ed* Dede Allen, Angelo
Corrao
☆ Judge Reinhold, Meg Tilly, Cleavant Derricks,
Harvey Keitel, Joe Mantegna, Jacques D'Amboise,
Amy Wright, John Turturro, James Tolkan, Fred
Gwynne

Off Limits: see *Saigon*

Off Limits
US · 1953 · 89m · bw
Paramount (Harry Tugend)
GB title: *Military Policemen*
A boxing manager trains a young fighter in the
military police.
Flat star comedy.

w Hal Kanter, Jack Sher *d* George Marshall
ph Peverell Marley *m* Van Cleave
☆ Bob Hope, Mickey Rooney, Marilyn Maxwell,
Marvin Miller

Off the Beaten Track: see *Behind the Eight*
Ball

Off the Dole
GB · 1935 · 89m · bw
Mancunian
An amateur detective catches burglars.
Artless comedy shot on a minuscule budget; it helped to
make George Formby a star.
wd Arthur Mertz
☆ George Formby, Beryl Formby, Constance
Shotter, Dan Young

Off the Record
US · 1939 · 71m · bw
Warner
A star reporter exposes the mob's use of youngsters
as spotters in the gambling racket.
Predictable crime support.
w Niven Busch, Lawrence Kimble, Earl Baldwin
d James Flood
☆ Pat O'Brien, Joan Blondell, Bobby Jordan, Alan
Baxter, Morgan Conway
'Stereotype dualler.' – *Variety*

Offbeat *
GB · 1960 · 72m · bw
British Lion/Northiam (M. Smedley Aston)
An MI5 undercover man finds himself
sympathizing with a gang of robbers and falling in
love with one of them.
Sharply observed thriller which gets a bit glum in
dealing with its rather contrived 'switch'.
w Peter Barnes *d* Cliff Owen *ph* Geoffrey
Faithfull *m* Ken Jones
☆ William Sylvester, Mai Zetterling, Anthony
Dawson, John Meillon, John Phillips, Victor
Brooks, Joseph Furst, Neil McCarthy, Harry Baird

The Offence *
GB · 1972 · 113m · DeLuxe
United Artists/Tantallon (Denis O'Dell)
A tough police inspector bullies a suspected child
molester.
Tortuous psychological study on the fringe of hysteria;
good performances.
w John Hopkins *play This Story of Yours* by John
Hopkins *d* Sidney Lumet *ph* Gerry Fisher
m Harrison Birtwistle
☆ Sean Connery, Trevor Howard, Ian Bannen,
Vivien Merchant

Office Killer
US · 1997 · 83m · Technicolor
Strand/Good Machine/Kardana/Swinsky (Christine
Vachon, Pamela Koffler)
Problems escalate on a magazine when a copy
editor accidentally electrocutes a writer and
discovers that she enjoys killing.
Dimly lit experimental movie, directed by a fashionable
photographer, that has all the attraction of the most
inept 'B' movie ever.
w Elise MacAdam, Tom Kalin, Todd Haynes
d Cindy Sherman *ph* Russell Fine *m* Evan Lurie
pd Kevin Thompson *ed* Merrill Stern
☆ Carol Kane, Molly Ringwald, Jeanne
Tripplehorn, Barbara Sukowa, Michael Imperioli,
David Thornton, Mike Hodge, Alice Drummond
'Deep-sixed by klutzy direction, mostly
sophomoric performances and a script so flat it
isn't even laughably bad, *Office Killer* sinks like a
stone.' – *Derek Elley, Variety*
† The film was a low-budget production, costing
$300,000.

Office Space **
US · 1999 · 89m · DeLuxe
TCF (Michael Rotenberg, Daniel Rappaport)
📼 ▦ 🎧
After a visit to an occupational hypnotherapist
goes wrong, a downhearted computer programmer
ceases to care about his boring job.
Witty demolition of corporate culture, deftly skewering
all the petty nuisances of office routine.
wd Mike Judge *animated shorts* Milton by Mike
Judge *ph* Tim Suhrstedt *m* John Frizzell
pd Edward McAvoy *ed* David Rennie
☆ Ron Livingston, Jennifer Aniston, Stephen
Root, Gary Cole, John C. McGinley, Diedrich

Bader, David Herman, Ajay Naidu, Michael
McShane, Richard Riehle
'This satirical comedy about white-collar wage-
slavery is amusing and accessible enough to have
wide-ranging appeal.' – *Joe Leydon, Variety*

An Officer and a Gentleman *
US · 1982 · 126m · Metrocolor
Paramount/Lorimar (Martin Elfand)
📼 ▦ 📀 🎧
A potential officer suffers thirteen weeks of agony
at the Naval Aviation Officer Candidate School.
Old-hat stuff given a fresh look and some smart acting.
w Douglas Day Stewart *d* Taylor Hackford
ph Donald Thorin *m* Jack Nitzsche *pd* Philip M.
Jefferies
☆ Richard Gere, Debra Winger, *Louis Gossett Jnr*,
David Keith, Lisa Blount, Lisa Eilbacher
'Shamelessly manipulative, but whether the
manipulations are funny, dramatic or tear-
jerking, it knows exactly what and how to
deliver.' – *Sunday Telegraph*
† John Travolta turned down the lead because 'I
was just more interested in pursuing my actual life
as a jet pilot than my film life as a jet pilot'.
⚵ *Louis Gossett Jnr* (as supporting actor); *song*
'Up Where We Belong' by Jack Nitzsche, Buffy
Sainte-Marie (*m*), Will Jennings (*ly*)
⚵ Debra Winger; original screenplay; editing
(Peter Zinner); music

The Official Version **
Argentina · 1985 · 115m · Eastmancolor
Virgin/Almi/HistoriasCinematograficas/Progress
Communications (Marcelo Pineyro)
📼 ▦ 📀
original title: *La Historia Official*
aka: *The Official Story*
A teacher begins to realize that her adopted
daughter was probably the child of parents
murdered by the regime under which she lives.
Strong and moving drama of the stirrings of a political
conscience.
w Aida Bortnik, Luis Puenzo *d* Luis Puenzo
ph Felix Monti *m* Atilio Stampone *ad* Abel
Facello *ed* Juan Carlos Macias
☆ Hector Alterio, Norma Aleandro, Chela Ruiz,
Chunchuna Villafane, Hugo Arana, Patricio
Contreras
⚵ best foreign film
⚵ screenplay

Offret: see *The Sacrifice*

Oggi a Me … Domani a Te!: see *Today It's*
Me, Tomorrow You!

Oh Dad, Poor Dad, Mamma's Hung You
in the Closet and I'm Feelin' So Sad
US · 1966 · 86m · Technicolor
Paramount/Seven Arts (Ray Stark, Stanley Rubin)
▦
A dead father helps his son to get married despite
his mother's influence to the contrary.
Zany black comedy which never really worked on the
stage, let alone the screen.
w Ian Bernard *play* Arthur Kopit *d* Richard
Quine *ph* Geoffrey Unsworth *m* Neal Hefti
☆ Rosalind Russell, Jonathan Winters, Robert
Morse, Hugh Griffith, Barbara Harris, Lionel
Jeffries, Cyril Delevanti, Hiram Sherman

Oh, Daddy!
GB · 1935 · 77m · bw
Gaumont-British/Gainsborough (Michael Balcon)
Aristocratic and abstemious members of the
League of Purity are converted to pleasure by a trip
to London.
A not very successful transfer of a stage play to the
screen, though the stars occasionally show why they
were so admired by their theatre audiences.
w Michael Powell, Austin Melford *play* Franz
Arnold, Ernst Bach *d* Graham Cutts, Austin
Melford *ph* Mutz Greenbaum (Max Greene)
m/ly Sam Coslow *md* Louis Levy *ad* Ernö
Metzner *ed* Charles Frend
☆ Leslie Henson, Frances Day, Robertson Hare,
Barry Mackay, Marie Löhr, Alfred Drayton, Tony
de Lungo, Daphne Courtney

Oh Doctor
US · 1937 · 67m · bw
Universal
A rich hypochondriac is the target of confidence
tricksters.

Moderate star comedy.
d Edmund Grainger
☆ Edward Everett Horton, Donrue Leighton, Eve Arden, Thurston Hall, William Demarest
'Smooth dialogue keeps this hokey picture from going completely corkscrew.' – Variety

Oh! For a Man!: see Will Success Spoil Rock Hunter?

'It's an almighty laugh!'
Oh, God *
♠♠ US   1977   104m   Technicolor
Warner (Jerry Weintraub)
▥▥ ▤ ℚ
A bewildered supermarket manager is enlisted by God to prove to the world that it can only work if people try.
Overlong but generally amiable reversion to the supernatural farces of the forties: its success seems to show that people again need this kind of comfort.
w Larry Gelbart novel Avery Corman d Carl Reiner ph Victor Kemper m Jack Elliott
☆ George Burns, John Denver, Ralph Bellamy, Donald Pleasence, Teri Garr, William Daniels, Barnard Hughes, Paul Sorvino, Barry Sullivan, Dinah Shore, Jeff Corey, David Ogden Stiers
'Undeniably funny and almost impossible to dislike.' – Tom Milne, MFB
'Basically a single-joke movie: George Burns is God in a football cap.' – Pauline Kael, New Yorker
& Larry Gelbart

Oh God Book Two
♠♠ US   1980   94m   Technicolor
Warner (Gilbert Cates)
▥▥ ▤
God enlists a child to remind people that he is still around.
Crass sequel with sentiment replacing jokes.
w Josh Greenfeld, Hal Goldman, Fred S. Fox, Seaman Jacobs, Melissa Miller d Gilbert Cates ph Ralph Woolsey m Charles Fox pd Preston Ames ed Peter E. Berger
☆ George Burns, Suzanne Pleshette, David Birney, Louanne, Howard Duff, Hans Conried, Wilfrid Hyde-White

Oh God, You Devil
US   1984   96m   Technicolor
Warner (Robert M. Sherman)
▥▥ ▤ ℚ
A struggling musician sells his soul to the devil in exchange for success.
A comic version of Faust, appended to the two films in which George Burns played God; he now puts on the other hat to fairly, but not very, comic effect.
w Andrew Bergman d Paul Bogart ph King Baggot m David Shire pd Peter Wooley ed Andy Zall
☆ George Burns, Ted Wass, Ron Silver, Roxanne Hart, Eugene Roche

Oh Heavenly Dog
US   1980   103m   DeLuxe
Mulberry Square/TCF
▤
A private eye is reincarnated as a dog and solves his own murder.
Witless fantasy comedy, an uncredited remake of You Never Can Tell which also rates as a Benji movie with curious additions of sex and profanity. A total muddle.
w Rod Browning, Joe Camp d Joe Camp
☆ Chevy Chase, Jane Seymour, Omar Sharif, Robert Morley, Alan Sues

Oh Men! Oh Women!
US   1957   90m   Eastmancolor   Cinemascope
TCF (Nunnally Johnson)
A psychoanalyst discovers that his wife is involved with two of his patients.
Scatty Broadway comedy which strains the patience.
wd Nunnally Johnson play Edward Chodorov ph Charles G. Clarke m Cyril Mockridge
☆ David Niven, Ginger Rogers, Dan Dailey, Barbara Rush, Tony Randall
'The ugliest sort of fun.' – Observer
'Cinemascope discovers a solution to the problem of filling its wide screen; the characters spend most of their time full length on the psychoanalyst's couch.' – Sunday Times

Oh Mr Porter ****
♠♠   GB   1937   84m   bw
GFD/Gainsborough (Edward Black)
The stationmaster of an Irish halt catches gun-runners posing as ghosts.
Marvellous star comedy showing this trio of comedians at their best, and especially Hay as the seedy incompetent. The plot is borrowed from The Ghost Train, but each line and gag brings its own inventiveness. A delight of character comedy and cinematic narrative.
w Marriott Edgar, Val Guest, J. O. C. Orton story Frank Launder d Marcel Varnel ph Arthur Crabtree md Louis Levy
☆ Will Hay, Moore Marriott, Graham Moffatt, Dave O'Toole, Dennis Wyndham
'That rare phenomenon: a film comedy without a dud scene.' – Peter Barnes, 1964
'Behind it lie the gusty uplands of the British music hall tradition, whose rich soil the British film industry is at last beginning to exploit.' – Basil Wright

Oh Rosalinda!
GB   1955   105m   Technicolor   Cinemascope
ABP/Powell and Pressburger
A playboy in four-power Vienna plays a practical joke on four officers and the flirtatious wife of one of them.
Lumbering attempt to modernize Die Fledermaus, unsuitably wide-screened and totally lacking the desired Lubitsch touch. A monumental step in the decline of these producers, and a sad stranding of a brilliant cast.
wd Michael Powell, Emeric Pressburger ph Christopher Challis m Johann Strauss ad Hein Heckroth
☆ Anton Walbrook, Michael Redgrave, Anthony Quayle, Mel Ferrer, Dennis Price, Ludmilla Tcherina

Oh What a Lovely War **
GB   1969   144m   Technicolor   Panavision
Paramount/Accord (Brian Duffy, Richard Attenborough)
A fantasia with music on World War I.
A brave all-star attempt which comes off only in patches; the pier apparatus from the stage show really doesn't translate, the piece only works well when it becomes cinematic, as in the recruiting song and the final track-back from the graves. But there are many pleasures, as well as yawns, along the way.
w Len Deighton stage show Joan Littlewood, Charles Chilton d Richard Attenborough ph Gerry Turpin m various md Alfred Ralston pd Don Ashton
☆ Ralph Richardson, Meriel Forbes, John Gielgud, Kenneth More, John Clements, Paul Daneman, Joe Melia, Jack Hawkins, John Mills, Maggie Smith, Michael Redgrave, Laurence Olivier, Susannah York, Dirk Bogarde, Phyllis Calvert and also Vanessa Redgrave
'This musical lampoon is meant to stir your sentiments, evoke nostalgia, and make you react to the obscenity of battles and bloodshed, and apparently it does all that for some people.' – New Yorker, 1977
'A naïve, sentimental, populist affair, using many (too many) clever devices yet making the same old simplistic statements.' – John Simon
'An overlong and rarely cinematic musical satire that ladles its anti-war message on by the bucketload.' – Time Out, 1984
❂ cinematography; production design; Laurence Olivier

Oh, What a Night
Canada   1992   93m   colour
Norstar (Peter Simpson)
▤
In the 50s, a teenager moves with his father to live in Ontario and becomes infatuated with a married woman.
Routine drama of teenage fumblings to a soundtrack of gentler hits of the period.
w Richard Nielsen d Eric Till ph Brian R. R. Hebb m Ian Thomas ad David Moe ed Susan Shipton
☆ Corey Haim, Barbara Williams, Keir Dullea, Genevieve Bujold, Robbie Coltrane, Andrew Miller

Oh You Beautiful Doll *
US   1949   93m   Technicolor
TCF (George Jessel)
Fred Fisher wants to write opera but is more successful with pop songs.
Standard turn-of-the-century biopic, very pleasantly handled and performed.
w Albert and George Lewis d John M. Stahl ph Harry Jackson md Alfred Newman
☆ S. Z. Sakall, Mark Stevens, June Haver, Charlotte Greenwood, Jay C. Flippen, Gale Robbins

O'Hara's Wife
US   1982   87m   DeLuxe
David-Panzer
▤
A widower is helped by his wife's ghost.
Rather icky sentimental comedy.
w James Nasella, William S. Bartman d William S. Bartman
☆ Ed Asner, Mariette Hartley, Jodie Foster, Perry Lang, Tom Bosley, Ray Walston

Oil for the Lamps of China *
US   1935   98m   bw
Warner (Robert Lord)
The career in China of an American oil company representative.
Adequate general audience picture from a bestseller.
w Laird Doyle novel Alice Tisdale Hobart d Mervyn Le Roy ph Tony Gaudio m Heinz Roemheld md Leo F. Forbstein
☆ Pat O'Brien, Josephine Hutchinson, Jean Muir, Lyle Talbot, Arthur Byron, John Eldredge, Henry O'Neill, Donald Crisp
'Long and choppy version of a best-seller novel. Little marquee strength will probably mean light returns.' – Variety
'Far above average in performance, direction and content.' – John Baxter, 1968
† Remade 1941 as Law of the Tropics.

OK Connery: see Operation Kid Brother

Okay America
US   1932   80m   bw
Universal
GB title: Penalty of Fame
A brash reporter saves a politician's daughter from kidnapping.
Okay melodrama remade in 1939 as Risky Business.
w William Anthony McGuire d Tay Garnett
☆ Lew Ayres, Maureen O'Sullivan, Louis Calhern, Walter Catlett, Edward Arnold

O-Kay for Sound *
GB   1937   85m   bw
GFD/Gainsborough (Edward Black)
The Crazy Gang runs amok in a film studio.
Patchy farce with music hall talents of the time.
w Marriott Edgar, Val Guest, R. P. Weston, Bert Lee d Marcel Varnel ph Jack Cox m/ly Michael Carr, Jimmy Kennedy md Louis Levy pd Vetchinsky ed R. E. Dearing
☆ Bud Flanagan, Chesney Allen, Jimmy Nervo, Teddy Knox, Charlie Naughton, Jimmy Gold, Fred Duprez, Enid Stamp-Taylor, Graham Moffatt, Meinhart Maur, H. F. Maltby, Peter Dawson, The Radio Three, The J. Sherman Fisher Girls

Okinawa
US   1952   67m   bw
Columbia
Adventures of the gun crew of a Pacific destroyer.
Routine war actioner with much newsreel padding.
w Jameson Bewer, Arthur Ross, Leonard Stern d Leigh Jason ph Henry Freulich m Mischa Bakaleinikoff
☆ Pat O'Brien, Richard Denning, Cameron Mitchell, Rhys Williams

'A picture straight from the heart of America!'
Oklahoma! **
♠♠ US   1955   143m   Technicolor   Todd-AO
Magna/Rodgers and Hammerstein (Arthur Hornblow Jnr)
▥▥ ▥▥ ▤ ℚ ⓓ 🎧
A cowboy wins his girl despite the intervention of a sinister hired hand.
Much of the appeal of the musical was in its simple timeworn story and stylized sets; the film makes the first merely boring and the latter are replaced by standard scenery, not even of Oklahoma. The result is efficient rather than startling or memorable.
w Sonya Levien, William Ludwig book Oscar Hammerstein play Green Grow the Rushes by Lynn Riggs d Fred Zinnemann ph Robert Surtees m Robert Russell Bennett, Jay Blackton, Adolph Deutsch pd Oliver Smith ed Gene Ruggiero, George Boemler songs Richard Rodgers, Oscar Hammerstein II
☆ Gordon MacRae, Shirley Jones, Rod Steiger, Gloria Grahame, Charlotte Greenwood, Gene Nelson, Eddie Albert
♬ music score
& Robert Surtees; editing

'A story of wooden derricks, iron men, and a defiant woman!'
Oklahoma Crude *
US   1973   111m   Technicolor
Columbia/Stanley Kramer
▤
In 1913, a drifting oil man stops to help a girl develop her rig.
Dour, downbeat melodrama with restricted action and much bad language; within its lights quite entertaining, but odd.
w Marc Norman d Stanley Kramer ph Robert Surtees m Henry Mancini pd Alfred Sweeney
☆ Faye Dunaway, George C. Scott, John Mills, Jack Palance, Woodrow Parfrey

The Oklahoma Kid **
US   1939   80m   bw
Warner (Samuel Bischoff)
▤
During the settlement of the Cherokee Strip a cowboy avenges the unjust lynching of his father.
Competent but slightly disappointing star Western memorable for the clash in this guise of its protagonists, more usually seen as gangsters.
w Warren Duff, Robert Buckner, Edward E. Paramore d Lloyd Bacon ph James Wong Howe m Max Steiner
☆ James Cagney, Humphrey Bogart, Rosemary Lane, Donald Crisp, Harvey Stephens, Charles Middleton, Edward Pawley, Ward Bond
'Its b.o. potency will depend on Cagney's name and draw, rather than story or production, neither of which is commendable.' – Variety
'There's something entirely disarming about the way he has tackled horse opera, not pretending for a minute to be anything but New York's Jimmy Cagney all dressed up as a Robin Hood of the old west.' – Frank Nugent

The Oklahoma Woman
US   1956   72m   bw   SuperScope
ARC/Sunset (Roger Corman)
After six years in jail, a gunfighter returns home in search of a quiet life to find that his former girlfriend is taking over the town.
Cliché-ridden Western that follows a familiar story with no sign of enthusiasm.
w Lou Rusoff d Roger Corman ph Fred West m Ronald Stein ed Ronald Sinclair
☆ Richard Denning, Peggie Castle, Cathy Downs, Touch Connors, Martin Kingsley, Tudor Owen, Jonathan Haze, Richard Miller, Edmund Cobb

The Oklahoman
US   1956   78m   DeLuxe   Cinemascope
Walter Mirisch/Allied Artists
▤
A widowed doctor becomes the subject of gossip when he takes an Indian girl for his housekeeper.
Rather curious domestic Western which erupts into action sequences but devotes too much time to talk and romance.
w Daniel B. Ullman d Francis D. Lyon ph Carl Guthrie m Hans Salter
☆ Joel McCrea, Barbara Hale, Brad Dexter, Gloria Talbott, Michael Pate

Old Acquaintance **
US   1943   110m   bw
Warner (Henry Blanke)
Two jealous lady novelists interfere in each other's love lives.
A dated but rather splendid battle of the wild cats, with two stars fighting their way through a plush production and a rather overlong script.
w John Van Druten, Lenore Coffee play John Van Druten d Vincent Sherman ph Sol Polito m Franz Waxman

☆ *Bette Davis, Miriam Hopkins, Gig Young, John Loder, Dolores Moran, Philip Reed, Roscoe Karns, Anne Revere*

'The odd thing is that the two ladies and the director can make the whole business look fairly intelligent, detailed and plausible; and that on the screen such trash can seem, even, mature and adventurous.' – *James Agee*
'Trashy fun, on an unusually literate level.' – *New Yorker, 1978*

Old and New: see *The General Line*

Old Bill and Son
GB 1941 96m bw
GFD/Legeran Films/London Films (Josef Somlo, Harold Boxall)
Too old for active duty, a veteran follows his son to Flanders.
Ineffective screen version of a popular newspaper strip.
w Bruce Bairnsfather, Ian Dalrymple *cartoons* Bruce Bairnsfather d Ian Dalrymple ph Georges Périnal md Muir Mathieson ed Charles Crichton
☆ Morland Graham, John Mills, Mary Clare, Renée Houston, Rene Ray, Roland Culver

Old Bones of the River *
GB 1938 90m bw
GFD/Gainsborough (Edward Black)
A teacher in Africa accidentally quells a native rising.
Tediously funny star comedy; enough said.
w Marriott Edgar, Val Guest, J. O. C. Orton *character* Edgar Wallace d Marcel Varnel ph Arthur Crabtree m Louis Levy ad Vetchinsky
☆ Will Hay, Moore Marriott, Graham Moffatt, Robert Adams, Jack Livesey

Old Boyfriends *
US 1978 103m Technicolor
Edward R. Pressman Productions (Paul Schrader)
▨ ⊚
A divorcee survives a nervous breakdown and goes on a journey of her past life to find out where she went wrong.
Low-key and somehow rather flat romantic odyssey, with interesting sequences and characters muted by the director's jaundiced eye.
w Paul and Leonard Schrader d Joan Tewkesbury ph William A. Fraker m David Shire
☆ Talia Shire, Richard Jordan, John Belushi, Keith Carradine, John Houseman, Buck Henry, Bethel Leslie

The Old Curiosity Shop: see *Mister Quilp* (1975)

The Old Curiosity Shop *
🎞 GB 1934 95m bw
BIP (Walter C. Mycroft)
The lives of a gambler and his granddaughter are affected by a miserly dwarf.
Heavy-going Dickens novel given reasonably rich production and well enough acted; sentimentality prevented a remake until the unsuccessful Mister Quilp (qv) in 1975.
w Margaret Kennedy, Ralph Neale *novel* Charles Dickens d Thomas Bentley ph Claude Friese-Greene
☆ Hay Petrie, Ben Webster, Elaine Benson, Beatrice Thompson, Gibb McLaughlin, Reginald Purdell, Polly Ward

'Beware The Night!'
The Old Dark House ****
US 1932 71m bw
Universal (Carl Laemmle Jnr)
Stranded travellers take refuge in the house of a family of eccentrics.
Marvellous horror comedy filled with superb grotesques and memorable lines, closely based on a Priestley novel but omitting the more thoughtful moments. A stylist's and connoisseur's treat.
w Benn W. Levy, R. C. Sherriff *novel* Benighted by J. B. Priestley d James Whale ph Arthur Edeson ad Charles D. Hall ed Clarence Kolster
☆ Melvyn Douglas, Charles Laughton, Raymond Massey, Boris Karloff, Ernest Thesiger, Eva Moore, Gloria Stuart, Lillian Bond, Brember Wills, John Dudgeon (Elspeth Dudgeon)

'Somewhat inane, it's a cinch for trick ballyhooing. Better for the nabes than the big keys.' – *Variety*
'An unbridled camp fantasy directed with great wit.' – *Charles Higham*
'Each threat as it appears is revealed to be burlap and poster paint … despite storm, attempted rape and a remarkable final chase, the film is basically a confidence trick worked with cynical humour by a brilliant technician.' – *John Baxter, 1968*
'Basically a *jeu d'esprit* in which comedy of manners is edged into tragedy of horrors, the film never puts a foot wrong.' – *Tom Milne, MFB, 1978*

'The ghost doesn't walk in this family – it runs riot!'
The Old Dark House *
GB 1962 86m Eastmancolor
Columbia/Hammer/William Castle
An American accepts an invitation to visit Femm Manor and finds the inhabitants either mad or homicidal.
A travesty which has nothing to do with the 1932 film and possesses no merit of its own. The cast is left floundering.
w Robert Dillon d William Castle ph Arthur Grant m Benjamin Frankel
☆ Tom Poston, Janette Scott, Robert Morley, Joyce Grenfell, Mervyn Johns, Fenella Fielding, Peter Bull

Old Dracula: see *Vampira*

'Come and meet a grand old sinner!'
Old English
US 1930 87m bw
Warner
In order to provide for his grandchildren, a financier makes certain illegal arrangements which involve his prearranged death.
Satisfying pattern play arranged for its star.
w Walter Anthony, Maude Howell *play* John Galsworthy d Alfred E. Green
☆ George Arliss, Leon Janney, Doris Lloyd, Betty Lawford, Ivan Simpson
'Will call for most careful placement by chains and indies to draw the class trade it will only appeal to.' – *Variety*

Old Enough
US 1984 91m colour
Silverfilm (Dina Silver)
▨
During one summer, a rich girl learns about life from a poor girl.
A dull movie about the first slow stirrings of adolescence.
wd Marisa Silver ph Michael Ballhaus m Julian Marshall pd Jeffrey Townsend ed Mark Burns
☆ Sarah Boyd, Rainbow Harvest, Neill Barry, Danny Aiello, Fran Brill

Old Gringo
US 1989 120m DeLuxe
Columbia TriStar (Lois Bonfiglio)
▨ ▧ ⊚ ⌒
The writer Ambrose Bierce and an American schoolteacher become involved in the Mexican revolution of Pancho Villa.
Confused romantic drama that attempts large gestures and bungles even small ones.
w Aida Bortnik, Luis Puenzo *novel* Gringo Viejo by Carlos Fuentes d Luis Puenzo ph Felix Monti m Lee Holdridge pd Stuart Wurtzel, Bruno Rubeo ed Juan Carlos Macias, William Anderson, Glenn Farr
☆ Jane Fonda, Gregory Peck, Jimmy Smits, Patricio Contreras, Jenny Gago, Gabriela Roel, Sergio Calderon
† The film cost $25m and took around $2m at the US box-office.

Old Hutch
US 1936 80m bw
MGM
An idler finds a fortune but can't spend it because everybody knows he hasn't worked for years.
Satisfactory star comedy.
w George Kelly d J. Walter Ruben
☆ Wallace Beery, Elizabeth Patterson, Eric Linden, Cecilia Parker, Donald Meek, Virginia Grey
'Hasn't the backbone usually associated with Wallace Beery's vehicles. A nice light comedy

which will doubtless garner fair box office.' – *Variety*

Old Iron
GB 1938 80m bw
TW Productions/British Lion
A shipping magnate disowns his son for marrying against his will, but a car accident reconciles them.
Very boring drama, an odd choice for this star, who can't cope with it.
w Ben Travers d Tom Walls
☆ Tom Walls, Eva Moore, Cecil Parker, Richard Ainley, David Tree, Enid Stamp-Taylor
'An embarrassing little stage comedy of parental affection, shot hurriedly from the front as you would shoot a charging lion.' – *Graham Greene*

The Old Lady Who Walked in the Sea
France 1991 94m colour
Gala/Blue Dahlia/SFC/A2/Little Bear/JM Productions (Gérard Jourd'hui)
▧ ▨
original title: La vieille qui marchait dans la mer
Two aged confidence tricksters fall out after they take on a young apprentice in crime.
A defiantly tasteless and foul-mouthed comedy that somehow manages to charm as well, mainly due to Moreau's imperious performance.
w Dominique Roulet, Laurent Heynemann *novel* San Antonio d Laurent Heynemann ph Robert Alazraki m Philippe Sarde pd Valérie Grall ed Jacques Comets
☆ Jeanne Moreau, Michel Serrault, Luc Thuillier, Geraldine Danon, Jean Bouchaud, Marie-Dominique Aumont, Hester Wilcox
'A film to test the audience's patience.' – *Geoff Brown, The Times*
'Tasteless, vulgar and even badly shot.' – *Derek Malcolm, Guardian*

The Old Maid **
US 1939 95m bw
Warner (Henry Blanke)
▧ ▨ ⊚
When her suitor is killed in the Civil War, an unmarried mother lets her childless cousin bring up her daughter as her own.
A 'woman's picture' par excellence, given no-holds-barred treatment by all concerned but a little lacking in surprise.
w Casey Robinson *play* Zoe Akins *novel* Edith Wharton d Edmund Goulding ph Tony Gaudio m Max Steiner md Leo F. Forbstein
☆ Bette Davis, Miriam Hopkins, George Brent, Jane Bryan, Donald Crisp, Louise Fazenda, James Stephenson, Jerome Cowan, William Lundigan, Rand Brooks
'Stagey, sombre and generally confusing fare. Must aim for the femme trade chiefly.' – *Variety*
'It is better than average and sticks heroically to its problem, forsaking all delights and filling a whole laundry bag with wet and twisted handkerchiefs.' – *Otis Ferguson*
'The picture isn't bad, but it trudges along and never becomes exciting.' – *New Yorker, 1977*

The Old Man and the Sea *
US 1958 89m Technicolor
Warner/Leland Hayward
⌒
An old fisherman dreams of hooking a great fish.
Expensive but poor-looking and stultifyingly dull one-character drama with variable production effects, a low key Moby Dick. Interesting but not effective.
w Peter Viertel *novella* Ernest Hemingway d John Sturges m James Wong Howe, Floyd Crosby, Tom Tutweiler, Larna Boren m Dimitri Tiomkin
☆ Spencer Tracy, Felipe Pazos, Harry Bellaver
'A literary property about as suited for the movie medium as *The Love Song of J. Alfred Prufrock.*' – *Time*
'A strange amalgam of practically unassisted acting, good camerawork and editing, and a lot of special effects.' – *Ernest Callenbach, Film Quarterly*
'Tracy struggles valiantly with the endless monologues … misguided in the extreme.' – *Time Out, 1984*
'This is not a picture audiences are going to tear down the doors to see.' – *Motion Picture Herald*
† It was remade as a TV film in 1990, starring Anthony Quinn.
🏆 Dimitri Tiomkin
👤 James Wong Howe; Spencer Tracy

Old Man Rhythm
US 1935 75m bw
Radio
A wealthy businessman becomes a college freshman to prevent his son marrying a gold-digger.
Amiable, relentlessly cheerful musical entertainment that passes the time pleasantly.
w Sig Herzig, Ernest Pagano, H. W. Hanemann d Edward Ludwig ph Nick Musuraca m/ly Lewis Gensler, Johnny Mercer md Roy Webb ch Hermes Pan ad Van Nest Polglase ed George Crone
☆ Charles Buddy Rogers, George Barbier, Barbara Kent, Grace Bradley, Betty Grable, Eric Blore, Erik Rhodes, John Arledge, Johnny Mercer, Donald Meek

Old Mother Riley
This Irish washerwoman with flailing arms and a nice line in invective was a music hall creation of Arthur Lucan, a variation of a pantomime dame. His wife Kitty McShane played Mother Riley's daughter, and despite personal difficulties they were top of the bill for nearly 30 years. Their first film was Stars on Parade, a collection of music-hall acts, in 1935.
The films were very cheaply made and the padding is difficult to sit through, but Lucan at his best is a superb comedian: they were made for small independent companies such as Butcher's and usually directed by Maclean Rogers.
1937 Old Mother Riley
1938 Old Mother Riley in Paris
1939 Old Mother Riley MP, Old Mother Riley Joins Up
1940 Old Mother Riley in Business, Old Mother Riley's Ghosts
1941 Old Mother Riley's Circus
1942 Old Mother Riley in Society
1943 Old Mother Riley Detective, Old Mother Riley Overseas
1944 Old Mother Riley at Home
1947 Old Mother Riley's New Venture
1949 Old Mother Riley's Jungle Treasure
1950 Old Mother Riley Headmistress (qv)
1952 Mother Riley Meets the Vampire

Old Mother Riley Headmistress
GB 1950 75m bw
Renown (Harry Reynolds)
Old Mother Riley, annoyed that her daughter has been unfairly sacked as a music teacher, buys the school.
A lacklustre comedy that fails to capitalize on Arthur Lucan's anarchic knockabout skills, insisting on a sympathetic mother–daughter relationship rather than the antagonistic one of his music-hall act.
w John Harlow, Ted Kavanagh *story* Jackie Marks, Con West d John Harlow ph James Wilson md George Melachrino ad C. Wilfred Arnold ed Douglas Myers
☆ Arthur Lucan, Kitty McShane, Willer Neal, Cyril Smith, C. Denier Warren, Enid Hewit, Paul Sheridan, Harry Herbert, The Luton Girls' Choir

The Old Woman Who Walked in the Sea: see *The Old Lady Who Walked in the Sea*

Old Yeller *
🎞 US 1957 83m Technicolor
Walt Disney
▨ ⊚
The love of a boy for his dog.
Archetypal family movie set in a remote rural area.
w Fred Gipson, William Tunberg *novel* Fred Gipson d Robert Stevenson ph Charles P. Boyle m Oliver Wallace
☆ Dorothy McGuire, Fess Parker, Tommy Kirk, Kevin Corcoran, Jeff York, Chuck Connors

The Oldest Profession
France/West Germany/Italy 1967 115m
Eastmancolor
Gibe/Francoriz/Rialto/Rizzoli
▨ ⊚
Six sketches about prostitution.
Very variable portmanteau, with moments of interest towards the end.
w Ennio Flaiano, Daniel Boulanger, Georges and André Tabet, Jean Aurenche, Jean-Luc Godard d Franco Indovina, Mauro Bolognini, Philippe de Broca, Michel Pfleghar, Claude Autant-Lara, Jean-Luc Godard

---

☆ Michele Mercier, Elsa Martinelli, Jeanne Moreau, Jean-Claude Brialy, Raquel Welch, Nadia Gray, Anna Karina

'You dastard! Get thee hence or I shall smite thee in the puss!'

The Old-Fashioned Way *

US   1934   74m   bw

Paramount/ (William Le Baron)

Adventures of The Great McGonigle and his troupe of travelling players.

Period comedy tailored for its star and incorporating fragments of The Drunkard. Not so funny as it might be, but essential for students.

w Garnett Weston, Jack Cunningham, Charles Bogle (W. C. Fields) d William Beaudine ph Benjamin Reynolds m Harry Revel

☆ W. C. Fields, Joe Morrison, Judith Allen, Jan Duggan, Jack Mulhall, Baby Leroy

Oleanna

US   1994   89m   DuArt

Samuel Goldwyn/Channel 4/Bay Kinescope (Patricia Wolff, Sarah Green)

▤ ⌕

An unhappy and pedantic professor is accused of sexually harassing a female student, who finds herself unable to understand the course he is teaching.

A controversial and successful two-character play transfers poorly to the screen, where the performances seem too aggressive to compel attention; it is less to do with sexual or male–female relationships than with an exploration of how we use language and what we mean by what we say.

wd David Mamet play David Mamet ph Andrzej Sekula m Rebecca Pidgeon ed Barbara Tulliver

☆ William H. Macy, Debra Eisenstadt

'This film never finds the magic balance between genre convention and sociopolitical currents. Its relevance to sexual harassment is on the same level as "The Hand That Rocks the Cradle's" analysis of contemporary babysitting.' – Leonard Klady, *Variety*

'Much much more than a musical!'

Oliver! ***

🏃 GB   1968   146m   Technicolor
Panavision 70

Columbia/Warwick/Romulus (John Woolf)

▤ ▦ ⌕ ◎ ⌒

A musical version of *Oliver Twist*.

The last, perhaps, of the splendid film musicals which have priced themselves out of existence; it drags a little in spots but on the whole it does credit both to the show and the original novel, though eclipsed in style by David Lean's straight version.

w Vernon Harris play Lionel Bart novel Charles Dickens d Carol Reed ph Oswald Morris m Lionel Bart md John Green ch Onna White pd John Box ed Ralph Kemplen

☆ Ron Moody, Oliver Reed, Harry Secombe, Mark Lester, Shani Wallis, Jack Wild, Hugh Griffith, Joseph O'Conor, Leonard Rossiter, Hylda Baker, Peggy Mount, Megs Jenkins

'Only time will tell if it is a great film but it is certainly a great experience.' – *Joseph Morgenstern*

'There is a heightened discrepancy between the romping jollity with which everyone goes about his business and the actual business being gone about … such narrative elements as the exploitation of child labour, pimping, abduction, prostitution and murder combine to make Oliver! the most non-U subject ever to receive a U certificate.' – *Jan Dawson*

♣ best picture; Carol Reed; John Green; Onna White; sound

♫ Vernon Harris; Oswald Morris; Ron Moody; Jack Wild; costumes (Phyllis Dalton); editing

Oliver and Company *

🏃 US   1988   74m   Metrocolor

Warner/Walt Disney/Silver Screen Partners III

▤ ▦ ⌒

A kitten becomes friends with a gang of criminal dogs and their human master.

Episodic film, short on charm, that only now and then provides glimpses of stylish animation.

w Jim Cox, Timothy J. Disney, James Mangold novel Oliver Twist by Charles Dickens d George Scribner m J. A. C. Redford ad Dan Hansen ed Jim Melton, Mark Hester

---

☆ Featuring the voices of Joey Lawrence, Bill Joel, Cheech Marin, Richard Mulligan, Roscoe Lee Browne, Sheryl Lee Ralph, Dom DeLuise, Taurean Blacque, Carl Weintraub, Robert Loggia, Natalie Gregory, William Glover, Bette Midler

Oliver the Eighth

US   1933   20m   bw

Hal Roach

Ollie goes on a blind date, and the lady turns out to be homicidal.

Star farce which never quite rises to the occasion; pleasant fooling but no more.

w anon d Lloyd French ph Art Lloyd ed Bert Jordan

☆ Stan Laurel, Oliver Hardy, Mae Busch, Jack Barty

Oliver Twist ****

🏃🏃 GB   1948   116m   bw

GFD/Cineguild (Ronald Neame)

▤ ▦ ⌕ ◎ ⌒

A foundling falls among thieves but is rescued by a benevolent old gentleman.

Simplified, brilliantly cinematic version of a voluminous Victorian novel, beautiful to look at and memorably played, with every scene achieving the perfect maximum impact.

w David Lean, Stanley Haynes novel Charles Dickens d David Lean ph Guy Green m Arnold Bax pd John Bryan

☆ Alec Guinness, Robert Newton, Francis L. Sullivan, John Howard Davies, Kay Walsh, Anthony Newley, Henry Stephenson, Mary Clare, Gibb McLaughlin, Diana Dors

'A thoroughly expert piece of movie entertainment.' – *Richard Winnington*

'A brilliant, fascinating movie, no less a classic than the Dickens novel which it brings to life.' – *Time*

Oliver's Story

US   1978   92m   Technicolor

Paramount (David V. Picker)

▤

A sequel to *Love Story*, showing how Oliver succumbed to depression but finally found another girlfriend.

Love means never having to watch this trendy rubbish.

w Erich Segal, John Korty d John Korty ph Arthur Ornitz m Francis Lai, Lee Holdridge

☆ Ryan O'Neal, Candice Bergen, Nicola Pagett, Edward Binns, Ray Milland

Olivier, Olivier **

France   1992   109m   Eastmancolor

Gala/Oliane/A2 (Marie-Laure Reyre)

▤ ▦ ▦ ⌕ ⌒

A middle-class family is thrown into confusion when a 15-year-old male prostitute claims to be the son who vanished six years earlier.

Engrossing examination of identity, credulity and family harmony.

w Agnieszka Holland, Yves Lapointe, Régis Debray d Agnieszka Holland ph Bernard Zitzermann m Zbigniew Preisner pd Helene Bourgy ed Isabelle Lorente

☆ François Cluzet, Brigitte Roüan, Jean-François Stévenin, Grégoire Colin, Marina Golovine, Frédéric Quiring

'What could have been a deadly mysterious tale becomes modestly intriguing, almost prosaic.' – *Geoff Brown, The Times*

'A seemingly simple but intriguing and ultimately powerful film.' – *Variety*

Olly Olly Oxen Free

🏃🏃 US   1978   93m   Metrocolor

Rico Lion (Richard A. Colla)

aka: *The Great Balloon Adventure*

A junkyard proprietress helps two young children to launch a decrepit hot-air balloon.

Simpleminded children's adventure with a surprising star.

w Eugene Poinc d Richard A. Colla ph Gayne Rescher m Bob Alcivar pd Peter Wooley

☆ Katharine Hepburn, Kevin McKenzie, Dennis Dimster

Los Olvidados *

Mexico   1951   88m   bw

Utramar/Oscar Dancigers

aka: *The Young and the Damned*

A good boy is contaminated by the young thugs in Mexico City's slums, and both he and his tormentor die violently.

Sober but penetrating analysis of social conditions leading to violence. The film was widely acclaimed, yet its very proficiency and excellent photography tend to glamorize its subject. Compare, however, the Hollywood resolutions of Dead End, on a similar subject.

w Luis Buñuel, Luis Alcoriza, Oscar Dancigers d Luis Buñuel ph Gabriel Figueroa m Gustavo Pitaluga

☆ Alfonso Mejia, Miguel Inclan, Estela Inda, Roberto Cobo

'I shall not put *Los Olvidados* among the films I have most enjoyed; but I am far from sure that it should not go among the monuments of the cinema.' – *Dilys Powell*

Olympische Spiele ***

Germany   1936   225m   bw

Leni Riefenstahl

An account of the Berlin Olympic Games.

This magnificent film is in no sense a mere reporting of an event. Camera movement, photography and editing combine with music to make it an experience truly olympian, especially in the introductory symbolic sequence suggesting the birth of the games. It was also, dangerously, a hymn to Nazi strength.

ph Hans Ertl, Walter Franz and 42 others m Herbert Windt d/ed Leni Riefenstahl assistant Walter Ruttman

'Here is the camera doing superbly what only the camera can do: refashioning the rhythms of the visible; of the moment seen.' – *Dilys Powell*

† Part 1 runs to 118m, and Part 2 to 107m.

The Omaha Trail

US   1942   62m   bw

MGM

The laying of train track across the west causes Indian wars.

Brisk second-feature Western with good production values.

w Jesse Lasky Jnr, Hugo Butler d Edward Buzzell

☆ James Craig, Dean Jagger, Edward Ellis, Chill Wills, Donald Meek, Pamela Blake, Howard da Silva

'One thousand years ago, Omar Khayyam was a poet, a scientist and military leader so great that an army of Assassins dedicated to world domination fell before his genius!'

Omar Khayyam

🏃🏃 US   1956   101m   Technicolor
Vistavision

Paramount (Frank Freeman Jnr)

The Persian poet and philosopher defends his Shah against the Assassins.

Clean but dull Arabian Nights fantasy with pantomime sets and no humour.

w Barre Lyndon d William Dieterle ph Ernest Laszlo m Victor Young

☆ Cornel Wilde, Michael Rennie, Raymond Massey, John Derek, Yma Sumac, Sebastian Cabot, Debra Paget

L'Ombre du Doute: see A Shadow of a Doubt

The Omega Man *

US   1971   98m   Technicolor   Panavision

Warner/Walter Seltzer

▤ ▦ ⌕

In 1977 a plague resulting from germ warfare has decimated the world's population; in Los Angeles, one man wages war against loathsome carriers of the disease.

'Realistic' version of a novel which was about vampires taking over, and was previously filmed unsatisfactorily as The Last Man on Earth. This nasty version rises to a few good action sequences but is bogged down by talk in between.

w John William Corrington, Joyce H. Corrington novel I am Legend by Richard Matheson d Boris Sagal ph Russell Metty m Ron Grainer

☆ Charlton Heston, Rosalind Cash, Anthony Zerbe

'Good morning. You are one day closer to the end of the world!'

The Omen **

US   1976   111m   DeLuxe   Panavision

TCF (Harvey Bernhard)

▤ ▦ ⌕ ⌒

The adopted child of an ambassador to Great Britain shows unnerving signs of being diabolically inspired.

Commercially successful variation on The Exorcist, quite professionally assembled and more enjoyable as entertainment than its predecessor.

w David Seltzer d Richard Donner ph Gil Taylor m Jerry Goldsmith

☆ Gregory Peck, Lee Remick, David Warner, Billie Whitelaw, Leo McKern, Harvey Stevens, Patrick Troughton, Anthony Nicholls, Martin Benson

'A cut above the rest in that it has an ingenious premise, a teasingly labyrinthine development, a neat sting in its tail, and enough confidence in its own absurdities to carry them off.' – *David Robinson, The Times*

'Dreadfully silly … its horrors are not horrible, its terrors are not terrifying, its violence is ludicrous.' – *New York Times*

'More laughs than an average comedy.' – *Judith Crist*

'I did it strictly for the money.' – *David Seltzer*

† See *Damien: Omen II* and *The Final Conflict*.

†† Gregory Peck inherited his role from Charlton Heston, who turned it down.

♣ Jerry Goldsmith

♫ song 'Ave Satani'

Omen IV: The Awakening

US   1991   97m   colour

TCF/FNM (Harvey Bernhard)

▤ ⌕ ⌒

A wealthy couple adopt a young girl who turns out to be the daughter of the Anti-Christ.

An American TV movie, virtually rehashing The Omen, that was given a cinema release elsewhere, it has all the sins of a film made for the small screen, looking cheap and clearly intended for audiences with brief attention spans.

w Brian Taggert d Jorge Montesi, Dominique Othenin-Girard ph Martin Fuhrer m Jonathan Sheffer pd Richard Wilcox ed Frank Irvine

☆ Faye Grant, Michael Woods, Michael Lerner, Madison Mason, Asia Vieira

'This mainly serves to remind you that, silly though they were, the earlier films were at least quality entertainment. Further sequels would be as welcome as a plague of locusts.' – *Kim Newman, Empire*

'While pic offers a few creepy moments, its structure is so convoluted that it's sheer hell to follow.' – *Variety*

On a Clear Day You Can See Forever *

US   1970   129m   Technicolor   Panavision

Paramount (Howard Koch)

▤ ▦ ⌕

A psychiatric hypnotist helps a girl to stop smoking, and finds that in trances she remembers previous incarnations.

Romantic musical which tries, and fails, to substitute wispy charm for its original Broadway vitality. There are compensations.

w Alan Jay Lerner play Alan Jay Lerner d Vincente Minnelli ph Harry Stradling m Burton Lane

☆ Barbra Streisand, Yves Montand, Bob Newhart, Larry Blyden, Jack Nicholson, Simon Oakland

On an Island with You

US   1948   104m   Technicolor

MGM (Joe Pasternak)

A film actress on location in the South Seas is chased by a naval officer.

Below par musical which far outstays its welcome.

w Dorothy Kingsley, Dorothy Cooper, Charles Martin, Hans Wilhelm d Richard Thorpe ph Charles Rosher md George Stoll

☆ Esther Williams, Peter Lawford, Jimmy Durante, Ricardo Montalban, Cyd Charisse, Xavier Cugat and his Orchestra

---

On Approval ***

GB 1943 80m bw
(GFD)

An Edwardian duke and an American heiress plan a chaperoned trial marriage in a remote Scottish castle.
Sparkling comedy of manners made even more piquant by careful casting and mounting; a minor delight.
w Clive Brook, Terence Young *play* Frederick Lonsdale d Clive Brook ph C. Friese-Greene m William Alwyn
☆ Clive Brook, Beatrice Lillie, Googie Withers, Roland Culver, O. B. Clarence, Lawrence Hanray, Hay Petrie
'Totally diverting, highly cinematic.' – *NFT, 1974*
'There has probably never been a richer, funnier anthology of late-Victorian mannerisms.' – *Time*
'I enjoyed it so thoroughly that I have to fight off superlatives.' – *James Agee*
† Also filmed in 1930 by Tom Walls for Herbert Wilcox, with Walls, Yvonne Arnaud, Winifred Shotter and Edmund Breon.

On Borrowed Time *

US 1939 98m bw
MGM (Sidney Franklin)

An old man refuses to die and chases Death up the apple tree.
Amiable, very American fantasy with much sentiment and several effective moments.
w Alice Duer Miller, Frank O'Neill, Claudine West *novel* Lawrence Edward Watkin d Harold S. Bucquet ph Joseph Ruttenberg m Franz Waxman
☆ Lionel Barrymore, Bobs Watson, Beulah Bondi, Cedric Hardwicke, Una Merkel, Ian Wolfe, Philip Terry, Eily Malyon
'General audiences may cotton to the novelty … artistically fine prestige production.' – *Variety*
'A weird, wild, totally unpredictable fantasy with dream sequences more like Buñuel than anything in the cinema.' – *John Russell Taylor, 1965*

On Connaît la Chanson: see *Same Old Song*

On Dangerous Ground

US 1951 82m bw
RKO (John Houseman)

A tough cop falls in love with the blind sister of a mentally defective murderer.
Pretentious Hollywood film noir in the Gabin manner, partly redeemed by its glossy surface.
w A. I. Bezzerides *novel* George Butler d Nicholas Ray ph George E. Diskant m Bernard Herrmann
☆ Robert Ryan, Ida Lupino, Ward Bond, Ed Begley, Cleo Moore, Charles Kemper

'His battle to save the Alaskan wilderness and protect its people can only be won…'

On Deadly Ground

US 1994 101m Technicolor
Warner/Seagal/Nasso (Steven Seagal, Julius R. Nasso, A. Kitman Ho)

A former CIA agent protects the Alaskan environment against a wicked oil mogul.
Risible action movie in which the pollution-count is high, particularly since Seagal's notion of saving the environment is to destroy it and everyone who stands in his way.
w Ed Horowitz, Robin U. Russin d Steven Seagal ph Ric Waite m Basil Poledouris pd William Ladd Skinner ed Robert Ferreti, Don Brochu
☆ Steven Seagal, Michael Caine, Joan Chen, John C. McGinley, R. Lee Ermey, Shari Shattuck, Billy Bob Thornton, Richard Hamilton, Chief Irvin Brink
'A vanity production parading as a social statement. It nonetheless has enough sound, fury and flash to satisfy the action crowd who have propped up Seagal's career.' – *Variety*
'Seagal, of course, remains exactly himself – a human bullet winging its way towards the flabby guts of the baddies. But he seems to be getting a little older now, and the martial arts are not as spectacular.' – *Derek Malcolm*

On Dress Parade

US 1939 62m bw
Warner

The Dead End Kids go to military school.
Cleaned-up comedy-drama, the last for the Kids before they split up.
w Tom Reed, Charles Belden d William Clemens
☆ Billy Halop, Leo Gorcey, Huntz Hall, Bobby Jordan, Gabriel Dell, Bernard Punsley, John Litel, Frankie Thomas
'It just doesn't ring true. Dualler.' – *Variety*

On Friday at Eleven

West Germany/France/Italy 1960 93m bw
Corona/Criterion/Erredi (Alexander Gruter)
aka: *The World in My Pocket*

A cold-hearted gang plans to rob a heavily armoured American army truck.
Unsurprising but vaguely unpleasant thriller with nary a character left alive at the end.
w Frank Harvey *novel* James Hadley Chase d Alvin Rakoff ph Vaclav Vich m Claude Bolling
☆ Rod Steiger, Nadja Tiller, Peter Van Eyck, Jean Servais, Ian Bannen

'Growing up isn't easy at any age'

On Golden Pond ***

US 1981 109m colour Panavision
ITC/IPC (Bruce Gilbert)

An 80-year-old, his wife and his daughter spend a holiday at their New England lakeside cottage.
A film remarkable not so much for what it is – a well-acted, decent screen presentation of a rather waffling and sentimental play – as for the fact that in the sophisticated eighties enough people paid to see it to make it a box-office record-breaker. This was mainly due to affection for its star, whose last film it was, but also to an American desire for a reversion to the old values of warmth and humanity after the sex and violence which the screen had lately been offering.
w Ernest Thompson *play* Ernest Thompson d Mark Rydell ph Billy Williams m Dave Grusin
☆ Henry Fonda, Katharine Hepburn, Jane Fonda, Doug McKeon, Dabney Coleman
'Moments of truth survive some cloying contrivance; Rydell directs on bended knees.' – *Sight and Sound*
'Two of Hollywood's best-loved veterans deserve a far better swansong than this sticky confection.' – *Time Out*
'The kind of uplifting twaddle that traffics heavily in rather basic symbols: the gold light on the pond stands for the sunset of life, and so on.' – *Pauline Kael, New Yorker*
🎐 Ernest Thompson; Henry Fonda; Katharine Hepburn
🅰 best film; Mark Rydell; editing (Robert L. Wolfe); Dave Grusin; Jane Fonda; Billy Williams; best actress (Katharine Hepburn)
🅱 Katharine Hepburn

On Her Majesty's Secret Service **

🎬 GB 1969 140m Technicolor Panavision
UA/Eon/Danilaq (Harry Saltzman, Albert R. Broccoli)

James Bond tracks down master criminal Blofeld in Switzerland.
Perhaps to compensate for no Sean Connery and a tragic ending, the producers of this sixth Bond opus shower largesse upon us in the shape of no fewer than four protracted and spectacular climaxes. Splendid stuff, but too much of it, and the lack of a happy centre does show.
w Richard Maibaum *novel* Ian Fleming d Peter Hunt ph Michael Reed, Egil Woxholt, Roy Ford, John Jordan m John Barry pd Syd Cain
☆ George Lazenby, Diana Rigg, Telly Savalas, Ilse Steppat, Gabriele Ferzetti, Yuri Borienko, Bernard Lee, Lois Maxwell

'Put on your straw boater and *Cuddle Up A Little Closer!*'

On Moonlight Bay **

US 1951 95m Technicolor
Warner (William Jacobs)

Family crises, to do with growing up and young love, in a 1917 Indiana town.
Pleasant musical, competently made, from the Penrod stories, with the emphasis switched to big sister.
w Melville Shavelson, Jack Rose *stories* Booth Tarkington d Roy del Ruth ph Ernest Haller md Ray Heindorf
☆ Doris Day, Gordon MacRae, Leon Ames, Rosemary de Camp, Billy Gray
† See also *By the Light of the Silvery Moon*, a companion piece.

On My Way to the Crusades I Met a Girl Who…: see *The Chastity Belt*

On Our Merry Way *

US 1948 107m bw
Miracle Productions (Benedict Bogeaus, Burgess Meredith)
aka: *A Miracle Can Happen*

A reporter is urged by his wife to dig up some human interest stories.
Frail compendium of anecdotes which barely work.
w Laurence Stallings *story* Arch Oboler d King Vidor, Leslie Fenton (also John Huston, George Stevens, uncredited) ph Joseph August, Gordon Avil, John Seitz, Edward Cronjager m Heinz Roemheld md David Chudnow, Skitch Henderson
☆ Burgess Meredith, Paulette Goddard, Fred MacMurray, Hugh Herbert, James Stewart, Dorothy Lamour, Victor Moore, Henry Fonda, William Demarest

On Our Selection

Australia 1932 99m bw
Australasian Films

The life of the Rudd family in rural Queensland.
Predictable plot complications and loveable characters.
w Bert Bailey, Ken G. Hall d Ken G. Hall
☆ Bert Bailey, Fred McDonald, Alfreda Bevan, Jack McGowan
† Subsequent Rudd adventures included *Dad and Dave Come to Town* (1938) and *Dad Rudd M.P.* (1940).

On Stage Everybody

US 1945 65m bw
Universal

A vaudevillian helps youngsters put on a radio show.
Tired musical support.
w Warren Wilson, Oscar Brodney d Jean Yarbrough
☆ Jack Oakie, Peggy Ryan, Johnny Coy, Julie London, Otto Kruger

On Such a Night

US 1937 71m bw
Emmanuel Cohen/Paramount

Gangsters get caught in a Mississippi flood.
Confusing action yarn which fizzles out before it gets going.
w Doris Malloy, William Lipman, and various hands d E. A. Dupont
☆ Grant Richards, Roscoe Karns, Karen Morley, Eduardo Ciannelli, Alan Mowbray, Robert McWade
'So many baffling twists that the thread of the narrative is soon lost.' – *Variety*

On Such a Night *

GB 1955 37m Eastmancolor
Screen Audiences/Rank

An American is initiated into the splendours of Glyndebourne Opera.
Modestly pleasing documentary with fictionalized bookends.
w Paul Dehn d Anthony Asquith
☆ David Knight, Josephine Griffin, Marie Lohr

'The tops in swank! The smoothest in rhythm! The greatest in stars! The newest in love! The fastest in dancing! The last word in entertainment!'

On the Avenue **

US 1937 89m bw
TCF (Gene Markey)

An heiress rages because she is being satirized in a revue, but later falls in love with the star.
Bright musical which keeps moving and uses its talents wisely.
w Gene Markey, William Conselman d Roy del Ruth ph Lucien Andriot m/ly Irving Berlin ch Seymour Felix
☆ Dick Powell, Madeleine Carroll, The Ritz Brothers, George Barbier, Alice Faye, Walter Catlett, Joan Davis, E. E. Clive

'An amusing revue, with a pleasant score and a disarming informality in its production to lure us into liking it.' – *New York Times*
† Revamped as *Let's Make Love* (qv)
🎵 'He Ain't Got Rhythm'; 'The Girl on the Police Gazette'; 'This Year's Kisses'; 'I've Got My Love to Keep Me Warm'. The title song was dropped before release.

On the Beach **

US 1959 134m bw
United Artists/Stanley Kramer

When most of the world has been devastated by atomic waste, an American atomic submarine sets out to investigate.
Gloomy prophecy which works well in spasms but is generally too content to chat rather than imagine. A solid prestige job nevertheless.
w John Paxton, James Lee Barrett *novel* Nevil Shute d Stanley Kramer ph Giuseppe Rotunno, Daniel Fapp m Ernest Gold pd Rudolph Sternad ed Frederic Knudtson
☆ Gregory Peck, Ava Gardner, Fred Astaire, Anthony Perkins, Donna Anderson, John Tate, Lola Brooks
'Its humanism is clearly of the order that seeks the support of a clamorous music score. The characters remain little more than spokesmen for timid ideas and Salvation Army slogans, their emotions hired from a Hollywood prop room; which is all pretty disturbing in a film about nothing less than the end of the world.' – *Robert Vas*
🅱 Ernest Gold; editing

On the Beat

🎬 GB 1962 105m bw
Rank (Hugh Stewart)

A Scotland Yard car park attendant manages to capture some crooks and become a policeman.
Busy but flat comedy vehicle, never very likeable.
w Jack Davies d Robert Asher ph Geoffrey Faithfull m Philip Green
☆ Norman Wisdom, Jennifer Jayne, Raymond Huntley, David Lodge, Esma Cannon, Terence Alexander

On the Black Hill *

GB 1988 117m colour
BFI/Channel 4/British Screen

Twin brothers grow up on a Welsh hill farm.
Unsentimental and episodic narrative of limited lives, but not without its longueurs.
wd Andrew Grieve *novel* Bruce Chatwin ph Thaddeus O'Sullivan m Robert Lockhart ad Jocelyn James ed Scott Thomas
☆ Mike Gwilym, Robert Gwilym, Bob Peck, Gemma Jones, Jack Walters, Nesta Harris, Huw Toghill, Gareth Toghill

On the Buses

🎬 GB 1971 88m Technicolor
EMI/Hammer (Ronald Woolfe, Ronald Chesney)

Women drivers cause trouble at a bus depot.
Grotesque, ham-handed farce from a TV series which was sometimes funny; this is merely vulgar.
w Ronald Woolfe, Ronald Chesney d Harry Booth ph Mark MacDonald m Max Harris
☆ Reg Varney, Doris Hare, Anna Karen, Michael Robbins, Stephen Lewis
† *Mutiny on the Buses* followed in 1972 and *Holiday on the Buses* in 1973. Both were deplorably witless.

On the Carpet: see *Little Giant*

On the Double *

US 1961 92m Technicolor Panavision
Paramount/Dena-Capri (Jack Rose)

During World War II, an American private is asked to impersonate a British intelligence officer.
From the plot and the talents it seems one might start laughing at this while still in the queue, but in fact most of it goes sadly awry and it never quite comes to the boil.
w Jack Rose, Melville Shavelson d Melville Shavelson ph Harry Stradling, Geoffrey Unsworth m Leith Stevens
☆ Danny Kaye, Dana Wynter, Wilfrid Hyde-White, Diana Dors, Margaret Rutherford, Allan Cuthbertson, Jesse White

On the Fiddle *

GB 1961 97m bw
Anglo-Amalgamated/S. Benjamin Fisz
US title: *Operation Snafu*
A wide boy and a slow-witted gypsy have comic and other adventures in the RAF.
Curious mixture of farce and action, more on American lines than British, but quite entertainingly presented.
w Harold Buchman *novel Stop at a Winner* by R. F. Delderfield d Cyril Frankel ph Ted Scaife m Malcolm Arnold
☆ Alfred Lynch, Sean Connery, Cecil Parker, Wilfrid Hyde-White, Kathleen Harrison, Alan King, Eleanor Summerfield, Eric Barker, Terence Longdon, John Le Mesurier, Harry Locke

On the Night of the Fire *

GB 1939 94m bw
GFD/G & S (Josef Somlo)
US title: *The Fugitive*
A barber kills the blackmailer of his wife.
Dour little drama, rather unusual for pre-war British studios.
w Brian Desmond Hurst, Terence Young *novel* F. L. Green d Brian Desmond Hurst ph Gunther Krampf
☆ Ralph Richardson, Diana Wynyard, Romney Brent, Mary Clare, Henry Oscar, Frederick Leister
'The kind of film either liked very much or very little ... absorbingly entertaining, and b.o. should profit considerably by word of mouth.' – *Variety*

On the Riviera **

US 1951 90m Technicolor
TCF (Sol C. Siegel)
A cabaret artist is persuaded to pose as a philandering businessman.
Remake of Folies Bergère and That Night in Rio (see also On the Double); disliked at the time and accused of tastelessness, it now seems smarter and funnier than comparable films of its era.
w Valentine Davies, Phoebe and Henry Ephron d Walter Lang ph Leon Shamroy m Alfred Newman ad Lyle Wheeler, Leland Fuller
☆ Danny Kaye, Corinne Calvet, Gene Tierney, Marcel Dalio, Jean Murat
♫ Alfred Newman; art direction

On the Run

Hong Kong 1988 96m colour
Bo Ho/Mobile (Raymond Chow)
A cop and the hit-woman who killed his wife go on the run from a gang of corrupt and violent policemen who are dealing in heroin.
Brutal, hard-boiled thriller with a great deal of slaughter and not much plausibility.
wd Alfred Cheung m Lam Man Yee pd Chen Yu ad Kih Chung Man, Loo Kah Hiu
☆ Yuen Biao, Patricia Ha, Kao Fei, Yuen Wah, Loh Lieh, Chan Yoke Lin
'More than just good Hong Kong noir, it is good film noir.' – *Jim Morton, Sex and Zen & A Bullet in the Head*

On the Threshold of Space

US 1956 96m Eastmancolor Cinemascope
TCF (William Bloom)
The USAF medical corps explores human reactions at high altitudes.
Semi-documentary flagwaver with dreary domestic asides; very dated now, and of no particular nostalgic interest.
w Simon Wincelberg, Francis Cockrell d Robert D. Webb ph Joe MacDonald m Lyn Murray
☆ Guy Madison, Virginia Leith, John Hodiak, Dean Jagger, Warren Stevens

On the Town ****

👫 US 1949 98m Technicolor
MGM (Arthur Freed)
Three sailors enjoy 24 hours' leave in New York.
Most of this brash location musical counts as among the best things ever to come out of Hollywood; the serious ballet towards the end tends to kill it, but it contains much to be grateful for.
w Betty Comden, Adolph Green *ballet Fancy Free* by Leonard Bernstein ph Harold Rosson md Lennie Hayton, Roger Edens d/ch Gene Kelly, Stanley Donen songs various

☆ Gene Kelly, Frank Sinatra, Jules Munshin, Vera-Ellen, Betty Garrett, Ann Miller, Tom Dugan, Florence Bates, Alice Pearce
'A film that will be enjoyed more than twice.' – *Lindsay Anderson*
'So exuberant that it threatens at moments to bounce right off the screen.' – *Time*
'The speed, the vitality, the flashing colour and design, the tricks of timing by which motion is fitted to music, the wit and invention and superlative technical accomplishment make it a really exhilarating experience.' – *Richard Mallett, Punch*
♫ Lennie Hayton, Roger Edens

On the Twelfth Day *

GB 1956 23m Eastmancolor
George K. Arthur/Bahamian
A balletic presentation of the song about the 12 days of Christmas, with plenty of maids a'milking and lords a'leaping.
A refreshing and extravagant novelty.
w James Matthews, Val Valentine d Wendy Toye ph Arthur Grant pd Ronald Searle
☆ Wendy Toye, Franklin Bennett, David O'Brien

On the Waterfront ****

US 1954 108m bw
Columbia/Sam Spiegel
After the death of his brother, a young stevedore breaks the hold of a waterfront gang boss.
Intense, broody dockside thriller with 'method' performances; very powerful of its kind, and much imitated.
w Budd Schulberg *novel* Budd Schulberg d Elia Kazan ph Boris Kaufman m Leonard Bernstein ad Richard Day ed Gene Milford
☆ Marlon Brando, Eva Marie Saint, Lee J. Cobb, Rod Steiger, Karl Malden, Pat Henning, Leif Erickson, James Westerfield, John Hamilton
TERRY (MARLON BRANDO): 'It was you, Charley. You and Mickey. Like the night the two of you's come in the dressing room and says, "Kid, this ain't your night. We're going for the price on Wilson." It ain't my night. I'd of taken Wilson apart that night! I was ready. Remember the early rounds throwing them combinations? So what happens? This bum Wilson he gets the title shot. Outdoors in the ball park! And what do I get? A couple of bucks and a one-way ticket to Palookaville.'
'It was you, Charley. You was my brother. You should have looked out for me instead of making me take them dives for the short end money.'
CHARLEY (ROD STEIGER): 'I always had a bet down for you. You saw some money.'
TERRY: 'See! You don't understand! I could've been a contender. I could've had class and been somebody. Real class. Instead of a bum. It was you, Charley.'
'An uncommonly powerful, exciting and imaginative use of the screen by gifted professionals.' – *New York Times*
'A medley of items from the Warner gangland pictures of the thirties, brought up to date.' – *Steven Sondheim, Films in Review*
🏆 best picture; Budd Schulberg; Elia Kazan; Boris Kaufman; Richard Day; Marlon Brando; Eva Marie Saint; editing
🏆 Leonard Bernstein; Lee J. Cobb; Rod Steiger; Karl Malden
🎬 Marlon Brando

On the Yard

US 1979 102m Technicolor
Midwest (Joan Micklin Silver)
In a tough jail, the controlling convict finds his authority challenged by a wife-killer and a new guard captain.
Bleak drama of prison life, conveying the futility of existence inside, but not much else.
w Malcolm Braly *novel* Malcolm Braly d Raphael D. Silver ph Alan Metzger m Charles Gross ad Leon Harris ed Evan Lottman
☆ John Heard, Thomas Waites, Mike Kellin, Richard Bright, Joe Grifasi, Lane Smith, Richard Hayes

On Top of Old Smoky

US 1953 60m bw
Columbia/Gene Autry (Armand Schaefer)
Gene Autry is mistaken for a Texas Ranger when he intervenes in a row between freight operators and a young woman operating a toll road.
Amiable light Western that ambles along, arousing mild interest as it goes.
w Gerald Geraghty d George Archainbaud ph William Bradford md Mischa Bakaleinikoff ad George Brooks ed James Sweeney
☆ Gene Autry, Smiley Burnette, Gail Davis, Grandon Rhodes, Sheila Ryan, Kenne Duncan, Cass County Boys, Champion

On Trial

US 1939 60m bw
Warner
A man kills his wife's lover and is put on trial for murder.
Dozy film version of a once sensational play.
w Don Ryan *play* Elmer Rice d Terry Morse
☆ John Litel, Margaret Lindsay, Edward Norris, James Stephenson
'Strictly dual fodder, talking along for an hour without going anywhere.' – *Variety*

On Wings of Song: see *Love Me Forever*

On with the Show

US 1929 98m Technicolor (two-colour)
Warner
Crude early talkie musical revue with historical interest.
w Robert Lord *play Shoestring* by Humphrey Pearson d Alan Crosland ph Tony Gaudio ch Larry Ceballos songs Grant Clarke, Harry Akst
☆ Betty Compson, Louise Fazenda, Sally O'Neil, Joe E. Brown, Ethel Waters, Arthur Lake

On Your Toes *

US 1939 94m bw
Warner (Robert Lord)
Backstage jealousies at the ballet.
Smooth film version of a top Broadway show of its time.
w Jerry Wald, Richard Macaulay *play* George Abbott d Ray Enright ph James Wong Howe, Sol Polito m/ly Richard Rodgers, Lorenz Hart
☆ Vera Zorina, Eddie Albert, Alan Hale, Frank McHugh, James Gleason, Donald O'Connor, Gloria Dickson
'Box office prospects appear to be pretty good, but more than the average campaigning should be indulged.' – *Variety*

Once a Crook

GB 1941 81m bw
TCF
A publican with a shady past helps his son who is in trouble with the law.
Low-key character comedy for two stars who would benefit from a greater tendency to farce.
w Roger Burford *play* Evadne Price, Ken Attiwill d Herbert Mason
☆ Gordon Harker, Sydney Howard, Frank Pettingell, Carla Lehmann, Bernard Lee, Kathleen Harrison, Cyril Cusack

Once a Jolly Swagman *

GB 1948 100m bw
GFD/Wessex (Ian Dalrymple)
US title: *Maniacs on Wheels*
A factory worker becomes a speedway rider.
Competent sporting drama of no particular interest.
w William Rose, Jack Lee d Jack Lee ph H. E. Fowle m Bernard Stevens
☆ Dirk Bogarde, Renée Asherson, Bonar Colleano, Bill Owen

Once a Lady

US 1931 65m bw
Paramount
An illegitimate baby grows up to meet her mother without recognizing her.
A plot that was often tried out during the early thirties, seldom more boringly than on this occasion.
w Zoe Akins, Samuel Hoffenstein *play The Second Life* by Rudolf Bernauer, Rudolf Oesterreicher d Guthrie McClintic
☆ Ruth Chatterton, Ivor Novello, Jill Esmond, Geoffrey Kerr, Doris Lloyd
'Another crying towel special.' – *Variety*

Once a Sinner

US 1930 71m bw
Fox
A girl criminal reforms but almost loses the love of her new boyfriend when he finds out about her past.
Transparent melodrama, strictly for indulgent ladies.
w George Middleton d Guthrie McClintic ph Arthur L. Todd
☆ Dorothy Mackaill, Joel McCrea, John Halliday, C. Henry Gordon, Ilka Chase, Clara Blandick, George Brent
'Slow drama that needs plenty of support.' – *Variety*

Once a Sinner

GB 1950 80m bw
John Argyle/Butcher
A girl with a shady past finds her husband is being threatened by her ex-partner.
Uninteresting character melodrama which defeats its lightweight stars.
w David Evans *novel Irene* by Ronald Marsh d Lewis Gilbert ph Frank North m Ronald Binge
☆ Pat Kirkwood, Jack Watling, Joy Shelton, Sydney Tafler, Thora Hird

Once a Thief

US 1965 107m bw Panavision
MGM/Cipra/RN/Fred Engel (Jacques Bar)
An ex-convict is hounded by a vengeful cop.
Glum crime melodrama gleamingly photographed but otherwise quite routine.
w Zekial Marko d Ralph Nelson ph Robert Burks m Lalo Schifrin
☆ Alain Delon, Ann-Margret, Van Heflin, Jack Palance, John Davis Chandler

Once a Thief

Hong Kong 1991 108m colour
Milestone (Linda Kuk, Terence Chang)
original title: *Zongheng Sihai*
A criminal gang of two men and a woman, stealing paintings in France, decide to take their revenge after they are double-crossed by their mentor.
A mix of crime caper and romantic comedy, of minimal appeal other than to aficionados of its cultish director's delight in unlikely violence.
w John Woo, Clifton Ko, Janet Chun d John Woo ph Poon Hang Seng m Violet Lam ad James Leung ed David Wu
☆ Chow Yun-Fat, Leslie Cheung, Cherie Chung
'Packed with so many hilarious, violent action sequences that it becomes silly sophomoric fun.' – *Variety*
† It was given a US makeover in 1995 to emerge as *John Woo's Once a Thief* (qv).

Once Around **

US 1991 114m colour
Universal/Cinecom (Amy Robinson, Griffin Dunne)
Urged by her loving family to marry, a thirtyish woman chooses as a husband a brash and vulgar salesman who does not win their approval.
Perceptive drama of the swings and roundabouts of marital and family life.
w Malia Scotch Marmo d Lasse Hallstrom ph Theo Van de Sande m James Horner ad David Gropman ed Andrew Monshein
☆ Richard Dreyfuss, Holly Hunter, Danny Aiello, Laura San Giacomo, Gena Rowlands, Roxanne Hart, Griffin Dunne
'An intelligently engaging domestic comedy-drama.' – *Variety*

Once Before I Die

US 1966 97m Eastmancolor
F.8 Productions (John Derek)
In the Philippines, after a Jap aerial attack, a cavalry major's girlfriend causes complications in her bids to escape.
Mildly hilarious action melodrama in which the star's superstructure is made the focus of the action.
w Vance Skarstedt d John Derek ph Arthur Arling m Emmanuel Vardi
☆ Ursula Andress, John Derek, Richard Jaeckel, Rod Lauren

'Mark Kendell just found out that his one-night stand has been around for centuries.'

Once Bitten
US 1985 93m Metrocolor
Villard-Wald-Hilderbrand

Teenage sex problems are complicated by a visiting vampiress who needs the blood of a virgin three times before Hallowe'en.
Dispiriting attempt to mix genres without even a tinge of talent or sophistication.
w David Hines, Jeffrey Hause, Jonathan Roberts d Howard Storm
☆ Lauren Hutton, Jim Carrey, Karen Kopins, Cleavon Little
'Mr Storm might have found his ideas for the tone of this movie written on high school locker walls.' – *People*

Once in a Blue Moon
US 1936 65m bw
Paramount

Adventures of an innocent abroad in contemporary Russia.
Would-be satire which was seen by very few people indeed.
wd Ben Hecht, Charles MacArthur
☆ Jimmy Savo, Nikita Balieff, Whitney Bourne, Cecilia Loftus
'A dud. The exhibitors who are kidded into playing it won't be very happy afterwards.' – *Variety*
† Produced in 1934.

Once in a Lifetime *
US 1933 80m bw
Universal (Carl Laemmle Jnr)

How a script was sold in old-time Hollywood.
Half good-humoured, half-scathing satire on Hollywood; technique dated, content still amusing.
w Seton I. Miller play Moss Hart, George S. Kaufman d Russell Mack ph George Robinson
☆ Jack Oakie, Sidney Fox, Aline MacMahon, Russell Hopton, ZaSu Pitts, Louise Fazenda, Gregory Ratoff, Onslow Stevens
'Idol-smashing satire, strictly for the initiated.' – *Variety*

Once in Paris
US 1978 100m TVC Color
Frank D. Gilroy

A naïve American writer is introduced to the delights of Paris by a worldly chauffeur and an amorous British noblewoman.
A movie that adds up to very little, but pleases along the way.
wd Frank D. Gilroy
☆ Wayne Rogers, Gayle Hunnicutt, Jack Lenoir, Philippe March, Tanya Lopert

'The darkest alleys of love among the international set!'

Once Is Not Enough
US 1975 122m Movielab Panavision
Paramount/Sujac/Aries (Howard W. Koch)

aka: *Jacqueline Susann's Once Is Not Enough*
The daughter of a movie producer is corrupted by his circle.
Old-fashioned jet-set melodrama with new-fashioned sexual novelties.
w Julius J. Epstein novel Jacqueline Susann d Guy Green ph John A. Alonzo m Henry Mancini pd John DeCuir
☆ Kirk Douglas, Alexis Smith, David Janssen, George Hamilton, Melina Mercouri, Gary Conway, Brenda Vaccaro, Deborah Raffin
⚡ Brenda Vaccaro

Once More My Darling
US 1949 92m bw
Universal (Joan Harrison)

A young girl is romantically pursued by an older man.
Tame comedy.
w Robert Carson d Robert Montgomery ph Franz Planer m Elizabeth Firestone
☆ Robert Montgomery, Ann Blyth, Jane Cowl, Taylor Holmes, Charles McGraw

Once More with Feeling
GB 1960 92m Technicolor
Columbia/Stanley Donen

The volatile private life of an orchestral conductor.

Thin comedy from a West End play, something between a shouting match and a fashion show.
w Harry Kurnitz play Harry Kurnitz d Stanley Donen ph Georges Périnal md Muir Mathieson pd Alexander Trauner
☆ Yul Brynner, Kay Kendall, Geoffrey Toone, Maxwell Shaw, Mervyn Johns, Martin Benson, Gregory Ratoff

Once to Every Woman
US 1934 70m bw
Columbia

A young doctor saves a patient's life by pushing his ailing chief aside during an operation.
Tedious, routine hospital stuff.
w Jo Swerling story A. J. Cronin d Lambert Hillyer
☆ Walter Connolly, Ralph Bellamy, Fay Wray, Mary Carlisle, Walter Byron
'A programmer which won't make the grade in key houses.' – *Variety*

Once Upon a Crime
US 1992 94m Technicolor
Entertainment/Troublemakers/Dino de Laurentiis

Two Americans in Europe, hoping to collect a reward for finding a valuable dog, are suspected of murdering the animal's owner.
Hysterically unamusing comedy, performed in a frantic style.
w Charles Shyer, Nancy Myers, Steve Kluger story Rodolfo Sonego d Eugene Levy ph Giuseppe Rotunno m Richard Gibbs pd Pier Luigi Basile ed Patrick Kennedy
☆ John Candy, James Belushi, Cybill Shepherd, Sean Young, Richard Lewis, Ornella Muti, Giancarlo Giannini, George Hamilton, Joss Ackland
'An overacted, unfunny, unexciting comedy-thriller.' – *Philip French, Observer*
'The film gives the impression of having been assembled, at great haste and in a state of panic, from bits and pieces left over from several other "international comedies".' – *Philip Kemp, Sight and Sound*
'Abysmal comedy.' – *Variety*
† A remake of *Crimen*, directed by Mario Camerini in 1960.

Once Upon a Dream
GB 1948 84m bw
Triton/Rank

An officer's wife has a romantic dream about her husband's batman, and comes to believe it true.
Very wispy comedy which does none of its principals any good.
w Patrick Kirwan, Victor Katona d Ralph Thomas
☆ Googie Withers, Griffith Jones, Guy Middleton, Raymond Lovell, Hubert Gregg

Once Upon a Forest
👫 US 1992 71m CFI color
TCF/Hanna-Barbera/HTV (David Kirschner, Jerry Mills)

After toxic waste destroys their environment, a mouse, a mole and a hedgehog have two days to find herbs that will save the life of their friend, a badger.
Dull and unimaginative animated movie that is unlikely to engage anyone's attention.
w Mark Young, Kelly Ward story Rae Lambert d Charles Grosvenor m James Horner pd Carol Holman Grosvenor, Bill Proctor ed Pat A. Foley
☆ Featuring the voices of Michael Crawford, Ben Vereen, Ellen Blain, Ben Gregory, Paige Gosney, Elizabeth Moss, Paul Elding, Janet Waldo
'It might, just, be of mild interest to the very young. But most kids, you suspect, are unregenerate sadists who will run a mile from something so earnestly improving.' – *Sheila Johnston, Independent*
'One long yawn.' – *Geoff Brown, The Times*

Once Upon a Honeymoon *
US 1942 116m bw
RKO (Leo McCarey)

An American radio correspondent and an ex-burlesque queen cheat the Nazis – and her husband – in Europe during World War II.
Smooth but curious mixture of comedy and drama, a satisfactory but unmemorable star vehicle.

w Sheridan Gibney, Leo McCarey d Leo McCarey ph George Barnes m Robert Emmett Dolan
☆ Cary Grant, Ginger Rogers, Walter Slezak, Albert Dekker, Albert Bassermann, Ferike Boros, Harry Shannon
'The attempt to play for both laughs and significance against a terrifying background of Nazi aggression is on the whole a little disappointing.' – *Newsweek*

Once Upon a Horse
US 1958 85m bw Cinemascope
Universal (Hal Kanter)

Two cowboys steal a herd of cattle but can't afford to feed them.
Unprepossessing comedy vehicle for a team which found success only on television.
wd Hal Kanter ph Arthur Arling ad Robert Clatworthy
☆ Dan Rowan, Dick Martin, Martha Hyer, Leif Erickson, Nita Talbot, James Gleason

Once Upon a Thursday: see *The Affairs of Martha*

Once Upon a Time *
👫 US 1944 89m bw
Columbia (Louis Edelman)

A luckless producer makes a sensation out of a boy and his dancing caterpillar.
Thin whimsical comedy, too slight to come off given such standard treatment, but with nice touches along the way.
w Lewis Meltzer, Oscar Saul radio play My Client Curley by Norman Corwin, Lucille F. Herrmann d Alexander Hall ph Franz Planer m Frederick Hollander
☆ Cary Grant, Janet Blair, James Gleason, Ted Donaldson, Howard Freeman, William Demarest, Art Baker, John Abbott
'There just isn't enough material here for a full-length feature.' – *Philip T. Hartung*
'It would be nice to see some screen fantasy if it were done by anyone with half a heart, mind and hand for it. But when the studios try to make it, duck and stay hid till the mood has passed.' – *James Agee*

'As boys they said they would die for each other. As men, they did.'

Once Upon a Time in America ****
US 1984 228m Technicolor
Warner/Embassy/Ladd/PSO (Arnon Milchan)

The lives of four gangsters between 1922 and 1968.
Vast, sprawling, violent crime saga that is both the epitome and summation of gangster movies, a powerful, almost operatic drama of waste and despair.
w Leonardo Benvenuti, Piero de Bernardi, Enrico Medioli, Franco Arcalli, Franco Ferrini, Sergio Leone novel The Hoods by David Aaronson ('Harry Grey') d Sergio Leone ph Tonino Delli Colli m Ennio Morricone ed Nino Baragli
☆ Robert DeNiro, James Woods, Elizabeth McGovern, Treat Williams, Tuesday Weld, Burt Young, Danny Aiello, William Forsythe
'It is, finally, a heart-breaking story of mutual need. By matching that need with his own need to come to terms with his own cultural memories, Leone has made his most oneiric and extraordinary film.' – *Tony Rayns, MFB*
🎵 music

Once Upon a Time in China *
Hong Kong 1991 140m colour
Film Workshop 1 (Zhen Wen Huai, Tsui Hark)

original title: *Wong Fei Hung*
Concerned about the growing Western influences in China, a martial master finds himself arrayed against a combination of triads, English, Americans selling the locals into slavery and prostitution, and government officials.
Anti-West martial arts movie, notable for the vigour and speed of its many scenes of fighting action.
w Tsui Hark, Yuan Zao Zhi, Liang Yao Min, Deng Bi Yan d Tsui Hark ph Chong Zhi Wen, Bill Huang, Arthur Huang, Ardy Chan m James Wong, Dai Le Ming pd David Luo, Jin Yang Xiang ed Mak Zhi Shang
☆ Jet Li, Yuan Biao, Rosamund Kwan, Ken Chung, Jacky Cheung, Wu Ma, Liu Xun, Yuan Xian Ren

Once Upon a Time in the West ***
Italy/US 1969 165m Techniscope
Paramount/Rafran/San Marco (Fulvio Morsella)

A lonely woman in the old west is in danger from a band of gunmen.
Immensely long and convoluted epic Western marking its director's collaboration with an American studio and his desire to make serious statements about something or other. Beautifully made, empty, and very violent.
w Sergio Leone, Sergio Donati d Sergio Leone ph Tonino Delli Colli m Ennio Morricone
☆ Henry Fonda, Claudia Cardinale, Jason Robards, Charles Bronson, Gabriele Ferzetti, Keenan Wynn, Paolo Stoppa, Lionel Stander, Jack Elam, Woody Strode
† This film has the longest credits of all: they sprawl through the first twelve minutes.

Once Were Warriors ***
New Zealand 1994 103m Eastmancolor
Entertainment/Communicado/NZFC/Avalon/New Zealand On Air (Robin Scholes)

In Auckland, a Maori woman attempts to bring up her children, including a bookish daughter and a son attracted to street gangs, and to cope with her unemployed, heavy-drinking and violent husband.
A powerfully emotional and often disturbing drama of the dispossessed, making its points with sledgehammer force, but also giving a place to the tenderness and pride that exist within a family forced to the edges of society.
w Riwia Brown novel Alan Duff d Lee Tamahori ph Stuart Dryburgh m Murray Grindley, Murray McNabb pd Michael Kane ed Michael Horton
☆ Rena Owen, Temuera Morrison, Mamaengaroa Kerr-Bell, Julian Arahanga, Taungaroa Emile, Rachael Morris, Joseph Kairau, Clifford Curtis
'Unflinchingly scans the domestic tragedy which can be found in any culture where hope is a luxury no one can afford.' – *Time*
'It's certainly operatic in style and melodramatic in concept. It shouldn't work as well as it does. But by flinging caution to the winds, it winds up mightily effective.' – *Derek Malcolm, Guardian*
† It took more money at the New Zealand box-office than any other film so far.

One Against Seven: see *Counterattack*

The One and Only
US 1978 98m Movielab
Paramount/First Artists (Steve Gordon, David V. Picker)

A stage-struck egomaniac finds success at the expense of happiness with his wife.
Uneasy mixture of farce and sentiment intended as a star vehicle, but not a very successful one.
w Steve Gordon d Carl Reiner ph Victor J. Kemper m Patrick Williams
☆ Henry Winkler, Kim Darby, Gene Saks, William Daniels, Polly Holiday, Herve Villechaize, Harold Gould, Richard Lane

The One and Only Genuine Original Family Band
👫 US 1968 110m Technicolor
Disney

Adventures of a Republican family at the 1888 convention.
Long and rather muddled family comedy with politics and music; not a winner anywhere.
w Lowell S. Hawley book Laura Bower Van Nuys d Michael O'Herlihy
☆ Walter Brennan, Buddy Ebsen, John Davidson, Lesley Ann Warren, Janet Blair, Kurt Russell, Richard Deacon

One Armed Boxer
Hong Kong 1972 97m Eastmancolor
Cathay/Champion (Raymond Chow)

original title: *Dop Bey Kuan Wan*
A young boxer seeks revenge after he loses an arm in a fight against a gang leader and his assorted thugs, each expert in a different martial art.
Little more than a series of fight sequences, which are well choreographed and will no doubt appeal to fans of the genre.
wd Wang Yu ph Mo Shen Ku m Wang Fu Ling, Wang Ping ed Cheng Hung Min

☆ Wang Yu, Tang Shin, Tien Yeh, Lung Fei, Wu Tung Choo, Pan Chun Lin, San Mao

'The photography and cutting of the fights is, as usual, highly expert, with a splendid sense of movement.' – *MFB*

† The film was cut to 92m for its British release.

One Body Too Many

US 1944 74m bw
Pine-Thomas/Paramount
▦

An insurance salesman arrives at a spooky house to find his prospect murdered.
Comedy melodrama which could have been a lot funnier and more melodramatic; once more, the butler didn't do it.
w Winston Miller, Maxwell Shane d Frank McDonald
☆ Jack Haley, Bela Lugosi, Jean Parker, Bernard Nedell, Blanche Yurka, Douglas Fowley, Lyle Talbot

One Born Every Minute: see The Flim Flam Man

One Brief Summer

GB 1969 86m Eastmancolor
TCF/Twickenham (Guido Coen)
A wealthy man loses interest in his mistress and begins courting his daughter's friend.
Odd, downbeat melodrama with hints of incest; a sophisticated time-passer.
w Wendy Marshall *play Valkyrie's Armour* by Harry Tierney d John Mackenzie ph David MacDonald m Roger Webb
☆ Clifford Evans, Felicity Gibson, Jennifer Hilary, Jan Holden, Peter Egan, Fanny Carby, Richard Vernon, Brian Wilde

One Dangerous Night

US 1943 77m bw
Columbia (David Chatkin)
Reformed jewel thief The Lone Wolf is accused of the murder of a society blackmailer.
Entertaining, fast-paced little thriller, with the usual comedy of bumbling cops kept to the minimum.
w Donald Davis *story* Arnold Phillips, Max Nosseck d Michael Gordon ph L. W. O'Connell md M. W. Stoloff ad Lionel Banks ed Viola Lawrence
☆ Warren William, Eric Blore, Marguerite Chapman, Mona Barrie, Tala Birell, Margaret Hayes, Ann Savage, Thurston Hall, Warren Ashe

One Day in the Life of Ivan Denisovich *

GB 1971 105m Eastmancolor
Group W/Leontes/Norsk (Caspar Wrede)
▦ @▵
Life in a Siberian labour camp in 1950.
A fairly successful book adaptation, as far as mere pictures can cope with the harrowing detail.
w Ronald Harwood *novel* Alexander Solzhenitsyn d Caspar Wrede ph Sven Nykvist m Arne Nordheim
☆ Tom Courtenay, Espen Skjonberg, James Maxwell, Alfred Burke, Eric Thompson, Matthew Guinness
'The film's general air of earnestness deflects rather than stimulates involvement.' – *David Wilson*

One Deadly Summer *

France 1983 133m Eastmancolor
Premier/SNC/CAPAC/TFI (Christine Beytout)
▦ ▦
original title: *L'été Meurtrier*
A nineteen-year-old girl seduces a villager into marrying her as the first step in a long-delayed act of revenge.
Moody psychological thriller, an award-winner in France, that grows more engrossing as it continues.
w Sebastien Japrisot *novel* Sebastien Japrisot d Jean Becker ph Etienne Becker m Georges Delerue ad Jean-Claude Gallouin ed Jacques Witta
☆ Isabelle Adjani, Alain Souchon, Suzanne Flon, Jenny Clève, Michel Galabru, François Cluzet

One Desire

US 1955 94m Technicolor
U-I (Ross Hunter)
The romantic career of the lady owner of a gambling saloon.
Tawdry 1890s drama which never really gets going.

w Lawrence Roman, Robert Blees *novel Tacey Cromwell* by Conrad Richter d Jerry Hopper ph Maury Gertsman m Frank Skinner md Joseph Gershenson
☆ Anne Baxter, Rock Hudson, Julia Adams, Natalie Wood, Barry Curtis, William Hopper, Carl Benton Reid
'The standards of writing and characterization belong to a Victorian servant girl's paper-covered romance.' – *MFB*

One Exciting Night

GB 1944 89m bw
Columbia British
A singing welfare worker averts a plan to steal a Rembrandt.
Very ho-hum stuff for a very popular but histrionically untried star.
w Howard Irving Young, Peter Fraser, Margaret Kennedy, Emery Bonnet d Walter Forde
☆ Vera Lynn, Donald Stewart, Mary Clare, Frederick Leister, Richard Murdoch

One Eyed Jacks

US 1961 141m Technicolor Vistavision
Paramount/Pennebaker (Frank P. Rosenberg)
▦ ▦ @▵ @ @
An outlaw has a running battle with an old friend.
Grossly self-indulgent Western controlled (unwisely) by its star, full of solemn pauses and bouts of violence.
w Guy Trosper, Calder Willingham *novel The Authentic Death of Hendry Jones* by Charles Neider d Marlon Brando ph Charles Lang Jnr m Hugo Friedhofer
☆ Marlon Brando, Karl Malden, Pina Pellicer, Katy Jurado, Slim Pickens, Ben Johnson, Timothy Carey, Elisha Cook Jnr
'This is not the ordinary Western; not the ordinary good Western; not even the ordinary extraordinary Western … The figures and the background, the colour and the movement repeatedly unite in compositions of mesmerizing beauty.' – *Dilys Powell*
'The picture is of variable quality: it has some visual grandeur; it also has some bizarrely brutal scenes. It isn't clear why Brando made this peculiarly masochistic revenge fantasy, or whether he hoped for something quite different from what he finished with.' – *Pauline Kael*
⋔ Charles Lang Jnr

One False Move ***

US 1992 105m colour
Metro/I.R.S. Media (Jesse Beaton, Ben Myron)
▦ ▦ @▵ @
Two killers on the run with their black girlfriend head for a small town in Alabama where the local police chief and two big city detectives are waiting for them.
A tough, complex, suspenseful thriller-cum-road movie that also finds room to concern itself with relationships and racism.
w Billy Bob Thornton, Tom Epperson d Carl Franklin ph James L. Carter m Peter Haycock, Derek Holt pd Gary T. New ed Carole Kravetz
☆ Bill Paxton, Cynda Williams, Billy Bob Thornton, Michael Beach, Jim Metzler, Earl Billings, Natalie Canerday
'Gives film buffs that special jolt they're always looking for.' – *Jami Bernard, New York Post*
'A crime film that lifts you up and carries you along in an ominously rising tide of tension, building to an emotional pay-off of amazing power.' – *Roger Ebert*

One Fine Day

US 1996 109m DeLuxe
TCF/Fox 2000/Via Rosa (Lynda Obst)
▦ @▵ @
Two busy single parents fall in love with each other.
Bland and sentimental romantic comedy.
w Terrel Seltzer, Ellen Simon d Michael Hoffman ph Oliver Stapleton m James Newton Howard pd David Gropman ed Garth Craven
☆ Michelle Pfeiffer, George Clooney, Mae Whitman, Alex D. Linz, Charles Durning, Jon Robin Baitz, Ellen Greene, Joe Grifasi, Pete Hamill
'Made with the right breezy insouciance and performed with consummate flair and sexy star appeal.' – *Todd McCarthy, Variety*
⋔ song 'For the First Time' (m/ly James Newton Howard, Jud J. Friedman, Allan Dennis Rich)

One Flew over the Cuckoo's Nest ****

US 1975 134m DeLuxe
UA/Fantasy Films (Saul Zaentz, Michael Douglas)
▦ ▦ ▦ @▵ @ @ @ @
A cheerful immoralist imprisoned for rape is transferred for observation to a state mental hospital.
Wildly and unexpectedly commercial film of a project which had lain dormant for fourteen years, this amusing and horrifying film conveniently sums up anti-government attitudes as well as make love not war and all that. It's certainly impossible to ignore.
w Lawrence Hauben, Bo Goldman *novel Ken Kesey* d Milos Forman ph Haskell Wexler m Jack Nitzsche pd Paul Sylbert
☆ Jack Nicholson, Louise Fletcher, William Redfield, Will Sampson, Brad Dourif, Christopher Lloyd
'Lacks the excitement of movie art, but the story and the acting make the film emotionally powerful.' – *New Yorker*
† Kirk Douglas bought the rights to the book and starred in a Broadway adaptation of it, but he was unable to obtain backing for a film version. When Michael Douglas obtained finance from outside the movie industry, his father was too old to play the lead role. James Caan turned down the role. Louise Fletcher's role was turned down by Anne Bancroft, Angela Lansbury and Ellen Burstyn.
🏆 best picture; script; Milos Forman; Jack Nicholson; Louise Fletcher
⋔ Haskell Wexler; Jack Nitzsche; Brad Dourif
🏆 best picture; Milos Forman; Jack Nicholson; Louise Fletcher; Brad Dourif

One Foot in Heaven *

US 1941 108m bw
Warner (Robert Lord, Irving Rapper)
The small-town doings of a methodist minister.
Slow but pleasing chronicle, nicely assembled.
w Casey Robinson *biography* (of his father) Hartzell Spence d Irving Rapper ph Charles Rosher m Max Steiner
☆ Fredric March, Martha Scott, Beulah Bondi, Gene Lockhart, Elisabeth Fraser, Harry Davenport, Laura Hope Crews, Grant Mitchell, Moroni Olsen, Ernest Cossart, Jerome Cowan
'A clean, sweet, decent picture.' – *Cecilia Ager*
⋔ best picture

One Foot in Hell

US 1960 89m DeLuxe Cinemascope
TCF (Sydney Boehm)
The sheriff of a small Western town is secretly plotting revenge on the townfolk for their long-ago treatment of his wife.
Unusual Western suspenser with plenty of violent action and an extremely equivocal hero.
w Aaron Spelling, Sydney Boehm d James B. Clark m William C. Mellor m Dominic Frontière
☆ Alan Ladd, Dan O'Herlihy, Don Murray, Dolores Michaels, Barry Coe, Larry Gates, John Alexander

One for the Book: see The Voice of the Turtle

One Frightened Night

US 1935 67m bw
Mascot
▦
Relatives assemble in a spooky house in the hope of inheriting an old man's wealth.
Low-budget thriller that sometimes seems like a spoof of The Cat and the Canary.
w Wellyn Totman d Christy Cabanne ph Ernest Miller, William Nobles
☆ Charles Grapewin, Mary Carlisle, Arthur Hohl, Evalyn Knapp, Wallace Ford, Hedda Hopper, Lucien Littlefield, Regis Toomey, Rafaela Ottiano

One from the Heart *

US 1982 101m Metrocolor
Zoetrope Studios (Gray Frederickson, Fred Roos, Armyan Bernstein)
▦ ▦ @▵ @
On Independence Day in Las Vegas, a pair of lovers quarrel and make up.
Extraordinarily slim (for its cost) romantic fantasy which makes one wonder why, of all stories in the world, its creator chose this one. It does however boast attractive visuals.

w Armyan Bernstein, Francis Coppola d Francis Coppola ph Vittorio Storaro m Tom Waits pd Dean Tavoularis
☆ Frederic Forrest, Teri Garr, Raul Julia, Nastassja Kinski, Lainie Kazan, Harry Dean Stanton
'Giddy heights of visual imagination and technical brilliance are lavished on a wafer-thin story.' – *Variety*
'If this is the essence of cinema, then Salvador Dali is the essence of painting.' – *Sunday Times*
'A very beautiful film, the background of which totally drowns a wafer-thin plot. A musical non-musical, a spectacular nonspectacular, a fantasy with realist aspirations.' – *Guardian*
'Escapism running away with itself.' – *Standard*
⋔ original song score

One Good Cop

US 1991 105m colour
Hollywood/Silver Screen Partners IV (Laurence Mark)
▦ ▦ @▵
A policeman and his wife run into problems when they try to adopt the three young girls of his murdered partner.
Mundane and manipulative drama that is never arresting.
wd Heywood Gould ph Ralf Bode m David Foster, William Ross ad Sandy Veneziano ed Richard Marks
☆ Michael Keaton, René Russo, Anthony LaPaglia, Kevin Conway, Rachel Ticotin, Tony Plana, Benjamin Bratt
'Excruciating dialogue, stagnant ideas and acting more wooden than Sherwood Forest.' – *Sight and Sound*

One Good Turn

US 1931 20m bw
Hal Roach
✿
Two odd-job men see their benefactress rehearsing a play, and think she is really being evicted.
Moderate star comedy with nice moments.
w H. M. Walker d James W. Horne ph Art Lloyd ed Richard Currier
☆ Stan Laurel, Oliver Hardy, Mary Carr, Billy Gilbert, James Finlayson, Snub Pollard

One Good Turn

👪 GB 1954 90m bw
GFD/Two Cities (Maurice Cowan)
An orphan stays on to become an odd job man, and tries to raise money to buy an old car.
The star's second comedy is an almost unmitigated disaster, disjointed and depending too much on pathos.
w Maurice Cowan, John Paddy Carstairs, Ted Willis d John Paddy Carstairs ph Jack Cox m John Addison
☆ Norman Wisdom, Joan Rice, Shirley Abicair, Thora Hird, William Russell, Richard Caldicot

One Heavenly Night

US 1930 82m bw
Samuel Goldwyn
A flower girl in a Budapest music hall finds herself imitating the absent star.
Would-be-Lubitsch-like musical comedy which doesn't quite succeed in its pleasant aims.
w Sidney Howard *story* Louis Bromfield d George Fitzmaurice ph George Barnes, Gregg Toland
☆ Evelyn Laye, John Boles, Leon Errol, Lilyan Tashman, Hugh Cameron, Lionel Belmore
'It will satisfy the customers, but lacks the intrinsic quality that makes 'em talk and recommends it as an entertainment for big grosses.' – *Variety*

One Hour with You: see The Marriage

Circle (1924)

'Gayest screen event of the year!'
One Hour with You ***

US 1932 84m bw
Paramount (Ernst Lubitsch)
The affairs of a philandering Parisian doctor.
Superbly handled comedy of manners in Lubitsch's most inventive form, handled by a most capable cast. Unique entertainment of a kind which is, alas, no more.

---

w Samson Raphaelson *play* Only a Dream *by* Lothar Schmidt *d* George Cukor, Ernst Lubitsch *ph* Victor Milner *m* Oscar Straus, Richard Whiting *ad* Hans Dreier *ly* Leo Robin

☆ Maurice Chevalier, Jeanette MacDonald, Genevieve Tobin, Roland Young, Charles Ruggles, George Barbier

'Sure fire if frothy screen fare, cinch b.o. at all times.' – *Variety*

'A brand new form of musical entertainment … he has mixed verse, spoken and sung, a smart and satiric musical background, asides to the audience, and sophisticated dialogue, as well as lilting and delightful songs … The result is something so delightful that it places the circle of golden leaves jauntily upon the knowing head of Hollywood's most original director.' – *Philadelphia Inquirer*

† A remake of Lubitsch's silent success *The Marriage Circle.*

👑 best picture

One Hundred and One Dalmatians ***
👪 US 1961 79m Technicolor
Walt Disney
📽

The dogs of London help save puppies which are being stolen for their skins by a cruel villainess.
Disney's last really splendid feature cartoon, with the old flexible style cleverly modernized and plenty of invention and detail in the story line. The London backgrounds are especially nicely judged.
w Bill Peet *novel* Dodie Smith *d* Wolfgang Reitherman, Hamilton S. Luske, Clyde Geronimi *m* George Bruns

☆ Featuring the voices of Rod Taylor, Cate Bauer, Betty Lou Gerson, J. Pat O'Malley

'It has the freshness of the early short colour-cartoons without the savagery which has often disfigured the later feature-length stories.' – *Dilys Powell*

'When schools become war zones and both sides start taking casualties, what then?'
187
US 1997 119m DeLuxe
Warner/Anna K/Icon (Bruce Davey, Stephen McEveety)
📽 📽 ⛑

A New York teacher recovers from being stabbed by a pupil sufficiently to move to a Los Angeles school, where he reacts violently when he is threatened by some of his students.
Risible and confused melodrama, from which an audience can learn nothing and enjoy even less.
w Scott Yagemann *d* Kevin Reynolds *ph* Ericson Core *pd* Stephen Storer *ed* Stephen Semel
☆ Samuel L. Jackson, John Heard, Kelly Rowan, Clifton Gonzalez Gonzalez, Tony Plana, Karina Arroyave, Lobo Sebastian

'"A teacher wrote this movie," the final credit reads. It might have made more sense to hire a screenwriter.' – *Richard Williams, Guardian*

One Hundred Men and a Girl ***
👪 US 1937 84m bw
Universal (Joe Pasternak)
📽 ⛑

A young girl persuades a great conductor to form an orchestra of unemployed musicians.
Delightful and funny musical fable, an instance of the Pasternak formula of sweetness and light at its richest and best.
w Bruce Manning, Charles Kenyon, Hans Kraly *d* Henry Koster *ph* Joseph Valentine *m* Charles Previn *ed* Bernard W. Burton *songs* various
☆ Deanna Durbin, Adolphe Menjou, Leopold Stokowski, Alice Brady, Mischa Auer, Eugene Pallette, Billy Gilbert, Alma Kruger, Jed Prouty, Frank Jenks, Christian Rub

'Smash hit for all the family … something new in entertainment.' – *Variety*
'Apart from its value as entertainment, which is considerable, it reveals the cinema at its sunny-sided best.' – *New York Times.*
'An original story put over with considerable skill.' – *MFB*

👤 Charles Previn
👑 best picture; original story (Hans Kraly); editing

'This Time The Magic Is Real.'
101 Dalmatians
👪 US 1996 103m Technicolor Panavision
Buena Vista/Walt Disney/Great Oaks (John Hughes, Ricardo Mestres)
📽 📽 ⛑ 📺 🎧

After their owners marry, two dalmatians protect their numerous puppies from a fur-loving woman who wants to turn them into a fur coat.
Live-action remake of a successful animated feature which lacks the charm of the original.
w John Hughes *novel* The One Hundred and One Dalmatians *by* Dodie Smith *d* Stephen Herek *ph* Adrian Biddle *m* Michael Kamen *pd* Assheton Gorton *ed* Industrial Light and Magic; Jim Henson's Creature Shop
☆ Glenn Close, Jeff Daniels, Joan Plowright, Joely Richardson, Hugh Laurie, Mark Williams, John Shrapnel

'Relentlessly cuddlesome enough to make this, if not enchanting, then sufficiently chucklesome and likeable to send family audiences home with their tails wagging.' – *Angie Errigo, Empire*

One Hundred Per Cent Pure: see *The Girl from Missouri*

100 Rifles *
US 1969 109m DeLuxe
TCF/Marvin Schwartz
📽 📽

In war-torn Mexico, a black American sheriff and his prisoner become involved in a girl's fight for vengeance after her father's death.
Blood-soaked adventure with plenty of tough action and tight pace. A little too purposeful in its unpleasantness to be very entertaining.
w Clair Huffaker, Tom Gries *novel* Robert MacLeod *d* Tom Gries *ph* Cecilio Paniagua *m* Jerry Goldsmith
☆ Jim Brown, Raquel Welch, Burt Reynolds, Fernando Lamas, Dan O'Herlihy, Hans Gudegast

120 Days of Sodom
Italy/France 1975 117m Technicolor
PEA/PAA

After the Italian campaign of 1944, four local dignitaries marry each other's daughters, withdraw with a bevy of nubile girls to a mountain retreat, and tell each other sado-masochistic sexual adventures.
Thoroughly revolting and much banned piece with no perceptible point but a good deal of emetic detail.
wd Pier Paolo Pasolini *novel* Marquis de Sade *ph* Tonino delli Colli *ad* Dante Ferretti
☆ Paolo Bonacelli, Giorgio Cataldi, Uberto P. Quintavalle, Aldo Valetti

One in a Million **
👪 US 1936 94m bw
TCF (Raymond Griffith)
The daughter of a Swiss innkeeper becomes an Olympic ice-skating champion.
Sonja Henie's film debut shows Hollywood at its most professional, making entertainment out of the purest moonshine with considerable injections of novelty talent.
w Leonard Praskins, Mark Kelly *d* Sidney Lanfield *ph* Edward Cronjager *md* Louis Silvers *ch* Jack Haskell *songs* Sidney Mitchell, Lew Pollack
☆ Sonja Henie, Don Ameche, The Ritz Brothers, Jean Hersholt, Ned Sparks, Arline Judge, Dixie Dunbar, Borrah Minevitch and his Rascals, Montagu Love

'A very entertaining, adroitly mixed concoction of romance, music, comedy and skating … Miss Henie is a screen find.' – *Variety*
👤 Jack Haskell

One Is a Lonely Number *
US 1972 97m Metrocolor
MGM (Stan Margulies)
When her husband leaves her, a woman tries to develop new interests.
Satirical sentimental view of American divorce, with interesting moments.
w David Seltzer *novel* Rebecca Morris *d* Mel Stuart *ph* Michel Hugo *m* Michel Legrand
☆ Trish Van Devere, Monte Markham, Melvyn Douglas, Janet Leigh

One Little Indian
👪 US 1973 91m Technicolor
Walt Disney (Winston Hibler)
📽 📺

A cavalry corporal escapes from jail and falls in with a ten-year-old Indian.
Sentimental semi-Western, a bit dull for Disney apart from a camel.
w Harry Spalding *d* Bernard McEveety *ph* Charles F. Wheeler *m* Jerry Goldsmith
☆ James Garner, Vera Miles, Pat Hingle, Morgan Woodward, John Doucette

One Magic Christmas
👪 Canada 1985 88m DeLuxe
Silver Screen/Telefilm Canada/Walt Disney (Peter O'Brian, Fred Roos)
📽 ⛑

An angel interferes in the lives of a family with problems.
Decidedly downbeat Christmas fantasy: daddy gets drowned, mother is a nut, and the angel looks like a tramp. Santa Claus puts in an appearance for a happy finale, but It's a Wonderful Life should sue for plagiarism.
w Thomas Meecham *d* Phillip Borsos *ph* Frank Tidy *m* Michael Conway *pd* Bill Brodie *ed* Sidney Wolinsky
☆ Mary Steenburgen, Gary Basaraba, Harry Dean Stanton, Arthur Hill

One Man Mutiny: see *The Court Martial of Billy Mitchell*

One Man's Journey
US 1933 72m bw
RKO
The career of a rural doctor for whom fame arrives too late.
Pleasant, predictable, rather downbeat small-town drama.
w Lester Cohen, Sam Ornitz *story* Failure *by* Katharine Haviland Taylor *d* John Robertson
☆ Lionel Barrymore, May Robson, Dorothy Jordan, Joel McCrea, Frances Dee, David Landau, Samuel S. Hinds

'Carries sympathetic interest and appeal.' – *Variety*

One Man's Way *
US 1964 105m bw
UA
A crime reporter becomes a priest.
Rather self-conscious biography of Norman Vincent Peale, adequately assembled but containing no surprises.
w Eleanore Griffin, John W. Bloch *book* Minister to Millions *by* Arthur Gordon *d* Denis Sanders
☆ Don Murray, Diana Hyland, William Windom, Virginia Christine, Carol Ohmart

One Mile from Heaven
US 1937 68m bw
TCF
A girl reporter makes hay with the story of a black woman who is raising a white child.
Curious mixture of melodrama and wisecracking farce, with tap dancing from Bill Robinson thrown in.
w Lou Breslow, John Patrick *d* Allan Dwan
☆ Claire Trevor, Sally Blane, Douglas Fowley, Fredi Washington, Ralf Harolde

'Whether the theme fits into the popular groove is something to think about.' – *Variety*

'The most exciting adventure in a million years!'
One Million BC *
US 1940 80m bw
Hal Roach
📽 ⛑
GB title: *Man and His Mate*
aka: *The Cave Dwellers*
Life between warring tribes of primitive man in the stone age.
Impressive-looking but slow-moving grunt-and-groan epic originally based on D. W. Griffith's Man's Genesis and on which Griffith did some work. The totally unhistoric dinosaurs (which had disappeared long before man arrived) are impressively concocted by magnifying lizards.
w Mickell Novak, George Baker, Joseph Frickert *d* Hal Roach, Hal Roach Jnr, D. W. Griffith *ph* Norbert Brodine *m* Werner R. Heymann
☆ Victor Mature, Carole Landis, Lon Chaney Jnr, John Hubbard, Nigel de Brulier, Conrad Nagel
👑 Werner R. Heymann

'This is the way it was!'
One Million Years BC *
👪 GB 1966 100m Technicolor
Hammer (Michael Carreras)
📽

A vague remake of the above, with animated monsters.
Not badly done, with some lively action.
w Michael Carreras *d* Don Chaffey *ph* Wilkie Cooper *m* Mario Nascimbene
☆ John Richardson, Raquel Welch, Robert Brown, Percy Herbert, Martine Beswick

'Very easy to dismiss the film as a silly spectacle; but Hammer production finesse is much in evidence and Don Chaffey has done a competent job of direction. And it is all hugely enjoyable.' – *David Wilson*

One Minute to Zero
US 1952 105m bw
RKO (Edmund Grainger)
📽

In Korea a US colonel is evacuating American civilians but is forced to bomb refugees.
Flat war film with Something To Say and the star at his most humourless.
w Milton Krims, William Haines *d* Tay Garnett *ph* William E. Snyder *m* Victor Young *md* Constantin Bakaleinikoff
☆ Robert Mitchum, Ann Blyth, William Talman, Charles McGraw, Richard Egan

One More River *
US 1934 88m bw
Universal (James Whale)
GB title: *Over the River*
A wife runs away from her husband, and he sets detectives on her and her lover.
Old-fashioned, well made picturization of a novel.
w R. C. Sherriff *novel* John Galsworthy *d* James Whale *ph* John Mescall *m* W. Franke Harling
☆ Colin Clive, Diana Wynyard, C. Aubrey Smith, Jane Wyatt, Lionel Atwill, Mrs Patrick Campbell, Frank Lawton, Reginald Denny, Henry Stephenson, Alan Mowbray, E. E. Clive

'Galsworthy beautifully transmuted to the screen … Very British and ultra, but should prove nice enough b.o.' – *Variety*
'Taste, elegance, narrative drive and a deliberate nostalgia for the Galsworthy period.' – *Peter John Dyer, 1966*
'One of the finest courtroom episodes ever projected on a screen.' – *Motion Picture Herald*

One More Spring *
US 1935 87m bw
Fox (Winfield Sheehan)
Three strangers, in reduced circumstances due to the Depression, meet in Central Park and pool their resources.
Topical serio-comedy which looks pretty dated but still serves as a summation of American mid-thirties attitudes.
w Edwin Burke *novel* Robert Nathan *d* Henry King *ph* John Seitz *md* Arthur Lange
☆ Janet Gaynor, Warner Baxter, Walter Woolf King, Grant Mitchell, Jane Darwell, Roger Imhof, John Qualen, Dick Foran, Stepin Fetchit

'Whimsical comedy with plenty of laughs. Should do well.' – *Variety*

One More Time
GB 1969 93m DeLuxe
UA/Chrislaw-Tracemark (Milton Ebbins)
Two London club owners become involved with spies, gangsters and jewel-thieves.
The stars of the tedious Salt and Pepper are reunited for an even less amusing film.
w Michael Pertwee *d* Jerry Lewis *ph* Ernest Steward *m* Les Reed
☆ Peter Lawford, Sammy Davis Jnr, Esther Anderson, Maggie Wright

One More Tomorrow *
US 1946 89m bw
Warner (Henry Blanke)
A wealthy playboy marries a left-wing photographer and buys up her magazine.
An interesting but dated play fails to come to life because neither cast nor director seem to understand what it's about.
w Charles Hoffman, Catherine Turney, Julius J. and Philip G. Epstein *play* The Animal Kingdom *by* Philip Barry *d* Peter Godfrey *ph* Bert Glennon *m* Max Steiner

---

☆ Ann Sheridan, Dennis Morgan, Jack Carson, Alexis Smith, Jane Wyman, Reginald Gardiner, John Loder, Marjorie Gateson.

One More Train to Rob

US 1971 108m Technicolor
Universal (Robert Arthur)

A train robber comes out of prison and warily takes up with his old partners.
Undistinguished Western which tries to be funny and serious at the same time.
w Don Tait, Dick Nelson d Andrew V. McLaglen ph Alric Edens m David Shire
☆ George Peppard, Diana Muldaur, John Vernon, France Nuyen, Steve Sandor

One New York Night *

US 1935 80m bw
MGM (Bernard Hyman)
GB title: *The Trunk Mystery*

A young farmer in Manhattan on a visit finds a body in the hotel room next to his.
Slick comedy thriller very typical of its date and studio.
w Frank Davis *play* Edward Childs Carpenter d Jack Conway
☆ Franchot Tone, Una Merkel, Steffi Duna, Conrad Nagel, Charles Starrett, Harold Huber
'Sprightly devised murder mystery accounting for plenty of laughs … studded with multiple touches of production value.' – *Variety*
'A comedy of astonishing intelligence and finish … it ought to take its place immediately with the classics.' – *Graham Greene*

One Night in Lisbon

US 1941 97m bw
Paramount (Edward H. Griffith)

During World War II an American flyer falls for a British socialite who is being used by the government as a decoy for spies.
Flabby romantic comedy-drama which mostly wastes a good cast.
w Virginia Van Upp *play* There's Always Juliet by John Van Druten d Edward H. Griffith ph Bert Glennon m Sigmund Krumgold
☆ Madeleine Carroll, Fred MacMurray, Edmund Gwenn, Patricia Morison, Billie Burke, John Loder, Dame May Whitty, Reginald Denny, Billy Gilbert

One Night in the Tropics

US 1940 69m bw
Universal (Leonard Spigelgass)

Holidays on a Caribbean island lead to a double wedding.
Very lightweight comedy-musical notable only for introducing Abbott and Costello.
w Gertrude Purcell, Charles Grayson *play* Love Insurance by Earl Derr Biggers d A. Edward Sutherland ph Joseph Valentine md Charles Previn *songs* Oscar Hammerstein II, Jerome Kern, Otto Harbach, Dorothy Fields
☆ Allan Jones, Nancy Kelly, Bud Abbott, Lou Costello, Robert Cummings, Leo Carrillo, Peggy Moran, Mary Boland

One Night of Love **

US 1934 95m bw
Columbia (Harry Cohn)

An opera star rebels against her demanding teacher.
Light classical musical which was a surprising box-office success and brought Hollywood careers for Lily Pons, Gladys Swarthout, Miliza Korjus, etc.
w Dorothy Speare, Charles Beahan, S. K. Lauren, James Gow, Edmund North d Victor Schertzinger ph Joseph Walker m Victor Schertzinger, Gus Kahn md Pietro Cimini ed Gene Milford
☆ Grace Moore, Tullio Carminati, Lyle Talbot, Mona Barrie, Nydia Westman, Jessie Ralph, Luis Alberni, Jane Darwell
♪ score
† best picture; direction; Grace Moore; editing

One Night Stand

US 1994 92m Foto-Kem
New World/New Horizons/Schwartzman (Alida Camp)

aka: *Before the Night*

An unhappy, restless career woman falls for a man who picks her up in a night-club and discovers that he is suspected of murdering his wife.
Unconvincing and extremely boring romantic drama, along the lines of a TV soap opera, with trite dialogue.

---

w Marty Casella d Talia Shire ph Arthur Albert m David Shire pd Rusty Smith ed Jim Prior
☆ Ally Sheedy, A. Martinez, Frederic Forrest, Diane Salinger, Gina Hecht, Don Novello, Jodi Thelen, Robin Frates, Elsa Raven

'It was just one night that changed everything.'

One Night Stand *

US 1997 102m DeLuxe
Entertainment/New Line/Red Mullet (Mike Figgis, Annie Stewart, Ben Myron)

Visiting New York, a director of commercials spends the night with a woman he meets at his hotel, and finds he misses her when he returns home to his wife.
Slick, well-acted account of a burgeoning romance, but very forgettable.
wd Mike Figgis ph Declan Quinn m Mike Figgis pd Waldemar Kalinowski ed John Smith
☆ Wesley Snipes, Nastassja Kinski, Robert Downey Jnr, Ming-Na Wen, Kyle MacLachlan, Glenn Plummer, Amanda Donohoe, Thomas Haden Church, Julian Sands
'It's beautiful to look at, but shallow and trivial … flashy, phoney and as ephemeral as its title.' – *Alexander Walker, London Evening Standard*
† Joe Eszterhas was reportedly paid $3m for his original script, which was to have been directed by Adrian Lyne; Figgis rewrote it, keeping only the title and the plot device.
†† Wesley Snipes won the best actor award at the Venice Film Festival.

One Night with You

GB 1948 92m bw
Two Cities/Rank

An English girl and an Italian tenor, stranded by a train failure, are taken for forgers.
Rather frantic but occasionally amusing Italian-set comedy.
w Caryl Brahms, S. J. Simon d Terence Young ph André Thomas m Lambert Williamson
☆ Nino Martini, Patricia Roc, Hugh Wakefield, Bonar Colleano, Guy Middleton, Stanley Holloway, Irene Worth, Charles Goldner

One of Our Aircraft Is Missing *

GB 1941 102m bw
British National (Michael Powell, Emeric Pressburger)

A bomber is grounded after a raid and its crew is helped by the Dutch resistance.
Efficient propaganda piece which starts vigorously but gets bogged down in talk.
wd Michael Powell, Emeric Pressburger ph Ronald Neame ed David Lean
☆ Godfrey Tearle, Eric Portman, Hugh Williams, Bernard Miles, Hugh Burden, Emrys Jones, Googie Withers, Pamela Brown, Peter Ustinov, Joyce Redman, Hay Petrie, Robert Helpmann, Alec Clunes
§ script

One of Our Dinosaurs Is Missing *

US 1975 94m Technicolor
Walt Disney (Bill Walsh)

In the 1920s a strip of secret microfilm is smuggled out of China and hidden in a dinosaur's skeleton in the Natural History Museum.
Unexceptionable family comedy with everyone trying hard; somehow it just misses, perhaps because it is told through talk rather than cinematic narrative.
w Bill Walsh *novel* The Great Dinosaur Robbery by David Forrest d Robert Stevenson ph Paul Beeson m Ron Goodwin
☆ Helen Hayes, Peter Ustinov, Derek Nimmo, Clive Revill, Joan Sims, Bernard Bresslaw, Roy Kinnear, Deryck Guyler, Richard Pearson

One on One

US 1977 98m colour
Warner (Martin Hornstein)

An idealistic young basketball star finds life hard after he wins a scholarship to university.
Dull teen drama of a misfit making good.
w Robby Benson, Jerry Segal d Lamont Johnson ph Donald M. Morgan m Charles Fox ad Sherman Laudermilk ed Robbe Roberts
☆ Robby Benson, Annette O'Toole, G. D. Spradlin, Gail Strickland, Melanie Griffith

---

The One Piece Bathing Suit: see *Million Dollar Mermaid*

'Tis Pity She's a Whore **

Italy 1971 109m Technicolor
Miracle/Clesi (Silvio Clementelli)

original title: *Addio, Fratello Crudele*

A husband seeks revenge when he discovers that his wife is pregnant by her brother.
A gripping version of a Jacobean tragedy on the themes of obsessive love and jealousy.
w Giuseppe Patroni Griffi, Alfio Valdarnini, Carlo Carunchio *play* John Ford d Giuseppe Patroni Griffi ph Vittorio Storaro m Ennio Morricone ad Mario Ceroli ed Franco Arcalli
☆ Charlotte Rampling, Oliver Tobias, Fabio Testi, Antonio Falsi, Rik Battaglia, Angela Luce, Rino Imperio
'Magnificently expressive, as sensitive a transposition of the play as *Throne of Blood* was of *Macbeth*.' – *Tony Rayns, MFB*
'Too inclined to soft-focus ramblings through pretty countryside with characters' dubbed voices failing to match their lip movements. Odd but worthwhile.' – *Empire*
† The film was cut to 102m in its English version.

One Plus One

GB 1968 104m Eastmancolor
Connoisseur/Cupid (Michael Pearson, Iain Quarrier)

aka: *Sympathy for the Devil*

As the Rolling Stones rehearse their song 'Sympathy for the Devil', the film cuts between black militants, a television interview about revolution and its relationship with culture, and a bookshop where someone recites excerpts from *Mein Kampf*.
A confused revolutionary statement, with Godard trying to annex rock 'n' roll for his own impenetrable purposes. The last words in the film are the director's, stating that he is fed up and wants to go home; his audience is likely to have left earlier.
wd Jean-Luc Godard ph Tony Richmond m The Rolling Stones ed Ken Rowles
☆ Jean-Luc Godard, Sean Lynch, Mick Jagger, Keith Richard, Brian Jones, Charlie Watts, Bill Wyman, Anne Wiazemsky, Iain Quarrier, Frankie Dymon Jnr, Nike Arrighi
'Regardless of the effectiveness of certain scenes and sequences, one is left with the feeling that the film as a whole doesn't add up. But this is falling into the trap Godard has set for us: it is not meant to add up, and it won't.' – *Richard Roud, MFB*
† The producers increased Godard's cut by five minutes to 109m to include a full version of the Stones' song 'Sympathy for the Devil' at the end of the film.

One Rainy Afternoon *

US 1935 79m bw
Pickford-Lasky

In a cinema one afternoon, a gigolo kisses the wrong girl.
Rather heavy-handed light comedy with interesting credentials.
w Stephen Morehouse Avery, Maurice Hanline *play* Emeric Pressburger and René Pujal d Rowland V. Lee
☆ Francis Lederer, Ida Lupino, Roland Young, Hugh Herbert, Erik Rhodes, Mischa Auer
'Mr Lee has given a useful demonstration of how not to direct this kind of story: he has been remorselessly logical when he should have been crazy; his only idea of humour is speed and noise, not speed of thought or situation, but just literal speed of walking and talking.' – *Graham Greene, The Spectator*

One Spy Too Many

US 1966 102m Metrocolor
MGM/Arena (David Victor)

A modern-day Alexander the Great is foiled in his attempt to conquer the world.
Trivial spy caper, edited from episodes of the television series The Man from U.N.C.L.E.
w Dean Hargrove d Joseph Sargent ph Fred Koenekamp m Gerald Fried ad George W. Davis, Merrill Pye ed Henry Berman
☆ Robert Vaughn, David McCallum, Rip Torn, Dorothy Provine, Leo G. Carroll, David Opatoshu, David Sheiner

---

One Summer Love

US 1976 97m colour Panavision
AIP

aka: *Dragonfly*

A young man leaves mental hospital for his Connecticut home, only to find everyone there nuttier than he is.
Over-the-top melodrama.
w N. Richard Nash d Gilbert Cates
☆ Beau Bridges, Susan Sarandon, Mildred Dunnock, Michael B. Miller

One Sunday Afternoon **

US 1933 93m bw
Paramount (Louis D. Lighton)

In 1910, a Brooklyn dentist feels he has married the wrong girl, but discovers that his choice was the right one.
Pleasant period comedy drama which was twice remade: as The Strawberry Blonde (qv) and see below.
w William Slavens McNutt, Grover Jones *play* James Hagan d Stephen Roberts ph Victor Milner
☆ Gary Cooper, Frances Fuller, Fay Wray, Neil Hamilton, Roscoe Karns
'Still pitched in stage tempo and unfolds haltingly.' – *Variety*

One Sunday Afternoon

US 1948 90m Technicolor
Warner (Jerry Wald)

Pleasant but undistinguished musical remake of the above.
w Robert L. Richards d Raoul Walsh ph Sid Hickox, Wilfrid M. Cline md Ray Heindorf ad Anton Grot
☆ Dennis Morgan, Dorothy Malone, Janis Paige, Don DeFore, Ben Blue
'A lackadaisical and uninspired jaunt down memory lane.' – *New Yorker, 1978*

'You Talkin' to Me?'

US 1987 97m colour
UA/Second Generation (Michael Polaire)

A New York actor, obsessed with De Niro's performance in *Taxi Driver*, goes to Hollywood in search of fame and finds it working for a producer of right-wing and fundamentalist films.
An attempt to combine a semi-satirical drama about ambition and the laid-back ways of California with an attack on racism; it is moderately engaging but lacks coherence.
wd Charles Winkler ph Paul Ryan m Joel McNeely ad Alexandra Kicenik ed David Handman
☆ Jim Youngs, Faith Ford, Mykel T. Williamson, Bess Motta, Alan King, James Noble

The One that Got Away **

GB 1957 111m bw
Rank (Julian Wintle)

A German flyer, Franz von Werra, is captured and sent to various British prisoner-of-war camps, from all of which he escapes.
True-life biopic, developed in a number of suspense and action sequences, all very well done.
w Howard Clewes *book* Kendal Burt, James Leasor d Roy Baker ph Eric Cross m Hubert Clifford
☆ Hardy Kruger, Michael Goodliffe, Colin Gordon, Alec McCowen

'Til There Was You

US 1997 113m Technicolor
Paramount/Lakeshore (Penney Finkelman Cox, Tom Rosenberg, Alan Poul)

Two people, who are destined to fall in love, take a long time to meet one another.
Gaudy and charmless romantic comedy; it might have worked with a lighter touch.
w Winnie Holzman d Scott Winant ph Bobby Bukowski m Miles Goodman, Terence Blanchard pd Craig Stearns ed Richard Marks, Joanna Cappuccilli
☆ Jeanne Tripplehorn, Dylan McDermott, Sarah Jessica Parker, Jennifer Aniston, Ken Olin, Nina Foch, Christine Ebersole, Michael Tucker, Patrick Malahide
'A sorry recipe of stale ideas and sickly sweet smiles.' – *Sight and Sound*
'A tired piece of romantic cornball fare.' – *Variety*

♠ film suitable for family viewing ▦ VHS video-cassette for the British PAL system ▭ VHS video-cassette for the British PAL system in wide screen-format ✩ Video cassette in a computer-colourised version ▬ American NTSC video-cassette ✎ Laser disc

One Third of a Nation *
US   1939   79m   bw
Federal Theatre (Dudley Murphy)

A shopgirl persuades a landlord to tear down his dangerous slums and put up good buildings.
Naïve do-goodery, not too persuasively managed.
w Dudley Murphy, Oliver H. P. Garrett
play Arthur Arent *d* Dudley Murphy *ph* William Mellor *m* Nathaniel Shilkret

☆ Sylvia Sidney, Leif Erickson, Myron McCormick, Hiram Sherman, Sidney Lumet, Percy Waram

'No worse and rather better than a commensurate modest-budgeter essayed on the coast … the cinematic transition however seems to have almost wholly ditched the Federal Housing "living newspaper" purpose of the stage version, emphasizing the boy-meets-girl premise against the shocking slum background.' – *Variety*

1871
GB   1989   100m   Metrocolor
ICA/Looseyard/Film Four/La Sept/Palawood/Animatografo (Stewart Richards)
An Irish rebel, in love with an actress-cum-prostitute whom he is forced to share with an English aristocrat and spy, takes part in the doomed Paris Commune of 1871.
Blinkered and fussy look at a failed revolution.
w Terry James, James Leahy, Ken McMullen *d* Ken McMullen *ph* Elso Roque *m* Barrie Guard *pd* Paul Cheetham *ed* William Diver

☆ Roshan Seth, John Lynch, Timothy Spall, Alexandre de Sousa, Ian McNeice, Alan Braine, Maria João Toscano, Maria de Medeiros, Ana Padrao, Jacqueline Dankworth

'Another melancholy example of rigid radicalism lacking mainstream and popular sophistication.' – *Raymond Durgnat, Sight and Sound*
'Has all the elements of terrific television: romance, revolution, murder, a good cast and top-notch production values.' – *Variety*

'Centuries Before The Exploration Of Space, There Was Another Voyage Into The Unknown.'
1492: Conquest of Paradise **
US   1992   155m   colour   Panavision
Guild/Touchstone (Ridley Scott, Alain Goldman)
Columbus persuaded the Spanish court to back his expedition to reach the East by sailing west, but his attempts to live in peace with the natives in the New World are sabotaged by his followers.
A box-office flop, it is nevertheless a handsome-looking film and one that sustains one's interest throughout, despite some narrative ambiguity.
w Roselyne Bosch *d* Ridley Scott *ph* Adrian Biddle *m* Vangelis *pd* Norris Spencer *ed* William Anderson, Françoise Bonnot

☆ Gérard Depardieu, Armand Assante, Sigourney Weaver, Loren Dean, Angela Molina, Fernando Rey, Michael Wincott, Tcheky Karyo, Kevin Dunn, Frank Langella

1900 *
Italy/France/West Germany   1976   320m
Technicolor
TCF/PEA/Artistes Associés/Artemis (Alberto Grimaldi)
original title: *Novecento*
The political and personal vicissitudes of a noble Italian family between 1900 and 1945
Immensely long and heavy-going study of the rise of fascism in the form of a family saga. For specialists only.
w Bernardo Bertolucci, Franco Arcalli, Giuseppe Bertolucci *d* Bernardo Bertolucci *ph* Vittorio Storaro *m* Ennio Morricone *ad* Enzo Frigiero

☆ Burt Lancaster, Robert de Niro, Gérard Depardieu, Dominique Sanda, Donald Sutherland, Sterling Hayden

'Exasperatingly uneven, but its most powerful moments can't be matched by any movie since Godfather Two.' – *Time*
'Bertolucci tried to write a 19th-century novel on film: the result is appalling, yet it has the grandeur of a classic visionary folly.' – *New Yorker*
† The film was normally shown in two separate parts.

1984 *
GB   1955   91m   bw
Holiday (N. Peter Rathvon)
Europe has become the fascist state of Oceania, ruled by Big Brother; Winston Smith yearns for the old days, and is brainwashed.
The famous prophecy of a dehumanized future is followed with reasonable fidelity apart from the defiant ending, but the novel is too literary for cinematic success and the result is too often both downbeat and boring.
w William P. Templeton, Ralph Bettinson *novel* George Orwell *d* Michael Anderson *ph* C. Pennington Richards *m* Malcolm Arnold

☆ Michael Redgrave, Edmond O'Brien, Jan Sterling, David Kossoff, Mervyn Johns, Donald Pleasence

'Will ecstasy be a crime – in the terrifying world of the future?'
1984 *
GB   1984   110m   Eastmancolor
Umbrella/Rosenblum/Virgin (Simon Perry)
Winston Smith comes to love Big Brother after being brainwashed and taught Doublethink.
Pointless, perhaps, to make a prophetic film in the year it was supposed to be prophesying, but this version adds a few twists to Orwell's nightmarish original and is well if sometimes confusingly made.
wd Michael Radford *novel* George Orwell *m* Dominic Muldowney *pd* Allan Cameron *ed* Tom Priestley *d/ph* Roger Deakins

☆ John Hurt, Richard Burton, Suzanna Hamilton, Cyril Cusack, Gregor Fisher, James Walker

'A tale of unrelieved bleakness is told with relentless accuracy to Mr Orwell's novel, to which it is a kind of homage.' – *Quentin Crisp*

1941 *
US   1979   118m   Metrocolor
Panavision
Columbia/Universal/A-Team (John Milius)
Just after Pearl Harbor, a stray Japanese submarine terrorizes Hollywood.
Absurdly over-budgeted manic farce which substitutes noise for wit and slapstick for comedy; it fails on every level.
w Robert Zemeckis, Bob Gale *d* Steven Spielberg *ph* William A. Fraker *m* John Williams *pd* Dean Edward Mitzner

☆ Dan Aykroyd, Ned Beatty, John Belushi, Lorraine Gary, Murray Hamilton, Christopher Lee, Tim Matheson, Toshiro Mifune, Warren Oates, Robert Stack, Elisha Cook Jnr

'So overloaded with visual humour of rather monstrous nature that the feeling emerges that once you've seen ten explosions, you've seen them all.' – *Variety*
'Aimed at young audiences, who deserve better fun.' – *New Yorker*
'Its sheer relentless physicality, its elaborately orchestrated pointlessness on every other level, make it probably the purest demonstration of what it means to have two of the all-time commercial blockbusters to one's record and one's hands firmly on the fantasy machine.' – *Richard Combs, MFB*
'Spielberg intended it as "a stupidly outrageous celebration of paranoia" … audiences found it curiously unfunny and elephantine.' – *Les Keyser, Hollywood in the Seventies*
§ William A. Fraker

1969
US   1988   96m   colour
Entertainment/Atlantic (Daniel Grodnick, Bill Badalato)
As the Vietnam War gets under way, two small-town youths protest for peace.
A nostalgic wallow that never rises above cliché.
wd Ernest Thompson *ph* Jules Brenner *m* Michael Small *pd* Marcia Hinds *ed* William Anderson

☆ Robert Downey Jnr, Kiefer Sutherland, Bruce Dern, Mariette Hartley, Winona Ryder, Joanna Cassidy, Christopher Wynne

The One Thousand Plane Raid
US   1968   94m   DeLuxe
Oakwood/UA
An American colonel persuades top brass of the need for daylight bombing of Germany.
Reasonable routine war action drama.
w Donald S. Sanford *d* Boris Sagal

☆ Christopher George, Laraine Stephens, J. D. Cannon, Gary Marshall, Michael Evans, Ben Murphy

1776 *
US   1972   141m   Eastmancolor   Panavision
Columbia/Jack L. Warner
The thirteen American colonies prepare to declare their independence of Great Britain.
Plain, low-key filming of the successful Broadway musical showing the domestic lives of the historical figures concerned. Splendid moments alternate with stretches of tedium.
w Peter Stone *play* Peter Stone *d* Peter Hunt *ph* Harry Stradling Jnr *m/ly* Sherman Edwards *md* Ray Heindorf *ad* George Jenkins

☆ William Daniels, Howard da Silva, Ken Howard, Donald Madden, Blythe Danner
§ Harry Stradling Jnr

One Touch of Venus *
US   1948   82m   bw
Universal/Lester Cowan
In a fashionable department store, a statue of Venus comes to life and falls for a window dresser.
Pleasant satirical comedy, watered down from the Broadway original.
w Harry Kurnitz, Frank Tashlin *play* S. J. Perelman, Ogden Nash *d* William A. Seiter *ph* Franz Planer *ad* Bernard Herzbrun, Emrich Nicholson *songs* Kurt Weill

☆ Ava Gardner, Robert Walker, Eve Arden, Dick Haymes, Olga San Juan, Tom Conway

One, Two, Three **
US   1961   115m   bw   Panavision
United Artists/Mirisch/Pyramid (Billy Wilder)
An executive in West Berlin is trying to sell Coca Cola to the Russians while preventing his boss's daughter from marrying a communist.
Back to Ninotchka territory, but this time the tone is that of a wild farce which achieves fine momentum in stretches but also flags a lot in between, teetering the while on the edge of taste.
w Billy Wilder, I. A. L. Diamond *play* Ferenc Molnar *d* Billy Wilder *ph* Daniel Fapp *m* André Previn

☆ James Cagney, Horst Buchholz, Arlene Francis, Pamela Tiffin, Lilo Pulver, Howard St John, Leon Askin

'A sometimes bewildered, often wonderfully funny exercise in nonstop nuttiness.' – *Time*
'This first-class featherweight farce is a serious achievement.' – *Stanley Kauffmann*
§ Daniel Fapp

One Way Out
GB   1955   80m   bw
Rank/Major (John Temple-Smith)
A detective on the point of retirement is forced to cover up a crime to protect his daughter.
Pedestrian thriller that never rises above the commonplace.
w Jonathan Roche *story* John Temple-Smith, Jean Scott Rogers *d* Francis Searle *ph* Walter Harvey *ad* William Kellner *ed* Maurice Rootes

☆ Jill Adams, Eddie Byrne, Lyndon Brook, John Chandos, Olive Milbourne, Arthur Howard, Arthur Lowe

One Way Passage *
US   1932   69m   bw
Warner (Robert Lord)
On an ocean voyage, a dying girl falls in love with a crook going home to face a life sentence.
Pattern melodrama which stood Hollywood in good stead.
w Wilson Mizner, Joseph Jackson, Robert Lord *d* Tay Garnett *ph* Robert Kurrie *m* W. Franke Harling

☆ William Powell, Kay Francis, Frank McHugh, Aline MacMahon, Warren Hymer, Herbert Mundin, Roscoe Karns, Stanley Fields

'Will reach house averages for this time of year.' – *Variety*

† Remade as '*Til We Meet Again* (qv).
§ original story (Robert Lord)

One Way Pendulum
GB   1964   85m   bw
UA/Woodfall (Michael Deeley)
A suburban clerk leads a dream existence; his son teaches speak-your-weight machines to sing, while he sets an imaginary murder trial in motion.
A nonsense play (which has many adherents) resists the literalness of the camera eye.
w N. F. Simpson *play* N. F. Simpson *d* Peter Yates *ph* Denys Coop *m* Richard Rodney Bennett

☆ Eric Sykes, George Cole, Julia Foster, Jonathan Miller, Peggy Mount, Alison Leggatt, Mona Washbourne

One Way Street
US   1950   79m   bw
U-I/Leonard Goldstein (Sam Goldwyn Jnr)
A disillusioned doctor steals a fortune and hides out in a Mexican village, where he regains his self-respect.
Thin and pointless melodrama.
w Lawrence Kimble *d* Hugo Fregonese *ph* Maury Gertsman *m* Frank Skinner

☆ James Mason, Marta Toren, Dan Duryea, William Conrad, King Donovan, Jack Elam

'It is reported that James Mason chooses his own parts, and if this is true I have to report that he is a glutton for punishment.' – *Daily Herald*
'One of the dullest, most stupid films of the year.' – *Sunday Pictorial*

One Way to Love
US   1945   83m   bw
Burt Kelly/Columbia
A Chicago radio writer gets a chance in Hollywood.
Hit-and-miss romantic comedy which takes place largely on a westbound train.
w Joseph Hoffman, Jack Henley, Lester Lee, Larry Marks *d* Ray Enright

☆ Willard Parker, Marguerite Chapman, Hugh Herbert, Chester Morris, Jerome Cowan, Janis Carter

'Til We Meet Again
US   1940   99m   bw
Warner (David Lewis)
On a ship bound from Hong Kong to San Francisco, a dying woman falls for a crook about to be executed.
Stolid remake of One Way Passage (qv).
w Warren Duff *story* Robert Lord *d* Edmund Goulding *ph* Tony Gaudio *m* Ray Heindorf

☆ Merle Oberon, George Brent, Frank McHugh, Pat O'Brien, Geraldine Fitzgerald, Eric Blore, Binnie Barnes, Henry O'Neill, George Reeves
† Marlene Dietrich was originally scheduled for the lead.

One Wedding and Lots of Funerals: see *Leprechaun 2*

One Wild Moment: see *A Summer Affair*

One Wild Night
US   1938   63m   bw
John Stone/TCF
Four small-town citizens anxious for vacations away from their wives plot their own kidnapping.
Tolerable second feature comedy, but the plot might have been better developed.
w Charles Belden, Jerry Cady *d* Eugene Forde

☆ June Lang, Dick Baldwin, Lyle Talbot, J. Edward Bromberg, Sidney Toler, William Demarest, Andrew Tombes, Spencer Charters

One Wild Oat
GB   1951   78m   bw
Coronet/Eros
An old flame tries to blackmail a highly respectable solicitor.
Modest film version of a popular West End farce.
w Vernon Sylvaine, Lawrence Huntington *play* Vernon Sylvaine *d* Charles Saunders *ph* Robert Navarro *m* Stanley Black

☆ Robertson Hare, Stanley Holloway, Sam Costa, Andrew Crawford, Vera Pearce, Robert Moreton, Irene Handl

One Woman or Two: see *Une Femme ou Deux*

One Woman's Story: see *The Passionate Friends*

'From Alexander Pushkin's timeless masterpiece of love and obsession.'

Onegin *
GB/US   1998   106m   DeLuxe
Entertainment/Seven Arts/Baby/Protagonist (Ileen Maisel, Simon Bosanquet)
An aristocrat rejects the love of a young woman and lives to regret his action.
Sumptuous version of a classic tale of doomed love, but one that has an unwonted air of Anglo-Saxon repression about it; and Tyler is miscast.
w Peter Ettedgui, Michael Ignatieff *verse* novel Aleksandr Pushkin d Martha Fiennes ph Remi Adefarasin m Magnus Fiennes pd Jim Clay ed Jim Clark
☆ Ralph Fiennes, Liv Tyler, Toby Stephens, Lena Headey, Martin Donovan, Alun Armstrong, Harriet Walter, Irene Worth, Jason Watkins, Francesca Annis
'There's something frozen about her film, despite its immense decorative appeal.' – Adam Mars-Jones, *Times*
'Diminishes Alexander Pushkin's epic 19th-century novel ... into a cramped little soap opera whose two stars are painfully mismatched.' – Janet Maslin, *New York Times*

One-Trick Pony *
US   1980   98m   Technicolor
Warner (Michael Tannen)
A veteran rock musician attempts to hold on to his integrity as his career and marriage disintegrate.
An episodic account, broken by songs that carry, not always successfully, the movie's emotional weight; but the scenes detailing the business side of popular music, dealing with a crass DJ and an unsympathetic producer and record boss, have an authentic bitterness about them.
w Paul Simon d Robert M. Young ph Dick Bush m/ly Paul Simon pd David Mitchell ed Edward Beyer, Barry Malkin, David Ray
☆ Paul Simon, Blair Brown, Rip Torn, Joan Hackett, Allen Goorwitz (Garfield), Mare Winningham, Michael Pearlman, Lou Reed, Daniel Stern
† The film also includes performamces by the B-52s, Sam and Dave and the Lovin' Spoonful, and a brief appearance by Tiny Tim.

One-Way Ticket *
US   1935   66m   bw
Columbia
A convicted bank robber falls in love with the warden's daughter.
Prison break drama which seems to be trying to make a point but is not sure what.
w Vincent Lawrence, Joseph Anthony, Oliver H. P. Garrett, Grover Jones novel Ethel Turner d Herbert Biberman
☆ Lloyd Nolan, Walter Connolly, Peggy Conklin, Edith Fellows, Nana Bryant, Thurston Hall
'It is "different" at the cost of credulity.' – *Variety*

A One-Way Ticket: see *Un Pasaje de Ida*

Onibaba *
Japan   1964   104m   bw   Tohoscope
Kindai Eiga Kyokai/Tokyo Eiga
aka: *The Hole*
In medieval times on a remote marshy plain, mother and daughter live by killing stray soldiers and selling their armour, until daughter takes one for a lover and mother becomes jealous.
A kind of original horror legend is told by this strange, compelling piece with its frequent moments of nastiness. It remains, perhaps mercifully, unique.
wd Kaneto Shindo ph Kiyomi Juroda m Hikaru Hayashi
☆ Nobuko Otowa, Jitsuko Yoshimura, Kei Sato
'The film is the most ardent and unflinching celebration of sex. It shows with equal faithfulness the ecstasies of its fulfilment and the agonies of its frustration.' – John Simon

'What happened is true ... but the real crime is what happened after!'
The Onion Field
US   1979   126m   Eastmancolor
Black Marble (Walter Coblenz)
Two policemen are shot at by a manic killer, and the one who survives finds that he is suspected of cowardice and has to resign from the force.
Well meaning but lumbering case history. The author must carry the blame, as for once the picture was made exactly on his terms.
w Joseph Wambaugh novel Joseph Wambaugh d Harold Becker ph Charles Rosher m Eumir Deodato pd Brian Eatwell
☆ John Savage, James Woods, Franklyn Seales, Ted Danson, Ronny Cox, David Huffman

Onionhead
US   1958   110m   bw
Warner (Jules Schermer)
Adventures of a ship's cook in the US Coastguard.
Service comedy that must have seemed funnier in the US than in Britain.
w Nelson Gidding novel Weldon Hill d Norman Taurog ph Harold Rosson md Ray Heindorf
☆ Andy Griffith, Felicia Farr, Walter Matthau, Erin O'Brien, Joe Mantell, Ray Danton, Roscoe Karns, James Gregory, Tige Andrews
† An attempt to cash in on the success of *No Time for Sergeants.*

'Romance as glorious as the towering Andes!'
Only Angels Have Wings **
US   1939   121m   bw
Columbia (Howard Hawks)
Tension creeps into the relationships of the men who fly cargo planes over the Andes when a stranded showgirl sets her cap at the boss.
For an action film this is really too restricted by talk and cramped studio sets, and its theme was more entertainingly explored in Red Dust. Still, it couldn't be more typical of the Howard Hawks film world, where men are men and women have to be as tough as they are.
w Jules Furthman story Howard Hawks d Howard Hawks ph Joseph Walker, Elmer Dyer m Dimitri Tiomkin md Morris Stoloff
☆ Cary Grant, Jean Arthur, Rita Hayworth, Richard Barthelmess, Thomas Mitchell, Sig Rumann, Victor Kilian, John Carroll, Allyn Joslyn
'All these people did the best they could with what they were given – but look at it.' – *Otis Ferguson*

The Only Game in Town *
US   1969   113m   DeLuxe
TCF (Fred Kohlmar)
A Las Vegas chorus girl and a piano player have an unhappy life because of his gambling fever.
Uninteresting two-header from a play that would make it; no light relief, no action, and not even very good acting.
w Frank D. Gilroy play Frank D. Gilroy d George Stevens ph Henri Decaë m Maurice Jarre
☆ Elizabeth Taylor, Warren Beatty, Charles Braswell, Hank Henry
'It epitomizes the disaster the studio and star systems foist on films ... the only two-character tale around to cost $11 million.' – *Judith Crist*
† Frank Sinatra was originally cast but walked out after production started; Warren Beatty astonishingly chose to do this rather than *Butch Cassidy and the Sundance Kid.*

Only the Best: see *I Can Get It for You Wholesale*

'A comedy for anyone who's ever had a mother.'
Only the Lonely *
US   1991   104m   DeLuxe
TCF/Hughes Entertainment (John Hughes, Hunt Lowry)
A mother-dominated cop falls in love with a shy beautician at his neighbourhood undertakers.
Soft-centred, sentimental drama that lacks the courage to be convincing.
wd Chris Columbus ph Julio Macat m Maurice Jarre ch Monica Devereux pd John Muto ed Raja Gosnell

☆ John Candy, Maureen O'Hara, Ally Sheedy, Anthony Quinn, James Belushi, Kevin Dunn, Milo O'Shea, Bert Remsen, Macaulay Culkin
† It was Maureen O'Hara's first film for 20 years.

'On The Streets Survival Is The Only Law.'
Only the Strong
US   1993   96m   Eastmancolor
Rank/Polygram/Freestone/Davis (Samuel Hadida, Stuart S. Shapiro, Steven G. Menkin)
An expert in the Brazilian martial art of capoeira teaches it to a school's 12 toughest kids to give them self-respect.
Apart from its use of Brazil's dance-based method of beating opponents to pulp, a standard, forgettable film of its type, surprisingly given a cinema release.
w Sheldon Lettich, Luis Esteban d Sheldon Lettich ph Edward Pei m Harvey J. Mason pd J. Mark Harrington ed Stephen Semel
☆ Mark Dacascos, Geoffrey Lewis, Paco Christian Prieto, Stacey Travis, Todd Susman, Richard Coca
'I strained my neck just watching it, largely because I kept nodding off. I imagine Sheldon Lettich, the director, might have done so too. At any rate, he must have written it in a doze.' – *Derek Malcolm, Guardian*

'They were six and they fought like six hundred!'
Only the Valiant
US   1950   105m   bw
(Warner)
A tough cavalry officer in a lonely fort wins a battle against Indians.
Standard top-of-the-bill Western; competent but not very gripping.
w Edmund H. North, Harry Brown d Gordon Douglas ph Lionel Lindon m Franz Waxman
☆ Gregory Peck, Ward Bond, Gig Young, Lon Chaney Jnr, Barbara Payton, Neville Brand

Only Two Can Play ***
GB   1962   106m   bw
British Lion/Vale (Launder and Gilliat)
A much married assistant librarian in a Welsh town has an abortive affair with a councillor's wife.
Well characterized and generally diverting 'realistic' comedy which slows up a bit towards the end but contains many memorable sequences and provides its star's last good character performance.
w Bryan Forbes novel *That Uncertain Feeling* by Kingsley Amis d Sidney Gilliat ph John Wilcox m Richard Rodney Bennett ad Albert Witherick
☆ Peter Sellers, Mai Zetterling, Virginia Maskell, Richard Attenborough, Raymond Huntley, John Le Mesurier, Kenneth Griffith
'It has a kind of near-truth which is at once hilarious and faintly macabre.' – *Dilys Powell*

Only When I Larf *
GB   1968   103m   Eastmancolor
Paramount/Beecord (Len Deighton, Brian Duffy, Hugh Attwooll)
The adventures of three confidence tricksters.
Quite likeable but unmemorable 'with it' comedy of the sixties; the tricks are more amusing than the characterization.
w John Salmon novel Len Deighton d Basil Dearden ph Anthony Richmond m Ron Grainer
☆ Richard Attenborough, David Hemmings, Alexandra Stewart, Nicholas Pennell, Melissa Stribling, Terence Alexander, Edric Connor, Calvin Lockhart, Clifton Jones

Only When I Laugh *
US   1981   120m   Metrocolor
Columbia (Roger M. Rothstein, Neil Simon)
GB title: *It Hurts Only When I Laugh*
An alcoholic actress tries to rebuild her life.
Last desperate fling (one hopes) of the Neil Simon industry, dispensing in this case more bitter tears than laughs, and generally failing to stay the course.
w Neil Simon play *The Gingerbread Lady* by Neil Simon d Glenn Jordan ph David M. Walsh m David Shire
☆ Marsha Mason, Kristy McNichol, James Coco, Joan Hackett, David Dukes, John Bennett Perry
'One can almost hear the click of typewriter keys.' – *Geoff Brown, MFB*
§ Marsha Mason; James Coco (supporting actor); Joan Hackett (supporting actress)

Only Yesterday *
US   1933   105m   bw
Universal
An unmarried mother is seduced twice by the same man.
One that Ross Hunter didn't get around to remaking ... and a good job too.
w William Hurlbut, George O'Neill, Arthur Richman d John M. Stahl
☆ Margaret Sullavan, John Boles, Billie Burke, Reginald Denny, Edna May Oliver, Benita Hume
'The film needs little more praise than that it warrants its unusual length.' – *Variety*
† The original intention seems to have been to mirror recent history as in Frederick Lewis Allen's book of the same title.

Only You *
US   1994   108m   Technicolor
Columbia TriStar/Fried/Woods Films/Yorktown (Norman Jewison, Cary Wood, Robert N. Fried, Charles Mulvehill)
In Italy, a woman pursues the man she believes, on the evidence of a fortune teller, she is destined to marry and finds the love of her life.
Sugary, glossy, nostalgic romantic comedy that deliberately harks back to the 50s Roman Holiday, starring Audrey Hepburn and Gregory Peck, and which seems even more old-fashioned.
w Diane Drake d Norman Jewison ph Sven Nykvist m Rachel Portman pd Luciana Arrighi ed Stephen Rivkin
☆ Marisa Tomei, Robert Downey Jnr, Bonnie Hunt, Billy Zane, Joaquim de Almeida, Fisher Stevens
'Populated by characters who believe in pursuing their amorous destinies as long as it involves staying in five-star hotels, handsomely turned-out trifle has a healthy dose of highly calculated commercial appeal, especially to those who are ready to swallow cornball romance without worrying about excess sweets.' – Todd McCarthy, *Variety*

Ooh, You Are Awful *
GB   1972   97m   Eastmancolor
British Lion/Quintain (E. M. Smedley Aston)
US title: *Get Charlie Tully*
A London con man seeks a fortune, the clue to which is tattooed on the behind of one of several girls.
Amusing star vehicle with plenty of room for impersonations and outrageous jokes.
w John Warren, John Singer d Cliff Owen ph Ernest Steward m Christopher Gunning
☆ Dick Emery, Derren Nesbitt, Ronald Fraser, Pat Coombs, William Franklyn, Brian Oulton, Norman Bird

Open City **
Italy   1945   101m   bw
Minerva
original title: *Roma, Città Aperta*
Italian underground workers defy the Nazis in Rome towards the end of the war.
A vivid newsreel quality is achieved by this nerve-stretching melodrama in which all the background detail is as real as care could make it.
w Sergio Amidei, Federico Fellini d Roberto Rossellini ph Ubaldo Arata m Renzo Rossellini
☆ Aldo Fabrizi, Anna Magnani, Marcello Pagliero, Maria Michi
§ script

Open Season
US/Spain/Switzerland   1974   104m
Eastmancolor   Panavision
Impala/Arpa (George H. Brown, Jose S. Vicuna)
Three young criminals hunt human prey, but one of their victims takes his own revenge.
Rough, flashy, violent melodrama which pretends to have something to say but in fact is merely sensationalist.
w David Osborn, Liz Charles Williams d Peter Collinson ph Fernando Arribas m Ruggero Cini
☆ Peter Fonda, Cornelia Sharpe, John Phillip Law, Richard Lynch, Albert Mendoza, William Holden
'An offensive, gamy potboiler.' – *Variety*
'Both patience and the plot line are severely strained by the artiness Collinson frequently

indulges, with frozen shots to mark the moments of truth and a meaningless punctuation throughout of long shots, angles and flashes.' – *Tom Milne*

'Sometimes you can't wake from a nightmare, even if you do...'

Open Your Eyes **
Spain/France/Italy   1997   119m   colour
Redbus/Sogetel/El Escorpion/Alain Sarde/Lucky Red
original title: *Abre Los Ojos*
Explaining to a prison psychiatrist how he came to be accused of murder, a wealthy young man, hideously disfigured in a road crash that killed his companion, realises that he is trapped in a unreal life.
Clever, tricksy, games-playing thriller that deals with the confusions of reality and illusion, and the limits of personality.
w Alejandro Amenábar, Matteo Gil d Alejandro Amenábar ph Hans Burmann m Alejandro Amenábar, Mariano Marin ad Wolfgang Burmann ed Maria Elena Sainz de Rojas
☆ Eduardo Noriega, Penelope Cruz, Chete Lera, Fele Martinez, Najwa Nimri, Gérard Barray, Jorge de Juan
  'Ambitiously complex, disturbing and terrific-looking thriller.' – *Jonathan Holland, Variety*

Opening Night
US   1978   144m   Metrocolor
Faces Distribution (Al Ruban)
📼 🎞 ⊚
A Broadway actress is on the point of a nervous breakdown.
Interminable addition to the director's list of unwatchable personal films.
wd John Cassavetes ph Al Ruban m Bo Horwood
☆ Gena Rowlands, Ben Gazzara, John Cassavetes, Joan Blondell, Paul Stewart, Zohra Lampert, Laura Johnson
  'Shrill, puzzling, depressing and overlong.' – *Variety*

L'Opéra de Quat' Sous: see *Die Dreigroschenoper*

Opera do Malandro
Brazil   1986   105m   colour
Goldwyn/MK2/Austra/TF1 (Marin Karmitz, Ruy Guerra)
A pro-American pimp in pro-Nazi Brazil becomes involved with the daughter of his enemy, a corrupt night-club owner.
A South American treatment of Brecht's Threepenny Opera without Kurt Weill's music or much to recommend it.
w Chico Buarque, Orlando Senna, Ruy Guerra d Ruy Guerra ph Antonio Luis Mendes m Chico Buarque ed Mair Tavares, Ide Lacreta, Kenout Peltier
☆ Edson Celulari, Claudia Ohana, Elba Ramalho, Ney Latorraca, Fabio Sabag, J. C. Violla, Wilson Grey

Operation Amsterdam *
GB   1958   104m   bw
Rank/Maurice Cowan
📼
In 1940 spies are sent into Holland to prevent the invading Germans from finding Amsterdam's stock of industrial diamonds.
Semi-documentary war adventure, well mounted and played.
w Michael McCarthy, John Eldridge book *Adventure in Diamonds* by David Walker d Michael McCarthy ph Reg Wyer m Philip Green
☆ Peter Finch, Tony Britton, Eva Bartok, Alexander Knox, Malcolm Keen, Tim Turner, John Horsley, Melvyn Hayes, Christopher Rhodes

Operation Bullshine
GB   1959   84m   Technicolor
ABPC
In 1942, complications ensue when an ATS private suspects her husband of infidelity.
Flabby army comedy with a few laughs.
w Anne Burnaby, Rupert Lang, Gilbert Gunn d Gilbert Gunn ph Gilbert Taylor m Laurie Johnson
☆ Donald Sinden, Barbara Murray, Carole Lesley, Ronald Shiner, Naunton Wayne, Daniel Massey, Dora Bryan

Operation CIA
US   1965   90m   bw
Allied Artists
📼
An agent is rushed to Saigon to find a secret message which was never delivered.
Crude thick ear with a few suspenseful moments.
w Bill S. Ballinger, Peer J. Oppenheimer d Christian Nyby ph Richard Moore m Paul Dunlap
☆ Burt Reynolds, John Hoyt, Daniele Aubry, Kieu Chinh, Cyril Collick

Operation Condor
Hong Kong   1991   103m   colour
Golden Harvest/Golden Way (Raymond Chow)
original title: *Feiying Gaiwak*
aka: *The Armor of God II*
A Chinese explorer is hired by a Spanish aristocrat to find a hoard of Nazi gold buried in the Sahara Desert.
Genial and energetic martial arts movie, less effective than usual because the action is removed from its normal Hong Kong context, though no doubt its desert setting seemed exotic to its home audience.
w Jackie Chan, Edward Tang, Ma Mei-ping d Jackie Chan ph Arthur Wong m Peter Pau ad Oliver Wong, Eddie Ma, Lou Ka-yiu ed Peter Cheung
☆ Jackie Chan, Carol Cheng, Eva Cobo de Garcia, Shoko Ikeda
  'A breezy actioneer that's always watchable.' – *Variety*
† The film was the most expensive so far made in Hong Kong, at a cost of $15 million ($HK115).

Operation Crossbow *
GB   1965   116m   Metrocolor   Panavision
MGM/Carlo Ponti
📼 ⊙
aka: *The Great Spy Mission*
In World War II, trained scientists are parachuted into Europe to destroy the Nazi rocket-making plant at Peenemunde.
Unlikely, star-packed war yarn with more passing tragedy than most, all obliterated by a shoot-em-up James Bond finale.
w Richard Imrie (Emeric Pressburger), Derry Quinn, Ray Rigby d Michael Anderson m Erwin Hillier m Ron Goodwin ed Ernest Walter
☆ George Peppard, Tom Courtenay, John Mills, Sophia Loren, Lilli Palmer, Anthony Quayle, Patrick Wymark, Jeremy Kemp, Paul Henreid, Trevor Howard, Sylvia Sims, Richard Todd, Richard Johnson

Operation Daybreak *
US   1975   119m   Technicolor
Warner/Howard R. Schuster/American Allied (Carter de Haven)
In 1941, Czech patriots kill the hated Nazi Heydrich and are hunted down.
Curiously-timed evocation of wartime resistance adventures, too realistic for the squeamish and certainly not very entertaining despite a fair level of professionalism.
w Ronald Harwood novel *Seven Men at Daybreak* by Alan Burgess d Lewis Gilbert ph Henri Decaë m David Hentschel
☆ Timothy Bottoms, Martin Shaw, Joss Ackland, Nicola Pagett, Anthony Andrews, Anton Diffring, Carl Duering, Diana Coupland

Operation Disaster: see *Morning Departure*

Operation Dumbo Drop
🎬 US   1995   107m   colour
Buena Vista/Walt Disney (Diane Nabatoff, David Madden)
📼 ⊚
US soldiers in Vietnam have five days to deliver an elephant to villagers whose beast was killed by the Vietcong.
Amiable movie that ignores the realities of war for the story of an appealing animal.
w Gene Quintano, Jim Kouf story Jim Morris d Simon Wincer ph Russell Boyd m David Newman pd Paul Peters ed O. Nicholas Brown
☆ Danny Glover, Ray Liotta, Denis Leary, Doug E. Doug, Corin Nemec, Dinh Thien Le, Tcheky Karyo
  'A well-crafted and entertaining pic with broad, cross-generational appeal.' – *Variety*

Operation Eichmann
US   1961   94m   bw
Allied Artists
📼
After the war, the Nazi who exterminated six million Jews escapes from Europe but is eventually recaptured.
Crude exploitation item designed to cash in on Eichmann's trial, a documentary on which would have been much more interesting.
w Lewis Copley d R. G. Springsteen ph Joseph Biroc m Alex Alexander
☆ Werner Klemperer, Ruta Lee, Donald Buka, John Banner

Operation Kid Brother
Italy   1967   105m   Techniscope
Dario Sabatello
📼
aka: *OK Connery*
007's brother defeats an international mastermind with the help of a Scottish archery team.
Very elementary James Bond spoof, with a confusing array of old and new elements but less than the required minimum of style.
w Paolo Levi, Vincenzo Mannino, Carlo Tritto d Alberto de Martino ph Alejandro Ulloa m Ennio Morricone
☆ Neil Connery, Daniela Bianchi, Adolfo Celi, Bernard Lee, Lois Maxwell, Agata Flori
  'A grotesque parody of a parody ... bad enough to be hysterically funny.' – *MFB*
† Neil Connery is Sean's kid brother.

Operation Mad Ball *
US   1957   105m   bw
Columbia (Jed Harris)
American troops in Normandy are forbidden to fraternize with nurses, but a clandestine dance is arranged.
Madcap army farce which keeps promising to be funnier than it is.
w Arthur Carter, Jed Harris, Blake Edwards play Arthur Carter d Richard Quine ph Charles Lawton Jnr m George Duning
☆ Jack Lemmon, Ernie Kovacs, Kathryn Grant, Mickey Rooney, James Darren, Arthur O'Connell
  'A routine regimental farce, but fast and snafurious.' – *Time*

Operation Pacific *
US   1950   109m   bw
Warner (Louis F. Edelman)
📼 🎞
Adventures of a submarine commander in the Pacific war.
Routine war heroics, tolerably done but overstretched.
wd George Waggner ph Bert Glennon m Max Steiner
☆ John Wayne, Patricia Neal, Ward Bond, Scott Forbes, Phil Carey, Paul Picerni, William Campbell, Martin Milner

Operation Petticoat *
US   1959   124m   Eastmancolor
Universal/Granart (Robert Arthur)
📼 ⊙
During World War II, a crippled submarine is refloated by fair means and foul, and a party of nurses is taken aboard.
Flabby comedy with good moments, but not many.
w Stanley Shapiro, Maurice Richlin story Paul King, Joseph Stone d Blake Edwards ph Russell Harlan m David Rose
☆ Cary Grant, Tony Curtis, Joan O'Brien, Dina Merrill, Gene Evans, Arthur O'Connell, Richard Sargent
  'Grant is a living lesson in getting laughs without lines.' – *Variety*
⅄ story and screenplay

Operation Secret
US   1952   108m   bw
Warner (Henry Blanke)
A traitor in the French resistance movement shoots a colleague, and the wrong man is accused.
Belated World War II adventure which gives the impression of having been discarded by Errol Flynn.
w James R. Webb, Harold Medford d Lewis Seiler ph Ted McCord m Roy Webb
☆ Cornel Wilde, Steve Cochran, Paul Picerni, Karl Malden

Operation Snafu: see *On the Fiddle*

Operation St Peter's
Italy   1968   100m   colour
Paramount/Turi Vasile
Three thieves steal Michelangelo's *Pietà* and sell it for forty dollars to an American gangster.
Rather surprisingly watchable comedy chase, with the star parodying his past roles.
w Ennio de Concini, Adriano Baracco, Roberto Gianviti, Lucio Fulci d Lucio Fulci
☆ Edward G. Robinson, Lando Buzzanca, Heinz Ruhmann, Jean-Claude Brialy

Operation Thunderbolt *
Israel   1977   117m   Eastmancolor
Panavision
GS Films (Menahem Golan, Yoram Globus)

aka: *Entebbe: Operation Thunderbolt*
An account of the rescue of Israeli hostages from terrorists who have hijacked their plane to Entebbe.
Victory at Entebbe and Raid on Entebbe were made with all-star casts for American television. This home-grown account of a famous deed is more modest yet more authoritative.
w Clarke Reynolds d Menahem Golan ph Adam Greenberg m Dov Seltzer
☆ Klaus Kinski, Assaf Dayan, Ori Levy, Yehoram Geon, Mark Heath
⅄ best foreign film

Operation Undercover: see *Report to the Commissioner*

Operation X: see *My Daughter Joy*

Operator 13
US   1934   86m   bw
MGM/Cosmopolitan (Lucien Hubbard)
GB title: *Spy 13*
During the Civil War an actress becomes a Union spy.
Elaborate period romance with action highlights.
w Harry Thew, Zelda Sears, Eve Greene d Richard Boleslawski ph George Folsey m William Axt
☆ Marion Davies, Gary Cooper, Jean Parker, Katherine Alexander, Ted Healy, Russell Hardie, Henry Wadsworth, Douglass Dumbrille
  'Will please generally ... one of Davies' best.' – *Variety*
⅄ George Folsey

Opposing Force
US   1986   97m   DeLuxe
Orion (Tamar E. Glaser, Daniel A. Berk)

aka: *Hellcamp*
The brutal, power-crazed commandant of a simulated prison camp, run as part of a military escape-and-evasion exercise, loses control after he rapes the only woman on the course.
An unpleasant and unconvincing action movie, stupidly violent.
w Gil Cowan d Eric Karson ph Michael A. Jones m Marc Donahue pd Art Nicdao ed Mark Conte
☆ Tom Skerritt, Lisa Eichhorn, Anthony Zerbe, Richard Roundtree, Robert Wightman, John Considine

'You'll laugh, you'll cry, you'll be offended.'

The Opposite of Sex ***
US   1998   105m   Foto-Kem
Sony/Rysher (David Kirkpatrick, Michael Besman)
📼 🎞 ⊚
A teenager runs away from home, seduces her gay brother's boyfriend, and runs off with him to LA.
Tough, tart, smart movie, which makes fun of the usual rites-of-passage stories and has enough twists in its plot to provide a continual surprise.
wd Don Roos ph Hubert Taczanowski m Mason Daring pd Michael Clausen ed David Codron
☆ Christina Ricci, Martin Donovan, Lisa Kudrow, Lyle Lovett, Johnny Galecki, Ivan Sergei
  'A delight on every conceivable level.' – *Andy Medhurst, Sight and Sound*

The Opposite Sex
US   1956   116m   Metrocolor   Cinemascope
MGM (Joe Pasternak)
📼 🎞
A New York socialite divorces her unfaithful husband but finally takes him back.
Softened, musicalized version of The Women (qv); very patchy, shapeless, and not nearly sharp enough.

---

w Fay and Michael Kanin *play* Clare Boothe
d David Miller *ph* Robert Bronner *m* Nicholas
Brodszky *songs* Nicholas Brodszky, Sammy Cahn
☆ June Allyson, Dolores Gray, Joan Collins, Ann
Sheridan, Agnes Moorehead, Joan Blondell,
Barbara Jo Allen, Charlotte Greenwood

The Opposite Sex and How to Live with Them
US   1993   86m   CFI color
Spelling/Outlaw/Once Upon A Time (Stanley M.
Brooks, Robert Newmyer)
📼   ▤   ⊘
Two Jewish men court WASP women and insist on
discussing their attitudes at length with the
audience.
*An experience akin to being buttonholed by a bore in a
bar.*
w Noah Stern *d* Matthew Meshekoff *ph* Jacek
Laskus *m* Ira Newborn *pd* Alex Tavoularis
ed Adam Weiss
☆ Arye Gross, Courteney Cox, Kevin Pollak, Julie
Brown, Mitchell Ryan, Phil Bruns

The Optimists of Nine Elms *
👫   GB   1973   110m   Eastmancolor
Cheetah/Sagittarius (Adrian Gaye, Victor Lyndon)
Children of a London slum make friends with an
old busker.
*Gentle, sentimental, quite well-observed piece of
wistful melancholia, falsified by its star performance.*
wd Anthony Simmons *novel* Anthony Simmons
ph Larry Pizer *m* George Martin *co-w* Tudor
Gates
☆ Peter Sellers, Donna Mullane, John Chaffey,
David Daker, Marjorie Yates
   'Told with economy and sensitivity, this
   underrated film establishes Tony Simmons as a
   first-rate director and justifies the risk Sellers
   took in tackling a difficult role in an offbeat
   subject.' – Ken Russell, *Fire over England*

The Oracle
👫   GB   1952   83m   bw
Group Three (Colin Lesslie)
US title: *The Horse's Mouth*
A reporter discovers that a village well in Ireland
contains an oracle which can predict the future.
*Weak sub-Ealing comedy which aims to please and gets
a few laughs. All very British.*
w Patrick Campbell *d* C. M. Pennington-
Richards *ph* Wolfgang Suschitzky *m* Temple
Abady
☆ Robert Beatty, Virginia McKenna, Mervyn
Johns, Gilbert Harding

Orca – Killer Whale
👫   US   1977   92m   Technicolor
Panavision
Famous Films/Dino de Laurentiis (Luciano Vincenzoni)
📼   ▤   ⊘   🎧
Off Newfoundland, a killer whale takes revenge for
its mate's death.
*A rather unpleasant attempt to mix horror and thrills
with ecology: not very entertaining, and not for the
squeamish.*
w Luciano Vincenzoni, Sergio Donati *d* Michael
Anderson *ph* Ted Moore, J. Barry Herron
m Ennio Morricone
☆ Richard Harris, Charlotte Rampling, Will
Sampson, Keenan Wynn
   'The biggest load of cod imaginable.' – *Philip
   Bergson, Sunday Times*
   'There are more thrills to be had in the average
   dolphinarium.' – *Sight and Sound*

Orchestra Wives **
US   1942   97m   bw
TCF (William Le Baron)
📼   ▤   ⊘
A small town girl marries the trumpet player of a
travelling swing band.
*Fresh and lively musical of its period, full of first-class
music and amusing backstage backbiting.*
w Karl Tunberg, Darrell Ware *d* Archie Mayo
ph Lucien Ballard *md* Alfred Newman
☆ Ann Rutherford, George Montgomery, Lynn
Bari, *Glenn Miller and his Orchestra*, Carole Landis,
Jackie Gleason, Cesar Romero
   'A natural for any theatre that hasn't got an
   ironclad rule against jive.' – *Hollywood Reporter*
♪ song 'I've Got a Girl in Kalamazoo' (*m*Harry
Warren, *ly*Mack Gordon)

Orchids to You *
US   1935   74m   bw
Robert T. Kane/Fox
A florist pulls several strokes to prevent an
attorney from taking over her lease.
*Amusing comedy drama which failed through lack of
strong names.*
w William Hurlbut, Bartlett Cormack, Glenn
Tryon, Howard Estabrook *d* William A. Seiter
☆ John Boles, Jean Muir, Charles Butterworth,
Ruthelma Stevens, Arthur Lake, Spring Byington
   'One of those productions that just misses the
   top rung.' – *Variety*

Ordeal by Innocence
US   1985   88m   Eastmancolor
Cannon (Jenny Craven)
▤   ⊘
An explorer returning from an Antarctic trip
discovers that an acquaintance has been hanged
for murder, and he might have saved him.
*Rather dim Agatha Christie adaptation (though set in
her favourite Devon from her favourite book), with
workaday actors and a most unsuitable music score. By
the time the end comes, nobody could possibly care who
done it.*
w Alexander Stuart *d* Desmond Davis *ph* Billy
Williams *m* Dave Brubeck
☆ Donald Sutherland, Christopher Plummer, Faye
Dunaway, Sarah Miles, Ian MacShane, Diana
Quick, Annette Crosbie, Michael Elphick, Phoebe
Nicholls

Order of Death
Italian   1983   101m   colour
New Line/Virgin/RAI (Elda Ferri)
A corrupt cop and a cop-killer form a sado-
masochistic relationship.
*Confused personalities battle it out in an exaggerated,
bombastic psychological thriller.*
w Ennio de Concini, Hugh Fleetwood
novel Hugh Fleetwood *d* Roberto Faenza
ph Giuseppe Pinori *m* Ennio Morricone
ad Giantito Burchiellaro *ed* Nini Baragli
☆ Harvey Keitel, John Lydon, Nicole Garcia,
Leonard Mann, Sylvia Sidney, Carlo Romanelli,
Bob Kelly, Tony Mayer

Orders Are Orders
GB   1954   78m   bw
Group 3 (Donald Taylor)
Flabby update of *Orders Is Orders* with an
interesting cast below par.
w Donald Taylor, Geoffrey Orme *d* David
Paltenghi *ph* Arthur Grant *m* Stanley Black
☆ Peter Sellers, Brian Reece, Sid James, Tony
Hancock, Margot Grahame, Raymond Huntley,
Maureen Johnson, June Thorburn, Bill Fraser

Orders Is Orders *
GB   1933   88m   bw
Gaumont British (Michael Balcon)
An army barracks is disrupted when an American
film company gets permission to work there.
Breezy farce which pleased at the time.
w Leslie Arliss, Sidney Gilliat *play* Ian Hay,
Anthony Armstrong *d* Walter Forde *ph* Glen
MacWilliams
☆ Charlotte Greenwood, James Gleason, Cedric
Hardwicke, Cyril Maude, Ian Hunter, Ray Milland,
Jane Carr, Donald Calthrop, Eliot Makeham,
Wally Patch, Finlay Currie
   'A wow from start to finish.' – *Variety*

'They made this boy a cold-blooded killer!'
Orders to Kill *
GB   1958   111m   bw
British Lion/Lynx (Anthony Asquith, Anthony
Havelock-Allan)
During World War II a bomber pilot undertakes a
mission to parachute into occupied France and kill
a double agent, who turns out afterwards to have
been innocent.
*Strong, hard-to-take but well made war story about the
effect of war on conscience.*
w Paul Dehn *d* Anthony Asquith *ph* Desmond
Dickinson *m* Benjamin Frankel
☆ Paul Massie, Irene Worth, James Robertson
Justice, *Leslie French*, Eddie Albert, Lillian Gish,
John Crawford, Jacques Brunius, Lionel Jeffries
🏆 Paul Dehn; Irene Worth; Paul Massie (best
newcomer)

Ordet *
Denmark   1957   126m   bw
Palladium (Carl Theodor Dreyer)
📼   ▤
In a God-fearing village, a father and his three sons
have various religious experiences.
*Hard-to-take intellectual drama of the faith, very slow
and austere but strangely compelling.*
wd Carl Theodor Dreyer *ph* Henning Bendtsen
m Poul Schierbeck
☆ Henrik Malberg, Emil Hass Christensen,
Preben Lerdorff-Rye, Caj Kristensen

'A smash and grab masterpiece.'
Ordinary Decent Criminal
Ireland/GB/Germany/US   2000   90m
Technicolor
Icon/Little Bird/Tatfilm/Trigger
Street/Miramax/IFB/Greenlight/Filmstiftung (Jonathan
Cavendish)
🎧
In Dublin, a notorious criminal runs rings around
the police in a series of audacious thefts.
*Partly based on the true-life exploits of Martin Cahill,
this is a run-of-the-mill thriller with some unconvincing
casting.*
w Gerard Stembridge *d* Thaddeus O'Sullivan
ph Andrew Dunn *m* Damon Albarn *pd* Tony
Burrough *ed* William Anderson
☆ Kevin Spacey, Linda Fiorentino, Peter Mullan,
Stephen Dillane, Helen Baxendale, David
Hayman, Patrick Malahide, Gerard McSorley
   'You just feel like you've seen it all before.' – *Bob
   McCabe, Empire*
† A better film dealing with Martin Cahill is John
Boorman's *The General* (qv).

'Everything is in its proper place – except the past!'
Ordinary People ***
US   1980   124m   Technicolor
Paramount/Wildwood (Ronald L. Schwary)
📼   ▤   ⊘
The eldest son of a well-heeled American family is
drowned, and the survivors take stock and indulge
in recriminations.
*An actor's piece which on that level succeeds very well,
and accurately pins down a certain species of modern
American family.*
w Alvin Sargent *novel* Judith Guest *d* Robert
Redford *ph* John Bailey *m* Marvin Hamlisch
☆ Donald Sutherland, Mary Tyler Moore, Timothy
Hutton, Judd Hirsch, Elizabeth McGovern, M.
Emmet Walsh
   'This is an academic exercise in catharsis: it's
   earnest, it means to improve people, and it lasts
   a lifetime.' – *New Yorker*
🏆 best film; Alvin Sargent; Robert Redford;
Timothy Hutton
🏆 Mary Tyler Moore; Judd Hirsch (supporting
actor)

The Oregon Trail
US   1959   86m   DeLuxe   Cinemascope
TCF
A New York reporter in 1846 is sent to cover a
westward trek.
*Prototype settlers vs Indians Western with all the
expected incident.*
w Louis Vittes, Gene Fowler Jnr *d* Gene Fowler
Jnr *ph* Kay Norton *m* Paul Dunlap
☆ Fred MacMurray, William Bishop, Nina
Shipman, Gloria Talbott, Henry Hull, John
Carradine, Elizabeth Patterson

Orfeu Negro: see Black Orpheus

The Organization
US   1971   108m   DeLuxe
UA/Mirisch (Walter Mirisch)
▤
San Francisco policemen combat an international
drug smuggling organization.
*The third and weakest adventure of Virgil Tibbs, black
policeman of In the Heat of the Night. Absolutely
routine.*
w James R. Webb *d* Don Medford *ph* Joseph
Biroc *m* Gil Melle
☆ Sidney Poitier, Barbara McNair, Sheree North,
Gerald S. O'Loughlin

'Making sex safe again!'
Orgazmo
US   1997   90m   colour
October/Kuzui Enterprises/MDP/Avenging Conscience
(Fran Rubel Kuzui, Jason McHugh, Matt Stone)
📼   ▤   ⊘
A naïve Mormon actor is persuaded to take the
leading role of Captain Orgazmo in a pornographic
movie.
*Drear and feeble send-up of porn and superheroes that
is enough to give comedy a bad name.*
wd Trey Parker *ph* Kenny Gioseffi *m* Paul Robb
pd Tristan Paris Bourne *ed* Trey Parker, Michael
R. Miller
☆ Trey Parker, Dian Bachar, Robyn Lynne,
Michael Dean Jacobs, Ron Jeremy, Andrew W.
Kemler
   'Patchy, clumsy and almost unwatchable. The
   laughs are few, and feebly silly at best.' – *Mark
   Sinker, Sight and Sound*
   'Massively inventive and spiked with perversely
   wicked humor.' – *Emanuel Levy, Variety*

Orient Express *
US   1934   71m   bw
Fox
Various stories conflict on the Orient Express.
*Moderately successful multi-drama in the wake of
Grand Hotel.*
w Paul Martin, Carl Hovey, Oscar Levant,
William Conselman *novel* Graham Greene
d Paul Martin
☆ Heather Angel, Ralph Morgan, Norman Foster,
Herbert Mundin, Una O'Connor, Irene Ware,
Dorothy Burgess
   'Rather too much story all of a sudden; auditors
   may be lulled to quiet by the easy, non-exciting
   early action.' – *Variety*

Oriental Dream: see Kismet (1944)

Original Gangstas *
US   1996   98m   DeLuxe
Orion/Po' Boy (Fred Williamson)
📼   ▤   ⊘
A former gang leader, now a respected football
coach, returns home to recruit some old friends to
deal with the violent criminals who shot his father,
a shopkeeper in Gary, Indiana, described as 'the
city with the highest murder rate in the USA'.
*Some of the originators of the blaxploitation movies of
the 70s return in a brash, energetic action movie,
fuelled by a righteous anger at urban degradation, mob
rule, and the specious platitudes of politicians.*
w Aubrey Rattan *d* Larry Cohen *ph* Carlos
Gonzalez *m* Vladimir Horunzhy *pd* Elayne
Barbara Ceder *ed* David Kern, Peter B. Ellis
☆ Fred Williamson, Jim Brown, Pam Grier,
Richard Roundtree, Paul Winfield, Isabel Sanford,
Ron O'Neal, Robert Forster, Charles Napier,
Wings Hauser, Frank Pesce, Dru Down, Shyheim
   'Everyone involved gets a job done without
   much fuss and with the cool savvy that makes
   the film a satisfying diversion.' – *Variety*

Orion's Belt
Norway   1985   103m   Eastmancolor
Enterprise/Filmeffekt (Dag Alveberg, Petter Borgli)
original title: *Orions Belte*
Three sailors discover a Soviet spy station.
Plodding Cold War thriller.
w Richard Harris *novel* Jon Michelet *d* Ola
Solum *ph* Harald Paalgard *m* Geir Bohren, Bent
Aserud *ad* Harald Egede-Nissen *ed* Bjorn
Breigutu, Yngve Refseth
☆ Helge Jordal, Sverre Anker Ousdal, Hans Ola
Sorlie, Kjersti Holmen, Vidar Sandem, Nils
Johnson

Orlando **
GB/Russia/France/Italy/Netherlands   1992   93m
Eastmancolor
Electric/Adventure
Pictures/Lenfilm/Mikado/Sigma/British Screen
(Christopher Sheppard)
📼   ▤   ⊘   🎧
In a life that lasts for 400 years, a male favourite of
Queen Elizabeth I undergoes a sex change and
becomes a 20th-century woman.
*A divertingly different romp, amusing and occasionally
provocative in its examination of identity and gender.*
wd Sally Potter *novel* Virginia Woolf *ph* Alexsei
Rodionov *m* David Motion, Sally Potter *pd* Ben
Van Os, Jan Roelfs *ed* Herve Schneid

☆ Tilda Swinton, Billy Zane, Lothaire Bluteau, John Wood, Charlotte Valandrey, Heathcote Williams, Quentin Crisp, Peter Eyre, Thom Hoffman, Jimmy Somerville, Dudley Sutton, Anna Healy

'Exciting, wonderfully witty entertainment for discriminating auds.' – *Variety*

⅄ Ben Van Os, Jan Roelfs; costume design (Sally Potter)

L'Oro di Napoli: see *Gold of Naples*

O'Rourke of the Royal Mounted: see *Saskatchewan*

Orphans

US 1987 120m colour
Lorimar

Two outcast brothers have their lives transformed by a gangster.
Photographed talk-piece which could hope for few takers among the general audience: one for actor-fanciers.
w Lyle Kessler *play* Lyle Kessler *d* Alan J. Pakula *ph* Donald McAlpine *m* Michael Small
☆ Albert Finney, Matthew Modine, Kevin Anderson, John Kellogg

'Are Your Parents A Burden?'

Orphans **

GB 1999 95m colour
Downtown/Channel 4 (Frances Higson)

Three brothers and their handicapped sister mourn the death of their mother in Glasgow.
A raw-edged, energetic, dark comedy of working-class life in Glasgow; it takes some imaginative risks as it veers between knockabout comedy and stark tragedy.
wd Peter Mullan *ph* Grant Scott Cameron *m* Craig Armstrong *pd* Campbell Gordon *ed* Colin Monie
☆ Gary Lewis, Douglas Henshall, Rosemarie Stevenson, Stephen McCole, Frank Gallagher, Malcolm Shields

'The milk of human kindness hasn't merely soured in Peter Mullan's transcendentally nasty comedy … It has so poisoned the air of Glasgow that its clammy atmosphere seems charged with petty malice.' – *Stephen Holden, New York Times*

'Can a woman love more than one man?'

Orphans of the Storm *

US 1921 124m bw silent
D. W. Griffith

Two sisters are caught up in the French revolution of 1789.
Half melodrama, half epic, this celebrated film survives chiefly by its careful attention to historical detail and by the excitement of its crowd scenes.
w D. W. Griffith *play* Adolph Ennery *d* D. W. Griffith *ph* Henrick Sartov
☆ Lillian Gish, Dorothy Gish, Joseph Schildkraut, Lucile La Verne, Morgan Wallace, Frank Puglia, Creighton Hale

'There is scarcely a scene or an effect in the entire production that is not beautiful to look upon, and there is scarcely a moment that is not charged with intense dramatic power.' – *Robert E. Sherwood, Life*

Orphée ***

France 1949 112m bw
André Paulvé 1/Films du Palais Royal

Death, represented by a princess, falls in love with Orpheus, a poet, and helps him when he goes into hell in pursuit of his dead love.
Fascinating poetic fantasy which may have been finally unintelligible but was filled to overflowing with memorable scenes and cinematic tricks, from the entry to the hereafter through a mirror to intercepted code messages such as 'L'oiseau compte avec ses doigts'. The closest the cinema has got to poetry.
wd Jean Cocteau *play* Jean Cocteau *ph* Nicolas Hayer *m* Georges Auric *ad* Jean d'Eaubonne
☆ Jean Marais, François Périer, Maria Casarès, Marie Déa, Edouard Dermithe, Juliette Greco

'It is a drama of the visible and the invisible … I interwove many myths. Death condemns herself in order to help the man she is duty bound to destroy. The man is saved but Death dies: it is the myth of immortality.' – *Jean Cocteau*

† See the sequel *Le Testament d'Orphée*.
†† The film was dedicated to its designer Christian Bérard (1902–49).

Oscar

♈♈ US 1991 109m Technicolor
Warner/Touchstone/Silver Screen Partners IV (Leslie Belzberg)

A gangster who is trying to reform attempts to sort out the marital problems of his daughters.
Leaden attempt at a screwball comedy, and one that sinks under its own witlessness.
w Michael Barrie, Jim Mulholland *play* Claude Magnier *d* John Landis *ph* Mac Ahlberg *m* Elmer Bernstein *pd* Bill Kenney *ed* Dale Beldin, Michael R. Miller
☆ Sylvester Stallone, Ornella Muti, Kirk Douglas, Peter Riegert, Chazz Palminteri, Vincent Spano, Marisa Tomei, Tim Curry, Don Ameche, Yvonne DeCarlo, Linda Gray

'Zany farce generates a fair share of laughs but still probably remains too creaky a conceit for modern audiences to go for in a big way.' – *Variety*

† Magnier's play was first filmed in France in 1967, directed by Eduardo Molinaro and starring Louis de Funes.

The Oscar *

US 1966 118m Pathécolor
Paramount/Greene-Rouse (Russel Rouse)

On the night of the Academy Awards his friend recalls a heel's rise to stardom.
Squalid, sensationalist account of Hollywood mores; one hopes it isn't quite true.
w Harlan Ellison, Russel Rouse, Clarence Greene *novel* Richard Sale *d* Russel Rouse *ph* Joseph Ruttenberg *m* Percy Faith
☆ Stephen Boyd, Elke Sommer, Tony Bennett, Eleanor Parker, Milton Berle, Joseph Cotten, Jill St John, Edie Adams, Ernest Borgnine, Ed Begley, Walter Brennan, Broderick Crawford, James Dunn, Peter Lawford, Edith Head and also Hedda Hopper, Merle Oberon, Bob Hope, Frank Sinatra

'This is the sort of film that only Hollywood could make, and on that level it is preposterously enjoyable.' – *David Wilson*

'That true movie rarity – a picture that attains a perfection of ineptitude quite beyond the power of words to describe.' – *Richard Schickel*

Oscar and Lucinda **

Australia 1997 132m Atlab Pamavision
Fox/AFFC/Meridian (Robin Dalton, Timothy White)

A gambling-mad English missionary makes one last bet with a wealthy Australian woman: that he can transport a glass chapel she has designed to a remote part of the country.
An imaginative, flawed attempt to encompass a strange and obsessive drama of the varieties of faith.
w Laura Jones *novel* Peter Carey *d* Gillian Armstrong *ph* Geoffrey Simpson *m* Thomas Newman *pd* Luciana Arrighi *ed* Nicholas Beauman
☆ Ralph Fiennes, Cate Blanchett, Ciaran Hinds, Tom Wilkinson, Richard Roxburgh, Clive Russell, Barry Otto, Geoffrey Rush

Oscar Wilde **

GB 1959 96m bw
Vantage (William Kirby)

Scandal strikes Oscar Wilde through his involvement with Lord Alfred Douglas.
Competent, well acted version of well-known events of the 1890s, with Morley in his original stage role; generally more satisfactory than The Trials of Oscar Wilde which was shot simultaneously.
w Jo Eisinger *d* Gregory Ratoff *ph* Georges Périnal *m* Kenneth V. Jones
☆ Robert Morley, John Neville, Phyllis Calvert, Ralph Richardson, Dennis Price, Alexander Knox, Edward Chapman, Martin Benson, Robert Harris, Henry Oscar, William Devlin

O'Shaughnessy's Boy

US 1935 88m bw
MGM

A circus performer is reunited with the son his wife took away in childhood.
Shameless sentiment which failed to repeat for its stars the success of The Champ.

w Leonard Praskins, Otis Garrett *d* Richard Boleslawski
☆ Wallace Beery, Jackie Cooper, Leona Maricle, Sara Haden, Henry Stephenson, Spanky, MacFarland

'Far too much crying. Good production will help.' – *Variety*

Ososhiki: see *Death Japanese Style*

Ossessione **

Italy 1942 135m bw
ICI

A wanderer falls for the wife of an innkeeper and they murder him, but fate takes a hand.
Unofficial remake of The Postman Always Rings Twice, barely released outside Italy. A powerful melodrama credited with starting the neo-realist school.
w Antonio Pietrangeli, Giuseppe de Santis, Gianni Puccini, Luchino Visconti, Mario Alicata *d* Luchino Visconti *ph* Aldo Tonti, Domenico Scala *m* Giuseppe Rosati
☆ Massimo Girotti, Clara Calamai, Elio Marcuzzo

† Other versions: *Le Dernier Tournant* (France 1939); *The Postman Always Rings Twice* (US 1945); *The Postman Always Rings Twice* (US 1981).

Ostatni Etap: see *The Last Stage*

The Osterman Weekend

US 1983 102m DeLuxe
Davis-Panzer/Fox

A CIA chief tries to convince a powerful TV journalist that several of his trusted informants are Soviet agents.
Convoluted bloodbath with absolutely nothing new in its locker.
w Alan Sharp, Ian Masters *novel* Robert Ludlum *d* Sam Peckinpah *ph* John Coquillon *m* Lalo Schifrin
☆ Rutger Hauer, John Hurt, Burt Lancaster, Craig T. Nelson, Dennis Hopper, Chris Sarandon, Meg Foster, Helen Shaver

'A competent, professional, but thoroughly impersonal meller.' – *Variety*

Otac Na Sluăbenom Putu: see *When Father Was Away On Business*

Otello *

US/Italy 1986 120m Eastmancolor
Cannon/RAI (John Thompson, Fulvio Lucisano)

An adaptation of Verdi's opera, based on Shakespeare's play.
A visually splendid transcription, which however did not hit the mark with audiences.
wd Franco Zeffirelli *ph* Ennio Guarnieri *m* Giuseppe Verdi *ed* Peter Taylor, Franca Silvi
☆ Placido Domingo, Katia Ricciarelli, Justino Diaz, Petra Malakova
♟ costumes (Anna Anni, Maurizio Millenotti)

Othello *

US/France 1951 91m bw
Mercury/Films Marceau (Orson Welles)

Shakespeare's play as rearranged by Orson Welles at the start of his European wanderings; modest budget, flashes of brilliance, poor technical quality, variable acting.
Not really the best way to film Shakespeare.
wd Orson Welles *play* William Shakespeare *ph* Anchise Brizzi, George Fanto, Obadan Troania, Roberto Fusi, G. Araldo *m* Francesco Lavagnino, Alberto Barberis *ad* Alexander Trauner
☆ Orson Welles, Michael MacLiammoir, Fay Compton, Robert Cook, Suzanne Cloutier, Michael Laurence, Hilton Edwards, Doris Dowling
† Michael MacLiammoir's book *Put Money in Thy Purse* is a witty account of the sporadic, poverty-stricken making of the film.

Othello *

GB 1965 166m Technicolor Panavision
BHE (Richard Godwin)

A record of the National Theatre production, disappointing in terms of cinema but a valuable record of a famous performance.
d Stuart Burge *ph* Geoffrey Unsworth *md* Richard Hampton

☆ Laurence Olivier, Frank Finlay, Joyce Redman, Maggie Smith, Derek Jacobi, Robert Lang, Anthony Nicholls

'What the director does is keep the camera moving among the actors with the most intelligent precision.' – *Observer*
⅄ Laurence Olivier; Frank Finlay; Joyce Redman; Maggie Smith

'Envy greed jealousy and love.'

Othello *

US 1995 124m Technicolor
Columbia/Castle Rock/Dakota/Imminent (Luc Roeg, David Barron)

A black soldier woos, wins and loses the love of his life.
A good-looking version of Shakespeare's play but hampered by some inadequate speaking of the verse. Othello is robbed of much of his charisma by having his speeches, the means by which he won Desdemona, cut short. Branagh survives the experience best.
wd Oliver Parker *ph* David Johnson *m* Charlie Mole *pd* Tim Harvey *ed* Tony Lawson
☆ Laurence Fishburne, Irene Jacob, Kenneth Branagh, Nathaniel Parker, Michael Maloney, Anna Patrick, Nicholas Farrell, Indra Ove

'Colorful and intimate production is relatively conventional and unremarkable as an interpretation, but is well performed by its two male leads and clearly staged and enunciated for ready comprehension by a mass audience.' – *Todd McCarthy, Variety*

'Pitched at audiences as a sort of psychological thriller about sexual jealousy: *Basic Instinct* with better dialogue and a handkerchief instead of an ice pick.' – *Tom Shone, Sunday Times*

† The film's trailer went: 'In the time of heroes there was but one great general. His bravery in battle was legendary, his devotion to his love unchallenged. His name was Othello. Under the cover of darkness and against her father's will, he took Desdemona into his heart. The great general and his true love were secretly wed. Some men die for glory, some men fight for love. One man lives for revenge. His was the soul of a traitor, and the opportunity he seized will change their lives forever…'

†† Only a third of Shakespeare's dialogue remains in this version. The director explained, 'I thought it would be interesting to make it more of a punchy, pacey number.'

The Other *

US 1972 100m DeLuxe
TCF/Rex-Benchmark (Tom Tryon)

A boy insists that his dead twin is responsible for several unexplained deaths.
Subtle family ghost story for intellectuals; a bit pretentious and restrained for popular success.
w Tom Tryon *novel* Tom Tryon *d* Robert Mulligan *m* Robert Surtees *m* Jerry Goldsmith *pd* Albert Brenner
☆ Uta Hagen, Diana Muldaur, Chris Connelly, Victor French

Other Halves

New Zealand 1984 95m Eastmancolor
Oringham/Galatea (Tom Finlayson, Dean Hill)

A middle-class woman, recovering from a breakdown and the end of her marriage, falls for a homeless and delinquent 16-year-old Maori youth.
Confused melodrama of racial intolerance and an unlikely love affair, unconvincing for the most part.
w Sue McCauley *novel* Sue McCauley *d* John Laing *ph* Leon Narbey *m* Don McGlashan *pd* Robert Gillies *ed* Harley Oliver
☆ Lisa Harrow, Mark Pilisi, Clare Clifford, Bruce Purchase, Emma Piper, Paul Gittins, John Bach

'Her every exciting moment was an unforgettable experience!'

The Other Love

US 1947 96m bw
Enterprise (David Lewis)

At a Swiss sanatorium, a lady concert pianist who is dying falls in love with her doctor.
Fairly icky 'woman's picture' with uncomfortable performances.
w Ladislas Fodor, Harry Brown *story* Erich Maria Remarque *d* André de Toth *ph* Victor Milner *m* Miklos Rozsa

---

⊙ Digital Video Disc Region 2 ⊙ Digital Video Disc Region 1 ♪ Soundtrack released on compact disc ☆ Cast in approximate order of importance † Points of interest ♫ Notable songs ♟ Academy Award ⅄ Academy Award nomination ⍟ BAFTA

☆ Barbara Stanwyck, David Niven, Richard Conte, Gilbert Roland, Joan Lorring, Lenore Aubert

Other Men's Women

US   1931   70m   bw
Warner
A train driver falls for his partner's wife.
Stilted heavy-breathing melodrama.
w William K. Wells d William A. Wellman
☆ Grant Withers, James Cagney, Mary Astor, Joan Blondell, Regis Toomey
'Good railroad melo for the lesser run theatres.' – *Variety*

'Meet Larry the Liquidator. Arrogant. Greedy. Self-centered. Ruthless. You gotta love the guy.'
Other People's Money *

US   1991   101m   Technicolor
Warner/Yorktown (Norman Jewison, Ric Kidney)
▨   ▦   ◎~
A selfish asset-stripper attempts to take over an old-established company and its attractive young lawyer.
Entertaining comedy of the conflict between big-city and small-town values in the modern manner: that is, greed wins.
w Alvin Sargent *play* Jerry Sterner d Norman Jewison ph Haskell Wexler m David Newman pd Philip Rosenberg ed Lou Lombardo, Michael Pacek, Hubert de la Bouillerie
☆ Danny DeVito, Gregory Peck, Penelope Ann Miller, Piper Laurie, Dean Jones, R. D. Call, Mo Gaffney, Bette Henritze

'The romance of passion and power!'
The Other Side of Midnight

US   1977   166m   DeLuxe   Panavision
TCF/Frank Yablans, Martin Ransohoff (Howard W. Koch Jnr)
▨
Before and after World War II a young Parisienne courts an American flyer, but her tycoon husband eventually exacts a grim revenge on both of them.
Turgid and interminable adaptation of a best-seller, with no likeable characters and several unpleasant sequences.
w Herman Raucher, Daniel Taradash *novel* Sidney Sheldon d Charles Jarrott ph Fred J. Koenekamp m Michel Legrand pd John DeCuir
☆ Marie-France Pisier, John Beck, Susan Sarandon, Raf Vallone, Clu Gulager, Christian Marquand
'After 166 minutes the feeling that one has actually lived through it all is a little too real for comfort.' – *David Badder, MFB*
'A fatuous, money-spinning film from the fatuous, money-spinning book.' – *New Yorker*
'Right down to the nonsense title, this epic of schlock restores the era of *Now Voyager* ... the movie equivalent of a good bad read.' – *Time Out*

'Once in your life – may someone love you like this!'
The Other Side of the Mountain

US   1975   102m   Technicolor
Universal/Filmways/Larry Peerce (Edward S. Feldman)
▨
GB title: *A Window to the Sky*
A girl skiing champion is paralysed by polio.
Maudlin tearjerker based on a real case; altogether too much of a good thing.
w David Seltzer *book* A *Long Way Up* by E. G. Valens d Larry Peerce ph David M. Walsh m Charles Fox
☆ Marilyn Hassett, Beau Bridges, Belinda Montgomery, Nan Martin, William Bryant, Dabney Coleman
♫ song 'Richard's Window' (mCharles Fox, lyNorman Gimbel)

'For everyone who believes in happy endings!'
The Other Side of the Mountain Part Two

US   1977   99m   Technicolor
Universal/Filmways (Edward S. Feldman)
▦
Crippled skier Jill Kinmont becomes a teacher and falls in love again.
More true-life weepie material spun out from the first successful film; the sequel is quickly forgettable.
w Douglas Day Stewart d Larry Peerce ph Ric Waite m Lee Holdridge

☆ Marilyn Hassett, Timothy Bottoms, Nan Martin, Belinda J. Montgomery

'A love story for the romantically challenged.'
The Other Sister

US   1999   129m   Technicolor   Panavision
Buena Vista/Touchstone (Mario Iscovich, Alexandra Rose)
▨   ▦   ◎   ◯~
In San Francisco, two mentally retarded young people fall in love.
Manipulative, sentimental romantic tale that resembles a couple of episodes from a TV soap opera.
w Garry Marshall, Bob Brunner, Alexandra Rose, Blair Richwood d Garry Marshall ph Dante Spinotti m Rachel Portman pd Stephen J. Lineweaver ed Bruce Green
☆ Juliette Lewis, Diane Keaton, Tom Skerritt, Giovanni Ribisi, Poppy Montgomery, Sarah Paulson, Linda Thorson, Joe Flanigan, Juliet Mills, Hector Elizondo
'The sentiments are so perniciously calculated to extract tears that it left me stone cold.' – *James Christopher, Times*

'The Heart Is Deceitful, Who Can Know It?'
Other Voices, Other Rooms *

US   1995   98m   colour
Dowtown/Golden Eye (Peter Wentworth, David Rocksavage)
▦
A teenage boy is summoned by his cousin to a Southern mansion where his father lies paralysed.
Muted gothic romance, a work of intense, somewhat precious imagination that does not translate well to the screen.
w Sara Flanigan, David Rocksavage *novel* Truman Capote d David Rocksavage ph Paul Ryan m Chris Hajian pd Amy McGary ed Cynthia Scheider
☆ Lothaire Bluteau, Anna Thomson, David Speck, April Turner, Frank Taylor, Leonard Watkins, Audrey Dollar, Elizabeth Byler, Moses Gibson, Bob Kingdom
'A torturous experience at best.' – *Film Review*

Otley **

GB   1968   91m   Technicolor
Columbia/Open Road (Bruce Cohn Curtis)
An inoffensive Londoner falls in with spies and murderers.
Semi-spoof comedy thriller taking in James Bondery and the swinging London set. Generally pretty funny, but not entirely certain of its own motives.
w Ian La Frenais, Dick Clement *novel* Martin Waddell d Dick Clement ph Austin Dempster m Stanley Myers
☆ Tom Courtenay, Romy Schneider, Alan Badel, James Villiers, Leonard Rossiter, Freddie Jones, James Bolam, Fiona Lewis

Otto e Mezzo: see Eight and a Half

Our Betters *

US   1933   83m   bw
RKO (David O. Selznick)
An American woman in London finds her titled husband is unfaithful and sets about causing society scandals.
Dimly adapted West End success makes an interesting but unamusing film.
w Jane Murfin, Harry Wagstaff Gribble *play* W. Somerset Maugham d George Cukor ph Charles Rosher m Max Steiner
☆ Constance Bennett, Violet Kemble Cooper, Alan Mowbray, Gilbert Roland, Phoebe Foster, Charles Starrett, Grant Mitchell, Anita Louise, Minor Watson, Hugh Sinclair
'It's all very English and so sophisticated ... they will really have to go for Constance Bennett to go for this picture.' – *Variety*
'One of those familiar dreams of high life in which we are asked to admire even while we condemn the superb immorality of our almost godlike betters.' – *The Times*

Our Blushing Brides: see Our Dancing Daughters

Our Daily Bread *

US   1934   80m   bw
(UA)
▨   ▦   ◎~
A young couple in the Depression inherit a broken-down farm and make it work.
A rather drab sequel to The Crowd, with an irrigation ditch finale in clear imitation of Eisenstein.
w Elizabeth Hill *story* King Vidor d King Vidor ph Robert Planck m Alfred Newman
☆ Karen Morley, Tom Keene, John Qualen, Barbara Pepper, Addison Richards
'Regardless of the scepticism on the matter of box office, and its chances seem thin, it ranks as a fine effort.' – *Variety*
'With the arrival of the ditchdigging sequence, all that has gone before seems but buildup for this compelling climax.' – *Eileen Bowser, Film Notes, 1969*
† Vidor so desperately wanted to make the film that, discovering its theme to be unpopular with sponsors, he pawned everything he owned to finance it.

Our Dancing Daughters *

US   1928   86m   bw   silent
MGM/Cosmopolitan (Hunt Stromberg)
▦
A wild young socialite knows when to stop, and makes a good marriage; her friend doesn't and falls to her death while drunk.
Mild exploitation piece of its time which swept Joan Crawford to stardom after her dance in her underwear.
w Josephine Lovett d Harry Beaumont ph George Barnes
☆ Joan Crawford, John Mack Brown, Dorothy Sebastian, Anita Page, Nils Asther
† Sequels: *Our Modern Maidens* (silent, 1929) with JC, Rod La Rocque, Douglas Fairbanks Jnr, Anita Page, w Josephine Lovett; *Our Blushing Brides* (sound, 1930) with JC, Robert Montgomery, Anita Page, Dorothy Sebastian, Raymond Hackett, w Bess Meredyth and John Howard Lawson. Neither was remarkable.
♫ Josephine Lovett; George Barnes

Our Fighting Navy

GB   1937   75m   bw
Herbert Wilcox
US title: *Torpedoed*
In South America, a British naval captain saves the consul's daughter from a revolutionary.
Tuppenny blood heroics, unconvincingly staged.
w 'Bartimeus', Guy Pollock, H. T. Bishop, Gerald Elliott, Harrison Owens d Norman Walker
☆ Robert Douglas, H. B. Warner, Noah Beery, Richard Cromwell, Hazel Terry, Esme Percy

Our Girl Friday

GB   1953   87m   Eastmancolor
Renown
▨   ▦
US title: *The Adventures of Sadie*
Four shipwrecked survivors are washed up on a desert island.
Coy sex comedy for the family; pretty unbearable.
wd Noel Langley ph Wilkie Cooper m Ronald Binge
☆ Kenneth More, Joan Collins, George Cole, Robertson Hare, Hermione Gingold, Walter Fitzgerald

Our Hearts Were Growing Up

US   1946   83m   bw
Daniel Dare/Paramount
Our two heroines experience their college days during the roaring twenties.
Rather stiffly made but fitfully amusing sequel to the above.
w Norman Panama, Melvin Frank d William D. Russell
☆ Gail Russell, Diana Lynn, Brian Donlevy, James Brown, William Demarest, Bill Edwards, Billy DeWolfe, Sara Haden

Our Hearts Were Young and Gay *

US   1944   81m   bw
Paramount (Sheridan Gibney)
Two well-to-do flappers of the twenties find fun and romance in Paris.
A pleasant, undemanding piece of nostalgia based on a popular biography.

w Sheridan Gibney *book* Cornelia Otis Skinner, Emily Kimbrough d Lewis Allen ph Theodor Sparkuhl m Werner Heymann
☆ Gail Russell, Diana Lynn, Charles Ruggles, Dorothy Gish, Beulah Bondi, James Brown, Bill Edwards, Jean Heather

Our Hospitality ***

US   1923   70m   bw   silent
Metro/Buster Keaton (Joseph M. Schenck)
▨   ▦   ◎~
Around 1850, a Southerner returns home to claim his bride and finds himself in the middle of a blood feud.
Charming rather than hilarious star comedy with a splendid ancient train and at least one incredible stunt by the star.
w Jean Havez, Joseph Mitchell, Clyde Bruckman d Buster Keaton, Jack Blystone ph Elgin Lessley, Gordon Jennings
☆ Buster Keaton, Natalie Talmadge, Joe Keaton, Buster Keaton Jnr
'A novelty mélange of dramatics, low comedy, laughs and thrills ... one of the best comedies ever produced.' – *Variety*

Our Leading Citizen

US   1939   87m   bw
George Arthur/Paramount
A philosophical lawman tries to deal with labour unrest in his community.
Another attempt to make a star out of a character who appealed only in rural districts.
w John C. Moffitt *stories* Irvin S. Cobb d Alfred Santell
☆ Bob Burns, Susan Hayward, Joseph Allen, Charles Bickford, Elizabeth Patterson, Clarence Kolb, Paul Guilfoyle
'Confusing and burdensome script ... programme supporter.' – *Variety*

Our Little Girl

⋔⋔   US   1935   63m   bw
Fox (Edward Butcher)
A doctor's daughter brings her parents together.
One of the child star's thinner and more sentimental vehicles.
w Stephen Morehouse Avery, Allen Rivkin, Jack Yellen *story* Heaven's Gate by Florence Leighton Pfalzgraf d John Robertson ph John Seitz md Oscar Bradley
☆ Shirley Temple, Joel McCrea, Rosemary Ames, Lyle Talbot, Erin O'Brien-Moore
'She should easily satisfy her following and assure business.' – *Variety*

Our Man Flint *

US   1965   108m   DeLuxe   Cinemascope
TCF (Saul David)
▦   ◎~   ◯
An American secret agent and super stud fights an organization bent on controlling the world through its weather.
Comic strip imitation of James Bond; in its wild way the first instalment scored as many laughs, but the sequel, In Like Flint (qv), quickly ended the series.
w Hal Fimberg, Ben Starr d Daniel Mann ph Daniel L. Fapp m Jerry Goldsmith
☆ James Coburn, Lee J. Cobb, Gila Golan, Edward Mulhare, Benson Fong, Sigrid Valdis
'Despite the fact that everyone from designers to actors seems to be having a ball, the film somehow goes over the edge of parody – ultimately it looks suspiciously like a case of wish-fulfilment.' – *John Gillett*

Our Man in Havana *

GB   1959   112m   bw   Cinemascope
Columbia/Kingsmead (Carol Reed)
A British vacuum cleaner salesman in Havana allows himself to be recruited as a spy, and wishes he hadn't.
The wry flavour of the novel does not really translate to the screen, and especially not to the wide screen, but a few lines and characters offer compensation.
w Graham Greene *novel* Graham Greene d Carol Reed ph Oswald Morris m Hermanos Deniz Cuban Rhythm Band
☆ Alec Guinness, Noël Coward, Burl Ives, Maureen O'Hara, Ernie Kovacs, Ralph Richardson, Jo Morrow, Paul Rogers, Grégoire Aslan, Duncan Macrae
'The main weakness is the absence of economic, expressive cutting and visual flow. As a result ... stretches of dialogue become tedious to watch;

and the essential awareness of the writer's shifting tensions yields disappointingly to the easier mannerisms of any conventional comedy-thriller.' – Peter John Dyer

Our Man in Marrakesh
GB 1966 92m Technicolor
Harry Alan Towers
US title: Bang Bang, You're Dead
A tourist becomes involved with gangsters.
Thin comedy-thriller with exotic locations.
w Peter Yeldham d Don Sharp ph Michael Reed m Malcolm Lockyer
☆ Tony Randall, Senta Berger, Terry-Thomas, Herbert Lom, Wilfrid Hyde-White, Grégoire Aslan, Klaus Kinski

Our Miss Brooks
US 1955 85m bw
Warner
A lady teacher finds that the professor to whom she is engaged is tied to mother's apron strings.
Verbose comedy considerably less funny than the TV series from which it was spun off.
w Al Lewis, Joseph Quillan d Al Lewis
☆ Eve Arden, Gale Gordon, Robert Rockwell, Don Porter, Jane Morgan, Richard Crenna, Nick Adams

Our Miss Fred *
GB 1972 96m Technicolor
EMI/Willis World Wide (Josephine Douglas)
In World War II France, an actor escapes in women's clothes when his troupe is captured by the Nazis.
A carefully nurtured vehicle for Britain's top female impersonator somehow doesn't come off; celluloid both constrains his range and reveals his inadequacies.
w Hugh Leonard d Bob Kellett ph Dick Bush m Peter Greenwell
☆ Danny La Rue, Alfred Marks, Lance Percival, Lally Bowers, Frances de la Tour, Walter Gotell

Our Modern Maidens: see Our Dancing Daughters

Our Mother's House
GB 1967 105m Metrocolor
MGM/Filmways (Jack Clayton)
When mother dies, seven children, who don't want to go to an orphanage, bury her in the garden. Then their ne'er-do-well father turns up.
Unpleasant and rather boring melodrama, too silly to have much dramatic impact.
w Jeremy Brooks, Haya Harareet novel Julian Gloag d Jack Clayton ph Larry Pizer m Georges Delerue
☆ Dirk Bogarde, Margaret Brooks, Pamela Franklin, Mark Lester, Yootha Joyce, Anthony Nicholls
'The children begin to display an alarming variety of accents ... and when Dirk Bogarde enters, doing a rich Bill Sykes act as the long lost wicked father to a predominantly genteel family, the whole structure collapses.' – Tom Milne
'Clayton succeeds where upstarts have failed in capturing the essence of the horror-suspense film – and that is the realization that the monsters among us are human.' – Judith Crist

Our Neighbours the Carters
US 1939 85m bw
Paramount
A small-town pharmacist is so poor that he considers an offer from a wealthy friend to adopt one of his children.
A small-town saga of smiles and tears, much appreciated at the time.
w S. K. Lauren, Renaud Hoffman d Ralph Murphy
☆ Fay Bainter, Frank Craven, Genevieve Tobin, Edmund Lowe
'Neatly set up as a programmer for the family trade.' – Variety

Our Relations ***
👬 US 1936 65m bw
Hal Roach/Stan Laurel Productions
📀 📼 ⊙↷ ✧
Two sailors entrusted with a diamond ring get mixed up with their long lost and happily married twin brothers.

A fast-moving comedy which contains some of Laurel and Hardy's most polished work as well as being their most satisfying production.
w Richard Connell, Felix Adler, Charles Rogers, Jack Jevne story The Money Box by W. W. Jacobs d Harry Lachman ph Rudolph Maté
☆ Stan Laurel, Oliver Hardy, James Finlayson, Alan Hale, Sidney Toler, Daphne Pollard, Iris Adrian, Noel Madison, Ralf Harolde, Arthur Housman

Our Story
France 1984 111m Eastmancolor
Artificial Eye/Adel Productions/Sara Films-A2 (Alain Sarde)
original title: Notre Histoire
A boozy traveller falls for a beautiful woman he meets on a train.
Sub-Buñuel surrealism that is an irritant rather than a pleasure.
wd Bertrand Blier ph Jean Penzer m Martinu, Beethoven, Schubert and others ad Bernard Evien ed Claudine Merlin
☆ Alain Delon, Nathalie Baye, Michel Galabru, Geneviève Fontanel, Jean-Pierre Darroussin, Gérard Darmon

'The story of a love affair that lasted a lifetime!'

Our Town **
US 1940 90m bw
Principal Artists/Sol Lesser
📼
Birth, life and death in a small New Hampshire community.
One of the main points of the play, the absence of scenery, is abandoned in this screen version, and the graveyard scene has to be presented as a dream, but the film retains the narrator and manages to make points of its own while absorbing the endearing qualities which made the play a classic.
w Thornton Wilder, Frank Craven, Harry Chantlee play Thornton Wilder d Sam Wood ph Bert Glennon m Aaron Copland pd William Cameron Menzies
☆ Frank Craven, William Holden, Martha Scott, Thomas Mitchell, Fay Bainter, Guy Kibbee, Beulah Bondi, Stuart Erwin
'You can nearly smell things cooking, and feel the night air.' – Otis Ferguson
⚖ best picture; Aaron Copland; Martha Scott; art direction

Our Very Own
US 1950 93m bw
Samuel Goldwyn
A girl is shocked to discover that she is adopted.
Another Goldwyn foray into chintzy, middle-class, small-town America, but not a winning example.
w F. Hugh Herbert d David Miller ph Lee Garmes m Victor Young sp Richard Day
☆ Ann Blyth, Farley Granger, Joan Evans, Jane Wyatt, Ann Dvorak, Donald Cook, Natalie Wood, Gus Schilling, Phyllis Kirk

Our Vines Have Tender Grapes *
US 1945 105m bw
MGM (Robert Sisk)
📼
Life in a Norwegian farm community in southern Wisconsin.
Unexceptionable family picture produced in MGM's best manner.
w Dalton Trumbo novel George Victor Martin d Roy Rowland ph Robert Surtees m Bronislau Kaper
☆ Edward G. Robinson, Margaret O'Brien, James Craig, Agnes Moorehead, Jackie 'Butch' Jenkins, Morris Carnovsky, Frances Gifford, Sara Haden

Our Wife *
👫 US 1931 20m bw
Hal Roach
Stan helps Ollie to elope.
Good standard star comedy with a rather disappointing third sequence as three people try to get into a car designed for one.
w H. M. Walker d James W. Horne ph Art Lloyd ed Richard Currier
☆ Stan Laurel, Oliver Hardy, James Finlayson, Jean London, Ben Turpin, Charley Rogers

Our Wife
US 1941 95m bw
Columbia (John M. Stahl)
A composer is romantically torn between a lady scientist and his own ex-wife.
Middling romantic comedy of a kind very familiar at the time.
w P. J. Wolfson play Lillian Day, Lyon Mearson d John M. Stahl ph Franz Planer m Leo Shuken
☆ Melvyn Douglas, Ruth Hussey, Ellen Drew, Charles Coburn, John Hubbard, Harvey Stephens

Ourselves Alone
GB 1936 87m bw
British International
An Irish colleen has a brother in the IRA and a lover in the British Army.
Rather tired hawking of a theme already treated in Beloved Enemy.
w Dudley Leslie, Marjorie Jeans, Dennis Johnstone play Dudley Sturrock, Noel Scott d Brian Desmond Hurst, Walter Summers
☆ Antoinette Cellier, Niall MacGinnis, John Lodge, John Loder, Clifford Evans
'Will find tough sledding because of the subject matter.' – Variety
'One of the silliest pictures which even an English studio has yet managed to turn out.' – Graham Greene, The Spectator

Out Cold
US 1989 92m CFI color
Hemdale (George G. Braunstein, Ron Hamady)
📀 📼 ⊙↷
Believing that he has inadvertently killed his partner, a butcher covers up the crime with the help of the widow, who is the real murderer.
Limp comedy that quickly runs out of ideas.
w Leonard Glasser, George Malko d Malcolm Mowbray ph Tony Pierce-Roberts m Michel Colombier pd Linda Pearl ed Dennis M. Hill
☆ John Lithgow, Teri Garr, Randy Quaid, Bruce McGill, Lisa Blount, Alan Blumenfeld, Morgan Paull, Barbara Rhoades

Out for Justice
US 1991 91m Technicolor Panavision
Warner (Steven Seagal, Arnold Kopelson)
📀 📼 ⊙↷ ⊙ ↷
In Brooklyn, a cop hunts down the drug-crazed killer who murdered his best friend.
Despite the title, our hero is out for revenge, and the bloodier the better. The familiar theme is played out with the maximum amount of violence.
w David Lee Henry d John Flynn ph Ric Waite m David Michael Frank pd Gene Rudolf ed Robert A. Ferretti, Donald Brochu
☆ Steven Seagal, William Forsythe, Jerry Orbach, Jo Champa, Shareen Mitchell, Sal Richards, Gina Gershon, Jay Acovone
'Steven Seagal should snap off another hefty chunk of box-office with this latest lame-brained excuse to showcase his bone-breaking talents.' – Variety

Out in Fifty
US 1999 100m CFI
Amco/Urban (Ami Artzi, BoJesse Christopher, Scott Leet)
📀 📼 ↷
After he gets out of prison, an ex-convict is stalked by the vengeful LA cop whose wife he accidentally killed.
Another giant step in the disintegration of Rourke's career: you cannot go much lower, in cinematic terms, than starring in this crude, posturing, self-indulgent and badly-acted and -scripted thriller.
wd BoJesse Christopher, Scott Leet ph Sharon Meir m Steve Edwards pd Linda Keil ed Ross Guidici
☆ Mickey Rourke, BoJesse Christopher, Nina Ofenböck, Nikki Bokal, Scott Leet, Peter Greene, Christina Applegate, Alexis Arquette, Balthazar Getty, James Avery, Abraham Benrubi

Out of Africa **
US/GB 1985 150m Rank Colour Technovision
Mirage/Sydney Pollack
📀 📼 ⊙↷ ⊙ ↷
In 1914 Karen Blixen arrives in Africa for a marriage of convenience with a German baron who ignores her; a white hunter remedies the situation.

Heavy going but critically lauded transcription of a semi-classic which ambles along for an extremely long time without really getting anywhere.
w Kurt Luedtke, from writings of 'Isak Dinesen' (Karen Blixen) d Sydney Pollack ph David Watkin m John Barry pd Stephen Grimes ed Frederic Steinkamp, William Steinkamp
☆ Meryl Streep, Robert Redford, Klaus Maria Brandauer, Michael Kitchen, Michael Gough
'It's a long way to go for a downbeat ending.' – Variety
'The film purrs pleasantly along like one of its own big cats.' – Sight and Sound
⚖ best picture; direction; photography; music; art direction; adapted screenplay; sound
⚑ Meryl Streep; Klaus Maria Brandauer (supporting actor); editing
☒ Kurt Luedtke; David Watkin

Out of Order *
West Germany 1984 88m colour
Laura/Mutoskop (Thomas Schühly, Matthias Deyle)
original title: Abwärts
In an office block at night, four people are trapped in a lift with an alarm system that does not work.
Well-made, moderately gripping thriller, although it might have been better with a few more people trapped, to provide more variation on what threatens to stay close to cliché for most of its length.
w Carl Schenkel, Frank Göhre d Carl Schenkel ph Jacques Steyn m Jacques Zwart ed Norbert Herzner
☆ Götz George, Renee Soutendijk, Wolfgang Kieling, Hannes Jaenicke, Kurt Raab

Out of Rosenheim: see Bagdad Café

Out of Season *
GB 1975 90m Technicolor
EMI/Lorimar (Robert Enders, Merv Adelson)
📼
One winter in an English seaside resort, an old love is rekindled.
Restrained sexual fireworks in the old French manner, well enough done with excellent atmosphere but a shade overlong and marred by the need to indulge in modern tricks such as a deliberately ambiguous ending.
w Reuben Bercovitch, Eric Bercovici d Alan Bridges ph Arthur Ibbetson m John Cameron
☆ Cliff Robertson, Vanessa Redgrave, Susan George, Edward Evans

Out of Sight ***
US 1998 123m DeLuxe
Universal/Jersey (Danny de Vito, Michael Shamberg, Stacey Sher)
📀 📼 ⊙↷ ⊙ ↷
A bank robber and a federal marshal fall for each other, despite being on opposite sides of the law.
A thriller disguised as a romantic comedy, acted and directed with the necessary light touch.
w Scott Frank novel Elmore Leonard d Steven Soderbergh ph Elliot Davis m Cliff Martinez pd Gary Frutkoff ed Anne V. Coates
☆ George Clooney, Jennifer Lopez, Vingh Rhames, Don Cheadle, Dennis Farina, Albert Brooks
'There's no getting away with the simplicity of its success – great script based on a good book, good actors working with great characters, a great director empowered to be great again.' – Ian Nathan, Empire
⚑ Scott Frank; Anne V. Coates

Out of the Blue
GB 1931 88m bw
BIP
An aristocrat's daughter loves the radio singer who is engaged to her sister.
Dated frou-frou with interesting talent.
w R. P. Weston, Frank Miller, Bert Lee play Little Tommy Tucker by Caswell Garth and Desmond Carter d Gene Gerrard, John Orton ph Ernest Palmer, Arthur Crabtree m Vivian Ellis
☆ Jessie Matthews, Gene Gerrard, Kay Hammond, Kenneth Kove, Binnie Barnes

Out of the Blue
US 1947 86m bw
Eagle Lion
📼 ⊙↷
A Greenwich village artist thinks a girl who has passed out in his apartment is dead, and tries to hide the body.
Tasteless and very unfunny farce.

w Vera Caspary, Walter Bullock, Edward Eliscu *d* Leigh Jason
☆ George Brent, Carole Landis, Ann Dvorak, Turhan Bey, Virginia Mayo, Elizabeth Patterson, Julia Dean, Richard Lane

Out of the Blue
Canada   1980   94m   colour
(Leonard Yakir, Gary Jules Jouvenat)
📼 ▤
A wayward teenage punk, with a drug-addicted mother and a drunken, sexually abusive ex-convict for a father, finds her life unendurable.
At least she can count herself fortunate that she didn't have to sit through this film.
w Leonard Yakir, Brenda Nelson *d* Dennis Hopper *ph* Marc Champion *m* Tom Lavin, Neil Young *ad* David Hiscox *ed* Doris Dyck
☆ Linda Manz, Dennis Hopper, Sharon Farrell, Don Gordon, Raymond Burr

Out of the Clouds
GB   1954   88m   Eastmancolor
Ealing (Michael Balcon, Michael Relph)
Several personal stories mesh against a background of London airport during a fog.
A dull compendium of stories with a background of documentary detail which is now fascinating because it's so dated.
w John Eldridge, Michael Relph *novel* John Fores *d* Michael Relph, Basil Dearden *ph* Paul Beeson *m* Richard Addinsell
☆ Anthony Steel, Robert Beatty, David Knight, Margo Lorenz, James Robertson Justice, Eunice Gayson, Isabel Dean, Gordon Harker, Bernard Lee, Michael Howard, Marie Lohr, Esma Cannon, Abraham Sofaer
'The film relies considerably on small-time players and marginal incidents; the detail, however, never looks like adding up to a satisfactory whole.' – *Penelope Houston*

Out of the Dark
US   1988   89m   colour
Medusa/Zel Films (Zane W. Levitt)
▤ 🔍
Cops investigate a series of sex-related murders by a man dressed as a clown.
Camp horror film, full of sniggers at its own nastiness.
w J. Gregory de Felice, Zane W. Levitt *d* Michael Schroeder *ph* Julio Macat *m* Paul F. Antonelli, David Wheatley *pd* Robert Schulenberg *ed* Mark Manos
☆ Cameron Dye, Karen Black, Lynn Danielson, Karen Witter, Tracey Walter, Silvana Gallardo, Bud Cort, Geoffrey Lewis, Divine, Paul Bartel, Tab Hunter

Out of the Fog *
US   1941   86m   bw
Warner (Henry Blanke)
Gangsters move in to terrorize an innocent Brooklyn family.
Standard exploration of a situation which became routine.
w Robert Rossen, Jerry Wald, Richard Macaulay *play* The Gentle People *by* Irwin Shaw *d* Anatole Litvak *ph* James Wong Howe
☆ Ida Lupino, John Garfield, Thomas Mitchell, Eddie Albert, George Tobias, Aline MacMahon, Jerome Cowan, John Qualen, Leo Gorcey
'Has succeeded in converting a disappointing stage work into a vastly entertaining motion picture.' – *New York Herald Tribune*

'You're no good and neither am I. We deserve each other!'
Out of the Past **
US   1947   97m   bw
RKO (Warren Duff)
📼 ▤ 🔍
GB title: Build My Gallows High
A private detective is hired by a hoodlum to find his homicidal girlfriend; he does, and falls in love with her.
Moody film noir with Hollywood imitating French models; plenty of snarling and a death-strewn climax.
w Geoffrey Homes *novel* Build My Gallows High *by* Geoffrey Homes *d* Jacques Tourneur *ph* Nicholas Musuraca *m* Roy Webb
☆ *Robert Mitchum, Jane Greer, Kirk Douglas,* Rhonda Fleming, Richard Webb, Steve Brodie, Virginia Huston, Dickie Moore
'Is this not an outcrop of the national masochism induced by a quite aimless, newly industrialized

society proceeding rapidly on its way to nowhere?' – *Richard Winnington*
'Mitchum is so sleepily self-confident with the women that when he slopes into clinches you expect him to snore in their faces.' – *James Agee*

'The First Film Made In Outer Space.'
Out of the Present *
Germany/France/Belgium/Russia   1995   96m   colour
Downtown/Bremer Institut/Fernsehen (Elke Peters)
A documentary about life on the Russian Mir space station in the early 90s.
Using film shot by Sergei Krikalev, who spent ten months aboard Mir, this is a fascinating glimpse of a confined life in space.
wd Andrei Ujica *ph* Vadim Yusov *m* Johann Strauss, Peter Lazonby *ed* Ralf Henninger, Heldi Leihbecher
☆ Anatoli Artesbarski, Sergei Krikalev, Helen Sharman, Viktor Afanasiev, Musa Monarov

'The laugh-a-minute lowdown on the birth of swoon!'
Out of this World
US   1945   96m   bw
Paramount (Sam Coslow)
A Western Union messenger becomes a hit crooner and a national phenomenon.
Very mild comedy with the gimmick that Bing Crosby dubbed the singing.
w Walter de Leon, Arthur Phillips *d* Hal Walker *ph* Stuart Thompson *m* Victor Young
☆ Eddie Bracken, Veronica Lake, Diana Lynn, Cass Daley, Parkyakarkus, Donald MacBride, Florence Bates, Carmen Cavallero

'When they take you for an out-of-towner, they really take you.'
The Out of Towners *
US   1970   98m   Movielab
Paramount/Jalem (Paul Nathan)
▤ 🔍
An executive and his wife fly into New York for an interview, but their encounter with the city is a mounting series of traumatic disasters.
A love-hate relationship with a city demonstrated by a resident is something of an in-joke and becomes increasingly hysterical and unsympathetic, but there are bright moments in this company.
w Neil Simon *d* Arthur Hiller *ph* Andrew Laszlo *m* Quincy Jones
☆ Jack Lemmon, Sandy Dennis
'Technically the sloppiest as well as the most witlessly uncomfortable movie for some time.' – *Roger Greenspun, New York Times*

Out on a Limb
US   1992   83m   DeLuxe
Universal/Interscope (Michael Hertzberg)
📼 ▤ 🔍
Asked by her teacher to describe her summer vacation, a young girl tells a story involving mistaken indentity, kidnapping, murder and romance.
Witless black farce, neatly plotted but with a hapless, wimpish hero and a leaden pace.
w Daniel Goldin, Joshua Goldin *d* Francis Veber *ph* Donald E. Thorin *m* Van Dyke Parks *pd* Stephen Marsh *ed* Glenn Farr
☆ Matthew Broderick, Jeffrey Jones, Heidi Kling, John C. Reilly, Courtney Peldon, Nancy Lenehan, Marian Mercer, David Margulies, Michael Monks

Out to Sea
US   1997   109m   DeLuxe
TCF (John Davis, David T. Friendly)
📼 ▤
A gambler in search of a wealthy wife signs on as a dance host aboard a luxury liner and tricks his brother-in-law into accompanying him on the cruise.
Nostalgic, old-fashioned comedy that provides a modicum of amusement.
w Robert Nelson Jacobs *d* Martha Coolidge *ph* Lajos Koltai *m* David Newman *pd* James Spencer *ed* Anne V. Coates
☆ Jack Lemmon, Walter Matthau, Dyan Cannon, Gloria Delaney, Brent Spiner, Elaine Stritch, Hal Linden, Donald O'Connor, Edward Mulhare, Rue McClanahan
'Mildly amusing and unabashedly retrograde trifle that, except for a few naughty words, resembles glossy studio product of a generation or so ago.' – *Joe Leydon, Variety*

Outback *
Australia   1970   109m   Technicolor
NlT/Group W (George Willoughby)
A young teacher becomes involved in the rougher side of life in a remote Australian village.
A convincingly brutal picture of a community whose interests range from homosexuality to a bloody kangaroo hunt.
w Evan Jones *novel* Wake in Fright *by* Kenneth Cook *d* Ted Kotcheff *ph* Brian West *m* John Scott
☆ Gary Bond, Donald Pleasence, Chips Rafferty

Outback
Australia/US   1989   94m   colour
Samuel Goldwyn/Burrowes (John Sexton)
In Australia at the turn of the century, a wealthy American entrepreneur and a drover both risk everything for the love of a young heiress threatened by an unscrupulous landowner.
Opulent period drama, enjoyable enough in its lush, romantic way but populated by stock characters.
w John Sexton *d* Ian Barry *ph* Ross Berryman *m* Mario Millo *pd* Owen Paterson *ed* Henry Dangar
☆ Jeff Fahey, Tushka Bergen, Steven Vidler, Richard Moir, Shane Briant, Drew Forsythe, Sandy Gore

'An animal carries a deadly virus ... And the greatest medical crisis in history begins.'
'Try to remain calm.'
Outbreak
US   1995   127m   Technicolor
Warner/Punch (Arnold Kopelson, Wolfgang Petersen, Gail Katz)
📼 ▤ 🔍 🎧
A US Army expert saves the world from a deadly virus that spreads from Africa to the States and his own gung-ho generals.
An increasingly risible thriller that begins well and then becomes a fevered exercise in sub-James Bond heroics, with a military villain straight out of a comic book.
w Laurence Dworet, Robert Roy Pool *d* Wolfgang Petersen *ph* Michael Ballhaus *m* James Newton Howard *pd* William Sandell *ed* Neil Travis, Lynzee Klingman, William Hoy *sp* John Frazier; Boss Film Studios
☆ Dustin Hoffman, Rene Russo, Morgan Freeman, Kevin Spacey, Cuba Gooding Jnr, Donald Sutherland, Patrick Dempsey, Zakes Mokae, Malick Bowens
'The entire film has been put together with such skill and attention to viewer excitement that audiences will readily swallow the whole enchilada without a burp. A highly topical and alarming cautionary tale that's been socked over for maximum visceral impact.' – *Todd McCarthy, Variety*
'A pallid epic about an appalling epidemic.' – *Time*
† Five other screenwriters worked uncredited on the script: Neil Jiminez, Ted Tally, Jeb Stuart, Carrie Fisher and Dan Gilroy.

The Outcast: *see Man in the Saddle*

The Outcast
US   1954   87m   Trucolor
Republic (Herbert J. Yates)
▤
A cowboy returns home to claim the ranch his uncle stole from him.
Fast-paced Western that relies on non-stop action to distract attention from its clichéd narrative.
w John K. Butler, Richard Wormser *story* Todhunter Ballard *d* William Witney *ph* Reggie Lanning *m* R. Dale Butts *ad* Frank Arrigo *ed* Tony Martinelli
☆ John Derek, Joan Evans, Jim Davis, Slim Pickens, Harry Carey Jnr

Outcast Lady
US   1934   79m   bw
MGM
GB title: A Woman of the World
A spoilt rich girl goes from man to man but helps her drunken brother.
Modest remake of the Garbo vehicle A Woman of Affairs.
w Zoe Akins *novel* The Green Hat *by* Michael Arlen *d* Robert Z. Leonard

☆ Constance Bennett, Hugh Williams, Mrs Patrick Campbell, Elizabeth Allan, Henry Stephenson, Leo G. Carroll

'Even her love was primitive!'
Outcast of the Islands **
GB   1951   102m   bw
London Films (Carol Reed)
A shiftless trader finds a secret Far Eastern trading post where he can be happy – but even here he becomes an outcast.
An interesting but not wholly successful attempt to dramatize a complex character study. It looks great and is well acted.
w William Fairchild *novel* Joseph Conrad *d* Carol Reed *ph* John Wilcox *m* Brian Easdale
☆ *Trevor Howard,* Ralph Richardson, Kerima, Robert Morley, Wendy Hiller, George Coulouris, Frederick Valk, Wilfrid Hyde-White, Betty Ann Davies
'The script is so overwhelmed by the narrative itself that the characters and relationships fail to crystallize ... while the handling is often intelligent, ingenious, and has its effective moments, no real conception emerges.' – *Gavin Lambert*
'Its sordidness is not veneered by the usual lyricism of Hollywood.' – *London Evening News*
'The most powerful film ever made in this country.' – *Observer*

The Outcasts of Poker Flat
US   1937   68m   bw
RKO (Robert Sisk)
Four undesirables are run out of town and stuck in a mountain cabin during a snowstorm.
Overstretched anecdote with a predictably downbeat finale and not much action.
w John Twist, Harry Segall *story* Bret Harte *d* Christy Cabanne *ph* Robert de Grasse
☆ Preston Foster, Jean Muir, Van Heflin

The Outcasts of Poker Flat
US   1952   80m   bw
TCF (Julian Blaustein)
Good-looking but equally undramatic remake of the above.
w Edmund H. North *d* Joseph M. Newman *ph* Joseph LaShelle *m* Hugo Friedhofer
☆ Dale Robertson, Anne Baxter, Cameron Mitchell, Miriam Hopkins
'Fails badly either as dramatic or as western fare ... best where two features prevail.' – *Variety*

The Outfit *
US   1974   103m   Metrocolor
MGM (Carter de Haven)
📼
A bank robber comes out of prison to discover that gangsters have murdered his brother and intend to kill him.
Slick, tough thriller with slick, tough dialogue and performances to match; the taut direction maintains suspense even when the action becomes predictable.
wd John Flynn *novel* Richard Stark *ph* Bruce Surtees *m* Jerry Fielding *ad* Tambi Larsen *ed* Ralph E. Winters
☆ Robert Duvall, Karen Black, Joe Don Baker, Robert Ryan, Timothy Carey, Richard Jaeckel, Sheree North, Felice Orlandi, Joanna Cassidy, Elisha Cooke

'Even in space, the ultimate enemy is man!'
'On Jupiter's moon, something deadly is happening!'
Outland
GB   1981   109m   Technicolor   Panavision
Warner/Ladd (Richard A. Roth)
📼 ▤ 🔍 💿 🎧
The marshal of a mining base on the third moon of Jupiter waits for hired killers to arrive from Earth and try to assassinate him.
Ludicrous, over-plotted outer-space version of High Noon, in such thick colour that the action is hard to follow.
wd Peter Hyams *ph* Stephen Goldblatt *m* Jerry Goldsmith *pd* Philip Harrison
☆ Sean Connery, Peter Boyle, Frances Sternhagen, James B. Sikking, Kika Markham, Clarke Peters
'Acres of footage are expended on the same old dreary electronic gadgetry and the same old hollowly echoing metalwork sets.' – *Tom Milne, MFB*

🏃 film suitable for family viewing   📼 VHS video-cassette for the British PAL system   ▤ VHS video-cassette for the British PAL system in wide screen-format   💿 Video cassette in a computer-colourised version   ▥ American NTSC video-cassette   🔍 Laser disc

'Action! Thrills! Sensations! Primitive Love!'

The Outlaw *
US 1943 126m bw
Howard Hughes
◉ ▦ ◎
Billy the Kid, Doc Holliday and Pat Garrett meet up at a way station and quarrel over a half-breed girl.
Half-baked Western with much pretentious chat and the main interest squarely focused on the bosom of the producer's new discovery. This aspect kept censorship ballyhoo going for six years before the film was finally released in truncated form, and audiences found it not worth the wait, though it does look good.
w Jules Furthman d Howard Hughes ph Gregg Toland md Victor Young
☆ Jack Beutel, Jane Russell, Thomas Mitchell, Walter Huston
'A Western employing every ingredient ever used in this brand of production, but in such a naive fashion that you will laugh – not with the picture but at it.' – *Ewart Hodgson, News of the World*
† Despite the controversy, the British Board of Film Censors gave the film a 'U' certificate, which meant that children could see it.

Outlaw Blues
US 1977 101m Technicolor
Warner/Fred Weintraub–Paul Heller (Steve Tisch)
▦
An ex-con finds that a singing star has stolen his song.
Fashionable comedy-melodrama with no great entertainment value despite action scenes towards the end.
w B. W. L. Norton d Richard T. Heffron ph Jules Brenner m Charles Bernstein
☆ Peter Fonda, Susan Saint James, John Crawford, James Callahan, Michael Lerner

The Outlaw Josey Wales *
US 1976 135m DeLuxe Panavision
Warner/Malpaso (Robert Daley)
◉ ▦ ◎ ◎ ◠
A Westerner gradually avenges the death of his wife at the hands of bandits.
Bloodthirsty actioner in the star's usual mould; likely to prove unintentionally funny for hardened addicts.
w Phil Kaufman, Sonia Chernus novel Gone to Texas by Forrest Carter d Clint Eastwood ph Bruce Surtees m Jerry Fielding
☆ Clint Eastwood, Chief Dan George, Sondra Locke, John Vernon, Bill McKinney
'If only the actors hadn't got in the way of the scenery, it would have been a very beautiful film indeed.' – *Benny Green, Punch*
♫ Jerry Fielding

'They fell in love 24 years ago … and in the next 24 hours they'll remember why.'
The Out-of-Towners
US 1999 91m colour
Paramount (Robert Cort, David Madden, Robert Evans, Teri Schwartz)
◠
A long-time married couple visit New York, where everything goes wrong except their feelings for one another.
Lamentably dull remake of a comedy that left much to be desired the first time around.
w Marc Lawrence play Neil Simon d Sam Weisman ph John Bailey m Marc Shaiman pd Ken Adam ed Kent Beyda
☆ Steve Martin, Goldie Hawn, John Cleese, Mayor Rudolph Giuliani
'So feeble and unfocused as to make the Farrelly brothers of There's Something about Mary appear to have been suckled at the bosom of Aristophanes.' – *Lawrence Van Gelder, New York Times*

Outpost in Malaya: see The Planter's Wife

Outpost in Morocco
US 1949 92m bw
Joseph N. Ermolieff
A romantic Foreign Legion officer falls for the daughter of an enemy Arab.
Despite authentic locations and the cooperation of the Legion this is a stolid piece of work, too dull even for children's matinees.
w Charles Grayson, Paul de St Columbe d Robert Florey ph Lucien Andriot

☆ George Raft, Akim Tamiroff, Marie Windsor, John Litel, Eduard Franz

Outrage
US 1950 75m bw
Filmmakers (Collier Young)
A girl who has been raped is almost unhinged by the experience.
Well-meaning low-budgeter, thin in entertainment value.
w Ida Lupino, Collier Young, Malvin Wald d Ida Lupino ph Archie Stout m Paul Sawtell md Constantin Bakaleinikoff pd Harry Horner
☆ Mala Powers, Tod Andrews, Robert Clarke, Raymond Bond, Lilian Hamilton
'An unconvincing mixture of sensationalism, sentiment and half-baked sociology.' – *MFB*

The Outrage *
US 1964 97m bw Panavision
MGM/Harvest/February/Ritt/Kayos (A. Ronald Lubin)
Conflicting views of a Western murder.
Wildly ineffective remake of Rashomon, with everyone strangely overacting and little sense of the West as it is normally depicted.
w Michael Kanin d Martin Ritt ph James Wong Howe m Alex North
☆ Paul Newman, Edward G. Robinson, Laurence Harvey, Claire Bloom, William Shatner, Albert Salmi

Outrageous Fortune *
US 1987 100m DeLuxe
Touchstone/Interscope (Ted Field, Robert Cort)
◉ ▦ ◎ ◎
Two disparate women are in love with the same man, who is wanted by the CIA and the KGB.
Chase comedy with sex elements and plenty going on: old-fashioned jokes wrapped up in a modern package.
w Leslie Dixon d Arthur Hiller ph David M. Walsh m Alan Silvestri pd James D. Vance
☆ Shelley Long, Bette Midler, Peter Coyote, Robert Prosky, John Schuck
'Really a risqué film for a conservative audience.' – *Daily Variety*

The Outriders
US 1950 93m Technicolor
MGM (Richard Goldstone)
Three Confederate soldiers escape from a Yankee prison camp.
Competent star Western with solid production values.
w Irving Ravetch d Roy Rowland ph Charles Schoenbaum m André Previn
☆ Joel McCrea, Arlene Dahl, Barry Sullivan, Claude Jarman Jnr, Ramon Novarro

The Outside Man **
France/Italy 1972 104m DeLuxe
United Artists/Cité Films/Mondial TE.FI (Jacques Bar)
▦
original title: *Un Homme est Mort*
After he has killed a Mafia boss in Los Angeles to pay off his debts, a Frenchman discovers that he is to be killed and goes on the run from his assassin.
Well-made thriller full of unexpected twists and turns, with some intriguing set-pieces, including a shoot-out at a funeral.
w Jean-Claude Carrière, Jacques Deray, Ian McLellan Hunter d Jacques Deray ph Terry K. Meade, Silvano Ippoliti m Michel Legrand pd Marvin March ed Henri Lanoe, William K. Chulack
☆ Jean-Louis Trintignant, Ann-Margret, Roy Scheider, Angie Dickinson, Georgia Engel, Felice Orlandi, Talia Shire
'A neat, intriguing thriller which never gets ambitions above its station.' – *Tom Milne, MFB*

Outside the Law
US 1930 76m bw
Universal
A girl becomes involved between two crooks planning a bank robbery.
Incompetent early talkie with some familiar talents all at sea.
w Tod Browning, Garrett Fort d Tod Browning
☆ Mary Nolan, Edward G. Robinson, Owen Moore, Edwin Sturgis
'One of the worst examples of claptrap since sound came in … no continuity and the director lets the cast run wild.' – *Variety*

The Outsider: see The Guinea Pig (1948)

The Outsider
GB 1931 93m bw
Cinema House/MGM
A 'quack' osteopath is finally able to make a surgeon's crippled daughter walk.
Cast-iron theatre and a fairly successful quota quickie which was also released in America.
w Harry Lachman, Alma Reville play Dorothy Brandon d Harry Lachman ph Günther Krampf ad Wilfred Arnold
☆ Harold Huth, Joan Barry, Norman McKinnel, Frank Lawton, Mary Clare

The Outsider
GB 1939 90m bw
ABPC
Sturdy remake of the above.
w Dudley Leslie d Paul Stein
☆ George Sanders, Mary Maguire, Frederick Leister, Peter Murray Hill, Kathleen Harrison
'Up-to-date and should appeal to popular-priced audiences.' – *Variety*

The Outsider
US 1961 108m bw
U-I (Sy Bartlett)
Ira Hayes, a simple Red Indian, becomes a war hero but cannot reconcile himself to living in a white society.
Prolonged biopic which proves a shade too much for an eager star; it's all earnest and mildly interesting but not cinematically compulsive.
w Stewart Stern d Delbert Mann ph Joseph LaShelle m Leonard Rosenman
☆ Tony Curtis, James Franciscus, Bruce Bennett, Gregory Walcott, Vivian Nathan, Edmund Hashim, Stanley Adams

The Outsider *
France 1983 95m Eastmancolor
Cerito/Ariane (Dominique Rigaux)
original title: *Le Marginal*
A tough and reckless Parisian cop runs into trouble when he is sent to Marseille to sort out the local drug smugglers.
Fast-moving low-life thriller, with a maverick hero patterned after Dirty Harry, but much dirtier.
w Jacques Deray, Jean Herman d Jacques Deray ph Xaver Schwarzenberger m Ennio Morricone ad Eric Moulard ed Albert Jurgenson
☆ Jean-Paul Belmondo, Henry Silva, Carlos Sotto Mayor, Pierre Vernier, Maurice Barrier, Tcheky Karyo, Claude Brosset

The Outsiders: see Bande à Part (1964)

The Outsiders
♟♟ US 1983 91m Technicolor
Panavision
Zoetrope/Warner
◉ ▦ ▦ ◎ ◎ ◠
A young punk leads a high school gang against another rather higher in the social scale.
Oddball youth melodrama, a curious choice for a director with big successes behind him.
w Katherine Knutsen Rowell novel S. E. Hinton d Francis Ford Coppola ph Stephen H. Burum m Carmine Coppola pd Dean Tavoularis
☆ Matt Dillon, Ralph Macchio, C. Thomas Howell, Patrick Swayze, Rob Lowe, Emilio Estevez, Tom Cruise
'No more than a well-acted teen film.' – *Motion Picture Guide*

Outward Bound *
US 1930 82m bw
Warner
Passengers on a strange liner discover that they are all dead and heading for purgatory.
Early sound version of a popular twenties play which does not translate too well to cinematic forms and now seems very dated apart from a couple of performances; remade as Between Two Worlds (qv).
w J. Grubb Alexander play Sutton Vane d Robert Milton ph Hal Mohr
☆ Leslie Howard, Douglas Fairbanks Jnr, Alec B. Francis, Helen Chandler, Beryl Mercer, Alison Skipworth, Montagu Love, Dudley Digges
'Intelligentsia subject that must be spotted carefully … seems to lack the essentials of mass entertainment.' – *Variety*

Over Her Dead Body: see Enid Is Sleeping

Over My Dead Body
US 1942 67m bw
Walter Morosco/TCF
A writer plans commercial success by pleading guilty to an imaginary crime, but truth is stranger than fiction.
Over-talkative crime comedy.
w Edward James novel James O'Hanlon d Mal St Clair
☆ Milton Berle, Mary Beth Hughes, Reginald Denny, Frank Orth, J. Pat O'Malley

Over She Goes *
GB 1937 74m bw
ABPC
An old friend helps a nobleman to thwart a blackmailer.
Lively comedy vehicle for a forgotten star.
w Elizabeth Meehan, Hugh Brooke play Stanley Lupino d Graham Cutts ph Otto Kanturek m Billy Mayerl
☆ Stanley Lupino, Laddie Cliff, Gina Malo, Claire Luce, Max Baer, Sally Gray, Syd Walker

Over the Brooklyn Bridge
US 1983 106m Metrocolor
Golan-Globus
▦
Misadventures of a family-ridden Jewish restaurant owner in New York.
Frantic ethnic comedy with an unsympathetic hero.
w Arnold Somkin d Menahem Golan ph Adam Greenberg m Pino Donaggio
☆ Elliott Gould, Margaux Hemingway, Sid Caesar, Shelley Winters, Burt Young, Carol Kane
'The film's lip service to liberalism is offset by a blatantly sexist storyline.' – *Ruth Baumgarten, MFB*

Over the Edge *
US 1979 95m colour
Orion (George Litto)
▦
In a new Colorado development, bored, affluent teenagers go on the rampage.
Slick, violent movie about the disaffected young that for some reason never found a responsive audience.
w Charlie Hass, Tom Hunter d Jonathan Kaplan ph Andrew Davis m Sol Kaplan pd Jim Newport ed Robert Bargere
☆ Michael Kramer, Pamela Ludwig, Matt Dillon, Vincent Spano, Tom Fergus, Harry Northup, Ellen Geer
'Sensationally effective … exploitation movie. In their opportunistic way, the fellows who made it get at the social truths and middle-class nightmares more effectively than most "responsible" filmmakers would.' – *David Denby, New York*

Over the Hill
US 1931 87m bw
Fox
An ageing mother is sent to the poorhouse by her hard-hearted older son, but rescued by her ne'er-do-well younger one.
Sound remake of a silent success which in 1920 made a star of Mary Carr, who thereafter specialized in playing dear old ladies.
w Tom Barry, Jules Furthman poems Will Carleton d Henry King
☆ James Dunn, Sally Eilers, Mae Marsh, Edward Crandall, James Kirkwood
'There isn't a single overacted scene and there isn't a sequence that doesn't reach straight to the heart.' – *Variety*

Over the Hill *
Australia 1993 102m colour
Rank/Village Roadshow/Glasshouse (Robert Caswell, Bernard Terry)
◉ ▦ ◎
The adventures in the Australian outback of a 60-year-old American widow, who flees from a dull life in Maine to visit her estranged and ambitious daughter in Sydney.
A gentle road movie, enjoyably done, about a woman's refusal to give up on life.
w Robert Caswell book Alone in the Australian Outback by Gladys Taylor d George Miller ph David Connell m David McHugh pd Graham 'Grace' Walker ed Henry Dangar
☆ Olympia Dukakis, Sigrid Thornton, Derek Fowlds, Bill Kerr, Steve Bisley, Martin Jacobs, Gerry Connolly, Andrea Moore

Over the Moon

GB   1940   78m   Technicolor   London Films
(Alexander Korda)
▣

A poor girl comes into a fortune but this does not help her romance with a proud young doctor.
Insubstantial comedy which turns itself into a European travelogue before petering out.
w Anthony Pelissier, Arthur Wimperis, Alec Coppel d Thornton Freeland ph Harry Stradling m Mischa Spoliansky
☆ Merle Oberon, Rex Harrison, Ursula Jeans, Robert Douglas, Louis Borell, Zena Dare, Peter Haddon, David Tree
† Made in 1937–8, but not released.

Over the River: see One More River

Over the Top

US   1987   93m   Metrocolor   Panavision
Cannon (Menaham Golan, Yoram Globus)
▣ ▤ ◔ ⌒

An arm wrestler tries to win the love of his son.
Mundane melodrama which its star couldn't carry.
w Stirling Silliphant, Sylvester Stallone d Menahem Golan ph David Gurfinkel m Giorgio Moroder pd James Schoppe ed Don Zimmerman, James Symons
☆ Sylvester Stallone, Robert Loggia, Susan Blakely, Rick Zumwalt, David Mendenhall
'Routinely made in every respect.' – *Daily Variety*

Over the Wall

US   1938   72m   bw
Warner

A man wrongly convicted of murder fights the prison system.
Predictable semi-documentary thriller from the prolific pen of Warden Lewis E. Lawes; just an efficient second feature.
w Crane Wilbur, George Bricker d Frank MacDonald
☆ Dick Foran, John Litel, June Travis, Dick Purcell, Veda Ann Borg, George E. Stone
'Authentic melodrama, headed for nice biz.' – *Variety*

Over Twenty-One

US   1945   102m   bw
Columbia (Sidney Buchman)

A famous lady screenwriter copes with wartime domestic problems while her husband is off at the war.
Thin star comedy based on Ruth Gordon's play about her own predicament; not for the wider audience, and not very good anyway.
w Sidney Buchman play Ruth Gordon

d Alexander Hall ph Rudolph Maté m Marlin Skiles
☆ Irene Dunne, Alexander Knox, Charles Coburn, Jeff Donnell, Lee Patrick, Phil Brown, Cora Witherspoon

Overboard

👪 US   1987   112m   colour
UIP/MGM (Alexandra Rose, Anthea Sylbert)
▣ ▤ ◔ ◎

An heiress suffering from amnesia is claimed as a wife by a carpenter with three kids.
Mild amusement is provided by a predictable comedy.
w Leslie Dixon d Garry Marshall ph John A. Alonzo m Alan Silvestri ad James Shanahan, Jim Dultz ed Dov Hoenig, Sonny Baskin
☆ Goldie Hawn, Kurt Russell, Edward Herrmann, Katherine Helmond, Roddy McDowall, Michael Hagerty, Jeffrey Wiseman

Overdrive

US   1997   95m   Foto-Kem
Pacific Trust/Libra (Cheryl Parnell, Darin Spillman)
An out-of-control racing driver becomes involved with a secret agent who is being stalked by the spy she is attempting to blackmail.
A truly terrible thriller that commits the crimes of being dull, amoral and cliché-ridden.
w Malcolm Stephens d Lev L. Spiro ph Christopher Baffa ed Dan Holland
☆ Steve Guttenberg, Robert Wagner, Kaela Dobkin, Stephen Meadows, Richard Arquette, Frantz Turner, Alex Hyde-White

The Overlanders **

👪 Australia   1946   91m   bw
Ealing (Ralph Smart)
▤

In 1943 a drover saves a thousand head of cattle from the Japanese by taking them two thousand miles across country.
Attractive, easy-going semi-Western, the first and best of several films made by Ealing Studios in Australia.
wd Harry Watt ph Osmond Borradaile m John Ireland
☆ Chips Rafferty, John Nugent Hayward, Daphne Campbell
'Let us congratulate Harry Watt on the absence of kangaroos and camp-fire songs, items which few directors could have resisted.' – *Richard Winnington*

Overlord *

GB   1975   83m   bw
EMI/Jowsend (James Quinn)
An eighteen-year-old is called up in early 1944 and

killed in the D-Day landings.
Semi-documentary recreating a time in history (with much aid from newsreels) but making no discernible point. Interesting, though.
w Stuart Cooper, Christopher Hudson d Stuart Cooper ph John Alcott m Paul Glass
☆ Brian Stirner, Davyd Harries, Nicholas Ball, Julie Neesam

Owd Bob *

👪 GB   1938   78m   bw
GFD/Gainsborough (Edward Black)
US title: *To the Victor*
A Cumberland farmer's faithful dog is accused of killing sheep.
Sentimental yarn with good location backgrounds; the plot was later reused as Thunder in the Valley.
w Michael Hogan, J. B. Williams novel Alfred Olivant d Robert Stevenson ph Jack Cox md Louis Levy
☆ Will Fyffe, John Loder, Margaret Lockwood, Moore Marriott, Graham Moffatt, Wilfred Walter, Elliot Mason

'When she starts mixing business with pleasure, she goes out of business'

The Owl and the Pussycat *

US   1970   96m   Eastmancolor   Panavision
Columbia/Rastar (Ray Stark)
▣ ▤ ◔

A bookstore assistant reports a fellow tenant for prostitution, and when she is evicted she moves in with him.
Wacky, bawdy double act which starts promisingly but outstays its welcome. A solid step forward in permissiveness, with kinky behaviour as well as four-letter words.
w Buck Henry play Bill Manhoff d Herbert Ross ph Harry Stradling, Andrew Laszlo m Richard Halligan
☆ Barbra Streisand, George Segal, Robert Klein, Allen Garfield
'If computers ever turn out romantic comedies, the results will look like this.' – *Stanley Kauffmann*

The Ox **

Sweden/Norway/Denmark   1992   92m
Eastmancolor
Artificial Eye/Sweetland (Jean Doumanian)
▣ ▤ ◔
original title: *Oxen*
In a time of famine, a man kills his employer's ox in order to feed his starving family and is condemned to hard labour in prison for life.

A harrowing and humane story of hardship and forgiveness, much in the Bergman manner and as visually striking as you'd expect from a great cinematographer in his directorial debut.
w Sven Nykvist, Lasse Summanen d Sven Nykvist ph Sven Nykvist m Greig and others pd Peter Høimark ed Lasse Summanen
☆ Max von Sydow, Stellan Skarsgård, Ewa Fröling, Erland Josephson, Liv Ullmann
'Much more than just another snowy Scandinavian tale, this infuses its bleakness with tenderness and compassion while remaining a million miles away from sentimentality.' – *Empire*
🏆 best foreign film

The Ox-Bow Incident **

US   1943   75m   bw
TCF (Lamar Trotti)
▤ ◔

GB title: *Strange Incident*
A cowboy is unable to prevent three wandering travellers being unjustly lynched for murder.
Stark lynch law parable, beautifully made but very depressing.
w Lamar Trotti novel Walter Van Tilburg Clark d William Wellman ph Arthur Miller m Cyril Mockridge
☆ Henry Fonda, Henry Morgan, Jane Darwell, Anthony Quinn, Dana Andrews, Mary Beth Hughes, William Eythe, Harry Davenport, Frank Conroy
'Realism that is as sharp and cold as a knife.' – *Frank S. Nugent, New York Times*
'Very firm, respectable, and sympathetic; but I still think it suffers from rigor artis.' – *James Agee*
🏆 best picture

Oxen: see The Ox

Oxford Blues

US   1984   97m   colour
Winkast/Baltic Industrial (Peter Kohn, David Wimbury)
▤ ◔

A Los Angeles casino worker wins enough to finance an Oxford education.
Sexed-up version of A Yank at Oxford; only tolerable when the tone gets close to the original.
wd Robert Boris ph John Stanier m John Du Prez
☆ Rob Lowe, Ally Sheedy, Alan Howard, Amanda Pays, Julian Sands, Julian Firth, Michael Gough, Aubrey Morris

---

P

'Gun in one hand – woman in the other!'
P.J.
US 1967 109m Techniscope
Universal (Edward J. Montagne)
GB title: New Face in Hell
A down-at-heel private eye takes a job as bodyguard to a boorish businessman.
Routine thick ear with a predictable turnabout plot.
w Philip Reisman Jnr story Edward J. Montagne d John Guillermin ph Loyal Griggs m Neal Hefti
☆ George Peppard, Gayle Hunnicutt, Raymond Burr, Susan St James, Coleen Gray, Jason Evers, Wilfrid Hyde-White, Severn Darden
'Enough action to keep you from noticing that the plot doesn't make any sense.' – *Judith Crist*

P.K. and the Kid
US 1982 89m CFI color
Sunn Classic (Joe Roth)
A teenager, running away from her brutal step-father, goes on the road with a contestant heading for the world arm-wrestling championships in Los Angeles.
Mundane teen pic with too much concentration on the world's least photogenic sport.
w Neal Barbera d Lou Lombardo ph Ed Koons m James Horner pd Chet Allen ed Tony Lombardo
☆ Paul Le Mat, Molly Ringwald, Alex Rocco, Charles Hallahan, John Di Santi, Fionnula Flanagan, Bert Remsen, Leigh Hamilton, Esther Rolle

'A killer and a girl – trapped in America's first air raid!'
Pacific Blackout
US 1942 76m bw
Paramount (Sol C. Siegel)
An inventor escapes from jail and proves his innocence during a practice air raid blackout.
Minor melo which proved profitably topical, being released shortly after the Japanese attack on Pearl Harbor.
w Lester Cole, W. P. Lipscomb d Ralph Murphy ph Theodor Sparkuhl
☆ Robert Preston, Martha O'Driscoll, Philip Merivale, Eva Gabor, Louis Jean Heydt, Thurston Hall

Pacific Destiny
GB 1956 97m Eastmancolor Cinemascope
James Lawrie
Experiences of a British colonial servant in the South Seas.
Pleasant episodic drama which needed a firmer hand all round.
w Richard Mason autobiography A Pattern of Islands by Sir Arthur Grimble d Wolf Rilla ph Martin Curtis m James Bernard
☆ Denholm Elliott, Susan Stephen, Michael Hordern

Pacific Heights *
US 1990 104m DeLuxe
Fox/Morgan Creek (Scott Rudin, William Sackheim)
A young couple let part of their house to a dangerously unbalanced tenant.
A suburban horror that rapidly goes over the top into unconvincing melodrama.
w Daniel Pyne d John Schlesinger ph Amir Mokri m Hans Zimmer pd Neil Spisak ed Mark Warner, Steven Ramirez
☆ Melanie Griffith, Matthew Modine, Michael Keaton, Mako, Nobu McCarthy, Laurie Metcalf, Carl Lumbly, Dorian Harewood, Luca Bercovici, Tippi Hedren

Pacific Liner
US 1938 73m bw
RKO
Cholera breaks out on a ship bound from Shanghai to San Francisco.
Rather a depressing melodrama with all the action below decks, and very slow at that.
w John Twist, Anthony Coldeway, Henry Roberts Symonds d Lew Landers
☆ Victor McLaglen, Chester Morris, Wendy Barrie, Alan Hale, Barry Fitzgerald, Halliwell Hobbes, Cy Kendall
'Drab melodrama with little of interest to hold attention.' – *Variety*
♫ music (Robert Russell Bennett)

Pacific Rendezvous
US 1942 76m bw
MGM
A coding expert breaks up an enemy spy ring.
Competent propaganda potboiler, rehashed from the rather smarter Rendezvous, which was set one war earlier.
w Harry Kurnitz, P. J. Wolfson, George Oppenheimer d George Sidney
☆ Lee Bowman, Jean Rogers, Mona Maris, Carl Esmond, Paul Cavanagh, Blanche Yurka

Paciorki Jednego Rózańca: see The Beads of One Rosary

The Pack
US 1977 99m colour
Warner (Fred Weintraub, Paul Heller)
Abandoned dogs on a remote island turn on holidaymakers.
The Birds becomes The Dogs; competently made but unsurprising thriller.
wd Robert Clouse novel Dave Fisher ph Ralph Woolsey m Lee Holdridge ed Peter Berger sp Milton Rice
☆ Joe Don Baker, Hope Alexander Willis, Richard B. Shull, R. G. Armstrong

Pack Up Your Troubles *
US 1931 68m bw
Hal Roach
Two World War I veterans try to look after their late pal's orphan daughter.
Patchy comedy vehicle in which too many gags are not fully thought out or timed.
w H. M. Walker d George Marshall, Ray McCarey ph Art Lloyd ed Richard Currier
☆ Stan Laurel, Oliver Hardy, Donald Dillaway, Mary Carr, Charles Middleton, Dick Cramer, James Finlayson, Tom Kennedy, Billy Gilbert

Pack Up Your Troubles *
US 1939 75m bw
TCF
GB title: We're in the Army Now
Exploits in Flanders of three zany soldiers.
Good slapstick antics in an unfamiliar venue.
w Lou Breslow, Owen Francis d H. Bruce Humberstone
☆ The Ritz Brothers, Jane Withers, Joseph Schildkraut, Lynn Bari, Stanley Fields
'A pretty good programmer in the B division.' – *Variety*

The Package
US 1989 108m DeLuxe
Rank/Orion (Beverly J. Camhe, Tobie Haggerty)
An army sergeant discovers an assassination plot after the escape of a prisoner he is escorting.
Unconvincing and melodramatic thriller that rarely grips the attention.
w John Bishop d Andrew Davis ph Frank Tidy m James Newton Howard pd Michael Levesque ed Don Zimmerman, Billy Weber
☆ Gene Hackman, Joanna Cassidy, Tommy Lee Jones, Dennis Franz, Reni Santoni, Pam Grier, Chelcie Ross, Ron Dean, Kevin Crowley

The Pad, and How to Use It *
US 1966 86m Technicolor
Universal (Ross Hunter)
A shy young man has his first date.
Pleasant, odd little comedy apparently made in emulation of The Knack.
w Thomas C. Ryan, Ben Starr play The Private Ear by Peter Shaffer d Brian G. Hutton ph Ellsworth Fredericks m Russ Garcia
☆ Brian Bedford, James Farentino, Julie Sommars, Edy Williams, Nick Navarro

Paddy O'Day
US 1935 73m bw
TCF (Sol M. Wurtzel)
An Irish child emigrates to America to find that her mother has died.
One of the more satisfactory vehicles for a child star maintained by the studio as an antidote to the cuter antics of Shirley Temple.
w Lou Breslow, Edward Eliscu story Sonya Levien d Lewis Seiler ph Arthur Miller m Harry Akst, Troy Sanders
☆ Jane Withers, Pinky Tomlin, Rita Hayworth, Jane Darwell, Francis Ford

Paddy the Next Best Thing
US 1933 75m bw
Fox
Adventures of an Irish tomboy in New York.
Modest star comedy from a popular play.
w Edwin Burke play Gertrude Page d Harry Lachman ph John Seitz
☆ Janet Gaynor, Warner Baxter, Walter Connolly, Harvey Stephens, Margaret Lindsay
'Easy entertainment: excellent, wholesome and amusing.' – *Variety*

Padella Calibro 38: see Panhandle Calibre 38

Padre Padrone ***
Italy 1977 113m Eastmancolor
Radiotelevisione Italia (Tonino Paoletti)
aka: Father and Master
The author recounts how he grew up with a violent and tyrannical father.
A vivid chunk of autobiography with food for thought on several levels, and a clever piece of film-making to boot.
wd Paolo Taviani, Vittorio Taviani book Gavino Ledda ph Mario Masini md Egisto Macchi
☆ Omero Antonutti, Saverio Marconi, Marcella Michelangeli

The Pagan
US 1929 85m bw
MGM
A South Sea islander falls for the daughter of a white trader.
Highly commercial star vehicle apparently made as an afterthought to White Shadows in the South Seas.
w Dorothy Farnum d W. S. Van Dyke
☆ Ramon Novarro, Renee Adoree, Dorothy Janis, Donald Crisp

Pagan Lady
US 1931 70m bw
Columbia
A nice American boy in Havana falls for a girl who is no better than she should be.
Sultry melodrama reminiscent of Rain but of no intrinsic merit.
w Ben Glazer play William Dubois d John Francis Dillon

☆ Evelyn Brent, Conrad Nagel, Charles Bickford, Roland Young, William Farnum
'Something of a lightweight; the storm is quite the best thing in the picture.' – *Variety*

Pagan Love Song
US 1950 76m Technicolor
MGM (Arthur Freed)
An American schoolteacher marries a Tahitian girl.
Very mild musical potboiler using familiar talents.
w Robert Nathan, Jerry Davis d Robert Alton ph Charles Rosher m Harry Warren ly Arthur Freed
☆ Esther Williams, Howard Keel, Rita Moreno, Minna Gombell

Page Miss Glory *
US 1935 90m bw
Warner/Cosmopolitan
A con man wins a beauty contest with a composite photograph of a non-existent girl.
Amusing comedy-musical, unjustly forgotten.
w Delmer Daves, Robert Lord play Joseph Schrank, Philip Dunning d Mervyn Le Roy ph George Folsey m/ly Harry Warren, Al Dubin
☆ Dick Powell, Marion Davies, Frank McHugh, Pat O'Brien, Mary Astor, Lyle Talbot, Patsy Kelly, Allen Jenkins, Barton MacLane

'All The Adventure Your Imagination Can Hold.'
The Pagemaster
US 1994 75m colour
TCF/Turner (David Kirschner, Paul Gertz)
A timid child takes refuge in a library and, changed into a cartoon figure, has to undergo three tests of courage before he can go home.
Intended as an encouragement for children to read books, the movie's more likely effect is to discourage them from going to the cinema; the lack of imagination in the script is deadening to the spirit as Long John Silver, Dr Jekyll and Mr Hyde and others join in dull animated adventures.
w David Casci, David Kirschner, Ernie Contreras d Joe Johnston, Maurice Hunt (animation director) ph Alexandra Gruszynski m James Horner pd Gay Lawrence, Valeria Ventura ed Roy Forge Smith
☆ Macaulay Culkin, Christopher Lloyd, Ed Begley Jnr, Mel Harris and also the voices of Patrick Stewart, Whoopi Goldberg, Frank Welker, Leonard Nimoy
'Plays like a slickly produced afternoon special and should be limited in its appeal to the youngest of kids.' – *Brian Lowry, Variety*

Pagliacci *
GB 1936 92m colour
Trafalgar
US title: A Clown Must Laugh
A jealous clown kills his wife and her lover.
A surprising British enterprise of the time which did fairly well at the box-office, presumably because of the colour.
w Monckton Hoffe, Roger Burford, Ernest Betts opera Ruggiero Leoncavallo d Karl Grune ph Otto Kanturek pd Oscar Werndorff ly John Drinkwater
☆ Richard Tauber, Steffi Duna, Diana Napier, Arthur Margetson, Esmond Knight, Jerry Verno

Pagliacci *
Italy 1948 104m bw
Itala Film/Titanus (Mario Bisi)
The leader of a theatrical troupe kills his wife and her lover after he realizes that the performance they are staging resembles his own situation.
A slightly clumsy attempt to open up the opera by filming it in the open air and casting actors in the

leading roles, with their singing dubbed. Worth seeing for the acting and singing of Tito Gobbi, who appears as the Prologue, as Nedda's would-be lover Tonio, and as her lover Silvio.

w Anton Giulio Majano, Mario Costa, Carlo Castelli d Mario Costa ph Mario Bava md Giuseppe Morelli ad Ottavio Scotti ed Otello Colangeli

☆ Tito Gobbi, Afro Poli (singing by Galliano Masini), Gina Lollobrigida (singing by Onella Fineschi), Filippo Morucci (singing by Gino Sinimberghi)

Paid *
US   1930   80m   bw
MGM
GB title: Within the Law
A woman sent to prison unjustly plots revenge on those responsible.
Reliable melodrama with the heroine eventually forgiving and forgetting.
w Charles MacArthur, Lucien Hubbard play Within the Law by Bayard Veiller d Sam Wood ph Charles Rosher
☆ Joan Crawford, Kent Douglass, Robert Armstrong, Marie Prévost, John Miljan, Polly Moran

Paid in Full
US   1949   105m   bw
Paramount/Hal B. Wallis
A woman is responsible for the death of her sister's child, and becomes pregnant herself in the knowledge that giving birth will be fatal to her.
Stolid, contrived tearjerker.
w Robert Blees, Charles Schnee d William Dieterle ph Leo Tover m Victor Young
☆ Lizabeth Scott, Diana Lynn, Robert Cummings, Eve Arden, Ray Collins, Frank McHugh, Stanley Ridges, Louis Jean Heydt
'Aimed straight at the lachrymal glands, if it can be said to be aimed at anything. The dialogue is appalling.' – C. A. Lejeune

A Pain in the A–: see L'Emmerdeur

'Ben and pardner shared everything – even their wife!'

Paint Your Wagon *
⚇⚇ US   1969   164m   Technicolor
Panavision 70
Paramount/Alan Jay Lerner (Tom Shaw)
⚇⚇ ▦ ⚏ ⚇
During the California Gold Rush, two prospectors set up a Mormon menage with the same wife.
Good-looking but uncinematic and monumentally long version of an old musical with a new plot and not much dancing. There are minor pleasures, but it really shouldn't have been allowed.
w Paddy Chayefsky musical play Alan Jay Lerner, Frederick Loewe d Joshua Logan ph William A. Fraker md Nelson Riddle pd John Truscott
☆ Lee Marvin, Clint Eastwood, Jean Seberg, Harve Presnell, Ray Walston
'One of those big movies in which the themes are undersized and the elements are juggled around until nothing fits together right and even the good bits of the original show you started with are shot to hell.' – Pauline Kael
† Jean Seberg's singing was dubbed by Anita Gordon.
♫ Nelson Riddle

Painted Angels
GB/Canada   1998   109m   colour
Artificial
Eye/Shaftesbury/Greenpoint/Heartland/British Screen
(Ann Scott, Christine Jennings, Stephen Onda)
⚇⚇
Five prostitutes lead tawdry lives in a frontier-town brothel in the American West of the 1870s.
Glum portrait of unhappy working women in desperate circumstances; its depiction may well be accurate, but it is not involving.
w Anna Mottram, Jon Sanders d Jon Sanders ph Gerald Packer m Douglas Finch pd Hayden Griffin ed Maysoon Pachachi
☆ Brenda Fricker, Kelly McGillis, Meret Becker, Bronagh Gallagher, Lisa Jakub, Anna Mottram, Josiah Wu, Kent Allan

Painted Boats
GB   1945   63m   bw
Ealing
US title: The Girl on the Canal
Romance among the bargees.
Excessively thin location drama, which nevertheless has an early place in the Ealing tradition.
w Louis MacNeice, Michael McCarthy d Charles Crichton
☆ Jenny Laird, Bill Blewett, Robert Griffith, May Hallatt

Painted Desert
US   1938   59m   bw
RKO (Bert Gilroy)
▦
A rancher becomes a miner for romantic reasons but has to overcome a crooked banker and his followers.
A B-Western with B-picture acting and direction. A remake of a 1931 movie starring William Boyd, it contains footage from the earlier film.
w John Rathmell, Oliver Drake story Jack Cunningham d David Howard ph Harry Wild md Roy Webb ad Van Nest Polglase ed Frederic Knudtson
☆ George O'Brien, Laraine Day, Ray Whitley, Fred Kohler Snr, Stanley Fields, William V. Mong, Maude Allen

Painted Heart
US   1992   90m   colour
Metro Tartan/Second Son (Mark Pollard, Randall Poster)
⚇⚇
A house-painter suspects that his boss is the Lipstick Murderer, who kills old men and paints their faces.
Determinedly eccentric movie of small-town America, slow-moving whimsy in which even the sane residents behave in an odd manner.
wd Michael Taav ph Robert Yeoman m John Wesley Harding, Jeff Charbonneau pd Mark Friedberg ed Nancy Richardson
☆ Will Patton, Bebe Neuwirth, Casey Siemaszko, Robert Pastorelli, Mark Boone Jnr, Richard Hamilton, Jayne Haynes
'It's ultimately hopelessly self-indulgent, and a little bit like watching paint dry.' – David Richardson, Film Review

The Painted Smile
GB   1962   60m   bw
Planet/Mancunian (Tom Blakeley)
US title: Murder Can Be Deadly
A student who goes out for a celebration in a night-club becomes involved in a murder.
Dreary thriller that makes little sense, and is sadly lacking in suspense or interest.
w Pip and Jane Baker idea Brock Williams d Lance Comfort ph Basil Emmot m Martin Slavin ad George Provis ed John Trumper
☆ Liz Fraser, Kenneth Griffith, Tony Wickert, Ray Smith, Nanette Newman, David Hemmings, Harold Berens, Peter Reynolds, Craig Douglas

The Painted Veil *
US   1934   84m   bw
MGM (Hunt Stromberg)
In China, a doctor's wife gives up her lover to join her husband fighting an epidemic.
Soulful melodrama which seemed much more acceptable in this version than in the summer stock style remake The Seventh Sin.
w John Meehan, Salka Viertel, Edith Fitzgerald novel W. Somerset Maugham d Richard Boleslawski ph William Daniels m Herbert Stothart
☆ Greta Garbo, George Brent, Herbert Marshall, Warner Oland, Jean Hersholt
'Confused and slow, but extra heavy name cast should get it by.' – Variety

Painted Woman
US   1932   73m   bw
Fox
A floozie stranded on a South Sea island resists offers of help from several men.
Another variation on Rain, and not the best.
w Guy Bolton, Leon Gordon novel After the Rain by A. C. Kennedy d John Blystone
☆ Spencer Tracy, Peggy Shannon, William 'Stage' Boyd, Irving Pichel, Raul Roulien

'It's hard to see how the studio figured a good picture would result from the material at hand.' – Variety

Painting the Clouds with Sunshine
US   1951   86m   Technicolor
Warner (William Jacobs)
Three singing sisters go to Las Vegas in search of rich husbands.
Yet another revamp of the original Gold Diggers (qv), and not a very lively one.
w Harry Clork, Roland Kibbee, Peter Milne d David Butler ph Wilfred Cline
☆ Virginia Mayo, Gene Nelson, Dennis Morgan, S. Z. Sakall, Lucille Norman, Tom Conway

A Pair of Briefs
GB   1961   90m   bw
Rank/Betty E. Box-Ralph Thomas
Barristers Tony and Frances fall in love while opposing each other in court.
Adam's Rib need have no fears; this is the palest of imitations.
w Nicholas Phipps play How Say You by Harold Brooke, Kay Bannerman d Ralph Thomas ph Ernest Steward m Norrie Paramor
☆ Michael Craig, Mary Peach, Brenda de Banzie, James Robertson Justice, Roland Culver, Liz Fraser, Ron Moody, Jameson Clark, Charles Heslop

Paisà *
Italy   1946   115m   bw
Foreign Film Productions/OFI
⚇⚇
Six episodes in the Battle of Italy between 1943 and 1945.
More important historically than dramatically, Paisà was always a somewhat disappointing experience, especially as the earlier episodes are stronger than the later ones. Like Open City, it was partly improvised and had a gritty documentary quality.
w Federico Fellini, Roberto Rossellini d Roberto Rossellini ph Otello Martelli m Renzo Rossellini
☆ William Tubbs, Gar Moore, Maria Michi and non-professionals
'It brings to the picture of war a pity at once savage and tender which is quite foreign to the studio-made film – or, come to that, the contemporary documentary film.' – Dilys Powell
♫ script

The Pajama Game ***
⚇⚇ US   1957   101m   Warnercolor
Warner/George Abbott
⚇⚇ ▦ ⚏
Workers in a pajama factory demand a pay rise, but their lady negotiator falls for the new boss.
Brilliantly conceived musical on an unlikely subject, effectively concealing its Broadway origins and becoming an expert, fast-moving, hard-hitting piece of modern musical cinema.
w George Abbott, Richard Bissell book Seven and a Half Cents by Richard Bissell d Stanley Donen ph Harry Stradling ch Bob Fosse songs Richard Adler, Jerry Ross
☆ Doris Day, John Raitt, Eddie Foy Jnr, Reta Shaw, Carol Haney

The Pajama Girl Case (dubbed)
Italy/Spain   1978   105m   colour
Capitol (Giorgio Salvioni)
⚇⚇
original title: La Ragazza dal Pigiama Giallo
aka: Pyjama Girl
A retired police inspector goes back to work to solve the murder of an unknown woman found on a beach.
Dull thriller, with Milland looking as though he would rather be somewhere else.
wd Flavio Mogherini ph Carlo Carlini m Riz Ortolani pd Franco Velchi ed Adriani Tagliavia
☆ Ray Milland, Dalila Di Lazzaro, Michele Placido, Howard Ross, Ramiro Oliveros, Rod Mullinar, Mel Ferrer

Pajama Party
US   1964   85m   Pathécolor   Panavision
AIP (James Nicholson, Samuel Z. Arkoff)
▦
A Martian, a scout for an invasion of Earth, changes his mind after meeting some partying teenagers.
The beach party formula as usual, except that the beach is abandoned in this bland teen mix of romance and forgettable songs.

w Louis M. Heyward d Don Weis ph Floyd Crosby m Les Baxter m/ly Guy Hemric, Jerry Styner ch David Winters ad Daniel Haller ed Fred R. Feitshans, Eve Newman
☆ Tommy Kirk, Annette Funicello, Elsa Lanchester, Buster Keaton, Harvey Lembeck, Jesse White, Jody McCrea, Dorothy Lamour, Candy Johnson
† It was a follow-up to Bikini Beach and was followed by Beach Blanket Bingo (qqv).

Pal Joey **
US   1957   109m   Technicolor
Columbia/Essex-Sidney (Fred Kohlmar)
⚇⚇ ▦ ⚏ ⚇
The rise of a night-club entertainer who is also a heel.
Smart musical which begins very brightly indeed but slides off alarmingly into conventional sentiment.
w Dorothy Kingsley play John O'Hara stories John O'Hara d George Sidney ph Harold Lipstein ad Walter Holscher ed Viola Lawrence, Jerome Thomas songs Richard Rodgers, Lorenz Hart
☆ Frank Sinatra, Rita Hayworth, Kim Novak, Bobby Sherwood, Hank Henry, Elizabeth Patterson, Barbara Nichols
† Rita Hayworth's singing was dubbed by Jo Ann Greer, and Kim Novak's by Trudy Erwin.
♫ Walter Holscher; editing

Pale Rider
US   1985   115m   Technicolor   Panavision
Warner/Malpaso (Clint Eastwood)
⚇⚇ ▦ ⚏ ⚇
Harassed gold prospecting families are helped by a mysterious avenger.
Unreeling like a supernatural Shane, this is a violent and pretentious Western with nothing to be pretentious about.
w Michael Butler, Dennis Shryack d Clint Eastwood ph Bruce Surtees m Lennie Niehaus pd Edward Carfagno ed Joel Cox
☆ Clint Eastwood, Michael Moriarty, Carrie Snodgress, Christopher Penn, Richard Dysart, Richard Kiel

The Paleface ***
⚇⚇ US   1948   91m   Technicolor
Paramount (Robert L. Welch)
▦ ⚏
Calamity Jane undertakes an undercover mission against desperadoes, and marries a timid dentist as a cover.
Splendid wagon train comedy Western with the stars in excellent form.
w Edmund Hartman, Frank Tashlin d Norman Z. McLeod ph Ray Rennahan m Victor Young
☆ Bob Hope, Jane Russell, Robert Armstrong, Iris Adrian, Robert Watson, Jackie Searl, Joe Vitale, Clem Bevans, Charles Trowbridge
† Sequel: Son of Paleface (qv); remake, The Shakiest Gun in the West (1968).
♪ song 'Buttons and Bows' (m Jay Livingston, ly Ray Evans)

The Pallbearer
US   1996   97m   DeLuxe
Miramax (Jeffrey Abrams, Paul Webster)
⚇⚇ ▦ ⚏ ⚇
An unemployed graduate, asked to be the pallbearer at the funeral of a friend whom he cannot remember, is seduced by the dead youth's mother.
A limp comedy that owes much to The Graduate, but remains no more than a very pale shadow of that film.
w Jason Katims, Matt Reeves d Matt Reeves ph Robert Elswit m Stewart Copeland pd Robert Standefer ed Stan Salfas
☆ David Schwimmer, Gwyneth Paltrow, Michael Rapaport, Toni Collette, Barbara Hershey, Carol Kane, Michael Vartan, Bitty Schram
'A passably entertaining seriocomedy.' – Variety
† The film flopped, taking $5.7m at the US box-office.

The Palm Beach Story ***
US   1942   88m   bw
Paramount (Paul Jones)
▦ ⚏
The wife of a penurious engineer takes off for Florida to set her sights on a millionaire.
Flighty comedy, inconsequential in itself, but decorated with scenes, characters and zany touches typical of its creator, here at his most brilliant if uncontrolled.

---

wd Preston Sturges *ph* Victor Milner *m* Victor Young

☆ *Claudette Colbert*, Joel McCrea, Rudy Vallee, Mary Astor, Sig Arno, Robert Warwick, Torben Meyer, Jimmy Conlin, William Demarest, Jack Norton, Robert Greig, Roscoe Ates, Chester Conklin, Franklin Pangborn, Alan Bridge and also *Robert Dudley*

HACKENSACKER (RUDY VALLEE): 'That's one of the tragedies of this life, that the men most in need of a beating up are always enormous.'

WEENIE KING (ROBERT DUDLEY): 'Anyway, I'd be too old for you. Cold are the hands of time that creep along relentlessly, destroying slowly but without pity that which yesterday was young. Alone, our memories resist this disintegration and grow more lovely with the passing years. That's hard to say with false teeth.'

'Surprises and delights as though nothing of the kind had been known before … farce and tenderness are combined without a fault.' – *William Whitebait*

'Minus even a hint of the war … packed with delightful absurdities.' – *Variety*

Palm Springs
US 1936 74m bw
Paramount
GB title: *Palm Springs Affair*

An elderly Englishman becomes a gambler in order to give his daughter the appropriate upbringing.
Slight romantic comedy which gave a young Englishman a foothold in Hollywood.
w Joseph Fields *d* Aubrey Scotto
☆ David Niven, Sir Guy Standing, Frances Langford, Ernest Cossart, Spring Byington

Palm Springs Affair: see *Palm Springs*

Palm Springs Weekend
US 1963 100m Technicolor
Warner (Michael Hoey)
◉ 🔲

Various holidaymakers at Palm Springs get romantically involved.
Youth-oriented farce, better produced than most but basically a depressing experience.
w Earl Hamner Jnr *d* Norman Taurog *ph* Harold Lipstein *m* Frank Perkins
☆ Troy Donahue, Ty Hardin, Connie Stevens, Stefanie Powers, Robert Conrad, Jack Weston, Andrew Duggan

'In A Town This Bad It's No Use Being Good.'

Palmetto
US/Germany 1998 114m Technicolor
Panavision
Warner/Castle Rock/Rialto (Mathias Wendlandt)
◉ ◉ ⊚

An ex-journalist is hired by a seductive woman to stage the kidnapping of her daughter so that she can extort money from the girl's father, a dying millionaire.
A laboured attempt at a film noir, which is taken at too leisurely a pace to provide any thrills or suspense.
w E. Max Frye *novel Just Another Sucker* by James Hadley Chase *d* Volker Schlondorff *ph* Thomas Kloss *m* Klaus Dolinger *pd* Clare Jenora Bowin *ed* Peter Przygodda
☆ Woody Harrelson, Elisabeth Shue, Gina Gershon, Rolf Hoppe, Marc Rapaport, Chloe Sevigny, Tom Wright, Marc Macauley
'May well have coined a new genre: the unthriller.' – *Gaby Wood, Guardian*
'The film deserves a new subgenre of its own, that of sitcom noir.' – *Edward Porter, Sunday Times*

Palmy Days
US 1932 77m bw
Samuel Goldwyn
Shady fortune tellers find a willing stooge.
Dated star comedy.
w Eddie Cantor, Morrie Ryskind, David Freedman, Keene Thompson *d* A. Edward Sutherland *ph* Gregg Toland *ch* Busby Berkeley
☆ Eddie Cantor, Charlotte Greenwood, Charles Middleton, George Raft, Walter Catlett
'Heavily hoked but funny throughout.' – *Variety*

Palooka
US 1934 80m bw
Reliance (Edward Small)
🔲

GB title: *The Great Schnozzle*

An eccentric manager makes a prizefighter of a country cousin.
Fairly amusing first-feature version of the strip cartoon hero Joe Palooka.
w Jack Jevne, Arthur Kober, Gertrude Purcell *strip* Ham Fisher *d* Ben Stoloff
☆ Jimmy Durante, Stuart Erwin, Lupe Velez, Marjorie Rambeau, Robert Armstrong, Mary Carlisle, William Cagney, Thelma Todd
'A laugh riot, the nearest approach to a Marx picture that's been around.' – *Variety*

Palookaville *
US 1995 92m DuArt
Metrodome/Playhouse International/Samuel Goldwyn/Redwave (Uberto Pasolini)
◉ 🔲

In New Jersey, three unemployed young men turn to crime with unpredictable results.
Amiable comic drama of incompetents failing to cope with the cost and problems of living.
w David Epstein *d* Alan Taylor *ph* John Thomas *m* Rachel Portman *pd* Anne Stuhler *ed* David Leonard
☆ William Forsythe, Vincent Gallo, Adam Trese, Gareth Williams, Lisa Gay Hamilton, Bridget Ryan, Kim Dickens
'A refreshing and hilarious alternative to the cool-guys-with-guns flick.' – *Empire*

Paltoquet
France 1986 92m colour
Artificial Eye/Elefilm/Erato/Soprofilm/TF1/Sofia/Sofima (Rosalinde Damamme)

A detective tries to discover which habitué of a seedy bar, with its shiftless waiter, is a killer.
Intellectual thriller in which film theory has precedence over practice, resulting in tedium.
wd Michel Deville *novel On A Tué Pendant L'Escale* by Franz-Rudolf Falk *ph* André Diot *m* Dvořák, Janáček *pd* Thierry Leproust *ed* Raymonde Guyot
☆ Jeanne Moreau, Michel Piccoli, Fanny Ardant, Daniel Auteuil, Richard Bohringer, Philippe Léotard, Claude Piéplu, Jean Yanne

Panama Hattie
US 1942 79m bw
MGM (Arthur Freed)
🔲

A showgirl in Panama helps to capture Nazis.
Dim film version of a Broadway musical, stripped of most of its music and more like a Maisie comedy.
w Jack McGowan, Wilkie Mahoney *musical play Herbert Fields, B. G. de Sylva, Cole Porter d* Norman Z. McLeod *ph* George Folsey *md* George Stoll
☆ Ann Sothern, Dan Dailey, Red Skelton, Marsha Hunt, Rags Ragland, Virginia O'Brien, Alan Mowbray, Ben Blue, Carl Esmond

Pan-Americana *
US 1945 85m bw
RKO (Sid Rogell)
A New York magazine sends editors around South America to choose the prettiest girl of each nation.
Slick, mindless musical with good numbers.
w Lawrence Kimble *d* John H. Auer *ph* Frank Redman *md* Constantin Bakaleinikoff *ch* Charles O'Curran
☆ Audrey Long, Phillip Terry, Robert Benchley, Eve Arden, Ernest Truex, Marc Cramer

Pancho Villa
Spain 1971 93m Technicolor
Granada Films (Bernard Gordon)
🔲

In 1916 Villa is rescued from execution and starts a reign of terror.
Mexican banditry played half for laughs and half for real; not a very successful compromise.
w Julian Halevy *d* Eugenio Martin *ph* Alejandro Ulloa *m* Anton Garcia-Abril
☆ Telly Savalas, Clint Walker, Chuck Connors

Pandora and the Flying Dutchman *
GB 1950 122m Technicolor
Romulus (Albert Lewin)
🔲

A cold but beautiful American woman in Spain falls for a mystery man who turns out to be a ghostly sea captain; she dies so as to be with him.
Pretentious, humourless, totally unpersuasive fantasy of the kind much better done in Portrait of Jennie. The writer-director wears Omar Khayyam's moving finger to the bone, and the actors look thoroughly unhappy; even the colour is a bit thick.
wd Albert Lewin *ph* Jack Cardiff *m* Alan Rawsthorne *ad* John Bryan
☆ James Mason, Ava Gardner, Harold Warrender, Nigel Patrick, Sheila Sim, Mario Cabre, John Laurie, Pamela Kellino, Marius Goring
'Conspicuous in its confident assumption of scholarship and its utter poverty of imagination and taste.' – *C. A. Lejeune*
'It might have been enjoyably silly but for Lewin's striving to be classy and an air of third-rate decadence that hangs about it. This is an Anglo-American co-production and one of the occasions, I think, when we might be generous and let Hollywood have all the credit.' – *Richard Winnington*

Pandora's Box *
Germany 1929 97m bw silent
Nero Film
◉ 🔲

original title: *Die Büchse der Pandora*
aka: *Lulu*

A woman murders her lover, becomes a prostitute, and is murdered in London by Jack the Ripper.
Oddball fantasy on a few favourite German themes: very watchable, and benefiting from its star performance.
w G. W. Pabst, Laszlo Wajda *plays 'Erdgeist' and 'Pandora's Box'* by Franz Wedekind *d* G. W. Pabst *ph* Günther Krampf
☆ *Louise Brooks*, Fritz Kortner, Franz Lederer, Gustav Diessl
'A disconnected melodramatic effusion.' – *Mordaunt Hall, New York Times*
† Remade in Austria in 1962 as *No Orchids for Lulu*, with Nadja Tiller.

Panhandle
US 1948 84m bw
Champion-Edwards/Allied Artists
A reformed gunman avenges the murder of his brother.
Solid co-feature Western.
w Blake Edwards, John C. Champion *d* Lesley Selander *ph* Harry Neumann
☆ Rod Cameron, Cathy Downs, Reed Hadley, Anne Gwynne, Blake Edwards

Panhandle Calibre 38 (dubbed)
Italy 1972 90m SPES colour
Cinegai (F. T. Gay)

original title: *Padella Calibro 38*

An ageing gunslinger and his convent-educated son are hired to take a million dollars of Confederate gold across bandit-filled country.
Coarse, slapstick spaghetti Western, taken at a very leisurely tempo.
w Mario Amendola, Massimo Franciosa, Luisa Montagnana, Toni Secchi *d* Toni Secchi *ph* Giorgio Regis *m* Franco Micalizzi *ad* Luciano Puccini *ed* Luciano Anconetani
☆ Scott Holden, Delia Boccardo, Keenan Wynn, Giorgio Trestini, Mimmo Palmara, Franco Fabrizi, Philippe Leroy

Panic Button
US 1963 98m bw
Gorton Associates
A has-been film star is hired by gangsters to star in a film which must lose money; but it wins the Venice Festival award.
Artless and padded comedy with good moments provided by an intriguing cast.
w Hal Biller *d* George Sherman *ph* Enzo Serafin *m* Georges Garvarentz
☆ Maurice Chevalier, Akim Tamiroff, Jayne Mansfield, Eleanor Parker, Michael Connors

The Panic in Needle Park
US 1971 110m DeLuxe
Gadd Productions (Dominick Dunne)
◉ 🔲

Drug addiction problems in a New York ghetto.
Vivid, intimate but overlong and unsympathetic account of a junkie and his mistress.
w Joan Didion, John Gregory Dunne *novel* James Mills *d* Jerry Schatzberg *ph* Adam Holender *m* none
☆ Al Pacino, Kitty Winn, Alan Vint, Richard Bright, Kiel Martin

Panic in the Parlor: see *Sailor Beware (1956)*

Panic in the Streets ***
US 1950 96m bw
TCF (Sol C. Siegel)
🔲 ◎▨

On the New Orleans waterfront, public health officials seek a carrier of bubonic plague.
Semi-documentary suspenser in the Naked City manner; location Hollywood at its best.
w Richard Murphy, Edward and Edna Anhalt *d* Elia Kazan *ph* Joe MacDonald *m* Alfred Newman
☆ *Richard Widmark*, Jack Palance, Paul Douglas, Barbara Bel Geddes, Zero Mostel
'Elia Kazan directs this tough and unique story with the speed, imagination and ruthlessness that it needs.' – *Milton Shulman*
'A model of what an action story should be … every department is admirably handled.' – *Richard Mallett, Punch*
🏆 original story (Edward and Edna Anhalt)

Panic in Year Zero *
US 1962 93m bw Cinemascope
AIP (Lou Rusoff, Arnold Houghland)
Adventures of a family on a fishing trip in the mountains when Los Angeles is blasted by a nuclear attack.
Mildly interesting catalogue of predictable events – thugs, looting, fear of fall-out – in a simple-minded script finishing with a hopeful meeting of the UN.
w Jay Simms, John Morton *d* Ray Milland *ph* Gil Warrenton *m* Les Baxter
☆ Ray Milland, Jean Hagen, Frankie Avalon, Joan Freeman

Panic on the Trans-Siberian Express: see *Horror Express*

Pánico en el Transiberiano: see *Horror Express*

Panique *
France 1946 98m bw
Filmsonor
A respectable man knows who committed a murder, and the murderer cunningly swings the blame onto him.
Careful suspenser with a twist ending.
w Charles Spaak, Julien Duvivier *novel* Georges Simenon *d* Julien Duvivier *ph* Nicolas Hayer
☆ *Michel Simon*, Viviane Romance, Paul Bernard
'Whether you like it or not, you may be forced to agree that it's a near-perfect movie.' – *Pauline Kael, 1972*

Panther
US 1995 124m DeLuxe/bw
Polygram/Working Title/Tribeca/MVP (Mario Van Peebles, Melvin Van Peebles, Preston L. Holmes)
◉ 🔲 ⊚ 🎧

A black Vietnam veteran recalls his role in the Black Panther Party, which was formed in the mid-60s and soon faced infiltration and attacks by the FBI, culminating in the Bureau's involvement in introducing cheap heroin to the ghettos.
A melodramatic account of the black rights struggle and the highly publicized activities of the Panthers which abandons fact to indulge in wild fiction, to the detriment of the film.
w Melvin Van Peebles *novel* Melvin Van Peebles *d* Mario Van Peebles *ph* Eddie Pei *m* Stanley Clarke *pd* Richard Hoover *ed* Earl Watson
☆ Kadeem Hardison, Bokeem Woodbine, Joe Don Baker, Courtney B. Vance, Tyrin Turner, Marcus Chong, James Russo, Chris Rock, Richard Dysart, M. Emmet Walsh, Jenifer Lewis, Wesley Johnson, Nefertiti
'A crudely schematic propaganda thriller.' – *Alexander Walker*

The Panther's Claw

US 1942 73m bw
PRC

Thatcher Colt solves a blackmail case which ends in murder.
Unassuming but efficient second-feature mystery.
w Martin Mooney, Anthony Abbott d William Beaudine
☆ Sidney Blackmer, Byron Foulger, Rick Vallin

Panther's Moon: see Spy Hunt

Paoda Shuang Deng: see Red Firecracker, Green Firecracker

Papa's Delicate Condition

US 1963 98m Technicolor
Paramount/Amro (Jack Rose)

At the turn of the century in a small Texas town an amiable family man gets into scrapes when he drinks too much.
Basically pleasing period comedy which suffers from slow, stiff treatment.
w Jack Rose book Corinne Griffith d George Marshall ph Loyal Griggs m Joseph J. Lilley
☆ Jackie Gleason, Glynis Johns, Charles Ruggles, Charles Lane, Laurel Goodwin, Juanita Moore, Elisha Cook Jnr, Murray Hamilton
♟ song 'Call Me Irresponsible' (mJames Van Heusen, lySammy Cahn)

'They put together New York's fastest moving newspaper. They search for truth, they strive for justice … then print what they can get away with.'
'Never let the truth get in the way of a good story.'

The Paper **

US 1994 112m DeLuxe
Universal/Imagine (Brian Grazer, Frederick Zollo)

A day in the life of the metropolitan editor of a struggling New York tabloid, who has to sort out career and family problems, which include a job offer from a better paper, an emasculating managing editor and an anxious and pregnant wife.
Entertaining, though soft-centred, slice of journalism, but lacking that occupation's bracing cynicism, and somewhat remote from reality.
w David Koepp, Stephen Koepp d Ron Howard ph John Seale m Randy Newman pd Todd Hallowell ed Daniel Hanley, Michael Hill
☆ Michael Keaton, Glenn Close, Marisa Tomei, Robert Duvall, Randy Quaid, Jason Alexander, Spalding Gray, Catherine O'Hara, Lynne Thigpen
'Howard may take on large, semi-serious topics, but he always intends to make cotton candy of them in the end.' – *Michael Atkinson, Sight and Sound*
'It naturally lacks the edge of the *great* media farces, but there's a lot of sparkling fun to be had.' – *Angie Errigo, Empire*
♟ song 'Make Up Your Mind'

Paper Bullets

US 1941 69m bw
King Brothers/PRC

Three orphanage pals grow up to be involved in crime.
Fast-moving second feature.
w Martin Mooney d Phil Rosen
☆ Joan Woodbury, Jack La Rue, Alan Ladd, Linda Ware, Vince Barnett, Gavin Gordon, John Archer

The Paper Chase **

US 1973 111m DeLuxe Panavision
TCF (Robert C. Thompson, Rodrick Paul)

A Harvard law graduate falls in love with the divorced daughter of his tetchiest professor.
A thoughtful analysis of attitudes to learning turns into just another youth movie.
wd James Bridges novel John Jay Osborn Jnr ph Gordon Willis m John Williams
☆ Timothy Bottoms, Lindsay Wagner, John Houseman, Graham Bickel
'A slightly unfocused account of conformism and milk-mild rebellion on the campus.' – *Sight and Sound*
'A worthy film which engages the eye and the brain.' – *Benny Green, Punch*
♟ John Houseman
ℬ James Bridges (as writer)

Paper Lion

US 1968 105m colour
Stuart Millar/United Artist

The training of a professional football player.
Rather single-minded sporting biography from a book by George Plimpton.
w Lawrence Roman d Alex March
☆ Alan Alda, Lauren Hutton, David Doyle, Sugar Ray Robinson

'Trust me. I'm a doctor.'

Paper Mask **

GB 1990 105m colour
Enterprise/Film Four International (Christopher Morahan)

A hospital porter pretends to be a doctor.
Chilling and enjoyable small-scale thriller.
w John Collee d Christopher Morahan ph Nat Crosby m Richard Harvey pd Caroline Hanania ed Peter Coulson
☆ Paul McGann, Amanda Donohoe, Frederick Treves, Tom Wilkinson, Barbara Leigh-Hunt, Jimmy Yuill, Mark Lewis Jones, John Warnaby, Alexandra Mathie

'As P. T. Barnum put it, "There's a sucker born every minute".'

Paper Moon **

US 1973 103m bw
Paramount/Saticoy (Peter Bogdanovich)

In the American midwest in the thirties, a bible salesman and a plain little girl make a great con team.
Unusual but overrated comedy, imperfectly adapted from a very funny book, with careful but disappointing period sense and photography. A lot more style and gloss was required.
w Alvin Sargent novel Addie Pray by Joe David Brown d Peter Bogdanovich ph Laszlo Kovacs m popular songs and recordings
☆ Ryan O'Neal, Tatum O'Neal, Madeline Kahn, John Hillerman
'I've rarely seen a film that looked so unlike what it was about.' – *Stanley Kauffmann*
'At its best the film is only mildly amusing, and I'm not sure I could recall a few undeniable highlights if pressed on the point.' – *Gary Arnold*
'Bogdanovich once again deploys the armoury of nostalgia with relentless cunning to evoke the threadbare side of American life forty years ago … one of those rare movies which engages at least two of the senses.' – *Benny Green, Punch*
'It is so enjoyable, so funny, so touching that I couldn't care less about its morals.' – *Daily Telegraph*
♟ Tatum O'Neal
ℬ Alvin Sargent; Madeline Kahn

Paper Orchid

GB 1949 86m bw
Ganesh/Columbia

A girl reporter is suspected of murdering an actor.
Mystery programmer which did not displease.
w Val Guest novel Arthur La Bern d Roy Baker
☆ Hugh Williams, Hy Hazell, Sidney James, Garry Marsh, Andrew Cruickshank, Ivor Barnard, Walter Hudd

Paper Tiger

GB 1975 99m Technicolor
Maclean and Co (Euan Lloyd)

An ageing Englishman becomes tutor to the son of the Japanese ambassador in a Pacific state, and finds he has to live his heroic fantasies in reality.
Uneasy adventure comedy drama which might, given more skilled handling, have been much better than it is.
w Jack Davies d Ken Annakin ph John Cabrera m Roy Budd
☆ David Niven, Toshiro Mifune, Hardy Kruger, Ando, Ivan Desny, Irene Tsu, Miiko Taka, Ronald Fraser, Jeff Corey
'Makes no demands, except on 99 minutes of our time.' – *Michael Billington, Illustrated London News*

'He's hard, tough… and doesn't give a XXXX for anything… except romantic novels.'

Paperback Hero *

Australia 1998 97m colour
AFFC/Paperback (Lance W. Reynolds, John Winter)

A truck driver who lives in the outback persuades a waitress to pose as the author of a best-selling romantic novel that he has written.
Amiable, though predictable, romantic comedy, with a few sideswipes at macho attitudes on the way.
wd Antony J. Bowman ph David Burr m Burkhard Dallwitz pd Jon Dowding ed Veronika Jenet
☆ Claudia Karvan, Hugh Jackman, Angie Milliken, Andrew S. Gilbert, Jeanie Drynan, Bruce Venables, Barry Rugless, Tony Barry
'The pace is slow, the plot is predictable and all the characters are cardboard cutouts.' – *Cosmo Landesman, Sunday Times*

Paperhouse

GB 1988 92m Technicolor
Vestron/Working Title (Tim Bevan, Sarah Radcliffe)

An 11-year-old girl has fainting fits which take her into a dangerous fantasy world that resembles her drawings.
Slow-moving, shallow fantasy.
w Matthew Jacobs novel Marianne's Dream by Catherine Storr d Bernard Rose ph Mike Southon m Hans Zimmer, Stanley Myers pd Gemma Jackson ed Dan Rae
☆ Charlotte Burke, Ben Cross, Glenne Headly, Elliott Spiers, Gemma Jones

Papillon *

US 1973 150m Technicolor Panavision
Papillon Partnership/Corona/General Production Co (Robert Dorfmann)

Filmed autobiography of life on Devil's Island.
Overlong and rather dreary film of a bestseller; it determinedly rubs the audience's nose in ordure from the start, and the final successful escape is one try too many.
w Dalton Trumbo, Lorenzo Semple Jnr book Henri Charrière d Franklin Schaffner ph Fred Koenekamp m Jerry Goldsmith
☆ Steve McQueen, Dustin Hoffman, Victor Jory, Don Gordon, Anthony Zerbe, George Coulouris, Woodrow Parfrey
'A 2½-hour epic trampling the corn growing round the theme of man's inhumanity to man.' – *Sight and Sound*
'Papillon offers torture as entertainment but winds up making entertainment a form of torture … a tournament of brutality unrelieved by imagination.' – *Paul D. Zimmermann*
'So overloaded with details that the stars are almost lost in exposition, repetition and unfocused drama.' – *Judith Crist, 1977*
'So solemn one would think it the story of a pope at the very least.' – *New Yorker, 1980*
ℬ Jerry Goldsmith

Parachute Battalion

US 1941 75m bw
Howard Benedict/RKO

Three boys go through parachute training school.
Propaganda quickie.
w John Twist and Major Hugh Fite d Leslie Goodwins
☆ Robert Preston, Nancy Kelly, Edmond O'Brien, Harry Carey, Buddy Ebsen, Paul Kelly, Richard Cromwell, Robert Barrat
'It would make a nice educational short, but as feature material it rates in the secondary dual category.' – *Variety*

Parachute Jumper

US 1932 70m bw
Warner

Ex-flying Marines out of a job fall in with gangsters.
Easy-going adventure yarn with agreeable players.
w Rian James, John Francis Larkin d Alfred E. Green
☆ Douglas Fairbanks Jnr, Bette Davis, Leo Carrillo, Claire Dodd, Frank McHugh, Harold Huber
'Breezy treatment of a not very brilliant yarn.' – *Variety*

Parade *

France/Sweden 1974 85m Technicolor
Gray Film/Sveriges Radio

Jacques Tati introduces a series of acts in a small-scale circus.
Pleasant, sometimes boring variety show, to be included in the Tati canon for completeness; it does include some of his unique pieces of mime.
wd Jacques Tati ph Jean Badal, Gunnar Fischer m Charles Dumont
'A curious, unresolved envoi.' – *John Pym, MFB*
'Moments of great good humour and flashes of incomparable magic.' – *Sight and Sound*

The Paradine Case **

US 1947 115m bw
Selznick

A barrister falls in love with his client, who is suspected of murder.
A stodgy and old-fashioned script is given gleaming treatment; this and the acting make it seem better thirty years later than it did on release.
w David O. Selznick novel Robert Hichens d Alfred Hitchcock ph Lee Garmes m Franz Waxman
☆ Gregory Peck, Alida Valli, Ann Todd, Louis Jourdan, Charles Laughton, Charles Coburn, Ethel Barrymore, Leo G. Carroll
'This is the wordiest script since the death of Edmund Burke.' – *James Agee*
'The characters and their problems don't make much imprint on a viewer; if you can't remember whether you've seen the picture or not, chances are you did and forgot it.' – *New Yorker, 1976*
† Original choices were Olivier instead of Peck, Garbo instead of Valli, and Robert Newton instead of Jourdan.
ℬ Ethel Barrymore

Paradise *

US 1991 110m Technicolor
Buena Vista/Touchstone/Touchwood Pacific Partners I/Interscope/Jean-François Lepetit (Scott Kroopf, Patrick Palmer)

A ten-year-old boy makes friends with a young girl when he goes to spend the summer with a childless couple.
Sentimentality is kept at bay for the most part and charm predominates in a gently effective narrative.
wd Mary Agnes Donoghue ph Jerzy Zielinski m David Newman pd Evelyn Sakash, Marcia Hinds ed Eva Gardos, Debra McDermott
☆ Melanie Griffith, Don Johnson, Elijah Wood, Thora Birch, Sheila McCarthy, Eve Gordon, Louise Latham, Greg Travis, Sarah Trigger, Richard K. Olsen
'Excellent ensemble acting and a feel-good payoff to this bittersweet tale could produce a sleeper hit.' – *Variety*
† A remake of Le Grand Chemin (qv), directed in 1987 by Jean-Loup Hubert.

Paradise Alley

US 1978 107m Technicolor
Universal/Force Ten (John F. Roach, Ronald A. Suppa)

The adventures of three wrestling brothers in New York's Hell's Kitchen during the forties.
Fashionable update of the City for Conquest school, not in itself very interesting despite amusing bits.
wd Sylvester Stallone ph Laszlo Kovacs m Bill Conti pd John W. Corso
☆ Sylvester Stallone, Kevin Conway, Anne Archer, Joe Spinell, Armand Assante, Lee Canalito

Paradise for Three

US 1937 78m bw
MGM

GB title: *Romance for Three*

A businessman goes to Germany to find out how the workers live.
An interesting premise leads inevitably into a flimsy romantic comedy.
w George Oppenheimer, Harry Ruskin d Edward Buzzell
☆ Robert Young, Frank Morgan, Mary Astor, Edna May Oliver, Florence Rice, Reginald Owen, Henry Hull, Sig Rumann, Herman Bing

---

Paradise for Two

GB 1937 77m bw

Günther Stapenhorst/Denham

US title: *Gaiety Girls*

A millionaire posing as a reporter is asked to pose as a millionaire.

Cheerful comedy-romance.

w Robert Stevenson, Arthur Macrae d Thornton Freeland ph Gunther Krampf m Mischa Spoliansky ad Vincent Korda, Shamoon Nadir ed E. B. Jarvis

☆ Jack Hulbert, Patricia Ellis, Arthur Riscoe, Googie Withers, Sydney Fairbrother, Wylie Watson, David Tree

Paradise Hawaiian Style

US 1965 91m Technicolor

Paramount/Hal Wallis/Joseph H. Hazen

▣ ▤

An amorous airline pilot returns to Hawaii and sets up a helicopter service.

Mindless musical vehicle for an increasingly resistible star.

w Allan Weiss, Anthony Lawrence d Michael Moore ph W. Wallace Kelley md Joseph J. Lilley

☆ Elvis Presley, Suzanna Leigh, James Shigeta, Irene Tsu

Paradise Lagoon: see *The Admirable Crichton*

'Courage echoes forever.'

Paradise Road *

Australia/US 1997 115m colour

Panavision

TCF/YTC/Village Roadshow (Sue Milliken, Greg Coote)

▣ ▤ ⊛ ⌒

During the Second World War, women survivors of a shipwreck are imprisoned by the Japanese; some keep their morale high by forming a vocal orchestra.

Based on a true story, this should be more affecting than it is; it is too often shallow and manipulative to be moving.

wd Bruce Beresford story David Giles, Martin Meader diaries by Betty Jeffrey in White Coolies ph Peter James m Ross Edwards pd Herbert Pinter ed Tim Wellburn

☆ Glenn Close, Pauline Collins, Cate Blanchett, Frances McDormand, Julianna Margulies, Jennifer Ehle, Wendy Hughes, Johanna Ter Steege, Elizabeth Spriggs, Clyde Kusatsu

'This powerful account of female friendship and bonding under the most cruel conditions lacks the narrative focus and dramatic shapeliness to generate emotional excitement.' – *Emanuel Levy, Variety*

Paradisio

GB 1962 82m bw/tinted

Jacques Henrici

An Oxford professor chases across Europe in search of the creators of special X-ray sunglasses, followed by Russian spies.

Feeble, leering farce that serves as an excuse for some discreet female nudity from a cast identified only as '20 international beauties'.

w Lawrence Zeitlin, Henri Haile, Jacques Henrici d Henri Haile ph Claude Ballanger, Wolf Schneider, Donald Rodine, Kurt Kriger, M. Barcarol, Raphael Giello m John Bath ed Edouard de Tuko

☆ Arthur Howard, Eva Wagener

The Parallax View ***

US 1974 102m Technicolor Panavision

Paramount/Gus/Harbour/Doubleday (Alan J. Pakula)

Witnesses to a political assassination are systematically killed, despite the efforts of a crusading journalist.

Stylish, persuasive political thriller with a downbeat ending; the villains win.

w David Giler, Lorenzo Semple Jnr novel Loren Singer d Alan J. Pakula ph Gordon Willis m Michael Small

☆ Warren Beatty, Paula Prentiss, William Daniels, Hume Cronyn, Walter McGinn

'Pakula at his best … the test sequence is one of the most celebrated, manipulating the audience as it bombards Beatty's psyche.' – *Les Keyser, Hollywood in the Seventies*

'It is terribly important to give an audience a lot of things they may not get as well as those they will, so that finally the film does take on a

texture and is not just simplistic communication.' – *Alan J. Pakula*

Paramount on Parade *

US 1930 102m bw (Technicolor sequence)

Paramount (Elsie Janis)

▤

A revue featuring Paramount contract stars.

A ragged affair by any standard, but worth a look for a couple of Chevalier's numbers.

w various d Dorothy Arzner, Otto Brower, Edmund Goulding, Victor Heerman, Edwin H. Knopf, Rowland V. Lee, Ernst Lubitsch, Lothar Mendes, Victor Schertzinger, Edward Sutherland, Frank Tuttle ph Harry Fischbeck, Victor Milner m various

☆ Richard Arlen, Jean Arthur, George Bancroft, Clara Bow, Nancy Carroll, Ruth Chatterton, Maurice Chevalier, Gary Cooper, Leon Errol, Kay Francis, Harry Green, Mitzi Green, Dennis King, Fredric March, Nino Martini and also Jack Oakie, Charles 'Buddy' Rogers, Lillian Roth, Fay Wray, Clive Brook, Warner Oland, Eugene Pallette, William Powell

'Pip revue packed with laughs and talent.' – *Variety*

'It ran for less than two hours but I came out of the theater several years older.' – *Robert Benchley*

Paranoia

Italy/Spain 1969 88m Technicolor

Techniscope

Eagle/Tritone/Medusa/D.I.A.

aka: *A Quiet Place to Kill*

A jealous wife plots to murder her philandering husband with the help of his former wife.

Lacklustre thriller that seemingly failed to engage the interest of director or cast.

w Rafael Romero Marchent, Marcello Coscia, Bruno di Geronimo d Umberto Lenzi ph Guglielmo Mancori m Gregorio Garcia Segura ad Wolfgang Burmann ed Antonio Ramirez, Enzo Alabiso

☆ Carroll Baker, Jean Sorel, Marina Coffa, Anna Proclemer, Alberto Dalbes

'A sun-struck little thriller so listlessly plotted – between Majorca beach and luxury poolside – that not even the occasional homicide can shake its mildly enervated holiday air.' – *Richard Combs, MFB*

† The film was cut to 77m on its British release.

'Suddenly, she knew the lips burning on hers did not belong to any normal man!'

Paranoiac *

GB 1963 80m bw Cinemascope

U-I/Hammer (Anthony Hinds)

An heiress is saved from a suicide attempt by a young man claiming to be her dead brother.

A complex maze of disguise, mistaken identity, family curses and revelations of something nasty in the woodshed, out of Psycho by Taste of Fear. Not very good in itself, but interesting in its borrowings.

w Jimmy Sangster d Freddie Francis ph Arthur Grant m Elisabeth Lutyens

☆ Oliver Reed, Janette Scott, Alexander Davion, Sheila Burrell, Liliane Brousse, Maurice Denham, John Bonney

Les Parapluies de Cherbourg **

🎬 France/West Germany 1964 92m

Eastmancolor

Parc/Madeleine/Beta

▣ ▤ ⊛ ⌒

aka: *The Umbrellas of Cherbourg*

A shopgirl loves a gas station attendant. He goes on military service; she finds she is pregnant and marries for security. Years later they meet briefly by accident.

Unexpected, charming, pretty successful screen operetta with only sung dialogue. Careful acting and exquisite use of colour and camera movement paste over the thinner sections of the plot.

wd Jacques Demy ph Jean Rabier m Michel Legrand, Jacques Demy ad Bernard Evein

☆ Catherine Deneuve, Anne Vernon, Nino Castelnuovo

'Poetic neo-realism.' – *Georges Sadoul*

'We are told that in Paris the opening night audience wept and the critics were ecstatic. It would have made a little more sense the other way round.' – *John Simon*

§ best foreign film; script; Michel Legrand, Jacques Demy; song 'I Will Wait for You'

'The First Futuristic Monster Movie In 3-D!'

Parasite

US 1982 85m Metrocolor StereoVision 3-D

Embassy/Charles Band

▣ ▤ ⊛ ⌒

In a post-holocaust 1992, a scientist battles to control a virulent flesh-eating parasite he has developed.

Silly sci-fi horror, in which three-dimensional effects take precedence over sense and logic.

w Alan J. Adler, Michael Shoob, Frank Levering d Charles Band ph Mac Ahlberg m Richard Band ad Pamela B. Warner ed Brad Arensman sp parasite effects: Stan Winston, James Kagel, Lance Anderson

☆ Robert Glaudini, Demi Moore, Luca Bercovici, James Davidson, Vivian Blaine, Al Fann, Tom Villard, Scott Thomson

† The film was a hit, owing mainly to its excellent 3-D and scenes such as one in which, in close-up so that it was right in the viewer's face, blood oozes out of the end of a pipe on which a man is impaled. A sequel was announced but never, so far, made.

The Parasite Murders

Canada 1974 87m colour

Target/Cinepix/Canadian Film Development Corp.

(Ivan Reitman)

▣ ▤

aka: *Shivers*

US title: *They Came from Within*

Parasites that turn people into diseased sex maniacs infect the inhabitants of a luxury hotel.

Bloody and violent horror movie, the first to explore its director's obsession with the alteration of the human body from one form to another.

wd David Cronenberg ph Robert Saad ad Erla Gliserman ed Patrick Dodd sp Joe Blasco

☆ Paul Hampton, Joe Silver, Lynn Lowry, Allan Migicovsky, Susan Petrie, Barbara Steele, Ronald Mlodzik

'A fresh and diverting variation of a hoary entertainment formula.' – *Richard Combs, MFB*

'I was saying "I love sex, but I love sex as a venereal disease. I am syphilis. I am enthusiastic about it, but in a very different way from you".' – *David Cronenberg*

Paratrooper: see *The Red Beret*

Pardners

🎬 US 1956 88m Technicolor

Vistavision

Paramount (Paul Jones)

An incompetent idiot goes west and accidentally cleans up the town.

Stiff Western star burlesque, a remake of Rhythm on the Range.

w Sidney Sheldon d Norman Taurog ph Daniel Fapp songs Sammy Cahn, Jimmy Van Heusen

☆ Dean Martin, Jerry Lewis, Agnes Moorehead, Lori Nelson, John Baragrey, Jeff Morrow, Lon Chaney Jnr

Pardon Mon Affaire *

France 1977 108m Eastmancolor

Gaumont/La Guéville (Daniel Deschamps)

▤ ⌒

aka: *Un Eléphant ça Trompe Enormément*

A middle-aged married man discovers that he is a very unsuccessful adulterer.

Unsubtle comedy that was successful in France, though it does not travel well.

w Jean-Loup Dabadie, Yves Robert d Yves Robert ph René Mathelin m Vladimir Cosma ad Jean-Pierre Kohut-Svelko ed Gérard Pollicand

☆ Jean Rochefort, Claude Brasseur, Guy Bedos, Victor Lanoux, Daniele Delorme, Anny Duperey

† The film was remade by Hollywood as *The Woman In Red* (qv), directed by Gene Wilder.

Pardon My Past *

US 1945 88m bw

Columbia

A man unwittingly takes on the problems of his double, a shady playboy.

Amusing mistaken identity comedy.

w Earl Felton, Karl Kamb d Leslie Fenton ph Russell Metty m Dimitri Tiomkin

☆ Fred MacMurray, Marguerite Chapman, Akim Tamiroff, Rita Johnson, William Demarest, Harry Davenport

Pardon My Rhythm

US 1944 61m bw

Bernard W. Burton/Universal

A kid orchestra participates in a national radio contest.

We have all been here before.

w Val Burton, Eugene Conrad d Felix Feist

☆ Gloria Jean, Mel Tormé, Patric Knowles, Evelyn Ankers, Marjorie Weaver, Walter Catlett, Bob Crosby and his orchestra

Pardon Us *

🎬 US 1931 55m bw

Hal Roach

▣ ▤ ⊛ ⌒ ✿

aka: *Jailbirds*

Two zany bootleggers find themselves in and out of prison.

Patchy star comedy which finds the boys on the whole not in quite their best form.

w H. M. Walker d James Parrott ph George Stevens ed Richard Currier

☆ Stan Laurel, Oliver Hardy, Wilfred Lucas, Walter Long, James Finlayson

'Their first full-length, with not over two reels of value.' – *Variety*

† Boris Karloff replaced Walter Long in the French version of the film.

The Parent Trap *

🎬 US 1961 129m Technicolor

Walt Disney (George Golitzen)

▤ ⌒

Twin daughters of separated parents determine to bring the family together again.

Quite bright but awesomely extended juvenile romp.

wd David Swift novel Das Doppelte Lottchen by Erich Kästner ph Lucien Ballard m Paul Smith

☆ Hayley Mills, Maureen O'Hara, Brian Keith, Charles Ruggles, Leo G. Carroll, Una Merkel, Joanna Barnes, Cathleen Nesbitt, Ruth McDevitt, Nancy Kulp

The Parent Trap *

🎬 US 1998 127m

Buena Vista/Disney (Charles Shyer)

▣ ▤

Twins separated when very young discover each other and decide to bring together again their divorced parents.

Overlong remake that is on the bland side, but also bright and cheerful.

w David Swift, Nancy Meyers, Charles Shyer book Das Doppelte Lottchen by Erich Kastner d Nancy Meyers ph Dean A. Cundey m Alan Silvestri pd Dean Tavoularis ed Stephen A. Rotter

☆ Lindsay Lohan, Dennis Quaid, Natasha Richardson, Elaine Hendrix, Lisa Ann Walter, Simon Kunz, Polly Holliday, Maggie Wheeler, Ronnie Stevens

'Slick, sentimental and exceptionally well cast.' – *Variety*

Parenthood **

US 1989 99m DeLuxe Panavision

UIP/Imagine Entertainment (Brian Grazer)

▣ ▤ ⊛ ⌒

Three generations of fathers and sons try to come to terms with each other.

Expertly packaged, frequently funny, sometimes accurate, but more often sentimental, study of paternal relationships (maternal relationships are defined in terms of the absence of a father).

w Lowell Ganz, Babaloo Mandel d Ron Howard ph Donald McAlpine m Randy Newman pd Todd Hallowell ed Michael Hill, Daniel Hanley

☆ Steve Martin, Tom Hulce, Rick Moranis, Martha Plimpton, Keanu Reeves, Jason Robards, Mary Steenburgen, Dianne Wiest

§ Dianne Wiest; song 'I Love To See You Smile' (m/lRandy Newman)

Parents

US 1988 82m colour

Vestron/Parents Productions (Bonnie Palef-Woolf)

▤ ⌒

A child in small-town America of the 1950s discovers that his parents are cannibals.

Black comedy all the more unsettling because of its resolutely suburban setting.

w Christopher Hawthorne d Bob Balaban ph Ernest Day, Robin Vidgeon m Angelo

Badalamenti, Jonathan Elias *ad* Andris
Hausmanis *ed* Bill Pankow
☆ Randy Quaid, Mary Beth Hurt, Sandy Dennis,
Bryan Madorsky, Juno Mills-Cockell, Kathryn
Grody, Deborah Rush, Graham Jarvis
'The most interesting and exciting directorial
debut that I have encountered in some time – a
"failure" that most recent successes seem
like cold mush.' – *Jonathan Rosenbaum, Chicago
Reader*

Les Parents Terribles **

France   1948   98m   bw
Sirius
Life with a family in which the children are as
neurotic as the parents.
*Alternately hilarious and tragic, this is a fascinating
two-set piece of filmed theatre, with every performance
a pleasure.*
wd Jean Cocteau *play* Jean Cocteau *ph* Michel
Kelber *m* Georges Auric *ad* Christian Bérard,
Guy de Gastyne
☆ Jean Marais, Yvonne de Bray, Gabrielle Dorziat,
Marcel André, Josette Day
† In 1953 a curious and unsatisfactory British
version was made by Charles Frank under the title
Intimate Relations, with Marian Spencer, Russell
Enoch, Ruth Dunning, Harold Warrender and Elsy
Albiin.

Le Parfum d'Yvonne *

France   1994   89m   colour
Artificial Eye/Lambart/Zoulou/CECR-A/M6 (Thierry de
Ganay)
🔲 🎧
aka: *Yvonne's Perfume*
A man remembers a holiday by Lake Geneva,
when he was avoiding service in the Algerian war,
one that changed his life after he became involved
with a beautiful actress and her reckless friend, an
elderly homosexual doctor.
*Slight, leisurely, bitter-sweet romance among the idle,
set against the background of privilege.*
wd Patrice Leconte *novel* Villa Triste by Patrick
Modiano *ph* Eduardo Serra *m* Pascal Estève
ad Ivan Maussion *ed* Joëlle Hache
☆ Jean-Pierre Marielle, Hippolyte Girardot, Sandra
Majani, Richard Bohringer, Paul Guers, Corinne
Marchand, Philippe Magnan
'Good playing, particularly from Marielle, some
fine widescreen camerawork and a certain sense
of melancholy, even as the gaiety is outlined,
prevents the film falling into bathos. But it's a
near thing.' – *Derek Malcolm, Guardian*
'Stunningly lensed widescreen memoir captured
at the intersection of insouciance and longing.' –
Variety

Paris

US   1929   88m   bw/colour
Warner
An American stage star, her fiancé, her partner
and her mother-in-law-to-be converge on the
Champs Elysées.
*Shaky musical with interesting talent, but bereft of its
original Cole Porter score.*
w Hope Loring *d* Clarence Badger
☆ Irene Bordoni, Jack Buchanan, Louise Closser
Hale, Jason Robards

Paris after Dark

US   1943   85m   bw
TCF
GB title: *The Night Is Ending*
In wartime Paris a doctor leads the resistance
forces.
Propaganda potboiler, quite neatly made and cast.
w Howard Buchman *d* Leonide Moguy
ph Lucien Andriot
☆ George Sanders, Philip Dorn, Brenda Marshall,
Marcel Dalio, Madeleine LeBeau

Paris Belongs to Us

France   1961   140m   bw
AJYM/Films du Carrosse (Roland Nonia)
original title: *Paris Nous Appartient*
A student becomes involved with a group
unsuccessfully rehearsing a Shakespearean play
who fear a conspiracy to take over the world.
*Overlong, often pretentious and famously amateurish,
Rivette's first feature reflects an adolescent despair of
the future.*
w Jacques Rivette, Jean Gruault *d* Jacques
Rivette *ph* Charles Bitsch *m* Philippe Arthuys
ed Denise de Casablanca

☆ Betty Schneider, Gianni Esposito, Françoise
Prévost, Daniel Crohem, François Maistre, Jean-
Marie Robain, Hans Lucas, Jean-Claude Brialy

Paris Blues *

US   1961   98m   Technicolor
UA/Pennebaker/Diane/Jason/Monica/Monmouth (Sam
Shaw)
🔲 🎧
Two jazz musicians have romantic problems in
Paris.
*Semi-serious mini-drama with emphasis on the music;
one is not quite sure what the actors thought they were
up to.*
w Jack Sher, Irene Kamp, Walter Bernstein
novel Harold Flender *d* Martin Ritt *ph* Christian
Matras *m* Duke Ellington
☆ Paul Newman, Joanne Woodward, Sidney
Poitier, Louis Armstrong, Diahann Carroll, Serge
Reggiani, Barbara Laage
'All wrong from beginning to end.' – *Sidney
Poitier*
🎵 Duke Ellington

Paris by Night

GB   1988   103m   Eastmancolor
Virgin/British Screen/Film Four International/Zenith
Harassed by personal problems, a Conservative MP
in the European Parliament is driven to extreme
actions.
*Unsatisfactory political drama, intended to expose
social and moral hypocrisies but rarely rising above
melodrama.*
wd David Hare *ph* Roger Pratt *m* Georges
Delerue *pd* Anthony Pratt *ed* George Akers
☆ Charlotte Rampling, Michael Gambon, Robert
Hardy, Iain Glen, Jane Asher, Andrew Ray, Niamh
Cusack, Jonathan White, Linda Bassett, Robert
Flemyng, Robert David MacDonald

Paris Calling

US   1941   95m   bw
Universal/Charles K. Feldman
When the Nazis invade Paris, a woman discovers
that her husband is a traitor.
Totally predictable flagwaver.
w Benjamin Glazer, Charles Kaufman *d* Edwin L.
Marin *ph* Milton Krasner *m* Richard Hageman
☆ Elisabeth Bergner, Basil Rathbone, Randolph
Scott, Gale Sondergaard, Lee J. Cobb, Eduardo
Ciannelli, Charles Arnt

Paris Express: see The Man Who Watched Trains Go By

'Sometimes the most erotic place to go is inside
yourself.'
Paris France

Canada   1993   105m   Eastmancolor/bw
Feature Film/Alliance/Lightshow (Eric Norlen, Allan
Levine)
🔲
A writer comes between a publisher and his wife.
*An absurd mishmash of sex and literary musings,
resembling a pornographer's fantasy of the artistic life in
which coupling and writing are seen as complementary
activities.*
w Tom Walmsley *novel* Tom Walmsley *d* Gerard
Ciccoritti *ph* Barry Stone *m* John McCarthy
pd Marian Wihak *ed* Roushell Goldstein
☆ Leslie Hope, Peter Outerbridge, Victor
Ertmanis, Dan Lett, Raoul Trujillo
'A pretentiously steamy piece of Canadian
erotica.' – *Derek Malcolm, Guardian*
'An unerotic bonkathon chock-full of
unintentional laughs, hysterical performances
and flaccid members.' – *Film Review*

Paris Holiday *

US   1957   101m   Technirama
UA/Tolda (Bob Hope)
📼
An American comedian meets a French one in
Paris, and both have narrow escapes because their
script contains the clue to a gang of counterfeiters.
*Amiable location romp with the stars in pretty good
form.*
w Edmund Beloin, Dean Riesner *d* Gerd Oswald
ph Roger Hubert *m* Joseph J. Lilley
☆ Bob Hope, Fernandel, Anita Ekberg, Martha
Hyer, André Morell, Maurice Teynac, Jean Murat,
Preston Sturges

Paris Honeymoon

US   1938   85m   bw
Paramount
An American in Paris persuades his fiancée to
forget a French nobleman.
Candy floss musical for star fans.
w Frank Butler, Don Hartman *d* Frank Tuttle
ph Karl Struss *m/ly* Leo Robin *md* Boris Morros
☆ Bing Crosby, Franciska Gaal, Akim Tamiroff
'Entertaining offering that will click
substantially at the box office.' – *Variety*

Paris in Spring

US   1935   81m   bw
Paramount
GB title: *Paris Love Song*
Four visitors change partners in the romantic city.
Predictable romance with good ingredients.
w Samuel Hoffenstein, Franz Schulz, Keene
Thompson *play* Dwight Taylor *d* Lewis Milestone
☆ Mary Ellis, Tullio Carminati, Lynne Overman,
Ida Lupino
'In everything except the unhappy choice of
narrative it comes close to being an ideal
production.' – *Variety*

Paris Interlude

US   1934   72m   bw
MGM
American newspapermen hang out in a Paris bar.
*Aimless comedy-drama which fails to achieve the
intended mood of world-weariness.*
w Wells Root *play* All Good Americans by S. J.
and Laura Perelman *d* Edwin L. Marin
☆ Madge Evans, Otto Kruger, Robert Young, Una
Merkel, Ted Healy, Louise Henry, Edward Brophy
'60 minutes instead of 72 would still have left
something to be desired – further cutting.' –
Variety

Paris Is Burning **

US   1990   78m   colour
ICA/OffWhite (Jennie Livingston)
🔲 🔍
Documentary about gay black men who compete
for prizes at drag balls.
*Fascinating glimpse of an enclosed world, reported with
insight and sensitivity.*
d Jennie Livingston *ph* Paul Gibson *ed* Jonathan
Oppenheim
☆ Paris Dupree, Andre Christian, Dorian Corey,
Pepper Labeija, Willi Ninja
'A masterpiece of underworld reportage.' – *Sight
and Sound*

Paris Love Song: see Paris in Spring

Paris Model

US   1953   88m   bw
Albert Zugsmith/Columbia
Stories involving four copies of the same Paris
gown.
*Depressing dramatic package with production values at
a low ebb and some pleasant talents going awry.*
w Robert Smith *d* Alfred E. Green *ph* William
Bradford *m* Albert Glasser
☆ Paulette Goddard, Eva Gabor, Marilyn
Maxwell, Barbara Lawrence, Tom Conway, Leif
Erickson, Florence Bates, Cecil Kellaway, Robert
Hutton
'Wasn't it dreadful?' – *Marilyn Maxwell*

Paris Nous Appartient: see Paris Belongs to Us

Paris Qui Dort *

France   1923   40m   bw   silent
Films Diamant (Maurice Diamant-Berger)
aka: *The Crazy Ray*
A mad scientist invents a ray which brings
everyone but six people in Paris to a halt.
*Mildly entertaining semi-professional comedy showing
several of its director's most engaging traits.*
ph Maurice Défassiaux, Paul Guichard *wd/ed* René
Clair
☆ Henri Rollan, Albert Préjean, Marcel Vallée,
Madeleine Rodrigue

Paris, Texas **

West Germany/France   1984   148m   colour
Road Movies/Argos (Don Guest, Anatole Dauman)
🔲 📼 🔍
After separating from his wife a man goes missing
and is later found in the small town where he was
born.

*Long, enigmatic but generally fascinating puzzle-
without-a-solution, about people who never find what
they want.*
w Sam Shepard *d* Wim Wenders *ph* Robby
Müller *m* Ry Cooder
☆ Harry Dean Stanton, Dean Stockwell, Aurore
Clement, Hunter Carson, Nastassja Kinski,
Bernhard Wicki
† Filmed in English.
⑰ best director

Paris Trout **

US   1991   99m   CFI color   Panavision
Palace/Viacom (Frank Konigsberg, Larry Sanitsky)
🔲 📼 🔍
In the 1940s, in a small town in Georgia, a bigoted
white store-owner is amazed to be tried for
shooting a black girl and wounding her mother in a
dispute over a car.
*Powerful if predictable drama of racial hatred and a
disintegrating marriage, though not helped by a
portentous voice-over narration.*
w Pete Dexter *novel* Pete Dexter *d* Stephen
Gyllenhaal *ph* Robert Elswit *m* David Shire
pd Richard Sherman *ed* Harvey Rosenstock
☆ Dennis Hopper, Barbara Hershey, Ed Harris,
Ray McKinnon, Tina Lifford, Darnita Henry, Eric
Ware, Ronreaco Lee, Gary Bullock

Paris Underground

US   1945   97m   bw
(UA)
GB title: *Madame Pimpernel*
Two women caught in Paris when the Nazis invade
continue their resistance activities.
Artificial and not very exciting flagwaver.
w Boris Ingster, Gertrude Purcell *novel* Etta
Shiber *d* Gregory Ratoff *ph* Lee Garmes
m Alexander Tansman
☆ Constance Bennett, Gracie Fields, George
Rigaud, Kurt Kreuger, Leslie Vincent
'Mainly trash, involving enough handsome
young men, in various poses of gallant gratitude,
to satisfy Mae West in her prime.' – *James Agee*
🎵 Alexander Tansman

Paris Vu Par... **

France   1965   98m   colour
Films du Losange/Les Films du Cyprès/Barbet
Schroeder
🔲 📼
aka: *Six in Paris*
Six short stories set in different parts of Paris: in
Douchet's 'Saint Germain-des-Prés', an American
girl is seduced by appearances. In Rouch's 'Gard du
Nord', a discontented wife is offered the freedom
that she thinks she desires. In Pollet's 'Rue St
Denis', a dull dishwasher takes a prostitute back to
his dingy flat. In Rohmer's 'Place de l'étoile', a
fastidious shirt-salesman thinks he has killed
someone in a roadside brawl. In Godard's
'Montparnasse et Levallois', a girl believes she has
mixed up telegrams sent to her two lovers. In
Chabrol's 'La Muette Chabrol', a young boy buys
ear-plugs to avoid listening to his parents' quarrel
and so misses a vital cry for help.
*Enjoyable, ironic anecdotes by six French 'New Wave'
directors, originally shot in 16mm using hand-held
cameras and natural lighting to achieve an
appropriately offhand style.*
wd Jean Douchet; Jean Rouch; Jean-Daniel Pollet;
Eric Rohmer; Jean-Luc Godard; Claude Chabrol
ph Nestor Almendros; Etienne Becker; Alain
Levent; Albert Maysles; Jean Rabier *ed* Jacqueline
Raynal
☆ Barbara Wilkind, Jean-François Chappey, Jean-
Pierre Andréani; Nadine Ballot, Barbet Schroeder,
Gilles Quéant; Micheline Dax, Claude Melki;
Jean-Michel Rouzière, Marcel Gallon; Joanna
Shimkus, Philippe Hiquily, Serge Davri; Stéphane
Audran, Gilles Chusseau, Claude Chabrol

Paris When It Sizzles

US   1963   110m   Technicolor
Paramount (Richard Quine, George Axelrod)
📼
A film writer tries out several script ideas with his
secretary as heroine and himself as hero or villain.
*As a French film called La Fête à Henriette this was a
charming whimsy, but Hollywood made it heavy-
handed and boring, especially as no one in it seems to
be having much fun.*
w George Axelrod *screenplay* Julien Duvivier,
Henri Jeanson *d* Richard Quine *ph* Charles Lang
Jnr *m* Nelson Riddle

☆ William Holden, Audrey Hepburn, Grégoire Aslan, Noël Coward, Raymond Bussières

'The new script embalms the original instead of reviving it.' – *Stanley Kauffmann, New Republic*

Park Row *

US 1952 83m bw
UA/Samuel Fuller

Conflict breaks out between two newspapers in 1886 New York.

Earnest but flat low-budgeter of a rather unusual kind.

wd Samuel Fuller ph Jack Russell m Paul Dunlap ad Theobold Holsopple

☆ Gene Evans, Mary Welch, Bela Kovacs, Herbert Heyes, Forrest Taylor

Parker

GB 1984 97m colour
Moving Picture Company (Nigel Stafford-Clark)

A British businessman turns up after claiming to have been kidnapped in Munich, but the police don't necessarily believe him.

Suspense thriller hampered by overblown bits of ambivalence which prevent sympathy from lodging in any quarter.

w Trevor Preston d Jim Goddard ph Peter Jessop m Richard Hartley

☆ Bryan Brown, Cherie Lunghi, Kurt Raab, Bob Peck, Beate Finkh

Parlor, Bedroom and Bath

US 1931 72m bw
MGM
▦ 💿

GB title: *Romeo in Pyjamas*

A mild-mannered husband has trouble when he becomes a landlord.

Rather flatfooted farce, on a par with the star's other talkies.

w Richard Schayer, Robert Hopkins play Charles W. Bell, Mark Swan d Edward Sedgwick

☆ Buster Keaton, Charlotte Greenwood, Reginald Denny, Cliff Edwards

'Funny, clean enough for kids, and generally well made.' – *Variety*

† The film was largely shot on location in Keaton's own house.

'As though torn from life's pages!'

Parnell *

US 1937 115m bw
MGM (John M. Stahl)

A 19th-century Irish politician comes to grief through his love for a married woman.

Well made but miscast biopic, a resounding thud at the box-office.

w John Van Druten, S. N. Behrman play Elsie T. Schauffler d John M. Stahl ph Karl Freund m William Axt

☆ Clark Gable, Myrna Loy, Edmund Gwenn, Edna May Oliver, Alan Marshal, Donald Crisp, Billie Burke, Berton Churchill, Donald Meek, Montagu Love, George Zucco

'Dull and overlong historical drama ... word of mouth is likely to be poor.' – *Variety*
'A singularly pallid, tedious and unconvincing drama.' – *Frank Nugent*
'Poor though the picture may be, it is pleasing to think how clean a film magnate's wish-fulfilments are, how virginal and high-minded the tawdry pathetic human past becomes when the Mayers and Goldwyns turn the magic ring.' – *Graham Greene*

Parole, Inc

US 1948 71m bw
Orbit/Eagle Lion
▦

A racketeer arranges to spring hardened criminals from the state prison.

Routine crime stuff, quite efficiently handled.

w Sherman Lowe d Alfred Zeisler ph Gilbert Warrenton m Alexander Laszlo

☆ Michael O'Shea, Turhan Bey, Evelyn Ankers, Virginia Lee, Lyle Talbot

Parrish

US 1961 137m Technicolor
Warner (Delmer Daves)

A young tobacco plantation worker has an ample sex life and the luck to become boss.

Predictable trudge through scenes from a bestselling novel, less offensive than most such adaptations.

wd Delmer Daves novel Mildred Savage ph Harry Stradling m Max Steiner

☆ Troy Donahue, Claudette Colbert, Karl Malden, Dean Jagger, Connie Stevens, Diane McBain, Sharon Hugueny

Parsifal **

West Germany 1982 255m colour
Artificial Eye/Gaumont/TMS
📼

Cinematic version of Wagner's opera of the knights of the Holy Grail.

Imaginative treatment, set around the composer's death mask, with a youth and a girl playing Parsifal; its actors are dubbed by singers.

d Hans Jürgen Syberberg ph Igor Luther m Richard Wagner md Armin Jordan ed Jutta Brandstaedter, Marianne Fehrenberg

☆ Michael Kutter, Karin Krick, Edith Clever, Armin Jordan, Robert Lloyd, Aage Haugland, Martin Sperr and also the voices of Rainer Goldberg, Yvonne Minton and Wolfgang Schöne

The Parson of Panamint

US 1941 84m bw
Paramount (Harry Sherman)

A gold-rush mountain town is corrupted by success until a two-fisted parson puts things right.

Middling Western morality play.

w Harold Shumate, Adrian Scott novel Peter B. Kyne d William McGann ph Russell Harlan m Irvin Talbot

☆ Charles Ruggles, Ellen Drew, Phillip Terry, Joseph Schildkraut, Henry Kolker, Janet Beecher, Paul Hurst

Une Partie de Campagne ***

France 1936 40m bw
Pantheon/Pierre Braunberger
aka: *A Day in the Country*

Around 1880, a Parisian tradesman and his family picnic one Sunday in the country, and one of the daughters falls in love.

An unfinished film which was much admired for its local colour, like an impressionist picture come to life.

wd Jean Renoir story Guy de Maupassant ph Claude Renoir, Jean Bourgoin m Joseph Kosma

☆ Sylvia Bataille, Georges Darnoul, Jane Marken, Paul Temps

'Nothing can tarnish the intense lyrical simplicity underlaid with an aching irony and made almost unbearable by the yearning musical score of Kosma. This is everybody's lost love.' – *Richard Winnington*

Une Partie de Plaisir *

France 1975 100m colour
La Boétie/Sunchild/Gerico (André Génoves)
📼

The analysis of a divorce.

Bitter comedy drama, with the director's usual scriptwriter playing out his own life story. A little too incestuous for its own good, but with striking moments.

w Paul Gegauff d Claude Chabrol ph Jean Rabier m Beethoven, Brahms, Schubert ad Guy Littaye ed Jacques Gaillard

☆ Paul Gegauff, Danielle Gegauff, Paula Moore, Michel Valette, Cecile Vassort, Pierre Santini

Parting Glances *

US 1986 90m DuArt
Rondo (Yoran Mandel, Arthur Silverman)
▦

A gay couple, one of whom is going to work in Africa, spend their last day together with friends.

A low-key drama of love, death and companionship in a community haunted by the fear of death; it was one of the first movies to confront the trauma of AIDS.

wd Bill Sherwood ph Jacek Laskus pd John Loggia

☆ Richard Ganoung, John Bolger, Steve Buscemi, Kathy Kinney, Adam Nathan, Yolande Bavan, Patrick Tull

'Is skilfully constructed and artfully shot, and boasts impressive acting.' – *MFB*

† Bill Sherwood died of AIDS in 1990.

Parting Shots

GB 1998 98m colour
UIP/Scimitar/Michael Winner
📼

Told that he has only six weeks to live, a photographer decides to kill all the people who have humiliated him.

An extravagant waste of talent; with a miscast lead and a leaden script, it reworks the director's Death Wish *as a comedy, but isn't as funny.*

w Michael Winner, Nick Mead d Michael Winner ph Ousama Rawi m Les Reed pd Crispian Sallis ed Chris Barnes, Arnold Crust (Michael Winner)

☆ Chris Rea, Felicity Kendall, Bob Hoskins, Ben Kingsley, Joanna Lumley, Oliver Reed, Diana Rigg, John Cleese, Gareth Hunt, Peter Davison, Patrick Ryecart, Nicky Henson, Edward Hardwicke

'Sucks on every conceivable level. Its technical ineptitude and dramatic impotence simply beggar belief.' – *Andrew Collins, Empire*
'A thoroughbred contender for the crown "Worst Film Ever Made".' – *Observer*

Partners

US 1982 98m Movielab
Titan (Aaron Russo)
📼 ▦

Two Los Angeles police officers, one straight and one gay, investigate the murder of a homosexual.

Uneasy comedy-melodrama of somewhat mysterious purpose.

w Francis Veber d James Burrows ph Victor J. Kemper m Georges Delerue

☆ John Hurt, Ryan O'Neal, Kenneth McMillan, Robyn Douglass, Jay Robinson

Partners in Crime

US 1937 66m bw
Paramount

A private eye stumbles on a plot to victimize the reform candidate in a local election.

Reliable second feature with few surprises.

w Garnett Weston novel Kurt Steel d Ralph Murphy

☆ Lynne Overman, Roscoe Karns, Muriel Hutchinson, Anthony Quinn, Inez Courtney, Charles Halton, Lucien Littlefield

'A cockeyed affair, perforated with surprises.' – *Variety*

The Party *

🎭 US 1968 98m DeLuxe Panavision
UA/Mirisch/Geoffrey (Blake Edwards)
▦ 💿

An accident-prone Indian actor is accidentally invited to a swank Hollywood party and wrecks it.

Would-be Tatiesque comedy of disaster, occasionally well-timed but far too long for all its gloss.

w Blake Edwards, Tom and Frank Waldman d Blake Edwards ph Lucien Ballard m Henry Mancini pd Fernando Carrere

☆ Peter Sellers, Claudine Longet, Marge Champion, Fay McKenzie, Steve Franken, Buddy Lester

'One thing the old movie makers did know is that two reels is more than enough of this stuff.' – *Wilfred Sheed*
'It is only rarely that one laughs or even smiles; mostly one just chalks up another point for ingenuity.' – *Tom Milne*

The Party and the Guests *

Czechoslovakia 1966 71m bw
Barrandov Studio
original title: *O Slavnosti A Hostech*

A reluctant guest at an outdoor birthday and wedding party refuses to join in the celebrations.

Biting political allegory on the nature of tyranny.

w Ester Krumbachová, Jan Nĕcaronmec d Jan Nĕmec ph Jaromir Šofr m Karel Mares

☆ Helena Pejsková, Jana Pracharova, Zdena Skvorecká, Pavel Bosek, Karel Mares, Evald Schorm, Jan Klusak, Jiři Nĕmec, Wan Vyskocil

Party Girl

US 1958 98m Metrocolor Cinemascope
MGM/Euterpe (Joe Pasternak)
▦ 💿

In twenties Chicago, a lawyer wins a girl from a gangster.

Heavy-handed Scarface-style saga which at one time won a curious reputation for being a satire.

w George Wells d Nicholas Ray ph Robert Bronner m Jeff Alexander

☆ Robert Taylor, Cyd Charisse, Lee J. Cobb, John Ireland, Kent Smith, Claire Kelly, Corey Allen

Party, Party

GB 1983 98m colour
A & M Records

A teenager throws a drunken party while his parents are out.

Ghastly British rubbish: no plot and nothing to laugh at at all, just young people making asses of themselves.

w Daniel Peacock, Terry Winsor d Terry Winsor ph Syd Macartney

☆ Daniel Peacock, Karl Howman, Perry Fenwick, Sean Chapman, Phoebe Nicholls, Caroline Quentin

Party Wire

US 1935 70m bw
Columbia

Small-town gossipers listen in on party wires and draw the wrong conclusions.

Multi-stranded comedy-drama; not important but quite pleasant.

w Ethel Hill, John Howard Lawson, Bruce Manning d Erle C. Kenton

☆ Jean Arthur, John Qualen, Helen Lowell, Charley Grapewin, Clara Blandick, Maude Eburne

'Entertaining for the family trade.' – *Variety*

The Party's Over

GB 1963 94m bw
Tricastle (Anthony Perry)

An American girl joins a group of Chelsea beatniks and dies in a fall from a balcony; her father investigates.

Tasteless and boring swinging London trash which became notorious when its producers (Rank) disowned it because it features a party at which a man makes love to a dead girl. An unattractive display of moral squalor.

w Marc Behm d Guy Hamilton ph Larry Pizer m John Barry

☆ Oliver Reed, Eddie Albert, Ann Lynn, Louise Sorel

Pas de Problème: see *No Problem!*

Un Pasaje de Ida

Dominican Republic 1988 90m colour
Producciones Testimonio (Agliberto Melendez)
aka: *A One-Way Ticket*

A ship's captain, who is smuggling 40 men to America, panics when police come aboard to search the vessel.

A competent exposé of high-level corruption and low-level greed which gains some resonance from its harrowing climax, based as it is on a true story.

w Agliberto Melendez, Adelso Cass, Danilo Taveras d Agliberto Melendez ph Pedro Guzman Cordero m Rafael Solano pd Orlando Menicucci ed Pericles Mejia

☆ Horacio Veloz, Miguel Buccarelli, Victor Checo, Felix German, Pepito Guerra, Nini German, Giovanni Cruz, Delta Soto

Pasazerka: see *Passenger*

Pascali's Island *

GB 1988 104m Metrocolor
Virgin/Avenue Pictures/Initial/Film Four International
📼 ▦ 💿

On an Aegean island, a Turkish spy and an English con man attempt to double-cross one another.

Elegant period drama full of an understated sexual tension.

wd James Dearden novel Barry Unsworth ph Roger Deakins m Loek Dikker pd Andrew Mollo ed Edward Marnier

☆ Ben Kingsley, Charles Dance, Helen Mirren, Stefan Gryff, George Murcell, Nadim Sawalha, T. P. McKenna, Sheila Allan

Pasqualino Settebellezze: see *Seven Beauties*

The Passage

GB 1978 98m Eastmancolor Technovision
Hemdale/Passage/Lester Goldsmith-Maurice Binder (John Quested)
🎧

A Basque shepherd guides a scientist and his family from occupied France over the mountains into Spain.

Routine war suspenser given an unnecessary taint of sadism. Only those addicted to unpleasant detail will enjoy it.

w Bruce Micolaysen *novel* The Perilous Passage by Bruce Micolaysen d J. Lee Thompson ph Michael Reed m Michael J. Lewis

☆ Anthony Quinn, James Mason, Malcolm McDowell, Patricia Neal, Kay Lenz, Paul Clemens, Christopher Lee

Le Passage du Rhin: see *The Crossing of the Rhine*

Passage Home

GB 1955 102m bw
GFD/Group Films (Julian Wintle)

In 1931, tensions run high on a merchant ship when the captain accepts an attractive girl as passenger from South America.

Obvious melodrama complete with drunken captain and storm at sea; not badly done if it must be done at all.

w William Fairchild *novel* Richard Armstrong d Roy Baker ph Geoffrey Unsworth m Clifton Parker

☆ Peter Finch, Anthony Steel, Diane Cilento, Cyril Cusack, Geoffrey Keen, Hugh Griffith, Duncan Lamont, Bryan Forbes, Gordon Jackson, Michael Craig

A Passage to India **

GB 1984 163m Technicolor
EMI/John Brabourne-Richard Goodwin/HBO/John Heyman/Edward Sands

An English girl in India accuses an Indian doctor of rape.

Another film about India under the Raj seems somewhat redundant after The Jewel in the Crown, Gandhi and The Far Pavilions, but at least under David Lean's direction this is intelligent and good to look at.

novel E. M. Forster ph Ernest Day m Maurice Jarre pd John Box wd/ed David Lean

☆ Judy Davis, Alec Guinness, Victor Banerjee, Peggy Ashcroft, James Fox, Nigel Havers, Richard Wilson, Antonia Pemberton, Michael Culver, Art Malik

🏆 Peggy Ashcroft (supporting actress); music

A best picture; direction; Judy Davis; adapted screenplay; photography; editing; art direction

🎬 Peggy Ashcroft

Passage to Marseilles *

US 1944 110m bw
Warner (Hal B. Wallis)

Convicts escape from Devil's Island and join the Free French.

A rare example of a film boasting flashbacks within flashbacks within flashbacks, this confusing if sometimes entertaining all-star saga is done to death by its unconvincing flagwaving endpapers which prevent it from being at all comparable with Casablanca, as was clearly intended.

w Casey Robinson, Jack Moffitt *story* Charles Nordhoff, James Hall d Michael Curtiz ph James Wong Howe m Max Steiner

☆ Humphrey Bogart, Michèle Morgan, Claude Rains, Philip Dorn, Sydney Greenstreet, Peter Lorre, Helmut Dantine, George Tobias, John Loder, Victor Francen, Eduardo Ciannelli

'Invincibly second rate.' – *Richard Mallet, Punch*

Passage West

US 1951 81m Technicolor
Pine-Thomas/Paramount

Religious pioneers headed west are menaced by escaped convicts.

Entertaining minor Western.

w Lewis R. Foster, Nedrick Young d Lewis R. Foster ph Loyal Griggs m Mahlon Merrick

☆ John Payne, Dennis O'Keefe, Arleen Whelan, Peter Hanson

Passager de la Pluie: see *Rider on the Rain*

Passed Away

US 1992 96m Technicolor
Hollywood/Touchwood (Larry Brezner, Timothy Marx)

After his elderly father dies, and the family gathers for a wake, the eldest son decides it is time to take risks with his life.

Mundane domestic comedy, too predictable to be enjoyable; like its central character it settles for safety and familiarity.

wd Charlie Peters ph Arthur Albert m Richard Gibbs pd Catherine Hardwicke ed Harry Keramidas

☆ Bob Hoskins, Blair Brown, Tim Curry, Frances McDormand, William Petersen, Pamela Reed, Peter Riegert, Maureen Stapleton, Nancy Travis, Jack Warden

Passenger *

Poland 1963 63m bw Dyaliscope
Kadr

original title: Pasazerka

A German woman on a liner sees a woman she thinks she recognizes, and realizes that it is one of her charges when she was an official in a concentration camp.

Minor but effective character drama, in essence an investigation of guilt. The director died during its making, so some scenes are replaced by still photographs.

wd Andrzej Munk *play* Zofia Posmysz-Piasecka ph Krzysztof Winiewicz

☆ Aleksandra Slaska, Anna Ciepielewska

'I used to be somebody else; but I traded myself in...'

The Passenger *

Italy/France/Spain 1975 119m Metrocolor
MGM/CCC/Concordia/CIPI (Carlo Ponti)

aka: Profession: Reporter

A TV reporter in a desert hotel changes identities with a dead man and finds he is now an African gun runner being drawn irresistibly towards his own death.

Pretty much in the style of Blow Up, but this time with no frills of fashion or nudity to bring the public in. After this, Antonioni was given up by the commercial cinema.

w Mark Peploe, Peter Wollen, Michelangelo Antonioni d Michelangelo Antonioni ph Luciano Tovoli md Ivan Vandor

☆ Jack Nicholson, Maria Schneider, Jenny Runacre, Ian Hendry

'A film of real romance, depth and power ... the very quintessence of cinema.' – *Michael Billington, Illustrated London News*

'He's an ex-cop with a bad mouth, a bad attitude, and a bad seat. For the terrorists on flight 163 ... he's very bad news.'

Passenger 57

US 1992 84m Technicolor
Warner (Lee Rich, Dan Paulson, Dylan Sellers)

An ex-cop goes into action when terrorists hijack his plane.

A Die Hard-style thriller, entertaining enough although inevitably predictable.

w David Loughery, Dan Gordon, Stewart Raffill d Kevin Hooks m Mark Irwin m Stanley Clarke pd Jaymes Hinkle ed Richard Nord

☆ Wesley Snipes, Bruce Payne, Tom Sizemore, Alex Datcher, Bruce Greenwood, Robert Hooks, Elizabeth Hurley, Michael Horse

'About as fresh as an in-flight meal. Even so, it has a certain appetizing quality about it.' – *Guardian*

Passe-Passe: see *Quicker than the Eye*

Passing Clouds: see *Spellbound*

The Passing of the Third Floor Back *

GB 1935 90m bw
Gaumont (Ivor Montagu)

A Christ-like visitor stays at a London boarding house and changes the lives of the inmates.

Competent film version of a famous, sentimental, dated play.

w Michael Hogan, Alma Reville *play* Jerome K. Jerome d Berthold Viertel ph Curt Courant m Hubert Bath

☆ Conrad Veidt, René Ray, Anna Lee, Frank Cellier, Mary Clare, Beatrix Lehmann, Cathleen Nesbitt, Sara Allgood

'Drawing power of the book, the play, the picturization and the star should, on form, be invincible.' – *Variety*

'The pious note has been toned down, the milk of human kindness has been agreeably watered, and the types in the small London private hotel are observed with malicious realism.' – *Graham Greene*

Passion: see *Madame Dubarry (1919)*

Passion

US 1954 84m Technicolor
Benedict Bogeaus/RKO

Jealousy erupts between ranchers in Spanish California.

Peculiarly titled Western of no merit whatsoever.

w Beatrice A. Dresher, Joseph Leytes d Allan Dwan ph John Alton m Louis Forbes

☆ Yvonne de Carlo, Cornel Wilde, Raymond Burr, Lon Chaney Jnr, Rodolfo Acosta, John Qualen

Passion *

France 1982 88m Eastmancolor
Artificial Eye/Sonimage/Sara Films/A2/Film et Video Productions (Alain Sarde)

A Polish film director has an affair with the wife of a factory owner who is trying to cope with a threatened strike.

Visually complex examination of film-making, work, love and betrayal.

wd Jean-Luc Godard ph Raoul Coutard m Ravel, Mozart and others ad Serge Marzolff

☆ Isabelle Huppert, Hanna Schygulla, Michel Piccoli, Jerzy Radziwilowicz, László Szabó, Jean-François Stevenin, Patrick Bonnel, Sophie Loucachevsky

Passion Fish

US 1992 134m DuArt
Atchafalaya (Sarah Green, Maggie Renzi)

A new nurse with problems of her own gives a crippled TV actress a reason to live.

A well-acted but constricting domestic drama.

wd John Sayles ph Roger Deakins m Mason Daring pd Dan Bishop, Dianna Freas ed John Sayles

☆ Mary McDonnell, Alfre Woodard, David Strathairn, Vondie Curtis-Hall, Nora Dunn, Sheila Kelley, Angela Bassett, Leo Burmester

'Pic has a measure of charm, plenty of validity and some fine scenes, but lacks the intensity that would have made it galvanizing or transcendent.' – *Variety*

A Mary McDonnell; John Sayles

Passion Flower

US 1930 78m bw
MGM

Two rich girls marry beneath them.

Tedious romantic drama about class and true love.

w Martin Flavin, L. E. Johnson, Edith Fitzgerald *novel* Kathleen Norris d William de Mille

☆ Kay Francis, Kay Johnson, Charles Bickford, Lewis Stone, ZaSu Pitts, Dickie Moore, Winter Hall

'A flock of talent, but talent doesn't always count on a marquee.' – *Variety*

A Passion for Murder

Canada 1992 92m colour
The Fare/Actra (Robert Vince, Vonnie von Helmont)

aka: Black Ice

Following the death of the corrupt politician who was her lover, a female secret agent enlists the help of a friendly taxi driver when she is stalked by a killer from the CIA.

A chase thriller taken at a too-leisurely pace, and demonstrating too great an interest in the passing landscape, to maintain much suspense.

w Arne Olsen, John Alan Schwartz d Neill Fearnley ph David Geddes m Asmin Bahtia pd Deanna Rhode ed Alan Lee

☆ Joanna Pacula, Michael Nouri, Michael Ironside, Lee J. Campbell, Victor Cowie, Mickey Jones

'When nature divides, the spirit unites.'

Passion in the Desert *

US 1997 93m colour
Fine Line/Roland (Jamil Dehlavi, Lavinia Currier)

Lost in the Sahara, a Napoleonic officer forms a loving relationship with a female leopard.

An unusual and imaginative movie that manages without much dialogue to raise philosophical questions of man's place within the natural world.

w Lavinia Currier, Martin Edmunds *novella* Honoré de Balzac d Lavinia Currier ph Alexei Rodionov m Joseph Nieto pd Amanda McArthur ed Nicolas Gaster

☆ Ben Daniels, Michel Piccoli, Paul Meston, Kenneth Collard, Nadi Odeh

'If You Go Down To The Woods Tonight...'

The Passion of Darkly Noon

GB/Germany/Belgium 1995 101m colour
Entertainment/Fugitive/Die Hauskunst/Keytsman (Dominic Anciano, Frank Henschke, Alain Keytsman)

A 17-year-old runaway from a strict religious community is given shelter by a carpenter and the woman he lives with.

Portentous and overwrought fable, involving incest and murder, full of symbols that will no doubt mean something to someone.

wd Philip Ridley ph John de Borman m Nick Bicât pd Hubert Pouillé ed Leslie Healey

☆ Brendan Fraser, Ashley Judd, Viggo Mortensen, Loren Dean, Grace Zabriskie, Lou Myers, Kate Harper

'Looks and sounds like a B-movie with symbolic pretensions.' – *Derek Malcolm, Guardian*

The Passion of Joan of Arc ****

France 1928 110m bw silent
Société Générale des Films

original title: La Passion de Jeanne d'Arc

On her last day on Earth, Joan of Arc is subjected to five increasingly threatening interrogations before being burned at the stake.

Austerely moving drama, using close-ups to give intense scrutiny to Joan and her accusers, drawing in the audience to become involved in the action.

w Carl Dreyer, Joseph Delteil d Carl Dreyer ph Rudolph Maté ad Hermann Warm, Jean Hugo ed Carl Dreyer

☆ Renée Falconetti, Eugène Silvain, Maurice Schutz, Michel Simon, Antonin Artaud, Louis Ravet, André Berley, Jean d'Yid

'One of the greatest of all movies ... Falconetti's Joan may be the finest performance ever recorded on film.' – *Pauline Kael*

'Isn't worth a dollar to any commercial regular picture theatre in the US.' – *Variety*

† Lilian Gish was first considered for the role of Joan. Falconetti never made another film. After its first showing the film was cut by the French authorities and was banned by the British until 1930.

The Passionate Friends **

GB 1948 91m bw
GFD/Cineguild (Ronald Neame)

US title: *One Woman's Story*

A woman marries an older man, then meets again her young lover.

A simple and obvious dramatic situation is tricked out with flashbacks and the inimitable high style of its director to make a satisfying entertainment.

w Eric Ambler *novel* H. G. Wells d David Lean ph Guy Green m Richard Addinsell

☆ Ann Todd, Trevor Howard, Claude Rains, Betty Ann Davies, Isabel Dean, Arthur Howard, Wilfrid Hyde-White

'Mr Lean plants his clues with the certainty of a master of the detective story, and heightens their effect with a sure handling of camera and sound track.' – *The Times*

† Ronald Neame began as director, but was replaced by David Lean, his partner in Cineguild, and instead took over the role of producer from Eric Ambler. Lean replaced Marius Goring with Trevor Howard.

The Passionate Plumber

US 1932 73m bw
MGM

A woman hires a professional lover to fend off the man she really loves but thinks she shouldn't have.

Much revamped farce version of a comedy made straight in 1927 and 1942. All flopped, but this is the worst.

w Laurence E. Johnson *play* Her Cardboard Lover by Frederick Lonsdale d Edward Sedgwick

☆ Buster Keaton, Jimmy Durante, Irene Purcell, Polly Moran, Gilbert Roland, Mona Maris, Maude Eburne

'Another lay-me-down-to-sleeper for box offices.' – *Variety*

The Passionate Sentry: see *Who Goes There?*

The Passionate Stranger

GB   1956   97m   bw/Eastmancolor

British Lion/Beaconsfield (Peter Rogers, Gerald Thomas)

US title: *A Novel Affair*

A lady novelist bases a character on her virile chauffeur; he reads the book and thinks she fancies him.

Feeble comedy, half of it consisting of a dramatization of the heroine's very dull novel.

w Muriel and Sydney Box d Muriel Box ph Otto Heller m Humphrey Searle

☆ Ralph Richardson, Margaret Leighton, Carlo Justini, Patricia Dainton, Marjorie Rhodes, Thorley Walters, Frederick Piper

Passionate Summer

GB   1958   104m   Eastmancolor

Briar/Kenneth Harper

A divorced headmaster at a Jamaican school is loved by three women.

Silly melodrama with splendid backgrounds ruined by poor colour.

w Joan Henry novel *The Shadow and the Peak* by Richard Mason d Rudolph Cartier ph Ernest Steward m Angelo Lavagnino

☆ Virginia McKenna, Bill Travers, Yvonne Mitchell, Alexander Knox, Ellen Barrie, Carl Mohner

'The climactic hurricane does little to dispel the overall feeling of emotional suffocation.' – *MFB*

Passione d'Amore

Italy/France   1982   119m   Eastmancolor

Connoisseur/Rizzoli Films/Massfilm/Marceau Cocinor (Franco Committou, Gino Santarelli)

A neurotic and unattractive woman becomes infatuated with a handsome young army captain.

Turgid 19th-century melodrama.

w Ruggero Maccari, Ettore Scola novel *Fosca* by Ignio Ugo Tarchetti d Ettore Scola ph Claudio Ragona m Armando Trovagoli ad Fiorenzo Senese ed Raimondo Crociani

☆ Valeria D'Obici, Bernard Giraudeau, Jean-Louis Trintignant, Massimo Girotti, Bernard Blier, Laura Antonelli

Passport to Destiny

US   1943   65m   bw

RKO (Herman Schlom)

During the Second World War, a London charlady takes her scrubbing brush and bucket and makes her way to Berlin to assassinate Hitler, protected by her dead husband's lucky charm.

One of the silliest movies ever made, even by the standards of wartime propaganda: the risible narrative makes no sense at all, though Lanchester acts as if her life depended upon her performance.

w Val Burton, Muriel Roy Bolton d Ray McCarey ph Jack Mackenzie m Roy Webb md C. Bakaleinikoff ad Albert D'Agostino, Jack Okey ed Robert Swink

☆ Elsa Lanchester, Gordon Oliver, Lenore Aubert, Lionel Royce, Fritz Feld, Joseph Vitale, Gavin Muir, Lloyd Corrigan, Anita Bolster, Lumsden Hare

† Charles Laughton appears in a photograph as Elsa Lanchester's husband.

Passport to Fame: see *The Whole Town's Talking*

Passport to Hell

US   1932   72m   bw

Fox

A woman tainted by scandal moves from country to country and marries a German commandant in the Cameroons to avoid internment.

Reasonably lively drama which ends less well than it began.

w Bradley King, Leon Gordon, Harry Hervey d Frank Lloyd

☆ Elissa Landi, Paul Lukas, Warner Oland, Alexander Kirkland, Donald Crisp

'Not a de luxer; Broadway spotted because of the product shortage.' – *Variety*

Passport to Pimlico ****

†† GB   1949   84m   bw

Ealing (E. V. H. Emmett)

Part of a London district is discovered to belong to Burgundy, and the inhabitants find themselves free of rationing restrictions.

A cleverly detailed little comedy which inaugurated the best period of Ealing, its preoccupation with suburban man and his foibles. Not exactly satire, but great fun, and kindly with it.

w T. E. B. Clarke d Henry Cornelius ph Lionel Banes m Georges Auric

☆ Stanley Holloway, Margaret Rutherford, Basil Radford, Naunton Wayne, Hermione Baddeley, John Slater, Paul Dupuis, Jane Hylton, Raymond Huntley, Betty Warren, Barbara Murray, Sydney Tafler

'One of the most felicitous and funny films since the age of the René Clair comedies.' – C. A. Lejeune

† The film was based on a genuine news item. The Canadian government presented to the Netherlands the room in which Princess Juliana was to bear a child.

⚖ T. E. B. Clarke

Passport to Shame

GB   1959   88m   bw

United/Cory/Eros

US title: *Room 43*

A taxi driver rescues his girl from the white slave business.

Would-be seamy melodrama which just about serves its purpose.

w Patrick Alexander d Alvin Rakoff ph Jack Asher m Ken Jones

☆ Eddie Constantine, Diana Dors, Odile Versois, Herbert Lom, Brenda de Banzie, Robert Brown

Passport to Suez

US   1943   71m   bw

Columbia (Wallace MacDonald)

In Alexandria, the Lone Wolf foils Nazi spies who steal British plans that will enable them to destroy the Suez canal.

An over-complicated minor thriller, more interested in propaganda than suspense.

w John Stone story Alden Nash d André de Toth ph L. W. O'Connell md M. W. Stoloff ad Lionel Banks ed Mel Thorsen

☆ Warren William, Eric Blore, Ann Savage, Robert Stanford, Sheldon Leonard, Lloyd Bridges, Gavin Muir

† It was André de Toth's first feature in the US. According to *Fragments*, his autobiography, he was told 'the script stinks, but do the best you can'. The film had a seven-day shooting schedule and he finished it seven days late.

Passport to Treason

GB   1956   80m   bw

Mid Century/Eros

A detective traces the death of his colleague to fascists working within an alleged peace group.

Stock melodramatic situations straightforwardly presented make this a watchable support.

w Kenneth Hales, Norman Hudis d Robert S. Baker ph Monty Berman m Stanley Black

☆ Rod Cameron, Lois Maxwell, Clifford Evans, John Colicos, Ballard Berkeley

The Password Is Courage *

GB   1962   116m   bw

MGM/Andrew and Virginia Stone

In Europe during World War II, Sgt-Major Charles Coward has a career of escapes and audacious anti-Nazi exploits.

Lively, slightly over-humorous account of one man's war, well mounted and shot entirely on location.

wd Andrew L. Stone biography John Castle ph David Boulton

☆ Dirk Bogarde, Maria Perschy, Alfred Lynch, Nigel Stock, Reginald Beckwith

'The experiences are, it seems, mainly true but they do not seem so.' – *Guardian*

Past Midnight

US   1991   96m   Foto-Kem

Cinetel (Lisa M. Hansen)

A social worker begins an affair with a paroled prisoner, convicted of murdering his pregnant wife.

Utterly predictable thriller, taken at a slow pace that does nothing to disguise its deficiencies.

w Frank Norwood d Jan Eliasberg ph Robert Yeoman m Steve Barteck pd Sharon Seymour ed Christopher Rouse

☆ Rutger Hauer, Natasha Richardson, Clancy Brown, Guy Bond, Ernie Lively, Tom Wright

Pastor Hall *

GB   1940   97m   bw

Charter (John Boulting)

The story of a German village pastor shot for denouncing the Nazis. Inspired by the life of Martin Niemöller (1892–1984), who survived eight years in concentration camps.

A courageous film of its time, not very interesting dramatically or cinematically.

w Leslie Arliss, Haworth Bromley, Anna Reiner play Ernst Toller d Roy Boulting ph Max Greene

☆ Wilfrid Lawson, Nova Pilbeam, Seymour Hicks, Marius Goring, Percy Walsh, Brian Worth, Peter Cotes, Hay Petrie

'Not much meat on her, but what there is is cherce!'

Pat and Mike **

US   1952   95m   bw

MGM (Lawrence Weingarten)

A small-time sports promoter takes on a female intellectual multi-champion.

A comedy which amuses because of its star playing, but doesn't really develop. All very easy going, with guest appearances from sporting personalities.

w Ruth Gordon, Garson Kanin d George Cukor ph William Daniels m David Raksin

☆ Spencer Tracy, Katharine Hepburn, Aldo Ray, William Ching, Sammy White, Jim Backus, Phyllis Povah

'They do not, like the Lunts, give the impression of a rigid calculated effect; rather, they complement and stimulate each other.' – *MFB*

⚖ script

Pat Garrett and Billy the Kid

US   1973   106m   Metrocolor   Panavision

MGM (Gordon Carroll)

Blood-spattered version of a Western legend, with violence always to the fore, accentuated by the impossibility of listening to the dialogue because of poor direction and recording.

w Rudolph Wurlitzer d Sam Peckinpah ph John Coquillon m Bob Dylan

☆ James Coburn, Kris Kristofferson, Bob Dylan, Richard Jaeckel, Katy Jurado, Slim Pickens, Chill Wills, Jason Robards Jnr

'A sombre, intense, downbeat essay on the truth behind the legend and the legend behind the truth.' – *Sight and Sound*

'Shows what Peckinpah can do when he doesn't put his mind to it.' – *Stanley Kauffmann*

'A rash adventure in inadvertent self-parody.' – *William S. Pechter*

'Ambitious, erotic, peculiarly unrealized...' – *Pauline Kael, New Yorker*

'Laughter is contagious.'

Patch Adams

US   1998   115m   DeLuxe

Universal/Blue Wolf-Farrell/Minoff-Bungalow 78 (Barry Kemp, Mike Farrell, Marvin Minoff, Charles Newirth)

A doctor discovers that clowning promotes health, and sets up his own hospital to prove it.

Cloyingly sweet drama that is based on a true story but here bears no resemblance to any reality; it is merely an opportunity for Williams to be alternately manic and misty-eyed.

w Steve Oedekerk book *Gesundheit – Good Health Is a Laughing Matter* by Hunter Doherty Adams with Maureen Mylander d Tom Shadyac ph Phedon Papamichael m Marc Shaiman pd Linda DeScenna ed Don Zimmerman

☆ Robin Williams, Daniel London, Monica Potter, Philip Seymour Hoffman, Bob Gunton, Peter Coyote, Josef Sommer, Irma P. Hall, Frances Lee McCain, Harvey Presnell, Daniella Kuhn, Jake Bowen, Michael Jeter, Harold Gould, Richard Kiley

'A comedy that neglects the humble task of making an audience laugh in favour of the more vainglorious task of delivering a 90-minute lecture on the positive benefits laughter has for your kidneys.' – *Tom Shone, Sunday Times*

⚖ Marc Shaiman

A Patch of Blue *

US   1965   105m   bw   Panavision

MGM/Pandro S. Berman

A blind girl who lives in a slum is helped by a Negro with whom she falls in love without realizing his colour.

Polished tearjerker with racial overtones; nicely done for those who can take it.

wd Guy Green novel *Be Ready with Bells and Drums* by Elizabeth Kata ph Robert Burks m Jerry Goldsmith

☆ Sidney Poitier, Elizabeth Hartman, Shelley Winters, Wallace Ford, Ivan Dixon, Elisabeth Fraser, John Qualen

⚑ Shelley Winters

⚖ Robert Burks; Jerry Goldsmith; Elizabeth Hartman

'He wants YOU to have his baby!'

Paternity

US   1981   93m   Movielab

Paramount (Jerry Tokofsky)

A middle-aged bachelor decides to father a son via a hired mother, who will then return the child to him.

Tastelessly up-dated Hollywood romance with predictable complications. Not worth sitting through.

w Charlie Peters d David Steinberg ph Bobby Byrne m David Shire

☆ Burt Reynolds, Beverly D'Angelo, Norman Fell, Paul Dooley, Elizabeth Ashley, Lauren Hutton, Juanita Moore

Pather Panchali ****

India   1955   115m   bw

Government of West Bengal

In a small Bengal village, the son of a would-be writer grows up in poverty and tragedy before setting off with what remains of the family to seek a living in Benares.

A remarkable first film of a director now famous, showing that people are much the same though the details of their daily lives may be different. The pace may be slow but the content is mainly absorbing.

wd Satyajit Ray novels Bhibuti Bashan Bannerjee ph Subrata Mitra m Ravi Shankar

☆ Kanu Banerjee, Karuna Banerjee, Uma Das Gupta, Subir Bannerjee, Chunibala

'It has been left to the Indian cinema to give us a picture of a childhood which preserves under the shadow of experience not only its innocence but its gaiety.' – *Dilys Powell*

† The film was the first part of a trilogy and was followed by *Aparajito* (1956) and *The World of Apu* (1959).

Pathfinder **

†† Norway   1987   86m   colour

Guild/Filmkameratene/Norsk Film (John M. Jacobson)

original title: *Ofelas*

A gang of ruthless raiders capture a 16-year-old boy and force him to lead them to his village so that they may plunder it.

Based on an ancient Lapp folk-tale, this is a simple, direct, marvellously exciting adventure shot in a snow-and ice-bound landscape.

wd Nils Gaup ph Erling Thurmann-Andersen m Nils-Aslak Valkeapaa pd Harald Egede-Nissen ed Niels Pagh Andersen

☆ Mikkel Gaup, Nils Utsi, Svein Scharffenberg, Helgi Skulason, Sverre Porsanger, Svein Birger Olsen

⚖ best foreign film

Paths of Glory ****

US   1957   86m   bw

UA/Bryna (James B. Harris)

In 1916 in the French trenches, three soldiers are courtmartialled for cowardice.

Incisive melodrama chiefly depicting the corruption and incompetence of the high command; the plight of the soldiers is less interesting. The trench scenes are the most vivid ever made, and the rest is shot in genuine castles, with resultant difficulties of lighting and recording; the overall result is an overpowering piece of cinema.

w Stanley Kubrick, Calder Willingham, Jim Thompson novel Humphrey Cobb d Stanley Kubrick ph Georg Krause m Gerald Fried

☆ *Kirk Douglas, Adolphe Menjou, George Macready, Wayne Morris, Richard Anderson, Ralph Meeker, Timothy Carey*
'A bitter and biting tale, told with stunning point and nerve-racking intensity.' – *Judith Crist*
'Beautifully performed, staged, photographed, cut and scored.' – *Colin Young*

The Patient Vanishes: see *This Man Is Dangerous*

Patrick

Australia 1978 110m colour
AIFC (Anthony I. Ginnane, Richard Franklin)
▦

A new nurse discovers that an apparently comatose young man, hospitalized after killing his mother and her lover, possesses psychic powers that can kill those he dislikes.
Slick but derivative thriller, well enough done in its low-budget way but lacking suspense as well as originality.
w Everett de Roche d Richard Franklin ph Don McAlpine m Brian May ad Leslie Binns ed Edward McQueen-Mason
☆ Susan Penhaligon, Robert Helpmann, Rod Mullinar, Bruce Barry, Julia Blake, Helen Hemingway, Robert Thompson
'The film's intrinsic interest is minimal.' – *MFB*
† The US release ran for 96m.

Patrick the Great *

US 1944 88m bw
Universal (Howard Benedict)
An actor whose career is waning is jealous of his young son.
Slick teenage family comedy, virtually a one-man show for O'Connor.
w Jane Hall, Bertram Millhauser, Dorothy Bennett, Frederick Kohner, Ralph Block d Frank Ryan ph Frank Redman m Hans Salter
☆ Donald O'Connor, Donald Cook, Peggy Ryan, Frances Dee, Eve Arden, Thomas Gomez, Gavin Muir, Andrew Tombes

The Patriot **

US 1928 110m bw silent
Paramount (Ernst Lubitsch)
Mad Czar Paul I is assassinated by his chief adviser for the good of the state.
Historical melodrama with a good many comedy touches: the director makes the most of both aspects, but they don't in the end hang together despite bravura acting.
w Hans Kraly novel Alfred Neumann d Ernst Lubitsch ph Bert Glennon ad Hans Dreier
☆ Emil Jannings, Lewis Stone, Florence Vidor, Neil Hamilton
'I believe this picture the most suggestive we ever ran. Just another reason why we need censorship. Small-town exhibitors need clean pictures.' – *Ohio exhibitor's report in Motion Picture Herald*
🏆 Hans Kraly
☆ best picture; Ernst Lubitsch; Lewis Stone; Hans Dreier

The Patriot

West Germany 1979 120m bw/colour
The Other Cinema/Kairos Film/ZDF (Alexander Kluge)
original title: *Die Patriotin*
A schoolteacher looks for new ways of presenting the history of Germany.
Intellectually austere examination of Germany's past and future, using newsreels, commentary and documentary footage; as cinema it is inert and condescending.
wd Alexander Kluge ph Thomas Mauch, Jörg Schmidt-Reitwein, Werner Lring, Gunther Hörmann ed Beate Mainka-Jellinghaus
☆ Hannelore Hoger, Alfred Edel, Alexander von Eschwege, Hans Heckel, Beate Holle, Curt Jürgens, Dieter Mainka, Willi Münch

The Patriot

US 1986 88m Foto-Kem
Crown International/Patriot (Michael Bennett)
A former commando, now a diver on oil rigs, rejoins the navy to track down terrorists who have stolen some nuclear warheads.
Dull and jingoistic action movie which is always predictable, and also clumsy and contrived.

w Andy Ruben, Katt Shea Ruben d Frank Harris ph Frank Harris m Jay Ferguson ad Brad Einhorn ed Richard E. Westover
☆ Gregg Henry, Simone Griffeth, Michael J. Pollard, Jeff Conaway, Stack Pierce, Leslie Nielsen

'Not for honour. Not for country. For his wife and child.'

Patriot Games

US 1992 117m Technicolor Panavision
UIP/Paramount (Mace Neufeld, Robert Rehme)
▦ 🎦 ⊙ ⊘ 🎧
In London, a former CIA agent shoots an IRA terrorist in a street battle and becomes a target for the organization's revenge on his return to the States.
Muddled and melodramatic, it relies on nationalistic clichés and violent set-pieces rather than narrative coherence; it is certainly not for posterity.
w W. Peter Iliff, Donald Stewart, Steven Zaillian novel Tom Clancy d Phillip Noyce ph Donald McAlpine m James Horner pd Joseph Nemec III ed Neil Travis, William Hoy
☆ Harrison Ford, Anne Archer, Patrick Bergin, Sean Bean, Thora Birch, James Fox, Samuel L. Jackson, Polly Walker, J. E. Freeman, James Earl Jones, Richard Harris, Hugh Fraser, David Threlfall, Alun Armstrong
'A star turn and smart action sequences enliven an otherwise abstract film.' – *Time*
'It flounders from one absurdity to another, with results that are hilarious when they aren't insulting.' – *Adam Mars-Jones, Independent*
'Mindless, morally repugnant and ineptly directed to boot.' – *Variety*

El Patrullero: see *Highway Patrolman*

The Patsy *

US 1928 80m bw silent
MGM (Irving Thalberg)
GB title: *The Politic Flapper*
Tired of being taken for granted, a girl puts on a surprising show for her family.
Amusing comedy which, in sound, might have made Miss Davies a bigger star than she ever became.
w Agnes Christine Johnston play Barry Connors d King Vidor
☆ Marion Davies, Marie Dressler, Lawrence Gray, Del Henderson, Jane Winton
'Marion Davies is in my opinion Filmland's Funniest Female, the only one I would mention in the same breath as Charlie Chaplin.' – *A. P. Herbert, Punch*

The Patsy *

US 1964 101m Technicolor
Paramount/Jerry Lewis (E. J. Glucksman)
▦ 🎦 ⊙
Hollywood executives try to mould a bellboy to replace a deceased comedian.
A few mildly funny scenes scarcely atone for a long raucous comedy in which the star upstages his betters.
wd Jerry Lewis ph Wallace Kelley m David Raksin
☆ Jerry Lewis, Everett Sloane, Peter Lorre, John Carradine, Phil Harris, Hans Conried, Ina Balin

'Inside the skyscraper jungle! Ruthless men and ambitious women clawing for control of a billion-dollar empire!'

Patterns ***

US 1956 88m bw
UA/Jed Harris, Michael Myerberg
▦
GB title: *Patterns of Power*
The tough boss of a New York corporation forces a showdown between a young executive and the older ineffectual man who he hopes will resign.
Tense little boardroom melodrama with domestic asides, one of the best of the filmed TV plays of the mid-fifties.
w Rod Serling play Rod Serling d Fielder Cook ph Boris Kaufman
☆ Van Heflin, Everett Sloane, Ed Begley, Beatrice Straight, Elizabeth Wilson

Patterns of Power: see *Patterns*

Patti Rocks *

US 1987 87m colour
Premier/FilmDallas (Gwen Field, Gregory M. Cummins)
▦
A married man takes an old, but estranged, friend on a long car ride to the home of his pregnant girlfriend.
Low-budget movie concentrating on character development, though the likelihood of the slobbish male and the sensitive woman ever being attracted to one another seems remote.
w David Burton Morris, Chris Mulkey, John Jenkins, Karen Landry d David Burton Morris ph Gregory M. Cummins m Doug Maynard ad Charlotte Whitaker ed Gregory M. Cummins
☆ Chris Mulkey, John Jenkins, Karen Landry, David L. Turk, Stephen Yoakam

'Nobody ever won a war by dying for his country. He won it by making the other poor dumb bastard die for his country!'

Patton ***

US 1969 171m DeLuxe Dimension 150
TCF (Frank McCarthy)
▦ 🎦 ⊙ 🎧
GB title: *Patton – Lust for Glory*
World War II adventures of an aggressive American general.
Brilliantly handled wartime character study which is also a spectacle and tries too hard to have it both ways, but as a piece of film-making is hard to beat.
w Francis Ford Coppola, Edmund H. North d Franklin Schaffner ph Fred Koenekamp m Jerry Goldsmith ad Urie McCleary, Gil Parrondo ed Hugh S. Fowler
☆ George C. Scott, Karl Malden, Michael Bates, Stephen Young, Michael Strong, Frank Latimore
'Here is an actor so totally immersed in his part that he almost makes you believe he is the man himself.' – *John Gillett*
🏆 best picture; script; Franklin Schaffner; George C. Scott; art direction; editing; sound (Douglas Williams, Don Bassman)
☆ Fred Koenekamp; Jerry Goldsmith; special visual effects

Patton – Lust for Glory: see *Patton*

Patty Hearst *

US/GB 1988 104m DeLuxe
Entertainment/Atlantic Entertainment/Zenith (Marvin Worth)
🎦 ⊙ 🎧
After being kidnapped and imprisoned by a revolutionary group, a wealthy, privileged teenager joins in their terrorist activities.
Based on fact, though impressionistic in approach, it concerns itself, not always successfully, with questions of identity and personal responsibility.
w Nicholas Kazan book Every Secret Thing by Patricia Campbell Hearst with Alvin Moscow d Paul Schrader ph Bojan Bazelli, Stuart Barbee m Scott Johnson pd Jane Musky ed Michael R. Miller
☆ Natasha Richardson, William Forsythe, Ving Rhames, Frances Fisher, Jodi Long, Olivia Barash, Dana Delany, Marek Johnson, Kitty Swink, Peter Kowanko

Paula: see *Framed (1947)*

Paula

US 1952 80m bw
Columbia (Buddy Adler)
GB title: *The Silent Voice*
A barren wife causes a boy's deafness in an accident; she cures and adopts him.
Adequate woman's picture, a vehicle for a star and a luxuriant wardrobe.
w James Poe, William Sackheim d Rudolph Maté ph Charles Lawton Jnr m George Duning
☆ Loretta Young, Kent Smith, Alexander Knox, Tommy Rettig

Paulie

🏃 US 1998 91m Technicolor
DreamWorks/Mutual Film (Mark Gordon, Gary Levinsohn, Allison Lyon Segan)
▦ 🎦 ⊙
A wisecracking parrot explains to a cleaner how he came to be shut in the basement of an LA animal-study institute.

Intermittently enjoyable movie, though its style may not suit the kids for whom it is presumably intended.
w Laurie Craig d John Roberts ph Tony Pierce-Roberts m John Debney pd Dennis Washington ed Bruce Cannon sp animatronics: Stan Winston
☆ Gena Rowlands, Tony Shalhoub, Cheech Marin, Bruce Davison, Jay Mohr, Trini Alvarado, Buddy Hackett, Hallie Kate Eisenberg, Matt Craven
'The script, intent on fable status, cannot stop wading into territory and language unsuitable for toddlers.' – *Geoff Brown, The Times*

Pauline at the Beach **

France 1983 94m colour
Gala/Les Films Du Losange/Les Films Ariane (Margaret Menegoz)
▦ 🎦 ⊙
original title: *Pauline à la Plage*
A young girl observes her older cousin's disastrous holiday romances.
Delicately witty, eminently civilized entertainment.
wd Eric Rohmer ph Nestor Almendros m Jean-Louis Valero ed Cécile Decugis
☆ Arielle Dombasle, Amanda Langlet, Pascal Greggory, Féodor Atkine, Simon de la Brosse, Rosette

Paura e Amore: see *Three Sisters*

Paura nella Città dei Morti Viventi: see *City of The Living Dead*

The Pawnbroker **

US 1965 114m bw
Landau-Unger (Worthington Miner)
▦ 🎦 ⊙
A Jew in slummy New York is haunted by his experiences in Nazi prison camps.
Engrossing, somewhat over-melodramatic character study, generally well done.
w David Friedkin, Morton Fine novel Edward Lewis Wallant d Sidney Lumet ph Boris Kaufman m Quincy Jones
☆ Rod Steiger, Brock Peters, Geraldine Fitzgerald, Jaime Sanchez, Thelma Oliver, Juano Hernandez
'Might have been a great film had the director been able to restrain his dual tendency towards artiness and towards slickness.' – *Judith Crist*
'The film is trite, and you can see the big pushes for powerful effects, yet it isn't negligible.' – *Pauline Kael*
🏆 Rod Steiger
🏆 Rod Steiger

Paws *

🏃 GB/Australia 1997 84m Atlab
Polygram/AFFC/Latent Image/NSWFTO (Andrena Finlay, Vicki Watson)
A Jack Russell terrier with the power of speech leads his new-found family to hidden wealth.
Pleasant, tail-wagging family film that is eager to please.
w Harry Crips d Karl Zwicky ph Geoff Burton m Mario Millo pd Stephen Jones-Evans ed Nicholas Holmes sp D-Film Services
☆ Billy Connolly, Nathan Cavaleri, Emile Francois, Jon Petruzzi, Caroline Gillmer, Rachel Blake, Sandy Gore, Norman Kaye
'It's really quite lovable, not to mention fully housebroken of anything that might disturb younger viewers.' – *Leslie Felperin, Sight and Sound*

Pay or Die! *

US 1960 109m bw
Allied Artists (Richard Wilson)
▦
In 1906, a New York Italian police detective forms a special squad to combat the Black Hand.
Tough, convincing period melodrama.
w Richard Wilson, Bertram Millhauser d Richard Wilson ph Lucien Ballard m David Raksin ad Fernando Carrere
☆ Ernest Borgnine, Alan Austin, Zohra Lampert, Robert F. Simon, Renata Vanni

'Get Ready To Root For The Bad Guy.'

Payback

US 1999 101m DeLuxe
Paramount/Icon (Bruce Davey)
▦ 🎦 ⊙ 🎧
Betrayed by his fellow crooks, a robber decides to get his revenge and his share of the loot.

🏃 film suitable for family viewing 🎦 VHS video-cassette for the British PAL system 🎬 VHS video-cassette for the British PAL system in wide screen-format ♢ Video cassette in a computer-colourised version ▦ American NTSC video-cassette ⊙ Laser disc

Ugly, brutish thriller with drawn-out scenes of gratuitous violence.

w Brian Helgeland, Terry Hayes *story* The Hunter by Richard Stark *d* Brian Helgeland *ph* Ericson Core *m* Chris Boardman *pd* Richard Hoover *ed* Kevin Stitt

☆ Mel Gibson, Gregg Henry, Maria Bello, Deborah Kara Unger, David Paymer, Bill Duke, Jack Conley, William Devane, Kris Kristofferson, John Glover, Lucy Alexis Liu

'A passable, intermittently enjoyable entertainment.' – *Variety*

'What one word might best describe *Payback*. How about "loathsome"?' – *Stephen Holden, New York Times*

† John Boorman's 1967 *Point Blank* (qv) is based on the same novel.

†† Gibson, whose company produced the movie, had a quarter of it remade by an unnamed director because he thought Helgeland's version lacked impact. In order to achieve its dark look, an image of the film in black and white was overlaid on the colour print.

Payday
US 1972 103m colour
Cinerama/Pumice/Fantasy (Ralph J. Gleason)
An over-age pop singer has personal problems which erupt into violence.
Well made, dislikeable melodrama.
w Don Carpenter *d* Daryl Duke *ph* Richard C. Glouner *m* Ed Bogas
☆ Rip Torn, Ahna Capri, Elayne Heilveil, Michael C. Gwynne
'Explores the Nashville-centered world of country with an easy authenticity which makes this nothing like a repetition of what has been before.' – *Charles Champlin*

Paydirt: see There Goes the Neighborhood

Paying the Penalty: see Underworld

Payment Deferred *
US 1932 75m bw
MGM (Irving Thalberg)
A man desperate for money poisons his wealthy nephew.
Watchable photographed play.
w Ernest Vajda, Claudine West *play* Jeffrey Dell *d* Lothar Mendes *ph* Merritt Gerstad
☆ Charles Laughton, Maureen O'Sullivan, Ray Milland, Dorothy Peterson, Verree Teasdale, Billy Bevan, Halliwell Hobbes
'In spite of its excellence, it will probably prove indifferent box office.' – *Variety*

Payment on Demand *
US 1951 90m bw
RKO/Jack H. Skirball
A happy wife and mother is appalled when her husband asks for a divorce.
A star suffers her way through luxury to a happy ending; good enough stuff for its intended audience.
w Bruce Manning, Curtis Bernhardt *d* Curtis Bernhardt *ph* Leo Tover *m* Victor Young
☆ Bette Davis, Barry Sullivan, Jane Cowl, Kent Taylor, Betty Lynn, John Sutton, Frances Dee, Otto Kruger
'An absolutely typical Joan Crawford picture except that Bette Davis happens to be in the Joan Crawford part.' – *Richard Mallett, Punch*

The Payoff
US 1943 74m bw
PRC/Jack Schwarz
A star reporter nabs the killer of a prosecuting attorney.
A fading star in a role he had played several times before.
w Edward Dein *d* Arthur Dreifuss
☆ Lee Tracy, Tom Brown, Tina Thayer, Evelyn Brent, Jack La Rue

Payroll *
GB 1961 105m bw
Anglo Amalgamated/Lynx (Norman Priggen)
Small-time crooks snatch £100,000, but after the getaway things begin to go wrong.
Tense, vivid, thoroughly predictable Rififi-style thriller, handled with solid professionalism.
w George Baxt *novel* Derek Bickerton *d* Sidney Hayers *ph* Ernest Steward *m* Reg Owen

☆ Michael Craig, Billie Whitelaw, Françoise Prévost, Kenneth Griffith, William Lucas, Tom Bell, Barry Keegan, Joan Rice, Glyn Houston

PCU
US 1994 95m DeLuxe
TVF (Paul Schiff)
A freshman at Port Chester University becomes involved with a group of students fighting the pervading atmosphere of political correctness and sensitivity to others.
Crude and boisterous romp for the young and unstudious.
w Adam Leff, Zak Penn *d* Hart Bochner *ph* Reynaldo Villalobos *m* Steve Vai *pd* Steven Jordan *ed* Nicholas C. Smith
☆ Jeremy Piven, Chris Young, David Spade, Megan Ward, Sarah Trigger, Jon Favreau, Jake Busey, Jessica Walter

'In the fall of 1997, every nuclear device in the world will be accounted for ... Except one.'
The Peacemaker
US 1997 123m Technicolor 'Scope
DreamWorks (Walter Parkes, Branko Lustig)
An American scientist and a military agent reluctantly team up to track down a stolen nuclear warhead in New York.
Frantic attempt at a topical thriller, set against the background of Russian gangsters and Bosnian unrest; it fails to deliver.
w Michael Schiffer *article* Leslie Cockburn, Andrew Cockburn *d* Mimi Leder *ph* Dietrich Lohmann *m* Hans Zimmer *pd* Leslie Dilley *ed* David Rosenbloom
☆ George Clooney, Nicole Kidman, Marcel Iures, Alexander Baluev, Rene Medvesek, Gary Werntz, Randall Batinkoff, Jim Haynie, Armin Mueller-Stahl
'Another machine-tooled slab of Hollywood brutality.' – *Sunday Times*
'Standard action-film stuff.' – *Time*
† It was the first release from the new studio DreamWorks SKG (initials which stand for Steven Spielberg, Jeffrey Katzenberg and David Geffen).

Peach O'Reno
US 1931 66m bw
RKO-Pathé
Two incompetent lawyers work on a divorce case.
Burlesque-style comedy with cabaret asides. Thin stuff.
w Ralph Spence, Tim Whelan *d* William Seiter
☆ Bert Wheeler, Robert Woolsey, Dorothy Lee, Joseph Cawthorn, Cora Witherspoon, Zelma O'Neal
'Less than average; low comedy laughs for the minor spots.' – *Variety*

The Pearl *
US/Mexico 1948 72m bw
RKO/Oscar Dancigers
In a remote Mexican village, a simple shell diver finds a pearl of great price, but finds his life complicated as a result.
A fable which at the time seemed to have considerable quality, being the first Mexican film to receive international distribution.
w John Steinbeck, Emilio Fernandez, Jack Wagner *d* Emilio Fernandez *ph* Gabriel Figueroa *m* Antonio Diaz Conde
☆ Pedro Armendariz, Maria Elena Marques, Alfonso Bedoya

'The Master Minds Tackle The Master Crimes!'
The Pearl of Death **
US 1944 67m bw
Universal (Howard S. Benedict)
When a valuable pearl is stolen, Sherlock Holmes has only his own cleverness to blame; but he redeems himself by trapping 'The Creeper'.
An amusing picturization of Doyle's The Six Napoleons, with the addition of a horror figure; it plays very well and is certainly among the best of this series.
w Bertram Millhauser *d* Roy William Neill *ph* Virgil Miller *m* Paul Sawtell
☆ Basil Rathbone, Nigel Bruce, Dennis Hoey, Miles Mander, Rondo Hatton, Evelyn Ankers

Peau d'Espion: see To Commit A Murder

La Peau Douce: see Silken Skin

The Pebble and the Penguin
US 1995 74m Technicolor
Warner/Don Bluth Ireland (Russell Boland)
A shy penguin searches for the perfect pebble to give to his intended.
Unadventurous animated film that lacks a captivating story, substituting a string of unconnected episodes of varying interest.
w Rachel Koretsky, Steve Whitestone *d* Don Bluth *m* Mark Watters *m/ly* Barry Manilow, Bruce Sussman
☆ Featuring the voices of: Martin Short, Annie Golden, Tim Curry, James Belushi, Shani Wallis, Scott Bullock
'A sweet, enjoyable romantic tale more likely to succeed as an afternoon diversion on home video than on the big screen.' – *Variety*

Pecker
US 1998 87m Technicolor
Fine Line/Polar Entertainment (John Fiedler, Mark Tarlov)
A Baltimore amateur photographer, who takes snapshots of his friends, is fêted by the New York art establishment, while the subjects of his work are humiliated.
Blandly camp satire on big-city tastes and people, though what it offers in its place is even less enticing.
wd John Waters *ph* Robert Stevens *m* Stewart Copeland *pd* Vincent Peranio *ed* Janice Hampton
☆ Edward Furlong, Christina Ricci, Lili Taylor, Mary Kay Place, Martha Plimpton, Brendan Sexton III, Mark Joy, Mink Stole, Lili Taylor
'A pleasant but ephemeral spoof that may disappoint Waters' hardcore fans while not recruiting many new devotees.' – *Emanuel Levy, Variety*

Peck's Bad Boy
US 1934 70m bw
Fox/Sol Lesser
Adventures of a well-intentioned but accident-prone boy in a midwestern town.
Old-fashioned American juvenile classic, modestly well done.
w Bernard Schubert, Marguerite Roberts *story* G. W. Peck *d* Edward Cline
☆ Jackie Cooper, Jackie Searl, Dorothy Peterson, Thomas Meighan
† Previously made in 1921 with Jackie Coogan. Cline also directed a sequel, *Peck's Bad Boy with the Circus* starring Tommy Kelly, in 1938.

Peeper
US 1975 87m DeLuxe Panavision
TCF/Chartoff-Winkler (Ron Buck)
In 1947 Los Angeles, a poor British private eye gets into trouble when he seeks a man's lost daughter.
Semi-spoofing Chandleresque caper which is never quite funny or quite thrilling enough.
w D. M. Richter *novel* Deadfall by Keith Laumer *d* Peter Hyams *ph* Earl Rath *m* Richard Clements
☆ Michael Caine, Natalie Wood, Kitty Winn, Thayer David, Liam Dunn
'Flimsy whimsy.' – *Variety*

'More horrible than horror! More terrible than terror!'
Peeping Tom *
GB 1959 109m Eastmancolor
Anglo Amalgamated/Michael Powell
A film studio focus puller is obsessed by the lust to murder beautiful women and photograph the fear on their faces.
Thoroughly disagreeable suspenser, a kind of compendium of the bad taste the director showed in flashes during his career.
w Leo Marks *d* Michael Powell *ph* Otto Heller *m* Brian Easdale
☆ Carl Boehm, Moira Shearer, Anna Massey, Maxine Audley, Esmond Knight, Michael Goodliffe, Shirley Anne Field, Jack Watson
'Perhaps one would not be so disagreeably affected by this exercise in the lower regions of the psychopathic were it handled in a more bluntly debased fashion.' – *Dilys Powell*

'Of enormous and deserved reputation.' – *Time Out, 1982*

Pee-wee's Big Adventure *
US 1985 92m colour
Mainline/Aspen Film Society/Robert Shapiro
Pee-wee Herman loses his red bicycle and goes looking for it.
Starring an American TV comedian who acts like a small child, this offbeat, episodic comedy has some amusing moments.
w Phil Hartman, Paul Reubens, Michael Varhol *d* Tim Burton *ph* Victor J. Kemper *m* Danny Elfman *pd* David L. Snyder *ed* Billy Weber
☆ Paul Reubens, Elizabeth Daily, Mark Holton, Diane Salinger, Judd Omen, Jon Harris, Carmen Filpi, Tony Bill, James Brolin, Morgan Fairchild
'This slapstick fantasy has the bouncing-along inventiveness of a good cartoon.' – *Pauline Kael, New Yorker*

Peg o' My Heart
US 1933 86m bw
MGM
To the concern of his family, an English nobleman falls for an Irish colleen.
Half-hearted version of a famous lavender-tinted stage hit previously filmed in the twenties with its original star Laurette Taylor; but by 1933 its time was past.
w Frances Marion *play* J. Hartley Manners *d* Robert Z. Leonard
☆ Marion Davies, Onslow Stevens, Alan Mowbray, Robert Greig, Irene Browne, J. Farrell MacDonald, Juliette Compton
'Just an 86-minute Irish monologue ... undeservedly flattered by an almost perfect production.' – *Variety*

Peg of Old Drury *
GB 1935 76m bw
British and Dominions/Herbert Wilcox
The romance of 18th-century actress Peg Woffington with David Garrick.
Primitive but vivacious historical romp with adequate star performances.
w Miles Malleson *play* Masks and Faces by Charles Reade, Tom Taylor *d* Herbert Wilcox *ph* F. A. Young
☆ Anna Neagle, Cedric Hardwicke, Jack Hawkins, Margaretta Scott, Hay Petrie
'I never tired of Miss Neagle's physical appearance, which was as pretty as a Chelsea figure. The whole film indeed is very pretty, with the sentiment neatly handled. But prettiness is a quality one wants, if at all, in small quantities.' – *Graham Greene, The Spectator*

Peggy Sue Got Married **
US 1986 104m DeLuxe
Tri-Star/Rastar (Paul R. Gurian)
A disillusioned woman goes to her 25th high school reunion and finds herself reliving her young life.
It plays like an extended Twilight Zone, but with plenty of interesting details to back up an excellent leading performance.
w Jerry Leichtling, Arlene Sarner *d* Francis Coppola *ph* Jordan Cronenweth *m* John Barry *pd* Dean Tavoularis *ed* Barry Malkin
☆ Kathleen Turner, Nicolas Cage, Barry Miller, Catherine Hicks, Maureen O'Sullivan, Leon Ames, Helen Hunt, Don Murray, Barbara Harris, Kevin J. O'Connor
'Provocative, well acted, stylish and uneven.' – *Variety*
⅄ Jordan Cronenweth; Theodora Van Runkle (costumes); Kathleen Turner

Peking Express
US 1951 90m bw
Paramount/Hal B. Wallis
In communist China, an assortment of people are aboard a train which is diverted by outlaws.
Pot-boiling remake of Shanghai Express (qv); an adequate time-passer.
w John Meredyth Lucas *d* William Dieterle *ph* Charles Lang *m* Dimitri Tiomkin
☆ Joseph Cotten, Corinne Calvet, Edmund Gwenn, Marvin Miller
'Lacks flavour or distinction.' – *Leonard Maltin*

The Peking Medallion

Italy/Germany/France 1966 87m Technicolor
CCC/Criterion/Senior (Artur Brauner)
original title: Il Sigillo di Pechino
US title: The Corrupt Ones
A freelance photographer searches for buried treasure while fighting off the attentions of two rival gangs.
Routine chase thriller with a cast that tries to get the most out of a pedestrian script.
w Brian Clemens story Ladislas Fodor d James Hill ph Heinz Pehlke m Georges Garvarentz ad Hans-Jürgen Kiebach ed Alfred Srp
☆ Robert Stack, Elke Sommer, Nancy Kwan, Christian Marquand, Werner Peters, Maurizio Arena, Dean Heyde, Marisa Merlini

Two Supreme Court Justices have been assassinated. One lone law student has stumbled upon the truth. An investigative journalist wants her story. Everyone else wants her dead.'

The Pelican Brief

US 1993 141m Technicolor
Warner (Alan J. Pakula, Pieter Jan Brugge)
▦ ▤ ◿ ◉ ◠
A law student is stalked by hitmen after she speculates on the reasons behind the killings of two leading judges.
Mundane chase movie, a paranoid thriller that rarely rings true and mainly consists of Julia Roberts being chased but not caught. Her fans may enjoy it.
wd Alan J. Pakula novel John Grisham ph Stephen Goldblatt m James Horner pd Philip Rosenberg ed Tom Rolf, Trudy Ship
☆ Julia Roberts, Denzel Washington, Sam Shepard, John Heard, Tony Goldwyn, James B. Sikking, William Atherton, Robert Culp, Stanley Tucci, Hume Cronyn, John Lithgow
'This crackling thriller will have a long, prosperous box-office flight.' – Variety
'Pakula allows everyone to be briefly implicated, with menace poured on by the gallon, but fails to raise a spark of interest.' – Lizzie Francke, Sight and Sound

Pelle Erobreren: see Pelle the Conqueror

Pelle the Conqueror ****

Denmark/Sweden 1987 150m colour
Curzon/Danish Film Institute/Swedish Film Institute/Svensk Filmindustri/Per Holst
▦ ▤ ◿ ◠
original title: Pelle Erobreren
In the early 1900s, the young son of a Swedish immigrant worker enduring hardship on a Danish farm learns to be self-sufficient.
Winner of the Palme D'Or at the Cannes Film Festival in 1988, it matches an epic scope with domestic detail in a finely acted, beautifully photographed movie.
wd Bille August novel Martin Andersen Nexö ph Jörgen Persson m Stefan Nilsson pd Anna Asp ed Janus Billeskov Jansen
☆ Max von Sydow, Pelle Hvenegaard, Erik Paaske, Kristina Tornqvist, Morten Jørgensen, Alex Strøbye, Astrid Villaume, Björn Granath
† It was released on video in two versions, one subtitled, one dubbed by American actors.
♟ best foreign film
& Max von Sydow

The Penalty

US 1941 81m bw
MGM (Jack Chertok)
The son of a gangster is regenerated by farm life and turns against his father.
Antediluvian sweetness and light which wastes a good cast.
w Harry Ruskin, John C. Higgins d Harold S. Bucquet ph Harold Rosson m David Snell
☆ Edward Arnold, Lionel Barrymore, Marsha Hunt, Robert Sterling, Gene Reynolds

Penalty of Fame: see Okay America

Pendulum *

US 1969 102m Technicolor
Columbia/Pendulum (Stanley Niss)
▤ ◿
A convicted murderer and rapist is freed on appeal and kills the wife of the detective who arrested him.
Heavy-going police melodrama, efficient but not very interesting.
w Stanley Niss d George Schaefer ph Lionel Lindon m Walter Scharf

☆ George Peppard, Jean Seberg, Richard Kiley, Charles McGraw, Robert F. Lyons, Madeleine Sherwood

Penelope

US 1966 98m Metrocolor Panavision
MGM/Euterpe (Joe Pasternak, Arthur Loew Jnr)
The wife of a bank vice-president is a bank robber and kleptomaniac.
Would-be cute comedy which only sickens one for wasting its talent.
w George Wells novel E. V. Cunningham d Arthur Hiller ph Harry Stradling m Johnny Williams
☆ Natalie Wood, Ian Bannen, Dick Shawn, Peter Falk, Jonathan Winters, Lila Kedrova, Lou Jacobi, Norma Crane, Arthur Malet, Jerome Cowan

Penguin Pool Murder

US 1932 70m bw
RKO (Kenneth Macgowan)
A spinster schoolteacher helps a police inspector solve the murder of a man found floating in the penguin pool.
Enjoyable minor mystery with the emphasis on the tart relationship between teacher and cop.
w Willis Goldbeck novel Stuart Palmer story Lowell Brentano d George Archinbaud ph Henry Gerrard m Max Steiner ed Jack Kitchin
☆ Edna May Oliver, James Gleason, Robert Armstrong, Mae Clarke, Donald Cook, Edgar Kennedy, Clarence H. Wilson, James Donlan, Gustav von Seyffertitz
† It was the first of three films featuring Edna Mae Oliver as Hildegarde Withers, and was followed by Murder on the Blackboard and Murder on a Honeymoon (qqv).

Penitentiary

US 1938 78m bw
Columbia
▤
A district attorney becomes prison warden, and his daughter falls for a convict.
Scene-for-scene remake of The Criminal Code (qv) but considerably less dynamic.
w Fred Niblo Jnr, Seton I. Miller play Martin Flavin d John Brahm
☆ Walter Connolly, John Howard, Jean Parker, Robert Barrat, Marc Lawrence, Arthur Hohl, Paul Fix

Penn of Pennsylvania

GB 1941 79m bw
British National (Richard Vernon)
▤
US title: The Courageous Mr Penn
Persecuted Quakers leave England for America.
Stodgily fictionalized history.
w Anatole de Grunwald book William Penn by C. E. Vulliamy d Lance Comfort ph Ernest Palmer
☆ Clifford Evans, Deborah Kerr, Denis Arundell, Aubrey Mallalieu, Henry Oscar, Max Adrian

Pennies from Heaven

US 1936 81m bw
Columbia (Emanuel Cohen)
▤
A wanderer protects a homeless little girl from the truant officer.
Mild star musical, lucky enough to have a hit title song.
w Jo Swerling novel The Peacock Feather by Katharine Leslie Moore story William Rankin d Norman Z. McLeod ph Robert Pittack m Arthur Johnston
☆ Bing Crosby, Edith Fellows, Madge Evans, Donald Meek, Louis Armstrong and his band
& song 'Pennies from Heaven' (mArthur Johnson, lySidney Mitchell)

Pennies from Heaven △

US 1981 108m Metrocolor
MGM/Hera (Nora Kaye, Herbert Ross)
▦ ▤ ◿
In 1934 Chicago, a sheet music salesman consoles himself for his drab and tragic life by fantasies induced by his songs.
The essence of Dennis Potter's British TV serial was hard enough to get at; transposed to America it becomes unattractive nonsense, and the song sequences are not even well staged despite the enormous expense.

w Dennis Potter d Herbert Ross ph Gordon Willis md Marvin Hamlisch, Billy May pd Ken Adam
☆ Steve Martin, Bernadette Peters, Christopher Walken, Jessica Harper, John McMartin
'All flash and style and no heart.' – Roger Ebert
& Dennis Potter

Penny Gold

GB 1973 90m colour
Fanfare (George H. Brown)
Police investigate the murder of a young woman involved in dealing in rare stamps.
Direly unimaginative thriller, all dull talk and no action; any audience is likely to have anticipated its final twist within the first ten minutes.
w David Osborn, Liz Charles-Williams d Jack Cardiff ph Ken Hodges m John Scott ad Bert Davey ed John Trumper
☆ James Booth, Francesca Annis, Nicky Henson, Joss Ackland, Richard Heffer, Sue Lloyd, Joseph O'Conor, Una Stubbs, Penelope Keith

Penny Paradise

GB 1938 72m bw
ATP (Basil Dean)
A tugboat captain thinks he has won the football pools; but the coupon wasn't posted.
An old, old story, put over with modest effectiveness.
w Tommy Thompson, W. L. Meade, Thomas Browne d Carol Reed ph Ronald Neame, Gordon Dines m/ly Harry Parr-Davies, Harry O'Donovan ad Wilfrid Shingleton ed Ernest Aldridge
☆ Edmund Gwenn, Betty Driver, Jimmy O'Dea, Maire O'Neill, Jack Livesey

Penny Points to Paradise

GB 1951 77m bw
Advance/Adelphi
A pools winner takes cash but nearly loses it to a forger.
Abysmally made comedy, only interesting as an early teaming of the Goons.
w John Ormonde d Tony Young ph Bert Mason m Spike Milligan
☆ Harry Secombe, Peter Sellers, Spike Milligan, Alfred Marks, Bill Kerr, Freddie Frinton, Paddie O'Neil

The Penny Pool

GB 1937 85m bw
Mancunian (John Blakeley)
A store foreman tries to cheat one of the workers out of her football pool winnings.
Threadbare comedy, subtitled 'A Merry Musical Burlesque', with musical interludes that preserve the slapstick music-hall act of Duggie Wakefield, which does not wear well, and some of the lesser performers of the era, including a yodelling accordion band.
w Arthur Mertz d George Black Jnr ph James Burger m Julian Niman m/ly Arthur Mertz, Albert Stanbury ad George Ward ed B. Bayley
☆ Duggie Wakefield, Billy Nelson, Chuck O'Neil, Jack Butler, Tommy Fields, Luanne Shaw, Charles Sewell, Harry Terry, Howard Douglas

Penny Princess

GB 1952 94m Technicolor
Rank/Conquest (Frank Godwin)
A New York shopgirl inherits a tiny European state and boosts its economy by marketing a mixture of cheese and schnapps.
Thin, spoofy comedy with mild moments of fun.
wd Val Guest ph Geoffrey Unsworth m Ronald Hammer
☆ Dirk Bogarde, Yolande Donlan, A. E. Matthews, Anthony Oliver, Edwin Styles, Reginald Beckwith, Kynaston Reeves, Peter Butterworth, Laurence Naismith, Mary Clare, Desmond Walter-Ellis

Penny Serenade *

US 1941 120m bw
Columbia (Fred Guiol)
▦ ▤ ◿ ◠
Courtship, marriage and the death of two children are recollected by a woman contemplating divorce.
Well-played but uneasy film which veers suddenly and disconcertingly from light comedy into tragedy.
w Morrie Ryskind d George Stevens ph Joseph Walker m W. Franke Harling
☆ Cary Grant, Irene Dunne, Beulah Bondi, Edgar Buchanan, Ann Doran

'To make something out of very little, and that so near at hand, is one of the tests of artistry.' – Otis Ferguson
'A tear compeller showing how Cary Grant and Irene Dunne lose first their own baby and then the one they adopt. Which, as Lady Bracknell would certainly have observed, looks like carelessness.' – James Agate
& Cary Grant

Penrod and Sam

US 1937 68m bw
Warner
Exploits of a club for juvenile sleuths.
Start of a second feature series which had little to do with the original period characters but was generally well received. Later the same year came Penrod and his Twin Brother, and in 1938 Penrod's Double Trouble.
w Lillie Hayward, Hugh Cummings from the characters created by Booth Tarkington d William McGann
☆ Billy Mauch, Frank Craven, Spring Byington, Craig Reynolds, Charles Halton
'Should serve as a nucleus for swell exploitation tie-ups.' – Variety
† There had been an earlier version in 1931, starring Leon Janney; and the family turned up again in the Doris Day musicals On Moonlight Bay and By the Light of the Silvery Moon.

'The Most Challenging Sport Has Just Become The Deadliest Game.'

Pentathlon

Germany 1994 97m Foto-Kem
First Independent/Live/PFG (Martin E. Caan, Dolph Lundgren)
▦ ▤
The East German Olympic pentathlon gold medallist defects to the US, where, following the fall of the Berlin Wall, he is followed by his former trainer and a gang of neo-Nazi assassins.
Risible melodrama which swiftly runs out of ideas; you keep thinking it cannot get any worse, but it does, with David Soul cackling manfully as the villain of the piece.
w William Stadiem, Gary McDonald, Gary DeVore, Bruce Malmuth d Bruce Malmuth ph Misha Suslov m David Spear pd Jaymes Hinkle ed Richard Nord, Joseph Gutowski
☆ Dolph Lundgren, David Soul, Renee Coleman, Daniel Riordan, David Drummond, Philip Bruns, Roger E. Mosley

Penthouse *

US 1933 90m bw
MGM/Hunt Stromberg
▤ ◿
GB title: Crooks in Clover
When he outlives his usefulness to the underworld, a lawyer is framed for murder.
Sprightly murder comedy-drama which plays like a try-out for The Thin Man.
w Frances Goodrich, Albert Hackett d W. S. Van Dyke
☆ Warner Baxter, Myrna Loy, C. Henry Gordon, Nat Pendleton, Charles Butterworth, George E. Stone
'Well-sustained crime solution with smashing climax and arresting title.' – Variety

The Penthouse

GB 1967 96m Eastmancolor
Paramount/Tahiti (Harry Fine)
Illicit lovers in an unfinished block of flats are terrorized by intruders.
Thoroughly objectionable and unpleasant melodrama with no attractive characters and no attempt to explain itself.
wd Peter Collinson play The Meter Man by J. Scott Forbes ph Arthur Lavis m John Hawkesworth
☆ Suzy Kendall, Terence Morgan, Tony Beckley, Norman Rodway, Martine Beswick
'Pornography in Pinter's clothing.' – MFB

The People against O'Hara *

US 1951 102m bw
MGM (William H. Wright)
◿
An ex-alcoholic defence lawyer sacrifices himself to prove his client's innocence.
Formula drama, well made and entertainingly performed, with snatches of bright dialogue.
w John Monks Jnr novel Eleazar Lipsky d John Sturges ph John Alton m Carmen Dragon

---

☆ Spencer Tracy, Diana Lynn, Pat O'Brien, John Hodiak, James Arness, Arthur Shields, Eduardo Ciannelli, Louise Lorimer

The People Next Door

US 1970 93m DeLuxe
Avco Embassy (Herb Brodkin)

Suburban parents have trouble with their drug-addicted teenage daughter.
Hysterical melodrama with good credentials.
w J. P. Miller TV play J. P. Miller d David Greene ph Gordon Willis m Don Sebesky
☆ Eli Wallach, Julie Harris, Hal Holbrook, Cloris Leachman, Stephen McHattie, Nehemiah Persoff
'As unlovely a picture of suburban living as one is likely to see.' – *Judith Crist*

People on Sunday *

Germany 1929 72m bw silent
Filmstudio 1929
original title: *Menschen am Sonntag*
Two couples spend a day in Berlin's countryside.
Influential semi-documentary with fascinating credits.
w Billy Wilder, Curt Siodmak d Robert Siodmak, Fred Zinnemann, Edgar G. Ulmer ph Eugen Schüfftan
☆ Brigitte Borchert, Christl Ehlers, Annie Schreyer

The People that Time Forgot

♠♠ GB 1977 90m Technicolor
AIP/Amicus (John Dark)

Major McBride tries to rescue his old friend from a prehistoric island on which he disappeared in 1916.
Tepid sequel to The Land that Time Forgot: even the dinosaurs don't rise to the occasion.
w Patrick Tilley d Kevin Connor ph Alan Hume m John Scott pd Maurice Carter
☆ Patrick Wayne, Sarah Douglas, Dana Gillespie, Doug McClure, Thorley Walters, Shane Rimmer, Tony Britton

'They'll devour everything but your screams.'
The People under the Stairs *

US 1991 102m DeLuxe
UIP/Universal/Alive (Marianne Maddalena, Stuart M. Besser)

A 13-year-old boy discovers that the wealthy couple he attempts to rob have imprisoned in their cellar kidnapped youths who have become damaged mutants.
An effective horror film, or possibly a less effective allegory about the exploitation of the urban poor.
wd Wes Craven ph Sandi Sissel m Don Peake pd Bryan Jones ed James Coblentz, Tom Walls sp Image Engineering Inc.
☆ Brandon Adams, Everett McGill, Wendy Robie, A. J. Langer, Ving Rhames, Sean Whalen, Bill Cobbs, Kelly Jo Minter, Jeremy Roberts
'This revival of the plot-driven, exhausting, funny-pointed, suspense-horror picture is a welcome change.' – *Kim Newman, Sight and Sound*

The People vs. Larry Flynt ***

US 1996 130m Technicolor Panavision
Columbia TriStar/Ixtlan/Phoenix (Oliver Stone, Janet Yang, Michael Hausman)

A poor Kentucky boy grows up to be a successful publisher of porn magazines, and takes his fight to protect his business and freedom of speech to the Supreme Court.
Biopic of the publisher of Hustler that also manages to be a witty, engaging portrait of the extremes and excesses – sexual, religious, judicial and political – of modern American society.
w Scott Alexander, Larry Karaszewski d Milos Forman ph Philippe Rousselot m Thomas Newman pd Patrizia von Brandenstein ed Christopher Tellefsen
☆ Woody Harrelson, Courtney Love, Edward Norton, James Cromwell, Crispin Glover, James Carville, Brett Harrelson, Donna Hanover
'That Forman has found the raucous, satirical side of Larry Flynt's story doesn't surprise us; that he has uncovered its pathos, and something that could even be considered its patriotism, is a stunning achievement.' – *David Ansen, Newsweek*

'Makes it OK to take your brain to the movies again. Not just OK, but necessary; you'll need all the skepticism and relish for irony that you can muster.' – *Joe Morgenstern, Wall Street Journal*
'For all its virtues of writing, direction and performance, the film still leaves a brackish taste in the mouth and seems very much less than wholly satisfactory.' – *Derek Malcolm, Guardian*
† Larry Flynt himself appears as the judge who sentenced him early in his career to 25 years' imprisonment on charges of obscenity and links to organized crime.
& Milos Forman; Woody Harrelson

People Will Talk

US 1935 60m bw
Paramount
Mr and Mrs Wilton try to patch up their daughter's failing marriage.
Slight domestic comedy with popular leads.
w Herbert Fields, Sophie Kerr, F. Hugh Herbert d Al Santell
☆ Charles Ruggles, Mary Boland, Leila Hyams, Dean Jagger, Edward Brophy
'Strictly light summer fare and not solid enough to stand alone.' – *Variety*

People Will Talk **

US 1951 110m bw
TCF (Darryl F. Zanuck)

A surgeon's unorthodox psychological methods cause jealousy among his colleagues, especially when he falls in love with a pregnant patient.
Oddly entertaining jumble of melodrama, comedy, romance, speeches and a little mystery, all quite typical of its director.
wd Joseph L. Mankiewicz play Dr Praetorius by Curt Goetz ph Milton Krasner md Alfred Newman
☆ Cary Grant, Jeanne Crain, Finlay Currie, Hume Cronyn, Walter Slezak, Sidney Blackmer, Basil Ruysdael
'A picture so mature and refreshingly frank as to hold that an erring young woman might be rewarded with a wise and loving mate is most certainly a significant milestone in the moral emancipation of American films.' – *New York Times*

'The Most Fabulous Fun Show Ever On The Screen! So Hilarious! So Heartwarming! You'll Glow All Over!'
Pepe

♠♠ US 1960 195m Eastmancolor Cinemascope
Columbia/George Sidney (Jacques Gelman)
A Mexican peasant in Hollywood gets help from the stars.
Feeble and seemingly endless extravaganza in which the boring stretches far outnumber the rest, and few of the guests have anything worthwhile to do.
w Dorothy Kingsley, Claude Binyon d George Sidney ph Joe MacDonald md Johnny Green ed Viola Lawrence, Al Clark
☆ Cantinflas, Dan Dailey, Shirley Jones, Ernie Kovacs, Jay North, William Demarest, Michael Callan, Maurice Chevalier, Bing Crosby, Richard Conte, Bobby Darin, Sammy Davis Jnr, Jimmy Durante, Zsa Zsa Gabor, Judy Garland and also Hedda Hopper, Joey Bishop, Peter Lawford, Janet Leigh, Jack Lemmon, Kim Novak, André Previn, Donna Reed, Debbie Reynolds, Greer Garson, Edward G. Robinson, Cesar Romero, Frank Sinatra, Billie Burke, Tony Curtis, Dean Martin, Charles Coburn
'A joyous production crammed with delightful entertainment.' – *New York Daily News*
& Joe MacDonald; Johnny Green; song 'Faraway Part of Town' (mAndré Previn, ly Dory Langdon); editing

Pépé le Moko **

France 1936 90m bw
Paris Film

A Parisian gangster lives in the Algerian casbah where the police can't get at him; but love causes him to emerge and be shot.
Romantic melodrama modelled on the American gangster film but with a decided poetic quality all its own: the Americans promptly paid it the compliment of remaking it as the not-too-bad Algiers.
w Henri Jeanson, Roger d'Ashelbe novel Roger d'Ashelbe (Henri La Barthe) d Julien Duvivier

ph Jules Kruger m Vincent Scotto ad Jacques Krauss
☆ Jean Gabin, Mireille Ballin, Gabriel Gabrio, Lucas Gridoux
'One of the most compelling of all French films.' – *New Yorker, 1977*
'Perhaps there have been pictures as exciting on the thriller level ... but I cannot remember one which has succeeded so admirably in raising the thriller to a poetic level.' – *Graham Greene*

Pepi, Luci, Bom

Spain 1980 80m colour
Metro/Figaro (Pepon Corominas)

original title: *Pepi, Luci, Bom y otras chicas del montón*
A woman raped by a policeman takes her revenge by encouraging his wife to form a lesbian relationship with a sadistic singer.
Almodóvar's first full-length feature attempts to shock and surprise with a kitsch mix of sex, cruelty and eccentricity.
wd Pedro Almodóvar ph Paco Femenia ed Pepe Salcedo
☆ Carmen Maura, Félix Rotaeta, Olvido 'Alaska' Gara, Eva Siva, Diego Alvarez, Pedro Almodóvar
'The roots of Almodóvar's down-and-dirty, intentionally amoral and often disgusting films are abundant in *Pepi, Luci, Bom*.' – *Variety*

Perceval Le Gallois

France 1978 140m colour Panavision
Les Films du Losange/Barbet Schroeder/FR3/ARD/SSR/RAI/Gaumont (Margaret Menegoz)

A naïve Welsh youth becomes a knight at the court of King Arthur and meets the Fisher King.
This is less a film than an interesting, though not engrossing, illustrated accompaniment, against stylized backgrounds, to a long medieval poem.
wd Eric Rohmer poem Chrétien de Troyes ph Nestor Almendros m Guy Robert ad Jean-Pierre Kohut-Svelko ed Cecile Decugis
☆ Fabrice Luchini, André Dussollier, Solange Boulanger, Catherine Schroeder, Francisco Orozco, Deborah Nathan, Pascale Ogier
'Combines real people and real horses with toy castles and small, stylized trees, and the effect is just the opposite of what Rohmer could have wanted: it's cute. And it's cute for only a short time because nothing can be cute for a long time.' – *Stanley Kauffmann*

Percy

GB 1971 103m Eastmancolor
Anglo EMI/Welbeck (Betty E. Box)

After an unfortunate accident, a young man undergoes a successful penis transplant, and sets out to discover who the donor was.
Barrage of phallic jokes, some quite funny, but mostly as witless as the whole idea.
w Hugh Leonard novel Raymond Hitchcock d Ralph Thomas ph Ernest Steward m Ray Davies
☆ Hywel Bennett, Elke Sommer, Denholm Elliott, Britt Ekland, Cyd Hayman

Percy's Progress

GB 1974 101m Eastmancolor
EMI (Betty E. Box)

US title: *It's Not the Size that Counts*
A chemical causes impotence in all males except the owner of the first transplanted penis.
Percy dug deep, but this is really the bottom of the barrel.
w Sid Colin d Ralph Thomas ph Tony Imi m Tony Macauley
☆ Leigh Lawson, Elke Sommer, Denholm Elliott, Judy Geeson, Harry H. Corbett, Vincent Price, Adrienne Posta, Julie Ege, James Booth

Perdita Durango

Spain/Mexico 1997 126m colour 'Scope
Sogetel/Lolafilms/Mirador/Canal+/Imcine (Andres Vicente Gomez)

A whore teams up with a drug dealer for a life of crime and murder.
Energetic, sex-obsessed thriller that would have benefited by being much shorter; it falls short of the mythic status it aims for.

w Barry Gifford, Jorge Guerricaechevarria, David Trueba, Alex de la Iglesia novel *59 Degrees and Raining: The Story of Perdita Durango* by Barry Gifford d Alex de la Iglesia ph Flavio Martinez Labiano m Simon Boswell pd Jose Luis Arrizabalaga, Arturo Garcia ed Teresa Font
☆ Rosie Perez, Javier Bardem, Harley Cross, Aimee Graham, James Gandolfini, Screamin' Jay Hawkins, Carlos Bardem, Santiago Segura, Don Stroud, Alex Cox
'A well-scripted, well-directed and mostly enjoyable story.' – *Empire*

The Perez Family

US 1995 113m DeLuxe
Film Four/Samuel Goldwyn (Michael Nozik, Lydia Dean Pilcher)

After 20 years in a Cuban jail, a former plantation owner goes to Miami to be reunited with his family, but finds a new life instead.
Uncertain domestic drama, with comic undertones, about breaking free from the past.
w Robin Swicord novel Christine Bell d Mira Nair ph Stuart Dryburgh m Alan Silvestri pd Mark Friedberg ed Robert Estrin
☆ Marisa Tomei, Alfred Molina, Chazz Palminteri, Anjelica Huston, Trini Alvarado, Celia Cruz, Diego Wallraff, Angela Lanza
'A disappointingly messy picture that seldom finds its dramatic or emotional core.' – *Variety*

'Health clubs – more sex than sweat?'
Perfect

US 1985 115m Technicolor
Columbia/Delphi III (James Bridges)

An aerobics instructor (female) meets a reporter (male) doing a story on health clubs, but it isn't love at first sight.
Nervy, unattractive drama which didn't find an audience.
w Aaron Latham, James Bridges d James Bridges ph Gordon Willis m Ralph Burns
☆ John Travolta, Jamie Lee Curtis, Anne de Salvo, Marilu Henner, Laraine Newman
'Guilty of the sins it condemns – superficiality, manipulation and smugness.' – *Variety*

A Perfect Couple *

US 1979 112m DeLuxe
TCF/Lions Gate (Robert Altman)
A middle-aged Greek much dependent on his family meets a jazz singer through a dating service.
A free-speaking update of Marty, featuring the Altman repertory company; intelligent sequences are muffled by the familiar Altman messiness of approach.
w Robert Altman, Allan Nicholls d Robert Altman ph Edmond L. Koons md Tom Pierson, Tony Berg
☆ Paul Dooley, Marta Heflin, Titos Vandis, Belita Moreno, Henry Gibson, Dimitra Arliss
'Has the usual Altman assets: technical deftness, idiosyncrasy, unexpected subject. But the deftness rattles around in a vacuum, the idiosyncrasy – because unsupported in theme or dynamics – degenerates quickly into egotism, and the unexpected subject is so poorly developed that it quickly becomes sterile.' – *Stanley Kauffmann*

Perfect Day *

♠♠ US 1929 20m bw
Hal Roach

Various problems delay a family's departure for a picnic.
Technically a most adept star comedy but its repetition can annoy.
w Hal Roach, Leo McCarey, H. M. Walker d James Parrott ed Richard Currier
☆ Stan Laurel, Oliver Hardy, Edgar Kennedy
† The picnic was originally to have occupied the second reel, but the departure gags swelled to occupy the entire footage.

Perfect Friday *

GB 1970 95m Eastmancolor
London Screenplays/Sunnymede (Jack Smith)
A bank manager engages aristocratic help to rob his own bank.
Middling comedy caper.
w Anthony Greville-Bell, J. Scott Forbes d Peter Hall ph Alan Hume m Johnny Dankworth pd Terence Marsh ed Rex Pyke

☆ Stanley Baker, Ursula Andress, David Warner, Patience Collier, T. P. McKenna, David Waller, Joan Benham, Julian Orchard

The Perfect Furlough

US   1958   93m   Eastmancolor   Cinemascope

U-I (Robert Arthur)

≣

GB title: *Strictly for Pleasure*

To help morale at a remote Arctic army unit, one of the men is selected to enjoy the perfect leave in Paris on behalf of the others.

Amiable farce which entertains while it's on but is quickly forgotten.

w Stanley Shapiro   d Blake Edwards   ph Philip Lathrop   m Frank Skinner

☆ Tony Curtis, Janet Leigh, Elaine Stritch, Keenan Wynn, Troy Donahue, King Donovan, Linda Cristal

The Perfect Gentleman

US   1935   73m   bw

MGM

GB title: *The Imperfect Lady*

A retired officer helps an actress make a comeback.

Genial comedy which didn't quite work well enough to make an English variety star popular on both sides of the Atlantic.

w Edward Childs Carpenter   d Tim Whelan

☆ Cicely Courtneidge, Frank Morgan, Heather Angel, Herbert Mundin, Henry Stephenson

The Perfect Marriage

US   1946   88m   bw

Paramount/Hal B. Wallis

On their tenth wedding anniversary, a happy couple have a row and start divorce proceedings.

Wispy comedy, unmemorable and rather tiresome.

w Leonard Spigelgass   play   Samson Raphaelson   d Lewis Allen   ph Russell Metty   m Frederick Hollander

☆ David Niven, Loretta Young, Eddie Albert, Nona Griffith, Virginia Field, Jerome Cowan, Rita Johnson, Charles Ruggles, Nana Bryant, ZaSu Pitts

'Another film about disillusionment and reconciliation in a mansion with constant evening dress.' – *Sunday Times*

A Perfect Murder

US   1998   105m   Technicolor

Warner (Arnold Kopelson, Anne Kopelson, Christopher Mankiewicz, Peter Macgregor-Scott)

⊞ **≣** **ⓖ** **∩**

To kill his wealthy wife a husband hires the artist and ex-convict with whom she is having an affair.

Slick, glossy thriller that fails to involve an audience on an emotional level.

w Patrick Smith Kelly   play   *Dial M for Murder* by Frederick Knott   d Andrew Davis   ph Dariusz Wolski   m James Newton Howard   pd Philip Rosenberg   ed Dennis Virkler, Dov Hoenig

☆ Michael Douglas, Gwyneth Paltrow, Viggo Mortensen, David Suchet, Sarita Choudhury, Constance Towers, Michael P. Moran, Novella Nelson

'A fast-moving, logically thought-out and beautifully crafted thriller … both psychologically and socially sharp.' – *Philip French, Observer*

'An artistic misdemeanor.' – *Variety*

† Knott's play was filmed by Alfred Hitchcock as *Dial M for Murder* (qv).

The Perfect Murder

India   1988   95m   colour

Enterprise/Merchant Ivory (Wahid Chowhan)

A Bombay detective investigates an attempted murder, with a little diamond smuggling on the side.

Keating's fictional Inspector Ghote transfers poorly to the screen in a film that is more slapstick than thriller.

w Naseeruddin Shah, H. R. F. Keating   novel H. R. F. Keating   d Zafar Hai   ph Walter Lassally   m Richard Robbins   pd Kiran Patki, Sartaj Noorani   ed Charles Rees

☆ Naseeruddin Shah, Stellan Skarsgard, Dalip Tahil, Madhur Jaffrey, Sakeena Jaffrey, Dinshaw Daji

The Perfect Snob

US   1941   63m   bw

Walter Morosco/TCF

A woman tosses her daughter at millionaires. The girl settles on a poor boy … who turns out to be a millionaire after all.

Predictable comedy with competent cast.

w Lee Loeb, Harold Buchman   d Ray McCarey

☆ Charles Ruggles, Charlotte Greenwood, Lynn Bari, Cornel Wilde, Anthony Quinn, Alan Mowbray

'…They Thought He Was A "Mamma's Boy" … But When He Broke Loose! … Wow!'

The Perfect Specimen

US   1937   82m   bw

Warner (Harry Joe Brown)

The grandmother of a rich young man brings him up uncontaminated by the world, but when a girl crashes her car into his fence he proves fitted to deal with the situation.

Fantasticated comedy a long way after Mr Deeds and too slow by half.

w Norman Reilly Raine, Lawrence Riley, Brewster Morse, Fritz Falkenstein, Samuel Hopkins Adams   d Michael Curtiz   ph Charles Rosher

☆ Errol Flynn, Joan Blondell, Hugh Herbert, Edward Everett Horton, May Robson, Dick Foran, Beverly Roberts, Allen Jenkins

'Upper bracket comedy for the family trade.' – *Variety*

Perfect Strangers: see *Blind Alley (1984)*

Perfect Strangers **

GB   1945   102m   bw

MGM/London Films (Alexander Korda)

US title: *Vacation from Marriage*

A downtrodden clerk and his dowdy wife go to war, and come back unrecognizably improved.

Pleasant comedy with good actors; but the turnabout of two such caricatures really strains credibility.

w Clemence Dane, Anthony Pelissier   d Alexander Korda   ph Georges Périnal   m Clifton Parker

☆ Robert Donat, Deborah Kerr, Glynis Johns, Ann Todd, Roland Culver, Elliot Mason, Eliot Makeham, Brefni O'Rorke, Edward Rigby

'War is supposed to be the catalyst, the sportsman's bracer; and the film's chief weakness is its failure to show the briefly exalted couple sinking back, uncontrollably, under their peacetime stone.' – *James Agee*

'It glows with laughter and honest sentiment.' – *New York Times*

🎞 original story (Clemence Dane)

'They met by chance, and once they kissed, they knew they never should have!'

Perfect Strangers

US   1950   87m   bw

Warner (Jerry Wald)

GB title: *Too Dangerous to Love*

Two jurors on a murder case fall in love.

Talkative, unlikely, and rather boring potboiler.

w Edith Sommer   play   *Ladies and Gentlemen* by Charles MacArthur, Ben Hecht   d Bretaigne Windust   ph Peverell Marley   m Leigh Harline

☆ Ginger Rogers, Dennis Morgan, Thelma Ritter, Margalo Gillmore, Howard Freeman, Alan Reed, Paul Ford, George Chandler

Perfect Understanding *

GB   1933   80m   bw

Gloria Swanson British Pictures Ltd

A couple agree to marry on condition that they will never disagree with each other.

Silly comedy with a unique star combination looking acutely uncomfortable.

w Miles Malleson, Michael Powell   d Cyril Gardner   ph Curt Courant

☆ Gloria Swanson, Laurence Olivier, John Halliday, Nigel Playfair, Michael Farmer, Genevieve Tobin, Nora Swinburne

'Dull and talky picture, done in the uninspiring British style.' – *Variety*

The Perfect Weapon

US   1991   85m   Technicolor

Paramount (Mark DiSalle, Pierre David)

⊞ **≣** **ⓠ**

A Kenpo karate expert returns home to avenge the death of his friend at the hands of the drug-dealing Korean mafia.

The usual revenge plot and the usual fight sequences of American martial arts movies are done with a small attempt at style, but otherwise it is strictly an assembly-line product.

w David C. Wilson   d Mark DiSalle   ph Russell Carpenter   m Gary Chang   pd Curtis A. Schnell   ed Wayne Wahrman

☆ Jeff Speakman, John Dye, Mako, James Hong, Mariska Hargitay, Dante Basco, Beau Starr, Seth Sakai, Clyde Kusatsu, Cary-Hiroyuki Tagawa

† The British TV version runs for 65m.

A Perfect Weekend: see *The St Louis Kid*

The Perfect Woman *

GB   1949   89m   bw

GFD/Two Cities (George and Alfred Black)

A girl changes places with her inventor uncle's robot woman.

Described as a romp, this is in fact a pretty good farce, very fast moving and well played after the usual expository start.

w George Black, Bernard Knowles, J. B. Boothroyd   play   Wallace Geoffrey, Basil Mitchell   d Bernard Knowles   ph Jack Hildyard   m Arthur Wilkinson

☆ Patricia Roc, Nigel Patrick, Stanley Holloway, David Hurst, Miles Malleson, Irene Handl

A Perfect World *

US   1993   138m   Technicolor   Panavision

Warner/Malpaso (Mark Johnson, David Valdes)

⊞ **≣** **ⓠ** **∩**

A father–son relationship develops between an escaped convict and the seven-year-old boy he takes as a hostage.

A very American mix of male bonding, road movie and thriller that every now and then reveals a few signs of originality.

w John Lee Hancock   d Clint Eastwood   ph Jack N. Green   m Lennie Niehaus   pd Henry Bumstead   ed Joel Cox, Ron Spang

☆ Kevin Costner, Clint Eastwood, Laura Dern, T. J. Lowther, Keith Szarabajka, Leo Burmester, Paul Hewitt, Bradley Whitford

'A somber, subtly nuanced study of an escaped con's complex relationship with an abducted boy that carries a bit too much narrative flab for its own good.' – *Variety*

'As jarring and fundamentally goofy as the movie is, it never feels like an ordinary, generic Hollywood product: at every moment, there's something to gape at – sometimes in admiration, often in disbelief.' – *Terrence Rafferty, New Yorker*

Perfectly Normal *

Canada   1990   105m   colour

Palace/Bialystock & Bloom/Téléfilm Canada/BSB/Skyhost/British Screen (Michael Burns)

⊞ **≣**

An ice hockey-playing brewery worker teams up with a dubious chef to open an operatic restaurant.

Bizarre comedy of eccentric lives in a small-town setting.

w Eugene Lipinski, Paul Quarrington   d Yves Simoneau   m Richard Gregoire   pd Anne Pritchard   ed Ronald Sanders

☆ Robbie Coltrane, Michael Riley, Deborah Duchene, Eugene Lipinski, Jack Nichols, Elizabeth Harpur, Patricia Gage, Kenneth Welsh

'The movie is too eager to be loved, but has its moments.' – *Philip French, Observer*

Performance ***

GB   1970   105m   Technicolor

Warner/Goodtimes (Donald Cammell)

⊞ **≣** **ⓠ** **∩**

A vicious gangster moves in with an ex-pop star.

Dense, Pinterish melodrama about alter egos.

w Donald Cammell   d Nicolas Roeg, Donald Cammell   ph Nicolas Roeg   m Jack Nitzsche   md Randy Newman

☆ James Fox, Mick Jagger, Anita Pallenberg, Michèle Breton, Stanley Meadows, Allan Cuthbertson

'A humourless, messy mixture of crime and decadence and drug-induced hallucination.' – *New Yorker, 1980*

'You don't have to be a drug addict, pederast, sado-masochist or nitwit to enjoy it, but being one or more of these things would help.' – *John Simon*

Perfume of the Cyclone: see *Night of the Cyclone*

Péril: see *Death in a French Garden*

Péril en la Demeure: see *Death in a French Garden*

Perilous Holiday

US   1946   89m   bw

Columbia

A newly acquainted couple become involved with counterfeiters in Mexico City.

Passable comedy-crime programme filler.

w Robert Carson, Roy Chanslor   d Edward H. Griffith

☆ Pat O'Brien, Ruth Warrick, Alan Hale, Minna Gombell

A Perilous Journey

US   1953   87m   bw

Republic (W. J. O'Sullivan)

A party of women sail to the California goldfields to sell themselves into marriage.

Reasonably lively action drama.

w Richard Wormser   novel   *The Golden Tide* by Virgie Roe   d R. G. Springsteen   ph Jack Marta   m Victor Young

☆ Vera Ralston, David Brian, Charles Winninger, Scott Brady, Virginia Grey, Ben Cooper

The Perils of Pauline *

🏋 US   1947   96m   Technicolor

Paramount (Sol C. Siegel)

ⓐ

The career of silent serial queen Pearl White.

An agreeable recreation of old time Hollywood, with plenty of slapstick chases but a shade too much sentiment also.

w P. J. Wolfson   d George Marshall   ph Ray Rennahan   md Robert Emmett Dolan

☆ Betty Hutton, John Lund, Billy de Wolfe, William Demarest, Constance Collier, Frank Faylen, William Farnum, Paul Panzer, Snub Pollard, Creighton Hale, Chester Conklin, James Finlayson, Hank Mann, Bert Roach, Francis McDonald and also Chester Clute

'People who can accept such stuff as solid gold have either forgotten a lot, or never knew first-rate slapstick when they saw it, twenty or thirty years ago, when it was one of the wonders of the world.' – *James Agee*

𝄞 song 'I Wish I Didn't Love You So' (*m/ly* Frank Loesser)

Period of Adjustment

US   1962   122m   bw   Panavision

MGM/Marton (Lawrence Weingarten)

A Korean War veteran has the shakes and his sexual adequacy is affected, as his wife furiously discovers.

Comedy of maladjustment, tolerably witty but unsuitably widescreened.

w Isobel Lennart   play   Tennessee Williams   d George Roy Hill   ph Paul C. Vogel   m Lyn Murray

☆ Tony Franciosa, Jane Fonda, Jim Hutton, Lois Nettleton

Les Perles de la Couronne *

France   1937   118m   bw

Serge Sandburg/Tobis

The history over four centuries of seven pearls given by Pope Clement VII to Catherine de Medici.

Generally amusing series of historical sketches in Guitry's inimitable style.

w Sacha Guitry   d Sacha Guitry, Christian-Jaque

☆ Sacha Guitry, Renée Saint-Cyr, Lyn Harding, Percy Marmont, Arletty, Claude Dauphin, Raimu, Jean-Louis Barrault, Jacqueline Delubac

'Headed to bring in returns both at home and abroad.' – *Variety*

† The picture tried, but failed, to be intelligible without sub-titles to all language-speakers.

Permanent Midnight

US   1998   85m   DeLuxe

Artisan (Jane Hamsher, Don Murphy)

≣ **ⓐ** **∩**

A successful TV scriptwriter becomes a heroin addict, to the detriment of his relationships and career.

Based on an autobiography, a glum account of enslavement to drugs.

wd David Veloz   book   Jerry Stahl   ph Robert Yeoman   m Daniel Licht   pd Jerry Fleming   ed Steven Weisberg, Cara Silverman

---

🏋 film suitable for family viewing   **⊞** VHS video-cassette for the British PAL system   **⊞** VHS video-cassette for the British PAL system in wide screen-format   ✪ Video cassette in a computer-colourised version   **≣** American NTSC video-cassette   **ⓠ** Laser disc

☆ Ben Stiller, Elizabeth Hurley, Mario Bello, Owen Wilson, Lourdes Benedicto, Cheryl Ladd, Peter Greene, Janeane Garofalo, Jerry Stahl
'Exactly the kind of affliction-of-the-week babble the talented Stahl rails against in his bestselling memoir.' – *Glenn Lovell, Variety*

Permanent Record
US 1988 91m Technicolor
Paramount (Frank Mancuso Jnr)
⬜ ▤ ◎

The unexpected suicide of a popular high school student has a traumatic effect on his friends.
Well-meaning but dull drama of teenage angst.
w Jarre Fees, Alice Liddle, Larry Ketron d Marisa Silver ph Frederick Elmes m Joe Strummer pd Michel Levesque ed Robert Brown
☆ Keanu Reeves, Alan Boyce, Michelle Meyrink, Jennifer Rubin, Barry Corbin, Kathy Baker, Pamela Gidley, Richard Bradford

Permission to Kill
US/Austria 1975 97m Technicolor
Panavision
Warner/Sascha (Paul Mills)
▤

British agents try to stop a communist returning home from the west.
Prolonged, confusing and boring spy melodrama in which everyone looks understandably glum.
w Robin Estridge novel Robin Estridge d Cyril Frankel ph Freddie Young m Richard Rodney Bennett
☆ Bekim Fehmiu, Dirk Bogarde, Ava Gardner, Timothy Dalton, Frederic Forrest
'Pretentious political mishmash.' – *MFB*

Permissive
GB 1970 86m colour
Shonteff Films (Jack Shulton)
⬜

A provincial girl goes to London and becomes a groupie.
Dull exploitation movie of sex and rock, with too much footage given over to uninteresting groups of the period.
w Jeremy Craig Dryden d Lindsay Shonteff ph John C. Taylor m Forever More, Comus ed Jackson J. Bowdell
☆ Maggie Stride, Gay Singleton, Gilbert Wynne, Debbie Bowen, Robert Daubigny, Titus Groan, Nicola Austin
'Probably because of the shoestring budget, the squalor of life on the streets comes across quite well.' – *David McGillivray, Dark Side*

Perri **
👣 US 1957 75m Technicolor
Walt Disney (Winston Hibler)
The life of a squirrel.
Disney's first True Life Fantasy, in which live footage of animals is manipulated against artificial backgrounds to produce an effect as charming and unreal as a cartoon.
w Ralph Wright, Winston Hibler novel Felix Salten d Ralph Wright ph various m Paul Smith
🎵 Paul Smith

Persecution
GB 1974 96m Eastmancolor
Fanfare/Tyburn (Kevin Francis)
⬜ ▤
US title: *The Terror of Sheba*
aka: *The Graveyard*
A rich American woman in England is hated by her son and fearful that her murky past will be revealed.
Rich but not engrossing nonsense, somewhat à la Baby Jane, with hazy script and stolid production.
w Robert B. Hutton, Rosemary Wootten d Don Chaffey ph Ken Talbot m Paul Ferris
☆ Lana Turner, Ralph Bates, Olga Georges-Picot, Trevor Howard, Suzan Farmer, Ronald Howard, Patrick Allen
'Gives off the unmistakable odour of damp mothballs.' – *Michael Billington, Illustrated London News*

The Persecution and Assassination of Jean-Paul Marat: see *The Marat/Sade*

Persona ****
Sweden 1966 81m bw
Svensk Filmindustri (Lars-Owe Carlberg)

A nurse begins to identify with her mentally ill patient, and herself has a nervous breakdown.
Intense clinical study presented in a very complex cinematic manner which tends to obscure the main theme while providing endless fascination for cinéastes.
wd Ingmar Bergman ph Sven Nykvist m Lars Johan Werle ad Bibi Lindström
☆ Liv Ullmann, Bibi Andersson, Margaretha Krook, Gunnar Björnstrand
'Reactions have ranged from incomprehension to irritation with what is dismissed as a characteristic piece of self-indulgence on Bergman's part – Bergman talking to himself again.' – *David Wilson, MFB*
'A puzzling, obsessive film that Bergman seems not so much to have worked out as to have torn from himself.' – *New Yorker, 1977*

Personal Affair
GB 1953 83m bw
Rank/Two Cities (Anthony Darnborough)
A schoolmaster and his neurotic wife run into trouble when a girl pupil develops a crush on him.
Preposterous domestic drama making much ado about nothing.
w Lesley Storm play Lesley Storm d Anthony Pelissier ph Reg Wyer m William Alwyn
☆ Leo Genn, Gene Tierney, Glynis Johns, Pamela Brown

Personal Best
US 1982 122m Technicolor
Warner (Robert Towne)

A female Olympic track star has a lesbian relationship.
So what, is the response to two numbing hours of tedium.
wd Robert Towne ph Michael Chapman m Jack Nitzsche
☆ Mariel Hemingway, Scott Glenn, Patrice Donnelly, Kenny Moore, Jim Moody
'There's an undercurrent of flabbergasted awe in this celebration of women's bodies, and everything in the movie is physically charged.' – *Pauline Kael, New Yorker*

Personal Choice: see *Beyond the Stars*

Personal Column: see *Pièges (1939)*

Personal Column: see *Lured*

Personal Maid's Secret
US 1935 60m bw
Warner/Bryan Foy
A maid's financial tips keep her master and mistress solvent.
Modest comedy which was well liked at the time.
w F. Hugh Herbert, Lillie Hayward story Lillian Day d Arthur Greville Collins
☆ Ruth Donnelly, Anita Louise, Warren Hull, Margaret Lindsay, Frank Albertson, Arthur Treacher

Personal Property *
US 1937 84m bw
MGM (John W. Considine Jnr)

GB title: *The Man in Possession*
An American widow in England, in financial straits, falls for the bailiff sent to keep an eye on her.
Moderate star comedy which still amuses.
w Hugh Mills, Ernest Vajda play *The Man in Possession* by H. M. Harwood d W. S. Van Dyke II ph William Daniels m Franz Waxman
☆ Jean Harlow, Robert Taylor, Reginald Owen, Una O'Connor, Henrietta Crosman, E. E. Clive, Cora Witherspoon, Barnett Parker
'Harmless boudoir farce, for the undergraduates.' – *Variety*

Personal Services *
GB 1987 105m Eastmancolor
Zenith (Tim Bevan)
⬜ ▤
Adventures of a London madam.

Rather astonishing study of British attitudes to sex; not for Aunt Edna, but with a fair measure of interest for many.
w David Leland d Terry Jones ph Roger Deakins ed George Akers
☆ Julie Walters, Alec McCowen, Shirley Stelfox, Danny Schiller, Victoria Hardcastle

The Personality Kid
US 1934 70m bw
Warner
A prizefighter becomes intoxicated by his own success and ignores his faithful wife.
Mediocre filler wasting reliable stars.
w F. Hugh Herbert, Erwin Gelsey, Gene Towne, Graham Baker d Alan Crosland
☆ Pat O'Brien, Glenda Farrell, Claire Dodd, Henry O'Neill, Robert Gleckler, Thomas Jackson
'Rates poorly: strictly cuffo yarn.' – *Variety*

'She's the woman behind the killer behind the gun!'
Persons in Hiding *
US 1939 71m bw
Paramount
A bored girl absconds with gangsters and becomes a public enemy.
Interesting programmer which led to several sequels using the same book as source; this one was vaguely inspired by the story of Bonnie and Clyde.
w William R. Lipman, Horace McCoy book J. Edgar Hoover d Louis King ph Harry Fischbeck m Boris Morros
☆ Patricia Morison, J. Carrol Naish, Lynne Overman, William Henry, Helen Twelvetrees, William Frawley
'Strong supporter for the duals … will depend entirely on rep of J. Edgar Hoover to attract.' – *Variety*
'A little on the tame side, but distinguished by the presence of a crooked and merciless heroine.' – *Graham Greene*

Persons Unknown *
Italy 1958 105m bw
Lux/Vides/Cinecittà (Franco Cristaldi)
⬜ ▤
original title: *I Soliti Ignoti*
US title: *Big Deal on Madonna Street*
Adventures of a gang of incompetent thieves, who get arrested more often than they get away, and finally, elaborately drill through a wall into the bank … only to find it's the wrong wall and they are in another room of the same flat.
Spoof black comedy working up to an elaborate take-off of Rififi; a great success in Italy and the USA, mildly received elsewhere.
w Age Scarpelli, Suso Cecchi d'Amico, Mario Monicelli d Mario Monicelli ph Gianni di Venanzo m Piero Umiliani
☆ Vittorio Gassman, Renato Salvatori, Toto, Marcello Mastroianni, Memmo Carotenuto, Carla Gravina, Rossana Rory

Persons Unknown
US 1996 99m Foto-Kem
Metro/Tartan/Guild/Promark/Spectacor/Videal (David Lancaster)
A crooked ex-cop helps two sisters who are being hunted down by Colombian drug dealers.
A downbeat thriller, set among sleazy two-timers; only occasional moments elevate it out of the ordinary.
w Craig Smith d George Hickenlooper ph Richard Crudo m Ed Tomney pd Jerry Fleming ed Suzanne Pettit
☆ Joe Mantegna, Kelly Lynch, Naomi Watts, J. T. Walsh, Xander Berkeley, Jon Favreau
'For those who like their thrillers hard-boiled, *Persons Unknown* is about as tough as it gets.' – *Jake Hamilton, Empire*

'It's never too late for true love.'
Persuasion *
GB 1995 102m colour
BBC-TV/WGBH/Boston and Millesime/France2 (Fiona Finlay)
⬜ ▤ ◎ ⊙ ⊙
A naval officer and the woman who was persuaded to reject his proposal some years before get a second chance at romance.
A lively but coarse adaptation that strives too hard to avoid gentility and to add action to a largely static, domestic drama.
w Nick Dear novel Jane Austen d Roger Michell ph John Daly m Jeremy Sams pd William Dudley ed Kate Evans

☆ Amanda Root, Ciaran Hinds, Susan Fleetwood, Corin Redgrave, Fiona Shaw, John Woodvine, Samuel West, Phoebe Nicholls, Judy Cornwell
'A Jane Austen movie that is never pretty and only occasionally charming; instead it is troubled, astringent and touched with melancholy – not unlike the novel.' – *Anthony Lane, New Yorker*
† The film was originally made for BBC-TV and later given a cinema release.

La Perversa Caricia De Satan: see *The Devil's Kiss*

The Pest
US 1997 82m DeLuxe
Columbia TriStar/Bubble Factory (Sid, John and Bill Sheinberg)
▤
A con man tries a multitude of disguises to escape from a gang of Scottish crooks, and a big-game hunter who plans to hunt him.
A cartoon-style comic variation on The Most Dangerous Game, featuring frenetic gags that depend for their humour on flatulence and vomit.
w David Bar Katz d Paul Miller ph Roy H. Wagner m Kevin Kiner pd Rodger E. Maus ed Ross Albert, David Rawlins
☆ John Leguizamo, Jeffrey Jones, Edoardo Ballerini, Freddy Rodriguez, Tommy Townsend, Aries Spears, Joe Morton, Charles Hallahan

Pet Sematary
US 1989 103m Technicolor Panavision
UIP/Paramount (Richard P. Rubinstein)
⬜ ▤ ◎ 🎧
A doctor and his family move into a house near a burial ground where the dead can be brought back to life.
Turgid horror, lacking in suspense and excitement.
w Stephen King novel Stephen King d Mary Lambert ph Peter Stein m Elliot Goldenthal pd Michael Z. Hanan ed Michael Hill, Daniel Hanley
☆ Dale Midkiff, Fred Gwynne, Denise Crosby, Brad Greenquist, Michael Lombard, Miko Hughes, Blaze Berdahl
'If all the usual excesses of the genre are well exercised, King's old-dark-house clichés have come up with far more edge and shine than he deserved.' – *Philip Strick, MFB*

'Raise some hell.'
Pet Sematary Two
US 1992 100m DuArt
Paramount (Ralph S. Singleton)
⬜ ▤ ◎
A father and son move to a new house, next to a cemetery where the dead can be resurrected.
Nasty little shocker, with no redeeming features.
w Richard Outten novel Stephen King d Mary Lambert ph Russell Carpenter m Mark Governor pd Michelle Minch ed Tom Finan sp Peter Chesney, Steve Johnson
☆ Edward Furlong, Anthony Edwards, Clancy Brown, Jared Rushton, Darlanne Fluegel, Jason McGuire, Sarah Trigger, Lisa Waltz
'About 50% better than its predecessor, which is to say it's not very good at all.' – *Variety*
'A complete waste of time.' – *Nigel Floyd, The Dark Side*

Pétain
France 1992 133m colour
Gala/Mod/France 2 (Jacques Kirsner)
⬜
In 1940, the ageing Marshall Pétain becomes the leader of France; in Vichy, he makes peace with the invading German army and, under the influence of Laval, collaborates with the Nazis.
Mundane biopic that plods through the facts without making them seem particularly relevant.
w Jean-Pierre Marchand book Marc Ferro d Jean Marboeuf ph Dominique Bouilleret m Georges Garvarentz pd Jerome Clément ed Anne-France Lebrun
☆ Jacques Dufilho, Jean Yanne, Jean-Pierre Cassel, Jean-Claude Dreyfus, Antoinette Moya, Julie Marboeuf, Ludwig Haas
'A major accomplishment. Taboo-breaking and ideologically irreproachable pic about Vichy and its legacy is a clear and nuanced – and long overdue – view of crucial French history. Unfailingly cinematic, intelligently structured

and beautifully cast, pic is essential viewing for Gallic auds and deserves to be shown everywhere.' – *Variety*

'The film plods along, serenely untroubled by anything that would justify its 133 minutes. Quiet days in Vichy indeed.' – *Sheila Johnston, Independent*

'The story of a jazz-man of the wide-open 20s ... caught in the crossfire of its blazing .38s!'

Pete Kelly's Blues *

US   1955   95m   Warnercolor   Cinemascope
(Warner) Mark VII Ltd (Jack Webb)

Jazz musicians in the twenties get involved with gangsters.
Minor cult film, mainly for the score; dramatically it is not exactly compelling.
w Richard L. Breen d Jack Webb ph Harper Goff m Sammy Cahn, Ray Heindorf, Arthur Hamilton, Matty Matlock
☆ Jack Webb, Edmond O'Brien, Janet Leigh, Peggy Lee, Andy Devine, *Ella Fitzgerald*, Lee Marvin, Martin Milner
'Concerned with striking attitudes and establishing an atmosphere rather than developing anything very coherent in the way of narrative ... one remains aware of an over-deliberate straining after effect.' – *Penelope Houston*
⍟ Peggy Lee

'Honeymoon's over – time to get married!'

Pete 'n Tillie *

US   1972   100m   Technicolor   Panavision
Universal (Julius J. Epstein)
The tragi-comic marriage of two eccentrics.
Curious: plain drama treated as comedy, with surprisingly satisfactory results, but not an example to be followed.
w Julius J. Epstein novel *Witch's Milk* by Peter de Vries d Martin Ritt ph John Alonzo m John T. Williams
☆ Walter Matthau, Carol Burnett, Geraldine Page, René Auberjonois, Barry Nelson, Henry Jones
'For the most part an amusing, moving, sentimental comedy. The wisecracks stay on this side of human possibility – that is, we don't feel, as we do so often with Neil Simon, that the characters have private gag writers in their homes.' – *Stanley Kauffmann*
⍟ Julius J. Epstein; Geraldine Page
Ⓥ Walter Matthau

'The most beautiful romance in all modern literature!'

Peter Ibbetson *

US   1935   85m   bw
Paramount (Louis D. Lighton)
Childhood sweethearts meet again as adults, are separated when he is imprisoned for her husband's murder, but are reunited in heaven.
Downright peculiar romantic fantasy, even more oddly cast, but extremely well produced.
w Vincent Lawrence, Waldemar Young, Constance Collier novel *George du Maurier* d Henry Hathaway ph Charles Lang m Ernst Toch
☆ Gary Cooper, Ann Harding, Ida Lupino, John Halliday, Douglass Dumbrille, Virginia Weidler, Dickie Moore, Doris Lloyd
'In a day and a world hard-boiled and realistic Paramount hopes to sell a picture about dreams and beauty and love. It just isn't in the cards.' – *Variety*
'A triumph of surrealist thought.' – *André Breton*
'One of the world's ten best films.' – *Luis Buñuel*
⍟ Ernst Toch

Peter Pan ***

👭 US   1953   76m   Technicolor
Walt Disney
Three London children are taken into fairyland by a magic flying boy who cannot grow up.
Solidly crafted cartoon version of a famous children's play; not Disney's best work, but still miles ahead of the competition.
d Wilfred Jackson, Clyde Geronimi, Hamilton Luske m Oliver Wallace supervisor Ben Sharpsteen
☆ Featuring the voices of Bobby Driscoll, Kathryn Beaumont, Hans Conried, Bill Thompson, Heather Angel
'A painful travesty.' – *C. A. Lejeune*

Peter Rabbit and the Tales of Beatrix Potter: see Tales of Beatrix Potter

Peter the Great *

USSR   1937   96m   bw
Lenfilm
The rise to power of the famous autocrat.
Standard Russian first feature with plenty of action and striking composition, but not really memorable.
w Alexei Tolstoy, Vladimir Petrov d Vladimir Petrov
☆ Nikolai Simonov, Nikolai Cherkassov, Alla Tarasova, M. Zharov
'Surprisingly strong: a cinch in Russian-languagers.' – *Variety*

'A comedy about love, friendship and other natural disasters.'

Peter's Friends **

GB   ·1992   101m   Technicolor
Entertainment/Renaissance/Samuel Goldwyn/Channel 4 (Kenneth Branagh)

A decade after they left university, a group of former friends get together for a New Year's reunion at a country mansion.
A British variation on The Big Chill that is a good deal chillier, with a cast too familiar from innumerable television comedies to be entirely convincing in their roles.
w Martin Bergman, Rita Rudner d Kenneth Branagh ph Roger Lanser m Gavin Greenaway pd Tim Harvey ed Andrew Marcus
☆ Kenneth Branagh, Alphonsia Emmanuel, Stephen Fry, Hugh Laurie, Phyllida Law, Alex Lowe, Rita Rudner, Tony Slattery, Imelda Staunton, Emma Thompson, Richard Briers
'Well written, beautifully performed and highly entertaining.' – *Derek Malcolm, Guardian*
'A lot more work is called for all round before these likeable people produce something worthy to be called disposable film entertainment.' – *Adam Mars-Jones, Independent*
'Awful, with glimpses of wit. The script is hopelessly schematic: one long, drawing-room chat in which people dish each other, then leave the room so they can be talked about.' – *Richard Corliss, Time*

The Peterville Diamond

GB   1942   85m   bw
Warner (A. H. Salomon)
A bored wife revives her husband's interest by cultivating the advances of a jewel thief.
Modest comedy-drama, smoothly presented: the same play formed the basis of Dieterle's Jewel Robbery.
w Brock Williams, Gordon Wellesley play *Jewel Robbery* by Ladislas Fodor d Walter Forde ph Basil Emmott md Jack Beaver
☆ Anne Crawford, Donald Stewart, Renee Houston, Oliver Wakefield, Charles Heslop, William Hartnell, Felix Aylmer, Charles Victor

Pete's Dragon

👭 US   1977   127m   Technicolor
Walt Disney (Ron Miller, Jerome Courtland)
In Maine in 1900, a nine-year-old boy escapes from grasping foster-parents with his pet dragon, which no one but himself can see.
A kind of juvenile rewrite of Harvey. The dragon is drawn (rather poorly) and the human characters are not exactly three-dimensional. A long way from Mary Poppins.
w Malcolm Marmorstein story Seton I. Miller, S. S. Field d Don Chaffey ph Frank Phillips md Irwin Kostal ch Onna White animation Ken Anderson songs Al Kasha, Joel Hirschhorn
☆ Sean Marshall, Mickey Rooney, Jim Dale, Helen Reddy, Red Buttons, Shelley Winters, Jim Backus, Joe E. Ross, Ben Wrigley
'For a Disney film it's terribly badly made, in parts so clumsy that it looks like the work of the Burbank Amateur Camera Club.' – *Barry Took, Punch*
⍟ music; song 'Candle on the Water'

La Petite Bande **

👭 France   1983   91m   colour
Squirrel/Gaumont-Stand'Art/FR3/Hamster Productions (Denis Mermet)
A gang of English children stow away to France where they cause mayhem and save the world from a gang of wicked adults before ending up on a desert island.

Lively and subversive entertainment intended for children.
w Gilles Perrault, Michel Deville, Yan Appas, Joan Népami d Michel Deville ph Claude Lecompte m Edgar Cosma pd Michel Guyot, Régis Des Plas ed Raymonde Guyot
☆ Andrew Chandler, Hélène Dassule, Nicole Palmer, Hamish Scrimgeour, Katherine Scrimgeour, Nicolas Sireau, Rémi Usquin, Valérie Gauthier

La Petite Voleuse *

France   1988   109m   Fujicolour
Pathé/Orly Films/Renn Productions/Ciné Cinq/Les Films du Carrosse/Sedif (Jean-José Richer)
A young girl becomes the lover and accomplice of a thief.
Moderately engaging account of a defiant, amoral outlaw determined to make her own way in the world.
w François Truffaut, Claude de Givray d Claude Miller ph Dominique Chapuis ad Jean-Pierre Kohut Svelko ed Albert Jurgenson
☆ Charlotte Gainsbourg, Didier Bazace, Simon de la Brosse, Raoul Billerey, Chantal Banlier, Nathalie Cardone, Clotilde de Bayser

Les Petites Filles Modèles

France   1971   88m   Eastmancolor
Plan-Film/Studio du Dragon/Labrador/Tanagra (Louis Duchesne)

aka: *Good Little Girls*
The amorous adventures of a wealthy aristocratic widow and her two nubile daughters.
Lively comic carry-on, updating a novel about well-brought-up young girls behaving badly.
w François de Bernis novel *Comtesse de Ségur* d Jean-Claude Roy ph Claude Saunier m Maurice Lecoeur ed Florence Eymon
☆ Jessica Dorn, Marie-Georges Pascal, Cathy Reghin, Sylvie Lafontaine, Michèle Girardon, Bella Darvi, Béatrice Arnac, François Guerin, Dominique Paturel
'This crudely unsubtle adaptation, which reduces the story to the level of a mild exploitation picture, full of coy nudity and doubles entendres, and made without any grace or humour.' – *John Gillett, MFB*

The Petrified Forest **

US   1936   83m   bw
Warner (Henry Blanke)

Travellers at a way station in the Arizona desert are held up by gangsters.
Rather faded melodrama (it always was), which is important to Hollywood for introducing such well used figures as the poet idealist hero and the gangster anti-hero, and for giving Bogart his first meaty role.
Otherwise, the settings are artificial, the acting theatrical, the development predictable and the dialogue pretentious.
w Charles Kenyon, Delmer Daves play *Robert E. Sherwood* d Archie Mayo ph Sol Polito md Leo F. Forbstein
☆ Leslie Howard, Bette Davis, Humphrey Bogart, Genevieve Tobin, Dick Foran, Joe Sawyer, Porter Hall, Charley Grapewin
ALAN SQUIER (LESLIE HOWARD): 'Let there be killing. All this evening I've had a feeling of destiny closing in.'
JACKIE (JOE SAWYER): 'Now, just behave yourself and nobody'll get hurt. This is Duke Mantee, the world-famous killer, and he's hungry.'
'Marquee draft should offset the philosophic meanderings which minimize appeal.' – *Variety*
'Drama slackens under the weight of Mr Sherwood's rather half-baked philosophy.' – *Alistair Cooke*
'There is good dramatic material here, but Mr Sherwood doesn't see his play as certain things happening, but as ideas being expressed, "significant" cosmic ideas ... Life itself, which crept in during the opening scene, embarrassed perhaps at hearing itself so explicitly discussed, crept out again, leaving us only with the symbols, the too pasteboard desert, the stunted cardboard studio trees.' – *Graham Greene*
† Remade as *Escape in the Desert* (qv).

Petticoat Fever

US   1936   80m   bw
MGM (Frank Davis)
A girl and her stuffy fiancé crash land their plane in sub-Arctic Labrador and are helped by a wireless operator who has not seen a woman for two years.
Pert, slightly unusual comedy which comes off pretty well.
w Harold Goldman play *Mark Reed* d George Fitzmaurice ph Ernest Haller m William Axt
☆ Robert Montgomery, Myrna Loy, Reginald Owen, Winifred Shotter

Petticoat Pirates

GB   1961   87m   Technicolor   CinemaScope
Gordon L. T. Scott/ABPC

Women naval officers mutiny and take a nervous male stoker with them.
Uncertain comedy fantasy.
w Lew Schwartz, Charlie Drake d David MacDonald ph Gilbert Taylor m Stanley Black
☆ Charlie Drake, Cecil Parker, Anne Heywood, John Turner, Maxine Audley, Thorley Walters

The Petty Girl

US   1950   88m   Technicolor
Columbia (Nat Perrin)
GB title: *Girl of the Year*
A calendar artist takes a staid college professor as his model, and causes a scandal.
Witless comedy musical which barely lingers in the memory.
w Nat Perrin story Mary McCarthy d Henry Levin ph William Snyder m George Duning songs Harold Arlen, Johnny Mercer
☆ Robert Cummings, Joan Caulfield, Melville Cooper, Elsa Lanchester, Audrey Long, Mary Wickes, Frank Orth

Petulia *

US   1968   105m   Technicolor
Warner/Petersham (Raymond Wagner)

A doctor's life is disrupted by his meeting and loving a kooky girl who has family problems.
Swinging London melodrama which happens to be set in San Francisco. All very flashy, and occasionally arresting or well acted, but adding up to nothing.
w Lawrence B. Marcus novel *Me and the Arch Kook Petulia* by John Haase d Richard Lester ph Nicolas Roeg m John Barry
☆ George C. Scott, Julie Christie, Richard Chamberlain, Joseph Cotten, Arthur Hill, Shirley Knight, Kathleen Widdoes, Pippa Scott
'A sad and savage comment on the ways we waste our time and ourselves in upper-middle-class America.' – *Richard Schickel*
'A soulless, arbitrary, attitudinizing piece of claptrap.' – *John Simon*

Peur sur la Ville: see Night Caller

'Everybody in this town hides behind plain wrappers!'

Peyton Place **

US   1957   157m   DeLuxe   Cinemascope
TCF (Jerry Wald)

Sex, frustration and violence ferment under the placid surface of a small New England town.
Well-made film of what was at the time a scandalous bestseller, one of the first to reveal those nasty secrets of 'ordinary people'.
w John Michael Hayes novel *Grace Metalious* d Mark Robson ph William Mellor m Franz Waxman
☆ Lana Turner, Arthur Kennedy, Hope Lange, Lee Philips, Lloyd Nolan, Diane Varsi, Russ Tamblyn, Terry Moore, Barry Coe, David Nelson, Betty Field, Mildred Dunnock, Leon Ames, Lorne Greene
⍟ best picture; John Michael Hayes; Mark Robson; William Mellor; Lana Turner; Arthur Kennedy; Hope Lange; Diane Varsi, Russ Tamblyn

Phaedra *

US/Greece   1961   116m   bw
UA/Melinafilm (Jules Dassin)
A tycoon's wife falls in love with her stepson.
Ludicrous, awesomely folly-filled attempt to modernize and sex up Greek tragedy.
wd Jules Dassin ph Jacques Natteau m Mikis Theodorakis

☆ Melina Mercouri, Anthony Perkins, Raf Vallone, Elizabeth Ercy

'Unfortunately unforgettable.' – *John Simon*

'If this one doesn't scare you ... you're already dead!'

Phantasm
US 1979 90m Technicolor
Avco Embassy
📼 ▦ 🎧

A 16-year-old has nightmares which seem to come true.

Cleverly assembled horror comic with many nasty moments. Not for the squeamish, and with no real merit except the power to frighten.

wd Don Coscarelli (who was 20 at the time) ph Don Coscarelli ed Don Coscarelli

☆ Michael Baldwin, Bill Thornbury, Reggie Bannister, Angus Scrimm

Phantasm II
US 1988 97m colour
Guild/Starway International (Roberto A. Quezada)
📼 ▦ 🎧

A creature from another dimension who brings corpses back to life is thwarted by a teenager and his old adversary.

In the nine years separating this sequel from the original, its director has retained his ability to shock but still cannot tell a story convincingly.

wd Don Coscarelli ph Dayn Okada m Fred Myrow, Christopher L. Stone pd Philip J. C. Duffin ed Peter Teschner

☆ James Le Gros, Reggie Bannister, Angus Scrimm, Paula Irvine, Samantha Phillips, Kenneth Tigar, Ruth C. Engel, Mark Anthony Major, Rubin Kushner

'A slick-looking but uninvolving, uncertain picture.' – *MFB*

The Phantom
🎭 US/Australia 1996 100m DeLuxe
Paramount/Ladd Company/Village Roadshow (Robert Evans, Alan Ladd Jnr)
📼 ▦ 🎬 🎧

A pirate's plan to make himself dictator of America by obtaining three skulls with supernatural powers is thwarted by a masked hero.

A limp action movie featuring a dull super-hero, this is below-par Saturday matinee stuff.

w Jeffrey Boam comic strip Lee Falk d Simon Wincer ph David Burr m David Newman pd Paul Peters ed O. Nicholas Brown, Bryan H. Carroll

☆ Billy Zane, Kristy Swanson, Treat Williams, Catherine Zeta Jones, James Remar, Jon Teney, Cary-Hiroyuki Tagawa, Patrick McGoohan, Bill Smitrovich, Samantha Eggar

'Brings a light touch to appealingly old-fashioned action material, creating a fast-moving yarn.' – *Variety*

The Phantom Baron: see *Le Baron Fantôme*

The Phantom Carriage: see *Thy Soul Shall Bear Witness*

The Phantom Fiend: see *The Lodger*

Phantom Killer
US 1942 57m bw
A. W. Hackel/Monogram

A young district attorney uncovers an ingenious criminal ruse by twin brothers.

Better-than-average crime filler.

w Karl Brown d William Beaudine

☆ Dick Purcell, Joan Woodbury, John Hamilton, Warren Hymer, J. Farrell MacDonald, Mantan Moreland

Phantom Lady **
US 1944 87m bw
Universal (Joan Harrison)

A man is accused of murder and his only alibi is a mysterious lady he met in a bar.

Odd little thriller which doesn't really hold together but is made for the most part with great style.

w Bernard C. Schoenfeld novel William Irish d Robert Siodmak ph Woody Bredell m Hans Salter

☆ Franchot Tone, Alan Curtis, Ella Raines, Elisha Cook Jnr, Fay Helm, Andrew Tombes

The Phantom Light
GB 1935 76m bw
Gaumont British/Gainsborough (Jerome Jackson)

A new keeper takes over at a remote Welsh lighthouse which is reputed to be haunted.

An old-fashioned and stagey melodrama, a sort of seafaring Ghost Train, which defeats the director's best efforts to create something more realistic.

w Ralph Smart, J. Jefferson Farjeon, Austin Melford play The Haunted Light by Evadne Price, Joan Roy Byford d Michael Powell ph Roy Kellino md Louis Levy ad A. Vetchinsky ed D. N. Twist

☆ Binnie Hale, Gordon Harker, Donald Calthrop, Milton Rosmer, Ian Hunter, Herbert Lomas

Phantom Love: see *Ai No Borei*

Phantom of 42nd Street
US 1945 58m bw
PRC/Mooney-Herman

A young Broadway star is suspected when her uncle is murdered backstage.

Lightweight but amiable mystery.

w Milton Raison d Albert Herman

☆ Dave O'Brien, Kay Aldridge, Alan Mowbray, Frank Jenks, Jack Mulhall

Phantom of Crestwood *
US 1932 77m bw
RKO (David O. Selznick)
🎬

Murder strikes when a blackmailer assembles her victims.

Lively mystery with spoof elements.

w Bartlett Cormack, J. Walter Ruben d J. Walter Ruben ph Henry Gerrard m Max Steiner

☆ Ricardo Cortez, H. B. Warner, Anita Louise, Karen Morley, Pauline Frederick, Robert McWade, Skeets Gallagher

'Below the deluxe classification it should give a good account of itself.' – *Variety*

The Phantom of Liberty ***
France 1974 104m Eastmancolor
Fox-Rank/Greenwich (Serge Silberman)
📼

original title: *Le Fantôme de la Liberté*

Surrealist episodes in the lives of various loosely linked individuals that range from a firing squad in 1808 to modern-day Paris where a dead woman phones her brother to offer him consolation and the police prepare to suppress a revolt.

A hit and miss affair in its treatment of middle-class hypocrisies, often funny, but sometimes no more than bizarre, although you keep watching, just to see what happens next.

w Luis Buñuel, Jean-Claude Carrière d Luis Buñuel ph Edmond Richard ad Pierre Guffroy ed Hélène Plemiannikov

☆ Monica Vitti, Jean-Claude Brialy, Michel Piccoli, Jean Rochefort, Adolfo Celi, Michel Lonsdale, Adriana Asti, Bernard Verley, Maxence Mailfort, Muni, Philippe Brigaud

'A magnificent film ... one of Buñuel's masterpieces.' – *Tom Milne, Sight and Sound*

'Buñuel has a great spare, tonic style, but the domesticated surrealism of this picture has no sting and no after-effect. The film drifts out of your head before it's over.' – *Pauline Kael, New Yorker*

Phantom of Paris
US 1931 73m bw
MGM

A magician proves by a complex plan that he did not kill his fiancée's father.

Unusual but tortuous thriller which fails to thrill.

w Bess Meredyth, John Meehan, Edwin Justus Mayer d John S. Robertson

☆ John Gilbert, Leila Hyams, Ian Keith, C. Aubrey Smith, Lewis Stone, Jean Hersholt

'It isn't Gilbert that makes the picture, it makes itself. Merits above-average gross.' – *Variety*

Phantom of the Opera ***
US 1925 94m bw (Technicolor sequence)
silent
Universal
📼 ▦ 🎬

A disfigured man in a mask abducts the prima donna of the Paris Opera House to his lair in the sewers below.

Patchy but often splendid piece of Grand Guignol which not only provided its star with a famous role but was notable for its magnificent visual style.

w Raymond Schrock, Elliott Clawson novel Gaston Leroux ph Charles Van Enger, Virgil Miller ad Dan Hall

☆ Lon Chaney, Mary Philbin, Norman Kerry, Gibson Gowland

'The greatest inducement to nightmare that has yet been screened.' – *Variety*

† The chase was directed by Edward Sedgwick.

†† In 1930 an 89m talkie version was issued (L), with approximately 35% dialogue which had been recorded by the surviving actors, and some new footage.

Phantom of the Opera
GB 1962 90m Technicolor
U-I/Hammer (Anthony Hinds)
📼 ▦ 🎬

A disfigured composer lurks beneath an opera house with his hunchbacked assistant and kidnaps the singer he loves to coach her in a leading role.

Stodgy remake with the accent on shock. Its box-office failure was attributed to treating the phantom too sympathetically.

w John Elder (Anthony Hinds) d Terence Fisher ph Arthur Grant m Edwin Astley md John Hollingsworth ad Bernard Robinson, Don Mingaye ed Alfred Cox

☆ Herbert Lom, Edward de Souza, Heather Sears, Thorley Walters, Michael Gough, Ian Wilson, Martin Miller, John Harvey, Miriam Karlin

'The only shock is that the British, who could have had a field day with this antique, have simply wafted it back with a lick and a promise.' – *New York Times*

Phantom of the Opera
US 1989 93m colour
Castle Premier/21st Century/Breton Film (Harry Alan Towers)
▦ 🎬 🎧

Struck on the head, a singer finds herself back in Victorian England, where she falls under the influence of a disfigured musical genius who has sold his soul to the devil.

Undistinguished variation on a familiar story, cashing in on the popularity of the actor who plays 'Freddy' in the Nightmare On Elm Street series.

w Duke Sandefur, Gerry O'Hara d Dwight H. Little ph Elemer Ragalyi m Misha Segal ad Tivadar Bertalan ed Charles Bornstein

☆ Robert Englund, Jill Schoelen, Alex Hyde-White, Bill Nighy, Terence Harvey, Stephanie Lawrence, Nathan Lewis, Peter Clapham

The Phantom of the Opera *
🎭 US 1943 92m Technicolor
Universal (George Waggner)
📼 ▦ 🎬

A shy violinist, obsessed with a chorus girl, haunts the sewers of the opera house after he is disfigured by having acid thrown in his face by a jealous rival.

This version of the familiar story is more decorous and gentlemanly than most, with much attention paid to the music, but it certainly has its moments.

w Erich Taylor, Samuel Hoffenstein d Arthur Lubin ph Hal Mohr, W. Howard Greene m Edward Ward ad John B. Goodman, Alexander Golitzen

☆ Claude Rains, Nelson Eddy, Susanna Foster, Edgar Barrier, Leo Carrillo, J. Edward Bromberg, Jane Farrar, Hume Cronyn

'A grand and gaudy entertainment.' – *Manchester Guardian*

🏆 Hal Mohr, W. Howard Greene; John B. Goodman, Alexander Golitzen; Edward Ward

Phantom of the Paradise *
US 1974 91m Movielab
TCF/Pressman Williams (Edward R. Pressman)
▦ 🎬 🎧

A modern satirical remake of *Phantom of the Opera* in rock opera terms, set in a pop music palace.

Not bad in spots, but it doesn't really know where it's going.

wd Brian de Palma ph Larry Pizer m Paul Williams pd Jack Fisk

☆ Paul Williams, William Finley, Jessica Harper, George Memmoli, Gerrit Graham

'Too broad in its effects and too bloated in style to cut very deeply as a parody ... closer to the anything goes mode of a Mad magazine lampoon.' – *Richard Combs*

🎵 Paul Williams

Phantom of the Rue Morgue
US 1954 84m Warnercolor 3-D
Warner (Henry Blanke)

In old Paris, a killer of pretty girls turns out to be an ape.

Dull revamping of a rather dull story, with boring characters and little horror.

w Harold Medford, James R. Webb story Murders in the Rue Morgue by Edgar Allan Poe d Roy del Ruth ph Peverell Marley m David Buttolph

☆ Karl Malden, Claude Dauphin, Steve Forrest, Patricia Medina, Allyn McLerie, Dolores Dorn

The Phantom President *
US 1932 78m bw
Paramount

A fast-talking quack doubles for a lacklustre presidential candidate.

A likely but in fact unsuccessful film début for a famous Broadway star: many points of interest.

w Walter de Leon, Harlan Thompson d Norman Taurog ph David Abel songs Richard Rodgers, Lorenz Hart

☆ George M. Cohan, Claudette Colbert, Jimmy Durante, George Barbier, Sidney Toler, Jameson Thomas, Paul Hurst, Alan Mowbray

'A lot of smart stuff is packed into the footage ... should do well without threatening to rate itself a smash.' – *Variety*

'For anyone who cares about American theatrical history, it's an indispensable record of Cohan's style.' – *New Yorker, 1978*

Phantom Ship: see *The Mystery of the Marie Celeste*

The Phantom Strikes: see *The Gaunt Stranger*

The Phantom Tollbooth
🎭 US 1969 89m Metrocolor
MGM/Animation/Visual Arts (Abe Levitow, Les Goldman)
📼 ▦

A bored young boy, oblivious to his surroundings, is transported into a world of the imagination, where words and numbers battle for supremacy.

A witty, literate children's story, depending on wordplay, becomes a conventional animated film, constraining the antic imagination of Chuck Jones.

w Chuck Jones, Sam Rosen novel Norton Juster d Chuck Jones, Abe Levitow (animation); David Monahan (live action) ph Lester Shorr m Dean Elliott m/ly Norman Gimbel, Lee Pockriss, Paul Vance pd Maurice Noble ed Jim Faris

☆ Butch Patrick and also the voices of Mel Blanc, Daws Butler, Candy Candido, Hans Conried, June Foray, Patti Gilbert

'Chuck Jones and Abe Levitow have approached Juster with an appalling condescension – manifested partly in the snail's pace and constant over-emphasis, and partly in the sickening cuteness, reminiscent of Disney at his worst.' – *Tom Milne, MFB*

Phar Lap
🎭 Australia 1983 118m colour
Panavision
TCF/Michael Edgley International (John Sexton)
📼 ▦

GB title: *Phar Lap – Heart of a Nation*

The story of a crack racehorse which was the talk of the world in the early thirties but died of a mysterious disease.

The film, though adequately textured, won't win any races.

w David Williamson d Simon Wincer ph Russell Boyd m Bruce Rowland

☆ Tom Burlinson, Martin Vaughan, Judy Morris, Celia de Burgh, Ron Liebman, Vincent Ball

'The day the earth was turned into a cemetery!'

Phase IV *
GB 1973 84m Technicolor
Paramount/Alced (Paul B. Radin)
📼 ▦

In the Arizona desert, ants attack a scientific installation.

Oddly effective if repulsive science fiction; the ants are all the more unpleasant because they stay the normal size.

w Mayo Simon d Saul Bass ph Dick Bush m Brian Gascoigne

☆ Nigel Davenport, Lynne Frederick, Michael Murphy, Alan Gifford

---

'Sin City of Alabama!'

The Phenix City Story *

US   1955   100m   bw

Allied Artists (Sam Bischoff, David Diamond)

A young lawyer fights the racketeers who control his town.

Goodish example of the semi-documentary melodramas of small-town corruption which swarmed out of Hollywood following the Kefauver investigations.

w Crane Wilbur, Dan Mainwaring d Phil Karlson ph Harry Neumann m Harry Sukman

☆ Richard Kiley, *Edward Andrews*, John McIntire, Kathryn Grant

Phenomena: see *Creepers*

'Some Things In Life Just Can't Be Explained.'

Phenomenon

US   1996   124m   Technicolor   Panavision

Buena Vista/Touchstone (Barbara Boyle, Michael Taylor)

A dim-witted mechanic becomes a genius after he is knocked out by seeing a bright light in the sky.

Sentimental weepie with the message that it's good to conform.

w Gerald DiPego d Jon Turteltaub ph Phedon Papamichael m Thomas Newton pd Garreth Stover ed Bruce Green

☆ John Travolta, Kyra Sedgwick, Forest Whitaker, Jeffrey DeMunn, Robert Duvall, Richard Kiley, Brent Spiner

'Suggests that, in late-20th-century America, to work at gaining knowledge is to be weird – a freak to be feared. The film would be unbearable were Travolta not so consistently charming.' – *Ken Tucker, Entertainment Weekly*

'Don't Say it. See it!'

Phffft

US   1954   91m   bw

Columbia (Fred Kohlmar)

The title refers to the sound of an expiring match; the story tells of a couple who get divorced and try to find out what they have been missing.

Champagne comedy with no bubbles.

w George Axelrod d Mark Robson ph Charles Lang m Frederick Hollander

☆ Jack Lemmon, Judy Holliday, Kim Novak, Jack Carson, Luella Gear, Donald Randolph, Donald Curtis, Merry Anders

'At best, moderate entertainment.' – *Saturday Review*

'No One Would Take On His Case ... Until One Man Was Willing To Take On The System.'

Philadelphia **

US   1993   125m   Technicolor

TriStar/Clinca Estetica (Edward Saxon, Jonathan Demme)

A successful homosexual lawyer with AIDS sues his firm for unfair dismissal after he is sacked for 'an attitude problem'.

A feel-good film about AIDS, set within a standard Hollywood courtroom drama; it is well made and absorbing, given its limits.

w Ron Nyswaner d Jonathan Demme ph Tak Fujimoto m Howard Shore pd Kristi Zea ed Craig McKay

☆ Tom Hanks, Denzel Washington, Jason Robards, Mary Steenburgen, Antonio Banderas, Ron Vawter, Robert Ridgely, Charles Napier, Joanne Woodward

'An ideal film for people who have never known anyone with AIDS ... extremely well-made message picture.' – *Variety*

'The film ultimately becomes a documentary on the ravages of AIDS – and on the masochistic machismo of Method acting.' – *Richard Corliss, Time*

'A heartbreakingly mediocre film. It's dishonest, it's often legally, medically and politically inaccurate, and it breaks my heart that I must say it's simply not good enough and I'd rather people not see it at all.' – *Larry Kramer*

🎬 Tom Hanks; song 'Streets of Philadelphia' (m/ly Bruce Springsteen)

🎵 Ron Nyswaner; song 'Philadelphia' (m/ly Neil Young); make-up

The Philadelphia Experiment *

US   1984   101m   CFI color

New World/Cinema Group (Joel B. Michaels, Douglas Curtis)

Seamen on a 1943 destroyer fall through a time warp into 1984, and have one hell of a job getting back.

Science fiction, Outer Limits/Final Countdown style; quite watchable, and technically proficient, but the claim that it was based on an actual incident seems a bit tall.

w William Gray, Michael Janover book William I. Moore, Charles Berlitz d Stewart Raffill ph Dick Bush m Ken Wannberg ad Chris Campbell ed Neil Travis, William Hoy

☆ Michael Paré, Nancy Allen, Eric Christmas, Bobby Di Cicco, Louise Latham

The Philadelphia Experiment 2

US   1993   97m   colour

Trimark (Mark Levinson, Doug Curtis)

An experiment goes wrong and a modern bomber-plane goes through the space-time continuum into a place of dictatorship and concentration camps.

Undemanding action fare that does little with its science-fiction elements.

w Kevin Rock, Nick Paine d Stephen Cornwell ph Ronn Schmidt m Gerald Couriet pd Armin Ganz ed Nina Gilberti sp Frank Ceglia

☆ Brad Johnson, Marjean Holden, Gerrit Graham, James Greene, Geoffrey Blake, Cyril O'Reilly, John Christian Grass

'An old idea, passably reworked.' – *Sight and Sound*

† The film was released direct to video in Britain.

'Uncle Leo's bedtime story for you older tots! The things they do among the playful rich – oh, boy!'

The Philadelphia Story ****

US   1940   112m   bw

MGM (Joseph L. Mankiewicz)

A stuffy heiress, about to be married for the second time, turns human and returns gratefully to number one.

Hollywood's most wise and sparkling comedy, with a script which is even an improvement on the original play. Cukor's direction is so discreet you can hardly sense it, and all the performances are just perfect.

w Donald Ogden Stewart play Philip Barry d George Cukor ph Joseph Ruttenberg m Franz Waxman ad Cedric Gibbons

☆ Katharine Hepburn, Cary Grant, James Stewart, Ruth Hussey, Roland Young, John Halliday, Mary Nash, Virginia Weidler, John Howard, Henry Daniell

'There are just not enough superlatives sufficiently to appreciate this show.' – *Hollywood Reporter*

'An exceptionally bright job of screenplay writing ... though films like this do little to advance the art of motion pictures, they may help to convince some of the more discerning among cultural slugabeds that when movies want to turn their hand to anything, they can turn it.' – *Otis Ferguson*

† Cary Grant donated his salary to war relief.

🎬 Donald Ogden Stewart; James Stewart

🎵 best picture; George Cukor; Katharine Hepburn; Ruth Hussey

Philo Vance

The smooth sleuth created by S. S. Van Dine was a popular film hero of the thirties, for several different companies and several different actors. As a series it was very variable indeed.

1929 The Canary Murder Case (Paramount: William Powell), The Greene Murder Case (Paramount: William Powell)

1930 The Bishop Murder Case (MGM: Basil Rathbone), The Benson Murder Case (Paramount: William Powell)

1933 The Kennel Murder Case (qv) (Warner: William Powell)

1934 The Dragon Murder Case (Warner: Warren William)

1935 The Casino Murder Case (MGM: Paul Lukas)

1936 The Garden Murder Case (MGM: Edmund Lowe)

1937 Night of Mystery (Paramount: Grant Richards), The Scarab Murder Case (British: Wilfrid Hyde-White)

1939 The Gracie Allen Murder Case (Paramount: Warren William), Calling Philo Vance (Warner: James Stephenson)

1947 Philo Vance Returns (PRC: William Wright), Philo Vance's Gamble (PRC: Alan Curtis), Philo Vance's Secret Mission (PRC: Alan Curtis)

Der Philosoph

West Germany   1988   83m   colour

Mainline/Moana Film Produktion (Rudolf Thome)

aka: *Three Women in Love*

A writer finds three women to love and look after him.

Updating of Greek myth to male fantasy.

wd Rudolf Thome ph Reinhold Vorschneider m Hanno Rinne ad Eve Schaenen ed Dörte Völz-Mannarell

☆ Johannes Herrschmann, Adriana Altaras, Friederike Tiefenbacher, Claudia Matschulla, Jürgen Wink, Werner Gerber, Anton Rey

Phobia

Canada   1980   90m   colour

Borough Park (Zale Magder)

Five volunteer phobics, released from jail for experiments, are killed one by one.

Unprepossessing whodunnit with horror touches but none of the style one might expect from its director.

w Lew Lehman, Jimmy Sangster, Peter Bellwood d John Huston ph Reginald H. Morris m Andre Gagnon

☆ Paul Michael Glaser, John Colicos, Susan Hogan, Alexandra Stewart, David Bolt

'The androids on Titus 4 have taken over the asylum.'

Phoenix

US   1995   96m   colour

Triad (Jimmy Lifton, Dan Bates, Troy Cook)

An élite team, sent down to a mining planet to deal with revolting androids, discovers that things are not what they seem.

Unoriginal action movie with dull dialogue, clichéd characters and a predictable plot.

w Jimmy Lifton, Troy Cook d Troy Cook ph T. Alexander m Lisa Bloom pd James Scanlon ed Paulette Renée Victor sp Stargate Films

☆ Brad Dourif, Billy Drago, Stephen Nichols, Denice Duff, Peter Murnik, William Sanderson, Robert Gossett, Betsy Soo

Phone Call from a Stranger

US   1952   96m   bw

TCF (Nunnally Johnson)

Of four airplane acquaintances, only one survives a crash; he visits the families of the others.

Four stories with an unlikely link. (The compendium craze, which had started in 1948 with Quartet, was now straining itself.) Nothing to remember except Miss Davis.

w Nunnally Johnson d Jean Negulesco ph Milton Krasner m Franz Waxman

☆ Bette Davis, Gary Merrill, Michael Rennie, Shelley Winters, Keenan Wynn, Evelyn Varden, Warren Stevens, Craig Stevens

'A cinematic party line on which several conversations are going at once, none of them coming across very distinctly.' – *Time*

The Photograph *

Greece/France   1986   120m   colour

Two expatriate Greeks living in Paris encourage each other's hopes for the future with tragic results.

Dour, skilfully made film of people unable to alter the trajectory of their lives.

wd Nicos Papatakis ph Aris Stavrou m Christodoulos Chalaris

☆ Aris Retsos, Christos Tsangas

'Another World ... As Close As The Beat Of Your Heart.'

Photographing Fairies *

GB   1997   104m   Technicolor

Entertainment/Starry Night/Polygram (Michele Camarda)

A photographic expert, devastated by the death of his wife and his experiences in the First World War, investigates photographs of fairies taken by two young girls and concludes that they are genuine.

An odd, obsessive film, about love and death and how people cope with loss; while not entirely successful, it has its moments.

w Nick Willing, Chris Harrald novel Steve Szilagyi d Nick Willing ph John de Borman m Simon Boswell pd Laurence Dorman ed Sean Barton

☆ Toby Stephens, Ben Kingsley, Emily Woof, Frances Barber, Philip Davis, Rachel Shelley, Edward Hardwicke, Hannah Bould

'The cinematic equivalent of the well-made play, the made-for-television film. It's intriguing, occasionally moving, but to magnify its impact it would be better seen on the smaller screen.' – *Nick Kimberley, Sight and Sound*

† The story of the Cottingley Fairies was also the basis for another film, *Fairytale: A True Story* (qv).

†† The script for the film is said to have gone through 23 drafts.

Photos Scandale

France   1968   69m   Eastmancolor

Tanagra/Impex

A detective investigates when wealthy businessmen are blackmailed after their daughters are photographed in compromising situations.

Ludicrous, illogical soft-porn thriller, so clichéd that its trench-coated, cigarette-smoking private eye rarely removes his hat, even when making love; it is the sort of film in which a character can complain, with a straight face, of someone being 'more puritanical than all the Popes put together'.

wd Patrick Aubin ph Pierre Robes m Gary Sandeur

☆ Marcel Charvey, Muriel Montosse, Sandra Flower, Sylvie Schmidt, Brigitte Lahaie

Physical Evidence

US   1988   99m   colour

Rank/Columbia (Martin Ransohoff)

An ex-cop, accused of murder, begins to have doubts about the female lawyer hired to defend him.

Dull thriller with an unnecessarily convoluted plot.

w Bill Phillips story Steve Ransohoff, Bill Phillips d Michael Crichton ph John A. Alonzo m Henry Mancini pd Dan Yarhi ed Glenn Farr

☆ Burt Reynolds, Theresa Russell, Ned Beatty, Kay Lenz, Ted McGinley, Tom O'Brien, Kenneth Welsh, Ray Baker, Ken James, Michael P. Moran

'The whole exercise, while never quite collapsing, contrives to look and sound peculiarly futile.' – *Philip Strick, MFB*

'Faith in chaos.'

Pi **

US   1998   85m   bw

Live Entertainment/Truth & Soul/Harvest/Plantain/Protozoa (Eric Watson)

An obsessive mathematician seeks to find a number that will explain the universe.

Gripping, clever theological and psychological thriller, which is less about explanations than observing varieties of monomania in action.

wd Darren Aronofsky ph Matthew Libatique m Clint Mansell pd Matthew Marraffi ed Oren Sach

☆ Sean Gullette, Mark Margolis, Ben Shenkman, Pamela Hart, Stephen Pearlman, Samia Shoaib

'If his film leaves one unsatisfied, it's still remarkable to what extent Aronofsky has rendered the cerebral kinetically intense. The film's imaginative, diverse images create a mind's-eye urban claustrophobia; such intensity may exhaust over 85 minutes' course, but it's never less than impressive.' – *Dennis Harvey, Variety*

Il Piacere: see *The Pleasure*

The Piano ****

Australia   1993   120m   Eastmancolor

Entertainment/CIBY 2000/Jan Chapman

A mute Scottish widow travels with her young daughter for an arranged marriage to a landowner in New Zealand, where she is forced to leave her most-treasured possession, her piano, on a beach.

A complex drama of lust, love and a woman emerging from an emotional silence in a repressive community into a self-determined and fulfilled life; beautifully

photographed and impeccably acted, it is powerful and moving.

wd *Jane Campion* ph *Stuart Dryburgh* m *Michael Nyman* pd *Andrew McAlpine* ed *Veronika Jenet*

☆ Holly Hunter, Harvey Keitel, Sam Neill, Anna Paquin, Kerry Walker, Genevieve Lemon, Tungla Baker, Ian Mune

'A riveting excursion into 19th-century sexuality, a movie that takes the conventions of the Gothic romance and refracts them through a dark contemporary lens.' – *David Ansen, Newsweek*

'Not since the early days of cinema, when audiences trampled over each other towards the exit to avoid the train emerging from the screen, could I imagine the medium of film to be so powerful.' – *Lizzie Francke, Sight and Sound*

'An emotionally devastating tour de force, both heart-rending and heart-warming.' – *Film Review*

† The film shared the *Palme d'Or* as best film, and Holly Hunter won the award as best actress, at the Cannes Film Festival in 1993.

♟ Holly Hunter; Anna Paquin; Jane Campion (as writer)

♟ best picture; Jane Campion (as director); Stuart Dryburgh; Veronika Jenet; costume design (Janet Patterson)

♟ Holly Hunter; Andrew McAlpine

Piatka z Ulicy Barskiej: see *Five Boys from Barska Street*

Piccadilly *
GB 1929 105m bw silent
BIP (E. A. Dupont)

A club owner's fiancée is accused of killing his Chinese mistress.

Sub-Edgar Wallace melodrama, no longer watchable with a straight face.

w Arnold Bennett *d* E. A. Dupont *ph* Werner Brandes

☆ Gilda Gray, Anna May Wong, Jameson Thomas, Cyril Ritchard, Ellen Pollock, Charles Laughton, Debroy Somers and his Band

† Sound added in 1930.

Piccadilly Incident *
GB 1946 102m bw
ABP (Herbert Wilcox)

During World War II, a girl believed drowned returns from the front to find her husband remarried.

The Enoch Arden theme again, and the first of the Wilcox-Neagle 'London' films, though untypically a melodrama with a sad ending. Efficient enough for its chosen audience.

w Nicholas Phipps *d* Herbert Wilcox *ph* Max Greene *m* Anthony Collins

☆ Anna Neagle, Michael Wilding, Michael Laurence, Frances Mercer, Coral Browne, A. E. Matthews, Edward Rigby, Brenda Bruce

† Michael Wilding was cast only after Rex Harrison and John Mills had proved unavailable.

Piccadilly Jim *
US 1936 100m bw
MGM (Harry Rapf)

A cartoonist helps his father to marry by making the bride's stuffy family objects of ridicule.

Amiable comedy with a diverting London setting.

w Charles Brackett, Edwin Knopf *novel* P. G. Wodehouse *d* Robert Z. Leonard *ph* Joseph Ruttenberg *m* William Axt

☆ Robert Montgomery, Madge Evans, Frank Morgan, Billie Burke, Eric Blore, Robert Benchley, Ralph Forbes, Cora Witherspoon, E. E. Clive

Piccadilly Third Stop
GB 1960 90m bw
Rank/Sydney Box/Ethiro (Norman Williams)

A smooth crook seduces the daughter of an eastern ambassador in London to gain entry to the embassy and rob it.

Boring and rather unpleasant thriller partly redeemed by a final chase through the Underground.

w Leigh Vance *d* Wolf Rilla *ph* Ernest Steward *m* Philip Green

☆ Terence Morgan, Yoko Tani, John Crawford, William Hartnell, Mai Zetterling, Dennis Price, Ann Lynn

Pick a Star
US 1937 76m bw
MGM/Hal Roach

An innocent girl in Hollywood achieves stardom with the help of a publicity man.

Perfectly awful Cinderella story with interesting glimpses behind the studio scenes and (if you can wait that long) a couple of good Laurel and Hardy sequences.

w Richard Flournoy, Arthur Vernon Jones, Thomas J. Dugan *d* Edward Sedgwick *ph* Norbert Brodine *m* Marvin Hatley, Arthur Morton *ed* William Terhune

☆ Rosina Lawrence, Jack Haley, Patsy Kelly, Mischa Auer, *Stan Laurel, Oliver Hardy*, Charles Halton, Lyda Roberti

'Part farce, part comedy, part musical and three parts dull.' – *Variety*

Pick Up
US 1933 80m bw
B. P. Schulberg/Paramount

A girl released from jail picks up with a truck driver, but her crooked husband reappears.

Sob story of the Peg's Paper type; a yawn.

w S. K. Lauren, Agnes Leahy, Vina Delmar *d* Marion Gering

☆ Sylvia Sidney, George Raft, William Harrigan, Lillian Bond

'Good title and cast, weakish film.' – *Variety*

Pick Up
US 1951 78m bw
Columbia (Hugo Haas)

A lonely middle-aged man falls for a tart who is interested only in his money.

Modest variation on The Blue Angel, the first of several second features made by Haas to feature himself as a second Emil Jannings. They got progressively more maudlin.

wd *Hugo Haas ph* Paul Ivano *m* Harold Byrns

☆ Hugo Haas, Beverly Michaels, Allan Nixon, Howland Chamberlin

The Pickle
US 1993 100m Technicolor/bw
Columbia (Paul Mazursky)

A middle-aged, once admired film director returns from France for the premiere of a science-fiction movie he made for the money, about farm boys who fly a giant cucumber to another planet.

Sour and self-referential movie about Hollywood; it's a measure of its failure that the deliberately banal excerpts from the sf movie are more entertaining than the soul-searchings of its central character.

wd *Paul Mazursky ph* Fred Murphy *m* Michel Legrand *pd* James Bissell *ed* Stuart Papp

☆ Danny Aiello, Dyan Cannon, Clotilde Courau, Shelley Winters, Barry Miller, Jerry Stiller, Chris Penn, Little Richard, Jodi Long, Rebecca Miller, Ally Sheedy

'Aims for comedy and poignance that never come, and feels wearily disenchanted and out of touch.' – *Todd McCarthy, Variety*

Pickpocket **
France 1959 80m bw
Lux

A lonely, compulsive pickpocket is redeemed through love.

Based on the themes of Dostoevsky's Crime and Punishment, an austere but moving and complex drama, notable for its scenes of thievery.

wd *Robert Bresson ph* Léonce-Henry Burel *m* Jean-Baptiste Lully *ed* Raymond Lamy

☆ Martin Lassalle, Marika Green, Pierre Leymarie, Jean Pelegri, Pierre Etaix, Kassagi, Dolly Scal, César Gattegno

'The style of the film is characteristic of the director. It is one of persistent concentration: the camera will not be deflected from its close stare at the silent face, the tense figure in the foreground, but this time the method defeats itself. In rejecting every irrelevant action, in ruthlessly refining away every decoration, Bresson has thrown away the motives as well.' – *Dilys Powell*

Pickup Alley: see *Interpol*

The Pick-Up Artist
US 1987 81m colour
TCF (David L. Macleod)

A smug, compulsively womanizing teacher falls for the daughter of an alcoholic in trouble with gangsters.

A romantic comedy short on laughs and romance; what excites the director is gambling, which is no fun either.

wd *James Toback ph* Gordon Willis *m* Georges Delerue *pd* Paul Sylbert *ed* David Bretherton, Angelo Corrao

☆ Molly Ringwald, Robert Downey Jnr, Dennis Hopper, Harvey Keitel, Danny Aiello, Mildred Dunnock, Victoria Jackson, Bob Gunton, Frederick Koehler

'Full of spangly good humor. In its own irrepressible way it's sustained. It's not heady enough, not a lift-off, but it's bright and convivial, like the sound of the sixties girl groups on the track. It keeps you laughing.' – *Pauline Kael*

'Anybody's back seat will do – as long as he's going her way!'

Pickup on 101
US 1972 93m Movielab
AIP

A lady hitchhiker picks up with an old hobo and an unemployed rock 'n' roller.

Sentimental rather than sensational is this small drama which starts slowly and goes nowhere.

w Anthony Blake *d* John Florea *ph* Brick Marquard *m* Stu Phillips

☆ Lesley Warren, Jack Albertson, Martin Sheen, Michael Ontkean

Pickup on South Street **
US 1953 80m bw
TCF (Jules Schermer)

A pickpocket steals a girl's wallet and finds himself up to his neck in espionage.

Over-rich mixture of crime, violence and anti-communism, smartly made without being very interesting.

wd *Samuel Fuller story* Dwight Taylor *ph* Joe MacDonald *m* Leigh Harline *ad* Lyle R. Wheeler, George Patrick *ed* Nick de Maggio

☆ Richard Widmark, Jean Peters, *Thelma Ritter*, Richard Kiley

† Remade 1968 as *Capetown Affair*.

♟ Thelma Ritter

The Pickwick Papers *
♙♙ GB 1952 115m bw
George Minter (Bob McNaught)

Various adventures of the Pickwick Club culminate in Mrs Bardell's suit for breach of promise.

Flatly conceived and loosely constructed Dickensian comedy; good humour and lots of well-known faces do not entirely atone for lack of artifice.

wd *Noel Langley ph* Wilkie Cooper *m* Antony Hopkins *ed* Fred Pusey

☆ *James Hayter, James Donald*, Donald Wolfit, Hermione Baddeley, Hermione Gingold, Kathleen Harrison, *Nigel Patrick*, Alexander Gauge, Lionel Murton

'As welcome as the sun in the morning and as British as a cup of tea.' – *Daily Mirror*

'A town – a stranger – and the things he does to its people! Especially its women!'

Picnic ***
US 1955 113m Technicolor Cinemascope
Columbia (Fred Kohlmar)

A brawny wanderer causes sexual havoc one summer in a small American town.

Seminal melodrama setting new directions for Hollywood and illustrating the side of life the Hardy family never showed. Generally quite compulsive despite some overacting.

w Daniel Taradash *play* William Inge *d* Joshua Logan *ph* James Wong Howe *m* George Duning *pd* Jo Mielziner *ad* William Flannery *ed* Charles Nelson, William A. Lyon

☆ *William Holden, Kim Novak*, Rosalind Russell, *Susan Strasberg*, Arthur O'Connell, Cliff Robertson, Betty Field, Verna Felton, Reta Shaw

'Mr Logan's idea of an outing in the corn country includes a choir of at least a hundred voices, a camera so alert that it can pick up the significance of the reflection of a Japanese lantern in a pool (futility, wistfulness, the general transience of life, as I get it) and a sound track let loose in the most formidable music I've heard in my time at the movies.' – *New Yorker*

♟ art direction; editing

♟ best picture; Joshua Logan; George Duning; Arthur O'Connell

'A recollection of evil...'

Picnic at Hanging Rock ****
Australia 1975 115m Eastmancolor
Picnic Productions/Australia Film Corporation (Hal and Jim McElroy)

In 1900, schoolgirls set out for a picnic; some disappear and are never found.

A film that ventures successfully into the mystic and bravely offers no answer to its central puzzle, just a question that continues to haunt the mind. Whether you want to regard it as a parable of sexual awakening or of colonial repression, it successfully retains its own mystery.

w Cliff Green *novel* Joan Lindsay *d* Peter Weir *ph* Russell Boyd *m* Bruce Smeaton

☆ Rachel Roberts, Dominic Guard, Helen Morse, Jacki Weaver, Vivean Gray, Kirsty Child

'Atmospherically vivid, beautifully shot, and palpably haunting.' – *Michael Billington, Illustrated London News*

'If this film had a rational and tidy conclusion, it would be a good deal less interesting. But as a tantalizing puzzle, a tease, a suggestion of forbidden answer just out of earshot, it works hypnotically and very nicely indeed.' – *Roger Ebert*

♟ Russell Boyd

'Hawaii, 1918. She left Japan for a man she had never met, in a new world she could not imagine ... America.'

Picture Bride
US 1995 95m Foto-Kem
Artificial Eye/Thousand Cranes/Miramax (Lisa Onodera, Cellin Glick)

An 18-year-old Japanese woman comes gradually to love the middle-aged man in Hawaii that she is tricked into marrying.

Effective domestic drama along predictable lines.

w Kayo Hatta, Mari Hatta *d* Kayo Hatta *ph* Claudio Rocha *m* Mark Adler *pd* Paul Guncheon *ed* Lynzee Klingman, Mallory Gottlieb

☆ Youki Kudoh, Akaira Takayama, Tamlyn Tomita, Cary-Hiroyuki Tagawa, Toshiro Mifune, Yoko Sugi

'However predictable the story-line, the film-makers succeed in making us care about the characters right from the start.' – *Philip Kemp, Sight and Sound*

Picture Mommy Dead
US 1966 88m Pathécolor
Embassy/Berkeley (Bert I. Gordon)

A girl who has been hospitalized following the death of her mother in a fire returns home to find, apparently, that her father's new wife is trying to kill her.

Twist-ending shocker with tired stars, from the tag end of the Baby Jane cycle.

w Robert Sherman *d* Bert I. Gordon *ph* Ellsworth Fredericks *m* Robert Drasnin

☆ Don Ameche, Martha Hyer, Zsa Zsa Gabor, Susan Gordon, Maxwell Reed, Signe Hasso, Wendell Corey

The Picture of Dorian Gray ***
US 1945 110m bw (Technicolor inserts)
MGM (Pandro S. Berman)

A Victorian gentleman keeps in the attic a picture of himself, which shows his age and depravity while he stays eternally young.

Elegant variation on Dr Jekyll and Mr Hyde, presented in portentous style which suits the subject admirably.

wd *Albert Lewin novel* Oscar Wilde *ph* Harry Stradling *m* Herbert Stothart *ad* Cedric Gibbons, Hans Peters

☆ *George Sanders*, Hurd Hatfield, Donna Reed, Angela Lansbury, Peter Lawford

SIR HENRY (GEORGE SANDERS): 'If I could get back my youth, I'd do anything in the world – except get up early, take exercise or be respectable.'

⊚ Digital Video Disc Region 2   ⊚ Digital Video Disc Region 1   ♫ Soundtrack released on compact disc   ☆ Cast in approximate order of importance   † Points of interest   ♫ Notable songs   ♟ Academy Award   ♟ Academy Award nomination   ♟ BAFTA sir henry: 'I apologize for the intelligence of my remarks, Sir Thomas, I had forgotten that you were a Member of Parliament.'

DORIAN (HURD HATFIELD): 'If only the picture could change and I could be always what I am now. For that, I would give anything. Yes, there's nothing in the whole world I wouldn't give. I'd give my soul for that.'

'Respectful, earnest, and, I'm afraid, dead.' – James Agee

'Loving and practised hands have really improved Wilde's original, cutting down the epigrammatic follow ... and rooting out all the preciousness which gets in the way of the melodrama.' – Richard Winnington

♟ Harry Stradling
♟ Angela Lansbury; art direction

'Kate always lived her life by the rules ... some rules were meant to be broken.'

Picture Perfect

US   1997   100m   Technicolor
TCF/3 Arts (Erwin Stoff)

In order to succeed in her job, a female advertising executive pretends to be engaged to a man she briefly met.
Slight, enervated romantic comedy that might have made a passable half-hour television sitcom.
w Arleen Sorkin, Paul Slansky, Glenn Gordon Caron d Glenn Gordon Caron ph Paul Sarossy m Carter Burwell pd Larry Fulton ed Robert Reitano
☆ Jennifer Aniston, Jay Mohr, Kevin Bacon, Olympia Dukakis, Illeana Douglas, Kevin Dunn, Faith Prince, Anne Twomey
'Too ineffectual to tickle either the funnybone or the heartstrings.' – *Variety*

The Picture Show Man *

👪 Australia   1977   98m   Eastmancolor
Limelight (Joan Long)
Adventures of a travelling picture show troupe in the 1920s.
Agreeably nostalgic incidents, not very dramatically connected.
w Joan Long d John Power ph Geoffrey Burton m Peter Best
☆ Rod Taylor, John Meillon, John Ewart, Harold Hopkins, Judy Morris, Patrick Cargill

The Picture Snatcher *

US   1933   77m   bw
Warner
An ex-racketeer just out of prison becomes a scandal photographer.
Lively star vehicle, interesting for period detail.
w Allen Rivkin, P. J. Wolfson d Lloyd Bacon ph Sol Polito md Leo F. Forbstein
☆ James Cagney, Ralph Bellamy, Patricia Ellis, Alice White, Ralf Harolde, Robert Emmett O'Connor, Robert Barrat
'A vulgar but generally funny collection of blackouts.' – *Time*
'Fast, snappy, tough and packed with action.' – *New York Herald Tribune*
† Remade 1947 as *Escape from Crime*, with Richard Travis.

Pidä Huivista Kiinni, Tatjana: see *Take Care of Your Scarf, Tatjana*

Pie in the Sky

US   1995   95m   Foto-Kem
New Line (Denise Shaw, Allan Mindel)

Boy obsessed with traffic meets girl, loses girl, gets girl.
An offbeat romantic comedy about an unlikely couple which attempts to overwhelm with its charm, which proves resistible well before the end.
wd Bryan Gordon ph Bernd Heinl m Michael Convertino pd Linda Pearl ed Colleen Halsey
☆ Josh Charles, Anne Heche, Peter Riegert, Christine Ebersole, Wil Wheaton, Christine Lahti, John Goodman, Bob Balaban
'For all its manifest flaws (structural, directional ✓ and dramatic), it serves as a cheeky reminder of how formulaic and orthodox most Hollywood teen romance flicks are.' – *Sight and Sound*

A Piece of the Action

US   1977   135m   Metrocolor
Warner/First Artists/Verdon (Melville Tucker)

Crooks are blackmailed into helping rebellious adolescents.
A black version, at immense length, of the hoodlum comedies in which the Dead End Kids so often featured. Not badly made, but out of date without being nostalgic.
w Charles Blackwell story Timothy March d Sidney Poitier ph Don Morgan m Curtis Mayfield
☆ Sidney Poitier, James Earl Jones, Bill Cosby, Denise Nicholas, Hope Clarke, Tracy Reed, Jason Evers, Marc Lawrence

The Pied Piper **

👪 US   1942   86m   bw
TCF (Nunnally Johnson)
An elderly man who hates children finds himself smuggling several of them out of occupied France.
Smart, sentimental, occasionally funny war adventure.
w Nunnally Johnson novel Nevil Shute d Irving Pichel ph Edward Cronjager m Alfred Newman
☆ Monty Woolley, Anne Baxter, Roddy McDowall, Otto Preminger, J. Carrol Naish, Lester Matthews, Jill Esmond, Peggy Ann Garner
♟ best picture; Edward Cronjager; Monty Woolley

The Pied Piper

👪 GB   1971   90m   Eastmancolor
Panavision
Sagittarius/Goodtimes (David Puttnam, Sanford Lieberson)
In 1349 a strolling minstrel rids Hamelin of a plague of rats.
Paceless, slightly too horrific, and generally disappointing fantasy, especially from this director; poor sets and restricted action.
w Jacques Demy, Mark Peploe, Andrew Birkin d Jacques Demy ph Peter Suschitsky m Donovan pd Assheton Gorton
☆ Donovan, Donald Pleasence, Michael Hordern, Jack Wild, Diana Dors, John Hurt

Pièges

France   1939   120m   bw
Speva (Michel Safra)
US title: *Personal Column*
aka: *Snares*
A dancer acts as a decoy to trap a serial killer murdering women who answer lonely hearts advertisements.
A thriller that finds it hard to accommodate murders and leave room for its debonair singing star.
w Jacques Companeez, Ernest Neuville, Simon Gantillon d Robert Siodmak m Michelet ad G. Wakhevitch ed Yvonne Martin
☆ Maurice Chevalier, Pierre Renoir, Marie Déa, Erich von Stroheim, Jean Temerson, André Brunot
† This was Siodmak's last French film before he left for Hollywood. It was remade in Hollywood in 1947 as *Lured* (qv), directed by Douglas Sirk.

Pier 13: see *Me and My Gal (1932)*

Pierre of the Plains

US   1942   66m   bw
MGM
Adventures of a cheerful trapper in Canada's northwest territory.
Unashamed second-feature version of a play which its producer, Edgar Selwyn, had written in 1907 and which had been filmed in 1918 (as Hearts of the Wild) and in 1922 (as Over the Border). (Selwyn was the man who once merged with Goldfish to form Goldwyn, a name which Goldfish then kept.)
w Bertram Millhauser, Lawrence Kimble d George B. Seitz
☆ John Carroll, Ruth Hussey, Bruce Cabot, Reginald Owen, Henry Travers, Evelyn Ankers

Pierrot Le Fou **

France/Italy   1968   110m   Eastmancolor
Techniscope
Rome/Paris/SNC (Renée Pigneres, Gerard Beytout)

Bored by his marriage, a Frenchman leaves his wife at a party and takes off with an old flame, now involved in gun-running and crime.
A pulp thriller re-told in terms of farce and artifice, and a playful and enjoyably intellectual romp through pop culture, though it is difficult to take it as seriously as its maker intended.
wd Jean-Luc Godard novel *Obsession* by Lionel White ph Raoul Coutard m Antoine Duhamel ad Pierre Guffroy ed Françoise Colin
☆ Jean-Paul Belmondo, Anna Karina, Dirk Sanders, Raymond Devos, Graziella Galvani
'Godard has reached a stage at which self-confidence and self-indulgence join hands to lead him into a disaster area.' – *Dilys Powell*
'Purports to be against a world of advertising and conspicuous consumption; yet what it offers as an alternative, the mindless, feckless, and finally feelingless relationship of its hero and heroine, is at least as repugnant.' – *John Simon*

The Pigeon that Took Rome

US   1962   101m   bw   Panavision
Paramount/Llenroc (Melville Shavelson)
American undercover agents are smuggled into Rome during the German occupation.
Heavy-going war comedy-drama with bright sequences countered by too little wit and too many voluble Italians.
wd Melville Shavelson novel *The Easter Dinner* by Donald Downes ph Daniel Fapp m Alessandro Cicognini
☆ Charlton Heston, Elsa Martinelli, Brian Donlevy, Harry Guardino, Baccaloni

Pigeons

US   1970   87m   Movielab
Saturn/Lois Holland Callaway/Plaza (Richard Lewis)
aka: *The Sidelong Glances of a Pigeon Kicker*
A Princeton graduate turned New York taxi driver thinks himself superior to all those he meets.
Dim would-be satirical drama making fun of conformity. With its pretentious and unlikeable protagonist, the fun is flat when it should be fizzy. Its style derives from the cycle of dull 'swinging London' movies, probably because of its British director.
w Ron Whyte novel *David Boyer* d John Dexter ph Urs Furrer m Pat Williams, Lee Holdridge, Edd Kaleroff, Chris Dedrick, Warren Marley ad Manny Gerard ed John Oettinger
☆ Jordan Christopher, Jill O'Hara, Robert Walden, William Redfield, Kate Reid, Lois Nettleton, Riggs O'Hara, Boni Enten, David Doyle, Elaine Stritch, Melba Moore, Pat Ast

Pigskin Parade

US   1936   93m   bw
TCF (Bogart Rogers)

GB title: *Harmony Parade*
A country farmer becomes a college football hero.
Livelier-than-average college comedy.
w Harry Tugend, Jack Yellen, William Conselman d David Butler ph Arthur Miller md David Buttolph songs Sidney Mitchell, Lew Pollack
☆ Stuart Erwin, Patsy Kelly, Jack Haley, Johnny Downs, Betty Grable, Arline Judge, Dixie Dunbar, Judy Garland, Tony Martin, Elisha Cook Jnr
♟ Stuart Erwin

The Pilgrim *

US   1923   38m   bw   silent
First National/Charles Chaplin
An escaped convict disguises himself as a minister and does a few good deeds.
Star comedy with more sentiment than laughter.
wd Charles Chaplin ph Rollie Totheroh
☆ Charles Chaplin, Edna Purviance, Kitty Bradbury, Mack Swain

Pilgrimage *

US   1933   95m   bw
Fox
A selfish mother sees the error of her ways when she makes a post-war journey to her son's grave.
Strong character study, put across with style.
w Dudley Nichols, Philip Klein, Barry Conners story I. A. R. Wylie d John Ford
☆ Henrietta Crosman, Heather Angel, Norman Foster, Marian Nixon, Maurice Murphy, Charley Grapewin, Hedda Hopper
'A natural for residential clienteles: mother love from a new angle.' – *Variety*

Pillars of the Sky

US   1956   95m   Technicolor   Cinemascope
U-I (Robert Arthur)
GB title: *The Tomahawk and the Cross*
An Indian scout and a missionary help bring peace between cavalry and Indians.
Modest Western, adequately done.

w Sam Rolfe novel *Frontier Fury* by Will Henry d George Marshall ph Harold Lipstein m Joseph Gershenson ad Alexander Golitzen, Bill Newberry ed Milton Carruth
☆ Jeff Chandler, Dorothy Malone, Ward Bond, Keith Andes, Lee Marvin, Sydney Chaplin, Michael Ansara, Willis Bouchey

The Pillow Book **

GB/Netherlands/France   1995   126m   colour
Film Four/Kasander & Wigman/Alpha/Woodline (Kees Kasander)

A Japanese woman with a fetish for being written upon takes an elaborate revenge on the homosexual publisher who humiliated her father.
A complex narrative that gives a sexual edge to the act of writing, it is ravishing to watch, especially in its split-screen recreations of pleasures listed in The Pillow Book of Sei Shonagon, but too often seems little more than an elaborate literary conceit.
wd Peter Greenaway ph Sacha Vierny pd Wilbert van Dorp, Andree Putman ed Chris Wyatt, Peter Greenaway
☆ Vivian Wu, Yoshi Oida, Ken Ogata, Hideko Yoshida, Ewan McGregor, Judy Ongg, Ken Mitsuishi
'Decidedly not everyone's cup of sake, but for Greenaway fans and filmgoers willing to be seduced by a mature and richly decorative slice of Asian culture, The Pillow Book will be a treat, albeit at times a demanding one.' – *David Stratton, Variety*

Pillow of Death

US   1945   66m   bw
Universal
A lawyer is suspected when his wife is murdered.
First fumbling story in the Inner Sanctum series, of which the title sequence was always the most entertaining portion.
w George Bricker d Wallace Fox
☆ Lon Chaney Jnr, Brenda Joyce, J. Edward Bromberg, Rosalind Ivan, Clara Blandick

Pillow Talk **

US   1959   110m   Eastmancolor
Cinemascope
Universal/Arwin (Ross Hunter, Martin Melcher)

Two people who can't stand each other fall in love via a party line.
Slightly elephantine romantic comedy which nevertheless contains a number of funny scenes and was notable for starting off the Hudson–Day partnership and a run of similar comedies which survived the sixties.
w Stanley Shapiro, Maurice Richlin, Russell Rouse, Clarence Greene d Michael Gordon ph Arthur E. Arling m Frank de Vol ad Richard H. Riedel
☆ Doris Day, Rock Hudson, Tony Randall, Thelma Ritter, Nick Adams, Julia Meade, Allen Jenkins, Marcel Dalio, Lee Patrick
♟ Stanley Shapiro, Maurice Richlin, Russell Rouse, Clarence Greene
♟ Frank de Vol; Doris Day; Thelma Ritter; art direction

Pillow to Post

US   1945   96m   bw
Warner (Alex Gottlieb)
A girl poses as a soldier's wife to get a hotel room.
World War II comedy on a familiar theme (The More the Merrier, Standing Room Only, The Doughgirls, etc). Uninspired.
w Charles Hoffman play *Pillar to Post* by Rose Simon Kohn d Vincent Sherman ph Wesley Anderson m Frederick Hollander
☆ Ida Lupino, Sydney Greenstreet, William Prince, Stuart Erwin, Ruth Donnelly, Barbara Brown, Frank Orth

The Pilot *

US   1979   92m   colour
Summit/New Line
A once great pilot insists on working despite an alcohol problem.
Not enough meat on the story bones is enough to ground this dismal drama, but the air scenes look terrific and the actors seem to believe in what they're doing.
wd Cliff Robertson novel *Robert P. Davis* ph Walter Lassally m John Addison

☆ *Cliff Robertson*, Frank Converse, Diane Baker, Gordon MacRae, Dana Andrews, Milo O'Shea

Pilot Number Five

US   1943   71m   bw
MGM (B. P. Fineman)

A pilot in the South Pacific volunteers for a desperate mission because – we learn in flashback – he hates fascists.

Rather unpalatable propaganda encased in dim drama.

w David Hertz d George Sidney ph Paul C. Vogel m Lennie Hayton

☆ Franchot Tone, Gene Kelly, Marsha Hunt, Van Johnson, Alan Baxter, Dick Simmons, Steve Geray

Pimpernel Smith **

GB   1941   121m   bw
British National (Leslie Howard)
▣

US title: *Mister V*
aka: *The Fighting Pimpernel*

A professor of archaeology goes into war-torn Europe to rescue refugees.

The Scarlet Pimpernel unassumingly and quite effectively brought up to date, with memorable scenes after a slow start.

w Anatole de Grunwald, Roland Pertwee, Ian Dalrymple d Leslie Howard ph Max Greene m John Greenwood

☆ *Leslie Howard*, Mary Morris, Francis L. Sullivan, Hugh McDermott, Raymond Huntley, Manning Whiley, Peter Gawthorne, David Tomlinson

'Funny, touching, imaginative, and enormously exciting.' – *C. A. Lejeune*

'Just an amusing piece of hokum.' – *Leslie Howard*

A Pin for the Butterfly *

GB/Czechoslovakia   1994   113m   colour
Heureka/Channel 4/British Screen/Skreba (James Crawford)

Life in the 50s under a Stalinist regime, as seen through the eyes of a young girl, who, unlike the adults around her, tries to tell the truth.

An uneven drama that begins in an exaggerated and grotesque style before settling for a more absorbing account of compromise and betrayal.

wd Hannah Kodicek ph Ivan Slapeta m Ilona Sekacz pd Jiri Matolin ed Kant Pan

☆ Joan Plowright, Ian Bannen, Hugh Laurie, Imogen Stubbs, Ian Hogg, Florence Hoath

'In a market crammed with bloody vengeance tales and erotica, *Pin* deserves points for its seriousness of purpose and willingness to make a tough family film.' – *Variety*

Pin Up Girl

US   1944   83m   Technicolor
TCF (William Le Baron)
▣   ⊚

A Washington secretary becomes a national celebrity when she meets a navy hero.

Adequate star flagwaver, mildly interesting for its new streamlined set designs.

w Robert Ellis, Helen Logan, Earl Baldwin story Libbie Block d Bruce Humberstone ph Ernest Palmer md Emil Newman, Charles Henderson ch Hermes Pan ad James Basevi, Joseph C. Wright songs James V. Monaco, Mack Gordon

☆ Betty Grable, John Harvey, Martha Raye, Joe E. Brown, Eugene Pallette, Dave Willock, Charles Spivak and his Orchestra

'A spiritless blob of a musical, and a desecration of a most inviting theme.' – *Bosley Crowther*

Pink Cadillac *

US   1989   122m   Technicolor
Warner/Malpaso (David Valdes)
▣   ▣   ⊚   ⌂

A bounty hunter goes in search of a mother who has disappeared with her baby and a pink Cadillac containing $250,000 belonging to a bunch of neo-Nazis.

Amiable, if somewhat aimless, comedy with unsubtle performances.

w John Eskow d Buddy Van Horn ph Jack N. Green m Steve Dorff pd Edward C. Carfagno ed Joel Cox

☆ Clint Eastwood, Bernadette Peters, Timothy Carhart, John Dennis Johnston, Michael Des Barres, Geoffrey Lewis

Pink Floyd The Wall *

GB   1982   95m   Metrocolor
MGM/Tin Blue/Goldcrest (Alan Marshall)
▣   ⊚

A washed-up pop star finds his life a mixture of fact and fiction, of reality and animation.

Dislikeable self-pitying dirge, accompanied by animation which will not be to everybody's taste but is sometimes brilliantly arranged.

w Roger Waters d Alan Parker ph Peter Biziou m Roger Waters animation designer Gerald Scarfe

☆ Bob Geldof, Christine Hargreaves, James Laurenson, Eleanor David, Kevin McKeon, Bob Hoskins

'A vacuous, bombastic and humourless piece of self-indulgence.' – *Steve Jenkins, MFB*

'Roger Waters flounders in woman-hating self-pity; Gerald Scarfe turns up particularly weedy examples of his animated savagery; and Alan Parker revels in the chance to make a feature-length TV commercial.' – *Sight and Sound*

The Pink Jungle

US   1968   104m   Techniscope
Universal/Cherokee (Stan Margulies)

A photographer and his model are stranded in a South American village and become involved in a diamond hunt.

Curious mixture of adventure and light comedy that works only in patches.

w Charles Williams novel *Snake Water* by Alan Williams d Delbert Mann ph Russell Metty m Ernie Freeman

☆ James Garner, Eva Renzi, George Kennedy, Nigel Green, Michael Ansara, George Rose

'Another backlot cheapie.' – *Robert Windeler*

'A unique experience in visual fantasy.'
Pink Narcissus

US   1971   102m   colour
Smerpix/Les Folies des Hommes
▣

A young hustler, trying to escape the sordid reality of his life, imagines a series of mainly masturbatory homosexual encounters: as a matador, a Roman slave, a harem boy in the tent of a sheik, a wood nymph, and as his own, ageing client.

A once-notorious gaudily coloured exploitation film aimed at gay audiences which is very much of its time, being almost a definitive example of camp and kitsch. It received its first large-scale British showing in a grainy video release in 1993.

w Anonymous d Anonymous ph Anonymous md Martin Jay Sadoff, Gary Goch ed Martin Jay Sadoff

☆ Bobby Kendall

'We are expected to be drooling, aroused, captivated – and weak enough to approve this celebration of the bottomless Narcissistic pit – instead of damning it as the oafish indulgence it really is. One would care less if it were content to be pornography, but instead it operates smugly within the "decadent" underground style of Anger et al.' – *Shock Xpress*

† Although the film and the video release list the producer, director and writer as anonymous, some prints credit 'Jim Bidgood' as director.

The Pink Panther **

👪   US   1963   113m   Technirama
UA/Mirisch (Martin Jurow)
▣   ▣   ⊚   ⌂

An incompetent *Sûreté* inspector is in Switzerland on the trail of a jewel thief called The Phantom.

Sporadically engaging mixture of pratfalls, Raffles, and Monsieur Hulot, all dressed to kill and quite palatable for the uncritical.

w Maurice Richlin, Blake Edwards d Blake Edwards ph Philip Lathrop m Henry Mancini ad Fernando Carrere animation De Patie-Freleng

☆ David Niven, Peter Sellers, Capucine, Claudia Cardinale, Robert Wagner, Brenda de Banzie, Colin Gordon

† Peter Ustinov had been offered the role of Clouseau first, but backed out. Inspector Clouseau later became a cartoon character and also provoked six sequels: *A Shot in the Dark, Inspector Clouseau, The Return of the Pink Panther, The Pink Panther Strikes Again, The Revenge of the Pink Panther* and *Son of the Pink Panther.*

♫ Henry Mancini

The Pink Panther Strikes Again *

👪   GB   1976   103m   DeLuxe   Panavision
United Artists/Amjo (Blake Edwards)
▣   ▣   ⊚   ⌂

After a nervous breakdown, Chief Inspector Dreyfus builds up a vast criminal organization devoted to the extermination of Inspector Clouseau.

Zany pratfall farce with signs of over-confidence since the success of The Return of the Pink Panther. But some gags are funny, despite a rather boring star.

w Frank Waldman, Blake Edwards d Blake Edwards ph Harry Waxman m Henry Mancini

☆ Peter Sellers, Herbert Lom, Colin Blakely, Leonard Rossiter, Lesley-Anne Down, Burt Kwouk

♫ song 'Come To Me' (*m*Henry Mancini, *ly*Don Black)

Pink String and Sealing Wax *

GB   1945   89m   bw
Ealing (Michael Balcon)

In 1880 Brighton, a publican's wife plans to have her husband poisoned.

Unusual, carefully handled period crime melodrama which needed a slightly firmer grip.

w Diana Morgan, Robert Hamer play Roland Pertwee d Robert Hamer ph Richard S. Pavey m Norman Demuth

☆ Googie Withers, Mervyn Johns, Gordon Jackson, Sally Ann Howes, Mary Merrall, John Carol, Catherine Lacey, Garry Marsh

The Pink Telephone

France   1975   93m   colour
Gaumont International/Les Productions 2000 (Alain Poire)

aka: *Le Téléphone Rose*

An old-fashioned, provincial businessman becomes involved with an expensive Parisian call-girl.

Satire on big business, sexual politics and middle-aged angst that runs out of steam before the end.

w Francis Véber d Edouard Molinaro ph Gérard Hameline m Vladimir Cosma pd Robert Sussfeld, Michel Choquet ed Robert and Monique Isnardon

☆ Mireille Darc, Pierre Mondy, Michel Lonsdale, Daniel Ceccaldi, Françoise Prevost, Gérard Hérold

'She passed for white!'
Pinky **

US   1949   102m   bw
TCF (Darryl F. Zanuck)

In the American South, a Negro girl who passes for white has romantic problems.

Rather blah problem picture which seemed brave at the time; a highly professional piece of work nevertheless.

w Philip Dunne, Dudley Nichols novel *Quality* by Cid Ricketts Summer d Elia Kazan ph Joe MacDonald m Alfred Newman

☆ Jeanne Crain, Ethel Barrymore, Ethel Waters, William Lundigan, Basil Ruysdael, Nina Mae McKinney, Frederick O'Neal, Evelyn Varden

'It has about as much daring as a cheese-mite. It is careful to affront no particular section of the public, to draw no particular conclusion, to outrage no particular code of cinema ethics, to challenge no particular box-office convention.' – *C. A. Lejeune*

⅋ Jeanne Crain; Ethel Barrymore; Ethel Waters

'Out of a dream world into yours!'
Pinocchio ****

👪   US   1940   77m   Technicolor
Walt Disney
▣   ▣   ⊚   ⌂

The blue fairy breathes life into a puppet, which has to prove itself before it can turn into a real boy.

Charming, fascinating, superbly organized and streamlined cartoon feature without a single second of boredom.

m/ly Leigh Harline, Ned Washington, Paul J. Smith supervisors Ben Sharpsteen, Hamilton Luske

☆ Featuring the voices of Dickie Jones, Christian Rub, Cliff Edwards, Evelyn Venable, Walter Catlett, Frankie Darro

'A film of amazing detail and brilliant conception.' – *Leonard Maltin*

'A work that gives you almost every possible kind of pleasure to be got from a motion picture.' – *Richard Mallett, Punch*

'The limits of the animated cartoon have been blown so wide open that some of the original wonder of pictures has been restored.' – *Otis Ferguson*

⅃ Leigh Harline, Ned Washington, Paul J. Smith (*m*); song 'When You Wish Upon a Star' (*m*Leigh Harline, *ly*Ned Washington)

Pinocchio and the Emperor of the Night

👪   US   1987   90m   colour
Palace/Filmation (Lou Scheimer)
▣   ⊚

Pinocchio continues his adventures as a real boy.

Sugary confection that cannot stand comparison with Disney's classic.

w Robby London d Hal Sutherland m Anthony Marinelli, Brian Banks songs Will Jennings, Barry Mann, Steve Tyrell

☆ Featuring the voices of Ed Asner, Lana Beeson, Tom Bosley, Linda Gary, Scott Grimes, James Earl Jones, Rickie Lee Jones, Don Knotts

Pioneer Builders: see *The Conquerors*

Pippi in the South Seas (dubbed)

Sweden/Germany   1974   100m   Movielab
Beta/Iduna/K B Nordart (Olle Nordemar)

Pippi, a girl with superhuman strength, sets off with two friends to rescue her father who has been captured by pirates.

An atrocious children's film, cheap and shoddy and so badly dubbed as to be unwatchable.

novel Astrid Lindgren d Olle Hellbom ph Kalle Bergholm m George Riedel ed Jan Persson, Jutte Schweden

☆ Inger Nilsson, Maria Persson, Par Sundberg, Alfred Schieske, Wolfgang Volz, Nikolaus Schilling

Pippi Longstocking

👪   Sweden/Germany/Canada   1997   78m   colour
Optimum/Nelvana/TFC/Iduna (Hasmi Giakoumis, Merle-Anne Ridley)

Thieves try to steal the gold belonging to the strongest girl in the world, who sets up home alone while waiting for the return of her sea-faring father.

Yet another dud film made from a favourite children's book, with substandard animation and a dull story.

w Catherine Stackelberb, Ken Sobol, Frank Nissen books Astrid Lindgren d Clive Smith m Anders Berglund ad Clive Powsey ed Noda Tsamardos

☆ Featuring voices of: Melissa Altro, Catherine O'Hara, Dave Thomas, Gordon Pinsent, Wayne Robson, Carole Pope, Richard Binsley, Rick Jones

'Here, Pippi's dislike of conformity, attractive on the printed page, seems selfish and tiresome rather than spirited.' – *Sight and Sound*

'Lost River Lake was a thriving resort – until they discovered...'
Piranha *

US   1978   92m   Metrocolor
New World (Roger Corman, Jeff Schechtman, Jon Davison)
▣   ▣

A mad doctor's stock of man-eating fish is accidentally released into the local rivers.

Slightly spoofy thriller with a high death rate and a better than usual script. On the whole, an improvement on Jaws.

w John Sayles d Joe Dante ph Jamie Anderson m Pino Donaggio sp Jon Berg

☆ Bradford Dillman, Heather Menzies, Kevin McCarthy, Bruce Gordon, Barbara Steele, Keenan Wynn, Dick Miller

'They bred the ultimate killing machine ... Now you're not safe OUT of the water!'
Piranha II: The Spawning

Italy/US   1982   94m   Technicolor
Columbia/Chako (Chako van Leevwew, Jeff Schechtman)
▣   ⊚

aka: *Piranha II: Flying Killers*

Holiday-makers are attacked by mutant flying fish.

Feeble low-budget sequel, the first feature of a director who went on to make more successful action movies, including Terminator and Terminator 2.

w H. A. Milton d James Cameron m Roberto D'Ettore Piazzoli m Steve Powder ed Robert Silvi

☆ Tricia O'Neil, Steve Marachuk, Lance Henriksen, Ricky G. Paull, Ted Richert, Leslie Graves

The Pirate **

US   1948   102m   Technicolor
MGM (Arthur Freed)

In a West Indian port, a girl imagines that a wandering player is a famous pirate, who in fact is her despised and elderly suitor.
Minor MGM musical with vivid moments and some intimation of the greatness shortly to come; all very set-bound, but the star quality is infectious.
w Albert Hackett, Frances Goodrich *play* S. N. Behrman d Vincente Minnelli *m/ly* Cole Porter *md* Lennie Hayton ph Harry Stradling
☆ Gene Kelly, Judy Garland, Walter Slezak, Gladys Cooper, Reginald Owen, George Zucco, the Nicholas Brothers
♪ Lennie Hayton

The Pirate Movie

Australia   1982   105m   Colorfilm
Fox/Joseph Hamilton International

A girl dreams herself back into *The Pirates of Penzance* but changes some of the details.
Galumphing fantasy which suggests that Australian film-makers had better stick to Botany Bay, Gallipoli and sheep shearing.
w Trevor Farrant d Ken Annakin ph Robin Copping *pd* Tony Woollard *ed* Kenneth W. Zemke
☆ Kristy McNichol, Christopher Atkins, Ted Hamilton, Bill Kerr, Maggie Kirkpatrick, Garry Macdonald
'The slapstick and the swordplay are as ineptly choreographed as the production numbers.' – *Kim Newman, MFB*

Pirates

France/Tunisia   1986   124m   Eclaircolor
Panavision
Cannon/Carthago/Accent Dominco (Tarak Ben Ammar)

A British buccaneer, cast adrift on a raft, is taken aboard a Spanish galleon and causes mayhem.
A disaster from a director who should never be allowed to attempt comedy. This one is revolting when it is not a crashing bore.
w Gerard Brach, Roman Polanski d Roman Polanski ph Witold Sobocinski m Philippe Sarde
☆ Walter Matthau, Damien Thomas, Richard Pearson, Roy Kinnear, Ferdy Mayne, Charlotte Lewis
† The galleon, which cost 8 million dollars, was not wasted. It was given to the municipality of Cannes and became a tourist attraction.
♪ costumes (Anthony Powell)

Pirates of Blood River *

GB   1961   84m   Technicolor
Hammerscope
Hammer (Anthony Nelson Keys)
Pirates in search of gold terrorize a Huguenot settlement.
Land-locked blood and thunder for tough schoolboys.
w John Hunter, John Gilling d John Gilling ph Arthur Grant
☆ Christopher Lee, Andrew Keir, Kerwin Mathews, Glenn Corbett, Peter Arne, Oliver Reed, Marla Landi, Michael Ripper

Pirates of Monterey

US   1947   72m   Technicolor
Paul Malvern/Universal-International
A Spanish girl goes to California to marry a soldier but is romanced by an outlaw.
Predictable action hokum.
w Sam Hellman, Margaret Buell Wilder d Alfred Werker
☆ Maria Montez, Rod Cameron, Mikhail Rasumny, Philip Reed, Gilbert Roland, Gale Sondergaard, Tamara Shayne, Robert Warwick

The Pirates of Penzance

GB   1982   112m   Technicolor   Panavision
Universal (Joseph Papp, Timothy Burrill)

An adaptation of the Gilbert and Sullivan operetta in the form of the Joseph Papp Broadway revival.
What was tolerably pretty and witty on the stage is a great bore on wide film.
wd Wilford Leach ph Douglas Slocombe m Gilbert and Sullivan pd Elliott Scott ed Anne V. Coates

☆ Kevin Kline, Angela Lansbury, Linda Ronstadt, George Rose, Tony Azito, Rex Smith
'Not the slightest trace of imagination.' – *MFB*
'Anyone who thinks Gilbert and Sullivan indestructible should see this.' – *Observer*

Pirates of Tortuga

US   1961   97m   DeLuxe   Cinemascope
Sam Katzman/TCF
In the 17th-century Caribbean, a privateer is ordered by the king to go undercover and rout Sir Henry Morgan.
Listless swashbuckler with inferior talent.
w Melvin Levy, Jesse L. Lasky Jnr, Pat Silver d Robert D. Webb
☆ Ken Scott, Dave King, Letitia Roman, John Richardson, Robert Stephens, Edgar Barrier

Pirates of Tripoli

US   1955   72m   Technicolor
Columbia (Sam Katzman)
A pirate captain comes to the aid of an oriental princess.
More akin to the Arabian Knights than Blackbeard, but not bad for a double-biller.
w Allen March d Felix Feist ph Henry Freulich md Mischa Bakaleinikoff
☆ Paul Henreid, Patricia Medina, Paul Newland, John Miljan, Lillian Bond

Pisma Myortovovo Cheloveka: see *Letters from a Dead Man*

A Pistol for Ringo *

Italy/Spain   1965   99m   colour
PCM/Balcázar (Alberto Pugliese, Luciano Ercoli)
original title: *Una Pistola per Ringo*
A wandering gunman goes to the aid of a Texan family whose ranch has been taken over by Mexican bandits.
Above-average spaghetti Western, much influenced by the work of John Ford and Howard Hawks.
wd Duccio Tessari ph Francisco Marin m Ennio Morricone ad Juan Alberto Soler ed Lucia Quaglia
☆ Giuliano Gemma, Fernando Sancho, Hally Hammond (Lorella de Luca), Nieves Navarro, Antonio Casas, Jorge Martin
† It was followed by a sequel, *The Return of Ringo* (qv).

Pistola di Deo: see *God's Gun*

The Pit and the Pendulum *

US   1961   85m   Pathécolor   Panavision
AIP/Alta Vista (Roger Corman)

Lovers plan to drive her brother mad; he responds by locking them in his torture chamber.
The centrepiece only is borrowed from Poe; the rest is lurid but mostly ineffective. Still, its commercial success started the Poe cycle of the sixties.
w Richard Matheson d Roger Corman ph Floyd Crosby m Les Baxter
☆ Vincent Price, Barbara Steele, John Kerr
'As in *House of Usher*, the quality of the film is its full-blooded feeling for Gothic horror – storms and lightning, mouldering castles and cobwebbed torture chambers, bleeding brides trying to tear the lids from their untimely tombs.' – *David Robinson*

Pit of Darkness

GB   1962   76m   bw
Butcher's
A man returns home to discover that he has been missing for three weeks.
Tame and implausible amnesiac thriller, acted without much conviction.
wd Lance Comfort novel *To Dusty Death* by Hugh McCutcheon ph Basil Emmot m Martin Slavin ad John Earl ed John Trumper
☆ William Franklyn, Moira Redmond, Bruno Barnabe, Leonard Sachs, Nigel Green, Humphrey Lestocq, Anthony Booth, Nanette Newman, Michael Balfour

Pitch Black

US   2000   108m   colour
UIP/Gramercy/Interscope (Tom Engelman)
After their spaceship crashes on an unknown planet, the survivors, who include a hardened killer, find that it is too hot to move except at night, when the place is crawling with fierce creatures.
Essentially a 'B' movie with few pretensions, this delivers a few shocks efficiently enough, but is otherwise in need of a better script and a bigger budget.
w Jim Wheat, Ken Wheat, David Twohy d David Twohy ph David Eggby m Graeme Revell pd Graham 'Grace' Walker ed Rick Shaine sp Patrick Tatopoulos
☆ Radha Mitchell, Vin Diesel, Cole Hauser, Keith David, Lewis Fitz-Gerald, Claudia Black, Rhiana Griffith, John Moore, Simon Burke
'Mildly scary but not particularly engaging on any other level.' – *Emanuel Levy, Variety*

Pitfall

US   1948   85m   bw
Samuel Bischoff

An insurance investigator proves easy prey for a grasping woman.
Modest suspenser, quite efficiently made.
w Jay Dratler novel Jay Dratler d André de Toth ph Harry Wild md Louis Forbes
☆ Dick Powell, Lizabeth Scott, Jane Wyatt, Raymond Burr, John Litel, Byron Barr, Ann Doran

Pittsburgh

US   1942   91m   bw
Universal (Charles K. Feldman)

A coal miner's daughter has two loves, all of them trying to improve their social status as Pittsburgh becomes a world centre of steel production.
Routine melodrama ending as a flagwaver, and allowing none of its stars any opportunity.
w Kenneth Gamet, Tom Reed d Lewis Seiler ph Robert de Grasse m Hans Salter
☆ Marlene Dietrich, Randolph Scott, John Wayne, Frank Craven, Louise Allbritton, Shemp Howard, Ludwig Stossel, Thomas Gomez

Pixote **

Brazil   1981   127m   colour
Palace/Embrafilme

A 10-year-old living on the streets of São Paulo tries to survive by pimping, drug-dealing and murder.
Grim and sensational exposé of a social problem, using actual homeless children to add to its reality.
w Hector Babenco, Jorge Duran novel *Infancia dos Mortos* by José Louzeiro d Hector Babenco ph Rodolfo Sanches m John Neschling ad Clovis Bueno ed Luiz Elias
☆ Fernando Ramos da Silva, Jorge Julião, Gilberto Moura, Edilson Lino, Zenildo Oliveira Santos, Claudio Bernardo, Marilia Pera, José Nilson Dos Santos

The Pizza Triangle: see *Jealousy Italian Style*

'They do it in the name of love!'
A Place for Lovers

US   1969   102m   colour
MGM
A dying American fashion designer retires to her Italian villa and has a high old time with an Italian engineer.
Incomparably crass tearjerker which seems eager to offer too many morals about life and love and art.
w Peter Baldwin, Ennio de Concini, Tonino Guerra, Julian Halevy, Cesare Zavattini d Vittorio de Sica
☆ Faye Dunaway, Marcello Mastroianni, Caroline Mortimer, Karin Engh
'The most God-awful piece of pseudo-romantic slop I've ever seen.' – *Roger Ebert, Chicago Sun Times*
'The worst movie I have seen all year and possibly since 1926.' – *Charles Champlin, L.A. Times*
'The five scriptwriters who supposedly worked on the film must have spent time enough at the watercooler to flood a camel.' – *Time*

'Seldom has the screen so captured the fire and fever of today's youth! Seldom has a film boasted three such exciting star performances!'
A Place in the Sun **

US   1951   122m   bw
Paramount/George Stevens

A poor young man, offered the chance of a rich wife, allows himself to be convicted and executed for the accidental death of his former fiancée.
Overblown, overlong and over-praised melodrama from a monumental novel of social guilt; sometimes visually striking, this version alters the stresses of the plot and leaves no time for sociological detail. A film so clearly intended as a masterpiece could hardly fail to be boring.
w Michael Wilson, Harry Brown novel *An American Tragedy* by Theodore Dreiser d George Stevens ph William C. Mellor m Franz Waxman ad Hans Dreier, Walter Tyler ed William Hornbeck
☆ Montgomery Clift, Elizabeth Taylor, Shelley Winters, Anne Revere, Keefe Brasselle, Fred Clark, Raymond Burr, Frieda Inescort, Shepperd Strudwick, Kathryn Givney, Walter Sande
'An almost incredibly painstaking work ... mannered enough for a very fancy Gothic murder mystery. This version gives the story a modern setting, but the town is an arrangement of symbols of wealth, glamour and power versus symbols of poor, drab helplessness – an arrangement far more suitable to the thirties than to the fifties.' – *Pauline Kael*
♟ script; George Stevens; William C. Mellor; Franz Waxman; editing
♪ best picture; Montgomery Clift; Shelley Winters

A Place of One's Own **

GB   1944   92m   bw
GFD/Gainsborough (R. J. Minney)
In Edwardian times, an old house is taken over by an elderly couple, and their young companion is possessed by the spirit of a murdered girl.
Charming little ghost story, not quite detailed enough to be totally effective.
w Brock Williams novel Osbert Sitwell d Bernard Knowles ph Stephen Dade m Hubert Bath md Louis Levy
☆ James Mason, Barbara Mullen, Margaret Lockwood, Dennis Price, Helen Haye, Michael Shepley, Dulcie Gray, Moore Marriott
'A fine piece of work ... gripping, marvellous, outstanding, eerie, perky, beautiful, lovely and different.' – *C. A. Lejeune*
'One comes away with an impression of elegance which has not so far been frequent in the British cinema.' – *Dilys Powell*

A Place to Go

GB   1963   86m   bw
British Lion/Excalibur (Michael Relph, Basil Dearden)
A young man depressed by his urban environment turns to crime.
Panorama of London low life, efficiently varied and well made but not in any way memorable. It Always Rains on Sunday, fifteen years earlier, wears better.
w Michael Relph, Clive Exton novel *Bethnal Green* by Michael Fisher d Basil Dearden ph Reg Wyer m Charles Blackwell
☆ Rita Tushingham, Mike Sarne, Doris Hare, John Slater, Bernard Lee, Barbara Ferris, Roy Kinnear

Place Vendôme **

France/Belgium/GB   1998   118m   colour
Technovision
Artificial Eye/TF1/l'Etang/Alhena/Angel's Co. (Alain Sarde)

The alcoholic widow of a near-bankrupt jeweller tries to protect the business from its importunate creditors.
Elegant, intriguing French thriller that provides Deneuve with probably her best role for years, as a pressured woman recovering her dignity and abilities.
w Jacques Fieschi, Nicole Garcia d Nicole Garcia ph Laurent Dailland m Richard Robbins ad Thierry Flamand ed Luc Barnier, Francoise Bonnot cos Nathalie du Roscoat, Elisabeth Tavernier
☆ Catherine Deneuve, Jean-Pierre Bacri, Emmanuelle Seigner, Jacques Dutronc, Bernard Fresson, François Berléand, Philippe Clévenot

---

'A rhinestone rather than a gem, this is a drama that looks sophisticated and deep, but proves hollow.' – *Angie Errigo, Empire*

Places in the Heart

US 1984 111m Technicolor
Tri-Star/Delphi (Arlene Donovan)

In 1935 Texas, the sheriff's widow struggles to maintain the family farm.
All-American saga with asides including the Ku Klux Klan; though based on the author's recollections of childhood, it all seems predictable.
wd Robert Benton ph Nestor Almendros m John Kander pd Gene Callahan
☆ Sally Field, Lindsay Crouse, Ed Harris, Amy Madigan, John Malkovich, Danny Glover
'Basically just another calculated tug at the heartstrings.' – *Tom Milne, MFB*
🏆 Sally Field; original screenplay
🏆 best picture; John Malkovich (supporting actor); Lindsay Crouse (supporting actress); direction

Plaff! Or Too Afraid of Life *

Cuba 1988 92m colour
Metro/ICAIC (Ricardo Avila)
original title: *Desmasiado Miedo A La Vida, O Plaff*
A superstitious mother tries to get rid of her scientific daughter-in-law.
Deliberately ramshackle political comedy – the beginning of the film is kept to the end – which is not without a certain surrealist charm.
w Daniel Chavarría, Juan Carlos Tabío d Juan Carlos Tabío ph Julio Valdés ad Raúl Oliva ed Roberto Bravo, Osvaldo M. Donatien
☆ Daisy Granados, Thais Valdés, Luis Alberto Garcia, Raúl Pamares, Alicia Bustamente, Jorge Cao
'A wittily cynical exercise in alienation which oozes awkwardness and provokes uncomfortable laughter.' – *MFB*

La Plage des Enfants Perdus: see *The Beach of Lost Children*

The Plague Dogs

🏃 GB/US 1982 103m Technicolor
Nepenthe Productions

Two dogs escape from a research laboratory and are in danger of infecting the country with a deadly virus.
Misguided and woefully overlong attempt to preach a message through a cartoon. Like Watership Down, it needs the printed word and is deflected by the inevitably cuddly look of the animated animals.
wd Martin Rosen novel Richard Adams
☆ Featuring the voices of John Hurt, James Bolam, Christopher Benjamin, Judy Geeson, Barbara Leigh-Hunt

The Plague of the Zombies *

GB 1965 91m Technicolor
Hammer (Anthony Nelson Keys)

A voodoo-practising Cornish squire raises zombies from the dead and uses them to work his tin mine.
They don't explain why he didn't simply hire the living; apart from that this is Hammer on its better side, with a charming elderly hero and good suspense sequences.
w Peter Bryan d John Gilling ph Arthur Grant m James Bernard
☆ *André Morell, John Carson, Diane Clare, Brook Williams, Jacqueline Pearce, Alex Davion, Michael Ripper*
'Visually the film is splendid ... the script manages several offbeat strokes.' – *MFB*

Plain Clothes

US 1988 98m CFI color
Paramount (Richard Wechsler, Michael Manheim)

After his brother is accused of murdering a teacher, a cop, who is suspended from the force, decides to go undercover as a high-school student to find the real killer.
An occasionally amusing comedy, though it is doubtful whether there are enough laughs, or even smiles, to make watching it worthwhile.
w A. Scott Frank d Martha Coolidge ph Daniel Hainey m Scott Wilk pd Michel Levesque ed Patrick Kennedy, Edward Abroms
☆ Arliss Howard, Suzy Amis, George Wendt, Diane Ladd, Seymour Cassel, Larry Pine, Jackie Gayle, Abe Vigoda, Robert Stack

'Grandest love story ever told!'

The Plainsman **

US 1936 113m bw
Paramount/Cecil B. de Mille

The life of Wild Bill Hickok and his friends Buffalo Bill and Calamity Jane.
Standard big-scale 30s Western; narrative lumpy, characters idealized, spectacle impressive, technical credits high.
w Waldemar Young, Lynn Riggs, Harold Lamb d Cecil B. de Mille ph Victor Milner, George Robinson m George Antheil md Boris Morros
☆ Gary Cooper, James Ellison, Jean Arthur, Charles Bickford, Helen Burgess, Porter Hall, Paul Harvey, Victor Varconi
'It should do all right for business, ranging from big to good, possibly irregular in spots.' – *Variety*
'Certainly the finest western since *The Virginian*; perhaps the finest western in the history of the film.' – *Graham Greene*
† The story was remade as a TV movie in 1966, with Don Murray.

The Plainsman and the Lady

US 1946 84m bw
Republic

In 1847, the Pony Express is threatened by stagecoach owners.
Moderate Western for family consumption.
w Richard Wormser d Joseph Kane
☆ William Elliott, Gail Patrick, Vera Ralston, Joseph Schildkraut

Le Plaisir *

France 1952 97m bw
Stera/CCFC

Three stories by Guy de Maupassant, about the search for pleasure: 'Le Masque', 'La Maison Tellier', 'Le Modèle'.
Stylish but rather subdued compendium, with no highlights to stay in the memory.
w Jacques Natanson, Max Ophuls d Max Ophuls ph Christian Matras, Philippe Agostini m Joe Hajos ad Max Ophuls
☆ Claude Dauphin, Gaby Morlay; Madeleine Renaud, Danielle Darrieux, Ginette Leclerc, Jean Gabin, Pierre Brasseur; Simone Simon, Daniel Gélin
'An attractive theme tune, good performances, and the pleasure itself of virtuosity.' – *Gavin Lambert, MFB*
🏆 art direction

'There comes a time in every man's life when he just can't believe his eyes!'

Plan 9 from Outer Space

US 1958 79m bw
Wade Williams Productions (Edward D. Wood Jnr)

aka: *Grave Robbers from Outer Space*
Space people try to resurrect the Earth's dead and turn them against the world.
Inept mini-budgeter often hailed as the worst film ever made. It is certainly among the most boring.
wd Edward D. Wood Jnr ph William C. Thompson md Gordon Zahler ad Tom Kemp sp Charles Duncan
☆ Bela Lugosi, Tor Johnson, Gregory Walcott, Mona McKinnon, Vampira, Lyle Talbot
SAMPLE DIALOGUE: 'One thing's sure, Inspector Clay's dead. Murdered. And somebody's responsible.'
† Lugosi died after four days of shooting and is mostly represented by a double, who keeps his cape up so that it covers his face.

Planes, Trains and Automobiles *

US 1987 93m colour
UIP/Paramount (John Hughes)

An advertising executive, trying to get home for Thanksgiving, finds many obstacles hampering his progress, including an insufferable companion.
Cheerful farce that allows some room for characterization.
wd John Hughes ph Don Peterman m Ira Newborn pd John W. Corso ed Paul Hirsch
☆ Steve Martin, John Candy, Michael McKean, Kevin Bacon, Dylan Baker, Carol Bruce, Olivia Burnette, Diana Douglas, William Windom

'Somewhere in the universe, there must be something better than man!'

Planet of the Apes ***

🏃 US 1968 119m DeLuxe Panavision
TCF/Apjac (Mort Abrahams)

Astronauts caught in a time warp land on a planet which turns out to be Earth in the distant future, when men have become beasts and the apes have taken over.
Stylish, thoughtful science fiction which starts and finishes splendidly but suffers from a sag in the middle. The ape make-up is great.
Sequels, in roughly descending order of interest, were:
1969 Beneath the Planet of the Apes
1970 Escape from the Planet of the Apes
1972 Conquest of the Planet of the Apes
1973 Battle for the Planet of the Apes.
A TV series followed in 1974, and a cartoon series in 1975.
w Michael Wilson, Rod Serling novel *Monkey Planet* by Pierre Boulle d Franklin Schaffner ph Leon Shamroy m Jerry Goldsmith
☆ *Charlton Heston, Roddy McDowall, Kim Hunter, Maurice Evans, James Whitmore, James Daly, Linda Harrison*
'One of the most telling science fiction films to date.' – *Tom Milne*
🏆 make-up (John Chambers)
🏆 Jerry Goldsmith; costumes (Morton Haack)

The Planter's Wife

GB 1952 91m bw
Rank/Pinnacle (John Stafford)
US title: *Outpost in Malaya*
original title: *White Blood*
Malaya under the terrorists. A wife is planning to leave but changes her mind after she and her husband defend their home in a siege.
Superficial studio-bound melodrama unworthy of its subject but a good star vehicle.
w Peter Proud, Guy Elmes d Ken Annakin ph Geoffrey Unsworth m Allan Gray
☆ Claudette Colbert, Jack Hawkins, Ram Gopal, Jeremy Spenser, Tom Macauley, Helen Goss

Platinum Blonde *

US 1931 92m bw
Columbia

A newspaper reporter falls for an heiress.
Limp romantic comedy with interesting performances: the film which established Jean Harlow.
w Robert Riskin, Jo Swerling story Harry E. Chandler, Doug Churchill d Frank Capra ph Joseph Walker
☆ *Robert Williams, Loretta Young, Jean Harlow, Halliwell Hobbes, Reginald Owen*
'A programmer that fully entertains, is laughy and represents what cast, dialogue and direction can do with a lean story.' – *Variety*

Platinum High School

US 1960 96m bw
MGM (Red Doff)
GB title: *Rich, Young and Deadly*
A father investigates his son's death at a military academy for rich juvenile delinquents.
Hilarious serial-like melodrama with the worm turning to some effect.
w Robert Smith d Charles Haas ph Russell Metty m Van Alexander
☆ Mickey Rooney, Dan Duryea, Terry Moore, Warren Berlinger, Yvette Mimieux, Conway Twitty, Elisha Cook Jnr, Richard Jaeckel

'The first casualty of war is innocence.'

Platoon **

US 1986 120m CFI color
Hemdale/Arnold Kopelson

Experiences of infantrymen during the Vietnam war.
Not badly done in the style of Bataan (plus brutality and gore). One would have thought it too late to do it at all, but the American public made it a box-office hit.
wd Oliver Stone ph Robert Richardson m Georges Delerue ed Claire Simpson
☆ Tom Berenger, Willem Dafoe, Charlie Sheen, Forest Whitaker, Francesco Quinn
'It is fundamentally an entirely formulaic war movie, more "artistic" than many of its genre but true to conventions in both characters and narrative.' – *Judith Williamson, New Statesman*

🏆 best picture; Oliver Stone as director; Claire Simpson
🏆 Tom Berenger, Willem Dafoe; Oliver Stone for original screenplay; Robert Richardson
🏆 Oliver Stone (as director)

Play Dirty *

GB 1969 118m Technicolor Panavision
UA/Lowndes (Harry Saltzman)
During World War II, a squad of ex-criminals is given the job of destroying an enemy oil depot in North Africa.
Small-scale Dirty Dozen with would-be ironic twists; well made entertainment for the stout-hearted.
w Lotte Colin, Melvyn Bragg d André de Toth ph Edward Scaife m Michel Legrand
☆ Michael Caine, Nigel Davenport, Nigel Green, Harry Andrews, Bernard Archard, Daniel Pilon

Play It Again Sam *

US 1972 86m Technicolor Panavision
Paramount/APJAC/Rollins-Joffe (Arthur P. Jacobs)

A neurotic film critic is abandoned by his wife and seeks fresh companionship, with help from the shade of Humphrey Bogart.
Random comedy for star fans, mainly quite lively and painless.
w Woody Allen play Woody Allen d Herbert Ross ph Owen Roizman m Billy Goldenberg
☆ Woody Allen, Diane Keaton, Jerry Lacy, Susan Anspach

Play It as It Lays

US 1972 94m Technicolor Panavision
Universal
An unsuccessful actress takes stock of her wrecked life.
With-it melodrama which audiences preferred to be without.
w Joan Didion, John Gregory Dunne novel Joan Didion d Frank Perry
☆ Anthony Perkins, Tuesday Weld, Tammy Grimes, Adam Roarke, Ruth Ford

Play It Cool

GB 1962 81m bw
Independent Artists/Coronado (David Deutsch)
An unsuccessful rock group, twisting around London's clubs, saves an heiress from the clutches of an unscrupulous singer.
A slight, unsubtle comedy hampered by a lack of memorable songs, and intended to showcase the talents of Britain's best Elvis-styled rocker, which do not extend to acting; other singers featured include Helen Shapiro, Bobby Vee, Danny Williams, Shane Fenton and the Fentones, and Jimmy Crawford.
w Jack Henry d Michael Winner ph Reginald Wyer m Norrie Paramor m/ly Norrie Paramor, Richard B. Rowe, Bernard Jewry, Norman Newell, Ron Fraser, Bob Barratt, Larry Parnes ad Lionel Couch ed Tristam Cones
☆ Billy Fury, Michael Anderson Jnr, Dennis Price, Richard Wattis, Ray Brooks, Maurice Kaufman, Peter Barkworth, Max Bacon, Lionel Blair

Play Me Something

GB 1989 72m bw/colour
BFI/Film Four International/Scottish Film Production Fund/Grampian TV (Kate Swan)
On a small Scottish island, a group of passengers waiting for a plane listen to a story about an Italian peasant leaving his village to go to Venice.
An intellectual endeavour that never quite comes alive on the screen.
w John Berger, Timothy Neat story *Once in Europe* by John Berger d Timothy Neat ph Chris Cox m Jim Sutherland ad Annette Gillies ed Russell Fenton
☆ Lucia Lanzarini, Charlie Barron, John Berger, Hamish Henderson, Tilda Swinton, Stewart Ennis, Robert Carr, Liz Lochhead

'The scream you hear may be your own!'

Play Misty for Me *

US 1971 102m Technicolor
Universal/Malpaso (Robert Daley)

A radio disc jockey is pestered by a girl who turns out to be homicidally jealous.
Smartly made if over-extended psycho melodrama with good suspense sequences and a fair quota of shocks.
w Jo Heims, Dean Reisner d Clint Eastwood ph Bruce Surtees m Dee Barton

---

☆ Clint Eastwood, Jessica Walter, Donna Mills, John Larch

The Playboy: see *Kicking the Moon Around*

'Maurice brings a new kind of love to you!'
Playboy of Paris
US 1930 82m bw
Paramount
A waiter inherits a million but finds he can't leave his job, so he becomes a playboy by night only.
Rather rickety star vehicle which demands attention only when he is on screen.
w Percy Heath play *The Little Café* by Tristan Bernard d Ludwig Berger
☆ Maurice Chevalier, Frances Dee, O. P. Heggie, Stuart Erwin, Eugene Pallette
'Light, amusing farce story doesn't help and may hurt … Chevalier's the only draw.' – *Variety*

'In a small community, love is never a private affair.'
The Playboys *
GB 1992 109m Technicolor
Samuel Goldwyn/Green Umbrella (William P. Cartlidge, Simon Perry)
▥ ▦ ⊕
In an Irish village in the 1950s, the alcoholic local policeman and a strolling player both fall in love with an unmarried mother.
A soap opera-style narrative of thwarted love, of interest mainly for its performances.
w Shane Connaughton, Kerry Crabbe d Gillies MacKinnon ph Jack Conroy m Jean-Claude Petit pd Andy Harris ed Humphrey Dixon
☆ Albert Finney, Aidan Quinn, Robin Wright, Milo O'Shea, Alan Devlin, Niamh Cusack, Niall Buggy, Adrian Dunbar
'A heartbreak tragedy wrapped up inside an ingratiating comedy.' – *Alexander Walker, London Evening Standard*

The Player **
US 1992 124m DeLuxe
Guild/Avenue (David Brown, Michael Tolkin, Nick Wechsler)
▥ ▦ ⊕ ◉ ⌂
A Hollywood studio executive gets away with murder.
A deft and dazzling satire on the film industry – witty, surprising and intelligent.
w Michael Tolkin novel Michael Tolkin d Robert Altman ph Jean Lepine m Thomas Newman pd Stephen Altman ed Geraldine Peroni
☆ Tim Robbins, Greta Scacchi, Fred Ward, Whoopi Goldberg, Peter Gallagher, Brion James, Cynthia Stevenson, Vincent D'Onofrio, Dean Stockwell, Richard E. Grant, Sydney Pollack
'The movie has the exhilarating nonchalance of the director's seventies classics, and its tone is volatile, elusive: with breathtaking assurance, it veers from psychological-thriller suspense to goofball comedy to icy satire.' – *Terrence Rafferty, New Yorker*
† The film featured more than 60 stars playing themselves, including Harry Belafonte, James Coburn, Peter Falk, Teri Garr, Angelica Huston, Jack Lemmon, Nick Nolte, Burt Reynolds, Julia Roberts, Susan Sarandon, Rod Steiger and Bruce Willis.
♫ Robert Altman; Michael Tolkin; Geraldine Peroni
▼ Robert Altman; Michael Tolkin

Players: see *The Club*

Players
US 1979 120m Metrocolor
Paramount (Robert Evans)
▦
A pro tennis player is trained for top stardom by a sculptress with a mysterious past.
Entirely uninvolving romantic drama stretched around a Wimbledon match; slickness does not compensate for a gaping hole at the centre.
w Arnold Schulman d Anthony Harvey ph James Crabe m Jerry Goldsmith pd Richard Sylbert
☆ Ali MacGraw, Dean-Paul Martin, Maximilian Schell, Pancho Gonzalez

The Players Club
US 1998 104m DeLuxe
New Line (Patricia Charbonnet)
▥ ▦
A single mother works as a stripper to pay her way through college.
Energetic, uneven drama with a comic tone and an uncertain attitude towards sex and gender.
wd Ice Cube ph Malik Sayeed m Hidden Faces pd Dina Lipton ed Suzanne Hines
☆ Lisa Raye, Bernie Mac, Monica Calhoun, A. J. Johnson, Ice Cube, Alex Thomas, Jamie Foxx, Chrystale Wilson, Adele Givens, Larry McCoy
'A messy but lively B-movie that recalls the more spirited comedic dramas of the '70s blaxploitation era.' – *Joe Leydon, Variety*

Playgirl
US 1954 85m bw
Universal-International
A small-town girl becomes a good-time girl in the big city.
Totally unsurprising melodrama.
w Robert Blees d Joseph Pevney ph Carl Guthrie m Joseph Gershenson
☆ Shelley Winters, Barry Sullivan, Colleen Miller, Gregg Palmer, Richard Long, Kent Taylor

The Playgirl and the War Minister: see *The Amorous Prawn*

'To live and love in LA.'
Playing By Heart
US 1998 121m DeLuxe Panavision
Buena Vista/Miramax/Intermedia/Morpheus/Hyperion (Willard Carroll, Meg Liberman, Tom Wilhite)
▥ ▦ ⌂
In Los Angeles, a group of loosely-connected people look for love.
Garrulous romantic drama that never quite conveys true emotion.
wd Willard Carroll ph Vilmos Zsigmond m John Barry pd Melissa Stewart ed Pietro Scalia
☆ Gillian Anderson, Angelina Jolie, Madeleine Stowe, Anthony Edwards, Ryan Phillippe, Gena Rowlands, Sean Connery, Dennis Quaid, Ellen Burstyn, Jay Mohr, Jon Stewart, Patricia Clarkson, Nastassja Kinski
'A rather wearisome and sentimental film, with uneven acting.' – *Peter Bradshaw, Guardian*

Playing God
US 1997 94m DeLuxe
Blue Dolphin/Touchstone/Beacon (Marc Abraham, Laura Bickford)
▥ ▦ ⊕ ◉
A disgraced, drug-addicted surgeon goes to work for a gangster.
A lugubrious central performance sinks this sluggish, predictable thriller.
w Mark Haskell Smith d Andy Wilson ph Anthony B. Richmond m Richard Hartley pd Naomi Shohan ed Louise Rubacky
☆ David Duchovny, Timothy Hutton, Angelina Jolie, Michael Massee, Peter Stormare, Andrew Tiernan, Gary Dourdan, John Hawkes
'This trashy thriller aspires to flip black comedy but manages only moments of unintentional hilarity.' – *Liese Spencer, Sight and Sound*

Playmates *
US 1941 96m bw
RKO (Cliff Reid)
For the sake of a lucrative radio contract, John Barrymore agrees to turn bandleader Kay Kyser into a Shakespearian actor.
Barrymore's last film is a weird comedy concoction, awesome in its waste of his talents but fairly funny in a high school kind of way.
w James V. Kern d David Butler ph Frank Redman songs James Van Heusen, Johnny Burke
☆ Kay Kyser and his Band, John Barrymore, Ginny Simms, Lupe Velez, May Robson, Patsy Kelly, Peter Lind Hayes, George Cleveland

Playtime *
▥▥ France 1968 152m Eastmancolor
70mm
Specta Films (René Silvera)
▥ ▦
Hulot and a group of American tourists are bewildered by life in an airport, a business block and a restaurant.
Incredibly extended series of sketches, none of which is devastatingly funny. The irritation is that the talent is clearly there but needs control.
w Jacques Tati, Jacques Lagrange d Jacques Tati ph Jean Badal, Andreas Winding m Francis Lemarque pd Eugène Roman
☆ Jacques Tati, Barbara Dennek, Jacqueline Lecomte, Henri Piccoli
'Tati still seems the wrong distance from his audience: not so far that we cannot see his gifts, not close enough so that they really touch.' – *Stanley Kauffmann*
'How sad that the result of all this, though it includes a great deal of intermittent pleasure, comes at times so dangerously close to boredom.' – *Brenda Davies, MFB*
'A series of brilliant doodles by an artist who has earned the right to indulge himself on such a scale.' – *Alexander Walker*

Plaza Suite *
US 1971 114m Technicolor
Paramount (Howard B. Koch)
▥▥
Three sketches set in the same suite at New York's Plaza Hotel, with Walter Matthau appearing in all three but in different character.
A highly theatrical entertainment which was bound to seem flattened on the screen, but emerges with at least some of its laughs intact.
w Neil Simon play Neil Simon d Arthur Hiller ph Jack Marta m Maurice Jarre
☆ Walter Matthau, Maureen Stapleton, Barbara Harris, Lee Grant, Louise Sorel
† In the play, Maureen Stapleton played all three female roles.

'Nothing is as simple as black and white.'
Pleasantville **
US 1998 124m DeLuxe/bw
New Line/Larger Than Life (Gary Ross, Jon Kilik, Robert J. Degus, Steven Soderbergh)
▥▥ ▦ ⊕
Two colourful teenagers of the 90s are sucked back through the television into the black-and-white, hygienic world of a 50s sitcom.
Engaging fantasy that makes fun of the repressions and restrictions of the past, takes pleasure in the uncertainties of living, and uses special effects with wit.
wd Gary Ross ph John Lindley m Randy Newman pd Jeannine Oppewall ed William Goldenberg
☆ Tobey Maguire, Jeff Daniels, Joan Allen, William H. Macy, J. T. Walsh, Don Knotts, Reese Witherspoon
'A provocative, complex and surprisingly anti-nostalgic parable wrapped in the beguiling guise of a commercial high-concept comedy.' – *Joe Leydon, Variety*
♫ Randy Newman; Jeannine Oppewall; Judianna Makovsky (costumes)

Please Believe Me
US 1950 87m bw
MGM (Val Lewton)
An English girl inherits an American ranch and is chased by a millionaire, a con man and a lawyer.
Dullsville comedy which failed to establish its star in America.
w Nathaniel Curtis d Norman Taurog ph Robert Planck m Hans Salter
☆ Deborah Kerr, Robert Walker, Mark Stevens, Peter Lawford, James Whitmore, Spring Byington

Please Don't Eat the Daisies
US 1960 111m Metrocolor Panavision
MGM (Joe Pasternak)
▦ ⊕
The family of a drama critic move to the country.
Thin, obvious comedy, all dressed up but with nowhere to go.
w Isobel Lennart book Jean Kerr d Charles Walters ph Robert Bronner m David Rose
☆ Doris Day, David Niven, Janis Paige, Spring Byington, Patsy Kelly, Richard Haydn, Jack Weston, John Harding, Margaret Lindsay

Please Murder Me
US 1956 78m bw
DCA (Donald Hyde)
An attorney defends an accused murderess, at great cost to himself.
Adequate Poverty Row suspenser with a foreseeable trick ending.

w Al C. Ward, Donald Hyde d Peter Godfrey ph Allen Stensvold
☆ Angela Lansbury, Raymond Burr, Dick Foran, John Dehner, Lamont Johnson, Denver Pyle

Please Sir
▥▥ GB 1971 101m Eastmancolor
Rank/LWI/Leslie Grade (Andrew Mitchell)
The masters and pupils of Fenn Street school go on an annual camp.
Grossly inflated, occasionally funny big-screen version of the TV series.
w John Esmonde, Bob Larbey d Mark Stuart ph Wilkie Cooper m Mike Vickers
☆ John Alderton, Deryck Guyler, Joan Sanderson, Noel Howlett, Eric Chitty, Richard Davies

Please Teacher
GB 1937 75m bw
Associated British
An heir tries to find his bequest in the country house he has sold as a girls' school.
Cheerful star farce with songs.
wd Stafford Dickens musical K. R. G. Browne, R. P. Weston
☆ Bobby Howes, René Ray, Vera Pearce, Wylie Watson, Bertha Belmore, Lyn Harding
'Plenty of laughs.' – *Variety*

Please Turn Over
GB 1959 87m bw
Beaconsfield/Anglo Amalgamated
A teenager writes a sexy best-seller clearly featuring her family and friends.
Acceptable but uninspired comedy from a West End success.
w Norman Hudis play *Book of the Month* by Basil Thomas d Gerald Thomas ph Ted Scaife m Bruce Montgomery
☆ Ted Ray, Jean Kent, Leslie Phillips, Joan Sims, Julia Lockwood, Charles Hawtrey, Lionel Jeffries

The Pleasure (dubbed)
Italy 1985 94m colour
Filmirage
▥▥
original title: *Il Piacere*
In 30s Venice a woman models herself on her dead mother in order to lose her virginity to her mother's aristocratic lover.
Dreary sub-pornographic nonsense, with the cast appearing as bored as its likely spectators.
w Homerus S. Zweitag, Clyde Anderson d Joe D'Amato (Aristide Massaccesi) ph Aristide Massaccesi m Cluster ad Italo Focacci ed Franco Alessandre
☆ Steve Wyler, Laura Gemser, Isabelle Andréa Guzon, Marco Mattioli, Lillie Carati
† The version released in British cinemas ran for 90m.

The Pleasure Garden
GB/Germany 1925 74m bw silent
Gainsborough/Emelka (Michael Balcon, Erich Pommer)
A chorus girl marries a rich colonial who goes native.
Boring melodrama with a few touches typical of its director, whose first film it is.
w Eliot Stannard novel Oliver Sandys d Alfred Hitchcock ph Baron Ventimiglia
☆ Virginia Valli, John Stuart, Miles Mander, Carmelita Geraghty

The Pleasure Girls
GB 1965 88m bw
Compton Tekli (Harry Fine)
Girl flatmates in London have trouble with their boyfriends.
The road to ruin sixties style, hackneyed but quite well observed.
wd Gerry O'Hara ph Michael Reed m Malcolm Lockyer
☆ Ian McShane, Francesca Annis, Tony Tanner, Klaus Kinski, Mark Eden, Suzanna Leigh

The Pleasure of His Company
US 1961 114m Technicolor
Paramount/Perlberg-Seaton
An ageing playboy arrives unexpectedly in San Francisco for his daughter's wedding.
Tame family comedy, very flatly adapted from the stage; dressed to kill, but with no narrative or cinematic drive.

w Samuel Taylor *play* Samuel Taylor, Cornelia Otis Skinner *d* George Seaton *ph* Robert Burks *m* Alfred Newman

☆ Fred Astaire, Lilli Palmer, Debbie Reynolds, Charles Ruggles, Tab Hunter, Gary Merrill, Harold Fong

'Smart comedy in its most diluted form.' – *MFB*

'Do Men Deserve Everything They Get?'

The Pleasure Principle

GB   1991   100m   Metrocolor
Palace/Psychology News (David Cohen)

A medical journalist, divorced from his lesbian wife, tries to keep three affairs on the go at once.
Flaccid farce of sexual misadventures, performed with perfunctory interest.

wd David Cohen *ph* Andrew Speller *m* Sonny Southon *pd* Cecilia Brereton *ed* Joe McAllister
☆ Peter Firth, Lynsey Baxter, Haydn Gwynne, Lysette Anthony, Sara Mair-Thomas, Ian Hogg, Francesca Folan, Liam McDermott

'A refreshing light comedy that simply asks its audience to lie back and enjoy.' – *Variety*
'It does not stimulate as it simulates and is essentially a throwback to those sleazy British soft-core comedies of the mid-Seventies.' – *Philip French, Observer*
† The film was made for £200,000, which its producer-director borrowed from his bank.

The Pleasure Seekers

US   1964   107m   DeLuxe   Cinemascope
TCF (David Weisbart)

Three girls in Madrid find boyfriends.
Dim remake of Three Coins in the Fountain, adequate but unstimulating on all levels.

w Edith Sommer *d* Jean Negulesco *ph* Daniel L. Fapp *m* Lionel Newman, Alexander Courage
☆ Ann-Margret, Tony Franciosa, Carol Lynley, Gene Tierney, Brian Keith, Gardner McKay, Isobel Elsom
♫ Lionel Newman, Alexander Courage

Plein Soleil **

France/Italy   1960   115m   colour
Paris/Panitalia/Titanus (Robert and Raymond Hakim)

aka: *Purple Noon*
aka: *Lust for Evil*

Hired to bring a rich friend back home to his father, a young wastrel decides to kill him instead and assume his identity.
Sparkling variation on an American film noir, glowing in the Mediterranean sun and maintaining suspense as well as a sense of sexual ambiguity.

w René Clément, Paul Gégauff *novel* The Talented Mr Ripley by Patricia Highsmith *d* René Clément *ph* Henri Decaë *m* Nino Rota *ad* Paul Bertrand *ed* Françoise Javet
☆ Alain Delon, Marie Laforêt, Maurice Ronet, Elvire Popesco, Erno Crisa, Frank Latimore, Bill Kearns

'All it has going for it is this sensuous kicky atmosphere: you feel as if you're breathing something beautiful and rotten.' – *Pauline Kael*
† Highsmith's novel was remade in 2000 by Anthony Minghella under its original title, *The Talented Mr Ripley* (qv).

Plenty *

US   1985   124m   Technicolor   Panavision
TCF/RKO/Edward R. Pressman

After World War II, the career of a neurotic society woman has parallels with the problems of western Europe.
Heavy-going allegory which should have stayed on the stage.

w David Hare *play* David Hare *d* Fred Schepisi *ph* Ian Baker *m* Bruce Smeaton *pd* Richard MacDonald *ed* Peter Honess
☆ Meryl Streep, Charles Dance, Tracey Ullman, John Gielgud, Sting, Ian McKellen, Sam Neill

'The press tell us that this film is an allegory of the fall of the British Empire. No wonder it is dreary!' – *Quentin Crisp*

The Plot Against Harry

US   1969   81m   bw
Electric/Contemporary/King Screen (Robert Young, Michael Roemer)

Out of jail on parole, a gangster finds that business and his family are not what they were.

Put on the shelf for twenty years before its eventual release and hailed by some as a comic masterpiece, it turns out to be a moderately amusing movie that shows its age.

wd Michael Roemer *ph* Robert Young *m* Frank Lewin *ad* Howard Mandel *ed* Maurice Schell
☆ Martin Priest, Ben Lang, Maxine Woods, Henry Nemo, Jacques Taylor, Jean Leslie, Ellen Herbert, Sandra Kazan

'Harry's wit looks less deadpan than stone dead.' – *Kevin Jackson, Independent*

The Plot Thickens

US   1936   69m   bw
RKO/William Sistrom

A murder proves to be connected with an art swindle.
Another minor case for Hildegarde Withers.

w Clarence Upson Young, Jack Townley *novel* Stuart Palmer *d* Ben Holmes
☆ James Gleason, ZaSu Pitts, Owen Davis Jnr, Louise Latimer

The Plot to Kill Roosevelt: see *Teheran*

The Plough and the Stars *

US   1936   72m   bw
RKO (Cliff Reid, Robert Sisk)

In 1916, a Dublin marriage is threatened by the husband's appointment as commander of the citizen army.
Rather elementary film version of the play about the Troubles; interesting for effort rather than performance, and for the talent involved.

w Dudley Nichols *play* Sean O'Casey *d* John Ford *ph* Joseph August *m* Roy Webb
☆ Barbara Stanwyck, Preston Foster, Barry Fitzgerald, Denis O'Dea, Eileen Crowe, F. J. McCormick, Arthur Shields, Una O'Connor, Moroni Olsen, J. M. Kerrigan, Bonita Granville

'Skilfully made but not impressive as a money entry.' – *Variety*

The Ploughman's Lunch ***

GB   1983   107m   colour
Goldcrest/Greenpoint/AC & D (Simon Relph, Ann Scott)

Media people find their cynicism deepened after the Falklands War.
Tough and intelligent, with nice observation and twists of detail.

w Ian McEwan *d* Richard Eyre *ph* Clive Tickner *m* Dominic Muldowney
☆ Jonathan Pryce, Tim Curry, Rosemary Harris, Frank Finlay, Charlie Dore, David de Keyser, Nat Jackley

'You don't have to agree with it, but you can't ignore it.' – *Daily Mail*
'It quietly and persuasively suggests that we get precisely the media we deserve.' – *Guardian*

Plovec: see *The Swimmer*

The Plow that Broke the Plains **

US   1936   28m   bw
Resettlement Administration Film Unit

The story of how overcultivation of America's Great Plains resulted in the Dust Bowl.
Classic documentary which inevitably means less now than it did at the time but is still an impressive counterpoint to The Grapes of Wrath.

wd Pare Lorentz *m* Virgil Thomson

Pluck of the Irish: see *Great Guy*

Plucking the Daisy (dubbed) *

France   1956   100m   bw
EGE/Hoche

original title: *En Effeuillant la Marguerite*
aka: *Mam'selle Striptease*

A general's daughter is forced to become a striptease performer in order to raise some much-needed money.
Pleasing comedy, designed to show off the body of Brigitte Bardot, at which it succeeds admirably.

w Marc Allégret, Roger Vadim *d* Marc Allégret *ph* Louis Page *m* Paul Misraki *ad* Alexandre Trauner *ed* Suzanne de Troeve
☆ Brigitte Bardot, Daniel Gélin, Robert Hirsch, Darry Cowl, Nadine Tallier, Mischa Auer

Plunder *

GB   1930   98m   bw
Herbert Wilcox/British and Dominions

Two society friends turn jewel thieves to help an heiress.
Primitive talkie version of a Ben Travers farce which veered towards melodrama but had a successful stage revival at the National Theatre in 1978; valuable as a record of the original performances.

w W. P. Lipscomb *d* Tom Walls *ph* Freddie Young
☆ Tom Walls, Ralph Lynn, Robertson Hare, Winifred Shotter, Sydney Lynn, Ethel Coleridge

'Just a photographic record of the stage success.' – *Variety*

Plunder of the Sun *

US   1953   81m   bw
Warner (Robert Fellows)

Various criminal elements seek buried treasure among the Mexican Aztec ruins.
Interestingly located, well made, unconvincingly scripted melodrama, yet another borrowing from The Maltese Falcon.

w Jonathan Latimer *novel* David Dodge *d* John Farrow *ph* Jack Draper *m* Antonio D. Conde
☆ Glenn Ford, Diana Lynn, Francis L. Sullivan, Patricia Medina, Sean McClory, Douglass Dumbrille, Eduardo Noriega

The Plunderers

US   1948   87m   bw
Republic

An undercover cavalry officer becomes friends with an outlaw who saves his life.
Routine Western, just about watchable.

w Gerald Geraghty, Gerald Drayson Adams *d* Joseph Kane
☆ Rod Cameron, Ilona Massey, Adrian Booth

The Plunderers

US   1960   94m   bw
Allied Artists/August (Joseph Pevney)

In the old west, four juvenile delinquents take over a town.
The Wild One in period dress. Nothing in particular.

w Bob Barbash *d* Joseph Pevney *ph* Eugene Polito *m* Leonard Rosenman
☆ Jeff Chandler, John Saxon, Ray Stricklyn, Roger Torrey, Dee Pollock, Marsha Hunt, Dolores Hart, Jay C. Flippen, James Westerfield

'They rob the rich and … that's it.'

Plunkett & Macleane

GB   1999   101m   Technicolor
Polygram/Working Title/Arts Council (Tim Bevan, Eric Fellner, Rupert Harvey)

In 18th-century London, a highwayman teams up with a penurious aristocrat to rob the rich.
A period romp with all the class and style of a Carry On movie, though its humour is on a lower level; crass, anachronistic and trivial, it has the narrative coherence of a pop video.

w Robert Wade, Neil Purvis, Charles McKeown *screenplay* Selwyn Roberts *d* Jake Scott *ph* John Mathieson *m* Craig Armstrong *pd* Norris Spencer *ed* Oral Norrie Ottey
☆ Robert Carlyle, Jonny Lee Miller, Liv Tyler, Ken Stott, Michael Gambin, Alan Cumming, Iain Robertson, Tommy Flanagan, Stephen Walters, James Thornton, Terence Rigby

'Was this film part of some new experiment to test the lower limits of audience expectation to see how little we would accept, and how much its makers could get away with? Talk about daylight robbery.' – *Tom Shone, Sunday Times*

La Plus Longue Nuit du Diable: see *The Devil's Nightmare*

Plymouth Adventure *

US   1952   105m   Technicolor
MGM (Dore Schary)

The Pilgrim Fathers sail from Plymouth on the *Mayflower* and spend their first months ashore on the coast of America.
Well-meaning schoolbook history, totally unconvincing and very dull despite obvious effort all round. One or two of the actors have their moments.

w Helen Deutsch *novel* Ernest Gebler *d* Clarence Brown *ph* William Daniels *m* Miklos Rozsa

☆ Spencer Tracy, Gene Tierney, Van Johnson, Leo Genn, Dawn Addams

'It demonstrates how Hollywood can dull down as well as jazz up history.' – *Judith Crist, 1973*

Pocahontas

US   1995   81m   Technicolor
Buena Vista/Walt Disney (James Pentecost)

Pocahontas falls in love with the British settler Captain John Smith and saves him from death.
Bad history, indifferent animation, dull songs, and an unexciting story all combine to produce a poor film, a disappointment after Disney's recent return to top form, though it still drew the crowds at the box-office and Disney stores.

w Carl Binder, Susannah Grant, Philip Lazebnik *idea* Mike Gabriel *d* Mike Gabriel, Eric Goldberg *m* Hawk Pope *m/ly* Alan Menken, Stephen Schwartz *md* Danny Troob, David Friedman *ad* Michael Giaimo *ed* H. Lee Patterson
☆ Featuring the voices of: Irene Bedard, Judy Kuhn, Mel Gibson, David Ogden Stiers, John Kassir, Russell Means, Christian Bale, Linda Hunt, Danny Mann, Billy Connolly

'Disney's fable of an arcadian American history wrecked by incursions from the Old World is obviously a means of allaying a bad conscience, while voicing xenophobic resentments about corrupt Europeans.' – *Roy Porter, Sunday Times*
'Pleasant to look at, and it will probably satisfy very small kiddies, but virtually everything in the movie is as generic as the two hygienic lovers.' – *Owen Gleiberman, Entertainment Weekly*
'The dullest Disney animation for years.' – *Empire*
† Twelve people contributed to the film's story.
†† The film took more than $317m at the box-office worldwide.
††† In real life Pocahontas was 12 when she met the 27-year-old Smith. She became the wife of a member of her tribe before leaving him when she converted to Christianity to marry John Rolfe, who took her and their son to England, where she died of smallpox.
♪ Alan Menken (score and music), Stephen Schwartz (lyrics); song 'Colors of the Wind' (*m/ly* Alan Menken, Stephen Schwartz)

Pocket Money

US   1972   100m   Technicolor
First Artists/Coleytown (John Foreman)

Two slow-thinking Arizona cowboys try to make money herding cattle.
Peculiar modern Western comedy drama which doesn't work.

w Terrence Malick *novel* Jim Kane by J. K. S. Brown *d* Stuart Rosenberg *ph* Laszlo Kovacs *m* Alex North
☆ Paul Newman, Lee Marvin, Strother Martin, Kelly Jean Peters, Wayne Rogers

Pocketful of Miracles

US   1961   136m   Technicolor   Panavision
UA/Franton (Frank Capra)

Kindly gangsters help an old apple seller to persuade her long lost daughter that she is a lady of means.
Boring, overlong remake of Lady for a Day, showing that Capra's touch simply doesn't work on the wide screen, that his themes are dated anyway, and that all the fine character actors in Hollywood are a liability unless you find them something to do.

w Hal Kanter, Harry Tugend *story* Damon Runyon *scenario* Robert Riskin *d* Frank Capra *ph* Robert Bronner *m* Walter Scharf
☆ Bette Davis, Glenn Ford, Hope Lange, Arthur O'Connell, Peter Falk, Thomas Mitchell, Edward Everett Horton, Sheldon Leonard, Barton MacLane, Jerome Cowan, Fritz Feld, Snub Pollard, David Brian, Ann-Margret, John Litel and also Jay Novello, Willis Bouchey, George E. Stone, Mike Mazurki, Jack Elam, Mickey Shaughnessy, Peter Mann, Frank Ferguson

'The effect is less one of whimsy than of being bludgeoned to death with a toffee apple.' – *Peter John Dyer*
'The story has enough cracks in it for the syrup to leak through.' – *Playboy*
♫ title song (*m* James Van Heusen, *ly* Sammy Cahn); Peter Falk

Poetic Justice

US 1993 109m Technicolor
Columbia TriStar (Steve Nicolaides, John Singleton)
📼 ▤ ◷ ⍟ 🎧

In South Central Los Angeles, a poetry-writing beautician, upset by the murder of her boyfriend, becomes involved with a mailman and his young daughter.
A disappointing second film from the director of Boyz N The Hood, much closer to a conventional soap opera and with a clumsy and contrived narrative.
wd John Singleton ph Peter Lyons Collister m Stanley Clarke pd Keith Brian Burns ed Bruce Cannon
☆ Janet Jackson, Tupac Shakur, Regina King, Joe Torry, Tyra Ferrell, Roger Guenveur Smith, Maya Angelou, Billy Zane, Lori Petty
'The film still deals too much in stereotypes to be convincing, and can't get away from the fact that it needs a stronger storyline than this to be properly effective.' – Derek Malcolm, Guardian

Poet's Pub

GB 1949 79m bw
GFD/Aquila (Donald B. Wilson)

A rowing blue takes over a Tudor inn and discovers a priceless jewelled gauntlet, the wearer of which is kidnapped during the performance of a pageant.
Very thin, naïve treatment of a whimsical novel. The last film to use the Independent Frame process.
w Diana Morgan novel Eric Linklater d Frederick Wilson ph George Stretton m Clifton Parker
☆ Derek Bond, Rona Anderson, Barbara Murray, Leslie Dwyer, Joyce Grenfell

Poil de Carotte ***

France 1932 94m bw
Legrand Majestic/Marcel Vandal-Charles Delac
aka: The Redhead

A red-haired boy, neglected by his father and tormented by his mother, attempts suicide.
A moving and unsentimental account of childhood, notable for the performances of Baur and Lynen as father and son.
wd Julien Duvivier story Jules Renard ph Armand Thirard m Alexandre Tansman ed Marthe Poncin
☆ Harry Baur, Robert Lynen, Catherine Fonteney, Louis Gouthier, Simone Aubry, Colette Segall, Christiane Dor
† The British censors banned the film for a time and in America it was restricted to adult audiences. Duvivier had made a silent version of the story in 1925. There were less successful remakes by Paul Mesnier in 1951 and Henri Graziani in 1973.

Point Blank *

US 1967 92m Metrocolor Panavision
MGM/Judd Bernard, Irwin Winkler
📼 ▤

A gangster takes an elaborate revenge on his cheating partner.
Extremely violent gangster thriller, well shot on location and something of a cult, but with irritating pretentiousness and obscure plot points.
w Alexander Jacobs, David Newhouse, Rafe Newhouse novel The Hunter by Richard Stark d John Boorman ph Philip Lathrop m Johnny Mandel
☆ Lee Marvin, Angie Dickinson, Keenan Wynn, Carroll O'Connor, Lloyd Bochner, Michael Strong, John Vernon, Sharon Acker
'The fragmentation was necessary to give the characters and the situation ambiguity, to suggest another meaning beyond the immediate plot.' – John Boorman
† The Outfit (qv) is a kind of sequel/reprise.

'Every Friendship Has Its Limits. Every Man Has His Breaking Point. Together They Take Adventure Past The Point Of No Return.'
Point Break *

US 1991 122m DeLuxe
TCF/Largo/Tapestry (Peter Abrams, Robert L. Levy)
📼 ▤ ◷

An FBI agent goes undercover among Californian surfers and skydivers to investigate a series of bank robberies.
Ridiculous thriller, with convoluted and unbelievable plot and a great deal of masculine posturing.
w W. Peter Iliff d Kathryn Bigelow ph Donald Peterman m Mark Isham pd Peter Jamison ed Howard Smith, Scott Conrad, Burt Lovitt

☆ Patrick Swayze, Keanu Reeves, Gary Busey, Lori Petty, John McGinley, James Le Gros, John Philbin, Bojesse Christopher, Julian Reyes
'Acts like a huge, nasty wave, picking up viewers for a few major thrills but ultimately grinding them into the sand via overkill and absurdity.' – Variety

'The Government Gave Her A Choice. Death. Or Life As An Assassin. Now, There's No Turning Back.'
Point of No Return

US 1993 108m Technicolor Panavision
Warner (Art Linson)
📼 ▤ ◷ ⍟

GB title: The Assassin

A drug addict captured by the police during a robbery is given a choice between dying or becoming a government assassin.
A remake of the French movie Nikita which apes the original in virtually every respect, yet fails to match it in interest; it says much about Hollywood, and American attitudes to subtitles, that such a pointless exercise should ever have been carried out.
w Robert Getchell, Alexandra Seros d John Badham ph Michael Watkins m Hans Zimmer, Nick Glennie-Smith pd Philip Harrison ed Frank Morriss
☆ Bridget Fonda, Gabriel Byrne, Dermot Mulroney, Miguel Ferrer, Harvey Keitel, Olivia D'Abo, Richard Romanus, Geoffrey Lewis
'A soulless, efficiently slavish remake.' – Variety

Pointed Heels

US 1929 61m bw (colour sequence)
Paramount

A theatrical producer loves a musical comedy star but loses her to a young composer.
Predictable backstage drama.
w Florence Ryerson, John V. A. Weaver story Charles Brackett d A. Edward Sutherland
☆ William Powell, Fay Wray, Helen Kane, Phillips Holmes, Richard 'Skeets' Gallagher, Eugene Pallette
'Moderate business likely for a light comedy that choked on too big a mouthful.' – Variety

'The Film That Shocked America! Denounced As "Obscene" and "Pornographic" by the Moral Majority.'
Poison *

US 1990 85m colour/bw
Mainline/Bronze Eye (Christine Vachon)
📼 ▤

Three stories are interwoven: 'Hero', in which a seven-year-old boy kills his father and flies away; 'Homo', in which a jealous prisoner rapes another; 'Horror', in which a doctor creates a serum containing the sex drive, drinks it and becomes a monster.
Cleverly dealing with deviance, sexual and social, and inspired by the work of Jean Genet, it ranges in style from the risible to the repugnant.
wd Todd Haynes ph Maryse Alberti m James Bennett pd Sarah Stollman ed James Lyons, Todd Haynes
☆ 'Hero': Edith Meeks, Millie White, Buck Smith, Anne Giotta;, 'Homo': Scott Renderer, James Lyons, John R. Lombardi, Tony Pemberton, Andrew Harpending, Tony Gigante;', 'Horror': Larry Maxwell, Susan Norman, Al Quagliata, Michelle Sullivan
'A provocative look at societal outcasts and twisted behavior that can be read in ways both artistic and political.' – Variety
'A whole that is often uneven but, in less than 90 minutes, says more about desire and transgression than most more straightforward movies on that theme.' – Derek Malcolm, Guardian

Poison Ivy

US 1992 89m colour
New Line (Andy Ruben)
📼 ▤ ◷

A teenage schoolgirl decides she wants the father of her best friend, which means getting rid of his invalid wife.
A heady brew of incest, lesbianism, drunkenness and death which quickly goes flat.
w Katt Shea Ruben, Andy Ruben d Katt Shea Ruben ph Phedon Papamichael m Aaron Davies pd Virginia Lee ed Gina Mittleman
☆ Drew Barrymore, Sara Gilbert, Tom Skerritt, Cheryl Ladd

'Will make audiences itch to get out of the theater and into the open.' – Variety
'The film, distinguished by a complete absence of thrills, is too turgid even to qualify as camp.' – Stephen Farber, Movieline

Poison Pen *

GB 1939 79m bw
ABP (Walter C. Mycroft)

A village community is set at odds by a writer of vindictive anonymous letters.
Effective minor drama, with good location atmosphere.
w Doreen Montgomery, William Freshman, N. C. Hunter, Esther McCracken play Richard Llewellyn d Paul Stein
☆ Flora Robson, Reginald Tate, Robert Newton, Ann Todd, Geoffrey Toone, Belle Chrystal, Edward Chapman, Edward Rigby
'Sordid theme makes it doubtful film fare.' – Variety
'A lamentably artificial piece.' – Richard Mallett, Punch

Pokémon: The First Movie

👪 Japan/US 1999 75m DeLuxe
Warner/Pikachu Project '98-Shogakukan/4Kids (Norman J. Grossfeld, Choji Yoshikawa, Tomoyuki Igarashi, Takemoto Mori)
▤

A Pokémon trainer is invited to a championship match on an island, and discovers that it is a trap set by Mewto, a rogue Pokémon who plans to rule the world.
A critic-proof movie: the millions of Pokémon collectors will love it; all others will cringe from a poorly animated, incomprehensible, confusing story featuring oddly unpleasant creatures (and that's just the strangely-drawn human participants).
w Takeshi Shudo (English adaptation: Norman J. Grossfeld, Michael Haigney, John Touhey) characters created by Satoshi Tajiri d Kunihiko Yuyama (English adaptation d Michael Haigney) ph Hisao Shirai m Ralph Schuckett, John Loeffle ed Toshio Henmi, Yutaka Ito
☆ Featuring voices of: Veronica Taylor, Philip Bartlett, Rachael Lillis, Eric Stuart, Addie Blaustein, Ikue Otani
'Humourless, boring, impenetrable and with animation of such staggeringly low quality that it constitutes an insult to cinemagoers of all ages.' – Peter Bradshaw, Guardian
† The film took more than $85.5m at the US box office.

Pokjaniye, Monanieba: see Repentance

Pokolenie: see Generation

Police *

France 1985 113m colour Panavision
Artificial Eye/Gaumont/TF1
📼 ▤

A tough and bigoted cop, investigating Tunisian drug-dealers, falls for a suspect.
Well-directed thriller, filmed in documentary style, that was a box-office hit in France, though it offers nothing that has not been seen before.
w Catherine Breillat, Sylvie Danton, Jacques Fieschi, Maurice Pialat d Maurice Pialat ph Luciano Tovoli m Henryk Mikolaj Gorecki ad Constantin Mejinksy ed Yann Dedet, Helene Viard, Nathalie Letrosne
☆ Gérard Depardieu, Sophie Marceau, Richard Ancanina, Pascale Rocard, Sandrine Bonnaire, Franck Karoul, Jonathan Leina

'Call them what you like. Just don't call them when you're in trouble!'
Police Academy

👪 US 1984 96m Technicolor
Paul Maslansky/Ladd Company/Warner Brothers
📼 ▤ ◷

The mayor of an American city lifts all restrictions on entry to the police force.
Appallingly unfunny series of snippets about police training, like an American Carry On with few jokes leading to a punch line and occasional resorting to dirty bits.
w Neal Israel, Pat Proft, Hugh Wilson d Hugh Wilson
☆ Steve Guttenberg, Kim Cattrall, G. W. Bailey, Bubba Smith, Donovan Scott, George Gaynes
'Hit or miss comic juvenilia … pure popcorn fantasy fodder.' – Paul Taylor, MFB

Police Academy 2: Their First Assignment

👪 US 1985 87m Technicolor
Warner/Ladd (Paul Maslansky)
📼 ▤

The new recruits foil attempts from an ambitious lieutenant to take over command.
An unambitious and dull sequel.
w Barry Blaustein, David Sheffield d Jerry Paris ph James Crabe m Robert Folk pd Trevor Williams ed Bob Wyman
☆ Steve Guttenberg, Bubba Smith, David Graf, Michael Winslow, Art Metrano, Marion Ramsey, George Gaynes

Police Academy 3: Back in Training

👪 US 1986 82m colour
Warner (Paul Maslansky)
📼 ▤ ◷

Rival police academies vie for survival.
Plodding comedy that recycles a few familiar, unfunny routines.
w Gene Quintano d Jerry Paris ph Robert Saad m Robert Folk pd Trevor Williams ed Bud Malin
☆ Steve Guttenberg, Bubba Smith, David Graf, Michael Winslow, Marion Ramsey, Leslie Easterbrook, George Gaynes, Bobcat Goldthwait, Art Metrano

Police Academy 4: Citizens on Patrol

👪 US 1987 87m colour
Warner (Paul Maslansky)
📼 ▤ ◷

A police commandant attempts to involve ordinary people in law enforcement.
A feeble comedy that makes it impossible to understand the apparent popularity of this turgid series.
w Gene Quintano d Jim Drake ph Robert Saad m Robert Folk pd Trevor Williams ed David Rawlins
☆ Steve Guttenberg, Bubba Smith, David Graf, Michael Winslow, Sharon Stone, Leslie Easterbrook, Bobcat Goldthwait, George Gaynes
'Carries the banner of tasteless humor … to new heights of insipidness.' – Variety

Police Academy 5: Assignment: Miami Beach

👪 US 1988 90m colour
Warner (Paul Maslansky)
📼 ▤ ◷

Cops on holiday in Miami help foil a gang of jewel thieves.
Witlessness reaches a new low in a comedy devoid of laughs.
w Stephen J. Curwick d Alan Myerson ph Jim Pergola m Robert Folk pd Trevor Williams ed Hubert de la Bouillerie
☆ Matt McCoy, Janet Jones, George Gaynes, G. W. Bailey, Rene Auberjonois, Bubba Smith, David Graf, Michael Winslow, Leslie Easterbrook

Police Academy 6: City Under Siege

👪 US 1989 84m Technicolor
Warner (Paul Maslansky)
📼 ▤ ◷

The police squad track down a criminal mastermind responsible for a massive crime wave.
Farcical, broadly acted comedy that does raise an occasional smile.
w Stephen J. Curwick d Peter Bonerz ph Charles Rosher Jnr m Robert Folk pd Tho E. Azzari ed Hubert de la Bouillerie
☆ Bubba Smith, David Graf, Michael Winslow, Leslie Easterbrook, Marion Ramsey, Lance Kinsey, Matt McCoy, Bruce Mahler, G. W. Bailey, George Gaynes, Kenneth Mars

Police Academy 7: Mission to Moscow

👪 US 1994 83m colour
Warner (Paul Maslansky)
📼 ▤

Members of the Police Academy go to Moscow to deal with the Russian mafia's plans to take over the world.
Witless romp that is by far the worst of the series, and they don't come any worse than that.
w Randolph Davis, Michele S. Chodos d Alan Metter ph Ian Jones m Robert Folk pd Frederic Weiler ed Denise Hill, Suzanne Hines
☆ George Gaynes, Michael Winslow, David Graf, Leslie Easterbrook, G. W. Bailey, Charlie Schlatter, Christopher Lee, Ron Perlman, Claire Forlani
'An inept, geriatric romp that's for completists only.' – Variety
† The film flopped at the box-office.

Police Dog
GB 1955 70m bw
Westridge (Harold Huth)
A policeman trains a stray to become a police dog and tracks down the thief who murdered his friend.
Semi-documentary on the theme that our police dogs are wonderful; Christopher Lee makes a brief appearance as a frightened constable.
wd Derek Twist ph Cedric Williams md Bretton Byrd ad Duncan Sutherland ed Gordon Pilkington
☆ Joan Rice, Tim Turner, Sandra Dorne, Charles Victor, Nora Gordon, Cecil Brock, John Le Mesurier, James Gilbert, Christopher Lee, Rex III

Police Force: see Police Story (1985)

Police Story (dubbed) *
Hong Kong 1985 85m colour
Golden Harvest/Paragon (Leonard Ho)
🖭 ▤ ⊙⌇
original title: *Jingcha Gushi*
US title: *Police Force*
A cop is given the task of guarding a witness who is the girlfriend of a drug-dealing gangster.
Standard cops and robbers martial arts mayhem, enlivened by some spectacular stunts and chases.
w Edward Tang d Jackie Chan ph Cheung Yiu Joe m Kevin Bassingson ad Oliver Wong ed Peter Cheung
☆ Jackie Chan, Brigitte Lin, Maggie Cheung, Cho Yuen, Bill Tung, Kenneth Tong
† The film was cut by 15 minutes for its release on video cassette.

Police Story II (dubbed)
Hong Kong 1988 92m colour
Golden Harvest/Paragon (Leonard Ho)
🖭 ▤
Demoted to traffic cop, a former detective is re-instated to combat a gang extorting money from big business.
The mixture as before: elaborately choreographed fights and broad comedy, but lacking the set-pieces of the first film.
w Jackie Chan, Edward Tang d Jackie Chan ph Cheung Yiu Joe, Lee Yau Tong m Michael Lai pd Oliver Wong ed Peter Cheung
☆ Jackie Chan, Maggie Cheung, Bill Tung, Lam Kwok Hung, Charles Chao, Cho Yuen

Police Story III: Supercop
Hong Kong 1992 93m colour
Golden Way (Willie Chan, Tang King-Sung)
🖭 ▤ ⊙⌇
An undercover Hong Kong cop infiltrates a gang of drug smugglers with the aid of the Chinese police and a glamorous inspector.
Some spectacular stunts add interest to a familiar story, which is given an extra topical twist with its references to the takeover of Hong Kong by mainland China.
w Tang King-Sung, Ma Mei-Ping, Lee Wei-Yee d Stanley Tong ph Lam Kwok-Wah m Lee Chung Sing ad Oliver Wong ed Cheung Yaeo-Chung, Cheung Kai Fei
☆ Jackie Chan, Michelle Yeaoh, Maggie Cheung, Tsang Kong, Yuen Wah, Lo Lieh
'An okay adventure.' – *Variety*

The Polish Bride **
Netherlands 1998 90m
Artificial Eye/Motel/IJswater/VPRO (Marc Bary, Ilana Netiv, Jeroen Beker, Frans van Gestel)
🖭
original title: *De Poolse Bruid*
A farmer shelters a fugitive Polish woman, on the run from her brutal employers.
A spare film, of affection developing between two isolated people amid a flat landscape. The dialogue is minimal, but much is conveyed by simple gestures; it yields quiet pleasures.
w Kees van de Hulst d Karim Traidia ph Jacques Laureys m Fons Merkies ad Anne Winterink ed Chris Teerink
☆ Jaap Spijkers, Monic Hendricks, Rudi Falkenhagen, Roef Ragas, Hakim Traidia, Soraya Traidia
'The surprise is how tightly all-of-a-piece it is, and, from the first to the last shot, how totally absorbing.' – *Alexander Walker, London Evening Standard*

Polish Wedding
US 1978 107m DeLuxe
Fox Searchlight/Lakeshore (Tom Rosenberg, Julia Chasman, Geoff Stier)
🖭 ▤ ⌇
Tensions erupt in a large working-class Polish family in Detroit when the only daughter becomes pregnant.
Boisterous comic drama, full of a forced vitality and soap opera situations; its cast tries hard to elevate it above triteness.
wd Theresa Connelly ph Guy Dufaux m Luis Bacalov pd Kara Lindstrom ed Curtiss Clayton, Suzanne Fenn
☆ Lena Olin, Gabriel Byrne, Claire Danes, Adam Trese, Mili Avital, Daniel Lapaine, Steven Petrarca, Jeffrey Nordling, Ramsey Krull, Rade Serbedzija
'A movie of gratifying small moments, some of which are hilariously funny and charged with healthy eroticism.' – *Emanuel Levy, Variety*

The Politic Flapper: see The Patsy

Politics
US 1931 71m bw
MGM
Two small-town women get into politics to fight racketeers.
Scrappy star comedy which probably seemed funnier at the time.
w Robert E. Hopkins, Wells Root, Zelda Sears, Malcolm Stuart Boylan d Charles F. Reisner
☆ Marie Dressler, Polly Moran, Roscoe Ates, Karen Morley, William Bakewell, John Miljan
'Loaded with technical faults, but it has too many laugh moments to fail to sock the b.o.' – *Variety*

Polly Fulton: see BF's Daughter

Polly of the Circus
US 1932 72m bw
MGM (Paul Bern)
A trapeze artiste falls for the local minister, but incurs disapproval from his bishop.
Elementary romance reminiscent of silent drama.
w Carey Wilson play Margaret Mayo d Alfred Santell ph George Barnes m William Axt
☆ Marion Davies, Clark Gable, C. Aubrey Smith, Raymond Hatton, David Landau, Maude Eburne, Guinn Williams, Ray Milland
'Frail entertainment with both leads miscast.' – *Variety*

Pollyanna *
🎎 US 1960 134m Technicolor
Walt Disney (George Golitzen)
▤ ⊙⌇
A 12-year-old orphan girl cheers up the grumps of the small town where she comes to live.
Well cast but overlong and rather humourless remake of a children's classic from an earlier age.
wd David Swift novel Eleanor Porter ph Russell Harlan m Paul Smith ad Carroll Clark, Robert Clatworthy
☆ Hayley Mills, Jane Wyman, Karl Malden, Nancy Olson, Adolphe Menjou, Donald Crisp, Agnes Moorehead, Richard Egan, Kevin Corcoran, James Drury, Reta Shaw, Leora Dana
'Even Hayley Mills can neither prevent one from sympathizing with the crusty aunts, hermits, vicars and hypochondriacs who get so forcibly cheered up, nor from feverishly speculating whether films like this don't run the risk of inciting normally kind and gentle people into certain excesses of violent crime – child murder, for instance.' – *MFB*
🎖 special award to Hayley Mills for 'the most outstanding juvenile performance'

'It knows what scares you!'
Poltergeist **
US 1982 114m Metrocolor Panavision
MGM/SLM (Steven Spielberg)
🖭 ▤ ⊙⌇ ⊙ ⌇
Suburban life is disrupted when through her TV set a young girl releases unpleasant forces from the cemetery over which the modern estate was built.
Skilful but dramatically thin and sometimes rather nasty horror movie in which the producer's hand seems often to have controlled the director's. Misjudgment must be the reason that it was not the huge success intended.
w Steven Spielberg, Michael Grais, Mark Victor d Tobe Hooper ph Matthew F. Leonetti m Jerry Goldsmith ed Michael Kahn
☆ JoBeth Williams, Craig T. Nelson, Beatrice Straight, Dominique Dunne, Oliver Robbins
♫ music, visual effects (Richard Edlund, Michael Wood, Bruce Nicholson)

Poltergeist II
US 1986 90m Metrocolor Panavision
MGM-UA/Freddie Fields/Victor-Grais
🖭 ▤ ⊙⌇ ⌇
The family from *Poltergeist* is in for more trouble when Grandma dies and they begin receiving phone messages from the other side.
More pointless spine-shivering: good technical effects but no message of any kind, not even entertainment.
w Mark Victor, Michael Grais d Brian Gibson ph Andrew Laszlo pd Ted Haworth
☆ JoBeth Williams, Craig T. Nelson, Heather O'Rourke, Oliver Robins, Julian Beck

Poltergeist III
US 1988 98m Astrocolor
UIP/MGM-UA (Barry Bernardi)
▤ ⊙⌇ ⌇
A young child living in Chicago is haunted by an evil ghost who takes her and others into another dimension.
Lacklustre sequel, with only the occasional effective shock to recommend it.
w Gary Shearman, Brian Taggert d Gary Shearman ph Alex Nepomniaschy m Joe Renzetti pd Paul Eads ed Ross Albert
☆ Tom Skerritt, Nancy Allen, Heather O'Rourke, Zelda Rubinstein, Lara Flynn Boyle, Kip Wentz, Richard Fire

Polyester
US 1981 86m colour Odorama
New Line (John Waters)
🖭 ▤
A Baltimore housewife with a dysfunctional family finds true love elsewhere.
Camp comedy, where the fun, such as it is, lies in the exaggerated performances.
wd John Waters ph David Insley m Chris Stein, Michael Kamen ad Vincent Paranio ed Charles Roggero
☆ Divine, Tab Hunter, Edith Massey, Mink Stole, David Samson, Joni Ruth White, May Garlington, Stiv Bators, Ken King, Hans Kramm

Ponette *
France 1996 97m colour
Les Films Alain Sarde/Rhône-Alpes Cinéma
🖭 ▤ ⌇
A four-year-old girl tries to come to terms with the death of her mother in a car crash.
An unsettling film, partly because of doubts over the methods used to extract such an astonishing, emotional, tearful performance from its young protagonist, but also because of the harshness it exhibits – all the adults behave inappropriately – and its final lurch into banal fantasy.
wd Jacques Doillon ph Caroline Champetier m Philippe Sarde ad Henri Berthon ed Jacqueline Lecompte
☆ Victoire Thivisol, Marie Trintignant, Claire Nebout, Xavier Beauvois, Matiaz Bureau Caton, Delphine Schiltz, Léopoldine Serre, Luckie Royer, Carla Ibled, Antoine du Merle
'A magical, poetic and, at times, surreal psychological study of a child's emotional landscape.' – *Helen Van Kruyssen, Film Review*
† Victoire Thivisol won the best actress award at the Venice Film Festival in 1996.

Pontiac Moon
US 1994 107m DeLuxe
Paramount (Robert Schaffel, Youssef Vahabzadeh)
In 1969, a teacher, worried about his agoraphobic wife's effect on his young son, decides to drive him on a 1,776-mile journey, which will bring his Pontiac car's mileage up to 238,857 miles, the distance to the moon, and so celebrate the Apollo landing and moonwalk.
Flimsy road movie that settles for easy sentimentality.
w Finn Taylor, Jeffrey Brown d Peter Medak ph Thomas Kloss m Randy Edelman pd Jeffrey Beecroft ed Anne V. Coates
☆ Ted Danson, Mary Steenburgen, Ryan Todd, Eric Schweig, Cathy Moriarty, Max Gail, Lisa Jane Persky
'Inane whimsy.' – *Sight and Sound*

Pontius Pilate
Italy/France 1961 100m Technicolor
Glomer Film/Lux (Enzo Merolle)
original title: *Ponzio Pilato*
Pontius Pilate runs into political and personal problems while trying to govern Israel.
Pilate's love-life is given prominence over Jesus's trial and crucifixion, although both receive standard Italian sword-and-sandals treatment to reduce them to banality. Barrymore doubles as Judas and Jesus (who is seen only from the back).
w Gino de Santis, Ivo Perilli, Oreste Biancoli, Gian Paolo Callegari, Guglielmo Santangelo, Josette France, Guy Elmes d Irving Rapper ph Massimo Dallamano m A. Francesco Lavagnino
☆ Jean Marais, Jeanne Crain, Basil Rathbone, Letitia Roman, John Drew Barrymore, Massimo Serato

Pony Express *
US 1953 101m Technicolor
Paramount (Nat Holt)
▤
In 1860 Buffalo Bill Cody and Wild Bill Hickok are sent to establish pony express stations across California.
Standard Western which tells a factual tale adequately if rather slowly.
w Charles Marquis Warren d Jerry Hopper ph Ray Rennahan m Paul Sawtell
☆ Charlton Heston, Forrest Tucker, Rhonda Fleming, Jan Sterling

Pony Soldier
US 1952 82m Technicolor
TCF (Samuel G. Engel)
GB title: *MacDonald of the Canadian Mounties*
The Mounties settle the hash of Canadian Indian renegades who have been causing trouble on the American border.
Mediocre outdoor adventure.
w John C. Higgins d Joseph M. Newman ph Harry Jackson m Alex North
☆ Tyrone Power, Cameron Mitchell, Robert Horton, Thomas Gomez, Penny Edwards, Adeline de Walt Reynolds

Ponzio Pilato: see Pontius Pilate

Pookie: see The Sterile Cuckoo

Pool of London
GB 1950 85m bw
Ealing (Michael Relph)
A smuggling sailor gets involved in murder.
Routine semi-documentary police thriller with locations in London docks decorating a standard piece of thick ear.
w Jack Whittingham, John Eldridge d Basil Dearden ph Gordon Dines m Jack Addison
☆ Bonar Colleano, Susan Shaw, Earl Cameron, Renée Asherson, Moira Lister, Max Adrian, James Robertson Justice, Joan Dowling
'Done with such imagination, humour and visual attractiveness as to hold the pleased attention of all who like to use their eyes and their ears.' – *Richard Mallett, Punch*

De Poolse Bruid: see The Polish Bride

Poor Cow *
GB 1967 101m Eastmancolor
Anglo Amalgamated/Vic/Fenchurch (Joe Janni)
🖭
The dismal life of a young London mother who lives in squalor with her criminal husband.
Television-style fictional documentary determined to rub one's nose in the mire. Innovative and occasionally striking but not very likeable.
w Nell Dunn, Ken Loach novel Nell Dunn d Ken Loach ph Brian Probyn m Donovan
☆ Carol White, Terence Stamp, John Bindon, Kate Williams, Queenie Watts
'A superficial, slightly patronizing excursion into the nether realms of social realism.' – *Jan Dawson*

Poor Little Rich Girl *
US 1936 79m bw
TCF (Darryl F. Zanuck)
▤
A child is separated from her father and joins a radio singing act.

Pleasing star vehicle with all the expected elements, adapted from a Mary Pickford vehicle of 1917.
w Sam Hellman, Gladys Lehman, Harry Tugend d Irving Cummings ph John Seitz songs Mack Gordon, Harry Revel
☆ Shirley Temple, Jack Haley, Alice Faye, Gloria Stuart, Michael Whalen, Sara Haden, Jane Darwell, Claude Gillingwater, Henry Armetta

Pop Always Pays

US 1940 65m bw
RKO/Bert Gilroy
Pop promises to match his future son-in-law's savings, but runs into a business slump.
Minor comedy which accelerates into frantic farce, but the star was always funnier at two-reel length.
w Charles E. Roberts d Leslie Goodwins ph Jack MacKenzie md Paul Sawtell
☆ Leon Errol, Dennis O'Keefe, Adele Pearce, Walter Catlett, Marjorie Gateson, Tom Kennedy

Pope Joan

GB 1972 132m Eastmancolor Panavision
Big City Productions/Kurt Unger
aka: The Devil's Impostor
The legend of a ninth-century German semi-prostitute who discovered a vocation to preach and was made Pope.
Uninspiring pageant, brutish and rather silly, full of would-be medieval sensationalism.
w John Briley d Michael Anderson ph Billy Williams m Maurice Jarre pd Elliott Scott
☆ Liv Ullmann, Trevor Howard, Olivia de Havilland, Maximilian Schell, Keir Dullea, Robert Beatty, Franco Nero, Patrick Magee

'In the tradition of the great religious epics, Ben Hur, The Greatest Story Ever Told and 9* Weeks, comes a film that breaks all Ten Commandments and a few laws of nature.'

The Pope Must Die

GB 1991 99m colour
Palace/Michael White/Miramax/British Film/Film Four (Stephen Woolley)
◙ ▤
US title: The Pope Must Diet
Through an error, a former car mechanic, rock singer and inept priest becomes Pope and tries to clean up a Vatican infiltrated by the Mafia.
Farcical and misfiring comedy, a poor attempt at a parody of gangster films.
w Peter Richardson, Pete Richens d Peter Richardson ph Frank Gell m Anne Dudley, Jeff Beck pd John Ebden ed Katharine Wenning
☆ Robbie Coltrane, Beverly D'Angelo, Herbert Lom, Alex Rocco, Paul Bartel, Balthazar Getty, William Hootkins, Robert Stephens, Annette Crosbie, Steve O'Donnell, John Sessions

The Pope of Greenwich Village

US 1984 120m Metrocolor
MGM UA/Koch-Kirkwood (Benjy Rosenberg)
◙ ▤ ◐
In New York, Charlie and his cousin Paulie become thieves and fall foul of the Mafia.
Back again to the mean streets of the east side, but with nothing at all new to add to the scores of indistinguishable real-life melodramas of this kind.
w Vincent Patrick novel Vincent Patrick d Stuart Rosenberg ph John Bailey m Dave Grusin pd Paul Sylbert
☆ Eric Roberts, Mickey Rourke, Daryl Hannah, Geraldine Page, Kenneth McMillan, Tony Musante, M. Emmet Walsh, Burt Young
🎝 Geraldine Page (supporting actress)

Popeye

🏃🏃 US 1980 114m colour
Paramount/Disney (Robert Evans)
◙ ▤ ◐
Popeye returns to Sweethaven in search of the father who abandoned him.
Lamentable attempt by an ill-chosen director to humanize and sentimentalize a celebrated cartoon character who doesn't get into the expected physical action until the film is nearly over.
w Jules Feiffer, from characters created by E. C. Segar d Robert Altman ph Giuseppe Rotunno m/ly Harry Nilsson pd Wolf Kroeger
☆ Robin Williams, Shelley Duvall, Ray Walston, Paul Dooley
'The picture doesn't come together, and much of it is cluttered, squawky, and eerily unfunny.' – *Pauline Kael, New Yorker*

Popi *

US 1969 113m DeLuxe
UA/Leonard Films (Herbert B. Leonard)
▤
Adventures of a cheerful inhabitant of New York's Puerto Rican ghetto.
Ethnic comedy-drama of the kind that has since found its way in abundance into American TV series. Very competently done for those who like it, e.g. Puerto Ricans.
w Tina and Lester Pine d Arthur Hiller ph Ross Lowell m Dominic Frontière
☆ Alan Arkin, Rita Moreno, Miguel Alejandro, Ruben Figuero
'An appropriately disenchanted view of an immigrant's struggling ambitions in the Promised Land.' – *Richard Combs*

Popiol y Diament: see Ashes and Diamonds

Poppy *

US 1936 74m bw
Paramount (Paul Jones)
An itinerant medicine-seller sets up his stall in a small town where his daughter falls in love with the mayor's son.
Clumsily but heavily plotted vehicle for W. C. Fields, who as usual has great moments but seems to rob the show of its proper pace.
w Waldemar Young, Virginia Van Upp play Dorothy Donnelly d A. Edward Sutherland ph William Mellor m Frederick Hollander
☆ W. C. Fields, Rochelle Hudson, Richard Cromwell, Granville Bates, Catherine Doucet, Lynne Overman, Maude Eburne
'Antique hokum trussed up for a Fields vehicle.' – *Literary Digest*
'To watch Mr Fields, as Dickensian as anything Dickens ever wrote, is a form of escape for poor human creatures: we who are haunted by pity, by fear, by our sense of right and wrong, who are tongue-tied by conscience, watch with envious love this free spirit robbing the gardener of ten dollars, cheating the country yokels by his own variant of the three-card trick, faking a marriage certificate, and keeping up all the time, in the least worthy and the most embarrassing circumstances, his amazing flow of inflated sentiments.' – *Graham Greene, The Spectator*

Porgy and Bess *

US 1959 138m Technicolor Todd-AO
Columbia/Samuel Goldwyn
A slum girl falls in love with a crippled beggar.
Negro opera about the inhabitants of Catfish Row; full of interest for music lovers, but not lending itself very readily to screen treatment.
w N. Richard Nash play Porgy by DuBose and Dorothy Heyward libretto DuBose Heyward d Otto Preminger ph Leon Shamroy m George Gershwin md André Previn, Ken Darby ch Hermes Pan ly DuBose Heyward, Ira Gershwin
☆ Sidney Poitier, Dorothy Dandridge, Sammy Davis Jnr, Pearl Bailey, Brock Peters, Diahann Carroll, Clarence Muse
† Diahann Carroll's vocals were dubbed by Loulie Jean Norman, Dorothy Dandridge's by Adele Addison, and Sidney Poitier's by Robert McFerrin.
👤 André Previn, Ken Darby
🎝 Leon Shamroy

'Bold! blunt! blustering! the battle picture without equal!'

Pork Chop Hill *

US 1959 97m bw
United Artists/Melville/Lewis Milestone
▤ ◐
The Americans in Korea take a vital hill but the colonel in command finds it difficult to hold.
Ironic war film with vivid spectacle separated by much talk.
w James R. Webb d Lewis Milestone ph Sam Leavitt m Leonard Rosenman pd Nicolai Remisoff
☆ Gregory Peck, Harry Guardino, George Shibata, Woody Strode, James Edwards, Rip Torn, George Peppard, Barry Atwater, Robert Blake

Porky's

Canada 1982 98m colour
Melvin Simon/Astral Bellevue Pathé/Porky's Productions/ (Don Carmody, Bob Clark)
◙ ▤ ◐
In Florida in the early fifties, high school boys try to get into a local brothel.
Ghastly teenage goings-on taking cinema bad taste just about as far as it will get.
wd Bob Clark ph Reginald H. Morris m Carl Zittrer, Paul Zaza pd Reuben Freed
☆ Dan Monahan, Mark Herrier, Wyatt Knight, Roger Wilson, Kim Cattrall, Art Hindle, Wayne Maunder, Alex Karras, Nancy Parsons
'It is difficult to say which is the more depressing: the technical expertise with which this mind-numbing tripe has been put together, or its great success at the US box office.' – *Jo Imeson, MFB*
'One of those movies that makes you weep for the state of the contemporary commercial cinema – and, even more, for the gullibility of the public that pays to see it.' – *Margaret Hinxman, Daily Mail*
† Porky's 2 followed in 1983 and was even worse. 1985 brought Porky's Revenge, about which there is nothing to be said.

Porridge *

GB 1979 93m Eastmancolor
Black Lion/Witzend
◙
US title: Doing Time
Two convicts at Slade Prison become unwilling participants in a break-out.
Genial expansion of a successful TV series to the big screen; alas, as usual the material is stretched to snapping point, and the welcome irony of the original becomes sentimentality. Still, the film is a valuable record of memorable characters.
w Dick Clement, Ian La Frenais d Dick Clement ph Bob Huke md Terry Oates
☆ Ronnie Barker, Richard Beckinsale, Fulton Mackay, Brian Wilde, Peter Vaughan, Geoffrey Bayldon, Julian Holloway

Port Afrique

GB 1956 92m Technicolor
David E. Rose/Columbia
In Morocco, an American pilot solves the shooting of his wife.
Tropical variation on The Maltese Falcon and The Blue Dahlia; not much cop on its own account.
w Frank Partos, John Cresswell novel Bernard Victor Dyer d Rudolph Maté ph Wilkie Cooper m Malcolm Arnold
☆ Phil Carey, Pier Angeli, Dennis Price, Eugene Deckers, James Hayter, Rachel Gurney, Anthony Newley

Port of Call *

Sweden 1948 99m bw
Svensk Filmindustri
original title: Hamnstad
A sailor who quits the sea begins an affair with a lonely and unhappy girl recently released from reform school.
A tough and perceptive drama of class, conventions and relationships, particularly a destructive one between mother and daughter, shot in a documentary style against a background of docks.
wd Ingmar Bergman story Olle Länsberg ph Gunnar Fischer m Erland von Koch ad Nils Svenwall ed Oscar Rosander
☆ Nine Christine Jönsson, Bengt Eklund, Berta Hall, Mimi Nelson, Birgitta Valberg, Sif Ruud, Else Merete Heiberg

Port of New York *

US 1949 82m bw
Eagle Lion (Aubrey Schenck)
▤
A woman narcotics smuggler determines to betray her colleagues to the authorities.
Good routine semi-documentary thick ear, notable for an early appearance by Yul Brynner as villain-in-chief.
w Eugene Ling d Laslo Benedek ph George E. Diskant m Sol Kaplan
☆ Scott Brady, Richard Rober, K. T. Stevens, Yul Brynner

Port of Seven Seas *

US 1938 81m bw
MGM (Henry Henigson)
Love on the Marseilles waterfront.

Stagey Hollywoodization of Pagnol's Marius trilogy: some vigour shows through.
w Preston Sturges d James Whale ph Karl Freund m Franz Waxman
☆ Wallace Beery, Frank Morgan, Maureen O'Sullivan, John Beal, Jessie Ralph, Cora Witherspoon
'Genuine and touching drama … strong solo biller.' – *Variety*

Port of Shadows: see Quai des Brumes

Porte des Lilas *

France/Italy 1957 95m bw
Filmsonor/Rizzoli (Jacques Plante)
aka: Gate of Lilacs
A gangster on the run shelters in a poor quarter of Paris, but his treachery is his undoing.
Atmospheric comedy-drama put across with the expected style but providing very little to wake at.
w René Clair, Jean Aurel novel La Grande Ceinture by René Fallet d René Clair ph Robert Le Fèbvre m Georges Brassens
☆ Pierre Brasseur, Georges Brassens, Henri Vidal, Dany Carrel, Raymond Bussières, Amedée, Alain Bouvette

Les Portes de la Nuit *

France 1946 106m bw
Pathé Cinema
🎧
aka: Gates of Night
Various people in post-war Paris are drawn into a pattern woven by Destiny – who appears as a melancholy tramp.
A polished piece of post-war gloom, and the archetype of all films noirs of the period. The beginning, also, of its director's decline.
w Jacques Prévert d Marcel Carné ph Philippe Agostini m Joseph Kosma ad Alexander Trauner
☆ Pierre Brasseur, Yves Montand, Nathalie Nattier, Serge Reggiani, Jean Vilar, Saturnin Fabre, Mady Berry, Dany Robin
† One of the few films to have been based on a ballet – Le Rendezvous by Prévert. Oddly enough its realistic scenes of daily life are among its most successful elements.

Les Portes Tournantes: see The Revolving Doors

'From the pages of Faith Baldwin's greatest story comes this tense, moving drama of a woman who faced the world, alone, for love…'

Portia on Trial *

US 1937 83m bw
Republic
GB title: The Trial of Portia Merriman
A lady lawyer uses her skills in the courtroom to right the personal wrongs done to her years before.
Efficient tearjerker, Madame X style, and one of the comparatively big productions Republic occasionally tried.
w Sam Ornitz, E. E. Paramore Jnr novel Faith Baldwin d George Nicholls Jnr m Alberto Colombo
☆ Frieda Inescort, Walter Abel, Neil Hamilton, Heather Angel, Ruth Donnelly, Barbara Pepper, Clarence Kolb
'A distinguished production: exploitation required to overcome title and no-name handicap.' – *Variety*
🎝 Alberto Colombo

Portnoy's Complaint

US 1972 101m Technicolor Panavision
Warner/Chehnault (Ernest Lehman)
▤
A young New York Jewish boy has mother and masturbation problems.
Foolhardy attempt to film a fashionably sensational literary exercise; one of Hollywood's last attempts – thank goodness – to be 'with it'.
wd Ernest Lehman novel Philip Roth ph Philip Lathrop m Michel Legrand
☆ Richard Benjamin, Karen Black, Lee Grant, Jack Somack, Jill Clayburgh, Jeannie Berlin
'The spectator is forced into the doubly uncomfortable position of a voyeur who can't actually see anything.' – *Jan Dawson*

Portrait from Life

GB   1948   90m   bw

GFD/Gainsborough (Antony Darnborough)

US title: *The Girl in the Painting*

In an art gallery, a German professor recognizes a portrait as that of his daughter, lost during the war in Germany, and after a search discovers her to have been an amnesiac under the protection of a leading Nazi.

Tolerable melodrama with similarities to The Seventh Veil (the girl has to choose between four men).

w Frank Harvey Jnr, Muriel and Sydney Box
d Terence Fisher ph Jack Asher m Benjamin Frankel

☆ Mai Zetterling, Robert Beatty, Guy Rolfe, Herbert Lom, Patrick Holt

Portrait in Black *

US   1960   113m   Eastmancolor

U-I/Ross Hunter

An elderly shipping tycoon is murdered by his wife and doctor, but they are blackmailed.

Absurd old-fashioned melodrama of dark doings among the idle rich. Quite entertaining for addicts.

w Ivan Goff, Ben Roberts d Michael Gordon
ph Russell Metty m Frank Skinner

☆ Lana Turner, Anthony Quinn, Richard Basehart, Anna May Wong, Lloyd Nolan, Sandra Dee, John Saxon, Ray Walston, Virginia Grey

'Connoisseurs of the higher tosh should find it irresistible.' – *Penelope Houston*

Portrait in Smoke: see Wicked as They Come

Portrait of a Hitman: see Jim Buck

The Portrait of a Lady *

GB/US   1996   144m   Technicolor   Panavision

Polygram/Propaganda (Monty Montgomery, Steve Golin)

🔲 ▤ ◎ ⦵ ♎

In Europe in the 1870s, an American heiress makes an unhappy marriage.

Cool and uninvolving version of a classic novel which never quite gets to grips with its drama of a woman who unexpectedly loses her independence to a domineering husband, not helped by the miscasting of its central roles.

w Laura Jones novel Henry James d Jane Campion ph Stuart Dryburgh m Wojciech Kilar
pd Janet Patterson ed Veronika Jenet

☆ Nicole Kidman, John Malkovich, Martin Donovan, Barbara Hershey, Mary-Louise Parker, Shelley Winters, Richard E. Grant, Shelley Duvall, Viggo Mortensen, Christian Bale, John Gielgud

'Like a Merchant Ivory movie where there's nothing you'd want to buy; it's one of those movies where I want Pauly Shore to suddenly run on-screen and start rubbing himself against someone.' – *Libby Gelman-Waxner, Premiere*

⧓ Barbara Hershey; Jane Patterson (costumes)

Portrait of a Mobster

US   1961   108m   bw

Warner

The career of twenties gangster Dutch Schultz.

Over-familiar, warmed over racketeering stuff with no particular edge or style.

w Howard Browne d Joseph Pevney ph Eugene Polito m Max Steiner

☆ Vic Morrow, Leslie Parrish, Peter Breck, Ray Danton, Norman Alden, Ken Lynch

† Danton also played the title role in *The Rise and Fall of Legs Diamond* (qv).

Portrait of a Sinner: see The Rough and the Smooth

Portrait of Alison *

GB   1955   84m   bw

Anglo-Amalgamated/Insignia (Frank Godwin)

aka: *Postmark for Danger*

A journalist dies while investigating an international smuggling ring, and his brother takes up the case.

Solidly carpentered mystery with all the twists expected from this source.

w Guy Green, Ken Hughes radio serial Francis Durbridge d Guy Green ph Wilkie Cooper
m John Veale

☆ Robert Beatty, Terry Moore, William Sylvester, Josephine Griffin, Geoffrey Keen, Allan Cuthbertson, Henry Oscar

Portrait of Clare

GB   1950   98m   bw

ABPC (Leslie Landau)

In 1900, a woman looks back on her three marriages.

High school novelette for easily pleased female audiences.

w Leslie Landau, Adrian Arlington novel Francis Brett Young d Lance Comfort ph Günther Krampf ad Don Ashton

☆ Margaret Johnston, Richard Todd, Robin Bailey, Ronald Howard, Mary Clare, Marjorie Fielding, Anthony Nicholls, Lloyd Pearson

Portrait of Jennie ***

US   1948   86m   bw (tinted sequence)

David O. Selznick

🔲 ▤ ◎

GB title: *Jennie*

A penniless artist meets a strange girl who seems to age each time he sees her; they fall in love and he discovers that she has long been dead, though she finally comes to life once more during a sea storm like the one in which she perished.

A splendid example of the higher Hollywood lunacy: a silly story with pretensions about life and death and time and art, presented with superb persuasiveness by a first-class team of actors and technicians.

w Peter Berneis, Paul Osborn, Leonard Bernovici novel Robert Nathan d William Dieterle ph Joseph August m Dimitri Tiomkin, after Debussy ad J. McMillan Johnson ed William Morgan, Gerald Wilson

☆ Jennifer Jones, Joseph Cotten, Ethel Barrymore, David Wayne, Lillian Gish, Henry Hull, Florence Bates

PROLOGUE: 'Since time began man has looked into the awesome reaches of infinity and asked the eternal questions: What is time? What is life? What is space? What is death? Through a hundred civilizations, philosophers and scientists have come together with answers, but the bewilderment remains … Science tells us that nothing ever dies but only changes, that time itself does not pass but curves around us, that the past and the future are together at our side for ever. Out of the shadows of knowledge, and out of a painting that hung on a museum wall, comes our story, the truth of which lies not on our screen but in your hearts.'

JENNIE'S SONG: 'Where I come from, nobody knows … And where I'm going, everything goes … The wind blows The sea flows … And nobody knows…'

EBEN (JOSEPH COTTEN): 'I want you, not dreams of you.'

JENNIE (JENNIFER JONES): 'There is no life, my darling, until you love and have been loved. And then there is no death.'

'Easily the Selznick masterpiece, rich in superb performances, tasteful direction and superb photography.' – *Motion Picture Herald*

'One of the most exquisite fantasy films ever made … a milieu rich in visual and aural imagery … a sensuous evocation of time and timelessness.' – *Cinefantastique*

'Though the story may not make sense, the pyrotechnics, joined to the dumbfounded silliness, keep one watching.' – *New Yorker, 1976*

🏆 special effects

⧓ Joseph August

'Auteur. Couturier. Actor. Author. Shopper. Friend.'
'Whatever they do, they do with style.'

Portraits Chinois

France/GB   1996   123m   colour

Film Four/IMA/U&GC/France2/Polar (Georges Benyoun)

♎

An English fashion designer in Paris loses her boyfriend and her job to a newcomer.

The tangled love lives of twentysomethings, in which art is shown as mirroring life, something this slight movie significantly fails to do.

w Martine Dugowson, Peter Chase d Martine Dugowson ph Antoine Roch m Peter Chase
ad Pierre Guffroy ed Martine Barraque, Noëlle Boisson

☆ Helena Bonham Carter, Romane Bohringer, Marie Trintignant, Elsa Zylberstein, Yvan Attal, Sergio Castellitto, Jean-Philippe Ecoffey, Jean-Claude Brialy

'A smart look at the way we live. Sassy as hell and funny in a covert way, it's terrific.' – *Marianne Gray, Film Review*

The Poseidon Adventure **

US   1972   117m   DeLuxe   Panavision

TCF/Kent (Irwin Allen)

🔲 ▤ ◎ ♎

A luxury liner is capsized, and trapped passengers have to find their way to freedom via an upside down.

Tedious disaster movie which caught the public fancy and started a cycle. Spectacular moments, cardboard characters, flashes of imagination.

w Stirling Silliphant, Wendell Mayes novel Paul Gallico d Ronald Neame ph Harold Stine
m John Williams pd William Creber

☆ Gene Hackman, Ernest Borgnine, Shelley Winters, Red Buttons, Carol Lynley, Leslie Nielsen, Arthur O'Connell, Pamela Sue Martin, Roddy McDowall, Eric Shea, Jack Albertson, Stella Stevens

'The script is the only cataclysm in this waterlogged *Grand Hotel*.' – *New Yorker*

† See also: *Beyond the Poseidon Adventure*.

🎵 song 'The Morning After' (m/ly Al Kasha, Joel Hirschhorn)

⧓ Harold Stine; John Williams; Shelley Winters

🏆 Gene Hackman

Posse **

US   1975   93m   Technicolor   Panavision

Paramount/Bryna (Kirk Douglas)

▤ ◎ ♎

A US marshal seeking higher office vows to capture a railroad bandit, but the tables are smartly turned.

Unusual minor Western, quite pleasing in all departments and neither mindless nor violent.

w William Roberts, Christopher Knopf d Kirk Douglas ph Fred Koenekamp m Maurice Jarre

☆ Kirk Douglas, Bruce Dern, Bo Hopkins, James Stacy, Luke Askew, David Canary

Posse

GB/US   1993   111m   Technicolor

Rank/Polygram/Working Title (Preston Holmes, Jim Steel)

🔲 ▤ ◎ ♎

In the 1890s, a group of black cowboys defeat the Ku Klux Klan and other dastardly whites.

An undistinguished Western in the Italian manner, but lacking style and substance.

w Sy Richardson, Dario Scardapane d Mario Van Peebles ph Peter Menzies Jnr m Michel Colombier pd Catherine Hardwicke ed Mark Conte, Seth Flaum

☆ Mario Van Peebles, Stephen Baldwin, Charles Lane, Tiny Lister, Big Daddy Kane, Billy Zane, Blair Underwood, Melvin Van Peebles, Tone Loc, Isaac Hayes

'Races through its paces with little attention to nuance or characterization, but its action, hip attitude, and cool cast should score with youthful general auds as well as blacks.' – *Variety*

Posse from Hell

US   1961   89m   Technicolor

Universal-International

Four killers escape from jail and take over a town.

Moderate Western programmer with more violence than usual.

w Clair Huffaker novel Clair Huffaker d Herbert Coleman ph Clifford Stine m Joseph Gershenson

☆ Audie Murphy, John Saxon, Zohra Lampert, Vic Morrow, Robert Keith

Possessed *

US   1931   76m   bw

MGM

▤

A factory girl goes to New York in search of riches.

Reasonably gutsy Depression melodrama which moves at a fair pace.

w Lenore Coffee play The Mirage by Edgar Selwyn d Clarence Brown ph Oliver T. Marsh

☆ Joan Crawford, Clark Gable, Wallace Ford, Skeets Gallagher, Frank Conroy, Marjorie White, John Miljan

'Lots of luxury; lots of charm; lots of smooth talk about courage and marriage and what women want.' – *James R. Quirk*

'You'll be possessed by its love madness!'

Possessed

US   1947   108m   bw

Warner (Jerry Wald)

🔲 ▤ ◎

An emotionally unstable nurse marries her employer but retains a passionate love for an engineer whom she kills when he does not respond.

Extremely heavy, almost Germanic, flashback melodrama with everyone tearing hammer and tongs at the rather ailing script. Fun if you're in that mood, and an interesting example of the American film noir of the forties.

w Silvia Richards, Ranald MacDougall novel One Man's Secret by Rita Weiman d Curtis Bernhardt ph Joseph Valentine m Franz Waxman

☆ Joan Crawford, Raymond Massey, Van Heflin, Geraldine Brooks, Stanley Ridges, John Ridgely, Moroni Olsen

'Acting with bells on.' – *Richard Winnington*

'Miss Crawford performs with the passion and intelligence of an actress who is not content with just one Oscar.' – *James Agee*

⧓ Joan Crawford

Possession

France/West Germany   1981   127m   colour

Oliane/Marianne/Soma (Marie-Laure Reyre)

🔲 ▤ ◎

An unhappy woman leaves her husband and lover and gives birth to a monster.

Extraordinary horror movie pitched at a level of hysteria and, with its setting of a divided Berlin, no doubt is intended as an allegory, though of what, among the blood and gore, attitudinizing and demented performances, is anybody's guess.

wd Andrzej Zulawski ph Bruno Nuytten
m Andrzej Korzynski, Art Phillips ad Holger Gross sp Carlo Rambaldi

☆ Isabelle Adjani, Sam Neill, Margit Carstensen, Heinz Bennent, Johanna Hofer, Michael Hogben, Shaun Lawton

† It was released in the US in a 97m version.

†† Isabelle Adjani was adjudged best actress in the French equivalent of the Oscars in 1982.

The Possession of Joel Delaney

US   1971   108m   Eastmancolor

ITC/Haworth (George Justin)

A wealthy New York divorcee tries to save her brother from death at the hands of a Puerto Rican occult group who believe in ritual murder and demonic possession.

Unpleasant, frightening and overlong horror film with some kind of message struggling to get out but precious little entertainment value.

w Matt Robinson, Grimes Grice novel Ramona Stewart d Waris Hussein ph Arthur J. Ornitz
m Joe Ragoso

☆ Shirley MacLaine, Perry King, Lisa Kohane, David Elliott

'Some see the film as a political allegory; I see it as a piece of political tosh.' – *Michael Billington, Illustrated London News*

Postcards from America *

US/GB   1995   93m   colour

Islet/Channel 4/Normal (Christine Vachon, Craig Paul)

🔲 ▤

Adapted from two semi-autobiographical books by an artist and writer who died from AIDS in 1992, this fragmentary work concentrates on a loveless childhood with a violent father and adult years as a petty thief and hustler.

A highly stylized, episodic account of a man's remembrance of his search for affection and love and finding only disappointment and disease; the approach emphasizes the alienation of not only the protagonist, but of his audience.

wd Steve McLean novels Close to the Knives and Memories that Smell Like Gasoline by David Wojnarowicz ph Ellen Kuras m Stephen Endelman pd Thérèse Deprez ed Elizabeth Gazzara

☆ James Lyons, Michael Tighe, Olmo Tighe, Michael Imperiolo, Michael Ringer, Maggie Low

Postcards from the Edge *

US   1990   101m   Technicolor

Columbia (Mike Nichols, John Calley)

🔲 ▤ ◎

A drug-addicted actress is forced to live with her unstable mother, an ageing film star.

Entertaining parade of Hollywood egos, enjoyable providing you do not take it seriously.

w Carrie Fisher *novel* Carrie Fisher *d* Mike Nichols *ph* Michael Ballhaus *m* Carly Simon *pd* Patrizia von Brandenstein *ed* Sam O'Steen
☆ Meryl Streep, Shirley MacLaine, Dennis Quaid, Gene Hackman, Richard Dreyfuss, Rob Reiner, Mary Wickes, Conrad Bain, Annette Bening, Simon Callow

'Packs a fair amount of emotional wallop in its dark-hued comic take on a chemically dependent Hollywood mother and daughter.' – *Variety*

👤 Meryl Streep; original song 'I'm Checkin' Out' (*m/ly* Shel Silverstein)

'A shy postman didn't stand a chance with the island's most beautiful woman until the great poet of love gave him the courage to follow his dreams ... and the words to win her heart.'

Il Postino **

Italy/France 1994 100m Eastmancolor
Buena Vista/Cecchi Gori/Tiger/Pentafilm/Mediterraneo/Blue Dahlia/Canal
🔲 📼 🎧
aka: The Postman

An Italian postman is inspired by the exiled Chilean poet Pablo Neruda to woo and win a beautiful woman.
A gentle comedy that gains a great deal from Troisi's contained performance, which illumines the sometimes clumsy narrative, so that it becomes genuinely moving despite its obvious manipulation.
w Anna Pavignano, Michael Radford, Furio Scarpelli, Giacomo Scarpelli, Massimo Troisi *novel* Il Postino di Neruda by Antonio Skarmeta *d* Michael Radford *ph* Franco di Giacomo *m* Luis Enrique Bacalov *pd* Lorenzo Baraldi *ed* Roberto Perpignani
☆ Massimo Troisi, Philippe Noiret, Maria Grazia Cucinotta, Linda Moretti, Renato Scarpa, Anna Bonaiuto, Bruno Alessandro

'A tender and wistful comedy.' – *Kenneth Turan, Los Angeles Times*

† Massimo Troisi died of a heart attack within days of finishing the film.

🏆 Luis Enrique Bacalov
👤 best picture; Michael Radford; Massimo Troisi; screenplay adaptation
🎬 best foreign-language film; Michael Radford

The Postman: see *Il Postino* (1994)

The Postman

US 1997 177m Technicolor Panavision
Warner/Tig (Jim Wilson, Steve Tisch, Kevin Costner)
🔲 📼 ⊘ ⊘ 🎧
In 2013, after a world war, a man tries to keep scattered communities together by setting up a postal service.
An apocalyptic Western, lost in a wilderness of its own making.
w Eric Roth, Brian Helgeland *novel* David Brin *d* Kevin Costner *ph* Stephen Windon *m* James Newton Howard *pd* Ida Random *ed* Peter Boyle
☆ Kevin Costner, Will Patton, Larenz Tate, Olivia Williams, James Russo, Daniel von Bargen, Tom Petty, Scott Bairstow

'A rare epic film that is actually about something.' – *Variety*
'This lacks both the visual and verbal stimuli to keep you watching for three hours.' – *David Eimer, Empire*

† The film cost $80m and took around $17.4m at the US box-office.

The Postman Always Rings Twice *

US 1946 113m bw
MGM (Carey Wilson)
🔲 📼 ⊛
A guilty couple murder her husband but get their come-uppance.
Pale shadow of Double Indemnity, efficient but not interesting or very suspenseful.
w Harry Ruskin, Niven Busch *novel* James M. Cain *d* Tay Garnett *ph* Sidney Wagner *m* George Bassman
☆ Lana Turner, John Garfield, Cecil Kellaway, Hume Cronyn, Leon Ames, Audrey Totter, Alan Reed

'It was a real chore to do *Postman* under the Hays Office, but I think I managed to get the sex across.' – *Tay Garnett*

'You will feel the heat!'
'Their love was a war that destroyed!'

The Postman Always Rings Twice *

US 1981 121m Metrocolor
Lorimar/Northstar International (Charles Mulvehill, Bob Rafelson)
🔲 📼 📼 ⊛ ⊘
A remake of the above with more heavy breathing and some table-ending.
Not otherwise any better, but an interesting measure of the times.
w David Mamet *novel* James M. Cain *d* Bob Rafelson *ph* Sven Nykvist *m* Michael Small *pd* George Jenkins *ed* Graeme Clifford
☆ Jack Nicholson, Jessica Lange, John Colicos, Michael Lerner, John P. Ryan, Anjelica Huston

'Too cheerless to be erotic, too charmless to be titillating.' – *Margaret Hinxman, Daily Mail*

Postman's Knock *

🚻 GB 1961 88m bw
MGM (Ronald Kinnoch)
A village postman is transferred to London, finds life and work bewildering, but captures some crooks and ends up a hero.
Mildly amusing star vehicle rising to good comic climaxes.
w John Briley, Jack Trevor Story *d* Robert Lynn *ph* Gerald Moss *m* Ron Goodwin
☆ Spike Milligan, Barbara Shelley, Wilfrid Lawson

Postmark for Danger: see *Portrait of Alison*

Postmortem

US 1997 105m Foto-Kem
Imperial/Filmwerks/Wild Side (Gary Schmoeller, Tom Karnowski)
🔲 ⊘
A depressed, heavy-drinking, best-selling author, a former San Francisco homicide detective, moves to Glasgow, where his help is sought in catching a serial killer.
Downbeat thriller, shot in sickly hues of blue, green and orange, and noteworthy only for lacking its director's usual action-packed, explosive manner.
w John Lowry Lamb, Robert McDonnell *d* Albert Pyun *ph* George Mooradian *m* Tony Riparetti *pd* Pat Campbell *ed* Natasha Gjurokovic
☆ Charles Sheen, Michael Halsey, Ivana Milicevic, Stephen McCole, Gary Lewis

Il Posto: see *The Job*

The Pot Carriers

GB 1962 84m bw
Associated British
A sensitive young man is debased by prison routine.
Odd little comedy-drama with comedy moments seeming to set the mood.
w T. J. Morrison, Mike Watts *play* Mike Watts *d* Peter Graham Scott *ph* Erwin Hillier *m* Stanley Black
☆ Paul Massie, Ronald Fraser, Carole Lesley, Dennis Price, Paul Rogers, Davy Kaye, Eddie Byrne

Pot Luck *

GB 1936 71m bw
Gainsborough (Michael Balcon)
A Scotland Yard inspector enlists the aid of department store staff to recover a stolen Chinese vase.
Surprisingly not from a stage original, this action farce gets better as it goes along and finds time for a quick spoof of The Old Dark House.
w Ben Travers *d* Tom Walls *ph* Roy Kellino, Arthur Crabtree *md* Louis Levy
☆ Tom Walls, Ralph Lynn, Robertson Hare, Diana Churchill, Gordon James, Martita Hunt

'There is too much melodrama, too little Hare, and, of course, as always to my mind, too much Lynn, too much of the scaly tortoise face and hollow imbecility.' – *Graham Greene*

Pot o' Gold

US 1941 87m bw
Globe/James Roosevelt
GB title: The Golden Hour
A radio giveaway show finds work for idle musicians.
Thin Capraesque comedy which needed more determined handling.

w Walter de Leon *d* George Marshall *ph* Hal Mohr *m* Lou Forbes
☆ James Stewart, Paulette Goddard, Horace Heidt, Charles Winninger, Mary Gordon, Frank Melton, Jed Prouty

Pote tin Kyriaki: see *Never on Sunday*

Potemkin: see *The Battleship Potemkin*

Potomok Chingis-Khana: see *Storm over Asia*

Poulet au Vinaigre: see *Cop au Vin*

Powaqqatsi *

US 1988 97m colour
Cannon/Golan-Globus (Mel Lawrence, Godfrey Reggio, Lawrence Taub)
🔲 📼 🎧
Montage of images of back-breaking labour in the Third World.
A sequel to Koyaanisqatsi, silent apart from the hypnotic score, its beautifully composed images detract from the undignified labour it shows.
w Godfrey Reggio, Ken Richards *d* Godfrey Reggio *ph* Graham Berry, Leonidas Zourdoumis *m* Philip Glass *ed* Iris Cahn, Alton Walpole

Powder

US 1995 112m Technicolor
Buena Vista/Hollywood/Caravan (Roger Birnbaum, Daniel Grodnik)
🔲 📼 ⊛ 🎧
When an old man dies, locals discover the existence of his freakish grandson, a hairless, white-skinned boy with strange powers and a powerful intellect.
A familiar story of a misunderstood teenager, tricked out with some hocus-pocus of mysterious powers, and undermined by its sentimentality.
wd Victor Salva *m* Jerzy Zielinski *m* Jerry Goldsmith *pd* Waldemar Kalinowski *ed* Dennis M. Hill
☆ Mary Steenburgen, Sean Patrick Flanery, Lance Henriksen, Jeff Goldblum, Brandon Smith, Bradford Tatum, Susan Tyrrell

'Features some fine performances, an imaginative premise and a couple of go-for-broke emotional scenes. But the muddled script plays like a first draft, the continuity is jagged and the climax is a cop-out of sappy mysticism.' – *Joe Leydon, Variety*

Powder River

US 1953 77m Technicolor
TCF
A marshal finds that an embittered doctor is the killer he is seeking.
Satisfactory programmer, more of a suspense drama than a Western.
w Geoffrey Holmes (Daniel Mainwaring) *novel* Stuart Lake *d* Louis King *ph* Edward Cronjager *m* Lionel Newman
☆ Rory Calhoun, Cameron Mitchell, Corinne Calvet, Penny Edwards, Carl Betz, John Dehner

Powder Town

US 1942 79m bw
RKO
A scientist in a munitions plant comes into conflict with a tough foreman.
Propaganda action programmer.
w David Boehm, Vicki Baum *novel* Max Brand *d* Rowland V. Lee
☆ Victor Mclaglen, Edmond O'Brien, June Havoc

Power: see *Jew Suss* (1934)

Power

US 1986 111m Technicolor
TCF/Lorimar/Polar (Reene Schisgal, Mark Tarlov)
A political PR man takes on an industrialist of dubious background.
Slick and punchy but somewhat unnecessary investigation of corruption in the media, an American version of The Ploughman's Lunch.
w David Himmelstein *d* Sidney Lumet *ph* Andrzej Bartkowiak *m* Cy Coleman *pd* Peter Larkin *ed* Andrew Mondshein
☆ Richard Gere, Julie Christie, Gene Hackman, Kate Capshaw, Denzel Washington, E. G. Marshall, Beatrice Straight, Fritz Weaver, Michael Learned

The Power *

US 1967 109m Metrocolor Cinemascope
MGM/George Pal
Scientists researching into human endurance are menaced by one of their number who has developed the ability to kill by will power.
Interesting but finally unexciting and exasperating science fiction which badly lacks a gimmick one can actually see.
w John Gay *novel* Frank M. Robinson *d* Byron Haskin *ph* Ellsworth Fredericks *m* Miklos Rozsa
☆ Michael Rennie, George Hamilton, Suzanne Pleshette, Nehemiah Persoff, Earl Holliman, Arthur O'Connell, Aldo Ray, Barbara Nichols, Yvonne de Carlo, Richard Carlson, Gary Merrill, Ken Murray, Miiko Taka, Celia Lovsky

'The movie takes itself very seriously. We don't have to.' – *Robert Windeler*

The Power and the Glory *

US 1933 76m bw
Fox (Jesse L. Lasky)
The flashback story of a tycoon who rose from nothing and was corrupted by power.
Often noted as a forerunner of Citizen Kane, this is in fact a disappointing film with a very thin script and a general sense of aimlessness. 'Presented in narratage' meant that the characters voice their unspoken thoughts. Most interesting for its credits.
w Preston Sturges *d* William K. Howard *ph* James Wong Howe
☆ Spencer Tracy, Colleen Moore, Ralph Morgan, Helen Vinson

'Débuting at two dollars on Broadway. Not two dollars but decidedly above-average film fare. Packs plenty of appeal, even with a not too punch marquee cast.' – *Variety*

The Power and the Prize *

US 1956 98m bw Cinemascope
MGM (Nicholas Nayfack)
An ambitious company executive is criticized by his president for wanting to marry a European refugee, but the other executives support him.
Unconvincing big business fairy tale which passes the time competently enough, though Taylor is a humourless hero.
w Robert Ardrey *novel* Howard Swiggett *d* Henry Koster *ph* George Folsey *m* Bronislau Kaper
☆ Robert Taylor, Elisabeth Mueller, Mary Astor, Burl Ives, Charles Coburn, Cedric Hardwicke

'He's had to fight all his life. Now he's fighting for theirs.'

The Power of One

US 1991 127m Technicolor
Warner (Arnon Milchan)
🔲 📼 ⊛ 🎧
In South Africa in the 1930s, an English boy, who witnesses the brutality of the Afrikaners and is taught boxing by a black prisoner, decides to dedicate his life to the cause of racial equality.
Sentimental and unconvincing account of an African childhood, with Rocky-like moments thrown in for good measure.
w Robert Mark Kamen *novel* Bryce Courtenay *d* John G. Avildsen *ph* Dean Semler *m* Hans Zimmer, Lebo M *pd* Roger Hall *ed* John G. Avildsen
☆ Stephen Dorff, John Gielgud, Armin Mueller-Stahl, Morgan Freeman, Guy Witcher, Simon Fenton

'Crude, patronising and mawkish, sure, but rescued by excellent performances, beautiful landscape photography, and hard-to-argue-with themes of natural justice, delivered with a punch.' – *Angie Errigo, Empire*

Power of the Press

US 1943 63m bw
Columbia
The owner of a New York paper kills to maintain its isolationist line.
Hard-hitting melodrama which overdoes the propaganda.
w Samuel Fuller, Robert D. Andrews *d* Lew Landers
☆ Lee Tracy, Guy Kibbee, Otto Kruger, Gloria Dickson

Power Play

GB/Canada 1978 109m colour
Robert Cooper/Canada United Kingdom (Christopher Dalton)
📼

In a mythical country, a tank commander joins the leaders of a coup d'état only to doublecross them.
Uninteresting mixture of violent action and verbosity.
wd Martyn Burke ph Ousama Rawi m Ken Thorne
☆ Peter O'Toole, David Hemmings, Donald Pleasence, Barry Morse

The Power Within

US 1995 97m colour
(Joseph Merhi, Richard Pepin)
📼

A high-school student is all that prevents a vicious thief from obtaining an ancient ring that will give him immense power.
Violent, teenage wish fulfilment about a nerd who takes on the bad guys.
w Jacobsen Hart, Scott McAboy d Art Camacho ph Ken Blakey m Jim Halfpenny pd Chris Blocker ed Chris Worland
☆ Ted Jan Roberts, Karen Valentine, Keith Coogan, John O'Hurley, Gerald Okamura, Tracy Lindsey, P.J. Soles, Ed O'Ross, Jacob Parker, William Zabka

The Powers Girl

US 1942 92m bw
UA/Charles R. Rogers
GB title: *Hello Beautiful*
Girls come to New York to become models for John Robert Powers.
Extremely thin and forgettable musical.
w Edwin Moran, Harry Segall book John Robert Powers d Norman Z. McLeod ph Stanley Cortez md Louis Silvers
☆ George Murphy, Anne Shirley, Carole Landis, Alan Mowbray, Dennis Day, Benny Goodman and his Orchestra, Mary Treen

Powwow Highway

UK 1988 91m Technicolor
Handmade (Jan Wieringa)
📼

A militant American Indian leaves the reservation with his simple friend to make a long journey to rescue his sister, imprisoned on a trumped-up drugs charge.
Rambling road movie that comes to the conclusion that it is morally justifiable for the exploited to lie, cheat and steal.
w Janet Heaney, Jean Stawarz novel David Seals d Jonathan Wacks ph Toyomichi Kurita m Barry Goldberg pd Cynthia Sowder ed Hilarie Roope
☆ A. Martinez, Gary Farmer, Joanelle Nadine Romero, Geoff Rivas, Roscoe Born, Wayne Waterman, Margo Kane, Amanda Wyss, Sam Vlanos
   'Settles for the affirmations of the buddy movie, without achieving either a consistently manic tone or a convincing balance between character, humour and suspense.' – *Farrah Anwar, MFB*

'Falling in love is the trickiest spell of all.'

Practical Magic

US 1998 105m Technicolor
Warner/Village Roadshow/Di Novi/Fortis
📼 ▤ ◉ ⊙ ⌒
Two young witches deal with an ancient curse that any man who falls in love with them will die.
Like one of those spells where you throw everything into a cauldron and stir hopefully, this has ingredients of a feminist tract, a romantic comedy, a thriller, and domestic drama; nothing works.
w Robin Swicord, Akiva Goldsman, Adam Brooks novel Alice Hoffman d Griffin Dunne ph Andrew Dunn m Alan Silvestri pd Robin Standefer ed Elizabeth Kling, Craig McKay sp Cinesite Digital Studios
☆ Sandra Bullock, Nicole Kidman, Dianne Wiest, Stockard Channing, Aidan Quinn, Goran Visnic, Evan Rachel Wood, Alexandra Astrip, Mark Feuerstein
   'A chick movie with multiple personality disorder.' – *Angie Errigo, Empire*

Practically Yours

US 1944 89m bw
Paramount (Mitchell Leisen)
A war hero comes back after being supposed dead, and finds himself with a fiancée he never met.

Silly romantic comedy which never gets going.
w Norman Krasna d Mitchell Leisen ph Charles Lang Jnr m Victor Young
☆ Claudette Colbert, Fred MacMurray, Gil Lamb, Cecil Kellaway, Robert Benchley, Rosemary de Camp, Tom Powers, Jane Frazee

'It Started With A Kiss.'

Prague *

GB/France 1991 89m Eastmancolor
Winstone/BBC/Constellation/UGC Hachette-Premiere/British Screen/Canal (Christopher Young)
A Scot goes to Prague in search of a wartime newsreel that will reveal information about his mother and her family.
Moderately interesting account of a shared European past that illumines the present, but lacking narrative drive.
wd Ian Sellar ph Darius Khondji m Jonathan Dove pd Jiri Matolin ed John Bloom
☆ Alan Cumming, Sandrine Bonnaire, Bruno Ganz, Raphael Meiss, Henri Meiss, Hana Gregorova
   'A decent Euro-movie that makes good use of the idea of film as collective memory.' – *Philip French, Observer*
   'Comes across like a collection of ideas for a Euro co-production to be lensed in a photogenic city rather than an accomplished vital picture.' – *Variety*

Prancer *

👣 US 1989 102m Film House colour
Orion/Nelson/Cineplex Odeon (Raffaella de Laurentiis)
📼 ▤ ◉
The eight-year-old daughter of a widowed, taciturn, near-bankrupt farmer takes care of an injured reindeer which she believes belongs to Father Christmas.
Pleasing family drama that for the most part avoids cuteness and sentimentality.
w Greg Taylor d John Hancock ph Misha Suslov m Maurice Jarre pd Chester Kaczenski ed Dennis O'Connor
☆ Sam Elliott, Rebecca Harrell, Cloris Leachman, Rutanya Alda, Abe Vigoda, Ariana Richards, Michael Constantine

A Prayer for the Dying

GB 1987 107m Metrocolor
Peter Snell/Samuel Goldwyn Co
An ex-IRA gunman feels unable to silence a priest witness of a killing, and confesses his sins instead.
Convoluted melodrama which kills its chances as a thriller by striving to say something meaningful.
w Edmund Ward, Martin Lynch novel Jack Higgins d Mike Hodges (who disowned the version released) m Bill Conti
☆ Mickey Rourke, Bob Hoskins, Alan Bates, Sammi Davis, Christopher Fulford

Prayer of the Rollerboys

US 1990 94m colour
First Independent/Gaga/Fox Lorber/Academy/JVC/TV Tokyo (Robert Mickelson)
📼 ▤ ◉ ⌒
In a future bankrupt America, a youth, working undercover for the police, infiltrates a vicious gang of young, skating drug dealers.
Dull, paranoid science fiction aimed at a teenage audience.
w W. Peter Iliff d Rick King ph Phedon Papamichael m Stacy Widelitz pd Thomas A. Walsh ed Daniel Loewenthal
☆ Corey Haim, Patricia Arquette, Christopher Collet, J. C. Quinn, Julius Harris, Devin Clark, Mark Pellegrino, Morgan Weisser
   'Offers blood-pumping entertainment in a pulpy, cartoonish mode.' – *Variety*

The Preacher's Wife

US 1996 124m Technicolor
Buena Vista/Touchstone/Samuel Goldwyn
📼 ▤ ◉ ⊙ ⌒
An angel helps sort out the troubled marriage of a preacher.
Bland and gruesomely sentimental comedy that is out of touch with the modern world, and lacks the charm to persuade an audience otherwise; its sole point seems to have been to sell the soundtrack songs by Houston.
w Nat Maudlin, Allan Scott d Penny Marshall ph Miroslav Ondricek m Hans Zimmer pd Bill Groom ed Stephen A. Rotter, George Bowers

☆ Denzel Washington, Whitney Houston, Courtney B. Vance, Gregory Hines, Jenifer Lewis, Loretta Devine, Lionel Ritchie
   'Marshall's marshmallow world and her heavy-handedness in trying so hard to win your approval every step of the way simply grate on the nerves.' – *Alan Jones, Film Review*
† It is a remake of *The Bishop's Wife* (qv), directed by Henry Koster in 1947 and starring Cary Grant.
♫ Hans Zimmer

Preaching to the Perverted

GB 1997 100m Fujicolour
Victor/Cyclops (Stuart Urban)
📼
The young aide to a campaigning, puritanical politician infiltrates a London sex club run by an American dominatrix.
Fetishistic images predominate in this coarse and dispiriting satire that may appeal to masochists: certainly, watching it is torture.
wd Stuart Urban ph Sam McCurdy m Maya and Magnus Fiennes pd James Hendy ed Julian Rodd
☆ Guinevere Turner, Christien Anholt, Tom Bell, Julie Graham, Julian Wadham, Ricky Tomlinson, Georgina Hale, Sue Johnston, Roger Lloyd Pack, Keith Allen
   'The film's impact is blunted by the decision to downplay its serious intent in favour of a comic approach which aims at satire, but swiftly descends into Carry On territory.' – *Sheila Johnston, Screen International*
† The credits include 'Ms Turner's Nipple Double', 'Ms Turner's Tongue Double', 'Ms Graham's Bottom Double' and 'Mr Anholt's Nipple Double', as well as the statement: 'The Producers wish to point out that no animals were improperly treated during the making of this motion picture; however, all the submissives were.'

Precinct 45: Los Angeles Police: see The New Centurions

Pred dozdot: see Before the Rain

Predator

US 1987 107m DeLuxe
TCF/Lawrence Gordon/Joel Silver/John Davis
📼 ▤ ◉ ⌒
An allied military rescue team gets into trouble in South America.
Lethargic action thriller with unpleasant moments.
w Jim and John Thomas d John McTiernan ph Donald McAlpine, Leon Sanchez m Alan Silvestri pd John Vallone ed John F. Link, Mark Helfrich
☆ Arnold Schwarzenegger, Carl Weathers, Bill Duke, Elpidia Carrillo, Jesse Ventura

Predator 2

US 1990 108m DeLuxe
Fox/Lawrence Gordon/Joel Silver/John Davis
📼 ▤ ◉ ⌒
A heavily armed alien killer visits Earth.
Violent and gore-filled, filmed in a frenetic style that soon wearies.
w Jim Thomas, John Thomas d Stephen Hopkins ph Peter Levy m Alan Silvestri pd Lawrence G. Paull ed Mark Goldblatt
☆ Danny Glover, Gary Busey, Ruben Blades, Maria Conchita Alonso, Bill Paxton, Kevin Peter Hall
   'In terms of overall excitement, it outdoes its first safari in start-to-finish hysteria.' – *Variety*

Prefontaine

US 1997 107m Technicolor
Buena Vista/Hollywood (Irby Smith, Jon Lutz, Mark Doonan, Peter Gilbert)
▤ ◉ ⌒
Biopic of the record-breaking American athlete who died young.
Documentary-style movie that never quite gets to grips with the charismatic track star, who liked to run from the front but never had the time to live up to his own high expectations.
w Steve James, Eugene Corr d Steve James ph Peter Gilbert m Mason Daring pd Carol Winstead Wood ed Peter Frank
☆ Jared Leto, R. Lee Ermey, Ed O'Neill, Amy Locane, Lindsay Crouse, Laurel Holloman, Breckin Meyer, Brian McGovern, Kurtwood Smith, Peter Anthony Jacobs

'The film never strays sufficiently beyond the straight-line narrative to allow the potential character relationships to breathe or take on much resonance.' – *Todd McCarthy, Variety*
† *Without Limits* (qv), another biopic of Prefontaine, was released in 1998.

Prehistoric Women: see Slave Girls

Prelude to a Kiss

US 1992 106m DuArt
TCF (Michael Gruskoff, Michael I. Levy)
📼 ▤ ◉ ⌒
After his bride kisses a mysterious old man at her wedding, her husband discovers that she has become a stranger to him.
An oddly uncompelling romantic fantasy; charm is laid on with a trowel, but it is otherwise thin and unconvincing.
w Craig Lucas play Craig Lucas d Norman René ph Stefan Czapsky m Howard Shore pd Andrew Jackness ed Stephen A. Rotter
☆ Alec Baldwin, Meg Ryan, Kathy Bates, Ned Beatty, Patty Duke, Sydney Walker, Stanley Tucci
   'Back in the 1930s or '40s, this sort of sophisticated, literary-oriented treatment of a simple romantic idea would have been the norm. Today's general audiences, however, may be put off by the quick-witted talk and mildly confused by the central device.' – *Todd McCarthy, Variety*
† The play ran on Broadway in 1990, with Alec Baldwin playing the same role. Alec Guinness was originally offered the role of the old man. It was released direct to video in Britain in 1994.

Prelude to Fame

GB 1950 88m bw
Rank/Two Cities (Donald B. Wilson)
The health of a child musical prodigy is endangered by an ambitious woman who pushes him to the top.
Banal drama with classical music, generally overacted by the adults.
w Robert Westerby, Bridget Boland story Young Archimedes by Aldous Huxley d Fergus McDonell ph George Stretton ad Fred Pusey ed Sid Hayers
☆ Jeremy Spenser, Guy Rolfe, Kathleen Ryan, Kathleen Byron, James Robertson Justice, Henry Oscar, Rosalie Crutchley

Prelude to War ***

US 1943 53m bw
US Signal Corps (Frank Capra)
First in the Why We Fight series.
A brilliant assemblage of newsreel, diagrams, and March of Time techniques which pointed a new way for documentary.
   'There isn't a dull second.' – *Variety*

The Premature Burial

US 1961 81m Eastmancolor Panavision
AIP (Roger Corman)
▤ ◉
A man afraid of being buried alive suffers just that fate, but later comes to and wreaks revenge on his tormentors.
Gloomy Gothic horror based vaguely on Edgar Allan Poe: the ultimate in graveyard ghoulishness.
w Charles Beaumont, Ray Russell d Roger Corman ph Floyd Crosby m Ronald Stein ad Daniel Haller
☆ Ray Milland, Heather Angel, Hazel Court, Richard Ney, Alan Napier, John Dierkes

Premiere

GB 1938 71m bw
ABPC
The principal backer of a stage show is shot during the first performance.
Slightly unusual mystery drama.
w F. McGrew Willis d Walter Summers ph Otto Kanturek m Peter Fenn
☆ John Lodge, Judy Kelly, Joan Marion, Hugh Williams, Edmund Breon, Steven Geray, Edward Chapman

---

◎ Digital Video Disc Region 2   ◉ Digital Video Disc Region 1   ⌒ Soundtrack released on compact disc   ☆ Cast in approximate order of importance   † Points of interest   ♫ Notable songs   🏆 Academy Award   👤 Academy Award nomination   🏆 BAFTA

'It's Halloween Night All Over Again ... Be Warned.'

The Premonition

Sweden　1992　114m　colour

Svensk Filmindustri (Waldemar Bergendahl)

🖭

original title: *Svart Lucia*

aka: *Black Lucia*

A girl's dreams of sex and death, which she records in her diary, begin to come true on the longest night of the year.

A psychological thriller with voyeuristic overtones, stronger on disturbing images than narrative interest; it owes much to American examples, from Hitchcock to Carpenter.

w Carina Rydberg, Rumle Hammerich d Rumle Hammerich ph Jens Fischer m Jacob Groth pd Gert Wibe ed Camilla Skousen

☆ Tova Magnusson, Lars Green, Agneta Ekmanner, Figge Norling, Björn Kjellman, Liv Alsterland, Malin Berghagen, Niklas Hjulström

'More interested in atmosphere than action, with character insights instead of suspense, this isn't going to satisfy fans of Freddy and Jason.' – *Kim Newman, Empire*

Préparez Vos Mouchoirs: see *Get Out Your Handkerchiefs*

Present Arms: see *Leathernecking*

Presenting Lily Mars *

US　1943　104m　bw

MGM (Joe Pasternak)

A girl from the sticks hits it big on Broadway.

No, the plot wasn't new, but some of the numbers were nice.

w Richard Connell, Gladys Lehman novel Booth Tarkington d Norman Taurog ph Joseph Ruttenberg md George Stoll

☆ Judy Garland, Van Heflin, Fay Bainter, Richard Carlson, Marta Eggerth, Spring Byington, Bob Crosby and his band, Tommy Dorsey and his band

The President Vanishes

US　1934　80m　bw

Walter Wanger (Paramount)

GB title: *Strange Conspiracy*

The president of the US agrees to drop out of sight for a few days, pretending to have been kidnapped, so that his country will not be drawn into a European war.

Reasonably intriguing political fantasy with good production and performances.

w Lynn Starling, Carey Wilson, Cedric Worth novel anonymous d William A. Wellman

☆ Arthur Byron, Janet Beecher, Paul Kelly, Peggy Conklin, Rosalind Russell, Sidney Blackmer, Walter Kingsford, Charley Grapewin, Edward Arnold

'Provocative topical meller, but likely to be spotty.' – *Variety*

The President's Analyst *

US　1967　104m　Technicolor　Panavision

Paramount/Panpiper (Stanley Rubin)

A psychiatrist who has been asked to treat the president is pursued by spies of every nationality.

Wild political satirical farce which finally unmasks as its chief villain the telephone company. Laughs along the way, but it's all rather too much.

wd Theodore J. Flicker ph William A. Fraker m Lalo Schifrin pd Pato Guzman

☆ James Coburn, Godfrey Cambridge, Severn Darden, Joan Delaney, Pat Harrington, Eduard Franz, Will Geer

'Free-wheeling, outrageous and very funny, laced with a sophisticated zaniness that is sheer delight.' – *Judith Crist*

The President's Lady *

US　1953　96m　bw

TCF (Sol C. Siegel)

An account of the early career of Andrew Jackson, a lawyer whose frail wife died shortly after he became president.

Well-produced political historical romance.

w John Patrick novel Irving Stone d Henry Levin ph Leo Tover m Alfred Newman ad Lyle Wheeler, Leland Fuller

☆ Charlton Heston, Susan Hayward, John McIntire, Fay Bainter, Carl Betz

'History plays a curious second fiddle to love's old sweet song.' – *New York Times*

👤 art direction

The Presidio

US　1988　98m　Technicolor　Panavision

UIP/Paramount (D. Constantine Conte)

🖭 🖭 📀 📀

An army officer and a former cop, who are old adversaries, investigate a murder at an army base.

Tame and uninvolving action movie.

w Larry Ferguson d Peter Hyams ph Peter Hyams m Bruce Broughton pd Albert Brenner ed James Mitchell, Diane Adler, Beau Barthel-Blair

☆ Sean Connery, Mark Harmon, Meg Ryan, Jack Warden, Mark Blum, Dana Gladstone, Jenette Goldstein, Marvin J. McIntyre, Don Calfa, John DiSanti

Press for Time

GB　1966　102m　Eastmancolor

Rank/Ivy/Titan (Robert Hartford Davis, Peter Newbrook)

🖭

The prime minister's grandson is a newspaper seller, and is quietly promoted to be a journalist in a seaside town where it is thought he can do no harm.

The star's last comedy in his original style; competent but nothing special.

w Norman Wisdom, Eddie Leslie novel *Yea Yea Yea* by Angus McGill d Robert Asher ph Peter Newbrook m Mike Vickers

☆ Norman Wisdom, Derek Bond, Angela Browne, Derek Francis, Noel Dyson, Peter Jones, David Lodge

Pressure Point *

US　1962　89m　bw

UA/Larcas/Stanley Kramer

A black prison psychiatrist has longstanding trouble with a violent racist inmate.

Curious, quite compelling case history, told in pointless and confusing flashback; sharply made and photographed, melodramatically acted.

w Hubert Cornfield, S. Lee Pogostin d Hubert Cornfield ph Ernest Haller m Ernest Gold

☆ Sidney Poitier, Bobby Darin, Peter Falk, Carl Benton Reid

Prestige

US　1932　71m　bw

RKO

A woman follows her fiancé to a Malayan prison colony where he is on the staff, and finds he has become an alcoholic.

Tediously stilted romantic melodrama which seems at least twice as long as its actual running time.

w Francis Edward Faragoh novel *Lips of Steel* by Harry Hervey d Tay Garnett ph Lucien Andriot md Arthur Lange

☆ Ann Harding, Melvyn Douglas, Adolphe Menjou, Guy Bates Post, Clarence Muse

'Attraction. Desire. Deception. Murder. No one is ever completely innocent.'

Presumed Innocent **

US　1990　127m　DuArt

Warner/Mirage (Sydney Pollack, Mark Rosenberg)

🖭 🖭 📀 📀 🎧

A public prosecutor is accused of murdering a colleague.

Gripping courtroom drama in which very little is what it seems.

w Frank Pierson, Alan J. Pakula novel Scott Turow d Alan J. Pakula ph Gordon Willis m John Williams pd George Jenkins ed Evan Lottman

☆ Harrison Ford, Brian Dennehy, Raul Julia, Bonnie Bedelia, Paul Winfield, Greta Scacchi, John Spencer, Joe Grifasi, Sab Shimono, Jesse Bradford

'A demanding, disturbing javelin of a courtroom murder mystery.' – *Variety*

'The fashion world laid bare.'

Prêt-à-Porter

US　1994　133m　Technicolor　Panavision

Buena Vista/Miramax (Robert Altman)

🖭 🖭 📀 📀 📀 🎧

aka: *Ready to Wear*

Journalists and fashion designers converge upon Paris for the week of ready-to-wear fashion shows.

About as revealing of the cut-throat world of the fashion business as the Emperor's new clothes, this wastes a great many talents on a ramshackle affair, connected neither to the fantasy nor the reality of the world it depicts; it needed a much stronger narrative structure to knit together its disparate elements.

w Robert Altman, Barbara Shulgasser d Robert Altman ph Pierre Mignot, Jean Lépine m Michel Legrand pd Stephen Altman ed Geraldine Peroni

☆ Anouk Aimée, Lauren Bacall, Kim Basinger, Michael Blanc, Sophia Loren, Marcello Mastroianni, Anne Canovas, Jean-Pierre Cassel, Rossy de Palma, François Cluzet, Rupert Everett, Teri Garr, Richard E. Grant, Sally Kellerman, Ute Lemper and also Linda Hunt, Lyle Lovett, Stephen Rea, Tim Robbins, Julia Roberts, Jean Rochefort, Tracey Ullman, Forest Whitaker

'A flaccid mess, missing its easy targets. It is also undiluted Altman – a movie that sums up his attitude toward actors, audiences, the press, humanity. When one hears the word contempt, one thinks of Robert Altman.' – *Richard Corliss, Time*

'A supremely slack satire on the fashion business.' – *Adam Mars-Jones, Independent*

Pretty Baby *

US　1950　92m　bw

Warner (Harry Kurnitz)

🖭 📀

A girl finds it easier to get a seat on the subway if she is carrying a (dummy) baby, but gets into complications when she meets a baby food king.

Silly but quite pleasant comedy variation on Bachelor Mother.

w Everett Freeman, Harry Kurnitz d Bretaigne Windust ph Peverell Marley m David Buttolph

☆ Betsy Drake, Edmund Gwenn, Dennis Morgan, Zachary Scott, William Frawley

Pretty Baby **

US　1978　109m　Metrocolor

Paramount (Louis Malle)

🖭 📀

A 12-year-old girl grows up in a New Orleans brothel in the 1910s.

A teasing exploration of adult hypocrisies as seen through the eyes of a child, beautifully composed in the manner of French paintings of the period.

w Polly Platt, Louis Malle d Louis Malle ph Sven Nykvist md Jerry Wexler

☆ Keith Carradine, Susan Sarandon, Brooke Shields, Francis Faye, Antonio Fargas

'The picture is too rotten to be worth much of a fuss; it's worth just enough attention to show why it's rotten.' – *Stanley Kauffmann*

👤 Jerry Wexler

Pretty in Pink

US　1986　96m　Technicolor

Paramount (Lauren Shuler-Donner)

🖭 🖭 📀 🎧

A pretty girl from the wrong side of the tracks begins to find herself when she goes to a classy high school.

Slick but not very interesting look at the insecurities of American adolescents.

w John Hughes d Howard Deutch ph Tak Fujimoto m Michael Gore

☆ Molly Ringwald, Harry Dean Stanton, Jon Cryer, Andrew McCarthy, Annie Potts

Pretty Ladies

US　1925　70m　bw　silent

MGM

The husband of a Broadway actress leaves her for a chorus girl.

Heavy-going melodrama with a star who later turned comedienne and a couple of stars-to-be playing bits.

w Adela Rogers St Johns d Monta Bell

☆ ZaSu Pitts, Tom Moore, Norma Shearer, Lilyan Tashman, Conrad Nagel, George K. Arthur, Myrna Loy, Joan Crawford

Pretty Maids All in a Row

US　1971　95m　Metrocolor

MGM (Gene Roddenberry)

High school girl students are being murdered by their guidance counsellor.

Uneasy murder comedy with few laughs, casting its star as a most unlikely villain. An interesting if unsuccessful attempt to be different.

w Gene Roddenberry novel Francis Pollini d Roger Vadim ph Charles Rosher m Lalo Schifrin

☆ Rock Hudson, Angie Dickinson, Telly Savalas, Roddy McDowall, Keenan Wynn

Pretty Poison *

US　1968　89m　DeLuxe

TCF/Lawrence Turman/Mollino (Marshal Backlar, Noel Black)

🖭

A psychotic arsonist enlists the aid of a teenager but soon discovers she is kinkier than he and has murder in mind.

Bizarre black comedy-melodrama, quite successfully mixed and served.

w Lorenzo Semple Jnr novel *She Let Him Continue* by Stephen Geller d Noel Black ph David Quaid m Johnny Mandel

☆ Anthony Perkins, Tuesday Weld, Beverly Garland, John Randolph, Dick O'Neill, Clarice Blackburn

Pretty Polly

GB　1967　102m　Techniscope

Universal/George W. George, Frank Granat

US title: *A Matter of Innocence*

On a world tour with her vulgar aunt, a timid maiden finds romance in Singapore.

Slight romantic fable decked out with travel guide backgrounds and at odds with the cynicism of the short story from which it originates.

w Keith Waterhouse, Willis Hall story Noël Coward d Guy Green ph Arthur Ibbetson m Michel Legrand

☆ Hayley Mills, Trevor Howard, Shashi Kapoor, Brenda de Banzie, Dick Patterson, Peter Bayliss, Patricia Routledge, Dorothy Alison

'It came and went this winter, leaving a slight trace of camphor and old knitting needles.' – *Wilfrid Sheed*

Pretty Village Pretty Flame ***

Serbia　1996　129m　colour　'Scope

Guild Pathé/Cobra/RTV/MCRC (Goran Bjelogrlic, Dragan Bjelogrlic, Nikola Kojo, Milko Josifov)

🖭 🖭 🇺🇸

original title: *Lepa Sela Lepo Gore*

Two friends from boyhood, one Serbian, the other Muslim, find themselves on opposite sides in a civil war.

An angry, bitter film about the madness of the conflict that overwhelmed Yugoslavia, shifting back and forth in time to illumine the lives of those caught up in the craziness.

w Vanja Bulic, Srdan Dragojevic, Nikola Pejakovic d Srdan Dragojevic ph Dusan Joksimovic m Aleksandar Sasa Habic pd Milenko Jeremic ed Petar Markovic

☆ Dragan Bjelogrlic, Nikola Kojo, Dragan Maksimovic, Velimir Bata Zivojlinovic, Zoran Cvijanovic, Milorad Mandic, Dragan Petrovic

'It's enough to know this one has plenty of action, a witty script, buckets of blood, a couple of sex scenes and is pretty darned good.' – *Jake Hamilton, Empire*

Pretty Woman *

US　1990　119m　Technicolor

Buena Vista/Touchstone (Arnon Milchan, Steven Reuther)

🖭 🖭 📀 📀 📀 🎧

A wealthy workaholic asset stripper picks up a hooker and invites her to spend a week with him.

Shameless Hollywood concoction of romance and glossy fantasy that was an immense popular success in 1990, proving that there remains an insatiable demand for escapist fairy tales.

w J. F. Lawton d Garry Marshall ph Charles Minsky m James Newton Howard pd Albert Brenner ed Priscilla Nedd

☆ Richard Gere, Julia Roberts, Ralph Bellamy, Jason Alexander, Laura San Giacomo, Hector Elizondo

'Despite its obvious flaws, Garry Marshall's sentimental pic hits the right emotional targets to shape up as a monster hit.' – *Variety*

👤 Julia Roberts

'The Extraterrestrial Triangle'

Prey

GB　1977　85m　Eastmancolor

Supreme/Tymar (Terence Marcel, David Wimbury)

🖭

An alien, who likes to eat the flesh of humans, takes over the body of a young man and is invited to stay the night by two lesbians, one of whom is a murderer.

Absurd mix of sexploitation and science fiction, treated with the utmost seriousness by director and cast.

w Max Cuff *story* Quinn Donoghue *d* Norman J. Warren *ph* Derek V. Brown *m* Ivor Slaney *ad* Hayden Pearce *ed* Alan Jones

☆ Glory Annen, Sally Faulkner, Barry Stokes, Sandy Chinney, Eddie Stacey

'Shabby low-budget exploitation pic with a ludicrous storyline.' – *Sight and Sound*

† The version released in the British cinemas was cut to 83m.

A Price above Rubies

US   1998   116m   DeLuxe

Film4/Miramax (Lawrence Bender, John Penotti)

📷 ▦

An Orthodox Jewish wife feels oppressed by the Brooklyn community she inhabits, and seeks freedom elsewhere.

An earnest soap opera with a feminist slant, as a woman seeks her identity in a male-dominated world.
wd Boaz Yakin *ph* Adam Holender *m* Lesley Barber *pd* Dan Leigh *ed* Arthur Coburn

☆ Renee Zellweger, Christopher Eccleston, Glenn Fitzgerald, Allen Payne, Julianna Margulies, Kathleen Chalfant, Edie Falco, John Randolph, Kim Hunter, Jackie Ryan, Shelton Dane

'It's an awful big dung-heap to wade through for those small gems.' – *Ceri Thomas, Total Film*

The Price of Fear

US   1956   79m   bw

Universal-International (Howard Christie)

A lady hit-and-run driver falls for a man on the run from racketeers but plans to give him away in order to save herself.

Vaguely unpleasing programmer in which nobody is sympathetic.
w Robert Tallman *d* Abner Biberman *ph* Irving Glassberg *md* Joseph Gershenson

☆ Merle Oberon, Lex Barker, Charles Drake, Gia Scala, Warren Stevens

Prick up Your Ears **

GB   1987   108m   Eastmancolor

Zenith/Civilhand (Andrew Brown)

📷 ▦

The life and violent death of Joe Orton, playwright.

Raunchy homosexual saga of a writer who became a cult figure with the sophisticated; treatment full of vigour for those who can take the pace.
w Alan Bennett *biography* John Lahr *d* Stephen Frears *ph* Oliver Stapleton *m* Stanley Myers *pd* Hugo Luczyc-Wyhowski

☆ Gary Oldman, Alfred Molina, Vanessa Redgrave, Wallace Shawn, Julie Walters, James Grant

'Five charming sisters on the gayest, merriest manhunt that ever snared a bewildered bachelor! Girls! take a lesson from these husband hunters!'

Pride and Prejudice ***

US   1940   116m   bw

MGM (Hunt Stromberg)

📷 ▦ 📀 ◉

An opinionated young lady of the early 19th century wins herself a rich husband she had at first despised for his pride.

A pretty respectable version of Jane Austen's splendid romantic comedy, with a generally excellent cast; full of pleasurable moments.
w Aldous Huxley, Jane Murfin *play* Helen Jerome *novel* Jane Austen *d* Robert Z. Leonard *ph* Karl Freund *m* Herbert Stothart *ad* Cedric Gibbons, Paul Groesse

☆ *Laurence Olivier*, Greer Garson, Edmund Gwenn, Mary Boland, Melville Cooper, Edna May Oliver, Karen Morley, Frieda Inescort, Bruce Lester, Edward Ashley, Ann Rutherford, Maureen O'Sullivan, E. E. Clive, Heather Angel, Marsha Hunt

'The most deliciously pert comedy of old manners, the most crisp and crackling satire in costume that we can remember ever having seen on the screen.' – *Bosley Crowther*

'Animated and bouncing, the movie is more Dickens than Austen; once one adjusts to this, it's a happy and carefree viewing experience.' – *New Yorker, 1980*

🏆 art direction

The Pride and the Passion *

👫 US   1957   131m   Technicolor

Vistavision

UA/Stanley Kramer

▦ 🎧

In 1810 Spain a British naval officer helps Spanish guerrillas, by reactivating an old cannon, to win their fight against Napoleon.

Stolid, miscast adventure spectacle, its main interest being the deployment of the gun across country by surging throngs of peasants.
w Edna and Edward Anhalt *novel* The Gun by C. S. Forester *d* Stanley Kramer *ph* Franz Planer *m* Georges Antheil

☆ Cary Grant, Sophia Loren, Frank Sinatra, Theodore Bikel, John Wengraf, Jay Novello, Philip Van Zandt

'The whirr of the cameras often seems as loud as the thunderous cannonades. It evidently takes more than dedication, cooperative multitudes and four million dollars to shoot history in the face.' – *Time*

Pride of Kentucky: see *The Story of Seabiscuit*

The Pride of St Louis

US   1952   93m   bw

TCF (Jules Schermer)

📷

The life of baseball star Dizzy Dean, who injured himself and became a commentator.

Sporting biopic of clearly restricted interest; modestly well done.
w Herman J. Mankiewicz *d* Harmon Jones *ph* Leo Tover *m* Arthur Lange

☆ Dan Dailey, Joanne Dru, Richard Haydn, Richard Crenna, Hugh Sanders

🏆 original story (Guy Trosper)

Pride of the Bowery

US   1941   61m   bw

Savoy/Monogram/Banner (Sam Katzman)

The East Side Kids go to a Civilian Conservation Corps camp, so that Muggsy can train for a boxing championship; but, in trying to help a friend, he is accused of theft.

One of the Kids' less comic and more earnest efforts, emphasizing good works rather than their usual high spirits.
w George Plympton *story* Steven Clensos, William Lively *d* Joseph H. Lewis *ph* Robert Kline *md* Lange and Porter *ed* Robert Golden

☆ Leo Gorcey, Bobby Jordan, Kenneth Howell, Mary Ainslee, Bobby Stone, Donald Haines, David Gorcey, Sunshine Sammy Morrison, Kenneth Harlan, Nick Stuart, Lloyd Ingraham

Pride of the Marines *

US   1945   120m   bw

Warner (Jerry Wald)

GB title: *Forever in Love*

The story of Marine Al Schmid, blinded while fighting the Japanese.

Over-dramatic, sudsy biopic which is well enough mounted to carry quite an impact in the flagwaving Hollywood style.
w Albert Maltz *d* Delmer Daves *ph* Peverell Marley *m* Franz Waxman

☆ John Garfield, Eleanor Parker, Dane Clark, John Ridgely, Rosemary de Camp, Ann Doran, Warren Douglas, Tom D'Andrea

'Long drawn out and never inspired, but very respectably honest and dogged.' – *James Agee*

🏆 Albert Maltz

'The most wonderful story America ever took to its heart!'

The Pride of the Yankees *

US   1942   128m   bw

Samuel Goldwyn

📷 ▦ 📀 ◉

The story of the baseball star Lou Gehrig, who died of amytropic lateral sclerosis at the height of his powers.

Standard sporting biopic ending on Gehrig's famous speech to the crowd; emotion covers the film's other deficiencies.
w Jo Swerling, Herman J. Mankiewicz *story* Paul Gallico *d* Sam Wood *ph* Rudolph Maté *m* Leigh Harline *ad* William Cameron Menzies *ed* Daniel Mandell

☆ Gary Cooper, Teresa Wright, Babe Ruth, Walter Brennan, Dan Duryea, Elsa Janssen, Ludwig Stossel, Virginia Gilmore

'A simple, tender, meticulous and explicitly narrative film … a real saga of American life, homey, humorous, sentimental, and composed in patient detail.' – *New York Times*

† In order to show Cooper batting left-handed, the prints were reversed for these sequences. Elsewhere in the movie, he is right-handed.

👤 Daniel Mandell

🏆 best picture; script; Paul Gallico; Rudolph Maté; Leigh Harline; Gary Cooper; Teresa Wright

'In A World Of Rituals, In A Place Of Secrets, A Man Must Choose Between Keeping The Faith And Exposing The Truth.'

'One man is about to challenge two thousand years of tradition.'

Priest **

GB   1994   109m   colour

Electric/BBC/Polygram (George Faber, Josephine Ward)

📷 ▦ 📀

A young Catholic priest goes to work in a working-class Liverpool parish where his faith and his ability to deal with problems are tested and his homosexuality is made public.

Powerful drama examining the attitudes of the Catholic hierarchy to sexuality and social ills which is didactic and sometimes lacking in logic – the young priest, priggish and disapproving of sexual activity, cruises a gay bar for a pick-up with the accustomed ease of an habitué of such places – but compelling viewing, nevertheless.
w Jimmy McGovern *d* Antonia Bird *ph* Fred Tammes *m* Andy Roberts *pd* Raymond Langhorn *ed* Susan Spivey

☆ Linus Roache, Tom Wilkinson, Cathy Tyson, Robert Carlyle, James Ellis, Lesley Sharp, Robert Pugh, Christine Tremarco

'Can only be really recommended to people who have never heard the phrases "piss off" and "out of my diocese" in the same sentence, and are anxious to rectify the omission.' – *Adam Mars-Jones, Independent*

'What the film delivers is naked emotion and a powerful sense of drama that often strays into melodrama. What it fails to do is make you think, since it's so intent on telling us what to think itself.' – *Derek Malcolm, Guardian*

† The US Catholic League for Religious and Civil Rights condemned the film as 'designed to stick it to the Catholic Church' and attempted to prevent its distribution. French Catholics also attempted to have it banned.

'Their extravagant romance was more tempestuous than anything he wrote!'

Priest of Love

GB   1981   125m   colour

Ronceval/Milesian (Stanley J. Seeger)

📷 ▦

The last years of D. H. Lawrence, when his books were banned and he was seeking warmer climes to help his TB.

An extremely disappointing film, seeming to consist of aimless travelling by fractious people who never have anything interesting to say. Stilted in all departments.
w Alan Plater *d* Christopher Miles *ph* Ted Moore *m* Joseph James

☆ Ian McKellen, Janet Suzman, Helen Mirren, Penelope Keith, Jorge Rivero, John Gielgud

'Miles was assigned himself a missionary role but he is just not up to the task.' – *Jill Forbes, MFB*

The Priest's Wife (dubbed)

Italy/France   1970   106m   Technicolor

Warner/Champion/ECF (Carlo Ponti)

original title: *La Moglie del Prete*

A pop singer seduces a priest who attempts to save her from suicide.

Dreary treatment of the topical theme of celibacy.
w Ruggero Maccari, Bernardino Zapponi *d* Dino Risi *ph* Alfio Contini *m* Armando Trovaioli *ad* Gianni Polidori *ed* Alberto Gallitti

☆ Sophia Loren, Marcello Mastroianni, Venantino Venantini, Jacques Stany, Pippo Starnazza

'Vulgar, fence-sitting charade.' – *John Gillett, MFB*

† The film was cut to 103m on its British release.

Prima della Rivoluzione: see *Before the Revolution*

'Sooner or later a man who wears two faces forgets which one is real.'

Primal Fear

US   1996   129m   DeLuxe

UIP/Paramount/Rysher (Gary Lucchesi)

📷 ▦ 📀 ◉

A slick lawyer defends a shy choirboy accused of murdering an archbishop.

An implausible thriller with a twist at its end, but one that diminishes all that has gone before, so that an audience is more likely to feel cheated than surprised.
w Steve Shagan, Ann Biderman *novel* William Diehl *d* Gregory Hoblit *ph* Michael Chapman *m* James Newton Howard *pd* Jeannine Oppewall *ed* David Rosenbloom

☆ Richard Gere, Laura Linney, John Mahoney, Alfre Woodard, Frances McDormand, Edward Norton, Terry O'Quinn, Andre Braugher

'This frail thriller has a clean, unfussed-over look – which is about all one can say for it.' – *Peter Matthews, Sight and Sound*

🏆 Edward Norton

'What Went Down On The Way To The Top.'

Primary Colors **

US   1998   143m   DeLuxe   'Scope

Universal/Mutual/Icarus (Mike Nichols)

📷 ▦ 📀 ◉

A manipulative and womanizing governor from a Southern state, aided by his tough-talking wife, runs for the job of President of the United States.

A tart, knowing account of American politics, based on a bestselling novel that was itself based on Bill Clinton's first presidential campaign; it both entertains and, in its exposure of the backstage mechanics of massaging public opinion, appals.
w Elaine May *novel* Anonymous (Joe Klein) *d* Mike Nichols *ph* Michael Ballhaus *m* Ry Cooder *pd* Bo Welch *ed* Arthur Schmidt

☆ John Travolta, Emma Thompson, Billy Bob Thornton, Adrian Lester, Maura Tierney, Paul Guilfoyle, Larry Hagman, Kathy Bates, Diane Ladd, Caroline Aaron, Mykelti Williamson

'Frequently funny, wonderfully performed, eerily evocative of recent history and gratifyingly blunt in its assessment of what it takes to get to the top in modern American politics, pic also lacks something crucial at its center that prevents it from being an entirely credible portrait of its subject.' – *Todd McCarthy, Variety*

🏆 Kathy Bates; Elaine May

🏆 Elaine May

Prime Cut

US   1972   91m   Technicolor   Panavision

Cinema Center (Joe Wizan)

▦

A Kansas gangster incurs the wrath of his Chicago bosses, and a hired killer is sent to eliminate him.

Gory cat-and-mouse chase melodrama with no interest save its excesses.
w Robert Dillon *d* Michael Ritchie *ph* Gene Polito *m* Lalo Schifrin

☆ Gene Hackman, Lee Marvin, Angel Tompkins, Sissy Spacek

The Prime Minister *

GB   1941   109m   bw

Warner (Max Milder)

Episodes in the life of Disraeli.

Modestly budgeted historical pageant notable only for performances.
w Brock Williams, Michael Hogan *d* Thorold Dickinson *ph* Basil Emmott

☆ John Gielgud, Diana Wynyard, Will Fyffe, Stephen Murray, Owen Nares, Fay Compton, Lyn Harding, Leslie Perrins

The Prime of Miss Jean Brodie *

GB   1969   116m   DeLuxe

TCF (Robert Fryer)

📷

A sharp-minded Edinburgh schoolmistress of the thirties is a bad influence on her more easily-swayed pupils.

Interesting but slackly handled and maddeningly played character drama.
w Jay Presson Allen *novel* Muriel Spark *d* Ronald Neame *ph* Ted Moore *m/ly* Rod McKuen *pd* John Howell

☆ Maggie Smith, Robert Stephens, Pamela Franklin, Celia Johnson, Gordon Jackson, Jane Carr

'The novel lost a good deal in its stage simplification, and loses still more in its movie reduction of that stage version.' – *John Simon*

👤 Maggie Smith

🎵 song 'Jean' (m/ly Rod McKuen)

🏆 Maggie Smith; Celia Johnson

The Primitives

GB   1962   65m   bw

Rank/Border (Negus Fancey)

A night-club dance group double as jewel thieves.

Dire comedy thriller that is never more than unwatchable.

w Moris Farhi, Alfred Travers d Alfred Travers ph Michael Reed m Edmundo Ros ad William Kellner ed Alfred Cox

☆ Jan Holden, Rio Fanning, Bill Edwards, George Mikell, Terence Fallon, Derek Ware, Peter Hughes, George Roderick

The Primrose Path

US   1940   92m   bw

RKO (Gregory La Cava)

The youngest of a family of shanty-town prostitutes falls in love with an honest hamburger stand proprietor.

Downright peculiar melodrama for its day and age, and not very entertaining either, spending most of its time being evasive.

w Allan Scott, Gregory La Cava play Robert Buckner, Walter Hart novel *February Hill* by Victoria Lincoln d Gregory La Cava ph Joseph H. August m Werner Heymann

☆ Ginger Rogers, Joel McCrea, Marjorie Rambeau, Henry Travers, Miles Mander, Queenie Vassar, Joan Carroll

'The story isn't good enough, the direction isn't sincere enough, to give any pain to the lumps in the throat which its designers obviously had in mind.' – *Richard Mallett, Punch*

👤 Marjorie Rambeau

'In One Thrill-Packed Night You'll Live The Adventures Of A Lifetime!'

The Prince and the Pauper *

👪 US   1937   118m   bw

Warner (Robert Lord)

In Tudor London, young Edward VI changes places with a street urchin who happens to be his double.

Well-produced version of a famous story; it never quite seems to hit the right style or pace, but is satisfying in patches.

w Laird Doyle novel Mark Twain d William Keighley ph Sol Polito m Erich Wolfgang Korngold

☆ Errol Flynn, Claude Rains, Billy Mauch, Bobby Mauch, Henry Stephenson, Barton MacLane, Alan Hale, Eric Portman, Montagu Love, Lionel Pape, Halliwell Hobbes, Fritz Leiber

'Lavish but not convincing. Doubtful box office: the commercial aspect seems wholly concerned in the timeliness of a Coronation sequence and the name of Errol Flynn. It is not enough.' – *Variety*

The Prince and the Pauper *

👪 Panama   1977   121m   Technicolor

Panavision

International Film Production/Ilya and Alexander Salkind (Pierre Spengler)

US title: *Crossed Swords*

Young Edward VI changes place with a beggar, who helps to expose a traitor.

Moderately well-made swashbuckler with an old-fashioned air, not really helped by stars in cameo roles or by the poor playing of the title roles.

w George MacDonald Fraser novel Mark Twain d Richard Fleischer ph Jack Cardiff m Maurice Jarre pd Anthony Pratt ad Tony Pratt ed Ernest Walter

☆ Mark Lester, Oliver Reed, Raquel Welch, Ernest Borgnine, George C. Scott, Rex Harrison, David Hemmings, Charlton Heston, Harry Andrews, Murray Melvin, Julian Orchard

The Prince and the Showgirl *

GB   1957   117m   Technicolor

Warner/Marilyn Monroe Productions (Laurence Olivier)

In London for the 1911 coronation, a Ruritanian prince picks up a chorus girl and they come to understand and respect each other.

Heavy-going comedy, rich in production values but weak in dramatic style and impact.

w Terence Rattigan play *The Sleeping Prince* by Terence Rattigan d Laurence Olivier ph Jack Cardiff m Richard Addinsell pd Roger Furse ad Carmen Dillon

☆ Laurence Olivier, Marilyn Monroe, Sybil Thorndike, Richard Wattis, Jeremy Spenser, Esmond Knight, Rosamund Greenwood, Maxine Audley

† Colin Clark's book *The Prince, the Showgirl and Me* is an entertaining account of the behind-the-screen story of the making of the film, as seen from the viewpoint of its 3rd assistant director.

Prince of Darkness

US   1987   101m   colour

Guild/Alive (Larry Franco)

Scientists are called in by a priest to deal with a canister containing the spirit of Satan.

Risible horror that never arouses any interest.

w Martin Quatermass (John Carpenter) d John Carpenter m Gary B. Kibbe m John Carpenter, Alan Howarth pd Daniel Lomino ed Steve Mirkovich

☆ Donald Pleasence, Victor Wong, Lisa Blount, Dennis Dun, Jameson Parker, Susan Blanchard, Anne Howard, Ann Yen, Ken Wright

'The Power Is Real. The Story Is Forever. The Time Is Now.'

The Prince of Egypt **

US   1998   97m   colour

DreamWorks (Penney Finkelman Cox, Sandra Rabins)

In Ancient Egypt, the baby Moses escapes death, is adopted by the Queen, and grows up to lead the Israelites from slavery.

An animated feature that mistakenly apes the epic spectacle of a Cecil B. de Mille – while a real cast of thousands or vast sets may appeal, the effect is diminished when drawn, since anything is possible with pencil and paper. For a rival to Disney, it sticks very close to that studio's prevailing style of pop musicals.

w Philip LaZebnik d Brenda Chapman, Steve Hickner, Simon Wells m Hans Zimmer

m/ly Stephen Schwartz pd Darek Gogol ed Nick Fletcher

☆ Featuring the voices of: Val Kilmer, Ralph Fiennes, Michelle Pfeiffer, Sandra Bullock, Jeff Goldblum, Danny Glover, Patrick Stewart, Helen Mirren, Steve Martin, Martin Short

'Epic storytelling on the grandest scale. Big imagery, big themes, big emotions – all met head-on and accomplished triumphantly within a film that is in essence a live action movie – more precisely, a Steven Spielberg live action movie – with cartoon.' – *Ian Freer, Empire*

🎵 song 'When You Believe' (m/ly Stephen Schwartz)

🏆 Stephen Schwartz, Hans Zimmer

'A saga of scoundrels in a century of infamy!'

Prince of Foxes *

US   1949   107m   bw

TCF (Sol. C. Siegel)

A wandering adventurer in medieval Italy gets mixed up with the Borgias.

Good-looking historical fiction with a slight edge to it.

w Milton Krims novel Samuel Shellabarger d Henry King ph Leon Shamroy m Alfred Newman

☆ Tyrone Power, Orson Welles, Wanda Hendrix, Felix Aylmer, Everett Sloane, Katina Paxinou, Marina Berti

'Plot, counterplot, action and vengeance.' – *MFB*

'This pretentious chapter of pseudo-history never rises above the merely spectacular, hovers mostly around the conventionally banal, and descends once to the unpardonably crude.' – *Richard Mallett, Punch*

🏆 Leon Shamroy

Prince of Jutland

Denmark/France/Germany/Netherlands/GB   1994   107m   colour

Allarts/Ariane/Woodline/Eurimages/Roses/Kenneth Madsen

A prince avenges the death of his father.

Given the talents involved, a disappointing version of the story of Hamlet, based on the original legend from The Exploits of the Danes, written early in the 13th century by the secretary to the Archbishop of Lund.

w Gabriel Axel, Erik Kjersgard book Saxo Grammaticus d Gabriel Axel ph Henning Kristiansen m Per Norgaard pd Sven Wichmann ed Jean-François Naudon

☆ Gabriel Byrne, Helen Mirren, Christian Bale, Tony Haygarth, Steven Waddington, Freddie Jones, Brian Cox, Kate Beckinsale

'Looks like a made-for-TV film, meandering from the mildly diverting to the mundane.' – *Sight and Sound*

The Prince of Pennsylvania *

US   1988   93m   Technicolor

Palace/New Line Cinema (Joan Fishman)

A rebellious teenager has problems with his father.

Sensitive, downbeat tale of a boy's alienation from his family that avoids easy conclusions.

wd Ron Nyswaner ph Frank Prinzi m Thomas Newman pd Tony Corbett ed William Scharf

☆ Fred Ward, Keanu Reeves, Bonnie Bedelia, Amy Madigan, Jeff Hayenga, Tracey Ellis, Joseph de Lisi, Jay O. Sanders, Kari Keegan

Prince of Pirates

👪 US   1953   80m   Technicolor

Columbia (Sam Katzman)

A young prince of the Netherlands turns pirate when his brother allies with the Spanish invader.

Fast-moving costume potboiler with lavish use of action scenes from Joan of Arc.

w John O'Dea, Samuel Newman d Sidney Salkow ph Henry Freulich md Mischa Bakaleinikoff

☆ John Derek, Barbara Rush, Carla Balenda, Whitfield Connor, Edgar Barrier

Prince of Players *

US   1955   102m   DeLuxe   Cinemascope

TCF (Philip Dunne)

Episodes in the life of actor Edwin Booth, brother of the man who killed Abraham Lincoln.

Earnest but ham-fisted biopic more notable, as a Hollywood entertainment, for its dollops of straight Shakespeare than for any dramatic interest.

w Moss Hart book Eleanor Ruggles d Philip Dunne ph Charles G. Clarke m Bernard Herrmann

☆ Richard Burton, Eva Le Gallienne, Maggie McNamara, John Derek, Raymond Massey, Charles Bickford, Elizabeth Sellars, Ian Keith

Prince of Shadows: see *Beltenebros*

Prince of the City *

US   1981   167m   Technicolor

Warner/Orion (Jay Presson Allen)

A New York policeman on the drug beat is induced to inform on his corrupt colleagues.

Punishingly long police semi-documentary based on real events and apparently filmed with a political motive. Excellent acting and production detail do not prevent the enterprise from seeming like a half-speed version of Serpico.

w Jay Presson Allen, Sidney Lumet book Robert Daley d Sidney Lumet

☆ Treat Williams, Jerry Orbach, Don Billett, Richard Foronjy, Carmine Caridi, Kenny Marino

🏆 screenplay

Prince of Thieves

👪 US   1948   72m   bw

Sam Katzman/Columbia

Robin Hood saves a nobleman's intended from Baron Tristram.

Tatty second-feature version of a legendary figure.

w Maurice Tombragel d Howard Bretherton

☆ Jon Hall, Patricia Morison, Alan Mowbray, Michael Duane, Adele Jergens

'A story about the memories that haunt us, and the truth that sets us free.'

The Prince of Tides **

US   1991   132m   Technicolor

Columbia/Barwood/Longfellow (Barbra Streisand, Andrew Karsch)

A married psychiatrist falls in love with the unhappy brother of her catatonic patient.

Excellent performances enliven a lushly romantic melodrama.

w Pat Conroy, Becky Johnston novel Pat Conroy d Barbra Streisand ph Stephen Goldblatt m James Newton Howard pd Paul Sylbert ed Don Zimmerman

☆ Barbra Streisand, Nick Nolte, Blythe Danner, Kate Nelligan, Jeroen Krabbé, Melinda Dillon, George Carlin, Jason Gould, Brad Sullivan

'Has a passion seldom found in contempo US films and a quality not usually associated with Barbra Streisand – self-effacement.' – *Variety*

'This phoney overblown movie … is the king of soaps.' – *Philip French, Observer*

🏆 film; Nick Nolte; Kate Nelligan; Pat Conroy, Becky Johnston; Stephen Goldblatt; James Newton Howard; Paul Sylbert

Prince Valiant *

👪 US   1954   100m   Technicolor

Cinemascope

TCF (Robert L. Jacks)

The son of the exiled king of Scandia seeks King Arthur's help against the usurper, and becomes involved in a court plot.

Agreeable historical nonsense for teenagers, admittedly and sometimes hilariously from a comic strip.

w Dudley Nichols comic strip Hal Foster d Henry Hathaway ph Lucien Ballard m Franz Waxman

☆ Robert Wagner, James Mason, Debra Paget, Janet Leigh, Sterling Hayden, Victor McLaglen, Donald Crisp, Brian Aherne, Barry Jones, Primo Carnera

Prince Valiant

👪 US/GB/Ireland/Germany   1997   91m   colour   Super 35

Entertainment/Paramount/Constantin/Lakeshore/Legacy (Carsten Lorenz)

The adventures of Prince Valiant, Sir Gawain's royal squire, against the Vikings in the time of King Arthur.

A lively, old-fashioned medieval romp, in appropriate comic-book style, but one that may not have much appeal these days.

w Michael Frost Beckner, Anthony Hickox, Carsten Laurenz comic strip Harold R. Foster d Anthony Hickox ph Roger Lanser m David Bergeaud pd Crispian Sallis ed Martin Hunter

☆ Stephen Moyer, Katherine Heigl, Thomas Kretschmann, Edward Fox, Udo Kier, Warwick Davis, Gavan O'Herlihy, Ben Pullen, Walter Gotell, Zach Galligan, Chesney Hawkes, Joanna Lumley, Ron Perlman, Anthony Hickox

The Prince Who Was a Thief

👪 US   1951   88m   Technicolor

U-I (Leonard Goldstein)

An Arabian Nights prince is lost as a baby and brought up by thieves, but finally fights back to his rightful throne.

Given the synopsis, any viewer can write the script himself. Standard eastern Western romp.

w Gerald Drayson Adams, Aeneas Mackenzie story Theodore Dreiser d Rudolph Maté ph Irving Glassberg m Hans Salter

☆ Tony Curtis, Piper Laurie, Everett Sloane, Jeff Corey

The Princess *

Hungary   1982   113m   bw

Cinegate/Tarsulas Studio/Mafilm (Pal Erdoss)

original title: *Adj Király Katonát!*

A 15-year-old girl moves to Budapest to discover that life is tougher than she expected.

Downbeat, documentary-style examination of a teenager facing a succession of disappointments; the film, though, manages to suggest that there is hope for the future.

w Istvan Kardos d Pál Erdöss ph Ferenc Pap, Lajos Koltai, Gabor Szabo pd Andras Gyurki ed Klara Majoros

☆ Erika Ozda, Andrea Szendrei, Denes Diczhazi, Arpad Toth, Juli Nyako, Lajos Soltis

---

The Princess and the Goblin
👫 GB/Hungary 1992 111m colour
Entertainment/Siriol/Pannonia/SC4/NHK Enterprises
(Robin Lyons)
📀 🎬 🎧

A miner's son saves a princess from being
kidnapped by goblins.
*Uninteresting animated feature, with a dull fairy-tale
plot dully executed.*
w Robin Lyons *novel* George MacDonald
d József Gémes *ph* Arpad Lessecry, Gyergy Verga,
Ede Pagner, Nick Smith, Pete Turner, Steve
Turner, Andreas Klawsz *m* István Lerch
ed Magda Hap
☆ Featuring the voices of: Joss Ackland, Claire
Bloom, Roy Kinnear, Sally Ann Marsh, Rik
Mayall, Peggy Mount, Peter Murray, Victor
Spinetti, Mollie Sugden
'A potentially charming medieval cartoon let
down by so-so technique and unimaginative
plotting.' – *Variety*

The Princess and the Pirate *
👫 US 1944 94m Technicolor
Samuel Goldwyn (Don Hartman)
🎬 🎧

An impostor is on the run from a vicious pirate.
*Typical star costume extravaganza with fewer laughs
than you'd expect.*
w Don Hartman, Melville Shavelson, Everett
Freeman *d* David Butler *ph* William Snyder,
Victor Milner *m* David Rose *ad* Ernst Fegte
☆ Bob Hope, Virginia Mayo, Victor McLaglen,
Walter Slezak, Walter Brennan, Marc Lawrence,
Hugo Haas, Maude Eburne
'From start to finish, Hope dominates the action
with well-timed colloquial nifties.' – *Variety*
𝄞 David Rose; Ernst Fegte

The Princess Bride *
👫 US 1987 98m DeLuxe
Act III (Andrew Scheinmann, Rob Reiner)
📀 🎬 🎧

Grandfather tells a fairy tale of good and evil.
*Rather strained fantasy with occasional bright
moments.*
w William Goldman *novel* William Goldman
d Rob Reiner *ph* Adrian Biddle *m* Mark
Knopfler *pd* Norman Garwood
☆ Cary Elwes, Mandy Patinkin, Chris Sarandon,
Christopher Guest, Peter Falk, Wallace Shawn
𝄞 song 'Storybook Love'

'She was everything they dreamed of ... And nothing
they expected.'

Princess Caraboo *
US 1994 97m colour
Entertainment/Beacon/TriStar/J&M/Longfellow/Artisa
n (Andy Karsch, Simon Bosanquet)
📀 🎬 🎧

In the early 18th century, a woman found
wandering in Devon claims to be a Javanese
princess who has escaped from pirates and is taken
up by the aristocracy.
*A moderately entertaining comedy of identity that has
its basis in fact and is blessed with a better cast than it
deserves, even if their performances are well below their
best.*
w Michael Austin, John Wells *d* Michael Austin
ph Freddie Francis *m* Richard Hartley
pd Michael Howells *ed* George Akers
☆ Phoebe Cates, Jim Broadbent, Wendy Hughes,
Kevin Kline, John Lithgow, Stephen Rea, Peter
Eyre, Roger Lloyd Pack, John Sessions, John Lynch
'Delve deeper into this period meringue and the
whole concoction deflates into fluffy
nothingness.' – *Colin Brown, Screen International*

Princess Charming
GB 1934 78m bw
Gainsborough
A Ruritanian revolution forces a princess to escape
in disguise.
Light operetta with an intriguing cast.
w L. DuGarde Peach, Arthur Wimperis, Lauri
Wylie *play* Alexandra by F. Martos *d* Maurice
Elvey *ph* Max Greene *songs* Ray Noble, Max
Kester
☆ Evelyn Laye, Yvonne Arnaud, George
Grossmith, Max Miller, Henry Wilcoxon, Ivor
Barnard, Francis L. Sullivan
'Still just below the peak of excellence for which
Hollywood is noted.' – *Variety*

The Princess Comes Across *
US 1936 76m bw
Paramount (Arthur Hornblow Jnr)
A starstruck Brooklyn girl makes a transatlantic
liner voyage disguised as a princess, and finds
herself involved in a murder mystery.
Zany comedy thriller with plenty of jokes.
w Walter de Leon, Francis Martin, Frank Butler,
Don Hartman, Philip MacDonald *novel* Louis
Lucien Rogger *d* William K. Howard *ph* Ted
Tetzlaff *m* Phil Boutelje
☆ Carole Lombard, Fred MacMurray, Alison
Skipworth, Douglass Dumbrille, William Frawley,
Porter Hall, George Barbier, Lumsden Hare, Sig
Rumann, Mischa Auer, Tetsu Komai

Princess of the Nile
US 1954 71m Technicolor
TCF
An Egyptian princess of the middle ages leads her
country against the invasion of a bedouin prince.
Lethargic costume piece with hopelessly miscast actors.
w Gerald Drayson Adams *d* Harmon Jones
ph Lloyd Ahern *m* Lionel Newman
☆ Debra Paget, Michael Rennie, Jeffrey Hunter,
Dona Drake, Edgar Barrier, Jack Elam, Lee Van
Cleef

Princess O'Hara
US 1935 79m bw
Universal
In her father's memory a girl steals the racehorse he
loved.
*Sentimental comedy from Damon Runyon, later
remade for Abbott and Costello as It Ain't Hay. Not
up to much in either version.*
w Doris Malloy, Harry Clork *d* David Burton
☆ Jean Parker, Chester Morris, Leon Errol, Vince
Barnett, Henry Armetta, Ralph Remley, Clara
Blandick
'Poor construction limits this one's chances ...
not likely to go above average grosses.' – *Variety*

Princess O'Rourke
US 1943 94m bw
Warner (Hal B. Wallis)
An ace pilot falls for a princess and causes
diplomatic complications.
*Very thin wartime comedy with a propaganda ending
involving Franklin Roosevelt.*
wd Norman Krasna *ph* Ernest Haller *m* Frederick
Hollander
☆ Olivia de Havilland, Robert Cummings,
Charles Coburn, Jack Carson, Jane Wyman, Harry
Davenport, Gladys Cooper, Minor Watson, Curt
Bois
👤 Norman Krasna (as writer)

Princesse de l'Erotisme: see *Virgin among
the Living Dead*

Il Principe Di Homburg *
Italy 1996 85m Eastmancolor
Filmalbatross/Istituto Luce (Pier Giorgio Bellocchio)
aka: *The Prince of Homburg*
A headstrong cavalry commander is condemned to
death for disobeying orders.
*Intriguing psychological drama, somewhat
underpowered in this version; its theme—that discipline
and obedience matter more than individual liberty—
lacks popular appeal.*
wd Marco Bellocchio *play* Heinrich von Kleist
ph Giuseppe Lanci *m* Carlo Crivelli *md* Rinaldo
Muratori *pd* Giantito Burchiellaro *ed* Francesca
Calvelli
☆ Andrea Di Stefano, Barbara Bobulova, Toni
Bertorelli, Anita Laurenzi, Fabio Camilli, Gianluigi
Fogacci, Italo Dall'Orto, Bruno Corazzari

Priorities on Parade
US 1942 79m bw
Sol C. Siegel/Paramount
Members of a swing band get jobs in a munitions
factory.
Inept propaganda musical.
w Art Arthur, Frank Loesser *d* Albert S. Rogell
☆ Ann Miller, Johnnie Johnston, Jerry Colonna,
Betty Jane Rhodes, Vera Vague, Eddie Quillan,
The Debonaires
'Manifestly just another of the misfortunes of
war.' – *Variety*

La Prise de Pouvoir par Louis XIV: see *The
Rise of Louis XIV*

Prison: see *The Devil's Wanton*

Prison
US 1988 103m colour
Entertainment/Empire (Irwin Yablans)
🎬 🎧
The spirit of a long-dead prisoner returns for
revenge against the prison's new governor.
*Energetic horror movie, re-animating all the clichés of
prison dramas.*
w C. Courtney Joyner *story* Irwin Yablans
d Renny Harlin *ph* Michael Ballhaus *m* Richard
Band, Christopher Stone *pd* Phillip Duffin
ed Ray Lovejoy
☆ Viggo Mortensen, Chelsea Field, Lane Smith,
Lincoln Kilpatrick, Tom Everett, Ivan Kane

Prison Farm
US 1938 69m bw
Paramount
A girl denounces her boyfriend when he is wanted
for robbery and murder.
*Good example of this studio's tour of criminals and
penal institutions.*
w Eddie Welch, Robert Yost, Stuart Anthony
d Louis King *ph* Harry Fishbeck *md* Boris Morros
ed Edward Dmytryk
☆ Lloyd Nolan, Shirley Ross, John Howard, J.
Carrol Naish, Porter Hall, Anna Q. Nilsson, Esther
Dale, May Boley
'First-rate entertainment despite lightweight star
names.' – *Variety*

Prison without Bars
GB 1938 80m bw
Columbia/London Films (Arnold Pressburger)
The newest inmate of a reform school for girls vies
with the superintendent for the love of the doctor.
*Basically paperback trash, this film of a notorious
original was shot in three languages, but the English
version at least omitted the lesbianism, except by
implication. Cinematically it was without style.*
w Hans Wilhelm, Margaret Kennedy, Arthur
Wimperis *play* Prison sans Barreau by Gina Kaus,
E. and O. Eis, Hilde Koveloff *d* Brian Desmond
Hurst *ph* Georges Périnal *m* John Greenwood
ad Vincent Korda *ed* Charles Crichton
☆ Edna Best, Corinne Luchaire, Barry K. Barnes,
Mary Morris, Lorraine Clewes, Martita Hunt,
Glynis Johns

The Prisoner *
GB 1955 91m bw
(Columbia) Facet/London Independent Producers
(Vivian A. Cox)
🎬
In a European totalitarian state, a Cardinal is
tortured and brainwashed.
*Virtually a two-character talkpiece from an offbeat play
which should have stayed in the theatre.*
w Bridget Boland *play* Bridget Boland *d* Peter
Glenville *ph* Reg Wyer *m* Benjamin Frankel
☆ Alec Guinness, Jack Hawkins, Wilfrid Lawson,
Kenneth Griffith, Ronald Lewis, Raymond
Huntley

'An undercover cop. An investigation. A mistake ...
he's dead meat.'

The Prisoner (dubbed) *
Hong Kong 1991 91m colour
Golden Harvest/Blaine & Blake (Jimmy Wang Yu)
📀
An episodic film set in a tough prison ruled by
thuggish warders, where an undercover cop is sent
to discover the assassin of his elderly mentor, a
prisoner keeps escaping to see his young son, and a
gangster arrives to murder the man who
accidentally killed his brother.
*Interlocking plots give this downbeat martial arts movie
a greater narrative appeal than most of its kind, though
its morality is hardly endearing and Jackie Chan fans
may be disappointed that he plays only a minor role,
despite his star billing.*
w Fu Li, Yeh Yuen Chin *d* Chu Yen Ping *m* Fu
Lap *ad* Cheung Sau Ping *ed* Chow Tak Yeung
☆ Jackie Chan, Andy Lau, Samo Hung, Tony
Leung, Jimmy Wang Yu, Ko Chuen Hsiung, Tao
Chung Hwa
'Surprisingly good entertainment.' – *Impact*
'Unsurprising but enjoyable chop-sockey fodder.'
– *Sight and Sound*

Prisoner of Rio
Brazil 1988 105m colour
Palace/Doisirmaos Producioes (Klaus Pagh, Michael
Lunderskoff)
A British policeman goes to Brazil to bring back to
justice one of the Great Train Robbers.
*Special pleading on behalf of Ronald Biggs, one of the
thieves involved in the robbery in 1963, which even he
may find embarrassing to watch.*
w Lech Majewski, Ronald Biggs, Julia Frankel
d Lech Majewski *ph* George Mooradian *m* Luis
Bonfa, Hans Zimmer, Luciano Perrone *ad* Oscar
Ramos *ed* Darren Kloomok
☆ Steven Berkoff, Paul Freeman, Peter Firth,
Florinda Bolkan, Jose Wilker, Zeze Mota, Desmond
Llewelyn, Breno Mello

'And you think you've got problems?'

The Prisoner of Second Avenue *
US 1975 98m Technicolor Panavision
Warner (Melvin Frank)
🎬 🎧
A New York clerk and his wife are driven to
distraction by the problems of urban living.
*Gloomier-than-usual (from this author) collection of
one-liners which almost turns into a psychopathic
melodrama and causes its amiable leading players to
overact horrendously.*
w Neil Simon *play* Neil Simon *d* Melvin Frank
ph Philip Lathrop *m* Marvin Hamlisch
☆ Jack Lemmon, Anne Bancroft, Gene Saks,
Elizabeth Wilson

The Prisoner of Shark Island **
US 1936 95m bw
TCF (Darryl F. Zanuck)
The story of the doctor who treated the assassin of
President Lincoln.
*Well-mounted historical semi-fiction with excellent
detail.*
w Nunnally Johnson *d* John Ford *ph* Bert Glennon
md Louis Silvers
☆ Warner Baxter, Gloria Stuart, Joyce Kay, Claude
Gillingwater, Douglas Wood, Harry Carey, Paul
Fix, John Carradine
'Strong film fare for men; will have to be sold for
femme appeal.' – *Variety*
'A powerful film, rarely false or slow,
maintaining the relentless cumulative pressure,
the logical falling of one thing into another,
until the audience is included in the movement
and carried along with it in some definite
emotional life that is peculiar to the art of
motion pictures at its best.' – *Otis Ferguson*

Prisoner of the Mountains **
Russia/Kazakhstan 1996 99m colour
Metro/Tartan/Karavan/BG (Boris Giller, Sergei Bodrov)
📀 🎬 🎧
original title: *Kavkazskii Plennik*
In the Caucasus, two Russian soldiers escape from
their Muslim captors, who want to exchange them
for a prisoner held by the Russians.
*An engaging and tragic account of growing respect and
affection across ethnic divides by people trapped in a
conflict they simply wish to survive.*
w Arif Aliev, Sergei Bodrov, Boris Giller *d* Sergei
Bodrov *m* Leonid Desiatnikov *pd* Valerii Kostrin
ed Olga Grinshpun, Vera Kruglova, Alan Baril
☆ Oleg Men'shikov, Sergei Bodrov Jnr, Susanna
Mekhralieva, Dzhemal Sikharulidze, Alesandr
Bureev, Valentina Fedotova, Aleksei Zharkov
'A powerful war story, with confused loyalties
and moral codes at its centre.' – *Film Review*
𝄞 foreign film

Prisoner of the Volga
Italy/France 1959 102m Eastmancolor
Fidès/Transmonde/Rialto (Arnaldo Genoino)
original title: *I Battellieri del Volga*
aka: *The Boatmen*
A cavalry officer discovers that his newly married
wife is pregnant as the result of being raped
by his commanding officer.
Revenge melodrama of an unremarkable kind.
w Mario Damiani, Arnaldo Genoino
screenplay Salka Viertel, Al Lyx *d* Viktor
Tourjansky, Arnaldo Genoino *ph* Mario Montuori
m Norbert Glanzberg *ed* Roberto Cinquini
☆ John Derek, Elsa Martinelli, Dawn Adams,
Gert Frobe, Charles Vanel, Ingmar Zeisberg, Rik
Battaglia, Feodor Chaliapin Jnr

Prisoner of War

US 1954 81m bw
MGM (Henry Berman)

Life in a communist prison camp in Korea.
Sensational propaganda, reduced to comic strip level.
w Allen Rivkin d Andrew Marton ph Robert
Planck m Jeff Alexander
☆ Ronald Reagan, Steve Forrest, Dewey Martin,
Oscar Homolka, Robert Horton, Paul Stewart,
Henry Morgan, Stephen Bekassy
'It presents its catalogue of horrors in a manner
unworthy of the cause it attempts to uphold.' –
John Gillett

'The Immortal Lovers All The World Loves!'

The Prisoner of Zenda ****

🏋 US 1937 101m bw
David O. Selznick
▦ 🇺🇸 ◎

An Englishman on holiday in Ruritania finds
himself helping to defeat a rebel plot by
impersonating the kidnapped king at his
coronation.
*A splendid schoolboy adventure story is perfectly
transferred to the screen in this exhilarating
swashbuckler, one of the most entertaining films to
come out of Hollywood.*
w John Balderston, Wells Root, Donald Ogden
Stewart novel Anthony Hope d John Cromwell
ph James Wong Howe m Alfred Newman ad Lyle
Wheeler
☆ Ronald Colman, Douglas Fairbanks Jnr,
Madeleine Carroll, David Niven, Raymond
Massey, Mary Astor, C. Aubrey Smith, Byron
Foulger, Montagu Love
'The most pleasing film that has come along in
ages.' – *New York Times*
'One of those rare movies that seem, by some
magic trick, to become more fascinating and
beguiling with each passing year.' – *John Cutts,
1971*
† Previously filmed in 1913 and 1922.
⅋ Alfred Newman; Lyle Wheeler

The Prisoner of Zenda *

🏋 US 1952 100m Technicolor
MGM (Pandro S. Berman)
▦ 🇺🇸 ◎

A costly scene-for-scene remake which only goes
to show that care and discretion are no match for
the happy inspiration of the original.
w John Balderston, Noel Langley, Donald Ogden
Stewart d Richard Thorpe ph Joseph Ruttenberg
m Alfred Newman
☆ Stewart Granger, James Mason, Deborah Kerr,
Robert Coote, Robert Douglas, Jane Greer, Louis
Calhern, Francis Pierlot, Lewis Stone
† Donald Ogden Stewart, blacklisted during the
50s, had his name restored to the writing credits in
1999.

The Prisoner of Zenda

🏋 US 1979 108m Technicolor
Universal (Walter Mirisch)
🇺🇸

Palpably uneasy version of the above which teeters
between comedy and straight romance, with barely
a moment of real zest creeping in. The star is way
off form in both roles.
w Dick Clement, Ian La Frenais d Richard Quine
ph Arthur Ibbetson m Henry Mancini pd John J.
Lloyd
☆ Peter Sellers, Lynne Frederick, Lionel Jeffries,
Elke Sommer, Gregory Sierra, Stuart Wilson,
Jeremy Kemp, Catherine Schell, Simon Williams,
Norman Rossington, John Laurie
'Flatly directed, leadenly unfunny.' – *Paul Taylor,
MFB*

Prisoners of the Casbah

🏋 US 1953 78m Technicolor
Columbia (Sam Katzman)

An Eastern princess and her lover take refuge from
the evil Grand Vizier in the Casbah, a haven for
outcasts.
*Inept sword and sandal actioner; you can almost smell
the Turkish delight.*
w DeVallon Scott d Richard Bare ph Henry
Freulich m Mischa Bakaleinikoff
☆ Gloria Grahame, Cesar Romero, Turhan Bey,
Nestor Paiva

Private Affairs

US 1940 74m bw
Universal

A girl with problems seeks out the father she has
never met.
Thin comedy with a pleasant cast.
w Charles Grayson, Leonard Spigelgass, Peter
Milne story Walter Green d Albert S. Rogell
☆ Nancy Kelly, Robert Cummings, Roland Young,
Hugh Herbert, Montagu Love, Jonathan Hale

'All women take to men who have the appearance of
wickedness!'

The Private Affairs of Bel Ami *

US 1946 119m bw
UA/David L. Loew (Ray Heinz)
🇺🇸

In 1890s Paris, a career journalist climbs to fame
over the ruined lives of his friends.
*Tame and stuffy adaptation of an incisive novel, rather
poorly produced.*
wd Albert Lewin novel Guy de Maupassant
ph Russell Metty m Darius Milhaud
☆ George Sanders, Angela Lansbury, Ann
Dvorak, Frances Dee, John Carradine, Hugo Haas,
Marie Wilson, Albert Basserman, Warren William

Private Angelo

GB 1949 106m bw
Pilgrim (Peter Ustinov)

An Italian soldier hates war and spends World War
II on the run from both sides.
Listless satirical comedy that just isn't funny enough.
w Peter Ustinov, Michael Anderson novel Eric
Linklater d Peter Ustinov ph Erwin Hillier
☆ Peter Ustinov, Godfrey Tearle, Robin Bailey,
Maria Denis, Marjorie Rhodes, James Robertson
Justice, Moyna McGill

Private Benjamin

US 1980 110m Technicolor
Warner/Hawn-Myers-Shyer-Miller
▦ 🇺🇸 ◎ ◎

A well-heeled Jewish widow, at a crossroads in her
life, joins the army.
*Half-assed attempt at combining slapstick, character
study, sentiment, sex and a recruiting poster. Some
funny moments don't really make it worth sitting
through.*
w Nancy Meyers, Charles Shyer, Harvey Miller
d Howard Zieff ph David M. Walsh m Bill Conti
☆ Goldie Hawn, Eileen Brennan, Armand
Assante, Robert Webber, Sam Wanamaker,
Barbara Barrie, Harry Dean Stanton
⅋ screenplay; Goldie Hawn; Eileen Brennan
(supporting actress)

Private Buckaroo

US 1942 68m bw
Universal
🇺🇸

The difficulties of putting on shows for soldiers.
*Slaphappy second feature worth preserving for the
talent.*
w Edmund Kelso, Edward James d Edward Cline
☆ The Andrews Sisters, Harry James and his
Orchestra, Joe E. Lewis, Donald O'Connor, Peggy
Ryan, Huntz Hall, Ernest Truex, Shemp Howard

A Private Conversation ***

USSR 1983 96m colour
Contemporary/Mosfilm
original title: *Bez Svidetelei*
aka: *Without Witnesses*

A party hack visits his ex-wife for an evening of
recrimination and raking over the past.
*A two-character movie in the limited setting of a small
flat, but one that succeeds in its searing portrait of a
failed marriage and a wasted life.*
w Nikita Mikhalkov, Sofia Prokofieva, Ramiz
Fataliev play Sofia Prokofieva d Nikita
Mikhalkov ph Pavel Lebeshev m Eduard
Artemiev ad Alexander Adabashian, Igor
Makarov, Alexander Samulekin
☆ Mikhail Ulyanov, Irina Kupchenko

The Private Files of J. Edgar Hoover *

US 1978 112m Movielab
AIP/Larco (Larry Cohen)
🇺🇸 ♻

The supposedly true facts of the career of the
longtime head of the FBI.
Unreliable exposé with some interesting bits.
wd Larry Cohen ph Paul Glickman m Miklos
Rozsa

☆ Broderick Crawford, José Ferrer, Michael Parks,
Ronee Blakley, Rip Torn, Celeste Holm, Dan
Dailey, Raymond St Jacques, Howard Da Silva,
June Havoc, John Marley, Andrew Duggan, Lloyd
Nolan

A Private Function ***

GB 1984 94m colour
Handmade (Mark Shivas)
▦

In 1947 Yorkshire, a doctor and his family secretly
fatten an unlicensed pig.
*Sharply-detailed comedy typical of its author, but less
likeable than many.*
w Alan Bennett d Malcolm Mowbray ph Tony
Pierce-Roberts m John Du Prez pd Stuart Walker
ed Barrie Vince
☆ Michael Palin, Maggie Smith, Denholm Elliott,
Richard Griffiths, Tony Haygarth, Liz Smith, John
Normington
🏆 Maggie Smith; Liz Smith (supporting actress);
Denholm Elliott (supporting actor)

Private Hell 36 *

US 1954 81m bw
Filmakers
🇺🇸 ◎

Two cops on a robbery trail find the loot and keep
it for themselves.
*Predictable but stylish film noir, still moderately
watchable.*
w Collier Young, Ida Lupino d Don Siegel
ph Burnett Guffey m Leith Stevens
☆ Ida Lupino, Steve Cochran, Howard Duff,
Dean Jagger, Dorothy Malone

Private Izzy Murphy

US 1926 80m bw silent
Warner

A Jewish boy loves a Catholic girl.
*Dreary variant on Abie's Irish Rose, popular enough
for a 1927 sequel called* Sailor Izzy Murphy.
w Philip Lonergan d Lloyd Bacon
☆ George Jessel, Patsy Ruth Miller, Vera Gordon

Private Lessons

US 1981 87m Metrocolor
Barry & Enright (R. Ben Efraim)
🇺🇸

When his father goes away on business, a rich 15-
year-old boy is left in the care of a seductive
housekeeper and a crooked chauffeur.
Tedious mixture of schoolboy smut and feeble comedy.
w Dan Greenburg novel *Philly* by Dan Greenburg
d Alan Myerson ph Jan de Bont ad Linda Pearl
ed Fred Chulack
☆ Sylvia Kristel, Howard Hesseman, Eric Brown,
Patrick Piccininni, Ed Begley Jnr, Pamela Bryant,
Meredith Baer, Dan Greenburg

Private Life *

USSR 1982 104m colour
Contemporary/Mosfilm
original title: *Chastnaya Zhizn*

A businessman, retiring in his fifties, discovers that
he has drifted away from his wife and children.
*Perceptive, occasionally ponderous, study of a man in
crisis.*
w Anatoly Grebnyev, Yuli Raizman d Yuli
Raizman ph Nikolai Olonovsky ad Tatyana
Lapshina
☆ Mikhail Ulyanov, Iya Savvina, Irina Gubanova,
Tatyana Dogileva, Aleksei Blokhin, Elena
Sanayeva, Liliya Gritsenko
⅋ best foreign film

The Private Life of Don Juan

GB 1934 90m bw
London Films (Alexander Korda)
▦ 🇺🇸

In 17th-century Spain, the famous lover fakes
death and makes a comeback in disguise.
*Lacklustre frolic by an overage star through dismal sets.
The production was meant to extend the success of* The
Private Life of Henry VIII, *but totally failed to do so.*
w Lajos Biro, Frederick Lonsdale play Henri
Bataille d Alexander Korda ph Georges Périnal
m Ernst Toch
☆ Douglas Fairbanks, Merle Oberon, Binnie
Barnes, Benita Hume, Joan Gardner, Melville
Cooper, Athene Seyler, Owen Nares
'Technically it has so much in its favour that it's
too bad it doesn't promise solid b.o. attraction.' –
Variety

'One of those ideas that never really take off.' –
New Yorker, 1977

'The things I do for England!'

The Private Life of Henry VIII ***

🏋 GB 1933 97m bw
London Films (Alexander Korda)
▦ 🇺🇸 ◎

How Henry beheaded his second wife and acquired
four more.
*This never was a perfect film, but certain scenes are
very funny and its sheer sauciness established the
possibility of British films making money abroad, as
well as starting several star careers. It now looks very
dated and even amateurish in parts.*
w Lajos Biro, Arthur Wimperis d Alexander Korda
ph Georges Périnal m Kurt Schroeder
☆ Charles Laughton, Elsa Lanchester, Robert
Donat, Merle Oberon, Binnie Barnes, Franklin
Dyall, Miles Mander, Wendy Barrie, Claud Allister,
Everley Gregg
'Among the best anywhere and by far the top
British picture … figures a sock entry, especially
for the best houses.' – *Variety*
♟ Charles Laughton
⅋ best picture

The Private Life of Sherlock Holmes ***

GB 1970 125m DeLuxe Panavision
UA/Phalanx/Mirisch/Sir Nigel (Billy Wilder)
▦ 🇺🇸 ◎

A secret Watson manuscript reveals cases in which
Sherlock Holmes became involved with women.
*What started as four stories is reduced to two, one
brightly satirical and the other no more than a careful
and discreet recreation, with the occasional jocular
aside, of the flavour of the stories themselves. A very
civilized and pleasing entertainment except for the
hurried rounding-off which is a let-down.*
w Billy Wilder, I. A. L. Diamond d Billy Wilder
ph Christopher Challis m Miklos Rozsa
ad Alexander Trauner ed Ernest Walter
☆ Robert Stephens, Colin Blakely, Genevieve Page,
Clive Revill, Christopher Lee, Catherine Lacey,
Stanley Holloway
'Affectionately conceived and flawlessly
executed.' – *NFT, 1974*
'Wilder's least embittered film, and by far his
most moving. Great.' – *Time Out, 1984*

Private Lives *

US 1931 82m bw
MGM (Albert Lewin)
🇺🇸 ◎

Ex-marrieds desert their intended new spouses to
try each other again.
*An essentially theatrical comedy, and a great one,
seems somewhat slow-witted on film.*
w Hans Kraly, Richard Schayer play Noël Coward
d Sidney Franklin ph Ray Binger
☆ Norma Shearer, Robert Montgomery, Reginald
Denny, Una Merkel, Jean Hersholt
'Stars are a big asset to this parlour comedy
which will amuse the women more than the
men.' – *Variety*
'For polish, few comedies of the thirties can
equal this early alliance of cinema and stage.' –
John Baxter, 1968

The Private Lives of Elizabeth and
Essex **

🏋 US 1939 106m Technicolor
Warner (Robert Lord)
▦ 🇺🇸

reissue title: *Elizabeth the Queen*

Elizabeth I falls in love with the Earl of Essex, but
events turn him into a rebel and she has to order
his execution.
*Unhistorical history given the grand treatment; a
Hollywood picture book, not quite satisfying
dramatically despite all the effort.*
w Norman Reilly Raine, Aeneas Mackenzie
play *Elizabeth the Queen* by Maxwell Anderson
d Michael Curtiz ph Sol Polito, W. Howard
Greene m Erich Wolfgang Korngold ad Anton
Grot
☆ Bette Davis, Errol Flynn, Olivia de Havilland,
Donald Crisp, Vincent Price, Alan Hale, Henry
Stephenson, Henry Daniell, Leo G. Carroll,
Nanette Fabray, Robert Warwick, John Sutton
'Solid box office material, with fine grosses and
holdovers indicated … in all technical
departments, picture has received topnotch
investiture.' – *Variety*

🏋 film suitable for
family viewing   ▦ VHS video-cassette for
the British PAL system   ▦ VHS video-cassette for the British
PAL system in wide screen-format   ♻ Video cassette in a computer-
colourised version   🇺🇸 American NTSC video-cassette   ◎ Laser disc

'A rather stately, rigorously posed and artistically technicolored production.' – Frank S. Nugent

🎵 Sol Polito, W. Howard Greene; Erich Wolfgang Korngold; Anton Grot

The Private Navy of Sergeant O'Farrell

US   1968   92m   Technicolor
Hope Enterprises (John Beck)

After World War II, military personnel congregate on an island which has been by-passed by hostilities.

Nothing much wrong with the plot, but at this time in his career Hope seemed unable to do anything right, and the film was barely released.

wd Frank Tashlin ph Alan Stensvold m Harry Stikman

☆ Bob Hope, Gina Lollobrigida, Phyllis Diller, Jeffrey Hunter, Mylene Demongeot, Henry Wilcoxon

Private Number

US   1936   80m   bw
TCF (Raymond Griffith)
GB title: *Secret Interlude*

A wealthy young man keeps a secret of his marriage to a housemaid.

Warmed-over class melodrama previously filmed in 1930 as Common Clay. Adequate within its lights.

w Gene Markey, William Conselman play *Common Clay* by Cleves Kinkead d Roy del Ruth ph Peverell Marley m Louis Silvers

☆ Loretta Young, Robert Taylor, Basil Rathbone, Patsy Kelly, Marjorie Gateson, Paul Harvey, Monroe Owsley, John Miljan

'He turned on everyone who tuned in!'

Private Parts

US   1997   109m   DeLuxe
Paramount/Rysher (Ivan Reitman)
📀 💿 🎵 📀 @

New York radio personality Howard Stern tells how, although he wants to be loved by everyone, he is always misunderstood.

Unlikable, self-regarding biopic of a notorious 'shock jock', famed for his outrageousness, though there's little evidence of it in this anodyne confection, in which he is about as abrasive as cotton wool; he limits himself to a few farting jokes and a great deal of mock humility.

w Len Blum, Michael Kalesniko book *Howard Stern* d Betty Thomas ph Walt Lloyd m Van Dyke Parks pd Charles Rosen ed Peter Teschner

☆ Howard Stern, Robin Quivers, Mary McCormack, Fred Norris, Paul Giamatti, Gary Dell'Abate, Jackie Martling, Carol Alt

'The Stern on display here wants to go Hollywood and so has turned in a bland cookie-cutter biopic about a vulnerable, misunderstood young man eager to make it in showbiz.' – Mark Steyn, Spectator

Private Potter

GB   1962   89m   bw
MGM/Ben Arbeid

A young soldier is court-martialled for cowardice but claims he had a vision of God.

Stilted morality play, unpersuasively made and acted.

w Ronald Harwood TV play Ronald Harwood d Caspar Wrede ph Arthur Lavis m George Hall

☆ Tom Courtenay, Mogens Wieth, Ronald Fraser, James Maxwell, Ralph Michael, Brewster Mason

The Private Secretary

GB   1935   70m   bw
Twickenham

A clerical gentleman is duped into protecting a rich young idler from his creditors.

Moderately effective filming of a popular stage farce from a German original.

w Arthur Macrae, George Broadhurst, H. Fowler Mear play *Van Moser* d Henry Edwards

☆ Edward Everett Horton, Barry Mackay, Judy Gunn, Oscar Asche, Sydney Fairbrother, Alastair Sim, Michael Shepley

The Private War of Major Benson

US   1955   105m   Technicolor   Cinemascope
U-I (Howard Pine)

A soldier with outspoken views is sent to cool off as commander of a military academy run by an order of nuns.

Cute and sentimental nonsense with unlikely situations, a martinet becoming soft-centred and a happy-ever-after finale.

w William Roberts, Richard Alan Simmons d Jerry Hopper ph Harold Lipstein m Henry Mancini, Herman Stein

☆ Charlton Heston, Julie Adams, Tim Hovey, William Demarest, Tim Considine, Sal Mineo, Nana Bryant, Milburn Stone, Mary Field

🎵 original story (Bob Mosher, Joe Connelly)

The Private Wore Skirts: see *Never Wave at a WAC*

'She loved a man who did not exist – except in her own private world!'

Private Worlds *

US   1935   84m   bw
Paramount (Walter Wanger)

Romance among the doctors at a mental hospital.

Melodrama treated with what was at the time unexpected seriousness.

w Lynn Starling novel *Phyllis Bottome* d Gregory La Cava ph Leon Shamroy m Heinz Roemheld

☆ Claudette Colbert, Charles Boyer, Joel McCrea, Joan Bennett, Helen Vinson, Esther Dale, Samuel S. Hinds

'Fine but not too artistic production … woman's picture of fair b.o. potentialities.' – Variety

🎵 Claudette Colbert

A Private's Affair

US   1959   92m   DeLuxe   Cinemascope
TCF (David Weisbart)

Three army recruits form a close harmony trio and get into various scrapes.

Thin service comedy for the 'new' youth audience.

w Winston Miller d Raoul Walsh ph Charles G. Clarke m Cyril Mockridge

☆ Sal Mineo, Christine Carere, Barry Coe, Barbara Eden, Gary Crosby, Terry Moore, Jim Backus, Jessie Royce Landis

Privates on Parade *

GB   1982   113m   colour
Handmade (Simon Relph)

Farcical and serious incidents in the lives of an army concert party in 1948 Singapore.

Rather heavy-handed comedy with much bad language and an overdose of effeminacy; on the whole no funnier than It Ain't Half Hot, Mum.

w Peter Nichols play *Peter Nichols* d Michael Blakemore ph Ian Wilson m Denis King

☆ John Cleese, Denis Quilley, Michael Elphick, Nicola Pagett, Bruce Payne, Joe Melia

Private's Progress ***

GB   1956   97m   bw
British Lion/Charter (Roy Boulting)
📀

An extremely innocent young national serviceman is taught a few army dodges and becomes a dupe for art thieves.

Celebrated army farce with satirical pretensions; when released it had something to make all Britain laugh.

w Frank Harvey, John Boulting novel *Alan Hackney* d John Boulting ph Eric Cross m John Addison

☆ Ian Carmichael, Terry-Thomas, Richard Attenborough, Dennis Price, Peter Jones, William Hartnell, Thorley Walters, Ian Bannen, Jill Adams, Victor Maddern, Kenneth Griffith, Miles Malleson, John Le Mesurier

Prividenie, Kotoroe ne Vozvrashchaetsya: see *The Ghost That Never Returns*

Privilege *

GB   1967   103m   Technicolor
Universal/Worldfilm/Memorial (John Heyman)

The publicity campaign for a pop star turns him into a religious messiah.

Rather hysterical fable for our time, undeniably forceful in spots and yawnful in others.

w Norman Bogner story *Johnny Speight* d Peter Watkins ph Peter Suschitzky m Mike Leander

☆ Paul Jones, Jean Shrimpton, Mark London, Max Bacon, Jeremy Child, James Cossins, Victor Henry

'Everything in it goes wrong, and one can do little but catalogue the failures.' – MFB

Privileged *

GB   1982   96m   Technicolor
ITC/The Oxford Film Company (Richard Stevenson)

Oxford undergraduates rehearsing *The Duchess of Malfi* become involved in sexual intrigues which result in suicide.

Highly unusual because made and funded by the students themselves, this melodrama has vivid patches but generally lacks a professional eye.

w Michael Hoffman, David Woollcombe, Rupert Walters d Michael Hoffman ph Fiona Cunningham Reid m Rachel Portman ad Peter Schwabach ed Derek Goldman

☆ Robert Woolley, Diana Katis, Hugh Grant, Victoria Studd, James Wilby

Le Prix du Danger: see *The Prize of Peril*

The Prize ***

US   1963   135m   Metrocolor   Panavision
MGM/Roxbury (Pandro S. Berman)
📀

In Stockholm during the Nobel Prize awards, a drunken American author stumbles on a spy plot.

Whatever the original novel is like, the film is a Hitchcock pastiche which works better than most Hitchcocks: suspenseful, well characterized, fast moving and funny from beginning to end.

w Ernest Lehman novel *Irving Wallace* d Mark Robson ph William Daniels m Jerry Goldsmith

☆ Paul Newman, Elke Sommer, Edward G. Robinson, Diane Baker, Kevin McCarthy, Leo G. Carroll, Micheline Presle

A Prize of Arms

GB   1961   105m   bw
British Lion/Interstate (George Maynard)

An ex-army officer and an explosives expert plan to steal an army payroll.

Standard, pacy caper melodrama offering nothing at all new.

w Paul Ryder d Cliff Owen ph Gilbert Taylor m Robert Sharples

☆ Stanley Baker, Tom Bell, Helmut Schmid, John Phillips

A Prize of Gold

GB   1955   100m   Technicolor
Columbia/Warwick (Phil C. Samuel)

An American army sergeant in Berlin decides to steal a cargo of Nazi loot.

Routine caper thriller with sentimental leanings.

w Robert Buckner, John Paxton novel *Max Catto* d Mark Robson ph Ted Moore m Malcolm Arnold

☆ Richard Widmark, Mai Zetterling, Nigel Patrick, George Cole, Donald Wolfit, Andrew Ray, Joseph Tomelty, Karel Stepanek

The Prize of Peril

France/Yugoslavia   1983   88m   Eastmancolor
Brent Walker/Swanie Productions/ TF1/UGC/Top 1/Avala (Norbert Saada)
original title: *Le Prix du Danger*

A man volunteers to enter a TV contest, where the prize goes to the person who can survive being hunted across Paris by armed killers.

An interesting idea, badly executed.

w Yves Boisset, Jean Curtelin story *Robert Sheckley* d Yves Boisset ph Pierre-William Glenn m Vladimir Cosmo ad Aleksandar Milovic ed Michelle David

☆ Gérard Lanvin, Michel Piccoli, Marie-France Pisier, Bruno Cremer, Andréa Ferréol, Jean Rougerie, Jean-Claude Dreyfus

The Prizefighter and the Lady

US   1933   102m   bw
MGM (Hunt Stromberg)
📀 @
GB title: *Every Woman's Man*

A boxer falls for a high-class gangster's girl.

Plodding romantic melodrama, popular because it starred a real boxer.

w John Meehan, John Lee Mahin d W. S. Van Dyke ph Lester White m David Snell

☆ Myrna Loy, Max Baer, Otto Kruger, Walter Huston, Jack Dempsey, Primo Carnera

'Freak Max Baer starrer, a picture that entertains in high-pressure manner.' – Variety

🎵 original story (Frances Marion)

Prizzi's Honor *

US   1985   129m   DeLuxe
ABC/John Foreman
📀 💿

Male and female hired killers for Mafia families fall in love before each are assigned to 'hit' each other.

Critically lauded but puzzling and unsatisfactory black comedy which takes far too long to get going, is muddled in narrative, and leaves an unpleasant taste.

w Richard Condon, Janet Roach novel *Richard Condon* d John Huston ph Andrzej Bartkowiak m Alex North pd Dennis Washington ed Rudi and Kaja Fehr

☆ Jack Nicholson, Kathleen Turner, Robert Loggia, William Hickey, John Randolph, Anjelica Huston

'Certainly one of the most curious films to kick off the summer season by an American major.' – Variety

🏆 Anjelica Huston (supporting actress)

🎵 best picture; direction; Jack Nicholson; William Hickey; adapted screenplay; editing

🏆 adapted screenplay

Problem Child

👪 US   1990   81m   DeLuxe
UIP/Universal/Imagine Entertainment (Robert Simonds)
📀 💿 🎵 @

A badly behaved boy is adopted by a small-town couple.

Broadly played, predictable comedy of mayhem and misunderstandings.

w Scott Alexander, Larry Karaszewski d Dennis Dugan ph Peter Lyons Collister m Miles Goodman pd George Costello ed Daniel Hanley, Michael Hill

☆ John Ritter, Jack Warden, Michael Oliver, Gilbert Gottfried, Amy Yasbeck, Michael Richards, Peter Jurasik, Charlotte Akin

'Universal took a step in the right direction by whittling it down to just 81 minutes but didn't go far enough. The studio should have excised another 75 minutes and released this unbelievable mess as a short.' – Variety

'Now, Junior has a brand new friend. He's bad. She's worse.'

Problem Child 2

👪 US   1991   91m   DeLuxe
UIP/Universal/Imagine (Robert Simonds)
📀 💿 🎵 @

An ill-behaved boy decides that his father should marry the mother of his friend, a badly behaved girl.

Nasty-minded, witless slapstick with an anal fixation.

w Scott Alexander, Larry Karaszewski d Brian Levant ph Peter Smokler m David Kitay pd Maria Caso ed Lois Freeman-Fox, Robert P. Seppey

☆ John Ritter, Michael Oliver, Jack Warden, Laraine Newman, Amy Yasbeck, Ivyann Schwan, Gilbert Gottfried, Paul Wilson

'No seam of bad taste is left unmined as the screenwriters sink to impossibly low depths in pursuit of anything vaguely resembling a laugh.' – Mark Salisbury, Empire

Le Procès: see *The Trial*

Procès de Jeanne d'Arc **

France   1962   65m   bw
Agnès Delahaie
aka: *The Trial of Joan of Arc*

Joan of Arc is tried for heresy at the University of Paris and, under pressure from the English, burned at the stake.

An austere, almost ritualistic retelling of the trial, based on the actual documents and eye-witness accounts; its non-judgmental approach, letting the drama speak for itself, is ultimately more moving and engrossing than the usual sensationalist approaches.

wd Robert Bresson ph Léonce-Henry Burel m Francis Seyrig ad Pierre Charbonnier ed Germaine Artus

☆ Florence Carrez, Jean-Claude Fourneau, Roger Honorat, Marc Jacquier, Jean Gillibert, Michel Herubel, André Régnier, Arthur Le Bau

'Little good can be said about Bresson's catatonic Trial of Joan of Arc.' – John Simon

'Terse, spare, and oddly perfunctory.' – Pauline Kael

† The film won the Special Jury Prize at the Cannes Film Festival of 1962.

The Prodigal
US 1931 76m bw
MGM
The scion of a Southern plantation becomes a tramp.
Pleasant minor musical with a star who never really caught on.
w Bess Meredyth, Wells Root d Harry Pollard
☆ Lawrence Tibbett, Esther Ralston, Roland Young, Cliff Edwards, Purnell Pratt, Hedda Hopper, Stepin Fetchit
'Between average and good ... should top the normal gross.' – *Variety*

'The story of woman's beauty and man's temptation!'
The Prodigal
US 1955 115m Eastmancolor
Cinemascope
MGM (Charles Schnee)
The son of a Hebrew farmer falls for the high priestess of a pagan cult.
Wildly apocryphal 'biblical' story of obvious expensiveness but no merit.
w Maurice Zimm d Richard Thorpe ph Joseph Ruttenberg m Bronislau Kaper
☆ Lana Turner, Edmund Purdom, Louis Calhern, James Mitchell, Walter Hampden, Francis L. Sullivan, Joseph Wiseman, Audrey Dalton, Taina Elg, Neville Brand, Cecil Kellaway
'A few lines of dialogue derive from the Bible; the rest is pure Hollywood, but Hollywood in its mood of sham solemnity when even the unintentional jokes are not funny.' – *MFB*
'A costume stinker ... it should have played Disneyland!' – *Lana Turner*

The Prodigal Son (dubbed)
Hong Kong 1981 90m colour
Paragon (Raymond Chow)
A spoilt, rich young man, determined to become a kung fu master, attaches himself to a fighter who is also the star of a Chinese opera troupe, with fatal results for many.
By Western standards, an unsettling mix of broad comedy and bloody violence, but done with some style.
w Samo Hung, Wong Bing Yiu d Samo Hung ph Lau Kwun Wai m Frankie Chan, Chan Pui Lap ad Chien Sum ed Cheung Yiu Chung
☆ Samo Hung, Yuen Biao, Frankie Chan, Lam Chen Ying, Chung Fat, Dick Wai, Wai Pak, Chan Lung

The Producers *
US 1968 88m Pathécolor
Avco /Springtime/Crossbow (Sidney Glazier)
A Broadway producer seduces elderly widows to obtain finance for his new play, sells 25,000 per cent in the expectation that it will flop, and is horrified when it succeeds.
Dismally unfunny satire except for the play itself, Springtime for Hitler, which is neatly put down. This has, however, become a cult film, so that criticism is pointless.
wd Mel Brooks ph Joseph Coffey m John Morris
☆ Zero Mostel, Gene Wilder, Kenneth Mars, Estelle Winwood, Renee Taylor, Dick Shawn
'Over and over again promising ideas are killed off, either by over-exposure or bad timing.' – *Tom Milne*
'An almost flawless triumph of bad taste, unredeemed by wit or style.' – *Arthur Schlesinger Jnr*
🏃 Mel Brooks (as writer)
🎭 Gene Wilder

Profession: Reporter: see *The Passenger*

The Professional: see *Leon (1994)*

The Professional
France 1981 111m colour
Les Films Ariane/Cerito (Alain Belmondo)
original title: *Le Professionnel*
A French hitman, betrayed by his superiors, escapes from an African prison to seek revenge by carrying out his original assignment.
Routine action adventure, influenced by spaghetti Westerns; it has its occasional moments, including a car chase around the steps of Paris.
w Georges Lautner, Jacques Audiard, Michel Audiard novel *Death of a Thin-Skinned Animal* by Patrick Alexander d Georges Lautner ph Henri Decae m Ennio Morricone ad Eric Moulard ed Michelle David
☆ Jean-Paul Belmondo, Jean Desailly, Marie-Christine Descouard, Cyrielle Claire, Robert Hossein, Elisabeth Marconi, Jean-Louis Richard, Michel Beaune

A Professional Gun: see *The Mercenary*

Professional Soldier
US 1936 75m bw
TCF (Darryl F. Zanuck)
A kidnapper befriends the young prince who is his victim.
Predictable, polished family film.
w Gene Fowler, Howard Ellis Smith story Damon Runyon d Tay Garnett ph Rudolph Maté m Louis Silvers
☆ Victor McLaglen, Freddie Bartholomew, Constance Collier, Gloria Stuart, Michael Whalen
'Some of the sequences are amusing; some of the action is very fast. But fundamentally the story is not believable.' – *Variety*

Professional Sweetheart
US 1933 70m bw
RKO (Merian C. Cooper)
GB title: *Imaginary Sweetheart*
A radio 'purity girl' seeks some real life romance.
Modestly smart comedy of no lasting merit.
w Maurine Watkins d William Seiter ph Edward Cronjager m Max Steiner
☆ Ginger Rogers, Betty Furness, Gregory Ratoff, Sterling Holloway, Frank McHugh, ZaSu Pitts, Allen Jenkins, Norman Foster, Edgar Kennedy, Franklin Pangborn
'After a fast start this radio satire loses a lot of ground ... but comedy's there all the way.' – *Variety*

The Professionals **
US 1966 123m Technicolor Panavision
Columbia/Pax (Richard Brooks)
Skilled soldiers of fortune are hired by a millionaire rancher to get back his kidnapped wife.
Strong-flavoured star Western with good suspense sequences.
wd Richard Brooks novel *A Mule for the Marquesa* by Frank O'Rourke ph Conrad Hall m Maurice Jarre
☆ Burt Lancaster, Lee Marvin, Robert Ryan, Jack Palance, Ralph Bellamy, Claudia Cardinale, Woody Strode
'After the *Lord Jim* excursion, it is good to see Brooks back on his own professional form, filming the tight, laconic sort of adventure which usually seems to bring out the best in Hollywood veterans.' – *Penelope Houston*
'It has the expertise of a cold old whore with practised hands and no thoughts of love.' – *Pauline Kael, 1968*
🎭 Richard Brooks (as writer and as director); Conrad Hall

Professor Beware *
US 1938 93m bw
Paramount
A staid professor finds himself on the run across America in pursuit of an Egyptian artefact.
Slow-starting comedy with only moments of the comedian at his best.
w Delmer Daves, Jack Cunningham story Crampton Harris, Francis M. and Marian B. Cockrell d Elliott Nugent ph Archie Stout
☆ Harold Lloyd, Phyllis Welch, Raymond Walburn, Lionel Stander, William Frawley, Thurston Hall, Cora Witherspoon, Sterling Holloway
'Both Lloyd and the audience are out of breath after 3000 miles cross country, but most of it is exhaustion from laughing.' – *Variety*

Professor Mamlock **
USSR 1938 100m bw
Lenfilm
The leading surgeon of a Berlin hospital is driven to attempt suicide because he is a Jew.
Ironic in all kinds of ways, this quite devastating film was a unique attack by one government on a neighbouring one.
w Friedrich Wolf, Adolph Minkin, Herbert Rappaport d Adolph Minkin, Herbert Rappaport
☆ Sergei Mezhinski, E. Nikitina, Oleg Zhakov, Nina Shaternikova, Vasili Merkuriev

'An arresting picture which is sure to arouse strenuous comment.' – *Variety*
'The theme of a story should never be expressed so plainly; argument is valueless in fiction unless it is dramatic and individualized.' – *Graham Greene, The Spectator*

Profondo Rosso: see *Deep Red*

Profundo Carmesi: see *Deep Crimson*

Progeny
US 1998 100m colour
Fries (Jack F. Murphy, Henry Seggerman)
A Californian doctor fears that his wife is going to give birth to an alien baby.
Slow-paced psychological horror with some gruesome moments; after a long, dull opening, it becomes more interesting and suspenseful.
w Aubrey Solomon, Stuart Gordon d Brian Yuzna ph James Hawkinson m Steven Morrell pd Anthony Tremblay ed Christopher Roth, Harry B. Miller III sp make-up: Anthony C. Ferrante; visual fx: Marcus Keys; creature: Screaming Mad George
☆ Arnold Vosloo, Jillian McWhirter, Brad Dourif, Lindsay Crouse, Wilford Brimley, Willard E. Pugh, David Wells

The Program
US 1993 114m colour
Buena Vista/Touchstone/Samuel Goldwyn (Samuel Goldwyn Jnr)
A college coach, faced with losing his job unless his team improves, recruits some dubious new players.
The problems of college football have never seemed less interesting; the movie retains a slight anthropological interest for audiences outside North America.
w David S. Ward, Aaron Latham d David S. Ward ph Victor Hammer m Michel Colombier pd Albert Brenner ed Paul Seydor, Kimberly Ray
☆ James Caan, Halle Berry, Omar Epps, Craig Sheffer, Kristy Swanson, Abraham Benrubi, Duane Davis, Andrew Bryniarski, J. Leon Pridgen II

Il Proiezionista: see *The Inner Circle*

Project A *
Hong Kong 1984 108m colour
Golden Harvest (Leonard K. C. Ho)
In 1903 a Chinese coastguard quits the force in order to track down pirates that his superiors tolerate.
One of the better kung-fu movies, mixing humour with spectacular stunts and frenetically choreographed fights.
wd Jackie Chan
☆ Jackie Chan, Samo Hung, Li Hai Sheng, Yuan Baio

Project A-Ko (dubbed)
Japan 1986 120m colour
Soeishinsha/APPP (Kazufumu Nomura)
While aliens try to kidnap her, a 16-year-old girl with superhuman powers fights a rival for the friendship of another girl.
Bizarre animated parody of high-tech science fantasy and high-school romance.
w Yuji Moriyama, Katsuhiko Nishijima, Tomoko Kawasaki d Katsuhiko Nishijima sp Takafumi Arai m Richie Zito, Joey Carbone, Toji Akasaka ad Shinji Kimura
☆ Featuring the voices of: Stacey Gregg, Denica Fairman, Julia Brahms, Marc Smith, Jay Benedict, Lisa Ross

Project M 7: see *The Net*

Project X *
US 1968 97m Technicolor
Paramount/William Castle
In the year 2118, a man is scientifically induced to think he lives in the 1960s so that he can recover a lost secret.
Fearsomely complex science fiction, cheaply made but on the whole intriguingly imagined.
w Edmund Morris novel Leslie P. Davies d William Castle ph Harold Stine m Van Cleave
☆ Christopher George, Greta Baldwin, Henry Jones, Monte Markham, Harold Gould

Project X
US 1987 108m DeLuxe
TCF (Walter F. Parkes, Lawrence Lasker)
A pilot rebels when he is assigned a new job teaching chimps to fly and then discovers the real purpose of the project.
An odd little film that raises questions about the morality of experimenting on animals and then retreats into fantasy instead of confronting them. Some attractive performances from the apes hardly compensate.
w Stanley Weiser d Jonathan Kaplan ph Dean Cundey m James Horner pd Lawrence G. Paull ed O. Nicholas Brown
☆ Matthew Broderick, Helen Hunt, Bill Sadler, Johnny Ray McGhee, Jonathan Stark, Robin Gammell, Stephen Lang, Jean Smart

The Projected Man
GB 1966 90m Technicolor Techniscope
Compton (John Croydon, Maurice Foster)
A scientist working on a matter transmitter experiments on himself and turns monster.
Low-budget shocker with a narrative that owes more than a little to The Fly; the acting and direction are ponderous at best, and the subplot, involving love and jealousy, is uninteresting.
w John C. Cooper, Peter Bryan story Frank Quattrocchi d Ian Curteis ph Stanley Pavey m Kenneth V. Jones ad Peter Mullins ed Derek Holding sp Flo Nordhoff, Robert Hedges, Mike Hope
☆ Mary Peach, Norman Wooland, Derek Farr, Bryant Haliday, Ronald Allen, Tracey Crisp, Derrick de Marney, Sam Kydd, Gerard Heinz

The Promise
GB 1969 98m Eastmancolor
Commonwealth United/Howard and Wyndham
Two young men and a girl share a flat after the 1942 siege of Leningrad; thirteen years later, their dreams of life considerably modified, they meet again and change partners.
Talky and too carefully budgeted screen version of a somewhat pretentious play.
w Michael Hayes play Aleksei Arbuzov d Michael Hayes ph Brendan Stafford m Iwan Williams pd William McCrow
☆ Ian McKellen, John Castle, Susan Macready, Mary Jones, David Mettheim

The Promise
US 1979 97m Technicolor Panavision
Universal (Fred Weintraub, Paul Heller)
GB TV title: *Face of a Stranger*
A young man fails to recognize his lost love when her face has been rebuilt after an accident.
Rambling teenage variation on Random Harvest, not very well done and about forty years behind its proper times.
w Garry Michael White d Gilbert Cates ph Ralph Woolsey m David Shire
☆ Kathleen Quinlan, Stephen Collins, Beatrice Straight, Laurence Luckinbill, William Prince
'Appalling romantic tushery by any standards.' – *Tom Milne, MFB*
🎵 song 'I'll Never Say Goodbye' (mDavid Shire, lyAlan and Marilyn Bergman)

The Promise *
Germany/France 1994 110m Eastmancolor
Artificial Eye/Bioskop/Odessa/MH/WDR (Eberhard Junkersdorf)
original title: *Das Versprechen*
Lovers are separated for more than 20 years by the Berlin Wall.
Slow-moving, intermittently engaging, small-scale drama of the effect of the Cold War on individual lives.
w Peter Schneider, Margarethe von Trotta idea Francesco Laudadio d Margarethe von Trotta ph Franz Rath m Jürgen Knieper pd Martin Dostal ed Suzanne Baron
☆ Meret Becker, Corinna Harfouch, Anian Zollner, August Zirner, Susann Ugé, Eva Mattes, Jean-Yves Gaultier
'Plods doggedly through the bitter years, underlining its metaphorical points heavy-handedly.' – *George Perry*

Promise at Dawn

US/France 1970 102m DeLuxe
Avco/Nathalie (Jules Dassin)

The boyhood of novelist Romain Gary and the last years of his fearsome Russian Jewish actress mother with whom he traipses around Europe.

Scrappy star vehicle and unnecessary biopic in a variety of indulgent styles.

w Jules Dassin *play First Love* by Samuel Taylor
d Jules Dassin *ph* Jean Badal *m* Georges Delerue
☆ Melina Mercouri, Assaf Dayan

Promise Her Anything

GB 1966 97m Technicolor
Seven Arts (Stanley Rubin)

A mail order movie maker falls for a young French widow in the next flat.

Scatty comedy set in Greenwich Village and aiming in vain for a kind of frantic bohemian charm, with a baby as deus ex machina.

w William Peter Blatty *d* Arthur Hiller
ph Douglas Slocombe *m* Lyn Murray
☆ Warren Beatty, Leslie Caron, Hermione Gingold, Lionel Stander, Robert Cummings, Keenan Wynn, Cathleen Nesbitt

'Good-natured bounce the picture has, but the going gets mighty bumpy and frantic in this harmless story.' – *New York Times*

Promised Land

US 1988 103m colour
Vestron/Wildwood/Oxford Film Company

Two high-school friends meet a couple of years later, when one is a cop and the other a robber.
Atmospheric, downbeat tale of thwarted hopes.

wd Michael Hoffman *ph* Ueli Steiger, Alexander Gruszynski *m* James Newton Howard *pd* Eugenio Zanetti *ed* David Spiers
☆ Kiefer Sutherland, Meg Ryan, Jason Gedrick, Tracy Pollan, Googy Gress, Deborah Richter

Promises in the Dark

US 1979 115m Metrocolor
Warner/Orion (Jerome Hellman)

A young girl dies of cancer.
Depressing and not particularly well done case history, a curious enterprise in view of the hundreds of television movies relentlessly exploring the same field.

w Loring Mandel *d* Jerome Hellman *ph* Adam Holender *m* Leonard Rosenman
☆ Marsha Mason, Ned Beatty, Susan Clark, Michael Brandon, Kathleen Beller, Paul Clemens

The Promoter: see *The Card*

'Before Love Comes Trust. Before Trust Comes...'
Proof **

Australia 1991 90m colour
Artificial Eye/House & Moorhouse Films/Australian Film Commission/Film Victoria (Lynda House)

A blind photographer spurns the love of his housekeeper and forms a friendship with a restaurant worker who describes his photographs to him.
A complex story of betrayal that was a notable debut for its director.

wd Jocelyn Moorhouse *ph* Martin McGrath
m Not Drowning, Waving *pd* Patrick Reardon
ed Ken Sallows
☆ Hugo Weaving, Genevieve Picot, Heather Mitchell, Jeffrey Walker, Daniel Pollock, Frankie J. Holden, Frank Gallacher, Saskia Post

'An imaginative ethical and psychological drama that is as gripping as a thriller.' – *Philip French, Observer*

'One of this or any year's most confident and original writer-director debuts ... a breakthrough in concept and technique.' – *Alexander Walker, London Evening Standard*

'It lives. Don't move. Don't breathe. There's nowhere to run. It will find you.'
Prophecy

US 1979 102m Movielab Panavision
Paramount (Robert L. Rosen)

In rural Maine, mercury poisoning produces huge animal mutants.
Unpleasant ecological shocker with no particular talent in evidence.

w David Seltzer *d* John Frankenheimer *ph* Harry Stradling Jnr *m* Leonard Rosenman *pd* William Craig Smith
☆ Talia Shire, Robert Foxworth, Armand Assante, Richard Dysart

The Prophecy

US 1995 96m colour
Neo Motion (Joel Soisson)

aka: *God's Army*

A former priest turned detective discovers that the angel Gabriel is revolting against God and, to help with strategy, is seeking the soul of a dead general that has been hidden in a living girl.
Bizarre low-budget chase thriller that is enjoyable in an over-the-top way; it's helpful to discover that bad angels wear black leather trousers.

wd Gregory Widen *ph* Bruce D. Johnson, Richard Clabaugh *m* David C. Williams *pd* Clark Hunter *ed* Sonny Baskin *sp* Jor van Kline
☆ Christopher Walken, Elias Koteas, Eric Stoltz, Virginia Madsen, Moriah Snyder, Amanda Plummer, Viggo Mortensen, Adam Goldberg

'An occult freakshow so inert it seems to have been pasted together out of stock footage.' – *Owen Gleiberman, Entertainment Weekly*

'One man gave up everything he owned. The other, everything he believed in.'
The Proposition

US 1998 110m Technicolor
Polygram/Interscope (Ted Field, Diane Nabatoff, Scott Kroopf)

In Boston in the 30s, a man falls in love with the wife of an impotent lawyer after he is hired to impregnate her.
A lurid melodrama of sudden deaths, overwhelming passions and a priest behaving badly, it hovers on the edge of risibility.

w Rick Ramage *d* Lesli Linka Glatter *ph* Peter Sova *m* Stephen Endelman *pd* David Brisbin *ed* Jacqueline Cambas
☆ Kenneth Branagh, Madeleine Stowe, William Hurt, Neil Patrick Harris, Robert Loggia, Josef Sommer, Blythe Danner, David Byrd

'The Proposition is an offer most people will be able to refuse.' – *Todd McCarthy, Variety*

The Proprietor

GB/France/Turkey/US 1996 113m Fujicolour
Warner/Merchant Ivory/Ognon/Fez (Humbert Balsan, Donald Rosenfeld)

A Jewish writer returns from New York to buy a hotel in Paris as a means of investigating her past and her mother's death at the hands of the Nazis.
Unsuccessful and meandering exploration of multiculturalism; it never quite comes into focus, whether dealing with highbrow or with popular culture.

w Jean-Marie Besset, George Trow, Andrew Litvak *d* Ismail Merchant *ph* Larry Pizer *m* Richard Robbins *pd* Bruno Santini, Kevin Thompson *ed* William Webb
☆ Jeanne Moreau, Sean Young, Sam Waterston, Christopher Cazenove, Nell Carter, Jean-Pierre Aumont, Austin Pendleton

'For once, even Moreau's magic is not enough to save a film.' – *George Perry*

Proshchanie: see *Farewell*

Prosperity

US 1932 90m bw
MGM

Mothers-in-law disagree about the marriage of their children.
Reliable comedy of the Depression, marking the last teaming of its popular stars.

w Eve Greene, Zelda Sears *d* Sam Wood
☆ Marie Dressler, Polly Moran, Anita Page, Norman Foster, Henry Armetta

'Sure-fire money picture ... could stand a little cutting but on the whole it's a workmanlike production.' – *Variety*

Prospero's Books **

Netherlands/France/Italy 1991 120m colour
Palace/Allarts/Cinea/Camera One/Penta/Elsevier Vendex/Film Four/VPRO/Canal Plus/NHK (Kees Kasander, Denis Wigman)

Abandoned with his daughter on an island, the former Duke of Milan invokes a storm to wreck the ship carrying those who betrayed him and so regain his dukedom.
A free and exuberant adaptation of Shakespeare, using the techniques of High Definition Television and computer technology to create dense, rich, bookish images and with Gielgud speaking virtually all of the verse. It may be best watched on video, where you can rewind the film or freeze-frame images to take it all in.

wd Peter Greenaway *play The Tempest* by William Shakespeare *ph* Sacha Vierny *m* Michael Nyman *pd* Ben van Os, Jan Roelfs *ed* Marina Bodbyl
☆ John Gielgud, Michael Clark, Michel Blanc, Erland Josephson, Isabelle Pasco, Tom Bell, Kenneth Cranham, Mark Rylance, Gérard Thoolen, Pierre Bokma, Michiel Romeyn

'An intellectually and erotically rampaging meditation on the arrogance and value of the artistic process.' – *Variety*

'A remarkable feast, taking in the video revolution at one level and a highly literate interpretation of Shakespeare at another. Nothing quite like it has been seen before, let alone from a British director.' – *Derek Malcolm, Guardian*

Prostitute

GB 1980 96m colour
Kestrel (Tony Garnett)

A provincial tart moves into the West End.
Downbeat, supposedly realistic documentary drama which ends up being depressing but not in the least titillating.

wd Tony Garnett *ph* Charles Stewart *m* The Gangsters
☆ Eleanor Forsythe, Kate Crutchley, Kim Lockett, Nancy Samuels

'There's something funny going on in the world of diplomacy!'
Protocol

US 1984 96m Technicolor
Warner (Anthea Sylbert)

A cocktail waitress thwarts an assassination and becomes a career diplomat.
Star comedy with Something to Say and not much to laugh at; a step down even from Private Benjamin.

w Buck Henry *d* Herbert Ross *ph* William A. Fraker *m* Basil Poledouris *pd* Bill Malley *ed* Paul Hirsch
☆ Goldie Hawn, Chris Sarandon, Gail Strickland, Richard Romanus, André Gregory, Cliff de Young

Prototype

US 1992 94m colour
Filmtown (Gian-Carlo Scandiuzzi, Phillip Roth)

In Los Angeles in the 21st century, a cripple is transformed into an indestructible cybernetic robot in order to eliminate the last of the Omegas, human beings altered to become the new leaders of civilization.
Post-apocalyptic science fiction, cheap in every respect, indifferently acted and where the future looks much like the present, only dirtier and with no-smoking rules relaxed.

wd Phillip Roth *ph* Mark W. Gray *m* Emilio Kauderer *ed* Daniel Lawrence
☆ Lane Lenhart, Robert Tossberg, Brenda Swanson, Paul Coulj, Mitchell Cox, Sebastien Scandiuzzi

'Dingy visuals, murky scripting, vague characters and a lack of actual action render the whole thing remarkably unexciting.' – *Empire*

The Proud and Profane

US 1956 112m bw Vistavision
Paramount (William Perlberg)

In the Pacific War a Roman Catholic widow falls for a tough lieutenant colonel. ('My pleasure is physical; my men call me The Beast.')
Unlikely romantic melodrama with a certain amount of plain speaking, otherwise routine.

wd George Seaton *novel The Magnificent Bastards* by Lucy Herndon Crockett *ph* John F. Warren *m* Victor Young *ad* Hal Pereira, A. Earl Hedrick
☆ William Holden, Deborah Kerr, Thelma Ritter, Dewey Martin, William Redfield
⚱ art direction

The Proud and the Beautiful

France 1953 90m bw
C.I.C.C./Chrysaor/Iena/Reforma (Louis Wipf, Felipe Subervielle)

original title: *Les Orgueilleux*
aka: *The Proud Ones*

In a small Mexican town, a drunken doctor is redeemed by the love of a tourist unexpectedly detained by the sudden death of her husband from a contagious disease.
Ineffably silly, poorly acted and unconvincing romance.

w Jean Aurenche, Yves Allegret *novel L'Amour Rédempteur* by Jean-Paul Sartre *d* Yves Allegret *ph* Alex Phillips *m* Paul Misraki *ad* Gunther Gerszo *ed* Claude Nicole
☆ Michele Morgan, Gérard Philipe, Victor Manuel Mendoza, Carlos Lopez Moctezuma, Michele Cordoue, Andre Toffel, Arturo Soto Rangel
⚱ Jean-Paul Sartre

The Proud Ones: see *The Proud and the Beautiful (1953)*

The Proud Ones

US 1956 94m Eastmancolor Cinemascope
TCF (Robert L. Jacks)

A marshal cleans up a crooked town despite the hazards of his own physical disability and a deputy who hates him.
Entertaining though rather foolishly scripted Western.

w Edmund North, Joseph Patracca *d* Robert D. Webb *ph* Lucien Ballard *m* Lionel Newman
☆ Robert Ryan, Jeffrey Hunter, Virginia Mayo, Robert Middleton

'One has only to look at a first-rate Western to recognise the makeshift quality of The Proud Ones.' – *Dilys Powell*

The Proud Ones *

France 1980 118m Eastmancolor
Gala/Production Bela/TF1 (Georges de Beauregard)

original title: *Le Cheval d'Orgueil*

In the early years of the century, a young boy grows up in a peasant community in Brittany.
Lovingly observed and glossy exercise in nostalgia, ravishing to look at, but somewhat stilted.

w Daniel Boulanger, Claude Chabrol *book* Pierre-Jakez Helias *d* Claude Chabrol *ph* Jean Rabier *m* Pierre Jansen *ad* Hilton McConnico *ed* Monique Fardoulis
☆ Jacques Dufilho, Bernadette Lesache, François Cluzet, Ronan Hubert, Paul Leperson, Pierre Le Rumeur, Michel Blanc

The Proud Rebel

US 1958 103m Technicolor
MGM/Sam Goldwyn Jnr

After the Civil War, a Southerner wanders the Yankee states in search of a doctor to cure his mute son; he falls for a lady farmer and his son finds his voice at a crucial moment.
Pretty dim family Western for pretty dim families; everything happens precisely according to plan.

w Joseph Patracca, Lillie Hayward *d* Michael Curtiz *ph* Ted McCord *m* Jerome Moross
☆ Alan Ladd, Olivia de Havilland, David Ladd, Dean Jagger, Cecil Kellaway, Harry Dean Stanton, Henry Hull, John Carradine, James Westerfield

The Proud Valley *

GB 1939 76m bw
Ealing (Sergei Nolbandov)

A black stoker helps unemployed Welsh miners reopen their pits.
Neat little propaganda drama.

w Roland Pertwee, Louis Golding, Jack Jones *d* Pen Tennyson *ph* Roy Kellino, Glen MacWilliams *m* Ernest Irving
☆ Paul Robeson, Edward Chapman, Edward Rigby, Rachel Thomas, Simon Lack, Clifford Evans, Allan Jeayes

'The direction of the quiet documentary scenes is good, but Mr Pen Tennyson, who may have been handicapped by an undistinguished cast and a wobbly script, seems ill at ease with drama.' – *Graham Greene, The Spectator*

Providence *
France/Switzerland 1977 107m Eastmancolor
Action Film/Société Française de Production/FR3/Citel
(Philippe Dussart)
📼 ▆ ⌒
A famous-writer, dying, spends a painful night in
unpleasant and sometimes fantastic recollections of
his sons and their women; but the reality, when
they come to lunch next day, is somewhat
different.
*Despite its cast and other credits, this is a repellent and
not too well acted study in the lack of communication,
told at undue length and in turgid colour.*
w David Mercer d Alain Resnais ph Ricardo
Aronovich m Miklos Rozsa ad Jacques Saulnier
☆ John Gielgud, Dirk Bogarde, Ellen Burstyn,
David Warner, Elaine Stritch
    'The movie is peculiarly fastidious and static: you
    feel as if it were going to dry up and blow away.'
    – New Yorker

La Provinciale: see *A Girl from Lorraine*

The Prowler *
US 1950 92m bw
Horizon (Sam Spiegel)
A discontented wife thinks she sees a prowler and
calls a cop; they have an affair and murder her
husband.
*Another variant on Double Indemnity and The
Postman Always Rings Twice; the script is terse and
the actors well-handled.*
w Hugo Butler d Joseph Losey ph Arthur Miller
m Lyn Murray
☆ Van Heflin, Evelyn Keyes, John Maxwell,
Katharine Warren
    'A film in which the spectator is repelled by the
    characters, finds in them no curiosity of nature
    to overcome his repugnance, and is therefore
    indifferent to their fate; and I call that a
    nauseating film.' – Dilys Powell
    'A rivetingly cool, clean thriller.' – NFT, 1973

Prudence and the Pill *
GB 1968 92m DeLuxe
TCF/Kenneth Harper, Ronald Kahn
A girl borrows her mother's contraceptive pills and
replaces them with aspirin, causing no end of
complications.
*Self-consciously naughty sex comedy with a long
dénouement and some stiff patches to affect one's
enjoyment of the brighter moments.*
w Hugh Mills play Hugh Mills d Fielder Cook
ph Ted Moore m Bernard Ebbinghouse
☆ David Niven, Deborah Kerr, Edith Evans, Keith
Michell, Robert Coote, Irina Demick, Joyce
Redman, Judy Geeson
    'Everybody winds up pregnant to clutter the
    earth, apparently, with people as obnoxious as
    their progenitors.' – Judith Crist

Przesluchnie: see *Interrogation*

Psyche 59
GB 1964 94m bw
Columbia/Troy/Schenck (Philip Hazelton)
A wife recovers from blindness after realizing that
her husband is in love with her sister.
*Pretentious melodrama with stuffy dialogue, pompous
direction and irritating characters.*
w Julian Halevy novel Françoise de Ligneris
d Alexander Singer ph Walter Lassally
m Kenneth V. Jones
☆ Patricia Neal, Curt Jurgens, Samantha Eggar,
Ian Bannen, Beatrix Lehmann

Psychic Killer
US 1975 90m
Avco Embassy (Mardi Rustam)
▆
A man released from an asylum kills those who put
him there by the power of his mind.
*Low-budget exploitation movie that draws heavily on
Hitchcock, even if it substitutes heavy-handedness for
his teasing style.*
w Mike Angel, Greydon Clark, Raymond Danton
d Raymond Danton ph Herb Pearl m William
Kraft ad Joel Leonard ed Mike Brown
☆ Jim Hutton, Paul Burke, Julie Adams,
Nehemiah Persoff, Neville Brand, Aldo Ray, Della
Reese, Rod Cameron

'The screen's master of suspense moves his camera
into the icy blackness of the unexplained!'
'Don't give away the ending – it's the only one we
have!'

Psycho **
US 1960 109m bw
Shamley/Alfred Hitchcock
📼 ▆ ⌒ ⦿ ⌒
At a lonely motel vicious murders take place and
are attributed to the manic mother of the young
owner.
*Curious shocker devised by Hitchcock as a tease and
received by most critics as an unpleasant horror piece in
which the main scene, the shower stabbing, was
allegedly directed not by Hitchcock but by Saul Bass.
After enormous commercial success it achieved classic
status over the years; despite effective moments of
fright, it has a childish plot and script, and its interest is
that of a tremendously successful confidence trick,
made for very little money by a TV crew.*
w Joseph Stefano novel Robert Bloch d Alfred
Hitchcock (and Saul Bass) ph John L. Russell
m Bernard Herrmann ad Joseph Hurley, Robert
Clatworthy
☆ Anthony Perkins, Vera Miles, John Gavin, Janet
Leigh, John McIntire, Martin Balsam, Simon
Oakland
    'Probably the most visual, most cinematic
    picture he has ever made.' – Peter Bogdanovich
    'I think the film is a reflection of a most
    unpleasant mind, a mean, sly, sadistic little
    mind.' – Dwight MacDonald
† When asked by the press what he used for the
blood in the bath, Mr Hitchcock said: 'Chocolate
sauce.'
†† This is the whole text of Hitchcock's trailer, in
which he audaciously wandered round the sets and
practically gave away the entire plot: Here we have
a quiet little motel, tucked away off the main
highway, and as you see perfectly harmless looking,
whereas it has now become known as the scene of
a crime … This motel also has an adjunct, an old
house which is, if I may say so, a little more sinister
looking. And in this house the most dire, horrible
events took place. I think we can go inside because
the place is up for sale – though I don't know who
would buy it now. In that window in the second
floor, the one in front, that's where the woman was
first seen. Let's go inside. You see, even in daylight
this place looks a bit sinister. It was at the top of
these stairs that the second murder took place. She
came out of that door and there met the victim at
the top. Of course in a flash there was the knife,
and in no time the victim tumbled and fell with a
horrible crash … I think the back broke
immediately it hit the floor. It's difficult to describe
the way … the twisting of the … I won't dwell on
it. Come upstairs. Of course the victim, or should I
say victims, hadn't any idea of the kind of people
they'd be confronted with in this house. Especially
the woman. She was the weirdest and the most …
well, let's go into her bedroom. Here's the woman's
room, still beautifully preserved. And the imprint
of her body on the bed where she used to lie. I
think some of her clothes are still in the wardrobe.
(He looks, and shakes his head.) Bathroom. This
was the son's room but we won't go in there
because his favourite spot was the little parlour
behind the office in the motel. Let's go down there.
This young man … you have to feel sorry for him.
After all, being dominated by an almost maniacal
woman was enough to … well, let's go in. I suppose
you'd call this his hideaway. His hobby was
taxidermy. A crow here, an owl there. An
important scene took place in this room. There
was a private supper here. By the way, this picture
has great significance because … let's go along into
cabin number one. I want to show you something
there. All tidied up. The bathroom. Oh, they've
cleaned all this up now. Big difference. You should
have seen the blood. The whole place was … well,
it's too horrible to describe. Dreadful. And I tell
you, a very important clue was found here. (Shows
toilet.) Down there. Well, the murderer, you see,
crept in here very slowly – of course, the shower
was on, there was no sound, and …
Music wells up fiercely, shower curtain swishes
across, blackout.
Voice: The picture you must see from the
beginning – or not at all.
Janet Leigh's book Psycho: Behind the Scenes of the
Classic Thriller (1995) chronicles the making of the
film.
🎞 Alfred Hitchcock; John L. Russell; Janet Leigh;
art direction

'A New Vision Of The Most Frightening Movie
Experience Of All Time.'
Psycho
US 1998 104m DeLuxe
Universal/Imagine (Brian Grazer, Gus Van Sant)
📼 ▆ ⦿ ⌒
A mother's boy murders a woman who visits his
isolated motel.
*A genuine curiosity, though, unfortunately, not a very
interesting one: a remake of Hitchcock's thriller that
hardly deviates from the original, except that it is in
colour, the acting is inferior, and the content is a little
tired.*
w Josef Stefano novel Robert Bloch d Gus Van
Sant ph Chris Doyle m Bernard Herrmann,
Danny Elfman pd Tom Foden ed Amy
Duddleston
☆ Vince Vaughn, Julianne Moore, Viggo
Mortensen, William H. Macy, Anne Heche
    'This version isn't a sacrilege – it's just pointless.'
    – Anthony Quinn, Independent
    'However low-yield the shift in meaning Van
    Sant accomplishes proves to be, it's enough to
    justify the experiment: same film, different
    meaning. Where Hitchcock's Norman is
    conclusively Other, Van Sant's is one of us.' –
    Gavin Smith, Sight and Sound

'It's 22 years later and Norman Bates is coming
home!'
Psycho 2 *
US 1983 113m Technicolor
Universal/Oak (Hilton A. Green)
📼 ▆ ⦿ ⌒
Despite protests from the sister of one of his
victims, Norman Bates is released after 22 years in
a mental institution … and the murders begin
again.
*A reasonably inventive sequel, if on the gory side. It
probably holds the record for the longest delayed follow-
up.*
w Tom Holland d Richard Franklin ph Dean
Cundey m Jerry Goldsmith pd John W. Corso
☆ Anthony Perkins, Vera Miles, Meg Tilly, Robert
Loggia, Dennis Franz
    'It's all very well having your tongue in your
    cheek, but it helps to have a brain in your head.'
    – Sunday Times

Psycho 3
US 1986 93m colour
Universal/Hilton A. Green
📼 ▆ ⌒
A suicidal novice flees after unwittingly causing
the death of another nun, and takes refuge at the
Bates Motel.
*More variations on the original Psycho murders, with
invention wearing a bit thin by now.*
w Charles Edward Pogue d Anthony Perkins
ph Bruce Surtees m Carter Burwell pd Henry
Bumstead ed David Blewitt
☆ Anthony Perkins, Diana Scarwid, Jeff Fahey,
Roberta Maxwell

Psycho Sex Fiend: see *Scream … and Die!*

Psycho-Circus: see *Circus of Fear*

Psychomania
GB 1972 91m Technicolor
Benmar (Andrew Donally)
▆
A Hells Angels motor cyclist commits suicide and
returns from the dead an invulnerable monster.
*Arrant nonsense of the macabre sort, sometimes
irresistibly amusing.*
w Armand d'Usseau d Don Sharp ph Ted Moore
m David Whitaker
☆ George Sanders, Nicky Henson, Beryl Reid,
Robert Hardy

The Psychopath
GB 1966 83m Techniscope
Paramount/Amicus (Milton Subotsky)
Men are found dead in London, each with a doll
beside him.
*Complicated horror thriller in which the actors go
further over the top the more the plot winds down.*
w Robert Bloch d Freddie Francis ph John
Wilcox m Philip Martell
☆ Patrick Wymark, Margaret Johnston, John
Standing, Alexander Knox, Judy Huxtable, Don
Borisenko, Thorley Walters, Colin Gordon

PT 109
US 1963 140m Technicolor Panavision
Warner (Brian Foy)
📼 ▆ ⌒
Adventures of president-to-be John F. Kennedy
when he was a naval lieutenant in the Pacific
during World War II.
*Extraordinarily protracted and very dull action story
which seems to have been overawed by its subject.*
w Richard L. Breen d Leslie H. Martinson
ph Robert Surtees m William Lava, David
Buttolph
☆ Cliff Robertson, Ty Hardin, James Gregory,
Robert Blake

Puberty Blues
Australia 1982 81m Eastmancolor
Panavision
Limelight
▆
Teenage girls aim to become beach groupies.
*Both repellent and boring, this mindless sex movie has
little more to offer than the beach extravaganzas of the
sixties.*
w Margaret Kelly novel Kathy Lette, Gabrielle
Carey d Bruce Beresford ph Donald McAlpine
pd David Copping
☆ Nell Schofield, Jad Capelja, Geoff Rhoe, Tony
Hughes, Sandy Paul

Public Access
US/Japan 1993 87m DeLuxe
Cinemabeam (Kenneth Kokin, Adam Ripp)
📼 ▆
An new broadcaster in town begins a telephone
chat show that causes intense controversy.
*An interesting film that promises more than it delivers:
it hovers tensely on the edge of revelation for most of its
length, but then ends disappointingly.*
w Christopher McQuarrie, Michael Feit Dougan,
Bryan Singer d Bryan Singer ph Bruce Douglas
Johnson m John Ottman pd Jan Sessler ed John
Ottman
☆ Ron Marquette, Dina Brooks, Burt Williams,
Larry Maxwell, Charles Kavanaugh, Brandon
Boyce
    'Serious-minded and bounces around some
    provocative ideas, but is vague about such
    important matters as key story points,
    motivation and overriding theme.' – Todd
    McCarthy, Variety
    'It's an arresting beginning, shot in a baroque
    style that defies a puny budget.' – Adam Mars-
    Jones, Independent

Public Deb Number One
US 1940 80m bw
TCF
A waiter spanks a spoiled society girl at a
communist rally, and accepts a job which makes
him a capitalist.
Lively comedy packed with familiar faces.
w Karl Tunberg, Darrell Ware d Gregory Ratoff
☆ Brenda Joyce, George Murphy, Ralph Bellamy,
Elsa Maxwell, Mischa Auer, Charles Ruggles,
Maxie Rosenbloom, Berton Churchill, Franklin
Pangborn, Hobart Cavanaugh, Lloyd Corrigan,
Elisha Cook Jnr

'Drama that hurls a mighty challenge to all
humanity!'
The Public Enemy *
US 1931 84m bw
Warner
📼 ▆ ⌒ ⌒
GB title: Enemies of the Public
Two slum boys begin as bootleggers, get too big for
their boots, and wind up dead.
*Although it doesn't figure as a narrative, this early
gangster film still has vivid and startling scenes and was
most influential in the development of the urban
American crime film.*
w Harvey Thew story Kubec Glasmon, John
Bright d William Wellman ph Dev Jennings
m David Mendoza
☆ James Cagney, Edward Woods, Jean Harlow,
Joan Blondell, Beryl Mercer, Donald Cook, Mae
Clarke, Leslie Fenton
    'Roughest, most powerful and best gang picture
    to date. So strong as to be repulsive in some
    aspects, plus a revolting climax. No strong cast
    names but a lot of merit.' – Variety
    'The real power of The Public Enemy lies in its
    vigorous and brutal assault on the nerves and in

the stunning acting of James Cagney.' – *James Shelley Hamilton*

'A postscript said that the producers wanted to "depict honestly an environment that exists today in certain strata of American life, rather than glorify the hoodlum or the criminal". The film had a different effect: Cagney was playful and dynamic, and so much more appealing than the characters opposed to him that audiences rooted for him in spite of themselves.' – *Martin Quigley Jnr, 1970*

'What not many people know is that right up to two days before shooting started, I was going to play the good guy, the pal. Edward Woods played it in the end.' – *James Cagney*

  Kubec Glasmon, John Bright

Public Enemy's Wife
US 1936 78m bw
Warner (Sam Bischoff)
GB title: *G-Man's Wife*

A girl agrees to marry an escaped convict so that the FBI can track him down.
Lower-berth gangster thrills culminating in a chase climax; neatly enough done.
w Abem Finkel, Harold Buckley *story* David O. Selznick, P. J. Wolfson *d* Nick Grinde *ph* Ernest Haller

☆ Pat O'Brien, Margaret Lindsay, Robert Armstrong, Cesar Romero, Dick Foran, Dick Purcell

† Remade as *Bullets for O'Hara* (1942).

The Public Eye: see *Follow Me*

'Murder. Scandal. Crime. No matter what he was shooting, Bernzy never took sides he only took pictures … Except once.'

The Public Eye
US 1992 99m colour
UIP/Universal (Sue Baden-Powell)

A tabloid newspaper photographer becomes involved with a beautiful woman who runs a night-club and is in trouble with the Mafia.
A modern attempt at a film noir set in the 1940s that works only intermittently.
wd Howard Franklin *ph* Peter Suschitzky *m* Mark Isham *pd* Marcia Hinds-Johnson *ed* Evan Lottman *sp* Industrial Light and Magic

☆ Joe Pesci, Barbara Hershey, Stanley Tucci, Jerry Adler, Jared Harris, Richard Riehle, Bryan Travis Smith

'Never quite takes off, either as romantic melodrama or as a consideration of one very eccentric man's means of self-expression.' – *Vincent Canby, New York Times*

† The film was based in part on the New York photographer Weegee, whose book of photographs of the seamier side of life inspired the movie *The Naked City* (qv).

Public Hero Number One
US 1935 89m bw
MGM (Lucien Hubbard)

A G-man goes undercover to track down the Purple Gang.
Moderate thick ear dating from the time when studios tried to smother public outcry against gangster films by presenting the cop as the hero.
w Wells Root *d* J. Walter Ruben *ph* Gregg Toland

☆ Chester Morris, Jean Arthur, Joseph Calleia, Lionel Barrymore, Paul Kelly, Lewis Stone, Paul Hurst

'Rates with the best of the G-men pictures.' – *Variety*
'The best picture on criminal life I've seen.' – *Otis Ferguson*

Puerto Escondido
Italy 1993 125m colour
Mayfair/Pentafilm/Colorado (Maurizio Totti, Mario and Vittorio Cecchi Gori)

A Milanese bank manager drops out and goes to Mexico after seeing a policeman murder a colleague and then try to kill him, but his troubles follow him.
Amiable comedy, but one that never comes close to making any point, other than a vague approval of escapism.
w Enzo Monteleone, Diego Abatantuono, Gabriele Salvatores *d* Gabriele Salvatores *ph* Italo Petriccione *m* Mauro Pagani, Federico de

Robertis *ad* Marco Belluzzu, Alejandro Olmas *ed* Nino Baragli

☆ Diego Abatantuono, Valeria Golino, Claudio Bisio, Renato Carpentieri, Antonio Catania

'So drawn out it will take a very mellow-minded viewer not to lose patience with the cartoonish characters and their unconnected adventures.' – *Variety*

Pufnstuf
US 1970 98m Technicolor
Universal/Krofft Enterprises

A dejected boy is led by his talking flute on a talking boat to Living Island, full of strange but friendly animals in fear of an incompetent witch.
Amalgam of a TV series using life-size puppets to project a mildly pleasing variation on The Wizard of Oz, *without quite achieving the right blend of wit and charm.*
w John Fenton Murray, Si Rose *d* Hollingsworth Morse *ph* Kenneth Peach *m* Charles Fox *ad* Alexander Golitzen

☆ Jack Wild, Billie Hayes, Martha Raye, Mama Cass

I Pugni in Tasca: see *Fists in the Pocket*

Pulp *
GB 1972 95m colour
UA/Klinger-Caine-Hodges (Michael Klinger)

An ex-funeral director now living in the Mediterranean as a successful pulp fiction writer gets involved with gangsters and weirdos.
Occasionally funny pastiche which sorely lacks shape and is sustained by guest appearances and zany ideas.
wd Mike Hodges *ph* Ousama Rawi *m* George Martin

☆ Michael Caine, Mickey Rooney, Lizabeth Scott, Lionel Stander, Nadia Cassini, Al Lettieri, Dennis Price

'Various eccentrics act out their "turns", but never quite lift a light comedy-thriller through the more playful and productive inversions of parody.' – *Richard Combs*

Pulp Fiction ***
US 1994 153m DeLuxe Panavision
Buena Vista/Miramax/A Band Apart/Jersey (Lawrence Bender)

Four interlocking stories with unexpected twists involve a gangster, his two hitmen, his wife, a mysterious briefcase, and a boxer who refuses to throw a fight after being paid to do so.
Clever, witty, violent celebration of junk culture, drawing rather too heavily on past thrillers but blessed with some excellent performances which crackle with menace.
w Quentin Tarantino, Roger Avary *d* Quentin Tarantino *ph* Andrzej Sekula *pd* David Wasco *ed* Sally Menke

☆ John Travolta, Samuel L. Jackson, Uma Thurman, Harvey Keitel, Tim Roth, Amanda Plummer, Ving Rhames, Maria de Madeiros, Eric Stoltz, Rosanna Arquette, Christopher Walken, Bruce Willis

'Tarantino's adrenaline rush of an American melodrama is a brash dare to Hollywood filmmakers in their current slough of timidity. Let's see, he says, if you can be this smart about going this far.' – *Time*
'A spectacularly entertaining piece of pop culture.' – *Todd McCarthy, Variety*
'A very funky, American sort of pop masterpiece, improbable, uproarious, with bright colors and danger and blood right on the surface.' – *David Denby, New York*

† In a poll conducted by the *Sunday Times* in April 1995, its readers voted it the seventh-best film of all time, and Tarantino the seventh-best director, ahead of Martin Scorsese, Orson Welles and Stanley Kubrick but behind David Lean, Alfred Hitchcock, Michael Curtiz, Billy Wilder and Francis Ford Coppola.

  Quentin Tarantino, Roger Avary (screenplay)
  best picture; Quentin Tarantino; John Travolta; Samuel L. Jackson; film editing

Quentin Tarantino, Roger Avary; Samuel L. Jackson

Pulse
US 1988 95m DeLuxe
Columbia/Aspen (Patricia A. Stallone)

Visiting his father, a small boy discovers that there is a malevolent force affecting the electrical equipment in the home.
Tepid thriller, a tame variation on Poltergeist.
wd Paul Golding *ph* Peter Lyons Collister *m* Jay Ferguson *pd* Holger Gross *ed* Gib Jaffe

☆ Joey Lawrence, Cliff de Young, Roxanne Hart, Charles Tyner, Myron Healey

Pummaro
Italy 1990 102m Video Lux
Numero Uno/RAI/Cineuropa '92 (Claudio Bonivento)

A Ghanaian studying to be a doctor travels around Italy looking for his brother, who, after working in Naples, is on the run from the police and the Camorra.
A bleak, episodic account of the lives of immigrant workers and the dispossessed, which modulates into a melodramatic interracial romance; drama is too often replaced by earnestness.
w Sandro Petraglia, Stefano Rulli, Michele Placido *d* Michele Placido *ph* Vilko Filac *m* Lucio Dalla, Mauro Malavasi *ad* Lorenzo Baraldi *ed* Ruggero Mastroianni

☆ Thywill A. K. Amenya, Pamela Villoresi, Jacqueline Williams, Gerardo Scala, Nicola di Pinto, Franco Interlenghi

Pump Up the Volume *
US 1990 105m
New Line/SC Entertainment (Rupert Harvey, Sandy Stern)

A discontented student starts his own pirate radio station.
Loud and raucous and aimed at an audience that reveres rebellion and rock music.
wd Allan Moyle *ph* Walt Lloyd *md* Nicole Freegard *pd* Bruce Bolander *ed* Robert Fiore *ph* Robert Fiore *m* Michael Small *ed* Larry Silk, Geof Bartz
Ric Keeley, Kurt Hathaway

☆ Christian Slater, Ellen Greene, Annie Ross, Samantha Mathis, Scott Paulin

'It could appeal not only to '90s teens, but to sympathetic young adults who remember the stormy passage through adolescence.' – *Variety*

Pumping Iron **
US 1976 81m colour
White Mountain Films (George Butler, Jerome Gary)

Documentary on body-builders' contest for the title of Mr Olympia.
Well-observed study in competitiveness and obsession that first brought Arnold Schwarzenegger to the general attention.
book *Pumping Iron* by Charles Gaines, George Butler *d* George Butler, Robert Fiore *ph* Robert Fiore *m* Michael Small *ed* Larry Silk, Geof Bartz

☆ Arnold Schwarzenegger, Louis Ferrigno, Natty and Victoria Ferrigno, Mike Katz, Franco Columbu

Pumping Iron II: The Women *
US 1984 107m colour
Blue Dolphin/Cinecom (George Butler)

Documentary on a 1983 contest and its preliminaries in Las Vegas, with the male judges trying to decide at what point musculation ceases to be feminine.
Enjoyable and sometimes witty, though it has an air of contrivance about it.
w Charles Gaines, George Butler *book Pumping Iron II: The Unprecedented Women* by Charles Gains, George Butler *d* George Butler *ph* Dyanna Taylor *m* David McHugh, Michael Montes *ed* Paul Barnes, Susan Crutcher, Jane Kurson

☆ Lori Bowen, Carla Dunlop, Bev Francis, Rachel McLish, Kris Alexander, Lydia Cheng

The Pumpkin Eater ***
GB 1964 118m bw
Columbia/Romulus (James Woolf)

A compulsive mother (of eight children) finds her third marriage rocking when she gets evidence of her husband's affairs.
Brilliantly made if basically rather irritating kaleidoscope of vivid scenes about silly people, all quite recognizable as sixties Londoners; very well acted.
w Harold Pinter *novel* Penelope Mortimer *d* Jack Clayton *ph* Oswald Morris *m* Georges Delerue

☆ Anne Bancroft, Peter Finch, James Mason, Maggie Smith, Cedric Hardwicke, Richard Johnson, Eric Porter

'There never was a film so rawly memorable.' – *Evening Standard*
'It is solid, serious, intelligent, stylish. It is also, for the most part, quite dead.' – *The Times*
'It plays like a house afire.' – *Time*

  Anne Bancroft
  Anne Bancroft; Oswald Morris

Pumpkinhead *
US 1988 86m Technicolor
UA (Howard Smith, Richard C. Weinman)
aka: *Vengeance: The Demon*

A farmer summons an earth demon to destroy the teenagers who accidentally kill his son and finds that he gets more than he expected.
Effective and chilling little shocker, gaining much from the intensity of Henriksen's performance and from its superior monster.
w Mark Patrick Carducci, Gary Gerani *poem* Ed Justin *d* Stan Winston *ph* Bojan Bazelli *m* Richard Stone *pd* Cynthia Kay Charette *ed* Marcus Manton *sp* Alec Gillis, Richard Landon, Shane Patrick Mahan, John Rosengrant, Tim Woodruff Jnr

☆ Lance Henriksen, Jeff East, John DiAguino, Kimberly Ross, Joel Hoffman, Cynthia Bain, Kerry Remsen

'An elegant and unforgettable tale of backwoods terror that will keep you enthralled.' – *John McCarty, Splatter Movie Guide*

† A dull sequel, *Pumpkinhead II* (aka *The Revenge of Pumpkinhead II: Blood Wings*), followed in 1993, directed by Jeff Burr and starring Ami Dolenz and Andrew Robinson; it was released on video.

The Punch and Judy Man *
GB 1962 96m bw
(ABP) Macconkey (Gordon L. T. Scott)

A seashore children's entertainer tries and fails to establish himself as an important citizen.
Melancholy comedy of failure which did not please its star's adherents and indeed just missed the style it was seeking.
w Philip Oakes, Tony Hancock *d* Jeremy Summers *ph* Gilbert Taylor *m* Derek Scott, Don Banks

☆ Tony Hancock, Sylvia Syms, Ronald Fraser, Barbara Murray, John Le Mesurier, Hugh Lloyd

'Dying's easy. Comedy's hard'

Punchline *
US 1988 122m DeLuxe
Columbia TriStar (Daniel Melnick, Michael Rachmil)

A housewife and aspiring stand-up comedienne is helped by another comedian with personality problems.
A serious look at the business of being funny.
wd David Seltzer *ph* Reynaldo Villalobos *m* Charles Gross *pd* Jack Degovia *ed* Bruce Green

☆ Sally Field, Tom Hanks, John Goodman, Mark Rydell, Kim Greist, Paul Mazursky, Pam Matteson

'Is there a limit to revenge?'

The Punisher
Australia 1989 90m Eastmancolor
Castle Premier/New World International/Marvel Entertainment (Robert Mark Kamen)

A former policeman, who lives in the sewers, takes revenge on the gangsters who killed his family.
Undistinguished, excessively violent action movie based on a comic-book character.
w Robert Mark Kamen, Boaz Yakin *d* Mark Goldblatt *ph* Ian Baker *m* Dennis Dreith *pd* Norma Moriceau *ed* Tim Wellburn

☆ Dolph Lundgren, Louis Gossett Jnr, Jeroen Krabbe, Kim Miyori, Bryan Marshall, Nancy Everhard, Barry Otto, Brian Rooney, Zoshka Mizak, Todd Boyce

The Punk and the Princess
GB 1993 96m Technicolor
Feature Film/Videodrome/M2 (Mike Sarne, Robin Mahoney)
aka: *The Punk*

A young punk leaves home and falls in love with a wealthy American actress.

An odd little fable, vaguely updating Romeo and Juliet, which strings together a series of incidents of interest to its presumed audience – rows with parents and pub fights predominating – and does not bother with characterization or motivation.

wd Mike Sarne novel The Punk by Gideon Sams ph Alan M. Trow m Claudia Sarne, Charlie Creed-Miles, Nigel Powell ed Gwyn Jones, Matthew Salkeld

☆ Charlie Creed-Miles, Vanessa Hadaway, David Shawyer, Jess Conrad, Yolanda Mason, Jacqueline Skarvellis, Peter Miles

'Featuring some of the most unforgivably trite "street" dialogue, contrived working-class relationships and one-dimensional performances from its two leads, it's difficult to see, post-Slacker generation, exactly where its appeal might lie.' – Karen McLuskey, Empire

† The film is based on a novel written by a 14-year-old.

Puppet Master

US 1990 90m colour
Full Moon (Hope Perello)
⊞ ▤ ⌕ ♫

Four psychics who go to investigate strange happenings at an isolated hotel find themselves being attacked by living puppets.

A twist on the Frankenstein story, with some clever special effects adding a little interest to the usual slasher narrative.

w Joseph G. Collodi story Charles Band, Kenneth J. Hall d David Schmoeller ph Sergio Salvati m Richard Band pd John Myhre ed Tom Meshelski sp David Allen Productions

☆ Paul Le Mat, Irene Miracle, Matt Roe, Kathryn O'Reilly, Robert Frates, Merrya Small, William Hickey

Puppet Master II

US 1991 88m DeLuxe
Full Moon (David DeCoteau, John Schouweiler)
⊞ ▤ ⌕ ♫

Puppets who have been brought to life, each with their own special weapon, stalk and slay a group of psychic researchers staying in a supposedly haunted hotel.

All that distinguishes this sequel from the original is the addition of some new puppets with different and gory ways of killing. They, unlike the remainder of the cast, are effectively animated.

w David Pabian story Charles Band d David Allen m Thomas F. DeNove m Richard Band pd Kathleen Coates ed Peter Teschner, Bert Glatstein sp David Allen, David Barton, Steve Neill

☆ Elizabeth MacClellan, Collin Bernsen, Gregory Webb, Charlie Spradling, Steve Welles, Jeff Weston, Nita Talbot

'Gruesome thrills.' – Variety

The Puppet Masters *

US 1994 108m Technicolor
Hollywood Pictures (Ralph Winter)
⊞ ▤ ⌕

aka: Robert A. Heinlein's The Puppet Masters
Parasitical aliens, who share the same mind, invade the Earth and begin to take over the population.

Slick low-budget science-fiction thriller, done with a little style and more intelligence than usual, though the three Invasion of the Bodysnatchers movies have made the narrative somewhat familiar.

w Ted Elliott, Terry Rossio, David S. Goyer novel Robert A. Heinlein d Stuart Orme ph Clive Tickner m Colin Towns pd Daniel A. Lomino ed William Goldenberg

☆ Donald Sutherland, Eric Thal, Julie Warner, Keith David, Will Patton, Richard Belzer, Marshall Bell, Yaphet Kotto

'A thoroughly undistinguished if inoffensive telling of Heinlein's classic tale.' – Variety
'Deliriously entertaining.' – Sight and Sound

† The film was released direct to video in Britain.

Puppet on a Chain *

GB 1970 98m Technicolor
Big City (Kurt Unger)

An American Interpol agent hunts down drug smugglers in Amsterdam.

Sadistic adventure thriller, a toughened version of James Bond, climaxing in a splendid boat chase through Amsterdam.

w Alistair MacLean, Don Sharp, Paul Wheeler novel Alistair MacLean d Geoffrey Reeve, Don

Sharp ph Jack Hildyard, Skeets Kelly m Piero Piccioni

☆ Sven Bertil Taube, Barbara Parkins, Patrick Allen, Alexander Knox, Vladek Sheybal

'One suspects that a marionette also sat in for Alistair MacLean.' – Judith Crist

'There is always someone pulling the strings.'

The Puppetmaster **

Taiwan 1993 142m colour
Electric Pictures/Nian Dai (Qiu Fusheng)
⊞

original title: Hsimeng Rensheng

A Chinese boy grows to manhood and becomes a celebrated puppeteer during the 50-year occupation of Taiwan by the Japanese, which finished at the end of the Second World War.

An austere biopic, narrated by the 84-year-old Li Tienlu himself, exploring with restraint the life of an actor and puppetmaster during interesting times. The often motionless camera, the long takes and the lack of close-ups frame the action in a theatrical way, celebrating a life full of harshness, and an ancient and vanishing culture, without nostalgia.

w Wu Nianzhen, Zhu Tianwen story Li Tienlu d Hou Hsiao-Hsien ph Lee Pingbin m Chen Mingzhang, Zhang Hongda pd Zhan Hongzhi ed Liao Qingsong

☆ Li Tienlu, Lim Giong, Chen Kuizhong

'Those not attuned to Hou's distanced, controlled style will be turned off; enthusiasts, however, will relish its greater refinement, painterly visuals and deeply humanistic style.' – Derek Elley, Variety

'Stubbornly sluggish and as serious as a final-term dissertation.' – Empire

Pure Country

US 1992 112m Technicolor
Warner/Jerry Weintraub
⊞ ▤ ⌕ ♫

A country singer grows tired of showbiz trappings and tries to return to his roots.

Rambling and pleasant enough meander through an urban jungle and a rural paradise, though only likely to interest fans of its star.

w Rex McGee d Christopher Cain ph Richard Bowen m Steve Dorff pd Jeffrey Howard ed Jack Hofstra

☆ George Strait, Lesley Ann Warren, Isabel Glasser, Kyle Chandler, John Doe, Rory Calhoun, Molly McClure

'An effective vehicle for amiable country star George Strait.' – Variety

The Pure Hell of St Trinian's *

🏃 GB 1960 94m bw
Hallmark/Tudor (Frank Launder, Sidney Gilliat)

After the girls burn down St Trinian's, a dubious headmaster offers to create a new school for them.

Bright comedy performances from some of the best of character actors add a gloss to familiar material.

w Frank Launder, Sidney Gilliat, Val Valentine d Frank Launder ph Gerald Gibbs m Malcolm Arnold ed Thelma Connell

☆ Cecil Parker, Joyce Grenfell, George Cole, Thorley Walters, Irene Handl, Eric Barker, Dennis Price, Raymond Huntley, Julie Alexander

Pure Luck

US 1991 96m DeLuxe
Universal/Silver Lion (Lance Hool, Sean Daniel)
⊞ ▤ ⌕ ♫

A cop and his hapless assistant go to Mexico in search of a missing accident-prone heiress.

Broad and unsubtle comedy that relies for its humour on obvious and mistimed slapstick; it never rises above well-intentioned mediocrity.

w Herschel Weingrod, Timothy Harris d Nadia Tass ph David Parker m Jonathan Sheffer, Danny Elfman pd Peter Wooley ed Billy Weber

☆ Martin Short, Danny Glover, Sheila Kelley, Sam Wanamaker, Scott Wilson, Harry Shearer, Jorge Russek

† It is a remake of the French Le Chevre, directed by François Veber.

The Purple Gang

US 1960 85m bw
Allied Artists

In Detroit during prohibition a gang of juvenile delinquents become as powerful as the gangsters.

Unpleasant detail mars this cops-and-robbers subject; twenty years later it would have been even more of a shocker, but it's bad enough as it is.

w Jack DeWitt d Frank McDonald ph Ellis Carter m Paul Dunlap

☆ Robert Blake, Barry Sullivan, Elaine Edwards, Marc Cavell, Jody Lawrance, Susie Marquette, Paul Dubov

'The "Inside Japan" Story Of Yanks Bombing Tokyo ... Taken Jap Prisoners ... Put On Trial For "Murder"!'

The Purple Heart *

US 1944 99m bw
TCF (Darryl F. Zanuck)
⊞ ▤

American prisoners of war in Japan are tried and executed.

Relentlessly sombre flagwaver, extremely persuasively presented.

w Jerome Cady, Darryl F. Zanuck d Lewis Milestone ph Arthur Miller m Alfred Newman

☆ Dana Andrews, Richard Conte, Farley Granger, Kevin O'Shea, Sam Levene, Don Barry, Richard Loo

'It is unusually edged, well organized and solidly acted. But I feel extremely queasy watching fiction – especially persuasive fiction – which pretends to clarify facts that are not clear, and may never become so.' – James Agee

Purple Heart Diary

US 1951 73m bw
Columbia (Sam Katzman)
GB title: No Time for Tears

Entertainers tour war zones and bring various comforts.

Sentimental piece which the USO picked up as useful propaganda.

w William Sackheim d Richard Quine ph William Whitley m Ross Di Maggio

☆ Frances Langford, Ben Lessy, Tony Romano, Judd Holdren

Purple Hearts

US 1984 116m Technicolor Panavision
Warner/The Ladd Company (Sidney J. Furie)
⊞ ▤

In Vietnam, a naval surgeon falls for a nurse but the course of true romance is interrupted by the war.

Conventional war heroics with time out for a trite love story; it gets sillier as it goes on.

w Rick Natkin, Sidney J. Furie d Sidney J. Furie ph Jan Kiesser m Robert Folk ad Francisco Balangue ed George Grenville

☆ Ken Wahl, Cheryl Ladd, Stephen Lee, Annie McEnroe, Paul McCrane, Cyril O'Reilly, David Harris, R. Lee Ermey, Drew Snyder

The Purple Mask

🏃 US 1955 82m Technicolor
Cinemascope
U-I (Howard Christie)

In 1802 Paris the Royalist resistance to Napoleon is led by the mysterious Purple Mask, who also disguises himself as a foppish dandy.

Cheeky rewrite of The Scarlet Pimpernel, with plenty of gusto but not much style.

w Oscar Brodney d Bruce Humberstone ph Irving Glassberg m Joseph Gershenson

☆ Tony Curtis, Dan O'Herlihy, Colleen Miller, Gene Barry, Angela Lansbury, George Dolenz, John Hoyt

'Sir Percy, one feels, would have personally conducted this lot to the guillotine.' – MFB

The Purple Monster Strikes

US 1945 bw serial: 15 eps
Republic

A Martian kills a great scientist and enters his body.

Early example of unpleasant aliens, a precursor of It Came from Outer Space and Invasion of the Body Snatchers.

d Spencer Bennet, Fred Brannon

☆ Dennis Moore, Linda Stirling, Roy Barcroft

Purple Noon: see Plein Soleil

Purple People Eater

🏃 US 1988 91m colour
MPCA/Vertex (Brad Krevoy, Steve Stabler)

A purple one-eyed alien helps a lonely boy learn confidence by forming a rock group and helping elderly people threatened with eviction from their homes.

Feeble kids' film based on a witless novelty hit of the late 50s; an embarrassment for all those involved.

wd Linda Shayne ph Peter Deming m Dennis Dreith pd Stephen Greenberg ed Cari Ellen Coughlin song Sheb Wooley

☆ Ned Beatty, Shelley Winters, Neil Patrick Harris, Peggy Lipton, James Houghton, John Brumfield, Chubby Checker, Little Richard, Sheb Wooley

The Purple Plain *

GB 1954 100m Technicolor
GFD/Two Cities (John Bryan)

During the Burma campaign, a Canadian squadron leader regains his shattered nerves during an arduous trek across country.

Psychological study and eastern adventure combined; not the best of either, but a potent crowd-puller.

w Eric Ambler novel H. E. Bates d Robert Parrish ph Geoffrey Unsworth m John Veale

☆ Gregory Peck, Maurice Denham, Win Min Than, Lyndon Brook, Brenda de Banzie, Bernard Lee, Anthony Bushell, Ram Gopal

The Purple Rose of Cairo *

US 1984 82m DeLuxe
Orion/Jack Rollins-Charles H. Joffe (Robert Greenhut)
⊞ ▤ ⌕

In the thirties, a film-struck woman is confronted in reality by the hero of her dreams.

Amusing but slight comedy: several good jokes, but in sum no more than an elongated sketch.

wd Woody Allen ph Gordon Willis m Dick Hyman pd Stuart Wurtzel ed Susan E. Morse

☆ Mia Farrow, Jeff Daniels, Dianne Wiest, Van Johnson, Zoe Caldwell, John Wood, Milo O'Shea

🎬 best picture, original screenplay

Pursued *

US 1947 101m bw
(Warner) United States (Milton Sperling)
▤ ⌕ ♫

A revenge-seeking cowboy accidentally causes a tragedy in his adopted family.

Glum, good-looking revenge Western.

w Niven Busch d Raoul Walsh ph James Wong Howe m Max Steiner

☆ Robert Mitchum, Teresa Wright, Judith Anderson, Dean Jagger, Alan Hale, Harry Carey Jnr

Pursuit

US 1935 73m bw
Lucien Hubbard-Ned Marin/MGM

A child is kidnapped, and several people want the reward for restoring him.

Rather frantic chase thriller with insufficient variety.

w Wells Root, Lawrence G. Blochman d Edwin L. Marin

☆ Chester Morris, Sally Eilers, Scotty Beckett, Henry Travers, C. Henry Gordon, Dorothy Peterson, Harold Huber

The Pursuit of D. B. Cooper

US 1981 100m Metrocolor
Polygram (Daniel Wigutow, Michael Taylor)
▤ ⌕

A skyjacker bails out with his loot and is chased by various people after the reward.

Fantasy variation on a real case which was never solved; of no interest whatever despite the talent involved.

w Jeffrey Alan Fiskin book Free Fall by J. D. Reed d Roger Spottiswoode (also John Frankenheimer, Buzz Kulik) ph Harry Stradling Jnr m James Horner pd Preston Ames

☆ Robert Duvall, Treat Williams, Kathryn Harrold, Ed Flanders, Paul Gleason, R. G. Armstrong

'Doubtless a law-enforcement ploy to lure the skyjacker out of hiding: surely after seeing this mess he will want to surface and sue somebody.' – Variety

The Pursuit of Happiness

US 1934 75m bw
Paramount (Arthur Hornblow Jnr)

In 1776 Connecticut a Puritan maid falls for a Hessian soldier.

Mildly pleasing romantic comedy centring on the ancient practice of 'bundling' in which betrothed couples might sleep together fully clothed.

w Stephen Morehouse Avery, Jack Cunningham, J. P. McEvoy, Virginia Van Upp play Lawrence Langner, Armina Marshall d Alexander Hall ph Karl Struss

☆ Francis Lederer, Joan Bennett, Charles Ruggles, Mary Boland, Walter Kingsford, Minor Watson
'A comedy that will entertain and merits business.' – *Variety*

The Pursuit of Happiness *
US 1970 98m Eastmancolor
Columbia/TA Films/Norton-Simon (David Susskind)
📀
A New York college dropout is sent to prison after a hit and run accident.
Smooth, watchable but empty youth movie.
w Sidney Carroll, George L. Sherman d Robert Mulligan ph Dick Kratina m Dave Grusin
☆ Michael Sarrazin, Barbara Hershey, Robert Klein, Ruth White, E. G. Marshall, Arthur Hill

Pursuit of the Graf Spee: see The Battle of the River Plate

Pursuit to Algiers
US 1945 65m bw
Universal (Roy William Neill)
Sherlock Holmes guards the young king of Ruritania on a sea voyage.
After an amiably lunatic first reel, this settles down as one of the dullest of the series, but it never entirely taxes the patience.
w Leonard Lee d Roy William Neill ph Paul Ivano m Hans Salter md Edgar Fairchild
☆ Basil Rathbone, Nigel Bruce, Martin Kosleck, Marjorie Riordan, Rosalind Ivan, John Abbott, Frederic Worlock, Morton Lowry

Pusher *
Denmark 1996 110m colour
Metrodome/Balboa (Henrik Danstrup)
📀
In Copenhagen, a heroin dealer is prepared to cheat anyone in order to pay off his debt to a local gangster.
A week in the life of a loser, a tough and gritty account of a trapped, petty criminal going round in ever-diminishing circles, fiercely directed.
w Nikolas Winding Refn, Jens Dahl d Nikolas Winding Refn ph Morten Soborg m various pd Kim Lovetand Julebaek ed Anne Osterud
☆ Kim Bodnia, Zlatko Buric, Laura Drasbaek, Slavko Labovic, Mads Mikkelsen, Peter Anderson, Vanja Bajicic
'Brutal, upsetting and impressive in its refusal to tart itself up with the modish tricks of Quentin Tarantino or Abel Ferrara. There are no cute monologues here. No one has the time to indulge in existential reveries.' – *Richard Williams, Guardian*

Pushing Tin **
US 1999 124m DeLuxe Super 35
TCF/Fox 2000, Regency (Art Linson)
📀 📀 🎧
Rivalry develops between a top, long-established New York air-traffic controller and a newcomer.

Often engrossing social comedy set in a fascinating environment, with two men giving each other, and their wives, a bumpy ride; unfortunately it crash-lands half-an-hour before it ends.
w Glen Charles, Les Charles article *Something's Got to Give* by Darcy Frey d Mike Newell ph Gale Tattersall m Anne Dudley pd Bruno Rubeo ed Jon Gregory
☆ John Cusack, Billy Bob Thornton, Cate Blanchett, Angelina Jolie, Tina Leary, Kurt Fuller, Matt Ross, Jerry Grayson, Michael Willis
'An adherence to the conventions of slick Hollywood comedy-drama goes down as smoothly as a bout of clear air turbulence.' – *Simon Braund, Empire*
'One of the most consistently enjoyable US films of the year.' – *Andrew O'Hehir, Sight and Sound*

Pushover *
US 1954 91m bw
Columbia (Jules Schermer)
📀
An honest policeman involves himself in murder for loot.
Another variation on Double Indemnity, smoothly carpentered as the first appearance of newly-groomed star Kim Novak. The events of a night were familiar and watchable.
w Roy Huggins novels *The Night Watch* by Thomas Walsh, *Rafferty* by William S. Ballinger d Richard Quine ph Lester B. White m Arthur Morton
☆ Fred MacMurray, Kim Novak, Phil Carey, Dorothy Malone, E. G. Marshall

Puss och Kram: see Hugs and Kisses

Pussycat Alley: see The World Ten Times Over

Pussycat, Pussycat, I Love You
US 1970 100m DeLuxe
UA/Three Pictures (Jerry Bresler)
A sex-mad writer tells a doctor how he lost his wife to a film-star.
Tedious chase comedy that goes nowhere in particular.
wd Rod Amateau ph Tonino Delli Colli m Lalo Schifrin ad Toni Sarzi-Braga d Larry Heath
☆ Ian McShane, Anna Calder-Marshall, Severn Darden, Joyce Van Patten, John Gavin, Beba Loncar
'The gags, both visual and verbal, strain and creak, giving the impression of being made up on the spur of the moment.' – *David McGillivray, MFB*

Putney Swope *
US 1969 85m bw/Eastmancolor
Contemporary/Herald
A black adman takes over an agency, renaming it Truth and Soul Inc. and staffing it with black militants.

Anarchic, intermittently funny comedy, stuffed with jokes at the expense of most institutions.
wd Robert Downey ph Gerald Cotts m Charley Cuva ad Gary Weist ed Bud Smith
☆ Arnold Johnson, Antonio Fargas, Laura Greene, Eric Krupnik, Pepi Hermine, Ruth Hermine
'Visual graffiti of this order don't merit public exposure.' – *David Wilson, MFB*

Puttin' on the Ritz
US 1930 88m bw (colour sequence)
UA/Joseph M. Schenck (John W. Considine Jnr)
A has-been vaudevillian gets a second chance but succumbs to the demon rum.
Primitive early musical melodrama valuable only as an example of the work of its star.
w John W. Considine Jnr d Edward Sloman ph Ray June ad William Cameron Menzies
☆ Harry Richman, Joan Bennett, James Gleason, Aileen Pringle, Lilyan Tashman, Purnell Pratt
'Entertaining backstage story with ultra production values.' – *Variety*

Putting Pants on Philip *
🎬🎬 US 1927 20m bw silent
Hal Roach
A respectable man meets his randy Scottish nephew who wears nothing under his kilt.
Early star comedy, allegedly their first as a team but before their more recognizable characteristics had developed. Not at all bad in its way, though developing into one long chase.
w H. M. Walker d Clyde Bruckman
☆ Laurel and Hardy, Sam Lufkin, Harvey Clark

Puzzle of a Downfall Child
US 1970 104m Technicolor
Universal/Newman-Foreman
Fantasy reminiscences of a top fashion model.
Pretentious, fashionable, seemingly interminable collage of sex and high living.
w Adrien Joyce (Carole Eastman) d Jerry Schatzberg ph Adam Holender m Michael Small
☆ Faye Dunaway, Barry Primus, Viveca Lindfors, Barry Morse, Roy Scheider

Pygmalion ****
GB 1938 96m bw
Gabriel Pascal
📀 📀
A professor of phonetics takes a bet that he can turn a Cockney flower seller in six months into a lady who can pass as a duchess.
Perfectly splendid Shavian comedy of bad manners, extremely well filmed and containing memorable lines and performances; subsequently turned into the musical My Fair Lady (qv). One of the most heartening and adult British films of the thirties.
w Anatole de Grunwald, W. P. Lipscomb, Cecil

Lewis, Ian Dalrymple play *Bernard Shaw* d Anthony Asquith, Leslie Howard ph Harry Stradling m Arthur Honegger ad Laurence Irving ed David Lean
☆ Leslie Howard, Wendy Hiller, Wilfrid Lawson, Scott Sunderland, Marie Lohr, David Tree, Esmé Percy, Everley Gregg, Jean Cadell
HIGGINS (LESLIE HOWARD): 'Yes, you squashed cabbage leaf, you disgrace to the noble architecture of these columns, you incarnate insult to the English language, I can pass you off as the Queen of Sheba.'
HIGGINS: 'Where the devil are my slippers, Eliza?'
'Ought to have big potentialities in the US, with some cutting … An introductory title briefly gives the source of the play, which was Shakespeare's *Pygmalion*. (!)' – *Variety*
'An exhibition of real movie-making – of a sound score woven in and out of tense scenes, creating mood and tempo and characterization.' – *Pare Lorentz*
'Every possible care has been taken in the presentation of what may well prove to have a significant effect on future British film production, for it is live, human entertainment, flawlessly presented and making an obvious appeal to all kinds of audiences.' – *The Cinema*
🏆 Bernard Shaw; Ian Dalrymple, Cecil Lewis, W. P. Lipscomb
🏅 best picture; Leslie Howard; Wendy Hiller

Pyjama Girl: see The Pajama Girl Case

Pyrates
US 1991 95m colour
Rank/Act III/Mixed Breed (Jonathan Furie)
📀 📀
The passion of two lovers is so incendiary that they literally set the world alight.
Odd and risible little movie, with a great deal of uninteresting chat about love.
wd Noah Stern ph Janusz Kaminski m Peter Himmelman pd Sherman Williams ed Gib Jaffe
☆ Kevin Bacon, Kyra Sedgwick, Bruce Martyn Payne, Kristin Dattilo

A Pyromaniac's Love Story
US 1995 94m Technicolor
Buena Vista/Hollywood (Mark Gordon)
📀 📀 📀
After the neighbourhood baker's shop burns down, many people confess to starting the fire.
Genial, gently farcical fable of love that becomes too whimsical for its own good.
w Morgan Ward d Joshua Brand ph John Schwartzman m Rachel Portman pd Dan Davis ed David Rosenbloom
☆ William Baldwin, John Leguizamo, Sadie Frost, Erika Eleniak, Michael Lerner, Mike Starr, Julio Oscar Mechoso, Joan Plowright, Armin Mueller-Stahl, Richard Crenna

Q

Q & A *
US 1990 132m Technicolor
Virgin/Regency/Odyssey (Arnon Milchan, Burtt Harris)
An inexperienced assistant D.A. investigates the killing of a Puerto Rican crook by a veteran policeman and uncovers widespread corruption.
Increasingly ponderous and predictable drama of an innocent struggling in a moral quicksand.
w/d Sidney Lumet *novel* Judge Edwin Torres
ph Andrzej Bartkowiak *m* Ruben Blades
pd Philip Rosenberg *ed* Richard Cirincione
☆ Nick Nolte, Timothy Hutton, Armand Assante, Patrick O'Neal, Lee Richardson, Luis Guzman, Charles Dutton, Jenny Lumet, Paul Calderon
'One is left reflecting sadly on the miscalculations … that make a film which opens with the bang of a superb first half gradually tail away to a whimper.' – *Tom Milne, MFB*

Q Planes **
GB 1939 82m bw
Harefield/London Films (Irving Asher, Alexander Korda)
US title: *Clouds over Europe*
A secret ray helps spies to steal test aircraft during proving flights.
Lively comedy thriller distinguished by a droll leading performance.
w Ian Dalrymple, Brock Williams, Jack Whittingham, Arthur Wimperis *d* Tim Whelan *ph* Harry Stradling *md* Muir Mathieson
☆ Ralph Richardson, Laurence Olivier, Valerie Hobson, George Merritt, George Curzon, Gus McNaughton, David Tree
'A bright vigorous little picture, and Mr Richardson's Major is the brightest thing in it. You should see it. You'll like it. It has savour.' – *C. A. Lejeune*

Q – The Winged Serpent **
US 1982 93m colour Panavision
Larco/Larry Cohen
aka: *The Winged Serpent*
An ex-con on the run finds a monstrous Aztec god, a flying serpent, nesting in the spire of the Chrysler building.
Quirky, above-average horror film with flashes of brightness.
w/d Larry Cohen *ph* Fred Murphy *m* Robert O. Ragland *ed* Armand Lebowitz
☆ Michael Moriarty, Candy Clark, David Carradine, Richard Roundtree, James Dixon

Qiu Ju Da Guansi: see *The Story of Qiu Ju*

Qiuyue: see *Autumn Moon*

Quackser Fortune Has a Cousin in the Bronx *
US 1970 90m Eastmancolor
UMC (John H. Cushingham)
An Irish layabout strikes up an acquaintance with an American student.
Likeable if plotless Dublin comedy, pleasantly photographed.
w Gabriel Walsh *d* Waris Hussein *ph* Gil Taylor *m* Michael Dress
☆ Gene Wilder, Margot Kidder, Eileen Colgan, Seamus Ford

Quadrophenia
GB 1979 120m Eastmancolor
Brent-Walker/Polytel (Roy Baird, Bill Curbishley)
A drama of bitter rivalry between Mods and Rockers on the Brighton beaches in 1964.

What passed for a successful musical at the end of the seventies is typified by this violent, screaming and wholly unattractive amalgam of noise, violence, sex and profanity.
w Dave Humphries, Martin Stellman, Franc Roddam *d* Franc Roddam *ph* Brian Tufano *m* The Who *md* John Entwistle, Pete Townshend *pd* Simon Holland *ed* Mike Taylor
☆ Phil Daniels, Mark Wingett, Philip Davis, Leslie Ash, Garry Cooper, Toyah Wilcox, Sting

Quai des Brumes ***
France 1938 89m bw
Rabinovitch
US title: *Port of Shadows*
An army deserter rescues a girl from crooks but is killed before they can escape.
Artificial, set-bound, but at the time wholly persuasive melodrama which became one of the archetypal French films of the thirties, its doomed lovers syndrome not being picked up by Hollywood until after World War II.
w Jacques Prévert *novel* Pierre MacOrlan *d* Marcel Carné *ph* Eugen Schüfftan *m* Maurice Jaubert *ad* Alexander Trauner
☆ Jean Gabin, Michèle Morgan, Michel Simon, Pierre Brasseur
'Unity of space, time and action give the film a classical finish.' – *Georges Sadoul*
'The sort of powerful and joyless film that the French do so well – a study in foetid atmosphere, in which the one beauty is its uncompromising honesty.' – *C. A. Lejeune*
† The plot was in fact almost identical with that of *Pépé le Moko*. The romantic pessimism of these films, plus *Le Jour Se Lève*, so suited the mood of France that Vichy officials later said: 'If we have lost the war it is because of *Quai des Brumes*.'

Quai des Orfèvres *
France 1947 105m bw
Majestic
A music hall artiste is accused of murdering the man he took to be seducing his mistress.
The equivalent of many a British Scotland Yard thriller, but a good one, with excellent acting, atmosphere and suspense.
w Henri-Georges Clouzot, Jean Ferry *novel* Légitime Défense by Stanislas-André Steeman *d* Henri-Georges Clouzot *ph* Armand Thirard *m* Francis Lopez
☆ Louis Jouvet, Bernard Blier, Suzy Delair, Pierre Larquey, Simone Rennant
'The wonder of *Quai des Orfèvres* is the way Clouzot has pricked it with life.' – *Guardian*
'A stunningly well made entertainment.' – *New Yorker, 1982*

'Two love experts in a daring game of hearts!'
Quality Street *
US 1937 84m bw
RKO (Pandro S. Berman)
When an officer returns from the Napoleonic wars, he does not recognize his sweetheart, whose beauty has faded, so she masquerades as her own capricious niece.
Fairly successful attempt to capture on screen the essence of Barrie whimsy; everyone tries hard, anyway.
w Mortimer Offner, Allan Scott *play* J. M. Barrie *d* George Stevens *ph* Robert de Grasse *m* Roy Webb
☆ Katharine Hepburn, Franchot Tone, Fay Bainter, Eric Blore, Cora Witherspoon, Estelle Winwood, Florence Lake, Joan Fontaine
'Hepburn and Tone unable to instil any life, and little entertainment, into this old-timer from legit … one for the bonnet and shawl trade.' – *Variety*

'It is strictly a self-propelled picture, tearing breathlessly, even hysterically, through Barrie's quizzical account of a man-hunt … But we were exhausted by the intensity of Miss Hepburn's concentration on it. Her Phoebe needs a neurologist far more than a husband. Such flutterings and jitterings and twitchings, such hand-wringings and mouth-quiverings, such runnings-about and eyebrow-raisings have not been on the screen in many a moon.' – *Frank Nugent, New York Times*
'Actually quite repulsive.' – *Katharine Hepburn*
† Previously made by MGM in 1927 (silent), with Marion Davies and Conrad Nagel; directed by Sidney Franklin.
♫ Roy Webb

Quante Volte… Quella Notte: see *Four Times That Night*

Quantez
US 1957 80m Eastmancolor Cinemascope
Universal-International
Robbers hiding for the night in a frontier town become involved in an Indian attack.
Curious, slow-paced attempt to redo The Gunfight with inferior materials; not a profitable experience.
w R. Wright Campbell *d* Harry Keller *ph* Carl Guthrie *m* Herman Stein
☆ Fred MacMurray, Dorothy Malone, James Barton, Sydney Chaplin, John Gavin, John Larch, Michael Ansara

Quantrill's Raiders
US 1958 68m DeLuxe Cinemascope
Allied Artists (Ben Schwalb)
A Southern agent seeks the help of Quantrill's gang to attack an army arsenal at Lawrence, Kansas, and regrets it.
Uninteresting, conventional Western with a flimsy narrative and dull characterization.
w Polly James *d* Edward Bernds *ph* William Whitley *m* Marlin Skiles *ad* David Milton *ed* William Austin
☆ Steve Cochran, Diane Brewster, Leo Gordon, Gale Robbins, Will Wright, Kim Charney, Myron Healey

The Quare Fellow
GB 1962 90m bw
BLC/Bryanston (Anthony Havelock-Allan)
Life in a Dublin prison when two men are to be hanged, as experienced by a new young warder.
Watered-down version of a rumbustious stage tragicomedy, with not much but the gloom left.
w/d Arthur Dreifuss *play* Brendan Behan *ph* Peter Hennessey *m* Alexander Faris
☆ Patrick McGoohan, Sylvia Syms, Walter Macken, Dermot Kelly, Hilton Edwards

Quartet ***
GB 1948 120m bw
GFD/Gainsborough (Anthony Darnborough)
Four stories introduced by the author.
This entertaining production began the compendium fashion (Full House, Phone Call from a Stranger, etc.) and is fondly remembered, though all the stories had softened endings and the middle two did not work very well as drama. Subsequent Maugham compilations were Trio and Encore (both qv).
The Facts of Life:
d Ralph Smart *ph* Ray Elton with Basil Radford, Naunton Wayne, Mai Zetterling, Jack Watling, James Robertson Justice
The Alien Corn:
d Harold French *ph* Ray Elton with Dirk Bogarde, Françoise Rosay, Raymond Lovell, Honor Blackman, Irene Browne
The Kite:
d Arthur Crabtree *ph* Ray Elton with George Cole,

Hermione Baddeley, Susan Shaw, Mervyn Johns, Bernard Lee
The Colonel's Lady:
d Ken Annakin *ph* Reg Wyer with Cecil Parker, Linden Travers, Nora Swinburne, Ernest Thesiger, Felix Aylmer, Henry Edwards, Wilfrid Hyde-White
w R. C. Sherriff *stories* W. Somerset Maugham *m* John Greenwood

Quartet *
GB/France 1981 101m GTC colour
TCF/Merchant Ivory (Ismail Merchant, Jean Pierre Mahot de la Querantonnais)
In 1927 Paris, a convict's wife finds herself part of a *ménage à trois*.
Slow-moving, good-looking study of characters in a milieu; as usual with films from this stable, it has nothing to please the majority.
w Ruth Prawer Jhabvala *novel* Jean Rhys *d* James Ivory *ph* Pierre Lhomme *m* Richard Robbins
☆ Isabelle Adjani, Maggie Smith, Alan Bates, Anthony Higgins

'See women defiled by monsters from outer space! Men turned killers by mysterious power more incredible than anything today's science or fiction ever imagined!'
Quatermass and the Pit **
GB 1967 97m Technicolor
Hammer/Anthony Nelson Keys
US title: *Five Million Years to Earth*
Prehistoric skulls are unearthed during London Underground excavations, and a weird and deadly force makes itself felt.
The third film of a Quatermass serial is the most ambitious, and in many ways inventive and enjoyable, yet spoiled by the very fertility of the author's imagination: the concepts are simply too intellectual to be easily followed in what should be a visual thriller. The climax, in which the devil rears over London and is 'earthed', is satisfactorily harrowing.
w Nigel Kneale TV *serial* Nigel Kneale *d* Roy Ward Baker *ph* Arthur Grant *m* Tristram Cary
☆ Andrew Keir, James Donald, Barbara Shelley, Julian Glover, Duncan Lamont, Edwin Richfield, Peter Copley

'You Can't Escape It! Nothing Can Destroy It! It's Coming For You From Space To Wipe All Living Things From The Face Of The Earth! Can It Be Stopped?'
The Quatermass Experiment **
GB 1955 82m bw
Exclusive/Hammer (Anthony Hinds)
US title: *The Creeping Unknown*
When a rocketship returns from space, two of its three crew members have disappeared and the third is slowly taken over by a fungus which thrives on blood.
Intelligent science fiction based on a highly successful BBC TV serial; the film version is generally workmanlike despite its obvious low budget.
w Richard Landau, Val Guest *serial* Nigel Kneale *d* Val Guest *ph* Jimmy Harvey
☆ Brian Donlevy, Jack Warner, Margia Dean, Richard Wordsworth, David King Wood, Thora Hird, Gordon Jackson

Quatermass II **
GB 1957 85m bw
Hammer (Anthony Hinds)
US title: *Enemy from Space*
A research station operating under military secrecy is supposed to be making synthetic foods, but is in fact an acclimatization centre for invaders from outer space.

Simplified version of a TV serial, a bit stodgy in the talk scenes, but building into sequences of genuine alarm and based on an idea of lingering persuasiveness.
w Nigel Kneale, Val Guest *serial* Nigel Kneale d Val Guest *ph* Gerald Gibbs *m* James Bernard
☆ Brian Donlevy, John Longden, Sidney James, Bryan Forbes, William Franklyn, Charles Lloyd Pack, Percy Herbert, Tom Chatto

Quatre Aventures de Reinette et Mirabelle: see *Four Adventures of Reinette and Mirabelle*

Les Quatre Cents Coups: see *The Four Hundred Blows*

I Quattro dell'Ave Maria: see *Ace High*

Quattro Passi fra le Nuvole: see *Four Steps in the Clouds*

Que He Hecho Yo Para Merecer Esto?: see *What Have I Done to Deserve This?*

Que la Bête Meure ***
France/Italy 1969 110m colour
La Boétie/Rizzoli (André Génovés)
📀 ▤
US title: *This Man Must Die*
aka: *The Beast Must Die; Killer!*
A father decides to find and murder the hit-and-run driver who killed his young son.
A complex and engrossing psychological study that ignores the thriller aspects of the story to concentrate on relationships of love and hatred, with a memorable performance from Yanne as an uncouth villain.
w Paul Gégauff *novel* The Beast Must Die by Nicholas Blake d Claude Chabrol *ph* Jean Rabier *m* Pierre Jansen, Brahms *ad* Guy Littaye *ed* Jacques Gaillard
☆ Michel Duchaussoy, Caroline Cellier, Jean Yanne, Anouk Ferjac, Marc di Napoli, Maurice Pialat, Jean-Louis Maury, Louise Chevalier, Guy Marly
'The movie is so attenuated and unhurried that it dies on the screen.' – *Pauline Kael*

Quebec
US 1951 85m Technicolor
Paramount
▤
The wife of the loyalist governor of Quebec is in love with the leader of the rebels.
Ho-hum period actioner with some pretty backgrounds and not much personality.
w Alan Le May d George Templeton *ph* W. Howard Greene *m* Van Cleave
☆ Corinne Calvet, John Barrymore Jnr, Barbara Rush, Patric Knowles, John Hoyt, Arnold Moss

'She's so excitingly good when she's so wonderfully bad!'
Queen Bee *
US 1955 95m bw
Columbia (Jerry Wald)
📀
A wealthy woman has a compulsion to dominate everyone around her.
Claustrophobic Southern-set melodrama obviously created for its star.
wd Ranald MacDougall *novel* Edna Lee *ph* Charles Lang *m* George Duning *md* Morris Stoloff
☆ Joan Crawford, Barry Sullivan, Betsy Palmer, John Ireland, Lucy Marlow, William Leslie, Fay Wray
♫ Charles Lang

Queen Christina ***
US 1933 101m bw
MGM (Walter Wanger)
📀 ▤ 📀⌃
The queen of 17th-century Sweden, distressed at the thought of a political marriage, goes wandering through her country in men's clothes and falls in love with the new Spanish ambassador.
The star vehicle par excellence, superb to look at and one of its star's most fondly remembered films. Historically it's nonsense, but put across with great style.
w Salka Viertel, H. M. Harwood, S. N. Behrman d Rouben Mamoulian *ph* William Daniels *m* Herbert Stothart

☆ Greta Garbo, John Gilbert, Ian Keith, Lewis Stone, C. Aubrey Smith, Reginald Owen, Elizabeth Young
ANTONIO (JOHN GILBERT): 'It's all a question of climate. You cannot serenade a woman in a snowstorm. All the graces in the art of love – elaborate approaches that will make the game of love amusing – can only be practised in those countries that quiver in the heat of the sun.'
CHRISTINA (GRETA GARBO): 'I have been memorizing this room. In the future, in my memory, I shall live a great deal in this room.'
'The shortcomings, such as they are, are so far overshadowed by the potency of the premier satellite, the sterling support, the Mamoulian montage and the Behrman crisp dialogue that they're relatively unimportant; for Christina is cinch b.o.' – *Variety*
'Garbo, as enchanting as ever, is still enveloped by her unfathomable mystery.' – *Photoplay*
'An unending series of exceptional scenes.' – *Modern Screen*
† The leading male role was announced in turn for Leslie Howard, Franchot Tone, Nils Asther, Bruce Cabot and Laurence Olivier: Garbo turned them all down.

Queen Elizabeth *
France 1912 35m bw silent
Histrionic Film
original title: *Les Amours de la Reine Elisabeth*
Scenes from the life of the queen.
Abysmally boring now, this film is important in several ways. It is our best record of Sarah Bernhardt. It was immensely successful throughout the world. It made cinema interesting to all classes, not just the hoi polloi. It made the fortunes of Adolph Zukor, who bought it cheaply and went on to found Paramount Pictures. (Bernhardt is said to have remarked to him: 'You have put me in pickle for all time!')
w Eugène Moreau d Henri Desfontaines, Louis Mercanton
☆ Sarah Bernhardt, Lou Tellegen

Queen Kelly **
US 1928 100m bw silent
United Artists/Gloria Productions/Joseph Kennedy
📀 ▤ 📀⌃
A convent girl goes to the bad, is ill-used by a prince, becomes a white slave in Africa but finally inherits a fortune.
Sexually-oriented extravaganza, the last great folly of its director but never finished by him. Various versions exist: in all of them individual scenes are more entertaining than the whole. Extracts were shown in Sunset Boulevard.
wd Erich von Stroheim *ph* Gordon Pollock, Paul Ivano, Ben Reynolds. *m* Adolf Tandler *ad* Harry Miles
☆ Gloria Swanson, Walter Byron, Seena Owen
† The version released on video in 1994 is the European version of 1931, which runs for 115m.

Queen Margot: see *La Reine Margot*

Queen of Atlantis: see *L'Atlantide*

Queen of Destiny: see *Sixty Glorious Years*

Queen of Hearts *
GB 1936 80m bw
ATP (Basil Dean)
A working girl poses as a socialite and wins a matinée idol.
Stalwart romantic comedy with its star slightly more glamorized than usual.
w Clifford Grey, H. F. Maltby, Douglas Furber, Anthony Kimmins, Gordon Wellesley d Monty Banks *ph* John W. Boyle *md* Ernest Irving *ad* J. Elder Wills
☆ Gracie Fields, John Loder, Enid Stamp Taylor, Fred Duprez, Edward Rigby, Hal Gordon

Queen of Hearts *
👥 GB 1989 112m colour
Enterprise/TVS Films/Nelson Entertainment/Film Four International/Telso International (John Hardy)
▤ 📀⌃
A ten-year-old, part of a large and happy Italian family living in London, watches while his father risks everything by gambling.
Odd and ultimately unsatisfactory mix of fantasy and reality, contrasting Italian warmth and British cool to the detriment of both.

w Tony Grisoni d Jon Amiel *ph* Mike Southon *m* Michael Convertino *pd* Jim Clay *ed* Peter Boyle
☆ Vittorio Duse, Joseph Long, Anita Zagaria, Eileen Way, Vittorio Amandola, Roberto Scateni, Stefano Spagnoli, Alec Bregonzi

Queen of Outer Space
US 1958 79m DeLuxe Cinemascope
Allied Artists (Ben Schwalb)
▤
The man-hating Queen of Venus is thwarted in her plans to destroy the Earth with a powerful ray by astronauts who crash-land on the planet.
Ludicrously inept science fiction that borrows from Flight to Mars, World without End *and* Forbidden Planet *for many of its props and special effects. No film that casts a heavily accented Zsa Zsa Gabor as a Venusian scientist in sequins, silk and gold high heels can have been intended as entirely serious, but most of the laughter is at the expense of the acting, dialogue and aliens, who look as if they have just stepped out of a chorus line.*
w Charles Beaumont *story* Ben Hecht d Edward Bernds *ph* William Whitley *m* Marlin Skiles *ad* David Milton *ed* William Austin
☆ Zsa Zsa Gabor, Eric Fleming, Dave Willock, Laurie Mitchell, Lisa Davis, Patrick Waltz, Paul Birch, Barbara Darrow, Marilyn Buferd

The Queen of Spades **
GB 1948 96m bw
ABP/World Screen Plays (Anatole de Grunwald)
▤
A Russian officer tries to wrest from an ancient countess the secret of winning at cards, in return for which he has sold his soul to the devil; but she dies of fright and haunts him.
Disappointingly slow-moving but splendidly atmospheric recreation of an old Russian story with all the decorative stops out; the chills when they come are quite frightening, the style is impressionist and the acting suitably extravagant.
w Rodney Ackland, Arthur Boys *novel* Alexander Pushkin d Thorold Dickinson *ph* Otto Heller *m* Georges Auric *ad* Oliver Messel
☆ Anton Walbrook, Edith Evans, Ronald Howard, Yvonne Mitchell, Mary Jerrold
'The photography is adventurous, the cutting imaginative and the sets startling.' – *Evening Standard*
'It is fine to come across such distinguished filmcraft.' – *Evening News*

The Queen of Spies: see *Joan of Ozark*

Queen of the Mob *
US 1940 61m bw
Paramount
A murderess and her three sons are captured by the FBI.
Pacy crime melodrama from the Persons in Hiding *series, based on the exploits of Ma Barker.*
w Horace McCoy, William Lipman d James Hogan *ph* Theodor Sparkuhl
☆ Blanche Yurka, Ralph Bellamy, Jack Carson, Richard Denning, Paul Kelly, J. Carrol Naish, Jeanne Cagney, William Henry, James Seay, Hedda Hopper

Queen of the Nile: see *Nefertite, Queen of the Nile*

Queen of the Pirates (dubbed)
Italy 1960 80m colour
Max
A sea captain and his swashbuckling daughter become pirates in order to resist the rule of a local tyrant.
Silly period romp, dubbed into dialogue even more clichéd than its plot ('Belay there, you swabs,' says the captain to his crew); its main purpose seems to have been to put Canale into tight-fitting breeches.
d Mario Costa *ph* Raffaele Masciocchi *ed* Renato Cinquinni
☆ Gianna Maria Canale, Massimo Serato, Scilla Gabel, Livio Lorenzon, Moira Orfei, Paul Muller

Queen of the Road
Australia 1984 96m colour
JNP (James Davern)
A daughter inherits trouble when she takes over her father's truck haulage business.
A dull comedy of mishap and misadventure, interspersed with country and western songs and

relying for the most part on the old joke (though it may be new to Australia) that women are poor drivers.
w Tom Mitchell d Bruce Best *ph* Joseph Pickering *m* Mike Perjanik *ad* Michael Ralph *ed* Zsolt Kollanyi
☆ Joanne Samuel, Amanda Muggleton, Shane Worthington, Jonathan Sweet, Chris Hession

The Queen's Guards
GB 1960 112m Technicolor Cinemascope
TCF/Imperial (Michael Powell)
Reminiscences during trooping the colour of father and son guardsmen.
Incredibly old-fashioned family melodrama complete with skeleton in family closet, despite its date it has a decidedly pre-war air, except that it might have been more smartly done then.
w Roger Milner d Michael Powell *ph* Gerald Turpin *m* Brian Easdale
☆ Raymond Massey, Daniel Massey, Robert Stephens, Ursula Jeans, Judith Stott, Elizabeth Shepherd, Duncan Lamont, Ian Hunter, Jack Watling
'This flagwaving museum piece would be distressing if it weren't so inept … [the actors] battle manfully with dialogue and characters as dated as a Crimean cavalry charge. The film could scarcely be taken as a tribute to the Guards except, just possibly, by elderly aunts in Cheltenham.' – *MFB*

The Queen's Husband: see *The Royal Bed*

Queens Logic *
US 1991 116m DeLuxe
New Visions (Stuart Oken, Russ Smith)
📀 ▤ 📀⌃ ⌂
Friends from boyhood offer each other support and succour at a moment of marital crisis.
Energetically acted domestic drama that covers familiar ground but does so in an enjoyably high-spirited manner.
w Tony Spiridakis *story* Tony Spiridakis, Joseph W. Savino d Steve Rash *ph* Amir Mokri *m* Joe Jackson *pd* Edward Pisoni *ed* Patrick Kennedy
☆ Kevin Bacon, Linda Fiorentino, John Malkovich, Joe Mantegna, Ken Olin, Tony Spiridakis, Tom Waits, Chloe Webb, Jamie Lee Curtis
'This deadpan midlife crisis comedy-drama is undeniably compulsive in its simplified TV fashion, thanks to a cleverly worked script and some heartening acting.' – *John Lyttle, Independent*

Queimada!
France/Italy 1968 132m DeLuxe
PEA/PPA (Alberto Grimaldi)
📀
aka: *Burn!*
A diplomat is sent to a Caribbean island to break the Portuguese sugar monopoly and becomes involved with revolutionaries.
An indigestible attempt to combine adventure with the film of ideas; very tedious.
w Franco Solinas, Giorgio Arlorio d Gillo Pontecorvo *ph* Marcello Gatti *m* Ennio Morricone
☆ Marlon Brando, Renato Salvatori, Norman Hill, Evaristo Marquez

'Theirs was a time of love and violence!'
Quentin Durward *
👥 GB 1955 101m Eastmancolor Cinemascope
MGM (Pandro S. Berman)
aka: *The Adventures of Quentin Durward*
An elderly English lord sends his nephew to woo a French lady on his behalf; but the boy falls in love with her himself.
Haphazardly constructed and produced, but quite enjoyable, period romp, with a bold black villain and several rousing set-pieces including a final set-to on bell ropes.
w Robert Ardrey *novel* Sir Walter Scott d Richard Thorpe *ph* Christopher Challis *m* Bronislau Kaper *ed* Ernest Walter
☆ Robert Taylor, Kay Kendall, Robert Morley, Alec Clunes, Marius Goring, Wilfrid Hyde-White, Ernest Thesiger, Duncan Lamont, Harcourt Williams, Laya Raki, George Cole

Querelle
West Germany/France 1982 108m
Eastmancolor
Planet/Albatross/Gaumont
A homosexual sailor has a mystical quest which involves murder.
Overheated fantasy which may have something to say to gays, but not much to other audiences.
wd Rainer Werner Fassbinder book Jean Genet
ph Xaver Schwarzenberger m Peer Raben
☆ Brad Davis, Franco Nero, Jeanne Moreau, Laurent Malet

The Quest
US 1996 95m DeLuxe 'Scope
Universal/MDP (Moshe Diamant)
A petty thief takes part in a martial arts championship in Tibet in the 20s.
Trivial martial arts flick, serving up the same old narrative as usual; this time it is woodenly directed as well as acted.
w Steve Klein, Paul Mones story Frank Dux, Jean-Claude Van Damme d Jean-Claude Van Damme ph David Gribble m Randy Edelman pd Steve Spence ed John F. Link, William J. Meshover
☆ Jean-Claude Van Damme, Roger Moore, James Remar, Janet Gunn, Jack McGee, Aki Aleong, Abdel Qissi, Louis Mandylor
'Dull stuff, except perhaps for martial-arts fanatics.' – George Perry

Quest for Camelot
↟↟ US 1998 86m Technicolor
Warner (Dalisa Cooper Cohen)
GB title: The Magic Sword: Quest for Camelot
The daughter of a murdered knight goes in search of King Arthur's sword Excalibur, which has been stolen and lost in a magic forest.
Like Mulan, this is one of the current cycle of animated movies with heroines who take on male roles; maybe boys no longer watch cartoons, which in this case is the sensible option.
w Kirk de Micco, William Schifrin, Jacqueline Feather, David Seidler novel The King's Damosel by Vera Chapman d Frederick Du Chau ph Mark Dinicola m Patrick Doyle pd Steve Pilcher ed Stanford C. Allen
☆ Featuring the voices of: Jessalyn Gilsig (sung by Andrea Corr), Cary Elwes (sung by Bryan White), Gary Oldman, Eric Idle, Don Rickles, Jane Seymour, Celine Dion, Pierce Brosnan (sung by Steve Perry), Bronson Pinchot, Jaleel White, Gabriel Byrne, John Gielgud
♫ song 'The Prayer' (m Carole Bayer Sager, David Foster, l Carole Bayer Sager, David Foster, Tony Renis, Alberto Testa)

Quest for Fire
Canada/France 1981 100m Bellevue-Pathé
Panavision
ICC/Cine Trail/Belstar/Stephan (Michael Gruskoff)
Eighty thousand years ago, a primitive tribe uses the discovery of fire to defeat its enemies.
Scientifically cosseted but sometimes unintentionally funny attempt to make us care about the problems of primitive man. Lively sequences are separated by longueurs.
w Gérard Brach novel La Guerre du Feu by J. H. Rosny d Jean-Jacques Annaud ph Claude Agostini m Philippe Sarde pd Guy Comtois, Brian Morris special language Anthony Burgess body movement Desmond Morris
☆ Everett McGill, Ron Perlman, Rae Dawn Chong, Nameer El-Kadi

'He had seen her, felt her touch, knew she existed...'
Quest for Love
GB 1971 90m Eastmancolor
Rank/Peter Rogers Productions (Peter Eton)
After an explosion during an experiment, a young physicist finds himself living a different life, in love with a dying girl; returning to normal, he finds the girl and saves her.
Pleasing variation on Berkeley Square, quite well staged and played.
w Terence Feely story Random Quest by John Wyndham d Ralph Thomas ph Ernest Steward m Eric Rogers

☆ Tom Bell, Joan Collins, Denholm Elliott, Laurence Naismith, Lyn Ashley

A Question of Adultery
GB 1958 84m bw
Eros/Connaught Place/Raymond Stross
When a husband is discovered to be sterile, his wife suggests artificial insemination, but when she seems to have a lover he institutes divorce proceedings.
Opportunist melodrama from the headlines. Not even interesting then.
w Anne Edwards play Breach of Marriage by Dan Sutherland d Don Chaffey ph Stephen Dale m Philip Green
☆ Julie London, Anthony Steel, Basil Sydney, Donald Houston, Anton Diffring, Andrew Cruickshank, Conrad Phillips, Kynaston Reeves

A Question of Silence *
Netherlands 1982 96m colour
C.O.W./Sigma Films (Matthijs van Heijningen)
original title: De Stilte Rond Christine M
A lawyer, defending three women who commit a gratuitous act of murder of a male boutique owner, claims that their action is the result of masculine oppression.
Stylish feminist thriller that skilfully wraps its propagandist message.
wd Marleen Gorris ph Frans Bromet m Lodewijk de Boer, Martijn Hasebos ad Harry Ammerlaan ed Hans van Dongen
☆ Edda Barends, Nelly Frijda, Henriette Tol, Cox Habbema, Eddy Brugman, Hans Croiset, Erik Plooyer

'The Wild West Just Got A Little Wilder'
The Quick and the Dead *
US 1995 108m Technicolor
Columbia TriStar (Joshua Donen, Allen Shapiro, Patrick Markey)
Gunmen and one vengeful woman congregate in a Western town run by a psychotic killer for a gunfighting contest in which the winner is the last man left alive.
The Western genre taken to a logical conclusion: as a succession of quick-draw contests; the influence here is Sergio Leone, to which the director adds his trademark convulsive camerawork.
w Simon Moore d Sam Raimi ph Dante Spinotti m Alan Silvestri pd Patrizia von Brandenstein ed Pietro Scalia
☆ Gene Hackman, Sharon Stone, Leonardo DiCaprio, Russell Crowe, Tobin Bell, Roberts Blossom, Lance Henriksen, Pat Hingle, Gary Sinise, Woody Strode
'Take it as parody or take it seriously, the effect is the same: extreme boredom.' – Geoff Brown, The Times
'The definitive postmodern, postfeminist, post-what-have-you western – for what it's worth.' – Premiere

Quick Before It Melts
US 1964 97m Metrocolor Panavision
MGM/Biography (Douglas Lawrence, Delbert Mann)
A journalist is sent to cover a naval enterprise in the Antarctic, and gets a scoop despite his shyness.
Noisy service comedy with precious little plot.
w Dale Wasserman novel Philip Benjamin d Delbert Mann ph Russell Harlan m David Rose
☆ George Maharis, Robert Morse, Anjanette Comer, James Gregory, Howard St John, Janine Gray, Michael Constantine
'The combination of romantic dalliance, service high jinks and hectic journalism remains uniformly flat all through.' – MFB

Quick Change
US 1990 88m DuArt Panavision
Warner/Devoted (Robert Greenhut, Bill Murray)
Two men and a woman stage a flawless bank robbery and then have trouble making their getaway from New York.
Farcical comedy taken at a decorous pace and with the joke of an escalating series of disasters too often mistimed to produce any amusement.
w Howard Franklin novel Jay Cronley d Howard Franklin, Bill Murray ph Michael Chapman m Randy Edelman ad Speed Hopkins ed Alan Heim

☆ Bill Murray, Geena Davis, Randy Quaid, Jason Robards, Bob Elliott, Kimberleigh Aarn, Ron Ryan, Brian McConnachie, Jack Gilpin

The Quick Gun
US 1964 88m Techniscope
Admiral/Columbia
A gunfighter gets an icy welcome when he returns home to claim his father's farm.
Standard Western with the hero redeemed and elected sheriff at the end.
w Robert E. Kent d Sidney Salkow ph Lester Shorr m Richard La Salle
☆ Audie Murphy, Merry Anders, James Best, Ted de Corsia, Walter Sande, Frank Ferguson

Quick Let's Get Married
US 1965 100m colour
Golden Eagle (William Marshall)
aka: The Confession, Seven Different Ways
The voice of a sneak thief in a ruined church is taken by an unwed mother as a miracle.
Downright peculiar mishmash wasting interesting stars; an independent production by Rogers and husband in Jamaica.
w Allan Scott d William Dieterle ph Robert Bronner m Michael Colicchio
☆ Ginger Rogers, Ray Milland, Barbara Eden, Walter Abel, Cecil Kellaway, Elliott Gould, Michael Ansara, David Hurst

Quick Millions *
US 1931 69m bw
Fox
An ambitious truck driver becomes a ruthless racketeer.
Fast-moving, otherwise naïve early gangster melodrama notable for Tracy's first star performance.
w Courteney Terrett, Rowland Brown, John Wray d Rowland Brown ph Joseph August
☆ Spencer Tracy, Marguerite Churchill, Sally Eilers, Robert Burns, John Wray, George Raft
'This film is in the money. Ranks with the best of the gangster items.' – Variety

Quicker than the Eye
France/Switzerland 1988 92m Fujicolour
Condor/Crocodile/SRG/ZDF/ORF/Paul-Boris Lobadowsky/William Hartman (Peter-Christian Fueter)
original title: Passe-Passe
In Switzerland, a gang of ruthless assassins, hired to kill the president of an African country, plan to use an American magician as their cover.
Uninteresting and uninvolving thriller, with a cast coasting through the convolutions of the plot.
w Joseph Morhaim, Nicolas Gessner novel Claude Cueni d Nicolas Gessner ph Wolfgang Treu m George Garvarentz pd Max Stubenrauch ed Daniela Roderer
☆ Ben Gazzara, Mary Crosby, Jean Yanne, Robert Linesol, Catherine Jarrett, Eb Lottimer, Wolfram Berger, Dinah Hinz, Ivan Desny

Quicksand
US 1950 79m bw
UA/Mort Briskin
A garage mechanic gets involved in crime for the sake of an unworthy girl.
Lower-case melodrama of no notable merit.
w Robert Smith d Irving Pichel ph Lionel Lindon ad Boris Leven
☆ Mickey Rooney, Jeanne Cagney, Barbara Bates, Peter Lorre

The Quiet American *
US 1957 122m bw
UA/Figaro (Joseph L. Mankiewicz)
An American in Saigon has naïve ideas for ending the war; he saves the life of a journalist who for various reasons becomes jealous and is duped into betraying the American to the communists.
Semi-successful excursion into the territory of Graham Greene, who as in Brighton Rock has allowed his ironic ending to be totally re-emphasized, here making the film anti-communist instead of anti-American.
wd Joseph L. Mankiewicz novel Graham Greene ph Robert Krasker m Mario Nascimbene
☆ Michael Redgrave, Audie Murphy, Claude Dauphin, Giorgia Moll, Bruce Cabot, Fred Sadoff, Richard Loo

Quiet Days in Clichy
France/Italy/Germany 1989 100m colour
ItalFrance (Lawrence Schiller)
original title: Jours Tranquilles à Clichy
An elderly American writer recalls the sexual encounters of his youth.
Curiously passionless and unconvincing movie set in an art director's idea of decadent pre-war Paris, not helped by the casting of the bland McCarthy as Miller; it is better on politics than sex.
w Ugo Leonzio, Claude Chabrol novel Henry Miller d Claude Chabrol ph Jean Rabier m Matthieu Chabrol, Luigi Ceccarelli, Jean-Michel Bernard ad Marco Dentici ed Monique Fardoulis
☆ Andrew McCarthy, Nigel Havers, Barbara de Rossi, Stephanie Cotter, Isolde Barth, Eva Grimaldi, Anna Galiena, Stephane Audran, Elide Melli

The Quiet Earth *
New Zealand 1985 94m colour
Cinepro/Pillsbury Films (Sam Pillsbury, Don Reynolds)
After an experiment goes disastrously wrong, a suicidal scientist wakes to discover that he appears to be the only person left alive in the world.
An intriguing and often witty exercise in apocalyptic science fiction, with an unconventional approach.
w Bill Baer, Bruno Lawrence, Sam Pillsbury novel Craig Harrison d Geoff Murphy ph James Bartle m John Charles pd Josephine Ford ed Michael Horton
☆ Bruno Lawrence, Alison Routledge, Peter Smith

The Quiet Man *
US 1952 129m Technicolor
Republic/Argosy (John Ford, Merian C. Cooper)
An Irish village version of The Taming of the Shrew, the tamer being an ex-boxer retired to the land of his fathers and in need of a wife. Archetypal John Ford comedy, as Irish as can be, with everything but leprechauns and the Blarney Stone on hand.
Despite some poor sets the film has a gay swing to it, much brawling vigour and broad comedy, while the actors all give their roistering best.
w Frank Nugent story Maurice Walsh d John Ford ph Winton C. Hoch, Archie Stout m Victor Young
☆ John Wayne, Maureen O'Hara, Barry Fitzgerald, Victor McLaglen, Ward Bond, Mildred Natwick, Francis Ford, Arthur Shields, Eileen Crowe, Sean McClory, Jack MacGowran
'Ford's art and artifice … are employed to reveal a way of life – stable, rooted, honourable, purposeful in nature's way, and thereby rhythmic. Everyone is an individual, yet everyone and everything has a place.' – Henry Hart, Films in Review
♟ John Ford; Winton C. Hoch, Archie Stout
♟ best picture; Frank Nugent, Victor McLaglen

A Quiet Place to Kill: see Paranoia

Quiet Please, Murder *
US 1943 70m bw
TCF (Ralph Dietrich)
Nazis and art thieves cause a high death rate in a public library.
Unusual, stylish second feature.
wd John Larkin m Joe MacDonald m Arthur Lange md Emil Newman
☆ George Sanders, Kurt Katch, Gail Patrick, Richard Denning, Lynne Roberts, Sidney Blackmer, Byron Foulger
SAMPLES OF QUIRKY DIALOGUE: PATRICK TO SANDERS: 'How many butterflies did you torture since lunch, hoping one would turn on you?'
SANDERS: 'I am a punishment in your life. Your conscience demands it. The unconscious instinct to punish ourselves sometimes becomes self-destructive. The way we live is a constant threat to our own security. We love it. Giving and taking pain.'
PATRICK: 'You hate because you fear love – and the thought of desiring.'

Quiet Wedding *
GB 1940 80m bw
Paramount/Conqueror (Paul Soskin)
Middle-class wedding preparations are complicated by family guests.

A semi-classic British stage comedy is admirably filmed with a splendid cast.
w *Terence Rattigan, Anatole de Grunwald*
play *Esther McCracken* d *Anthony Asquith*
☆ Margaret Lockwood, Derek Farr, A. E. Matthews, Marjorie Fielding, Athene Seyler, Peggy Ashcroft, Margaretta Scott, Frank Cellier, Roland Culver, Jean Cadell, David Tomlinson, Bernard Miles
  'A completely unpretentious and charming film, the components of which are as delicately balanced as the mechanism of a watch.' – *New York Times*
  'No subtlety of glance, movement or dialogue has been missed, no possible highlight omitted.' – *MFB*
† Production was halted five times when bombs fell on the studio.
†† Remade as *Happy is the Bride* (qv).

Quiet Weekend
GB 1946 92m bw
Associated British (Warwick Ward)
The Royds spend a weekend at their country cottage and get involved with poachers.
Trivial and poorly-made sequel, not up to the standard of Quiet Wedding as a comic study of British types.
w *Victor Skutezky* play *Esther McCracken*
d *Harold French* ph *Eric Cross*
☆ Derek Farr, Marjorie Fielding, George Thorpe, Frank Cellier

Quigley Down Under
US 1990 120m colour Panavision
UIP/Pathé (Stanley O'Toole, Alexandra Rose)
◉ ▦ 🎧
In 1860s Australia, an American hired gun is outlawed after quarrelling with his employer, a violent British cattle rancher.
Apart from its outback setting, a conventional and unoriginal Western, given perfunctory treatment.
w *John Hill* d *Simon Wincer* ph *David Eggby*
m *Basil Poledouris* pd *Ross Major* ed *Peter Burgess*
☆ Tom Selleck, Laura San Giacomo, Alan Rickman, Chris Haywood, Ron Hadrick, Tony Bonner, Jerome Ehlers, Conor McDermottroe, Roger Ward, Ben Mendelsohn, Steve Dodd

'Potters along for two hours juggling cardboard figures and contrived situations that might have strayed in from some Hollywood potboiler of the 50s.' – *Geoff Brown, MFB*
† The script was originally written in the 1970s for Steve McQueen.

The Quiller Memorandum *
GB 1966 105m Eastmancolor Panavision
Rank/Ivan Foxwell/Carthay
▦
A British secret service man is sent to Berlin to combat a neo-Nazi organization.
Disappointingly thin but smooth and watchable spy story.
w *Harold Pinter* novel *The Berlin Memorandum* by Adam Hall (Elleston Trevor) d *Michael Anderson*
ph *Erwin Hillier* m *John Barry*
☆ George Segal, Max von Sydow, Alec Guinness, Senta Berger, George Sanders, George Helpmann, Robert Flemyng
  'In disposing of most of the storyline Pinter has virtually thrown out the baby with the bathwater; all that remains is a skeleton plot which barely makes sense and is totally lacking in excitement.' – *Brenda Davies*
  'Harold Pinter wrote the screenplay and for each word of dialogue there has to be a separate scene involving several different camera angles, which is perhaps why they asked him to do it as the story is pretty thin.' – *J. A., Illustrated London*

The Quince Tree Sun **
Spain 1992 137m Eastmancolor
Artificial Eye/Maria Moreno
◉
original title: *El Sol del Membrillo*
aka: *Dream of Light*
Painter Antonio López meticulously prepares a canvas and his subject: a tree of yellow, ripening quinces in the morning sun. The documentary then follows his progress through ten weeks, struggling against the fading light and unsympathetic weather, reminiscing and talking to friends, eventually abandoning his original oil painting and making a drawing instead.
A slow but absorbing examination of the process of artistic creation.

d *Victor Erice* ph *Javier Aguirresarobe, Angel Luis Fernéndez* m *Pascal Gaigne* ed *Juan Ignacio San Mateo*
  'What might have proven a poignant statement on life and art unfortunately runs so long impact is diluted.' – *Variety*

Quingchun Ji: see *Sacrificed Youth*

Quintet
US 1979 118m DeLuxe
TCF/Lions Gate (Robert Altman)
▦
In an icebound city of the future, citizens play a death game and a survivor hunts down a killer who plays for real.
Dismayingly pretentious claptrap which did its star's career no good at all.
w *Frank Barhydt, Robert Altman, Patricia Resnick* d *Robert Altman* ph *Jean Boffety* m *Tom Pierson*
pd *Leon Ericksen*
☆ Paul Newman, Vittorio Gassman, Fernando Rey, Bibi Andersson, Brigitte Fossey, Nina Van Pallandt
  'I find it mysterious, exciting, tenacious.' – *Dilys Powell, Punch*
  'Paralyzingly stupid.' – *Stanley Kauffmann*

'Fifty million people watched, but no one saw a thing.'

Quiz Show **
US 1994 132m Technicolor
Buena Vista/Hollywood/Wildwood/Baltimore (Robert Redford, Michael Jacobs, Julian Krainin, Michael Nozik)
◉ ▦ 🎧 ◉ ◉
In the 50s, the producers of TV's most popular quiz show fix the results in search of higher ratings and are exposed.
A smart and gripping drama of media corruption, based on fact and revealing inequities of class and culture that retain their power today.
w *Paul Attanasio* book *Remembering America: A Voice from the Sixties* by Richard N. Goodwin
d *Robert Redford* ph *Michael Ballhaus* m *Mark Isham* pd *Jon Hutman* ed *Stu Linder*
☆ John Turturro, Ralph Fiennes, Rob Morrow, Paul Scofield, David Paymer, Hank Azaria,

Christopher McDonald, Griffin Dunne, Mira Sorvino, Martin Scorsese
  'It hums along like a well-constructed farce, and its crazy momentum carries it over the bumps of social significance.' – *Terrence Rafferty, New Yorker*
  'Something that's fast becoming a rarity: an entertaining, funny, intelligent studio picture.' – *Sheila Johnston, Independent*
🏆 best picture; Robert Redford; Paul Scofield; Paul Attansio
🎖 Paul Attansio

'In making this film, MGM feel privileged to add something of permanent value to the cultural treasure house of mankind...'
'Ancient Rome is going to the dogs, Robert Taylor is going to the lions, and Peter Ustinov is going crazy!'

Quo Vadis **
🏛 US 1951 171m Technicolor
MGM (Sam Zimbalist)
◉ ▦ 🎧
A Roman commander under Nero falls in love with a Christian girl and jealous Poppea has them both thrown to the lions.
Spectacular but stagey and heavy-handed Hollywood version of a much-filmed colossus which shares much of its plot line with The Sign of the Cross. Three hours of solemn tedium with flashes of vigorous acting and a few set-pieces to take the eye; but the sermonizing does not take away the bad taste of the emphasis on physical brutality.
w *John Lee Mahin, S. N. Behrman, Sonya Levien* novel *Henryk Sienkiewicz* d *Mervyn Le Roy*
ph *Robert Surtees, William V. Skall* m *Miklos Rozsa* ad *Cedric Gibbons, Edward Carfagno, William Horning* ed *Ralph E. Winters*
☆ Robert Taylor, Deborah Kerr, *Peter Ustinov, Leo Genn, Patricia Laffan*, Finlay Currie, Abraham Sofaer, Marina Berti, Buddy Baer, Felix Aylmer, Nora Swinburne, Ralph Truman, Norman Wooland
🏆 best picture; Robert Surtees, William V. Skall; Miklos Rozsa; Peter Ustinov; Leo Genn; art direction; editing

R

'Three years ago Rabbit Angstrom ran out to buy his wife cigarettes. He hasn't come back yet...'

Rabbit, Run
US 1970 94m Technicolor Panavision
Warner (Howard Kreitsek)

A man leaves his pregnant wife for a prostitute.
Uninteresting sex melodrama without any of the wit which distinguishes the book; hard to sit through.
w Howard B. Kreitsek *novel* John Updike *d* Jack Smight *ph* Philip Lathrop *m* Ray Burton, Brian King
☆ James Caan, Anjanette Comer, Arthur Hill, Jack Albertson, Carrie Snodgress

Rabbit Test
US 1978 84m colour
Avco Embassy (Edgar Rosenberg)
■ ▦

A man becomes pregnant.
Dreary and tasteless film, the nadir of comedy.
w Jay Redack, Joan Rivers *d* Joan Rivers
ph Lucien Ballard *m* Peter Carpenter, Mike Post
ad Robert Kinoshita *ed* Stanford C. Allen
☆ Billy Crystal, Joan Prather, Alex Rocco, Doris Roberts, Edward Ansara, Imogene Coca, Jane Connell, Keene Curtis, Roddy McDowall, Sheree North, Joan Rivers

The Rabbit Trap *
US 1959 76m bw
UA/Canon (Harry Kleiner)

A hardworking draughtsman finally defies his boss and completes his holiday with his family.
Watchable minor drama just about marking the end of Hollywood's infatuation with TV plays which had begun with Marty; the moral and family problems of ordinary people were beginning to prove a shade lacking in excitement.
w J. P. Miller *TV play* J. P. Miller *d* Philip Leacock
ph Irving Glassberg *m* Jack Marshall
☆ Ernest Borgnine, Bethel Leslie, David Brian, Kevin Corcoran

Rabid
Canada 1976 91m colour
Alpha/Cinepix/Dibar/Famous Players (Dan Goldberg)
▥ ▦

aka: Rage

After extensive intestinal surgery, a woman develops a taste for human blood, infecting her victims with a form of rabies.
Gory though stylish horror about predatory sexuality that features a star of pornographic movies and has gained a cult following.
wd David Cronenberg *ph* René Verzier *m* Ivan Reitman *ad* Claude Marchand *ed* Jean Lafleur
sp Art Griswold
☆ Marilyn Chambers, Frank Moore, Joe Silver, Howard Ryshpan, Patricia Gage, Susan Roman

Rabid Grannies
Belgium/US 1988 88m colour
Troma/Star Pictures Nr 1 (James Desert, Jonathan Rambert)
▦

Two elderly aunts (there is not a granny to be seen) invite their family to a birthday celebration and, under demonic influence, proceed to murder them.
Exceptionally silly and unpleasant, gore-filled horror.
wd Emmanuel Kervyn *ph* Hugo Labye *m* Pierre-Damien Castelain, Jean-Bruno Castelain *pd* Luc Bertrand *ed* Philippe Ravoet
☆ Elie Lison, Catherine Aymerie, Jacques Mayar, Françoise Moens, Robert du Bois, Florine Elslande, Guy Van Riet, Françoise Lamoureux

Race for the Yankee Zephyr
♈ New Zealand/Australia 1981 108m
Eastmancolor Panavision
Enterprise/Hemdale/Pact/First City (David Hemmings, Antony I. Ginnane, John Barnett)
▤ ☊

Adventurers discover an American aircraft wrecked in 1944, and argue over the loot without knowing that it contains a 50-million-dollar payroll.
Very moderate adventure story distinguished only by good locations.
w Everett de Roche *d* David Hemmings
ph Vincent Monton *m* Brian May
☆ Ken Wahl, Lesley Ann Warren, Donald Pleasence, George Peppard, Bruno Lawrence, Robert Bruce

Race Gang: see *The Green Cockatoo*

Race Street
US 1948 79m bw
RKO (Nat Holt)
▦

A bookie vows revenge when his pal is killed by an extortionist gang, but discovers that his girlfriend is married to the leader.
Routine thick ear, quite adequately handled.
w Martin Rackin *story* Maurice Davis *d* Edwin L. Marin *ph* J. Roy Hunt *m* Roy Webb
☆ George Raft, Marilyn Maxwell, William Bendix, Frank Faylen, Henry Morgan, Gale Robbins

Race with the Devil
US 1975 88m DeLuxe
TCF/Saber/Maslansky (Wes Bishop)
▤

Holidaymakers witness a black mass and are pursued by the diabolists.
Silly melodrama which resolves into a wild car chase and much violence.
w Lee Frost, Wes Bishop *d* Jack Starrett
ph Robert Jessup *m* Leonard Rosenman
☆ Peter Fonda, Warren Oates, Loretta Swit, Lara Parker, R. G. Armstrong

'Why do you need a woman when death is your mistress every afternoon?'
'A love story that hurtles full speed across the barriers of convention!'

The Racers
US 1955 112m DeLuxe Cinemascope
TCF (Julian Blaustein)
GB title: *Such Men Are Dangerous*

A Monte Carlo Rally contestant is financed by an attractive lady gambler.
Routine racing car melodrama, totally unmemorable but impersonally efficient.
w Charles Kaufman *novel* Hans Ruesch *d* Henry Hathaway *ph* Joe MacDonald *m* Alex North
☆ Kirk Douglas, Bella Darvi, Gilbert Roland, Cesar Romero, Lee J. Cobb, Katy Jurado, Charles Goldner, George Dolenz

Rachel and the Stranger *
US 1948 92m bw
RKO (Richard H. Berger)
▤ ▦

A widowed farmer first feels real love for the new wife he bought when an attractive stranger seems likely to take her away from him.
Modestly appealing romantic drama in a Western setting.
w Waldo Salt *stories* Rachel; Neighbor Sam by Howard Fast *d* Norman Foster *ph* Maury Gertsman *m* Roy Webb *m/ly* Roy Webb, Waldo Salt *md* Constantin Bakaleinikoff *ad* Albert S. D'Agostino, Walter E. Keller, Jack Okey *ed* Les Milbrook *cos* Edith Head

☆ Loretta Young, Robert Mitchum, William Holden, Gary Gray, Tom Tully, Sara Haden, Frank Ferguson, Walter Baldwin
♫ Just Like Me; Oh He, oh Hi, oh Ho; Summer Song; Along Came A Tall Dark Stranger; Foolish Pride; Rachel

The Rachel Papers
GB 1989 95m colour
Virgin/Initial Film and Television/Longfellow Pictures (Andrew S. Karsch)
▥ ▦

A would-be Oxford University student has an on-and-off affair with an American girl.
Bungled attempt at a contemporary comedy of manners.
wd Damian Harris *novel* Martin Amis *ph* Alex Thomson *m* Chaz Jankel, David Storrs
pd Andrew McAlpine *ed* David Martin
☆ Dexter Fletcher, Ione Skye, Jonathan Pryce, James Spader, Bill Paterson, Shirley Anne Field, Michael Gambon, Lesley Sharp, Jared Harris, Aubrey Morris

Rachel, Rachel **
US 1968 101m Eastmancolor
Warner/Kayos (Paul Newman)

Events in the life of a middle-aged schoolmistress in a small New England town.
Appealing and freshly observed study of a limited personality in a small community.
w Stewart Stern *novel* A Jest of God by Margaret Laurence *d* Paul Newman *ph* Gayne Rescher *m* Jerome Moross
☆ Joanne Woodward, Estelle Parsons, James Olson, Kate Harrington, Donald Moffat, Geraldine Fitzgerald, Bernard Barrow
'It could all very easily degenerate into a woman's weepy; and the fact that it doesn't is due largely to Newman's refusal to treat Manawaka as another Peyton Place.' – *Jan Dawson*
'It tends to verge on dullness, but something always saves it.' – *John Simon*
♟ best picture; Stewart Stern; Joanne Woodward; Estelle Parsons

Rachel River
US 1987 90m DuArt
American Playhouse/Marx/Smolan (Timothy Marx)
▤

A radio journalist tries to cope with an impoverished life in a small Minnesota town with her two children and an unhelpful ex-husband.
Unpretentious, folksy drama dealing with everyday happenings in an undemandingly nostalgic manner.
w Judith Guest *stories* Carol Bly *d* Sandy Smolan *ph* Paul Elliott *m* Arvo Pärt *pd* David Wasco *ed* Susan Crutcher
☆ Pamela Reed, Viveca Lindfors, Zeljko Ivanek, James Olson, Craig T. Nelson, Alan North, Jo Henderson, Jon DeVries

Racing with the Moon
US 1984 108m Movielab
Paramount/Jaffe-Lansing (Alain Bernheim, John Kohn)
▥ ▤ ▦

In 1942 California, two young men await induction into the Marines and say goodbye to their girlfriends.
Disappointing flashback by people who fail to capture the spirit of the time, and replace it by conventional boy–girl teenage antics.
w Steven Kloves *d* Richard Benjamin *ph* John Bailey *m* Dave Grusin *pd* David L. Snyder
☆ Sean Penn, Elizabeth McGovern, Nicolas Cage, John Karlen, Max Showalter

The Rack
US 1956 100m bw
MGM (Arthur M. Loew Jnr)

A veteran of the Korean War is courtmartialled for collaborating with the enemy under torture.
Dullish courtroom melodrama overstretched from a TV play.
w Stewart Stern *play* Rod Serling *d* Arnold Laven *ph* Paul Vogel *m* Adolph Deutsch
☆ Paul Newman, Walter Pidgeon, Edmond O'Brien, Lee Marvin, Cloris Leachman, Wendell Corey

The Racket *
US 1951 88m bw
RKO/Edmund Grainger
▤ ▦

Police break up the empire of a powerful gangster.
Oddly timed and rather weak remake of the 1928 film; glossy but very old-fashioned in treatment.
w William Wister Haines *play* Bartlett Cormack *d* John Cromwell *ph* George E. Diskant
md Constantin Bakaleinikoff
☆ Robert Ryan, Robert Mitchum, Ray Collins, Lizabeth Scott, William Talman

Racket Busters
US 1938 71m bw
Warner (Samuel Bischoff)

A gangster aiming to take over a trucking enterprise is opposed by the special prosecutor's office.
Routine cops and robbers, still very watchable but also forgettable.
w Robert Rossen, Leonardo Bercovici *d* Lloyd Bacon *ph* Arthur Edeson *m* Adolph Deutsch
☆ George Brent, Humphrey Bogart, Gloria Dickson, Allen Jenkins, Walter Abel, Penny Singleton, Henry O'Neill

Rackety Rax
US 1932 65m bw
Fox

Gangster methods are applied to college football.
Stiff burlesque which didn't transfer well from the printed page.
w Ben Markson, Lou Breslow *novel* Joel Sayre *d* Alfred Werker
☆ Victor McLaglen, Greta Nissen, Nell O'Day, Alan Dinehart, Allen Jenkins

Radio City Revels
US 1938 90m bw
RKO

A songwriter can work only in his sleep.
A wisp of plot is the peg for a very moderate revue.
w Matt Brooks, Eddie Davis, Anthony Veiller, Mortimer Offner *d* Ben Stoloff *ph* J. Roy Hunt *md* Victor Baravalle *ch* Hermes Pan
☆ Bob Burns, Jack Oakie, Kenny Baker, Victor Moore, Ann Miller, Milton Berle, Helen Broderick, Jane Froman, Buster West, Richard Lane
'Should do well at b.o., but no smash.' – *Variety*

Radio Days **
US 1987 85m DuArt
Orion (Robert Greenhut)
▥ ▤ ▦ ☊

At the beginning of World War II, families near New York are affected by what they hear on the radio.
Shapeless montage of funny bits, best appreciated by those who lived through the time at somewhere near the place.
wd Woody Allen *ph* Carlo di Palma *pd* Santo Loquasto *ed* Susan E. Morse *m/ed* Dick Hyman
☆ Mia Farrow, Dianne Wiest, Seth Green, Julie Kavner, Josh Mostel, Michael Tucker, Wallace Shawn
'One of his most purely entertaining pictures.' – *Daily Variety*

♈ film suitable for family viewing　　▥ VHS video-cassette for the British PAL system　　▤ VHS video-cassette for the British PAL system in wide screen-format　　✪ Video cassette in a computer-colourised version　　▦ American NTSC video-cassette　　☊ Laser disc

   best original screenplay; art direction (Speed Hopkins)
▽ Santo Loquasto

'Powered By Imagination.'
Radio Flyer
US 1992 113m Technicolor Panavision
Columbia/Stonebridge Entertainment (Lauren Schuler-Donner)
◉ ▦ ◎ ♫

A father tells his sons how, when he was young, he and his small brother decided to build a flying machine in an attempt to escape from their increasingly violent stepfather.
An uneasy mix of fantasy and reality that remains stolidly earthbound.
w David Mickey Evans d Richard Donner ph Laszlo Kovacs m Hans Zimmer ad J. Michael Riva ed Stuart Baird, Dallas Puett
☆ Lorraine Bracco, John Heard, Elijah Wood, Joseph Mazello, Adam Baldwin, Ben Johnson, Tom Hanks (uncredited)
   'A film one would like to like more.' – *Variety*
† Originally, David Mickey Evans was assigned to direct with Rosanna Arquette playing the mother, but that production was abandoned. The film was released direct to video in Britain.

Radio On
GB 1979 101m bw
BFI/Road Movies (Keith Griffiths)
A disc-jockey in a biscuit factory makes a haphazard journey from London to Bristol to discover the circumstances of his brother's death.
Inconsequential road movie that can barely summon up any interest in its characters; it is much influenced by the films of Wim Wenders, who was its associate producer.
wd Chris Petit ph Martin Schafer ad Susannah Buxton ed Anthony Sloman
☆ David Beames, Lisa Kreuzer, Sandy Ratcliff, Andrew Byatt, Sue Jones, Sting
   'For all its German and American antecedents, however, *Radio On* remains peculiarly English in its concerns and atmosphere. It is in fact one of the most distinguished attempts by a native film-maker to contain all those influences and emerge with a firm sense of its own identity.' – *Richard Combs*

Radio Parade of 1935
GB 1934 96m bw (colour sequence)
BIP (Walter C. Mycroft)
US title: *Radio Follies*
Amateur talent makes it big for a radio station.
Historically interesting revue which unfortunately requires its comic lead to play straight.
w Jack Davies, Paul Perez, Arthur Woods, James Bunting d Arthur Woods ph Claude Friese-Greene
☆ Will Hay, Helen Chandler, Clifford Mollison, Davy Burnaby, The Western Brothers, Alfred Drayton, Lily Morris, Nellie Wallace, Clapham and Dwyer, Claude Dampier, Ronald Frankau, Ted Ray, Beryl Orde, Stanelli

Radio Stars on Parade
US 1945 69m bw
RKO/Ben Stoloff
Agents fix up a show despite threats from gangsters.
Slim excuse for a revue including talent popular at the time.
w Robert E. Kent, Monte Brice d Leslie Goodwins
☆ Wally Brown, Alan Carney, Frances Langford, Don Wilson, Tony Romano, Rufe Davis, Sheldon Leonard, Ralph Edwards, Skinnay Ennis and his band

Radioland Murders
US 1994 108m Rank Colour
Universal/Lucasfilm (Rick McCallum, Fred Roos)
◉ ▦ ◎ ♫

In 1939, a series of murders disrupts the opening night of a new radio network and an attempt by a writer to win back his estranged wife.
Fitfully engaging exercise in nostalgia, but as easy to switch off as it is to switch on.
w Willard Huyck, Gloria Katz, Jeff Reno, Ron Osborn story George Lucas d Mel Smith ph David Tattersall m Joel McNeely pd Gavin Bocquet ed Paul Trejo

☆ Mary Stuart Masterson, Brian Benben, Ned Beatty, George Burns, Brion James, Michael McKean, Christopher Lloyd, Scott Michael Campbell, Stephen Tobolowsky, Corbin Bernsen, Michael Lerner, Bobcat Goldthwait
   'A well-intentioned but annoying shrill exercise virtually devoid of romance, suspense or wit.' – *Brian Lowry, Variety*

Rafferty and the Gold Dust Twins
US 1975 92m Technicolor Panavision
Warner/Gruskoff-Venture-Linson

A drifter encounters two female vagrants who force him at gunpoint to drive them to New Orleans and get him into various adventures.
Indulgent and unattractive 'road' movie which despite occasional amusing incident gets nowhere very slowly.
w John Kaye d Dick Richards ph Ralph Woolsey m Artie Butler
☆ Alan Arkin, Sally Kellerman, MacKenzie Phillips, Alex Rocco, Charlie Martin Smith, Harry Dean Stanton, John McLiam

Raffles *
US 1930 72m bw
UA/Samuel Goldwyn
A gentleman thief decides to go straight, but then agrees to carry out a final robbery to save a suicidal schoolfriend from disgrace.
Colman's performance adds a touch of elegance to a staid but still entertaining, wittily scripted light-hearted drama.
w Sidney Howard novel The Amateur Cracksman by E. W. Hornung d Harry D'Abbadie D'Arrast, George Fitzmaurice ph George S. Barnes, Gregg Toland ad W. Cameron Menzies, Park French ed Stuart Heisler
☆ Ronald Colman, Kay Francis, David Torrence, Frederick Kerr, Bramwell Fletcher, John Rogers, Wilson Benge, Alison Skipworth, Frances Dade
† The film's on-screen credits do not include the name of its director. Harry D'Arrast was fired by Goldwyn because he was playing the scenes too fast for the producer's liking and was replaced by Fitzmaurice. The film made a profit of $200,000.

Raffles *
US 1939 72m bw
Samuel Goldwyn
Raffles the famous cricketer is also a compulsive and daring amateur thief.
Slight, modernized version of the turn-of-the-century stories; very palatable, but it could have been better.
w John Van Druten, Sidney Howard novel Raffles the Amateur Cracksman by E. W. Hornung d Sam Wood ph Gregg Toland m Victor Young
☆ David Niven, Olivia de Havilland, Dudley Digges, May Whitty, Douglas Walton, Lionel Pape, E. E. Clive, Peter Godfrey
   'Fair remake … moderate b.o. potential.' – *Variety*
† This was virtually a scene-for-scene remake of the 1930 Goldwyn version starring Ronald Colman, Kay Francis and Alison Skipworth. It was written by Sidney Howard and George Fitzmaurice.

Rag Doll
GB 1960 67m bw
Mancunian (Tom Blakeley)
US title: *Young, Willing and Eager*
A 17-year-old runs away to Soho, where she gets a job as a waitress in a shady club and falls in love with a singer.
A melodramatic cautionary tale, given a little life by the playing of some expert character actors propping up the young leads.
w Brock Williams, Derry Quinn d Lance Comfort ph Basil Emmott m Martin Slavin ad John Earl ed Peter Pitt
☆ Jess Conrad, Christina Gregg, Hermione Baddeley, Kenneth Griffith, Patrick Magee, Patrick Jordan, Michael Wynne

Ragan
Spain 1968 90m Movielab
Westside International (Sidney Pink)
An American pilot, a former mercenary, is hired to help overthrow the government of a small country.
Glossy but dull thriller, a low-budget, low-talent attempt at a Bond-style entertainment.
w Howard Berk, Sidney Pink d Gilbert Lee Kay ph Antonio Macasoli m Nico Fidenco, G. Dell'orso ed Tony Ramirez

☆ Ty Hardin, Antonella Lualdi, Gustavo Rojo, Jack Stewart, Rossella Como, Joe Caffarell, Dick Palace

La Ragazza dal Pigiama Giallo: see *The Pajama Girl Case*

Rage
US 1966 103m Technicolor
Columbia/Joseph M. Schenck/Cinematografico Jalisco (Gilberto Gazcon)
A drunken doctor finds a new will to live during a difficult journey to avert a rabies epidemic.
Pattern melodrama with no surprises, but gripping most of the way.
w Teddi Sherman, Gilberto Gazcon, Fernando Mendez d Gilberto Gazcon ph Rosalio Solano m Gustavo Cesar Carreon
☆ Glenn Ford, Stella Stevens, David Reynoso, Armando Silvestre

Rage
US 1972 99m DeLuxe Panavision
Warner (Fred Weintraub)
▦
A father takes revenge when his son dies after a chemical warfare accident.
Well-meaning but turgid and boring melodrama.
w Philip Friedman, Dan Kleinman d George C. Scott ph Fred Koenekamp m Lalo Schifrin
☆ George C. Scott, Richard Basehart, Martin Sheen, Barnard Hughes, Stephen Young
   'Sluggish, tired and tiring.' – *Variety*

Rage at Dawn
US 1955 86m Technicolor
RKO/Nat Holt
▦
Detectives stage a fake train robbery to attract the evil Reno brothers.
Very moderate Western programmer.
w Horace McCoy d Tim Whelan ph Ray Rennahan m Paul Sawtell
☆ Randolph Scott, Forrest Tucker, J. Carrol Naish, Mala Powers, Edgar Buchanan, Ray Teal

'Looks Can Kill.'
The Rage: Carrie 2
US 1999 101m DeLuxe/bw
MGM/UA/Red Bank (Paul Monash)
♫
A teenage girl who is humiliated at school discovers that she has appalling telekinetic powers.
A sequel that recycles the original movie with no understanding of what made it effective.
w Rafael Moreu d Katt Shea ph Donald M. Morgan m Danny P. Harvey pd Peter Jamison ed Richard Nord
☆ Emily Bergl, Jason London, Dylan Bruno, J. Smith-Cameron, Amy Irving, Zachery Ty Bryan, John Doe, Gordon Clapp, Rachel Blanchard, Charlotte Ayanna, Justin Urich
   'An uninspired update with video cameras, sexual frankness, margaritas and tattoos.' – *Anita Gates, New York Times*
   'Abysmal.' – *Variety*

A Rage in Harlem **
GB 1991 108m DeLuxe
Palace/Miramax (Stephen Woolley, Kerry Boyle)
◉ ▦ ◎ ♫
In 1950s Harlem, a gullible undertaker's assistant gives refuge to a gangster's mistress with a trunkful of gold.
Lively, entertaining, fast-paced tongue-in-cheek thriller.
w John Toles-Bey, Bobby Crawford novel Chester Himes d Bill Duke ph Toyomichi Kurita m Elmer Bernstein pd Steven Legler ed Curtis Clayton
☆ Forest Whitaker, Gregory Hines, Robin Givens, Zakes Mokae, Danny Glover, Badja Djola, John Toles-Bey, Ron Taylor, Samm-Art Williams
   'Many will be turned off by the excessive bloodshed, but the fine cast keeps the pic watchable.' – *Variety*
   'Enjoyable though it is, Bill Duke's mix of brisk action, sexy innuendo and cameo-studded comedy takes considerable liberties with the spirit of Himes' Harlem.' – *Jonathan Romney, Sight and Sound*

Rage in Heaven
US 1941 82m bw
MGM (Gottfried Reinhardt)
An unstable millionaire becomes jealous of his wife and arranges his own death so that her supposed lover will be suspected.
Stilted melodrama with the stars more or less at sea.
w Christopher Isherwood, Robert Thoeren novel James Hilton d W. S. Van Dyke II ph Oliver T. Marsh m Bronislau Kaper
☆ Robert Montgomery, Ingrid Bergman, George Sanders, Lucile Watson, Oscar Homolka, Philip Merivale, Matthew Boulton, Aubrey Mather
   'Nothing happens but the obvious, and that only after a long and confused struggle.' – *Otis Ferguson*
† Directors Robert Sinclair and Richard Thorpe also worked on the film, which was sabotaged by Robert Montgomery giving a deliberately monotonous performance because he felt affronted by not being consulted over the script. The writers added a speech by a psychiatrist commenting on the listlessness of Montgomery's character in order to explain his acting.

The Rage of Paris *
US 1938 78m bw
Universal (B. G. de Sylva)
▦
Confidence tricksters invest their money in a French girl who is out to nail a millionaire.
If memory serves right, an amusingly amoral trifle in the best style of its year.
w Bruce Manning, Felix Jackson d Henry Koster
☆ Danielle Darrieux, Douglas Fairbanks Jnr, Louis Hayward, Mischa Auer, Helen Broderick, Harry Davenport, Samuel S. Hinds, Mary Martin
   'Smart comedy of first-run calibre … a finished and polished job.' – *Variety*

'The names and the places didn't matter – only when!'
A Rage to Live
US 1965 101m bw Panavision
UA/Mirisch (Lewis J. Rachmil)
The unhappy college and married life of a nymphomaniac.
Well made but deliberately 'daring' case history which becomes too obvious and silly.
w John T. Kelley novel John O'Hara d Walter Grauman ph Charles Lawton m Nelson Riddle
☆ Suzanne Pleshette, Bradford Dillman, Ben Gazzara, Peter Graves, Bethel Leslie, James Gregory, Ruth White
   'Stuff like this needs the exuberance of grand opera; sadly, all it gets here is a blue note.' – *MFB*

Raggedy Ann and Andy *
♠♠ US 1977 85m Movielab Panavision
Lester Osterman (Richard Horner)
Toys come to life and have their own adventures while their owner is absent.
Attractive fully animated cartoon feature in which only the central story is lacking in pace and humour.
w Patricia Thackray, Max Wilk stories Johnny Gruelle d Richard Williams m Joe Raposo

Raggedy Man
US 1981 94m Technicolor
Universal/William D. Wittliff, Burt Weissbourd
▦ ◎
In 1944, a small-town switchboard operator and her two children are protected by a mysterious stranger.
Curious and quite unnecessary melodrama of some skill but very dubious appeal.
w William D. Wittliff d Jack Fisk ph Ralf Bode m Jerry Goldsmith ed Edward Warschilka
☆ Sissy Spacek, Eric Roberts, Sam Shepard, William Sanderson, Tracey Walter, R. G. Armstrong
   'Despite the casual, unhurried pace of the film, it doesn't seem to observe much.' – *Richard Combs, MFB*

The Raggedy Rawney *
GB 1987 103m Technicolor
Virgin/HandMade (Bob Weis)
◉ ▦
An army deserter disguises himself as a woman and joins a group of wandering gypsies.
Downbeat rural tale, providing cold comfort.

---

w Bob Hoskins, Nicole de Wilde d Bob Hoskins ph Frank Tidy m Michael Kamen pd Jiri Matolin ed Alan Jones

☆ Bob Hoskins, Dexter Fletcher, Zoe Nathenson, Zoe Wanamaker, David Hill, Ian Dury, Ian McNeice, Veronica Clifford, Gawn Grainger, Jim Carter

Raging Bull ****

US   1980   119m   bw/colour
UA/Chartoff-Winkler
📼 📼 ▥ ◷ ⦿ ⦿

The rise to fame of an unlikeable middle-weight boxer, based on the autobiography of Jake La Motta.

Tough, compelling, powerfully made ringside melodrama. A poll of American critics voted it the best movie of the 1980s.

w Paul Schrader, Mardik Martin d Martin Scorsese ph Michael Chapman m from library sources pd Gene Rudolf

☆ Robert DeNiro, Cathy Moriarty, Joe Pesci, Frank Vincent, Nicholas Colasanto

'Scorsese makes pictures about the kind of people you wouldn't want to know.' – *Variety*
'A bravura display of cinematic skill.' – *Daily Mail*

⬛ editing (Thelma Schoonmaker); Robert DeNiro
⦿ best film; best direction; Cathy Moriarty; Joe Pesci; Michael Chapman
▽ editing

The Raging Moon *

GB   1970   111m   Technicolor
EMI (Bruce Cohn Curtis)
📼 📼

aka: *Long Ago Tomorrow*

A love affair develops between two inmates of a home for the physically handicapped.

Appealing romantic drama which nearly became a big commercial success.

wd Bryan Forbes novel Peter Marshall ph Tony Imi m Stanley Myers

☆ Malcolm McDowell, Nanette Newman, Georgia Brown, Bernard Lee, Gerald Sim, Michael Flanders

The Raging Tide

US   1951   93m   bw
U-I (Aaron Rosenberg)

A San Francisco gangster stows away on a fishing trawler and redeems himself when he perishes saving the life of a fisherman.

Fearfully old-fashioned seafaring melodrama, rather well made.

w Ernest K. Gann novel *Fiddler's Green* by Ernest K. Gann d George Sherman ph Russell Metty m Frank Skinner

☆ Richard Conte, Charles Bickford, Shelley Winters, Stephen McNally, Alex Nicol, Jesse White, John McIntire

Raging Waters: see Green Promise

Una Ragione per Vivere e Una per Morire: see A Reason to Live, a Reason to Die

The Ragman's Daughter

GB   1972   94m   Technicolor
TCF/Penelope (Harold Becker)

A Nottingham layabout falls in love with an exciting middle-class girl; they fail to overcome parental opposition and she is killed in a road accident.

Wispy drama framed in pointless flashbacks; done on the cheap, it never seems to get anywhere and even fails to use its locations to advantage.

w Alan Sillitoe story Alan Sillitoe d Harold Becker ph Michael Seresin m Kenny Clayton

☆ Simon Rouse, Victoria Tennant, Patrick O'Connell, Leslie Sands

'What a time it was, an incredible time, a good time, a bad time...'

Ragtime *

US   1981   155m   Technicolor   Todd-AO
Ragtime/Sunley (Dino de Laurentiis)
▥ ⦿

Just before World War I, various Americans are affected by world events, and a chapter of accidents turns a placid Negro into a revolutionary.

The fascinating patchwork of the novel has been virtually abandoned in favour of its least interesting episode, which is even further drawn out by the decision to bring on the aged James Cagney as a comic

turn not in the novel. The early sequences show what might have been.

w Michael Weller novel E. L. Doctorow d Milos Forman ph Miroslav Ondricek m Randy Newman ad John Graysmark, Patrizia von Brandenstein, Anthony Reading

☆ James Olson, Mary Steenburgen, James Cagney, Pat O'Brien, Elizabeth McGovern, Howard E. Rollins Jnr, Brad Dourif, Moses Gunn, Kenneth McMillan, Donald O'Connor

'It's limp ... it always seems to be aiming about halfway toward the effects that Doctorow achieved in his literary extravaganza.' – *New Yorker*
'The book, despite its defects, was funny, radical and angry. The film, despite its virtues, is solemn, liberal and passive.' – *Sunday Times*

† The film cost 32 million dollars and took eleven.

⦿ screenplay; Miroslav Ondricek; Randy Newman; Elizabeth McGovern (supporting actress); Howard E. Rollins Jnr; art direction; song 'One More Hour'

The Raid *

US   1954   83m   Technicolor
TCF (Robert L. Jacks)

In 1864 six confederate soldiers escape from a union prison, and from a Canadian refuge carry out a revenge raid on a small Vermont town.

Interesting little action drama, crisply characterized and plotted, and based on a historical incident.

w Sydney Boehm story *Affair at St Albans* by Herbert Ravenal Sass d Hugo Fregonese ph Lucien Ballard m Roy Webb

☆ Van Heflin, Anne Bancroft, Richard Boone, Lee Marvin, Tommy Rettig, Peter Graves, Douglas Spencer, Will Wright, John Dierkes

Raid on Rommel

US   1971   99m   Technicolor
Universal (Harry Tatelman)
📼 📼

In North Africa during World War II, a British officer releases prisoners of war and leads them in an assault on Tobruk.

Dispirited low-budget actioner apparently first intended for television.

w Richard Bluel d Henry Hathaway ph Earl Rath m Hal Mooney

☆ Richard Burton, John Colicos, Clinton Greyn, Wolfgang Preiss

The Raiders: see Riders of Vengeance (1952)

The Raiders

US   1964   75m   Technicolor
Revue/Universal

Cattle drovers enlist the aid of famous Western characters to persuade the railroad company to extend its line through dangerous country.

Slightly oddball Western with endearing moments amid the miscalculations.

w Gene L. Coon d Herschel Daugherty ph Bud Thackery m Morton Stevens

☆ Robert Culp, Judi Meredith, James McMullan, Brian Keith, Alfred Ryder, Simon Oakland

Raiders of the Lost Ark ***

👪 US   1981   115m   Metrocolor
Panavision
Paramount/Lucasfilm (Frank Marshall)
📼 📼 ⦿ ⦾

In the thirties, an American archaeologist and explorer beats the Nazis to a priceless artefact, the magical box containing fragments of the stones on which God wrote his laws.

Commercially very successful, this attempted wrap-up of the Saturday morning serials of two generations ago spends a great deal of money and expertise on frightening us rather than exciting us; in Dolby sound the experience is horrendous. Second time round, one can better enjoy the ingenious detail of the hero's exploits and ignore the insistence on unpleasantness; still, there are boring bits in between, and the story doesn't make a lot of sense.

w Lawrence Kasdan d Steven Spielberg ph Douglas Slocombe m John Williams pd Norman Reynolds

☆ Harrison Ford, Karen Allen, Ronald Lacey, Paul Freeman, John Rhys-Davies, Denholm Elliott

'Both de trop and not enough.' – *Sight and Sound*
'Children may well enjoy its simple-mindedness, untroubled by the fact that it looks so shoddy and so uninventive.' – *Observer*

'Kinesthetically, the film gets to you, but there's no exhilaration, and no surge of feeling at the end.' – *Pauline Kael, New Yorker*
'An out of body experience, a movie of glorious imagination and breakneck speed that grabs you in the first shot, hurtles you through a series of incredible adventures, and deposits you back in reality two hours later – breathless, dizzy, wrung-out, and with a silly grin on your face.' – *Roger Ebert*

† Tom Selleck was the first choice for the lead, but was tied up with his TV series *Magnum*.
†† It was followed by two sequels: *Indiana Jones and the Temple of Doom* and *Indiana Jones and the Last Crusade* (qqv).

⬛ editing (Michael Kahn); visual effects
⦿ best picture; Steven Spielberg; Douglas Slocombe; John Williams
▽ Norman Reynolds

Railroaded *

US   1947   72m   bw
Charles F. Reisner/Eagle Lion
▥ ⦾

A detective is on the trail of a ruthless mobster.

A new post-war toughness was evident in this sharply made second feature.

w John C. Higgins, Gertrude Walker d Anthony Mann ph Guy Roe m Alvin Levin

☆ John Ireland, Sheila Ryan, Hugh Beaumont, Jane Randolph, Ed Kelly, Charles D. Brown

Rails into Laramie

US   1954   81m   Technicolor
Universal-International

Railway construction is hampered in Laramie by a salon keeper who keeps the workers too happy.

Solid co-feature Western, quite enjoyable.

w D. D. Beauchamp, Joseph Hoffman d Jesse Hibbs m Maury Gertsman md Joseph Gershenson

☆ John Payne, Dan Duryea, Mari Blanchard, Barton MacLane, Harry Shannon, Lee Van Cleef

'A film for adults to take their children, too!'
The Railway Children ***

👪 GB   1970   108m   Technicolor
EMI (Robert Lynn)
▥

Three Edwardian children and their mother move into Yorkshire when their father is imprisoned as a spy, and have adventures on the railway line while helping to prove his innocence.

Fresh and agreeable family film with many pleasing touches to compensate for its meandering plot.

wd Lionel Jeffries novel E. Nesbit ph Arthur Ibbetson m Johnny Douglas

☆ Dinah Sheridan, William Mervyn, Jenny Agutter, Bernard Cribbins, Iain Cuthbertson, Gary Warren, Sally Thomsett

'There are passages in Mr Jeffries' deliberately nostalgic film which may appeal more to sensitive parents than to their bloodthirsty offspring. But everybody, I hope, will enjoy the playing.' – *Dilys Powell*

Rain *

US   1932   92m   bw
UA/Art Cinema Corporation (Joseph Schenck)
▥

Stranded passengers in Pago Pago during an epidemic include a prostitute and a missionary who lusts after her.

Early talkie version of a much filmed story; interesting but not very entertaining now that the sensational aspects have worn off.

w Maxwell Anderson play John Colton, Clemence Randolph story W. Somerset Maugham d Lewis Milestone ph Oliver T. Marsh m Alfred Newman

☆ Joan Crawford, Walter Huston, William Gargan, Beulah Bondi, Matt Moore, Guy Kibbee, Walter Catlett

'A b.o. disappointer. Only the play's rep and Joan Crawford's personal pull will save it.' – *Variety*

† Other versions: *Sadie Thompson* (1928) with Gloria Swanson; *Miss Sadie Thompson* (1953) (qv).

Rain Man **

US   1988   133m   DeLuxe
UIP/United Artists/Guber-Peters (Mark Johnson)
📼 📼 ⦾ ▥ ⦾ ⦾

A fast-talking salesman discovers, on his father's death, that he has an autistic elder brother.

An intelligent road movie, but one that does not move far enough from more conventional buddy-buddy movies.

w Ronald Bass, Barry Morrow d Barry Levinson ph John Seale m Hans Zimmer pd Ida Random ed Stu Linder, Thomas R. Moore

☆ Dustin Hoffman, Tom Cruise, Valeria Golino, Jerry Molen, Jack Murdock, Michael D. Roberts, Ralph Seymour, Lucinda Jenney, Bonnie Hunt

⬛ best picture; best director; best original screenplay; Dustin Hoffman
⦿ best original score; best cinematography; best film editing; best art direction

Rain or Shine *

US   1930   90m   bw
Columbia (Harry Cohn)

A circus performer puts on a one-man show in an attempt to stop it from closing.

A musical comedy translated to the screen without its songs as a showcase for the acrobatic, slack-wire and juggling talents of its star, a Broadway comedian famous for his wide smile and nonsense patter.

w Jo Swerling, Dorothy Howell musical comedy James Gleason, Maurice Marks d Frank Capra ph Joe Walker md Bakaleinikoff ed Maurice Wright

☆ Joe Cook, Louise Fazenda, Joan Peers, William Collier Jnr, Tom Howard

The Rain People

US   1969   101m   Technicolor
Warner/American Zoetrope (Bart Patton, Ronald Colby)

A depressed housewife leaves home, drives across country, and picks up a mentally retarded hitch-hiker who tries to protect her.

Slow, pretentious character drama which strains after art but only presents an unedifying study of failure.

wd Francis Ford Coppola ph Wilmer Butler m Ronald Stein

☆ Shirley Knight, James Caan, Robert Duvall, Tom Aldredge, Marya Zimmet

'The rain people are people made of rain and when they cry they disappear because they cry themselves away.' – *sample dialogue*

Rainbow

👪 GB/Canada   1995   101m
Technicolor/bw   Digital High Definition
First Independent/Winchester (Rainbow)/Filmline/Screen Partners (Robert Sidaway, Nicolas Clermont)
📼 ▥

Children steal gold from a rainbow, which causes colour to drain from the world with disastrous results.

Heavy-handed, didactic children's film that strives for a fairy-tale quality, but too frequently falls flat.

w Ashley Sidaway, Robert Sidaway d Bob Hoskins ph Freddie Francis m Alan Reeves pd Claude Paré ed Ray Lovejoy

☆ Bob Hoskins, Dan Aykroyd, Saul Rubinek, Jacob Tierney, Willy Lavenda, Jonathan Schuman, Eleanor Misrahi

'It would be hard to find a more charmless fable than this leaden patience-tester which gets everything wrong from the whimsical atmosphere striven for to the light touch so desperately needed to make the completely hopeless humour work.' – *Alan Jones, Film Review*

† It is the first film to be shot in Digital High Definition video.

The Rainbow *

GB   1988   111m   Technicolor
Vestron (Ken Russell)
📼 ▥ ⦾ ⦾

Determined to be independent, a farmer's daughter rejects her lover to go to university.

Over-simplified version of the novel, but watchable enough.

w Ken Russell, Vivian Russell novel D. H. Lawrence d Ken Russell ph Billy Williams m Carl Davis pd Luciana Arrighi ed Peter Davies

☆ Sammi Davis, Paul McGann, Amanda Donohoe, Christopher Gable, David Hemmings, Glenda Jackson, Dudley Sutton, Jim Carter, Judith Paris, Ken Colley

---

👪 film suitable for family viewing   📼 VHS video-cassette for the British PAL system   📼 VHS video-cassette for the British PAL system in wide screen-format   ⦿ Video cassette in a computer-colourised version   ▥ American NTSC video-cassette   ⦾ Laser disc

'The siren of the sarongs is calling you!'

Rainbow Island

US   1944   95m   Technicolor

Paramount (I. D. Leshin)

A white girl brought up by her doctor father on a Pacific island is pursued by three sailors escaping from the Japanese.

Cheerful spoof of the sarong cycle with the star seeing the joke; otherwise a silly service farce with South Sea trimmings.

w Walter de Leon, Seena Owen, Arthur Phillips d Ralph Murphy ph Karl Struss m Roy Webb songs Burton Lane, Ted Koehler

☆ Dorothy Lamour, Eddie Bracken, Gil Lamb, Barry Sullivan, Forrest Orr, Anne Revere, Reed Hadley, Marc Lawrence

The Rainbow Jacket

GB   1954   99m   Technicolor

Ealing (Michael Relph)

A boy jockey is blackmailed into losing a big race.

Disappointing racecourse drama which packs in all the expected ingredients.

w T. E. B. Clarke d Basil Dearden ph Otto Heller m William Alwyn

☆ Kay Walsh, Bill Owen, Edward Underdown, Robert Morley, Wilfrid Hyde-White, Charles Victor, Honor Blackman, Sidney James

'Probably the best racing film ever made.' – C. A. Lejeune

Rainbow on the River

US   1936   83m   bw

Sol Lesser (RKO)

After the Civil War, an orphan is brought up by a Black mammy and later discovered to be rich.

Sentimental drama with songs from its boy star; not much, but popular.

w Earle Snell, William Hurlbut story Mrs C. V. Jamison d Kurt Neumann

☆ Bobby Breen, May Robson, Charles Butterworth, Louise Beavers, Alan Mowbray, Benita Hume, Henry O'Neill

'Phoney and over-sugared sentimentality.' – Variety

Rainbow round My Shoulder

US   1952   78m   Technicolor

Columbia

A society girl breaks into show business.

Agreeable light musical for the easily pleased.

w Blake Edwards, Richard Quine d Richard Quine

☆ Frankie Laine, Billy Daniels, Charlotte Austin, Arthur Franz, Ida Moore, Lloyd Corrigan

Raining Stones **

GB   1993   91m   colour

First Independent/Parallax/Channel 4 (Sally Hibbin)

📀 🎞 ⊚

An unemployed Catholic father tries to raise the money to buy a communion dress for his seven-year-old daughter.

A realistic drama about working-class lives, absorbing, richly detailed and welcome as one of the few British films of recent years to concern itself with contemporary, everyday life and its problems.

w Jim Allen d Ken Loach ph Barry Ackroyd m Stewart Copeland pd Martin Johnson ed Jonathan Morris

☆ Bruce Jones, Julie Brown, Gemma Phoenix, Ricky Tomlinson, Tom Hickey, Mike Fallon, Ronnie Ravey, Lee Brennan

'The film contains more truth and humor than many a large-screen picture, and is sure to captivate audiences who seek it out.' – Variety

The Rainmaker: see *John Grisham's The Rainmaker (1997)*

The Rainmaker

US   1956   121m   Technicolor   Vistavision

Paramount/Hal B. Wallis (Paul Nathan)

🎞 ⊚ 🎧

In 1913 Kansas, a fake rainmaker has more success melting the heart of a confirmed spinster.

Such a whimsical play is too talky to make a good movie, especially as the actors are over-age, their performances are mannered, the dialogue seems interminable and the production is too stagey.

w N. Richard Nash play N. Richard Nash d Joseph Anthony ph Charles Lang Jnr m Alex North

☆ Katharine Hepburn, Burt Lancaster, Wendell Corey, Lloyd Bridges, Earl Holliman, Cameron Prud'homme, Wallace Ford

🎵 Alex North; Katharine Hepburn

The Rainmakers

US   1935   79m   bw

RKO

Fake rainmakers are chased by midwestern farmers to California, where they get involved in an irrigation scheme.

Slow-paced comedy with a train chase finale which comes too late.

w Grant Garrett, Leslie Goodwins d Fred Guiol

☆ Bert Wheeler, Robert Woolsey, Dorothy Lee, Berton Churchill, George Meeker

'May appeal mildly to their fans, but won't make new business.' – Variety

The Rains Came ***

US   1939   103m   bw

TCF (Harry Joe Brown)

High-class parasites in India during the Raj redeem themselves when a flood disaster strikes.

Wholly absorbing disaster spectacular in which the characterization and personal plot development are at least as interesting as the spectacle, and all are encased in a glowingly professional production.

w Philip Dunne, Julien Josephson novel Louis Bromfield d Clarence Brown ph Arthur Miller m Alfred Newman ed Barbara McLean sp Fred Sersen

☆ Myrna Loy, George Brent, Tyrone Power, Brenda Joyce, Maria Ouspenskaya, Joseph Schildkraut, H. B. Warner, Nigel Bruce, Mary Nash, Jane Darwell, Marjorie Rambeau, Henry Travers

'A big box-office picture with the advantage of a new locale.' – Variety

'It would be difficult to improve on the direction, the outbreak of the monsoon, a curtain billowing in the breeze, a lamp casting the shadow of lattice work against white silk, servants scattering for cover…' – Charles Higham, 1972

'Slick Hollywood film-making at its professional best.' – Channel 4, 1982

† Myrna Loy was third choice after Dietrich and Lamarr; Brent second choice after Ronald Colman.

🎵 Alfred Newman; editing

The Rains of Ranchipur

US   1955   104m   Eastmancolor   Cinemascope

TCF (Frank Ross)

Dismal remake of *The Rains Came*, with bored actors and inferior production, all the character of the original being wiped out by badly processed wide-screen spectacle.

w Merle Miller d Jean Negulesco ph Milton Krasner m Hugo Friedhofer

☆ Lana Turner, Fred MacMurray, Richard Burton, Joan Caulfield, Eugenie Leontovich, Michael Rennie

Raintree County

US   1957   166m   Technicolor   Panavision (Camera 65)

MGM (David Lewis)

🎞 ⊚ 🎧

During the Civil War a Southern belle gets the man she thinks she wants, but subsequently finds life as a schoolmaster's wife boring.

Dreary attempt by MGM to out-do Gone with the Wind, with neither characters nor plot one third as interesting and the production values merely expensive.

w Millard Kaufman novel Ross Lockridge d Edward Dmytryk ph Robert Surtees m Johnny Green ad William A. Horning, Urie McCleary

☆ Montgomery Clift, Elizabeth Taylor, Eva Marie Saint, Nigel Patrick, Lee Marvin, Rod Taylor, Agnes Moorehead, Walter Abel, Jarma Lewis, Tom Drake, Gardner McKay, Rhys Williams

🎵 Johnny Green; Elizabeth Taylor; art direction

Raise Ravens *

Spain   1975   115m   colour

Elias Querejeta

📀 🎞

original title: *Cria Cuervos*

aka: *Cria!*

A woman remembers her life as a child, when she may have caused the death of her philandering father.

Elliptical story of childhood and of women trapped in a world dominated by men; it is never less than watchable, but its meaning, possibly obliquely political, remains obscure.

wd Carlos Saura ph Teo Escamilla m Federico Mompoli ad Rafael Palmero ed Pablo G. del Amo

☆ Geraldine Chaplin, Monica Randall, Florinda Chico, Ana Torrent, Conchi Perez, Maite Sanchez, Josefina Diaz, German Cobos, Hector Alterio, Mirta Miller

'Saura has succeeded in conjuring up, with many nice touches, a picture of childhood which is finely balanced between reality and sentimentality.' – John Pym, MFB

† The film won the Special Jury Prize at the 1976 Cannes Film Festival.

'China, 1920's. One master, four wives … One fate.'

Raise the Red Lantern **

Hong Kong   1991   125m   Eastmancolor

Palace/Era/China Film (Chiu Fu-Sheng)

📀 🎞 ⊚ 🎧

original title: *Dahong Denglong Gaogao Gua*

A young woman, who has become the fourth wife of a rich merchant, finds herself in competition with his other wives for her husband's favour.

Cool study of sexual politics and the subjugation of women.

w Ni Zhen story Su Tong d Zhang Yimou ph Zhao Fei m Zhao Jiping ad Cao Jiuping, Dong Huamiao ed Du Yuan

☆ Gong Li, Ma Jingwu, He Caifei, Cao Cuifeng, Jin Shuyuan, Kong Li, Ding Weimin, Cui Zhigang, Chu Xiao

🎵 best foreign film

🏆 best foreign film

Raise the Roof

GB   1930   77m   bw

BIP

An actress is bribed to sabotage a touring show.

Early talkie which retains surprising freshness.

w Walter Summers, Philip MacDonald d Walter Summers

☆ Betty Balfour, Maurice Evans, Jack Raine, Sam Livesey, Ellis Jeffreys

† Credited as the first British musical.

Raise the Titanic!

US   1980   122m   DeLuxe

Lord Grade/Martin Starger (William Frye)

📀 🎞

Assorted Americans try to recover rare minerals from the wreck of the ship which sank in the North Atlantic in 1912.

Heavy-going exploiter with little action and even less plot.

w Adam Kennedy, Eric Hughes novel Clive Cussler d Jerry Jameson ph Matthew F. Leonetti m John Barry pd John F. DeCuir second unit ph Rex Metz underwater ph Bob Steadman

☆ Jason Robards, Richard Jordan, Alec Guinness, David Selby, Anne Archer, J. D. Cannon

'Hits new depths hitherto unexplored by the worst of Lew Grade's overloaded ark melodramas. This one wastes a potentially intriguing premise with dull scripting, a lacklustre cast, laughably phony trick work and clunky direction that makes *Voyage of the Damned* seem inspired by comparison.' – Variety

'The longer it all goes on, the more one hopes that, if they ever do raise the *Titanic*, they'll heave the film overboard to replace it.' – Guardian

† The film cost 40 million dollars and took 7 million.

A Raisin in the Sun *

US   1961   128m   bw

Columbia/Paman – Doris (David Susskind, Philip Rose)

📀 🎞

The life of a struggling black family in a cramped Chicago flat.

Earnest but claustrophobic play-on-film which long outstays its welcome but contains good performances.

w Lorraine Hansberry play Lorraine Hansberry d Daniel Petrie ph Charles Lawton Jnr m Laurence Rosenthal

☆ Sidney Poitier, Ruby Dee, Claudia McNeil, Diana Sands, Ivan Dixon, John Fiedler, Lou Gossett

Raising a Riot

GB   1955   90m   Technicolor

British Lion/Wessex (Ian Dalrymple, Hugh Perceval)

With his wife away, a naval officer tries to cope with his three lively children while staying with his elderly father in a derelict windmill.

Sentimental domestic comedy that goes for easy laughs and misses most of them.

w Ian Dalrymple, Hugh Perceval novel Alfred Toombs d Wendy Toye ph Christopher Challis m Bruce Montgomery md Muir Mathieson ad Joseph Bato ed Albert Rule

☆ Kenneth More, Shelagh Fraser, Ronald Squire, Olga Lindo, Jan Miller, Nora Nicholson, Lionel Murton, Mandy, Gary Billings, Fusty Bentine, Robin Brown

Raising Arizona *

US   1987   94m   DuArt

Circle Films/TCF

📀 🎞 ⊚ 🎧

In the American heartlands, a petty crook falls for the lady cop who regularly checks him into jail.

Zany collection of incidents which scarcely welds itself into a story but offers a few laughs along the way.

w Ethan and Joel Coen d Joel Coen ph Barry Sonnenfeld m Carter Burwell

☆ Nicolas Cage, Holly Hunter, Trey Wilson, John Goodman, William Forsythe

'When Jenny cheated on her husband, he didn't just leave … he split.'

Raising Cain

US   1992   92m   colour

UIP/Universal (Gale Anne Hurd)

📀 🎞 ⊚ 🎧

A psychologist develops multiple personalities, including that of a murderous twin brother.

Risible thriller, stuffed full of shock moments that hamper the narrative flow, and growing increasingly ridiculous throughout; it fails to repay its huge debt to Peeping Tom and to Hitchcock.

wd Brian de Palma ph Stephen H. Burum m Pino Donaggio pd Doug Kraner ed Paul Hirsch, Bonnie Koehler, Robert Dalva

☆ John Lithgow, Lolita Davidovich, Steven Bauer, Frances Sternhagen, Gregg Henry, Tom Bower, Mel Harris, Teri Austin, Gabrielle Carteris

'Scandalously prodigal with its loose ends and red herrings, and scandalously unfair with its narrative let-outs.' – Sight and Sound

'A superficial, often risible, exercise in pure aesthetics that's likely to turn off mainstream audiences, spelling a fast flop.' – Variety

Raising the Wind

🎬🎬 GB   1961   91m   colour

GHW/Anglo Amalgamated (Peter Rogers)

US title: *Roommates*

Misadventures of students at a music academy.

A Carry On in all but name, from the same stable; good moments among the dross.

w Bruce Montgomery d Gerald Thomas ph Alan Hume m Bruce Montgomery

☆ James Robertson Justice, Leslie Phillips, Kenneth Williams, Sidney James, Paul Massie, Liz Fraser, Eric Barker, Jennifer Jayne, Geoffrey Keen, Esma Cannon

The Rake's Progress *

GB   1945   123m   bw

GFD/Individual (Frank Launder, Sidney Gilliat)

US title: *Notorious Gentleman*

The career of a cheerful ne'er-do-well playboy of the thirties.

The road to ruin played for light comedy, with silly endpapers in which, quite out of character, the rake becomes a war hero. Generally good production, witty script.

w Frank Launder, Sidney Gilliat story Val Valentine d Sidney Gilliat ph Wilkie Cooper m William Alwyn pd David Rawnsley

☆ Rex Harrison, Lilli Palmer, Margaret Johnston, Godfrey Tearle, Griffith Jones, Guy Middleton, Jean Kent, Marie Lohr, Garry Marsh, David Horne, Alan Wheatley

'Bright, witty and finished.' – Richard Winnington

† In the American version Harrison crowned the Martyrs' Memorial not with a chamber pot but with a top hat.

Rally Round the Flag Boys

US   1958   106m   DeLuxe   Cinemascope
TCF (Leo McCarey)
▣

A small community protests at the siting nearby of a missile base.

Raucous service and sex comedy which becomes frenetic without ever being very funny.

w Claude Binyon, Leo McCarey *novel* Max Shulman *d* Leo McCarey *ph* Leon Shamroy *m* Cyril Mockridge

☆ Paul Newman, Joanne Woodward, Joan Collins, Jack Carson, Dwayne Hickman, Tuesday Weld, Gale Gordon, Murvyn Vye

'She has been quite promiscuous since early childhood. She has absolutely no control over her sexual impulses. Miss Rosebud has arrived!'

Rambling Rose ★★

US   1991   112m   DuArt/DeLuxe
Guild/Carolco (Renny Harlin)
▣   ▤   ⌖   ⊚   ⌒

During the Depression, a boy becomes infatuated with a sexually-free young woman who comes to work at his home.

Gripping domestic drama that gains from its period setting.

w Calder Willingham *novel* Calder Willingham *d* Martha Coolidge *ph* Johnny E. Jensen *m* Elmer Bernstein *pd* John Vallone *ed* Steven Cohen

☆ Laura Dern, Robert Duvall, Diane Ladd, Lukas Haas, John Heard, Kevin Conway, Robert Burke, Lisa Jakub, Evan Lockwood, Matt Sutherland

'A quiet, unassertive picture, very literary in the memories it evokes, full of universal insights into family life, and performed with delicacy by all concerned.' – *Philip French, Guardian*

⌑ Laura Dern; Diane Ladd

Rambo: First Blood Part Two

US   1985   92m   Technicolor   Panavision
Anabasis Investments NV/Buzz Feitshans
▣   ▤   ⌖   ⊚   ⌒

A special ops veteran is sent to spring POWs in Vietnam.

Absurdly overwrought comic strip action which shamefully once again caught the mood of America at the time of its release.

w Sylvester Stallone, James Cameron *d* George Pan Cosmatos *ph* Jack Cardiff *m* Jerry Goldsmith

☆ Sylvester Stallone, Richard Crenna, Charles Napier, Julia Nickson, Steven Berkoff

'One mounting fireball … risible production, comic book heroics.' – *Variety*

Rambo III

US   1988   101m   Technicolor
Columbia TriStar/Carolco (Buzz Feitshans)
▣   ▤   ⌖   ⊚   ⌒

Rambo invades Afghanistan to rescue a friend captured by the Soviet forces.

More ludicrously melodramatic heroics, with Stallone as a one-man army defeating the massed forces of the enemy.

w Sylvester Stallone, Sheldon Lettich *d* Peter MacDonald *ph* John Stanier *m* Jerry Goldsmith *pd* Bill Kenney *ed* James Symons, Andrew London, O. Nicholas Brown, Edward Warschilka

☆ Sylvester Stallone, Richard Crenna, Marc de Jonge, Kurtwood Smith, Spiros Focas, Sasson Gabai

† Russel Mulcahy began directing the film but left after a few days. It was the most expensive film made to that date, costing in excess of $60 million.

Ramona

US   1936   90m   Technicolor
TCF (Sol M. Wurtzel)

A half-breed girl and an Indian chief's son combat the greed of white pioneers.

Old-fashioned, stuffy adventure romance, much filmed in silent days.

w Lamar Trotti *novel* Helen Hunt Jackson *d* Henry King *ph* William Skall, Chester Lyons *m* Alfred Newman

☆ Loretta Young, Don Ameche, Kent Taylor, Pauline Frederick, Jane Darwell, Katherine de Mille, Victor Kilian, John Carradine

Rampage

US   1963   98m   Technicolor
Warner Seven Arts/Talbot (William Fadiman)

Two white hunters love the same girl; one releases a tiger to harm the other, but it escapes.

Silly, unconvincing, old-style melodrama in which even the animals seem to overact.

w Robert Holt, Marguerite Roberts *novel* Alan Caillou *d* Phil Karlson *ph* Harold Lipstein *m* Elmer Bernstein

☆ Robert Mitchum, Jack Hawkins, Elsa Martinelli, Sabu, Emile Genest

The Ramparts We Watch ★

US   1940   87m   bw
RKO/Louis de Rochemont

A typical American family exemplifies the need for military preparedness.

A feature acted by amateurs, produced by the March of Time unit; interesting rather than influential, as it still took Pearl Harbor to bring the Americans into the war.

w Robert Richards, Cedric B. Worth *d* Louis de Rochemont

'It enters the fray with frankness in its favour.' – *Variety*

'A woman is soft and warm … and deadlier than steel!'

Ramrod

US   1947   94m   bw
(MGM) Enterprise (Harry Sherman)
▤

A predatory lady ranch owner hires a tough foreman and her ruthlessness causes several deaths and a stampede.

Ho-hum minor Western with fading stars.

w Jack Moffitt, Graham Baker, Cecile Kramer *story* Luke Short *d* André de Toth *ph* Russell Harlan *m* Adolph Deutsch *pd* Lionel Banks *ed* Sherman A. Rose

☆ Veronica Lake, Joel McCrea, Preston Foster, Charles Ruggles, Donald Crisp, Arleen Whelan, Lloyd Bridges

Ran ★★★★

Japan   1985   161m   colour
Herald-Ace/Nippon-Herald/Greenwich (Masato Hara, Serge Silberman)
▣   ▤   ⌖   ⊚   ⌒

A Japanese version of *King Lear*, with three sons instead of three daughters.

Predictable bloodshed and tremendous style are evident in this oriental epic from a master hand at the age of 75.

w Akira Kurosawa, Hideo Oguni, Masato Ide *d* Akira Kurosawa *ph* Takao Saito *m* Toru Takemitsu

☆ Tatsuya Nakadai, Satoshi Terao, Jinpachi Nezu, Daisuke Ryu

'Prepare to be astonished … a towering achievement in any language.' – *People*

⬘ costumes (Emi Wada)
⌑ direction, photography, art direction
▥ best foreign film

Rancho De Luxe

US   1974   95m   DeLuxe
UA/EK (Anthony Ray)
▤   ⌒

Cheerful cattle rustlers go on a binge and end up in prison.

Modern anti-everything Western; it's anti-entertainment as well.

w Thomas McGuane *d* Frank Perry *ph* William A. Fraker *m* Jimmy Buffett

☆ Sam Waterston, Jeff Bridges, Elizabeth Ashley, Charlene Dallas, Clifton James, Slim Pickens

'Where anything goes … for a price!'

Rancho Notorious

US   1952   89m   Technicolor
RKO/Fidelity (Howard Welsch)
▣   ▤

A cowboy seeking revenge for his girlfriend's murder follows a clue to a lonely ranch run by a saloon singer.

Curious Western which seems to have been intended as another Destry Rides Again but is made in a hard inflexible style which prevents it from appealing.

w Daniel Taradash *d* Fritz Lang *ph* Hal Mohr *m* Hugo Friedhofer *md* Emil Newman

☆ Marlene Dietrich, Arthur Kennedy, Mel Ferrer, Gloria Henry, William Frawley, Jack Elam

'Every luxury you might ask of a western is in lavish supply – except entertainment value.' – *Alton Cook*

'Those In The Know, Know.'

Rancid Aluminium

GB   2000   91m   colour   Super 35
Entertainment/Fiction Factory (James Hawes, Mike Parker, Mike Thomas)

When his close friend inherits the family business, an envious accountant decides to take over the company with the financial aid of Russian gangsters.

Rancid it is, so bad that it won't even become a cult movie.

w James Hawes *d* Ed Thomas *ph* Tony Imi *m* John Hardy *pd* Hayden Pearce *ed* Chris Lawrence

☆ Joseph Fiennes, Rhys Ifans, Tara Fitzgerald, Sadie Frost, Steven Berkoff, Keith Allen, Dani Behr, Andrew Howard, Nick Moran, Barry Foster

'A stupid, unfunny and self-satisfied film that should be avoided at all costs.' – *Cosmo Landesman, Sunday Times*

'By universal consent, it is the worst film ever made in the UK. People who have seen it belong to an exclusive club. They cannot speak about the film, they simply shudder at its mention.' – *Jacques Peretti, Guardian*

The Randolph Family: see *Dear Octopus*

Random Harvest ★★★

US   1942   126m   bw
MGM (Sidney Franklin)
▤   ⌒

A shell-shocked officer in the 1914–18 war escapes from an asylum, marries a music hall singer and is idyllically happy until a shock makes him remember that he is the head of a noble family. His wife, whom he does not now remember, dutifully becomes his secretary and years later another shock brings memory and happiness back.

A silly enough story works remarkably well in this rather splendid, no holds barred, roses round the door romance in Hollywood's best style with incomparable stars. A triumph of the Peg's Paper syndrome, and hugely enjoyable because it is done so enthusiastically.

w Claudine West, George Froeschel, Arthur Wimperis *novel* James Hilton *d* Mervyn Le Roy *ph* Joseph Ruttenberg *m* Herbert Stothart *ad* Cedric Gibbons, Randall Duell

☆ Ronald Colman, Greer Garson, Susan Peters, Philip Dorn, Reginald Owen, Henry Travers, Margaret Wycherly, Bramwell Fletcher, Arthur Margetson

'I would like to recommend this film to those who can stay interested in Ronald Colman's amnesia for two hours and who could with pleasure eat a bowl of Yardley's shaving soap for breakfast.' – *James Agee*

'A strangely empty film … its characters are creatures of fortune, not partisans in determining their own fates.' – *Bosley Crowther, New York Times*

'It is cast with pearly players in every part. Its pedigreed plot is savoured with just the right mixture of ups and downs, ecstasy and well-bred anguish, implausibility and psyche. And it moves towards its climax with the measured tread and nicely timed emotional bumps of a Hearst Cosmopolitan serial. It is perhaps the clearest example of the year of how a studio possessing lion's shares of movie-making capital and ingratiating talent can mate these two to synthesize a magnificent neuter, which will predictably bring in vast box office returns with which to produce more neuters.' – *John McManus, PM*

⌑ best picture; script; Mervyn Le Roy; Herbert Stothart; Ronald Colman; Susan Peters; art direction

'In a perfect world, they never would have met.'

Random Hearts

US   1999   133m   DeLuxe
Columbia/Rastar/Mirage (Sydney Pollack, Marykay Powell)
▣   ⊚   ⌒

When his wife is killed in a plane crash, a cop discovers that she was with her lover, and goes to meet the widow of the man with whom she was having an affair.

Run-of-the-mill romance of an odd couple, thrown together by chance; it is difficult to summon up much interest in their doings.

w Kurt Luedtke, Darryl Ponicsan *novel* Warren Adler *d* Sydney Pollack *ph* Philippe Rousselot

m Dave Grusin *pd* Barbara Ling *ed* William Steinkamp

☆ Harrison Ford, Kristin Scott Thomas, Charles S. Dutton, Bonnie Hunt, Dennis Haysbert, Sydney Pollack, Richard Jenkins, Paul Guilfoyle, Susanna Thompson, Peter Coyote, Dylan Baker

'An ideal rainy day matinee attraction for well-to-do ladies of a certain age.' – *Todd McCarthy, Variety*

'Dismal.' – *Times*

Randy Rides Alone

US   1934   53m   bw
Monogram/Lone Star (Paul Malvern)

An undercover agent unmasks a murdering outlaw, who is disguised as a dumb storekeeper, Matt the Mute. He also gets the girl.

Quickie Western with some of the trappings of a detective story, including secret hiding places and a portrait whose eyes move.

w Lindsley Parsons *d* Harry Fraser *ph* Archie Stout *ed* Carl Pierson

☆ John Wayne, Alberta Vaughn, George Hayes, Yakima Canutt, Earl Dwire

Rangers of Fortune

US   1940   79m   bw
Paramount (Dale Van Every)

Three amiable gun-runners clean up a south-west town.

Good reliable Western with star appeal.

w Frank Butler *d* Sam Wood

☆ Fred MacMurray, Albert Dekker, Gilbert Roland, Patricia Morison, Joseph Schildkraut, Dick Foran, Betty Brewer

Rango

US   1931   70m   bw
Paramount

An old man and a boy in Sumatra go about their business of killing tigers.

Faded semi-documentary by the man who was about to direct King Kong.

wd Ernest B. Schoedsack

☆ Claude King, Douglas Scott

Rangoon: see *Beyond Rangoon*

'He faced a decision that someday may be yours to make!'

Ransom ★

US   1955   104m   bw
MGM (Nicholas Nayfack)

A rich man takes desperate measures to rescue his son from a kidnapper.

Solid but overlong suspenser, virtually a vehicle for a star at his twitchiest and most dogged.

w Cyril Hume, Richard Maibaum *d* Alex Segal *ph* Arthur E. Arling *m* Jeff Alexander

☆ Glenn Ford, Donna Reed, Leslie Nielsen, Juano Hernandez, Robert Keith

Ransom ★

GB   1975   98m   Eastmancolor
Lion International (Peter Rawley)
⌒

aka: *The Terrorists*

A British ambassador to Scandinavia is kidnapped by terrorists and a Norwegian security chief gives chase.

Topical but unconvincing action thriller with unfamiliar detail; builds up to exciting sequences but is quickly forgotten.

w Paul Wheeler *d* Caspar Wrede *ph* Sven Nykvist *m* Jerry Goldsmith

☆ Sean Connery, Ian McShane, Norman Bristow, John Cording, Isabel Dean, William Fox, Robert Harris

'Someone Is Going To Pay.'

Ransom ★

US   1996   120m   Technicolor
Buena Vista/Touchstone (Brian Grazer, Scott Rudin, B. Kipling Hagopian)
▣   ▤   ⌖   ⊚   ⌒

Realizing that his kidnapped son is unlikely to be returned to him alive, a millionaire offers the ransom money as a reward for the capture of the criminals.

A moderately tense psychological thriller, competently made but only passably interesting.

w Richard Price *story* Alexander Ignon *d* Ron Howard *ph* Piotr Sobocinski *m* James Horner *pd* Michael Corenblith *ed* Dan Hanley, Michael Hill

☆ Mel Gibson, Rene Russo, Gary Sinise, Delroy Lindo, Lili Taylor, Liev Schreiber, Evan Handler, Donnie Wahlberg, Dan Hedaya

'A crackerjack thriller with some unusually tasty plot twists.' – *Todd McCarthy, Variety*
'Watchable, made with a highly professional gloss, has a decent performance from a major star, and is pretty forgettable.' – *Derek Malcolm, Guardian*

† It is a remake of the 1956 film written by Cyril Hume and Richard Maibum, starring Glenn Ford, Donna Reed and Leslie Nielsen, and directed by Alex Segal, who had previously directed it as a TV play.

Rapa Nui *
US   1994   107m   Technicolor   Panavision
Entertainment/Majestic/Tig/Newcomm (Kevin Costner, Jim Wilson)

🔲 ▤ ℚ ∩

In the 1680s, on what was later known as Easter Island, antagonism between warring clans and the island's two classes – nobles and labourers – flares during a dangerous annual race in which young men swim through shark-infested waters to bring back an egg from a nearby island.
Unconvincing, exotic epic which dithers between being a conventional love story and a conventional ecological fable; it looks splendid but is let down by its often banal dialogue and varying styles of acting.
w Tim Rose Price, Kevin Reynolds *d* Kevin Reynolds *ph* Stephen Windon *m* Stewart Copeland *pd* George Liddle *ed* Peter Boyle
☆ Jason Scott Lee, Esai Morales, Sandrine Holt, George Henare, Zac Wallace, Nathaniel Lees, Eru Potaka-Dewes, Pete Smith, Rawiri Paratene

'Looks very much like an act of cinematic folly, a wacky anthropological adventure staged on a grand scale and filmed in obviously difficult and inhospitable circumstances. It's more of a guilty pleasure than a satisfying movie experience.' – *Variety*
'Almost no movie last year was more unintentionally funny, nor more wrongheaded.' – *Stephen Rebello, Movieline*

† The movie, despite its lack of expensive stars, cost more than $20m. Filming on the remote Easter Island was, said Kevin Reynolds, 'a nightmare'.

The Rape of Malaya: see *A Town Like Alice*

Rapid Fire
US   1992   95m   DeLuxe
TCF (Robert Lawrence)

🔲 ▤ ℚ ∩

After a Chinese college student is witness to a mob murder he has no alternative but to help the FBI bust two international drugs rings.
Cliché-ridden action movie whose only point of interest is that it stars Bruce Lee's son, although he has yet to acquire his father's charisma.
w Alan McElroy *story* Cindy Cirile, Alan McElroy *d* Dwight H. Little *ph* Ric Waite *m* Christopher Young *pd* Ron Foreman *ed* Gib Jaffe
☆ Brandon Lee, Powers Boothe, Nick Mancuso, Raymond J. Barry, Kate Hodge, Tzi Ma, Tony Longo, Michael Paul Chan, Dustin Nguyen

'A clumsily plotted, clumsily choreographed and clumsily acted attempt at combining a hard-nosed cop thriller with an old-fashioned martial arts fable.' – *Geoffrey Macnab, Sight and Sound*

Rapture
US/France   1965   104m   bw
International Classics/TCF (Christian Ferry)
A mentally unstable girl has a tragic romance with a fugitive murderer.
Gloomy all the way, and if it's art it needs explaining.
w Stanley Mann *novel* Rapture in My Rags by Phyllis Hastings *d* John Guillermin *ph* Marcel Grignon
☆ Patricia Gozzi, Dean Stockwell, Melvyn Douglas, Gunnel Lindblom

The Rapture **
US   1991   100m   DeLuxe
Electric/New Line/Wechsler/Tenenbaum/Parker

🔲 ▤ ℚ

Tiring of her empty and promiscuous life, a telephone operator turns to fundamentalist religion and, claiming she has received a message from

God, heads for the desert with her young daughter to await the Second Coming.
A clever and thought-provoking movie which overturns expectations – the apparently mad and neurotic turn out to be right in their predictions – but finally seems to side with an individual's right to justice at all costs.
wd Michael Tolkin *ph* Bojan Bazelli *m* Thomas Newman *pd* Robert Standefer *ed* Suzanne Fenn
☆ Mimi Rogers, David Duchovny, Patrick Bauchau, Kimberly Cullum, Terri Hanauer, Dick Anthony Williams, James Le Gros

'The film is long on empathy, short on insight.' – *Philip French, Observer*
'A complex and intellectual horror story tackling a thorny subject in a manner simply guaranteed to offend almost everyone at some point.' – *Kim Newman, Empire*

The Rare Breed
US   1966   97m   Technicolor   Panavision
Universal (William Alland)

▤

An English bull is taken by its woman owner to St Louis to breed with American longhorns, and various frictions are caused among the ranchers.
Amusing Western idea which misses fire by not coming down firmly as either drama or comedy; it does however pass the time amiably enough.
w Ric Hardman *d* Andrew V. McLaglen *ph* William H. Clothier *m* Johnny Williams
☆ James Stewart, Maureen O'Hara, Brian Keith, Juliet Mills, Don Galloway, David Brian, Jack Elam, Ben Johnson

Rascals
US   1938   77m   bw
TCF
A rich young man and a girl suffering from amnesia join a gypsy troupe.
Absurdly cast and plotted semi-musical with a certain liveliness to keep it going.
w Robert Ellis, Helen Logan *d* H. Bruce Humberstone
☆ Jane Withers, Borrah Minevitch and his Rascals, Robert Wilcox, Rochelle Hudson, Steffi Duna

'In the main amusing and entertaining.' – *Variety*

Rashomon ****
Japan   1951   83m   bw
Daiei (Jingo Minoura)

🔲 ▤ ℚ ∩

aka: *In the Woods*
In medieval Japan, four people have different versions of a violent incident when a bandit attacks a nobleman in the forest.
Indescribably vivid in itself, and genuinely strange (one of the versions is told by a ghost), Rashomon reintroduced Japanese films to the world market and was remade (badly) in Hollywood as The Outrage.
wd Akira Kurosawa *story* Inside a Bush by Ryunosuke Akutagawa *ph* Kazuo Matsuyama *m* Takashi Matsuyama *ad* H. Motsumoto
☆ Toshiro Mifune, Machiko Kyo, Masayuki Mori, Takashi Shimura

'A masterpiece, and a revelation.' – *Gavin Lambert, MFB*

🏆 best foreign film
👑 art direction

Raskolnikov *
Germany   1923   80m   bw   silent
Neumann (Robert Wiene)
A student kills a pawnbroker and is hounded by a police inspector until he confesses.
Interesting adaptation of Crime and Punishment with some of the expressionist aspects of the same director's The Cabinet of Dr Caligari.
wd Robert Wiene *ph* Willy Godberger *ad* Andre Andreyev
☆ Gregory Khmara, Michael Tarkhanov, Pavel Pavlov, Vera Toma

Rasputin: see *Agony*

Rasputin and the Empress *
US   1932   133m   bw
MGM (Irving Thalberg)

GB title: *Rasputin the Mad Monk*
The story of the last years of the Russian court, when a sinister monk gained influence over the empress.
An unhappy film which was besieged by lawsuits and never generated much drama of its own despite starring

the three Barrymores, who all seemed to be acting in separate rooms. *Production values are the most impressive thing about it.*
w Charles MacArthur *d* Richard Boleslawski *ph* William Daniels *m* Herbert Stothart *ad* Cedric Gibbons, Alexander Toluboff *ed* Tom Held
☆ John Barrymore, Ethel Barrymore, Lionel Barrymore, Diana Wynyard, Ralph Morgan, C. Henry Gordon, Edward Arnold, Jean Parker, Gustav von Seyffertitz, Anne Shirley

† The lawsuit was by Prince Youssoupoff (portrayed as Chegodieff), who claimed that although he did kill Rasputin his wife was never raped. He was awarded one million dollars.
👑 Charles MacArthur

Rasputin the Mad Monk: see *Rasputin and the Empress (1932)*

Rasputin the Mad Monk
GB   1966   92m   DeLuxe   CinemaScope
Warner-Pathé/Hammer/7 Arts (Anthony Nelson-Keys)

🔲

A recapitulation of well-known events with fictional trimmings.
Dreary excuse for its star to go berserk.
w John Elder *d* Don Sharp *ph* Michael Reed *m* Don Banks *pd* Bernard Robinson *ed* James Needs, Roy Hyde
☆ Christopher Lee, Barbara Shelley, Richard Pasco, Francis Matthews, Renee Asherson

The Rat *
GB   1937   72m   bw
Herbert Wilcox/Imperator
A Parisian thief takes the blame for murder, but is saved by the socialite who loves him.
Rather smart talkie version of a well-worn theatrical hit, previously filmed in 1925 as a silent, with Ivor Novello as star.
w Hans Rameau, Marjorie Gaffney, Miles Malleson and Romney Brent *play* Ivor Novello, Constance Collier *d* Jack Raymond
☆ Anton Walbrook, Ruth Chatterton, Rene Ray, Beatrix Lehmann, Felix Aylmer, Mary Clare

Le Rat des Villes et le Rat des Champs **
France   1927   14m   bw
Tobis Klangfilm

🔲

A country rat visits Paris and finds life too hectic for his rural tastes.
Witty exercise in stop-motion animation, brilliantly done for its time and notable for its ballet danced by two rats.
wd Ladislaw Starewicz *m* Georges Tzipine *ad* Jacques Natanson

† The film has been released on video with the feature-length *The Tale of the Fox* (qv) and four other shorts under the title *Ladislaw Starewicz: Selected Films.*

The Rat Race *
US   1960   105m   Technicolor
Paramount/Perlberg-Seaton
A young jazz musician and a dance hall hostess share a flat and face the adversities of New York.
A kind of sour fairy tale of the big city which has neither enough jokes nor enough incident but purveys the kind of charm that grows on one despite oneself.
w Garson Kanin *play* Garson Kanin *d* Robert Mulligan *ph* Robert Burks *m* Elmer Bernstein
☆ Tony Curtis, Debbie Reynolds, Jack Oakie, Kay Medford, Don Rickles

'The New Yorkers of *The Rat Race* – noisy soft-hearted landlady, philosophical bartender, backchatting taxi driver – are as familiar as the settings of shabby apartment house and quiet little bar across the street. Film makers no longer need to invent here – they simply move in for a few weeks.' – *Penelope Houston*

Ratboy
👥👥   US   1986   104m   Technicolor
Warner/Malpaso

▤

A half-rodent alien gets the anticipated rough treatment when he visits Earth.
Clint Eastwood's favourite co-star was given leave to make the film of her choice, but the choice is inexplicable in the wake of so many other E.T. imitations.

w Rob Thompson *d* Sondra Locke *ph* Bruce Surtees *m* Lennie Niehaus
☆ Sondra Locke, Robert Townsend, Christopher Hewett, Larry Hankin

Ratcatcher **
GB/France   1999   93m   colour
Pathé (Gavin Emerson)
In 1970s Glasgow, a boy feels guilty about causing the death of a friend by drowning, and dreams of moving from his tenement slum to a new housing estate on the edge of the city.
Glum drama of family life enlivened by a lyrical visual approach.
wd Lynne Ramsay *ph* Alwin Küchler *m* Rachel Portman *pd* Jane Morton *ed* Lucia Zucchetti
☆ William Eadie, Tommy Flanagan, Mandy Matthews, Michelle Stewart, Lynne Ramsay Jnr, Leanne Mullen, John Miller, Jackie Quinn

'A must-see: a wonderful film from a brilliant director.' – *Peter Bradshaw, Guardian*
🎖 Lynne Ramsay (best newcomer)

Rationing
US   1943   93m   bw
MGM (Orville Dull)
A small-town shopkeeper is frustrated by wartime restrictions.
Amiable comedy for established stars.
w William Lipman, Grant Garrett, Harry Ruskin *d* Willis Goldbeck
☆ Wallace Beery, Marjorie Main, Donald Meek, Howard Freeman, Connie Gilchrist

Raton Pass
US   1951   84m   bw
Warner (Saul Elkins)
GB title: *Canyon Pass*
A greedy wife swindles her husband out of his share in their ranch.
Unusual Western melodrama; quite entertaining.
w Tom Blackburn, James Webb *d* Edwin L. Marin *ph* Wilfred M. Cline *m* Max Steiner
☆ Dennis Morgan, Patricia Neal, Steve Cochran, Scott Forbes, Dorothy Hart

Rattle of a Simple Man
GB   1964   95m   bw
Sydney Box (William Gell)

🔲

A shy football supporter in London spends the night with a tart for a bet.
Archetypal farcical situation with sentiment added to string it out to twice its proper length. Production values modest but adequate.
w Charles Dyer *play* Charles Dyer *d* Muriel Box *ph* Reg Wyer *m* Stanley Black
☆ Harry H. Corbett, Diane Cilento, Thora Hird, Charles Dyer

The Raven: see *Le Corbeau (1943)*

The Raven *
US   1935   61m   bw
Universal

🔲 ▤ ℚ

A doctor obsessed by Poe-inspired torture devices transforms a gangster on the run into a hideous mutant.
Silly but quite effective horror film with memorable sequences.
w David Boehm *d* Lew Landers *ph* Charles Stumar *md* Gilbert Kurland
☆ Bela Lugosi, Boris Karloff, Samuel S. Hinds, Irene Ware, Lester Matthews

'Maintains Universal's high batting average with the shockers … should come through with nice grosses.' – *Variety*

The Raven *
US   1963   86m   Pathécolor   Panavision
AIP/Alta Vista (Roger Corman)

▤ ℚ

Two 15th-century conjurors fight a deadly duel of magic.
The rather splendid duel is a long time coming; the preliminaries are largely confined to chat in a single set, and the random jokes do not quite atone for the boredom.
w Richard Matheson *d* Roger Corman *ph* Floyd Crosby *m* Les Baxter
☆ Vincent Price, Peter Lorre, Boris Karloff, Hazel Court, Jack Nicholson

'Edgar Allan Poe might turn over in his grave at this nonsensical adaptation of his immortal poem, but audiences will find the spooky goings-on a cornpop of considerable comedic dimensions.' – *Variety*

Ravenous

US   1999   100m   DeLuxe   'Scope
TCF/Fox 2000/ (Adam Fields, David Heyman)
▦ 🎧

In the mid-19th century, an isolated army outpost is commanded by a cannibal who initiates others in the addictive eating of human flesh.
Grisly drama that veers between black comedy and horror while remaining an unappetizing stew.
w Ted Griffin d Antonia Bird ph Anthony B. Richmond m Michael Nyman, Damon Albarn pd Bryce Perrin ed Neil Farrell
☆ Guy Pearce, Robert Carlyle, Jeremy Davies, Jeffrey Jones, John Spencer, Stephen Spinella, Neal McDonough, David Arquette
'A bigger mystery than anything in the plot is why fine actors like Guy Pearce and Robert Carlyle chose this shoddy vehicle as a showcase.' – *Stephen Farber, Movieline*
† Directors Milcho Manchevski and Raja Gosnell both worked on the film before Antonia Bird became involved.

Raw Courage

US   1984   90m   colour
Adams Apple/Sandy Howard (Ronny Cox, Robert L. Rosen)
aka: *Courage*
Three long-distance runners are attacked by a fanatical group of would-be soldiers in the New Mexican desert.
A land-locked, brain-dead variation on Deliverance, notably short on thrills.
w Ronny Cox, Mary Cox d Robert L. Rosen ph F. Pershing Flynn m Johnny Harris pd Don Nunley ed Steven Polivka
☆ Ronny Cox, Art Hindle, M. Emmet Walsh, Tim Maier, Lois Chiles, William Russ, Lisa Sutton

Raw Deal

US   1948   78m   bw
Reliance/Eagle Lion
A convict is helped by his girlfriend to escape, and the police chase them across country.
Fairly violent crime melodrama which holds the attention.
w Leopold Atlas, John C. Higgins d Anthony Mann
☆ Dennis O'Keefe, Claire Trevor, Marsha Hunt, John Ireland, Raymond Burr

Raw Deal

US   1986   106m   Technicolor   JDC Wide Screen
De Laurentiis/International (Martha Schumacher)
▦ ▦ ◎ ◉ ◎ 🎧
An ex-FBI man is recruited to infiltrate Chicago's biggest mob.
Violent crime hokum with momentary amusements.
w Gary M. DeVore, Norman Wexler d John Irvin ph Alex Thomson m Cinemascore
☆ Arnold Schwarzenegger, Kathryn Harrold, Sam Wanamaker, Paul Shenar, Ed Lauter, Darren McGavin, Joe Regalbuto
'Comic book crime meller suffers from an irredeemable script' – *Variety*

Raw Edge

US   1956   76m   Technicolor
Universal-International (Albert Zugsmith)
A rancher's workers plan to kill him.
Tense, fairly adult Western.
w Harry Essex, Robert Hill d John Sherwood ph Maury Gertsman ad Alexander Golitzen
☆ Rory Calhoun, Yvonne de Carlo, Mara Corday, Rex Reason, Neville Brand

Raw Meat: see *Death Line*

Raw Wind in Eden

US   1958   93m   Eastmancolor   Cinemascope
U-I (William Alland)
A model is stranded on a Sardinian island, and falls in love with a mysterious American who turns out to be a disillusioned millionaire.
Wish-fulfilment woman's picture with the occasional relief of a smart line.
w Elizabeth and Richard Wilson d Richard Wilson ph Enzo Serafin m Hans Salter

☆ Esther Williams, Jeff Chandler, Carlos Thompson, Rossana Podesta, Eduardo de Filippo, Rik Battaglia

Rawhead Rex

US   1987   86m   colour
Empire/Alpine/Paradise/Green Man (Kevin Attew, Don Hawkins)
▦ ◎
In Ireland a farmer unwittingly releases a primitive demon, which immediately goes on the rampage.
Ineffectual, low-budget horror.
w Clive Barker d George Pavlou ph John Metcalfe ad Lee Huntingford ed Andy Horvitch
☆ David Dukes, Kelly Piper, Ronan Wilmot, Niall Toibin, Heinrich von Schellendoft, Niall O'Brian

Rawhide **

US   1950   86m   bw
TCF (Samuel G. Engel)
TV title: *Desperate Siege*
Four escaped convicts terrorize a stagecoach stop.
Good suspense Western with excellent technical credits.
w Dudley Nichols d Henry Hathaway ph Milton Krasner m Sol Kaplan
☆ Tyrone Power, Susan Hayward, Hugh Marlowe, Jack Elam, Dean Jagger, George Tobias, Edgar Buchanan, Jeff Corey

The Rawhide Years

US   1956   85m   Technicolor
Universal International (Stanley Rubin)
A poor but honest riverboat gambler clears himself of a murder charge with the aid of a con man.
Run-of-the-mill but amiable-enough Western, with Curtis more convincing as a card sharp than as a cowboy.
w Earl Felton, Robert Presnell Jnr, D. D. Beauchamp novel Norman A. Fox d Rudolph Maté ph Irving Glassberg m Frank Skinner, Hans J. Salter md Joseph Gershenson ad Alexander Golitzen, Richard H. Riedel ed Russell Schoengarth
☆ Tony Curtis, Colleen Miller, Arthur Kennedy, William Demarest, William Gargan, Peter Van Eyck, Minor Watson, Donald Randolph, Robert Wilke

Le Rayon Vert: see *The Green Ray*

Razorback

Australia   1984   95m   colour   Panavision
UAA/Western (Hal McElroy)
▦ ◎
In a small outback town a man is tried for the murder of his grandson, actually carried off by a wild boar.
Grim images of Australian life pepper this cross between Jaws and the dingo baby case. Not, as they say, for the squeamish.
w Everett de Roche novel Peter Brennan d Russell Mulcahy ph Dean Semler m Iva Davies pd Bryce Walmsley ed William Anderson
☆ Gregory Harrison, Arkie Whiteley, Bill Kerr, Chris Haywood

'Between love and hatred there is a line as sharp as a razor's edge!'

The Razor's Edge *

US   1946   146m   bw
TCF (Darryl F. Zanuck)
▦ ▦ ◎ 🎧
A well-to-do young man spends the years between the wars first idling, then looking for essential truth.
The novel was an empty parable with amusing trimmings. In the film the trimmings seem less amusing, but the presentation is glossy.
w Lamar Trotti novel W. Somerset Maugham d Edmund Goulding ph Arthur Miller m Alfred Newman ad Richard Day, Nathan Juran
☆ Tyrone Power, Gene Tierney, Clifton Webb, Herbert Marshall, John Payne, Anne Baxter, Lucile Watson, Frank Latimore, Elsa Lanchester, Fritz Kortner
'I like Somerset Maugham when he's looking through keyholes or down cracks, not at vistas.' – *Richard Winnington*
'Almost as irresistibly funny and terrible as The Fountainhead.' – *Pauline Kael, 70s*
† Maugham has a different source for his title, in the shape of an Oriental proverb, probably invented: 'The sharp edge of a razor is difficult to

pass over; thus the wise say that the path to salvation is hard.'
🎭 Anne Baxter
♟ best picture; Clifton Webb; art direction

The Razor's Edge

US   1984   128m   colour
Columbia (Robert P. Marucci, Harry Benn)
▦ ◎
An unlikely remake which came into being because the star persuaded the studio to do it, then failed in his attempt to convey the necessary spirituality. As for the rest, the time is out of joint (except for Denholm Elliott).
w John Byrum, Bill Murray d John Byrum ph Peter Hannan m Jack Nitzsche pd Philip Harrison ed Peter Boyle
☆ Bill Murray, Denholm Elliott, Theresa Russell, Catherine Hicks, James Keach, Peter Vaughan, Faith Brook

Reach for Glory *

GB   1962   86m   bw
Columbia/Blazer (John Kohn, Jud Kinberg)
During World War II, evacuee boys play war games and a German refugee is accidentally killed.
Grim and unpalatable parable, competently rather than excitingly made.
w John Rae novel The Custard Boys by John Rae d Philip Leacock ph Bob Huke m Bob Russell
☆ Kay Walsh, Harry Andrews, Michael Anderson Jnr, Oliver Grimm, Alexis Kanner, Martin Tomlinson, Richard Vernon

Reach for the Sky *

👪 GB   1956   135m   bw
Rank/Pinnacle (Daniel M. Angel)
▦ ▦ ◎
Douglas Bader loses both legs in a 1931 air crash, learns to walk on artificial limbs and flies again in World War II.
Box-office exploitation of one man's personal heroism, adequately but not inspiringly put together with many stiff upper lips and much jocular humour.
wd Lewis Gilbert book Paul Brickhill ph Jack Asher m John Addison
☆ Kenneth More, Muriel Pavlow, Lyndon Brook, Lee Patterson, Alexander Knox, Dorothy Alison, Sydney Tafler, Howard Marion Crawford
'It is least successful in what should be exciting action.' – *Dilys Powell*
🏆 best British film

Reaching for the Moon

US   1931   90m   bw
United Artists (Douglas Fairbanks)
▦
On a transatlantic liner, a new cocktail has a sensational effect on a mild-mannered hero.
Very flimsy comedy with songs and some athletic stunts for its hero.
wd Edmund Goulding ph Ray June song Irving Berlin
☆ Douglas Fairbanks, Bebe Daniels, Edward Everett Horton, Claud Allister, Jack Mulhall, Bing Crosby
'Not a smash entry, but should do moderately and perhaps a little better than that.' – *Variety*

'You'll love them as much as they love each other!'

Reaching for the Sun

US   1941   90m   bw
Paramount
A clam digger who needs an outboard motor goes to work in a Detroit car plant.
Easygoing comedy, too muted to recommend itself widely.
w W. L. River novel Wessel Smitter d William Wellman
☆ Joel McCrea, Ellen Drew, Eddie Bracken, Albert Dekker

'Sing! Swing! Youth Has Its Fling!'

Ready, Willing and Able

US   1937   93m   bw
Warner (Samuel Bischoff)
Two songwriters import an English leading lady for their new show.
Lightweight star musical with no outstanding qualities except a number in which girls dance on the keys of a huge typewriter.
w Sig Herzig, Jerry Wald, Warren Duff d Ray Enright ph Sol Polito ch Bobby Connolly songs Johnny Mercer, Richard Whiting

☆ Ruby Keeler, Ross Alexander, Lee Dixon, Wini Shaw, Jane Wyman, Allen Jenkins
'Too many numbers and a slow script.' – *Variety*
♟ Bobby Connolly

The Real Blonde *

US   1997   105m   colour
Paramount/Lakeshore (Marcus Viscidi, Tom Rosenberg)
▦ ▦ ◉
Two struggling actors in troubled relationships make good at work and home.
Enjoyable satire on such easy targets as fashion photographers and TV soap opera stars.
wd Tom DiCillo m Frank Prinzi m Jim Farmer pd Christopher A. Nowak ed Camilla Toniolo
☆ Matthew Modine, Catherine Keener, Daryl Hannah, Maxwell Caulfield, Elizabeth Berkley, Marlo Thomas, Bridgette Wilson
'Winds up a cartoonish satire on a cartoonish world – form and content in perfect unison.' – *Xan Brooks, Sight and Sound*

Real Genius

US   1985   104m   Metrocolor   Panavision
TriStar/Delphi III (Brian Grazer)
A 15-year-old scientific prodigy joins a think-tank of whizz kids who are being unwittingly exploited by the military.
Slickly directed youth movie that abandons any seriousness in favour of anarchic slapstick comedy; its message appears to be that too much intelligence is bad for you.
w Neal Israel, Pat Proft, Peter Torokvei d Martha Coolidge ph Vilmos Zsigmond m Thomas Newman pd Josan F. Russo ed Richard Chew
☆ Val Kilmer, Gabe Jarret, Michelle Meyrink, William Atherton, Patti D'Arbanville, Robert Prescott

'Always outnumbered! Never outfought!'
'One of the most stunning dramas of love and courage ever brought to the screen!'

The Real Glory *

US   1939   96m   bw
Samuel Goldwyn
▦
Soldiers of fortune help the American Army to quell a terrorist uprising in the Philippines just after the Spanish-American War.
Well made Gunga Dinnery.
w Jo Swerling, Robert R. Presnell d Henry Hathaway ph Rudolph Maté m Alfred Newman ad James Basevi
☆ Gary Cooper, David Niven, Broderick Crawford, Andrea Leeds, Reginald Owen, Kay Johnson, Russell Hicks, Vladimir Sokoloff
'Moro uprisings, guerrilla warfare, cholera epidemics, and fancy exhibitions of inhuman cruelty are the frame against which an innocuous melodramatic yarn is told.' – *Variety*
'The same sort of picture as Gunga Din.' – *Richard Mallett, Punch*
'Recommended to adolescents of all ages.' – *New Statesman*
'In times like these, we question the wisdom of rattling the bones in Yankee imperialism's closet.' – *Daily Worker*

The Real Howard Spitz *

👪 GB/Canada   1997   101m   colour
The Mob/Metrodome/Images/TMN (Paul Brooks, Christopher Zimmer)
A child-hating author finds success when he writes a book about a cow detective with the aid of a young girl in search of her father.
Pleasant children's film with a light, comic touch.
w Jurgen Wolff d William Jean ph Glen Macpherson m David A. Hughes, John Murphy pd Chris Townsend ed Pia Di Ciaula
☆ Kelsey Grammer, Amanda Donohoe, Joseph Rutten, Patrick McKenna, Genevieve Tessier, Kay Tremblay
'A worthy small-scale alternative to summer heavyweights.' – *Empire*

Real Life *

US   1979   99m   colour
Paramount (Penelope Spheeris)
▦
A self-centred film-maker moves in with an average family in order to make a documentary about them.

Clever satire on a certain style of television programme, but the joke is over-stretched.

w Albert Brooks, Monica Johnson, Harry Shearer d Albert Brooks ph Eric Saarinen m Mort Lindsay ad Linda Marder, Linda Spheeris ed David Finfer

☆ Albert Brooks, Charles Grodin, Frances Lee McCain, J. A. Preston, Matthew Tobin, Jennings Lang

Real Life

GB 1983 92m colour
Entertainment/The Real Life Partnership (Mike Dinseen)

An estate agent's assistant with a vivid imagination becomes involved in thefts.

Clumsy, witless comedy which quickly bores.

w Francis Megahy, Bernie Cooper d Francis Megahy ph Peter Jessop m David Mindel pd John White ed Peter Delfgou

☆ Rupert Everett, Cristina Raines, Norman Beaton, Warren Clarke, Isla Blair, James Faulkner

'Try as one may to look sympathetically on this brand of independent British venture, the resolute lack of wit or style wipes the indulgent smile from one's lips early on, and it never returns.' – Guardian

'She's the only one who can break into a bank that holds $18m, but it's not for the money.'

The Real McCoy

US 1993 101m Technicolor
Capella (Martin Bregman, Willi Baer, Michael S. Bregman)

A reluctant cat burglar is forced to rob a bank by a gangster who kidnaps her young son.

There is nothing original here, merely a competent director and cast going through familiar routines with moderate enthusiasm.

w William Davies, William Osborne d Russell Mulcahy ph Denis Crossan m Brad Fiedel pd Kim Colefax ed Peter Honess

☆ Kim Basinger, Val Kilmer, Terence Stamp, Gailard Sartain, Zach English, Raynor Scheine

'Provides scant suspense, and the final bank job doesn't blaze any trails for anyone who's seen caper movies. Similarly, the payoff may satisfy the undemanding, but most viewers will have seen it coming a mile off.' – Variety

Real Men

US 1987 96m Metrocolor
United Artists (Martin Bregman)

An unpredictable CIA agent recruits a timid insurance clerk to deliver a message to friendly aliens while rival agents attempt to kill them both.

Dim though frenetic comedy that provides nothing but tedium.

wd Dennis Feldman ph John A. Alonzo m Miles Goodman ad William J. Cassidy, James Allen ed Malcolm Campbell, Glenn Farr

☆ James Belushi, John Ritter, Barbara Barrie, Bill Morey, Isa Andersen, Gale Barle, Mark Herrier

'A Comedy About Love In The '90s.'

Reality Bites *

US 1994 99m colour
Universal/Jersey (Danny DeVito, Michael Shamberg)

Four friends, newly graduated, try to survive in the real world in Houston; one makes a video documentary of their lives and becomes emotionally involved with another, an articulate rock musician, and with an ambitious TV executive.

Up-to-the-minute details of life among the recently 20, but so timely in its references it already seems old-fashioned; its love story is very familiar, though it may seem new to the recently adult.

w Helen Childress d Ben Stiller ph Emmanuel Lubezki m Karl Wallinger pd Sharon Seymour ed Lisa Churgin

☆ Winona Ryder, Ethan Hawke, Ben Stiller, Janeane Garofalo, Steve Zahn, Swoosie Kurtz, Joe Don Baker, John Mahoney, Harry O'Reilly, Barry Sherman

'Patchy stuff at the best of times and irritatingly off-the-wall at its worst. Reality only occasionally bites, and then with none too sharp teeth.' – Derek Malcolm, Guardian

'The old, old love triangle tangle, dressed by Gap and styled by MTV.' – Angie Errigo, Empire

'Death is just the beginning!'

Re-Animator

US 1985 86m DeLuxe
Entertainment/Empire International (Brian Yuzna)

When a crazy scientist brings people back to life, they come back violent.

Gross and grisly horror comic which amused some critics.

w Dennis Paoli, William J. Norris, Stuart Gordon story Herbert West – Re-animator by H. P. Lovecraft d Stuart Gordon ph Mac Ahlberg, Stephen Sealy m Richard Band ad R. A. Burns, Charles Nixon ed Lee Percy

☆ Jeffrey Combs, Bruce Abbott, Barbara Crampton, David Gale

'For those with a strong sense of humour, and a stomach stronger still.' – Sunday Times

'A cheap smell of excess.' – Observer

Re-Animator 2

US 1989 96m colour
Medusa/Wildstreet (Paul White, Keith Walley, Hidetaka Konno)

aka: Bride of Re-Animator

A scientist, building himself a woman from spare parts, is attacked by the re-animated remnants of his previous experiments.

The mixture much as before, and gaining nothing from the repetition.

w Woody Keith, Rick Fry story H. P. Lovecraft d Brian Yuzna ph Rick Fichter m Richard Band pd Philip J. C. Duffin ed Peter Teschner

☆ Bruce Abbott, Claude Earl Jones, Fabiana Udenio, David Gale, Kathleen Kinmont, Jeffrey Combs, Mel Stewart, Michael Strasser, Irene Forrest

'Yet another example of a sequel that is content to rehash all the ingredients of the first film without ever gelling in the way that made the original work.' – MFB

'Man against terrifying monster – in the most spectacular underwater scenes ever filmed!'

Reap the Wild Wind **

US 1942 124m Technicolor
Paramount/Cecil B. de Mille

Seafaring salvage engineers fight over a Southern belle.

Georgia-set period adventure; intended as another Gone with the Wind, it simply doesn't have the necessary, but on its level it entertains solidly, climaxing with the famous giant squid fight.

w Alan le May, Jesse Lasky Jnr, Charles Bennett d Cecil B. de Mille ph Victor Milner, Dewey Wrigley, William V. Skall m Victor Young ad Hans Dreier, Roland Anderson

☆ Ray Milland, John Wayne, Paulette Goddard, Raymond Massey, Robert Preston, Lynne Overman, Susan Hayward, Charles Bickford, Walter Hampden, Louise Beavers, Martha O'Driscoll, Hedda Hopper

'The essence of all his experience, the apogee of all his art, and as jamfull a motion picture as has ever played two hours upon a screen.' – Howard Barnes, New York Herald Tribune

† The underwater scenes were filmed in the Santa Monica Pan Pacific Marine Museum, which had a pool 100 feet long and 50 feet wide. The 50-foot giant squid was operated by a 24-button electronic keyboard

& photography; art direction

Rear Window ****

US 1954 112m Technicolor
Paramount/Alfred Hitchcock

A news photographer, confined to his room by a broken leg, sees a murder committed in a room on the other side of the court.

Artificial but gripping suspense of an unusual kind; with such restricted settings, all depends on the script and the acting, and they generally come up trumps.

w John Michael Hayes novel Cornell Woolrich d Alfred Hitchcock ph Robert Burks m Franz Waxman

☆ James Stewart, Grace Kelly, Raymond Burr, Judith Evelyn, Wendell Corey, Thelma Ritter

& John Michael Hayes; Alfred Hitchcock; Robert Burks

A Reason to Live, a Reason to Die

(dubbed)
Italy/France/Spain 1972 96m colour Scope K-Tel/Sancrosiap-Terza/Europrodis/Atlantida/Corona (Michael Billingsley)

original title: Una Ragione per Vivere e Una per Morire

In the American Civil War, a Union colonel recruits seven desperadoes, all due to be executed, for a daring raid to recapture a Confederate fort.

An unexciting cut-rate variation on The Dirty Dozen.

w Tonino Valerii, Ernesto Gastaldi d Tonino Valerii ph Alejandro Ulloa m Riz Ortolani ed Franklin Boll

☆ James Coburn, Telly Savalas, Bud Spencer (Carlo Pedersoli), Ralph Goodwin, Joseph Mitchell, Robert Burton, William Spofford

'A colourless, perfunctory gloss on a text that the director and scriptwriters might assume their audiences to know by heart.' – MFB

† The film was cut to 91m on its British release.

Rebecca ****

US 1940 130m bw
David O. Selznick

The naïve young second wife of a Cornish landowner is haunted by the image of his glamorous first wife Rebecca.

The supreme Hollywood entertainment package, set in Monte Carlo and Cornwall, with generous helpings of romance, comedy, suspense, melodrama and mystery, all indulged in by strongly-drawn characters, and directed by the English wizard from a novel which sold millions of copies. It really couldn't miss, and it didn't.

w Robert E. Sherwood, Joan Harrison novel Daphne du Maurier d Alfred Hitchcock ph George Barnes m Franz Waxman ad Lyle Wheeler ed Hal C. Kern

☆ Laurence Olivier, Joan Fontaine, George Sanders, Judith Anderson, Nigel Bruce, Gladys Cooper, Florence Bates, Reginald Denny, C. Aubrey Smith, Melville Cooper, Leo G. Carroll, Leonard Carey

NARRATOR: 'Last night I dreamed I went to Manderley again...'

FAVELL (GEORGE SANDERS) TO MRS DE WINTER: 'I say, marriage with Max is not exactly a bed of roses, is it?'

MRS DANVERS (JUDITH ANDERSON): 'You're overwrought, madam. I've opened a window for you. A little air will do you good. Why don't you go? Why don't you leave Manderley? He doesn't need you. He's got his memories. He doesn't love you – he wants to be alone again with her. You've nothing to stay for. You've nothing to live for, have you, really? Look down there. It's easy, isn't it? Why don't you? Go on, go on. Don't be afraid...'

MAXIM (LAURENCE OLIVIER): 'You thought I loved Rebecca? You thought that? I hated her. Oh, I was carried away by her – enchanted by her, as everyone was – and when I was married, I was told I was the luckiest man in the world. She was so lovely, so accomplished, so amusing. "She's got the three things that really matter in a wife," everyone said, "breeding, brains and beauty." And I believed them completely. But I never had a moment's happiness with her. She was incapable of love, or tenderness, or decency.'

'A carefully considered trying out of the superior technical resources at Hitchcock's disposal.' – George Perry, 1965

'Hitchcock fans will have to put up with a surprising lack of the characteristic Hitchcock improvisations in the way of salty minor personages and humorous interludes, and satisfy themselves with a masterly exhibition of the Hitchcock skill in creating suspense and shock with his action and his camera.' – National Board of Review

'Riveting and painful – a tale of fear and guilt, class and power.' – Time Out, 1988

'Hitch kept me off balance, much to his own delight ... he would constantly tell me that no one thought I was very good except himself.' – Joan Fontaine

† Original casting thoughts, all rejected, were Ronald Colman, William Powell and Leslie Howard for Maxim; Anne Baxter, Margaret Sullavan, Loretta Young, Vivien Leigh and Olivia de Havilland (for the second Mrs de Winter).

🏆 best picture; George Barnes

& script; Alfred Hitchcock; Franz Waxman; Laurence Olivier; Joan Fontaine; Judith Anderson; Lyle Wheeler; Hal C. Kern

Rebecca of Sunnybrook Farm

US 1932 75m bw
Fox

A rural glad girl wins over her dour aunt and reforms an atheist.

Routine sound remake of the children's classic in a 1921 silent version in which Mary Pickford starred.

w S. N. Behrman, Sonya Levien novel Kate Douglas Wiggin and Charlotte Thompson d Alfred Santell

☆ Marian Nixon, Ralph Bellamy, Mae Marsh, Louise Closser Hale, Alan Hale, Charlotte Henry

Rebecca of Sunnybrook Farm

US 1938 80m bw
TCF (Raymond Griffith)

A child performer becomes a pawn in the fight to exploit her talents on radio.

Unrecognizable revamping of a famous story makes a very thin star vehicle.

w Karl Tunberg, Don Ettlinger novel Kate Douglas Wiggin and Charlotte Thompson d Allan Dwan ph Arthur Miller m Arthur Lange songs various

☆ Shirley Temple, Randolph Scott, Jack Haley, Gloria Stuart, Phyllis Brooks, Helen Westley, Slim Summerville, Bill Robinson

'More fitting title would be Rebecca of Radio City ... a weak story, indifferently directed and acted.' – Variety

Rebecca's Daughters *

GB/Germany 1991 97m colour
Mayfair/Palace/Rebecca's Daughters/Astralma Erste Filmproduktions/Delta/BBC Wales/British Screen (Chris Sievernich)

In the 19th century, Welsh farmers form gangs dressed in women's clothes to protest against unfair toll-gate charges imposed by the local aristocracy.

Ramshackle caper, ripely performed and occasionally amusing.

w Guy Jenkin, Karl Francis story based on a screenplay by Dylan Thomas d Karl Francis ph Russ Walker m Rachel Portman pd Ray Price ed Roy Sharman

☆ Peter O'Toole, Paul Rhys, Joely Richardson, Keith Allen, Simon Dormandy, Dafydd Hywel, Sue Roderick

'An irresistible period romp.' – Variety

Rebel

Australia 1985 89m colour
Village Roadshow (Phillip Emanuel)

In wartime Sydney, a singer shelters a deserter from the US Marines.

Dim romance, punctuated by some dull song and dance routines.

w Michael Jenkins, Bob Herbert play No Names, No Pack Drill by Bob Herbert d Michael Jenkins ph Peter James m Chris Neal m/ly Peter Best pd Brian Thomson ed Michael Honey

☆ Matt Dillon, Debbie Byrne, Bryan Brown, Bill Hunter, Ray Barrett, Julie Nihill

The Rebel *

GB 1960 105m Technicolor
Associated British (W. A. Whitaker)

US title: Call Me Genius

A suburban businessman goes to Paris to become an artist.

A kind of farcical The Moon and Sixpence, insufficiently well tailored to the requirements of a very specialized comic, but occasionally diverting none the less.

w Alan Simpson, Ray Galton d Robert Day ph Gilbert Taylor m Frank Cordell

☆ Tony Hancock, George Sanders, Paul Massie, Margit Saad, Grégoire Aslan, Dennis Price, Irene Handl, Mervyn Johns, Peter Bull, John Le Mesurier, Nanette Newman, Oliver Reed, John Wood

'The more prosaic the setting, the funnier Hancock seems; transplanted into a conventionally silly screen art world, he is submerged among the other grotesques.' – Penelope Houston

---

Rebel in Town
US   1956   78m   bw
Bel Air/UA
A bank robber accidentally kills a small boy and is hunted down by the father.
Surprisingly stark Western with no particular merit.
w Danny Arnold d Alfred Werker ph Gordon Avil m Les Baxter
☆ John Payne, John Smith, Ruth Roman, J. Carrol Naish, Ben Cooper

The Rebel Nun: see *Flavia the Heretic*

Rebel Rousers
US   1969   78m   colour
Paragon International (Martin B. Cohen)
An architect and his pregnant lover are terrorized by a gang of bikers in a small Arizona town.
Typical low-budget biker movie, lacking any originality but peopled by actors who went on to better films later.
w Abe Polsky, Michael Kars, Martin B. Cohen d Martin B. Cohen ph Leslie Kouvacs, Glen Smith m William Loose ed Thor Brooks
☆ Cameron Mitchell, Diane Ladd, Bruce Dern, Jack Nicholson, Harry Dean Stanton, Neil Burstyn, Lou Procopo, Earl Finn, Phil Carey

The Rebel Son
GB   1939   90m   bw
London Films Omnia (E. C. Molinier, Charles David)
A Tartar leader's son falls in love with the daughter of the opposing leader.
Resistible grafting of the Romeo and Juliet story into the barbarians of the Steppes, with much carousing and threatened violence surrounding a good central performance. It includes much footage from a 1936 French film, Taras Bulba, directed by Alexis Granowsky.
w Adrian Brunel story Gogol d Alexis Granowsky, Adrian Brunel ph Franz Planer, Bernard Browne
☆ Harry Baur, Patricia Roc, Roger Livesey, Anthony Bushell, Joan Gardner
'After half an hour the joke had gone on long enough and I left. A man in the audience was remarking slowly, with some of Dr Johnson's weight, "I am still wondering what the reason for the existence of this film can be".' – *Graham Greene, The Spectator*

'The bad boy from a good family!'
Rebel without a Cause **
US   1955   111m   Warnercolor   Cinemascope
Warner (David Weisbart)
The adolescent son of a well-to-do family gets into trouble with other kids and the police.
The first film to suggest that juvenile violence is not necessarily bred in the slums, this somewhat dreary melodrama also catapulted James Dean to stardom as the prototype fifties rebel.
w Stewart Stern story Nicholas Ray d Nicholas Ray ph Ernest Haller m Leonard Rosenman
☆ James Dean, Natalie Wood, Jim Backus, Sal Mineo, Ann Doran, Dennis Hopper
ŏ original story (Nicholas Ray); Natalie Wood; Sal Mineo

Rebound
US   1931   88m   bw
RKO-Pathé
A woman tries to forgive her husband when he is jilted by a girlfriend.
A sophisticated stage comedy presented with the minimum of alteration.
w Horace Jackson play Donald Ogden Stewart d E. H. Griffith
☆ Ina Claire, Robert Williams, Robert Ames, Myrna Loy, Hedda Hopper, Louise Closser Hale
'A splendidly made picture which will delight smart audiences.' – *Variety*

'The biggest musical show of the century, with a throbbing love story as exciting as its title!'
Reckless
US   1935   96m   bw
MGM (David O. Selznick)
A theatrical agent loves the glamorous star he represents, but she marries a drunken millionaire.
Remarkably flat backstage melodrama with music, based on the life of Libby Holman.
w P. J. Wolfson d Victor Fleming ph George Folsey md Edward Ward songs various

☆ Jean Harlow, William Powell, Franchot Tone, May Robson, Ted Healy, Nat Pendleton, Rosalind Russell, Henry Stephenson
'Several sets of dramatic premises are established and then permitted to wander aimlessly, making the 93 minutes seem much longer than that.' – *Variety*

Reckless Kelly
Australia   1993   94m   Eastmancolor
Panavision
Warner/Yahoo Serious
A modern Ned Kelly battles to save his home from bankers and greedy developers.
A rambling but enjoyable anti-British comedy.
wd Yahoo Serious, David Roach, Warwick Ross, Lulu Serious d Yahoo Serious ph Kevin Hayward m Tommy Tycho ed David Roach, Robert Gibson, Antony Gray
☆ Yahoo Serious, Melora Hardin, Alexei Sayle, Hugo Weaving, Tracy Mann, Kathleen Freeman
'Full of ideas and nonsense but short on genuine laughs and zest.' – *Variety*
† The British video release ran for 76m.

The Reckless Moment *
US   1949   82m   bw
Columbia (Walter Wanger)
A woman accidentally kills her daughter's would-be seducer, and is then trailed by a blackmailer.
Uninteresting melodrama electrified by Ophuls's direction, which might have been applied to something more worthwhile.
w Henry Garson, R. W. Soderborg novel The Blank Wall by Elizabeth Sanxay Holding d Max Ophuls ph Burnett Guffey m Hans Salter md Morris Stoloff
☆ Joan Bennett, James Mason, Geraldine Brooks, Henry O'Neill, Shepperd Strudwick
'Swift, sure narrative and solidly pleasurable detail.' – *Richard Winnington*

The Reckoning **
GB   1969   108m   Technicolor
Columbia/Ronald Shedlo (Hugh Perceval)
A tough London executive with a Liverpool-Irish background has a brutal streak and a self-destructive urge, but goes on narrowly averting misfortune.
Interesting melodrama of a man disgusted with both bourgeois and working-class values; slickly made and fast-moving.
w John McGrath novel The Harp That Once by Patrick Hall d Jack Gold ph Geoffrey Unsworth m Malcolm Arnold
☆ Nicol Williamson, Rachel Roberts, Paul Rogers, Zena Walker, Ann Bell, Gwen Nelson, J. G. Devlin

Recoil
GB   1953   79m   bw
Eros/Tempean (Robert S. Baker, Monty Berman)
A woman decides to track down the jewel thief who robbed and killed her father.
Mundane and clichéd thriller, full of implausibilities.
wd John Gilling ph Monty Berman m Stanley Black ad Wilfred Arnold ed Sid Hayers
☆ Kieron Moore, Elizabeth Sellars, Edward Underdown, John Horsley, Robert Raglan, Ethel O'Shea, Martin Benson, Tony Pelly, Michael Kelly

Recollections of the Yellow House
Portugal   1989   119m   colour
Invicta (João Pedro Bénard, Joaquim Pinto)
original title: *Recordações da Casa Amarela*
Life in a Lisbon boarding house, where a middle-aged voyeur and fetishist goes slowly mad.
Despite its billing as 'a Portuguese comedy', a drawn-out, downbeat movie that strives too hard for significance.
wd João César Monteiro ph José Antonio Loureiro m Schubert, Vivaldi ad Luis Monteiro ed Helena Alvez, Claudio Martinez
☆ Manuela de Freitas, João César Monteiro, Sabina Sacchi, Teresa Calado, Ruy Furtado, Henrique Viana, Luis Miguel Cintra

Recordações da Casa Amarela: see
Recollections of the Yellow House

The Red Badge of Courage **
US   1951   69m   bw
MGM (Gottfried Reinhardt)
A youth called up during the Civil War gets his first taste of battle.
Fresh, poetic, but dramatically unsatisfactory filming of a classic American novel. The story of its production is fascinatingly told in Picture, a book by Lillian Ross.
wd John Huston novel Stephen Crane ph Harold Rosson m Bronislau Kaper
☆ Audie Murphy, Bill Mauldin, Douglas Dick, Royal Dano, John Dierkes, Andy Devine, Arthur Hunnicutt

Red Ball Express
US   1952   83m   bw
U-I (Aaron Rosenberg)
A supply column runs from the Normandy beachhead to Patton's army on the outskirts of Paris.
Standard war adventure, not too convincingly mounted but providing the usual excitements.
w John Michael Hayes d Budd Boetticher ph Maury Gertsman
☆ Jeff Chandler, Sidney Poitier, Alex Nicol, Judith Braun, Hugh O'Brian, Jack Kelly, Jack Warden

The Red Balloon ****
France   1955   34m   Technicolor
Films Montsouris
A lonely boy finds a balloon which becomes his constant companion and finally lifts him to the skies.
Absorbing and quite perfectly timed fantasy, one of the great film shorts.
wd Albert Lamorisse ph Edmond Sechan m Maurice Le Roux
☆ Pascal Lamorisse
⬩ best original screenplay

The Red Baron: see *Von Richthofen and Brown*

The Red Beret
GB   1953   88m   Technicolor
Warwick (Irving Allen, Albert R. Broccoli)
US title: *Paratrooper*
In 1940, an American with a guilt complex joins the British paratroopers.
Routine war action flagwaver; good battle scenes, rubbish in between.
w Richard Maibaum, Frank Nugent book Hilary St George Saunders d Terence Young ph John Wilcox m John Addison
☆ Alan Ladd, Susan Stephen, Leo Genn, Harry Andrews, Donald Houston, Anthony Bushell, Patric Doonan, Stanley Baker, Lana Morris

Red Canyon
US   1949   82m   Technicolor
Universal (Leonard Goldstein)
A cowboy drifter sets out to corral a famous wild stallion.
Old-fashioned family Western.
w Maurice Geraghty novel Zane Grey d George Sherman ph Irving Glassberg m Walter Scharf
☆ Howard Duff, George Brent, Ann Blyth, Edgar Buchanan, John McIntire, Chill Wills, Jane Darwell, Lloyd Bridges

The Red Circle (dubbed) *
France/Italy   1970   102m   colour
Corona (Robert Dorfmann)
original title: *Le Cercle Rouge*
An ex-convict teams up with a criminal on the run and a former police marksman to steal jewels from a shop equipped with a high-tech security system.
Dark, grim thriller with downbeat ending, enlivened by the central set-piece of the robbery itself.
wd Jean-Pierre Melville ph Henri Decae m Eric de Marsan ad Theo Meurisse
☆ Alain Delon, André Bourvil, Gian Maria Volonte, Yves Montand, Paul Crauchet, François Périer

Red Corner
US   1997   122m   DeLuxe
MGM (Jon Avnet, Jordan Kerner, Charles B. Mulvehill, Rosalie Swedlin)
While trying to set up a television satellite deal in China, an American lawyer is framed for murder.

Unconvincing mix of courtroom thriller and action-man antics, despite its footage secretly shot in Beijing.
w Robert King d Jon Avnet ph Karl Walter Lindenlaub m Thomas Newman pd Richard Sylbert ed Peter E. Berger
☆ Richard Gere, Bai Ling, Bradley Whitford, Byron Mann, Peter Donat, Robert Stanton, Tsai Chin, James Hong
'A ludicrous but humourless anti-Chinese diatribe thriller … self important tosh.' – *Angie Errigo, Empire*

The Red Danube
US   1950   119m   bw
MGM (Carey Wilson)
In occupied Vienna, citizens are being returned to Russia against their will.
Tedious and silly Red-baiting cold war charade.
w Gina Kaus, Arthur Wimperis novel Vespers in Vienna by Bruce Marshall d George Sidney ph Charles Rosher m Miklos Rozsa ad Cedric Gibbons, Hans Peters
☆ Ethel Barrymore, Walter Pidgeon, Janet Leigh, Peter Lawford, Francis L. Sullivan, Angela Lansbury, Louis Calhern, Melville Cooper
ŏ art direction

Red Dawn
US   1984   114m   Metrocolor
MGM-UA/Valkyrie (Buzz Feitshans, Barry Beckerman)
Russians lead a violent invasion into Colorado and are wiped out by the locals.
Ludicrous and somewhat dangerous Cold War throwback with little entertainment value to commend it. Violent teenage nonsense.
w Kevin Reynolds, John Milius d John Milius ph Ric Waite m Basil Poledouris pd Jackson de Govia ed Thom Noble
☆ Patrick Swayze, C. Thomas Howell, Lea Thompson, Charlie Sheen, Darren Dalton, Jennifer Grey, Ben Johnson, Harry Dean Stanton, Ron O'Neal, Vladek Sheybal, Powers Boothe

The Red Desert *
Italy/France   1964   116m   Eastmancolor
Duemila/Federiz (Angelo Rizzoli)
original title: *Il Deserto Rosso*
A wife suffers from depression, and a brief affair with her husband's friend doesn't help.
Elongated character study, very talkative but rather decoratively designed with the same subtle use of colour in an urban landscape as was seen later in Blow Up.
w Michelangelo Antonioni, Tonino Guerra d Michelangelo Antonioni ph Carlo di Palma m Giovanni Chionetti
☆ Monica Vitti, Richard Harris, Carlos Chionetti
'The beauty is stationary, painterly; and the arresting image precisely arrests and retards the already moribund thrust of the film.' – *John Simon*
'Boredom in Ravenna, and it seeps into the viewer's bones.' – *Pauline Kael, New Yorker, 1984*

'He treated her rough – and she loved it!'
Red Dust ***
US   1932   86m   bw
MGM (Hunt Stromberg)
On a rubber plantation in Indo-China, the overseer is pursued by his engineer's bride but himself falls for a stranded prostitute.
Vigorous romantic melodrama with echoes of Rain; remade as Congo Maisie (1940) and Mogambo (1954).
w John Lee Mahin play Wilson Collison d Victor Fleming ph Harold Rosson
☆ Clark Gable, Jean Harlow, Mary Astor, Gene Raymond, Donald Crisp, Tully Marshall, Forrester Harvey
'Lots of pash, sex and undress … an exhib's delight and a cinch for fancy takings. Done so expertly it almost overcomes the basic script shortcomings.' – *Variety*
'Gable and Harlow have full play for their curiously similar sort of good-natured toughness.' – *Time*
† The Gable role was first announced for John Gilbert.
†† Scenes showing the shooting of Red Dust are included in Bombshell.

ᛐᛐ film suitable for family viewing　　ᗕ VHS video-cassette for the British PAL system　　ᗕ VHS video-cassette for the British PAL system in wide screen-format　　✿ Video cassette in a computer-colourised version　　◼ American NTSC video-cassette　　ꙩ Laser disc

'An Explosive Love Story'

Red Firecracker, Green Firecracker **

China/Hong Kong 1993 115m colour
Electric/Yung/Xi'an Studio/Beijing Salon (Çhan Chun-Keung, Yong Naiming)

original title: *Paoda Shuang Deng*

An artist begins an affair with a young woman who is also head of a thriving family business, making fireworks – but before he can marry her, he has to' compete in a firework contest with a rival suitor.
An enjoyably exotic story of romance and thwarted love, colourful and exciting and visually arresting.
w Da Ying *novel* Feng Jicai d He Ping ph Yang Lun m Zhao Jiping ad Qian Yunxiu ed Yuan Hong
☆ Ning Jing, Wu Gang, Zhao Xiaorui, Gao Yang, Xu Zhengyum, Zhao Liang
'A beguilingly mad tale of illicit passion and sacrifice.' – *Lizzie Francke, Guardian*

Red Garters **

US 1954 91m Technicolor
Paramount (Pat Duggan)

Various familiar types congregate in the Western town of Paradise Lost, and settle matters by the Code of the West.
Amusing Western musical spoof slightly deadened by its pretty but finally boring theatrically stylized scenery. Songs are catchy, performances good natured.
w Michael Fessier d George Marshall ph Arthur E. Arling m Joseph J. Lilley ad Hal Pereira, Roland Anderson songs Jay Livingston, Ray Evans
☆ Rosemary Clooney, Guy Mitchell, Gene Barry, Jack Carson, Pat Crowley, Cass Daley, Frank Faylen, Reginald Owen
'A musical of considerable freshness and gaiety.' – *MFB*
♬ art direction

Red Headed Woman *

US 1932 74m bw
MGM (Albert Lewin)

A shopgirl marries the boss but is rejected in his social circles.
Unconvincing but occasionally entertaining melodrama.
w Anita Loos *novel* Katharine Brush d Jack Conway ph Harold Rosson
☆ Jean Harlow, Chester Morris, Lewis Stone, Leila Hyams, Una Merkel, Henry Stephenson, Charles Boyer, May Robson
'Gingery treatment of a controversial subject that is bound to engage femme interest.' – *Variety*

Red Heat *

US 1988 104m Technicolor
Columbia TriStar/Carolco/Lone Wolf/Oak (Walter Hill, Gordon Carroll)

A Russian and a Chicago cop team up against an international gang of drug smugglers.
Fast-moving action movie, but one that offers only a minor variation on the standard plot of ill-assorted partners.
w Harry Kleiner, Walter Hill, Troy Kennedy Martin d Walter Hill ph Matthew F. Leonetti pd John Vallone ed Freeman Davies, Carmel Davies, Donn Aron
☆ Arnold Schwarzenegger, James Belushi, Peter Boyle, Ed O'Ross, Larry Fishburne, Gina Gershon, Richard Bright, J. W. Smith, Brent Jennings

The Red House *

US 1947 100m bw
(UA) Thalia (Sol Lesser)

A moody farmer's guilty obsession with an old house in the woods is that he murdered his parents in it.
Psycho-like suspense melodrama, too extended for comfort and too restricting for the actors, but effective in spurts.
wd Delmer Daves *novel* George Agnew Chamberlain ph Bert Glennon m Miklos Rozsa
☆ Edward G. Robinson, Judith Anderson, Lon McCallister, Allene Roberts, Rory Calhoun, Julie London, Ona Munson

The Red Inn *

France 1951 95m bw
Memnon

original title: *L'Auberge Rouge*

In 1833, stagecoach travellers stay at a remote inn, where the owners intend to rob and murder them.
Extreme black farce which manages to be pretty funny for those who can take this kind of thing: even the survivors of the night's massacre fall down a ravine.
w Jean Aurenche, Pierre Bost d Claude Autant-Lara ph André Bac m René Cloërc ad Max Douy
☆ Fernandel, Françoise Rosay, Carette, Grégoire Aslan

Red Kiss: see *Rouge Baiser*

The Red Light

US 1949 83m bw
UA/Pioneer (Roy Del Ruth)

An industrialist tracks down his brother's murderer.
Competent routine detection piece with engaging clues.
w George Callahan, Charles Grayson story This Guy Gideon by Donald Barry d Roy Del Ruth ph Bert Glennon m Dimitri Tiomkin ad F. Paul Syles ed Richard Heermance
☆ George Raft, Virginia Mayo, Raymond Burr, Gene Lockhart, Henry Morgan, Henry Arthur Franz, Barton MacLane, Ken Murray

Red Line 7000

US 1965 110m Technicolor
Paramount/Laurel (Howard Hawks)

The career and loves of a stock car racer.
Very routine romantic actioner full of the director's favourite situations but failing to find any fresh slant.
w George Kirgo d Howard Hawks ph Milton Krasner m Nelson Riddle
☆ James Caan, Laura Devon, Gail Hire, Charlene Holt, John Robert Crawford

Red Lips: see *Sadisterotica*

The Red Menace

US 1949 87m bw
Republic

GB title: *The Enemy Within*

A discontented war veteran is preyed on by communists.
An odd piece of anti-Red propaganda to come from an action studio, but it had some effect on thinking at the time.
w Albert DeMond, Gerald Geraghty d R. G. Springsteen ph John MacBurnie m Nathan Scott
☆ Robert Rockwell, Hanne Axman, Shepard Menken
'It waves the flag at the proper times and is an okay melodrama on other points.' – *Variety*
† The cast was deliberately chosen from unknowns.

Red Mountain

US 1951 84m Technicolor
Paramount/Hal B. Wallis

A Confederate captain joins Quantrell's Raiders but is horrified by their brutality.
Fast-moving action Western.
w John Meredyth Lucas, George W. George, George F. Slavin d William Dieterle ph Charles Lang Jnr m Franz Waxman
☆ Alan Ladd, Lizabeth Scott, Arthur Kennedy, John Ireland, Jeff Corey, James Bell

'The World Torn Asunder By A Threat From Outer Space!'

Red Planet Mars

US 1952 87m bw
UA/Donald Hyde, Anthony Veiller

Americans and Russians both tune in to Mars and learn that it is a powerful Christian planet; the news causes first panic, then a religious revival and a determination to live more harmoniously on Earth.
Lunatic farrago that has to be seen to be believed.
w Anthony Veiller, John L. Balderston d Harry Horner ph Joseph Biroc m Mahlon Merrick md David Chudnow ad Charles D. Hall
☆ Herbert Berghof, Peter Graves, Andrea King, Marvin Miller

The Red Pony

US 1949 88m Technicolor
Republic (Lewis Milestone)

When his pet pony dies after an illness, a farmer's son loses faith in his father.
Sincere but rather obvious little fable which although capably made does not make inspiring film drama.
w John Steinbeck d Lewis Milestone ph Tony Gaudio m Aaron Copland pd Nicolai Remisoff
☆ Myrna Loy, Robert Mitchum, Peter Miles, Louis Calhern, Shepperd Strudwick, Margaret Hamilton

Red River **

US 1948 133m bw
UA/Monterey (Howard Hawks)

How the Chisholm Trail was developed as a cattle drive.
Brawling Western, a bit serious and long drawn out but with splendid action sequences.
w Borden Chase, Charles Schnee d Howard Hawks ph Russell Harlan m Dimitri Tiomkin ed Christian Nyby
☆ John Wayne, Montgomery Clift, Joanne Dru, Walter Brennan, Coleen Gray, John Ireland, Noah Beery Jnr, Harry Carey Jnr
† It was remade as a TV film in 1988, directed by Richard Michaels and starring James Arness, Bruce Boxleitner and Gregory Harrison.
♬ original story (Borden Chase); editing

'Death is a $10,000 Bullet.'

Red Rock West *

US 1992 98m DeLuxe
Rank/Red Rock (Sigurjon Sighvatsson, Steve Golin)

A drifter who arrives in a small town is mistaken for a hitman and hired by both a husband and a wife to kill the other.
Enjoyable, blackly comic thriller with plenty of twists and turns.
w John Dahl, Rick Dahl d John Dahl ph Marc Reshovsky m William Olvis pd Robert Pearson ed Scott Chestnut
☆ Nicolas Cage, Lara Flynn Boyle, Dennis Hopper, J. T. Walsh, Craig Reay, Vance Johnson, Robert Apel
'Though it vaguely resembles a droll Buñuel construction, it owes much to the hard-boiled thrillers of the 1940s, albeit with a very large tongue-in-cheek quotient.' – *Variety*
'Very entertaining, doesn't detain you long, and has total confidence in its cinematic convictions.' – *Derek Malcolm, Guardian*

Red Salute *

US 1935 78m bw
Reliance (Edward Small)

aka: *Runaway Daughter*

GB title: *Arms and the Girl*

A college girl with communist leanings takes a cross country trip with an American soldier.
Odd little romantic comedy modelled on It Happened One Night; it was picketed for its inconsequential attitude to politics.
w Humphrey Pearson, Manuel Seff d Sidney Lanfield ph Robert Planck
☆ Barbara Stanwyck, Robert Young, Hardie Albright, Cliff Edwards, Ruth Donnelly, Gordon Jones, Henry Kolker
'Tepid comedy romance wrapped up in a preachment against campus agitators who oppose militarism.' – *Variety*

Red Scorpion

US 1989 102m DeLuxe
Shapiro Glickenhaus (Jack Abramoff)

A Russian agent's assignment is to assassinate the leader of a group of African terrorists.
Incompetent action movie that staggers from one dull moment to another with a complete lack of conviction.
w Arne Olsen d Joseph Zito ph João Fernandes m Jay Chattaway pd Ladislav Wilhelm ed Daniel Loewenthal sp John Evans; make-up: Tom Savini
☆ Dolph Lundgren, M. Emmet Walsh, Al White, T. P. McKenna, Carmen Argenziano, Alex Cohen, Brion James

Red Scorpion 2

US 1994 90m colour
August/Northwood (Robert Malcolm)

A government agent recruits an élite group of soliders to recover the legendary spear of destiny, which is in the possession of a neo-fascist businessman and his gang of violent skinheads.
Frenetic action film, drawing some of its inspiration from The Dirty Dozen, though it operates on a far lower level.
w Troy Bolotnick, Barry Victor d Michael Kennedy ph Curtis Petersen m George Blondheim pd Brent Thomas ed Gary Zubeck
☆ Matt McColm, John Savage, Jennifer Rubin, Michael Ironside, Michael Covert, Real Andrews, George Touliatos
'Contains almost non-stop fights, explosions, shooting and general mayhem, certainly enough to keep the action crowd moderately happy.' – *Variety*

The Red Shoes ****

GB 1948 136m Technicolor
GFD/The Archers (Michael Powell, Emeric Pressburger)

A girl student becomes a great ballet star but commits suicide when torn between love and her career.
Never was a better film made from such a penny plain story so unpersuasively written and performed; the splendour of the production is in the intimate view it gives of life backstage in the ballet world with its larger-than-life characters. The ballet excerpts are very fine, and the colour discreet; the whole film is charged with excitement.
wd Michael Powell, Emeric Pressburger ph Jack Cardiff m Brian Easdale pd Hein Heckroth ed Reginald Mills
☆ Anton Walbrook, Moira Shearer, Marius Goring, Robert Helpmann, Albert Basserman, Frederick Ashton, Leonide Massine, Ludmilla Tcherina, Esmond Knight
'In texture, like nothing the British cinema has ever seen.' – *Time Out, 1981*
🏆 Brian Easdale; Hein Heckroth
♬ best picture; original story (Michael Powell, Emeric Pressburger); editing

Red Skies of Montana

US 1952 99m Technicolor
TCF (Samuel G. Engel)

aka: *Smoke Jumpers*

Tension among firefighting crews in the mountains of Montana.
Adequate, routine action melodrama with semi-documentary touches.
w Harry Kleiner d Joseph M. Newman ph Charles G. Clarke m Sol Kaplan
☆ Richard Widmark, Jeffrey Hunter, Constance Smith, Richard Boone, Richard Crenna

'A man's desperation – a woman's passion – a boy's awakening – a girl's desire!'

Red Sky at Morning

US 1970 113m Technicolor
Universal/Hal Wallis

During World War II the family of an officer on active service find life in New Mexico not what they've been used to.
Peyton Place by any other name, well produced but of little real interest.
w Marguerite Roberts *novel* Richard Bradford d James Goldstone ph Vilmos Zsigmond m Billy Goldenberg
☆ Claire Bloom, Richard Thomas, Richard Crenna, Catherine Burns, Desi Arnaz Jnr, John Colicos, Harry Guardino

Red Sonja

US 1985 89m Metrocolor
MGM-UA/Thorn EMI (Christian Ferry)

In the times of sword and sorcery, Sonja avenges her sister's death and deposes an evil queen.
Absolute comic strip nonsense: even the monsters look mechanical.
w Clive Exton, George MacDonald Fraser stories Robert E. Howard d Richard Fleischer ph Giuseppe Rotunno m Ennio Morricone pd Danilo Donati ed Frank J. Urioste
☆ Brigitte Nielsen, Arnold Schwarzenegger, Sandahl Bergman, Paul Smith, Ronald Lacey

---

Red Sorghum ***

China   1987   92m   Eastmancolor
Palace/Xi'an Film Studio (Li Changqing)
📺 🔲

original title: *Hong Gaoliang*

A man recalls his grandparents' love affair and
violent times.

*Exuberant tragi-comic folk tale, told with immense
panache.*

w Chen Jianyu, Zhu Wei, Mo Yan d Zhang
Yimou ph Gu Changwei m Zhao Jiping ad Yang
Gang ed Du Yuan
☆ Gong Li, Jiang Wen, Teng Rujun, Liu Ji, Qian
Ming, Ji Chunhua, Zhai Chunhua

'A rough, proletarian belch of a film, a gleeful
assertion of peasant vitality, founded on amoral
(but fully justified) acts of transgression' – *Tony
Rayns, MFB*

The Red Squirrel **

Spain   1993   114m   colour
Sogetel (Ricardo Garcia Arrojo)
📺 🔍

original title: *La Ardilla Roja*

A suicidal rock musician invents a new identity as
her lover for a woman who crashes her motorcycle
and, as a result, apparently loses her memory.

*An intriguing playful comedy of identity and
commitment, memory and imagination, directed with a
light touch.*

wd Julio Medem ph Gonzalo Fernandez Berridi
m Alberto Iglesias ed Maria Elena Sainz de Rozas
☆ Emma Suarez, Nancho Novo, Maria Barranco,
Karra Elejalde, Carmelo Gomez, Cristina Marcos,
Monica Molina, Ana Gracia

'A pleasingly complex film – it's a love story, a
mystery, a comedy – which is an unnerving,
thought-provoking mix of the commonplace and
the surreal, the sinister and the comic.' – *Yvette
Huddleston, Empire*

Red Sun

France/Italy/Spain   1971   108m   Eastmancolor
Corona/Oceania/Balcazar (Robert Dorfman)
🔲 ⊘

In 1870 Arizona, an outlaw is forced to accompany
a Japanese samurai to recover a ceremonial sword
which his partner has stolen.

*Unusual but generally ineffective Western with a
fashionable international cast.*

w Laird Koenig, D. B. Petitclerc, W. Roberts, L.
Roman d Terence Young ph Henri Alekan
m Maurice Jarre
☆ Charles Bronson, Toshiro Mifune, Alain Delon,
Ursula Andress, Capucine

'A nice exotic item ruined by suburban
direction.' – *Sight and Sound*

Red Sundown

US   1956   81m   Technicolor
Universal-International (Albert Zugsmith)

A gunslinger becomes a deputy and tames a lawless
town.

Elementary Western action piece, not unentertaining.

w Martin Berkeley story *Black Trail* by Lewis B.
Patten d Jack Arnold ph William Snyder
m Hans J. Salter
☆ Rory Calhoun, Martha Hyer, Dean Jagger,
Robert Middleton, James Millican, Grant Williams

The Red Tent *

Italy/USSR   1970   121m   Technicolor
Paramount/Vides/Mosfilm (Franco Cristaldi)
🔲 🔍

The story of General Nobile's ill-fated 1928
expedition by dirigible to the Arctic.

*Stiffly-conceived international spectacular with one
striking sequence but not much good cheer.*

w Ennio de Concini, Richard Adams d Mikhail
Kalatozov ph Leonid Kalashnikov m Ennio
Morricone
☆ Peter Finch, Sean Connery, Hardy Kruger,
Claudia Cardinale, Mario Adorf, Massimo Girotti

Red Tomahawk

US   1967   80m   Technicolor
A. C. Lyles/Paramount

The small town of Deadwood is caught up in the
aftermath of Little Big Horn.

*Talkative Western filled with old faces, as is this
producer's wont.*

w Steve Fisher d R. G. Springsteen ph W.
Wallace Kelley m Jimmie Haskell

☆ Howard Keel, Joan Caulfield, Broderick
Crawford, Scott Brady, Wendell Corey, Richard
Arlen, Tom Drake

The Red Violin *

Canada/Italy   1998   130m   colour
Film4/New Line/Téléfilm Canada/Rhombus
Media/Mikado/Sidecar (Niv Fichman)
📺 🔲 ⊘ 🎧

A violin, which was the last work of a master
craftsman, travels through various hands until the
present time, when it is the star attraction in an
auction.

*An episodic movie on the power of music that holds the
interest for the most part, though a romantic and
miscast interlude in England nearly ruins the pleasure it
provides.*

w Don McKellar, François Girard d François
Girard ph Alain Dostie m John Corigliano
pd François Séguin ed Gaëtan Huot
☆ Samuel L. Jackson, Don McKellar, Carlo
Cecchi, Irene Grazioli, Jean-Luc Bideau, Christoph
Koncz, Jason Flemyng, Greta Scacchi, Sylvia
Chang, Liu Zi Feng, Colm Feore, Monique
Mercure

'Fails on a number of counts, mostly because the
individual stories aren't very gripping.' – *David
Stratton, Variety*

👤 John Corigliano

Red Wagon

GB   1933   107m   bw
BIP (Walter C. Mycroft)

Passions mount in a travelling circus. Gypsies and
jealousies are the ingredients of a melodrama
aimed at the international market.

It failed.

w Roger Burford, Edward Knoblock, Arthur
Woods novel *Lady Eleanor Smith* d Paul Stein
ph Jack Cox md Kurt Schroeder ed Leslie
Norman
☆ Charles Bickford, Raquel Torres, Greta Nissen,
Don Alvarado, Anthony Bushell, Paul Graetz,
Jimmy Hanley, Frank Pettingell, Francis L.
Sullivan

Redbeard *

Japan   1965   165m   bw   Tohoscope
Toho-Kurosawa
🔲 🔍

original title: *Akahige*

Problems of a 19th-century doctor. Almost a
Japanese version of *The Citadel*: Kurosawa himself
called it 'a monument to goodness in man'.

Rather heavy-going, but sporadically compelling.

w Masato Ide, Hideo Oguni, Akira Kurosawa
novel Shugoro Yamamoto d Akira Kurosawa
ph A. Nakai, T. Saito m M. Sato
☆ Toshiro Mifune, Yuzo Kayama

'A three-hour excursion into nineteenth-century
hospital soap opera; a mediocre enough script,
but beautifully directed and flawlessly acted.' –
John Simon

Redemption

US   1930   82m   bw
MGM

A man thought dead commits suicide rather than
interrupt his wife's new life.

*Elaborate but unsuccessful talkie début of a waning
star; very hard going.*

w Dorothy Farnum, Edwin Justus Mayer
novel *The Living Corpse* by Leo Tolstoy d Fred
Niblo
☆ John Gilbert, Renee Adoree, Eleanor
Boardman, Conrad Nagel

The Redhead: see *Poil de Carotte*

Redneck

Italy/GB   1972   87m   colour
Crawford/CIAC/Sterle (Michael Lester, Silvio
Narizzano)

original title: *Senza Ragione*

Two crooks on the run steal a car and discover that
it contains a teenage boy.

*Dull chase film that wanders around the Italian
countryside to little effect.*

w Win Wells, Masolino D'Amico story Rafael
Sanchez Campoy d Silvio Narizzano ph Giorgio
Tonti m Maurizio Catalano ad Arrigo Equini
ed Thom Noble
☆ Franco Nero, Telly Savalas, Mark Lester, Ely
Galleani, Duilio Del Prete, Maria Michi

'Not since *Gone with the Wind* has there been a
great romantic epic like it!'

Reds ***

US   1981   196m   Technicolor
Paramount (Warren Beatty)
📺 🔲 🔍 🎧

The last years of John Reed, an American writer
who after stormy romantic vicissitudes goes with
his wife to Russia and writes *Ten Days That Shook
the World*.

*Interminably long but full of quality, this immensely
detailed work was a most unlikely project to succeed in
the eighties, but its very strangeness enabled it to break
even.*

w Warren Beatty, Trevor Griffiths d Warren
Beatty ph Vittorio Storaro m Stephen Sondheim
pd Richard Sylbert
☆ Warren Beatty, Diane Keaton, Edward
Herrmann, Jerzy Kosinski, Jack Nicholson,
Maureen Stapleton, Paul Sorvino
👤 Warren Beatty (as director); Vittorio Storaro;
Maureen Stapleton (supporting actress)
👤 best picture; screenplay; editing (Dede Allen,
Craig McKay); Warren Beatty (as actor); Diane
Keaton; Jack Nicholson
Ⓣ best supporting actor (Jack Nicholson); best
supporting actress (Maureen Stapleton)

Reducing

US   1931   73m   bw
MGM

The proprietress of a beauty parlour sends for an
old family servant to help her.

*Loosely plotted comedy consisting largely of slapstick in
a Turkish bath.*

w Willard Mack, Beatrice Banyard d Charles F.
Reisner
☆ Marie Dressler, Polly Moran, Anita Page,
Lucien Littlefield, Sally Eilers

'Rough and tumble hoke comedy addressed to
the banana peel sense of humour.' – *Variety*

Reed – México Insurgente **

Mexico   1971   106m   bw
Salvador Lopez/Ollin y Asociados

Reporting the Mexican revolution in 1913,
American journalist John Reed learns to identify
with the oppressed.

*A low-key documentary-style account of Reed's
conversion to political action, eschewing mock-heroics
and enhanced by sepia photography.*

wd Paul Leduc ph Alexis Grivas
☆ Claudio Obregón, Ernesto Gómez Cruz,
Eduardo López Rojas, Juan Angel Martinez, Carlos
Castañón

Reefer and the Model *

Ireland   1988   93m   Technicolor
Metro/Berber Films (Lelia Doolan)
📺

A former IRA man, his trawler-owning friends, and
a pregnant girl he picks up, attempt a bank robbery
to raise money.

*Raffishly enjoyable thriller, though its attempt to
explain the political context of modern Ireland lacks
resonance.*

wd Joe Comerford ph Breffni Byrne m Johnny
Duhan pd John Lucas ed Sé Merry
☆ Ian McElhinney, Eve Watkinson, Carol
Scanlan, Birdy Sweeney, Sean Lawlor, Ray
McBride

Reefer Madness

US   1936   67m   bw
Motion Picture Ventures/G & H (George A. Hirliman)
📺 🔲 ⊘

aka: *The Burning Question*
aka: *Tell Your Children*

Clean-cut kids tread the downward path to fast
cars, sex and murder after smoking marijuana.

*Direly made, low-budget, unsophisticated, sensational
exposé that reveals much about attitudes of the period;
as a film its value is nil, though the maniacal acting
may provide some amusement.*

w Arthur Hoerl, Paul Franklin story Lawrence
Meade d Louis Gasnier ph Jack Greenhalgh
md Abe Meyer ad Robert Priestley ed Carl
Pierson
☆ Dorothy Short, Kenneth Craig, Lillian Miles,
Dave O'Brien, Thelma White, Carleton Young,
Warren McCullom, Pat Royale, Joseph Royale
† The film opens with the foreword: 'The motion
picture you are about to witness may startle you. It
would not have been possible, otherwise, to
sufficiently emphasize the frightful toll of the new

drug menace which is destroying the youth of
America in alarmingly-increasing numbers.
Marihuana is that drug – a violent narcotic – an
unspeakable scourge – The Real Public Enemy
Number One! Its first effect is sudden, violent,
uncontrollable laughter; then come dangerous
hallucinations – space expands – time slows down,
almost stands still … fixed ideas come next,
conjuring up monstrous extravagances – followed
by emotional disturbances, the total inability to
direct thoughts, the loss of all power to resist
physical emotions … leading finally to acts of
shocking violence … ending often in incurable
insanity. In picturing its soul-destroying effects no
attempt was made to equivocate. The scenes and
incidents, while fictionalized for the purposes of
this story, are based upon actual research into the
results of Marihuana addiction. If their stark reality
will make you *think*, will make you aware that
something *must be done* to wipe out this ghastly
menace, then the picture will not have failed in its
purpose … Because the dreaded Marihuana may be
reaching forth next for your son or daughter … or
yours … or YOURS!'

'He took them hostage. They drove him crazy.'

The Ref

US   1994   93m   Technicolor
Buena Vista/Touchstone/Don Simpson/Jerry
Bruckheimer (Ron Bozman, Richard LaGravenese, Jeff
Weiss)
📺 🔲 🔍 🎧

GB title: *Hostile Hostages*

At Christmas, a bad-tempered cat burglar on the
run takes hostage an argumentative yuppie couple
whose marriage is in difficulties.

*Misfiring black comedy; what might have been a
bracing alternative to* It's a Wonderful Life, *a sort of*
What a Lousy Existence, *too often leaves a sour
taste, although it has a few moments.*

w Richard LaGravenese, Marie Weiss d Ted
Demme ph Adam Kimmel m David A. Stewart
pd Dan Davis ed Jeffrey Wolf
☆ Denis Leary, Judy Davis, Kevin Spacey, Robert
J. Steinmiller Jnr, Glynis Johns, Richard Bright,
Raymond J. Barry

'Unrelenting rough language, bitter, caustic
humor and unbearable grotesqueries in place of
characters seem unlikely elements to generate
feel-good numbers for Simpson-Bruckheimer's
first production for Disney.' – *Variety*

'It's all part of the American Dream.'

The Reflecting Skin

GB   1990   95m   Technicolor
Virgin/Fugitive Features/BBC Films/British
Screen/Zenith (Dominic Anciano, Ray Burdis)
📺 🔲 🔍

A young boy suspects a strange woman of having
killed his friends.

*Grotesque, death-obsessed movie, directed at a
somnambulistic pace, though it found admirers at
several film festivals.*

wd Philip Ridley ph Dick Pope m Nick Bicat
ad Rick Roberts ed Scott Thomas
☆ Viggo Mortensen, Lindsay Duncan, Jeremy
Cooper, Sheila Moore, Duncan Fraser, David
Longworth, Robert Koons, David Bloom

'The film strains for poetic resonance: a puffed-
up frog trying to pass as a prince.' – *Independent*
'This is American Grand Guignol orchestrated
by a foreigner with a frightening idea of how the
mysteries of the adult world seem to the highly
imaginative but still relatively innocent young.'
– *Guardian*

Reflection of Fear

US   1971   90m   Eastmancolor
Columbia (Howard B. Jaffe)
🔲

A retarded teenage girl kills her mother and her
grandmother.

Psycho thriller of little interest or suspense.

w Edward Hume, Lewis John Carlino novel *Go to
Thy Deathbed* by Stanton Forbes d William A.
Fraker ph Laszlo Kovacs m Fred Myrow
☆ Robert Shaw, Mary Ure, Signe Hasso, Sondra
Locke, Mitch Ryan

Reflections in a Golden Eye *

US   1967   108m   Technicolor
Warner Seven Arts (Ray Stark)
🔲

Repressions at a peacetime army camp in Georgia.
A private soldier rides nude on horseback, a major

---

has the hots for him, the major's wife has an affair with their neighbour, whose wife has cut off her nipples with garden shears.
A film as idiotic as its story line, but smoothly marshalled so that at least it's more amusing than boring.
w Chapman Mortimer, Gladys Hill *novel* Carson McCullers d John Huston ph Aldo Tonti m Toshiro Mayuzumi pd Stephen Grimes
☆ Marlon Brando, Elizabeth Taylor, Brian Keith, Julie Harris, Robert Forster, Zorro David
'One feels trapped in a huge overheated hothouse containing nothing but common snapdragons. Pedestrian, crass, and uninvolving to the point of repellence.' – *John Simon*
'Nothing more than nutty people and pseudo porn.' – *Judith Crist*

The Reformer and the Redhead *
US 1950 90m bw
MGM (Norman Panama, Melvin Frank)
A small-town reform candidate abandons his crooked protector and wins under his own steam, helped by the daughter of the zoo superintendent.
Scatty sub-Capra comedy with a lightweight script but good production and playing.
wd Norman Panama, Melvin Frank ph Ray June m David Raksin
☆ Dick Powell, June Allyson, Cecil Kellaway, David Wayne, Ray Collins, Robert Keith, Marvin Kaplan

'Somewhere in America a woman is being terrorized by a major domestic appliance.'
'Just when you thought it was safe to go back into the kitchen.'
The Refrigerator
US 1991 86m colour
Avenue D (Christopher Oldcorn)
Two newlyweds move from Ohio to New York and rent an apartment with a carnivorous refrigerator.
Camp horror movie, satirizing suburban domesticity and consumerism, but done without any wit or style.
w Nicholas Jacobs, Christopher Oldcorn, Philip Dolin d Nicholas Jacobs ph Paul Gibson m Don Peterkofsky, Adam Roth, Chris Burke pd Therese Deprez ed P. J. Pesce, Suzanne Pillsbury, Christopher Oldcorn, Nicholas Jacobs
☆ David Simonds, Julia McNeal, Phyllis Sanz, Angel Caban, Nena Segal, Jaime Rojo, Alex Trisano
'Smart, quirky horror spoof. Slick-looking production delivers its thrills with enough laughs to promise a cult following.' – *Variety*

Regain: see *Harvest*

Regalo di Natale: see *Christmas Present*

Regarde les Hommes Tomber: see *See How They Fall*

Regarding Henry
US 1991 108m Technicolor
UIP/Paramount (Scott Rudin, Mike Nichols)
A tough lawyer, who loses most of his faculties in a shooting, becomes a much nicer person as he recovers.
Sentimental fable that fails to convince.
w Jeffrey Abrams d Mike Nichols ph Giuseppe Rotunno m Hans Zimmer pd Tony Walton ed Sam O'Steen
☆ Harrison Ford, Annette Bening, Bill Nunn, Mikki Allen, Donald Moffat, Aida Linares, Elizabeth Wilson, Robin Bartlett, Bruce Altman, Rebecca Miller

Regeneration **
GB/Canada 1997 110m colour
Artificial Eye/Norstar/Telefilm Canada/SFPF/GFF (Allan Scott, Peter R. Simpson)
In 1917, in order to nullify his growing opposition to the war, the poet Siegfried Sassoon is sent to a Scottish psychiatric hospital treating shell-shocked officers.
Excellently acted, sensitively directed drama of the impact of war; but there is a stilted quality to the script that keeps it earthbound.
w Allan Scott *novel* Pat Barker d Gillies MacKinnon ph Glen MacPherson m Mychael Danna pd Andy Harris ed Pia di Ciaula

☆ Jonathan Pryce, James Wilby, Jonny Lee Miller, Stuart Bunce, Tanya Allen, John Neville
'Dignified but uninvolving.' – *Variety*

La Règle du Jeu ***
France 1939 113m bw
La Nouvelle Edition Française (Claude Renoir)
aka: The Rules of the Game
A count organizes a weekend shooting party which results in complex love intrigues among servants as well as masters.
Celebrated satirical comedy with a uniquely bleak outlook.
w Jean Renoir, Carl Koch d Jean Renoir ph Jean Bachelet, Alain Renoir m Joseph Kosma, Roger Desormières ad Eugène Lourié, Max Douy ed Marguerite Renoir, Marthe Huguet
☆ Marcel Dalio, Nora Gregor, Jean Renoir, Mila Parély, Julien Carette, Gaston Modot, Roland Toutain
'It is a question of panache, of preserving a casual indifference to the workings of fate.' – *The Times*
'How brilliantly Renoir focuses the confusion! The rather fusty luxury of the chateau, the constant mindless slaughter of wild animals, the minuets of adultery and seduction, the gavottes of mutual hatred or mistrust…' – *Basil Wright, 1972*
† The film was originally banned as indicting the corruption of France, and during the war the negative was destroyed during an air raid; but eventually a full version was pieced together from various materials.

Reign of Terror: see *The Black Book*

The Reincarnation of Peter Proud
US 1974 104m Technicolor
Avco Embassy/Bing Crosby (Frank P. Rosenberg)
A history professor is troubled by recurring dreams of his former existence.
Hysterical psychic melodrama which pretty well ruins its own chances by failing to explain its plot.
w Max Ehrlich *novel* Max Ehrlich d J. Lee-Thompson ph Victor J. Kemper m Jerry Goldsmith
☆ Michael Sarrazin, Jennifer O'Neill, Margot Kidder, Cornelia Sharpe, Paul Hecht
'It may well be the silliest approach to the subject in any medium … all flashbacks trampling the action with the finesse of a rogue elephant.' – *Tom Milne*

'She was the daughter of a King, the sister of a King, the wife of a King … and the lover of an enemy.'
La Reine Margot **
France/Germany/Italy 1994 162m colour
Guild/Renn/France 2/DA/NEF/Degeto/RCS
In 1572, the sister of the Catholic King of France reluctantly agrees to marry the Protestant Duke of Navarre, an event that leads to the Saint Bartholomew's Day Massacre of Protestants and causes turmoil in the kingdom.
Engagingly vivid account of power struggles on personal, political and religious levels, involving bloodshed, poison, lust and betrayal.
w Danièle Thompson, Patrice Chereau *novel* Alexandre Dumas d Patrice Chereau ph Philippe Rousselot m Goran Bregovic pd Richard Peduzzi, Olivier Radot ed François Gédiger, Hélène Viard
☆ Isabelle Adjani, Daniel Auteuil, Jean-Hugues Anglade, Vincent Perez, Virna Lisa, Dominique Blanc, Pascal Greggory, Asia Argento, Jean-Claude Brialy
'A tempestuous, lavish and intelligently thought-out account of the Saint Bartholomew's Day Massacre and its aftermath, marinated in gore and lovingly trimmed with the finest brocade.' – *Jonathan Romney, Guardian*
♟ costume design

Reise der Hoffnung: see *Journey of Hope*

The Reivers *
US 1969 111m Technicolor Panavision
Cinema Center/Duo/Solar (Irving Ravetch)
In Mississippi at the turn of the century a hired hand borrows the new family auto for a trip into

Memphis with the grandson of the family and a black stablehand.
Pleasant but insubstantial yarn of more gracious days; most attractive to look at, it entertains gently without ever reaching a point.
w Irving Ravetch, Harriet Frank Jnr *novel* William Faulkner d Mark Rydell ph Richard Moore m John Williams
☆ Steve McQueen, Sharon Farrell, Will Geer, Rupert Crosse, Mitch Vogel, Michael Constantine, Juano Hernandez, Clifton James
♟ John Williams; Rupert Crosse

Relentless
US 1948 93m Technicolor
Columbia (Eugene B. Rodney)
A cowboy framed for murder must clear himself before the posse catches up with him.
Brisk Western copy of The 39 Steps.
w Winston Miller d George Sherman ph Edward Cronjager m Marlin Skiles
☆ Robert Young, Marguerite Chapman, Willard Parker, Barton MacLane, Will Wright

Relentless
US 1989 93m Foto-Kem
New Line (Howard Smith)
The son of a disgraced LA cop turns serial killer.
A formulaic thriller with occasional moments that lift it out of the very mundane.
w Jack T. D. Robinson d William Lustig ph James Lemmo m Jay Chattaway pd Gene Abel ed David Kern
☆ Judd Nelson, Robert Loggia, Meg Foster, Leo Rossi, Patrick O'Brien, Ken Lerner, Mindy Seeger

'Some Things Are Best Left Undiscovered.'
The Relic
US 1997 110m DeLuxe Panavision
Paramount/Cloud Nine/Pacific Western (Sam Mercer, Gale Anne Hurd)
Crates shipped from the Brazilian jungle to a Chicago museum contain a brain-eating monster.
A standard monster movie, done with a certain amount of relish but no originality.
w Amy Jones, John Raffo, Rick Jaffa *novel* Douglas Preston, Lincoln Child d Peter Hyams ph Peter Hyams m John Debney pd Philip Harrison ed Steven Kemper sp Stan Winston; VIFX
☆ Penelope Ann Miller, Tom Sizemore, Linda Hunt, James Whitmore, Clayton Rohner, Chi Muoi Lo, Lewis Van Bergen
'A B-movie shocker in an expensive suit.' – *George Perry*

The Reluctant Astronaut
US 1967 101m Technicolor
Universal (Edward J. Montagne)
By a series of accidents a man with vertigo becomes an astronaut.
Feeble vehicle for a comedian briefly popular.
w Jim Fritzell, Everett Greenbaum d Edward J. Montagne ph Rexford Wimpey m Vic Mizzy
☆ Don Knotts, Leslie Nielsen, Joan Freeman, Jesse White, Jeanette Nolan, Arthur O'Connell

The Reluctant Débutante *
US 1958 96m Metrocolor Cinemascope
MGM/Avon (Pandro S. Berman)
A noble couple have difficulty in steering their American-educated daughter through the intricacies of the London season.
A slight but pleasing British comedy has become a rather strident example of lend-lease, but still affords minor pleasures.
w William Douglas Home *play* William Douglas Home d Vincente Minnelli ph Joseph Ruttenberg md Eddie Warner ad Jean d'Aubonne
☆ Rex Harrison, Kay Kendall, Sandra Dee, Peter Myers, Angela Lansbury, John Saxon, Diane Clare

The Reluctant Dragon **
†† US 1941 72m Technicolor
Walt Disney
A tour of the Disney Studios affords some glimpses of how cartoons are made.
Amiable pot-pourri of cartoon shorts (Baby Weems, How to Ride a Horse and the title story) linked by a studio tour of absorbing interest.

w various d Alfred Werker (live action), various
☆ Robert Benchley, Frances Gifford, Nana Bryant

Reluctant Heroes *
GB 1951 80m bw
Byron (Henry Halstead)
Comedy of national servicemen and their misdemeanours.
Simple-minded army farce which was popular for years as play and film.
w Colin Morris *play* Colin Morris d Jack Raymond ph James Wilson
☆ Brian Rix, Ronald Shiner, Derek Farr, Christine Norden, Larry Noble

The Reluctant Widow
GB 1950 91m bw
Rank/Two Cities (Gordon Wellesley)
During the Napoleonic wars a governess is co-opted as a spy.
Thin romantic drama which despite nice art direction never really sparks into life.
w Gordon Wellesley, J. B. Boothroyd *novel* Georgette Heyer d Bernard Knowles ph Jack Hildyard ad Carmen Dillon
☆ Jean Kent, Guy Rolfe, Kathleen Byron, Paul Dupuis, Lana Morris, Julian Dallas, Peter Hammond, Andrew Cruickshank

The Remains of the Day **
GB/US 1993 134m Technicolor
Columbia/Merchant Ivory (Ishmail Merchant, Mike Nichols, John Calley)
A butler comes to realize that his lifelong respect for, and loyalty to, his aristocratic master was misplaced.
An artful, nicely composed study in repressed emotions, stiff upper lips and class attitudes; in the final analysis, though, it seems no more than P. G. Wodehouse re-played as tragedy.
w Ruth Prawer Jhabvala *novel* Kazuo Ishiguro d James Ivory ph Tony Pierce-Roberts m Richard Robbins pd Luciana Arrighi ed Andrew Marcus
☆ Anthony Hopkins, Emma Thompson, James Fox, Christopher Reeve, Peter Vaughan, Hugh Grant, Michel Lonsdale, Tim Piggot-Smith, Patrick Godfrey
'Continuously absorbing, but lacks the emotional resonance that would have made it completely satisfying.' – *Variety*
'This luxuriously mounted and often brilliantly engineered adaptation … could well be the producer and director team Merchant Ivory's most comprehensive success. It unquestionably deserves to be.' – *Derek Malcolm, Guardian*
♟ Anthony Hopkins; Emma Thompson; James Ivory; best picture; Ruth Prawer Jhabvala; Richard Robbins; Luciana Arrighi; costume design (Jenny Beavan, John Bright)
♛ Anthony Hopkins

Remains to Be Seen
US 1953 88m bw
MGM (Arthur Hornblow Jnr)
The manager of an apartment house finds a dead body, and before the police arrive someone sticks a knife into it.
Flabby comedy-thriller giving the cast little to work on.
w Sidney Sheldon *play* Howard Lindsay, Russel Crouse d Don Weis ph Robert Planck md Jeff Alexander
☆ June Allyson, Van Johnson, Angela Lansbury, Louis Calhern, John Beal, Dorothy Dandridge

'By thunderation, I'll show America how to get tough!'
The Remarkable Andrew *
US 1942 80m bw
Paramount (Richard Blumenthal)
A young municipal bookkeeper is framed by local politicians but helped by the ghost of Andrew Jackson and friends.
Pleasant, rather faded, whimsical comedy which also managed to be propaganda for the war effort.
w Dalton Trumbo d Stuart Heisler ph Theodor Sparkuhl m Victor Young
☆ William Holden, Ellen Drew, Brian Donlevy, Rod Cameron, Richard Webb, Porter Hall, Frances Gifford, Nydia Westman, Montagu Love
'About all that comes through in the juxtaposition of these lithograph characters over modern Shale City is Franklin's delight over the

electric light and Jackson's alarm over the radio.'
– *John McManus, PM*

The Remarkable Mr Kipps: see *Kipps*

The Remarkable Mr Pennypacker
US 1958 87m Technicolor Cinemascope
TCF (Charles Brackett)
A Pennsylvania businessman leads two lives with
two separate families.
*Feeble and obvious period comedy of bigamy; very few
laughs.*
w Walter Reisch *play* Liam O'Brien *d* Henry
Levin *ph* Milton Krasner *m* Leigh Harline
☆ Clifton Webb, Dorothy McGuire, Charles
Coburn, Ray Stricklyn, Jill St John, Ron Ely, David
Nelson

Rembrandt ****
GB 1936 85m bw
London Films (Alexander Korda)
🏴
Episodes in the life of the 17th-century painter.
*Austerely comic, gently tragic character piece, superbly
staged and photographed, with a great performance at
its centre.*
w Lajos Biro, June Head, Carl Zuckmayer
d Alexander Korda *ph* Georges Périnal, Richard
Angst *m* Geoffrey Toye
☆ Charles Laughton, Elsa Lanchester, Gertrude
Lawrence, Edward Chapman, Walter Hudd, Roger
Livesey, Herbert Lomas, Allan Jeayes, Sam Livesey,
Raymond Huntley, John Clements
  'Never exciting, and only partly believable ... a
  feature film without a story plot.' – *Variety*
  'Amazingly full of that light which the great
  master of painting subdued to his supreme
  purpose.' – *James Agate*
  'The film is ruined by lack of story and
  continuity; it has no drive. Like *The Private Life
  of Henry the Eighth* it is a series of unrelated
  tableaux.' – *Graham Greene*

Remember?
US 1939 83m bw
MGM (Milton Bren)
A newly married couple do not get on, so a friend
gives them a potion which makes them lose their
memories and fall in love all over again.
*Silly, witless comedy which did no good for anyone
concerned.*
w Corey Ford, Norman Z. McLeod *d* Norman Z.
McLeod *ph* George Folsey *m* Edward Ward
☆ Robert Taylor, Greer Garson, Lew Ayres, Billie
Burke, Reginald Owen, George Barbier, Henry
Travers, Richard Carle, Laura Hope Crews,
Halliwell Hobbes, Sig Rumann
  'Many bright episodes contrast with some bumpy
  and over-dialogued stretches.' – *Variety*

Remember Last Night? **
US 1936 80m bw
Universal
Socialites with hangovers find that murder was
committed during their party.
*Ingenious but overlong mixture of styles: farce, Thin
Man comedy, murder mystery, satire, fantasy. Very
well worth looking at.*
w Harry Clork, Dan Totheroh, Doris Malloy
novel The Hangover Murders by Adam Hobhouse
d James Whale *ph* Joseph Valentine *m* Franz
Waxman
☆ Robert Young, Edward Arnold, Arthur
Treacher, Constance Cummings, Robert
Armstrong, Sally Eilers, Reginald Denny, Ed
Brophy, Jack La Rue, Gustav von Seyffertitz,
Gregory Ratoff
  'It will be hard to sell because it is hard to
  understand ... the basic story can scarcely be
  followed, while the superficial gloss of phoney
  sophistication neither fits a narrative in which
  four murders and two suicides are recorded, nor
  carries conviction of itself.' – *Variety*
  'Parodying the detective thriller in a dazzling
  cascade of gags, this brilliant divertissement
  eventually takes off into pure surrealism.' – *Tom
  Milne, MFB, 1974*

Remember Me?
GB 1997 81m Metrocolor
Film Four/Talisman (Alan Shallcross, Alan Wright)
📺
A suburban couple's life is turned upside down
when they are visited by the wife's former

boyfriend, a charmer who is being hounded by his
creditors.
*A limp sitcom that looks and sounds as if it were quick-
frozen in the 50s and now partially thawed out.*
w Michael Frayn *d* Nick Hurran *ph* David Odd
m Michael Kamen, Ed Shearmur *pd* Christopher
Bradshaw *ed* John Wilson
☆ Robert Lindsay, Rik Mayall, Imelda Staunton,
Brenda Blethyn, James Fleet, Haydn Gwynne,
Natalie Walker, Tim Matthews
  'It's a disaster: a prehistoric burial mound of
  farcical clichés beyond even this talented cast's
  power to excavate.' – *Alexander Walker, London
  Evening Standard*

Remember My Name *
US 1978 94m DeLuxe
Columbia/Lion's Gate (Robert Altman)
After twelve years in prison, a woman takes calm
revenge on the man who allowed her to take the
blame for his crime.
*Basically reminiscent of a Barbara Stanwyck vehicle of
the forties, this interesting film is finally too concerned
to strike on all levels, including satire, social awareness
and fashionable pessimism.*
wd Alan Rudolph *ph* Tak Fujimoto *ed* Thomas
Walls, William A. Sawyer *songs* Alberta Hunter
☆ Geraldine Chaplin, Anthony Perkins, Moses
Gunn, Berry Berenson, Jeff Goldblum

Remember That Face: see *The Mob*

Remember the Day *
US 1941 86m bw
TCF (William Perlberg)
An elderly schoolteacher recollects her past life.
Pleasant sentimental drama, very well mounted.
w Tess Schlesinger, Frank Davis, Allan Scott
play Philo Higley *d* Henry King *ph* George
Barnes *m* Alfred Newman
☆ Claudette Colbert, John Payne, Shepperd
Strudwick, Jane Seymour, Anne Revere, Frieda
Inescort

Remember the Night *
US 1940 94m bw
Paramount (Mitchell Leisen)
An assistant district attorney takes a lady shoplifter
home with him for Christmas.
*Eccentric but winning blend of comedy, romance and
drama, deftly mixed by master chefs.*
w Preston Sturges *d* Mitchell Leisen *ph* Ted Tetzlaff
m Frederick Hollander
☆ Barbara Stanwyck, Fred MacMurray, Beulah
Bondi, Elizabeth Patterson, Sterling Holloway,
Paul Guilfoyle, Willard Robertson
  'Rarely has such a theme been so smoothly
  advanced and so pleasantly played out to so
  sensible and credible a conclusion.' – *New York
  Times*

Remembrance
GB 1982 117m Eastmancolor
Channel 4/Colin Gregg
Young sailors in Plymouth enjoy a last night's leave
before a six-month tour of duty with the NATO
forces.
*A few slices of what in the eyes of film-makers passes
for realism these days: boozing, violence and bad
language. The film seems to make no point and
certainly doesn't entertain, though the components are
slickly enough assembled.*
w Hugh Stoddart *d* Colin Gregg *ph* John
Metcalfe *m* various pop performances *ed* Peter
Delfgou
☆ John Altman, Al Ashton, Martin Barrass, Nick
Dunning, Sally Jane Jackson, David John, Peter
Lee-Wilson, Kenneth Griffith
  'A clear and disheartening case of ambition
  exceeding grasp.' – *Geoff Brown, MFB*

Remo Williams: The Adventure Begins
US 1985 121m DeLuxe
Orion/Dick Clark, Larry Spiegel, Mel Bergman
📺 🏴 💿 🎧
GB title: *Remo: Unarmed and Dangerous*
A New York cop is recruited by the CIA to learn
martial arts which will help him to fight an evil
arms manufacturer.
*Po-faced and oddly unlikeable, this elaborate adventure
movie never really finds a style, and is dislocated by a
middle section in which our hero is taught by an elderly
Korean.*
w Christopher Wood *novels Destroyer* series by
Richard Sapir, Warren Murphy *d* Guy Hamilton

ph Andrew Laszlo *m* Craig Safan *pd* Jackson de
Govia
☆ Fred Ward, Joel Grey, Wilford Brimley, J. A.
Preston, Charles Cioffi, Kate Mulgrew, George Coe

Remorques *
France 1941 80m bw
MAIC
US title: *Stormy Waters*
A tugboat captain falls in love with a mysterious
woman but remains faithful to his invalid wife.
Effective, minor, romantic melodrama.
w Jacques Prévert, André Cayatte *novel* Roger
Vercel *d* Jean Grémillon *ph* Armand Thirard,
Louis Née *m* Roland Manuel
☆ Jean Gabin, Michèle Morgan, Madeleine
Renaud, Fernand Ledoux

Renaissance Man
US 1994 129m Technicolor
Guild/Cinergi (Sara Colleton, Elliot Abbott, Robert
Greenhut)
📺 💿
An out-of-work ad-man is employed to teach some
of the army's dimmest recruits and gives them a
sense of self-esteem.
*Soft-centred comedy that marches along predictable
tracks and has little to do with the realities of teaching
or army service; as recruiting propaganda, it no doubt
serves a purpose.*
w Jim Burnstein *d* Penny Marshall *ph* Adam
Greenberg *m* Hans Zimmer *pd* Geoffrey Kirkland
ed George Bowers, Battle Davis
☆ Danny DeVito, Gregory Hines, James Remar,
Cliff Robertson, Stacey Dash, Lillo Brancato Jnr,
Kadeem Hardison, Richard T. Jones, Mark
Wahlberg
  'Warm-hearted humanism is glopped all over
  Renaissance Man in the hopes we won't notice
  that the story makes no sense.' – *Richard Schickel,
  Time*
  † Mark Wahlberg is better known as rapper Marky
  Mark.

Rendezvous: see *Darling How Could You?* (1951)

Rendezvous
US 1935 106m bw
MGM (Lawrence Weingarten)
A decoding expert breaks an enemy spy ring.
*Agreeable light romantic comedy drama with an
espionage plot.*
w Bella and Samuel Spewack *novel Black
Chamber* by Herbert Yardley *d* William K. Howard
ph William Daniels *m* William Axt
☆ William Powell, Rosalind Russell, Binnie
Barnes, Lionel Atwill, Cesar Romero, Samuel S.
Hinds, Henry Stephenson, Frank Reicher
  'Another chill-and-chuckle play aiming at the
  Thin Man trade and scoring a bull's-eye.' –
  Variety

Rendez-Vous **
France 1985 83m colour
Cannon/T Films/A2 (Alain Terzian)
📺 💿
A provincial actress, trying for success in Paris,
becomes involved with a self-destructive actor.
*Stylish drama of young hopefuls that won the best
director award at the Cannes Film Festival in 1985.*
w André Téchiné, Olivier Assayas *d* André
Téchiné *ph* Renato Berta *m* Philippe Sarde
pd Jean-Pierre Kohut Svelko *ed* Martine
Giordano
☆ Juliette Binoche, Lambert Wilson, Wadeck
Stanczak, Jean-Louis Trintignant, Dominique
Lavanant

Rendezvous 24
US 1946 70m bw
TCF (Sol M. Wurtzel)
American secret agents track down post-war Nazis
who are working on atomic explosions from a
remote base in the Harz mountains.
*Routine thick ear despite claims of timeliness; as such,
quite tolerable.*
w Aubrey Wisberg *d* James Tinling
☆ William Gargan, Maria Palmer, Pat O'Moore,
David Leonard, Kurt Katch, Herman Bing

Rendezvous at Midnight
US 1935 60m bw
Universal
A police commissioner investigates the murder of
his predecessor.

*Modest mystery co-feature which wastes time up front
on a fashion show.*
w Gladys Unger *play The Silver Fox* by Gaetano
Sazlo *d* Christy Cabanne
☆ Ralph Bellamy, Valerie Hobson, Catherine
Doucet, Irene Ware, Helen Jerome Eddy
  'The woeful lack of action drags it down.' –
  Variety

Rendezvous de Juillet **
France 1949 110m bw
UGC-SNEG (René G. Vuattoux)
A group of young people in post-war St Germain-
des-Prés plan an expedition to the Congo.
*Highly likeable series of impressions of interesting
people, a little indeterminate and possibly dated now,
but in its time extremely fresh and vital.*
wd Jacques Becker *ph* Claude Renoir *m* Jean
Wiener, Mezz Mezzrow
☆ Daniel Gelin, Maurice Ronet, Brigitte Auber,
Pierre Trabaud, Nicole Courcel

Les Rendezvous du Diable **
France 1958 80m colour
Union Générale Cinématographique/Jacques
Constant/Haroun Tazieff
aka: *Volcano*
Adventures of a Belgian volcanologist.
*Daring exploits on the rims of the world's most active
volcanoes, including Etna and Stromboli in eruption.
Fascinating footage is urbanely presented.*
m Marius-François Gaillard *wd/ph* Haroun Tazieff
  'Beauty blends with horror, romantic grandeur
  with fear.' – *MFB*

Rendez-vous in Paris *
France 1995 98m colour
Artificial Eye/Mayfair/Compagnie Eric Rohmer/Canal
(Françoise Etchegaray)
Three tales of meetings: in the first, a law student
discovers that her boyfriend is seeing another
woman; in the second, a man tries to persuade a
woman to leave her lover for him; in the third, an
artist, showing a tourist around Paris, is attracted
by a woman in one of the galleries
*Three casual accounts of accidental meetings between
men and women and the impossibility of successful
relationships between them; the stories are deceptively
slight, conveying more than at first appears*
wd Eric Rohmer *ph* Diane Baratier *ed* Mary
Stephen
☆ Clara Beller, Antoine Basler, Mathias Megard,
Judith Chancel, Malcolm Conrath
  'Far from his greatest, but still has his familiar
  gracenotes.' – *Sunday Times*

Rendezvous with Annie
US 1946 89m bw
Republic
An American soldier in England goes absent
without leave to see his wife in New York, an
exploit which later nearly loses him a fortune.
*An engaging comedy idea filmed with insufficient wit,
this gets by on charm.*
w Mary Loos, Richard Sale *d* Allan Dwan
☆ Eddie Albert, Faye Marlowe, C. Aubrey Smith

Réne La Canne *
France/Italy 1977 98m Telecolor
Président/Rizzoli (Jacques-Eric Strauss)
📺
During the Second World War a French policeman
and a thief defy the Germans; after it, they find
themselves in friendly rivalry.
*Broad and sometimes blackish farce which amuses
mainly by the expert and stylized comedy performances
of the two male leads.*
w Jacques Rouffio, Francis Girod *novel* Roger
Borniche *d* Francis Girod *ph* Aldo Tonti
m Ennio Morricone *ad* Jean-Jacques Caziot
ed Eva Zora
☆ Gérard Depardieu, Sylvia Kristel, Michel
Piccoli, Stefano Patrizi, Riccardo Garrone, Jacques
Jouanneau, Jean Rigaux, Orchidea de Santis,
Venantino Venantini, Valerie Mairesse, Jean
Carmet

Renegade
Italy 1987 90m colour
Paloma/Cinecittà (Lucio Bompani)
A modern-day itinerant cowboy promises to look
after the knowing 14-year-old son of an imprisoned
friend.

Comic Western that ambles in an easy-going, unmemorable manner from one mild joke, usually involving a punch-up, to another. Its only novelty is that, instead of the cavalry, Hells Angels ride to the rescue.

w Mark Barboni d E. B. Clucher (Enzo Barboni) ph Alfio Contini m Mauro Paoluzzi pd Carlo Simi ed Eugene Alabiso

☆ Terence Hill (Mario Girotti), Robert Vaughn, Ross Hill, Norman Bowler, Beatrice Palme, Lisa Ann Rubin, Donal Hodson

Renegade

US 1993 95m Foto-Kem

Cannell Entertainment

An ex-cop turned bounty hunter joins an organization that stages fights to the death in order to discover what happened to his brother, who disappeared 17 years earlier.

Risible action adventure with muscle-bound acting and dialogue, and padded out with some irrelevant scenes of love-making between extras.

w Stephen J. Cannell, Nick Corea d Ralph Hemecker, R. Marvin ph Kenneth L. Gibb m Roger Neill ad Michel Levesque ed John W. Carr, Skip Robinson

☆ Lorenzo Lamas, Branscombe Richmond, Kathleen Kinmont, Charles Napier, Madison Mason, Stephen J. Cannell, Marjean Holden, Danny Wells, Mitchell Ryan, Martin Kove

Renegade Girls: see Caged Heat

Renegades

US 1930 84m bw

Fox

A disgraced French officer becomes a hero of the Foreign Legion.

Satisfying romantic melodrama of its period.

w Jules Furthman novel André Armandy d Victor Fleming

☆ Warner Baxter, Myrna Loy, Bela Lugosi, Noah Beery, C. Henry Gordon, Gregory Gaye

'Everyone in the picture dies in the last few feet.' – Variety

Renegades

US 1946 88m Technicolor

Columbia

An outlaw's son tries in vain to go straight.

Unsurprising but efficient bill-topping Western of its day.

w Melvin Levey, Francis Faragoh d George Sherman

☆ Evelyn Keyes, Larry Parks, Willard Parker, Edgar Buchanan

Renegades

US 1989 105m colour

Virgin/Morgan Creek/Interscope Communications (David Madden)

A cop and an Indian team up to recover a stolen sacred lance.

Run-of-the-mill action movie in which nothing memorable occurs.

w David Rich d Jack Sholder ph Phil Meheux m Michael Kamen pd Carol Spier ed Caroline Biggerstaff

☆ Kiefer Sutherland, Lou Diamond Phillips, Jami Gertz, Rob Knepper, Bill Smitrovich, Peter MacNeill

Reno

US 1939 72m bw

RKO

As Reno becomes a great city for gambling and divorce, a lawyer becomes a gambling hall proprietor.

Mildly interesting romantic drama in a flashback format.

w John Twist, Ellis St Joseph d John Farrow

☆ Richard Dix, Gail Patrick, Anita Louise, Paul Cavanagh, Laura Hope Crews, Louis Jean Heydt, Hobart Cavanaugh, Charles Halton

'Capable handling of an interesting story against a colourful background.' – Variety

Rent-a-Cop

US 1988 96m colour

Kings Road (Raymond Wagner)

A tough policeman, who loses his job when a drug arrest goes wrong, teams up with a prostitute to track down a vicious killer.

Dull and violent thriller, in which Reynolds's laid-back cop and Minnelli's hyper-active hooker fail to achieve any noticeable rapport.

w Dennis Shryack, Michael Blodgett d Jerry London ph Giuseppe Rotunno m Jerry Goldsmith pd Tony Masters ed Robert Lawrence

☆ Burt Reynolds, Liza Minnelli, James Remar, Richard Masur, Dionne Warwick, Bernie Casey, Robby Benson, John Stanton

Rentadick

GB 1972 94m Eastmancolor

Rank/Paradine/Virgin (Ned Sherrin)

Incompetent private eyes become involved in the battle for a deadly nerve gas.

Ineffective crazy comedy which never takes shape, preferring to aim barbs of satire in all directions.

w John Wells, John Fortune d Jim Clark ph John Coquillon m Carl Davis

☆ James Booth, Richard Briers, Julie Ege, Donald Sinden

Repeat Performance *

US 1947 93m bw

Eagle Lion/Aubrey Schenck

People in trouble find they can repeat the previous year.

Adequate flashback fantasy, very dated now.

w Walter Bullock d Alfred L. Werker ph Lew O'Connell m George Antheil

☆ Louis Hayward, Joan Leslie, Tom Conway, Richard Basehart, Virginia Field

Repentance ***

USSR 1984 155m colour

Cannon/Sovexportfilm/Gruziafilm

original title: Pokjaniye, Monanieba

A woman explains to a court why she keeps exhuming the body of the town's long-serving and much respected mayor.

A bleak and blackly humorous account of a society's complicity in a rule of terror; Abuladze uses dreams and other non-realistic techniques to create a biting allegory of the corruption of a society by Stalinism.

w Nana Djanelidze, Tengiz Abuladze, Rezo Kveselava d Tengiz Abuladze ph Mikhail Agranovich m Nana Djanelidze pd Georgy Mikeladze ed Guliko Omadze

☆ Avtandil Makharadze, Ia Ninidze, Merab Ninidze, Zeinab Botsvadze, Ketevan Abuladze, Edisher Giorgobiani, Kakhi Kavsadze, Nino Zakariadze

† The film did not receive a release until 1987. It was the third part of a trilogy that began with The Plea (1968) and The Wishing Tree (1976).

'Kill Or Be Replaced.'

The Replacement Killers

US 1998 86m Technicolor Panavision

Columbia/WCG (Brad Grey, Bernie Brillstein)

A Chinese hitman, hired by an Asian gangster in New York to kill the young son of a cop, becomes a target himself when he decides that it is one death too many.

A not-too-successful attempt to make an American star out of a Hong Kong one, which is not helped by his rudimentary grasp of English, and action sequences that are less effective than those of his home-grown movies.

w Ken Sanzel d Antoine Fuqua ph Peter Lyons Collister m Harry Gregson-Williams pd Naomi Shohan ed Jay Cassidy

☆ Chow Yun-Fat, Mira Sorvino, Michael Rooker, Jürgen Prochnow, Kenneth Tsang, Til Schweiger, Danny Trejo

'This mechanical effort is studied rather than heartfelt and will disappoint aficionados and thwart potential fans.' – Leonard Klady, Variety

Repo Man *

US 1984 92m DeLuxe

Universal/Edge City (Peter McCarthy, Jonathan Wacks)

A repossessor of cars finds himself on the run from all manner of dangers.

Nightmarish film noir with nods to many predecessors and some elements of black fantasy.

wd Alex Cox ph Robby Müller m Tito Larriva, Steven Hufsteter

☆ Harry Dean Stanton, Emilio Estevez, Tracey Walter, Olivia Barash, Sy Richardson, Susan Barnes

'The saltiest, sweetest, most sublimely sleazy tickle in the Los Angeles ribs. If it doesn't convulse you with belly laughs, then you're a stiff.' – Carrie Rickey, Boston Herald

Report from the Aleutians **

US 1943 45m colour

US Signal Corps

American forces live under tough conditions on a group of Arctic islands from which they raid Japanese bases.

Simple and somewhat overlong, but still one of the better US documentaries to come out of World War II.

wd and narrated by John Huston; additional narration by Walter Huston

Report to the Commissioner

US 1974 112m Metrocolor

UA/M. J. Frankovich

GB title: Operation Undercover

A policeman's son follows in father's footsteps but finds life around Times Square dismaying.

Realistic, concerned crime melodrama with nothing very new to say.

w Abby Mann, Ernest Tidyman novel James Mills d Milton Katselas ph Mario Tosi m Elmer Bernstein

☆ Michael Moriarty, Yaphet Kotto, Susan Blakely, Hector Elizondo, Tony King, Michael McGuire

'A clear also-ran in the police thriller stakes.' – Verina Glaessner

'A bit too full of sweat and frenzy.' – Michael Billington, Illustrated London News

Repossessed

US 1990 84m CFI color

Guild/First Class films (Steve Wizan)

Attempting an exorcism on television, a priest struggles to control a demon intent on possessing the entire viewing audience.

Raucous parody of The Exorcist, crammed with jokes, most of them juvenile.

wd Bob Logan ph Michael D. Margulies m Charles Fox pd Shay Austin ed Jeff Freeman

☆ Linda Blair, Ned Beatty, Leslie Nielsen, Anthony Starke, Thom J. Sharp, Lana Schwab

'Clunking, but the jokes are just about numerous enough to stifle the groans.' – Sight and Sound

Reprieve: see Convicts Four

The Reptile *

GB 1966 90m Technicolor

Warner-Pathé/Hammer (Anthony Nelson-Keys)

A Cornish village is terrified by several mysterious and unpleasant deaths; it turns out that the daughter of the local doctor, victim of a Malayan sect, periodically turns into a deadly snake.

Silly horror story most effectively filmed as a mixture of chills, detection and good characterization.

w John Elder d John Gilling ph Arthur Grant m Don Banks pd Bernard Robinson ed James Needs, Roy Hyde

☆ Noel Willman, Jennifer Daniel, Ray Barrett, Jacqueline Pearce, Michael Ripper, John Laurie, Marne Maitland

Repulsion **

GB 1965 105m bw

Compton/Tekli (Gene Gutowski)

A Belgian manicurist in London is driven by pressures into neurotic withdrawal; terrified above all by sex, she locks herself up in her gloomy flat and murders her boyfriend and landlord when they try to approach her.

Weird, unmotivated but undeniably effective Grand Guignol in the form of a case history; little dialogue, which is just as well as the director at that time clearly had no ear for the language.

w Roman Polanski, Gerard Brach d Roman Polanski ph Gilbert Taylor m Chico Hamilton

☆ Catherine Deneuve, Ian Hendry, John Fraser, Patrick Wymark, Yvonne Furneaux

'An unashamedly ugly film, but as a lynx-eyed view of a crumbling mind it is a masterpiece of the macabre.' – Daily Mail

Reputation: see Lady with a Past

Requiem for a Heavyweight *

US 1962 87m bw

Columbia (David Susskind)

GB title: Blood Money

The last bouts of a prizefighter who will not realize his career is over.

Tough, effective melodrama, extremely well acted.

w Rod Serling TV play Rod Serling d Ralph Nelson ph Arthur J. Ornitz m Laurence Rosenthal

☆ Anthony Quinn, Jackie Gleason, Mickey Rooney, Julie Harris, Stan Adams, Madame Spivy, Jack Dempsey, Cassius Clay

Requiem for a Vampire (dubbed)

France 1971 95m colour

Les Films A.B.C. (Jean Rollin)

original title: Requiem pour un Vampire

aka: Virgins and Vampires

Two young gun-toting girls on the run from killers take refuge in a ruined chateau where vampires live.

Stylish, dreamlike fantasy, with little dialogue, intermingled with scenes of sex and sadism that have no connection to the main narrative; the music is unpleasantly obtrusive.

wd Jean Rollin ph Renan Polles m Pierre Raph ed Michel Patient

☆ Marie-Pierre Castel, Mireille D'Argent, Philippe Gasté, Dominique, Louise Dhour, Paul Bisciglia

'You will get more out of this if you abandon all foolish misconceptions of discovering a coherent plotline and any form of characterisation. Rollin makes these things up as he goes along and to enjoy them you have to get into the same "anything goes" spirit. I always find a stiff drink helps fortify the critical faculties.' – The Dark Side

† The British video release runs for 78m.

Requiem for Dominic: see Requiem für Dominic

Requiem für Dominic **

Austria 1990 90m

Terra Film/OFF/ORF (Norbert Blecha)

aka: Requiem for Dominic

An exiled Romanian scientist returns to his home town of Timisoara to investigate the death of a friend accused of mass murder.

Based on a true story and filmed where the events happened, the documentary style thriller achieves a horrific truth by incorporating actual footage of the accused man as he lay dying.

w Michael Kohlmeier, Felix Mitterer d Robert Dorhelm ph Hans Selikovsky m Harald Kloser ed Ingrid Koller

☆ Felix Mitterer, Viktoria Schubert, August Schmolzer, Angelica Schutz, Antonia Rados, Nikolas Vogel, Georg Hoffman-Ostenhorf, Werner Prinz, Georg Metzenrad

'The most remarkable political thriller since Z ... nail-biting cinema' – Variety

Requiescant: see Kill and Pray

La Resa dei Conti: see The Big Gundown

The Rescue

US 1988 98m colour

Touchstone/Silver Screen Partners III (Laura Ziskin)

A group of American teenagers in South Korea set out to rescue their fathers, imprisoned in North Korea as spies.

Ludicrous film, of a quite stupifying banality, which even its intended audience of gung-ho 13-year-olds are likely to treat with the derision it deserves.

w Jim Thomas, John Thomas d Ferdinand Fairfax ph Russell Boyd m Bruce Broughton pd Maurice Cain ed David Holden, Carroll Timothy O'Meara ☆ Kevin Dillon, Christine Harnos, Marc Price, Ned Vaughn, Ian Giatti, Charles Haid, Edward Albert, Mel Wong

The Rescuers *
👫👫 US 1977 77m Technicolor
Walt Disney (Ron Miller)
📼 ▦ 💿

The Mouse Rescue Aid Society volunteers to bring back a girl lost in a swamp.
Feature-length cartoon which, while by no means as bad as some of Disney's very routine seventies product, still seems light years away from his classics of the thirties.
w Larry Clemmons, Ken Anderson stories Margery Sharp d Wolfgang Reitherman, John Lounsbery, Art Stevens m Artie Butler ☆ Featuring the voices of Bob Newhart, Eva Gabor, Geraldine Page, Joe Flynn, Jim Jordan, John McIntire
'The people who really need rescuing are the Disney animators and cameramen.' – *Time Out*
'It's no *Snow White* but there are long moments when its inventiveness and skill are entirely captivating. I have only this one lingering doubt: if you are going to put this amount of effort into a movie shouldn't you have more at the end than a snappy collection of 330,000 drawings and a bill for six million dollars?' – *Barry Took, Punch*
♬ song 'Someone's Waiting for You' (mSammy Fain, lyCarol Conners, Ayn Robbins)

The Rescuers Down Under **
👫👫 US 1990 77m Technicolor
Warner/Walt Disney/Silver Screen Partners IV (Thomas Schumacher)
📼 ▦ 💿 ◉

The mouse Rescue Aid Society goes to help a trapped eagle and a boy in Australia.
Slick, lively and enjoyable animated feature, an improvement on the original.
w Jim Cox, Karey Kirkpatrick, Byron Simpson, Joe Ranft d Hendel Butoy, Mike Gabriel m Bruce Broughton ad Maurice Hunt ed Michael Kelly, Mark Hester
☆ Featuring the voices of Bob Newhart, Eva Gabor, John Candy, Tristan Rogers, Adam Ryen, George C. Scott, Wayne Robson, Douglas Seale, Frank Walker, Peter Firth, Billy Barty
'Comes on like an Indiana Jones movie which has been reconceived as animation and then proceeded to push back that medium's technical boundaries.' – *Sight and Sound*

Reserved for Ladies: see Service for Ladies

'Let's go to work.'
Reservoir Dogs ***
US 1991 99m colour
Rank/Live America/Dog Eat Dog (Lawrence Bender)
📼 ▦ 🇺🇸 💿 ◉ ◉

While one of their number bleeds to death after a bungled robbery, the rest of the gang, hiding out in a warehouse, try to discover what went wrong.
Brilliant, if sometimes repellent, gangster movie; notably violent, it is also a tense and exciting examination of male egos on a collision course.
wd Quentin Tarantino ph Andrzej Sekula pd David Wasco ed Sally Menks
☆ Harvey Keitel, Tim Roth, Michael Madsen, Chris Penn, Steve Buscemi, Lawrence Tierney, Randy Brooks, Kirk Baltz, Eddie Bunker, Quentin Tarantino
'An astute mix of wit and cynicism which washes down its melodramatic excesses with sly satire on the blood-and-guts elements of the crime movie, this is a film of considerable acuity and power.' – *Kim Newman, Sight and Sound*
'Undeniably juicy, with its salty talk and gunplay, film is nihilistic but not resonantly so, giving it no meaning outside the immediate story and characters. Pic is impressive, but impossible to love.' – *Variety*
'No one should go to see *Reservoir Dogs* without prior thought. But what they will see is a riveting treatment on the theme of betrayal set in an urban wasteland that murders hope and makes redemption virtually impossible.' – *Derek Malcolm, Guardian*
† Quentin Tarantino has acknowledged that the film was influenced by Hong Kong director Ringo

Lam's *City on Fire*, as well as by Stanley Kubrick's *The Killing* and Joseph Sargent's *The Taking of Pelham 123.*

Restless: see The Beloved

'Torn from the blazing pages of Texas history!'
The Restless Breed
US 1957 81m Eastmancolor by Pathé
National Pictures (Edward L. Alperson)
🇺🇸

The son of a secret service agent arrives in a frontier town to avenge his father's death.
Standard star Western full of expected elements.
w Steve Fisher d Allan Dwan ph John Boyle m Edward L. Alperson Jnr
☆ Scott Brady, Anne Bancroft, Jay C. Flippen, Jim Davis, Rhys Williams

Restless Natives
GB 1985 89m Technicolor
Thorn EMI/Oxford Film Company (Rick Stevenson)
📼

Two young idlers set up as modern highwaymen, robbing American visitors on coach tours; to their surprise, they become a tourist attraction.
Irritatingly patchy and amoral comedy which wastes a potentially interesting idea.
w Ninian Dunnett d Michael Hoffman ph Oliver Stapleton m Stuart Adamson pd Adrienne Atkinson ed Sean Barton
☆ Vincent Friell, Joe Mullaney, Teri Lally, Ned Beatty, Robert Urquhart

The Restless Years
US 1959 86m bw Cinemascope
Universal-International
A small-town dressmaker tries to prevent her daughter from discovering that she is illegitimate.
Antediluvian sudser with second-string talent.
w Edward Anhalt play Teach Me How to Cry by Patricia Joudry ☆ John Saxon, Sandra Dee, Margaret Lindsay, Luana Patten, Virginia Grey

Restoration *
US 1996 118m colour
Buena Vista/Segue/Avenue/Oxford Film Company (Cary Brokaw, Andy Paterson, Sarah Ryan Black)
📼 ▦ 💿

A young doctor falls out of favour with Charles II when he agrees to an unconsummated marriage with one of the king's mistresses but then desires her.
A sumptuous costume drama of one man's redemption, set against the excesses of the 1660s and such events as the Plague and the Great Fire of London. Underlying it, though, is a puritanical dislike of sex. (And, in reality, Charles II was happy to share his many mistresses with all-comers.)
w Rupert Walters novel Rose Tremain d Michael Hoffman ph Oliver Stapleton m James Newton Howard ☆ Eugenio Zanetti ed Garth Craven
☆ Robert Downey Jnr, Sam Neill, David Thewlis, Polly Walker, Meg Ryan, Ian McKellen, Hugh Grant, Ian McDiarmid, Mary Macleod
⚱ Eugenio Zanetti; costume design (James Acheson)

Resurrected *
GB 1989 92m colour
Hobo/St Pancras Films/Film Four International/British Screen (Tara Prem, Adrian Hughes)
A soldier believed killed in the Falklands War turns up alive after the fighting is over and is accused of being a deserter.
Effective and dramatic examination of patriotism and the aftermath of battle.
w Martin Allen d Paul Greengrass ph Ivan Strasburg m John Keane pd Chris Burke ed Dan Rae
☆ David Thewlis, Tom Bell, Rita Tushingham, Michael Pollitt, Rudi Davies, William Hoyland, Ewan Stewart, Christopher Fulford, David Lonsdale

Resurrection
US 1931 81m bw
Universal
In 1870s Russia, a peasant girl is seduced by a prince and bears his child.
Unremarkable version of a much-filmed melodrama.
w Finis Fox novel Leo Tolstoy d Edwin Carewe ph Robert B. Kurrle, Al Green m Dimitri Tiomkin

☆ Lupe Velez, John Boles, Nance O'Neil, William Keighley, Rose Tapley
† See also: *We Live Again.*

Resurrection
US 1980 103m Technicolor
Universal (Renee Missel, Howard Rosenman)
▦

A woman who has escaped death in a car crash finds herself miraculously able to heal others.
Curious modern parable with nowhere to go; even religious reactionaries may find it rather boring.
w Lewis John Carlino d Daniel Petrie ph Mario Tosi m Maurice Jarre
☆ Ellen Burstyn, Sam Shepard, Richard Farnsworth, Eva LeGallienne, Roberts Blossom, Clifford David
♀ Ellen Burstyn; Eva LeGallienne (supporting actress)

'Get right to the source of the fear.'
Resurrection Man *
GB 1998 102m Rank Colour
Polygram/Revolution (Andrew Eaton)
📼

In Belfast in the mid-70s, a psychopath leads a gang of Loyalists into a Catholic killing spree.
Grim and bloody portrait of a born killer who is as much influenced by James Cagney's gangster antics as by any political convictions; the film, too, is shackled by movie conventions.
w Eoin McNamee novel Eoin McNamee d Marc Evans ph Pierre Aim m David Holmes, Gary Burns, Keith Tenniswood pd Mark Tildesley ed John Wilson
☆ Stuart Townsend, Geraldine O'Rawe, James Nesbitt, Brenda Fricker, John Hannah, James Ellis, Sean McGinley, Derek Thompson, Zara Turner, B. J. Hogg
'The film leaves you with a feeling of having been on an occasionally unguided tour of an abattoir.' – *Richard Falcon, Sight and Sound*

Le Retour de Martin Guerre: see The Return of Martin Guerre

Le Retour du Grand Blond: see Return of the Tall Blond

Retreat, Hell!
US 1952 95m bw
(Warner) United States (Milton Sperling)
Adventures of a Marine unit in the Korean War.
Standard war film.
w Milton Sperling, Ted Sherdeman d Joseph H. Lewis ph Warren Lynch m William Lava
☆ Frank Lovejoy, Richard Carlson, Anita Louise, Russ Tamblyn

Retribution
US 1988 108m colour
Medusa/Unicorn/Renegade (Guy Magar)
▦ 💿 🎧

A shy artist is possessed by the vengeful spirit of a murderer.
Gory, predictable and fussily frenetic horror movie.
w Guy Magar, Lee Wasserman d Guy Magar ph Gary Thieltges m Alan Howarth pd Robb Wilson King ed Guy Magar
☆ Dennis Lipscomb, Leslie Wing, Suzanne Snyder, Jeff Pomerantz, George Murdock, Pamela Dunlap, Susan Peretz

Return from the Ashes *
GB 1965 104m bw Panavision
UA/Mirisch (J. Lee-Thompson)
A woman returns from Dachau to find that her husband is living with her step-daughter and that they plan to murder her.
Broken-backed thriller melodrama, the first half of which is quite irrelevant to the second. The whole is modestly inventive for those who don't mind a mixture of Enoch Arden, Psycho and Dial M for Murder with a touch of the concentration camps and a background of post-war misery.
w Julius J. Epstein novel Hubert Monteilhet d J. Lee-Thompson ph Christopher Challis m Johnny Dankworth
☆ Ingrid Thulin, Maximilian Schell, Samantha Eggar, Herbert Lom

Return from the River Kwai
GB 1988 101m colour
Rank/Screenlife Establishment (Kurt Unger)
📼

An American pilot teams up with a British officer to try to prevent the Japanese taking prisoners of war back to Japan.
Rambling adventure movie that has no connection, other than its title, with The Bridge on the River Kwai.
w Sargon Tamini, Paul Mayersberg book Joan Blair, Clay Blair Jnr d Andrew V. McLaglen ph Arthur Wooster m Lalo Schifrin pd Michael Stringer ed Alan Strachan
☆ Edward Fox, Denholm Elliott, Christopher Penn, Tatsuya Nakadai, George Takei, Nick Tate, Timothy Bottoms, Michael Dante, Richard Graham

Return from Witch Mountain
👫👫 US 1978 93m Technicolor
Walt Disney (Ron Miller, Jerome Courtland)
▦

A brother and sister from outer space come back to Earth for a vacation and are used by crooks for their own purposes.
Acceptable sequel to Escape from Witch Mountain, with improved special effects.
w Malcolm Marmorstein d John Hough ph Frank Phillips m Lalo Schifrin sp Eustace Lycett, Art Cruickshank, Danny Lee
☆ Bette Davis, Christopher Lee, Ike Eisenmann, Kim Richards, Jack Soo

Return Home
Australia 1989 90m colour
Musical Films/Film Victoria/Australian Film Commission (Cristina Pozzan)
Unhappy with his life, a successful insurance broker returns to his home town to visit his brother who runs a garage.
Amiable domestic drama that comes to few conclusions slowly.
wd Ray Argall ph Mandy Walker ad Kerith Holmes ed Ken Sallows
☆ Dennis Coard, Frankie J. Holden, Ben Mendelsohn, Micki Camilleri

The Return of a Man Called Horse *
US 1976 125m DeLuxe Panavision
UA/Sandy Howard/Richard Harris

The English nobleman of *A Man Called Horse* goes back to the West to save his adopted Indian tribe from extinction.
Another 'realistic' action adventure with torture highlights; nicely made, but not for the squeamish.
w Jack de Witt d Irvin Kershner ph Owen Roizman m Laurence Rosenthal
☆ Richard Harris, Gale Sondergaard, Geoffrey Lewis, Bill Lucking, Jorge Luke
'Maintains a tidy balance between nausea and boredom.' – *Judith Crist*
† At 17 minutes, this pre-title sequence must be the longest so far.

Return of a Stranger
GB 1937 69m bw
Sun/Premier
US title: *The Face Behind the Scar*
A chemist's elopement with his boss's daughter runs into problems when he is accused of murder.
Stilted melodrama, both in performance and direction; too often it suggests a view from the stalls of a provincial repertory theatre.
w Reginald Long, Akos Tolnay play Rudolf Lothar d Victor Hanbury ph James Wilson m Jack Beaver ad Jack Hallward, Philip Balcombe ed Ralph Thomas
☆ Ellis Jeffreys, Athole Stewart, Cecil Ramage, Griffith Jones, Rosalyn Boulter, Sylvia Marriot, James Harcourt, Tarver Penna

The Return of Bulldog Drummond
GB 1934 71m bw
BIP
Drummond forms a society to oust crooked foreigners from Britain.
Thin Drummond exploit with traces of the original Fascism.
wd Walter Summers novel The Black Gang by 'Sapper' ph Jack Parker ad John Mead
☆ Ralph Richardson, Ann Todd, Francis L. Sullivan, Claud Allister, Joyce Kennedy, Pat Aherne

---

👫👫 film suitable for family viewing   📼 VHS video-cassette for the British PAL system   ▦ VHS video-cassette for the British PAL system in wide screen-format   ✿ Video cassette in a computer-colourised version   🇺🇸 American NTSC video-cassette   💿 Laser disc

The Return of Captain Invincible

Australia   1982   91m   Eastmancolor
Panavision
Seven Keys/Willarra

An American superhero is discovered in the back streets of Sydney, a down-and-out drunk; but his skills are needed for the fight against Mr Midnight.

Occasionally agreeable spoof which for most of its length is too frantic.

w Steven E. de Souza, Andrew Gaty   d Philippe Mora

☆ Alan Arkin, Christopher Lee, Kate Fitzpatrick, Bill Hunter, Michael Pate, John Bluthal

The Return of Count Yorga

US   1971   97m   Movielab
AIP/Peppertree (Michael Macready)

Count Yorga falls in love with an orphan while killing most of the orphanage's other inhabitants.

A second instalment that is as amateurish as the first, though also suffering from the belief that a great deal of screaming is automatically scary; its tempo remains so somnambulistic that it is closer to a zombie movie than a conventional tale of vampires.

w Bob Kelljan, Yvonne Wilder   d Bob Kelljan   ph Bill Butler   m Bill Marx   ed Fabien Tordjmann, Laurette Odney

☆ Robert Quarry, Mariette Hartley, Roger Perry, Yvonne Wilder, Tom Toner, Rudy DeLuca, Philip Frame, George Macready, Walter Brooke

The Return of Dr X *

US   1939   62m   bw
Warner (Bryan Foy)

A modern vampire terrorizes the city.

Minor thriller which doesn't get going till the last reel; only notable for Bogart's appearance as the monster. Nothing to do with Dr X.

w Lee Katz   novel The Doctor's Secret by William J. Makin   d Vincent Sherman   ph Sid Hickox   m Bernhard Kaun

☆ Dennis Morgan, Rosemary Lane, Wayne Morris, Humphrey Bogart, Olin Howland, John Litel

The Return of Dracula *

US   1958   77m   bw
UA/Gramercy (Jules V. Levy, Arthur Gardner)
GB title: *The Fantastic Disappearing Man*

A European vampire makes his way to an American small town in the guise of a refugee Iron Curtain painter.

Quite nicely made low-budget horror film with a good balance of the supernatural and the ordinary.

w Pat Fielder   d Paul Landres   ph Jack MacKenzie   m Gerald Fried

☆ Francis Lederer, Norma Eberhardt, Ray Stricklyn, Jimmy Baird, John Wengraf

The Return of Frank James *

US   1940   92m   Technicolor
TCF (Darryl F. Zanuck)

A sequel to *Jesse James* (qv).

Moody, nicely photographed Western in which Jesse's brother avenges his murder.

w Sam Hellman   d Fritz Lang   ph George Barnes, William V. Skall   m David Buttolph

☆ Henry Fonda, Gene Tierney, Jackie Cooper, Henry Hull, John Carradine, J. Edward Bromberg, Donald Meek, Eddie Collins, George Barbier

'I doubt if any character was ever as lily white as that of Frank James here, but that is a present from the Hays Office to you, and anyway the part is played by Henry Fonda. Durn if I don't like that boy.' – *Otis Ferguson*

The Return of Martin Guerre *

France   1982   123m   Fujicolour
Palace/Marcel Dassault/SFP

original title: *Le Retour de Martin Guerre*

In the 16th century, a man comes to a French village claiming to be the one who left his wife and child eight years before. Complaints are laid that he is an impostor …

Mildly intriguing story which falls apart because one is never sure where the film's sympathies lie.

w Jean-Claude Carrière, Daniel Vigne   d Daniel Vigne   ph André Neau   m Michel Portal   ad Alain Negre   ed Denise de Casabianca

☆ Gérard Depardieu, Nathalie Baye, Sylvie Meda, Maurice Barrier

'By far the most enigmatic film seen in London this year.' – *Sunday Times*

'A plodding, confusing narrative that neither does proper justice to the story nor really teases out the complex historical, moral and psychological issues which it raises.' – *Observer*

The Return of Monte Cristo *

US   1946   92m   bw
Columbia/Edward Small-Grant Whytock
GB title: *Monte Cristo's Revenge*

The grandson of the original count is framed and sent to Devil's Island, but escapes.

Very tolerable action romp of its time, with a fair troupe of actors enjoying themselves.

w George Bruce, Alfred Neumann, Kurt Siodmak   d Henry Levin   ph Charles Lawton Jnr   m Lucien Moraweck

☆ Louis Hayward, Barbara Britton, George Macready, Una O'Connor, Henry Stephenson, Steve Geray, Ray Collins, Ludwig Donath, Ivan Triesault

The Return of October

US   1948   89m   Technicolor
Columbia
GB title: *A Date with Destiny*

A girl's inheritance is contested on the grounds that she thinks a horse is the reincarnation of her Uncle Willie.

Thin whimsy which leaves its stars with egg on their faces.

w Norman Panama, Melvin Frank   d Joseph H. Lewis   ph William Snyder   m George Duning

☆ Glenn Ford, Terry Moore, Dame May Whitty, James Gleason, Albert Sharpe

The Return of Peter Grimm

US   1935   82m   bw
RKO

A strong-minded family man returns as a ghost to see how his family is getting on without him.

Fairly satisfying fantasy with good performances.

w Francis Edward Faragoh   play David Belasco   d George Nicholls Jnr

☆ Lionel Barrymore, Helen Mack, Edward Ellis, Donald Meek

'Sombre fantasy … pretty dull and boresome.' – *Variety*

† Previously filmed in 1926 with Alec B. Francis and Janet Gaynor.

The Return of Ringo (dubbed) **

Italy/Spain   1965   96m   Eastmancolor
Golden Era/Mediterranee/Rizzoli/Balcázar (Alberto Pugliese, Luciano Ercoli)
original title: *Il Ritorno di Ringo*

Returning home after the Civil War, a man discovers that the town, including his family and home, have been taken over by a Mexican bandit.

Superior spaghetti Western that allows room for character development among the usual baroque touches.

w Duccio Tessari, Fernando Di Leo   d Duccio Tessari   ph Francisco Marin   m Ennio Morricone   ad Juan Alberto Soler   ed Lucia Quaglia

☆ Giuliano Gemma, Fernando Sancho, Hally Hammond (Lorella de Luca), Nieves Navarro, Antonio Casas, Pajarito, Jorge Martin

† The movie was a sequel to *A Pistol for Ringo* (qv).

Return of Sabata (dubbed)

Italy/France/West Germany   1971   88m
Technicolor   Techniscope
UA/PEA/Artistes Associés/Artemis (Alberto Grimaldi)

original title: *E Tornato Sabata … Hai Chiuso un'Altra Volta*

The gunfighter Sabata is double-crossed by an old friend in his search for gold but emerges victorious as usual.

Almost a repeat of the original film, except that it now lacks the element of surprise and has little else to offer.

w Renato Izzo, Gianfranco Parolini   d Frank Kramer (Gianfranco Parolini)   ph Sandro Mancori   m Marcello Giombini   ad Luciano Puccini   ed Gianfranco Parolini, Salvatore Aventario

☆ Lee Van Cleef, Reiner Schöne, Annabella Incontrera, Gianni Rizzo, Gianpiero Albertini, Pedro Sanchez (Ignazio Spalla)

'Fairly run-of-the-mill Spaghetti Western, with the usual quota of menacing close-ups and modish camera angles.' – *Alistair Whyte, MFB*

† The film was a sequel to *Sabata* (qv). It was originally released in Italy at 107m.

Return of Superfly

US   1990   95m   colour
Crash Pictures (Sig Shore, Anthony Wisdom)

A former drug-dealer decides to destroy his old gang.

Dull and violent sequel that hits a new low.

w Anthony Wisdom   d Sig Shore   ph Anghel Decca   m Curtis Mayfield   pd Jeremie Frank   ed John Mullen

☆ Nathan Purdee, Margaret Avery, Leonard Thomas, Christopher Curry

'Shore brings no style or humor to a routine portrayal of New York's drug underground.' – *Variety*

Return of the Ape Man: see *The Ape Man*

The Return of the Bad Men

US   1948   90m   bw
RKO (Nat Holt)

A farmer tries to reform the female leader of a terrorist outlaw gang, but she is killed in a bank raid.

Standard, well-shot Western which contrives to introduce a number of well-known historical bandits.

w Charles O'Neal, Jack Natteford, Luci Ward   d Ray Enright   ph J. Roy Hunt   m Roy Webb   md Constantin Bakaleinikoff

☆ Randolph Scott, Robert Ryan, Anne Jeffreys, Jacqueline White, Steve Brodie

'Riding to greater glory as the gay O. Henry hero!'

The Return of the Cisco Kid

US   1939   70m   bw
TCF (Kenneth MacGowan)

The Kid escapes a Mexican firing squad into Arizona and defeats swindlers.

Modest Western with plenty of zip.

w Milton Sperling   d Herbert I. Leeds

☆ Warner Baxter, Lynn Bari, Cesar Romero, Henry Hull, Kane Richmond, C. Henry Gordon, Robert Barrat

'Substantial fare for adventure audiences.' – *Variety*

The Return of the Corsican Brothers: see *Bandits of Corsica*

Return of the Dragon: see *The Way of the Dragon*

The Return of The Evil Dead

Spain   1973   91m   Eastmancolor
London International/Ancla Century (Roman Plana)

original title: *El Ataque de los Muertos sin Ojos*

Devil-worshipping Knights Templar, blinded and killed by villagers in the Middle Ages, rise from their graves to slaughter the locals and a visiting American.

Gruesome but dull horror movie, one of a series featuring the dead Knights.

wd Amando de Ossorio   ph Miguel F. Mila   m Tony Abril   ed Joseph Anthony

☆ Tony Kendal, Fernando Sancha, Esther Rey, Lone Fleming, Frank Blake

'Blood-Curdling Giant Fly-Creature Runs Amok!'
'Scream At The Human Terror Created By Atoms Gone Wild!'
'Scream At Ghastly Fly Monster As He Keeps A Love Tryst!'
'Scream At The Desperate Search For The Fly With A Heart Of A Man!'

Return of the Fly

US   1959   80m   bw
TCF (Bernard Glasser)

The son of the original fly man meets the same fate as his father.

Cheerless follow-up.

wd Edward Bernds   ph Brydon Baker   m Paul Sawtell, Bert Shefter

☆ Vincent Price, Brett Halsey, John Sutton, David Frankham, Dan Seymour

Return of the Frontiersman

US   1950   74m   Technicolor
Warner

A man escapes from prison to prove himself innocent of the bank robbery for which he was convicted.

Goodish double-bill Western with no surprises.

w Edna Anhalt   d Richard Bare   ph J. Peverall Marley   m David Buttolph

☆ Gordon MacRae, Julie London, Rory Calhoun, Fred Clark, Edwin Rand

Return of the Jedi *

US   1983   132m   DeLuxe   Panavision
TCF/Lucasfilm (Howard Kazanjian)

'Episode 6' of the *Star Wars* serial: our heroes combat Darth Vader and Jabba the Hutt.

More expensive fantasy for the world's children of all ages, especially the undemanding ones.

w Lawrence Kasdan, George Lucas   d Richard Marquand   ph Alan Hume   m John Williams   pd Norman Reynolds

☆ Mark Hamill, Harrison Ford, Carrie Fisher, Billy Dee Williams, Anthony Daniels, Peter Mayhew, Kenny Baker

'I admire the exquisite skill and talent which have been poured into these films, while finding the concepts behind these gigantic video games in the sky mindlessly tedious.' – *Margaret Hinxman, Daily Mail*

'An impersonal and rather junky piece of moviemaking.' – *Pauline Kael, New Yorker*

'Only the effects are special.' – *Sight and Sound*

⅄ John Williams; art direction

'They're back – and they're hungry!'

The Return of The Living Dead

US   1985   90m   DeLuxe
Tom Fox/Hemdale/Orion

The army is called in to repel a zombie onslaught.

Cult horror movie hailed by some as a black comedy, but likely to repel most audiences.

wd Dan O'Bannon   story Rudy Ricci, John Russo, Russell Streiner   m Jules Brenner   pd Matt Clifford   ed Robert Gordon

☆ Clu Gulager, James Karen, Don Calfa, Thom Mathews

'Back From The Dead And Hungry For More.'

Return of The Living Dead III

US   1993   105m   Foto-Kem
Trimark/Bandai Visual/Ozla (Gary Schmoeller, Brian Yuzna)

A youth who spies on an experiment to revive the dead decides to bring his girlfriend back to life when she is killed in a motorcycle accident.

A Romeo and Juliet for the splatter generation: an extremely gory movie of flesh-eating zombies, aimed unerringly at the teens and twenties with its narrative of young love gone awry; it is slickly done, though its scenes with blood-spattered, mutilated bodies and decaying corpses are not for the squeamish.

w John Penney   d Brian Yuzna   ph Gerry Lively   m Barry Goldberg   pd Anthony Tremblay   ed Christopher Roth   sp Steve Johnson, Tim Ralston, Kevin Brennan, Christopher Nelson, Wayne Toth

☆ Mindy Clarke, J. Trevor Edmond, Kent McCord, Sarah Douglas, James T. Callahan, Mike Moroff, Sal Lopez, Basil Wallace

'A pedestrian and gruesome, but never really scary, story.' – *Variety*

'The best of the series so far, with a back-to-basics scenario that goes for solid scares rather than splatter spoofery … one of the best zombie movies since the glory days of George Romero.' – *The Dark Side*

† The film was released direct to video in Britain in an uncut version. For the American cinema release, which runs for 97m, some of the bloodier scenes were removed.

Return of The Living Dead Part II

US   1987   89m   Photolab
Guild/Lorimar/Greenfox (Tom Fox)

Brain-eating zombies attack a small town.

Dismal horror movie, unable to raise chills or laughs.

wd Ken Wiederhorn   ph Robert Elswit   m J. Peter Robinson, Vladimir Horunzhy   ad Dale Allan Pelton   ed Charles Bornstein

☆ James Karen, Thom Mathews, Dana Ashbrook, Marsha Dietlein, Suzanne Snyder, Philip Bruns, Michael Kenworthy, Thor Van Lingen, Jason Hogan

'The film is typical of the juvenile, enervating would-be-comic approach adopted by too many horror movies in the late 80s.' – *Kim Newman, MFB*

The Return of the Musketeers

👫👫 GB/France/Spain 1989 101m colour
Entertainment/Timoth Burrill Productions/Fildebroc-Cine 5/Iberoamericana (Pierre Spengler)
📼 🎞 📀

The daughter of Milady de Winter vows vengeance on the Musketeers who were responsible for her mother's execution.
A sequel to The Four Musketeers, it is a lacklustre affair of four middle-aged failures attempting to redeem themselves.
w George MacDonald Fraser *novel Vingt Ans Après* by Alexandre Dumas d Richard Lester ph Bernard Lutic m Jean-Claude Petit pd Gil Parrondo ed John Victor Smith
☆ Michael York, Oliver Reed, Frank Finlay, C. Thomas Howell, Kim Cattrall, Geraldine Chaplin, Roy Kinnear, Christopher Lee, Philippe Noiret, Richard Chamberlain, Eusebio Lazaro, Alan Howard, Jean-Pierre Cassel

The Return of the Pink Panther *

GB 1974 113m DeLuxe Panavision
UA/Jewel/Pimlico/Mirisch/Geoffrey (Blake Edwards)
📼 🎞 📀

When the Pink Panther diamond – national treasure of the Eastern state of Lugash – is once again stolen, bungling Inspector Clouseau is called in.
Rehash of jokes from The Pink Panther (qv), not bad in parts but a rather tedious whole.
w Frank Waldman, Blake Edwards d Blake Edwards ph Geoffrey Unsworth m Henry Mancini
☆ Peter Sellers, Christopher Plummer, Herbert Lom, Catherine Schell, Peter Arne, Peter Jeffrey, Grégoire Aslan, David Lodge, Graham Stark
'The film never comes fully to the boil, but simmers in a series of self-contained, self-destructing little set pieces.' – *Richard Combs*
'The first film in history to be upstaged by its own credit titles.' – *Benny Green, Punch*

The Return of the Scarlet Pimpernel *

GB 1937 94m bw
London Films (Alexander Korda, Arnold Pressburger)
Sir Percy Blakeney saves his wife and other French aristos from the guillotine.
Predictable, stylish revolutionary romance, much thinner in plot and performance than its predecessor.
w Lajos Biro, Arthur Wimperis, Adrian Brunel d Hans Schwarz ph Mutz Greenbaum m Arthur Benjamin
☆ Barry K. Barnes, Sophie Stewart, Margaretta Scott, James Mason, Henry Oscar, Francis Lister, Anthony Bushell

Return of the Seven

US 1966 95m Technicolor Panavision
UA/Mirisch/CB (Ted Richmond)
🎞 📀 🎬
The seven gunmen, slightly reconstituted, fight again to rescue some kidnapped farmers.
The mixture as before (see The Magnificent Seven); adequate but scarcely inspired.
w Larry Cohen d Burt Kennedy ph Paul Vogel m Elmer Bernstein
☆ Yul Brynner, Robert Fuller, Julian Mateos, Warren Oates, Claude Akins, Virgilio Teixeira, Emilio Fernandez, Jordan Christopher, Fernando Rey
🎵 Elmer Bernstein

The Return of the Soldier *

GB 1982 102m Technicolor
Brent Walker/Barry R. Cooper (Ann Skinner, Simon Relph)
🎞
In 1916, a shellshocked soldier returns home, able to remember his old sweetheart but not his wife.
Overcast and heavy-handed treatment of a classy novella.
w Hugh Whitemore *novel* Rebecca West d Alan Bridges ph Stephen Goldblatt m Richard Rodney Bennett pd Luciana Arrighi

☆ Alan Bates, Ann-Margret, Julie Christie, Glenda Jackson, Jeremy Kemp, Edward de Souza, Frank Finlay, Jack May, Ian Holm
'The film has nowhere to go except into rhetorical bluster about class distinctions.' – *Tom Milne, MFB*

Return of the Swamp Thing

US 1989 85m DeLuxe
Medusa/Lightyear Entertainment/J & M Entertainment (Benjamin Melniker, Michael E. Uslan)
📼 🎞 📀
A mad scientist is thwarted from using his step-daughter in genetic experiments by a vegetable monster.
Ineffectual and relentlessly jokey approach to a comic-book hero.
w Derek Spencer, Grant Morris d Jim Wynorski ph Zoran Hochstatter m Chuck Cirino pd Robb Wilson King ed Leslie Rosenthal
☆ Louis Jourdan, Heather Locklear, Sarah Douglas, Dick Durock, Joey Sagal, Ace Mask, Chris Doyle, Daniel Taylor

Return of the Tall Blond *

France 1974 89m colour
Fox-Rank/Gaumont/De la Gueville (Alain Poiré, Yves Robert)
🎞
original title: Le Retour du Grand Blond
A violinist is once again caught up in rivalry between the police and the secret service.
Enjoyable, gently humorous sequel that lives up to the original.
w Francis Veber, Yves Robert d Yves Robert ph René Mathelin m Vladimir Cosma pd Guy Blanc ed Ghislaine Desjonquières, Françoise London
☆ Pierre Richard, Mireille Darc, Jean Carmet, Jean Rochefort, Michel Duchaussoy, Paul Le Person, Colette Castel
'The film never loses its light-hearted humour.' – *MFB*
† A sequel to *Le Grand Blond avec une Chaussure Noire.*

The Return of the Terror

US 1934 65m bw
Warner
A scientist feigns insanity to avoid prosecution for murder, and escapes to his old sanatorium, where murder strikes again.
Barnstorming murder mystery borrowing its title and nothing else from Edgar Wallace.
w Eugene Solow, Peter Milne d Howard Bretherton
☆ John Halliday, Mary Astor, Lyle Talbot, Frank McHugh, Irving Pichel, J. Carrol Naish
'Formula mystery, but speedy.' – *Variety*

'Terrifying! Paralysing! Horrifying!'
The Return of the Vampire *

US 1943 69m bw
Columbia (Sam White)
🎞 📀
Dracula reappears amid the London blitz.
Surprisingly well made and complexly plotted horror film; it looks good and only lacks humour. The wolf man, however, is a regrettable intrusion.
w Griffin Jay d Lew Landers ph John Stumar, L. J. O'Connell m Mario Castelnuovo-Tedesco md Morris Stoloff
☆ Bela Lugosi, Nina Foch, Frieda Inescort, Miles Mander, Matt Willis, Roland Varno, Ottola Nesmith

Return to Glennascaul *

Eire 1951 23m bw
Dublin Gate Theatre
Orson Welles gives a man a lift and is told a gentle ghost story.
Neither very satisfying nor very well done, this little film deserves a niche in history because of the talents involved. It was apparently made during one of the many intervals in the filming of Othello.
wd Hilton Edwards *narrator* Orson Welles
🎵 short film

Return to Macon County

US 1975 89m Movielab
AIP/Macon Service Company (Eliot Schick)
In the fifties, two wandering youths pick up a waitress and have serious trouble with a manic policeman in America's unfriendliest area.

Slam-bang sequel to Macon County Line, rather unintentionally comic.
wd Richard Compton ph Jacques Marquette m Robert O. Ragland
☆ Nick Nolte, Don Johnson, Robin Mattson, Robert Viharo

Return to Oz

👫👫 US 1985 110m Technicolor
Walt Disney/Silver Screen Partners (Paul Maslansky)
📼 📀 🎬
Dorothy has traumas because of her Oz experiences, and suffers further nightmares under shock treatment.
A weird way to treat a children's classic, the result being a movie which appealed strongly to nobody except, possibly, the producer. The Disney people should have known better.
w Walter Murch, Gill Dennis d Walter Murch ph David Watkin m David Shire
☆ Fairuza Balk, Jean Marsh, Nicol Williamson, Piper Laurie, Matt Clark, Emma Ridley
'Astonishingly sombre, melancholy, and sadly unengaging.' – *Variety*
'Without musical numbers this narrative seems a perilously thin journey with no particular purpose.' – *Time Out*

Return to Paradise *

US 1953 109m Technicolor
UA/Aspen (Theron Warth)
A peace seeker settles on a tiny South Sea island and leaves when his wife dies; he returns after World War II with his daughter.
Curious idyll, slow but not displeasing.
w Charles Kaufman *novel* James Michener d Mark Robson ph Winton Hoch m Dimitri Tiomkin
☆ Gary Cooper, Barry Jones, Roberta Haynes, Moira MacDonald

'Give up three years of their lives or give up the life of their friend. They have eight days to decide.'
Return to Paradise

US 1998 111m colour
Polygram/Propaganda/Tetragram (Alain Bernheim, Steve Golin)
📼 🎞 📀 💿
Two American men, who discover that their friend is about to be executed for drug offences in Malaysia, have to choose between letting him die or returning to testify, and facing possible imprisonment themselves.
A drama of total predictability; it raises moral issues only to avoid resolving them.
w Wesley Strick, Bruce Robinson screenplay Pierre Jolivet, Olivier Schatzky d Joseph Ruben ph Reynaldo Villalobos m Mark Mancina pd Bill Groom ed Andrew Mondshein, Craig McKay
☆ Vince Vaughn, Anne Heche, Joaquin Phoenix, David Conrad, Vera Farmiga, Nick Sandow, Jada Pinkett Smith
'Disappointingly conventional treatment of an intriguing story that could have used either more narrative zing or greater thematic complexity.' – *Todd McCarthy, Variety*
† It is a remake of the 1989 French film *Force Majeure* (qv).

Return to Peyton Place *

US 1961 122m DeLuxe Cinemascope
TCF/API (Jerry Wald)
Constance Mackenzie's daughter writes a novel about Peyton Place and falls in love with her publisher.
More closets are unlocked, more skeletons fall out; for addicts, the sequel does not disappoint, and it's all very glossy.
w Ronald Alexander d José Ferrer ph Charles G. Clarke m Franz Waxman
☆ Jeff Chandler, Carol Lynley, Eleanor Parker, Mary Astor, Robert Sterling, Luciana Paluzzi, Brett Halsey, Tuesday Weld
'Enough soap suds to pollute the Mississippi along with the mind.' – *Judith Crist, 1973*

Return to Snowy River

Australia 1988 97m colour Panavision
Burrowes Film Group/Hoyts
📼 🎞 📀
aka: *The Man from Snowy River Part II*
aka: *The Untamed*
Returning home with a herd of horses, a restless young rancher finds that he is resented by the more conventional settlers, who plan to dispossess him of his land.
Stolid sequel to a local success; an uninspired drama which does not have much to offer other than a great many horses.
w John Dixon, Geoff Burrowes d Geoff Burrowes ph Keith Wagstaff m Bruce Rowland pd Leslie Binns ed Gary Woodyard
☆ Tom Burlinson, Sigrid Thornton, Brian Dennehy, Nicholas Eadie, Bryan Marshall, Mark Hembrow, Rhys McConnochie, Peter Cummins

Return to the Blue Lagoon

US 1991 98m Technicolor
Columbia TriStar/Price (William A. Graham)
📼 🎞 📀
A mother, her daughter and an orphaned boy are washed up on a desert island; the girl and boy grow to adulthood and fall in love.
A sequel that, once it has disposed of the adult, is virtually a remake of the 1980 version and no better the second time around.
w Leslie Stevens *novel The Garden of God* by Henry de Vere Stacpoole d William A. Graham ph Robert Steadman m Basil Poledouris pd Jon Dowding ed Ronald J. Fagan
☆ Milla Jovovich, Brian Krause, Lisa Pelikan, Courtney Phillips

Return to Yesterday

GB 1940 68m bw
Ealing
A bored Hollywood star seeks anonymity in a seaside repertory company.
Mild comedy, not without interest.
w Robert Stevenson, Roland Pertwee, Angus MacPhail *play Goodness How Sad* by Robert Morley d Robert Stevenson ph Ronald Neame m Ernest Irving
☆ Clive Brook, Anna Lee, Dame May Whitty, Hartley Power, Milton Rosmer, David Tree, Olga Lindo

Reuben, Reuben *

US 1982 101m CFI color
Saltair/Taft (Walter Shenson)
A drunken British poet upsets a New England community.
Oddball comedy at which one laughs without much enthusiasm.
w Julius J. Epstein *play Spofford* by Herman Shumlin *novel Peter de Vries* d Robert Ellis Miller ph Peter Stein m Billy Goldenberg pd Peter Larkin
☆ Tom Conti, Kelly McGillis, Roberts Blossom, Cynthia Harris, Joel Fabiani
🎵 Tom Conti; adaptation

Reunion

US 1936 83m bw
Darryl Zanuck/TCF
GB title: *Hearts in Reunion*
When a doctor retires, the townsfolk reunite him with many of the children he has brought into the world.
Tiresome second attempt to cash in on the Dionne Quintuplets, who make several appearances.
w Sam Hellman, Gladys Lehman, Sonya Levien d Norman Taurog
☆ Jean Hersholt, Rochelle Hudson, Helen Vinson, Slim Summerville, J. Edward Bromberg, Sara Haden
'Too episodic to command interest or supply suspense.' – *Variety*
† A sequel to *The Country Doctor.*

Reunion

France/West Germany/GB 1989 110m colour
Rank/Les Films Ariane/FR3/NEF/CLG/TAC (Anne Françoise)
📼 📀
original title: *L'Ami Retrouvé*
Returning to Germany as an old man, a Jewish lawyer recalls a schoolboy friendship destroyed by the Nazis' anti-Semitism.

Minimally scripted, ploddingly directed and lacking in emotional weight.
w Harold Pinter *novel* Reunion by Fred Uhlman d Jerry Schatzberg *ph* Bruno de Keyzer *m* Philippe Sarde *pd* Alexandre Trauner *ed* Martine Barraque
☆ Jason Robards, Christien Anholt, Samuel West, Françoise Fabian, Maureen Kerwin, Barbara Jefford, Dorothea Alexander, Frank Baker, Tim Barker
'A tedious re-exploration of already over-charted territory.' – *Tom Milne, MFB*

Reunion in France
US 1942 104m bw
MGM (Joseph L. Mankiewicz)
GB title: *Mademoiselle France*
A selfish Parisian dress designer gradually realizes that her world has changed when the Nazis invade and she is asked to help an American flyer.
Action flagwaver which tries also to be a woman's picture and goes pretty soppily about it.
w Jan Lustig, Marvin Borowsky, Marc Connelly *story* Ladislas Bus-Fekete d Jules Dassin *ph* Robert Planck *m* Franz Waxman
☆ Joan Crawford, John Wayne, Philip Dorn, Reginald Owen, Albert Basserman, John Carradine, Ann Ayars, J. Edward Bromberg, Henry Daniell, Moroni Olsen, Howard da Silva
'Miss Crawford isn't making all the sacrifices implied in the script … Dressing like a refugee is certainly not in her contract.' – *New York Herald Tribune*

Reunion in Vienna *
US 1933 100m bw
MGM
A long-exiled nobleman tries to take up an old romance even though the lady is married.
Lacklustre adaptation of a play which must have style; the performances remain interesting.
w Ernest Vajda, Claudine West *play* Robert E. Sherwood d Sidney Franklin *ph* George Folsey *m* William Axt
☆ John Barrymore, Diana Wynyard, Frank Morgan, May Robson, Eduardo Ciannelli, Una Merkel, Henry Travers
'Unlikely money film outside a few of the larger cities.' – *Variety*
ಠ George Folsey

Reveille With Beverly *
US 1943 78m bw
Columbia (Sam White)
A girl disc jockey runs a programme for soldiers.
Thin excuse for a musical, but the result was pretty popular.
w Howard J. Green, Jack Henley, Albert Duffy d Charles Barton
☆ Ann Miller, William Wright, Dick Purcell, Franklin Pangborn, Tim Ryan, Larry Parks

Revenge: see *Blood Feud* (1979)

Revenge
GB 1971 89m Eastmancolor
Rank/Peter Rogers Productions (George H. Brown)
When children are raped and murdered in a north country town, two men take the law into their own hands.
Crude melodrama set in Cold Comfort Farm country; efficient but unrewarding.
w John Kruse d Sidney Hayers *ph* Ken Hodges *m* Eric Rogers
☆ Joan Collins, Sinead Cusack, James Booth, Ray Barrett, Kenneth Griffith

Revenge
US 1989 124m DeLuxe Panavision
Columbia TriStar/Raster (Hunt Lowry, Stanley Rubin)
Left for dead by a jealous husband, a former pilot seeks revenge and reunion with his lover.
Brutal, shallow thriller that is too predictable to be enjoyable.
w Jim Harrison, Jeffrey Fiskin *novel* Jim Harrison d Tony Scott *ph* Jeffrey Kimball *m* Jack Nitzsche *pd* Michael Seymour, Benjamin Fernandez *ed* Chris Lebenzon, Michael Tronick
☆ Kevin Costner, Anthony Quinn, Madeleine Stowe, Tomas Milian, Joaquin Martinez, James Gammon, Jesse Corti, Sally Kirkland, Miguel Ferrer

Revenge at El Paso: see *Ace High*

Revenge Is My Destiny
US 1971 95m colour
Gold Key (Toby Ross)
A one-eyed hero returns from Vietnam to discover that his hated wife is missing; he goes looking for her.
Drab thriller with less than adequate script, direction and performances.
w Mardik Martin d Joseph Adler *ph* Ares Parshalis Demertzis *m* Stu Phillips, Richard Markowitz *ad* Paul Moore *ed* Joseph Adler, Charles Carrubba
☆ Chris Robinson, Sidney Blackmer, Elisa Ingram, Joe E. Ross, John Lodge, Patricia Rainier, Willie Pastrano

Revenge of Billy the Kid
GB 1992 87m Colour
Powerhouse Pictures/Montage (Tim Dennison)
A carnivorous monster, the offspring of a goat and a farmer, kills off his father's family.
Grotesque and disgusting low-budget horror comedy, obsessed with rape, bestiality and the nastier bodily functions. A credit for 'Flatulence Artists' sets the tone.
w Tim Dennison, Jim Groom, Richard Matthews d Jim Groom *ph* David Read *m* Tony Flynn
☆ Michael Balfour, Samantha Perkins, Jackie D. Broad, Trevor Peake, Bryan Heeley, Norman Mitchell, Dean Williamson, Michael Ripper
'Amateurish horror spoof made on a tiny budget and with even less wit or intelligence.' – *Sight and Sound*

'If you go alone – you'll find yourself running all the way home!'

The Revenge of Frankenstein
GB 1958 89m Technicolor
Columbia/Hammer (Anthony Hinds)
Baron Frankenstein evades the guillotine and makes a new creature with the brain of a homicidal dwarf.
Dullish horror farrago with a few indications of quirkish humour.
w Jimmy Sangster, Hurford Janes d Terence Fisher *ph* Jack Asher *m* Leonard Salzedo *pd* Bernard Robinson *ed* James Needs, Alfred Cox
☆ Peter Cushing, Michael Gwynn, Oscar Quitak, Francis Matthews, Eunice Gayson, John Welsh, Lionel Jeffries, Richard Wordsworth, Charles Lloyd Pack, John Stuart, Arnold Diamond
† This second Hammer Frankenstein set the tone for the rest; see *The Curse of Frankenstein*.

Revenge of the Blood Beast: see *She Beast*

Revenge of the Dead: see *Night of the Ghouls*

Revenge of the Gladiators: see *Fire over Rome*

Revenge of the Nerds
US 1984 90m DeLuxe
TCF/Interscope (Ted Field, Peter Samuelson)
College freshmen decide to fight back when they are evicted from their dormitories and mocked by the football team and rejected by the fraternities.
Raucous comedy for the intellectually challenged.
w Steve Zacharias, Jeff Buhai *story* Tim Metcalfe, Miguel Tejada-Flores d Jeff Kanew *ph* King Baggot *m* Thomas Newman *pd* James L. Schoppe *ed* Alan Balsam
☆ Robert Carradine, Anthony Edwards, Ted McGinley, Bernie Casey, Julia Montgomery, John Goodman
† It was followed by two lesser sequels: *Revenge of the Nerds II: Nerds in Paradise*, directed by Joe Roth in 1987; *Revenge of the Nerds III: The Next Generation*, directed for TV by Roland Mesa in 1992.

Revenge of the Pink Panther
US 1978 98m Technicolor Panavision
UA/Blake Edwards
Inspector Clouseau tracks down a drug-smuggling industrialist.
Feeble addition to a series which was always too pleased with itself.
w Frank Waldman, Ron Clark, Blake Edwards d Blake Edwards *ph* Ernie Day *m* Henry Mancini
☆ Peter Sellers, Herbert Lom, Robert Webber, Dyan Cannon, Burt Kwouk, Paul Stewart, Robert Loggia, Graham Stark

Revenge of the Vampire: see *Mask of Satan*

Revenge of the Zombies
US 1943 61m bw
Lindsley Parsons/Monogram
A Nazi scientist in Mexico tries to convert an army of the dead for Hitler's use.
Unpersuasive horror cheapie.
w Edmund Kelso, Van Norcross d Steve Sekely
☆ John Carradine, Robert Lowery, Gale Storm, Veda Ann Borg, Mantan Moreland

The Revengers
US 1972 108m DeLuxe Panavision
Cinema Center/Martin Rackin
A rancher gathers a posse to hunt down the Indians who have allegedly murdered his wife and family.
Standard major Western with a dismal script which echoes The Dirty Dozen and The Wild Bunch: sometimes repulsive, seldom exciting.
w Wendell Mayes d Daniel Mann *ph* Gabriel Torres *m* Pino Calvi
☆ William Holden, Ernest Borgnine, Susan Hayward, Woody Strode, Roger Hanin

Revengers' Comedies
GB/France 1997 82m Technicolor
J&M/BBC/Arts Council/France 2/Artisan/IMA (Simon Bosanquet)
Two suicidal strangers agree to take revenge on each other's nemesis.
Despite the efforts of an accomplished cast, this is a lumpy comedy of a dull man who finds himself ill-at-ease in eccentric, upper-middle-class society.
wd Malcolm Mowbray *play* Alan Ayckbourn *ph* Romain Winding *m* Alexandre Desplat *pd* Stuart Walker *ed* Barrie Vince
☆ Sam Neill, Helena Bonham-Carter, Kristin Scott Thomas, Rupert Graves, Martin Clunes, Steve Coogan, John Wood, Liz Smith, Anita Dobson, Charlotte Coleman

Reversal of Fortune **
US 1990 111m Technicolor
Warner/Shochiku Fuji/Sovereign Pictures/Edward R. Pressman, Oliver Stone
A European aristocrat, found guilty of attempting to murder his wealthy American wife, hires a brilliant lawyer to mount an appeal against the sentence.
Based on a true story, it combines the appeal of court-room drama with a prurient curiosity about the lives of the very rich.
w Nicholas Kazan *book* Alan Dershowitz d Barbet Schroeder *ph* Luciano Tovoli *m* Mark Isham *pd* Mel Bourne *ed* Lee Percy
☆ Glenn Close, Jeremy Irons, Ron Silver, Annabella Sciorra, Uta Hagen, Fisher Stevens, Christine Baranski, Jack Gilpin, Stephen Mailer
'A classy piece of filmmaking.' – *Variety*
▲ Jeremy Irons
ಠ Barbet Schroeder; Nicholas Kazan

The Revolt of Job **
Hungary 1983 98m colour
Mafilm Tarsulas Filmstudio/Hungarian TV/ZDF
original title: *Jób Lázadása*
A young Christian orphan is adopted by a Jewish farmer and his wife, who fear the coming of the Nazis.
Touching, understated film, told from the perspective of the child, which gives a freshness and poignancy to a familiar theme.
w Katalin Petényi, Imre Gyöngyössi, Barna Kabay d Imre Gyöngyössi, Barna Kabay *ph* Gábor Szabó *m* Zoltán Jeney
☆ Ference Zenthe, Hédi Temessy, Gábor Fehér, Péter Rudolf, Leticia Cano, Gregor Henry
ಠ best foreign-language film

The Revolt of Mamie Stover
US 1956 93m Eastmancolor Cinemascope
TCF (Buddy Adler)
A dance hall girl leaves San Francisco for Honolulu, makes money there but reforms for love of a rich novelist.
Absurdly bowdlerized and boring film version of a novel about a sleazy prostitute; hardly worth making at all in this form, especially as the cast seems well capable of a raunchier version.
w Sydney Boehm *novel* William Bradford Huie d Raoul Walsh *ph* Leo Tover *m* Hugo Friedhofer
☆ Jane Russell, Agnes Moorehead, Richard Egan, Joan Leslie

The Revolt of the Praetorians (dubbed)
Italy 1964 90m Technicolor Technoscope
FIA
original title: *La Rivolta dei Pretoriani*
The leader of the Praetorian guard doubles as the Red Wolf, the masked leader of a revolt against the vicious and autocratic rule of the emperor Domitian.
Typical undistinguished sword-and-sandals historical romp.
w Gianpaolo Callegari d Alfonso Brescia *ph* Pierludovico Pavoni *m* Carlo Franci *ad* Piervittorio Marchi *ed* Nella Nannuzzi
☆ Richard Harrison, Moira Orfei, Giuliano Gemma, Piero Lulli, Aldo Cecconi, Paola Pitti
† The film's American star, Richard Harrison, turned down the lead in *A Fistful of Dollars*, which went to Clint Eastwood instead.

Revolution
US 1985 125m Technicolor
Warner/Goldcrest/Viking (Irwin Winkler)
A trapper becomes involved in the American War of Independence and with the aristocratic daughter of a loyalist.
A mouse of a movie, despite its epic pretensions; the narrative has been swallowed by incoherent set-pieces and the period setting falters under the Method acting of its star.
w Robert Dillon d Hugh Hudson *ph* Bernard Lutic *m* John Corigliano *pd* Assheton Gorton *ed* Stuart Baird
☆ Al Pacino, Donald Sutherland, Nastassja Kinski, Joan Plowright, Dave King, Steven Berkoff, John Wells, Annie Lennox, Dexter Fletcher, Richard O'Brien
'Hudson has thrown what doubtless started as a perfectly straightforward script to the winds and marched off in search of images that would somehow galvanise the whole show into life. But as his camera stumbles through the smoke, fire, and mobs of expensively costumed extras it's clear he's not going to find them.' – *David Ehrenstein*

The Revolutionary
US 1970 101m Technicolor
(UA) Pressman-Williams (Edward R. Pressman)
Episodes in the life of a revolutionary, from distributing leaflets to attempted assassination.
A rather casual study of one man's radicalism, in no particular time or place; no doubt of great interest to other revolutionaries.
w Hans Königsberger d Paul Williams *ph* Brian Probyn *m* Michael Small
☆ Jon Voight, Jennifer Salt, Robert Duvall

The Revolving Doors
France/Canada 1988 102m colour
Gala/Malofilm/Canal Plus (René Malo, Francyne Morin)
original title: *Les Portes Tournantes*
A dying woman recalls her earlier life, marriage and musical ambitions.
Slight but quite enjoyable bout of nostalgia, heavy on period charm.
w Jacques Savoie, Francis Mankiewicz d Francis Mankiewicz *ph* Thomas Vamos *m* François Dompierre *ad* Anne Pritchard *ed* André Corriveau
☆ Monique Spaziani, Gabriel Arcand, Miou-Miou, François Methe, Jacques Penot, Françoise Faucher, Jean-Louis Roux, Remy Girard, Charles Reiner
'This lumbering tale of thwarted mother-love seems even more bereft of sense than sensibility.' – *Derek Malcolm, Guardian*

The Reward
US 1965 92m DeLuxe Cinemascope
TCF/Aaron Rosenberg
A mixed group of adventurers set out across the desert to capture a murderer; but thieves fall out.

Pretentious and talky melodrama which quickly scuttled its director's chances in Hollywood. Little action, obvious outcome, attractive Death Valley locations.
w Serge Bourgignon, Oscar Mullard
novel Michael Barrett d Serge Bourgignon ph Joe MacDonald m Elmer Bernstein
☆ Max von Sydow, Efrem Zimbalist Jnr, Yvette Mimieux, Gilbert Roland, Emilio Fernandez, Henry Silva

'Emotions clash in a crescendo of drama!'

Rhapsody

US 1954 116m Technicolor
MGM (Lawrence Weingarten)
📼

A wealthy woman affects the lives of two quite different musicians, each of whom has his weakness.
Tedious romantic drama which vainly attempted a smart veneer but boasted a splendid musical soundtrack.
w Fay and Michael Kanin *novel Maurice Guest* by Henry Handel Richardson d Charles Vidor
ph Robert Planck md Johnny Green, Bronislau Kaper *piano* Claudio Arrau *violin* Michael Rabin
☆ Elizabeth Taylor, Vittorio Gassman, John Ericson, Louis Calhern, Michael Chekhov, Barbara Bates, Celia Lovsky, Richard Hageman

Rhapsody in August *

Japan 1990 97m colour
Palace/Shochiku/Akira Kurosawa
🔊

original title: *Hachigatsu-no-Kyoshikyoku*
A grandmother, prompted by her grandchildren and a visit from her Japanese-American nephew, recalls the death of her husband when the atomic bomb was dropped on Nagasaki.
A small-scale but ponderous plea for an understanding of the past.
wd Akira Kurosawa *novel Nabe-no-Naka* by Kiyoko Murata ph Takao Saito, Masaharu Ueda m Shinichiro Ikebe ad Yoshiro Muraki ed Akira Kurosawa
☆ Richard Gere, Sachiko Murasé, Hisashi Igawa, Narumi Kayashima, Tomoko Ohtakara, Mitsunori Isaki, Toshié Negishi, Choichiro Kawarasaki, Hidetaka Yoshioka, Mié Suzuki

Rhapsody in Blue **

US 1945 139m bw
Warner (Jesse L. Lasky)
📼 📀

The life story of composer George Gershwin.
No more trustworthy on factual matters than other Hollywood biopics of its era, this rather glum saga at least presented the music and the performers to excellent advantage.
w Howard Koch, Elliot Paul *story* Sonya Levien d Irving Rapper ph Sol Polito (musical numbers: Ernest Haller, Merritt B. Gerstad) md Leo Forbstein, Max Steiner ch Le Roy Prinz
ad Anton Grot, John Hughes
☆ Robert Alda, Joan Leslie, Alexis Smith, Charles Coburn, Julie Bishop, Albert Basserman, Oscar Levant, Herbert Rudley, Rosemary de Camp, Morris Carnovsky, Al Jolson, Paul Whiteman, George White, Hazel Scott
'With no story at all, this two-hour concert of Gershwin music would be well worth the price of admission' – *Daily Mail*
† Joan Leslie's songs were dubbed by Louanne Hogan.
♪ Ray Heindorf, Max Steiner

Rhinestone

US 1984 111m DeLuxe
TCF/Howard Smith, Marvin Worth
📼 📀

A night-club singer bets her obnoxious employer that she can turn a cab driver into a star.
Crude and witless Pygmalion variation with unsympathetic leads.
w Phil Alden Robinson, Sylvester Stallone d Bob Clark ph Timothy Galfas m Dolly Parton
☆ Dolly Parton, Sylvester Stallone, Richard Farnsworth, Ron Leibman, Tim Thomerson
'You'd have thought we all got together and decided how we could fastest ruin our careers.' – *Sylvester Stallone*

Rhino

US 1964 91m Metrocolor
MGM/Ivan Tors (Ben Chapman)
A scientist working with white rhinos is joined by an unscrupulous big game hunter.
Inoffensive African adventure.
w Art Arthur, Arthur Weiss d Ivan Tors ph Sven Persson, Lamar Boren m Lalo Schifrin
☆ Harry Guardino, Robert Culp, Shirley Eaton

Rhinoceros

US 1974 101m Eastmancolor
AFT/American Express/Cinevision/Ely Landau
In an American town, an alcoholic clerk is horrified to see his friends all turning into rhinoceroses.
An unsuccessful absurdist play about the pressures of conformity has become a somewhat absurd movie, though there is a little pleasure to be found in the comic interaction of Mostel and Wilder.
w Julian Barry *play* Eugene Ionesco d Tom O'Horgan ph James Crabe m Galt MacDermot pd Jack Martin Smith ed Bud Smith
☆ Gene Wilder, Zero Mostel, Karen Black, Joe Silver, Robert Weil, Marilyn Chris, Lou Cutell

Rhodes: see *Rhodes of Africa*

Rhodes of Africa *

GB 1936 91m bw
Gaumont (Geoffrey Barkas)
📼
US title: *Rhodes*
A rough-hewn diamond miner becomes Prime Minister of Cape Colony.
Heavy-going but generally interesting historical drama shot on location.
w Michael Barringer, Leslie Arliss, Miles Malleson *book* Sarah Millin d Berthold Viertel ph Bernard Knowles m Hubert Bath
☆ Walter Huston, Oscar Homolka, Basil Sydney, Peggy Ashcroft, Frank Cellier, Bernard Lee, Lewis Casson
'One of the better English-made pictures ... should do all right even if it doesn't get the women.' – *Variety*
'Solid, worthy, humourless, it unrolls its eleven well-bred reels with all the technical advantages of 1936.' – *Graham Greene*

Rhubarb

US 1951 94m bw
Paramount (Perlberg-Seaton)
A millionaire leaves his fortune, including a baseball team, to a wild ginger cat, which means problems for his publicity agent.
Typical scatty farce of the early fifties, held together by the splendid performance of the disdainful feline in the title role rather than by any special merit in the handling.
w Dorothy Reid, Francis Cockrell *novel* H. Allen Smith d Arthur Lubin ph Lionel Lindon m Van Cleave
☆ Ray Milland, Jan Sterling, Gene Lockhart, William Frawley

Rhubarb

👫 GB 1969 37m Technicolor
ABPC/Avalon
📼
Various village notables congregate on the golf course.
Virtually silent comedy (nobody says anything but 'rhubarb') which could have been very funny with better jokes. A TV remake in 1979 was however much worse.
wd Eric Sykes
☆ Harry Secombe, Eric Sykes, Jimmy Edwards, Hattie Jacques, Gordon Rollins, Graham Stark, Kenneth Connor

Rhythm of the Islands

US 1943 60m bw
Universal (Bernard Burton)
A rather dull South Sea island sets itself up to attract tourists.
Moderate musical programmer, one of many from this studio during the war.
w Oscar Brodney, M. M. Musselman d Roy William Neill
☆ Allan Jones, Jane Frazee, Andy Devine, Ernest Truex, Marjorie Gateson, Mary Wickes
'Acceptably fulfils its purpose of providing an hour's diverting footage for dual support in the general runs.' – *Variety*

Rhythm on the Range *

US 1936 87m bw
Paramount (Benjamin Glazer)
A hired hand saves the boss's daughter when she is kidnapped by local badmen.
Easy-going musical comedy with a Western background, later remade as Pardners (qv).
w John C. Moffett, Sidney Salkow, Walter de Leon, Francis Martin d Norman Taurog ph Karl Struss *songs* various
☆ Bing Crosby, Martha Raye, Frances Farmer, Bob Burns, Lucile Watson, Samuel S. Hinds, George E. Stone, Warren Hymer
'Bing Crosby as a cowboy; Bing Crosby crooning a prize bull to sleep on a freight car; Bing Crosby more than ever like Walt Disney's Cock Robin; it needs some stamina to be a film reviewer.' – *Graham Greene*

Rhythm on the River *

US 1940 92m bw
Paramount (William Le Baron)
📼 📀
A song writer employs 'ghosts' to produce his music and lyrics; they discover this fact and go into business for themselves.
Cheerful musical with strong billing.
w Dwight Taylor, Billy Wilder, Jacques Théry d Victor Schertzinger ph Ted Tetzlaff m Johnny Burke, James V. Monaco
☆ Bing Crosby, Mary Martin, Basil Rathbone, Oscar Levant, Oscar Shaw, Charley Grapewin, William Frawley
♪ song 'Only Forever'

Rhythm Romance: see *Some Like It Hot (1939)*

Rhythm Serenade

GB 1943 87m bw
Columbia British (Ben Henry)
During the Second World War, a teacher who starts a day nursery so that mothers can work in a munitions factory falls in love with a commando recovering from a breakdown.
Sentimental little flag-waver with a few songs thrown in.
w Basil Woon, Marjorie Deans d Gordon Wellesley ph Erwin Hillier, Geoffrey Faithfull md Harry Bidgood ad George Provis ed Alan Jaggs
☆ Vera Lynn, Peter Murray-Hill, Julien Mitchell, Charles Victor, Jimmy Jewel, Ben Warris, Irene Handl, Jimmy Clitheroe, Joan Kemp Welch

Rhythm Thief

US 1994 88m bw
Film Crash (Jonathan Starch)
A hustler who makes a living on the streets selling bootleg tapes is pursued by violent punk rockers and a girl who was in a mental home with his mother.
There is talent on show here, but in the unloveliest of settings and among blank, alienated, strung-out, drugged denizens of the streets, whose horizons are limited to getting through the day.
w Matthew Harrison, Christopher Grimm d Matthew Harrison ph Howard Krupa m Danny Brenner, Hugh O'Donovan, John L. Horn, Kevin Okerlund ad Daniel Fisher ed Matthew Harrison
☆ Jason Andrews, Eddie Daniels, Kevin Corrigan, Kimberly Flynn, Sean Hagerty, Mark Alfred, Christopher Cooke, Bob McGrath
'No-budget New York item gets stronger as it moves confidently forward, weaving together the lives of some very desperate Lower East Siders before reaching a quietly devastating close.' – *Ken Eisner, Variety*
† The film was shot in 11 days.

Rice People *

Cambodia/France 1994 130m colour
Gala/JBA/Thelma/La Sept/TSR (Jacques Bidou)
original title: *Neak Sre*
aka: *Les Gens de la Rizière*
When her husband dies suddenly, the wife of a Cambodian rice farmer tries to tend the crops as well as looking after her seven daughters.
Elegantly shot, low-key drama that can be rewarding if you submit to its slow, seasonal rhythms.
w Rithy Panh, Eve Deboise *novel Ranju Sepanjang Jalan* by Shahnon Ahmad d Rithy Panh ph Jacques Bouquin m Marc Marder ad Nhean Chamnaul ed Andrée Davanture, Marie-Christine Rougerie

☆ Peng Phan, Mom Soth, Chhim Naline, Va Simorn, Meas Daniel, Phang Chamroeun, Sophy Sodany, Muong Danyda
'Hard to enthuse about so much noble suffering. But it's occasionally fascinating, all the same, as a window on a very different world.' – *Sheila Johnston, Independent*

'From the very beginning, they knew they'd be friends to the end. What they didn't count on was everything in between!'

Rich and Famous

US 1981 117m Metrocolor
MGM/Jaquet/William Allyn
📼 📀
Two girlfriends meet again years after college; one has become a famous highbrow novelist, and with her help the other becomes a lowbrow one.
Unattractively sexed-up remake of Old Acquaintance, with even more talk than the original, and much less style.
w Gerald Ayres d George Cukor ph Don Peterman, Peter Eco m Georges Delerue pd Jan Scott ed John F. Burnett
☆ Candice Bergen, Jacqueline Bisset, David Selby, Hart Bochner, Steven Hill, Meg Ryan
'A sadly dispiriting occasion ... a jumbled conflation of The Group and a female version of Carnal Knowledge.' – *Tim Pulleine, MFB*
† The director was 82 when the film was shot, which must be some kind of record.

Rich and Strange *

GB 1931 83m bw
BIP (John Maxwell)
📼 📀
US title: *East of Shanghai*
A young couple come into money and take a trip around the world.
Slight, agreeable early talkie with a few Hitchcock touches.
w Alma Reville, Val Valentine, Alfred Hitchcock *novel* Dale Collins d Alfred Hitchcock ph Jack Cox, Charles Martin m Hal Dolphe
☆ Henry Kendall, Joan Barry, Percy Marmont, Betty Amann, Elsie Randolph
'Hitchcock, being Britain's D. W. Griffith, according to the press agents around here, usually gets a rave as his pictures take the screen. Here's one where the admirers will have difficulty knowing what to say.' – *Variety*
'Perhaps his bravest failure.' – *George Perry, 1965*

The Rich Are Always with Us

US 1932 73m bw
Warner (Sam Bischoff)
A socialite determines on a divorce but her new love is annoyed by her concern for her ex-husband.
Cocktail drama of a kind which totally disappeared from the screen.
w Austin Parker *novel* E. Pettit d Alfred E. Green m Ernest Haller m W. Franke Harling
☆ Ruth Chatterton, George Brent, John Miljan, Bette Davis, Adrienne Doré, Mae Madison, Robert Warwick
'Chiefly a femme picture ... the title's appropriateness is as obscure as the wisdom of so metaphoric a label for a flicker.' – *Variety*

The Rich Full Life: see *Cynthia*

Rich in Love

US 1992 105m DeLuxe Panavision
UPI/MGM (Richard D. Zanuck/Lili Fini Zanuck)
📼 📼 📀 📀
A teenage schoolgirl tries to keep the family together as her father begins to disintegrate after her mother leaves home suddenly, and her pregnant sister arrives with her new husband.
Meandering domestic drama, an attempt at a character study which fails because its participants distinctly lack character, cleaving only to the obvious and expected.
w Alfred Uhry *novel* Josephine Humphreys d Bruce Beresford ph Peter James m Georges Delerue pd John Stoddart ed Mark Warner
☆ Albert Finney, Jill Clayburgh, Kathryn Erbe, Kyle MacLachlan, Piper Laurie, Ethan Hawke, Suzy Amis, Alfre Woodard
'It could play on television tomorrow, and no-one would find anything amiss, save perhaps the ratings dropping precipitously as the audience drifted away in search of something more than genteel good taste.' – *John Harkness, Sight and Sound*

Rich Kids

US 1979 96m Technicolor
Lion's Gate/UA (George W. George, Michael Hausman)

An adolescent boy and girl are mildly corrupted by the behaviour of their parents.

Spasmodically interesting comedy-drama which seems ill at ease among the rich and alternates between exploitation, satire and whimsy.

w Judith Ross d Robert M. Young ph Ralf D. Bode m Craig Doerge

☆ Trini Alvarado, Jeremy Levy, Kathryn Walker, John Lithgow, Terry Kiser, David Selby

Rich Man, Poor Girl

US 1938 72m bw
MGM

Consternation takes a white-collar family when a millionaire takes a fancy to one of its daughters.

Unexciting comedy-drama vaguely modelled on You Can't Take It With You.

w Joseph Fields, Jerome Chodorov play Edith Ellis d Reinhold Schünzel

☆ Lew Ayres, Ruth Hussey, Robert Young, Don Castle, Guy Kibbee, Lana Turner, Rita Johnson

'Lightweight in marquee strength but should build through word of mouth.' – *Variety*

Rich Man's Folly

US 1931 80m bw
Paramount

A rich man has no time for his children.

Curious updating of Dickens's Dombey and Son; not really a success.

w Grover Jones, Edward Paramore Jnr d John Cromwell ph David Abel

☆ George Bancroft, Frances Dee, Robert Ames, Juliette Compton, Dorothy Peterson

'Splendid cast and serviceable product anywhere.' – *Variety*

The Rich Man's Wife

US 1996 94m Technicolor
Buena Vista/Hollywood/Caravan (Roger Birnbaum, Julie Bergman Sender)

An unhappily married woman discovers that her lover had her husband killed by an unstable stranger.

Predictable thriller, told in flashback, that never carries conviction.

wd Amy Holden Jones ph Haskell Wexler m John Frizzell, James Newton Howard pd Jeannine Oppewall ed Wendy Greene Bricmont

☆ Halle Berry, Christopher McDonald, Clive Owen, Peter Greene, Charles Hallahan, Frankie Faison, Clea Lewis

'A lady-and-the-psycho yarn so generic it might have been constructed by computer printout.' – *Godfrey Cheshire, Variety*

Rich, Young and Deadly: see *Platinum High School*

Rich, Young and Pretty

US 1951 95m Technicolor
MGM (Joe Pasternak)

A Texas rancher takes his young daughter to Paris, where she meets her real mother.

Moderate musical.

w Dorothy Cooper, Sidney Sheldon d Norman Taurog ph Robert Planck m Nicholas Brodszky ch Nick Castle ly Sammy Cahn

☆ Danielle Darrieux, Wendell Corey, Jane Powell, Fernando Lamas, Vic Damone

♪ song 'Wonder Why' (mNicholas Brodszky, lySammy Cahn)

Richard III ***

GB 1955 161m Technicolor Vistavision
London Films (Laurence Olivier)

Shakespeare's play about Richard Crookback, his seizure of the throne and his defeat at Bosworth.

Theatrical but highly satisfying filming of a splendidly melodramatic view of history. Interesting but not fussy camera movement, delightful sets (followed by a disappointingly 'realistic' battle) and superb performances.

w William Shakespeare (adapted by Laurence Olivier, Alan Dent, with additions) d Laurence

Olivier ph Otto Heller m William Walton pd Roger Furse ad Carmen Dillon

☆ Laurence Olivier, Claire Bloom, Ralph Richardson, Cedric Hardwicke, Stanley Baker, Alec Clunes, John Gielgud, Mary Kerridge, Pamela Brown, Michael Gough, Norman Wooland, Helen Haye, Patrick Troughton, Clive Morton, Andrew Cruickshank

'Wherever the play was loose-jointed or ill-fitting, Sir Laurence has been its tinker and its tailor, but never once its butcher.' – *Paul Dehn, News Chronicle*

⛓ Laurence Olivier

🎬 best film; best British film; Laurence Olivier

'I can smile ... and murder while I smile.'

Richard III ***

GB 1995 105m Technicolor
UA/British Screen/First Look (Liza Katselas Pare, Stephen Bayly)

In a fascist England of the 30s, the King's younger brother murders his way to the throne and attempts to hold it as civil war rages.

A fast-moving, pared-down version of Shakespeare that remains true to much of the play's poetry, concentrating on political manoeuvre and successfully translating the action to a modern setting.

w Ian McKellen play William Shakespeare stage production Richard Eyre d Richard Loncraine ph Peter Biziou m Trevor Jones pd Tony Burrough ed Paul Green

☆ Ian McKellen, Annette Bening, Jim Broadbent, Robert Downey Jnr, Nigel Hawthorne, Kristin Scott Thomas, Maggie Smith, John Wood, Adrian Dunbar, Dominic West

'A superb political thriller in an England that is a subtly distorting mirror of reality – or a reality adjacent to our own.' – *Peter Holland, TLS*

'A fast, exuberant, violent ride.' – *Variety*

⛓ Tony Burrough; costume design (Shuna Harwood)

Richer than the Earth: see *The Whistle at Eaton Falls*

The Richest Girl in the World

US 1934 80m bw
RKO (Pandro S. Berman)

A millionairess changes places with her secretary to find a man who will love her for herself.

Rose-coloured romance, remade in 1944 as Bride by Mistake.

w Norman Krasna d William A. Seiter ph Nick Musuraca md Max Steiner

☆ Miriam Hopkins, Joel McCrea, Fay Wray, Henry Stephenson, Reginald Denny, Beryl Mercer

'Eighty minutes of unerring entertainment ... a pip picture for Miriam Hopkins.' – *Variety*

⛓ Norman Krasna

The Richest Man in Town

US 1941 70m bw
Columbia (Jack Fier)

A small-town newspaper publisher feuds with an old friend over his prepared obituary of the latter.

A fragment of Americana with an unfinished feel.

w Farnya Foss, Jerry Sackheim d Charles Barton

☆ Frank Craven, Edgar Buchanan, Eileen O'Hearn, Roger Pryor, Tom Dugan

'Five buddies, one butler, and a dog on an adventure so big ... Even the world's richest kid can't afford to miss it.'

Richie Rich

👨👧 US 1994 95m colour
Warner/Silver Pictures/Davis Entertainment (Joel Silver, John Davis)

A wealthy 12-year-old, aided by his poorer friends, saves his parents when they are threatened by a murderous employee.

Unexceptional entertainment aimed at a young audience; it might keep them quiet for half an hour or so.

w Tom S. Parker, Jim Jennewein story Neil Tolkin, based on characters appearing in Harvey Comics d Donald Petrie ph Don Burgess m Alan Silvestri pd James Spencer ed Malcolm Campbell

☆ Macaulay Culkin, John Larroquette, Edward Herrmann, Jonathan Hyde, Christine Ebersole, Michael McShane

'Decently crafted but oddly charmless.' – *Variety*

'He's a cop accused of murder. The only person who knows he's innocent is the psycho who wants him dead.'

'This is one case that's going to be settled out of court.'

Ricochet

US 1991 102m colour
First Independent/Summit/Silver (Joel Silver, Michael Levy)

Seeking revenge, a murderer sets out to frame the one-time cop, now an assistant district attorney, who put him inside.

Depressingly violent and unpleasant thriller.

w Steven E. de Souza story Fred Dekker, Menno Meyjes d Russell Mulcahy ph Peter Levy m Alan Silvestri pd Jay Hinkle ed Peter Honess

☆ Denzel Washington, John Lithgow, Ice T, Kevin Pollak, Lindsay Wagner, Mary Ellen Trainor, Josh Evans, Victoria Dillard

'If you don't flinch when power tools are being abused and can swallow ridiculous plot points if more dynamite action is only a minute away, then this is a good bet for an entertaining night out.' – *Kim Newman, Empire*

Ricochet Romance

US 1954 80m bw
Universal (Robert Arthur)

The new cook transforms a dude ranch which had been allowed to run down.

Modest programme filler on well-established lines.

w Kay Lennard d Charles Lamont ph George Robinson md Joseph Gershenson

☆ Marjorie Main, Chill Wills, Rudy Vallee, Pedro Gonzales-Gonzales, Alfonso Bedoya, Ruth Hampton

The Riddle of the Sands *

👨👧 GB 1978 102m Eastmancolor Panavision
Rank/Worldmark (Drummond Challis)

In 1901 a British yachtsman in the North Sea hits upon a German trial invasion.

Rather too placid adaptation of a semi-classic adventure story in which too little happens to make a rousing action film; points of interest along the way, though.

w Tony Maylam, John Bailey novel Erskine Childers d Tony Maylam ph Hazel Peiser m Howard Blake

☆ Michael York, Simon MacCorkindale, Jenny Agutter, Alan Badel, Jurgen Andersen

The Riddle of the Stinson *

Australia 1988 95m colour
Kennedy Miller (Terry Hayes, George Miller, Doug Mitchell)

In 1937, a farmer goes to the rescue of survivors of a plane crash in inaccessible country.

A pleasant period picture, based on fact and told in direct and simple manner.

w Tony Morphett d Chris Noonan ph Geoffrey Simpson m Jim Conway, Colin Watson pd Owen Paterson ed Frans Vandenburgh

☆ Norman Kaye, Richard Roxburgh, Helen O'Connor, Esben Storm, Huw Williams, Susan Lyons

Ride a Crooked Mile *

US 1938 70m bw
Paramount (Jeff Lazarus)

An ex-Cossack cattle hijacker is disappointed when jailed to find that his son will not help him escape.

Lively crime melodrama with an unusual twist.

w Ferdinand Reyher, John C. Moffitt d Alfred E. Green

☆ Akim Tamiroff, Leif Erickson, Frances Farmer, Lynne Overman, John Miljan, Vladimir Sokoloff

'Fine melodrama, handicapped by lack of cast strength and so-so title.' – *Variety*

Ride a Crooked Trail

US 1958 88m Eastmancolor Cinemascope
Universal-International (Howard Pine)

A crook takes refuge in a small town and becomes its honest marshal.

One we've heard before, and seen better done.

w Borden Chase d Jesse Hibbs ph Harold Lipstein

☆ Audie Murphy, Walter Matthau, Gia Scala, Henry Silva

The Ride Back *

US 1957 79m bw
UA/Associates and Aldrich (William Conrad)

A lawman arrests an outlaw wanted for murder, but has the problem of getting him back to base.

Slightly offbeat low-budget Western, well enough done if it had to be done at all.

w Anthony Ellis d Allen H. Miner ph Joseph Biroc m Frank de Vol

☆ Anthony Quinn, William Conrad, George Trevino, Lita Milan

Ride beyond Vengeance

US 1966 100m Technicolor
Columbia/Tiger/Goodson/Todman/Sentinel/Fenady

A young Westerner, accused of cattle rustling and branded, vows revenge.

Dourly brutal but studio-bound and very padded Western; if there is any entertainment value it doesn't emerge for more than a few moments.

w Andrew J. Fenady novel The Night of the Tiger by Al Dewlen d Bernard McEveety ph Lester Shorr m Richard Markowitz

☆ Chuck Connors, Michael Rennie, Kathryn Hays, Claude Akins, Bill Bixby, Paul Fix, Gary Merrill, Joan Blondell, Gloria Grahame, Ruth Warrick, Arthur O'Connell, Frank Gorshin, James MacArthur

† Probably intended as a TV movie and found too violent.

Ride Clear of Diablo

US 1954 80m Technicolor
Universal-International (John W. Rogers)

A young man seeking vengeance on his father's murderer becomes deputy to a sheriff hired to kill him too.

Lively enough star Western.

w George Zuckerman d Jesse Hibbs ph Irving Glassberg m Joseph Gershenson

☆ Audie Murphy, Dan Duryea, Susan Cabot, Abbe Lane, Russell Johnson, Paul Birch, Jack Elam

Ride 'Em Cowboy

US 1941 82m bw
Universal (Alex Gottlieb)

Two hot dog vendors find themselves working on an Arizona dude ranch.

Slick but routine comedy star vehicle with no outstanding sequences.

w True Boardman, John Grant d Arthur Lubin ph John W. Boyle m Frank Skinner songs Don Raye, Gene de Paul

☆ Bud Abbott, Lou Costello, Dick Foran, Anne Gwynne, Samuel S. Hinds, Richard Lane, Johnny Mack Brown, Ella Fitzgerald

Ride Him Cowboy

US 1932 55m bw
Warner

GB title: *The Hawk*

A cowboy saves Duke, a temperamental horse, from being shot for murder, tames the beast and tracks down the real killer.

Enjoyable, fast-moving low-budget Western, the first in which Wayne displayed star quality.

w Scott Mason story Kenneth Perkins d Fred Allen

☆ John Wayne, Ruth Hall, Otis Harlan, Henry B. Walthall, Harry Gribbon, Duke

† The film was a remake of the silent *The Unknown Cavalier*, made in 1926 and starring Ken Maynard.

Ride in the Whirlwind *

US 1965 82m colour
Jack H. Harris/Proteus (Jack Nicholson, Monte Hellman)

Three cowhands are mistaken for outlaws by a vengeful posse.

Grim and talkative Western about lives trapped by circumstance.

w Jack Nicholson d Monte Hellman ph Gregory Sandor m Robert Drasnin ad James Campbell

☆ Cameron Mitchell, Millie Perkins, Jack Nicholson, Katherine Squire, George Mitchell, Rupert Crosse, Harry Dean Stanton

---

Ride Lonesome
US 1959 73m Eastmancolor Cinemascope
Columbia

A bounty hunter catches a killer as bait to trap the criminal's brother against whom he plots vengeance.
Mildly suspenseful Western, rather lost on the wide screen.
w Burt Kennedy d Budd Boetticher ph Charles Lawton Jnr m Heinz Roemheld
☆ Randolph Scott, Karen Steele, Pernell Roberts, James Best, James Coburn, Lee Van Cleef

Ride Out for Revenge
US 1957 79m bw
Bryna/UA (Norman Retchin)

Gold is discovered on land to which the army is moving Indians, and this causes second thoughts.
Low-key, rather brooding Western which aims to be different.
w Norman Retchin d Bernard Girard ph Floyd Crosby m Leith Stevens
☆ Rory Calhoun, Lloyd Bridges, Gloria Grahame, Joanne Gilbert, Vince Edwards

Ride the High Country **
US 1962 94m Metrocolor Cinemascope
MGM (Richard E. Lyons)
GB title: *Guns in the Afternoon*

Two retired lawmen help transport gold from a mining camp to the bank, but one has ideas of his own.
Thoughtful Western graced by ageing star presences; generally well done.
w N. B. Stone Jnr d Sam Peckinpah ph Lucien Ballard m George Bassman
☆ Joel McCrea, Randolph Scott, Edgar Buchanan, Mariette Hartley, James Drury
'A nice little conventional unconventional Western.' – *Stanley Kauffmann*

'The movie that rocked the debutantes – down to their last martini!'

Ride the High Iron
US 1957 74m bw
Columbia (William Self)

A war veteran gets into the seamier side of public relations.
Curious little urban melodrama with a high moral tone, like a cut-price Sweet Smell of Success.
w Milton Gelman d Don Weis ph Joe Novak m Melvyn Leonard
☆ Don Taylor, Raymond Burr, Sally Forrest
† Originally made for TV.

Ride the Man Down
US 1952 90m Trucolor
Republic

The death of a rancher sets off a bitter fight for his lands.
Flat and uninteresting Western melodrama.
w Mary McCall Jnr story Luke Short d Joe Kane ph Jack Marta m Ned Freeman
☆ Brian Donlevy, Ella Raines, Rod Cameron, Forrest Tucker, Barbara Britton, James Bell, Chill Wills, J. Carrol Naish, Jim Davis

Ride the Pink Horse *
US 1947 101m bw
U-I (Joan Harrison)

An ex-serviceman visits a New Mexican town in search of the gangster who killed his buddy.
Dour, complex melodrama with a certain amount of style but not enough substance.
w Charles Lederer novel Dorothy B. Hughes d Robert Montgomery ph Russell Metty m Frank Skinner
☆ Robert Montgomery, Wanda Hendrix, Andrea King, Thomas Gomez, Fred Clark, Art Smith
'One of a kind: no one in his right mind would imitate it.' – *Pauline Kael, 70s*
§ Thomas Gomez

Ride the Wild Surf
👫 US 1964 101m Eastmancolor
Columbia/Jana (Jo and Art Napoleon)

Surf riders go to Hawaii and find romance.
Pleasant, overlong, open air fun and games.
w Jo and Art Napoleon d Don Taylor ph Joseph Biroc m Stu Phillips
☆ Fabian, Shelley Fabares, Tab Hunter, Barbara Eden

The Ride to Hangman's Tree
US 1967 90m Technicolor
Universal (Howard Christie)

Three bandits never quite manage to reform.
Easy-going Western, played on the light side in a vein later developed in Butch Cassidy and the Sundance Kid.
w Luci Ward, Jack Natteford, William Bowers d Alan Rafkin ph Gene Polito m Frank Skinner md Joseph Gershenson ad Alexander Golitzen, John F. McCormack ed Gene Palmer
☆ Jack Lord, James Farentino, Don Galloway, Melodie Johnson, Richard Anderson

Ride, Vaquero
US 1953 90m Anscocolor
MGM (Stephen Ames)

Ranchers settling in New Mexico after the Civil War cause some natives to turn bandit; one of them has a mysterious American associate called Rio.
Very mildly interesting Western with the stars rather swamping a humourless script.
w Frank Fenton d John Farrow ph Robert Surtees m Bronislau Kaper
☆ Robert Taylor, Ava Gardner, Howard Keel, Anthony Quinn, Charlita

'In a No-man's Land between North and South, You didn't fight for the Blue or the Grey... You fought for your friends and family.'

Ride With The Devil **
US 1999 138m DeLuxe Panavision
Entertainment/Universal/Good Machine (Ted Hope, Robert Colesberry, James Schamus)

In Missouri in the 1860s, a youth goes with his friends to join the Southern irregular forces and participates in the massacre of the Kansas town of Lawrence.
Dour, beautifully photographed semi-western, a harsh drama of idealism corrupted and redeemed; it ably shows the futility of war, as both sides commit atrocities and betrayals, but might have benefited from a maturer point of view than that of its youthful participants.
w James Schamus novel Woe to Live On by Daniel Woodrell d Ang Lee ph Frederick Elmes m Mychael Danna pd Mark Friedberg ed Tim Squyres cos Marit Allen
☆ Skeet Ulrich, Tobey Maguire, Jewel, Jeffrey Wright, Simon Baker, Jonathan Rhys Meyers, James Caviezel, Thomas Guiry, Tom Wilkinson, Jonathan Brandis, Matthew Faber, Stephen Mailer, John Ales
'A masterpiece that is also one of the finest films touching on the Civil War.' – *Philip French, Observer*
'The focus is diffused among too many characters, some of them so poorly defined as to be indistinguishable.' – *Stephen Farber, Movieline*

Le Rideau Cramoisi: see *The Crimson Curtain*

Rider from Tucson
US 1950 60m bw
RKO (Herman Scholm)

Two rodeo performers ride to Colorado to be at a friend's wedding and find that they must first rescue his bride-to-be.
Standard second-feature Western that jogs along in an unmemorable manner.
w Ed Earl Repp d Lesley Selander ph Nicholas Musuraca m Paul Sawtell ad Albert S. D'Agostino, Walter E. Keller ed Robert Swink
☆ Tim Holt, Richard Martin, Elaine Riley, Douglas Fowley, Veda Ann Borg, Robert Shayne

Rider on a Dead Horse
US 1962 72m bw
Allied Artists

A prospector murders one partner for his gold and tries to pin the blame on the other.
Watchable minor Western with good use of location.
w Stephen Longstreet d Herbert L. Strock ph Frank Phillips
☆ John Vyvyan, Bruce Gordon, Kevin Hagen, Lisa Lu

Rider on the Rain
France/Italy 1969 119m colour
Joseph E. Levine, Serge Silberman

original title: *Passager de la Pluie*
A woman shoots her rapist and then tries to conceal the crime.
Routine, fairly implausible thriller that owes much to Hitchcock.
w Sebastien Japrisot d René Clément ph Andreas Winding m Francis Lai ad Pierre Guffroy
☆ Charles Bronson, Marlène Jobert, Annie Cordy, Jill Ireland, Gabriele Tinti, Jean Gaven, Jean Piat, Corinne Marchand

Riders in the Sky
US 1949 70m bw
Columbia/Gene Autry (Armand Schaefer)

A former investigator for a county attorney, who decides to become a rancher, finds himself pitted against the ruthless boss of a small town.
Built around a hit song (for Vaughn Monroe), a leisurely minor Western of no particular interest.
w Gerald Geraghty story Herbert A. Woodbury d John English ph William Bradford md Mischa Bakaleinikoff ad Harold MacArthur ed Henry Batista
☆ Gene Autry, Champion, Pat Buttram, Gloria Henry, Mary Beth Hughes, Robert Livingston, Steve Darrell, Alan Hale Jnr, Tom London

Riders of Destiny
US 1933 54m bw
Monogram/Lone Star (Paul Malvern)

An undercover agent goes West to investigate small ranchers being swindled out of their water rights.
A dramatically crude and inert Western, with Wayne looking decidedly uncomfortable when strumming a guitar on horseback as the heroic 'Singin' Sandy'.
wd Robert N. Bradbury ph Archie Stout ed Carl Pierson
☆ John Wayne, Cecilia Parker, Forrest Tucker, George Hayes, Al St John, Heinie Conklin, Yakima Canutt, Earl Dwire
† Wayne's singing was dubbed by Jack Kirk.

Riders of the Purple Sage
US 1931 58m bw
Fox

A rootin', tootin' cowboy traps a villain and weathers a stampede and an avalanche.
Good standard Western previously filmed in 1918 with William Farnum and in 1925 with Tom Mix. This version was premièred on the wide screens of the period.
novel Zane Grey d Hamilton McFadden
☆ George O'Brien, Marguerite Churchill, Noah Beery, Yvonne Pelletier, Stanley Fields
'Srill a good Western and okay outside the de luxers.' – *Variety*

Riders of Vengeance
US 1952 80m Technicolor
Universal-International (William Alland)
GB title: *The Raiders*

During the California gold rush, a prospector takes revenge on a local dictator.
Standard Western themes against a colourful background.
w Polly James, Lillie Hayward d Lesley Selander ph Carl Guthrie
☆ Richard Conte, Barbara Britton, Viveca Lindfors, Hugh O'Brian, Morris Ankrum, William Reynolds, Dennis Weaver

Riders to the Stars *
US 1954 81m Color Corporation
UA/Ivan Tors

Rocket scientists investigate the problems of cosmic bombardment.
Enjoyably straightforward science fiction with no monsters or political problems; it has decided historic interest as a record of what scientists in 1954 thought rocket travel would be like.
w Curt Siodmak d Richard Carlson ph Stanley Cortez m Harry Sukman
☆ Richard Carlson, Herbert Marshall, William Lundigan, Dawn Addams, Martha Hyer, Robert Karnes, Lawrence Dobkin

Ridicule **
France 1996 103m colour
Electric/Epithète/Cinéa/France 3 (Gilles Legrand, Frédérick Brillion/Philippe Carcassonne)

In the 1780s, a minor aristocrat arrives at the court of Louis XVI at Versailles seeking help to improve his peasants' lives, only to discover that the only quality valued is the exercise of wit.
Enjoyable period extravaganza on the power of language to make and break careers, and a portrait of a corrupt culture in its final decadence.
w Remi Waterhouse, Michel Fessler, Eric Vicaut d Patrice Leconte ph Thierry Arbogast m Antoine Duhamel pd Ivan Maussion ed Joëlle Hache
☆ Fanny Ardant, Charles Berling, Bernard Giraudeau, Judith Godrèche, Jean Rochefort, Carlo Brandt
'Resplendent and terrific entertainment.' – *Film Review*
§ foreign-language film
◎ Foreign film

'It's a rootin', tootin', six-gun shootin' musicalallapalooza!'

Riding High
US 1943 88m Technicolor
Paramount (Fred Kohlmar)
GB title: *Melody Inn*

A burlesque queen goes home to Arizona and helps ranchers by performing at a dude ranch.
Dim formula musical with exuberance but neither wit nor style.
w Walter de Leon, Arthur Phillips, Art Arthur play Ready Money by James Montgomery d George Marshall m Karl Struss, Harry Hallenberger md Victor Young
☆ Dorothy Lamour, Dick Powell, Victor Moore, Gil Lamb, Cass Daley, Bill Goodwin, Rod Cameron, Glenn Langan, Andrew Tombes, Tim Ryan, Douglas Fowley, Milt Britton and his Band

Riding High *
US 1950 112m bw
Paramount (Frank Capra)

An easygoing racing man forsakes the chance of wealth to train his beloved horse for the Imperial Derby.
The director's familiar ingredients – farce, sentimentality, fast cutting, nice people and a lot of noise – seem a shade too tried and tested in this remake of his 1934 success Broadway Bill. Despite the cast, the result is only moderately entertaining.
w Robert Riskin d Frank Capra ph George Barnes, Ernest Laszlo m James Van Heusen ly Johnny Burke
☆ Bing Crosby, Coleen Gray, Charles Bickford, Raymond Walburn, James Gleason, Oliver Hardy, Frances Gifford, William Demarest, Ward Bond, Clarence Muse, Percy Kilbride, Harry Davenport, Margaret Hamilton, Douglass Dumbrille, Gene Lockhart

Riding Shotgun
US 1954 75m Warnercolor
Warner

A shotgun stagecoach guard carries on a long vendetta against an outlaw.
Routine Western excitements, played mainly indoors.
w Tom Blackburn d André de Toth ph Bert Glennon m David Buttolph
☆ Randolph Scott, Wayne Morris, Joan Weldon, Joe Sawyer, James Millican, Charles Bronson, James Bell

Rien Ne Va Plus
France/Switzerland 1997 106m colour
Artificial Eye/MK2/TF1/CAB/CDE

A couple of confidence tricksters have a love-hate relationship with one another.
Casual, slightly comic movie that Chabrol has called autobiographical, though he must have led a more interesting life than the ones that he here puts on the screen.
wd Claude Chabrol ph Eduardo Serra m Matthieu Chabrol ad Françoise Benoît-Fresco ed Monique Fardoulis
☆ Isabelle Huppert, Michel Serrault, François Cluzet, Jean-François Balmer, Jackie Berroyer, Jean Benguigui, Mony Dalmes, Thomas Chabrol

'There's little mystery, and surprisingly little humanity either, in a film that's finally as dead and dated as the wretched pop *chanson* that ends it.' – *Jonathan Romney, Sight and Sound*

Riff Raff *
US 1935 90m bw
MGM (Irving Thalberg)
A con man and his wife end up on the wrong side of the law.
Modest comedy drama that never quite sparks.
w Frances Marion, H. W. Haneman, Anita Loos
d J. Walter Ruben ph Ray June m Edward Ward
☆ Jean Harlow, Spencer Tracy, Joseph Calleia, Una Merkel, Mickey Rooney, Victor Kilian, J. Farrell MacDonald
'It ain't art, but it's box office.' – *Variety*

Riff Raff *
US 1947 80m bw
RKO (Nat Holt)
A dying man hands a Panama City con man a map to valuable oil deposits, and various shady people are after it.
Rather heavy but well made comedy-drama with some striking scenes.
w Martin Rackin d Ted Tetzlaff ph George E. Diskant m Roy Webb
☆ Pat O'Brien, Walter Slezak, Anne Jeffreys, Percy Kilbride, Jerome Cowan

'Those that live on the edge sometimes fall.'
Riff-Raff **
GB 1990 95m colour
BFI/Parallax (Sally Hibbin)
Labourers on a building site take revenge on their employers when one of them is killed in an accident.
Successful blend of wit and naturalism, although the overlapping dialogue in many regional accents can be hard to follow at times.
w Bill Jesse d Ken Loach ph Barry Ackroyd m Stewart Copeland pd Martin Johnson ed Jonathan Morris
☆ Robert Carlyle, Emer McCourt, Jimmy Coleman, George Moss, Ricky Tomlinson, David Finch, Richard Belgrave, Ade Sapara, Derek Young, Bill Moores
'A wonderfully entertaining account of life on the margins in London that combines laughter and tears, delivering its message in an intimate and subtle way.' – *Screen International*
† The film was turned down by Britain's major distributors. It received a limited release after winning an award as the best European film of the year and receiving the International Critics Prize at the Cannes Film Festival.

Rififi **
France 1955 116m bw
Indus/Pathé/Prima
original title: *Du Rififi chez les Hommes*
After an elaborate raid on a jewellery store, thieves fall out and the caper ends in bloodshed.
A film with much to answer for, in the form of hundreds of imitations showing either detailed accounts of robberies (Topkapi, Gambit) or gloomy looks at the private lives of criminals. At the time it seemed crisp and exciting, and the 25-minute silent robbery sequence is quite something.
w René Wheeler, Jules Dassin, Auguste le Breton *novel* Auguste le Breton d Jules Dassin ph Philippe Agostini m Georges Auric
☆ Jean Servais, Carl Mohner, Robert Manuel, Marie Sabouret, Perlo Vita (Jules Dassin)
'I sometimes ask myself whether so much of the film is silent because of my own lack of French.' – *Jules Dassin*
† Several 'sequels' were made using the word *rififi* (criminal argot for 'trouble') in the title, but in plot terms they were entirely unrelated.

The Rift: see *La Grieta*

Riget: see *The Kingdom*

The Right Approach
US 1961 92m bw Cinemascope
TCF (Oscar Brodney)
A Hollywood opportunist tries to make it as a star.

A potentially witty Hollywood story is sabotaged by a style which is as naïve as it is dismal; and Mr Vaughan's hopes of stardom unfairly ended right here.
w Fay and Michael Kanin *play* Garson Kanin d David Butler ph Sam Leavitt m Dominic Frontière
☆ Frankie Vaughan, Martha Hyer, Juliet Prowse, Gary Crosby, David MacLean, Jesse White, Jane Withers

Right Cross *
US 1950 90m bw
MGM (Armand Deutsch)
A boxing champion injures his hand and has to abandon his career.
Rather dull sporting melodrama with a Mexican background, saved by good production values.
w Charles Schnee d John Sturges ph Norbert Brodine m David Raksin
☆ Dick Powell, June Allyson, Lionel Barrymore, Ricardo Montalban

The Right Stuff *
US 1983 193m Technicolor
Warner/Ladd (Irwin Winkler, Robert Chartoff)
Test pilots are recruited and trained as astronauts.
A reasonably factual account of the Mercury programme: extremely well made but somehow too brash and inhuman to provide much entertainment. An unexpected commercial flop.
wd Philip Kaufman *book* Tom Wolfe ph Caleb Deschanel m Bill Conti pd Geoffrey Kirkland ed Glenn Farr, Lisa Fruchtman, Stephen A. Rotter, Douglas Stewart, Tom Rolf
☆ Sam Shepard, Scott Glenn, Ed Harris, Dennis Quaid, Fred Ward, Barbara Hershey, Kim Stanley, Veronica Cartwright
🏆 Bill Conti; editing; sound; sound editing
🏅 best picture; Sam Shepard; Caleb Deschanel

The Right to Live *
US 1935 75m bw
Warner
GB title: *The Sacred Flame*
Someone in the family mercifully kills a crippled war hero.
Uninspired rendering of Somerset Maugham's play The Sacred Flame, previously filmed under its own title in 1929 (with Pauline Frederick, Henrietta Crosman).
w Ralph Block d William Keighley
☆ George Brent, Colin Clive, Josephine Hutchinson, Peggy Wood, C. Aubrey Smith, Leo G. Carroll, Halliwell Hobbes

The Right to Love: see *Brainwashed (1972)*

The Right to Love *
US 1930 79m bw
Paramount
A mother has a strong affinity with her illegitimate daughter who is a missionary on the other side of the world.
Curious mystic melodrama which adds a twist to popular mother-love devices. Technically it introduced the Bell light valve which improved sound reproduction, and also the Dunning process which improved the presentation of dual roles. (The star played mother and daughter.)
w Zoe Akins *novel* Brook Adams by Susan Glaspell d Richard Wallace ph Charles Lang
☆ Ruth Chatterton, Paul Lukas, David Manners, Irving Pichel, George Baxter
'A profound and thoughtful romantic drama treated with utmost refinement of sophistication and still possessing elements which will appeal to the broadest kind of screen audience.' – *Variety*
🏅 Charles Lang

Rikky and Pete *
Australia 1988 107m colour
UA/Cascade (Nadia Tass, David Parker)
An irresponsible, cop-hating inventor and his sister, a singer and geologist, leave home and head for a remote mining town, pursued by an obsessive policeman.
Unsuccessful comedy, over-elaborate and heavy-handed with its jokes, and seemingly uncertain as to its point.
w David Parker d Nadia Tass ph David Parker m Eddie Rayner m/ly Philip Judd pd Josephine Ford ed Ken Sallows

☆ Stephen Kearney, Nina Landis, Tetchie Agbayani, Bill Hunter, Bruno Lawrence, Bruce Spence, Lewis Fitz-Gerald, Dorothy Alison

The Ring *
GB 1927 116m bw
BIP (John Maxwell)
Two boxers vie for the love of a woman.
Early Hitchcock that shows his already developed skill for deft story-telling; it was the first of his films to reveal his individuality as a director.
w Alfred Hitchcock, Alma Reville, Eliot Stannard d Alfred Hitchcock ph John J. Cox ad C. Wilfred Arnold
☆ Carl Brisson, Lilian Hall Davis, Ian Hunter, Forrester Harvey, Harry Terry, Gordon Harker, Billy Wells
'Succeeds in that very rare accomplishment of being the purest film art and a fine popular entertainment.' – *Evening News*
† The version released on video runs for 73m.

The Ring
US 1952 79m bw
King Brothers
A young Mexican becomes a prizefighter in the hope of winning greater respect for Mexican-Americans.
Well-meant low-budget programmer.
w Irving Shulman d Kurt Neumann ph Russell Harlan m Herschel Burke Gilbert
☆ Gerald Mohr, Lalo Rios, Rita Moreno, Robert Arthur

Ring of Bright Water *
GB 1969 107m Technicolor
Palomar/Brightwater (Joseph Strick)
A civil servant buys a pet otter and moves to a remote cottage in the western Highlands.
Disneyesque fable for animal lovers, from a bestselling book.
w Jack Couffer, Bill Travers *book* Gavin Maxwell d Jack Couffer ph Wolfgang Suschitzky m Frank Cordell
☆ Bill Travers, Virginia McKenna, Peter Jeffrey, Roddy McMillan, Jameson Clark

Ring of Fear
US 1954 88m Warnercolor Cinemascope
Warner/Wayne-Fellows (Robert M. Fellows)
A homicidal maniac returns to the circus where he used to work and causes various 'accidents.'
Tediously predictable circus melodrama with a curious but not very likeable cast.
w Paul Fix, Philip MacDonald, James Edward Grant d James Edward Grant ph Edwin DuPar m Emil Newman, Arthur Lange
☆ Clyde Beatty, Pat O'Brien, Mickey Spillane, Sean McClory, Marian Carr, John Bromfield, Pedro Gonzalez Gonzalez, Emmett Lynn

Ring of Fire
US 1961 90m Metrocolor
MGM/Andrew and Virginia Stone
An Oregon sheriff is kidnapped by teenage delinquents but manages to lead them into both a police trap and a forest fire.
Outdoor action thriller with a plot which is ludicrously unconvincing in detail, though the fire scenes impress.
wd Andrew L. Stone ph William H. Clothier m Duane Eddy
☆ David Janssen, Joyce Taylor, Frank Gorshin, Joel Marston

Ring of Spies *
GB 1963 90m bw
British Lion (Leslie Gilliatt)
US title: *Ring of Treason*
How the Portland spy ring was tracked down.
Documentary drama, rather less intriguing, somehow, than the actual facts; but the sheer thought of spies in the suburbs keeps interest going.
w Frank Launder, Peter Barnes d Robert Tronson ph Arthur Lavis
☆ Bernard Lee, Margaret Tyzack, David Kossoff, Nancy Nevinson, William Sylvester

Ring of Treason: see *Ring of Spies*

Ring Up the Curtain: see *Broadway to Hollywood*

The Ringer *
GB 1952 78m bw
BL/London (Hugh Perceval)
A dangerous criminal known only as The Ringer threatens to kill the crooked lawyer responsible for his sister's death.
Artful old-fashioned mystery, quite well restaged, and in fact the best extant example of filmed Wallace.
w Val Valentine *play and novel* Edgar Wallace d Guy Hamilton ph Ted Scaife m Malcolm Arnold
☆ Donald Wolfit, Mai Zetterling, Herbert Lom, Greta Gynt, William Hartnell, Norman Wooland
† The play was also filmed in 1931 with Patric Curwen, Franklin Dyall and Gordon Harker; and in 1938 as *The Gaunt Stranger* (qv).

'Thanksgiving is about sharing ... blow by blow.'
Ringmaster
US 1998 90m DeLuxe
Artisan/Kushner-Locke (Steve Stabler, Gary Goldstein, Jerry Springer, Brad Jenkel, Gina Rugolo-Judd)
Fans of a trashy TV talk show petition to appear on the programme, to expose the sexual misbehaviour of those close to them.
With the host of a trashy TV talk show playing a similar fictional creation, this seems a completely redundant movie; it is certainly not a watchable one.
w John Bernstein d Neil Abramson ph Russell J. Lyster m Kennard Ramsey pd Dorian Vernaccio, Deborah Raymond ed Suzanne Hines
☆ Jerry Springer, Jaime Pressly, William McNamara, Molly Hagan, John Capodice, Wendy Raquel Robinson, Michael Jai White, Michael Dudikoff
'As Springer well knows, however, you can't go broke overestimating the bad taste of the American public, so perhaps paying customers do exist who will find this feature funner 'n' a lesbian mud-wrestling match.' – *Dennis Harvey, Variety*

Ringo and His Golden Pistol (dubbed)
Italy 1966 88m Eastmancolor
MGM/Sanson (Joseph Fryd)
original title: *Johnny Oro*
A Mexican bounty hunter is chased across the border to a small law-abiding town by bandits and Apaches seeking revenge.
Stylish spaghetti Western, though its invincible hero comes near to being a bore.
w Adriano Bolzoni, Franco Rossetti d Sergio Corbucci ph Riccardo Pallottini m Carlo Savina ad Carlo Simi ed Otello Colangeli
☆ Mark Damon, Valeria Fabrizi, Franco Derosa, Giulia Rubini, Loris Loddi, Ettore Manni
† For its US release, the name of the original was changed to take advantage of the success of Duccio Tessari's *A Pistol for Ringo* (qv).

Rings on Her Fingers *
US 1942 85m bw
TCF (Milton Sperling)
The front girl for a couple of confidence tricksters falls in love with their first victim.
Lively comedy which drags into drama in its second half.
w Ken Englund d Rouben Mamoulian ph George Barnes m Cyril Mockridge
☆ Gene Tierney, Henry Fonda, Laird Cregar, Spring Byington, Shepperd Strudwick, Frank Orth, Henry Stephenson, Marjorie Gateson

Ringside Maisie
US 1941 96m bw
MGM (J. Walter Ruben)
GB title: *Cash and Carry*
A showgirl becomes involved with a reluctant boxer and his manager.
Bright, slight comedy that slides unconvincingly into melodrama and never recovers.
w Mary C. McCall Jnr d Edwin L. Marin ph Charles Lawton m David Snell ad Cedric Gibbons
☆ Ann Sothern, George Murphy, Robert Sterling, Virginia O'Brien, Natalie Thompson, Margaret Moffat, Maxie Rosenbloom

Rio

US 1939 78m bw
Universal
A crooked financier escapes from Devil's Island to join his wife in Rio, only to find she has been unfaithful.
Modest but well made melodrama.
w Stephen Morehouse Avery, Frank Partos, Edwin Justus Mayer, Aben Kandel, Jean Negulesco d John Brahm ph Hal Mohr m Frank Skinner md Charles Previn
☆ Basil Rathbone, Victor McLaglen, Sigrid Gurie, Robert Cummings, Leo Carrillo, Billy Gilbert, Irving Bacon, Irving Pichel
'A fair programmer with a blend of romance and adventure … should stand up satisfactorily as a top dualler in most situations.' – *Variety*

Rio Bravo **

US 1959 141m Technicolor
Warner/Armada (Howard Hawks)
A wandering cowboy and a drunken sheriff hold a town against outlaws.
Cheerfully overlong and slow-moving Western in which everybody, including the director, does his thing. All very watchable for those with time to spare, but more a series of revue sketches than an epic.
w Jules Furthman, Leigh Brackett d Howard Hawks m Russell Harlan m Dimitri Tiomkin
☆ John Wayne, Dean Martin, Ricky Nelson, Angie Dickinson, Walter Brennan, Ward Bond, John Russell, Pedro Gonzalez Gonzalez, Claude Akins, Harry Carey Jnr, Bob Steele
'After we finished we found we could have done it a lot better … and that's why we went ahead and made *El Dorado*.' – *Howard Hawks*
† More or less remade in 1966 as *El Dorado* and in 1970 as *Rio Lobo*.

Rio Conchos *

US 1964 107m DeLuxe Cinemascope
TCF (David Weisbart)
Two thousand rifles are stolen from an army command post and traced to the hide-out of a former Confederate colonel who wants to continue the Civil War.
Good standard Western which shares much of its story line with The Comancheros.
w Clair Huffaker, Joseph Landon novel Clair Huffaker d Gordon Douglas ph Joe MacDonald m Jerry Goldsmith
☆ Richard Boone, Edmond O'Brien, Stuart Whitman, Tony Franciosa

Rio Grande *

US 1950 105m bw
Republic/Argosy (John Ford, Merian C. Cooper)
A Cavalry unit on the Mexican border in the 1880s conducts a vain campaign against marauding Indians.
Thin Ford Western on his favourite theme, with too many pauses for song, too many studio sets, and too little plot. Aficionados, however, will find much to admire.
w James Kevin McGuinness story James Warner Bellah d John Ford ph Bert Glennon m Victor Young
☆ John Wayne, Maureen O'Hara, Ben Johnson, Claude Jarman Jnr, Harry Carey Jnr, Chill Wills, J. Carrol Naish, Victor McLaglen

Rio Lobo *

US 1970 114m Technicolor
Cinema Center (Howard Hawks)
A Union colonel near the end of the Civil War recovers a gold shipment and exposes a traitor.
Rambling Western with traces of former glory, enjoyable at least for its sense of humour.
w Leigh Brackett, Burton Wohl d Howard Hawks ph William Clothier m Jerry Goldsmith
☆ John Wayne, Jorge Rivero, Jennifer O'Neill, Jack Elam, Victor French, Chris Mitchum, Mike Henry

Rio Rita

US 1929 135m bw and Technicolor
RKO (William Le Baron)
Romance on a ranch near the Mexican border.
Very early talkie version of a popular Broadway operetta of the twenties; historical interest only.

w Luther Reed, Russell Mack book Guy Bolton, Fred Thomson, as produced by Florenz Ziegfeld d Luther Reed ph Robert Kurrk, Lloyd Knechtel md Victor Baravalle songs Harry Tierney, Joe McCarthy
☆ Bebe Daniels, John Boles, Bert Wheeler, Robert Woolsey, Dorothy Lee, Don Alvarado, George Renavent

Rio Rita

US 1942 91m bw
MGM (Pandro S. Berman)
Flat-footed remake bringing in Nazi spies.
Poor comedy even by Abbott and Costello standards.
w Richard Connell, Gladys Lehman d S. Sylvan Simon ph George J. Folsey m Herbert Stothart
☆ Bud Abbott, Lou Costello, John Carroll, Kathryn Grayson, Tom Conway, Barry Nelson

Riot

US 1968 98m Technicolor
Paramount/William Castle
While the warden is away, thirty-five convicts take over a state penitentiary and are violently subdued.
Strikingly bloody melodrama set in an actual prison in Arizona; well made, but less entertaining than Cagney and Raft used to be.
w James Poe novel Frank Elli d Buzz Kulik ph Robert B. Hauser m Christopher Komeda
☆ Gene Hackman, Jim Brown, Ben Carruthers, Mike Kellin, Gerald O'Loughlin, Clifford David

Riot in Cell Block Eleven *

US 1954 80m bw
Allied Artists/Walter Wanger
In a big American prison three convicts seize their guards, free the other prisoners and barricade themselves in their block.
Socially concerned low-budgeter, quite nicely made and persuasive of the need for prison reform.
w Richard Collins d Don Siegel ph Russell Harlan m Herschel Burke Gilbert
☆ Neville Brand, Emile Meyer, Frank Faylen, Leo Gordon, Robert Osterloh, Paul Frees, Don Keefer
'As a compassionate, angry, unsensational account of an episode of violence it makes considerably more impact than many of the overblown melodramas currently in fashion.' – *Penelope Houston*

Ripoux contre ripoux: see *Le Cop 2*

Riptide *

US 1934 90m bw
MGM (Irving Thalberg)
A British diplomat weds a Manhattan chorus girl, but she later falls for an old flame.
Elegantly set, star-packed drawing-room drama which somehow didn't click.
wd Edmund Goulding ph Ray June m Herbert Stothart
☆ Norma Shearer, Robert Montgomery, Herbert Marshall, Mrs Patrick Campbell, Skeets Gallagher, Ralph Forbes, Lilyan Tashman, Helen Jerome Eddy, George K. Arthur, Halliwell Hobbes
'Has all the earmarks of box office … a commendable job all round.' – *Variety*

The Rise and Fall of Legs Diamond

US 1960 101m bw
Warner/United States (Milton Sperling)
The career of a New York hoodlum of the twenties.
Inspired, like King of the Roaring Twenties, by the TV success of The Untouchables, this was part of a brief attempt by Warner to recapture its pre-war gangster image. Alas, stars and style were equally lacking.
w Joseph Landon d Budd Boetticher ph Lucien Ballard m Leonard Rosenman
☆ Ray Danton, Karen Steele, Elaine Stewart, Jesse White, Simon Oakland, Robert Lowery, Warren Oates, Judson Pratt

The Rise and Rise of Michael Rimmer

GB 1970 101m Technicolor
Warner/David Frost (Harry Fine)
An efficiency expert takes over an advertising agency and is soon an MP, a cabinet minister, and PM.
Satirical comedy which quickly goes overboard and is only occasionally funny; it does, however, mark the

final death throes of the swinging sixties, and the changeover to Monty Python.
w Peter Cook, John Cleese, Kevin Billington, Graham Chapman d Kevin Billington ph Alex Thomson m John Cameron
☆ Peter Cook, John Cleese, Arthur Lowe, Denholm Elliott, Ronald Fraser, Vanessa Howard, George A. Cooper, Harold Pinter, James Cossins, Roland Culver, Dudley Foster, Julian Glover, Dennis Price, Ronnie Corbett

Rise and Shine

US 1941 93m bw
TCF (Mark Hellinger)
A dumb but brilliant football player is kidnapped by the other side.
Drab collegiate comedy, disappointing considering the credits.
w Herman J. Mankiewicz novel My Life and Hard Times by James Thurber d Allan Dwan ph Edward Cronjager m Emil Newman songs Leo Robin, Ralph Rainger
☆ Linda Darnell, Jack Oakie, George Murphy, Walter Brennan, Milton Berle, Sheldon Leonard, Donald Meek, Ruth Donnelly, Donald MacBride, Raymond Walburn, Emma Dunn

The Rise of Catherine the Great: see *Catherine the Great*

The Rise of Helga: see *Susan Lenox, Her Fall and Rise*

The Rise of Louis XIV **

France 1966 100m Eastmancolor
ORTF (Pierre Gout)
original title: *La Prise de Pouvoir par Louis XIV*
The young King of France asserts his power through the use of fashion, style and spectacle.
A complex study of power, shot in a direct, semi-documentary manner, with much use of a zoom lens.
w Jean Gruault story Philippe Erlanger d Roberto Rossellini ph Georges Leclerc, Jean-Louis Picavet ad Maurice Valay ed Armand Ridel
☆ Jean-Michel Patte, Raymond Jourdan, Silvagni, Katharine Renn, Dominique Vincent, Pierre Barrat
'Even the fact that it was made as a spectacular for French television does not quite justify its singular vapidity and pointlessness.' – *John Simon*
† The film was first shown on French TV before being given a cinema release.

Rising Damp

GB 1980 98m colour
ITC/Black Lion (Roy Skeggs)
The amorous and conniving landlord of a slum boarding house develops a passion for one of his tenants.
A useful reminder of a TV sitcom worth remembering, but handicapped by restriction of action, paucity of plot and the overlength usual in film versions of such things, not to mention the premature death of its original co-star Richard Beckinsale.
w Eric Chappell d Joe McGrath ph Frank Watts m David Lindup
☆ Leonard Rossiter, Frances de la Tour, Don Warrington, Denholm Elliott, Christopher Strauli

'Unforgettably John Ford's finest film!'

The Rising of the Moon

Eire 1957 81m bw
Warner/Four Provinces (Lord Killanin)
Three Irish short stories.
Curiously dull John Ford portmanteau with the Abbey players.
w Frank Nugent stories Frank O'Connor, Malcolm J. McHugh, Lady Gregory d John Ford ph Robert Krasker m Eamonn O'Gallagher narrator Tyrone Power
☆ Maureen Connell, Eileen Crowe, Cyril Cusack, Maureen Delany, Donal Donnelly, Frank Lawton, Edward Lexy, Jack MacGowran, Denis O'Dea, Jimmy O'Dea, Noel Purcell

'A collision of East and West. A conspiracy of seduction and murder. A battle between tradition and power. Business is war.'

Rising Sun

US 1993 129m DeLuxe
TCF (Peter Kaufman)
Two cops, one an expert in Japanese culture, investigate the murder of a prostitute in the

boardroom of a Japanese corporation's new Los Angeles headquarters.
Turgid thriller, revealing paranoid feelings about the Japanese in America but not much else to engage the interest.
w Philip Kaufman, Michael Crichton, Michael Backes novel Michael Crichton d Philip Kaufman ph Michael Chapman m Toru Takemitsu, Richard Marriott pd Dean Tavoularis ed Stephen A. Rotter, William S. Scharf
☆ Sean Connery, Wesley Snipes, Harvey Keitel, Cary-Hiroyuki Tagawa, Kevin Anderson, Mako, Ray Wise, Stan Egi, Stan Shaw, Tia Carrere, Steve Buscemi
'The myth in *Rising Sun* is that found in most late 20th-century boysy genre films – the battle to prove white (or sometimes these days, black) male superiority in a world in which extreme male violence is constant, natural, and inevitable … one sits in the cinema feeling spattered by something false and degrading' – *Marilyn French*
'Even if the director was keen on doing a thriller exercise, his creative instincts don't seem to have been fully ignited.' – *Variety*

Risky Business

US 1939 67m bw
Universal
A crusading radio columnist tracks down a kidnapper.
Tolerable crime programmer.
w Charles Grayson from a previous script by William Anthony McGuire d Arthur Lubin
☆ George Murphy, Dorothea Kent, Eduardo Ciannelli, Leon Ames, El Brendel, John Wray
'It will garner nice business in city spots, where they like their melodrama realistic.' – *Variety*

'Joel was a perfectly ordinary high-school virgin with two perfectly ordinary obsessions: SEX and MONEY'

Risky Business

US 1983 99m Technicolor
Tisch-Avnet/Geffen
A 17-year-old is left in charge of his parents' house and fills it with pimps and prostitutes … a lucrative business.
Would-be outrageous teenage comedy which is pretty well made but soon wears out its welcome.
wd Paul Brickman ph Reynaldo Villalobos, Bruce Surtees m Tangerine Dream pd William J. Cassidy ed Richard Chew
☆ Tom Cruise, Rebecca de Mornay, Joe Pantoliano, Richard Masur, Bronson Pinchot, Curtis Armstrong, Nicholas Pryor

Riso Amaro: see *Bitter Rice*

Rita, Sue and Bob Too *

GB 1987 95m Eastmancolor
Mainline/Umbrella/British Screen/Film Four (Sandy Lieberson)
Schoolgirl babysitters are introduced to sex by their employer on the way home.
Raunchy yet appealing study of British attitudes to sex, in the tradition of Letter to Brezhnev.
w Andrea Dunbar plays The Arbour and Rita, Sue And Bob Too by Andrea Dunbar d Alan Clarke ph Ivan Strasburg m Michael Kamen pd Len Huntingford ed Stephen Singleton
☆ Michelle Holmes, Siobhan Finneran, George Costigan, Lesley Sharp

Il Ritorno di Ringo: see *The Return of Ringo*

Los Ritos Sexuales del Diablo: see *Black Candles*

The Ritz *

US 1976 90m Technicolor
Warner/Courtyard (Denis O'Dell)
A comedy of mistaken identities in a gay New York turkish bath.
An adaptation of a stage success which doesn't seem nearly as funny as it thinks it is; but some of it does work.
w Terrence McNally play Terrence McNally d Richard Lester ph Paul Wilson m Ken Thorne pd Phillip Harrison
☆ Jack Weston, Rita Moreno, Jerry Stiller, Kaye Ballard, Bessie Love, George Coulouris, F. Murray Abraham, Treat Williams

---

The River *

India 1951 87m Technicolor
Oriental/International/Theatre Guild (Kenneth McEldowney)

Episodes in the life of a small English community living on the banks of the Ganges.

A slight and surprising work from this director, superbly observed and a pleasure to watch but dramatically very thin.

w Rumer Godden, Jean Renoir *novel* Rumer Godden d Jean Renoir ph Claude Renoir m M. A. Partha Sarathy pd Eugene Lourié

☆ Nora Swinburne, Esmond Knight, Arthur Shields, Adrienne Corri

† Renoir's assistant was Satyajit Ray.

The River

US 1984 122m Technicolor
Universal/Edward Lewis

The Garveys battle flood waters to save the family farm.

Old-fashioned rural drama, at times reminiscent of Way Down East plus a dash of symbolism. A surprise in 1984, and not a very pleasant one, despite or because of its political awareness.

w Robert Dillon, Julian Barry d Mark Rydell ph Vilmos Zsigmond m John Williams pd Charles Rosen ed Sidney Levin

☆ Mel Gibson, Sissy Spacek, Shane Bailey, Becky Jo Lynch, Scott Glenn, Billy Green Bush

⬧ Sissy Spacek; photography; music; sound

The River *

Taiwan 1997 115m colour
BFI/Central (Hsu Li-Kong, Chiu Shun-Ching)

original title: Heliu

In Taipei, a youth becomes ill after playing the part of a drowned corpse in a movie and seeks treatment in vain.

A downbeat account of a family emotionally distant from one another; nothing much happens for most of the film, and audiences will either go with the slow-moving flow or find its lack of resolution intensely irritating.

w Tsai Ming-Liang, Yang Pi-Ying, Tsai Yi-Chun d Tsai Ming-Liang ph Liao Pen-Jung pd Tony Lan ed Chen Sheng-Chang, Lei Chen-Ching

☆ Miao Tian, Li Kangsheng, Lu Xiaolin, Ann Hui, Chen Xiangqi

'It's a film that requires a tremendous amount of patience and concentration from the viewer, taking its leave from inaction, not movement. Occasionally tiresome, meaning is very much left to personal interpretation.' – James Mottram, Film Review

† The film won the Silver Bear at the Berlin Film Festival.

River Lady

US 1948 78m Technicolor
Universal-International

The beautiful owner of a Mississippi gambling boat tries to buy up all her rivals.

Routine romantic drama.

w D. D. Beauchamp, William Bowers *novel* Houston Branch, Frank Waters d George Sherman ph Irving Glassberg m Paul Sawtell

☆ Yvonne de Carlo, Rod Cameron, Dan Duryea, Helena Carter, Lloyd Gough, Florence Bates, John McIntire

River of No Return *

US 1954 91m Technicolor Cinemascope
TCF (Stanley Rubin)

During the California gold rush a widower and his 10-year-old son encounter a saloon singer with a gold claim.

Cheerful, clichéd star Western designed to exploit the splendours of early Cinemascope, and very adequate for this purpose.

w Frank Fenton d Otto Preminger ph Joseph LaShelle m Cyril Mockridge md Lionel Newman

☆ Robert Mitchum, Marilyn Monroe, Tommy Rettig, Rory Calhoun, Murvyn Vye

The River Rat

US 1984 93m Technicolor
Paramount/Sundance/Larson Rickman (Bob Larson)

During a river journey on a raft to escape from a dishonest parole officer, a just-released convict tries to form a relationship with the young daughter he has never known.

A domestic drama that is never more than moderately effective.

wd Tom Rickman ph Jan Kiesser m Mike Post pd John J. Lloyd ed Dennis Virkler

☆ Tommy Lee Jones, Nancy Lea Owen, Brian Dennehy, Martha Plimpton

A River Runs through It *

US 1992 123m Technicolor
Guild/Allied Filmmaker/Columbia (Robert Redford, Patrick Markey)

Two brothers, whose relationship with each other is often troubled, find shared pleasure in fly-fishing.

A soothingly nostalgic movie, often graceful but more often sluggish.

w Richard Friedenberg *story* Norman Maclean d Robert Redford ph Philippe Rousselot m Mark Isham pd Jon Hutman ed Lynzee Klingman, Robert Estrin

☆ Craig Sheffer, Brad Pitt, Tom Skerritt, Brenda Blethyn, Emily Lloyd, Edie McClurg, Stephen Shellen, Nicole Burdette, Susan Traylor

'Old-fashioned, literary and restrained … but its concerns are too refined, gentle and, finally, unexciting to stir the masses.' – Variety

'Cool, allusive and, in the best sense, poetic movie, rich in unforced metaphors and feelings.' – Richard Schickel, Time

'As a film, it has all the virtues except tension, which is unfortunately like saying that a watch would be a good timekeeper if the mainspring wasn't bust.' – Adam Mars-Jones, Independent

🏆 Philippe Rousselot

⬧ Richard Friedenberg; Mark Isham

'The vacation is over.'

The River Wild *

US 1994 111m DeLuxe Panavision
UIP/Turman-Foster (David Foster, Lawrence Turman)

A family on a white-water rafting expedition is forced to help armed robbers escape their pursuers.

Predictable action drama, made with some skill but too obvious in its plotting to create much suspense.

w Denis O'Neill d Curtis Hanson ph Robert Elswit m Jerry Goldsmith pd Bill Kenney ed Joe Hutshing, David Brenner

☆ Meryl Streep, Kevin Bacon, David Strathairn, Joseph Mazzello, John C. Reilly, Benjamin Bratt

'So formulaic that the picture is never more than moderately exciting; you can see round every bend in this river.' – Terrence Rafferty, New Yorker

'Streep goes down-market and down-river … The things Hollywood stars have to do to get back into the mainstream sometimes.' – Derek Malcolm, Guardian

Riverboat Rhythm

US 1946 65m bw
RKO

A Mississippi riverboat captain is financially embarrassed.

Very mild comedy with the star in dual roles.

w Robert Faber, Charles Roberts d Leslie Goodwins

☆ Leon Errol, Walter Catlett, Glenn Vernon, Marc Cramer, Jonathan Hale, Joan Newton

River's Edge **

US 1986 99m Metrocolor
Palace/Hemdale (Sarah Pillsbury, Midge Sanford)

After a teenager murders his girlfriend, his friends wonder what action they should take.

A gripping drama of teenage alienation.

w Neal Jimenez d Tim Hunter ph Frederick Elmes m Jurgen Knieper pd John Muto ed Howard Smith, Sonya Sones

☆ Crispin Glover, Keanu Reeves, Ione Skye, Daniel Roebuck, Dennis Hopper, Joshua Miller

'An unusually downbeat and depressing youth pic.' – Variety

'This brilliant, messy little picture, another triumph for the independent film movement, should cause people to argue and celebrate for

years – argue over how it could have been done better, celebrate that it was done at all.' – David Denby, New York

The River's Edge

US 1956 87m Eastmancolor Cinemascope
TCF (Benedict Bogeaus)

A fugitive bank robber forces a farmer to guide him over the mountains into Mexico.

Sluggish open-air character melodrama.

w Harold J. Smith d Allan Dwan ph Harold Lipstein m Lou Forbes

☆ Ray Milland, Anthony Quinn, Debra Paget, Byron Foulger

River's End

US 1930 74m bw
Warner

A Mountie dies chasing his man, who then impersonates him.

Popular, contrived, outdoor thriller, previously filmed in 1922 with Lewis Stone, and subsequently in 1940 with Dennis Morgan (this version became known as Double Identity).

w Charles Kenyon *story* James Oliver Curwood d Michael Curtiz

☆ Charles Bickford, Evalyn Knapp, J. Farrell MacDonald, ZaSu Pitts, David Torrence

La Rivière du Hibou: see Incident at Owl Creek

The Road: see La Strada

Road Agent

US 1941 69m bw
Universal

Three cowboys are released from jail so that they can capture an outlaw gang.

Feeble 'B'-movie Western with a couple of forgettable songs thrown in.

w Morgan Cox, Arthur Strawn, Maurice Tombragel *story* Sherman Lowe, Arthur St Clare d Charles Lamont ph Jerome Ash md H. J. Salter ad Jack Otterson ed Frank Gross

☆ Dick Foran, Leo Carillo, Andy Devine, Anne Gwynne, Samuel S. Hinds, Richard Davis, Anne Nagel, Morris Ankrum

The Road Back **

US 1937 105m bw
Universal (James Whale)

After World War I, German soldiers go home to problems and disillusion.

A major work, intended as a sequel to All Quiet on the Western Front. Despite impressive sequences, it doesn't quite reach inspiring heights.

w R. C. Sherriff, Charles Kenyon *novel* Erich Maria Remarque d James Whale ph John Mescall, George Robinson m Dimitri Tiomkin ad Charles D. Hall

☆ Richard Cromwell, John King, Slim Summerville, Andy Devine, Barbara Read, Louise Fazenda, Noah Beery Jnr, Lionel Atwill, John Emery, Etienne Girardot, Spring Byington, Laura Hope Crews

'Big and frequently effective, but a let-down in toto … does not compare with All Quiet in quality or power.' – Variety

'They call it an all-star cast and that means there isn't a single player of any distinction to be picked out of the herd … It might be funny if it wasn't horrifying. This is America seeing the world in its own image.' – Graham Greene

† The film is said to have been extensively reshot after protests from the German consul in Los Angeles. No 35mm negative now exists, as it reverted to Remarque and was lost.

Road Games

Australia 1981 110m colour
Avco Embassy/Barber International/Quest (Richard Franklin)

A long-distance truck-driver unwittingly picks up a murderer on the run.

Tolerable but overlong road thriller.

w Everett de Roche d Richard Franklin ph Vincent Monton m Brian May pd John Dowding ed Edward McQueen-Mason

☆ Stacy Keach, Jamie Lee Curtis, Marion Edwards, Grant Page

Road Gang

US 1936 60m bw
First National

GB title: Injustice

Penal corruption and brutality in a Southern state is exposed by the Chicago Sun.

A rough ride over familiar ground.

w Abem Finkel, Dalton Trumbo, Harold Buckley d Louis King

☆ Donald Woods, Carlyle Moore Jnr, Kay Linaker, Harry Cording, Marc Lawrence

The Road Home

US 1989 116m colour
Rank/Orion (Howard Rosenman, Thomas Baer)

aka: Lost Angels

A rebellious youth is sent to a private institution for the problem children of the wealthy.

Confused and unconvincing picture of teenage traumas.

w Michael Weller d Hugh Hudson ph Juan Ruiz-Anchia m Philippe Sarde pd Assheton Gorton ed David Gladwell

☆ Donald Sutherland, Adam Horovitz, Amy Locane, Don Bloomfield, Celia Weston, Graham Beckel, Patricia Richardson, Ron Frazier, Joseph d'Angerio

'What is wrong with it, apart from a rather overblown style which is never hard-edged enough, is the depiction of the rebellion itself which seems too predicated on adult perfidy to be entirely true.' – Derek Malcolm, Guardian

Road House

GB 1934 76m bw
Gaumont (Michael Balcon)

A barmaid helps to track down a murderer.

Mild comedy melodrama with music.

w Austin Melford, Leslie Arliss *play* Walter Hackett d Maurice Elvey m Leslie Rowson

☆ Violet Loraine, Gordon Harker, Emlyn Williams, Aileen Marson, Hartley Power, Stanley Holloway, Marie Lohr

Road House *

US 1948 95m bw
TCF (Edward Chodorov)

A road house owner is jealous of his manager and frames him for murder.

Dated but watchable film noir of its era, with all characters cynical or homicidal.

w Edward Chodorov d Jean Negulesco ph Joseph LaShelle m Cyril Mockridge

☆ Richard Widmark, Ida Lupino, Cornel Wilde, Celeste Holm

Road House *

US 1989 114m DeLuxe Panavision
UIP/United Artists/Star Partners II/Silver Pictures (Joel Silver)

A kung fu expert, who is hired to clean up a saloon, incurs the enmity of a local racketeer.

Rowdy action movie that provides unthinking enjoyment.

w David Lee Henry, Hilary Henkin d Rowdy Herrington ph Dean Cundey ad William J. Durrell Jnr ed Frank J. Urioste, John F. Link

☆ Patrick Swayze, Kelly Lynch, Sam Elliott, Ben Gazzara, Marshall Teague, Julie Michaels, Red West, Sunshine Parker, Jeff Healey

'Very nearly a perfect exploitation movie.' – MFB

Road Show *

US 1941 86m bw
Hal Roach

A young man wrongly committed to an insane asylum escapes with another inmate and joins a travelling circus.

Engaging scatty comedy on familiar Roach lines which suffers from lame pacing but manages some likeable moments.

w Arnold Belgard, Harry Langdon, Mickell Novak *novel* Eric Hatch d Gordon Douglas ph Norbert Brodine m George Stoll

☆ John Hubbard, Adolphe Menjou, Carole Landis, Patsy Kelly, George E. Stone

---

Road to Bali *

🏃 US 1952 91m Technicolor
Paramount (Harry Tugend)
▤

In and around the South Seas, with colour making the sets obvious and the gags only tediously funny.
The team's zest was also flagging.
w Frank Butler, Hal Kanter, William Morrow d Hal Walker ph George Barnes md Joseph J. Lilley songs Johnny Burke, Jimmy Van Heusen
☆ Bob Hope, Bing Crosby, Dorothy Lamour, Murvyn Vye, Peter Coe

The Road to Corinth: see La Route de Corinthe

Road to Denver

US 1955 90m Trucolor
Republic
An honest ranch hand gets into trouble when he tries to help his lawless brother.
Uninspired Western which just about passes the time.
w Horace McCoy, Allen Rivkin story Bill Gulick d Joe Kane ph Reggie Lanning m R. Dale Butts
☆ John Payne, Lee J. Cobb, Skip Homeier, Mona Freeman, Ray Middleton, Andy Clyde, Lee Van Cleef

The Road to Frisco: see They Drive by Night

The Road to Glory *

US 1936 103m bw
TCF (Darryl F. Zanuck)
Adventures of a French regiment in World War I.
Meticulously produced war movie which bears comparison with All Quiet on the Western Front.
w Joel Sayre, William Faulkner d Howard Hawks ph Gregg Toland m Louis Silvers
☆ Fredric March, Warner Baxter, Lionel Barrymore, June Lang, Gregory Ratoff, Victor Kilian, John Qualen, Julius Tannen, Leonid Kinskey

Road to Hong Kong

GB 1962 91m bw
UA/Melnor (Melvin Frank)
▤ ◎〜
Curious, slightly dismal-looking attempt to continue the series in a British studio and on a low budget.
A few good gags, but it's all very tired by now, and the space fiction plot makes it seem more so.
w Norman Panama, Melvin Frank d Norman Panama ph Jack Hildyard m Robert Farnon pd Roger Furse
☆ Bob Hope, Bing Crosby, Dorothy Lamour, Joan Collins, Robert Morley, Walter Gotell, Felix Aylmer, David Niven, Frank Sinatra, Dean Martin, Jerry Colonna, Peter Sellers

The Road to Hope: see Il Cammino della Speranza

The Road to Life *

USSR 1930 100m bw
Mejrabpom
Moscow street children are rounded up and reformed.
A kind of Russian prequel to the Dead End Kids, *presented with much style.*
wd Nikolai Ekk
☆ Mikhail Zharov, Maria Gonfa, Tsifan Kyrla
'Judged purely as entertainment the film recedes quickly, as do most Russian films.' – Variety

'Where the human wreckage of the seven seas foregather, this powerful tale of love and intrigue is told!'

Road to Mandalay

US 1926 77m bw silent
MGM
Two eastern planters quarrel over a girl.
Potboiling star vehicle.
w Elliott Clawson, Herman Mankiewicz d Tod Browning
☆ Lon Chaney, Lois Moran, Owen Moore, Henry B. Walthall

Road to Morocco **

🏃 US 1942 83m bw
Paramount (Paul Jones)
▣ ▤ ◎〜 ⊘
Hollywood Arab palaces, a captive princess, topical gags and talking camels.

---

w Frank Butler, Don Hartman d David Butler ph William C. Mellor md Victor Young songs Johnny Burke, Jimmy Van Heusen
☆ Bob Hope, Bing Crosby, Dorothy Lamour, Anthony Quinn, Dona Drake
'A bubbly spontaneous entertainment without a semblance of sanity.' – Variety
'It would be difficult to find a screen pantomime with better wartime credentials.' – Kine Weekly
'This is the screwiest picture I've ever been in.' – Camel
ß script

The Road to Reno

US 1938 69m bw
Universal
A rancher won't give his wife the divorce she thinks she wants.
Combination comedy, drama, romance and horse opera which doesn't gel.
w Roy Chanslor, Adele Comandini, Brian Marlow novel I. A. R. Wylie d S. Sylvan Simon
☆ Randolph Scott, Hope Hampton, Glenda Farrell, Helen Broderick, Alan Marshal, Samuel S. Hinds

Road to Rio **

🏃 US 1947 100m bw
Paramount (Daniel Dare)
▤
Guest stars are given their head, plot intrudes again in the shape of a hypnotized heiress, and the style is more constrained (but still funny).
w Edmund Beloin, Jack Rose d Norman Z. McLeod ph Ernest Laszlo md Robert Emmett Dolan songs Johnny Burke, Jimmy Van Heusen
☆ Bob Hope, Bing Crosby, Dorothy Lamour, Gale Sondergaard, Frank Faylen, the Wiere Brothers, the Andrews Sisters
'Enough laughs to pass the time easily and to remind you how completely, since sound came in, the American genius for movie comedy has disintegrated.' – James Agee
ß Robert Emmett Dolan

Road to Ruin

US/France 1992 90m colour
Chrysalide/Canal+/Movie Group/RTBF (Monique Annaud)
▤
After he pretends to be poor in order to test a model's love for him, a millionaire businessman is bankrupted by his partner and sets out to regain his fortune and the woman's love.
Slick, glossy, extremely shallow romantic comedy that prefers implausibility to reality.
w Eric Anjou story Richard Gitelson, Eric Freiser d Charlotte Brandstrom ph Jean-Yves Le Mener m John Goldstein ad Bertrand Seitz ed Michele Robert-Lauliac
☆ Peter Weller, Carey Lowell, Michel Duchaussoy, Nathalie Auffret

The Road to Salina

France/Italy 1971 96m colour Panavision
Robert Dorfmann
▤
original title: Quando il Sola Scotta
The proprietress of a roadside café recognizes a drifter as her long-lost son.
Boring emotional drama stymied by the multi-language problem.
w Georges Lautner, Pascal Jardin, Jack Miller novel Maurice Cury d Georges Lautner ph Maurice Fellons m Bernard Gérard, Ian Anderson
☆ Rita Hayworth, Mimsy Farmer, Robert Walker Jnr, Ed Begley, Sophie Hardy

Road to Singapore

US 1931 70m bw
Warner
A doctor's wife is caught with her lover, and her life falls to pieces.
Tensions among the oriental upper crust: very dated and not very convincing.
w J. Grubb Alexander play Roland Pertwee d Alfred E. Green
☆ William Powell, Louis Calhern, Doris Kenyon, Marian Marsh, Alison Skipworth

---

'THE 'ROAD' SERIES'

Road to Singapore *

🏃 US 1940 84m bw
Paramount (Harlan Thompson)
▣ ▤ ◎〜
Two rich playboys swear off women until they quarrel over a Singapore maiden.
The first Hope-Crosby-Lamour 'road' picture is basically a light romantic comedy and quite forgettable; the series got zanier as it progressed.
w Don Hartman, Frank Butler story Harry Hervey d Victor Schertzinger ph William C. Mellor m Victor Young
☆ Bing Crosby, Bob Hope, Dorothy Lamour, Charles Coburn, Judith Barrett, Anthony Quinn, Jerry Colonna
'A deft blend of romance and comedy, songs and fisticuffs.' – Picture Show
'Two of the most congenially harmonized performances caught by the camera in recent years.' – Motion Picture Herald
† The script was originally designed for Fred MacMurray and Jack Oakie, who weren't available; then for Burns and Allen, who turned it down.

Road to Utopia **

🏃 US 1945 89m bw
Paramount (Paul Jones)
▣ ▤
The Klondike gold rush, with all the previous gag styles in good order, capped by a cheeky epilogue and constant explanatory narration by Robert Benchley.
w Norman Panama, Melvin Frank d Hal Walker ph Lionel Lindon m Leigh Harline songs Johnny Burke, Jimmy Van Heusen
☆ Bob Hope, Bing Crosby, Dorothy Lamour, Douglass Dumbrille, Hillary Brooke, Jack La Rue
ß script

'A Comedy Of The Heart And Other Organs.'

The Road to Wellville *

US 1994 120m Technicolor
J&M/Beacon/Dirty Hands (Alan Parker, Armyan Bernstein, Robert Colesberry)
▣ ▤ ◎〜 🎧
In the early 1900s, a couple whose marriage is in difficulties visit a famous sanatarium, run by Dr Kellogg, in a town full of get-rich-quick merchants hoping to cash in on the fad for healthy living and invented foods, such as cornflakes.
A film quite unlike any other in its exuberant account of the quirky methods of the health industry; Hopkins brings toothy menace to the role of Kellogg, but the screenplay fatally softens the darkly satirical tone of its source, bringing it closer in spirit to a Carry On *movie.*
wd Alan Parker novel T. Coraghessen Boyle ph Peter Biziou m Rachel Portman pd Brian Morris ed Gerry Hambling
☆ Anthony Hopkins, Bridget Fonda, Matthew Broderick, John Cusack, Dana Carvey, Michael Lerner, Colm Meaney, John Neville, Lara Flynn Boyle
'Amusing without being particularly funny, and not especially involving in terms of its characters or melodrama, Alan Parker's unzipped cereal comedy is more something to gape at in wonderment, so persistently odd and unusual are its setting and tone.' – Todd McCarthy, Variety
'One of the most intricately tiresome movies ever made.' – David Denby, New York
'Like its hero, it's possessed of an awesome oddity that is finally rather endearing. In an era of Big Mac movies, the occasional nut cutlet can come as a tonic relief.' – Sheila Johnston, Independent

Road to Zanzibar **

🏃 US 1941 92m bw
Paramount (Paul Jones)
▤ ◎〜
The trio on safari in Africa, with *Hellzapoppin* gags breaking in and an anything-goes atmosphere.
w Frank Butler, Don Hartman d Victor Schertzinger ph Ted Tetzlaff m Victor Young songs Johnny Burke, Jimmy Van Heusen
☆ Bob Hope, Bing Crosby, Dorothy Lamour, Una Merkel, Eric Blore, Luis Alberni, Douglass Dumbrille
'The funniest thing I've seen on the screen in years. Years.' – Otis Ferguson

The Road Warrior: see Mad Max 2

Roadblock *

US 1951 73m bw
RKO (Lewis J. Rachmil)
An insurance investigator plans a million-dollar robbery after falling for a woman who wants a rich life.
Minor film noir, about the corruption of an honest man, with slick dialogue ('Happiness can't buy you money') and an effective finale along the Los Angeles riverbed.
w Steve Fisher, George Bricker story Richard Landau, Geoffrey Homes d Harold Daniels ph Nicholas Musuraca m Paul Sawtell md Constantin Bakaleinikoff ad Albert D'Agostino, Walter E. Keller ed Robert Golden
☆ Charles McGraw, Joan Dixon, Lowell Gilmore, Louis Jean Heydt, Milburn Stone, Joseph Crehan

Roadhouse 66

US 1984 90m colour
Atlantic (Scott M. Rosenfelt, Mark Levinson)
A motorist and his down-at-heel hitchhiker are stuck in a small town when their car breaks down.
Uninteresting drama, lacking verve and originality.
w Galen Lee, George Simpson d John Mark Robinson ph Tom Ackerman m Gary Scott pd Chester Kaczenski ed Jay Lash Cassidy
☆ Willem Dafoe, Judge Reinhold, Karen Lee, Kate Vernon, Stephen Elliott

Roadhouse Nights *

US 1930 71m bw
Paramount
A reporter exposes a gangster operating from a country night-club.
Experimental mingling of elements which later become very familiar.
w Garrett Fort story Ben Hecht d Hobart Henley ph William Steiner
☆ Helen Morgan, Charles Ruggles, Fred Kohler, Jimmy Durante, Fuller Mellish Jnr

Roadside Prophets

US 1992 96m CFI color
Electric/New Line (Peter McCarthy, David Swinson)
▣ ▤ ◎〜 🎧
A biker sets off across country to scatter the ashes of his friend in a place where he had been happy.
A punkish road movie, mainly peopled by the sort of eccentrics you would take back-roads to avoid; an Easy Rider *for the 90s it isn't.*
wd Abbe Wool story David Swinson ph Tom Richmond m Pray For Rain, John Doe pd J. Rae Fox ed Nancy Richardson
☆ John Doe, David Anthony Marshall, Adam Horovitz, Barton Heyman, John Cusack, Jennifer Balgobin, Ellie Raab, David Carradine, Timothy Leary, Arlo Guthrie
'With its unfashionable adherence to the idealism of 60s drop-out cinema and occasional deadpan belly laughs, this is well worth travelling along with for an hour and a half.' – Kim Newman, Empire

Roald Dahl's Matilda

🏃 US 1996 100m Technicolor
Columbia TriStar/Jersey (Danny DeVito, Michael Shamberg, Stacey Sher, Liccy Dahl)
▣ ▤ ◎〜 ⊘
The precocious daughter of horrid parents uses her powers of telekinesis to frighten her headmistress.
Sour little black comedy, celebrating childish wish-fulfilment; adults may find it tough going.
w Nicholas Kazan, Robin Swicord novel Roald Dahl d Danny DeVito ph Stefan Czapsky m David Newman pd Bill Brzeski ed Lynzee Klingman, Brent White
☆ Danny DeVito, Rhea Perlman, Embeth Davidtz, Pam Ferris, Mara Wilson, Paul Reubens, Tracey Walter, Brian Levinson
'This is strongish stuff, funny and bitter in turn and not entirely softened by its feel-good ending.' – Derek Malcolm, Guardian

Roar *

🏃 US 1981 102m colour Panavision
Noel Marshall/Banjiro Uemura
A research biologist lives in the African bush with assorted wild animals. He is expecting his family, but they arrive a day early when he is out …
A rather silly story takes in some of the most remarkable animal photography on record, and there is a sub-plot involving villainous game hunters.

---

wd Noel Marshall *ph* Jan de Bont *m* Dominic Frontière

☆ Noel Marshall, Tippi Hedren, and family

† The Marshalls live with their 150 lions and other wild animals in a ranch near Los Angeles. During production the film, which eventually cost 17 million dollars, was halted by flood, fire, epidemic and injury.

Roar of the Dragon

US 1932 70m bw
Radio

Passengers in a Chinese river boat are menaced by bandits.

Curious water-set version of Shanghai Express, with a good cast its best recommendation.

w Howard Estabrook *story* George Kibbee Turner, Merian C. Cooper, Jane Bigelow *d* Wesley Ruggles *ph* Edward Cronjager *md* Max Steiner

☆ Richard Dix, Edward Everett Horton, Gwili Andre, ZaSu Pitts, Arline Judge, Dudley Digges, C. Henry Gordon

'The land of the free gone wild! The heyday of the hotcha! The shock-crammed days G-men took ten whole years to lick!'

The Roaring Twenties ***

US 1939 106m bw
Warner (Hal B. Wallis)
◉ ▣ ⓐ

A World War I veteran returns to New York, innocently becomes involved in bootlegging, builds up an empire and dies in a gang war.

Among the last of the Warner gangster cycle, this was perhaps the best production of them all, despite the familiar plot line: stars and studio were in cracking form.

w Jerry Wald, Richard Macaulay, Robert Rossen *story* Mark Hellinger *d* Raoul Walsh, Anatole Litvak *ph* Ernest Haller *m* Heinz Roemheld

☆ James Cagney, Humphrey Bogart, Priscilla Lane, Jeffrey Lynn, Gladys George, Frank McHugh, Paul Kelly, Elizabeth Risdon

† The James Cagney character was based on Larry Fay, who was Texas Guinan's partner, and Gladys George is clearly Guinan herself.

†† Walsh replaced Litvak as director during filming.

'Honour made him a man. Courage made him a hero. History made him a legend.'

Rob Roy **

US 1995 139m DeLuxe
UIP/UA/Talisman (Peter Broughan, Richard Jackson)
◉ ▣ ⓐ

In the early 1700s, Rob Roy McGregor turns outlaw rather than act dishonourably, as the English demand.

Enjoyably old-fashioned adventure among the heather, though it is the villains who get the best lines.

w Alan Sharp *d* Michael Caton-Jones *ph* Karl Walter Lindenlaub *m* Carter Burwell *pd* Assheton Gorton *ed* Peter Honess

☆ Liam Neeson, Jessica Lange, John Hurt, Tim Roth, Eric Stoltz, Andrew Keir, Brian Cox, Brian McCardie, Gilbert Martin, Vicki Masson

'Gives more pleasure than you think you might get, despite its length and empty patches. It's an epic that at least tries for some sort of authenticity and rises to the main occasion with some bravura.' – *Derek Malcolm, Guardian*

'Profoundly mediocre.' – *Empire*

✍ Tim Roth
🎬 Tim Roth

Rob Roy the Highland Rogue

↟↟ GB 1953 81m Technicolor
Walt Disney (Perce Pearce)
▣

After the defeat of the clans in the 1715 rebellion, their leader escapes and after several adventures is granted a royal pardon.

A kind of Scottish Robin Hood, so stiffly acted and made that it might as well – or better – be a cartoon.

w Lawrence E. Watkin *d* Harold French *ph* Guy Green *m* Cedric Thorpe Davie

☆ Richard Todd, Glynis Johns, James Robertson Justice, Michael Gough, Finlay Currie, Geoffrey Keen, Archie Duncan

Robbers' Roost

US 1955 82m DeLuxe
UA (Leonard Goldstein)

An honest cowboy is employed by cattle rustlers and strives to clear his name.

Fair Western programmer.

w John O'Dea, Sidney Salkow, Maurice Geraghty *novel* Zane Grey *d* Sidney Salkow *ph* Jack Draper *m* Paul Dunlap

☆ George Montgomery, Richard Boone, Sylvia Findley, Bruce Bennett, Peter Graves, Warren Stevens, William Hopper

Robbery *

GB 1967 113m Eastmancolor
Joseph E. Levine/Oakhurst (Michael Deeley, Stanley Baker)
▣

Criminals conspire to rob the night mail train from Glasgow.

Heavy-going fictionalized account of the famous train robbery of 1963; best seen as standard cops and robbers, with some good chase sequences.

w Edward Boyd, Peter Yates, George Markstein *d* Peter Yates *ph* Douglas Slocombe *m* Johnny Keating

☆ Stanley Baker, James Booth, Frank Finlay, Joanna Pettet, Barry Foster, William Marlowe, Clinton Greyn, George Sewell

Robbery under Arms

GB 1957 99m Eastmancolor
Rank (Joe Janni)

In 19th-century Australia, two farming brothers join the notorious outlaw Captain Starlight.

Howlingly dull film version of a semi-classic adventure novel; a rambling story with no unity of viewpoint is saved only by excellent photography.

w Alexander Baron, W. P. Lipscomb *novel* Rolf Boldrewood *d* Jack Lee *ph* Harry Waxman *m* Matyas Seiber

☆ Peter Finch, David McCallum, Ronald Lewis, Maureen Swanson, Jill Ireland, Laurence Naismith, Jean Anderson

Robbery under Arms

Australia 1985 141m colour
Jock Blair/South Australia Film Corporation
♫

Adventures of two young followers of the highwayman Captain Starlight.

Uninteresting cut-down of a TV mini-series; earlier versions were made in 1907, 1911, 1920 and 1957 (above).

w Graeme Koetsveld, Tony Morphett *novel* Rolf Boldrewood *d* Ken Hannam, Donald Crombie

☆ Sam Neill, Steven Vidler, Christopher Cummins, Liz Newman, Ed Devereaux

'The miracle story of all time!'

The Robe **

US 1953 135m Technicolor Cinemascope
TCF (Frank Ross)
◉ ▣ ⓐ ♫

Followers and opponents of Jesus are affected by the robe handed down by him at his crucifixion.

The first film in Cinemascope was, surprisingly, a biblical bestseller, but the crowded Roman sets hid most of the flaws in the process. The film itself was competent and unsurprising in the well-tried Sign of the Cross manner.

w Philip Dunne *novel* Lloyd C. Douglas *d* Henry Koster *ph* Leon Shamroy *m* Alfred Newman *ad* Lyle Wheeler, George W. Davis

☆ Richard Burton, Jean Simmons, Michael Rennie, Victor Mature, Jay Robinson, Torin Thatcher, Dean Jagger, Richard Boone, Betta St John, Jeff Morrow, Ernest Thesiger, Dawn Addams

'The film, then, is the usual vulgarising stuff; and to judge CinemaScope on this evidence would be unfair. The weaknesses of the system are obvious.' – *Dilys Powell*

† Power was originally cast in the Burton role, and Burt Lancaster in Mature's.

🏆 art direction

🏆 best picture; Leon Shamroy; Richard Burton

Robert A. Heinlein's The Puppet Masters: see The Puppet Masters

Roberta *

US 1935 105m bw (Technicolor sequence)
RKO (Pandro S. Berman)
▣ ⓐ ♫

An American inherits a Parisian fashion house.

Thin and remarkably flatly-handled musical romance of the old school, charged only by the occasional appearances in supporting roles of Astaire and Rogers, then on the brink of stardom.

w Jane Murfin, Sam Mintz, Allan Scott *play* Otto Harbach *book* Alice Duer Miller by Gowns by Roberta *d* William A. Seiter *ph* Edward Cronjager *m* Jerome Kern *md* Max Steiner *ch* Fred Astaire *ad* Van Nest Polglase

☆ Irene Dunne, Fred Astaire, Ginger Rogers, Randolph Scott, Helen Westley, Claire Dodd, Victor Varconi, Torben Meyer

'Musical picture-making at its best – fast, smart, good-looking and tuneful.' – *Variety*

† Remade as *Lovely to Look At* (qv).

✍ song 'Lovely to Look At' (*m*Jerome Kern, *ly*Dorothy Fields, Jimmy McHugh)

Robin and Marian *

US 1976 107m Technicolor
Columbia/Rastar (Dennis O'Dell)
◉ ▣

Robin Hood returns from the Crusades and finds conditions in Britain depressing; he finally conquers the evil Sheriff but dies in the attempt.

A kind of serious parody of medieval life, after the fashion of The Lion in Winter but much glummer; in fact, nothing to laugh at at all.

w James Goldman *d* Richard Lester *ph* David Watkin *m* John Barry *pd* Michael Stringer

☆ Sean Connery, Audrey Hepburn, Robert Shaw, Ronnie Barker, Nicol Williamson, Richard Harris, Denholm Elliott, Kenneth Haigh, Ian Holm, Bill Maynard, Esmond Knight, Peter Butterworth

'Surface realism only hides a core of mush, suddenly revealed when the hero and heroine settle down for love-making in a field of corn.' – *Geoff Brown*

'Whimsical jokiness is a bit hard to reconcile with the final plunge into sacrificial romance.' – *Michael Billington, Illustrated London News*

Robin and the Seven Hoods *

US 1964 123m Technicolor Panavision
Warner/PC (Howard W. Koch, William H. Daniels)
◉ ▣ ⓐ

A spoof of the Robin Hood legend set in gangland Chicago of the twenties.

Too flabby by far to be as funny as it thinks it is, this farrago of cheerful jokes has effective moments and lively routines, but most of them are nearly swamped by flat treatment and the wide screen.

w David Schwartz *d* Gordon Douglas *ph* William H. Daniels *m* Nelson Riddle *songs* Sammy Cahn, James Van Heusen

☆ Frank Sinatra, Dean Martin, Bing Crosby, Sammy Davis Jnr, Peter Falk, Barbara Rush, Edward G. Robinson, Victor Buono, Barry Kelley, Jack La Rue, Allen Jenkins, Sig Rumann, Hans Conried

✍ Nelson Riddle; song 'My Kind of Town' (*m*James Van Heusen, *ly*Sammy Cahn)

Robin Hood **

↟↟ US 1922 127m bw silent
Douglas Fairbanks
◉ ▣

Robin Hood combats Prince John and the Sheriff of Nottingham.

An elaborate version of the legend which featured some of Hollywood's most celebrated sets and allowed the star to perform a selection of exhilarating stunts.

w Douglas Fairbanks *d* Allan Dwan *ph* Arthur Edeson *ad* Wilfrid Buckland, Irvin J. Martin

☆ Douglas Fairbanks, Wallace Beery, Alan Hale, Enid Bennett

'The high water mark of film production. It did not grow from the bankroll, it grew from the mind.' – *R. E. Sherwood*

'A story book picture, as gorgeous and glamorous a thing in innumerable scenes as the screen has yet shown … thrilling entertainment for the whole family group.' – *National Board of Review*

† See also *The Adventures of Robin Hood* and *The Story of Robin Hood and his Merrie Men*.

Robin Hood

↟↟ US 1973 83m Technicolor
Walt Disney (Wolfgang Reitherman)
◉ ▣ ⓐ

Alarmingly poor cartoon feature with all the characters 'played' by animals; songs especially dim and treatment quite lifeless.

w Larry Clemmons, Ken Anderson, others *d* Wolfgang Reitherman

☆ Featuring the voices of Brian Bedford, Peter Ustinov, Terry-Thomas, Phil Harris, Andy Devine, Pat Buttram

✍ song 'Love' (*m*George Bruns, *ly*Floyd Huddleston)

Robin Hood

↟↟ US 1991 104m colour
TCF/Working Title (Sarah Radclyffe, Tim Bevan)
◉ ▣ ⓐ ⓓ ♫

Condemned for saving a poacher, a Saxon nobleman, Robert Hode, becomes the outlaw Robin Hood.

Dully facetious re-telling of a familiar tale.

w Mark Allen Smith, John McGrath *d* John Irvin *ph* Jason Lehel *m* Geoffrey Burgon *pd* Austen Spriggs *ed* Peter Tanner

☆ Patrick Bergin, Uma Thurman, Jurgen Prochnow, Edward Fox, Jeroen Krabbé, Owen Teale, David Morrissey, Alex North, Gabrielle Reidy

'The film increasingly comes to resemble a 1960s Hammer cheapie.' – *Sight and Sound*

Robin Hood: Men in Tights

US 1993 102m DeLuxe
TCF/Brooksfilms/Gaumont (Mel Brooks)
◉ ▣ ⓐ

Robin Hood escapes from prison in the Holy Land to return to England and fight against the tyranny of the Sheriff of Rottingham with the help of his merry men, including Will Scarlett O'Hara and Rabbi Tuckman.

An uninventive parody of Kevin Costner's commercially successful retelling as the outlaw of Sherwood Forest; the Costner version is the funnier.

w Mel Brooks, J. David Shapiro, Evan Chandler *d* Mel Brooks *ph* Michael D. O'Shea *m* Hummie Mann *pd* Roy Forge Smith *ed* Steven E. Rivkin

☆ Cary Elwes, Richard Lewis, Roger Rees, Amy Yasbeck, Tracey Ullman, Mel Brooks, Dom DeLuise, Dick Van Patten, Isaac Hayes, Patrick Stewart

'A return to the wild anarchic scatological comedies that made Mel Brooks a marquee name around the world.' – *Variety*

'Doesn't so much lampoon *Prince of Thieves* as try to rise on its jerkin-tails – what is it that he thinks he is adding when he takes off a film?' – *Adam Mars-Jones*

'To say it's feeble would be to give it the benefit of quite a few doubts. It's very feeble indeed.' – *Derek Malcolm*

Robin Hood of El Dorado *

US 1936 86m bw
MGM

Joaquin Murieta turns bandit to avenge himself on the men who killed his wife.

Whitewashed biopic of a notorious Western desperado, played mainly for action and light relief.

w William Wellman, Melvin Levy, Joseph Calleia *d* William Wellman

☆ Warner Baxter, Bruce Cabot, Margo, Eric Linden, J. Carrol Naish, Ann Loring

Robin Hood: Prince of Thieves *

↟↟ US 1991 143m Technicolor
Warner/Morgan Creek (John Watson, Pen Densham, Richard B. Lewis)
◉ ▣ ⓐ ⓓ ♫

Returning from the Crusades to discover that his father has been killed by the Sheriff of Nottingham, Robin of Locksley becomes an outlaw to get his revenge.

A glum version, with little sense of community among the outlaws and an odd mix of acting styles. But it found great favour with the public, becoming one of the most commercially successful films of the year.

w Pen Densham, John Watson *d* Kevin Reynolds *ph* Douglas Milsome *m* John Blakeley *pd* John Graysmark *ed* Peter Boyle

☆ Kevin Costner, Morgan Freeman, Mary Elizabeth Mastrantonio, Christian Slater, Alan Rickman, Sean Connery (uncredited), Geraldine McEwan, Michael McShane, Brian Blessed, Michael Wincott, Nick Brimble

✍ song '(Everything I Do) I Do For You' (*m*Michael Kamen, *ly*Bryan Adams, Robert John Lange)

🎬 Alan Rickman

Robinson Crusoe: see The Adventures of Robinson Crusoe

Robinson Crusoe and the Tiger

👫 Mexico 1969 110m Eastmancolor
Avant/Avco Embassy

Simple but extremely handsome version of the famous story, with the addition of a tiger which Crusoe takes as a pet.

w Mario Marzac, Rene Cardona Jnr *novel* Daniel Defoe d Rene Cardona Jnr ph Alex Phillips, Luis Medina m Raul Lavista

☆ Hugo Stieglitz, Ahui

Robinson Crusoe on Mars **

US 1964 110m Techniscope
Paramount/Devonshire (Aubrey Schenck)
▦ ⚝

An astronaut lands on Mars and learns to survive until rescue comes.

Remarkably close to Defoe (Man Friday being a refugee in an interplanetary war) this is an absorbing, entertaining and well-staged piece of science fiction, strikingly shot in Death Valley.

w Ib Melchior, John C. Higgins d Byron Haskin ph Winton C. Hoch m Van Cleave ad Hal Pereira, Arthur Lonergan sp Lawrence Butler

☆ Paul Mantee, Adam West, Vic Lundin

'Here comes a pleasant surprise, a piece of science fiction based on valid speculation … modest yet provocative.' – *Time*

Robinson Crusoeland

👫 France/Italy 1950 98m bw
Sirius/Franco-London/Fortezza
▦

aka: *Atoll K*
aka: *Escapade; Utopia*

Stan and Ollie inherit an island in the Pacific, but uranium is discovered on it.

Laurel and Hardy's last film is a dispiriting mess, and the less said about it the better.

w John Klorer, Frederick Kohner, Rene Wheeler, Pierro Tellini d Leo Joannon, John Berry ph Armand Thirard, Louis Née m Paul Misraki ad Roland Quignon ed Raymond Isnardon

☆ Stan Laurel, Oliver Hardy, Suzy Delair, Max Elloy

Robinson in Space *

GB 1997 81m colour
BBC/BFO/Koninck (Keith Griffiths)
▦

A man is commissioned to make a study of the problem of present-day Britain.

A film that consists of a sequence of carefully framed shots of Britain's less enticing sights – run-down factories, motorways and the detritus of industrial life – with an oblique commentary, on the relationship between the narrator and the man he accompanies on his travels, which gains its effect by often having little direct connection with what is shown.

wd Patrick Keiller ph Patrick Keiller ed Larry Sidor

☆ Paul Scofield

'Like leafing through a picture album with someone bombarding you with facts over your shoulder.' – *Derek Elley, Variety*

† The film is a continuation of the director's *London* (qv).

'Part man. Part machine. All cop.'

Robocop ***

US 1987 103m DuArt
Rank/Orion (Arne Schmidt)
▦ ▦ ⚝ ◎ ⌒

Detroit in the future: a badly injured cop is reconstructed by science, and defeats the forces of evil.

Gleefully dark vision of the future, directed with flair, although the violence goes over the top towards the end. It gained a best director award at the Sitges Film Festival and a special award for excellence at the 16th Fantasy Film Festival at Avoriaz.

w Edward Neumeier, Michael Miner d Paul Verhoeven ph Jost Vacano m Basil Poledouris pd William Sandell ad Frank J. Urioste

☆ Peter Weller, Nancy Allen, Ronny Cox, Kurtwood Smith, Dan O'Herlihy, Miguel Ferrer

'The greatest science-fiction film since Metropolis' – *Ken Russell*
'A comic book film that's definitely not for kids.' – *Daily Variety*
'Very violent and very funny.' – *Time Out*
'Essentially, it's just a hipper, more bam-bam version of the law-and-order hits of the seventies … The picture keeps telling you that its brutishness is a terrific turn-on, and maybe it is if

you're hooked on Wagnerian sci-fi comic books.' – *Pauline Kael, New Yorker*
⚒ editing (Frank J. Urioste)

Robocop 2

US 1990 118m DuArt
Rank/Orion (Jon Davison)
▦ ▦ ⚝ ⌒

Robocop goes into battle against Robocop 2, a vicious cyborg with the brain of a criminal drug-addict.

Stupefyingly frenetic sequel with none of the panache or wit of the original.

w Frank Miller, Walon Green d Irvin Kershner ph Mark Irwin m Leonard Rosenman pd Peter Jamison ad Pam Marcotte ed William Anderson

☆ Peter Weller, Nancy Allen, Dan O'Herlihy, Belinda Bauer, Tom Noonan, Gabriel Damon, Felton Perry, Willard Pugh

'The level of constant violence, with noisy sound effects, explosions and hundreds of thousands of rounds fired by automatic weaponry, is at first arresting but ultimately numbing and boring.' – *Variety*
'If you like to stagger away from a film feeling numb and slightly sick, this one's for you.' – *Empire*

Robocop 3

US 1993 104m DuArt
Orion (Patrick Crowley)
▦ ▦ ⚝ ⌒

Robocop is caught in a fight between a controlling Japanese corporation and the poor it is trying to evict to build a new city.

Inspiration is sadly lacking here in a film aimed at an audience of early teens; all that can be said in its favour is that it contains less violence than its predecessor.

w Frank Miller, Fred Dekker d Fred Dekker ph Gary B. Kibbe m Basil Poledouris pd Hilda Stark ed Bert Lovitt sp Jeff Jarvis

☆ Robert John Burke, Nancy Allen, Rip Torn, John Castle, Jill Hennessy, Mako, Robert DoQui

'A cluttered, nasty exercise that seems principally intent on selling action figures.' – *Variety*

† A *Robocop* television series followed in 1994.

Rocco and His Brothers **

Italy/France 1960 180m bw
Titanus/Les Films Marceau (Goffredo Lombardo)
▦ ▦ ⚝

A peasant family moves into Milan, and each of its five brothers has his problems.

Massive portmanteau of realistic stories, a bit hard to take despite its undoubted brilliance.

w Luchino Visconti, Suso Cecchi d'Amico, Vasco Pratolini d Luchino Visconti ph Giuseppe Rotunno m Nino Rota

☆ Alain Delon, Renato Salvatori, Annie Girardot, Katina Paxinou, Roger Hanin, Paolo Stoppa, Suzy Delair, Claudia Cardinale

'Joins the band of films which, these last months, have given one new hope for the cinema.' *Dilys Powell*

'Alcatraz. Only one man has ever broken out. Now five million lives depend upon two men breaking in.'

The Rock

US 1996 136m Technicolor Panavision
Buena Vista/Hollywood (Don Simpson, Jerry Bruckheimer)
▦ ▦ ⚝ ◎ ◎ ⌒

A top agent and a convict combine forces to break into Alcatraz, where a renegade general threatens to destroy San Francisco.

Ludicrously over-the-top thriller, filmed and edited in frenetic bursts of action for those with short attention spans; the narrative lacks logic, with explosions used to distract attention from its shortcomings.

w David Weisberg, Douglas S. Cook, Mark Rosner d Michael Bay ph John Schwartzman m Nick Glennie-Smith, Hans Zimmer pd Michael White ed Richard Francis-Bruce sp Dream Quest Images

☆ Sean Connery, Nicolas Cage, Ed Harris, Michael Biehn, William Forsythe, David Morse, John Spencer, John C. McGinley

'Hollywood appears to have developed a new definition of the comedy thriller: not a thriller that's also funny, but one with a plot so stupid that it can only be played for laughs.' – *John Wrathall, Sight and Sound*
'The movie is so relentless and assaultive it runs roughshod over its own characters.' – *Owen Gleiberman, Entertainment Weekly*

† The film was among the box-office successes of 1996, taking more than $134m at the US box-office and a further $195m worldwide.
†† Apart from the credited screenwriters, Dick Clement and Ian La Frenais worked on Connery's dialogue, and Jonathan Hensleigh, Aaron Sorkin and Quentin Tarantino also contributed to the script.
⚒ sound

Rock a Bye Baby

US 1958 107m Technicolor Vistavision
Paramount (Jerry Lewis)

A film star asks her devoted schoolday admirer to look after her triplets by a secret marriage.

Tasteless jazzing-up of The Miracle of Morgan's Creek by talents distinctly unsympathetic.

wd Frank Tashlin ph Haskell Boggs m Walter Scharf

☆ Jerry Lewis, Marilyn Maxwell, Reginald Gardiner, Salvatore Baccaloni, Hans Conried, Isobel Elsom, James Gleason, Ida Moore, Connie Stevens

Rock All Night

US 1957 65m bw
AIP (Roger Corman)

Two gangsters hide out in a pub and hold its customers hostage.

Talky, cheap rock movie, with some occasionally bright dialogue, and a single set in which heavy drinkers philosophise and listen to a few indifferent musical numbers; at least, it doesn't take itself too seriously.

w Charles B. Griffith wd Richard Corman story David P. Harmon ph Floyd Crosby md Buck Ram ad Robert Kinosenta ed Frank Sullivan

☆ Dick Miller, Russell Johnson, Abby Dalton, Jeanne Cooper, Robin Morse, Mel Welles, Richard Cutting, Chris Alcaide, Jonathan Haze, Bruno Ve Sota, The Platters, The Blockbusters, Nora Hayes

♫ I'm Sorry; He's Mine; Rock All Night; I Wanna Rock Now; Rock and Roll Guitar; The Great Pretender; I Guess I Won't Hang Around Here Any More

Rock around the Clock *

👫 US 1956 74m bw
Columbia (Sam Katzman)
▦

A band playing a new form of music – rock 'n' roll – becomes a nationwide sensation.

A cheap second feature with guest artists, this cheerful little movie deserved at least a footnote in the histories because it spotlights the origins and the leading purveyors of rock 'n' roll. It also caused serious riots in several countries. A sequel in 1957, Don't Knock the Rock, was merely cheap.

w Robert E. Kent, James B. Gordon d Fred F. Sears ph Benjamin H. Kline

☆ Bill Haley and the Comets, the Platters, Little Richard, Tony Martinez and his Band, Freddie Bell and the Bellboys, Johnny Johnston, Alan Freed, Lisa Gaye, Alix Talton

Rock Hudson's Home Movies **

US 1992 63m video
Mark Rappaport

A semi-documentary, in which an actor playing the role of Rock Hudson comments on film clips of the real Hudson, looking at his performances from a gay perspective.

A witty deconstruction of Hudson's masculine and heterosexual screen image and the constraints and evasions of Hollywood movies in the 1950s and 60s.

wd Mark Rappaport ph Mark Daniels ed Mark Rappaport

☆ Eric Farr

'Shatters the false image of the movies so completely that you wonder how it ever lasted so long.' – *Premiere*

Rock 'n' Roll Cop

Hong Kong 1994 90m colour
Sky Point

original title: *Sang Gong Yatho Tungchap Fan*

Two incompatible cops – a guitar-playing loner from Hong Kong and an uptight disciplinarian from mainland China – combine forces to go after a violent gang that divides its time between the two territories.

*Frenetically violent action movie, frequently incoherent and often unpleasantly sadistic, that looks forward to the absorption of Hong Kong into China in 1997;

despite the heroics, both police forces here seem remarkably incompetent at catching criminals.*

w Lou Bing d Che Kirk Wong ph Ko Tsiu-lam m Tsung Ding-yat ad Eddie Ma ed Kam Ma

☆ Anthony Wong, Wu Hsing-Kuo, Yu Wing-kwong, Carrie Ng, Chan Ming-tsing

'The action sequences deliver.' – *Variety*

Rock 'n' Roll High School *

US 1979 93m colour
New World (Michael Finnell)
▦ ⚝ ⌒

High-school students rebel against an oppressive principal.

A tongue-in-cheek, sometimes self-conscious update of a 1950s rock movie, retaining and enjoying every cliché.

w Russ Dvonch, Joseph McBride, Richard Whitley story Allan Arkush, Joe Dante d Allan Arkush ph Dean Cundey m The Ramones ad Marie Kordus ed Larry Bock, Gail Werbin

☆ P. J. Soles, Vincent Van Patten, Clint Howard, Dey Young, Mary Woronov, Paul Bartel, Dick Miller, Grady Sutton

Rock Rock Rock

US 1957 83m bw
Vanguard (Max J. Rosenberg, Milton Subotsky)

Two girls are rivals for the love of a high-school rock singer.

Poorly written and ineptly acted low-budget movie exploiting the popularity of rock 'n' roll. It consists mainly of a series of performances that have nothing to do with the narrative, which are either by second-string performers – the appalling Ivy Schulman, Cirino and The Bowties, Jimmy Cavallo and His House Rockers, The Three Chuckles, The Moonglows – or better ones such as Chuck Berry, The Flamingos, Frankie Lymon and LaVern Baker performing second-rate material.

w Milton Subotsky d Will Price ph Morris Hartzband md Milton Subotsky ad Paul M. Heller ed Blandine Hafela

☆ Tuesday Weld, Teddy Randazzo, Jacqueline Kerr, Ivy Schulman, Alan Freed, Fran Manfred, Jack Collins, Carol Moss

† Rock singer Johnny Burnette (1934–64) is featured in his only screen performance.
†† Connie Francis dubbed Tuesday Weld's two songs.

Rockabye

US 1932 70m bw
Radio

A great actress who has scratched her way up is unhappy because of frustrated mother love.

One of many tearjerkers of its type produced in the first three years of the thirties: it doesn't travel well across the decades.

w Jane Murfin, Kubec Glasmon play Lucia Bronder d George Cukor

☆ Constance Bennett, Joel McCrea, Paul Lukas, Walter Pidgeon, Jobyna Howland, Walter Catlett

'Moderate grosser, best for the neighbourhood mats.' – *Variety*

Rock-a-Doodle

👫 GB 1990 74m Technicolor
Rank/Goldcrest/Sullivan Bluth (Don Bluth, Gary Goldman, John Pomeroy, Robert Enrietto)
▦ ▦ ⚝ ◎ ⌒

A farmboy, transformed into a cat by a wicked owl, travels to the big city to persuade a rock-singing rooster to return home and make the sun shine again.

Excellent animation is rendered pointless by a poor and confusing narrative.

w David N. Weiss story Don Bluth, David N. Weiss, John Pomeroy, T. J. Kuenster, David Steinberg, Gary Goldman d Don Bluth m Robert Folk, T. J. Kuenster pd David Goetz ed Bernard Caputo, Fiona Trayler, Lisa Dorney, Joe Gall

☆ Featuring the voices of Phil Harris, Glen Campbell, Eddie Deezen, Kathryn Holcomb, Toby Scott Ganger, Stan Ivar, Christian Hoff, Jason Marin, Christopher Plummer, Sandy Duncan

Rockers

Jamaica 1978 100m colour
Jesse Burton Stone (Patrick Hulsey)

A hard-up Rastafarian reggae drummer plans an elaborate revenge when big-city gangsters steal the motorbike that was going to make his fortune.

There's an air of authenticity about this slight and often charming narrative of life on the streets of Jamaica,

---

frequently interrupted for music, but it is also casual to the point of amateurishness.
wd Theodoros Bafaloukos ph Peter Sova m Kiddus-I, Jacob Miller and the Inner Circle, Burning Spear, Gregory Isaacs, Peter Tosh, Rockers All Stars ad Lilly Kilvert ed Susan Steinberg
☆ Leroy (Horsemouth) Wallace, Richard Hall, Monica Craig, Marjorie Norman, Jacob Miller, Gregory Isaacs, Winston Rodney, Frank Dowding
† The credits include 'Keeper of The Peace'.

The Rocket Man
US   1954   79m   bw
TCF
A visitor from outer space gives a magic ray gun to an orphan boy and tells him to use it only for good.
Elementary fantasy with amusing moments.
w Lenny Bruce, Jack Henley d Oscar Rudolph ph John F. Seitz m Lionel Newman
☆ Charles Coburn, George 'Foghorn' Winslow, Spring Byington, Anne Francis, John Agar

Rocket to the Moon: see *Cat Women of the Moon*

The Rocketeer
↟↟ US   1991   108m   Technicolor
Panavision
Walt Disney/Silver Screen Partners IV (Lawrence Gordon, Charles Gordon, Lloyd Levin)
▣ ▤ ⊚ ⊚ ⌒
In 1938 a racing pilot finds a one-man rocket pack which he uses to foil a Nazis' attempt at world domination.
Tame attempt at a period adventure that never gets off the ground.
w Danny Bilson, Paul de Meo graphic novel Dave Stevens d Joe Johnston ph Hiro Narita m James Horner pd Jim Bissell ed Arthur Schmidt sp Jon G. Belyeu
☆ Bill Campbell, Jennifer Connelly, Alan Arkin, Timothy Dalton, Paul Sorvino, Terry O'Quinn, Ed Lauter, James Handy
   'This high-octane, high-flying, live-action comic strip has been machine-tooled into agreeable lightweight summer fare.' – *Variety*

Rockets Galore
GB   1958   94m   Technicolor
Rank (Basil Dearden)
US title: *Mad Little Island*
The Scottish island of Todday resists the installation of a rocket-launching site.
Amiable but disappointingly listless sequel to Whisky Galore.
w Monja Danischewsky novel Compton Mackenzie d Michael Relph ph Reg Wyer m Cedric Thorpe Davie
☆ Jeannie Carson, Donald Sinden, Roland Culver, Noel Purcell, Ian Hunter, Duncan Macrae, Jean Cadell, Carl Jaffe, Gordon Jackson, Catherine Lacey

Rocketship XM *
US   1950   79m   bw
Lippert (Kurt Neumann)
▣ ▤ ⊚
An expedition to the moon lands by accident on Mars.
The first post-war space adventure is sheer hokum, quite likeable for its cheek though not for its cheap sets.
wd Kurt Neumann ph Karl Struss m Ferde Grofe
☆ Lloyd Bridges, Osa Massen, John Emery, Hugh O'Brian
   'The message of Rocketship X-M is clear: never take a lady as your fuel expert on a trip into interstellar space.' – *C. A. Lejeune*

The Rocking Horse Winner *
GB   1949   90m   bw
Rank/Two Cities (John Mills)
▤
A boy discovers he can predict winners while riding an old rocking horse; his mother's greed has fatal results.
A very short story is fatally over-extended and becomes bathetic; but the production is solid and the film deserves a mark for trying.
wd Anthony Pelissier story D. H. Lawrence ph Desmond Dickinson m William Alwyn ad Carmen Dillon
☆ John Mills, Valerie Hobson, John Howard Davies, Ronald Squire, Hugh Sinclair, Cyril Smith
   'Fails as an interpretation of D. H. Lawrence. But as a skilful piece of narrative with excellent

technical qualities it is well worth a visit.' – *Dilys Powell, Britain Today*

'His whole life was a million-to-one shot!'
Rocky ***
↟↟ US   1976   119m   Technicolor
UA/Chartoff-Winkler (Gene Kirkwood)
▣ ▤ ⊚ ⊚ ⌒
A slightly dimwitted Philadelphia boxer makes good.
Pleasantly old-fashioned comedy-drama with rather unattractive characters in the modern manner. Despite the freshness, on the whole Marty is still preferable.
w Sylvester Stallone d John G. Avildsen ph James Crabe m Bill Conti
☆ Sylvester Stallone, Burgess Meredith, Talia Shire, Burt Young, Carl Weathers, Thayer David
♟ best picture; John G. Avildsen
⚜ Sylvester Stallone (as writer); song 'Gonna Fly Now' (mBill Conti, lyCarol Connors, Ayn Robbins); Sylvester Stallone (as actor); Burgess Meredith; Talia Shire; Burt Young

The Rocky Horror Picture Show ***
GB   1975   100m   Eastmancolor
TCF (Michael White)
▣ ▤ ⊚ ⌒
A couple, whose car breaks down on a dark and stormy night, take refuge in an old, dark mansion where a mad scientist is trying to make the perfect man.
A spoof of horror and science-fiction movies, based on a hit musical, and notable mainly for the high-energy performance of Tim Curry, repeating his stage success as a transvestite transsexual from Transylvania.
w Richard O'Brien, Jim Sharman play The Rocky Horror Show by Richard O'Brien d Jim Sharman ph Peter Suschitzky m Richard O'Brien pd Brian Thomson ed Graeme Clifford
☆ Tim Curry, Susan Sarandon, Barry Bostwick, Richard O'Brien, Patricia Quinn, Little Nell, Jonathan Adams, Peter Hinwood, Meatloaf, Charles Gray
   'A self-consciously slick rendition of the original material, shorn of the song reprises, staged and performed with evident delight in having larger and more lavish sets to move around in.' – *Tony Rayns, MFB*
   'A quite wonderful mixture of spoof horror and sci-fi.' – *Empire*
† The film was a failure on its first release but later became a cult phenomenon at midnight screenings, with audiences dressed as the characters and chanting their dialogue.

Rocky II
↟↟ US   1979   119m   Technicolor
UA/Irwin Winkler, Robert Chartoff
▣ ▤ ⊚ ⊚ ⌒
After success comes failure; then Rocky marries his sweetheart and works for another big fight.
Over-inflated but under-nourished sequel with absolutely nothing new to offer.
wd Sylvester Stallone ph Bill Butler m Bill Conti
☆ Sylvester Stallone, Talia Shire, Burt Young, Carl Weathers, Burgess Meredith

'A Fighter. A Lover. A Legend. The Greatest Challenge.'
Rocky III
↟↟ US   1982   99m   Technicolor
United Artists/Chartoff-Winkler (James D. Brubaker)
▣ ▤ ⊚ ⌒
Rocky is challenged by a brutal slugger who beats him at the first match …
Unnecessary regurgitation of bits and pieces from the first two Rocky movies.
wd Sylvester Stallone ph Bill Butler m Bill Conti pd William J. Cassidy ed Don Zimmerman, Mark Warner
☆ Sylvester Stallone, Talia Shire, Burt Young, Burgess Meredith, Carl Weathers, Tony Burton, Mr T, Hulk Hogan
   'The time has surely come for Rocky Balboa to take the final count.' – *Tom Milne, MFB*
   'The first Rocky was primitive in a relatively innocent way. This picture is primitive too, but it's also shrewd and empty and inept.' – *New Yorker*
⚜ original song 'Eye of the Tiger' by Jim Peterik and Frankie Sullivan III

Rocky IV
↟↟ US   1985   91m   Metrocolor
MGM/UA/Winkler-Chartoff
▣ ▤ ⊚ ⊚ ⌒
Rocky takes on a Russian champion.
Hilarious, hysterical, would-be allegorical, this is the pits; but it took a lot of money.
wd Sylvester Stallone ph Bill Butler m Vince DiCola, Bill Conti pd Bill Kenney ed Don Zimmerman, John W. Wheeler
☆ Sylvester Stallone, Dolph Lundgren, Carl Weathers, Talia Shire, Burt Young, Brigitte Nielsen
   'Ludicrous rubbish, but efficient with it.' – *Shaun Usher, Daily Mail*

Rocky Mountain
US   1950   83m   bw
Warner (William Jacobs)
A Confederate horseman gets involved in an Indian war.
Routine star Western with unusual tragic ending.
w Winston Miller, Alan le May d William Keighley ph Ted McCord m Max Steiner
☆ Errol Flynn, Patrice Wymore, Scott Forbes, Guinn Williams, Slim Pickens

Rocky Mountain Mystery
US   1935   64m   bw
Paramount
An engineer solves a number of murders at a radium mine.
Routine whodunnit in an unfamiliar setting. Mrs Leslie Carter provides a rare screen appearance, and just as well to judge from her performance
w Edward E. Paramore Jnr novel Golden Dreams by Zane Grey d Charles Barton
☆ Randolph Scott, Charles Chic Sale, Mrs Leslie Carter, Kathleen Burke, Ann Sheridan
   'Good entertainment in spite of minor shortcomings.' – *Variety*

'Where does a champion go when he takes off the gloves?'
Rocky V
↟↟ US   1990   104m   DeLuxe
UIP/United Artists/Star Partners III (Robert Chartoff, Irwin Winkler)
▣ ▤ ⊚ ⌒
Rocky, suffering, unsurprisingly, from brain-damage, takes on a young protégé.
The series continues its steep, downward spiral into insipid nonsense.
w Sylvester Stallone d John G. Avildsen ph Steven Poster m Bill Conti pd William J. Cassidy ed John G. Avildsen, Michael N. Knue
☆ Sylvester Stallone, Talia Shire, Burt Young, Sage Stallone, Burgess Meredith, Tommy Morrison, Richard Gant, Tony Burton
† Stallone's original ending had Rocky dying in his moment of final triumph.

Roger & Me **
US   1989   90m   DuArt
Warner/Dog Eat Dog Films/Michael Moore
▣ ▤ ⌒
A journalist attempts to interview the chairman of General Motors about his decision to close its factory in the town where the company began and so put thousands of people out of work.
Entertaining, blackly comic (though not always accurate) documentary on the human cost of big business.
wd Michael Moore ph Christopher Beaver, John Prusak, Kevin Rafferty, Bruce Schermer ed Wendy Stanzler, Jennifer Beman
   'A fascinating account of blue collar life unable to come to terms with the clouding of the American Dream they are perpetually adjured to believe in.' – *Derek Malcolm, Guardian*

Roger Touhy, Gangster
US   1944   73m   bw
TCF
GB title: *The Last Gangster*
An associate of Al Capone is finally cornered by the FBI.
Unsurprising, competent cops-and-robbers melodrama, based more or less on fact.
w Crane Wilbur, Jerry Cady d Robert Florey
☆ Preston Foster, Victor McLaglen, Lois Andrews, Kent Taylor, Anthony Quinn, Henry Morgan

Rogue Cop
US   1954   92m   bw
MGM (Nicholas Nayfack)
A police detective is on the payroll of a crime syndicate.
Uncompelling star melodrama.
w Sydney Boehm novel William P. McGivern d Roy Rowland ph John Seitz m Jeff Alexander
☆ Robert Taylor, George Raft, Janet Leigh, Steve Forrest, Anne Francis
   'Another of the sour, disillusioned crime stories which have recently been coming into fashion.' – *Penelope Houston*
⚜ John Seitz

The Rogue Song *
US   1930   115m   Technicolor
MGM (Lionel Barrymore)
A bandit wins the hand of a Russian princess.
Primitive early sound operetta, not salvaged by a few Laurel and Hardy scenes added as an afterthought.
w Frances Marion, John Colton operetta Gypsy Love by Franz Lehàr, Robert Bodansky d Lionel Barrymore, Hal Roach ph Percy Hilburn, C. Edgar Schoenbaum m Dimitri Tiomkin ed Margaret Booth
☆ Lawrence Tibbett, Catherine Dale Owen, Florence Lake, Judith Vosselli, Nance O'Neil, Stan Laurel, Oliver Hardy
   'Slow unto dullness outside of Tibbett's singing; Laurel and Hardy names draw but their comedy is very weak.' – *Variety*
† No print is known to exist, but in 1980 the sound track was issued on record.
⚜ Lawrence Tibbett

Rogue Trader
GB/US   1998   101m   colour
Pathé/Granada/Newmarket/David Paradine (James Dearden, Paul Raphael, Janette Day)
▣ ▤ ⊚
An English merchant banker, working in Singapore, gains a reputation as a financial genius while losing millions of dollars.
A biopic, of a man who ruined one of London's most venerable merchant bankers, that should have made a perfect morality play on modern day values, but instead settles for a tabloid approach that explains and illumines nothing.
wd James Dearden book Rogue Trader: How I Brought Down Barings Bank and Shook the Financial World by Nicholas Leeson and Edward Whitley ph Jean-François Robin m Richard Hartley pd Alan MacDonald ed Catherine Creed
☆ Ewan McGregor, Anna Friel, Yves Beneyton, Betsy Brantley, Caroline Langrishe, Nigel Lindsay, Tim McInnerney, Irene Ng, Lee Ross, Simon Shepherd, John Standing
   'Truly awful.' – *Guardian*

Rogue's March
US   1953   84m   bw
MGM (Leon Gordon)
A British army officer is unjustly accused of espionage but becomes a hero in India.
Victorian comedy adventure set on a never-never frontier. Not much.
w Leon Gordon d Allan Davis ph Paul C. Vogel m Alberto Colombo
☆ Peter Lawford, Richard Greene, Janice Rule, Leo G. Carroll, John Abbott, Patrick Aherne

Rogues of Sherwood Forest *
↟↟ US   1950   80m   Technicolor
Columbia (Fred M. Packard)
Robin Hood's son helps the barons to force the signing of Magna Carta.
Satisfactory action adventure.
w George Bruce d Gordon Douglas ph Charles Lawton Jnr m Heinz Roemheld, Arthur Morton
☆ John Derek, Diana Lynn, George Macready, Alan Hale, Paul Cavanagh, Lowell Gilmore, Billy House

Rogues' Regiment
US   1948   86m   bw
Universal-International (Robert Buckner)
An intelligence man joins the French Foreign Legion in Saigon to track down an ex-Nazi.
Keen but rather muddled actioner.
w Robert Buckner d Robert Florey ph Maury Gertsman m Daniele Amfitheatrof
☆ Dick Powell, Marta Toren, Vincent Price, Stephen McNally

Le Roi de Coeur: see *King of Hearts*

Rojin Z: see *Roujin Z*

Roller Boogie

US   1979   103m   colour
United Artists (Bruce Cohn Curtis)

▣

With the help of an expert roller-skater, a poor little rich girl foils a crooked businessman who is trying to take over the local roller disco.
A silly and trivial attempt to cash in on a teenage craze, with much skating to unmemorable songs; it has nothing to recommend it, least of all the leading performances.
w Barry Schneider *story* Irwin Yablans d Mark L. Lester *ph* Dean Cundey m Bob Esty m/ly Bob Esty, Michele Aller, Michael Brooks *ad* Keith Michl *ed* Howard Kunin
☆ Linda Blair, Jim Bray, Beverly Garland, Roger Perry, James Van Patten, Kimberly Beck, Sean McClory, Mark Goddard

Rollerball *

US   1975   129m   Technicolor   Scope
UA/Norman Jewison

▣ ▣ ◎ ◎

In the 21st century an ultra-violent game is used to release the anti-social feelings of the masses.
A one-point parable, and an obvious point at that, is stretched out over more than two hours of violence in which the rules of the game are not even explained. A distinctly unlikeable film.
w William Harrison d Norman Jewison *ph* Douglas Slocombe *md* André Previn *pd* John Box
☆ James Caan, John Houseman, Ralph Richardson, Maud Adams, John Beck, Moses Gunn
'A classic demonstration of how several millions of dollars can be unenjoyably wasted.' – *Jonathan Rosenbaum*
🏆 John Box

Rollercoaster

US   1977   118m   Technicolor   Panavision
Sensurround
Universal (Jennings Lang)

▣ ▣ ◎ ◐

A saboteur blows up rollercoasters if his blackmail demands are not met.
Limp, unsuspenseful, would-be spectacular in which a stalwart cast struggles with inane dialogue and situations.
w Richard Levinson, William Link d James Goldstone *ph* David M. Walsh m Lalo Schifrin
☆ George Segal, Timothy Bottoms, Richard Widmark, Susan Strasberg, Harry Guardino, Henry Fonda

Rolling Thunder

US   1977   94m   DeLuxe
AIP (Norman T. Herman)

▣ ◎

A former prisoner of war in Vietnam seeks revenge on the killers of his wife and son.
Moderate action thriller, although its use of the Vietnam War seems opportunistic rather than apposite.
w Heywood Gould, Paul Schrader d John Flynn *ph* Jordan Cronenweth m Barry DeVorzon *ad* Steve Burger *ed* Frank P. Keller
☆ William Devane, Tommy Lee Jones, Linda Haynes, Lisa Richards, Dabney Coleman, James Best

Rollover

US   1981   115m   Technicolor   Panavision
Orion/IPC (Bruce Gilbert)

▣

The widow of a murdered bank president exposes various kinds of financial chicanery on an international scale.
So complexly plotted as to be virtually unintelligible, this slick romantic melodrama was caviare to the general despite its stars.
w David Shaber d Alan J. Pakula *ph* Giuseppe Rotunno, William Garroni m Michael Small
☆ Jane Fonda, Kris Kristofferson, Hume Cronyn, Josef Sommer, Bob Gunton

Roma: see *Fellini's Roma*

Roma, Città Aperta: see *Open City*

Le Roman de Renard: see *The Tale of the Fox*

Le Roman d'un Tricheur *

France   1936   83m   bw
Cinéas
aka: *The Story of a Cheat*

A reformed elderly cardsharp writes his memoirs.
First person singular comedy, a tour de force in which only the narrator speaks, the rest use pantomime only.
wd Sacha Guitry *ph* Marcel Lucien
☆ Sacha Guitry, Marguerite Moreno, Serge Grave

Roman Holiday **

US   1953   118m   bw
Paramount (William Wyler)

▣ ▣ ▣

A princess on an official visit to Rome slips away incognito and falls in love with a newspaperman.
Wispy, charming, old-fashioned romantic comedy shot in Rome and a little obsessed by the locations; one feels that a studio base would have resulted in firmer control of the elements. The stars, however, made it memorable.
w Ian McLellan Hunter, John Dighton d William Wyler *ph* Franz Planer, Henri Alekan m Georges Auric *ad* Hal Pereira, Walter Tyler *ed* Robert Swink
☆ Gregory Peck, Audrey Hepburn, Eddie Albert, Hartley Power, Harcourt Williams
'While Capra, or in a different way Lubitsch, could have made something wholly enjoyable from it, it would seem that Wyler's technique is now too ponderously inflexible for such lightweight material.' – *MFB*
† Dalton Trumbo, then a blacklisted writer, was the actual author of the original story, although Ian McLellan Hunter received the credit for it.
🏅 original story (Ian McLellan Hunter); Audrey Hepburn; costumes (Edith Head)
🏆 best picture; script; William Wyler; photography; Eddie Albert; art direction; editing
🏆 Audrey Hepburn

Roman Scandals **

US   1933   93m   bw
Samuel Goldwyn

A troubled young man dreams himself back in ancient Rome.
Musical farce which is not only pretty entertaining on its own account but remains interesting for a number of reasons; as its star's best vehicle, for its Depression bookends, as a spoof on The Sign of the Cross and the inspiration of scores of other comedies in which the heroes dreamed themselves back into other times. Note also the musical numbers, the chariot race finale, and the rare appearance of Ruth Etting.
w William Anthony McGuire, George Oppenheimer, Arthur Sheekman, Nat Perrin *story* George S. Kaufman, Robert E. Sherwood d Frank Tuttle *ph* Gregg Toland m Alfred Newman *ch* Busby Berkeley *chariot sequence* Ralph Cedar *songs* Harry Warren (m), Al Dubin, L. Wolfe Gilbert (ly)
☆ Eddie Cantor, Gloria Stuart, Ruth Etting, Edward Arnold, Alan Mowbray, Verree Teasdale
'An extraordinary rigmarole containing everything from chariot races to a torch song.' – *Time*

The Roman Spring of Mrs Stone *

GB   1961   104m   Technicolor
Warner Seven Arts/AA (Louis de Rochemont)

▣

A widowed American actress in Rome begins to drift into lassitude and moral decline.
Vivien Leigh gets degraded again in this rambling novella complete with mysterious dark stranger waiting at the end. Nice to look at, and occasionally compelling, but unsuccessful as a whole.
w Gavin Lambert *novel* Tennessee Williams d José Quintero *ph* Harry Waxman m Richard Addinsell *pd* Roger Furse *ad* Herbert Smith
☆ Vivien Leigh, Warren Beatty, Lotte Lenya, Jeremy Spenser, Coral Browne, Ernest Thesiger
'The slightly sweet smell of decay hovers over everything. Although its very subject matter limits this film and smothers it slightly, it is quietly and sincerely made.' – *New York Herald Tribune*
🏅 Lotte Lenya

Romance *

US   1930   76m   bw
MGM

▣

A clergyman falls in love with the opera singer mistress of an industrialist.
Simple-minded romantic drama with the star not at her best; but an interesting example of 'high class' romance of the time.
w Bess Meredyth, Edwin Justus Mayer *play* Edward Sheldon d Clarence Brown *ph* William Daniels
☆ Greta Garbo, Lewis Stone, Gavin Gordon, Elliott Nugent, Clara Blandick, Florence Lake, Henry Armetta
'A first-run hit of the sort that won't miss.' – *Variety*
🏅 Clarence Brown; Greta Garbo

Romance **

France   1999   99m   colour
Blue Light/Flach/CB/ARTE (Jean-François Lepetit)

▣

Frustrated by her partner's refusal to make love to her, a schoolteacher embarks on a series of affairs.
A movie that caused controversy because of its scenes of explicit sexual activity, some of which involved the well-endowed porn star Siffredi; otherwise it is one of those films, typical of France, in which a woman's search for sexual emancipation causes her to be abused by men. Finally, it becomes a twisted drama of revenge.
wd Catherine Breillat *ph* Yorgos Arvanitis m Raphael Tidas, DJ Valentin *pd* Frédérique Belvaux *ed* Agnès Guillemot
☆ Caroline Trousselard, Sagamore Stévenin, François Berléand, Rocco Siffredi, Reza Habouhossein, Fabien de Jomaron, Emma Colberti, Ashley Wanninger
'What makes the film as a whole so odd is that the sexual acts are the only realistic things in it. If this is a landmark in cinema, it's strangely stranded.' – *Adam Mars-Jones, Times*

Romance and Riches: see *The Amazing Quest of Ernest Bliss*

Romance for Three: see *Paradise for Three*

Romance in Flanders

GB   1937   73m   bw
Franco-London/British Lion
US title: *Romance on the Western Front*
Two sergeants fall for a Belgian farmer's daughter; she marries the one she doesn't love, thinking the other is dead.
Rose-coloured romantic hokum, of no sustaining interest.
w Harold Simpson *book* Mario Fort, Ralph E. Vanloc d Maurice Elvey
☆ Paul Cavanagh, Marcelle Chantal, Garry Marsh, Olga Lindo, Alastair Sim

Romance in Manhattan

US   1934   78m   bw
RKO

▣

A New York girl helps a Czech immigrant to find work in the metropolis.
Slim, sentimental movie novelette without a touch of sophistication.
w Jane Murfin, Edward Kaufman d Stephen Roberts
☆ Ginger Rogers, Francis Lederer, Arthur Hohl, J. Farrell MacDonald, Eily Malyon, Donald Meek

Romance in the Dark

US   1938   78m   bw
Paramount
A famous baritone helps a singing servant to get famous.
Musical romance for the carriage trade, with apparently more comedy asides than were originally intended.
w Frank Partos, Anne Morrison Chapin d H. C. Potter
☆ Gladys Swarthout, John Boles, John Barrymore, Claire Dodd, Fritz Field, Curt Bois
'Biz will be good, if no wow. Boles and Barrymore will give some tug to the tide against the turnstiles.' – *Variety*

Romance in the Rain

US   1934   74m   bw
Universal
A girl from the slums wins a Cinderella contest and falls for the press agent.
Lightweight romantic concoction which pleased at the time.
w Barry Trivers, Gladys Unger, John V. A. Weaver, Sig Herzig, Jay Gorney d Stuart Walker
☆ Roger Pryor, Heather Angel, Victor Moore, Esther Ralston, Ruth Donnelly, Christian Rub

Romance is Sacred: see *The King and the Chorus Girl*

Romance of a Horse Thief

US/Yugoslavia   1971   100m   Technicolor
Allied Artists/Jadran/Emmanuel L. Wolf (Gene Gutowski)

In a Polish village in 1904 there is dismay when horses are commandeered by Cossacks for service in the Russo-Japanese war.
Nostalgic Jewish drama which ends up rather like Fiddler on the Roof without the music.
w David Opatoshu, based on his father Joseph's novel d Abraham Polonsky *ph* Piero Portalupisisic m Mort Shuman
☆ Yul Brynner, Eli Wallach, Jane Birkin, Oliver Tobias, Lainie Kazan, David Opatoshu

The Romance of Rosy Ridge

US   1947   103m   bw
MGM (Jack Cummings)

After the Civil War, farmers make their own peace.
Mild period romance with everything settled by a betrothal.
w Lester Cole *novel* Mackinlay Kantor d Roy Rowland *ph* Sidney Wagner m George Bassman
☆ Van Johnson, Thomas Mitchell, Janet Leigh, Selena Royle, Marshall Thompson, Dean Stockwell
'Rustic charm spread through it like molasses.' – *Douglas Eames*

Romance on the High Seas *

US   1948   99m   Technicolor
Warner (Alex Gottlieb, George Amy)

▣ ◎

GB title: *It's Magic*
Various romances mesh on an ocean voyage.
Lightweight musical which introduces Doris Day and generally manages to keep afloat.
w Julius J. and Philip G. Epstein, I. A. L. Diamond d Michael Curtiz *ph* Elwood Bredell m Ray Heindorf *songs* Jule Styne, Sammy Cahn
☆ Jack Carson, Janis Paige, Don Defore, Doris Day, Oscar Levant, S. Z. Sakall, Eric Blore, Franklin Pangborn, Fortunio Bonanova
🏅 Ray Heindorf; song 'It's Magic' (m Jule Styne, ly Sammy Cahn)

Romancing the Stone *

🏕 US   1984   106m   DeLuxe   Panavision
TCF/El Corazon (Michael Douglas)

▣ ▣ ◎

A best-selling lady romance novelist gets more than she bargained for when she tries to find her kidnapped sister in Colombia.
Spoof adventure thriller which takes too long to get going and then finds it has nowhere to go. But commercial...
w Diane Thomas d Robert Zemeckis *ph* Dean Cundey m Alan Silvestri *pd* Lawrence G. Paull *ed* Donn Cambern, Frank Morriss
☆ Michael Douglas, Kathleen Turner, Danny DeVito, Zack Norman, Alfonso Arau
'The picture has a bravura opening and a jolly kind of movement, but it becomes too slambang.' – *Pauline Kael, New Yorker*
🏅 Donn Cambern, Frank Morriss

Romanoff and Juliet *

US   1961   103m   Technicolor
U-I/Pavla (Peter Ustinov)

Both Americans and Russians woo the tiny country of Concordia, and war threatens while the ambassadors' children fall in love.
Despite the author's wit this pattern comedy became something of a bore as a stylized stage piece, and the film is not smartly enough handled to be anything but a yawn; the humour never becomes cinematic.
wd Peter Ustinov *play* Peter Ustinov *ph* Robert Krasker m Mario Nascimbene *ad* Alexander Trauner

---

☆ Peter Ustinov, Sandra Dee, John Gavin, Akim Tamiroff, Tamara Shayne, John Phillips, Alix Talton, Peter Jones

The Romantic Age

GB 1949 86m bw
Pinnacle – Rank
US title: *Naughty Arlette*

A precocious French student sets her cap at the art teacher.
Fluffy farce in which all the adults behave like children; not well regarded.

w Edward Dryhurst, Peggy Barwell *novel* Serge Weber *d* Edmond T. Greville *ph* Hone Glendining *m* Charles Williams
☆ Mai Zetterling, Hugh Williams, Margot Grahame, Petula Clark, Carol Marsh, Raymond Lovell, Paul Dupuis

Romantic Comedy

US 1983 102m Metrocolor
MGM-UA/Taft Entertainment/The Mirisch Corporation (Walter Mirisch, Morton Gottlieb)

A Broadway playwright and a New England schoolteacher have a creative partnership that is more personal than professional.
Tedious film version of a play which wallows in autobiography.

w Bernard Slade *play* Bernard Slade *d* Arthur Hiller *ph* David M. Walsh *m* Marvin Hamlisch *pd* Alfred Sweeney
☆ Dudley Moore, Mary Steenburgen, Frances Sternhagen, Janet Eilber, Robyn Douglass, Ron Leibman

'When a movie's production notes wax lyrical about the pile of the living room carpet, one senses that they're in trouble.' – *Nick Roddick, MFB*

The Romantic Englishwoman *

GB 1975 116m Eastmancolor
Dial/Meric-Matalon (Daniel M. Angel)

A discontented woman, holidaying at Baden Baden, falls in love with a stranger while her husband completes a novel on the same theme.
Almost as ambiguous as Last Year in Marienbad, this annoying film wastes good actors in a script which hovers uncertainly between fantasy, melodrama and reality, intending one supposes to make humourless and obvious comparisons between romance and life.

w Tom Stoppard, Thomas Wiseman *novel* Thomas Wiseman *d* Joseph Losey *ph* Gerry Fisher *m* Richard Hartley
☆ Glenda Jackson, Michael Caine, Helmut Berger, Marcus Richardson, Kate Nelligan, René Kolldehoff, Michel Lonsdale

'The central trio bite off their lines, play deviously with hypocrisies and humiliations, and seem slightly aware that they're creations by artifice out of artificiality.' – *Penelope Houston*
'An itsy-bitsy, fragmented film that seems less than the sum of its parts.' – *Michael Billington, Illustrated London News*

Rome Adventure

US 1962 119m Warnercolor
Warner
GB title: *Lovers Must Learn*

A pretty American librarian goes to Rome to learn about love, and does.
Sluggish and overstretched travelogue with dollops of arch romance; hard to take.

wd Delmer Daves *novel* Irving Fineman *ph* Charles Lawton Jnr *m* Max Steiner
☆ Suzanne Pleshette, Troy Donahue, Angie Dickinson, Rossano Brazzi, Constance Ford, Chad Everett

Rome Express ***

GB 1932 94m bw
Gaumont (Michael Balcon)

Thieves and blackmail victims are among the passengers on an express train.
Just a little faded now as sheer entertainment, this remains the prototype train thriller from which The Lady Vanishes, Murder on the Orient Express and a hundred others are all borrowed; and it also spawned a myriad movies in which strangers are thrown together in dangerous situations. Technically it still works very well, though the script needs modernizing.

w Clifford Grey, Sidney Gilliat, Frank Vosper, Ralph Stock *d* Walter Forde *ph* Gunther Krampf
☆ Conrad Veidt, Gordon Harker, Esther Ralston, Joan Barry, Harold Huth, Cedric Hardwicke, Donald Calthrop, Hugh Williams, Finlay Currie, Frank Vosper, Muriel Aked, Eliot Makeham
HARKER: 'Discretion is the better part of Wagons Lits.'

'A first class craftsman's job.' – *Basil Wright*
'Technically, and in a sense intellectually speaking, this film puts Forde into Class A1.' – *Cinema Quarterly*
† Remade 1948 as *Sleeping Car to Trieste* (qv).

Romeo and Juliet: see *William Shakespeare's Romeo and Juliet (1996)*

'The greatest love drama, the mightiest entertainment of our time.'

Romeo and Juliet *

US 1936 127m bw
MGM (Irving Thalberg)

Hollywood Shakespeare with a super production and a rather elderly cast.
Not entertaining in the strict sense, but full of interest.

w Talbot Jennings *d* George Cukor *ph* William Daniels *m* Herbert Stothart *ad* Cedric Gibbons, Frederic Hope, Edwin B. Willis
☆ Leslie Howard, Norma Shearer, John Barrymore, Basil Rathbone, Edna May Oliver, Henry Kolker, C. Aubrey Smith, Violet Kemble-Cooper, Robert Warwick, Virginia Hammond, Reginald Denny, Ralph Forbes, Andy Devine, Conway Tearle

'Unimaginative, coarse-grained, a little banal, it is frequently saved – by Shakespeare – from being a bad film.' – *Graham Greene*
'It is impossible to realize how bad this film was unless you reflect on how good it might have been.' – *Alberto Cavalcanti*
† Fredric March, Robert Donat and Robert Montgomery all refused the lead before Leslie Howard accepted.
⬥ best picture; Norma Shearer; Basil Rathbone; art direction

Romeo and Juliet

GB 1954 138m Technicolor
Rank/Verona (Joe Janni, Sandro Ghenzi)

Good-looking but extremely boring version shot on Italian locations with quite unacceptable leads.
wd Renato Castellani *ph* Robert Krasker *m* Roman Vlad
☆ Laurence Harvey, Susan Shentall, Aldo Zollo, Enzo Fiermonte, Flora Robson, Mervyn Johns, Sebastian Cabot, Lydia Sherwood, Giulio Garbinetti, Nietta Zocchi, Bill Travers, Norman Wooland, John Gielgud

Romeo and Juliet *

⬆ GB 1968 152m Technicolor
Paramount/BHE/Verona/Dino de Laurentiis (Anthony Havelock-Allan, John Brabourne, Richard Goodwin)

The with-it version for modern youngsters.
Unfortunately the admirably rapid style does not suit the verse, and long before the much-deferred end the thing becomes just as tiresome as the other versions.

w Franco Brusati, Masolino D'Amico *d* Franco Zeffirelli *ph* Pasquale de Santis *m* Nino Rota
☆ Leonard Whiting, Olivia Hussey, John McEnery, Michael York, Pat Heywood, Milo O'Shea, Paul Hardwick, Natasha Parry, Antonio Pierfederici, Esmeralda Ruspoli, Bruce Robinson, Roberto Bisacco, Laurence Olivier as prologue speaker

'A large gold watch should be tossed to Zeffirelli for his part in reversing the movies' reputation for emasculating the classics.' – *Newsweek*
🏆 Pasquale de Santis; costumes (Danilo Donati)
⬥ best picture; Franco Zeffirelli

Romeo in Pajamas: see *Parlor, Bedroom and Bath*

Romeo Is Bleeding

US 1993 108m DeLuxe
Rank/Polygram/Working Title (Hilary Henkin)

A cop, who takes bribes from the crooks he investigates while trying to keep his wife and his mistress happy, is assigned to protect a sexy hitwoman on the run from his gangster friends; it proves to be a recipe for mayhem.
Hectic, delirious thriller in which violence takes precedence over character and plot.

w Hilary Henkin *d* Peter Medak *ph* Dariusz Wolski *m* Mark Isham *pd* Stuart Wurtzel *ed* Walter Murch
☆ Gary Oldman, Lena Olin, Annabella Sciorra, Juliette Lewis, Roy Scheider, David Proval, Will Patton

'This heavy dose of ultra-violent neo-noir gives Gary Oldman a face-first trip through the gutter that would make Mickey Rourke drool, but the far-fetched plotting eventually goes so far over the top that pic flirts with inventing a new genre of film noir camp.' – *Variety*

Romero

US 1989 105m DeLuxe
Warner/Paulist Pictures (Ellwood E. Kieser)

An apolitical priest is transformed by events into an archbishop who vigorously opposes El Salvador's government-sanctioned death squads.
Low-key biopic that tends to pussyfoot around its subject.

w John Sacret Young *d* John Duigan *ph* Geoff Burton *m* Gabriel Yared *ad* Francisco Magallon *ed* Frans Vandenburg
☆ Raul Julia, Richard Jordan, Ana Alicia, Eddie Velez, Alejandro Bracho, Tony Plana, Harold Gould, Lucy Reina

Rommel, Desert Fox: see *The Desert Fox*

Romper Stomper *

Australia 1992 92m Eastmancolor
Seon/Australian Film Commission/Film Victoria (Daniel Scharf, Ian Pringle)

In Melbourne, Nazi-loving skinheads battle with a Vietnamese gang.
A violent excursion into Australian low-life and one that refrains from any implied comment on the anti-social action it presents.

wd Geoffrey Wright *ph* Ron Hagen *m* John Clifford White *pd* Steven Jones-Evans *ed* Bill Murphy
☆ Russell Crowe, Daniel Pollock, Jacqueline McKenzie, Alex Scott, Leigh Russell

'Swiftly turns into another from the seemingly endless conveyor belt of debut moviemakers who use street violence as their calling card and a hand-held camera to conceal their other deficiencies of talent, imagination or personal vision.' – *Alexander Walker, London Evening Standard*
'Art house patrons are likely to be turned off by the brutally depicted violence and dominant antisocial behaviour … Pic is well acted and directed with a certain slickness, but rarely has there been such a disturbing, essentially misconceived pic.' – *Variety*

Romuald et Juliette *

France 1989 112m colour
Gala/Cinéa/Eniloc/FR3 (Jean-Louis Piel, Philippe Carcassonne)

A managing director, whose business is being sabotaged by disgruntled colleagues, is saved by his cleaner.
Amusing comedy of ineffectual men and strong women.

wd Coline Serreau *ph* Jean-Noël Ferragut *ad* Jean-Marc Stehle *ed* Catherine Renault
☆ Daniel Auteuil, Firmine Richard, Pierre Vernier, Maxime Leroux, Gilles Privat, Muriel Combeau, Catherine Salviat

Romy and Michele's High School Reunion

US 1997 91m Technicolor
Buena Vista/Bungalow 78 (Laurence Mark)

Two flatmates in their 20s, who have missed out on success, decide to go to their high-school reunion to be rich and famous.
A movie about humiliation at school and undeserved success after which is too rooted in American rituals and manners to mean much anywhere else.

w Robin Schiff *d* David Mirkin *ph* Reynaldo Villalobos *m* Steve Bartek *pd* Mayne Berke *ed* David Finfer

☆ Mira Sorvino, Lisa Kudrow, Janeane Garofalo, Alan Cumming, Julia Campbell, Mia Cottet, Kristen Bauer

'Desperately uncertain in tone and able to generate only sporadic laughs, pic decks out its meager story of revenge and comeuppance with a vulgar, flashy shimmer that will no doubt attract teenage girls.' – *Todd McCarthy, Variety*

La Ronde ***

France 1950 100m bw
Sacha Gordine

In 1900 Vienna, an elegant compère shows that love is a merry-go-round: prostitute meets soldier meets housemaid meets master meets married woman meets husband meets midinette meets poet meets actress meets officer meets prostitute meets soldier …
Superb stylized comedy with a fine cast, subtle jokes, rich decor and fluent direction; not to mention a haunting theme tune.

w Jacques Natanson, Max Ophuls *novel* Arthur Schnitzler *d* Max Ophuls *ph* Christian Matras *m* Oscar Straus
☆ Anton Walbrook, Simone Signoret, Serge Reggiani, Simone Simon, Daniel Gélin, Danielle Darrieux, Fernand Gravey, Odette Joyeux, Jean-Louis Barrault, Isa Miranda, Gérard Philipe

'One of the most civilized films to have come from Europe in a long time.' – *Gavin Lambert, MFB*
'A film that drags on and on by what seems like geometric progression.' – *John Simon, 1968*
⬗ script
⬥ best film

La Ronde

France 1964 110m Eastmancolor
Franscope
Robert and Raymond Hakim

Vulgarization of the above, reset in Paris in 1913.
The lack of a compère vastly reduces the number of jokes.

w Jean Anouilh *d* Roger Vadim *ph* Henri Decaë *m* Michel Magne
☆ Marie Dubois, Claude Giraud, Anna Karina, Jean-Claude Brialy, Jane Fonda, Maurice Ronet, Catherine Spaak, Bernard Noel, Francine Bergé, Jean Sorel

'Loyalty Is Bought. Betrayal Is A Way Of Life…'

Ronin

US 1998 121m DeLuxe Panavision
UA/FGM (Frank Mancuso Jnr)

Six undercover agents, who are recruited to steal a briefcase by Irish revolutionaries, betray one another.
Involved and implausible thriller, though there's some pleasure to be gained from watching the cast out-tough one another.

w J. D. Zeik, Richard Weisz (David Mamet) *d* John Frankenheimer *ph* Robert Fraisse *m* Elia Cmiral *pd* Michael Z. Hanan *ed* Tony Gibbs
☆ Robert de Niro, Jean Réno, Natascha McElhone, Stellan Skarsgard, Sean Bean, Skipp Sudduth, Michael Lonsdale, Jan Triska, Jonathan Pryce

'Can be watched as appreciatively for its hard-boiled performances as for its visceral excitement.' – *Janet Maslin, New York Times*

Rooftops

US 1989 95m DeLuxe
Fox/New Vision/Koch Company (Howard W. Koch)

Teenagers living on the roofs of an old tenement building combine to fight a vicious drug dealer.
Uninteresting teen movie, involving unlikeable characters.

w Terence Brennan *story* Allan Goldstein *d* Robert Wise *ph* Theo Van de Sande *m* Michael Kamen *pd* Jeannine C. Oppewall *ed* William Reynolds
☆ Jason Gedrick, Troy Beyer, Eddie Velez, Tisha Campbell, Alexis Cruz, Allen Payne, Steve Love, Rafael Baez, Jaime Tirelli

'Words fail me where this absurd piece of tuppence-coloured fantasy is concerned.' – *Derek Malcolm, Guardian*

◎ Digital Video Disc Region 2   ◉ Digital Video Disc Region 1   ⌒ Soundtrack released on compact disc   ☆ Cast in approximate order of importance   † Points of interest   ♫ Notable songs   🏆 Academy Award   ⬥ Academy Award nomination   ▽ BAFTA

Rookery Nook ★★
GB 1930 107m bw
British and Dominions (Herbert Wilcox)
A nervous husband on holiday tries to hide a runaway girl who has asked for protection against her stepfather.
Primitive talkie technique cannot entirely conceal the brilliance of the original Aldwych farce team in their most enduring vehicle.
w Ben Travers *play* Ben Travers d Tom Walls ph Dave Kessan
☆ Ralph Lynn, Tom Walls, Robertson Hare, Winifred Shotter, Mary Brough, Ethel Coleridge, Griffith Humphreys, Margot Grahame
'As a talker it is the best specimen so far made on this side.' – *Variety*

'He took a new kid and made a hero out of him.'
The Rookie
US 1990 121m Technicolor
Warner/Malpaso (Howard Kazanjian, Steven Siebert, David Valdes)
⬛ ≡ ⌾
Ageing cop teaches his new young partner how to act tough.
Dreary, amoral and cliché-ridden slog through all-too-familiar territory.
w Boaz Yakin, Scott Spiegel d Clint Eastwood ph Jack N. Green m Lennie Niehaus ed Joel Cox
☆ Clint Eastwood, Charlie Sheen, Raul Julia, Sonia Braga, Tom Skerritt, Lara Flynn Boyle, Pepe Serna, Marco Rodriguez, Pete Randall
'Overlong, sadistic and stale even by the conventions of the buddy pic genre.' – *Variety*
'Clint Eastwood has forgotten how to make popular entertainment.' – *Philip French, Observer*

Rookie of the Year
↑↑ US 1993 103m Technicolor
TCF (Robert Harper)
⬛ ≡ ⌾
A young boy, who can throw a ball at great speed after an accident to his arm, becomes a pitcher for the Chicago Cubs baseball team, turning them from losers to winners.
A soft-centred wish-fulfilment fantasy for young baseball fans which offers little to those not enraptured by the sport.
w Sam Harper d Daniel Stern ph Jack N. Green m Bill Conti pd Steven Jordan ed Donn Cambern, Raja Gosnell
☆ Gary Busey, Thomas Ian Nicholas, Albert Hall, Amy Morton, Dan Hedaya, Eddie Bracken, Daniel Stern, Bruce Altman, John Candy (uncredited)
'Rife with humor and sentimentality but is just one run away from the game-winning score.' – *Variety*

Rookies: see *Buck Privates (1941)*

Rookies
US 1927 75m bw silent
MGM
Army adventures of a tough sergeant and a bumbling recruit.
Popular comedy of its day which established a new team of Dane and Arthur.
w Byron Morgan d Sam Wood
☆ Karl Dane, George K. Arthur, Marceline Day, Louise Lorraine, Tom O'Brien

Rookies Come Home: see *Buck Privates Come Home*

Room at the Top ★★★
GB 1958 117m bw
Remus (John and James Woolf)
≡
An ambitious young clerk causes the death of his real love but manages to marry into a rich family.
Claimed as the first British film to take sex seriously, and the first to show the industrial north as it really was, this melodrama actually cheats on both counts but scene for scene is vivid and entertaining despite a weak central performance.
w Neil Paterson *novel* John Braine d Jack Clayton ph Freddie Francis m Mario Nascimbene
☆ Laurence Harvey, Simone Signoret, Heather Sears, Donald Wolfit, Ambrosine Philpotts, Donald Houston, Raymond Huntley, John Westbrook, Allan Cuthbertson, Hermione Baddeley, Mary Peach

'A drama of human drives and torments told with maturity and precision.' – *Stanley Kauffmann*
🏆 Neil Paterson; Simone Signoret
⅋ best picture; Jack Clayton; Laurence Harvey; Hermione Baddeley
🎬 best picture; best British picture; Simone Signoret

Room for One More
US 1952 95m bw
Warner (Henry Blanke)
aka: *The Easy Way*
A married couple adopt several underprivileged children.
Slightly mawkish family movie redeemed by star performances.
w Jack Rose, Melville Shavelson d Norman Taurog ph Robert Burks m Max Steiner
☆ Cary Grant, Betsy Drake, Lurene Tuttle, Randy Stuart, George Winslow

The Room of Words
Italy 1989 97m Kodak Color
Filmirage/Wind Film
⬛
Anaïs Nin falls in love with writer Henry Miller and his wife June.
Inept on every level, lacking any sense of period or place (despite a streetcar named Desire) and concentrating on artfully shot lesbian love scenes. It is also saddled with an obtrusive and unsympathetic score and the near incomprehensible English of Martine Brochard as Anaïs Nin.
w Franco Molè *play* Franco Molè d Joe D'Amato ph Giancarlo Ferrando m Gianni Silano ed Kathleen Stratton
☆ Martine Brochard, David Brandon, Linda Carol, Ron Gural, Colette de La Croix

Room Service ★
US 1938 78m bw
RKO (Pandro S. Berman)
⬛ ≡ ⌾
Penniless theatricals find ways of staying in a hotel until they can find a backer.
Claustrophobic Broadway farce unsuitably adapted for the Marx Brothers, who are constrained by having to play characters with a passing resemblance to human beings.
w Morrie Ryskind *play* John Murray, Allen Boretz d William A. Seiter ph Russell Metty m Roy Webb
☆ Groucho Marx, Chico Marx, Harpo Marx, Lucille Ball, *Donald MacBride*, Frank Albertson, Ann Miller, Philip Loeb
'A natural for the box office … the change of pace is a good idea.' – *Variety*
'It should also be noted … that there is a scene in which a turkey is chased around a room. Not everybody will care for this.' – *MFB*
† Remade as *Step Lively (qv).*

A Room with a View ★★★
GB 1985 115m colour
Merchant Ivory/Goldcrest (Ismail Merchant)
⬛ ≡ ⌾
An innocent Edwardian girl travelling in Italy has her eyes opened to real life and romance.
Competent, unexciting equivalent of a television classic mini-series which so perfectly filled a need as to become a runaway commercial success.
w Ruth Prawer Jhabvala *novel* E. M. Forster d James Ivory ph Tony Pierce-Roberts m Richard Robbins pd Gianna Quaranta, Brian Ackland-Snow ed Humphrey Dixon
☆ Maggie Smith, Denholm Elliott, Helena Bonham Carter, Julian Sands, Daniel Day-Lewis, Simon Callow, Judi Dench, Rosemary Leach, Rupert Graves
'Quality-starved filmgoers will welcome it.' – *Variety*
🏆 art direction; adapted screenplay; costumes (Jenny Beavan, John Bright)
⅋ James Ivory as director; Tony Pierce-Roberts; best picture; Maggie Smith; Denholm Elliott
🎬 best picture; production design; Maggie Smith; Judi Dench

Roommates
US 1995 108m Technicolor
Buena Vista/Polygram/Interscope (Ted Field, Scott Kroopf, Robert W. Cort)
A young doctor learns the important lessons of life through his grandfather, a retired baker, who moves in with him.
Low-key domestic soap opera, strong on charm but outstaying its welcome.
w Max Apple, Stephen Metcalfe d Peter Yates ph Mike Southon m Elmer Bernstein pd Dan Bishop ed John Tintori
☆ Peter Falk, D. B. Sweeney, Julianne Moore, Jan Rubes, Frankie Faison, Noah Fleiss, Joyce Reehling, Ellen Burstyn
'Goes down painlessly but hasn't much flavor or substance.' – *Variety*

Rooney ★
GB 1958 88m bw
Rank (George H. Brown)
Adventures of a bachelor Irish dustman.
Moderately charming, though unconvincing, Dublin comedy.
w Patrick Kirwan *novel* Catherine Cookson d George Pollock ph Christopher Challis m Philip Green
☆ John Gregson, Barry Fitzgerald, Muriel Pavlow, June Thorburn, Noel Purcell, Marie Kean, Liam Redmond, Jack MacGowran, Eddie Byrne

Rooster Cogburn ★
↑↑ US 1975 108m Technicolor
Panavision
Universal (Paul Nathan)
⬛ ≣ ⌾ ⌾
An elderly marshal after a gang of outlaws is helped by the Bible-thumping daughter of a priest.
Disappointing Western too obviously patterned after True Grit and The African Queen. Having had the idea for outrageous star casting, the producers obviously decided erroneously that the film would make itself.
w Martin Julien d Stuart Millar ph Harry Stradling Jnr m Laurence Rosenthal
☆ John Wayne, Katharine Hepburn, Anthony Zerbe, Richard Jordan, John McIntire, Strother Martin
'Like one of those infuriating exhibition bouts in which two resilient old pros bob, weave and spar without ever landing any punches.' – *Michael Billington, Illustrated London News*
† 'Martin Julien' allegedly covers the writing talents of Hal Wallis, his wife Martha Hyer, and some friends.

The Root of All Evil
GB 1946 110m bw
Gainsborough
A jilted woman becomes unscrupulous in business in order to get even with her ex-boyfriend.
Incredible farrago with a star ill at ease.
wd Brock Williams *novel* J. S. Fletcher
☆ Phyllis Calvert, Michael Rennie, John McCallum, Moore Marriott, Brefni O'Rorke, Hazel Court, Edward Rigby

The Roots of Heaven ★
US 1958 125m Eastmancolor
Cinemascope
TCF/Darryl F. Zanuck
A white man in central Africa dedicates himself to prevent the slaughtering of elephants.
Curiously patchy version of a novel which was a strange choice for filming; so many side issues are introduced that at times it takes on the look of another jolly safari adventure.
w Romain Gary, Patrick Leigh-Fermor *novel* Romain Gary d John Huston ph Oswald Morris m Malcolm Arnold
☆ Trevor Howard, Juliette Greco, Errol Flynn, Eddie Albert, Orson Welles, Paul Lukas, Herbert Lom, Grégoire Aslan, Friedrich Ledebur, Edric Connor
'The Huston who did Sierra Madre would have lighted his cigar with this script.' – *Stanley Kauffmann*

Rope ★★
US 1948 80m Technicolor
Transatlantic (Sidney Bernstein, Alfred Hitchcock)
⬛ ≡ ⌾
Two homosexuals murder a friend for the thrill of it and conceal his body in a trunk from which they

serve cocktails to a party including his father and girlfriend.
An effective piece of Grand Guignol on the stage, this seemed rather tasteless when set in a New York skyscraper, especially when the leading role of the investigator was miscast and Hitch had saddled himself with the ten-minute take, a short-lived technique which made the entire action (set in one room) cinematically continuous (and dizzy-making). Of considerable historic interest, nevertheless.
w Arthur Laurents *play* Patrick Hamilton d Alfred Hitchcock ph Joseph Valentine, William V. Skall md Leo F. Forbstein theme Francis Poulenc
☆ James Stewart, John Dall, Farley Granger, Joan Chandler, Cedric Hardwicke, Constance Collier, Edith Evanson, Douglas Dick
'It was a limiting use of the medium, and parts of the film were unbearably tedious.' – *George Perry, 1965*

'A mighty story of savage greed and sultry love!'
Rope of Sand ★
US 1949 105m bw
Paramount (Hal B. Wallis)
Various factions seek hidden diamonds in a prohibited South African area.
Ham-fisted adventure story which suggests at times that a violent parody of Casablanca was intended. The stars carry it through.
w Walter Doniger d William Dieterle ph Charles Lang m Franz Waxman
☆ Burt Lancaster, Paul Henreid, Claude Rains, Peter Lorre, Corinne Calvet, Sam Jaffe

Rosa Luxemburg ★★
West Germany 1986 112m colour
Bioskop/Pro-Jekt/Regina Ziegler/Bärenfilm (Eberhard Junkersdorf)
≡
Biopic of the Polish-born socialist revolutionary and martyr (1871–1919) who was involved in political activity in Germany, including founding its Communist party, imprisoned for her activities, and murdered by the militia in Berlin.
Impressive, well-acted account, from a feminist viewpoint, of an impassioned life, based on Rosa Luxemburg's own writings, which limits its historical perspective but brings into sharp focus her own beliefs and feelings in reaction to the events of her time.
wd Margarethe von Trotta ph Franz Rath m Nicolas Economou ad Bernd Lepel, Karel Vacek ed Dagmar Hirtz
☆ Barbara Sukowa, Daniel Olbrychski, Otto Sander, Doris Schade, Hannes Jaenicke, Adelheid Arndt, Jürgen Holtz
'Often comes close to a conventional bio-pic which traces a star's career from success to tragic decline.' – *MFB*
† Barbara Sukowa's performance won her the award for best actress at the Cannes Film Festival in 1986.

'The entertainment world is ablaze!'
Rosalie ★
US 1937 118m bw
MGM (William Anthony McGuire)
≡
A college football hero falls for an incognito Balkan princess.
Ambitious light musical with a wispy plot but satisfying numbers.
w William Anthony McGuire *play* William Anthony McGuire, Guy Bolton d W. S. Van Dyke ph Oliver T. Marsh m Herbert Stothart songs Cole Porter
☆ Nelson Eddy, Eleanor Powell, Frank Morgan, Ray Bolger, Ilona Massey, Reginald Owen, Edna May Oliver, Jerry Colonna
'The most lavish, ornate, tinselled and glittering production which has come from Hollywood.' – *Variety*

Rosalie Goes Shopping
West Germany 1989 93m colour
Mainline/Pelemele (Percy Adlon, Eleonore Adlon)
⬛ ≡ ⌾
A German housewife, living in Arizona with her large family, uses credit card frauds to keep them supplied with the good things of life.
Slight comedy of consumerism that relies too heavily on the charm of its performers.
w Percy Adlon, Eleonore Adlon, Christopher Doherty d Percy Adlon ph Bernd Heinl ad Stephen Lineweaver ed Heiko Hinders

☆ Marianne Sägebrecht, Brad Davis, Judge Reinhold, William Harlander, Erika Blumberger, Patricia Zehentmayr, John Hawkes, Alex Winter, Courtney Kraus

The Rosary Murders

US   1987   105m   colour
Laurel-Mihalich/Samuel Goldwyn

◉ ℚ ◠

In Detroit, murders are committed by someone with a grudge against the Catholic Church.
Lax thriller with a priest detective.
w Elmore Leonard, Fred Walton d Fred Walton
☆ Donald Sutherland, Charles Durning, Josef Sommer, Belinda Bauer

'She gave ... and gave ... and gave ... until there was nothing left to give!'

The Rose

US   1979   134m   DeLuxe
TCF (Tony Ray)

◉ ▦ ℚ ◠

Drink and drugs cause the decline and death of a famous rock singer.
An unattractive, hysterical, foul-mouthed show business biopic roughly based on Janis Joplin, this does afford an undisciplined night-club talent a role to get her teeth into.
w Bill Kerby, Bo Goodman d Mark Rydell
ph Vilmos Zsigmond md Paul A. Rothchild
pd Richard MacDonald
☆ Bette Midler, Alan Bates, Frederic Forrest, Harry Dean Stanton, Barry Primus
⛤ Frederic Forrest; Bette Midler

The Rose and the Sword: see *Flesh and Blood* (1985)

Rose Marie *

US   1936   113m   bw
MGM (Hunt Stromberg)

▦ ℚ

A Canadian Mountie gets his man – and a lady.
Backwoods romance from a stage success, filmed mostly on location and quite successfully.
w Frances Goodrich, Albert Hackett, Alice Duer Miller play Otto Harbach, Oscar Hammerstein II
d W. S. Van Dyke ph William Daniels m Rudolf Friml md Herbert Stothart songs various
☆ Nelson Eddy, Jeanette MacDonald, James Stewart, Reginald Owen, Allan Jones, Gilda Gray, George Regas, Alan Mowbray, Robert Greig, Una O'Connor, David Niven, Herman Bing
'An operatic honey with MacDonald and Eddy for the tungstens.' – *Variety*
† Previously filmed in 1928 – and see below.

Rose Marie

US   1954   115m   Technicolor   Cinemascope
MGM (Mervyn Le Roy)

◉ ▦ ℚ

Dull remake with stodgy handling and poor sets.
w Ronald Millar d Mervyn Le Roy ph Paul C. Vogel md Georgie Stoll ch Busby Berkeley
☆ Howard Keel, Ann Blyth, Fernando Lamas, Bert Lahr, Marjorie Main, Ray Collins

'The wildcat of the west has the outlaws in her gunsights!'

Rose of Cimarron

US   1952   72m   Natural Color
TCF (Edward L. Alperson)

A girl tracks down the killers of her Indian foster-parents.
Routine lower-berth Western.
w Maurice Geraghty d Harry Keller ph Karl Struss
☆ Mala Powers, Jack Buetel, Bill Williams, Jim Davis

Rose of the Rancho

US   1935   83m   bw
Paramount (William LeBaron)

Spanish settlers in California fight landgrabbers.
Romantic musical with interesting if seldom-used talent.
w Frank Partos, Charles Brackett, Arthur Sheekman, Nat Perrin, Harlan Thompson, Brian Hooker play Richard Walton Tully, David Belasco
d Marion Gering
☆ John Boles, Gladys Swarthout, Willie Howard, Charles Bickford, Herb Williams, H. B. Warner
'A fandango mustang meller ... a tango version of a bronc opera.' – *Variety*

'Song by song ... scene by scene ... the thrill grows greater!'

Rose of Washington Square **

US   1939   86m   bw
TCF (Darryl Zanuck)

Tribulations of a Broadway singer in love with a worthless husband.
Revamping of the Fanny Brice story; smartly done, but the material interpolated for Jolson is what makes the film notable.
w Nunnally Johnson story John Larkin, Jerry Horwin d Gregory Ratoff ph Karl Freund
m Louis Silvers songs various
☆ Alice Faye, Tyrone Power, Al Jolson, Hobart Cavanaugh, William Frawley, Joyce Compton, Louis Prima and his band
'This is Jolson's picture ... the rest is also-ran.' – *Variety*
'Jolson's singing is something for the memory book.' – *New York Times*
† Fanny Brice sued TCF for 75,000 dollars for invasion of privacy; the defendants settled.

'The boldest story of love you have ever been permitted to see!'

The Rose Tattoo

US   1955   117m   bw   Vistavision
Paramount/Hal B. Wallis

▦ ℚ

A Sicilian woman on the gulf coast is tormented by the infidelity of her dead husband, but a brawny truckdriver makes her forget him.
Heavily theatrical material, unsuited to the big screen for all the powerful acting (or perhaps because of it).
w John Michael Hayes play Tennessee Williams
d Daniel Mann m James Wong Howe m Alex North ad Hal Pereira, Tambi Larsen ed Warren Low
☆ Anna Magnani, Burt Lancaster, Marisa Pavan, Ben Cooper, Virginia Grey, Jo Van Fleet
⛤ James Wong Howe; Anna Magnani; art direction
⛤ best picture; Alex North; Marisa Pavan; editing
⛤ Anna Magnani

Roseanna McCoy

US   1949   89m   bw
Samuel Goldwyn

◉

In old Virginia the Hatfields and the McCoys continue their feud with tragic results.
Hillbilly Romeo and Juliet saga, a shade too cornfed despite the credits.
w John Collier d Irving Reis ph Lee Garmes
m David Buttolph
☆ Joan Evans, Farley Granger, Charles Bickford, Raymond Massey, Richard Basehart, Aline MacMahon

'A romantic comedy about the things we do for love'

Roseanna's Grave

US/GB   1996   98m   Technicolor   Panavision
Polygram/Fine Line/Spelling (Paul Trijbits, Alison Owen, Dario Poloni)

◉ ▦ ◠

aka: *For Roseanna*

As the last plots in the graveyard of an Italian town are filled, a husband is anxious to secure one for his dying wife by ensuring that everyone else stays alive.
Moribund comedy that dithers between sentimentality and farce, and finally settles for soft-centred romance.
w Saul Turteltaub d Paul Weiland ph Henry Braham m Trevor Jones pd Rod McLean
ed Martin Walsh
☆ Jean Reno, Mercedes Ruehl, Polly Walker, Mark Frankel, Luigi Diberti, Roberto della Casa, Giovanni Pallavicino, Jorge Krimer
'A lightweight movie that constantly finds itself balancing between genuine whimsy and forced comedy.' – *Bob McCabe, Empire*

Les Roseaux Sauvages **

France   1993   102m   colour
Gala/Ima/Alain Sarde

▦ ⊘

aka: *The Wild Reeds*

In the early 60s, as the Algerian War comes to an end, provincial French schoolboys experiment with sex and political action.
A stylish evocation of adolescence, sensitively handled.
w André Techiné, Gilles Taurand, Olivier Massart
d André Techiné ph Jeanne Lapoirie pd Pierre Soula ed Martine Giordano

☆ Elodie Bouchez, Gael Morel, Stephane Rideau, Frederic Gorny, Michele Moretti
'Politics and post-pubescent sex are the interlocking elements in this well-crafted and sober study of provincial French youth in the early 1960s.' – *Alexander Walker, London Evening Standard*

Rosebud

US   1975   126m   Eastmancolor   Panavision
UA/Otto Preminger

Five girls of wealthy families are kidnapped by the Palestine Liberation Army.
Overlong topical suspenser which goes awry by not being very suspenseful, and by packing in too many irrelevant satirical jibes.
w Erik Lee Preminger novel Joan Hemingway, Paul Bonnecarrere d Otto Preminger ph Denys Coop m Laurent Petitgirard titles Saul Bass
☆ Peter O'Toole, Richard Attenborough, Cliff Gorman, Claude Dauphin, John V. Lindsay, Peter Lawford, Raf Vallone, Adrienne Corri

Roseland *

US   1977   103m   colour
Cinema Shares/Merchant Ivory (Ismail Merchant)

▦

Generation after generation, the lonely and the loving come to a New York ballroom.
Pleasantly intentioned slice-of-life drama which is rather slackly written and handled, with unprofessionalism showing through at several points.
w Ruth Prawer Jhabvala d James Ivory ph Ernest Vincze m Michael Gibson
☆ Geraldine Chaplin, Teresa Wright, Lou Jacobi, Don de Natale, Louise Kirkland, Helen Gallagher, Joan Copeland, Conrad Janis, Lilia Skala, Christopher Walken
'Typically discreet and dull film from Merchant-Ivory ... what one might call over-decorous.' – *Time Out, 1984*

Roselyne and the Lions **

⚲ France   1989   137m   colour
Palace/Cargo Films/Gaumont (Jean-Jacques Beineix)

◉

original title: *Roselyne et les Lions*

Two trainee lion tamers fall in love and run away to join a circus.
Charming, dreamlike boy-meets-girl romance.
w Jean-Jacques Beineix, Jacques Forgeas, Thierry Le Portier d Jean-Jacques Beineix ph Jean-François Robin m Reinhardt Wagner ad Carlos Conti ed Marie Castro-Brechignac, Annick Baly, Danielle Fillios, Oswald Bargero
☆ Isabelle Pasco, Gérard Sandoz, Philippe Clevenot, Gunter Meisner, Wolf Harnisch, Gabriel Monnet, Jacques Le Carpentier, Dimitro Furdui

Rosemary's Baby **

US   1968   137m   Technicolor
Paramount/William Castle

◉ ▦ ℚ

After unwittingly becoming friendly with diabolists, an actor's wife is impregnated by the Devil.
Seminal gothic melodrama which led in due course to the excesses of The Exorcist; in itself well done in a heavy-handed way, the book being much more subtle.
wd Roman Polanski novel Ira Levin ph William Fraker m Krzysztof Komeda pd Richard Sylbert
☆ Mia Farrow, John Cassavetes, Ruth Gordon, Sidney Blackmer, Patsy Kelly, Ralph Bellamy, Maurice Evans, Angela Dorian, Elisha Cook, Charles Grodin
'It may not be for the very young, and perhaps pregnant women should see it at their own risk.' – *Motion Picture Herald*
'Tension is sustained to a degree surpassing Alfred Hitchcock at his best.' – *Daily Telegraph*
† William Castle, the producer, is glimpsed outside a phone booth.
†† A TV sequel followed: *Look What Happened to Rosemary's Baby.*
⛤ Ruth Gordon
⛤ Roman Polanski (as writer)

Rosencrantz and Guildenstern Are Dead *

US   1990   118m   Technicolor
Hobo/Brandenburg (Michael Brandman, Emanuel Azenburg)

◉ ▦ ℚ

Two courtiers are summoned to Elsinore by the King of Denmark to discover why Prince Hamlet is behaving so strangely.
A celebrated stage play, and gloss on Shakespeare, transfers awkwardly to the screen.
wd Tom Stoppard play Tom Stoppard ph Peter Biziou m Stanley Myers pd Vaughan Edwards
ed Nicolas Gaster
☆ Gary Oldman, Tim Roth, Richard Dreyfuss, Joanna Roth, Iain Glen, Donald Sumpter, Joanna Miles, Ljubo Zecevic, Ian Richardson, Sven Medvesck
'Stoppard's adaptation, at a shade under two hours, is too long, too slow, and ponderous when it is trying to be humorous.' – *Sight and Sound*

Rosetta ***

Belgium/France   1999   94m   colour
Artificial Eye/Les Films du Fleuve/RTBF/ARP (Luc and Jean-Pierre Dardenne, Michele and Laurent Petin)

In a Belgian industrial town, a young unemployed woman, living on a caravan site with her alcoholic mother, dreams of leading a normal life.
Intense, gritty drama concentrating almost entirely on a woman's desperate search for some small acceptance from a hostile world; it gains immeasurably from its unforced central performance.
wd Luc and Jean-Pierre Dardenne ph Alain Marcoen m Jean-Pierre Cocco ad Igor Gabriel ed Marie-Hélène Dozo
☆ Emilie Dequenne, Fabrizio Rongione, Anne Yernaux, Olivier Gourmet
'A stunning and remarkable achievement... It is a film whose grace and lyricism has earned it, simply, the status of classic: something of real greatness.' – *Peter Bradshaw, Guardian*
'An unforgiving piece of hard-boiled cinema-verite...desperately moving and desperately depressing.' – *James Christopher, Times*
† At the 1999 Cannes Film Festival, the film won the Palme d'Or , and Emilie Dequenne was awarded the prize for best actress.

Rosie

US   1967   98m   Techniscope
Universal/Ross Hunter (Jacque Mapes)

A rich woman spends wildly and her daughters try to have her committed to safeguard their inheritance.
Hopelessly muddled comedy drama which flits from one mood to the other without making a success of either.
w Samuel Taylor play Ruth Gordon French original Les Joies de la Famille by Philippe Heriat
d David Lowell Rich ph Clifford Stine m Lyn Murray
☆ Rosalind Russell, Brian Aherne, Sandra Dee, Vanessa Brown, Audrey Meadows, James Farentino, Leslie Nielsen, Margaret Hamilton, Reginald Owen, Juanita Moore, Virginia Grey
'A mawkish mixture of Auntie Mame and King Lear.' – *MFB*

Rosie the Riveter

US   1944   75m   bw
Armand Schaefer/Republic

▦

GB title: *In Rosie's Room*

Warplant workers have to share rooms in a boarding house.
Easy-going wartime comedy.
w Jack Townley, Aleen Leslie story Dorothy Curnow Handley d Joseph Santley
☆ Jane Frazee, Frank Albertson, Vera Vague, Frank Jenks, Lloyd Corrigan, Frank Fenton, Maude Eburne, Carl 'Alfalfa' Switzer

Rote Lippen: see *Sadisterotica*

Rotten to the Core

GB   1965   88m   bw   Panavision
BL-Tudor (Roy Boulting)

Ex-convicts plan an army payroll robbery.
Routine caper comedy, unsuitably widescreened, with a few good jokes along the way.
w Jeffrey Dell, Roy Boulting, John Warren, Len Heath d John Boulting ph Freddie Young
m Michael Dress ad Alex Vetchinsky ed Teddy Darvas

☆ Anton Rodgers, *Thorley Walters*, Eric Sykes, Kenneth Griffith, Charlotte Rampling, Ian Bannen, Avis Bunnage, Raymond Huntley, Dudley Sutton, Victor Maddern

† The original title, *Rotten to the Corps*, was more apt but plainly seemed too subtle.

Rouge **

Hong Kong   1987   93m   colour
ICA/Golden Harvest/Golden Way (Jackie Chan)
📼 ■ ⊘

original title: *Yanzhi Kou*
More than 50 years after she killed herself in the mid-30s, the ghost of a courtesan enlists the aid of a journalist to search for the lover with whom she made a suicide pact.
An exotic, bitter-sweet romance of a lost past and its contrast with a radically altered present, acted with style and directed with visual panache.
w Lee Bihua, Qiu-Dai Anping *novel* Lee Bihua d Stanley Kwan *ph* Bill Wong *m* Michael Lai *ad* Piao Ruomu, Horace Ma *ed* Peter Cheung
☆ Anita Mui, Leslie Cheung, Alex Man, Emily Chu, Irene Wan, Patrick Tse, Wang Fu
   'Seems assured of its status as a classic.' – *Tony Rayns, Sight and Sound*

Rouge Baiser *

France/Germany   1985   112m   Fujicolour
Stephan/A2/Farena/C&H/Aldo Lado
aka: *Red Kiss*
A 15-year-old Jewish girl growing up in 50s Paris has her faith in Communism shaken but begins to appreciate the power of love.
One of the rare films to take politics seriously, as it follows one person's disillusionment with ideology.
w Vera Belmont, Guy Konopnicki, David Milhaud d Vera Belmont *ph* Raymond Suarez *m* Jean-Marie Senia *ed* Martine Giordano
☆ Charlotte Valandrey, Lambert Wilson, Marthe Keller, Laurent Terzieff, Gunther Lamprecht, Laurent Arnal, Elsa Lunghini

Le Rouge et le Noir *

France/Italy   1954   170m   Eastmancolor
Franco London/Documento
aka: *Scarlet and Black*
A carpenter's son becomes a private tutor, seduces his master's wife and is sent to study for the priesthood …
Massive attempt to conquer an unfilmable novel. Some enjoyable scenes and décor are the best it can offer.
w Jean Aurenche, Pierre Bost, Claude Autant-Lara *novel* Stendhal d Claude Autant-Lara *ph* Michel Kelber *m* René Cloërc *ad* Max Douy
☆ Gérard Philipe, Danielle Darrieux, Antonella Lualdi, Jean Martinelli

The Rough and the Smooth

GB   1959   99m   bw
Renown (George Minter)
US title: *Portrait of a Sinner*
An archaeologist about to marry the niece of a press lord falls for a mysterious nymphomaniac.
Preposterous melodrama about unreal people; its very excesses become enjoyable for those who can stay the course.
w Audrey Erskine-Lindop, Dudley Leslie *novel* Robin Maugham d Robert Siodmak *ph* Otto Heller *m* Douglas Gamley *md* Muir Mathieson
☆ Tony Britton, Nadja Tiller, William Bendix, Natasha Parry, Norman Wooland, Donald Wolfit, Tony Wright, Adrienne Corri, Joyce Carey
   'The script is never even on nodding terms with life, and tries to make up for this deficiency by a candidly explosive vocabulary which gives the production a weirdly old-fashioned air.' – *MFB*

Rough Company: see *The Violent Men*

Rough Cut

US   1980   112m   Movielab
Paramount/David Merrick
■ ⊘
A retiring Scotland Yard inspector spars with a jewel thief and finally changes sides.
Dated comedy which required a much lighter touch in all departments.
w Francis Burns *novel* Touch the Lion's Paw by Derek Lambert d Don Siegel *ph* Frederick Young *m* Nelson Riddle, from Duke Ellington themes *pd* Ted Haworth

☆ Burt Reynolds, Lesley-Anne Down, David Niven, Timothy West, Patrick Magee, Joss Ackland
   'All surface smartness without a single structural idea.' – *Richard Combs, MFB*

Rough Diamonds

Australia   1994   88m   colour
ITC/Forest Home/AFFC/Film Queensland/Beyond/Southern Star (Damien Parer)
A rancher and a country and western singer fall in love after she helps him win an award with his champion bull.
Dreary little star vehicle for Donovan, though even his fans may have difficulty in staying awake until the end.
w Donald Crombie, Christopher Lee d Christopher Lee *ph* John Stokes *pd* Georgina Greenhill *ed* Wayne Le Clos
☆ Jason Donovan, Angie Milliken, Peter Phelps, Max Cullen, Jocelyn Gabriel, Hayley Toomey, Kit Taylor, Lee James
   'Probably pitched at undemanding early teens but it's hard to tell; it's the sort of film where jolly banjo music breaks out whenever a fist fight does.' – *Jonathan Romney, Guardian*
   'Donovan fans will probably enjoy this fluff, and they are welcome to it.' – *Sheila Johnston, Independent*

Rough Magic

GB/France   1995   105m   Technicolor
TCF/UGC/Recorded Picture (Laurie Parker, Delan Baldwin)
A reporter, hired by a millionaire to find his missing fiancée, who has magic powers, tracks her down to Mexico and falls in love with her.
An odd fantasy, in which a fire-breathing heroine vomits up her heart and turns an adversary into a sausage; its absurdities do not hold the attention for long.
w Robert Mundy, William Brookfield, Clare Peploe *novel* Miss Shumway Waves a Wand by James Hadley Chase d Clare Peploe *ph* John J. Campbell *m* Richard Hartley *pd* Waldemar Kalinowski *ed* Suzanne Fenn
☆ Bridget Fonda, Russell Crowe, Jim Broadbent, D. W. Moffet, Paul Rodriguez, Euva Anderson
   'A peculiar and often uncomfortable mixture of romantic caper, farce and film noir.' – *Empire*

Rough Night in Jericho

US   1967   97m   Techniscope
Universal (Martin Rackin)
■ ⊘
A stagecoach man rids a cattle town of a villain.
Totally uninteresting star Western with glum performances.
w Sidney Boehm, Marvin H. Albert *novel* The Man in Black by Marvin H. Albert d Arnold Laven *ph* Russell Metty *m* Don Costa
☆ George Peppard, Dean Martin, Jean Simmons, John McIntire, Slim Pickens, Don Galloway, Brad Weston

Rough Shoot *

GB   1952   86m   bw
Raymond Stross
US title: *Shoot First*
A retired US officer in Dorset thinks he has shot a poacher – but the dead man is a spy, and someone else shot him.
Minor Hitchcock-style thriller with a climax in Madame Tussaud's. Generally efficient and entertaining.
w Eric Ambler *novel* Geoffrey Household d Robert Parrish *ph* Stan Pavey *md* Hans May
☆ Joel McCrea, Evelyn Keyes, Marius Goring, Roland Culver, Frank Lawton, Herbert Lom

Rough, Tough and Ready

US   1945   64m   bw
Alexis Thurn-Taxis/Columbia
Two members of the Army engineers' port repair service fall out over a girl.
A faint echo of the old Flagg and Quirt comedies.
w Edward T. Lowe *d* Del Lord
☆ Victor McLaglen, Chester Morris, Veda Ann Borg, Jean Rogers

Roughly Speaking *

US   1945   117m   bw
Warner (Henry Blanke)
Oddball, overlong domestic drama about father's wild and impractical schemes.

w Louise Randall Pierson *book* Louise Randall Pierson d Michael Curtiz *ph* Joseph Walker *m* Max Steiner
☆ Rosalind Russell, Jack Carson, Robert Hutton, Jean Sullivan, Alan Hale, Donald Woods, Andrea King, Ray Collins, Kathleen Lockhart

Roughshod

US   1949   88m   bw
RKO (Richard H. Berger)
Two cowboys journeying to California with a herd of horses come up against villains intent on revenge.
Likeable old-fashioned Western.
w Geoffrey Homes, Hugo Butler *d* Mark Robson *ph* Joseph F. Biroc *m* Roy Webb
☆ Robert Sterling, Gloria Grahame, Claude Jarman Jnr, John Ireland, Jeff Donnell, Martha Hyer

Roujin Z *

Japan   1991   80m   colour
Manga/Tokyo Theaters/TV Ashahi/Sony (Yasuhito Nomura, Yasuku Kazama, Yoshiaki Motoya)
📼
original title: *Rojin Z*
A robotic bed becomes possessed by the spirit of the dead wife of an elderly man chosen to test it and develops a will of its own.
An odd, satirical animated film, written by the creator of Akira, about the effect of technology and the dangers of militarism. The animation is sometimes poor, but the themes give it an interest beyond anime's usual teenage audience.
w Katsuhiro Otomo *d* Kiroyuki Kitakubo *m* Fumi Itakura *ad* Hiroshi Sasaki *ed* Eiko Nishiide
☆ Featuring the voices of Allan Wagner, Toni Barry, Barbara Barnes, Adam Henderson, Jana Carpenter, Ian Thompson
   'Shot through with wry humour, genuine tenderness and inventive action.' – *Manga Mania*

Round Midnight **

France   1986   133m   Eastmancolor
Warner/Little Bear/PECF (Irwin Winkler)
📼 ■ ⊘ 🎧
A black American jazz musician spends his last days in Paris.
A jazz buff's tribute to Bud Powell and Lester Young; acclaimed by the critics but essentially a film for minorities.
w Bertrand Tavernier, David Rayfiel *d* Bertrand Tavernier *ph* Bruno de Keyzer *m* Herbie Hancock *md* Herbie Hancock *pd* Alexandre Trauner
☆ Dexter Gordon, François Cluzet, Gabrielle Haker, John Berry, Martin Scorsese
🏆 Herbie Hancock
🎭 Dexter Gordon

Rounders

US   1998   121m   DeLuxe   'Scope
Buena Vista/Miramax/Spanky (Joel Stillerman, Ted Demme)
📼 ■ ⊘ 🎧
The ups and downs, in love and cards, of a young poker player.
A romantic thriller on predictable lines that is unable to make playing cards seem a life-or-death situation.
w David Levien, Brian Koppelman *d* John Dahl *ph* Jean-Yves Escoffier *m* Christopher Young *pd* Rob Pearson *ed* Scott Chestnut
☆ Matt Damon, Edward Norton, John Turturro, Famke Janssen, Gretchen Moll, John Malkovich, Martin Landau
   'As dull and mechanical as poker itself is to the uninitiated.' – *Edward Yardley, Sight and Sound*

The Rounders

US   1965   85m   Metrocolor   Panavision
MGM (Richard E. Lyons)
Two modern cowboys mean to settle down but never get around to it.
Pale comedy Western which never gets going.
wd Burt Kennedy *novel* Max Evans *ph* Paul C. Vogel *m* Jeff Alexander
☆ Henry Fonda, Glenn Ford, Chill Wills, Sue Ane Langdon, Edgar Buchanan
   'One of those utterly relaxed comedies that make ideal entertainment where there's tender loving care every step of the way and no sweat.' – *Judith Crist*

Roustabout

US   1964   101m   Techniscope
Hal B. Wallis
📼 ■ ⊘
A wandering tough guy joins a travelling carnival.
Dreary star vehicle momentarily salvaged by its co-star.
w Allan Weiss, Anthony Lawrence *d* John Rich *ph* Lucien Ballard *m* Joseph L. Lilley
☆ Elvis Presley, Barbara Stanwyck, Sue Ane Langdon, Joan Freeman, Leif Erickson

La Route de Corinthe *

France/Italy/Greece   1967   90m   Eastmancolor
La Boëtie/CGFC/Orion (André Génovés)
📼
aka: *The Road to Corinth*
The wife of a secret agent, accused of killing her husband in Greece, goes in search of the real killer.
Engaging, lightweight thriller, a parody of the espionage genre, which is stylishly shot against some superb Greek locations.
w Claude Brûlé, Daniel Boulanger *novel* Claude Rank d Claude Chabrol *ph* Jean Rabier *m* Pierre Jansen *ed* Jacques Gaillard
☆ Jean Seberg, Maurice Ronet, Christian Marquand, Michel Bouquet, Saro Urzi, Antonio Passalia, Claude Chabrol
   'Flimsy, forgettable stuff.' – *Sight and Sound*

A Row of Crows: see *A Climate for Killing*

Rowing with the Wind *

Spain/Norway   1987   94m   colour
Ditirambo (Andres Vincente Gomez)
Mary Shelley recalls her elopement with Shelley, their meeting with Byron and her creation of Frankenstein.
A glossy death-haunted romantic melodrama, with Frankenstein's monster popping up throughout as a reminder of mortality; a few startling images, such as a meeting between a giraffe and a cardinal in a Venetian palace, spice the familiar story.
wd Gonzalo Suarez *ph* Carlos Suarez *m* Alejandro Masso *ad* Wolfgang Burman *ed* José Salcedo
☆ Hugh Grant, Lizzy McInnerny, Valentine Pelka, Elizabeth Hurley, José Luis Gomez, Virginia Mataix, Ronan Vibert, José Carlos Rivas, Bibi Andersen
† Other films on a similar theme include *Gothic*, *Haunted Summer* and *Frankenstein Unbound* (qqv).

Roxanne *

🏃🏃 US   1987   107m   DeLuxe
Columbia/Michael Rachmil, Daniel Melnick
📼 ■ ⊘ 🎧
An ugly man writes love letters for his friend … but true love will find a way.
Zany modernization of Rostand's Cyrano de Bergerac, funny in spots but way overlong.
w Steve Martin *d* Fred Schepisi *ph* Ian Baker *m* Bruce Smeaton *pd* Jack DeGovia
☆ Steve Martin, Daryl Hannah, Rick Rossovich, Shelley Duvall, John Kapelos, Fred Willard, Michael J. Pollard

'The low down story of a high class gal!'
Roxie Hart **

US   1942   72m   bw
TCF (Nunnally Johnson)
A twenties showgirl confesses for the sake of publicity to a murder of which she is innocent.
Crowded Chicago burlesque which now seems less funny than it did but is full of smart moments.
w Nunnally Johnson *play* Chicago by Maurine Watkins d William Wellman *ph* Leon Shamroy *m* Alfred Newman
☆ Ginger Rogers, George Montgomery, Adolphe Menjou, Lynne Overman, Nigel Bruce, Spring Byington, Sara Allgood, William Fawley
   'A masterpiece of form, of ensemble acting, of powerhouse comedy and scripting.' – *NFT, 1974*
   'Why then, am I not in the aisles all the time? Is it possible that Ginger Rogers, by overplaying the brainless little creature, destroys some of the plausibility and therefore some of the fun? Maybe; I can offer no other explanation of my moments of repose, straight-faced and in my stall.' – *Dilys Powell*
† The play was also filmed in 1927 under its original title, with Phyllis Haver.

Royal African Rifles

†† US 1954 75m Cinecolor
Allied Artists
GB title: *Storm over Africa*

In British East Africa in 1914, a lieutenant tracks down a consignment of stolen guns.
Mini-budgeted Boy's Own Paper heroics; quite enjoyable on its level.

w Dan Ullman d Lesley Selander ph Ellis Carter m .Paul Dunlap
☆ Louis Hayward, Veronica Hurst, Michael Pate, Angela Greene, Steve Geray, Bruce Lester

The Royal Bed

US 1931 74m bw
RKO
GB title: *The Queen's Husband*

The king and queen of a European country lead their own private lives.
Insufficient wit graces this would-be daring romantic drama from a Broadway hit.

w J. Walter Ruben play *The Queen's Husband* by Robert E. Sherwood d Lowell Sherman
☆ Mary Astor, Lowell Sherman, Nance O'Neil, Anthony Bushell, Robert Warwick

Royal Cavalcade

GB 1935 104m bw
BIP

A chronicle of the events of the reign of King George V.
Thoroughly embarrassing jubilee tribute, of historical interest only.

w Marjorie Deans, Val Gielgud, Eric Maschwitz, Holt Marvel d Marcel Varnel, Thomas Bentley, Herbert Brenon, Norman Lee, Walter Summers, Will Kellino ph Brian Langley, Leslie Rowson, Phil Grindrod, Jack Cox, Horace Wheddon md Idris Lewis
☆ Marie Lohr, Hermione Baddeley, Esme Percy, John Mills, Reginald Gardiner, Syd Walker, Seymour Hicks, Owen Nares, Matheson Lang, George Robey, Florrie Forde, many others

A Royal Divorce

GB 1938 85m bw
Herbert Wilcox/Imperator

Napoleon Bonaparte in 1809 marries a widow whose reputation isn't exactly spotless.
Heavy comedy or light drama, take your pick; not exactly riveting as either.

w Miles Malleson novel *Josephine* by Jacques Thery d Jack Raymond
☆ Pierre Blanchar, Ruth Chatterton, Frank Cellier, Carol Goodner, George Curzon, John Laurie, Jack Hawkins

The Royal Family of Broadway *

US 1930 82m bw
Paramount
GB title: *Theatre Royal*

The off-stage escapades of a famous family of actors.
Fairly funny lampoon of the Barrymores, primitively staged and very talky but still entertaining for those in the joke.

w Herman J. Mankiewicz, Gertrude Purcell play George S. Kaufman, Edna Ferber d George Cukor, Cyril Gardner ph George Folsey
☆ Fredric March, Henrietta Crosman, Ina Claire, Mary Brian, Charles Starrett, Frank Conroy
'Lionel does not come into the burlesque at all, and I can quite believe that he is the most damaged of the entire family.' – *James Agate*
'Stagebound and awkward, but great fun anyway.' – *New Yorker, 1977*
⅄ Fredric March

Royal Flash

†† GB 1975 118m Technicolor
TCF/Two Roads (David V. Picker, Denis O'Dell)
▬

A Victorian bully and braggart has various adventures in Europe and Ruritania.
A rather unsatisfactory romp which takes pot shots at every 19th-century person and object in the encyclopaedia, but is never as funny as it intends to be.

w George Macdonald Fraser novel George Macdonald Fraser d Richard Lester ph Geoffrey Unsworth m Ken Thorpe pd Terence Marsh
☆ Malcolm McDowell, Oliver Reed, Alan Bates, Florinda Bolkan, Britt Ekland, Lionel Jeffries, Tom Bell, Joss Ackland, Leon Greene, Richard Hurndall, Alastair Sim, Michael Hordern

Royal Flush: see *Two Guys from Milwaukee*

The Royal Hunt of the Sun

GB 1969 121m Technicolor
Security Pictures (Eugene Frenke, Philip Yordan)
Ⓓ

How the Spanish soldier Pizarro on his South American trek overcame the Inca god-king Atahualpa.
Deadly literal rendering with nothing to replace the play's theatrical splendour, resembling nothing so much as an opera without the music.

w Philip Yordan play Peter Shaffer d Irving Lerner ph Roger Barlow m Marc Wilkinson
☆ Robert Shaw, Christopher Plummer, Nigel Davenport, Michael Craig, Leonard Whiting, Andrew Keir, James Donald, Percy Herbert, Alexander Davion

A Royal Scandal

US 1945 94m bw
TCF (Ernst Lubitsch)
GB title: *Czarina*

The illicit loves of Catherine the Great.
Censored romps around some chilly court sets; very few moments of interest, and none of the style of the silent version Forbidden Paradise.

w Edwin Justus Mayer play Lajos Biro, Melchior Lengyel d Otto Preminger ph Arthur Miller m Alfred Newman
☆ Tallulah Bankhead, Charles Coburn, Anne Baxter, William Eythe, Vincent Price, Mischa Auer, Sig Rumann, Vladimir Sokoloff
'Nothing is one-tenth well enough done, and all the laughs are played for at their cheapest, far down the ramp.' – *James Agee*

Royal Wedding

US 1951 93m Technicolor
MGM (Arthur Freed)
▬ ▬ ◎ ▬
GB title: *Wedding Bells*

Journalists congregate in London for the royal wedding.
Thin musical with acceptable numbers.

w Alan Jay Lerner d Stanley Donen ph Robert Planck md Johnny Green songs Alan Jay Lerner, Burton Lane
☆ Fred Astaire, Jane Powell, Sarah Churchill, Peter Lawford, Keenan Wynn
♫ song 'Too Late Now' (mBurton Lane, lyAlan Jay Lerner)

RPM (Revolutions Per Minute)

US 1970 97m colour
Columbia/Stanley Kramer
▬

At an American college, a middle-aged professor teaches liberal ideas.
Dim, thankfully forgotten addition to the Strawberry Statement cycle.

w Erich Segal d Stanley Kramer ph Michel Hugo, Perry Botkin Jnr m Barry de Vorzon
☆ Anthony Quinn, Ann-Margret, Gary Lockwood, Paul Winfield, Alan Hewitt

Ruba al Prossimo Tua: see *A Fine Pair*

Ruby

US 1992 DeLuxe
Rank/Propaganda (Sigurjon Sighvatsson, Steve Golin)
▬ ▬ ◎ ▬

A shady night-club owner kills Lee Harvey Oswald, assassin of President Kennedy, in order to expose a plot by the Mafia and the CIA to murder the President.
Muddled, small-scale, mainly fictional conspiracy movie that confuses the issues it attempts to explain.

w Stephen Davis play *Love Field* by Stephen Davis d John MacKenzie ph Phil Meheux m John Scott pd David Brisbin ed Richard Trevor
☆ Danny Aiello, Sherilyn Fenn, Frank Orsatti, Jeffrey Nordling, Jane Hamilton, Maurice Bernard, Joe Viterelli, Robert S. Telford

Ruby and Rata

New Zealand 1990 113m colour
Preston-Laing/NZFC

An uneasy relationship develops between an elderly woman and her tenant, an unemployed would-be rock singer with a small son.
Uninteresting domestic drama, presumably intended as a comedy.

w Graeme Tetley d Gaylene Preston ph Leon Narbey m Jonathan Crayford pd Robert Gillies ed Paul Sutorius
☆ Yvonne Lawley, Vanessa Rare, Lee Mete-Kingi, Simon Barnett

Ruby Cairo

US 1992 111m Technicolor
Entertainment/Majestic (Lloyd Phillips)
▬ ◎

After her husband is reported killed in a car crash, his hard-up wife discovers that he has a fortune hidden in bank accounts across the world.
Dull thriller, which doubles as an attractive travelogue.

w Robert Dillon, Michael Thomas d Graeme Clifford ph Laszlo Kovacs m John Barry pd Richard Sylbert ed Caroline Biggerstaff
☆ Andie MacDowell, Liam Neeson, Viggo Mortensen, Jack Thompson, Paul Spencer, Chad Power, Monica Mikala
'An old-fashioned Yank-in-Europe mystery-adventure that squanders an interesting cast.' – *Variety*
'Nothing but a plot and the plot nothing but predictable.' – *Sight and Sound*

'Dangerous ... destructive ... deadly to love!'

Ruby Gentry

US 1952 82m bw
Joseph Bernhard/King Vidor
▬ ▬

A tempestuous girl, brought up as a boy in the Carolina swamps, has a love-hate relationship with a local aristocrat, revenges herself on the people who scorn her, loses her lover in a swamp shooting, and becomes a sea captain.
Richly absurd sex melodrama typical of its director and star yet not very entertaining.

w Silvia Richards d King Vidor ph Russell Harlan m Heinz Roemheld ad Dan Hall
☆ Jennifer Jones, Charlton Heston, Karl Malden, Josephine Hutchinson

Ruby in Paradise

US 1993 114m DuArt
Mainline/Ruby in Paradise/A Full Crew/Say Yea
▬ ▬

A young woman leaves home to seek life and love and ends up in an out-of-season holiday resort.
A deliberately small-scale movie, focussing its attention on minor matters and the frequently dull intricacies of everyday living.

wd Victor Nuñez ph Alex Vlacos m Charles Engstrom pd John Iacovelli ed Victor Nuñez
☆ Ashley Judd, Todd Field, Bentley Mitchum, Allison Dean, Dorothy Lyman, Betsy Douds, Felicia Hernandez, Sharon Lewis
'Very well played, very well set and directed with a sharp eye for detail.' – *Derek Malcolm, Guardian*

'Two hippies come back from 1969 to get the bad news...'

Rude Awakening

US 1989 101m Technicolor
Rank (Aaron Russo)
▬ ▬ ◎

Two hippies return to New York after twenty years in Central America.
Weak ecological and political farce.

w Neil Levy, Richard LaGravenese d Aaron Russo, David Greenwalt ph Tom Sigel m Jonathan Elias pd Mel Bourne ed Paul Fried
☆ Cheech Marin, Eric Roberts, Julie Hagerty, Robert Carradine, Buck Henry, Louise Lasser, Cindy Williams

Rudy

†† US 1993 116m Technicolor
Columbia TriStar (Robert N. Fried, Cary Woods)
▬

An undersized youth is determined to play football for the University of Nôtre Dame.
Based on a true story, a likeable, though predictable and overly sentimental, story of success against the odds.

w Angelo Pizzo d David Anspaugh ph Oliver Wood m Jerry Goldsmith pd Robb Wilson King ed David Rosenbloom
☆ Sean Astin, Ned Beatty, Charles Dutton, Lili Taylor, Jason Miller, Robert Prosky, Greta Lind, Jon Favreau
'A film that hits all the right emotional buttons, it's an intelligent, sentimental drama that lifts an audience to its feet cheering.' – *Leonard Klady, Variety*
'Appears to confirm the basic premise of the American dream – that you can do anything if you try hard enough. Its appeal is almost incomprehensible out of America.' – *Nick Hasted, Sight and Sound*

Rudyard Kipling's Jungle Book: see *The Jungle Book (1942)*

Rudyard Kipling's Jungle Book *

†† US 1994 111m Technicolor
Buena Vista/Walt Disney (Edward S. Feldman, Raju Patel)
▬ ▬ ◎

The adventures of Mowgli, an Indian boy brought up by jungle animals.
Enjoyable children's adventure, closer to Indiana Jones than to Kipling, but with enough action and animals to keep it interesting.

w Stephen Sommers, Ronald Yanover, Mark D. Geldman d Stephen Sommers ph Juan Ruiz Anchia m Basil Poledouris pd Allan Cameron ed Bob Ducsay
☆ Jason Scott Lee, Cary Elwes, Lena Headey, Sam Neill, John Cleese, Jason Flemyng, Stefan Kalipha, Ron Donachie
'An engrossing, bloodthirsty family fable that's an edge-of-the-seater for all over-tens.' – *Tom Hutchinson, Film Review*

Rue Cases Nègres **

France 1983 106m Fujicolour
Artificial Eye/Orion Classics/Su Ma Fa/Orca/NEF Diffusion (Jean-Luc Ormieres)
▬ ▬ ◎
US title: *Sugar Cane Alley*
aka: *Black Shack Alley*

In Martinique in the 1930s, a woman sacrifices herself so that her grandson can escape from poverty through education.
Moving and evocative account of colonial life, tinged with nostalgia but marked by some full-blooded performances.

wd Euzhan Palcy novel Joseph Zobel ph Dominique Chapuis m Groupe Malavoi ad Hoang Thanh At, Romul Eloise ed Marie-Joseph Yoyotte
☆ Garry Cadenat, Darling Legitimus, Douta Seck, Joby Bernabe, Francisco Charles, Marie-Jo Descas, Marie-Ange Farot

Rue de l'Estrapade *

France 1953 95m bw
Cinephonic/SGGC/Filmsonor
aka: *Françoise Steps Out*

A young Parisienne suspects her husband of having an affair.
Lightly likeable domestic comedy in the vein of Edouard et Caroline, but not quite up to its standard.

w Annette Wademant d Jacques Becker ph Marcel Grignon m Georges Van Parys, Marguerite Monnot
☆ Louis Jourdan, Anne Vernon, Daniel Gelin, Jean Servais, Micheline Dax

'Five comedy stars in a five-star comedy!'

Ruggles of Red Gap **

US 1935 90m bw
Paramount (Arthur Hornblow Jnr)
▬ ◎

A British butler has a startling effect on the family of an American rancher who takes him out west.
A famous comedy which seemed hilarious at the time but can now be seen as mostly composed of flat spots; the performances however are worth remembering.

w Walter de Leon, Harlan Thompson, Humphrey Pearson novel Harry Leon Wilson d Leo McCarey ph Alfred Gilks
☆ Charles Laughton, Mary Boland, Charles Ruggles, ZaSu Pitts, Roland Young, Leila Hyams, James Burke, Maude Eburne, Lucien Littlefield
'Plenty of marquee strength, and dynamite on the inside. An A1 comedy.' – *Variety*
'A sane, witty, moving and quite unusual picture of Anglo-American relations.' – *C. A. Lejeune*
'The most heart-warming comedy of the season ... there is about it a sympathetic and even a patriotic quality which is touching.' – *Literary Digest*
'The archetypal film they don't make any more, partly because comedy has now grown too raucous to favour the quiet drollery of players like Charlie Ruggles and Mary Boland, partly

because even McCarey himself had trouble after the thirties separating sentiment from sentimentality.' – *Time Out, 1980*
† Remade as *Fancy Pants* (qv).
✥ best picture

The Rugrats Movie **
🏃 US 1999 79m DeLuxe
Paramount/Nickelodeon (Arlene Klasky, Gabor Csupo)
A gang of small children, attempting to return the new baby brother of their leader to hospital, become lost in a forest which is full of unfriendly animals.
Fast-moving, lively animated feature, based on a TV series, that takes an infant's-eye view of the adult world to extremes.
w David N. Weiss, J. David Stem d Norton Virgien, Igor Kovalyov m Mark Mothersbaugh ad Dima Malanitchev ed John Bryant
☆ Featuring the voices of: E. G. Daily, Christine Cavanaugh, Kath Soucie, Cheryl Case, Tara Charendoff, Melanie Chartoff, Jack Riley, Joe Alaskey, Phil Proctor, Cree Summer, Michael Bell, Tress MacNeille, Busta Rhymes, Whoopi Goldberg, David Spade
'Witty, sophisticated and, in its depiction of very young children as a wild bunch with bad attitude and faces like over-boiled potatoes, it's hard to fault.' – *Alexander Walker, London Evening Standard*

Rulers of the Sea *
US 1939 96m bw
Paramount (Frank Lloyd)
Problems surround the first steamship voyage across the Atlantic.
Well-made period action drama.
w Talbot Jennings, Frank Cavett, Richard Collins d Frank Lloyd ph Theodor Sparkuhl, Archie Stout m Richard Hageman
☆ Douglas Fairbanks Jnr, Margaret Lockwood, Will Fyffe, Montagu Love, George Bancroft, Mary Gordon, Alan Ladd
'Timely in content and grand for exploitation. In the British Empire it will be greeted as inspirational entertainment.' – *Variety*

The Rules of the Game: see La Règle du Jeu

The Ruling Class *
GB 1972 155m DeLuxe
Keep Films (Jules Buck, Jack Hawkins)
The fetishistic Earl of Gurney is succeeded by his mad son Jack who believes he is God.
An overlong satirical play with brilliant patches is hamfistedly filmed but boasts some bright performances. The hits are as random as the misses, however.
w Peter Barnes *play* Peter Barnes d Peter Medak ph Ken Hodges m John Cameron
☆ Peter O'Toole, Harry Andrews, Arthur Lowe, Alastair Sim, Coral Browne, Michael Bryant
'This irritating and unsatisfying film is worth being irritated and unsatisfied by.' – *Stanley Kauffmann*
✥ Peter O'Toole

'This is the dance of love!'
Rumba *
US 1935 71m bw
Paramount (William Le Baron)
A society girl has a yen for a Broadway hoofer.
Streamlined star vehicle which attempts to recapture the success of Bolero (qv).
w Howard J. Green d Marion Gering ph Ted Tetzlaff
☆ Carole Lombard, George Raft, Margo, Lynne Overman, Monroe Owsley, Iris Adrian, Gail Patrick, Samuel S. Hinds, Jameson Thomas

Rumble Fish
US 1983 94m bw (with colour inserts)
Universal/Zoetrope (Fred Roos, Douglas Claybourne)
A Tulsa teenager survives local gang violence and while working in a petshop sees himself in the rumble fish, which fights even its own image in a glass.
Glum piece of self-absorption by a director going rapidly downhill.

w Francis Ford Coppola *novel* S. E. Hinton ph Stephen H. Burum m Stewart Copeland pd Dean Tavoularis ed Barry Malkin
☆ Matt Dillon, Mickey Rourke, Diane Lane, Dennis Hopper, Diana Scarwid

Rumble in the Bronx
Hong Kong 1995 105m colour
Golden Harvest (Leonard K. C. Ho)
In New York, a Hong Kong cop helps a Chinese woman whose supermarket is threatened by a biker gang.
Moderate martial arts action with a few comic moments; the film is calculated to appeal to Western audiences, though Chan always seems at his best on his home ground.
w Edward Tang *story* Stanley Tong, Ma Mei-ping d Stanley Tong ph Jingle Ma m J. Peter Robinson ad Oliver Wong ed Peter Cheung
☆ Jackie Chan, Anita Mui, Bill Tung, Yip Fong-wa, Bai Cheun-wai
'An enjoyable comedy-actioner whose ooh-aah moments are mostly confined to the last few reels.' – *Variety*

Run
US 1990 91m Technicolor
Buena Vista/Hollywood (Raymond Wagner)
An accident-prone law student is hunted by crooked cops and robbers when he accidentally causes the death of a gangster's son.
Inane thriller, with a less than sympathetic protagonist, that amounts to little more than a series of car chases and crashes.
w Dennis Shryack, Michael Blodgett d Geoff Burrowes ph Bruce Surtees m Phil Marshall pd John Willett ed Jack Hofstra
☆ Patrick Dempsey, Kelly Preston, Ken Pogue, James Kidnie, Sean McCann

Run for Cover *
US 1955 92m Technicolor Vistavision
Paramount (William H. Pine)
An ex-convict becomes innocently involved in a train robbery.
Adequate star Western.
w William C. Thomas *story* Harriet Frank Jnr, Irving Ravetch d Nicholas Ray ph Daniel Fapp md Howard Jackson
☆ James Cagney, Viveca Lindfors, John Derek, Jean Hersholt, Grant Withers, Ernest Borgnine, Jack Lambert

Run for the Sun
US 1956 99m Technicolor Superscope
UA/Russ-Field (Harry Tatelman)
Crashlanding in the Mexican jungle, a disillusioned author and a lady journalist find themselves at the mercy of renegade Nazis.
Tame remake of The Most Dangerous Game with Count Zaroff replaced by Lord Haw-Haw. Sluggish plot development mars the action.
w Dudley Nichols, Roy Boulting d Roy Boulting ph Joseph LaShelle m Fred Steiner
☆ Richard Widmark, Jane Greer, Trevor Howard, Peter Van Eyck

A Run for Your Money *
GB 1949 83m bw
Ealing (Leslie Norman)
Welsh Rugby supporters have various adventures on their one day in London.
Slight, bright, British chase comedy with characterizations as excellent as they are expected.
w Richard Hughes, Charles Frend, Leslie Norman d Charles Frend ph Douglas Slocombe m Ernest Irving
☆ Alec Guinness, Meredith Edwards, Moira Lister, Donald Houston, Hugh Griffith, Clive Morton, Joyce Grenfell

Run Lola Run ***
Germany 1998 80m colour
Columbia TriStar/Bavaria/German Independents/X Filme/ (Stefan Arndt)
original title: Lola Rennt
A girl has 20 minutes in which to save her boyfriend from death, after he loses a bag of money belonging to a drug dealer.
Exhilarating, speedy thriller which provides three alternative versions of events, depending on tiny incidents which precipitate different consequences; it's a

witty demonstration of the vagaries of cause and effect and the unpredictability of life.
wd Tom Tykwer ph Frank Griebe m Tom Tykwer, Johnny Klimek, Reinhold Hei ad Alexander Manasse ed Mathilde Bonnefoy
☆ Franka Potente, Moritz Bleibtreu, Herbert Knaup, Armin Rohde, Joachim Krol, Nina Petri, Heino Ferch
'That Tykwer maintains our flow of empathy while demonstrating and exploiting the potential of interactive cinema manqué is, in itself, an awesome achievement.' – *Richard Falcon, Sight and Sound*
'This stylish, hugely likeable bit of adrenaline-pumped Euro-nonsense should shatter the illusions of those convinced that all subtitled fare is musty, wordy and dull.' – *Caroline Westbrook, Empire*

'A Rebel's Hate ... A Woman's Undying Love!'
Run of the Arrow *
US 1957 85m Technicolor RKOscope
Global (Samuel Fuller)
An ex-Civil War soldier is captured by Indians and accepted by them, but sickened by their violence.
Bloody little Western in the accustomed Fuller vein.
wd Samuel Fuller ph Joseph Biroc m Victor Young
☆ Rod Steiger, Sarita Montiel, Charles Bronson, Tim McCoy, Ralph Meeker
'Just an ordinary cavalry-Indian film, conspicuous for a lot of raw blood-letting.' – *Bosley Crowther*

'Sometimes, the most daring step to freedom is out the front door.'
The Run of the Country
GB/Ireland 1995 108m Technicolor Panavision
Rank/Castle Rock/One Two Nine (Peter Yates, Ruth Boswell)
An Irish policeman in a small town near the border with Northern Ireland has problems with his teenage son.
A domestic drama that skirts round the Irish troubles but uses them as a backdrop to an unilluminating account of young love and its aftermath.
w Shane Connaughton *novel* Shane Connaughton d Peter Yates ph Mike Southon m Cynthia Millar pd Mark Geraghty ed Paul Hodgson
☆ Albert Finney, Matt Keeslar, Victoria Smurfit, Anthony Brophy, David Kelly, Dearbhla Molloy
'A bog-standard rite-of-passage film.' – *Sheila Johnston, Independent*

A Run on Gold: see Midas Run

Run Silent Run Deep *
US 1958 93m bw
UA/Hecht-Hill-Lancaster (William Schorr)
Antagonisms flare up between the officers of a US submarine in Tokyo Bay during World War II
Competent, unsurprising war actioner trading on its stars.
w John Gay d Robert Wise ph Russell Harlan m Franz Waxman
☆ Clark Gable, Burt Lancaster, Jack Warden, Brad Dexter, Nick Cravat, Joe Maross, H. M. Wynant
'Mostly good sea fights. Otherwise it's damn the torpedoes, half speed ahead.' – *Time*

Run Wild, Run Free *
🏃 GB 1969 98m Technicolor
Columbia/Irving Allen (John Danischewsky)
A mute boy living on Dartmoor gains self-confidence through the love of animals.
Rather vaguely developed family film with agreeable sequences.
w David Rook *novel The White Colt* by David Rook d Richard C. Sarafian ph Wilkie Cooper m David Whitaker
☆ John Mills, Sylvia Syms, Mark Lester, Bernard Miles, Gordon Jackson, Fiona Fullerton

The Runaround *
US 1946 100m bw
Universal (Joseph Gershenson)
Two rival detectives are hired to find a missing heiress.

Peripatetic comedy on the lines of It Happened One Night; unexpectedly enjoyable.
w Arthur T. Horman, Sam Hellman d Charles Lamont ph George Robinson m Frank Skinner
☆ Rod Cameron, Broderick Crawford, Ella Raines, Samuel S. Hinds, Frank McHugh, George Cleveland

Runaway
US 1984 100m Metrocolor Panavision
Tri-Star/Michael Crichton (Michael Rachmil)
An electronics wizard sets a half-perfected robot on the rampage.
Simple-minded comedy-melodrama which feels as though it ought to have been played entirely for laughs.
wd Michael Crichton ph John A. Alonzo m Jerry Goldsmith pd Douglas Higgins ed Glenn Farr
☆ Tom Selleck, Cynthia Rhodes, Gene L. Simmons, Kirstie Alley, Stan Shaw

'Catch her if you can.'
Runaway Bride *
US 1999 116m Technicolor Panavision
Paramount/Touchstone/Interscope/Lakeshore (Ted Field, Tom Rosenberg, Scott Kroopf, Robert Cort)
A sacked newspaper columnist goes to find the thrice-bolting bride who cost him his job.
A romantic comedy in search of a better script; this one manages to make both of its protagonists unsympathetic.
w Josann McGibbon, Sara Parriott d Garry Marshall ph Stuart Dryburgh m James Newton Howard pd Mark Friedberg ed Bruce Green cos Albert Wolsky
☆ Julia Roberts, Richard Gere, Joan Cusack, Hector Elizondo, Rita Wilson, Paul Dooley, Christopher Meloni, Donal Logue
'Director Garry Marshall specialises in this kind of schmaltz. This time, though, the trademark warm glow only highlights the script's awesome deficiences.' – *Andrew O'Hagan, Daily Telegraph*
'An ultracommercial mainstream romantic comedy that delivers all the laughs and smiles it intends to.' – *Todd McCarthy, Variety*
† The film grossed more than $155m at the US box-office.

The Runaway Bus *
GB 1954 78m bw
Eros/Conquest-Guest (Val Guest)
Passengers at London Airport are fogbound, and a relief bus driver takes some of them to Blackbushe. Incognito among them are robbers and detectives ...
Vaguely plotted variation on The Ghost Train, with fair production, a good smattering of jokes, and a hilarious view of a great airport in its earlier days.
wd Val Guest m Stan Pavey m Ronald Binge
☆ Frankie Howerd, Margaret Rutherford, George Coulouris, Petula Clark, Terence Alexander, Toke Townley, Belinda Lee

Runaway Daughter: see Red Salute

'Once it starts, nothing can stop it!'
Runaway Train *
US 1985 111m Rank Colour
Cannon/Northbrook (Menahem Golan, Yoram Globus)
Prison breakers escape into the Alaskan wilderness and commander a train which can't stop.
Violent, foul-mouthed melodrama with no interest beyond breathtaking photography of the speeding train. Its general pretentiousness, perhaps, is also something to experience.
w Djordje Milicevic, Paul Zindel, Edward Bunker, from screenplay by Akira Kurosawa d Andrei Konchalovsky ph Alan Hume m Trevor Jones pd Stephen Marsh
☆ Jon Voight, Eric Roberts, Rebecca DeMornay, Kyle T. Heffner
'The most exciting epic since *The Road Warrior*.' – *Variety*
'Nervy, exciting violence; immaculate, metallic camerawork; unstoppable pace.' – *Sight and Sound*
✥ Jon Voight; Eric Roberts (supporting actor); editing

The Runner

Iran 1984 94m colour

Electric/Studio of the Voice and Portrait of the Islamic Revolution of Iran (Fatholah Dalili)

original title: *Dawandeh*

A 13-year-old orphan makes his living on the streets of a Gulf port while learning to outdistance his peers.

Unsparing but repetitious account of childhood poverty.

w Amir Naderi, Behruz Gharibpur d Amir Naderi ph Firuz Malekzadeh pd Gholam Reza Ramezani ed Bahram Beyza'i

☆ Majid Nirumand, Musa Torkizadeh, A. Gholamzadeh, Reza Ramezani

The Runner Stumbles

US 1979 110m CFI color

Melvin Simon Productions (Stanley Kramer)

▤

In the mid-twenties, a Catholic priest is accused of the murder of a nun for whom he had felt a strong romantic attraction.

Musty exhumation of a genuine case which has little dramatic interest and even less wider significance. Good acting does not atone.

w Milan Stiff *play* Milan Stiff d Stanley Kramer ph Laszlo Kovacs m Ernest Gold pd Alfred Sweeney Jnr

☆ Dick Van Dyke, Kathleen Quinlan, Maureen Stapleton, Ray Bolger, Tammy Grimes, Beau Bridges

'The reanimated corpse of middlebrow Hollywood pretension ... funereal pacing, portentous low angles and symbolic overkill.' – *Paul Taylor, MFB*

Runners

GB 1983 106m colour

Goldcrest (Barry Hanson)

▥

Distraught parents try to trace their missing children in London.

Heavy-going realistic drama with apparent inner meanings which are not brought to the surface.

w Stephen Poliakoff d Charles Sturridge ph Howard Atherton m George Fenton pd Arnold Chapkis

☆ James Fox, Kate Hardie, Jane Asher, Eileen O'Brien, Ruti Simon

Running

Canada 1979 103m colour

Universal (Robert Cooper, Ronald Cohen)

▥

A man in his 30s who has failed in his work and marriage decides that he can succeed as an Olympic marathon runner.

Slight drama with rather too much footage of our hero running through city streets to the accompaniment of syrupy music to maintain any interest in its conventional and sentimental narrative.

wd Steven Hilliard Stern ph Laszlo George m André Gagnon pd Roy Forge Smith ed Kurt Kirschler

☆ Michael Douglas, Susan Anspach, Lawrence Dane, Eugene Levy, Charles Shamata, Philip Akin, Jim McKay

Running Brave

US 1983 106m colour

ITC/Englander Productions

▤ ◎

A young Sioux from the reservation faces the pressures of the white world and becomes an Olympic runner.

The terrible punning title is the best thing in this very predictable piece of do-goodery, which would just about have passed muster as a TV movie.

w Henry Bean, Shirl Hendryx d D. S. Everett ph François Protat m Mike Post pd Carol Spier ed Tony Lower, Earle Herden

☆ Robby Benson, Pat Hingle, Claudia Cron, Jeff McCracken

'This is in essence a propaganda film for the American way, masked as a piece of liberal sentiment, and I distrust it thoroughly.' – *Observer*

Running Cool

US 1993 106m colour

Paramount (Beverly Sebastian)

▥ ▤

Two bikers go to help a wildlife-loving friend in a small South Carolina town, whose swampland is threatened by the reckless son of a ruthless developer.

Overlong, cliché-ridden action movie with an environmental message, providing you can accept that 400 bikers improve an environment.

w Ferd & Beverly Sebastian d Ferd Sebastian ph Ferd Sebastian m Robert Etoll ed Ralph Clemente

☆ Andrew Divoff, Tracy Sebastian, Dedee Pfeiffer, James Gammon, Paul Gleason, Arlen Dean Snyder, Bubba Baker

'Time is running out for him!'

The Running Man *

GB 1963 103m Technicolor Panavision

Columbia/Peet (Carol Reed, John R. Sloan)

A private airline pilot fakes an accident and disappears, leaving his wife to collect the insurance and meet him in Spain.

Flabby, expensive suspenser; both plot and character take a back seat to scenic views.

w John Mortimer *novel* The Ballad of the Running Man *by* Shelley Smith d Carol Reed ph Robert Krasker m William Alwyn

☆ Laurence Harvey, Alan Bates, Lee Remick, Felix Aylmer, Eleanor Summerfield, Allan Cuthbertson

'There seems to be something about the panoramic screen that seduces film-makers into filling it with irrelevant local colour and drawing the whole proceedings out to a length that matches its width.' – *Brenda Davies*

The Running Man

US 1987 101m colour

Rank/Braveworld (Tim Zinnemann, George Linder)

▥ ▤ ◎ ◉ ◠

In the future, a convict, framed on a murder charge, takes part in a TV game show in which he is hunted through Los Angeles by expert killers.

Fast-moving action movie, full of violence and some dubious jokes.

w Steven E. de Souza *novel* Stephen King d Paul Michael Glaser ph Thomas Del Ruth m Harold Faltermeyer pd Jack T. Collis ed Mark Roy Warner, Edward A. Warschilka, John Wright

☆ Arnold Schwarzenegger, Maria Conchita Alonso, Yaphet Kotto, Jim Brown, Jesse Ventura, Erland Van Lidth, Marvin J. McIntyre, Mick Fleetwood, Richard Dawson

Running on Empty

US 1988 116m Technicolor

Warner/Lorimar/Double Play (Amy Robinson, Griffin Dunne)

▥ ▤ ◎ ◉

A teenager, whose parents are long-time political activists on the run from the FBI, tries to live his own life as a budding musician.

Mundane family drama that fails to illuminate the problems it describes.

w Naomi Foner d Sidney Lumet ph Gerry Fisher m Tony Mottola pd Philip Rosenberg ed Andre Mondshein

☆ Christine Lahti, River Phoenix, Judd Hirsch, Jonas Abry, Martha Plimpton, Ed Crowley, L. M. Kit Carson, Steven Hill, Augusta Dabney, David Margulies

♟ best original screenplay; River Phoenix

Running Scared

GB 1972 98m Technicolor Panavision

Paramount/Wigan/Hemmings/O'Toole (Gareth Wigan)

A university student is generally condemned for allowing his friend to commit suicide; eventually he takes his own life.

Depressing and rather pointless exercise in death wish complicated by a doomed love affair.

w Clive Exton, David Hemmings *novel* Gregory MacDonald d David Hemmings ph Ernest Day m Michael J. Lewis

☆ Robert Powell, Gayle Hunnicutt, Barry Morse, Stephanie Bidmead, Edward Underdown, Maxine Audley, Georgia Brown

Running Scared

US 1986 106m Metrocolor Panavision

MGM-UA/Turman-Foster (Peter Hyams)

▥ ▤ ◎ ◠

Accident-prone Chicago cops nevertheless succeed in getting their man.

Crime comedy-melodrama of a type seen far too often before.

w Gary DeVore, Jimmy Huston d Peter Hyams ph Peter Hyams m Rod Temperton pd Albert Brenner

☆ Gregory Hines, Billy Crystal, Steven Bauer, Joe Pantoliano, Tracy Reed, Darlanne Fluegel

La Rupture *

Belgium/France/Italy 1970 125m

Eastmancolor

Contemporary/Films de la Boétie (André Genovès)

▥

aka: *The Breakup*

A mother who wants custody of her young son after she divorces her drug-addicted husband finds herself in conflict with her ruthless and powerful father-in-law.

Enjoyable thriller in which innocence triumphs over experience.

wd Claude Chabrol *novel* Charlotte Armstrong ph Jean Rabier m Pierre Jansen

☆ Stéphane Audran, Jean-Pierre Cassel, Michel Bouquet, Jean-Claude Drouot, Annie Cordy, Jean Carmet, Michel Duchaussoy, Catherine Rouvel

'The director, who can indubitably be very subtle if he chooses, is pleased this time to wallow in the obvious, but to do so with a fine cinematic judgement.' – *Gordon Gow, Films and Filming*

'How far do they go before they've gone too far?'

Rush *

US 1992 120m DeLuxe Panavision

MGM/Zanuck (Richard D. Zanuck)

▥ ▤ ◎ ◠

In the 1970s two undercover narcotics cops become drug addicts.

Unrelenting, though skilfully made, tale of degradation and despair.

w Pete Dexter *book* Kim Wozencraft d Lili Fini Zanuck ph Kenneth MacMillan m Eric Clapton pd Paul Sylbert ed Mark Warner

☆ Jason Patric, Jennifer Jason Leigh, Sam Elliott, Max Perlich, Gregg Allman, Tony Frank

'Downbeat nature of this addiction saga may be too intense and draining for general audiences, but resounding implications of the subject are bound to touch a nerve.' – *Variety*

'The Fastest Hands in the East versus the Biggest Mouth in the West.'

Rush Hour *

US 1998 98m DeLuxe

New Line (Arthur Sarkissian, Roger Birnbaum, Jonathan Glickman)

▥ ▤ ◎ ◉ ◉ ◠

A Chinese detective joins a disgraced LA cop in tracking down a master criminal.

A movie designed to package Chan for US audiences, in which it succeeds, providing some sharply written exchanges along with his usual blend of comedy, fights and extraordinary stunts.

w Jim Kouf, Ross Lamanna d Brett Ratner ph Adam Greenberg m Lalo Schifrin pd Robb Wilson King ed Mark Helfrich

☆ Jackie Chan, Chris Tucker, Tom Wilkinson, Elizabeth Peña, Philip Baker Hall, Mark Rolston, Tzi Ma, Rex Linn, Ken Leung, Chris Penn, Julia Hsu

'A frankly formulaic but raucously entertaining action comedy.' – *Joe Leydon, Variety*

'All's fair when love is war.'

Rushmore *

US 1998 93m DeLuxe Panavision

Buena Vista/Touchstone/American Empirical (Barry Mendel, Paul Schiff)

▥ ▤

A precocious 15-year-old student and a wealthy businessman compete for the attentions of a school teacher.

Quirky comedy of adolescent ambition and adult resignation that has its moments, but loses its way long before the end.

w Wes Anderson, Owen Wilson d Wes Anderson ph Robert Yeoman m Mark Mothersbaugh pd David Wasco ed David Moritz

☆ Jason Schwartzman, Bill Murray, Olivia Williams, Seymour Cassel, Brian Cox, Mason Gamble, Sara Tanaka, Stephen McCole, Ronnie McCawley, Keith McCawley, Connie Nielsen, Kim Terry

'A genre-defying marvel, switching between outrageous humour and genuine pathos at a moment's notice.' – *Peter Bradshaw, Guardian*

'Made to be treasured: it feels like an immediate American classic.' – *Richard Kelly, Sight and Sound*

The Russia House *

US 1990 123m Technicolor

UIP/Pathé Entertainment (Paul Maslansky, Fred Schepisi)

▥ ▤ ◎ ◠

A publisher, acting as a go-between for western intelligence and a Soviet scientist, finds life complicated by love.

Intelligent but sluggish thriller with few surprises.

w Tom Stoppard *novel* John Le Carré d Fred Schepisi ph Ian Baker m Jerry Goldsmith pd Richard MacDonald ad Roger Cain ed Peter Honess

☆ Sean Connery, Michelle Pfeiffer, Roy Scheider, James Fox, John Mahoney, Michael Kitchen, J. T. Walsh, Ken Russell, David Threlfall, Klaus Maria Brandauer

'An absorbing but muted yarn of romance and political intrigue.' – *Variety*

Russian Roulette

US 1975 90m Eastmancolor

ITC/Elliott Kastner/Bulldog

Real and fake secret agents shoot it out when the Russian premier is about to visit Vancouver.

Fast-moving but impossible to follow vacation thriller which resolves itself into a series of chases.

w Tom Ardies, Stanley Mann, Arnold Margolin *novel* Kosygin is Coming *by* Tom Ardies d Lou Lombardo ph Brian West m Michael J. Lewis

☆ George Segal, Gordon Jackson, Denholm Elliott, Cristina Raines, Richard Romanus, Louise Fletcher, Nigel Stock

'A stale, mechanical espionage caper that wastes its star.' – *Kevin Thomas*

'Why the crazy title? If we told you, you'd only laugh!'

The Russians Are Coming, The Russians Are Coming *

US 1966 126m DeLuxe Panavision

UA/Mirisch (Norman Jewison)

▤ ◎

Russian submariners make a forced landing on a Connecticut holiday island and cause panic.

'Daring' cold war comedy which turns out to be of the most elementary and protracted nature, saved from boredom only by a few cameos.

w William Rose *novel* The Off-Islanders *by* Nathaniel Benchley d Norman Jewison ph Joseph Biroc m Johnny Mandel

☆ Carl Reiner, Eva Marie Saint, Alan Arkin, John Phillip Law, Paul Ford, Tessie O'Shea, Brian Keith, Jonathan Winters, Theodore Bikel, Ben Blue

'Rather amiable, though the film, like its title, seems to repeat most things twice.' – *Sight and Sound*

♟ best picture; William Rose; Alan Arkin

Russicum

Italy 1987 112m colour Cinemascope

Columbia TriStar/TigerCinematographica/RAI/Mario Cecchi Gori, Vittorio Cecchi Gori

▤

Investigating the death of an American nun in Rome, a diplomat discovers a plot to prevent the Pope visiting Russia.

Dull, lifeless thriller in which it becomes difficult to discover who is doing what to whom.

w Valerio Riva, Robert Balchus, Pasquale Squitieri *novel* I Mercedi del Diavolo *by* Enzo Russo d Pasquale Squitieri ph Giuseppe Tinelli m Renato Serio ad Emilio Baldelli ed Mauro Bonanni

☆ F. Murray Abraham, Treat Williams, Danny Aiello, Rita Rusic, Luigi Montini, Robert Balchus, Nigel Court, Leopoldo Mastelloni, Rossano Brazzi

'Clearly destined to drop straight into the dustiest oubliette in film history.' – *Tom Milne, MFB*

Rustler's Rhapsody *

US 1985 88m Metrocolor Panavision

Paramount/Impala/Tesauro (David Giler, Walter Hill)

▥ ▤ ◎

A 'B' Western hero of 1940s movies copes with a more modern and colourful world where life is no longer a matter of simple black and white.

An affectionate parody of cowboy clichés, though the joke begins to wear thin before the final shoot-out.

---

wd Hugh Wilson ph José Luis Alcaine m Steve Dorff pd Gil Parrondo ed John Victor Smith ☆ Tom Berenger, G. W. Bailey, Marilu Henner, Fernando Rey, Andy Griffith, Sela Ward

'Love betrayed them – power destroyed them!'
Ruthless *
US   1948   104m   bw
Eagle Lion/Arthur S. Lyons
📼

A conniver breaks several lives on his way to the top.
Rich melodrama with some entertaining moments.
w S. K. Lauren, Gordon Kahn *novel* Prelude to Night by Dayton Stoddert d Edgar G. Ulmer ph Bert Glennon m Werner Janssen
☆ Zachary Scott, Sydney Greenstreet, Diana Lynn, Louis Hayward, Martha Vickers, Lucille Bremer, Edith Barrett, Raymond Burr, Dennis Hoey

'Beginning pictures at the end
Is, I'm afraid, the modern trend.
But I'd find *Ruthless* much more winning
If it could end at the beginning.' – C. A. *Lejeune*

Ruthless People *
US   1986   93m   DeLuxe
Touchstone/Silver Screen Partners II/Wagner-Lancaster
📼 ▦ ℚ⌇ ᴖ

Comic kidnappers find they have on their hands a troublesome woman whose husband won't pay for her return.
Raucous comedy which packs a few good laughs before wearing out its welcome.
w Dale Launer d Jim Abrahams, David and Jerry Zucker ph Jan DeBont m Michel Colombier
☆ Danny DeVito, Bette Midler, Judge Reinhold, Helen Slater, Anita Morris, Bill Pullman

RX Murder
GB   1958   85m   bw   Cinemascope
TCF
aka: *Family Doctor*
The doctor of a small seaside resort has had four wives die on him. Could it be murder?
Modest mystery with an obvious outcome.
wd Derek Twist *novel* The Deeds of Dr Deadcert by Joan Fleming ph Arthur Grant m John Wooldridge
☆ Marius Goring, Rick Jason, Lisa Gastoni, Mary Merrall, Vida Hope, Phyllis Neilson-Terry, Frederick Leister, Nicholas Hannen

Ryan's Daughter **
GB   1970   206m   Metrocolor   Panavision 70
MGM/Faraway (Anthony Havelock-Allan)
📼 ▦ ℚ⌇ ᴖ

1916 Ireland: a village schoolmaster's wife falls for a British officer.
A modestly effective pastoral romantic melodrama, stretched on the rack of its director's meticulous film-making technique and unnecessarily big budget. A beautiful, impressive, well-staged and well-acted film but not really four hours' worth of drama.
w Robert Bolt d David Lean ph Frederick A. Young m Maurice Jarre pd Stephen Grimes (who created an entire village)
☆ Sarah Miles, Robert Mitchum, Chris Jones, John Mills, Trevor Howard, Leo McKern
'Instead of looking like the money it cost to make, the film feels like the time it took to shoot.' – *Alexander Walker*
'Gush made repectable by millions of dollars tastefully wasted.' – *Pauline Kael*
🏆 Frederick A. Young; John Mills
⚐ Sarah Miles

S.F.W. *

US 1994 96m Eastmancolor
Rank/A&M/Propaganda (Dale Pollock)
⬜ ⬜ @. ⊙

A fast-food chef becomes a celebrity because of his cool reaction to surviving being taken hostage by a terrorist group: 'So fucking what?'
Sharp and cynical drama of empty lives and the media that consume them.
w Danny Rubin, Jefery Levy d Jefery Levy ph Peter Deming m Graeme Revell pd Eve Cauley ed Lauren Zuckerman
☆ Stephen Dorff, Reese Witherspoon, Jake Busey, Joey Lauren Adams, Pamela Gidley, David Barry Gray
'Levy's message creaks with typical Generation X griping. But as contrived as it may be, he hits many of the right buttons.' – *Empire*

S.I.S. – Extreme Justice: see *Extreme Justice*

S.O.B.

US 1981 121m Metrocolor Panavision
Lorimar/Geoffrey (Blake Edwards, Tony Adams)
⬜ @.

A Hollywood director goes bananas when his much-touted epic is a fiasco, and decides to remake it as a sex picture.
Tasteless, vulgar and unfunny comedy, with everybody shouting at once and most of the jokes about vomiting, farting and funerals. Julie Andrews, who is made to bare her breasts, could surely use it as grounds for divorce.
wd Blake Edwards ph Harry Stradling Jnr m Henry Mancini
☆ Julie Andrews, Richard Mulligan, Robert Preston, William Holden, Robert Vaughn, Robert Webber, Larry Hagman, Shelley Winters, Marisa Berenson, Loretta Swit, Craig Stevens, Robert Loggia
'One feels that this in-house comedy was in some way intended as a purge and not an entertainment.' – *John Pym, MFB*
'At best the humour is cheap and at worst unnecessarily vulgar.' – *Margaret Hinxman, Daily Mail*
† S.O.B., it seems, stands no longer for Son of a Bitch but for Standard Operational Bullshit.

S*P*Y*S

GB 1974 100m Technicolor
Dymphana/C-W/American Film Properties (Irwin Winkler, Robert Chartoff)
⬜

Clumsy CIA agents in Paris come across a list of KGB agents in China.
Surprisingly dull and unfashionable parade of comic spy clichés; the talents involved obviously intended something closer to M*A*S*H.
w Malcolm Marmorstein, Lawrence J. Cohen, Fred Freeman d Irvin Kershner ph Gerry Fisher m John Scott
☆ Elliott Gould, Donald Sutherland, Zouzou, Joss Ackland, Kenneth Griffith, Vladek Sheybal
'Seems to have arrived several years too late to find its true niche.' – *Sight and Sound*

Saadia

US 1953 87m Technicolor
MGM (Albert Lewin)

A young French doctor in the Sahara has trouble with the local witch doctor.
Pretentious and ill-considered multi-national romance from the champion of Omar's Rubaiyat.
wd Albert Lewin novel Echec au Destin by Francis D'Autheville ph Christopher Challis m Bronislau Kaper
☆ Cornel Wilde, Mel Ferrer, Rita Gam, Michel Simon, Wanda Rotha, Cyril Cusack, Marcel Poncin, Peter Bull

Sabata *(dubbed)* *

Italy 1969 106m Technicolor Techniscope
UA/PEA/Delphos (Alberto Grimaldi)
⬜ ⬜

original title: *Ehi, Amico ... C'e Sabata, Hai Chiuso*
An inventive bounty hunter attempts to find the brains behind a bank robbery.
Stylish over-the-top spaghetti Western.
w Gianfranco Parolini, Renato Izzo d Frank Kramer (Gianfranco Parolini) ph Sandro Mancori m Marcello Giombini ad Carlo Simi ed Edmondo Lozzi
☆ Lee Van Cleef, William Berger, Franco Ressel, Linda Veras, Pedro Sanchez (Ignazio Spalla), Gianni Rizzo
'A certain cold-blooded ingenuity provides a substitute for inspiration in this colourful but extended anthology of Italian Western clichés.' – *Richard Combs, MFB*
† The film was followed by two sequels, *The Bounty Hunters* and *Return of Sabata* (qqv).

Sabotage ***

GB 1936 76m bw
Gaumont British (Michael Balcon, Ivor Montagu)
⬜ ⬜

US title: *A Woman Alone*
The proprietor of a small London cinema is a dangerous foreign agent.
Unattractively plotted but fascinatingly detailed Hitchcock suspenser with famous sequences and a splendidly brooding melodramatic atmosphere.
w Charles Bennett, Ian Hay, Helen Simpson, E. V. H. Emmett novel The Secret Agent by Joseph Conrad d Alfred Hitchcock ph Bernard Knowles md Louis Levy
☆ Oscar Homolka, Sylvia Sidney, John Loder, Desmond Tester, Joyce Barbour, Matthew Boulton
'Tightly packed, economical, full of invention and detail.' – *NFT, 1961*
'The cleverest picture Alfred Hitchcock has made since the arrival of the talkies. It is also, to me, the least likeable of them all ... Discreet directors don't kill schoolboys and dogs in omnibuses. Believe me, it isn't done.' – *C. A. Lejeune*

Sabotage

Canada 1996 99m colour
Imperial/Applecreek (Andy Emilio)

An FBI agent and a bodyguard discover corruption and cover-ups when they investigate the murder of a senator.
Routine action fodder, with a typically paranoid plot that makes little sense but provides opportunities for gunfights and explosions.
w Rick Filon, Michael Stokes d Tibor Takacs ph Curtis Petersen m Guy Zerafa pd Ian Hall ed Craig Nisker
☆ Mark Dasascos, Carrie Anne Moss, Graham Greene, Tony Todd, John Neville, Heidi Von Palleske, James Purcell

Saboteur ***

US 1942 108m bw
Universal (Frank Lloyd, Jack H. Skirball)
⬜ @.

A war worker unjustly suspected of sabotage flees across the country and unmasks a spy ring.
Flawed Hitchcock action thriller, generally unsatisfactory in plot and pace but with splendid sequences at a ball, in Radio City Music Hall, and atop the Statue of Liberty.
w Peter Viertel, Joan Harrison, Dorothy Parker story Alfred Hitchcock d Alfred Hitchcock ph Joseph Valentine m Frank Skinner md Charles Previn
☆ Robert Cummings, Priscilla Lane, Otto Kruger, Alan Baxter, Alma Kruger, Norman Lloyd
'It throws itself forward so rapidly that it allows slight opportunity for looking back.' – *New York Times*

'The drama of a nation stirred to action, of a people's growing realization of themselves and their responsibilities.' – *Motion Picture Herald*
† Hitchcock wanted for the three leading roles Gary Cooper, Barbara Stanwyck and Harry Carey, but all refused or were unavailable.

'World War II espionage adventure and human lives have never before been combined so explosively!'
The Saboteur, Code Name Morituri *

US 1965 122m bw
TCF/Arcola/Colony (Aaron Rosenberg)
⬜

aka: *Morituri*
aka: *The Saboteur*
In 1942 a German pacifist working for the allies is actually a German spy.
Dreary as a whole, suspenseful in snatches, this shipboard melodrama is full of irrelevancies and is in any case played much more seriously than the matter demands.
w Daniel Taradash novel Werner Jeorg Kosa d Bernhard Wicki ph Conrad Hall m Jerry Goldsmith
☆ Yul Brynner, Marlon Brando, Trevor Howard, Janet Margolin
⍟ Conrad Hall

The Sabre and the Arrow: see *Last of the Comanches*

Sabre Jet

US 1953 96m Cinecolor
Krueger Productions/UA

A US Air Force colonel in Korea has trouble with his career-hunting wife as well as with the enemy.
Propaganda cheapie with a few stirring aerial moments.
w Dale Eunson, Katherine Albert d Louis King ph Charles Van Enger m Herschel Burke Gilbert
☆ Robert Stack, Coleen Gray, Richard Arlen, Julie Bishop, Leon Ames, Amanda Blake

Sabrina *

US 1954 113m bw
Paramount (Billy Wilder)
⬜ ⬜ @.

GB title: *Sabrina Fair*
The chauffeur's daughter is wooed by both her brother employers.
Superior comedy, rather uneasily cast.
w Billy Wilder play Samuel Taylor d Billy Wilder ph Charles Lang Jnr m Frederick Hollander ad Hal Pereira, Walter Tyler
☆ Humphrey Bogart, William Holden, Audrey Hepburn, Walter Hampden, John Williams, Martha Hyer, Joan Vohs, Marcel Dalio
'This is never less than a glittering entertainment, but somehow a certain measure of lead has found its way into the formula.' – *Time*
† Cary Grant was sought for the role played by Bogart.
⍟ Billy Wilder (as writer and director); Charles Lang Jnr; Audrey Hepburn; art direction

'You are cordially invited to the most surprising merger of the year.'
Sabrina

US 1995 127m DeLuxe
UIP/Paramount/Constellation/Mirage/Sandollar (Sydney Pollack, Scott Rudin)
⬜ ⬜ @. ⊙

A chauffeur's daughter is loved by both a playboy and his workaholic millionaire brother.
A waste of effort for all concerned: the story seems tired, the performances are inferior, the romance and comedy have been dissipated, and there is very little left to engage the attention, other than to wonder why anyone should want to remake the Wilder version.
w Barbara Benedek, David Rayfiel play Samuel Taylor d Sydney Pollack ph Giuseppe Rotunno

m John Williams pd Brian Morris ed Frederic Steinkamp
☆ Harrison Ford, Julia Ormond, Greg Kinnear, Nancy Marchand, John Wood, Richard Crenna, Angie Dickinson, Lauren Holly, Fanny Ardant
'Has plenty of innocent pleasure to impart in a time when movies tend to appeal to our basic instincts, and satisfyingly fills in the emotional holes left by the original.' – *Ian Nathan, Empire*
⍟ John Williams; song 'Moonlight' (mJohn Williams, lyAlan and Marilyn Bergman)

Sabrina Fair: see *Sabrina*

The Sacred Flame: see *The Right to Live*

The Sacrifice *

Sweden 1986 149m Eastmancolor/bw
Swedish Film Institute/SVT2/Film Four/Argos/Sandrew/Josephson & Nykvist (Katinka Farago)
⬜ ⬜ @. ⊙

original title: *Offret*
A writer, who dreams that a nuclear war has begun, promises God that he will renounce his home, his family and speech if the world can return to normal.
A brilliantly filmed but obscure and confusing parable that does not easily yield its meaning.
wd Andrei Tarkovsky ph Sven Nykvist m J. S. Bach, folk music ad Anna Asp ed Andrei Tarkovsky, Michel Leszczylowski
☆ Erland Josephson, Susan Fleetwood, Valerie Mairesse, Allan Edwall, Gudrün Gísladóttir, Sven Wollter, Filippa Franzén
⍟ best foreign film

Sacrificed Youth *

China 1985 96m colour
Artificial Eye/Peking Youth Studio (Zhao Yamin)
original title: *Quingchun Ji*
During the Cultural Revolution, a young student is sent from her family in the city to work on a remote farm.
Touching, quietly elegant account of a girl growing to adulthood.
wd Zhang Nuanxin story There Was That Beautiful Place by Zhang Manling ph My Deyuan, Deng Wei m Liu Suola, Qu Xiaosong pd Li Yonxin, Wang Yanjin ed Zhao Qihua
☆ Li Fengxu, Feng Yuanzheng, Song Tao, Guo Jianguo, Yu Da

The Sad Sack

US 1957 98m bw Vistavision
Paramount (Paul Nathan)
⬜

Adventures of an army misfit.
Resistible star comedy.
w Edmund Beloin, Nate Monaster cartoon George Baker d George Marshall ph Loyal Griggs m Walter Scharf
☆ Jerry Lewis, David Wayne, Phyllis Kirk, Peter Lorre, Joe Mantell, Gene Evans, George Dolenz, Liliane Montevecchi, Shepperd Strudwick

Saddle the Wind *

US 1958 84m Metrocolor Cinemascope
MGM (Armand Deutsch)

A reformed gunman's young brother gets into bad company.
Modestly effective, humourless Western drama.
w Rod Serling d Robert Parrish ph George J. Folsey m Elmer Bernstein ad William J. Horning, Malcolm Brown ed John McSweeney Jnr
☆ Robert Taylor, John Cassavetes, Julie London, Donald Crisp, Charles McGraw, Royal Dano, Richard Erdman

---

Saddle Tramp

US 1950 76m Technicolor
Universal-International

A wandering cowboy adopts four orphan children and after various adventures marries the eldest of them.

Mild family Western for star-fanciers.

w Harold Shumate d Hugo Fregonese ph Charles Boyle m Joseph Gershenson

☆ Joel McCrea, Wanda Hendrix, John Russell, John McIntire, Jeanette Nolan, Russell Simpson

Sadie McKee *

US 1934 88m bw
MGM (Lawrence Weingarten)

A maid at various times loves her master, a young ne'er-do-well, and a middle-aged millionaire.

Solidly carpentered millgirl's romance of the period.

w John Meehan story Vina Delmar d Clarence Brown ph Oliver T. Marsh m William Axt

☆ Joan Crawford, Franchot Tone, Gene Raymond, Edward Arnold, Esther Ralston, Jean Dixon, Leo Carrillo, Akim Tamiroff

'The stuff the fans cry for.' – *Hollywood Reporter*

Sadie Thompson *

US 1928 95m bw silent
Gloria Swanson

In the South Seas, a fire-and-brimstone missionary is attracted to a prostitute.

Steamy, much-filmed melodrama (see Rain, Miss Sadie Thompson). This version has long been unavailable for revaluation.

w C. Gardner Sullivan story Rain by W. Somerset Maugham d Raoul Walsh ph George Barnes, Robert Kurrle ad William Cameron Menzies

☆ Gloria Swanson, Lionel Barrymore, Blanche Frederici, Charles Lane, Florence Midgley, Raoul Walsh

'It's stirring and ironic and funny. You couldn't ask more.' – *Photoplay*

⅋ George Barnes; Gloria Swanson

Sadisterotica (dubbed)

Germany/Spain 1967 80m colour
Aquila/Montana (Adrian Hoven)

aka: *Red Lips*
aka: *Rote Lippen*

A female private detective, hired to find a missing woman, discovers that her disappearance is linked to a reclusive artist.

Ridiculous thriller, poorly acted and directed, and badly dubbed; the disjointed narrative may be caused by cuts to remove some of its moments of nudity or could be due to the director's usual incompetence.

w Luis Revenga, Jesus Franco d Jesus Franco ph Jorge Herrero, Franz Hofer m Jerry Van Rooyen ad Carlos Viudes, Graf Pilati

☆ Janine Renauld, Rossana Yanni, Chris Howland, Alexander Engel, Marcello Arriota, Manuel Otero, Adrian Hoven

'Her hungry heart beat to tom-tom rhythm!'

Safari

US 1940 82m bw
Paramount (Anthony Veiller)

A disillusioned girl goes to Africa with her sportsman fiancé, but falls for the hired white hunter.

We had heard that before, even in 1940. Moderate time-passer.

w Delmer Daves story Paul Hervey Fox d Edward H. Griffith

☆ Douglas Fairbanks Jnr, Madeleine Carroll, Tullio Carminati, Billy Gilbert, Muriel Angelus, Lynne Overman

Safari

GB 1956 91m Technicolor Cinemascope
Warwick (Adrian Worker)

A white hunter falls in love with the wife of his employer and luckily the latter is killed by the Mau Mau.

Feeble adventure story exploiting political tensions.

w Anthony Veiller d Terence Young ph John Wilcox, Fred Ford, Ted Moore m William Alwyn

☆ Victor Mature, Janet Leigh, Roland Culver, John Justin, Earl Cameron, Liam Redmond, Orlando Martins

'In the 21st Century Nobody Is...'

Safe **

US 1995 118m colour
Metro Tartan/American Playhouse/Chemical/Good Machine/Kardana/Channel 4/Arnold Semler (Christine Vachon, Lauren Zalaznick)

A house-proud housewife begins to develop allergies to most aspects of modern life and moves to a New Age desert refuge for the chemically sensitive.

A studiously detached account of the effects on an individual of a mysterious ailment, which may simply be life itself; beneath its placid surface, it packs an unexpected power.

wd Todd Haynes ph Alex Nepomniaschy m Ed Tomney pd David Bomba ed James Lyons

☆ Julianne Moore, Xander Berkeley, Dean North, Julie Burgess, Ronnie Farer, Jodie Markell

'The film's neutral tone isn't easy, but it makes for a movie that is exceptional in both style and content and it addresses pressing problems with very considerable intelligence and skill.' – *Derek Malcolm, Guardian*

Safe Men

US 1998 88m Technicolor
UIP/Andell/Blue Guitar (Andrew Hauptman, Ellen Bonfman, Jeffrey Clifford, Jonathan Cohen)

Gangsters recruit two layabouts, mistaking them for expert safe-breakers.

A jokey blend of crime caper and romantic comedy, lightweight but occasionally amusing.

wd John Hamburg ph Michael Barrett m Theodore Shapiro pd Anthony Gasparro ed Suzanne Pillsbury, Scott Smith

☆ Sam Rockwell, Steve Zahn, Mark Ruffalo, Josh Pais, Paul Giamatti, Michael Schmidt, Christina Kirk, Harvey Fierstein, Michael Lerner

'Tepid tangle of half-baked buffoonery.' – *Alan Jones, Film Review*

Safe Passage

US 1994 96m DeLuxe
Entertainment/Pacific Western (Gale Anne Hurd)

Six sons and their estranged father gather at their mother's home when they fear that their brother, a Marine, may have been killed in an explosion in the Sinai Desert.

A domestic drama that follows a familiar and well-trodden path, really never rising above the level of soap opera, though the cast do their best to make it all seem fresh and original.

w Deena Goldstone novel Ellyn Bache d Robert Allan Ackerman ph Ralf Bode m Mark Isham pd Dan Bishop ed Rick Shaine

☆ Susan Sarandon, Sam Shepard, Robert Sean Leonard, Sean Astin, Marcia Gay Harden, Nick Stahl, Jason London, Matt Keeslar, Philip Bosco

'Aside from a few nicely tetchy scenes, there is nothing in this lugubrious film worth committing to.' – *Geoff Brown, The Times*

The Safecracker

GB 1958 96m bw
MGM/Coronado (David E. Rose)

A safecracker is released to help in a commando raid during World War II.

One-twelfth of a dirty dozen, with a long indecisive lead-up and not much pull as drama or comedy.

w Paul Monash story Rhys Davies d Ray Milland ph Gerald Gibbs m Richard Rodney Bennett ed Ernest Walter

☆ Ray Milland, Barry Jones, Jeanette Sterke, Victor Maddern, Ernest Clark, Cyril Raymond, Melissa Stribling

Safety Last ***

US 1923 70m bw silent
Harold Lloyd

A small-town boy goes to the big city and to impress his girlfriend enters a contest to climb a skyscraper.

Marvellous star comedy which set a new standard not only in sight gags but in the comedy-thrill stunts which became Lloyd's stock-in-trade.

w Harold Lloyd, Sam Taylor, Tim Whelan, Hal Roach d Sam Taylor, Fred Newmeyer ph Walter Lundin

☆ Harold Lloyd, Mildred Davis, Noah Young

The Saga of Anatahan

Japan 1953 90m bw
Daiwa

During the Pacific war, castaways on a remote island kill each other for the sake of one woman.

A curious footnote to its director's career, this mannered film is entirely in Japanese with English commentary, and does not recommend itself to western audiences.

m Akira Ifukube wd/ph Josef von Sternberg

The Saga of Hemp Brown

US 1958 80m colour CinemaScope
Universal (Gordon Kay)

A blameless cavalry lieutenant, dishonourably discharged from the army, sets out to track down the man who caused his disgrace.

Unoriginal western in which the confrontation between hero and villain is re-staged several times to diminishing effect.

w Bob Williams story Bernard Girard d Richard Carlson ph Philip Lathrop m Joseph Gershenson ad Alexander Golitzen, Robert E. Smith ed Tony Martinelli

☆ Rory Calhoun, Beverly Garland, John Larch, Russell Johnson, Fortunio Bonanova, Allan Lane, Morris Ankrum

Sagebrush Trail

US 1933 58m bw
Monogram/Lone Star (Paul Malvern)

Falsely imprisoned for murder, a cowboy escapes from jail to discover the real killer.

Routine Western with the occasional spectacular stunt.

w Lindsley Parsons d Armand Schaefer ph Archie Stout ed Carl Pierson

☆ John Wayne, Nancy Shubert, Lane Chandler, Yakima Canutt, Henry Hall, Wally Wales, Bob Burns

Sahara **

US 1943 97m bw
Columbia (Harry Joe Brown)

During the retreat from Tobruk a group of men of mixed nationality find water for themselves and harass the Nazis.

Good, simple war actioner with a realistic feel and strong characters deployed in melodramatic situations.

w John Howard Lawson, Zoltan Korda story Philip MacDonald d Zoltan Korda ph Rudolph Maté m Miklos Rozsa

☆ Humphrey Bogart, Bruce Bennett, Lloyd Bridges, Rex Ingram, J. Carrol Naish, Dan Duryea, Kurt Kreuger

'It borrows, chiefly from the English, a sort of light-alloy modification of realism which makes the traditional Hollywood idiom seem as obsolete as a minuet.' – *James Agee*

'The tank keeps rolling, picking up strays along the way until it has a full Hollywood ethnic complement.' – *Pauline Kael, 70s*

⅋ Rudolph Maté; J. Carrol Naish

Sahara

US 1984 111m Metrocolor
MGM-UA/Cannon (Menahem Golan, Yoram Globus)

In the 1920s, an heiress who competes in a trans-Sahara rally in a car made by her father's company is kidnapped by a lecherous Arab sheik.

Laughably bad and unoriginal romantic adventure, given a perfunctory treatment by all concerned.

w James R. Silke d Andrew V. McLaglen ph David Gurfinkel, Armando Nannuzzi m Ennio Morricone ad Luciano Spadoni ed Michael Duthie

☆ Brooke Shields, Lambert Wilson, Horst Buchholz, John Rhys-Davies, Ronald Lacey, John Mills, Steve Forrest

'Lamentably low on excitement, laughs and passion.' – *Variety*

Said O'Reilly to McNab

GB 1937 83m bw
Gainsborough

US title: *Sez O'Reilly to McNab*

A rich Scot is afflicted by an Irish con man.

Lively ethnic comedy, a good vehicle for two stars.

w Leslie Arliss, Marriott Edgar story Howard Irving Young d William Beaudine ph Arthur Crabtree

☆ Will Mahoney, Will Fyffe, Ellis Drake, Sandy McDougal

'Most hinterland exhibs have the quakes and headaches when it comes time on their sked to play a British film, but here's one, if sold along American lines, which may be found acceptable to the patrons in most places.' – *Variety*

'It's dynamite – when these two come together in the powderkeg city of the Far East!'

Saigon

US 1947 93m bw
Paramount (P. J. Wolfson)

Veteran airmen in Saigon are offered half a million to help in a robbery.

Tired studio-set star actioner.

w P. J. Wolfson, Arthur Sheekman d Leslie Fenton ph John Seitz m Robert Emmett Dolan

☆ Alan Ladd, Veronica Lake, Douglas Dick, Wally Cassell, Luther Adler, Morris Carnovsky, Mikhail Rasumny

Saigon

US 1988 102m colour
Fox (Alan Barnette)

aka: *Off Limits*

Two cops in Saigon track down a mass murderer of Vietnamese prostitutes.

Violent thriller for those with a boredom threshold as high as the body count.

w Christopher Crowe, Jack Thibeau d Christopher Crowe ph David Gribble m James Newton Howard pd Dennis Washington ed Douglas Ibold

☆ Willem Dafoe, Gregory Hines, Fred Ward, Amanda Pays, Scott Glenn, Kay Tong Lim, David Alan Grier

Saikaku Ichidai Onna: see *The Life of Oharu*

Sail a Crooked Ship

US 1961 88m bw
Columbia/Philip Barry Jnr

A shipowner unwittingly takes on a crew of crooks intending to use the boat as a getaway after a bank robbery.

Flimsy comedy sustained by a star comedian.

w Ruth Brooks Flippen, Bruce Geller novel Nathaniel Benchley d Irving Brecher ph Joseph Biroc m George Duning

☆ Robert Wagner, Ernie Kovacs, Dolores Hart, Carolyn Jones, Frank Gorshin

Sailing Along

GB 1938 90m bw
Gaumont-British (Michael Balcon)

A girl barge hand meets an impresario and becomes a dancing star.

Rather deadly British musical romance with the star not at her best, the supporting talents wasted, and a generally heavy hand in evidence.

wd Sonnie Hale ph Glen MacWilliams m/ly Arthur Johnston, Maurice Sigler ad Alfred Junge

☆ Jessie Matthews, Roland Young, Barry Mackay, Jack Whiting, Noel Madison, Alastair Sim, Athene Seyler, Frank Pettingell

Sailor Beware

US 1952 103m bw
Paramount/Hal B. Wallis

Martin and Lewis in the navy.

Unlovable star antics.

w James Allardice, Martin Rackin play Kenyon Nicholson, Charles Robinson d Hal Walker ph Daniel L. Fapp m Joseph J. Lilley

☆ Dean Martin, Jerry Lewis, Corinne Calvet, Marion Marshall, Robert Strauss, Leif Erickson

Sailor Beware *

GB 1956 80m bw
Romulus (Jack Clayton)

US title: *Panic in the Parlor*

A young sailor has trouble with his mother-in-law-to-be.

Plain but adequate film version of a successful lowbrow stage farce about an archetypal female dragon.

w Philip King, Falkland L. Cary play Philip King, Falkland L. Cary d Gordon Parry ph Douglas Slocombe m Peter Akister

☆ Peggy Mount, Esma Cannon, Cyril Smith, Shirley Eaton, Ronald Lewis

'It's the music-hall mother-in-law joke inflated to gigantic proportions.' – *Times*

The Sailor from Gibraltar

GB 1967 89m bw

Lopert (Oscar Lewenstein, Neil Hartley)

A mysterious woman searching for her lost lover meets a man determined to abandon his mistress.

A dry and unimaginative movie, with a good cast seemingly all at sea.

w Christopher Isherwood, Don Magner, Tony Richardson *novel* Marguerite Duras *d* Tony Richardson *ph* Raoul Coutard *m* Antoine Duhamel *ad* Marilena Aravantinou *ed* Anthony Gibbs

☆ Jeanne Moreau, Ian Bannen, Vanessa Redgrave, Zia Moyheddin, Hugh Griffith, Orson Welles, Eleanor Bron, John Hurt

Sailor of the King: see *Single-Handed*

The Sailor Takes a Wife

US 1945 91m bw

MGM

A sailor on leave gets married and finds he has acquired a few problems.

Rather self-consciously cute sentimental comedy, proficiently staged.

w Anne Chapin, Whitfield Cook *play* Chester Erskine *d* Richard Whorf

☆ June Allyson, Robert Walker, Reginald Owen, Hume Cronyn, Eddie Anderson, Audrey Totter, Gerald Oliver Smith

'He gave his soul to the sea and his heart to a woman! Their love will arouse you – their story will disturb you – the ending will startle you!'

'Like the act of love, this film must be experienced from beginning to end!'

The Sailor Who Fell from Grace with the Sea

GB 1976 105m Technicolor

AVCO/Sailor Company (Martin Poll)

A precocious boy interferes with his widowed mother's affair with a sailor by castrating the latter.

Weird and unattractive sex fantasy set in Dartmouth of all places and not helped by tiresome sex scenes.

wd Lewis John Carlino *novel* Gogo No Eiko by Yukio Mishima *ph* Douglas Slocombe *m* John Mandel

☆ Sarah Miles, Kris Kristofferson, Jonathan Kahn, Margo Cunningham, Earl Rhodes

'This everyday tale of torture, scopophilia, copulation, masturbation, dismemberment and antique dealing deserves to be traded back to the Japs and made required viewing for timorous kamikaze pilots.' – *Benny Green, Punch*

The Sailor's Return

GB 1978 100m colour

Euston Films

A Victorian seaman returns to his native village with a black bride, and opens a pub.

Lame-paced and highly predictable yarn of prejudice and doomed love, assembled with almost no cinematic flair.

w James Saunders *novel* David Garnett *d* Jack Gold

☆ Tom Bell, Shope Sodeinde, Elton Charles, Mick Ford, Clive Swift

† As a theatrical film it found no takers, and in GB was first shown on television in 1980.

Sailors Three **

GB 1940 86m bw

Ealing (Culley Forde)

US title: *Three Cockeyed Sailors*

Drunken sailors capture a German battleship by mistake.

Low service comedy which keeps moving, is brightly played and reaches a good standard. Sequel: Fiddlers Three (qv).

w Angus Macphail, John Dighton, Austin Melford *d* Walter Forde *ph* Gunther Krampf *md* Ernest Irving

☆ Tommy Trinder, Claude Hulbert, Michael Wilding, Carla Lehmann, Jeanne de Casalis, James Hayter, John Laurie

The Saint

Leslie Charteris's famous character, the reformed British gentleman crook who becomes a Robin Hood of crime, has been most popular in the long-running sixties TV series starring Roger Moore. *The film series (qqv) which featured him never seemed to hit quite the right note, and now seems slow. All were*

made for RKO, who later switched allegiance to THE FALCON (qv).

1938 The Saint in New York
1939 The Saint Strikes Back, The Saint in London
1940 The Saint's Double Trouble, The Saint Takes Over
1941 The Saint in Palm Springs, The Saint's Vacation, The Saint Meets the Tiger
1953 The Saint's Return (US: The Saint's Girl Friday)

Louis Hayward played the role in the first and last; Hugh Sinclair in Vacation and Tiger; George Sanders in the rest. In 1997, Val Kilmer starred in a big-budget remake, *The Saint* (qv), though the alienated character he portrayed bore little resemblance to Charteris's original.

The Saint

US 1997 116m Rank Colour

Paramount/Rysher (David Brown, Robert Evans, William J. MacDonald, Mace Neufeld)

🔲 🔲 ◉ 🎧

A millionaire crook, sent to obtain a formula for cheap energy, falls in love with the female research scientist who discovered it.

An action adventure that commits the unforgivable sin of being dull. There are attempts to reposition Charteris's suave hero as a man with a troubled past, in the manner of the modern version of Batman, and to turn him into another James Bond. Both fail, for while Kilmer's Saint is described as 'a master of disguise', he seems more a ham actor in search of a role.

w Jonathan Hensleigh, Wesley Strick *d* Phillip Noyce *ph* Phil Meheux *m* Graeme Revell *pd* Joseph Nemec III *ed* Terry Rawlings

☆ Val Kilmer, Elisabeth Shue, Rade Serbedzija, Valery Nikolaev, Henry Goodman, Alun Armstrong, Michael Byrne, Evgeny Lazarev, Irena Apeximova, Lev Prigunov, Charlotte Cornwell

'One unholy mess.' – *Sunday Times*

'With his array of comic voices and false moustaches, Kilmer would be more suited to a summer season at the Southend Cliffs Pavilion than a Hollywood movie.' – *Ryan Gilbey, Independent*

St Benny the Dip

US 1951 79m bw

Danzigers

GB title: *Escape If You Can*

Gamblers learn to escape the law by dressing as priests, but circumstance converts them to good works.

Unfunny comedy notable only for its cast.

w John Roeburt *d* Edgar G. Ulmer *ph* Don Malkames *m* Robert Stringer

☆ Freddie Bartholomew, Roland Young, Dick Haymes, Lionel Stander, Nina Foch

'The passion burns deep!'

St Elmo's Fire

US 1985 108m Metrocolor

Columbia/Lauren Shuler

🔲 🔲 ◉ 🎧

A group of college graduates drift apart as realities impinge on their lives.

Nobody explained why audiences should want to interest themselves in such a group of objectionable people; and they didn't.

w Joel Schumacher, Carl Kurlander *d* Joel Schumacher *ph* Stephen H. Burum *m* David Foster

☆ Rob Lowe, Demi Moore, Andrew McCarthy, Judd Nelson, Ally Sheedy, Emilio Estevez, Mare Winningham, Martin Balsam

The Saint in London

US 1939 72m bw

RKO (William Sistrom)

The Saint exposes a gang of forgers.

Amiable thriller, with Sanders coasting along with charm.

w Lynn Root, Frank Fenton *story* The Million Pound Day by Leslie Charteris *d* John Paddy Carstairs *ph* Claude Friese-Greene *m* Harry Acres *ad* Wilfred Arnold *ed* Douglas Robertson

☆ George Sanders, Sally Gray, David Burns, Gordon McLeod, Athene Seyler, Henry Oscar, John Abbott, Ballard Berkeley

The Saint in New York *

US 1938 71m bw

RKO (William Sistrom)

🔲

New York police ask the Saint for help in dealing with a crime wave.

Slick, enjoyable programmer, the success of which led to the series of films featuring the Saint, though Hayward only returned to the role for the last film in the sequence.

w Charles Kaufman, Mortimer Offner *novel* Leslie Charteris *d* Ben Holmes *ph* Joseph August, Frank Redman *ad* Van Nest Polglase, Perry Ferguson *ed* Harry Marker

☆ Louis Hayward, Kay Sutton, Sig Rumann, Jonathan Hale, Jack Carson, Paul Guilfoyle, Frederick Burton, Ben Welden

The Saint in Palm Springs

US 1941 65m bw

RKO (Howard Benedict)

The Saint, wanted for murder and in possession of some rare stamps, turns the tables on a criminal gang.

Undistinguished time-waster, with cast and director showing only scant enthusiasm for their tasks.

w Jerry Cady *story* Leslie Charteris *d* Jack Hively *ph* Harry Wild *m* Roy Webb *ad* Van Nest Polglase *ed* George Hively

☆ George Sanders, Wendy Barrie, Jonathan Hale, Paul Guilfoyle, Linda Hayes, Ferris Taylor, Harry Shannon, Eddie Dunn

'He's clean! He's mean! He's the go-between!'

St Ives

US 1976 93m Technicolor

Warner (Pancho Kohner, Stanley Canter)

🔲

An ex-police reporter gets involved in a complex murder puzzle.

Soporific suspenser with every tired situation in the book.

w Barry Beckerman *novel* The Procane Chronicle by Oliver Bleeck *d* J. Lee-Thompson *ph* Lucien Ballard *m* Lalo Schifrin

☆ Charles Bronson, Harry Guardino, John Houseman, Jacqueline Bisset, Maximilian Schell, Harris Yulin, Dana Elcar, Elisha Cook Jnr

'Much cross-cutting of the sort where the only events you care less about than the ones you cut from are the ones you cut to.' – *John Simon*

'People make love for so many crazy reasons – why shouldn't money be one of them?'

Saint Jack

US 1979 115m colour

New World/Shoals Creek/Playboy/Copa de Oro (Roger Corman)

🔲

An American wanderer in Singapore finds his metier as a pimp.

Whimsical, loquacious black comedy which failed to set its wavering director back on the firm ground he needed.

w Peter Bogdanovich, Howard Sackler, Paul Theroux *novel* Paul Theroux *d* Peter Bogdanovich *ph* Robby Muller *m* various

☆ Ben Gazzara, Denholm Elliott, James Villiers, Joss Ackland, Rodney Bewes, Mark Kingston, Lisa Lu, George Lazenby, Peter Bogdanovich

Saint Joan

GB 1957 110m bw

Wheel (Otto Preminger)

🔲 ◉

Glumly assembled screen version of the brilliantly argumentative play about the Maid of Orleans.

Plenty of talent, but neither wit nor style.

w Graham Greene *play* Bernard Shaw *d* Otto Preminger *ph* Georges Périnal *m* Mischa Spoliansky *pd* Roger Furse

☆ Jean Seberg, Anton Walbrook, Richard Widmark, John Gielgud, Felix Aylmer, Harry Andrews, Richard Todd

St Louis Blues *

US 1939 92m bw

Paramount (Jeff Lazarus)

A Broadway musical star finds new fame down south.

Moderate star entertainment with good guest artists.

w John C. Moffitt, Malcolm Stuart Boylan, Frederick Hazlitt Brennan *d* Raoul Walsh

ph Theodor Sparkuhl *songs* Frank Loesser, Burton Lane

☆ Dorothy Lamour, Lloyd Nolan, Tito Guizar, Jerome Cowan, Jessie Ralph, William Frawley, the King's Men, Matty Melneck and his Orchestra

'It doesn't quite jell but will suffice as passable divertissement.' – *Variety*

St Louis Blues

US 1958 93m bw VistaVision

Paramount (Robert Smith)

W. C. Handy, son of a black Memphis preacher, becomes a blues composer.

Unsurprising biopic with some good music and the usual strained plot about father's disapproval of the new music.

w Robert Smith, Ted Sherdeman *d* Allen Reisner *ph* Haskell Boggs *md* Nelson Riddle

☆ Nat King Cole, Eartha Kitt, Pearl Bailey, Cab Calloway, Mahalia Jackson, Ruby Dee, Juano Hernandez, Ella Fitzgerald

The St Louis Kid

US 1934 67m bw

Warner (Sam Bischoff)

GB title: *A Perfect Weekend*

A hot-headed truck driver takes the side of milk farmers in a trade dispute.

Modest star action comedy with a fair amount to amuse.

w Seton I. Miller, Warren Duff *d* Ray Enright *ph* Sid Hickox

☆ James Cagney, Patricia Ellis, Hobart Cavanaugh, Spencer Charters, Addison Richards

'Jimmy in another slugger role, with results this time not so satisfactory.' – *Variety*

St Martin's Lane *

GB 1938 85m bw

Mayflower (Erich Pommer)

🔲

US title: *Sidewalks of London*

A middle-aged busker falls in love with a brilliant girl dancer who becomes a star.

Well-made romantic drama with star performances and interesting theatrical background.

w Clemence Dane *d* Tim Whelan *ph* Jules Kruger *m* Arthur Johnston

☆ Charles Laughton, Vivien Leigh, Rex Harrison, Tyrone Guthrie, Larry Adler, Gus MacNaughton

'In its choice of subject, its overwhelming interest in character and its introspective, uncompromising treatment, it is experimental in a courageous fashion.' – *Film Weekly*

The Saint Meets the Tiger

US 1943 70m bw

RKO

The Saint is pitted against a resourceful gangster and gold smuggler.

Feeble little thriller with Sinclair proving an inadequate substitute for Sanders in the title role.

w Leslie Arliss, Wolfgang Wilhelm, James Seymour *novel* Meet the Tiger by Leslie Charteris *d* Paul L. Stein *ph* Robert Krasker *ad* Paul Sheriff *ed* Ralph Kemplen

☆ Hugh Sinclair, John Slater, Gordon McLeod, Clifford Evans, Wylie Watson, Charles Victor

The Saint of Fort Washington

US 1993 108m Technicolor

(David V. Picker, Nessa Hyams)

🔲 🔲 ◉

Two homeless people, a young schizophrenic drifter and a black Vietnam veteran, help each other survive on the streets.

A well-meaning but bland piece of escapism, romanticizing the dispossessed.

w Lyle Kessler *d* Tim Hunter *ph* Frederick Elmes *m* James Newton Howard *pd* Stuart Wurtzel *ed* Howard Smith

☆ Danny Glover, Matt Dillon, Rick Aviles, Nina Siemaszko, Joe Seneca, Ving Rhames

'The sort of worthy project big-name stars tackle to earn artistic and social brownie points between megabuck sequels.' – *Kim Newman, Empire*

The Saint Strikes Back

US 1939 67m bw

RKO (Robert Sisk)

🔲

The Saint goes to San Francisco to save the father of a female friend from being framed for murder.

◉ Digital Video Disc Region 2   ◉ Digital Video Disc Region 1   🎧 Soundtrack released on compact disc   ☆ Cast in approximate order of importance   † Points of interest   🎵 Notable songs   🏆 Academy Award   🏅 Academy Award nomination   🏆 BAFTA

Enjoyable minor thriller, which made the most of Sanders's world-weary charm.
w John Twist novel Angels of Doom by Leslie Charteris d John Farrow ph Frank Redman md Roy Webb ad Van Nest Polglase, Albert S. D'Agostino ed Jack Hively
☆ George Sanders, Barry Fitzgerald, Wendy Barrie, Jonathan Hale, Jerome Cowan, Edward Gargan

The Saint Takes Over
US 1940 69m bw
RKO (Howard Benedict)
The Saint comes to the aid of his friend, Inspector Fernack, who has been framed by crooked gamblers.
Pleasant, fast-moving, though undistinguished, little thriller.
w Lynn Root, Frank Fenton d Jack Hively ph Frank Redman md Roy Webb ad Van Nest Polglase ed Desmond Marquette
☆ George Sanders, Wendy Barrie, Jonathan Hale, Paul Guilfoyle, Morgan Conway

The St Valentine's Day Massacre
US 1967 99m DeLuxe Panavision
TCF/Los Altos (Roger Corman)
The twenties gang war between Al Capone and Bugs Moran.
The director's first big studio film is disappointing; stagey, poorly developed, unconvincing-looking and overacted.
w Howard Browne d Roger Corman ph Milton Krasner m Fred Steiner md Lionel Newman
☆ Jason Robards Jnr, George Segal, Ralph Meeker, Jean Hale, Clint Ritchie, Joseph Campanella, Richard Bakalyan, David Canary, Bruce Dern, Harold J. Stone, Kurt Kreuger, John Agar, Alex D'Arcy

'You'll love every illegal inch of 'em!'
The Sainted Sisters
US 1948 89m bw
Paramount (Richard Maibaum)
Two New York con girls find themselves taken in by the inhabitants of the small town in which they are hiding out.
Unfunny period comedy which misses on all cylinders.
w Harry Clork d William D. Russell ph Lionel Lindon m Van Cleave
☆ Veronica Lake, Joan Caulfield, Barry Fitzgerald, William Demarest, George Reeves, Beulah Bondi, Chill Wills, Darryl Hickman
'Lake, Caulfield, and a swarm of clichés, pleasantly kidded in a manner derived from Preston Sturges.' – James Agee

Saints and Sinners
GB 1948 85m bw
London Films/BLPA (Leslie Arliss)
An ex-convict comes back to his home town to prove that those who condemned him were fools or knaves.
Curious slice of Irish whimsy mixed with Ealing comedy; not very satisfactory.
w Paul Vincent Carroll, Leslie Arliss d Leslie Arliss ph Osmond Borradaile m Philip Green ad Wilfred Shingleton ed David Newhouse
☆ Kieron Moore, Christine Norden, Sheila Manahan, Michael Dolan, Maire O'Neill, Noel Purcell

The Saint's Double Trouble
US 1940 68m bw
RKO (Cliff Reid)
The Saint discovers that a jewel thief is his double.
Lacklustre thriller that fails to make much of Sanders playing both sides of the law.
w Ben Holmes story Leslie Charteris d Jack Hively ph J. Roy Hunt md Roy Webb ed Theron Warth
☆ George Sanders, Helene Whitney, Jonathan Hale, Bela Lugosi, Thomas W. Ross

The Saint's Girl Friday: see The Saint's Return

The Saint's Return
GB 1954 73m bw
RKO/Royal/Hammer (Anthony Hinds, Julian Lesser)
US title: The Saint's Girl Friday
The Saint goes after a gang of gamblers who have murdered a former girlfriend.

Effective programmer, though the concept was beginning to seem more than a little dated and old-fashioned.
w Allan MacKinnon d Seymour Friedman ph Walter Harvey m Ivor Slaney ad J. Elder Wills ed James Needs
☆ Louis Hayward, Naomi Chance, Sydney Tafler, Charles Victor, Jane Carr, Harold Lang, Diana Dors
† The US release ran for 68m.

The Saint's Vacation
US 1941 60m bw
RKO (William Sistrom)
Holidaying in Switzerland, the Saint outwits spies searching for a secret code.
Moderate thriller, though missing the piquancy that Sanders's personality added to the routine nature of the enterprise.
w Leslie Charteris, Jeffrey Dell novel Getaway by Leslie Charteris d Leslie Fenton ph Bernard Knowles md Bretton Byrd ad Paul Sheriff ed Al Barnes
☆ Hugh Sinclair, Sally Gray, Cecil Parker, Arthur Macrae, Leueen MacGrath, Felix Aylmer, Ivor Barnard

Saiyu-ki: see Alakazam the Great

Salaam Bombay! **
India/France/GB 1988 114m colour
Mainline/Mirabai Films/NFDC/Cadrage/La SEPT/Channel 4 (Mira Nair)
Street life in an Indian city among pimps, prostitutes, drug peddlers and addicts, as seen by a tea-boy abandoned by his mother.
Poignant, well-observed narrative of small treacheries and smaller hope, acted by a mainly amateur cast.
w Sooni Taraporevala d Mira Nair ph Sandi Sissel m L. Subramaniam pd Mitch Epstein ed Barry Alexander Brown
☆ Shafiq Syed, Raghubir Yadav, Nana Patekar, Irshad Hasni, Aneeta Kanwar, Hansa Vithal
'A notable debut.' – MFB

Le Salaire de la Peur: see The Wages of Fear

The Salamander
US/GB/Italy 1981 101m colour
Grade/William R. Foreman (Paul Maslansky)
A colonel in army intelligence thwarts a fascist takeover of Italy.
Lurid melodrama with an inane script.
w Robert Katz, Rod Serling novel Morris West d Peter Zinner ph Marcello Gatti m Jerry Goldsmith pd Giantito Burchiellaro ed Claudio Cutry
☆ Franco Nero, Anthony Quinn, Martin Balsam, Sybil Danning, Christopher Lee, Cleavon Little, Paul Smith, John Steiner, Claudia Cardinale, Eli Wallach

'For this woman men would commit every sin ... every sacrilege.'
Salambo
Italy 1959 95m DeLuxe Cinemascope
Fidès/Stella
aka: The Loves of Salammbo
The love affair between the daughter of a Carthaginian general and the leader of a mercenary army does not run smoothly.
A cut-price epic with an inadequate central performance.
w John Blamy, Barbara Schmers novel Salammbo by Gustave Flaubert d Sergio Grieco ph Piero Portalupi m Alexandre Derenevsky
☆ Jeanne Valérie, Edmund Purdom, Jacques Sernas, Arnoldo Foà, Kamala Devi, Charles Fawcett, Ricardo Garrone
† After the fiasco of Cleopatra, 20th Century-Fox abandoned its plans to produce a film of Flaubert's novel starring Gina Lollobrigida, and instead bought the rights to this production, which it released in 1962 in a version cut to 72m.

Salem's Lot: The Movie *
US 1979 112m colour Panavision
Warner/Serendipity Productions (Richard Kobritz)
A writer returns to his small hometown to discover that it is being taken over by vampires.

Effective horror movie, cut from a 200 minute two-part TV mini-series.
w Paul Monash novel Stephen King d Tobe Hooper ph Jules Brenner m Harry Sukman pd Mort Rabinowitz ed Carol Sax, Tom Pryor
☆ David Soul, James Mason, Lance Kerwin, Bonnie Bedelia, Lew Ayres, Julie Cobb, Elisha Cook, George Dzundza, Ed Flanders, Kenneth McMillan

Salesman **
US 1969 95m bw
Maysles Films
A team of salesmen, urged on by their aggressive manager, sell Bibles door to door to Catholics mostly reluctant to buy.
Fascinating cinema-verité documentary, especially in the contrast between the sales convention, with its sanctimonious hyperbole, and the actual experiences on the road.
d Albert and David Maysles, Charlotte Zwerin ph Albert Maysles ed David Maysles, Charlotte Zwerin
'The film tries to be at once tough and sentimental, mocking and sympathetic ... They have stumbled onto something much bigger than they realize: a condemnation – however fragmented, fortuitous, and even inept – of the human condition, of man himself; but also of a society plagued by superstition, idiotic competitiveness, and stultifying materialism.' – John Simon

Sally
US 1930 90m Technicolor
Warner
A waitress makes it to the lights of Broadway.
Lightweight musical play, previously filmed in 1925 with Colleen Moore and Leon Errol, here the basis of an elaborate colour production with its original star, who however did not take too kindly to the camera.
w Waldemar Young play Guy Bolton, Jerome Kern d John Francis Dillon ph Dev Jennings, E. E. Schoenbaum ch Larry Ceballos ad Jack Okey
☆ Marilyn Miller, Joe E. Brown, Alexander Gray, T. Roy Barnes, Pert Kelton, Ford Sterling
♫ Jack Okey

Sally and St Anne
US 1952 90m bw
U-I (Leonard Goldstein)
When an Irish-American family is threatened with eviction, the daughter appeals to St Anne for help.
Whimsical comedy, quite nimbly performed.
w James O'Hanlon, Herb Meadow d Rudolph Maté ph Irving Glassberg m Frank Skinner
☆ Ann Blyth, Edmund Gwenn, Hugh O'Brian, John McIntire, Jack Kelly

Sally in Our Alley *
GB 1931 77m bw
ATP/Basil Dean
Poor girl loves wounded soldier.
Early talkie drama with music which made Gracie Fields a star and gave her a theme song.
w Miles Malleson, Archie Pitt, Alma Reville play The Likes of 'Er by Charles McEvoy d Maurice Elvey ph Robert G. Martin, Alex Bryce
☆ Gracie Fields, Ian Hunter, Florence Desmond, Ivor Barnard
'The songs are just numbers, the general standard nothing to shout about.' – Variety

Sally, Irene and Mary
US 1938 86m bw
TCF (Gene Markey)
Three girls try to break into show business.
Simple-minded romantic comedy-musical, well enough done.
w Harry Tugend, Jack Yellen d William A. Seiter ph Peverell Marley md Arthur Lange
☆ Alice Faye, Tony Martin, Fred Allen, Jimmy Durante, Gregory Ratoff, Joan Davis, Marjorie Weaver, Gypsy Rose Lee
'Palatable light entertainment that is no Pulitzer prizer but prize b.o.' – Variety

Sally of the Sawdust
US 1925 78m bw silent
Paramount/United Artists
A circus juggler and faker tries to prevent his daughter from discovering that she is adopted.

Silent version of the stage hit Poppy, remade under its own title in 1936 (qv). In both versions W. C. Fields takes over the whole show (not to one's entire satisfaction) and the director's name in this case should not lead one to expect a film of significance, as he seems to have been glad of the work.
w Forrest Halsey play Dorothy Donnelly d D. W. Griffith
☆ W. C. Fields, Carol Dempster, Alfred Lunt, Effie Shannon, Erville Alderson

Salmonberries
Germany 1991 95m DeLuxe
Electric/PeleMele (Eleonore Adlon)
A mysterious and parentless young woman is attracted to a middle-aged German woman, working as a librarian in a small Alaskan mining town.
A somewhat glum and claustrophobic account of thwarted lives.
w Percy Adlon, Felix O. Adlon d Percy Adlon ph Tom Sigel m Bob Telson pd Amadeus Capra ed Conrad Gonzalez
☆ k. d. lang, Rosel Zech, Chuck Connors, Jane Lind, Oscar Kawagley, Wolfgang Steinberg, Christel Merian
'An exhaustingly slow-moving tale which makes for trying viewing.' – Empire

Salo: see 120 Days of Sodom

Salome
US 1923 80m bw silent
Nazimova
Almost unendurable as an entertainment, this stylized silent provided a famous role for its star against backgrounds in Aubrey Beardsley style, and is much illustrated in film histories. The New Yorker commented on a 1980 revival: 'The movie looks better in stills than when one actually sees it, but a folly like this should probably be experienced.'
play Oscar Wilde drawings Aubrey Beardsley d Charles Bryant ad Natacha Rambova cos Natacha Rambova
☆ Nazimova, Mitchell Lewis, Nigel de Brulier

'The supreme screen achievement of our time!'
Salome
US 1953 103m Technicolor
Columbia/Beckworth (Buddy Adler)
Princess Salome of Galilee eludes her licentious stepfather, falls in love with a secret Christian, and leaves home when her dancing fails to save the life of John the Baptist.
Distorted biblical hokum with an interesting cast frozen into unconvincing attitudes.
w Harry Kleiner, Jesse Lasky Jnr d William Dieterle ph Charles Lang m George Duning md Daniele Amfitheatrof ad John Meehan
☆ Rita Hayworth, Charles Laughton, Stewart Granger, Judith Anderson, Cedric Hardwicke, Alan Badel, Basil Sydney, Maurice Schwartz, Rex Reason, Arnold Moss
'Pomp and splendour are paraded across the screen as a background to the story's combination of sex and religion.' – Variety

Salome Where She Danced *
US 1945 90m Technicolor
Universal (Walter Wanger, Alexander Golitzen)
During the Austro-Prussian war a dancer is suspected of being a spy and flees to Arizona, where she affects the lives of the citizenry.
Absurdly plotted and stiffly played romantic actioner whose sheer creakiness made it a minor cult film.
w Laurence Stallings story Michael J. Phillips d Charles Lamont ph Hal Mohr, W. Howard Green m Edward Ward
☆ Yvonne de Carlo, Rod Cameron, Albert Dekker, David Bruce, Walter Slezak, Marjorie Rambeau, J. Edward Bromberg, Abner Biberman, John Litel, Kurt Katch
'I gratefully salute it as the funniest dead-pan parody I have ever seen.' – James Agee

Salome's Last Dance
GB 1987 90m Technicolor
Vestron/Jolly Russell Productions (Penny Corke)
Oscar Wilde watches a production of his banned play, Salome, acted by prostitutes in a brothel.

Coarse and clumsy treatment, all excess and no moderation, though some found it entertaining.
wd Ken Russell play Salome by Oscar Wilde ph Harvey Harrison md Richard Cooke, Ray Beckett ad Michael Buchanan ed Timothy Gee
☆ Glenda Jackson, Stratford Johns, Nickolas Grace, Douglas Hodge, Imogen Millais-Scott, Denis Lill, Ken Russell
'An outstanding film marking a new career bent for film-maker Russell.' – *Variety*

Salon Kitty

France/Germany/Italy 1978 127m colour
TCF/Coralta/S.R.L./Cinema Seven (Giulio Barigia, Ermanno Donati)
🔲
In 1939, a Nazi army officer takes over a Berlin brothel and installs spying devices and prostitutes loyal to the party to report on their clients.
A voyeuristic movie with a gloating nastiness about it that is thoroughly dislikeable.
w Ennio de Concini, Maria Pia Fusco, Tinto Brass d Tinto Brass ph Silvano Ippoliti m Fiorenzo Caspi pd Ken Adam ed Luciana di Russo, Fiorenza Muller
☆ Helmut Berger, Ingrid Thulin, Teresa Ann Savoy, Bekim Fehmiu, John Ireland, Tina Aumont

Saloon Bar *

GB 1940 76m bw
Ealing (Michael Balcon)
A murder is solved during an evening in a pub.
Amusing, well-made little suspenser from a West End success.
w Angus MacPhail, John Dighton play Frank Harvey d Walter Forde ph Ronald Neame md Ernest Irving
☆ Gordon Harker, Elizabeth Allen, Mervyn Johns, Joyce Barbour, Anna Konstam, Judy Campbell, Norman Pierce, Alec Clunes, Felix Aylmer, Mavis Villiers, Torin Thatcher, O. B. Clarence
'The detail has been sought lovingly and with exactitude … this is a modest and endearing film.' – *New Statesman*

Salsa

US 1988 99m TVC Color
Cannon/Menahem Golan, Yoram Globus
🔲 ◎⌐
A motor mechanic is determined to become the best salsa dancer.
A few energetic dance routines break up a weak narrative and some sub-standard acting.
w Boaz Davidson, Tomas Benitez, Shepherd Goldman story Boaz Davidson, Eli Tabor d Boaz Davidson ph David Gurfinkel pd Mark Hastings ed Alain Jakubowicz
☆ Robby Rosa, Rodney Harvey, Magali Alvarado, Miranda Garrison, Moon Orona, Angela Alvarado, Loyda Ramos, Valente Rodriguez

Salt and Pepper

GB 1968 101m DeLuxe
UA/Chrislaw/Tracemark (Milton Ebbins)
Soho night-club proprietors solve a murder.
Infuriating throwaway star vehicle in the dregs of swinging London. The two stars teamed up again in an even worse film, One More Time (1970).
w Michael Pertwee d Richard Donner ph Ken Higgins m Johnny Dankworth
☆ Sammy Davis Jnr, Peter Lawford, Michael Bates, Ilona Rodgers, John Le Mesurier, Graham Stark, Ernest Clark

Salt on Our Skin

Germany/France/Canada 1992 106m colour
Warner/Neue Constantin/Torii/Telescene/RTL Plus/Canal (Bernd Eichinger, Martin Moszkowicz)
🔲
A sophisticated half-French woman remembers a youthful love affair in Scotland with the son of a local farmer, which she resumed a decade later.
A dull romantic drama of minimal interest and credibility.
w Andrew Birkin, Bee Gilbert novel Les Vaisseaux du Coeur by Benoîte Groult d Andrew Birkin ph Dietrich Lohmann m Klaus Doldinger pd Jean-Baptiste Tard, Robert Laing ed Dagmar Hirtz
☆ Greta Scacchi, Vincent D'Onofrio, Anais Jeanneret, Hanns Zischler, Barbara Jones, Rolf Illic, Petra Berndt, László Kish, Claudine Auger
'An old-fashioned weepie.' – *Variety*

Salt to the Devil: see *Give Us This Day*

Salty O'Rourke

US 1945 100m bw
Paramount/E. D. Leshin
A racetrack con man is reformed by a schoolteacher.
Very moderate and overlong star vehicle.
w Milton Holmes d Raoul Walsh ph Theodor Sparkuhl m Robert Emmett Dolan
☆ Alan Ladd, Gail Russell, William Demarest, Bruce Cabot, Spring Byington, Stanley Clements
♪ Milton Holmes

Saludos Amigos *

🎥🎥 US 1943 43m Technicolor
Walt Disney
🔲
Donald Duck has various South American adventures with a parrot named Joe Carioca.
Basically a naïve implementation of the good neighbour policy, but with flashes of brilliant animation and some mingling of live-action with cartoon.
production supervisor Norman Ferguson
'Self-interested, belated ingratiation embarrasses me, and Disney's famous cuteness, however richly it may mirror national infantilism, is hard on my stomach.' – *James Agee*
♪ music (Edward H. Plumb, Paul J. Smith, Charles Wolcott); title song (mCharles Wolcott, lyNed Washington)

Salut l'Artiste (dubbed) **

France/Italy 1973 97m Eastmancolor
Gaumont/De La Guéville/Euro-Internazionale (Alain Poiré, Yves Robert)
🔲
GB title: *The Bit Player*
After his mistress walks out, an unsuccessful actor tries to return to his wife and children but finds life too complicated.
Adroit and witty comedy, performed with insouciant skill.
w Jean-Loup Dabadie, Yves Robert d Yves Robert ph Jean Penzer m Vladimir Cosma ad Theo Meurisse ed Ghislaine Desjonquières
☆ Marcello Mastroianni, Françoise Fabian, Jean Rochefort, Carla Gravina, Xavier Gelin, Evelyne Buyle

Salute for Three

US 1943 75m bw
Paramount
An all-girl orchestra opens a canteen for servicemen.
Modest, middling propaganda musical with minimum talents.
w Davis Anderson, Curtis Kenyon, Hugh Wedlock Jnr and Howard Snyder d Ralph Murphy
☆ Betty Jane Rhodes, Macdonald Carey, Dona Drake and her orchestra, Marty May, Lorraine and Rognan

Salute John Citizen

GB 1942 98m bw
British National (Wallace Orton)
A clerk and his family suffer cheerfully through the blitz.
Modest, competent propaganda piece.
w Clemence Dane, Elizabeth Baron novel Mr Bunting at War by Robert Greenwood d Maurice Elvey ph James Wilson
☆ Edward Rigby, Stanley Holloway, George Robey, Mabel Constanduros, Jimmy Hanley, Dinah Sheridan, Peggy Cummins, Stewart Rome

The Salute of the Jugger

Australia 1989 91m Technicolor
Virgin/Handistrom/Kamisha Corporation/Kings Road Entertainment
🔲 🔲 ◎⌐
In the future, a group of outcasts challenges a big city team to a violent sports contest.
Derivative and pallid low-budget science fiction movie of little interest.
wd David Peoples ph David Eggby m Todd Boekelheide pd John Stoddart ed Richard Francis-Bruce
☆ Rutger Hauer, Delroy Lindo, Anna Katarina, Vincent Phillip D'Onofrio, Gandhi McIntyre, Justin Monju, Aaron Martin, Joan Chen

Salute to the Marines

US 1943 101m Technicolor
MGM (John Considine Jnr)
A sergeant-major struggles to get his family out of the Philippines when the Japs attack.

Recruiting poster heroics with comedy interludes.
w Wells Root, George Bruce story Robert Andrews d S. Sylvan Simon ph Charles Schoenbaum, W. Howard Green m Lennie Hayton
☆ Wallace Beery, Fay Bainter, Marilyn Maxwell, William Lundigan, Keye Luke, Reginald Owen, Ray Collins, Noah Beery, Russell Gleason

Salvador *

US 1986 123m colour
Hemdale/Gerald Green, Oliver Stone
🔲 🔲 ◎⌐ ◎ ⌒
Adventures of an American photo-journalist in Central America.
Drama torn from the headlines; it should perhaps have stayed there, as few people proved to be interested in paying to see it. One cannot, however, deny its brilliant if superficial technical command.
w Oliver Stone, Richard Boyle d Oliver Stone ph Robert Richardson m Georges Delerue
☆ James Woods, James Belushi, Michael Murphy, John Savage
'As raw, difficult, compelling, unreasonable, reckless and vivid as its protagonist.' – *Variety*
♪ best original screenplay; James Woods

The Salvation Hunters **

US 1925 65m bw silent
Academy Photoplays (Josef von Sternberg, George K. Arthur)
Among the mud flats of San Pedro, a boy wins his girl from a brute.
Mini-budgeted minor classic whose very artiness and pretentiousness were keys to its director's later development.
wd Josef von Sternberg ph Josef von Sternberg, Edward Gheller
☆ George K. Arthur, Georgia Hale, Bruce Guerin
'Audience reaction was: even our lives are not so drab as this, and if they are we don't want to know about it. Asked to comment on the failure of a film he had praised so highly, Chaplin said, "Well, you know I was only kidding. They all take everything I say so seriously. I thought I'd praise a bad picture and see what happened."' – *Richard Griffith and Arthur Mayer, The Movies*

Salvation Nell

US 1931 83m bw
Tiffany
A wronged girl sinks lower and lower until she joins the Salvation Army.
One thinks it must have been meant as a spoof, but apparently not.
w Selma Stein, Walter Woods play Edward Sheldon d James Cruze
☆ Helen Chandler, Ralph Graves, Sally O'Neil, Jason Robards, Dewitt Jennings
'It probably will be livelier in the States, where the Mme Cloquette scene is not cut out.' – *Variety*

Salvatore Giuliano *

Italy 1961 125m bw
Lux/Vides/Galatea (Franco Cristaldi)
The bullet-ridden body of key Sicilian Mafia leader Giuliano triggers flashbacks to his complex and brutal career.
Vivid, sometimes obscure, politically oriented melodrama based on fact. Undoubtedly a local classic, but not an easy film to appreciate.
w Francesco Rosi, Suso Cecchi d'Amico, Enzo Provenzale, Franco Solinas d Francesco Rosi ph Gianni di Venanzo m Piero Piccioni
☆ Frank Wolff, Salvo Randone, Federico Zardi
'Epic reportage in the twentieth-century manner of a society reminiscent of some backward corner of the nineteenth century.' – *Peter John Dyer, MFB*

The Salzburg Connection

US 1972 93m DeLuxe Panavision
TCF (Ingo Preminger)
🔲
An American lawyer on holiday in Salzburg finds himself suspected by spies of both sides.
Turgid, routine action thriller with attractive locations.
w Oscar Millard novel Helen MacInnes d Lee H. Katzin ph Wolfgang Treu md Lionel Newman
☆ Barry Newman, Anna Karina, Klaus-Maria Brandauer, Karen Jensen, Wolfgang Preiss
'So dull you can't tell the CIA agents from the neo-Nazis or double agents – or the inept actors

---

from the blocks and stones in the handsome Austrian locales.' – *Judith Crist*

Sam Whiskey

US 1969 96m DeLuxe
UA/Brighton (Jules Levy, Gardner, Arnold Laven)
An itinerant gambler is paid to recover a fortune in gold bars from the bottom of a Colorado river.
Easy-going but rather slackly handled Western.
w William W. Norton d Arnold Laven ph Robert Moreno m Herschel Burke Gilbert
☆ Burt Reynolds, Clint Walker, Ossie Davis, Angie Dickinson, Rick Davis, William Schallert

Samba Traoré

Burkina Faso/France 1992 85m colour
De La Plaine/De L'Avenir/Waka/A2 (Christophe Chesson, Joseph Traoré)
After robbing a petrol station, a man returns to his village and marries, but cannot escape the consequences of his act.
A pleasant but undramatic tale of strong women and weak men, told in a leisurely fashion.
w Idrissa Ouédraogo, Jacques Arhex, Santiago Amigoréna d Idrissa Ouédraogo ph Pierre Laurent Chenieux, Mathieu Vadepied m Faton Cahen, Lamine Konté ad Yves Brover ed Joelle Dufour
☆ Bakary Sangaré, Mariam Kaba, Irene Tassembedo, Abdoulaye Komboudri, Moumouri Compaoré, Sibidou Ouédraogo

Same Old Song

France/Switzerland/Italy/GB 1997 122m colour
Pathé/Arena/Camera One/France 2/Vega/Greenpoint Films (Bruno Pesery)
🔲 🔲
original title: *On Connaît la Chanson*
Six characters in search of love and luxury apartments.
Claiming inspiration from the work of English playwright Dennis Potter, this has the cast expressing their feelings by lip-synching to popular songs or, at any rate, songs popular in France; it gives a little lift to an otherwise conventional romantic comedy.
w Agnes Jaoui, Jean-Pierre Bacri d Alain Resnais ph Renato Berta m Bruno Fontaine ad Jacques Saulnier ed Hervé de Luze
☆ Pierre Arditi, Sabine Azema, Jean-Pierre Bacri, André Dussollier, Agnes Jaoui, Lambert Wilson, Jane Birkin, Jean-Paul Roussillon
'A comedy that's amiable enough but nothing exceptional.' – *Philip Kemp, Sight and Sound*

'The story of the longest-run date in the history of non-marriage!'

Same Time, Next Year *

US 1978 119m colour
Universal/Walter Mirisch, Robert Mulligan
🔲 ◎⌐
An illicit affair is carried on for twenty-five years, the couple confining themselves to one annual meeting in a hotel.
Careful film version of a smash Broadway comedy; the flimsiness of the premise is well concealed, but it remains a one-set play.
w Bernard Slade play Bernard Slade d Robert Mulligan m Robert Surtees m Marvin Hamlisch pd Henry Bumstead
☆ Ellen Burstyn, Alan Alda
♪ Bernard Slade; Robert Surtees; Ellen Burstyn; song 'The Last Time I Felt Like This' (mMarvin Hamlisch, lyAlan and Marilyn Bergman)

Sammy and Rosie Get Laid *

GB 1987 100m colour
Cinecom/Film Four (Tim Bevan, Sarah Radclyffe)
🔲 ◎⌐ ⌒
A young Pakistani accountant in London is confused by the return of his long-lost father, and vice versa.
Those who liked the harsh conflicts of My Beautiful Laundrette will get similar frissons from this; others will be as confused as the characters.
w Hanif Kureishi d Stephen Frears ph Oliver Stapleton m Stanley Myers ed Mick Audsley
☆ Shashi Kapoor, Claire Bloom, Ayub Khan Din, Frances Barber, Roland Gift
'This is a film standing on important territory, confronting important issues, and trying to say important things. But its supreme failure as a film is that, frankly, I don't give a damn whether

---

Sammy and Rosie get laid.' – *Judith Williamson, New Statesman*

Sammy Going South *
🏃🏃 GB 1963 128m Eastmancolor
Cinemascope
Bryanston (Hal Mason)
US title: *A Boy Ten Feet Tall*
A 10-year-old boy is orphaned in Port Said and hitch-hikes to his aunt in Durban.
Disappointing family-fodder epic in which the mini-adventures follow each other too predictably.
w Denis Cannan *novel* W. H. Canaway
d Alexander Mackendrick *ph* Erwin Hillier
m Tristram Cary
☆ Fergus McClelland, Edward G. Robinson, Constance Cummings, Harry H. Corbett

'A story as timeless and tumultuous as the violent age it spreads before you!'

Samson and Delilah
US 1949 128m Technicolor
Paramount/Cecil B. de Mille
📼 🎥 📀
Delilah, rejected by religious strong man Samson, cuts his hair and delivers him to his enemies.
Absurd biblical hokum, stodgily narrated and directed, monotonously photographed and edited, and notable only for the 30-second destruction of the temple at the end.
w Jesse L. Lasky Jnr, Fredric M. Frank d Cecil B. de Mille ph George Barnes m Victor Young
ad Walter Tyler
☆ Hedy Lamarr, Victor Mature, Angela Lansbury, George Sanders, Henry Wilcoxon, Olive Deering, Fay Holden, Russ Tamblyn
'To ignore so enormous, over-coloured, over-stuffed, flamboyant an "epic" would be almost as absurd as taking it seriously.' – *Richard Mallett, Punch*
'Perhaps de Mille's survival is due to the fact that he decided in his movie nonage to ally himself with God as his co-maker and get his major scripts from the Bible, which he has always handled with the proprietary air of a gentleman fondling old love letters.' – *New Yorker*
🏆 art direction
🏅 George Barnes; Victor Young

The Samurai ***
France 1967 95m colour
Filmel/CICC/Fida (Raymond Borderie, Eugene Lepicier)
📼
original title: *Le Samourai*
US title: *The Godson*
A hired assassin who lives by a code of self-sufficiency betrays himself by falling in love with the woman who witnessed his murder of a night-club owner.
Moodily atmospheric, engrossing, low-key thriller with minimal dialogue, shot in tones of greys and blues.
wd Jean-Pierre Melville ph Henri Decaë
m François de Roubaix pd Georges Casati
ad François de Lamothe ed Monique Bonnot, Yo Maurette
☆ Alain Delon, François Périer, Nathalie Delon, Caty Rosier, Jacques Le Roy, Michel Boisrond, Robert Favart
† A dubbed version released in Britain in 1971 ran for 86m.

San Antone
US 1952 90m bw
Republic
During the Civil War a Texas rancher antagonizes an army lieutenant.
Very routine, competent Western without any moment of inspiration.
w Steve Fisher *novel* *Golden Herd* by Curt Carroll
d Joe Kane ph Bud Thackery m R. Dale Butts
☆ Rod Cameron, Forrest Tucker, Arleen Whelan, Katy Jurado, Rodolfo Acosta

San Antonio *
US 1945 109m Technicolor
Warner (Robert Buckner)
📼 🎥
A cowboy incurs the jealousy of a saloon owner.
Typically thinly plotted Warner star Western which works well enough sequence by sequence, climaxing with a fight in the deserted Alamo.
w Alan le May, W. R. Burnett d David Butler
ph Bert Glennon m Max Steiner ad Ted Smith

☆ Errol Flynn, Alexis Smith, Paul Kelly, Victor Francen, S. Z. Sakall, John Litel, Florence Bates, Robert Shayne, Monte Blue, Robert Barrat
🎵 song 'Some Sunday Morning' (mRay Heindorf, M. K. Jerome, lyTed Koehler); Ted Smith

San Demetrio London *
GB 1943 105m bw
Ealing (Robert Hamer)
📼
In 1940, the survivors of a crippled tanker bring it back home.
Rather flat and dated propaganda piece which seemed much more vivid at the time.
w Robert Hamer, Charles Frend story F. Tennyson Jesse d Charles Frend ph Ernest Palmer, Roy Kellino m John Greenwood
☆ Walter Fitzgerald, Mervyn Johns, Ralph Michael, Robert Beatty, Charles Victor, Frederick Piper, Gordon Jackson
'In many ways a model for war films.' – *Dilys Powell*

San Diego I Love You *
US 1944 83m bw
Universal (Michael Fessier, Ernest Pagano)
A family travels to San Diego to promote father's inventions.
Pleasing, easy-come-easy-go comedy full of memorable incident and characterization.
w Michael Fessier, Ernest Pagano d Reginald Le Borg ph Hal Mohr m Hans Salter
☆ Louise Allbritton, Edward Everett Horton, Jon Hall, Eric Blore, Buster Keaton, Irene Ryan

'She fell in love with the toughest guy on the toughest street in the world!'

San Francisco ****
US 1936 117m bw
MGM (John Emerson, Bernard Hyman)
📼 🎥 📀
The loves and career problems of a Barbary Coast saloon proprietor climax in the 1906 earthquake.
Incisive, star-packed, superbly-handled melodrama which weaves in every kind of appeal and for a finale has some of the best special effects ever conceived.
w Anita Loos story Robert Hopkins d W. S. Van Dyke ph Oliver T. Marsh m Edward Ward
md Herbert Stothart montage John Hoffman title song Bronislau Kaper
☆ Clark Gable, Spencer Tracy, Jeanette MacDonald, Jack Holt, Jessie Ralph, Ted Healy, Shirley Ross, Al Shean, Harold Huber
'Prodigally generous and completely satisfying.' – *Frank S. Nugent*
🏅 best picture; Robert Hopkins; W. S. Van Dyke; Spencer Tracy

San Francisco Docks
US 1940 64m bw
Marshall Grant/Universal
A man accused of killing a crooked politician proves he didn't do it.
Curiously pretentious melodrama with suggestions of Group Theater style; not for the action buffs, or anybody else.
w Stanley Crea Rubin, Edmund L. Hartmann
d Arthur Lubin
☆ Burgess Meredith, Irene Hervey, Raymond Walburn, Barry Fitzgerald, Robert Armstrong, Lewis Howard

'Between the sea and the Sierras stood the brawling gateway to gold!'

The San Francisco Story *
US 1952 90m bw
Warner/Fidelity-Vogue (Howard Welsch)
In 1856, a wanderer bound for China stops in San Francisco to get involved in politics.
Lively melodrama with good period feel.
w D. D. Beauchamp *novel* Richard Summers
d Robert Parrish ph John Seitz m Paul Dunlap
md Emil Newman
☆ Joel McCrea, Yvonne de Carlo, Sidney Blackmer, Florence Bates

San Quentin *
US 1937 70m bw
Warner (Sam Bischoff)
A convict's sister loves the warden.
Standard tough prison melodrama, competently done.
w Peter Milne, Humphrey Cobb story John Bright, Robert Tasker d Lloyd Bacon ph Sid Hickox m Heinz Roemheld, David Raksin

☆ Pat O'Brien, Ann Sheridan, Humphrey Bogart, Barton MacLane, Joseph Sawyer, Veda Ann Borg
'Fairly good appeal but will need pushing.' – *Variety*

San Quentin
US 1946 66m bw
RKO
A convict starts a movement for the rehabilitation of prisoners after release, but despite himself is caught up in a prison break.
Tolerable support of a familiar kind.
w Lawrence Kimble, Arthur A. Ross, Howard J. Green d Gordon Douglas ph Frank Redman
m Paul Sawtell
☆ Lawrence Tierney, Barton MacLane, Marian Carr, Raymond Burr, Joe Devlin

Sanctuary
US 1960 90m bw Cinemascope
TCF (Richard D. Zanuck)
The governor's daughter is seduced by a bootlegger, and her life goes from one tragedy to another.
Confused adaptation of unadaptable material, full of pussyfoot daring but little sense.
w James Poe *novel* William Faulkner d Tony Richardson ph Ellsworth Fredericks m Alex North
☆ Lee Remick, Bradford Dillman, Yves Montand, Odetta, Harry Townes, Howard St John, Reta Shaw, Strother Martin

'This is the story of the men on the USS *San Pablo* who disturbed the sleeping dragon of China as the world watched in breathless terror.'

The Sand Pebbles *
US 1966 193m DeLuxe Panavision
TCF/Argyle/Solar (Robert Wise)
📼 📀 🎥
In 1926 an American gunboat patrolling the Yangtze river gets involved with Chinese warlords.
Confused action blockbuster with Vietnam parallels for those who care to pick them up; pretty thinly stretched entertainment despite the tons of explosive.
w Robert Anderson *novel* Richard McKenna
d Robert Wise ph Joseph MacDonald m Jerry Goldsmith
☆ Steve McQueen, Candice Bergen, Richard Attenborough, Richard Crenna, Marayat Andriane, Mako, Larry Gates, Simon Oakland
'If it had been done twenty years ago, it would have been fast and unpretentious, with some ingeniously faked background shots … and we would never have asked for larger historical meanings.' – *Pauline Kael*
🏅 best picture; Joseph MacDonald; Jerry Goldsmith; Steve McQueen; Mako

Sanders: see *Death Drums along the River*

Sanders of the River *
GB 1935 98m bw
London (Alexander Korda)
🎥
US title: *Bosambo*
Problems of a British colonial servant in keeping peace among the tribes.
Much-caricatured African adventure of the very old school, helped by Robeson's personality.
w Lajos Biro, Jeffrey Dell *stories* Edgar Wallace
d Zoltan Korda ph Georges Perinal, Osmond Borrodaile, Louis Page m/ly Mischa Spoliansky, Arthur Wimperis md Muir Mathieson ed Charles Crichton
☆ Leslie Banks, Paul Robeson, Nina Mae McKinney, Robert Cochran, Martin Walker, Richard Grey
'It will interest those who are sincerely interested in the cinema as an art form, but it will suffer the hazards of all pioneers.' – *Variety*
† The film's opening credits included the description: 'Africa … Tens of millions of natives under British rule, each tribe with its own chieftain, governed and protected by a handful of white men whose everyday work is an unsung saga of courage and efficiency. One of them was Commissioner Sanders.'

The Sandlot
🏃🏃 US 1993 101m colour
TCF/Island World
📼 🎥 📀
GB title: *The Sandlot Kids*
In the early 60s, an 11-year-old boy makes new friends with kids playing baseball in a sandlot and passes a personal test of courage by retrieving a valuable ball from a fearsome dog.
Pleasant, undemanding entertainment for the young, a nostalgic evocation of an idealized time.
w David Mickey Evans, Robert Gunter d David Mickey Evans ph Anthony B. Richmond
m David Newman pd Chester Kaczenski
ed Michael A. Stevenson
☆ Tom Guiry, Mike Vitar, Patrick Renna, Marty York, Chauncey Leopardi, Denis Leary, Karen Allen, James Earl Jones, Art La Fleur
'It leaves the odd impression of not only starring 12-year-olds, but being made by one.' – *Nick Hasted, Sight and Sound*

Sandokan against the Leopard of Sarawak
🏃🏃 Italy 1964 94m Eastmancolor
Totalscope
Liber (Ottavio Poggi)
Three years after recovering his kingdom of Sarawak, Sandokan rescues his bride-to-be after she is kidnapped by the ambitious son of the former ruler.
A gaudy, plodding, low-brow adventure, short on thrills and likely to irritate many with its insistence that men have stronger wills than women.
w Deriso Arpad, Luigi Capuano *novel* Emilio Salgari d Luigi Capuano *ad* Giancarlo Bartolini Salimbeni, Ernest Kronberg ed Antonietta Zita
☆ Ray Danton, Guy Madison, Franca Bettoja, Mario Petri, Alberto Farnese, Mino Doro, Giulio Marchetti, Aldo Bufi-Landi
† It was a sequel to *Sandokan Fights Back* (qv).

Sandokan Fights Back
🏃🏃 Italy/West Germany 1964 96m colour
Liber/Eichberg (Ottavio Poggi)
A Malaysian pirate discovers that he is the rightful Rajah of Sarawak and decides to regain his kingdom.
Inept and trivial adventure, devoid of thrills.
w Arpad de Riso, Luigi Capuano *novel* Emilio Salgari d Luigi Capuano ph Adalberto Albertini
ed Antonietta Zita
☆ Ray Danton, Guy Madison, Franca Bettoja, Mino Doro
† It was followed by a sequel, *Sandokan against the Leopard of Sarawak* (qv).

Sandokan the Great
🏃🏃 Italy/France/Spain 1963 114m
Techniscope
Filmes/CCF/Ocean
🎥
The son of the Sultan of Borneo wages jungle war against the oppressive British.
A curious mixture of Tarzan and Robin Hood, this character appeared in several adventures before expiring; the first chapter is the best, or least worst.
w Fulvio Gicca, Umberto Lenzi *novel* Emilio Salgari d Umberto Lenzi ph Aurelio Gutierrez Larraya, Angelo Lotti m Giovanni Fusco
☆ Steve Reeves, Genevieve Grad, Rik Battaglia, Andrea Bosic

The Sandpiper
US 1965 116m Metrocolor Panavision
MGM/Filmways (John Calley)
📼 🎥 🎧
An artist lives with her illegitimate son in a Monterey beach shack; when she is forced to send the boy to school he attracts the attention of the minister in charge.
Absurd novelettish love story basically copied from The Garden of Allah; pretty seascapes are the most rewarding aspect.
w Dalton Trumbo, Michael Wilson d Vincente Minnelli ph Milton Krasner m Johnny Mandel
☆ Elizabeth Taylor, Richard Burton, Eva Marie Saint, Charles Bronson, Robert Webber
'Straight Louisa May Alcott interlarded with discreet pornographic allusions.' – *John Simon*
'Sex-on-the-sand soap opera.' – *Robert Windeler*
🏅 song 'The Shadow of Your Smile' (mJohnny Mandel, lyPaul Francis Webster)

'My name is Stryker. Sgt John M. Stryker. You're gonna be my squad!'

Sands of Iwo Jima *
US 1949 109m bw
Republic (Edmund Grainger)
▣ ▤ ⌨

During World War II in the Pacific, a tough sergeant of marines moulds raw recruits into fighting men but is himself shot by a sniper.
Celebrated star war comic, still quite hypnotic in its flagwaving way.
w Harry Brown, James Edward Grant d Allan Dwan ph Reggie Lanning m Victor Young ed Richard L. Van Enger
☆ John Wayne, John Agar, Adele Mara, Forrest Tucker, Arthur Franz, Julie Bishop, Richard Jaeckel
'The battle sequences are terrifyingly real ... but the personal dramatics make up a compendium of war-picture clichés.' – *Variety*
'Say what you like about the sentimental flavour of war pictures such as this, there's no denying they keep you in your seat.' – *Richard Mallett, Punch*
⅋ Harry Brown (original story); John Wayne; editing

Sands of the Desert
👫 GB 1960 92m Technicolor
Associated British
▣

A diminutive travel agent goes out to investigate a desert holiday camp which has suffered from sabotage.
Limp star comedy with poor studio work and meandering script.
wd John Paddy Carstairs ph Gilbert Taylor m Stanley Black
☆ Charlie Drake, Peter Arne, Sarah Branch, Raymond Huntley, Peter Illing, Harold Kasket

Sands of the Kalahari
GB 1965 119m Technicolor Panavision
Pendennis (Cy Endfield, Stanley Baker)

Survivors of a plane crash trek across the desert and are menaced by baboons and each other.
Hysterical melodrama with predictable heebie-jeebies by all concerned and the baddie finally left to the mercy of the monkeys. For hardened sensationalists.
wd Cy Endfield novel William Mulvihill ph Erwin Hillier m Johnny Dankworth
☆ Stanley Baker, Stuart Whitman, Harry Andrews, Susannah York, Theodore Bikel, Nigel Davenport, Barry Lowe

The Sandwich Man *
👫 GB 1966 95m Eastmancolor
Rank/Titan (Peter Newbrook)

In the course of a walking day around London a sandwich man encounters many of his eccentric acquaintances.
Spurned when it was first released, this comedy variety show, mostly in mime, can now be seen to be of a kind popularized by TV, and may have been simply ahead of its time. It certainly seems funnier than it did.
w Michael Bentine, Robert Hartford-Davis d Robert Hartford-Davis ph Peter Newbrook m Mike Vickers
☆ Michael Bentine, Dora Bryan, Suzy Kendall, Norman Wisdom, Harry H. Corbett, Bernard Cribbins, Ian Hendry, Stanley Holloway, Alfie Bass, Diana Dors, Ron Moody, Wilfrid Hyde-White, Donald Wolfit, Max Bacon, Fred Emney and also Frank Finlay, Peter Jones, Michael Medwin, Ronnie Stevens, John Le Mesurier, Sydney Tafler, John Junkin, Warren Mitchell

Sandy Gets Her Man
US 1940 65m bw
Universal (Burt Kelly)

A councilman's baby gets involved in the rival claims of police and fire departments for the best funding.
Rather complex excuse for a slight family comedy.
w Sy Bartlett, Jane Storm d Otis Garrett, Paul Gerard Smith
☆ Baby Sandy, Stuart Erwin, Edgar Kennedy, Una Merkel, William Frawley, Edward Brophy

Sandy Is a Lady
US 1940 62m bw
Universal (Burt Kelly)

A baby is responsible for her father's promotion.
Third of a series featuring the gurgling infant introduced in East Side of Heaven. (The others: Little Accident, Unexpected Father, Sandy Gets

Her Man.) *This one is an excuse for slapstick comedy situations.*
w Charles Grayson d Charles Lamont
☆ Baby Sandy, Butch and Buddy, Eugene Pallette, Nan Grey, Tom Brown, Mischa Auer, Billy Gilbert, Edgar Kennedy

Sandy Takes a Bow: see *Unexpected Father*

Le Sang d'un Poète: see *The Blood of a Poet*

Sang Gong Yatho Tungchap Fan: see *Rock'N'Roll Cop*

Sangaree
US 1953 95m Technicolor 3-D
Paramount/Pine-Thomas

Trouble ensues when a plantation owner wills his wealth to the son of a slave.
Period skulduggery rather hammily presented.
w David Duncan novel Frank G. Slaughter d Edward Ludwig ph Lionel Lindon, W. Wallace Kelley m Lucien Cailliet
☆ Fernando Lamas, Arlene Dahl, Patricia Medina, Francis L. Sullivan, Charles Korvin, Tom Drake, John Sutton, Willard Parker, Lester Matthews

Sango Malo *
Cameroon/Burkina Faso 1991 93m colour
Les Films Terre Africaine/Cameroun Radio and TV/FODIC/DIPROCI (Emmanuel Toko)

An idealistic schoolteacher in his first job angers village leaders and his punitive and conservative headmaster by ignoring traditional ways and putting the emphasis on practical education.
A tough and complex view of Cameroonian village life, in which there are no heroes.
wd Bassek Ba Kobhio novel Sango Malo – Le Maître du Canton by Bassek Ba Kobhio ph Joseph Guerin m Francis Bebey ad François Bollo ed Marie-Jeanne Kanyala
☆ Jérome Bolo, Marcel Mvondo II, Edwige Ntongon è Zock, Jean Minguele, Jimmy Biyong, Henriette Fenda
'Offers a valuable look at the harsh realities of life in this little-seen land. But despite a relatively lively script, pic is unable to sustain its initially fast pace.' – *Variety*

Sanjuro **
Japan 1962 96m bw Tohoscope
Toho/Kurosawa (Tomoyuki Tanaka, Ryuzo Kikushima)
▣ ▤ ⌨

original title: *Tsubaki Sanjuro*

A ronin, or wandering samurai, inspires some young and rebellious warriors to fight against corruption.
Deftly enjoyable drama, spiced with wit and humanity, and tinged with sadness for its lone and homeless hero.
w Ryuzo Kikushima, Hideo Oguni, Akira Kurosawa novel Shugoro Yamamoto d Akira Kurosawa ph Fukuzo Koizumi m Masaru Sato ad Yoshio Muraki
☆ Toshiro Mifune, Tatsuya Nakadai, Yuzo Kayama, Akihiko Hirata, Kunie Tanaka
'The most autumnal of Kurosawa's Japanese Westerns.' – *Nigel Andrews*
† Despite the change in name, the ronin played by Mifune is the same character who appeared in the earlier *Yojimbo* (qv).

Sans Lendemain *
France 1940 83m bw
Gregor Rabinovitch/Cine Alliance

A night-club hostess with a mysterious past is troubled when an old lover turns up.
Moody melodrama in the Quai des Brumes tradition.
w Jean Wilhelm, Max Colpet d Max Ophuls
☆ Edwige Feuillère, Georges Rigaud, Georges Lannes, Paul Azais

Sans Toit ni Loi: see *Vagabonde*

Sansho the Bailiff ***
Japan 1954 132m bw
Daiei (Masaichi Nagata)
▣ ⌨

original title: *Sansho dayu*

In medieval Japan, a provincial governor is exiled for trying to protect the peasants from exploitation; following him seven years later, his wife is forced into prostitution and his son and daughter bought as slaves by the ruthless Sansho.

A tough tale of oppression and injustice, sacrifice and redemption, told simply but with great skill, the beauty of its images alleviating some of the narrative's harshness, but not its power.
w Fuji Yahiro, Yoshikata Yoda novel Ogai Mori d Kenji Mizoguchi ph Kazuo Miyagawa m Fumio Hayasaka ad Kasaku Ito ed Mitsuji Miyata
☆ Eitaro Shindo, Kinuyo Tanaka, Yoshiaki Hanayagi, Kyoko Kagawa, Akitaka Kono, Keiko Enami, Masahiko Kato
† The film was awarded a Silver Lion at the Venice Film Festival in 1955.

Santa Claus
👫 GB 1985 112m Rank Colour
Panavision
Alexander Salkind (Ilya Salkind, Pierre Spengler)
▣ ▤ ⌨

An old woodcutter is given immortality by the elves and turned into Santa Claus; in modern times, he goes to New York to rescue a discontented elf from the clutches of a demon toymaker.
Utterly charmless treatment of an extremely vague legend, with the two halves entirely failing to coalesce and the level of invention low throughout.
w David Newman d Jeannot Szwarc ph Arthur Ibbetson m Henry Mancini pd Anthony Pratt ed Peter Hollywood
☆ David Huddleston, Dudley Moore, John Lithgow, Judy Cornwell, Christian Fitzpatrick, Burgess Meredith
'For children of all ages, but it skews best towards infancy or senility.' – *Variety*

The Santa Clause
👫 US 1994 95m colour
Buena Vista/Walt Disney (Brian Reilly, Jeffrey Silver, Robert Newmyer)
▣ ▤ ⓐ ⓐ ⌨

When Santa Claus falls off the roof of his house, an advertising executive takes over and discovers he is stuck with the job.
A pleasant though far from hilarious comedy that seems uncertain whether it's intended for kids or adults and is unlikely to prove memorable for either audience.
w Leonard Benvenuti, Steve Rudnick d John Pasquin ph Walt Lloyd m Michael Convertino pd Carol Spier ed Larry Bock
☆ Tim Allen, Judge Reinhold, Wendy Crewson, Eric Lloyd
'Allen can mug with the best of them, but his straight material is found wanting. Like a latter-day Bob Hope, he can't transcend his popular persona.' – *Denis Seguin, Screen International*

Santa Fe
US 1951 89m Technicolor
Columbia (Harry Joe Brown)

After the Civil War, the eldest of four westbound brothers tries to prevent the others from becoming outlaws.
Regulation star Western, with action sequences a little under par.
w Kenneth Gamet d Irving Pichel ph Charles Lawton Jnr m Paul Sawtell
☆ Randolph Scott, Jerome Courtland, Janis Carter, Peter Thompson, John Archer, Warner Anderson, Roy Roberts

Santa Fe Passage
US 1955 89m Trucolor
Republic

An Indian-hating scout with a bad record is hired to transport arms to Santa Fe.
Rough-and-ready brawling Western with very little going for it.
w Lillie Hayward d William Witney ph Bud Thackery m R. Dale Butts
☆ John Payne, Rod Cameron, Faith Domergue, Slim Pickens, Leo Gordon

'The thundering story that challenges all filmdom to match its excitement!'

Santa Fe Trail **
US 1940 110m bw
Warner (Robert Fellows)
▣ ▤ ⓐ ⌨

A cavalry officer is responsible for the final capture of John Brown.
The most solemn Western from star or studio has impressive patches amid routine excitements.
w Robert Buckner d Michael Curtiz ph Sol Polito m Max Steiner

☆ Errol Flynn, Olivia de Havilland, Raymond Massey, Ronald Reagan, Alan Hale, Van Heflin, Gene Reynolds, Henry O'Neill

'Forget everything you have ever seen!'

Santa Sangre
Italy 1989 123m colour
Mainline/Produzioni Intersound (Claudio Argento)
▣ ▤ ⌨

An armless, but far from harmless, mother forces her demented son to use his arms and hands as substitutes for her own, severed by her jealous husband.
Phantasmagoria of images of death and mutilation that, despite their occasional visual flamboyance, signify very little.
w Robert Leoni, Alejandro Jodorowsky, Claudio Argento d Alejandro Jodorowsky ph Daniele Nannuzzi m Simon Boswell pd Alejandro Luna ed Mauro Bonanni
☆ Axel Jodorowsky, Blanca Guerra, Guy Stockwell, Thelma Tixou, Sabrina Dennison, Adan Jodorowski, Faviola Elenka Tapia, Teo Jodorowsky

Santee
US 1972 93m colour
Vagabond (Deno Paoli, Edward Platt)
▤

A boy goes west to find his father and befriends the bounty hunter who has killed him.
Personable, violent Western with adequate style and performances.
w Brand Bell d Gary Nelson ph Donald Morgan m Don Randi
☆ Glenn Ford, Michael Burns, Dana Wynter, Jay Silverheels, Harry Townes, John Larch

Santiago
US 1956 92m Warnercolor Cinemascope
Warner (Martin Rackin)
GB title: *The Gun Runner*

A Mississippi paddle-boat sets out for Cuba with a consignment of guns for the rebels.
Stiff period actioner of no particular merit.
w Martin Rackin, John Twist d Gordon Douglas ph John Seitz m David Buttolph
☆ Alan Ladd, Rossana Podesta, Lloyd Nolan, Chill Wills, Paul Fix, L. Q. Jones, Frank de Kova

The Saphead *
US 1920 70m bw silent
Metro/Buster Keaton
▤ ⓐ

A shy young man reads a manual on how to win the modern girl.
Interesting early star comedy: quite winning in its way, but without the spectacular moments which were a feature of his later films.
w June Mathis play The New Henrietta by Winchell Smith, Victor Mapes d Herbert Blache ph Harold Wenstrom
☆ Buster Keaton, Beula Booker, William H. Crane, Irving Cummings

Sapphire **
GB 1959 92m Eastmancolor
Rank/Artna (Michael Relph)

Scotland Yard solves the murder of a black music student.
Efficient police thriller with a strong race angle.
w Janet Green d Basil Dearden ph Harry Waxman m Philip Green
☆ Nigel Patrick, Michael Craig, Yvonne Mitchell, Paul Massie, Bernard Miles, Olga Lindo, Earl Cameron, Gordon Heath, Robert Adams
'A dandy murder mystery – taut, tantalizing and beautifully done.' – *Judith Crist, 1980*
Ⓥ best British film

Saps at Sea
👫 US 1940 60m bw
Hal Roach
▣ ▤ ⓐ ✿

Ollie needs a rest after working in a horn factory, so he and Stan take a boating holiday but are kidnapped by a gangster.
Disappointing star comedy with gags too few and too long drawn out.
w Charles Rogers, Harry Langdon, Gil Pratt, Felix Adler d Gordon Douglas ph Art Lloyd m Marvin Hatley

---

⊚ Digital Video Disc Region 2   ⊚ Digital Video Disc Region 1   ⌨ Soundtrack released on compact disc   ☆ Cast in approximate order of importance   † Points of interest   ♫ Notable songs   ⓛ Academy Award   ⅋ Academy Award nomination   Ⓥ BAFTA

☆ Stan Laurel, Oliver Hardy, James Finlayson, Dick Cramer, Ben Turpin

Saraband: see *Saraband for Dead Lovers*

Saraband for Dead Lovers *

GB   1948   96m   Technicolor
Ealing (Michael Relph)

🎞

US title: *Saraband*

The tragic love affair of Konigsmark and Sophie Dorothea, wife of the Elector of Hanover who later became George I of England.
Gloomy but superb-looking historical love story; it just misses being a memorable film.
w John Dighton, Alexander Mackendrick *novel* Helen Simpson *d* Basil Dearden, Michael Relph *ph* Douglas Slocombe *m* Alan Rawsthorne *ad* Jim Morahan, William Kellner, Michael Relph
☆ Stewart Granger, Joan Greenwood, Françoise Rosay, Flora Robson, Peter Bull
'Suspense, romance, interest and excitement in full measure.' – *MFB*
& art direction

The Saracen Blade

👫👫   US   1954   76m   Technicolor
Columbia (Sam Katzman)
In the 13th century a young Italian crusader devotes himself to avenging the murder of his father.
Cut-price swashbuckler full of unintentional laughs and therefore quite watchable.
w DeVallon Scott, George Worthing Yates *novel* Frank Yerby *d* William Castle *ph* Henry Freulich *m* Mischa Bakaleinikoff
☆ Ricardo Montalban, Betta St John, Rick Jason, Carolyn Jones, Michael Ansara

'The Sound of Freedom.'
'Her story will move you. Her struggle will change you. Her spirit will inspire you.'

Sarafina!

👫👫   South Africa   1992   116m   Agfacolor
Warner/Ideal/Distant Horizon/Videovision/Ariane/VPI/BBC (Anant Singh, David M. Thompson)

🎞 🎞 📀 🎧

A South African schoolgirl in Soweto realizes she has to fight for freedom, following the example of her history teacher and her mother – and learning from her own experiences when she is imprisoned and tortured.
An odd mix of musical and near-documentary realism that obstinately fails to comes to life on the screen.
w William Nicholson, Mbongeni Ngema *musical* Mbongeni Ngema *d* Darrell James Roodt *ph* Mark Vincente *m* Stanley Myers *ch* Michael Peters, Mbongeni Ngema *ed* Peter Hollywood, Sarah Thomas
☆ Leleti Khumalo, Whoopi Goldberg, Miriam Makeba, John Kani, Dumisani Diamini, Mbongeni Ngema, Sipho Kunene
'If one is prepared to forgive it its large measure of amateurishness and naivety, and is braced for the distress inherent in the subject matter, this can be cautiously recommended as a vivid testament to the unacceptable circumstances in which too many children grow up.' – *Angie Errigo, Empire*

Sarah and Son

US   1930   85m   bw
Paramount (David O. Selznick)
A widow seeks the baby her husband took away from her.
Mother love saga; soppy but with good credits.
w Zoe Akins *novel* Timothy Shea *d* Dorothy Arzner *ph* Charles Lang
☆ Ruth Chatterton, Fredric March, Fuller Mellish Jnr, Gilbert Emery, Doris Lloyd
'Madame X with a slightly varied theme. Photography and recording par.' – *Variety*
& Ruth Chatterton

Saratoga *

US   1937   102m   bw
MGM (Bernard H. Hyman)

🎞 📀

A bookmaker helps the daughter of a horse breeder.
Forgettable racetrack drama notable chiefly as the last film of Jean Harlow who died before it was completed.

w Anita Loos, Robert Hopkins *d* Jack Conway *ph* Ray June *m* Edward Ward
☆ Clark Gable, Jean Harlow, Lionel Barrymore, Frank Morgan, Walter Pidgeon, Una Merkel, Cliff Edwards, George Zucco, Jonathan Hale
'Glib, forthright, knowing and adroit.' – *Time*
'Surefire box office, and tastefully produced.' – *Variety*

'Their times were violent – and so was their love!'

Saratoga Trunk *

US   1943   135m   bw
Warner (Hal B. Wallis)
A notorious woman comes back to New Orleans and falls for a cowboy helping a railroad combine against their rivals.
Curious, unsatisfactory, miscast and overlong film version of a bestseller; there are enjoyable sequences, but it simply fails to come alive.
w Casey Robinson *novel* Edna Ferber *d* Sam Wood *ph* Joseph St Amaad *m* Max Steiner
☆ Ingrid Bergman, Gary Cooper, Flora Robson, Jerry Austin, Florence Bates, John Warburton, John Abbott, Curt Bois, Ethel Griffies
'It lacks a logical pattern of drama and character … a piece of baggage labelled solely for the stars.' – *Bosley Crowther*
& Flora Robson

Sarraounia *

Burkina Faso   1986   121m   Fujicolour Technovision
Les Films Soleil (Med Hondo)
An African warrior queen resists white colonization of her country.
Based on actual events in the 1890s in what is now Nigeria, an ambitious, if flawed, attempt at an epic of repression and power politics.
w Med Hondo, Abdoulaye Mamani, Abdoul War *book* Abdoulaye Mamani *d* Med Hondo *ph* Guy Famechon *m* Pierre Akendengue *pd* Jacques D'Ovidio *ed* Marie-Therese Boiché
☆ Ai Keita, Jean-Roger Milo, Feodor Atkine, Didier Sauvegrain, Roger Mirmont, Luc-Antoine Diquaro, Jean-Pierre Castaldi, Tidjani Ouedraogo
'An alternative to mainstream cinema which is both exhilarating and accessible … cinema-goers will be surprised how much they enjoy it.' – *Judith Williamson, New Statesman*

Sartana

Italy/West Germany   1968   97m   Telecolor Paris-Etoile/Widescreen (Aldo Addobbati)
A mysterious stranger thwarts the plans of gangs of ruthless killers and gains a fortune in gold.
Uninteresting spaghetti Western with an invulnerable hero, notable only for its high body count and its contrived yet clichéd details, ranging from an eccentric coffin-maker to a cackling villain, deaths accompanied by the sound of a tinkling, musical watch, and a gunfighter who shoots a four-barrelled pistol.
w Renato Izzo, Gianfranco Parolini, Werner Hauff *story* Luigi de Santis, Fabio Piccioni, Adolfo Cagnacci *d* Frank Kramer (Gianfranco Parolini) *ph* Sandro Mancori *m* Piero Piccioni *ad* Giorgio Desideri *ed* Edmundo Lozzi
☆ John Garko (Gianni Garko), William Berger, Sydney Chaplin, Klaus Kinski, Gianni Rizzo, Fernando Sancho, Andrew Scott, Carlo Tamberlani, Franco Pesce, Heidi Fisher

Saskatchewan

US   1954   87m   Technicolor
U-I (Aaron Rosenberg)
GB title: *O'Rourke of the Royal Mounted*
A mountie helps the lady survivor of an Indian attack.
Standard star actioner.
w Gil Doud *d* Raoul Walsh *ph* John Seitz *m* Hans Salter
☆ Alan Ladd, Shelley Winters, J. Carrol Naish, Hugh O'Brian, Robert Douglas, Richard Long, Jay Silverheels

The Satan Bug *

US   1965   114m   DeLuxe Panavision
UA/Mirisch/Kappa (John Sturges)

🎞

At a top-secret desert research station, one scientist is a traitor, and a deadly virus has been stolen for use by a mad millionaire.
Slow-moving, portentous, gadget-filled actioner which looks good but seldom stimulates.

w James Clavell, Edward Anhalt *novel* Alistair MacLean *d* John Sturges *ph* Robert Surtees *m* Jerry Goldsmith
☆ George Maharis, Richard Basehart, Anne Francis, Dana Andrews, Ed Asner

Satan Met a Lady *

US   1936   74m   bw
Warner (Henry Blanke)
Various crooks and a private detective pursue a rare artifact.
Perversely rewritten version of The Maltese Falcon (qv). Fascinating but not really successful.
w Brown Holmes *d* William Dieterle *ph* Arthur Edeson *m* Leo F. Forbstein
☆ Bette Davis, Warren William, Alison Skipworth, Arthur Treacher, Wini Shaw, Marie Wilson, Porter Hall
'One lives through it in constant expectation of seeing a group of uniformed individuals appear suddenly from behind the furniture and take the entire cast into protective custody.' – *Bosley Crowther*

Satan Never Sleeps

US/GB   1962   126m   DeLuxe   Cinemascope
TCF/Leo McCarey
GB title: *The Devil Never Sleeps*
In the late forties in China, Catholic missionaries defy the communists.
Failed anti-Red imitation of Inn of the Sixth Happiness with the priests from Going My Way. Has to be seen to be believed.
w Claude Binyon, Leo McCarey *d* Leo McCarey *ph* Oswald Morris *m* Richard Rodney Bennett
☆ Clifton Webb, William Holden, France Nuyen, Weaver Lee, Athene Seyler, Martin Benson
'For all its superficial smirk of piety, this is just a prurient, soft-soapy and holy water version of the spicy story about the lonely missionary and the beautiful native girl.' – *Time*

The Satanic Rites of Dracula

GB   1973   88m   Technicolor
Hammer (Roy Skeggs)

🎞 🎞

US title: *Count Dracula and His Vampire Bride*
When vampires infest London, a property speculator proves to be Dracula himself.
Intriguingly plotted screamer with more mystery than horror.
w Don Houghton *d* Alan Gibson *ph* Brian Probyn *m* John Cacavas *ad* Lionel Couch *ed* Chris Barnes *sp* Les Bowie
☆ Peter Cushing, Christopher Lee, Michael Coles, William Franklyn, Freddie Jones, Richard Vernon, Patrick Barr
'Shot with the kind of flashy anonymity that one expects of a TV series.' – *David Pirie, MFB*

Satan's Skin: see *Blood on Satan's Claw*

'Never told till now! The world's most guarded secret!'

Satellite in the Sky

GB   1956   85m   Warnercolor   Cinemascope
Warner/Tridelta/Danziger
A rocketship is ordered to lose a tritonium bomb in space, but the device attaches itself to the side of the ship.
Boringly talkative low-budget science fiction with ideas beyond its station but not enough talent to put them over.
w John Mather, J. T. McIntosh, Edith Dell *d* Paul Dickson *ph* Georges Périnal *m* Albert Elms
☆ Kieron Moore, Lois Maxwell, Donald Wolfit, Bryan Forbes, Jimmy Hanley, Alan Gifford

Satisfaction

US   1988   96m   DeLuxe
TCF/NBC (Aaron Spelling, Alan Greisman)

🎞 📀 🎧

aka: *The Girls of Summer*
A rock band – three women, one man – win a summer residency and find romance, or sex, at a smart club.
Inconsequential teen drama providing no entertainment and sub-standard rock.
w Charles Purpura *d* Joan Freeman *ph* Thomas Del Ruth *m* Michel Colombier *ed* Joel Goodman
☆ Justine Bateman, Liam Neeson, Trini Alvarado, Scott Coffey, Britta Phillips, Julia Roberts, Debbie Harry

Saturday Island

GB   1951   102m   Technicolor
Coronado (David E. Rose)
US title: *Island of Desire*
In 1943 a supply boat is torpedoed and a Canadian nurse finds romance on a desert island with a US marine and a one-armed RAF pilot.
Unlikely, conversational, old-fashioned love story.
wd Stuart Heisler *novel* Hugh Brooke *ph* Oswald Morris *m* William Alwyn
☆ Linda Darnell, Tab Hunter, Donald Gray

Saturday Night and Sunday Morning ****

GB   1960   89m   bw
Bryanston/Woodfall (Harry Salzman, Tony Richardson)

🎞

A Nottingham factory worker is dissatisfied with his lot, gets into trouble through an affair with a married woman, but finally settles for convention.
Startling when it emerged, this raw working-class melodrama, with its sharp detail and strong comedy asides, delighted the mass audience chiefly because of its strong central character thumbing his nose at authority. Matching the mood of the times, and displaying a new attitude to sex, it transformed British cinema and was much imitated.
w Alan Sillitoe *novel* Alan Sillitoe *d* Karel Reisz *ph* Freddie Francis *m* Johnny Dankworth
☆ Albert Finney, Shirley Anne Field, Rachel Roberts, Bryan Pringle, Norman Rossington, Hylda Baker
'Here is a chance for our own new wave.' – *Evening Standard*
† Warwickshire never showed the film because the producers refused to delete two love scenes. David Kingsley of British Lion said: 'We are not prepared to agree that a film of outstanding importance and merit should be re-edited by the Mrs Grundys of the Warwickshire County Council. It is fortunate for the world that Warwickshire's greatest and often bawdy son, William Shakespeare, was not subject in his day to the restrictions of prim and petty officialdom.'
🏆 best British film; Albert Finney; Rachel Roberts

Saturday Night at the Palace *

South Africa   1987   90m   colour
Intertrade (Robert Davies)
An embittered, unemployed white vents his anger on the black manager of an all-night diner.
Tough drama of racial antagonism, based on a true story, with a slow start and a rousing, if overly theatrical, conclusion.
w Paul Slabolepsy, Bill Flynn *play* Paul Slabolepsy *d* Robert Davies *ph* Robert Davies *ad* Wayne and Sandy Attrill *ed* Lena Farugia, Carla Sandrock
☆ Bill Flynn, John Kani, Paul Slabolepsy

Saturday Night Fever ***

US   1977   119m   Movielab
Paramount/Robert Stigwood (Milt Felsen)

🎞 🎞 📀 🎧

Italian roughnecks in Brooklyn live for their Saturday night disco dancing, and one of them falls in love with a girl who makes him realize there are better things in life.
Foul-mouthed, fast-paced slice of life which plays like an updated version of Marty except that all the characters seem to have crawled from under stones. The slick direction, fast editing and exciting dance numbers do something to take away the sour taste.
w Norman Wexler *story* Nik Cohn *d* John Badham *ph* Ralf D. Bode *m* David Shire *pd* Charles Bailey *ed* David Rawlins *songs* Barry, Robin and Maurice Gibb (and others), performed by the Bee Gees
☆ John Travolta, Karen Lynn Gorney, Barry Miller, Joseph Cali, Paul Pape, Bruce Ornstein
'A stylish piece of contemporary anthropology, an urban safari into darkest America, a field study of the mystery cults among the young braves and squaws growing up in North Brooklyn.' – *Alan Brien, Sunday Times*
& John Travolta

Saturday Night Out

GB   1963   96m   bw
Compton-Tekli
Five sailors spend an overnight leave in London.
Portmanteau drama in which all elements are equally uninteresting.

---

w Donald and Derek Ford d Robert Hartford-Davis ph Peter Newbrook m Robert Richards
☆ Bernard Lee, Heather Sears, John Bonney, Francesca Annis, Erika Remberg, Colin Campbell, David Lodge

Saturday's Children
US 1940 101m bw
Warner (Henry Blanke)
An impractical young inventor marries an ambitious young woman, but depressed finances lead to discord.
Glum, dated rehash of a 1929 silent; watchable but not compelling.
w Julius J. and Philip G. Epstein play Maxwell Anderson d Vincent Sherman ph James Wong Howe
☆ John Garfield, Claude Rains, Anne Shirley, Lee Patrick, George Tobias, Roscoe Karns, Elizabeth Risdon, Berton Churchill
† The story was also made in 1935 as *Maybe It's Love*, with Ross Alexander, Henry Travers and Gloria Stuart; William McGann directed without flair.

Saturday's Hero
US 1951 110m bw
Columbia (Sidney Buchman)
GB title: *Idols in the Dust*
A poor boy wins a football scholarship but finds his value to the college is purely commercial and he isn't given time to learn anything.
A spirited attack on the American sporting system, but a dull and overlong film.
w Millard Lampell, Sidney Buchman novel *The Hero* by Millard Lampell d David Miller ph Lee Garmes m Elmer Bernstein
☆ John Derek, Donna Reed, Sidney Blackmer, Alexander Knox, Elliott Lewis, Howard St John

Saturn 3
GB 1980 87m colour
ITC/Transcontinental (Stanley Donen)
▦▦ ⊙ ⊚
A maniac builds a robot on a remote space station, and they both go berserk.
Rather unpleasant blend of space fiction, horror and suspense, with some nasty detail and a general feeling that the actors wish they were elsewhere.
w Martin Amis story John Barry d Stanley Donen ph Billy Williams m Elmer Bernstein pd Stuart Craig
☆ Kirk Douglas, Farrah Fawcett, Harvey Keitel, Ed Bishop

Satyricon *
Italy/France 1969 129m DeLuxe
Panavision
UA/PAA/PEA (Alberto Grimaldi)
▦▦ ▦▦ ⊚
aka: *Fellini Satyricon*
Sexual adventures of a Roman student.
Garish, sporadically enjoyable sketches on a very thin thread of plot: a more benevolent version of the usual Fellini nightmare.
w Federico Fellini, Bernardino Zapponi d Federico Fellini ph Giuseppe Rotunno m Nino Rota, Ilhan Mimaroglu, Tod Dockstader, Andrew Rudin pd Danilo Donati
☆ Martin Potter, Hiram Keller, Salvo Randone, Max Born
'A picaresque satire in fragments … a series of tableaux which carry the poetry visually at the price of coherence.' – Mike Wallington, MFB
'Part of the gradual decomposition of what once was one of the greatest talents in film history … a gimcrack, shopworn nightmare.' – John Simon
⌷ Federico Fellini (as director)

Le Sauvage
France/Italy 1978 107m Eastmancolor
Lira/PAI (Raymond Danon)
A business executive has opted out of life to be alone on a desert island, but on his last night in the city accidentally helps a runaway heiress who follows him.
A promising and amusing start is squandered in the tedious island sequences of this patchy romantic comedy, which does however leave one with a sense of freshness and optimism rare in the cinema of the seventies.
w Jean-Paul Rappeneau, Elizabeth Rappeneau, Jean-Loup Dabadie d Jean-Paul Rappeneau ph Pierre Lhomme m Michel Legrand

☆ Yves Montand, Catherine Deneuve, Luigi Vannucchi, Dana Wynter

Sauve Qui Peut (La Vie) *
France/Switzerland 1980 87m colour
Sara/MK2/Saga/Sonimage/CDIC/ZDF/SSR/ORF
⌑
aka: *Slow Motion*
US title: *Every Man for Himself*
The lives of three people cross: a country girl who becomes a prostitute in the city, a woman leaving the city for a rural life, and her lover, who is not sure where he wants to be.
Godard's return to more commercial cinema is intermittently interesting, but lacks the challenge and playfulness of his best work.
w Anne-Marie Miéville, Jean-Claude Carrière d Jean-Luc Godard ph William Lubtchansky, Renato Berta, Jean-Bernard Menoud m Gabriel Yared ad Romain Goupil ed Anne-Marie Miéville, Jean-Luc Godard
☆ Isabelle Huppert, Jacques Dutronc, Nathalie Baye, Roland Amstutz, Anna Baldaccini, Fred Personne

The Savage
US 1952 95m Technicolor
Paramount (Mel Epstein)
A white boy grows up with Indians and later suffers from divided loyalties.
Solemn, rather tedious but well produced Western.
w Sydney Boehm novel L. L. Foreman d George Marshall ph John F. Seitz m Paul Sawtell
☆ Charlton Heston, Susan Morrow, Peter Hanson, Joan Taylor, Richard Rober, Don Porter

The Savage Eye *
US 1959 68m bw
City Film Corporation (Ben Maddow, Joseph Strick, Sidney Meyers)
An unhappily married young woman takes a jaundiced view of life around her in Los Angeles.
The wisp of plot is merely an excuse to present a documentary exposé of the seamier side of life in America's most eccentric city, with its faith healers and revellers. Much of it is fascinating, though the film is not a cohesive whole and the would-be poetic commentary falls on its face.
ph Jack Couffer, Haskell Wexler, Helen Levitt m Leonard Rosenman wd/ed Ben Maddow, Joseph Strick, Sidney Meyers
☆ Barbara Baxley, Gary Merrill, Herschel Bernardi
'The picture is funny, pathetic, cruel, terrible; and it is worth going miles to see.' – Dilys Powell, Sunday Times

The Savage Guns
US/Spain 1961 83m Metrocolor
Cinemascope
Capricorn/Tecisa/MGM (Jimmy Sangster)
After the Civil War, an American rancher settles in Mexico but finds his pacifist principles tested by bandits.
Unappealing, stodgy Western with the Hammer horror team rather curiously cast as co-producers.
w Edmund Morris d Michael Carreras ph Alfredo Fraile m Anton Garcia Abril
☆ Richard Basehart, Don Taylor, Alex Nicol, Jose Nieto, Fernando Rey

Savage Hearts
GB 1996 111m colour
August/Wavepower Navigation/Bratton (Keith Hayley)
▦▦
Told she has six months to live, a young woman steals £2m from an aristocratic drug dealer and goes on a spending spree, aided and hampered by a con man and a prostitute.
Drearily incompetent thriller, poorly acted, scripted and directed; the narrative twists and turns without going anywhere interesting.
wd Mark Ezra ph James Aspinall m Dominic Crawford-Collins, Basil Moore-Asfouri pd Jenny Chartres ed Andrea MacArthur
☆ Jamie Harris, Maryam D'Abo, Myriam Cyr, Richard Harris, Stephen Marcus, Angus Deayton, Jerry Hall, Julian Fellowes

The Savage Innocents
GB/France/Italy 1960 107m SuperTechnirama 70
Joseph Janni/Magic Film/Playart/Gray Films (Maleno Malenotti)
aka: *Ombre Bianchi*
Trials of an Eskimo and his wife in Canada's frozen north.
Conscientious, determined and very boring account of Eskimo life played by actors talking pidgin English. Not a success despite the magnificent photography.
w Nicholas Ray novel *Top of the World* by Hans Ruesch d Nicholas Ray, Baccio Bandini ph Aldo Tonti, Peter Hennessy m Angelo Lavagnino
☆ Anthony Quinn, Yoko Tani, Marie Yang, Peter O'Toole, Carlo Justini, Anna May Wong, Lee Montague, Ed Devereaux
† The Anna May Wong in the cast is not the famous silent star.

'Don't Bother To Hide … He's Already Inside.'

The Savage Intruder
US 1973 90m Movielab
Congdon Films (Donald Wolfe)
▦▦
A former Hollywood star hires as a nurse a psychopathic killer who dismembers middle-aged women.
Gruesome thriller, which borrows from Night Must Fall and Sunset Boulevard and is inept when it is not unpleasant.
wd Donald Wolfe ph John A. Morrill m Stu Phillips pd Norman Houlé ed Hatwig Deeb
☆ Miriam Hopkins, John David Garfield, Gale Sondergaard, Florence Lake, Lester Matthews, Riza Royce, Joe Besser, Minta Durfee, Virginia Wing
† The film was cut to 85m for its British video release.

Savage Islands
⌖⌖ New Zealand 1983 94m colour
Paramount (Lloyd Phillips, Rob Whitehouse)
On the morning of his execution, a pirate recalls rescuing a beautiful Englishwoman from a rival brigand.
Standard adventure fare, given a slight novelty by being set in the era of steam warships.
w John Hughes, David Odell story Lloyd Phillips d Ferdinand Fairfax ph Tony Imi m Trevor Jones pd Maurice Cain ed John Shirley
☆ Tommy Lee Jones, Michael O'Keefe, Max Phipps, Jenny Seagrove, Bruce Allpress, Grant Tilley

Savage Messiah *
GB 1972 103m Metrocolor
MGM/Russ-Arts (Ken Russell)
The life together (1910–14) of the 18-year-old painter Gaudier and 38-year-old Sophie Brzeska.
Intense, fragmentary art film about two eccentrics; would have better suited TV.
w Christopher Logue book H. S. Ede d Ken Russell ph Dick Bush m Michael Garrett pd Derek Jarman
☆ Dorothy Tutin, Scott Anthony, Helen Mirren, Lindsay Kemp, Michael Gough, John Justin

'1986. Passion, Rage, Liberty and Love.'

Savage Nights *
France 1992 126m colour
Banfilm Ter/La Sept/Erre/Canal/Sofinergie II/CNC (Nella Banfi)
▦▦ ⌑
original title: *Les Nuits Fauves*
A bisexual cameraman begins an affair with a 17-year-old girl without telling her he is HIV positive; she finds it impossible to share him with others.
A rawly emotional film about sex, love and death and rootless, excitement-seeking young people, often hysterical in tone and curiously uninvolving.
wd Cyril Collard novel *Les Nuits Fauves* by Cyril Collard ph Manuel Téran m Cyril Collard and others ed Lise Beaulieu
☆ Cyril Collard, Romane Bohringer, Carlos Lopez, Corine Blue, Claude Winter, René-Marc Bini, Maria Schneider, Clémentine Célarié
'The movie finally confounds everyone's best intentions, including the audience's. It is both sensational and sentimentalized. It ricochets from one lurid fresco to another.' – Richard Corliss, Time
† Cyril Collard died of AIDS in 1993, four days before his film won French César awards for best film, best first film, best female newcomer (Romane Bohringer) and best editing.

Savage Pampas
Spain/Argentina/US 1967 108m
Eastmancolor Superpanorama
Jaime Prados-Dasa-Sam Bronston
In 19th-century Argentina the commander of an isolated fort finds that a bandit is bribing his men to desert.
Densely plotted semi-Western, sometimes good to look at but slow and lugubrious.
w Hugo Fregonese, John Melson d Hugo Fregonese ph Marcel Berenguer m Waldo de los Rios
☆ Robert Taylor, Ron Randell, Ty Hardin, Rosenda Monteros, Marc Lawrence

Savage Princess: see Aan

Savage Sam *
⌖⌖ US 1962 104m Technicolor
Walt Disney (Bill Anderson)
The youngest son of a homesteading family has a troublesome dog which redeems itself by tracking down Apaches.
Folksy boy-and-dog Western, good of its kind, with adequate suspense and scenery.
w Fred Gipson, William Tunberg d Norman Tokar ph Edward Colman m Oliver Wallace
☆ Brian Keith, Tommy Kirk, Kevin Corcoran, Dewey Martin, Jeff York
'A cadet edition of the best of Ford.' – MFB

Savage Wilderness
US 1956 98m Technicolor Cinemascope
Columbia (William Fadiman)
GB title: *The Last Frontier*
An Indian-hating fort commander puts himself and his charges in jeopardy.
Standard Western with good performances and excellent action scenes.
w Philip Yordan, Russell S. Hughes novel *The Gilded Rooster* by Richard Emery Roberts d Anthony Mann ph William Mellor m Leigh Harline
☆ Victor Mature, Robert Preston, Guy Madison, Anne Bancroft, James Whitmore, Peter Whitney

Savages
US 1972 106m colour
Angelika/Merchant-Ivory (Joseph Saleh)
Forest wanderers take over a deserted mansion and begin to feel its civilizing influence.
Mild fable which needed a Buñuel to do it justice; a few lively moments.
w George Swift Trow, Michael O'Donoghue d James Ivory ph Walter Lassally m Joe Raposo
☆ Lewis J. Stadlen, Anne Francine, Thayer David, Salome Jens, Neil Fitzgerald
'Adds up to a disappointing and indigestible blend of flip anthropological metaphor, sophomoric gags and intentional or unintentional visual nods to other directors.' – Nigel Andrews, MFB

'Juggle the books. Set fire to the factory. Supply women for the clients. Harry Stoner will do anything to get one more season.'

Save the Tiger *
US 1973 100m Movielab
Paramount/Jalem/Filmways/Cirandinha (Steve Shagan)
▦▦ ⊚
A middle-aged businessman regrets the slack morality of modern America.
Self-adulatory drama which really has little point but gets a few marks for meaning well and for vivid scenes.
w Steve Shagan d John G. Avildsen ph Jim Crabe m Marvin Hamlisch
☆ Jack Lemmon, Jack Gilford, Laurie Heineman, Norman Burton, Thayer David
'A scathing indictment of the US, of materialism, war, marriage – the works. Wordy, literate and deeply felt.' – NFT, 1974
'Not a very good movie but it's rather a brave one, a serious-minded examination of some of the least interesting aspects of the failed American Dream.' – Vincent Canby, New York Times
⌸ Jack Lemmon
⌷ Steve Shagan; Jack Gilford

Saving Grace
US 1986 112m Technicolor Technovision
Columbia/Embassy (Herbert F. Solow)
▤▤ ⊚ ⌑
A Pope escapes from office to meet the real people.

The trouble with this movie is, he learns nothing by doing so.

w Joaquin Montana *novel* Celia Gittelson d Robert M. Young *ph* Reynaldo Villalobos

☆ Tom Conti, Fernando Rey, Erland Josephson, Giancarlo Giannini, Donald Hewlett

'More sleeping draught than balm for the spirits.' – *Sight and Sound*

'The mission is a man.'
Saving Private Ryan ***
US 1998 169m Technicolor
Paramount/Amblin/Mutual (Steven Spielberg, Ian Bryce, Mark Gordon, Gary Levinsohn)

After surviving the D-Day landings, eight soldiers are sent on a special mission to bring back a private, the only survivor of four brothers, who is somewhere behind enemy lines.
Two battles, the opening sequence on the Omaha beach and a later one in a ruined town, are virtuoso demonstrations of the director's art; in between, though, the film settles for a standard platoon-in-peril routine familiar from other war movies.
w Robert Rodat d Steven Spielberg *ph* Janusz Kaminski m John Williams *pd* Tom Sanders *ed* Michael Kahn

☆ Tom Hanks, Edward Burns, Tom Sizemore, Jeremy Davies, Vin Diesel, Adam Goldberg, Barry Pepper, Giovanni Ribisi, Matt Damon, Dennis Farina, Ted Danson, Harve Presnell, Harrison Young

'As powerful, devastating, memorable and moving as movies get.' – *Ian Freer, Empire*
'One of the greatest war movies ever made.' – *James Cameron-Wilson, Film Review*
† The film took more than $460m at the box-office worldwide.
▮ Steven Spielberg; Janusz Kaminski; Michael Kahn; sound; sound effects editing
⸸ best picture; Tom Hanks; Robert Rodat; John Williams; Tom Sanders; make-up
▼ visual effects; sound

'Hope is worth fighting for.'
'He's fighting a war he doesn't believe in, hoping to find something he does.'
Savior
US 1998 103m DeLuxe Panavision
First Independent/Initial Entertainment (Oliver Stone, Janet Yang)

An American mercenary, fighting for the Serbians in Bosnia, helps deliver the baby of a woman raped by Muslims and tries to get them both to safety, while threatened by both sides in the civil war.
Topical and melodramatic war movie that simplifies a complex situation in order to make an obvious point.
w Robert Orr d Peter Antonijevic *ph* Ian Wilson m David Robbins *pd* Vladislav Lasic *ed* Ian Crafford, Gabriella Cristiani

☆ Dennis Quaid, Nastassja Kinski, Stellan Skarsgard, Natasa Ninkovic, Sergej Trifunovic, Nebojsa Glogovac, Vesna Trivalic

'Grim but engrossing pic ... has little going for it commercially but is an impressive addition to the war-as-existential-battlefield genre that dates back to the '50s.' – *Derek Elley, Variety*

Saviour of the Soul
Hong Kong 1992 90m colour
Team Work (Andy Lau)

In the 21st century, a city soldier tries to protect the woman he loves from a ruthless criminal, Silver Fox, who has supernatural powers.
A movie in comic-book style, with little in the way of comprehensible narrative; it relies instead on immature notions of romantic love, and outbursts of spectacular, well-choreographed and violent action to compensate for its paper-thin characterizations.
w Kar-Wai Wong d Yuen Kwai, David Lai

☆ Andy Lau, Anita Mui, Aaron Kwok

'*The Water Margin* is crossed with manga and *Blade Runner* in this imaginative sci-fi action movie.' – *Sight and Sound*
† The English subtitles are often in a language all their own: 'We'll treat him some nutrious soup'; 'It's useless to have force, but should have brain!'; and 'I think you are guest so I give you some face.'

Sawdust and Tinsel *
Sweden 1953 95m bw
Svensk Filmindustri

aka: *The Naked Night*
original title: *Gycklarnas Afton*
The owner of a travelling circus leaves his mistress for his separated wife, and is challenged to fight by the mistress's new lover.
Powerfully-made yet rather pointless melodrama about unpleasant people.
wd Ingmar Bergman *ph* Sven Nykvist m Karl-Birger Blomdahl

☆ Harriet Andersson, Ake Grönberg, Hasse Ekman, Annika Tretow

'One of the extremely rare instances of a film's elements all blending perfectly.' – *John Simon*

The Saxon Charm
US 1948 88m bw
Universal (Joseph Sistrom)

A Broadway impresario dominates the lives of those around him.
Rather heavy-going comedy drama which could have done with more malicious wit; allegedly based on Jed Harris.
wd Claude Binyon *novel* Frederick Wakeman *ph* Milton Krasner m Walter Scharf

☆ Robert Montgomery, Susan Hayward, John Payne, Audrey Totter, Henry Morgan, Harry von Zell, Cara Williams, Chill Wills, Heather Angel

Say Anything... *
US 1989 100m DeLuxe
TCF (Polly Platt)

A student whose ambition it is to become a kick-boxer dates a beautiful and brainy girl, to the distress of her father.
Better than average teenage romance, deft and sometimes witty.
wd Cameron Crowe *ph* Laszlo Kovacs m Richard Gibbs, Anne Dudley, Nancy Wilson *pd* Mark Mansbridge *ed* Richard Marks

☆ John Cusack, Ione Skye, John Mahoney, Lili Taylor, Amy Brooks, Pamela Segall, Jason Gould, Joan Cusack, Lois Chiles

'One of the best films of 1989 – a film that is really about something, that cares deeply about the issues it contains – and yet it also works wonderfully as a funny, warmhearted romantic comedy.' – *Roger Ebert*

'My husband has a memory that you can never share – he can remember me when I was nineteen'
Say Hello to Yesterday
GB 1970 92m Eastmancolor
Josef Shaftel (William Hill)

A middle-aged married woman goes to London for shopping and is pursued by a strange young man whom she allows to seduce her.
Unattractive 'with it' romantic drama with a swinging London setting, a long way after Brief Encounter.
w Alvin Rakoff, Peter King d Alvin Rakoff *ph* Geoffrey Unsworth m Riz Ortolani

☆ Jean Simmons, Leonard Whiting, *Evelyn Laye*, John Lee, Jack Woolgar

Say It in French
US 1938 67m bw
Paramount

A golf champion marries a French girl, but on his return, in order to help his father's finances, has to pretend to be marrying a rich girl, so his wife pretends to be a maid.
Thin comedy which has a job to sustain its short running time.
w Frederick Jackson *play* Jacques Deval d Andrew L. Stone

☆ Ray Milland, Olympe Bradna, Irene Hervey, Janet Beecher, Mary Carlisle, Holmes Herbert, Erik Rhodes

'The harder it strives for hare-brained badinage, the more laboured it becomes.' – *Variety*

Say It with Flowers (A Human Story) *
GB 1934 71m bw
Real Art (Julius Hagen)

Traders in a London street market rally round when a flower-seller becomes too ill to work.
A mix of music-hall jokes and a documentary on Cockney life which, for all its caricatures, reveals more about the everyday life of its time than many more
ambitious films. It has not only acquired the fascination of a social document but also gives a rare glimpse of several music-hall performers: Charles Coburn (singing 'The Man Who Broke the Bank at Monte Carlo'), Marie Kendall (singing 'Did Your First Wife Ever Do That?' and 'Just Like the Ivy'), and Florrie Forde (reprising her hits 'Lassie from Lancashire', 'Has Anybody Here Seen Kelly', 'Hold Your Hand Out Naughty Boy', 'Oh, Oh Antonio' and 'Down at the Old Bull and Bush').
w H. Fowler Mear *story* William Orton d John Baxter *ph* Sydney Blythe *md* Colin Wark *ad* James A. Carter *ed* Michael C. Chorlton

☆ Mary Clare, Ben Field, George Carney, Mark Daly, Edgar Driver, Freddie Watts, Edwin Ellis, Wilson Coleman

Say It with Songs
US 1929 89m bw
Warner

A radio singer accidentally kills a man and is jailed for manslaughter.
Miscalculated star vehicle with a few good moments among the sentiment and melodrama.
w Darryl F. Zanuck, Joseph Jackson, Harvey Gates d Lloyd Bacon *ph* Lee Garmes

☆ Al Jolson, Davey Lee, Marian Nixon, Fred Kohler, Holmes Herbert
† Though Jolson was paid half a million dollars to do it, the film was a tremendous flop. The songs were again by De Sylva, Brown and Henderson, but 'Little Pal' was not another 'Sonny Boy'.

Say One for Me
US 1959 117m DeLuxe Cinemascope
TCF/Bing Crosby (Frank Tashlin)

Adventures of a parish priest in New York's theatrical quarter.
Unconvincing, unattractive imitation of Going My Way which counters bad taste with religiosity.
w Robert O'Brien d Frank Tashlin *ph* Leo Tover *md* Lionel Newman *songs* Sammy Cahn, James Van Heusen

☆ Bing Crosby, Robert Wagner, Debbie Reynolds, Ray Walston, Les Tremayne, Connie Gilchrist, Frank McHugh, Joe Besser, Sebastian Cabot

'Tasteless and disturbing.' – *Variety*
⸸ Lionel Newman

'I am not allowed to love. But I will love you if that is your desire!'
Sayonara **
US 1957 147m Technirama
Goetz Pictures-Pennebaker (William Goetz)

An American air force major in Tokyo after the war falls in love with a Japanese actress.
A lush travelogue interrupted by two romances, one tragic and one happy. A great success at the time, though mainly of interest to Americans; now vaguely dated.
w Paul Osborn *novel* James A. Michener d Joshua Logan *ph* Ellsworth Fredericks m Franz Waxman *ad* Ted Haworth *ed* Arthur P. Schmidt, Philip W. Anderson

☆ Marlon Brando, Miyoshi Umeki, Miiko Taka, Red Buttons, Ricardo Montalban, Patricia Owens, Kent Smith, Martha Scott, James Garner
▮ Miyoshi Umeki; Red Buttons; art direction
⸸ best picture; Paul Osborn; Joshua Logan; Ellsworth Fredericks; Marlon Brando; editing

Scalawag
US/Italy 1973 93m Technicolor
Bryna/Inex-Oceania (Anne Douglas)

Mexico 1840: a one-legged pirate and a boy try to trace a hidden treasure.
Flagrant reworking of Treasure Island, heavily overdone by stars and rhubarbing extras alike.
w Albert Maltz, Sid Fleischman d Kirk Douglas *ph* Jack Cardiff m John Cameron

☆ Kirk Douglas, Mark Lester, Neville Brand, Don Stroud, Lesley-Anne Down, Phil Brown

The Scalphunters *
US 1968 102m DeLuxe Panavision
UA/Bristol/Norlan (Levy-Gardner-Laven)

An old cowboy and a black ex-slave track down a gang who kill Indians for their scalps.
Vigorous, aimless, likeable comedy Western with the emphasis on brawling.
w William Norton d Sydney Pollack *ph* Duke Callaghan, Richard Moore m Elmer Bernstein

☆ Burt Lancaster, Ossie Davis, Telly Savalas, Shelley Winters, Nick Cravat, Paul Picerni

'It is the sort of frolic where bodies litter the ground, but you know they'll get up and draw their pay. And where even a villain can crack a joke without losing face.' – *Robert Ottaway*

The Scamp
GB 1957 90m bw
Minter/Renown (James H. Lawrie)

A couple decide to adopt a lovable but mischievous boy.
Amiable minor film, a vehicle for a child actor who had made an impression in Smiley (qv) the year before, a success he was never to recapture.
wd Wolf Rilla *play* Charlotte Hastings *ph* Freddie Francis m Francis Chagrin *ad* Elven Webb *ed* Bernard Gribble

☆ Colin Petersen, Richard Attenborough, Dorothy Alison, Terence Morgan, Jill Adams, Sam Kydd, Margaretta Scott, Geoffrey Keen, Charles Lloyd Pack

Scandal *
GB 1988 115m Fujicolour
Palace/Miramax/British Screen (Stephen Woolley)

A showgirl's sexual relationships with a leading British politician and a Russian diplomat cause a major upset.
Leaden account of the British scandal of the 1960s involving Christine Keeler, osteopath Stephen Ward and John Profumo, a Conservative Minister.
w Michael Thomas d Michael Caton-Jones *ph* Mike Molloy m Carl Davis *pd* Simon Holland *ed* Angus Newton

☆ John Hurt, Joanne Whalley-Kilmer, Ian McKellen, Bridget Fonda, Leslie Phillips, Britt Ekland, Daniel Massey, Roland Gift, Jeroen Krabbé

Scandal at Scourie
US 1953 90m Metrocolor
MGM (Edwin H. Knopf)

The wife of the Protestant reeve of a Scottish-Canadian Protestant community adopts a Catholic child.
Sentimental whimsy with no holds barred, but with rather jaded acting and production.
w Norman Corwin, Leonard Spigelgass, Karl Tunberg d Jean Negulesco *ph* Robert Planck m Daniele Amfitheatrof

☆ Greer Garson, Walter Pidgeon, Agnes Moorehead, Arthur Shields, Philip Ober, Donna Corcoran

A Scandal in Paris *
US 1946 100m bw
UA/Arnold Pressburger

aka: *Thieves' Holiday*
Adventures of Vidocq, a 19th-century rogue who became Paris chief of police.
The actors look uneasy in their costumes, and the sets are cardboard, but there is fun to be had from this light comedy-drama.
w Ellis St Joseph d Douglas Sirk *ph* Guy Roe m Hanns Eisler

☆ George Sanders, Signe Hasso, Carole Landis, Akim Tamiroff, Gene Lockhart

Scandal Sheet
US 1931 77m bw
Paramount

A newspaper editor with principles prints scandal involving his wife.
Dated star drama.
w Vincent Lawrence, Max Marcin d John Cromwell

☆ George Bancroft, Kay Francis, Regis Toomey, Clive Brook

Scandal Sheet
US 1939 67m bw
Columbia

A ruthless publisher sacrifices himself to save his son.
Uninteresting star quickie.
w Joseph Carole d Nick Grinde

☆ Otto Kruger, Ona Munson, Edward Norris

Scandal Sheet

US 1952 81m bw
Columbia (Edward Small)
GB title: The Dark Page

An editor has to allow his star reporter to expose a murderer – himself.

Obvious, reasonably holding melodrama with familiar characters.

w Ted Sherdeman, Eugene Ling, James Poe *novel* Samuel Fuller *d* Phil Karlson *ph* Burnett Guffey *m* George Duning

☆ Broderick Crawford, John Derek, Donna Reed, Rosemary de Camp, Henry O'Neill, Henry Morgan

Scandal Street

US 1938 63m bw
Paramount

The arrival in a small town of an innocent young girl causes gossip which leads to murder.

Satisfactory mini-drama for the easily pleased.

w Bertram Millhauser, Eddie Welch *story* Vera Caspary *d* James Hogan

☆ Lew Ayres, Louise Campbell, Roscoe Karns, Porter Hall, Virginia Weidler, Edgar Kennedy, Elizabeth Patterson

'A curiously beguiling little hodge-podge.' – *Variety*

Le Scandale: see The Champagne Murders

Scandalous!

GB 1984 92m Technicolor
Hemdale/Raleigh/Angeles Cinema Investors (Arlene Sellers, Alex Winitsky)

A TV reporter becomes involved with two con artists, who seem to have some connection with the murder of his wife.

Frantic black comedy which never even begins to be funny.

w Rob Cohen, John Byrum *d* Rob Cohen *ph* Jack Cardiff *m* Dave Grusin *pd* Peter Mullins

☆ Robert Hays, John Gielgud, Pamela Stephenson, M. Emmet Walsh, Nancy Wood, Jim Dale

Scandalous John

♛♛ US 1971 117m Technicolor
Walt Disney (Bill Walsh)

The elderly owner of a derelict ranch resists all efforts to close him up.

Unsatisfactory Disney attempt to capture a more adult audience than usual; overlong, repetitious and dreary.

w Bill Walsh, Don da Gradi *novel* Richard Gardner *d* Robert Butler *ph* Frank Phillips *m* Rod McKuen

☆ Brian Keith, Alfonso Arau, Michele Carey, Rick Lenz, Henry Morgan, Simon Oakland

'Their thoughts can kill!'

Scanners

Canada 1980 103m Eastmancolor
Filmplan International (Claude Heroux)

Certain people are found to be telepathic 'scanners' able to lock at will into other people's nervous systems. This has the occasional result of blowing apart the other people's heads.

Overlong science fiction which concentrates on the nastier elements.

wd David Cronenberg *ph* Mark Irwin *m* Howard Shore

☆ Jennifer O'Neill, Patrick McGoohan, Stephen Lack, Lawrence Dane, Michael Ironside

Scanners II: The New Order

Canada 1991 104m colour
Malofilm (René Malo)

A corrupt police chief attempts to use people with frightening telepathic powers for his own ends.

Effective sequel with several exploding heads.

w B. J. Nelson *d* Christian Duguay *ph* Rodney Gibbons *m* Marty Simon *pd* Richard Tassé *ed* Yves Langlois *sp* Michael Smithson

☆ David Hewlett, Yvan Ponton, Deborah Raffin, Isabelle Majias, Raoul Trujillo, Tom Butler, Vlasta Vrana

'A first class imitation of the mind-blowing original.' – *Variety*

Scanners III: The Takeover

Canada 1992 101m colour
Republic/Malofilm (Rene Malo)

An experimental drug turns a female scanner into a power-hungry killer.

The intriguing notion of the first film has now become an excuse for a horror movie indistinguishable from, and no more distinguished than, a hundred others.

w B. J. Nelson, Julie Richard, David Preston, Christian Duguay *d* Christian Duguay *ph* Hughes de Haeck *m* Marty Simon *pd* Michael Joy *ed* Yves Langlois *sp* Mike Maddi

☆ Liliana Komorowska, Valerie Valois, Steve Parrish, Colin Fox, Daniel Pilon, Michel Perron, Harry Hill

'A technically slick, relatively mindless thriller.' – *Variety*

The Scapegoat *

GB 1959 92m bw
MGM/Du Maurier-Guinness (Dennis Van Thal)

A quiet bachelor on a French holiday is tricked into assuming the identity of a lookalike aristocrat who wants to commit a murder.

Disappointing adaptation of a good story, with much evidence of re-cutting and an especially slack middle section.

w Gore Vidal, Robert Hamer *novel* Daphne du Maurier *d* Robert Hamer *ph* Paul Beeson *m* Bronislau Kaper

☆ Alec Guinness, Bette Davis, Irene Worth, Nicole Maurey, Pamela Brown, Geoffrey Keen

'A disaster.' – *Daphne du Maurier*

The Scar

US 1948 83m bw
Eagle-Lion (Bryan Foy, Paul Henreid)

aka: Hollow Triumph

A fugitive kills his psychoanalyst double and takes his place, but is caught for the double's crimes.

Cheap suspense thriller with no suspense and no surprises.

w Daniel Fuchs *novel* Murray Forbes *d* Steve Sekely *ph* John Alton *m* Sol Kaplan

☆ Joan Bennett, Paul Henreid, Eduard Franz, Leslie Brooks, John Qualen, Mabel Paige, Herbert Rudley

Scaramouche **

♛♛ US 1952 115m Technicolor
MGM (Carey Wilson)

A young man disguises himself as an actor to avenge the death of his friend at the hands of a wicked marquis.

Cheerful swashbuckler set in French revolutionary times, first filmed in the twenties with Ramon Novarro. MGM costume production at somewhere near its best.

w Ronald Millar, George Froeschel *novel* Rafael Sabatini *d* George Sidney *ph* Charles Rosher *m* Victor Young *ad* Cedric Gibbons, Hans Peters

☆ Stewart Granger, Mel Ferrer, Eleanor Parker, Janet Leigh, Henry Wilcoxon, Nina Foch, Lewis Stone, Robert Coote, Richard Anderson

† The sword fight, at 6½ minutes, is credited with being the longest in cinema history.

Scarecrow *

US 1973 112m Technicolor Panavision
Warner (Robert M. Sherman)

Two of the world's losers hitch-hike across America.

Well-shot but eventually dreary parable of friendship, a pedestrian Easy Rider.

w Garry Michael White *d* Jerry Schatzberg *ph* Vilmos Zsigmond *m* Fred Myrow

☆ Gene Hackman, Al Pacino

'Here's a picture that manages to abuse two American myths at once – the Road and the Male Pair.' – *Stanley Kauffmann*

The Scarecrow *

New Zealand 1981 88m colour
Oasis/New Zealand National Film Unit (Rob Whitehouse)

In a small town in the early fifties, a strange chain of events is set in motion by the disappearance of six chickens.

A curious mix of sinister atmosphere which seems mystical and sinister events which are all too real. Interesting but unsatisfying, both as a murder mystery and as a study in evil.

w Michael Heath, Sam Pillsbury *novel* Ronald Hugh Morrieson *d* Sam Pillsbury *ph* James Bartle *m* Schtung

☆ John Carradine, Tracy Mann, Jonathan Smith, Daniel McLaren, Denise O'Connell, Anne Flannery

Scared Stiff

US 1945 65m bw
Paramount/Pine-Thomas

A timid reporter stumbles over a murder on a bus and finds the culprit before the sheriff arrives.

Tedious comedy mystery.

w Geoffrey Homes, Maxwell Shane *d* Frank McDonald

☆ Jack Haley, Ann Savage, Barton MacLane, Veda Ann Borg, George E. Stone, Lucien Littlefield

'They're making a spook-tacle of themselves!'

Scared Stiff

US 1953 108m bw
Paramount (Hal B. Wallis)

Night-club entertainers get involved with a girl who has inherited a spooky castle off the Cuban coast.

Stretched-out remake of The Ghost Breakers; the last half hour, being closest to the original, is the most nearly funny.

w Herbert Baker, Walter de Leon, Ed Simmons, Norman Lear *d* George Marshall *ph* Ernest Laszlo *md* Joseph J. Lilley

☆ Dean Martin, Jerry Lewis, Lizabeth Scott, Carmen Miranda, George Dolenz, Dorothy Malone, William Ching, Jack Lambert

Scared to Death

US 1947 65m Cinecolor
Golden Gate

A corpse explains how it came to be dead.

Eccentric mystery set in a sanatorium presided over by a mad doctor; the green-tinged colour adds to the atmosphere.

w Walter Abbott *d* Christy Cabanne *ph* Marcel Le Picard *m* Carl Hoefle *ad* Harry Reif *ed* George McGuire

☆ Bela Lugosi, Douglas Fowley, Joyce Compton, George Zucco, Nat Pendleton, Angelo Rossitto, Molly Lamont

† It was released on DVD together with Devil Bat (qv).

The Scarf

US 1951 86m bw
UA/Gloria (I. G. Goldsmith)

A man escapes from a lunatic asylum and proves himself innocent of the crime for which he was committed.

Glum and pretentious murder mystery with a pictorial style to match its flowery dialogue.

wd E. A. Dupont *ph* Franz Planer *m* Herschel Burke Gilbert

☆ John Ireland, Mercedes McCambridge, Emlyn Williams, James Barton, Lloyd Gough, Basil Ruysdael

'I'm going to run the whole works. There's only one law: do it first, do it yourself, and keep doing it!'

Scarface ****

US 1932 99m bw
Howard Hughes

aka: The Shame of a Nation

The life and death of a Chicago gangster of the twenties.

Obviously modelled on Al Capone, with an incestuous sister thrown in, this was perhaps the most vivid film of the gangster cycle, and its revelling in its own sins was not obscured by the subtitle, The Shame of a Nation.

w Ben Hecht, Seton I. Miller, John Lee Mahin, W. R. Burnett, Fred Pasley *novel* Armitage Trail *d* Howard Hawks *ph* Lee Garmes, L. W. O'Connell *m* Adolph Tandler, Gus Arnheim

☆ Paul Muni, Ann Dvorak, George Raft, Boris Karloff, Osgood Perkins, Karen Morley, C. Henry Gordon, Vince Barnett, Henry Armetta, Edwin Maxwell

'Presumably the last of the gangster films, on a promise, it is going to make people sorry that there won't be any more. Should draw wherever it can play.' – *Variety*

'More brutal, more cruel, more wholesale than any of its predecessors.' – *James Shelley Hamilton*

'Because it was so close to the actual events, it possesses a kind of newsreel quality which cannot be recaptured or imitated. It vibrates with the impact of things that were real and deeply felt.' – *National Film Theatre programme, 1961*

† On original release added scenes showed Tony tried, convicted and hanged, though since Muni is never seen, it appears that they were an afterthought made when he was not available.

Scarface

US 1983 170m Technicolor Panavision
Universal (Martin Bregman)

Absurdly brutalized version of the above, with detailed violence and a superabundance of foul language. Scarface has now become an emigré Cuban, and the film seems to want to make a political statement.

w Oliver Stone *d* Brian de Palma *ph* John A. Alonzo *m* Giorgio Moroder

☆ Al Pacino, Steven Bauer, Michelle Pfeiffer, Mary Elizabeth Mastrantonio, Robert Loggia, Paul Shenar, Harris Yulin

The Scarface Mob *

US 1958 96m bw
Desilu (Quinn Martin)

Al Capone's empire thrives while he is in Alcatraz, and prohibition agent Eliot Ness recruits a tough squad to fight the gangsters.

Though released theatrically, this was in effect a pilot film for the successful TV series The Untouchables, well enough done within its limits.

w Paul Monash *novel* The Untouchables by Eliot Ness *d* Phil Karlson *ph* Charles Straumer *m* Wilbur Hatch

☆ Robert Stack, Neville Brand, Keenan Wynn, Barbara Nichols, Joe Mantell, Pat Crowley, Bruce Gordon, Paul Picerni, Abel Fernandez

Scarlet and Black: see Le Rouge et le Noir

Scarlet Angel

US 1952 81m Technicolor
U-I (Leonard Goldstein)

A saloon hostess presents herself to a wealthy family as their dead son's wife.

Modest, satisfactorily plotted picture with action interludes.

w Oscar Brodney *d* Sidney Salkow *ph* Russell Metty *m* Joseph Gershenon

☆ Yvonne de Carlo, Rock Hudson, Richard Denning, Henry O'Neill, Amanda Blake

The Scarlet Blade *

GB 1963 82m Technicolor Hammerscope
Hammer (Anthony Nelson-Keys)
US title: The Crimson Blade

In 1648, a Cromwellian colonel plans to hang every royalist rebel.

Adequate swashbuckler.

wd John Gilling *ph* Jack Asher *m* Gary Hughes *pd* Bernard Robinson *ed* John Dunsford

☆ Lionel Jeffries, Oliver Reed, Jack Hedley, June Thorburn, Duncan Lamont

The Scarlet Buccaneer: see Swashbuckler

The Scarlet Claw **

US 1944 74m bw
Universal (Roy William Neill)

Grisly revenge murders take place in the fog-bound Canadian village of Le Mort Rouge.

Possibly the best of the modernized Sherlock Holmes series, with a plot hastily borrowed from The Hound of the Baskervilles.

w Edmund L. Hartmann, Roy William Neill *d* Roy William Neill *ph* George Robinson *m* Hans Salter *md* Paul Sawtell

☆ Basil Rathbone, Nigel Bruce, Miles Mander, Gerald Hamer, Paul Cavanagh, Kay Harding, Arthur Hohl

The Scarlet Coat

US 1955 99m Eastmancolor Cinemascope
MGM (Nicholas Nayfack)

During the American War of Independence, an American officer deserts to the British in order to unmask a traitor.

Rather talky historical actioner with too much time spent on friendship and romance.

w Karl Tunberg d John Sturges ph Paul C. Vogel m Conrad Salinger

☆ Cornel Wilde, Michael Wilding, George Sanders, Anne Francis, Robert Douglas, Bobby Driscoll, John McIntire

Scarlet Dawn *
US 1932 76m bw
Warner (Hal Wallis)
During the Russian revolution, an exiled aristocrat loves a serving maid.
Heavy-going romantic drama distinguished by stylish direction and sets.

w Niven Busch, Erwin Gelsey, Douglas Fairbanks Jnr novel Revolt by Mary McCall Jnr d William Dieterle ph Ernest Haller ad Anton Grot

☆ Douglas Fairbanks Jnr, Nancy Carroll, Lilyan Tashman, Guy Kibbee, Sheila Terry, Frank Reicher
'The story starts off to get somewhere but fails to arrive.' – *Variety*

'Based on a private diary of Catherine the Great!'
'The screen's reigning beauty in a wild pageant of barbaric splendour!'
'A cavalcade of fury led by a woman of fire!'
The Scarlet Empress ***
US 1934 109m bw
Paramount
A fantasia on the love life of Catherine the Great.
A marvellous, overwhelming, dramatically insubstantial but pictorially brilliant homage to a star; not to everyone's taste, but a film to remember.

w Manuel Komroff d Josef von Sternberg ph Bert Glennon md W. Franke Harling, John M. Leipold, Milan Roder ad Hans Dreier, Peter Ballbusch, Richard Kollorsz cos Travis Banton

☆ Marlene Dietrich, John Lodge, Sam Jaffe, Louise Dresser, C. Aubrey Smith, Gavin Gordon, Jameson Thomas
'She's photographed behind veils and fishnets, while dwarfs slither about and bells ring and everybody tries to look degenerate.' – *New Yorker, 1975*
'A ponderous, strangely beautiful, lengthy and frequently wearying production.' – *Mordaunt Hall, New York Times*

The Scarlet Hour
US 1955 93m bw Vistavision
Paramount (Michael Curtiz)
A bored wife persuades her lover to turn thief; her husband misconstrues the situation and is accidentally killed.
Complex suspenser designed to introduce new talent; rather too smooth, and pretty boring.

w Rip van Ronkel, Frank Tashlin, Meredyth Lucas d Michael Curtiz ph Lionel Lindon m Leith Stevens

☆ Carol Ohmart, Tom Tryon, James Gregory, Jody Lawrance, E. G. Marshall, Elaine Stritch

The Scarlet Letter *
US 1926 90m bw silent
MGM/Jury
In Puritan New England, the mother of an illegitimate child wears the scarlet A (for adulteress) for years rather than reveal that her lover was the village priest.
Celebrated 17th-century melodrama, quite powerfully made in the best silent tradition, but of little intrinsic interest for modern audiences.

w Frances Marion novel Nathaniel Hawthorne d Victor Sjostrom ph Henrik Sartov ad Cedric Gibbons

☆ Lillian Gish, Lars Hanson, Karl Dane, Henry B. Walthall

† Other versions include the following: US 1910, US 1911, US 1913, US 1917, US 1920, GB 1922, US 1934, Germany 1971, US (TV) 1979.

The Scarlet Letter
US 1934 70m bw
Darmour/Majestic
A lightened version with an attempt at comedy relief.
Not in any way remarkable.

w Leonard Fields, David Silverstein d Robert G. Vignola

☆ Colleen Moore, Hardie Albright, Henry B. Walthall, William Farnum, Alan Hale

'When intimacy is forbidden and passion is a sin, love is the most defiant crime of all.'
The Scarlet Letter
US 1995 135m Technicolor
Entertainment/Hollywood/Lightmotive/Allied Stars/Cinergi/Moving Pictures (Roland Joffé, Andrew G. Vajna)
In 17th-century Massachusetts, a settler's wife gives birth to an illegitimate daughter but refuses to name the father of her child.
Hilariously bad period drama, loosely based on Hawthorne's original, with little sense of history or decorum; it respresents Hollywood at its most crass and unthinking.

w Douglas Day Stewart novel Nathaniel Hawthorne d Roland Joffé ph Alex Thomson m John Barry pd Roy Walker ed Thom Noble

☆ Demi Moore, Gary Oldman, Robert Duvall, Robert Prosky, Edward Hardwicke, Joan Plowright, Roy Dotrice, Dana Ivey, Lisa Joliff-Andoh
'A campy period piece of pseudo-erotica. It should wear a brand mark all right – but not the letter "A" (for adulteress, and the accompanying spiritual penance). More appropriate would be the letter "V" (for video, which is its only hope of earthly salvation).' – *Alexander Walker*
'Provides all the usual incidental pleasures to be had from Hollywood's frequent bear hugs with great literature – unmappable migrations of thees and thines, an extra with an arrow through his neck who simply will not drop out of sight until he has caught the camera's eye, and – my favourite, this – a proud young Indian beauty with bikini marks. Absolute bliss.' – *Tom Shone, Sunday Times*
'A ponderous overstuffed package. Moore brandishes her scarlet letter snootily, as if she'd been forced to wear something from last year's fashion collections.' – *Owen Gleiberman, Entertainment Weekly*
† The film was not given a press show when it opened in Britain.

The Scarlet Pimpernel ***
GB 1934 98m bw
London Films (Alexander Korda)
In the early days of the French revolution, an apparently foppish Englishman leads a daring band in rescuing aristocrats from the guillotine.
First-class period adventure with a splendid and much imitated plot, strong characters, humour and a richly detailed historical background.

w Robert E. Sherwood, Sam Berman, Arthur Wimperis, Lajos Biro novel Baroness Orczy d Harold Young ph Harold Rosson m Arthur Benjamin

☆ Leslie Howard, Merle Oberon, Raymond Massey, Nigel Bruce, Bramwell Fletcher, Anthony Bushell, Joan Gardner, Walter Rilla
'Excellent British import that will do business.' – *Variety*
'One of the most romantic and durable of all swashbucklers.' – *New Yorker, 1976*
'A triumph for the British film world.' – *Sunday Times*
† Some scenes were directed by Alexander Korda, others by Rowland Brown.
†† The story was remade as *The Elusive Pimpernel* (qv) and in 1982 in a TV version starring Anthony Andrews. See also *The Return of the Scarlet Pimpernel.*

'I've been wanting to laugh in your face ever since I met you. You're old and ugly and I'm sick of you – sick, sick, sick!'
Scarlet Street **
US 1945 103m bw
(Universal) Walter Wanger (Fritz Lang)
A prostitute is murdered by her client and her pimp is executed for the crime.
Daring but rather gloomy Hollywood melodrama, the first in which a crime went unpunished (though the culprit was shown suffering remorse). Interesting and heavily Teutonic, but as entertainment not a patch on the similar but lighter The Woman in the Window, which the same team had made a year previously.

w Dudley Nichols play La Chienne by George de la Fouchardière (filmed by Jean Renoir in 1932) d Fritz Lang ph Milton Krasner m Hans Salter ad Alexander Golitzen

☆ Edward G. Robinson, Joan Bennett, Dan Duryea, Jess Barker, Margaret Lindsay, Rosalind Ivan, Samuel S. Hinds, Arthur Loft
'The director unerringly chooses the right sound and image to assault the spectator's sensibilities.' – *C. A. Lejeune*

The Scarlet Thread
GB 1950 84m bw
Nettlefold/Butcher
Jewel thieves take refuge in a Cambridge college.
Flabby melodrama featuring emergent young talent.

w A. R. Rawlinson play A. R. Rawlinson, Moie Charles d Lewis Gilbert ph Geoffrey Faithfull m Kenneth D. Morrison

☆ Kathleen Byron, Laurence Harvey, Sydney Tafler, Arthur Hill, Dora Bryan

The Scarlet Tunic
GB 1998 91m Fujicolour
Indy/Scarlet/Bigger Picture/Scorpio (Zygi Kamasa, Daniel Figuero)
An English farmer's daughter falls for a handsome German cavalry officer, who is planning to desert from his regiment.
A mundane period romantic drama, worthy but dull.

w Mark Jenkins, Colin Clements, Stuart St Paul story The Melancholy Hussar of the German Legion by Thomas Hardy d Stuart St Paul ph Malcolm McLean m John Scott pd Richard Elton ed Don Fairservice

☆ Jean-Marc Barr, Emma Fielding, Simon Callow, Jack Shepherd, John Sessions, Lynda Bellingham, Thomas Lockyer
'A nicely made film with no surprises.' – *Guardian*
† The film was made for £500,000.

Scars of Dracula
GB 1970 96m Technicolor
Hammer/EMI (Aida Young)
A young man on the run finds himself an unwitting guest of Count Dracula.
Overpadded vampire saga, its few effective moments stemming directly from the original novel.

w John Elder d Roy Ward Baker ph Moray Grant m James Bernard ad Scott MacGregor ed James Needs

☆ Christopher Lee, Dennis Waterman, Christopher Matthews, Jenny Hanley, Patrick Troughton, Michael Gwynn, Bob Todd

Scattergood Baines
US 1941 69m bw
RKO
The new owner of a small-town hardware store takes an interest in his fellow men.
First of several second features featuring the exploits of a likeable busybody.

w Michael L. Simmons, Edward T. Lowe stories Clarence Budington Kelland d Christy Cabanne

☆ Guy Kibbee, Carol Hughes, John Archer, Emma Dunn
† The succeeding episodes were as follows: *Scattergood Pulls the Strings*, 1941; *Scattergood Meets Broadway*, 1941; *Scattergood Rides High*, 1942; *Scattergood Survives a Murder*, 1942; *Cinderella Swings It*, 1943.

Scavenger Hunt
US 1979 116m DeLuxe
TCF/Melvin Simon
A rich man leaves a fortune to the member of his family who can collect most of the useless objects in a list provided.
Depressing cheapjack imitation of Kramer's It's a Mad Mad Mad Mad World, which itself was not free from fault.

w Steven A. Vail, Henry Harper d Michael Schultz ph Ken Lamkin m Billy Goldenberg

☆ Richard Benjamin, James Coco, Scatman Crothers, Cloris Leachman, Cleavon Little, Roddy McDowall, Robert Morley, Richard Mulligan, Tony Randall, Dirk Benedict, Vincent Price
'Loud, obnoxious, and above all unfunny.' – *Variety*

Lo Sceicco Bianco: see *The White Sheik*

A Scene at the Sea *
Japan 1991 101m colour
ICA/Totsyu/Office Kitano (Masayuki Mori, Takio Yoshida)
original title: *Ano Natsu, Ichiban Shizukana Umi*
A deaf and dumb garbage collector tries to become a champion surfer, with the aid of his girlfriend, who is also a deaf-mute.
A restrained, heartfelt movie of momentary redemption; it is austere throughout, and its ambiguous ending leaves a sense of loss.

wd Takeshi Kitano ph Katsumi Yanagishima m Joe Hisaishi ed Takeshi Kitano

☆ Kurodo Maki, Hiroko Oshima, Sabu Kawahara
'A 'miniature' with huge emotional and even philosophical resonance.' – *Tony Rayns, Sight and Sound*

Scener Ur Ett äktenskap: see *Scenes from a Marriage*

Scenes from a Mall
US 1990 87m DuArt Panavision
Warner/Touchstone/Silver Screen Partners IV (Paul Mazursky)
Preparing to celebrate their sixteenth wedding anniversary, a Los Angeles couple confess their recent affairs while on a shopping spree.
An unsuccessful comic teaming in a wordy celebration of conspicuous consumption.

w Roger L. Simon, Paul Mazursky d Paul Mazursky ph Fred Murphy m Marc Shaiman pd Pato Guzman ed Stuart Pappé

☆ Bette Midler, Woody Allen, Bill Irwin, Daren Firestone, Rebecca Nickels, Paul Mazursky

Scenes from a Marriage ***
Sweden 1973 168m colour
Cinematograph (Ingmar Bergman)
original title: *Scener Ur Ett äktenskap*
After ten years of marriage, a husband announces to his wife that he is leaving her because he has fallen in love with someone else; over the next ten years they continue to meet and examine their relationship.
Bergman edited the film into feature length from six 50-minute episodes made for television, and the structure of the original remains, with each episode given its own title, moving from Innocence and Panic, with an apparently happy marriage on display, to In the Middle of the Night in a Dark House Somewhere in the World, with the couple, by now remarried to other partners, seeking solace with each other. The time-span gives the characters room to develop: the husband from complacency to wry understanding, the wife from subservience to individuality. It is an unsparing and detailed examination of a relationship, marked by more pain than pleasure, but reaching a hopeful conclusion; it is also, despite its claustrophobic style, of a succession of close-ups of talking heads, rivetting cinema.

wd Ingmar Bergman ph Sven Nykvist m none ed Björn Thulin ed Siv Lundgren

☆ Liv Ullmann, Erland Josephson, Bibi Andersson, Jan Malmsjö, Gunnel Lindblom, Anita Wall
'Shows how habit and conciliatory effort erode communication. But it is ultimately an optimistic film, suggesting that beyond the hell of a return to zero, the knowledge of one's absolute separateness from others can lead through despair to a glowing fulfilment.' – *Jan Dawson, MFB*

Scenes from the Class Struggle in Beverly Hills
US 1989 103m CFI color
Rank/North Street Films/Cinecom Entertainment (Amir J. Malin, Ira Deutchman)
Two servants bet that they can seduce the other's mistress, both of whom have sexual problems of their own.
Bed-hopping black-tinged comedy that never goes quite far enough to be funny.

w Bruce Wagner story Paul Bartel, Bruce Wagner d Paul Bartel ph Steven Fierberg m Stanley Myers pd Alex Tavoularis ed Alan Toomayan

☆ Jacqueline Bisset, Ray Sharkey, Mary Woronov, Robert Beltran, Ed Begley Jnr, Wallace Shawn, Arnetia Walker, Paul Bartel, Paul Mazursky, Rebecca Schaeffer

---

🏌 film suitable for family viewing   📼 VHS video-cassette for the British PAL system   📼 VHS video-cassette for the British PAL system in wide screen-format   ☼ Video cassette in a computer-colourised version   ▤ American NTSC video-cassette   ◎~ Laser disc

'Col. Frank Slade has a very special plan for the weekend. It involves travel, women, good food, fine wine, the tango, chauffeured limousines and a loaded forty-five. And he's bringing Charlie along for the ride.'

Scent of a Woman *
US 1992 157m DeLuxe
UIP/Universal/City Lights (Martin Brest)
▦ ▤ ◎ ◉ ◯

A blind former soldier shows a high-school student how to enjoy life.
Sentimental drama showcasing a flamboyant over-the-top performance from Pacino.
w Bo Goldman d Martin Brest ph Donald E. Thorin m Thomas Newman pd Angelo Graham ed William Steinkamp
☆ Al Pacino, Chris O'Donnell, James Rebhorn, Gabrielle Anwar, Philip S. Hoffman, Richard Venture
'Essentially a two-character piece that goes on nearly an hour too long, Martin Brest's latest boasts good writing, filmmaking and performances, but far too much of each.' – *Variety*
† The film was suggested by the Italian movie *Profumo di Donna*, directed in 1974 by Dino Risi from the novel *Il Buio e il Miele* by Giovanni Arpino.
♣ Al Pacino
⚖ Best picture; Martin Brest; Bo Goldman

The Scent of Green Papaya **
France 1993 104m colour
Artificial Eye/Lazennec/La Sept/Canal
▦ ▤ ◎ ◉ ◯

original title: *Mùi Du Du Xanh*
In Saigon in the 50s, a young village girl grows up as she works as a maid for a family where the mother struggles to bring up her sons in the absence of their father.
Gentle, well-observed domestic drama, crafted with care and visual style.
wd Tran Anh Hung ph Benoît Delhomme m Tiêt Ton-That ad Alain Nègre ed Nicole Dedieu, Jean-Pierre Roques
☆ Yên-Khê Tran Nu, Man San Lu, Thi Lôc Truong, Anh Hoa Nguyen, Hoa Hôi Vuong, Ngoc Trung Tran
'Although visually more rigorous, Hung's movie in some ways recalls the early works of Indian helmer Satyajit Ray in its portrayal of childhood dreams and the invisible walls between kids and adults.' – *Variety*
'Marries nature and artifice, taking the graceful shape of an Oriental character that grows, like a cherry tree, into ever larger meaning as pen-strokes are slowly added.' – *Kathleen Murphy, Film Comment*
⚖ best foreign film

'First they moved (1895)! Then they talked (1927)! Now they smell!'

Scent of Mystery *
US 1959 125m Technicolor Cinerama
(70mm)
Cinerama/Mike Todd Jnr
aka: *Holiday in Spain*
An Englishman on holiday in Spain protects a mysterious girl.
More of a travelogue than a thriller, but worth a note as the cinema's first 'smellie'. A process called Smell-o-Vision released appropriate odours throughout the auditorium...
w William Rose d Jack Cardiff ph John von Kotze m Mario Nascimbene
☆ Denholm Elliott, Peter Lorre, Beverly Bentley, Paul Lukas, Liam Redmond, Leo McKern, Peter Arne, Mary Laura Wood, Elizabeth Taylor
† The first film to credit its providers of shoe polish.

Scent of Passion (dubbed)
Italy 1990 84m Telecolor
Film 90
▦

A choreographer, dissatisfied by his relationships with dancers, decides to find a woman he can mould to his taste and picks up a vagrant from the streets.
Glossy, silly and empty movie that uses the trappings of culture – the work of a classic writer and the ballet – for a great deal of macho posturing and, by the women, breast-baring; not so much a vision of Gautier's belief in art for art's sake as an example of soft porn for money's sake.

w Leandro Lucchetti novel *Violette* by Theophile Gautier d Pasquale Fanetti ph (uncredited) m Donimak, Lindok ad Vlado Perkovic ed Cesare Bianchini
☆ Malú, Angeles Lopez Barea, Giancarlo Teodori, Zvonco Zrncic, Suada Herak, Melita Turisic, Mircea Hurdubea

Die Schaukel: see *The Swing*

'The List Is Life. The Man Was Real. The Story Is True.'

Schindler's List ****
US 1993 195m bw/colour
Universal/Amblin (Steven Spielberg, Gerald R. Molen, Branko Lustig)
▦ ▦ ▤ ◎ ◯

During the Second World War, an Austrian businessman persuades the Nazis to let him use Jewish slave labour in his factory; and then, with the money he earns, bribes a brutal SS commandant to save 1,100 Jews from the concentration camps.
A brilliantly realized, fiercely controlled and restrained treatment of a true story, using monochrome photography for the most part to achieve a documentary feel; harsh and compassionate, it avoids sentimentality until the end. It marks not only a notable achievement, but Spielberg's coming of age as an adult film-maker.
w Steven Zaillian novel *Schindler's Ark* by Thomas Keneally d Steven Spielberg ph Janusz Kaminski m John Williams pd Allan Starski ed Michael Kahn
☆ Liam Neeson, Ben Kingsley, Ralph Fiennes, Caroline Goodall, Jonathan Sagalle, Embeth Davidtz, Malgosha Gebel, Shmulik Levy, Mark Ivanir
'Evinces an artistic rigor and unsentimental intelligence unlike anything the world's most successful filmmaker has demonstrated before.' – *Variety*
'The elevated downer of the decade.' – *Richard Corliss, Time*
'He captures images of experience that most of us thought we would never see represented adequately on the screen. This is by far the finest, fullest dramatic (i.e. nondocumentary) film ever made about the Holocaust.' – *Terrence Rafferty, New Yorker*
'Indiana Jones in the Cracow Ghetto.' – *Will Tremper, Die Welt*
♣ best film; Steven Spielberg; Steven Zaillian; Janusz Kaminski; Michael Kahn; John Williams; Allan Starski
⚖ Liam Neeson; Ralph Fiennes; costume design (Anna Biedrzycka-Sheppard); make-up
Ⓥ best film; adapted screenplay; Steven Spielberg; Ralph Fiennes; Janusz Kaminski; John Williams

Schizo
GB 1976 109m Technicolor
Columbia-Warner/Pete Walker
▦ ▤

aka: *Amok*
aka: *Blood of the Undead*
A series of bloody murders result when a famous ice-skater announces that she is to be married.
An unsuccessful attempt at a slick and surprising thriller; the twist in the plot is obvious from the beginning.
w David McGillivray d Pete Walker ph Peter Jessop m Stanley Myers ad Chris Burke ed Alan Brett
☆ Lynne Frederick, John Leyton, Stephanie Beacham, John Fraser, Jack Watson, Queenie Watts, John McEnery, Colin Jeavons
'Deprived of any support from the script this time, Pete Walker's direction, all thump, scream and cut as shadows lurk and doorknobs turn – with each cliché heralded by a triumphant tremolo or bass boom from the score – reduces the whole thing to risible absurdity.' – *Tom Milne, MFB*

Die Schlangengrube und das Pendel: see *The Blood Demon*

School for Husbands
GB 1937 71m bw
Wainwright (Richard Wainwright)
A romantic novelist annoys the husbands of his adoring fans.
Would-be champagne comedy which bubbles pretty well for most of its length.
w Frederick Jackson, Gordon Aherry, Austin Melford play Frederick Jackson d Andrew Marton ph Phil Tannura

☆ Rex Harrison, Henry Kendall, Romney Brent, Diana Churchill, June Clyde

The School for Scandal
GB 1930 73m Raycol Colour
Albion Film Syndicate
Two brothers have characters opposite to their appearances.
Doomed attempt to film the famous 18th-century comedy of manners.
w Jean Jay play Richard Brinsley Sheridan d Maurice Elvey
☆ Madeleine Carroll, Basil Gill, Henry Hewitt, Ian Fleming
'Its value in the States looks like exactly nothing.' – *Variety*

School for Scoundrels *
GB 1960 94m bw
ABP/Guardsman (Hal E. Chester)
▦
A failure reports to the College of One-Upmanship and his life is transformed.
Amusing trifle, basically a series of sketches by familiar comic actors.
w Patricia Mayes, Hal E. Chester books Stephen Potter d Robert Hamer ph Erwin Hillier m John Addison
☆ Ian Carmichael, Alastair Sim, Terry-Thomas, Janette Scott, Dennis Price, Peter Jones, Edward Chapman, John Le Mesurier

School for Secrets
GB 1946 108m bw
Rank/Two Cities (George H. Brown, Peter Ustinov)
US title: *Secret Flight*
The boffins who invented radar find themselves in a little war action of their own.
An unsatisfactory entertainment which, with the best intentions, shuffles between arch comedy, character drama, war action and documentary, doing less than justice to any of these aspects.
wd Peter Ustinov ph Jack Hildyard m Alan Rawsthorne
☆ Ralph Richardson, Raymond Huntley, Richard Attenborough, Marjorie Rhodes, John Laurie, Ernest Jay, David Tomlinson, Finlay Currie

School for Unclaimed Girls: see *The Smashing Bird I Used to Know*

School Ties *
US 1992 107m DeLuxe
Paramount (Stanley R. Jaffe, Sherry Lansing)
▤ ◎ ◯
In the mid-1950s a Jewish boy conceals his religion when he wins a scholarship to an exclusive school rife with anti-Semitism.
A slickly directed, well-acted, moderately gripping drama.
w Dick Wolf, Darryl Ponicsan d Robert Mandel ph Freddie Francis m Maurice Jarre pd Jeannine Claudia Oppewall ed Jerry Greenberg, Jacqueline Cambas
☆ Brendan Fraser, Matt Damon, Chris O'Donnell, Randall Batinkoff, Andrew Lowery, Amy Locane, Ed Lauter
'Gives a multifaceted, nuanced look at the roots of prejudice and self-denial.' – *Variety*

Das Schreckliche Mädchen: see *The Nasty Girl*

Schtonk!
Germany 1992 111m colour
Artificial Eye/Bavarian Film/WDR (Gunter Rohrbach, Helmut Dietl)
▦ ▤
A forger decides to fake Hitler's diaries to sell to a collector of Nazi memorabilia and enlists the aid of a journalist.
The heavy-handed farcical treatment of an hilarious true story provides little amusement, although it was a great success in its home country.
w Helmut Dietl, Ulrich Limmer d Helmut Dietl ph Xaver Schwarzenberger m Konstantin Wecker ad Götz Weidner, Benedikt Herforth ed Tanja Schmidbauer
☆ Götz George, Uwe Ochsenknecht, Christiane Hörbiger, Rolf Hoppe, Dagmar Manzel, Veronica Ferres, Rosemarie Fendel
'This crude, overacted account of the Hitler diaries scandal is largely of sociological interest,

an occasion for sporadic chuckles rather than sustained laughter.' – *Philip French, Observer*
⚖ foreign language film

Schweik's New Adventures
GB 1943 84m bw
Eden Films
An unassuming Czechoslovakian writer gently kids the Nazi occupiers and manages to save some of his friends from the concentration camp.
Curious English attempt to film a popular Czechoslovakian character; it made mildly effective wartime propaganda, though few went to see it.
w Karel Lamac, Con West novel Jaroslav Hasek d Karel Lamac
☆ Lloyd Pearson, George Carney, Julien Mitchell, Richard Attenborough, Margaret McGrath

Schwestern oder die Balance des Glücks: see *Sisters or the Balance of Happiness*

Sciuscià: see *Shoeshine*

Scorchers
US 1991 82m colour
Rank/Goldcrest/FilmWorks (Morrie Eisenman, Richard Hellman)
▦
In a sleazy bar, a prostitute sorts out a wife's marital problems while nearby a newly-wed couple have troubles of their own.
Risibly decadent movie, set in a town of misfits.
wd David Beaird play David Beaird ph Peter Deming m Carter Burwell pd Bill Eigenbrodt ed David Garfield
☆ Faye Dunaway, Denholm Elliott, James Earl Jones, Emily Lloyd, Jennifer Tilly, James Wilder, Anthony Geary, Leland Crooke, Luke Perry
'An uncomfortable mix of melodrama, sentimentality and failed farce.' – *Empire*

Scorching Winds: see *Garm Hava*

'When Scorpio wants you, there is nowhere to hide!'

Scorpio
US 1972 114m Technicolor
UA/Scimitar (Walter Mirisch)
▤
CIA agents doublecross each other.
Incredibly complex spy thriller in which it's difficult to know, or care, who's following whom. The brutalities, however, are capably staged.
w David W. Rintels, Gerald Wilson d Michael Winner ph Robert Paynter m Jerry Fielding
☆ Burt Lancaster, Alain Delon, Paul Scofield, John Colicos, Gayle Hunnicutt, J. D. Cannon
'Strictly zoom and thump.' – *Sight and Sound*
'Relying on moments of violence for effect, Winner directs with typically crass abandon.' – *Time Out, 1984*

Scorsese x 4: see *The Big Shave, ItalianAmerican, It's Not Just You Murray!, What's A Nice Girl Like You Doing in a Place Like This?*

'Protection Is The Job, Justice Is The Goal, Death Is The Price.'

La Scorta **
Italy 1993 92m Technicolor
Claudio Bonivento
▦ ▤
aka: *The Escort*
Following the assassination by the Sicilian Mafia of a judge, a team of carabinieri is assigned to protect his replacement.
Tough, timely and suspenseful thriller about political corruption in Italy, based on truth and close in style to American gangster movies.
w Graziano Diana, Simona Izzo d Ricky Tognazzi ph Alessio Gelsini m Ennio Morricone ad Mariangela Capuano ed Carla Simoncelli
☆ Claudio Amendola, Enrico Lo Verso, Carlo Cecchi, Ricky Memphis, Tony Sperandeo, Francesca D'Aloja, Angelo Infanti, Leo Gullotta
'This finds a gripping, even uplifting, human story inside its depiction of oppressive and omnipresent evil.' – *Kim Newman, Empire*

Scotch on the Rocks: see *Laxdale Hall*

Scotland Yard
US 1941 68m bw
TCF (Sol M. Wurtzel)
The Nazis capture a London banker and use his double to turn funds over to them.

Outlandish spy melodrama which certainly keeps the interest.
w Samuel G. Engel, John Balderston play Deniston Clift d Norman Foster ph Virgil Miller m Emil Newman
☆ Nancy Kelly, Edmund Gwenn, Henry Wilcoxon, John Loder, Melville Cooper, Gilbert Emery, Norma Varden

Scotland Yard Investigator
US   1945   68m   bw
Republic (George Blair)
Frenchmen attempt to steal the Mona Lisa from its wartime home in the National Gallery.
Very passable programme filler with stalwart actors enjoying themselves.
w Randall Faye d George Blair
☆ Sir Aubrey Smith, Erich von Stroheim, Stephanie Bachelor, Forrester Harvey, Richard Fraser, Frederick Worlock

Scott of the Antarctic **
👫 GB   1948   111m   Technicolor
Ealing (Sidney Cole)
🔲
After long preparation, Captain Scott sets off on his ill-fated 1912 expedition to the South Pole.
The stiff-upper-lip saga par excellence; inevitable knowledge of the end makes it pretty downbeat, and the actors can only be sincere; but the snowscapes, most of them artificial, are fine.
w Ivor Montagu, Walter Meade, Mary Hayley Bell d Charles Frend ph Geoffrey Unsworth, Jack Cardiff, Osmond Borradaile m Ralph Vaughan Williams
☆ John Mills, James Robertson Justice, Derek Bond, Harold Warrender, Reginald Beckwith, Kenneth More, James McKechnie, John Gregson

The Scoundrel **
US   1935   74m   bw
Paramount (Ben Hecht, Charles MacArthur)
A famous writer dies; his ghost comes back to find the meaning of love.
Unique thirties supernatural melodrama with barbs of dated wit despatched by a splendid cast. Nonsense, but great nonsense.
wd Ben Hecht, Charles MacArthur ph Lee Garmes m George Antheil
☆ Noël Coward, Alexander Woollcott, Julie Haydon, Stanley Ridges, Eduardo Ciannelli
'Good Hotel Algonquin literati stuff, but not for the Automat trade.' – *Variety*
'An unmistakable whiff from a gossip column world which tries hard to split the difference between an epigram and a wisecrack.' – *William Whitebait*
'Practically flawless drama. It's arty, but if this is art, let us have more of it.' – *Photoplay*
'An impudent work ... but there are brains in it, and observation, and even a kind of stunted poetry.' – *Observer*
† Helen Hayes and Edna Ferber made cameo appearances.
▌ original story

The Scoundrel *
France/Italy/Rumania   1971   100m
Eastmancolor
Cinecenta/Gaumont/Rizzoli/BFP (Alain Poiré)
🔲
original title: *Mariés de L'An Deux*
The adventures in the 1790s of a Frenchman who returns from America to divorce his wife and then decides he wants to stay married.
Enjoyable and hectic swashbuckling period romp in which true love triumphs after a great number of death-defying moments.
w Jean-Paul Rappeneau, Claude Sautet, Maurice Clavel, Daniel Boulanger d Jean-Paul Rappeneau ph Claude Renoir m Michel Legrand ad Alexandre Trauner, Will Holt ed Pierre Gillette
☆ Jean-Paul Belmondo, Marlène Jobert, Michel Auclair, Sami Frey, Laura Antonelli, Pierre Brasseur

Scram! *
👫 US   1932   20m   bw
Hal Roach
🔲
Two vagrants are ordered out of town but by a series of misadventures are found drunk with the judge's wife.

Generally sprightly star comedy culminating in a marathon laughing session.
w H. M. Walker d Ray McCarey ed Richard Currier
☆ Stan Laurel, Oliver Hardy, Arthur Housman, Rychard Cramer, Vivien Oakland

Scream *
US   1996   110m   CFI color   Panavision
Buena Vista/Miramax/Dimension (Cary Woods, Cathy Konrad)
🔲 ▤ 🔈 👁 🎧
A serial killer with an extensive knowledge of horror movies begins to murder teenage girls.
A knowing romp through the conventions of slasher movies, but one that also manages to scare as well; it is most likely to appeal to those familiar with the genre, who will appreciate its parodies.
w Kevin Williamson d Wes Craven ph Mark Irwin m Marco Beltrami pd Bruce Alan Miller ed Patrick Lussier sp Frank Seglia; make-up: Robert Kurtzman, Greg Nicotero, Howard Berger
☆ Drew Barrymore, Neve Campbell, Skeet Ulrich, Courteney Cox, Rose McGowan, David Arquette
'An ingeniously unsettling tribute to the splatterific teen horror films of the '80s.' – *Owen Gleiberman, Entertainment Weekly*
'Just about every effect in the picture is predictable.' – *Herschell Gordon Lewis*

'Someone has taken their love of *sequels* one step too far.'
Scream 2 *
US   1997   120m   Foto-Kem   Panavision
Miramax/Dimension/Konrad (Cathy Konrad, Marianne Maddalena)
🔲 ▤ 🔈 👁 🎧
Attending the première of a movie based on their experiences with a serial killer, two students become the first victims of a copycat murderer.
Another dose of knowing, self-referential horror movie lore that finally twists back on itself with a killer who claims to have been corrupted by movies; it's very ingenious, but it's still junk.
w Kevin Williamson d Wes Craven ph Peter Deming m Marco Beltrami pd Robert Ziembicki ed Patrick Lussier
☆ David Arquette, Neve Campbell, Courteney Cox, Sarah Michelle Gellar, Jamie Kennedy, Jerry O'Connell, Jada Pinkett, Liev Schreiber, David Warner, Laurie Metcalf
'Visceral, witty and appropriately redundant, the sequel has a winning commercial recipe that's certain to cook up excellent returns in all areas.' – *Leonard Klady, Variety*

'The Third and Final chapter in the trilogy that made you laugh, and made you Scream.'
Scream 3
US   2000   116m   DeLuxe
Buena Vista/Konrad (Cathy Konrad, Kevin Williamson, Marianne Maddalena)
👁 🎧
The cast of a horror film *Stab 3* are killed off one by one.
A sequel so self-referential that audiences who have not seen the first two movies in the series will be at a loss to understand what is happening; but, then those who didn't see the earlier Screams will want to miss this one, too.
w Ehren Kruger d Wes Craven ph Peter Deming m Marco Beltrami pd Bruce Alan Miller ed Patrick Lussier
☆ David Arquette, Neve Campbell, Courteney Cox Arquette, Patrick Dempsey, Scott Foley, Lance Henriksen, Matt Keeslar, Jenny McCarthy, Emily Mortimer, Parker Posey, Deon Richmond, Liev Schreiber, Heather Matarazzo, Carrie Fisher, Kevin Smith and also Roger Corman
'So tediously knowing that it ceases to be an entertainment. It becomes simply an extended raft of film references, as chilling as a draughty lavatory seat and as sexy as number crunching.' – *James Christopher, Times*

Scream ... and Die!
GB   1973   99m   Eastmancolor
Variety/Blackwater (Diana Daubeney)
aka: *Psycho Sex Fiend*
A model fears that she may be murdered after witnessing an unidentifiable man in black stab a girl to death in a remote country mansion.
Trivial thriller that sets out to titillate, but fails miserably.

w Derek Ford d Joseph Larraz (José Larraz) ph Trevor Wrenn m Terry Warr ad John Hoesli ed Roy Deverell
☆ Andrea Allan, Karl Lanchbury, Maggie Walker, Peter Forbes-Robertson, Judy Matheson, Annabella Wood, Alex Leppard
'At heart just another sexploitation film posing as a thriller.' – *Tom Milne, MFB*

'Triple distilled horror ... as powerful as a vat of boiling acid!'
Scream and Scream Again *
GB   1969   94m   Eastmancolor
AIP/Amicus (Milton Subotsky, Max J. Rosenberg)
🔲 ▤
Murders are traced to superhuman composite beings created by a mad scientist.
Energetic and well-staged though rather humourless shocker.
w Christopher Wicking *novel The Disorientated Man* by Peter Saxon d Gordon Hessler ph John Coquillon m David Whittaker ad Don Mingaye
☆ Vincent Price, Christopher Lee, Peter Cushing, Alfred Marks, Anthony Newlands, David Lodge, Peter Sallis

Scream, Blacula, Scream
US   1973   96m   Movielab
Gala/AIP (Joseph T. Naar)
🔲 ▤
A 19th-century African vampire is brought back to life.
Routine horror movie of little interest, a lacklustre sequel to Blacula (qv).
w Joan Torres, Raymond Koenig, Maurice Jules d Bob Kelljan ph Isodore Mankofsky m Bill Marx ad Alfeo Bocchicchio ed Fabian Tordjmann sp Jack de Bron
☆ William Marshall, Pam Grier, Don Mitchell, Michael Conrad, Richard Lawson, Lynne Moody, Beverly Gill, Bernie Hamilton
'Will excite only the most undemanding audiences.' – *MFB*

Scream for Help
US   1984   90m   colour
Miracle/Lorimar/Videoform (Michael Winner)
A teenager becomes convinced that her stepfather is trying to murder her mother.
Crude splatter movie which the director presumably undertook as a joke.
w Tom Holland d Michael Winner ph Robert Paynter, Dick Kratina m Howard Blake ad Tony Reading ed Christopher Barnes
☆ Rachael Kelly, David Brooks, Marie Masters, Rocco Sisto, Lolita Lorre
'Over the moronic characterization, daft dialogue, inept performances and opportunistic camerawork, music has been poured like a constant stream of cold gravy, making a sound that on occasion resembles, not inappropriately, a growling stomach.' – *Philip Strick, MFB*

A Scream in the Dark
US   1943   53m   bw
Republic (George Sherman)
A private eye tracks down a constant widow with a trail of dead husbands.
Lightweight mystery which might have been better.
w Gerald Schnitzer, Anthony Coldeway *novel The Morgue Is Always Open* by Jerome Odlum d George Sherman
☆ Robert Lowery, Marie McDonald, Edward S. Brophy, Wally Vernon, Hobart Cavanaugh, Jack La Rue, Elizabeth Russell

Scream of Fear: see *Taste of Fear*

Scream of Stone *
Germany/France/Canada   1991   105m   colour
SERA/A2/Les Films Stock/ZDF/Canal Plus/Telefilm Canada/Lucky Red/RAI2 (Walter Saxer)
A young climber challenges an older one to tackle the most difficult mountain in the world in Patagonia.
Spectacular photography compensates for a muddled narrative about obsessive people.
w Hans-Ulrich Klenner, Walter Saxer *story* Reinhold Messner d Werner Herzog ph Rainer Klausmann, Herbert Raditschnig m Ingram Marshall, Alan Lamb pd Juan Santiago ed Suzanne Baron
☆ Vittorio Mezzogiorno, Mathilda May, Stefan Glowacz, Brad Dourif, Donald Sutherland

'While it does feature some spectacular mountain photography in an area of the world few will ever see first-hand, the dramatic and psychological aspects remain so obscure as to become silly.' – *Variety*

Screamers *
US/Canada/Japan   1996   107m   colour
Triumph/Fuji Eight/Fries/Allegro (Tom Berry, Franco Battista)
🔲 ▤ 🔈 👁 🎧
In 2078, on the planet Sirius 6B, an alliance of mine-workers and scientists invents killer robots to win a war against a corrupt and authoritarian mining corporation.
Paranoid science fiction, bleak in tone but interesting in its speculations about intelligent machines and violent people; judging by the soundtrack song, rock music will regress in the future.
w Dan O'Bannon, Miguel Tejada-Flores *story Second Variety* by Philip K. Dick d Christian Duguay ph Rodney Gibbons m Normand Corbeil pd Perri Gorrara ed Yves Langlois sp Ernest Faring; Richard Ostiguy
☆ Peter Weller, Roy Dupuis, Jennifer Rubin, Andy Lauer, Ron White, Charles Powell, Liliana Komorowska
† Dick's original story, published in 1953, was set on Earth, with a war between UN forces and the Soviet Union.

The Screaming Dead: see *Dracula – Prisoner of Frankenstein*

Screaming Mimi
US   1958   79m   bw
Sage/Columbia (Harry Joe Brown, Robert Fellows)
After being sexually assaulted a dancer comes to believe she has committed murder ... and later we learn that she has.
Sub-Freudian melodrama on the comic strip level.
w Robert Blees *book* Frederic Brown d Gerd Oswald ph Burnett Guffey md Mischa Bakaleinikoff
☆ Anita Ekberg, Phil Carey, Harry Townes, Gypsy Rose Lee, Romney Brent, Alan Gifford, Red Norvo

Scrooge *
👫 GB   1935   78m   bw
Twickenham (Julius Hagen)
▤
A miser reforms after ghosts haunt him on Christmas Eve.
Acceptable unambitious version with interesting performances.
w Seymour Hicks, H. Fowler Mear *novel* Charles Dickens d Henry Edwards ph Sidney Blythe, William Luff
☆ Seymour Hicks, Donald Calthrop, Athene Seyler, Oscar Asche, Barbara Everest, Maurice Evans, C. V. France, Marie Ney
† Seymour Hicks starred in a silent version in 1913.

Scrooge ***
👫 GB   1951   86m   bw
Renown (Brian Desmond Hurst)
🔲 ▤ 🔈 ✛
US title: *A Christmas Carol*
By far the best available version of the classic parable; casting, art direction, pace and general handling are as good as can be.
w Noel Langley d Brian Desmond Hurst ph C. Pennington-Richards m Richard Addinsell
☆ Alastair Sim, Mervyn Johns, Kathleen Harrison, Jack Warner, Michael Hordern, Hermione Baddeley, George Cole, Miles Malleson

Scrooge *
👫 GB   1970   113m   Technicolor
Panavision
Cinema Center/Waterbury (Robert H. Solo)
🔲 ▤ 🔈
Dim musical version, darkly coloured and quite lost on the wide screen; but it has its macabre moments of trick photography.
d Ronald Neame ph Oswald Morris pd Terry Marsh w/m/ly Leslie Bricusse
☆ Albert Finney, Michael Medwin, Alec Guinness, Edith Evans, Kenneth More, David Collings, Laurence Naismith, Kay Walsh
† Richard Harris and Rex Harrison were both sought before Finney was signed.

👫 film suitable for family viewing   🔲 VHS video-cassette for the British PAL system   ▤ VHS video-cassette for the British PAL system in wide screen-format   ✛ Video cassette in a computer-colourised version   🔈 American NTSC video-cassette   👁 Laser disc

♬ song 'Thank You Very Much' (m/ly Leslie Bricusse); original score; art direction; costume design (Margaret Furse)

Scrooged *
♙♙ US 1988 101m Technicolor
Paramount/Mirage (Richard Donner, Art Linson)
▣ ▤ ◔ ◌

Updated version of Dickens's *A Christmas Carol*, centring on the president of a New York television company.
Energetic and sometimes genuinely scary seasonal entertainment for modern kids.
w Mitch Glazer, Michael O'Donoghue d Richard Donner ph Michael Chapman m Danny Elfman pd J. Michael Riva
☆ Bill Murray, Karen Allen, John Forsythe, Robert Mitchum, John Houseman, Lee Majors

Scrubbers
GB 1982 93m Eastmancolor
Handmade (Don Boyd)
▤

Sensational events in a girls' borstal.
Wild-eyed melodrama which seems to serve no sort of purpose and is certainly not entertaining.
w Roy Minton, Jeremy Watt, Mai Zetterling d Mai Zetterling ph Ernest Vincze m Michael Hurd
☆ Amanda York, Chrissie Cotterill, Elizabeth Edmonds, Kate Ingram, Honey Bane, Eva Motley

Scudda Hoo, Scudda Hay
US 1948 98m Technicolor
TCF (Walter Morosco)
GB title: *Summer Lightning*

A farmer's son is more interested in girls than in the welfare of his two mules.
Antediluvian rural romance for the simple-minded.
wd F. Hugh Herbert *novel* George Agnew Chamberlain ph Ernest Palmer m Cyril Mockridge
☆ June Haver, Lon McCallister, Walter Brennan, Anne Revere, Natalie Wood, Robert Karnes, Henry Hull, Tom Tully, Marilyn Monroe

Scum *
GB 1979 97m Eastmancolor
GTO/Berwick Street Films (Clive Parsons, Davina Belling)
▣ ▤ ◌

Injustices in a Borstal institution lead to a riot.
Gorily overstated view of boys' prison life from the inside, with the camera gloating over each violent close-up. (The original TV play had been made, then banned, by the BBC.)
w Roy Minton d Alan Clarke ph Phil Meheux ad Judith Lang ed Mike Bradsell
☆ Ray Winstone, Mick Ford, Julian Firth, John Blundell

The Sea Bat
US 1930 69m bw
MGM

Mexican fishermen compete to kill a deadly sting-ray.
The Jaws of its time; box-office hokum.
w Bess Meredyth and John Howard Lawson d Wesley Ruggles
☆ Charles Bickford, Raquel Torres, Nils Asther, John Miljan, Gibson Gowland, Boris Karloff

The Sea Beast *
US 1926 125m bw silent
Warner

In this version of *Moby Dick*, Ahab gets to settle down at the end with his lady love.
Memorable sea scenes and a star performance.
w Bess Meredyth d Millard Webb
☆ John Barrymore, Dolores Costello, George O'Hara, Mike Donlin, Sam Baker

The Sea Chase *
US 1955 117m Warnercolor Cinemascope
Warner (John Farrow)
▣ ▤ ◔

In 1939 a German freighter tries to make it from Sydney harbour back to Germany.
Unusual but not very compelling naval melodrama, chiefly because the leads are miscast.
w James Warner Bellah, John Twist *novel* Andrew Geer d John Farrow ph William Clothier m Roy Webb

☆ John Wayne, Lana Turner, David Farrar, Lyle Bettger, Tab Hunter, James Arness, Dick Davalos, John Qualen
'A film compounded of monotonously familiar ingredients.' – *Penelope Houston*

Sea Devils
US 1937 88m bw
RKO
▤

Exploits of the ice patrols of the US Coast Guard.
Flagwaving action hokum for popular stars.
w Frank Wead, John Twist, P. J. Wolfson d Ben Stoloff ph J. Roy Hunt, Joseph August md Roy Webb
☆ Victor McLaglen, Preston Foster, Ida Lupino, Donald Woods

Sea Devils
GB 1953 90m Technicolor
Coronado (David E. Rose)
▣

Spies prevent Napoleon's invasion of England.
Cheerful, forgettable swashbuckler.
w Borden Chase d Raoul Walsh ph Wilkie Cooper m Richard Addinsell
☆ Yvonne de Carlo, Rock Hudson, Maxwell Reed, Denis O'Dea, Michael Goodliffe, Bryan Forbes, Ivor Barnard, Arthur Wontner

Sea Fury
GB 1958 97m bw
Rank (Benjamin Fisz)

Rivalry strikes up between an old and a young sailor on tugboats plying between Spain and England.
Shapeless, leery melodrama with strong performances and an exciting storm-at-sea climax.
w John Kruse, Cy Endfield d Cy Endfield ph Reg Wyer m Philip Green
☆ Stanley Baker, Victor McLaglen, Luciana Paluzzi, Grégoire Aslan, Francis de Wolff, David Oxley, Rupert Davies, Robert Shaw
'They stand side by side. Young and old. Rich and poor. They gather together for a single purpose. Survival.'

The Sea Gull *
GB 1968 141m Technicolor
Warner/Sidney Lumet

Loves and hates on a 19th-century Russian estate.
Rather heavily star-studded, but certainly proficient film version of a Chekhov favourite.
w Moura Budberg *play* Anton Chekhov d Sidney Lumet ph Gerry Fisher m none pd Tony Walton
☆ James Mason, Simone Signoret, Vanessa Redgrave, David Warner, Harry Andrews, Ronald Radd, Eileen Herlie, Kathleen Widdoes, Denholm Elliott, Alfred Lynch
'The camera cannot capture the hollowness of space, the oppressive immovableness of a seemingly harmless enclosure, stasis settling on everything like a fine, corrosive dust.' – *John Simon*
'If you miss it, you will owe yourself an apology!'

The Sea Hawk ***
♙♙ US 1940 122m bw
Warner (Hal B. Wallis), Henry Blanke)
▣ ▤ ♬ ◌

Elizabeth I encourages one of her most able captains to acts of piracy against the Spanish.
Wobbly-plotted but stirring and exciting seafaring actioner, with splendid battle and duel scenes.
w Seton I. Miller, Howard Koch d Michael Curtiz ph Sol Polito m Erich Wolfgang Korngold ad Anton Grot
☆ Errol Flynn, Flora Robson, Brenda Marshall, Henry Daniell, Claude Rains, Donald Crisp, Alan Hale, Una O'Connor, James Stephenson, Gilbert Roland, William Lundigan
'Endless episodes of court intrigue tend to diminish the effect of the epic sweep of the high seas dramatics.' – *Variety*
♫ Erich Wolfgang Korngold; Anton Grot
'A man who loved as ruthlessly as he ruled. A woman whose indiscretions cost a lifetime of happiness!'

The Sea of Grass
US 1947 131m bw
MGM (Pandro S. Berman)

A cattle tycoon is so obsessed by his work that he alienates his family.

Brooding, overlong semi-Western with an unexpected cast.
w Marguerite Roberts, Vincent Lawrence *novel* Conrad Richter d Elia Kazan ph Harry Stradling m Herbert Stothart
☆ Spencer Tracy, Katharine Hepburn, Melvyn Douglas, Phyllis Thaxter, Robert Walker, Edgar Buchanan, Harry Carey, Ruth Nelson, James Bell
'In spite of all the sincerity and talent involved, an epically dreary film.' – *Time*
'The only film I ever made that I'm truly ashamed of.' – *Elia Kazan*

Sea of Lost Ships
US 1953 85m bw
Republic

The US Coast Guard saves a passenger ship from an iceberg.
Scrappy, semi-documentary account punctuated by rough action highlights.
w Steve Fisher d Joe Kane ph Reggie Lanning m R. Dale Butts
☆ Walter Brennan, John Derek, Wanda Hendrix, Richard Jaeckel, Barton MacLane, Darryl Hickman

Sea of Love **
US 1989 112m DeLuxe Panavision
Universal (Martin Bregman, Louis A. Stroller)
▣ ▤ ◔ ◎ ◉ ◌

A New York cop, suffering a mid-life crisis, falls in love with the chief suspect of a series of murders of men advertising in lonely hearts columns.
Effective urban thriller, though the emphasis is more on the romance than in discovering whodunnit.
w Richard Price d Harold Becker ph Ronnie Taylor m Trevor Jones pd John Jay Moore ed David Bretherton
☆ Al Pacino, Ellen Barkin, John Goodman, William Hickey, Michael Rooker, Richard Jenkins

Sea of Sand *
GB 1958 98m bw
Rank/Tempean (Robert Baker, Monty Berman)
▤
US title: *Desert Patrol*

Just before Alamein an Eighth Army desert group plans to destroy one of Rommel's last petrol dumps.
Good standard war suspenser.
w Robert Westerby d Guy Green ph Wilkie Cooper m Clifton Parker
☆ Richard Attenborough, John Gregson, Vincent Ball, Percy Herbert, Michael Craig, Barry Foster, Andrew Faulds, Dermot Walsh

Sea of Silence: see *La Mer Cruelle*

The Sea Shall Not Have Them
GB 1954 93m bw
Eros/Daniel M. Angel
▣ ▤

Survivors of a seaplane crash await rescue in a dinghy.
Rather dim computerized compendium of flashback mini-dramas.
w Lewis Gilbert, Vernon Harris d Lewis Gilbert ph Stephen Dade m Malcolm Arnold
☆ Dirk Bogarde, Michael Redgrave, Bonar Colleano, Jack Watling, Anthony Steel, Nigel Patrick, James Kenney, Sydney Tafler, George Rose

The Sea Wall: see *This Angry Age*

'One of the most challenging stories of faith ever told! What happened out there ... in the surging vastness of the Indian Ocean?'

Sea Wife
GB 1957 82m DeLuxe Cinemascope
TCF/Sumar (André Hakim)

Survivors of a shipwreck near Singapore in 1942 are rescued, not before the bosun has fallen in love with the only lady, not knowing she is a nun.
Flashbacked, uncertain, intermittently effective film of a popular minor novel.
w George K. Burke *novel* Sea Wyf by J. M. Scott d Bob McNaught ph Ted Scaife m Kenneth V. Jones, Leonard Salzedo
☆ Richard Burton, Joan Collins, Basil Sydney, Cy Grant

The Sea Wolf **
US 1941 90m bw
Warner (Henry Blanke)
▣ ▤

Survivors of a ferry crash in San Francisco Bay are picked up by a psychopathic freighter captain who keeps them captive.
Much filmed action suspenser which in this version looks great but overdoes the talk.
w Robert Rossen *novel* Jack London d Michael Curtiz ph Sol Polito m Erich Wolfgang Korngold
☆ Edward G. Robinson, Alexander Knox, Ida Lupino, John Garfield, Gene Lockhart, Barry Fitzgerald, Stanley Ridges, David Bruce, Howard da Silva
'A Germanic, powerful work almost devoid of compromise.' – *Charles Higham, 1972*
† Other versions appeared in 1913, with Hobart Bosworth; in 1920, with Noah Beery; in 1925, with Ralph Ince; in 1930, with Milton Sills; in 1950 (as *Barricade*, turned into a Western), with Raymond Massey; in 1958 (as *Wolf Larsen*), with Barry Sullivan; and in 1975 (Italian), as *Wolf of the Seven Seas*, with Chuck Connors.

The Sea Wolves *
GB/US/Switzerland 1980 122m Eastmancolor
Richmond-Lorimar-Varius (Euan Lloyd)
▣ ▤ ◎

In 1943, elderly British territorials living in India dispose of a Nazi transmitter in neutral Goa.
Mildly larkish Boy's Own Paper adventure with a somewhat geriatric air; an interesting 1980 throwback to the films of 1950.
w Reginald Rose *novel* Boarding Party by James Leasor d Andrew McLaglen ph Tony Imi m Roy Budd
☆ Gregory Peck, Roger Moore, Trevor Howard, David Niven, Barbara Kellerman, Patrick Macnee, Patrick Allen, Bernard Archard, Faith Brook, Martin Benson, Allan Cuthbertson, Kenneth Griffith, Donald Houston, Glyn Houston, Percy Herbert and also Patrick Holt, Terence Longdon, John Standing, Michael Medwin
'As a genre – the arterio-sclerotic war movie – it'll never catch on.' – *Time Out*
† The film was dedicated to Earl Mountbatten after his assassination.

Seagulls over Sorrento
GB 1954 92m bw
MGM (John Boulting)
US title: *Crest of the Wave*

Life on a naval research station on a small Scottish island.
A long-running British service comedy has been Americanized to little effect, but it remains just about watchable.
w Frank Harvey, Roy Boulting *play* Hugh Hastings d Roy Boulting ph Gilbert Taylor m Miklos Rozsa
☆ Gene Kelly, John Justin, Bernard Lee, Sidney James, Jeff Richards, Patric Doonan, Patrick Barr

Seal Island: see *The Living Desert*

Sealed Cargo *
US 1951 90m bw
RKO (Warren Duff)

In 1943, an American fishing-boat captain, sailing to Newfoundland, becomes suspicious of the captain of a wrecked schooner he discovers.
Enjoyable and atmospheric wartime thriller, maintaining its sense of mystery and suspense to the end.
w Dale Van Every, Oliver H. P. Garrett, Roy Huggins *novel* The Gaunt Woman by Edmund Gilligan d Alfred Werker ph George E. Diskant m Roy Webb pd J. McMillan Johnson ad Albert S. D'Agostino ed Ralph Dawson
☆ Dana Andrews, Carla Balenda, Claude Rains, Philip Dorn, Onslow Stevens, Skip Homeier, Eric Feldary, J. M. Kerrigan, Arthur Shields, Morgan Farley

Sealed Lips: see *After Tonight*

'What is the truth about fraternization?'

Sealed Verdict
US 1948 83m bw
Paramount (Robert Fellows)

An American officer in Germany falls in love with the ex-girlfriend of a Nazi war criminal.
Routine melodrama, as boring as it sounds.

---

w Jonathan Latimer *novel* Lionel Shapiro
d Lewis Allen *ph* Leo Tover *m* Hugo Friedhofer
☆ Ray Milland, Florence Marly, Broderick Crawford, John Hoyt, John Ridgely, Ludwig Donath

Seance on a Wet Afternoon *
GB 1964 121m bw
Rank/Allied Film Makers (Richard Attenborough, Bryan Forbes)
▇▇▇

A fake medium persuades her husband to kidnap a child so that she can become famous by revealing its whereabouts in a trance.
Overlong character melodrama in which the suspense is better than the psychopathology. A mannered performance from the lady, a false nose from the gentleman, and a general air of gloom.
wd Bryan Forbes *ph* Gerry Turpin *m* John Barry
☆ Kim Stanley, Richard Attenborough, Nanette Newman, Patrick Magee
'Not only a psychological suspense thriller but also a top-notch crime-and-detection tale and, above all, a horror film.' – *Judith Crist*
🎭 Kim Stanley
🏆 Richard Attenborough

The Search *
US/Switzerland 1948 105m bw
MGM/Praesens Film (Lazar Wechsler)
▇▇▇

An American soldier in Germany cares for a war orphan.
Vivid semi-documentary post-war drama which falls down in its elementary dramatics but sent audiences home wiping away tears.
w Richard Schweizer, David Wechsler, Paul Jarrico
d Fred Zinnemann *ph* Emil Berna *m* Robert Blum
☆ Montgomery Clift, Aline MacMahon, Ivan Jandl, Wendell Corey
'Far and away the most touching film we have seen for years.' – *C. A. Lejeune*
🏅 original story (Richard Schweizer, David Wechsler); Ivan Jandl (special award for outstanding juvenile performance)
🎭 script; Fred Zinnemann; Montgomery Clift

'You never saw so many skins you'd like to touch!'
Search for Beauty
US 1934 77m bw
Paramount
A physical culture magazine sponsors an international contest for beauties of both sexes.
Mildly amusing extravaganza staking its popularity on girls in bathing dress.
w Claude Binyon, Sam Hellman, Frank Butler and others *play* Schuyler E. Gray, Paul R. Milton
d Erle C. Kenton
☆ Larry 'Buster' Crabbe, Ida Lupino, Toby Wing, James Gleason, Robert Armstrong, Gertrude Michael, Roscoe Karns
'A couple of years ago so many girls in abbreviated dress would have been enough for one picture ... but they've seen massed pulchritude quite often lately, so the girls here are just trimmings.' – *Variety*

The Search for Bridey Murphy *
US 1956 84m bw Vistavision
Paramount (Pat Duggan)
▇▇▇

A Colorado businessman and amateur hypnotist finds a lady neighbour so good a subject that he is able to delve into her previous incarnation as a long-dead Irish peasant.
Adequately presented with alienation effects, but mainly consisting of two-shots and fuzzy flashbacks, this treatment of an actual case (subsequently discredited) works up to a fine pitch of frenzy when the subject seems unable to come back from her previous life.
wd Noel Langley *book* Morey Bernstein *ph* John F. Warren *m* Irvin Talbot
☆ Teresa Wright, Louis Hayward, Kenneth Tobey, Nancy Gates, Richard Anderson

'He had to find her ... he had to find her...'
The Searchers ****
US 1956 119m Technicolor Vistavision
Warner/C. V. Whitney (Merian C. Cooper)
▇▇ ▇▇ ▇▇ 🔄 ☯

A Confederate war veteran tracks down the Indians who have slaughtered his brother and sister-in-law and carried off their daughter.

Disturbing Western of obsession and racism which has become Ford's most influential film, in which Wayne gives his most ambiguous performance, being no longer a simple gung-ho hero, but a tormented loner out of step with his society. Its themes of loss and reconciliation are echoed in many films that followed.
w Frank S. Nugent *novel* Alan le May *d* John Ford *ph* Winton C. Hoch *m* Max Steiner
☆ John Wayne, Jeffrey Hunter, Natalie Wood, Vera Miles, Ward Bond, John Qualen, Henry Brandon, Antonio Moreno
'You can read a lot into it, but it isn't very enjoyable.' – *Pauline Kael, 70s*

Searching for Bobby Fischer
👪 US 1993 110m DeLuxe
Paramount/Mirage (Scott Rudin, William Horberg)
▇▇ ▇▇▇

GB title: Innocent Moves
A father discovers that his seven-year-old son is a chess prodigy.
An off-beat film that concentrates on the father–son relationship, although it does attempt the impossible of making chess games visually exciting and accessible to non-players.
wd Steven Zaillian *book* Fred Waitzkin *ph* Conrad L. Hall *m* James Horner *pd* David Gropman *ed* Wayne Wahrman
☆ Joe Mantegna, Max Pomeranc, Ben Kingsley, Joan Allen, Laurence Fishburne, Michael Nirenberg, Robert Stephens, David Paymer
'Earnest and well-acted.' – *Variety*
🎭 Conrad L. Hall

'What strange power could drive this man from the lips of the woman he married to the arms of the woman he loved?'
The Searching Wind *
US 1946 107m bw
Paramount (Hal B. Wallis)
Affairs of an American diplomat in Europe during the thirties.
Earnest melodrama which would have been better timed six years earlier. Excellent production, though.
w Lillian Hellman *play* Lillian Hellman
d William Dieterle *ph* Lee Garmes *m* Victor Young *ad* Hans Drier, Franz Bachelin
☆ Robert Young, Sylvia Sidney, Ann Richards, Douglas Dick, Dudley Digges, Albert Basserman, Dan Seymour

The Seashell and the Clergyman *
France 1928 30m bw silent
(Producer unknown)
A clergyman is afflicted by sexual torments.
Celebrated surrealist short with memorable images and a great deal of confusion.
w Antonin Artaud *d* Germaine Dulac *ph* Paul Guichard
☆ Alix Allin
† In GB the film was banned by the censor with the famous comment: 'It is so cryptic as to have no apparent meaning. If there is a meaning, it is doubtless objectionable.'

Season of Passion: see Summer of the Seventeenth Doll

Season of the Witch
US 1973 89m colour
Latent Image (Nancy M. Romero)
▇▇

aka: *Jack's Wife*
aka: *Hungry Wives*
A housewife, bored by the sameness of her domestic routine, turns to witchcraft, which leads in turn to murder.
A low-budget satirical take on the horrors of suburbia, often imaginatively photographed and edited, but fatally sabotaged by its rudimentary acting and frequently naïve script.
wd George A. Romero *ph* George A. Romero *m* Steve Gorn *ed* George A. Romero
☆ Jan White, Ray Laine, Anne Muffly, Joedda McClain, Virginia Greenwald, Bill Thunhurst, Neil Fisher, Shirlee Strasser
'A strange experimental film, with an unmistakeable (but amateurish) aura of Bergman.' – *David Pirie, Time Out*
† The British video release in 1994 ran for 104m.

The Seaweed Children: see Malachi's Cove

Sebastian
GB 1968 100m Eastmancolor
Paramount/Maccius (Herb Brodkin, Michael Powell)
▇▇▇

An Oxford professor and code expert is appointed to the secret service.
Mildly spoofy spy yarn: style but not much substance.
w Gerald Vaughan-Hughes *story* Leo Marks
d David Greene *ph* Gerry Fisher *m* Jerry Goldsmith *pd* Wilfred Shingleton
☆ Dirk Bogarde, John Gielgud, Lilli Palmer, Susannah York, Janet Munro, Margaret Johnston, Nigel Davenport, Ronald Fraser
'One of the problems with this kind of movie is the enormous pressure put on the audience to have a good time over practically nothing.' – *Renata Adler*

Sebastian
Norway/Sweden 1995 84m colour
Mefistofilm/Miramar/Nordisk (Peter Vennerod, Hansi Mandoki, Lars Kolvig)
A 16-year-old boy has problems coming to terms with his homosexuality.
A no-problem movie, about a boy whose lifestyle is accepted without many qualms by those around him; the lack of real conflict leads to blandness.
w Svend Wam, Peter Vennerod, Hansi Mandoki, Per Källberg *novel* Svart Cayal by Per Knutsen
d Svend Wam *ph* Per Källberg *m* various
ad Crispin Gerholt *ed* Einar Egeland
☆ Hampus Björck, Nicolai Cleve Broch, Ewa Fröling, Helge Jordal, Rebecka Hamse, Lena Olander

Sebastiane *
GB 1976 86m colour
Megalovision/Cinegate/Disctac (James Waley, Howard Malin)
Sebastian, a soldier and former favourite banished to a remote outpost by the Emperor Diocletian, is executed by his commander when he refuses his sexual advances.
Unusual semi-improvised feature in which the dialogue is in Latin with English subtitles. It was the first British film to deal openly with homosexual desire.
w Derek Jarman, James Waley *d* Derek Jarman, Paul Humfress *ph* Peter Middleton *m* Brian Eno *pd* Derek Jarman *ed* Paul Humfress
☆ Leonardo Treviglio, Barney James, Neil Kennedy, Richard Warwick, Donald Dunham, Ken Hicks, Lindsay Kemp
'The most promising sign of new film life in independent narrative cinema in this country in many, many years.' – *Tony Rayns, MFB*

Second Best
GB/US 1994 105m Technicolor
Warner/Regency/Alcor/Fron/Monarchy (Sarah Radclyffe)
▇▇ ▇▇▇ ☯ 🎧

An introverted Welsh postman adopts a young boy with problems.
Small-scale domestic drama of male bonding that remains too inert to engage attention.
w David Cook *novel* David Cook *d* Chris Menges *ph* Ashley Rowe *m* Simon Boswell *pd* Michael Howells *ed* George Akers
☆ William Hurt, Chris Cleary Miles, Keith Allen, Prunella Scales, Jane Horrocks, Alan Cumming, John Hurt, Alfred Lynch, Doris Hare, Nerys Hughes, Jodhi May
'So modest in its aim and achievement that it will be exceedingly difficult to drum up much audience interest in seeing it.' – *Variety*

Second Best Bed
GB 1938 74m bw
Capitol
A magistrate is suspected of adultery.
Cheerful star comedy with a touch of sophistication.
w Ben Travers *d* Tom Walls *ph* Jack Cox
md Van Phillips
☆ Tom Walls, Jane Baxter, Veronica Rose, Carl Jaffe, Greta Gynt

The Second Best Secret Agent in the Whole Wide World: see Licensed to Kill

Second Chance
US 1953 82m Technicolor 3-D
RKO (Edmund Grainger)
▇▇▇
In South America, a professional killer stalks a gangster's moll.

Comic strip antics with a climax on a stalled cable car.
w Oscar Millard, Sydney Boehm *story* D. M. Marshman Jnr *d* Rudolph Maté *ph* William Snyder *m* Roy Webb
☆ Robert Mitchum, Linda Darnell, Jack Palance, Reginald Sheffield, Roy Roberts

Second Chorus
US 1940 84m bw
Paramount (Boris Morros)
▇▇ ▇▇ 🔄
Two trumpeters and their lady manager hit Broadway.
Mild musical.
w Elaine Ryan, Ian Mclellan Hunter, Frank Cavett
d H. C. Potter *ph* Theodor Sparkuhl *m* Artie Shaw *songs* various
☆ Fred Astaire, Burgess Meredith, Paulette Goddard, Charles Butterworth, Artie Shaw and his Band, Frank Melton, Jimmy Conlin
🎵 Artie Shaw; song 'Love of my Life' (*m*Artie Shaw, *ly*Johnny Mercer)

Second Class Mail
GB 1984 4m colour
NFTS
▇▇
A woman sends away by mail order for an inflatable husband.
A delightful joke, told at the perfect length.
wd Alison Snowden
🏅 animated short

'The greatest combination of talent ever gathered in one show!'
Second Fiddle
US 1939 86m bw
TCF (Gene Markey)
A Minnesota skating schoolteacher goes to Hollywood and becomes a star.
Routine star vehicle.
w Harry Tugend *d* Sidney Lanfield *ph* Leon Shamroy *md* Louis Silvers *songs* Irving Berlin
☆ Sonja Henie, Tyrone Power, Edna May Oliver, Rudy Vallee, Mary Healy, Lyle Talbot, Alan Dinehart
🏅 song 'I Poured My Heart into a Song' (*m*/*ly*Irving Berlin)

The Second Greatest Sex
US 1955 87m Technicolor Cinemascope
U-I (Albert J. Cohen)
Western women emulate Lysistrata to stop their men from feuding.
Flat attempt to cash in on Seven Brides for Seven Brothers; some good acrobatic dancing but no style.
w Charles Hoffman *d* George Marshall *ph* Wilfrid M. Cline *md* Joseph Gershenson *ch* Lee Scott
☆ Jeanne Crain, George Nader, Bert Lahr, Kitty Kallen, Paul Gilbert, Keith Andes, Mamie Van Doren, Tommy Rall

Second Honeymoon
US 1937 79m bw
TCF (Raymond Griffith)
A man tries to win back his ex-wife.
Moderate star romantic comedy.
w Kathryn Scola, Darrell Ware *story* Philip Wylie *d* Walter Lang *ph* Ernest Palmer *m* David Buttolph
☆ Tyrone Power, Loretta Young, Stuart Erwin, Claire Trevor, Marjorie Weaver, Lyle Talbot, J. Edward Bromberg

The Second Mrs Tanqueray
GB 1952 75m bw
Vandyke (Roger Proudlock)
A Victorian society widower marries a notorious lady.
Stiff-backed penny-pinching version of an interestingly antiquated play.
play Arthur Wing Pinero *d* Dallas Bower
ph Gerald Gibbs
☆ Pamela Brown, Hugh Sinclair, Ronald Ward, Virginia McKenna, Andrew Osborn

Second Thoughts
US 1982 98m Movielab
Turman-Foster/EMI
▇▇▇

A lady lawyer gets into complex trouble when she bails out her inconsiderate lover from a Santa Fe jail.

An absurd series of situations is played for drama rather than comedy, and the feminist flag is frequently waved. The result is an unlikeable muddle.

w Steve Brown d Lawrence Turman ph King Baggot m Henry Mancini

☆ Lucie Arnaz, Craig Wasson, Ken Howard, Anne Schedeen

'Alternately dull and risible.' – Chris Auty, MFB

The Second Time Around
US 1961 99m DeLuxe Cinemascope
TCF/Cummings/Harman (Jack Cummings)

In 1912 Arizona, a widow stands for sheriff and has plenty of choice for a husband.

Light-hearted Western fun mixed with family sentimentality.

w Oscar Saul, Cecil Van Heusen novel Richard Emery Roberts d Vincent Sherman ph Ellis W. Carter m Gerald Fried

☆ Debbie Reynolds, Steve Forrest, Andy Griffith, Juliet Prowse, Thelma Ritter, Ken Scott, Isobel Elsom

'Keep a lemon handy for sucking to ward off an attack of the terminal cutesies.' – Judith Crist, 1973

The Second Victory
GB 1986 112m Rank Colour
Lelaleuka/J and M (Gerald Thomas)

In Austria after World War II, British occupation forces try to keep order in face of unrest following the murder of a sergeant.

Curiously timed return to the Third Man era, with a plotline unlikely to appeal to modern filmgoers; technical resources adequate rather than inspired.

w Morris West novel Morris West d Gerald Thomas

☆ Anthony Andrews, Helmut Griem, Max von Sydow, Mario Adorf, Birgit Doll

The Second Woman
US 1950 91m bw
United Artists/Cardinal (Mort Briskin)

GB title: Ellen

An architect, apparently paranoic, is proved to be the victim of a revenge plot.

Tolerable semi-star melodrama with a deliberate film noir look.

w Robert Smith d James V. Kern ph Hal Mohr md Nat Finston

☆ Robert Young, Betsy Drake, John Sutton, Florence Bates, Morris Carnovsky, Henry O'Neill

The Second-Floor Mystery
US 1930 56m bw
Warner

Correspondents through an agony column find themselves enmeshed in mystery and murder.

Burlesque whodunnit which seemed a smart trick at the time.

w Joseph Jackson novel The Agony Column by Earl Derr Biggers d Roy del Ruth

☆ Loretta Young, Grant Withers, H. B. Warner, Claire McDowell, John Loder

Seconds **
US 1966 106m bw
Paramount/Joel/Gibraltar (Edward Lewis)

A secret organization sells a special service to the jaded rich; apparent death followed by physical rejuvenation.

An intriguing half-hour is followed by a glum new life for our hero, capped by a horrifying finale in which, dissatisfied, he learns he is to become one of the corpses necessary to the organization's continuance.

w Lewis John Carlino novel David Ely d John Frankenheimer ph James Wong Howe m Jerry Goldsmith titles Saul Bass

☆ Rock Hudson, John Randolph, Will Geer, Salome Jens, Jeff Corey, Richard Anderson, Murray Hamilton, Wesley Addy

'A really horrifying piece of science fiction that burns its way into your mind like a gnawing headache.' – Sunday Express

'An ending that is one of the most terrifying episodes I have ever seen on the screen.' – Daily Express

⅋ James Wong Howe

'A nursery crime of epic proportions...'

The Secret Adventures of Tom Thumb **
GB 1993 60m colour
Bolex Brothers/BBC Bristol/La Sept/Manga/Lumen (Richard 'Hutch' Hutchison)

A freakish tiny child, taken from his parents to a laboratory full of mutants, escapes into a rubbish dump inhabited by small people much like himself. A squalid, predatory and unlovely universe is brilliantly created using a mix of live action, pixilation and stop-motion animation. The images are of decay and dissolution and disturbing in their detail (a laboratory technician's rubber gloves covered in bristles, a crucified Father Christmas, a man catching and eating a moth). The overall effect is of a wayward originality.

wd Dave Borthwick ph Dave Borthwick, Frank Passingham m John Paul Jones, Startled Insects pd Dave Borthwick ed Dave Borthwick

☆ Nick Upton, Deborah Collard, Frank Passingham, John Schofield, Mike Gifford, Robert Heath, George Brandt

'Brilliantly achieved but not one for the delectation of the feelgood brigade.' – Derek Malcolm, Guardian

Secret Agent **
GB 1936 83m bw
Gaumont British (Michael Balcon, Ivor Montagu)

A reluctantly recruited spy is ordered to kill a man.

Unsatisfactory in casting and writing, this Hitchcock suspenser nevertheless has many typically amusing moments.

w Charles Bennett play Campbell Dixon story Ashenden by Somerset Maugham d Alfred Hitchcock ph Bernard Knowles md Louis Levy

☆ John Gielgud, Robert Young, Peter Lorre, Madeleine Carroll, Percy Marmont, Lilli Palmer, Florence Kahn

'As uncommon as it is unsentimentally cruel.' – Peter John Dyer, 1964

'Many sequences which show Hitchcock at his very best: the fake funeral, the murder on the mountainside, the riverside café, and the climax in a chocolate factory.' – NFT, 1961

'How unfortunate it is that Mr Hitchcock, a clever director, is allowed to produce and even to write his own films, though as a producer he has no sense of continuity and as a writer he has no sense of life. His films consist of a series of small "amusing" melodramatic situations: the murderer's button dropped on the baccarat board; the strangled organist's hands prolonging the notes in the empty church; the fugitives hiding in the bell tower when the bell begins to swing. Very perfunctorily he builds up to these tricky situations ... and then drops them.' – Graham Greene

'Hitch said he was offering me Hamlet in modern dress. But when we came to make it, all the psychological interest was dissipated.' – John Gielgud

The Secret Agent
GB 1996 95m Technicolor
Fox/Capitol (Norma Heyman)

aka: Joseph Conrad's The Secret Agent

In Victorian London, a double agent is ordered by his Russian masters to commit a terrorist act: blowing up the Greenwich Observatory.

Wan, drably understated version of Conrad's novel of small-time revolutionaries.

wd Christopher Hampton novel Joseph Conrad ph Denis Lenoir m Philip Glass pd Caroline Amies ed George Akers

☆ Bob Hoskins, Patricia Arquette, Gérard Depardieu, George Spelvin, Jim Broadbent, Christian Bale, Eddie Izzard, Elizabeth Spriggs, Peter Vaughan, Julian Wadham, Robin Williams (uncredited)

'Appropriately gloomy and grim, but these are not qualities that will recommend it to most audiences.' – Variety

† Conrad's novel was also filmed by Alfred Hitchcock as Sabotage (qv).

The Secret Agent Club
US 1996 90m Foto-Kem
Marquee/Starlight/Secret Agent/Hit (Brian Shuster, James Ian Lifton)

A gang of kids led by the son of a secret agent defeat the baddies who steal a deadly laser gun.

Dismal action film for a young audience, which tones down the violence somewhat, but remains as morally dubious as its adult counterparts.

w Rory Johnson d John Murlowski ph S. Douglas Smith m Jan Hammer pd James Scanlon ed Leslie Rosenthal

☆ Hulk Hogan, Richard Moll, Matthew McCurley, Edward Albert, Lyman Ward, James Hong, Barry Bostwick, Lesley-Anne Down

'A film with few pretentions to quality and scant interest in stimulating or engaging grown-ups.' – Sight and Sound

Secret Agent of Japan
US 1942 72m bw
TCF

A female British agent tangles with Japanese in the Shanghai international settlement.

Standard propaganda filler with caricature Japs.

w John Larkin d Irving Pichel

☆ Preston Foster, Lynn Bari, Noel Madison, Sen Yung, Janis Carter, Steve Geray, Kurt Katch

'Behind a locked door – the relentless evil of his past!'

Secret Beyond the Door
US 1948 98m bw
Universal/Walter Wanger (Fritz Lang)

An heiress marries a moody millionaire with a death fixation, and comes to think of herself as his next potential victim.

Silly melodrama with much chat and little suspense.

w Silvia Richards story Rufus King d Fritz Lang ph Stanley Cortez m Miklos Rozsa

☆ Joan Bennett, Michael Redgrave, Anne Revere, Barbara O'Neil, Natalie Schafer, Paul Cavanagh

'A dog-wagon Rebecca with a seasoning of psychiatrics.' – Otis L. Guernsey Jnr

'Lang gets a few wood-silky highlights out of this sow's ear, but it is a hopeless job and a worthless movie.' – James Agee

The Secret Bride
US 1935 63m bw
Warner

GB title: Concealment

A District Attorney is secretly married to the daughter of the politician he is trying to convict.

Dismal melodrama, tritely scripted.

w Tom Buckingham, F. Hugh Herbert, Mary McCall Jnr play Concealment by Leonard Ide d William Dieterle ph Ernest Haller

☆ Barbara Stanwyck, Warren William, Glenda Farrell, Grant Mitchell, Arthur Byron, Henry O'Neill, Douglass Dumbrille

'Fast moving melodrama, well above average.' – Variety

Secret Ceremony
GB 1969 109m Eastmancolor
Universal/World Films/Paul M. Heller (John Heyman, Norman Priggen)

A prostitute mothers a young girl with a strange past.

Nuthouse melodrama for devotees of the director.

w George Tabori short story Marco Denevi d Joseph Losey ph Gerry Fisher m Richard Rodney Bennett

☆ Elizabeth Taylor, Robert Mitchum, Mia Farrow, Pamela Brown, Peggy Ashcroft

'This piece of garbage is so totally ridiculous that I can't imagine why anyone would want to be in it, let alone see it.' – Rex Reed

Secret Command
US 1944 92m bw
Columbia (Phil L. Ryan)

An ex-foreign correspondent goes undercover at a shipyard to track down saboteurs.

Routine wartime thick ear.

w Roy Chanslor story The Saboteurs by John and Ward Hawkins d Eddie Sutherland ph Franz Planer m Paul Sawtell

☆ Pat O'Brien, Carole Landis, Chester Morris, Ruth Warrick, Barton MacLane, Tom Tully, Wallace Ford, Howard Freeman

Secret Défense
France/Switzerland/Italy 1997 173m colour
Artificial Eye/La Sept/T&C (Martine Marignac, Christian Lambert)

A scientist's investigation into the death of her father leads to more deaths, accidental and deliberate.

An overlong, over-complicated thriller of tangled relationships.

w Pascal Bonitzer, Emmanuelle Cuau, Jacques Rivette d Jacques Rivette ph William Lubtchansky m Hesperion XX ad Manu de Chavigny ed Nicole Lubtchansky

☆ Sandrine Bonnaire, Jerzy Radziwilowicz, Laure Marsac, Grégoire Colin, Bernadette Giraud, Micheline Herzog, Sara Louis, Mark Saporta

'Patience is needed to watch the film and some may argue is not rewarded by the conclusion. My reply: watch more the unfurling than the answer.' – James Mottram, Film Review

Secret Flight: see School for Secrets

The Secret Four: see The Four Just Men (1939)

The Secret Four: see Kansas City Confidential (1952)

Secret Friends
GB 1991 97m Metrocolor
Feature/Whistling Gypsy/Film Four (Rosemarie Whitman)

On a train journey an artist hovers between dreams and reality as he imagines that his wife is a killer and that he has murdered his mistress.

Confusing account of a mid-life crisis in which it is difficult to separate fantasy from real life and hardly worth the effort of working out which is which.

wd Dennis Potter novel Ticket to Ride by Dennis Potter ph Sue Gibson m Nicholas Russell-Pavier pd Gary Williamson ed Clare Douglas

☆ Alan Bates, Gina Bellman, Frances Barber, Tony Doyle, Joanna David, Colin Jeavons, Rowena Cooper

'A tough ride for a very small return: the cramped and narcissistic anguish of a middle-aged male as seen in Potter passim.' – Sheila Johnston, Independent

'It is time that Potter pulled the communication cord on this particular train of thought.' – Jonathan Romney, Sight and Sound

The Secret Fury
US 1950 86m bw
RKO (Jack H. Skirball, Bruce Manning)

A successful pianist is deliberately driven insane by her fiancé.

Derivative melodrama of no great interest.

w Lionel House d Mel Ferrer ph Leo Tover m Roy Webb md Constantin Bakaleinikoff

☆ Claudette Colbert, Robert Ryan, Jane Cowl, Paul Kelly, Philip Ober, Elizabeth Risdon, Doris Dudley

The Secret Game: see Les Jeux Interdits

The Secret Garden *
⚤ US 1949 92m bw (Technicolor sequence)
MGM (Clarence Brown)

An orphan girl goes to stay with her moody uncle and brightens up the lives of those around her.

Subdued, richly produced, rather likeable Victorian fable with the same moral as The Bluebird and The Wizard of Oz: happiness is in your own back yard.

w Robert Ardrey novel Frances Hodgson Burnett d Fred M. Wilcox ph Ray June m Bronislau Kaper

☆ Margaret O'Brien, Herbert Marshall, Gladys Cooper, Elsa Lanchester, Dean Stockwell, Brian Roper

'Uneven, but oddly and unexpectedly interesting.' – Richard Mallett, Punch

'Let's have more pictures in this kindly vein.' – Picturegoer

'The timeless tale of a special place where magic, hope and love grow.'

The Secret Garden **

US   1993   101m   Technicolor
Warner/American Zoetrope (Fred Fuchs, Fred Roos, Tom Luddy)

A young, lonely, orphaned girl, sent to live with her aristocratic uncle, helps her invalid cousin back to life.
A charming version of the classic children's story, deftly made, though its appeal may be too tame for today's audiences.
w Caroline Thompson *novel* Frances Hodgson Burnett d Agnieszka Holland *ph* Roger Deakins *m* Zbigniew Preisner *pd* Stuart Craig *ed* Isabelle Lorente
☆ Maggie Smith, Kate Maberly, Heydon Prowse, Andrew Knott, Laura Crossley, John Lynch, Walter Sparrow, Irene Jacob
'Executed to near perfection in all artistic departments, this superior adaptation of the perennial favorite novel will find its core public among girls but should prove satisfying enough to a range of audiences.' – *Variety*

The Secret Heart

US   1946   97m   bw
MGM (Edwin H. Knopf)
A widow has problems with her emotionally disturbed daughter.
Old-fashioned woman's picture.
w Whitfield Cook, Anne M. Chapin *story* Rose Franken, William Brown Meloney d Robert Z. Leonard *ph* George Folsey *m* Bronislau Kaper
☆ Claudette Colbert, Walter Pidgeon, June Allyson, Robert Sterling, Marshall Thompson, Elizabeth Patterson, Richard Derr, Patricia Medina
'"There are three things you can't hide," says Walter Pidgeon in one of his bantering moments; "love, smoke, and a man riding a camel." I would add a fourth – that old MGM touch.' – *Richard Winnington*

Secret Interlude: see *The View From Pompey's Head* (1955)

Secret Interlude: see *Private Number* (1936)

'The daring plan – the staggering odds – the incredible five!'

The Secret Invasion

US   1964   98m   DeLuxe   Panavision
UA/San Carlos (Gene Corman)
During World War II five convicted criminals become commandos.
Cut price Dirty Dozen, quite well made and exciting.
w R. Wright Campbell d Roger Corman *ph* Arthur E. Arling *m* Hugo Friedhofer
☆ Stewart Granger, Raf Vallone, Henry Silva, Mickey Rooney, Edd Byrnes, William Campbell, Peter Coe

The Secret Life of an American Wife **

US   1968   92m   DeLuxe
TCF/Charlton (George Axelrod)
A bored suburban housewife sets out to seduce a movie star.
Sympathetic comedy of sixties suburban manners.
wd George Axelrod *ph* Leon Shamroy *m* Billy May
☆ Walter Matthau, Anne Jackson, Patrick O'Neal, Edy Williams
'Both a first-class satire on American mores and a compassionate study of wish-fulfilment.' – *NFT, 1970*

The Secret Life of Sergei Eisenstein **

Italy/GB   1987   58m   bw/colour
Polivideo/SSR-RTSI/BFI
Documentary on the life and work of the great Russian director.
Told in the first person, and drawing on Eisenstein's own words, this is a revealing portrait of a revolutionary artist in a hurry, one that gains from using excerpts from the films to illustrate the events of his life.
w Gian Carlo Bertelli, Pier Marco De Santi *writings of* Sergei M.Eisenstein d Gian Carlo Bertelli *m* Graziano Mandozzi *ed* Pedro Del Rey
☆ Paul Vaughan

The Secret Life of Walter Mitty **

US   1947   110m   Technicolor
Samuel Goldwyn
A mother's boy dreams of derring-do, and eventually life catches up with fiction.
This pleasantly remembered star comedy, though it never had much to do with Thurber, can now be seen to have missed most of its opportunities, though the nice moments do tend to compensate.
w Ken Englund, Everett Freeman *story* James Thurber d Norman Z. McLeod *ph* Lee Garmes *m* David Raksin
☆ Danny Kaye, Virginia Mayo, Boris Karloff, Florence Bates, Fay Bainter, *Thurston Hall*, Ann Rutherford, Gordon Jones, Reginald Denny

Secret Meeting: see *Marie Octobre*

Secret Mission

GB   1942   94m   bw
GFD/Marcel Hellman/Excelsior
During World War II four British Intelligence officers are landed in occupied France to discover the truth about German defences.
Stilted war suspenser.
w Anatole de Grunwald, Basil Bartlett, Terence Young *d* Harold French *ph* Bernard Knowles *m* Mischa Spoliansky
☆ Hugh Williams, Carla Lehmann, James Mason, Roland Culver, Nancy Price, Michael Wilding, Percy Walsh

Secret Motive: see *The London Blackout Murders*

The Secret of Blood Island

GB   1964   84m   Technicolor
U-I/Hammer (Anthony Nelson Keys)
A girl parachutist secret agent is smuggled into a Japanese POW camp and out again.
Absurd blood and thunder, almost perversely enjoyable – but not quite.
w John Gilling d Quentin Lawrence *ph* Jack Asher *m* James Bernard
☆ Barbara Shelley, Jack Hedley, Charles Tingwell, Bill Owen, Lee Montague

The Secret of Convict Lake *

US   1951   83m   bw
TCF (Frank P. Rosenberg)
In the 1870s, escaped convicts take over a California town.
Brooding, snowy, set-bound Western melodrama; predictable but watchable.
w Oscar Saul d Michael Gordon *ph* Leo Tover *m* Sol Kaplan *md* Lionel Newman
☆ Glenn Ford, Gene Tierney, Ann Dvorak, Ethel Barrymore, Zachary Scott, Barbara Bates, Cyril Cusack, Jeanette Nolan, Ruth Donnelly

The Secret of Madame Blanche

US   1933   85m   bw
MGM
The woman who takes the blame for murder committed by a young man is the mother he never knew.
Or, Madame X unofficially revisited: all-stops-out melodrama very typical of its time.
w Frances Goodrich, Albert Hackett *play The Lady* by Martin Brown d Charles Brabin
☆ Irene Dunne, Phillips Holmes, Lionel Atwill, Douglas Walton, Jean Parker, Una Merkel

The Secret of My Success

GB   1965   105m   Metrocolor   Panavision
MGM/Andrew and Virginia Stone
A village policeman follows his mother's dictum that he should not think ill of others, and accidentally goes from success to success.
Flabby portmanteau comedy full of in-jokes and flat-footed farce; satire is not evident.
wd Andrew L. Stone *ph* David Boulton *m* Lucien Cailliet and others *md* Roland Shaw
☆ James Booth, Lionel Jeffries, Amy Dalby, Stella Stevens, Honor Blackman, Shirley Jones, Joan Hickson

The Secret of My Success *

US   1987   110m   DeLuxe
Universal/Rastar (Herbert Ross)
A country cousin in New York is determined to hit the big time.
An amiable melange of familiar situations with just a touch of Midnight Cowboy and a sharp edge to some of the writing; but not enough to keep its star at the top.
w Jim Cash, Jack Epps, A. J. Carothers d Herbert Ross *ph* Carlo Di Palma *m* David Foster
☆ Michael J. Fox, Helen Slater, Richard Jordan, Margaret Whitton, John Pankow, Christopher Murney
'A bedroom farce with a leaden touch, a corporate comedy without teeth.' – *Daily Variety*

The Secret of Nimh *

US   1982   82m   Technicolor
Aurora/Don Bluth
Forced out of her cosy field, a widowed mouse seeks the help of Nicodemus, king of the rat pack.
Animated cartoon by Disney artists who rejected that company's declining standards and set up their own factory. Alas, though they have the skills, the narrative they have chosen needed refining.
w Don Bluth, John Pomeroy, Gary Goldman, Will Finn *novel Mrs Frisby and the Rats of Nimh* by Robert C. O'Brien d Don Bluth *m* Jerry Goldsmith
☆ Featuring the voices of: Elizabeth Hartman, Derek Jacobi, Dom DeLuise, John Carradine, Peter Strauss, Aldo Ray, Edie McClurg, Wil Wheaton
'Vintage techniques are proudly invoked, but the story desperately needs loving care.' – *Sight and Sound*

'Between Land And Sea There Is A Place Where Myths Are Real...'

The Secret of Roan Inish

US   1993   102m   DeLuxe
Metro Tartan/Skerry/Jones Entertainment (John Sloss, Glenn R. Jones, Peter Newman)
In Ireland, a young girl persuades her family to move to a seal-haunted island off the Donegal coast, where their ancestors once lived.
A Celtic myth, of loss and salvation, told with some sensitivity; but it is likely to leave modern audiences unmoved.
wd John Sayles *novel Secret of the Ron Mor Skerry* by Rosalie K. Fry *ph* Haskell Wexler *m* Mason Daring *pd* Adrian Smith *ed* John Sayles
☆ Mick Lally, Eileen Colgan, John Lynch, Jeni Courtney, Richard Sheridan, Cillian Byrne
'Hard to get through even as myth and even harder to contemplate as a contribution to any relevant form of Irish culture.' – *Derek Malcolm, Guardian*

The Secret of Santa Vittoria *

US   1969   140m   Technicolor   Panavision
UA/Stanley Kramer
In 1945 an Italian village hides its wine from the occupying Germans.
Expected, exhausting epic comedy with everyone talking at once.
w William Rose, Ben Maddow *novel* Robert Crichton d Stanley Kramer *ph* Giuseppe Rotunno *m* Ernest Gold
☆ Anthony Quinn, Anna Magnani, Virna Lisi, Hardy Kruger, Sergio Franchi, Renato Rascel
'A brainless farrago of flying rolling pins and rotten vegetables, filled with the kind of screaming, belching, eye-rolling fictional Italians only Stanley Kramer could invent.' – *Rex Reed*
♫ Ernest Gold

The Secret of St Ives

US   1949   76m   bw
Columbia
During the Napoleonic War, a French prisoner-of-war escapes from Edinburgh Castle, only to be accused of murder.
Modest swashbuckler with a somewhat lacklustre atmosphere.
w Eric Taylor *story* Robert Louis Stevenson d Phil Rosen *ph* Henry Freulich *m* Mischa Bakaleinikoff
☆ Richard Ney, Vanessa Brown, Henry Daniell, Aubrey Mather

The Secret of Stamboul

GB   1936   93m   bw
Wainwright
reissue title: *The Spy in White*
An English adventurer foils a Turkish revolution.
Pale rendering of a full-blooded best-seller.
w Richard Wainwright, Howard Irving Young, Noel Langley *novel The Eunuch of Stamboul* by Dennis Wheatley d Andrew Marton
☆ Valerie Hobson, Frank Vosper, James Mason, Kay Walsh, Peter Haddon

The Secret of the Blue Room

US   1933   66m   bw
Universal
An heiress's three suitors all volunteer to spend the night in the haunted room of her mansion.
Murderous malarkey without the courage of its convictions.
w William Hurlbut d Kurt Neumann
☆ Lionel Atwill, Gloria Stuart, Paul Lukas, Edward Arnold, Onslow Stevens, Robert Barrat, Elizabeth Patterson
'Americanization of a German mystery yarn which ought to do well in the smaller spots.' – *Variety*
† Remade in 1938 as *The Missing Guest* and in 1944 as *Murder in the Blue Room*.

The Secret of the Incas

US   1954   101m   Technicolor
Paramount (Mel Epstein)
Various adventurers seek a priceless Inca jewel.
Boys' Own Paper yarn which sounds a good deal more exciting than it is: too much talk and a few choice studio backcloths drop the tension alarmingly, and the script lacks humour and conciseness.
w Ranald MacDougall, Sydney Boehm d Jerry Hopper *ph* Lionel Lindon *m* David Buttolph
☆ Charlton Heston, Robert Young, Thomas Mitchell, Nicole Maurey, Yma Sumac, Glenda Farrell, Michael Pate

The Secret of the Loch

GB   1934   80m   bw
ABFD/Bray Wyndham
A diver thinks he finds a prehistoric monster in Loch Ness.
Mildly amusing exploitation item following the 1934 rebirth of interest in the old legend.
w Charles Bennett, Billie Bristow d Milton Rosmer *ph* Jimmy Wilson *m* Peter Mendoza
☆ Seymour Hicks, Nancy O'Neil, Gibson Gowland, Frederick Peisley, Rosamund John, Ben Field

'Run for your life! You must find the secret before it finds you!'

The Secret Partner *

GB   1961   91m   bw
MGM (Michael Relph)
A blackmailing dentist is visited by a mysterious hooded stranger who forces him to rob one of his businessman victims.
Complex puzzle thriller, neatly made in sub-Hitchcock style.
w David Pursall, Jack Seddon d Basil Dearden *ph* Harry Waxman *m* Philip Green
☆ Stewart Granger, Haya Harareet, Bernard Lee, Hugh Burden, Melissa Stribling, Norman Bird, Conrad Phillips

The Secret People *

GB   1951   96m   bw
Ealing (Sidney Cole)
European refugees in London during the thirties become members of a ring of anarchists.
Downbeat political melodrama which pleased neither the masses nor the highbrows, despite plaudits for sensitive direction and performances.
w Thorold Dickinson, Wolfgang Wilhelm d Thorold Dickinson *ph* Gordon Dines *m* Roberto Gerhard
☆ Valentina Cortese, Serge Reggiani, Audrey Hepburn, Charles Goldner, Megs Jenkins, Irene Worth, Athene Seyler, Reginald Tate
'The tension and power of the film make it one of the most remarkable British productions for some time.' – *Penelope Houston*
'That *Secret People*, despite the creative agonies recorded by Mr Lindsay Anderson [in a book on the making of the film] should turn out to be a confused, unco-ordinated spy thriller concealing a tentative message deep down below some

---

strained effects of style is another tragedy of British film hopes.' – *Richard Winnington*

Secret Places
GB 1984 98m Eastmancolor
Rank/Skreba/Virgin (Simon Relph, Ann Skinner)
🇺🇸

At the beginning of the Second World War an English schoolgirl forms a close relationship with another boarder, a refugee from Germany.
Psychological drama that is too sensitive for its own good, so that it seems more attenuated than intense.
wd Zelda Barron *novel* Janice Elliott *ph* Peter MacDonald *m* Michel Legrand *ed* Laurence Mery-Clark
☆ Marie-Therese Relin, Tara MacGowran, Claudine Auger, Jenny Agutter, Cassie Stuart, Anne-Marie Gwatkin, Klaus Barner, Sylvia Coleridge

The Secret Rapture *
GB 1993 96m colour
Oasis/Greenpoint/Channel 4 (Simon Relph)
🇬🇧 🇺🇸 📀

Following the death of their father, two sisters become deadly rivals.
An only partially successful adaptation of a stage play, one that softens the political aspects of the original to concentrate on the personal, a melodramatic study of self-destruction.
w David Hare *play* David Hare *d* Howard Davies *ph* Ian Wilson *m* Richard Hartley *pd* Barbara Gosnold *ed* George Akers
☆ Juliet Stevenson, Joanne Whalley-Kilmer, Penelope Wilton, Alan Howard, Neil Pearson, Robert Stephens, Hilton McRae, Robert Glenister
'A relentless, humourless movie – and one that ultimately fails to move.' – *Robin Brooks, Empire*

Secret Service
US 1931 67m bw
RKO

During the Civil War a Yankee officer goes behind enemy lines and falls in love with a Southern girl.
Sluggish romantic adventure.
w Bernard Schubert *play* William Gillette *d* J. Walter Ruben
☆ Richard Dix, Shirley Grey, William Post Jnr, Gavin Gordon
'Dix does a good character. It's all the picture has.' – *Variety*

Secret Service of the Air
US 1939 61m bw
Warner

A government agent tracks down smugglers.
Serial-like thrills and comedy, adequately presented.
w Raymond Schrock *d* Noel Smith
☆ Ronald Reagan, Eddie Foy Jnr, John Litel, Ila Rhodes, James Stephenson
'No marquee names, but a better than average story of its kind.' – *Variety*

The Secret Six *
US 1931 83m bw
MGM

A syndicate of businessmen finance two reporters to get evidence against a gang of bootleggers.
Solidly carpentered gangster thriller.
w Frances Marion *d* George Hill *ph* Harold Wenstrom
☆ Wallace Beery, Lewis Stone, Clark Gable, John Mack Brown, Jean Harlow, Marjorie Rambeau, Paul Hurst, Ralph Bellamy, John Miljan
'A gangster talker too rough, crude and familiar. In big cities it may pull the roughneck trade ... but the vocalized expression for it will be adverse.' – *Variety*

'It's not who you con – it's how you do it!'
The Secret War of Harry Frigg
US 1967 109m Techniscope
Universal/Albion (Hal E. Chester)

In 1943 a private engineers the escape of five captured generals.
Unattractive war comedy; slow, uninventive and overlong.
w Peter Stone, Frank Tarloff *d* Jack Smight *ph* Russell Metty *m* Carlo Rustichelli
☆ Paul Newman, John Williams, Sylva Koscina, Andrew Duggan, Tom Bosley, Charles D. Gray, Vito Scotti, James Gregory

The Secret Ways *
US 1961 112m bw
U-I/Heath (Richard Widmark)

An American reporter is recruited to rescue a scholar from communist Hungary.
Pretentious Iron Curtain melodrama, quite good to look at but overlong and no Third Man.
w Jean Hazelwood *novel* Alistair MacLean *d* Phil Karlson *ph* Max Greene *m* Johnny Williams
☆ Richard Widmark, Sonja Ziemann, Charles Regnier, Walter Rilla, Howard Vernon, Senta Berger

Secret Wedding **
Argentina/Netherlands 1989 95m colour
Allarts/Cogurccio/Cinéphile (Lujan Pflaum)
original title: Boda Secreta

Returning home after 13 years unjustly imprisoned in Buenos Aires, a man discovers that no one is prepared to recognize him, not even the woman he loves.
A gripping tale of political persecution, underscored by an unhappy romance.
wd Alejandro Agresti *ph* Ricardo Rodriguez *m* Paul Michael Van Brugge *pd* Juan Collini *ed* Rene Wiegmans
☆ Tito Haas, Mirtha Busnelli, Sergio Poves Campos, Nathan Pinzon, Flora Bloise, Elio Marchi

Secrets *
US 1933 85m bw
UA (Mary Pickford)

A pioneering couple sticks together despite the husband's infidelities.
Curiously mixed-up star vehicle, part romantic comedy, part Western, part sob-stuff. Interesting rather than entertaining.
w Frances Marion *play* Rudolf Besier, May Edginton *d* Frank Borzage
☆ Mary Pickford, Leslie Howard, C. Aubrey Smith, Blanche Friderici, Doris Lloyd, Ned Sparks
'Singularly uneven ... but at least the story is given fine production and interesting playing.' – *Variety*
'You can be sure you won't make any mistake by taking the family to see it.' – *Photoplay*
† Norma Talmadge starred in a 1923 silent version.

Secrets
Australia/New Zealand 1992 91m colour/bw
Victorian International/Avalon/NFU (Michael Pattinson)

In 1964, at the beginning of the Beatles' tour of Australia, five teenagers become trapped in the basement of the group's hotel.
A 'teen movie stretched beyond its limits; the director does not seem to know what to do with his ill-assorted group, once they are stuck in a cramped setting, other than let them talk too much.
w Jan Sardi *m* Michael Pattinson *ph* David Connell *m* Dave Dobbyn *pd* Kevin Leonard-Jones *ed* Peter Carrodus
☆ Beth Champion, Malcolm Kennard, Dannii Minogue, Willa O'Neill, Noah Taylor
'Pleasurable low-key entertainment.' – *Variety*

Secrets and Lies ***
GB 1995 141m Metrocolor
Film Four/CiBy 2000/Thin Man/Channel 4 (Simon Channing-Williams)
🇬🇧 🇺🇸 📀

A successful black woman goes in search of her real mother, and discovers that she is white, unmarried and working-class.
Deft and sometimes moving portrait of a family finding redemption through the sharing of its secrets, though some of the performances teeter on the edge of caricature; it was much admired, particularly away from Britain, where audiences gave it less attention than it deserved.
wd Mike Leigh *ph* Dick Pope *m* Andrew Dickson *pd* Alison Chitty *ed* Jon Gregory
☆ Timothy Spall, Phyllis Logan, *Brenda Blethyn*, Claire Rushbrook, *Marianne Jean-Baptiste*, Elizabeth Berrington, Michele Austin, Lee Ross
'A beautifully constructed sentimental melodrama, with none of the rough edges that Mike Leigh has insisted on in the past. The only mystery is that Leigh should have come up with so classic a humanist product after proclaiming for so long that things could never be so simple.' – *Adam Mars-Jones, Independent*

'The movie, for all its appeal, is naggingly sanctimonious. It's *Guess Who's Coming to Dinner* for the culturally correct '90s.' – *Owen Gleiberman, Entertainment Weekly*
† It won the Palme d'Or, and Brenda Blethyn received the best actress award, at the Cannes Film Festival in 1996.
🏆 best picture; Mike Leigh (as writer and director); Brenda Blethyn; Marianne Jean-Baptiste
🏆 best British film; Mike Leigh (as writer); Brenda Blethyn

Secrets of a Secretary
US 1931 76m bw
Paramount

A social secretary discovers that her ex-husband is blackmailing her employer's daughter.
Peg's Paper romance of a heroine who rises above her many problems.
w Dwight Taylor, Charles Brackett *d* George Abbott
☆ Claudette Colbert, Herbert Marshall, George Metaxa, Mary Boland, Berton Churchill

Secrets of a Soul **
Germany 1926 95m bw silent
UFA/Hans Neumann

A chemist develops a knife phobia, has hallucinations, and tries to cut his wife's throat.
A lesson in elementary psychology which was innovatory at the time and survives as cinema for its stylish and impressionist use of visual techniques.
w Colin Ross, Hans Neumann, G. W. Pabst *d* G. W. Pabst *ph* Guido Seeber, Curt Oertel, Robert Lach
☆ Werner Krauss, Jack Trevor, Ruth Weyher, Pawel Pawlow

Secrets of an Actress
US 1938 70m bw
Warner

A star actress falls for one of her backers, a married architect.
High-life suffering of a familiar kind: it satisfied the Peg's Paper audience.
w Milton Krims, Rowland Leigh, Julius J. Epstein *d* William Keighley
☆ Kay Francis, George Brent, Ian Hunter, Gloria Dickson, Isabel Jeans, Peggy Singleton
'Miss Francis may be able to live up to all requirements except an acrobatic dance on the toes, but it's no use hitching race horses to milk wagons.' – *Variety*

Secrets of G32: see Fly By Night

Secrets of Scotland Yard
US 1944 68m bw
Republic (George Blair)

A British secret service man is impersonated by his Nazi twin brother.
Likeable absurdities with a strong cast.
w Denison Clift *novel Room 40, O.B.* by Denison Clift *d* George Blair
☆ C. Aubrey Smith, Edgar Barrier, Stephanie Bachelor, Lionel Atwill, Henry Stephenson, John Abbott, Walter Kingsford, Martin Kosleck

Secrets of the French Police
US 1932 55m bw
RKO

The Sûreté tracks down a hypnotist and murderer.
Rather wildly-imagined suspenser with points of interest.
w Samuel Ornitz, Robert Tasker *d* Edward Sutherland
☆ Gwili André, Frank Morgan, Gregory Ratoff, Murray Kinnell, John Warburton
'Hodge-podge of melodramatics ... hardly enough for the de luxers.' – *Variety*

Secrets of the Phantom Caverns
GB 1984 90m colour
Adams Apple (Sandy Howard, Robert D. Bailey)
aka: What Waits Below

Anthropologists and soldiers exploring a cave system in Latin America discover a lost albino tribe living underground.
Totally inept fantasy from beginning to end.
w Christy Marx, Robert Vincent O'Neil *story* Ken Barnett *d* Don Sharp *ph* Virgil Harper *m* Michael Rubini, Denny Jaeger *ad* Stephen Marsh *ed* John R. Bowey
☆ Robert Powell, Lisa Blount, Richard Johnson, Anne Heywood, A. C. Weary, Timothy Bottoms

Secrets of the Underground
US 1943 70m bw
Republic

The proprietor of a fashionable gown shop is a Nazi agent.
Nifty second feature on predictable wartime lines.
w Robert Tasker, Geoffrey Homes *d* William Morgan
☆ John Hubbard, Virginia Grey, Lloyd Corrigan, Miles Mander, Ben Welden

Secrets of Women: see Waiting Women

'Satan has chosen his victims. The battle with evil has begun.'
The Sect *
Italy 1991 115m Technicolor
Penta/ADC (Mario and Vittorio Cecchi Gori, Dario Argento)
📀
original title: La Setta

A schoolteacher becomes accidentally involved with a group of devil worshippers who practise ritual human sacrifice.
Elegant, eerie and suspenseful horror with some gruesome moments.
w Dario Argento, Giovanni Romoli, Michele Soavi *d* Michele Soavi *ph* Raffaele Mertes *m* Pino Donaggio *pd* M. Antonello Geleng *ed* Franco Fraticelli
☆ Kelly Curtis, Herbert Lom, Tomas Arana, Maria Angela Giordano, Michel Adatte, Carla Cassola, Angelika Maria Boeck, Giovanni Lombardo Radice, Niels Gullov
'Soavi's dreamlike direction and enticing eye for design lend an air of gravitas to an otherwise workaday storyline, while a few choice moments of grisly gore ensure that diehard horror fans will not be disappointed.' – *Sight and Sound*

Sedmikrasky: see Daisies

'There are many ways to be seduced. Fame ... power ... love!'
The Seduction of Joe Tynan *
US 1979 107m Technicolor
Universal (Martin Bregman)
🇺🇸 📀

A young senator alienates his wife when he sacrifices his principles for advancement.
Fairly arresting political character drama with strong narrative and acting.
w Alan Alda *d* Jerry Schatzberg *ph* Adam Holender *m* Bill Conti
☆ Alan Alda, Barbara Harris, Meryl Streep, Melvyn Douglas, Rip Torn, Carrie Nye, Charles Kimbrough

The Seduction of Julia: see Adorable Julia

Seduction: The Cruel Woman
West Germany 1985 84m colour
Out on a Limb/Hyäne (Elfi Mikesch, Monika Treut)
📀
original title: Verführung: die Grausame Frau

A dominatrix displays varieties of sado-masochistic sex in public and private.
Elegant, subversive film of limited appeal which ignores more normal sexual erotic and fetishistic variations, but the subject is treated with an obsessiveness that can seem risible to those who do not share its concerns.
wd Elfi Mikesch, Monika Treut *novel Venus in Furs* by Leopold von Sacher-Masoch *ph* Elfi Mikesch *m* Maran Gosov *ad* Manfred Blösser, Klaus Weinrich *ed* Renata Merck
☆ Mechthild Grossmann, Udo Kier, Sheila McLaughlin, Carola Regnier, Peter Weibel, Georgette Dee
'A dark and disturbing movie.' – *Sight and Sound*

See America Thirst
US 1930 71m bw
Universal

Two hoboes become involved with rum runners.
Poorly constructed talkie début for a silent comedian who never made it.
w Edward Luddy, Vin Moore, C. J. Horwin *d* W. J. Craft
☆ Harry Langdon, Slim Summerville, Bessie Love, Mitchell Lewis, Stanley Fields
'Direction shows silent technique throughout, and is unmindful of the talkie advent. Rub is that this system got reversed in the important sequences.' – *Variety*

See Here Private Hargrove *
US 1944 102m bw
MGM (George Haight)
Adventures of a raw recruit in the US army.
Standard transcription of a humorous bestseller which did its best to make the war painless for Americans.
w Harry Kurnitz *book* Marion Hargrove
d Wesley Ruggles *ph* Charles Lawton *m* David Snell
☆ Robert Walker, Donna Reed, Robert Benchley, Keenan Wynn, Bob Crosby, Ray Collins, Chill Wills, Grant Mitchell
† Sequel 1945: *What Next, Corporal Hargrove?*

See How They Fall **
France 1993 100m colour 'Scope
MIHK/Bloody Mary/France3/CEC (Didier Haudepin)
🎧
original title: Regarde les Hommes Tomber
A crippled con man teaches criminal ways to an amoral young protégé who betrays him.
Dark, deftly made thriller with more than a hint of Jean Genet about it in its concentration on homosexual desire, degradation and death.
w Alain Le Henry, Jacques Audiard *novel* Triangle by Terry White *d* Jacques Audiard *ph* Gérard Sterin *m* Alexandre Desplat *pd* Jacques Rouxel *ed* Juliette Welfling
☆ Jean-Louis Trintignant, Jean Yanne, Mathieu Kassovitz, Bulle Ogier, Christine Pascal, Yvon Back

See How They Run
GB 1955 84m bw
Winwell (BL)
A country vicarage gets lively when several miscreants pretend to be the vicar.
Reliable stage farce which doesn't get the laughs on screen.
w Leslie Arliss, Roy Miller, Val Valentine *play* Philip King *d* Leslie Arliss *ph* Ken Talbot *m* John Bath
☆ Ronald Shiner, Greta Gynt, James Hayter, Wilfrid Hyde-White, Dora Bryan, Richard Wattis, Viola Lyel

See My Lawyer
US 1945 67m bw
Universal
Comedians try to get out of a night-club commitment by insulting the customers.
Thin vehicle for a team that wasn't going anywhere: too many variety acts got in their way.
w Edmund L. Hartmann, Stanley Davis *d* Edward Cline
☆ Ole Olsen, Chic Johnson, Grace McDonald, Franklin Pangborn, Alan Curtis, Noah Beery Jnr, Ed Brophy

See No Evil: see *Blind Terror*

See No Evil, Hear No Evil *
US 1989 102m Technicolor
Columbia TriStar (Marvin Worth)
📼 🎞️ 🔍
Suspected of murder, two friends, one deaf and the other blind, go in pursuit of the real killer.
Halting comedy that is not worth watching.
w Earl Barret, Arne Sultan, Eliot Wald, Andrew Kurtzman, Gene Wilder *d* Arthur Hiller *ph* Victor J. Kemper *m* Stewart Copeland *pd* Robert Gundlach *ed* Robert C. Jones
☆ Richard Pryor, Gene Wilder, Joan Severance, Kevin Spacey, Alan North, Anthony Zerbe, Louis Giambalvo, Kirsten Childs

See You in Hell Darling: see *An American Dream*

See You in the Morning *
US 1988 119m Metrocolor
Warner/Lorimar (Alan J. Pakula)
📼 🎞️ 🔍
A divorced psychiatrist begins an affair with an insecure widow with two young children.
Enjoyable, though hardly memorable, study of confused relationships.
wd Alan J. Pakula *ph* Donald McAlpine *m* Michael Small *pd* George Jenkins *ed* Evan Lottman
☆ Jeff Bridges, Alice Krige, Farrah Fawcett, Drew Barrymore, Lukas Haas, David Dukes, Frances Sternhagen, George Hearn, Theodore Bikel, Macaulay Culkin

Seed
US 1931 96m bw
Universal
A husband leaves his family to become a novelist, but returns ten years later.
Long-drawn-out domestic drama whose few virtues have not weathered the years.
w Gladys Lehman *novel* Charles G. Norris *d* John Stahl
☆ John Boles, Genevieve Tobin, Lois Wilson, Raymond Hackett, Bette Davis, ZaSu Pitts
'Good woman's picture that will strike generous b.o. anywhere.' – *Variety*

The Seekers
GB 1954 90m Eastmancolor
GFD/Fanfare (George H. Brown)
📼
US title: Land of Fury
In 1820 a British sailor and his family emigrate to New Zealand.
Stilted epic which never gains the viewer's sympathy or interest.
w William Fairchild *d* Ken Annakin *ph* Geoffrey Unsworth *m* William Alwyn
☆ Jack Hawkins, Glynis Johns, Inia Te Wiata, Noel Purcell, Kenneth Williams, Laya Raki

Seemabadha: see *Company Limited*

Seems Like Old Times *
US 1980 102m Metrocolor
Columbia/Ray Stark
📼 🎞️ 🔍
An innocently involved bank robber takes refuge with his ex-wife, a lady lawyer married to the district attorney.
Nostalgic farce which doesn't quite live up to the old skills and often bogs down in talk. Funny moments, though.
w Neil Simon *d* Jay Sandrich *ph* David M. Walsh *m* Marvin Hamlisch *pd* Gene Callahan
☆ Goldie Hawn, Chevy Chase, Charles Grodin, Robert Guillaume, Harold Gould, George Grizzard

Il Segno di Zorro: see *The Mark of Zorro (1963)*

Sei Donne per l'Assassino: see *Blood and Black Lace*

Sei Sei Vivo, Spara!: see *Django, Kill!*

Seize the Day *
US 1986 93m colour
Learning in Focus (Chiz Schultz)
In the mid-50s a salesman who quits his job meets rejection and disillusion at every turn.
A movie faithful to the book, but its relentless portrait of a man's disintegration and humiliation is much less easy to bear on the screen than it was on the page.
w Ronald Ribman *novel* Saul Bellow *d* Fielder Cook *ph* Eric Van Haren Noman *m* Elizabeth Swados *pd* John Robert Lloyd *ed* Sidney Katz, Rachel Igel
☆ Robin Williams, Joseph Wiseman, Jerry Stiller, Glenne Headly, William Hickey, Tony Roberts, Tom Aldredge
† The film was made for TV. Saul Bellow has a walk-on role as a man in a hotel corridor.

Sélect Hotel
France 1996 82m colour
MIHK/Climax (Francisco Guiterrez)
📼 🔍
Some denizens of a Parisian flophouse – a drug-addicted prostitute, her thieving brother and pimp – go about their miserable lives.
A depressing portrait of hopeless lives, lived on the edge of danger, which are viewed with sympathy and a disdain for conventional existence.
wd Laurent Bouhnik *ph* Gilles Henry *m* Jérôme Coullet *ad* Isabelle Millet *ed* Jacqueline Mariani, Clémence Bielov
☆ Julie Gayet, Jean-Michel Fête, Serge Blumental, Sabine Bail, Eric Aubrahn, Emmanuelle Rozes, Michel Gondoin
'Hardly a comfortable night at the pictures, this is an extraordinarily powerful but utterly draining piece of cinema.' – *Giala Murray, Empire*

A Self-Made Hero **
France 1995 106m colour
Artificial Eye/Alicélo/Lumière/France 3/M6/Initial (Patrick Godeau)
📼 🎧
original title: Un Héros Très Discret
After the liberation of France, a cowardly and simple-minded fantasist reinvents himself as a hero of the Resistance.
Sharply political comedy of assumed identity and innocence – imagine a cross between Candide and Captain of Kopenick – which casts a beady and entertaining eye over French attitudes to the recent past.
w Alain Le Henry, Jacques Audiard *novel* Jean-François Deniau *d* Jacques Audiard *ph* Jean-Marc Fabre *m* Alexandre Desplat *ad* Michel Vandestien *ed* Juliette Welfling
☆ Mathieu Kassovitz, Anouk Grinberg, Sandrine Kiberlain, Jean-Louis Trintignant, Albert Dupontel, Nadia Barentin, Bernard Bloch
'Half comic and half in deadly earnest – a political film seemingly determined to cause offence by questioning both orthodox history and those who made it.' – *Derek Malcolm, Guardian*

The Selling of America: see *Beer*

The Sellout
US 1951 82m bw
MGM (Nicholas Nayfack)
A newspaper exposes a corrupt administration.
Competent melodrama with no surprises.
w Charles Palmer *d* Gerald Mayer *ph* Paul Vogel *m* David Buttolph
☆ Walter Pidgeon, John Hodiak, Audrey Totter, Thomas Gomez, Everett Sloane, Cameron Mitchell, Karl Malden, Paula Raymond

The Sellout
GB/Italy 1975 102m colour
Warner/Oceanglade/Amerifilm (Josef Shaftel)
Russians and Americans lure a double agent to Jerusalem in order to eliminate him.
Unsmiling spy melodrama with a complex plot, a bagful of clichés and some unnecessarily unpleasant violence.
w Judson Kinberg, Murray Smith *d* Peter Collinson *ph* Arthur Ibbetson *m* Mike Green, Colin Frechter
☆ Richard Widmark, Oliver Reed, Gayle Hunnicutt, Sam Wanamaker, Vladek Sheybal, Ori Levy, Assaf Dayan

La Semana del Asesino: see *Cannibal Man*

Seminole
US 1953 86m Technicolor
Universal-International (Howard Christie)
A West Point graduate goes to Florida to make peace with the Indians.
Slightly unusual but not very interesting semi-Western with the usual clichés.
w Charles K. Peck Jnr *d* Budd Boetticher *ph* Russell Metty *md* Joseph Gershenson
☆ Rock Hudson, Anthony Quinn, Barbara Hale, Richard Carlson, Hugh O'Brian, Russell Johnson, Lee Marvin, James Best

Semi-Tough *
US 1977 107m DeLuxe
UA/David Merrick
📼 🎞️ 🔍
The manager's daughter decides between two star members of a football team.
Rambling satiric comedy which takes jabs at various states of mind in America today, notably the fashionable forms of self-help therapy. Much of it comes off quite well.
w Walter Bernstein *novel* Dan Jenkins *d* Michael Ritchie *ph* Charles Rosher Jnr *m* Jerry Fielding
☆ Burt Reynolds, Kris Kristofferson, Jill Clayburgh, Bert Convy, Robert Preston, Lotte Lenya, Roger E. Mosley

The Senator Was Indiscreet *
US 1947 95m bw
U-I (Nunnally Johnson)
📼
GB title: Mr Ashton Was Indiscreet
A foolish politician determines to become president and hires a press agent.

Satirical political farce which hurls its shafts wide and doesn't seem to mind how few of them hit.
w Charles MacArthur *story* Edwin Lanham *d* George S. Kaufman *ph* William Mellor *m* Daniele Amfitheatrof
☆ William Powell, Ella Raines, Peter Lind Hayes, Ray Collins, Arleen Whelan, Allen Jenkins, Hans Conried, Charles D. Brown

Send Me No Flowers *
US 1964 100m Technicolor
U-I/Martin Melcher (Harry Keller)
📼 🔍
A hypochondriac mistakenly thinks he is dying and tries to provide another spouse for his wife.
A timeworn farcical situation is handled in the glossy Doris Day manner; it all starts quite brightly but gradually fizzles out.
w Julius Epstein *play* Norman Barrasch, Carroll Moore *d* Norman Jewison *ph* Daniel Fapp *m* Frank de Vol *ad* Alexander Golitzen, Robert Clatworthy
☆ Doris Day, Rock Hudson, Tony Randall, Paul Lynde, Clint Walker, Hal March, Edward Andrews

The Seniors
US 1977 87m Metrocolor
CSI (Stanley Shapiro, Carter de Haven)
📼
Four college students discover a way to become rich by making prostitution respectable.
Exploitative comedy, mixing teenage wish-fulfilment with black but unfunny farce.
w Stanley Shapiro *d* Rod Amateau *ph* Robert Jessup *ed* Guy Scarpitta
☆ Jeffrey Byron, Gary Imhoff, Dennis Quaid, Lou Richards, Rocky Flintermann, Priscilla Barnes, Alan Reed

La Señora *
Spain 1987 103m colour
ICA/Virginia (Jonni Bassiner)
Sexually frustrated by a loveless marriage, an aristocratic woman finds temporary happiness with her gardener.
Moderately engrossing melodrama of sex and class.
w Jordi Cadena, Silvia Tortosa *novel* Antoni Mus *d* Jordi Cadena *ph* José G. Galisteo *m* J. M. Pagan *pd* Joseph Maria Espada *ed* Amat Carreras
☆ Silvia Tortosa, Hermann Bonnin, Luis Merlo, Fernando Guillén-Cuervo, Jeaninne Mestre, Alfonso Guirao

Sensation
GB 1936 67m bw
BIP (Walter Mycroft)
A village barmaid is murdered and only our reporter hero sees the wider implications.
Presentable murder mystery.
w Dudley Leslie, Marjorie Deans, William Freshman *play* Murder Gang by Basil Dean, George Munro *d* Brian Desmond Hurst *ph* Walter Harvey
☆ John Lodge, Diana Churchill, Francis Lister, Joan Marion, Margaret Vyner, Athene Seyler, Richard Bird
'The genuine situation is lost in false trials, in an absurd love story, in humour based on American films, and in the complete unreality of the "murder gang".' – *Graham Greene*

Sensations of 1945
US 1944 87m bw
Andrew L. Stone
Father and son disagree over the handling of their publicity agency.
Slim plot holds together a ragbag of variety acts, some quite choice.
w Dorothy Bennett *d* Andrew L. Stone *ph* Peverell Marley, John Mescall *md* Mahlon Merrick
☆ Eleanor Powell, W. C. Fields, Sophie Tucker, Dennis O'Keefe, Eugene Pallette, C. Aubrey Smith, Lyle Talbot, Dorothy Donegan, Cab Calloway and his band, Woody Herman and his band
♪ Mahlon Merrick

Sense and Sensibility **
GB/US 1995 136m Technicolor
Columbia/Mirage (Lindsay Doran)
📼 🔍 🎞️ 💿 🎧
Two sisters hope for suitable husbands when they, their younger sister and widowed mother lose their

home and money and are forced to move into a small cottage.

A high-spirited romance that is a joy to watch; Emma Thompson's casting as Elinor (who is a 19-year-old in the book) slightly undermines Austen's intent, but does not reduce the pleasure the film provides.

w Emma Thompson *story* Jane Austen *d* Ang Lee *ph* Michael Coulter *m* Patrick Doyle *pd* Luciana Arrighi *ed* Tim Squyres

☆ Emma Thompson, Alan Rickman, *Kate Winslet*, Hugh Grant, James Flett, Harriet Walter, Gemma Jones, Elizabeth Spriggs, Robert Hardy, Greg Wise, *Hugh Laurie*, Imelda Staunton, Imogen Stubbs, Emile François

'Luminously brings to life Austen's vision of the dance of the sexes. The final romantic epiphany is a stunner, at once rapturous and funny.' – *Owen Gleiberman, Entertainment Weekly*

'It is still a pleasant shock to see a film so divested of precious charm in favour of humour, dramatic force and the kind of romance that isn't merely sentimental.' – *Derek Malcolm, Guardian*

† It won the Golden Bear as the best film at the 1996 Berlin Film Festival.

🏆 Emma Thompson (adapted screenplay)

🏆 best picture; Emma Thompson (as actress); Kate Winslet; Michael Coulter; Patrick Doyle; costume design (Jenny Beavan, John Bright)

🏆 best film; Emma Thompson (as actress); Kate Winslet

Senso *

Italy 1953 115m Technicolor
Lux
📀 〰️

aka: *The Wanton Countess (cut version)*

In 1866 Venice a noblewoman falls in love with an officer of the invading Austrian army, but finally denounces him.

The melodramatic plot is less important than the portrait of a period, for this is an expensive film in the grand style, often breathtaking to look at.

w Luchino Visconti, Suso Cecchi d'Amico and others *story* Camilla Botto *d* Luchino Visconti *ph* G. R. Aldo, Robert Krasker *m* Anton Bruckner *ad* Ottavio Scotti

☆ Alida Valli, Farley Granger, Massimo Girotti, Christian Marquand

The Sensualist

Japan 1992 54m colour
Ren Usami, Tsunemasa Hatano, Zuza Hagiwara

A merchant, whose life is dedicated to lust, aids a tailor who has wagered his manhood on bedding a courtesan at their first meeting.

A rarity: an animated film intended for an adult audience. The images, based on traditional Japanese woodcuts, are attractive; the inconsequential narrative less so.

w Eiichi Yamamoto *novel* Saikaku Ihara *d* Yukio Abe *ph* Minoru Fujita *m* Keiju Ishikawa *ad* Yukio Abe *ed* Kenichi Takashima

Sentimental Journey

US 1946 94m bw
TCF (Walter Morosco)

An actress who knows she is dying arranges for a little orphan girl to take her place in her husband's affections.

Hollywood's most incredible three-handkerchief picture; nicely made, but who dared to write it?

w Samuel Hoffenstein, Elizabeth Reinhardt *story* Nelia Gardner White *d* Walter Lang *ph* Norbert Brodine *m* Cyril Mockridge

☆ Maureen O'Hara, John Payne, William Bendix, Cedric Hardwicke, Glenn Langan, Mischa Auer, Connie Marshall, Kurt Kreuger

'In twenty years of filmgoing I can't remember being so slobbered at: the apotheosis of the weepie.' – *Richard Winnington*

'It may not be for the critics, but who are critics? Just a lot of Joes, with passes.' – *Variety*

† Remade as *The Gift of Love* (qv).

'Doomed to guard the gates of Hell forever!'
The Sentinel

US 1976 92m Technicolor
Universal/Jeffrey Konvitz
📀

A disturbed girl in an old apartment house is haunted by walking corpses: the house turns out to be the gateway to hell and she its appointed sentinel.

Vulgarly modish rip-off of several fashionable themes, notably Rosemary's Baby and The Exorcist.

w Michael Winner, Jeffrey Konvitz *novel* Jeffrey Konvitz *d* Michael Winner *ph* Dick Kratina *m* Gil Melle

☆ Chris Sarandon, Cristina Raines, Martin Balsam, John Carradine, José Ferrer, Ava Gardner, Arthur Kennedy, Burgess Meredith, Sylvia Miles, Deborah Raffin, Eli Wallach, Jerry Orbach

'Moral or ironic points are hard to discern in the eye-wrenching flux of a Michael Winner movie, which drifts and zooms across its polished people and places in a continual caressing motion, as crudely excitatory as any sex movie when the climaxes are approaching.' – *Richard Combs, MFB*

'A man with a face that looks like chicken giblets, a naked whore with a mouse on her thigh, a cat devouring a canary and Sylvia Miles in a tight leotard – these are some of the highlights of *The Sentinel*, a perfect film for those who like to slow down and look at traffic accidents.' – *Janet Maslin, Newsweek*

Senza Ragione: see Redneck

Separate Beds: see The Wheeler Dealers

Separate Lives

US 1995 101m colour
Interscope/Trimark (Mark Amin, Diane Nabatoff, Guy Reidel)

A psychology professor with a split personality fears she may have committed a murder.

Dully derivative thriller, offering nothing that has not been done rather better in the past.

w Steven Pressfield *d* David Madden *ph* Kees Van Oostrum *m* William Olvis *pd* Bernt Capra *ed* Janice Hampton

☆ James Belushi, Linda Hamilton, Vera Miles, Elisabeth Moss, Drew Snyder, Mark Lindsay Chapman, Marc Poppel, Elizabeth Arlen

'A thinly plotted and tiresomely formulaic drama.' – *Variety*

Separate Tables **

US 1958 98m bw
UA/Hecht-Hill-Lancaster (Harold Hecht)
📀

Emotional tensions among the boarders at a British seaside guest house.

The genteel melodramas seem less convincing on the Hollywood screen than they did on the London stage, but the handling is thoroughly professional.

w Terence Rattigan, John Gay *play* Terence Rattigan *d* Delbert Mann *ph* Charles Lang *m* David Raksin

☆ Burt Lancaster, Rita Hayworth, *David Niven*, Deborah Kerr, *Wendy Hiller*, Gladys Cooper, Cathleen Nesbitt, Felix Aylmer, Rod Taylor, Audrey Dalton, May Hallatt

🏆 David Niven; Wendy Hiller

🏆 best picture; script; Charles Lang; David Raksin; Deborah Kerr

La Séparation *

France 1994 88m colour
Guild/Renn/France2/DA/MCV/Canal (Claude Berri)
📀

An unmarried couple, who have a young child, begin to drift apart.

A buttoned-up account of the breakdown of a relationship, given intensity by the acting of its two protagonists.

w Dan Franck, Christian Vincent *novel* Dan Franck *d* Christian Vincent *ph* Denis Lenoir *m* Bach *ad* Christian Vallerin *ed* François Ceppi

☆ Isabelle Huppert, Daniel Auteuil, Jérôme Deschamps, Karin Viard, Laurence Lerel, Louis Vincent, Nina Morato

Seppuku: see Hara Kiri

September

US 1987 83m DuArt/DeLuxe
Orion (Jack Rollins, Charles H. Joffe)
📀 📀

Enclosed family drama: Allen in his melancholy Bergman mode.

wd Woody Allen *ph* Carlo Di Palma *m* various *ad* Speed Hopkins *ed* Susan E. Morse

☆ Denholm Elliott, Dianne Wiest, Mia Farrow, Elaine Stritch, Sam Waterston

'The debts to Chekhov are everywhere.' – *Variety*

September Affair

US 1950 104m bw
Paramount (Hal B. Wallis)
📀 〰️

Two married people fall in love and a plane crash in which they are reported dead gives them their chance.

Turgid romantic melodrama, not very well made despite the background tour of Capri; what made it a hit was the playing of the old Walter Huston record of the title song.

w Robert Thoeren *d* William Dieterle *ph* Charles B. Lang *m* Victor Young

☆ Joseph Cotten, Joan Fontaine, Françoise Rosay, Jessica Tandy, Robert Arthur, Jimmy Lydon

'A smooth surface mirrors the film's essential superficiality.' – *Penelope Houston*

September Storm

US 1960 110m DeLuxe Cinemascope 3-D
TCF/Alco (Edward L. Alperson)

A New York model and two adventurers search for sunken treasure off an uncharted Mediterranean island.

Thin actioner originally intended to marry 3-D and Cinemascope, but failed to do so.

w W. R. Burnett *novel* The Girl in the Red Bikini by Steve Fisher *d* Byron Haskin *ph* Jorge Stahl Jnr, Lamar Boren *m* Edward L. Alperson Jnr

☆ Joanne Dru, Mark Stevens, Robert Strauss

Sequestro di Persona: see Island of Crime

Sequoia

US 1934 73m bw
MGM

A girl living in the High Sierras defends wild animals from hunters.

Refreshingly unusual outdoor drama with good location photography.

w Ann Cunningham, Sam Armstrong, Carey Wilson *d* Chester Franklin *ph* Chester Lyons

☆ Jean Parker, Russell Hardie, Samuel S. Hinds, Paul Hurst

'It was unlikely that either Miss Parker or the deer would eat the puma, but I hung on hoping that the puma would eat the deer or Miss Parker.' – *James Agate*

SER *

USSR 1989 75m colour
Artificial Eye/Mosfilm (Victor Trakhtenberg)
aka: *Freedom is Paradise*

A boy escapes from reform school to find his father who is also a prisoner.

Simple, understated and gripping account of the dispossessed.

wd Sergei Bodrov *ph* Yuri Skirtladze *m* Alexander Raskatov *pd* Velery Kostrin *ed* Valentina Kulagina

☆ Volodya Kozyrev, Alexander Bureyev, Svetlana Gaitan, Vitautas Tomkus

'It may not be too great a hope to see in its spare approach a hitherto under-explored way forward for Russian, or even Soviet, cinema.' – *Verina Glaessner, MFB*

Serena

GB 1962 62m bw
Butcher's (John I. Phillips)

A Scotland Yard detective investigating a murder discovers that the victim is not who he thought it was.

A neat but somewhat plodding mystery with a clever twist at the end.

w Reginald Hearne, Edward and Valerie Abraham *d* Peter Maxwell *ph* Stephen Dade *m* John Gregory *ad* George Provis *ed* Allan Morrison

☆ Patrick Holt, Emrys Jones, Honor Blackman, Bruce Beeby, John Horsley, Vi Stevens, Gerry Duggan, Benedicta Leigh, Wally Patch

Serenade: see Broadway Serenade (1939)

Serenade

US 1956 121m Warnercolor
Warner (Henry Blanke)

A vineyard worker becomes a successful opera singer and is desired by two women.

Cliché success story with plot taking second place to singing.

w Ivan Goff, Ben Roberts, John Twist *novel* James M. Cain *d* Anthony Mann *ph* Peverell Marley *md* Ray Heindorf *songs* Nicholas Brodszky (m), Sammy Cahn (ly)

☆ Mario Lanza, Joan Fontaine, Sarita Montiel, Vincent Price, Joseph Calleia, Harry Bellaver, Vince Edwards, Silvio Minciotti

The Sergeant

US 1968 108m Technicolor
Warner/Robert Wise (Richard Goldston)

France, 1952. In a dreary army camp, a tough army sergeant in a guilt complex is brought face to face with his own homosexuality.

Well-made but very ponderous and limited melodrama which could have been told in half the time.

w Dennis Murphy *play* Dennis Murphy *d* John Flynn *ph* Henri Persin *m* Michel Mayne

☆ Rod Steiger, John Phillip Law, Frank Latimore, Ludmila Mikael

'The funniest foul-up of the space age!'
Sergeant Deadhead

US 1965 89m CFI color
AIP (James H. Nicholson, Samuel Z. Arkoff)

An army sergeant is accidentally sent into orbit and undergoes a personality change.

Clumsy comedy partially redeemed by its supporting players.

w Louis M. Heyward *d* Norman Taurog *ph* Floyd Crosby *m* Les Baxter

☆ Frankie Avalon, Deborah Walley, Fred Clark, Cesar Romero, Eve Arden, Gale Gordon, Buster Keaton, Harvey Lembeck, John Ashley

Sergeant Madden

US 1939 78m bw
MGM (J. Walter Ruben)

A policeman's son becomes a gangster.

Routine crime melodrama with sentimental trimmings, quite untypical of its director.

w Wells Root *story* A Gun in His Hand by William A. Ulman *d* Josef von Sternberg *ph* John Seitz *m* William Axt

☆ Wallace Beery, Tom Brown, Alan Curtis, Laraine Day, Fay Holden, Marc Lawrence, Marion Martin

'Good programme drama, geared to supply strong support in the key duals.' – *Variety*

Sergeant Rutledge *

US 1960 111m Technicolor
Warner/John Ford (Willis Goldbeck, Patrick Ford)
📀

In 1881 a black army sergeant is on trial for rape and murder, but his defence counsel reveals the real culprit.

Flashback Western; not the director's best, but generally of some interest.

w James Warner Bellah, Willis Goldbeck *d* John Ford *ph* Bert Glennon *m* Howard Jackson

☆ Woody Strode, Jeffrey Hunter, Constance Towers, Willis Bouchey, Billie Burke, Carleton Young, Juano Hernandez, Mae Marsh

Sergeant Steiner

West Germany 1979 115m Eastmancolor
Panavision
Palladium/Rapidfilm (Arlene Sellers, Alex Winitsky)
📀

aka: *Breakthrough*

The German sergeant hero of *Cross of Iron* survives the Western Front and involvement in an anti-Hitler conspiracy.

Somewhat bloodless though interesting sequel to an exceptionally nasty war film, with an international cast aiming at better box-office.

w Tony Williamson *d* Andrew McLaglen *ph* Tony Imi *m* Peter Thomas

☆ Richard Burton, Robert Mitchum, Curt Jurgens, Rod Steiger, Helmut Griem, Michael Parks

Sergeant York **

US 1941 134m bw
Warner (Jesse L. Lasky)
📀 📀 〰️

The story of a gentle hillbilly farmer who became a hero of World War I.

Standard real-life fiction given the big treatment; a key Hollywood film of its time in several ways.

w Abem Finkel, Harry Chandlee, Howard Koch, John Huston *d* Howard Hawks *ph* Sol Polito *m* Max Steiner *ad* John Hughes *ed* William Holmes

☆ Gary Cooper, Joan Leslie, Walter Brennan, George Tobias, David Bruce, Stanley Ridges, Margaret Wycherly, Dickie Moore, Ward Bond
'I hardly think the effect is any different from that of a parade, with colours and a band; it is stirring and it is too long; there are too many holdups and too many people out of step, and your residue of opinion on the matter is that it will be nice to get home and get your shoes off.' – *Otis Ferguson*
'It has all the flavour of true Americana, the blunt and homely humour of backwoodsmen and the raw integrity peculiar to simple folk.' – *Bosley Crowther, New York Times*
👤 Gary Cooper
🏆 best picture; script; Howard Hawks; Sol Polito; Max Steiner; Walter Brennan; Margaret Wycherly; John Hughes; William Holmes

Sergeants Three
US 1961 112m Technicolor Panavision
(UA) Essex-Claude (Frank Sinatra)
Just after the Civil War three cavalry sergeants, with the help of an ex-slave bugler, dispose of some hostile Indians.
High-spirited but exhausting parody of Gunga Din, with bouts of unfunny bloodthirstiness separated by tedious slabs of dialogue.
w W. R. Burnett d John Sturges ph Winton Hoch, Carl Guthrie m Billy May
☆ Frank Sinatra, Dean Martin, Peter Lawford, Sammy Davis Jnr, Joey Bishop, Henry Silva, Ruta Lee
'The participants have a better time than the onlookers.' – *Judith Crist, 1973*

Serial *
US 1980 91m Movielab
Paramount/Sidney Beckerman
📼 ▤
Well-heeled Californians in a high suburban community go in for various cults and fashions.
Amusing satire on everything from Peyton Place to Bob and Carol and Ted and Alice. Just a little late in coming, that's all.
w Rich Eustis, Michael Elias novel Cyra McFadden d Bill Persky ph Rexford Metz m Lalo Schifrin
☆ Martin Mull, Tuesday Weld, Jennifer McAllister, Sam Chew Jnr, Sally Kellerman, Nita Talbot, Bill Macy, Christopher Lee, Pamela Bellwood, Peter Bonerz, Tom Smothers

'A loving mother. A caring wife. A model citizen. So what's the problem?'
Serial Mom *
US 1994 89m Technicolor
Guild/Savoy/Polar (John Fiedler, Mark Tarlov)
📼 📼 ▤ ⊙
A devoted home-loving wife and mother becomes famous after she murders everyone who upsets her by not behaving as she expects.
Mildly amusing one-sick-joke movie, given a little spark by Turner's comic turn as the killer mother.
wd John Waters ph Robert M. Stevens m Basil Poledouris pd Vincent Peranio ed Janice Hampton, Erica Huggins
☆ Kathleen Turner, Sam Waterston, Ricki Lake, Matthew Lillard, Mary Jo Catlett, Patricia Hearst, Mink Stole, Suzanne Somers
'There is something insubstantial about Waters' satire of sit-com suburbia.' – *Kim Newman, Sight and Sound*

Serious Charge
GB 1959 99m bw
Alva (Mickey Delamar)
A small-town troublemaker, accused by his priest of being responsible for the death of a young girl, amuses himself by accusing the priest of making homosexual advances.
A sensational play of its time makes a dull film despite earnest performances.
w Guy Elmes, Mickey Delamar play Philip King d Terence Young ph Georges Périnal m Leighton Lucas
☆ Anthony Quayle, Andrew Ray, Sarah Churchill, Irene Browne, Percy Herbert, Cliff Richard

The Serpent
France/Italy/Germany 1974 124m colour
Films La Boetie (Henri Verneuil)
▤
A top KGB official defects to the West.
Complicated, humourless, multi-lingual spy capers.
w Henri Verneuil, Gilles Perrault novel Pierre Nord d Henri Verneuil ph Claude Renoir m Ennio Morricone
☆ Yul Brynner, Henry Fonda, Dirk Bogarde, Philippe Noiret, Farley Granger, Virna Lisi

The Serpent and the Rainbow
US 1987 98m DuArt
UIP/Universal (David Ladd, Doug Claybourne)
📼 📼 ⊙ ☍
A scientist travels to Haiti to investigate zombies.
Standard horror film, designed to shock, in which it succeeds.
w Richard Maxwell, A. R. Simoun book Wade Davis d Wes Craven ph John Lindley m Brad Fiedel pd David Nichols ed Glenn Farr
☆ Bill Pullman, Cathy Tyson, Zakes Mokae, Paul Winfield, Brent Jennings, Conrad Roberts, Badja Djola, Theresa Merritt, Michael Gough

The Serpent's Egg *
West Germany/US 1977 120m Eastmancolor
Rialto-Dino de Laurentiis
▤
An American trapeze artist has a hard time in Berlin at the time of Hitler's rise to power.
More of a curate's egg, really, with a poor leading performance and too many lapses into nastiness, but much incidental interest of the kind one associates with the director.
wd Ingmar Bergman ph Sven Nykvist m Rolf Wilhelm pd Rolf Zehetbauer
☆ David Carradine, Liv Ullmann, Gert Frobe, James Whitmore, Heinz Bennent
'A crackpot tragedy: everything is strained, insufficient, underfelt.' – *New Yorker*

Serpent's Lair
US 1995 90m DeLuxe
Kushner-Locke/WarnerVision/Castel (Vlad Paunescu)
▤
A businessman is seduced by an irresistible and sexually voracious succubus.
Risible exploitation movie, barely competent on any level.
w Marc Rosenberg d Jeffrey Reiner ph Feliks Parnell m Vinny Golia pd Stuart Blatt ed Virginia Katz
☆ Jeff Fahey, Lisa B., Heather Medway, Anthony Palermo, Kathleen Noone, Jack Kehler, Patrick Bauchau, Taylor Nichols

Serpico *
US 1973 130m Technicolor
Paramount/Artists Entertainment Complex/Dino de Laurentiis (Martin Bregman)
▤ ⊙ ☍
A New York cop reveals police corruption and is eventually forced to leave the country.
A harrowing true story played with authentic gloom and violence.
w Waldo Salt, Norman Wexler book Peter Maas d Sidney Lumet ph Arthur J. Ornitz m Mikis Theodorakis
☆ Al Pacino, John Randolph, Jack Kehoe, Biff McGuire
'There's nothing seriously wrong with *Serpico* except that it's unmemorable, and not even terribly interesting while it's going on.' – *Stanley Kauffmann*
🏆 script; Al Pacino

The Servant **
GB 1963 116m bw
Elstree/Springbok (Joseph Losey, Norman Priggen)
📼 📼
A rich, ineffectual young man is gradually debased and overruled by his sinister manservant and his sexy 'sister'.
Acclaimed in many quarters on its first release, this downbeat melodrama now seems rather naïve and long drawn out; its surface gloss is undeniable, but the final orgy is more risible than satanic.
w Harold Pinter novel Robin Maugham d Joseph Losey ph Douglas Slocombe m Johnny Dankworth
☆ Dirk Bogarde, James Fox, Sarah Miles, Wendy Craig, Catherine Lacey, Richard Vernon

'Moodily suggestive, well acted, but petering out into a trickle of repetitious unmeaningful nastiness.' – *John Simon*
📼 Dirk Bogarde; James Fox; Douglas Slocombe

Servants' Entrance
US 1934 88m bw
Fox
A maid falls in love with a chauffeur.
Upstairs downstairs style comedy drama; passable.
w Samson Raphaelson novel Sigrid Boo d Frank Lloyd ph Hal Mohr m Arthur Lange
☆ Janet Gaynor, Lew Ayres, Walter Connolly, G. P. Huntley Jnr, Sig Rumann, Louise Dresser, Astrid Allwyn, Ned Sparks
'Capable production, directing and casting manages to make it fair entertainment.' – *Variety*

Service De Luxe *
US 1938 85m bw
Universal
Adventures of the members of a super-secretarial agency.
Very tolerable but uninspired comedy which doesn't really allow its acting talent full rein.
w Gertrude Purcell, Leonard Spigelgass d Rowland V. Lee ph George Robinson
☆ Constance Bennett, Vincent Price, Charles Ruggles, Helen Broderick, Mischa Auer, Halliwell Hobbes
'A speedy comedy-drama … will hold its own as a leadoff attraction in the keys.' – *Variety*

Service for Ladies
GB 1932 93m bw
Paramount (Alexander Korda)
US title: *Reserved for Ladies*
A waiter has a way with his rich lady clients.
Tenuous satirical comedy, a variation on the American silent The Grand Duchess and the Waiter.
w Eliot Crawshay-Williams, Lajos Biro novel *The Head Waiter* by Ernst Vajda d Alexander Korda m Percival Mackey ad Alfred Junge ed Harold Young
☆ Leslie Howard, George Grossmith, Benita Hume, Elizabeth Allan, Morten Selten, Cyril Ritchard, Martita Hunt, Merle Oberon
'Too talky and English for general American consumption.' – *Variety*

Set It Off *
US 1996 122m DeLuxe
Entertainment/New Line/Peak (Dale Pollock, Oren Koules)
📼 ▤ ⊙ ☍ ⊙ ☊
In Los Angeles, four women with money and other troubles become bank robbers.
Tough action film in a blaxploitation style updated with female bonding; quite fun in its regressive way.
w Kate Lanier, Takashi Bufford d F. Gary Gray ph Marc Reshovsky m Christopher Young pd Robb Wilson-King ed John Carter sp Tom Bellissimo
☆ Jada Pinkett, Queen Latifah, Vivica A. Fox, John C. McGinley, Kimberly Elise, Blair Underwood, Anna Maria Horsford
'Applies a gender twist to the familiar formula of hold-ups, car chases and shootouts, but makes many sacrifices to plausibility.' – *George Perry*

The Set Up ***
US 1949 72m bw
RKO (Richard Goldstone)
▤ ☍
An ageing boxer refuses to pull his last fight, and is beaten up by gangsters.
One of the most brilliant little films noirs of the late forties; thoroughly studio-bound, yet evoking a brilliant feeling for time and place. Photography, direction, editing, acting are all of a piece.
w Art Cohn poem Joseph Moncure March d Robert Wise ph Milton Krasner md Constantin Bakaleinikoff
☆ Robert Ryan, Audrey Totter, George Tobias, Alan Baxter, Wallace Ford

La Setta: see The Sect

The Settlement
Australia 1983 100m colour
Queensland Film Corporation/Robert Bruning
In Queensland in the 1950s, two drifters outrage locals when they set up house with a prostitute.
Small, enjoyable movie, with the accent on character and humour.

w Ted Roberts d Howard Rubie ph Ernest Clark m Sven Libaek ad John Watson ed Henry Dangar
☆ Bill Kerr, John Jarratt, Lorna Lesley, Tony Barry, Katy Wild, David Downer, Elaine Cusick, Alan Cassell

Seul contre Tous *
France 1998 81m colour 'Scope
Alliance/Cinémas de la Zone/Lovestreams/CNC (Gaspar Noé)
aka: *I Stand Alone*
An unemployed butcher beats up his pregnant mistress and returns to his haunts in the slums of Paris to seek work, and to be reunited with the mute daughter he abandoned.
Bleak study in alienation that uses shock tactics – sudden pans or zooms and a percussive soundtrack, a warning towards the end that you have 30 seconds to leave the cinema – to keep its audience alert. It is impressive in demonstrating how much can be achieved with minimal means, but the ending is a cop-out, and, like Zola, Noé piles up the malignancies until they become unintentionally funny.
wd Gaspar Noé ph Dominique Colin ed Lucille Hadzihalilovic, Gaspar Noé
☆ Philippe Nahon, Frankye Pain, Blandine Lenoir, Martine Audrain
'Probes as relentlessly into the psychology of nihilism as any movie has ever attempted.' – *Stephen Holden, New York Times*
'An ultra-widescreen slice of jaundice that creates its own unrelentingly tawdry, hermetic universe.' – *Lisa Nesselson, Variety*
† Excerpts from a pornographic film being watched by the protagonist were shown blurred in the UK version.

'Seven deadly sins. Seven ways to die.'
Seven ***
US 1995 127m DeLuxe Panavision
Entertainment/New Line (Arnold Kopelson, Phyllis Carlyle)
📼 📼 ▤ ⊙ ⊙ ⊙ ☊
A detective nearing retirement and his temperamental young replacement track down a serial killer who is working his way through the seven deadly sins.
A tense, involving thriller that rises above the somewhat predictable schematics of its screenplay and its central situation to reach a surprisingly downbeat conclusion; it depicts the city as a paradise lost, and its inhabitants as mostly beyond redemption.
w Andrew Kevin Walker d David Fincher ph Darius Khondji m Howard Shore pd Arthur Max ed Richard Francis-Bruce
☆ Brad Pitt, Morgan Freeman, Richard Roundtree, R. Lee Ermey, John C. McGinley, Julie Araskog, Kevin Spacey, Gwyneth Paltrow
'Dark, grim and terrific … this weirdly off-kilter suspenser goes well beyond the usual police procedural or killer-on-the-rampage yarn.' – *Todd McCarthy, Variety*
🏆 Richard Francis-Bruce

Seven Angry Men *
US 1954 90m bw
Allied Artists (Vincent M. Fennelly)
In Kansas, John Brown determines to abolish slavery by violence.
Low-budget, intensely felt little biopic of the celebrated 19th-century fanatic and his sons.
w Daniel B. Ullman d Charles Marquis Warren ph Ellsworth Fredericks m Carl Brandt
☆ Raymond Massey, Jeffrey Hunter, Larry Pennell, Debra Paget, Leo Gordon, John Smith, James Best, Dennis Weaver

Seven Beauties *
Italy 1975 115m Technicolor
Medusa (Lina Wertmuller, Giancarlo Giannini, Arrigo Colombo)
📼 ▤ ⊙ ⊙
original title: *Pasqualino Settebellezze*
An incorrigible survivor manages to get through the rigours of World War II and scarcely notices the damage to his honour.
Candide-like mixture of farce and satire with the addition of a good deal of unpleasantness. Less meaningful abroad than on its home ground.
wd Lina Wertmüller ph Tonino Delli Colli m Enzo Jannacci
☆ Giancarlo Giannini, Fernando Rey, Shirley Stoler, Piero di Iorio

---

'A stunning piece of work. Wertmüller proves here more brilliantly than before she is a somewhat erratic but individual, strong, fierce talent.' – *Stanley Kauffmann*

♣ Lina Wertmüller (as writer and as director); best foreign film; Giancarlo Giannini

'I now pronounce you – men and wives!'

Seven Brides for Seven Brothers **

US   1954   104m   Anscocolor   Cinemascope
MGM (Jack Cummings)

In the Old West, seven hard-working brothers decide they need wives, and carry off young women from the villages around.

Disappointingly studio-bound Western musical, distinguished by an excellent score and some brilliant dancing, notably the barn-raising sequence.

w Frances Goodrich, Albert Hackett *story* Sobbin' Women by Stephen Vincent Benet d Stanley Donen ph George Folsey m Adolph Deutsch, Saul Chaplin ch Michael Kidd ed Ralph E. Winters *songs* Johnny Mercer, Gene de Paul
☆ Howard Keel, Jane Powell, Jeff Richards, Russ Tamblyn, Tommy Rall, Howard Petrie, Marc Platt, Jacques d'Amboise, Matt Mattox

'It does have a plot, it does have imagination, it fairly explodes into life, and many discerning people will find the dance arrangements – exact, insidious, acrobatic, graceful, slipped in as if they were a natural development of the story – wildly exciting.' – *C. A. Lejeune*

♔ Adolph Deutsch, Saul Chaplin
♣ best picture; script; George Folsey; editing

Seven Chances **

US   1925   69m   bw   silent
Buster Keaton/Joseph M. Schenck

A meek young man finds that he is to inherit seven million dollars if he is married within a few hours.

Slim and rather slow comedy which builds to a fine climax as the hero is pursued first by hordes of women and then by rolling boulders.

w Clyde Bruckman, Jean Havez, Joseph A. Mitchell *play* Roi Cooper Megrue d Buster Keaton ph Elgin Lessley, Byron Houck
☆ Buster Keaton, Ruth Dwyer, Ray Barnes, Snitz Edwards

† The rocks sequence, which makes the film, was added only after a disappointing sneak preview.

'The sword and the cross battle for California's soul!'

Seven Cities of Gold *

US   1955   103m   DeLuxe   Cinemascope
TCF (Robert D. Webb, Barbara McLean)

In 1796, a Spanish expedition sets out from Mexico to annex California, but with it goes Father Junipero Serra ...

A semi-historical, semi-religious Western which ends up not being much of anything but has interesting sequences.

w Richard L. Breen, John C. Higgins *novel* Isabelle Gibson Ziegler d Robert D. Webb ph Lucien Ballard m Hugo Friedhofer
☆ Michael Rennie, Richard Egan, Anthony Quinn, Rita Moreno, Jeffrey Hunter, Eduardo Noriega, John Doucette

Seven Days in May ***

US   1964   120m   bw
Seven Arts/Joel/John Frankenheimer (Edward Lewis)

An American general's aide discovers that his boss intends a military takeover because he considers the President's pacifism traitorous.

Absorbing political mystery drama marred only by the unnecessary introduction of a female character. Stimulating entertainment.

w Rod Serling *novel* Fletcher Knebel, Charles W. Bailey II d John Frankenheimer ph Ellsworth Fredericks m Jerry Goldsmith
☆ Kirk Douglas, Burt Lancaster, Fredric March, Ava Gardner, Martin Balsam, Edmond O'Brien, George Macready, John Houseman

'A political thriller which grips from start to finish.' – *Penelope Houston*
'It is to be enjoyed without feelings of guilt, there should be more movies like it, and there is nothing first class about it.' – *John Simon*
'In the best tradition of the suspense thriller, with the ultimate thrill our awareness of its actual potential.' – *Judith Crist*

'An entertainment, in Graham Greene's sense of the word, and an intelligent one.' – *MFB*
† In 1994, it was remade as a TV movie, *The Enemy Within*, starring Forest Whitaker and Sam Waterston.
♣ Edmond O'Brien

Seven Days Leave

US   1929   83m   bw
Paramount (Louis D. Lighton)
GB title: *Medals*

A London charlady 'adopts' a soldier, and both their lives are changed.

Sentimental melodrama which suited the times and confirmed Cooper's stardom.

w John Farrow, Dan Totheroh *play* The Old Lady Shows Her Medals by J. M. Barrie d Richard Wallace ph Charles Lang
☆ Gary Cooper, Beryl Mercer, Daisy Belmore, Nora Cecil, Tempe Piggott, Arthur Hoyt, Basil Radford

Seven Days Leave

US   1942   87m   bw
RKO (Tim Whelan)

In order to inherit a hundred thousand dollars, a soldier must marry within a week.

Cheerful frivolity featuring radio stars of the time.

w William Bowers, Ralph Spence, Curtis Kenyon, Kenneth Earl d Tim Whelan ph Robert de Grasse md Roy Webb *songs* Frank Loesser, Jimmy McHugh
☆ Lucille Ball, Victor Mature, Harold Peary, Mary Cortes, Ginny Simms, Ralph Edwards, Peter Lind Hayes, Marcy McGuire, Wallace Ford

Seven Days to Noon **

GB   1950   94m   bw
London Films (Roy Boulting)

A professor engaged on atomic research threatens to blow up London unless his work is brought to an end.

Persuasively understated suspense piece which was subsequently much copied, so that it now seems rather obvious.

w Frank Harvey, Roy Boulting, Paul Dehn, James Bernard d John Boulting ph Gilbert Taylor m John Addison
☆ Barry Jones, Olive Sloane, André Morell, Joan Hickson, Sheila Manahan, Hugh Cross, Ronald Adam, Marie Ney

'A first rate thriller that does not pretend to a serious message, but yet will leave a query in the mind.' – *Richard Winnington*
'A film of great tension and excitement with a climax that is reached after breathless suspense.' – *Star*
♔ Paul Dehn, James Bernard (motion picture story)

The Seven Deadly Sins *

France/Italy   1952   150m   bw
Franco London/Costellazione

The master of ceremonies introduces seven stories and an epilogue.

Among the most successful compendiums of its kind, partly because of cast and credits and partly because it came when French naughtiness was appealing to a wide international audience.

w Jean Aurenche, Pierre Bost, Roberto Rossellini, Leo Joannon, Carlo Rim, Diego Fabbri, Liana Ferri, Eduardo de Filippo, Charles Spaak, Turi Vaselle, René Wheeler d Eduardo de Filippo, Jean Dréville, Yves Allégret, Roberto Rossellini, Carlo Rim, Claude Autant-Lara, Georges Lacombe
☆ Gérard Philipe, Isa Miranda, Eduardo de Filippo, Noel-Noel, Louis de Funès, Viviane Romance, Frank Villard, Henri Vidal, Michèle Morgan, Françoise Rosay

Seven Different Ways: see Quick Let's Get Married

Seven Doors to Death

US   1944   60m   bw
Alfred Stern/PRC

The owners of six exclusive shops and an apartment house are all murder suspects.

Flabby little bottom-biller which never gets going.

wd Elmer Clifton
☆ Chick Chandler, June Clyde, George Meeker, Gregory Gay, Edgar Dearing

Seven Faces of Dr Lao *

👪👪   US   1964   100m   Metrocolor
MGM/George Pal

An elderly Chinaman with a penchant for spectacular disguise solves the problems of a Western desert town.

A pleasant idea and excellent production are submerged in a sloppily sentimental and verbose script.

w Charles Beaumont *novel* The Circus of Dr Lao by Charles G. Finney d George Pal ph Robert Bronner m Leigh Harline *make-up* William Tuttle
☆ Tony Randall, Arthur O'Connell, John Ericson, Barbara Eden, Noah Beery Jnr, Lee Patrick, Minerva Urecal, John Qualen

Seven Footsteps to Satan

US   1929   70m   bw
Warner

A rich recluse plays an elaborate and macabre joke on his niece and nephew.

Richly-designed but dramatically disappointing haunted house spoof.

w Richard Bee d Benjamin Christensen
☆ Thelma Todd, Creighton Hale, Sheldon Lewis, Ivan Christie, Sojin

Seven Golden Men *

Italy/France/Spain   1965   91m   Eastmancolor
Atlantica/PUF/Asfilm/Warner

Seven master criminals plot to rob a bank of its gold.

Simple-minded but slickly handled caper story with many visual pleasures.

wd Marco Vicario
☆ Rossana Podesta, Philippe Leroy, Gastone Moschin, Gabriele Tinti

† A sequel, *Seven Golden Men Strike Again*, was less successful.

Seven Hills of Rome

US/Italy   1957   104m   Technirama
MGM/Titanus (Lester Welch)

An American singer in Italy is pursued by the fiancée with whom he has quarrelled.

Thin travelogue with several halts for the star to sing; production very patchy.

w Art Cohn, Giorgio Prosperi d Roy Rowland ph Tonino Delli Colli md George Stoll
☆ Mario Lanza, Renato Rascel, Marisa Allasio, Peggie Castle

711 Ocean Drive *

US   1950   102m   bw
Columbia (Frank N. Seltzer)

A wireless expert is drawn into the bookie racket.

Overlong but vigorous crime exposé melodrama with excellent location sequences, notably a climax on Hoover Dam.

w Richard English, Francis Swann d Joseph M. Newman ph Franz Planer m Sol Kaplan
☆ Edmond O'Brien, Joanne Dru, Otto Kruger, Don Porter, Sammy White, Dorothy Patrick, Barry Kelley, Howard St John

Seven Keys to Baldpate *

US   1935   69m   bw
RKO

A novelist retiring to a lonely inn for inspiration finds it full of criminals and damsels in distress.

An old theatrical warhorse with a trick ending, also filmed in 1929 (with Richard Dix; Variety said 'it all happens like a synopsis of what might have occurred') and in 1947 with Philip Terry. There was also a horror variation in 1982, House of the Long Shadows (qv). None was as satisfying as a good stage production.

play George M. Cohan *story* Earl Derr Biggers d William Hamilton, Edward Killy ph Robert de Grasse
☆ Gene Raymond, Margaret Callahan, Eric Blore, Grant Mitchell, Moroni Olsen, Henry Travers

'Too much conversation and too little action.' – *Variety*
† The 1935 version at least will be found to have lost its trick ending, without which it ends lamely. A curious executive decision.

The Seven Little Foys *

US   1955   95m   Technicolor   Vistavision
Paramount (Jack Rose)

The story of a family vaudeville act.

Routine showbiz biopic, a little heavy on the syrup.

w Melville Shavelson, Jack Rose d Melville Shavelson ph John F. Warren md Joseph J. Lilley
☆ Bob Hope, Milly Vitale, George Tobias, Angela Clarke, Herbert Heyes, James Cagney
† Milly Vitale's singing was dubbed by Viola Vonn.
♣ script

Seven Men from Now

US   1956   78m   Warnercolor
Batjac (Andrew V. McLaglen, Robert E. Morrison)

A sheriff seeks revenge when his wife is killed by bandits.

Good Western programmer.

w Burt Kennedy d Budd Boetticher ph William H. Clothier m Henry Vars
☆ Randolph Scott, Gail Russell, Lee Marvin, Walter Reed, Don Barry, John Larch

Seven Miles from Alcatraz

US   1942   62m   bw
RKO (Herman Schlom)

Prison escapees take over an offshore lighthouse.

Compact melodrama with the lifers heroically catching spies.

w Joseph Krumgold, John D. Klorer d Edward Dmytryk
☆ James Craig, Bonita Granville, Frank Jenks, Cliff Edwards, George Cleveland, Tala Birell, John Banner

The Seven Minutes

US   1971   102m   DeLuxe
TCF (Russ Meyer)

A bookseller is arrested for distributing an obscene novel, and many people are unexpectedly involved in the court case.

A fascinating piece of old-fashioned hokum, full of 'daring' words and cameo performances.

w Richard Warren Lewis *novel* Irving Wallace d Russ Meyer ph Fred Mandl m Stu Phillips
☆ Wayne Maunder, Marianne MacAndrew, Yvonne de Carlo, Phil Carey, Jay C. Flippen, Edy Williams, Lyle Bettger, Ron Randell, David Brian, Charles Drake, John Carradine, Harold J. Stone

Seven Nights in Japan

GB/France   1976   104m   Eastmancolor
EMI-Marianne (Lewis Gilbert)

The heir to the British throne has shore leave in Tokyo and falls in love with a geisha.

Tediously daring romance with a banal script which seems over impressed by its own barely-existent controversial qualities.

w Christopher Wood d Lewis Gilbert ph Henri Decaë m David Hentschel
☆ Michael York, Hidemi Aoki, James Villiers, Peter Jones, Charles Gray

The Seven Per Cent Solution

US   1976   114m   Technicolor
Universal (Herbert Ross)

Dr Watson lures Sherlock Holmes to Vienna so that Professor Freud can cure him of persecution complex and cocaine addiction.

Drearily serious spoof with only a glimmer of the required style and a totally miscast Holmes.

w Nicholas Meyer *novel* Nicholas Meyer d Herbert Ross ph Oswald Morris m John Addison pd Ken Adam
☆ Nicol Williamson, Robert Duvall, Alan Arkin, Vanessa Redgrave, Laurence Olivier, Jeremy Kemp, Samantha Eggar, Joel Grey, Charles Gray, Georgia Brown, Regine

'Sorrily botched all-star extravaganza.' – *Sight and Sound*
'Comes into the category of hit and myth ... A heavyweight spoof in which Sherlock Holmes is placed under hypnosis by Sigmund Freud. The audience is then placed under hypnosis by director Herbert Ross.' – *Michael Billington, Illustrated London News*
♣ script

The Seven Samurai ****

Japan   1954   155m   bw
Toho (Shojiro Motoki)

original title: *Shichi-nin no Samurai*

16th-century villagers hire samurai to defend their property against an annual raid by bandits.

Superbly strange, vivid and violent medieval adventure which later served as the basis for the Western The

---

Magnificent Seven *and the science-fiction film* Battle Beyond the Stars.
w Akira Kurosawa, Shinobu Hashimoto, Hideo Oguni d Akira Kurosawa ph Asaichi Nakai m Fumio Hayasaka ad Takashi Matsuyama
☆ Toshiro Mifune, Takashi Shimura, Kuninori Kodo

'It is as sheer narrative, rich in imagery, incisiveness and sharp observation, that it makes its strongest impact … It provides a fascinating display of talent, and places its director in the forefront of creative film-makers of his generation.' – *Gavin Lambert, Sight and Sound*
'This, on the surface, is a work of relentless, unmitigated action, as epic as any film ever made, and, again on the surface, sheer entertainment. Yet it is also an unquestionable triumph of art.' – *John Simon*
⧗ art direction

Seven Seas to Calais

US/Italy 1962 103m Eastmancolor Cinemascope
MGM/Adelphia (Paolo Moffa)
In 1577, Sir Francis Drake follows the Spanish treasure route.
Ho-hum swashbuckler with a background of schoolboy history.
w Filippo Sanjust d Rudolph Maté ph Giulio Gianini m Franco Mannino
☆ Rod Taylor, Keith Michell, Irene Worth, Anthony Dawson, Basil Dignam

Seven Sinners *

GB 1936 70m bw
Gaumont (Michael Balcon)
US title: *Doomed Cargo*
Gunrunners wreck trains to cover traces of murder.
Fascinatingly dated comedy suspenser with excellent sub-Hitchcock sequences, the whole thing having a strong flavour of The 39 Steps.
w Frank Launder, Sidney Gilliat, L. DuGarde Peach, Austin Melford play *The Wrecker* by Arnold Ridley, Bernard Merivale d *Albert de Courville* m Mutz Greenbaum (Max Greene)
☆ Edmund Lowe, Constance Cummings, Thomy Bourdelle, Henry Oscar, Felix Aylmer, Allan Jeayes, O. B. Clarence

Seven Sinners *

US 1940 86m bw
Universal (Joe Pasternak)
▦ ⧗
GB title: *Café of Seven Sinners*
A cabaret singer is deported from several South Sea islands for causing too many fights among the naval officers.
Ho-hum hokum with an amiable cast and a good-natured final free-for-all.
w John Meehan, Harry Tugend d Tay Garnett ph Rudolph Maté m Frank Skinner
☆ Marlene Dietrich, John Wayne, Albert Dekker, Broderick Crawford, Mischa Auer, Billy Gilbert, Oscar Homolka, Anna Lee, Samuel S. Hinds

'Nothing to worry about, unless you happen to be in the theatre, watching it go from fairly good to worse than worse.' – *Otis Ferguson*

Seven Sweethearts

US 1942 98m bw
MGM (Joe Pasternak)
Seven daughters must marry in sequence, eldest first.
Period musical frou-frou inspired by Pride and Prejudice. *So light it almost floats.*
w Walter Reisch, Leo Townsend d Frank Borzage ph George Folsey m Franz Waxman
☆ Kathryn Grayson, Marsha Hunt, Van Heflin, Cecilia Parker, S. Z. Sakall, Peggy Moran, Isobel Elsom, Diana Lewis, Donald Meek, Louise Beavers

Seven Thieves *

US 1960 102m bw Cinemascope
TCF (Sidney Boehm)
▦
An elderly crook conceives a last plan to rob the Monte Carlo casino.
Routine caper story, efficiently presented with some humour.
w Sydney Boehm novel *Lions at the Kill* by Max Catto d Henry Hathaway ph Sam Leavitt m Dominic Frontière
☆ Edward G. Robinson, Rod Steiger, Joan Collins, Eli Wallach, Michael Dante, Alexander Scourby, Berry Kroeger, Sebastian Cabot

'Christ, it was supposed to be a fun film, and Steiger is far, far from having a sense of humour.' – *Henry Hathaway*

Seven Thunders

GB 1957 100m bw
Rank (Daniel M. Angel)
US title: *The Beasts of Marseilles*
In wartime Marseilles, escaped POWs are helped by a doctor who turns out to have sinister intent.
Slow chiller which telegraphs its surprises but gets by on good production values.
w John Baines novel Rupert Croft-Cooke d Hugo Fregonese ph Wilkie Cooper m Antony Hopkins
☆ James Robertson Justice, Stephen Boyd, Kathleen Harrison, Anna Gaylor, Tony Wright, Eugene Deckers, Rosalie Crutchley

Seven Waves Away

GB 1956 95m bw
Columbia/Copa (John R. Sloan)
US title: *Abandon Ship*
After the sinking of a luxury liner, the officer in charge of a lifeboat has to make life or death decisions.
Initially gripping but finally depressing open sea melodrama derived from Souls at Sea *and later remade for TV as* The Last Survivors.
wd Richard Sale ph Wilkie Cooper m Arthur Bliss
☆ Tyrone Power, Mai Zetterling, Lloyd Nolan, Stephen Boyd, Moira Lister, James Hayter, Marie Lohr, Moultrie Kelsall, Noel Willman, Gordon Jackson, Clive Morton, John Stratton

'Eventually one is bludgeoned into a grudging admiration for the film's staying power.' – *Peter John Dyer*
'It jabs at your entrails with a cold unrelenting spear.' – *New York Times*

Seven Ways from Sundown

US 1960 87m Eastmancolor
Universal-International
A Texas Ranger befriends an outlaw, but has twinges of conscience.
Straightforward character Western with the inevitable shootout finale.
w Clair Huffaker d Harry Keller
☆ Audie Murphy, Barry Sullivan, Venetia Stevenson, John McIntire, Kenneth Tobey

'Love, lust, courage and cowardice! Faith, fury and sacrifice!'

Seven Women *

US 1966 100m Metrocolor Panavision
MGM/John Ford/Bernard Smith
⧗
In 1935, an isolated Chinese mission staffed by American women is overrun by bandits.
Dusty melodrama which might have appealed in the thirties but was quite out of tune with the sixties. Well enough made and acted, but a strange choice for Ford's last film.
w Janet Green, John McCormick story *Chinese Finale* by Norah Lofts d John Ford ph Joseph LaShelle m Elmer Bernstein
☆ Anne Bancroft, Flora Robson, Margaret Leighton, Sue Lyon, Mildred Dunnock, Betty Field, Anna Lee, Eddie Albert, Mike Mazurki, Woody Strode, Irene Tsu

The Seven Year Itch *

US 1955 105m DeLuxe Cinemascope
TCF (Charles K. Feldman, Billy Wilder)
▦ ▦ ⧗
A married man has a fling with the girl upstairs.
An amusing theatrical joke, with dream sequences like revue sketches, Is really all at sea on the big screen, especially as the affair remains unconsummated, but direction and performances keep the party going more or less.
w Billy Wilder, George Axelrod play George Axelrod d Billy Wilder ph Milton Krasner m Alfred Newman
☆ Tom Ewell, Marilyn Monroe, Sonny Tufts, Evelyn Keyes, Robert Strauss, Oscar Homolka, Marguerite Chapman, Victor Moore

Seven Years in Tibet *

US 1997 139m Technicolor Panavision
Entertainment/Mandalay/Reperage and Vanguard/Applecross (Jean-Jacques Annaud, John H. Williams, Iain Smith)
▦ ⧗ ⧗ ⧗ ⧗ 🎧
Escaping from a British prisoner-of-war camp in India, an Austrian mountaineer makes it through the Himalayas to the forbidden Tibetan city of Lhasa, where he becomes friends with the Dalai Lama.
Uninvolving epic that looks much better than it sounds.
w Becky Johnston book Heinrich Harrer d Jean-Jacques Annaud ph Robert Fraisse m John Williams pd At Hoang ed Noëlle Boisson
☆ Brad Pitt, David Thewlis, B. D. Wong, Mako, Danny Denzongpa, Victor Wong, Ingeborga Dapkunaite, Jamyang Jamsho Wangchuk

'A glossy, good-natured travelogue with modest philosophical pretensions.' – *Mark Kermode, Sight and Sound*

Seventeen

US 1940 76m bw
Paramount (Stuart Walker)
Adolescent problems of a midwestern small-town boy.
Old-fashioned family entertainment, smartly cast and filmed.
w Agnes Christine Johnston, Stuart Palmer novel Booth Tarkington d Louis King
☆ Jackie Cooper, Betty Field, Otto Kruger, Ann Shoemaker, Norma Nelson

Seventh Cavalry

US 1956 75m Technicolor
Columbia (Harry Joe Brown)
An officer accused of cowardice volunteers to bring back General Custer's body after Little Big Horn.
Lively co-feature with a good traditional action climax.
w Peter Packer story Glendon F. Swarthout d Joseph H. Lewis ph Ray Rennahan m Mischa Bakaleinikoff
☆ Randolph Scott, Barbara Hale, Jay C. Flippen, Jeanette Nolan, Frank Faylen

The Seventh Cross **

US 1944 112m bw
MGM (Pandro S. Berman)
▦
Seven Germans escape from a concentration camp, and the Nazis threaten to execute them all. Just one escapes.
Impressive melodrama, brilliantly limiting its escape/suspense story to studio sets. Old style Hollywood production at its best; but a rather obviously contrived story.
w Helen Deutsch novel Anna Seghers d Fred Zinnemann ph Karl Freund m Roy Webb ad Cedric Gibbons, Leonid Vasian
☆ Spencer Tracy, Signe Hasso, Hume Cronyn, Jessica Tandy, Agnes Moorehead, Felix Bressart, George Macready, George Zucco
⧗ Hume Cronyn

The Seventh Curse

Hong Kong 1986 93m colour
Paragon (Leonard K. C. Ho)
▦
A doctor seeks a cure for a deadly curse put upon him by a sorcerer after he saves a woman in Thailand from being sacrificed to a living skeleton.
Risible fantasy that begins as a violent action movie before it settles for a delirious mix of horror and science fiction, with low-budget monsters, lashings of gore and not much sense.
w I. Kuang d Lan Wei-tsang
☆ Chow Yun-Fat, Chin Siu Ho, Maggie Cheung, Dick Wei, Elvis Tsui

The Seventh Dawn

GB 1964 123m Technicolor
UA/Holden/Charles K. Feldman (Karl Tunberg)
In the early fifties a Malayan rubber planter finds that his best friend is a leading terrorist.
Doom-laden romantic adventure drama with a lot of suffering and too little entertainment value.
w Karl Tunberg novel *The Durian Tree* by Michael Keon d Lewis Gilbert ph Freddie Young m Riz Ortolani
☆ William Holden, Tetsuro Tamba, Capucine, Susannah York, Michael Goodliffe, Allan Cuthbertson, Maurice Denham

'Echoes of *The Ugly American, Love Is a Many-Splendored Thing*, and many another adventure East of Sumatra, with every character running absolutely true to form.' – *MFB*
'An interminable melange of political, racial and romantic clichés, with performances and dialogue as overripe as the jungle setting.' – *Judith Crist, 1973*

Seventh Day, Eighth Night **

Czechoslovakia 1969 108m bw
Filmowe Studio Barrandov (Vera Kadlecova)
original title: *Den Sedmy – Osma Noc*
Following the disappearance of the station master, a village is panicked into believing that it is facing danger from an unknown enemy.
Savage, black political farce of intimidation and betrayal that was withheld for several years by the Czech authorities.
w Zdenek Mahler, Evald Schorm d Evald Schorm ph Vaclav Hanus m Jan Klusak pd Karel Lier
☆ Jaroslav Wagner-Kleuka, Jan Kacer, Jana Markova, Kveta Fialova, Ljuba Skorepova, Josef Bek

'Lovers Who Lift Your Heart To The Skies … In The Tenderest Romance Of Our Time!'

Seventh Heaven **

US 1927 93m bw silent
Fox (William Fox)
A Paris sewer worker shelters a war waif, marries her and after idyllic happiness goes off to war, returning blinded.
All softness, sweetness and light, a very typical – and attractive – film of its director and a big influence on Hollywood's European period.
w Benjamin Glazer play Austin Strong d Frank Borzage ph Ernest Palmer, J. A. Valentine ad Harry Oliver
☆ Janet Gaynor, Charles Farrell, Gladys Brockwell, David Butler
⧍ Benjamin Glazer; Frank Borzage; Janet Gaynor
⧗ best picture; Harry Oliver

Seventh Heaven *

US 1937 102m bw
TCF (Raymond Griffith)
Dewy-eyed remake; the mood is antediluvian but the production impresses.
w Melville Baker d Henry King ph Merritt Gerstad m Louis Silvers ad William Darling
☆ James Stewart, Simone Simon, Jean Hersholt, Gale Sondergaard, J. Edward Bromberg, Gregory Ratoff, John Qualen, Victor Kilian, Sig Rumann, Mady Christians

'A romance that can stand another telling … the older element will join in making it a bracer for the box office.' – *Variety*

The Seventh Seal ****

Sweden 1957 95m bw
Svensk Filmindustri (Allan Ekelund)
▦ ▦ ⧗ ⧗
original title: *Det Sjunde Inseglet*
Death comes for a knight, who challenges him to a game of chess while he tries to show illustrations of goodness in mankind: but Death takes them all away in the end.
A modestly budgeted minor classic which, because of its international success and its famous shots, is seldom analysed in detail. It is kept going by its splendid cinematic feel and its atmosphere is that of a dark world irrationally sustained by religion.
wd Ingmar Bergman ph Gunnar Fischer m Erik Nordgren
☆ Max von Sydow, Bengt Ekerot, Gunnar Bjornstrand, Nils Poppe, Bibi Andersson, Gunnel Lindblom

'The most extraordinary mixture of beauty and lust and cruelty, Odin-worship and Christian faith, darkness and light.' – *Alan Dent, Illustrated London News*
'You know where they dance along the horizon? We'd packed up for the evening and were about to go home. Suddenly I saw a cloud, and Fischer swung his camera up. Some actors had gone, so grips had to stand in. The whole scene was improvised in ten minutes flat.' – *Ingmar Bergman*

The Seventh Sign

US 1988 95m colour
Columbia Tri-Star/Interscope (Ted Field, Robert Cort)
📷 🇺🇸 @. ⊚ ⌂

A pregnant mother fears that the birth of her baby will signal the end of the world.

Apocalyptic thriller that is too silly to be enjoyable on any level.

w Clifford Green, Ellen Green d Carl Schultz ph Juan Ruiz-Anchia m Jack Nitzsche pd Stephen Marsh ed Caroline Biggerstaff
☆ Jürgen Prochnow, Demi Moore, Michael Biehn, Peter Friedman, John Taylor, John Heard

The Seventh Sin

US 1957 94m bw Cinemascope
MGM (David Lewis)
⌂

A faithless wife accompanies her bacteriologist husband to fight a Chinese cholera epidemic, and regains her self-respect.

Tatty remake of a Garbo vehicle which was dated even in 1934. (See The Painted Veil.)

w Karl Tunberg novel The Painted Veil by Somerset Maugham d Ronald Neame ph Ray June m Miklos Rozsa
☆ Eleanor Parker, Bill Travers, George Sanders, Jean-Pierre Aumont, Françoise Rosay

The Seventh Survivor

GB 1941 75m bw
British National

Survivors of a shipwreck gather in a lighthouse and discover that one of them is a Nazi agent.

Adequate mystery potboiler, comparable with Hitchcock's talkier Lifeboat.

w Michael Barringer d Leslie Hiscott
☆ Linden Travers, Austin Trevor, John Stuart, Martita Hunt, Frank Pettingell, Jane Carr, Felix Aylmer, Wally Patch, Henry Oscar

The Seventh Veil **

GB 1945 94m bw
Theatrecraft/Sydney Box/Ortus
📷

A concert pianist is romantically torn between her psychiatrist, her guardian, and two other fellows.

A splendid modern melodrama in the tradition of Jane Eyre and Rebecca; it set the seal of moviegoing approval on psychiatry, classical music, and James Mason, and is it the most utter tosh.

w Muriel and Sydney Box d Compton Bennett ph Reg Wyer m Benjamin Frankel
☆ James Mason, Ann Todd, Herbert Lom, Albert Lieven, Hugh McDermott, Yvonne Owen, David Horne, Manning Whiley

'An example of the intelligent, medium-priced picture made with great technical polish which has represented for Hollywood the middle path between the vulgar and the highbrow.' – *Spectator*

'A popular film that does not discard taste and atmosphere.' – *Daily Mail*

'A rich, portentous mixture of Beethoven, Chopin, Kitsch and Freud.' – *Pauline Kael, 1968*

'An odd, artificial, best sellerish kind of story, with reminiscences of Trilby and Jane Eyre and all their imitations down to Rebecca.' – *Richard Mallett, Punch*

'Maybe, with a few veils stripped away, all of us have a fantasist inside who gobbles up this sadomasochistic sundae.' – *Pauline Kael, 70s*
🎖 script

The Seventh Victim *

US 1943 71m bw
RKO (Val Lewton)
🇺🇸 @.

A girl goes to New York in search of her sister, who is under the influence of Satanists.

Much praised but in effect rather boring little thriller, with rather stately acting and ponderous direction and dialogue. Censorship made the plot so obscure that it's difficult to follow.

w Charles O'Neal, De Witt Bodeen d Mark Robson ph Nicholas Musuraca m Constantin Bakaleinikoff
☆ Kim Hunter, Tom Conway, Jean Brooks, Hugh Beaumont, Erford Gage, Isabel Jewell, Evelyn Brent

'It is the almost oppressive mood, the romantic obsession with death-in-life, which dominates the film.' – *NFT, 1973*
† Note the use in the first scene of the staircase from *The Magnificent Ambersons*.

The Seventh Voyage of Sinbad *

🎦 US 1958 89m Technicolor
Columbia/Morningside (Charles Schneer)
📷 🇺🇸 @. ⌂

Sinbad seeks a roc's egg which will restore his fiancée from the midget size to which an evil magician has reduced her.

Lively fantasy with narrative drive and excellent effects.

w Kenneth Kolb d Nathan Juran ph Wilkie Cooper m Bernard Herrmann sp Ray Harryhausen
☆ Kerwin Mathews, Kathryn Grant, Torin Thatcher, Richard Eyer, Alec Mango

70,000 Witnesses

US 1932 69m bw
Harry Joe Brown/Paramount

A football star is murdered in the middle of a game.

Okay for sports fans, but not much of a murder mystery.

w Garrett Fort, P. J. Wolfson, Allen Rivkin novel Cortland Fitzsimmons d Ralph Murphy
☆ Phillips Holmes, Johnny Mack Brown, Charles Ruggles, Dorothy Jordan, J. Farrell MacDonald, Lew Cody

'Will make money and please … enough comedy interwoven to satisfy on laughs alone.' – *Variety*

'They take the third degree one step further!'

The Seven-Ups

US 1973 103m DeLuxe
TCF/Philip D'Antoni
🇺🇸 @.

Gangsters are hunted down by a secret force of the New York police.

Formulary realistic rough stuff in the wake of The French Connection.

w Albert Ruben, Alexander Jacobs d Philip D'Antoni ph Urs Furrer m Don Ellis
☆ Roy Scheider, Victor Arnold, Jerry Leon, Tony Lo Bianco, Richard Lynch

Several Interviews on Personal Problems **

USSR 1979 94m colour
Gruziafilm

original title: *Neskolko Intervyu Po Lichnyam Voprosam*

A busy journalist spends her time sorting out other people's problems while failing to solve her own domestic difficulties.

Interspersed with interviews with Soviet women on their lives, it provides a compassionate, witty look at the situation of women in Russia.

w Zaira Arsenishvili, Erlom Akhvlediani, Lana Gogoberidze d Lana Gogoberidze ph Nugzar Erkomaishvili m Gia Kanchell
☆ Sofiko Chiaureli, Gia Badridze, Ketevan Orakhelashvili, Janri Lolashvili, Salome Kancheli, Ketevan Bochorishvili, Noutsa Alexi-Meskhshvili

A Severed Head *

GB 1970 98m Technicolor
Columbia/Winkast (Alan Ladd Jnr)

A wine merchant has a long-standing affair which he thinks is secret, but is annoyed when his wife tries the same game.

Unwisely boisterous screen version of a slyly academic novel; tolerably sophisticated for those who don't know the original.

w Frederic Raphael novel Iris Murdoch d Dick Clement ph Austin Dempster m Stanley Myers pd Richard Macdonald
☆ Lee Remick, Richard Attenborough, Ian Holm, Claire Bloom, Jennie Linden, Clive Revill

Severed Ties

US 1991 90m colour
Fangoria Films (Christopher Webster)
📷

A mad, mother-dominated scientist grows himself a new arm from plasma taken from a serial killer and a lizard, with predictable results.

Unbelievably cheap, would-be comic horror, by far the worst film its two stars have ever made (and they have appeared in some appalling ones), devoid of style or invention, and taking its plot from half a dozen better movies.

w John Nystrom, Henry Dominic story Damon Santostefano, David A. Casci d Damon Santostefano ph Geza Sincovics m Daniel Licht pd Don Day ed Richard Roberts sp KNB Effects

☆ Oliver Reed, Elke Sommer, Garrett Morris, Johnny Legend, Denise Wallace, Roger Perkovich, Bekki Vallin, Billy Morrisette

'Combo of grotesque gore effects and over-the-top acting is a winning one.' – *Variety*

Sex and the Single Girl

US 1964 114m Technicolor
Warner/Richard Quine/Reynard (William T. Orr)
🇺🇸

A journalist worms his way into the life of a lady sexologist in order to unmask her – but guess what.

Coy sex comedy with noise substituting for wit and style, all pretence being abandoned in a wild chase climax.

w Joseph Heller, David R. Schwartz book Helen Gurley Brown d Richard Quine ph Charles Lang Jnr m Neal Hefti
☆ Natalie Wood, Tony Curtis, Henry Fonda, Lauren Bacall, Mel Ferrer, Fran Jeffries, Edward Everett Horton, Otto Kruger

'For those willing to devote two hours of their lives to a consideration of Natalie Wood's virginity.' – *Judith Crist, 1973*

Sex and the Vampire: see Le Frisson des Vampires

sex, lies and videotape **

US 1989 100m CFI color
Virgin/Outlaw Productions (Robert Newmyer, John Hardy)
📷 🇺🇸 @. ⊚ ⌂

An old college friend, who likes to videotape interviews with women about their sexual experiences, visits a couple whose marriage is in difficulties.

Witty, intelligent conversation piece that won the Palme D'Or for best film at the Cannes Film Festival.

wd Steven Soderbergh ph Walt Lloyd m Cliff Martinez ad Joanne Schmidt ed Steve Soderbergh
☆ James Spader, Andie MacDowell, Peter Gallagher, Laura San Giacomo, Ron Vawter
🎖 best original screenplay

Sex Life in a Convent: see Behind Convent Walls

The Sex Life of a Female Private Eye: see Big Zapper

The Sex Thief

GB 1973 89m Eastmancolor
LMG/Ocarina/Drumbeat/Rainbow (Michael Style, Teddy White)
📷

A writer turns cat burglar by night, making love to the women he robs.

Low-budget sex quickie, better acted and with brighter dialogue than average for the genre.

w Edward Hyde (Michael Armstrong) d Martin Campbell ph Grenville Middleton m Mike Vickers ad Anthony Noble ed Rex Graves
☆ David Warbeck, Diane Keen, Terence Edmond, Linda Coombes, Michael Armstrong, Christopher Neil, Christopher Biggins, James Aubrey

'Tawdry, ridiculous fare, only marginally redeemed by its own self-mocking humour.' – *Sight and Sound*

Sextette *

US 1978 91m Metrocolor
Briggs and Sullivan (Warren G. Toub)
🇺🇸

The honeymoon of a Hollywood film star is interrupted by her previous husbands.

An amazing last stab at her old métier by an 86-year-old ex-star. It doesn't work, of course, and most of it is embarrassing, but the attempt is in itself remarkable.

w Herbert Baker play Mae West d Ken Hughes ph James Crabe m Artie Butler
☆ Mae West, Tony Curtis, Ringo Starr, Dom DeLuise, Timothy Dalton, George Hamilton, Alice Cooper, Rona Barrett, Walter Pidgeon, George Raft

Sexton Blake and the Hooded Terror

GB 1938 70m bw
George King

A millionaire is unmasked as the head of a criminal gang.

Rather unyielding series melodrama, chiefly interesting for the casting of Tod Slaughter as Blake's Moriarty.

w A. R. Rawlinson d George King ph H. M. Glendining md Jack Beaver ad Philip Bawcombe ed John Seabourne
☆ George Curzon, Tod Slaughter, Greta Gynt, Charles Oliver, David Farrar, Tony Sympson

TERROR: 'You little fool! Don't you realise that the game is up? The Black Quorum has seen through your treacheries. I alone can save you from their revenge!'

GIRL: 'I'd rather die.'
† Other Sexton Blake movies, all cheaply made by British independents, include six 1928 two-reelers starring Langhorne Burton: *Sexton Blake and the Bearded Doctor* and *Sexton Blake and the Mademoiselle*, both 1935, both with Curzon; *Meet Sexton Blake* and *The Echo Murders*, both 1943, both with David Farrar; and *Murder on Site Three*, 1963 with Geoffrey Toone.

The Sexual Life of the Belgians 1950–1978 *

Belgium 1994 63m colour
Metro Tartan/Transatlantic (Jan Bucquoy)
📷

original title: *La Vie Sexuelle des Belges 1950–1978*

The sexual experiences of a Flemish man, from babyhood to a failed marriage and what appears to be his most enjoyable relationship, with an inflatable doll.

An odd little comedy of repression and release that claims to be autobiographical; it is subversive in a downbeat way.

wd Jan Bucquoy ph Michel Baudour m Francis de Smet pd Nathalie André, Nicole Lenoir ed Matyas Veress
☆ Jean-Henri Compère, Noé Francq, Isabelle Legros, Sophie Schneider, Pascale Binneri, Michele Shor

'There's a wonderful sense of abandon to this light, titillating comedy.' – *Empire*

Sgt Bilko

US 1996 94m DeLuxe
Universal/Imagine/Entertainment (Brian Grazer)
📷 🇺🇸 @. ⊚ ⌂

Sergeant Bilko outsmarts an old rival, an army major.

Dull and miscast comedy, one that only makes the original television series seem, in retrospect, better than it was.

w Andy Breckman d Jonathan Lynn ph Peter Sova m Alan Silvestri pd Lawrence G. Paull ed Tony Lombardo
☆ Steve Martin, Dan Aykroyd, Phil Hartman, Glenne Headly, Daryl Mitchell, Max Casella, Eric Edwards, Dan Ferro

'This misconceived venture could just give a laugh or two to those who have never seen the original, but those who have may curse the day Martin was born.' – *Derek Malcolm, Guardian*

'A terrible film … has no visual wit, a pathetically scrappy script and the usual "pop-noodle" soundtrack of disparate songs. Oh, and Dan Aykroyd's Colonel Hall is as much an insult to Paul Ford's magnificent creation as this whole episode is a piss-stain on Phil Silvers's pedestal.' – *Kim Newman, Sight and Sound*
† The original TV series was first titled *You'll Never Get Rich*, then was known as *The Phil Silvers Show*, running from 1955 to 1959, and retitled *Sgt Bilko* when it was syndicated. Created by Nat Hiken, who named its hero after his favourite baseball player, Steve Bilko, it starred Phil Silvers as Bilko, supported by Paul Ford as his commanding officer and Elisabeth Fraser as his girlfriend.

Sgt Pepper's Lonely Hearts Club Band

🎦 US 1978 111m Technicolor
Panavision
Universal/Robert Stigwood (Dee Anthony)
🇺🇸 @.

A family band finds a new sound despite the activities of villains.

Oddball hotch-potch of middle-aged comedy and youth nostalgia in an American small-town setting. Some moments please, but most of it simply doesn't gel.

w Henry Edwards d Michael Schultz ph Owen Roizman m various (mostly the Beatles) pd Brian Eatwell
☆ Peter Frampton, Barry Gibb, Robin Gibb, Maurice Gibb, George Burns, Frankie Howerd, Donald Pleasence, Paul Nicholas, Sandy Farina, Alice Cooper, Steve Martin, Earth Wind and Fire

---

'Another of those films which serve as feature-length screen advertising for an album.' – *Variety*

Sh! The Octopus
US 1937 54m bw
First National
Lamebrain detectives fight a giant octopus in a lighthouse.
Footling remake of The Gorilla (qv).
w George Bricker d William McGann
☆ Hugh Herbert, Allen Jenkins, Marcia Ralston, John Eldredge, George Rosener
'This bit of grist for the double-feature mills is so feeble even the actors seem embarrassed.' – *Variety*

Shack Out on 101 *
US 1955 80m bw
AA/William F. Broidy
A waitress at a café near a research establishment unmasks two spies.
Modest suspenser which seemed at the time to have some fresh and realistic attitudes.
w Ed and Mildred Dein d Ed Dein ph Floyd Crosby m Paul Dunlap
☆ Frank Lovejoy, Lee Marvin, Keenan Wynn, Terry Moore, Whit Bissell

Shadey
GB 1985 106m colour
Larkspur/Otto Plashkes
A bankrupt car mechanic will do almost anything to finance his sex change operation.
Weird, utterly unprovoked and unmotivated black comedy which confounded all comers.
w Snoo Wilson d Philip Saville ph Roger Deakins m Colin Towns
☆ Anthony Sher, Billie Whitelaw, Patrick Macnee, Leslie Ash, Bernard Hepton, Larry Lamb, Katherine Helmond

The Shadow
GB 1933 74m bw
UA/Real Art (Julius Hagen)
A police hunt for a murderous blackmailer leads to the Chief Commissioner's house.
Old-fashioned whodunnit that looks like a stage production transferred intact to the screen.
w H. Fowler Mear, Terence Egan, Donald Stuart d George A. Cooper ph Sydney Blythe ad James A. Carter ed Jack Harris
☆ Henry Kendall, Elizabeth Allan, Felix Aylmer, John Turnbull, Cyril Raymond

'The Glamour. The Mystery. The Danger.'
The Shadow
US 1994 107m DeLuxe
UIP (Martin Bregman, Willi Baer)
In the 30s, a former criminal-turned-vigilante with psychic powers battles in New York against a descendant of Genghis Khan who plans to destroy the city and rule the world.
A dim attempt to revive a forgotten hero of pulp fiction, radio and a little-regarded cinema serial of the 40s; the period setting looks good but the story is thin and the result forgettable.
w David Koepp d Russell Mulcahy ph Stephen H. Burum m Jerry Goldsmith pd Joseph Nemec III ed Peter Honess
☆ Alec Baldwin, Penelope Ann Miller, John Lone, Peter Boyle, Ian McKellen, Tim Curry, Jonathan Winters, Sab Shimono
'A helpful how-to guide for Hollywood producers who are looking to make expensive bad movies.' – *Mo Ryan, Cinescape*

Shadow Conspiracy
US 1997 103m Technicolor Panavision
Buena Vista/Hollywood/Cinergi (Terry Collis)
A White House aide is the only person who can save the President from assassination.
Risibly silly chase movie that fails to do more than amuse by its presumption.
w Adi Hasak, Ric Gibbs d George P. Cosmatos ph Buzz Feitshans IV m Bruce Broughton pd Joe Alves ed Robert A. Ferretti
☆ Charlie Sheen, Donald Sutherland, Linda Hamilton, Stephen Lang, Ben Gazzara, Nicholas Turturro, Sam Waterston, Henry Strozier, Theodore Bikel, Gore Vidal
'One of those misfires that is so bad it's funny.' – *Variety*

Shadow in the Sky
US 1951 78m bw
MGM (William H. Wright)
A shell-shocked marine moves from a psychiatric hospital to live with his sister.
Low-key drama, plainly but quite well done, though of little continuing interest.
w Ben Maddow d Fred M. Wilcox ph George Folsey m Bronislau Kaper
☆ Ralph Meeker, Nancy Davis, James Whitmore, Jean Hagen

Shadow Makers
US 1989 127m Technicolor
UIP/Paramount (Tony Garnett)
aka: *Fat Man and Little Boy*
The army and scientists clash when working on a project to develop the first atom bomb.
A significant moment in history is rendered mundane in a damp squib of a film.
w Bruce Robinson, Roland Joffe d Roland Joffe ph Vilmos Zsigmond m Ennio Morricone pd Gregg Fonseca ed Françoise Bonnot
☆ Paul Newman, Dwight Schultz, Bonnie Bedelia, John Cusack, Laura Dern, Ron Frazier, John C. McGinley, Natasha Richardson, Ron Vawter

'The Good Guys Don't Always Wear Black.'
The Shadow Men
US 1997 91m colour
Promark/Spectacor (Steve Beswick)
After a family report an experience with a UFO they are menaced by pale men dressed entirely in black.
A low-budget, low-enterprise reworking of themes from Men in Black and the TV series The X Files, with small rewards.
w Eric Miller, Justin Stanley d Timothy Bond ph Frank Byers pd Cecil Gentry ed Barry Zetlin
☆ Eric Roberts, Sherilyn Fenn, Dean Stockwell

Shadow of a Doubt ***
US 1943 108m bw
Universal (Jack H. Skirball)
A favourite uncle comes to visit his family in a small Californian town. He is actually on the run from police, who know him as the Merry Widow murderer.
Hitchcock's quietest film is memorable chiefly for its depiction of small-town life; but the script is well written and keeps the suspense moving slowly but surely.
w Thornton Wilder, Sally Benson, Alma Reville story Gordon McDonell d Alfred Hitchcock ph Joe Valentine m Dimitri Tiomkin
☆ Joseph Cotten, Teresa Wright, Hume Cronyn, Macdonald Carey, Patricia Collinge, Henry Travers, Wallace Ford
'Some clever observation of rabbity white-collar life which, in spite of a spacious sweetness, is the best since It's a Gift.' – *James Agee*
† Remade in 1959 as *Step Down to Terror*, with Charles Drake.
†† A lacklustre TV version was made in 1991, starring Mark Harmon and directed by Karen Arthur.
ठ original story

A Shadow of a Doubt **
France 1992 106m colour CinemaScope
CIBY 2000/TF1 (Patrick Lancelot)
original title: *L'Ombre du Doute*
An 11-year-old girl claims that her father is sexually abusing her, but he denies it and his wife believes him.
Complex, emotionally charged film that catches the confusion of a child caught between reality and fantasy, in a situation too difficult for her to deal with; it tackles its difficult subject-matter without sensationalism, concentrating on the love-hate relationship between father and daughter and its repercussions on other members of the family.
w Aline Issermann, Martine Fadier-Nisse, Frederique Gruyer d Aline Issermann ph Darius Khondji m Reno Isaac ad Cyr Boitard ed Hervé Schneid
☆ Mireille Perrier, Alain Bashung, Sandrine Blancke, Emmanuelle Riva, Michel Aumont, Luis Issermann, Roland Bertin, Dominique Lavanant, Thierry L'hermitte

'This sensitive and emotionally powerful film does an extremely good job with material that has a good many pitfalls.' – *Derek Malcolm, Guardian*

Shadow of a Woman
US 1946 78m bw
Warner (William Jacobs)
A woman suspects her husband of trying to murder his son by a former marriage.
Poor melodrama on Love from a Stranger lines.
w Whitman Chambers, C. Graham Baker d Joseph Santley ph Bert Glennon m Adolph Deutsch
☆ Andrea King, Helmut Dantine, Don McGuire, Richard Erdman, William Prince

Shadow of Doubt
US 1935 71m bw
MGM
An actress suspected of murder is cleared by the efforts of her fiancé's aunt.
Routine mystery with a strong part for a new character actress from England.
w Wells Root, Arthur Somers Roche d George B. Seitz
☆ Ricardo Cortez, Virginia Bruce, Constance Collier, Arthur Byron, Isabel Jewell, Regis Toomey, Edward Brophy
'Passable murder mystery.' – *Variety*

Shadow of Fear
GB 1963 60m bw
Butcher's (John I. Phillips)
An American oilman, returning to London from Baghdad, is caught up in espionage.
Mundane and stupid programmer, ploddingly directed.
w Ronald Liles, James O'Connolly story Decoy, Be Damned by T. F. Fotherby d Ernest Morris ph Walter J. Harvey m Martin Slavin ad Wilfred Arnold ed Henry Richardson
☆ Paul Maxwell, Clare Owen, Anita West, John Sutton, John Arnatt, Eric Pohlmann, Alan Tilvern, Reginald Marsh

Shadow of the Cat
GB 1961 79m bw
U-I/BHP (Jon Penington)
A cat appears to wreak vengeance on those who murdered its mistress.
Tolerable old dark house shocker with an amusing theme not too well sustained.
w George Baxt d John Gilling ph Alec Grant m Mikis Theodorakis
☆ André Morell, William Lucas, Barbara Shelley, Conrad Phillips, Alan Wheatley, Vanda Godsell, Richard Warner, Freda Jackson

Shadow of the Eagle
GB 1950 92m bw
Valiant (Anthony Havelock-Allan)
In 1770, a Russian envoy to Venice falls for the princess he is supposed to kidnap.
Limp swashbuckler based on a deservedly shadowy corner of European history.
w Doreen Montgomery, Hagar Wilde d Sidney Salkow ph Erwin Hillier m Hans May
☆ Richard Greene, Valentina Cortese, Greta Gynt, Binnie Barnes, Charles Goldner, Walter Rilla

Shadow of the Wolf
Canada/France 1993 112m Sonolab Color Cinemascope
Vision/Transfilm/Eiffel/Canal (Claude Leger)
aka: *Agaguk*
In the 1930s, an Eskimo, banished for his hatred of white men, becomes an outcast who has to learn to fend for himself.
Simple-minded rites-of-passage drama of a man pitted against the elements.
w Rudy Wurlitzer, Evan Jones, David Milhaud novel Yves Theriault d Jacques Dorfmann ph Billy Williams m Maurice Jarre pd Wolf Kroeger ed Françoise Bonnot
☆ Lou Diamond Phillips, Toshiro Mifune, Jennifer Tilly, Bernard-Pierre Donnadieu, Donald Sutherland
'Pic is too simple-minded and clichéd for adults, but probably too rough for kids.' – *Variety*
† The film, which cost around $30 million, was the most expensive Canadian production so far. It was released direct to video in Britain.

Shadow on the Wall
US 1949 84m bw
MGM (Robert Sisk)
A child is traumatized by the accidental witnessing of the murder of her unpleasant stepmother.
Forgettable melodramatic suspenser.
w William Ludwig d Pat Jackson ph Ray June m André Previn
☆ Ann Sothern, Zachary Scott, Gigi Perreau, Nancy Davis, Kristine Miller, John McIntire

The Shadow on the Window
US 1957 73m bw
Columbia (Jonie Taps)
Three teenage thugs break into a lonely house, murder its owner and hold a girl hostage.
Routine crime programmer, rather boringly unravelled.
w Leo Townsend, David Harmon d William Asher ph Kit Carson m George Duning
☆ Betty Garrett, Phil Carey, John Barrymore Jnr, Corey Allen, Gerald Saracini

Shadow Warrior: see *Kagemusha*

'He thought that magic only existed in books, and then he met her.'
Shadowlands ***
GB 1993 131m colour Scope
UIP/Showlands/Spelling/Pirce/Savoy (Richard Attenborough, Brian Eastman)
The emotionally repressed C. S. Lewis, Oxford don and famous writer of children's books and works of popular theology, enters into a marriage of convenience with an American woman, whom he grows to love, only to learn that she has terminal cancer.
Impeccably acted and directed drama of emotional risk and the pain and joy it can bring.
w William Nicholson play William Nicholson d Richard Attenborough ph Roger Pratt m George Fenton pd Stuart Craig ed Lesley Walker
☆ Anthony Hopkins, Debra Winger, John Wood, Edward Hardwicke, Joseph Mazzello, Julian Fellowes, Roddy Maude-Roxby, Michael Denison, Peter Firth
'A mature film for grown-ups.' – *Variety*
'Reticent is the word for Richard Attenborough's film version. But that's a virtue, not a defect, when the setting is English academia (no one has more persuasively captured its manners) and your subject is mortality.' – *Richard Corliss, Time*
'The picture isn't actually very good; it's just a tearjerker with clumsy interpolations of theology.' – *Terrence Rafferty, New Yorker*
'A beautifully crafted movie that gleams like a newly-made antique.' – *Philip French, Observer*
† William Nicholson first wrote the story as a play for BBC TV and then adapted it for the stage before it became a film. Despite Hopkins's Welsh accent, Lewis was an Ulsterman, born in Belfast.
ठ Debra Winger; William Nicholson

Shadows *
US 1959 81m bw
Cassavetes/Cassel/Maurice McEndree
Two blacks and their sister find their identities in Manhattan.
16mm realistic drama which began a new and essentially dreary trend of grainily true-life pictures with improvised dialogue and little dramatic compression.
w the cast d John Cassavetes ph Erich Kollmar m Charles Mingus
☆ Ben Carruthers, Lelia Goldoni, Hugh Hurd, Rupert Crosse, Anthony Ray
'I don't so much object to its mindlessness as to its formlessness, regardless of the practical excuses that may be advanced for its rambling incoherence.' – *William S. Pechter*
'A picture of startling immediacy and shocking power.' – *Robert Hatch, Nation*
'We were improvising … every scene was very simple. They were predicated on people having problems that were overcome with other problems. At the end of the scene another problem would come in and overlap.' – *John Cassavetes*

Shadows and Fog *

US 1991 86m bw
Columbia TriStar/Orion (Jack Rollins, Charles Joffe)
▦ ▤ @.

In a town where a circus has come to visit, a timid individual is forced by his neighbours to join vigilantes trying to trap a murderer.
An occasionally witty excursion into the world of German expressionist movies of the 20s.
wd Woody Allen ph Carlo Di Palma m Kurt Weill pd Santo Loquasto ed Susan E. Morse
☆ Woody Allen, Mia Farrow, John Malkovich, Madonna, Donald Pleasence, Lily Tomlin, Jodie Foster, Kathy Bates, John Cusack, Kate Nelligan, Julie Kavner, Fred Gwynne
'Is Allen confronting his inability to treat history, or anything else, as tragedy rather than farce? The film is a serious joke, possibly reflecting on German re-unification, and it has an unpleasant aftertaste.' – *Philip French, Observer*

Shadows of our Forgotten Ancestors *

USSR 1964 100m bw/colour
Dovzhenko Film Studios
▦

original title: *Teni Zabytykh Predkov*
A youth falls in love with the daughter of the rich landowner who killed his father.
A story of a doomed love, told in the form of a folk-tale, episodic and highly coloured.
w Sergo Paradjanov, Ivan Chendei d Sergo Paradjanov ph Y. Ilyenko m M. Sorik
☆ Ivan Nikolaichuk, Larisa Kadochnikova, Tatiana Bestayeva, Spartak Bagashvili

Shadows of the Peacock

Australia 1987 94m colour
Laughing Kookaburra (Jane Scott)
▤

After discovering her husband's infidelity, a politician's wife asserts her independence by going to Thailand and falling for a Balinese dancer.
Slight, bitter-sweet romance, acted and directed at a somnambulistic pace.
w Jan Sharp, Anne Brooksbank d Phillip Noyce ph Peter James m William Motzing pd Judith Russell ed Frans Vandenburg
☆ Wendy Hughes, John Lone, Rod Mullinar, Peta Toppano, Steven Jacobs, Gillian Jones

Shady Lady

US 1945 90m bw
Universal
An elderly cardsharp is persuaded to help the district attorney nab others of his kind.
Poorish comedy which offers its star little support.
w Curt Siodmak, Gerald Geraghty and M. M. Musselman d George Waggner
☆ Charles Coburn, Ginny Simms, Robert Paige, Martha O'Driscoll, Alan Curtis

Shaft *

US 1971 100m Metrocolor
MGM/Shaft Productions (Joel Freeman)
▦ ▤ @.

A black private eye finds himself at odds with a powerful racketeer.
Violent, commercial action thriller which spawned two sequels and a tele-series as well as stimulating innumerable one more violent imitations.
w Ernest Tidyman, John D. F. Black d Gordon Parks ph Urs Furrer m Isaac Hayes
☆ Richard Roundtree, Moses Gunn, Charles Cioffi, Christopher St John
'Relentlessly supercool dialogue, all throwaway colloquialisms and tough Chandlerian wisecracks.' – *MFB*
♪ title song (m/ly Isaac Hayes)
♫ Isaac Hayes (musical score)

Shaft in Africa

US 1973 112m Metrocolor Panavision
MGM/Shaft Productions (Roger Lewis)
Shaft is kidnapped by an Ethiopian emir who wants to track down a gang of slavers.
More miscellaneous violence, rather shoddily assembled, with a few good jokes.
w Stirling Silliphant d John Guillermin ph Marcel Grignon m Johnny Pate ad John Stoll ed Max Benedict
☆ Richard Roundtree, Frank Finlay, Vonetta McGee

Shaft's Big Score!

US 1972 105m Metrocolor Panavision
MGM/Shaft Productions (Richard Lewis, Ernest Tidyman)
▤

Shaft avenges the death of a friend and comes up against the numbers racket.
Violent footage and an incomprehensible plot. No one, least of all the director, shows any interest in the narrative, which is ignored for a succession of action-packed set-pieces, finally settling down into a long chase sequence, in which our hero can dispose of all the villains without anyone trying to make sense of the plot.
w Ernest Tidyman d Gordon Parks ph Urs Furrer m Gordon Parks ad Emanuel Gerard ed Harry Howard
☆ Richard Roundtree, Moses Gunn, Joseph Mascolo, Kathy Imrie, Wally Taylor, Julius W. Harris, Drew Bundini Brown
'Self-conscious, contrived, ambitious and sluggish.' – *Variety*

Shag

GB 1988 100m colour
Palace/Hemdale (Stephen Woolley, Julia Chasman)
▦ ▤ @. ♪

Four girls go to the beach for fun and boys.
Set in the 1960s, it is an attempt, successful enough in its inane way, to revive the style of the teen movies of the time.
w Robin Swicord, Lanier Laney, Terry Sweeney d Zelda Barron ph Peter MacDonald pd Buddy Cone ed Laurence Mery Clark
☆ Phoebe Cates, Scott Coffey, Bridget Fonda, Annabeth Gish, Page Hannah, Robert Rusler, Tyrone Power III, Jeff Yagher

The Shaggy DA

♠♠ US 1976 92m Technicolor
Walt Disney (Ron Miller)
▤

A magic ring enables a young lawyer to become a talking dog and thus expose corruption.
Rather feeble sequel to The Shaggy Dog, with overtones of Watergate.
w Don Tait d Robert Stevenson ph Frank Phillips m Buddy Baker sp Eustace Lycett, Art Cruickshank, Danne Lee
☆ Dean Jones, Tim Conway, Suzanne Pleshette, Jo Anne Worley, Vic Tayback, Keenan Wynn, Dick Van Patten

The Shaggy Dog *

♠♠ US 1959 101m bw
Walt Disney (Bill Walsh)
▤

A small boy turns into a big shaggy dog and catches some crooks.
Simple-minded, overlong Disney comedy for kids and their indulgent parents; good laughs in the chase scenes.
w Bill Walsh, Lillie Hayward novel The Hound of Florence by Felix Salten d Charles Barton ph Edward Colman m Paul Sawtell
☆ Fred MacMurray, Jean Hagen, Tommy Kirk, Cecil Kellaway, Annette Funicello, Tim Considine, Kevin Corcoran, Alexander Scourby

Shake Hands with Murder

US 1944 61m bw
American Productions/PRC
Bailbondsmen get involved in murder.
Tolerable little mystery for the bottom of the bill.
w John T. Neville, Martin Mooney d Albert Herman ph Robert Cline md Lee Zahler
☆ Frank Jenks, Iris Adrian, Douglas Fowley, Jack Raymond

Shake Hands with the Devil *

Eire 1959 110m bw
UA/Troy/Pennebaker (Michael Anderson)
In 1921 Dublin a surgeon is the secret leader of the IRA, and comes to cherish violence as an end rather than a means.
Downbeat action melodrama, politically very questionable but well made.
w Ivan Goff, Ben Roberts novel Rearden Connor d Michael Anderson ph Erwin Hillier m William Alwyn
☆ James Cagney, Glynis Johns, Don Murray, Dana Wynter, Michael Redgrave, Sybil Thorndike, Cyril Cusack, Niall MacGinnis, Richard Harris, Ray McAnally, Noel Purcell

Shake, Rattle & Rock!

US 1956 75m bw
AIP (James H. Nicholson, Samuel Z. Arkoff)
A small-town disc jockey demands a public trial after a vigilante committee is set up to ban rock 'n' roll.
Enjoyable-enough exploitation movie in a familiar groove, notable for the musical performances of Joe Turner ('Lipstick, Powder And Paint') and Fats Domino ('Ain't That A Shame', 'I'm In Love Again'), and Margaret Dumont, Groucho Marx's old adversary, as a killjoy.
w Lou Rusoff d Edward L. Cahn ph Frederick E. West m Alexander Courage ad Don Ament ed Robert S. Eisen, Charles Gross Jnr
☆ Touch Connors, Lisa Gaye, Sterling Holloway, Raymond Hatton, Paul Dubov, Douglass Dumbrille, Clarence Kolb, Margaret Dumont, Frank Jenks, Percy Helton, Tommy Charles, Fats Domino, Annita Ray, Joe Turner

Shakedown: see *Blue Jean Cop* (1988)

Shakedown

US 1950 80m bw
U-I (Ted Richmond)
A ruthless press photographer becomes a blackmailer.
Routine crime melodrama, adequately done.
w Alfred Lewis, Martin Goldsmith d Joseph Pevney ph Irving Glassberg m Joseph Gershenson
☆ Howard Duff, Brian Donlevy, Anne Vernon, Peggy Dow, Lawrence Tierney, Bruce Bennett

The Shakedown

GB 1959 92m bw
Rank/Alliance/Ethiro (Norman Williams)
A Soho vice boss photographs prominent people in compromising situations and blackmails them.
A semi-remake set in the squalid London so beloved of film makers at the time, before it became 'swinging'. Of no interest or entertainment value.
w Leigh Vance d John Lemont ph Brendan J. Stafford m Philip Green
☆ Terence Morgan, Hazel Court, Donald Pleasence, Bill Owen, Robert Beatty, Harry H. Corbett, Gene Anderson, Eddie Byrne

Shaker Run

New Zealand 1985 90m colour
Laurelwood/Aviscom/Mirage (Igo Kantor, Larry Parr)
▤ @.

Two American stunt car drivers help a girl who for the best political reasons has stolen a deadly virus.
Harebrained excuse for car chases against beautiful scenery; quite exhausting.
w James Kouf Jnr, Henry Fownes, Bruce Morrison d Bruce Morrison ph Kevin Hayward m Stephen McCurdy
☆ Cliff Robertson, Leif Garrett, Lisa Harrow, Shane Briant

Shakespeare in Love ***

US 1998 113m DeLuxe
UIP/Miramax/Universal/Bedford Falls (David Parfitt, Donna Gigliotti, Harvey Weinstein, Edward Zwick, Mark Norman)
▦ ▤ @ @ ♪

Shakespeare, suffering writer's block over his new work, Romeo and Ethel, the Pirate's Daughter, is inspired when he falls in love with a cross-dressing heiress.
If movies be the food of love, then there's an excess of it in this delightful romantic comedy, a clever romp that makes witty use of theatrical conventions and Shakespeare's own works; it is not only in love with love, but with the power of theatre.
w Marc Norman, Tom Stoppard d John Madden ph Richard Greatrex m Stephen Warbeck pd Martin Childs ed David Gamble
☆ Gwyneth Paltrow, Joseph Fiennes, Geoffrey Rush, Colin Firth, Ben Affleck, Judi Dench, Rupert Everett, Simon Callow, Jim Carter, Martin Clunes, Antony Sher, Imelda Staunton, Tom Wilkinson, Mark Williams
'A ripely emotional comedy fantasia.' – *David Denby, New Yorker*
'A great success, bawdy, silly, handsome, brainy and energetic.' – *Ian Nathan, Empire*
† The day after the Oscar ceremony, its US box-office income increased by 42 per cent.

†† Judi Dench, winner of the Oscar as best supporting actress, was on-screen for eight minutes.
††† Daniel Day-Lewis and Julia Roberts were the first choices for the roles played by Joseph Fiennes and Gwyneth Paltrow.
♠ best picture; Gwyneth Paltrow; Judi Dench; Marc Norman, Tom Stoppard; Stephen Warbeck; Martin Childs; Sandy Powell (costumes)
♧ John Madden; Geoffrey Rush; Richard Greatrex; David Gamble; make-up; sound
♉ best film; Judi Dench; Geoffrey Rush; David Gamble

Shakespeare Wallah *

India 1965 125m bw
Merchant Ivory (Ismail Merchant)
▤

A troupe of English actors find their Indian tour interrupted by romance.
Interesting but sluggish drama on an unusual subject. Not by any means a classic, but it set off this partnership on an enduring wave of critical acclaim and public indifference.
w Ruth Prawer Jhabvala, James Ivory d James Ivory ph Subrata Mitra m Satyajit Ray
☆ Felicity Kendal, Shashi Kapoor, Laura Liddell, Geoffrey Kendal, Madhur Jaffrey, Utpal Dutt
'Touched by brilliance, marked throughout by grace, it is a quiet film that allows one to perceive the ironies and the poignancy of a time of transition.' – *Judith Crist*

Shakha Proshakha: see *Branches of the Tree*

The Shakiest Gun in the West

♠♠ US 1967 101m Technicolor
Universal (Edward J. Montagne)
▤ @.

A cowardly dentist becomes a Western hero.
Dreary farce, an unsubtle remake of The Paleface.
w Jim Fritzell, Everett Greenbaum d Alan Rafkin ph Andrew Jackson m Vic Mizzy
☆ Don Knotts, Barbara Rhoades, Jackie Coogan, Don Barry

'Sex. Love. Marriage. Infidelity. Happiness. Success. Friendship. Trust. Babies. Work. Deadlines. Parents. Dreams. Money. Hopes. Fears. Secrets. Growing Up. Hanging Out. Hanging In.'

Shaking the Tree

US 1990 107m Astor Color
Hobo/Reality (Robert J. Wilson)
▦ ▤

The lives of a group of old schoolfriends go through changes as they gather for a Christmas reunion.
Tedium sets in early in this examination of the dull lives of uninteresting people.
w Duane Clark, Steven Wilde d Duane Clark ph Ronn Schmidt m David E. Russo ed Martin L. Bernstein
☆ Arye Gross, Gale Hansen, Doug Savant, Steven Wilde, Courteney Cox, Christina Haag
'Lackluster tale of four childhood buddies generates little interest despite competent technical credits all-around and some nice acting turns. The who-cares factor is simply too high.' – *Variety*

Shalako

GB 1968 118m Technicolor Franscope
Kingston/Dimitri de Grunwald (Euan Lloyd)
▦ ▤

New Mexico, 1880: a cowboy acts as guide to European aristocratic big game hunters, but the Indians become annoyed and attack.
A cute idea is given routine treatment; though packed with stars, the action never becomes very exciting despite incidental brutalities.
w J. J. Griffith, Hal Hopper, Scot Finch novel Louis L'Amour d Edward Dmytryk ph Ted Moore m Robert Farnon
☆ Sean Connery, Brigitte Bardot, Jack Hawkins, Stephen Boyd, Peter Van Eyck, Honor Blackman, Eric Sykes, Alexander Knox, Woody Strode, Valerie French

Shall We Dance? **

US 1937 116m bw
RKO (Pandro S. Berman)
▦ ▤ @.

Dancing partners pretend to be married but are not; until they both get the same idea.

A light musical which was full of good things but nevertheless began the decline of Astaire-Rogers films; repetition was obvious, as was ostentation for its own sake, and the audience was expecting too much.
w Allan Scott, Ernest Pagano d Mark Sandrich ph David Abel m/ly George and Ira Gershwin md Nathaniel Shilkret ad Van Nest Polglase
☆ Fred Astaire, Ginger Rogers, Edward Everett Horton, Eric Blore, Harriet Hoctor, Jerome Cowan, Ketti Gallian, Ann Shoemaker

'Another holdover musical in the Astaire-Rogers string ... it has everything it needs in production.' – Variety
♫ song 'They Can't Take That Away From Me'

'He's An Overworked Accountant. She's An Accomplished Dancer. Passion Is About To Find Two Unlikely Partners.'

Shall We Dance? ★★
Japan   1995   119m   colour
Buena Vista/Altamura/Daiei/NTV/Hakuhodo/Nippon Shuppan (Yasuyoshi Tokuma)
An office worker, bored by his job and his marriage, joins a ballroom dancing class.
Charming comedy that makes the familiar seem extraordinarily exotic.
wd Masayuki Suo ph Naoki Kayano m Yoshikazu Suo pd Kyoko Heya ed Junichi Kikuchi
☆ Koji Yakusho, Tamiyo Kusakari, Naoto Takenaka, Eriko Watanabe, Akira Emoto, Yu Tokui, Hiromasa Taguchi, Reiko Kasamura, Hideko Hara

'An enormously sweet-tempered comedy.' – Alexander Walker
† It became the most successful Japanese film shown in the USA.

'What's a little murder between friends?'
Shallow Grave ★★
GB   1994   92m   colour
Rank/Figment/Channel 4/Glasgow Film Fund (Andrew Macdonald)
Three flatmates, who discover that their new tenant has died leaving a suitcase full of money, decide to dispose of the body and keep the cash.
Energetic, fast-moving thriller that maintains its breathless pace to the end and is done with great panache, almost enough to overlook its faults of unconvincing character shifts, unlikely plot developments and its final burst of insufficiently motivated and gratuitous violence.
w John Hodge d Danny Boyle ph Brian Tufano m Simon Boswell pd Kave Quinn ed Masahiro Hirakubo
☆ Kerry Fox, Christopher Eccleston, Ewan McGregor, Ken Stott, Keith Allen, Colin McCredie

'A British thriller of great assurance and fair accomplishment.' – Adam Mars-Jones, Independent
'A masterpiece of creepy terror.' – Stephen Farber, Movieline
⊽ best British film

Shame ★★
Australia   1987   94m   Eastmancolor
Metro/Barron Films/UAA Films (Damien Parer, Paul D. Barron)
A female lawyer uncovers a series of rapes in a small town.
Powerful indictment of male bonding and aggression.
w Beverly Blankenship, Michael Brindley d Steve Jodrell ph Joseph Pickering m Mario Millo pd Phil Peters ed Kerry Regan
☆ Deborra-Lee Furness, Tony Barry, Simone Buchanan, Gillian Jones, Peter Aanensen, Margaret Ford, David Franklin, Bill McClusky

The Shame of a Nation: see Scarface

Shampoo ★
US   1975   110m   Technicolor
Columbia/Persky-Bright/Vista (Warren Beatty)
A Beverly Hills hairdresser seduces his most glamorous clients.
Ugly little sex farce with few laughs but much dashing about and bad language. Its setting on election eve 1968 has made some people think it a political satire.
w Robert Towne, Warren Beatty d Hal Ashby ph Laszlo Kovacs m Paul Simon

☆ Warren Beatty, Julie Christie, Lee Grant, Goldie Hawn, Jack Warden, Tony Bill, Jay Robinson, Carrie Fisher, Brad Dexter

'It has the bursting-with-talent but fuzziness-of-effect aspect of a movie made by a group of friends for their own amusement.' – Richard Combs
♟ Lee Grant
ᐔ script; Jack Warden

Shamus
US   1972   98m   Eastmancolor
Columbia/Robert M. Weitman
A private eye is hired by a wealthy man to recover stolen jewels and find a murderer.
A forties retread with seventies violence; junky stuff, with a few laughs for buffs who can spot the in-jokes.
w Barry Beckerman d Buzz Kulik ph Victor J. Kemper m Jerry Goldsmith
☆ Burt Reynolds, Dyan Cannon, John Ryan, Joe Santos, Giorgio Tozzi, Ron Weyland

'Very hectic, very vividly New York and as idiotic as Reynolds' physical resiliency.' – Judith Crist

Shane ★★★
♟♟ US   1953   118m   Technicolor
Paramount (George Stevens)
A mysterious stranger helps a family of homesteaders.
Archetypal family Western, but much slower and statelier than most, as though to emphasize its own quality, which is evident anyway.
w A. B. Guthrie Jnr novel Jack Schaefer d George Stevens ph Loyal Griggs m Victor Young
☆ Alan Ladd, Jean Arthur, Van Heflin, Jack Palance, Brandon de Wilde, Ben Johnson, Edgar Buchanan, Emile Meyer, Elisha Cook Jnr, John Dierkes

'A kind of dramatic documentary of the pioneer days of the west.' – MFB
'Westerns are better when they're not too self-importantly self-conscious.' – New Yorker, 1975
'Stevens managed to infuse a new vitality, a new sense of realism into the time-worn story through the strength and freshness of his visuals.' – Arthur Knight
♟ Loyal Griggs
ᐔ best picture; A. B. Guthrie Jnr; George Stevens; Jack Palance; Brandon de Wilde

Shangai Joe (dubbed)
Italy/West Germany   1974   96m   colour
CBA/Divina (Ennio Onorati)
A Chinese stranger protects peasants and townspeople from a crooked businessman and his gang.
Spaghetti Western with the added ingredient of martial arts; together with its broadly comic tone, the combination results in rather too many slapstick punch-ups.
w Bitto Albertini, Carlo Alberto Alfieri story Mariano Caiano, Luigi Russo d Bitto Albertini ph Pier Luigi Santi m Mario Chiara ad Riccardo Domenici ed Fausto Ulisse
☆ Klaus Kinski, Cheen Lie, Karin Field, Tommy Polgar, Claudio Giorgi, Paolo Casella, Tom Felleghy, Fortunato Rena

Shanghai
US   1935   77m   bw
(Paramount)
A visiting American lady falls in love with a half caste.
Romantic drama programmer.
w Gene Towne, Graham Baker, Lynn Starling d James Flood ph James Van Trees
☆ Loretta Young, Charles Boyer, Warner Oland, Alison Skipworth, Fred Keating, Charles Grapewin, Walter Kingsford

Shanghai Express ★★★
US   1932   84m   bw
Paramount
A British officer and his old flame meet on a train which is waylaid by Chinese bandits.
Superbly pictorial melodrama which set the pattern for innumerable train movies to come, though none matched its deft visual quality and few sketched in their characters so neatly. Plot and dialogue are silent style, but refreshingly so.

w Jules Furthman d Josef von Sternberg ph Lee Garmes m W. Franke Harling ad Hans Dreier
☆ Marlene Dietrich, Clive Brook, Warner Oland, Anna May Wong, Eugene Pallette, Lawrence Grant, Louise Closser Hale, Gustav von Seyffertitz
LILY (MARLENE DIETRICH): 'It took more than one man to change my name to Shanghai Lily.'

'Good programme picture bolstered by the Dietrich name ... Excellent camerawork overcomes really hoke melodramatic story.' – Variety
'A limited number of characters, all meticulously etched, highly atmospheric sets and innumerable striking photographic compositions.' – Curtis Harrington, 1964
♟ Lee Garmes
ᐔ best picture; Josef von Sternberg

'Shanghai. Where Almost Anything Can Happen ... And Does!'
The Shanghai Gesture ★
US   1941   90m   bw
Arnold Pressburger (Albert de Courville)
The proprietress of a Shanghai gambling casino taunts her ex-husband by showing him his daughter in a state of degradation; but he proves that the girl is her daughter also.
An ancient theatrical shocker was completely bowdlerized and chopped into nonsense for the screen; but the director's hand showed in the handling of the vast casino set.
w Josef von Sternberg, Geza Herczeg, Karl Vollmoeller, Jules Furthman play John Colton d Josef von Sternberg ph Paul Ivano m Richard Hageman ad Boris Leven
☆ Ona Munson, Victor Mature, Walter Huston, Gene Tierney, Albert Basserman, Phyllis Brooks, Maria Ouspenskaya, Eric Blore, Ivan Lebedeff, Mike Mazurki

'The effect of a descent into a maelstrom of iniquity.' – Curtis Harrington, 1962
'In spite of all the changes necessitated by the Hays Office, seldom have decadence and sexual depravity been better suggested on the screen.' – Richard Roud, 1966
'Hilariously, awesomely terrible.' – New Yorker, 1977
ᐔ Richard Hageman; Boris Leven

Shanghai Madness
US   1933   63m   bw
Fox
A naval officer is cashiered in Shanghai and gets mixed up with Communists.
Weakish melodrama which goes the long way round to a happy ending.
w Frederick Hazlitt Brennan, Austin Parker, Gordon Wellesley d John G. Blystone
☆ Spencer Tracy, Fay Wray, Ralph Morgan, Eugene Pallette, Herbert Mundin

'Okay generally but in big spots will need stage support.' – Variety

Shanghai Surprise
GB   1986   97m   Technicolor
HandMade/Vista/John Kohn
A lady missionary hires an adventurer to track down a stack of opium before it falls into the wrong hands.
Astonishingly abysmal adventure romance set rather uncertainly in the 1937 Orient. Nothing matches the so-called talents involved.
w John Kohn, Robert Bentley novel Faraday's Flowers by Tony Kenrick d Jim Goddard ph Ernest Vincze m George Harrison, Michael Kamen
☆ Madonna, Sean Penn, Paul Freeman, Richard Griffiths

'A silly little trifle which wouldn't even have passed muster as a 1930s programmer.' – Variety

'In 1930's Shanghai violence was not the problem. It was the solution.'
Shanghai Triad ★★
Hong Kong   1995   108m   colour
Electric/Shanghai Studio/Alpha/UGC-Images/La Sept (Jean-Louis Piel)
original title: Yao a Yao Yao dao Waipo Qiao
In the 30s, a young country boy goes to work for a gangster's mistress and becomes a witness to a power struggle involving another gang member and a rival triad.

A skilled and colourful account of corruption and betrayal, which avoids on-screen violence for the most part in order to concentrate on its devastating aftermath.
w Bi Feiyu novel Gang Law by Li Xiao d Zhang Yimou ph Lu Yue m Zhang Guangtian pd Cao Jiuping ed Du Yuan
☆ Gong Li, Li Baotian, Wang Xiaoxiao, Li Xuejian, Sun Chun, Fu Biao, Chen Shu, Liu Jiang

'Oozes a confidence that carries the viewer almost without pause to its shocking climax and ironic close.' – Derek Elley, Variety
♟ Lu Yue

Shaolin Martial Arts (dubbed)
Hong Kong   1987   112m   colour   Shaw Scope
Shaw Brothers/Chang's Film Co. (Run Run Shaw)
Followers of the Shaolin school of kung-fu, feared as rebels, are threatened with extinction by the authorities, with the aid of the rival Manchu faction and their two invincible fighters.
Period action film, somewhat staid and old-fashioned by present-day standards but moderately entertaining, with its succession of grumpy, taciturn old men teaching the young how to fight.
w I Kuang, Chang Cheh d Chang Cheh ph Kung Mu-To ed Kuo Ting-Hung
☆ Fu Sheng, Chi Kuan-Chun, Chen I-Ling, Liu Chia Hui, Tang Yen Tsan, Li Chen-Piao, Liang Chia-Jen, Wang Lung-Wei

Shark
US/Mexico   1969   88m   Eastmancolor
Heritage/Cinematografica Calderon
A gunrunner in the Sudan becomes involved with unscrupulous divers after wrecks.
Tepid adventure yarn allegedly damaged by recutting but showing very little sign of original talent.
w Samuel Fuller, John Kingsbridge novel His Bones Are Coral by Victor Canning d Samuel Fuller ph Raul Martinez Solares m Rafael Moroyoqui
☆ Burt Reynolds, Arthur Kennedy, Barry Sullivan, Silvia Pinal, Enrique Lucero

The Sharkfighters
US   1956   72m   Technicolor Cinemascope
(UA) Formosa (Samuel Goldwyn Jnr)
To save the lives of flyers forced down into the sea, navy scientists experiment with a shark repellent.
Straightforward semi-documentary with suspenseful action sequences.
w Lawrence Roman, John Robinson d Jerry Hopper ph Lee Garmes m Jerome Moross
☆ Victor Mature, Karen Steele, James Olson, Claude Akins

Shark's Treasure ★
♟♟ US   1974   95m   DeLuxe
UA/Symbol (Cornel Wilde)
Treasure hunters seek buried gold in the Caribbean where sharks abound.
Fairly thrilling action hokum.
wd Cornel Wilde ph Jack Atcheler, Al Giddings m Robert O. Ragland
☆ Cornel Wilde, Yaphet Kotto, John Neilson, David Canary, Cliff Osmond

'Wilde maintains his reputation for making the most likeable bad movies around.' – Tom Milne

'Some cops are good at opening a case. Sharky knows how to finish one.'
Sharky's Machine
US   1981   120m   Technicolor
Warner/Orion/Deliverance (Hank Moonjean)
A vice squad policeman builds up a new team.
Exceptionally violent cop thriller on the lines of Dirty Harry.
w Gerald Di Pego novel William Diehl d Burt Reynolds ph William A. Fraker md Al Capps
☆ Burt Reynolds, Vittorio Gassman, Brian Keith, Charles Durning, Earl Holliman, Bernie Casey, Henry Silva, Rachel Ward

Sharpshooters
US   1938   63m   bw
TCF
Adventures of a newsreel cameraman who saves a young prince from kidnapping.
Serial-like action and comedy very palatably blended: the first of a short series.

♟♟ film suitable for family viewing   ▦ VHS video-cassette for the British PAL system   ▦ VHS video-cassette for the British PAL system in wide screen-format   ♻ Video cassette in a computer-colourised version   ▤ American NTSC video-cassette   ᐔ Laser disc

w Robert Ellis, Helen Logan d James Tinling
☆ Brian Donlevy, Lynn Bari, Wally Vernon, John King, Douglass Dumbrille, C. Henry Gordon, Sidney Blackmer

'A standard programmer to entertain, and a natural for the juve trade.' – *Variety*

Shatter

GB 1974 90m colour
Hammer (Michael Carreras, Vee King Shaw)
▨

US title: Call Him Mr Shatter
A professional assassin is marked for death by his former employer in Hong Kong.
Botched attempt to combine a thriller with the style of a kung fu movie.
w Don Houghton d Michael Carreras ph Brian Probyn, John Wilcox, Roy Ford m David Lindup ed Eric Boyd-Perkins
☆ Stuart Whitman, Ti Lung, Peter Cushing, Anton Diffring, Lily Li

'Murder Is Never An Accident.'
Shattered *

US 1991 98m Technicolor
Palace/Capella/Davis Entertainment (Wolfgang Petersen, John Davis, David Korda)
▨ ▤ ◎.

Recovering from a car crash that left him with no memory and facial injuries that required plastic surgery, a property developer hires a private eye to discover more about his past.
Clever, unsettling mystery that keeps an audience guessing until the end.
wd Wolfgang Petersen *novel* The Plastic Nightmare by Richard Neely ph Laszlo Kovacs m Angelo Badalamenti pd Gregg Fonseca ed Hannes Nikel, Glenn Farr
☆ Tom Berenger, Greta Scacchi, Bob Hoskins, Joanne Whalley-Kilmer, Corbin Bernsen, Debi A. Monahan, Bert Robario, Scott Getlin, Kellye Nakahara

'A solidly entertaining plot-driven thriller which, although it requires an initial act of faith from its audience, rewards them with an intelligent, satisfying mystery.' – *Nigel Floyd, Sight and Sound*

'Fear can hold you prisoner. Hope can set you free.'
The Shawshank Redemption *

US 1994 142m Technicolor
Rank/Castle Rock (Niki Marvin)
▨ ▤ ◎ ◎ ◠

A banker, wrongly imprisoned for 20 years, and a murderer serving a life sentence revenge themselves on the prison warden who exploits them.
A melodrama of wasted lives and male bonding with a twist ending, more enjoyable for the performances than the narrative, which veers unpredictably between toughness and sentimentality.
wd Frank Darabont *novel* Stephen King ph Roger Deakins m Thomas Newman pd Terence Marsh ed David Francis-Bruce
☆ Tim Robbins, Morgan Freeman, Bob Gunton, William Sadler, Clancy Brown, James Whitmore, Gil Bellows, Mark Rolston, Jeffrey DeMunn

'The movie burns with dubious ardor. No one could disagree with its point of view. No one is likely to be much interested either.' – *David Denby, New York*

'An extremely satisfying entertainment.' – *Entertainment Weekly*
⌕ best picture; Morgan Freeman; Frank Darabont; cinematography; film editing; Thomas Newman

'Young and beautiful for 500 years – and wicked every one of them!'
She *

⚥ US 1935 89m bw
RKO (Merian C. Cooper)
▤

Ancient papers lead a Cambridge professor and his friends to the lost city where dwells a queen who cannot die – until she falls in love.
The producers have the right spirit for this Victorian fantasy, but tried too hard to emulate the mood of their own King Kong, and it was a mistake to transfer the setting from Africa to the Arctic. One for connoisseurs, though.
w Ruth Rose, Dudley Nichols *novel* H. Rider Haggard d Irving Pichel, Lansing G. Holden ph J. Roy Hunt m Max Steiner ch Benjamin Zemach
☆ Randolph Scott, Nigel Bruce, Helen Gahagan

'Beautiful production, but story dubious for discriminating adults.' – *Variety*
'To an unrepentant Haggard fan it does sometimes seem to catch the thrill as well as the childishness of his invention.' – *Graham Greene*
'A spectacle of magnificent proportions with the decadent effluvium of the tomb period.' – *Photoplay*
'The stagey décor of Kor is in the art deco style of Radio City Music Hall, and you keep expecting the Rockettes to turn up.' – *Pauline Kael, 70s*
⌕ Benjamin Zemach

She

⚥ GB 1965 105m Technicolor Hammerscope
ABP/Hammer (Michael Carreras, Aida Young)
▨

Flat, uninventive and tedious remake which reverts to Africa but does nothing else right; it ignores the essential Cambridge prologue and ignores all suggestions of fantasy.
w David T. Chantler *novel* H. Rider Haggard d Robert Day ph Harry Waxman m James Bernard ad Robert Jones, Don Mingaye ed James Needs, Eric Boyd-Perkins
☆ Peter Cushing, Ursula Andress, Christopher Lee, John Richardson, Bernard Cribbins, André Morell, Rosenda Monteros

She Beast

Italy 1965 76m Eastmancolor 'Scope
Leith (Paul M. Maslansky)
original title: La Sorella di Satana
aka: Sister of Satan/Revenge of the Blood Beast
The spirit of a witch killed in the eighteen century possesses the body of an Englishwoman on her honeymoon in Transylvania.
A powerful opening, set in the past, gives way to a modern horror comedy, which is uncertain in tone and hampered by its low budget.
w Michael Byron (Michael Reeves) d Mike Reeves ph G. Gengarelli m Ralph Ferraro ed Nera Omri
☆ Barbara Steele, John Karlsen, Ian Ogilvy, Mel Welles, Jay Riley, Richard Watson, Ed Randolph, Peter Grippe, Lucrezia Love, Tony Antonelli

She Couldn't Say No

US 1952 89m bw
RKO (Robert Sparks)
▤

GB title: Beautiful But Dangerous
An heiress returns to the town of her childhood to distribute anonymous gifts to those who had helped her.
Moderate Capraesque comedy which doesn't quite come off.
w D. D. Beauchamp, William Bowers, Richard Flournoy d Lloyd Bacon ph Harold J. Wild m Roy Webb
☆ Jean Simmons, Robert Mitchum, Arthur Hunnicutt, Edgar Buchanan, Wallace Ford, Raymond Walburn

She Couldn't Take It *

US 1935 89m bw
Columbia (B. P. Schulberg)
A rich old reprobate meets a gangster in prison and puts him in charge of his rebellious family.
Little-known crazy comedy with touches of melodrama; not a success, but with interesting elements.
w Gene Towne, Oliver H. P. Garrett *story* Graham Baker d Tay Garnett ph Leon Shamroy
☆ George Raft, Joan Bennett, Walter Connolly, Billie Burke, Lloyd Nolan, Wallace Ford, Alan Mowbray, Donald Meek

The She Creature

US 1956 77m bw
AIP/Golden State (Alex Gordon)
An evil hypnotist regresses his subject back through time to summon up a murderous prehistoric monster from the sea.
Unusual B movie that concentrates less on the monster and more on its exploitation by a corrupt businessman.
w Lou Rusoff *story* Jerry Zigmond d Edward L. Cahn ph Frederick E. West m Ronald Stein ad Don Ament ed Ronald Sinclair
☆ Chester Morris, Tom Conway, Cathy Downs, Lance Fuller, Ron Randell, Frieda Inescort, Marla English

'Beautiful production, but story dubious for discriminating adults.' – *Variety*

She Didn't Say No!

GB 1958 97m Technicolor
GW Films (Sergei Nolbandov)
A young Irish widow has five illegitimate children, each by a different father.
Coyly daring comedy full of stage Oirishisms and obvious jokes, a few of which work.
w T. J. Morison, Una Troy *novel* We Are Seven by Una Troy d Cyril Frankel ph Gilbert Taylor m Tristram Cary
☆ Eileen Herlie, Jack MacGowran, Perlita Neilson, Niall MacGinnis, Ian Bannen

She Done Him Wrong ***

US 1933 68m bw
Paramount (William Le Baron)
▨ ◎.

A lady saloon keeper of the Gay Nineties falls for the undercover cop who is after her.
As near undiluted Mae West as Hollywood ever came: fast, funny, melodramatic and pretty sexy; also a very atmospheric and well-made movie.
w Mae West *play* Diamond Lil by Mae West (with help on the scenario from Harry Thew, John Bright) d Lowell Sherman ph Charles Lang *songs* Ralph Rainger (m), Leo Robin (ly)
☆ Mae West, Cary Grant, Owen Moore, Gilbert Roland, Noah Beery, David Landau, Rafaela Ottiano, Rochelle Hudson, Dewey Robinson

'Only alternative to a strong drawing cast, nowadays if a picture wants business, is strong entertainment. This one has neither.' – *Variety*
⌕ best picture

She Freak

US 1967 87m colour
David F. Friedman
▨
aka: Alley of Nightmares
A waitress leaves a diner, joins a carnival, marries a freak-show operator and ends up as a sideshow attraction.
Cheap and feeble exploitation movie that takes what little inspiration it has from Tod Browning's Freaks (qv); much of the film was shot without sound and, despite its brevity, is padded out with a great many irrelevant shots of fairground activities.
w David F. Friedman d Byron Mabe ph Bill Troiano m Billy Allen ed Byron Mabe
☆ Claire Brennen, Lee Raymond, Lynn Courtney, Bill McKinney, Claude Smith, Ben Moore, Felix Silla, Bill Bagdad

She Gets Her Man *

US 1945 73m bw
Universal (Warren Wilson)
A country girl in New York tracks down a blowgun murderer.
Disarming mystery farce which tries every slapstick situation known to gag writers, and gets away with it.
w Warren Wilson, Clyde Bruckman d Erle C. Kenton ph Jerry Ash
☆ Joan Davis, William Gargan, Leon Errol, Milburn Stone, Russell Hicks

She Got Her Man: see Maisie (Maisie Gets Her Man)

She Has What It Takes

US 1943 66m bw
Colbert Clark/Columbia
A small-time singer masquerades as the long-lost daughter of a famous stage star.
An excuse for musical padding, for indulgent audiences.
w Paul Yawitz d Charles Barton
☆ Jinx Falkenburg, Tom Neal, Constance Worth, Joe King, The Radio Rogues, The Vagabonds

She Killed in Ecstasy

West Germany 1970 86m colour
Cinerama/Tele-Cine (Rudolph Herzog Jnr)
▨
original title: Sie Tötete in Ekstase
The widow of a doctor, who killed himself after being struck off for experimenting on human embryos, takes revenge on those responsible for his expulsion.
A rarity from this director: a movie with an almost coherent narrative; unfortunately, it is an uninteresting one, being merely a peg on which to hang a few unimaginatively shot scenes of female nudity.
wd Frank Hollman (Jésus Franco) *m* Manuel Merino m Manfred Hübler, Siegfried Schwab ed Clarissa Ambach

☆ Horst Tappert, Susann Korda, Fred Williams, Paul Müller, Howard Vernon, Ewa Stroemberg

She Knew All the Answers

US 1941 84m bw
Charles R. Rogers/Columbia
Prevented by his uncle from marrying a playboy, a chorine falls for the uncle.
Mildly merry comedy which came and went without being noticed.
w Harry Segall, Kenneth Earl, Curtis Kenyon *story* Jane Allen d Richard Wallace
☆ Joan Bennett, Franchot Tone, John Hubbard, Eve Arden, William Tracy

She Learned about Sailors

US 1934 82m bw
Fox
In Shanghai, a couple get married so that they will be permitted to leave; back home, they're not sure they want an annulment.
Mild comedy with music.
w William Conselman, Henry Johnson *story* Randall H. Faye d George Marshall
☆ Alice Faye, Lew Ayres, Harry Green, Frank Mitchell, Jack Durant

'The hi-de-hi of higher education!'
She Loves Me Not *

US 1934 85m bw
Paramount (Benjamin Glazer)
A showgirl murder witness takes refuge in a men's college.
Larky musical farce later remade as True to the Army and How to be Very Very Popular; this first version is perhaps the most nearly amusing.
w Ben Glazer *play* Howard Lindsay *novel* Edward Hope d Elliott Nugent ph Charles Lang *songs* various
☆ Bing Crosby, Miriam Hopkins, Kitty Carlisle, Edward Nugent, Lynne Overman, Henry Stephenson, Warren Hymer, George Barbier
⌕ song 'Love in Bloom' (mRalph Rainger, lyLeo Robin)

She Married an Artist

US 1938 78m bw
Columbia
A wife becomes jealous of her husband's models.
Very mild romantic comedy.
w Avery Strakosch, Delmer Daves, Gladys Lehman d Marion Gering
☆ John Boles, Frances Drake, Albert Dekker

She Married Her Boss

US 1935 90m bw
Columbia
A secretary marries her boss and finds herself taken for granted.
Pleasant but rather thin romantic comedy with amiable stars.
w Sidney Buchman d Gregory La Cava ph Leon Shamroy
☆ Claudette Colbert, Melvyn Douglas, Raymond Walburn, Edith Fellows, Jean Dixon, Katherine Alexander

She Played with Fire: see Fortune is a Woman

She Shall Have Murder

GB 1950 90m bw
Concanen/IFD
A law clerk helps to solve the murder of an elderly client.
Old-fashioned light comedy whodunnit, the equivalent of reading a Crime Club thriller.
w Allan Mackinnon *novel* Delano Ames d Daniel Birt ph Robert Navarro m Eric Spear
☆ Rosamund John, Derrick de Marney, Mary Jerrold, Felix Aylmer, Joyce Heron, Beatrice Varley

She Shall Have Music

GB 1935 91m bw
Twickenham (Julius Hagen)
A band leader helps prevent dirty doings at sea.
A story that is no more than an excuse for a series of dull production numbers by Jack Hylton's Band and assorted singers.
w H. Fowler Mear, Arthur Macrae *story* Paul England d Leslie Hiscott ph Sydney Blythe, William Luff ad James Carter
☆ Claude Dampier, June Clyde, Jack Hylton

◉ Digital Video Disc Region 2   ◉ Digital Video Disc Region 1   ◠ Soundtrack released on compact disc   ☆ Cast in approximate order of importance   † Points of interest   ♫ Notable songs   ⌕ Academy Award   ⌕ Academy Award nomination   ▨ BAFTA

She Wanted a Millionaire
US   1932   74m   bw
Fox
A girl spurns her childhood sweetheart for a rich man who turns out to be dangerous.
Curious comedy-melodrama which confuses its watchers.
w Sonya Levien *story* William Anthony McGuire d John G. Blystone
☆ Joan Bennett, Spencer Tracy, James Kirkwood, Una Merkel, Dorothy Peterson

'Beauty or beast? Woman or monster?'

She Wolf of London
US   1946   61m   bw
Universal
GB title: *The Curse of the Allenbys*
A girl thinks she must be the family werewolf.
Risibly inept semi-horror melodrama with a highly implausible solution and poor production.
w George Bricker d Jean Yarbrough
☆ June Lockhart, Don Porter, Sara Haden, Lloyd Corrigan, Dennis Hoey, Martin Kosleck

She Wore a Yellow Ribbon **
US   1949   103m   Technicolor
RKO/Argosy (John Ford, Merian C. Cooper)
Problems of a cavalry officer about to retire.
Fragmentary but very enjoyable Western with all Ford ingredients served piping hot.
w Frank Nugent, Laurence Stallings *story* James Warner Bellah d John Ford ph Winton C. Hoch m Richard Hageman
☆ *John Wayne, Joanne Dru, John Agar, Ben Johnson, Harry Carey Jnr, Victor McLaglen, Mildred Natwick, George O'Brien, Arthur Shields*
🎬 Winton C. Hoch

She Wouldn't Say Yes
US   1945   87m   bw
Columbia
A lady psychiatrist falls for the subject of an experiment.
Star comedy vehicle which falls rather flat.
w Laszlo Gorog, William Thiele, Virginia Van Upp, John Jacoby, Sarett Tobias d Alexander Hall
☆ Rosalind Russell, Lee Bowman, Charles Winninger, Adele Jergens

She Wrote the Book
US   1946   72m   bw
Universal
A lady professor imagines herself to be the glamorous femme fatale heroine of a lurid novel.
Adventures of a female Walter Mitty; one of the star's better comedies.
w Warren Wilson, Oscar Brodney d Charles Lamont
☆ Joan Davis, Mischa Auer, Jack Oakie, Kirby Grant, John Litel, Gloria Stuart, Thurston Hall

She-Devil
US   1989   99m   DuArt
Rank/Orion (Jonathan Brett, Susan Seidelman)
An unattractive housewife takes her revenge when her husband leaves her for a glamorous romantic novelist.
Unsuccessful and bland adaptation of the sour comedy of the original.
w Barry Strugatz, Mark R. Burns *novel The Life and Loves of a She-Devil* by Fay Weldon d Susan Seidelman ph Oliver Stapleton m Howard Shore pd Santo Loquasto ed Craig McKay
☆ Meryl Streep, Roseanne Barr, Ed Begley Jnr, Sylvia Miles, Linda Hunt, Elisebeth Peters, Bryan Larkin, A. Martinez

'Guts As Hard As The Steel Of Their 'Hogs'!'

She-Devils On Wheels
US   1968   83m   colour
Mayflower Pictures/Herschell Gordon Lewis
A gang of female bikers indulge in sex and violence, including the decapitation of a rival male biker.
Ineptly written, poorly acted, photographed and directed – a sort of inferior home movie – it reveals that a cult reputation is not necessarily an indication of talent.
w Louise Downe d Herschell Gordon Lewis ph Roy Collodi m Larry Wellington pd Robert Enrietto ed Richard Brinkman

☆ Betty Connell, Nancy Lee Noble, Christie Wagner, Rodney Bedell

'When paradise became a battleground, she led the fight for survival!'

Sheena, Queen of the Jungle
🎪 US   1984   115m   Metrocolor
Panavision
Columbia/Delphi II (Paul Aratow)
Orphaned when her explorer parents are killed, a white girl is raised by an African tribe.
Female Tarzan stuff from a comic strip, smoothly made but too rough and slightly too sexy for the family audience which must have been intended.
w David Newman, Lorenzo Semple Jnr d John Guillermin ph Pasqualino de Santis m Richard Hartley
☆ Tanya Roberts, Ted Wass, Donovan Scott

The Sheep Has Five Legs *
France   1954   96m   bw
Raoul Ploquin
original title: *Le Mouton a Cinq Pattes*
A town seeking publicity tries to bring together the five quintuplet grandsons of its oldest inhabitant.
Mildly saucy star vehicle which was in fact most notable for introducing Fernandel to an international audience.
w Albert Valentin d Henri Verneuil ph Armand Thirard m Georges Van Parys
☆ Fernandel, Françoise Arnoul, Delmont, Paulette Dubost, Louis de Funès
§ original story

The Sheepman *
US   1958   91m   Metrocolor   Cinemascope
MGM (Edmund Grainger)
A tough sheep farmer determines to settle in a cattle town.
Easy-going Western with humorous moments.
w William Bowers, James Edward Grant d George Marshall m Robert Bronner m Jeff Alexander
☆ Glenn Ford, Shirley MacLaine, Leslie Nielsen, Mickey Shaughnessy, Edgar Buchanan
§ script

'When an Arab sees a woman he wants, he takes her!' – *ancient Arabian proverb*
'A photoplay of tempestuous love between a madcap English beauty and a bronzed Arab chief!'

The Sheik *
US   1921   73m   bw   silent
Famous Players-Lasky/George Melford
An English heiress falls for a desert chieftain.
Archetypal romantic tosh which set the seal on Valentino's superstardom.
w Monte M. Katterjohn *novel* E. M. Hull d George Melford ph William Marshall
☆ *Rudolph Valentino, Agnes Ayres, Adolphe Menjou, Walter Long, Lucien Littlefield*
† *Son of the Sheik*, released in 1926, was even more popular.

The Sheik Steps Out
US   1937   68m   bw
Republic (Herman Schlom)
A modern sheik has a riotous time in the big city.
Uninventive spoof of the Valentino myth.
w Adele Buffington, Gordon Kahn d Irving Pichel ph Jack Marta md Alberto Colombo
☆ Ramon Novarro, Lola Lane, Gene Lockhart, Kathleen Burke, Stanley Fields
'Novarro in a comeback start. An action picture of the desert for the lower half of the duals.' – *Variety*

She'll Be Wearing Pink Pajamas
GB   1985   90m   Eastmancolor
Virgin/Pink Pajamas/Film Four International (Tara Prem, John Goldschmidt)
Women go on an outdoor survival course.
Basically an excuse for a lot of female nattering; it might have seemed more appealing under a more sensible title.
w Eva Hardy d John Goldschmidt ph Clive Tickner m John Du Prez pd Colin Pocock ed Richard Key
☆ Julie Walters, Anthony Higgins, Jane Evers, Janet Henfrey, Paula Jacobs

She'll Have to Go
GB   1962   90m   bw
Anglo-Amalgamated/Asher Brothers
US title: *Maid to Murder*
Two brothers plan to murder the woman who has inherited their home; when they meet her, both decide to marry her.
A ponderous farce: instead of the needed lightness of touch, there is a great deal of mugging from its cast, who are all determined to let the audience know it's meant to be funny.
w Ian Stuart Black, John Waterhouse *play We Must Kill Toni* by Ian Stuart Black d Robert Asher ph Jack Asher m Philip Green ed Gerry Hambling
☆ Bob Monkhouse, Alfred Marks, Hattie Jacques, Anna Karina, Dennis Lotis, Clive Dunn, Peter Butterworth, Graham Stark, Hugh Lloyd, Harry Locke

'A woman's dangerous and erotic journey beneath...'

The Sheltering Sky **
GB/Italy   1990   138m   Technicolor
Technovision
Palace/Sahara Company/TAO Film/Recorded Picture Company/Aldrich Group (Jeremy Thomas)
An American couple wander through North Africa in search of themselves.
Austere, stunningly photographed movie that yields rewards if approached on its own terms.
w Mark Peploe, Bernardo Bertolucci *novel* Paul Bowles d Bernardo Bertolucci ph Vittorio Storaro m Ryuichi Sakamoto, Richard Horowitz pd Gianni Silvestri ed Gabriella Cristiani
☆ Debra Winger, John Malkovich, Campbell Scott, Jill Bennett, Timothy Spall, Eric Vu-An, Amina Annabi, Philippe Morier-Genoud, Paul Bowles
'It refuses to indulge those who believe movies should be easy and edifying, with characters worth snuggling up to.' – *Richard Corliss, Time*

Shenandoah **
US   1965   105m   Technicolor
Universal (Robert Arthur)
How the American Civil War affected the lives of a Virginia family.
Surprisingly hard-centred and moving semi-Western for the family; excellent performances and well-controlled mood.
w James Lee Barrett d Andrew V. McLaglen ph William Clothier m Frank Skinner md Joseph Gershenson
☆ James Stewart, Rosemary Forsyth, Doug McClure, Glenn Corbett, Katharine Ross, Philip Alford

Shepherd of the Hills *
US   1941   98m   Technicolor
Paramount/Jack Moss
Ozarkian backwoodsmen enjoy their lifestyle except for the intrusions of the revenue men and a mysterious stranger.
Early colour adaptation of a long-favourite American story, deliberately styled for rural audiences.
w Grover Jones, Stuart Anthony *novel* Harold Bell Wright Jnr d Henry Hathaway ph Charles Lang Jnr, W. Howard Greene m Gerard Carbonara
☆ John Wayne, Betty Field, Harry Carey, Beulah Bondi, James Barton, Samuel S. Hinds, Marjorie Main, Ward Bond, Marc Lawrence, John Qualen, Fuzzy Knight

The Sheriff of Fractured Jaw
🎪 GB   1958   103m   Eastmancolor
Cinemascope
TCF/Daniel M. Angel
A London gunsmith in the old west accidentally becomes a hero.
Tame, predictable comedy with a clear lack of invention.
w Arthur Dales d Raoul Walsh ph Otto Heller m Robert Farnon
☆ Kenneth More, Jayne Mansfield, Robert Morley, Ronald Squire, David Horne, Henry Hull, Eynon Evans, Bruce Cabot, William Campbell

Sherlock Holmes
The innumerable Sherlock Holmes films are noted in *Filmgoer's Companion*, and in this volume the appropriate films are listed under their own titles

including the modernized dozen made in the forties by Universal, starring Basil Rathbone as Holmes and Nigel Bruce as Watson. These followed on from Fox's two period pieces, *The Hound of the Baskervilles* and *The Adventures of Sherlock Holmes* (qv). The series started and ended somewhat lamely but several of the episodes remain highly enjoyable, for performances and dialogue rather than plot or pacing. All but the first were directed by Roy William Neill.

1942 Sherlock Holmes and the Voice of Terror (d John Rawlins, with Reginald Denny, Thomas Gomez), Sherlock Holmes and the Secret Weapon (L)* (with Lionel Atwill as Moriarty)
1943 Sherlock Holmes in Washington (V)* (with Henry Daniell, George Zucco), Sherlock Holmes Faces Death (V, L)** (with Halliwell Hobbes, Dennis Hoey)
1944 Sherlock Holmes and the Spider Woman (V)** (with Gale Sondergaard, Dennis Hoey), The Scarlet Claw** (with Gerald Hamer), The Pearl of Death** (with Miles Mander, Dennis Hoey, Rondo Hatton)
1945 The House of Fear* (with Aubrey Mather, Dennis Hoey), The Woman in Green (L)* (with Henry Daniell as Moriarty), Pursuit to Algiers (with Martin Kosleck)
1946 Terror by Night (V)* (with Alan Mowbray), Dressed to Kill (GB title: Sherlock Holmes and the Secret Code (V); with Patricia Morison)

Sherlock Holmes: see *The Adventures of Sherlock Holmes (1939)*

Sherlock Holmes *
US   1932   68m   bw
Fox
Moriarty brings Chicago gangsters into London.
Interesting but rather unsatisfactory Holmes adventure.
w Bertram Milhauser d William K. Howard ph George Barnes
☆ Clive Brook, Reginald Owen, Ernest Torrence, Miriam Jordan, Alan Mowbray, Herbert Mundin
'Old-fashioned artificial stage play with modern trimmings that only muddle it. The interpolated modern gangster angle will mystify the mugs who go for underworld and it's a late day to offer the Conan Doyle thing straight to educated clienteles.' – *Variety*

Sherlock Holmes and the Secret Code: see *Dressed to Kill (1946)*

Sherlock Holmes and the Secret Weapon *
US   1942   68m   bw
Universal (Howard Benedict)
Sherlock Holmes saves a stolen bombsight from Nazi agents.
Slightly stiff modernized Holmes story with amusing ingredients.
w Edward T. Lowe, W. Scott Darling, Edmund L. Hartmann, vaguely based on *The Dancing Men* by Sir Arthur Conan Doyle d Roy William Neill ph Les White m Frank Skinner
☆ Basil Rathbone, Nigel Bruce, Lionel Atwill, Dennis Hoey, Karen Verne, William Post Jnr, Mary Gordon

Sherlock Holmes and the Spider Woman: see *Spider Woman*

Sherlock Holmes and the Voice of Terror
US   1942   65m   bw
Universal (Howard Benedict)
Sherlock Holmes unmasks a Lord Haw Haw in the war cabinet.
Fairly risible first entry in the modernized series, with a Hollywood view of London and a singular haircut for the star.
w Lynn Riggs *story His Last Bow* by Sir Arthur Conan Doyle d John Rawlins ph Woody Bredell m Frank Skinner
☆ Basil Rathbone, Nigel Bruce, Hillary Brooke, Reginald Denny, Evelyn Ankers, Montagu Love, Thomas Gomez, Mary Gordon

Sherlock Holmes: Dressed to Kill: see *Dressed to Kill (1946)*

Sherlock Holmes Faces Death **
US 1943 68m bw
Universal (Roy William Neill)
📀 &

Weird murders occur in a convalescent home for retired officers.
One of the better entries in this rather likeable modernized series; fairly close to the original story except that the events don't make a lot of sense.
w Bertram Millhauser *story The Musgrave Ritual* by Sir Arthur Conan Doyle d Roy William Neill ph Charles Van Enger m Hans Salter
☆ Basil Rathbone, Nigel Bruce, Hillary Brooke, Milburn Stone, Halliwell Hobbes, Arthur Margetson, Dennis Hoey, Gavin Muir, Frederic Worlock, Olaf Hytten, Gerald Hamer, Mary Gordon, Vernon Downing

Sherlock Holmes in Washington *
US 1943 70m bw
Universal (Howard Benedict)
📀

Sherlock Holmes flies west and prevents Nazi spies from grabbing a microfilmed document concealed in a match folder.
Moderate adventure in the modernized series, with a good beginning and end but a sag in the middle.
w Bertram Millhauser, Lynn Riggs d Roy William Neill ph Lester White m Frank Skinner
☆ Basil Rathbone, Nigel Bruce, Henry Daniell, George Zucco, Marjorie Lord, John Archer, Gavin Muir

Sherlock Junior **
👫 US 1924 45m bw silent
Metro/Buster Keaton (Joseph M. Schenck)
📀 📀 &

A film projectionist, unjustly accused of stealing a watch, has dreams of being a great detective.
Fast-moving, gag-filled comedy which ranks among its star's best.
w Clyde Bruckman, Jean Havez, Joseph Mitchell ph Elgin Lessley, Byron Houck d/ed Buster Keaton
☆ Buster Keaton, Kathryn McGuire, Ward Crane, Joseph Keaton

'There's more to attraction than meets the eye.'
She's All That
US 1999 96m DeLuxe
Miramax/Tapestry/Film Colony (Peter Abrams, Robert L. Levy, Richard N. Gladstein)
📀 📀

Smarting after losing his girlfriend, a high school student bets that he can make even the unlikiest girl into the prom queen.
Familiar variation on Pygmalion, the sort of tale that has been a staple of romantic comedies for generations; all that happens here is that it is combined with equally familiar high-school clichés.
w R. Lee Fleming Jnr d Robert Iscove ph Francis Kenny m Stewart Copeland pd Charles Breen ed Casey O Rohrs
☆ Freddie Prinze Jnr, Rachael Leigh Cook, Matthew Lillard, Paul Walker, Jodi Lyn O'Keefe, Kevin Pollak, Anna Paquin, Kieran Culkin, Elden Henson, Usher Raymond, Kimberly 'Lil' Kim' Jones, Gabrielle Union, Dule Hill
'Feels like it could have been made by a team of septuagenarians from the glory days of American Intl. Pictures. The overall mood is one of condescension to the milieu, the material and teen filmgoers.' – *Godfrey Cheshire, Variety*

She's Got Everything
US 1937 70m bw
RKO
A young woman in debt meets a stuffed shirt coffee planter.
Mild comedy which never seems to jell despite the talent assembled.
w Harry Segall, Maxwell Shane d Joseph Santley
☆ Ann Sothern, Gene Raymond, Victor Moore, Helen Broderick, Parkyakarkus, Billy Gilbert

She's Gotta Have It
US 1986 84m bw/colour
40 Acres And A Mule Filmworks (Shelton J. Lee)
📀 📀 & 🎧

Three men woo the same woman.
Smart, but ultimately tiresome, comedy as the men explain one-by-one and then together why each would make the perfect lover.
wd Spike Lee ph Ernest Dickerson m Bill Lee pd Wynn Thomas ed Spike Lee

☆ Tracy Camilla Johns, Tommy Redmon Hicks, John Canada Terrell, Raye Dowell, Joie Lee, Spike Lee

She's My Lovely: see Get Hep to Love

She's Out of Control
US 1989 95m CFI color
Columbia TriStar/Weintraub Entertainment (Stephen Deutsch)
📀 📀 & 🎧

A widower follows the advice of a psychiatrist in trying to control the sex life of his teenage daughter.
Lifeless and singularly witless comedy.
w Seth Winston, Michael J. Nathanson d Stan Dragoti ph Donald Peterman m Alan Silvestri pd David L. Snyder ed Dov Hoenig
☆ Tony Danza, Catherine Hicks, Wallace Shawn, Dick O'Neill, Ami Dolenz, Laura Mooney, Derek McGrath, Dana Ashbrook
'The movie begins shakily and ends feebly, but, in between, is often sharp and funny.' – *Philip French, Observer*

'The story of one outrageous woman. Caught between two men. Both of them certain of one thing...'
She's So Lovely
US/France 1997 97m colour
Miramax/Clyde is Hungry/Hachette (Rene Cleitman)
📀 📀

A wife and mother is forced to choose between her husband and her violent former husband, who has been released from a mental institution after ten years.
An unconvincing triangular love story with overheated performances; the script was written more than 20 years ago and it shows its age.
w John Cassavetes d Nick Cassavetes ph Thierry Arbogast m Joseph Vitarelli pd David Wasco ed Petra Van Oeffelen
☆ Sean Penn, Robin Wright Penn, John Travolta, Harry Dean Stanton, Debi Mazar, James Gandolfini, Gena Rowlands, Kelsey Mulrooney
'A vastly uneven, only intermittently enjoyable film.' – *Variety*

'A film about love, marriage, happiness ... and the little distractions in between.'
She's the One *
US 1996 96m DeLuxe Panavision
TCF/Good Machine/Marlboro (Ted Hope, James Schamus, Edward Burns)
📀 📀 & 🎧

Two brothers with marital problems come to blows before they resolve their troubles.
Much in the vein of Burns's first film, The Brothers McMullen (qv), this explores the interaction between members of a family, in which women provide the catalyst for some soul-searching.
wd Edward Burns ph Frank Prinzi m Tom Petty pd William Barclay ed Susan Graef
☆ Jennifer Aniston, Maxine Bahns, Edward Burns, Cameron Diaz, John Mahoney, Mike McGlone, Anita Gillette
'While it is never quite as funny or sassy as its credentials promise, it still makes for an easy-going diversion.' – *Empire*

'She shakes the student body like it's never been shook before!'
She's Working Her Way through College
US 1952 101m Technicolor
Warner (William Jacobs)
A burlesque queen goes to college and brings out the beast in an English professor.
Limp and vulgar musical remake of a well-liked play and film; just about gets by as a lowbrow timekiller.
w Peter Milne *play The Male Animal* by James Thurber, Elliott Nugent d Bruce Humberstone ph Wilfrid Cline md Ray Heindorf ch Le Roy Prinz *songs* Sammy Cahn, Vernon Duke
☆ Virginia Mayo, Ronald Reagan, Don Defore, Gene Nelson, Phyllis Thaxter, Patrice Wymore
† Sequel 1953: *She's Back on Broadway.*

The She-Wolf
US 1931 90m bw
Universal
A woman gets rich but neglects her children.
Talkative filmed play, almost redeemed by its star performance.

w Winifred Dunn *play Mother's Millions* by Winifred Dunn d James Flood
☆ May Robson, James Hall, Lawrence Gray, Frances Dade

Shichi-nin no Samurai: see Seven Samurai

Shidi Chuma: see The Young Master

Shiloh
👫 US 1996 93m colour
Utopia/Carl Borack/Zeta (Zane W. Levitt, Dale Rosenbloom)
📀 📀

A young boy takes care of a runaway beagle, owned by a cruel hunter.
Amiable, predictable tale of puppy love.
wd Dale Rosenbloom *novel* Phyllis Reynolds Naylor ph Frank Byers m Joel Goldsmith pd Amy Ancona ed Mark Westmore
☆ Michael Moriarty, Rod Steiger, Blake Heron, Scott Wilson, Bonnie Bartlett, Ann Dowd

Shine ***
Australia/GB 1996 105m Cinevex
Buena Vista/AFFC/Momentum/SAFC/Film Victoria (Jane Scott)
📀 📀 & ⊚ ⊚ 🎧

A promising classical pianist, dominated by his anxious and repressive father, suffers a mental breakdown, from which he is eventually rescued by an unexpected love.
Moving, superbly acted drama of tragedy and redemption that brilliantly evokes a man's alienation from his roots and his disintegration, as well as his re-emergence into the world.
w Jan Sardi *story* Scott Hicks d Scott Hicks ph Geoffrey Simpson m David Hirschfelder pd Vicki Niehus ed Pip Karmel
☆ Geoffrey Rush, Armin Mueller-Stahl, Noah Taylor, Lynn Redgrave, Googie Withers, Sonia Todd, Nicholas Bell, John Gielgud, Chris Haywood
'A throwback to the best of old-fashioned Hollywood movies, able to move an audience without insulting it in the process.' – *Kenneth Turan, Los Angeles Times*
† The film is based on the life of pianist David Helfgott, who embarked on an international concert tour following the film's release, and also played at the Oscars award ceremony in 1997.
†† It won nine Australian Film Institute awards, including best picture, best director, best actor (Geoffrey Rush) and best original screenplay.
👤 Geoffrey Rush
& best picture; Scott Hicks (as director and writer); Jan Sardi; Armin Mueller-Stahl; David Hirschfelder; Pip Karmel
🏆 Geoffrey Rush

Shine on Harvest Moon *
US 1944 112m bw (Technicolor sequence)
Warner (William Jacobs)
The life and times of vaudeville singer Nora Bayes.
Standard ragtime biopic, very adequately made.
w Sam Hellman, Richard Weil, Francis Swan, James Kern d David Butler ph Arthur Edeson md Heinz Roemheld
☆ Ann Sheridan, Dennis Morgan, Jack Carson, Irene Manning, S. Z. Sakall, Marie Wilson, Robert Shayne

The Shining *
GB 1980 119m colour
Warner/Stanley Kubrick
📀 📀 &

Under the influence of a desolate hotel where murders had occurred, a caretaker goes berserk and threatens his family.
Uninteresting ghost story sparked by meticulous detail and sets but finally vitiated by overlength and an absurdly over-the-top star performance.
w Stanley Kubrick, Diane Johnson *novel* Stephen King d Stanley Kubrick ph John Alcott m Bela Bartok (on record) pd Roy Walker
☆ Jack Nicholson, Shelley Duvall, Danny Lloyd, Barry Nelson, Scatman Crothers, Philip Stone
'The truly amazing question is why a director of Kubrick's stature would spend his time and effort on a novel that he changes so much it's barely recognizable, taking away whatever originality it possessed while emphasizing its banality. The answer presumably is that Kubrick was looking for a "commercial" property he could impose his own vision on, and Warners, not having learned

its lesson with Barry Lyndon, was silly enough to let him do it.' – *Variety*
'A grandiose horror tale which consumes itself, snake-like, swallowing its own tail in a series of narrowing spirals.' – *Sunday Times*

The Shining Hour
US 1938 76m bw
MGM
A night-club dancer marries a gentleman farmer, but has trouble with his family.
Overcast melodrama with insufficient basic interest in the characters.
w Ogden Nash, Jane Murfin *play* Keith Winter d Frank Borzage
☆ Joan Crawford, Melvyn Douglas, Margaret Sullavan, Robert Young, Fay Bainter, Allyn Joslyn, Hattie McDaniel
'A confused jumble of cross-purpose motivations and situations that fail entirely to arouse interest.' – *Variety*

'He needed to trust her with his secret. She had to trust him with her life.'
Shining Through
US 1992 132m Panavision
TCF/Peter V. Miller Investment Corp/Sandollar (Howard Rosenman, Carol Baum)
📀 📀 & 🎧

A secretary recalls how she fell in love with a lawyer and became an American spy in wartime Berlin.
Glossily romantic thriller, not only soft-centred but also coated in marshmallow.
wd David Seltzer *novel* Susan Isaacs ph Jan de Bont m Michael Kamen pd Anthony Pratt ed Craig McKay
☆ Michael Douglas, Melanie Griffith, Liam Neeson, Joely Richardson, John Gielgud
'Little more than a big, brassy Hallmark card with a World War II backdrop.' – *Variety*
'Fun, in an extravagant, hopelessly retrograde fashion.' – *Janet Maslin, New York Times*

Shining Victory
US 1941 80m bw
Warner (Robert Lord)
A psychiatrist is torn between love and duty.
Adequate romantic programmer.
w Howard Koch, Anne Froelick *play Jupiter Laughs* by A. J. Cronin d Irving Rapper ph James Wong Howe m Max Steiner
☆ James Stephenson, Geraldine Fitzgerald, Donald Crisp, Barbara O'Neil, Montagu Love, Sig Rumann

Shinjuku Dorobo Nikki: see Diary of a Shinjuku Thief

Ship Ahoy
US 1942 95m bw
MGM (Jack Cummings)
📀
On a trip to Puerto Rico, a tap dancer is enlisted as a spy.
Tepid musi-comedy.
w Harry Clork d Eddie Buzzell ph Leonard Smith md George Stoll ad Merrill Pye
☆ Eleanor Powell, Red Skelton, Bert Lahr, Virginia O'Brien, William Post Jnr, James Cross

Ship Café
US 1935 65m bw
Harold Hurley/Paramount
A singing stoker wins a rich girl.
Musical star vehicle of the lower class.
w Harlan Thompson, Herbert Fields d Robert Florey
☆ Carl Brisson, Arline Judge, Mady Christians, William Frawley, Eddie Davis

Ship of Fools ***
US 1965 150m bw
Columbia/Stanley Kramer
📀 &
In 1933 a German liner leaves Vera Cruz for Bremerhaven with a mixed bag of passengers.
Ambitious, serious, quite fascinating slice-of-life shipboard multi-melodrama. Capable mounting, memorable performances and a bravura finale erase memories of padding and symbolic pretensions.
w Abby Mann *novel* Katherine Anne Porter d Stanley Kramer ph Ernest Laszlo m Ernest Gold

☆ Vivien Leigh, Simone Signoret, Oskar Werner, Heinz Ruhmann, José Ferrer, Lee Marvin, Elizabeth Ashley, Michael Dunn, George Segal, Jose Greco, Charles Korvin, Alf Kjellin, Werner Klemperer, John Wengraf, Lilia Skala and also Karen Verne

GLOCKEN (MICHAEL DUNN): 'My name is Karl Glocken, and this is a ship of fools. I'm a fool. You'll meet more fools as we go along. This tub is packed with them. Emancipated ladies and ballplayers. Lovers. Dog lovers. Ladies of joy. Tolerant Jews, Dwarfs. All kinds. And who knows – if you look closely enough, you may even find yourself on board!'

'When you're not being hit over the head with the symbolism, you're being punched in the stomach by would-be inventive camera work while the music score unremittingly fills your nostrils with acrid exhalations.' – *John Simon*

'There is such wealth of reflection upon the human condition, so subtle an orchestration of the elements of love and hate, that it is not fair to tag this with the label of any other film.' – *New York Times*

🕴 Ernest Laszlo

🏆 best picture; Abby Mann; Simone Signoret; Oskar Werner; Michael Dunn

The Ship that Died of Shame

GB 1955 91m bw

Ealing (Michael Relph)

📼

The wartime crew of a motor gunboat buy the vessel and go into postwar business as smugglers.
Thin and rather obvious melodramatic fable.
w John Whiting, Michael Relph, Basil Dearden *novel* Nicholas Monsarrat *d* Basil Dearden *ph* Gordon Dines *m* William Alwyn
☆ Richard Attenborough, George Baker, Bill Owen, Virginia McKenna, Roland Culver, Bernard Lee, Ralph Truman, John Chandos

'A sentimental fantasy tacked on to a basically conventional thriller.' – *Penelope Houston*

A Ship to India *

Sweden 1947 102m bw

Sveriges Folkbiografer (Lorens Marmstedt)

original title: *Skepp Till Indialand*

aka: *The Land of Desire*

A hunchbacked sailor, returning after seven years at sea and searching for the woman he loved, recalls how the affair began after his father, a bullying tugboat captain, brought her aboard.
Despite the movie's low-budget origins, a sombre, claustrophobic and complex study of relationships and damaged lives which builds to a hopeful ending.
wd Ingmar Bergman *play* Martin Soederhjelm *ph* Goran Strindberg *m* Erland von Koch *ad* O. A. Lundgren *ed* Tage Holmberg
☆ Holger Lowenadler, Anna Lindahl, Birger Malmsten, Gertrud Fridh, Naemi Briese, Hjordis Pettersson

The Ship Was Loaded: see *Carry On Admiral*

Shipbuilders

GB 1943 89m bw

British National

A cavalcade of the problems of a Clydeside tycoon in the thirties.
Plodding propaganda piece ending with masters and unions working for Britain.
w Gordon Wellesley, Stephen Potter, Reginald Pound *d* John Baxter
☆ Clive Brook, Morland Graham, Finlay Currie, Maudie Edwards

Shipmates Forever

US 1935 124m bw

Warner

An admiral's son disappoints his dad by preferring song and dance to the navy.
Very stretched light musical without any overpowering talents.
w Delmer Daves *d* Frank Borzage
☆ Dick Powell, Ruby Keeler, Lewis Stone, Ross Alexander, Eddie Acuff, Dick Foran

Ships with Wings *

GB 1941 103m bw

Ealing (S. C. Balcon)

📼

Aircraft carriers prepare for World War II.
Historically interesting, dramatically insubstantial flagwaver.

---

w Sergei Nolbandov, Patrick Kirwan, Austin Melford, Diana Morgan *d* Sergei Nolbandov *ph* Max Greene, Eric Cross, Roy Kellino, Wilkie Cooper *m* Geoffrey Wright
☆ John Clements, Leslie Banks, Jane Baxter, Ann Todd, Basil Sydney, Edward Chapman, Hugh Williams, Frank Pettingell, Michael Wilding

Shipyard Sally

GB 1939 79m bw

TCF (Edward Black)

A barmaid persuades a shipyard owner to reopen.
Sub-Ealing style comedy with music which manages to bring in management and man as well as waving a flag or two.
w Karl Tunberg, Don Ettlinger *d* Monty Banks *ph* Otto Kanturek
☆ Gracie Fields, Sydney Howard, Morton Selten, Norma Varden, Oliver Wakefield

'This picture has the embarrassment of a charade where you don't know the performers well.' – *Graham Greene*

The Shiralee *

GB 1957 99m bw

Ealing (Jack Rix)

An Australian swagman leaves his wife and takes to the road with his small daughter.
Episodic character comedy-drama throwing a fairly sharp light on the Australian scene.
w Neil Paterson, Leslie Norman *novel* D'Arcy Niland *d* Leslie Norman *ph* Paul Beeson *m* John Addison
☆ Peter Finch, Dana Wilson, Elizabeth Sellars, George Rose, Russell Napier, Niall MacGinnis, Tessie O'Shea

Shirley Valentine **

US 1989 108m Technicolor

UIP/Paramount (Lewis Gilbert)

📼 📼 🔎 🎧

A bored housewife abandons her husband to enjoy a holiday romance in Greece.
Enjoyably old-fashioned movie, with some entertaining monologues on her narrow existence from its heroine.
w Willy Russell *play* Willy Russell *d* Lewis Gilbert *ph* Alan Hune *m* Willy Russell, George Hatzinassios *pd* John Stoll *ed* Lesley Walker
☆ Pauline Collins, Tom Conti, Julia McKenzie, Alison Steadman, Joanna Lumley, Sylvia Sims, Bernard Hill
🏆 Pauline Collins; song 'The Girl Who Used to be Me' (*m*Marvin Hamlisch; *l*Alan and Marilyn Bergman)
🎭 Pauline Collins

Shivers: see *The Parasite Murders*

Shoah ***

France 1985 566m colour

Aleph/Historia

📼 📼

Massive documentary history of the Holocaust, using survivors' testimony and some reenactment but no historical footage.
d Claude Lanzmann
† Part 1 is 274m, Part 2 292m.

Shock

US 1946 70m bw

TCF

📼

A girl in a hotel sees a murder committed, and an elaborate plan is concocted to silence her.
Flat treatment ruins a good suspense situation.
w Eugene Ling *d* Alfred Werker *ph* Glen MacWilliams, Joe MacDonald *m* David Buttolph
☆ Vincent Price, Lynn Bari, Frank Latimore, Annabel Shaw

'Extreme improbabilities and a general lack of finish.' – *MFB*

The Shock *

France 1982 95m colour Panavision

Sara Films/T. Films (Charlotte Fraisse)

original title: *Le Choc*

A professional killer finds himself in trouble with his boss when he decides to retire.
Slick, glossy romantic thriller that is enjoyable providing you can stomach its amorality or believe that Catherine Deneuve could be the wife of a turkey farmer.
w Alain Delon, Dominique Robelet, Claude Veillot, Robin Davis *novel* La Position du Tireur Couché by Jean-Patrick Manchette *d* Robin Davis

---

ph Pierre-William Glenn *m* Philippe Sarde *ad* Serge Douy *ed* Thierry Derocles
☆ Alain Delon, Catherine Deneuve, Philippe Leotard, Etienne Chicot, Jean-Louis Richard, Catherine Leprince, François Perrot

Shock Corridor **

US 1963 101m bw (colour sequence)

Leon Fromkess/Sam Firks (Samuel Fuller)

📼 📼 🔎 🎧

A journalist gets himself admitted to a mental asylum to solve the murder of an inmate.
Sensational melodrama, a cinematic equivalent of the yellow press, and on that level quite lively.
wd Samuel Fuller *ph* Stanley Cortez *m* Paul Dunlap
☆ Peter Breck, Constance Towers, Gene Evans, James Best, Hari Rhodes, Philip Ahn

'A minor masterpiece' – *Derek Malcolm, Guardian*

'Killing is easy. Getting away with it is murder'

A Shock to the System

US 1990 87m DuArt

Medusa/Corsair (Patrick McCormick)

📼 📼

Passed over for promotion and bored by his wife, a marketing executive turns to murder to resolve his difficulties.
Lacklustre black comedy.
w Andrew Klavan *novel* Simon Brett *d* Jan Egleson *ph* Paul Goldsmith *m* Gary Chang *pd* Howard Cummings *ed* Peter C. Frank, William A. Anderson
☆ Michael Caine, Elizabeth McGovern, Peter Riegert, Swoosie Kurtz, Will Patton, Jenny Wright, John McMartin, Barbara Baxley, Haviland Morris, Philip Moon

'A study of personal psychosis and corporate ruthlessness that is at once mordantly comic and chillingly controlled.' – *Nigel Floyd, MFB*

Shock Treatment

US 1964 94m bw

Warner (Aaron Rosenberg)

Murders are committed in a mental institution.
Tasteless thriller, not even very arresting as a yarn.
w Sydney Boehm *d* Denis Sanders *ph* Sam Leavitt *m* Jerry Goldsmith
☆ Lauren Bacall, Roddy MacDowall, Carol Lynley, Ossie Davis, Stuart Whitman, Douglass Dumbrille

'Trust me, I'm a doctor.'

Shock Treatment

GB 1982 95m Technicolor

TCF (John Goldstone)

An innocent young couple are trapped on a bizarre TV game show.
A sort of sequel to The Rocky Horror Show (qv), featuring the same hapless hero and heroine, but lacking any spark of originality. It also failed to attract its predecessor's cult following.
w Richard O'Brien, Jim Sharman *d* Jim Sharman *ph* Mike Molloy *m* Richard Hartley, Richard O'Brien *pd* Brian Thomson *ed* Richard Bedford
☆ Jessica Harper, Cliff de Young, Richard O'Brien, Patricia Quinn, Charles Gray, Nell Campbell, Ruby Wax, Barry Humphries, Rik Mayall

Shocker

US 1989 110m Foto-Kem

Guild/Alive Films/Carolco International (Marianne Maddalena, Barin Kumar)

📼 📼 🔎 🎧

The spirit of a mass murderer survives his execution.
Mundane horror, lacking any spark of originality and obviously patterned on the director's Nightmare On Elm Street.
wd Wes Craven *ph* Jacques Haitkin *m* William Goldstein *ad* Randy Moore *ed* Andy Blumenthal
☆ Michael Murphy, Peter Berg, Cami Cooper, Mitch Pileggi, John Tesh, Heather Langenkamp, Jessica Craven, Richard Brooks

The Shocking Miss Pilgrim

US 1946 85m Technicolor

TCF (William Perlberg)

In 1894 Boston, a lady typist (stenographer) fights for women's rights.
Period comedy with music; not nearly as sharp as it thinks it is.

---

wd George Seaton *ph* Leon Shamroy *md* David Raksin *ad* James Basevi, Boris Leven
songs George and Ira Gershwin
☆ Betty Grable, Dick Haymes, Anne Revere, Allyn Joslyn, Gene Lockhart, Elizabeth Patterson, Arthur Shields, Elizabeth Risdon

Shockproof

US 1949 79m bw

Columbia (S. Sylvan Simon)

A parole officer falls in love with his protégée and becomes corrupted.
Predictable programmer with a few pleasant touches.
w Helen Deutsch, Samuel Fuller *d* Douglas Sirk *ph* Charles Lawton Jnr *m* George Duning
☆ Cornel Wilde, Patricia Knight, John Baragrey, Esther Minciotti, Howard St John, Russell Collins

The Shoes of the Fisherman **

US 1968 157m Metrocolor Panavision

MGM (George Englund)

📼 🎧

After twenty years as a political prisoner, a Russian bishop becomes Pope.
Predigested but heavy-going picturization of a bestseller; big budget, big stars, big hopes. In fact a commercial dud, with plenty of superficial interest but more dramatic contrivance than religious feeling.
w John Patrick, James Kennaway *novel* Morris West *d* Michael Anderson *ph* Erwin Hillier *m* Alex North *ad* Edward Carfagno, George W. Davis *ed* Ernest Walter
☆ Anthony Quinn, David Janssen, Laurence Olivier, Oskar Werner, John Gielgud, Barbara Jefford, Leo McKern, Vittorio de Sica, Clive Revill, Paul Rogers

'A splendidly decorated curate's egg.' – *MFB*
🏆 Alex North

Shoeshine **

Italy 1946 90m bw

Alfa (Paolo W. Tamburella)

📼

original title: *Sciuscià*

In Nazi-occupied Rome two shoeshine boys become involved in black marketeering, with tragic consequences.
Not especially rewarding to watch now, this was a key film in the development of Italian neo-realism.
w Cesare Zavattini, Sergio Amidei, Adolfo Franci, C. G. Viola *d* Vittorio de Sica *ph* Anchise Brizzi, Elio Paccara
☆ Franco Interlenghi, Rinaldo Smordoni

'It is filled in every scene with an awareness of the painful complexity of even simple evil.' – *James Agee*
🏆 special award
🏆 script

Shogun Assassin *

Japan/US 1980 86m Fujicolour Tohoscope

Facelift/Katsu (Shintaro Katsu, Hisaharu Matsubara, David Weisman)

📼 📼 🔎

A disgraced shogun executioner seeks revenge for the murder of his wife.
Dubbed and edited for American consumption from the first two films in a Japanese series featuring Lone Wolf, a comic-book character and the hero of the goriest martial arts films so far made, it concentrates on the violence.
w Kazuo Koike, Robert Houston, David Weisman *d* Kenji Misumi, Robert Houston *ph* Chishi Makiura *m* Hideakira Sakurai, Mark Lindsay, W. Michael Lewis *ad* Akira Naito *ed* Toshio Taniguchi, Lee Percy
☆ Tomisaburo Wakayama, Masahiro Tomikawa, Kayo Matsuo, Minoru Ohki, Shoji Kobayashi, Shia Kishida, Akihiro Tomikawa

'No one bleeds like this unless they have garden hoses for veins.' – *Roger Ebert*

Shogun Warrior

Japan 1991 105m colour

Sanyo/Sho Productions/Mayeda/Sho Kosugi

📼 🎧

US title: *Journey of Honor*

In the 17th century a samurai travels from Japan to Spain to buy flintlock rifles to give his side the advantage in a clan war to decide the ruler of the country.
Enjoyable, action-filled romp mixing martial arts, swashbuckling, pirates, assassins and a little romance.

---

w Nelson Gidding, Sho Kosugi d Gordon Hessler ph John Connor m John Scott pd Adrian Gorton ed Bill Butler

☆ Sho Kosugi, David Essex, Kane Kosugi, Christopher Lee, Norman Lloyd, Ronald Pickup, John Rhys-Davies, Polly Walker, Dylan Kussman, Miwa Takada, Nijiko Kiyokawa, Toshiro Mifune

Shokutaku No Nai Ie: see *The Empty Table*

Shoot First: see *Rough Shoot*

Shoot the Moon *
US   1981   123m   Metrocolor
MGM (Alan Marshall)
▦   ◎

The family is affected when well-heeled parents decide to split up.
A halfway decent actors' piece which doesn't really justify its time or leave affectionate memories behind. In essence it adds nothing except noise to what was being done in this field forty years ago.
w Bo Goldman d Alan Parker ph Michael Seresin m no credit pd Geoffrey Kirkland
☆ Albert Finney, Diane Keaton, Karen Allen, Peter Weller, Dana Hill, Leora Dana
'Despite their superficial sophistication, these are immature creatures playing grown-up games which would be thought childish in Bugsy Malone.' – *Sunday Times*

Shoot the Pianist *
France   1960   80m   bw   Dyaliscope
Films de la Pléiade (Pierre Braunberger)
▦   ▦   ◎

original title: *Tirez sur le Pianiste*
A bar-room piano player becomes involved with gangsters and his girlfriend is killed.
Fair copy of an American film noir, not especially interesting except for its sharp observation.
w Marcel Moussy, François Truffaut novel *Down There* by David Goodis d François Truffaut ph Raoul Coutard m Jean Constantin, Georges Delerue
☆ Charles Aznavour, Nicole Berger, Marie Dubois, Michèle Mercier, Albert Rémy
'Pictorially it is magnificent, revealing Truffaut's brilliant control over his images; emotionally, it is all a little jejeune.' – *John Gillett, MFB*

Shoot the Works
US   1934   82m   bw
Albert Lewis/Paramount
A band leader and a gossip columnist stage a fake feud.
Anaemic Hollywood version of a rather sharp Broadway play which in this form means less than nothing.
w Howard J. Green, Claude Binyon play *The Great Magoo* by Ben Hecht, Gene Fowler d Wesley Ruggles
☆ Jack Oakie, Ben Bernie, Dorothy Dell, Arline Judge, Alison Skipworth, Roscoe Karns, William Frawley, Paul Cavanagh, Lew Cody

Shoot to Kill
US   1988   110m   colour
Touchstone/Silver Screen Partners III (Ron Silverman, Daniel Petrie Jnr)
▦   ◎

UK title: *Deadly Pursuit*
An FBI agent and a guide track down a killer who is hiding in the mountains.
Moderately suspenseful, though unmemorable, thriller.
w Harv Zimmell, Michael Burton, Daniel Petrie Jnr d Roger Spottiswoode ph Michael Chapman m John Scott pd David Sylbert ed Garth Craven, George Bowers
☆ Sidney Poitier, Tom Berenger, Kirstie Alley, Clancy Brown, Frederick Coffin, Richard Masur, Andrew Robinson, Kevin Scannell

The Shooter
US   1994   104m   Technicolor
Polygram/Adelson/Muraglia
Sladek/Newmarket/Baumgarten (Paul Pompian, Silvio Muraglia)
A US marshal goes to Prague to arrest the hit-woman who killed the Cuban ambassador in New York and falls for her instead.
Risible action drama with a narrative that follows familiar patterns of paranoia and conspiracy.
w Yves Andre Martin, Meg Thayer, Billy Ray d Ted Kotcheff ph Fernando Arguelles

m Stefano Mainetti pd Brian Eatwell ed Ralph Brunjes
☆ Dolph Lundgren, Maruschka Detmers, Assumpta Serna, Gavan O'Herlihy, John Ashton, Simon Andreu
'A fairly perfunctory post-cold-war exercise with not too much thought expended on plot logic.' – *Sunday Times*

The Shooting
US   1966   82m   DeLuxe
Santa Clara (Jack Nicholson, Monte Hellman)
▦   ◎

An ex-bounty hunter is trailed by a hired killer.
Simplistic semi-professional Western which achieves some power despite poor technical quality and a deliberately obscure ending.
w Adrien Joyce d Monte Hellman ph Gregory Sandor m Richard Markowitz
☆ Warren Oates, Will Hutchins, Jack Nicholson, Millie Perkins

Shooting Fish *
GB   1997   109m   Technicolor   Super 35
Entertainment/Fox/Winchester/Gruber Brothers/Arts Council/Tomboy (Richard Holmes, Glynis Murray)
▦   ▦   ◎

Two young con men who set out to cheat their way to owning a stately home find love instead.
An engagingly acted, hectic farce that loses its way and becomes increasingly desperate in its search for laughs.
w Stefan Schwartz, Richard Holmes d Stefan Schwartz ph Henry Braham m Stanislas Syrewicz pd Max Gottlieb ed Alan Strachan
☆ Dan Futterman, Stuart Townsend, Kate Beckinsale, Nickolas Grace, Peter Capaldi, Annette Crosbie, Jane Lapotaire, Phyllis Logan, Claire Cox
'An unashamed crowd-pleaser weakened by a third act that suffers from plot overload.' – *Derek Elley, Variety*

The Shooting Party *
GB   1984   96m   Technicolor
Edenflow/Geoff Reeve (Peter Dolman)
▦   ◎

In 1913 Sir Randolph Nettleby invites guests for a weekend at his country estate, but the coming war is foretold in their behaviour.
Mild little symbolic play which provides the expected minor pleasures.
w Julian Bond novel *Isabel Colegate* d Alan Bridges ph Fred Tammes m John Scott
☆ James Mason, Edward Fox, Dorothy Tutin, John Gielgud, Gordon Jackson, Cheryl Campbell, Robert Hardy

Shooting Stars *
GB   1928   80m   bw   silent
British Instructional (H. Bruce Woolf)
The wife of a film star puts real bullets in a prop gun but her lover is killed by mistake.
Late silent drama with comedy touches: its main interest lies in its behind-the-scenes background and in the emergence of a new director.
w John Orton, Anthony Asquith d Anthony Asquith, A. V. Bramble ph Karl Fisher
☆ Annette Benson, Brian Aherne, Donald Calthrop, Wally Patch, Chili Bouchier

The Shootist *
US   1976   100m   Technicolor   Panavision
Paramount/Frankovich-Self
▦   ▦   ◎

In 1901, a dying ex-gunfighter arrives in a small town to set his affairs in order.
Impressive semi-Western melodrama, very well written and acted all round; the kind of solidly entertaining and thoughtful movie one imagined they didn't make any more.
w Miles Hood Swarthout, Scott Hale novel Glendon Swarthout d Don Siegel ph Bruce Surtees m Elmer Bernstein
☆ John Wayne, Lauren Bacall, James Stewart, Ron Howard, Bill McKinney, Richard Boone, John Carradine, Scatman Crothers, Harry Morgan, Hugh O'Brian, Sheree North
'Just when it seemed that the western was an endangered species, due for extinction because it had repeated itself too many times, Wayne and Siegel have managed to validate it once more.' – *Arthur Knight*
'Watching this film is like taking a tour of Hollywood legends.' – *Frank Rich*

'Three fast guns against one determined man!'
Shootout
US   1971   94m   Technicolor
Universal (Hal B. Wallis)
After seven years in prison, a bank robber seeks out his betrayer.
Routine, flatly-handled revenge Western.
w Marguerite Roberts novel *The Lone Cowboy* by Will James d Henry Hathaway ph Earl Rath m Dave Grusin
☆ Gregory Peck, Pat Quinn, Robert F. Lyons, Susan Tyrrell, Jeff Corey, James Gregory, Rita Gam

Shootout at Medicine Bend
US   1957   87m   bw
Warner
Three ex-soldiers clean up a corrupt community.
Entertaining Western programmer.
w John Tucker Battle, D. D. Beauchamp d Richard Bare
☆ Randolph Scott, James Craig, Angie Dickinson, James Garner, Gordon Jones

The Shop around the Corner **
US   1940   97m   bw
MGM (Ernst Lubitsch)
▦   ◎

In a Budapest shop, the new floorwalker and a girl who dislikes him find they are pen pals.
Pleasant period romantic comedy which holds no surprises but is presented with great style.
w Samson Raphaelson play *Parfumerie* by Miklos Laszlo d Ernst Lubitsch ph William Daniels m Werner Heymann
☆ James Stewart, Margaret Sullavan, Frank Morgan, Joseph Schildkraut, Sara Haden, Felix Bressart, William Tracy
'It's not pretentious but it's a beautiful job of picture-making, and the people who did it seem to have enjoyed doing it just as much as their audiences will enjoy seeing it.' – *James Shelley Hamilton*
'An agreeably bittersweet example of light entertainment.' – *Charles Higham, 1972*
'One of the most beautifully acted and paced romantic comedies ever made in this country.' – *New Yorker, 1978*
† Remade as *In the Good Old Summertime* (qv).

The Shop at Sly Corner
GB   1946   92m   bw
Pennant (George King)
US title: *Code of Scotland Yard*
An antique dealer who is also a fence kills a blackmailer in order to shield his daughter.
Competent but stagey version of a West End success, giving full rein to a bravura star performance.
w Katherine Strueby play *Edward Percy* d George King ph Hone Glendinning m George Melachrino
☆ Oscar Homolka, Muriel Pavlow, Derek Farr, Manning Whiley, Kenneth Griffith, Kathleen Harrison, Garry Marsh, Irene Handl

The Shop on Main Street *
Czechoslovakia   1965   128m   bw
Ceskoslovensky Film
▦   ◎

original title: *Obchod na Korze*
aka: *The Shop on the High Street*
During the German invasion of Czechoslovakia, a well-meaning carpenter tries to shield an old Jewish lady, but his own rough treatment kills her.
A rather obvious sentimental fable, developed at too great length, but with bravura acting.
w Ladislav Grosman, Jan Kadar, Elmar Klos d Jan Kadar, Elmar Klos ph Vladimir Novotny m Zdenek Liska
☆ Ida Kaminska, Jozef Kroner, Hana Slivkova, Martin Holly
'Overlong, derivative, ploddingly directed.' – *John Simon*
🏆 best foreign film
🏆 Ida Kaminska

The Shop on the High Street: see *The Shop on Main Street*

'No one leaves without paying...'
Shopping
GB   1994   107m   colour
Rank/Channel 4/Polygram/Kazui/WMG/Impact (Jeremy Bolt)
As soon as he leaves prison, a young thief reverts to his old ways of stealing cars, ram-raiding (smash-and-grab raids on stores using a car as a battering-ram) and taunting the police.
An unconvincing drama of urban disaffection, set in the near future and concentrating on action without much attempt at even rudimentary character portrayal; it presents no more than a collection of attitudes posing as rootless teenagers, though it does have energy.
wd Paul Anderson ph Tony Imi m Barrington Pheloung pd Max Gottlieb ed David Stiven
☆ Sadie Frost, Jude Law, Sean Pertwee, Fraser James, Sean Bean, Marianne Faithfull, Jonathan Pryce
'Though the subject is torn from the headlines, this is hardly social realism ... As an all-action carquake, this is flawed by budgetary stinginess. There is also a problem with the cast: Law and Frost look less like homeless desperadoes than slumming models.' – *Kim Newman, Empire*
'So obsessed with its own hipness that it ends up being totally embarrassing.' – *Sight and Sound*

Shopworn Angel *
US   1928   90m   bw   part-talkie
Paramount (Louis D. Lighton)
A showgirl meets a naïve young soldier off to war and forsakes her man about town.
Hard-boiled, soft-centred romantic drama remade as below and later as That Kind of Woman (qv).
w Howard Estabrook, Albert Shelby Le Vino play *Private Pettigrew's Girl* by Dana Burnet d Richard Wallace ph Charles Lang
☆ Nancy Carroll, Gary Cooper, Paul Lukas, Emmett King

Shopworn Angel *
US   1938   85m   bw
MGM (Joseph L. Mankiewicz)
Smooth, close remake of the above.
w Waldo Salt d H. C. Potter ph Joseph Ruttenberg m Edward Ward montage Slavko Vorkapich
☆ Margaret Sullavan, James Stewart, Walter Pidgeon, Hattie McDaniel, Sam Levene

Short Circuit *
👥   US   1986   98m   Metrocolor
Panavision
Rank/PSO (David Foster, Lawrence Turman)
▦   ▦   ◎

An electric shock transforms a military robot into a creature with a mind of its own.
Amusing, if predictable comedy that owes much to E.T.
w S. S. Wilson, Brent Maddock d John Badham ph Nick McLean m David Shire ad Dianne Wager ed Frank Morriss
☆ Ally Sheedy, Steve Guttenberg, Fisher Stevens, Austin Pendleton, G. W. Bailey, Brian McNamara, Tim Blaney

Short Circuit 2
👥   US   1988   110m   Technicolor
Columbia TriStar (David Foster, Lawrence Turman, Gary Foster)
▦   ▦   ◎

At large in the big city, a robot with human sensibilities is fooled into helping jewel thieves.
Ineffectual sequel, lacking in laughs and bungling the action.
w S. S. Wilson, Brent Maddock d Kenneth Johnson ph John McPherson m Charles Fox pd Bill Brodie ed Conrad Buff
☆ Fisher Stevens, Michael McKean, Cynthia Gibb, Jack Weston, Dee McCafferty, David Hemblen, Tim Blaney

Short Cut to Hell
US   1957   89m   Vistavision
Paramount (A. C. Lyles)
A racketeer hires a gunman to commit a double murder, then double-crosses him.
Rough and ready remake of This Gun for Hire (qv), less arresting than the original.
w Ted Berkeman, Raphael Blau, W. R. Burnett novel *A Gun for Sale* by Graham Greene d James Cagney ph Haskell Boggs md Irvin Talbot

☆ Robert Ivers, Georgeann Johnson, William Bishop, Murvyn Vye

Short Cuts ***
US 1993 188m colour Panavision
Artificial Eye/Spelling/Fine Line/Avenue (Cary Brokaw)
📼 📼 🇺🇸 📾 ⊚ 🎧

In Los Angeles, the lives of nine dysfunctional, suburban couples intertwine.
An excellent, continually fascinating examination of people living on the edge, cut off from the truth of their emotions. The complexity of the cross-cutting between one scene and another is brilliantly achieved; what mars the film is its tendency to melodrama, particularly in its treatment of an alcoholic jazz singer and her equally disturbed cello-playing daughter.
w Robert Altman, Frank Barhydt story Raymond Carver d Robert Altman ph Walt Lloyd m Mark Isham pd Stephen Altman ed Geraldine Peroni
☆ Andie MacDowell, Bruce Davison, Jack Lemmon, Zane Cassidy, Julianne Moore, Matthew Modine, Anne Archer, Fred Ward, Jennifer Jason Leigh, Chris Penn, Joseph C. Hopkins, Josette Macario, Robert Downey Jnr, Madeleine Stowe, Tim Robbins and also Lily Tomlin, Tom Waits, Frances McDormand, Peter Gallagher, Annie Ross, Lori Singer, Lyle Lovett, Buck Henry
'Altman has used Carver's stories as a vehicle for presenting a vast panorama of life problems that are humorous, grim and absurd in equal measure. Viewer interest in the goings-on is generated not by artificial melodrama or hyped-up filmmaking technique, but by the recognition factor of the human foibles on display.' – *Todd McCarthy, Variety*
'A victory both as a summation of Altman's unflattering, but not unloving, view of American society, and an epic piece of cinema of innate daring and imagination.' – *Derek Malcolm, Guardian*
'A film with no dud line, flawed performance or slick piece of editing in all its 188 minutes … Only at a second viewing can one fully appreciate the magnificence of the film's grand design, which is the presentation of life as a mutually shared tragi-comedy.' – *Philip French, Observer*
Ⅎ Robert Altman (as director)

Short Encounters *
USSR 1967 95m bw
Odessa Feature Film Studio
original title: *Korotkie Vstrechi*

Two women, one a bureaucrat, the other a young country girl, recall their love for the same man, a footloose geologist.
An innocuous love story, it was banned for 20 years by the Soviet authorities because of the attitudes it displays towards sex and social misdemeanours.
w Kira Muratova, Leonid Zhukhovitsky d Kira Muratova ph G. Kariuk m Oleg Karavaichuk
☆ Nina Ruslanova, Vladimir Vysotsky, Kira Muratova

A Short Film about Killing ****
Poland 1988 84m colour
Gala/Film Unit 'Tor'/Zespoly Filmowe (Ryszard Chutkowski)
📼 📼
original title: *Krótki Film O Zabijaniu*

A disenchanted youth who commits a bungled and motiveless murder is defended by an idealistic lawyer opposed to capital punishment.
Powerful and unremittingly bleak, but unforgettable in its condemnation of killing, whether criminal or judicial. It is one of the Decalogues, a series of films on the ten commandments made for television.
w Krzysztof Piesiewicz, Krzysztof Kieslowski d Krzysztof Kieslowski ph Slawomir Idziak m Zbigniew Preisner ad Halina Dobrowolska ed Ewa Small
☆ Miroslaw Baka, Krzysztof Globisz, Jan Tesarz, Zbigniew Zapasiewicz

A Short Film about Love **
Poland 1988 87m colour
Gala/Polish Film Producers' Corporation (Ryszard Chutkowski)
📼
original title: *Krótki Film O Milosci*

A teenager spies on the sexual activities of a woman who lives opposite his flat.
Grim but gripping film on the impossibility of love.

w Krzysztof Piesiewicz, Krzysztof Kieslowski d Krzysztof Kieslowski ph Witold Adamek m Zbigniew Preisner pd Halina Dobrowolska ed Ewa Smal
☆ Grazyna Szapolowska, Olaf Lubaszenko, Stefania Iwinska, Piotr Machalica, Artur Barcis

Short Fuse: see Good to Go

'Getting killed isn't as easy as it looks'
Short Time
US 1987 102m colour
Rank/Gladden Entertainment/Touchstone (Todd Black)
📼 📼 📾

Discovering he has a fatal disease and wanting to die on active service so his family can collect on his insurance policy, an ageing cop volunteers for dangerous assignments.
A comedy suffering from a terminal lack of laughs.
w John Blumenthal, Michael Berry d Gregg Champion ph John Connor m Ira Newborn pd Michael Bolton ed Frank Morriss
☆ Dabney Coleman, Matt Frewer, Teri Garr, Barry Corbin, Joe Pantoliano, Xander Berkeley, Rob Roy

Shot in the Dark
GB 1933 53m bw
Real Art (Julius Hagen)

A golfing rector solves the murder of an eccentric who was hated by his relatives.
A country-house melodrama of a very old-fashioned kind, moderately enjoyable as an example of English acting styles of the time.
w George Pearson, Terence Egan novel Gerard Fairlie d George Pearson ph Ernest Palmer ad James A. Carter ed Lister Laurance
☆ Jack Hawkins, Michael Shepley, Dorothy Boyd, O. B. Clarence, Davy Burnaby, Russell Thorndike, Margaret Yarde, A. Bromley Davenport

A Shot in the Dark *
US 1964 101m DeLuxe Panavision
UA/Mirisch/Geoffrey (Blake Edwards)
📼 📼 📾

A woman is accused of shooting her lover; accident-prone Inspector Clouseau investigates.
Further adventures of the oafish, Tatiesque clodhopper from The Pink Panther; mildly funny for those in the mood for pratfalls.
w Blake Edwards, William Peter Blatty d Blake Edwards ph Christopher Challis m Henry Mancini pd Michael Stringer
☆ Peter Sellers, Elke Sommer, George Sanders, Herbert Lom, Tracy Reed, Graham Stark

Shotgun
US 1954 81m Technicolor
Allied Artists
📾

A deputy marshal avenges the death of his boss.
Rather violent Western with a few unusual angles.
w Clark E. Reynolds, Rory Calhoun d Lesley Selander ph Ellsworth J. Fredricks m Carl Brandt
☆ Sterling Hayden, Zachary Scott, Yvonne de Carlo, Guy Prescott, Robert Wilke

Should Ladies Behave?
US 1933 90m bw
MGM

A young girl falls for her aunt's lover.
Brittle comedy of manners which transferred poorly from Broadway with a star well over the top.
w Sam and Bella Spewack play The Vinegar Tree by Paul Osborn d Harry Beaumont
☆ Alice Brady, Lionel Barrymore, Conway Tearle, Katherine Alexander, Halliwell Hobbes, Mary Carlisle

Should Married Men Go Home?
US 1928 20m bw silent
Hal Roach

Tribulations on the golf course end in a mud-slinging contest.
Goodish star slapstick, but the preliminary domestic scene is the funniest.
w Leo McCarey, James Parrott, H. M. Walker d James Parrott ph George Stevens ed Richard Currier
☆ Stan Laurel, Oliver Hardy, Edgar Kennedy, Kay Deslys

Shoulder Arms *
US 1918 24m bw silent
Charles Chaplin/First National

A soldier in the trenches dreams of winning the war single-handedly.
A comedy which meant a great deal at the time of its release but now provides precious little to laugh at.
wd Charles Chaplin ph Rollie Totheroh
☆ Charles Chaplin, Edna Purviance, Sydney Chaplin, Henry Bergman, Albert Austin

Shout
👫 US 1991 89m DeLuxe
Universal (Robert Simonds)
📼 📼 📾 📾 🎧

In the early 50s, a rebellious teenager, sent to a strict Texan boys' home, falls for the tough warden's daughter and learns to love rock 'n' roll, as taught by the new music teacher.
Ludicrous teen melodrama that even its target audience is likely to find condescending and immature.
w Joe Gayton d Jeffrey Hornaday ph Robert Brinkmann m Randy Edelman pd William F. Matthews ed Seth Flaum
☆ James Walters, John Travolta, Heather Graham, Richard Jordan, Linda Fiorentino, Scott Coffey, Glenn Quinn, Gwyneth Paltrow

The Shout *
GB 1978 87m colour
Rank/Recorded Picture (Jeremy Thomas)
📾

A man who may be mad claims that, like the old Aborigine magicians, he can kill by shouting.
Curiously gripping but ultimately pointless fable, very well done to little purpose.
w Michael Austin, Jerzy Skolimowsky story Robert Graves d Jerzy Skolimowsky ph Mike Molloy m Rupert Hine, Anthony Banks, Michael Rutherford
☆ Alan Bates, Susannah York, John Hurt, Robert Stephens, Tim Curry
'Poorly acted, incoherent and unendurably loud.' – *Pauline Kael, New Yorker*

Shout at the Devil *
GB 1976 147m Technicolor Panavision
Tonav (Michael Klinger)
📾

In 1913 Zanzibar, a hard-drinking American and an old Etonian Englishman join forces to rout a brutal German commissioner who resents their poaching ivory in his territory.
The main characters are respectively repellent, effete, and just plain nasty, but the action scenes are vivid and the production is mainly notable as an expensive old-fashioned British film made at a time when there were few British films of any kind.
w Wilbur Smith, Stanley Price, Alastair Reid novel Wilbur Smith d Peter Hunt ph Mike Reed m Maurice Jarre
☆ Lee Marvin, Roger Moore, Barbara Parkins, René Kolldehoff, Ian Holm, Karl Michael Vogler, Maurice Denham, Jean Kent, Robert Lang, Murray Melvin, George Coulouris
'Elephantine plod through the action highlights of a best seller.' – *Sight and Sound*

Show Business ***
US 1944 92m bw
RKO (Eddie Cantor)
📼 📾 📾

The careers of four friends in vaudeville.
Lively low-budget period musical which probably presents the best picture of what old-time vaudeville was really like; a lot of fun when the plot doesn't get in the way.
w Joseph Quillan, Dorothy Bennett d Edwin L. Marin ph Robert de Grasse, Vernon L. Walker m George Duning md Constantin Bakaleinikoff ch Nick Castle
☆ Eddie Cantor, Joan Davis, George Murphy, Constance Moore, Don Douglas, Nancy Kelly
'Bits of archaic vaudeville which give off a moderately pleasant smell of peanuts and cigar smoke.' – *James Agee*

Show Girl in Hollywood
US 1930 77m bw (colour sequence)
First National

Adventures of a New York girl on the west coast.
Comedy with music; it seems content to wallow in supposed Hollywood glamour without contributing much by way of wit or storyline.

w Harvey Thew, James A. Starr, J. P. McEvoy d Mervyn Le Roy
☆ Alice White, Jack Mulhall, Blanche Sweet, Ford Sterling, John Miljan, Herman Bing

The Show Goes On
GB 1937 93m bw
ATP (Basil Dean)

A mill girl becomes a star singer with the help of a dying composer.
An attempt to turn Gracie Fields into a serious performer, this was not much enjoyed by her fans.
w Austin Melford, Anthony Kimmins, E. G. Valentine d Basil Dean ph Jan Stallich
☆ Gracie Fields, Owen Nares, Edward Rigby, John Stuart, Horace Hodges, Amy Veness, Cyril Ritchard

Show Me Love: see Fucking Amal

A Show of Force
US 1990 93m Technicolor
Paramount/Golden Harvest (John Strong)
📼 📾

In 1978, a TV reporter investigates the death of two left-wingers campaigning for an independent Puerto Rico who were apparently murdered with the connivance of the FBI.
Unconvincing mix of exposé and thriller, for all its supposed basis in fact; its gloss, glibness and reliance on formula film-making render it highly suspect.
w Evan Jones, John Strong book Murder Under Two Flags by Anne Nelson d Bruno Barreto ph James Glennon m Georges Delerue pd William J. Cassidy ed Henry Richardson, Sonya Polansky
☆ Amy Irving, Andy Garcia, Lou Diamond Phillips, Robert Duvall, Kevin Spacey, Erik Estrada, Juan Fernandez

'In Vitaphone, it eclipses the sun in splendour!'
Show of Shows **
US 1929 128m Technicolor
Warner (Darryl F. Zanuck)

A big musical show put on by Warner contract artists.
Primitive early talkie, of vital historical interest but mostly photographed from a seat in the stalls.
d John G. Adolfi ph Barney McGill w/m various
☆ Frank Fay, H. B. Warner, Monte Blue, Lupino Lane, Ben Turpin, Chester Morris, Ted Lewis and his band, Georges Carpentier, Patsy Ruth Miller, Beatrice Lillie, Winnie Lightner, Irene Bordoni, Myrna Loy, Douglas Fairbanks Jnr, John Barrymore and also Betty Compson
'Colour photography of the crudest, most garish kind, the resulting impression being that a child of seven has been let loose with a shilling box of paints.' – *James Agate*

Show People
US 1928 80m bw silent
MGM
📾

A naïve young actress makes it in Hollywood.
Historically important comedy with cameo appearances by many stars of the time.
w Wanda Tuchock, Agnes Christine Johnston, Laurence Stallings d King Vidor
☆ Marion Davies, William Haines

Show Them No Mercy *
US 1935 76m bw
TCF (Raymond Griffith)

GB title: Tainted Money
Kidnappers are rounded up by G-men.
Lively crime thriller typical of its time.
w Kubec Glasmon, Henry Lehrman d George Marshall ph Bert Glennon m David Buttolph
☆ Rochelle Hudson, Cesar Romero, Bruce Cabot, Edward Norris, Edward Brophy, Warren Hymer
'Direct, surely dramatic, inevitable and full of terror.' – *Otis Ferguson*

Showboat ***
US 1936 110m bw
Universal (Carl Laemmle Jnr)
📾

Lives and loves of the personnel on an old-time Mississippi showboat.
Great style and excellent performances mark this version, which still suffers from longueurs in the middle followed by the rapid passage of many years to provide a happy ending.

---

w Oscar Hammerstein II *book* Oscar Hammerstein II for the Broadway musical *novel* Edna Ferber *d* James Whale *ph* John Mescall *m* Jerome Kern *ly* Oscar Hammerstein II

☆ Irene Dunne, Allan Jones, Helen Morgan, Paul Robeson, Charles Winninger, Hattie McDaniel, Donald Cook, Sammy White

'For three quarters of its length good entertainment: sentimental, literary, but oddly appealing.' – *Graham Greene*

† A primitive talkie version of *Showboat*, now lost, was made in 1929.

†† Before Allan Jones was cast, Walter Pidgeon, Robert Taylor, John Boles, Fredric March and Nelson Eddy were all considered.

Showboat **
US 1951 108m Technicolor
MGM (Arthur Freed)
⬛ 🟦 ▤ ⌕ ⊙ 🎧

Vigorous remake with good ensemble dancing; otherwise inferior to the 1936 version.

w John Lee Mahin, George Wells, Jack McGowan *d* George Sidney *ph* Charles Rosher *md* Conrad Salinger, Adolph Deutsch *ch* Robert Alton

☆ Kathryn Grayson, *Howard Keel*, Ava Gardner, William Warfield, *Joe E. Brown*, Robert Sterling, Marge Champion, Gower Champion, Agnes Moorehead

† Ava Gardner's singing was dubbed by Annette Warren.

♫ Charles Rosher; Conrad Salinger, Adolph Deutsch

Showdown
US 1963 79m Technicolor
Universal
▤

Two wandering cowboys become involved with a criminal.
Below-par Western with little action and rather boring characters.

w Bronson Howitzer *d* R. G. Springsteen *ph* Ellis Carter *m* Hans J. Salter

☆ Audie Murphy, Charles Drake, Harold J. Stone, Kathleen Crowley, Skip Homeier, L. Q. Jones, Strother Martin

Showdown
US 1972 99m Technicolor Todd-AO 35
Universal (George Seaton)

A sheriff finds that his old friend is leader of an outlaw gang.
Routine star Western adequately done.

w Theodore Taylor *d* George Seaton *ph* Ernest Laszlo *m* David Shire

☆ Rock Hudson, Dean Martin, Susan Clark, Donald Moffat, John McLiam

The Showdown
US 1950 86m bw
Republic

A trail boss seeks revenge on his brother's killer.
Routine Western with a touch of mystery.

w Richard Wormser and Dan Gordon *d* Darrell and Stuart McGowan *ph* Reggie Lanning *m* Stanley Wilson

☆ Wild Bill Elliott, Marie Windsor, Walter Brennan, Henry Morgan, William Ching, Rhys Williams

Showdown at Abilene
US 1956 80m Technicolor
Universal-International

A shellshocked Civil War veteran, returning home to find his girl married, reluctantly takes a job as sheriff.
Fairly lively Western remade eleven years later as Gunfight in Abilene.

w Berne Giler *novel* Gun Shy by Clarence Upson Young *d* Charles Haas

☆ Jock Mahoney, David Janssen, Martha Hyer, Lyle Bettger, Grant Williams

Showdown in Little Tokyo
US 1991 77m Technicolor
Warner (Mark L. Lester, Martin E. Caan)
⬛ 🟦 ▤ ⌕

A cop takes revenge on the Japanese gangster who killed his parents.
Cheap, but not particularly cheerful, action nonsense, in which no one seems to have minded that the script was banal, perhaps because the money appears to have

been spent on sound effects of bodies being hit and bones breaking.

w Stephen Glantz, Caliope Brattlestreet *d* Mark L. Lester *ph* Mark Irwin *m* David Michael Frank *pd* Craig Stearns *ed* Steven Kemper, Robert A. Ferretti

☆ Dolph Lundgren, Brandon Lee, Carey-Hiroyuki Tagawa, Tia Carrere, Toshiro Obata, Philip Tan

'By-the-numbers revenge stuff, although screenplay skips a lot of numbers, the better to focus on nonstop and generally unimaginative action sequences.' – *Variety*

Showgirl in Hollywood
US 1930 80m bw and Technicolor
Warner

A girl singer is spotted and trained for movie stardom.
Naïve look behind the studio scenes, historically fascinating but dramatically dull.

w Harvey Thew, James A. Starr *novel* Hollywood Girl by J. P. McEvoy *d* Mervyn LeRoy

☆ Alice White, Jack Mulhall, Blanche Sweet, Ford Sterling, John Miljan, Herman Bing

'Leave Your Inhibitions At The Door.'

Showgirls
US 1995 131m Technicolor Clairmont
Guild/United Artists/Chargeurs/Carolco (Alan Marshall, Charles Evans)
⬛ 🟦 ▤ ⌕

A Las Vegas stripper has ambitions to be slightly more than a lap dancer.
A prurient and voyeuristic display which its director apparently saw as an updated version of the Hollywood musical; but the routines on display are invariably tawdry, all the characters are dim, exploited and exploitative, the script is composed of the stalest clichés, and the acting is barely competent.

w Joe Eszterhas *d* Paul Verhoeven *ph* Jost Vacano *m* David A. Stewart *pd* Allan Cameron *ed* Mark Goldblatt, Mark Helfrich

☆ Elizabeth Berkley, Kyle MacLachlan, Gina Gershon, Glenn Plummer, Robert Davi, Alan Rachins, Gina Ravera

'A very shallow and ultimately rather silly film.' – *Derek Malcolm, Guardian*

'Beyond teasing, titillation and an abundant display of female flesh in various stages of undress, there is very little reason for *Showgirls* to exist. The plot is wobbly, the acting one short step ahead of amateurish and what passes for dialogue is a mere collection of turgid lines.' – *Anna Maria Bahiana, Screen International*

'Akin to being keelhauled through a cesspool, with sharks swimming alongside.' – *Todd McCarthy, Variety*

† Only one of the 14 leading British critics, and two out of 34 critics in Chicago, New York and Los Angeles, liked the film. It received an NC-17 certificate in the US, an 18 certificate in Britain with 15 seconds cut, a 12 certificate in France, and was banned in Ireland. Paul Verhoeven recut the film for its US video release.

†† The film flopped at the US box-office, taking around $20m.

The Show-Off
US 1934 80m bw
MGM

A girl's blundering new husband alienates his in-laws and nearly wrecks his brother-in-law's career.
Surefire satirical comedy-drama from a Broadway staple, this low-budget item gave MGM a new star.

w Herman Mankiewicz *play* George Kelly *d* Charles Riesner

☆ Spencer Tracy, Madge Evans, Clara Blandick, Henry Wadsworth, Grant Mitchell, Lois Wilson

† The play had been filmed twice in silent days by Paramount, and turned up again in 1946 as a Red Skelton vehicle.

Showtime: see Gaiety George

The Shrieking: see Hex

The Shrike
US 1955 88m bw
U-I (Aaron Rosenberg)

A brilliant theatre man has a nervous breakdown because his wife is a vindictive harpy.
Theatrical two-hander, aridly filmed, of little interest except to show that both stars are capable of sustained emotional acting.

w Ketti Frings *play* Joseph Kramm *d* José Ferrer *ph* William Daniels *m* Frank Skinner *titles* Saul Bass

☆ José Ferrer, June Allyson, Joy Page, Jacqueline de Wit, Kendall Clark

'The film is unvaryingly paced, the result, one feels, of a respectable but far from invigorating honesty of purpose.' – *MFB*

Shrunken Heads
US 1994 86m Foto-Kem
Full Moon (Charles Band)
⬛ 🟦

A Haitian witch doctor in America shrinks the heads of three teenagers killed by local thugs and turns them into avenging, flying monsters.
Bizarre comic horror that never quite achieves the atmosphere it needs to work.

w Matthew Bright *idea* Charles Band *d* Richard Elfman *ph* Stephen McNutt *m* Richard Band, Danny Elfman (title theme) *pd* Milo *ed* Charles Simmons *sp* Alchemy fx; Paul Gentry

☆ Meg Foster, Julius Harris, Aeryk Egan, Becky Herbst

'A promising idea ruined by shoddy production values and an inadequate script.' – *Sight and Sound*

Shuanglong Hui: see Twin Dragons

The Shuttered Room
GB 1967 110m Technicolor
Warner/Troy-Schenck (Philip Hazelton)

Returning to her childhood home on an island off the New England coast, a girl and her husband are subjected to terror and violence.
Stretched out suspenser which looks good and is carefully made but fails in its effort to combine the menace of teenage yobboes with that of the monster lurking upstairs.

w D. B. Ledrov, Nathaniel Tanchuck *story* H. P. Lovecraft, August Derleth *d* David Greene *ph* Ken Hodges *m* Basil Kirchin

☆ Gig Young, Carol Lynley, Flora Robson, Oliver Reed, William Devlin

Shy People *
US 1987 120m colour
Cannon/Menahem Golan, Yoram Globus
▤ ⌕ 🎧

A glamorous journalist, who researches into her family, traces some isolated relatives to the bayous of Louisiana.
Off-beat melodrama that has a queasy fascination.

w Gérard Brach, Marjorie David, Andrei Konchalovsky *d* Andrei Konchalovsky *ph* Chris Menges *m* Tangerine Dream *pd* Stephen Marsh *ed* Alain Jakubowicz

☆ Jill Clayburgh, Barbara Hershey, Martha Plimpton, Merritt Butrick, John Philbin, Don Swayze, Pruitt Taylor Vince

Une Si Jolie Petite Plage *
France 1948 91m bw
CICC (Emile Darbon)
aka: *Such a Pretty Little Beach*

A murderer returns to the small seaside town where he spent his childhood, befriends the maid at the hotel, and after a few days kills himself.
A melancholy anecdote which works both as a character study and pictorially.

w Jacques Sigurd *d* Yves Allégret *ph* Henri Alekan *m* Maurice Thiriet

☆ Gérard Philipe, Jean Servais, Madeleine Robinson, Jane Marken, Carette

'Shows fine craftsmanship and is beautifully sensitive to place and atmosphere.' – *Gavin Lambert, MFB*

Si Può Fare ... Amigo: see The Big and the Bad

Si Tous les Gars du Monde... *
France 1956 108m bw
Ariane/Filmsonor/Francinex (Alexandre Mnouchkine)
aka: *Race for Life*

When members of a French trawler crew fall ill in mid-Atlantic, amateur radio operators around the world arrange rescue.
Well-meaning realistic melodrama with a hands-across-the-sea message.

w Jacques Remy *d* Christian-Jaque *ph* Armand Thiraud *m* Georges Van Parys

☆ Andre Valmy, Jean Gaven, Doudou-Babet, Jean-Louis Trintignant

Si Tutte le Donne del Mondo: see Kiss the Girls and Make Them Cry

Sib: see The Apple (1997)

'It was not sex it was *good*!'

Sibling Rivalry
US 1990 88m colour
First Independent/Castle Rock/Nelson
⬛ 🟦 ▤ ⌕

Complications ensue after an unhappy wife, advised by her sister to have an affair, goes to bed with her sister's husband.
Broad farce of marital upset that causes an occasional smile.

w Martha Goldhirsh *d* Carl Reiner *ph* Reynaldo Villalobos *m* Jack Elliott *pd* Jeannine C. Oppewall *ed* Bud Molin

☆ Kirstie Alley, Bill Pullman, Carrie Fisher, Jami Gertz, Scott Bakula, Frances Sternhagen, John Randolph, Sam Elliott, Ed O'Neill, Paul Benedict

'In opting for romantic comedy rather than the black variety, the picture has grave problems of mood which are never resolved.' – *Philip French, Observer*

The Sicilian
US 1987 146m Technicolor
Fox/Gladden Entertainment (Michael Cimino, Joann Carelli)
⬛ 🟦 ▤ ⌕ 🎧

The Sicilian bandit Salvatore Giuliano, who robs the rich in order to give to the poor, is betrayed by his own men.
Over-long and with a cast that lack authenticity as Sicilians, the movie rarely rises above incoherence.

w Steve Shagan *novel* Mario Puzo *d* Michael Cimino *ph* Alex Thomson *m* David Mansfield *pd* Wolf Kroeger *ed* Françoise Bonnot

☆ Christophe Lambert, Terence Stamp, Joss Ackland, John Turturro, Richard Bauer, Barbara Sukowa, Ray McAnally, Aldo Ray

The Sicilian Cross
Italy 1976 92m colour
Aetos (Manolo Bolognini, Luigi Borghese)
US title: *Street People*
original title: *Gli Esecutori*

A Mafia investigator and his racing-driver buddy set out to discover the person responsible for double-crossing a gang leader by hiding heroin in a crucifix sent from Sicily to the United States.
Conventional thriller, composed of shoot-outs and car chases, in which it is difficult to remember, or care, who is doing what to whom.

w Ernest Tidyman, Randal Kleiser, Gianfranco Bucceri, Roberto Leoni, Gian Franco Bucceri, Nicola Badalucco, Maurizio Lucidi *story* Gianfranco Bucceri, Roberto Leoni *d* Maurizio Lucidi *ph* Aiace Parolin *m* Luis Enriquez *ad* Gastone Carsetti *ed* Renzo Lucidi

☆ Roger Moore, Stacy Keach, Ivo Garrani, Fausto Tozzi, Ennio Balbo, Rosemarie Lindt, Ettore Manni

'The uneasy pairing of Moore and Stacy Keach suggests, however, that Maurizio Lucidi intended to enter his picture in the even less inspired Starsky and Hutch stakes.' – *MFB*

The Sicilians
GB 1964 69m bw
Butcher's (John I. Phillips)

British police and an American embassy official investigate the kidnapping of the son of a Mafia gangster who testified against his bosses.
Plodding and convoluted thriller of little interest, other than the unsuccessful attempt by low-budget film-makers to suggest foreign locations.

w Ronald Liles, Reginald Hearne *d* Ernest Morris *ph* Geoffrey Faithfull *m* John Gregory *ch* Pamela Devis *ad* Harry White *ed* Henry Richardson

☆ Robert Hutton, Reginald Marsh, Ursula Howells, Alex Scott, Susan Denny, Robert Ayres, Eric Pohlmann, Patricia Hayes, Warren Mitchell, Michael Balfour

Sick
US 1997 90m colour
Kirby Dick/Peter Norton/Art Matters

Documentary on Bob Flanagan, an artist and self-styled Supermasochist, who had the incurable disease cystic fibrosis and used suffering as the basis

of his life, involved in a sado-masochistic relationship, and work.
Despite Flanagan's joy in life and his humour, this is a painful film to face, not only in his performances but in the final moments of his life, caught on video and still photographs; it remains a curiosity.
d Kirby Dick *ph* Jonathan Dayton, Kirby Dick, Sheree Rose, Geza Sinkovics *m* Blake Leyh *ed* Kirby Dick, Dody Dorn
☆ Bob Flanagan, Sheree Rose

Sid and Nancy
GB 1986 111m colour
Zenith/Initial (Eric Feliner)
📼 ▤ ⚙ 🎧
An account of the self-destruction of the leader of a punk rock group and his American girlfriend.
Some have said stimulating, most have preferred revolting. Consensus, an example of the dregs to which cinema has been reduced.
w Alex Cox, Abbe Wool *d* Alex Cox *ph* Roger Deakins *m* The Pogues
☆ Gary Oldman, Chloe Webb, David Hayman
'The dialogue is extremely rough, the settings sordid, the theme of wasted lives depressing.' – *Variety*
'Relentlessly whingeing performances and a lengthy slide into drugs, degradation and death make this a solemnly off-putting moral tract.' – *Sight and Sound*

Siddharta
US 1972 94m Eastmancolor Panavision
Columbia-Warner/Lotus (Conrad Rooks)
A young Brahmin leaves his comfortable home to join a band of itinerant holy men.
Despite its visual charm, a dull, though faithful, version of the book.
wd Conrad Rooks *novel* Hermann Hesse *ph* Sven Nykvist *m* Hemanta Kuma *ad* Malcolm Golding *ed* Willy Kemplen
☆ Shashi Kapoor, Simi Garewal, Rommesh Sharma, Pincho Kapoor, Amrik Singh, Zul Vellani, Shanti Hiranand, Kunal Kapoor

Side by Side
GB 1975 84m Technicolor
GTO (Drummond Challis)
When a magistrate orders that one of a town's two rundown night-clubs will have to close in a month, the rival owners search for new acts to boost their chances of remaining open.
A ramshackle comedy mainly designed as a showcase for a succession of bland pop groups; in between the songs, the narrative includes, for no good reason, an old music-hall slapstick routine and some occasionally funny moments from Terry-Thomas as a seedy entrepreneur. Performances from groups such as Fox have also gained a measure of hilarity over the years.
w Garry Chambers, Ron Inkpen, Peter James, Bruce Beresford *d* Bruce Beresford *ph* Harvey Harrison *m* Hello, Mac and Katie Kisson, Bob Kerr's Whoopee Band, Desmond Dekker and the Israelites *ad* Terry Gough *ed* Ray Lovejoy
☆ Terry-Thomas, Barry Humphries, Stephanie de Sykes, Billy Boyle, Dave Mount, Frank Thornton, Jennifer Guy
'The exuberant vulgarity which characterised Bruce Beresford's Barry McKenzie movies is wholly absent from this abysmal comedy.' – *MFB*

Side Out
US 1990 100m colour
Tri-Star/Aurora/Then/Jay Wesson (Gary Foster)
📼 ▤ 🎧
A young would-be lawyer goes to California to work for his uncle, but prefers professional volleyball.
Trivial 'teen picture built around a game that may be fun to play, but is hell to watch.
w David Thoreau *d* Peter Israelson *ph* Ron Garcia *m* Jeff Lorber *pd* Dan Lomino *ed* Conrad Buff
☆ C. Thomas Howell, Peter Horton, Courtney Thorne-Smith, Harley Jane Kozak, Christopher Rydell, Terry Kiser
'Anodyne Californian whimsy which celebrates beach culture and the body beautiful.' – *Sight and Sound*

Side Street
US 1950 83m bw
MGM (Sam Zimbalist)
A petty thief finds himself involved with big-time crooks.

Well-made but rather boring crime melodrama with an excellent car chase finale.
w Sydney Boehm *d* Anthony Mann *ph* Joseph Ruttenberg *m* Lennie Hayton
☆ Farley Granger, Cathy O'Donnell, James Craig, Paul Kelly, Jean Hagen, Edmon Ryan, Paul Harvey

Side Streets
US 1934 63m bw
First National
GB title: *A Woman in Her Thirties*
A lady furrier takes pity on a sailor, and finally marries him, only to find that he has a past.
Strange, rather tedious, and quite unconvincing character drama.
w Manuel Seff *story* Ann Garrick, Ethel Hill *d* Alfred E. Green
☆ Aline MacMahon, Paul Kelly, Ann Dvorak, Helen Lowell, Henry O'Neill, Marjorie Gateson

'It's the hottest day in the real New York.'
Side Streets
US 1998 131m Technicolor
First Independent/Merchant Ivory/Cornerstone (Bruce Weiss)
A day in the New York life of five immigrants, who are all struggling to make a living.
Ambitious but meandering account of the diversity of city life on one stifling day; but the characters stubbornly refuse to come to life.
w Lynn Nottage, Tony Gerber *d* Tony Gerber *ph* Russell Lee Fine *m* Evan Lurie *pd* Stephen McCabe *ed* Kate Williams
☆ Valeria Golino, Shashi Kapoor, Leon, Art Malik, Shabana Azmi, Mirjana Jokovic, Miho Nikaldo, Marc Tissot, John Ortiz
'Very, very long and dull.' – *Peter Bradshaw, Guardian*

Sidekicks
👪 US 1993 100m colour
Gallery (Don Carmody)
An asthmatic teenager escapes his unhappiness by day-dreams of heroic acts at the side of his hero, Chuck Norris.
A movie for young audiences, who may be able to share the fantasies on offer.
w Don Thompson, Lou Illar *d* Aaron Norris *ph* João Fernandes *m* Alan Silvestri *pd* Reuben Freed *ed* David Rawlins, Bernard Weiser
☆ Chuck Norris, Beau Bridges, Jonathan Brandis, Mako, Julia Nickson-Soul, Joe Piscopo, Danica McKellar

Sidewalk Stories *
US 1989 97m bw
Palm (Charles Lane)
A homeless street artist looks after a little girl after her father is killed by muggers.
Whimsical, almost silent movie with deft musical accompaniment; its lightness of touch almost disguises its underlying anger on behalf of the dispossessed.
wd Charles Lane *ph* Bill Dill *m* Marc Marder *pd* Lyn Pinezich *ed* Anne Stein, Charles Lane
☆ Charles Lane, Nicole Alysia, Sandye Wilson, Darnell Williams, Trula Hoosier, Michael Baskin, George Riddick

Sidewalks of London: see St Martin's Lane

Sidewalks of New York *
US 1931 73m bw
MGM (Lawrence Weingarten)
▤
The playboy owner of some tenement apartments falls in love with the daughter of one of the tenants.
Interesting rather than wholly successful early sound comedy which marked the beginning of Keaton's decline; he was not allowed full control and the comedy scenes are thinly spaced.
w George Landy, Paul Gerard Smith, Eric Hatch, Robert E. Hopkins *d* Jules White, Zion Myers *ph* Leonard Smith
☆ Buster Keaton, Anita Page, Cliff Edwards, Frank Rowan

Sie Tötete in Ekstase: see She Killed in Ecstasy

The Siege
US 1998 116m DeLuxe Super 35
TCF (Lynda Obst, Edward Zwick)
📼 ▤ 🎧
Martial law is declared after Arab terrorists begin to explode bombs in New York.

Hysterical political melodrama, which will leave most audiences outside the USA feeling decidedly queasy.
w Lawrence Wright, Menno Meyjes, Edward Zwick *d* Edward Zwick *ph* Roger Deakins *m* Graeme Revell *pd* Lilly Kilvert *ed* Steven Rosenblum
☆ Denzel Washington, Annette Bening, Bruce Willis, Tony Shalhoub, Sami Bouajila, David Proval
'The filmmakers peddle fear and then try to claim the moral high ground; the treatment is foolish, confused and borderline irresponsible.' – *David Denby, New Yorker*

The Siege at Red River
US 1954 86m Technicolor
TCF/Panoramic (Leonard Goldstein)
During the American Civil War a Confederate agent behind northern lines defeats a treacherous helper and escapes to the South.
Modest, generally watchable, and quite forgettable Western.
w Sydney Boehm *d* Rudolph Maté *ph* Edward Cronjager *m* Lionel Newman
☆ Van Johnson, Joanne Dru, Richard Boone, Milburn Stone, Jeff Morrow, Craig Hill

The Siege of Pinchgut
GB 1959 104m bw
Ealing (Eric Williams)
US title: *Four Desperate Men*
Escaped convicts take over a small island in Sydney harbour.
Disappointingly obvious location melodrama with routine excitements.
w Harry Watt, Jon Cleary *d* Harry Watt *ph* Gordon Dines *m* Kenneth V. Jones
☆ Aldo Ray, Heather Sears, Neil McCallum, Victor Maddern, Carlo Justini

The Siege of Sidney Street *
GB 1960 92m bw Dyaliscope
Midcentury (Robert S. Baker, Monty Berman)
An account of the anarchists who infiltrated London in 1912.
Detailed but not dramatically absorbing historical reconstruction with unsatisfactory fictional trimmings.
w Jimmy Sangster, Alexander Baron *m* Stanley Black *d/ph* Robert S. Baker, Monty Berman
☆ Peter Wyngarde, Donald Sinden, Nicole Berger, Kieron Moore, Leonard Sachs, Tutte Lemkow

'He used the power of the universe 2,500 years ago to destroy the Roman invaders.'
The Siege of Syracuse
Italy/France 1959 115m Eastmancolor Dyaliscope
Glomer/Galatea/Lyre (Giovanni Laterza, Armando Grottini)
original title: *L'Assedio di Siracusa*
Scientist meets slave girl, scientist loses slave girl, scientist gets slave girl while saving his city from the Romans.
Colourful epic that successfully mixes action and romance; directed with verve it is one of the better examples of its kind.
w Pietro Francisci, Giorgio Graziosi, Ennio de Concini *d* Pietro Francisci *ph* Carlo Carlini *m* Angelo Francesco Lavagnino *pd* Ottavio Scotti *ed* Nino Baragli
☆ Rossano Brazzi, Tina Louise, Sylva Koscina, Enrico Maria Salerno, Gino Cervi, Alberto Farnese
† The film was released in the US in 1962 in a dubbed version that runs for 96m.

The Siege of the Saxons
👪 GB 1963 85m Technicolor
Columbia/Ameran (Jud Kinberg)
When King Arthur is ill, the Saxons plot his overthrow but are foiled by a handsome outlaw.
Comic strip adventure with action highlights borrowed from older and better films.
w John Kohn, Jud Kinberg *d* Nathan Juran *ph* Wilkie Cooper, Jack Willis *m* Laurie Johnson
☆ Ronald Lewis, Janette Scott, Ronald Howard, Mark Dignam, John Laurie, Richard Clarke, Jerome Willis

Sierra
US 1950 83m Technicolor
Universal (Michael Kraike)
A father, accused of a crime he did not commit, hides out in the hills with his son.
Dim Western, routinely directed and with little conviction in the performances.

w Edna Anhalt, Milton Gunzburg *novel* The Mountains Are My Kingdom by Stuart Hardy *d* Alfred E. Green *ph* Russell Metty *m* Walter Scharf *ad* Bernard Herzbrun, Robert Boyle *ed* Ted Kent
☆ Wanda Hendrix, Audie Murphy, Dean Jagger, Burl Ives, Richard Rober, Anthony (Tony) Curtis, Sara Allgood, James Arness
'Worth its weight in manure. A really lousy western.' – *Clive Hirschhorn, The Universal Story*
† It was a remake of *Forbidden Valley* (qv).

Siesta
US 1987 100m colour
Palace/Lorimar (Gary Kurfirst)
📼 ▤ ⚙ 🎧
An amnesiac skydiver, visiting her former lover in Spain, is implicated in a murder.
Pretentious, deliberately obscure movie where there is little reward for working out what is happening.
w Patricia Louisianna Knop *novel* Patrice Chaplin *d* Mary Lambert *ph* Bryan Loftus *m* Miles Davis *pd* John Beard *ed* Glen Morgan
☆ Ellen Barkin, Gabriel Byrne, Julian Sands, Isabella Rossellini, Martin Sheen, Alexei Sayle, Grace Jones, Jodie Foster

Il Sigillo di Pechino: see The Peking Medallion

The Sign of Four
GB 1932 75m bw
ATP
Sherlock Holmes clears up a mystery including a hidden fortune, a secret pact, revenge from the east, and a pygmy who blows poison darts through a pipe.
Very acceptable version of the famous story, previously filmed as a silent.
w W. P. Lipscomb, John Paddy Carstairs *novel* Sir Arthur Conan Doyle *d* Graham Cutts *ph* Robert de Grasse, Robert G. Martin *md* Ernest Irving
☆ Arthur Wontner, Ian Hunter, Isla Bevan, Miles Malleson, Herbert Lomas, Roy Emerton

'A picture which will proudly lead all the entertainments the world has ever seen!'
'Like a shining light – the simple faith that was mightier than a pagan empire!'
The Sign of the Cross ***
US 1932 123m bw
Paramount (Cecil B. de Mille)
In the days of Nero, a Roman officer is converted to Christianity.
A heavily theatrical play becomes one of de Mille's most impressive films, the genuine horror of the arena mingling with the debauched humour of the court. A wartime prologue added in 1943 prolongs the film without improving it.
w Waldemar Young, Sidney Buchman *play* Wilson Barrett *d* Cecil B. de Mille *ph* Karl Struss *m* Rudolph Kopp
☆ Fredric March, Elissa Landi, Charles Laughton, Claudette Colbert, Ian Keith, Harry Beresford, Arthur Hohl, Nat Pendleton
'A beautiful film to watch … a triumph of popular art. – *Charles Higham, 1972*
'However contemptible one may find de Mille's moralizing, it is impossible not to be impressed by The Sign of the Cross.' – *John Baxter, 1968*
'De Mille's bang-them-on-the-head-with-old-orgies-and-imperilled-virginity style is at its ripest.' – *New Yorker, 1976*
'Preposterous, but the laughter dies on the lips.' – *NFT, 1974*
'This slice of "history" has it all: Laughton's implicitly gay Nero fiddling away while an impressive miniature set burns, Colbert bathing up to her nipples in asses' milk, Christians and other unfortunates thrown to a fearsome menagerie, much suggestive slinking about in Mitchell Leisen's costumes, much general debauchery teetering between the sadistic and the erotic. Not for people with scruples.' – *Geoff Brown, Time Out, 1980*
🎞 Karl Struss

Sign of the Gladiator
Italy/France/West Germany 1959 84m
Eastmancolor Dyaliscope
Glomer Film/Lyre-Lux/Tele Film (Rino Merolle)
original title: *Nel Segno di Roma*
Zenobia, Queen of Syria, revolts against Roman rule but falls in love with the consul sent to destroy her.

An early, dull example of Italy's 'sword and sandal' cycle, lacking the genre's saving spectacle
w F. Thellung, F. de Feo, Sergio Leone, G. Mangione, Guido Brignone d Guido Brignone, Riccardo Freda (battle scenes) ph Luciano Trasatti m A. Francesco Lavagnino ad Ottavio Scotti ed Nino Baragli
☆ Anita Ekberg, Georges Marchal, Folco Lulli, Jacques Sernas, Lorella de Luca, Alberto Farnese, Chelo Alonso

'Against his ruthless pagan lusts – the power of a woman's love!'

The Sign of the Pagan

👫 US 1954 92m Technicolor
Cinemascope
U-I (Albert J. Cohen)
Attila the Hun is defeated by the Romans.
Historic horse opera, rather cheaply done.
w Oscar Brodney, Barre Lyndon d Douglas Sirk ph Russell Metty m Frank Skinner, Hans Salter
☆ Jeff Chandler, Jack Palance, Rita Gam, Ludmilla Tcherina, Jeff Morrow, George Dolenz, Eduard Franz, Alexander Scourby

The Sign of the Ram

US 1948 84m bw
Columbia (Irving Cummings Jnr)
A selfish invalid interferes in her family's affairs.
Stultifying melodrama in the wake of Guest in the House, devised for the unfortunate Miss Peters who was crippled after an accident. Poor production values don't help.
w Charles Bennett d John Sturges ph Burnett Guffey m Hans Salter
☆ Susan Peters, Alexander Knox, Peggy Ann Garner, May Whitty

Signal 7

US 1983 92m colour
Myron/Taylor/New Front/Alliance
Two middle-aged taxi drivers, with aspirations to be actors, reminisce about their lives and hopes.
Semi-improvised slice of life, although you wouldn't necessarily want to ride in either of the protagonists' cabs.
w Signal 7 Group (Victoria Bennett, Hildy Burns, Steve Burns, Roy Kissin, Sara Morris, Rob Nilsson, David Schickele) d Rob Nilsson ph Geoff Schaaf, Tomas Tucker m Andy Narell ed Richard Harkness
☆ Bill Ackridge, Dan Leegant

Le Signe du Lion *

France 1959 90m bw
AJYM Films/Claude Chabrol (Jean Cotet)
aka: The Sign of Leo
An American composer living in Paris mistakenly believes he has inherited a fortune and is reduced to penury as a result.
Rohmer's first feature, a lively slice-of-life among French bohemians, but spoiled by its unlikely ending.
w Eric Rohmer, Paul Gegauff d Eric Rohmer ph Nicolas Hayer m Louis Saguer ed Anne-Marie Cotret
☆ Jess Hahn, Michèle Girardon, Van Doude, Paul Bisciglia, Gilbert Edard, Stéphane Audran, Jean Le Poulain

La Signora della Notte: see Lady of the Night

Signore e Signori: see The Birds, the Bees and the Italians

Signpost to Murder

US 1964 74m bw Panavision
MGM/Martin (Lawrence Weingarten)
A convicted murderer escapes after ten years and a lonely wife promises to help him.
Tricksy mystery set in a never-never English village.
w Sally Benson play Monte Doyle d George Englund ph Paul C. Vogel m Lyn Murray
☆ Joanne Woodward, Stuart Whitman, Edward Mulhare, Alan Napier, Murray Matheson

Signs of Life *

West Germany 1968 90m bw
Werner Herzog
original title: Lebenszeichen
During the Second World War, a German soldier, sent to a small Greek island to guard a fortress while he recovers from a wound, is maddened by the peace and boredom of the place.

A coolly dispassionate account of an individual's breakdown when faced with the apparent meaningless of existence.
wd Werner Herzog story Der tolle Invalide auf dem Fort Ratonneau by Achim von Arnim m Thomas Mauch m Stavros Xarchakos ed Beate Mainke-Jellinghaus, Maxi Mainke
☆ Peter Brogle, Wolfgang Reichmann, Julio Pinheiro, Athina Zacharopoulou, Wolfgang von Ungern-Sternberg, Wolfgang Stumpf
'A limpidly clear meditation on life shrivelling under a self-imposed oppression.' – Richard Combs, MFB

The Silence *

Sweden 1963 96m bw
Svensk Filmindustri
🖭 ▦ 🎧
original title: Tystnaden
Of two women in a large hotel in a foreign city where the military are dominant, one masturbates while the other sleeps with a barman.
Bergman may know what this was all about, but it's a certainty that no one else did: so everyone thought it must be very clever and went to see it. Superficially, as usual, it is careful and fascinating.
wd Ingmar Bergman ph Sven Nykvist m from Bach
☆ Ingrid Thulin, Gunnel Lindblom
'There is not enough forward thrust, not enough momentum to unite the specific points, the complementary but discrete images. The pearls are there, but the string is too weak to hold them.' – John Simon

Le Silence est d'Or *

France 1947 99m bw
Pathé/RKO Radio (René Clair)
In 1906 a comedian becomes a film producer and as a result falls into an affair with a young girl.
Somehow not an important film, but quite a delightful one, especially for its local colour and for the combination of Clair and Chevalier up to their old tricks.
wd René Clair ph Armand Thirard m Georges Van Parys
☆ Maurice Chevalier, François Périer, Marcelle Derrien

The Silence of Dean Maitland

Australia 1934 97m bw
Cinesound (Ken G. Hall)
A clergyman sires an illegitimate baby, kills the girl's father and allows another man to be convicted.
Once sensational stuff which almost caused an Australian scandal.
w Gayne Dexter, Edmund Barclay d Ken G. Hall
☆ John Longden, Charlotte Francis, Jocelyn Howarth, Patricia Minchin

Silence of the Hams

Italy/US 1993 81m Foto-Kem
Polygram/Thirtieth Century Wolf/Berlusconi (Ezio Greggio, Julie Corman)
🖭
A woman who steals money from her boss spends the night in a motel, where she is murdered in the shower; an FBI agent and a private eye investigate.
An inept attempt by a popular Italian television comic to cash in on the market for dumb, lazy spoofs of popular movies, though this one harks back to Hitchcock's Psycho, with Balsam sadly parodying his original role, more than to Silence of the Lambs.
wd Ezio Greggio ph Jacques Haitkin m Parmer Fuller pd Jim Newport ed Robert Barrere, Andy Horvitch
☆ Ezio Greggio, Dom DeLuise, Billy Zane, Joanna Pacula, Charlene Tilton, Martin Balsam, Stuart Pankin, John Astin, Phyllis Diller, Bubba Smith, Shelley Winters, Henry Silva
'Even if you smirked at the title, don't waste another second of your life.' – Sight and Sound
† Joe Dante, John Carpenter, John Landis and Mel Brooks also appear in cameo roles, poor things.

Silence of the Lambs ***

US 1990 118m Technicolor Panavision
Rank/Orion/Strong Heart/Demme (Edward Saxon, Kenneth Utt, Ron Bozman)
🖭 ▦ 🎦 ⑨ 🎧
A young female FBI agent seeks the aid of an imprisoned serial killer and psychiatrist, Hannibal 'The Cannibal' Lecter, to track down another mass murderer.

Tense, exciting and sometimes gruesome thriller, suspenseful enough to make you overlook its essential absurdities. Hopkins plays the role of the devious Lecter with lip-smacking relish.
w Ted Tally novel Thomas Harris d Jonathan Demme ph Tak Fujimoto m Howard Shore pd Kristi Zea ed Craig McKay
☆ Jodie Foster, Anthony Hopkins, Scott Glenn, Ted Levine, Anthony Heald, Lawrence A. Bonney, Kasi Lemmons, Lawrence J. Wrentz, Frankie Faison, Roger Corman
HANNIBAL LECTER: 'I do wish we could chat longer, but I'm having an old friend for dinner.'
'A mesmerizing thriller that will grip audiences from first scene to last.' – Variety
'A sombre masterpiece' – Sight and Sound
'An exceptionally good film, perhaps this fine director's best, in which the horror genre is elevated into the kind of cinema that can at least be argued about as a treatise for its unsettling times.' – Derek Malcolm, Guardian
👤 film; Jonathan Demme; Anthony Hopkins; Jodie Foster; Ted Tally
♫ editing; sound
🏆 Anthony Hopkins; Jodie Foster

Silence of the North

Canada 1981 94m colour
Universal (Canada) (Murray Shostak)
🎧
In 1919 a city girl is courted by a trapper and joins him in the north country.
Nicely filmed but utterly predictable romantic melodrama, based on a biography but not carrying much conviction. D. W. Griffith would have liked it.
w Patricia Louisianna Knop book Olive Fredrickson, Ben East d Allan Winton King ph Richard Leiterman m Allan MacMillan
☆ Ellen Burstyn, Tom Skerritt, Gordon Pinsent, Jennifer McKinney

'Follow his secret from bedroom to bedlam, with guns, girls and dynamite!'

The Silencers *

US 1966 103m Technicolor
Columbia/Irving Allen (Jim Schmerer)
Adventures of a sexy secret agent.
Or, James Bond sent up rotten. Plenty of fun along the way, with in-jokes and characters like Lovey Kravezit, but the plot could have done with more attention, and the sequels (Murderers Row, The Ambushers, Wrecking Crew) were uncontrolled disaster areas.
w Oscar Saul novel Donald Hamilton d Phil Karlson ph Burnett Guffey m Elmer Bernstein
☆ Dean Martin, Stella Stevens, Victor Buono, Daliah Lavi, Cyd Charisse, Robert Webber, James Gregory, Nancy Kovack
'The dullest, dirtiest thud excreted by the sex-and-sadism spoofs of Bondism.' – Judith Crist

The Silences of the Palace *

France/Tunisia 1994 127m colour
ICA/Mat/Cinetelefilms/Magfilm (Ahmed Baha, Eddine Attia, Richard Magnien)
🖭
A singer returns to the Tunisian palace where she was brought up by her mother, a servant and mistress of the king, and recalls her past life.
A leisurely, careful drama of women trapped within a social system that denies them freedom over their own lives.
wd Moufida Tlatli ph Youssef Ben Youssef m Anouar Brahem ad Claude Bennys, Mondher Dhrif ed Moufida Tlatli, Camille Cotte, Kerim Hammouda
☆ Ahmel Hedhili, Hend Sabri, Najia Ouerghi, Ghalia Lecroix, Sami Bouajila, Kamel Fazaa
'Honourable, but a little torpid – better on the textures of feudal life than storytelling.' – Kevin Jackson, Independent
'This is, at heart, a Stella Dallas story set in the shimmering reflections of royal life before any revolution.' – Time

The Silent Battle

GB 1939 84m bw
Pinebrook (Anthony Havelock-Allan)
A French agent battles revolutionaries in the Balkans.
Unconvincing spy stuff with an uncertain tone.
w Wolfgang Wilhelm, Rodney Ackland novel Jean Bommart d Herbert Mason
☆ Rex Harrison, Valerie Hobson, John Loder, Muriel Aked, John Salew, George Devine

Silent Dust *

GB 1948 82m bw
ABP/Independent Sovereign (Nat Bronsten)
A baronet builds a memorial to his son who has apparently been killed in action, but the son turns up and proves to be an absolute bounder.
Effective stage melodrama, quite neatly filmed.
w Michael Pertwee play The Paragon by Roland and Michael Pertwee d Lance Comfort ph Wilkie Cooper m Georges Auric
☆ Sally Gray, Derek Farr, Stephen Murray, Nigel Patrick, Seymour Hicks

The Silent Enemy

GB 1958 112m bw
Romulus (Bertram Ostrer)
🖭
The World War II exploits of a naval frogman in the Mediterranean.
Stereotyped naval underwater adventures, adequately presented.
wd William Fairchild book Commander Crabb by Marshall Pugh ph Egil Woxholt, Otto Heller m William Alwyn
☆ Laurence Harvey, John Clements, Michael Craig, Dawn Addams, Sidney James, Alec McCowen, Nigel Stock

'A Savage Crime. A Silent Witness.'

Silent Fall

US 1994 101m Technicolor
Warner/Morgan Creek (James G. Robinson)
🖭 🖭 🎦 🎧
An autistic nine-year-old is the only witness to his parents' brutal murder.
Dull thriller, silly when it is not predictable and cheap in its use of autism for such a trivial end.
w Akiva Goldsman d Bruce Beresford ph Peter James m Stewart Copeland pd John Stoddart
☆ Richard Dreyfuss, Linda Hamilton, John Lithgow, J. T. Walsh, Ben Faulkner, Liv Taylor, Zahn McClarnon
'Nothing could save this film from being mediocre at best.' – Derek Malcolm, Guardian
'For a thriller about the life of the mind, this one is chock-full of cheap thinking.' – Tom Shone, Sunday Times

The Silent Flute

US 1978 95m colour
Volare (Richard St Johns)
In a martial arts tournament, a hero is chosen to challenge the wizard Zetan.
Curiously mystical adventure allegory with an unhelpful title. Not too bad for those in the mood.
w Stirling Silliphant, Stanley Mann d Richard Moore ph Ronnie Taylor m Bruce Smeaton
☆ Jeff Cooper, David Carradine, Roddy McDowall, Christopher Lee, Eli Wallach

Silent Movie *

👫 US 1976 87m DeLuxe
TCF/Crossbow (Michael Hertzberg)
🖭 🖭 🎦
An alcoholic producer gets the idea that a silent movie would be a great novelty, and tries to get stars to take part.
Fairly lively spoof with the talents concerned in variable form. The shortage of laughter made it a hit in the seventies, but at no time does it approach the Keaton or Laurel and Hardy level.
w Mel Brooks, Ron Clark, Rudy de Luca, Barry Levinson d Mel Brooks ph Paul Lohmann m John Morris
☆ Mel Brooks, Marty Feldman, Dom DeLuise, Bernadette Peters, Sid Caesar, Harold Gould, Fritz Feld, Harry Ritz, Henny Youngman
† guest stars Anne Bancroft, Paul Newman, Burt Reynolds, James Caan, Liza Minnelli, Marcel Marcea.
†† Marcel Marceau utters the only word in the movie, which is 'Non'.

Silent Night, Evil Night: see Black Christmas

The Silent Partner

Canada 1978 105m colour
Carolco (Garth H. Drabinsky)
🖭 🎦
A bank teller foils an attempted raid and steals the money himself.
A suspense thriller of a familiar kind; it might have been entertaining but elects instead to be unpleasant.

w Curtis Hanson *novel* *Think of a Number* by Anders Bodelsen d Daryl Duke ph Stephen Katz m Oscar Peterson

☆ Christopher Plummer, Elliott Gould, Susannah York, Celine Lomez, Michael Kirby

The Silent Passenger

GB   1935   75m   bw

Phoenix

Lord Peter Wimsey clears a man of a murder charge.

Not an unappealing presentation of Dorothy Sayers's famous detective, though he is presented as too much the silly ass and the story is weak.

w Basil Mason *story* Dorothy L. Sayers d Reginald Denham ph Jan Stallich

☆ Peter Haddon, John Loder, Mary Newland, Austin Trevor, Donald Wolfit, Leslie Perrins, Robb Wilton

Silent Running *

US   1971   90m   Technicolor

Universal/Michel Gruskoff

⊞ ▦ ℚ ◈

Members of a space station crew in 2001 are space gardening to replenish nuclear-devastated Earth.

Sombre futuristic fantasy, well made but slow and muddled in development.

w Deric Washburn, Michael Cimino, Steve Bochco d Douglas Trumbull ph Charles F. Wheeler m Peter Schickele

☆ Bruce Dern, Cliff Potts, Ron Rifkin, Jesse Vint

Silent Scream *

GB   1989   85m

BFI/Film Four International (Paddy Higson)

Jailed for the murder of a bartender, a depressive prisoner, dying from an overdose of drugs, recalls his past life.

Based on the writings and life of Larry Winters, who was transferred to a prison where he was encouraged to be creative, the film's hallucinatory style too often obscures its intentions.

w Bill Beech, Jane Beech d David Hayman ph Denis Crossan m Callum McNair pd Andy Harris ed Justin Krish

☆ Iain Glen, Paul Samson, Andrew Barr, Kenneth Glenaan, Steve Hotchkiss, John Murtagh, Bobby Carlyle, Tom Watson, Julie Graham

'I felt as if someone had handed me a bag of jumbled jigsaw pieces and told me to make up my own picture.' – *Philip French, Observer*

The Silent Stranger: see Step Down to Terror

Silent Tongue

US   1993   101m   colour

Entertainment/Belbo/Alive (Carolyn Pfeiffer, Ludi Boeken)

⊞ ▦ ℚ

A horse-dealer sets out to buy as a new wife for his son the daughter of a alcoholic quack; after her twin sister dies in childbirth; the two girls were born as the result of their father's rape of a mute Indian woman.

A portentous, heavily symbolic melodrama that might have been more effective on the stage or on the page; certainly, the ripe over-acting of the cast is no help to understanding its point.

wd Sam Shepard ph Jack Conroy m Patrick O'Hearn pd Cary White ed Bill Yahraus

☆ Richard Harris, Sheila Tousey, Alan Bates, River Phoenix, Dermot Mulroney, Tantoo Cardinal, Jeri Arredondo

'The whole thing looks like one of those moody philosophical westerns they used occasionally to make before the genre ran out of both ideas and box-office appeal.' – *Derek Malcolm, Guardian*

The Silent Touch

GB/Poland/Denmark   1992   96m   colour

Mayfair/Tor/Mark Forstater

A Polish music student goes to Denmark to encourage a composer who has not written a note for 40 years to complete his work.

A curious fable about creativity, which precisely lacks that quality.

w Peter Morgan, Mark Wadlow *story* Krzysztof Zanussi, Edward Zebrowski d Krzysztof Zanussi ph Jaroslaw Zamojda m Wojciech Kilar pd Ewa Braun ed Mark Denys

☆ Max von Sydow, Lothaire Bluteau, Sarah Miles, Sofie Grabol, Aleksander Bardini, Peter Hesse Overgaard, Lars Lunoe

---

'A great score, von Sydow's performance and a number of delightful moments do not compensate for the ludicrous plot which fails to fully engage the imagination.' – *Empire*

The Silent Village **

GB   1943   35m   bw

Humphrey Jennings/Ministry of Information

Harrowing depiction, by the members of a Welsh village, of what happened to the Czech population of Lidice after the assassination of Heydrich.

A chilling documentary at the time, this little classic has kept its kick.

wd Humphrey Jennings ed Stewart McAllister

Silent Voice: see Amazing Grace and Chuck

The Silent Voice: see The Man Who Played God (1932)

The Silent Voice: see Paula (1952)

The Silent Witness

US   1932   73m   bw

Fox

A man confesses to murder in order to protect his son.

Solid courtroom stuff of its day, built for a new star who never quite made it.

play Jack de Leon and Jack Celestin d Marcel Varnel, R. L. Hough

☆ Lionel Atwill, Helen Mack, Greta Nissen, Bramwell Fletcher, Alan Mowbray

'A gripping talker that rates well above most of the creep releases.' – *Variety*

The Silent Woman

France   1989   96m   colour

Antenne 2/Son et Lumière

A doctor finds her isolated country home invaded by three assassins, who plan to kill her after she witnesses their murder of a politician, and a lunatic who escapes from a nearby asylum.

Suspenseful, though silly, thriller in which the hitmen behave with surprising stupidity.

w Jean-Claude Carrière, Joyce Bunuel d Joyce Bunuel m François Breant

☆ Marie-Christine Barrault, Véronique Genest, Pierre Clementi

The Silk Hat Kid

US   1935   70m   bw

Fox (Joseph Engel)

A settlement housekeeper accepts help from a racketeer.

Thin little drama, perfunctorily played.

w Edward Eliscu, Lou Breslow, Dore Schary *story* Gerald Beaumont d H. Bruce Humberstone

☆ Lew Ayres, Mae Clarke, Paul Kelly, Ralf Harolde, William Harrigan

'It hasn't the story nor the entertainment weight to lift it out of the double feature classification.' – *Variety*

Silk Stockings *

US   1957   116m   Metrocolor   Cinemascope

MGM (Arthur Freed)

⊞ ▦ ℚ ◈

A Russian composer in Paris agrees to write music for a Hollywood film; a lady commissar is sent to get him back.

Musical rewrite of Ninotchka via a Broadway show; good moments but generally very stretched.

w Leonard Gershe, Leonard Spigelgass play George S. Kaufman, Leueen McGrath, Abe Burrows *original play* Melchior Lengyel d Rouben Mamoulian ph Robert Bronner m/ly Cole Porter md André Previn

☆ Fred Astaire, Cyd Charisse, Peter Lorre, Janis Paige, George Tobias, Jules Munshin, Joseph Buloff

† Cyd Charisse's singing was dubbed by Carole Richards.

The Silken Affair

GB   1956   96m   bw

Dragon (Fred Feldkamp)

An accountant decides to live it up, and finds himself on trial for manipulating the firm's books.

Unsatisfactory mix of comedy and fantasy, with a dim plot and virtually no comic ideas.

w Robert Lewis Taylor d Roy Kellino ph Gilbert Taylor m Peggy Stuart

☆ David Niven, Genevieve Page, Wilfrid Hyde-White, Ronald Squire, Beatrice Straight, Howard Marion Crawford, Dorothy Alison

---

Silken Skin **

France   1964   118m   bw

Films du Carrosse/SEDIF

⊞

original title: *La Peau Douce*

A middle-aged married man leaves his wife for an attractive young girl, but the latter leaves him and his wife shoots him.

Carefully balanced mixture of comedy and melodrama which rings almost every possible change on the theme of adultery and does so with wit.

w François Truffaut, Jean-Louis Richard d François Truffaut ph Raoul Coutard m Georges Delerue

☆ Jean Desailly, Françoise Dorléac, Nelly Benedetti

'Very funny, very touching, very wise about human beings.' – *New York Herald Tribune*

Silkwood *

US   1983   131m   Technicolor

ABC (Mike Nichols, Michael Hausman)

⊞ ▦ ○ ℚ

The true story, more or less, of a girl worker in a nuclear processing plant who mysteriously dies in an accident just before she is going to talk to a reporter about a safety problem.

Despite the historical interest of the case, it is too simple to merit a film of this length, which is filled with pregnant pauses and romantic asides. Nor are the actors quite so charismatic as they think they are.

w Nora Ephron, Alice Arlen d Mike Nichols ph Miroslav Ondricek m Georges Delerue pd Patrizia von Brandenstein

☆ Meryl Streep, Cher, Kurt Russell, Craig T. Nelson, Diana Scarwid, Fred Ward

'A movie with a preordained conclusion but nowhere to go ... it submerges what could have been its most telling points in a kind of concentrated soap opera.' – *Richard Combs, MFB*

§ Meryl Streep; Cher; direction; screenplay; editing (Sam O'Steen)

Silver Bears

GB   1977   113m   Technicolor

EMI/Raleigh (Arlene Sellers, Alex Winitsky)

⊞ ▦

A Las Vegas money man invests money in various European outlets and makes a killing.

Extraordinarily complex financial jape which tries the patience of all but financiers.

w Peter Stone *novel* Paul Erdman d Ivan Passer ph Anthony Richmond m Claude Bolling

☆ Michael Caine, Louis Jourdan, Cybill Shepherd, Stephane Audran, David Warner, Tom Smothers, Martin Balsam, Charles Gray

Silver Blaze

GB   1937   70m   bw

Twickenham (Julius Hagen)

▦

US title: *Murder at the Baskervilles*

Sherlock Holmes clears a racehorse of having killed its trainer.

Not the best of the Holmes series, but this is a very satisfying Holmes.

w Arthur Macrae, H. Fowler Mear *story* Sir Arthur Conan Doyle d Thomas Bentley ph Sydney Blythe ad James Carter

☆ Arthur Wontner, Ian Fleming, Lyn Harding, Judy Gunn, Lawrence Grossmith, Arthur Macrae

The Silver Brumby

🎠 Australia   1993   92m   colour

Media World/AFFC (John Tatoulis, Colin J. South)

A foal grows up to become a stallion and leader of a herd of wild horses, only to be hunted by a ruthless man.

Despite some excellent photography, the slight and uninteresting narrative makes it heavy going even for horse lovers.

w John Tatoulis, Jon Stephens, Elyne Mitchell *book* Elyne Mitchell d John Tatoulis ph Mark Gilfedder m Tassos Ioannides pd Phil Chambers ed Peter Burgess

☆ Caroline Goodall, Russell Crowe, Ami Daemion, Johnny Raaen

'A superbly crafted family film for animal lovers.' – *Variety*

Silver Bullet

US   1985   95m   Technicolor

Paramount/Dino de Laurentiis (Martha Schumacher)

⊞ ▦ ℚ

Murders at Tarker's Mill turn out to be the work of a werewolf.

Dreary, unimaginative rendition of a theme that was more entertaining in 1941.

w Stephen King *novelette* Cycle of the Werewolf by Stephen King d Daniel Attias ph Armando Nannuzzi m Jay Chattaway

☆ Corey Haim, Gary Busey, Megan Follows, Everett McGill

'It's a Stephen King filmette from his novelette which may sell some tickettes but not without regrettes.' – *Variety*

'I bid you seek the lost silver cup ... for sin is rising like the swollen rivers!'

'Against the broad canvas of history's mad era of splendour and seduction – here is the story of the sacred cup of silver that challenged the iron sword of tyranny – the mighty struggle to possess it – and the loves and the faith that triumphed in humanity's darkest hour!'

The Silver Chalice

US   1954   142m   Warnercolor   Cinemascope

Warner (Victor Saville)

⊞

Adventures of a slave freed by Luke the apostle to fashion a chalice to hold the cup used at the Last Supper.

Po-faced biblical hokum, slower and deadlier than most, with howlingly bad casting and direction. On reflection, interesting things are being attempted with limbo set design, but in this sea of boredom the attempt only raises an eyebrow.

w Lesser Samuels *novel* Thomas B. Costain d Victor Saville ph William V. Skall m Franz Waxman pd Rolf Gerard

☆ Paul Newman, Pier Angeli, Jack Palance, Virginia Mayo, Walter Hampden, Joseph Wiseman, Alexander Scourby, Lorne Greene, Michael Pate, E. G. Marshall

§ William V. Skall; Franz Waxman

Silver City

US   1951   90m   Technicolor

Paramount (Nat Holt)

GB title: *High Vermilion*

A mining assayer helps a farmer and his daughter protect the ore found on their land.

Standard Western programmer with plenty of action

w Frank Gruber *story* Luke Short d Byron Haskin ph Ray Rennahan m Paul Sawtell

☆ Yvonne de Carlo, Edmond O'Brien, Barry Fitzgerald, Richard Arlen, Gladys George, Laura Elliott, Edgar Buchanan, John Dierkes

Silver City *

Australia   1984   102m   Eastmancolor

Artificial Eye/Limelight Productions (Joan Long)

▦

Arriving in Australia in 1949, a Polish woman is sent to a camp where she has an affair with another, married immigrant.

Sharp study of bigotry and hostility undercut by a limp romance.

w Sophia Turkiewicz, Thomas Keneally d Sophia Turkiewicz ph John Seale m William Motzing ad Igot Nay ed Don Saunders

☆ Gosia Dobrowolska, Ivar Kants, Anna Jemison, Steve Bisley, Debra Lawrance, Ewa Brok, Joel Cohen, Tim McKenzie, Dennis Miller, Annie Byron

'Works best as a sociological study of cultural clash.' – *Brian McFarlane, Australian Cinema 1970–1985*

The Silver Cord

US   1933   74m   bw

RKO (Pandro S. Berman)

A young wife threatens to leave her husband because of his excessive devotion to his mother.

Stilted version of an old theatrical warhorse.

w Jane Murfin play Sidney Howard d John Cromwell ph Charles Rosher

☆ Irene Dunne, Joel McCrea, Laura Hope Crews, Frances Dee, Eric Linden, Helen Cromwell

The Silver Darlings

GB   1947   84m   bw

Holyrood

Hebridean islanders take to herring fishing as a last chance to avoid emigration.

Uneventful island mood piece which lacks the poetic quality which might have made it memorable.
w Clarence Elder *novel* Neil Gunn d Clarence Elder, Clifford Evans
☆ Clifford Evans, Helen Shingler, Carl Bernard, Norman Shelley, Simon Lack, Hugh Griffith

Silver Dollar *
US 1932 84m bw
Warner

A poor farmer goes to Colorado for the gold rush, strikes it rich, and learns that money doesn't bring happiness.
Packed biopic of one H. A. W. Tabor, an excellent star vehicle.
w Carl Erickson, Harvey Thew d Alfred E. Green ph James Van Trees m Milan Roder
☆ Edward G. Robinson, Bebe Daniels, Aline MacMahon, Jobyna Howland, Robert Warwick, Russell Simpson
'Historical subject admirably done as to its variety but not so strong on its commercial side.' – *Variety*

Silver Dream Racer
GB 1980 111m Eastmancolor Panavision
Rank/David Wickes (Rene Dupont)

A garage mechanic becomes a racing motorcyclist and is killed at the peak of success.
One wonders who can have thought there was any box-office appeal in this cliché-ridden, derivative, flashily made update of the Road to Ruin.
wd David Wickes ph Paul Beeson m David Essex
☆ David Essex, Beau Bridges, Cristina Raines, Harry H. Corbett, Lee Montague, Clarke Peters
'Watching this grotesque hotch-potch of implausible characters being shunted through improbable situations is uncannily akin to being assaulted by a non-stop stream of TV commercials.' – *Tom Milne, MFB*

The Silver Fleet *
GB 1943 87m bw
GFD/Archers (Michael Powell, Emeric Pressburger, Ralph Richardson)

In occupied Holland, a shipping magnate destroys his new U-boat and himself and his Nazi mentors with it.
Slow-starting, rather stilted melodrama which when it gets into its stride provides good acting and gripping propaganda.
wd Vernon Sewell, Gordon Wellesley ph Erwin Hillier
☆ Ralph Richardson, Esmond Knight, Googie Withers, Beresford Egan, Frederick Burtwell, Kathleen Byron

Silver Lode *
US 1954 80m Technicolor
Benedict Bogeaus/RKO

A respected citizen of Silver Lode proves that the marshal who rides into town on his wedding day to accuse him of murder is a civilian bent on revenge.
Broody little Western melodrama, not half bad.
w Karen de Wolf d Allan Dwan ph John Alton m Louis Forbes
☆ John Payne, Dan Duryea, Lizabeth Scott, Dolores Moran, Emile Meyer, Robert Warwick

Silver Queen *
US 1942 80m bw
UA/Harry Sherman

A chivalrous Western gambler rescues a girl from the wiles of a villain.
Standard romantic melodrama mainly set in saloons.
w Bernard Schubert, Cecile Kramer d Lloyd Bacon m Russell Harlan m Victor Young ad Ralph Berger
☆ George Brent, Priscilla Lane, Bruce Cabot, Lynne Overman, Eugene Pallette, Janet Beecher, Guinn Williams, Roy Barcroft
& Victor Young; Ralph Berger

Silver River *
US 1948 110m bw
Warner (Owen Crump)

A ruthless gambler becomes powerful but loses everything because of his character defects.
Meandering Western drama with a few good highlights dissipated by long chunks of character building and a rehash of the David and Bathsheba story.

w Stephen Longstreet, Harriet Frank Jnr d Raoul Walsh ph Sid Hickox m Max Steiner
☆ Errol Flynn, Ann Sheridan, Thomas Mitchell, Bruce Bennett, Tom D'Andrea, Barton MacLane, Monte Blue, Alan Bridge

Silver Skates
US 1942 73m bw
Monogram (Lindsley Parsons)

A touring ice revue is lapsing into debt.
Novelties on ice occupy more screen time than the story, which is just as well. Competent small-scale musical filler.
w Jerry Cady d Leslie Goodwins
☆ Kenny Baker, Patricia Morison, Belita, Frick and Frack

Silver Streak *
US 1976 113m DeLuxe
TCF/Martin Ransohoff, Frank Yablans

On a trans-continental train, a young publisher discovers a murder and is at the mercy of the culprits.
Rather like an update of a Bob Hope comedy-thriller with a whiff of sex, this amiable spoof goes on too long, brings in a second comic too late, and ends with fashionable but irrelevant violence.
w Colin Higgins d Arthur Hiller ph David M. Walsh m Henry Mancini pd Alfred Sweeney
☆ Gene Wilder, Jill Clayburgh, Richard Pryor, Patrick McGoohan, Ned Beatty, Clifton James, Ray Walston, Richard Kiel
'Nineteen-seventies performers are trapped in this fake thirties mystery comedy, which is so inept you can't even get angry.' – *New Yorker*

The Silver Streak *
US 1934 85m bw
RKO

A streamlined train makes its first run from Chicago to Boulder Dam, where a victim of infantile paralysis must be got into an iron lung.
Historically interesting melodrama which seldom pauses for breath.
w H. W. Hanemann, Jack O'Donnell, Roger Whately d Tommy Atkins ph J. Roy Hunt md Alberto Colombo
☆ Sally Blane, Charles Starrett, Hardie Albright, William Farnum, Irving Pichel, Arthur Lake, Edgar Kennedy
'Pretty absurd, yet exciting and fast ... there's scarcely a stunt known to the railroad picture formula that hasn't been employed.' – *Variety*

Silverado *
US 1985 132m Technicolor Super Techniscope
Lawrence Kasdan

In the 1880s, various pioneers try to establish a future in the west.
Interesting but not wholly successful attempt to revive in one movie various Western myths and legends; a little more conscious humour might have helped.
w Lawrence and Mark Kasdan d Lawrence Kasdan ph John Bailey m Bruce Broughton pd Ida Random ed Carol Littleton
☆ Kevin Kline, Scott Glenn, Kevin Costner, Danny Glover, John Cleese, Rosanna Arquette, Brian Dennehy, Linda Hunt, Jeff Goldblum
'Less like the film westerns of imagination and more like something more common. Maybe it was that way in real life.' – *Variety*
& music

Simba
GB 1955 99m Eastmancolor
GFD/Group Film (Peter de Sarigny)

An English farmer in Kenya fights the Mau Mau.
Savagely topical melodrama which tends to cheapen a tragic situation.
w John Baines d Brian Desmond Hurst ph Geoffrey Unsworth m Francis Chagrin
☆ Dirk Bogarde, Donald Sinden, Virginia McKenna, Basil Sydney, Marie Ney, Joseph Tomelty, Earl Cameron, Orlando Martins

Simon *
US 1980 97m Technicolor
Warner/Orion (Louis A. Stroller, Martin Bregman)

Corrupt scientists brainwash a psychology professor into thinking he's from another planet.
Solemn comic fantasy which doesn't seem to make much of a point and only superficially entertains, but is well made and well acted.
wd Marshall Brickman ph Adam Holender m Stanley Silverman pd Stuart Wurtzel
☆ Alan Arkin, Madeline Kahn, Austin Pendleton, Judy Graubart, William Finley, Fred Gwynne

Simon and Laura *
GB 1955 91m Technicolor Vistavision
GFD/Group Films (Teddy Baird)

The actors who play husband and wife in a TV series are married in reality and hate each other, a fact that shows in the live Christmas episode.
Adequate film of a reasonably sophisticated West End comedy; good lines and performances.
w Peter Blackmore *play* Alan Melville d Muriel Box ph Ernest Steward m Benjamin Frankel
☆ Peter Finch, Kay Kendall, Ian Carmichael, Alan Wheatley, Richard Wattis, Muriel Pavlow, Maurice Denham, Hubert Gregg

Simon Birch
US 1998 113m Technicolor
Buena Vista/Hollywood/Caravan (Laurence Mark, Roger Birnbaum)

A man remembers the diminutive childhood friend who caused the death of his mother and changed his life.
Maudlin tale, manipulative and melodramatic for the most part; its story of loss and redemption never convinces.
wd Mark Steven Johnson *suggested by novel* A Prayer for Owen Meany by John Irving ph Aaron E. Schneider m Marc Shaiman pd David Chapman ed David Finfer
☆ Ian Michael Smith, Joseph Mazzello, Ashley Judd, Oliver Platt, David Strathairn, Dana Ivey, Hildie Grove, Jim Carrey, Jan Hooks
'Though routinely slick, feature grows more irksome as it goes along — the lack of any genuinely felt emotions communicated makes later melodrama come off as shameless contrivance.' – *Dennis Harvey, Variety*
† Unhappy at the adaptation, John Irving insisted that the film's credit should read 'suggested by' his novel, and that the name of his central character should be changed.

Simon of the Desert **
Mexico 1965 45m bw
Gustavo Alatriste

original title: Simón del Desierto
A holy man, following the example of St Simeon Stylites by living at the top of a column in the desert, is tempted by the Devil in the shape of a woman.
Intriguing and amusing fable on the nature of goodness, though it does not come to a satisfactory conclusion.
w Luis Buñuel, Julio Alejandro d Luis Buñuel ph Gabriel Figueroa m Raul Lavista ed Carlos Savage Jnr
☆ Claudio Brook, Silvia Pinal, Enrique Alvarez Felix, Hortensia Santoveña, Francisco Reiguera, Luis Aceves Castañeda, Enrique Garcia Alvarez
'It is Buñuel at his best: stylite and stylist face each other from their respective pedestals.' – *John Simon*
† The film was intended to be at least twice as long, but many scenes, including a visit from the Emperor of Byzantium, had to be cut when the producer ran out of money. Buñuel has said that it was the reason that the film's ending is somewhat abrupt.

Simon the Swiss: see Le Voyou

'How Much Can Three Friends Share?'
Simpatico *
US/France 1999 106m DeLuxe
Alliance/Emotion/Canal (Dan Lupovitz, Timm Oberwelland, Jean-Francois Fonlupt)

A multimillionaire racehorse owner discovers that a seedy boyhood friend is about to expose their dubious past.

A muted, melancholy drama of men being overtaken and destroyed by unnecessary guilt; the acting is a pleasure to watch.
w Matthew Warchus, David Nicholls *play* Sam Shepard d Matthew Warchus ph John Toll m Stewart Copeland pd Amy Ancona ed Pasquale Buba
☆ Nick Nolte, Jeff Bridges, Sharon Stone, Catherine Keener, Albert Finney, Shawn Hatosy, Liam Waite, Kimberly Williams
'Thoughtful and appealing entertainment.' – *Variety*

'There is no such thing as adventure and romance. There's only trouble and desire.'
Simple Men *
GB/US 1992 105m Technicolor
Metro/Zenith/American Playhouse/Fine Line/Film Four/BIM (Ted Hope, Hal Hartley)

A petty crook and his brother search for their father, a former radical baseball star who has been on the run since the 60s.
Off-beat, occasionally amusing road movie that goes nowhere very interesting. It is too determinedly eccentric to be effective, but incidental pleasures include a fight between a nun and a policeman and a sheriff desperately searching for the meaning of life.
wd Hal Hartley m Michael Spiller m Ned Rifle pd Daniel Ouellette ed Steve Hamilton
☆ Robert Burke, William Sage, Karen Sillas, Elina Löwensohn, Martin Donovan, Mark Chandler Bailey, Chris Cooke
'Effortlessly manages to encompass social comment and satire as it oscillates between the comic and the absurd with a stylish self-confidence.' – *Mark Salisbury, Empire*

'Sometimes good people do evil things.'
A Simple Plan ***
US 1998 120m colour
Paramount/Mutual/Savoy (James Jacks, Adam Schroeder)

Outside a small Minnesota town, three friends stumble across a bag containing $4.4m dollars in a crashed plane, and decide to keep the money.
A deft, chilling thriller of corruption and greed, charting an inexorable slide from integrity to betrayal and worse.
w Scott B.Smith *novel* Scott B. Smith d Sam Raimi ph Alar Kivilo m Danny Elfman pd Patrizia von Brandenstein ed Arthur Coburn, Eric L. Beason
☆ Bill Paxton, Billy Bob Thornton, Bridget Fonda, Brent Briscoe, Gary Cole, Becky Ann Baker, Chelcie Ross, Jack Walsh
'Marvellously nuanced and beautifully acted.' – *Andrew Sarris*
& Billy Bob Thornton; Scott B. Smith

'Michael McCann Is About To Find Wealth Beyond His Imagination ... A Real Family.'
A Simple Twist of Fate *
US 1994 106m colour
Buena Vista/Touchstone (Ric Kidney)

A reclusive and miserly furniture-maker redeems himself when he adopts a small and abandoned girl.
A not entirely successful attempt to make the plot of Eliot's Victorian novel work in a modern setting, but it has its moments.
w Steve Martin *novel* Silas Marner by George Eliot d Gillies MacKinnon ph Andrew Dunn m Cliff Edelman pd Andy Harris ed Humphrey Dixon
☆ Steve Martin, Gabriel Byrne, Laura Linney, Catharine O'Hara, Stephen Baldwin, Byron Jennings, Michael des Barres, Amelia Campbell, Kellen Crosby
'A faithful, heartfelt, somber piece about family and responsibility.' – *Variety*

A Simple Wish
US 1997 90m DeLuxe
Universal/Bubble Factory (Sid Sheinberg, Bill Sheinberg, Jon Sheinberg)

An incompetent fairy godfather has problems making a child's wish come true.
Sickly whimsy that is over-reliant on special effects.
w Jeff Rothberg m Michael Ritchie ph Ralf Bode m Bruce Broughton pd Stephen Hendrickson ed William Scharf sp Greg Cannom

☆ Martin Short, Kathleen Turner, Mara Wilson, Robert Pastorelli, Amanda Plummer, Francis Capra, Ruby Dee, Teri Garr, Alan Campbell

'A case of talent adrift on an ocean of cutesy kids material.' – *Empire*

Simply Irresistible

US/Germany 1999 96m DeLuxe
TCF/Monarchy/Regency (John Fiedler, Jon Amiel, Joseph M. Carracciolo Jnr)

An indifferent cook, who suddenly produces great food with the aid of a magic crab, attracts a businessman with an interest in restaurants.
Dire and risible romantic comedy, quite bereft of any magic.

w Judith Roberts, Elisabeth Robinson d Mark Tarlov ph Robert Stevens m Gil Goldstein pd John Kasarda, William Barclay ed Paul Karasick

☆ Sarah Michelle Gellar, Sean Patrick Flanery, Patricia Clarkson, Dylan Baker, Larry Gilliard Jnr, Christopher Durang, Betty Buckley, Olek Krupa, Amanda Peet, Alex Draper

'Simply excruciating.' – *Empire*

Sin: see *The Beloved*

Sin Compasión *

Peru/Mexico/France 1994 120m DuArt
Gala/Inca/Aramanta/CiBy 2000 (Francisco J. Lombardi)
aka: *No Mercy*

A poor, idealistic student confesses murdering a wealthy old woman and her husband to a priest.
An updated version of the original, taken at a too-leisurely pace that allows attention to slacken.

w Augusto Cabada *novel* Crime and Punishment by Feodor Dostoevsky d Francisco J. Lombardi ph Pili Flores Guerra m Leopoldo La Rosa pd Cecilia Montiel ed Luis Barrios

☆ Diego Bertie, Adriana Davila, Jorge Chiarella, Hernan Romero, Marcello Rivera, Mariells Trejos, Carlos Onetto

'The complicated moral universe inhabited by Dostoevsky's characters seems a long way indeed from this gallery of one-dimensionality.' – *Sight and Sound*

The Sin of Harold Diddlebock: see *Mad Wednesday*

The Sin of Madelon Claudet

US 1931 74m bw
MGM (Harry Rapf)
GB title: *The Lullaby*

A mother is separated from her illegitimate baby.
Sob stuff for a rising star: hilarious now.

w Charles MacArthur *play* Edward Knoblock d Edgar Selwyn

☆ Helen Hayes, Robert Young, Neil Hamilton, Lewis Stone, Marie Prevost, Cliff Edwards, Jean Hersholt, Karen Morley

'Natural sobber for women and grosses ... but you don't have to go back as far as *Madame X* to find a parallel for the plot.' – *Variety*

♟ Helen Hayes

Sin Town

US 1942 74m bw
Universal (George Waggner)

Two confidence tricksters arrive in a Western town and solve a murder.
Members of the studio repertory company in a passable Western discarded by Marlene Dietrich.

w Gerald Geraghty, W. Scott Darling, Richard Brooks d Ray Enright m Hans Salter

☆ Constance Bennett, Broderick Crawford, Leo Carrillo, Anne Gwynne, Patric Knowles, Andy Devine, Ward Bond, Ralf Harolde

Sinbad and the Eye of the Tiger

👫 GB 1977 113m Metrocolor
Columbia/Andor (Charles H. Schneer, Ray Harryhausen)
📺 📺 📼 ◎

Sinbad frees a city from a wicked woman's spell.
Lumpish sequel to a sequel: even the animated monsters raise a yawn this time.

w Beverley Cross d Sam Wanamaker ph Ted Moore m Roy Budd sp Ray Harryhausen

☆ Patrick Wayne, Taryn Power, Jane Seymour, Margaret Whiting, Patrick Troughton

Sinbad the Sailor

👫 US 1947 117m Technicolor
RKO (Stephen Ames)
📺 ◎

Sinbad sets off on his eighth voyage to find the lost treasure of Alexander.
Well-staged but humourless Arabian Nights swashbuckler.

w John Twist d Richard Wallace ph George Barnes m Roy Webb

☆ Douglas Fairbanks Jnr, Walter Slezak, Maureen O'Hara, Anthony Quinn, George Tobias, Jane Greer, Mike Mazurki, Sheldon Leonard

'Is there a public for this twopence-coloured rubbish. For me, it belongs to the Christmas theatre, with a principal boy in tights.' – *Stephen Watts, Sunday Express*

Since You Went Away ***

US 1944 172m bw
David O. Selznick
📺 ◎ 🎧

When hubby is away at the war, his wife and family adopt stiff upper lips.
Elaborate flagwaving investigation of the well-heeled American home front in World War II, with everyone brimming with goodwill and not a dry eye in the place. Absolutely superbly done, if it must be done at all, and a symposium of Hollywood values and techniques of the time.

w David O. Selznick *book* Margaret Buell Wilder d John Cromwell ph Stanley Cortez m Max Steiner pd William L. Pereira ad Mark-Lee Kirk ed Hal C. Kern, James E. Newcom

☆ Claudette Colbert, Joseph Cotten, Jennifer Jones, Shirley Temple, Agnes Moorehead, Monty Woolley, Lionel Barrymore, Guy Madison, Robert Walker, Hattie McDaniel, Craig Stevens, Keenan Wynn, Albert Basserman, Nazimova, Lloyd Corrigan

PREFACE: 'This is the story of the unconquerable fortress – the American home, 1943.'

'A deft, valid blend of showmanship, humour, and yard-wide Americanism.' – *James Agee*

'The whole litany of that middle-class synthetic emotionalism, meticulously annotated over a decade by tough and sentimental experts, has been procured for us.' – *Richard Winnington*

'A rather large dose of choking sentiment.' – *Bosley Crowther*

'It is not an average US reality. It is an average US dream.' – *Time*

'Selznick wrote the script himself, intending his story to be moving and simple, along epic lines; the result is pedestrian in a peculiarly grandiose manner.' – *Pauline Kael, 70s*

† Jennifer Jones's marriage to Robert Walker had broken down just before shooting began, which added awkwardness to their love scenes together, especially as the ever-present Selznick was then busily courting Jones. Cinematographer George Barnes was replaced during filming.

♟ Max Steiner

♟ best picture; Stanley Cortez; Claudette Colbert; Jennifer Jones; Monty Woolley; art direction; editing

Sincerely Yours

US 1955 115m Warnercolor
Warner (Henry Blanke)
📺 ◎

A concert pianist goes deaf and retires to his penthouse, but with the help of binoculars lipreads the humble folk below. Helping them anonymously gives him courage to have an operation.
Absurd updating for a modern non-star of a creaky old George Arliss vehicle The Man Who Played God.

w Irving Wallace d Gordon Douglas ph William H. Clothier *musical advisor* George Liberace

☆ Liberace, Joanne Dru, Dorothy Malone, Alex Nicol, William Demarest

'Drenched in coy bathos to the point of embarrassment.' – *Films and Filming*

'Given sufficient intoxication, you could find this movie amusing.' – *Saturday Review*

La Sindrome di Stendhal: see *The Stendhal Syndrome*

Sinful Davey

GB 1968 95m Eastmancolor Panavision
UA/Mirisch/Webb (William N. Graf)

In 1821 a young Scotsman determines to become a criminal like his father, but falls in love.

Thin imitation of Tom Jones, highly implausible but played with some zest.

w James R. Webb *autobiography* David Haggart d John Huston ph Ted Scaife, Freddie Young m Ken Thorne pd Stephen Grimes

☆ John Hurt, Pamela Franklin, Nigel Davenport, Ronald Fraser, Robert Morley, Maxine Audley, Noel Purcell

Sing

👫 US 1988 98m Technicolor
Columbia TriStar (Craig Zadan)
📺 ◎

Students at a school faced with closure organise a singing and dancing competition.
Dim, cliché-ridden movie that offers little, even for its target audience of the young and undemanding.

w Dean Pitchford d Richard Baskin ph Peter Sova m Jay Gruska pd Carol Spier ed Bud Smith, Jere Huggins, Scott Smith

☆ Lorraine Bracco, Peter Dobson, Jessica Steen, Louise Lasser, George DiCenzo, Patti LaBelle, Susan Peretz

'Remarkably old-fashioned.' – *MFB*

Sing and Be Happy

US 1937 67m bw
TCF (Milton H. Feld)

A young man is too irresponsible to work in his father's advertising agency.
A wisp of a plot with some wisps of music attached; nothing to remember next day.

w Ben Markson, Lou Breslow, John Patrick d James Tinling

☆ Tony Martin, Leah Ray, Joan Davis, Chick Chandler, Helen Westley, Allan Lane, Berton Churchill

'This musical will require plenty of exploitative pressure by exhibs.' – *Variety*

Sing As We Go ***

GB 1934 80m bw
ATP (Basil Dean)

An unemployed millgirl gets various holiday jobs in Blackpool.
A splendid, pawky star vehicle which is also the best picture we have of industrial Lancashire in the thirties. Great fun.

w J. B. Priestley, Gordon Wellesley d Basil Dean ph Robert G. Martin

☆ Gracie Fields, John Loder, Frank Pettingell, Dorothy Hyson, Stanley Holloway

'We have an industrial north that is bigger than Gracie Fields running around a Blackpool fun fair.' – *C. A. Lejeune*

Sing Baby Sing *

US 1936 87m bw
TCF (Darryl F. Zanuck)

A drunken Shakespearian actor sets his sights on a night-club singer.
Reasonably hilarious take-off on the John Barrymore-Elaine Barrie affair, with several Fox contractees fooling to the top of their bent with the help of good musical numbers.

w Milton Sperling, Jack Yellen, Harry Tugend d Sidney Lanfield ph Peverell Marley md Louis Silvers *songs* various

☆ Alice Faye, Adolphe Menjou, Gregory Ratoff, Patsy Kelly, Ted Healy, The Ritz Brothers, Montagu Love, Dixie Dunbar

♟ song 'When Did You Leave Heaven?' (mRichard Whiting, lyWalter Bullock)

Sing, Boy, Sing

US 1958 91m bw Cinemascope
TCF (Henry Ephron)

A rock and roll star comes close to a nervous breakdown because of an unscrupulous manager and a revivalist grandfather.
Fairly painless vehicle for a singing star.

w Claude Binyon d Henry Ephron ph William C. Mellor m Lionel Newman

☆ Tommy Sands, Edmond O'Brien, John McIntire, Lili Gentle, Nick Adams, Josephine Hutchinson

Sing Me a Love Song

US 1936 78m bw
Cosmopolitan/First National

A reformed playboy starts at the bottom as a clerk in his father's department store.
Thin but mildly pleasing musical with good comedy support.

w Sig Herzig, Jerry Wald, Harry Sauber d Ray Enright

☆ James Melton, Patricia Ellis, Hugh Herbert, ZaSu Pitts, Allen Jenkins, Nat Pendleton, Ann Sheridan, Walter Catlett, Hobart Cavanaugh, Charles Halton

'Story isn't much and the dialogue fails to sparkle, yet there's a constant stream of laughs.' – *Variety*

'The god-darnedest family in the whole USA!'

Sing You Sinners **

US 1938 88m bw
Paramount (Wesley Ruggles)

The adventures of a happy-go-lucky family and their racehorse.
Cheerful family musical with amiable cast and good tunes.

w Claude Binyon d Wesley Ruggles ph Karl Struss md Boris Morros *songs* James V. Monaco, Johnny Burke

☆ Bing Crosby, Donald O'Connor, Fred MacMurray, Elizabeth Patterson, Ellen Drew, John Gallaudet

'Homespun, down to earth, and as natural as eggs for breakfast.' – *Variety*

Sing Your Worries Away

US 1941 71m bw
RKO (Cliff Reid)
📺

A debt-ridden songwriter has a girlfriend unaware of a huge pending inheritance.
Rather ribby comedy material which adds up to very little.

w Monte Brice d Edward Sutherland

☆ Bert Lahr, Buddy Ebsen, June Havoc, Patsy Kelly, Sam Levene, Margaret Dumont

Singapore Woman

US 1941 65m bw
Warner (Harlan Thompson)

A slightly fallen woman is redeemed by a plantation owner.
Hasty and uninteresting remake of the Bette Davis vehicle Dangerous.

w Laird Doyle d Jean Negulesco

☆ Brenda Marshall, David Bruce, Virginia Field, Jerome Cowan, Rose Hobart, Heather Angel

Un Singe en Hiver: see *A Monkey in Winter*

The Singer Not the Song

GB 1960 132m colour Cinemascope
Rank (Roy Baker)
📺

In an isolated Mexican town a priest defies an outlaw who oddly respects him.
Lengthy character drama with little action or humour but a great deal of moody introspection and a suggestion of homosexuality.

w Nigel Balchin *novel* Audrey Erskine Lindop d Roy Baker ph Otto Heller m Philip Green

☆ John Mills, Dirk Bogarde, Mylene Demongeot, John Bentley, Laurence Naismith, Eric Pohlmann

'A rewarding film, as startling as a muffled scream from the subconscious.' – *Peter John Dyer*

Singin' in the Rain ****

👫 US 1952 102m Technicolor
MGM (Arthur Freed)
📺 ◎ 🎧 ◎

When talkies are invented, the reputation of one female star shrivels while another grows.
Brilliant comic musical, the best picture by far of Hollywood in transition, with the catchiest tunes, the liveliest choreography, the most engaging performances and the most hilarious jokes of any musical.

w Adolph Green, Betty Comden ph Harold Rosson m Nacio Herb Brown md Lennie Hayton d/ch Gene Kelly, Stanley Donen ly Arthur Freed

☆ Gene Kelly, Donald O'Connor, Debbie Reynolds, Millard Mitchell, Jean Hagen, Rita Moreno, Cyd Charisse, Douglas Fowley

'Perhaps the most enjoyable of all movie musicals.' – *New Yorker, 1975*

♟ Lennie Hayton; Jean Hagen

The Singing Fool **

US 1928 110m bw
Warner
◎

A successful singer goes on the skids when his small son dies.

Early talkie musical, a sensation because of its star's personality, but a pretty maudlin piece of drama.

w C. Graham Baker *play* Leslie S. Barrows
d Lloyd Bacon *ph* Byron Haskin *songs* Lew Brown, Ray Henderson, B. G. de Sylva

☆ Al Jolson, Davey Lee, Betty Bronson, Josephine Dunn, Arthur Housman

'Obvious and tedious as the climax is, when the black-faced comedian stands before the camera and sings "Sonny Boy" you know the man is greater, somehow, than the situation, the story or the movie.' – *Pare Lorentz*

The Singing Kid

US   1936   83m   bw
Warner (Robert Lord)
⊙

A cocky night-club singer takes a talented juvenile under his wing.
Routine star vehicle most notable for a string of standards sung by him right after the credits.

w Warren Duff, Pat C. Flick *d* William Keighley *ph* George Barnes *md* Leo F. Forbstein *songs* E. Y. Harburg, Harold Arlen

☆ Al Jolson, Sybil Jason, Allen Jenkins, Lyle Talbot, Edward Everett Horton, Beverly Roberts, Claire Dodd

The Singing Marine

US   1937   107m   bw
Warner

A marine singer wins a talent contest and success goes to his head.
Light musical of very little interest save two dance sequences by Busby Berkeley.

w Delmer Daves *d* Ray Enright

☆ Dick Powell, Doris Weston, Jane Darwell, Hugh Herbert, Lee Dixon, Dick Wesson, Allen Jenkins, Jane Wyman, Larry Adler

The Singing Musketeer: see The Three Musketeers (1939)

The Singing Nun

US   1966   98m   Metrocolor   Panavision
MGM (Jon Beck)
▤

Adventures of a nun who takes her music to the outside world.
Icky musical drama based on a true character.

w Sally Benson, John Furia *d* Henry Koster *ph* Milton Krasner *md* Harry Sukman *songs* Soeur Sourire

☆ Debbie Reynolds, Greer Garson, Ricardo Montalban, Agnes Moorehead, Chad Everett, Katharine Ross, Ed Sullivan, Juanita Moore
♫ Harry Sukman

The Singing Sheriff

US   1944   60m   bw
Universal (Bernard W. Burton)

A New York singer inadvertently becomes sheriff of a town threatened by the gang of a crooked lawyer.
Bizarre comic minor Western, interspersed with songs and vaudeville acts, culminating in a courtroom scene in which the prosecutor sings a demand for the death penalty: 'Yeah, yeah, hang him on the hickory/Yeah, yeah, rid him of his trickery/Yeah, yeah, hang him on the hickory/We want to see him swing,' goes the chorus, in which all the court joins in.

w Henry Blankford, Eugene Conrad *story* John Grey *d* Leslie Goodwins *ph* Charles Van Enger *md* Sam Freed Jnr *ad* John B. Goodman, Abraham Grossman

☆ Bob Crosby, Fay McKenzie, Fuzzy Knight, Iris Adrian, Samuel S. Hinds, Edward Norris, Doodles Weaver, Spade Colley and his Orchestra

A Single Life

Australia   1985   108m   colour
AFT (Hugh Rule)

Desperate to have a child, an unmarried woman begins an affair with her married boss.
Unsatisfactory domestic drama in which the characters' actions seem dictated solely by the whims of the authors.

w Mark Poole, John Power *m* John Power *ph* Vladimir Osherov *m* Brett Goldsmith *pd* Chris Kennedy *ed* Ian Lang

☆ Tina Bursill, Steven Jacobs, Jane Clifton, Pamela Rabe, Tony Rickards, Esben Storm

'Allie's new roommate is about to borrow a few things without asking. Her clothes. Her boyfriend. Her life.'
'Living with a roommate can be murder.'

Single White Female *

US   1992   108m   Technicolor
Columbia TriStar/Columbia (Barbet Shroeder)
⊞ ▤ ⊙ ⊙

A young Manhattan businesswoman finds that her new flatmate is taking over her life.
Well-done thriller, but its subject-matter is too familiar from too many recent films to cause much in the way of a frisson.

w Don Roos *novel* SWF Seeks Same by John Lutz *d* Barbet Schroeder *ph* Luciano Tovoli *m* Howard Shore *pd* Milena Canonero *ed* Lee Percy

☆ Bridget Fonda, Jennifer Jason Leigh, Steven Weber, Peter Friedman, Stephen Tobolowsky

'It is saddening to see a fine filmmaker courting the crowds by trashing his talent.' – *Geoff Brown, The Times*

Single-Handed *

GB/US   1953   83m   bw
TCF (Frank McCarthy)
US title: *Sailor of the King*

The action of a Canadian seaman, who was born as the result of an affair between a naval officer and a woman he meets on a train during the First World War, results in the destruction of a German battleship during World War II.
Deft drama of wartime action, an effective flag-waver with its theme of courage and leadership through the generations.

w Valentine Davies *novel* Brown on Resolution by C. S. Forester *d* Roy Boulting *ph* Gilbert Taylor *m* Clifton Parker *md* Muir Mathieson *ad* Alec Vetchinsky *ed* Alan Osbiston

☆ Jeffrey Hunter, Michael Rennie, Wendy Hiller, Bernard Lee, Peter Van Eyck, Victor Maddern, John Horsley, Patrick Barr, Robin Bailey

† The film was made with two endings, with the first audiences asked to vote on which they preferred: in one, the most dramatically effective, our hero dies and his mother receives his posthumous medal; in the other, he survives and unknowingly meets his father. The latter version is the most common, though prints showing both endings survive.

†† C. S. Forester's novel was first filmed in 1935 under the title *Forever England*, directed by Walter Forde with an action sequence directed by Anthony Asquith, and starring John Mills and Betty Balfour.

Singles *

US   1992   99m   Technicolor
Warner/Atkinson/Knickerbocker (Cameron Crowe, Richard Hashimoto)
⊞ ▤ ⊙ ⊙ ♫

The young occupants of an apartment block in Seattle fall in and out of love.
A meandering movie of singles attempting to become couples in order to occupy their empty lives; it is slight, but perceptive.

wd Cameron Crowe *ph* Ueli Steiger *m* Paul Westerberg *pd* Stephen Lineweaver

☆ Bridget Fonda, Campbell Scott, Kyra Sedgwick, Sheila Kelley, Jim True, Matt Dillon, Ally Walker, Eric Stoltz, Tom Skerritt

'The movie gets nowhere in particular, but the leading performances are immensely attractive.' – *Philip French, Observer*
'Superbly scripted, cast and scored, pic is a natural for the partner-hunting twentysomething crowd and should easily cross over to thirtysomething singles or couples primed to laugh at the dating syndrome.' – *Variety*

Singleton's Pluck: see Laughterhouse

The Sinister Man *

GB   1961   60m   bw
Anglo Amalgamated/Merton Park (Jack Greenwood)
The murder of an Oxford scholar is linked to archaeological relics which are coveted for political purposes.
Very tolerable minor thriller in the Edgar Wallace series: short, sharp and snappy.

w Robert Banks Stewart *d* Clive Donner *ph* Bert Mason *m* Charles Blackwell

☆ Patrick Allen, John Bentley, Jacqueline Ellis, Eric Young, Arnold Lee, John Glyn-Jones, William Gaunt, Wilfrid Brambell

'Personal! Powerful! Human! Heroic!'

Sink the Bismarck! **

GB   1960   97m   bw   Cinemascope
TCF/John Brabourne
⊞ ▤ ⊙

In 1941, Britain's director of naval operations arranges the trapping and sinking of Germany's greatest battleship.
Tight little personal drama which would have been better on a standard screen, as its ships are plainly models and much of the footage stretched-out newsreel. Nevertheless, a good example of the stiff-upper-lip school.

w Edmund H. North *d* Lewis Gilbert *ph* Christopher Challis *m* Clifton Parker *md* Muir Mathieson

☆ Kenneth More, Dana Wynter, Karel Stepanek, Carl Mohner, Laurence Naismith, Geoffrey Keen, Michael Hordern, Maurice Denham, Esmond Knight

Sinner Take All

US   1937   74m   bw
MGM (Lucien Hubbard, Sam Marx)
Members of a family are murdered one by one.
Moderate puzzler with a reporter sharing solving honours with the police.

w Leonard Lee, Walter Wise *novel* Murder of a Wanton by Whitman Chambers *d* Errol Taggart

☆ Bruce Cabot, Margaret Lindsay, Joseph Calleia, Stanley Ridges, Vivienne Osborne, Charley Grapewin, Edward Pawley, George Zucco

'Above the usual whodunit average ... able to make its way alone in the less exacting spots.' – *Variety*

Sinners' Holiday: see Christmas Eve (1947)

Sinner's Holiday

US   1930   55m   bw
Warner

A fairground barker loves the daughter of a penny arcade owner, but is framed by her brother.
Early talkie quickie using Broadway talent, and introducing James Cagney to the screen. It still has vigour if little else.

w Harvey Thew, George Rosener *play* Penny Arcade by Marie Baumer *d* John G. Adolfi *ph* Ira Morgan

☆ Grant Withers, Evalyn Knapp, James Cagney, Joan Blondell, Lucille La Verne, Warren Hymer, Noel Madison

Sinners in Paradise

US   1938   65m   bw
Universal (Ken Goldsmith)
▤

Air travellers are wrecked on a South Sea island.
Much ado about very little, and a grave disappointment from its director.

w Lester Cole, Harold Buckley, Louis Stevens *d* James Whale

☆ Madge Evans, John Boles, Bruce Cabot, Marion Martin, Gene Lockhart, Charlotte Wynters, Nana Bryant

'Melodrama sufficiently lurid to be cut into several parts and released as a serial.' – *Variety*

Sinners in the Sun

US   1932   69m   bw
Paramount

A young couple break up; each has romantic adventures, but eventually they come together again.
Blah comedy-drama with the defects of its period.

w Vincent Lawrence, Waldemar Young, Samuel Hoffenstein, Mildred Cram *d* Alexander Hall

☆ Carole Lombard, Chester Morris, Adrienne Allen, Alison Skipworth, Walter Byron, Cary Grant

'Only high-powered selling will aid a dull and poorly-handled story.' – *Variety*

The Sins of Rachel Cade

US   1961   123m   Technicolor
Warner (Henry Blanke)

An American missionary nurse in the Belgian Congo falls in love with a crashed flyer and has a baby.
Romantic melodrama which starts like The Nun's Story *and ends like* Peg's Paper; *competent on its level.*

w Edward Anhalt *novel* Charles Mercer *d* Gordon Douglas *ph* Peverell Marley *m* Max Steiner

☆ Angie Dickinson, Roger Moore, Peter Finch, Errol John, Woody Strode, Juano Hernandez, Frederick O'Neal, Mary Wickes

Sins of Rome: see Spartacus (1952)

'Sometimes The Most Dangerous Journey Is Into Your Past.'

Sioux City

US   1994   100m   Foto-Kem
Cabin Fever/Facet (Brian Rox, Jane Ubell)
⊞ ▤ ⊙
GB video title: *Ultimate Revenge*

A Lakota Indian youth, adopted as a baby by a Jewish couple, investigates the murder of his real mother, who had invited him to visit her, and rediscovers his roots.
Dull thriller on an interesting theme of cultural identity.

w L. Virginia Browne *d* Lou Diamond Phillips *ph* James W. Wrenn *m* Christopher Lindsey *pd* Rando Schmook *ed* Christopher Rouse, Mark Fitzgerald

☆ Lou Diamond Phillips, Salli Richardson, Melinda Dillon, Ralph Waite, Bill Allen, Adam Roarke, Gary Farmer

'An undistinguished mystery-thriller that's criminally short on mystery and thrills.' – *Joe Leydon, Variety*

Sir Henry at Rawlinson End

GB   1980   71m   bw
Charisma (Tony Stratton Smith)
⊞

A grossly eccentric English aristocrat lays a family ghost.
Weirdly isolated, semi-professional comedy with elements of everything from Ealing to Monty Python.

w Vivian Stanshall, Steve Roberts *radio play* Vivian Stanshall *d* Steve Roberts *ph* Martin Bell *m* Vivian Stanshall *pd* Alistair Bowtell *ed* Chris Rose

☆ Trevor Howard, Patrick Magee, Denise Coffey, J. G. Devlin, Vivian Stanshall

Siren of Atlantis: see L'Atlantide

Siren of Bagdad

US   1953   72m   Technicolor
Columbia (Sam Katzman)
A travelling magician helps reinstate a deposed sultan.
Flippant oriental extravaganza aiming at the Hope-Crosby style but falling sadly short of it.

w Robert E. Kent *d* Richard Quine *ph* Henry Freulich *m* Mischa Bakaleinikoff

☆ Paul Henreid, Patricia Medina, Hans Conried, Charlie Lung

La Sirène du Mississippi: see The Mississippi Mermaid

'A Seductive New Comedy.'

Sirens *

Australia/GB   1994   94m   colour
Buena Vista/WGM/AFFC/British Screen/Samson/Sarah Radclyffe (Sue Milliken)
⊞ ▤ ⊙

The repressed wife of an English vicar learns to lose her inhibitions when the couple visit the Australian painter Norman Lindsay and his Bohemian entourage of free-living models.
A light-hearted and lightweight summertime clash of attitudes and cultures, enjoyable without being particularly memorable.

wd John Duigan *ph* Geoff Burton *m* Rachel Portman *pd* Roger Ford *ed* Humphrey Dixon

☆ Hugh Grant, Tara Fitzgerald, Sam Neill, Elle Macpherson, Portia de Rossi, Kate Fischer, Pamela Rabe, Ben Mendelsohn, Mark Gerber, Tom Polson

'A deliciously sexy and hedonistic comedy of morals and manners.' – *Variety*
'The kind of attractive, fluent period film which those who swear by James Ivory will appreciate.' – *Derek Malcolm, Guardian*

Sirocco

US   1951   98m   bw
Columbia/Santana (Robert Lord)
▤ ⊙

In 1925 Damascus, an American runs guns for the rebels.
Tedious romantic drama in the Casablanca vein but with none of the magic.

---

w A. I. Bezzerides, Hans Jacoby *novel* Coup de Grâce by Joseph Kessel *d* Curtis Bernhardt *ph* Burnett Guffey *m* George Antheil

☆ Humphrey Bogart, Marta Toren, Lee J. Cobb, Everett Sloane, Gerald Mohr, Zero Mostel, Onslow Stevens

'No Sex. No Booze. No Men. No Way.'

Sister Act *

👫 US 1992 100m Technicolor
Buena Vista/Touchstone/Touchwood Pacific Partners (Teri Schwartz)
📼 ▤ 🔎 🎧

A singer on the run from the Mafia takes refuge in a convent and transforms its choir.
Cheerful and modest comedy, though lacking in wit and with a plot that makes little sense. It was the surprise hit of 1992, ranking fourth at the box-office.
w Joseph Howard *d* Emile Ardolino *ph* Adam Greenberg *m* Marc Shaiman *pd* Jackson DeGovia *ed* Richard Halsey
☆ Whoopi Goldberg, Maggie Smith, Kathy Najimy, Wendy Makkena, Mary Wickes, Harvey Keitel, Bill Nunn, Robert Miranda, Richard Portnow
'The film isn't a divine comedy, and it's not satisfyingly profane either. But it generates a few laughs. It's got a good beat, and you can dance to it.' – *Michael Sragow, New Yorker*
'Offers the kind of cute, synthetic uplift usually found in television commercials and casts its nun characters as walking sight gags rather than real people.' – *Janet Maslin, New York Times*
'A truly awful film, pretending to be audacious but in fact pandering to every facile assumption in the book.' – *Derek Malcolm, Guardian*

Sister Act 2: Back in the Habit

👫 US 1993 106m Technicolor
Cinemascope
Buena Vista/Touchstone (Scott Rudin, Dawn Steel)
📼 ▤ 🔎 🎧

A Las Vegas singer agrees to dress as a nun to teach singing at a ghetto school that is in trouble.
Distressingly dire comedy, sickly and silly; it is smug and patronizing in its attitudes to the problems of inner-city life and not at all amusing.
w James Orr, Jim Cruickshank, Judi Ann Mason *d* Bill Duke *ph* Oliver Wood *m* Miles Goodman *pd* John DeCuir Jnr *ed* John Carter, Pem Herring, Stuart Pappé
☆ Whoopi Goldberg, Kathy Najimy, Barnard Hughes, Mary Wickes, James Coburn, Maggie Smith, Wendy Makkena, Lauryn Hill, Sheryl Lee Ralph
'Two trips to the convent is one too many.' – *Variety*
'If *Sister Act 2* is how Hollywood rewards success, how does it punish failure?' – *Adam Mars-Jones, Independent*
† Kathy Najimy's singing was dubbed by Andrea Robinson

Sister Kenny *

US 1946 116m bw
RKO (Dudley Nichols)
▤ 🔎

The career of a nurse who instigated treatment for polio.
Standard, well-done biopic.
w Dudley Nichols, Alexander Knox, Mary McCarthy *d* Dudley Nichols *ph* George Barnes *m* Alexander Tansman
☆ Rosalind Russell, Alexander Knox, Dean Jagger, Philip Merivale, Beulah Bondi, Dorothy Peterson
† From the autobiography of Australian nurse Mary Kenny: *And They Shall Walk.*
🏆 Rosalind Russell

Sister My Sister *

GB 1994 104m colour
Arrow/Film Four/British Screen/NFH (Norma Heyman)
▤

In France in the 30s, two sisters who work as maids in the same strict household begin an incestuous affair and start acting strangely.
Claustrophobic upstairs/downstairs tragedy, in which the only escape seems to be through violence.
w Wendy Kesselman *play* My Sister in This House by Wendy Kesselman *d* Nancy Meckler *ph* Ashley Rowe *m* Stephen Warbeck *pd* Caroline Amies *ed* David Stiven
☆ Julie Walters, Joely Richardson, Jodhi May, Sophie Thursfield

'A small-scale film with some powerful moments' – *Variety*
'A piece of cinema of almost stifling intensity and formidably acted throughout.' – *Derek Malcolm, Guardian*
† The same true-life story was the basis of Jean Genet's play *The Maids*, which was filmed in 1974 (qv).

Sister of Satan: see *She Beast*

Sisters *

US 1973 92m colour
British Lion/Pressman-Williams Enterprises (Edward R. Pressman)
▤ 🎧

GB title: *Blood Sisters*
A Siamese twin takes on the personality of her deranged and dead sister.
The plots of Alfred Hitchcock's Psycho and Rear Window are both raided for this effective, if derivative, shocker.
w Brian de Palma, Louisa Rose *d* Brian de Palma *ph* Gregory Sandor *m* Bernard Herrmann *pd* Gary Weist *ed* Paul Hirsch
☆ Margot Kidder, Jennifer Salt, Charles Durning, Bill Finley, Lisle Wilson, Barnard Hughes
'A long way from being the brilliant thriller the ads say it is, but its limp technique doesn't seem to matter to the people who want their gratuitous gore. The movie supplies it, but why is there so much gratuitous dumbness, too?' – *Pauline Kael, New Yorker*
'A distinctly uneasy blend of that brand of unprincipled exploitation that makes horror out of madness and birth abnormality.' – *MFB*

Sisters *

US 1988 93m colour
UIP/MGM/Oxford Film Company (Andy Paterson, Mark Bentley)
US title: *Some Girls*
An American student who goes to spend Christmas with the Catholic family of his girlfriend in Quebec finds himself looking after her dying grandmother.
Mildly amusing comedy of cultural misunderstandings.
w Rupert Walters *d* Michael Hoffman *ph* Ueli Steiger *m* James Newton Howard *pd* Eugenio Zanetti *ed* David Spiers
☆ Patrick Dempsey, Jennifer Connelly, Sheila Kelley, Lance Edwards, Lila Kedrova, Florinda Bolkan, Andre Gregory, Ashley Greenfield

The Sisters *

US 1938 98m bw
Warner (Hal B. Wallis)
▤

The marriages of three sisters from a small Montana town.
Well-made potboiler for women; it even brings in the San Francisco earthquake, and the star teaming is piquant to say the least.
w Milton Krims *novel* Myron Brinig *d* Anatole Litvak *ph* Tony Gaudio *m* Max Steiner
☆ Bette Davis, Errol Flynn, Anita Louise, Ian Hunter, Donald Crisp, Beulah Bondi, Jane Bryan, Alan Hale, Dick Foran, Henry Travers, Patric Knowles, Lee Patrick, Harry Davenport
'Worth seeing for the adroit period direction and the fragile, pop-eyed acting of Miss Bette Davis.' – *Graham Greene*

Sisters or The Balance of Happiness *

West Germany 1979 95m colour
Blue Dolphin/Bioskop Film/WDR (Eberhard Junkersdorf)
original title: *Schwestern oder Die Balance des Glücks*
Two sisters, one an executive secretary, the other a biology student whom she supports and stifles, grow ever more dependent upon each other.
Troubling, claustrophobic study of damaging family relationships.
wd Margarethe von Trotta *ph* Franz Rath, Thomas Schwan *m* Konstantin Wecker *ad* Winifred Hennig *ed* Annette Dorn
☆ Jutta Lampe, Gudrun Gabriel, Jessica Früh, Konstantin Wecker, Heinz Bennet

Sisters under the Skin

US 1934 65m bw
Columbia
An older man loses his mistress to a bohemian composer.

Surprise, surprise: and the screenplay does not enliven the situation.
w Jo Swerling, S. K. Lauren *d* David Burton
☆ Frank Morgan, Elissa Landi, Joseph Schildkraut, Doris Lloyd, Clara Blandick, Samuel S. Hinds
'Mild flicker of obvious triangle story texture.' – *Variety*

Sitcom

France 1998 79m colour
Alliance/Fidélité/Canal+ (Olivier Delbosc, Marc Missonnier)
📼

After their father brings home a white rat, a family disintegrates; so he apparently kills them all.
A film determined to shock by its stew of seduction and incest; but it is simply silly.
wd François Ozon *ph* Yorik Le Saux *m* Eric Neveux *ad* Angelique Puron *ed* Dominique Petrot
☆ Evelyne Dandry, François Marthouret, Marina de Van, Adrien de Van, Stephane Rideau, Lucia Sanchez, Julien-Emmanuel Eyoum Deido, Jean Douchet
'This childish film is intended to shock, but is merely tedious.' – *Philip French, Observer*

Sitting Bull

US 1954 106m Eastmancolor
Cinemascope
United Artists/W. R. Frank/Televoz of Mexico
▤

Despite the massacre of Custer's men, a cavalry officer strives to establish a relationship with Sitting Bull.
Sloppy and undernourished Western epic in abysmal colour, not helped by Mexicans pretending to be Indians.
w Jack de Witt, Sidney Salkow *d* Sidney Salkow *ph* Charles Van Enger, Victor Herrera *m* Raoul Kraushaar
☆ Dale Robertson, Mary Murphy, J. Carrol Naish, Iron Eyes Cody, John Litel, William Hopper, Douglas Kennedy

Sitting Ducks

US 1978 88m DeLuxe
Sunny Side Up (Meira Atta Dor)
▤

Two men steal a fortune and abscond to Miami with two women who turn out to have a contract on them.
Endlessly talkative sex comedy from a practitioner who scorns built-up gags. The kind of movie that puts people off movies.
wd Henry Jaglom *ph* Paul Glickman *m* Richard Romanus
☆ Michael E. Jaglom, Zack Norman, Patrice Townsend, Irene Forrest, Richard Romanus, Henry Jaglom

Sitting in Limbo

Canada 1986 95m colour
NFBC (David Wilson, John N. Smith)
In Montreal, a black teenager discovers she is pregnant and goes to live with her caring but irresponsible boyfriend.
Low-key slice-of-life drama, focusing on the divide between single mothers and the men who father their children, and mainly notable for presenting a black working-class community not often seen in Canadian films.
w David Wilson, John N. Smith *d* John N. Smith *ph* Barry Perles, Andreas Poulsson *ed* David Wilson
☆ Pat Dillon, Fabian Gibbs, Sylvie Clarke, Debbie Grant, Compton McLean, Millicent Dillon, Ronald Lang

Sitting Pretty

US 1933 85m bw
Paramount (Charles R. Rogers)
Two songwriters strike it rich in Hollywood.
Cheerful comedy musical, interesting for its backgrounds.
w Jack McGowan, S. J. Perelman, Lou Breslow *d* Harry Joe Brown *ph* Milton Krasner *songs* Mack Gordon, Harry Revel
☆ Jack Oakie, Jack Haley, Ginger Rogers, Thelma Todd, Gregory Ratoff, Lew Cody, Harry Revel, Mack Gordon
'Should please all over.' – *Variety*

Sitting Pretty ***

US 1948 84m bw
TCF (Samuel G. Engel)
A young couple acquire a most unusual male baby sitter, a self-styled genius who sets the neighbourhood on its ears by writing a novel about it.
Out of the blue, a very funny comedy which entrenched Clifton Webb as one of Hollywood's great characters and led to two sequels, Mr Belvedere Goes to College and Mr Belvedere Rings the Bell (qv).
w F. Hugh Herbert *novel* Belvedere by Gwen Davenport *d* Walter Lang *ph* Norbert Brodine *m* Alfred Newman
☆ Clifton Webb, Robert Young, Maureen O'Hara, Richard Haydn, Louise Allbritton, Ed Begley, Randy Stuart, Larry Olsen
🏆 Clifton Webb

Sitting Target

GB 1972 92m Metrocolor
MGM (Barry Kulick)
A violent killer escapes from jail and seeks revenge on those who 'shopped' him.
Rough, tough action thriller; passes the time for hardened addicts.
w Alexander Jacobs *novel* Lawrence Henderson *d* Douglas Hickox *ph* Ted Scaife *m* Stanley Myers *pd* Jonathan Barry
☆ Oliver Reed, Jill St John, Edward Woodward, Frank Finlay, Ian McShane, Freddie Jones, Robert Beatty

Situation Hopeless But Not Serious

US 1965 97m bw
Paramount/Castle (Gottfried Reinhardt)
In 1944, two American flyers are captured by a friendly, lonely mild-mannered German, who keeps them in his cellar and hasn't the heart to tell them when the war is over ...
Flat little comedy which leaves a talented cast no room for manoeuvre.
w Silvia Reinhardt *novel* The Hiding Place by Robert Shaw *d* Gottfried Reinhardt *ph* Kurt Hasse *m* Harold Byrne
☆ Alec Guinness, Robert Redford, Mike Connors, Anita Hoefer

Six Black Horses

US 1962 80m Eastmancolor
Universal-International
A girl hires a gunslinger and a horse thief to escort her across Indian territory.
Rather glum Western programmer.
w Burt Kennedy *d* Harry Keller
☆ Audie Murphy, Dan Duryea, Joan O'Brien, George Wallace, Roy Barcroft

Six Bridges to Cross

US 1955 96m bw
U-I (Aaron Rosenberg)
The criminal career of a young hoodlum in Boston in the thirties.
Public Enemy reprise with a sentimental veneer, smooth but uninteresting.
w Sydney Boehm *novel* They Stole Two and a Half Million Dollars and Got Away with It by Joseph F. Dineen *d* Joseph Pevney *ph* William Daniels *m* Joseph Gershenson
☆ Tony Curtis, George Nader, Julie Adams, Jay C. Flippen, Sal Mineo, Jan Merlin

Six Day Bike Rider

US 1934 69m bw
Warner (Sam Bischoff)
One of life's failures impresses his girl by entering a cycling contest.
One of the star's stronger comedy vehicles.
w Earl Baldwin *d* Lloyd Bacon *ph* Warren Lynch
☆ Joe E. Brown, Maxine Doyle, Frank McHugh, Gordon Westcott

'After This Week In Paradise, They're Going To Need A Vacation.'

Six Days, Seven Nights

US 1998 101m Technicolor Panavision
Touchstone/Caravan/Northern Lights (Ivan Reitman, Wallis Nicita, Roger Birnbaum)
📼 ▤ 🔎 🎧

En route to Tahiti, a pilot makes an emergency landing and strands himself and his passenger, a New York fashion editor, on an unknown island.

A romantic comedy so obvious in its outcome that an audience can sleep through most of it without missing anything of interest.
w Michael Browning d Ivan Reitman
ph Michael Chapman m Randy Edelman pd J. Michael Riva ed Sheldon Kahn, Wendy Greene Bricmont
☆ Harrison Ford, Anne Heche, David Schwimmer, Temuera Morrison
'Plagued with a hackneyed screenplay (which borrows from so many films you'll lose count), this lame romantic comedy falls to pieces within six minutes and seven seconds.' – *Judy Sloane, Film Review*

Six Days, Six Nights **
France   1994   98m   colour
New Light/France 3 (Alexandre Arcady)
original title: *A la Folie*
An unhappily married art teacher envies her sister's success as an artist and her happy new relationship with a boxer.
Deft and intriguing drama of sibling rivalry and destructive passions.
wd Diane Kurys ph Fabio Conversi m Michael Nyman pd Tony Egry ed Luc Barnier
☆ Anne Parillaud, Béatrice Dalle, Patrick Aurignac, Bernard Verley, Alain Chabat, Jean-Claude de Goros, Marie Guillard

'For Paul, every person is a new door to a new world.'
Six Degrees of Separation **
US   1993   111m   DeLuxe
MGM/Maiden Movies/New Regency (Fred Schepisi, Arnon Milchan)
A young man arrives on the doorstep of a wealthy and sophisticated New York couple claiming to be mugged and convinces them that he is a friend of their children and the son of Sidney Poitier.
Witty, complex, always engrossing study of identity and more; the key moment comes as the con man lectures his captive audience, complacent in their belief in themselves and their understanding of culture, on the death of the imagination – and fools them.
w John Guare play John Guare d Fred Schepisi ph Ian Baker m Jerry Goldsmith pd Patrizia von Brandenstein ed Peter Honess
☆ Stockard Channing, Will Smith, Donald Sutherland, Mary Beth Hurt, Bruce Davison, Heather Graham, Anthony Michael Hall, Eric Thal, Richard Masur, Ian McKellen
'This is a wonderful play about the capacity of the ever-so-slightly guilty haves to be gulled rotten by those have-nots who have yet got the wit to deceive them. But, being American, it has only the vaguest of ideas about the political implications of what it shows. Which is why the film tails off startlingly at the end, almost disappearing up its own elegant backside.' – *Derek Malcolm, Guardian*
'Always entertains, looks elegant, never mangles its source material, and gives movie audiences that rare commodity: something to think about.' – *Geoff Brown, The Times*
† The title refers to the belief that each person in the world can trace a connection by friendship or acquaintance to any other person which will involve no more than six intermediary links, that everyone is thus joined by a maximum of six degrees of separation to everyone else.

Six Hours to Live *
US   1932   78m   bw
Fox
A scientist revives a diplomat for six hours so that his murderer can be traced.
Fanciful hokum set at a Geneva peace conference.
w Bradley King story Gordon Morris, Morton Barteaux d William Dieterle
☆ Warner Baxter, John Boles, Miriam Jordan, Irene Ware, George Marion
'A strong box office title which together with an aggressive sales campaign should bring picture into the money.' – *Variety*

633 Squadron *
GB   1964   94m   Technicolor   Panavision
UA/Mirisch (Cecil F. Ford)
In 1944 Mosquito aircraft try to collapse a cliff overhanging a munitions factory in a Norwegian fjord.

Standard war heroics with enough noise and disorder to keep most audiences hypnotized.
w James Clavell, Howard Koch novel Frederick E. Smith d Walter Grauman ph Ted Scaife, John Wilcox m Ron Goodwin
☆ Cliff Robertson, George Chakiris, Maria Perschy, Harry Andrews, Donald Houston, Michael Goodliffe

Six in Paris: see *Paris Vu Par...*

Six Inches Tall: see *Attack of the Puppet People*

Six Lessons from Madame La Zonga
US   1941   62m   bw
Universal
A Cuban night-club proprietress causes mix-ups on a pleasure boat.
Witless vehicle for two stars popular at another studio in the Mexican Spitfire series.
w Stanley Rubin, Marion Orth, Larry Rhine, Ben Chapman d John Rawlins
☆ Lupe Velez, Leon Errol, William Frawley, Helen Parrish, Charles Lang, Eddie Quillan, Quinn Williams

'Their first honeymoon was so much funThey're off to have another one!'
Six of a Kind *
US   1934   69m   bw
Paramount
Comic adventures of six people driving across America.
Minor comedy which doesn't come off as a whole but adequately displays the talents of its stars.
w Walter de Leon, Harry Ruskin d Leo McCarey ph Henry Sharp m Ralph Rainger
☆ Charles Ruggles, Mary Boland, W. C. Fields, Alison Skipworth, George Burns, Gracie Allen
'Another pleasing film ... it reminds the Englishman of Three Men in a Boat.' – *E. V. Lucas, Punch*
'Old-fashioned farce that gets a lot of laughs. Better for duals than de luxers.' – *Variety*

Six Pack
US   1982   110m   DeLuxe
TCF/Lion Share (Michael Trikilis)
A loner stock car driver finds himself fathering six orphan kids.
Old-fashioned family picture built around a country singer.
w Mike Marvin, Alex Matter d Daniel Petrie ph Mario Tosi m Charles Fox
☆ Kenny Rogers, Diane Lane, Erin Gray, Barry Corbin

6,000 Enemies
US   1939   61m   bw
MGM (Lucien Hubbard)
A district attorney is framed for a prison stretch and finds himself hated by every convict inside.
Formula support climaxing in a prison break: well enough done.
w Bertram Millhauser d George B. Seitz
☆ Walter Pidgeon, Rita Johnson, Paul Kelly, Nat Pendleton, Harold Huber, Grant Mitchell
'Prison meller with action aplenty.' – *Variety*

Six Weeks
US   1982   107m   Metrocolor
Polygram (Peter Guber, Jon Peters)
A lady cosmetics tycoon whose ten-year-old daughter is dying of leukaemia enlists the aid of a politician to make what's left of her life a triumph.
Icky tearjerker on the lines of The Christmas Tree. Everything is done to make it palatable, but it won't be many people's cup of bromide.
w David Seltzer novel Fred Mustard Stewart d Tony Bill m Michael D. Margulies m Dudley Moore ad Hilyard Brown ed Stu Linder
☆ Dudley Moore, Mary Tyler Moore, Katherine Healy, Shannon Wilcox, Bill Calvert
'Very sleek and very sickmaking.' – *Observer*
† Nick Nolte and Audrey Hepburn were originally to have starred. Sylvester Stallone also turned down the lead.

Sixteen Candles *
US   1985   95m   Technicolor
Universal (Hilton A. Green)
A teenage girl, pursued by one boy and pursuing another, finds her 16th birthday being overlooked by her family.
Mildy amusing comedy of teenage life, from a 'teen's viewpoint, though reaffirming conventional family values.
wd John Hughes ph Bobby Byrne m Ira Newborn pd John W. Corso ed Edward Warschilka
☆ Molly Ringwald, Justin Henry, Michael Schoeffling, Haviland Morris, Gedde Watanabe, Anthony Michael Hall, Paul Dooley, John Cusack, Joan Cusack, Jami Gertz
'It doesn't amount to much, and it's certainly not to be confused with a work of art, but the young writer-director John Hughes has a knack for making you like the high-school-age characters better each time you hear them talk.' – *Pauline Kael, New Yorker*

Sixth Happiness *
GB   1997   98m   Metrocolor
BFI/BBC/Kennedy Mellor (Tatiana Kennedy)
The autobiography of a boy born with brittle bone disease, growing older in Bombay of the 60s.
With Kanga playing a fictional version of himself from early childhood, this is a necessarily stylized, episodic account of the formative influences of a writer; the tone is lightly confessional, verging on the satirical in its portrait of people maintaining a British way of life against all odds.
w Firdaus Kanga novel Trying to Grow by Firdaus Kanga d Waris Hussein ph James Welland m Dominique Le Gendre pd Lynne Whiteread ed Laurence Méry-Clark
☆ Firdaus Kanga, Souad Faress, Khodus Wadia, Ashen Bhatti, Indira Varma, Nina Wadia, Nisha K. Nahar, Roger Hammond, Sabira Merchant
'Pic has idiosyncratic characters and situations that never come to life thanks to flat-footed execution.' – *Dennis Harvey, Variety*

'They're lifting the game to a higher level.'
The Sixth Man
US   1997   107m   colour
Touchstone/Mandeville (David Hoberman)
The ghost of a dead basketball player comes to the aid of his brother's team.
Trivial comedy which for the most part seems to elevate cheating to the aim of the game; though more unforgivable than its dubious morality is its lack of genuine humour.
w Christopher Reed, Cynthia Carle d Randall Miller ph Michael Ozier m Marcus Miller pd Michael Bolton ed Eric Sears
☆ Marlon Wayans, Kadeem Hardison, David Paymer, Michael Michele, Kevin Dunn, Harold Sylvester, Vladimir Cuk, Travis Ford
'Dim slapstick in a cloying comedy which adds nothing new to a now moribund formnula.' – *Sight and Sound*

The Sixth Sense ***
US   1999   107m   Technicolor
Buena Vista/Hollywood/Spyglass (Frank Marshall, Kathleen Kennedy, Barry Mendel)
A child psychologist begins to treat a disturbed young boy, who can see the dead.
Spooky movie with a twist ending that changes the focus of what has gone before; it's both clever and disturbing, maintaining a haunting atmosphere that keeps its audience off-balance.
wd M. Night Shyamalan ph Tak Fujimoto m James Newton Howard pd Larry Fulton ed Andrew Mondshein sp make-up fx: Stan Winston Studio; visual fx: Dream Quest Images
☆ Bruce Willis, Toni Collette, Olivia Williams, Haley Joel Osment, Donnie Wahlberg, Glenn Fitzgerald, Mischa Barton, Trevor Morgan, Bruce Norris
'Moody, low-key and semi-pretentious effort is ominous without being scary or suspenseful for most of its running time.' – *Todd McCarthy, Variety*
'A preposterous piece of work.' – *Adam Mars-Jones, Times*

† The film was a box-office success, taking more than $276m at the US box-office, and earning Willis an estimated $50m.
⚇ picture; Haley Joel Osment; Toni Collette; M. Night Shyamalan (as director); M. Night Shyamalan (as writer); Andrew Mondshein

'68
US   1988   98m   colour
Entertainment/New World (Dale Djerassi, Isabel Maxwell, Steven Kovacs)
A Hungarian immigrant experiences problems with his children as he opens a restaurant in San Francisco in the mid-1960s.
The movie's background, with its emphasis on the political events of the time, overwhelms its insufficiently developed characters.
wd Steven Kovacs ph Daniel Lacambre ad Joshua Koral ed Cari Coughlin
☆ Eric Larsen, Robert Locke, Sandor Tecsi, Anna Dukasz, Neil Young

Sixty Glorious Years **
GB   1938   95m   Technicolor
Imperator (Herbert Wilcox)
US title: *Queen of Destiny*
Scenes from the life of Queen Victoria.
A stately pageant apparently composed of material which couldn't be fitted into the previous year's black-and-white success Victoria the Great. Fascinating, though the camerawork is not very nimble.
w Robert Vansittart, Miles Malleson, Charles de Grandcourt d Herbert Wilcox ph Frederick A. Young
☆ Anna Neagle, Anton Walbrook, C. Aubrey Smith, Walter Rilla, Charles Carson, Felix Aylmer, Lewis Casson
'One of the most artistic and expensive films made in England.' – *Variety*
† The two films were edited together in 1943 to make a new selection called *Queen Victoria*, and in the process the original negatives were accidentally destroyed, so that both films now have to be printed from unattractive dupes.

Det Sjunde Inseglet: see *The Seventh Seal*

Skateboard
US   1977   95m   Technicolor
Universal
A small-time theatrical agent in trouble builds up a professional skateboard team.
Unsatisfactory exploitation item which devotes more time to its plot than to its sport.
w Richard A. Wolf, George Gage d George Gage ph Ross Kelsay m Mark Snow
☆ Allen Garfield, Kathleen Lloyd, Leif Garrett, Richard Van Der Wyk

Skepp Till Indialand: see *A Ship to India*

Sketch Artist
US   1992   86m   Foto-Kem
Motion Picture Corp of America (Brad Krevoy, Steve Stabler)
A police artist sketching a witness's description of a murderer finds that he has produced a drawing of his wife.
A slick little thriller, enjoyable enough on its own limited terms.
w Michael Angeli d Phedon Papamichael ph Wally Pfister m Mark Isham pd Phedon Papamichael Snr ed Carole Kravetz
☆ Jeff Fahey, Sean Young, Frank McRae, Tcheky Karyo, James Tolkan, Charlotte Lewis, Drew Barrymore

'Pray they never have to rescue YOU ... !'
Ski Patrol
US   1989   92m   DeLuxe
Entertainment/Epic/Sarlui/Diamant/Paul Maslansky (Phillip B. Goldfine, Donald L. West)
A developer attempts to sabotage the safety record of a ski resort.
Broad farce in the style of the Police Academy series and no funnier.
w Steven Long Mitchell, Craig W. Van Sickle d Richard Correll ph John Stephens m Bruce Miller pd Fred Weiler ed Scott Wallace

☆ Roger Rose, Yvette Nipar, T. K. Carter, Leslie Jordan, Paul Feig, Sean Gregory Sullivan, Corbin Timbrook, George Lopez, Ray Walston

The Ski Raiders
US   1972   90m   Technicolor   Panavision
Warner (Edward L. Rissien)
aka: *Snow Job*
An alpine ski instructor devises a scheme to rob a bank.
Very medium caper thriller with a breathtaking opening sequence.
w Ken Kolb, Jeffrey Bloom d George Englund ph Gabor Pogany, Willy Bogner m Jacques Loussier
☆ Jean Claude Killy, Cliff Potts, Vittorio de Sica, Daniele Gaubert

Ski School
Canada   1991   88m   colour
Movie Store Entertainment/Rose & Ruby (Damian Lee)
Rival groups of skiers try to sabotage each other.
Crass comedy that is mainly an excuse for ski stunts and the cavortings of skimpily clad bimbos.
w David Mitchell d Damian Lee ph Curtis Petersen, Roxanne Di Santo m Steven Hunter ad Craig MacMillan ed Robert Gordon
☆ Dean Cameron, Tom Breznahan, Patrick Laborteaux, Mark Thomas Miller, Darlene Vogel, Charlie Spradling

Skidoo
US   1968   98m   Technicolor   Panavision
Paramount/Sigma (Otto Preminger)
Active and reformed gangsters get involved with hippies and preach universal love.
Abysmal mishmash with top talent abused; clearly intended as satirical farce, but in fact one of the most woebegone movies ever made.
w Doran William Cannon d Otto Preminger ph Leon Shamroy m Harry Nilsson
☆ Jackie Gleason, Carol Channing, Groucho Marx, Frankie Avalon, Fred Clark, Michael Constantine, Frank Gorshin, John Phillip Law, Peter Lawford, Burgess Meredith, George Raft, Cesar Romero, Mickey Rooney
'Unspeakable.' – *Michael Billington, Illustrated London News*

Skin & Bone
US   1995   110m   Foto-Kem
Film Research (Claudia Hoover, Gardner Monks)
Hopeful Hollywood actors work as male prostitutes for an escort agency, satisfying the fantasies of their clients.
A relentlessly downbeat slice of violent low life, dimly photographed.
wd Everett Lewis ph Fernando Arguelles m Geoff Harper, Mark Jan Wlodarkiewicz ed Everett Lewis
☆ B. Wyatt, Alan Boyce, Nicole Dillenberg, Garret Scullin, Chad Kula, Susannah Melvoin
'This 16mm production offers hardly any incentives to viewing: one must continually peer through a smog of blurry, underlit cinematography to make out the rudiments of the images, and long stretches of dialogue are rendered semi-inaudible by the traffic noise.' – *Peter Matthews, Sight and Sound*

Skin Deep
US   1989   101m   Technicolor   Panavision
Braveworld/Fox/Morgan Creek/BECO (Tony Adams)
A best-selling author devotes his time to booze and women.
Shallow comedy too much in love with its unprepossessing hero.
wd Blake Edwards ph Isidore Mankofsky pd Rodger Maus ed Robert Pergament
☆ John Ritter, Vincent Gardenia, Alyson Reed, Joel Brooks, Julianne Phillips, Chelsea Field, Peter Donat, Don Gordon, Nina Foch
'Edwards' undeniable personal obsessions are winding up as bland, uniform, nothing-in-particular films like this.' – *Kim Newman, MFB*

The Skin Game
GB   1932   85m   bw
BIP (John Maxwell)
A landowner hates his self-made neighbour.
Stiff picturization of a well-known stage play.

w Alfred Hitchcock, Alma Reville play John Galsworthy d Alfred Hitchcock ph Jack Cox
☆ Edmund Gwenn, John Longden, Jill Esmond, C. V. France, Helen Haye, Phyllis Konstam, Frank Lawton

The Skin Game *
US   1971   102m   Technicolor   Panavision
Warner/Cherokee (Harry Keller)
A white and a black con man have near escapes in many a Western town.
Amusing comedy Western with good pace and a few shafts of wit.
w Peter Stone, Richard Alan Simmons d Paul Bogart ph Fred Koenekamp m David Shire
☆ James Garner, Lou Gossett, Susan Clark, Brenda Sykes, Ed Asner, Andrew Duggan, Henry Jones, Neva Patterson

Skinheads
US   1988   93m   colour
Greydon Clark
aka: *Skinheads: The Second Coming of Hate*
A gang of neo-Nazis hunt down a couple who witnessed their slaughter of a café owner and her customers.
Unpleasant low-budget shocker, badly written, hammily acted and dully directed. Despite his star billing, Connors sensibly makes a brief appearance.
w David Reskin, Greydon Clark d Greydon Clark ph Nicholas von Sternberg m Dan Slider ad Doug Abrahamson ed Travis Clark
☆ Chuck Connors, Barbara Bain, Brian Brophy, Jason Culp, Elizabeth Sagal

Skippy *
US   1931   88m   bw
Paramount
The young son of a local health inspector makes friends in the slums.
Standard, blameless family entertainment.
w Joseph L. Mankiewicz, Norman McLeod comic strip Percy Crosby d Norman Taurog ph Karl Struss
☆ Jackie Cooper, Robert Coogan, Mitzi Green, Jackie Searl, Willard Robertson
'A great kid talker, but not for kids only ... if there is such a thing as being 100% inhuman, only then is it possible for anyone to dislike *Skippy* as entertainment.' – *Variety*
♟ Norman Taurog
♟ best picture; script; Jackie Cooper

Skirts Ahoy
US   1952   105m   Technicolor
MGM (Joe Pasternak)
Three girls join the navy and get their men.
Musical recruiting poster, quite devoid of interest.
w Isobel Lennart d Sidney Lanfield ph William Mellor m Harry Warren ch Nick Castle ly Ralph Blane
☆ Esther Williams, Vivian Blaine, Joan Evans, Barry Sullivan, Keefe Brasselle, Dean Miller, Debbie Reynolds, Bobby Van, Billy Eckstine

Skrivanci Na Niti: see *Larks on a String*

The Skull
GB   1965   83m   Techniscope
Paramount/Amicus (Milton Subotsky)
The skull of the Marquis de Sade haunts two antiquarians.
Clodhopping horror with very visible wires.
w Milton Subotsky story Robert Bloch d Freddie Francis ph John Wilcox m Elisabeth Lutyens
☆ Peter Cushing, Christopher Lee, Patrick Wymark, Jill Bennett, Nigel Green, Michael Gough, George Coulouris

Skullduggery
US   1969   105m   Technicolor   Panavision
Universal (Saul David)
Archaeologists and adventurers clash on a trek in New Guinea.
Fashionable oddball adventure about the discovery of an unspoiled primitive tribe; the elements don't jell.
w Nelson Gidding d Gordon Douglas ph Robert Moreno m Oliver Nelson

☆ Burt Reynolds, Susan Clark, Roger C. Carmel, Paul Hubschmid, Chips Rafferty, Alexander Knox, Edward Fox, Wilfrid Hyde-White, Rhys Williams

Sky Bandits
GB   1986   93m   Rank Colour
London Front Ltd (Richard Herland)
aka: *Gunbus*
Adventures of World War I flyers.
An attempt at a light-hearted Hell's Angels. It misfires on all cylinders.
w Thom Keyes d Zoran Perisic ph David Watkin m Alfie Kabilje pd Tony Woollard ed Peter Tanner
☆ Scott McGinnis, Jeff Osterhage, Ronald Lacey, Miles Anderson, Valerie Steffen, Ingrid Held, Adrian Dunbar

Sky Bride
US   1932   75m   bw
Paramount
An aerial barnstormer loses his nerve after an accident.
Formula melodrama with aerobatics.
w Joseph L. Mankiewicz, Agnes Brand Leahy, Grover Jones d Stephen Roberts
☆ Richard Arlen, Jack Oakie, Virginia Bruce, Robert Coogan, Charles Starrett
'Lack of romantic interest is somewhat of a handicap to a conventional air plot with a suspensive finish.' – *Variety*

Sky Devils
US   1931   89m   bw
Caddo/Howard Hughes
Two draft dodgers find themselves heroes of the Army Air Corps in World War I France.
Little-seen but unremarkable adventure comedy in the Flagg and Quirt tradition.
w Joseph Moncure March, Edward Sutherland d Edward Sutherland ph Tony Gaudio md Alfred Newman ch Busby Berkeley
☆ Spencer Tracy, William Boyd, Ann Dvorak, George Cooper, Billy Bevan, Forrester Harvey
'A hodge-podge of all the laugh war stuff ... and how they want something to laugh about right now. Psychologically and in a material way, it should do nicely.' – *Variety*

Sky Full of Moon
US   1952   73m   bw
MGM (Sidney Franklin Jnr)
A rodeo cowboy wins money and a showgirl in Las Vegas.
Ambling comedy with an agreeable air of innocence.
wd Norman Foster ph Ray June m Paul Sawtell
☆ Carleton Carpenter, Jan Sterling, Keenan Wynn

Sky Giant
US   1938   80m   bw
RKO (Robert Sisk)
Romance and adventure at a flying school.
Unremarkable melodrama with expected heroics.
w Lionel Houser d Ken Landers
☆ Richard Dix, Joan Fontaine, Chester Morris, Harry Carey, Paul Guilfoyle
'Good for the lighter weight first run houses and the upper berth of double deckers.' – *Variety*

Sky Pirates
Australia   1986   89m   Colorfilm   Panavision
John Lamond Motion Pictures (John Lamond, Michael Hirsh)
A pilot foils a crazed squadron leader attempting to obtain the three parts of an ancient stone that will provide him with unlimited power.
Silly and thrill-free adventure with an over-complicated narrative which amounts to no more than a feeble imitation of the Indiana Jones movies.
w John Lamond d Colin Eggleston ph Garry Wapshott m Brian May pd Kristian Fredrickson ed John Lamond, Michael Hirsh sp Dennis Nicholson
☆ John Hargreaves, Meredith Phillips, Max Phipps, Bill Hunter, Simon Chilvers, Alex Scott

'He'll try anything once ... even if it's impossible!'

Sky Riders *
US   1976   91m   DeLuxe   Todd-AO 35
TCF (Terry Morse Jnr)
In Athens, the family of an American businessman is kidnapped by terrorists and rescued by hang-gliders led by a soldier of fortune.
Old-fashioned actioner with new-fashioned political concern.
w Jack de Witt, Stanley Mann, Garry Michael White, Hall T. Sprague, Bill McGaw d Douglas Hickox ph Ousama Rawi m Lalo Schifrin
☆ James Coburn, Susannah York, Robert Culp, Charles Aznavour, Werner Pochath, Kenneth Griffith, Harry Andrews

Sky West and Crooked
GB   1965   102m   Eastmancolor
Rank/John Mills (Jack Hanbury)
US title: *Gypsy Girl*
A mentally retarded girl falls in love with a gypsy.
Eccentric rural melodrama with echoes of Cold Comfort Farm and Les Jeux Interdits. Interesting, but scarcely a runaway success.
w Mary Hayley Bell, John Prebble d John Mills ph Arthur Ibbetson m Malcolm Arnold
☆ Hayley Mills, Ian McShane, Laurence Naismith, Geoffrey Bayldon, Annette Crosbie, Norman Bird
'Behind the overwhelming feyness of it all lurk assumptions which in cold blood look almost sinister.' – *MFB*

Skyjacked *
US   1972   101m   Metrocolor   Panavision
MGM/Walter Seltzer
A Boeing 707 on a flight from Los Angeles to Minneapolis is forced by a mad bomber to fly to Moscow.
Shamelessly hackneyed aeroplane adventure with quite enjoyable elements.
w Stanley R. Greenberg novel Hijacked by David Harper d John Guillermin ph Harry Stradling Jnr m Perry Botkin Jnr
☆ Charlton Heston, Yvette Mimieux, James Brolin, Claude Akins, Jeanne Crain, Rosey Grier, Walter Pidgeon, Leslie Uggams

Skylark
US   1941   94m   bw
Paramount (Mark Sandrich)
A wife decides on her fifth anniversary that she is tired of being secondary to her husband's career, and needs a fling.
Formula matrimonial comedy; plenty of talent but no sparkle.
w Z. Myers play Samson Raphaelson d Mark Sandrich ph Charles Lang m Victor Young
☆ Claudette Colbert, Ray Milland, Brian Aherne, Binnie Barnes, Walter Abel, Grant Mitchell, Mona Barrie, Ernest Cossart

Skyliner
US   1949   61m   bw
Lippert/William Stephens
The FBI nabs a spy on a transcontinental plane.
Second feature chiefly interesting for its setting.
w Maurice Tombragel d William Berke ph Carl Berger m Raoul Kraushaar
☆ Richard Travis, Pamela Blake, Rochelle Hudson, Steve Geray, Greg McClure

The Sky's the Limit
GB   1937   79m   bw
Jack Buchanan
A sacked aircraft designer suddenly finds himself in demand.
Amiable star musical.
w Jack Buchanan, Douglas Furber d Lee Garmes and Jack Buchanan
☆ Jack Buchanan, Mara Loseff, William Kendall, David Hutcheson, H. F. Maltby, Athene Seyler, Sara Allgood

The Sky's the Limit *
US   1943   89m   bw
RKO (David Hempstead)
A flyer on leave meets and falls for a news photographer.
Thin musical with incidental compensations.

---

w Frank Fenton, Lynn Root d Edward H. Griffith ph Russell Metty m Leigh Harline md Leo F. Forbstein

☆ Fred Astaire, Joan Leslie, *Robert Benchley*, Robert Ryan, Elizabeth Patterson

† Joan Leslie's singing was dubbed by Sally Sweetland.

♫ Leigh Harline; song 'My Shining Hour' (mHarold Arlen, lyJohnny Mercer)

Skyscraper Souls
US 1932 100m bw
MGM

In an office building, several personal dilemmas interlock.

Portmanteau drama in the Grand Hotel mould, and quite comparable.

w C. G. Sullivan, Elmer Harris book Faith Baldwin d Edgar Selwyn

☆ Warren William, Maureen O'Sullivan, Verree Teasdale, Gregory Ratoff, Jean Hersholt, Norman Foster, Anita Page, George Barbier, Wallace Ford, Hedda Hopper

Slab Boys *
GB 1997 97m Technicolor
Channel 4/Skreba/Wanderlust (Simon Relph, Lauren Lowenthal)

In 50s Scotland, three working-class teenagers mixing paints in a carpet factory dream of a better life.

An interesting attempt to find an appropriate visual style for two plays that worked better on the stage; the power and passion are too often dissipated and the result has the quaintness of a period piece.

wd John Byrne plays *The Slab Boys and Cuttin' a Rug by John Byrne ph* Seamus McGarvey m Jack Bruce pd Luana Hanson ed John Macdonnell

☆ Robin Lang, Duncan Ross, Russell Barr, Bill Gardiner, Louise Berry, Anna Massey, Tom Watson, Moray Hunter, David O'Hara

'A whole lot of energy and visual design going nowhere special.' – *Variety*

Slacker **
US 1991 97m colour
Feature/Detour (Richard Linklater)

In Austin, Texas, young people wandering the streets confide to the camera their odd beliefs and attitudes, including the avoidance of careers.

Leisurely, lackadaisical feature of oddballs that exerts a certain bemused fascination.

wd Richard Linklater ph Lee Daniel m Buffalo Gals, Triangle Mallet Apron, The Texas Instruments ad Debbie Pastor ed Scott Rhodes

☆ Richard Linklater, Rudy Basquez, Jean Caffeine, Jan Hockey, Stephan Hockey, Mark James

'A film of quirky, unpredictable and oddly poetic charm.' – *Philip Kemp, Sight and Sound*

'One of the freshest independent films to come along in some time, but because of its non-narrative, non-characterization approach, film won't be to all tastes.' – *Variety*

Slade: see *Jack Slade*

Slam *
US 1998 100m colour
Trimark/Off Line (Henri Kessler, Marc Levin, Richard Stratton)

Thrown into prison, a black poet uses his art to persuade others that violence solves nothing.

Earnest drama, in a semi-documentary style, on the power of rap to change macho attitudes.

w Richard Stratton, Marc Levin, Sonja Sohn, Saul Williams d Marc Levin ph Marc Benjamin ed Emir Luis

☆ Saul Williams, Sonja Sohn, Bonz Malone

'Emotionally powerful and technically innovative.' – *Variety*

Slam Dunk Ernest
US 1995 92m colour
Emshell (George Horie, Stacy Williams)

A dimwitted handyman becomes a basketball wizard when he puts on some magic shoes.

Dimwitted, heavy-handed slapstick comedy of little appeal.

w John R. Cherry III, Daniel Butler d John Cherry ph David Geddes m Mark Adler pd Chris August ed Craig Bassett, Chris Ellis

☆ Jim Varney, Cylk Cozart, Miguel A. Nunez Jnr, Lester Barrie, Colin Lawrence, Richard Leacock, Jay Brazeau, Kareem Abdul-Jabbar

† The film was released direct to video.

Slamdance
US 1987 99m colour
Zenith Productions/Island Pictures (Rupert Harvey, Barry Opper)

A newspaper cartoonist is framed for a murder by a corrupt cop.

Silly, convoluted mish-mash of a thriller.

w Don Opper d Wayne Wang ph Amie Mokri m Mitchell Froom pd Eugenio Zanetti ed Lee Percy

☆ Tom Hulce, Mary Elizabeth Mastrantonio, Virginia Madsen, Millie Perkins, Don Opper, Adam Ant, John Doe, Robert Beltran, Judith Barsi, Harry Dean Stanton

Slander
US 1956 81m bw
MGM (Armand Deutsch)

Revelations about a film star in a scandal magazine lead to blackmail and murder.

Unlikely melodrama, routinely assembled, based on the Confidential Magazine lawsuits.

w Jerome Weidman d Roy Rowland ph Harold J. Marzerati m Jeff Alexander

☆ Van Johnson, Ann Blyth, Steve Cochran, Marjorie Rambeau, Harold J. Stone

Slap Shot *
US 1977 124m Technicolor
Universal/Robert J. Wunsch, Stephen Friedman

The wily player-coach of a fading ice hockey team finds ways, including dirty play, of keeping it going.

Violent, foul-mouthed comedy which works as it goes but leaves a bad taste in the mouth.

w Nancy Dowd d George Roy Hill ph Victor Kemper, Wallace Worsley md Elmer Bernstein

☆ Paul Newman, Michael Ontkean, Lindsay Crouse, Jennifer Warren, Strother Martin

'Fast, noisy, profane … gets you laughing, all right, but you don't necessarily enjoy yourself.' – *New Yorker*

'Both indulgent and moralizing, the self-consciously racy script ends up looking merely opportunistic.' – *Time Out*

Slattery's Hurricane
US 1949 87m bw
TCF (William Perlberg)

Loves of a storm-spotting pilot with the US Weather Bureau in Florida.

Forgettable programmer with good storm sequences.

w Herman Wouk, Richard Murphy novel Herman Wouk d André de Toth ph Charles G. Clarke m Cyril Mockridge

☆ Richard Widmark, Linda Darnell, Veronica Lake, John Russell, Gary Merrill, Walter Kingsford

Slaughter
US 1972 90m DeLuxe Todd-AO 35
AIP/Slaughter United (Monroe Sachson)

A black Vietnam veteran hunts down the underworld syndicate which killed his mother and father.

Hectic crime yarn with a pitilessly violent hero and not enough style to relieve the unappetizing monotony.

w Mark Hanna, Don Williams d Jack Starrett ph Rosanio Solano m Luchi de Jesus

☆ Jim Brown, Rip Torn, Don Gordon, Cameron Mitchell

'The cast perform their trigger-happy tasks with all the passionate conviction of a team of well-oiled robots.' – *Jan Dawson*

Slaughter on Tenth Avenue
US 1957 103m bw
U-I (Albert Zugsmith)

The New York DA's office investigates union murders on the docks.

Uninteresting imitation of On the Waterfront.

w Lawrence Roman novel *The Man Who Rocked the Boat* by William J. Keating, Richard Carter d Arnold Laven ph Fred Jackman m Richard Rodgers

☆ Richard Egan, Jan Sterling, Dan Duryea, Julie Adams, Walter Matthau, Charles McGraw, Sam Levene, Mickey Shaughnessy, Harry Bellaver

Slaughter Trail
US 1951 78m Cinecolor
RKO (Irving Allen)

Three outlaws cause trouble between white man and Indian.

Rough-hewn Western strung together by verses of a ballad.

w Sid Kuller d Irving Allen ph Jack Greenhalgh ad George Van Marter ed Fred Allen

☆ Brian Donlevy, Gig Young, Virginia Grey, Andy Devine, Robert Hutton

Slaughterhouse Five *
US 1972 104m Technicolor
Universal/Vanadas (Paul Monash)

A suburban optometrist has nightmare space/time fantasies involving Nazi POW camps and a strange futuristic planet.

Interesting but infuriating anti-war fantasy for intellectuals.

w Stephen Geller novel Kurt Vonnegut Jnr d George Roy Hill ph Miroslav Ondricek m J. S. Bach, performed by Glen Gould pd Henry Bumstead

☆ Michael Sacks, Ron Leibman, Eugène Roche, Sharon Gans, Valerie Perrine, Sorrell Booke, John Dehner

'A lot of good makings in this picture; but very little is made.' – *Stanley Kauffmann*

Slaughter's Big Rip-Off
US 1973 93m Movielab Todd-AO 35
AIP (Monroe Sachson)

Still on the run from gangsters who have killed his best friend, Slaughter violently disposes of a number of adversaries.

More routine black violence, a rampage of senseless brutality against sunny Los Angeles backgrounds.

w Charles Johnson d Gordon Douglas ph Charles Wheeler m James Brown, Fred Wesley

☆ Jim Brown, Ed MacMahon, Brock Peters, Don Stroud

Slave Girl
US 1947 79m Technicolor
U-I (Michael Fessier, Ernest Pagano)

In the early 1800s, a diplomat is sent to Tripoli to ransom sailors held by the power-mad potentate.

Criticism would be superfluous; when the film was finished it was obviously so bad that executives ordered the addition of a talking camel and other Hellzapoppin-type jokes in order to turn it into a comedy.

w Michael Fessier, Ernest Pagano d Charles Lamont ph George Robinson, W. Howard Greene m Milton Rosen

☆ George Brent, Yvonne de Carlo, Albert Dekker, Broderick Crawford, Lois Collier, Andy Devine, Carl Esmond, Arthur Treacher

Slave Girls
GB 1968 74m Technicolor Cinemascope
Hammer (Aida Young)

US title: *Prehistoric Women*

A hunter seeking white rhinoceros finds himself in a lost valley ruled by a tribe of women.

Feebly preposterous comic strip farrago without the saving grace of humour.

w Henry Younger (Michael Carreras) d Michael Carreras m Michael Reed m Carlo Martelli ad Robert Jones ed Jim Needs, Roy Hyde

☆ Michael Latimer, Martine Beswick, Edina Ronay, Carol White

'The Highest Love … The Lowest Men The Seven Seas Have Ever Known.'

Slave Ship **
US 1937 92m bw
TCF (Darryl F. Zanuck)

An American slave captain decides to become respectable but finds a mutiny on his hands.

Well-made adventure movie in the old tradition, a model of studio production.

w Sam Hellman, Lamar Trotti, Gladys Lehman novel George S. King story William Faulkner d Tay Garnett ph Ernest Palmer m Alfred Newman

☆ Wallace Beery, Warner Baxter, Elizabeth Allen, Mickey Rooney, George Sanders, Jane Darwell, Joseph Schildkraut, Arthur Hohl, Minna Gombell,

Billy Bevan, Francis Ford, Edwin Maxwell, J. Farrell MacDonald, Paul Hurst, Holmes Herbert

'Plenty of action and de luxe scenic trimmings … good box office blood and thunder.' – *Variety*

Slave Women of Corinth: see *Aphrodite, Goddess of Love*

Slaves
US 1969 110m Eastmancolor
Slaves Company/Theatre Guild/Walter Reade (Philip Langner)

In 1850 Kentucky a slave stands up for his rights and plans escape.

Well-meaning but muddled and old-fashioned melodrama, hardly well enough done to raise comparison with Gone with the Wind.

wd Herbert J. Biberman ph Joseph Brun m Bobby Scott

☆ Stephen Boyd, Ossie Davis, Dionne Warwick, Shepperd Strudwick, Nancy Coleman, David Huddleston, Gale Sondergaard

Slaves of New York
US 1989 125m Technicolor
Columbia TriStar/Hendler-Merchant Ivory/Ismail Merchant, Gary Hendler

Trendy young artists and fashion designers in New York fall in and out of love.

Inconsequential movie that is unable to get to grips with its insubstantial characters.

w Tama Janowitz stories Tama Janowitz d James Ivory ph Tony Pierce-Roberts m Richard Robbins pd David Gropman ed Katherine Wenning

☆ Bernadette Peters, Madeleine Potter, Adam Coleman Howard, Nick Corri, Charles McCaughan, Jonas Abry, Tama Janowitz

Slayground
GB 1983 89m Technicolor
EMI/Jennie and Co. (John Dark, Gower Frost)

A rich man hires an assassin to track down a criminal who accidentally killed his daughter.

One of those tedious and violent films in which the criminal wins out; slickness seems to make it worse.

w Trevor Preston novel Richard Stark d Terry Bedford ph Stephen Smith, Herb Wagreich m Colin Towns pd Keith Wilson

☆ Peter Coyote, Mel Smith, Billie Whitelaw, Philip Sayer, Bill Luhrs

'A disappointingly lame front runner for the new EMI stable.' – *Philip Strick, MFB*

SLC Punk!
US/Australia 1999 98m colour Panavision
Columbia TriStar/Beyond/Blue Tulip (Sam Maydew, Peter Ward)

In Salt Lake City, a clever student gives up being a punk to go to Harvard.

Aimless movie, directed in a frenetic style, of failed rebellion and middle-class conformity, with an unsympathetic protagonist who won't stop talking.

wd James Merendino ph Greg Littlewood pd Charlotte Malmloff ed Esther P. Russel

☆ Matthew Lillard, Michael Goorjian, Annabeth Gish, Jennifer Lien, Christopher McDonald, Devon Sawa, Jason Segel, Summer Phoenix, James Duval, Til Schweiger, Adam Pascal, Chiara Barzini, Kevin Breznahan

'Thematically barren, visually bland and stylistically bland, SLC Punk! is, no bones about it, a bad movie.' – *Rupert Laight, Film Review*

Sleep My Love *
US 1948 96m bw
UA/Mary Pickford (Charles 'Buddy' Rogers, Ralph Cohn)

A man plots to murder his wife, but is foiled.

Thin suspenser, rather splendidly photographed in the expressionist manner.

w St Clair McKelway, Leo Rosten novel Leo Rosten d Douglas Sirk ph Joseph Valentine m Rudy Schrager

☆ Claudette Colbert, Don Ameche, Robert Cummings, Rita Johnson, George Coulouris, Hazel Brooks, Keye Luke, Raymond Burr

'After all, what are friends for?'

Sleep with Me *

US   1994   94m   Foto-Kem
First Independent/August/Paribas/Revolution
(Michael Steinberg, Roger Hedden, Eric Stoltz)
⬛ ▦ ⚲

A couple who have been living together decide to get married; then the wife has a brief affair with their best friend.
An episodic film about self-obsessed young people in social settings, with each section written by a different hand; it offers little that is fresh, apart from Tarantino's monologue on the gay subtext of Top Gun, *but there are moments of nice observation along the way.*
w Duane Dell'Amico, Roger Hedden, Neal Jimenez, Joe Keenan, Rory Kelly, Michael Steinberg d Rory Kelly ph Andrzej Sekula m David Lawrence pd Randy Eriksen ed David Moritz
☆ Eric Stoltz, Meg Tilly, Craig Sheffer, Todd Field, Dean Cameron, Susan Traylor, Thomas Gibson, Adrienne Shelly, Quentin Tarantino
'A comedy so laid back that at times it faces atrophy.' – *Sheila Johnston, Independent*

'A love story about two people who hate each other!'

Sleeper *
👫 US   1973   88m   DeLuxe
UA/Jack Rollins, Charles Joffe (Jack Grossberg)
⬛ ▦ ⚲

A health food store owner is deep frozen after an operation and wakes two hundred years in the future.
Predictable star vehicle with an agreeable string of bright gags.
w Woody Allen, Marshall Brickman d Woody Allen ph David M. Walsh m Woody Allen pd Dale Hennesy
☆ Woody Allen, Diane Keaton, John Beck, Mary Gregory
'Verbal and visual gags rain down like hailstones.' – *Michael Billington, Illustrated London News*

'Four friends made a mistake that changed their lives forever.'

Sleepers
US   1996   147m   Technicolor
Polygram/Warner/Propaganda/Baltimore (Barry Levinson, Steve Golin)
⬛ ▦ ⚲ ◉ ⚲

With the aid of a journalist and a lawyer, two petty gangsters get away with the murder of a sadistic guard who abused the four of them when they were teenagers in a reform home.
Allegedly based on a true incident, this nevertheless has the insubstantiality of pulp fiction, as just another example of the modern cycle of unexceptional, amoral vigilante thrillers.
wd Barry Levinson book Lorenzo Carcaterra ph Michael Ballhaus m John Williams pd Kristi Zea ed Stu Linder
☆ Kevin Bacon, Robert DeNiro, Dustin Hoffman, Bruno Kirby, Jason Patric, Brad Pitt, Brad Renfro, Ron Eldard, Billy Crudup, Vittorio Gassman, Minnie Driver
'Stylish, lurid, yet insubstantial film.' – *Sight and Sound*
♫ John Williams

The Sleepers: see Little Nikita

The Sleeping Beauty *
👫 US   1959   75m   Technirama 70
Walt Disney (Ken Peterson)
⬛ ▦ ⚲ ⚲

Rather stodgy, unwisely Cinemascoped feature cartoon of the old legend; very fashionable and detailed, but somehow lifeless.
d Clyde Geronimi md George Bruns pd Don da Gradi, Ken Anderson
☆ Featuring the voices of Mary Costa, Bill Shirley, Eleanor Audley, Verna Felton, Barbara Jo Allen, Barbara Luddy
'The drawings on the whole suggest a combination of *New Yorker*, comic horror strip and chocolate box – the special Disney chocolate box assortment with hard centres and soft centres.' – *C. A. Lejeune*
♫ George Bruns

Sleeping Car
GB   1933   82m   bw
Gaumont (Michael Balcon)
A woman on the run pretends to marry a sleeping car attendant, then finds they really are married.
Artificial comedy with interesting cast from London stage.
w Franz Schultz d Anatole Litvak ph Günther Krampf, Glen MacWilliams
☆ Madeleine Carroll, Ivor Novello, Laddie Cliff, Kay Hammond, Claud Allister, Stanley Holloway

The Sleeping Car Murders *
France   1965   95m   bw   Cinemascope
PECF (Julien Derode)
original title: *Compartiment Tueurs*
When the overnight express from Marseilles reaches Paris, a girl is found dead in the sleeping car.
Rather long-winded whodunnit with an unlikely solution: a good pace helps, however, as do skilful borrowings from American police films of the forties.
wd Costa-Gavras novel Sebastien Japrisot ph Jean Tournier m Michel Magne
☆ Yves Montand, Simone Signoret, Pierre Mondy, Catherine Allégret, Jacques Perrin, Jean-Louis Trintignant, Michel Piccoli

Sleeping Car to Trieste *
GB   1948   95m   bw
GFD/Two Cities (George H. Brown)
▦
Spy melodrama, a slow-starting but generally entertaining remake of *Rome Express* (qv).
w Allan Mackinnon d John Paddy Carstairs ph Jack Hildyard m Benjamin Frankel
☆ Albert Lieven, Jean Kent, David Tomlinson, David Hutcheson, Rona Anderson, Paul Dupuis, Finlay Currie, Alan Wheatley, Derrick de Marney, Grégoire Aslan, Hugh Burden

The Sleeping Cardinal
GB   1931   84m   bw
Twickenham (Julius Hagen)
Sherlock Holmes exposes a smuggling ring.
Slow-paced but interesting adaptation, vaguely based on The Empty House.
w Cyril Twyford, H. Fowler Mear stories Sir Arthur Conan Doyle d Leslie Hiscott
☆ Arthur Wontner, Ian Fleming, Norman McKinnel, Jane Welsh, Louis Goodrich

The Sleeping City *
US   1950   85m   bw
U-I (Leonard Goldstein)
A policeman disguises himself as a medical student to learn more about a murder in a general hospital.
A location melodrama of modest excellence.
w Jo Eisinger d George Sherman ph William Miller m Frank Skinner
☆ Richard Conte, Richard Taber, Coleen Gray, John Alexander, Peggy Dow, Alex Nicol

The Sleeping Tiger
GB   1954   89m   bw
Anglo-Amalgamated/Insignia (Victor Hanbury)
▦
A psychiatrist overpowers a criminal and takes him home as a guinea pig; the criminal then falls in love with the psychiatrist's wife.
Turgid and unconvincing melodrama, a thoroughgoing bore.
w Harold Buchman, Carl Foreman novel Maurice Moiseiwitch d Joseph Losey ph Harry Waxman m Malcolm Arnold
☆ Dirk Bogarde, Alexander Knox, Alexis Smith, Hugh Griffith, Maxine Audley, Glyn Houston, Billie Whitelaw
'There is a splendour about this film, which has one of the most absurdly extravagant plots on record, and never flinches from it.' – *Gavin Lambert*

'She changed her name. Her looks. Her life. All to escape the most dangerous man she's ever met. Her husband.'

Sleeping with the Enemy
US   1990   99m   DeLuxe
TCF (Leonard Goldberg)
⬛ ▦ ⚲ ⚲

In order to leave her violent husband, a wife fakes her own death and takes a new identity.
Uninvolving thriller that is never original enough to overcome its predictability.
w Ronald Bass novel Nancy Price d Joseph Ruben ph John W. Lindley m Jerry Goldsmith pd Doug Kraner ed George Bowers
☆ Julia Roberts, Patrick Bergin, Kevin Anderson, Elizabeth Lawrence, Kyle Secor, Claudette Nevins, Tony Abatemarco, Marita Geraghty, Harley Venton
'A glossy combination of secondhand showing-off-Julia scenes from Pretty Woman and secondhand scares from The Stepfather.' – *Pauline Kael, New Yorker*

'What if someone you never met, someone you never saw, someone you never knew was the only someone for you?'

Sleepless in Seattle *
US   1993   105m   Technicolor
TriStar (Gary Foster)
⬛ ▦   ⚲   ⚲

After his mother dies, an eight-year-old boy confides to a radio phone-in that he wants to find someone for his father to marry; the call is heard by an intrigued journalist, worried about her engagement to a dull man.
Enjoyable romantic comedy, although its overall tone is excessively sweet.
w Nora Ephron, David S. Ward, Jeff Arch d Nora Ephron ph Sven Nykvist m Marc Shaiman pd Jeffrey Townsend ed Robert Reitano
☆ Tom Hanks, Meg Ryan, Ross Malinger, Rita Wilson, Victor Garber, Tom Riis Farrell, Carey Lowell, Bill Pullman
'This shamelessly romantic comedy ... delivers ample warmth and some explosively funny moments.' – *Variety*
♫ Nora Ephron, David S. Ward, Jeff Arch; song 'A Wink and a Smile' (m Marc Shaiman, ly Ramsey McLean)

Sleepwalkers
US   1992   89m   Technicolor
Columbia TriStar/Columbia/ION (Mark Victor, Michael Grais, Nabeel Zahid)
⬛ ▦   ⚲

A mother and son, shape-shifting monsters, move into a new community.
Ridiculous horror, lacking suspense, sense or the slightest ability to shock or scare.
w Stephen King d Mick Garris ph Rodney Charters m Nicholas Pike pd John DeCuir Jnr ed O. Nicholas Brown sp Apogee Productions
☆ Brian Krause, Mädchen Amick, Alice Krige, Jim Haynie, Cindy Pickett, Ron Perlman, Lyman Ward, Dan Martin, John Landis, Joe Dante, Stephen King, Clive Barker, Tobe Hooper
'Piffle.' – *Sheila Johnston, Independent*
'This technically proficient, surprisingly gory but utterly nonsensical movie is billed as the first screenplay written by horror novelist Stephen King expressly for the screen. Unfortunately, this hardly rates as a recommendation.' – *Nigel Floyd, Sight and Sound*

'Heads will roll.'

Sleepy Hollow *
US   1999   105m   DeLuxe
Paramount/Mandalay/American Zoetrope (Scott Rudin, Adam Schroeder)
⚲

An effete New York constable goes to a village to solve a series of beheadings by a mysterious figure.
This is yet another 'B' movie with pretensions, a big-budget Hammer-styled horror. It succeeds only on the level of design and atmosphere; the narrative creaks, and the performances tend to eccentricity for no good purpose.
w Andrew Kevin Walker, Kevin Yagher ph Emanuel Lubezki m Danny Elfman pd Rick Heinrichs ed Chris Lebenzon sp Industrial Light & Magic; Kevin Yagher cos Colleen Atwood
☆ Johnny Depp, Christina Ricci, Miranda Richardson, Michael Gambon, Casper Van Dien, Jeffrey Jones, Christopher Lee, Richard Griffiths, Ian McDiarmid, Michael Gough, Christopher Walken, Lisa Marie, Steven Waddington, Claire Skinner, Alun Armstrong
'As beautifully crafted a film as anyone could ever hope to see.' – *Todd McCarthy, Variety*
'A film with no theatrical core and no integrity in the writing, acting or storytelling. The jokes aren't funny. The tone is uncertain. It invokes nothing real or fantastic.' – *Mick LaSalle, San Francisco Chronicle*
♫ Rick Heinrichs
♫ Emmanuel Lubezki; Colleen Atwood
⚲ Rick Heinrichs, Colleen Atwood

The Slender Thread *
US   1965   98m   bw
Paramount/Athene (Stephen Alexander)
▦

A volunteer social worker tries to prevent a woman from committing suicide while police track her down from their phone conversations.
Acceptable star melodrama, curiously artificially styled.
w Stirling Silliphant d Sydney Pollack ph Loyal Griggs m Quincy Jones
☆ Anne Bancroft, Sidney Poitier, Steven Hill, Telly Savalas

'Think of the crime ... then go one step further ... If it was murder, where's the body? If it was for a woman, which woman? If it's only a game, why the blood?'

Sleuth *
GB   1972   139m   colour
Palomar (Morton Gottlieb)
⬛ ▦ ⚲ ⚲

A successful thriller writer invents a murder plot which rebounds on himself.
Well-acted version of a highly successful piece of stage trickery; despite hard work all round it seems much less clever and arresting on the screen, and the tricks do show.
w Anthony Shaffer play Anthony Shaffer d Joseph L. Mankiewicz ph Oswald Morris m John Addison
☆ Laurence Olivier, Michael Caine
♫ Joseph L. Mankiewicz; John Addison; Laurence Olivier; Michael Caine

Sliding Doors *
GB/US   1998   108m   Technicolor
Paramount/Miramax (Sydney Pollack, Philippa Braithwaite, William Horberg)

Two possible lives unfold for a public relations executive: in one, she misses the train that would have taken her home in time to discover her boyfriend in their bed with his former girlfriend; in the other, she catches the train.
A formally clever, occasionally charming romance; the problem is that instead of one not very interesting existence, we witness two.
wd Peter Howitt ph Remi Adfarasin m David Hirschfelder pd Maria Djurokovic ed John Smith
☆ Gwyneth Paltrow, John Hannah, John Lynch, Jeanne Tripplehorn, Zara Turner, Douglas McFerran, Paul Brightwell, Nina Young, Virginia McKenna
'Pulls off the rare fusion of a clever, almost philosophical conceit with a comedy-drama which packs a satisfying emotional punch.' – *Demetrios Matheou, Premiere*
'You're watching two things at the same time: a great idea for a film, and the actual film unfolding in front of you. Who knows? In another life, it could have been great.' – *Tom Shone, Sunday Times*

A Slight Case of Murder *
US   1938   85m   bw
Warner (Sam Bischoff)
When a beer baron tries to go legitimate his colleagues attempt to kill him, but end up shooting each other.
Amusing black farce, remade to less effect as Stop, You're Killing Me (qv).
w Earl Baldwin, Joseph Schrank play Damon Runyon, Howard Lindsay d Lloyd Bacon ph Sid Hickox m M. K. Jerome, Jack Scholl
☆ Edward G. Robinson, Jane Bryan, Willard Parker, Ruth Donnelly, Allen Jenkins, John Litel, Harold Huber, Edward Brophy, Bobby Jordan
'Nothing funnier has been produced by Hollywood for a long time ... a mirthful and hilarious whimsy.' – *Variety*
'The complications crazily mount, sentiment never raises its ugly head, a long nose is made at violence and death.' – *Graham Greene*

Slightly French
US   1948   81m   bw
Columbia (Irving Starr)
A film director in trouble passes off a Bowery-born carnival dancer as an exotic French star.
Rather tedious comedy which lively performances can't sustain.
w Karen de Wolf d Douglas Sirk m George Duning

☆ Dorothy Lamour, Don Ameche, Janis Carter, Jeanne Manet, Willard Parker

'Her heart belongs to daddy, and she calls everybody daddy!'

Slightly Honorable
US 1940 85m bw
UA/Walter Wanger (Tay Garnett)

Lawyer partners set out to break a crime syndicate.
Fair crime thriller which can't decide whether it's comedy or drama.
w John Hunter Lay, Robert Tallman, Ken Englund *novel* Send Another Coffin *by* F. G. Presnell d Tay Garnett *ph* Merritt Gerstad *m* Werner Janssen
☆ Pat O'Brien, Broderick Crawford, Edward Arnold, Eve Arden, Claire Dodd, Ruth Terry, Bernard Nedell, Alan Dinehart, Douglass Dumbrille, Ernest Truex
'The story skips along without deftness between serious drama and comedy, and winds up in the aggregate as a whatsit.' – *Variety*

Slightly Scarlet
US 1930 72m bw
Paramount

Two jewel thieves outwit a malicious mastermind.
Somewhat effete comedy-drama in a long bygone style.
w Howard Estabrook, Joseph L. Mankiewicz, Percy Heath d Louis Gasnier, Edwin H. Knopf
☆ Clive Brook, Evelyn Brent, Paul Lukas, Eugene Pallette, Helen Ware, Virginia Bruce, Henry Wadsworth, Claud Allister
'Fair general programme feature.' – *Variety*

Slightly Scarlet
US 1956 92m Technicolor Superscope (RKO)

The mayor's secretary loves the leader of a criminal gang.
Competent but uninteresting crime romance.
w Robert Blees *novel* James A. Cain d Allan Dwan *ph* John Alton *m* Louis Forbes
☆ Arlene Dahl, John Payne, Rhonda Fleming, Kent Taylor, Ted de Corsia
'So complicated that it is difficult to sort out which characters are supposed to be sympathetic.' – *MFB*

Slim
US 1937 85m bw
Warner

Electric linesmen argue about their work and their women.
A reworking of Tiger Shark which itself later became Manpower; competent action stuff.
w William Wister Haines d Ray Enright
☆ Pat O'Brien, Margaret Lindsay, Henry Fonda, Stuart Erwin, J. Farrell MacDonald, Jane Wyman
'A comedy drama which will do all right without setting off fireworks.' – *Variety*

Slim Carter
US 1957 82m Eastmancolor
Universal-International

A playboy is signed up by a Hollywood studio and required to change his image.
Curious sentimental comedy which might have worked with stronger casting.
w Montgomery Pittman d Richard H. Bartlett *ph* Ellis Carter *m* Herman Stein
☆ Jock Mahoney, Julie Adams, Tim Hovey, William Hopper, Ben Johnson, Barbara Hale

Sling Blade **
US 1996 136m CFI color
Miramax/Shooting Gallery (Brandon Rosser, David L. Bushell)

A simple-minded man goes to live with a widow and her unhappy son in a small Southern town, after leaving the mental hospital where he was incarcerated for 25 years for murdering his mother and her lover.
Slow-paced tragedy, notable for some fine, detailed performances, and marred by its remorseless predictability.
wd Billy Bob Thornton *ph* Barry Markowitz *m* Daniel Lanois *pd* Clark Hunter *ed* Hughes Winborne
☆ Billy Bob Thornton, Dwight Yoakam, J. T. Walsh, John Ritter, Lucas Black, Natalie Canderday, Robert Duvall, Jim Jarmusch

† The film began as a short, *Some Call It a Sling Blade*, which was directed by George Hickenlooper.
🏆 Billy Bob Thornton (as writer)
🏆 Billy Bob Thornton (as actor)

'A Tale Of Exploration, Imagination, And Inspiration.'
The Slingshot **
Sweden 1993 101m colour
Columbia TriStar/AB/SVT Kanal/Nordisk/SFI (Waldemar Bergendahl)

original title: Kådisbellan

A Jewish boy, the son of a crippled socialist, grows up in Stockholm in the 1920s, trying to make money by selling slingshots made from scrap metal and condoms, which his mother sells under the counter in her tobacconist shop, and taking revenge on his sadistic teacher.
A wry and charming story of childhood, family life and resilience, filmed with exuberance, capturing the past in loving detail.
wd Ake Sandgren *novel* Roland Schutt *m* Björn Isfält *pd* Lasse Westfelt *ed* Grete Moldrup
☆ Jesper Salen, Stellan Skarsgard, Basia Frydman, Niclas Olund, Ernst-Hugo Jaregard, Reine Brynolifsson
'This is the sort of film that has little real dramatic flow or narrative drive, but relies instead on its slightly picaresque characters and a certain sad but not unfunny charm to carry it through.' – *Derek Malcolm, Guardian*
† It won the Swedish Academy award as best picture.

'You'll forget every love story you ever saw – or sang to!'
The Slipper and the Rose *
🎭 GB 1976 146m Technicolor Panavision
Paradine Co-Productions (David Frost, Stuart Lyons)

The story of Cinderella.
The elements are charming, but the treatment is fussy yet uninventive and the film is immensely overlong and lacking in magic and wit. Alas, not the renaissance of the family film that was hoped for.
w Bryan Forbes, Robert and Richard Sherman d Bryan Forbes *ph* Tony Imi *pd* Ray Simm *songs* Robert and Richard Sherman
☆ Richard Chamberlain, Gemma Craven, Kenneth More, Michael Hordern, Edith Evans, Annette Crosbie, Margaret Lockwood, Christopher Gable, Julian Orchard, Lally Bowers, John Turner
'The tunes, I'm afraid, go in one ear and out the other; and, as Dr Johnson said of *Paradise Lost*, no man wished it a minute longer.' – *Michael Billington, Illustrated London News*
🎵 music; song 'He Danced with Me'

Slipstream
🎭 GB 1989 102m Eastmancolor
Entertainment/Entertainment Film Productions (Gary Kurtz)

In a post-holocaust future, an android learns human feelings while being hunted by a policeman and woman.
Futuristic chase movie, a little lacking in imagination.
w Tony Kayden *story* Bill Bauer d Steven M. Lisberger *ph* Frank Tidy *m* Elmer Bernstein *pd* Andrew McAlpine *ed* Terry Rawlings
☆ Mark Hamill, Bob Peck, Bill Paxton, Kitty Aldridge, Eleanor David, Ben Kingsley, F. Murray Abraham, Robbie Coltrane

Slither *
US 1972 96m Metrocolor
MGM/Talent Associates/Jack Sher

An ex-con, some gangsters, and a few mobile homes are involved in a chase across California for some hidden loot.
Wackily with-it comedy-thriller ranging from violence to slapstick, the former always undercut into the latter. Pretty funny, once you get the idea.
w W. D. Richter d Howard Zieff *ph* Laszlo Kovacs *m* Tom McIntosh
☆ James Caan, Peter Boyle, Sally Kellerman, Louise Lasser

'You Like To Watch Don't You.'
Sliver
US 1993 108m DeLuxe
Paramount (Robert Evans)

A woman moves into an apartment block where the tenants are being murdered and discovers that its owner maintains a video surveillance of every room in the building.
A voyeuristic thriller, no doubt intended to be erotic but only succeeding in being dull.
w Joe Eszterhas *novel* Ira Levin d Phillip Noyce *ph* Vilmos Zsigmond *m* Howard Shore *pd* Paul Sylbert *ed* Richard Francis-Bruce, William Hoy
☆ Sharon Stone, William Baldwin, Tom Berenger, Polly Walker, Colleen Camp, Amanda Foreman, Martin Landau, C. C. H. Pounder
'All flash and no sizzle.' – *Variety*

Slow Dancing in the Big City
US 1978 110m Technicolor
UA/CIP (Michael Levee, John G. Avildsen)

A New York newspaper columnist is affected by a dying eight-year-old drug addict and an ailing girl ballet dancer.
Warner in the 30s might have got away with this corn, but in 1978, played against a realistic backdrop, it seems merely silly and indigestible, its title as pretentious as its use of four-letter words.
w Barra Grant d John G. Avildsen *ph* Ralf D. Bode *m* Bill Conti
☆ Paul Sorvino, Anne Ditchburn, Nicolas Coster, Anita Dangler
'The earnestness and shamelessness of the director are so awesome that if the picture fails as romance, it succeeds as camp.' – *New Yorker*

Slow Motion: see Sauve Qui Peut (La Vie)

'Take it from Vivian ... the biggest problem in the country isn't money or drugs. It's breasts.'
Slums of Beverly Hills
US 1998 90m DeLuxe
Fox Searchlight/South Fork (Michael Nozik, Stan Wlodkowski)

In the mid-70s, an adolescent girl observes her hard-up single father's attempts to maintain a family life in Beverly Hills.
Coarse, semi-autobiographical comedy that resembles a TV sitcom with ideas above its station.
wd Tamara Jenkins *ph* Tom Richmond *m* Rolfe Kent *pd* Dena Roth *ed* Pamela Martin
☆ Alan Arkin, Marisa Tomei, Natasha Lyonne, Kevin Corrigan, Eli Marienthal, David Krumholtz, Jessica Walter, Carl Reiner, Rita Moreno
'Everything is delivered with such a heavy hand that you want to grab the movie and its makers by the shoulders and give them all a good shake.' – *James Cameron-Wilson, Film Review*

Smack and Thistle *
GB 1990 90m Technicolor
Channel 4/Working Title (Sarah Cellan Jones, Alison Jackson)

A former convict, chased by police and gangsters after he gains possession of an MP's stolen briefcase containing details of shady deals, falls in love with an upper-class heroin addict.
A fast-paced thriller, with a little romance thrown in, acted and directed with verve.
wd Tunde Ikoli *ph* Peter Sinclair *m* Colin Towns *pd* Hugo Luczyc-Wyhowski *ed* Angus Newton
☆ Charlie Cain, Rosalind Bennett, Patrick Malahide, Connie Booth, Rudolph Walker, John Elmes, James Saxon, Geoffrey Palmer, Trevor Laird, Thomas Craig

The Small Back Room **
GB 1949 106m bw
London Films/The Archers

US title: Hour of Glory

A bomb expert with a lame foot and a drink problem risks his life dismantling a booby bomb and returns to his long-suffering girlfriend.
Rather gloomy suspense thriller with ineffective personal aspects but well-made location sequences and a fascinating background of boffins at work in post-war London.
wd Michael Powell, Emeric Pressburger *novel* Nigel Balchin *ph* Christopher Challis *m* Brian Easdale
☆ David Farrar, Kathleen Byron, Jack Hawkins, Leslie Banks, Robert Morley, Cyril Cusack

'The film as a whole can be recommended as unusually adult entertainment, notable for some admirable writing and acting.' – *Campbell Dixon*
'An exceptionally well-told story.' – *Dilys Powell*

Small Change *
France 1976 105m Eastmancolor
Films du Carosse/Artistes Associés (Marcel Berbert, Roland Thenot)

original title: L'Argent de Poche

Linked incidents affecting a class of small boys in provincial France.
Competent if rather ordinary little portmanteau which one can't imagine adults actually paying to see.
w François Truffaut, Suzanne Schiffman d François Truffaut *ph* Pierre-William Glenn *m* Maurice Jaubert
☆ Geory Desmouceaux, Philippe Goldman, Claudio Deluca
'Aside from the arrant sentimentality of much of Truffaut's text, the picture is depressed by the self-imitation of his film-making: the opening iris-in, the wipes. His eye for color has never been worse.' – *Stanley Kauffmann*

A Small Circle of Friends
US 1980 112m Technicolor
United Artists

Adventures of Harvard men at the end of the sixties.
Comedy, sex, politics and melodrama are all ploughed into this tiresome and predictable mixture.
w Ezra Sacks d Rob Cohen *ph* Michael Butler *m* Jim Steinman
☆ Brad Davis, Karen Allen, Jameson Parker, Shelley Long, John Friedrich
'Sacks' recreation of his college days relies on a mistaken belief that an audience will love his characters as much as they love each other.' – *John Pym, MFB*

Small Faces **
GB 1995 108m colour
Guild/BBC/Glasgow Film Fund/Skyline (Billy MacKinnon, Steve Clark-Hall)

In the 60s, three Glaswegian brothers become involved in gang warfare.
An involving, toughly humorous drama of dawning maturity, high spirited and rooted in reality.
w Billy MacKinnon, Gillies MacKinnon d Gillies MacKinnon *ph* John de Borman *m* John Keane *pd* Zoe Macleod *ed* Scott Thomas
☆ Ian Robertson, Joseph McFadden, J. S. Duffy, Laura Fraser, Garry Sweeney, Clare Higgins, Kevin McKidd, Mark McConnochie
'Consummately crafted, surprisingly delicately acted by its young cast, it surely stands alongside Bill Douglas's trilogy and Bill Forsyth's *Gregory's Girl* as one of the great Scottish evocations of youth.' – *Geoffrey Macnab, Sight and Sound*

Small Hotel
GB 1957 59m bw
Associated British/Welwyn (Robert Hall)

An elderly head waiter at the Jolly Fiddler resists the area manager's attempts to get rid of him.
Mild entertainment enlivened by some expert comedy performances from Harker, Handl and Loder.
w Wilfred Eades *play* Rex Frost d David MacDonald *ph* Norman Warwick *md* Louis Levy *ad* Terence Verity *ed* Seymour Logie
☆ Gordon Harker, Marie Lohr, John Loder, Irene Handl, Francis Matthews, Billie Whitelaw, Ruth Trouncer, Frederick Schiller, Derek Blomfield, Janet Munro

The Small Miracle: see Never Take No for an Answer

Small Soldiers *
US 1998 110m Technicolor Panavision
UPI/DreamWorks/Universal/Amblin (Mike Finnell, Colin Wilson)

Prototypes of toy soldiers, equipped with a redundant military microprocessor, come to life and besiege a family.
A quirky satire on militarism and big business overwhelmed by its own technological prowess in creating lifelike toys that caricature a liking for violence.

---

w Gavin Scott, Adam Rifkin, Ted Elliott, Terry Rossio *d* Joe Dante *ph* Jamie Anderson *m* Jerry Goldsmith *pd* William Sandell *ed* Marshall Harvey, Michael Thau
☆ Kirsten Dunst, Gregory Smith, Jay Mohr, Phil Hartman, Kevin Dunn, Denis Leary, David Cross, Ann Magnuson, Wendy Schaal, Alexandra Wilson, Dick Miller, Robert Picardo and also the voices of: Tommy Lee Jones, Frank Langella, Ernest Borgnine, Jim Brown, Bruce Dern, George Kennedy, Clint Walker, Christopher Guest, Sarah Michelle Gellar, Christina Ricci
'While pic's sense of a toy store turned upside down, courtesy of dazzling f/x, will draw young viewers, ultimately the film's mean-spiritedness and serious underpinnings will turn off its core audience.' – *Leonard Klady, Variety*

Small Time
US   1991   88m   bw
Panorama (Norman Loftis)
📼
A petty criminal tries to survive among the crooks, hustlers and prostitutes of Harlem.
Gritty, downbeat drama of a doomed life, filmed in a documentary style.
wd Norman Loftis *ph* Michael C. Miller *m* Arnold Bieber *pd* Nancy Evangelista *ed* Marc Cohen
☆ Richard Barboza, Carolyn Kinebrew, Scott Ferguson, Keith Allen, Jane Williams

Small Town Girl *
US   1936   90m   bw
MGM (Hunt Stromberg)
A girl traps a handsome stranger into offering marriage when he's drunk, then sets out to win him when he's sober.
Thin but adequate romantic comedy, a good example of MGM's production line of the mid-thirties, with established star and character players helping upcoming talents.
w John Lee Mahin, Edith Fitzgerald *novel* Ben Ames Williams *d* William A. Wellman *ph* Oliver Marsh, Charles Rosher *m* Edward Ward
☆ Janet Gaynor, Robert Taylor, James Stewart, Binnie Barnes, Frank Craven, Elizabeth Patterson, Lewis Stone, Andy Devine, Isabel Jewell, Charley Grapewin, Robert Greig, Agnes Ayres

Small Town Girl *
US   1952   93m   Technicolor
MGM (Joe Pasternak)
📼 💿
Musical remake of the above.
Willing hands make the most of it, but the songs are not the best.
w Dorothy Cooper, Dorothy Kingsley *d* Leslie Kardos *ph* Joseph Ruttenberg *md* André Previn *ch* Busby Berkeley *songs* Leo Robin, Nicholas Brodszky
☆ Jane Powell, Farley Granger, *Bobby Van,* Ann Miller, Robert Keith, Billie Burke, S. Z. Sakall, Fay Wray, Nat King Cole
♫ song 'My Flaming Heart'

A Small Town in Texas
US   1976   96m   colour
AIP
📼
An ex-convict returns to his home town seeking revenge on those who framed him.
Unpleasant shock thriller with much violence.
w William Norton *d* Jack Starrett *ph* Robert Jessup *m* Charles Bernstein
☆ Susan George, Timothy Bottoms, Bo Hopkins, Art Hindle

The Small Voice *
GB   1948   83m   bw
British Lion/Constellation (Anthony Havelock-Allan)
US title: *Hideout*
Escaped convicts hold up a playwright and his wife in their country cottage.
Gripping, well-characterized version of a very well worn plot.
w Derek Neame, Julian Orde *novel* Robert Westerby *d* Fergus McDonell *ph* Stan Pavey
☆ James Donald, Valerie Hobson, Howard Keel, David Greene, Michael Balfour, Joan Young

The Small World of Sammy Lee
GB   1962   107m   bw
Bryanston/Seven Arts/Ken Hughes (Frank Godwin)
A small-time Soho crook tries desperately to raise money to pay off threatening bookies.
Overlong 'realist' comedy-melodrama based on a TV play and filled with low-life 'characters'; vivid but cursed with a tedious hero.
wd Ken Hughes *TV play* Ken Hughes *ph* Wolfgang Suschitzky *m* Kenny Graham *ad* Seamus Flannery
☆ Anthony Newley, Julia Foster, Robert Stephens, Wilfrid Brambell, Warren Mitchell, Miriam Karlin, Kenneth J. Warren

The Smallest Show on Earth *
GB   1957   81m   bw
British Lion/Launder and Gilliat (Michael Relph)
US title: *Big Time Operators*
Two young marrieds inherit a decayed cinema and make it pay.
Amiable caricature comedy with plenty of obvious jokes and a sentimental attachment to old cinemas but absolutely no conviction, little plot, and a very muddled sense of the line between farce and reality.
w William Rose, John Eldridge *d* Basil Dearden *ph* Douglas Slocombe *m* William Alwyn
☆ Bill Travers, Virginia McKenna, Margaret Rutherford, Bernard Miles, Peter Sellers, Leslie Phillips, Francis de Wolff

Smalltime
GB   1996   60m   colour
BFI/Big Arty (Shane Meadows)
💿
Two petty crooks – 'we rob from the rich and sell it to the poor, half-price' – attempt to carry out a big robbery in a run-down suburb of a northern city.
A low-budget slice of low life, about a bunch of losers who use a supermarket trolley as their getaway vehicle; entertaining, and occasionally perceptive, in a desultory way.
wd Shane Meadows *ph* Helene Whitehall *m* Gavin Clarke *ed* David Wilson
☆ Mat Hand, Dena Smiles, Shane Meadows, Gena Kawecka, Jimmy Hynd, Leon Lammond, Tim Cunningham, Dominic Dillon

Smart Blonde *
US   1936   57m   bw
Warner
A female reporter beats the cops to the solution of a murder.
Slick second feature, first in the Torchy Blane series.
w Don Ryan, Kenneth Gamet, Frederick Nebel *d* Frank McDonald
☆ Glenda Farrell, Barton MacLane, Wini Shaw, Craig Reynolds, Addison Richards, Jane Wyman
'Fairly well paced with gunplay, an amount of smart talk, but no mountings to mention.' – *Variety*

Smart Girl
US   1935   78m   bw
Paramount (Walter Wanger)
Girls left orphaned and penniless get their men – each other's.
Very mild comedy.
w Frances Hyland, Wilson Collison *d* Aubrey Scotto
☆ Ida Lupino, Kent Taylor, Gail Patrick, Joseph Cawthorn, Sidney Blackmer, Pinky Tomlin

Smart Girls Don't Talk
US   1948   81m   bw
Warner
A society girl rats on her gangster boyfriend after her brother has been killed.
Flatly handled underworld melodrama, as uninteresting as its cast.
w William Sackheim *d* Richard Bare
☆ Virginia Mayo, Bruce Bennett, Robert Hutton, Richard Rober, Tom D'Andrea

'A fool in love! A sap for women!'
Smart Money
US   1931   67m   bw
Warner
A gambler hits the big time but finally goes to jail.
Rather ordinary crime drama, a distinct letdown for its star after Little Caesar.
w Kubec Glasmon, John Bright *story* Lucien Hubbard, Joseph Jackson *d* Alfred E. Green *ph* Robert Kurrie

☆ Edward G. Robinson, James Cagney, Evalyn Knapp, Ralf Harolde, Noel Francis, Margaret Livingston, Boris Karloff, Billy House
'It will have no trouble upholding its title at the box office.' – *Variety*
† This film marks the only teaming of Robinson and Cagney.
♀ Lucien Hubbard, Joseph Jackson

Smart Woman
US   1948   93m   bw
Monogram (Hal E. Chester)
A crafty lady lawyer becomes romantically involved with a crusading district attorney.
What to Monogram was a high-class production would have been a very routine programmer from anyone else.
w Alvah Bessie, Louis Morheim, Herbert Margolis *d* Edward A. Blatt *ph* Stanley Cortez *m* Louis Gruenberg *md* Constantin Bakaleinikoff
☆ Constance Bennett, Brian Aherne, Barry Sullivan, Michael O'Shea, James Gleason, Otto Kruger, Isobel Elsom, Taylor Holmes, John Litel

Smash and Grab
GB   1937   76m   bw
GFD/Jack Buchanan
US title: *Larceny Street*
A detective's wife helps him track down a criminal mastermind.
Agreeable star comedy.
w Ralph Spence *d* Tim Whelan *ph* Roy Clark, Henry Harris
☆ Jack Buchanan, Elsie Randolph, Arthur Margetson, Antony Holles, Zoe Wynn, Edmund Willard, David Burns

Smash Palace *
New Zealand   1981   108m   colour
Aardvark Films
💿 💿
The owner of a car-wrecking business goes to pieces when his wife leaves him.
Downbeat character study of the kind of psychopath who doesn't arouse much sympathy; but the film is well mounted.
wd Roger Donaldson *ph* Graeme Cowley *m* Sharon O'Neill
☆ Bruno Lawrence, Anna Jemison, Keith Aberdein, Greer Robson
'May be the most melodramatic but also the most acutely motivated film yet about divorce.' – *Richard Schickel, Time*

The Smashing Bird I Used to Know
GB   1969   95m   colour
Titan (Peter Newbrook)
aka: *School for Unclaimed Girls*
aka: *House of Unclaimed Women*
A schoolgirl suffering from guilt over the death of her father is sent to a remand home after stabbing her mother's lecherous boyfriend.
Sensationalist treatment of a trite story.
w John Peacock *d* Robert Hartford-Davis *ph* Peter Newbrook *m* Bobby Richards *ad* Bruce Grimes *ed* Don Deacon
☆ Madeline Hinde, Renee Asherson, Dennis Waterman, Patrick Mower, Faith Brook, Janina Faye, David Lodge, Maureen Lipman, Derek Fowlds, Megs Jenkins

Smashing the Money Ring
US   1939   57m   bw
First National/Warner (Bryan Foy)
The Secret Service investigates gambling ships.
Fast-moving serial-like action.
w Anthony Coldeway, Raymond Schrock *d* Terry Morse
☆ Ronald Reagan, Eddie Foy Jnr, Margot Stevenson, Charles D. Brown

Smashing the Rackets
US   1938   69m   bw
RKO (B. P. Fineman)
An FBI agent turned special prosecutor cleans up the city.
Lively 'B' movie with a sensational, tabloid approach, though its campaign against slot machines dates it somewhat.
w Lionel Hauser *story* Forrest Davis *d* Lew Landers *ph* Nicholas Musuraca *md* Frank Tours *pd* Van Nest Polglase *ed* Harry Marker

☆ Chester Morris, Frances Mercer, Rita Johnson, Bruce Cabot, Edward Pawley, Joseph de Stefani, Kay Sutton, Ben Welden

Smashing Time
GB   1967   96m   Eastmancolor
Paramount/Partisan/Carlo Ponti (Roy Millichip)
Two north country girls have farcical adventures in swinging London, including paint squirting and pie throwing.
Horrendous attempt to turn two unsuitable actresses into a female Laurel and Hardy; plenty of coarse vigour but no style or sympathy.
w George Melly *d* Desmond Davis *ph* Manny Wynn *m* John Addison
☆ Rita Tushingham, Lynn Redgrave, Ian Carmichael, Anna Quayle, Michael York, Irene Handl, Jeremy Lloyd

Smash-up, The Story of a Woman
US   1947   113m   bw
Universal-International (Walter Wanger)
📼
GB title: *A Woman Destroyed*
The story of a lady alcoholic.
Tedious distaff side of The Lost Weekend.
w John Howard Lawson *d* Stuart Heisler *ph* Stanley Cortez *m* Daniele Amfitheatrof
☆ Susan Hayward, Lee Bowman, Eddie Albert, Marsha Hunt, Carl Esmond, Carleton Young, Charles D. Brown
♀ original story (Dorothy Parker, Frank Cavett); Susan Hayward

Smile ***
US   1975   113m   DeLuxe
UA (Michael Ritchie)
📼 💿
A bird's eye view of the Young Miss America pageant in a small California town.
A witty series of sketches in the form of a drama-documentary or satirical mosaic. Highly polished fun for those who can stay the course.
w Jerry Belson *d* Michael Ritchie *ph* Conrad Hall *m* various
☆ Bruce Dern, Barbara Feldon, Michael Kidd, Geoffrey Lewis, Nicholas Pryor
'A beady, precise, technically skilful movie.' – *Michael Billington, Illustrated London News*

A Smile Like Yours
US   1997   98m   DeLuxe
Paramount/Rysher (David Kirkpatrick, Tony Amatullo)
Without discussing it with her husband, a wife tries hard to have a baby.
Somnolent attempt at a romantic comedy, in which it is difficult to feel much sympathy for either of the leading characters.
w Kevin Meyer, Keith Samples *d* Keith Samples *ph* Richard Bowen *m* William Ross *pd* Garreth Stover *ed* Wayne Wahrman
☆ Greg Kinnear, Lauren Holly, Joan Cusack, Jay Thomas, Jill Hennessy, Christopher McDonald, Donald Moffat, France Nuyen, Marianne Muellerleile
'Flat and formulaic, this painfully charmless romantic comedy is destined to disappear quickly after its halfhearted theatrical release.' – *Joe Leydon, Variety*
† Shirley MacLaine appears uncredited.

Smiles of a Summer Night ***
Sweden   1955   105m   bw
Svensk Filmindustri
💿 📼 💿
original title: *Sommarnattens Leende*
A country lawyer meets again a touring actress who was once his mistress, and accepts an invitation for him and his young wife to stay at her mother's country home for a weekend.
Comedy of high period manners with an admirable detached viewpoint and elegant trappings. It later formed the basis of Stephen Sondheim's A Little Night Music, a stage musical which was later filmed.
wd Ingmar Bergman *ph* Gunnar Fischer *m* Erik Nordgren *ad* P.A. Lundgren *ed* Oscar Rosander
☆ Gunnar Bjornstrand, Eva Dahlbeck, Ulla Jacobsson, Harriet Andersson, Margit Carlqvist, Naima Wifstrand, Jarl Kulle

---

Smiley *

GB 1956 97m Technicolor
Cinemascope
TCF/London Films (Anthony Kimmins)

An adventurous Australian boy has various adventures and finally gets the bicycle he wants.
An open-air 'William'-type story for children, quite nicely made and generally refreshing. Smiley Gets a Gun was a less effective sequel.

w Moore Raymond, Anthony Kimmins *novel* Moore Raymond d Anthony Kimmins ph Ted Scaife, Russ Wood m William Alwyn ☆ Colin Petersen, Ralph Richardson, Chips Rafferty, John McCallum

Smiley Gets a Gun

Australia 1958 90m Technicolor
Cinemascope
Canberra Films

Smiley is promised a rifle if he can keep out of trouble.
Unexceptional sequel.

w Anthony Kimmins, Rex Rienits d Anthony Kimmins ph Ted Scaife m Wilbur Sampson ☆ Keith Calvert, Bruce Archer, Sybil Thorndike, Chips Rafferty

Smilin' Through *

US 1932 97m bw
MGM (Irving Thalberg)

Three generations of complications follow when a Victorian lady is accidentally killed by a jealous lover on her wedding day.
Archetypal sentimental romantic drama, wholly absorbing to the mass audience and extremely well done; originally a 1922 Norma Talmadge vehicle.

w Ernest Vajda, Claudine West, Donald Ogden Stewart, J. B. Fagan *play* Jane Cowl, Jane Murfin d Sidney Franklin ph Lee Garmes m William Axt ☆ Norma Shearer, Leslie Howard, Fredric March, O. P. Heggie, Ralph Forbes, Beryl Mercer

'A big women's picture of tear-drawing power, done with satisfying sincerity by a cast which spells money.' – *Variety*

'A sensitive and beautiful production distinguished by excellent settings and rich photography.' – *New York Mirror*

♟ best picture

Smilin' Through *

US 1941 100m Technicolor
MGM (Victor Saville)

Flat but adequate remake of the above.

w Donald Ogden Stewart, John Balderston d Frank Borzage ph Leonard Smith m Herbert Stothart ☆ Jeanette MacDonald, Gene Raymond, Brian Aherne, Ian Hunter, Frances Robinson, Patrick O'Moore

Smiling Along: see Keep Smiling

The Smiling Ghost

US 1941 71m bw
Warner

A girl reporter solves a haunted house mystery.
Moderate comedy chiller with plenty going on.

w Kenneth Gamet d Lewis Seiler ph Arthur Todd ☆ Alexis Smith, Wayne Morris, Brenda Marshall, Alan Hale, Willie Best, David Bruce, Helen Westley, Richard Ainley

'His intimate and roguish romance will break your heart – with love and laughter!'

The Smiling Lieutenant **

US 1931 88m bw
Paramount (Ernst Lubitsch)

A Viennese guards officer leaves his mistress to become consort to a visiting princess.
A sophisticated soufflé in Lubitsch's best style, naughty but quite nice, with visual effects largely replacing dialogue.

w Ernest Vajda, Samson Raphaelson *operetta* A Waltz Dream d Ernst Lubitsch ph George Folsey m Oscar Straus md Adolph Deutsch ☆ Maurice Chevalier, Miriam Hopkins, Claudette Colbert, Charles Ruggles, George Barbier, Elizabeth Patterson

'Will delight smart audiences and figures to be liked well enough by the average fan. A good but not a smash picture.' – *Variety*

'All the shrewd delights that were promised in *The Love Parade* all realized with an economy and sureness that give it a luster which no other American-made comedy satire has achieved. One must look to *Le Million* to find its peer.' – *Richard Watts, New York Post*

♟ best picture

'Snow covers everything ... except the truth.'

Smilla's Feeling for Snow *

Germany/Denmark/Sweden 1997 121m
colour Panavision
TCF/Constantin/Greenland/Bavaria (Bernd Eichinger, Martin Moszkowicz)

In Copenhagen, a woman investigates the apparently accidental death of her neighbour's young son.
A stilted thriller based on a bestselling book; it never quite settles down to deliver on its promise.

w Ann Biderman *novel* Miss Smilla's Feeling for Snow by Peter Hoeg d Bille August ph Jörgen Persson m Harry Gregson-Williams pd Anna Asp ed Janus Billeskov-Jansen ☆ Julia Ormond, Gabriel Byrne, Richard Harris, Vanessa Redgrave, Robert Loggia, Jim Broadbent, Mario Adorf, Bob Peck, Tom Wilkinson, Emma Croft, Peter Capaldi

'An exceedingly sleek and handsome thriller.' – *Variety*

Smithereens *

US 1982 90m colour
Susan Seidelman

Obsessed with becoming manager of a punk rock band, a young girl in New York drifts through a series of unsatisfactory encounters.
Unblinking account of empty lives, well done but ultimately depressing.

w Susan Seidelman, Ron Nyswaner, Peter Askin d Susan Seidelman ph Chirine El Khadem m Glenn Mercer, Bill Million pd Franz Harland ed Susan Seidelman ☆ Susan Berman, Brad Rinn, Richard Hell, Roger Jet

Smoke *

US 1995 112m DuArt
Miramax/Nippon (Greg Johnson, Peter Newman, Hisami Kuriowa, Kenzo Hurikoshi)

The interlinked lives of customers who frequent a Brooklyn cigar store.
Pleasantly anecdotal and articulate account of lives shifted and altered by chance and coincidence, the way lives are.

w Paul Auster d Wayne Wang ph Adam Holender m Rachel Portman pd Kalina Ivanov ed Maisie Hoy ☆ William Hurt, Harvey Keitel, Forest Whitaker, Harold Perrineau Jnr, Victor Argo, Erica Gimpel, Clarice Taylor, Malik Yoba, Mary Ward, Jared Harris

'Plenty of smoke but not a great deal of fire.' – *Variety*

† As filming finished, another film in the same style, *Blue in the Face* (qv), was quickly made, also featuring Keitel as the cigar store owner.

Smoke Jumpers: see Red Skies of Montana

Smoke Signal

US 1955 88m Technicolor
U-I (Howard Christie)

A small band of cavalry, together with their prisoner, an officer accused of treason and murder, attempt to escape marauding Indians by travelling down a dangerous, uncharted river.
A Western that abandons dry land for boats, but still manages to tell a familiar story of redemption and romance.

w George F. Slavin, George W. George d Jerry Hopper ph Clifford Stine md Joseph Gershenson ad Alexander Golitzen, Richard H. Riedel ed Milton Carruth ☆ Dana Andrews, Piper Laurie, Rex Reason, Milburn Stone, William Talman, Douglas Spencer, Gordon Jones, William Schallert

Smokescreen

GB 1964 66m bw
Butcher's (John I. Phillips)

An insurance assessor solves a murder.

Minor thriller with a little more individuality than many second features.

wd Jim O'Connolly ph Jack Mills m Johnny Gregory ad Peter Mullins ed Henry Richardson ☆ Peter Vaughan, John Carson, Yvonne Romain, Gerald Flood, Glynn Edwards, John Glyn-Jones, Sam Kydd, Deryck Guyler, Penny Morrell, David Gregory

Smokey and the Bandit *

US 1977 97m Technicolor
Universal/Rastar (Robert L. Levy)

A Georgia bootlegger on a mission picks up a girl in distress and is chased by her irate sheriff fiancé.
Frantic chase comedy full of car crashes and low lines: a surprise box-office smash.

w James Lee Barrett, Charles Shyer, Alan Mandel d Hal Needham ph Bobby Byrne m Bill Justis, Jerry Reed, Art Feller ☆ Burt Reynolds, Jackie Gleason, Sally Field, Jerry Reed, Mike Henry, Pat McCormick, Paul Williams

Smokey and the Bandit II

US 1980 101m Technicolor
Universal/Rastar/Mort Engelberg

GB title: Smokey and the Bandit Ride Again

A trucker is hired to take a pregnant elephant to the Republican convention.
More mindless chasing and crashing, with even less wit than before and rather more wholesale destruction.

w Jerry Belson, Brock Yates d Hal Needham ph Michael Butler md Snuff Garrett ☆ Burt Reynolds, Jackie Gleason, Sally Field, Jerry Reed, Dom DeLuise, Paul Williams

Smokey and the Bandit III

US 1983 88m Technicolor
Mort Engelberg/Universal

Sheriff Justice mistakes an innocent driver for his old enemy.
A rather random car chase movie, obviously the last of a short line.

w Stuart Birnbaum, David Dashev d Dick Lowry ph James Pergola m Larry Cansler ad Ron Hobbs ed Byron Brandt, David Blewitt, Christopher Greenbury ☆ Jackie Gleason, Jerry Reed, Mike Henry, Pat McCormick, Burt Reynolds (cameo)

'A patchwork of arbitrary mayhem.' – *Variety*

Smokey and the Bandit Ride Again: see Smokey and the Bandit II

Smokey and the Goodtime Outlaws

US 1978 88m CFI color
Howco (Tommy Amato)

Two dim-brained country singers go to Nashville in search of fame.
A stupefying mix of car chases, bar-room brawls and country-and-western music, put together with little evidence of sense or style.

w Frank Dobbs, Bob Walsh *story* Jesse Turner d Alex Grasshoff m Mauro Bruno ed Geoffrey Rowland ☆ Jesse Turner, Dennis Fimple, Slim Pickens, Diane Sherill, Marcie Barkin, Hope Summers, Don Sherman

Smoking/No Smoking **

France 1993 146m colour
Mainline/Arena/Camera One/France 2 (Bruno Persey, Michel Seydoux)

Happenings to do with love and death in a Yorkshire village, the outcome of which is dependent upon whether or not the wife of the local headmaster decides to give up smoking.
An unusual and engaging cinematic experience, based on a sequence of eight plays which each had two possible endings. Here the two films, which can be watched in any order, provide 12 varying conclusions, dependent upon earlier actions, but each ending in a graveyard. Yorkshire has never looked quite as it does in this French studio re-creation, but the film does provide for some virtuoso acting from its two stars, who play 17 parts between them.

w Jean-Pierre Bacri, Agnes Jaoui *play* Intimate Exchanges by Alan Ayckbourn d Alain Resnais ph Renato Berta m John Pattison pd Jacques Saulnier ed Albert Jurgenson ☆ Sabine Azéma, Pierre Arediti

'Just about perfect within the boundaries it sets itself.' – *Variety*

Smoky

US 1946 87m Technicolor
TCF (Robert Bassler)

An especially independent horse virtually runs the ranch on which he lives.
Family saga of the great outdoors, well enough assembled.

w Dwight Cummins, Lillie Hayward, Dorothy Yost *novel* Will James d Louis King ph Charles Clarke m David Raksin md Emil Newman ☆ Fred MacMurray, Anne Baxter, Burl Ives, Bruce Cabot, Esther Dale

† The story was also made by Fox in 1933 with Victor Jory, and in 1966 with Fess Parker.

Smooth as Silk

US 1946 64m bw
Universal (Jack Bernhard)

When his girlfriend jilts him, a criminal lawyer plans to murder her new sweetheart.
Watchable supporting feature.

w Dane Lussier, Kerry Shaw d Charles Barton ☆ Kent Taylor, Virginia Grey, Jane Adams, Milburn Stone, John Litel

Smooth Talk

US 1985 92m colour
Nepenthe/American Playhouse/Goldcrest (Martin Rosen)

A mixed-up 15-year-old girl has a dangerous encounter with a mildly psychopathic male.
Unattractive scenario about thoroughly dislikeable people.

w Tom Cole *story* Joyce Carol Oates d Joyce Chopra ph James Glennon m Bill Payne, Russ Kunkel, George Massenburg md James Taylor pd David Wasco ed Patrick Dodd ☆ Treat Williams, Laura Dern, Mary Kay Place, Levon Helm

The Smugglers: see The Man Within

Smultronstället: see Wild Strawberries

SNAFU

US 1945 85m bw
Columbia

GB title: Welcome Home

Middle-class parents rescue their difficult 15-year-old son from the army, then wish they hadn't.
Predictable, well-greased comedy of a rebellious teenager.

w Louis Solomon, Harold Buchman *play* Louis Solomon, Harold Buchman d Jack Moss ph Franz Planer m Paul Sawtell ☆ Robert Benchley, Vera Vague, Conrad Janis, Nanetta Parks

† The title can be bowdlerized as 'Situation Normal, All Fouled Up'.

'A Shocking Movie From The World's Most Sensational Director!'

Snake Eyes

US 1993 104m DeLuxe
Rank/Cecchi Gori/Maverick (Mary Kane)

aka: Dangerous Game

A film director making a movie about a marriage on the rocks, with an abusive husband who berates and beats his wife for abandoning their sex- and drug-filled life, discovers that reality begins to mirror the fiction.
A confused film that swiftly disappears up its own pretensions; it has the air of a semi-improvised piece, but the relentless soul-searchings of the characters, and their identification with the roles they play, seem hardly worthwhile when the film they are making is even worse than the 'reality' the audience is watching; self-indulgent is a polite way of describing the result.

w Nicholas St John d Abel Ferrara ph Ken Kelsch m Joe Delia pd Alex Tavoularis ed Anthony Redman ☆ Harvey Keitel, Madonna, James Russo, Nancy Ferrara, Reilly Murphy

'As long as you go with it, it seduces you into playing along with its circuit of sex, drugs, anger, confusion, fear and deception. If you let go, it becomes easy to ask why you should bother watching these brittle, self-engrossed people whose unmitigated self-disgust is not simply depressing but irritating.' – *Amanda Lipman, Sight and Sound*

'Another abrasive, confrontational downer likely to appeal only to a marginal audience.' – *Variety*

'Believe everything except your eyes.'

Snake Eyes *

US 1998 99m DeLuxe Panavision
Buena Vista/DeBart (Brian de Palma)

A corrupt cop investigates the shooting of a senior politician at a championship boxing match.
An implausible thriller on the theme of surveillance, with broad acting and some impressive directorial flourishes that keep the adrenalin flowing.
w David Koepp d Brian de Palma ph Stephen H. Burum m Ryuichi Sakamoto pd Anne Pritchard ed Bill Pankow sp Industrial Light & Magic
☆ Nicolas Cage, Gary Sinise, John Heard, Carla Gugino, Stan Shaw, Kevin Dunn, Michael Rispoli, Joel Fabiani, Luis Guzman, David Anthony Higgins
'Wispy threads of dramatic plausibility and character involvement unravel completely by the time of the incredibly silly final reel.' – *Todd McCarthy, Variety*

The Snake Pit **

US 1948 108m bw
TCF (Anatole Litvak, Robert Bassler)

A girl becomes mentally deranged and has horrifying experiences in an institution.
A headline-hitting film which made a stirring plea for more sympathetic treatment of mental illness. Very well made, and arrestingly acted, but somehow nobody's favourite movie.
w Frank Partos, Millen Brand novel Mary Jane Ward d Anatole Litvak ph Leo Tover m Alfred Newman
☆ Olivia de Havilland, Leo Genn, Mark Stevens, Celeste Holm, Glenn Langan, Leif Erickson, Beulah Bondi, Lee Patrick, Natalie Schafer
'A film of superficial veracity that requires a bigger man than Litvak; a good film with bad things.' – *Herman G. Weinberg*
† The British censor insisted on a foreword explaining that everyone on the film was an actor and that conditions in British mental hospitals were unlike those depicted.
⟁ best picture; script; Anatole Litvak; Alfred Newman; Olivia de Havilland

Snares: see *Pièges*

'We could tell you what it's about. But then, of course, we would have to kill you.'

Sneakers **

US 1992 125m DeLuxe
UIP/Universal (Walter F. Parkes, Lawrence Lasker)

A group of oddball experts is hired to recover from a criminal mastermind an electronic device that can penetrate the government's most secure computer systems.
Enjoyable caper that pleasantly passes a couple of hours.
w Phil Alden Robinson, Lawrence Lasker, Walter F. Parkes d Phil Alden Robinson ph John Lindley m James Horner pd Patrizia von Brandenstein ed Tom Rolf
☆ Robert Redford, Dan Aykroyd, Ben Kingsley, Mary McDonnell, River Phoenix, Sidney Poitier, David Strathairn, James Earl Jones, Stephen Tobolowsky
'The mainstream pleasures it affords should appeal to just about all audience segments, save perhaps ultra-sophisticates and low-brow teens.' – *Variety*
'This isn't really a serious film. It's over-stretched and under-characterised, but watchable for all that if you don't find the techno aspects too depressing.' – *Derek Malcolm, Guardian*

Sniper *

US 1993 98m colour
Columbia TriStar/Baltimore (Robert L. Rosen)

An experienced Marine sniper is joined by a novice on a dangerous assignment in Panama.
Familiar ingredients are expertly mixed to create a tense action picture.
w Michael Frost Beckner, Crash Leyland d Luis Llosa ph Bill Butler m Gary Chang pd Herbert Pinter ed Scott Smith

☆ Tom Berenger, Billy Zane, J. T. Walsh, Aden Young, Ken Radley, Reinaldo Arenas, Carlos Alvarez, Roy Edmonds
'An expertly directed, yet ultimately unsatisfying psychological thriller.' – *Variety*

The Sniper **

US 1952 87m bw
Columbia/Stanley Kramer (Edna and Edward Anhalt)

A psychopath kills a succession of blondes with a high-powered rifle.
Semi-documentary police drama which was quite startling and influential when released but seems quite routine now.
w Harry Brown d Edward Dmytryk ph Burnett Guffey m George Antheil
☆ Adolphe Menjou, Arthur Franz, Gerald Mohr, Richard Kiley, Frank Faylen, Marie Windsor
⟁ original story (Edna and Edward Anhalt)

Snitch

US 1998 93m colour
Filmline/Phoenician/Clinica Estetico/Tribeca/Spanky/Apostle (Joel Stillerman, Ted Demme, Jim Serpico, Nicolas Clermont, Elie Samaha)
aka: *Noose*

In Boston, a group of petty crooks discover that there is no honour among thieves.
Gritty drama of dead-end lives, well enough acted but inconsequential.
w Mike Armstrong d Ted Demme ph Adam Kimmel pd Ruth Ammon ed Jeffrey Wolf
☆ Denis Leary, Jason Barry, Billy Crudup, John Diehl, Greg Dulli, Noah Emmerich, Ian Hart, Famke Janssen, Colm Meaney, Martin Sheen, Jean Tripplehorn

The Snorkel

GB 1958 90m bw
Columbia/Hammer (Michael Carreras)

A man murders his wife and is given away by his observant young stepdaughter.
Tenuous suspenser which outstays its welcome.
w Peter Myers, Jimmy Sangster, Anthony Dawson d Guy Green ph Jack Asher ad John Stoll ed James Needs, Bill Lenney
☆ Peter Van Eyck, Betta St John, Mandy Miller, William Franklyn, Grégoire Aslan

'Roads closed. Schools shut. Rules were made to be frozen!'

Snow Day

🏃 US 2000 89m DeLuxe
Paramount/Nickelodeon (Albie Hecht, Julia Pistor)
⌑

A failing weather forecaster and his dysfunctional family have their problems solved during an unexpected fall of snow.
Amiable, unexceptional comedy of family troubles and 'teen love.
w Will McRobb, Chris Viscardi d Chris Koch ph Robbie Greenberg m Steve Bartek pd Leslie McDonald ed David Finfer
☆ Chris Elliott, Mark Webber, Jean Smart, Schuyler Fisk, Iggy Pop, Pam Grier, Chevy Chase, John Schneider, Zena Grey, Claire Bonner
'A family film that's about as fluffy as fresh powder…mixes a cast of familiar faces with bright new talent in an unremarkable, innocuous package.' – *Lael Loewenstein, Variety*

Snow Job: see *The Ski Raiders*

Snow Treasure

US 1968 95m Eastmancolor
Sagittarius (Irving Jacoby)

In Nazi-occupied Norway a teenage boy finds gold hidden in the snow; an underground agent helps him get it to safety.
Curiously undernourished but attractively made adventure film.
w Irving Jacoby, Peter Hansen novel Marie McSwigan d Irving Jacoby ph Sverre Bergli m Egil Monn-Iversen
☆ James Franciscus, Paul Anstad, Paoul Oyen, Randi Borch

Snow White: A Tale of Terror

GB/US 1996 100m colour
Polygram/Interscope (Tom Engelman)

A young girl takes refuge with seven gold miners when her wicked stepmother, jealous of her beauty, tries to kill her.

An interesting attempt to take the familiar story of Snow White back to its Gothic and grotesque roots; unfortunately, it is not successful, just something to frighten the children.
w Tom Szollosi, Deborah Serra story The Brothers Grimm d Michael Cohn ph Mike Southon m John Ottman pd Gemma Jackson ed Ian Crafford
☆ Sigourney Weaver, Sam Neill, Gil Bellows, Taryn Davis, David Conrad, Brian Glover, Monica Keena, Anthony Brophy, Frances Cuka
'Cloaked thickly with an oppressive, unsettling atmosphere, the film succeeds by drawing deep, fearful uncertainty from its ambiguity.' – *Darren Bignall, Empire*

Snow White and the Seven Dwarfs ****

🏃 US 1937 82m Technicolor
Walt Disney

Disney's first feature cartoon, a mammoth enterprise which no one in the business thought would work. The romantic leads were wishy-washy but the splendid songs and the marvellous comic and villainous characters turned the film into a worldwide box-office bombshell which is almost as fresh today as when it was made.
w Ted Sears, Otto Englander, Earl Hurd, Dorothy Ann Blank, Richard Creedon, Dick Richard, Merrill de Maris, Webb Smith, from the fairy tale by the brothers Grimm m Frank Churchill, Leigh Harline, Paul Smith supervising d David Hand songs Larry Morey, Frank Churchill
☆ Featuring the voices of Adriana Caselotti, Harry Stockwell, Lucille La Verne, Billy Gilbert
'The first full-length animated feature, the turning point in Disney's career, a milestone in film history, and a great film.' – *Leonard Maltin*
'Sustained fantasy, the animated cartoon grown up.' – *Otis Ferguson*
'The sort of film that happens once in a generation. It is as necessary a part of our film upbringing as The Birth of a Nation or The Jazz Singer. Crude, tentative, and born of compromise it may be, but it is still history in the making.' – *C. A. Lejeune*
† Adriana Caselotti (1916–97) was the voice of Snow White, chosen after 150 teenagers, including Deanna Durbin, had auditioned for the role. Snow White's appearance was based on dancer Marjorie Belcher, who was later better known as Marge Champion.
⚐ Special Award to Walt Disney for 'a significant screen innovation'. He was given one Oscar and seven miniature statuettes.
⟁ Frank Churchill, Leigh Harline, Paul Smith

Snow White and the Three Clowns: see Snow White and the Three Stooges

Snow White and the Three Stooges *

🏃 US 1961 107m DeLuxe
Cinemascope
(TCF) Chanford (Charles Wick)

GB title: *Snow White and the Three Clowns*
The old story retold as a vehicle for a champion skater and three veteran clowns.
Surprisingly tolerable as a holiday attraction, once you get over the shock.
w Noel Langley, Elwood Ullman d Walter Lang ph Leon Shamroy m Lyn Murray ad Jack Martin Smith, Maurice Ransford
☆ Carol Heiss, Moe Howard, Larry Fine, Joe de Rita, Edson Stroll, Patricia Medina, Guy Rolfe, Buddy Baer, Edgar Barrier

Snowball Express

🏃 US 1972 99m Technicolor
Walt Disney (Ron Miller)

An insurance accountant inherits a dilapidated skiing hotel in the Colorado Rockies.
Uninspired family comedy with slapstick on the snow slopes.
w Don Tait, Jim Parker, Arnold Margolin novel Château Bon Vivant by Frankie and John O'Rear d Norman Tokar ph Frank Phillips m Robert F. Brunner
☆ Dean Jones, Nancy Olson, Henry Morgan, Keenan Wynn, Mary Wickes, Johnny Whittaker
'As wholesome and bland as that old American favourite the peanut butter and jelly sandwich.' – *MFB*

Snowbound

GB 1948 87m bw
GFD/Gainsborough

Various people congregate at a ski hut in the Swiss Alps; all are after buried Nazi loot.
A rather foolish story which provides little in the way of action but at least assembles a fine crop of character actors.
w David Evans, Keith Campbell novel The Lonely Skier by Hammond Innes d David MacDonald ph Stephen Dade
☆ Robert Newton, Dennis Price, Herbert Lom, Stanley Holloway, Marcel Dalio, Mila Parely, Guy Middleton

'Out of one masterpiece, another has been created!'

The Snows of Kilimanjaro **

US 1952 117m Technicolor
TCF (Darryl F. Zanuck)

A hunter lies wounded in Africa and while waiting for help looks back over his life and loves.
Hollywood version of a portable Hemingway, with reminiscences of several novels stirred into a lush and sprawling mix of action and romance, open spaces and smart salons. A big popular star film of its time, despite constricted and unconvincing characters.
w Casey Robinson story Ernest Hemingway d Henry King ph Leon Shamroy m Bernard Herrmann ad Lyle Wheeler, John DeCuir
☆ Gregory Peck, Susan Hayward, Ava Gardner, Hildegard Neff, Leo G. Carroll, Torin Thatcher, Marcel Dalio
'A naïve kind of success story with a conventional boy-meets-lots-of-girls plot.' – *Karel Reisz*
'The succinct and vivid qualities associated with Hemingway are rarely evoked, and what has been substituted is for the most part meandering, pretentious and more or less maudlin romance.' – *Newsweek*
⟁ Leon Shamroy; art direction

So Big *

US 1932 80m bw
Warner (Lucien Hubbard)

A schoolteacher marries a farmer, has trouble with her son, falls in love with a sculptor.
Watchable, superficial, top-talented adaptation of a best-seller, first filmed in 1925 with Colleen Moore.
w J. Grubb Alexander, Robert Lord novel Edna Ferber d William Wellman ph Sid Hickox m W. Franke Harling
☆ Barbara Stanwyck, George Brent, Dickie Moore, Guy Kibbee, Bette Davis, Hardie Albright
'Too long getting started, and only has moments towards the end … somewhat of a bore for the major part of its footage.' – *Variety*

So Big

US 1953 101m bw
Warner (Henry Blanke)

By the time this inflated remake came along, the story was just too corny despite careful production.
w John Twist d Robert Wise ph Ellsworth Fredericks m Max Steiner
☆ Jane Wyman, Sterling Hayden, Richard Beymer, Nancy Olson, Steve Forrest, Elisabeth Fraser, Martha Hyer

So Bright the Flame: see The Girl in White

So Close to Life **

Sweden 1958 84m bw
Nordisk Tonefilm
original title: *Nära Livet*
aka: *Brink of Life*

In a maternity ward of a Stockholm hospital, three women reach a turning point in their lives.
A bleak and austere drama of life and death and the randomness of existence, given vigour and intensity by the acting of the women at its centre.
w Ingmar Bergman, Ulla Isaksson story Det vängila, värdiga by Ulla Isaksson d Ingmar Bergman ph Max Wilén ad Bibi Lindström ed Carl-Olov Skeppstedt
☆ Eva Dahlbeck, Ingrid Thulin, Bibi Andersson, Barbro Hiort af Ornäs, Erland Josephson, Max von Sydow, Gunnar Sjöberg
† Ingmar Bergman won the award as best director, and Eva Dahlbeck, Ingrid Thulin, Bibi Andersson and Barbro Hiort af Ornäs were collectively awarded the best actress prize at the 1958 Cannes Film Festival.

So Dark the Night *
US 1946 71m bw
Columbia
A detective tracks down a murderer whom he finds to be himself.
Smart second feature with a likeable leading performance.
w Aubrey Wisberg, Martin Berkeley, Dwight Babcock d Joseph H. Lewis ph Burnett Guffey m Hugo Friedhofer
☆ Steven Geray, Ann Codee, Micheline Cheirel

So Dear to My Heart *
US 1948 84m Technicolor
Walt Disney
📀 🎬
Life on a country farm in 1903
Live action nostalgia with a few cartoon segments; well enough done, but mainly appealing to well brought up children.
w John Tucker Battle novel Midnight and Jeremiah by Sterling North d Harold Schuster ph Winton C. Hoch m Paul Smith
☆ Burl Ives, Beulah Bondi, Harry Carey, Luana Patten, Bobby Driscoll
🎵 song 'Lavender Blue' (mEliot Daniel, lyLarry Morey)

So Ends Our Night *
US 1941 120m bw
UA (David L. Loew, Albert Lewin)
Refugees from Nazi Germany are driven from country to country and meet persecution everywhere.
Worthy but rather drab and unconvincing melodrama from the headlines.
w Talbot Jennings novel Flotsam by Erich Maria Remarque d John Cromwell ph William Daniels m Louis Gruenberg
☆ Fredric March, Margaret Sullavan, Glenn Ford, Frances Dee, Anna Sten, Erich von Stroheim, Joseph Cawthorn, Leonid Kinskey, Alexander Granach, Sig Rumann
'It ought to be a great picture but it isn't.' – *Archer Winsten, New York Post*
🎵 Louis Gruenberg

So Evil My Love *
GB 1948 100m bw
Paramount (Hal B. Wallis)
A missionary's widow is enticed into a life of crime and immorality by a scoundrelly artist.
Curious Victorian melodrama with a Wildean flavour; doesn't quite come off.
w Leonard Spigelgass, Ronald Millar novel Joseph Shearing d Lewis Allen ph Max Greene m Victor Young, William Alwyn
☆ Ray Milland, Ann Todd, Geraldine Fitzgerald, Leo G. Carroll, Raymond Huntley, Martita Hunt, Moira Lister, Raymond Lovell, Muriel Aked, Finlay Currie, Hugh Griffith
'There's only one thing that can keep them apart – the seven-foot thing she's married to!'

So Fine *
US 1981 91m Technicolor
Warner/Lobell – Bergman (Mike Lobell)
🇺🇸
A professor of literature trying to save his father from gangsters becomes involved in strange adventures.
Weirdly titled action comedy which tries to be far too clever for its own good.
wd Andrew Bergman ph James A. Contner m Ennio Morricone
☆ Ryan O'Neal, Jack Warden, Mariangela Melato, Richard Kiel, Fred Gwynne, Mike Kellin
'A visual insult, crudely lighted and framed, and jumping out at you.' – *Pauline Kael, New Yorker*

So Goes My Love *
US 1946 88m bw
U-I (Jack H. Skirball, Bruce Manning)
GB title: *A Genius in the Family*
The domestic life of inventor Hiram Maxim.
Formula period family film with pleasant moments.
w Bruce Manning, James Clifden d Frank Ryan ph Joseph Valentine m Hans Salter
☆ Myrna Loy, Don Ameche, Rhys Williams, Bobby Driscoll, Richard Gaines

'For Harriet, the honeymoon was her best yet. For Charles, it was a pain in the neck.'

So I Married an Axe Murderer
US 1993 92m Technicolor
TriStar/Fried/Woods Films
📀 📺 🎬 🎧
A poet suspects that his newly married wife, a butcher, is a serial killer of husbands.
Slight and slightly amusing comedy, parodying Hitchcock with some sophistication and moderate success.
w Robbie Fox d Thomas Schlamme ph Julio Macat m Bruce Broughton pd John Graysmark ed Richard Halsey, Colleen Halsey
☆ Mike Myers, Nancy Travis, Anthony LaPaglia, Amanda Plummer, Brenda Fricker, Matt Doherty, Charles Grodin, Phil Hartman
'A hip slice of life about the dilemma of marital commitment with just a pinch of Hitchcock providing a cutting edge. Fueled by an anarchic style and a winning cast, it looks like an appealing commercial prospect.' – *Variety*
'An inconsequential, light-hearted black comedy populated by San Francisco eccentrics.' – *Philip French, Observer*

So Little Time *
GB 1952 88m bw
ABP/Mayflower (Aubrey Baring, Maxwell Setton)
In occupied Belgium an aristocratic lady falls in love with a Nazi colonel.
Doomed love story with musical accompaniment; tolerable but slow.
w John Cresswell d Compton Bennett ph Oswald Morris m Robert Gill
☆ Marius Goring, Maria Schell, Gabrielle Dorziat, Barbara Mullen

So Long at the Fair *
GB 1950 86m bw
Rank/Gainsborough/Sydney Box (Betty E. Box)
During the 1889 Paris Exposition a girl books into a hotel with her brother, and next day finds that he has totally disappeared and his existence is denied by all concerned.
Straightforward version of an old yarn which has turned up in such varied forms as The Lady Vanishes and Bunny Lake is Missing. This modest production is pleasant enough but badly lacks drive.
w Hugh Mills, Anthony Thorne d Terence Fisher, Anthony Darnborough ph Reginald Wyer m Benjamin Frankel ad Cedric Dawe
☆ Jean Simmons, Dirk Bogarde, David Tomlinson, Marcel Poncin, Cathleen Nesbitt, Honor Blackman, Betty Warren, Felix Aylmer, André Morell

'A foxhole was her honeymoon hotel!'
'The first great story of our women at the fighting front!'

So Proudly We Hail *
US 1943 125m bw
Paramount (Mark Sandrich)
The self-sacrifice of war nurses in the Pacific.
Fairly harrowing and well-meant but studio-bound and unconvincing flagwaver.
w Allan Scott d Mark Sandrich ph Charles Lang m Miklos Rozsa
☆ Claudette Colbert, Paulette Goddard, Veronica Lake, George Reeves, Barbara Britton, Walter Abel, Sonny Tufts, John Litel
'Probably the most deadly accurate picture ever made of what war looks like through the lenses of a housewives' magazine romance.' – *James Agee*
'The stars are devotedly, almost gallantly, deglamorized and dishevelled but they cannot escape the smell of studio varnish.' – *Richard Winnington*
🎵 Allan Scott; Charles Lang; Paulette Goddard

'The flower of southern chivalry dewed with the shining glory of a woman's tears!'

So Red the Rose *
US 1935 82m bw
Paramount (Douglas MacLean)
The life of a Southern family during the Civil War.
Quiet, pleasing historical romance.
w Laurence Stallings, Maxwell Anderson, Edwin Justus Mayer novel Stark Young d King Vidor ph Victor Milner m W. Franke Harling
☆ Margaret Sullavan, Randolph Scott, Walter Connolly, Elizabeth Patterson, Janet Beecher, Robert Cummings

'Certain to go better in the Dixie belt than north, but okay on average.' – *Variety*

So This Is London
GB 1939 89m bw
TCF
An American magnate visits his English rival, and romance springs up between their children.
Brightish comedy with a fair scattering of funny lines.
w William Conselman, Ben Travers, Tom Phipps, Douglas Furber d Thornton Freeland ph Otto Kanturek
☆ Robertson Hare, Alfred Drayton, George Sanders, Berton Churchill, Fay Compton, Carla Lehmann, Stewart Granger, Ethel Revnell, Gracie West

So This Is Love *
US 1953 101m Technicolor
Warner (Henry Blanke)
GB title: *The Grace Moore Story*
Events leading up to Grace Moore's debut at the Metropolitan Opera in 1928.
Acceptable musical biopic full of the usual Hollywood contrivances.
w John Monks Jnr autobiography Grace Moore d Gordon Douglas ph Robert Burks md Ray Heindorf, Max Steiner ch Le Roy Prinz ad Edward Carrere
☆ Kathryn Grayson, Merv Griffin, Joan Weldon, Walter Abel, Rosemary de Camp, Jeff Donnell, Douglas Dick, Mabel Albertson, Fortunio Bonanova

So This Is New York *
US 1948 78m bw
Enterprise/Stanley Kramer
In 1919 some country cousins who have come into money have a big time in the gay city.
Curious, sporadically effective, silent-style comedy which doesn't quite come off.
w Carl Foreman, Herbert Baker novel The Big Town by Ring Lardner d Richard Fleischer ph Jack Russell m Dimitri Tiomkin
☆ Henry Morgan, Rudy Vallee, Hugh Herbert, Bill Goodwin, Virginia Grey, Dona Drake, Leo Gorcey

So This Is Paris *
US 1954 96m Technicolor
U-I (Albert J. Cohen)
🇺🇸
Three American sailors on leave in Paris meet girls and help war orphans.
Very thin imitation of On the Town, bogged down by sentimentality and lack of sparkle. The musical numbers, however, are not bad.
w Charles Hoffman d Richard Quine ph Maury Gertsman md Joseph Gershenson ch Gene Nelson, Lee Scott
☆ Tony Curtis, Gloria de Haven, Gene Nelson, Corinne Calvet, Paul Gilbert, Mara Corday, Allison Hayes

So Well Remembered *
GB 1947 114m bw
RKO/Alliance (Adrian Scott)
🎬
The ambitious daughter of a mill-owner marries a rising politician but almost ruins his life.
Rather routine treatment of a three-decker north country novel; humdrum incident and unsympathetic characters, but full of minor British virtues.
w John Paxton novel James Hilton d Edward Dmytryk ph Frederick A. Young
☆ John Mills, Martha Scott, Trevor Howard, Patricia Roc, Richard Carlson
'The occasional slackness of narrative is atoned for by a strongly communicated sense of place: the mean streets shining with rain, the sullen suffocated houses.' – *Dilys Powell, Sunday Times*

Soak the Rich *
US 1935 74m bw
Paramount (Ben Hecht, Charles MacArthur)
A rebellious rich girl is cured when she is rescued from kidnapping.
Smartly written social comedy-melodrama.
wd Ben Hecht, Charles MacArthur ph Leon Shamroy
☆ Walter Connolly, John Howard, Mary Taylor, Lionel Stander, Ilka Chase
'Hecht and MacArthur have not been very successful in their attempts to gauge public opinion … inadequate entertainment.' – *Variety*

Soapdish *
US 1991 97m Technicolor
UIP/Paramount (Aaron Spelling, Alan Greisman)
📀 📺 🎬 🎧
A jealous co-star tries to sabotage the popularity of America's most popular star of a daily soap-opera.
Fitfully amusing parody of a TV soap, but one that failed to find much of an audience.
w Robert Harling, Andrew Bergman d Michael Hoffman ph Ueli Steiger m Alan Silvestri pd Eugenio Zanetti ed Garth Craven
☆ Sally Field, Kevin Kline, Robert Downey Jnr, Whoopi Goldberg, Carrie Fisher, Cathy Moriarty, Teri Hatcher, Paul Johansson, Elisabeth Shue, Garry Marshall
'An amiable comedy with enough one-liners to keep the chuckles coming regularly.' – *Sight and Sound*

Social Register
US 1934 71m bw
Columbia (William de Mille)
A chorus girl fights the prejudices of her in-laws to be.
Dull and obvious romantic drama mainly notable for its cast, and for the star who failed to make a comeback.
w Clara Beranger, Anita Loos, John Emerson d Marshall Neilan
☆ Colleen Moore, Charles Winninger, Pauline Frederick, Alexander Kirkland, Robert Benchley, Ross Alexander
'Good players lost in a trite story.' – *Variety*

Society
US 1989 99m colour
Medusa/Society Productions/Wild Street Pictures (Keith Walley)
📀 📺
A student discovers that his wealthy parents and friends are shape-shifting monsters who devour the poor.
Weird allegory of class warfare that contains stomach-turning special effects.
w Woody Keith, Rick Fry d Brian Yuzna ph Rick Fichter m Mark Ryder, Phil Davies pd Mathew C. Jacobs ed Peter Teschner sp Screaming Mad George
☆ Bill Warlock, Devin DeVasquez, Evan Richards, Ben Meyerson, Charles Lucia, Connie Danese, Patrice Jennings
'One of the most extraordinary genre debuts of the 80s.' – *MFB*

Society Doctor
US 1935 63m bw
MGM (Lucien Hubbard)
GB title: *After Eight Hours*
A doctor's modern ideas incur hostility: he goes into private practice, but returning to the hospital is wounded by a gangster and supervises his own operation under spinal anaesthetic.
Melodramatic hokum with most attention going to the second male lead, the young and rising Robert Taylor.
w Sam Marx, Michael Fessier novel The Harbor by Theodore Reeves d George B. Seitz ph Lester White m Oscar Radin
☆ Chester Morris, Virginia Bruce, Robert Taylor, Billie Burke, Raymond Walburn, Henry Kolker,' William Henry

Society Girl
US 1932 72m bw
Fox
A prizefighter falls for a society girl.
Weak melodrama whose best scenes are in the ring.
w Charles Benhan, Elmer Harris play John Larkin Jnr d Sidney Lanfield
☆ James Dunn, Spencer Tracy, Peggy Shannon, Walter Byron, Marjorie Gateson
'Falls short of first-rate classification.' – *Variety*

Society Lawyer
US 1939 77m bw
MGM (John W. Considine Jnr)
A lawyer is embarrassed by the gratitude of a racketeer.
Tolerable co-feature with class production.
w Frances Goodrich, Albert Hackett, Leon Gordon, Hugo Butler d Edwin L. Marin
☆ Walter Pidgeon, Virginia Bruce, Leo Carrillo, Eduardo Ciannelli, Lee Bowman, Herbert Mundin
'Fairish murder mystery with sophisticated background. For duals.' – *Variety*

Sodom and Gomorrah

Italy/France   1963   154m   colour
Titanus/S. N. Pathé (Goffredo Lombardo, Joseph E. Levine)

Lot and the Hebrews become involved in a Helamite plan to take over the rich sinful cities of Sodom and Gomorrah.

Dreary biblical blood-and-thunder; an international muddle, tedious in the extreme outside a few hilariously misjudged moments.

w Hugo Butler, Giorgio Prosperi d Robert Aldrich ph Silvano Ippoliti, Cyril Knowles m Miklos Rozsa ad Ken Adam

☆ Stewart Granger, Stanley Baker, Pier Angeli, Anouk Aimée, Rossana Podesta

Sofie *

Denmark/Norway/Sweden   1992   152m   colour
Arrow/Nordisk/Norsk/Svensk Filmindustri (Lars Kolvig)

In Copenhagen in the 1890s, a Jewish woman is forced by her family to reject her non-Jewish admirer and move away from the city to marry a cousin who goes slowly mad.

A well-acted, home, domestic saga that follows changing attitudes across three generations, from Sofie's parents, anxious to be anonymous in a larger society while preserving their own way of life, to Sofie, wanting to break away but unable to do so, to her son, who rejects the old traditions; it is nevertheless at its most affecting when depicting the pleasures of Sofie's parents rather than the miseries of her own mismatch.

w Liv Ullmann, Peter Poulsen novel Mendel Philipsen and Son by Henri Nathansen d Liv Ullmann ph Jörgen Persson m Peter Hoimark ed Grete Moldrup

☆ Karen-Lise Mynster, Ghita Norby, Erland Josephson, Jesper Christensen, Torben Zeller, Henning Moritzen, Stig Hoffmeyer, Kirsten Rolffes

'Lurches regrettably towards the gratuitous miserablism of Bergmanesque stereotype.' – *Sight and Sound*

Soft Beds, Hard Battles

GB   1973   107m   colour
Rank/Charter (John Boulting)
US title: *Undercovers Hero*

Inhabitants of a Paris brothel help to win World War II.

Ragbag of poor sketches and dirty jokes, with the star in several ineffective roles including Hitler.

w Leo Marks, Roy Boulting d Roy Boulting ph Gil Taylor m Neil Rhoden

☆ Peter Sellers, Lila Kedrova, Curt Jurgens, Gabriella Licudi, Jenny Hanley

Soft Deceit

Canada   1994   91m   colour
Chesler/Perlmutter (Lewis B. Chester, T. A. Baird, Jorge Montesi)

A female special agent offers to spring a master thief from prison in an attempt to recover the $6m he stole from the Catholic Church.

Slick, trivial, pulp thriller, with softboiled dialogue and a narrative that is predictably implausible.

w Jorge Montesi, Roy Sallows d Jorge Montesi ph Philip Linzey m Ian Thomas pd Harold Thrasher ed George Roulston

☆ Patrick Bergin, Kate Vernon, John Wesley Shipp, Gwynyth Walsh, Nigel Bennett, Ted Dykstra, Damir Andrei

'A Motorvated Comedy.'
'They're going to make it. Nothing will stop them now...'

Soft Top, Hard Shoulder *

GB   1992   95m   colour
Feature/Road Movie Productions (Richard Holmes)

An unsuccessful Scottish artist living in London has 36 hours to drive to Glasgow in his ancient car so that he can share in the family fortune; on the way he picks up a female hitch-hiker.

Amiable, soft-centred road movie with an affection for eccentricity.

w Peter Capaldi d Stefan Schwartz ph Henry Braham m Chris Rea pd Sonja Klaus ed Derek Trigg

☆ Peter Capaldi, Frances Barber, Catherine Russell, Jeremy Northam, Richard Wilson, Peter Ferninando, Simon Callow, Phyllis Logan

'The initial novelty of this particular roadshow ultimately pales.' – *Empire*

Soigne Ton Gauche *

France   1937   12m   bw
Cady (Fred Orain)

A boxing training session in a village ends in chaos.

A gentle short comedy from Tati, revealing his pleasure in the eccentric details of life.

w Jean Marie Huard d René Clément m Jean Yatove

☆ Jacques Tati, Max Martell, Robur Cliville

† It was released on video together with *L'école des Facteurs* and *Cours du Soir* under the title *Tati Shorts.*

Sol Madrid

US   1968   90m   Metrocolor   Panavision
MGM/Gershwin-Kastner (Hall Bartlett)
GB title: *The Heroin Gang*

An undercover narcotics agent is assigned to track down an elusive Mafia executive.

Humdrum, predictable, brutishly violent international crime caper.

w David Karp novel Fruit of the Poppy by Robert Wilder d Brian G. Hutton ph Fred Koenekamp m Lalo Schifrin

☆ David McCallum, Telly Savalas, Stella Stevens, Ricardo Montalban, Rip Torn, Pat Hingle, Paul Lukas, Perry Lopez, Michael Ansara

Solamente Nero: see *The Bloodstained Shadow*

Solange Du da bist: see *As Long as You're Near Me*

Solar Crisis

US/Japan   1992   107m   DeLuxe
Trimark/Gakken/NHK (Richard Edlund, James Nelson, Morris Morishima)

A power-crazed industrialist plans to sabotage Earth's last hope: a spaceship carrying an anti-matter bomb to the sun in order to prevent a massive flare from burning up the planet.

Dire science-fiction extravaganza; the banality of the plot is exceeded only by the stupidity of the dialogue.

w Joe Gannon, Crispan Bolt novel Takeshi Kawata d Alan Smithee (Richard Sarafian) ph Russ Carpenter m Maurice Jarre, Michael Boddicker pd George Jenson ed Richard Trevor sp Neil Krepela

☆ Tim Matheson, Charlton Heston, Peter Boyle, Annabel Schofield, Corin 'Corky' Nemec, Tetsuya Bessho, Jack Palance, David Ursin, Brenda Bakke, Paul Williams

† The movie cost $35 million. It was released direct to video in Britain.

Solar Warriors

US   1986   94m   colour
MBM/Brooksfilms (Irene Walzer, Jack Frost Sanders)
US title: *Solarbabies*

In a future world where water is scarce, a gang of roller-skating teenagers rebel against authority with the aid of a mystic ball.

Ludicrous science fiction adventure that lacks invention, style and plausibility.

w Walon Green, Douglas Anthony Metrov d Alan Johnson ph Peter MacDonald m Maurice Jarre pd Anthony Pratt ed Conrad Buff

☆ Richard Jordan, Jami Gertz, Jason Patric, Lukas Haas, James Le Gros, Claude Brooks, Peter DeLuise, Sarah Douglas, Charles Durning

Solarbabies: see *Solar Warriors*

'The planet where nightmares come true...'

Solaris ***

USSR   1972   165m   Sovcolor   'Scope
Mosfilm

A psychologist is sent to investigate the many deaths in a space station orbiting a remote planet.

Heavy-going but highly imaginative space fiction in which the menaces are ghosts materialized from the subjects' guilty pasts. The technology is superbly managed, but the whole thing is rather humourless.

w Andrei Tarkovsky, Friedrich Gorenstein novel Stanislaw Lem d Andrei Tarkovsky ph Vadim Yusov m Eduard Artemyev

☆ Natalya Bondarchuk, Donatas Banionis, Yuri Yarvet

The Soldier and the Lady *

US   1937   85m   bw
RKO (Pandro S. Berman)
GB title: *Michael Strogoff*

In Napoleonic times, a messenger from the Czar sees more trouble than he expected.

Mildly ambitious swashbuckler from a story much remade in Europe; the elements jelled quite well in the Hollywood fashion.

w Mortimer Offner, Anthony Veiller, Anne Morrison Chapin novel Jules Verne d George Nicholls Jnr ph Joseph H. August

☆ Anton Walbrook, Elizabeth Allan, Akim Tamiroff

'Spectacle film lacking strength and names. Will have its troubles.' – *Variety*

† Exteriors were taken from a German/French film of 1936, *Courier to the Czar* (*Der Kurier des Zaren*), also starring Anton Walbrook.

'Stained with the blood of the innocent!'

Soldier Blue *

US   1970   114m   Technicolor   Panavision
Avco (Gabriel Katzka, Harold Loeb)

A paymaster's detachment of the US cavalry is attacked by Indians seeking gold, and two white survivors trek through the desert.

Extremely violent 'anti-violence' Western with a particularly nauseating climax following clichés all the way. From a director with pretensions.

w John Gay novel Arrow in the Sun by Theodore V. Olsen d Ralph Nelson ph Robert Hauser m Roy Budd

☆ Candice Bergen, Peter Strauss, Donald Pleasence

'One is more likely to be sickened by the film itself than by the wrongs it tries to right.' – *Tom Milne*

Soldier in the Rain

US   1963   87m   bw
AA/Cedar/Solar (Martin Jurow)

Two army sergeants have wild plans for their demob, but one dies.

Curious sentimental tragi-comedy which misfires on all cylinders.

w Blake Edwards, Maurice Richlin novel William Goldman d Ralph Nelson ph Philip Lathrop m Henry Mancini

☆ Steve McQueen, Jackie Gleason, Tuesday Weld, Tony Bill, Tom Poston, Ed Nelson, John Hubbard

Soldier of Fortune *

US   1955   96m   DeLuxe   Cinemascope
TCF (Buddy Adler)

When a photographer disappears in Red China, his wife comes to Hong Kong to institute a search, enlists the aid of an amiable smuggler.

Cheerful Boy's Own Paper adventure romance with attractive locations and some silly anti-Red dialogue.

w Ernest K. Gann novel Ernest K. Gann d Edward Dmytryk ph Leo Tover m Hugo Friedhofer

☆ Clark Gable, Susan Hayward, Gene Barry, Alex D'Arcy, Michael Rennie, Tom Tully, Anna Sten, Russell Collins, Leo Gordon

'A very good adventure film but not one of the Gable smashes.' – *Hollywood Reporter*

Soldier of Fortune (dubbed)

Italy/France   1976   90m   colour
Mondial/Cite/J. Leitienne/Labrador/Impexci
original title: *Humungus Hector*

A wandering Italian soldier and his small troop defeat an invading French army.

Comic epic, a good-natured, though undistinguished, romp through the past.

w Castellano, Pipolo, Franco Verucci, Pasquale Festa Campanile d Pasquale Festa Campanile ph Marcello Masciocchi m Guido and Maurizio de Angelis ad Pier Luigi Pizzi ed Mario Morra

☆ Bud Spencer (Carlo Pedersoli), Franco Agostini, Enzo Cannavale, Frederic de Pasquale, Jacques Dufilho, Andrea Ferreol

'The city of lights. A famous American author and the decade that changed a generation ... forever.'

A Soldier's Daughter Never Cries *

GB   1998   127m   Technicolor
Capitol/Merchant Ivory/British Screen (Ismail Merchant)

In the mid-60s, an unhappy young girl grows up in Paris and the USA.

Based on a semi-autobiographical novel by the daughter of writer James Jones, this is a rewarding domestic drama of an out-of-the-ordinary family, coping with their status as outsiders.

w James Ivory, Ruth Prawer Jhabvala novel Kayle Jones d James Ivory ph Jean-Marc Fabre m Richard Robbins pd Jacques Bufnoir, Pat Garner ed Noëlle Boisson

☆ Kris Kristofferson, Barbara Hershey, Leelee Sobieski, Jesse Bradford, Anthony Roth Costanzo, Dominique Blanc, Jane Birkin, Virginie Ledoyen, Samuel Gruen, Luisa Conlon, Isaac de Bankole

'Nicely mounted, superbly acted picture, which should appeal to the art crowd that has supported Merchant Ivory productions over the last two decades.' – *Emanuel Levy, Variety*

Soldiers of the King

GB   1933   80m   bw
Gainsborough (Michael Balcon)

A guards lieutenant causes trouble when he wants to marry a music hall star.

Sprightly star vehicle with all talents in good form.

w J. O. C. Orton, Jack Hulbert, W. P. Lipscomb story Douglas Furber d Maurice Elvey ph Leslie Rowson md Louis Levy

☆ Cicely Courtneidge, Edward Everett Horton, Anthony Bushell, Frank Cellier, Dorothy Hyson, Leslie Sarony

A Soldier's Story *

US   1984   101m   Metrocolor
Columbia/Delphi (Norman Jewison, Patrick Palmer)

In 1944 Louisiana, a hated sergeant at a small army post is shot dead.

Investigative melodrama on the old lines of Boomerang; quite watchable and well acted.

w Charles Fuller play Charles Fuller d Norman Jewison ph Russell Boyd m Herbie Hancock

☆ Howard E. Rollins Jnr, Adolph Caesar, Art Evans, David Alan Grier, David Harris, Denzel Washington

⅄ best picture; Adolph Caesar (supporting actor); adapted screenplay

A Soldier's Tale

US   1988   94m   colour
Mirage/Atlantic (Larry Parr)

A sergeant in the British Army tries to protect a young woman accused of being a collaborator by the French Resistance.

Bleak wartime drama of love and lust that never quite convinces.

w Grant Hindin Miller, Larry Parr novel M. K. Joseph d Larry Parr ph Alun Bollinger m John Charles pd Ivan Maussion ed Mike Horton

☆ Gabriel Byrne, Marianne Basler, Paul Wyett, Maurice Garrel, Benoit Regent, Jacques Mathou, Judge Reinhold

Soldiers Three

US   1951   87m   bw
MGM (Pandro S. Berman)

Adventures of three roistering British officers on the North-West Frontier.

A kind of unofficial remake of Gunga Din without the title character; one suspects it was meant seriously and found to be so bad that the only way out was strenuously to play it for laughs.

w Marguerite Roberts, Tom Reed, Malcolm Stuart Boylan d Tay Garnett ph William Mellor m Adolph Deutsch

☆ Stewart Granger, David Niven, Robert Newton, Walter Pidgeon, Cyril Cusack, Greta Gynt, Frank Allenby, Robert Coote, Dan O'Herlihy

'Kipling fans will probably have a fit but my guess is that it will have most people in fits of laughter.' – *Daily Mail*

Il sole anche di notte: see *Night Sun*

The Solid Gold Cadillac **

US 1956 99m bw
Columbia (Fred Kohlmar)
⬚

A very minor stockholder upsets the crooked board of a large corporation.

Vaguely Capraesque comedy which begins brightly but peters out; performances sustain passing interest.

w Abe Burrows play George S. Kaufman, Howard Teichmann d Richard Quine ph Charles Lang m Cyril Mockridge ad Ross Bellah

☆ Judy Holliday, Paul Douglas, John Williams, Fred Clark, Hiram Sherman, Neva Patterson, Ralph Dumke, Ray Collins, Arthur O'Connell

& art direction

'What would happen if your lover could read your mind?'

Solitaire for Two

GB 1994 106m Eastmancolor
Entertainment/Solitaire (Gary Sinyor, Richard Holmes)
⬚ ⬚

A psychologist dates a woman who is able to read the minds of the men around her, who all seem to be thinking the same thing.

A botched romantic comedy, with neither the wit nor the cast to carry off its underdeveloped central conceit.

wd Gary Sinyor ph Henry Braham m David A. Hughes, John Murphy pd Carmel Collins ed Ewa J. Lind

☆ Mark Frankel, Amanda Pays, Roshan Seth, Jason Isaacs, Maryam D'Abo, Annette Crosbie

'A still-born attempt at a latter-day Hawksian comedy.' – Variety

The Solitaire Man *

US 1933 68m bw
MGM

Crooks doublecross each other on a Paris–London aeroplane.

Smart little comedy with top talent.

w James Kevin McGuinness play Bella and Samuel Spewack d Jack Conway

☆ Herbert Marshall, Elizabeth Allan, Mary Boland, Lionel Atwill, May Robson, Ralph Forbes

'Diverting crook melodrama in the drawing room manner ... a lot better than the grosses it will probably get.' – Variety

I Soliti Ignoti: see Persons Unknown

'Their tragedy was to fall in love.'

Solomon and Gaenor *

GB 1998 104m DeLuxe
Film4/S4C/Arts Council/APT (Sheryl Crown)
⬚

In the early 1900s, a Jewish salesman and a Welsh woman fall in love, to the dismay of both their families.

A sometimes moving story of star-crossed lovers encountering racial prejudices.

wd Paul Morrison ph Nina Kellgren m Ilona Sekacz d Hayden Pearce ed Kant Pan

☆ Ioan Gruffudd, Nia Roberts, Sue Jones Davies, William Thomas, Mark Lewis Jones, Maureen Lipman, David Horovitch, Cyril Shaps

'Beautifully photographed and confidently directed, with powerful and affecting performances.' – Peter Bradshaw, Guardian

& foreign film

'Only once in 3000 years – anything like it!'

Solomon and Sheba

↟↟ US 1959 142m Super Technirama 70
UA/Edward Small (Ted Richmond)
⬚ ⬚ ⬚. ⌒

When David names his younger son as heir, his older son plots revenge.

Dullish biblical spectacle, alternating between pretentiousness and cowboys and Indians.

w Anthony Veiller, Paul Dudley, George Bruce story Crane Wilbur d King Vidor ph Frederick A. Young m Mario Nascimbene ad Richard Day, Alfred Sweeney

☆ Yul Brynner, Gina Lollobrigida, George Sanders, Marisa Pavan, David Farrar, John Crawford, Laurence Naismith, Alejandro Rey, Harry Andrews

'Penance is due.' – Hollis Alpert

'Watch out it doesn't put you to sleep.' – New York Times

Sombrero

US 1953 103m Technicolor
MGM (Jack Cummings)

Two Mexican villages feud over the burial place of a famous poet.

Rather self-consciously unusual musical which never catches fire but certainly keeps one watching its incredible mixture of music and melodrama.

w Norman Foster, Josefina Niggli novel A Mexican Village by Josefina Niggli d Norman Foster ph Ray June m Leo Arnaud

☆ Ricardo Montalban, Pier Angeli, Yvonne de Carlo, Nina Foch, Cyd Charisse, Rick Jason, Jose Greco, Thomas Gomez, Kurt Kasznar, Walter Hampden, John Abbott

'Staggering is the only word for the hokum of this extraordinary film.' – Gavin Lambert

Some Call It Loving

US 1973 103m Technicolor
Pleasant Pastures/James B. Harris
⬚

A young man buys a 'sleeping beauty' at a fair but is sorry when he wakes her up.

Fashionable fantasy, amplified from a slender, winning short story.

wd James B. Harris story Sleeping Beauty by John Collier ph Mario Tosi m Richard Hazard

☆ Zalman King, Carol White, Tisa Farrow, Richard Pryor, Veronica Anderson

Some Came Running

US 1958 136m Metrocolor Cinemascope
MGM/Sol C. Siegel
⬚ ⬚ ⬚. ⌒

A disillusioned writer returns after service to his home town and takes up with a gambler and a prostitute.

Strident and rather pointless melodrama with solid acting and production values.

w John Patrick, Arthur Sheekman novel James Jones d Vincente Minnelli ph William H. Daniels m Elmer Bernstein

☆ Frank Sinatra, Dean Martin, Shirley MacLaine, Martha Hyer, Arthur Kennedy, Nancy Gates, Leora Dana

& song 'To Love and Be Loved' (mJames Van Heusen, lySammy Cahn); Shirley MacLaine; Martha Hyer; Arthur Kennedy

Some Girls: see Sisters

Some Girls Do

GB 1969 93m Eastmancolor
Rank/Ashdown (Betty E. Box)

Bulldog Drummond traces the sabotage of a supersonic airliner to a gang of murderous women.

Abysmal spoof melodrama in the swinging sixties mould; a travesty of a famous character.

w David Osborn, Liz Charles-Williams d Ralph Thomas ph Ernest Steward m Charles Blackwell

☆ Richard Johnson, Daliah Lavi, Beba Loncar, James Villiers, Sydne Rome, Robert Morley, Maurice Denham, Florence Desmond, Ronnie Stevens

Some Kind of a Nut

US 1969 89m DeLuxe
UA/Mirisch/TFT/DFI (Walter Mirisch)

When a bank teller grows a beard because of an unsightly bee sting, he is thought to be flouting authority and his whole life changes.

Laboured, cliché-ridden anti-establishment comedy, a waste of the talent involved.

wd Garson Kanin ph Burnett Guffey, Gerald Hirschfeld m Johnny Mandel

☆ Dick Van Dyke, Angie Dickinson, Rosemary Forsyth, Zohra Lampert, Elliott Reid, Dennis King

Some Kind of Hero

US 1981 97m Movielab
Paramount (Howard W. Koch)
⬚ ⬚ ⌒

After six years as a prisoner of the Vietcong, an army veteran returns home to find his life no bed of roses.

Weird mixture of comedy and melodrama which simply doesn't jell, especially when it tries to get earnest.

w James Kirkwood, Robert Boris novel James Kirkwood d Michael Pressman ph King Baggot m Patrick Williams ad James L. Schoppe ed Christopher Greenbury

☆ Richard Pryor, Margot Kidder, Ray Sharkey, Ronny Cox, Lynne Moody, Olivia Cole

Some Kind of Wonderful

US 1987 95m Technicolor Panavision
Paramount (John Hughes)
⬚ ⬚ ⬚. ⌒

Girl meets boy, boy meets another girl, boy loses girl, boy gets first girl.

Teen romance pandering to its target audience: all adults are stupid and repressive, and maturity and wisdom are to be found among the young. Its appeal will be limited to the immature.

w John Hughes d Howard Deutch ph Jan Kiesser m Stephen Hague, John Musser pd Josan Russo ed Bud Smith, Scott Smith

☆ Eric Stoltz, Mary Stuart Masterson, Craig Sheffer, John Ashton, Lea Thompson, Elias Koteas, Maddie Corman

'The killer-diller of all swing shows!'

Some Like It Hot

US 1939 65m bw
Paramount (William C. Thomas)
TV reissue title: Rhythm Romance

A sideshow owner runs out of money.

Very mild comedy, one of several which helped to establish Hope's star potential.

w Lewis R. Foster play Wilkie C. Mahoney, Ben Hecht, Gene Fowler d George Archainbaud ph Karl Struss

☆ Bob Hope, Shirley Ross, Una Merkel, Gene Krupa, Richard Denning

'Turned out deliberately to catch the jitterbug devotees ... will satisfy moderately.' – Variety

† The play, The Great Magoo, was previously filmed in 1934 as Shoot the Works.

Some Like It Hot ****

↟↟ US 1959 122m bw
UA/Mirisch (Billy Wilder)
⬚ ⬚ ⌒

Two unemployed musicians accidentally witness the St Valentine's Day Massacre and flee to Miami disguised as girl musicians.

A milestone of film comedy which keeps its central situation alive with constant and fresh invention; its wit, combined with a sense of danger, has rarely been duplicated and never equalled.

w Billy Wilder, I. A. L. Diamond d Billy Wilder ph Charles Lang Jnr m Adolph Deutsch ad Ted Howarth

☆ Jack Lemmon, Tony Curtis, Marilyn Monroe, Joe E. Brown, George Raft, Pat O'Brien, Nehemiah Persoff, George E. Stone, Joan Shawlee

'A comedy set in the Prohibition era, with transvestism, impotence, role confusion, and borderline inversion – and all hilariously innocent, though always on the brink of really disastrous double-entendre.' – Pauline Kael

'Most of the time Billy Wilder's new piece – a farce blacker than is common on the American screen – whistles along at a smart, murderous pace.' – Dilys Powell

'Hectic slapstick, smartass movie parodies, sexist stereotyping, crass one-liners, and bad taste galore.' – Time Out, 1984

& script; Billy Wilder (as director); Charles Lang Jnr; Jack Lemmon; art direction

ⓥ Jack Lemmon

Some Like It Sexy

GB 1969 89m Eastmancolor
Donwin (Donovan Winter)
⬚

aka: Come Back Peter

A butcher's boy dreams of a series of sexual conquests, changing his personality to suit each woman.

Dull, though slickly made, exploitation film, which could have done with more variation in its interminable scenes of unadventurous love-making.

wd Donovan Winter ph Ian D. Struthers, Gus Coma ed Donovan Winter

☆ Christopher Matthews, Yolande Turner, Valerie St Hélène, Annabel Leventon, Penny Riley, Erika Bergmann, Maddy Smith, Mary and Madeleine Collinson, Nicola Pagett

† The version released in the cinemas ran for 65m.

Some Mother's Son

US/Ireland 1996 112m colour
Rank/Castle Rock/Turner/Hell's Kitchen (Jim Sheridan, Arthur Lappin, Edward Burke)
⬚ ⬚ ⌒

In Northern Ireland, a schoolteacher is drawn into political activism when her son is arrested by the British and put into prison, where, following the lead of Bobby Sands, he is among those who go on hunger strike.

A bleak drama, based on the events in 1981 when ten men starved themselves to death; that reality overwhelms this fiction, which does no more than recreate the tragedy through the reactions of two mothers.

w Terry George, Jim Sheridan d Terry George ph Geoffrey Simpson m Bill Whelan pd David Wilson ed Craig McKay

☆ Helen Mirren, Fionnula Flanagan, Aiden Gillen, David O'Hara, John Lynch, Tom Hollander, Tim Woodward, Ciaran Hinds

'The action is dominated by the realities of domestic violence, prison life and a prolonged hunger strike, all of which rate as box office negatives.' – Todd McCarthy, Variety

Some People

GB 1962 93m Eastmancolor
Vic Films (James Archibald)

Troublesome teenage factory workers are helped by a church organist and become model citizens.

Bland propaganda for the Duke of Edinburgh's Award scheme for young people, quite acceptably presented, with pop music ad lib.

w John Eldridge d Clive Donner ph John Wilcox m Ron Grainer

☆ Kenneth More, Ray Brooks, Annika Wells, David Andrews, Angela Douglas, David Hemmings, Harry H. Corbett

Some Will, Some Won't

GB 1969 90m Technicolor
ABP/Transocean (Giulio Zampi)
⬚

In order to inherit under an eccentric will, four people have to perform tasks out of character.

Thin remake of Laughter in Paradise (qv); funny moments extremely few.

w Lew Schwartz d Duncan Wood ph Harry Waxman m Howard Blake

☆ Ronnie Corbett, Thora Hird, Michael Hordern, Leslie Phillips, Barbara Murray, James Robertson Justice, Dennis Price, Wilfrid Brambell, Eleanor Summerfield, Arthur Lowe

Somebody Killed Her Husband

US 1978 96m Movielab
Columbia/Melvin Simon (Martin Poll)

The title tells what happened when an unhappily married young mother falls in love.

Very thin suspense comedy which starts as it ends, uncertainly.

w Reginald Rose d Lamont Johnson ph Andrew Laszlo, Ralf D. Bode m Alex North pd Ted Howarth

☆ Farrah Fawcett-Majors, Jeff Bridges, John Wood, Tammy Grimes, John Glover, Patricia Elliott

Somebody Loves Me

US 1952 97m Technicolor
Paramount/Perlberg-Seaton

First successful in San Francisco at earthquake time, Blossom Seeley climbs to Broadway success with her partner Benny Fields, then retires to become his wife.

Adequate, unsurprising star musical of the second or third rank.

wd Irving Brecher ph George Barnes songs Jay Livingston, Ray Evans

☆ Betty Hutton, Ralph Meeker, Robert Keith, Adele Jergens, Billie Bird, Sid Tomack, Ludwig Stossel

'She Was Worth Living For ... Worth Killing For...'

Somebody to Love *

US 1994 103m Foto-Kem
Entertainment/Lumiere/Initial (Lila Cazes)
⬚ ⬚

A dancer in a sleazy Los Angeles club, who hopes to become a film star, has problems with the men in her life.

Confused and unfocused drama of showbiz hopefuls whose ambitions are greater than their talents; there are occasional pleasures to be had.

w Sergei Bodrov, Alexandre Rockwell d Alexandre Rockwell ph Robert Yeoman m Mader pd J. Rae Fox ed Elena Maganini

☆ Rosie Perez, Harvey Keitel, Anthony Quinn, Michael DeLorenzo, Steve Buscemi, Sam Fuller, Stanley Tucci

'Rarely fires on more than one cylinder at a time.' – Variety

† The film was inspired by Fellini's *Cabiria* (qv) and the character played by Giulietta Masina.

Somebody Up There Likes Me *
US   1956   112m   bw
MGM (Charles Schnee)

An East Side kid with reform school experience becomes middleweight boxing champion of the world.
A sentimental fantasia on the life of Rocky Graziano, expertly blending violence, depression, prizefight sequences and fake uplift.
w Ernest Lehman d Robert Wise ph Joseph Ruttenberg m Bronislau Kaper ad Cedric Gibbons, Malcolm F. Brown ed Albert Akst
☆ Paul Newman, Pier Angeli, Everett Sloane, Eileen Heckart, Sal Mineo, Joseph Buloff, Harold J. Stone, Robert Loggia
🎞 Joseph Ruttenberg; art direction
🎞 editing

Someone at the Door
GB   1936   74m   bw
BIP (Walter Mycroft)
The new owner of a spooky house invents a murder which seems to come true.
Derivative but quite amusing comedy thriller.
w Jack Davies, Marjorie Deans play Dorothy and Campbell Christie d Herbert Brenon ph Bryan Langley
☆ Billy Milton, Aileen Marson, Noah Beery, Edward Chapman, Hermione Gingold, John Irwin
† Remade in 1950 with Michael Medwin, Yvonne Owen and Garry Marsh; directed by Francis Searle; for Hammer.

Someone Behind the Door
France   1971   97m   colour
Miracle/Lira Film/Comaccio/SNC (Raymond Danon)
🔲 🔍
original title: *Quelqu'un derrière la Porte*
aka: *Two Minds for Murder*
A brain surgeon takes a psychopathic patient home and tries to make him commit murder.
Adequate but somehow unexciting suspenser.
w Mark Boehm, Jacques Robert novel Jacques Robert d Nicolas Gessner ph Pierre Lhomme m Georges Garvarentz
☆ Charles Bronson, Anthony Perkins, Jill Ireland, Henri Garcia

Someone Else's America *
France/Germany/GB   1995   93m   Fujicolour
Film Four/Mact/Intrinsica/Lichtblick/Stefi 2 (Antonie de Clermont-Tonnerre, David Rose, Helga Bähr)
original title: *L'Amérique des autres*
In Brooklyn, a struggling Spanish bar-owner helps the family of his best friend, illegal immigrants who arrive unexpectedly from Montenegro.
A ramshackle film, set in the gap between life as it is at the bottom of the heap and the American dream, which has a few telling moments.
w Gordan Mihic d Goran Paskaljevic ph Yorgos Arvanitis m Andrew Dickson ad Wolf Seesselberg ed William Diver
☆ Tom Conti, Miki Manojlovic, Maria Casarès, Zorka Manojlovic, Sergej Trifunovic, Jose Ramon Rosario, Lanny Flaherty
'Sentimental, eccentric and quietly funny.' – *Sight and Sound*

Someone to Love *
US   1987   105m   DeLuxe
ICA/International Rainbow/Jagfilm (M. H. Simonsons)
🔲 🔍
On Valentine's Day, a director throws a party for his single and divorced friends and questions them on camera about their attitudes to love and relationships.
Little more than a succession of turns by various actors and actresses, but intermittently interesting and notable for Welles's final appearance on film, bringing it to an end with a shout of 'Cut!'
wd Henry Jaglom ph Hanania Baer ed Henry Jaglom
☆ Orson Welles, Henry Jaglom, Andrea Marcovicci, Michael Emil, Sally Kellerman, Oja Kodar, Stephen Bishop, Dave Frishberg

Someone to Watch Over Me *
US   1987   106m   DeLuxe
Columbia/Thierry de Ganay
🔲 🔍
A New York cop falls for the witness he must protect from a vicious killer.
Lively thriller with slick technicalities.
w Howard Franklin d Ridley Scott ph Steven Poster m Michael Kamen pd Jim Bissell
☆ Tom Berenger, Mimi Rogers, Lorraine Bracco, Jerry Orbach, John Rubinstein, Andreas Katsulas
'Stylish and romantic ... manages to triumph over several hard-to-swallow plot developments.' – *Daily Variety*

Something about Love
Canada   1988   93m   colour
Allegro/NFBC (Franco Battista, Tom Berry, Stefan Wodoslawsky)
A Hollywood producer returns home to reconcile with his father, who is suffering from Alzheimer's disease.
Mundane domestic drama that never gets to grips with its subject.
w Tom Berry, Stefan Wodoslawsky d Tom Berry ph Rodney Gibbons m Lou Forestieri ad Guy Lalande ed Franco Battista
☆ Stefan Wodoslawsky, Jan Rubes, Jennifer Dale, Ron James, Leonore Zann, Diana Reis

Something Big
US   1971   108m   Technicolor
Cinema Center/Stanmore and Penbar (Andrew V. McLaglen)
A retiring cavalry colonel has a last battle with his old enemy.
Wry serio-comic Western in the Ford tradition.
w James Lee Barrett d Andrew V. McLaglen ph Harry Stradling Jnr m Marvin Hamlisch
☆ Dean Martin, Brian Keith, Honor Blackman, Carol White, Ben Johnson, Albert Salmi, Denver Pyle

Something for Everyone *
US   1970   110m   colour
National General (John Flaxman)
🔲
GB title: *Black Flowers for the Bride*
A young con man insinuates himself into the household of a widowed Austrian countess.
Unusual black comedy which doesn't quite come off.
w Hugh Wheeler novel *The Cook* by Harry Kressing d Harold Prince ph Walter Lassally m John Kander
☆ Angela Lansbury, Michael York, Anthony Corlan, Heidelinde Weis
'Nothing much for anyone, actually.' – *New Yorker*

Something for the Birds
US   1952   81m   bw
TCF (Samuel G. Engel)
An elderly fraud is of help to a Washington girl trying to save a bird sanctuary.
Derivative, competent but slightly boring political whimsy on Capra lines.
w I. A. L. Diamond, Boris Ingster d Robert Wise ph Joseph LaShelle m Sol Kaplan
☆ Edmund Gwenn, Victor Mature, Patricia Neal, Larry Keating, Christian Rub

Something for the Boys
US   1944   87m   Technicolor
TCF (Irving Starr)
A Southern plantation is turned into a retreat for army wives.
Modest musical, vaguely based on a Broadway success.
w Robert Ellis, Helen Logan, Frank Gabrielson musical comedy Cole Porter, Herbert and Dorothy Fields d Lewis Seiler ph Ernest Palmer m Cyril Mockridge title song Cole Porter other songs Harold Adamson, Jimmy McHugh
☆ Carmen Miranda, Michael O'Shea, Vivian Blaine, Phil Silvers, Sheila Ryan, Perry Como, Glenn Langan, Cara Williams

Something in the Wind
US   1947   89m   bw
U-I (Joseph Sistrom)
A lady disc jockey is mistaken for her aunt, who has been seeing too much for the heirs' liking of a wealthy old man.
Poorish star musical comedy.
w Harry Kurnitz, William Bowers d Irving Pichel
☆ Deanna Durbin, Donald O'Connor, John Dall, Charles Winninger, Helena Carter

Something Money Can't Buy
GB   1952   82m   bw
Rank/Vic (Joe Janni)
After World War II a young couple find civilian life difficult and dreary, but finally start a catering and secretarial business.
Weakly contrived comedy which makes nothing of its possibilities and is limply handled all round.
w Pat Jackson, James Landsdale Hodson d Pat Jackson ph C. Pennington-Richards m Nino Rota
☆ Patricia Roc, Anthony Steel, A. E. Matthews, Moira Lister, David Hutcheson, Michael Trubshawe, Diane Hart, Charles Victor, Henry Edwards

Something of Value
US   1957   113m   bw
MGM (Pandro S. Berman)
A young African with many English friends is initiated into the Kikuyu.
An attempt to see all sides in the case of the African ritual murders of the fifties; bloodthirsty and unconvincing as well as dull.
wd Richard Brooks novel Robert Ruark ph Russell Harlan m Miklos Rozsa
☆ Rock Hudson, Sidney Poitier, Dana Wynter, Wendy Hiller, Robert Beatty, Juano Hernandez, William Marshall, Walter Fitzgerald, Michael Pate

'Believe in Love. Believe in Life. Believe in Yourself. Believe in Miracles.'
Something to Believe In
GB/Germany   1997   113m   colour   'Scope
Warner/Grade/Kirch (John Hough)
A female croupier, given two months to live, goes to Italy in search of a miracle cure, and falls in love with a concert pianist.
Risibly sentimental weepie, extraordinarily old-fashioned in its attitudes and approach.
w John Goldsmith, John Hough d John Hough ph Tony Pierce Roberts m Lalo Schifrin pd Nello Giorgetti ed Peter Tanner
☆ William McNamara, Maria Pitillo, Tom Conti, Maria Schneider, Ian Bannen, Robert Wagner, Jill St John, Roddy McDowall
'Simply defies credulity.' – *Guardian*
'A movie this stupid could change your life forever.' – *Independent*

Something to Hide
GB   1971   99m   Eastmancolor
Avton (Michael Klinger)
🔲
A civil servant has a row with his wife, kills her and buries her body on the Isle of Wight.
Unpleasant and uninteresting melodrama demanding a hysterical performance from its star. Pleasant photography is its only asset.
wd Alastair Reid novel Nicholas Monsarrat ph Wolfgang Suschitzky m Roy Budd, Jack Fishman
☆ Peter Finch, Colin Blakely, John Stride, Shelley Winters, Linda Hayden, Harold Goldblatt

Something to Live For
US   1952   89m   bw
Paramount (George Stevens)
A commercial artist member of Alcoholics Anonymous falls for a dipsomaniac actress but refuses to break up his marriage.
Glossy romantic melodrama with some style but no depth; the casting makes it seem like a sequel to The Lost Weekend.
w Dwight Taylor d George Stevens ph George Barnes m Victor Young
☆ Ray Milland, Joan Fontaine, Teresa Wright, Richard Derr, Douglas Dick
'The victory over alcohol becomes a somewhat woebegone business.' – *Penelope Houston*
† Completed in 1950, but not released until later.

Something to Shout About
US   1943   93m   bw
Columbia (Gregory Ratoff)
A press agent tries to get rid of an untalented star.
Tolerable musical comedy.
w Fred Shiller, Lou Breslow, Edward Eliscu, George Owen d Gregory Ratoff md Morris Stoloff songs Cole Porter

☆ Don Ameche, Janet Blair, William Gaxton, Perry Como
🎞 Morris Stoloff; song 'You'd Be So Nice to Come Home To'

Something to Sing About *
US   1937   90m   bw
Grand National (Zion Myers)
🔲 🔍
A New York bandleader decides to take a fling at Hollywood.
Lightweight but reasonably pleasing musical, made by the star as an independent during a rift with his studio, Warner.
w Austin Parker ph John Stumar md Constantin Bakaleinikoff d/songs Victor Schertzinger
☆ James Cagney, Evelyn Daw, Mona Barrie, William Frawley, Gene Lockhart
'A first-class comedy with music; will please everywhere.' – *Variety*
🎞 Victor Schertzinger

Something to Talk About
US   1995   106m   Technicolor
Warner/Spring Creek (Anthea Sylbert, Paula Weinstein)
🔲 🔍 🔍
A wife discovers that her husband has been having an affair and throws him out of the house; her mother-in-law follows her example.
Vacuous and glossy romantic comedy which emphasizes that the wealthy also suffer, though in greater comfort than the rest of us.
w Callie Khouri d Lasse Hallström ph Sven Nykvist m Hans Zimmer, Graham Preskett pd Mel Bourne ed Mia Goldman
☆ Julia Roberts, Dennis Quaid, Robert Duvall, Gena Rowlands, Kyra Sedgwick, Brett Cullen, Haley Aull, Muse Watson
'Bland one moment and barbed the next ... dithers on like compulsive conversationalists who take twice as long as necessary to say what they want to say.' – *Variety*

Something Wicked This Way Comes *
US   1983   95m   Technicolor
Walt Disney/Bryna (Peter Vincent Douglas)
🔲 🔍 🎧
A sinister carnival with a power over time and age visits a small town in Illinois.
A curious departure for the Disney studio is this grim fairy tale from a novel which was probably intractable. In the cinema, this is the sort of film very lucky to find an audience despite its good qualities.
w Ray Bradbury novel Ray Bradbury d Jack Clayton ph Stephen H. Burum m James Horner pd Richard MacDonald
☆ Jason Robards, Jonathan Pryce, Diane Ladd, Pam Grier, Royal Dano, Vidal Peterson, Shawn Carson

Something Wild
US   1961   112m   bw
(UA) Prometheus (George Justin)
A girl's life and attitudes change after she is raped, and she moves in with a garage mechanic.
A bit of a wallow, with much method acting but no clear analysis of the central relationship.
w Jack Garfein, Alex Karmel novel *Mary Ann* by Alex Karmel d Jack Garfein ph Eugene Schufftan m Aaron Copland ad Richard Day
☆ Carroll Baker, Ralph Meeker, Mildred Dunnock, Charles Watts, Martin Kosleck, Jean Stapleton

Something Wild
US   1986   113m   colour
Orion/Religioso Primitiva Du Art (Jonathan Demme, Kenneth Utt)
🔲 🔍 🎧
Two irresponsible young people find themselves on the run from police and criminals.
Unremarkable melodrama with trendy musical trappings.
w E. Max Frye d Jonathan Demme ph Tak Fujimoto m John Cale, Laurie Anderson
☆ Jeff Daniels, Melanie Griffith, Ray Liotta, Margaret Colin

Sometimes a Great Notion *
US 1971 114m Technicolor Panavision
Universal/Newman-Foreman

GB title: *Never Give an Inch*

In a small Oregon township, trouble is caused by an independent family of lumberjacks.
Freewheeling but unsatisfactorily eccentric comedy-melodrama which never quite jells but has flashes of individuality.
w John Gay *novel* Ken Kesey *d* Paul Newman *ph* Richard Moore *m* Henry Mancini
☆ Paul Newman, Henry Fonda, Lee Remick, Michael Sarrazin, Richard Jaeckel, Linda Lawson, Cliff Potts
♫ song 'All His Children' (*m*Henry Mancini, *ly*Alan and Marilyn Bergman); Richard Jaeckel

Somewhere I'll Find You *
US 1942 108m bw
MGM (Pandro S. Berman)

Brother war correspondents quarrel over a girl and later find her in Indo-China smuggling Chinese babies to safety.
Absurd but satisfactory star vehicle of the second rank, with the theme designed to prepare America for war.
w Marguerite Roberts *story* Charles Hoffman *d* Wesley Ruggles *ph* Harold Rosson *m* Bronislau Kaper
☆ Clark Gable, Lana Turner, Robert Sterling, Patricia Dane, Reginald Owen, Lee Patrick, Charles Dingle, Rags Ragland, William Henry

Somewhere in England
GB 1940 79m bw
Mancunian (John E. Blakeley)

High jinks among army recruits staging a show.
One of a series of misshapen and badly made regional comedies which afflicted British cinemas in the forties and should be mentioned for their immense popularity, their new-style vulgarity (later to be refined by the Carry On series) and their highly popular stars.
w Arthur Mertz, Roney Parsons *d* John E. Blakeley *ph* Geoffrey Faithfull
☆ Frank Randle, Harry Korris, Robbie Vincent, Winki Turner, Dan Young
† Subsequently released, or allowed to escape, between 1941 and 1949 were *Somewhere in Camp*, *Somewhere on Leave*, *Somewhere in Civvies* and *Somewhere in Politics*.

Somewhere in France: see *The Foreman Went to France*

Somewhere in Sonora
GB 1933 58m bw
Warner

A cowboy goes to the aid of his friend, whose son has been kidnapped by an outlaw gang.
John Wayne once more steps into Ken Maynard's boots in a remake of the silent star's unremarkable 1927 Western.
w Joe Roach *novel* *Somewhere South in Sonora* by Will L. Comfort *d* Mack V. Wright
☆ John Wayne, Henry B. Walthall, Shirley Palmer, Paul Fix, Ann Faye, Billy Franey, Ralph Lewis, Frank Rice, J. P. McGowan

Somewhere in the Night *
US 1946 111m bw
TCF (Anderson Lawler)

An amnesiac war veteran tries to discover his true identity and discovers he is a crook with much-wanted information.
Overlong suspenser with a tentative film noir atmosphere. A few nice touches partly atone for a tediously conversational plot.
w Howard Dimsdale, Joseph L. Mankiewicz *story* *The Lonely Journey* by Marvin Borowsky *d* Joseph L. Mankiewicz *ph* Norbert Brodine *m* David Buttolph
☆ John Hodiak, Nancy Guild, Lloyd Nolan, Richard Conte, Josephine Hutchinson, Fritz Kortner

Somewhere in Time *
US 1980 104m Technicolor
Universal/Rastar (Stephen Deutsch)

A playwright falls in love with the photograph of an actress, and finds a way back in time to meet her.

Rather a charming variation on Berkeley Square, but hardly a theme to do well in the hardnosed eighties.
w Richard Matheson *novel* *Bid Time Return* by Richard Matheson *d* Jeannot Szwarc *ph* Isidore Mankofsky *m* John Barry *pd* Seymour Klate *ed* Jeff Gourson *cos* Jean-Pierre Dorleac
☆ Christopher Reeve, Christopher Plummer, Jane Seymour, Teresa Wright, Bill Erwin, George Voskovec, Susan French, John Alvin
'A charming, witty, passionate romantic drama.' – *Variety*
♫ Jean-Pierre Dorleac

Somewhere on Leave
GB 1942 96m bw
Mancunian/F. W. Baker and John E. Blakeley

New recruits in the Army go to spend a weekend in a stately home.
Low-budget comedy that switches from some low comedy music-hall routines and anarchic acrobatic fun from Randle to a stilted, badly acted romance by the young leads; it has a few amusing moments.
w Roney Parsons, Anthony Toner *d* John E. Blakeley, Arthur Mertz *md* Percival Mackey *ad* W. J. Hemsley *ed* E. Richards
☆ Frank Randle, Harry Korris, Dan Young, Robbie Vincent, Toni Lupino, Pat McGrath, Tonie Edgar Bruce

Somewhere Tomorrow
US 1983 87m colour
Blue Marble (Robert Wiemer, Glenn Kershaw)

After watching *Topper* on TV, a girl falls in love with the ghost of a boy killed in a plane crash.
Forgettable teenage romance, over-sentimental for all but the very sweet-toothed.
w*d* Robert Wiemer *ph* Glenn Kershaw *m* Paul Baillargeon *ad* Richard Hoover, Ruth Ammon *ed* Peter Hammer
☆ Sarah Jessica Parker, Nancy Addison, Tom Shea, Rick Weber, Paul Bates

Sommaren med Monika: see *Summer with Monika*

Sommarlek: see *Summer Interlude*

Sommarnattens Leende: see *Smiles of a Summer Night*

Sommersby
US/France 1993 113m Technicolor
Warner/Regency/Canal (Arnon Milchan, Steven Reuther)

After the American Civil War, a man who returns home after a gap of seven years is suspected of being an impostor.
Lush costume piece that never comes to terms with the ambiguity of its story.
w Nicholas Meyer, Sarah Kernochan *d* Jon Amiel *ph* Philippe Rousselot *m* Danny Elfman *pd* Bruno Rubeo *ed* Peter Boyle
☆ Richard Gere, Jodie Foster, Bill Pullman, James Earl Jones, Lanny Flaherty, William Windom, Wendell Wellman, Brett Kelley
'Fails to generate any sense of tragedy or passion, preferring to remain at a distance to the story, mistaking seriousness for profundity and aloofness for sophistication.' – *Jason Drake, Sight and Sound*
† It is a remake of the French film *The Return of Martin Guerre* (qv).

Son of a Gunfighter
US/Spain 1964 90m Metrocolor
Cinemascope
Zurbano/MGM (Lester Welch)

A young Westerner stalks the outlaw responsible for his mother's death.
Tolerable international Western.
w Clarke Reynolds *d* Paul Landres *ph* Manuel Berenguer *md* Frank Barber
☆ Russ Tamblyn, Kieron Moore, James Philbrook, Fernando Rey

Son of Ali Baba
†† US 1952 75m Technicolor
U-I (Leonard Goldstein)

A cadet of the military academy outwits a wicked caliph.
Routine Arabian Nights hokum.

w Gerald Drayson Adams *d* Kurt Neumann *ph* Maury Gertsman *m* Joseph Gershenson
☆ Tony Curtis, Piper Laurie, Susan Cabot, Victor Jory

Son of Blob: see *Beware! The Blob*

Son of Captain Blood
†† Italy/Spain 1962 95m Eastmancolor
Dyaliscope
CCM/BP/Harry Joe Brown

Captain Blood's son routs his father's enemies.
Lively swashbuckler with the original star's son rather unhappily cast.
w Mario Caiano *d* Tulio Demicheli *ph* Alejandro Ulloa *m* Angelo Francesco Lavagnino
☆ Sean Flynn, Ann Todd, Jose Nieto, John Kitzmiller

Son of Dr Jekyll
US 1951 77m bw
Columbia

Dr Jekyll's son worries about developing a split personality, but discovers that his father's supposed friend Dr Lanyon is the spanner in the works.
Irresistibly silly elaboration of a famous story; no thrills but several good unintentional laughs.
w Mortimer Braus, Jack Pollexfen *d* Seymour Friedman *ph* Henry Freulich *m* Paul Sawtell
☆ Louis Hayward, Alexander Knox, Jody Lawrance, Lester Matthews, Paul Cavanagh, Gavin Muir, Rhys Williams

'Searing the screen with new terror!'

Son of Dracula *
US 1943 80m bw
Universal (Ford Beebe)

A mysterious stranger named Alucard, with a penchant for disappearing in puffs of smoke, turns up on a Southern plantation.
Stolid series entry with a miscast lead; nicely handled moments.
w Eric Taylor *d* Robert Siodmak *ph* George Robinson *m* Hans Salter
☆ Lon Chaney Jnr, Louise Allbritton, Robert Paige, Samuel S. Hinds, Evelyn Ankers, Frank Craven, J. Edward Bromberg
† The title cheats: he isn't the son of, but the old man himself …

Son of Flubber
†† US 1963 100m bw
Walt Disney

An inventor tries out a rain-making machine that goes wrong.
Mildly silly comedy with a couple of amusing moments.
d Robert Stevenson *ph* Edward Colman *m* George Bruns
☆ Fred MacMurray, Nancy Olson, Keenan Wynn, Tommy Kirk, Ed Wynn, Charlie Ruggles, Leon Ames, William Demarest, Paul Lynde
† It was a sequel to *The Absent-Minded Professor* (qv).

'The black shadows of the past bred this half-man, half-demon!'

Son of Frankenstein *
US 1939 99m bw
Universal (Rowland V. Lee)

The old baron's son comes home and starts to dabble, with the help of a broken-necked and vindictive shepherd.
Handsomely mounted sequel to Bride of Frankenstein and the last of the classic trio. The monster is less interesting, but there are plenty of other diversions, including the splendid if impractical sets.
w Willis Cooper *d* Rowland V. Lee *ph* George Robinson *m* Frank Skinner *ad* Jack Otterson
☆ Basil Rathbone, Boris Karloff, Bela Lugosi, Lionel Atwill, Josephine Hutchinson, Donnie Dunagan, Emma Dunn, Edgar Norton, Lawrence Grant
'Rather strong material for the top keys, picture will still garner plenty of bookings in the secondary first runs along the main stem.' – *Variety*
'The slickness of production gives a kind of refinement to the horrific moments and a subtlety to the suspense.' – *Film Weekly*

Son of Fury *
†† US 1942 102m bw
TCF (William Perlberg)

An 18th-century Englishman is deprived of his inheritance, flees to a South Sea island but comes back seeking restitution.
Elaborate costumer which suffers from loss of suspense during the central idyll. Much to enjoy along the way.
w Philip Dunne *novel* *Benjamin Blake* by Edison Marshall *d* John Cromwell *ph* Arthur Miller *m* Alfred Newman
☆ Tyrone Power, Gene Tierney, George Sanders, Frances Farmer, Roddy McDowall, John Carradine, Elsa Lanchester, Dudley Digges, Harry Davenport, Halliwell Hobbes
† Remade as *Treasure of the Golden Condor* (qv).

Son of Godzilla
†† Japan 1967 86m colour
Toho Company (Tomoyuki Tanaka)

Intrepid scientists, experimenting with the weather on a remote island, battle against back projections of spiders and a giant mantis as a motherless son is born to Godzilla.
Standard monster hokum, with actors in rubber suits trampling on model buildings.
w Shinichi Sekizawa, Kazue Shiba *d* Jun Fukuda *ph* Kazuo Yamada *m* Masaru Sato *ad* Takeo Kita *ed* Ryohei Fujii
☆ Tadeo Takashima, Bibari Maeda, Akira Kubo, Akihiko Hirata, Kenji Sahara, Yoshio Tsuchiya

Son of Kong *
†† US 1933 69m bw
RKO (Merian C. Cooper)

After Kong has wrecked New York, producer Carl Denham flees from his creditors and finds more monsters on the old island.
Hasty sequel to the splendid King Kong; the results were so tame and unconvincing that the film was sold as a comedy, but it does have a few lively moments after four reels of padding.
w Ruth Rose *d* Ernest B. Schoedsack *ph* Eddie Linden, Vernon Walker, J. O. Taylor *m* Max Steiner *sp* Willis O'Brien
☆ Robert Armstrong, Helen Mack, Frank Reicher, John Marston, Victor Wong
'The sequel to and wash-up of the King Kong theme, consisting of salvaged remnants from the original production … the punch is no longer there.' – *Variety*

Son of Lassie
†† US 1945 100m Technicolor
MGM (Samuel Marx)

A dog follows its young master to the war and helps settle the hash of a few Nazis.
Silly dog story, the first sequel to Lassie Come Home; far too slow to start with, then packed with serial-like action.
w Jeanne Bartlett *d* S. Sylvan Simon *ph* Charles Schoenbaum *m* Herbert Stothart
☆ Peter Lawford, Donald Crisp, June Lockhart, Nigel Bruce, Leon Ames, Nils Asther
'Good old sentimental hokum.' – *Variety*

Son of Monte Cristo *
†† US 1940 102m bw
(UA)

The masked avenger who quashes a dictatorship in 1865 Lichtenstein is none other than the son of Edmond Dantes.
Cheerful swashbuckler of the second class.
w George Bruce *d* Rowland V. Lee *ph* George Robinson *m* Edward Ward *ad* John DuCasse Schulze
☆ Louis Hayward, Joan Bennett, George Sanders, Florence Bates, Lionel Royce, Montagu Love, Clayton Moore, Ralph Byrd
♫ art direction

Son of Paleface *
†† US 1952 95m Technicolor
(Paramount) Bob Hope (Robert L. Welch)

A tenderfoot and a government agent compete for the attentions of a lady bandit.
Gagged-up sequel to The Paleface; much of the humour now seems self-conscious and dated in the

Road tradition which it apes, but there are still moments of delight.

w Frank Tashlin, Joseph Quillan, Robert L. Welch d Frank Tashlin ph Harry J. Wild m Lyn Murray ☆ Bob Hope, Roy Rogers, Jane Russell, Trigger, Douglass Dumbrille, Harry von Zell, Bill Williams, Lloyd Corrigan

♬ song 'Am I in Love' (m/ly Jack Brooks)

Son of Robin Hood

👫 GB 1958 77m Eastmancolor
Cinemascope
TCF/Argo (George Sherman)

Robin's daughter joins with the Regent's brother to overthrow the Black Duke.

Empty-headed romp, more or less in the accepted tradition.

w George George, George Slavin d George Sherman ph Arthur Grant m Leighton Lucas ☆ David Hedison, June Laverick, David Farrar, Marius Goring, Philip Friend, Delphi Lawrence, George Coulouris, George Woodbridge

Son of Sinbad *

👫 US 1955 88m Technicolor
Superscope
RKO (Robert Sparks)

Sinbad and Omar Khayyam are imprisoned by the Caliph but escape with the secret of green fire.

Arabian Nights burlesque, mainly quite bright, with the forty thieves played by harem girls.

w Aubrey Wisberg, Jack Pollexfen d Ted Tetzlaff ph William Snyder m Victor Young ☆ Dale Robertson, Vincent Price, Sally Forrest, Lili St Cyr, Mari Blanchard, Leon Askin, Jay Novello

Son of the Gods

US 1930 90m bw
First National

A Chinaman falls in love with a white girl ... but turns out not to be a Chinaman after all.

Antediluvian miscegenation melodrama with an unconvincing twist.

w Bradley King novel Rex Beach d Frank Lloyd ☆ Richard Barthelmess, Constance Bennett, Geneva Mitchell, E. Alyn Warren

'High-class general programme release.' – Variety

'Clumsy has a colour all its own.'

Son of the Pink Panther

US 1993 93m DeLuxe
MGM/UA/Filmauro (Tony Adams)

A French policeman, the illegitimate son of Inspector Clouseau, hinders the investigation of the kidnapping of a princess by terrorists.

Benigni, a natural clown with splendidly fractured English, was an ideal choice, if one had to be made, to take over the role of a bumbling policeman in the Pink Panther series – but that had already become lacking in inspiration during Peter Sellers's time and now its condition is terminal; even natural clowns need good material.

w Blake Edwards, Steve Sunshine, Madeline Sunshine d Blake Edwards ph Dick Bush m Henry Mancini pd Peter Mullins ed Robert Pergament ☆ Roberto Benigni, Herbert Lom, Debrah Farentino, Claudia Cardinale, Robert Davi, Burt Kwouk, Graham Stark, Oliver Cotton, Anton Rodgers

'A tired pastiche of recycled sketches and gags.' – Variety

'An eye feast of virile action, colourful settings and glowing climaxes!'

The Son of the Sheik *

US 1926 74m bw silent
(UA)

Ahmed protects a dancing girl from a band of renegades.

Tongue-in-cheek desert romp which was probably its star's best film. He plays a dual role of father and son.

w Frances Marion, George Marion Jnr, Frederick Gresac d George Fitzmaurice m (1934 sound version) Jack Ward ☆ Rudolph Valentino, Vilma Banky, Agnes Ayres

'The very picture for which the world's wife, mother and daughter have been waiting!' – Louella Parsons

---

'We expect every fan in the country to be saying: It is Rudy's best. We can never forget him.' – Photoplay

Sonatine

Canada 1983 92m colour
Corporation Image/M & M (Pierre Gendron)

Two teenage girls form tentative relationships with older men before joining in a public suicide pact.

Trite tale of teenagers unable to make contact with a wider world than themselves.

wd Micheline Lanctôt ph Guy Dufaux m François Lanctôt ed Louise Surprenant ☆ Pascale Bussieres, Marcia Pilote, Pierre Fauteux, Kliment Dentchev

Sonatine *

Japan 1993 93m colour
ICA/Bandai/Shochiku Dai-ichi Kogyo (Masayuki Mori, Hisao Nabeshima, Takio Yoshida)

A violent Tokyo gangster, sent to intervene in a gang war in Okinawa, realizes that he has made a mistake and, after relaxing at the seaside with his gang, faces a final showdown.

An odd gangster movie, violent and downbeat, but also veering away from the genre into casual moments of fun and games.

wd Takeshi Kitano ph Katsumi Yanagishima m Joe Hisaishi ad Osamu Sasaki ed Takeshi Kitano ☆ 'Beat' Takeshi (Takeshi Kitano), Aya Kokumai, Tetsu Watanabe, Masanobu Katsumura, Susumu Terashima, Ren Ohsugi, Tonbo Zushi, Kenichi Yajima

'Pic's combo of dry humor, sudden bursts of violence, and world-weary romanticism will take a while to build for first-time viewers of Kitano's movies, and the jigsaw of plot and characters only takes recognisable shape about halfway in.' – Variety

Söndags Barn: see Sunday's Children

The Son-Daughter

US 1932 79m bw
MGM

True love among the San Francisco Chinese is affected by warring Tongs.

Ill-advised oriental romance which failed to please.

w Claudine West, Leon Gordon, John Goodrich play David Belasco, George Scarborough d Clarence Brown ☆ Ramon Novarro, Helen Hayes, Lewis Stone, Warner Oland, Ralph Morgan, H. B. Warner, Louise Closser Hale

'Old-time stuff, moving slowly and laboriously towards a sad climax.' – Variety

The Song and Dance Man

US 1936 72m bw
TCF

A vaudeville dancer goes on the skids but turns up when his former partner needs him.

Hokey backstage drama with interesting detail.

w Maude Fulton play George M. Cohan d Allan Dwan ☆ Paul Kelly, Claire Trevor, Michael Whalen, Ruth Donnelly, James Burke

A Song Is Born *

US 1948 113m Technicolor
Samuel Goldwyn

Flat remake of Ball of Fire (qv), graced by an array of top-flight musical talent.

w Harry Tugend d Howard Hawks ph Gregg Toland m Hugo Friedhofer md Emil Newman songs Don Raye, Gene de Paul ☆ Danny Kaye, Virginia Mayo, Hugh Herbert, Steve Cochran, Felix Bressart, J. Edward Bromberg, Mary Field, Ludwig Stossel, Louis Armstrong, Charlie Barnet, Benny Goodman, Lionel Hampton, Tommy Dorsey, Mel Powell

Song o' My Heart

US 1930 85m bw
Fox

A professional singer looks after the orphaned children of his former love.

A thin story is the excuse for a great tenor to sing eleven songs.

w Tom Barry, J. J. McCarthy d Frank Borzage ☆ John McCormack, Maureen O'Sullivan, John Garrick, J. M. Kerrigan, Alice Joyce

---

'A simple tale charmingly told ... sitting through it is no hardship.' – Variety

'We're going to see Jennifer Jones again in...'

The Song of Bernadette **

US 1943 156m bw
TCF (William Perlberg)

A peasant girl has a vision of the Virgin Mary at what becomes the shrine of Lourdes.

Hollywood religiosity at its most commercial; but behind the lapses of taste and truth is an excellent production which was phenomenally popular and created a new star.

w George Seaton novel Franz Werfel d Henry King ph Arthur Miller m Alfred Newman ad James Basevi, William Darling ed Barbara McLean ☆ Jennifer Jones, William Eythe, Charles Bickford, Vincent Price, Lee J. Cobb, Gladys Cooper, Anne Revere, Roman Bohnen, Patricia Morison, Aubrey Mather, Charles Dingle, Mary Anderson, Edith Barrett, Sig Rumann

PROLOGUE: 'For those who believe in God, no explanation is necessary. For those who do not believe in God, no explanation is possible.'

'A tamed and pretty image, highly varnished, sensitively lighted, and exhibited behind immaculate glass, the window at once of a shrine and of a box office.' – James Agee

'It contains much to conciliate even the crustiest and most prejudiced objector.' – Richard Mallett, Punch

♟ Arthur Miller; Alfred Newman; Jennifer Jones; James Basevi, William Darling
♬ best picture; George Seaton; Henry King; Charles Bickford; Gladys Cooper; Anne Revere; Barbara McLean

Song of Ceylon **

GB 1934 40m bw
Ceylon Tea Board (John Grierson)

A pictorial, almost sensuous, but not very informative documentary in four sections: 'The Buddha', 'The Virgin Island', 'The Voices of Commerce', 'The Apparel of a God'. Its influence was immense.

m Walter Leigh wd/ph Basil Wright

Song of Freedom *

GB 1936 80m bw
Hammer (J. Fraser Passmore)

A black London docker becomes an opera singer, then goes to Africa to free the tribe of which he has discovered himself to be the head.

A weird fable but a good star vehicle and a surprisingly smart production for the time.

w Fenn Sherie, Ingram d'Abbes, Michael Barringer, Philip Lindsay d J. Elder Wills ph Eric Cross ☆ Paul Robeson, Elizabeth Welch, George Mozart, Esmé Percy

'The direction is distinguished but not above reproach, the story is sentimental and absurd, and yet a sense stays in the memory of an unsophisticated mind fumbling on the edge of simple and popular poetry.' – Graham Greene

Song of India

US 1949 77m bw
Columbia (Albert S. Rogell)

An Indian prince protects his land against a big game hunter.

Not much singing, but lots of animals and a fight with knives: tolerable programme filler.

w Art Arthur, Kenneth Perkins d Albert S. Rogell ☆ Sabu, Gail Russell, Turhan Bey, Anthony Caruso, Aminta Dyne, Fritz Leiber

Song of Love *

US 1947 118m bw
MGM (Clarence Brown)

The story of Clara and Robert Schumann and their friend Johannes Brahms.

Dignified musical biopic which unfortunately falls into most of the pitfall clichés of the genre. Dull it may be, but it looks good and the music is fine.

w Ivan Tors, Irmgard von Cube, Allen Vincent, Robert Ardrey d Clarence Brown ph Harry Stradling md Bronislau Kaper ad Cedric Gibbons piano Artur Rubinstein

---

☆ Katharine Hepburn, Paul Henreid, Robert Walker, Henry Daniell, Leo G. Carroll, Elsa Janssen, Gigi Perreau

'This is how Brahms and the Schumanns might very possibly have acted if they had realized that later on they would break into the movies.' – Time

Song of Norway *

US 1970 141m DeLuxe Super Panavision 70
ABC/Andrew and Virginia Stone

A fantasia on the life of Grieg.

Multinational hodgepodge, mostly in the Sound of Music style but with everything from cartoons to Christmas cracker backgrounds. Quite watchable, and the landscapes are certainly splendid.

wd Andrew Stone play Homer Curran stage musical Milton Lazarus (book), Robert Wright, George Forrest (m/ly) ph Davis Boulton md Roland Shaw ad William Albert Havemeyer ed Virginia Lively Stone ☆ Toralv Maurstad, Florence Henderson, Christina Schollin, Frank Porretta, Harry Secombe, Edward G. Robinson, Robert Morley, Elizabeth Larner, Bernard Archard, Oscar Homolka, Richard Wordsworth

Song of Russia

US 1944 107m bw
MGM (Joe Pasternak)

An American symphony conductor is in Russia when hostilities begin, and watches the citizens' war effort with admiration.

A terrible big-budget film which followed the wartime propaganda line but five years later was heavily criticized by the Unamerican Activities Committee (for the wrong reasons).

w Paul Jarrico, Richard Collins d Gregory Ratoff ph Harry Stradling m Herbert Stothart ☆ Robert Taylor, Susan Peters, John Hodiak, Robert Benchley, Felix Bressart, Michael Chekhov, Darryl Hickman

'Film makers have evolved a new tongue – the broken accent deriving from no known language to be used by foreigners on all occasions.' – Richard Winnington

'MGM performs the neatest trick of the week by leaning over backward in Russia's favour without once swaying from right to left.' – Newsweek

Song of Scheherezade

US 1947 107m Technicolor
Universal (Edward Kaufman)

In 1865 naval cadet Rimsky-Korsakov falls in love with a dancer.

Yet another composer takes a drubbing in this dull and unconvincing hodgepodge.

wd Walter Reisch ph Hal Mohr, William V. Skall md Miklos Rozsa ch Tilly Losch ad Jack Otterson ☆ Yvonne de Carlo, Jean-Pierre Aumont, Brian Donlevy, Eve Arden, Charles Kullman, John Qualen, Richard Lane, Terry Kilburn

'One of the world's great love stories comes to the star who can make it live!'

Song of Songs

US 1933 89m bw
Paramount (Rouben Mamoulian)

A German peasant girl falls for a sculptor but marries a lecherous baron.

Pretentious romantic nonsense, made fairly palatable by the director's steady hand.

w Leo Birinsky, Samuel Hoffenstein play Edward Sheldon novel Das hohe Lied by Herman Sudermann d Rouben Mamoulian ph Victor Milner m Karl Hajos, Milan Rodern ad Hans Dreier ☆ Marlene Dietrich, Brian Aherne, Lionel Atwill, Alison Skipworth, Hardie Albright

'An ornate and irresistible slice of outright hokum.' – Peter John Dyer, 1966

'From the moment she heard this strange, compelling music of love – she was lost!'

Song of Surrender

US 1949 93m bw
Paramount (Richard Maibaum)

In turn-of-the-century New England, a sophisticated visitor from New York falls for the wife of the museum curator.

Ho-hum romantic drama, well enough presented.

👫 film suitable for family viewing   📼 VHS video-cassette for the British PAL system   📼 VHS video-cassette for the British PAL system in wide screen-format   ♻ Video cassette in a computer-colourised version   🎞 American NTSC video-cassette   💿 Laser disc

w Richard Maibaum *d* Mitchell Leisen
ph Daniel L. Fapp *m* Victor Young
☆ Wanda Hendrix, Claude Rains, Macdonald Carey, Andrea King, Henry Hull, Elizabeth Patterson, Art Smith

Song of the City
US 1937 73m bw
MGM (Lucien Hubbard)
Italian fisherfolk in San Francisco pull a socialite out of the bay and make a man of him.
Unlikely and unlovable moral tale, full of warmhearted simple people.
w Michael Fessier *d* Errol Taggart
☆ Margaret Lindsay, Jeffrey Dean, J. Carrol Naish, Nat Pendleton, Stanley Morner, Edward Norris
'Elemental stuff with some nice photography but needs bolstering for b.o. allure.' – *Variety*

Song of the Eagle
US 1933 65m bw
Paramount (Charles S. Rogers)
Racketeers try to control the supply of beer both after and during prohibition.
Tolerable crime/family saga which becomes sentimental.
w Casey Robinson, Willard Mack, Gene Towne, Graham Baker *d* Ralph Murphy
☆ Charles Bickford, Richard Arlen, Jean Hersholt, Mary Brian, Louise Dresser, George E. Stone, Andy Devine
'Fairly good programmer and timely. What hurts is the title. Remember Animal Kingdom.' – *Variety*

Song of the Islands *
US 1942 75m Technicolor
TCF (William Le Baron)
On a South Sea island, the daughter of an Irish beachcomber falls for the son of an American cattle king.
Wispy musical with agreeable settings and lively songs.
w Joseph Schrank, Robert Pirosh, Robert Ellis, Helen Logan *d* Walter Lang *ph* Ernest Palmer *md* Alfred Newman *songs* various
☆ Betty Grable, Victor Mature, Jack Oakie, Thomas Mitchell, Hilo Hattie, Billy Gilbert, George Barbier

Song of the Open Road
US 1944 93m bw
UA (Charles R. Rogers)
A dissatisfied child movie star goes off to help volunteers to save a tomato crop.
Thin youth drama enlivened by a putting-on-a-show finale.
w Albert Mannheimer *d* S. Sylvan Simon
☆ Jane Powell, Bonita Granville, Jackie Moran, W. C. Fields, Edgar Bergen and Charlie McCarthy, Sammy Kaye and his orchestra
♬ Charles Previn (music direction); song 'Too Much in Love' (*m*Walter Kent, *ly*Kim Gannon)

Song of the Road *
GB 1937 73m bw
UK Films
Laid off when the firm they work for goes over to lorries, a man and his cart-horse travel through a Britain that is becoming mechanized, looking for work.
Sentimental, idealized account of a country at peace with itself and its institutions; it has a gentle charm in its narrative of a simple, honourable man putting the world to rights.
d John Baxter
☆ Bransby Williams, Ernest Butcher, Muriel George, Davy Burnaby, Tod Slaughter, John Turnbull

Song of the South *
👥 US 1946 94m Technicolor
Walt Disney (Perce Pearce)
On a long-ago Southern plantation, small boys listen to the Brer Rabbit stories from an elderly black servant.
Too much Uncle Remus and not enough Brer Rabbit, we fear, but children liked it. The cartoons were actually very good.
w Dalton Raymond *d* Harve Foster, Wilfred Jackson *ph* Gregg Toland *m* Daniele Amfitheatrof, Paul J. Smith, Charles Wolcott
cartoon credits various

☆ Ruth Warrick, Bobby Driscoll, James Baskett, Luana Patten, Lucile Watson, Hattie McDaniel
'The ratio of live to cartoon action is approximately two to one, and that is the ratio of the film's mediocrity to its charm.' – *Bosley Crowther*
♬ song 'Zip-a-Dee-Do-Dah' (*m*Allie Wrubel, *ly*Ray Gilbert); James Baskett (special award)
₰ Daniele Amfitheatrof, Paul J. Smith, Charles Wolcott

A Song to Remember **
US 1944 113m Technicolor
Columbia (Louis F. Edelman)
The life and death of Chopin and his liaison with George Sand.
Hilarious classical musical biopic which was unexpectedly popular and provoked a flood of similar pieces. As a production, not at all bad, but the script…
w Sidney Buchman *d* Charles Vidor *ph* Tony Gaudio, Allan M. Davey *md* Miklos Rozsa, Morris Stoloff *ad* Lionel Banks, Van Nest Polglase *ed* Charles Nelson *piano* José Iturbi
☆ Cornel Wilde, Merle Oberon, Paul Muni, Stephen Bekassy, Nina Foch, George Coulouris, Sig Arno, Howard Freeman, George Macready
'It is the business of Hollywood to shape the truth into box-office contours.' – *Richard Winnington*
'This glorious picture is a major event in film history.' – *Hollywood Reporter*
'As infuriating and funny a misrepresentation of an artist's life and work as I have seen.' – *James Agee*
₰ original story (Ernst Marischka); Tony Gaudio, Allen M. Davey; Miklos Rozsa, Morris Stoloff; Cornel Wilde; Charles Nelson

Song without End
US 1960 142m Eastmancolor
Cinemascope
Columbia (William Goetz)
The life and loves of Franz Liszt.
What worked at the box-office for Chopin failed disastrously for Liszt; famous people are turned into papier mâché dullards. Again, the production is elegance itself.
w Oscar Millard *d* Charles Vidor, George Cukor *ph* James Wong Howe *md* Morris Stoloff, Henry Sukman *ad* Walter Holscher *piano* Jorge Bolet
☆ Dirk Bogarde, Capucine, Genevieve Page, Patricia Morison, Ivan Desny, Martita Hunt, Lyndon Brook, Alex Davion
♬ Morris Stoloff, Henry Sukman

Songwriter
US 1984 94m Metrocolor
Tri-Star (Sydney Pollack)
Adventures of a country-music duo.
Very moderate entertainment which gives the impression of stars doing their own thing.
w Bud Shrake *d* Alan Rudolph *ph* Matthew Leonetti *m* Kris Kristofferson *pd* Joel Schiller *ed* Stuart Pappe
☆ Willie Nelson, Kris Kristofferson, Melinda Dillon, Rip Torn, Lesley Ann Warren, Richard C. Sarafian
₰ Kris Kristofferson (for music)

Son-in-Law
US 1993 95m Technicolor
Buena Vista/Hollywood Pictures (Michael Rotenberg, Peter M. Lenkov)
A girl takes her Californian boyfriend home to the family farm for Thanksgiving.
A sickly, oversweet comedy featuring an antic, unfunny comedian caught in direly predictable situations.
w Fax Bahr, Adam Small, Shawn Schepps *story* Patrick J. Clifton, Susan McMartin, Peter Lenkov *d* Steve Rash *ph* Peter Deming *m* Richard Gibbs *pd* Joseph T. Garrity *ed* Dennis M. Hill
☆ Pauly Shore, Carla Gugino, Lane Smith, Cindy Pickett, Mason Adams, Patrick Renna, Dennis Burkley
'You'd have to dig way back to the likes of Sleep 'n' Eat and the Bowery Boys' Huntz Hall to find a moron-funnyman persona as irksome as Pauly Shore's.' – *Variety*

Sono Otoko Kyobo ni Tsuki: see *Violent Cop*

Sons *
US 1989 88m DuArt
Pacific (Marc Toberoff)
Three warring brothers take their father, unable to speak or walk after a stroke, to Normandy to find the Frenchwoman he loved when he was a soldier during the Second World War.
Meandering, episodic movie of sibling conflicts with a few flashes of insight and originality.
w Alexandre Rockwell, Brandon Cole *d* Alexandre Rockwell *ph* Stefan Czapsky *m* Mader *pd* Virginia Fields *ed* Jay Freund
☆ William Forsythe, D. B. Sweeney, Robert Miranda, Samuel Fuller, Stéphane Audran, Judith Godreche, William Hickey, Jennifer Beals, Shirley Stoller, Bernard Fresson

'The first experiences of a young man in the mysteries of woman!'

Sons and Lovers ***
GB 1960 103m bw Cinemascope
TCF/Company of Artists/Jerry Wald
A Nottingham miner's son learns about life and love.
Well-produced and generally absorbing, if unsurprising, treatment of a famous novel.
w Gavin Lambert, T. E. B. Clarke *novel* D. H. Lawrence *d* Jack Cardiff *ph* Freddie Francis *m* Mario Nascimbene *ad* Tom Morahan
☆ Dean Stockwell, Trevor Howard, Wendy Hiller, Mary Ure, Heather Sears, William Lucas, Donald Pleasence, Ernest Thesiger
'An album of decent Edwardian snapshots.' – *Peter John Dyer*
'A rare, remarkable and courageous film.' – *Daily Herald*
♬ Freddie Francis
₰ best picture; script; Jack Cardiff; Trevor Howard; Mary Ure; art direction

Sons o' Guns
US 1936 79m bw
Warner
A Broadway dancer in uniform finds himself accidentally enlisted and sent to France.
Among the better comedies of this star.
w Julius J. Epstein, Jerry Wald *d* Lloyd Bacon
☆ Joe E. Brown, Joan Blondell, Eric Blore, Wini Shaw, Robert Barrat

The Sons of Katie Elder *
US 1965 122m Technicolor Panavision
Paramount/Hal B. Wallis (Paul Nathan)
At Katie Elder's funeral, her four troublesome wandering sons find themselves on the verge of further trouble.
Sluggish all-star Western with predictable highlights.
w Allan Weiss, William H. Wright, Harry Essex *d* Henry Hathaway *ph* Lucien Ballard *m* Elmer Bernstein
☆ John Wayne, Dean Martin, Michael Anderson Jnr, Earl Holliman, Martha Hyer, Jeremy Slate, James Gregory, George Kennedy, Paul Fix

Sons of the Desert ****
👥 US 1934 68m bw
Hal Roach
GB title: Fraternally Yours
Stan and Ollie want to go to a Chicago convention, but kid their wives that they are going on a cruise for health reasons.
Archetypal Laurel and Hardy comedy, unsurpassed for gags, pacing and sympathetic characterization.
w Frank Craven, Byron Morgan *d* William A. Seiter *ph* Kenneth Peach *m/ly* Marvin Hatley *ed* Bert Jordan
☆ Stan Laurel, Oliver Hardy, Charley Chase, Mae Busch, Dorothy Christie, Lucien Littlefield
'Funny all the way through.' – *New York Times*

Sons of the Musketeers: see *At Sword's Point*

Sons of the Sea: see *Atlantic Ferry (1941)*

Sons of the Sea
GB 1939 82m Dufaycolor
British Consolidated
Life at the Royal Naval College in Dartmouth.

Simple-minded recruiter with a top dressing of spy stuff: naïve but well liked at the time.
w Gerald Elliott, Maurice Elvey, D. William Woolf, George Barraud *d* Maurice Elvey
☆ Leslie Banks, Mackenzie Ward, Kay Walsh, Simon Lack, Cecil Parker, Ellen Pollock, Nigel Stock

Sophie's Choice *
US 1982 157m Technicolor
Universal/AFD/ITC/Keith Barish
In 1947, a Polish girl who has been in a concentration camp finds that her past still haunts her in New York.
Glum romantic drama about guilt and retribution, long and uncinematic as well as rather poorly done; but its intentions are doubtless honourable.
wd Alan J. Pakula *novel* William Styron *ph* Nestor Almendros *m* Marvin Hamlisch *pd* George Jenkins *ed* Evan Lottman
☆ Meryl Streep, Kevin Kline, Peter MacNicol, Rita Karin, Stephen D. Newman, Josh Mostel
'Handsome, doggedly faithful and astoundingly tedious.' – *Variety*
'Not boring, simply unilluminating. By the end, only one question remains: why did Pakula have to make this movie?' – *Sight and Sound*
♬ Meryl Streep
₰ screenplay (adaptation); cinematography; costume design; music

Sophie's Place: see *Crooks and Coronets*

Sorcerer
US 1977 121m Technicolor
Universal/Film Properties International (William Friedkin)
GB title: Wages of Fear
Volunteers are needed to drive nitro-glycerine to an outpost in the South American jungle.
Why anyone should have wanted to spend twenty million dollars on a remake of The Wages of Fear, do it badly, and give it a misleading title is anybody's guess. The result is dire.
w Walon Green *novel* Georges Arnaud (and the film by Henri-Georges Clouzot) *d* William Friedkin *m* John M. Stephens, Dick Bush *m* Tangerine Dream, Keith Jarrett, Charlie Parker *pd* John Box
☆ Roy Scheider, Bruno Cremer, Francisco Rabal, Amidou, Ramon Bieri
♬ sound

The Sorcerers
GB 1967 85m Eastmancolor
Tigon/Curtwel/Global (Patrick Curtis, Tony Tenser)
An old couple find a way of regaining their youth through hypnotizing a young man to do their bidding.
Rather slight but oddly memorable horror film, with an elegant old lady becoming the real monster.
w Michael Reeves, Tom Baker, John Burke *d* Michael Reeves *ph* Stanley Long *m* Paul Ferris
☆ Boris Karloff, Catherine Lacey, Ian Ogilvy, Elizabeth Ercy, Victor Henry, Susan George, Meier Tzelniker

Les Sorcières de Salem: see *The Witches of Salem*

La Sorella di Satana: see *She Beast*

Sorok Pervyi: see *The Forty First*

Sorority Girl
US 1957 61m bw
AIP/Sunset (Roger Corman)
A poor little rich college girl feels alienated from her mother and her contemporaries.
Corman's campus exploitation movie is positively middle-aged in its stodgy approach, with a cast that looks far too old and a script mouldering with aged clichés.
w Ed Waters *story* Leo Lieberman *d* Roger Corman *ph* Monroe P. Askins *m* Ronald Stein *ed* Charles Gross Jnr
☆ Susan Cabot, Dick Miller, Barboura O'Neill, June Kenney, Barbara Crane, Fay Baker, Jeanne Wood, Joan Lora

Sorrell and Son

GB 1933 97m bw

B and D/Herbert Wilcox

When his wife leaves them, a man devotes his life to his worthless son.

Fair picturization of a popular novel.

w Lydia Hayward *novel* Warwick Deeping d Jack Raymond ph Cyril Bristow

☆ H. B. Warner, Hugh Williams, Winifred Shotter, Margot Grahame, Donald Calthrop, Louis Hayward

'Insufficient in action for the average American screen devotee.' – *Variety*

† H. B. Warner played the same role in the silent version of 1927.

Sorrowful Jones

US 1949 88m bw

Paramount (Robert L. Welch)

A racetrack tout unofficially adopts an orphan girl.

Heavy-going sentimental comedy peopled by comic gangsters, a remake of Little Miss Marker with the emphasis changed.

w Melville Shavelson, Edmund Hartmann, Jack Rose *story* Damon Runyon d Sidney Lanfield ph Daniel L. Fapp m Robert Emmett Dolan

☆ Bob Hope, Lucille Ball, William Demarest, Bruce Cabot, Thomas Gomez, Tom Pedi, Houseley Stevenson, Mary Jane Saunders

The Sorrows of Satan *

US 1926 115m bw silent

Famous Players/Paramount

A struggling writer accepts success in the form of a fortune offered to him by a prince who is in fact Satan.

Smooth Faust derivative with a few choice scenes of special effects.

w Forrest Halsey, John Russell, George Hull *novel* Marie Corelli d D. W. Griffith (who didn't want to do it)

☆ Adolphe Menjou, Ricardo Cortez, Lya de Putti, Carol Dempster, Ivan Lebedeff

Sorry, Wrong Number **

US 1948 89m bw

Paramount (Hal B. Wallis, Anatole Litvak)

A bedridden neurotic woman discovers she is marked for murder and tries to summon help.

Artificial but effective suspenser, extended from a radio play.

w Lucille Fletcher *play* Lucille Fletcher d Anatole Litvak ph Sol Polito m Franz Waxman ed Warren Low

☆ Barbara Stanwyck, Burt Lancaster, Ann Richards, Wendell Corey, Ed Begley, Harold Vermilyea, Leif Erickson, William Conrad

'The people who made it ... have tried to do just one thing – to thrill. This they have triumphantly done.' – *James Monahan*

⧓ Barbara Stanwyck

SOS Iceberg *

US 1933 117m bw

Universal

A young scientist seeks to recover the records of the lost Wegener expedition to the Arctic.

At the time this was a spectacular semi-documentary, but it did no business.

w Tom Reed, Edwin H. Knopf d Tay Garnett

☆ Rod la Rocque, Leni Riefenstahl, Sepp Rist, Gibson Gowland

† The production was begun in Berlin and taken over by Universal when the producers ran out of money.

SOS Pacific *

GB 1959 91m bw

Rank/Sydney Box (John Nasht, Patrick Filmer-Sankey)

Survivors of a Pacific plane crash await rescue on a small island which is the site of an imminent H-bomb test.

Satisfactory open-air thick ear with strongly deployed types and a suspense climax.

w Robert Westerby d Guy Green ph Wilkie Cooper m Georges Auric

☆ Eddie Constantine, Pier Angeli, John Gregson, Richard Attenborough, Eva Bartok, Clifford Evans, Jean Anderson, Cec Linder

Soshun: see *Early Spring*

Sotto Gli Occhi Dell'Assassino: see *Tenebrae*

Le Souffle au Coeur ***

France/Italy/West Germany 1971 118m colour

NEF/Marianne Films/Video Films/Seitz (Maurice Urbain)

US title: *Murmur of the Heart*

aka: *Dearest Love*

Recovering from an illness at a spa, a 15-year-old boy overcomes his sexual problems after sleeping, almost inadvertently, with his mother.

A witty and observant study of middle-class attitudes to love, sex and adolescent traumas, with incest forming a minor theme.

wd Louis Malle ph Ricardo Aronovich m Gaston Frèche, Sidney Bechet, Henri Renaud, Charlie Parker pd Jean-Jacques Caziot, Philippe Turlure ed Suzanne Baron

☆ Léa Massari, Benoit Ferreux, Daniel Gelin, Michel Lonsdale, Ave Ninchi, Gila von Weitershausen

⧓ Louis Malle (writer)

Soul Food

US 1997 114m DeLuxe

TCF (Tracey E. Edmonds, Robert Teitel)

A family group, of three sisters and their husbands, begins to disintegrate when their mother sickens and dies.

An unimaginative, familiar domestic drama, set around a ritual of Sunday lunches, in which squabbling siblings are finally reconciled.

wd George Tillman ph Paul Elliott m Wendy Melvoin, Lisa Coleman pd Maxine Shepard ed John Carter

☆ Vanessa L. Williams, Vivica A. Fox, Nia Long, Michael Beach, Mekhi Phifer, Brandon Hammond, Jeffrey D. Sams, Gina Ravera, Irma P. Hall, Carl Wright

'A rich tapestry of characters and stories deftly woven together to create an engaging and satisfying drama. Colourful, observant and refreshingly free from cliché.' – *James Cameron-Wilson, Film Review*

Soul in the Hole *

US 1995 99m colour

Metrodome/Asphalt (Lilibert Foster)

In Brooklyn in 1993, an amateur coach leads his street basketball team to some famous victories.

An interesting documentary on a street culture that offers a means of escape from the ghetto.

d Danielle Gardner ph Paul Gibson ed Melissa Neidich

☆ Kenny Jones, Ed Smith, Gary Sims, Javone Moore, Braheen Cotton, Charles Jones, Dennis Miller

The Soul Kiss: see *A Lady's Morals*

Soul Man

US 1986 101m Technicolor Panavision

New World (Steve Tisch)

A white student tans his skin to win a black scholarship to law school.

Despite its premise, basically a farce of mistaken identities rather than a treatment of racism.

w Carol Black d Steve Miner ph Jeffrey Jur m Tom Scott pd Greg Fonseca ed David Finfer

☆ C. Thomas Howell, Rae Dawn Chong, Arye Gross, Melora Hardin, James B. Sikking, Leslie Nielsen, James Earl Jones

The Soul of a Monster

US 1944 61m bw

Columbia (Ted Richmond)

A rich man is saved from death by a female hypnotist, who keeps him under her spell.

Unusual but not very interesting thriller.

w Edward Dein d Will Jason

☆ Rose Hobart, George Macready, Jim Bannon, Jeanne Bates

'Out of the secret annals of the sea comes the strangest story ever told!'

Souls at Sea *

US 1937 93m bw

Paramount (Henry Hathaway)

In a 19th-century shipwreck an intelligence officer must save himself, and his mission, at the cost of other lives, and is courtmartialled.

A lively seafaring melodrama produced on a fairly impressive scale.

w Grover Jones, Dale Van Every d Henry Hathaway ph Charles Lang Jnr m Milan Roder, W. Franke Harling md Boris Morros ad Hans Dreier, Roland Anderson

☆ Gary Cooper, George Raft, Frances Dee, Henry Wilcoxon, Harry Carey, Olympe Bradna, Robert Cummings, Porter Hall, George Zucco, Virginia Weidler, Joseph Schildkraut, Gilbert Emery

'First rate slave ship adventure.' – *Variety*

⧓ Milan Roder, W. Franke Harling; art direction

The Sound and the Fury

US 1959 117m Eastmancolor

Cinemascope

TCF/Jerry Wald

A once proud Southern family has sunk low in finance and moral stature, and a stern elder son tries to do something about it.

Heavy melodrama with performances to match.

w Irving Ravetch, Harriet Frank Jnr *novel* William Faulkner d Martin Ritt ph Charles G. Clarke m Alex North

☆ Yul Brynner, Joanne Woodward, Margaret Leighton, Stuart Whitman, Ethel Waters, Jack Warden, Françoise Rosay, John Beal, Albert Dekker

'A fourth carbon copy of Chekhov in Dixie.' – *Stanley Kauffmann*

The Sound Barrier **

GB 1952 118m bw

London Films (David Lean)

US title: *Breaking the Sound Barrier*

An aircraft manufacturer takes risks with the lives of his family and friends to prove that the sound barrier can be broken.

Riveting, then topical, melodrama with splendid air sequences; a bit upper crust, but with well-drawn characters.

w Terence Rattigan d David Lean ph Jack Hildyard m Malcolm Arnold

☆ Ralph Richardson, Nigel Patrick, Ann Todd, John Justin, Dinah Sheridan, Joseph Tomelty, Denholm Elliott

'The most exciting film about the air that has ever been produced anywhere.' – *Daily Express*

'A peacetime film as exciting as any wartime one.' – *Sunday Dispatch*

⧓ Terence Rattigan

▽ best film; best British film; Ralph Richardson

The Sound of Fury: see *Try and Get Me*

The Sound of Music ***

⫰⫰ US 1965 172m DeLuxe Todd-AO

TCF/Argyle (Robert Wise)

In 1938 Austria, a trainee nun becomes governess to the Trapp family, falls in love with the widower father, and helps them all escape from the Nazis.

Slightly muted, very handsome version of an enjoyably old-fashioned stage musical with splendid tunes.

w Ernest Lehman *book* Howard Lindsay, Russel Crouse d Robert Wise ph Ted McCord m/ly Richard Rodgers, Oscar Hammerstein II md Irwin Kostal pd Boris Leven

☆ Julie Andrews, Christopher Plummer, Richard Haydn, Eleanor Parker, Peggy Wood, Anna Lee, Marni Nixon

'The success of a movie like *The Sound of Music* makes it even more difficult for anyone to try to do anything worth doing, anything relevant to the modern world, anything inventive or expressive' – *Pauline Kael, New Yorker*

'This last, most remunerative and least inspired, let alone sophisticated, of the Rodgers and Hammerstein collaborations is square and solid sugar. Calorie-counters, diabetics and grown-ups from eight to eighty had best beware.' – *Judith Crist*

'...sufficient warning to those allergic to singing nuns and sweetly innocent children.' – *John Gillett*

† Christopher Plummer's singing was dubbed by Bill Lee, and Peggy Wood's by Margery McKay.

⧓ best picture; Robert Wise; Irwin Kostal

⧓ Ted McCord; Julie Andrews; Peggy Wood

Sound Off

US 1952 83m Supercinecolor

Columbia (Jonie Taps)

An entertainer is recruited into the army and has predictable difficulties.

Dishevelled service farce with funny moments.

w Blake Edwards, Richard Quine d Richard Quine ph Ellis Carter m George Duning md Morris Stoloff

☆ Mickey Rooney, Anne James, Sammy White, John Asher, Gordon Jones

Sounder *

US 1972 105m DeLuxe Panavision

TCF/Radnitz-Mattel (Robert B. Radnitz)

During the 30s Depression, black sharecroppers in the deep South endure various tribulations.

Well made liberated family movie ... but not very exciting.

w Lonnie Elder III *novel* William H. Armstrong d Martin Ritt ph John Alonzo m Taj Mahal

☆ Paul Winfield, Cicely Tyson, Kevin Hooks, Carmen Mathews, James Best, Taj Mahal

⧓ best picture; Lonnie Elder III; Paul Winfield; Cicely Tyson

Le Soupirant: see *The Suitor*

Sour Grapes *

US 1998 91m Technicolor

Columbia/Castle Rock (Laurie Lennard)

Two cousins fall out after one wins a fruit-machine jackpot with money lent to him by the other.

An intermittently amusing, extended TV sitcom that is visually uninspiring but saved by some clever writing.

wd Larry David ph Victor Hammer pd Charles Rosen ed Priscilla Nedd-Friendly

☆ Steven Weber, Craig Bierko, Matt Keeslar, Karen Sillas, Robyn Peterman, Viola Harris, Orlando Jones, Jennifer Leigh Warren, Richard Gant, James MacDonald, Sonya Eddy, Philip Baker Hall, Ann Guilbert

'Catch it fast, because it bears all the hallmarks of a future cult classic.' – *Alan Jones, Film Review*

Soursweet **

GB 1988 111m colour

Curzon/First Film/British Screen/Zenith/Film Four International (Roger Randall-Cutler)

A Chinese couple living in London start their own small restaurant.

Affecting drama of immigrant life.

w Ian McEwan *novel* Timothy Mo d Mike Newell ph Michael Garfath m Richard Hartley pd Adrian Smith ed Mick Audsley

☆ Sylvia Chang, Danny An-Ning, Jodi Long, Speedy Choo, Han Tan, Soon-Teck Oh, William Chow

Sous le Ciel de Paris Coule la Seine

France 1951 111m bw

Regina Filmsonor (Pierre O'Connell and Arys Nisotti)

The adventures of a variety of characters during a day in Paris.

The director is back on his multi-story band wagon, but in this case the stories are undeveloped and the handling less than interesting.

w René Lefèvre, Julien Duvivier d Julien Duvivier ph Nicholas Hayer m Jean Winer

☆ Brigitte Auber, Jean Brochard, René Blancard, Paul Frankeur, Sylvie

'A hotchpotch of familiar story devices, camera tricks and picturesque characterizations and settings, bundled together with an old hand's facility.' – *MFB*

Sous le Soleil de Satan: see *Under Satan's Sun*

Sous les Toits de Paris *

France 1930 92m bw

Tobis (Frank Clifford)

A Parisian street singer falls in love with a girl, fights her lover, and proves himself innocent of theft.

⫰⫰ film suitable for family viewing   ▦ VHS video-cassette for the British PAL system   ▣ VHS video-cassette for the British PAL system in wide screen-format   ⟳ Video cassette in a computer-colourised version   ▬ American NTSC video-cassette   ⧓ Laser disc

Surprisingly serious and darkly lit little comedy-drama which, while well enough directed, hardly seems to merit its classic status.

w/d René Clair *ph* Georges Périnal *m* Armand Bernard *pd* Lazare Meerson

☆ Albert Préjean, Pola Illery, Gaston Modot, Edmond Gréville

'Real film fare of quality … a talker which is intelligible to any country.' – *Variety*

'It is far more movie than talkie, which exercises the imagination and rests the ear.' – *National Board of Review*

South **

GB   1919   81m   bw   silent

BFI

Documentary of Sir Ernest Shackleton's expedition to the Antarctic in 1914, when the crew of 28 and 70 dogs were marooned for nine months after their ship was first trapped, and then destroyed, by the sea ice.

Beautifully restored by the National Film and Television Archive, a fascinating report on an ill-fated journey, with some remarkable photography.

† Presenting a wonderful and true story of British pluck, self-sacrifice and indomitable courage displayed by a small party of men who set forth on a voyage of discovery into the hitherto unexplored lands and uncharted seas of the great Antarctic Continent.

South **

Argentina/France   1988   127m   colour

Cinesur/Pacific/Canal (Sabina Sigler)

original title: *Sur*

Released after five years, a political prisoner wanders the streets of his home town accompanied by the ghosts of his past.

Dream, fantasy, past and present merge into a powerful, elegiac account of tyranny and oppression, hope and despair.

w/d Fernando Solanas *ph* Felix Monti *m* Astor Piazzolla *pd* Fernando Solanas *ed* Juan Carlos Macias, Pablo Mari

☆ Susu Pecoraro, Miguel Angel Sola, Philippe Leotard, Lito Cruz, Ulises Dumont

† The film won Solanas the award for best director at the Cannes Film Festival in 1988.

The South **

Spain/France   1983   94m   colour

Connoisseur/Television EspanolaChloe/Elias Querejeta

original title: *El Sur*

A woman recalls her childhood in the late 1950s and her relationship with her unhappy father.

Delicate, poetic account of a child's view of adult experience.

w Jose Luis Lopez Linares *story* Adelaida Garcia Morales *d* Victor Erice *ph* Jose Luis Alcaine *ad* Antonio Belizon *ed* Pablo G. Del Amo

☆ Omero Antonutti, Lola Cardona, Aurore Clement, Sonsoles Arangueren, Iciar Bollain, Rafaela Aparicio, Germaine Montero, Maria Caro

South American George

GB   1941   93m   bw

Ben Henry/Columbia

An unsuccessful singer poses as a South American opera star.

Not among the star's best.

w Leslie Arliss, Norman Lee, Austin Melford *d* Marcel Varnel *ph* Arthur Crabtree

☆ George Formby, Linden Travers, Enid Stamp-Taylor, Jacques Brown, Felix Aylmer

South Central *

US   1992   99m   DeLuxe

Ixtlan/Monument/Enchantment (Janet Yang, William B. Steakley)

GB title: *South Central L.A.*

A black hoodlum, imprisoned for murder, discovers that his 10-year-old son has joined his old gang.

A well-acted but over-earnest account of a man's attempt to redeem his violent past.

w/d Steve Anderson *book* Crips by Donald Bakeer *ph* Charlie Lieberman *m* Tim Truman *pd* David Brian Miller, Marina Kieser *ed* Steve Nevius

☆ Glenn Plummer, Byron Keith Minns, LaRita Shelby, Kevin Best, Christian Coleman, Starletta Dupois, Ivory Ocean, Carl Lumbly

'Speaks eloquently to black kids desperately in need of straight talk. A profoundly moving story … It has the power to save lives.' – *Variety*

South of Algiers

GB   1952   95m   Technicolor

ABP/Mayflower (Aubrey Baring, Maxwell Setton)

US title: *The Golden Mask*

Archaeologists and thieves search the Sahara for a priceless mask.

Schoolboy adventure story with a straightforward plot and plenty of local colour.

w Robert Westerby *d* Jack Lee *ph* Oswald Morris *m* Robert Gill

☆ Van Heflin, Wanda Hendrix, Eric Portman, Charles Goldner, Jacques François, Jacques Brunius, Alec Mango, Marne Maitland

'A thousand thundering terrific thrills in a fight-swept tropic paradise!'

South of Pago Pago

US   1940   96m   bw

(UA) Edward Small (Erle C. Kenton)

Greedy white men seek riches in pearls by cheating and overworking the natives.

Slightly unfamiliar backgrounds and a fair supply of two-fisted action gave this romantic adventure drama plenty of box-office pull.

w George Bruce *d* Alfred E. Green *ph* John Mescall *m* Edward Ward

☆ Victor McLaglen, Jon Hall, Frances Farmer, Olympe Bradna, Gene Lockhart, Douglass Dumbrille, Francis Ford

South of St Louis

US   1948   88m   Technicolor

Warner (Milton Sperling)

Before the Civil War starts, Southern farmers are plagued by Union guerrillas.

Pretty good Western with plenty of action.

w Zachary Gold and James R. Webb *d* Ray Enright *ph* Karl Freund *m* Max Steiner

☆ Joel McCrea, Zachary Scott, Victor Jory, Douglas Kennedy, Dorothy Malone, Alexis Smith, Alan Hale

'Distinguished by the fact that all the good men wear bells on their spurs in contradistinction to the bad men. This determines character without benefit of acting, as well as making a jolly noise.' – C. A. *Lejeune*

South of Suez

US   1940   85m   bw

Warner

A diamond miner falls for the daughter of a man he is accused of murdering.

Watchable melodrama with pleasing actors.

w Barry Trivers *d* Lewis Seiler

☆ George Brent, Brenda Marshall, George Tobias, James Stephenson, Lee Patrick, Eric Blore, Cecil Kellaway

South of Tahiti

US   1941   75m   bw

Universal

GB title: *White Savage*

Four adventurers drift ashore on a tropical island.

Penny-pinching hokum without even the colour to make it watchable.

w Gerald Geraghty *d* George Waggner

☆ Brian Donlevy, Maria Montez, Broderick Crawford, Andy Devine, Henry Wilcoxon, H. B. Warner

South Pacific **

US   1958   170m   Technicolor   Todd-AO

Magna/S. P. Enterprises (Buddy Adler)

In 1943 an American navy nurse on a South Pacific island falls in love with a middle-aged French planter who becomes a war hero.

Overlong, solidly produced film of the musical stage hit, with great locations, action climaxes and lush photography (also a regrettable tendency to use alarming colour filters for dramatic emphasis).

w Paul Osborn, Richard Rodgers, Oscar Hammerstein II, Joshua Logan *stories* Tales of the South Pacific by James A. Michener *d* Joshua Logan *ph* Leon Shamroy *m/ly* Richard Rodgers, Oscar Hammerstein II *md* Alfred Newman, Ken Darby *ch* Le Roy Prinz

☆ Mitzi Gaynor, Rossano Brazzi, Ray Walston, John Kerr, France Nuyen, Juanita Hall

'What a monstrous visual riot! What a din!' – C. A. *Lejeune*

† Rossano Brazzi's singing was dubbed by Giorgio Tozzi, John Kerr's by Bill Lee and Juanita Hall's by Muriel Smith, even though she had sung the role of Bloody Mary in the Broadway production.

♫ Leon Shamroy; Alfred Newman, Ken Darby

South Park: Bigger Longer & Uncut **

US   1999   81m   DeLuxe

Paramount/Warner/Comedy Central/Scott Rudin/Trey Parker/Matt Stone (Trey Parker, Matt Stone)

After schoolkids sneak into an R-rated movie, featuring two foul-mouthed Canadian comedians, their mothers campaign for a war against Canada.

With humour often as crude as the animation, this is nevertheless a deft and witty demolition of many aspects of modern life, aimed particularly at all those who maintain double standards or tell others what to do and how to behave.

w Trey Parker, Matt Stone, Pam Brady *d* Trey Parker *m* Marc Shaiman *m/ly* Trey Parker, Marc Shaiman *ed* John Venzon

☆ Featuring voices of: Matt Stone, Trey Parker, Mary Kay Bergman, Isaac Hayes, George Clooney, Brent Spiner, Minnie Driver, Eric Idle

'The funniest, most risk-taking, most incisive movie of the summer.' – *Lisa Schwarzbaum, Entertainment Weekly*

'The most impressively vicious and nasty-minded film satire of the year.' – *Andrew Pulver, Guardian*

♫ Mountain Town; Uncle Fucka; Wendy's Song; It's Easy Mmmkay; Hell Isn't Good; Blame Canada; Kyle's Mom's a Bitch; What Would Brian Boitano Do?; Up There; I Can Change; I'm Super; Eyes of a Child

♪ song 'Blame Canada' (m/l Trey Parker, Marc Shaiman)

South Riding **

GB   1937   91m   bw

London Films (Alexander Korda, Victor Saville)

A schoolmistress in a quiet Yorkshire dale exposes crooked councillors and falls for the depressed local squire.

Dated but engrossing multi-drama from a famous novel; a good compact piece of film-making.

w Ian Dalrymple, Donald Bull *novel* Winifred Holtby *d* Victor Saville *ph* Harry Stradling *m* Richard Addinsell

☆ Ralph Richardson, Edna Best, Edmund Gwenn, Ann Todd, Glynis Johns, John Clements, Marie Lohr, Milton Rosmer, Edward Lexy

'Another artistic Korda film … lacking in a story of popular appeal.' – *Variety*

'A convincing and dramatic picture of English provincial life.' – *Film Weekly*

South Sea Sinner

US   1949   88m   bw

Universal-International

GB title: *East of Java*

On a South Sea island, a fugitive from justice is blackmailed by a café owner.

Hackneyed elements are strung together without much flair in this routine melodrama.

w Joel Malone, Oscar Brodney *d* Bruce Humberstone *ph* Maury Gertsman *m* Walter Scharf

☆ Macdonald Carey, Shelley Winters, Luther Adler, Helena Carter, Frank Lovejoy, Art Smith, Liberace

South Sea Woman

US   1953   99m   bw

Warner (Sam Bischoff)

Adventures of a fight-loving marine in the Pacific war.

Unlovable mixture of brawling, romancing and war-winning.

w Edwin Blum *play* William M. Rankin *d* Arthur Lubin *ph* Ted McCord *m* David Buttolph

☆ Burt Lancaster, Virginia Mayo, Chuck Connors, Arthur Shields, Barry Kelley, Leon Askin

Southern Comfort ****

US   1981   106m   DeLuxe

EMI/Phoenix/Cinema Group Venture (David Giler)

National Guardsmen on a routine exercise into swampland find themselves involved in a life-and-death struggle with the Cajun inhabitants.

Brilliant, compelling, tightly-constructed thriller that manages also to be an allegory of American involvement in Vietnam.

w Michael Kane, Walter Hill, David Giler *d* Walter Hill *ph* Andrew Laszlo *m* Ry Cooder

☆ Keith Carradine, Powers Boothe, Fred Ward, Franklyn Seales, T. K. Carter, Lewis Smith

'As an action director Walter Hill has a dazzling competence. Southern Comfort comes across with such immediacy that it had a near-hypnotic hold on me and I felt startled – brought up short – when it ended.' – *Pauline Kael, New Yorker*

'Africa explodes with a thousand surprises!'

The Southern Star *

GB/France   1968   105m   Technicope

Columbia/Eurofrance/Capitole (Roger Duchet)

In French West Africa in 1912, a penniless American finds a huge diamond which several crooks are after.

Quite a likeable adventure romp, with good suspense sequences and convincing jungle settings.

w David Pursall, Jack Seddon *novel* Jules Verne *d* Sidney Hayers *ph* Raoul Coutard *m* Georges Garvarentz

☆ George Segal, Ursula Andress, Orson Welles, Ian Hendry, Michael Constantine, Johnny Sekka, Harry Andrews

A Southern Yankee *

US   1948   90m   bw

MGM (Paul Jones)

GB title: *My Hero*

During the Civil War a Southern bellboy masquerades as a spy and finds himself behind enemy lines.

A rather feeble reworking of Buster Keaton's The General, with some excellent gags supervised by the master himself.

w Harry Tugend *d* Edward Sedgwick *ph* Ray June *m* David Snell

☆ Red Skelton, Brian Donlevy, Arlene Dahl, George Coulouris, Lloyd Gough, John Ireland, Minor Watson, Charles Dingle

'She was his woman! And he was her man! That's all they had to fight with – against the world, the flesh, and the devil!'

The Southerner ***

US   1945   91m   bw

(UA)

Problems of penniless farmers in the deep South.

Impressive, highly pictorial outdoor drama, more poetic than The Grapes of Wrath and lacking the acting strength.

w/d Jean Renoir *novel* Hold Autumn in Your Hand by George Sessions Perry *ph* Lucien Andriot *m* Werner Janssen

☆ Zachary Scott, Betty Field, *Beulah Bondi*, J. Carrol Naish, Percy Kilbride, Blanche Yurka, Norman Lloyd

'I cannot imagine anybody failing to be spellbound by this first successful essay in Franco-American screen collaboration.' – *Richard Winnington*

'You can smell the earth as the plough turns it up; you can sense the winter and the rain and the sunshine.' – C. A. *Lejeune*

† Some sources state that the script was by William Faulkner.

♪ Jean Renoir (as director); Werner Janssen

Southwest to Sonora: see *The Appaloosa*

Souvenir

GB   1987   93m   Technicolor

Curzon/Fancy Free/Geoff Reeve Pictures (Tom Reeve, James Reeve)

An elderly German living in New York returns to the French town where he was involved in a massacre of the inhabitants during the Second World War.

Unsuccessful and heavy-handed, it never comes close to exploring the themes of guilt and individual responsibility that it raises.

w Paul Wheeler *novel* The Pork Butcher by David Hughes *d* Geoffrey Reeve *ph* Fred Tammes *m* Tony Kinsey *pd* Morley Smith *ed* Bob Morgan

☆ Christopher Plummer, Catherine Hicks, Michael Lonsdale, Christopher Cazenove, Lisa Daniely, Jean Badin, Patrick Bailey

'Could be a bad joke about the type of international co-production which is made because the money, rather than the audience, can be found for it.' – *MFB*

Soylent Green *

US 1973 97m Metrocolor Panavision
MGM (Walter Seltzer, Russell Thatcher)
📼 ▥

In 2022, the population of New York exists in perpetual feud on synthetic foods; a policeman hears from his elderly friend about an earlier time when things were better.
Lively futuristic yarn with a splendid climax revealing the nature of the artificial food; marred by narrative incoherence and by direction which fails to put plot points clearly across.
w Stanley R. Greenberg *novel* Make Room, Make Room *by* Harry Harrison d Richard Fleischer ph Richard H. Kline m Fred Myrow
☆ Charlton Heston, *Edward G. Robinson*, Leigh Taylor-Young, Chuck Connors, Brock Peters, Joseph Cotten

The Space Children

US 1958 71m bw VistaVision
Paramount (William Alland)
Children at a rocket testing site sabotage equipment on the instructions of a strange pulsating object.
Naïve moral fable, not badly done on its level.
w Bernard Schoenfeld d Jack Arnold ph Ernest Laszlo m Van Cleave
☆ Adam Williams, Peggy Webber, Michel Ray, Jackie Coogan

Space Jam

US 1996 87m Technicolor
Warner (Ivan Reitman, Joe Medjuck, Daniel Goldberg)
📼 ▥ ⌖ ⊙ 🎧

After Bugs Bunny and other Looney Tunes characters are kidnapped by aliens, basketball star Michael Jordan comes to the rescue.
An unlovely mix of live action and animation, climaxing in a basketball game, which might have been passable had it been 80 minutes shorter. It is little more than a long commercial that, in the process, diminishes its cartoon stars, erasing their quirky individuality in favour of a bland and hectic banality.
w Leo Benvenuti, Steve Rudnick, Timothy Harris, Herschel Weingrod d Joe Pytka ph Michael Chapman m James Newton Howard pd Geoffrey Kirkland ed Sheldon Kahn
☆ Michael Jordan, Wayne Knight, Theresa Randle and also the voices of: Billy West, Bradley Baker, Danny DeVito
'Cute, rambunctious, generally amusing rather than outright funny, this clever mix of live action, highlighted by the unequaled skills of basketball superstar Michael Jordan, and animated Looney Tunes antics will be a must-see for kids.' – *Todd McCarthy, Variety*
'A lazy, cynical attempt to pitch the Warners characters (and the merchandising derived from them) at pre-teen black, or black-identified, punters. It's a hugely dispiriting film.' – *Jonathan Romney, Sight and Sound*
† The film was based on a commercial for Nike sneakers.

Space Master X-7

US 1958 71m bw Regalscope
Twentieth Century Fox (Bernard Glasser)
A space probe returns from Mars carrying a deadly fungus.
Dull science fiction, done on the cheap in a documentary style that fails to provide any much-needed urgency; the alien growth resembles an inanimate length of grey felt.
w George Worthing Yates, Daniel Mainwaring d Edward Bernds ph Brydon Baker m Josef Zimanich ad Harry Reif ed John F. Link
☆ Bill Williams, Lyn Thomas, Robert Ellis, Paul Frees, Rhoda Williams, Joan Barry, Carol Varga, Moe Howard

Space Raiders

👫 US 1983 82m colour
Millennium (Roger Corman)
▥

A space mercenary promises to help return a 10-year-old stowaway to his home planet.
Low-budget Star Wars rip-off for juvenile audiences, incorporating footage from Battle beyond the Stars.
wd Howard R. Cohen ph Alec Hirschfeld
☆ Vince Edwards, David Mendenhall, Patsy Pease, Thom Christopher, Dick Miller

Space Truckers

US/Ireland 1996 96m Technicolor
Goldcrest/Peter Newman/Interal/Mary Breen-Farrelly
📼 ▥

A maverick space trucker discovers that he is carrying a cargo of killer robots to take over the Earth.
Pulp science fiction of a very old-fashioned kind, done with tongue in cheek; not that that makes it any more enjoyable.
w Ted Mann d Stuart Gordon ph Mac Ahlberg m Colin Towns pd Simon Murton ed John Victor Smith sp Brian Johnson, Paul Gentry; bio-mechanicals: Screaming Mad George
☆ Dennis Hopper, Stephen Dorff, Debi Mazar, George Wendt, Vernon Wells, Barbara Crampton, Shane Rimmer, Charles Dance
'Amiable latenight trash.' – *Variety*

Spaceballs

👫 US 1987 96m Metrocolor
MGM/UA (Mel Brooks, Ezra Swerdlow)
📼 ▥ ⌖

A ruthless race is out to steal the air supply from the planet Druidia.
Flabby spoof of Star Wars, without any funny ideas.
w Mel Brooks, Thomas Meehan, Ronny Graham d Mel Brooks ph Nick McLean m John Morris pd Terence Marsh ed Conrad Buff IV
☆ Mel Brooks, John Candy, Rick Moranis, Bill Pullman, Daphne Zuniga, Dom DeLuise, John Hurt
'At its worst, it displays a colossal ego at work and humour better left to home movies.' – *Daily Variety*

SpaceCamp

👫 US 1986 107m DeLuxe Panavision
TCF/ABC (Patrick Bailey, Walter Coblenz)
▥ ⌖

Five teenagers attending a NASA summer camp are accidentally launched into space.
Tolerable entertainment for ten-year-olds, who may enjoy its empowerment of the young, and will be willing to overlook the ordinary special effects that include a rather irritating robot.
w Clifford Green, Ellen Green, Casey T. Mitchell story Patrick Bailey, Larry B. Williams d Harry Winer ph William A. Fraker m John Williams pd Richard MacDonald ed John W. Wheeler, Timothy Board
☆ Kate Capshaw, Lea Thompson, Kelly Preston, Larry B. Scott, Leaf Phoenix, Tate Donovan, Tom Skerritt, Barry Primus, Terry Quinn

Spaced Invaders

👫 US 1989 100m CFI color
Medusa/Smart Egg Pictures (Luigi Cingolani)
📼 ▥ ⌖

A spaceship load of inept Martians mistakenly try to conquer the Earth.
Inane spoof of the current cycle of science fiction films.
w Patrick Read Johnson, Scott Alexander d Patrick Read Johnson ph James L. Carter m David Russo pd Tony Tremblay ed Seth Gaven, Daniel Bross
☆ Douglas Barr, Royal Dano, Ariana Richards, J. J. Anderson, Gregg Berger, Fred Applegate, Patrika Darbo

Spacehunter: Adventures in the Forbidden Zone

US 1983 90m Metrocolor 3-D
Columbia/Delphi (Don Carmody, Andre Link, John Dunning)
📼 ▥ ⌖

In the 22nd century, a spaceship salvage expert lands on a long-forgotten planet to rescue three Earthwomen from the tyrants of Graveyard City.
Mindless and rather unattractive space fantasy, far less likeable than Flash Gordon.
w David Preston, Edith Rey, Dan Goldbert, Len Blum d Lamont Johnson ph Frank Tidy m Elmer Bernstein pd Jackson de Govia
☆ Peter Strauss, Molly Ringwald, Ernie Hudson, Andrea Marcovicci, Michael Ironside

The Spaceman and King Arthur

👫 US 1979 93m Technicolor
Walt Disney
US title: *Unidentified Flying Oddball*
An astronaut and his robot accidentally land themselves back at the court of King Arthur.
Mindless but occasionally funny rewrite of Mark Twain's A Connecticut Yankee.

w Don Tait d Russ Mayberry ph Paul Beeson m Ron Goodwin
☆ Dennis Dugan, Jim Dale, Ron Moody, Kenneth More, John Le Mesurier, Rodney Bewes, Robert Beatty

Spaceways

GB 1953 76m bw
Exclusive/Hammer (Michael Carreras)
A scientist is suspected of killing his wife and her lover and sending their bodies into space in Britain's first satellite.
Trite marital drama in a science-fiction setting, interesting only for its belief that the 1960s would bring the first manned space station.
w Paul Tabori, Richard Landau play Charles Eric Maine d Terence Fisher ph Reginald Wyer md Ivor Slaney ad J. Elder Wills ed Maurice Rootes sp The Trading Post
☆ Howard Duff, Eva Bartok, Alan Wheatley, Philip Leaver, Michael Medwin, Andrew Osborn, Cecile Chevreau

La Spada e la Croce: see *The Sword and the Cross*

The Spaniard's Curse

GB 1958 74m bw
Independent Film Distributors/Wentworth (Roger Proudlock)
A man wrongly convicted of murder pronounces an old Spanish death curse on the judge, prosecuting counsel, foreman of the jury and the killer.
A neat, well-plotted little thriller.
w Kenneth Hyde, Ralph Kemplen, Roger Proudlock story Edith Pargeter d Ralph Kemplen ph Arthur Grant m Lambert Williamson pd Tony Masters ed Stanley Hawkes
☆ Tony Wright, Lee Patterson, Michael Hordern, Susan Beaumont, Ralph Truman, Henry Oscar, Brian Oulton, Olga Dickie, Roddy Hughes, Joe Gibbons

Spanish Affair

US 1958 92m Technicolor Vistavision
Paramount/Nomad (Bruce Odlum)
An American architect in Madrid falls in love with his interpreter and is pursued by her lover.
Curiously plotless excuse for a travelogue, lushly photographed but not exactly gripping.
w Richard Collins d Don Siegel ph Sam Leavitt m Daniele Amfitheatrof
☆ Richard Kiley, Carmen Sevilla, Jose Guardiola

Spanish Fly

GB 1975 86m Technicolor
EMI (Peter James, Gerald Flint-Shipman)
📼

An Englishman in Majorca tries to improve a purchase of local wine by putting an aphrodisiac in it, with predictable results.
Crude, tatty comedy by people who should know better.
w Robert Ryerson d Bob Kellett ph Jack Atcheler m Ron Goodwin
☆ Terry-Thomas, Leslie Phillips, Graham Armitage, Frank Thornton, Sue Lloyd

The Spanish Gardener

GB 1956 97m Technicolor Vistavision
Rank (John Bryan)
The British consul in Spain is annoyed when his young son develops a strong friendship with the gardener.
Slow, understated study in human relationships which doesn't come off; any sexual relevance is well concealed.
w Lesley Storm, John Bryan novel A. J. Cronin d Philip Leacock ph Christopher Challis m John Veale
☆ Dirk Bogarde, Michael Hordern, Jon Whiteley, Cyril Cusack, Geoffrey Keen, Maureen Swanson, Lyndon Brook, Josephine Griffin, Bernard Lee, Rosalie Crutchley

The Spanish Main *

US 1945 101m Technicolor
RKO (Robert Fellows)
⌖

In the Caribbean, the fiancée of the Spanish viceroy is kidnapped by a pirate who determines to tame her before marrying her.
Slightly tongue-in-cheek pirate hokum; generally good value for the easily amused.

w George Worthing Yates, Herman J. Mankiewicz d Frank Borzage ph George Barnes m Hanns Eisler md Constantin Bakaleinikoff
☆ Paul Henreid, Maureen O'Hara, Binnie Barnes, Walter Slezak, John Emery, Barton MacLane, J. M. Kerrigan, Nancy Gates, Fritz Leiber, Jack La Rue, Mike Mazurki, Victor Kilian
♟ George Barnes

The Spanish Prisoner **

US 1997 112m Technicolor Panavision
Sweetland (Jean Doumanian)
📼 ▥

A paranoid scientist does not know whom to trust, among colleagues, friends and FBI, with his valuable formula.
A clever, intriguing game of double-cross and treble bluff that keeps the audience, as well as its characters, guessing throughout.
wd David Mamet ph Gabriel Beristain m Carter Burwell pd Tim Galvin ed Barbara Tulliver
☆ Campbell Scott, Rebecca Pidgeon, Steve Martin, Ricky Jay, Ben Gazzara, Felicity Huffman, Ed O'Neill
'Ingenious but glassily unengaging, like watching a game of chess at a distance of 100 metres.' – *Tom Shone, Sunday Times*
'Mamet plays his genre games with such elegant wit that no one should pine for the usual battering from galactic explosions.' – *Geoff Brown, The Times*

'A Darkly Humorous Suburban Tale Creeping Beyond Normality…'

Spanking the Monkey **

US 1995 106m colour
Metro Tartan/Buckeye/Swelter
📼 ▥ ⌖

A medical student is told by his father, a commercial traveller, that he must spend the summer looking after his mother, who has broken a leg in a suicide attempt.
Deft, witty and assured account of confused family relationships and a young man's search for his sexual identity, which leads to an incestuous relationship; it is an often dark work, but one about survivors.
wd David O. Russell m David Carbonara pd Susan Block ed Pamela Martin
☆ Jeremy Davies, Alberta Watson, Benjamin Hendrickson, Carlo Gallo, Matthew Puckett, Judette Jones
'A thought provoking movie that should not be allowed to disappear beneath this year's Dredds and Batmans.' – *Empire*
† The film won the Audience Award at the 1994 Sundance Film Festival.

Spare a Copper *

GB 1940 77m bw
Ealing
A police war reservist catches saboteurs.
One of the last good Formby comedies, with everything percolating as it should.
w Roger MacDougall, Austin Melford, Basil Dearden d John Paddy Carstairs ph Bryan Langley m Louis Levy
☆ George Formby, Dorothy Hyson, Bernard Lee, John Warwick, John Turnbull, George Merritt

Spare the Rod

GB 1961 93m bw
British Lion/Bryanston/Weyland (Victor Lyndon)
At an East End school, a novice master wins the confidence of tough pupils.
A British Blackboard Jungle, paving the way for To Sir with Love; not exciting on its own account.
w John Cresswell novel Michael Croft d Leslie Norman ph Paul Beeson m Laurie Johnson
☆ Max Bygraves, Geoffrey Keen, Donald Pleasence, Richard O'Sullivan, Betty McDowall, Eleanor Summerfield, Mary Merrall

'Her passion was a caged bird waiting to be set free…'

Sparrow

Italy 1993 106m colour
Rank/Polygram/Nippon (Mario Cecchi Gori, Vittorio Cecchi Gori)
Sent home because of a plague threatening the convent, a nun preparing for her final vows meets and falls in love with a young student.
A moody, period melodrama of a doomed love, given an operatic treatment and hindered by the fact that its

leading characters cannot portray the emotional upheavals required of them.
wd Franco Zeffirelli *novel* A Sparrow's Tale by Giovanni Verga *ph* Ennio Guarnieri *m* Claudio Cappani, Alessio Vlad *ed* Richard Marden
☆ Angela Bettis, Sinead Cusack, Johnathon Schaech, Vanessa Redgrave, John Castle, Valentina Cortese, Frank Finlay, Pat Heywood, Denis Quilley
'Dramatic, grand in scope, and tragic in its tale of unfulfilled love and lives. Unfortunately the plot is almost tortuously slow, and the film ends up neither emotionally nor intellectually gripping.' – *Karen Regelman, Variety*

Sparrows Can't Sing
GB 1962 94m bw
Elstree/Carthage (Donald Taylor)
📺
Returning after two years at sea, a sailor searches for his wife and threatens vengeance on her lover.
Relentlessly caricatured Cockney comedy melodrama, too self-conscious to be effective, and not at all likeable anyway.
w Stephen Lewis, Joan Littlewood *d* Joan Littlewood *ph* Max Greene *m* James Stevens
☆ James Booth, Barbara Windsor, Roy Kinnear, Avis Bunnage, George Sewell, Barbara Ferris, Murray Melvin, Arthur Mullard

Spartaco: see Spartacus (1952)

'Behold the splendor and fury of a city made with pleasure.'
Spartacus
Italy 1952 92m bw
RKO/Consorzio Spartacus
📺
original title: Spartaco
aka: Spartacus the Gladiator; Sins of Rome
After he rejects the advances of the daughter of a Roman general, a Thracian slave becomes a gladiator, and leads a revolt against Rome.
A version that substitutes a love affair and action for historical accuracy; it has good performances and splendid photography to recommend it.
w Jean Ferry, Mario Bori *d* Riccardo Freda *ph* Gabor Rogany *m* Renzo Rossellini
☆ Massimo Girotti, Lumilla Tcherina, Gianni Maria Canale, Yves Vincent, Vittorio Sanipoli, Carlo Ninchi
† The US version ran for 71m.

Spartacus **
👫 US 1960 196m Super Technirama 70
U-I/Bryna (Edward Lewis)
📺 🎬 ⊛ ◎ 🎧
The slaves of ancient Rome revolt and are quashed.
Long, well-made, downbeat epic with deeper than usual characterization and several bravura sequences.
w Dalton Trumbo *novel* Howard Fast *d* Stanley Kubrick *ph* Russell Metty *m* Alex North *pd* Alexander Golitzen *ed* Robert Lawrence
☆ Kirk Douglas, Laurence Olivier, Charles Laughton, Tony Curtis, Jean Simmons, Peter Ustinov, John Gavin, Nina Foch, Herbert Lom, John Ireland, John Dall, Charles McGraw, Woody Strode
'Everything is depicted with a lack of imagination that is truly Marxian.' – *Anne Grayson*
'A lot of first-rate professionals have pooled their abilities to make a first-rate circus.' – *Stanley Kauffmann*
'One comes away feeling rather revolted and not at all ennobled.' – *Alan Dent, Illustrated London News*
🎖 Russell Metty; Peter Ustinov; art direction
⚖ Alex North; editing

Spartacus the Gladiator: see Spartacus (1952)

'Born In Darkness. Sworn To Justice.'
Spawn
US 1997 97m DeLuxe
Entertainment/New Line/Todd McFarlane (Clint Goldman)
📺 🎬 ⊛ ◎ 🎧
An assassinated special agent is brought back to life with supernatural powers on condition that he leads the Devil's army to take over the world.
Exceptionally dreary, noisy nonsense that shows the cinema of mindless sensation at its worst: it makes little

narrative sense, displays no imagination in its repetitive action sequences, and is peopled by uninteresting characters.
w Alan McElroy *comic book* Todd McFarlane *d* Mark A.Z. Dippé *ph* Guillermo Navarro *m* Graeme Revell *pd* Philip Harrison *ed* Michael N. Knue *sp* Robert Kurtzman, Gregory Nicotero, Howard Berger; ILM
☆ John Leguizamo, Michael Jai White, Martin Sheen, Theresa Randle, Melinda Clarke, Miko Hughes, Sydni Beaudoin, Nicol Williamson, D. B. Sweeney
'Gives you the pleasurably junky sensation of living inside an apocalyptic videogame.' – *Owen Glieberman, Entertainment Weekly*
'If you're looking for a movie to restore your faith in superhero film-making, this sure as hell isn't the one.' – *Jason Caro, Film Review*

'A love story stormy as raging Arctic seas!'
Spawn of the North **
US 1938 110m bw
Paramount (Albert Lewin)
In 1890s Alaska, American fishermen combat Russian poachers.
Solidly carpentered all-star action melodrama, a sizzler of its day. Remade 1953 as Alaska Seas.
w Talbot Jennings, Jules Furthman *d* Henry Hathaway *ph* Charles Lang *m* Dimitri Tiomkin
☆ George Raft, Henry Fonda, Dorothy Lamour, John Barrymore, Akim Tamiroff, Louise Platt, Lynne Overman, Fuzzy Knight, Vladimir Sokoloff, Duncan Renaldo, John Wray
'The visual features are so realistic and terrifying that audiences will find complete satisfaction in the production.' – *Variety*
'This film has something which the cinema of bygone days used to supply as a matter of course – action and thrills, the quickened pulse and the lump in the throat.' – *Basil Wright*
'Rousing old-fashioned spectacle.' – *New York Times*
🎖 Special Award for special effects

Spawn of the Slithis
US 1978 86m Movielab
Paul Fabian/Stephen Traxler
A teacher of journalism investigates deaths in the neighbourhood and discovers a monster lurking in the local canals.
Low-budget shocker that is also bereft of originality or talent.
wd Stephen Traxler *ph* Robert Caramico *m* Steve Zuckerman *ad* Catherine Deeter *ed* Robert M. Ross
☆ Alan Blanchard, J. C. Claire, Dennis Lee Falt, Mello Alexandria, Win Condict

Speak Easily *
US 1932 83m bw
MGM (Lawrence Weingarten)
A professor inherits a Broadway musical and falls for the lure of the bright lights.
Interesting Keaton talkie at the point of his decline.
w Ralph Spence, Laurence E. Johnson *novel* Footlights by Clarence Budington Kelland *d* Edward Sedgwick *ph* Harold Wentstrom
☆ Buster Keaton, Jimmy Durante, Hedda Hopper

Speaking Parts
Canada 1989 92m colour
Recorded Releasing/Ego Film Arts/Telefilm Canada/Ontario Film Development Company/Academy Pictures/Film Four International
📺
A screenwriter and a hotel maid both fall in love with a gigolo who wants to be an actor.
Curious and ultimately unsatisfactory triangular drama of personalities who connect with each other mainly through the medium of video.
wd Atom Egoyan *ph* Paul Sarossy *m* Mychael Danna *ad* Linda Del Rosario *ed* Bruce McDonald
☆ Michael McManus, Arsinee Khanjian, Gabrielle Rose, Tony Nardi, David Hemblen, Patricia Collins

Special Agent
US 1935 74m bw
Cosmopolitan/Warner
A special investigator pretends to be a newspaperman.
Routine rough stuff, quite watchable.
w Laird Doyle, Abem Finkel *d* William Keighley

☆ Bette Davis, George Brent, Ricardo Cortez, Jack La Rue, Henry O'Neill, J. Carrol Naish
'Indifferent entertainment but Bette Davis may help.' – *Variety*

Special Delivery
US 1976 99m DeLuxe
TCF/Bing Crosby Productions (Richard Berg)
Three disabled Vietnam veterans rob a bank, and the consequences are complicated.
Unremarkable suspenser which takes itself too seriously.
w Don Gazzaniga *d* Paul Wendkos *ph* Harry Stradling Jnr *m* Lalo Schifrin
☆ Bo Svenson, Cybill Shepherd, Michael C. Gwynne, Vic Tayback, Sorrell Booke, Jeff Goldblum

'Killing Is His Profession. Revenge Is Her Goal. Together They Take On The Battle Against The Underworld Of Miami.'
The Specialist
US 1994 110m Technicolor
Warner (Jerry Weintraub)
📺 🎬 ⊛ ◎ 🎧
A woman seeking revenge infiltrates the gang that murdered her parents and hires an expert in explosives to kill them.
Trashily risible action movie, with the two stars kept far apart for much of the picture, for reasons that only become apparent when they are together.
w Alexandra Seros *suggested by* 'The Specialist' novels by John Shirley *d* Luis Llosa *ph* Jeffrey L. Kimball *m* John Barry *pd* Walter P. Martishius *ed* Jack Hofstra
☆ Sylvester Stallone, Sharon Stone, James Woods, Rod Steiger, Eric Roberts, Mario Ernesto Sanchez, Sergio Dore Jnr
'A pretty silly film. And it is capped by a sex scene involving Stone and Sylvester Stallone that has to be seen to be disbelieved.' – *Derek Malcolm, Guardian*
'Cheesecake meets beeake.' – *New Yorker*

'Two decades ago we sent a message to space. This is the reply...'
Species *
US 1995 108m DeLuxe Panavision
UIP/MGM (Fred Mancuso Jnr, Dennis Feldman)
📺 🎬 ⊛ 🎧
Scientists chase a half-human, half-alien girl who escapes from an experimental laboratory, concerned that she intends to mate and breed.
Enjoyable, fast-moving science-fiction thriller; it offers nothing new but presents a familiar tale with some style.
w Dennis Feldman *d* Roger Donaldson *ph* Andrzej Bartkowiak *pd* John Muto *ed* Conrad Buff *sp* visual effects: Richard Edlund; 'Sil' design: H. R. Giger
☆ Ben Kingsley, Michael Madsen, Alfred Molina, Forest Whitaker, Marg Helgenberger, Natasha Henstridge, Michelle Williams
'Think of it as Beach Blanket Alien – sure, it's dopey, but it's a guilty-pleasure pig-out.' – *Premiere*

Species II
US 1998 93m DeLuxe
UIP/MGM/FGM (Frank Mancuso Jnr)
📺 🎬 🎧
A woman who is part alien tracks down an astronaut on a killing spree who has returned from Mars infected with alien DNA.
A sequel that rings a few welcome changes on the original, and offers more fast-paced entertainment.
w Chris Brancato *d* Peter Medak *ph* Matthew F. Leonetti *m* Edward Shearmur *pd* Miljen Kreka Kljakovic *ed* Richard Nord *sp* Steve Johnson
☆ Michael Madison, Natasha Henstridge, Marg Helgenberger, Mykelti Williamson, George Dzundza, James Cromwell, Myriam Cyr, Sarah Wynter
'A carnival of the absurdly gruesome.' – *Philip Strick, Sight and Sound*

The Speckled Band
GB 1931 80m bw
B and D/Herbert Wilcox
📺
Sherlock Holmes saves an heiress from a horrible death.
Limp and overstretched version of Conan Doyle's story, interesting only for the actors.

w W. P. Lipscomb *d* Jack Raymond *ph* Freddie Young
☆ Raymond Massey, Athole Stewart, Lyn Harding, Angela Baddeley, Nancy Price

The Specter of the Rose *
US 1946 90m bw
Republic (Ben Hecht)
📺
A schizophrenic ballet dancer lives his role and nearly murders his wife.
A rather hilarious bid for culture: hard to sit through without laughing, but unique.
wd Ben Hecht *ph* Lee Garmes *m* Georges Antheil
☆ Viola Essen, Ivan Kirov, Michael Chekhov

The Spectre of Edgar Allan Poe
US 1972 86m Eastmancolor
Doverton/Cintel (Mohy Quandour)
📺
Poe visits an asylum where his beloved Lenore has been taken to recover from being buried alive and finds himself in a nightmare world of murder and monsters.
An intriguing notion is quickly done to death in an unimaginative production.
wd Mohy Quandour *story* Kenneth Hartford, Denton Foxx *ph* Robert Birchall *m* Allen D. Allen *ed* Abbas Amin *sp* Byrd Holland
☆ Robert Walker, Mary Grover, Cesar Romero, Tom Drake, Carol Ohmart

Speechless
US 1994 99m DeLuxe
MGM/Forge (Renny Harlin, Geena Davis)
📺 🎬 ⊛ 🎧
Two speech writers for rival candidates in a senatorial contest fall for each other.
Pleasant but unmemorable romantic comedy, cynical about politics and sentimental about love.
w Robert King *d* Ron Underwood *ph* Don Peterman *m* Marc Shaiman *pd* Dennis Washington *ed* Richard Francis-Bruce
☆ Michael Keaton, Geena Davis, Christopher Reeve, Bonnie Bedelia, Ernie Hudson, Charles Martin Smith, Gailard Sartain, Ray Baker, Mitchell Ryan
'Never achieves the madcap hilarity of the '40s romantic comedies it seeks to emulate, and some of the dramatic moments feel a bit forced.' – *Brian Lowry, Variety*

Speed ***
US 1994 115m DeLuxe Panavision
TCF (Mark Gordon)
📺 🎬 ⊛ ◎ 🎧
A mad bomber attempts to hold a city to ransom by planting a bomb on a bus which will explode if the vehicle's speed drops below 50 mph.
A fast, adrenalin-pumping action-packed thriller that achieves a high level of suspense; it works brilliantly well for the most part, even if the good guys cause more destruction than the bad, although it goes off the rails towards the end.
w Graham Yost *d* Jan de Bont *ph* Andrzej Bartkowiak *m* Mike Mancina *pd* Jackson de Govia *ed* John Wright
☆ Keanu Reeves, Dennis Hopper, Sandra Bullock, Joe Morton, Jeff Daniels, Alan Ruck, Glenn Plummer, Richard Lineback, Beth Grant, Hawthorne James, Carlos Carrasco
'A non-stop actioner that rarely pauses to take a breath. While highly derivative and mechanical in planning and execution, this high-octane thrillathon boasts more twists, turns and obstacles than the most hazardous video arcade road raceway.' – *Variety*
🎖 sound (Gregg Landaker, Steve Maslow, Bob Beemer, David R. R. MacMillan); sound effects editing (Stephen Hunter Flick)
⚖ editing
🎬 editing

'Rush Hour Hits The Water.'
Speed 2 – Cruise Control
US 1997 125m DeLuxe Panavision
TCF/Blue Tulip (Jan de Bont)
📺 🎬 ⊛ ◎ 🎧
A psychotic computer expert sabotages a cruise liner, whose passengers include a Los Angeles cop and his girlfriend.
A sequel so contrived and artificial that it swiftly sinks with all hands.

w Randall McCormick, Jeff Nathanson, Jan de Bont *d* Jan de Bont *ph* Jack N. Green *m* Mark Mancina *pd* Joseph Nemec III *ed* Alan Cody *sp* ILM; Rhythm and Hues

☆ Sandra Bullock, Jason Patric, Willem Dafoe, Temuera Morrison, Brian McCardie, Christine Firkins, Michael G. Hagerty, Colleen Camp, Lois Chiles, Bo Svenson

'Has no real logic, or characters or dramatic tension.' – *Derek Malcolm, Guardian*

'Suffers from a slender script, a tedious first reel and a routine villain.' – *Variety*

† It grossed more than $48m in the US, and $105m elsewhere.

Speed Zone

US/Canada 1989 95m Film House colour
Orion/Ruddy-Morgan/Entcorp (Murray Shostak)

aka: Cannonball Fever

When a police chief tries to stop the Cannonball Run by arresting the drivers, substitutes take over.
Dreary comedy, consisting of crude slapstick, tiresome car chases and cardboard characterizations; a few jokes might have helped.

w Michael Short *d* Jim Drake *ph* François Protat, Robert Saad *m* David Wheatley *ed* Michael Economou

☆ Melody Anderson, Peter Boyle, Donna Dixon, John Candy, Eugene Levy, Tim Matheson, Smothers Brothers, Shari Belafonte, Joe Flaherty, Matt Frewer, Mimi Kuzyk, Jamie Farr, Don Lake, Alyssa Milano, John Schneider and also Brooke Shields, Michael Spinks, Lee Van Cleef

† It is a sort of sequel to *The Cannonball Run* and *Cannonball Run II* (qqv).

Speedy **

👫 US 1928 90m bw silent
Paramount (Harold Lloyd)

A young man saves his girl's grandfather's trolley car business.
One of its star's most stylish comedies, and his last silent film, with a trolley car ride for climax.

w John Grey, Lex Neal, Howard Emmett Rogers, Jay Howe *d* Ted Wilde *ph* Walter Lundin

☆ Harold Lloyd, Ann Christy, Bert Woodruff, Brooks Benedict, Babe Ruth

🎗 Ted Wilde

The Spell of Amy Nugent: see *Spellbound* (1940)

Spellbinder

US 1988 99m colour
MGM/Indian Neck (Joe Wizan, Brian Russell)

A Los Angeles lawyer rescues a girl from a beating and finds himself confronting a murderous cult of devil worshippers.
Dreary occult drama, lacking any trace of magic, black or otherwise, and with a twist in the plot that will come as no surprise to anyone who has watched The Wicker Man.

w Tracy Tormé *d* Janet Greek *ph* Adam Greenberg *m* Basil Poledouris *pd* Rodger Maus *ed* Steve Mirkovich

☆ Timothy Daly, Kelly Preston, Audra Lindley, Cary-Hiroyuki Tagawa, Diana Bellamy, Anthony Crivello, Rick Rossovich

The Spellbinder

US 1939 68m bw
RKO

A criminal lawyer full of tricks finds himself on trial for murder.
Contrived courtroom drama tailored to its star.

w Thomas Lennon, Joseph A. Fields *d* Jack Hively

☆ Lee Tracy, Barbara Read, Patric Knowles, Allan Lane, Morgan Conway

'Average supporter for duals.' – *Variety*

Spellbound

GB 1940 82m bw
Pyramid Amalgamated (R. ●Murray Leslie)
aka: Passing Clouds
US title: *The Spell of Amy Nugent*

A young man is in despair when his fiancée dies, and nearly goes mad when a medium materializes her from the dead.
Very odd, very naive, but somehow rather winning.

w Miles Malleson *novel* The Necromancers by Robert Benson *d* John Harlow *ph* Walter Harvey

☆ Derek Farr, Vera Lindsay, Frederick Leister, Hay Petrie, Diana King, Felix Aylmer

Spellbound **

US 1945 111m bw
David O. Selznick

The new head of a mental institution is an impostor and an amnesiac; a staff member falls in love with him and helps him recall the fate of the real Dr Edwardes.
Enthralling and rather infuriating psychological mystery; the Hitchcock touches are splendid, and the stars shine magically, but the plot could have stood a little more attention.

w Ben Hecht, Angus MacPhail *novel* The House of Dr Edwardes by Francis Beeding *d* Alfred Hitchcock *ph* George Barnes *m* Miklos Rozsa *ad* James Basevi *dream sequence* Salvador Dali

☆ Ingrid Bergman, Gregory Peck, Leo G. Carroll, Michael Chekhov, Rhonda Fleming, John Emery, Norman Lloyd, Steve Geray

'Just about as much of the id as could be safely displayed in a Bergdorf Goodman window.' – *James Agee*

'Glossily produced and wildly improbable.' – *George Perry, 1965*

'Bergman's apple-cheeked sincerity has rarely been so out of place as in this confection whipped up by jaded chefs.' – *New Yorker, 1976*

🎵 Miklos Rozsa

🎗 best picture; Alfred Hitchcock; George Barnes; Michael Chekhov

Spencer's Mountain *

US 1963 121m Technicolor Panavision
Warner (Delmer Daves)

Life in rural America in the thirties with a poor quarry worker and his family of nine.
Sentimental rose-tinted hokum which later became TV's The Waltons. Expertly concocted, Hollywood style.

wd Delmer Daves *novel* Earl Hanmer Jnr *ph* Charles Lawton, H. F. Koenekamp *m* Max Steiner

☆ Henry Fonda, Maureen O'Hara, James MacArthur, Donald Crisp, Wally Cox, Mimsy Farmer, Lillian Bronson

'Outstanding for its smirking sexuality, its glorification of the vulgar, its patronizing tone, its mealymouthed piety.' – *Judith Crist*

Spendthrift

US 1936 80m bw
Paramount

A millionaire playboy runs out of cash.
Mild romantic comedy.

w Raoul Walsh, Bert Hanlon *story* Eric Hatch *d* Raoul Walsh *ph* Leon Shamroy *md* Boris Morros

☆ Henry Fonda, Pat Paterson, Mary Brian, George Barbier, Ed Brophy

Speriamo Che Sia Femmina: see *Let's Hope It's A Girl*

Spetters **

Netherlands 1980 115m Eastmancolor
Embassy/VSE (Joop Van Den Ende)

In a small town, three young men, two of them hoping to win a motor-cross biking championship, are all involved with a blonde sex siren who serves food from a mobile kitchen.
High energy melodrama, full of sex and violence, but eminently watchable.

w Gerard Soeteman *d* Paul Verhoeven *ph* Jöst Vacano *m* Ton Scherpenzeel *ad* Dick Schillemans *ed* Ine Schenkkan

☆ Hans Van Tongeren, Renee Soutendijk, Toon Agterberg, Maarten Spanjer, Marianne Boyer, Hugo Metsers, Kittye Courbois, Rutger Hauer, Jeroen Krabbé

'Terror Can Fill Any Space.'

Sphere

US 1998 133m Monaco Film Lab Arriflex
Warner/Baltimore/Constant/Punch (Michael Crichton, Andrew Wald, Barry Levinson)

A team of scientists investigate a mysterious alien sphere discovered on the ocean floor.
Like most American science-fiction movies of the 90s, this is merely an excuse for characters to explore their own inner space in an attempt to come to terms with themselves.

w Stephen Hauser, Paul Attanasio *story* Michael Crichton *d* Barry Levinson *ph* Adam Greenberg *m* Elliot Goldenthal *pd* Norman Reynolds *ed* Stu Linder *adaptation* Kurt Wimmer

☆ Dustin Hoffman, Sharon Stone, Samuel L. Jackson, Peter Coyote, Liev Schreiber, Queen Latifah, Marga Gomez

'An empty shell.' – *Variety*

Sphinx

US 1980 118m Technicolor Panavision
Warner/Orion (Stanley O'Toole)

Archaeologists in modern Cairo find clues to an ancient treasure.
Expensive penny dreadful which lurches about from comedy to horror but is often well worth looking at.

w John Byrum *novel* Robin Cook *d* Franklin J. Schaffner *ph* Ernest Day *m* Michael J. Lewis *pd* Terence Marsh

☆ Lesley-Anne Down, Frank Langella, Maurice Ronet, John Gielgud, Vic Tablian, Martin Benson, John Rhys-Davies

'A glossily-packaged exercise in random-selection box-office formulae.' – *Jo Imeson, MFB*

The Sphinx

US 1933 63m bw
Monogram

A murderer uses his deaf mute brother as an alibi.
Mildly ingenious low-budget thriller.

w Albert DeMond *d* Phil Rosen

☆ Lionel Atwill, Sheila Terry, Theodore Newton, Paul Hurst, Luis Alberni

'Fair returns are probable if dated properly.' – *Variety*

Spiceworld the Movie

GB 1997 92m Technicolor
Polygram/Icon/Fragile (Uri Fruchtman, Barnaby Thompson)

A week in the life of a pop group as they prepare for a concert at the Albert Hall.
Brash, lively movie aimed at the many fans of the Spice Girls, but one that is unlikely to convert others to the cause.

w Kim Fuller, Jamie Curtis *d* Bob Spiers *ph* Clive Tickner *m* Paul Hardcastle *pd* Grenville Horner *ed* Andrea MacArthur

☆ The Spice Girls (Mel B., Emma, Mel C., Geri, Victoria), Richard E. Grant, Alan Cumming, George Wendt, Claire Rushbrook, Mark McKinney, Richard O'Brien, Roger Moore, Barry Humphries, Meatloaf, Stephen Fry, Richard Briers, Bill Paterson

'A bright and breezy movie that's as timely but evanescent as the Cool Britannia culture it celebrates.' – *Derek Elley, Variety*

Spicy Rice: see *Dragon's Food*

The Spider

US 1931 65m bw
Fox

A theatre magician traps a killer.
Rather flat transcription of a play which in its original form took every advantage of the audience and other elements.

play Fulton Oursler, Lowell Brentano *d* William Cameron Menzies, Kenneth MacKenna

☆ Edmund Lowe, Howard Phillips, Lois Moran, George E. Stone, El Brendel

The Spider

GB 1939 81m bw
Admiral Films (Victor M. Greene)

A theatrical agent kills his partner on a train.
Barely competent murder thriller.

w Kenneth Horne, Reginald Long *novel* Henry Holt *d* Maurice Elvey

☆ Derrick de Marney, Diana Churchill, Cecil Parker, Jean Gillie, Frank Cellier, Allan Jeayes

The Spider and the Fly

GB 1949 95m bw
GFD/Maxwell Setton, Aubrey Baring

In 1913 a Parisian safecracker constantly outwits an inspector of the Sûreté, but war brings changes.
Coldly ironic comedy drama which really, regrettably, doesn't work.

w Robert Westerby *d* Robert Hamer *ph* Geoffrey Unsworth *m* Georges Auric

☆ Eric Portman, Guy Rolfe, Nadia Gray, George Cole, Edward Chapman, John Carol, Maurice Denham

'Not sufficiently exciting for a thriller, not quite sharp enough for a real drama of character.' – *Gavin Lambert, MFB*

'The Seductive Innocence of Lolita! The Savage Hunger of a Black Widow!'

Spider Baby

US 1964 80m bw
Admit One (Gil Lasky, Paul Monka)

aka: The Liver Eaters

A chauffeur takes care of the family whose members degenerate into cannibals as they grow older.
A low-budget horror with a cult reputation for its general ineptitude, which extends to Chaney singing the rock 'n' roll title song.

wd Jack Hill *ph* Alfred Taylor *m* Ronald Stein *ad* Ray Storey *ed* Elliot Fayad

☆ Lon Chaney Jnr, Carol Ohmart, Quinn Redeker, Mantan Moreland, Beverly Washburn, Mary Mitchell, Jill Banner, Sid Haig

'A sort of more perverse *Addams Family*, with genuinely grotesque humour and a unique cheesiness.' – *Kim Newman, Nightmare Movies*

Spider Woman **

US 1944 62m bw
Universal (Roy William Neill)

aka: Sherlock Holmes and the Spider Woman

A female Moriarty kills her victims with spiders so that she can collect on their insurance policies.
Lively episode in the modernized series, which packs in several suspenseful episodes borrowed from a variety of Conan Doyle originals.

w Bertram Millhauser *d* Roy William Neill *ph* Charles Van Enger *m* Hans Salter

☆ Basil Rathbone, Nigel Bruce, Gale Sondergaard, Dennis Hoey, Vernon Downing, Alec Craig, Mary Gordon

The Spider Woman Strikes Back

US 1946 59m bw
Universal (Howard Welsch)

An innocent girl is used as decoy by a conniving female criminal.
Boring crime filler, scarcely a worthy sequel to Spider Woman.

w Eric Taylor *d* Arthur Lubin *ph* Paul Ivano *md* Milton Rosen

☆ Gale Sondergaard, Brenda Joyce, Rondo Hatton, Milburn Stone, Kirby Grant, Hobart Cavanaugh

The Spider's Stratagem *

Italy 1970 97m Eastmancolor
Radiotelevisione Italiana/Red Film (Giovanni Bertolucci)

original title: Strategia del Ragno

Revisiting the village in the Po valley where his father was murdered by fascists in 1936, our gradually disillusioned hero learns that his father was really a traitor executed by his own men.
Elaborately mysterious puzzle play for intellectuals, with infinite shades of meaning which few will bother to explore. The atmosphere, however, is superbly caught.

w Bernardo Bertolucci, Eduardo de Gregorio, Marilu Parolini *story* The Theme of the Traitor and the Hero by Jorge Luis Borges *d* Bernardo Bertolucci *ph* Vittorio Storaro, Franco di Giacomo

☆ Giulio Brogi, Alida Valli, Tino Scotti, Pino Campanini

The Spider's Web

GB 1960 89m colour
Danzigers

A diplomat's wife has an unwanted corpse on her hands.
Fairly standard who-done-it played unwisely for comedy.

w Albert G. Miller, Eldon Howard *play* Agatha Christie *d* Godfrey Grayson *ph* Jimmy Wilson *m* Tony Crombie

☆ Glynis Johns, John Justin, Cicely Courtneidge, Jack Hulbert, Ronald Howard, David Nixon

---

Der Spiegel Ayna: see *The Mirror*

The Spies: see *Les Espions*

Spies Like Us
♟♟ US 1985 109m Technicolor
Warner (Brian Grazer, George Folsey Jnr)
⬚ ◉~ ◉
Bumbling bureaucrats are mistakenly chosen for a spy mission.
Inept attempts at humour fall flat throughout this dreary venture, which is as though Hope and Crosby had set out on the road to Morocco without a script.
w Dan Aykroyd, Lowell Ganz, Babaloo Mandel d John Landis ph Robert Paynter m Elmer Bernstein pd Peter Murton ed Malcolm Campbell
☆ Chevy Chase, Dan Aykroyd, Steve Forrest, Donna Dixon, Bruce Davison, William Prince, Bernie Casey

Spies of the Air
GB 1939 77m bw
British National (John Corfield)
A test pilot turns out to be an enemy agent.
Moderate programmer with an engaging cast.
w A. R. Rawlinson, Bridget Boland play *Official Secrets* by Jeffrey Dell d David MacDonald
☆ Barry K. Barnes, Roger Livesey, Joan Marion, Basil Radford, Felix Aylmer, John Turnbull, Henry Oscar

The Spikes Gang
US 1974 96m DeLuxe
UA/Mirisch/Duo/Sanford (Walter Mirisch)
Three boys shelter a bank robber and join his gang.
Doom-laden, violent Western with a few comic lines.
w Irving Ravetch, Harriet Frank Jnr novel *The Bank Robber* by Giles Tippette d Richard Fleischer ph Brian West m Fred Karlin
☆ Lee Marvin, Gary Grimes, Ron Howard, Charles Martin Smith, Arthur Hunnicutt, Noah Beery Jnr

Spin of a Coin: see *The George Raft Story*

La Spina Dorsale del Diavolo: see *The Deserter*

Spinout
US 1966 93m Metrocolor Panavision
MGM/Euterpe (Joe Pasternak)
⬚ ◉~ ◉
GB title: *California Holiday*
A carefree touring singer agrees to drive an experimental car in a road race.
Mild star musical which at least stays in the open air.
w Theodore J. Flicker, George Kirgo d Norman Taurog ph Daniel L. Fapp m Georgie Stoll
☆ Elvis Presley, Shelley Fabares, Carl Betz, Cecil Kellaway, Diane McBain, Deborah Walley, Jack Mullaney, Will Hutchins, Una Merkel

Spinster: see *Two Loves*

The Spiral Road
US 1962 145m Eastmancolor
U-I (Robert Arthur)
◉
In 1936 Java, an atheist medical man fights a leprosy epidemic and eventually becomes a missionary.
A long slog through jungle/religious clichés, with a hilariously musical star and an almost Victorian script.
w John Lee Mahin, Neil Paterson novel *Jan de Hartog* d Robert Mulligan ph Russell Harlan m Jerry Goldsmith
☆ Rock Hudson, Burl Ives, Geoffrey Keen, Gena Rowlands, Will Kuluva, Neva Patterson, Philip Abbott

The Spiral Staircase *
US 1945 83m bw
RKO (Dore Schary)
▤ ◉~
A small town in 1906 New England is terrorized by a psychopathic killer of deformed girls.
Archetypal old dark house thriller, superbly detailed and set during a most convincing thunderstorm. Even though the identity of the villain is pretty obvious, this is a superior Hollywood product.
w Mel Dinelli novel *Some Must Watch* by Ethel Lina White d Robert Siodmak ph Nicholas Musuraca m Roy Webb ad Albert S. D'Agostino, Jack Okey

☆ Dorothy McGuire, George Brent, Kent Smith, Ethel Barrymore, Rhys Williams, Rhonda Fleming, Gordon Oliver, Sara Allgood, James Bell
'A nice, cosy and well-sustained atmosphere of horror.' – *C. A. Lejeune*
⚥ Ethel Barrymore

The Spiral Staircase
GB 1975 89m Technicolor
Warner/Raven (Peter Shaw)
▤
Modernized remake of the above using virtually the same script, and apparently determined to prove how badly it can be presented.
w Andrew Meredith d Peter Collinson ph Ken Hodges m David Lindup
☆ Jacqueline Bisset, Christopher Plummer, Sam Wanamaker, Mildred Dunnock, Gayle Hunnicutt, Sheila Brennan, Elaine Stritch, John Ronane, Ronald Radd, John Phillip Law
'I don't think this needless remake is going to set anyone's flesh creeping, except at the vulgar flashiness of the whole enterprise.' – *Michael Billington, Illustrated London News*

The Spirit Is Willing
US 1966 100m Technicolor
Paramount/William Castle
A family finds that its holiday home is haunted by the ghosts of a *crime passionel.*
Overlong, overplayed and witless farce with virtually no opportunity well taken.
w Ben Starr novel *The Visitors* by Nathaniel Benchley d William Castle ph Hal Stine m Vic Mizzy
☆ Sid Caesar, Vera Miles, John McGiver, Cass Daley, John Astin, Mary Wickes, Jesse White

Spirit of Culver
US 1939 89m bw
Universal
A boy grows up at Culver Military Academy.
Very humdrum flagwaver combined with a last attempt to maintain stardom for two child performers.
w Nathanael West, Whitney Bolton d Joseph Santley
☆ Jackie Cooper, Freddie Bartholomew, Tim Holt, Henry Hull, Andy Devine, Gene Reynolds
'Mild entertainment for duals and kids.' – *Variety*

The Spirit of St Louis *
US 1957 135m Warnercolor Cinemascope
Warner (Leyland Hayward)
⬚ ◉~ ◉
In 1927 Charles Lindbergh flies a specially constructed plane 3,600 miles nonstop New York to Paris in 33½ hours.
Impeccably in its period, this needlessly Cinemascoped reconstruction can scarcely avoid dull patches since for long stretches its hero is on screen solo apart from a fly, and his monologues become soporific.
w Billy Wilder, Wendell Mayes book Charles Lindbergh d Billy Wilder ph Robert Burks, Peverell Marley m Franz Waxman
☆ James Stewart, Murray Hamilton, Marc Connelly

The Spirit of the Beehive *
Spain 1973 98m Eastmancolor
Elias Querejeta
⬚ ▤ ◉~
original title: *El Espíritu de la Colmene*
In 1940 in a remote village, two children see a travelling film show of Frankenstein, and their imaginations run riot; or do they?
Sensitive story of childish imagination, reminiscent of Jeux Interdits and yet very much its own vision.
w Francisco J. Querejeta d Victor Erice ph Luis Cuadrado m Luis de Pablo
☆ Fernando Fernan Gomez, Teresa Gimpera, Ana Torrent, Isabel Telleria

Spirit of the People: see *Abe Lincoln in Illinois*

Spirits of the Dead: see *Histoires Extraordinaires*

The Spiritualist: see *The Amazing Dr X*

Spite Marriage *
US 1929 77m bw silent
MGM/Buster Keaton (Lawrence Weingarten)
▤ ◉~
A tailor's assistant loves an actress, who marries him to spite someone else.
For a Keaton comedy from his great period, this is remarkably thin on invention, and its pleasures, though undeniable, are minor.
w Richard Schayer, Lew Lipton d Edward Sedgwick ph Reggie Lanning
☆ Buster Keaton, Dorothy Sebastian, Edward Earle, Leila Hyams

Spitfire: see *The First of the Few* (1942)

Spitfire *
US 1934 88m bw
RKO (Pandro S. Berman)
▤
An Ozark mountain girl believes herself to be a faith healer and is driven from the community.
Curious star melodrama with effective moments.
w Jane Murfin play *Trigger* by Lula Vollmer d John Cromwell ph Edward Cronjager m Max Steiner
☆ Katharine Hepburn, Robert Young, Ralph Bellamy, Martha Sleeper, Louis Mason
'The veins of the story carry thin milk rather than heavy corpuscles.' – *Variety*
'The picture would suggest that Katharine Hepburn is condemned to elegance, doomed to be a lady for the rest of her natural life, and that her artistry does not extend to the interpretation of the primitive or the uncouth. That her producers have not bothered to give her a scenario of any interest or quality is another aspect of the situation.' – *New Yorker*

The Spitfire Grill
US 1996 117m DeLuxe
Rank/Turner/Castle Rock/Gregory/Mendocino (Forrest Murray)
⬚ ▤ ◉~ ◉
aka: *Care of the Spitfire Grill*
The new waitress at a small-town diner, who served time for manslaughter, precipitates change and tragedy among the locals.
A minor melodrama among the dispossessed, soft at its centre, but strongly performed.
wd Lee David Zlotoff ph Robert Draper m James Horner pd Howard Cummings ed Margie Goodspeed
☆ Alison Elliott, Ellen Burstyn, Marcia Gay Harden, Will Patton, Kieran Mulroney, Gailard Sartain, John M. Jackson
'This view of café-society is too maudlin for its own good.' – *Tom Hutchinson, Film Review*

Spivs: see *I Vitelloni*

'She was the woman of his dreams. She had large dark eyes, a beautiful smile, and a great pair of fins.'
Splash! *
♟♟ US 1984 110m Technicolor
Touchstone/Buena Vista (Brian Grazer)
⬚ ▤ ◉~ ◉
A New York wholesaler on holiday off Cape Cod falls in love with a mermaid.
A kind of updated and mildly sexed-up Miranda: occasionally funny but far too long.
w Lowell Ganz, Babaloo Mandel, Bruce Jay Friedman, Brian Grazer d Ron Howard ph Don Peterman m Lee Holdridge
☆ Tom Hanks, Daryl Hannah, Eugene Levy, John Candy, Dody Goodman, Shecky Greene, Richard B. Shull, Howard Morris
'A typically Disney subject trying to be grown up.' – *Kim Newman, MFB*
'The picture is frequently on the verge of being more wonderful than it is ... more lyrical, a little wilder.' – *Pauline Kael, New Yorker*
⚥ screenplay

Splendor
US 1935 77m bw
Samuel Goldwyn
The son of a once-wealthy Park Avenue family marries a poor girl.
Dated romantic drama.
w Rachel Crothers play Rachel Crothers d Elliott Nugent ph Gregg Toland md Alfred Newman

☆ Joel McCrea, Miriam Hopkins, Helen Westley, Katherine Alexander, David Niven, Paul Cavanagh, Billie Burke, Arthur Treacher
'An unusually good production, but probably too quiet for the lesser spots.' – *Variety*
'A model of dramatic exposition, but it suffers from inaction and its theme is too commonplace.' – *New York Times*

Splendor *
Italy/France 1988 99m Cinecitta
Warner/Cecchi Gori/Tiger Cinematografica/Studio El/Gaumont/Generale d'Images/RAI (Mario Cecchi Gori, Vittorio Cecchi Gori)
A bankrupt small-town cinema owner remembers past glories.
Charming, gently nostalgic lament for movies as a communal experience.
wd Ettore Scola ph Luciano Tovoli m Armando Trovaioli ad Luciano Ricceri ed Francesco Malvestito
☆ Marcello Mastroianni, Massimo Troisi, Marina Vlady, Paolo Panelli, Pamela Villoresi, Giacomo Piperno, Massimo Bartocini

'Most pictures end in a theatre. This picture ends late at night in your heart.'
Splendor in the Grass *
US 1961 124m Technicolor
Warner/NBI (Elia Kazan)
⬚ ◉~
Adolescent love in a small Kansas town in the twenties.
Impressive though curiously unmemorable addition to a nostalgic young sex cycle which was already played out; production and performances well up to scratch.
w William Inge d Elia Kazan ph Boris Kaufman m David Amram
☆ Natalie Wood, Warren Beatty, Pat Hingle, Audrey Christie, Barbara Loden, Zohra Lampert, Sandy Dennis
'Less like a high-school version of *Summer and Smoke* than [like] an Andy Hardy story with glands.' – *Stanley Kauffmann*
🏆 William Inge
⚥ Natalie Wood

Splinters
GB 1929 82m bw
B and D (Herbert Wilcox)
Soldiers at the front in 1915 form a concert party.
Easy-going crowd-pleaser of its time.
w W. P. Lipscomb d Jack Raymond ph David Kesson m Carroll Gibbons
☆ Nelson Keys, Sydney Howard, Lew Lake, Hal Jones, Reg Stone
† Sequels, of roughly the same standard, included *Splinters in the Navy*, 1931, and *Splinters in the Air*, 1937; both with Sydney Howard.

The Split
US 1968 90m Metrocolor Panavision
MGM/Spectrum (Robert Chartoff, Irwin Winkler)
A black criminal plans to rob the Los Angeles Coliseum during a football match.
Busy, brutal crime thriller, well enough done but totally unsympathetic.
w Robert Sabaroff novel *The Seventh* by Richard Stark d Gordon Flemyng ph Burnett Guffey m Quincy Jones
☆ Jim Brown, Diahann Carroll, Ernest Borgnine, Julie Harris, Gene Hackman, Jack Klugman, Warren Oates, James Whitmore, Donald Sutherland

Split Image *
US 1982 111m Metrocolor Panavision
Polygram Pictures (Ted Kotcheff)
A normal middle-class college athlete becomes involved with a religious cult.
Effective melodrama about brainwashing.
w Scott Spencer, Robert Kaufman, Robert Mark Kamen d Ted Kotcheff ph Robert Jessup m Bill Conti pd Wolf Kroeger ed Jay Kamen
☆ Michael O'Keefe, Karen Allen, James Woods, Elizabeth Ashley, Brian Dennehy, Ronnie Scribner, Michael Sacks, Peter Fonda

Split Second
US 1953 85m bw
RKO (Edmund Grainger)
An escaped convict hides out with four hostages in an Arizona ghost town which has been cleared in preparation for an atom bomb test.

Routine suspenser.
w William Bowers, Irving Wallace d Dick Powell
ph Nicholas Musuraca m Roy Webb
☆ Stephen McNally, Alexis Smith, Jan Sterling, Keith Andes, Arthur Hunnicutt, Paul Kelly, Richard Egan, Robert Paige

Split Second
GB 1991 90m Eastmancolor
Entertainment/Challenge/Muse (Laura Gregory)
In 2008, in a flooded London, a cop goes after a serial killer who turns out to be a monster.
A gallant, if misguided, attempt to revive the man-in-a-rubber-suit school of horror movies.
w Gary Scott Thompson d Tony Maylam
ph Clive Tickner m Stephen Parsons, Francis Haines pd Chris Edwards ed Dan Rae
☆ Rutger Hauer, Kim Cattrall, Neil Duncan, Michael J. Pollard, Alun Armstrong, Peter Postlethwaite, Ian Dury, Roberta Eaton, Tony Steedman
'An extremely stupid monster film, boasting enough violence and special effects to satisfy less discriminating vid fans.' – *Variety*

Splitface: see Dick Tracy

Splitting Heirs
GB 1993 87m Technicolor
UIP/Prominent Features (Simon Bosanquet, Redmond Morris)
A city businessman, adopted by a Pakistani family, discovering that he, and not his best friend, is really the heir to the Dukedom of Bournemouth, decides to murder his rival.
Sad and trivial comedy, consisting of ineptly performed knockabout routines.
w Eric Idle d Robert Young ph Tony Pierce-Roberts m Michael Kamen pd John Beard
ed John Jympson
☆ Eric Idle, Rick Moranis, Barbara Hershey, Catherine Zeta Jones, John Cleese, Sadie Frost, Stratford Johns, Brenda Bruce, William Franklyn, Jeremy Clyde, Eric Sykes
'Breezy but lightweight comedy.' – *Variety*
'The pace and cheerful inanity of the picture may go some way to excusing its lack of wit and subtlety.' – *Geoffrey Macnab, Sight and Sound*

The Spoilers *
US 1930 86m bw
Paramount (Lloyd Sheldon)
In Alaska during the gold rush, crooked government officials begin despoiling the richest claims.
Early talkie version of a famous brawling saga.
w Bartlett Cormack, Agnes Brand Leahy
novel Rex Beach d Edward Carewe ph Harry Fischbeck
☆ Gary Cooper, William 'Stage' Boyd, Betty Compson, Kay Johnson, Harry Green, Slim Summerville
'Fair for a week in the de luxers, but made to order for the neighbourhoods and grinds everywhere.' – *Variety*

The Spoilers **
US 1942 87m bw
Universal (Frank Lloyd)
Two adventurers in the Yukon quarrel over land rights and a saloon entertainer.
Well-packaged mixture of saloon brawls, romance and adventure, much filmed as a silent.
w Lawrence Hazard, Tom Reed d Ray Enright ph Milton Krasner m Hans Salter ad Jack Otterson, John B. Goodman
☆ Marlene Dietrich, Randolph Scott, John Wayne, Margaret Lindsay, Harry Carey, Richard Barthelmess, George Cleveland, Samuel S. Hinds
'All concerned have kept their tongues firmly in their cheeks.' – *New York Times*
⅄ art direction

The Spoilers *
US 1955 82m Technicolor
U-I (Ross Hunter)
Adequate, unmemorable remake of the above.
w Oscar Brodney, Charles Hoffman d Jesse Hibbs ph Maury Gertsman m Joseph Gershenson
☆ Anne Baxter, Jeff Chandler, Rory Calhoun, Barbara Britton, Carl Benton Reid, Ray Danton, John McIntire, Raymond Walburn, Wallace Ford

Spoklenci slasti: see Conspirators of Pleasure

Spontaneous Combustion
US 1990 108m colour
Taurus (Jim Rogers)
The son of parents subjected to nuclear experiments discovers that he can set people on fire.
Direly ridiculous horror, a wet blanket of a movie, depressing and unimaginative.
w Tobe Hooper, Howard Goldberg d Tobe Hooper ph Levie Isaacks m Graeme Revell
ed David Kern
☆ Brad Dourif, Cynthia Bain, Jon Cypher, William Prince, Dey Young, Melinda Dillon, John Landis
'Silly beyond belief … a horror pic that literally goes up in flames.' – *Variety*

Spooks Run Wild
US 1941 65m bw
Monogram/Banner (Sam Katzman)
The East Side Kids are sent, against their will, to summer camp, where a killer is on the prowl.
Lively haunted-house comedy, with Lugosi providing a parody of his Count Dracula.
w Carl Foreman, Charles R. Marion, Jack Henley d Phil Rosen ph Marcel Le Picard ed Robert Golden
☆ Bela Lugosi, Leo Gorcey, Bobby Jordan, Huntz Hall, Sunshine Sammy Morrison, Dave O'Brien, David Gorcey, Angelo Rossitto

Spoorloos: see The Vanishing

Sport of a Nation: see The All-American

The Sport of Kings
GB 1931 98m bw
Gainsborough (Michael Balcon)
A strict JP inherits a bookie business.
Heavy-going adaptation of a stage comedy warhorse, which nevertheless paved the way for many screen farces of the thirties.
w Angus MacPhail play Ian Hay d Victor Saville ph Freddie Young
☆ Leslie Henson, Gordon Harker, Hugh Wakefield, Dorothy Boyd

Sporting Blood
US 1931 80m bw
MGM
A horse passes through various hands and finally wins the Kentucky Derby.
Unremarkable programme fodder.
w Charles Brabin, Wanda Tuchock, Willard Mack story Horseflesh by Frederick Hazlitt Brennan d Charles Brabin
☆ Clark Gable, Ernest Torrence, Madge Evans, Lew Cody, Marie Prevost
'Racetrack romance with a different twist and only name Clark Gable.' – *Variety*

Sporting Love
GB 1937 68m bw
British Lion/Hammer
Two owners of a bankrupt racing stable try to kidnap their prize horse which has been mortgaged.
Thin musical farce from a stage success.
w Fenn Sherie, Ingram D'Abbes play Stanley Lupino d J. Elder Wills ph Eric Cross
☆ Stanley Lupino, Laddie Cliff, Henry Carlisle, Edna Peel, Bobbie Comber

Spot: see Dogpound Shuffle

'It's the business.'
Spotswood *
Australia 1991 95m colour
Feature/Meridian/Smiley (Richard Brennan, Timothy White)
An English time-and-motion expert investigates a ramshackle shoe factory.
Pleasant comedy in the Ealing tradition of the little man against uncaring bureaucracy.
w Max Dann, Andrew Knight d Mark Joffe ph Ellery Ryan m Ricky Fataar pd Chris Kennedy ed Nicholas Beauman
☆ Anthony Hopkins, Ben Mendelsohn, Alwyn Kurts, Bruno Lawrence, Angela Punch McGregor, Russell Crowe, Toni Collette

'Glides along with a dry wit, a keen visual sense and a kindly heart.' – *Geoff Brown, The Times*

Spring and Port Wine
GB 1970 101m Technicolor
EMI/Memorial (Michael Medwin)
A Lancashire family runs into trouble when stern father insists that teenage daughter should eat a meal she refuses.
A popular old-fashioned stage comedy which simply doesn't work on film, partly from being set in a too-real town (Bolton) and partly because of a miscast lead.
w Bill Naughton play Bill Naughton d Peter Hammond ph Norman Warwick m Douglas Gamley pd Reece Pemberton
☆ James Mason, Diana Coupland, Susan George, Rodney Bewes, Hannah Gordon, Adrienne Posta, Arthur Lowe

Spring in Park Lane **
GB 1948 92m bw
Imperadio/Herbert Wilcox
A diamond merchant's niece falls for a footman who just happens to be an impoverished lord in disguise.
Flimsy but highly successful romantic comedy which managed to get its balance right and is still pretty entertaining, much more so than its sequel Maytime in Mayfair.
w Nicholas Phipps play Come Out of the Kitchen by Alice Duer Miller d Herbert Wilcox ph Max Greene m Robert Farnon
☆ Anna Neagle, Michael Wilding, Tom Walls, Nicholas Phipps, Peter Graves, Marjorie Fielding, Nigel Patrick, Lana Morris
'A never-failing dream of Olde Mayfaire and its eternally funny butlers and maids, its disguised lords and ladies.' – *Richard Winnington*
'A gag comedy which absolutely sparkles.' – *Picture Show*
'The best comedy any British studio has produced for more years than I care to remember.' – *News of the World*

Spring Madness
US 1938 66m bw
MGM
The romance of a Harvard man and a student in the nearby women's college.
Very thin comedy material, stretched to its tearing point.
w Edward Chodorov play Spring Dance by Philip Barry d S. Sylvan Simon
☆ Maureen O'Sullivan, Lew Ayres, Ruth Hussey, Burgess Meredith, Joyce Compton

Spring Meeting
GB 1940 93m bw
ABPC
In Ireland, an impecunious widow wants her son to marry the daughter of an old flame.
Staid film version of a comedy whose characters turned up again in Treasure Hunt.
w Walter C. Mycroft, Norman Lee play M. J. Farrell, John Perry d Walter C. Mycroft
☆ Nova Pilbeam, Basil Sydney, Henry Edwards, Sarah Churchill, Michael Wilding, Margaret Rutherford, Enid Stamp Taylor, Hugh McDermott

Spring Parade *
US 1940 89m bw
Universal (Joe Pasternak)
A single baker's assistant falls for a prince.
Pleasing, artificial Austrian frou-frou with star and support in good escapist form.
w Bruce Manning, Felix Jackson story Ernst Marischka d Henry Koster ph Joseph Valentine m Robert Stolz md Charles Previn
☆ Deanna Durbin, Robert Cummings, S. Z. Sakall, Mischa Auer, Henry Stephenson, Anne Gwynne, Butch and Buddy
⅄ Joseph Valentine; Charles Previn; song 'Waltzing in the Clouds' (mRobert Stolz, lyGus Kahn)

Spring Reunion
US 1956 79m bw
UA/Bryna (Jerry Bresler)
College classmates fall in love all over again at a reunion fifteen years later.
Romantic fiction for the middle-aged, performed with bare competence.
wd Robert Pirosh ph Harold Lipstein m Herbert Spencer, Earle Hagen

☆ Betty Hutton, Dana Andrews, Jean Hagen, Robert Simon, James Gleason, Laura La Plante, Irene Ryan

Spring Symphony
West Germany 1983 103m colour
Blue Dolphin/Allianz Filmproduktion/Peter Schamoni
original title: Frühlingssinfonie
Biopic of the love affair between the composer Robert Schumann and the pianist Clara Wieck.
Glossy and stolid plod through a decade that relies on the music to maintain interest.
wd Peter Schamoni ph Gerard Vandenberg m Schumann pd Alfred Hirschmeier ed Elfi Tillack
☆ Nastassja Kinski, Herbert Grönemeyer, Rolf Hoppe, André Heller, Bernhard Wicki, Gidon Kremer, Edda Seippel

Spring Tonic
US 1935 55m bw
Fox
An escaped tigress causes various farcical episodes.
Comedy extravaganza on modest lines, like a stretched-out two-reeler.
w Patterson McNutt, H. W. Hanemann play Man Eating Tiger by Ben Hecht, Rose Caylor d S. Sylvan Simon
☆ Lew Ayres, Claire Trevor, Walter Woolf King, ZaSu Pitts, Jack Haley, Tala Birell, Sig Rumann
'Hodge-podge of hokum that offers no hope to distraught exhibitors.' – *Variety*

'The gun … the girl … they made one man the equal of five!'
Springfield Rifle
US 1952 93m Warnercolor
Warner (Louis E. Edelman)
A Union officer gets himself cashiered, joins the Confederates as a spy, and unmasks a traitor.
Stolid Civil War Western with Grade-A production but not much individuality.
w Charles Marquis Warren, Frank Davis d André de Toth ph Edwin DuPar m Max Steiner
☆ Gary Cooper, Phyllis Thaxter, David Brian, Lon Chaney Jnr, Paul Kelly, Phil Carey, James Millican, Guinn Williams

Springtime for Henry
US 1935 73m bw
Fox (Jesse L. Lasky)
A rich man makes a vocation of woman chasing.
Modest version of a play which was toured for many years with Edward Everett Horton in the lead.
w Keene Thompson, Frank Tuttle play Benn W. Levy d Frank Tuttle
☆ Otto Kruger, Nancy Carroll, Nigel Bruce, Heather Angel, Herbert Mundin
'Farcical intent, but only a few snickers.' – *Variety*

Springtime in the Rockies
US 1942 91m Technicolor
TCF (William LeBaron)
Romances blossom on a mountain holiday.
Flimsily-plotted, studio-bound, absolutely routine musical.
w Walter Bullock, Ken Englund story Philip Wylie d Irving Cummings ph Ernest Palmer md Alfred Newman songs Mack Gordon, Harry Warren
☆ Betty Grable, John Payne, Carmen Miranda, Edward Everett Horton, Cesar Romero, Charlotte Greenwood, Frank Orth, Harry James and his Music Makers

Spy 13: see Operator 13

Spy for a Day
GB 1939 71m bw
Two Cities (Mario Zampi)
A farm hand is discovered to be the exact double of a spy.
The only screen vehicle for this 'gormless' comedian, and not a bad one.
w Anatole de Grunwald, Hans Wilhelm, Emeric Pressburger, Ralph Block, Tommy Thompson story Stacy Aumonier d Mario Zampi ph Bernard Knowles m Nikolaus Brodsky d David Lean
☆ Duggie Wakefield, Paddy Browne, Jack Allen, Albert Lieven, Nicholas Hannen, Gibb McLaughlin

---

Spy Hard

US 1996 81m Technicolor
Buena Vista/Hollywood (Rick Friedberg, Doug
Draizin, Jeffrey Konvitz)
⌖ ▤
Special agent WD-40 is assigned to defeat a mad
general who threatens to blow up the world.
*This scrapes the bottom of a genre that is now beyond
satirizing and no longer funny in itself; a ragbag of
feeble jokes ineffectually aimed at the Bond films, it
doesn't even attempt to hit its target.*
w Rick Friedberg, Dick Chudnow, Jason Friedberg,
Aaron Seltzer d Rick Friedberg ph John R.
Leonetti m Bill Conti pd William Creber
ed Eric Sears
☆ Leslie Nielsen, Nicollette Sheridan, Charles
Durning, Marcia Gay Harden, Barry Bostwick,
John Ales, Andy Griffith, Mason Gamble
'They should have called it *Dire Hard*.' – *Film
Review*
† Those appearing in cameo roles include Dr Joyce
Brothers, Ray Charles, Roger Clinton, Robert
Culp, Robert Guillaume, Hulk Hogan, Pat Morita
and Mr T.

Spy Hunt *

US 1950 74m bw
Universal (Ralph Dietrich)
GB title: Panther's Moon
Secret microfilm is stowed in the collar of one of
two panthers being transported out of Europe by
train for circus use.
Slick minor espionage thriller.
w George Zuckerman, Leonard Lee
novel Panther's Moon by Victor Canning d George
Sherman ph Irving Glassberg m Walter Scharf
md Joseph Gershenson
☆ Howard Duff, Marta Toren, Philip Friend,
Robert Douglas, Philip Dorn, Walter Slezak, Kurt
Kreuger

The Spy in Black **

GB 1939 82m bw
Harefield/Alexander Korda (Irving Asher)
⌖ ▤ ⌂
US title: U-Boat 29
In the Orkneys in 1917, German spies don't trust
each other.
*Unusual romantic melodrama which provided an
unexpectedly interesting romantic team.*
w Emeric Pressburger, Roland Pertwee *novel* J.
Storer Clouston d Michael Powell ph Bernard
Browne m Miklos Rozsa
☆ Conrad Veidt, Valerie Hobson, Hay Petrie, Helen
Haye, Sebastian Shaw, Marius Goring, June
Duprez, Athole Stewart, Cyril Raymond

Spy in the Pantry: see *Ten Days in Paris*

The Spy in White: see *The Secret of Stamboul*

Spy of Napoleon

GB 1936 101m bw
JH Productions
A dancer saves Louis Napoleon from assassination.
*Solidly mounted period piece without much sense of
humour.*
w L. DuGarde Peach, Frederick Merrick, Harold
Simpson *novel Baroness Orczy* d Maurice Elvey
ph Curt Courant m W. L. Trytel
☆ Richard Barthelmess, Dolly Haas, Frank Vosper,
Francis L. Sullivan, Lyn Harding, Henry Oscar

'Brace yourself for greatness!'
The Spy Who Came in from the Cold **

GB 1965 112m bw
Paramount/Salem (Martin Ritt)
▤ ⌂
A British master spy is offered a chance to get even
with his East German opponent by being
apparently sacked, disillusioned, and open for
recruitment.
*The old undercover yarn with trimmings of such sixties
malaises as death wish, anti-establishmentism and
racial problems. As a yarn, quite gripping till it gets too
downbeat, but very harshly photographed.*
w Paul Dehn, Guy Trosper *novel* John Le Carré
d Martin Ritt ph Oswald Morris m Sol Kaplan
pd Tambi Larsen
☆ Richard Burton, Claire Bloom, Oskar Werner,
Peter Van Eyck, Sam Wanamaker, Rupert Davies,
George Voskovec, Cyril Cusack, Michael Hordern,
Robert Hardy, Bernard Lee, Beatrix Lehmann
♪ Richard Burton

† best British film; Oswald Morris; Tambi Larsen;
Richard Burton

The Spy Who Loved Me

♛♛ GB 1977 125m Eastmancolor
Panavision
UA/Eon (Albert R. Broccoli)
⌖ ▤ ⌂ ◎ ♫
James Bond and a glamorous Russian spy combine
forces to track down and eliminate a
megalomaniac shipping magnate with an undersea
missile base.
*Witless spy extravaganza in muddy colour, with the
usual tired chases and pussyfoot violence but no new
gimmicks except a seven-foot villain with steel teeth.*
w Christopher Wood, Richard Maibaum
novel Ian Fleming d Lewis Gilbert ph Claude
Renoir m Marvin Hamlisch pd Ken Adam
☆ Roger Moore, Barbara Bach, Curt Jurgens,
Richard Kiel, Caroline Munro, Walter Gotell,
Bernard Lee, Lois Maxwell, George Baker,
Desmond Llewelyn, Edward de Souza, Sydney
Tafler
'The film, bearing no relation to its nominal
source, seems to do nothing more than
anthologize its forerunners.' – *Tim Pulleine, MFB*
♪ Marvin Hamlisch; song 'Nobody Does It Better'
(*m*Marvin Hamlisch, *ly*Carole Bayer Sager)

The Spy with a Cold Nose

GB 1966 93m Eastmancolor
Paramount/Associated London/Embassy (Robert
Porter)
A fashionable vet is blackmailed by MI5 into
inserting a radio transmitter into a bulldog.
*Rather painful, overacted and overwritten farce full of
obvious jokes masquerading as satire.*
w Ray Galton, Alan Simpson d Daniel Petrie
ph Kenneth Higgins m Riz Ortolani
☆ Lionel Jeffries, Laurence Harvey, Daliah Lavi,
Eric Sykes, Eric Portman, Colin Blakely, Denholm
Elliott, Robert Flemyng, Paul Ford, Bernard Lee,
June Whitfield, Bernard Archard

The Spy with My Face

US 1966 86m Metrocolor
MGM/Arena (Sam Rolfe)
Enemy spies use a double of Napoleon Solo in an
attempt to take over the world.
*An extended version of an episode from the television
series The Man from U.N.C.L.E., no better than the
others in the series and more confusing than most.*
w Clyde Ware, Joseph Calvelli *ph* Fred
Koenekamp m Morton Stevens *ad* George W.
Davis, Merrill Pye ed Joseph Dervin
☆ Robert Vaughn, David McCallum, Leo G.
Carroll, Michael Evans, Sharon Farrell

Spylarks: see *The Intelligence Men*

Squadron Leader X

GB 1942 100m bw
RKO (Victor Hanbury)
A Nazi hero poses as a British pilot but has
difficulty getting back home.
Tall war story with dreary romantic trimmings.
w Wolfgang Wilhelm, Miles Malleson d Lance
Comfort ph Mutz Greenbaum (Max Greene)
☆ Eric Portman, Ann Dvorak, Walter Fitzgerald,
Barry Jones, Henry Oscar, Beatrice Varley

The Squall

US 1929 105m bw
First National
A Hungarian gypsy girl attracts all the male
members of a farming family, and causes trouble.
*Perfectly awful melodrama made worse by early sound
techniques.*
w Bradley King *play* Jean Bart d Alexander
Korda
☆ Myrna Loy, Alice Joyce, Loretta Young,
Richard Tucker, Carroll Nye, ZaSu Pitts, Harry
Cording

The Square Circle *

India 1996 103m Eastmancolor
Blue Dolphin/Gateway (Pravesh Sippy)
▤
original title: Daayraa
A beautiful young girl, escaping from a gang of
kidnappers, disguises herself as a man and journeys
back to her village with the help of a transvestite
busker.

*A curiosity, but an interesting one – a melodrama
about gender, sexual differences and identity done in a
crowd-pleasing style.*
w Timeri N. Murari, Chitra Palekar, Shashank
Shanker, Amol Palekar, Kamlesh Pande
story Timeri N. Murari d Amol Palekar ph Debu
Deodhar m Anand-Milind pd Prem Pillai
ed Waman Bhosle
☆ Nirmal Pandey, Sonali Kulkarni, Faiyyaz,
Rekha Sahay, Nina Kulkarni, Hyder Ali
'A welcome and controversial diversion from the
hundreds of popular Bollywood movies released
each year.' – *Empire*

Square Dance *

♛♛ GB 1986 112m Metrocolor
NBC/Michael Nesmith/Island (Daniel Petrie)
▤
An awkward 13-year-old girl in rural Texas leaves
her gruff grandfather for a visit to the mother she
dislikes.
*Unremarkable but cohesive family drama which most
will feel they have seen before.*
w Alan Hines *novel* Alan Hines d Daniel Petrie
ph Jacek Laskus m Bruce Broughton pd Jan Scott
ed Bruce Green
☆ Jason Robards, Jane Alexander, Winona Ryder,
Rob Lowe, Deborah Richter

The Square Jungle

US 1955 85m bw
U-I (Albert Zugsmith)
A conceited boxer gets his come-uppance.
Tailor-made studio co-feature.
w George Zuckerman d Jerry Hopper ph George
Robinson m Heinz Roemheld
☆ Tony Curtis, Ernest Borgnine, Pat Crowley, Jim
Backus, Paul Kelly

The Square Peg *

GB 1958 89m bw
Rank (Hugh Stewart)
▤
An army recruit finds he is the double of a German
general.
*Slam-bang star slapstick, shorter than usual and with a
few jokes that can't fail.*
w Jack Davies d John Paddy Carstairs ph Jack
Cox m Philip Green
☆ Norman Wisdom, Honor Blackman, Edward
Chapman, Campbell Singer, Hattie Jacques, Brian
Worth, Terence Alexander

The Square Ring *

GB 1953 83m bw
Ealing (Michael Relph)
One night at a boxing stadium.
*An assortment of anecdotes does not constitute one of
Ealing's best films, but the competence level is high.*
w Robert Westerby, Peter Myers, Alec Grahame
play Ralph Peterson d Basil Dearden ph Otto
Heller md Dock Mathieson ad Jim Morahan
ed Peter Bezencenet
☆ Jack Warner, Robert Beatty, Maxwell Reed, Bill
Owen, Joan Collins, Kay Kendall, Bernadette
O'Farrell, Eddie Byrne, Sid James, Alfie Bass

The Squaw Man

US 1931 106m bw
MGM (Cecil B. de Mille)
GB title: The White Man
An Indian maiden saves the life of a British
aristocrat, bears his child and commits suicide.
*Third outing for a hoary miscegenation drama filmed in
1914 with Dustin Farnum and Red Wing, and in 1918
with Elliott Dexter and Ann Little. This talkie version
sank without trace.*
w Lucien Hubbard, Lenore Coffee *play* Edwin
Milton Royle d Cecil B. de Mille ph Harold
Rosson m Herbert Stothart
☆ Warner Baxter, Lupe Velez, Charles Bickford,
Eleanor Boardman, Roland Young, Paul Cavanagh,
Raymond Hatton
'Should be generally fair b.o. in the smaller
localities and perhaps not so hot for the diffident
big-town show shoppers.' – *Variety*

The Squeaker *

GB 1937 77m bw
UA/Denham Productions (Alexander Korda)
▤
US title: Murder on Diamond Row
A dangerous diamond fence is unmasked by a
discredited policeman.

*Typical Edgar Wallace who-is-it, performed with old-
fashioned bravura.*
w Edward O. Berkman, Bryan Wallace
novel Edgar Wallace d William K. Howard
ph Georges Périnal m Miklos Rozsa ad Vincent
Korda ed Russell Lloyd
☆ Edmund Lowe, Sebastian Shaw, Ann Todd,
Tamara Desni, Alastair Sim, Robert Newton,
Allan Jeayes, Stewart Rome
† Previously filmed in 1930, directed by Edgar
Wallace for British Lion; with Percy Marmont, Eric
Maturin, Anne Grey and Nigel Bruce.

The Squeeze

GB 1977 107m Technicolor
Warner/ Martinat (Stanley O'Toole)
An alcoholic ex-cop rescues his ex-wife from
kidnappers.
*Sleazy action thriller which despite efficient production
goes over the top in its search for unpleasant detail.*
w Leon Griffiths *novel* David Craig d Michael
Apted ph Dennis Lewiston m David Hentschel
☆ Stacy Keach, David Hemmings, Stephen Boyd,
Edward Fox, Carol White, Freddie Starr
'It provides action and moral ambiguity enough
to stock a Don Siegel thriller.' – *Richard Combs,
MFB*

Squibs *

GB 1935 77m bw
Twickenham
A Cockney flowergirl wins a sweepstake.
*Acceptable sound version of a series of rather naïve
silents which pleased the crowds in the early twenties
with the same star: they were Squibs, Squibs MP,
Squibs' Honeymoon and Squibs Wins the Calcutta
Sweep.*
w Michael Hogan, H. Fowler Mear *play* Clifford
Seyler, George Pearson d Henry Edwards
☆ Betty Balfour, Gordon Harker, Stanley
Holloway, Margaret Yarde, Michael Shepley

Squirm

US 1976 92m Movielab
AIP/The Squirm Company (Edgar Lansbury, Joseph
Beruh)
▤
A power cable cut in a storm turns worms into
maneaters.
*Revolting shocker with a few funny moments for those
who can take it.*
wd Jeff Lieberman ph Joseph Mangine m Robert
Prince
☆ John Scardino, Patricia Pearcy, R. A. Dow, Jean
Sullivan

Stablemates

US 1938 89m bw
MGM
A broken-down vet saves a stableboy's racehorse.
*Sentimental comedy vehicle for two masters of the
surreptitious tear.*
w Reginald Owen, William Thiele d Sam Wood
☆ Wallace Beery, Mickey Rooney, Margaret
Hamilton, Minor Watson, Marjorie Gateson

Stacy's Knights

US 1983 95m colour
Crown/American Twist/Golden Gators (JoAnn
Locktov, Freddy Sweet)
▤
A female blackjack player sets out to revenge her
partner's death.
*Mediocre thriller that owes its occasional television
screenings to the fact that its cast includes Costner in
his first leading role.*
w Michael Blake d Jim Wilson ph Raoul Lomas
m Norton Buffalo ad Florence Fellman
ed Bonnie Koehler
☆ Andra Millen, Kevin Costner, Eve Lilith, Mike
Reynolds, Ed Semenza, Don Hackstaff

Stage Door ***

US 1937 92m bw
RKO (Pandro S. Berman)
⌖ ▤ ⌂
Life in a New York theatrical boarding house for
girls.
*Melodramatic, sharply comedic, always fascinating
slice of stagey life from a Broadway hit; the
performances alone make it worth preserving.*
w Morrie Ryskind, Anthony Veiller *play* Edna
Ferber, George S. Kaufman d Gregory La Cava
ph Robert de Grasse m Roy Webb ad Van Nest
Polglase

☆ Katharine Hepburn, Ginger Rogers, Adolphe Menjou, Gail Patrick, Constance Collier, Andrea Leeds, Lucille Ball, Samuel S. Hinds, Jack Carson, Franklin Pangborn, Eve Arden

'It is a long time since we have seen so much feminine talent so deftly handled.' – Otis Ferguson

'Zest and pace and photographic eloquence.' – Frank S. Nugent, New York Times

'A rare example of a film substantially improving on a stage original and a remarkably satisfying film on all levels.' – NFT, 1973

'One of the flashiest, most entertaining comedies of the 30s, even with its tremolos and touches of heartbreak.' – Pauline Kael, 70s

⚱ best picture; script; Gregory La Cava; Andrea Leeds

'48 stars plus a great love story!'

Stage Door Canteen *

US 1943 132m bw
Sol Lesser (Barnett Briskin)
▦ ▦ ▬ ⌒

How the stars in New York entertained the armed forces during World War II.
Nothing as a film, mildly interesting as sociology and for some rarish appearances.
w Delmer Daves d Frank Borzage ph Harry Wild m Freddie Rich pd Harry Horner
☆ Cheryl Walker, Lon McCallister, Judith Anderson, Tallulah Bankhead, Ray Bolger, Katharine Cornell, Helen Hayes, George Jessel, Alfred Lunt, Harpo Marx, Yehudi Menuhin, Elliott Nugent, Cornelia Otis Skinner, Ethel Waters, May Whitty and also William Demarest, Gracie Fields, Katharine Hepburn, Gertrude Lawrence, Ethel Merman, Merle Oberon, Johnny Weissmuller, Edgar Bergen, Jane Cowl, Lynn Fontanne, Paul Muni, Gypsy Rose Lee, George Raft, etc; Count Basie, Benny Goodman, Xavier Cugat, Guy Lombardo, Kay Kyser and their bands

'A nice harmless picture for the whole family, and a goldmine for those who are willing to go to it in the wrong spirit.' – James Agee

⚱ Freddie Rich; song 'We Mustn't Say Goodbye' (mJames V. Monaco, lyAl Dubin)

Stage Fright *

GB 1950 110m bw
Warner/ABPC (Alfred Hitchcock)
▬ ⌒

A man is on the run for a backstage murder, and his girlfriend takes a job as maid to the great star he says is responsible.
Creaky Hitchcock thriller in which you can see all the joins and the stars seem stuck in treacle; but a few of the set-pieces work well enough.
w Whitfield Cook novel Man Running by Selwyn Jepson d Alfred Hitchcock ph Wilkie Cooper m Leighton Lucas
☆ Marlene Dietrich, Jane Wyman, Richard Todd, Alastair Sim, Michael Wilding, Sybil Thorndike, Kay Walsh, Miles Malleson

Stage Mother

US 1933 85m bw
MGM
The mother of a young actress is not above sacrificing her daughter for financial gain.
Wisecracking comedy-romance, rather similar to the later Gypsy.
w John Meehan, Bradford Ropes novel Bradford Ropes d Charles Brabin
☆ Alice Brady, Maureen O'Sullivan, Franchot Tone, Phillips Holmes, Ted Healy, C. Henry Gordon

'Packed with colour, not a little s.a., and certain of adequate b.o. attention.' – Variety

Stage Struck

US 1936 95m bw
Warner (Robert Lord)
Young people put on a show and become instant hits.
Dim musical oddly shorn of production numbers.
w Tom Buckingham, Pat C. Flick, Robert Lord ph Byron Haskin m Leo F. Forbstein d/ch Busby Berkeley songs Harold Arlen, E. Y. Harburg
☆ Dick Powell, Joan Blondell, Jeanne Madden, the Yacht Club Boys, Warren William, Frank McHugh

Stage Struck **

US 1957 95m Technicolor
RKO (Stuart Millar)
▦ ⌒

A young actress comes to New York intent on stardom …
Careful, slightly arid remake of Morning Glory marred by a tiresome central performance; good theatrical detail.
w Ruth and Augustus Goetz play Zoe Akins d Sidney Lumet ph Franz Planer m Alex North ad Kim Edgar Swados
☆ Susan Strasberg, Henry Fonda, Herbert Marshall, Joan Greenwood, Christopher Plummer

Stage to Thunder Rock

US 1964 89m Techniscope
Paramount/A.C. Lyles
An ageing sheriff takes a bank robber back to jail by stagecoach.
Acceptable lower-berth Western with the producer's usual roster of half-forgotten character actors.
w Charles Wallace d William F. Claxton ph W. Wallace Kelley m Paul Dunlap
☆ Barry Sullivan, Marilyn Maxwell, Scott Brady, Keenan Wynn, Allan Jones, Lon Chaney Jnr, John Agar, Wanda Hendrix, Anne Seymour, Robert Lowery

Stagecoach ****

US 1939 99m bw
(UA)
▦ ▬ ⌒

Various Western characters board a stagecoach in danger from an Indian war party.
What looked like a minor Western with a plot borrowed from Maupassant's Boule de suif, became a classic by virtue of the firm characterization, restrained writing, exciting climax and the scenery of Monument Valley. Whatever the reasons, it damn well works.
w Dudley Nichols story Stage to Lordsburg by Ernest Haycox d John Ford ph Bert Glennon m Richard Hageman, W. Frank Harling, John Leopold, Leo Shuken, Louis Gruenberg md Boris Morros ad Alexander Toluboff ed Otho Lovering, Dorothy Spencer
☆ Claire Trevor, John Wayne, Thomas Mitchell, George Bancroft, Andy Devine, Berton Churchill, Louise Platt, John Carradine, Donald Meek, Tim Holt, Chris-Pin Martin

'It displays potentialities that can easily drive it through as one of the surprise big grossers of the year.' – Variety
'The basic western, a template for everything that followed.' – John Baxter, 1968
'Grand Hotel on wheels.' – New Yorker, 1975
'A motion picture that sings a song of camera.' – Frank S. Nugent, New York Times
♟ music; Thomas Mitchell
⚱ best picture; John Ford; Bert Glennon; art direction; editing

Stagecoach

US 1966 114m DeLuxe Cinemascope
TCF/Martin Rackin
⌒

Absolutely awful remake of the above; costly but totally spiritless, miscast and uninteresting.
w Joseph Landon d Gordon Douglas ph William H. Clothier m Jerry Goldsmith
☆ Ann-Margret, Alex Cord, Bing Crosby, Van Heflin, Slim Pickens, Robert Cummings, Stefanie Powers, Michael Connors, Red Buttons, Keenan Wynn

The Stagecoach Kid

US 1949 63m bw
RKO (Herman Schlom)
In order to escape to the big city, a rancher's daughter disguises herself as a cowboy but then falls in love with a stagecoach owner.
Light-hearted Western, a pleasant if unmemorable programme-filler.
w Norman Houston d Lew Landers ph Nicholas Musuraca m Paul Sawtell ad Albert D'Agostino, Feild Gray ed Les Millbrook
☆ Tim Holt, Richard Martin, Jeff Donnell, Joe Sawyer, Thurston Hall, Carol Hughes, Robert Bray

Stagecoach to Dancer's Rock

US 1958 72m bw
Universal/Gray-Mac (Earl Bellamy)
Passengers on a long-distance stagecoach are abandoned in the desert when it is thought that one of them has smallpox.
Unusual minor Western, though it goes full gallop into melodrama rather than the character study it set out to be; Landau is here heavily under the influence of the Method approach to acting.
w Kenneth Darling d Earl Bellamy ph Ed Fitzgerald m Franz Steininger ad Leslie Thomas ed Budd Small
☆ Warren Stevens, Martin Landau, Jody Lawrance, Don Wilbanks, Del Moore, Bob Anderson, Judy Dan, Rand Brooks, Gene Roth

Staggered *

GB 1994 95m Technicolor
Entertainment/Big Deal (Philippa Braithwaite)
▦

Following a stag party, a toy demonstrator wakes up to find himself naked on a Scottish island, with three days to get home before his wedding.
Sporadically amusing, episodic movie that has its moments; it often borders on the obvious, but the acting and direction display a good sense of comic timing.
w Paul Alexander, Simon Braithwaite d Martin Clunes ph Simon Kossoff m Peter Brewis pd Iain Andrews ed Peter Delfgou
☆ Martin Clunes, Michael Praed, Sarah Winman, Sylvia Sims, Virginia McKenna, Griff Rhys Jones, Michael Medwin, John Forgeham, Anna Chancellor

'Sitcom-style humor, peopled by a large gallery of British eccentrics. Produces a steady flow of mild gags, but doesn't build a proper head of steam to go the distance as a feature.' – Derek Elley, Variety

Staircase *

US/France 1969 101m DeLuxe Panavision
TCF/Stanley Donen
The problems of two ageing homosexual hairdressers.
Unsatisfactorily opened-out and over-acted version of an effective two-hander play. Oddly made in France, so that the London detail seems all wrong.
w Charles Dyer play Charles Dyer d Stanley Donen ph Christopher Challis m Dudley Moore
☆ Richard Burton, Rex Harrison, Cathleen Nesbitt, Beatrix Lehmann

'The shape is smashed … no longer a graceful duet, it becomes a waddling tale, spattered with ugliness, that falls into the biggest sentimental trap for homosexual material: it pleads for pity.' – Stanley Kauffmann

Stairway to Heaven: see A Matter of Life and Death

Stakeout

US 1987 115m DeLuxe
Touchstone (Jim Kouf, Cathleen Summers)
▬ ⌒

One of two Seattle cops engaged in a long stakeout falls in love with a suspect.
Ho-hum policier with insufficient plot for its length.
w Jim Kouf d John Badham ph John Seale m Arthur B. Rubinstein pd Philip Harrison ed Tom Rolf, Michael Ripps
☆ Richard Dreyfuss, Emilio Estevez, Madeleine Stowe, Aidan Quinn, Dan Lauria

Stakeout on Dope Street *

US 1958 83m bw
Warner (Andrew J. Fenady)
Three young men find a briease containing heroin and are attacked by the gangsters who lost it.
Lively little crime morality, uneven but worth a look.
w Irwin Schwartz, Irvin Kershner, Andrew J. Fenady d Irvin Kershner ph Mark Jeffrey m Richard Markowitz
☆ Yale Wexler, Jonathan Haze, Morris Miller, Abby Dalton

Stalag 17 **

US 1953 120m bw
Paramount (Billy Wilder)
▦ ▦ ▬ ⌒

Comedy and tragedy for American servicemen in a Nazi prisoner-of-war camp.

High jinks, violence and mystery in a sharply calculated mixture; an atmosphere quite different from the understated British films on the subject.
w Billy Wilder, Edwin Blum play Donald Bevan, Edmund Trzinski d Billy Wilder ph Ernest Laszlo m Franz Waxman
☆ William Holden, Don Taylor, Otto Preminger, Robert Strauss, Harvey Lembeck, Richard Erdman, Peter Graves, Neville Brand, Sig Rumann

'A facility for continuous rapid-fire action which alternately brings forth the laughs and tingles the spine.' – Otis L. Guernsey Jnr
'Raucous and tense, heartless and sentimental, always fast-paced, it has already been assigned by critics to places on their lists of the year's ten best movies.' – Life
♟ William Holden
⚱ Billy Wilder (as director), Robert Strauss

Stalingrad **

Germany 1992 138m colour
Entertainment/Royal/Bavaria/BA/Perathon (Joseph Vilsmaier, Hanno Huth, Günter Rohrbach)
▦ ▦ ▬

German soldiers try to escape the horrors of war during and after the battle for Stalingrad.
An impressive, downbeat account, from the viewpoint of a lieutenant and his troop, of an attempt to survive the depredations of the harsh Russian winter and of their own officers.
w Johannes Heide, Jürgen Büsche, Joseph Vilsmaier d Joseph Vilsmaier ph Joseph Vilsmaier m Norbert J. Schneider pd Wolfgang Hundhammer, Jindrich Goetz ed Hannes Nikel
☆ Dominique Horwitz, Jochen Nickel, Sebastian Rudolph, Thomas Kretschmann, Martin Benrath, Dana Vavrova

'A unique movie in that it sticks so closely to its foot soldier heroes, enabling us to see very clearly what happens when a mad leader pushes them too far and too fast.' – Derek Malcolm, Guardian

Stalker *

USSR 1979 161m colour/bw
Mosfilm Unit 2
▦ ▬ ⌒

In the centre of an industrial wasteland there appears a mysterious zone where all normal laws of life are suspended.
Part political allegory, part personal fantasy, all very fascinating but rather hard tack for anybody in search of entertainment.
w Arkady Strugatsky, Boris Strugatsky story Arkady Strugatsky, Boris Strugatsky ph Aleksandr Knyazhinsky m Eduard Artemyev d/pd Andrei Tarkovsky
☆ Aleksandr Kaidanovsky, Anatoly Solonitsin, Nikolai Grinko, Alisa Freindlikh

The Stalker

US 1992 85m Foto-Kem
Concorde/New Horizons (Mike Elliott)
▦

In the aftermath of a San Francisco earthquake a woman finds herself imprisoned by her neighbourhood psychopath.
Typical product of Roger Corman's company, exploitative and topical, competent but uninspired.
w Mark Evan Schwartz story Rob Kerchner d Louis Morneau ph Mark Parry m Nigel Holton pd Stuart Blatt ed Glenn Garland
☆ Steve Railsback, Erika Anderson, Eb Lottimer, Burton Gilliam, Dick Miller

The Stalking Moon *

US 1968 109m Technicolor Panavision
National General/Stalking Moon Company (Alan J. Pakula)
▬

An ageing scout escorts home a white woman who has escaped from the Indians, and kills a murderous Apache.
Slow, thoughtful Western with effective moments.
w Alvin Sargent novel Theodore V. Olsen d Robert Mulligan ph Charles Lang m Fred Karlin
☆ Gregory Peck, Eva Marie Saint, Robert Forster, Frank Silvera

Stallion Road

US 1947 97m bw
Warner (Alex Gottlieb)
An outbreak of anthrax threatens a racing stable.
Routine romantic drama with sporting background.

w Stephen Longstreet d James V. Kern
ph Arthur Edeson m Frederick Hollander
☆ Ronald Reagan, Alexis Smith, Zachary Scott, Peggy Knudsen, Patti Brady, Harry Davenport, Frank Puglia

'The film, so free and fluent as long as it is talking horses, becomes curiously trite and turgid over the business of mating humans.' – C. A. Lejeune, Observer

Stamboul Quest

US 1934 88m bw
MGM (Walter Wanger)

During World War I, Germany's most notorious lady spy falls for an American medical student.
Modest variation on the true story twice filmed as Fräulein Doktor; standard Hollywood values.

w Herman J. Mankiewicz d Sam Wood ph James Wong Howe m Herbert Stothart
☆ Myrna Loy, George Brent, Lionel Atwill, C. Henry Gordon, Douglass Dumbrille, Mischa Auer

Stampeded: see The Big Land

Stan and George's New Life

Australia 1990 104m colour
Lea/AFC/Margot McDonald, Brian McKenzie

Bored with his life, and his quarrelling parents, a 40-year-old Melbourne barber gets a new job as a clerk in the weather bureau, where he marries into another dysfunctional family.
Drab drama of drabber lives, so low-key as to be virtually comatose.

w Brian McKenzie, Deborah Cox d Brian McKenzie ph Ray Argall m Michael Atkinson
ad Daryl Mills ed Edward McQueen-Mason
☆ Paul Chubb, John Bluthal, Julie Forsyth, Margaret Ford, Roy Baldwin, Bruce Alexander, Beverly Gardiner, Shapoor Baltiwallia

Stand Alone

US 1985 90m Metrocolor
Texas Star (Leon Williams)

A grandfather, a hero in the Second World War, is targeted by professional gangsters after he witnesses a murder in his local diner.
Dull and implausible drama, slow-moving, uninvolving and faintly risible.

w Roy Carlson d Alan Beattie ph Tom Richmond, Tim Suhrstedt m David Richard Campbell ad Pam Warner ed Fabien Tordjmann
☆ Charles Durning, Pam Grier, James Keach, Bert Remsen, Barbara Sammeth, Lu Leonard, Luis Contreras, Willard Pugh, Bob Tzudiker

Stand and Deliver **

US 1988 104m Foto-Kem
Warner/American Playhouse (Tom Musca)

A maths teacher at a tough high school persuades his class of violent pupils that education is an asset.
Based on facts, the engaging story wins out over the rudimentary cinematic style.

w Ramon Menendez, Tom Musca d Ramon Menendez ph Tom Richmond m Craig Safan ad Milo ed Nancy Richardson
☆ Edward James Olmos, Lou Diamond Phillips, Rosana de Soto, Andy Garcia, Ingrid Oliu, Karla Montana, Vanessa Marquez, Mark Eliot
⁑ Edward James Olmos

The Stand at Apache River

US 1953 77m Technicolor
Universal-International (William Alland)

Apaches attack a reservation when the army won't listen to reason.
Conventional Western with sympathy for the Indians.

w Arthur Ross d Lee Sholem ph Charles Boyle m Frank Skinner
☆ Stephen McNally, Julie Adams, Hugh Marlowe, Hugh O'Brian, Jack Kelly

Stand by for Action

US 1943 109m bw
MGM (Robert Z. Leonard, Orville O. Dull)
GB title: Cargo of Innocents

A Harvard graduate learns the realities of war on an old destroyer.
Studio-bound war heroics slurping into sentiment.

w George Bruce, Herman J. Mankiewicz, John L. Balderston d Robert Z. Leonard ph Charles Rosher m Lennie Hayton

☆ Robert Taylor, Charles Laughton, Brian Donlevy, Walter Brennan, Marilyn Maxwell, Henry O'Neill

Stand by Me *

US 1986 89m Technicolor/DeLuxe
Columbia/Act III

A boys' gang finds the body of a missing teenager.
Less macabre than its source would suggest, the film is mostly concerned with the friendships and tensions within the group; nostalgia for 50s childhood is nicely conveyed.

w Raynold Gideon, Bruce A. Evans story The Body by Stephen King d Rob Reiner ph Thomas Del Ruth m Jack Nitzsche pd Dennis Washington
☆ Wil Wheaton, River Phoenix, Corey Feldman, Jerry O'Connell, Kiefer Sutherland, Richard Dreyfuss
⁑ screenplay

Der Stand Der Dinge: see The State of Things

Stand Easy: see Down among the Z Men

'Hail! The conquering hero comes!'

Stand In *

US 1937 90m bw
Walter Wanger

An efficiency expert is sent to save a Hollywood studio from bankruptcy.
Amusing satire which could have done with sharper scripting and firmer control but is pleasantly remembered.

w Gene Towne, Graham Baker serial Clarence Budington Kelland d Tay Garnett ph Charles G. Clarke m Heinz Roemheld
☆ Leslie Howard, Joan Blondell, Humphrey Bogart, Alan Mowbray, Marla Shelton, C. Henry Gordon, Jack Carson, Tully Marshall

'A joyous and nonsensical Hollywood fantasia.' – Spectator

Stand Up and Be Counted *

US 1971 99m Eastmancolor
Columbia/Mike Frankovich

An international woman journalist returns to Denver and becomes involved in women's lib.
A glamoured-up flirtation with a fashionable theme, quite nicely done but instantly dated – and sociologically interesting.

w Bernard Slade d Jackie Cooper ph Fred Koenekamp m Ernie Wilkins
☆ Jacqueline Bisset, Stella Stevens, Steve Lawrence, Gary Lockwood, Loretta Swit, Lee Purcell, Madlyn Rhue

Stand Up and Cheer *

US 1934 80m bw
Fox (Winfield Sheehan)

The new US Secretary of Amusement attempts to shake the country's Depression blues by staging a mammoth revue.
Naïve propaganda, but the whole world was swept away to cloud nine – by Shirley Temple.

w Ralph Spence, Will Rogers, Philip Klein d Hamilton McFadden ph Ernest Palmer md Arthur Lange
☆ Warner Baxter, Madge Evans, Nigel Bruce, Stepin Fetchit, Frank Melton, Lila Lee, Ralph Morgan, James Dunn, Shirley Temple, John Boles, George K. Arthur

'Its intrinsic merits do not quite match its pretentiousness.' – Variety
'Impossible to file it away in an ordinary drawer marked "Stinkers". This one is extra, it is super, and it butters itself very thickly with the most obvious sort of topical significance.' – Otis Ferguson
† The original title was Fox Follies.

'They Built a New America with Glory and Guns ... They were MEN that Women Could Love!'

Stand Up and Fight *

US 1938 99m bw
MGM (Mervyn Le Roy)

A Southern aristocrat comes into conflict with a stagecoach operator used as transportation for stolen slaves.
Superior star action piece with plenty of vigorous brawls.

w James M. Cain, Jane Murfin, Harvey Ferguson d W. S. Van Dyke II ph Leonard Smith m William Axt
☆ Wallace Beery, Robert Taylor, Florence Rice, Helen Broderick, Charles Bickford, Barton MacLane, Charley Grapewin, John Qualen

'An action thriller that will please the muggs more than the dames ... should prove strong at the b.o.' – Variety

Stand Up Virgin Soldiers

GB 1977 90m Technicolor
Warner/Greg Smith/Maidenhead

More sexual adventures of National Servicemen in Singapore in 1950.
The Virgin Soldiers had a certain authenticity behind the fooling; this is a bawdy romp, and not a very efficient one.

w Leslie Thomas novel Leslie Thomas d Norman Cohen ph Ken Hodges m Ed Welch
☆ Nigel Davenport, Robin Askwith, George Layton, Robin Nedwell, Warren Mitchell, John Le Mesurier, Edward Woodward, Irene Handl

'The hilarious story of what a girl will do to get her boss a bed in Washington!'

Standing Room Only *

US 1944 83m bw
Paramount (Paul Jones)

Hotel rooms being hard to find in wartime Washington, a resourceful secretary hires herself and her boss as a servant couple.
Moderate romantic farce with a few good laughs.

w Darrell Ware, Karl Tunberg d Sidney Lanfield ph Charles Lang m Robert Emmett Dolan
☆ Paulette Goddard, Fred MacMurray, Edward Arnold, Roland Young, Hillary Brooke, Porter Hall, Clarence Kolb, Anne Revere

Stanley & Iris

US 1989 105m DuArt
UIP/MGM/Star Partners II (Arlene Sellers, Alex Winitsky)

A cook who loses his job because he is illiterate is taught to read by a sympathetic widow.
Dull, heavy-handed and sentimental, not even its stars can save it from tedium.

w Harriet Frank Jnr, Irving Ravetch novel Union Street by Pat Barker d Martin Ritt ph Donald McAlpine m John Williams pd Joel Schiller ed Sidney Levin
☆ Jane Fonda, Robert DeNiro, Swoosie Kurtz, Martha Plimpton, Harley Cross, Jamey Sheridan, Feodor Chaliapin

Stanley and Livingstone ***

US 1939 101m bw
TCF (Kenneth MacGowan)

An American journalist goes to Africa to find a lost Victorian explorer.
A prestige picture which played reasonably fair with history and still managed to please the masses.

w Philip Dunne, Julien Josephson d Henry King ph George Barnes m David Raksin, David Buttolph, Cyril Mockridge, Alfred Newman ad Thomas Little
☆ Spencer Tracy, Cedric Hardwicke, Richard Greene, Nancy Kelly, Walter Brennan, Charles Coburn, Henry Hull, Henry Travers, Miles Mander, Holmes Herbert

'Sound, worthy, interesting.' – Richard Mallett, Punch
'Most of the film consists of long shots of stand-ins moving across undistinguished scenery ... Mr Tracy is always a human being, but Sir Cedric is an elocution lesson, a handclasp.' – Graham Greene
'Holds box office promise for socko biz ... it's absorbing and adventurous drama.' – Variety

Stanno Tutti Bene **

Italy 1990 125m colour
Erre/Ariane (Angelo Rizzoli)

aka: Everybody's Fine

An elderly Sicilian decides to visit his five adult children living in various parts of Italy and finds that the reality does not live up to his expectations for them.
Bitter-sweet tale of muddling through life, elegantly acted and directed.

w Giuseppe Tornatore, Tonino Guerra d Giuseppe Tornatore ph Blasco Giurato

m Ennio Morricone ad Andrea Crisanti ed Mario Morra
☆ Marcello Mastroianni, Michele Morgan, Marino Cenna, Roberto Nobile, Valeria Cavali, Norma Martelli

'Liberally sprinkled with ideas that provide the viewer with periodic payoffs and laughs.' – Variety

Star! **

US 1968 194m DeLuxe Todd-AO
TCF/Robert Wise (Saul Chaplin)

Revue artist Gertrude Lawrence rises from poverty to international stardom and a measure of happiness.
Elephantiasis finally ruins this patient, detached, generally likeable recreation of a past theatrical era. In the old Hollywood style, it would probably have been even better on a smaller budget; but alas the star would still have been ill at ease with the drunken termagant scenes.

w William Fairchild d Robert Wise ph Ernest Laszlo md Lennie Hayton ch Michael Kidd pd Boris Leven
☆ Julie Andrews, Daniel Crenna, Michael Craig, Daniel Massey, John Collin, Robert Reed, Bruce Forsyth, Beryl Reid, Jenny Agutter
† Short version: Those Were the Happy Days.
†† The film cost 14 million and took four.
⁑ Ernest Laszlo; Lennie Hayton; title song (mJames Van Heusen, lySammy Cahn); Daniel Massey

'When the star fades, the woman is born!'
'The story of every woman who ever climbed the stairway to the stars – and found herself at the bottom looking up!'

The Star *

US 1952 91m bw
TCF/Bert E. Friedlob

A once famous Hollywood star is financially and psychologically on her uppers.
A movie apparently tailor-made for its star turns out to be a disappointingly plotless wallow.

w Katherine Albert, Dale Eunson d Stuart Heisler ph Ernest Laszlo m Victor Young
☆ Bette Davis, Sterling Hayden, Natalie Wood, Warner Anderson, Minor Watson
† The role was originally designed for Joan Crawford.
⁑ Bette Davis

Star 80

US 1983 103m Technicolor
Warner/Ladd (Wolfgang Glattes, Kenneth Utt)

The murder by her husband of Dorothy Stratten, the Playboy centrefold model.
Unappetizing recounting, made less palatable by flashy direction, of a story with no possible moral.

wd Bob Fosse ph Sven Nykvist m Ralph Burns pd Tony Walton ed Alan Heim
☆ Mariel Hemingway, Eric Roberts, Cliff Robertson, Carroll Baker, Roger Rees, Lisa Gordon, David Clennon, Josh Mostel

'A mishmash of embarrassments.' – Tom Milne, MFB
'Obviously intended as a cautionary tale for our times, with the beautiful dreamers and ruthless schemers peopling a colour supplement world of success.' – Sight and Sound

The Star Chamber

US 1983 109m DeLuxe Panavision
TCF/Frank Yablans

Judges get together to retry defendants who have been unjustly freed, and then have them executed by hired assassins.
A bit hard to swallow; also overlong and rather unpleasant.

w Roderick Taylor, Peter Hyams d Peter Hyams ph Richard Hannah m Michael Small pd Bill Malley
☆ Michael Douglas, Hal Holbrook, Yaphet Kotto, Sharon Gless, James B. Sikking, Joe Regalbuto

'Michael Winner territory with a veneer of conscience.' – Sight and Sound
'Small-screen material suffering from crippling inflation.' – Steve Jenkins, MFB

Star Dust *

US 1940 85m bw
TCF (Kenneth MacGowan)
A talent scout discovers a new Hollywood star.
Light, amusing studio comedy, a pleasing addition to Hollywood mythology.
w Robert Ellis, Helen Logan d Walter Lang
ph Peverell Marley m David Buttolph
☆ Linda Darnell, John Payne, Roland Young, Charlotte Greenwood, William Gargan, Mary Beth Hughes, Donald Meek, Jessie Ralph

A Star Is Born ***

US 1937 111m Technicolor
David O. Selznick
A young actress meets Hollywood success and marries a famous leading man, whose star wanes as hers shines brighter.
Abrasive romantic melodrama which is also the most accurate study of Hollywood ever put on film.
w Dorothy Parker, Alan Campbell, Robert Carson story William A. Wellman, based partly on 'What Price Hollywood' (1932) (qv) d William A. Wellman ph W. Howard Greene m Max Steiner
☆ Janet Gaynor, Fredric March, Adolphe Menjou, Lionel Stander, Andy Devine, May Robson, Owen Moore, Franklin Pangborn
  'One of those rare ones which everyone will want to see and talk about ... disproves the tradition that good pictures can't be made with a Hollywood background.' – *Variety*
  'Good entertainment by any standards.' – *Frank S. Nugent, New York Times*
  'A peculiar sort of masochistic self-congratulatory Hollywood orgy.' – *New Yorker, 1975*
  'The first colour job that gets close to what colour must eventually come to: it keeps the thing in its place, underlining the mood and situation of the story rather than dimming everything else out in an iridescent razzle-dazzle.' – *Otis Ferguson*
♫ original story; Special Award to W. Howard Greene for colour photography
♟ best picture; script; William A. Wellman; Janet Gaynor; Fredric March

'Fate raised her to fame – and killed the man she loved!'

A Star Is Born **

US 1954 181m Technicolor Cinemascope
Warner/Transcona (Sidney Luft)
Musical version of the above which begins very strongly and has two splendid performances, but suffers in the second half from a lack of writing strength and heavy post-production cutting. The numbers add very little except length.
w Moss Hart d George Cukor ph Sam Leavitt md Ray Heindorf ad Malcolm Bert, Gene Allen, Irene Sharaff
☆ Judy Garland, James Mason, Charles Bickford, Jack Carson, Tommy Noonan, Amanda Blake, Lucy Marlow
  'Maintains a skilful balance between the musical and the tear jerker.' – *Penelope Houston*
  'By far the best of all the films about life behind the cameras, the lights, the wind-machines, and the cocktail bars of Hollywood.' – *Dilys Powell*
† Cary Grant and Humphrey Bogart were both sought before James Mason was signed.
†† Ronald Haver's book A Star Is Born (1988) is an account of the making of the film and its 1983 restoration.
♟ Ray Heindorf; song 'The Man that Got Away' (mHarold Arlen, lyIra Gershwin); Judy Garland; James Mason; art direction

A Star Is Born *

US 1976 140m Metrocolor
Warner/Barwood/First Artists (Barbra Streisand, Jon Peters)
Interminable remake set in the pop world amid screaming crowds and songs at high decibel level; also an insufferable piece of showing off by the star. But some of the handling has style.
w John Gregory Dunne, Joan Didion, Frank Pierson d Frank Pierson ph Robert Surtees md Paul Williams pd Polly Platt
☆ Barbra Streisand, Kris Kristofferson, Paul Mazursky, Gary Busey

  'A clear case for the monopolies commission.' – *Michael Billington, Illustrated London News*
  'A bore is starred.' – *Village Voice*
♫ song 'Evergreen' (mBarbra Streisand, lyPaul Williams)
♟ Robert Surtees; Roger Kellaway (music underscoring)

Star Kid

US 1998 101m Foto-Kem
Entertainment/Trimark (Jennie Lew Tugend)
A young boy finds an alien cybersuit – a sort of living armour – which he wears first to punish his bullies, and then to protect the Earth from attack by a monster robot.
Pleasant, infantile science fiction of a familiar kind, offering harmless fantasies for the young.
wd Manny Coto ph Ronn Schmidt m Nicholas Pike pd C. J. Strawn ed Bob Ducsay
☆ Joseph Mazello, Joey Simmrin, Alex Daniels, Arthur Burghardt, Brian Simpson, Richard Gilliland
  'Should strike a responsive chord with pre-adolescent boys.' – *Variety*

The Star Maker *

US 1939 94m bw
Paramount (Charles R. Rogers)
A songwriter makes the big time by organizing kid acts.
Pleasant minor musical based on the career of Gus Edwards.
w Frank Butler, Don Hartman, Arthur Caesar d Roy del Ruth ph Karl Struss
☆ Bing Crosby, Louise Campbell, Linda Ware, Ned Sparks, Laura Hope Crews, Janet Waldo, Walter Damrosch
  'A rollicking filmusical, first-class entertainment.' – *Variety*

Star of Midnight *

US 1935 90m bw
RKO (Pandro S. Berman)
A New York attorney solves the disappearance of a leading lady.
Wisecracking, debonair murder mystery modelled on The Thin Man.
w Howard J. Green, Anthony Veiller, Edward Kaufman d Stephen Roberts ph J. Roy Hunt m Max Steiner
☆ William Powell, Ginger Rogers, Paul Kelly, Gene Lockhart, Ralph Morgan, Leslie Fenton, J. Farrell MacDonald
  'Too bad the title isn't more attractive, but the picture is excellent otherwise and should be a snappy grosser.' – *Variety*
  'It is all suavity and amusement, pistol shots and cocktails.' – *Graham Greene*
  'One of the best sophisticated comedy-mysteries in a period full of such films.' – *NFT, 1973*

The Star Packer

US 1934 60m bw
Monogram/Lone Star (Paul Malvern)
Investigating the murders of his three predecessors, a new sheriff and his Indian aide uncover the identity of an outlaw known as The Shadow.
Wayne as usual gets his man and the girl in a low-budget Western full of action and some novel stunts.
wd Robert N. Bradbury ph Archie Stout ed Carl Pierson
☆ John Wayne, Verna Hillie, George Hayes, Yakima Canutt, Billy Franey, Ed Parker, Earl Dwire, Tom Lingham

The Star Said No: see Callaway Went Thataway

The Star Spangled Girl

US 1971 92m colour
Paramount (Howard W. Koch)
A sweet old-fashioned girl is fought for by two young radicals.
Unamusingly 'with it' comedy from an unsuccessful play.
w Arnold Margolin, Jim Parker play Neil Simon d Jerry Paris ph Sam Leavitt m Charles Fox
☆ Sandy Duncan, Tony Roberts, Todd Susman, Elizabeth Allen

Star Spangled Rhythm ***

US 1942 99m bw
Paramount (Joseph Sistrom)
The doorman of Paramount Studios pretends to his sailor son that he is the big producer.
Frenetic farce involving most of the talent on Paramount's payroll and culminating in an 'impromptu' show staged for the navy. A good lighthearted glimpse of wartime Hollywood.
w Harry Tugend d George Marshall ph Leo Tover, Theodor Sparkuhl md Robert Emmett Dolan songs Johnny Mercer, Harold Arlen
☆ Betty Hutton, Eddie Bracken, Victor Moore, Walter Abel, Anne Revere, Cass Daley, Gil Lamb, Macdonald Carey, Bob Hope, Bing Crosby, Paulette Goddard, Veronica Lake, Dorothy Lamour, Vera Zorina, Fred MacMurray and also Ray Milland, Lynne Overman, Franchot Tone, Dick Powell, Walter Dare Wahl and Co, Cecil B. de Mille, Preston Sturges, Alan Ladd, Rochester, Katherine Dunham, Susan Hayward
† Veronica Lake's singing was dubbed by Martha Mears.
♟ Robert Emmett Dolan; song 'That Old Black Magic' (mHarold Arlen, lyJohnny Mercer)

'Resistance Is Futile.'

Star Trek: First Contact *

US 1996 110m DeLuxe
Paramount (Rick Berman)
Captain Jean-Luc Picard takes his Starship Enterprise back through time, chasing the Borg, a hive lifeform that wants to conquer the Earth by preventing the first contact with friendly aliens.
One for the fans, though it provides more action and excitement, as well as a hint of alien sex, than most of the series.
w Brannon Braga, Ronald D. Moore, Rick Berman d Jonathan Frakes ph Matthew F. Leonetti m Jerry Goldsmith pd Herman Zimmerman ed John W. Wheeler sp Industrial Light and Magic; make-up: Michael Westmore
☆ Patrick Stewart, Jonathan Frakes, Brent Spiner, LeVar Burton, Michael Dorn, Gates McFadden, Alfre Woodard, James Cromwell, Alice Krige
  'A smashingly exciting sci-fi adventure.' – *Variety*
  'A cheesy B-movie with a second-rate cast and plot and effects only marginally more special than the TV shows.' – *Screen International*
♟ Michael Westmore, Scott Wheeler, Jake Garber (make-up)

Star Trek: Generations *

US 1994 118m DeLuxe
UIP/Paramount (Rick Berman)
A mad scientist is willing to destroy worlds and ally with the Klingons to return to a strange joy-bringing ribbon of energy known as the Nexus.
A movie that will be remembered, if it is remembered, for marking the death of Captain Kirk and the arrival of Picard and other new cast members from the latest TV incarnation of the programme; what it really needs, if it is to appeal to more than the converted, is a better script.
w Ronald D. Moore, Brannon Braga, Rick Berman d David Carson ph John A. Alonzo m Dennis McCarthy pd Herman Zimmerman ed Peter Berger
☆ Patrick Stewart, William Shatner, Malcolm McDowell, Jonathan Frakes, Brent Spiner, LeVar Burton, Michael Dorn, Gates McFadden, Marina Sirtis, James Doohan, Walter Koenig, Whoopi Goldberg
  'Addressed primarily at cultists, and is not especially well plotted or directed.' – *Sheila Johnston, Independent*

Star Trek III: The Search for Spock

US 1984 105m Metrocolor
Panavision
Paramount/Cinema Group Venture (Harve Bennett)
Admiral Kirk discovers that Spock is not dead but has been reborn as a Vulcan child ...
Very silly, empty and unamusing follow-up.
w Harve Bennett d Leonard Nimoy ph Charles Correll m James Horner
☆ William Shatner, DeForest Kelley, James Doohan, Walter Koenig, Nichelle Nichols, Robert Hooks, Leonard Nimoy

'The Battle For Paradise Has Begun.'

Star Trek Insurrection

US 1998 105m colour 'Scope
Paramount (Rick Berman)
Captain Jean-Luc Picard discovers that the Federation is behaving unfairly towards a peaceful long-lived race, who face genocide.
A simple tale, of the sort that filled half an hour or less of television time, is here tricked out with special effects and rather more action; but it's still an example of more resulting in less.
w Michael Piller d Jonathan Frakes ph Matthew F. Leonetti m Jerry Goldsmith pd Herman Zimmerman ed Peter E. Berger sp make-up designer: Michael Westmore; Terry Frazee
☆ Patrick Stewart, Jonathan Frakes, Brent Spiner, LeVar Burton, Michael Dorn, Gates McFadden, Martina Sirtis, F. Murray Abraham, Donna Murphy, Anthony Zerbe, Gregg Henry, Daniel Hugh Kelly, Michael Welch
  'Little more than a glorified television episode.' – *New York Times*

Star Trek IV: The Voyage Home *

US 1986 119m Technicolor
Panavision
Paramount/Harve Bennett
GB title: *The Voyage Home: Star Trek IV*
The Enterprise crew are called home to face trial for mutiny: they find a very alien world.
The best of the series: it isn't saying much, but at least there are shreds of wit in the script.
w Harve Bennett, Steve Meerson, Peter Krikes, Nicholas Meyer d Leonard Nimoy ph Don Peterman m Leonard Rosenman pd Jack T. Collis ed Peter E. Berger
☆ William Shatner, Leonard Nimoy, DeForest Kelley, James Doohan, George Takei, Walter Koenig, Jane Wyatt, Catherine Hicks
♟ Don Peterman; Leonard Rosenman

'The human adventure is just beginning!'

Star Trek: The Motion Picture *

US 1979 132m Metrocolor
Panavision
Paramount (Gene Roddenberry)
In the 23rd century, Admiral Kirk resumes command of the Enterprise to combat an alien force.
And a surprisingly boring one. Vast sets and big-screen solemnity hardly make this more enjoyable than some of the TV episodes which got more tricks and philosophical fun into one-third of the length.
w Harold Livingston, Alan Dean Foster d Robert Wise ph Richard H. Kline, Richard Yuricich m Jerry Goldsmith pd Harold Michelson ed Todd Ramsey
☆ William Shatner, Leonard Nimoy, DeForest Kelley, Stephen Collins, Persis Khambatta
♟ Jerry Goldsmith; visual effects (Douglas Trumbull, John Dykstra and others); art direction

'At the end of the universe lies the beginning of vengeance!'

Star Trek: The Wrath of Khan

US 1982 114m Movielab
Panavision
Paramount (Harve Bennett)
The crew of the starship Enterprise counter the wiles of an evil genius on a distant planet.
Comic strip capers a long way from the controlled intelligence of some episodes of the TV series; but more entertaining than the first movie.
w Jack B. Sowards d Nicholas Meyer ph Gayne Rescher m James Horner pd Joseph R. Jennings
☆ William Shatner, Leonard Nimoy, Ricardo Montalban, DeForest Kelley, Ike Eisenmann
  'A pitiful snack for the eyes with some unappetizing crumbs left over for the mind to chew on.' – *Philip Strick, MFB*

Star Trek V: The Final Frontier

US 1989 107m Technicolor
Panavision
UIP/Paramount (Harve Bennett)
Captain Kirk goes in search of a legendary planet, said to be inhabited by God.
Mystic moments, tamely rendered, that indicate it is long after the time when the series should have been laid to rest.

---

w David Loughery *story* William Shatner, Harve Bennett, David Loughery *d* William Shatner *ph* Andrew Laszlo *m* Jerry Goldsmith *pd* Herman Zimmerman *ed* Peter Berger

☆ William Shatner, Leonard Nimoy, DeForest Kelley, James Doohan, Walter Koenig, Nichelle Nichols, George Takei, David Warner, Laurence Luckinbill

'The battle for peace has begun.'

Star Trek VI: The Undiscovered Country ★★

♠♠ US 1991 110m Technicolor
UIP/Paramount (Ralph Winter, Steven-Charles Jaffe)

Mr Spock attempts to solve the murder of a Klingon peace delegate after Captain Kirk and Dr McCoy are convicted of the crime.

The last voyage of the original crew of the Starship Enterprise turns out to be their finest hour and fifty minutes.

w Nicholas Meyer, Denny Martin Flynn *story* Leonard Nimoy, Lawrence Konner, Mark Rosenthal *d* Nicholas Meyer *ph* Hiro Narita *m* Cliff Eidelman *pd* Herman Zimmerman *ed* Ronald Roose, William Hoy *sp* Industrial Light and Magic

☆ William Shatner, Leonard Nimoy, DeForest Kelley, James Doohan, Walter Koenig, George Takei, Christian Slater, Kim Cattrall, Mark Lenard, Christopher Plummer, David Warner

'A lumbering and self-indulgent picture, dragged down at every turn by the weight of twenty-five years of illogical mediocrity, as if the series' notional science-fiction aspects pre-empted the need for characters, stories or a universe that made any dramatic sense.' *–Kim Newman, Sight and Sound*

'There are no signs of waning energy here, not even in an *Enterprise* crew that looks ever more ready for intergalactic rocking chairs.' *– Janet Maslin, New York Times*

Star Wars ★★★★

♠♠ US 1977 121m Technicolor
Panavision
TCF/Lucasfilm (Gary Kurtz)

A rebel princess in a distant galaxy escapes, and with the help of her robots and a young farmer overcomes the threatening forces of evil.

Flash Gordon rides again, but with timing so impeccably right that the movie became a phenomenon and one of the top grossers of all time. Good harmless fun, put together with style and imagination.

wd George Lucas *ph* Gilbert Taylor *m* John Williams *ad* John Barry *ed* Paul Hirsch, Marcia Lucas, Richard Chew *sp* Rick Baker, John Dykstra

☆ Mark Hamill, Harrison Ford, Carrie Fisher, Peter Cushing, Alec Guinness, Anthony Daniels, Kenny Baker, Dave Prowse, Phil Brown

'A great work of popular art, fully deserving the riches it has reaped.' *– Time*

'Acting in this movie I felt like a raisin in a giant fruit salad. And I didn't even know who the coconuts or the cantelopes were.' *– Mark Hamill*

'He intended his film, Lucas confesses, for a generation growing up without fairy tales. His target audience was fourteen years and younger … It was a celebration, a social affair, a collective dream, and people came again and again, dragging their friends and families with them.' *– Les Keyser, Hollywood in the Seventies*

'The loudness, the smash and grab editing and the relentless pacing drive every idea from your head, and even if you've been entertained you may feel cheated of some dimension – a sense of wonder, perhaps.' *– New Yorker, 1982*

'Heartless fireworks ignited by a permanently retarded director with too much clout and cash.' *– Time Out, 1984*

† The voice of Darth Vader was supplied by the uncredited James Earl Jones.

†† The film was re-released in 1997, with its sound remixed and digital technology used to improve battle sequences and the size of the city of Mos Eisley. Some unused footage from the original was added, together with computer animation, to show a meeting between Han Solo and Jabba the Hutt. It took more than $46m in the first week of its re-release, and became the first film to gross more than $400m at the US box-office.

♣ John Williams; John Barry; editing; costumes (John Mollo); visual effects (John Stears, John Dykstra and others); sound

☆ best picture; script; direction; Alec Guinness
♦ John Williams

Star Wars Episode I: The Phantom Menace ★★

♠♠ US 1999 116m DeLuxe
TCF/Lucasfilm (Rick McCallum)

Jedi knights come to the aid of the young queen of a peaceful planet, who is invaded by a powerful trade federation.

Having started the saga in the middle of things with the original Star Wars, there's a lot of static exposition here to explain what came after. The human actors tend to play supporting roles to the often dazzling special effects and computer-generated creatures; at times it seems little more than an illustrated toy catalogue for the 12-year-olds at which it is aimed. It is also the most critic-proof movie ever made.

wd George Lucas *ph* David Tattersall *m* John Williams *pd* Gavin Bocquet *ed* Paul Martin Smith *sp* ILM

☆ Liam Neeson, Ewan McGregor, Natalie Portman, Jake Lloyd, Pernilla August, Frank Oz, Ian McDiarmid, Oliver Ford Davies, Hugh Quarshie, Ahmed Best, Samuel L. Jackson, Ray Park, Peter Serafinowicz, Ralph Brown, Terence Stamp and also Brian Blessed, Sofia Coppola

'It is neither captivating nor transporting, for it lacks any emotional pull, as well as the sense of wonder and awe that marks the best works of sci-fi/fantasy.' *– Todd McCarthy, Variety*

'Brimming with dazzling special effects but short on dramatic focus.' *– John Hazleton, Screen International*

† The film set new records by taking $28.5m at the US box-office on its first day. It went on to take $430.4m in the US and a total of $920m around ther world.

♣ sound (Gary Rydstrom, Tom Johnson, Shawn Murphy, John Midgley); sound effects editing (Ben Burtt, Tom Bellfort); visual effects (John Knoll, Dennis Muren, Scott Squires, Rob Coleman)

The Star Witness ★

US 1931 68m bw
Warner

An old man witnesses a crime and is threatened by gangsters.

Pacy melodrama with good performances.

w Lucien Hubbard *d* William Wellman *ph* James Van Trees

☆ Walter Huston, Chic Sale, Grant Mitchell, Frances Starr, Sally Blane

'Plenty of action, laughs, and a tear.' *– Variety*
♦ Lucien Hubbard

Starcrash

US 1979 92m Metrocolor
Columbia/AIP/Film Enterprise (Nat Wachsberger, Patrick Wachsberger)

A spaceship pilot and her navigator are released from prison to find a kidnapped boy and, with the aid of a robot, defeat an evil dictator who wants to rule their world.

Science-fiction hokum of the silly kind, directed at a breathless pace and influenced by Star Wars, for its plot, and Barbarella, for its sex appeal.

w Luigi Cossi, Nat Wachsberger, R. A. Dillon *d* Lewis Coates (Luigi Cozzi) *ph* Roberto D'Ettorre Piazzoli, Paul Beeson *m* John Barry *pd* Aurelio Crugnola *ed* Sergio Montanari *sp* Armando Valcauda, Germano Natali, Ron Hays

☆ Marjoe Gortner, Caroline Munro, Christopher Plummer, David Hasselhoff, Robert Tessier, Joe Spinell, Nadia Cassini, Judd Hamilton, Hamilton Camp

'Show me a boy who never wanted to be a rock star – and I'll show you a liar'

Stardust

GB 1974 111m Technicolor
EMI/Goodtimes (David Puttnam, Sandy Lieberson)

The rise and fall of a pop singer.

Unappetizing rehash of Road to Ruin, pop music style.

w Ray Connolly *d* Michael Apted *ph* Tony Richmond *md* Dave Edmunds, David Puttnam

☆ David Essex, Adam Faith, Larry Hagman, Marty Wilde, Rosalind Ayres

Stardust Memories ★

US 1980 88m bw
UA/Jack Rollins, Charles H. Joffe (Robert Greenhut)

An increasingly melancholy comedian attends a retrospective of his work and is plagued by real and imaginary fears.

A plainly autobiographical work which, while amusing and moving in spots, marks it doubtful that the writer/director/star can even now shake off his obsessions.

wd Woody Allen *ph* Gordon Willis *m* Dick Hyman

☆ Woody Allen, Charlotte Rampling, Jessica Harper, Marie-Christine Barrault, Tony Roberts, Helen Hanft

'Its posturing pyrotechnics seem more the symptom of a crisis than its controlled expression.' *– Gilbert Adair, MFB*

Stargate

♠♠ US 1994 120m DeLuxe
Guild/Canal/Centropolis/Carolco (Joel B. Michaels, Oliver Eberle, Dean Devlin)

An Egyptologist discovers a gateway to another world where an alien intelligence rules over a slave kingdom of inhabitants descended from the ancient Egyptians; the American military goes through to bring them democracy and the atom bomb.

An old-fashioned gung-ho space opera, recycling threadbare themes, which unexpectedly found favour with the public.

w Roland Emmerich, Dean Devlin *d* Roland Emmerich *ph* Karl Walter Lindenlaub *m* David Arnold *pd* Holger Gross *ed* Michael Duthie, Derek Brechin *sp* Kleiser-Walczak Construction Company, Cinema Research Corporation, Available Light; creature effects: Patrick Tatopoulos

☆ Kurt Russell, James Spader, Jaye Davidson, Viveca Lindfors, Alexis Cruz, Mili Avital, Leon Rippy, John Diehl

'The movie, which does have a sort of cheeky energy, goes into narrative and cliché overload once the spacemen start exploring the unnamed planet – shall we call it Lucasland – where they set down.' *– Richard Schickel, Time*

'What this juvenile adventure has in spades is special effects and picturesque locations. What it lacks is an emotional link to make the Saturday afternoon he-man posturing palatable, or at least bearable.' *– Leonard Klady, Variety*

Starlift

US 1951 102m bw
Warner (Robert Arthur)

Movie stars entertain at Travis Air Base, where the boys are constantly leaving for Korea.

Insipid musical with even more insipid romantic interludes.

w John Klorer, Karl Kamb *d* Roy del Ruth *ph* Ted McCord *md* Ray Heindorf

☆ Janice Rule, Dick Wesson, Richard Webb, Howard St John, Doris Day, Gordon MacRae, Virginia Mayo, Gene Nelson, Ruth Roman, James Cagney, Gary Cooper, Phil Harris, Louella Parsons, Randolph Scott, Jane Wyman

Starlight Hotel ★

New Zealand 1987 90m
Recorded Releasing/Challenge Film Corp/NZ Film Commission (Finola Dwyer, Larry Parr)

Two runaways – one a rebellious child, the other a suspected murderer – team up on the road.

Slight but engaging story, with good period detail.

w Grant Hinden-Miller *novel* The Dream Monger *d* Sam Pillsbury *ph* Warrick Attewell *m* Andrew Hayes, Morton Wilson *pd* Mike Becroft *ad* Roger Guise *ed* Michael Horton

☆ Peter Phelps, Greer Robson, Marshall Napier, Alice Fraser

The Starmaker ★

Italy 1994 107m Technicolor Panavision
TCF/Cecchi Gori/Tiger/Sciarlò (Vittorio Cecchi Gori, Rita Cecchi Gori)

original title: L'Uomo delle Stelle

In Sicily in the mid-50s, a travelling con man offers townspeople the chance of stardom if they give him money to make a screen test.

A road movie about people's dreams and disappointments, too schematic to be entirely successful.

w Fabio Rinaudo, Giuseppe Tornatore *d* Giuseppe Tornatore *m* Ennio Morricone *pd* Francesco Bronzi *ed* Massimo Quaglia

☆ Sergio Castellitto, Tizana Lodato, Leopoldo Trieste, Nicola di Pinto, Franco Scaldati

'A gorgeously produced tourism commercial for the Italian island, this threadbare tale of a cocky con man's painful comeuppance has very little heart and, consequently, conjures few real emotions.' *– David Rooney, Variety*

Starman

US 1984 115m MGM Color
Columbia/Delphi (Larry J. Franco)

An alien arrives in Wisconsin and takes human form, falling in love with the widow of the man he impersonates.

Derivative but eccentric science-fiction fantasy with lapses of narrative and a general attempt to make the love story predominant over the hardware.

w Bruce A. Evans, Raynold Gideon *d* John Carpenter *ph* Donald M. Morgan *m* Jack Nitzsche *pd* Daniel Lomino *ed* Marion Rothman

☆ Jeff Bridges, Karen Allen, Charles Martin Smith, Richard Jaeckel, Robert Phalen, Tony Edwards

♦ Jeff Bridges

Staroye i Novoye: *see* The General Line

Stars and Bars

US 1988 94m DuArt/DeLuxe
Columbia (Sandy Lieberson)

Cliché Englishman's encounters with stereotyped Americans in search for long-lost Renoir painting.

w William Boyd *novel* William Boyd *d* Pat O'Connor *ph* Jerzy Zielinski *m* Stanley Myers *pd* Leslie Dilley, Stuart Craig *ed* Michael Bradsell

☆ Daniel Day-Lewis, Harry Dean Stanton, Martha Plimpton, Joan Cusack

'Unhappy mixture of farce and misdirected satire.' *– Variety*

Stars and Stripes Forever ★

US 1952 89m Technicolor
TCF (Lamar Trotti)

GB title: *Marching Along*

In the 1890s John Philip Sousa, a bandmaster who wants to write ballads, finds success as a writer of marches.

Low-key musical biopic with predictably noisy numbers.

w Lamar Trotti *autobiography* John Philip Sousa *d* Henry Koster *ph* Charles G. Clarke *md* Alfred Newman

☆ Clifton Webb, Debra Paget, Robert Wagner, Ruth Hussey, Finlay Currie, Roy Roberts, Lester Matthews

The Stars Are Singing

US 1952 99m Technicolor
Paramount (Irving Asher)

A Polish refugee girl illegally enters the US and becomes an opera star.

Painless Cinderella fantasy in which everybody sings.

w Liam O'Brien *d* Norman Taurog *ph* Lionel Lindon *m* Victor Young

☆ Anna Maria Alberghetti, Lauritz Melchior, Rosemary Clooney, Fred Clark, Mikhail Rasumny

The Stars Fell on Henrietta

US 1995 110m Technicolor Panavision
Warner/Malpaso/Butcher's Run (Clint Eastwood, David Valdes)

A woman remembers her childhood in the mid-30s, and the arrival of an eccentric, penniless wildcatter, who was convinced that there was oil on land belonging to her father, a poor Texan farmer.

Pleasant but unremarkable period drama of one man's determined struggle against constant humiliation, and his effect on the lives of others.

w Philip Railsback *d* James Keach *ph* Bruce Surtees *m* David Benoit *pd* Henry Bumstead *ed* Joel Cox

☆ Robert Duvall, Aidan Quinn, Frances Fisher, Brian Dennehy, Lexi Randall, Kaytlyn Knowles,

---

Francesca Ruth Eastwood, Billy Bob Thornton, Victor Wong

'A muted character piece of modest ambition and achievement.' – *Todd McCarthy, Variety*

Stars in My Crown *

US   1950   89m   bw

MGM (William H. Wright)

A two-gun parson brings peace to a Tennessee town after the Civil War.

Sentimental family Western, quite pleasantly made and performed.

w Margaret Fitts *novel* Joe David Brown
d Jacques Tourneur *ph* Charles Schoenbaum
m Adolph Deutsch

☆ Joel McCrea, Ellen Drew, Dean Stockwell, Juano Hernandez, James Mitchell, Lewis Stone, Alan Hale, Amanda Blake

The Stars Look Down **

GB   1939   110m   bw

Grafton (Isadore Goldschmidt)

The son of a coal miner struggles to become an MP.

Economically but well made social drama from a popular novel, with good pace and backgrounds.

w J. B. Williams, A. J. Cronin *novel* A. J. Cronin
d Carol Reed *ph* Max Greene *m* Hans May

☆ Michael Redgrave, Margaret Lockwood, Edward Rigby, Emlyn Williams, Nancy Price, Allan Jeayes, Cecil Parker, Linden Travers

'Dr Cronin's mining novel has produced a very good film – I doubt whether in England we have ever produced a better.' – *Graham Greene*

'A splendidly directed portrait of those who burrow for the black diamond in England's northland … the picture is mounted with exactness of detail and technique.' – *Variety*

Stars over Broadway

US   1935   89m   bw

Warner (Sam Bischoff)

Agent turns hotel porter into radio star.

Unremarkable musical, with unusual talent.

w Jerry Wald, Julius J. Epstein, Pat C. Flick
d William Keighley *ph* George Barnes *md* Leo F. Forbstein *ch* Busby Berkeley, Bobby Connolly *songs* Harry Warren, Al Dubin

☆ James Melton, Jane Froman, Pat O'Brien, Jean Muir, Frank McHugh, Marie Wilson, Frank Fay

'A far from inspired backstage yarn with pleasant dialogue and fancy trimmings.' – *Variety*

'Since his existence, man has ruled the Earth. In the future, the rules will change.'

Starship Troopers **

US   1997   129m   Technicolor

Buena Vista/TriStar/Touchstone (Jon Davison, Alan Marshall)

In the future, when the military rule an Earth facing an invasion from giant bug-like aliens, a group of friends become soldiers to fight the creatures on their own planet.

An uneasy and ambivalent movie: it attempts to subvert the intention of Heinlein's novel, which praises the notion of a military élite, yet remains true to the original's enjoyment of violent battles and military superiority; the cast suggest that individuality is a luxury the future cannot afford.

w Ed Neumeier *novel* Robert A. Heinlein *d* Paul Verhoeven *ph* Jost Vacano *m* Basil Poledouris *pd* Allan Cameron *ed* Mark Goldblatt, Caroline Ross *sp* Phil Tippett, Scott E. Anderson, Alec Gillis, John Richardson

☆ Caspar Van Dien, Dina Meyer, Denise Richards, Jake Busey, Neil Patrick Harris, Clancy Brown, Seth Gilliam, Patrick Muldoon, Michael Ironside, Rue McClanahan

'A spectacularly gung-ho sci-fi epic that delivers two hours of good, nasty fun.' – *Todd McCarthy, Variety*

'Would Paul Verhoeven kindly stop making movies?' – *Tom Shone, Sunday Times*

'The crowning achievement of Paul Verhoeven's film-making career to date.' – *Andrew O'Hehir, Sight and Sound*

† Robert Heinlein had to change publishers in order to get *Starship Troopers* published in 1959; the book was intended for a juvenile audience.

†† The film took around $55m at the US box-office.

♫ visual effects

Starstruck

Australia   1982   102m   colour

Palm Beach Pictures (David Elfick, Richard Brennan)

In a bid to keep open the family pub, a teenage boy makes a star of his young cousin.

Youth musical that does no more than transfer the usual backstage clichés to a punk and working-class setting.

w Stephen MacLean *d* Gillian Armstrong *ph* Russell Boyd *md* Mark Moffat *pd* Brian Thomson *ed* Nicholas Beauman

☆ Jo Kennedy, Ross O'Donovan, Margo Lee, Max Cullen, Pat Evison, John O'May, Ned Lander

Start Cheering

US   1938   78m   bw

Columbia

An actor's agent has problems when his potential star decides to go to college.

Fairly amusing low-budget musical with some surprises.

w Eugene Solow, Richard E. Wormser, Philip Rapp, Corey Ford *d* Albert S. Rogell

☆ Jimmy Durante, Walter Connolly, Joan Perry, Charles Starrett, the Three Stooges, Hal Leroy, Ernest Truex, Gertrude Niesen, Raymond Walburn, Broderick Crawford

'Longer on entertainment satisfaction than many of the more formidable pricers.' – *Variety*

Start the Revolution without Me *

US   1969   90m   Technicolor

Warner/Norbud (Norman Lear)

Two sets of twins get mixed up at the court of Louis XVI.

Historical spoof of the kind subsequently made familiar by Mel Brooks; the script might have suited Abbott and Costello better than these two actors.

w Fred Freeman, Lawrence J. Cohen *d* Bud Yorkin *ph* Jean Tournier *m* John Addison

☆ Donald Sutherland, Gene Wilder, Hugh Griffith, Jack MacGowran, Billie Whitelaw, Victor Spinetti, Ewa Aulin

Starting Over *

US   1979   106m   Movielab

Paramount/Century Associates (Alan J. Pakula, James L. Brooks)

A divorced man nearly goes back to his wife but finally plumps for a nursery school teacher.

Plain-speaking sex comedy-drama with accomplished stars giving rather more than the script is worth.

w James L. Brooks *novel* Dan Wakefield *d* Alan J. Pakula *ph* Sven Nykvist *m* Marvin Hamlisch *pd* George Jenkins

☆ Burt Reynolds, Jill Clayburgh, Candice Bergen, Charles Durning, Austin Pendleton

♫ Jill Clayburgh, Candice Bergen

State Fair **

US   1933   98m   bw

Fox (Winfield Sheehan)

Dad wants his prize pig to win at the fair, but the younger members of his family have romance in mind.

Archetypal family film, much remade but never quite so pleasantly performed.

w Paul Green, Sonya Levien *novel* Phil Stong *d* Henry King *ph* Hal Mohr *md* Louis de Francesco

☆ Will Rogers, Janet Gaynor, Lew Ayres, Sally Eilers, Norman Foster, Louise Dresser, Frank Craven, Victor Jory, Hobart Cavanaugh

'A pungent, good-humoured motion picture.' – *Pare Lorentz*

'Vigour, freshness and sympathy abound in its admittedly idealized fantasy treatment of small-town life.' – *Charles Higham, 1972*

♫ best picture; script

State Fair **

US   1945   100m   Technicolor

TCF (William Perlberg)

TV title: It Happened One Summer

Musical remake with an amiable cast and a rousing score.

w Oscar Hammerstein II *d* Walter Lang *ph* Leon Shamroy *m/ly* Richard Rodgers, Oscar Hammerstein II *md* Alfred Newman *ad* Lyle Wheeler, Lewis Creber *ed* J. Watson Webb

☆ Charles Winninger, Jeanne Crain, Dana Andrews, Vivian Blaine, Dick Haymes, Fay Bainter, Frank McHugh, Percy Kilbride, Donald Meek

'Surely the sort of theme that clamours for movie treatment. But no, say Twentieth Century Fox: let's make the fair look like a night club. Let's look around for stars of pristine nonentity. Let's screw the camera down to the studio floor. The result, "an epic that sings to the skies … with glorious, glamorous new songs".' – *Richard Winnington*

'Comes pretty close to being another Oklahoma.' – *Motion Picture Herald*

† Jeanne Crain's songs were dubbed by Louanne Hogan.

♫ song 'It Might As Well Be Spring'
♫ Alfred Newman

State Fair

US   1962   118m   DeLuxe Cinemascope

TCF (Charles Brackett)

Dullsville modernized version, condescending towards the rurals and peopled by unattractive youngsters.

w Richard Breen *d* José Ferrer *ph* William C. Mellor *md* Alfred Newman

☆ Pat Boone, Alice Faye, Tom Ewell, Pamela Tiffin, Ann-Margret, Bobby Darin, Wally Cox

State of Grace

US   1990   134m   DeLuxe   Panavision

Rank/Cinehaus/Orion (Ned Dowd, Randy Ostrow, Ron Rotholz)

In New York, an undercover cop returns to the district where he grew up in order to infiltrate an Irish gang that is about to make a deal with the Mafia.

Dull and plodding gangster movie.

w Dennis McIntyre *d* Phil Joanou *ph* Jordan Cronenweth *m* Ennio Morricone *pd* Patrizia von Brandenstein, Doug Kraner *ed* Claire Simpson

☆ Sean Penn, Ed Harris, Gary Oldman, Robin Wright, John Turturro, John C. Reilly, R. D. Call, Joe Vitorelli, Burgess Meredith, Deirdre O'Connell

'One of the more intriguing American thrillers of the year if only because it turns out to be dripping with old-fashioned romanticism as well as new-fangled violence.' – *Derek Malcolm, Guardian*

State of the Union ***

US   1948   110m   bw

MGM/Liberty Films (Frank Capra)

GB title: The World and His Wife

An estranged wife rejoins her husband when he is running for president.

Brilliantly scripted political comedy which unfortunately goes soft at the end but offers stimulating entertainment most of the way.

w Anthony Veiller, Myles Connolly *play* Howard Lindsay, Russel Crouse *d* Frank Capra *ph* George J. Folsey *m* Victor Young

☆ Spencer Tracy, Katharine Hepburn, Adolphe Menjou, Van Johnson, Angela Lansbury, Lewis Stone, Howard Smith, Raymond Walburn, Charles Dingle

'A triumphant film, marked all over by Frank Capra's artistry.' – *Howard Barnes*

The State of Things *

US/Portugal   1982   120m   bw

Artificial Eye/Road Movies/Pro-Ject/ZDF/Musidora/Film International (Chris Sievernich)

original title: Der Stand Der Dinge

A film director tracks down in Los Angeles the producer who abandoned him and his film crew in Portugal.

A sort of B movie about the making of a B movie and a reflection on the meaning of cinema, within the loose format of a thriller.

w Wim Wenders, Robert Kramer *d* Wim Wenders *ph* Henri Alekan, Martin Schafer, Fred Murphy *m* Jurgen Knieper *ad* Ze Branco *ed* Barbara von Weitershausen, Peter Przygodda

☆ Isabelle Weingarten, Rebecca Pauly, Patrick Bauchau, Paul Getty III, Samuel Fuller, Roger Corman, Allen Goorwitz

State Secret **

GB   1950   104m   bw

British Lion/London (Frank Launder, Sidney Gilliat)

US title: The Great Manhunt

In a Ruritanian country, spies pursue a surgeon, the only man who knows that the dictator is dead.

Hitchcockian chase comedy-thriller which is well detailed and rises to the heights on occasion.

wd Sidney Gilliat *novel* Appointment with Fear by Roy Huggins *ph* Robert Krasker *m* William Alwyn *ed* Thelma Myers

☆ Douglas Fairbanks Jnr, Glynis Johns, Herbert Lom, Jack Hawkins, Walter Rilla, Karel Stepanek, Carl Jaffe

'An admirably fast-moving diversion in the Hitchcock tradition.' – *Richard Mallett, Punch*

'One of the best thrillers a British studio (any studio, for that matter) has made for years.' – *Leonard Mosley*

State's Attorney *

US   1932   79m   bw

RKO

GB title: Cardigan's Last Case

A prosecuting counsel nearly pays the penalty for arrogance.

Good star melodrama.

w Rowland Brown, Gene Fowler *d* George Archainbaud

☆ John Barrymore, Jill Esmond, William Boyd, Helen Twelvetrees

'Good programme box office stuff if not particularly smashing.' – *Variety*

Static

US   1986   93m   colour

Necessity Films (Amy Ness)

An unemployed young man invents a device for displaying images of heaven on a television set, but he is the only one able to see them.

A desultory variation on the fable of the Emperor's new clothes, in which it is assumed that eccentricity is interesting and amusing; here, it isn't.

w Keith Gordon, Mark Romanek *d* Mark Romanek *ph* Jeff Jur *pd* Cynthia Sowder *ed* Emily Paine

☆ Keith Gordon, Amanda Plummer, Bob Gunton, Lily Knight, Barton Heyman, Reathel Bean

Station Six Sahara

GB   1962   101m   bw

British Lion/CCC/Artur Brauner (Victor Lyndon)

Five men working on a remote Saharan pipeline quarrel over the favours of an American girl whose car crashes nearby.

Raging old-fashioned melodrama with the courage of its lack of convictions.

w Bryan Forbes, Brian Clemens *d* Seth Holt *ph* Gerald Gibbs *m* Ron Grainer

☆ Carroll Baker, Ian Bannen, Peter Van Eyck, Denholm Elliott, Mario Adorf, Jorg Felmy, Biff McGuire

Station West

US   1948   91m   bw

RKO (Robert Sparks)

A saloon queen is the secret head of a gang of gold robbers.

Predictable but well-made Western patterned after Destry Rides Again.

w Frank Fenton, Winston Miller *novel* Luke Short *d* Sidney Lanfield *ph* Harry J. Wild *m* Heinz Roemheld

☆ Dick Powell, Jane Greer, Agnes Moorehead, Burl Ives, Tom Powers, Gordon Oliver, Steve Brodie, Guinn Williams, Raymond Burr, Regis Toomey

'The face was his … the body was his … but suddenly, Hello, Charlie!'

The Statue

GB   1970   89m   Eastmancolor

Cinerama/Josef Shaftel (Anis Nohra)

A languages professor is embarrassed when his sculptress wife makes an immense nude statue of him – with someone else's private parts.

Strained phallic comedy which doesn't even make the most of its one joke.

w Alec Coppel, Denis Norden *d* Rod Amateau *ph* Piero Portalupi *m* Riz Ortolani

☆ David Niven, Virna Lisi, Robert Vaughn, Ann Bell, John Cleese, Hugh Burden

Stay Away Joe

US 1968 102m Metrocolor Panavision
MGM (Douglas Lawrence)
▣▣ ▦ ◎.

An Indian rodeo rider returns to his reservation, makes several romantic conquests, and helps a government rehabilitation scheme.
Thin if surprising vehicle for a singing star; all rather tedious.

w Michael A. Hoey *novel* Dan Cushman *d* Peter Tewkesbury *ph* Fred Koenekamp *m* Jack Marshall
☆ Elvis Presley, Burgess Meredith, Joan Blondell, Katy Jurado, Thomas Gomez, Henry Jones, L. Q. Jones

Stay Hungry

US 1976 102m DeLuxe
UA/Outov (Harold Schneider, Bob Rafelson)

The heir to an Alabama estate annoys the locality by assembling a curious bunch of friends and making unexpected use of his money.
Rather obvious and pointless fable; well made but not very stimulating.

w Charles Gaines, Bob Rafelson *novel* Charles Gaines *d* Bob Rafelson *ph* Victor Kemper *m* Bruce Langhorne, Byron Berline
☆ Jeff Bridges, Sally Field, Arnold Schwarzenegger, R. G. Armstrong, Robert Englund, Roger E. Mosley
'The picture isn't just unsatisfying, it's a mess.' – *Stanley Kauffmann*

Stay Tuned

↟↟ US 1992 87m Technicolor
Warner/Morgan Creek (James G. Robinson)
▣▣ ▦ ◎. ◠

A couple are trapped in a cable television system run by the Devil.
An unsuccessful send-up of obsessive television viewing, mainly because it picks targets, such as Wayne's World, that are beyond parody.

w Tom S. Parker, Jim Jennewein *d* Peter Hyams *ph* Peter Hyams *m* Bruce Broughton *pd* Philip Harrison *ed* Peter E. Berger *sp* Rhythm and Hues Inc.
☆ John Ritter, Pam Dawber, Jeffrey Jones, David Tom, Heather McComb, Bob Dishy
'High class trash … redeemed by a manic script, good special effects and production values.' – *Sheila Johnston, Independent*
'A picture with nothing for everybody.' – *Variety*

'It's five years later for Tony Manero. The fever still burns!'

Staying Alive

US 1983 96m Metrocolor
Paramount/Robert Stigwood/Cinema Group Venture (Sylvester Stallone)
▣▣ ▦ ◎. ◠

Tony Manero becomes a Broadway dancer.
Fragile sequel to Saturday Night Fever, with some of its frenetic quality but none of its impact.

w Sylvester Stallone, Norman Wexler *d* Sylvester Stallone *ph* Nick McLean *m* Johnny Mandel, Robin Garb, others *m* Robert Boyle
☆ John Travolta, Cynthia Rhodes, Finola Hughes, Steve Inwood, Julie Bovasso
'By turns exhilarating and absurd.' – *Nick Roddick, MFB*
'Stallone doesn't bother much with character, scenes or dialogue. He just puts the newly muscle-plated Travolta in front of the camera, covers him with what looks like oil slick, and goes for the whambams.' – *Pauline Kael, New Yorker*

Staying Together

US 1989 91m CFI color
Hemdale (Joseph Fuery)
▣▣ ▦.

Three brothers growing up in a small town experience the pangs of requited love.
Exuberant but corny tale of family relationships.

w Monte Merrick *d* Lee Grant *ph* Dick Bush *m* Miles Goodman *pd* Stuart Wurtzel *ed* Katherine Wenning
☆ Sean Astin, Stockard Channing, Melinda Dillon, Jim Haynie, Levon Helm, Dinah Manoff, Dermot Mulroney, Tim Quill

'Whips up the clichés and homilies of American small-town melodrama without adding the slightest spice.' – *Geoff Brown, MFB*

'A tale of kidnapping, computer fraud and Morris Minors.'

The Steal

GB 1994 91m Eastmancolor
Warner/Poseidon (Gary Kurtz, Barbara Stone)

An English lawyer and an American computer hacker join forces to rob a corrupt bank.
A bungled attempt to revive the style of Ealing comedy, with little imagination and no attempt to update the genre to match changing social conditions.

wd John Hay *ph* Ronnie Taylor *m* Barry Kirsch *pd* Phil Robertson *ed* David Martin
☆ Alfred Molina, Helen Slater, Peter Bowles, Dinsdale Landen, Stephen Fry, Bryan Pringle, Patricia Hayes, Heathcote Williams
'Frighteningly inept and almost completely lacking in humour or thrills.' – *Empire*

Steal Big, Steal Little

US 1995 134m Technicolor
TCF/Chicago Pacific (Andrew Davis, Fred Caruso)
▣▣

Twins, one good, one bad, quarrel over the estate left to them by their adopted mother.
Appalling comedy that gets sillier by the minute, so that by its long-drawn-out conclusion, it is beyond belief; it receives the performances it deserves.

w Andrew Davis, Lee Blessing, Jeanne Blake, Teresa Tucker-Davies *d* Andrew Davis *ph* Frank Tidy *m* William Olvis *pd* Michael Haller *ed* Don Brochu, Tina Hirsch
☆ Andy Garcia, Alan Arkin, Rachel Ticotin, Joe Pantoliano, Holland Taylor, Ally Walker, David Ogden Stiers
'With its slapstick morality and cartoon characterisations, what this vastly unentertaining dud resembles most is an interminable episode of The Dukes of Hazzard, complete with the corpulent judges, their weak-minded sidekicks and gold-hearted crooks.' – *Liese Spencer, Sight and Sound*

'The Most Beautiful Place To Be Is Love.'

Stealing Beauty *

Italy/France/GB 1995 118m Technicolor
TCF/Fiction Cinematografica/Recorded Picture/UGC (Jeremy Thomas)
▣▣ ▦ ◎. ◠

A 19-year-old American girl visits her dead mother's artistic expatriate friends in Italy, determined to discover the identity of her biological father, and to lose her virginity.
Much inconsequential talk, determined ogling of Liv Tyler and languorous perambulations in the Tuscan landscape make for a pretty, but empty, film.

w Susan Minot *story* Bernardo Bertolucci *d* Bernardo Bertolucci *ph* Darius Khondji *m* Richard Hartley *pd* Gianni Silvestri *ed* Pietro Scalia
☆ Sinead Cusack, Jeremy Irons, Jean Marais, Donal McCann, D. W. Moffett, Stefania Sandrelli, Rachel Weisz, Liv Tyler, Carlo Cecchi, Joseph Fiennes, Jason Flemyng
'A richly satisfying chamber piece that is both literary and utterly contemporary.' – *Variety*
'The film is all taste and texture and nothing else. It melts in your mouth and fades from the screen like yesterday's gossip.' – *Tom Shone, Sunday Times*

Stealing Heaven

GB/Yugoslavia 1988 115m colour
Rank/Amy International/Jadran (Simon McCorkindale)
▣▣ ▦ ◎. ◠

The dying Heloise recalls her love-affair with Abelard.
Pasteboard reproduction of medieval life and love.

w Chris Bryant *novel* Marion Meade *d* Clive Donner *ph* Mikael Salomon *m* Nick Bicat *pd* Voytek Roman *ed* Michael Ellis
☆ Derek de Lint, Kim Thompson, Denholm Elliott, Bernard Hepton, Kenneth Cranham, Patsy Byrne, Cassie Stuart, Philip Locke, Rachel Kempson, Angela Pleasence, Yvonne Bryceland, Mark Jax

Stealing Home

US 1988 98m Technicolor
Warner/Mount (Thom Mount, Hank Moonjean)
▣▣ ▦ ◎. ◠

Returning home after the suicide of the woman he loved as a youth, a failed baseball player recalls their relationship.
Drab little domestic drama of unfulfilled hopes and desires.

wd Steven Kampmann, Will Aldis *ph* Bobby Byrne *m* David Foster *pd* Vaughan Edwards *ed* Antony Gibbs
☆ Mark Harmon, Blair Brown, Jonathan Silverman, Harold Ramis, William McNamara, Richard Jenkins, John Shea, Jodie Foster, Helen Hunt

Steamboat Bill Jnr *

↟↟ US 1928 71m bw silent
UA/Buster Keaton/Joseph Schenck

A student takes over his father's old Mississippi steamboat, and wins the daughter of his rival.
Rather flat comedy redeemed by a magnificent cyclone climax.

w Carl Harbaugh, Buster Keaton *d* Charles Riesner *ph* J. Devereaux Jennings, Bert Haines
☆ Buster Keaton, Ernest Torrence, Marion Byron

Steamboat Round the Bend *

US 1935 80m bw
TCF (Sol M. Wurtzel)

A Mississippi steamboat captain defeats his rival and finds evidence to clear his nephew of a murder charge.
Rather heavily-scripted star vehicle which sacrifices fun for atmosphere but is often good to look at.

w Dudley Nichols, Lamar Trotti *novel* Ben Lucien Burman *d* John Ford *ph* George Schneiderman *md* Samuel Kaylin
☆ Will Rogers, Anne Shirley, Eugene Pallette, John McGuire, Irvin S. Cobb, Berton Churchill, Stepin Fetchit, Roger Imhof, Raymond Hatton
'Will Rogers' final picture … in the money despite a drab theme.' – *Variety*

Steaming

GB 1985 95m colour
Paul Mills/World Film Services/Columbia
▣▣

Women in a rundown steam bath confide in each other.
Excessively dreary talk piece which apparently seemed crisper on the stage.

w Patricia Losey *play* Nell Dunn *d* Joseph Losey (his last film) *ph* Chris Challis
☆ Vanessa Redgrave, Sarah Miles, Diana Dors, Patti Love, Brenda Bruce
'It cannot be denied that it is very British. The humor is coarse and the outlook grim. It is the work of Nell Dunn and is a shameless feminist and socialist treatise. Whether these qualities rank as vices or virtues is, of course, a matter of taste.' – *Quentin Crisp*

Steel

US 1979 101m Movielab
Columbia/Panzer/Davis/Fawcett-Majors (Lee Majors)
▣▣

When a construction boss is killed, his daughter vows to complete his last project.
Flashy, foul-mouthed, but basically old-fashioned hokum climaxing in a race to complete before foreclosure.

w Leigh Chapman *d* Steve Carver *ph* Roger Shearman *m* Michel Colombier *pd* Ward Preston
☆ Lee Majors, Jennifer O'Neill, Art Carney, George Kennedy, Harris Yulin, Terry Kiser, Richard Lynch, Albert Salmi

Steel

↟↟ US 1997 97m Technicolor
Warner (Quincy Jones, David Salzman, Joel Simon)
A former army weapons expert devises a steel suit so that he can keep the streets free from teenage hoodlums.
Tepid, preachy action film, missing by miles its target audience of the young.

wd Kenneth Johnson *characters created by* Louise Simonson, Jon Bogdanove *m* Mark Irwin *m* Mervyn Warren *pd* Gary Wissner *ed* John F. Link
☆ Shaquille O'Neal, Annabeth Gish, Judd Nelson, Richard Roundtree, Irma P. Hall, Ray J., Charles Napier

'Too broad and episodic to attract anything other than the most undemanding crowd.' – *Leonard Klady, Variety*

The Steel Bayonet

GB 1957 85m bw Hammerscope
UA/Hammer (Michael Carreras)

During the assault on Tunis a battle-weary platoon holds a farm against enemy attack.
Dreary cliché-ridden war melodrama, peopled by all the usual types.

w Howard Clewes *d* Michael Carreras *ph* Jack Asher *m* Leonard Salzedo *ad* Ted Marshall *ed* Bill Lenny
☆ Leo Genn, Kieron Moore, Michael Medwin, Robert Brown, Michael Ripper, John Paul, Bernard Horsfall

Steel Magnolias *

US 1989 117m Technicolor
Columbia TriStar/Rastar/Ray Stark
▣▣ ▦ ◎. ◠

A group of women, who gather in a small-town beauty parlour, face up to life's vicissitudes.
Slickly made, sentimental account of marriage and motherhood that provides some meaty roles for the assembled actresses.

w Robert Harling *play* Robert Harling *d* Herbert Ross *ph* John A. Alonzo *m* Georges Delerue *pd* Gene Callahan, Edward Pisoni *ed* Paul Hirsch
☆ Sally Field, Dolly Parton, Shirley MacLaine, Daryl Hannah, Olympia Dukakis, Julia Roberts, Tom Skerritt, Sam Shepard
'A lush, excruciatingly elongated emotional wallow.' – *Tom Milne, MFB*
♟ Julia Roberts

Steel Town

US 1952 84m Technicolor
U-I (Leonard Goldstein)

A steel president's nephew joins the company as a furnace hand.
Routine drama with an unusual background.

w Gerald Drayson Adams, Lou Breslow *d* George Sherman *ph* Charles P. Boyle *m* Joseph Gershenson
☆ Ann Sheridan, John Lund, Howard Duff, James Best, Nancy Kulp

The Steel Trap *

US 1952 85m bw
TCF/Thor (Bert E. Friedlob)

An assistant bank manager steals half a million dollars from the vault but is troubled by conscience and manages to put it back before the loss is discovered.
Solidly competent little suspenser with plenty of movement.

wd Andrew Stone *ph* Ernest Laszlo *m* Dimitri Tiomkin
☆ Joseph Cotten, Teresa Wright, Jonathan Hale, Walter Sande

Steelyard Blues

US 1972 92m Technicolor
Warner/S. B. Productions (Tony Bill, Michael and Julia Phillips)
▣▣

An ex-con and his call-girl friend are an embarrassment to his DA brother.
Bits and pieces of anti-establishment comedy are tacked on to a thin plot; a few of them work.

w David S. Ward *d* Alan Myerson *ph* Laszlo Kovacs, Steven Larner *m* Nick Gravenites
☆ Donald Sutherland, Jane Fonda, Peter Boyle, Howard Hesseman

Stella

US 1990 109m colour
Rank/Samuel Goldwyn Company/Touchstone (David V. Picker)
▣▣ ▦ ◎.

A waitress makes sacrifices so that her illegitimate daughter can escape from the working class.
Outmoded soap opera that fails to achieve the tears provoked by the two earlier film versions.

w Robert Getchell *novel* Stella Dallas by Olive Higgins Prouty *d* John Erman *ph* Billy Williams *m* John Morris *pd* James Hulsey *ed* Jerrold L. Ludwig, Bud Molin, Lisa M. Citron
☆ Bette Midler, John Goodman, Trini Alvarado, Stephen Collins, Marsha Mason, Eileen Brennan, Linda Hart

'Bette Midler deserves better than this heap of cornball slush.' – *John Coldstream, Daily Telegraph*

Stella Dallas *
US   1925   110m   bw   silent
Samuel Goldwyn
An uncouth woman loses both husband and daughter.
Standard weepie complete with 'out into the cold cold snow' ending, but handled here with tact and discretion. A seminal film of its time.
w Frances Marion *novel* Olive Higgins Prouty d Henry King *ph* Arthur Edeson
☆ Belle Bennett, Ronald Colman, Lois Moran, Jean Hersholt, Douglas Fairbanks Jnr, Alice Joyce
'A sad film, but sad with the curious quality of sadness that leaves only happiness in its train. We, watching it, are happy to be so sad. We find here a vicarious courage; a fidelity and a generous understanding that by proxy become ours.' – C. A. Lejeune

Stella Dallas *
US   1937   106m   bw
Samuel Goldwyn
Fashionable remake with excellent talent; 1937 audiences came to sneer and stayed to weep.
w Victor Heerman, Sarah Y. Mason d King Vidor *ph* Rudolph Maté *m* Alfred Newman
☆ Barbara Stanwyck, John Boles, Anne Shirley, Barbara O'Neil, Alan Hale, Marjorie Main, Tim Holt
'A tear-jerker of A ranking. There are things about the story that will not appeal to some men, but no one will be annoyed or offended by it. And the wallop is inescapably there for femmes.' – *Variety*
† Goldwyn's premier choices for the lead were Ruth Chatterton and Gladys George.
⚜ Barbara Stanwyck; Anne Shirley

Stella Does Tricks *
GB   1996   99m   Metrocolor
BFI/Channel 4/Compulsive/Sidewalk (Adam Barker)
A Scottish teenage prostitute in London manages to escape from her abusive pimp and begins a relationship with a heroin addict.
Austerely truthful film of masculine exploitation, of people trapped in a cycle of deprivation; it is not without a bleak humour.
w A. L. Kennedy d Coky Giedroyc *ph* Barry Ackroyd *m* Nick Bicat *pd* Lynne Whiteread *ed* Budge Tremlett
☆ Kelly Macdonald, James Bolam, Hans Matheson, Ewan Stewart, Lindsay Henderson

The Stendhal Syndrome
Italy   1996   119m   Technicolor
Medusa/Cine 2000 (Dario Argento, Giuseppe Colombo)
original title: La Sindrome di Stendhal
A serial killer repeatedly rapes the female detective investigating him, who has the habit of fainting when confronted by great works of art.
Risible thriller that becomes increasingly silly; although its quota of gore is low by its director's standards, it has some unpleasant moments.
wd Dario Argento *inspired by* La Sindrome di Stendhal *by* Graziella Magherini *ph* Giuseppe Rotunno *m* Ennio Morricone *ad* Antonello Geleng *ed* Angelo Nicolini *sp* Sergio Stivaletti
☆ Asia Argento, Thomas Kretschmann, Marco Leonardi, Luigi Diberti, Paolo Bonacelli, Julien Lambroschini, John Quentin
'The film that finally proves beyond any reasonable argument that Dario Argento has finally lost it.' – *The Dark Side*

Step by Step *
US   1946   62m   bw
RKO (Sid Rogell)
The FBI gives chase to a young couple who may or may not have stolen government plans.
Trim second feature melodrama with nice touches.
w Stuart Palmer d Phil Rosen
☆ Lawrence Tierney, Anne Jeffreys, Lowell Gilmore, George Cleveland, Jason Robards

Step Down to Terror
US   1959   76m   bw
U-I (Joseph Gershenson)
GB title: The Silent Stranger
A man returns to his home town and is discovered to be a psychopathic killer on the run.
Dismal reworking of Shadow of a Doubt; strictly second feature stuff.
w Mel Dinelli, Czenzi Ormonde, Chris Cooper d Harry Keller *ph* Russell Metty *m* Joseph Gershenson
☆ Charles Drake, Colleen Miller, Rod Taylor, Josephine Hutchinson, Jocelyn Brando

Step Lively *
US   1944   88m   bw
RKO (Robert Fellows)
Gleaming musical remake of *Room Service* (qv); all very efficient if witless.
w Warren Duff, Peter Milne d Tim Whelan *ph* Robert de Grasse *md* Constantin Bakaleinikoff *ad* Albert S. D'Agostino, Carroll Clark *songs* Jule Styne, Sammy Cahn
☆ Frank Sinatra, George Murphy, Adolphe Menjou, Gloria de Haven, Anne Jeffreys, Walter Slezak, Eugene Pallette
⚒ art direction

Step Lively, Jeeves
US   1937   69m   bw
TCF (John Stone)
Two confidence tricksters attempt to persuade an English valet that he is heir to the fortune of Sir Francis Drake.
Broad and raucous farce with a gullible Jeeves who bears little resemblance to P. G. Wodehouse's creation of the imperturbable gentleman's gentleman.
w Frank Fenton, Lynn Root *story* Frances Hyland d Eugene Forde *ph* Daniel Clark *md* Samuel Kaylin *ad* Duncan Cramer *ed* Fred Allen
☆ Arthur Treacher, Patricia Ellis, Robert Kent, Alan Dinehart, George Givot, Helen Flint, Franklin Pangborn

Stepfather: see Beau-Père (1981)

The Stepfather
US   1986   88m   CFI color
Jay Benson/Vista/New World
A teenage girl discovers that her new stepfather is a psychopath who may make her his victim.
Well enough done but rather obvious suspenser on the lines of Love from a Stranger.
w Donald E. Westlake *story* Brian Garfield d Joseph Ruben *ph* John Lindley *m* Patrick Moraz
☆ Terry O'Quinn, Jill Schoelen, Shelley Hack, Charles Lanyer
'A one-joke movie, but the joke is wonderfully subversive ... It's not the culture's violence that drives people mad, but its fake harmony – especially the sunny world of TV sitcoms, where every crisis is handily resolved.' – *David Edelstein, Village Voice*

'There's Something You Should Know About My Past.'
Stepfather II
US   1989   86m   colour
ITC (Darin Scott, William Burr)
A mass murderer escapes from an asylum and sets up as a psychiatrist so that he can discover a ready-made family to take over.
A limp sequel that lacks suspense and offers no more than a predictable re-run of the original.
w John Auerbach d Jeff Burr *ph* Jacek Laskus *m* Jim Manzie, Pat Regan *pd* Byrnadette Disanto *ed* Pasquale A. Buba
☆ Terry O'Quinn, Meg Foster, Caroline Williams, Jonathan Brandis, Henry Brown, Mitchell Laurance
† It was followed by a made-for-TV movie, *Stepfather III*, which provided little variation on the original plot.

The Stepford Wives *
US   1974   115m   TVC Color
Fadsin/Palomar (Edgar J. Scherick)
A new wife in a commuter village outside New York finds all her female friends too good to be true

... because their husbands have had them replaced by computerized models.
An attractive idea which needs a much lighter and pacier touch but entertains in patches and shows agreeable sophistication.
w William Goldman *novel* Ira Levin d Bryan Forbes *ph* Owen Roizman *m* Michael Small *pd* Gene Callahan
☆ Katharine Ross, Paula Prentiss, Nanette Newman, Peter Masterson, Patrick O'Neal, Tina Louise, William Prince
'It was hard to tell Katharine Ross playing a robot from Katharine Ross playing a normal housewife.' – *Les Keyser, Hollywood in the Seventies*
'The first women's lib gothic – hardly the landmark the world had been waiting for.' – *Pauline Kael, New Yorker*

Stephen King's IT
US   1990   180m   colour
Lorimar (Matthew O'Connor)
Childhood friends gather after 30 years to rid their home town of a murderous evil spirit.
Overlong, indifferently acted, predictably scripted TV mini-series transferred to video.
w Lawrence D. Cohen, Tommy Lee Wallace *novel* IT by Stephen King d Tommy Lee Wallace *ph* Richard Leiterman *m* Richard Bellis *pd* Douglas Higgins *ed* Robert F. Shugrue, David Blangsted
☆ Harry Anderson, Dennis Christopher, Richard Masur, Annette O'Toole, Tim Reid, John Ritter, Richard Thomas, Tim Curry, Olivia Hussey

Stephen King's Thinner
US   1996   92m   DeLuxe
Paramount/Spelling (Richard P. Rubinstein, Mitchell Galin)
An overweight lawyer, who is cursed by a gypsy king after he has run over his daughter, begins to get thinner and thinner ...
Tedious little fable that claims to be about 'moral culpability', but simply shows its makers' lack of understanding and imagination.
w Tom Holland, Michael McDowell *novel* Stephen King d Tom Holland *ph* Kees Van Oostrum *m* Daniel Licht *pd* Laurence Bennett *ed* Marc Laub *sp* Greg Cannom
☆ Robert John Burke, Joe Mantegna, Michael Constantine, Lucinda Jenney, Kari Wuhrer, John Horton, Stephen King
'There's nothing particularly fresh in this routinely crafted, banally scripted and directed effort.' – *Leonard Klady, Variety*

Stepkids: see Big Girls Don't Cry ... They Get Even

'Be There For The Joy. Be There For The Tears. Be There For Each Other.'
Stepmom
US   1998   124m   Technicolor   Panavision
Columbia/1492 (Wendy Finerman, Chris Columbus, Mark Radcliffe, Michael Barnathan)
A divorced mother is scornful of her ex-husband's new girlfriend until she is diagnosed with cancer and needs help.
It is sometimes difficult to imagine what Hollywood scriptwriters would do without a terminal illness to fall back on: it provides opportunity for sentimentality, redemption, reconciliation and big gestures, all of which are too much in evidence here.
w Gigi Levangie, Jessie Nelson, Steven Rogers, Karen Leigh Hopkins, Ron Bass d Chris Columbus *ph* Donald M. McAlpine *m* John Williams *pd* Stuart Wurtzel *ed* Neil Travis
☆ Julia Roberts, Susan Sarandon, Ed Harris, Jena Malone, Liam Aiken, Lynn Whitfield, Darrell Larson, Mary Louise Wilson
'Tears are jerked with strenuously sincere calculation ... which sees some very talented thesps working over the most mawkish conventions as if they were freshly minted ... not a single cliché of the modern feel-good tragic melodrama genre has gone unturned, resulting in a soggy heart-tugger.' – *Todd McCarthy, Variety*

Steppin' in Society
US   1945   72m   bw
Republic (Joseph Bercholtz)
A judge is caught in a storm and takes refuge in a low club frequented by criminals.
Uncertain comedy which never really works.
w Bradford Ropes *novel* Marcel Arnac d Alexander Esway
☆ Edward Everett Horton, Gladys George, Ruth Terry, Robert Livingston, Jack La Rue, Lola Lane

'Your dreams are just a step away.'
Stepping Out
US   1991   110m   Technicolor
UIP/Paramount (Lewis Gilbert)
A tap-dance teacher attempts to prepare a class of amateurs for a charity performance.
Mundane and old-fashioned drama that lacks precision.
w Richard Harris *play* Richard Harris d Lewis Gilbert *ph* Alan Hume *m* Peter Matz *ch* Danny Daniels *pd* Peter Mullins *ed* Humphrey Dixon
☆ Liza Minnelli, Shelley Winters, Robyn Stevan, Jane Krakowski, Bill Irwin, Ellen Greene, Sheila McCarthy, Andrea Martin, Julie Walters, Carol Woods, Luke Reilly

'The man, the music, the murder.'
Stepping Razor Red X *
Canada   1992   92m   Fujicolour
Feature Film/SC Entertainment (Edgar Egger)
Documentary on the life and violent death, in 1987, of Jamaican Rastafarian reggae singer Peter Tosh, using some concert performances and tapes he recorded, which he intended to use as the basis of his autobiography, to be called *Red X*, after the cross in red ink he saw after his name on official documents, showing where he should put his signature, but which he interpreted as indicating that he was being singled out.
Interesting, if inconclusive, investigation of the reasons for Tosh's murder: was it a robbery or a politically motivated hit? Tosh's own, often bitter, paranoid and rambling commentary, couched in apocalyptical language, adds another layer of mystification.
wd Nicholas Campbell *ph* Edgar Egger *ed* Trevor Ambrose
'For all the stridency of his ideas and of his music, Peter Tosh remains a phantom beyond this film's grasp.' – *Sight and Sound*

Steptoe and Son
👪 GB   1972   98m   Technicolor
EMI/Associated London Films (Aida Young)
Harold gets married, mislays his wife but thinks he is a father.
Strained attempt to transfer the TV rag-and-bone comedy (which in the US became Sanford and Son) to the big screen. Not the same thing at all.
w Ray Galton, Alan Simpson d Cliff Owen *ph* John Wilcox *m* Roy Budd, Jack Fishman
☆ Wilfrid Brambell, Harry H. Corbett, Carolyn Seymour, Arthur Howard, Victor Maddern
† *Steptoe and Son Ride Again*, which followed in 1973, was even more crude and out of character.

Steptoe and Son Ride Again
GB   1973   99m   Technicolor
MGM/EMI/Associated London Films (Aida Young)
Sent out to buy a new horse, Harold spends the family savings on a greyhound that won't run.
Dim, coarse comedy that long overstays its welcome.
w Ray Galton, Alan Simpson d Peter Sykes *ph* Ernie Steward *m* Roy Budd, Jack Fishman, Ron Grainer *ad* Bernard Sarron *ed* Bernard Gribble
☆ Wilfrid Brambell, Harry H. Corbett, Diana Dors, Milo O'Shea, Neil McCarthy, Bill Maynard, George Tovey, Sam Kydd, Yootha Joyce, Henry Woolf, Geoffrey Bayldon, Frank Thornton
'Retains the trappings but none of the subtlety or intimacy of the original TV series ... sacrificed to the demands of the basic British screen comedy with its emphasis on lavatories, booze, breasts and (curiously enough) the hilarity of death.' – *Clyde Jeavons, MFB*

The Sterile Cuckoo
US   1969   107m   Technicolor
Paramount/Boardwalk (Alan J. Pakula)

🖭 @

GB title: *Pookie*

A talkative but insecure college girl has her first sexual adventures.

Rather tiresome comedy drama with good scenes; general handling far too restrained.

w Alvin Sargent *novel* John Nicholson d Alan J. Pakula *ph* Milton Krasner m Fred Karlin
☆ Liza Minnelli, Tim McIntire, Wendell Burton, Austin Green, Sandra Faison
♪ song 'Come Saturday Morning' (mFred Karlin, lyDory Previn); Liza Minnelli

Stevie *
US/GB   1978   102m   Technicolor
First Artists/Grand Metropolitan (Robert Enders)

🖭

An account of the uneventful life of poetess Stevie Smith, lived out mainly in a London suburb under the fear of death.

Claustrophobic showcase for a whimsical lady; interesting for some specialized audiences.

w Hugh Whitemore *play* Hugh Whitemore d Robert Enders *ph* Freddie Young m Marcus Gowers
☆ Glenda Jackson, Mona Washbourne, Trevor Howard, Alec McCowen

Stick
US   1985   109m   Technicolor
Universal/Jennings Lang (Robert Daley)

🖭 @

A hardboiled ex-con goes to Miami's low-life district in search of the man who killed his friend.

Wearisome crime melodrama with too many pauses for the hero's self-examination.

w Elmore Leonard, Joseph C. Stinson *novel* Elmore Leonard d Burt Reynolds *ph* Nick McLean m Barry de Vorzon, Joseph Conlan
☆ Burt Reynolds, Candice Bergen, George Segal, Charles Durning

'Plot is of the convoluted kind beloved by exhibitors since patrons can wander out for popcorn and come back without missing anything.' – *Variety*

The Stick Up
GB   1977   101m   colour
Backstage (Elliott Kastner, Danny O'Donovan)

In Devon in 1935, an American gives a lift to a café waitress and finds she is a thief on the run.

Numbingly peculiar comedy melodrama which tries too hard to have any chance of succeeding.

wd Jeffrey Bloom *ph* Michael Reed m Michael J. Lewis
☆ David Soul, Pamela McMyler, Johnny Wade, Michael Balfour

'The worst film of this or possibly any year.' – *Barry Took, Punch*

Sticky Fingers
US   1988   88m   DuArt
Virgin/Hightop/Spectrafilm (Catlin Adams, Melanie Mayron)

🖭 🖭

Two struggling musicians spend a fortune left with them for safe keeping by a drug dealer.

Lacklustre comedy without enough wit to keep it alive.

w Catlin Adams, Melanie Mayron d Catlin Adams *ph* Gary Thieltges m Gary Chang *ed* Bob Reitano
☆ Helen Slater, Melanie Mayron, Danitra Vance, Eileen Brennan, Carol Kane, Loretta Devine, Stephen McHattie, Christopher Guest

Stiff Upper Lips
GB   1997   94m   Metrocolor
Cavalier/Impact/Chrysalis/Yorkshire (Jeremy Bolt, Gary Sinyor)

An upper-class girl, who falls for a working-class boy, is taken by her aunt on trips to Italy and India.

A joke-stuffed send-up of Merchant Ivory's period dramas that occasionally raises a smile or three.

w Paul Simpkin, Gary Sinyor, Stephen Deitch, Richard Sparks d Gary Sinyor *ph* Simon Archer m David A. Hughes, John Murphy *pd* Mike Grant *ed* Peter Hollywood
☆ Peter Ustinov, Prunella Scales, Georgina Cates, Samuel West, Sean Pertwee, Brian Glover, Frank Finlay, Robert Portal, Richard Braine

'Terrible even as pastiche.' – *Gaby Wood, Guardian*

'It Will Scare The Hell Into You.'
Stigmata
US   1999   103m   colour
MGM (Frank Mancuso)

🖭 🖭 @ ⊙

A Catholic priest investigates when an irreligious Pittsburg hairdresser shows the weeping wounds of Christ on her hands and feet.

A good-looking, though irredeemably silly, horror movie that follows somewhat wanly in the footsteps of The Exorcist.

w Tom Lazarus, Rick Ramage d Rupert Wainwright *ph* Jeffrey L. Kimball m Billy Corgan, Elia Cmiral, Mike Garson *pd* Waldemar Kalinowski *ed* Michael R. Miller, Michael J. Duthie *sp* make-up: Ve Neill
☆ Patricia Arquette, Gabriel Byrne, Jonathan Pryce, Nia Long, Thomas Kopache, Rade Sherbedgia, Enrico Colantoni, Dick Latessa, Portia de Rossi, Patrick Muldoon, Ann Cusack

'Whips up an entertaining hysteria of stylistic overkill, tittersome dialogue and giddily outlandish situations.' – *David Rooney, Variety*

Stiletto
US   1969   99m   Berkeley-Pathé
Avco/Harold Robbins (Norman Rosemont)

A wealthy playboy racing driver is in fact a Mafia executioner.

Dreary, violent, fashionable Mafioso melodrama with international jet set trimmings.

w A. J. Russell *novel* Harold Robbins d Bernard Kowalski *ph* Jack Priestley m Sid Ramin
☆ Alex Cord, Britt Ekland, Barbara McNair, Patrick O'Neal, Joseph Wiseman, John Dehner, Eduardo Ciannelli, Roy Scheider

'Cardboard characters crumpled by a script which deals exclusively in clichés.' – *Sight and Sound*

'100 watts too loud. 50 pills too many. 20 years too late?'
Still Crazy **
GB/US   1998   95m   colour
Columbia (Amanda Marmot)

🖭 🖭

After 21 years away, a rock group of the 70s gets together again for a concert appearance.

Amiable comedy that pokes gentle fun at ageing rockers and their followers.

w Dick Clements, Ian La Frenais d Brian Gibson *ph* Ashley Rowe m Clive Langer *pd* Max Gottlieb *ed* Peter Boyle
☆ Stephen Rea, Billy Connolly, Jimmy Nail, Timothy Spall, Bill Nighy, Juliet Aubrey, Helena Bergström, Hans Matheson, Phil Daniels, Frances Barber, Phil Davis

'Though cinematically unadventurous, this is brilliantly observed and perfectly pitched. Every scene is a joy, every line one to remember.' – *Neil Jeffries, Empire*

Still of the Night *
US   1982   91m   Technicolor
MGM/UA (Arlene Donovan)

🖭 🖭

A psychiatrist finds himself in danger when one of his patients is murdered.

Hitchcock-style mystery melodrama with the villain fairly well concealed ... but somehow not very entertaining. The actors all take their characters too seriously.

w Robert Benton, David Newman d Robert Benton *ph* Nestor Almendros m John Kander *pd* Mel Bourne
☆ Roy Scheider, Meryl Streep, Jessica Tandy, Sara Botsford, Josef Sommer, Joe Grifasi

'A lifeless and frustrating muddle.' – *Steve Jenkins, MFB*

De Stilte Rond Christine M: see *A Question of Silence*

'All it takes is a little confidence!'
The Sting ***
US   1973   129m   Technicolor
Universal/Richard Zanuck, David Brown (Tony Bill, Michael S. Phillips)

🖭 🖭 @ ⊙

In twenties Chicago, two con men stage an elaborate revenge on a big time gangster who caused the death of a friend.

Bright, likeable, but overlong, unconvincingly studio-set and casually developed comedy suspenser cashing in on star charisma but riding to enormous success chiefly

---

on its tinkly music and the general lack of simple entertainment.

w David S. Ward d George Roy Hill *ph* Robert Surtees m Scott Joplin (arranged by Marvin Hamlisch) *ad* Henry Bumstead
☆ Paul Newman, Robert Redford, Robert Shaw, Charles Durning, Ray Walston, Eileen Brennan

'A visually claustrophobic, mechanically plotted movie that's meant to be a roguishly charming entertainment.' – *New Yorker*

'It demonstrates what can happen when a gifted young screenwriter has the good fortune to fall among professionals his second time out.' – *Judith Crist*

'A testament to the value of blue eyes and bright smiles.' – *Les Keyser, Hollywood in the Seventies*
🏆 best picture; David S. Ward; George Roy Hill; Marvin Hamlisch
🎗 Robert Surtees; Robert Redford

'The con is on – place your bets!'
The Sting 2
US   1983   102m   Technicolor
Universal (Jennings Lang)

🖭 @

Lonnegan plots his revenge on the two who stung him in twenties Chicago.

Boring reprise of an overrated movie: though efficiently made, it never catches fire, and the cast is indisputably a second team.

w David S. Ward d Jeremy Paul Kagan *ph* Bill Butler m Lalo Schifrin *pd* Edward C. Carfagno
☆ Jackie Gleason, Mac Davis, Karl Malden, Oliver Reed, Bert Remsen, Teri Garr

'The vivid minor characters have been squeezed into lifelessness by the python-like plot.' – *Tom Milne, MFB*
🎵 Lalo Schifrin

Stingaree
US   1934   76m   bw (colour sequence)
RKO (Pandro S. Berman)

An Australian outlaw of the eighties falls for a rancher's daughter.

Unexciting but unobjectionable piece of Robin Hoodery.

w Becky Gardiner *stories* E. W. Hornung d William A. Wellman *ph* James Van Trees m Max Steiner
☆ Irene Dunne, Richard Dix, Mary Boland, Conway Tearle, Andy Devine, Henry Stephenson, Una O'Connor, Reginald Owen, Snub Pollard, George Barraud

'Should bring medium results. It does not promise to rise to greater heights.' – *Variety*

Stir Crazy
US   1980   111m   Metrocolor
Columbia/Hannah Weinstein

🖭 🖭 @

Two New Yorkers heading for California to try their luck are wrongly convicted of a bank robbery but plan escape from prison.

Extended farce giving rather too free rein to its stars' potential for mugging, and polishing up every prison gag in the book.

w Bruce Jay Friedman d Sidney Poitier *ph* Fred Schuler m Tom Scott *pd* Alfred Sweeney
☆ Gene Wilder, Richard Pryor, Georg Stanford Brown, JoBeth Williams

A Stitch in Time
GB   1963   94m   bw
Rank (Hugh Stewart)

A butcher's boy goes into hospital and falls for a nurse.

Thin star slapstick; all one can say is that it's marginally preferable to Jerry Lewis.

w Jack Davies d Robert Asher *ph* Jack Asher m Philip Green
☆ Norman Wisdom, Edward Chapman, Jerry Desmonde, Jeanette Sterke, Jill Melford

Stockade
US   1990   97m   colour
Entertainment/Movie Group/Northern Lights Media Corporation (Richard Davis)

🖭 🖭 @

US title: *Count a Lonely Cadence*

A young soldier, sent to the stockade for brawling, is persecuted by a bigoted sergeant in charge.

Uninvolving prison drama.

w Dennis Shryack, Martin Sheen *novel* Count a Lonely Cadence by Gordon Weaver d Martin

---

Sheen *ph* Richard Leiterman m Georges Delerue *pd* Ian Thomas *ed* Martin Hunter
☆ Charlie Sheen, Martin Sheen, F. Murray Abraham, Larry Fishburne, Blu Mankuma, Michael Beach, Harry Stewart

'Predictably staged, glossily performed, erratically edited, and seems unable to conceal a mood of smug optimism.' – *Philip Strick, MFB*

The Stolen Children **
Italy/France   1992   114m   Technicolor
Mayfair/Erre/Alia/RAIDUE/Arena/Vega (Angelo Rizzoli, Stefano Munafo)

🖭

original title: *Il Ladro di Bambini*

A young cop travels across Italy to a children's home with an 11-year-old girl, forced to become a prostitute by her mother, and her younger brother.

Tough and compassionate movie that refuses to sensationalize its subject-matter, of adult and official indifference to the sufferings of the young.

w Sandro Petraglia, Stefano Rulli, Gianni Amelio d Gianni Amelio *ph* Tonino Nardi, Renato Tafuri m Franco Piersanti *pd* Andrea Crisanti *ed* Simona Paggi
☆ Enrico Lo Verso, Valentina Scalici, Giuseppe Ieracitano, Renato Carpentieri, Vitalba Andrea, Grignani, Massimo de Lorenzo

'Classical humanist cinema, almost in the neo-realist tradition.' – *Derek Malcolm, Guardian*
'Quiet, honest, admirably acted.' – *Philip French, Observer*

Stolen Face
GB   1952   72m   bw
Exclusive/Hammer (Michael Hinds)

Via plastic surgery a girl criminal is given another face, which produces a different kind of trouble.

Quickie melodrama which proved fairly popular because of its Hollywood stars.

w Martin Berkeley, Richard Landau d Terence Fisher *ph* Walter Harvey m Malcolm Arnold
☆ Paul Henreid, Lizabeth Scott, André Morell, John Wood, Susan Stephen, Mary Mackenzie, Arnold Ridley

Stolen Harmony
US   1935   79m   bw
Paramount

An ex-con becomes a saxophonist with a band and is suspected of a robbery.

Tedious mix-up of mayhem and music.

w Leon Gordon, Harry Ruskin, Claude Binyon, Lewis Foster d Alfred Werker
☆ George Raft, Ben Bernie, Grace Bradley, Iris Adrian, Lloyd Nolan, Ralf Harolde

'Once under way it provides some exciting entertainment; but the poor beginning isn't easily tossed off.' – *Variety*

Stolen Hearts: see *Two If by Sea*

'Its surprise finish will lift you to amazing emotional peaks!'
Stolen Heaven
US   1931   72m   bw
Paramount

A boy and girl decide to commit suicide after spending the twenty thousand dollars they've stolen, but neither can go through with it.

A very silly idea, ineptly presented.

w Dana Burnet d George Abbott
☆ Nancy Carroll, Phillips Holmes, Louis Calhern, Edward Keane

'It will range down from moderate figures.' – *Variety*

Stolen Heaven
US   1938   88m   bw
Paramount

Two jewel thieves in love are harboured on the run by an old concert pianist.

Sentimental melodrama which almost works, with its backing of classical piano pieces.

w Eve Greene, Frederick Jackson, Andrew L. Stone d Andrew L. Stone
☆ Gene Raymond, Olympe Bradna, Lewis Stone, Glenda Farrell, Porter Hall, Douglass Dumbrille

'Pleasing entertainment all the way.' – *Variety*

Stolen Holiday
US   1937   82m   bw
Warner

A model marries a fortune hunter to protect him from the law.

Slightly unusual romantic drama based on the career of Alexander Stavisky.
w Casey Robinson d Michael Curtiz
☆ Claude Rains, Kay Francis, Ian Hunter, Alison Skipworth, Charles Halton, Alex D'Arcy

Stolen Hours
GB   1963   97m   DeLuxe
UA/Mirisch/Barbican (Denis Holt)
An American divorcee with only a year to live falls in love with her surgeon.
Tired remake of Dark Victory; pleasant Cornish backgrounds.
w Jessamyn West d Daniel Petrie ph Harry Waxman m Mort Lindsey
☆ Susan Hayward, Michael Craig, Diane Baker, Edward Judd, Paul Rogers

Stolen Kisses *
France   1968   91m   Eastmancolor
Films du Carrosse/Artistes Associés (Marcel Berbert)
original title: *Baisers Volés*
An ineffective young man can find neither work nor love.
A pleasing, rather sad little comedy which has almost the feel of a Keaton; but one is not quite sure at the end what its creator intended.
w François Truffaut, Claude de Givray, Bernard Revon d François Truffaut ph Denys Clerval m Antoine Duhamel
☆ Jean-Pierre Léaud, Delphine Seyrig, Michel Lonsdale, Claude Jade
§ best foreign film

A Stolen Life *
GB   1939   91m   bw
(Paramount) Orion (Anthony Havelock-Allan)
In Brittany, a woman deceives her husband by exchanging identities with her dead twin.
An actress's showcase, quite satisfactorily mounted.
w Margaret Kennedy, George Barraud *novel* Karel J. Benes d Paul Czinner ph Philip Tannura m William Walton
☆ Elisabeth Bergner, Michael Redgrave, Wilfrid Lawson, Richard Ainley, Mabel Terry-Lewis, Clement McCallin

A Stolen Life *
US   1946   107m   bw
Warner (Bette Davis)
Enjoyable if slightly disappointing remake with New England backgrounds.
w Catherine Turney d Curtis Bernhardt ph Sol Polito, Ernest Haller m Max Steiner
☆ Bette Davis, Glenn Ford, Dane Clark, Walter Brennan, Charles Ruggles, Bruce Bennett, Peggy Knudsen, Esther Dale
'A distressingly empty piece of show-off.' – Bosley Crowther
'What I'm waiting for is a film about beautiful identical quintuplets who all love the same man.' – Richard Winnington

'Drugs, Sex And Murder.'
Stone Cold
US   1992   92m   DeLuxe
Columbia TriStar/Stone Group/Mace Neufeld/Yoram Ben Ami/Walter Doniger
A cop goes undercover in Mississippi to investigate a gang of violent bikers who have gone on a killing spree.
Standard action-movie stuff, but done with a little flair, despite its overblown climax.
w Walter Doniger d Craig R. Baxley ph Alexander Gruszynski m Sylvester Levay pd John Mansbridge, Richard Johnson ed Mark Helfrich, Larry Bock, Edward A. Warschilka Jnr
☆ Brian Bosworth, Lance Henriksen, William Forsythe, Arabella Holzbog, Sam McMurray, Richard Gant, David Tress
'Strictly six-pack fodder.' – Empire

Stone Cold Dead
Canada   1979   97m   Bellevue-Pathé
Ko-Zak (George Mendeluk, John Ryan)
A tough cop investigates the serial murders of prostitutes.
Beginning with a death, by gunshot in a shower, by a killer who photographs his victims, it attempts a few variations on very familiar themes but fails to establish any rhythm of its own; it also takes much suspension of disbelief to accept Paul Williams as a successful pimp.
wd George Mendeluk *novel* The Sin Sniper by Hugh Garner ph Dennis Miller m Paul James Zaza ed Martin Pepler
☆ Richard Crenna, Paul Williams, Linda Sorensen, Belinda J. Montgomery, Monique Mercure, George Chuvalo, Jennifer Dale, Frank Moore

'Take away his badge and he'd top the Ten Most Wanted list!' ·
The Stone Killer *
US   1973   96m   Technicolor
Columbia/Dino de Laurentiis (Michael Winner)
A brutal Los Angeles police detective takes on the Mafia.
Fast-moving amalgam of chases and violence with a downbeat hero.
w Gerald Wilson *novel* A Complete State of Death by John Gardner d Michael Winner ph Richard Moore m Roy Budd
☆ Charles Bronson, Martin Balsam, Ralph Waite, David Sheiner, Norman Fell
'Film-making as painting by numbers.' – Sight and Sound
'Keeps turning into exciting cinema, crude, often funny and sometimes quite brilliantly idiomatic. It may come as close to inspired primitivism as we are likely to get in the movies these days.' – Roger Greenspun, New York Times

'Between maleness and femaleness there is fabulousness.'
Stonewall *
GB   1996   98m   Technicolor
Metro Tartan/BBC (Christine Vachon, Ruth Caleb)
A gay man becomes radicalized when he moves from his small town to New York and eventually riots against the police when they raid the Stonewall bar, a seminal moment in the movement for homosexual liberation.
An engaging, low-budget drama of a revolt against oppression, often camp in style, with its focus on drag artistes, and celebrating an unexpected victory.
w Rikki Beadle Blair *book* Martin Duberman d Nigel Finch ph Chris Seager m Michael Kamen, Pat Seymour pd Therese DePrez ed John Richards
☆ Guillermo Diaz, Frederic Weller, Brendan Corbalis, Duane Boutté, Bruce MacVittie, Peter Ratray, Dwight Ewell, Matthew Faber
'The logistical problems of shooting a gay historical epic for peanuts must have been nightmarish; but, with all due sympathy, the fact remains, the filmmakers haven't solved them.' – Peter Matthews, Sight and Sound
'Its energy is positively blithe.' – Adam Mars-Jones, Independent

The Stooge
US   1952   100m   bw
Paramount/Hal B. Wallis
In 1930 a conceited song and dance man fails to realize that his moronic stooge is the act's real attraction.
Typical, and particularly resistible, Martin and Lewis concoction: whenever one thinks of laughing, a dollop of sentimentality comes along and promptly quashes the idea.
w Fred Finklehoffe, Martin Rackin d Norman Taurog ph Daniel L. Fapp m Joseph J. Lilley
☆ Dean Martin, Jerry Lewis, Polly Bergen, Marie McDonald, Eddie Mayehoff, Marion Marshall, Richard Erdman

Stop Me Before I Kill: see The Full Treatment

Stop! Or My Mom Will Shoot
US   1992   87m   DeLuxe
UIP/Universal/Northern Lights (Ivan Reitman, Joe Medjuck, Michael C. Gross)
The mother of a Los Angeles cop helps him solve a murder and get back together with his girlfriend.
Lamentable comedy, a failed attempt to extend Stallone's narrow range.
w Blake Snyder, William Osborne, William Davies d Roger Spottiswoode ph Frank Tidy m Alan Silvestri pd Charles Rosen ed Mark Conte, Lois Freeman-Fox
☆ Sylvester Stallone, Estelle Getty, JoBeth Williams, Roger Rees, Martin Ferrero, Gailard Sartain, Dennis Burkley

'One of those Hollywood films in which the flimsiest of plots buckles under the most obvious of concepts.' – Lizzie Franke, Sight and Sound

Stop Press Girl
GB   1949   78m   bw
Rank/Aquila
A girl finds she has the unconscious power to halt all machinery to a stop.
Weary comedy which has nowhere to go after its first silly idea.
w Basil Thomas, T. J. Morrison d Michael Barry
☆ Sally Ann Howes, Gordon Jackson, Basil Radford, Naunton Wayne, James Robertson Justice, Sonia Holm, Nigel Buchanan, Kenneth More

Stop You're Killing Me
US   1953   86m   Warnercolor
Warner (Louis F. Edelman)
At the end of prohibition a beer baron decides to go straight, but finds his house filled with the corpses of rival gangsters.
Frantic remake of A Slight Case of Murder with a few musical numbers added; all rather messy.
w James O'Hanlon d Roy del Ruth ph Ted McCord md Ray Heindorf
☆ Broderick Crawford, Claire Trevor, Virginia Gibson, Bill Hayes, Sheldon Leonard, Joe Vitale, Howard St John, Henry Morgan, Margaret Dumont

Stopover Forever
GB   1964   59m   bw
Associated British Pathé
An air hostess on holiday in Sicily believes that someone wants to murder her.
Mundane thriller with an unsympathetic heroine and nothing else to engage the attention.
w David Osborne d Frederic Goode ph William Jordan m Edwin Astley ed Ronald Glenister
☆ Ann Bell, Anthony Bate, Conrad Phillips, Bruce Boa, Julian Sherrier

Stopover Tokyo
US   1957   100m   Eastmancolor
Cinemascope
TCF (Walter Reisch)
An American spy in Tokyo seeks to capture a communist undercover man.
Sprawling espionage stuff with frequent halts for scenic tours.
w Richard L. Breen, Walter Reisch *novel* John P. Marquand d Richard L. Breen ph Charles G. Clarke m Paul Sawtell
☆ Robert Wagner, Joan Collins, Edmond O'Brien, Ken Scott, Larry Keating

Storia di una Monaca di Clausura: see Story of a Cloistered Nun

Stories from a Flying Trunk
👫👫   GB   1979   88m   Technicolor
EMI/Sands (John Brabourne, Richard Goodwin)
Three Hans Andersen stories are performed by stop frame animation and by ballet dancers dressed as vegetables.
Lugubrious attempt to repeat the success of Tales of Beatrix Potter; moments to make one smile, but on the whole a depressing experience.
wd Christine Edzard ph Robin Browne, Brian West m Gioacchino Rossini
☆ Murray Melvin, Ann Firbank, Johanna Sonnex, Tasneem Maqsood

Stork Bites Man
US   1948   67m   bw
Comet (Ralph Cohn, Buddy Rogers)
An apartment house manager has a pregnant wife and a baby-hating boss.
Threadbare farce, not enlivened by wit or pacing.
wd Cyril Endfield ph Robert Pittack m Raoul Kraushaar
☆ Jackie Cooper, Gene Roberts, Gus Schilling, Emory Parnell

The Stork Club
US   1945   98m   bw
Paramount (B. G. de Sylva)
A night-club hat-check girl saves an elderly millionaire from drowning.
Very light comedy with music, a great ad for a once famous night haunt.
w B. G. de Sylva, John McGowan d Hal Walker ph Charles Lang Jnr md Robert Emmett Dolan
☆ Betty Hutton, Barry Fitzgerald, Don Defore, Robert Benchley, Bill Goodwin, Iris Adrian, Mary Young, Mikhail Rasumny

The Storm
US   1930   76m   bw
Universal
An orphan girl left with a trapper becomes an object of jealousy between him and his partner.
Old-fashioned outdoor melodrama, previously filmed in 1916 and 1922. Not really talkie material.
w Wells Root *play* Langdon McCormick d William Wyler
☆ Lupe Velez, Paul Cavanagh, William Boyd, Alphonse Ethier
'A fairly good programmer ... the fight is a pip.' – Variety

The Storm
US   1938   79m   bw
Universal (Ken Goldsmith)
Tensions lead to violence among shipboard radio operators.
Lively action melodrama culminating in a storm at sea.
w Daniel Moore, Hugh King, Theodore Reeves d Harold Young
☆ Charles Bickford, Barton MacLane, Preston Foster, Tom Brown, Nan Grey, Andy Devine, Frank Jenks
'Good enough for the duals, but too weak for solo billing.' – Variety

Storm at Daybreak
US   1932   80m   bw
MGM
A fanciful reconstruction of events leading up to the Sarajevo assassination which precipitated World War I.
Unlikely melodrama with stars forced to overact; still, a rich and historically interesting slice of ham.
w Bertram Millhauser *play* Sandor Hunyady d Richard Boleslawski
☆ Walter Huston, Kay Francis, Nils Asther, Phillips Holmes, Eugene Pallette, C. Henry Gordon, Jean Parker
'A good cast unwisely spent on weak material: doubtful as a grosser.' – Variety

Storm Boy **
👫👫   Australia   1976   87m   colour
South Australian Film Corp (Matt Carroll)
A young boy, living in an isolated beachside shack with his misanthropic father, rears a pelican as a pet.
A pleasantly modest drama about a boy growing up and learning to come to terms with death and adult behaviour.
w Sonia Borg *novel* Storm Boy by Colin Thiele d Henri Safran ph Geoff Burton m Michael Carlos ad David Copping ed G. Turney-Smith
☆ Peter Cummins, David Gulpilil, Greg Rowe, Judy Dick, Tony Allison
'A beautifully crafted film for children.' – MFB

'Who really set the town aflame?'
Storm Center
US   1956   87m   bw
Columbia/Phoenix (Julian Blaustein)
A small-town librarian is dismissed when she refuses to remove a communist book from the shelves.
Formula anti-McCarthy melodrama originally designed for Mary Pickford's comeback; not very absorbing and rather dingily produced.
w Daniel Taradash, Elick Moll d Daniel Taradash ph Burnett Guffey m George Duning
☆ Bette Davis, Brian Keith, Kim Hunter, Paul Kelly, Joe Mantell

Storm Fear
US   1955   88m   bw
UA/Theodora (Cornel Wilde)
Three fugitives from justice hide in a mountain cabin, but all meet violent deaths.
Gloomy, strenuous melodrama, partly shot outdoors.
w Horton Foote *novel* Clinton Seeley d Cornel Wilde ph Joseph LaShelle m Elmer Bernstein
☆ Cornel Wilde, Jean Wallace, Dan Duryea, Lee Grant, Steven Hill, Dennis Weaver

Storm in a Teacup *
GB 1937 87m bw
Alexander Korda/Victor Saville

A national sensation ensues when a Scottish provost fines an old lady for not licensing her dog, and she refuses to pay.
Early Ealing-type comedy, a bit emaciated by later standards.
w Ian Dalrymple, Donald Bull *play Sturm im Wasserglass by Bruno Frank* d Ian Dalrymple, Victor Saville *ph* Max Greene *m* Frederic Lewis
☆ Vivien Leigh, Rex Harrison, Cecil Parker, Sara Allgood, Ursula Jeans, Gus McNaughton, Arthur Wontner

Storm over Africa: see Royal African Rifles

Storm over Asia *
USSR 1928 93m bw silent
Mezhrabpomfilm
📼 ▤

original title: *Potomok Chingis-Khana*
aka: *The Heir to Genghis Khan*
A Mongolian trapper is discovered to be descended from Genghis Khan and made puppet emperor of a Soviet province.
Curious yarn without much discernible point though with the usual patches of propagandizing. It certainly looks good.
w Osip Brik d V. I. Pudovkin *ph* A. L. Golovnya
☆ I. Inkizhinov, Valeri Inkizhinov, A. Dedintsev
'Fetid with propaganda and thematically ridiculous to any semi-intelligent audience. The more illiterate a man is in these Russian blurbs, the better his chances to make a name for himself in the Red World.' – *Variety*

Storm over Lisbon
US 1944 86m bw
Republic (George Sherman)
An international spy mastermind runs a Lisbon night-club and sells documents to the highest bidder.
Feeble copy of Casablanca.
w Doris Gilbert, Dane Lussier d George Sherman *ph* John Alton *m* Walter Scharf
☆ Vera Hruba Ralston, Erich von Stroheim, Richard Arlen, Eduardo Ciannelli, Otto Kruger, Robert Livingston, Mona Barrie, Frank Orth

Storm over the Andes
US 1935 82m bw
Universal (Maurice Pivar)
An American flyer helps Bolivia against Paraguay.
Thick-ear melodrama about a forgotten local war; soundly made of its kind.
w Eliot Gibbons, Laclede Christy, Frank Wead, Al de Mond, Eve Greene d Christy Cabanne
☆ Jack Holt, Antonio Moreno, Mona Barrie, Gene Lockhart, Grant Withers

Storm over the Nile
GB 1955 107m Technicolor Cinemascope
Independent/London (Zoltan Korda)
Feeble remake of *The Four Feathers* (qv), using most of that film's action highlights stretched out to fit the wide screen.
w R. C. Sherriff d Terence Young *ph* Ted Scaife, Osmond Borradaile *m* Benjamin Frankel
☆ Anthony Steel, Laurence Harvey, Ronald Lewis, Ian Carmichael, James Robertson Justice, Mary Ure, Geoffrey Keen, Jack Lambert, Ferdy Mayne, Michael Hordern
'The material appears not so much dated as fossilized within its period.' – *Penelope Houston*

Storm over Tibet
US 1951 87m bw
Columbia/Summit (Ivan Tors, Laslo Benedek)
An explorer steals a holy mask which brings bad luck.
Slight adventure yarn ingeniously built around an old German documentary.
w Ivan Tors, Sam Mayer d Andrew Marton *ph* George E. Diskant, Wallace Angst *m* Arthur Honegger
☆ Rex Reason, Diana Douglas, Myron Healey

Storm over Wyoming
US 1950 60m bw
RKO (Herman Schlom)
Two cowboys intervene in a range war between a rancher and a sheepman.
Fast-moving but standard stuff, with an over-familiar, no-surprises plot.
w Ed Earl Repp d Lesley Selander *ph* J. Roy Hunt *m* Paul Sawtell *ad* Albert S. D'Agostino, Feild Gray *ed* Robert Swink
☆ Tim Holt, Richard Martin, Noreen Nash, Richard Powers (Tom Keene), Betty Underwood, Bill Kennedy

Storm Warning *
US 1950 93m bw
Warner (Jerry Wald)
A New York model goes south to visit her sister, and finds that her brother-in-law is an oversexed brute and a Ku Klux Klan killer.
Heavy melodrama disguised as a social document; sufficiently arresting for its purposes.
w Daniel Fuchs, Richard Brooks d Stuart Heisler *ph* Carl Guthrie *m* Daniele Amfitheatrof
☆ Ginger Rogers, Doris Day, *Steve Cochran*, Ronald Reagan, Hugh Sanders, Raymond Greenleaf, Ned Glass

Stormy
👥 US 1935 67m bw
Universal (Henry MacRae)
Stable-boy meets horse, stable-boy loses horse, stable-boy gets horse, and girl.
A simple-minded, sentimental story for horse-lovers, though directed with sufficient energy to maintain interest; there are, for a 'B' movie, some spectacular scenes of wild horses.
w Ben Grauman Kohn, George Plympton *story* Cherry Wilson d Louis Friedlander (Lew Landers) *ph* Richard Fryer *md* Heinz Roemheld *ad* Ralph Berger *ed* Murray Seldeen
☆ Noah Beery Jnr, Jean Rogers, J. Farrell MacDonald, Raymond Hatton, Walter Miller, Fred Kohler, James Burtis, The Arizona Wranglers, Rex ('King of Wild Horses')
† The film opens with the statement: 'In the belief that in every heart abides the love of beauty in all things of the Universe, I dedicate this picture to my fellowmen of all nations. We have tried here to capture nature at her finest and manhood at its best. Set in the Painted Desert, of Arizona, "Stormy" combines for young and old the wonders of nature and the glory of human courage.'

Stormy Monday
GB 1987 93m colour
Palace/Moving Picture Company/Film Four International/Atlantic Entertainment/British Screen (Nigel Stafford-Clark)
📼 ▤ 🔊 🎧
An American gangster tries to put a Newcastle club-owner out of business.
Dull and implausible thriller of uninteresting characters.
wd Mike Figgis *ph* Roger Deakins *m* Mike Figgis *pd* Andrew McAlpine *ed* Dave Martin
☆ Melanie Griffith, Tommy Lee Jones, Sting, Sean Bean, James Cosmo, Mark Long, Brian Lewis
'An obscure, uninvolving and lethargic movie.' – *Kim Newman, MFB*

Stormy Waters: see Remorques

Stormy Weather
GB 1935 74m bw
Gainsborough (Michael Balcon)
📼
A top executive foils a blackmail racket in Chinatown.
Very presentable vehicle for the Aldwych team of farceurs.
w Ben Travers *play* Ben Travers d Tom Walls *ph* Philip Tannura *md* Louis Levy
☆ Tom Walls, Ralph Lynn, Robertson Hare, Yvonne Arnaud, Gordon James, Graham Moffatt

Stormy Weather ***
US 1943 77m bw
TCF (Irving Mills)
▤ 🔊 🎧
A backstage success story lightly based on the career of Bill Robinson.
Virtually a high-speed revue with all-black talent, and what talent! The production is pretty slick too.

w Frederick Jackson, Ted Koehler d Andrew Stone *ph* Leon Shamroy, Fred Sersen *md* Benny Carter *ch* Clarence Robinson
☆ Bill Robinson, Lena Horne, Fats Waller, Ada Brown, Cab Calloway, Katherine Dunham and her Dancers, Eddie Anderson, Flournoy Miller, The Nicholas Brothers, Dooley Wilson
'A first-rate show, a spirited divertissement ... a joy to the ear.' – *New York Times*
🎵 'There's No Two Ways about Love'; 'That Ain't Right'; 'Ain't Misbehavin'; 'Diga Diga Doo'; 'I Can't Give You Anything but Love'; 'Geechee Joe'; 'Stormy Weather'; 'My, My, Ain't That Somethin'?'

The Story of a Cheat: see Le Roman d'un Tricheur

Story of a Cloistered Nun (dubbed)
Italy 1973 90m colour
PAC Consorziate (Tonino Cervi)
📼
original title: *Storia di una Monaca di Clausura*
aka: *Diary of a Cloistered Nun*
In the 1600s, an aristocratic young woman is forced to become a nun when she refuses to marry the man chosen for her.
Turgid period drama, devoid of dramatic interest, with occasional interludes of unerotic love-making.
w Domenico Paolella, Antonio Cervi d Domenico Paolella *ph* Armando Nannuzzi *m* Piero Piccioni *ad* Pietro Filippone *ed* Amedeo Giomini
☆ Catherine Spaak, Suzy Kendall, Eleonora Giorgi, Martine Brochard, Ann Odessa, Antonio Falsi, Umberto Orsini
† The print quality of the British video release is poor.

Story of a Love Story
France/Italy 1973 110m colour
Franco-London/FLF/Robert Bradford/Euro International (Jud Kinberg)
aka: *Impossible Object*
A married middle-aged writer who finds it difficult to distinguish fiction from fact indulges in an affair with a woman whose husband is aware of her infidelity.
Meandering and rarely interesting account of the varieties of love; it lacks conviction and passion.
w Nicholas Mosley *Impossible Object by Nicholas Mosley* d John Frankenheimer *ph* Claude Renoir *m* Michel Legrand *pd* Alexandre Trauner *ed* Albert Jurgenson
☆ Alan Bates, Dominique Sanda, Michel Auclair, Evans Evans, Paul Crauchet, Lea Massari, Vernon Dobtcheff
† The film never received a cinema release.

The Story of a Woman
US/Italy 1969 101m Technicolor
Universal/Westward (Leonardo Bercovici)
A Swedish girl pianist in Rome falls in love with a fashionable doctor, then back in Sweden meets an American diplomat.
Intermezzo-type romantic drama with colour supplement trappings. Tolerable of its kind.
wd Leonardo Bercovici *ph* Piero Portalupi *m* John Williams
☆ Robert Stack, Bibi Andersson, James Farentino, Annie Girardot, Frank Sundstrom

The Story of Adèle H *
France 1975 98m Eastmancolor
Films du Carrosse/Artistes Associés (Marcel Berbert, Claude Miller)
▤ 🔊
In 1863, the daughter of Victor Hugo follows her lover to Nova Scotia.
Surprisingly slow and stilted version of a true story, though with a few of the expected subtleties.
w François Truffaut, Jean Gruault, Suzanne Schiffman d François Truffaut *ph* Nestor Almendros *m* Maurice Jaubert
☆ Isabelle Adjani, Bruce Robinson, Sylvia Marriott
👤 Isabelle Adjani

'America's most thrilling story! Of love so great and faith so strong that it inspired this man to endure ridicule, privation and hunger – to achieve the miracle of wings for the human voice!'

The Story of Alexander Graham Bell **
US 1939 97m bw
TCF (Kenneth MacGowan)
GB title: *The Modern Miracle*
The inventor of the telephone marries a deaf girl.
Acceptable history lesson with dullish principals but excellent production.
w Lamar Trotti d Irving Cummings *ph* Leon Shamroy *m* Louis Silvers
☆ Don Ameche, Henry Fonda, Loretta Young, Charles Coburn, Gene Lockhart, Spring Byington, Bobs Watson
'Production will need teasing to get the women.' – *Variety*

The Story of Dr Ehrlich's Magic Bullet: see Dr Ehrlich's Magic Bullet

The Story of Dr Wassell *
US 1944 140m Technicolor
Paramount/Cecil B. de Mille
The adventures of a naval doctor who heroically saved men during the Pacific war.
Long, slogging, glamorized account of real events which is typical de Mille and very unconvincing physically, but keeps one watching simply as a story.
w Alan le May, Charles Bennett *book* James Hilton d Cecil B. de Mille *ph* Victor Milner, William Snyder *m* Victor Young
☆ Gary Cooper, Laraine Day, Signe Hasso, Dennis O'Keefe, Carol Thurston, Carl Esmond, Paul Kelly, Stanley Ridges
'The director has taken a true story of heroism ... and jangled it into a cacophony of dancing girls, phoney self-sacrifice and melodramatic romance.' – *Howard Barnes*
'To be regretted beyond qualification. It whips the story into a nacreous foam of lies whose speciousness is only the more painful because Mr de Mille is so obviously free from any desire to alter the truth except for what he considers to be its own advantage.' – *James Agee*
'Close to the last word in honest understanding and convincing production.' – *Motion Picture Herald*

The Story of Esther Costello *
GB 1957 103m bw
Columbia/Romulus (James Woolf)
US title: *The Golden Virgin*
A blind Irish deaf mute girl is adopted by an American socialite and her plight becomes an international cause.
Rich melodrama develops from this unlikely premise and the star enjoys it hugely.
w Charles Kaufman *novel* Nicholas Monsarrat d David Miller *ph* Robert Krasker *m* Georges Auric
☆ Joan Crawford, Heather Sears, Rossano Brazzi, Ron Randell, Lee Patterson, Fay Compton, John Loder, Denis O'Dea, Sidney James, Maureen Delany
'A regular little *Titus Andronicus*, it abounds in fraud, embezzlement, suicide, murder and rape; all it wants is somebody baked in a pie.' – *Dilys Powell*
🏆 Heather Sears

The Story of GI Joe **
US 1945 108m bw
(UA) Lester Cowan (David Hall)
aka: *War Correspondent*
Journalist Ernie Pyle follows fighting men into the Italian campaign.
Slow, convincing, sympathetic war film with good script and performances; not by any means the usual action saga.
w Leopold Atlas, Guy Endore, Philip Stevenson *book* Ernie Pyle d William A. Wellman *ph* Russell Metty *m* Ann Ronell, Louis Applebaum
☆ Burgess Meredith, Robert Mitchum, Freddie Steele, Wally Cassell, Jimmy Lloyd, Jack Reilly
'It is humorous, poignant and tragic, an earnestly human reflection of a stern life and the dignity of man.' – *Thomas M. Pryor*
'A tragic and eternal work of art.' – *James Agee*
'One of the best films of the war.' – *Richard Mallett, Punch*
👤 script; music score; song 'Linda' (*m/ly* Ann Ronell); Robert Mitchum

---

The Story of Gilbert and Sullivan *

GB   1953   109m   Technicolor
British Lion/London Films (Frank Launder, Sidney Gilliat)

US title: *The Great Gilbert and Sullivan*

In 1875 a young composer named Arthur Sullivan and a librettist named William Gilbert come together under the auspices of Rupert D'Oyly Carte and write the Savoy Operas.

Light, accurate, well-cast and well-produced Victorian musical which somehow fails to ignite despite the immense talent at hand.

w Sidney Gilliat, Leslie Bailey d Sidney Gilliat ph Christopher Challis md Sir Malcolm Sargent pd Hein Heckroth

☆ Robert Morley, Maurice Evans, Peter Finch, Eileen Herlie, Dinah Sheridan, Isabel Dean, Wilfrid Hyde-White, Muriel Aked

'It is like a sound radio scrapbook, combined with a television passing show. It is bright, swift and bitty; faintly sentimental, enormously good-natured.' – *C. A. Lejeune*

The Story of Louis Pasteur ***

US   1936   85m   bw
Warner/Cosmopolitan (Henry Blanke)
♀

How the eminent 19th-century French scientist overcomes obstacles in finding cures for various diseases.

Adequate biopic which caused a sensation and started a trend; some of the others were better but this was the first example of Hollywood bringing schoolbook history to box-office life.

w Sheridan Gibney, Pierre Collings d William Dieterle ph Tony Gaudio m Bernhard Kaun, Heinz Roemheld

☆ Paul Muni, Josephine Hutchinson, Anita Louise, Donald Woods, Fritz Leiber, Henry O'Neill, Porter Hall, Akim Tamiroff, Walter Kingsford

'Probably limited b.o. but a creditable prestige picture.' – *Variety*

'What should be vital and arresting has been made hollow and dull … we are tendered something that is bright and stagey for something out of life.' – *Otis Ferguson*

'More exciting than any gangster melodrama.' – *C. A. Lejeune*

👤 original story; screenplay; Paul Muni
👥 best picture

'Men and their women from the beginning of creation! Never so vast an undertaking!'

The Story of Mankind

US   1957   100m   Technicolor
Warner/Cambridge (Irwin Allen)

A heavenly tribunal debates whether to allow man to destroy himself, and both the Devil and the Spirit of Man cite instances from history.

Hilarious charade, one of the worst films ever made, but full of surprises, bad performances, and a wide range of stock shots.

w Irwin Allen, Charles Bennett book Hendrik Van Loon d Irwin Allen ph Nicholas Musuraca m Paul Sawtell

☆ Ronald Colman, Vincent Price, Cedric Hardwicke, the Marx Brothers, Hedy Lamarr, Agnes Moorehead, Reginald Gardiner, Peter Lorre, Virginia Mayo, Charles Coburn, Francis X. Bushman

'A poor excuse to use a batch of available actors in some of the weirdest casting ever committed.' – *Newsweek*

'The script was bad to begin with and it worsened with daily changes. I remember one puzzled visitor asking Ronnie Colman, "Is this picture based on a book?", and he replied in that beautiful soft diction of his, "Yes. But they're only using the notes on the dust jacket."' – *Vincent Price*

The Story of Molly X

US   1949   82m   bw
Universal/International

When a criminal is killed, his wife masterminds the gang to find out who killed him.

Silly melodrama, generally ineptly presented.

wd Crane Wilbur ph Irving Glassberg m Milton Schwarzwald

☆ June Havoc, John Russell, Dorothy Hart, Elliott Lewis, Connie Gilchrist

The Story of Qiu Ju ***

China/Hong Kong   1992   100m   colour
Sil-Metropole/Beijing Film Academy Youth Film Studio (Ma Fung Kwok)
📼 ■ ⚬

The pregnant wife of a peasant appeals to higher authorities to force the village headman to apologize for injuring her husband.

Less flamboyant than the director's previous films, this takes a documentary-style approach to the story of a woman determined that principles must be upheld whatever the cost.

w Liu Heng novel Chen Yuanbin d Zhang Yimou ph Chi Xiaoning, Yu Xiaoqun m Zhao Jiping ad Cao Jiuping ed Du Yuan

☆ Gong Li, Lei Laosheng, Liu Peiqi, Yang Liuchun

'This simple, repetitive tale has a mesmerizing quality able to hook audiences from beginning to end.' – *Variety*

† The film won the Golden Lion award for best film and Gong Li won the award for best actress at the 1992 Venice Film Festival.

The Story of Robin Hood and his Merrie Men

👨‍👧 GB   1952   84m   Technicolor
Walt Disney (Perce Pearce)
■ ⚬

When Prince John starts a ruthless taxation campaign, Robert Fitzooth turns outlaw.

Fairly competent but quite forgettable version of the legend, softened for children.

w Lawrence E. Watkin d Ken Annakin ph Guy Green m Clifton Parker

☆ Richard Todd, Joan Rice, James Hayter, Hubert Gregg, James Robertson Justice, Martita Hunt, Peter Finch

The Story of Ruth

US   1960   132m   DeLuxe   Cinemascope
TCF (Samuel G. Engel)
■ ⚬

Ruth becomes the favourite of a pagan king but eventually flees to Israel.

Tedious, portentous bible-in-pictures, of virtually no interest or entertainment value.

w Norman Corwin d Henry Koster ph Arthur E. Arling m Franz Waxman

☆ Elana Eden, Peggy Wood, Viveca Lindfors, Stuart Whitman, Tom Tryon, Jeff Morrow, Thayer David, Eduard Franz

The Story of Seabiscuit

US   1949   98m   Technicolor
Warner (William Jacobs)
■

GB title: *Pride of Kentucky*

The success story of a racehorse.

Blue grass vapidities, the kind of family entertainment that drove the families away.

w John Taintor Foote d David Butler ph Wilfrid Cline md David Buttolph

☆ Shirley Temple, Barry Fitzgerald, Lon McCallister, Rosemary de Camp, Donald McBride, Pierre Watkin

The Story of Shirley Yorke

GB   1948   92m   bw
Nettlefold

A nobleman tries to blame his wife's nurse for her death by poison.

Lethargic version of a play previously filmed as Lord Camber's Ladies (qv).

w A. R. Rawlinson, Maclean Rogers and Kathleen Butler play *The Case of Lady Camber* by H. A. Vachell d Maclean Rogers

☆ Derek Farr, Dinah Sheridan, Margaretta Scott, John Robinson, Barbara Couper, Valentine Dyall

The Story of Temple Drake *

US   1933   71m   bw
Paramount (Ben Glazer)

A neurotic Southern flapper is abducted by gangsters, and likes it.

Deliberately shocking melodrama of its time, restructured from a notorious book later filmed under its own title. Very dated, but interesting.

w Oliver H. P. Garrett novel *Sanctuary* by William Faulkner d Stephen Roberts ph Karl Struss

☆ Miriam Hopkins, Jack La Rue, William Gargan, William Collier Jnr, Irving Pichel, Guy Standing, Elizabeth Patterson, Florence Eldridge

'Under Haysian ban the title of the novel can't be ballyhooed, but any whispering campaign about this is the picture's best b.o. asset. It has little else to commend it.' – *Variety*

The Story of Three Loves

US   1953   122m   Technicolor
MGM (Sidney Franklin)
♀

Three love stories concerning the passengers on a transatlantic liner.

Three bits of old-fashioned kitsch, one tragic, one whimsical, one melodramatic, all rather slow and dull though well produced.

w John Collier, Jan Lustig, George Froeschel d Gottfried Reinhardt, Vincente Minnelli ph Charles Rosher, Harold Rosson m Miklos Rozsa ad Cedric Gibbons, Preston Ames, Edward Carfagno, Gabriel Scognamillo

☆ Ethel Barrymore, James Mason, Moira Shearer, Pier Angeli, Leslie Caron, Kirk Douglas, Farley Granger, Agnes Moorehead, Zsa Zsa Gabor

👥 art direction

The Story of Us

US   1999   94m   DeLuxe
Warner/Castle Rock (Rob Reiner, Alan Zweibel, Jessie Nelson)
■

After 15 years of marriage and two children, a writer and his wife, a crossword compiler, decide to try a trial separation.

There's little sign of strain in the relationship Reiner shows us, so the ending will come as no surprise; but there's hardly any sign of pleasure, either, so the story is of the soporific bedtime sort.

w Alan Zweibel, Jessie Nelson d Rob Reiner ph Michael Chapman m Eric Clapton, Mark Shaiman pd Lilly Kilvert ed Robert Leighton, Alan Edward Bell

☆ Bruce Willis, Michelle Pfeiffer, Rob Reiner, Tim Matheson, Rita Wilson, Paul Reiser, Julie Hagerty, Colleen Rennison, Jake Sandvig, Jayne Meadows, Tom Poston, Betty White, Red Buttons

'As an ode to the ups and downs of middle-aged marriage, this arthritic suburban story is enough to make single people want to file for divorce.' – *Janet Maslin, New York Times*

The Story of Vernon and Irene Castle **

US   1939   93m   bw
RKO (George Haight, Pandro S. Berman)
■ ⚬

The story of a husband and wife dance team who had their first success in Paris and became influential international celebrities before he was killed as a flyer in World War I.

Pleasant understated musical with very agreeable dance sequences and a firm overall style. The last of the main stream of Astaire–Rogers musicals.

w Richard Sherman, Oscar Hammerstein II, Dorothy Yost books Irene Castle d H. C. Potter ph Robert de Grasse md Victor Baravalle ch Hermes Pan ad Van Nest Polglase

☆ Fred Astaire, Ginger Rogers, Edna May Oliver, Walter Brennan, Lew Fields, Etienne Girardot, Donald MacBride

'One of the best Astaire-Rogers musicals … a wealth of nostalgic appeal.' – *Variety*

† The title was devised and insisted on by Mrs Castle.

The Story of Will Rogers

US   1950   109m   Technicolor
Warner (Robert Arthur)

A wild west performer becomes a Ziegfeld star and pop philosopher.

Bland, unshaped biopic of one of American show business's best loved figures, who died in an air crash in 1935.

w Frank Davis, Stanley Roberts d Michael Curtiz ph Wilfrid M. Cline md Victor Young

☆ Will Rogers Jnr, Jane Wyman, James Gleason, Eddie Cantor, Carl Benton Reid

The Story on Page One

US   1960   123m   bw   Cinemascope
TCF/Company of Artists (Jerry Wald)

A lawyer undertakes the defence of a woman who with her lover is charged with the murder of her husband.

Long-drawn-out and not very interesting courtroom drama, performed and presented with some style.

wd Clifford Odets ph James Wong Howe m Elmer Bernstein

☆ Rita Hayworth, Tony Franciosa, Gig Young, Mildred Dunnock, Hugh Griffith, Sanford Meisner, Alfred Ryder

'A candidate's private moment can all too quickly become public record.'

Storyville

US   1992   113m   CFI color
Spelling/Davis (David Roe, Edward R. Pressman)
📼 ■ ⚬ ⚬

A rich young lawyer running for Congress and trying to discover why his father killed himself finds himself caught up in scandal and murder.

Overheated and muddled story of corruption with a narrative that depends on its central character behaving extremely stupidly throughout; an audience with any sense will keep well away.

w Mark Frost, Lee Reynolds novel *Juryman* by Frank Galbally and Robert Macklin d Mark Frost ph Ron Garcia m Carter Burwell pd Richard Hoover ed B. J. Sears

☆ James Spader, Joanne Whalley-Kilmer, Jason Robards, Charlotte Lewis, Michael Warren, Michael Parks, Chuck McCann, Charlie Haid, Chino Fats Williams, Woody Strode, Jeff Perry, Piper Laurie

'A straightforward and lacklustre potboiler, composed of disparate elements with little dynamic coherence.' – *Sight and Sound*

Stowaway *

US   1936   86m   bw
TCF (Earl Carroll, Harold Wilson)
📼

The orphan daughter of a Shanghai missionary stows away on an American pleasure ship.

Very good star vehicle in which Shirley performs some of her best musical numbers.

w William Conselman, Arthur Sheekman, Nat Perrin d William A. Seiter ph Arthur Miller md Louis Silvers songs Mack Gordon, Harry Revel

☆ Shirley Temple, Robert Young, Alice Faye, Eugene Pallette, Helen Westley, Arthur Treacher, J. Edward Bromberg, Astrid Allwyn

'No exhib worrying necessary for this one.' – *Variety*

Stowaway Girl: see Manuela

La Strada ***

Italy   1954   94m   bw
Ponti/de Laurentiis
📼 ♀

aka: *The Road*

A half-witted peasant girl is sold to an itinerant strong man and ill-used by him.

Curious attempt at a kind of poetic neo-realism, saved by style and performances.

w Federico Fellini, Ennio Flaiano, Tullio Pinelli d Federico Fellini ph Otello Martelli m Nino Rota

☆ Giulietta Masina, Anthony Quinn, Richard Basehart

👤 best foreign film
👥 script

Straight on Till Morning

GB   1972   96m   Technicolor
EMI/Hammer (Roy Skeggs)
■

A Liverpool girl in London meets a dangerous psychotic.

Unattractive suspenser, wildly directed.

w Michael Peacock d Peter Collinson ph Brian Probyn m Roland Shaw

☆ Rita Tushingham, Shane Briant, Tom Bell, Annie Ross, James Bolam

Straight out of Brooklyn

US   1991   83m   colour
Artificial Eye/Blacks N'Progress/American Playhouse (Matty Rich)
📼 ■ ⚬

Determined to escape the poverty that has engulfed his hard-working mother and drunken father, a young black man persuades his friends to rob some local hoodlums.

Interesting first feature of ghetto life from a teenaged director.

wd Matty Rich ph John Rosnell m Harold Wheeler ad Walter Meade ed Jack Haigis

☆ George T. Odom, Ann D. Sanders, Lawrence Gilliard Jnr, Barbara Sanon, Reana E. Drummond, Matty Rich, Mark Malone

---

👨‍👧 film suitable for family viewing   📼 VHS video-cassette for the British PAL system   ■ VHS video-cassette for the British PAL system in wide screen-format   ✧ Video cassette in a computer-colourised version   ■ American NTSC video-cassette   ⚬ Laser disc

'Not a glittering debut, but it does have a low-budget, first-time energy which sets it apart from much mainstream work.' – *Michael O'Pray, Sight and Sound*

'Rudimentary in every way, from writing to acting to camerawork, and covers all-too-familiar ground with no particular flair.' – *Variety*

Straight, Place and Show *

US 1938 66m bw

TCF

GB title: They're Off

Three pony-ride proprietors impersonate Russian jockeys to save a race.

Lively, unpretentious vehicle for three zanies, with a further bonus in its lead singer.

w M. M. Musselman, Allen Rivkin *play* Damon Runyon, Irving Caesar d David Butler

☆ The Ritz Brothers, Ethel Merman, Richard Arlen, Phyllis Brooks, George Barbier, Sidney Blackmer

The Straight Story ***

France/US 1999 111m FotoKem 'Scope

Buena Vista/Les Films Alain Sarde/Canal+/Picture Factory (Alain Sarde, Mary Sweeney, Neal Edelstein)

An elderly widower makes a 300 mile trip to see his ailing brother on the only transport available to him, a lawn mower.

A gentle, folksy road movie that takes its time but establishes a mood of quiet enjoyment for simple pleasures, mixed with a little regret for some past events; Farnsworth epitomises a man who knows his own worth and that of the others he meets on his journey.

w John Roach, Mary Sweeney d David Lynch ph Freddie Francis m Angelo Badalamenti pd Jack Fisk ed Mary Sweeney

☆ Richard Farnsworth, Sissy Spacek, Jane Galloway Heitz, Everett McGill, Jennifer Edwards-Hughes, John Farley, John Lordan, Harry Dean Stanton

'A lyrical poem to America's vast land and country folks.' – *Emanuel Levy, Variety*

'This must be the strangest road movie ever made, but it is also one of the most lovable.' – *Adam Mars-Jones, Times*

⅄ Richard Farnsworth

'Dreams do come true ... sometimes.'

Straight Talk

US 1992 91m Technicolor

Warner/Hollywood/Sandollar (Robert Chartoff, Fred Berner)

◫ ▤ @. ◠

An Arkansas dance teacher goes to Chicago to become a TV agony aunt.

Mundane romantic comedy tailored to the personality of Dolly Parton.

w Craig Bolotin, Patricia Resnick d Barnet Kellman ph Peter Sova m Brad Fiedel pd Jeffrey Townsend ed Michael Tronick

☆ Dolly Parton, James Woods, Griffin Dunne, Michael Madsen, Deirdre O'Connell, John Sayles, Teri Hatcher, Spalding Gray, Jerry Orbach, Philip Bosco

'Glib but sunny romantic comedy ... should be a B.O. winner.' – *Variety*

Straight Time

US 1978 114m Technicolor

Warner/First Artist/Sweetwall (Stanley Beck, Tim Zinnemann)

▤

A psychotic parolee fails to go straight.

Unappetizing social melodrama with an irresolute leading performance.

w Alvin Sargent, Edward Bunker, Jeffrey Boam *novel* No Beast So Fierce by Edward Bunker d Ulu Grosbard ph Owen Roizman m David Shire

☆ Dustin Hoffman, Theresa Russell, Gary Busey, Harry Dean Stanton

'One leaves the theatre hoping the character will die painfully and slowly in a hail of bullets.' – *Variety*

'Just keep saying to yourself – it's only a film, it's only a film!'

Strait Jacket

US 1963 92m bw

Columbia/William Castle

▤

A woman who murdered her faithless husband with an axe is released twenty years later, and more axe murders occur.

Dull and unattractive shocker in which all concerned lean over backwards to conceal the trick ending.

w Robert Bloch d William Castle ph Arthur E. Arling m Van Alexander

☆ Joan Crawford, Diane Baker, Leif Erickson, Howard St John, Rochelle Hudson, George Kennedy

Stranded

US 1935 73m bw

Warner

A woman working for Traveller's Aid meets an old school beau.

Much ado about nothing, the kind of movie that loses stars their reputations.

w Delmer Daves, Carl Erickson, Frank Wead, Ferdinand Reyher d Frank Borzage

☆ Kay Francis, George Brent, Patricia Ellis, Donald Woods, Robert Barrat, Barton MacLane

'Limited chances.' – *Variety*

Stranded

Canada 1991 88m colour

Libra/Erin (Christian Bruyere)

A woman trying to save her marriage goes to stay with her husband in an isolated lighthouse, near where her sister died mysteriously.

Cheap, nasty and stupid thriller, of no conceivable interest to anyone.

w Boon Collins, Stanley Park, Dan Vining, Deborah Wakeham story Daniel D. Williams d Paul Tucker ph Tobias Schliessler m Michael Conway Baker pd Richard Wilcox ed Jana Fritsch

☆ Deborah Wakeham, Ryan Michael, Stephen E. Miller, Blu Mankuma, Gabrielle Rose, Ric Reid

† The copyright notice on the credits is apposite: 'Erin Features No. 1 Ltd. in Bankruptcy'.

Stranded in Paris: see *Artists and Models Abroad*

The Strange Adventure of David Gray:
see *Vampyr*

The Strange Affair

GB 1968 106m Technicolor

Paramount (Howard Harrison, Stanley Mann)

A young London policeman finds that his superiors are almost as corrupt as the villains.

Stylishly made melodrama of despair, with a sexy nymphet heroine straight from swinging London. It all leaves a sour taste in the mouth.

w Stanley Mann *novel* Bernard Toms d David Greene ph Alex Thomson m Basil Kirchin

☆ Michael York, Jeremy Kemp, Susan George, Jack Watson, George A. Cooper

The Strange Affair of Uncle Harry

US 1945 82m bw

Universal (Joan Harrison)

▤ @.

aka: Uncle Harry

A man henpecked by his two sisters plans to murder one of them.

Stilted melodrama from an uninspired stage original, with a cop-out dream ending tacked on.

w Stephen Longstreet, Keith Winter *play* Thomas Job d Robert Siodmak ph Woody Bredell m Hans Salter

☆ George Sanders, Geraldine Fitzgerald, Ella Raines, Sara Allgood, Moyna MacGill, Samuel S. Hinds, Harry von Zell, Ethel Griffies

Strange Bargain

US 1949 68m bw

RKO (Sid Rogell)

▤

A lowly bookkeeper finds himself accomplice in an insurance swindle.

Watchable second feature suspenser.

w Lillie Hayward d Will Price ph Harry J. Wild

☆ Jeffrey Lynn, Henry Morgan, Martha Scott, Katherine Emery, Richard Gaines, Henry O'Neill

Strange Bedfellows

US 1965 99m Technicolor

U-I/Panama-Frank (Melvin Frank)

An American executive in London nearly divorces his fiery Italian wife.

Frantic sex comedy with picture postcard background; fatiguing rather than funny, but with minor compensations.

w Melvin Frank, Michael Pertwee d Melvin Frank ph Leo Tover m Leigh Harline

☆ Rock Hudson, Gina Lollobrigida, Gig Young, Edward Judd, Howard St John, Arthur Haynes, Dave King, Terry-Thomas

'The grind of predictable situations is further afflicted by considerable lapses in taste.' – *MFB*

Strange Boarders *

GB 1938 79m bw

GFD/Gainsborough (Edward Black)

A police detective postpones his honeymoon to book into a boarding house and discover which of the guests is a spy.

Quite engaging comedy-thriller in the Hitchcock mould, with entertaining performances and incidents.

w A. R. Rawlinson, Sidney Gilliat novel The Strange Boarders of Paradise Crescent by E. Phillips Oppenheim d Herbert Mason ph Jack Cox

☆ Tom Walls, Renee Saint-Cyr, Leon M. Lion, Googie Withers, C. V. France, Ronald Adam, Irene Handl, George Curzon, Martita Hunt

Strange Brew

US 1983 90m colour

MGM (Louis M. Silverstein)

▤ @.

Two dim-witted, beer-swilling Canadian brothers visit the Elsinore brewery in search of free drinks and, with the aid of some lunatics, thwart a plan to take over the world.

Offbeat but unamusing comedy, based on two characters from the SCTV Network television comedy series and borrowing much of its plot from Hamlet.

w Rick Moranis, Dave Thomas, Steven de Jarnatt d Dave Thomas, Rick Moranis ph Steven Poster m Charles Fox pd David L. Snyder ed Patrick McMahon

☆ Dave Thomas, Rick Moranis, Max von Sydow, Paul Dooley, Lynne Griffin, Angus MacInnes, Tom Harvey, Douglas Campbell

Strange Cargo *

US 1940 105m bw

MGM (Joseph L. Mankiewicz)

▤

Eight convicts escape from Devil's Island and are influenced by a Christ-like fugitive.

One of Hollywood's occasional lunacies; one doubts whether even the author knew the point of this cockamamy parable, but it was well produced and acted.

w Lawrence Hazard novel Not Too Narrow, Not Too Deep by Richard Sale d Frank Borzage ph Robert Planck m Franz Waxman

☆ Clark Gable, Joan Crawford, Ian Hunter, Peter Lorre, Paul Lukas, Albert Dekker, J. Edward Bromberg, Eduardo Ciannelli, Frederick Worlock

'Even the most hardened mystics may blush.' – *New Yorker, 1978*

The Strange Case of Clara Deane

US 1932 60m bw

Paramount

A young mother is unjustly convicted of a crime which she didn't commit and bids a tearful farewell to her child ...

Hilariously inept and theatrical rendering of a very outmoded play.

w Max Marcin play Arthur M. Brillant d Louis Gasnier, Max Marcin

☆ Wynne Gibson, Pat O'Brien, Frances Dee, Dudley Digges

'Strictly for the minors where the clientele is elderly and naive.' – *Variety*

The Strange Case of Doctor RX

US 1942 66m bw

Universal

A mysterious murderer eliminates criminals whom the law can't touch.

Inept semi-horror which wastes a good cast, as did the same author's Night Monster.

w Clarence Upson Young d William Nigh

☆ Lionel Atwill, Patric Knowles, Anne Gwynne, Samuel S. Hinds, Shemp Howard, Mona Barrie, Paul Cavanagh, Mantan Moreland

Strange Confession: see *The Imposter*

Strange Conquest: see *The Crime of Dr Hallet*

Strange Conspiracy: see *The President Vanishes*

'You know you want it.'

Strange Days

US 1995 145m DeLuxe Panavision

UIP/Lightstorm (James Cameron, Steven-Charles Jaffe)

◫ ▤ ▤ @. ◠

On the eve of the millennium, in the urban war zone that is Los Angeles in 1999, a former cop, who peddles an illegal form of virtual reality to eager customers, searches for his girlfriend, who has left him for a vicious gangster.

A thunderous, over-emphatic thriller of the near-future, when entertainment consists of experiencing other people's reality, from rape to murder; but under all the flash and frenetic activity is a narrative that was old when the world was much younger.

w James Cameron, Jay Cocks d Kathryn Bigelow ph Matthew F. Leonetti m Graeme Revell pd Lilly Kilvert ed Howard Smith sp Digital Domain

☆ Ralph Fiennes, Angela Bassett, Juliette Lewis, Tom Sizemore, Vincent D'Onofrio, Michael Wincott, Glenn Plummer

'Has a dazzling atmosphere of grunge futurism, but beneath its dark satire of audiovisual decadence lurks a naggingly conventional underworld thriller.' – *Owen Gleiberman, Entertainment Weekly*

'Terrifically hyped-up style will thrill many buffs, sci-fi and head trip elements will appeal to techies, and rough action and heavy racial angle will find a following among young ethnic viewers.' – *Todd McCarthy*

The Strange Death of Adolf Hitler *

US 1943 74m bw

Universal (Ben Pivar)

A stage impressionist murders the Führer and takes his place, steering Germany deliberately into losing the war.

One of the more eccentric curios of World War II, especially from a mundane studio like Universal. Once one recovers from the shock of its existence, the thing is moderately well done. See also The Magic Face.

w Fritz Kortner d James Hogan m Hans Salter

☆ Ludwig Donath, Gale Sondergaard, Fritz Kortner, George Dolenz

The Strange Door *

US 1951 81m bw

U-I (Ted Richmond)

▤

A young nobleman, passing through the one-way door of a castle, finds himself the prisoner of a madman.

Torture-chamber suspenser, adequately if rather tediously developed, with most of its interest reposing in the cast.

w Jerry Sackheim story The Sire de Maletroit's Door by Robert Louis Stevenson d Joseph Pevney ph Irving Glassberg m Hans Salter

☆ Charles Laughton, Boris Karloff, Michael Pate, Sally Forrest, Richard Stapley, Alan Napier

Strange Evidence

GB 1932 71m bw

Paramount/London Films (Alexander Korda)

When an invalid dies, his adulterous wife is suspected.

Mildly interesting quickie whodunnit.

w Miles Malleson story Lajos Biro d Robert Milton ph Robert Martin ed Stephen Harrison

☆ Leslie Banks, Carol Goodner, George Curzon, Frank Vosper, Norah Baring, Diana Napier

Strange Holiday

US 1945 61m bw

General Motors/Elite Pictures (Arch Oboler)

A man back from holiday discovers that American Nazis have taken over the country.

Over-talkative fantasy which barely scraped a release, especially since it was made in 1940 but not offered until five years later.

wd Arch Oboler ph Robert Surtees m Gordon Jenkins

☆ Claude Rains, Gloria Holden, Milton Kibbee, Bobbie Stebbins, Barbara Bate, Martin Kosleck

Strange Incident: see *The Ox Bow Incident*

'A woman suspected! A woman desired! A woman possessed!'

'The film in which you hear the characters think!'

Strange Interlude **
US 1932 110m bw
MGM (Irving Thalberg)

GB title: *Strange Interval*

Problems of an unfulfilled wife and her lover.
Surprising film version of a very heavy modern classic, complete with asides to the audience; very dated now, but a small milestone in Hollywood's development.
w Bess Meredyth, C. Gardner Sullivan *play* Eugene O'Neill d Robert Z. Leonard ph Lee Garmes
☆ Norma Shearer, Clark Gable, May Robson, Alexander Kirkland, Ralph Morgan, Robert Young, Maureen O'Sullivan, Henry B. Walthall

'Chiefly a reserved seat attraction, dubious for general release appeal.' – *Variety*

'A cinematic novelty to be seen by discerning audiences.' – *Film Weekly*

'More exciting than a thousand "action" movies.' – *Pare Lorentz*

Strange Interval: see *Strange Interlude*

Strange Intruder
US 1957 78m bw
AA (Lindsley Parsons)

A psychopathic ex-POW menaces the children of his dead friend's wife.
Gloomy second feature melodrama, rather well presented.
w David Evans, Warren Douglas *novel* Helen Fowler d Irving Rapper ph Ernest Haller m Paul Dunlap
☆ Edmund Purdom, Ida Lupino, Ann Harding, Jacques Bergerac, Carl Benton Reid

Strange Invaders *
US 1983 93m DeLuxe
EMI/Orion/Michael Laughlin (Walter Coblenz)

An Illinois town is taken over by beings from outer space.
Patchy but often amusing take-off of the Invasion of the Body Snatchers *genre.*
w William Condon, Michael Laughlin d Michael Laughlin ph Louis Horvath, Zoltan Vidor m John Addison pd Susanna Moore
☆ Paul Le Mat, Nancy Allen, Diana Scarwid, Michael Lerner, Louise Fletcher, Fiona Lewis, Kenneth Tobey

'Isn't so much a spoof of '50s sci-fi formulae as it is a running commentary on styles of cultural awareness.' – *Richard T. Jameson, Seattle Weekly*

Strange Lady in Town
US 1955 118m Warnercolor Cinemascope
Warner (Mervyn Le Roy)

Adventure of a woman doctor in 1880 Santa Fe.
Quaint Western drama which is never any more convincing than its star.
w Frank Butler d Mervyn Le Roy ph Harold Rosson m Dimitri Tiomkin
☆ Greer Garson, Dana Andrews, Cameron Mitchell, Lois Smith, Walter Hampden

'Fate drew them together and only murder can part them!'

'Whisper her name!'

The Strange Love of Martha Ivers **
US 1946 116m bw
Paramount/Hal B. Wallis

A murderous child becomes a wealthy woman with a spineless lawyer husband; the melodrama starts when an ex-boyfriend returns to town.
Irresistible star melodrama which leaves no stone unturned; compulsive entertainment of the old school.
w Robert Rossen d Lewis Milestone ph Victor Milner m Miklos Rozsa
☆ Barbara Stanwyck, Van Heflin, Kirk Douglas, Lizabeth Scott, Judith Anderson, Roman Bohnen
ஃ original story (Jack Patrick)

The Strange Love of Molly Louvain
US 1932 72m bw
Warner

A young mother has gone to the bad through men.
Hoary melodrama which the cast seem forever on the point of sending up.
w Maurine Watkins, Erwin Gelsey *play* The Tinsel Girl by Maurine Watkins d Michael Curtiz

☆ Lee Tracy, Ann Dvorak, Richard Cromwell, Guy Kibbee, Leslie Fenton, Frank McHugh

'A lightweight yarn which never takes a toehold to deliver a sock.' – *Variety*

The Strange Mr Gregory
US 1945 63m bw
Monogram (Louis Berkoff)

In pursuit of a murder fraud, a magician feigns his own death and poses as his brother.
Complex but watchable little crime thriller.
w Myles Connolly, Charles S. Belden d Phil Rosen
☆ Edmund Lowe, Jean Rogers, Don Douglas, Frank Reicher, Robert Emmett Keane

The Strange One *
US 1957 99m bw
Columbia/Sam Spiegel

GB title: *End as a Man*

A sadistic cadet causes trouble at a Southern military college.
A weird and unsavoury but rather compelling melodrama which unreels like a senior version of Tom Brown's Schooldays.
w Calder Willingham *novel* End as a Man by Calder Willingham d Jack Garfein ph Burnett Guffey m Kenyon Hopkins
☆ Ben Gazzara, George Peppard, Mark Richman, Pat Hingle, Arthur Storch, Paul Richards, Geoffrey Horne, James Olson

'The film's brilliance is in its persuasive depiction of a highly controversial, artificially organized world; its failure is to make any dramatic statement about it.' – *MFB*

The Strange Ones: see *Les Enfants Terribles*

A Strange Place to Meet: see *Drôle D'Endroit pour une Rencontre*

Strange Planet **
Australia 1999 96m colour
Redbus/AFFC/Strange Planet/Premium/Showtime/NSW Film & TV (Stavros Kazantzidis, Anastasia Sideris)

Three young women, who share a house, and three young men, partners in a law firm, all look for love in Sydney.
Engaging comedy, which follows six people from one New Year's Eve to another, though the two sets of friends do not meet each other for most of the year; there is a happy ending, though judging by the relationships that have gone before, it's likely to be a temporary one.
w Emma-Kate Croghan, Stavros Kazantzidis d Emma-Kate Croghan ph Justin Brickle pd Annie Beauchamp ed Ken Sallows
☆ Claudia Karvan, Naomi Watts, Tom Long, Aaron Jeffrey, Felix Williamson, Hugo Weaving, Marshall Napier

'An immensely likable romantic comedy.' – *Variety*

The Strange Woman
US 1946 100m bw
UA/Hunt Stromberg (Jack Chertok)

A scheming woman plays with the lives of three men.
Star wish-fulfilment; otherwise a hammy costume piece.
w Herb Meadows *novel* Ben Ames Williams d Edgar G. Ulmer ph Lucien Andriot m Carmen Dragon
☆ Hedy Lamarr, George Sanders, Louis Hayward, Gene Lockhart, Hillary Brooke

'Shock by incredible shock this ravaging death overruns the earth … menacing mankind with overwhelming chaos.'

'When men of different planets unite to combat the most loathsome peril the universe has ever known!'

Strange World of Planet X
GB 1957 75m bw
Eros Films (George Maynard)

US title: *Cosmic Monsters*

A mad scientist's experiments with magnetic fields cause insects to mutate into huge creatures with a taste for human flesh.
Risible science fiction with a great deal too much talk and the feeblest monsters to be found in any of the giant insect movies of the period.

w Paul Ryder *novel* Rene Ray d Gilbert Gunn ph Joe Ambor m Robert Sharples ad Bernard Sarron ed Francis Bieber
☆ Forrest Tucker, Gaby André, Martin Benson, Alec Mango, Wyndham Goldie, Hugh Latimer

The Stranger: see *The Intruder* (1961)

The Stranger: see *Agantuk* (1991)

The Stranger *
US 1946 95m bw
International (Sam Spiegel)

An escaped Nazi criminal marries an American woman and settles in a Connecticut village.
Highly unconvincing and artificial melodrama enhanced by directorial touches, splendid photography and no-holds-barred climax involving a church clock.
w Anthony Veiller *story* Victor Trivas, Decia Dunning d Orson Welles ph Russell Metty m Bronislau Kaper
☆ Edward G. Robinson, Orson Welles, Loretta Young, Philip Merivale, Richard Long, Konstantin Shayne

'Some striking effects, with lighting and interesting angles much relied on.' – *Bosley Crowther*

'A film of confused motivations and clumsy effects.' – *Basil Wright, 1972*
ஃ original story

The Stranger
US/Argentina 1987 83m DeLuxe
Columbia/Tusitala/Michael Nolin (Hugo Lamonica)

aka: *Mortifero*

Fleeing from witnessing three brutal murders, a woman crashes her car and forgets her identity; then the killers track her down …
Awkward thriller, acted with no great conviction, and only occasionally suspenseful or entertaining.
w Dan Gurskis d Adolfo Aristarain ph Horacio Maira m Craig Safan pd Abel Facello ed Eduardo Lopez
☆ Bonnie Bedelia, Peter Riegert, Barry Primus, David Spielberg, Ricardo Darin, Julio de Grazia, Cecilia Roth, Marcos Woinski

A Stranger among Us: see *Close to Eden*

Stranger at My Door
US 1956 85m bw
Republic (Sidney Picker)

A gunman takes refuge in the house of a preacher who tries to convert him.
Odd, sentimental little Western morality play, not badly presented.
w Barry Shipman d William Witney ph Bud Thackery m Dale Butts
☆ Macdonald Carey, Skip Homeier, Patricia Medina, Louis Jean Heydt

The Stranger Came Home
GB 1954 80m bw
Exclusive/Hammer (Michael Carreras)

US title: *The Unholy Four*

After being assaulted in the Far East, a financier loses his memory and does not return home until three years later, when murder ensues.
Muddled mystery quickie, only notable as the film which persuaded its star to retire.
w Michael Carreras *novel* Stranger at Home by George Sanders d Terence Fisher ph James Harvey m Ivor Slaney ed Bill Lenney
☆ Paulette Goddard, William Sylvester, Patrick Holt, Paul Carpenter, Russell Napier, Alvys Maben

The Stranger In Between: see *Hunted*

A Stranger in My Arms
US 1958 88m bw Cinemascope
U-I (Ross Hunter)

A test pilot falls in love with his dead friend's widow and helps her face up to her in-laws.
Dreary romantic drama.
w Peter Berneis *novel* And Ride a Tiger by Robert Wilder d Helmut Kautner ph William Daniels m Joseph Gershenson
☆ June Allyson, Jeff Chandler, Mary Astor, Sandra Dee, Charles Coburn, Conrad Nagel, Peter Graves

A Stranger in Town
US 1943 67m bw
MGM (Robert Sisk)

A supreme court judge on vacation finds himself sorting out crooked local politicians.
Interesting second feature with good cast and production values.
w Isobel Lennart, William Koslenko d Roy Rowland
☆ Frank Morgan, Richard Carlson, Jean Rogers, Porter Hall, Robert Barrat, Donald MacBride, Andrew Tombes, John Hodiak

A Stranger Is Watching
US 1981 92m Metrocolor
MGM-UA (Sidney Beckerman)

A small girl is terrified by the psychopath who raped and murdered her mother.
Unpleasant thriller in the modern manner.
w Earl Mac Rauch, Victor Miller *novel* Mary Higgins Clark d Sean S. Cunningham
☆ Kate Mulgrew, Rip Torn, James Naughton, Shawn Van Schreiber

The Stranger Left No Card **
GB 1952 23m bw
British Lion/Meteor (George Arthur)

A weirdly dressed eccentric comes to a small town and is accepted by the townspeople; but his real purpose is murder.
Smart little trick film which as a novelty has not been surpassed.
w Sidney Carroll d Wendy Toye ph Jonah Jones md Muir Mathieson
☆ Alan Badel, Cameron Hall, Eileen Way

Stranger on the Prowl
Italy/US 1952 82m bw
UA/CPCT (Noel Calef)

Italian title: *Imbarco a Mezzanotte*

GB title: *Encounter*

In an Italian port, a stranger helps a boy but is shot by the police.
Ineffective melodrama, a sad comedown for its star.
w Andrea Forzano (Ben Barzman) *story* Noel Calef d Andrea Forzano (Joseph Losey) ph Henri Alekan m G. C. Sonzogno ad Antonio Valente ed Thelma Connell
☆ Paul Muni, Joan Lorring, Vittorio Manunta, Aldo Silvani
† Both director and scriptwriter worked under a pseudonym owing to Hollywood's black-listing.

Stranger on the Third Floor *
US 1940 64m bw
RKO (Lee Marcus)

A reporter finds that he was wrong in the well-intentioned testimony which helps convict an innocent man for murder.
Stylish B feature with a striking dream scene and a curious fleeting performance by Lorre as the real murderer.
w Frank Partos d Boris Ingster ph Nicholas Musuraca m Roy Webb
☆ Margaret Tallichet, Peter Lorre, John McGuire, Charles Waldron, Elisha Cook Jnr, Charles Halton, Ethel Griffies

Stranger than Paradise *
US/Germany 1984 90m bw
Grokenberger/Cinesthesia/ZDF (Sara Driver)

The small adventures in America of a young Hungarian immigrant, her cousin and his friend.
Filmed in bleached-out black and white and not edited in the conventional sense – each take is shown complete and followed by a brief blackout before the next shot is shown – it focuses upon grungey lives in which nothing happens – and if it should, no one would notice; but it exerts a slight charm by its very waywardness.
wd Jim Jarmusch m Tom DiCillo m John Lurie ed Jim Jarmusch, Melody London
☆ John Lurie, Eszter Balint, Richard Edson, Cecilia Stark

'To think *Stranger than Paradise* was a knockout of a movie you'd have to tune in to its minimalism so passively that you lowered your expectations. The film is so hemmed in that it has the feel of a mousy East European comedy; it's like a comedy of sensory deprivation.' – *Pauline Kael, New Yorker*

'Full of a quirky character and irony that makes its central theme of American alienation seem extremely entertaining.' – *Derek Malcolm, Guardian*

A Stranger Walked In: see *Love from a Stranger*

'For him death has two faces – and he faces them both, alone!'

The Stranger Wore a Gun
US 1953 83m Technicolor 3-D
Columbia
▦

An honest adventurer finds that the man who once saved his life has become a stagecoach robber.
Routine Western with many objects hurled at the audience to show off the 3-D process.
w Kenneth Gamet *novel* John M. Cunningham
d André de Toth *ph* Lester White *md* Mischa Bakaleinikoff
☆ Randolph Scott, George Macready, Claire Trevor, Joan Weldon, Lee Marvin, Ernest Borgnine, Alfonso Bedoya

Strangers: see *Voyage to Italy*

Strangers All
US 1935 70m bw
RKO
A mother tries to keep the peace while her three unsuccessful sons – a shopkeeper, an actor and a political activist – quarrel about the worth of their callings and her daughter abandons her wealthy fiancé to marry a lawyer.
Sentimental family comedy-drama, enjoyable enough in its old-fashioned way if somewhat abrupt in its sudden ending.
w Milton Krims *play* Marie M. Bercovici
d Charles Vidor *ph* John W. Boyle *md* Roy Webb
ad Van Nest Polglase *ed* Jack Hively
☆ May Robson, Preston Foster, Florine McKinney, William Bakewell, James Bush, Samuel Hinds, Leon Ames

The Stranger's Hand
GB 1953 85m bw
Independent Film Producers/John Stafford, Peter Moore
aka: Mano della Straniero
A schoolboy is due to meet his father in Venice, but the father is kidnapped by enemy agents.
Rather tentative suspense thriller with a vague plot which seems to defeat an excellent cast.
w Guy Elmes, Giorgio Bassani *story* Graham Greene *d* Mario Soldati *ph* Enzo Serafin
m Nino Rota
☆ Trevor Howard, Richard O'Sullivan, Francis L. Sullivan, Alida Valli, Eduardo Ciannelli, Richard Basehart, Stephen Murray

Strangers in Good Company: see *The Company of Strangers*

Strangers in Love
US 1932 68m bw
Paramount
▦
A ne'er-do-well has some difficulties when he tries to step into his dead twin's shoes.
Predictable comedy-melodrama, quite well acted.
w Grover Jones, William Slavens McNutt
play The Shorn Lamb by William J. Locke
d Lothar Mendes
☆ Fredric March, Kay Francis, Stuart Erwin, Juliette Compton, George Barbier, Sidney Toler
'All the qualities that bespeak wide appeal.' – *Variety*

Strangers May Kiss
US 1931 82m bw
MGM
A sophisticated wife takes love and fidelity lightly.
Dated romantic drama.
w John Meehan *novel* Ursula Parrott *d* George Fitzmaurice *ph* William Daniels
☆ Norma Shearer, Robert Montgomery, Neil Hamilton, Marjorie Rambeau, Irene Rich
'Outstanding money picture. It'll sell itself.' – *Variety*

'It begins with the scream of a train whistle – and ends with screaming excitement!'
Strangers on a Train *
US 1951 101m bw
Warner (Alfred Hitchcock)
▦ ▤ ◉ ◠
A tennis star is pestered on a train by a psychotic who wants to swap murders, and proceeds to carry out his part of the bargain.
This quirky melodrama has the director at his best, sequence by sequence, but the story is basically unsatisfactory. It makes superior suspense entertainment, however.
w Raymond Chandler, Czenzi Ormonde
novel Patricia Highsmith *d* Alfred Hitchcock
ph Robert Burks *m* Dimitri Tiomkin *md* Ray Heindorf
☆ Farley Granger, *Robert Walker*, Ruth Roman, Leo G. Carroll, Patricia Hitchcock, *Marion Lorne*, Howard St John, Jonathan Hale, Laura Elliot
BRUNO (ROBERT WALKER): 'Some people are better off dead – like your wife and my father, for instance.'
'You may not take it seriously, but you certainly don't have time to think about anything else.' – *Richard Mallett, Punch*
'The construction seems a little lame, but Hitch takes delight in the set pieces.' – *Time Out, 1985*
† Remade 1970 as *Once You Kiss A Stranger*.
⅜ Robert Burks

The Stranger's Return
US 1933 89m bw
MGM
An old farmer disapproves of his granddaughter's affair with a married man.
An American view of Cold Comfort Farm country, too heavy to click at the box-office.
w Brown Holmes, Phil Stong *d* King Vidor
☆ Lionel Barrymore, Miriam Hopkins, Franchot Tone, Beulah Bondi, Stuart Erwin, Irene Hervey

Strangers When We Meet *
US 1960 117m Technicolor Cinemascope
Columbia/Bryna (Richard Quine)
A successful architect starts an affair with a beautiful married neighbour.
Beverly Hills soap opera with lots of romantic suffering in luxury. Lumpy but generally palatable.
w Evan Hunter *novel* Evan Hunter *d* Richard Quine *ph* Charles Lang Jnr *m* George Duning
☆ Kirk Douglas, Kim Novak, *Ernie Kovacs, Walter Matthau*, Barbara Rush, Virginia Bruce, Helen Gallagher, Kent Smith

The Strangler: see *East of Piccadilly (1940)*

The Strangler
US 1963 80m bw
AA
▤
An obese lab technician murders nurses who help his hated mother.
Modest, lively shocker.
w Bill S. Ballinger *d* Burt Topper *ph* Jacques Marquette *m* Marlin Skiles
☆ Victor Buono, David McLean, Ellen Corby, Diane Sayer

The Stranglers of Bombay
GB 1960 80m bw MegaScope
Columbia/Hammer (Anthony Nelson-Keys)
▦
In 1826 travellers are waylaid and sacrificially killed by a cult of stranglers.
Semi-historical parade of atrocities, repellent but scarcely exciting.
w David Z. Goodman *d* Terence Fisher
ph Arthur Grant *m* James Bernard *ad* Bernard Robinson, Don Mingaye *ed* James Needs, Alfred Cox
☆ Guy Rolfe, Allan Cuthbertson, Andrew Cruickshank, Marne Maitland, Jan Holden, George Pastell, Paul Stassino

Strapless
GB 1988 100m Technicolor
Virgin/Granada/Film Four International (Rick McCallum)
▦ ▤ ◉
Two sisters assert their independence after unsatisfactory relationships with men.
Uneasy blend of unbelievable romance and politics.

wd David Hare *ph* Andrew Dunn *m* Nick Bicat
pd Roger Hall *ed* Edward Marnier
☆ Blair Brown, Bruno Ganz, Bridget Fonda, Alan Howard, Michael Gough, Hugh Laurie, Suzanne Burden, Rohan McCullough

Strategic Air Command
US 1955 114m Technicolor Vistavision
Paramount (Samuel J. Briskin)
▤ ◉
A baseball player is recalled to air force duty.
Sentimental flagwaver featuring the newest jets of the fifties.
w Valentine Davies, Beirne Lay Jnr *d* Anthony Mann *ph* William Daniels *m* Victor Young
☆ James Stewart, June Allyson, Frank Lovejoy, Barry Sullivan, Alex Nicol, Bruce Bennett, Jay C. Flippen, James Millican, James Bell
⅜ original story (Beirne Lay Jnr)

The Stratton Story
US 1949 106m bw
MGM (Jack Cummings)
An amateur baseball enthusiast becomes a famous professional, but suffers an accident which involves the amputation of a leg.
Mild sentimental biopic, well made but not very interesting.
w Douglas Morrow, Guy Trosper *d* Sam Wood
ph Harold Rosson *m* Adolph Deutsch
☆ James Stewart, June Allyson, Frank Morgan, Agnes Moorehead, Bill Williams
† Van Johnson and Donna Reed were originally cast in the leading roles.
♟ original story (Douglas Morrow)

Strauss's Great Waltz: see *Waltzes from Vienna*

'The knock at the door meant the birth of one man and the death of seven others!'
Straw Dogs
GB 1971 118m Eastmancolor
Talent Associates/Amerbroco (Daniel Melnick)
▤ ▦ ◉
In a Cornish village, a mild American university researcher erupts into violence when taunted by drunken villagers who commit sustained assaults on himself and his wife. ·
Totally absurd, poorly contrived, hilariously overwritten Cold Comfort Farm melodrama with farcical violence.
w David Zelag Goodman, Sam Peckinpah
novel The Siege of Trencher's Farm by Gordon M. Williams *d* Sam Peckinpah *ph* John Coquillon
m Jerry Fielding
☆ Dustin Hoffman, Susan George, Peter Vaughan, David Warner, T. P. McKenna, Colin Welland
'Before the end you will have gasped and shuddered through an orgy of detailed rape, slaughter, arson and wanton destruction.' – *Cecil Wilson, Daily Mail*
'A magnificent piece of red-raw, meaty entertainment.' – *Ernest Betts, The People*
⅜ Jerry Fielding

'Distant Dreams and Passionate Lovers.'
Strawberry and Chocolate *
Cuba/Mexico/Spain 1993 111m colour
Metro Tartan/ICAIC/IMC/Telemadrid/Co. Tabasco (Miguel Mendoza)
▦ ▤ ◉ ◠
original title: Fresa y Chocolate
In Havana, a naïve and conformist university student, a Communist Party member, reluctantly becomes friends with a cultured homosexual, who is persecuted for his subversive views.
The first Cuban film to show homosexuality in a positive way is also concerned with more important matters than being gay; it is a playful attack on hidebound attitudes and prejudices and on a revolution that has gone stale, and a passionate plea for cultural diversity.
w Senel Paz *novel* El Lobo, el Bosque y el Hombre Nuevo by Senel Paz *d* Tomás Gutiérrez Alea, Juan Carlos Tabio *m* Mario Garcia Joya *m* José Maria Vitier *ad* Orlando Gonzalez *ed* Miriam Talavera, Osvaldo Donatien
☆ Jorge Perugorria, Vladimir Cruz, Mirta Ibarra, Francisco Gattorno, Joel Angelino, Marilyn Solaya
'This new comedy from Cuba is a gem. Filled with malicious swipes against the Castro regime, it's a provocative but very humane comedy about sexual opposites.' – *David Stratton, Variety*

† Juan Carlos Tabio helped with the direction when Alea became ill with cancer.
⅜ best foreign language film

The Strawberry Blonde *
US 1941 97m bw
Warner (William Cagney)
▤
A dentist in turn-of-the-century Brooklyn wonders whether he married the right woman.
Pleasant period comedy drama, a remake of One Sunday Afternoon *(qv).*
w Julius J. and Philip G. Epstein *d* Raoul Walsh
ph James Wong Howe *m* Heinz Roemheld
☆ James Cagney, Olivia de Havilland, *Rita Hayworth*, Alan Hale, George Tobias, Jack Carson, Una O'Connor, George Reeves
'It not only tells a very human story, it also creates an atmosphere, recreates a period.' – *New York Sun*
'A blithe, sentimental, turn-of-the-century buggy ride.' – *Time*
⅜ Heinz Roemheld

Strawberry Roan
GB 1945 84m bw
British National
A farmer weds a showgirl who ruins his life.
Rather glum rural drama with some style but little entertainment value.
w Elizabeth Baron *novel* A. G. Street *d* Maurice Elvey
☆ William Hartnell, Carol Raye, Walter Fitzgerald, Sophie Stewart, John Ruddock, Wylie Watson, Petula Clark

The Strawberry Statement
US 1970 109m Metrocolor
MGM/Robert Chartoff, Irwin Winkler
▤ ▦
Student rebels occupy a university administration building.
One of a short-lived group of student anti-discipline films of the early seventies, and about the most boring.
w Israel Horovitz *novel* James Simon Kunen
d Stuart Hagmann *ph* Ralph Woolsey *m* Ian Freebairn Smith
☆ Bruce Davison, Kim Darby, Bud Cort, Murray MacLeod

Streamers
US 1983 118m Movielab
Rank/Streamers International (Robert Altman, Nick J. Mileti)
▦ ▤ ◉
Tensions mount at a training camp for the 83rd Airborne Division.
Claustrophobic photographed play about generally worthless people.
w David Rabe *play* David Rabe *d* Robert Altman *ph* Pierre Mignot *pd* Wolf Kroeger
ed Norman Smith
☆ Matthew Modine, Michael Wright, Mitchell Lichtenstein, David Alan Grier, Guy Boyd, George Dzundza

'A thing of beauty is a joy for ever...'
Street Angel *
US 1928 101m bw part-talkie
Fox
An unwilling prostitute becomes a circus artiste.
A sentimental and tawdry tale becomes a vehicle for good typical work by director and stars.
w Marion Orth *play* Lady Cristallinda by Monckton Hoffe *d* Frank Borzage *ph* Ernest Palmer, Paul Ivano *ad* Harry Oliver
☆ Janet Gaynor, Charles Farrell, Henry Armetta, Guido Trento
♟ Janet Gaynor
⅜ Ernest Palmer; Harry Oliver

Street Corner
GB 1953 94m bw
Rank/LIP/Sydney Box (William MacQuitty)
US title: Both Sides of the Law
Days in the lives of the women police of Chelsea.
Patter-plotted female Blue Lamp; just about watchable.
w Muriel and Sydney Box *d* Muriel Box *ph* Reg Wyer *m* Temple Abady
☆ Rosamund John, Anne Crawford, Peggy Cummins, Terence Morgan, Barbara Murray, Sarah Lawson, Ronald Howard, Eleanor Summerfield, Michael Medwin

Street Fighter

US 1994 102m DeLuxe
UIP/Capcom (Edward R. Pressman, Kenzo Tsujimoto)

Street fighters set out to rescue hostages held by a mad dictator.

A popular video game is transferred to the screen with all its slam-bang excitement missing; it is presumably aimed at an easily satisfied audience of kids too young to play the game.

wd Steven E. de Souza ph William A. Fraker m Graeme Revell pd William Creber ed Dov Hoenig, Anthony Redman, Robert F. Shugrue, Ed Abroms, Donn Aron

☆ Jean-Claude Van Damme, Raul Julia, Kylie Minogue, Damian Chapa, Ming-Na Wen, Simon Callow, Roshan Seth, Wes Studi, Byron Mann

'Noisy, overblown and effects-laden and lacks sustained action or engaging characters.' – *Variety*

'I enjoyed making it but when I saw it, it was so bad both my wife and I walked out.' – *Roshan Seth*

Street Fleet: see D. C. Cab

Street Gang

US 1982 90m TVC Color Panavision
Film Ventures/Vigilante (William Lustig, Andrew Garroni)

aka: *Vigilante*

After his son is killed by a Puerto Rican gang, a factory worker joins a vigilante group to clean up the streets.

An unpleasant movie of rough justice that follows in the footsteps of Death Wish.

w Richard Vetere d William Lustig ph James Lemmo m Jay Chattaway pd Mischa Petrow ed Lorenzo Marinelli

☆ Robert Forster, Fred Williamson, Richard Bright, Rutanya Alda, Willie Colon, Joe Spinell, Carol Lynley, Woody Strode, Joseph Carberry

Street of Chance

US 1930 78m bw
Paramount (David O. Selznick)

A New York gambler gets his come-uppance.

Dullish family melodrama with gangsters as dei ex machina.

w Howard Estabrook, Lenore Coffee d John Cromwell ph Charles Lang

☆ William Powell, Kay Francis, Regis Toomey, Jean Arthur

'Strong exploitation can cinch this one. Strongly hints at recent murder of well-known gambler.' – *Variety*

℟ script

'Where women came to forget – one man came to remember!'

Street of Chance *

US 1942 74m bw
Burt Skelly/Sol C. Siegel/Paramount

An amnesia case discovers that he is wanted for murder.

The plot was fairly original at the time, and the treatment maintains interest.

w Garrett Fort story Cornell Woolrich d Jack Hively

☆ Burgess Meredith, Claire Trevor, Sheldon Leonard, Jerome Cowan, Frieda Inescort, Louise Platt

Street of Shadows

GB 1953 84m bw
Anglo Amalgamated/Merton Park (William H. Williams)

US title: *Shadow Man*

A Soho club-owner and his society girlfriend become mixed up in murder when the corpse of his mistress is discovered in his office.

Run-of-the-mill melodramatic thriller, with a better cast than it deserves.

wd Richard Vernon novel *The Creaking Chair* by Laurence Meynell ph Phil Grindrod m Eric Spear

☆ Cesar Romero, Kay Kendall, Simone Silva, Edward Underdown, Victor Maddern, John Penrose, Eileen Way, Bill Travers

Street of Shame *

Japan 1956 85m bw
Daiei (Masaichi Nagata)

original title: *Akasen Chitai*

Stories of women in a Tokyo brothel.

Unremarkable material executed with the style expected of the director.

w Masashige Narusawa d Kenji Mizoguchi ph Kazuo Miyagawa m Toshiro Mayazumi

☆ Machiko Kyo, Ayako Wakao, Aiko Mimasu

Street of Women

US 1932 59m bw
Warner

A property developer is torn between his wife and his mistress.

Choppily developed drama which starts haltingly and gets nowhere.

w Mary McCall Jnr novel Polan Banks d Archie Mayo

☆ Kay Francis, Alan Dinehart, Roland Young, Marjorie Gateson, Gloria Stuart

'Just a programme picture.' – *Variety*

Street People: see Sicilian Cross

Street Scene *

US 1931 80m bw
Samuel Goldwyn

In a New York slum street on a hot summer night, an adulterous woman is shot by her husband.

Slice-of-life drama from an influential play; never much of a film, and very dated.

w Elmer Rice play Elmer Rice d King Vidor ph George Barnes m Alfred Newman

☆ Sylvia Sidney, William Collier Jnr, Max Mantor, David Landau, Estelle Taylor, Russell Hopton

'Whenever the camera starts to focus on two or three characters, the plot thickens and *Street Scene* flies out the window; petty domestic tragedy supplants the original slice-of-life conception.' – *National Board of Review*

'As a commercial proposition it will cause talk and reap honours, but whether it will prove an exceptional box office attraction remains to be seen.' – *Variety*

The Street Singer

GB 1937 85m bw
British National

A musical comedy star is mistaken for a beggar by a girl with whom he falls in love.

Rather tiresome star vehicle.

w Reginald Arkell d Jean de Marguenat md Lew Stone

☆ Arthur Tracy, Margaret Lockwood, Arthur Riscoe, Hugh Wakefield

Street Smart

US 1987 95m TVC Color
Cannon (Menahem Golan, Yoram Globus)

A top journalist turns in a story that gets him involved with pimps and prostitutes.

Unpersuasive crime melodrama in which the star seems surprised to find himself.

w David Freeman d Jerry Schatzberg ph Adam Holender m Robert Irving pd Dan Leigh ed Priscilla Nedd

☆ Christopher Reeve, Kathy Baker, Mimi Rogers, Jay Patterson, Andre Gregory, Morgan Freeman

℟ Morgan Freeman

The Street with No Name *

US 1948 93m bw
TCF (Samuel G. Engel)

An FBI man goes undercover to unmask a criminal gang.

The oldest crime plot in the world, applied with vigour to the documentary realism of The House on 92nd Street and built around the Kiss of Death psychopathic character created by Richard Widmark.

w Harry Kleiner d William Keighley ph Joe MacDonald m Lionel Newman

☆ Richard Widmark, Mark Stevens, Lloyd Nolan, Barbara Lawrence, Ed Begley

† Remade 1955 as *House of Bamboo*.

A Streetcar Named Desire **

US 1951 122m bw
Warner/Elia Kazan (Charles K. Feldman)

A repressed Southern widow is raped and driven mad by her brutal brother-in-law.

Reasonably successful, decorative picture from a highly theatrical but influential play; unreal sets and atmospheric photography vaguely Sternbergian.

w Tennessee Williams play Tennessee Williams d Elia Kazan ph Harry Stradling m Alex North ad Richard Day

☆ Vivien Leigh, Marlon Brando, Kim Hunter, Karl Malden

† Two television versions followed, one in 1984 starring Ann-Margret and Treat Williams, and one in 1994 starring Jessica Lange and Alec Baldwin.

⚐ Vivien Leigh; Kim Hunter; Karl Malden

℟ best picture; Tennessee Williams; Elia Kazan; Harry Stradling; Alex North; Marlon Brando; Richard Day

🏆 Vivien Leigh

The Streetfighter: see Hard Times

Streets of Fire

US 1984 94m Technicolor
Universal/RKO/Hill-Gordon-Silver (Lawrence Gordon, Joel Silver)

A rock singer is kidnapped and a professional trouble shooter takes on the job of recovery.

Violent melodrama with an unsuccessful comic strip approach which fails to raise the material into the realm of myth.

w Walter Hill, Larry Gross d Walter Hill ph Andrew Laszlo m Ry Cooder pd John Vallone ed Freeman Davies, Michael Ripps

☆ Michael Paré, Diane Lane, Rick Moranis, Amy Madigan, Willem Dafoe

Streets of Gold *

US 1986 95m DeLuxe
TCF/James G. Robinson/Ufland-Roth

A disenchanted immigrant finds an unexpected road to success as a boxing coach for two streetwise kids.

Unappealing variation on the Rocky movies, good to look at but devoid of content.

w Heywood Gould, Richard Price, Tom Cole d Joe Roth ph Arthur Albert m Jack Nitzsche pd Marcos Flaksman ed Richard Chew

☆ Klaus Maria Brandauer, Adrian Pasdar, Wesley Snipes, Angela Molina

Streets of Laredo

US 1949 92m Technicolor
Paramount (Robert Fellows)

Two of three bandit friends become Texas Rangers.

Adequate star Western, a remake of The Texas Rangers.

w Charles Marquis Warren d Leslie Fenton ph Ray Rennahan m Victor Young

☆ William Holden, William Bendix, Macdonald Carey, Mona Freeman

Streets of New York

US 1939 72m bw
Monogram

The teenage owner of a newsstand studies law at night school.

Unconvincing street-life drama, an obvious vehicle for a boy star.

w Robert Andrews d William Nigh

☆ Jackie Cooper, Martin Spellman, George Cleveland, Dick Purcell

'Should do all right if not pointed too high.' – *Variety*

The Streetwalker: see La Marge

Strictly Ballroom ***

Australia 1992 94m Eastmancolor
Rank/M&A/Australian Film Finance Corp (Tristam Miall)

A would-be champion ballroom dancer, who incurs the wrath of the establishment by improvising his own steps, searches for a new partner in tune with his ideas.

Exuberant, charming, witty romance acted and directed with style and verve.

w Baz Luhrmann, Craig Pearce play N.I.D.A. stage production devised by its original cast story Baz Luhrmann, Andrew Bovell d Baz Luhrmann ph Steve Mason m David Hirschfelder ch John 'Cha Cha' O'Connell, Paul Mercurio pd Catherine Martin ed Jill Bilcock

☆ Paul Mercurio, Tara Morice, Bill Hunter, Pat Thomson, Gia Carides, Peter Whitford, Barry Otto, John Hannan, Sonia Kruger, Kris McQuade, Antonio Vargas, Armonia Benedito

'Bright, breezy and immensely likable musical-comedy.' – *Variety*

🏆 David Hirschfelder; Catherine Martin

Strictly Confidential: see Broadway Bill

Strictly Dishonourable

US 1951 94m bw
MGM (Melvin Frank, Norman Panama)

A young girl falls in love with a rakish Italian opera star; he is such a sentimentalist that he marries her.

Emasculated sentimental version of the sharp Preston Sturges comedy.

wd Norman Panama, Melvin Frank ph Ray June m Lennie Hayton

☆ Ezio Pinza, Janet Leigh, Millard Mitchell, Maria Palmer

† Previously filmed in 1931 by Universal, with Paul Lukas, Sidney Fox and Lewis Stone.

Strictly for Pleasure: see The Perfect Furlough

Strictly Unconventional: see The Circle

Strike ***

USSR 1924 70m bw silent
Goskino/Proletkult

A 1912 strike of factory workers is brutally put down by the authorities.

Brilliant propaganda piece with superbly cinematic sequences.

wd Sergei M. Eisenstein ph Edouard Tissé, Vassili Khvatov

☆ Grigori Alexandrov, Maxim Strauch, Mikhail Gomarov

Strike It Rich: see Loser Takes All

Strike Me Pink *

US 1935 104m bw
Samuel Goldwyn

A timid amusement park owner is threatened by crooks.

Acceptable star comedy with music.

w Frank Butler, Walter de Leon, Francis Martin d Norman Taurog ph Gregg Toland, Merritt Gerstad m Alfred Newman songs Harold Arlen, Lew Brown

☆ Eddie Cantor, Sally Eilers, Ethel Merman, William Frawley, Parkyakarkus

'At the box office both here and abroad the take will be big.' – *Variety*

Strike Up the Band *

US 1940 120m bw
MGM (Arthur Freed)

A high-school band takes part in a nationwide radio contest.

Rather tiresomely high-spirited musical with the stars at the top of their young form.

w Fred Finklehoffe, John Monks Jnr ph Ray June m Roger Edens d/ch Busby Berkeley ly Arthur Freed

☆ Judy Garland, Mickey Rooney, Paul Whiteman and his Orchestra, June Preisser, William Tracy, Larry Nunn

℟ Georgie Stoll, Roger Edens; song 'Our Love Affair' (m/ly Roger Edens, Georgie Stoll)

Striking Distance

US 1993 102m Technicolor
Columbia (Arnon Milchan, Tony Thomopoulos, Hunt Lowry)

A hard-drinking maverick cop tracks down the serial killer who murdered his father.

An unoriginal mix of car chases, tough cops and fist fights providing undemanding entertainment for the unthinking.

w Rowdy Herrington, Martin Kaplan d Rowdy Herrington ph Mac Ahlberg m Brad Fiedel

pd Greg Fonseca *ed* Pasquale Buba, Mark Helfrich
☆ Bruce Willis, Sarah Jessica Parker, Dennis Farina, Tom Sizemore, Brion James, Timothy Busfield, John Mahoney
'An OK action movie until it sinks under the weight of implausible plotting and over-the-top direction.' – *Brian Lowry, Variety*

The Strip *
US 1951 85m bw
MGM (Joe Pasternak)
A band drummer is accused of the murder of a racketeer.
Minor mystery melodrama intriguingly set on Sunset Strip, with jazz accompaniment.
w Allen Rivkin *d* Leslie Kardos *ph* Robert Surtees *m* George Stoll
☆ Mickey Rooney, Sally Forrest, William Demarest, James Craig, Kay Brown, Louis Armstrong, Earl Hines, Jack Teagarden
♫ song 'A Kiss To Build a Dream On' (*m/ly* Bert Kalmar, Harry Ruby, Oscar Hammerstein II)

'Today's army needs men of courage – honesty – integrity – ambition. Instead, they got John Winger...'
Stripes
US 1981 106m Metrocolor
Columbia (Ivan Reitman, Dan Goldberg)
A sergeant Hulka tries to train a platoon of misfit volunteers.
Ancient army wheezes dressed up with fashionable black comedy and sex, but no funnier than Carry On Sergeant.
w Len Blum, Dan Goldberg, Harold Ramis *d* Ivan Reitman *ph* Bill Butler *m* Elmer Bernstein
☆ Bill Murray, Harold Ramis, Warren Oates, P. J. Soles, John Larroquette, Sean Young

Stripper *
US 1986 90m colour
Arnon Milchan/Visionaire (Jerome Gary, Geof Bartz, Melvyn J. Estrin)
Strippers congregate in Las Vegas in 1984 to compete for the Golden G-string Award.
Interesting and saddening documentary on strippers, who talk of their art and pride in what they are doing, before performing their dispiriting routines in tacky clubs.
d Jerome Gary *ph* Edward Lachman *m* Buffy Sainte-Marie, Jack Nitzsche *ed* Geof Bartz, Bob Eisenhardt, Lawrence Silk

The Stripper *
US 1963 95m bw Cinemascope
TCF (Jerry Wald)
GB title: Woman of Summer
An ageing beauty queen returns to her Kansas hometown and has an affair with a 19-year-old garage hand.
Downbeat character melodrama typical of its time and its author; competent but sterile and rather tedious.
w Meade Roberts *play* A Loss of Roses *by* William Inge *d* Franklin Schaffner *ph* Ellsworth Fredericks *m* Jerry Goldsmith
☆ Joanne Woodward, Richard Beymer, *Claire Trevor*, Carol Lynley, Robert Webber, Louis Nye, Gypsy Rose Lee, Michael J. Pollard

'Some people get into trouble ... No matter what they wear.'
Striptease
US 1996 117m Technicolor
Rank/Castle Rock/Turner (Mike Lobell)
Investigating a murder involving a corrupt Congressman, a detective enlists the help of a single mother, who is working as a stripper to gain custody of her child.
Unsuccessful adaptation of a slick, witty thriller, fatally compromised by the casting of Demi Moore, whose requirements as a star run counter to the demands of the narrative.
wd Andrew Bergman *novel* Carl Hiaasen *ph* Stephen Goldblatt *m* Howard Shore *pd* Mel Bourne *ed* Anne V. Coates
☆ Demi Moore, Burt Reynolds, Armand Assante, Ving Rhames, Robert Patrick, Paul Guilfoyle, Jerry Grayson, Rumer Willis
'Sub-soft porn masquerading as a television custody drama – with jokes. Unfortunately it has

no idea of how to bring off this generic *ménage à trois*.' – *Linda Ruth Williams, Sight and Sound*

Striptease Lady: see *Lady of Burlesque*

Stroker Ace
US 1983 96m Technicolor Panavision
Universal/Warner (Hank Moonjean)
A top racing car driver is sponsored by the owner of a chain of fast-food restaurants.
Tediously leering comedy, with Reynolds repeating his over-familiar role as a macho ladies' man.
w Hugh Wilson, Hal Needham *novel* Stand On It *by* William Neely, Robert K. Ottum *d* Hal Needham *ph* Nick McLean *m* Al Capps *ad* Paul Peters *ed* Carl Kress, William Gordean
☆ Burt Reynolds, Ned Beatty, Jim Nabors, Parker Stevenson, Loni Anderson

Stromboli
Italy 1949 107m bw
RKO/Be-Ro (Roberto Rossellini)
A Lithuanian refugee accepts the protection of marriage to an Italian fisherman, but resents the barrenness and hostility of her life, especially when the local volcano erupts.
Sloppy melodrama with pretensions, interesting but not even attractive to the eye.
w Roberto Rossellini and others *d* Roberto Rossellini *ph* Otello Martelli *m* Renzo Rossellini
☆ Ingrid Bergman, Mario Vitale, Renzo Cesana
† The international version was cut to 81m.

'From the coolest city on the planet comes the hippest film of the year.'
Strong Language
GB 1999 80m bw/colour
Rumleyvision (Simon Rumley)
A group of twenty- and thirty-something Londoners discuss their lives, loves, likes and dislikes, and the event that links them together.
Fuzzily photographed confessions from a disparate group, given to the sort of monologues a barman might overhear on a bad night.
w Simon Rumley *ph* Armando Smit *m* David Conway, Laurence Elliot-Potter *pd* Joanna Cross *ed* Simon Rumley, Sasha Austen, Rick Moore
☆ David Groves, Paul Tonkinson, Tania Emery, Stuart Laing, Ricci Harnett, Kelly Marcell, Robyn Lewis, Julie Rice, Al Nedjari, Ruth Purser
'Absorbing and revealing as it heads to its conclusion and carves another notch in British cinema's innovative bedpost.' – *Film Review*

The Strong Man *
US 1926 75m bw (colour sequence) silent
First National/Harry Langdon
A war veteran returns and searches the city for his female penfriend.
Quite charming star comedy, probably Langdon's best.
w Frank Capra, Arthur Ripley, Hal Conklin, Robert Eddy *d* Frank Capra *ph* Elgin Lessley, Glenn Kershner
☆ Harry Langdon, Gertrude Astor, Tay Garnett

Stronger than Desire
US 1939 82m bw
MGM
A lawyer's wife gets into trouble and lets him try an innocent man for her crime.
Fast remake of Evelyn Prentice; a good half-bill.
w David Hertz, William Ludwig *d* Leslie Fenton
☆ Walter Pidgeon, Virginia Bruce, Ann Dvorak, Lee Bowman, Rita Johnson, Ilka Chase

Stronger than Fear: see *Edge of Doom*

The Strongest Man in the World
♠ US 1976 92m Technicolor
Walt Disney (Bill Anderson)
An accident in a science lab gives a student superhuman strength.
Formula comedy for older children.
w Joseph L. McEveety, Herman Groves *d* Vincent McEveety *ph* Andrew Jackson *m* Robert F. Brunner
☆ Kurt Russell, Joe Flynn, Eve Arden, Cesar Romero, Phil Silvers, Dick Van Patten, Harold Gould, William Schallert, James Gregory, Roy Roberts, Fritz Feld, Raymond Bailey, Eddie Quillan, Burt Mustin

Strongroom *
GB 1961 80m bw
Bryanston/Theatrecraft (Guido Coen)
Two car breakers plan a once-for-all bank robbery but get involved with potential murder when their hostages get locked in.
Suspenseful second feature with gloss and pace.
w Max Marquis, René Harris *d* Vernon Sewell *ph* Basil Emmott *m* Johnny Gregory
☆ Colin Gordon, Ann Lynn, Derren Nesbitt, Keith Faulkner

Stroszeck *
West Germany 1977 108m colour
Werner Herzog/ZDF
A crook, a prostitute and a friend move from Germany to what they hope will be the freedom of a mobile home in the United States; but everything goes wrong and they part company.
A simple narrative – described as 'a ballad' by its director – of a failed search for individuality and the exchange of one prison for another.
wd Werner Herzog *ph* Thomas Mauch, Ed Lachmann, Wolfgang Knigge, Stefano Guidi *m* Chet Atkins, Sonny Terry *ed* Beate Mainka-Jellinghaus
☆ Bruno S, Eva Mattes, Clemens Scheitz, Burkhard Driest, Alfred Edel, Norbert Grupe

The Struggle *
US 1931 88m bw
UA/D. W. Griffith
A New Yorker goes to the bad on bootleg liquor.
The director's last film reveals many of his old skills allied to a Victorian tract.
w Anita Loos, John Emerson *d* D. W. Griffith *ph* Joseph Ruttenberg
☆ Hal Skelly, Zita Johann, Charlotte Wynters, Jackson Halliday
'A dull and sodden rendering with old-time ranting and little drama ... just dull when it isn't in the highest degree maudlin.' – *Dwight MacDonald*
† It was based on The Drunkard by émile Zola.
†† The picture failed and was re-released as Ten Nights in a Bar-room.

Stryker
US/Philippines 1983 86m colour
New World/Cirio H. Santiago
In a world turned to desert by nuclear holocaust, gangs battle for water (though guns, ammunition, petrol and leatherwear remain in apparently endless supply).
Cheap and incompetent rip-off of Mad Max (qv).
w Howard R. Cohen *d* Cirio H. Santiago *ph* Ricardo Remias *m* Ed Gatchalian, Susan Justin *pd* Dimanlata *ed* Rudy Cabrales
☆ Steve Sandor, Andria Savio, William Ostrander, Michael Lane, Julie Gray, Monique St Pierre, Ken Metcalfe

Stuart Little **
♠ US 1999 92m DeLuxe
Columbia/Franklin/Waterman (Douglas Wick)
Promising their young son a little brother, a New York couple adopt a mouse, which annoys the family cat.
Clever, occasionally witty children's movie, seamlessly marrying live action and animation.
w M. Night Shyamalan, Greg Brooker *book* E.B. White *d* Rob Minkoff *ph* Guillermo Navarro *m/ly* Alan Silvestri *pd* Bill Brzeski *ed* Tom Finan *sp* John Dykstra; Jerome Chen
☆ Geena Davis, Hugh Laurie, Jonathan Lipnicki, Brian Doyle-Murray, Estelle Getty, Julia Sweeney, Dabney Coleman and also voices of: Michael J. Fox (Stuart Little), Nathan Lane, Chazz Palminteri, Steve Zahn, Jim Doughan, David Alan Grier, Jennifer Tilly, Bruno Kirby
'Sustains a lovely balance between enchantment and playfulness.' – *Stephen Holden, New York Times*
♫ visual effects (John Dykstra, Jerome Chen, Henry F. Anderson III, Eric Allard)

The Stud
GB 1978 90m colour
Brent Walker/Artoc (Edward D. Simons)
A millionaire's wife installs her lover as manager of a discotheque, but he becomes bored and wants a place of his own.
Life among the unpleasant rich. A surprise box-office success, richly undeserved.
w Jackie Collins *novel* Jackie Collins *d* Quentin Masters *ph* Peter Hannan *m* Biddu
☆ Joan Collins, Oliver Tobias, Sue Lloyd, Mark Burns, Doug Fisher, Walter Gotell
'Watching it is rather like being buried alive in a coffin stuffed with back numbers of Men Only.' – *Alan Brien*

The Student Prince
US 1954 107m Anscocolor Cinemascope
MGM (Joe Pasternak)
A prince studies in Heidelberg and falls for a barmaid.
Ruritanian operetta, lumpishly filmed, with Mario Lanza providing only the voice of the hero as he got too fat to play the part.
w William Ludwig, Sonya Levien *play* Old Heidelberg *by* Wilhelm Meyer-Foerster *operetta* Dorothy Donnelly *d* Richard Thorpe *ph* Paul C. Vogel *m* Sigmund Romberg *md* George Stoll
☆ Edmund Purdom, Ann Blyth, John Williams, Edmund Gwenn, S. Z. Sakall, John Ericson, Louis Calhern, Betta St John, Evelyn Varden
† Without the music, the play had been filmed at MGM in 1926, with Ramon Novarro and Norma Shearer under Ernst Lubitsch's direction.

Student Tour
US 1934 80m bw
MGM
A professor of philosophy chaperones a world tour by collegiates.
Very thin comedy yarn with songs.
w Ralph Spence, Philip Dunne *d* Charles F. Reisner
☆ Jimmy Durante, Charles Butterworth, Maxine Doyle, Phil Regan, Douglas Fowley, Betty Grable, Nelson Eddy
'Long, slow, and of mild entertainment appeal.' – *Variety*

The Studio Murder Mystery
US 1929 62m bw
Paramount
An actor is murdered on a film set.
Primitive talkie comedy mystery now interesting only for its studio backgrounds.
w Frank Tuttle *serial* the Edingtons *d* Frank Tuttle
☆ Neil Hamilton, Florence Eldridge, Warner Oland, Eugene Pallette, Fredric March, Doris Hill, Chester Conklin

Studs Lonigan
US 1960 95m bw
Longridge (Philip Yordan)
The growing up of an unlettered Chicago Irishman in the twenties.
Rough-and-ready version of a celebrated novel, not a bad try but insufficiently detailed to be any kind of classic.
w Philip Yordan *novel* James T. Farrell *d* Irving Lerner *ph* Arthur Feindel *m* Jerry Goldsmith
☆ Christopher Knight, Jack Nicholson, Frank Gorshin

A Study in Scarlet
US 1933 71m bw
KBS
Sherlock Holmes solves a mysterious murder.
Rather emaciated version of a spirited yarn.
w Robert Florey *story* Sir Arthur Conan Doyle *d* Edwin L. Marin
☆ Reginald Owen, Warburton Gamble, Anna May Wong, June Clyde, Alan Dinehart, Alan Mowbray
'Okay for secondary houses.' – *Variety*

A Study in Terror *

GB 1965 95m Eastmancolor
Compton-Tekli/Sir Nigel (Henry E. Lester)

▭ ▤ ◉

Sherlock Holmes discovers the identity of Jack the Ripper.

A reasonably good Holmes pastiche marred by a surfeit of horror and over-riotous local colour; quite literate, but schizophrenic.

w Donald and Derek Ford *novel* Ellery Queen d James Hill *ph* Desmond Dickinson *m* John Scott *ad* Alex Vetchinsky

☆ John Neville, Donald Houston, John Fraser, Robert Morley, Cecil Parker, Anthony Quayle, Barbara Windsor, Adrienne Corri, Judi Dench, Frank Finlay, Barry Jones, Kay Walsh, Georgia Brown

The Stuff

US 1985 93m Technicolor
New World (Paul Kurta)

▭

A monstrous yogurt-like goo eats people from the inside out.

Messy comedy-horror without benefit of much plotline.

wd Larry Cohen *ph* Paul Glickman *m* Anthony Guefen

☆ Michael Moriarty, Andrea Marcovicci, Paul Sorvino, Scott Bloom, Danny Aiello, Alexander Scourby

The Stunt Man *

US 1980 129m Metrocolor
Melvin Simon (Richard Rush)

▭ ▤ ◉

A Vietnam veteran on the run from the police finds refuge as a star stunt man for a sinister film director.

Overlong, curious, but sometimes compelling melodrama which entertains on the surface while its actual aims are harder to fathom.

w Lawrence B. Marcus *novel* Paul Brodeur d Richard Rush *ph* Mario Tosi *m* Dominic Frontière

☆ Peter O'Toole, Steve Railsback, Barbara Hershey, Allen Goorwitz, Alex Rocco, Sharon Farrell

'It's like one of those sets of Chinese boxes, each one with another box inside, growing smaller and smaller until finally there is nothing left at all.' – *Roger Ebert*

🏆 screenplay; Richard Rush; Peter O'Toole

Stunts *

US 1977 90m colour
New Line (Raymond Lafaro, William Panzer)

▤

The brother of a murdered stuntman takes his place in order to investigate the death.

Slick action thriller which capitalizes on the attraction of daring stunts.

w Barney Chen, Dennis Johnson *story* Michael Harpster, Raymond Lafaro, Robert Shaye d Mark L. Lester *ph* Bruce Logan *m* Michael Kamen *ed* Corky Ehlers

☆ Robert Forster, Fiona Lewis, Joanna Cassidy, Darrell Fetty, Bruce Glover, James Luisi

The Stupids

US 1995 94m Technicolor
Rank/Savoy/New Line/Imagine (Leslie Belzberg)

▤ 🎧

The dim father of a dimmer family tries to discover who is stealing his garbage.

Based on the characters from a successful series of children's books, this manages to be no more than a succession of crudely laborious slapstick jokes.

w Brent Forrester *books* James Marshall, Henry Allard d John Landis *ph* Manfred Guthe *m* Christopher Stone *pd* Phil Dagort *ed* Dale Beldin

☆ Tom Arnold, Jessica Lundy, Bug Hall, Alex McKenna, Mark Metcalf, Matt Keeslar, Christopher Lee

'Not quite bad enough to be laughable.' – *Derek Malcolm, Guardian*

† Directors making mercifully brief appearances include Mick Garris, David Cronenberg, Costa-Gavras, Robert Wise, Atom Egoyan, Norman Jewison and Gillo Pontecorvo.

The Subject Was Roses *

US 1968 107m Metrocolor
MGM (Edgar Lansbury)

A young war veteran finds he can't communicate with his parents, and vice versa.

Photographed play notable for its performances.

w Frank D. Gilroy *play* Frank D. Gilroy d Ulu Grosbard *ph* Jack Priestley

☆ Patricia Neal, Jack Albertson, Martin Sheen, Don Saxon, Elaine Williams

🧍 Jack Albertson

🧍 Patricia Neal

Submarine Command

US 1951 87m bw
Paramount (John Farrow, Joseph Sistrom)

A submarine officer who considers himself a coward becomes a hero in Korea.

Very routine soul-searching actioner.

w Jonathan Latimer d John Farrow *ph* Lionel Lindon *m* David Buttolph

☆ William Holden, Don Taylor, Nancy Olsen, William Bendix, Moroni Olson, Peggy Webber

Submarine D1

US 1937 93m bw
Cosmopolitan/Warner

Adventures of recruits in the naval submarine service.

Standard flagwaver of no intrinsic interest.

w Frank Wead, Warren Duff, Lawrence Kimble d Lloyd Bacon

☆ Pat O'Brien, George Brent, Wayne Morris, Frank McHugh, Doris Weston, Ronald Reagan, Henry O'Neill, Regis Toomey, Broderick Crawford

'An instructive and illuminating document … film waves its own flag, the best on earth, and with some exhibitor push it should do business.' – *Variety*

'Youth … Eager, Vital … Offers Its Life … Glorifies Its Ardent Love … In The Greatest Adventure Of The Great War!'

Submarine Patrol

US 1938 93m bw
TCF (Darryl Zanuck)

Recruits learn to handle sub-chasing boats at Annapolis.

Cheerful propaganda comedy-drama with familiar faces on hand and some good thrill sequences.

w Rian James, Darrell Ware, Jack Yellen *book* Ray Milholland d John Ford

☆ Richard Greene, Nancy Kelly, Preston Foster, George Bancroft, Slim Summerville, John Carradine, Henry Armetta, Warren Hymer, Elisha Cook Jnr, E. E. Clive, Ward Bond, George E. Stone

'Surefire film entertainment directed by a veteran who knows all the tricks.' – *Variety*

Submarine Raider

US 1942 65m bw
Wallace MacDonald/Columbia

An American sub learns too late about the attack on Pearl Harbor.

Stodgy wartime filler with unconvincing action sequences.

w Aubrey Wisberg d Lew Landers

☆ John Howard, Marguerite Chapman, Bruce Bennett, Warren Ashe

Submarine X-I

GB 1967 90m Eastmancolor
UA/Mirisch (John C. Champion)

A submarine commander in World War II trains men to attack the *Lindendorf* in midget submarines.

Belated quota quickie, routine in every department.

w Donald S. Sanford, Guy Elmes d William Graham *ph* Paul Beeson

☆ James Caan, Norman Bowler, David Sumner

Submarine Zone: see Escape to Glory

The Substitute

US 1996 103m Foto-Kem
Live Entertainment/Dinamo/H2 (Morrie Eisenman, Jim Steele)

▭ ▤ ◉ ◎ 🎧

When his girlfriend, a teacher, is beaten up by drug dealers involved with her school, a commando-turned-mercenary substitutes for her and sorts out the trouble with the aid of some old friends.

Proficiently made but empty drama composed of third-hand and fourth-rate elements that hardly warrant repetition: a deprived school, young hoodlums, large

men with big guns, and a narrative with more holes in it than its many dead. The explosive finale illustrates the maxim that in order to save the school, it was necessary to destroy it.

w Roy Frumkes, Rocco Simonelli, Alan Ormsby d Robert Mandel *ph* Bruce Surtees *m* Gary Chang *pd* Ron Foreman *ed* Alex Mackie

☆ Tom Berenger, Ernie Hudson, Diane Venora, Glenn Plummer, Marc Anthony, Raymond Cruz, Cliff de Young, Richard Brooks, William Forsythe

'A throwback to the mid-80s, when many films as tawdry as this used to get a cinema release.' – *Sight and Sound*

Subterfuge

GB 1968 86m Eastmancolor
Rank/Intertel (Peter Snell)

In London a CIA agent becomes involved with the wife of a British double-agent.

A routine retread of standard spy stories, crippled by its inexplicable narrative.

w David Whitaker d Peter Graham Scott *ph* Roy Garner, Albert Tolley *m* Cyril Ornadel *ad* Ron Fouracre *ed* Bill Lewthwaite

☆ Gene Barry, Joan Collins, Richard Todd, Tom Adams, Suzanna Leigh, Michael Rennie, Marius Goring, Colin Gordon

'A sad waste of several very capable players.' – *Brenda Davies, MFB*

'We are the new Bohemians!'

The Subterraneans

US 1960 89m Metrocolor Cinemascope
MGM (Arthur Freed)

The love affairs of San Francisco bohemians.

A boring oddity with lashings of eccentric behaviour and sexual hang-ups; MGM venturing very timidly outside its field.

w Robert Thom *novel* Jack Kerouac d Ranald MacDougall *ph* Joseph Ruttenberg *m* André Previn

☆ George Peppard, Leslie Caron, Janice Rule, Roddy McDowall, Anne Seymour, Jim Hutton

'He's an intergalactic Super Hero whose quest is to rid the Universe of evil-doers and combat the forces of darkness … But sometimes you gotta come down to Earth.'

Suburban Commando

👫 US 1991 90m DeLuxe
Entertainment/New Line (Howard Gottfried)

▭ ▤ ◉

An alien bounty-hunter takes a holiday on Earth and lodges with a suburban family.

Amiable, juvenile, low-brow comedy of no particular originality or distinction.

w Frank Capello d Burt Kennedy *ph* Patrick J. Swovelin *pd* Ivo Cristante, C. J. Strawn *ed* Sonny Baskin *sp* creature effects: Steve Johnson's XFX Productions

☆ Hulk Hogan, Christopher Lloyd, Shelley Duvall

'A sort of sickly lovechild of *Star Wars* (whose effects are reproduced on the cheap, and whose music is repeatedly plagiarized) and *Kindergarten Cop*.' – *Adam Mars-Jones, Independent*

Suburbia *

US 1983 99m colour
Suburbia Productions (Bert Dragin)

▤

aka: *The Wild Side*

A gang of rebellious teenagers leave home to set up their own community, arousing the antagonism of their parents.

Uncompromising account of unlovely LA punks and unlovelier adults that makes something personal out of standard teen-rebellion material.

wd Penelope Spheeris *ph* Timothy Suhrstedt *m* Alex Gibson *ad* Randy Moore *ed* Ross Albert

☆ Chris Pederson, Bill Coyne, Jennifer Clay, Timothy Eric O'Brien, Wade Walston, Mike B. The Flea, Maggie Ehrig, Grant Miner, Christina Beck

SubUrbia **

US 1996 121m Technicolor
Carlton/Castle Rock/Detour

▭ ▤ ◉

The return of a rock star to his home town precipitates a crisis among the three high-school friends he left behind.

Set in the car park of a convenience store, among disaffected twenty-or-so-year-olds, a darkly compelling take on stranded lives being thrown away.

w Eric Bogosian *play* Eric Bogosian d Richard Linklater *ph* Lee Daniel *m* Sonic Youth *pd* Catherine Hardwicke *ed* Sandra Adair

☆ Jayce Bartok, Amie Carey, Nicky Katt, Ajay Naidu, Parker Posey, Giovanni Ribisi, Samia Shoaib, Dina Spybey, Steve Zahn

'Truly great film-making combined with a truly great play.' – *Alan Jones, Film Review*

Subway

France 1985 104m colour CinemaScope
Gaumont/Films du Loup/TSF/TFI

▭ ▤ ◉

An eccentric hero on the run from thugs takes refuge overnight in the Paris Metro.

Oddball melodrama with more style than substance.

w Luc Besson and others d Luc Besson *ph* Carlo Varini *m* Eric Serra *ad* Alexandre Trauner

☆ Christophe Lambert, Isabelle Adjani, Richard Bohringer

Subway in the Sky

GB 1958 87m bw
Orbit (John Temple-Smith, Patrick Filmer-Sankey)

A Berlin cabaret star finds her landlady's ex-husband, a deserter, hiding in her apartment and sets out to prove his innocence of drug smuggling.

Tedious photographed play with precious few points of dramatic interest.

w Jack Andrews *play* Ian Main d Muriel Box *ph* Wilkie Cooper *m* Mario Nascimbene

☆ Hildegarde Neff, Van Johnson, Katherine Kath, Cec Linder, Albert Lieven, Edward Judd

Success at Any Price

US 1934 74m bw
RKO

A young man climbs to great business heights by crushing those around him, then attempts suicide when the crash comes.

Slackly handled drama with an unsympathetic hero.

w John Howard Lawson, Howard J. Green d J. Walter Ruben

☆ Douglas Fairbanks Jnr, Genevieve Tobin, Frank Morgan, Colleen Moore, Edward Everett Horton, Nydia Westman, Henry Kolker

'Episodic, unreasonable and anything but audience proof.' – *Variety*

Success Is the Best Revenge

GB/France 1984 91m Technicolor
De Vere/Gaumont (Jerzy Skolimowski)

▭ ▤

A Polish theatre director in London stages a symbolic show but alienates his son.

Another study of Polish exiles to follow Moonlighting, but this time with surrealist elements.

w Jerzy Skolimowski, Michael Lyndon d Jerzy Skolimowski *ph* Mike Fash *m* Stanley Myers, Hans Zimmer

☆ Michael York, Joanna Szczerbic, Michael Lyndon, Jerzy Skol, Michel Piccoli, John Hurt, Anouk Aimée, Jane Asher

A Successful Calamity

US 1931 75m bw
Warner

A millionaire discovers the true worth of his family when he pretends to be poor.

Good star vehicle which pleases despite its predictability.

w Maude Howell, Julien Josephson and Austin Parker *play* Clare Kummer d John G. Adolfi

☆ George Arliss, Mary Astor, Evelyn Knapp, Grant Mitchell, William Janney

Succubus (dubbed)

West Germany 1967 91m colour
Border/Trans American/Aquila (Adrian Hoven)

▭

original title: *Necronomicon – Getraumte Stunden*
aka: *Necronomicon*

A mysterious woman, who performs a night-club act that involves sex and sadism, is haunted by a past she cannot quite remember and fantasizes scenes of love-making and death.

An unholy mix of cut-rate surrealism, pretentious dialogue and incomprehensible narrative which has a vague connection with the legend of Faust; it will not bear close examination.

w Pier A. Caminneci d Jess (Jesús) Franco *ph* Robert Gaffron *m* Friedrich Gulda *md* Jerzy Van Rooyen *ad* Karl Heinz Mannchen *ed* Frizzi Schmidt

---

☆ Janine Reynaud, Jack Taylor, Howard Vernon, Nathalie Nort, Michel Lemoine, Pier A. Caminneci, Adrian Hoven

'An absurdly hit-or-miss affair, with scenes that have a certain bizarre appeal (shop window dummies coming to life) juxtaposed with others of crushing banality.' – David McGillivray, MFB

† The British release was cut to 81m.

Such a Gorgeous Kid Like Me: see *Une Belle Fille Comme Moi*

Such a Long Journey *
Canada/GB   1998   113m   colour
Optimum/Long Journey/Amy (Paul Stephens, Simon McCorkindale)
In Bombay during the 1970s, a Parsi bank clerk copes with family and other problems.
This saga of one man losing control of his life provides some intermittently interesting moments before it gives way to melodrama and sentimentality.
w Sooni Taraporevala *novel* Rohinton Mistry d Sturla Gunnarsson ph Jan Kiesser m Jonathan Goldsmith pd Nitin Desai ed Jeff Warren
☆ Om Puri, Roshan Seth, Naseeruddin Shah, Sam Dastor, Kurush Deboo, Vrajesh Hirjee, Shazneed Damania, Ranjit Chowdhry, Soni Razdan

'Heartfelt, humane and comic.' – *Empire*

Such a Pretty Little Beach: see *Une Si Jolie Petite Plage*

Such Good Friends *
US   1971   102m   Movielab
Paramount/Sigma (Otto Preminger)
A successful man has a mysterious illness and his wife enlists help from his friends.
Satirical parable which alternates between sex comedy and medical exposé; generally heavy-going but with good moments.
w Elaine May *novel* Lois Gould d Otto Preminger ph Gayne Rescher m Thomas Z. Shepard
☆ Dyan Cannon, James Coco, Jennifer O'Neil, Nina Foch, Laurence Luckinbill, Ken Howard, Burgess Meredith, Louise Lasser, Sam Levene, Rita Gam, Nancy Guild

Such Men Are Dangerous: see *The Racers (1955)*

Such Men Are Dangerous
US   1930   83m   bw
Fox
A crooked financier undergoes plastic surgery and leads a new life.
Phoney melodrama with slow pace and unconvincing details.
w Ernest Vajda, Elinor Glyn d Kenneth Hawks
☆ Warner Baxter, Catherine Dale Owen, Albert Conti, Hedda Hopper, Claud Allister, Bela Lugosi
'Will bore intelligent fans and impress even the gullible with its implausibilities.' – *Variety*

Such Women Are Dangerous
US   1934   81m   bw
Fox
Through circumstances an innocent man about town is accused of murder.
Mild drama which fails through slack handling.
w Jane Storm, Oscar M. Sheridan *story* Odd Thursday by Vera Caspary d James Flood
☆ Warner Baxter, Rosemary Ames, Rochelle Hudson, Mona Barrie, Herbert Mundin, Henrietta Crosman
'Just fair screen amusement.' – *Variety*

Sudba Cheloveka: see *Destiny of a Man*

'Action Goes Into Overtime.'
Sudden Death *
US   1995   110m   DeLuxe   Panavision
Universal/Signature/Baldwin Cohen (Moshe Diamant, Howard Baldwin)
◎ ▦ ◎~ ◠
A fire marshal deals with a gang who take the Vice-President hostage and demand a $1.7 billion ransom during an ice-hockey game.
Fast-paced action movie; it is mindless entertainment, but effectively delivers the requisite thrills and spills.
w Gene Quintano *story* Karen Baldwin d Peter Hyams ph Peter Hyams m John Debney pd Philip Harrison ed Steven Kemper

☆ Jean-Claude Van Damme, Powers Boothe, Raymond J. Barry, Whittni Wright, Ross Malinger, Dorian Harewood, Kate McNeil, Michael Gaston
'A whipcord-taut actioner that's bigger and better than its main star.' – *Variety*
'Tripe, but hard not to enjoy' – *Empire*

Sudden Fear **
US   1952   111m   bw
RKO/Joseph Kaufman
◎~ ◎
A playwright heiress finds that her husband is plotting to kill her.
Archetypal star suspenser, glossy and effectively climaxed.
w Lenore Coffee, Robert Smith d David Miller ph Charles Lang Jnr m Elmer Bernstein
☆ Joan Crawford, Jack Palance, Gloria Grahame, Bruce Bennett, Mike Connors
⅄ Charles Lang Jnr; Joan Crawford; Jack Palance

'Go on – make his day!'
Sudden Impact
US   1983   117m   Technicolor
Warner/Malpaso (Clint Eastwood)
▣◪ ▦ ◎~
San Francisco detective Harry Callahan goes after a lady killer of men who raped her.
Unattractive and overlong cop show featuring an increasingly tired Dirty Harry.
w Joseph C. Stinson d Clint Eastwood ph Bruce Surtees m Lalo Schifrin pd Edward Carfagno
☆ Clint Eastwood, Sondra Locke, Pat Hingle, Bradford Dillman, Paul Drake
'Eastwood presumably takes credit for such gems of authorial self-awareness as replacing the orang-outang of the *Which Way* films, with a farting dog.' – Paul Taylor, *MFB*
'To all those cowboy movies we saw in our youth, all those TV westerns and cop dramas and war movies, Dirty Harry has brought a great simplification: A big man, a big gun, a bad guy, and instant justice.' – Roger Ebert

Sudden Terror: see *Eyewitness (1970)*

Suddenly *
US   1954   75m   bw
UA/Robert Bassler
▣◪ ▦ ◎~ ◎
Gunmen take over a suburban house and plan to assassinate the President who is due to pass by.
Moderately effective minor suspenser with rather too much psychological chat.
w Richard Sale d Lewis Allen ph Charles G. Clarke m David Raksin
☆ Frank Sinatra, Sterling Hayden, James Gleason, Nancy Gates, Kim Charney

'What she doesn't know about spring – neither does Cupid!'
Suddenly It's Spring
US   1947   87m   bw
Paramount (Claude Binyon)
A WAC captain comes home to find that her husband wants a divorce.
Tired romantic comedy with no fizz at all.
w Claude Binyon d Mitchell Leisen ph Daniel L. Fapp m Victor Young
☆ Paulette Goddard, Macdonald Carey, Fred MacMurray, Arleen Whelan, Lillian Fontaine, Frank Faylen, Victoria Horne

Suddenly Last Summer *
GB   1959   114m   bw
Columbia/Horizon (Sam Spiegel)
▣◪ ▦ ◎~
A homosexual poet's young cousin goes mad when she sees him raped and murdered by beach boys.
Arty flashback talk-piece from a one-act play, padded out with much sub-poetic mumbo jumbo; it takes too long to get to the revelation, which is ambiguously presented anyway.
w Gore Vidal *play* Tennessee Williams d Joseph L. Mankiewicz ph Jack Hildyard m Buxton Orr, Malcolm Arnold pd Oliver Messel
☆ Katharine Hepburn, Elizabeth Taylor, Montgomery Clift, Albert Dekker, Mercedes McCambridge, Gary Raymond
'A short play turns into a ludicrous, lumbering horror movie.' – *New Yorker, 1978*
'I loathe this film, I say so candidly. To my mind it is a decadent piece of work, sensational,

barbarous and ridiculous.' – C. A. *Lejeune, Observer*
'A wholly admirable rendering into film of a work at once fascinating and nauseating, brilliant and immoral.' – *Arthur Knight*
⅄ Katharine Hepburn; Elizabeth Taylor; art direction

'Driven By The Love Of Two Women ... He Tore Continents Apart That Ships Might Sail The Desert!'
Suez *
US   1938   104m   bw
TCF (Gene Markey)
The career of French engineer Ferdinand de Lesseps, who built the Suez Canal.
Superbly mounted but rather undramatic fictionalized biopic.
w Philip Dunne, Julien Josephson *story* Sam Duncan d Allan Dwan ph Peverell Marley m David Raksin, David Buttolph, Cyril Mockridge md Louis Silvers
☆ Tyrone Power, Annabella, Loretta Young, J. Edward Bromberg, Joseph Schildkraut, Henry Stephenson, Sidney Blackmer, Maurice Moscovich, Sig Rumann, Nigel Bruce, Miles Mander, George Zucco, Leon Ames, Rafaela Ottiano
'It's a big film in its attempt, but it misses out on its epic aims.' – *Variety*
⅄ Peverell Marley; Louis Silvers

Sugar Cane Alley: see *Rue Cases Nègres*

Sugar Hill
US   1994   123m   DeLuxe
TCF/Beacon/South Street (Rudy Langlais, Gregory Brown)
▣◪ ▦ ◎~ ◠
Two brothers, successful drug dealers in Harlem, have a gang war on their hands, but one of them decides to give up the life that has made them rich because he has fallen in love with an actress.
Trite melodrama with flashbacks – to the death of his mother from an overdose of heroin, the shooting of his drug-dealing father by gangsters, and to his own academic prowess – designed to elicit sympathy for its guilt-ridden, thuggish protagonist; but he remains a blank and uninteresting one.
w Barry Michael Cooper d Leon Ichaso ph Bojan Bazelli m Terence Blanchard pd Michael Helmy ed Gary Carr
☆ Wesley Snipes, Michael Wright, Theresa Randle, Leslie Uggams, Larry Joshua, Sam Bottoms, Joe Dallesandro, Clarence Williams III, Abe Vigoda, Ernie Hudson
'At every level, this is a film falling short of conviction.' – *Sight and Sound*

Sugarbaby **
West Germany   1984   87m   colour
Electric/Pelemele film/BMI/Bayerischen Rundfunks (Eleonore Adlon)
▦
original title: *Zuckerbaby*
A fat woman pursues a handsome, married train driver whom she loves.
Enjoyable and witty romantic comedy.
wd Percy Adlon ph Johanna Heer m Dreier, Franz Erlmeier, Fritz Köstler, Paul Würges Combo pd Matthias Heller ed Jean-Claude Piroue
☆ Marianne Sägebrecht, Eisi Gulp, Toni Berger, Manuela Denz, Will Spindler, Hans Stadlbauer

Sugarfoot
US   1951   80m   Technicolor
Warner
TV title: *Swirl of Glory*
Two men meet on a train for Prescott, Arizona, and each determines to make the town his own.
Unusual but fatally sluggish Western.
w Russell Hughes *novel* Clarence Budington Kelland d Edwin L. Marin ph Wilfred Cline m Max Steiner
☆ Randolph Scott, Raymond Massey, Adele Jergens, S. Z. Sakall, Robert Warwick, Arthur Hunnicutt

'The true story of a girl who took on all of Texas ... and almost won.'
Sugarland Express *
US   1974   110m   Technicolor   Panavision
Universal (Richard Zanuck, David Brown)
▦ ◎~
A convict's wife persuades him to escape because their baby is being adopted, and they inadvertently

leave behind them a trail of destruction, ending in tragedy.
Mainly comic adventures with a bitter aftertaste, very stylishly handled.
w Hal Barwood, Matthew Robbins d Steven Spielberg ph Vilmos Zsigmond m John Williams
☆ Goldie Hawn, Ben Johnson, Michael Sacks, William Atherton
'Ace in the Hole meets Vanishing Point.' – *Sight and Sound*

The Suicide Club: see *Trouble for Two*

Suicide Squadron: see *Dangerous Moonlight*

Suite 16
GB/Belgium   1994   100m   colour
Feature Film/Corsan/Theorema (Paul Breuls)
◎
A wealthy voyeur in a wheelchair hires a young gigolo to seduce a woman and kill her while he listens.
A slick but hollow account of decadence and power, not far removed from the staple of Soho cinema clubs in its emphasis on sex.
w Charles Higson, Lise Mayer d Dominique Deruddere ph Jean-François Robin m Walter Hus ed Kant Pan
☆ Pete Postlethwaite, Antonie Kamerling, Geraldine Pailhas, Tom Jansen, Bart Siegers
'A pretty silly film from a director who has enough talent to stop farting about with semi-porn.' – Derek Malcolm, *Guardian*

The Suitor *
France   1962   85m   bw
CAPAC
original title: *Le Soupirant*
A nervous young man makes several attempts to get married.
The most successful feature of Pierre Etaix, a student of Tati: his jokes are more polished but in the end his own personality seems rather lacking.
w Pierre Etaix, Jean-Claude Carrière d Pierre Etaix ph Pierre Levant m Jean Paillaud
☆ Pierre Etaix, Laurence Lignères, France Arnell

The Sullivans *
US   1944   111m   bw
TCF (Sam Jaffe)
reissue title: *The Fighting Sullivans*
Five sons of the same family are killed in World War II.
Inspirational true story which had a wide appeal.
w Mary C. McCall Jnr d Lloyd Bacon ph Lucien Andriot m Alfred Newman
☆ Anne Baxter, Thomas Mitchell, Selena Royle, Edward Ryan, Trudy Marshall, John Campbell, James Cardwell, John Alvin, George Offerman Jnr, Roy Roberts
⅄ original story (Jules Schermer, Edward Doherty)

'There's no speed limit and no brake

When Sullivan travels with Veronica Lake!'
Sullivan's Travels ****
US   1941   90m   bw
Paramount (Paul Jones)
▦ ◎~
A Hollywood director tires of comedy and goes out to find real life.
Marvellously sustained tragi-comedy which ranges from pratfalls to the chain gang and never loses its grip or balance.
wd Preston Sturges ph John Seitz m Leo Shuken
☆ Joel McCrea, Veronica Lake, Robert Warwick, William Demarest, Franklin Pangborn, Porter Hall, Byron Foulger, Eric Blore, Robert Greig, Torben Meyer, Jimmy Conlin, Margaret Hayes
DEDICATION: 'To all the funny men and clowns who have made people laugh.'
'A brilliant fantasy in two keys – slapstick farce and the tragedy of human misery.' – James Agee
'The most witty and knowing spoof of Hollywood movie-making of all time.' – *Film Society Review*
'A deftly sardonic apologia for Hollywood make-believe.' – *New York Times*
'Reflecting to perfection the mood of wartime Hollywood, it danced on the grave of thirties social cinema.' – Eileen Bowser, 1969

The Sum of Us
Australia   1994   95m   colour
Southern Star/AFFC (Hal McElroy)
🎧
A widowed father and his gay son both search for other relationships.
Engaging performances are not enough to compensate for the longueurs in this small-scale, earnest and sentimental drama of male bonding and homophobia.
w David Stevens *play* David Stevens *d* Kevin Dowling, Geoff Burton *ph* Geoff Burton *m* Dave Faulkner *pd* Graham (Grace) Walker *ed* Frans Vandenburg
☆ Jack Thompson, Russell Crowe, John Polson, Deborah Kennedy

Summer: see *The Green Ray*

A Summer Affair *
France   1977   84m   Eastmancolor
Panavision
Gala/Renn Productions/Société Française de Production (Pierre Grunstein)
original title: Un Moment D'égarement
aka: One Wild Moment
A middle-aged man begins an affair with his best friend's teenage daughter when the two families go on holiday together.
Occasionally witty examination of the generation gap.
wd Claude Berri *ph* André Neau *m* Michel Stelio *ed* Jacques Witta
☆ Jean-Pierre Marielle, Victor Lanoux, Christine Dejoux, Agnes Soral, Martine Sarcey
† In 1984, the film was remade by Stanley Donen as *Blame It On Rio*.

'Bold ideas ... bolder people!'
Summer and Smoke
US   1961   118m   Technicolor   Panavision
Paramount/Hal B. Wallis
📼 🔵 🎧
In a small Mississippi town in 1916, the minister's spinster daughter nurses an unrequited love for the local rebel.
Wearisome screen version, in hothouse settings, of a pattern play about earthly and spiritual love.
w James Poe, Meade Roberts *play* Tennessee Williams *d* Peter Glenville *ph* Charles Lang Jnr *m* Elmer Bernstein *ad* Walter Tyler
☆ Geraldine Page, Laurence Harvey, Una Merkel, John McIntire, Pamela Tiffin, Rita Moreno, Thomas Gomez, Casey Adams, Earl Holliman, Lee Patrick, Malcolm Atterbury
🎘 Elmer Bernstein; Geraldine Page; Una Merkel

A Summer at Grandpa's **
Taiwan   1984   102m   colour
Marble Road (Chang Hwa-Kuen)
original title: Tung-Tung-te chia-ch'i
When his mother becomes seriously ill, a 12-year-old boy is sent with his small sister to stay with his grandfather in the country.
An episodic film of some charm, in part nostalgic for the idle pleasures of a holiday, and in part a comment on the world of adults as seen through the eyes of the disinterested young. The family is the bedrock of society, remarks a notary marrying a reluctant couple, but the family depicted here seems on the point of disintegration, surviving only by absorbing some antisocial behaviour.
w Chu Tien-Wen, Hou Hsiao-Hsien *d* Hou Hsiao-Hsien *ph* Chen K'un'hou *m* Edward Yang
☆ Wang Qiguang, Zhou Shengli, Gu Jun, Mei Fang, Lin Xiuling

Summer Holiday **
US   1948   92m   Technicolor
MGM (Arthur Freed)
📼 🔵
Life for a small-town family at the turn of the century.
Musical version of a famous play: excellent individual numbers, warm playing and sympathetic scenes, but a surprising lack of overall style.
w Frances Goodrich, Albert Hackett, Ralph Blane *play* Ah Wilderness by Eugene O'Neill *d* Rouben Mamoulian *ph* Charles Schoenbaum *md* Lennie Hayton *ch* Charles Walters *songs* Harry Warren, Ralph Blane
☆ Walter Huston, Mickey Rooney, Frank Morgan, Agnes Moorehead, Butch Jenkins, Selena Royle, Marilyn Maxwell, Gloria de Haven, Anne Francis
† The film was finished in 1946 and held back because it seemed unlikely to succeed.

Summer Holiday *
👫 GB   1962   109m   Technicolor
Cinemascope
ABP/Ivy (Kenneth Harper)
📼
Four young London Transport mechanics borrow a double-decker bus for a continental holiday.
Pacy, location-filmed youth musical with plenty of general appeal.
w Peter Myers, Ronnie Cass *d* Peter Yates *ph* John Wilcox *md* Stanley Black
☆ Cliff Richard, Lauri Peters, Melvyn Hayes, Una Stubbs, Teddy Green, Ron Moody, Lionel Murton, David Kossoff

Summer Interlude *
Sweden   1950   97m   bw
Svensk Filmindustri (Alan Ekelund)
📼 🔵
original title: Sommarlek
A prima ballerina remembers a happy summer she spent with a boy who was tragically killed.
Melancholy romance quite typical of its creator but with less density of meaning than usual.
w Ingmar Bergman, Herbert Grevenius *d* Ingmar Bergman *ph* Gunnar Fischer, Bengt Jarnmark *m* Erik Nordgren
☆ Maj-Britt Nilsson, Birger Malmsten, Alf Kjellin

Summer Lightning: see *Scudda Hoo, Scudda Hay*

Summer Lovers
US   1982   98m   Technicolor   Panavision
Orion (Mike Moder)
📼 🔵
A young man on holiday on a Greek island persuades his girlfriend that he needs a local girl as well.
A movie with little dialogue and less intelligence, just attractive locations, through which the three principals romp inanely to bubble-gum music. It might just pass muster on the level of a tourist brochure.
wd Randal Kleiser *ph* Timothy Galfas, Dimitri Papaconstandis *m* Basil Poledouris *pd* Bruce Weintraub *ed* Robert Gordon
☆ Peter Gallagher, Daryl Hannah, Valerie Quennessen, Barbara Rush, Carole Cook

Summer Madness: see *Summertime*

Summer Magic *
👫 US   1963   104m   Technicolor
Walt Disney (Ron Miller)
📼
Children help their widowed mother in 1912 Boston.
Amiable remake of Mother Carey's Chickens, irreproachably presented.
w Sally Benson *d* James Neilson *ph* William Snyder *m* Buddy Baker *songs* the Sherman Brothers
☆ Hayley Mills, Burl Ives, Dorothy McGuire, Darren McGavin, Deborah Walley, Una Merkel, Eddie Hodges, Michael J. Pollard

Summer Manoeuvres: see *Les Grandes Manoeuvres*

Summer of '42 *
US   1971   103m   Technicolor
Warner/Mulligan-Roth (Richard Alan Roth)
📼
Adolescents make sexual explorations on a New England island in 1942.
Well-observed indulgence in the new permissiveness.
w Herman Raucher *d* Robert Mulligan *ph* Robert Surtees *m* Michel Legrand
☆ Jennifer O'Neill, Gary Grimes, Jerry Houser, Oliver Conant, Lou Frizzell
🎗 Michel Legrand
🎘 Herman Raucher; Robert Surtees
📹 Michel Legrand

The Summer of Aviya *
Israel   1988   95m   colour
Mutual/HSA (Eitan Evan, Gila Almagor)
original title: Hakayitz Shel Aviya
A young girl's unhappy relationship with her disturbed mother comes to a head during a summer holiday.
Affecting, semi-autobiographical account of suffering in the aftermath of the Second World War.
w Eli Cohen, Gila Almagor, Chaim Buzaglo *novel* Gila Almagor *d* Eli Cohen *ph* David Gurfinkel *m* Shem-Tov Levi *ad* Yoram Shayer *ed* Tova Ne'eman
☆ Gila Almagor, Kaipo Cohen, Eli Cohen, Marina Rosetti, Avital Dicker, Dina Avrech
'Eli Cohen transforms the horror and trauma of the past and its excesses into a measured and humane expression of what can be achieved in the face of evil.' – *MFB*

'NYC '77. Disco In The Clubs. Panic In The Streets.'
Summer of Sam *
US   1999   142m   Technicolor
Downtown/Touchstone/40 Acres and a Mule (Jon Kilik, Spike Lee)
📼 🔵 🔵
A gang of Italian-Americans in the Bronx try to solve the mystery of a serial killer in the neighbourhood, during the hot summer of 1977.
The point of this shapeless ensemble piece seems to be a remark by a black woman that if the killer known as the Son of Sam had been black, there would have been riots in New York. Otherwise, it deals in minor panic and mishaps among stereotypical would-be mobsters; but not even the period detail is right.
w Victor Colicchio, Michael Imperioli, Spike Lee *d* Spike Lee *ph* Ellen Kuras *m* Terence Blanchard *pd* Therese DePrez *ed* Barry Alexander Brown *cos* Ruth E. Carter
☆ John Leguizamo, Adrien Brody, Mira Sorvino, Jennifer Esposito, Anthony LaPaglia, Bebe Neuwirth, Patti LuPone, Ben Gazarra, Joe Lisi, Michael Badalucco, Michael Rispoli, John Savage, Spike Lee
'A great little movie that has real heart and intelligence.' – *Cosmo Landesman, Sunday Times*
'An enormously energetic, flavourful film.' – *Kim Newman, Empire*

Summer of the Seventeenth Doll
US/Australia   1959   94m   bw
UA/Hecht-Hill-Lancaster (Leslie Norman)
US title: Season of Passion
Two cane-cutters on their annual city lay-off have woman trouble.
Miscast and unsatisfactory rendering of a good play; the humour has evaporated.
w John Dighton *play* Ray Lawler *d* Leslie Norman *ph* Paul Beeson *m* Benjamin Frankel
☆ Ernest Borgnine, John Mills, Angela Lansbury, Anne Baxter, Vincent Ball

A Summer Place
US   1959   130m .   Technicolor
Warner (Delmer Daves)
📼
Romantic summer adventures of teenagers and their elders on an island off the coast of Maine.
Sex among the idle rich: a routine piece of Hollywood gloss, bowdlerized from a bestseller.
wd Delmer Daves *novel* Sloan Wilson *ph* Harry Stradling *m* Max Steiner
☆ Richard Egan, Dorothy McGuire, Sandra Dee, Arthur Kennedy, Troy Donahue, Constance Ford, Beulah Bondi

Summer Rental
US   1985   93m   colour
Paramount (George Shapiro)
📼 📼 🔵
An accident-prone air traffic controller takes his family on a holiday where everything goes wrong.
Broad, lively comedy that relies too heavily on the skills and charm of Candy, though he almost manages to carry the picture.
w Jeremy Stevens, Mark Reisman *d* Carl Reiner *ph* Ric Waite *m* Alan Silvestri *pd* Peter Wooley *ed* Bud Molin
☆ John Candy, Richard Crenna, Rip Torn, Karen Austin, Kerri Green, Joey Lawrence, Aubrey Jene, John Larroquette

Summer School
US   1987   98m   Technicolor
Paramount (George Shapiro, Howard West)
📼 📼 🔵 🎧
A reluctant sports teacher, forced to give lessons in remedial English to even more reluctant students at summer school, makes a deal with his class.
Slight comedy that may amuse teenagers with nothing better to do with their time.
w Jeff Franklin, Stuart Birnbaum, David Dashev *d* Carl Reiner *ph* David M. Walsh *m* Danny Elfman *pd* David L. Snyder *ed* Bud Molin

☆ Mark Harmon, Kirstie Alley, Robin Thomas, Patrick Laborteaux, Courtney Thorne Smith, Dean Cameron, Gary Reilly

Summer Stock *
US   1950   109m   Technicolor
MGM (Joe Pasternak)
📼 🔵 🎧
GB title: If You Feel Like Singing
A theatre troupe takes over a farm for rehearsals, and the lady owner gets the bug.
Likeable but halting musical with the star's weight problems very obvious.
w George Wells, Sy Gomberg *d* Charles Walters *ph* Robert Planck *md* Johnny Green *ch* Nick Castle
☆ Judy Garland, Gene Kelly, Gloria de Haven, Carleton Carpenter, Eddie Bracken, Phil Silvers, Hans Conried
† June Allyson was to have starred, but became pregnant.

Summer Storm *
US   1944   106m   bw
(UA)
In 1912 Russia, a provincial judge falls for a local mancatcher.
One of Hollywood's occasional aberrations, an attempt to do something very European in typical west coast style. An interesting failure.
w Rowland Leigh *story* The Shooting Party by Anton Chekhov *d* Douglas Sirk *ph* Archie Stout *md* Karl Hajos
☆ George Sanders, Linda Darnell, Edward Everett Horton, Anna Lee, Hugo Haas, John Philiber, Sig Rumann, André Charlot
'There are bits of acting and photography which put it as far outside the run of American movies as it laudably tries to be. But most of it had for me the sporty speciousness of an illustrated drugstore classic.' – *James Agee*
🎘 Karl Hajos

A Summer Story
GB   1988   97m   colour
Warner/ITC (Danton Rissner)
📼 🎧
A lawyer recalls his love for a working-class country girl.
Stiff upper lip romance, pretty to look at but providing little else.
w Penelope Mortimer *story* The Apple Cart by John Galsworthy *d* Piers Haggard *ph* Kenneth MacMillan *m* Georges Delerue *pd* Leo Austin *ed* Ralph Sheldon
☆ James Wilby, Imogen Stubbs, Ken Colley, Sophie Ward, Susannah York, Jerome Flynn

Summer Vacation 1999
Japan   1988   90m   Eastmancolor
New Century/CBS-Sony (Yutaka Okada, Eiji Kishi)
original title: 1999 – Nen No Natsu Yasumi
Three adolescent boys spending the summer at an otherwise deserted school think their friend has returned from the dead when they are joined by a fourth boy who exactly resembles him.
Slow-moving, self-consciously poetic and finally ridiculous tale of repressed love and teenage angst, not helped by the fact that the boys are played by girls.
w Rio Kishida *d* Shusuke Kaneko *ph* Kenji Takama *m* Yuriko Nakamura *ad* Shu Yamaguchi
☆ Eri Miyajima, Tomoko Otakara, Miyuki Nakano, Rie Mizuhara

Summer Wishes, Winter Dreams *
US   1973   88m   Technicolor
Columbia/Rastar (Jack Brodsky)
📼
A neurotic New York housewife goes to pieces when her mother dies but finds a new understanding of her husband when she accompanies him on a trip to the World War II battlefields.
Menopausal melodrama, well observed but disappointingly wispy and underdeveloped.
w Stewart Stern *d* Gilbert Cates *ph* Gerald Hirschfeld *m* Johnny Mandel
☆ Joanne Woodward, Martin Balsam, Sylvia Sidney, Dori Brenner, Win Forman
🎘 Joanne Woodward; Sylvia Sidney
📹 Joanne Woodward

Summer with Monika *
Sweden 1952 97m bw
Svensk Filmindustri (Allan Ekelund)

📀 📼

original title: Sommaren med Monika
A wild, restless girl defies her parents and goes off with her boyfriend for an island holiday. Her subsequent pregnancy and motherhood don't in the least suit her, and the father is left alone with the baby.
Probably truthful but rather glum and unsophisticated drama of young love; not among Bergman's most interesting films.
wd Ingmar Bergman novel Per Anders Fogelstrom ph Gunnar Fischer m Erik Nordgren
☆ Harriet Andersson, Lars Ekborg

Summerfield
Australia 1977 91m Eastmancolor
Clare Beach/AFC/Victorian Film (Patricia Lovell)
A new schoolteacher arrives in an isolated community to find he faces hostility from the locals and a mystery concerning the fate of his predecessor.
A slick mystery story, although too slow and predictable to be engrossing.
w Cliff Green d Ken Hannam ph Mike Molloy m Bruce Smeaton ad Graham Walker ed Sara Bennett
☆ Nick Tate, John Waters, Elizabeth Alexander, Michelle Jarman, Charles Tingwell, Geraldine Turner

A Summer's Tale: see Conte d'été

Summertime ***
US 1955 99m Eastmancolor
London Films/Lopert Productions (Ilya Lopert)

📀 📼 🔊

GB title: Summer Madness
An American spinster has a holiday in Venice and becomes romantically involved.
Delightful, sympathetic travelogue with dramatic asides, great to look at and hinging on a single superb performance.
w David Lean, H. E. Bates play The Time of the Cuckoo by Arthur Laurents d David Lean ph Jack Hildyard m Sandro Cicognini
☆ Katharine Hepburn, Rossano Brazzi, Isa Miranda, Darren McGavin, Mari Aldon, André Morell
'The eye is endlessly ravished.' – Dilys Powell
⚟ David Lean; Katharine Hepburn

Summertree
US 1971 88m Eastmancolor
Warner/Bryna (Kirk Douglas)

📼

A bored student learns about life and becomes a Vietnam casualty.
Well-made, rather tedious character study; good social observation.
w Edward Hume, Stephen Yafa play Ron Cowen d Anthony Newley ph Richard C. Glouner m David Shire
☆ Michael Douglas, Brenda Vaccaro, Jack Warden, Barbara Bel Geddes

The Sun Also Rises **
US 1957 129m Eastmancolor
Cinemascope
TCF (Darryl F. Zanuck)
In Paris after World War I an impotent journalist meets a nymphomaniac lady of title, and they and their odd group of friends have various saddening adventures around Europe.
Not a bad attempt to film a difficult novel, though Cinemascope doesn't help and the last half hour becomes turgid. The Last Flight (qv) conveyed the same atmosphere rather more sharply.
w Peter Viertel novel Ernest Hemingway d Henry King ph Leo Tover m Hugo Friedhofer
☆ Tyrone Power, Ava Gardner, Errol Flynn, Eddie Albert, Mel Ferrer, Robert Evans, Juliette Greco, Gregory Ratoff, Marcel Dalio, Henry Daniell

The Sun Never Sets
US 1939 98m bw
Universal (Rowland V. Lee)
Two brothers in the African colonial service prevent a munitions baron from plunging the world into war.
Stiff upper lip melodrama, very dated.
w W. P. Lipscomb d Rowland V. Lee ph George Robinson m Frank Skinner md Charles Previn

☆ Basil Rathbone, Douglas Fairbanks Jnr, Virginia Field, Lionel Atwill, Barbara O'Neil, C. Aubrey Smith, Melville Cooper
'Confusing script and poor direction relegate this to lower duals … brightest thing is the title.' – Variety

The Sun Shines Bright **
US 1953 92m bw
Republic/Argosy (John Ford, Merian C. Cooper)

📀 📼

Forty years after the Civil War, the judge of a Kentucky town still has trouble quelling the Confederate spirit.
Mellow anecdotes of time gone by, scrappily linked but lovingly polished; a remake of a Will Rogers vehicle Judge Priest.
w Laurence Stallings stories Irwin S. Cobb d John Ford ph Archie Stout m Victor Young
☆ Charles Winninger, Arleen Whelan, John Russell, Stepin Fetchit, Milburn Stone, Grant Withers, Russell Simpson
'Passages of quite remarkable poetic feeling … alive with affection and truthful observation.' – Lindsay Anderson

Sun Valley Serenade *
US 1941 86m bw
TCF (Milton Sperling)

📀 📼 🔊

The band manager at an Idaho ice resort takes care of a Norwegian refugee.
Simple-minded musical which still pleases because of the talent involved.
w Robert Ellis, Helen Logan d H. Bruce Humberstone ph Edward Cronjager m Emil Newman songs Mack Gordon, Harry Warren
☆ Sonja Henie, Glenn Miller and his Orchestra, John Payne, Milton Berle, Lynn Bari, Joan Davis, The Nicholas Brothers, Dorothy Dandridge
⚟ Edward Cronjager; Emil Newman; song 'Chattanooga Choo-Choo' (mHarry Warren, lyMack Gordon)

Suna no Onna: see Woman of the Dunes

Sunbonnet Sue
US 1945 89m bw
Monogram/Scott R. Dunlap
In the 1890s, a Park Avenue matron objects to her niece singing in a Bowery saloon.
Old-fashioned family movie for the innocent-minded.
w Paul Gerard Smith, Bradford Ropes d Ralph Murphy
☆ Gale Storm, Phil Regan, Minna Gombell, George Cleveland, Raymond Hatton, Alan Mowbray
⚟ Edward J. Kay (music)

Sunburn
GB/US 1979 98m Technicolor
Hemdale/Bind Films (David Korda)

📼

An insurance investigator hires a model to act as his wife while he trails a suspected murderer in Acapulco.
All sun and skin and swirling cameras, this entire movie is a seventies cliché, but it provides some fitful amusement.
w John Daly, Stephen Oliver, James Booth novel The Bind by Stanley Ellin d Richard C. Sarafian ph Alex Phillips Jnr m John Cameron
☆ Farrah Fawcett, Charles Grodin, Art Carney, Joan Collins, William Daniels, John Hillerman, Eleanor Parker, Keenan Wynn

The Sunchaser
US 1996 122m Technicolor Panavision
Warner/Monarchy/Regency (Arnon Milchan, Michael Cimino, Larry Spiegel)

📀 📼

An ambitious doctor is kidnapped by a teenage convict, dying from cancer, and forced to travel to Arizona to find a Navajo medicine man.
Heavily symbolic road movie, travelling through photogenic landscapes but imbued with a second-hand mysticism.
w Charles Leavitt d Michael Cimino ph Doug Milsome m Maurice Jarre pd Victoria Paul ed Joe D'Augustine
☆ Woody Harrelson, Jon Seda, Anne Bancroft, Alexandra Tydings, Matt Mulhern, Talisa Soto, Richard Bauer, Victor Aaron

'A conceptually bold tale marked, in its execution, both by visceral intensity and dramatic sloppiness.' – Variety

'It's about three decent people. They will break your heart!'

Sunday, Bloody Sunday ***
GB 1971 110m DeLuxe
UA/Vectia (Joseph Janni)

📼 🔊

A young designer shares his sexual favours equally between two lovers of different sexes, a Jewish doctor and a lady executive.
Stylishly made character study with melodramatic leanings, rather self-conscious about its risky subject but, scene by scene, both adult and absorbing, with an overpowering mass of sociological detail about the way we live.
w Penelope Gilliatt d John Schlesinger ph Billy Williams m Ron Geesin pd Luciana Arrighi
☆ Glenda Jackson, Peter Finch, Murray Head, Peggy Ashcroft, Maurice Denham, Vivian Pickles, Frank Windsor, Tony Britton, Harold Goldblatt
'This is not a story about the loss of love, but about its absence.' – Roger Ebert
⚟ Penelope Gilliatt; John Schlesinger; Glenda Jackson; Peter Finch
⬚ best picture; John Schlesinger; Peter Finch; Glenda Jackson

'Their eyes met! Their lips questioned! Their arms answered!'

Sunday Dinner for a Soldier *
US 1944 86m bw
TCF (Walter Morosco)
A poor family living on a derelict Florida houseboat scrape together enough money to invite a soldier for a meal.
Sentimental little flagwaving romance, quite sympathetically presented and agreeably underacted.
w Wanda Tuchock, Melvin Levy d Lloyd Bacon ph Joe MacDonald m Alfred Newman
☆ Anne Baxter, John Hodiak, Charles Winninger, Anne Revere, Connie Marshall, Chill Wills, Bobby Driscoll, Jane Darwell
'Simple, true and tender, the best propaganda America has put out in the current year.' – Richard Winnington

Sunday in August: see Domenico d'Agosto

Sunday in New York *
US 1963 105m Metrocolor
MGM/Seven Arts (Everett Freeman)
Complications in the love life of a brother and sister, each of whom thinks the other is very moral.
Fresh, fairly adult sex comedy with New York backgrounds.
w Norman Krasna play Norman Krasna d Peter Tewkesbury ph Leo Tover m Peter Nero
☆ Cliff Robertson, Rod Taylor, Jane Fonda, Robert Culp, Jo Morrow, Jim Backus

Sunday in the Country
Canada 1975 92m colour Panavision
Quadrant/Impact (David M. Perlmutter)

📼

A righteous farmer decides to take the law into his own hands when three gun-happy bank robbers arrive at his home.
Uninteresting, brutal rural melodrama, done without finesse, and with both Pollard and Borgnine providing over-the-top performances that emphasize the pervading lack of reality; a sentimental title song is no help, either.
w Robert Maxwell, John Trent story David Main d John Trent ph Marc Champion m William McCauley, Paul Hoffert ad James Milton Parcher ed Tony Lower
☆ Ernest Borgnine, Michael J. Pollard, Hollis McLaren, Cec Linder, Louis Zorich, Vladimir Valenta, Al Waxman, Tim Henry, Murray Westgate

Sunday in the Country **
France 1984 94m Eastmancolor
Sara Films/Films A2/Little Bear (Alain Sarde)

📀 📼 🔊

original title: Un Dimanche à la Campagne
An elderly artist enjoys a Sunday visit from his family.
Delightful, slight and moving sketch for a drama, which gives nothing but pleasure yet is hard to recapture.

w Bertrand and Colo Tavernier novella Pierre Bost d Bertrand Tavernier ph Bruno de Keyzer m Gabriel Fauré
☆ Louis Ducreux, Sabine Azema, Michel Aumont, Geneviève Mnich, Monique Chaumette, Claude Winter

Sunday Too Far Away
Australia 1977 94m colour
South Australian Film Corporation

📼

Itinerant sheep shearers become involved in an industrial dispute.
Almost the archetypal Australian outback movie, good to look at but hard to care about.
w John Dingwall d Ken Hannam
☆ Jack Thompson, Max Cullen, Reg Lye, John Ewart

Sundays and Cybèle *
France 1962 110m bw Franscope
Terra/Fides/Orsa/Trocadéro (Romain Pinès)

original title: Cybèle ou les Dimanches de Ville d'Avray
An amnesiac ex-pilot strikes up a friendship with an abandoned 12-year-old girl, but the relationship is misunderstood and ends in tragedy.
A fashionable film of its time which now has little to offer: its director's reputation sagged alarmingly when he went to Hollywood.
w Serge Bourgignon, Antoine Tudal novel Bernard Echasseriaux d Serge Bourgignon ph Henri Decaë m Maurice Jarre
☆ Hardy Kruger, Nicole Courcel, Patricia Gozzi, Daniel Ivernel
'Studied charm and a creakingly melodramatic dénouement take the place of any serious attempt to probe the characters or situation … the film is so busily preoccupied with being as attractive, visually and sentimentally, as it possibly can, that it never has time to consider what it is being attractive about.' – Tom Milne, MFB
'Uneven but highly meritorious … a near-triumph of the intelligently mobile camera.' – John Simon
⬚ best foreign film
⚟ script; Maurice Jarre

Sunday's Children **
Sweden 1992 120m colour
Sandrews (Katinka Farago)
original title: Söndags Barn
During a summer holiday, an eight-year-old boy observes the difficulties of his parents' marriage; as a middle-aged man, he is forced to confront his relationship with his father.
Perceptive, delicately observed study of the tensions within family relationships, full of repressed emotion; it is a sort of sequel to The Best Intentions (qv).
w Ingmar Bergman d Daniel Bergman ph Tony Forsberg m Rune Gustafsson pd Sven Wichmann ed Darek Hodor
☆ Thommy Berggren, Lena Endre, Henrik Linnros, Jacob Leygraf, Anna Linnros, Malin Ek, Birgitta Valberg, Börje Ahlstedt
'Daniel Bergman gives this rambling memoir a shimmering, lyrical clarity, and his direction of the actors is extraordinary.' – Terrence Rafferty, New Yorker

Sundown
US 1941 91m bw
Walter Wanger

📼

The adopted daughter of an Arab trader assists British troops in Africa during World War II.
Artificial-looking romantic actioner with good cast.
w Barre Lyndon d Henry Hathaway ph Charles Lang m Miklos Rozsa ad Alexander Golitzen
☆ Gene Tierney, Bruce Cabot, George Sanders, Harry Carey, Joseph Calleia, Cedric Hardwicke, Carl Esmond, Reginald Gardiner
⚟ Charles Lang; Miklos Rozsa; Alexander Golitzen

The Sundowners **
GB/Australia 1960 133m Technicolor
Warner (Gerry Blatner)

In the twenties an Irish sheepdrover and his family travel from job to job in the Australian bush.

Easygoing, often amusing but lethargically developed family film with major stars somewhat ill at ease. Memorable sequences.

w Isobel Lennart *novel* Jon Cleary d Fred Zinnemann ph Jack Hildyard m Dimitri Tiomkin
☆ Robert Mitchum, Deborah Kerr, *Glynis Johns*, Peter Ustinov, Michael Anderson Jnr, Dina Merrill, Wylie Watson, Chips Rafferty

'For all Zinnemann's generous attention to character, the hints of longing, despair and indomitable spirit, the overall impression remains one of sheer length and repetition and synthetic naturalism.' – *Richard Winnington*
⚬ best picture; Isobel Lennart; Fred Zinnemann; Deborah Kerr; Glynis Johns

'In a world gone mad – a love story!'
Sunflower
France/Italy 1970 101m Technicolor
Champion/Concordia
📼 ⚬ ◗

A man and wife are separated during World War II.
Sudsy romantic drama, partly shot in Moscow but with no other redeeming feature.
w Tonino Guerra, Cesare Zavattini, Georgiy Mdivani d Vittorio de Sica m Henry Mancini
☆ Sophia Loren, Marcello Mastroianni, Lyudmila Savelyeva
⚬ Henry Mancini

Sunny *
US 1930 81m bw
Warner
A showgirl falls for a rich young man.
Tinny early musical notable for its star.
w Humphrey Pearson, Henry McCarthy *musical play* Otto Harbach, Oscar Hammerstein II, Jerome Kern d William A. Seiter ph Ernest Haller
☆ Marilyn Miller, Lawrence Grey, Jack Donahue, Mackenzie Ward, O. P. Heggie

Sunny *
US 1941 97m bw
RKO/Imperator (Herbert Wilcox)
Adequate remake of the above.
w Sig Herzig d Herbert Wilcox ph Russell Metty m Anthony Collins
☆ Anna Neagle, Ray Bolger, John Carroll, Edward Everett Horton, Frieda Inescort, Grace and Paul Hartman
⚬ Anthony Collins

Sunny Side Up *
US 1929 115m bw ('Multicolor' sequence)
Fox
📼 ⚬

A slum girl falls for the son of a rich Southampton family.
Typical early musical of the softer kind; rewarding for those who can project themselves back.
d David Butler ph Ernest Palmer w/m/ly B. G. de Sylva, Low Brown, Ray Henderson
☆ Janet Gaynor, Charles Farrell, El Brendel, Marjorie White, Sharon Lynn

Sunnyside *
US 1919 27m bw silent
First National/Charles Chaplin
The overworked odd job man at a country hotel has a pastoral dream.
Very mildly funny star comedy which was intended as a satire on the D. W. Griffith/Charles Ray type of rural drama then popular. It doesn't work in this vein either.
wd Charles Chaplin ph Rollie Totheroh
☆ Charles Chaplin, Edna Purviance, Tom Wilson, Albert Austin, Henry Bergman

Sunrise **
US 1927 97m bw silent
Fox
📼 🖵

A villager in love with a city woman tries to kill his wife but then repents and spends a happy day with her.
Lyrical melodrama, superbly handled: generally considered among the finest Hollywood productions of the twenties.
w Carl Mayer *novel* A Trip to Tilsit by Hermann Sudermann d F. W. Murnau ph Karl Struss, Charles Rosher m (sound version) Hugo Riesenfeld ad Rochas Gliese
☆ Janet Gaynor, George O'Brien, Margaret Livingston

OPENING TITLE: 'This story of a man and his wife is of nowhere and everywhere, you might hear it

anywhere and at any time.'
'It is filled with intense feeling and in it is embodied an underlying subtlety ... exotic in many ways for it is a mixture of Russian gloom and Berlin brightness.' – *Mordaunt Hall, New York Times*
'Not since the earliest, simplest moving pictures, when locomotives, fire engines and crowds in streets were transposed to the screen artlessly and endearingly, when the entranced eye was rushed through tunnels and over precipices on runaway trains, has there been such joy in motion as under Murnau's direction.' – *Louise Bogan, The New Republic*
'The story is told in a flowing, lyrical German manner that is extraordinarily sensual, yet perhaps too self-conscious, too fable-like, for American audiences.' – *Pauline Kael, 70s*
⚬ Karl Struss, Charles Rosher; Janet Gaynor; Unique and Artistic Picture
⚬ Rochas Gliese

Sunrise at Campobello *
US 1960 143m Technicolor
Warner/Dore Schary
📼 ⚬

The early life of Franklin Roosevelt, including his battle against polio and return to politics.
Static filming of a rather interesting Broadway success and of a memorable performance.
w Dore Schary *play* Dore Schary d Vincent J. Donehue ph Russell Harlan m Franz Waxman ad Edward Carrere
☆ Ralph Bellamy, Greer Garson, Ann Shoemaker, Hume Cronyn, Jean Hagen
⚬ Greer Garson; art direction

Sunset
US 1988 107m Technicolor Panavision
Columbia/Tri-Star/ML Delphi (Tony Adams)
📼 🖵 ⚬

In Hollywood as an adviser to a studio making a film of his life, Wyatt Earp teams up with cowboy star Tom Mix to solve a murder.
A comedy-thriller that misfires.
wd Blake Edwards *story* Rod Amateau ph Anthony B. Richmond m Henry Mancini pd Rodger Maus ed Robert Pergament
☆ Bruce Willis, James Garner, Malcolm McDowell, Mariel Hemingway, Kathleen Quinlan, Jennifer Edwards, Patricia Hodge, Richard Bradford, M. Emmet Walsh, Joe Dallesandro

'It happened in Hollywood ... a love story ... a drama real and ruthless, tender and terrifying!'
Sunset Boulevard ***
US 1950 110m bw
Paramount (Charles Brackett)
📼 🖵 ⚬

A luckless Hollywood scriptwriter goes to live with a wealthy older woman, a slightly dotty and extremely possessive relic of the silent screen.
Incisive melodrama with marvellous moments but a tendency to overstay its welcome; the first reels are certainly the best, though the last scene is worth waiting for and the malicious observation throughout is a treat.
w Charles Brackett, Billy Wilder, D. M. Marshman Jnr d Billy Wilder ph John F. Seitz m Franz Waxman ad Hans Dreier, John Meehan, Sam Comer ed Arthur Schmidt, Doane Harrison
☆ Gloria Swanson, William Holden, Erich von Stroheim, Fred Clark, Nancy Olson, Jack Webb, Lloyd Gough, Cecil B. de Mille, H. B. Warner, Anna Q. Nilsson, Buster Keaton, Hedda Hopper

'That rare blend of pungent writing, expert acting, masterly direction and unobtrusively artistic photography which quickly casts a spell over an audience and holds it enthralled to a shattering climax.' – *New York Times (T.M.P.)*
'Miss Swanson's performance takes her at one bound into the class of Boris Karloff and Tod Slaughter.' – *Richard Mallett, Punch*
'A weird, fascinating motion picture about an art form which, new as it is, is already haunted by ghosts.' – *Otis L. Guernsey Jnr, New York Herald Tribune*
'The most intelligent film to come out of Hollywood for years; lest the idea of intelligence in the cinema should lack allure, let me say that it is also one of the most exciting.' – *Dilys Powell*
† Montgomery Clift was to have played the role taken by William Holden, but decided against it at the last moment, because his real-life affair with an older woman, Libby Holman, was too close to the situation in the film.
⚬ script; Franz Waxman

⚬ best picture; Billy Wilder (as director); John F. Seitz; Gloria Swanson; William Holden; Erich von Stroheim; Nancy Olson; editing

Sunset Grill
US 1992 103m Foto-Kem
New Line/Movie Group (Faruque Ahmed)
🖵

An alcoholic ex-cop uncovers a trade in body parts when he investigates the murder of his estranged wife.
Bloody, over-ambitious thriller with a complex back-story that manages to dissipate most of the suspense and muddle of the narrative.
w Marcus Wright, Faruque Ahmed *story* Chip Walter d Kevin Connor ph Douglas Milsome m Ken Thorne pd Yuda Ako ed Barry Peters
☆ Peter Weller, Lori Singer, Stacy Keach, Alexandra Paul, John Rhys-Davies, Michael Anderson Jnr

Sunset in Vienna
GB 1937 73m bw
Herbert Wilcox
US title: *Suicide Legion*
An Italian cavalry officer finds that his wife's brother is a spy, and shoots him.
Dated romantic melodrama with music.
w Florence Tranter d Norman Walker
☆ Lilli Palmer, Tullio Carminati, John Garrick, Geraldine Hislop

'Three generations. One dream.'
Sunshine *
Alliance 1999 180m colour
Alliance/ISL/Kinowelt/Screen Ventures/DOR (Robert Lantos, Andras Hamori)
A Hungarian-Jewish family in Budapest survives through more than a hundred turbulent years, including periods of Austrian, Nazi and Stalinist domination.
A movie with an epic sweep, in which Fiennes plays three roles of successive heads of the family, men eager for success even if it means compromising religion and morality; unfortunately, the detailed, narrative exposition tends to overwhelm any character development.
w Istvan Szabo, Israel Horovitz d Istvan Szabo ph Lajos Koltai m Maurice Jarre ad Atilla Kovacs ed Dominique Fortin, Michael Arcand cos Pedro Moreno
☆ Ralph Fiennes, Rosemary Harris, Rachel Weisz, Jennifer Ehle, Molly Parker, Deborah Kara Unger, James Frain, John Neville, Miriam Margolyes, David de Keyser, Mark Strong, William Hurt, Bill Paterson, Rudiger Vogler
'The resulting dish is slightly stolid. Near the end of our epic journey we learn, "the purpose of life is... life itself", and the sense of anti-climax is palpable.' – *Julian Graffy, Sight and Sound*

'For the price of a movie, you'll feel like a million!'
The Sunshine Boys *
US 1975 111m Metrocolor
MGM/Rastar (Ray Stark)
📼 🖵 ⚬

Two feuding old vaudeville comedians come together for a television spot, and ruin it.
Over-extended sketch in which one main role is beautifully underplayed, the other hammed up, and the production lacks any kind of style. The one-liners are good, though.
w Neil Simon *play* Neil Simon d Herbert Ross ph David M. Walsh md Harry V. Lojewski
☆ Walter Matthau, *George Burns*, Richard Benjamin, Carol Arthur
'It's just shouting, when it needs to be beautifully timed routines.' – *New Yorker*
'They feud with ill-matched resources, and the movie's visual delights vanish with the title sequence.' – *Sight and Sound*
† George Burns stepped in when Jack Benny became ill and died.
†† In 1996 it was remade as a TV film starring Peter Falk and Woody Allen.
⚬ George Burns
⚬ Neil Simon; Walter Matthau

Sunshine Susie
GB 1931 87m bw
Gainsborough
A banker pretends to be a clerk in order to court a typist.

Viennese-set comedy which worked at the time but quickly dated.
w Angus MacPhail, Robert Stevenson, Victor Saville, Noel Wood-Smith *play* The Private Secretary by Franz Schultz d Victor Saville
☆ Renate Muller, Jack Hulbert, Owen Nares, Morris Harvey, Sybil Grove

Sunstruck
Australia 1972 92m Eastmancolor
Immigrant (Jack Neary, James Grafton)
A shy Welsh schoolmaster emigrates to the Australian outback.
Simple-minded, uninspired, predictable family comedy for star fans.
w Stan Mars d James Gilbert ph Brian West m Peter Knight
☆ Harry Secombe, Maggie Fitzgibbon, John Meillon, Dawn Lake

Il Suo Modo di Fari: see *The Girl Who Couldn't Say No*

Suor Omicidi: see *Killer Nun*

'The judge sentenced slumlord Louis Kritski to six months in his own building. He would have been better off in jail.'
The Super
US 1991 85m colour
Largo/JVC (Charles Gordon)
📼 🖵 ⚬

A New York landlord is forced to live in one of his slum properties.
A misfiring movie, comic when it should be serious, and sentimental the rest of the time.
w Sam Simon d Rod Daniel ph Bruce Surtees m Miles Goodman pd Kristi Zea ed Jack Hofstra
☆ Joe Pesci, Vincent Gardenia, Madolyn Smith-Osborne, Ruben Blades, Stacey Travis, Carole Shelley, Paul Benjamin
'A lesson, perhaps, that those movies that fail to get a theatrical release do, with the occasional exception, deserve the direct-to-video treatment.' – *Empire*
† The film was released direct to video in Britain.

The Super Cops
US 1974 94m Metrocolor
St Regis Films/UA
Two New York cops are suspended for breaking too many rules, but wage their private war on crime.
Low-life crime melodrama which plays effectively enough as a lighter-hearted Serpico.
w Lorenzo Semple Jnr *book* L. H. Whittemore d Gordon Parks Jnr ph Dick Kratina m Jerry Fielding
☆ Ron Leibman, David Selby, Sheila Frazier, Pat Hingle, Dan Frazer

Super Fuzz: see *Supersnooper*

'This Ain't No Game.'
Super Mario Brothers
👪 US 1993 104m Technicolor
Entertainment/Lightmotive/Allied/Cinergi (Jake Eberts, Roland Joffé)
📼 🖵 ◗

The Mario brothers, two plumbers, rescue a princess from a universe in another dimension, where reptilian humanoids, descended from dinosaurs, plan to rule both worlds.
An attempt to transfer a best-selling Nintendo video game to the screen; it doesn't work.
w Parker Bennett, Terry Runté, Ed Solomon, based on characters and concept created by Shigeru Miyamato, Takashi Tezuka d Rocky Morton, Annabel Jankel ph Dean Semler m Alan Silvestri pd David L. Snyder ed Caroline Ross sp Christopher Francis Woods, Patrick Tatopoulos
☆ Bob Hoskins, John Leguizamo, Dennis Hopper, Samantha Mathis, Fisher Stevens, Richard Edson, Rona Shaw, Dana Kaminski, Lance Henriksen
'There are plenty of gags, but not one laugh.' – *Variety*
'One and a half square miles of plywood went into the making of Super Mario Brothers, and that was just for the performances.' – *Sight and Sound*

Superdad

US 1974 95m Technicolor
Walt Disney

A lawyer is determined to rule the life of his teenage daughter.
Bumbling farce with frenzied and unattractive characters.
w Joseph L. McEveety d Vincent McEveety
ph Andrew Jackson m Buddy Baker
☆ Bob Crane, Barbara Rush, Kurt Russell, Joe Flynn, Kathleen Cody

Superfly

US 1972 98m Technicolor
Warner (Sig Shore)

The New York adventures of black cocaine peddlers.
'Sensational' comedy with violence in which the pushers exit laughing. Tedious and deplorable.
w Philip Fenty d Gordon Parks Jnr ph James Signorelli m Curtis Mayfield
☆ Ron O'Neal, Carl Lee, Sheila Frazier
'It suggests that New York is now nothing more than a concrete junkieyard.' – *Philip Strick*

Supergirl *

GB 1984 124m colour Panavision
Cantharus/Ilya Salkind (Timothy Burrill)

A Krypton power source falls into the hands of a power-hungry witch, and Supergirl is sent to retrieve it.
Playful comic strip spectacular which entertains in Wizard of Oz style for most of its way but was savaged by the critics.
w David Odell d Jeannot Szwarc ph Alan Hume m Jerry Goldsmith pd Richard MacDonald
☆ Helen Slater, Faye Dunaway, Peter O'Toole, Mia Farrow, Brenda Vaccaro, Peter Cook, Simon Ward, Marc McClure, Hart Bochner, David Healy

The Supergrass

GB 1985 105m colour
Recorded Releasing

The police unwisely believe that a boaster can lead them to a drug ring.
For those who enjoy the somewhat remote satirical humour of Channel 4's The Comic Strip.
w Pete Richens, Peter Richardson d Peter Richardson ph John Metcalfe m Keith Tippett
☆ Adrian Edmondson, Jennifer Saunders, Peter Richardson, Dawn French, Keith Allan, Robbie Coltrane, Alexei Sayle

Superman

US 1948 bw serial: 15 eps
Columbia

The man from Krypton who poses as mild-mannered Clark Kent combats The Spider Lady.
The subject makes this serial fairly lively – livelier in fact than the multi-million-dollar 1978 film.
d Spencer Bennet, Thomas Carr
☆ Kirk Alyn, Noel Neill, Tommy Bond, Carol Forman, George Meeker

'You'll believe a man can fly!'

Superman

US/GB 1978 142m colour
Panavision
Warner/Alexander Salkind (Pierre Spengler)

A baby saved from the planet Krypton when it explodes grows up as a newspaperman and uses his tremendous powers to fight evil and support the American way.
Long, lugubrious and only patchily entertaining version of the famous comic strip, with far too many irrelevant preliminaries and a misguided sense of its own importance.
w Mario Puzo, David Newman, Robert Benton, Leslie Newman d Richard Donner ph Geoffrey Unsworth m John Williams pd John Barry ed Stuart Baird sp various
☆ Christopher Reeve, Marlon Brando, Margot Kidder, Jackie Cooper, Glenn Ford, Phyllis Thaxter, Trevor Howard, Gene Hackman, Ned Beatty, Susannah York, Valerie Perrine
'Though one of the two or three most expensive movies made to date, it's cheesy-looking, and the plotting is so hit or miss that the story never seems to get started; the special effects are far

from wizardly and the editing often seems hurried and jerky just at the crucial points.' – *New Yorker*
'It gives the impression of having been made in panic – in fear that style or too much imagination might endanger its approach to the literal-minded.' – *Pauline Kael, New Yorker*
'The epitome of supersell.' – *Les Keyser, Hollywood in the Seventies*
† Reprehensible records were set by Brando getting three million dollars for a ten-minute performance (and then suing for a share of the gross); and by the incredible 7½-minute credit roll at the end.
†† Tiny roles were played by Noel Neill, who was Lois Lane in the TV series, and by Kirk Alyn, who was Superman in two serials.
♫ John Williams; editing; sound; visual effects

Superman 2

US 1980 127m Technicolor
Panavision
Warner/Alexander Salkind (Pierre Spengler)

Three renegade Kryptonians threaten Earth with a space bomb.
Half the first episode was devoted to a creaky and unnecessary setting up of plot and characters. This sequel is all the better for diving straight into action, but a classic it isn't, even of the comic strip kind.
w Mario Puzo, David Newman, Leslie Newman d Richard Lester ph Geoffrey Unsworth, Robert Paynter m Ken Thorne
☆ Christopher Reeve, Gene Hackman, Ned Beatty, Jackie Cooper, Sarah Douglas, Margot Kidder, Valerie Perrine, Susannah York, Terence Stamp, Jack O'Halloran, E. G. Marshall

Superman 3

GB 1983 125m colour Panavision
Dovemead/Cantharus (Pierre Spengler)

Synthetic Kryptonite warps Superman's character, but his conscience is reawakened by a plea from a small boy.
Sometimes humorous but overwritten and overacted variation on a tired theme. The special effects are the thing, but there's too much padding in between.
w David Newman, Leslie Newman d Richard Lester ph Robert Paynter m Ken Thorne pd Peter Murton
☆ Christopher Reeve, Richard Pryor, Jackie Cooper, Marc McClure, Annette O'Toole, Annie Ross, Pamela Stephenson, Robert Vaughn, Margot Kidder

Superman 4: The Quest for Peace

GB 1987 89m colour JDC
widescreen
Cannon

Superman determines that the world shall lay down its nuclear arms.
Stolid dialogue and poor technicalities are evident throughout what will surely be the last of the series.
w Lawrence Konner, Mark Rosenthal, Christopher Reeve d Sidney J. Furie
☆ Christopher Reeve, Gene Hackman, Jackie Cooper, Marc McClure, Sam Wanamaker, Mariel Hemingway, Margot Kidder

'Her heart cried out for love – yet her hands reached out to destroy!'

Supernatural *

US 1933 67m bw
Paramount (Victor and Edward Halperin)
A girl is possessed by the soul of a dead murderess.
Mad doctor nonsense, interestingly but not very successfully styled.
w Harvey Thew, Brian Marlow d Victor Halperin ph Arthur Martinelli
☆ Carole Lombard, H. B. Warner, Randolph Scott, Vivienne Osborne, Alan Dinehart
'A 65-minute ghost story that dies after the first half-hour.' – *Variety*

Supersnooper

Italy/US 1981 94m Technicolor
Columbia/Trans-Cinema TV (Maximilian Wolkoff)

aka: Super Fuzz
A Miami cop develops superhuman powers after being exposed to radiation.
Stolid comedy with poor special effects.

w Sergio Corbucci, Sabatino Giuffini d Sergio Corbucci ph Silvano Ippoliti m La Bionda pd Marco Dentici ed Eugene Ballaby
☆ Terence Hill (Mario Girotti), Ernest Borgnine, Joanne Dru, Marc Lawrence, Julie Gordon, Lee Sandman

Supervixens

US 1975 105m colour
Films International/September 19 (Russ Meyer)

Accused of the murder of his girlfriend, a garage mechanic goes on the run, pursued by a homicidal cop.
Inept, amateurish wallow in Meyer's simple-minded world of big-breasted nymphomaniacs and cuckolded men; film is, unfortunately, not one of Meyer's interests, but merely a means to what obsesses him.
wd Russ Meyer ph Russ Meyer m William Loose ad Michael Levesque ed Russ Meyer
☆ Shari Eubank, Charles Napier, Uschi Digard, Charles Pitts, Henry Rowland, Christy Hartburg, Sharon Kelly

Support Your Local Gunfighter

US 1971 92m DeLuxe
UA/Cherokee/Brigade (Bill Finnegan)

A con man jumps a train at a small mining town and is mistaken for a dreaded gunfighter.
Disappointing sequel to the following; just a couple of good jokes.
w James Edward Grant d Burt Kennedy ph Harry Stradling Jnr m Jack Elliott, Allyn Ferguson
☆ James Garner, Suzanne Pleshette, Joan Blondell, Jack Elam, Chuck Connors, Harry Morgan, Marie Windsor, Henry Jones, John Dehner

Support Your Local Sheriff **

US 1968 92m Technicolor
UA/Cherokee (William Bowers)

Gold is found near a Western village, and the resulting influx of desperate characters causes problems for the sheriff.
Amusing comedy, drawing on many Western clichés.
w William Bowers d Burt Kennedy ph Harry Stradling Jnr m Jeff Alexander
☆ James Garner, Joan Hackett, Walter Brennan, Jack Elam, Henry Morgan, Bruce Dern, Henry Jones
'It rejuvenates a stagnating genre by combining just the right doses of parody and affectionate nostalgia.' – *Jan Dawson*

Suppose They Gave a War and Nobody Came

US 1969 114m DeLuxe
Engel – Auerbach/ABC (Fred Engel)

Three accident-prone PROs try to give the army a good name in a town which wishes it would go away; they eventually cause panic by arriving at a dance in a tank.
Muddled farce which may have hoped to be satire.
w Don McGuire, Hal Captain d Hy Averback ph Burnett Guffey m Jerry Fielding
☆ Tony Curtis, Brian Keith, Ernest Borgnine, Ivan Dixon, Suzanne Pleshette, Tom Ewell, Bradford Dillman, Arthur O'Connell, Robert Emhardt, John Fiedler, Don Ameche

Sur: see South

El Sur: see The South

The Sure Thing

US 1985 94m DeLuxe
Roger Birnbaum/Monument/Embassy

Two uneasy couples travel west to California for Christmas.
Slightly unsettling youth comedy which, in the form of It Happened One Night, seems to be saying that friendship is more important than sex.
w Steven L. Bloom, Jonathan Roberts d Rob Reiner m Robert Elswit m Tom Scott
☆ John Cusack, Daphne Zuniga, Anthony Edwards, Boyd Gaines, Tim Robbins, Lisa Jane Persky, Viveca Lindfors
'Two sounds clash: old wine being poured into new bottles, and familiar barrels being scraped.' – *Philip French, Observer*

Surf Ninjas

US 1993 87m DeLuxe
Entertainment/New Line (Ezven Kolar)

Two Californian surfers discover that they are the rightful heirs to an island kingdom in the South China Sea, ruled by an evil dictator.
Jokey action film aimed at an audience too young to enjoy the real thing.
w Dan Gordon d Neal Israel m David Kitay pd Michael Novotny ed Tom Walls
☆ Leslie Nielsen, Ernie Reyes Jnr, Rob Schneider, Tone Loc, John Karlen, Ernie Reyes Snr, Kelly Hu
'Brain-dead though this film is, it has a certain goofy charm that's almost endearing.' – *Sight and Sound*

The Surfer

Australia 1988 94m colour
Night Flight (James M. Vernon, Frank Shields)
When a beach bum investigates the killing of a friend, he finds himself framed for murder, and embroiled with gangsters, crooked politicians and cops.
Low-budget thriller, directed with a certain nervy style but running out of energy before the end.
w David Marsh story Frank Shields d Frank Shields ph Michael Edols m Davood Tabrizi ed Greg Bell
☆ Gary Day, Gosia Dobrowolska, Rod Mullinar, Tony Barry, Gerard Maguire, Kris McQuade, Stephen Leeder

Surprise Package

GB 1960 100m bw
Columbia/Stanley Donen

An American gangster is deported to the same Mediterranean island as an exiled European king, whose crown gets stolen.
Flat and feeble comedy which defeats its stars.
w Harry Kurnitz novel Art Buchwald d Stanley Donen ph Christopher Challis m Benjamin Frankel
☆ Yul Brynner, Noël Coward, Mitzi Gaynor, Bill Nagy, Eric Pohlmann, George Coulouris, Warren Mitchell

Surrender

US 1931 69m bw
Fox

A French soldier in a German prison camp falls in love with a German girl at the nearby castle.
Flabby drama which seems constantly about to make symbolic points.
w S. N. Behrman, Sonya Levien play Axelle by Pierre Benoit d William K. Howard
☆ Warner Baxter, Leila Hyams, Ralph Bellamy, C. Aubrey Smith, William Pawley, Alexander Kirkland
'Anaemic picture product, not for A houses in big towns.' – *Variety*

Surrender

US 1987 95m TVC Color
Cannon (Aaron Spelling, Alan Greisman)

A writer with a history of unsatisfactory relationships with women falls for an artist who has had similar experiences with men.
Lacklustre attempt at a romantic comedy, taken at a snail's pace and with dialogue that fails to sparkle.
wd Jerry Belson ph Juan-Ruiz Anchia m Michel Colombier pd Lilly Kilvert ed Wendy Greene Bricmont
☆ Sally Field, Michael Caine, Steve Guttenberg, Peter Boyle, Jackie Cooper, Julie Kavner, Louise Lasser

Surrounded by Women: see Between Two Women

Survive

Mexico/US 1976 86m Technicolor
EMI/Robert Stigwood-Allan Carr/Conacine/Productora Filmica (Rene Cardona Jnr)

After a plane crash high in the Andes, surviving members of a rugby team resort to cannibalism in order to survive.
Unpleasant low-budget film, based on a true story and concentrating on the grislier aspects.
wd Rene Cardona Snr (English adaptation Martin Sherman) book Clay Blair Jnr ph Luis Medina m Gerald Fried ad A. L. de Guevara ed Marshall M. Borden

✫ Hugo Stiglitz, Norma Lazareno, Luz Aguilar, Fernando Larranaga, Lorenzo de Rodas, Luz Ma
'In its original form this low budget Mexican production clearly had little to offer: a sketchy script, feeble performances and scenes cloaked in fog which conveniently disguised polystyrene snow. Having been doctored in America for universal consumption, and fitted out with Dragnet-style commentary and limply banal dialogue, it is quite unbearable.' – *David McGillivray, MFB*
† The event was also the basis of the 1992 Hollywood movie *Alive* (qv).

Surviving Picasso
US/GB 1996 125m Technicolor
Warner/Merchant Ivory (Ismail Merchant, David L. Wolper)
📼 📼 ⊛ ◉
Françoise Gilot, an art student, becomes the mistress of Picasso and bears him two children before their relationship founders.
Dull biopic that wades through all the usual clichés of artistic life without once suggesting that it is dealing with characters of flesh and blood.
w Ruth Prawer Jhabvala *book Picasso: Creator and Destroyer* by Arianna Stassinopolous Huffington d James Ivory ph Tony Pierce-Roberts m Richard Robbins pd Luciana Arrighi ed Andrew Marcus
✫ Anthony Hopkins, Natascha McElhone, Julianne Moore, Joss Ackland, Peter Eyre, Jane Lapotaire, Joseph Maher, Bob Peck, Diane Venora, Joan Plowright
'A winner.' – *Variety*
'A film for middle-aged, middle-class people who know nothing about art.' – *Tracey Emin, Neon*

Surviving the Game
US 1994 96m DeLuxe
New Line/David Permut
📼
A homeless man turns the tables on six wealthy men who hunt him for sport.
This is yet another remake of Richard Connell's The Most Dangerous Game – and one that lacks drive or suspense as it strolls through very familiar territory.
w Eric Bernt d Ernest Dickerson ph Bojan Bazelli m Stewart Copeland pd Christiaan Wagener ed Sam Pollard
✫ Ice T, Rutger Hauer, Gary Busey, Charles S. Dutton, F. Murray Abraham, John C. McGinley, William McNamara, Jeff Corey
'Threadbare chase movie, which almost makes surviving the screening its own endurance test.' – *Variety*

The Survivors
US 1983 102m Metrocolor
Columbia-Delphi-Rastar-William Sackheim
📼 ⊛
An executive and a gas station attendant, both potential victims of a hit man, take refuge in the snowy mountains of Vermont.
Bewilderingly unfocused black comedy with some pleasant barbs along the way.
w Michael Leeson d Michael Ritchie ph Billy Williams m Paul Chihara pd Gene Callahan ed Richard A. Harris
✫ Walter Matthau, Robin Williams, Jerry Reed, James Wainwright, Kristen Vigard, Annie McEnroe

Susan and God *
US 1940 117m bw
MGM (Hunt Stromberg)
📼
GB title: *The Gay Mrs Trexel*
A flighty society woman gets religion but fails to practise what she preaches.
Unusual comedy-drama for MGM to tackle, but a fairly successful one for high-class audiences.
w Anita Loos play Rachel Crothers d George Cukor ph Robert Planck m Herbert Stothart
✫ Joan Crawford, Fredric March, Ruth Hussey, John Carroll, Rita Hayworth, Nigel Bruce, Bruce Cabot, Rita Quigley, Rose Hobart, Constance Collier, Gloria de Haven, Marjorie Main
'It's not a good comedy, but it has a certain fascination, because the theme is such an odd one for Hollywood to have attempted at all.' – *Pauline Kael, 70s*

'Thrill to them together!'
Susan Lenox, Her Fall and Rise *
US 1931 76m bw
MGM (Paul Bern)
GB title: *The Rise of Helga*
A farm girl flees to the city when her father tries to marry her off to a brute.
Moderate star melodrama with the star somewhat miscast.
w Wanda Tuchock *novel* David Graham Phillips d Robert Z. Leonard ph William Daniels
✫ Greta Garbo, Clark Gable, Jean Hersholt, John Miljan, Alan Hale
'A torrid romance that will fascinate the femmes.' – *Variety*
'If you like your romance spread thick, your passions strong and your Garbo hot, don't miss this.' – *Photoplay*
† The author of the book had been shot by a crank who disapproved of his treatment of women.

Susan Slade
US 1961 116m Technicolor
Warner (Delmer Daves)
An engineer brings his family back to San Francisco from Chile, and his teenage daughter runs into problems of the heart.
Stilted, busy sudser.
wd Delmer Daves *novel* Doris Hume ph Lucien Ballard m Max Steiner
✫ Connie Stevens, Troy Donahue, Dorothy McGuire, Lloyd Nolan, Brian Aherne, Natalie Schafer, Grant Williams, Bert Convy, Kent Smith

Susan Slept Here
US 1954 98m Technicolor
RKO (Harriet Parsons)
📼
The Hollywood scriptwriter of a film about youth problems agrees to look after a delinquent teenage girl.
Skittish, would-be piquant comedy; quite unattractive.
w Alex Gottlieb d Frank Tashlin ph Nicholas Musuraca md Leigh Harline songs Jack Lawrence, Richard Myers
✫ Dick Powell, Debbie Reynolds, Anne Francis, Glenda Farrell, Alvy Moore, Horace MacMahon
♫ song 'Hold My Hand'

Susannah of the Mounties *
👫 US 1939 78m bw
TCF (Kenneth MacGowan)
A little girl who is the only survivor of a wagon train massacre is looked after by the Canadian Mounties.
Adequate star action romance, Shirley's last real success.
w Robert Ellis, Helen Logan d William A. Seiter ph Arthur Miller md Louis Silvers
✫ Shirley Temple, Randolph Scott, Margaret Lockwood, J. Farrell MacDonald, Maurice Moscovich, Moroni Olsen, Victor Jory
'Strictly for the juvenile trade … illogical situations make it no more than a moderate fairy tale.' – *Variety*

Susan's Plan
US 1998 85m Foto-Kem
Kushner-Locke (Leslie Belzberg, Brad Wyman, John Landis)
📼 📼
A nursery teacher and her salesman lover hire two incompetents to kill her former husband so she can collect on his insurance.
Fast-paced but dreary farce, too bland in its approach to get any amusement from its theme of murder and greed.
wd John Landis ph Ken Kelsch m Peter Bernstein pd Stuart Blatt ed Nancy Morrison
✫ Natassja Kinski, Billy Zane, Michael Biehn, Rob Schneider, Lara Flynn Boyle, Carl Ballantine, Thomas Haden Church, Bill Duke, Lisa Edelstein, Sheree North, Dan Aykroyd

Suspect *
GB 1960 81m bw
British Lion/The Boulting Brothers
Government research chemists find a traitor in their midst.
Entertaining but fairly routine spy melodrama, shot on an experimental low budget but confined to lower berth bookings.

w Nigel Balchin *novel Sort of Traitors* by Nigel Balchin d Roy and John Boulting ph Max Greene md John Wilkes
✫ Tony Britton, Virginia Maskell, Peter Cushing, Ian Bannen, Raymond Huntley, Donald Pleasence, Thorley Walters, Spike Milligan, Kenneth Griffith
'A better standard of second feature film is badly needed, but the way to do it is not by making pictures which look as though they have strayed from TV.' – *Penelope Houston*

Suspect *
US 1987 121m colour
Columbia/Tri-Star (John Veitch)
📼 📼 ⊛ ◉
A public defender, with the aid of a member of the jury, uncovers high-level corruption when she defends a deaf-mute tramp accused of murder.
Despite its many implausibilities, a thriller that engages the attention.
w Eric Roth d Peter Yates ph Billy Williams m Michael Kamen pd Stuart Wurtzel ed Ray Lovejoy
✫ Cher, Dennis Quaid, Liam Neeson, John Mahoney, Joe Mantegna, Philip Bosco, E. Katherine Kerr, Fred Melamed, Lisbeth Bartlett, Paul D'Amato

'His was a strange secret! Hers was a strange love!'
The Suspect *
US 1944 84m bw
Universal (Islin Auster)
A henpecked husband kills his wife and is blackmailed.
Efficient studio-bound suspenser with theatrically effective acting.
w Bertram Millhauser *novel* James Ronald d Robert Siodmak ph Paul Ivano m Frank Skinner
✫ Charles Laughton, Henry Daniell, Rosalind Ivan, Ella Raines, Molly Lamont, Dean Harens
'High marks for tension, local colour, story.' – *William Whitebait*

Suspected Person
GB 1943 78m bw
Associated British
Thieves fall out and are tracked by police.
Slightly bitter crime drama which adequately filled half a bill.
wd Lawrence Huntington
✫ Clifford Evans, Patricia Roc, David Farrar, Robert Beatty

'Unmasking a beautiful woman's secret and unholy desires!'
Suspense
US 1946 103m bw
Monogram (Maurice and Frank King)
A tough guy crashes an ice palace and makes a play for the boss's skating star wife.
Heavy melodrama with skating interludes; remarkably similar in plot to the more famous Gilda. Chiefly remarkable as Monogram's most expensive film.
w Philip Yordan d Frank Tuttle ph Karl Struss
✫ Belita, Barry Sullivan, Albert Dekker, Bonita Granville, Eugene Pallette, George E. Stone, Leon Belasco

Suspicion **
US 1941 99m bw
RKO (Alfred Hitchcock)
📼 📼
A sedate young girl marries a playboy, and comes to suspect that he is trying to murder her.
Rather artificial and stiff Hitchcock suspenser, further marred by an ending suddenly switched to please the front office. Full of the interesting touches one would expect.
w Samson Raphaelson, Alma Reville, Joan Harrison *novel Before the Fact* by Francis Iles d Alfred Hitchcock ph Harry Stradling m Franz Waxman
✫ Joan Fontaine, Cary Grant, Nigel Bruce, Cedric Hardwicke, May Whitty, Isabel Jeans, Heather Angel, Leo G. Carroll
'The fact that Hitchcock throws in a happy end during the last five minutes, like a conjuror explaining his tricks, seems to me a pity; but it spoils the film only in retrospect, and we have already had our thrills.' – *William Whitebait, New Statesman*
🏆 Joan Fontaine
♫ best picture; Franz Waxman

'The only thing more terrifying than the last twelve minutes of this film is the first eighty!'
'Once you've seen it you will never again feel safe in the dark!'
Suspiria **
Italy 1976 97m Eastmancolor
Technovision
Seda Spettacoli (Claudio Argento)
📼 📼 📼 ⊛ ◉
A young American dance student arrives at dead of night at a continental academy where murder is the order of the day.
Psycho meets The Exorcist, with no holds barred: a genuinely scary thriller with gaudy visuals and a screaming sound track. A pyrotechnic display for those who can take it.
w Dario Argento, Daria Nicolodi d Dario Argento ph Luciano Tovoli m Dario Argento, Goblin
✫ Jessica Harper, Alida Valli, Joan Bennett, Stefania Casini, Udo Kier
'Thunderstorms and explicitly grotesque murders pile up as Argento happily abandons plot mechanics to provide a bravura display of his technical skill.' – *Time Out*

Sutter's Gold
US 1936 75m bw
Universal
During the California gold rush an immigrant has to fight for his rights when a strike starts on his land.
Patchily arresting Western which by costing much more than it should started the exit of Carl Laemmle from the chairman's office.
w Jack Kirkland, Walter Woods and George O'Neil d James Cruze
✫ Edward Arnold, Lee Tracy, Binnie Barnes, Katherine Alexander, Addison Richards, Montagu Love, John Miljan
† Most of the action footage was reused in a 1939 quickie, *Mutiny on the Blackhawk*.

'A thriller where nothing is black and white.'
Suture *
US 1993 96m bw
ICA/Scott McGehee, David Siegel
📼 📼 ⊛
A poor man suffering from amnesia after being injured in an explosion is mistaken for his wealthy half-brother and assumes his personality.
A stylish thriller, less concerned with the mechanics of a crime than questions of identity. Its main trick, as irritating as it is clever, is to have the two physically similar half-brothers played by very dissimilar actors, one white and the other black.
wd Scott McGehee, David Siegel ph Greg Gardiner m Cary Berger pd Kelly McGehee ed Lauren Zuckerman
✫ Dennis Haysbert, Mel Harris, Sab Shimono, Michael Harris, Dina Merrill
'An exceedingly smart and elegant American indie feature in a very unusual vein.' – *Variety*

Suzy *
US 1936 95m bw
MGM (Maurice Revnes)
📼
A French air ace of World War I marries an American showgirl; they then find that her former husband, thought dead, is still alive.
Proficient star comedy-drama with romance, action, comedy and a complex plot. A showcase for its stars.
w Dorothy Parker, Alan Campbell, Horace Jackson, Lenore Coffee *novel* Herbert Gorman d George Fitzmaurice ph Ray June m William Axt
✫ Jean Harlow, Cary Grant, Franchot Tone, Benita Hume, Lewis Stone
♫ song 'Did I Remember' (mWalter Donaldson, lyHarold Adamson)

Svart Lucia: see The Premonition

Svengali **
US 1931 81m bw
Warner
In 1890s Paris, a hypnotist turns a girl into a great opera singer but she does not reciprocate his love.
Victorian fantasy melodrama with a great grotesque part for the star and interesting artwork.
w J. Grubb Alexander *novel Trilby* by George du Maurier d Archie Mayo ph Barney McGill ad Anton Grot
✫ John Barrymore, Marian Marsh, Luis Alberni, Lumsden Hare, Donald Crisp, Paul Porcasi

---

'A slow and old-fashioned melodrama.' – *Variety*
'Barrymore never needed occult powers to be magnetic, but interest flags when he's offscreen.' – *New Yorker, 1978*

🎬 Barney McGill; Anton Grot

Svengali
GB 1954 82m Eastmancolor
Renown/Alderdale (Douglas Pierce)
▦

Flatulent remake which does have the virtue of following the original book illustrations but is otherwise unpersuasive.
wd Noel Langley *ph* Wilkie Cooper *m* William Alwyn *ad* Fred Pusey
☆ Donald Wolfit, Hildegarde Neff, Terence Morgan, Derek Bond, Paul Rogers, David Kossoff, Hubert Gregg, Noel Purcell, Alfie Bass, Harry Secombe

S.W.A.L.K.: see *Melody*

Swallows and Amazons
👫 GB 1974 92m Eastmancolor
EMI/Theatre Projects (Richard Pilbrow)
In the twenties four children have adventures in the Lake District.
Mild family film, great to look at but lacking in real excitement or style.
w David Wood *novel* Arthur Ransome *d* Claude Whatham *ph* Denis Lewiston *m* Wilfred Josephs
☆ Virginia McKenna, Ronald Fraser, Simon West, Sophie Neville, Zanna Hamilton, Stephen Grendon
'I have never read the Arthur Ransome classic but, if it is as dull as the film, I doubt I ever will … Everyone is frightfully prissy and well behaved.' – *Ken Russell, Fire over England*

Swamp Fire
US 1946 68m bw
Paramount/Pine-Thomas
The rehabilitation of a war veteran bar pilot in the treacherous waters at the mouth of the Mississippi.
Routine romantic melo, notable only as its star's only screen appearance in long trousers.
w Geoffrey Homes *d* William Pine
☆ Johnny Weissmuller, Buster Crabbe, Virginia Grey, Carol Thurston, Edwin Maxwell, Pedro de Cordoba

Swamp Thing
US 1981 91m Technicolor
UA/Swamp Films (Benjamin Melniker, Michael E. Uslan)
🔲 ▦ ◎~

A scientist, turned by accident into a cross between a man and a plant, battles against an evil colleague who wants to take over the world.
Less a horror pic, or a big-screen comic strip, more a sentimental story of vegetable love, it is about as interesting as watching grass grow.
wd Wes Craven *ph* Robin Goodwin *m* Harry Manfredini *ad* David Nichols, Robb Wilson King *ed* Richard Bracken *sp* William Munns
☆ Louis Jourdan, Adrienne Barbeau, Ray Wise, David Hess, Nicholas Worth, Don Knight
† It was followed by a sequel, *Return of The Swamp Thing* (qv).

Swamp Water **
US 1941 90m bw
TCF (Irving Pichel)
GB title: *The Man Who Came Back*
A fugitive holds out for years in the Okefenokee swamp, and affects the lives of the local township.
A strange little story, not very compelling as drama but with striking photography and atmosphere. Remade more straightforwardly as Lure of the Wilderness (qv).
w Dudley Nichols *story* Vereen Bell *d* Jean Renoir *m* Peverell Marley *m* David Buttolph
☆ Walter Huston, Walter Brennan, Anne Baxter, Dana Andrews, Virginia Gilmore, John Carradine, Eugene Pallette, Ward Bond, Guinn Williams
'So bad it's terrific.' – *Otis Ferguson*

The Swan *
US 1956 108m Eastmancolor
Cinemascope
MGM (Dore Schary)
▦ 🔲 ◎~
In 1910 Hungary, a girl of noble stock is groomed to marry the crown prince.

Interesting chiefly for a typical Hollywood reaction to a news event; about to lose their top star to a real life prince, MGM dusted off this old and creaky property for her last film. The star cast can't make much of it and the treatment is very heavy.
w John Dighton *play* Ferenc Molnar *d* Charles Vidor *ph* Robert Surtees *m* Bronislau Kaper *ad* Cedric Gibbons, Randall Duell
☆ Grace Kelly, Alec Guinness, Louis Jourdan, Agnes Moorehead, Jessie Royce Landis, Brian Aherne, Leo G. Carroll, *Estelle Winwood*, Robert Coote
'Balancing between artificial comedy and a no less artificial romantic theme, the film ultimately requires considerably greater finesse and subtlety in the handling.' – *Penelope Houston*

The Swan Princess
👫 US 1994 90m Technicolor
Columbia TriStar/International Nest/Rich Animal (Richard Rich, Jared F. Brown)
🎧

A wicked magician kidnaps a princess and turns her into a swan to force her to marry him.
Pleasant but unmemorable animated film, much in the Disney manner – its director is a former Disney animator – but lacking both charm and polish.
w Brian Nissen *d* Richard Rich *m* Lex de Azevedo *m/ly* David Zippel, Lex de Azevedo *ad* Mike Hodgson, James Coleman *ed* James Koford, Armetta Jackson-Hamlett
☆ Featuring the voices of: Jack Palance, Howard McGillin, Michelle Nicastro, John Cleese, Steven Wright, Steve Vinovich, Mark Harelik, James Arrington, Sandy Duncan
'Given the essential sentiment of the genre, it's decent value for the kids – not too frightening but possessed at least with a sense of magic and mystery in its better moments.' – *Derek Malcolm, Guardian*

Swanee River **
US 1939 84m Technicolor
TCF (Darryl F. Zanuck)
The life and loves of Stephen Foster.
Attractive, unsurprising family film in rich early colour, sparked by Jolson as E. P. Christy.
w John Taintor Foote, Philip Dunne *d* Sidney Lanfield *ph* Bert Glennon *md* Louis Silvers
☆ Don Ameche, *Al Jolson*, Andrea Leeds, Felix Bressart, Russell Hicks
'An unimpressive story: will hit profitable but not big b.o.' – *Variety*
🎬 Louis Silvers

'A murder … A lie … A secret shared.'
Swann *
GB/Canada 1996 95m colour
Guild/Shaftesbury/Greenpoint/Majestic/Norstar (Ann Scott, Christina Jennings)
In a small Canadian town, an American feminist arrives to research the life of a local poet, whose reputation is guarded by the librarian.
Teasing biographical mystery, given a heavy-handed treatment that obscures some of its meaning.
w David Young *novel* Carol Shields *d* Anna Benson Gyles *ph* Gerald Packer *m* Richard Rodney Bennett *pd* John Dondertman *ed* Robin Sales
☆ Miranda Richardson, Brenda Fricker, Michael Ontkean, David Cubitt, Sean McCann, John Neville, Sean Hewitt
'A gripping, affecting, deeply-felt film, wittily and compassionately scripted and superbly acted.' – *Philip Kemp, Sight and Sound*

Swann in Love **
France 1983 111m colour
Gaumont/FR3/SFPC/Bioskop/Films du Losange (Margaret Menegoz)
🔲 🔲
original title: *Un Amour de Swann*
An elegant Jew in 19th-century Paris society becomes obsessed by a beautiful demi-mondaine.
Reasonably successful attempt to film part of an unfilmable book. Comparisons with Letter from an Unknown Woman are inevitable.
w Peter Brook, Jean-Claude Carrière, Marie-Hélène Estienne, from the works of Marcel Proust *d* Volker Schlöndorff *ph* Sven Nykvist *m* Hans Werner Henze
☆ Jeremy Irons, Ornella Muti, Alain Delon, Fanny Ardant, Marie-Christine Barrault, Anne Bennent
'A film of more taste than vision.' – *Gilbert Adair, MFB*

'If you've read the original, forget it.' – *Volker Schlöndorff*
'A failure, maybe, but one that deserves to be seen.' – *Observer*

The Swarm
US 1978 116m Technicolor Panavision
Warner (Irwin Allen)
▦ ◎~
African killer bees menace the US.
Very obvious all-star disaster movie with risible dialogue. A box-office flop, probably because several TV movies had already tackled the same subject.
w Stirling Silliphant *novel* Arthur Herzog *d* Irwin Allen *ph* Fred J. Koenekamp *m* Jerry Goldsmith *sp* L. B. Abbott, Van Der Veer, Howard Jensen
☆ Michael Caine, Katharine Ross, Richard Widmark, Richard Chamberlain, Olivia de Havilland, Fred MacMurray, Ben Johnson, Lee Grant, José Ferrer, Patty Duke Astin, Slim Pickens, Bradford Dillman, Henry Fonda, Cameron Mitchell
'You could pass it all off as a sick joke, except that it cost twelve million dollars, twenty-two million bees, and several years of someone's life.' – *Guardian*
'The story is of a banality matched only by the woodenness of the acting.' – *Barry Took, Punch*

Swashbuckler *
👫 US 1976 101m Technicolor Panavision
Universal/Elliott Kastner (Jennings Lang)
▦ ◎~ ◎
GB title: *The Scarlet Buccaneer*
Rival pirates help a wronged lady.
Uninspired reworking of some old Errol Flynn ideas; the idea was pleasant, but the old style is sadly lacking.
w Jeffrey Bloom *d* James Goldstone *ph* Philip Lathrop *m* John Addison *pd* John Lloyd
☆ Robert Shaw, James Earl Jones, Peter Boyle, Geneviève Bujold, Beau Bridges, Geoffrey Holder
'This tacky pastepot job can't make up its mind whether it's serious, tongue-in-cheek, satirical, slapstick, burlesque, parody or travesty; but be assured it is all of the above.' – *Variety*
'The talented cast is left to play living statues, immobilized by dumb dialogue and awkward action.' – *Judith Crist*

Swedenhielms
Sweden 1935 90m bw
Svensk Filmindustri
A brilliant but spendthrift scientist, who has equally extravagant children, hopes that their troubles can be ended by his winning the Nobel Prize.
A domestic saga that never quite escapes from its theatrical origins; a superior soap opera kept buoyant by its performances.
w Stina Bergman *play* Hjalmar Bergman *d* Gustav Molander *ph* Ake Dahlquist *m* Eric Bengtson
☆ Gösta Ekman, Björn Berglund, Hakan Westergren, Tutta Rolf, Ingrid Bergman, Sigurd Wallen, Nils Eriksson, Karin Swanström

Sweeney! *
GB 1976 89m Technicolor
EMI/Euston (Ted Childs)
🔲🔲
Scotland Yard's Flying Squad investigates a suicide and uncovers an elaborate political blackmail scheme.
Enjoyable big screen version of a pacy, violent TV cop show.
w Ranald Graham *d* David Wickes *ph* Dusty Miller *m* Denis King
☆ John Thaw, Dennis Waterman, Barry Foster, Ian Bannen, Colin Welland, Michael Coles, Joe Melia

Sweeney 2
GB 1978 108m Technicolor
Euston Films (Ted Childs)
🔲🔲
The flying squad discovers that a series of armed bank robberies is being committed by a gang of expatriates who return from a luxurious Malta development for each caper.
Silly, sluggish and violent extension of thin material which would scarcely have made a good one-hour TV episode. There isn't even an exciting climax.

w Troy Kennedy Martin *d* Tom Clegg *ph* Dusty Miller *m* Tony Hatch
☆ John Thaw, Dennis Waterman, Barry Stanton, Denholm Elliott, Nigel Hawthorne, John Flanagan, David Casey

Sweeney Todd, the Demon Barber of Fleet Street *
GB 1936 68m bw
George King
▦
A barber kills his customers and makes them into 'mutton pies' for sale at the shop next door.
Decent version of a famous old melodrama; stilted as film-making, but preserving a swaggering star performance.
w Frederick Hayward, H. F. Maltby *play* George Dibdin-Pitt *d* George King *ph* Jack Parker *ad* Percy Bell *ed* John Seabourne
☆ Tod Slaughter, Bruce Seton, Eve Lister, Stella Rho, Ben Soutten, Johnny Singer, Eve Lister

Sweepings *
US 1933 77m bw
RKO
An ambitious Chicago merchant finds that his sons do not wish to emulate him.
Curious family melodrama based on fact; interesting but not exactly inspiring.
w Lester Cohen *novel* Lester Cohen *d* John Cromwell *ph* Edward Cronjager *m* Max Steiner
☆ Lionel Barrymore, Alan Dinehart, Eric Linden, William Gargan, Gloria Stuart, Gregory Ratoff
'Nothing to interest the women and a subject too sombre to interest the men.' – *Variety*

Sweet Adeline
US 1934 85m bw
Warner (Edward Chodorov)
▦
In the 1890s, the daughter of a beer garden owner attracts the attention of a composer and becomes a Broadway star.
Unexceptionable, and quite forgotten, adaptation of a pleasant, old-fashioned Broadway musical.
w Erwin S. Gelsey *play* Jerome Kern, Oscar Hammerstein II, Harry Armstrong, Dick Gerard *d* Mervyn Le Roy *ph* Sol Polito *m/ly* Jerome Kern, Oscar Hammerstein II *ch* Bobby Connolly *ad* Robert Haas
☆ Irene Dunne, Donald Woods, Ned Sparks, Hugh Herbert, Wini Shaw, Louis Calhern, Nydia Westman, Joseph Cawthorn
'As a production in the bigtime musical class, but strictly on merit it rates no better than fair.' – *Variety*

Sweet Aloes: see *Give Me Your Heart*

Sweet and Lowdown
US 1999 95m Technicolor
Columbia TriStar/Sweetland/Magnolia (Jean Doumanian)
▦ ◎ 🎧
In the 1930s, a self-obsessed jazz guitarist enjoys fame and misfortune.
Done in the style of a biopic, this is a delightfully inventive comedy, in love with the period and its music and able to communicate that emotion to its audience; the central performances of Penn, as the musician destructive of himself and others, and Samantha Morton, as his mute admirer, are excellent.
wd Woody Allen *ph* Zhao Fei *m* Dick Hyman *pd* Santo Loquasto *ed* Alisa Lepselter *cos* Laura Cunningham Bauer
☆ Sean Penn, Samantha Morton, Uma Thurman, Brian Markinson, Anthony LaPaglia, Gretchen Mol, Vincent Guastaferro, John Waters, Constance Schulman, Kellie Overbey
'Woody Allen's most delightful film in perhaps ten years.' – *Angie Errigo, Empire*
† Howard Alden dubbed Sean Penn's guitar playing.
🎬 Sean Penn; Samantha Morton

'A Promise Of Heaven. A Journey Into Hell.'
Sweet Angel Mine
GB/Canada 1996 88m colour
Optimum/HandMade/Mass Productions/ImagexBritish Screen/Telefilm Canada/NSFDC/Statescreen/Picture Palace (Sam Taylor, Christopher Zimmer)
🔲🔲
A Londoner, who goes to Novia Scotia to search for his long-lost father, stumbles across a remote farm occupied by three women.

Feeble horror with unconvincing characters, far-fetched narrative contrivances, and, after its slow-moving first half, a frenetic, gruesome finale.

w Sue Maheu, Tim Willocks *screenplay* Love's Executioners by Tim Willocks d Curtis Radclyffe ph Witold Stok m John McCarthy pd Maria Djurkovic ed Anne Sopel

☆ Oliver Milburn, Margaret Langrick, Anna Massey, Alberta Watson

'Isn't bad enough to be real fun and isn't good enough to convince on any level except the plain silly.' – *Derek Elley, Variety*

'He used love like most men use money!'

Sweet Bird of Youth *
US   1962   120m   Metrocolor   Cinemascope
MGM/Roxbury (Pandro S. Berman)

A Hollywood drifter brings an ageing glamour star back to his home town, but runs into revenge from the father of a girl he had seduced.
Emasculated version of an overwrought play with the author's usual poetic squalor; comatose patches alternate with flashes of good acting and diverting dialogue, but the wide screen and heavy colour don't direct the attention.

wd Richard Brooks *play* Tennessee Williams ph Milton Krasner m Harold Gellman md Robert Armbruster

☆ Paul Newman, Geraldine Page, Ed Begley, Mildred Dunnock, Rip Torn, Shirley Knight, Madeleine Sherwood

♦ Ed Begley

♢ Geraldine Page; Shirley Knight

'Love is what it's all about!'

Sweet Charity *
US   1969   149m   Technicolor   Panavision 70
Universal (Robert Arthur)

A New York taxi dancer dreams of love.
A revue-type musical bowdlerized from Fellini's Le notti di Cabiria accords ill with real New York locations, especially as its threads of plot come to nothing; but behind the camera are sufficient stylists to ensure striking success with individual numbers.

w Peter Stone *play* Neil Simon d Robert Fosse ph Robert Surtees m Cy Coleman md Joseph Gershenson ly Dorothy Fields

☆ Shirley MacLaine, Ricardo Montalban, John McMartin, Chita Rivera, Paula Kelly, Stubby Kaye, Sammy Davis Jnr

'The kind of platinum clinker designed to send audiences flying towards the safety of their television sets.' – *Rex Reed*

♢ Cy Coleman (as music director)

Sweet Dreams
US   1985   115m   Technicolor
Tri-Star/HBO/Silver Screen (Bernard Schwartz)

The effect on her marriage of the rise to success of folk singer Patsy Cline.
Pleasant, muted, unremarkable modern biopic.

w Robert Getchell d Karel Reisz ph Robbie Greenberg m Charles Gross

☆ Jessica Lange, Ed Harris, Ann Wedgeworth, David Clennon, James Staley

♢ Jessica Lange

'The Story Of Two Women's Struggle For Survival, Self-Respect And Hard Currency.'

Sweet Emma, Dear Böbe *
Hungary   1992   78m   Eastmancolor
Objektiv/Manfred Durniok Filmproduktion (Lajos Ovari, Gabriella Groz)

original title: édes Emma, Drága Böbe – Vazlatok, Aktok

Two young female teachers move to Budapest to work, sharing a tatty room together.
A well-made, engrossing study of glum lives.

w István Szabó, Andrea Veszits d István Szabó ph Lajos Koltai m Richard Schumann pd Attila Kovacs ed Eszter Kovacs

☆ Johanna Ter Steege, Eniko Börcsök, Peter Andorai

'The realities of day-to-day life in post-Communist Hungary are vividly brought to life in this compassionate, memorable film. Though the settings and narrative are understandably bleak, the treatment throbs with life and love, resulting in a most satisfying film.' – *Variety*
'The best movie to date about the way ordinary Central Europeans are experiencing the

cataclysmic changes following the collapse of Communism.' – *Philip French, Observer*

Sweet Hearts Dance
US   1988   101m   Technicolor
Columbia TriStar/Bright Star/Tri-Star ML Delphi Premier Productions (Jeffrey Lurie)

A small-town couple experience marital problems.
A drama of small incidents that never builds into a coherent whole.

w Ernest Thompson d Robert Greenwald ph Tak Fujimoto m Richard Gibbs pd James Allen ed Robert Florio, Janet Bartells

☆ Don Johnson, Susan Sarandon, Jeff Daniels, Elizabeth Perkins, Kate Reid, Justin Henry, Holly Marie Combs, Heather Coleman

The Sweet Hereafter ***
Canada   1997   112m   colour   Panavision
Electric/Speaking Parts/Alliance/Ego (Camelia Frieberg, Atom Egoyan)

A lawyer arrives in a small town to persuade parents, who are grieving over the deaths of 14 children killed in a school bus accident, to let him represent them.
A complex and compelling retelling of a tragic event, flashing back and forward in time to present the details of intertwined lives on the brink of disaster.

wd Atom Egoyan *novel* Russell Banks ph Paul Sarossy m Mychael Danna pd Philip Barker ed Susan Shipton

☆ Ian Holm, Maury Chaykin, Gabrielle Rose, Peter Donaldson, Bruce Greenwood, David Hemblen, Brooke Johnson, Arsinée Khanjian

'The cumulative impact is, by this director's standards, disappointingly uni-dimensional and almost banal.' – *Sheila Johnston, Screen International*
'A film of great scrupulousness and restraint, with few false notes.' – *Richard Williams, Guardian*

♢ Atom Egoyan (as director and as writer)

Sweet Kitty Bellairs
US   1930   60m   Technicolor
Warner

A romance of stagecoach days set in Bath.
A decided curiosity to come from this studio in Little Caesar days, and not a successful one.

w Hermann Harrison *play* David Belasco *novel* Agnes and Egerton Castle d Alfred E. Green

☆ Claudia Dell, Ernest Torrence, Walter Pidgeon, June Collyer, Perry Askam, Lionel Belmore, Flora Finch

'Artistic achievement, but weak on fan pull.' – *Variety*

Sweet Liberty
US   1986   107m   colour
Universal/Martin Bregman

A college professor is disgusted as he watches the Hollywood filming of his historical novel.
A good idea surprisingly wasted: the plot turns to tedium before the half-way mark.

wd Alan Alda ph Frank Tidy m Bruce Broughton pd Ben Edwards ed Michael Economou

☆ Alan Alda, Michael Caine, Michelle Pfeiffer, Lillian Gish, Bob Hoskins, Saul Rubinek, Lois Chiles, Lise Hilboldt

The Sweet Life: see La Dolce Vita

Sweet Lorraine *
US   1987   91m   colour
Autumn Pictures (Steve Gomer)

The owner of a rundown hotel in the Catskills has her granddaughter spend the summer working for her.
Gentle and charming film, strong on character.

w Michael Zettler, Shelly Altman d Steve Gomer ph Rene Ohashi m Richard Robbins pd David Gropman ed Laurence Solomon

☆ Maureen Stapleton, Trini Alvarado, Lee Richardson, John Bedford Lloyd, Freddie Roman

Sweet Music
US   1934   100m   bw
Warner

An orchestra leader and a girl singer spar a lot but finally make it up.

The slimmest of stories stretches over a few good numbers and some snappy dialogue; but it's all too long.

w Jerry Wald, Carl Erickson and Warren Duff d Alfred E. Green

☆ Rudy Vallee, Ann Dvorak, Ned Sparks, Helen Morgan, Allen Jenkins, Alice White, Robert Armstrong

Sweet November
US   1968   113m   Technicolor
Warner Seven Arts/Jerry Gershwin, Elliott Kastner

An English tycoon in New York meets a girl who takes a new lover every month because she hasn't long to live.
Irritating exercise in eccentric sentimentality, not helped by twitchy stars.

w Herman Raucher d Robert Ellis Miller ph Daniel L. Fapp m Michel Legrand

☆ Anthony Newley, Sandy Dennis, Theodore Bikel, Burr de Benning

Sweet Revenge: see Dandy the All-American Girl

The Sweet Ride
US   1967   110m   DeLuxe   Panavision
TCF (Joe Pasternak)

Surfers and drop-outs on a California beach have woman trouble.
Teenage melodrama, well produced but abysmal of content.

w Tom Mankiewicz *novel* William Murray d Harvey Hart ph Robert B. Hauser m Pete Rugolo

☆ Jacqueline Bisset, Tony Franciosa, Michael Sarrazin, Bob Denver, Michael Wilding

Sweet Rosie O'Grady *
US   1943   79m   Technicolor
TCF (William Perlberg)

A Police Gazette reporter tries to uncover the past of a musical comedy star.
Pleasant 1890s musical with plenty of zest but a lack of good numbers. A typical success of the war years.

w Ken Englund d Irving Cummings ph Ernest Palmer ch Hermes Pan ad James Basevi, Joseph C. Wright *songs* Mack Gordon, Harry Warren

☆ Betty Grable, Robert Young, Adolphe Menjou, Reginald Gardiner, Virginia Grey, Phil Regan, Sig Rumann, Hobart Cavanaugh, Alan Dinehart

† Remake of *Love Is News*; remade as *That Wonderful Urge.*

'This is the story of J.J. – but not the way he wants it told!'

Sweet Smell of Success ****
US   1957   96m   bw
UA/Norma/Curtleigh (James Hill)

A crooked press agent helps a megalomaniac New York columnist break up his sister's romance.
Moody, brilliant, Wellesian melodrama put together with great artificial style; the plot matters less than the photographic detail and the skilful manipulation of decadent characters, bigger than life-size.

w Clifford Odets, Ernest Lehman d Alexander Mackendrick ph James Wong Howe m Elmer Bernstein ad Edward Carrere

☆ Burt Lancaster, Tony Curtis, Martin Milner, Sam Levene, Susan Harrison, Barbara Nichols, Emile Meyer

'A sweet slice of perversity, a study of dollar and power worship.' – *Pauline Kael*

Sweet Sweetback Baad Asssss Song **
US   1971   97m   CFI color
Yeah

A black boy grows up in a brothel to become a womanizer and cop-killer.
Seminal, anarchic, anti-establishment movie that led to the blaxploitation boom of the 70s and beyond; it is fuelled by a righteous anger.

wd Melvin Van Peebles ph Bob Maxwell m Melvin Van Peebles ed Melvin Van Peebles

☆ Melvin Van Peebles, Rhetta Hughes, Simon Chuckster, John Amos, Hubert Scales, John Dullaghan, West Gale, Mario Van Peebles

'A slight, pale escape drama about a black man.' – *Vincent Canby, New York Times*
'Perhaps not the classic which some critics have proclaimed it, this is still an effective counterblast against racist violence and stereotyping.' – *Sight and Sound*

† Before listing individual performers, the credits begin: 'Starring The Black Community and Brer Soul.' The film is dedicated 'to all the Brothers and Sisters who have had enough of The Man.'

Sweet William
GB   1980   90m   Eastmancolor
Kendon

A London girl discovers that her American lover is constantly unfaithful.
A situation in search of a story makes this slight piece with its wry observations rather less memorable than the average TV play.

w Beryl Bainbridge *novel* Beryl Bainbridge d Claude Whatham ph Les Young md Marcus Dods pd Eileen Diss

☆ Sam Waterston, Jenny Agutter, Anna Massey, Daphne Oxenford, Arthur Lowe, Geraldine James

Sweetheart of the Campus
US   1941   64m   bw
Columbia (Jack Fier)

GB title: Broadway Ahead

A college principal objects to Ozzie Nelson's band playing at a nearby night spot.
Evanescent musical filler.

w Robert D. Andrews, Edmund Hartmann d Edward Dmytryk ph Franz F. Planer md M. W. Stoloff ad Lionel Banks ed William Lyon

☆ Ruby Keeler, Ozzie Nelson, Harriet Hilliard, Gordon Oliver, Don Beddoe, Kathleen Howard

Sweethearts **
US   1938   120m   Technicolor
MGM (Hunt Stromberg)

Two stars of the musical stage never stop fighting each other.
The lightest and most successful of the MacDonald/Eddy musicals, with an excellent script, production and cast.

w Dorothy Parker, Alan Campbell d W. S. Van Dyke ph Oliver Marsh, Allen Davey m Victor Herbert md Herbert Stothart

☆ Jeanette MacDonald, Nelson Eddy, Frank Morgan, Ray Bolger, Florence Rice, Mischa Auer, Fay Holden, Reginald Gardiner, Herman Bing, Allyn Joslyn, Raymond Walburn, Lucile Watson, Gene Lockhart

'It will disappoint because of length, and general lethargy and sameness of production values.' – *Variety*

♦ Special Award to Oliver Marsh and Allen Davey for 'colour photography'

♢ Herbert Stothart

Sweetie **
Australia   1989   100m   colour
Electric/Arena Film (John Maynard)

A woman with marital problems is visited by her unbalanced but exuberant sister.
Deliberately off-balance movie that explores the dynamic of family relationships and stifled lives.

w Gerard Lee, Jane Campion d Jane Campion ph Sally Bongers m Martin Armiger ad Peter Harris ed Veronika Haussler

☆ Genevieve Lemon, Karen Colston, Tom Lycos, Jon Darling, Dorothy Barry, Michael Lake, Andre Pataczek, Jean Hadgraft

Swell Guy
US   1946   86m   bw
Mark Hellinger/Universal-International

A war correspondent comes home to visit his family but turns out to be something of a heel.
Ironical drama which deserved better casting and handling.

w Richard Brooks *play* The Hero by Gilbert Emery d Frank Tuttle

☆ Sonny Tufts, Ann Blyth, Ruth Warrick, William Gargan, John Litel, Thomas Gomez, Millard Mitchell, Mary Nash

Swept from the Sea: see Amy Foster

'They had the pools – but he had their wives!'

The Swimmer *

US 1968 94m Technicolor
Columbia/Horizon/Dover (Frank Perry, Roger Lewis)
▣ ☍

A man clad only in trunks swims his way home via the pools of his rich friends, and arrives home to find that his success is a fantasy.
Strange but compelling fable, too mystifying for popular success, about the failure of the American dream. Annoyingly inexplicit, but well made and sumptuously photographed in a variety of Connecticut estates.
w Eleanor Perry *short stories* John Cheever
d Frank Perry, Sydney Pollack ph David L. Quaid
m Marvin Hamlisch
☆ Burt Lancaster, Janice Rule, Kim Hunter, Diana Muldaur, Cornelia Otis Skinner, Marge Champion

The Swimmer **

USSR 1981 105m bw/colour
Gruzia Film
original title: *Plovec*
A middle-aged man invades a film set to recount the exploits of his father and grandfather, famous swimmers who were cheated of their success.
The film's subtitle provides an indication of the contents: 'Twenty-two little stories from the life of three swimmers', but not the charm. It was banned by the Soviets for a time, presumably because of its celebration of individuality.
wd Irakli Kvirikadze ph Turam Tugshi
m Teimuraz Bakuradze
☆ Elgudza Burduli, Ruslan Mikaberidze, Baadur Tsuladze, Guram Pirtskhalava, Nana Kvachantiradze, Gia Lezhava, Imedo Kahkiani

Swimming to Cambodia **

US 1987 87m colour Panavision
Mainline/Cinecom International/The Swimming Co (R. A. Shafransky)
▣ ▦ ☍

An actor who played a bit part in *The Killing Fields* reminisces about his experiences in Thailand.
Witty and fascinating one-man show, skilfully filmed.
w Spalding Gray d Jonathan Demme ph John Bailey m Laurie Anderson pd Sandy McLeod
ed Carol Littleton
☆ Spalding Gray

Swimming with Sharks *

US 1995 93m colour
Starlight/Cineville/Neofight/Mama'z Boy (Steve Alexander, Joanne Moore)
▣ ▦

A new assistant to a tyrannical film studio executive turns the tables on his boss.
Tart black comedy on Hollywood excesses, one that enjoys the monsters it puts on display.
wd George Huang ph Steven Finestone m Tom Heil, Marco d'Ambrosio pd Veronika Merlin, Cecil Gentry ed Ed Marx
☆ Kevin Spacey, Frank Whaley, Benicio del Toro, Michelle Forbes, T. E. Russell, Roy Dotrice, Matthew Flynt
'A small, catty addendum to the cinema of office drudgery.' – *Tom Shone, Sunday Times*

The Swindlers: see Il Bidone

Swing

US 1998 98m CFI color
Entertainment/Kushner-Locke/Alpine (Su Lim, Louise Rosner)
In Liverpool, an ex-convict who learned to play the saxophone inside tries to form a swing band.
Dire would-be comedy that makes its many clichés seem even more dated than swing itself.
wd Nick Mead ph Ian Wilson m Ian Devaney
pd Richard Bridgland ed Norman Buckley
☆ Hugo Speer, Lisa Stansfield, Tom Bell, Rita Tushingham, Alexei Sayle, Paul Usher, Danny McCall, Clarence Clemons, Tom Georgeson
'The film, a light comedy, is clearly not meant to be deep, but its laziness makes it seem excessively shallow.' – *Edward Porter, Sunday Times*

The Swing **

West Germany 1983 133m colour
Pelemele Film/Roxy/Pro-Ject (Percy Adlon)
original title: *Die Schaukel*
In the 1930s an elderly novelist recalls her childhood with her exuberant brothers and sisters and improvident mother and father.
Charming and humorous evocation of family life.
wd Percy Adlon *novel* Annette Kolb d Percy Adlon ph Jürgen Martin m Peer Raben
☆ Anja Jaenicke, Rolf Illig, Christine Kaufmann, Lena Stolze, Joachim Bernhard, Susanne Herlet

Swing Fever

US 1943 80m bw
MGM
A bandleader uses hypnotism to train a boxer.
Witless farrago with sprightly musical numbers.
w Nat Perrin, Warren Wilson d Tim Whelan
☆ Kay Kyser and his band, Marilyn Maxwell, Nat Pendleton, William Gargan, Lena Horne

Swing High Swing Low **

US 1937 97m bw
Paramount (Arthur Hornblow Jnr)
▣

A talented trumpeter goes on a bender but is rescued by his wife.
Backstage comedy-drama, a beautifully cinematic version of a very tedious story also filmed as Dance of Life *(1929) and* When My Baby Smiles at Me *(1948).*
w Virginia Van Upp, Oscar Hammerstein II *play* Burlesque *by* George Manker Watters, Arthur Hopkins d Mitchell Leisen ph Ted Tetzlaff
m Victor Young md Boris Morros
☆ Carole Lombard, Fred MacMurray, Charles Butterworth, Jean Dixon, Dorothy Lamour, Harvey Stephens, Franklin Pangborn, Anthony Quinn
'No reason to believe it won't jam 'em at the gate … it's a cinch for the younger trade, and will satisfy general audience standards.' – *Variety*
'Enough concentrated filmcraft to fit out half a dozen of those gentlemen who are always dashing around in an independent capacity making just the greatest piece of cinema ever.' – *Otis Ferguson*

Swing Kids

🏠 US 1993 114m Technicolor
Buena Vista/Hollywood (Mark Gordon, John Bard Manulis)
▣ ▦ ☍ ☊

In Germany during the rise of the Nazis, a group of young men is trapped between the attractions of American swing music and the Hitler Youth.
An extremely peculiar movie, which makes little attempt at a period authenticity, apart from its music, and seems unlikely to appeal to any audience, least of all the young.
w Jonathan Marc Feldman d Thomas Carter
ph Jerzy Zielinski m James Horner pd Allan Cameron ed Michael R. Miller
☆ Robert Sean Leonard, Christian Bale, Frank Whaley, Barbara Hershey, Kenneth Branagh, Tushka Bergen, David Tom, Julia Stemberger
'Apart from its appealing young cast and period score, it has precious little to entice audiences.' – *Variety*

Swing Shift

US 1984 100m Technicolor
Warner/Lantana/Hawn-Sylbert/Jerry Bick
▣ ▦ ☍

During World War II, in her husband's absence at war, a woman factory hand has an affair with a co-worker.
Surprisingly dreary romantic drama on a subject which could at least have had a livelier surface despite the lack of surprise in what passes for plot.
w 'Rob Morton' (Ron Nyswaner, Bo Goldman, Nancy Dowd) d Jonathan Demme ph Tak Fujimoto m Patrick Williams pd Peter Jamison
ed Craig McKay
☆ Goldie Hawn, Kurt Russell, Christine Lahti, Fred Ward, Ed Harris
'Bland, muddled and inconclusive.' – *Steve Jenkins, MFB*
♟ Christine Lahti (supporting actress)

Swing, Teacher, Swing: see College Swing

Swing Time **

US 1936 103m bw
RKO (Pandro S. Berman)
▣ ▦ ☍

A dance team can't get together romantically because he has a commitment to a girl back home.
Satisfactory but unexciting musical vehicle for two stars at the top of their professional and box-office form.
w Howard Lindsay, Allan Scott d George Stevens
ph David Abel md Nathaniel Shilkret

ch Hermes Pan *songs* Jerome Kern, Dorothy Fields
☆ Fred Astaire, Ginger Rogers, Victor Moore, Helen Broderick, Eric Blore, Betty Furness, George Metaxa
♫ 'Pick Yourself Up'; 'A Fine Romance'; 'Never Gonna Dance'; 'The Way You Look Tonight'.
♟ song 'The Way You Look Tonight'
♟ Hermes Pan

Swing Your Lady *

US 1937 77m bw
Warner (Sam Bischoff)
A promoter gets involved in the problems of a hillbilly wrestler.
Minor comedy with some laughs.
w Joseph Schrank, Maurice Leo *story* Toehold on Artemus *by* H. R. Marsh d Ray Enright ph Arthur Edeson m Adolph Deutsch
☆ Humphrey Bogart, Louise Fazenda, Nat Pendleton, Frank McHugh, Penny Singleton, Allen Jenkins, Ronald Reagan, The Weaver Brothers and Elviry
'A comedy of not immense proportions, it is nevertheless a rollicking, considerably different laugh-piece which should do from average to good business everywhere.' – *Variety*

The Swinger

US 1966 81m Technicolor
Paramount/George Sidney
When a girl writer's wholesome stories are rejected, she pretends to have a naughty past.
With-it comedy which audiences preferred to be without.
w Lawrence Roman d George Sidney ph Joseph Biroc m Marty Paich
☆ Ann-Margret, Tony Franciosa, Robert Coote, Yvonne Romain, Horace MacMahon, Nydia Westman
'A hectically saucy mixture of lechery, depravity, perversion, voyeurism and girlie magazines … a heavy, witless pudding.' – *MFB*

'Get a nightlife.'
Swingers *

US 1996 96m DeLuxe
Miramax/Independent/Alfred Shay (Victor Simpkins)
▣ ▦ ☍ ⊚

Hung up on a failed love affair, a struggling comedian hopes for success in Hollywood, and parties with his friends.
Slick and very knowing movie about a bunch of losers; it is sometimes amusing, but its superficiality soon becomes wearing.
w Jon Favreau d Doug Liman ph Doug Liman
m Justin Reinhardt pd Brad Halvorson
ed Stephen Mirrione
☆ Jon Favreau, Vince Vaughn, Ron Livingston, Patrick Van Horn, Alex Desert, Deena Martin, Katherine Kendall, Heather Graham
'Engaging, refreshingly human in its humor and becomingly modest in its aspirations, this hip look at being out of it announces some promising new talent.' – *Todd McCarthy, Variety*
'So loaded with goodies that cinema-goers cannot really afford to miss it.' – *Marianne Gray, Film Review*

The Swinging Maiden: see The Iron Maiden

Swirl of Glory: see Sugarfoot

The Swiss Conspiracy

US/Germany 1975 88m colour
Baveria Atelier/Durham (Maurice Silverstein)
▣ ▦

When a blackmailer threatens to reveal the secret accounts of its wealthy clients, a Swiss bank hires an American former agent to investigate.
Dreary thriller, in which acting, direction and writing conspire to be as uninteresting as possible.
w Norman Klenman, Philip Saltzman, Michael Stanley d Jack Arnold ph W. P. Hassenstein
m Klaus Doldinger pd Rolf Zehetbauer
ed Murray Jordan
☆ David Janssen, Senta Berger, John Ireland, John Saxon, Anton Diffring, Arthur Brauss, Elke Sommer, Ray Milland

The Swiss Family Robinson

🏠 US 1940 93m bw
(RKO)
A shipwrecked family builds a new home on a desert island.

Pleasing low-budgeter.
w Gene Towne, Graham Baker, Walter Ferris
novel Johann Wyss d Edward Ludwig
ph Nicholas Musuraca
☆ Thomas Mitchell, Edna Best, Freddie Bartholomew, Tim Holt, Terry Kilburn
'In outlook, dialogue and manner it is frankly old-fashioned.' – *MFB*

The Swiss Family Robinson *

🏠 GB 1960 126m Technicolor
Panavision
Walt Disney (Bill Anderson, Basil Keys)
▣ ▦ ☍

Quite pleasing comedy adventure from the children's classic.
w Lowell S. Hawley d Ken Annakin ph Harry Waxman m William Alwyn
☆ John Mills, Dorothy McGuire, James MacArthur, Tommy Kirk, Kevin Corcoran, Janet Munro, Sessue Hayakawa, Cecil Parker

Swiss Miss *

🏠 US 1938 73m bw
(MGM)
▣ ▦ ✪

Two mousetrap salesmen in Switzerland run into trouble with a cook, a gorilla and two opera singers.
Operetta style vehicle which constrains its stars, since their material is somewhat below vintage anyway. Not painful to watch, but disappointing.
w James Parrott, Felix Adler, Charles Nelson
d John G. Blystone ph Norbert Brodine
m/ly Phil Charig, Arthur Quenzer md Marvin Hatley ed Bert Jordan
☆ Stan Laurel, Oliver Hardy, Walter Woolf King, Della Lind, Eric Blore
'Story, production, acting and direction suggest a revival of early sound filmusicals presented with stage technique.' – *Variety*

The Swissmakers

Switzerland 1978 108m Eastmancolor
Lyssy/Rex/Willora/Schoch/Ecco
Cases of a department investigating applicants for naturalization.
Amusing satirical comedy which presumably has more bite in its home territory.
w Rolf Lyssy, Christa Maerker d Rolf Lyssy
ph Fritz Maeder m Jonas Haefeli
☆ Walo Luond, Emil Steinberger, Beatrice Kessler

'For a ladykiller like Steve there was a fate worse than death: when he got to heaven they sent him back … with some modifications … It's tough being a woman in a man's world.'
Switch

US 1991 103m Technicolor Panavision
Columbia TriStar/Odyssey-Regency/HBO/Cinema Plus/LP/Beco (Tony Adams)
▣ ▦ ☍ ⊚

Murdered by old flames, a male chauvinist is sent back to Earth as a woman and told that he can live again if he can find a woman who likes him.
Bizarre farce that relies on the most obvious of sex-change jokes.
wd Blake Edwards ph Dick Bush m Henry Mancini pd Rodger Maus ed Robert Pergament
☆ Ellen Barkin, Jimmy Smits, JoBeth Williams, Lorraine Bracco, Tony Roberts, Perry King, Bruce Martyn Payne, Lysette Anthony, Victoria Mahoney
'A talented cast is wasted on a witless script.' – *Sunday Telegraph*

'The hunter is tracking the killer. But the killer is setting the trap.'
Switchback

US 1997 118m DeLuxe Panavision
Paramount/Rysher/Pacific Western (Gale Anne Hurd)
▣ ▦

An FBI agent searches for a serial killer, whose activities are causing problems to a Texan sheriff facing re-election.
A thriller that never quite comes to life; it might have worked better as a Western.
wd Jeb Stuart ph Oliver Wood m Basil Poledouris pd Jeff Howard ed Conrad Buff
☆ Dennis Quaid, Danny Glover, Jared Leto, R. Lee Ermey, Ted Levine, William Fichtner, Leo Burmester
'A standard thriller with a couple of novel touches.' – *Variety*

Switchblade Sisters

US 1975 89m Eastmancolor
Miramax/Rolling Thunder/Johnny Legend (John Prizer)

🎬 ⌖

aka: *The Jezebels*

A tough new girl in town becomes leader of a female gang.

Slick, violent exploitation movie of a familiar kind.

w F. X. Maier d Jack Hill ph Stephen Katz
m Medusa, Chuck Day, Richard Person
pd Robinson Royce, B. B. Neel ed Mort Tubor
☆ Robbie Lee, Joanne Nail, Monica Gayle, Asher Brauner, Chase Newhart, Marlene Clark, Kitty Bruce, Don Stark, Kate Murtagh

'Pic simply doesn't have a keen enough action or satiric edge to hold its head above water in the current marketplace.' – *Variety*, 1996

† The film was rereleased in the US in 1996 through Quentin Tarantino's distribution company.

The Switchboard Operator *

Yugoslavia 1969 70m bw
Avala

🎬

original title: *Ljubavni Slucaj*
US title: *Love Affair, or the Case of the Missing Switchboard Operator; aka: The Tragedy of a Switchboard Operator*

In Yugoslavia, an affair between a Hungarian-born post office worker and a Turkish rat-catcher ends in tragedy.

A collage that deftly mixes documentary, with a commentary from a sexologist and a criminologist, and fiction, with an account of a liaison that goes wrong, in which impulse and accident are as important as intent.

wd Dusan Makavejev ph Aleksander Petkovic
m Dusan Aleksic ad Vladislav Lazic ed Katarina Stojanovic
☆ Eva Ras, Slobodan Aligrudic, Ruzica Sokic, Miodrag Andric, Aleksander Kostic, Zivojin Aleksic

'Experimental, vividly performed, this is comic; tender fare, with a surprisingly dark undertow.' – *Sight and Sound*

Switching Channels *

US 1988 105m colour
Rank (Martin Ransohoff)

🎬 🎬 ⌖

A television reporter, leaving to be married, agrees to undertake one last assignment.

The third remake of The Front Page, this does not match the classic His Girl Friday, which, like this version, changed the sex of the hero, but it provides some amusement.

w Jonathan Reynolds play The Front Page by Ben Hecht, Charles MacArthur d Ted Kotcheff
ph François Protat m Michel Legrand pd Anne Pritchard ed Thom Noble
☆ Kathleen Turner, Burt Reynolds, Christopher Reeve, Ned Beatty, Henry Gibson, George Newbern, Al Waxman, Ken James

'Leopold and Loeb. The Perfect Crime. A Deadly Love Affair.'

Swoon *

US 1992 80m bw
Argos Films (Tom Kalin, Christine Vachon)

🎬 🎬 ⌖

In Chicago in 1924, two young middle-class homosexual Jews kidnap and kill a young boy as a demonstration of their criminal abilities.

An undeniably stylish account of the murders and murderers which may be closer to the real events and the couple's motivations than either of the other movie versions, Rope or Compulsion, but which is less effective as a film.

w Tom Kalin, Hilton Als d Tom Kalin ph Ellen Kuras m James Bennett ed Tom Kalin
☆ Daniel Schlachet, Craig Chester, Ron Vawter, Michael Kirby, Michael Stumm, Valda Z. Drabla, Natalie Stanford

'Kalin suggests that the couple internalised the homophobia and anti-Semitism around them into a pathological self-loathing but he doesn't show that process: his heroes seem simply born to be bad.' – *Sheila Johnston, Independent.*
'A determined attempt to reclaim a pair of notorious murderers on behalf of the gay community.' – *Philip French, Observer*
'Tom Kalin's brilliant debut feature presents history as you've always dreamed it might be: with personal, social and political perspectives all refracted through each other, and with a

burning sense of the need to know and understand more, and better.' – *Tony Rayns*

The Sword and the Cross

Italy 1960 93m Technicolor
Liber Films (Ottavio Poggi)

original title: *La Spada e la Croce*
aka: *Mary Magdalene*

In Jerusalem, Mary Magdalene, mistress of the High Priest's nephew, is kidnapped by Barabbas, falls in love with a Roman officer, is converted to Christianity, and witnesses her brother Lazarus being raised from the dead, as well as the crucifixion of Christ.

The scriptwriters' inventive way with the Bible is not matched by the acting or direction, which plod along familiar ways, showing more interest in profane than sacred love; Jesus has a walk-on role.

w Ottavio Poggi, Alessandro Continenza d Carlo Ludovico Bragaglia ph Marcello Masciocchi
m Roberto Nicolosi ed Renato Cinquini
☆ Yvonne de Carlo, Jorge Mistral, Rossana Podesta, Massimo Serato, Mario Girotti

† The film is shown on TV in a dubbed version.

The Sword and the Rose

GB 1952 91m Technicolor
Walt Disney (Perce Pearce)

🎬 🎬 ⌖

The romantic problems of young Mary Tudor.

Unhistorical charade not quite in the usual Disney vein, and not very good.

w Lawrence E. Watkin novel When Knighthood Was in Flower by Charles Major d Ken Annakin
ph Geoffrey Unsworth m Clifton Parker
☆ Richard Todd, Glynis Johns, James Robertson Justice, Michael Gough, Jane Barrett, Peter Copley, Rosalie Crutchley, Jean Mercure, D. A. Clarke-Smith

The Sword and the Sorcerer

🎬 US 1982 99m DeLuxe
Sorcerer Productions/Group One/Brandon Chase

A tyrant wins an idyllic kingdom with the help of an evil sorcerer; young Prince Talon gets it back.

Medieval magic and violence, laid on with a shovel; hopefully the last attempt to start an ill-fated cycle.

w Tom Karnowski, Albert Pyun, John Stuckmeyer
d Albert Pyun ph Joseph Mangine m David Whitaker
☆ Lee Horsley, Kathleen Beller, Simon MacCorkindale, George Maharis, Richard Lynch

Sword in the Desert

US 1949 100m bw
Robert Arthur/Universal

During World War II, Jewish refugees are smuggled to the Palestine coast.

Dim topical melodrama with an anti-British slant which caused international embarrassment.

w Robert Buckner d George Sherman ph Irving Glassberg m Frank Skinner
☆ Dana Andrews, Marta Toren, Jeff Chandler, Stephen McNally, Philip Friend

The Sword in the Stone **

🎬 US 1963 80m Technicolor
Walt Disney (Ken Peterson)

🎬 🎬 ⌖

In the Dark Ages, a young forest boy named Wart becomes King Arthur.

Feature cartoon with goodish sequences but disappointingly showing a flatness and economy of draughtsmanship.

w Bill Peet novel The Once and Future King by T. H. White d Wolfgang Reitherman m George Bruns songs The Sherman Brothers
♪ George Bruns

Sword of Ali Baba

🎬 US 1965 81m Technicolor
Universal

Ali Baba is forced from the royal court to become a king of thieves.

Cut-rate programme filler utilizing great chunks of Ali Baba and the Forty Thieves (twenty-one years older), with one actor, Frank Puglia, playing the same role in both films.

w Edmund Hartmann, Oscar Brodney d Virgil Vogel ph William Margulies m Frank Skinner
☆ Peter Mann, Jocelyn Lane, Peter Whitney, Gavin McLeod

Sword of Lancelot: see *Lancelot and Guinevere*

The Sword of Monte Cristo

🎬 US 1951 80m Supercinecolor
Edward L. Alperson

🎬

Virtuous rebels and a villainous minister all seek the fabulous treasure of Monte Cristo.

Rubbishy sequel apparently shot in somebody's back garden by people only recently acquainted with film techniques.

wd Maurice Geraghty ph Jack Greenhalgh
m Raoul Kraushaar
☆ George Montgomery, Paula Corday, Berry Kroeger, Robert Warwick, William Conrad

Sword of Sherwood Forest

🎬 GB 1960 80m Technicolor
Megascope
Columbia/Hammer/Yeoman (Richard Greene, Sidney Cole)

🎬 🎬

Robin Hood reveals the villainy of the Sheriff of Nottingham and the Earl of Newark.

This big-screen version of a popular TV series makes a rather feeble addition to the legend, but the actors try hard.

w Alan Hackney d Terence Fisher ph Ken Hodges m Alan Hoddinott
☆ Richard Greene, Peter Cushing, Richard Pasco, Niall MacGinnis, Jack Gwillim, Sarah Branch, Nigel Green

Sword of the Valiant

🎬 GB 1984 101m Fujicolour JDC
Wide Screen
Cannon (Michael Kagan, Philip M. Breen)

In the mythical middle ages, squire Gawain takes on a challenge from the magical Green Knight.

An unsatisfactory mixture of realism, fantasy and deadly seriousness. Spoofing might have worked better.

w Stephen Weeks, Philip M. Breen, Howard C. Pen d Stephen Weeks ph Freddie Young, Peter Hurst m Ron Geesin pd Maurice Fowler, Derek Nice ed Richard Marden, Barry Peters
☆ Miles O'Keeffe, Sean Connery, Trevor Howard, Leigh Lawson, Cyrielle Claire, Peter Cushing, Ronald Lacey, Lila Kedrova, John Rhys-Davies, Douglas Wilmer, Wilfrid Brambell

Swords of Blood: see *Cartouche*

The Swordsman

US 1947 80m Technicolor
Columbia

A young 18th-century Scot tries to end a family feud so that he can marry the girl of his choice.

Amiable costume programmer, quite forgettable but mostly enjoyable while it's on.

w Wilfred Pettitt d Joseph H. Lewis ph William Snyder m Hugo Friedhofer
☆ Larry Parks, Ellen Drew, George Macready

Sylvia

US 1964 115m bw
Paramount/Joseph E. Levine (Martin H. Poll)

A millionaire with a mysterious fiancée hires a detective to discover the truth about her past.

Improbable story of a high-minded prostitute, sluggishly narrated and variably acted.

w Sydney Boehm novel E. V. Cunningham
d Gordon Douglas ph Joseph Ruttenberg
m David Raksin
☆ Carroll Baker, George Maharis, Peter Lawford, Joanne Dru, Ann Sothern, Viveca Lindfors, Edmond O'Brien, Aldo Ray

'Maharis manages to suggest that he might be worth watching in a role worth acting in a movie worth making. Sylvia wasn't.' – *Judith Crist*

Sylvia **

New Zealand 1985 98m colour
Southern Light/Cinepro (Don Reynolds, Michael Firth)

🎬

In New Zealand, a wife of a headmaster at a village school encounters official opposition to her innovative methods of teaching Maori children to read.

An effective and moving low-key account, though full of repressed sexual feelings, based on the life and autobiographical books of writer Sylvia Ashton Warner.

w Michael Quill, F. Fairfax, Michael Firth
books Teacher and I Passed This Way by Sylvia Ashton Warner d Michael Firth ph Ian Paul
m Leonard Rosenman pd Gary Hansen
ed Michael Horton
☆ Eleanor David, Nigel Terry, Tom Wilkinson, Mary Regan, Martyn Sanderson, Terence Cooper, David Letch, Sarah Peirse

Sylvia and the Ghost *

France 1944 93m bw
Ecran Français/André Paulvé

original title: *Sylvie et la Fantôme*

A sixteen-year-old girl lives in her father's castle and is friendly with the ghost of a man killed in a duel fought for love of her grandmother.

Melancholy comedy which despite some charming moments somehow misses the expected style which would have made it a minor classic.

w Jean Aurenche play Alfred Adam d Claude Autant-Lara ph Philippe Agostini m René Cloerc
☆ Odette Joyeux, François Périer, Jacques Tati, Louis Salou, Jean Desailly

'A charming film, written, handled and acted with wit, feeling and a beautiful lightness of touch.' – *Gavin Lambert*

'She's a boy! It's Mr Hepburn to you!'

Sylvia Scarlett *

US 1935 94m bw
RKO (Pandro S. Berman)

🎬 ⌖

A girl masquerades as a boy in order to escape to France with her crooked father.

Strange, peripatetic English comedy-adventure which failed to ring any bells but preserves aspects of interest.

w Gladys Unger, John Collier, Mortimer Offner
novel Compton Mackenzie d George Cukor
ph Joseph August m Roy Webb
☆ Katharine Hepburn, Cary Grant, Edmund Gwenn, Brian Aherne, Lennox Pawle

'A story that's hard to believe. Dubious entertainment for the public.' – *Variety*
'It seems to go wrong in a million directions, but it has unusually affecting qualities.' – *New Yorker, 1978*
'A sprawling and ineffective essay in dramatic chaos.' – *Richard Watts Jnr, New York Herald Tribune*
'A tragic waste of time and screen talent.' – *Eileen Creelman, New York Sun*
'A much more polished comedy than most, and consistently engaging.' – *Winston Burdett, Brooklyn Daily Eagle*

Sylvie et la Fântome: see *Sylvia and the Ghost*

Sympathy for the Devil: see *One Plus One*

La Symphonie Fantastique *

France 1947 90m bw
L'Atelier Français

The life of Hector Berlioz.

Stately but uninspired biopic chiefly notable for its leading performance.

w J. P. Feydeau, H. A. Legrand d Christian-Jaque
☆ Jean-Louis Barrault, Renée Saint-Cyr, Jules Berry, Bernard Blier

La Symphonie Pastorale *

France 1946 105m bw
Les Films Gibe

A Swiss pastor takes in an orphan child who grows up to be a beautiful girl and causes jealousy between himself and his son.

Curious mountain tragedy, a great visual pleasure with its symbolic use of snow and water.

w Jean Delannoy, Jean Aurenche novel André Gide d Jean Delannoy ph Armand Thirard
m Georges Auric
☆ Pierre Blanchar, Michèle Morgan

Symphony of Six Million

US 1932 94m bw
RKO (Pandro S. Berman)

GB title: *Melody of Life*

A doctor drags himself from New York's slums to Park Avenue, but feels guilty and demoralized when he can't save the life of his own father.

Monumental tearjerker, not badly done.

w Bernard Schubert, J. Walter Ruben
novel Fannie Hurst d Gregory La Cava ph Leo Tover m Max Steiner

---

☆ Irene Dunne, Ricardo Cortez, Gregory Ratoff, Anna Appel, Noel Madison, Julie Haydon
'Picture of Jewish home life in the familiar Hurst style ... a good-looking picture without strongly marked cast names.' – *Variety*

Symptoms *
GB   1974   91m   Eastmancolor
SF/Finiton (Jean Dupuis)
aka: *The Blood Virgin*
A woman living in a remote and decaying mansion begins to show signs of madness.
Creepy thriller with lesbian undertones, stylishly directed.
w Joseph Larraz, Stanley Miller d Joseph Larraz (José Larraz) ph Trevor Mann m John Scott ad Kenneth Bridgeman ed Brian Smedley-Aston
☆ Angela Pleasence, Peter Vaughan, Lorna Heilbron, Nancy Nevinson, Ronald O'Neil, Raymond Huntley
   'Works more on the level of atmosphere than of ideas, but its psychological perceptions are unusually sophisticated for genre cinema.' – *David Pirie, MFB*

† The film was cut to 80m on its British cinema release.

Synanon
US   1965   106m   bw
Columbia/Richard Quine
GB title: *Get Off My Back*
Stories of the inmates of a voluntary Californian institution for the rehabilitation of drug addicts.
Well-intentioned but rather dreary case histories, unconvincingly dramatized. The house and its leader subsequently came in for much press criticism.
w Ian Bernard, S. Lee Pogostin d Richard Quine ph Harry Stradling m Neal Hefti
☆ Edmond O'Brien, Chuck Connors, Stella Stevens, Alex Cord, Eartha Kitt, Richard Conte, Barbara Luna
   'The real drug addicts who appear in the background are plumpish, greyish and utterly ordinary; but the fictional ones are glamorously handsome, and lead lives which are full of throbbing emotion and upset.' – *Tom Milne, MFB*

Syncopation *
US   1942   88m   bw
RKO/William Dieterle (Charles F. Glett)
The career of a young trumpeter parallels the development of jazz.
Somewhat disappointing musical considering the talents involved.
w Philip Yordan, Frank Cavett, Valentine Davies d William Dieterle
☆ Jackie Cooper, Adolphe Menjou, Bonita Granville, Connee Boswell, the Hall Johnson Choir, Benny Goodman, Harry James, Gene Krupa, Charlie Barnet
† Bonita Granville's piano playing was performed by Stan Wrightsman, and Jackie Cooper's cornet was dubbed by Bunny Berigan.

The System
US   1953   90m   bw
Warner (Sam Bischoff)
A crime leader is softened by love, and allows himself to be convicted.
Strange nonsense inspired by the Kefauver investigations into American society; neither edifying nor entertaining.
w Jo Eisinger d Lewis Seiler ph Edwin DuPar m David Buttolph
☆ Frank Lovejoy, Joan Weldon, Bob Arthur, Paul Picerni, Don Beddoe

The System
GB   1964   90m   bw
British Lion/Bryanston/Kenneth Shipman
US title: *The Girl-Getters*
Seaside layabouts have a system for collecting and sharing rich girl visitors, but one of the latter traps the leader at his own game.
Adequate sexy showcase for some looming talents; all very unattractive, but smoothly directed in a number of imitated styles.
w Peter Draper d Michael Winner ph Nicolas Roeg m Stanley Black
☆ Oliver Reed, Jane Merrow, Barbara Ferris, Julia Foster, Ann Lynn, Guy Doleman, Andrew Ray, David Hemmings, John Alderton, Derek Nimmo, Harry Andrews
   'A modest, skilful, charming, inconsequential, and fairly dishonest little picture, to be enjoyed and deprecated in roughly equal measure.' – *John Simon*

T

T. R. Baskin

US 1971 89m Technicolor
Paramount (Peter Hyams)
▆

GB title: *A Date with a Lonely Girl*
A businessman in Chicago meets an unhappy girl
who tells him her story of loneliness and lack of
communication.
Intolerable self-pitying mishmash with no place to go.
w Peter Hyams d Herbert Ross ph Gerald
Hirschfeld m Jack Elliott
☆ Candice Bergen, Peter Boyle, James Caan,
Marcia Rodd, Erin O'Reilly

Table for Five

US 1983 124m DeLuxe
CBS/Voight-Schaffel (Robert Schaffel)
▆▆ ▆ ◷

A divorced husband takes his children on a
European holiday and has to tell them that their
mother has been killed.
*Slow, sentimental domestic drama with attractive travel
backgrounds, like a TV movie writ large.*
w David Seltzer d Robert Lieberman ph Vilmos
Zsigmond m John Morris pd Robert F. Boyle
☆ Jon Voight, Richard Crenna, Marie-Christine
Barrault, Millie Perkins, Roxana Zal, Robby Kiger,
Son Hoang Bui, Maria O'Brien
'A family problem picture resolutely updated for
the eighties.' – *Robert Brown, MFB*

Tabu

US 1931 80m bw
Colorart Synchrotone
▆▆ ▆ ◷

The life of a young Tahitian pearl fisherman.
*The plot is used only to bring together the elements of a
superb travelogue, but the conflicts between the aims of
the two directors are clearly seen.*
wd F. W. Murnau, Robert Flaherty ph Floyd
Crosby, Robert Flaherty m Hugo Riesenfeld
'Never more than interesting … it is not going
to set anything on fire.' – *Variety*
⚲ Floyd Crosby

Tacones Lejanos: see High Heels

Ta'Det Som En Mand, Frue!: see Take It Like
a Man, Ma'am

Taffin

GB 1988 96m colour
Vestron (Peter Shaw)
▆▆ ▆ ◷

A debt collector battles with crooked developers
who want to build a chemical plant in an Irish
village.
Dull thriller that never rises above the mundane.
w David Ambrose d Francis Megahy ph Paul
Beeson m Stanley Myers, Hans Zimmer
pd William Alexander ed Rodney Holland, Peter
Tanner
☆ Pierce Brosnan, Alison Doody, Ray McAnally,
Jeremy Child, Patrick Bergin, Alan Stanford

Tagebuch einer Verliebten: see The Diary of
a Married Woman

Tagebuch einer Verlorenen: see Diary of a
Lost Girl

Taggart

US 1965 85m Technicolor
Universal
A young Western squatter avenges his parents'
murder but finds himself pursued by three
professional gunslingers.
Tough adult Western, quite well made.
w Robert Creighton Williams novel Louis
L'Amour d R. G. Springsteen ph William
Margulies m Herman Stein

☆ Tony Young, Dan Duryea, Dick Foran, Emile
Meyer, Elsa Cardenas, Jean Hale, David Carradine

Taiheiyo Hitoribochi: see Alone on the Pacific

Tail Spin

US 1938 83m bw
TCF (Harry Joe Brown)
The interwoven private lives of lady civilian air
pilots.
*Predictable romantic goings on; a tear, a smile, a song,
etc.*
w Frank Wead d Roy del Ruth ph Karl Freund
m Louis Silvers
☆ Alice Faye, Constance Bennett, Joan Davis,
Nancy Kelly, Charles Farrell, Jane Wyman, Kane
Richmond, Wally Vernon, Harry Davenport
'Story zooms and flutters to create many slow
spots in between the spectacular flying
sequences.' – *Variety*

Tainted Money: see Show Them No Mercy

Tai-Pan

US 1986 127m Technicolor JDC
Widescreen
Dino de Laurentiis (Raffaella de Laurentiis)
▆ ◷

Various problems afflict the leader of the European
community in Canton and Hong Kong.
*19th-century soap opera with 18th-century plotting and
dialogue.*
w John Briley, Stanley Mann novel James Clavell
d Daryl Duke ph Jack Cardiff m Maurice Jarre
pd Tony Masters
☆ Bryan Brown, Joan Chen, John Stanton, Tim
Guinee, Bill Leadbitter, Russell Wong
'Underneath all the gloss the film isn't really
about anything.' – *Variety*
'ith some movies, you're forever checking your
watch. With *Tai-Pan*, you'll be checking your
calendar.' – *People*
'Miniseries kitsch which shortchanges on
dramatic spectacle.' – *Sight and Sound*

Take a Giant Step

US 1958 100m bw
UA/Sheila/Hecht-Hill Lancaster (Julius J. Epstein)
A young black person brought up in a white town
feels ill at ease and runs into adolescent troubles.
*Well-meaning racial drama with good detail but no real
feeling.*
w Louis S. Peterson, Julius J. Epstein d Philip
Leacock ph Arthur Arling m Jack Marshall
☆ Johnny Nash, Estelle Hemsley, Ruby Dee,
Frederick O'Neal

Take a Girl Like You

GB 1970 101m Eastmancolor
Columbia/Albion (Hal E. Chester)
▆

A north country girl comes to teach in London
and has man trouble.
*Old-fashioned novelette with sex trimmings and neither
zest nor humour.*
w George Melly novel Kingsley Amis d Jonathan
Miller ph Dick Bush m Stanley Myers
☆ Hayley Mills, Oliver Reed, Noel Harrison,
Sheila Hancock, John Bird, Aimi MacDonald

Take a Letter, Darling **

US 1942 94m bw
Paramount (Fred Kohlmar)
GB title: *Green-Eyed Woman*
A woman executive hires a male secretary.
Smartish romantic comedy.
w Claude Binyon d Mitchell Leisen ph John
Mescall m Victor Young ad Hans Dreier, Roland
Anderson

☆ Rosalind Russell, Fred MacMurray, Macdonald
Carey, Constance Moore, Cecil Kellaway, Charles
Arnt, Kathleen Howard, Dooley Wilson
⚲ John Mescall; Victor Young; art direction

Take Care of My Little Girl

US 1951 93m Technicolor
TCF (Julian Blaustein)
A university freshwoman gets into trouble with her
sorority.
*Ho-hum exposé of college conventions, of routine
interest at best.*
w Julius J. and Philip G. Epstein novel Peggy
Goodwin d Jean Negulesco ph Harry Jackson
m Alfred Newman
☆ Jeanne Crain, Mitzi Gaynor, Dale Robertson,
Jean Peters, Jeffrey Hunter
'As is customary in college pictures, it appears
that Tri U recruits most of its strength from the
chorus.' – *Penelope Houston*

Take Care of Your Scarf, Tatjana *

Finland/Germany 1994 62m bw
ICA/Sputnik/Pandora/Suomen
Elokvasäätiö/Yleisradio/TV-1/Marianne Möller/Eila
Werning (Aki Kaurismäki)
original title: *Pidä Huivista Kiinni, Tatjana*
In the mid-60s, two dour and immature Finnish
men give a lift to two Russian women, who are
looking for love but are willing to settle for less.
*A quirky, downbeat road movie about the difficulties of
communication between the sexes, which can be taken
either as tragedy or comedy, depending on your mood
and point of view.*
w Aki Kaurismäki, Sakke Järvenpää d Aki
Kaurismäki ph Timo Salminen ad Kari Laine,
Markku Pätilä, Jukka Salmi ed Aki Kaurismäki
☆ Kati Outinen, Matti Pellonpää, Kirsi
Tykkyläinen, Mato Valtonen, Elina Salo
'Deserves to find an audience, because beneath
the offhand, casual approach is a moving and
funny film about relationships.' – *Variety*

Take Her, She's Mine *

US 1963 98m DeLuxe Cinemascope
TCF (Henry Koster)
A lawyer protects his teenage daughter from boys
and causes.
*Routine Hollywood family comedy with some laughs
and an agreeable cast.*
w Nunnally Johnson play Phoebe and Henry
Ephron d Henry Koster ph Lucien Ballard
m Jerry Goldsmith
☆ James Stewart, Sandra Dee, Robert Morley,
Audrey Meadows, Philippe Forquet, John McGiver

Take It Easy

France 1971 90m colour
Adel Productions (Alain Delon)
original title: *Doucement les Basses*
A Catholic priest, a former organist, living in an
isolated village, is visited by his wife, who he
thought had died eight years earlier, and discovers
she is now running a bordello.
*A broad comedy that fails to extract much fun from its
situation.*
w Pascal Jardin d Jacques Deray ph Jean-Jacques
Tarbes m Claude Bolling ad François de Lamotne
ed Paul Cayatte
☆ Alain Delon, Paul Meurisse, Nathalie Delon,
Julien Guiomar, Paul Préboist, André Pollet, Serge
Davri

Take It Like a Man, Ma'am *

Denmark 1975 96m colour
Rده Sister (Ilse M. Haugaard, Trine Hedman,
Annelise Hovinand)
original title: *Ta'Det Som En Mand, Frue!*
A bored middle-aged housewife dreams of the
sexual roles being reversed.
Mildly enjoyable feminist movie.

wd Elisabeth Rygard, Mette Knudsen, Li Vilstrup
ph Katia Forbert Petersen, Judy Irola, Lene Fog-
Moller, Leni Schou m Nina Larsen, Gudrun
Steen-Andersen, Maria Marcus ed Ann-Lis Lund
☆ Tove Maës, Bertha Quistgard, Asta Esper
Andersen, Birgit Brüel, Alf Lassen

Take It or Leave It

US 1944 68m bw
TCF
A sailor enters a quiz show to raise money for his
expectant wife.
*Thin link for a string of old movie clips which form the
questions; all from Fox films of course.*
w Harold Buchman, Snag Werris, Mac Benoff
d Ben Stoloff
☆ Phil Baker, Phil Silvers, Edward Ryan, Marjorie
Massow
† Performers shown in film clips include Shirley
Temple, the Ritz Brothers, Betty Grable, Alice
Faye, Sonja Henie, and Al Jolson.

Take Me High

GB 1973 90m Technicolor
EMI (Kenneth Harper)
A bank manager helps an unsuccessful restaurant
to launch a new hamburger.
*Jaded youth musical with no dancing but some zip and
bounce to commend it to mums and dads if not to its
intended young audience.*
w Christopher Penfold d David Askey
ph Norman Warwick m/songs Tony Cole
☆ Cliff Richard, Debbie Watling, Hugh Griffith,
George Cole, Anthony Andrews, Richard Wattis

Take Me Out to the Ball Game **

US 1949 93m Technicolor
MGM (Arthur Freed)
▆▆ ▆ ◷

GB title: *Everybody's Cheering*
A woman takes over a baseball team and the
players are antagonistic.
*Lively, likeable 1890s comedy musical which served as
a trial run for On the Town and in its own right is a
fast-moving, funny, tuneful delight with no
pretensions.*
w Harry Tugend, George Wells d Busby Berkeley
ph George Folsey md Adolph Deutsch
songs Betty Comden, Adolph Green, Roger Edens
☆ Gene Kelly, Frank Sinatra, Esther Williams,
Betty Garrett, Jules Munshin, Edward Arnold,
Richard Lane, Tom Dugan

Take Me to Town

US 1953 81m Technicolor
U-I (Ross Hunter)
The three sons of a backwoods widower import a
vaudeville artiste as their new mother.
*Old-fashioned family schmaltz containing every known
cliché professionally stitched into the plot.*
w Richard Morris d Douglas Sirk ph Russell
Metty m Joseph Gershenson
☆ Ann Sheridan, Sterling Hayden, Philip Reed,
Lee Patrick, Lee Aaker, Harvey Grant, Dusty
Henley

Take My Life **

GB 1947 79m bw
GFD/Cineguild (Anthony Havelock-Allan)
A man is suspected of murdering an ex-girlfriend,
and his wife journeys to Scotland to prove him
innocent.
*Hitchcock-style thriller with excellent detail and
performances.*
w Winston Graham, Valerie Taylor d Ronald
Neame ph Guy Green m William Alwyn
☆ Hugh Williams, Greta Gynt, Marius Goring,
Francis L. Sullivan, Rosalie Crutchley, Henry
Edwards, Ronald Adam
'An extremely confident and exciting British
thriller, with a story no less plausible than the

---

average made infinitely more plausible by the smooth narrative style.' – *Dilys Powell, Sunday Times*

Take My Tip
GB 1937 74m bw
Gaumont-British (Michael Balcon)
Lord Pilkington gets his revenge on a confidence trickster when they meet at a Dalmatian hotel.
Reasonably lively comedy musical adapted for the stars.
w Sidney Gilliat, Michael Hogan, Jack Hulbert d Herbert Mason ph Bernard Knowles *songs* Sam Lerner, Al Goodhart, Al Hoffman
☆ Jack Hulbert, Cicely Courtneidge, Frank Cellier, Harold Huth, Frank Pettingell, Robb Wilton, H. F. Maltby

Take One False Step *
US 1949 94m bw
U-I (Chester Erskine)
An innocent middle-aged man who has befriended a girl is hunted by the police when she is murdered.
Fairly absorbing and well-cast chase thriller in a minor key.
w Irwin Shaw, Chester Erskine *story* Night Call by Irwin and David Shaw d Chester Erskine ph Franz Planer m Walter Scharf
☆ William Powell, Shelley Winters, Marsha Hunt, Dorothy Hart, James Gleason, Felix Bressart, Art Baker, Sheldon Leonard

Take the High Ground
US 1953 101m Anscocolor
MGM (Dore Schary)
A tough sergeant trains army conscripts for action in Korea.
Very routine flagwaver.
w Millard Kaufman d Richard Brooks ph John Alton m Dimitri Tiomkin
☆ Richard Widmark, Karl Malden, Carleton Carpenter, Elaine Stewart, Russ Tamblyn, Jerome Courtland, Steve Forrest, Robert Arthur
⊗ Millard Kaufman

Take the Money and Run
US 1968 85m Technicolor
Palomar (Charles H. Joffe)
A social misfit becomes a bungling crook.
A torrent of middling visual gags, not the star's best vehicle.
wd Woody Allen ph Lester Shorr m Marvin Hamlisch
☆ Woody Allen, Janet Margolin, Marcel Hillaire

Take the Stage: see *Curtain Call at Cactus Creek*

Take This Job and Shove It
US 1981 106m colour
Avco Embassy/Cinema Group (Greg Blackwell)
A thrusting business executive discovers his social conscience when he returns to his home town to take over a run-down brewery.
Unoriginal but affable corn-belt comedy affirming small-town values.
w Barry Schneider *story* Jeffrey Bernini, Barry Schneider, from a song by David Allan Coe d Gus Trikonis ph James Devis m Billy Sherrill ad Jim Dultz ed Richard Belding
☆ Robert Hays, Barbara Hershey, David Keith, Art Carney, Tim Thomerson, Eddie Albert, Penelope Milford, Charlie Rich, Martin Mull

Taking Care of Business
US 1990 108m Technicolor
Warner/Hollywood Pictures/Silver Screen Partners IV (Geoffrey Taylor)
GB title: *Filofax*
A thief assumes the identity of an advertising executive whose Filofax he acquires.
Slow-moving comedy that fails to get much mileage from its tired central idea.
w Jill Mazursky, Jeffrey Abrams d Arthur Hiller ph David M. Walsh m Stewart Copeland pd Jon Hutman ed William Reynolds
☆ James Belushi, Charles Grodin, Anne DeSalvo, Loryn Locklin, Stephen Elliott, Hector Elizondo, Veronica Hamel
'Hiller brings his usual dogged persistence to bear, but it would take an alchemist's touch to turn *Filofax* into comic gold.' – *Geoff Brown, Sight and Sound*

The Taking of Pelham 123 *
US 1974 104m Technicolor Panavision
UA/Palomar/Palladium (Gabriel Katzka, Edgar J. Scherick)
Four ruthless gunmen hold a New York subway train to ransom and have an ingenious plan for escape.
Entertaining crime caper made less enjoyable by all the fashionable faults – the script is deliberately hard to follow and full of four letter words, the sound track hard to hear, and the visuals ugly.
w Peter Stone *novel* John Godey d Joseph Sargent ph Owen Roizman m David Shire
☆ Walter Matthau, Robert Shaw, Martin Balsam, Hector Elizondo, Earl Hindman, James Broderick
'Full of noise and squalling and dirty words used for giggly shock effects.' – *New Yorker*

Taking Off ***
US 1971 92m Movielab
Universal (Alfred W. Crown, Michael Hausman)
Suburban parents seek their errant daughter among the hippies, and gradually lose their own inhibitions.
Slight, formless, but amusing revue-style comment by a Czech director on the American scene.
w Milos Forman, John Guare, Jean-Claude Carrière, John Klein d Milos Forman ph Miroslav Ondricek
☆ Lynn Carlin, Buck Henry, Linnea Heacock

Tale of a Vampire
GB/Japan 1992 102m colour
State Screen/Tsuburaya Ezio/Furama (Simon Johnson)
A vampire in London is tracked down by the husband of his lost lover.
Slow-moving and gory account of an obsessive love.
w Shimako Sato, Jane Corbett d Shimako Sato ph Zubin Mistry m Julian Joseph pd Alice Normington ed Chris Wright sp Dave Watkins
☆ Julian Sands, Suzanna Hamilton, Kenneth Cranham, Marian Diamond, Michael Kenton, Catherine Blake, Mark Kempner, Nik Myers
'A flawed but impressive debut from a talent which deserves to be nurtured.' – *Mark Kermode, Sight and Sound*
'Is nailed to the floor by anaemic perfs from its two leads and a script that's all tease and no bite. Pic may build a small cult following among genre buffs but won't score many general converts.' – *Variety*

A Tale of Five Cities
GB 1951 99m bw
Grand National (Alexander Paal)
US title: *A Tale of Five Women*
An amnesiac American seeks clues to his past in Rome, Vienna, Paris, Berlin and London.
Tedious pattern drama remarkable only for its then untried cast.
w Patrick Kirwan, Maurice J. Wilson d Montgomery Tully ph Gordon Lang m Hans May
☆ Bonar Colleano, Gina Lollobrigida, Barbara Kelly, Lana Morris, Anne Vernon, Eva Bartok

A Tale of Five Women: see *A Tale of Five Cities*

A Tale of Springtime: see *Conte de Printemps*

The Tale of the Fox ***
🇫🇷 France 1931 65m bw
BFI/Wladyslaw Starewicz (Louis Nalpas, Roger Richebé)
original title: *Le Roman de Renard*
A cunning fox defeats all the other animals that unite to attack him.
A brilliant animated film, which with its British release in 1994 helped bring belated recognition to a master of the art.
w Wladyslaw Starewicz, Irène Starewicz, Jean Nohain, Antoinette Nordmann d Wladyslaw Starewicz m Vincent Scotto pd Wladyslaw Starewicz ed Laura Séjourné
☆ Featuring the voices of Claude Dauphin, Romain Bouquet, Sylvain Itkine, Léon Larive, Robert Seller, Edy Debray, Nicolas Amato

'His love challenged the flames of revolution!'
A Tale of Two Cities **
🇬🇧 US 1935 121m bw
MGM (David O. Selznick)
A British lawyer sacrifices himself to save another man from the guillotine.
Richly detailed version of the classic melodrama, with production values counting more than the acting.
w W. P. Lipscomb, S. N. Behrman *novel* Charles Dickens d Jack Conway ph Oliver T. Marsh m Herbert Stothart ed Conrad A. Nervig
☆ Ronald Colman, Elizabeth Allan, Basil Rathbone, Edna May Oliver, Blanche Yurka, Reginald Owen, Henry B. Walthall, Donald Woods, Walter Catlett, H. B. Warner, Claude Gillingwater, Fritz Leiber
'A screen classic … technically it is about as flawless as possible … it has been made with respectful and loving care.' – *Variety*
'A prodigiously stirring production … for more than two hours it crowds the screen with beauty and excitement.' – *New York Times*
† Originally prepared at Warner for Leslie Howard.
⊗ best picture; editing

A Tale of Two Cities *
🇬🇧 GB 1958 117m bw
Rank (Betty E. Box)
Modest but still costly remake with good moments but a rather slow pace.
w T. E. B. Clarke d Ralph Thomas ph Ernest Steward m Richard Addinsell
☆ Dirk Bogarde, Dorothy Tutin, Christopher Lee, Athene Seyler, Rosalie Crutchley, Ernest Clark, Stephen Murray, Paul Guers, Donald Pleasence, Ian Bannen, Cecil Parker, Alfie Bass
'Serviceable rather than imaginative.' – *MFB*

A Talent for Loving
US 1969 101m colour
Paramount (Walter Shenson)
Two generations of an international jet-setting family have woman trouble.
Little-seen melodrama apparently disowned by those who made it.
novel Richard Condon d Richard Quine
☆ Richard Widmark, Cesar Romero, Topol, Genevieve Page

Talent for the Game
US 1991 91m Technicolor
Paramount (Martin Elfand)
When a billionaire buys the team, a baseball scout tries to save his job by discovering a star pitcher.
Slow-moving drama that begins as an exposé of exploitation and corruption in sport before settling for a sentimental story of triumph against the odds.
w David Himmelstein, Tom Donnelly, Larry Ferguson d Robert M. Young ph Curtis Clark m David Newman pd Jeffrey Howard ed Arthur Coburn
☆ Edward James Olmos, Lorraine Bracco, Jamey Sheridan, Terry Kinney, Jeff Corbett

'How Far Would You Go To Become Someone Else?'
The Talented Mr Ripley **
US 1999 139m DeLuxe
Paramount/Miramax/Mirage/Timnick (William Horberg, Tom Sternberg)
Hired by a wealthy man to bring back his playboy son from Italy, a poor youth decides to kill him and assume his identity instead.
Glamorous thriller of class warfare and homosexual obsession, often engrossing but much too long.
wd Anthony Minghella *novel* Patricia Highsmith ph John Seale m Gabriel Yared pd Roy Walker ed Walter Murch cos Ann Roth, Gary Jones
☆ Matt Damon, Jude Law, Gwyneth Paltrow, Cate Blanchett, Philip Seymour Hoffman, Jack Davenport, James Rebhorn, Sergio Rubini, Philip Baker Hall, Rosario Fiorello, Stefania Rocca
'It ends up as a dismayingly unthrilling thriller and bafflingly unconvincing character study.' – *Peter Bradshaw, Guardian*
'There are diabolically smart surprises wherever you care to look in this glittering thriller.' – *Janet Maslin, New York Times*
† Highsmith's novel was first filmed in 1960 by René Clément under the title *Plein Soleil* (qv).

⊗ Jude Law; Anthony Minghella (as writer); Gabriel Yared; Roy Walker; Ann Roth, Gary Jones
🏆 Jude Law

Tales from the Crypt *
GB 1972 92m Eastmancolor
Metromedia/Amicus (Milton Subotsky)
Five people get lost in catacombs and are shown the future by a sinister monk who turns out to be Satan.
Fair ghoulish fun; a quintet of stories with a recognizable Amicus link.
w Milton Subotsky *comic strips* William Gaines d Freddie Francis ph Norman Warwick m Douglas Gamley
☆ Ralph Richardson, Geoffrey Bayldon, Peter Cushing, Joan Collins, Ian Hendry, Robin Phillips, Richard Greene, Barbara Murray, Roy Dotrice, Nigel Patrick, Patrick Magee

Tales from the Crypt: Demon Knight
US 1995 92m DeLuxe
UIP/Universal (Gilbert Adler)
A servant of the Devil attempts to obtain a key, protected by a Demon Knight, that will allow evil to triumph on Earth.
Comic-book horror, done with a modicum of style, though its episodic approach allows predictability to seep in.
w Ethan Reiff, Cyrus Voris, Mark Bishop d Ernest Dickerson ph Rick Bota m Ed Shearmur pd Christiaan Wagener ed Stephen Lovejoy sp Available Light; Scott Coulter; make-up: Todd Masters
☆ Billy Zane, William Sadler, Jada Pinkett, Brenda Bakke, C. C. H. Pounder, Dick Miller, Thomas Haden Church, John Schuck
'A fang-in-cheek horror thriller that likely will please fans and turn off non-devotees.' – *Variety*

Tales from the Crypt Presents Bordello of Blood
US 1996 87m DeLuxe
Universal (Gilbert Adler)
A preacher sets up a vampire-staffed brothel beneath a cemetery.
Derivative, tongue-in-cheek and gore-all-over-the-floor horror, aimed at an adolescent audience.
w A. L. Katz, Gilbert Adler *story* Bob Gale, Robert Zemeckis d Gilbert Adler ph Tom Priestly m Chris Boardman pd Gregory Melton ed Stephen Lovejoy
☆ Dennis Miller, Erika Eleniak, Angie Everhart, Chris Sarandon, Corey Feldman, Aubrey Morris, Phil Fondacaro, William Sadler, Whoopi Goldberg (uncredited)
'Another cheesy goulash of smart-alecky humor and full-bore gore, spiced with more shots of topless lovelies than you'd find in a '60s sexploitation flick.' – *Joe Leydon, Variety*

Tales from the Darkside: The Movie
US 1991 93m Technicolor
Columbia TriStar/Paramount (Richard P. Rubinstein, Mitchell Galin)
Facing being roasted in an oven for dinner, a small boy postpones the event by telling stories.
Bloody anthology of horrific anecdotes that fails to cohere.
Wraparound Story:
w Michael McDowell d John Harrison ph Robert Draper m Donald A. Rubinstein pd Ruth Ammon sp Dick Smith ed Harry B. Miller III with Deborah Harry, Matthew Lawrence
Lot 249:
w Michael McDowell *story* Arthur Conan Doyle d John Harrison ph Robert Draper m Pat Regan pd Ruth Ammon sp Dick Smith ed Harry B. Miller III with Christian Slater, Robert Sedgwick, Steve Buscemi, Donald Van Horn, Michael Deak
Cat from Hell:
w George Romero *story* Stephen King d John Harrison ph Robert Draper m Chaz Jankel pd Ruth Ammon sp Dick Smith ed Harry B. Miller III with David Johansen, Paul Greene, William Hickey
Lover's Vow:
w Michael McDowell d John Harrison ph Robert Draper m John Harrison pd Ruth Ammon sp Dick Smith ed Harry B. Miller III with James Remar, Ashton Wise, Philip Lenkowsky, Rae Dawn Chong

'The rending of flesh that punctuates each episode is so extravagantly disgusting that the senses are quickly stirred not to admiration but to apathy.' – *Philip Strick, Sight and Sound*

Tales of Beatrix Potter **

🏥 GB 1971 90m Technicolor
EMI (Richard Goodwin)
📼 ▦ 🎧

US title: *Peter Rabbit and the Tales of Beatrix Potter*
Children's stories danced by the Royal Ballet in animal masks.
A charming entertainment for those who can appreciate it, though hardly the most direct way to tell these stories.
w Richard Goodwin, Christine Edzard d Reginald Mills m Austin Dempster m Jacques Offenbach ch Frederick Ashton pd Christine Edzard masks Rotislav Doboujinsky

The Tales of Hoffman **

GB 1951 127m Technicolor
British Lion/London/Michael Powell, Emeric Pressburger
📼 ▦ 🔍

The poet Hoffman, in three adventures, seeks the eternal woman and is beset by eternal evil.
Overwhelming combination of opera, ballet, and rich production design, an indigestible hodgepodge with flashes of superior talent.
wd Michael Powell, Emeric Pressburger ph Christopher Challis m Jacques Offenbach md Sir Thomas Beecham (with the Royal Philharmonic Orchestra) pd Hein Heckroth
☆ Robert Rounseville, Robert Helpmann, Pamela Brown, Moira Shearer, Frederick Ashton, Leonide Massine, Ludmila Tcherina, Ann Ayars, Mogens Wieth
'The most spectacular failure yet achieved by Powell and Pressburger, who seem increasingly to dissipate their gifts in a welter of aimless ingenuity.' – *Gavin Lambert*
'An art director's picnic: I marvelled without being enthralled.' – *Richard Mallett, Punch*
'Enchanting, a labour of love.' – *Sunday Telegraph*
'It echoes the peak of the Victorian spirit.' – *Time*
🎨 art direction

Tales of Manhattan **

US 1942 118m bw
TCF (Boris Morros, Sam Spiegel)
Separate stories of a tail coat, which passes from owner to owner.
The stories are all rather disappointing in their different veins, but production standards are high and a few of the stars shine. A sequence starring W. C. Fields was deleted before release.
w Ben Hecht, Ferenc Molnar, Donald Ogden Stewart, Samuel Hoffenstein, Alan Campbell, Ladislas Fodor, Laslo Vadnay, Laszlo Gorog, Lamar Trotti, Henry Blankfort d Julien Duvivier ph Joseph Walker m Sol Kaplan
☆ Charles Boyer, Rita Hayworth, Thomas Mitchell;, Ginger Rogers, Henry Fonda, Cesar Romero, Gail Patrick, Roland Young;, Charles Laughton, Elsa Lanchester, Victor Francen, Christian Rub, Edward G. Robinson, George Sanders, James Gleason and also Paul Robeson, Ethel Waters, Eddie Anderson
† Duvivier was clearly chosen to make this film because of his success with the similar *Carnet de Bal*; he and Boyer went on to make the less successful *Flesh and Fantasy* on similar lines.

Tales of Mystery and Imagination: see *Histoires Extraordinaires*

Tales of Ordinary Madness

Italy/France 1981 108m Eastmancolor
English version
23 Giugno/Ginis (Jacqueline Ferreri)
📼 ▦ 🔍

A drunken poet is obsessed by sex but can't find a happy relationship with his women.
Outlandish, episodic wallow, mostly on Venice beach in California. Not for maiden aunts, and probably not for anyone else either.
w Marco Ferreri and others book *Erections, Ejaculations, Exhibitions and Tales of Ordinary Madness* by Charles Bukowski d Marco Ferreri ph Tonino Delli Colli m Philippe Sarde
☆ Ben Gazzara, Ornella Muti, Susan Tyrrell, Tanya Lopert, Katia Berger
'By turns repellent, naive and risible.' – *Sight*

Tales of Terror *

US 1962 90m Pathécolor Panavision
AIP (Roger Corman)
▦

'Morella': a dying girl discovers the mummified body of her mother. 'The Black Cat': a henpecked husband kills his wife and walls up the body. 'The Facts in the Case of M Valdemar': an old man is hypnotized at the moment of death.
Tolerable short story compendium, rather short on subtlety and style.
w Richard Matheson stories Edgar Allan Poe d Roger Corman ph Floyd Crosby m Les Baxter
☆ Vincent Price, Peter Lorre, Basil Rathbone, Debra Paget

Tales of the Taira Clan *

Japan 1955 108m Eastmancolor
Daiei
📼

original title: *Shin Heike Monogatari*
In the mid-1100s, an ambitious samurai becomes involved in the struggle for power between two royal courts and armed monks.
Deft, colourful, though stately, period movie of a seminal moment in Japanese history, when military power became paramount, that successfuly combines personal and dynastic dramas.
w Yoshikata Yoda, Masahige Narusawa, Kyuichi Tsuji novel Eiji Yoshikawa d Kenji Mizoguchi ph Kazuo Miyagawa m Fumio Hayasaka
☆ Raizo Ichikawa, Ichijiro Oya, Tatsuya Ishiguro, Michiyo Kogure, Eijiro Yanagi, Naritoshi Hayashi, Eitaro Shindo, Ichiro Sugau

'An orgy of the damned!'
Tales That Witness Madness

GB 1973 90m colour
Paramount/Amicus (Milton Subotsky, Norman Priggen)
Five ghostly tales linked by an old bookshop.
Extreme example of the Amicus compendiums.
w Jay Fairbank d Freddie Francis ph Norman Warwick m Bernard Ebbinghouse
☆ Jack Hawkins, Donald Pleasence, Georgia Brown, Donald Houston, Suzy Kendall, Peter McEnery, Joan Collins, Michael Jayston, Kim Novak, Michael Petrovitch, Mary Tamm

Talk About a Lady

US 1946 71m bw
Columbia
A country cousin comes to town and makes good.
Easy-going musical filler, better than some.
w Richard Weil, Ted Thomas d George Sherman
☆ Jinx Falkenburg, Forrest Tucker, Joe Besser, Trudy Marshall, Richard Lane, Stan Kenton and his orchestra

Talk About a Stranger *

US 1952 65m bw
MGM (Richard Goldstone)
In a small town, gossip is unjustly aroused over a mysterious stranger who is suspected of various crimes.
Unusual though rather naïve second feature, directed for more than its worth.
w Margaret Fitts novel Charlotte Armstrong d David Bradley ph John Alton m David Buttolph
☆ George Murphy, Nancy Davis, Lewis Stone, Billy Gray, Kurt Kasznar

Talk About Jacqueline

GB 1942 84m bw
Excelsior/Marcel Hellman
A girl is mistaken for her naughtier sister.
Thin, very British comedy with nowhere to go.
w Roland Pertwee, Marjorie Deans novel Katherine Holland d Harold French
☆ Hugh Williams, Carla Lehmann, Joyce Howard, Roland Culver, John Warwick, Mary Jerrold, Guy Middleton, Max Adrian

Talk of the Devil

GB 1936 78m bw
B and D
An impersonator pins a crooked deal on a magnate, who kills himself.
Glum drama chiefly notable as the first film to be shot at Pinewood Studios.
w Carol Reed, George Barraud, Anthony Kimmins d Carol Reed

☆ Ricardo Cortez, Sally Eilers, Basil Sydney, Randle Ayrton, Charles Carson

The Talk of the Town ***

US 1942 118m bw
Columbia (George Stevens, Fred Guiol)
📼 ▦ 🔍

A girl loves both a suspected murderer and the lawyer who defends him.
Unusual mixture of comedy and drama, delightfully handled by three sympathetic stars.
w Irwin Shaw, Sidney Buchman d George Stevens ph Ted Tetzlaff m Frederick Hollander ad Lionel Banks, Rudolph Sternad ed Otto Meyer
☆ Ronald Colman, Cary Grant, Jean Arthur, Edgar Buchanan, Glenda Farrell, Charles Dingle, Emma Dunn, Rex Ingram
'A rip-roaring, knock-down-and-drag-out comedy about civil liberties.' – *John T. McManus*
'Well tuned and witty, at its best when it sticks to the middle ground between farce and melodrama. The chief fault of the script is its excessive length and the fact that a standard lynching mob climax is followed by a prolonged anti-climax.' – *Newsweek*
'I can't take my lynching so lightly, even in a screwball. Still, I am all for this kind of comedy and for players like Arthur and Grant, who can mug more amusingly than most scriptwriters can write.' – *Manny Farber*
'Did the authors think they were writing a Shavian comedy of ideas? The ideas are garbled and silly, but the people are so pleasant that the picture manages to be quite amiable and high-spirited.' – *Pauline Kael, 70s*
'I knew it was going to come off all along: it didn't have that element of hazard in it. It was more of an understood flight with a take-off time and an arrival time and not too much headwind.' – *George Stevens*
† Two endings were filmed: the eventual choice of mate for Miss Arthur was determined by audience reaction at previews.
🎬 best picture; original story (Sidney Harmon); script; Ted Tetzlaff; Frederick Hollander; art direction; Otto Meyer

Talk Radio **

US 1988 109m DeLuxe
Fox/Cineplex Odeon/Ten-Four Productions (Edward R. Pressman, A. Kitman Ho)
📼 ▦ 🔍 🎧

Billed as 'the man you love to hate', the host of a radio talk-show, whose private life is a mess, courts trouble by abusing his listeners.
Powerful, virulent near-monologue of a mind at the end of its tether, filmed in an appropriately restless style.
w Eric Bogosian, Oliver Stone play Eric Bogosian, Ted Savinar book *Talked to Death: The Life and Murder of Alan Berg* by Stephen Singular d Oliver Stone ph Robert Richardson m Stewart Copeland pd Bruno Rubeo ed David Brenner, Joe Hutshing
☆ Eric Bogosian, Alec Baldwin, Ellen Greene, Leslie Hope, John C. McGinley, John Pankow, Michael Wincott

The Tall Blond Man with One Black Shoe: see *Le Grand Blond avec une Chaussure Noire*

Tall, Dark and Handsome

US 1941 78m bw
TCF
In 1929 Chicago, a gangster aspires to be a gentleman.
Moderate crime comedy.
w Karl Tunberg, Darrell Ware d H. Bruce Humberstone
☆ Cesar Romero, Virginia Gilmore, Charlotte Greenwood, Milton Berle, Sheldon Leonard
🎨 Karl Tunberg, Darrell Ware

The Tall Guy

GB 1989 92m Eastmancolor
Virgin/LWT/Working Title (Tim Bevan)
📼 ▦ 🔍

The stooge to a sadistic comedian tries for stardom on his own.
Lamentably unfunny comedy, ponderously directed.
w Richard Curtis d Mel Smith ph Adrian Biddle m Peter Brewis pd Grant Hicks ed Dan Rae

☆ Jeff Goldblum, Emma Thompson, Rowan Atkinson, Geraldine James, Emil Wolk, Kim Thomson, Harold Innocent, Anna Massey

The Tall Headlines

GB 1952 100m bw
Grand National/Raymond Stross
aka: *The Frightened Bride*
A family is affected when the eldest son is executed for murder.
Glum, boring, badly cast, badly written and generally inept melodrama.
w Audrey Erskine Lindop, Dudley Leslie novel Audrey Erskine Lindop d Terence Young ph C. M. Pennington-Richards m Hans May
☆ Flora Robson, Michael Denison, Mai Zetterling, Jane Hylton, André Morell, Dennis Price, Mervyn Johns, Naunton Wayne
'A falsity which will surely surprise even those familiar with the conventions of British middle-class cinema.' – *Lindsay Anderson*

Tall in the Saddle

US 1944 87m bw
RKO (Robert Fellows)
📼 ▦ 🔍

The newly-arrived ranch foreman finds that his boss has been murdered.
Quite a watchable, and forgettable, mystery Western.
w Michael Hogan, Paul J. Fix d Edwin L. Marin ph Robert de Grasse m Roy Webb md Constantin Bakaleinikoff
☆ John Wayne, Ella Raines, Ward Bond, George 'Gabby' Hayes, Audrey Long, Elizabeth Risdon, Don Douglas, Paul Fix, Russell Wade

Tall Man Riding

US 1955 83m Warnercolor
Warner
An adventurer feuds with a rancher but in the end marries his daughter.
Unremarkable star Western.
w Joseph Hoffman d Lesley Selander ph Wilfred Cline m Paul Sawtell
☆ Randolph Scott, Robert Barrat, Dorothy Malone, Peggie Castle, John Dehner

The Tall Men *

US 1955 122m DeLuxe Cinemascope
TCF (William A. Bacher, William B. Hawks)
📼 ▦ 🔍

After the Civil War, two Texans head north for the Montana goldfields.
Solid star Western.
w Sydney Boehm, Frank Nugent novel Clay Fisher d Raoul Walsh ph Leo Tover m Victor Young
☆ Clark Gable, Jane Russell, Robert Ryan, Cameron Mitchell, Juan Garcia, Harry Shannon, Emile Meyer
'A big action feast and value for anyone's money.' – *Newsweek*

Tall Story

US 1960 91m bw
Warner/Mansfield (Joshua Logan)
▦ 🔍

A college basketball player faces various kinds of trouble when he marries.
Dislikeable campus comedy with leading players miscast.
w Julius J. Epstein novel *The Homecoming Game* by Howard Nemoor d Joshua Logan ph Ellsworth Fredericks m Cyril Mockridge
☆ Anthony Perkins, Jane Fonda, Ray Walston, Anne Jackson, Marc Connelly, Murray Hamilton, Elizabeth Patterson

The Tall Stranger

US 1957 83m DeLuxe Cinemascope
Allied Artists
Cared for by wagon train pioneers after being mysteriously shot, a rancher tries to help them settle.
Fair star Western with some tough action.
w Christopher Knopf story Louis L'Amour d Thomas Carr ph Wilfred Cline m Hans J. Salter
☆ Joel McCrea, Virginia Mayo, Barry Kelley, Michael Ansara, Whit Bissell

---

🏥 film suitable for family viewing   📼 VHS video-cassette for the British PAL system   ▦ VHS video-cassette for the British PAL system in wide screen-format   🖵 Video cassette in a computer-colourised version   ▦ American NTSC video-cassette   🔍 Laser disc

The Tall T *
US 1957 78m Technicolor
Columbia/Scott-Brown (Harry Joe Brown)
🖭
Three bandits hold up a stagecoach and take a hostage, but are outwitted by a rancher.
Good small-scale suspense Western with plenty of action and a blood-spattered finale.
w Burt Kennedy d Budd Boetticher ph Charles Lawton Jnr m Heinz Roemheld
☆ Randolph Scott, Richard Boone, Maureen O'Sullivan, Arthur Hunnicutt, Skip Homeier, John Hubbard, Henry Silva

Tall Tale
†† US 1995 96m Technicolor
Panavision
Buena Vista/Walt Disney/Caravan (Joe Roth, Roger Birnbaum)
🖭 🖭 @.
A boy trying to save the family farm enlists the aid of legendary heroes Pecos Bill, Paul Bunyan and John Henry.
Pleasant children's fable, though it hasn't the quality to lift it beyond the mundane.
w Steven L. Bloom, Robert Rodat d Jeremiah Chechik ph Janusz Kaminski m Randy Edelman pd Eugenio Zanetti ad Richard Chew
☆ Patrick Swayze, Oliver Platt, Roger Aaron Brown, Nick Stahl, Scott Glenn, Stephen Lang, Jared Harris, Catherine O'Hara, Burgess Meredith (uncredited)
'A lavishly produced, robustly entertaining Old West fantasy.' – *Variety*

The Tall Target **
US 1951 78m bw
MGM (Richard Goldstone)
A discredited police officer tries to stop the assassination of Abraham Lincoln on a train to Washington.
Lively period suspenser with excellent attention to detail and much of the attraction of The Lady Vanishes. The plot slightly relaxes its hold before the end.
w George Worthing Yates, Art Cohn d Anthony Mann ph Paul C. Vogel ad Cedric Gibbons, Eddie Imazu
☆ Dick Powell, Adolphe Menjou, Paula Raymond, Marshall Thompson, Ruby Dee, Richard Rober, Will Geer, Florence Bates
'An intelligent minor picture which makes good use of its material.' – *MFB*

Tallinn Pimeduses: see *Darkness in Tallinn*

Ta'm e Guilass: see *A Taste of Cherry*

Tamahine
GB 1962 95m Technicolor Cinemascope
ABP (John Bryan)
The headmaster of a boys' school is visited by his glamorous half-caste Polynesian cousin.
Simple-minded school comedy with predictable situations.
w Denis Cannan novel Thelma Niklaus d Philip Leacock ph Geoffrey Unsworth m Malcolm Arnold
☆ John Fraser, Nancy Kwan, Dennis Price, Derek Nimmo, Justine Lord, James Fox, Coral Browne, Michael Gough, Allan Cuthbertson

The Tamarind Seed *
GB 1974 125m Eastmancolor Panavision
Jewel/Lorimar/Pimlico (Ken Wales)
🖭
While holidaying in Barbados, a British widow falls for a Russian attaché.
Old-fashioned romance which turns into a mild spy caper. A well-heeled time-passer.
wd Blake Edwards novel Evelyn Anthony ph Frederick A. Young m John Barry ad Harry Pottle ed Ernest Walter
☆ Julie Andrews, Omar Sharif, Sylvia Syms, Dan O'Herlihy, Anthony Quayle, Oscar Homolka
'A painless timekiller, but one wishes Miss Andrews didn't always give the impression that she had just left her horse in the hallway.' – *Michael Billington, Illustrated London News*

The Taming of the Shrew *
US 1929 68m bw
United Artists/Pickford/Elton
🖭 @.
A condensed version of the play which did not do much in its day for its stars' then declining reputations, but can now be watched with a fair measure of enjoyment.
w William Shakespeare, 'with additional dialogue by Sam Taylor' d Sam Taylor ph Karl Struss pd William Cameron Menzies, Laurence Irving
☆ Douglas Fairbanks, Mary Pickford, Edwin Maxwell, Joseph Cawthorn, Clyde Cook, Dorothy Jordan
† A 'widescreen' version was issued in 1976.

'In the war between the sexes, there always comes a time to surrender unconditionally!'
The Taming of the Shrew *
†† US 1967 122m Technicolor
Panavision
Columbia/Royal/FAI (Richard McWhorter)
🖭 @.
Petruchio violently tames his shrewish wife.
Busy version of one of Shakespeare's more proletarian comedies; the words in this case take second place to violent action and rioting colour.
w Suso Cecchi d'Amico, Paul Dehn, Franco Zeffirelli d Franco Zeffirelli ph Oswald Morris, Luciano Trasatti m Nino Rota
☆ Richard Burton, Elizabeth Taylor, Michael York, Michael Hordern, Cyril Cusack, Alfred Lynch, Natasha Pyne, Alan Webb, Victor Spinetti
'As entertainment Kiss Me Kate is infinitely better but then Cole Porter was a real artist and Burton is a culture vulture.' – *Wilfrid Sheed*
'The old warhorse of a comedy has been spanked into uproarious life.' – *Hollis Alpert*

Tam-Lin
GB 1971 106m Technicolor Panavision
Winkast (Jerry Gershwin, Elliott Kastner)
aka: *The Devil's Widow*
aka: *The Ballad of Tam-Lin*
A sinister, beautiful, middle-aged widow has a diabolic influence on the bright young people she gathers around her.
Self-indulgent melodrama which might have worked with a shorter running time and a tighter script; as it was, it sank almost without trace.
w William Spier poem Robert Burns d Roddy McDowall ph Willy Williams m Stanley Myers
☆ Ava Gardner, Ian MacShane, Richard Wattis, Cyril Cusack, Stephanie Beacham, David Whitman, Fabia Drake, Sinead Cusack, Joanna Lumley, Jenny Hanley

Tammy: see *Tammy and the Bachelor*

Tammy and the Bachelor *
US 1957 89m Technicolor Cinemascope
U-I (Ross Hunter)
🖭
GB title: *Tammy*
A backwoods tomboy falls for a stranded flyer.
Whimsical romance for middle America, which started Hollywood's last series of proletarian family appeal before the family was entirely forsaken for four letter words.
w Oscar Brodney stories Cid Ricketts Summer d Joseph Pevney ph Arthur E. Arling m Frank Skinner m Joseph Gershenson
☆ Debbie Reynolds, Walter Brennan, Leslie Nielsen, Mala Powers, Fay Wray, Sidney Blackmer, Mildred Natwick
♫ song 'Tammy' (m/ly Ray Evans, Jay Livingston)

Tammy and the Doctor
US 1963 88m Eastmancolor
U-I/Ross Hunter
🖭
Tammy leaves her riverboat to accompany an old lady who needs an operation in the big city.
More artless family fodder.
w Oscar Brodney d Harry Keller ph Russell Metty m Frank Skinner
☆ Sandra Dee, Peter Fonda, Macdonald Carey, Beulah Bondi, Margaret Lindsay, Reginald Owen, Adam West
'The aura of simple religion and naïve philosophy remains singularly charmless.' – *MFB*

Tammy and the Millionaire
US 1967 88m Technicolor
Universal
Tammy becomes a private secretary in the big city.
A re-edit from four half-hour TV shows; not at all watchable.
w George Tibbles d Sidney Miller, Leslie Goodwins, Ezra Stone
☆ Debbie Watson, Donald Woods, Dorothy Green, Denver Pyle, Frank McGrath

Tammy Tell Me True
US 1961 97m Eastmancolor
U-I (Ross Hunter)
Tammy gets a college education and charms all comers.
Sugar-coated sequel to the original.
w Oscar Brodney d Harry Keller ph Clifford Stine m Percy Faith
☆ Sandra Dee, John Gavin, Charles Drake, Virginia Grey, Beulah Bondi, Julia Meade, Cecil Kellaway, Edgar Buchanan
'The heroine appears to be not so much old-fashioned as positively retarded.' – *MFB*

Tampico
US 1944 75m bw
TCF (Robert Bassler)
A tanker captain picks up survivors from a torpedoed ship and finds himself involved with spies.
Very minor action melodrama, efficiently made.
w Kenneth Gamet, Fred Niblo Jnr, Richard Macaulay d Lothar Mendes ph Charles G. Clarke m David Raksin
☆ Edward G. Robinson, Lynn Bari, Victor McLaglen, Marc Lawrence, E. J. Ballentine, Mona Maris

Tampopo **
Japan 1986 117m colour Panavision
Itami Productions/New Century Producers (Juzo Itami, Yashushi Tamaoki, Seigo Hosogoe)
🖭 🖭 @. ⊚
Encouraged by a truck driver, a woman learns to become the best of noodle cooks.
Witty, affectionate, episodic celebration of food as nourishment, pleasure and aid to sexual enjoyment, contained within a parody of film genres, notably the Western.
wd Juzo Itami ph Masaki Tamura m Kinihiko Murai ad Takeo Kimura ed Akira Suzuki
☆ Tsutomu Yamazaki, Nobuko Miyamoto, Koji Yakuso, Ken Watanabe, Rikiya Yasouka

Tanganyika
US 1954 81m Technicolor
Universal-International
A 1900 settler finds that the African colony of his choice is terrorized by a murderer.
Curious blend of outdoor action and who-is-it; not at all bad.
w Richard Alan Simmons and William Sackheim d André de Toth ph Maury Gertsman m Joseph Gershenson
☆ Van Heflin, Howard Duff, Ruth Roman, Jeff Morrow, Joe Comadaore

Tangier
US 1946 74m bw
Universal-International
A dancer hunts for the Nazi war criminal responsible for her father's death.
You can tell returns had been bad from the fact that the queen of Technicolor was sentenced to monochrome, and in a two-bit Casablanca.
w M. M. Musselman, Monty Collins d George Waggner
☆ Maria Montez, Kent Taylor, Robert Paige, Sabu, Preston Foster, Louise Albritton, Reginald Denny, J. Edward Bromberg
'A comedy that keeps women hopping.'

Tango ***
France 1993 90m colour
Cinea/Hachette Premiere/TF1/Zoulou (Henri Brichetti)
🖭 ◎
A woman-hating judge arranges the murder of his nephew's wife by a husband he acquitted of killing his wife and her lover.
An outrageous black comedy and a witty examination of masculine and feminine attitudes to life. Style, and sprightly acting, carry the day.
w Patrice Leconte, Patrick Dewolf d Patrice Leconte ph Eduardo Serra m Angelique and Jean-Claude Nachon ad Ivan Maussion ed Genevieve Winding
☆ Philippe Noiret, Richard Bohringer, Thierry Lhermitte, Miou Miou, Judith Godreche, Carole Bouquet, Jean Rochefort
'A deliciously dark comedy.' – *Variety*

Tango *
Argentina/Spain/France/Germany 1998 115m colour
Metrodome/Pandora/Sono/Alama Ata (Luis A. Scalella, Carlos L. Mentasti, Juan C. Codazzi)
A theatre director, rehearsing his new show about the tango, begins to fall for the girlfriend of his backer, who becomes the star of the musical.
More a dance drama than a straightforward narrative, this combines reality and performance, rehearsal with documentary; it's a beguiling mix for the most part.
wd Carlos Saura ph Vittorio Storaro m Lalo Schifrin ad Emilio Basaldua ed Julia Juaniz
☆ Miguel Angel Sola, Cecilia Narova, Mia Maestro, Juan Carlos Copes, Carlos Rivarola, Sandra Ballesteros, Oscar Cardoza Ocampo, Martin Seefeld
'A film with plenty of sole but not much soul.' – *Empire*

Tango & Cash
US 1989 101m Technicolor Panavision
Warner/Jon Peters, Peter Guber
🖭 🖭 @. ◎
Two cops, one suave, the other dishevelled, are jailed on a false murder charge but escape to get their revenge.
Deliberately stylized, over-the-top action movie that never touches reality at any point and provides some unintentional amusement.
w Randy Feldman d Andrei Konchalovsky ph Donald E. Thorin m Harold Faltermeyer pd J. Michael Riva ed Hubert de La Bouillerie, Robert Ferretti
☆ Sylvester Stallone, Kurt Russell, Jack Palance, Teri Hatcher, Michael J. Pollard, Brion James, Geoffrey Lewis, James Hong, Robert Z'Dar

The Tango Lesson
GB/France/Argentina/Japan/Germany 1997 102m bw/colour
Artificial Eye/Adventure/OKCK/PIE/MDF/Imagica/Pandora/Cinema Projects/Sigma (Christopher Sheppard)
🖭 🖭
A British film director becomes obsessed with the tango and takes lessons from an Argentinian expert, but insists that she become the lead dancer.
A playful film about dance, which blurs the line between fact and fiction; ultimately, it means more to its director and star than to any audience.
wd Sally Potter ph Robby Müller m Sally Potter, Fred Frith ch Pablo Veron pd Carlos Conti ed Harvé Schneid
☆ Sally Potter, Pablo Veron, Gustavo Naveira, Fabian Salas, David Toole, Carolina Iotti
'In one and the same film, she's revived the Hollywood musical and taken by storm a tenaciously protected male citadel of the dance world.' – *Alexander Walker, London Evening Standard*
'A monumentally humourless, self-regarding picture.' – *Philip French, Observer*

Tank
US 1984 113m Metrocolor
Lorimar/Universal (Irwin Yablans)
🖭 @.
A retired army sergeant lovingly restores an old tank and uses it to secure justice for his wrongly imprisoned son.
Fairly lively if predictable American fantasy in which one just man stands up against the uncaring and/or corrupt mob.
w Dan Gordon d Marvin Chomsky ph Don Birnkrant m Lalo Schifrin pd Bill Kenney
☆ James Garner, Shirley Jones, C. Thomas Howell, Mark Herrier, Dorian Harewood, G. D. Spradlin
'Further dispiriting evidence of the new reactionary spirit of Reagan's America.' – *Tom Milne, MFB*

Tank Commando: see *Tank Commandos*

Tank Commandos

US   1959   79m   bw
AIP (Burt Topper)
GB title: *Tank Commando*

In Italy in 1944, a US Army demolition unit destroy an underwater bridge to prevent the Germans reinforcing their troops.
Low-budget war movie that tries for both sentimentality and melodrama and misses its targets; its death-roll is high but uninvolving because its characters never come to life.
w Burt Topper *ph* John Nickolaus Jnr *m* Ronald Stein *ad* Dan Haller *ed* Ronald Sinclair, Asa Clark
☆ Donato Farretta, Robert Barron, Maggie Lawrence, Wally Campo, Leo V. Metranga, Jack Sowards, Anthony Rich, Larry Hudson, Maria Monay

'In 2033, justice rides a tank and wears lip gloss.'
Tank Girl

US   1994   104m   DeLuxe
United Artists/Trilogy (Richard B. Lewis, Pen Densham, John Watson)

In the future, when the world has been devastated by collision with a comet and there is a continuous drought, Tank Girl, with the aid of mutant dogs and kangaroos, battles against a madman trying to monopolize the water supplies.
A muddled attempt to transfer the British comic strip by Alan Martin and Jamie Hewlett to the screen. It is all flash and no substance or narrative, lacking in imagination and presenting a future that is more familiar than most pasts; brief cartoon interludes suggest that an animated approach might have been more successful.
w Tedi Sarafian *d* Rachel Talalay *ph* Gale Tattersall *m* Graeme Revell *pd* Catherine Hardwicke *ed* James R. Symons
☆ Lori Petty, Ice T, Naomi Watts, Don Harvey, Reg E. Cathey, Scott Coffey, Malcolm McDowell, Jeff Kober
'It is not a movie, really, but a rock soundtrack with a bit of plot hanging on for dear life.' – *Tom Shone, Sunday Times*
'If Tank Girl were real she would have shot everyone rather than let this be released in her name.' – *Leslie Felperin*
† The title role was originally to have been played by Emily Lloyd.

Tank Malling

GB   1988   109m   Metrocolor
Cineplex/Parkfield Pictures/Pointlane Films (Glen Murphy, Jamie Foreman)
An investigative reporter is framed for murder.
Trivial thriller with a confusing plot and a silly denouement.
w James Marcus, Mick Southworth *d* Jamie Marcus *ph* Jason Lehel *m* Rick Fenn, Nick Mason *pd* Geoffrey Sharpe, Chris Cook *ed* Brian Peachey
☆ Ray Winstone, Jason Connery, Amanda Donohoe, Glen Murphy, Marsha Hunt, Peter Wyngarde, John Conteh, Terry Marsh, Nick Berry

Tanks a Million

US   1941   50m   bw
Hal Roach
An army recruit has a freak memory which keeps him out of trouble.
Acceptable programme filler.
w Paul Gerard Smith, Warren Wilson, Edward E. Seabrook *d* Fred Guiol
☆ William Tracy, James Gleason, Noah Beery Jnr, Joe Sawyer, Elyse Knox, Douglas Fowley
♫ Edward Ward (music)

The Tanks Are Coming

US   1951   90m   bw
Warner
A tough sergeant learns humility during the race to Berlin.
Tedious war drama which tries in vain to interest us in non-characters.
w Robert Hardy Andrews *story* Samuel Fuller *d* D. Ross Lederman, Lewis Seiler *ph* Edwin DuPar *m* William Lava
☆ Steve Cochran, Paul Picerni, Mari Aldon, Harry Bellaver, Philip Carey

Tap *

US   1989   101m   Technicolor   Panavision
Braveworld/Fox/Morgan Creek/BECO (Tony Adams)

A tap-dancer turned jewel-thief is persuaded to put on his dancing shoes again.
Its slight narrative is bolstered by an enjoyable celebration of the dying art of tap.
wd Nick Castle *ph* David Gribble *m* James Newton Howard *pd* Patricia Norris *ed* Patrick Kennedy
☆ Gregory Hines, Suzzanne Douglas, Sammy Davis Jnr, Savion Glover, Joe Morton, Dick Anthony Williams, Sandman Sims, Bunny Briggs, Steve Condos

Tap Roots

US   1948   109m   Technicolor
Universal-International (Walter Wanger)
A Southern family tries to remain neutral in the Civil War.
Minor Gone with the Wind saga, quite expensively produced but not very exciting.
w Alan le May *novel* James Street *d* George Marshall *m* Winton C. Hoch, Lionel Lindon *m* Frank Skinner
☆ Susan Hayward, Van Heflin, Boris Karloff, Julie London, Whitfield Connor

Taps

US   1981   126m   DeLuxe
TCF/Stanley Jaffe

Cadets at a military academy go on strike when the site is sold for development, and violence ensues.
Rather uninteresting moral fable, comparable with the British If. The moral attitudes are worked out on entirely predictable lines.
w Darryl Ponicsan, Robert Mark Kamen *novel* Father Sky by Devery Freeman *d* Harold Becker *ph* Owen Roizman *m* Maurice Jarre
☆ Timothy Hutton, George C. Scott, Ronny Cox, Sean Penn, Tom Cruise, Brendan Ward

'Even science was stunned!'
Tarantula

US   1955   80m   bw
U-I (William Alland)

Scientists working on an artificial food become grossly misshapen, and an infected spider escapes and grows to giant size.
Moderate monster hokum with the desert setting which became a cliché; the grotesque faces are more horrific than the spider, which seldom seems to touch the ground.
w Robert M. Fresco, Martin Berkeley *d* Jack Arnold *ph* George Robinson *md* Joseph Gershenson
☆ Leo G. Carroll, John Agar, Mara Corday, Nestor Paiva
'It's a great children's picture ... particularly for bad children. It'll scare hell out of the little monsters.' – *Hollywood Reporter*

'Now! add a motion picture to the wonders of the world!'
Taras Bulba *

US   1962   124m   Eastmancolor   Panavision
UA/H-H/Avala (Harold Hecht)

A cossack leader has bitter disagreements with his rebellious son.
Violent action epic based on a well-worn story; plenty of spectacular highlights.
w Waldo Salt, Karl Tunberg *novel* Nicolai Gogol *d* J. Lee-Thompson *ph* Joe MacDonald *m* Franz Waxman *pd* Edward Carrere
☆ Yul Brynner, Tony Curtis, Christine Kaufmann, Sam Wanamaker, Guy Rolfe, George Macready, Vladimir Sokoloff, Abraham Sofaer
♫ Franz Waxman

La Tarea

Mexico   1990   85m   colour
Metro/Clasa Films Mundiales (Pablo Barbachano, Francisco Barbachano)

aka: *Homework*
A husband and wife indulge in a sexual fantasy with the aid of a video camera.
Curiously uninvolving, voyeuristic movie that fails to illuminate its theme of sex in the cinema.

wd Jaime Humberto Hermosillo *ph* Toni Kuhn *m* Luis Arcaraz *ad* Laura Santa Cruz
☆ Maria Rojo, José Alonso, Xanic Zepeda, Christopher

Target

US   1985   117m   Technicolor
CBS/Richard Zanuck, David Brown

When his wife is kidnapped, an ex-spy goes back into action.
Lethargic, simple-minded, and often ludicrous melodrama: the intent seems to be to pile up as many clichés of the genre as the writers can remember.
w Howard Berk, Don Petersen *d* Arthur Penn *ph* Jean Tournier *m* Michael Small
☆ Gene Hackman, Matt Dillon, Gayle Hunnicutt, Josef Sommer, Guy Boyd, Herbert Berghof

Target for Scandal: see *Washington Story*

Target for Tonight ****

GB   1941   48m   bw
The Crown Film Unit

The story of a bombing raid over Germany.
Classic RAF semi-documentary, not quite so genuine as it seems since many scenes were re-created in the studio.
w Harry Watt, B. Cooper *d* Harry Watt
'It looks like a sure grosser ... one of the must-see films of 1941.' – *Variety*
🏆 Special AA

Target Harry

US   1969   81m   colour
ABC/Corman Company (Gene Corman)

aka: *How to Make It*
Various criminals try to discover the whereabouts of printing plates for banknotes that have gone missing from the Royal Mint.
Low budget variation on The Maltese Falcon with an uncharismatic cast. The director's name hides the identity of Roger Corman.
w Bob Barbash *d* Henry Neill *ph* Patrice Pouget *m* Les Baxter *pd* Sharon Compton *ed* Monte Hellman
☆ Vic Morrow, Suzanne Pleshette, Victor Buono, Cesar Romero, Stanley Holloway, Charlotte Rampling, Michael Ansara, Katy Fraysse, Fikret Hakan

Target Zero

US   1955   93m   bw
Warner (David Weisbart)
An infantry patrol in Korea is cut off behind enemy lines.
Routine battle exploits with a highly unlikely superimposed romance.
w Sam Rolfe *d* Harmon Jones *ph* Edwin DuPar *m* David Buttolph
☆ Richard Conte, Charles Bronson, Richard Stapley, Chuck Connors, L. Q. Jones, Peggie Castle

Targets *

US   1967   90m   Pathécolor
Peter Bogdanovich (Paramount)

An elderly horror film star confronts and disarms a mad sniper at a drive-in movie.
Oddball melodrama apparently meant to contrast real and fantasy violence; it doesn't quite work despite effective moments, and the low budget shows.
wd Peter Bogdanovich *story* Polly Platt *ph* Laszlo Kovacs *pd* Polly Platt
☆ Boris Karloff, Tim O'Kelly, James Brown, Sandy Baron

The Tarnished Angels

US   1957   91m   bw   Cinemascope
U-I (Albert Zugsmith)
A reporter falls in with a self-torturing family of circus air aces.
Unsatisfactory attempt to reunite the talents of Written on the Wind; a dull story, very boringly presented.
w George Zuckerman *novel* Pylon by William Faulkner *d* Douglas Sirk *ph* Irving Glassberg *m* Frank Skinner *md* Joseph Gershenson
☆ Rock Hudson, Robert Stack, Dorothy Malone, Jack Carson, Robert Middleton

'Married to a man she doesn't love! Loving a man she can't have! What does life hold for this pampered beauty of the drawing rooms?'
Tarnished Lady

US   1931   80m   bw
Paramount
Two society women and their lovers cross each other's paths.
Exaggerated melodrama which failed to justify the London stage reputation of its American star.
w Donald Ogden Stewart *d* George Cukor
☆ Tallulah Bankhead, Clive Brook, Phoebe Foster, Alexander Kirkland, Osgood Perkins, Elizabeth Patterson
'A poor picture that fits the straight grinds best. Heavy production but too ponderous to mean anything.' – *Variety*

Tars and Spars

US   1945   86m   bw
Columbia (Milton H. Bren)
Adventures of members of the Coast Guard's touring wartime revue.
Limp musical with interesting talent.
w John Jacoby, Sarett Tobias, Decla Dunning, Barry Trivers *d* Alfred E. Green
☆ Alfred Drake, Sid Caesar, Janet Blair, Marc Platt, Jeff Donnell

The Tartars

Italy   1960   105m   Technicolor   Totalscope
Lux (Riccardo Gualino)
Viking settlers on the Russian steppes fight Tartar invaders.
Action-packed comic strip.
d Richard Thorpe *ph* Amerigo Genarelli *m* Renzo Rossellini
☆ Orson Welles, Victor Mature, Folco Lulli, Arnoldo Foa

Tartu: see *The Adventures of Tartu*

Tarzan

The talkie *Tarzans* (qv) began with Johnny Weissmuller and tailed off from there. (See *Filmgoer's Companion* for the silents.) The 1932 version more or less followed the original Edgar Rice Burroughs novel, and all the MGM entries had a special vivid quality about them, but subsequently the productions, usually produced under the aegis of Sol Lesser, tailed off towards the standard of the TV series of the sixties starring Ron Ely. In the 80s, John Derek revived the series as a vehicle for his wife, and Hugh Hudson promised to return to Burroughs's original, but merely added some intellectual pretension of his own. In 1998, Casper Van Dien tried unsuccessfully to make the role his own.
1929 Tarzan the Tiger
1932 Tarzan the Ape Man
1933 Tarzan the Fearless
1934 Tarzan and His Mate
1935 The New Adventures of Tarzan
1936 Tarzan Escapes
1938 Tarzan's Revenge; Tarzan and the Green Goddess
1939 Tarzan Finds a Son
1941 Tarzan's Secret Treasure
1942 Tarzan's New York Adventure
1943 Tarzan Triumphs; Tarzan's Desert Mystery
1945 Tarzan and the Amazons
1946 Tarzan and the Leopard Woman
1947 Tarzan and the Huntress
1948 Tarzan and the Mermaids
1949 Tarzan's Magic Fountain
1950 Tarzan and the Slave Girl
1951 Tarzan's Peril
1952 Tarzan's Savage Fury
1953 Tarzan and the She-Devil (aka: *Tarzan Meets the Vampire*)
1955 Tarzan's Hidden Jungle
1957 Tarzan and the Lost Safari
1958 Tarzan's Fight for Life
1959 Tarzan's Greatest Adventure
1959 Tarzan the Ape Man
1960 Tarzan the Magnificent
1962 Tarzan Goes to India
1963 Tarzan's Three Challenges
1966 Tarzan and the Valley of Gold
1967 Tarzan and the Great River
1968 Tarzan and the Jungle Boy
1981 Tarzan the Ape Man
1984 Greystoke: The Legend of Tarzan, Lord of the Apes
1998 Tarzan and the Lost City

Tarzan ***

US 1999 88m Technicolor
Buena Vista/Walt Disney (Bonnie Arnold)
▣ ▤ ◎ ○

An orphaned baby, adopted by a great ape, grows up to discover that he is human, and becomes king of the apes.

Clever, fast-moving animated adventure that keeps the songs in the background so that they don't hold up the action; it proves there is still plenty of life left in traditional methods of animation, though it also makes use of some exciting computer-generated effects.

w Tab Murphy, Bob Tzudiker, Noni White, David Reynolds, Jeffrey Stepakoff *story* Tarzan and the Apes by Edgar Rice Burroughs d Kevin Lima, Chris Buck m Mark Mancina m/ly Phil Collins ad Daniel St Pierre ed Gregory Perler

☆ Featuring voices: Tony Goldwyn, Minnie Driver, Glenn Close, Brian Blessed, Nigel Hawthorne, Lance Henriksen, Wayne Knight, Alex D. Linz, Rosie O'Donnell

'The emphasis here is on trad storytelling made wondrous, and it works.' – *Ian Nathan, Empire*

♪ song 'You'll Be in My Heart' (m/l Phil Collins)

Tarzan and His Mate *

US 1934 105m bw
MGM (Bernard H. Hyman)
▤ ◎

Tarzan foils ivory poachers who are searching for the elephants' graveyard.

A slick adventure, for its time, with a carefree jungle couple and lots of lions and stampeding elephants.

w James K. McGuinness, Howard Emmett Rogers, Leon Gordon *story* Edgar Rice Burroughs d Cedric Gibbons ph Clyde DeVinna, Charles Clarke ad A. Arnold Gillespie ed Tom Held

☆ Johnny Weissmuller, Maureen O'Sullivan, Neil Hamilton, Paul Cavanagh, Forrester Harvey, William Stack

† Although Gibbons received the directorial credit, he was replaced early on by Jack Conway.

†† The Hays Office objected to the skimpy costume worn by O'Sullivan and the inference that she and Tarzan were not only living in the jungle, but also in sin. The later films turned her into a more respectable, all-American housewife with a tree-house to call home.

Tarzan and the Amazons

♈ US 1945 76m bw
RKO/Champion (Sol Lesser)

Tarzan goes to the aid of a tribe of Amazons threatened by gold hunters, though at first they do not welcome his help.

A moderately well-done adventure, but beginning to show signs of tiredness and lack of invention.

w Hans Jacoby, Marjorie L. Pfaelzer d Kurt Neumann ph Archie Stout md Paul Sawtell ad Walter Koessler ed Robert O. Crandall

☆ Johnny Weissmuller, Brenda Joyce, Johnny Sheffield, Henry Stephenson, Maria Ouspenskaya, Barton MacLane, Don Douglas

Tarzan and the Great River

♈ US/Switzerland 1967 88m
Eastmancolor Panavision
Paramount/Banner/Allfin (Sy Weintraub)

Tarzan tracks down the killers of his friend, a zoo director, with the aid of a lion and a chimpanzee.

Lacklustre adventure with an uncharismatic hero and, even by the standards of the series, stock characters and narrative.

w Bob Barbash, Lewis Reed d Robert Day ph Irving Lippman m William Loose ad Herbert Smith ed Anthony Carras, Edward Mann

☆ Mike Henry, Jan Murray, Manuel Padilla Jnr, Diana Millay, Rafer Johnson, Paulo Grazindo

Tarzan and the Green Goddess

♈ US 1938 72m bw
Principal/Burroughs-Tarzan (George W. Stout, Ashton Dearholt, Edgar Rice Burroughs)
▤

Tarzan travels to South America to ensure that a statue with strange powers is kept safe from thieves.

Dreary low-budget effort, with stilted acting and direction.

w Charles F. Royal *story* Edgar Rice Burroughs d Edward Kull ph Ernest F. Smith, Edward Kull ad Charles Clague ed Thomas Neff

☆ Herman Brix (Bruce Bennett), Ula Holt, Frank Baker, Dale Walsh, Harry Ernest, Don Castello, Lewis Sergent, Jiggs the Monkey

Tarzan and the Huntress

♈ US 1947 72m bw
RKO (Sol Lesser)

Tarzan fights off hunters who are stealing animals to restock zoos.

Pleasant-enough time-waster, recycling familiar material with a modicum of enthusiasm.

w Jerry Gruskin, Rowland Lee d Kurt Neumann ph Archie Stout m Paul Sawtell ad McClure Capps ed Merrill White

☆ Johnny Weissmuller, Brenda Joyce, Johnny Sheffield, Patricia Morison, Barton MacLane, John Warburton, Cheta

† It was Johnny Sheffield's last appearance in the role of Tarzan's adopted son. Two years later, he went on to star in his own series of a dozen jungle films, as Bomba the Jungle Boy (qv).

Tarzan and the Jungle Boy

♈ US/Switzerland 1968 90m
Eastmancolor Panavision
Paramount/Banner/Allfin (Robert Day)

Tarzan helps a journalist search for a young boy lost in the jungle seven years earlier.

A dull entry in the series, with not much action and a great deal of muscle flexing.

w Stephen Lord d Robert Gordon ph Ozen Sermet m William Loose ad Herbert Smith ed Milton Mann, Reg Browne

☆ Mike Henry, Alizia Gur, Ronald Gans, Rafer Johnson, Ed Johnson, Steven Bond

Tarzan and the Jungle Queen: see *Tarzan's Peril*

Tarzan and the Leopard Woman

US 1946 72m bw
RKO (Sol Lesser)

Investigating a massacre, apparently by leopards, Tarzan discovers a sinister tribe ruled by a pitiless queen.

Enjoyable hokum with camp overtones, though by this date it looked as though it was becoming increasingly difficult for Weissmuller to swing through the trees.

☆ Johnny Weissmuller, Johnny Sheffield, Brenda Joyce, Acquanetta, Edgar Barrier, Tommy Cook, Dennis Hoey

Tarzan and the Lost City

US 1998 84m Technicolor
Warner (Stanley Canter, Dieter Geissler, Michael Lake)

Tarzan abandons his wedding plans to stop an evil explorer, who is destroying the jungle and its inhabitants in a search for the city where civilization began.

Lacklustre attempt to revive the fortunes of the Ape-man, suffering from a bland hero, no imagination in the narrative or direction and no confidence in the source material.

w Bayard Johnson, J. Anderson Black *stories* Edgar Rice Burroughs d Carl Schenkel ph Paul Gilpin m Christopher Franke pd Herbert Pinter ed Harry Hitner

☆ Caspar Van Dien, Jane March, Steven Waddington, Winston Ntshona, Rapulana Seiphemo, Ian Roberts

'Comes across more like a sequel to *George of the Jungle*, but without the laughs.' – *Variety*

Tarzan and the Lost Safari

GB 1957 84m Technicolor Cinemascope
MGM/Sol Lesser (John Croydon)

Tarzan rescues the survivors of a plane crash who are threatened by a ruthless white hunter.

Effective adventure that gained from being shot on location and in colour.

w Montgomery Pittman, Lillie Hayward d Bruce Humberstone ph C. R. Pennington-Richards m Clifton Parker ad Geoffrey Drake ed William Lewthwaite

☆ Gordon Scott, Robert Beatty, Yolande Donlan, Betta St John, Wilfrid Hyde-White, George Coulouris, Peter Arne, Cheta

† It was the first Tarzan movie to be shot on African locations.

Tarzan and the Mermaids

US 1948 68m bw
RKO (Sol Lesser)

Tarzan goes to the aid of a pearl diver, one of a tribe threatened by a ruthless white trader.

Lively adventure that includes a fight with an octopus and gains from the expertise of Draper and Tiomkin.

w Carroll Young d Robert Florey ph Jack Draper md Dimitri Tiomkin ad McClure Capps ed Merrill White

☆ Johnny Weissmuller, Brenda Joyce, Linda Christian, John Lanenz, Fernando Wagner, Edward Ashley, George Zucco

† It was Weissmuller's final appearance in the role of Tarzan, though he stayed in the jungle to make 16 low-budget movies as the white hunter Jungle Jim (qv), which he followed with a 26-episode TV series.

Tarzan and the She-Devil

♈ US 1953 76m bw
RKO (Sol Lesser)

Tarzan is taken prisoner by ivory hunters.

A cheap and cheerless movie, with little action and much talk, incorporating stock footage.

w Karl Lamb, Carroll Young d Kurt Neumann ph Karl Struss md Paul Sawtell ad Carroll Clark ed Leon Barsha

☆ Lex Barker, Joyce MacKenzie, Monique Van Vooren, Raymond Burr, Tom Conway, Robert Bice, Mike Ross, Cheta

Tarzan and the Slave Girl

♈ US 1950 73m bw
RKO (Sol Lesser)

Tarzan rescues Jane from kidnap by a tribe whose women have died in an epidemic.

An unexciting adventure, in which the chimp steals the movie from his uninvolved co-stars.

w Hans Jacoby, Arnold Belgard d Lee Sholem ph Russell Harlan md Paul Sawtell ad Harry Horner ed Christian Nyby

☆ Lex Barker, Vanessa Brown, Robert Alda, Hurd Hatfield, Arthur Shields, Tony Caruso, Denise Darcel, Robert Warwick, Cheta

Tarzan and the Trappers

US 1958 74m colour
Sol Lesser
▤

Tarzan fights to save jungle creatures from ruthless trappers and treasure hunters.

Standard, undistinguished stuff, cut down from three episodes of an unsuccessful TV series.

w Frederick Schlick, Robert Leach d Charles Haas, Sandy Howard, H. Bruce Humberstone (uncredited) ph William Snyder, Alan Stensvold md Audrey Granville ad Ernst Fegte ed George A. Gittens

☆ Gordon Scott, Eve Brent, Rickie Sorenson, Leslie Bradley, Maurice Marsac, William Keene, Scatman Crothers

Tarzan and the Valley of Gold

US/Switzerland 1966 90m Eastmancolor Panavision
AIP/Banner/Allfin (Sy Weintraub)

Tarzan stops a ruthless crook stealing the treasure from a lost Aztec city.

Dull action with an earnest hero and little else to get excited about.

w Clair Huffaker d Robert Day ph Irving Lippman m Van Alexander ad José Rodriguez Granada ed Frank P. Keller

☆ Mike Henry, David Opatoshu, Manuel Padilla Jnr, Nancy Kovack, Don Megowan, Frank Brandstetter, Eduardo Noriega

† It was the first of Mike Henry's three movies as Tarzan.

Tarzan Escapes

US 1936 95m bw
MGM (Sam Zimbalist)
▤ ◎

Tarzan is captured by a white hunter, who plans to exhibit him in Britain.

The ape-man is beginning to be tamed into a more suburban way of life in this third outing, with much of the excitement and fun missing.

w Cyril Hume, John Farrow, Karl Brown d Richard Thorpe ph Leonard Smith ad E. E. Sheeley ed W. Donn Hayes

☆ Johnny Weissmuller, Maureen O'Sullivan, John Buckler, Benita Hume, William Henry, E. E. Clive, Cheta

† Nearly all the film was reshot after lukewarm audience reaction at previews.

Tarzan Finds a Son!

♈ US 1939 90m bw
MGM (Sam Zimbalist)
▤

Tarzan and Jane rescue and adopt a small boy, who is the only survivor of a plane crash.

The arrival of a five-year-old boy emphasizes that the series was being redirected towards juvenile audiences; on that level, it is moderately entertaining.

w Cyril Hume d Richard Thorpe ph Leonard Smith ad Cedric Gibbons, Urie McCleary ed Frank Sullivan, Gene Ruggiero

☆ Johnny Weissmuller, Maureen O'Sullivan, John Sheffield, Ian Hunter, Henry Stephenson, Frieda Inescort, Henry Wilcoxon

† The original script had O'Sullivan, who wanted to leave the series, dying; but Burroughs refused to allow his character to be killed off.

Tarzan Goes to India

US/GB/Switzerland 1962 86m Metrocolor Cinemascope
MGM/Banner/Allfin (Sy Weintraub)

Tarzan rescues a herd of elephants from floods caused by a new dam.

In an attempt to inject a little life into the series, the locale was shifted to India, but the result was no more than a cheap imitation of Elephant Boy.

w Robert Hardy Andrews, John Guillermin d John Guillermin ph Paul Beeson m Ken Jones, Ravi Shankar, Panchal Jaikishan ad George Provis ed Max Benedict

☆ Jock Mahoney, Mark Dana, Leo Gordon, Simi, Feroz Khan, Murad, Jai, Gajendra

Tarzan the Ape Man **

US 1932 99m bw
MGM
▤ ◎

Tarzan, Lord of the Jungle, falls in love with Jane, an American girl who is searching for the fabled elephants' graveyard with her explorer father.

The first sound version of Tarzan and still the best, despite its lack of sophistication; it is a tightly edited, action-packed adventure that retains its freshness and fantasy appeal.

w Cyril Hume, Ivor Novello *novel* Edgar Rice Burroughs d W. S. Van Dyke ph Harold Rosson, Clyde DeVinna ad Cedric Gibbons ed Ben Lewis, Tom Held

☆ Johnny Weissmuller, Neil Hamilton, Maureen O'Sullivan, C. Aubrey Smith, Doris Lloyd, Forrester Harvey, Ivory Williams

† Burroughs was paid $40,000 for the rights, though MGM were prepared to go to $100,000.

†† Hume named two of the jungle tribes Jocohnnies, after Joe Cohn, head of the production department, and Gibbonies, after Cedric Gibbons.

††† Tarzan's famous yell, heard for the first time in this movie, was created by Douglas Shearer using a combination of electronic methods and Weissmuller's shout played backwards.

Tarzan the Ape Man

♈ US 1959 82m Technicolor
MGM (Al Zimbalist)

A white hunter and his daughter discover a man raised by apes living in the African jungle.

Dire remake of the original film, incorporating tinted footage from it and earlier films.

w Robert Hill *story* Edgar Rice Burroughs d Joseph Newman ph Paul C. Vogel m S. Rogers ad Hans Peters, Malcolm Brown ed Gene Ruggiero

☆ Denny Miller, Joanna Barnes, Cesare Danova, Robert Douglas, Thomas Yangha

'The most exciting pair in the jungle!'

Tarzan the Ape Man

US 1981 112m Metrocolor
MGM/Svengali (Bo Derek)
▣ ▤ ◎

A young woman goes to Africa in search of her lost father, an explorer, and also finds Tarzan.

Tedium in the jungle: Derek simpers and prepares herself for wet T-shirt competitions, Harris rants and roars, O'Keeffe looks confused, and the result is certainly the worst of the Tarzan movies and possibly the most banal film so far made; even the animals give poor performances.

---

w Tom Rowe, Gary Goddard *novel* Edgar Rice Burroughs *d* John Derek *ph* John Derek, Wolfgang Dickmann *ad* Alan Roderick-Jones *ed* James B. Ling

☆ Bo Derek, Miles O'Keeffe, Richard Harris, John Phillip Law, Wilfrid Hyde-White, Akushula Selayah, Steven Strong

'The only apparent rationale of John Derek's resolutely sexist treatment of the old yarn is a besotted desire to celebrate his wife's physical attributes in various exotic settings and erotic costumes.' – Martyn Auty, *MFB*

Tarzan the Fearless

↟↟ US 1933 61m bw
Principal (Sol Lesser)
◉

Tarzan does battle with the worshippers of the jungle god Zar, in order to reunite a woman with her father.

A cheap and undistinguished rival to MGM's superior series, edited from the first four episodes of a 12-part serial.

w Basil Dickey, George Plympton *d* Robert Hill *ph* Harry Neumann, Joseph Brotherton *md* Abe Meyer *ed* Carl Himm

☆ Buster Crabbe, Jacqueline Wells, E. Alyn Warren, Edward Woods, Philo McCullough, Matthew Betz, Frank Lackteen, Mischa Auer

Tarzan the Magnificent

US 1960 88m Technicolor
Paramount/Solar (Sy Weintraub)
Tarzan escorts a criminal through the jungle to justice.

Tedious entry in a series that had run out of ideas and imagination; it might have been better had they gone back to Burroughs's original books for inspiration.

w Berne Giler, Robert Day *d* Robert Day *ph* Ted Scaife *m* Ken Jones *ad* Ray Simm *ed* Bert Rule

☆ Gordon Scott, Jock Mahoney, Betta St John, John Carradine, Lionel Jeffries, Alexandra Stewart, Carl Cameron, Charles Tingwell, Al Mulock

† It was Scott's last movie as Tarzan. He was replaced by Mahoney, who, confusingly, plays the villain here.

Tarzan the Tiger

US 1929 bw serial: 10 eps
Universal
Tarzan rescues Jane from slave traders.
Primitive talkie serial.
d Henry McRae
☆ Frank Merrill, Natalie Kingston, Lillian Worth, Al Ferguson

Tarzan Triumphs

US 1943 78m bw
RKO (Sol Lesser)
Tarzan defends the princess of a jungle city from attacking Germans.
Tarzan joins in the war effort in this very ordinary flag-waver.
w Carroll Young, Roy Chanslor *d* William Thiele *ph* Harry Wild *md* Paul Sawtell *pd* Harry Horner *ed* Hal Kern
☆ Johnny Weissmuller, Johnny Sheffield, Frances Gifford, Stanley Ridges, Sig Rumann, Pedro de Cordoba, Cheta

Tarzan's Deadly Silence

US 1970 88m colour
National General (Leon Benson)
Tarzan is faced by a mad colonel.
Edited from the TV series starring Ely, this is dull and uninspired stuff.
w Lee Erwin, Jack A. Robinson, John Considine, Tim Considine *d* Robert L. Friend, Lawrence Dobkin *ph* Abraham Vialla *m* Walter Greene *ed* Gabriel Torres
☆ Ron Ely, Manuel Padilla Jnr, Jock Mahoney, Woody Strode, Gregorio Acosta, Rudolph Charles, Nichelle Nichols

Tarzan's Desert Mystery

US 1943 70m bw
RKO/Principal (Sol Lesser)
Tarzan battles in the Sahara desert against Nazis, Arabs and giant spiders.
One of the more unusual films in the series: a delirious, incident-packed fantasy that made little sense, but provided unexpected thrills.
w Edward T. Lowe *story* Carroll Young *d* William Thiele *ph* Harry Wild, Russ Harlan

m Paul Sawtell *md* C. Bakaleinikoff *ad* Hans Peters *ed* Ray Lockert
☆ Johnny Weissmuller, Johnny Sheffield, Nancy Kelly, Otto Kruger, Joe Sawyer, Robert Lowery

Tarzan's Fight for Life

US 1958 86m Metrocolor
MGM (Sol Lesser)
Tarzan comes to the aid of a medical man threatened by the power of a witch doctor.
Cheap and dreadful studio-bound movie, lacking any sort of excitement.
w Thomas Hal Phillips *d* Bruce Humberstone *ph* William Snyder *m* Ernest Gold *ad* Ernst Fegte *ed* Aaron Stell
☆ Gordon Scott, Eve Brent, James Edwards, Carl Benton Reid, Woody Strode, Rickie Sorensen, Cheta

Tarzan's Greatest Adventure

GB 1959 85m Eastmancolor
Paramount/Solar (Sy Weintraub, Harvey Hayutin)
Tarzan pursues a ruthless boatload of killers who are in search of a diamond mine.
Brisk action-packed drama, with an effective mix of animals, explosions, villains and a little romance.
w Berne Giler, John Guillermin *story* Les Crutchfield *d* John Guillermin *ph* Ted Scaife *m* Douglas Gamley *ad* Michael Stringer *ed* Bert Rule
☆ Gordon Scott, Anthony Quayle, Sara Shane, Sean Connery, Niall MacGinnis, Scilla Gabel, Al Mulock

Tarzan's Hidden Jungle

US 1955 73m bw
RKO (Sol Lesser)
Tarzan saves the animals of the jungle from a ruthless hunter.
Moderate adventure that marked the advent of Scott in the title role.
w William Lively *d* Harold Schuster *ph* William Whitley *m* Paul Sawtell *ad* William Flannery *ed* Leon Barsha
☆ Gordon Scott, Vera Miles, Peter Van Eyck, Don Beddoe, Jester Hairston, Rex Ingram, Jack Elam, Cheta

Tarzan's Jungle Rebellion

US 1967 92m colour
National General (Steve Shagan)
Tarzan protects archaeologists who are investigating a burial ground from a hostile tribe.
Dreary little movie, cobbled together from episodes of a TV series.
w Jackson Gillis *d* William Whitney *ph* Abraham Vialla *m* Nelson Riddle *ad* José Rodriguez Granada *ad* Renn Reynolds
☆ Ron Ely, Manuel Padilla Jnr, Ulla Stromstedt, Sam Jaffe, William Marshall, Harry Lauter, Jason Evers

Tarzan's Magic Fountain *

↟↟ US 1949 73m bw
RKO (Sol Lesser)
Tarzan protects a fountain of youth from raiders.
Lively adventure in the footsteps of She and Lost Horizon.
w Curt Siodmak, Harry Chandlee *d* Lee Sholem *ph* Karl Struss *m* Alexander Laszlo *ad* McClure Capps *ed* Merrill White
☆ Lex Barker, Brenda Joyce, Evelyn Ankers, Albert Dekker, Charles Drake, Alan Napier, Henry Kulky

Tarzan's New York Adventure

US 1942 71m bw
MGM (Frederick Stephani)
▥ ◎~
Tarzan and Jane go to Manhattan to rescue their kidnapped son.
A little amusement is gained from the culture clash of Tarzan in an urban jungle, but one misses animals.
w Myles Connolly, William R. Lipman *d* Richard Thorpe *ph* Sidney Wagner *md* David Snell *ad* Cedric Gibbons *ed* Gene Ruggiero
☆ Johnny Weissmuller, Maureen O'Sullivan, Johnny Sheffield, Virginia Grey, Charles Bickford, Paul Kelly, Chill Wills, Russell Hicks, Mantan Moreland, Elmo Lincoln
† The urban jungle also served as a setting for *Tarzan in Manhattan*, starring Joe Ely, which was a pilot made in 1989 for a TV series that never materialized.

Tarzan's Peril

↟↟ US 1951 79m bw
RKO (Sol Lesser)
GB title: *Tarzan and the Jungle Queen*
Tarzan goes to the rescue of Jane and an embattled princess when gunrunners stir up a jungle war.
Standard stuff that gained from being filmed on location in Africa.
w Samuel Newman, Francis Swann, John Cousins *d* Byron Haskin *ph* Karl Struss *m* Michel Michelet *ad* John Meehan *ed* Jack Murray
☆ Lex Barker, Virginia Huston, George Macready, Douglas Fowley, Glen Anders, Frederick O'Neal, Dorothy Dandridge, Alan Napier

Tarzan's Revenge

US 1938 70m bw
TCF/Principal (Sol Lesser)
▥
Tarzan rescues a woman captured by a jungle ruler.
A minor movie with an absentee hero, as the movie concentrates on the plight of champion swimmer Eleanor Holm.
w Robert Lee Johnston, Jay Vann *story* Edgar Rice Burroughs *d* D. Ross Leterman *ph* George Meehan *m* Hugo Riesenfeld *ad* Lewis J. Rachmil *ed* Gene Milford
☆ Glenn Morris, Eleanor Holm, C. Henry Gordon, Hedda Hopper, George Meeker, Corbet Morris
† Glenn Morris was the 1936 Olympic decathlon champion. It was his only appearance in the role, acting not being among his talents.

Tarzan's Savage Fury

US 1952 80m bw
RKO/Principal (Sol Lesser)
Tarzan goes into action against crocodile and diamond hunters who threaten the lives of a boy and a local tribe.
Tame episode in the series, with a feeble script and little energy in the acting.
w Cyril Hume, Hans Jacoby, Shirley White *d* Cy Enfield *ph* Karl Struss *m* Paul Sawtell *ad* Walter Keller *ed* Frank Sullivan
☆ Lex Barker, Dorothy Hart, Patric Knowles, Charles Korvin, Tommy Carlton

Tarzan's Secret Treasure

US 1941 81m bw
MGM (B. P. Fineman)
▤ ◎~
Tarzan goes to the rescue of his son, who has been kidnapped by a tribe who want to sacrifice the boy.
Enjoyable adventure that manages some suspense and excitement, if beginning to lose much of the rough magic the series possessed in its earlier days.
w Myles Connolly, Paul Gangelin *d* Richard Thorpe *ph* Clyde de Vinna *m* David Snell *ad* Cedric Gibbons *ed* Gene Ruggiero
☆ Johnny Weissmuller, Maureen O'Sullivan, John Sheffield, Reginald Owen, Barry Fitzgerald, Tom Conway, Philip Dorn, Cordell Hickman, Cheta

Tarzan's Three Challenges

US 1963 92m Metrocolor
MGM/Sy Weintraub
Tarzan escorts the heir to the Thai throne across country to protect him from his wicked uncle.
An exotic location and a slick script gave a little fresh impetus to the series.
w Berne Giler, Robert Day *d* Robert Day *ph* Ted Scaife *m* Joseph Horovitz *ad* Wilfrid Shingleton *ed* Fred Burnley
☆ Jock Mahoney, Woody Strode, Earl Cameron, Tsuruko Kobayashi, Jimmy Jamal
† Mahoney was unwell during shooting.

'It's that rare kind of movie that lights the spark that lights the heart!'

Task Force

US 1949 116m bw (Technicolor sequences)
Warner (Jerry Wald)
An admiral about to retire recalls his struggle to promote the cause of aircraft carriers.
Stilted and long-drawn-out flagwaver with too much chat and action highlights borrowed from wartime newsreel.
wd Delmer Daves *ph* Robert Burks, Wilfrid M. Cline *m* Franz Waxman
☆ Gary Cooper, Walter Brennan, Jane Wyatt, Wayne Morris, Julie London, Bruce Bennett, Stanley Ridges, Jack Holt

A Taste of Cherry **

Iran 1997 98m colour
Artificial Eye/Abbas Kiarostami
▥
original title: *Ta'm e Guilass*
In Tehran, a middle-aged man, who plans to kill himself, seeks someone to bury him.
A teasing meditation on death and the simpler joys of life, told in a series of episodic meetings that never reach a conclusion; what matters is the journey, not the destination.
wd Abbas Kiarostami *ph* Homayon Payvar *ad* Hassan Yekta Panah *ed* Abbas Kiarostami
☆ Homayon Ershadi, Abdol Hossain Bagheri
'Filmed with the piercing intensity of a parable.' – *Variety*

A Taste of Excitement

GB 1968 99m Eastmancolor
Trio Films (George Willoughby)
An English girl holidaying on the Riviera suspects that someone is trying to kill her.
Standard frightened lady/'they won't believe me' mystery with enough twists to satisfy addicts.
w Brian Carton, Don Sharp *novel* Waiting for a Tiger *by* Ben Healey *d* Don Sharp *ph* Paul Beeson *m* Keith Mansfield
☆ Eva Renzi, David Buck, Peter Vaughan, Sophie Hardy, Paul Hubschmid, Kay Walsh

Taste of Fear **

GB 1961 82m bw
Columbia/Hammer (Jimmy Sangster)
US title: *Scream of Fear*
A crippled heiress visits her long-lost father and is haunted by his corpse.
Smartly tricked-out sub-Hitchcock screamer with sudden shocks among the Riviera settings and a plot which Hammer borrowed from Les Diaboliques and used again and again.
w Jimmy Sangster *d* Seth Holt *ph* Douglas Slocombe *m* Clifton Parker *ad* Tom Goswell *ed* James Needs, Eric Boyd Perkins
☆ Susan Strasberg, Ann Todd, Ronald Lewis, Christopher Lee, Leonard Sachs
'All those creaking shutters, flickering candles, wavering shadows and pianos playing in empty rooms still yield a tiny frisson.' – *Penelope Houston*
'It plays its particular brand of the three-card trick with ingenuity and without scruple.' – *The Times*

A Taste of Honey ***

GB 1961 100m bw
British Lion/Bryanston/Woodfall (Tony Richardson)
▥ ▤
Adventures of a pregnant Salford teenager, her sluttish mother, black lover and homosexual friend.
Fascinating offbeat comedy drama with memorable characters and sharply etched backgrounds.
w Shelagh Delaney, Tony Richardson *play* Shelagh Delaney *d* Tony Richardson *ph* Walter Lassally *m* John Addison
☆ Rita Tushingham, Dora Bryan, Murray Melvin, Robert Stephens, Paul Danquah
'Tart and lively around the edges and bitter at the core.' – *Peter John Dyer*
'Rich, full work, directed with an unerring sense of rightness.' – *New Yorker*
🏆 best British picture; Dora Bryan; Rita Tushingham; screenplay

Taste the Blood of Dracula

GB 1970 95m Technicolor
Warner/Hammer (Aida Young)
▥ ▤
A depraved peer involves three Victorian businessmen in the reactivation of Dracula.
Latterday vampire saga, initially lively but mainly dreary.
w John Elder (Anthony Hinds) *d* Peter Sasdy *ph* Arthur Grant *m* James Bernard *ad* Scott MacGregor *ed* Chris Barnes
☆ Christopher Lee, Geoffrey Keen, Gwen Watford, Linda Hayden, Peter Sallis, Anthony Corlan, John Carson, Ralph Bates

---

'You haven't met her yet and she already hates you.'

Tatie Danielle **
France 1990 112m colour
Palace/Téléma/FR3/Les Productions du Champ
Poirer/Sofica (Charles Gassot)

A malicious elderly woman creates problems when she moves in with her nephew's family.
Sharp and enjoyable black comedy.
w Florence Quentin d Etienne Chatiliez ph Philippe Welt m Gabriel Yared pd Geoffroy Larcher ed Catherine Renault
☆ Tsilla Chelton, Catherine Jacob, Isabelle Nanty, Neige Dolsky, Eric Pratt, Laurence Février, Virgine Pradal
'A tart comedy providing welcome Gallic relief to the saccharine Hollywood-endorsed stereotypes of the elderly as armchair dispensers of love and bromides.' – *Variety*

The Tattered Dress
US 1957 93m bw Cinemascope
U-I (Albert Zugsmith)
While conducting a murder defence, a criminal lawyer annoys a vindictive small-town sheriff, who plots revenge.
Silly melodrama which rapidly loses interest after a promising start.
w George Zuckerman d Jack Arnold ph Carl Guthrie m Frank Skinner
☆ Jeff Chandler, Jack Carson, Jeanne Crain, Gail Russell, George Tobias, Edward Andrews, Philip Reed

'Every great love leaves its mark!'

Tattoo
US 1980 103m Technicolor
Joseph E. Levine (Robert F. Colesberry)

A mad tattooist kidnaps a cover girl and tattoos her all over before forcing her to have sex. She kills him.
And not before time.
w Joyce Bunuel d Bob Brooks ph Arthur Ornitz m Barry de Vorzon pd Stuart Wurtzel
☆ Bruce Dern, Maud Adams, Leonard Frey, Rikke Borge
'*The Collector* crossed with *Ai No Corrida* ... a sensational package for the eighties confected from ideas half remembered from other films.' – *Mark Lefanu, MFB*

Tausend Augen: see *A Thousand Eyes*

Tawny Pipit *
GB 1944 85m bw
GFD/Two Cities (Bernard Miles)
The life of a village in wartime is disrupted when two rare birds nest in a local meadow.
Pleasant, thin little comedy, a precursor of the Ealing school.
wd Bernard Miles, Charles Saunders ph Eric Cross m Noel Mewton-Wood
☆ Bernard Miles, Rosamund John, Niall MacGinnis, Jean Gillie, Christopher Steele, Lucie Mannheim, Brefni O'Rorke, Marjorie Rhodes
'Almost unimaginably genteel.' – *James Agee*
'Not quite dry enough for the epicures nor sweet enough for the addicts.' – *C. A. Lejeune*
'Seldom does such a piece of unsophisticated charm and humour reach the screen.' – *New York Times*

Taxi!
US 1931 68m bw
Warner (Robert Lord)
Independent cab drivers defy a powerful trust.
Sassy comedy drama with plenty going on.
w Kubec Glasmon, John Bright play *The Blind Spot* by Kenyon Nicholson d Roy del Ruth ph James Van Trees md Leo Forbstein
☆ James Cagney, Loretta Young, George E. Stone, Guy Kibbee, David Landau, Leila Bennett, Matt McHugh
'As a deese, dem and dose, chip-on-the-shoulder, on-the-make example of young America the audience knows no better interpretation on the screen than that which Cagney gives it. The populace are now expectant of this player socking all and sundry including all the women in the cast.' – *Variety*
'A sordid but amusing observation on minor metropolitan endeavours.' – *Time*

Taxi
US 1952 77m bw
TCF (Samuel G. Engel)
A taxi driver helps a young mother find her husband, and falls for her himself.
Practised sentimental guff, Hollywoodized from the French film Sans Laisser d'Adresse.
w D. M. Marshman Jnr, Daniel Fuchs d Gregory Ratoff ph Milton Krasner m Leigh Harline
☆ Dan Dailey, Constance Smith, Neva Patterson, Blanche Yurka, Walter Woolf King

Taxi *
France 1998 89m colour Technovision
Metrodome/ARP/TF1/Canal+ (Michèle Pétin, Laurent Pétin)

Arrested for speeding, a reckless pizza delivery motorcyclist turned taxi driver is forced to help an incompetent cop attempt to catch a German gang of bank robbers, who have eluded capture with their high-speed getaways.
A hectic thriller, modelled on American gangster movies, that is irreverent about everything, particularly the police; it is fun in an uncomplicated way and has one splendid joke at the end of the final car chase.
w Luc Besson d Gérard Pirès m IAM ad Jean-Jacques Gernolle ed Véronique Lange
☆ Samy Naceri, Frédérick Diefenthal, Marion Cotillard, Emma Sjöberg, Manuela Gouray, Bernard Farcy, Georges Neri
'A one trick movie and, although it's short, you wouldn't wish it any longer.' – *Edward Porter, Sunday Times*
† It was released on video in both a dubbed and a subtitled version.
†† The film was a great commercial success in France, which resulted in a sequel, Taxi 2.

The Taxi Dancer
US 1926 64m bw silent
MGM
A Virginia girl in the big city rises from dime-a-dance joints to the big time.
Mildly suggestive star melodrama which promises more than it gives.
w A. P. Younger and Robert Terry Shannon d Harry Millarde
☆ Joan Crawford, Owen Moore, Douglas Gilmore, Marc McDermott, Gertrude Astor

Taxi Driver ****
US 1976 114m Metrocolor
Columbia/Italo-Judeo (Michael and Julia Philips)

A lonely Vietnam veteran becomes a New York taxi driver and allows the violence and squalor around him to explode in his mind.
The epitome of the sordid realism of the 70s, this unlovely but brilliantly made film haunts the mind and paints a most vivid picture of a hell on earth.
w Paul Schrader d Martin Scorsese ph Michael Chapman m Bernard Herrmann
☆ Robert DeNiro, Jodie Foster, Cybill Shepherd, Peter Boyle, Leonard Harris, Harvey Keitel
'I don't question the truth of this material. I question Scorsese's ability to lift it out of the movie gutters into which less truthful directors have trampled it.' – *Stanley Kauffmann*
† Schrader says the story was modelled after the diaries of would-be assassin Arthur Bremer.
♪ best picture; Bernard Herrmann; Robert DeNiro; Jodie Foster
▽ Bernard Herrmann; Jodie Foster

Taxi to the Toilet: see *Taxi Zum Klo*

Taxi Zum Klo *
West Germany 1981 92m colour
Laurens Straub, Frank Ripploh, Horst Schier

aka: *Taxi to the Toilet*
A homosexual schoolteacher, at odds with his home-loving partner, spends his spare time cruising lavatories, bars and parks in search of sex.
A semi-autobiographical film, saved from unpleasantness by its sense of humour. Its scenes of homosexual activity in grubby lavatories, seedy apartments and at a tacky drag ball may turn off all but the similarly inclined.
wd Frank Ripploh ph Horst Schier m Hans Wittstatt ed Marina Kunze, Mathias von Gunten
☆ Frank Ripploh, Bernd Broaderup, Orpha Termin, Peter Fahrni, Dieter Godde

'An admirable film, not least for tackling its subject with a warm sense of humour.' – *Films and Filming*

A Taxing Woman **
Japan 1987 130m colour Panavision
Itami Productions (Juzo Itami)

original title: *Marusa no onna*
A dedicated female tax inspector investigates the financial affairs of a crooked hotelier
Quirky, slyly observant comedy of greed that was a big hit in Japan.
wd Juzo Itami ph Yonezo Maeda
☆ Nobuko Miyamoto, Tsutomu Yamazaki, Masahiko Tsugawa, Hideo Murota, Mitsuko Sugino

'The year is 2020. He's mostly human. He's totally invincible ... until now.'

TC 2000
Canada 1993 90m colour
Shapiro Glickenhaus/Film One (Jalal Merhi)

In the future, when criminal gangs control a polluted world and the rich live in a heavily protected underground environment, a former cop saves the world for more dumb movies like this.
A dim rip-off of Robocop with elements of Blade Runner, done without wit or style, featuring a scantily clad female cyborg and an illogical narrative; even when outnumbered, the cop's preferred method of law enforcement is kick-boxing.
wd T. J. Scott story J. Stephen Maunder, Richard M. Samuels ph Curtis Petersen m Varouje ad Jasna Stefanovic ed Reid Dennison
☆ Bolo Yeung, Jalal Merhi, Billy Blanks, Bobbie Phillips, Matthias Hues, Ramsay Smith, Gregory Philpott, Harry Mok, Kelly Gallant

'Years from now, when you talk about this – and you will – be kind!'
'Even the most daring story can be brought onto the screen when done with courage, honesty and good taste.'

Tea and Sympathy
US 1956 122m Metrocolor Cinemascope
MGM (Pandro S. Berman)

A sensitive teenage schoolboy is scorned by his tougher classmates, but his housemaster's wife takes him in hand ...
Overblown and bowdlerized version of a quiet little Broadway play; impeccable production values, but no spark.
w Robert Anderson (and the Hays office) play Robert Anderson d Vincente Minnelli ph John Alton m Adolph Deutsch ad William A. Horning, Edward Carfagno ed Ferris Webster
☆ Deborah Kerr, John Kerr, Leif Erickson, Edward Andrews, Darryl Hickman, Norma Crane, Ollie
'...mounted for the screen as if it were a precious objet d'art in danger from rioting but miraculously saved. Besides being archaic, the film is a prodigiously silly fable, pulling the realities with which it deals dishonestly, systematically out of whack.' – *Parker Tyler*

Tea for Two *
US 1950 97m Technicolor
Warner (William Jacobs)

A nearly bankrupt financier promises his niece 25,000 dollars for her new musical show if she can say no to every question for twenty-four hours.
Tinkly, quite amusing light musical which has little to do with No No Nanette on which it is allegedly based.
w Harry Clork d David Butler ph Wilfrid Cline md Ray Heindorf ch Le Roy Prinz
☆ Doris Day, Gordon MacRae, Gene Nelson, Eve Arden, Billy de Wolfe, S. Z. Sakall, Bill Goodwin, Patrice Wymore

'A story of civilised disobedience.'

Tea with Mussolini *
GB/Italy 1999 116m Cinecitta
UIP/Medusa/Universal

An illegitimate Italian boy is looked after by a group of elderly English expatriates, living in Florence; when they are interned during the Second World War he helps them survive with the aid of a wealthy American.
A blandly old-fashioned, nostalgic wallow, in which its gaggle of actresses tame fascists with a withering glance, and are upstaged by the buildings and Tuscan landscapes.

w John Mortimer, Franco Zeffirelli book *Autobiography* by Franco Zeffirelli d Franco Zeffirelli ph David Watkin m Alessio Vlad, Stefano Arnaldi ad Carlo Centolavigna, Gioia Fiorella Mariani ed Tariq Anwar
☆ Judi Dench, Joan Plowright, Maggie Smith, Cher, Lily Tomlin, Baird Wallace, Charlie Lucas, Massimo Ghini, Paolo Seganti, Paul Checquer, Tessa Pritchard
'Suffers from a fatal lack of focus and emotional center, reducing potentially involving material to a succession of individual scenes.' – *Derek Elley, Variety*
'An old queen's film, awash with a rapt savouring of stellar femininity and endearingly predictable in its casting of inept but decorative young men.' – *Andy Medhurst, Sight and Sound*
▽ Maggie Smith

Teachers
US 1984 106m Metrocolor
MGM-UA (Aaron Russo)

A burnt-out teacher is drawn back to his ideas despite, or because of, apparent lunacy in the administration.
Wildly unconsidered black comedy which takes stabs at everything and hits nothing.
w W. R. McKinney d Arthur Hiller ph David M. Walsh m Sandy Gibson pd Richard MacDonald ed Don Zimmermann
☆ Nick Nolte, JoBeth Williams, Judd Hirsch, Ralph Macchio, Richard Mulligan, Allen Garfield, Royal Dano

Teacher's Pet *
US 1958 120m bw Vistavision
Paramount/Perlberg-Seaton (William Perlberg)

A tough city editor falls for a lady professor of journalism and enrols as a student.
Overlong one-joke comedy which quickly reneges on its early promise; but the principals play up divertingly.
w Fay and Michael Kanin d George Seaton ph Haskell Boggs m Roy Webb
☆ Clark Gable, Doris Day, Gig Young, Mamie Van Doren, Nick Adams
♪ Fay and Michael Kanin; Gig Young

The Teahouse of the August Moon *
US 1956 123m Metrocolor Cinemascope
MGM (Jack Cummings)

Okinawa 1944: a wily interpreter helps American troops succumb to the oriental way of life.
Adequate, well-acted screen version of a Broadway comedy which succeeded largely because of its theatricality. A few good jokes remain.
w John Patrick play John Patrick d Daniel Mann ph John Alton m Saul Chaplin
☆ Marlon Brando, Glenn Ford, Eddie Albert, Paul Ford, Machiko Kyo, Henry Morgan

Tears for Simon: see *Lost*

The Teckman Mystery
GB 1954 90m bw
British Lion/London Films/Corona (Josef Somlo)
An author commissioned to write the biography of a dead airman finds him very much alive and his own life in danger.
Peripatetic spy story with the twists expected of this author; all quite enjoyable.
w Francis Durbridge, James Matthews BBC serial Francis Durbridge d Wendy Toye ph Jack Hilyard m Clifton Parker
☆ Margaret Leighton, John Justin, Michael Medwin, Meier Tzelniker, Roland Culver, George Coulouris, Raymond Huntley, Duncan Lamont

Ted and Venus
US 1991 100m CFI color
Double Helix/LA Dreams (Randolf Turrow, William Talmadge)

A bearded Venice Beach poet loses control when his romantic approach to a local beauty is rejected.
Misguided whimsy that meanders all over the place without getting anywhere interesting.
w Paul Ciotti, Bud Cort d Bud Cort ph Dietrich Lohmann m David Robbins pd Lynn Christopher ed Katina Zinner
☆ Bud Cort, Jim Brolin, Kim Adams, Carol Kane, Woody Harrelson, Rhea Perlman, Martin Mull, Timothy Leary, Gena Rowlands

Teen Agent

🕇🕇 US 1991 88m Technicolor
Warner (Craig Zadan, Neil Meron)

📼 ▦ ◉. 🎧

aka: *If Looks Could Kill*

A student is mistaken for a CIA undercover agent and assigned to guard a top European politician.
Tired teenage copy of the James Bond formula of gags and gadgetry.

w Darren Star *story* Fred Dekker d William Dear ph Doug Milsome m David Foster pd Guy J. Comtois ed John F. Link, Mark Stevens
☆ Richard Grieco, Linda Hunt, Roger Rees, Robin Bartlett, Gabrielle Anwar, Geraldine James, Roger Daltrey

Teen Wolf

🕇🕇 US 1985 91m United Color
Entertainment/Atlantic (Mark Levinson, Scott Rosenfelt)

📼 ▦ ◉.

An ineffective college basketball player finds he is a hereditary werewolf, and in his altered form becomes a star.
Bewilderingly silly teenage variation on a famous legend, good-natured but totally empty.

w Joseph Loeb III, Matthew Weisman d Rod Daniel ph Tim Suhrstedt m Miles Goodman ed Lois Freeman-Fox
☆ Michael J. Fox, James Hampton, Scott Paulin, Susan Ursitti

Teen Wolf Too

🕇🕇 US 1987 94m colour
Entertainment/Atlantic (Kent Bateman)

📼 ▦ ◉.

A college student with a talent for boxing makes the most of the fact that he is a werewolf.
Drear comedy sequel that attempts to reprise the original with a leaden touch.

w R. Timothy Kring *story* Joseph Loeb III, Matthew Weisman d Christopher Leitch ph Jules Brenner m Mark Goldenberg ad Peg McClellan ed Steven Polivka, Kim Secrist, Harvey Rosenstock, Raja Gosnell
☆ Jason Bateman, Kim Darby, John Astin, Paul Sand, James Hampton, Mark Holton, Estee Chandler

Teenage Bad Girl: see My Teenage Daughter

Teenage Frankenstein: see I Was a Teenage Frankenstein

Teenage Gang Debs

US 1966 77m bw
Jode (Jerry Denby)

A young hoodlum's new girl causes his downfall and trouble among the members of his biker gang.
No-budget exploitation flick, notable only for its lack of any talent, and its reliance on the obvious.

w Hy Cahl d Sande N. Johnsen ph J. Denby m Steve Karmen ad Pat Follmer
☆ Diane Conti, Joey Naudic, John Batis, Linda Gale, Sandra Kane, Eileen Scott, Sue McManus, Robin Nolan, Linda Cambi, Lin Kennedy

Teenage Monster

US 1957 65m bw
Marquette Productions

📼

A meteor turns a home-loving teenager into a hairy rampaging monster.
Ridiculous monster movie, inept in every respect.

w Ray Buffum d Jacques Marquette ph Taylor Byars
☆ Anne Gwynne, Gloria Castillo, Stuart Wade, Gilbert Perkins, Steven Parker, Charles Courtney

'Mean. Green. And on the screen'

Teenage Mutant Ninja Turtles *

🕇🕇 US 1990 93m Technicolor
Virgin/Golden Harvest/Limelight (Kim Dawson, Simon Fields, David Chan)

📼 ▦ ◉. ⊘ 🎧

Pizza-loving, sewer-dwelling turtles and their rat guru, mutated into half-human creatures by radioactivity, battle against a gang of teenage martial arts experts led by an evil Japanese ninja.
Comic-book mayhem brought to the screen in the frenetic style of rock videos, it took more money at the box-office than any other independent film has ever done.

w Todd W. Langen, Bobby Herbeck, from comic-book characters created by Kevin Eastman and Peter Laird d Steve Barron ph John Fenner m John Du Prez pd Roy Forge Smith ed William Gordean, Sally Menke, James Symons sp creatures designed by Jim Henson's Creature Shop
☆ Judith Hoag, Elias Koteas, Josh Pais, Michelan Sisti, Leif Tilden, David Forman, James Sato

Teenage Mutant Ninja Turtles II: The Secret of the Ooze

🕇🕇 US 1991 87m colour
TCF/Golden Harvest (Thomas K. Gray, Kim Dawson, David Chan)

📼 ▦ ◉. 🎧

The four mutant ninja turtles go into battle against their arch-enemy Shredder and his two new monsters, a mutant dog and tortoise.
A tame sequel, seemingly aimed at the young audience that watches the anodyne animated TV cartoon versions of the four sewer-dwelling heroes.

w Todd W. Langen d Michael Pressman ph Shelly Johnson m John Du Prez pd Ray Forge Smith ed John Wright, Steve Mirkovich
☆ Paige Turco, David Warner, Michelan Sisti, Leif Tilden, Kenn Troum, Mark Caso, Kevin Clash, Ernie Reyes Jnr, François Chau

'If watching the first Turtles film was like chewing a good pizza, watching II is more like munching on the cardboard packaging, but – as fast food goes – even that can taste good enough in parts.' – *David Lusted, Sight and Sound*

Teenage Mutant Ninja Turtles III: The Turtles Are Back ... in Time

🕇🕇 US 1992 96m Technicolor
TCF/Golden Harvest/Clearwater (Thomas K. Gray, Kim Dawson, David Chan)

📼 ▦ ◉. 🎧

The turtles travel back to 17th-century Japan to rescue their friend.
The least of the adventures, a tired and aimless movie lacking in fun.

wd Stuart Gillard ph David Gurfinkel m John Du Prez pd Roy Forge Smith ed William D. Gordean, James R. Symons
☆ Elias Koteas, Paige Turco, Stuart Wilson, Sab Shimono, Vivian Wu, Mark Caso, Matt Hill, Jim Raposa, David Fraser, James Murray, Henry Hayashi

'A decided case of diminishing returns.' – *Variety*

Teenage Rebel

US 1956 94m bw Cinemascope
TCF (Charles Brackett)

A wealthy California woman is visited by her teenage daughter from a former marriage; the girl proceeds to make difficulties for everyone.
The first film in black-and-white Cinemascope is a tedious drama of unreal people.

w Walter Reisch, Charles Brackett play Edith Sommer d Edmund Goulding ph Joe MacDonald m Leigh Harline ad Lyle Wheeler, Jack Martin Smith
☆ Ginger Rogers, Michael Rennie, Mildred Natwick, Betty Lou Keim, Warren Berlinger, Louise Beavers, Irene Hervey
⚵ art direction

Teheran

GB 1947 86m bw
Pendennis
US title: *The Plot to Kill Roosevelt*

A correspondent in Iran foils an assassination plot.
Low-key blood and thunder; passable time-filler.

w Akos Tolnay, William Freshman d William Freshman, Giacomo Gentilomo
☆ Derek Farr, Marta Labarr, Manning Whiley, John Slater, John Warwick

'Your next phone call may be your last!'

Telefon *

US 1977 103m Metrocolor Panavision
MGM (James B. Harris)

A Russian agent is instructed to seek out and destroy a ring of hard liners who are opposing detente with the west.
Moderately watchable espionage capers with a slightly new twist.

w Peter Hyams, Stirling Silliphant *novel* Walter Wager d Don Siegel ph Michael Butler m Lalo Schifrin

☆ Charles Bronson, Lee Remick, Donald Pleasence, Tyne Daly, Alan Badel, Patrick Magee, Sheree North

The Telegraph Trail

US 1933 55m bw
Warner

📼 ▦

An army scout ensures supplies reach the men building the first telegraph line across the West.
A lacklustre Western, with action scenes lifted from the silent The Red Raiders made seven years earlier, though Wayne does get to wear a rather fetching fringed jacket.

w Kurt Kempler d Tenny Wright
☆ John Wayne, Marceline Day, Frank McHugh, Otis Harlan, Yakima Canutt, Albert J. Smith, Clarence Geldert

Le Téléphone Rose: see The Pink Telephone

Television Spy

US 1939 58m bw
Paramount

Enemy agents compete for the secret of long-range television transmission.
Watchable pocket thriller, with the hero and heroine getting acquainted only by television from a 3000-mile distance.

w Horace McCoy, William R. Lipman, Lillie Hayward d Edward Dmytryk
☆ William Henry, Judith Barrett, William Collier Snr, Anthony Quinn, Richard Denning, John Eldredge

'It may move slowly, but it does avoid the absurdity that goes with the average film crack at television.' – *Variety*

Tell England

GB 1931 88m bw
British Instructional
US title: *The Battle of Gallipoli*

In 1914, school chums join up and mostly die at Gallipoli.
Even the most patriotic audiences ended up roaring with laughter at this stiff-upper-lip charade.

w Anthony Asquith *novel* Ernest Raymond d Anthony Asquith, Gerald Barkas ph Jack Parker, Stanley Rodwell
☆ Carl Harbord, Fay Compton, Tony Bruce, Dennis Hoey, Gerald Rawlinson, Wally Patch

'Not likely to bring in any money.' – *Variety*

Tell It to a Star

US 1945 67m bw
Republic (Walter H. Goetz)

A cigarette girl in a Florida hotel aspires to be a vocalist.
The plot sets the level: minor musical.

w John K. Butler d Frank McDonald
☆ Ruth Terry, Robert Livingston, Alan Mowbray, Franklin Pangborn, Isabel Randolph

Tell It to the Judge

US 1949 87m bw
Columbia (Buddy Adler)

▦

A female candidate for judicial honours is suddenly re-attracted to her divorced husband.
Leaden farce, relying entirely on its stars.

w Nat Perrin, Devery Freeman, Roland Kibbee d Norman Foster ph Joseph Walker m Werner Heymann
☆ Rosalind Russell, Robert Cummings, Gig Young, Marie McDonald, Harry Davenport

Tell It to the Marines

US 1926 75m bw silent
MGM

A marine sergeant has an eventful time during training and in the Philippines.
Lively war action piece with a more or less straight role for its star.

w Richard Schayer d George Hill
☆ Lon Chaney, William Haines, Eleanor Boardman, Carmel Myers, Warner Oland

Tell Me a Riddle

US 1980 90m CFI color
Godmother/Filmways

A dying old woman, long a recluse, is reconciled with her family.
Adequate if not exciting treatment of a very downbeat subject.

w Joyce Eliason, Alev Lytle *novel* Tillie Olsen d Lee Grant
☆ Lila Kedrova, Melvyn Douglas, Brooke Adams, Dolores Dorn, Lili Valenty, Zalman King

Tell Me That You Love Me, Junie Moon

US 1969 113m Technicolor
Paramount/Sigma (Otto Preminger)

A disfigured girl, a homosexual paraplegic and an introvert epileptic set up house together.
Absurd tragicomedy which remains disturbingly icky in conception and execution.

w Marjorie Kellogg *novel* Marjorie Kellogg d Otto Preminger ph Boris Kaufman m Philip Springer
☆ Liza Minnelli, Ken Howard, Robert Moore, Kay Thompson, Leonard Frey, James Coco, Fred Williamson

'Like seeing a venerated senior citizen desperately trying to show he's in love with today by donning see-through clothes.' – *Michael Billington, Illustrated London News*
'It slushes us with sentimentality to the point past compassion.' – *Judith Crist*

Tell Me Tonight

GB/Germany 1932 91m bw
Herman Fellner-Josef Somlo/Cine Alliance
US title: *Be Mine Tonight*

An Italian tenor falls in love with a Swiss mayor's daughter, but complicates matters by pretending to be someone else.
Bilingual operetta, fondly remembered for its singing star.

w John Orton d Anatole Litvak
☆ Jan Kiepura, Sonnie Hale, Magda Schneider, Edmund Gwenn, Athene Seyler

Tell No Tales **

US 1939 68m bw
MGM (Edward Chodorov)

A managing editor seeks a big scoop to save his newspaper, and solves a kidnap-murder case.
Intriguingly written and handled second feature, with excellent pace, performance and entertainment value.

w Lionel Houser d Leslie Fenton ph Joseph Ruttenberg m William Axt
☆ Melvyn Douglas, Louise Platt, Gene Lockhart, Douglass Dumbrille, Zeffie Tilbury, Halliwell Hobbes

'Full of excellent detail, and the smallest part is a genuine character. Add these qualities to its pace and excitement and you have something well worth seeing.' – *Richard Mallett, Punch*

Tell Them Willie Boy is Here *

US 1969 97m Technicolor
Universal/Jennings Lang (Philip A. Waxman)

📼 ▦

In 1909 an Indian turned cowboy comes up against old prejudices and is pursued into the desert after an accidental death.
Boringly predictable story of white man's guilt, very professionally made.

wd Abraham Polonsky *novel* Willie Boy by Harry Lawton ph Conrad Hall m Dave Grusin
☆ Robert Redford, Robert Blake, Katharine Ross, Susan Clark, Barry Sullivan, Charles McGraw, Charles Aidman, John Vernon
🎬 Robert Redford; Katharine Ross

Tell Your Children: see Reefer Madness

Telling Lies in America

US 1997 101m DeLuxe 'Scope
Banner/Kazui/Ben Myron

📼 ▦ ⊘

In Cleveland in the early 60s, a teenager finds it difficult to adjust to life at home with his immigrant Hungarian father and to a corrupt wider world working for a bribe-taking rock disc jockey.
A semi-autobiographical rites-of-passage drama that never acquires enough significance to connect to a wider audience.

w Joe Eszterhas d Guy Ferland ph Reynaldo Villalobos m Nicholas Pike pd James Gelarden ed Jill Savitt
☆ Kevin Bacon, Brad Renfro, Maximilian Schell, Calista Flockhart, Paul Dooley, Jonathan Rhys Meyers, Luke Wilson

'Offers little to audiences that hasn't been served up in quantity in the past.' – *Variety*

Tema: see The Theme

🕇🕇 film suitable for family viewing   📼 VHS video-cassette for the British PAL system   ▦ VHS video-cassette for the British PAL system in wide screen-format   ⊘ Video cassette in a computer-colourised version   ▤ American NTSC video-cassette   ◉. Laser disc

The Temp

US   1993   95m   DeLuxe
Paramount/Columbus Circle (David Permut, Tom Engelman)

A temporary secretary works her way up the executive ladder.

A feeble and forgettable drama of office life.

w Kevin Falls d Tom Holland ph Steve Yaconelli m Frederic Talgorn pd Joel Schiller ed Scott Conrad

☆ Timothy Hutton, Lara Flynn Boyle, Dwight Schultz, Oliver Platt, Steven Weber, Colleen Flynn, Faye Dunaway

'Derivative, artificial and moronic are the first adjectives that come to mind to describe this concoction.' – *Variety*

Tempest

Italy/France/Yugoslavia   1958   123m
Technirama
(Paramount)

Adventures of a Russian ensign banished by Catherine the Great.

Expensive but sloppy epic which fails to generate much interest.

w Louis Peterson, Alberto Lattuada, Ivo Perelli novel *The Captain's Daughter* by Alexander Pushkin d Alberto Lattuada ph Aldo Tonti m Piero Piccioni

☆ Van Heflin, Geoffrey Horne, Silvana Mangano, Oscar Homolka, Viveca Lindfors, Robert Keith, Vittorio Gassman, Finlay Currie, Agnes Moorehead, Helmut Dantine, Laurence Naismith

'Most men dream their fantasies. Philip decided to live his!'

Tempest

US   1982   142m   DeLuxe
Columbia (Paul Mazursky)

An architect leaves his unfaithful wife and takes his daughter to live on a Greek island attended only by a half-witted shepherd.

Absurd attempt to update Shakespeare; any initial amusement quickly gives way to abject boredom.

w Paul Mazursky, Leon Capetanos d Paul Mazursky ph Don McAlpine m Stomu Yamashta pd Pato Guzman

☆ John Cassavetes, Gena Rowlands, Susan Sarandon, Vittorio Gassman, Raul Julia, Jerry Hardin, Molly Ringwald, Paul Stewart

'An aura of dottiness hangs over it … the fact remains that it is handsomely visualized and, within the limits of the material, excellently played.' – *Tim Pulleine, MFB*

The Tempest

GB   1980   95m   Eastmancolor
Boyd's Company

A punk version of Shakespeare's play; less horrendous than might have been supposed, but far from interesting in its own right.

wd Derek Jarman ph Peter Middleton m Wavemaker

☆ Heathcote Williams, Karl Johnson, Toyah Wilcox, Peter Bull, Richard Warwick, Elisabeth Welch

Tempos dificeis, este tempo: see *Hard Times*

Temptation

US   1946   92m   bw
Universal (Edward Small)

An archaeologist's wife takes to poisoning both her husband and her blackmailing lover.

Hoary Edwardian melodrama, unpersuasively restaged.

w Robert Thoeren novel *Bella Donna* by Robert Hichens d Irving Pichel ph Lucien Ballard m Daniele Amfitheatrof

☆ Merle Oberon, George Brent, Charles Korvin, Paul Lukas, Lenore Ulric, Arnold Moss, Ludwig Stossel, Gavin Muir, Ilka Gruning, André Charlot

Temptation Harbour

GB   1946   104m   bw
ABP (Victor Skutezky)

A railway signalman finds and keeps stolen money.

Well-presented but boringly predictable melodrama with an overwrought leading performance set against yards of studio fog.

w Victor Skutezky, Frederic Gotfurt, Rodney Ackland novel *Newhaven/Dieppe* by Georges Simenon d Lance Comfort

☆ Robert Newton, Simone Simon, William Hartnell, Marcel Dalio, Margaret Barton, Edward Rigby, Joan Hopkins, Charles Victor, Kathleen Harrison

The Temptress *

US   1927   80m   bw   silent
MGM

An immoral woman drives men to disgrace, murder and suicide.

No-holds-barred melodrama which, being Garbo's second American film, fully confirmed her stardom.

w Dorothy Farnum d Mauritz Stiller, Fred Niblo

☆ Greta Garbo, Antonio Moreno, Lionel Barrymore, Roy D'Arcy, Marc McDermott

Temptress Moon *

Hong Kong/China   1996   116m   colour
Artificial Eye/Tomson/Shanghai Film (Tong Cunlin, Hsu Feng)

original title: *Fengyue*

A successful Shanghai gigolo, ordered to seduce his wealthy sister-in-law and steal her fortune, falls in love with her instead.

A bombastic melodrama on the pains of requited and unrequited love, intermittently enjoyable.

w Shu Kei, Wang Anyi, Chen Kaige d Chen Kaige ph Christopher Doyle m Zhao Jiping ad Huang Qiagui ed Pei Xianzhi

☆ Leslie Cheung, Gong Li, Kevin Lin, He Seifei, Xie Tian, Zang Shi, David Wu

† Some 15 minutes from the director's Hong Kong release were cut on the orders of its US distributors Miramax, who also resubtitled it.

†† The director sacked three actresses before asking Gong Li to play the role.

'Just when he thought it was safe to go back in the water…'

'10'

US   1979   122m   Metrocolor   Panavision
Warner/Orion/Geoffrey (Blake Edwards, Tony Adams)

A sex-mad middle-aged composer marks his girls from one to ten according to their performance.

Randy farce which struck some, but not all, audiences as the funniest thing since sliced bread.

wd Blake Edwards ph Frank Stanley m Henry Mancini pd Rodger Maus

☆ Dudley Moore, Julie Andrews, Bo Derek, Robert Webber, Dee Wallace, Sam Jones

♪ Henry Mancini; song 'It's Easy to Say' (mHenry Mancini, lyRobert Wells)

Ten Cents a Dance

US   1931   75m   bw
Columbia

A dance hostess is desired by a rich man but marries a ne'er-do-well.

Rubbishy story inspired by a then-popular song.

w Jo Swerling d Lionel Barrymore

☆ Barbara Stanwyck, Monroe Owsley, Ricardo Cortez, Sally Blane, Blanche Friderici

'It lacks the magic of fancy that makes for universal entertainment.' – *Variety*

'The mightiest dramatic spectacle of all the ages!'

The Ten Commandments **

US   1923   150m   bw (part Technicolor)
silent
Paramount/Famous Players-Lasky (Cecil B. de Mille)

Moses leads the Israelites into the promised land in modern San Francisco; a story of two brothers shows the power of prayer and truth.

The two halves in fact are totally disconnected; but this is a de Mille spectacular and therefore beyond reproach, while as a Hollywood milestone it cannot be denied a place in the Hall of Fame.

w Jeanie MacPherson d Cecil B. de Mille ph Bert Glennon and others (colour, Ray Rennahan)

☆ Theodore Roberts, Richard Dix, Rod la Rocque, Edythe Chapman, Leatrice Joy, Nita Naldi

'It will last as long as the film on which it is recorded.' – *James R. Quirk, Photoplay*

'What a story it tells! What majesty it encompasses! What loves it unveils! What drama it unfolds!'

The Ten Commandments *

US   1956   219m   Technicolor
Vistavision
Paramount/Cecil B. de Mille (Henry Wilcoxon)

The life of Moses and his leading of the Israelites to the Promised Land.

Popular but incredibly stilted and verbose bible-in-pictures spectacle. A very long haul along a monotonous route, with the director at his pedestrian worst.

w Aeneas Mackenzie, Jesse L. Lasky Jnr, Jack Gariss, Fredric M. Frank d Cecil B. de Mille ph Loyal Griggs m Elmer Bernstein ad Hal Pereira, Walter H. Tyler, Albert Nozaki ed Anne Bauchens

☆ Charlton Heston, Yul Brynner, Edward G. Robinson, Anne Baxter, Nina Foch, Yvonne de Carlo, John Derek, H. B. Warner, Henry Wilcoxon, Judith Anderson, John Carradine, Douglass Dumbrille, Cedric Hardwicke, Martha Scott, Vincent Price and also Debra Paget

'De Mille not only moulds religion into a set pattern of Hollywood conventions; he has also become an expert at making entertainment out of it.' – *Gordon Gow, Films and Filming*

'The result of all these stupendous efforts? Something roughly comparable to an eight-foot chorus girl – pretty well put together, but much too big and much too flashy … What de Mille has really done is to throw sex and sand into the moviegoers' eyes for almost twice as long as anyone else has ever dared to.' – *Time*

♪ special effects (John Fulton)

⧫ best picture; Loyal Griggs; art direction; editing; sound; costumes (Edith Head and others)

Ten Days in Paris

GB   1939   82m   bw
Columbia/Irving Asher (Jerome J. Jackson)
US title: *Missing Ten Days*
aka: *Spy in the Pantry*

An amnesiac wakes up in Paris and finds he has been involved in espionage activities.

Modest, quite likeable little comedy suspenser.

w John Meehan Jnr, James Curtis novel *The Disappearance of Roger Tremayne* by Bruce Graeme d Tim Whelan ph Otto Kanturek m Miklos Rozsa

☆ Rex Harrison, Karen Verne, Leo Genn, Joan Marion, Antony Holles, John Abbott, Hay Petrie

Ten Days That Shook the World: see *October*

Ten Gentlemen from West Point **

US   1942   104m   bw
TCF (William Perlberg)

Adventures in Indian territory, and back at West Point, of the first recruits to that military academy in the early 1800s.

Likeable mixture of comedy and flagwaving adventure, with excellent production values and a dominating performance.

w Richard Maibaum, George Seaton d Henry Hathaway ph Leon Shamroy m Alfred Newman

☆ Laird Cregar, George Montgomery, Maureen O'Hara, John Sutton, Shepperd Strudwick, Victor Francen, Harry Davenport, Ward Bond, Douglass Dumbrille, Ralph Byrd, Louis Jean Heydt

⧫ Leon Shamroy

Ten Little Indians *

GB   1966   91m   bw
Tenlit (Harry Alan Towers)

Ten people, including two servants, invited to a remote house in the Austrian Alps are murdered one by one.

Fair copy of a classic whodunnit.

w Peter Yeldham, Harry Alan Towers novel *Agatha Christie* d George Pollock ph Ernest Steward m Malcolm Lockyer

☆ Wilfrid Hyde-White, Dennis Price, Stanley Holloway, Leo Genn, Shirley Eaton, Hugh O'Brian, Daliah Lavi, Fabian, Mario Adorf, Marianne Hoppe

† Made also in 1945 and 1975, as *And Then There Were None* (qv).

Ten Little Niggers: see *And Then There Were None (1945)*

Ten North Frederick *

US   1958   102m   bw   Cinemascope
TCF (Charles Brackett)

At the funeral of a local politico, his family and friends think back to the events of his life.

Small beer, but a generally adult and entertaining family drama despite a miscast lead.

wd Philip Dunne novel John O'Hara ph Joe MacDonald m Leigh Harline

☆ Gary Cooper, Geraldine Fitzgerald, Diane Varsi, Stuart Whitman, Suzy Parker, Tom Tully, Ray Stricklyn, John Emery

10.30 pm Summer

US/Spain   1966   85m   Technicolor
UA/Jorill/Argos (Jules Dassin, Anatole Litvak)

The neurotic Greek wife of an Englishman travelling in Spain becomes obsessed with a murderer on the run.

Preposterously overwrought romantic melodrama.

w Jules Dassin, Marguerite Duras novel Marguerite Duras d Jules Dassin ph Gabor Pogany m Christobel Halffter

☆ Peter Finch, Melina Mercouri, Romy Schneider, Julian Mateos

Ten Rillington Place **

GB   1971   111m   Eastmancolor
Columbia/Filmways (Leslie Linder)

An account of London's sordid Christie murders of the forties.

Agreeably seedy reconstruction of a cause célèbre, carefully built around the star part of a murderous aberrant landlord. Too long, however, and finally too lacking in detail.

w Clive Exton book Ludovic Kennedy d Richard Fleischer ph Denys Coop m Johnny Dankworth ed Ernest Walter

☆ Richard Attenborough, John Hurt, Judy Geeson, Pat Heywood, Isobel Black, Geoffrey Chater, André Morell, Robert Hardy

Ten Seconds to Hell

US   1959   93m   bw
UA/Hammer/Seven Arts (Michael Carreras)

Bomb disposal experts in post-war Berlin quarrel over a girl.

Boring, harsh, hollow melodrama, so artificially constructed that no one can possibly care who gets exploded.

w Robert Aldrich, Teddi Sherman novel *The Phoenix* by Lawrence Bachmann d Robert Aldrich ph Ernest Laszlo m Kenneth V. Jones ed James Needs, Henry Richardson

☆ Jack Palance, Jeff Chandler, Martine Carol, Robert Cornthwaite, Dave Willock, Wesley Addy

Ten Tall Men

US   1951   97m   Technicolor
Columbia/Norma (Harold Hecht)

A Foreign Legion patrol prevents a Riff attack.

Comic strip adventures, efficiently handled.

w Roland Kibbee, Frank Davis d Willis Goldbeck ph William Snyder m David Buttolph

☆ Burt Lancaster, Gilbert Roland, Kieron Moore, John Dehner, Jody Lawrance, George Tobias, Mike Mazurki

10 Things I Hate about You

US   1999   97m   colour
Buena Vista/Touchstone/Mad Chance/Janet Entertainment (Andrew Lazar)

A doctor refuses to let his younger daughter have dates until her older sister gets a boyfriend.

An attempt to make a teenage comedy out of Shakespeare's The Taming of the Shrew; it doesn't work.

w Karen McCullah Lutz, Kirsten Smith d Gil Junger ph Mark Irwin m Richard Gibbs pd Carol Winstead Wood ed O. Nicholas Brown

☆ Heath Ledger, Julia Stiles, Joseph-Gordon Levitt, Larisa Oleynik, David Krumholtz, Andrew Keegan, Susan May Pratt, Gabrielle Union, Larry Miller

'Lurches all over the map, encompassing dialogue both inspired and juvenile-tasteless. There's also middling slapstick, rampant product placement and awkward bits of earnest drama.' – *Dennis Harvey, Variety*

⊚ Digital Video Disc Region 2   ⊚ Digital Video Disc Region 1   ♫ Soundtrack released on compact disc   ☆ Cast in approximate order of importance   † Points of interest   ♫ Notable songs   ⧫ Academy Award   ⧫ Academy Award nomination   ⽥ BAFTA

Ten Thousand Bedrooms

US 1956 114m Metrocolor Cinemascope
MGM (Joe Pasternak)

An American millionaire finds romance when he buys a Rome hotel.

Old-fashioned, unfunny comedy sadly lacking pace and style.

w Laslo Vadnay, Art Cohn, William Ludwig, Leonard Spigelgass d Richard Thorpe ph Robert Bronner m George Stoll songs Nicholas Brodszky, Sammy Cahn

☆ Dean Martin, Eva Bartok, Anna Maria Alberghetti, Walter Slezak, Paul Henreid, Jules Munchin, Marcel Dalio

10 to Midnight

US 1983 102m Metrocolor
Cannon/Golan-Globus (Pancho Kohner, Lance Hool)

A sexual deficient kills girls who reject him, but is tracked down and shot by a cop who is the father of one of the threatened girls.

Crude and rather nasty vigilante melodrama.

w William Roberts d J. Lee-Thompson ph Adam Greenberg m Robert O. Ragland ad Jim Freiburger ed Peter Lee-Thompson

☆ Charles Bronson, Lisa Eilbacher, Andrew Stevens, Gene Davis, Geoffrey Lewis

'Too slow, slick and semi-respectable to live down to its inspirations.' – Kim Newman, MFB

Ten Wanted Men

US 1955 80m Technicolor
Columbia/Scott-Brown (Harry Joe Brown)

A rancher and his family are besieged by bandits in a lady's house.

Rather elementary but efficient and good-looking Western programmer.

w Kenneth Gamet story Irving Ravetch, Harriet Frank Jnr d Bruce Humberstone ph Wilfred Cline m Paul Sawtell

☆ Randolph Scott, Jocelyn Brando, Richard Boone, Alfonso Bedoya, Donna Martell, Skip Homeier

Ten Who Dared

✵✵ US 1960 92m Technicolor
Walt Disney (James Algar)

In 1869 a scientific expedition sets out to chart the Colorado River.

Tedious and unconvincing adventures.

w Lawrence E. Watkin journal Major John Wesley Powell d William Beaudine ph Gordon Avil m Oliver Wallace

☆ Brian Keith, John Beal, James Drury, R. G. Armstrong, Ben Johnson, L. Q. Jones

The Tenant

France 1976 126m Eastmancolor
Paramount/Marianne (Andrew Braunsberg)

original title: Le Locataire

A displaced person becomes convinced that his fellow lodgers are out to murder him.

Rather like a male version of the same director's Repulsion, this wearisome case history shows the total dissipation of whatever talent he once had.

w Gerard Brach, Roman Polanski novel Roland Topor d Roman Polanski ph Sven Nykvist m Philippe Sarde

☆ Roman Polanski, Melvyn Douglas, Isabelle Adjani, Shelley Winters, Jo Van Fleet, Lila Kedrova, Claude Dauphin

'It does not seem to have been designed as self-parody, but it certainly comes across that way.' – Janet Maslin, Newsweek

'A long-winded exercise in tedium and morbidity.' – Kevin Thomas, LA Times

Tender and Perverse Emanuelle (dubbed)

France 1973 75m colour
Brux Inter

After a neurotic pianist is murdered, police investigate her insanely jealous husband and many lovers.

Incompetent would-be erotic thriller, which contains a great deal of bare flesh, mainly of scenes of lesbian love-making shot in soft focus; all that can be said in its favour is that it lacks Franco's usual frenetic use of the zoom lens, but it contains most of his other faults, including poor acting and a needlessly complicated, tedious script.

w A. L. Mariaux, David Khunn (Jesús Franco) d J. P. Johnson (Jesús Franco) ph Stephen Rosenfeld, Alain Hardy m Daniel White ed Claude Gros

☆ Norma Castel, Jack Taylor, Lina Romay, Alice Arno (Marie-France Broquet), Monique Van Linden

Tender Comrade

US 1943 101m bw
RKO (David Hempstead)

Lady welders whose husbands are fighting men keep their chins up during World War II.

Dim tearjerker.

w Dalton Trumbo d Edward Dmytryk ph Russell Metty m Leigh Harline

☆ Ginger Rogers, Robert Ryan, Ruth Hussey, Patricia Collinge, Mady Christians, Kim Hunter, Jane Darwell

Tender Flesh: see Welcome to Arrow Beach

Tender Is the Night *

US 1961 146m DeLuxe Cinemascope
TCF (Henry T. Weinstein)

Adventures around Europe between the wars of a rich American psychiatrist who has married his patient.

Patchy, fairly literal transcription of a patently unfilmable novel about defiantly unreal people in what would now be the jet set. About half the result is superficially entertaining.

w Ivan Moffat novel F. Scott Fitzgerald d Henry King ph Leon Shamroy m Bernard Herrmann

☆ Jennifer Jones, Jason Robards Jnr, Joan Fontaine, Tom Ewell, Cesare Danova, Jill St John, Paul Lukas

♫ title song (mSammy Fain, lyPaul Francis Webster)

Tender Mercies *

US 1982 92m Movielab
EMI/Antron Media (Horton Foote, Robert Duvall)

An ex-alcoholic resumes his former career as a country and western singer.

Quiet, downbeat character study with scenic Texas backgrounds. Mildly impressive, but no real reason to go to the cinema.

w Horton Foote d Bruce Beresford ph Russell Boyd m George Dreyfus ad Jeannine Oppewall ed William Anderson

☆ Robert Duvall, Tess Harper, Betty Buckley, Wilford Brimley, Ellen Barkin, Allan Hubbard, Lenny von Dohlen

'It conceals its deficiencies behind heartfelt performances ... the construction is so rickety that it seems at times entirely to lack a plot.' – Kim Newman, MFB

♦ Robert Duvall; Horton Foote

⚘ best picture; Bruce Beresford; song 'Over You' (Austin Roberts, Bobby Hart)

The Tender Trap *

US 1955 111m Eastmancolor
Cinemascope
MGM (Lawrence Weingarten)

A smart New York agent has a way with women which annoys his friend; but Casanova gets his come-uppance when he sets his sights on an apparently naïve young actress.

Thin comedy with agreeable moments, not helped by the wide screen.

w Julius J. Epstein play Max Shulman, Robert Paul Smith d Charles Walters ph Paul Vogel m Jeff Alexander

☆ Frank Sinatra, Debbie Reynolds, David Wayne, Celeste Holm, Lola Albright, Carolyn Jones

♫ title song (mJames Van Heusen, lySammy Cahn)

The Tender Years

US 1947 81m bw
TCF (Edward L. Alperson)

A minister's son befriends a mistreated runaway dog.

Excessively sentimental tear-jerker that is mercifully short.

w Jack Jungmeyer Jnr, Arnold Belgard d Harold Schuster ph Henry Freulich m Dr Edward Kilenyi ad Arthur Lonergan ed Richard Farrell

☆ Joe E. Brown, Richard Lyon, Noreen Nash, Charles Drake, Josephine Hutchinson, James Millican, Griff Barnett

The Tenderfoot

US 1931 73m bw
Warner

Adventures of a cowboy in New York.

Slapstick version of George Kaufman's often-remade comedy The Butter and Egg Man; not remarkable in any way.

w Arthur Caesar, Monty Banks, Earl Baldwin d Ray Enright

☆ Joe E. Brown, Ginger Rogers, Lew Cody, Vivian Oakland, Robert Greig

'It ought to do well where they like lowdown comedy.' – Variety

Tenderloin

US 1928 88m bw
Warner

A dancer is accused of stealing a fortune and finds gangsters suddenly interested in her.

Primitive part-talkie (15 minutes of dialogue), unspeakably hammy to listen to though visually it had some inventiveness.

w Edward T. Lowe story Darryl Zanuck d Michael Curtiz

☆ Dolores Costello, Conrad Nagel, Mitchell Lewis, George E. Stone, Dan Wolheim

Tenderness of Wolves *

West Germany 1973 83m colour
Cinegate/Tango (Rainer Werner Fassbinder)

original title: Zärtlichkeit der Wölfe

In Hanover, a petty criminal seduces and kills young boys, drinking their blood and selling their bodies as meat.

A blackly comic re-telling of the true story of serial killer Fritz Haarmann, showing the influence of the company's mentor, Rainer Werner Fassbinder.

w Kurt Raab d Ulli Lommel ph Jürgen Jürges m Bach ad Kurt Raab ed Thea Eymèsz

☆ Kurt Raab, Jeff Roden, Margit Carstensen, Hannelore Tiefenbrunner, Wolfgang Schenck, Rainer Hauer, Rainer Werner Fassbinder, Jürgen Prochnow

Tendre Ennemie *

France 1938 66m bw
World Pictures

A woman's three dead lovers return to prevent her daughter from making a romantic mistake.

Decorative whimsy which is not among its director's best, but mildly amusing none the less.

w Max Ophuls, Kurt Alexander play L'Ennemie by A. P. Antoine d Max Ophuls

☆ Simone Berriau, Jacqueline Daix, Georges Vitray, Marc Valbel, Lucien Nat

'Story is sacrificed for camera angles ... weak even for the arties.' – Variety

Tendre Poulet: see Dear Inspector

Tenebrae (dubbed)

Italy 1982 101m colour
Anglo American/Sigma (Claudio Argento)

original title: Sotto Gli Occhi Dell'Assassino

US title: Unsane

As a thriller author promotes his latest work in Rome, there is a series of murders copying those in the book.

Gory serial killer movie with an intricate plot that confuses as much as it entertains.

w Dario Argento, George Kemp d Dario Argento ph Luciano Tovoli m Simonetti Pignatelli Morante ad Giuseppe Bassan ed Franco Fraticelli sp Giovanni Corridori

☆ John Saxon, Anthony Franciosa, Christian Borromeo, Mirella D'Angelo, Veronica Lario, Ania Pieroni, Eva Robins, Carola Stagnaro, Daria Nicolodi, John Steiner

'One is made all the more aware of the director's inability to match visual flair with anything worth watching.' – Philip Strick, MFB

† Four seconds were cut from the British video release.

Teni Zabytykh Predkov: see Shadows of Our Forgotten Ancestors

Tennessee Champ

US 1954 75m Anscocolor
MGM

The Lord helps a religious boxer to win a few fights.

Tedious sentimental square ring melodrama.

w Art Cohn d Fred M. Wilcox ph George Folsey m Conrad Salinger

☆ Earl Holliman, Dewey Martin, Keenan Wynn, Shelley Winters, Yvette Dugay

Tennessee Johnson *

US 1943 102m bw
MGM (J. Walter Ruben)

GB title: The Man on America's Conscience

The rise and the problems of President Andrew Johnson.

Sincere, straightforward, well-produced historical drama which failed to set the Thames – or the Hudson – on fire.

w John Balderston, Wells Root d William Dieterle ph Harold Rosson m Herbert Stothart

☆ Van Heflin, Ruth Hussey, Lionel Barrymore, Marjorie Main, Regis Toomey, Montagu Love, Porter Hall, Charles Dingle, J. Edward Bromberg

'Dieterle's customary high-minded, high-polished mélange of heavy touches and intelligent performances.' – James Agee

Tennessee's Partner

US 1955 87m Technicolor Superscope
RKO

A gambling queen and a tenderfoot are involved in a double cross which leads to murder.

Predictable Western.

w Milton Krims, D. D. Beauchamp, Graham Baker, Teddi Sherman story Bret Harte d Allan Dwan ph John Alton

☆ Ronald Reagan, John Payne, Rhonda Fleming, Coleen Gray

Tension

US 1950 91m bw
MGM (Robert Sisk)

A chemist plans the perfect murder of his wife's lover, loses his nerve, then finds himself suspected when the man is murdered after all.

Disappointing suspenser which starts well but outstays its welcome.

w Allen Rivkin d John Berry ph Harry Stradling m André Previn

☆ Richard Basehart, Audrey Totter, Barry Sullivan, Cyd Charisse, Lloyd Gough, Tom d'Andrea

Tension at Table Rock

US 1956 93m Technicolor
RKO

When a stagecoach station owner is killed, a gunman takes care of his small son and at the same time rids a town of outlaws.

All the clichés are in this one, fairly neatly amassed in corners labelled High Noon, Hondo and Shane.

w Winston Miller novel Frank Gruber d Charles Marquis Warren ph Joseph Biroc m Dimitri Tiomkin

☆ Richard Egan, Dorothy Malone, Cameron Mitchell, Angie Dickinson

Tentacles

Italy 1976 102m Technicolor Technovision
Esse Cinematografica (E. F. Doria)

A deadly menace which leaves its victims as skeletons washed up on the California beach turns out to be a giant octopus ...

Dreary Jaws rehash. Sadly there is no element of spoofing, it's all deadly serious.

w Jerome Max, Tito Carpi, Steve Carabatsos, Sonia Molteni d Oliver Hellman (Sonia Assonitis) ph Roberto d'Ettore Piazzoli m S. W. Cipriani

☆ Shelley Winters, John Huston, Bo Hopkins, Henry Fonda, Claude Akins, Cesare Danova, Delia Boccardo

Tenth Avenue Angel

US 1948 74m bw
MGM (Ralph Wheelright)

The little daughter of poor parents loses her faith in life.

Icky sentimental piece for a waning child star.

---

w Angna Enters, Craig Rice, Harry Ruskin, Eleanore Griffin d Roy Rowland ph Robert Surtees m Rudolph G. Kopp
☆ Margaret O'Brien, Angela Lansbury, George Murphy, Phyllis Thaxter, Rhys Williams, Warner Anderson, Audrey Totter, Connie Gilchrist

The Tenth Man
GB 1936 68m bw
BIP
A wife shows faith in her husband even though she knows him to be a crook.
Stock film version of one of Somerset Maugham's less pungent plays.
w Geoffrey Kerr, Dudley Leslie, Marjorie Deans, Jack Davies d Brian Desmond Hurst
☆ John Lodge, Antoinette Cellier, Aileen Marson, Clifford Evans, George Graves

The Tenth Victim
Italy/France 1965 92m Technicolor
Avco/CC Champion/Concordia (Carlo Ponti)
🎬
In the 21st century murder is legalized to avoid birth control and war, and ten killings bring a fabulous prize.
Science fiction satire which just about gets by.
w Tonino Guerra, Giorgio Salvioni, Ennio Flaiano, Elio Petri *story* The Seventh Victim by Robert Sheckley d Elio Petri ph Gianni di Venanzo m Piero Piccioni
☆ Ursula Andress, Marcello Mastroianni, Elsa Martinelli, Massimo Serato
'When one thinks of the number of gifted men who have labored to produce this wobbly jape, one is struck by the fact that, of all the arts, film can be the greatest waster of talents.' – *John Simon*

Tenue de Soirée *
France 1986 85m Eastmancolor
Panavision
Hachette Premiere/DD Productions/Cine Valse/Philippe Dussart
🎬
GB title: *Evening Dress*
aka: *Menage*
A husky burglar seduces the puny husband of a couple he involves in his criminal activities.
Anti-bourgeois comedy that tries too hard to be outrageous. Michel Blanc won the award for best actor at the Cannes Film Festival in 1986 for his performance as the timid husband.
wd Bertrand Blier ph Jean Penzer m Serge Gainsbourg pd Theobald Meurisse ed Claudine Merlin
☆ Gérard Depardieu, Michel Blanc, Miou-Miou, Michel Creton, Jean-François Stevenin, Mylène Demongeot, Caroline Sihol, Jean-Yves Berteloot, Bruno Cremer
'Never has there been a picture that made it more hideously clear that, even without the intervention of the police, crime does not pay and that sexual experimentation does not reward its practitioners with happiness.' – *Quentin Crisp*

Teorema: see *Theorem*

'A business on the line. A friendship on the edge. A woman caught in the middle.'
Tequila Sunrise
US 1988 115m DeLuxe
Warner/Mount Company (Tom Shaw)
🎬 🎬 🎬 🎧
A former drug-dealer, who is being tempted to get involved in one last major deal, and his friend, an undercover narcotics cop, compete for the same girl.
Wordy thriller in which everyone goes through the motions without much enthusiasm.
wd Robert Towne ph Conrad L. Hall m Dave Grusin pd Richard Sylbert ed Claire Simpson
☆ Mel Gibson, Michelle Pfeiffer, Kurt Russell, Raul Julia, J. T. Walsh, Arliss Howard, Arye Gross, Gabriel Damon
🎞 Conrad L. Hall

Teresa **
US 1950 101m bw
MGM (Arthur M. Loew)
A soldier with mother problems brings home an Italian bride.
Careful, sensitive, intelligent variation on a problem frequently considered by films of this period (Frieda, Fräulein, Japanese War Bride).

w Stewart Stern d Fred Zinnemann ph William J. Miller m Louis Applebaum
☆ Pier Angeli, John Ericson, Patricia Collinge, Richard Bishop, Peggy Ann Garner, Ralph Meeker, Bill Mauldin, Rod Steiger
🎞 original story (Arthur Hayes, Stewart Stern)

Term of Trial *
GB 1962 130m bw
Romulus (James Woolf)
An unsuccessful schoolmaster is accused of rape by a nymphomaniac schoolgirl he has scorned.
Rather flabby 'adult' drama, too schematic to be really interesting despite the best that acting can do.
wd Peter Glenville *novel* The Burden of Proof by James Barlow ph Oswald Morris m Jean-Michel Demasc ad Antony Woolgar
☆ Laurence Olivier, Sarah Miles, Simone Signoret, Hugh Griffith, Terence Stamp, Roland Culver, Frank Pettingell, Thora Hird, Dudley Foster, Norman Bird

'Harry Benson is a brilliant computer scientist. For three minutes a day, he is violently homicidal.'
The Terminal Man *
US 1974 104m colour
Warner (Mike Hodges)
🎬 🎬
A man, who has a computer implanted in his brain to control his murderous tendencies, discovers he enjoys the aftermath of his violent outbursts.
A moderately intriguing, modern variation on Frankenstein, done with a clinical style, in which scientists create a human monster that they cannot control.
wd Mike Hodges *novel* Michael Crichton ph Richard H. Kline ad Fred Harpman ed Robert Wolfe
☆ George Segal, Joan Hackett, Richard Dysart, Jill Clayburgh, Donald Moffat, Matt Clark
'Of all the bad sci-fi movies of the 70s, this one probably has the least charm.' – *Pauline Kael, New Yorker*

Terminal Station: see *Indiscretion of an American Wife*

Terminal Velocity
US 1994 102m colour
Buena Vista/Steep Hollow/Hollywood (Scott Kroopf, Tom Engelman)
🎬 🎬 🎬
A sky-diving instructor links up with an ex-KGB agent to recover a plane-load of gold bullion.
A slick but otherwise ordinary action movie with a preening hero and a few spectacular stunts.
w David Twohy d Deran Sarafian ph Oliver Wood m Joel McNeely pd David L. Snyder ed Frank J. Urioste
☆ Charlie Sheen, Natassja Kinski, James Gandolfini, Christopher MacDonald, Gary Bullock, Hans R. Howes, Melvin Van Peebles

The Terminator *
US 1984 108m CFI color
Orion/Hemdale/Pacific Western (Gale Anne Hurd)
🎬 🎬 🎬 🎬 🎧
An android from the future is sent back to the present time on a mission of extermination.
Slick, rather nasty but undeniably compelling comic book adventures.
w James Cameron, Gale Anne Hurd d James Cameron ph Adam Greenberg m Brad Fiedel ed Mark Goldblatt
☆ Arnold Schwarzenegger, Michael Biehn, Linda Hamilton, Paul Winfield, Rick Rossovich, Lance Henriksen

'It's Nothing Personal.'
Terminator 2: Judgment Day **
US 1991 135m CFI color
Guild/Carolco/Pacific Western/Lightstorm (James Cameron)
🎬 🎬 🎬 🎬 🎧
An android returns from the future to save a boy and his mother from a murderous shape-changing robot.
Thunderous, high-voltage action movie with dazzling special effects that provide a distraction from the often silly narrative.
w James Cameron, William Wisher d James Cameron ph Adam Greenberg m Brad Fiedel pd Joseph Nemec III ed Richard A. Harris, Mark Goldblatt, Conrad Buff sp Fantasy II Film Effects, Industrial Light and Magic

☆ Arnold Schwarzenegger, Linda Hamilton, Edward Furlong, Robert Patrick, Earl Boen, Joe Morton, S. Epatha Merkerson, Castulo Guerra
'A science-fiction film with verve, imagination and even a little wit.' – *Derek Malcolm, Guardian*
'A humongous, visionary parable that intermittently enthralls and ultimately disappoints. T2 is half of a terrific movie – the wrong half. For a breathless first hour, the film zips along in a textbook display of plot planting and showmanship. But then it stumbles over its own ambitions before settling for a conventional climax with a long fuse.' – *Richard Corliss, Time*
† Reportedly the most expensive film so far made, at a cost of $80–$100 million, it was the biggest box-office success of 1991, taking $112m in rentals in North America alone.
🏆 visual effects (Dennis Murren, Stan Winston, Gene Warren Jnr, Robert Skotak); make-up (Stan Winston, Jeff Dawn)
🎞 Adam Greenberg; editing

Terminus ***
GB 1961 30m bw
British Transport Films
Twenty-four hours in the life of Waterloo Station.
An excellent 'fly-on-the-wall' documentary which launched the feature film career of its director and is still both funny and moving.
wd John Schlesinger ph Ken Phipps, Robert Paynter m Ron Grainer

Terminus
France/West Germany 1986 83m colour
Fox/CAT/Films du Cheval de Fer/Initial Groupe/CLB/A2 (Anne François)
In the future, a driver takes over a computer-programmed truck from its dead owner in a dangerous race.
Virtually incomprehensible science fiction, cut from its original length of 110 minutes; even when it is understandable, it fails to grip.
w Pierre-William Glenn, Patrice Duvic *story* Alain Gillot d Pierre-William Glenn ph Jean-Claude Vicquery m David Cunningham ad Alain Challier ed Thierry Derocles
☆ Johnny Hallyday, Karen Allen, Jurgen Prochnow, Gabriel Damon, Julie Glenn, Louise Vincent

'Come To Laugh. Come To Cry. Come To Care. Come To Terms.'
Terms of Endearment **
US 1983 132m Metrocolor
Paramount (James L. Brooks)
🎬 🎬 🎬 🎧
An eccentric widow fends off suitors while interfering with her daughter's marriage; but all is forgiven when the daughter dies.
This shapeless film is little more than an excuse for actors and writer to show off, which they do to great excess; but parts of it are entertaining enough and it certainly impressed the Academy Award committee.
wd James L. Brooks *novel* Larry McMurtry ph Andrzej Bartkowiak m Michael Gore pd Polly Platt
☆ Shirley MacLaine, Jack Nicholson, Debra Winger, Danny DeVito, Jeff Daniels, John Lithgow
'An outsize sitcom and a crassly constructed slice of anti-feminism that contrives to rub liberal amounts of soap in the viewer's eyes.' – *Sight and Sound*
'There isn't a thing I would change.' – *Roger Ebert*
🏆 best picture; Shirley MacLaine; Jack Nicholson; direction; adaptation
🎞 John Lithgow; editing (Richard Marks); Michael Gore; art direction; Debra Winger

La Terra Trema *
Italy 1948 160m bw
Universalia
🎬
The life of a Sicilian fisherman and his family.
Seriously intended, carefully composed semi-documentary stressing the economic problems of the simple life. A commercial disaster: even the Italians couldn't understand the accents of the local actors.
wd Luchino Visconti ph G. R. Aldo m Luchino Visconti, Willy Ferrero
† The cast was drawn from the inhabitants of Aci Trezza, Sicily.

The Terra-Cotta Warrior *
Hong Kong 1990 111m Eastmancolor
Panavision
Art & Talent Group (Hon Pou Chu)
A soldier encased in clay and buried with his emperor comes back to life 3,000 years later to be re-united with his lover, reincarnated as an actress.
A familiar mix of the supernatural and martial arts, performed with verve.
w Lee Bik Wah d Ching Tung Yee ph Peter Pau m Joseph Koo pd Yee Chung Man ed Mak Chi Shin sp Tsui Hark
☆ Zhang Yimou, Gong Li, Yu Yung Kang

A Terrible Beauty
GB 1960 90m bw
UA/Raymond Stross
US title: *Night Fighters*
In a north Irish village, the IRA revive their activities on the outbreak of World War II.
Heavily Oirish melodrama with a muddled message.
w Robert Wright Campbell *novel* Arthur Roth d Tay Garnett ph Stephen Dade m Cedric Thorpe Davie
☆ Robert Mitchum, Anne Heywood, Dan O'Herlihy, Cyril Cusack, Richard Harris, Marianne Benet

The Terror
US 1928 82m bw
Warner
A mysterious killer lurks in the cellars of a country house.
Primitive talkie which attempted a few new styles but showed that more were needed, also that some silent actors could not make the transfer.
w Harvey Gates *play* Edgar Wallace *novel* Edgar Wallace d Roy del Ruth ph Barney McGill
☆ May McAvoy, Edward Everett Horton, Louise Fazenda, Alec B. Francis, John Miljan, Frank Austin
'The only terrible thing about this talkie Terror is its unnatural slowness … the characters speak as if they were dictating important letters.' – *A. P. Herbert, Punch*
'May be crude, but it is a maker of history. Something has been achieved here. A new chapter of film evolution is beginning. Today it is as foolish to argue that talking films cannot be successful as to declare that a man in London cannot possibly speak by telephone to a man in New York.' – *C. A. Lejeune*
† The first film without a single subtitle: all the credits were spoken.
†† *Return of the Terror* (US 1934) has little to do with it.

The Terror
GB 1938 73m bw
Associated British
Stilted remake of the above.
w William Freshman d Richard Bird
☆ Wilfrid Lawson, Arthur Wontner, Alastair Sim, Linden Travers, Bernard Lee, Henry Oscar

The Terror
US 1963 81m Pathécolor
AIP/Filmgroup (Roger Corman, Francis Ford Coppola)
🎬
A baron lives for twenty years in a creepy castle, mourning the death of his wife …
Shoddy horror improvised over a weekend on the set of The Raven. It looks it.
w Leo Gordon, Jack Hill d Roger Corman ph John Nickolaus m Ronald Stein
☆ Boris Karloff, Jack Nicholson, Sandra Knight, Dorothy Neumann

Terror Aboard
US 1933 70m bw
Paramount
Gruesome murders occur during a pleasure cruise.
Fair murder mystery.
w Harvey Thew, Manuel Seff d Paul Sloane
☆ Charles Ruggles, John Halliday, Shirley Grey, Neil Hamilton, Verree Teasdale, Jack La Rue

Terror by Night *
US 1946 60m bw
Universal (Howard Benedict)
🎬
Sherlock Holmes recovers a stolen jewel and solves a murder or two aboard a speeding train.

An amusing entry in the modernized series despite some bad support acting and hilarious interposed shots of the supposed scenery between London and Edinburgh.
w Frank Gruber d Roy William Neill ph Maury Gertsman m Hans Salter
☆ Basil Rathbone, Nigel Bruce, Dennis Hoey, Alan Mowbray, Renee Godfrey, Billy Bevan, Mary Forbes, Frederic Worlock

Terror from the Year 5000

US   1958   74m   bw
AIP (Robert J. Gurney Jnr)
GB title: *Cage of Doom*
A brash young entrepreneur who has invested in an experimental time machine inadvertently brings back a woman, disfigured by radiation, from the future.
A mix of sex and science fiction with a moral, effective enough in its low-budget way, though audiences have to wait a long time for the terror to arrive.
wd Robert J. Gurney Jnr ph Arthur Florman ed Dede Allen
☆ Ward Costello, Joyce Holden, Frederick Downs, John Stratton, Salome Jens, Fred Herrick

Terror House: see *The Night Has Eyes*

Terror in a Texas Town *

US   1958   81m   bw
UA/Frank N. Seltzer
A Swedish seaman arrives in a small Western town and avenges the death of his father.
Stylish second-feature Western, a genuine sleeper which holds the interest throughout.
w Ben L. Perry d Joseph H. Lewis ph Ray Rennahan m Gerald Fried
☆ Sterling Hayden, Sebastian Cabot, Carol Kelly, Eugene Martin, Ned Young

Terror in the Aisles

US   1984   82m   CFI color
TEM/Kaleidoscope/Universal
A compilation of fragments from mainly shock films, of no great interest even to film buffs because in most cases the scenes are wrenched out of context to fit a fatuous commentary.
w Margery Doppelt d Andrew Kuehn

Terror in the Haunted House

US   1958   81m   bw
Howco
aka: *My World Dies Screaming*
A bride finds that her honeymoon mansion is one about which she has been having recurring nightmares.
The plot has everything, even an axe murderer, but the treatment is soporific.
w Robert C. Dennis d Harold Daniels ph Frederick E. West m Darrell Calker
☆ Gerald Mohr, Cathy O'Donnell, William Ching, John Qualen, Barry Bernard

Terror in the Wax Museum

US   1973   94m   DeLuxe
Bing Crosby Productions/Fenady Associates (Andrew J. Fenady)
In Victorian London a waxworks owner is murdered …
Cheaply produced murder mystery (even the waxworks can't stand still) with horror asides and a cast of elderly hams.
w Jameson Brewer d Georg Fenady ph William Jurgensen m George Duning
☆ Ray Milland, Broderick Crawford, Elsa Lanchester, Louis Hayward, John Carradine, Shani Wallis, Maurice Evans, Patric Knowles

Terror of Mechagodzilla: see *Monsters from an Unknown Planet*

The Terror of Sheba: see *Persecution*

'Drug-crazed assassins carrying out their hate-filled ritual murders!'
The Terror of the Tongs

GB   1961   79m   Technicolor
BLC/Hammer/Merlin (Kenneth Hyman)
In 1910 Hong Kong a merchant avenges the death of his daughter at the hands of a villainous secret society.
Gory melodrama with dollops of screams, torture and vaguely orgiastic goings-on.

w Jimmy Sangster d Anthony Bushell ph Arthur Grant m James Bernard ad Bernard Robinson, Thomas Goswell ed Jim Needs, Eric Boyd-Perkins
☆ Geoffrey Toone, Christopher Lee, Yvonne Monlaur, Brian Worth, Richard Leech

The Terror of the Vampires: see *Le Frisson des Vampires*

Terror on a Train: see *Time Bomb*

Terror Train

Canada   1980   97m   DeLuxe
Fox/Triple T (Harold Greenberg)
Participants in a wild party aboard a train are decimated by a mysterious psychotic.
Shocks and blood in the Carpenter tradition, adequately mounted.
w T. Y. Drake d Roger Spottiswoode ph John Alcott m John Mills-Cockle pd Glenn Bydwell ed Anne Henderson
☆ Ben Johnson, Jamie Lee Curtis, David Copperfield, Hart Bochner

The Terroriser

Taiwan/Hong Kong   1986   109m   colour
ICA/Sunny Overseas Corporation/Golden Harvest (Lin Dengfei, Raymond Chow)
original title: *Kongbufenzi*
aka: *The Terrorizers*
A writer, whose marriage is going wrong, finds that life is beginning to resemble her latest novel.
Unconvincing melodrama with intellectual pretensions that makes little sense.
w Xiao Ye, Edward Yang d Edward Yang ph Zhang Zhan m Weng Xiaoliang ad Lai Mingtang ed Liao Qingsong
☆ Cora Miao, Li Liqun, Jin Shijie, Gu Baoming, Wang An, Liu Ming, You Anshun

The Terrorists: see *Ransom (1975)*

The Terrorizers: see *The Terroriser*

The Terry Fox Story

Canada   1983   97m   colour
ITC/CTV (Robert Cooper)
A young man dying of cancer has a leg amputated, but still runs across Canada in aid of research.
True it may be, but dramatically this is a one-note film with endless pretty pictures of countryside and in the foreground signs of failing health.
w Edward Hume d Ralph L. Thomas ph Richard Ciupka m Bill Conti ad Gavin Mitchell ed Ron Wisman
☆ Eric Fryer, Robert Duvall, Chris Makepeace, Rosalind Chao

Tess *

France-GB   1979   180m   colour
Renn-Burrill (Claude Berri)
A peasant girl tries to prove her noble heritage but finds herself with an illegitimate child.
Solid, unexciting version of the classic Wessex novel; a hard sell for 1980 audiences.
w Roman Polanski, Gerard Brach, John Brownjohn novel *Tess of the D'Urbervilles* by Thomas Hardy d Roman Polanski ph Geoffrey Unsworth, Ghislain Cloquet m Philippe Sarde pd Pierre Guffroy, Jack Stevens
☆ Nastassja Kinski, Leigh Lawson, Peter Firth, John Collin, David Markham, Richard Pearson
'It emerges without a hint of what might have drawn Polanski to the material.' – *Sight and Sound*
⚑ Geoffrey Unsworth, Ghislain Cloquet; art direction; costume design (Anthony Powell)
⚑ best film; Roman Polanski; Philippe Sarde
⚑ best photography

Tess of the Storm Country

US   1932   80m   bw
Fox
A retired sea captain's daughter loves the lord of the manor.
Antiquated tushery first filmed as a Mary Pickford silent.
w S. N. Behrman, Sonya Levien, Rupert Hughes novel Grace Miller White d Alfred Santell ph Hal Mohr
☆ Janet Gaynor, Charles Farrell, Dudley Digges, June Clyde, George Meeker

Tess of the Storm Country

US   1960   84m   colour   Cinemascope
TCF (Everett Chambers)
A Scottish girl moves to Pennsylvania and falls for a Mennonite farmer caught up in a dispute about a chemical works polluting the land.
An old-fashioned romantic drama, with a more modern ecological subplot, it is enjoyable and pleasing to the eye, though in no way memorable.
w Charles Lang novel Grace Miller White d Paul Guilfoyle ph James Wong Howe m Paul Sawtell, Bert Shefter ad John Mansbridge ed John Bushelman
☆ Diane Baker, Jack Ging, Lee Philips, Wallace Ford, Robert F. Simon, Bert Remsen, Archie Duncan, Nancy Valentine

'They're yours … in a heart-walloping love story!'
Test Pilot **

US   1938   118m   bw
MGM (Louis D. Lighton)
A brilliant but unpredictable test pilot is helped by his wife and his self-sacrificing friend.
A big box-office star vehicle of its time, still interesting as a highly efficient product.
w Waldemar Young, Vincent Lawrence story Frank Wead d Victor Fleming ph Ray June m Franz Waxman ed Tom Held
☆ Clark Gable, Myrna Loy, Spencer Tracy, Lionel Barrymore, Samuel S. Hinds, Marjorie Main, Gloria Holden
'B.o. potential of above-average calibre … could have been cut 10–15 minutes without spoiling.' – *Variety*
'The picture is so noisy with sure-fire elements – box office cast, violent excitement, glycerine tears and such – that it may be hard to keep the ear attuned to the quieter, more authentically human things in it.' – *James Shelley Hamilton*
⚑ best picture; Frank Wead; Tom Held

Testament *

US   1983   90m   CFI color
Entertainment Events/American Playhouse
A small California town is hit by a nuclear attack.
Probably better than the TV movie The Day After, *this was less well publicized and therefore lost out.*
w John Sacret Young story Carol Amen d Lynne Littman ph Steven Poster m James Horner
☆ Jane Alexander, William Devane, Ross Harris, Roxana Zal, Lukas Haas, Lilia Skala, Leon Ames
'After thirty years of learning to live with the Bomb, we still lack ways of conceiving the Unthinkable.' – *Sheila Johnston, MFB*
⚑ Jane Alexander

Testament

GB   1988   80m   Technicolor
Black Audio Film Collective/Channel 4 (Avril Johnson, Lina Gopaul)
Twenty years after the military coup that overthrew Nkrumah's government, a television interviewer returns to Ghana to try to interview Werner Herzog and to make sense of the past.
Part documentary, part fiction, it is too personal a film to mean much to the uncommitted.
wd John Akomfrah ph David Scott m Trevor Mathison ed Brand Thumin
☆ Tania Rogers, Evans Hunter, Emma Francis Wilson, Frank Parkes, Errol Shaker
'A richly allusive, evocative meditation on memory, history and identity, both national and personal.' – *MFB*

Le Testament d'Orphée *

France   1959   83m   bw
Editions Cinégraphiques (Jean Thullier)
aka: *The Testament of Orpheus*
The poet, as an 18th-century man, dies, enters spacetime, is revived, and seeks his identity.
Rather like a melancholy madman's Alice in Wonderland, this bizarre jumble has its fascinations but misses by a mile the arresting qualities of Orphée.
wd Jean Cocteau ph Roland Pointoizeau m Georges Auric and others
☆ Jean Cocteau, Edouard Dermithe, Maria Casarès, François Périer, Henri Crémieux, Yul Brynner, Jean-Pierre Léaud, Daniel Gélin, Jean Marais, Pablo Picasso, Charles Aznavour

The Testament of Dr Mabuse **

Germany   1933   122m   bw
Nero (Fritz Lang)
A sequel to *Dr Mabuse the Gambler*: the criminal mastermind dies in an asylum, and his assistant takes over his identity.
Fast-moving penny dreadful, alleged by its director to be a denouncing of the doctrines of Hitler, but showing little evidence of being more than a very slick entertainment.
w Thea von Harbou, Fritz Lang d Fritz Lang ph Fritz Arno Wagner m Hans Erdmann ad Karl Vollbrecht, Emil Hassler
☆ Rudolf Klein-Rogge, Otto Wernicke, Gustav Diessl
† On arrival in America Lang claimed that 'slogans of the Third Reich have been put into the mouths of criminals in the film'. Yet his wife, who co-scripted it, stayed behind as a confirmed Nazi.

The Testament of Orpheus: see *Le Testament d'Orphée*

La Teta y la Luna: see *The Tit and the Moon*

'Bizarre, Beautiful, Horrific…'
Tetsuo II: Bodyhammer **

Japan   1991   83m   colour
ICA/Kaiju Theatre/Toshiba EMI (Fuminori Shisido, Fumio Kurokawa)
A clerk, pursuing punks who have killed his son, mutates into a metallic man with built-in weaponry.
Bizarre but eminently watchable science-fiction fable.
wd Shinya Tsukamoto ph Shinya Tsukamoto, Fumikazu Oda, Katsunori Yokoyama ad Shinya Tsukamoto ed Shinya Tsukamoto
☆ Tomoroh Taguchi, Nobu Kanaoka, Shinya Tsukamoto, Keinosuke Tomioka, Sujin Kim, Min Tanaka
'Brain-blowing … this gruesome gore fest looks to be a solid click with the midnight crowd and metal fetishists.' – *Variety*

Tetsuo: The Iron Man *

Japan   1991   67m   bw
Kaijyu
After a metal fetishist is hit by a car, the driver begins to turn into a metallic man.
Weird science-fiction fantasy, by turns surreal and nasty, but displaying an unusual visual flair by its writer-director.
wd Shinya Tsukamoto ph Shinya Tsukamoto, Kei Fujiwara m Chu Ishikawa ed Shinya Tsukamoto
☆ Tomoroh Taguchi, Kei Fujiwara, Nobu Kanaoka, Shinya Tsukamoto, Naomasa Musaka, Renji Ishibashi
'For most viewers it will be the cinematic equivalent of being run over by a car and turning into a metal blob.' – *Variety*

Tevya the Milkman *

US   1939   93m   bw
Henry Ziskin
A Russian village milkman watches with awe as the pogroms begin to affect his people.
One of the best Yiddish films with the best Yiddish actor, this pleasing comedy-drama was the basis for the musical Fiddler on the Roof.
wd Maurice Schwartz story Sholem Aleichem
☆ Maurice Schwartz, Miriam Riselle, Rebecca Weintraub, Paula Lubelska

Tex and The Lord of the Deep

Italy   1985   96m   colour
Sacis/RAI (Giocchino Marano, José M. Rodriguez, Paola Bistolfi)
original title: *Tex e il Signore degli Abissi*
Tex Willer defeats an attempt to revive the Aztec empire in Mexico.
Last decadent gasp of the spaghetti Western, managing to combine cowboys and Indians with Kit Carson, a comic book hero, a scantily clad priestess, a fat man in a fez, a mummifying weapon and a volcanic eruption.
w Giorgio Bonelli, Gianfranco Clerici, Marcello Coscia, Duccio Tessari story Giovanni L. Bonelli d Duccio Tessari ph Pietro Morbidelli m Gianni Ferrio ad Antonello Geleng, Walter Patriarca ed Mirella Mercio, Lidia Bordi

---

☆ Giuliano Gemma, William Berger, Carlo Mucari, Isabel Russinova, Peter Berling, Flavio Bucci

The Texan

US 1930 79m bw

Paramount (Hector Turnbull)

The Llano Kid absolves his bandit past.

Early sound Western, an interesting curiosity.

w Daniel Nathan Rubin *story* The Double-Dyed Deceiver *by* O. Henry *d* John Cromwell *ph* Victor Milner

☆ Gary Cooper, Fay Wray, Emma Dunn, Oscar Apfel

'Few westerns are as well made and rate as high in every particular.' – *Variety*

'Love and glory on America's last frontier!'

The Texans

US 1938 92m bw

Paramount (Lucien Hubbard)

Problems of the post-Civil War years include new railroads, the Ku Klux Klan, and the new cattle drive routes.

Formula Western with fairly well staged excitements backing a routine romantic triangle.

w Bertram Millhauser, Paul Sloane, William Wister Haines *d* James Hogan *ph* Theodor Sparkuhl *m* Gerard Carbonara

☆ Joan Bennett, Randolph Scott, May Robson, Walter Brennan, Raymond Cummings, Raymond Hatton, Robert Barrat, Francis Ford

'Enough sweep and thrills to justify generally good business.' – *Variety*

Texas

US 1941 94m bw (released in sepia)

Columbia (Sam Bischoff)

▣

Two veteran Civil War Southerners head for Texas to set up a cattle business.

Western vehicle for two young stars, now very ordinary-looking.

w Horace McCoy, Lewis Meltzer, Michael Blankfort *d* George Marshall *ph* George Meehan

☆ William Holden, Glenn Ford, Claire Trevor, George Bancroft, Edgar Buchanan, Don Beddoe, Andrew Tombes, Addison Richards

'While spoofing a little along the way, it observes the etiquette and tradition of an accepted cinema form. It has rough riding, cattle rustling, shooting and a story that leaves out only the Indian raid and the rescue by the US Cavalry.' – *Christian Science Monitor*

Texas across the River

US 1966 101m Techniscope

Universal (Harry Keller)

A Texan, an Indian and a Spanish nobleman on the run from jealous rivals have various adventures.

Sloppy Western which seems to have had jokes added when someone realized it wasn't good enough to be taken seriously.

w Wells Root, Harold Greene, Ben Starr *d* Michael Gordon *ph* Russell Metty *m* Frank de Vol *md* Joseph Gershenson

☆ Dean Martin, Alain Delon, Joey Bishop, Rosemary Forsyth, Tina Marquand, Peter Graves, Andrew Prine, Michael Ansara

Texas Addio

Italy/Spain 1966 92m Eastmancolor

BRC/Estela (Manolo Bolognini)

▣ ○

aka: *The Avenger*

A man revenges his father's death.

Fast-paced, uncomplicated spaghetti Western; not very memorable.

w Franco Rossetti, Ferdinando Baldi *d* Ferdinando Baldi *ph* Enzo Barboni *m* Anton Garcia Abril *ad* Luigi Scaccianoce *ed* Sergio Montanari

☆ Franco Nero, Cole Kitosch, José Suarez, Elisa Montes, Livio Lorenzon, Hugo Blanco, José Guardiola

Texas, Brooklyn and Heaven

US 1948 76m bw

Robert S. Golden/United Artists

GB title: *The Girl from Texas*

A Texas boy meets a Texas girl in New York; after various eccentric encounters, they end up riding the range again.

Would-be Saroyanesque dalliance with odd characters which never begins to come off and has been abruptly edited into the bargain.

w Lewis Meltzer *story* Barry Benefield *d* William Castle

☆ Guy Madison, Diana Lynn, James Dunn, Lionel Stander, Florence Bates, Michael Chekhov, Margaret Hamilton, Moyna McGill, Irene Ryan, Roscoe Karns, William Frawley

Texas Carnival

US 1951 77m Technicolor

MGM (Jack Cummings)

▣ ◷

A fairground showman is mistaken for a millionaire and runs up debts.

Very thin comedy musical relying entirely on its stars.

w Dorothy Kingsley *d* Charles Walters *ph* Robert Planck *m* Harry Warren *ch* Hermes Pan *ly* Dorothy Fields

☆ Esther Williams, Red Skelton, Howard Keel, Ann Miller, Paula Raymond, Keenan Wynn, Tom Tully

The Texas Chainsaw Massacre

US 1974 81m CFI color

Vortex (Tobe Hooper)

▣ ◷ ◉

Visitors to a cemetery in rural Texas find their house occupied by a homicidal maniac.

Cheapjack horror thriller adapted from real events which also inspired Psycho. Nothing but shocks and gore, but the beginning of the wave of such deplorable movies which flooded the world's screens towards the end of the decade.

w Kim Henkel, Tobe Hooper *d* Tobe Hooper *ph* Daniel Pearl *m* Tobe Hooper, Wayne Bell

☆ Marilyn Burns, Allen Danziger, Paul A. Partain, William Vail

'An absolute must for all maniacs and blood drinkers in need of a few tips.' – *Benny Green, Punch*

'It's without any apparent purpose, unless the creation of disgust and fright is a purpose.' – *Roger Ebert*

The Texas Chainsaw Massacre Part 2

US 1986 95m TVC Color

Cannon (Menahem Golan, Yoram Globus)

▣ ◷

A family of Sweeney Todds lives in an abandoned Alamo theme park, and woe betide the stray visitor.

Splatter shocker on predictable lines.

w L. M. Kit Carson *d* Tobe Hooper *ph* Richard Kooris *m* Tobe Hooper, Jerry Lambert *pd* Cary White *ed* Alain Jakubowicz

☆ Dennis Hopper, Caroline Williams, Bill Johnson, Jim Siedow

Texas Lady

US 1955 85m Technicolor Superscope

RKO (Nat Holt)

▣

A lady newspaper owner runs an anti-corruption campaign.

Mild family Western.

w Horace McCoy *d* Tim Whelan *ph* Ray Rennahan *m* Paul Sawtell

☆ Claudette Colbert, Barry Sullivan, Greg Walcott, James Bell, Horace MacMahon, Ray Collins, Walter Sande, Douglas Fowley

'They wrote their story in words of fire!'

The Texas Rangers *

US 1936 95m bw

Paramount (King Vidor)

Three wandering ne'er-do-wells break up; two join the Texas Rangers and hunt down the third, who is an outlaw.

Pleasantly remembered star Western, later remade as The Streets of Laredo *(qv).*

w Louis Stevens *d* King Vidor *ph* Edward Cronjager

☆ Fred MacMurray, Jack Oakie, Lloyd Nolan, Jean Parker, Edward Ellis

† Another film called *The Texas Rangers* came from Columbia in 1952 and had a similar plot to the original; otherwise it was a shoddy piece of work in Supercinecolor, with George Montgomery and Jerome Courtland.

Texas Rangers Ride Again

US 1940 67m bw

Paramount

Modern Rangers capture cattle rustlers.

Second-feature 'sequel' with no relation to the original.

w William R. Lipman, Horace McCoy *d* James Hogan

☆ John Howard, Ellen Drew, Akim Tamiroff, May Robson, Broderick Crawford, Charley Grapewin, John Miljan, Anthony Quinn

Texas Terror

US 1935 58m bw

Monogram/Lone Star (Paul Malvern)

▣

A sheriff who believes he was responsible for the death of an old friend discovers the real culprit.

Mediocre Western, one of the least interesting of Wayne's early efforts, lacking the action and stunts that usually raised Malvern's productions above his low-budget rivals.

wd Robert N. Bradbury *ph* William Hyer *ed* Carl Pierson

☆ John Wayne, Lucile Browne, Leroy Mason, Fern Emmett, George Hayes, Buffalo Bill Jnr, John Ince

Texas to Tokyo: see *We've Never Been Licked*

'It's not a place ... it's a state of mind'

Texasville

US 1990 125m DeLuxe

Guild/Nelson Films/Cine-Source (Barry Spikings, Peter Bogdanovich)

▣ ◷

A middle-aged oil man faces difficulties with his wife and family and in his business.

A downbeat sequel, lacking in magic, to The Last Picture Show, *with its characters now much older and more miserable.*

wd Peter Bogdanovich *novel* Larry McMurtry *ph* Nicholas von Sternberg *pd* Phedon Papamichael *ed* Richard Fields

☆ Jeff Bridges, Cybill Shepherd, Annie Potts, Cloris Leachman, Timothy Bottoms, Eileen Brennan, Randy Quaid, Harvey Christiansen, Pearl Jones, Loyd Catlett

'Making a hash of trying to adapt McMurtry's extremely long and dense novel, Bogdanovich has simply thrown away the flesh and kept the bones.' – *Tom Milne, MFB*

Thank God It's Friday

US 1978 89m Metrocolor

Columbia/Motown/Casablanca (Rob Cohen)

▣ ◷

Problems of a disc jockey in a Hollywood disco.

Routine youth programmer, rather like Rock Around the Clock twenty years after.

w Barry Armyan Bernstein *d* Robert Klane *ph* James Crabe *m* various *pd* Tom H. John

☆ Valerie Landsburg, Terri Nunn, Chick Vennera, Donna Summer, The Commodores

♫ song 'Last Dance' (*m/ly* Paul Jabara)

Thank You All Very Much: see *A Touch of Love*

Thank You, Jeeves *

US 1936 57m bw

TCF (Sol M. Wurtzel)

A valet helps prevent his master from becoming involved in gun-running.

Competent second feature notable as Niven's first leading role; also one of the very few attempts to film Wodehouse.

w Joseph Hoffman, Stephen Gross *story* P. G. Wodehouse *d* Arthur Greville Collins *ph* Barney McGill *m* Samuel Kaylin

☆ David Niven, Arthur Treacher, Virginia Field, Lester Matthews, Colin Tapley

Thank You, Mr Moto

US 1938 67m bw

TCF

Mr Moto protects the tomb of Genghis Khan from unscrupulous treasure-hunters.

Slick and enjoyable small-scale thriller.

w Willis Cooper, Norman Foster *story* John P. Marquand *d* Norman Foster *ph* Virgil Miller *md* Samuel Kaylin *ad* Bernard Herzbrun, Albert Hogsett *ed* Irene Morra, Nick DeMaggio

☆ Peter Lorre, Thomas Beck, Pauline Frederick, Jayne Regan, Sidney Blackmer, Sig Rumann, John Carradine

Thank Your Lucky Stars ***

US 1943 127m bw

Warner (Mark Hellinger)

▣ ◷ ○

Eddie Cantor and his double get involved in planning a patriotic show.

All-star wartime musical with some unexpected turns and a generally funny script.

w Norman Panama, Melvin Frank, James V. Kern *d* David Butler *ph* Arthur Edeson *m/ly* Frank Loesser, Arthur Schwartz *md* Leo F. Forbstein *ch* Le Roy Prinz

☆ Eddie Cantor, Dennis Morgan, Joan Leslie, Edward Everett Horton, S. Z. Sakall, Humphrey Bogart, Jack Carson, Bette Davis, Olivia de Havilland, Errol Flynn, John Garfield, Alan Hale, Ida Lupino, Ann Sheridan, Dinah Shore and also George Tobias, Spike Jones and his City Slickers, Willie Best, Hattie McDaniel

'The loudest and most vulgar of the current musicals, it is also the most fun, if you are amused when show people kid their own idiom.' – *James Agee*

'An all-star show with the conspicuous flavour of amateur night at the studio.' – *New York Times*

'Everyone had a good time making it.' – *Motion Picture Herald*

♫ song 'They're Either Too Young or Too Old'

Thanks a Million **

US 1935 87m bw

TCF (Darryl F. Zanuck)

▣

A crooner runs for governor.

Smart, amusing political musical.

w Nunnally Johnson *d* Roy del Ruth *ph* Peverell Marley *m* Arthur Lange *m/ly* Arthur Johnston, Gus Kahn

☆ Dick Powell, Fred Allen, Ann Dvorak, Patsy Kelly, Phil Baker, Paul Whiteman and his band, the Yacht Club Boys, Benny Baker, Raymond Walburn, Alan Dinehart

'Socko filmusical for big grosses ... an example of canny showmanship and presentation.' – *Variety*

Thanks for Everything *

US 1938 70m bw

TCF (Darryl F. Zanuck)

Mr Average American is discovered, promoted and merchandized.

Very acceptable satirical comedy of the advertising world.

w Harry Tugend *d* William A. Seiter *ph* George Meehan *m* Abe Meyer

☆ Adolphe Menjou, Jack Haley, Jack Oakie, Arleen Whelan, Tony Martin, Binnie Barnes, George Barbier

'Light and breezy, a cinch for popular audience appeal.' – *Variety*

'The funniest film I can remember seeing for many months, with something of the old Kaufman touch.' – *Graham Greene*

Thanks for the Memory *

US 1938 75m bw

Paramount (Mel Shaver)

A smart novelist has trouble with his marriage.

Light, agreeable domestic comedy on familiar lines.

w Lynn Starling *play* Up Pops the Devil *by* Frances Goodrich, Albert Hackett *d* George Archainbaud *ph* Karl Struss *m* Boris Morros

☆ Bob Hope, Shirley Ross

'Although lightweight, it will please if not exactly boff them.' – *Variety*

Thark *

GB 1932 79m bw

British and Dominion (Herbert Wilcox)

The heir to an old mansion spends a night in it to prove it is not haunted.

Very funny Aldwych farce, plainly transferred to the screen with the original stage team intact. One's only regret is that it peters out at the end.

w Ben Travers *play* Ben Travers *d* Tom Walls *ph* F. A. Young

☆ Ralph Lynn, Tom Walls, Robertson Hare, Mary Brough, Claude Hulbert, Gordon James

'Scream after scream of laughter of the wobbling midriff variety.' – *Variety*

That Brennan Girl

US   1946   97m   bw
Republic
A young mother neglects her baby for the sake of a good time.
Absurdly padded-out moral tract.
w Doris Anderson d Alfred Santell
☆ Mona Freeman, James Dunn, William Marshall, June Duprez

That Certain Age *

US   1938   100m   bw
Universal (Joe Pasternak)
A girl gets a crush on an older man.
Pleasant, well-cast star musical for the family.
w Bruce Manning d Edward Ludwig ph Joseph Valentine songs Jimmy McHugh, Harold Adamson
☆ Deanna Durbin, Melvyn Douglas, Jackie Cooper, Irene Rich, Nancy Carroll, John Halliday, Juanita Quigley, Jackie Searl, Charles Coleman
'Certain for top grosses and extended runs.' – *Variety*
♫ song 'My Own'

That Certain Feeling

US   1956   102m   Technicolor   Vistavision
Paramount (Melvin Frank, Norman Panama)
An arrogant comic strip artist loses his touch and hires a 'ghost' – the ex-husband of his secretary/fiancée.
Arid comedy from a mild Broadway play, totally miscast and lacking any kind of interest.
w Norman Panama, Melvin Frank, I. A. L. Diamond, William Altman play King of Hearts by Jean Kerr, Eleanor Brooke d Norman Panama, Melvin Frank ph Loyal Griggs m Joseph J. Lilley
☆ Bob Hope, George Sanders, Eva Marie Saint, Pearl Bailey, Al Capp

'She got all the breaks – in her heart!'
That Certain Woman *

US   1937   91m   bw
Warner (Hal B. Wallis)
▦
A gangster's widow goes straight but runs into complex marriage trouble.
Self-sacrifice and mother love are rewarded by two convenient deaths and a happy ending in this routine romantic melodrama remade from a silent success.
wd Edmund Goulding original screenplay The Trespasser by Edmund Goulding ph Ernest Haller m Max Steiner
☆ Bette Davis, Henry Fonda, Ian Hunter, Anita Louise, Donald Crisp, Katherine Alexander, Mary Philips, Minor Watson
'Big-time cast in a well-made first run film.' – *Variety*

That Championship Season ^

US   1982   108m   Metrocolor
Cannon-Golan-Globus (Menahem Golan, Yoram Globus)
▦
Five rather unlikeable middle-aged men live by recreating the glory of a team basketball victory 25 years ago.
Unimaginative film version of a play which had dramatic strength but very limited general appeal. Rather less can be said of the film, as the acting shows a lack of team spirit.
wd Jason Miller play Jason Miller ph John Bailey m Bill Conti pd Ward Preston ed Richard Halsey
☆ Bruce Dern, Stacy Keach, Robert Mitchum, Martin Sheen, Paul Sorvino, Arthur Franz

That Cold Day in the Park

Canada   1969   115m   Eastmancolor
(Commonwealth United)
▦
A spinster invites a lonely wandering boy into her home, makes him a prisoner and becomes possessively jealous.
A companion piece to The Collector, rather better done for those who like morbid psychology.
w Gillian Freeman novel Richard Miles d Robert Altman ph Laszlo Kovacs m Johnny Mandel
☆ Sandy Dennis, Michael Burns, Susanne Benton, Luana Anders, John Garfield Jnr
'About as pretentious, loathsome and stupid as a film can get.' – *John Simon*

That Dangerous Age

GB   1949   98m   bw
London Films (Gregory Ratoff)
US title: *If This Be Sin*
Recovering from a breakdown, a KC discovers that his daughter wants to marry a man with whom his wife once had an affair.
Purple patch melodrama which sympathetic actors can't quite freshen up.
w Gene Markey play Autumn by Margaret Kennedy, Ilya Surgutchoff d Gregory Ratoff ph Georges Périnal m Mischa Spoliansky
☆ Roger Livesey, Myrna Loy, Peggy Cummins, Richard Greene, Elizabeth Allan, Gerard Heinz, Jean Cadell, G. H. Mulcaster

That Darn Cat! *

▦▦   US   1965   116m   Technicolor
Walt Disney (Bill Walsh, Ron Miller)
▦   ◎
A troublesome cat inadvertently helps to trail bank robbers.
Overlong but generally pleasing small-town comedy with well-paced sequences and a fascinating feline hero.
w The Gordons, Bill Walsh novel Undercover Cat by The Gordons d Robert Stevenson ph Edward Colman m Bob Brunner
☆ Hayley Mills, Dean Jones, Dorothy Provine, Roddy McDowall, Neville Brand, Elsa Lanchester, William Demarest, Frank Gorshin, Grayson Hall, Ed Wynn

That Darn Cat

▦▦   US   1997   89m   Technicolor
Buena Vista/Walt Disney (Robert Simonds)
▦
A girl solves the mystery of a missing woman with the aid of a cat.
Coarse and corny remake in an over-emphatic style.
w S. M. Alexander, L. A. Kareszewski novel Undercover Cat by Mildred and Gordon Gordon d Bob Spiers ph Jerzy Zielinski m Richard Kendall Gibbs pd Jonathan Carlson ed Roger Barton
☆ Christina Ricci, Doug E. Doug, Dean Jones, George Dzundza, Peter Boyle, Michael McKean, Bess Armstrong, Dyan Cannon, John Ratzenberger, Estelle Parsons
'A loud and largely charmless trifle.' – *Variety*

That Forsyte Woman *

US   1949   114m   Technicolor
MGM (Leon Gordon)
▦
GB title: *The Forsyte Saga*
The wife of an Edwardian man of property falls in love with her niece's fiancé.
Moderately successful American attempt to film the first part of a very British novel sequence; so genteel, however, that it becomes dull.
w Jan Lustig, Ivan Tors, James B. Williams novel A Man of Property by John Galsworthy d Compton Bennett ph Joseph Ruttenberg m Bronislau Kaper
☆ Greer Garson, Errol Flynn, Robert Young, Janet Leigh, Walter Pidgeon, Harry Davenport, Aubrey Mather

That Funny Feeling

US   1965   92m   Technicolor
U-I (Harry Keller)
A maid pretends she lives in her boss's apartment.
Makeshift romantic comedy which barely takes the attention even while it's on.
w David R. Schwartz d Richard Thorpe ph Clifford Stine m Joseph Gershenson
☆ Sandra Dee, Bobby Darin, Donald O'Connor, Nita Talbot, Larry Storch, Leo G. Carroll, James Westerfield

That Girl from Paris

US   1936   105m   bw
RKO (Pandro S. Berman)
▦
A Paris opera singer falls for a swing band leader and stows away on a transatlantic liner to be near him.
Comedy-accented musical romance: not bad but not memorable.
w P. J. Wolfson, Dorothy Yost, Jane Murfin d Leigh Jason m J. Roy Hunt m/ly Arthur Schwartz, Edward Heyman md Nathaniel Shilkret
☆ Lily Pons, Gene Raymond, Jack Oakie, Herman Bing, Lucille Ball, Mischa Auer, Frank Jenks

'When it's good it's very good, and when it's bad it's pretty awful.' – *Variety*

'Around her young heart she wore the scarlet letter of another woman's shame!'
That Hagen Girl

US   1947   83m   bw
Warner (Alex Gottlieb)
A girl is convinced she is the illegitimate daughter of her teacher.
Stale teenage drama with odd anti-establishment overtones.
w Charles Hoffman novel Edith Kneipple Roberts d Peter Godfrey ph Karl Freund m Franz Waxman
☆ Shirley Temple, Ronald Reagan, Rory Calhoun, Lois Maxwell, Dorothy Peterson, Charles Kemper, Conrad Janis, Harry Davenport
'Less a film than a series of false situations.' – *MFB*
'They shouldn't do such things to Shirley.' – *Bosley Crowther, New York Times*

That Hamilton Woman **

US   1941   128m   bw
Alexander Korda Films
▦   ▦   ◎
GB title: *Lady Hamilton*
The affair of Lord Nelson and Emma Hamilton.
Bowdlerized version of a famous misalliance; coldly made but quite effective scene by scene, with notable performances.
w Walter Reisch, R. C. Sherriff d Alexander Korda ph Rudolph Maté m Miklos Rozsa ad Vincent Korda
☆ Laurence Olivier, Vivien Leigh, Gladys Cooper, Alan Mowbray, Sara Allgood, Henry Wilcoxon, Halliwell Hobbes
'All its minor graces don't somehow add up to a major achievement … It is my impression that the film would have been a better job if it had stuck more to this man Nelson and bothered less about that woman Hamilton. These are not days when we have much patience for looking at history through the eyes of a trollop. And I am not at all sure that English people, who have been fighting for two years for something they like to call an ideal, will very much care for the implication that the future died with Nelson.' – *C. A. Lejeune*
♫ Rudolph Maté; Vincent Korda

That Kind of Woman

US   1959   92m   bw
Paramount/Ponti-Girosi
World War II remake of Shopworn Angel (qv); rather well made but basically dated and dull.
w Walter Bernstein d Sidney Lumet ph Boris Kaufman m Daniele Amfitheatrof
☆ Sophia Loren, Tab Hunter, George Sanders, Jack Warden, Barbara Nichols, Keenan Wynn
'The romantic reunion of Tab Hunter and Sophia Loren resembles nothing so much as a sea scout given a luxury liner for Christmas.' – *Peter John Dyer*

That Lady

GB   1955   100m   Eastmancolor
Cinemascope
TCF/Atlanta (Sy Bartlett)
A noble widow at the court of Philip II of Spain loves a minister but incurs the king's jealous hatred.
Tepid historical romance which never flows as a film should.
w Anthony Veiller, Sy Bartlett novel Kate O'Brien d Terence Young ph Robert Krasker m John Addison
☆ Olivia de Havilland, Gilbert Roland, Paul Scofield, Françoise Rosay, Dennis Price, Anthony Dawson, Robert Harris, Peter Illing, Christopher Lee
'Somehow, somewhere, one feels, something went very wrong.' – *MFB*
🎬 Paul Scofield (best newcomer)

That Lady in Ermine

US   1948   89m   Technicolor
TCF (Ernst Lubitsch)
Two generations of European noblewomen learn to repel invaders.
Cheerless musical comedy which never gets started, what with the director dying during production and unsuitable stars lost in tinselly sets; the result can have appealed to no one.

w Samson Raphaelson d Ernst Lubitsch, Otto Preminger m Leon Shamroy m Alfred Newman songs Leo Robin, Frederick Hollander
☆ Betty Grable, Douglas Fairbanks Jnr, Cesar Romero, Walter Abel, Reginald Gardiner, Harry Davenport
♫ song 'This is the Moment' (mFrederick Hollander, lyLeo Robin)

'When A No No Girl Meets A Go Go Man – Wham!!!'
That Lucky Touch

GB   1975   93m   Technicolor
Rank/Gloria (Dimitri de Grunwald)
During NATO war games in Brussels, a lady correspondent falls for an arms dealer.
Dim romantic farce which gives the impression of emanating from a dog-eared script written for the kind of stars who no longer shine.
w John Briley story Moss Hart d Christopher Miles ph Douglas Slocombe m John Scott
☆ Roger Moore, Susannah York, Lee J. Cobb, Shelley Winters, Jean-Pierre Cassel, Raf Vallone, Sydne Rome, Donald Sinden

That Mad Mr Jones: see *The Fuller Brush Man*

That Man Bolt

US   1973   103m   Technicolor
Universal (Bernard Schwarz)
Adventures of a professional black courier skilled in the martial arts.
Black Kung Fu hokum from a major company; tolerable of its debased kind.
w Quentin Werty, Charles Johnson d Henry Levin, David Lowell Rich ph Gerald Perry Finnerman m Charles Bernstein
☆ Fred Williamson, Bryon Webster, Miko Mayama, Teresa Graves
'Gives every indication of having been devised by a computer fed with a variety of ingredients currently thought to guarantee box office success.' – *John Raisbeck, MFB*

That Man from Rio

France/Italy   1964   120m   Eastmancolor
Ariane/Artistes Associés/Dear Film/Vides (Alexander Mnouchkine, Georges Danciger)
original title: *L'Homme de Rio*
An airforce pilot finds himself helping his girlfriend in a worldwide search for stolen statuettes.
Elaborate mock thriller which is never quite as much fun as those involved seem to think. It provoked several inferior sequels.
w J. P. Rappeneau, Ariane Mnouchkine, Daniel Boulanger, Philippe de Broca d Philippe de Broca ph Edmond Séchan m Georges Delerue
☆ Jean-Paul Belmondo, Jean Servais, Françoise Dorléac, Adolfo Celi, Simone Renant
'Fantasy takes over, with Belmondo outdoing Fairbanks in agility, Lloyd in cliffhanging, and Bond in indestructibility.' – *Brenda Davies, MFB*
♫ script

That Midnight Kiss

US   1949   98m   Technicolor
MGM (Joe Pasternak)
▦   ◎
An unknown becomes a great singing star.
Simple-minded vehicle for the first appearance of Mario Lanza.
w Bruce Manning, Tamara Hovey d Norman Taurog ph Robert Surtees m Bronislau Kaper
☆ Kathryn Grayson, Ethel Barrymore, Jose Iturbi, Mario Lanza, Keenan Wynn, J. Carrol Naish, Jules Munshin, Thomas Gomez, Marjorie Reynolds

That Night *

US   1957   88m   bw
Galahad (Himan Brown)
An overwhelmed TV writer has a heart attack, and recovers after a series of medical setbacks.
Impressive minor case history, hardly entertainment but quite arresting.
w Robert Wallace, Burton J. Rowles d John Newland ph Maurice Hartzband m Mario Nascimbene
☆ John Beal, Augusta Dabney, Shepperd Strudwick, Ralph Murphy

---

That Night

US 1992 89m Technicolor
Warner/Canal/Regency/Alcor (Arnon Milchan, Steven Reuther)

A small girl aids and abets a romance between two teenagers, a Catholic girl and the manager of a bowling alley.
An ungrossing rites-of-passage story, not helped by being told from the perspective of a knowing child.
wd Craig Bolotin *novel* Alice McDermott ph Bruce Surtees m David Newman pd Maher Ahmad ed Patricia Nedd-Friendly, Gregg London
☆ C. Thomas Howell, Helen Shaver, Juliette Lewis, Eliza Dushku, John Dossett, J. Smith-Cameron

That Night in London

GB 1933 78m bw
Paramount/London Films (Alexander Korda)
US title: Overnight
A bank clerk decides to steal money to have one final fling before he commits suicide.
Dim low-budget drama that wastes its star.
w Dorothy Greenhill, Arthur Wimperis d Rowland V. Lee m Robert Martin m Peter Mendoza ed Stephen Harrison
☆ Robert Donat, Pearl Argyle, Miles Mander, Lawrence Hanray, Roy Emmerton, Graham Soutten

That Night in Rio *

US 1941 90m Technicolor
TCF (Fred Kohlmar)
A night-club entertainer is paid to impersonate a lookalike count, but this causes complications with the countess.
Zippy musical based on a story first used in Folies Bergère (qv) and later in On the Riviera (qv).
w George Seaton, Bess Meredyth, Hal Long play Rudolph Lothar, Hans Adler d Irving Cummings ph Leon Shamroy md Alfred Newman songs Mack Gordon, Harry Warren
☆ Don Ameche, Alice Faye, Carmen Miranda, S. Z. Sakall, J. Carrol Naish, Curt Bois, Leonid Kinskey, Maria Montez
'An eye-filling and ear-filling musical comedy extravaganza.' – *Motion Picture Herald*

That Night in Varennes: see La Nuit de Varennes

That Night with You

US 1945 84m bw
Universal (Michael Fessier, Ernest Pagano)
A girl singer anxious to get on tells a producer that she is his illegitimate daughter.
Mindless farce with music, its gimmick being that all the songs are set to Tchaikovsky's music. Otherwise very dull.
w Michael Fessier, Ernest Pagano d William A. Seiter ph Woody Bredell
☆ Franchot Tone, Susanna Foster, David Bruce, Louise Allbritton, Buster Keaton, Irene Ryan, Jacqueline de Wit

That Obscure Object of Desire **

France/Spain 1977 103m Eastmancolor
Greenwich/Galaxie/In Cine (Serge Silberman)

A middle-aged gentleman suffers continual humiliations from the girl he loves.
Unrecognizable remake of a novel previously filmed as a vehicle for Dietrich and Bardot. Despite the tricking out with surrealist touches (the girl is played by two different actresses) it is not one of Buñuel's best, and amuses only on the surface.
w Luis Buñuel, Jean-Claude Carrière *novel* La Femme et le Pantin by Pierre Louys d Luis Buñuel ph Edmond Richard m from Richard Wagner
☆ Fernando Rey, Carole Bouquet, Angela Molina, Julien Bertheau
⚖ best foreign film; script

That Old Feeling

US 1997 105m DeLuxe
Universal/Bubble Factory/Boy of the Year/All Girl (Leslie Dixon, Bonnie Bruckheimer)

A divorced couple, each with a new partner, find that they are still attracted to one another when they meet at the wedding of their daughter, who is marrying a politician campaigning on family values.

A comedy constructed as a vehicle for Bette Midler, but, like the marriages on view here, it quickly breaks down.
w Leslie Dixon d Carl Reiner ph Steve Mason m Patrick Williams pd Sandy Veneziano ed Richard Halsey
☆ Bette Midler, Dennis Farina, Paula Marshall, Gail O'Grady, David Rasche, Jamie Denton, Danny Nucci
'Rekindles some fond memories of the sparks ignited between vintage feuding screen couples. But it also reminds us that current demands call for films to be less corny and schematic, more heartfelt and better focused.' – *Leonard Klady, Variety*

That Riviera Touch

GB 1966 98m Eastmancolor
Rank (Hugh Stewart)
Two tourists in the south of France get mixed up with jewel thieves.
Disappointing star comedy ending in a surfboard chase.
w S. C. Green, R. M. Hills, Peter Blackmore d Cliff Owen ph Otto Heller m Ron Goodwin
☆ Eric Morecambe, Ernie Wise, Suzanne Lloyd, Paul Stassino, Armand Mestral

That Summer of White Roses

GB/Yugoslavia 1989 103m colour
Amy International/Jadran (Simon MacCorkindale, Mike Mihalic)
In Yugoslavia in the last summer of the Second World War, a simple-minded lifeguard, who hides a woman and child from the Germans, finds that he is treated like a collaborator after he rescues the Nazi commandant from drowning.
A wartime drama that has no sense of urgency about it, nor much sense of anything; there is no resonance about the events depicted.
w Borislav Pekic, Rajko Grlic, Simon MacCorkindale *novel* Defence and the Last Days by Borislav Pekic d Rajko Grlic ph Tomislav Pinter m Brane Zivkovic, Junior Campbell, Mike O'Donnell ad Dinka Jericevic ed Damir F. German
☆ Tom Conti, Susan George, Rod Steiger, Alun Armstrong, John Gill, John Sharp, Geoffrey Whitehead
'Has a fine cast that is sadly under-stretched by a narrative which oscillates uncomfortably between the whimsical and the realist.' – *Jill Forbes, MFB*

'In every life there comes a time when that dream you dream becomes that thing you do.'

That Thing You Do! *

US 1996 108m DeLuxe
TCF/Clinica Estetico (Gary Goetzman, Jonathan Demme, Edward Saxon)

In the 60s, a beat group goes from the small to the big time before breaking up.
Sanitized 60s rock for those who grooved to Forrest Gump; nostalgia for a simpler, more innocent time (at least, as seen through Hanks's distorting lens) acts as a narrative sedative, though audiences may respond to its generalized warmth.
wd Tom Hanks ph Tak Fujimoto m Howard Shore m/ly Tom Hanks, Adam Schlesinger, Mike Miccirillo et al pd Victor Kempster ed Richard Chew
☆ Tom Everett Scott, Liv Tyler, Johnathon Schaech, Steve Zahn, Ethan Embry, Tom Hanks, Chris Isaak, Kevin Pollak, Jonathan Demme
'A bland, soft-centred, house-trained puppy of a film that begs to be loved.' – *Philip French, Observer*
'A lightweight but utterly loveable affair.' – *Empire*
⚖ song 'That Thing You Do!' (m/ly Adam Schlesinger)

That Touch of Mink **

US 1962 99m Eastmancolor Panavision
U-I/Granley/Arwin/Nob Hill (Stanley Shapiro, Martin Melcher)

Bachelor tycoon pursues virginal secretary.
Jaded sex comedy (or what passed for it in nudge-nudge 1962) enlivened by practised star performances and smart timing.
w Stanley Shapiro, Nate Monaster d Delbert Mann ph Russell Metty m George Duning
☆ Cary Grant, Doris Day, Gig Young, Audrey Meadows, Dick Sargent, John Astin

'Too often there's a hampering second-hand air about situation and joke. Throughout, the determination is to keep faith with the American sex mythology at all costs.' – Jack Pitman, Variety
⚖ script

That Uncertain Feeling *

US 1941 84m bw
UA/Sol Lesser (Ernst Lubitsch)

A wife with insomnia and hiccups befriends a wacky concert pianist who proceeds to move into her home.
Although Lubitsch had made this story before, as the silent Kiss Me Again, the elements didn't really jell in this version, which seemed silly rather than funny.
w Donald Ogden Stewart, Walter Reisch play Divorçons by Victorien Sardou, Emile de Najac d Ernst Lubitsch ph George Barnes m Werner Heymann pd Alexander Golitzen
☆ Merle Oberon, Melvyn Douglas, Burgess Meredith, Alan Mowbray, Olive Blakeney, Harry Davenport, Eve Arden, Sig Rumann
'Gay entertainment.' – *Picture Show*
⚖ Werner Heymann

That Was Then ... This Is Now

US 1985 102m TVC Color
Paramount/Media Ventures (Gary R. Lindberg, John M. Ondov)

Urban youths growing into manhood find the world a gloomy place.
Highly resistible chunk of pessimistic philosophizing with a few fights thrown in.
w Emilio Estevez *novel* S. E. Hinton d Christopher Cain ph Juan Ruiz-Anchia m Keith Olsen ad Chester Kaczenski ed Ken Johnson
☆ Emilio Estevez, Craig Sheffer, Kim Delaney, Jill Schoelen, Barbara Babcock, Morgan Freeman
'God save the kids who live in an S. E. Hinton novel. They're firecrackers waiting to go off.' – *Variety*

That Way with Women

US 1947 84m bw
Warner (Charles Hoffman)
A millionaire amuses himself by playing Cupid to a young couple.
Routine remake of The Millionaire: just about watchable.
w Leo Townsend d Frederick de Cordova ph Ted McCord m Frederick Hollander
☆ Sydney Greenstreet, Dane Clark, Martha Vickers, Alan Hale, Craig Stevens, Barbara Brown

That Woman Opposite

GB 1957 83m bw
Monarch (William Gell)
US title: City after Midnight
In a small French town, a killer returns to silence a witness.
Slow-paced semi-mystery, reasonably well done.
wd Compton Bennett *story* The Emperor's Snuff Box by John Dickson Carr ph Lionel Banes m Stanley Black
☆ Phyllis Kirk, Dan O'Herlihy, Wilfrid Hyde-White, Petula Clark, Jack Watling, William Franklyn, Margaret Withers

That Wonderful Urge

US 1948 82m bw
TCF (Fred Kohlmar)
A newspaperman is forced into marriage with a publicity-shy heiress.
Tepid romantic comedy, a remake of Love Is News (qv).
w Jay Dratler d Robert B. Sinclair ph Charles Clarke m Cyril Mockridge
☆ Gene Tierney, Tyrone Power, Reginald Gardiner, Arleen Whelan, Lucile Watson, Gene Lockhart, Porter Hall, Taylor Holmes

That'll Be the Day *

GB 1973 91m Technicolor
EMI/Goodtimes (David Puttnam, Sanford Lieberson)

In 1958, a young drifter becomes a fairground worker, and eventually walks out on his wife and family to become a pop star.
Spirited return to British realism, with well-sketched cameos, a likeable dour viewpoint, and a cheerful pop music background.

w Ray Connolly d Claude Whatham ph Peter Suschitzky md Ronald Leach
☆ David Essex, Ringo Starr, Rosemary Leach, James Booth, Billy Fury, Keith Moon, Rosalind Ayres
'As insubstantial as one of its own attempts at a statement.' – *Tony Rayns*

That's a Good Girl *

GB 1933 83m bw
British and Dominions (Herbert Wilcox)
A man about town seeks ways of making money.
Archetypal vehicle for a debonair song and dance man.
w Douglas Furber, Donovan Pedelty, Jack Buchanan d Jack Buchanan ph Freddie Young md Philip Braham
☆ Jack Buchanan, Elsie Randolph, Dorothy Hyson, Garry Marsh, Vera Pearce, William Kendall

That's Dancin'! **

US 1985 105m Metrocolor
MGM-UA/David Niven Jnr, Jack Haley Jnr

Selections from the golden age of the movie musical, featuring the likes of Fred Astaire, Gene Kelly, Eleanor Powell, Busby Berkeley.
Fascinating compilation which made little impact at the box-office.
narrators Gene Kelly, Sammy Davis Jnr, Mikhail Baryshnikov, Liza Minnelli, Ray Bolger

'Boy! do we need it now!'

That's Entertainment **

US 1974 137m Metrocolor 70mm (blown up)/scope
MGM (Daniel Melnick, Jack Haley Jnr)

Stars introduce some of their performances and other highlights from MGM's musical past.
A slapdash compilation which was generally very big at the box-office and obviously has fascinating sequences, though the narration is sloppily sentimental and the later wide-screen sequences let down the rest.
wd Jack Haley Jnr ph various m various
☆ Fred Astaire, Gene Kelly, Elizabeth Taylor, James Stewart, Bing Crosby, Liza Minelli, Donald O'Connor, Debbie Reynolds, Mickey Rooney, Frank Sinatra, Judy Garland, Esther Williams, Eleanor Powell, Clark Gable, Ray Bolger
'While many ponder the future of MGM, none can deny that it has one hell of a past.' – *Variety*
'It is particularly gratifying to get the key sequences from certain movies without having to sit through a fatuous storyline.' – *Michael Billington, Illustrated London News*
'No other film in town offers such a harvest of undiluted joy.' – *Sunday Express*

That's Entertainment! III **

US 1994 113m DeLuxe
MGM (Bud Friedgen, Michael J. Sheridan)

Former MGM stars introduce excerpts from 30 years of the studio's musicals, ranging from *The Hollywood Revue of 1929* to *Jailhouse Rock* and *Gigi*.
Enjoyable moments from the past, with fewer show-stopping numbers than the earlier films in this series, but adding some fascinating out-takes cut from such films as Easter Parade and Cabin in the Sky, contrasting the performance of Ava Gardner in Show Boat with what might have been had Lena Horne been allowed to play the role, and providing a glimpse of Judy Garland in the role of Annie Oakley before she was fired from Annie Get Your Gun.
d Bud Friedgen, Michael J. Sheridan m Marc Shaiman ed Bud Friedgen, Michael J. Sheridan
☆ June Allyson, Cyd Charisse, Lena Horne, Howard Keel, Gene Kelly, Ann Miller, Debbie Reynolds, Mickey Rooney, Esther Williams

That's Entertainment Part Two **

US 1976 133m Metrocolor 70mm (blown up)/scope
MGM (Saul Chaplin, Daniel Melnick)

More moments from MGM's successes, introduced by Astaire and Kelly, with comedy and drama sequences as well as musical.
An enjoyable rummage through the past, lacking a little coherence but providing plenty of nostalgic pleasures.
d Gene Kelly ph various *titles* Saul Bass
☆ Fred Astaire, Gene Kelly, Jeanette MacDonald, Nelson Eddy, the Marx Brothers, Stan Laurel, Oliver Hardy, Jack Buchanan, Judy Garland, Ann

Miller, Mickey Rooney, Oscar Levant, Bing
Crosby, Ann Miller, Louis Armstrong

That's Life!

US   1986   102m   DeLuxe   Panavision
Columbia/Paradise Cove/Ubilam (Tony Adams)
◼️   ◎~

An architect touching sixty, with a sick wife, pours
out all his fears of old age and mortality.
*Blake Edwards exposing himself again; the movie was
even shot in his own house. Somewhat embarrassing to
watch, and overwrought, it does have a few good
moments.*
w Milton Wexler, Blake Edwards d Blake
Edwards ph Anthony Richmond m Henry
Mancini
☆ Jack Lemmon, Julie Andrews, Sally Kellerman,
Robert Loggia, Jennifer Edwards
♫ song 'Life in a Looking Glass' (Mancini, Leslie
Bricusse)

That's My Boy

US   1951   98m   bw
Paramount/Hal B. Wallis (Cy Howard)

An athletic father tries to press his hypochondriac
teenage son into the same mould.
American college comedy of no international interest.
w Cy Howard d Hal Walker ph Lee Garmes
m Leigh Harline
☆ Dean Martin, Jerry Lewis, Eddie Mayehoff,
Ruth Hussey, Polly Bergen, John McIntire

That's My Man

US   1946   98m   bw
Republic (Frank Borzage)
GB title: *Will Tomorrow Ever Come?*

A racing man is reunited with his wife when their
son has pneumonia.
*A compendium of clichés, with everything but a title
card reading Came the Dawn. Of no real interest.*
w Steve Fisher, Bradley King d Frank Borzage
ph Tony Gaudio m Cy Feuer
☆ Don Ameche, Catherine McLeod, Roscoe
Karns, John Ridgely

That's My Wife *

🏃🏃 US   1929   20m   bw   silent
Hal Roach

Stan dresses up as Ollie's wife to impress his rich
uncle.
*Lesser-known star comedy which well sustains its basic
joke and includes some splendidly timed farce in a
restaurant.*
w Leo McCarey, H. M. Walker d Lloyd French
☆ Laurel and Hardy, Vivien Oakland, William
Courtright

That's Right, You're Wrong *

US   1939   91m   bw
RKO (David Butler)
◎~

A band leader gets a Hollywood contract but is
hated by the studio head.
*Typical of the nonsense musicals featuring Kay Kyser
and his radio Kollege of Musical Knowledge. The
movie background and self-spoofing made this first
attempt one of the best.*
w William Conselman, James V. Kern d David
Butler ph Russell Metty m George Duning
songs various
☆ Kay Kyser, Adolphe Menjou, Lucille Ball,
Dennis O'Keefe, May Robson, Edward Everett
Horton, Ish Kabibble, Ginny Simms, Roscoe
Karns, Moroni Olsen, Hobart Cavanaugh, Sheilah
Graham, Hedda Hopper
   'Moderate entertainment which will satisfy as a
   bill-topper.' – *Variety*

That's the Spirit

US   1945   87m   bw
Universal

A ghost comes back to tell his actress wife he
didn't desert her as she thought.
*Rather heavy comedy of the Here Comes Mr Jordan
school.*
w Michael Fessier, Ernest Pagano d Charles
Lamont
☆ Jack Oakie, Peggy Ryan, June Vincent, Gene
Lockhart, Andy Devine, Arthur Treacher, Irene
Ryan, Buster Keaton

That's Your Funeral

GB   1973   82m   colour
Rank/Hammer (Michael Carreras)

An undertaker mistakenly appropriates a coffin
containing cannabis which belongs to a rival
establishment.
*Moribund comedy of contrived double-entendres that
die on the lips of the cast.*
w Peter Lewis d John Robins ph David Holmes
m David Whitaker ad Scott MacGregor
ed Archie Ludski
☆ Bill Fraser, Raymond Huntley, David Battley,
John Ronane, Dennis Price, Sue Lloyd, Richard
Wattis, Roy Kinnear
   'Another nail in the British film industry's
   coffin, this grey comedy is depressingly unfunny
   even by TV spin-off standards.' – *Clyde Jeavons,
   MFB*

Theatre of Blood *

GB   1973   102m   DeLuxe
UA/Cineman (John Kohn, Stanley Mann)

A Shakespearean actor uses appropriate murder
methods on the various critics who have ridiculed
his performances.
*Spoof horror picture which goes too far with some sick
visuals; the idea and some of the performances are fine.*
w Anthony Greville-Bell d Douglas Hickox
ph Wolfgang Suschitzky m Michael J. Lewis
pd Michael Seymour
☆ Vincent Price, Diana Rigg, Ian Hendry, Harry
Andrews, Coral Browne, Robert Coote, Jack
Hawkins, Michael Hordern, Arthur Lowe, Robert
Morley, Dennis Price, Diana Dors, Joan Hickson,
Renée Asherson, Milo O'Shea and also Eric Sykes

Theatre of Death

GB   1966   91m   Techniscope
Pennea (Michael Smedley-Aston)
◼️
US title: *Blood Fiend*

Vampire-like murders in Paris are eventually
connected with a Grand Guignol theatre.
*Dreary backstage shocker with inadequate production
values.*
w Roger Marshall, Ellis Kadison d Sam Gallu
ph Gilbert Taylor m Elisabeth Lutyens
☆ Christopher Lee, Jenny Till, Lelia Goldoni,
Julian Glover, Ivor Dean, Evelyn Laye

Theatre Royal: see *The Royal Family of
Broadway (1930)*

Theatre Royal

GB   1943   92m   bw
British National

A revue and a theatre are saved by a sentimental
prop man.
Shapeless star comedy with music; not their best.
w Bud Flanagan, Austin Melford, Geoffrey Orme
d John Baxter
☆ Bud Flanagan, Chesney Allen, Peggy Dexter,
Lydia Sherwood, Horace Kenney, Marjorie Rhodes,
Finlay Currie

Their Big Moment

US   1934   68m   bw
RKO

Phoney mindreaders solve a murder mystery in a
spooky house.
Quite good, well-organized fun of its type.
w Arthur Caesar, Marion Dix, Walter Hackett
d James Cruze ph Harold Wenstrom md Max
Steiner
☆ ZaSu Pitts, Slim Summerville, William Gaxton,
Ralph Morgan, Bruce Cabot, Julie Haydon, Kay
Johnson
   'Should have fairly good audience strength.' –
   Variety

Their First Mistake **

🏃🏃 US   1932   20m   bw
Hal Roach
◉◉

Ollie decides to improve his marriage by adopting a
baby, only to find that his wife has left him.
*Sublimely silly but endearing star comedy with brilliant
passages of imbecilic conversation followed by well-
timed farce.*
w H. M. Walker d George Marshall ed Richard
Currier
☆ Stan Laurel, Oliver Hardy, Mae Busch, Billy
Gilbert, George Marshall

Their Purple Moment

🏃🏃 US   1928   20m   bw   silent
Hal Roach

Stan and Ollie go out on the town, only to
discover that Stan's wife has replaced his money
with grocery coupons.
*Minor star comedy with efficient but predictable
restaurant scenes ending in a pie fight.*
w H. M. Walker d James Parrott ph George
Stevens ed Richard Currier
☆ Stan Laurel, Oliver Hardy, Anita Garvin, Kay
Deslys, Tiny Sandford

Their Secret Affair: see *Top Secret Affair*

Thelma and Louise ***

US   1991   129m   DeLuxe   Panavision
UIP/Pathé Entertainment (Ridley Scott, Mimi Polk)
◉◉   ◼️   ◎~   ◍   🎧

Two women, off together on a weekend spree, go
on the run after one of them kills a man who tries
to rape the other.
*Timely, exuberant and off-beat feminist road movie
that manages to say something interesting about the
relationship between the sexes.*
w Callie Khouri d Ridley Scott ph Adrian
Biddle m Hans Zimmer pd Norris Spencer
ed Thom Noble
☆ Susan Sarandon, Geena Davis, Harvey Keitel,
Michael Madsen, Christopher McDonald, Stephen
Tobolowsky, Brad Pitt
   'An exhilarating feminist movie … that's
   designed to appeal to the outlaw lurking in all of
   us.' – *Philip French, Observer*
   'The first important American movie to plop
   two women in a car and send them careering
   down open Western roads with the cops in
   wheel-spinning pursuit. And it is the first to use
   sexism as the motivating force for their
   misdeeds.' – *Richard Schickel, Time*
♫ Callie Khouri
♫ Ridley Scott; Geena Davis; Susan Sarandon;
Adrian Biddle; editing

Thelma Jordan: see *The File on Thelma Jordan*

'Kill one and two others take its place! Don't turn
your back or you're doomed! And don't tell anyone
what Them are!'

Them! **

US   1954   94m   bw
Warner (David Weisbart)
◼️   ◎~

Atomic bomb radiation causes giant ants to breed
in the New Mexico desert.
*Among the first, and certainly the best, of the post-
atomic monster animal cycle, this durable thriller starts
with several eerie desert sequences and builds up to a
shattering climax in the Los Angeles sewers. A general
air of understatement helps a lot.*
w Ted Sherdeman story George Worthing Yates
d Gordon Douglas ph Sid Hickox m Bronislau
Kaper
☆ Edmund Gwenn, James Whitmore, Joan
Weldon, James Arness, Onslow Stevens
   'I asked the editor: How does it look? And he
   said: Fine. I said: Does it look honest? He said:
   As honest as twelve foot ants can look.' –
   Gordon Douglas

Them Thar Hills **

🏃🏃 US   1934   20m   bw
Hal Roach

Stan and Ollie go camping, drink from a well full
of moonshine whisky, and get drunk with another
camper's wife.
*Consistently funny star comedy culminating in a tit-
for-tat routine which was reprised in Tit for Tat the
following year.*
w Stan Laurel, H. M. Walker d Charles Rogers
ph Art Lloyd ed Bert Jordan
☆ Stan Laurel, Oliver Hardy, Charlie Hall, Mae
Busch, Billy Gilbert

The Theme *

USSR   1979   98m   colour
Mosfilm
◼️
original title: *Tema*

A depressed and famous middle-aged playwright,
who has settled for easy success, returns to the
town where he was born and falls in love with a
woman who has refused to compromise.
*A portrait of the artist as a failure, looking in vain for
redemption; its theme of artistic and personal freedom*

upset the Soviet authorities, who banned it for eight
years.
w Gleb Panfilov, Aleksander Cervinski d Gleb
Panfilov ph Leonid Kalashnikov m Vadim
Bibergan
☆ Inna Churikova, Michael Ulyanov, Stanislav
Lyubshin, Evgeny Vesnik, Sergei Nikonenko
† The film won the Golden Bear at the Berlin
Film Festival in 1987.

Themroc **

France   1972   110m   Eastmancolor
The Other Cinema/Filmanthrope/FDL (Jean-Claude
Bourlat)
◉◉

A depressed worker in a dead-end job suddenly
breaks free of all his restrictions, making love to his
sister and demolishing the walls of his apartment.
*An exuberant anti-authoritarian comedy, in which
normal dialogue is replaced by an invented language of
grunts and whistles.*
wd Claude Faraldo ph Jean-Marc Ripert ad C.
Lamarque ed Noun Serra
☆ Michel Piccoli, Béatrice Romand, Marilu Tolo,
Francesca R. Coluzzi, Patrick Dewaere, Miou-Miou
   'Succeeds in being poetic without being arty
   and, by using laughter as a critical tactic, in
   suggesting that revolution in a puritanical
   society ought to take a hedonistic form.' – *Jan
   Dawson, MFB*

Theodora Goes Wild *

US   1936   94m   bw
Columbia (Everett Riskin)

A small-town girl writes a titillating bestseller.
*Mildly crazy comedy which helped develop the trend for
stars performing undignified antics but today seems
rather slow and dated.*
w Sidney Buchman story Mary McCarthy
d Richard Boleslawski ph Joseph Walker
m Morris Stoloff ed Otto Meyer
☆ Irene Dunne, Melvyn Douglas, Thomas Mitchell,
Thurston Hall, Rosalind Keith, Spring Byington,
Elizabeth Risdon, Nana Bryant
   'The best light comedy since Mr Deeds.' –
   Graham Greene
♫ Irene Dunne; Otto Meyer

Theodore Rex

US   1995   92m   colour
New Line/J&M/Shooting Star (Richard Abramson, Sue
Baden-Powell)
◉◉   ◼️   ◎~

In the near future, when prehistoric animals have
been brought back to life and made almost human,
a cop teams up with a dinosaur to solve a murder.
*One of those films that you cannot believe ever got
made; its crassness is beyond criticism.*
wd Jonathan Betuel ph David Tattersall
m Robert Folk pd Walter Martishius ed Rick
Shaine, Steve Mirkovich sp dinosaurs: Criswell
Prods
☆ Whoopi Goldberg, Armin Mueller-Stahl, Juliet
Landau, Bud Cort, Stephen McHattie, Richard
Roundtree, George Newbern, Carol Kane
   'A bloated youth-appeal picture with
   disappointing effects and a very thin story.' –
   Leonard Klady, Variety
† The film, which cost $35m, was released direct
to video in the US after unsuccessful previews in
three cities. It received a cinema showing in some
countries, though in Britain it was also released
direct to video. Whoopi Goldberg did not want to
make the picture, appearing only after the threat of
legal action.

Theorem *

Italy   1968   98m   Eastmancolor
Aetos Film
◉◉   ◼️   🎧
original title: *Teorema*

A handsome young man arrives unexpectedly to
stay with a Milan industrialist and his family,
gratifying their desires but leaving them tragically
unhappy.
*Moderately amusing fable with the presumed intent of
decrying all universal panaceas, including Christianity.*
wd Pier Paolo Pasolini novel Pier Paolo Pasolini
ph Giuseppe Ruzzolini m Ennio Morricone
☆ Terence Stamp, Silvana Mangano, Massimo
Girotti, Anne Wiazemsky, Laura Betti

'If you're going to fall, make sure there's someone to catch you.'

The Theory of Flight

South Africa/GB 1998 99m DeLuxe
Buena Vista/Distant Horizon/BBC Films (Helena Spring, Ruth Caleb, David M. Thompson, Anant Singh)

A pilot is sentenced to work as a companion to a woman suffering from motor neurone disease, who is determined to lose her virginity before she dies.
Mawkish tale of an unlikely coupling that is a pain to watch.
w Richard Hawkins d Paul Greengrass ph Ivan Strasburg m Rolfe Kent pd Melanie Allen ed Mark Day
☆ Helena Bonham Carter, Kenneth Branagh, Gemma Jones, Holly Aird, Ray Stevenson
'A dire experience.' – *Guardian*

There Ain't No Justice

GB 1939 83m bw
Ealing (Michael Balcon)

A young boxer refuses to throw a fight.
Minor sporting drama, well praised at the time but later forgotten.
w Pen Tennyson, James Curtis, Sergei Nolbandov *novel* James Curtis d Pen Tennyson ph Mutz Greenbaum md Ernest Irving
☆ Jimmy Hanley, Edward Rigby, Mary Clare, Edward Chapman, Phyllis Stanley, Michael Wilding
'The whole picture breathes timidity and refinement.' – *Graham Greene*

There Goes My Heart

US 1938 81m bw
Hal Roach

A reporter is assigned to track down a runaway heiress.
Very pale imitation of It Happened One Night.
w Jack Jevne, Eddie Moran d Norman Z. McLeod ph Norbert Brodine m Marvin Hatley
☆ Fredric March, Virginia Bruce, Patsy Kelly, Nancy Carroll, Eugene Pallette, Claude Gillingwater, Arthur Lake, Harry Langdon, Etienne Girardot
'A comedy clicko … plenty of zip and zing.' – *Variety*
♫ Marvin Hatley

There Goes the Bride

GB 1980 91m Eastmancolor
Lonsdale (Martin Schute, Ray Cooney)
📀

A harassed advertising executive suffers hallucinations about a lifesize cardboard cut-out of a twenties flapper.
Embarrassingly witless and plotless revamp of innumerable better comedies in the Topper tradition; it has to be seen to be believed.
w Terence Marcel, Ray Cooney *play* Ray Cooney, John Chapman d Terence Marcel ph James Devis m Harry Robinson pd Peter Mullins
☆ Tom Smothers, Twiggy, Sylvia Syms, Martin Balsam, Michael Whitney, Geoffrey Sumner, Hermione Baddeley, Phil Silvers, Broderick Crawford, Jim Backus
'The whole thing would be laughable if it weren't so unfunny.' – *Gilbert Adair, MFB*

There Goes the Groom

US 1937 64m bw
RKO (Albert Lewis)

A young man comes back rich from the Alaskan gold fields and reminds an old girlfriend of her promise to marry him.
A well-played comedy which can't conceal its threadbare situations.
w S. K. Lauren, Dorothy Yost, Harold Kusell, David Garth d Joseph Santley
☆ Ann Sothern, Burgess Meredith, Mary Boland, Onslow Stevens, Louise Henry

There Goes the Neighborhood

US 1992 89m DeLuxe Panavision
Rank/Kings Road (Stephen Friedman)
📀 📼 🎬
aka: *Paydirt*

A prison psychologist and a gang of convicts go in search of a stolen fortune buried in a suburban basement.
Laboured farce with heavy-handed acting and direction which fails to raise a laugh.
wd Bill Phillips ph Walt Lloyd m David Bell pd Dean Tschetter ed Sharyn L. Ross

☆ Jeff Daniels, Catherine O'Hara, Hector Elizondo, Rhea Perlman, Judith Ivey, Harris Yulin, Jonathan Banks, Chazz Palminteri, Dabney Coleman
'A TV-inspired high concept and inept production values combine for an unappealing film sans redeeming qualities.' – *Variety*
† The film was released direct to video in Britain.

There Is Another Sun

GB 1951 95m bw
Nettlefold (Ernest G. Roy)
US title: *Wall of Death*

A fairground wall of death rider turns to crime.
Glum quickie which was oddly popular.
w Guy Morgan d Lewis Gilbert ph Wilkie Cooper m Wilfred Burns
☆ Maxwell Reed, Susan Shaw, Laurence Harvey, Hermione Baddeley, Leslie Dwyer

There Was a Crooked Man *

GB 1960 107m bw
UA/Knightsbridge (John Bryan)

An ex-safecracker outwits the crooked mayor of an industrial town.
Semi-happy attempt to humanize a knockabout clown; good supporting performances and production.
w Reuben Ship d Stuart Burge ph Arthur Ibbetson m Kenneth V. Jones
☆ Norman Wisdom, Andrew Cruickshank, Alfred Marks, Susannah York, Reginald Beckwith

There Was a Crooked Man *

US 1970 126m Technicolor Panavision
Warner Seven Arts (Joseph L. Mankiewicz)
📀 📼 🎬

In 1883 Arizona a murderer tries to escape from jail and recover hidden loot but is constantly thwarted by the sheriff who arrested him, now a warden.
Curious black comedy melodrama with lots of talent going nowhere in particular; hard to endure as a whole but with entertaining scenes.
w David Newman, Robert Benton d Joseph L. Mankiewicz ph Harry Stradling Jnr m Charles Strouse ad Edward Carrere
☆ Kirk Douglas, Henry Fonda, Hume Cronyn, Warren Oates, Burgess Meredith, John Randolph, Arthur O'Connell, Martin Gabel, Alan Hale
'This example of commercialized black comedy nihilism seems to have been an evil two-year-old, and it has been directed in the Grand Rapids style of moviemaking.' – *Pauline Kael, New Yorker*

There's a Girl in my Heart

US 1949 82m bw
Allied Artists (Arthur Dreifuss)

The attractive widow who owns a music hall finds the site in demand.
Slight, artificial but mildly pleasing musical extravaganza of the gay nineties.
w Arthur Hoerl, John Eugene Hasty d Arthur Dreifuss ph Philip Tanmura m Herschel Burke Gilbert
☆ Lee Bowman, Elyse Knox, Lon Chaney Jnr, Gloria Jean, Peggy Ryan, Ludwig Donath, Ray McDonald, Irene Ryan

There's a Girl in My Soup *

GB 1970 96m Eastmancolor
Columbia/Ascot (John Boulting)
📀 📼

A randy TV personality finds himself outpointed by a waif he picks up.
Flimsy screen version of a long-running sex comedy; some laughs, but the star is uncomfortably miscast.
w Terence Frisby *play* Terence Frisby d Roy Boulting ph Harry Waxman m Mike D'Abo
☆ Peter Sellers, Goldie Hawn, Tony Britton, Nicky Henson, John Comer, Diana Dors, Judy Campbell

There's Always a Woman *

US 1938 81m bw
Columbia

A private detective's wife beats him to the solution of a murder.
Amiably scatty crime comedy in the Thin Man tradition.
w Gladys Lehman, Wilson Collison d Alexander Hall

☆ Joan Blondell, Melvyn Douglas, Mary Astor, Frances Drake, Jerome Cowan, Robert Paige, Thurston Hall, Pierre Watkin
'Will provide general satisfaction as entertainment and as a grosser.' – *Variety*

There's Always Tomorrow

US 1934 86m bw
Universal

A depressed family man is cheered up by a former sweetheart.
Basically rather a dull drama, but with sincere performances which lift it.
w William Hurlbut *novel* Ursula Parrott d Edward Sloman
☆ Frank Morgan, Binnie Barnes, Lois Wilson, Louise Latimer, Alan Hale, Robert Taylor
'Attractive screen material, it weighs in for what looks like a favourable sprint for coin.' – *Variety*.
† Remade 1956 as *These Wilder Years*, with James Cagney and Barbara Stanwyck.

There's Always Tomorrow

US 1956 84m bw
Universal (Ross Hunter)

A married man falls for another woman.
Very flat variation on Brief Encounter, with stars going through mechanical paces.
w Bernard Schoenfeld *story* Ursula Parrott d Douglas Sirk ph Russell Metty m Herman Stein, Heinz Roemheld
☆ Barbara Stanwyck, Fred MacMurray, Joan Bennett, Pat Crowley, William Reynolds, Gigi Perreau, Jane Darwell
† Previously made by Universal in 1934 with Frank Morgan and Binnie Barnes.

There's No Business like Show Business **

👫 US 1954 117m DeLuxe
Cinemascope
TCF (Sol C. Siegel)
📀 📼 🎬 🎧

The life and times of a family of vaudevillians.
Mainly entertaining events and marvellous tunes make up this very Cinemascoped musical, in which the screen is usually filled with six people side by side.
w Phoebe and Henry Ephron d Walter Lang ph Leon Shamroy m Lionel Newman, Alfred Newman m/ly Irving Berlin ad John DeCuir, Lyle Wheeler
☆ Ethel Merman, Dan Dailey, Marilyn Monroe, Donald O'Connor, Johnny Ray, Mitzi Gaynor, Hugh O'Brian, Frank McHugh
'One of the saddening films which only occasionally live up to their huge promise.' – *Dilys Powell*
♫ original story (Lamar Trotti); Lionel Newman, Alfred Newman

There's Nothing Out There *

US 1991 90m colour
Valkhn (Victor Kanefsky)

Teenagers staying in an isolated mountain cabin are threatened by an alien monster.
Mildly amusing spoof of horror and science-fiction exploitation movies.
wd Rolfe Kanefsky ph Ed Hershberger m Christopher Thomas ed Victor Kanefsky sp Scott Hart; creature design: Ken Quinn
☆ Craig Peck, Wendy Bednarz, Mark Collver, Bonnie Bowers, John Carhart III, Claudia Flores, Jeff Dachis, Lisa Grant
'Tongue-in-cheeky thriller which takes dead aim at the clichés abounding in B and C list titles.' – *Variety*

There's Something about a Soldier

US 1943 81m bw
Columbia (Samuel Bischoff)

The destinies of five officer candidates at the Anti-Aircraft Training School.
Transparent recruiting poster dramatics.
w Horace McCoy, Barry Trivers d Alfred E. Green
☆ Tom Neal, Evelyn Keyes, Bruce Bennett, John Hubbard, Jeff Donnell, Frank Sully

'Be Offended. Be *Very* Offended.'

There's Something about Mary *

US 1998 118m DeLuxe
TCF (Frank Beddor, Michael Steinberg, Charles B. Wessler, Bradley Thomas)
📀 📼 🎬 🎧

Thirteen years after graduating, a man hires a private detective to find the girl he fancied at high school.
Broad comedy which draws attention to its tastelessness; it was among the biggest box-office successes of 1998.
w Ed Decter, John J. Strauss, Peter Farrelly, Bobby Farrelly d Bobby Farrelly, Peter Farrelly ph Mark Irwin m Jonathan Richman ad Arlan Jay Vetter ed Christopher Greenbury
☆ Cameron Diaz, Matt Dillon, Ben Stiller, Lee Evans, Chris Elliott, Lin Shaye, Jeffrey Tambor, Markie Post, Keith David, W. Earl Brown, Jonathan Richman
'It becomes clear that the real stars of Mary are the two grown men behind the camera, giggling triumphantly each time one of their actors says the word "dick".' – *Danny Leigh, Sight and Sound*

There's That Woman Again

US 1938 75m bw
Columbia

A district attorney is hampered by his meddlesome spouse.
Half-hearted follow-up to There's Always a Woman; the McMillan and Wife of its day.
w Philip G. Epstein, James Edward Grant, Ken Englund d Alexander Hall
☆ Melvyn Douglas, Virginia Bruce, Margaret Lindsay, Stanley Ridges, Gordon Oliver, Tom Dugan, Don Beddoe

Therese *

France 1986 91m colour
AFC/Films AZ/CNC

A 19th-century Normandy girl becomes a nun, dies at 24, and is canonized.
Straightforward, austere biographical account which weaves a curious spell.
wd Alain Cavalier ph Philippe Rousselot m Offenbach, Fauré
☆ Catherine Mouchet, Aurore Prieto, Sylvie Habault

These Are the Damned: see *The Damned*

These Dangerous Years

GB 1957 92m bw
Everest/Anna Neagle
US title: *Dangerous Youth*

A Liverpool teenage gang leader is called up and becomes a better guy.
Dim drama with music marking the debut of a singing star.
w John Trevor Story d Herbert Wilcox ph Gordon Dines m Stanley Black
☆ Frankie Vaughan, George Baker, Carole Lesley, Jackie Lane, Katherine Kath, Eddie Byrne, Kenneth Cope

These Foolish Things: see *Daddy Nostalgie*

These Glamour Girls

US 1939 78m bw
MGM

A drunken college student invites a dime-a-dance girl for a festive weekend with his snobbish friends.
Wincingly predictable romantic comedy-drama with no outstanding talent displayed from any quarter.
w Marion Parsonnet, Jane Hall d S. Sylvan Simon
☆ Lew Ayres, Lana Turner, Tom Brown, Richard Carlson, Jane Bryan, Anita Louise, Ann Rutherford, Marsha Hunt
'Silly situations and mawkish lines. A dualler.' – *Variety*

These Things Happen: see *Les Choses de la Vie*

These Thousand Hills

US 1958 96m Eastmancolor Cinemascope
TCF (David Weisbart)

A successful cattle rancher finds that his best friend is a rustler.
Large-scale but somehow unimpressive Western variant on The Virginian, cluttered with sub-plots.

w Alfred Hayes *novel* A. B. Guthrie Jnr
d Richard Fleischer *ph* Charles G. Clarke
m Leigh Harline
☆ Richard Egan, Stuart Whitman, Don Murray, Lee Remick, Albert Dekker, Harold J. Stone, Patricia Owens

These Three **
US   1936   93m   bw
Samuel Goldwyn
⬚⬚ ▤ ⬕

A lying schoolgirl accuses two schoolmistresses of scandalous behaviour.
Bowdlerized version of a famous play (instead of lesbianism we have extra-marital affairs). It worked well enough at the time but now seems dated; oddly enough when the play was filmed full strength in 1962 it didn't work at all.
w Lillian Hellman *play* The Children's Hour *by* Lillian Hellman d William Wyler *ph* Gregg Toland m Alfred Newman
☆ Merle Oberon, Miriam Hopkins, Joel McCrea, *Bonita Granville*, Catherine Doucet, Alma Kruger, Marcia Mae Jones, Margaret Hamilton, Walter Brennan
  'I have seldom been so moved by any fictional film … After ten minutes or so of the usual screen sentiment, quaintness and exaggeration, one began to watch with incredulous pleasure nothing less than life.' – *Graham Greene*
  ⅋ Bonita Granville

These Wilder Years
US   1956   91m   bw
MGM (Jules Schermer)
A wealthy industrialist returns to his home town to trace his illegitimate son.
Modest sentimental drama with practised stars.
w Frank Fenton d Roy Rowland *ph* George Folsey m Jeff Alexander
☆ James Cagney, Barbara Stanwyck, Walter Pidgeon, Betty Lou Keim, Don Dubbins, Edward Andrews

They All Died Laughing: see *A Jolly Bad Fellow*

They All Kissed the Bride
US   1942   86m   bw
Columbia (Edward Kaufman)
A woman executive falls in love with the crusading writer who is out to expose working conditions in her company.
No surprises are expected or provided in this very ho-hum romantic comedy.
w P. J. Wolfson d Alexander Hall *ph* Joseph Walker m Werner Heyman *md* Morris Stoloff
☆ Joan Crawford, Melvyn Douglas, Roland Young, Billie Burke, Allen Jenkins, Andrew Tombes, Helen Parrish, Mary Treen

They All Laughed *
US   1982   115m   Movielab
Time-Life/Moon (George Morfogen, Blaine Novak)
▤ ⬕
Three agency detectives fall in and out of love in the course of their duties.
It has the air of a somewhat misshapen and Americanized La Ronde, *with added suggestions of* On the Town, *but it adds up to very little and provides only a few laughs on the way.*
wd Peter Bogdanovich *ph* Robby Muller m various
☆ Audrey Hepburn, Ben Gazzara, John Ritter, Dorothy Stratten, Colleen Camp, Patti Hansen, George Morfogen, Blaine Novak
  'One tires of long looks that speak volumes, of endless successions of meeting cute.' – *John Pym, MFB*

They Call It Sin
US   1932   68m   bw
First National
GB title: The Way of Life
A Kansas girl joins a New York chorus and needs to be rescued from a villainous producer.
Ho-hum romantic drama without much substance.
w Lillie Hayward, Howard Green *novel* Alberta Steadman Eagan d Thornton Freeland
☆ Loretta Young, George Brent, Louis Calhern, David Manners, Una Merkel
  'It needs the sexy title to bolster a just so-so flicker.' – *Variety*

They Call Me Mister Tibbs!
US   1970   108m   DeLuxe
UA/Mirisch (Herbert Hirshman)
▤
A San Francisco police lieutenant suspects a crusading local minister of murder.
Flat, dispirited police melodrama with irrelevant domestic asides, a long way after In the Heat of the Night *which introduced the main character. (The Organization was the third and last in the so-called series.)*
w Alan R. Trustman, James R. Webb d Gordon Douglas *ph* Gerald Finnerman m Quincy Jones
☆ Sidney Poitier, Martin Landau, Barbara McNair, Anthony Zerbe, Jeff Corey, Juano Hernandez, Ed Asner

They Call Me Trinity (dubbed)
Italy   1970   100m   Technicolor   Techniscope
Avco/West (Italo Zingarelli)
⬚⬚ ⬕
original title: Lo Chiamavano Trinità
A gunman and his outlaw brother defend a Mormon settlement against a ruthless landowner.
Amiable spaghetti Western that parodies The Magnificent Seven *and ambles along in a pleasantly time-wasting way.*
wd E. B. Clucher (Enzo Barboni) *ph* Aldo Giordani m Franco Micalizzi *ad* Enzo Bulgarelli *ed* Giampiero Giunti
☆ Terence Hill (Mario Girotti), Bud Spencer (Carlo Pedersoli), Farley Granger, Steffen Zacharias, Dan Sturkie, Gisela Hahn
  'Highly engaging.' – *Sight and Sound*
† The British release ran for 93m.
†† It was followed by a sequel, *Trinity Is Still My Name* (qv).

They Came by Night
GB   1939   72m   bw
TCF
A jeweller pretends to be a crook in order to lure the men who killed his brother.
Smart little suspense yarn.
w Frank Launder, Sidney Gilliat, Michael Hogan, Roland Pertwee d Harry Lachman
☆ Will Fyffe, Phyllis Calvert, Anthony Hulme, George Merritt, Athole Stewart, John Glyn Jones

They Came from beyond Space
GB   1967   85m   Eastmancolor
Amicus (Max J. Rosenberg, Milton Subotsky)
▤
Disembodied aliens take over a team of scientists investigating a mysterious fall of meteors.
Implausible science fiction, lacking flair in acting, direction and writing and not helped by the change in locale from the original to an olde-worlde English setting.
w Milton Subotsky *novel* The Gods Hate Kansas *by* Joseph Millard d Freddie Francis *ph* Norman Warwick m James Stevens *pd* Bill Constable *ed* Peter Musgrave
☆ Robert Hutton, Jennifer Jayne, Zia Mohyeddin, Bernard Kay, Michael Gough, Geoffrey Wallace

They Came from Within: see *Shivers*

They Came to a City *
GB   1944   77m   bw
Ealing (Sidney Cole)
Assorted people find themselves outside the gates of a mysterious city.
The Outward Bound *format applied to postwar reconstruction, with characters deciding what kind of a world they want. Good talk and good acting, but not quite cinema.*
w Basil Dearden, Sidney Cole *play* J. B. Priestley d Basil Dearden *ph* Stan Pavey
☆ Googie Withers, John Clements, Raymond Huntley, Renée Gadd, A. E. Matthews, Mabel Terry-Lewis, *Ada Reeve*, Norman Shelley, Frances Rowe

They Came to Blow Up America
US   1943   73m   bw
TCF
An FBI man of German parentage goes to Nazi Germany and trains with a group of saboteurs who are arrested when they set foot in the US.
Tolerable propaganda potboiler.
w Aubrey Wisberg d Edward Ludwig
☆ George Sanders, Anna Sten, Ward Bond, Dennis Hoey, Sig Rumann, Ludwig Stossel

They Came to Cordura *
US   1959   123m   Technicolor   Cinemascope
Columbia/Goetz-Baroda (William Goetz)
▤ ⬕
In 1916 Mexico, six American military heroes are recalled to base, but the hardships of the journey reveal their true colours.
Watchable adventure epic, not so arresting as was intended but quite professional.
w Ivan Moffat, Robert Rossen *novel* Glendon Swarthout d Robert Rossen *ph* Burnett Guffey m Elie Siegmeister
☆ Gary Cooper, Rita Hayworth, Van Heflin, Richard Conte, Tab Hunter, Michael Callan, Dick York, Robert Keith

They Came to Rob Las Vegas *
Spain/France/Germany/Italy   1969   128m   Techniscope
Warner/Isasi/Capitoli/Eichberg/Franca
Criminals ambush a security truck in the Nevada desert.
Long-winded, flashily directed, gleamingly photographed, occasionally lively, frequently violent, finally tedious caper melodrama with a multi-lingual cast.
w Antonio Isasi, Jo Eisinger d Antonio Isasi *ph* Juan Gelpi m Georges Gavarentz
☆ Jack Palance, Lee J. Cobb, Elke Sommer, Gary Lockwood, Georges Geret, Jean Servais

They Dare Not Love
US   1941   76m   bw
Columbia (Sam Bischoff)
An Austrian prince flees the Nazis, but they force him to return and he has to leave his fiancée in America.
Curiously naïve romantic propaganda from this director; not at all memorable.
w Charles Bennett, Ernest Vajda d James Whale *ph* Franz Planer m Morris Stoloff
☆ George Brent, Martha Scott, Paul Lukas, Egon Brecher, Roman Bohnen, Edgar Barrier, Frank Reicher

They Died with Their Boots On **
US   1941   140m   bw
Warner (Robert Fellows)
⬚⬚ ▤ ⬕ 🎧
The life of General Custer and his death at Little Big Horn.
It seems it all happened because of an evil cadet who finished up selling guns to the Indians. Oh, well! The first half is romantic comedy, the second steels itself for the inevitable tragic outcome, but it's all expertly mounted and played in the best old Hollywood style.
w Wally Kline, Aeneas Mackenzie d Raoul Walsh *ph* Bert Glennon m Max Steiner
☆ Errol Flynn, Olivia de Havilland, Arthur Kennedy, Charles Grapewin, Anthony Quinn, Sydney Greenstreet, Gene Lockhart, Stanley Ridges, John Litel, Walter Hampden, Regis Toomey, Hattie McDaniel

They Drive by Night **
GB   1938   84m   bw
Warner (Jerome Jackson)
An ex-convict is helped by lorry drivers to solve the silk stocking murders of which he is suspected.
Excellent, little-seen British suspenser of the Hitchcock school.
w Derek Twist *novel* James Curtis d Arthur Woods *ph* Basil Emmott
☆ Emlyn Williams, Ernest Thesiger, Anna Konstam, Allan Jeayes, Antony Holles, Ronald Shiner
  'Dialogue, acting and direction put this picture on a level with the French cinema.' – *Graham Greene*

They Drive by Night **
US   1940   97m   bw
Warner (Mark Hellinger)
▤ ⬕
GB title: The Road to Frisco
A truck driver loses his brother in an accident, and in an attempt to improve his lot becomes involved with a scheming murderess.
Solid melodramatic entertainment which borrows the second half of its plot from Bordertown.
w Jerry Wald, Richard Macaulay *novel* Long Haul *by* A. I. Bezzerides d Raoul Walsh *ph* Arthur Edeson *md* Adolph Deutsch

☆ George Raft, Humphrey Bogart, *Ann Sheridan*, *Ida Lupino*, Gale Page, Alan Hale, Roscoe Karns, John Litel, Henry O'Neill, George Tobias

They Flew Alone *
GB   1941   103m   bw
RKO/Imperator (Herbert Wilcox)
US title: Wings and the Woman
The story of Amy Johnson and Jim Mollison, married flying pioneers of the thirties.
Adequate fictionalized history with interesting historical detail.
w Miles Malleson d Herbert Wilcox *ph* Frederick A. Young
☆ Anna Neagle, Robert Newton, Edward Chapman, Nora Swinburne, Joan Kemp-Welch, Charles Carson, Brefni O'Rorke

They Gave Him a Gun
US   1937   94m   bw
MGM (Harry Rapf)
Despite the efforts of his friend, a war-hardened veteran turns to crime and comes to a sticky end.
Dullish moral melodrama with its stars looking as though stuck in glue.
w Cyril Hume, Richard Maibaum, Maurice Rapf *novel* William Joyce Cowan d W. S. Van Dyke II *ph* Harold Rosson
☆ Spencer Tracy, Franchot Tone, Gladys George, Edgar Dearing, Mary Treen, Cliff Edwards
  'Meller overboard on grief. Does not sum up as having b.o. punch.' – *Variety*

They Go Boom
US   1929   20m   bw
Hal Roach
Stan's nocturnal efforts to cure Ollie's cold nearly bring down the house about their ears.
Average, rather protracted star comedy.
w Leo McCarey, H. M. Walker d James Parrott *ph* Art Lloyd, George Stevens *ed* Richard Currier
☆ Stan Laurel, Oliver Hardy, Charlie Hall

They Got Me Covered *
US   1943   93m   bw
Samuel Goldwyn
▤ ⬕
An incompetent foreign correspondent inadvertently breaks up a spy ring in Washington.
One of Hope's better and most typical comedy-thriller vehicles.
w Harry Kurnitz d David Butler *ph* Rudolph Maté m Leigh Harline
☆ Bob Hope, Dorothy Lamour, Otto Preminger, Lenore Aubert, Eduardo Ciannelli, Marion Martin, Donald Meek, Donald MacBride, Walter Catlett, John Abbott, Florence Bates, Philip Ahn

They Just Had to Get Married
US   1933   69m   bw
Universal
A butler and maid come into money and rise in the social scale.
Rather muddled comedy for star fans.
w Gladys Lehman, H. M. Walker *play* Cyril Harcourt d Edward Ludwig
☆ ZaSu Pitts, Slim Summerville, C. Aubrey Smith, Roland Young, Verree Teasdale, Fifi D'Orsay, Robert Greig, David Landau, Elizabeth Patterson
  'Not for big town first runs, but a booker's selection for B houses or less.' – *Variety*

They Knew Mr Knight
GB   1945   93m   bw
IP/GHW
A clerk and his family become rich, then poor, through listening to a speculator.
Slightly oddball domestic drama reminiscent of Priestley's Angel Pavement.
w Norman Walker, Victor MacClure *novel* Dorothy Whipple d Norman Walker *ph* Erwin Hillier
☆ Mervyn Johns, Alfred Drayton, Nora Swinburne, Joyce Howard, Joan Greenwood, Olive Sloane, Peter Hammond

They Knew What They Wanted **
US   1940   96m   bw
RKO (Erich Pommer)
▤
A waitress agrees by mail to marry a California-Italian vineyard owner, but is aghast when she

arrives to discover that he sent his handsome foreman's photograph.

First-rate minor drama, expertly handled by stars and production team alike.

w Robert Ardrey *play* Sidney Howard *d* Garson Kanin *m* Harry Stradling *m* Alfred Newman

☆ Charles Laughton, Carole Lombard, William Gargan, Harry Carey, Frank Fay

'For dialogue, acting, background and film creation it's a honey.' – *Otis Ferguson*

† Previous versions include *The Secret Love* (1928) with Pola Negri and *A Lady to Love* (1930) with Vilma Banky (and Edward G. Robinson).

& William Gargan

They Live

US 1988 94m DeLuxe Panavision
Guild/Alive Films (Larry Franco)

A labourer discovers that aliens are taking over the world, using subliminal advertising.

A standard action film with an uncertain tone, as if it started out to be something more interesting.

w Frank Armitage *story* Eight O'Clock in the Morning by Ray Nelson *d* John Carpenter *ph* Gary B. Kibbe *m* John Carpenter, Alan Howarth *ad* William J. Durrell Jnr, Daniel Lomino *ed* Gib Jaffe, Frank E. Jiminez

☆ Roddy Piper, Keith David, Meg Foster, George 'Buck' Flower, Peter Jason, Raymond St. Jacques, Jason Robards III

They Live by Night *

US 1948 96m bw
RKO (Dore Schary)

A young man imprisoned for an accidental killing escapes with two hardened criminals and is forced to take part in their crimes.

Well-made if basically uninteresting melodrama with a draggy romantic interest; its 'realistic' yet impressionist style drew attention on its first release, and it was remade in the seventies as Thieves Like Us *(qv).*

w Charles Schnee *novel* Edward Anderson *d* Nicholas Ray *ph* George E. Diskant *m* Leigh Harline *ed* Sherman Todd

☆ Farley Granger, Cathy O'Donnell, Howard da Silva, Helen Craig

'I recommend this film for the manner in which this love-story threads its way through the criminal scene like a white line on a dark road, and for the two wonderfully tender performances by the young principal players.' – *Paul Dehn*

They Loved Life: see Kanal

They Made Me a Criminal *

US 1939 92m bw
Warner (Benjamin Glazer)

When he thinks he has killed a boxing opponent, a young man flees to the west and settles on a farm.

Competent remake of The Life of Jimmy Dolan, *a tribute to the American way.*

w Sig Herzig *d* Busby Berkeley *ph* James Wong Howe *m* Max Steiner

☆ John Garfield, Claude Rains, Gloria Dickson, May Robson, Billy Halop, Bobby Jordan, Leo Gorcey, Huntz Hall, Gabriel Dell, Ann Sheridan

'Handsomely mounted and printed on sepia stock – all of which helps.' – *Variety*

They Made Me a Fugitive *

GB 1947 104m bw
Warner/Alliance (Nat Bronsten, James Carter)
US title: *I Became a Criminal*

An ex-RAF pilot is drawn into black marketeering. Framed for a killing, he escapes from Dartmoor and takes revenge on the gang leader.

Deliberately squalid thriller which began a fashion for British realism, but now seems only momentarily entertaining.

w Noel Langley *novel* A Convict Has Escaped by Jackson Budd *d* Alberto Cavalcanti *ph* Otto Heller

☆ Trevor Howard, Sally Gray, Griffith Jones, René Ray, Mary Merrall, Vida Hope, Ballard Berkeley, Phyllis Robins

'The direction and cutting, in a word, are masterly and must set up in anyone – even in one like myself who is inclined to be impatient with depravity unredeemed – an alert, uneasy, tingling excitement.' – *Alan Dent, News Chronicle*

They Made Me a Killer

US 1946 65m bw
Pine-Thomas/Paramount

A young man framed by bank robbers proves his innocence.

Elementary cops-and-robbers, not too badly presented for a second feature.

w Geoffrey Homes, Winston Miller, Kae Salkow, Owen Francis *d* William C. Thomas

☆ Robert Lowery, Barbara Britton, Frank Albertson, Lola Lane, James Bush

They Met in Argentina

US 1941 76m bw
RKO (Lou Brock)

A Texas oil millionaire sends his representative to buy a horse which has been winning races in Buenos Aires.

Thin romantic comedy in pursuance of the good neighbour policy.

w Jerry Cady, Lou Brock, Harold Daniels *d* Leslie Goodwins, Jack Hively

☆ Maureen O'Hara, James Ellison, Alberto Vila, Buddy Ebsen, Robert Barrat, Joseph Buloff

They Met in Bombay *

US 1941 86m bw
MGM (Hunt Stromberg)

Jewel thieves on the run in the East fall in love.

A rather unusual romantic comedy chase which provides pretty satisfactory star entertainment.

w Edwin Justus Mayer, Anita Loos, Leon Gordon *d* Clarence Brown *ph* William Daniels *m* Herbert Stothart

☆ Clark Gable, Rosalind Russell, Peter Lorre, Reginald Owen, Jessie Ralph, Matthew Boulton, Eduardo Ciannelli, Luis Alberni

They Met in the Dark

GB 1943 104m bw
Rank (Marcel Hellman)

A Blackpool theatrical agent is really a master spy.

Elementary spy romance with a richly villainous performance from Tom Walls.

w Anatole de Grunwald, Miles Malleson, Basil Bartlett, Victor MacClure, James Seymour *novel* The Vanishing Corpse by Anthony Gilbert *d* Karel Lamac

☆ Tom Walls, Joyce Howard, James Mason, Phyllis Stanley, Edward Rigby, Ronald Ward, David Farrar

They Might be Giants *

US 1972 88m Technicolor
Universal/Paul Newman, John Foreman

A lawyer imagines he is Sherlock Holmes, and is taken in hand by Dr Mildred Watson.

Curious fantasy comedy which rather tentatively satirizes modern life and the need to retreat into unreality. Mildly pleasing entertainment for intellectuals.

w James Goldman *play* James Goldman *d* Anthony Harvey *ph* Victor Kemper *m* John Barry

☆ George C. Scott, Joanne Woodward, Jack Gilford, Lester Rawlins

They Only Kill Their Masters *

US 1972 98m Metrocolor
MGM (William Belasco)

A village police chief doggedly solves a series of murders.

Atmospheric, serio-comic murder mystery with a cast of old hands.

w Lane Slate *d* James Goldstone *ph* Michel Hugo *m* Perry Botkin Jnr

☆ James Garner, Katharine Ross, Hal Holbrook, June Allyson, Harry Guardino, Tom Ewell, Peter Lawford, Ann Rutherford, Chris Connelly, Edmond O'Brien, Art Metrano, Arthur O'Connell

They Passed This Way: see Four Faces West

'The lovers of *The Caine Mutiny* have a picture all their own!'

They Rode West

US 1954 84m Technicolor
Columbia

A cavalry doctor at a frontier fort gets into trouble by trying to help the Indians.

Western programmer whose sights are higher than its achievement.

w De Vallon Scott, Frank Nugent *d* Phil Karlson *ph* Charles Lawton Jnr *m* Paul Sawtell

☆ Robert Francis, Donna Reed, May Wynn, Phil Carey, Onslow Stevens, Jack Kelly

They Shall Have Music

👪 US 1939 105m bw
Samuel Goldwyn

GB title: *Melody of Youth*

Jascha Heifetz conducts a charity concert to help a music school for slum children.

Formula family film given the best possible production.

w John Howard Lawson, Irmgard von Cube *d* Archie Mayo *ph* Gregg Toland *md* Alfred Newman

☆ Joel McCrea, Jascha Heifetz, Andrea Leeds, Gene Reynolds, Walter Brennan, Porter Hall, Terry Kilburn, Diana Lynn (Dolly Loehr)

'A natural for the musically minded ... elemental and surefire audience appeal.' – *Variety*

& Alfred Newman

They Shoot Horses, Don't They? ***

US 1969 129m DeLuxe Panavision
Palomar/Chartoff-Winkler-Pollack

Tragedy during a six-day marathon dance contest in the early thirties.

An unrelievedly harrowing melodrama about dreary people, confused by 'flashforwards' but full of skilled technique, entertaining detail, and one brilliant performance.

w James Poe, Robert E. Thompson *novel* Horace McCoy *d* Sydney Pollack *ph* Philip Lathrop *m* John Green *md* John Green, Albert Woodbury *pd* Harry Horner

☆ Gig Young, Jane Fonda, Susannah York, Michael Sarrazin, Red Buttons, Bonnie Bedelia, Bruce Dern

COMPERE (GIG YOUNG): 'There can only be one winner, folks, but isn't that the American way?'

'Although *They Shoot Horses, Don't They?* does not, as a whole, reach the domain of art, many of its aspects and an aura that lingers on establish it as a true and eminent cinematic achievement.' – *John Simon*

🏆 Gig Young

& script; John Green, Albert Woodbury; Sydney Pollack; Jane Fonda; Susannah York

🎬 Susannah York

They Were Expendable *

US 1945 135m bw
MGM (John Ford)

Life in and around motor torpedo boats in the Pacific War.

Long drawn out flagwaver with some nice moments.

w Frank Wead *book* William L. White *d* John Ford *ph* Joseph H. August *m* Herbert Stothart

☆ John Wayne, Robert Montgomery, Donna Reed, Jack Holt, Ward Bond, Marshall Thompson, Leon Ames, Cameron Mitchell, Jeff York

'For what seems at least half its dogged, devoted length all you have to watch is men getting on or off PT boats and other men watching them do so. But this is made so beautiful and so real that I could not feel one foot of the film was wasted.' – *James Agee*

They Were Not Divided *

GB 1950 102m bw
Rank/Two Cities (Earl St. John)

The life of a Guards officer is paralleled with that of his American friend; they both die on a reconnaissance during the advance on Berlin.

Odd mixture of barrack room comedy, semi-documentary action, propaganda and the most appalling sentimentality. No one questioned it at the box-office, though.

wd Terence Young *ph* Harry Waxman *m* Lambert Williamson *ed* Ralph Kemplen, Vera Campbell

☆ Edward Underdown, Ralph Clanton, Helen Cherry, Stella Andrews, Michael Brennan, Michael Trubshawe, R. S. M. Brittain

'It is a rather curious experience to see a film made with all the best trappings of realism containing so many of the clichés of the studio.' – *Gavin Lambert*

'Rides off in so many directions as to be beyond toleration ... an empty, fumbling and evasive film.' – *Richard Winnington*

They Were Sisters

GB 1945 115m bw
GFD/Gainsborough (Harold Huth)

The problems of three married sisters.

Flatly handled multi-melodrama, the chief attraction being 'wicked' James Mason as a sadist.

w Roland Pertwee *novel* Dorothy Whipple *d* Arthur Crabtree *ph* Jack Cox *m* Louis Levy

☆ James Mason, Phyllis Calvert, Dulcie Gray, Hugh Sinclair, Anne Crawford, Peter Murray Hill, Pamela Kellino

They Who Dare

GB 1953 107m Technicolor
British Lion/Mayflower (Aubrey Baring, Maxwell Setton)

During World War II a group of British soldiers are sent on a raiding expedition to Rhodes.

Grimmish war actioner with plenty of noise but not much holding power.

w Robert Westerby *d* Lewis Milestone *ph* Wilkie Cooper *m* Robert Gill

☆ Dirk Bogarde, Denholm Elliott, Akim Tamiroff, Gérard Oury, Eric Pohlmann, Alec Mango

They Won't Believe Me *

US 1947 95m bw
RKO (Joan Harrison)

A playboy finds himself on trial for murder because of his philandering with three women.

Unusual suspenser with Hitchcock touches; quite neatly packaged, complete with twist ending.

w Jonathan Latimer *d* Irving Pichel *ph* Harry J. Wild *m* Roy Webb

☆ Robert Young, Susan Hayward, Rita Johnson, Jane Greer, Tom Powers, Don Beddoe, Frank Ferguson

'Talk and die! Until now their lips were frozen with fear!'

They Won't Forget ***

US 1937 94m bw
Warner (Mervyn Le Roy)

The murder of a girl in a Southern town leads to a lynching.

Finely detailed social drama, a classic of American realism; harrowing to watch.

w Robert Rossen, Aben Kandel *novel* Death in the Deep South by Ward Greene *d* Mervyn Le Roy *ph* Arthur Edeson, Warren Lynch *m* Adolph Deutsch *md* Leo F. Forbstein

☆ Claude Rains, Gloria Dickson, Edward Norris, Otto Kruger, Allyn Joslyn, Linda Perry, Elisha Cook Jnr, Lana Turner, Cy Kendall, Elizabeth Risdon

'Not only an honest picture, but an example of real movie-making.' – *Pare Lorenz*

They're a Weird Mob

Australia 1966 112m colour
Williamson-Powell

An Italian journalist goes to Australia and doesn't get on at first.

Patchy comedy from a local best-seller.

w Richard Imrie (Emeric Pressburger) *novel* Nino Culotta by John O'Grady *d* Michael Powell *ph* Arthur Grant *m* Alan Bonstead

☆ Walter Chiari, Clare Dunne, Chips Rafferty, Alida Chelli, Ed Devereaux, John Meillon

They're Off: see Straight, Place and Show

Thicker than Water

👪 US 1935 20m bw
Hal Roach

Ollie spends his savings on a grandfather clock which is promptly destroyed by a passing truck.

Well made but slightly tiresome star comedy, the last short ever made featuring Stan and Ollie.

w Stan Laurel *d* James W. Horne *ph* Art Lloyd *ed* Ray Snyder

☆ Stan Laurel, Oliver Hardy, Daphne Pollard, James Finlayson, Charlie Hall

---

Thief

US 1981 123m Astrocolor
United Artists/Michael Mann/Caan Productions

🎞 ■ ◑ ⊘ ⌒

GB title: Violent Streets

A high-class thief's professional life is contrasted with his personal problems.

And at far too great a length, with the additional problem that few people are really interested. A slick but empty melodrama.

wd Michael Mann *novel The Home Invaders* by Frank Hohimer *ph* Donald Thorin *m* Tangerine Dream *pd* Mel Bourne

☆ James Caan, Tuesday Weld, Willie Nelson, James Belushi

'It promises too much and delivers too little.' – *Richard Combs, MFB*

The Thief *

US 1952 86m bw
Harry M. Popkin (Clarence Greene)

■

A nuclear physicist is on the run from the FBI, who suspect him of being a spy.

Curious attempt to produce a thriller with no dialogue whatever; parts are well done, but the strain eventually shows, as the makers are not quite clever enough to flesh out the trickery with human interest.

w Clarence Greene, Russel Rouse *d* Russel Rouse *ph* Sam Leavitt *m* Herschel Gilbert

☆ Ray Milland, Martin Gabel, Rita Gam, Harry Bronson, John McKutcheon

♫ Herschel Gilbert

The Thief ***

Russia/France 1997 97m colour
NTV Profit/Le Pont/Roissy (Igor Tolstunov)

🎞

original title: Vor

At the end of the Second World War, a fatherless boy gradually discovers that the soldier he and his mother love is a deserter, a cheat and a thief.

Compassionate, acutely observed study in love, betrayal and childhood disillusionment that also manages to find humour in painful situations.

wd Pavel Chukhrai *ph* Vladimir Klimov *m* Vladimir Dashkevich *pd* Victor Petrov *ed* Marina Dobrianskaja, Natalia Kucerenko

☆ Vladimir Mashkov, Ekaterina Rednikova, Misha Philipchuk, Dima Chigarev, Amalia Mordvinova, Lidia Savchenko

The Thief of Bagdad ***

🕇🕇 US 1924 135m bw silent
Douglas Fairbanks

■ ◑ ⊘ ⌒

In old Bagdad, a thief uses magic to outwit the evil Caliph.

Celebrated silent version of the old fable, its camera tricks a little timeworn now but nevertheless maintaining the air of a true classic by virtue of its leading performance and driving narrative energy.

w Lotta Woods, Douglas Fairbanks *d* Raoul Walsh *ph* Arthur Edeson *m* Mortimer Wilson *ad* William Cameron Menzies

☆ Douglas Fairbanks, Snitz Edwards, Charles Belcher, Anna May Wong, Julanne Johnston, Etta Lee, Brandon Hurst, Sojin

'An entrancing picture, wholesome and compelling, deliberate and beautiful, a feat of motion picture art which has never been equalled.' – *New York Times*

'Here is magic. Here is beauty. Here is the answer to cynics who give the motion picture no place in the family of the arts … a work of rare genius.' – *James Quirk, Photoplay*

The Thief of Baghdad ****

🕇🕇 GB 1940 109m Technicolor
London Films (Alexander Korda)

■ ◑ ⌒

A boy thief helps a deposed king thwart an evil usurper.

Marvellous blend of magic, action and music, the only film to catch on celluloid the overpowering atmosphere of the Arabian Nights.

w Miles Malleson, Lajos Biro *d* Michael Powell, Ludwig Berger, Tim Whelan *ph* Georges Périnal, Osmond Borradaile *m* Miklos Rozsa *ad* Vincent Korda *sp* Lawrence Butler

☆ Conrad Veidt, Sabu, John Justin, June Duprez, Morton Selten, Miles Malleson, Rex Ingram, Mary Morris

ABU (SABU): 'I'm Abu the thief, son of Abu the thief, grandson of Abu the thief, most unfortunate of ten sons with a hunger that yearns day and night…'

AGED KING (MORTON SELTEN): 'This is the Land of Legend, where everything is possible when seen through the eyes of youth.'

'The true stuff of fairy tale.' – *Basil Wright*

'Both spectacular and highly inventive.' – *NFT, 1969*

'Magical, highly entertaining, and now revalued by Hollywood moguls Lucas and Coppola.' – *Time Out, 1980*

🏆 Georges Périnal; Vincent Korda

♫ Miklos Rozsa

The Thief of Baghdad

🕇🕇 Italy/France 1960 100m Eastmancolor
Cinemascope
Titanus/Lux

■

A very moderate remake in the form of an action star vehicle.

w Augusto Frassinetti, Filippo Sanjust, Bruno Vailati *d* Arthur Lubin *ph* Tonino delli Colli *m* Carlo Rustichelli

☆ Steve Reeves, Georgia Moll, Arturo Dominici

The Thief of Baghdad

🕇🕇 GB/France 1978 102m colour
Columbia/Palm Films/Victorine (Aida Young)

🎞 ■

A prince outwits an evil Grand Vizier to win the daughter of the Caliph of Baghdad.

Colourful but unexciting retelling of the familiar tale; made for television, it was given a theatrical release in Britain.

w A. J. Carothers, Andrew Birkin *d* Clive Donner *ph* Denis Lewiston *m* John Cameron *ad* Edward Marshall *ed* Peter Tanner

☆ Roddy McDowall, Kabir Bedi, Frank Finlay, Terence Stamp, Peter Ustinov, Marina Vlady, Pavla Ustinov, Daniel Emilfork, Ian Holm

'A sadly hangdog affair … The general aura of disaster, in fact, is mitigated only by Terence Stamp's clever portrayal of the Wazir as a perambulating corpse.' – *MFB*

† The British video release ran for 86m.

Thief of Damascus

US 1952 78m Technicolor
Columbia/Sam Katzman

The wicked ruler of Damascus is deposed by his own general, in league with Sinbad, Aladdin, and Scheherezade.

Mindless bosh, interesting only for its liberal use of scenes from Joan of Arc; the mind boggles at the costume compromise.

w Robert E. Kent *d* Will Jason *ph* Ellis W. Carter *m* Mischa Bakaleinikoff

☆ Paul Henreid, Lon Chaney Jnr, Jeff Donnell, John Sutton, Elena Verdugo

Thief of Hearts

US 1984 100m Metrocolor Panavision
Paramount (Don Simpson, Jerry Bruckheimer)

■ ◑

A burglar begins an obsessive affair with a woman whose intimate diary he steals.

Plodding, glossily vacuous thriller with an over-obtrusive disco score.

wd Douglas Day Stewart *ph* Andrew Laszlo *m* Giorgio Moroder *ad* Edward Richardson *ed* Tom Rolf

☆ Steven Bauer, Barbara Williams, John Getz, George Wendt, David Caruso, Christine Ebersole

The Thief Who Came to Dinner

US 1973 105m DeLuxe
Warner/Tandem (Bud Yorkin)

A computer analyst determines to become a jewel thief.

Tedious comedy aping the Raffles school but saddled with a complex plot and listless script.

w Walter Hill *novel* Terence L. Smith *d* Bud Yorkin *ph* Philip Lathrop *m* Henry Mancini

☆ Ryan O'Neal, Jacqueline Bisset, Warren Oates, Jill Clayburgh, Charles Cioffi

Thieves: see *Les Voleurs*

Thieves Fall Out

US 1941 72m bw
First National/Warner

An old lady lends her grandson money to start his business, but he has to rescue her when she's kidnapped.

Fairly amusing goings-on to fill the lower half of a bill.

w Charles Grayson, Ben Markson *play* Irving Gaumont, Jack Sobel *d* Ray Enright

☆ Jane Darwell, Eddie Albert, Joan Leslie, Alan Hale, William T. Orr, John Litel, Anthony Quinn, Edward Brophy

Thieves' Highway **

US 1949 94m bw
TCF (Robert Bassler)

A truck driver tracks down the racketeers who cheated and maimed his father.

Glossy, highly professional thick ear shedding a convincing light into one of America's less salubrious corners.

w A. I. Bezzerides *novel Thieves' Market* by A. I. Bezzerides *d* Jules Dassin *ph* Norbert Brodine *m* Alfred Newman

☆ Richard Conte, Valentina Cortesa, Lee J. Cobb, Jack Oakie, Millard Mitchell, Joseph Pevney, Barbara Lawrence, Hope Emerson

'You will never be able to eat an apple again without calling up visions of trickery, mayhem, vandalism and violent death.' – *New York Times*

'The action sequences are brilliantly done.' – *Daily Mail*

Thieves' Holiday: see *A Scandal in Paris*

Thieves Like Us *

US 1974 123m DeLuxe
United Artists/Jerry Bick-George Litto (Robert Eggenwiler)

🎞 ■

Three convicts break jail, and the youngest is attracted to the daughter of the farmer who helps them escape.

Gloomy romantic melodrama, agreeably set in the thirties and feelingly acted, but otherwise inferior to the much shorter version released in the forties as They Live by Night.

w Calder Willingham, Joan Tewkesbury, Robert Altman *novel* Edward Anderson *d* Robert Altman *ph* Jean Boffety *m* various songs *ed* Lou Lombardo

☆ Keith Carradine, Shelley Duvall, John Schuck, Bert Remsen, Louise Fletcher, Tom Skerritt

The Thin Blue Line **

US 1988 101m DuArt
BFI/Third Floor/American Playhouse (Mark Lipson)

Documentary that set out, successfully, to prove the innocence of a man found guilty of the murder of a Dallas policeman in 1976.

Gripping, excellently structured investigative journalism.

d Errol Morris *ph* Stefan Czapsky, Robert Chappell *m* Philip Glass *ed* Paul Barnes

'A powerful and thrillingly strange movie.' – *Terrence Rafferty, New Yorker*

'Your eyes will open wide with wonder!'
'The picture you dreamed someday you'd see … lovely to look at, lovelier still as you listen!'

Thin Ice *

US 1937 78m bw
TCF (Raymond Griffith)

GB title: Lovely to Look At

A skating instructress at an Alpine resort falls in love with a visiting prince.

Light-hearted musical vehicle for Hollywood's newest novelty – a skating star.

w Boris Ingster, Milton Sperling *novel Der Komet* by Attilla Orbok *d* Sidney Lanfield *ph* Robert Planck, Edward Cronjager *md* Louis Silvers *ch* Harry Losee *songs* Lew Pollack, Sidney Mitchell

☆ Sonja Henie, Tyrone Power, Arthur Treacher, Raymond Walburn, Joan Davis, Sig Rumann, Alan Hale, Melville Cooper

'She's a flash of winter lightning, a great combination of muscle and music, a Pavlova on ice … production wallop is the staging of three elaborate ice ballets.' – *Variety*

♫ Harry Losee

Thin Ice

GB 1994 92m colour
ICA/Dangerous to Know (Fiona Cunningham Reid, Martien Coucke)

A white heterosexual woman becomes the lover and skating partner of a black lesbian ice skater who wants to compete in the Gay Games in New York.

The film's subtitle – 'Passion of the Pink Rink' – says it all: it is a simple, romantic story on ice.

w Geraldine Sherman, Fiona Cunningham Reid *d* Fiona Cunningham Reid *ph* Belinda Parsons *m* Claire Van Kampen, Richard Allen, Pete Baikie *pd* Patricia Boulter *ed* Rodney Sims

☆ Charlotte Avery, Sabra Williams, James Dreyfus, Clare Higgins, Guy Williams, Barbara New, Suzanne Bertish, Ian McKellen

'A horribly fluffy, naïve thing that falls into all the 1980s clichés of gay cinema.' – *Jonathan Romney, Guardian*

'She's had it with bad boys. Now it's time to get even.'

A Thin Line between Love & Hate

US 1996 108m DeLuxe
Entertainment/New Line/Savoy (Douglas McHenry, George Jackson)

🎞 ■ ◑ ⊘ ⌒

A philanderer finds himself in trouble when he breaks off an affair with a vengeful woman.

A comic variation on Fatal Attraction, an influence acknowledged by its makers, and with an equally misogynistic tone; the result is not pleasant, especially when coupled to the self-indulgent style of its director and star.

w Martin Lawrence, Bentley Kyle Evans, Kenny Buford, Kim Bass *d* Martin Lawrence *ph* Francis Kenny *m* Roger Troutman *pd* Simon Dobbin *ed* John Carter

☆ Martin Lawrence, Lynn Whitfield, Regina King, Bobby Brown, Della Reese, Malinda Williams, Daryl Mitchell, Roger E. Mosley

'There may be a thin line between love and hate, but the boundary separating this film and romantic comedy is as wide as the Gobi desert.' – *Stephen Amidon, Sunday Times*

'A laugh tops every thrilling moment!'

The Thin Man ***

US 1934 93m bw
MGM/Cosmopolitan (Hunt Stromberg)

■

In New York over Christmas, a tipsy detective with his wife and dog solves the murder of an eccentric inventor.

Fast-moving, alternately comic and suspenseful mystery drama developed in brief scenes and fast wipes. It set a sparkling comedy career for two stars previously known for heavy drama, it was frequently imitated, and it showed a wisecracking, affectionate married relationship almost for the first time.

w Frances Goodrich, Albert Hackett *novel Dashiell Hammett d* W. S. Van Dyke *ph* James Wong Howe *m* William Axt

☆ William Powell, Myrna Loy, Maureen O'Sullivan, Nat Pendleton, Minna Gombell, Edward Ellis, Porter Hall, Henry Wadsworth, William Henry, Harold Huber, Cesar Romero, Edward Brophy

'A strange mixture of excitement, quips and hard-boiled sentiment … full of the special touches that can come from nowhere but the studio, that really make the feet a movie walks on.' – *Otis Ferguson*

† Sequels, on the whole of descending merit, included the following, all made at MGM with the same star duo: 1936: *After the Thin Man* (V*, L; 110m). 1939: *Another Thin Man* (V*, L; 102m). 1941: *Shadow of the Thin Man* (V*, L; 97m). 1944: *The Thin Man Goes Home* (V*, L; 100m). 1947: *Song of the Thin Man* (V*, L; 86m).

♫ best picture; script; W. S. Van Dyke; William Powell

The Thin Red Line

US 1964 99m bw Cinemascope
Security/ACE (Sidney Harmon)

🎞 ■

Raw recruits land on Guadalcanal and most of them are killed.

Weary, routine, realistic war drama.

w Bernard Gordon *novel* James Jones *d* Andrew Marton *ph* Manuel Berenguer *m* Malcolm Arnold

---

🕇🕇 film suitable for family viewing   🎞 VHS video-cassette for the British PAL system   ■ VHS video-cassette for the British PAL system in wide screen-format   ⊘ Video cassette in a computer-colourised version   ■ American NTSC video-cassette   ◑ Laser disc

☆ Keir Dullea, Jack Warden, James Philbrook, Kieron Moore

'Every Man Fights His Own War.'
The Thin Red Line ***
US 1998 170m Technicolor Panavision
TCF/Fox 2000/Phoenix (Robert Michael Geisler, John Roberdeau, Grant Hill)
🔲 ▤ @~ 𝄞

In 1943, a group of American soldiers, fighting the Japanese on Guadalcanal, are ordered to take a heavily defended position.
A ruminative war movie, with much voice-over, and often depending for its viewpoint on sound and the visual contrast between the lush landscapes and the mess the soldiers make of it. War is seen as an aberration, an intrusion on a natural paradise.
wd Terrence Malick *novel* James Jones *ph* John Toll *m* Hans Zimmer *pd* Jack Fisk *ed* Billy Weber, Leslie Jones, Saar Klein
☆ Sean Penn, Adrien Brody, Jim Caviezel, Ben Chaplin, George Clooney, John Cusack, Woody Harrelson, Elias Koteas, Jared Leto, Dash Mihok, Tim Blake Nelson, Nick Nolte, John C. Reilly, Larry Romano, John Savage and also John Travolta, Arie Verveen, Miranda Otto
  'A complex, highly talented work marked by intellectual and philosophical ambitions that will captivate some critics and serious viewers as well as by an abstract nature, emotional remoteness and lack of dramatic focus that will frustrate mainstream audiences.' – *Todd McCarthy, Variety*
  'The film sprawls, gets lost and occasionally delivers visual poetry, the kind that could have been greatly helped by tighter editing.' – *Janet Maslin, New York Times*
🧍 best picture; Terrence Malick (as director and writer); John Toll; Hans Zimmer; Billy Weber, Leslie Jones, Saar Klein; sound

The Thing **
US 1951 87m bw
RKO/Winchester (Howard Hawks)
🔲 ▤ @~
GB title: *The Thing from Another World*
A US scientific expedition in the Arctic is menaced by a ferocious being they inadvertently thaw out from a spaceship.
Curiously drab suspense shocker mainly set in corridors, with insufficient surprises to sustain its length. It does, however, contain the first space monster on film, and is quite nimbly made, though it fails to use the central gimmick from its original story.
w Charles Lederer *story* Who Goes There? by J. W. Campbell Jnr *d* Christian Nyby (with mysterious help, either Hawks or Orson Welles) *ph* Russell Harlan *m* Dimitri Tiomkin *ad* Albert S. D'Agostino, John Hughes *ed* Roland Gross
☆ Robert Cornthwaite, Kenneth Tobey, Margaret Sheridan, William Self, Dewey Martin, James Arness, Douglas Spencer, Robert Nichols
LAST SPEECH OF FILM: 'I bring you warning – to every one of you listening to the sound of my voice. Tell the world, tell this to everyone wherever they are: watch the skies, watch everywhere, keep looking – watch the skies!'
  'There seems little point in creating a monster of such original characteristics if he is to be allowed only to prowl about the North Pole, waiting to be destroyed by the superior ingenuity of the US Air Force.' – *Penelope Houston*
  'A monster movie with pace, humour and a collection of beautifully timed jabs of pure horror.' – *NFT, 1967*

'Man is the warmest place to hide!'
The Thing
US 1982 109m Technicolor Panavision
Universal/Lawrence Turman, David Foster
🔲 ▤ @~ 𝄞

Working in the Antarctic, a group of American scientists thaw out the frozen body of an alien.
A remake using the basis of the original story (the thing conceals itself within each of the characters in turn) but filled with revolting detail which alienated many audiences.
w Bill Lancaster *story* Who Goes There? by John W. Campbell Jnr *d* John Carpenter *ph* Dean Cundey *m* Ennio Morricone *pd* John J. Lloyd *ed* Todd Ramsay *sp* Albert Whitlock
☆ Kurt Russell, A. Wilford Brimley, T. K. Carter, David Clennon, Richard Dysart, Richard Masur,

Keith David, Charles Hallahan, Peter Maloney, Donald Moffat

The Thing Called Love
US 1993 110m DeLuxe
Paramount (John Davis)
🔲 ▤ @~ 𝄞

A young New York woman goes to Nashville to join other hopefuls trying to become country and western stars.
An insipid failure of a film, a thin drama strung out long after it has ceased to entertain.
w Carol Heikkinen *d* Peter Bogdanovich *ph* Peter James *pd* Michael Seymour *ed* Terry Stokes
☆ River Phoenix, Samantha Mathis, Dermot Mulroney, Sandra Bullock, K. T. Oslin, Trisha Yearwood, Anthony Clark, Webb Wilder, Earl Poole Ball
  'It's like a home movie in more ways than one; Phoenix looks drunk or tranquillised most of the time, and shows none of the gifts he once had to burn … The film is quite stupendously aimless, with a lousy plot and even worse dialogue.' – *Sunday Times*
  'Phoenix's performance is perceivably off-kilter – at best strange in a Methody mumbo-jumbo kind of way, at worst downright creepy. Camouflaged as a greasy-haired wreck with a cobra-lidded gaze, he lurches from lucidity to functionally impaired, mumbling throughout. All of this, however, is unfair baggage with which to saddle Bogdanovich's formulaic musical drama, a film which otherwise registers as a wispy but mostly enjoyable romantic fable.' – *Matt Mueller, Empire*
† The film was released direct to video in Britain, although it also received a brief showing at the National Film Theatre. It was River Phoenix's last film to be released, though he later made *Dark Blood*, which was abandoned following his death. Bogdanovich joined the film at a relatively late stage, replacing the original director.

The Thing from Another World: see The Thing (1951)

'The doctor blew it – he transplanted a white bigot's head onto a soul brother's body!'
The Thing with Two Heads
US 1972 89m colour
AIP
A racist brain surgeon with terminal cancer arranges to have his head transplanted on to the body of a convict; but the convict turns out to be black.
Bad taste comedy-horror with a great many frantic action sequences. Beyond criticism.
w Lee Frost, Wes Bishop, James Gordon White *d* Lee Frost *ph* Jack Steely *m* Robert O. Ragland
☆ Ray Milland, Rosey Grier, Roger Perry, William Smith
  'Every bit as preposterous as it sounds.' – *LA Times*

Things Are Looking Up
GB 1935 78m bw
Gaumont
A circus horsewoman has to pose as her schoolmistress sister.
Lively star vehicle for an oddly matched team.
w Stafford Davies, Con West *d* Albert de Courville
☆ Cicely Courtneidge, William Gargan, Max Miller, Mary Lawson, Dick Henderson, Dick Henderson Jnr, Judy Kelly, Suzanne Lenglen, Vivien Leigh

Things Are Tough All Over
US 1982 92m Metrocolor Panavision
Columbia/C & C Brown (Howard Brown)
🔲 ▤ @~

Two layabouts are hired by Arabs to drive a limousine containing five million dollars to Las Vegas.
Dire and inane comedy, full of racist jokes.
w Cheech Marin, Tommy Chong *d* Thomas K. Avildsen *ph* Bobby Byrne *m* Gaye Delorme *pd* Richard Tom Sawyer *ed* Dennis Dolan
☆ Richard 'Cheech' Marin, Tommy Chong, Shelby Fields, Rikki Marin, Evelyn Guerrero, John Steadman, Rip Taylor

Things Change **
US 1988 100m DuArt
Columbia TriStar/Filmhaus (Michael Hausman)
🔲 ▤

An incompetent crook is given the task of guarding for a week an elderly shoemaker who has agreed to go to jail in place of the leading gangster he resembles.
Gently comic anecdote, delicately played.
w David Mamet, Shel Silverstein *d* David Mamet *ph* Juan Ruiz Anchia *m* Alaric Jans *pd* Michael Merritt *ed* Trudy Ship
☆ Don Ameche, Joe Mantegna, Robert Prosky, J. J. Johnston, Ricky Jay, Mike Nussbaum, Jack Wallace, Dan Conway

The Things of Life: see Les Choses de la Vie

Things to Come ****
GB 1936 113m bw
London Films (Alexander Korda)
War in 1940 is followed by plague, rebellion, a new glass-based society, and the first rocketship to the moon.
Fascinating, chilling and dynamically well-staged vignettes tracing mankind's future. Bits of the script and acting may be wobbly, but the sets and music are magnificent, the first part of the prophecy chillingly accurate, and the whole mammoth undertaking almost unique in film history.
w H. G. Wells *book* The Shape of Things to Come by H. G. Wells *ph* Georges Périnal *m* Arthur Bliss *ad* Vincent Korda *sp* Harry Zech, Ned Mann *d/pd* William Cameron Menzies
☆ Raymond Massey, Edward Chapman, Ralph Richardson, Margaretta Scott, Cedric Hardwicke, Sophie Stewart, Derrick de Marney, John Clements
CABAL (RAYMOND MASSEY): 'It is this or that – all the universe or nothing. Which shall it be, Passworthy? Which shall it be?'
THEOTOCOPULOS (CEDRIC HARDWICKE): 'What is this progress? What is the good of all this progress onward and onward? We demand a halt. We demand a rest … an end to progress! Make an end to this progress now! Let this be the last day of the scientific age!'
  'Successful in every department except emotionally. For heart interest Mr Wells hands you an electric switch … It's too bad present-day film distribution isn't on a Wells 2040 basis, when the negative cost could be retrieved by button pushing. It's going to be harder than that. It's going to be almost impossible.' – *Variety*
  'An amazingly ingenious technical accomplishment, even if it does hold out small hope for our race … the existence pictured is as joyless as a squeezed grapefruit.' – *Don Herold*
  'A leviathan among films … a stupendous spectacle, an overwhelming, Dorean, Jules Vernesque, elaborated Metropolis, staggering to eye, mind and spirit, the like of which has never been seen and never will be seen again.' – *Sunday Times*

'They Can Die Quickly Or They Can Die Slowly But They Have To Die.'
Things to Do in Denver When You're Dead **
US 1995 114m CFI color
Woods Entertainment (Cary Woods)
🔲 ▤ @~ 𝄞

A reformed criminal, asked by the local crime boss to carry out one last job, recruits a gang of helpers who have seen better days and bungles the mission with deadly results.
An interesting and stylish thriller, but one that is too determinedly quirky, with its gallery of eccentric gangsters, to be entirely enjoyable.
w Scott Rosenberg *d* Gary Fleder *ph* Elliot Davis *m* Michael Convertino *pd* Nelson Coates *ed* Richard Marks
☆ Andy Garcia, Christopher Lloyd, William Forsythe, Bill Nunn, Treat Williams, Jack Warden, Steve Buscemi, Fairuza Balk, Gabrielle Anwar, Christopher Walken

Think Fast, Mr Moto *
US 1937 66m bw
TCF
Mr Moto goes on a long cruise from San Francisco to Shanghai to solve a case of diamond smuggling.

Enjoyable, quick-moving comedy thriller, the first in the series featuring Peter Lorre as the mild-mannered Japanese detective skilled in disguises and at judo.
w Howard Ellis Smith, Norman Foster *story* J. P. Marquand *d* Norman Foster *ph* Harry Jackson *md* Samuel Kaylin *ad* Lewis Creber *ed* Alex Troffey
☆ Peter Lorre, Virginia Field, Thomas Beck, Sig Rumann, Murray Kinnell, John Rogers, Lotus Long, George Cooper, J. Carrol Naish

The Third Alibi
GB 1961 68m bw
Grand National/Eternal (Maurice J. Wilson)
A wife takes action when she discovers that her husband plans to kill her so that he can marry her sister.
Enjoyable minor thriller, somewhat stolidly directed.
w Maurice J. Wilson, Montgomery Tully *play* A Moment of Blindness by Pip Baker, Jane Baker *d* Montgomery Tully *ph* James Harvey *m* Don Banks *md* Philip Martell *ad* William Hutchinson *ed* Jim Connock
☆ Laurence Payne, Patricia Dainton, Jane Griffiths, Edward Underdown, John Arnatt, Humphrey Lestocq, Lucy Griffiths, Cleo Laine

The Third Day
US 1965 119m Technicolor Panavision
Warner (Jack Smight)
An amnesiac learns that he is a rich unpopular tycoon facing a major crisis.
Glum melodrama which suggests domestic mystery but provides only interminable chat.
w Burton Wohl, Robert Presnell Jnr *novel* Joseph Hayes *d* Jack Smight *ph* Robert Surtees *m* Percy Faith
☆ George Peppard, Elizabeth Ashley, Roddy McDowall, Herbert Marshall, Mona Washbourne, Robert Webber, Charles Drake, Sally Kellerman, Arte Johnson, Vincent Gardenia

Third Finger Left Hand
US 1940 96m bw
MGM (John W. Considine Jnr)
A lady fashion editor fends off unwanted suitors by saying she is already married, but a commercial artist trumps this card by claiming to be the long lost husband of her invention.
Cheerful but overstretched romantic comedy.
w Lionel Houser *d* Robert Z. Leonard *ph* George Folsey *m* David Snell
☆ Myrna Loy, Melvyn Douglas, Lee Bowman, Bonita Granville, Raymond Walburn, Felix Bressart, Sidney Blackmer

The Third Generation
West Germany 1979 111m colour
Tango/Pro-Ject/FDA (Harry Baer)
original title: *Die dritte Generation*
A Berlin executive becomes the victim of a gang of terrorists.
Realistic melodrama, curiously muted in its satire and its anger, watchable more as an entertainment than as a polemic.
wd Rainer Werner Fassbinder *ph* Rainer Werner Fassbinder *m* Peer Raben *ed* Juliane Lorenz
☆ Volker Spengler, Bulle Ogier, Harry Baer, Eddie Constantine, Udo Kier, Hanna Schygulla

The Third Key: see The Long Arm

The Third Man ****
GB 1949 100m bw
British Lion/London Films/David O. Selznick/Alexander Korda (Carol Reed)
🔲 ▤ @~ ⊙

An unintelligent but tenacious writer of Westerns arrives in post-war Vienna to join his old friend Harry Lime, who seems to have met with an accident … or has he?
Totally memorable and irresistible romantic thriller. Stylish from the first to the last, with inimitable backgrounds of zither music and war-torn buildings pointing up a then-topical black market story full of cynical characters but not without humour. Hitchcock with feeling, if you like.
w Graham Greene *d* Carol Reed *ph* Robert Krasker *m* Anton Karas *ed* Oswald Hafenrichter
☆ Joseph Cotten, Trevor Howard, Alida Valli, Orson Welles, Bernard Lee, Wilfrid Hyde-White, Ernst Deutsch, Siegfried Breuer, Erich Ponto, Paul Hoerbiger
HARRY LIME (ORSON WELLES): 'Look down there. Would you really feel any pity if one of those dots

stopped moving for ever? If I offered you twenty thousand pounds for every dot that stopped, would you really, old man, tell me to keep my money, or would you calculate how many dots you could afford to spare? Free of income tax, old man, free of income tax. It's the only way to save money nowadays.'

LIME: 'In Italy for thirty years under the Borgias they had warfare, terror, murder and bloodshed, but they produced Michelangelo, Leonardo da Vinci and the Renaissance. In Switzerland, they had brotherly love; they had five hundred years of democracy and peace – and what did that produce? The cuckoo clock.'

'Sensitive and humane and dedicated, [Reed] would seem to be enclosed from life with no specially strong feelings about the stories that come his way other than that they should be something he can perfect and polish with a craftsman's love.' – *Richard Winnington*
'Reaffirms Carol Reed as our foremost film-maker and one of the best three or four in the world' – *Fred Majdalany*
'Crammed with cinematic plums which could do the early Hitchcock proud.' – *Time*

🏛 Robert Krasker
🎞 Carol Reed; editing

Third Man on the Mountain

👪👪   GB   1959   103m   Technicolor
Walt Disney (Bill Anderson)

🖭

In 1865 a Swiss dishwasher dreams of conquering the local mountain, and befriends a distinguished mountaineer.
Handsomely photographed boys' adventure story.
w Eleanore Griffin *novel* Banner in the Sky by James Ramsay Ullman d Ken Annakin ph Harry Waxman, George Tairraz m William Alwyn
☆ James MacArthur, Michael Rennie, Janet Munro, James Donald, Herbert Lom, Laurence Naismith, Walter Fitzgerald, Nora Swinburne

'The story of a man searching for a killer – who might even be himself!'
The Third Secret

GB   1964   103m   bw   Cinemascope
TCF/Hubris (Robert L. Joseph)

A psychiatrist apparently commits suicide; a patient who has relied on his strength finds the truth by interviewing other patients.
Pretentious package of short stories, only one of which is relevant to the frame (yet another one featuring Patricia Neal was shot but discarded); full of philosophical conversations on a Thames mudbank and other absurdities, but well enough put together.
w Robert L. Joseph d Charles Crichton ph Douglas Slocombe m Richard Arnell
☆ Stephen Boyd, Pamela Franklin, Jack Hawkins, Richard Attenborough, Rachel Kempson, Diane Cilento, Paul Rogers, Freda Jackson
'An unappealing and irritatingly muddled scribble of a film, thoroughly lacking in suspense, veracity and justification.' – *MFB*

Third Time Lucky

GB   1948   91m   bw
Alliance-Anglofilm (Mario Zampi)

A woman explains how her involvement with a professional gambler led to a killing.
Unconvincing drama, dully directed, of love conquering a low-life addiction.
w Gerald Butler *novel* They Cracked Her Glass Slipper by Gerald Butler d Gordon Parry ph Cedric Williams m Stanley Black ad Ivan King ed Giulio Zampi
☆ Glynis Johns, Dermot Walsh, Charles Goldner, Harcourt Williams, Yvonne Owen, Helen Haye, Ballard Berkeley, Harold Berens, John Stuart

The Third Voice **

US   1959   80m   bw   Cinemascope
TCF (Maury Dexter, Hubert Cornfield)

A woman kills her wealthy lover and an accomplice impersonates him through a series of complex negotiations.
Superstylish minor thriller, with a plot fascinating as it unfolds and a climax which is only a slight letdown.
wd Hubert Cornfield *novel* All the Way by Charles Williams ph Ernest Haller m Johnny Mandel
☆ Edmond O'Brien, Laraine Day, Julie London

Third World Cop

Jamaica   1999   98m   colour
Optimum/Palm/Hawk's Nest (Carolyn Pfeiffer)

Two friends from childhood meet again in Kingston, Jamaica: one has become a policeman, the other a gangster.
Ramshackle thriller with a slight charm, when you can understand what is being said.
w Chris Browne, Suzanne Fenn, Chris Salewicz d Chris Browne ph Richard Lannaman m Wally Badarou, Sly & Robbie pd Richard Lannaman ed Suzanne Fenn
☆ Winston Bell, Carl Bradshaw, Mark Danvers, Paul Campbell, Audrey Reid, Lenford Salmon
'Resolutely local in its language and setting so you can tune into its idiosyncratic pleasures even though you've seen virtually the same stock characters in crime movies since the 40s.' – *Peter Curran, Sight and Sound*

Thirst: see *Three Strange Loves*

The Thirst of Baron Blood: see *Baron Blood*

Thirteen *

USSR   1937   90m   bw
Mosfilm

Red Army soldiers are trekking from well to well through the desert. When help arrives only one is left.
Russian adventure film which was supposedly copied from The Lost Patrol but itself inspired Sahara. Good stuff, anyway.
w L. Prout, Mikhail Romm d Mikhail Romm

13 East Street

GB   1952   71m   bw
Eros/Tempean (Robert S. Baker, Monty Berman)
A policeman goes undercover to expose a gang of hijackers.
Average 'B' movie with a narrative robbed of suspense by being told in flashback at a press conference.
w John Gilling, Carl Nystrom *story* Robert S. Baker d Robert S. Baker ph Monty Berman m John Lanchbery ad Andrew Mazzei ed Gerald Landau
☆ Patrick Holt, Sandra Dorne, Sonia Holm, Robert Ayres, Dora Bryan, Michael Balfour, Hector MacGregor, Michael Brennan

Thirteen Ghosts

US   1960   88m   bw (colour sequence)
Columbia/William Castle

🖭

A penniless scholar inherits a haunted house.
Childish thriller for which the audience was issued with a 'ghost viewer' (anaglyph spectacles) so that they could see the 'spirits'. The gimmick was called Illusion-O.
w Robb White d William Castle ph Joseph Biroc m Von Dexter
☆ Charles Herbert, Jo Morrow, Martin Milner, Rosemary de Camp, Donald Woods, Margaret Hamilton

'Hurtling through space, eight people live fifteen dangerous, unforgettable hours!'
Thirteen Hours by Air *

US   1936   80m   bw
Paramount (E. Lloyd Sheldon)

A transcontinental plane is hijacked by an ex-convict.
Solidly carpentered minor thriller which is also an interesting record of the early days of commercial aviation.
w Bogart Rogers, Kenyon Nicholson d Mitchell Leisen ph Theodor Sparkuhl
☆ Fred MacMurray, Joan Bennett, ZaSu Pitts, Alan Baxter, Fred Keating, Brian Donlevy, John Howard, Ruth Donnelly, Dean Jagger
'Belongs to that rather tiresome genre, of which the formula is too familiar to excite and too unrealistic to entertain, now that the novelty of a thriller worked out in the cramped surroundings of a train, hotel or 'plane has worn off.' – *Graham Greene*

13 Rue Madeleine *

US   1947   95m   bw
TCF (Louis de Rochemont)

🖭🖭

Four trained American espionage agents locate a Nazi rocket site in France.
Semi-documentary spy stuff in the tradition of The House on 92nd Street but rather less satisfactory despite excellent technique.
w John Monks Jnr, Sy Bartlett d Henry Hathaway ph Norbert Brodine m David Buttolph md Alfred Newman
☆ James Cagney, Annabella, Richard Conte, Frank Latimore, Walter Abel, Melville Cooper, Sam Jaffe, Blanche Yurka
'Far and away the roughest, toughest spy chase yet gleaned from the bulging files of the OSS.' – *Time*
'I stole the plot of The Virginian and used it. I'd always wanted to make that story anyway.' – *Henry Hathaway*
'It carries the kick of a mule.' – *Kine Weekly*
† Rex Harrison rejected the role taken by Cagney.

The 13th Warrior *

US   1999   103m   Technicolor   Panavision
Buena Vista /Touchstone (John McTiernan, Michael Crichton, Ned Dowd)

🖭🖭   🖭   ⟳

An Arab poet is forced to join a band of Viking warriors bent on defeating a mysterious, marauding tribe of cannibals who are rampaging through the land.
Rollicking and gory historical romp, of a kind not seen since The Vikings; despite its claims to be based on fact, it is not to be taken seriously.
w William Wisher, Warren Lewis *novel* Eaters of the Dead by Michael Crichton ph Peter Menzies Jnr m Jerry Goldsmith pd Wolf Kroeger ed John Wright
☆ Antonio Banderas, Diane Venora, Dennis Storhoi, Vladimir Kulich, Omar Sharif, Anders T. Andersen, Richard Bremmer, Tony Curran, Mischa Hausserman, Neil Maffin, Asbjorn Riis, Clive Russell, Daniel Southern
'An old-fashioned potboiler with half-baked serious intentions sprinkled about.' – *Todd McCarthy, Variety*
† The film was made in 1997, but not released for two years.

'This is where evil lurks!'
13 West Street *

US   1962   80m   bw
Columbia/Ladd Enterprises (William Bloom)
An engineer is attacked on the street by teenage hoodlums and becomes obsessed by revenge.
Competent, darkly photographed, rather dislikeable little thriller, a kind of trial run for Death Wish.
w Bernard Schoenfeld, Robert Presnell Jnr d Philip Leacock ph Charles Lawton Jnr m George Duning
☆ Alan Ladd, Rod Steiger, Dolores Dorn, Michael Callan, Kenneth MacKenna, Margaret Hayes

Thirteen Women

US   1932   73m   bw
RKO

One of thirteen boarding school graduates is trying to murder the others.
Thin mystery which wastes its cast.
w Bartlett Cormack *novel* Tiffany Thayer d George Archainbaud
☆ Ricardo Cortez, Irene Dunne, Myrna Loy, Jill Esmond, Florence Eldridge, Julie Haydon, Marjorie Gateson, C. Henry Gordon

The Thirteenth Chair

US   1929   85m   bw
MGM

A medium holds a seance to unmask a murderer.
Effective though now very dated chiller from a Broadway hit.
w Elliott Clawson *play* Bayard Veiller d Tod Browning
☆ Margaret Wycherly, Bela Lugosi, Holmes Herbert, Conrad Nagel, Leila Hyams
'Playgoer type will get more enjoyment from it than the moviegoer.' – *Variety*
† The same studio remade the vehicle in 1936 with Dame May Whitty, Henry Daniell, Holmes Herbert – again – Elissa Landi and Lewis Stone; the director was George B. Seitz.

'You can go there even though it doesn't exist.'
The Thirteenth Floor

US   1999   106m   colour
Columbia/Centropolis (Roland Emmerich, Ute Emmerich, Marco Webber)

🖭🖭   🖭   ⟳

A computer expert investigates the murder of his boss who appears to have been able to travel back in time, or to have inhabited a computer-generated simulation of the past.
Confusing science-fiction, involving time travel into the past and the future; the problem is, nothing very interesting happens there, or in the present.
w Josef Rusnak, Ravel Centeno-Rodriguez *novel* Simulacron 3 by Daniel Galouye d Josef Rusnak ph Wedigo von Schultzendorff ed Henry Richardson
☆ Craig Bierko, Armin Mueller-Stahl, Gretchen Mol, Vincent D'Onofrio, Dennis Haysbert, Steven Schub, Jeremy Roberts
'Time — and movie trends — have passed it by, while its attempts at conveying a simulated cyber-reality are an extremely mixed bag.' – *Robert Koehler, Variety*

The Thirteenth Guest

US   1932   70m   bw
Monogram (M. H. Hoffman)

🖭

A haunted house, a will at midnight, and a frightened lady.
Archetypal comedy thriller, shot on Poverty Row but still watchable.
w Frances Hyland, Arthur Hoerl *novel* Armitage Trail d Albert Ray ph Harry Neumann, Tom Galligan
☆ Ginger Rogers, Lyle Talbot, J. Farrell MacDonald, James Eagles, Eddie Phillips, Erville Alderson
'For all classes of houses a positive money maker.' – *Variety*

The Thirteenth Letter *

US   1951   85m   bw
TCF (Otto Preminger)
A small French-Canadian town suffers from an outbreak of poison pen letters.
Moderate transcription of a memorable French film, Le Corbeau; in this version the events seem all too predictable and the performances dull.
w Howard Koch d Otto Preminger ph Joseph LaShelle m Alex North
☆ Charles Boyer, Linda Darnell, Constance Smith, Michael Rennie, Françoise Rosay, Judith Evelyn

–30–

US   1959   96m   bw
Warner/Mark VII (Jack Webb)
GB title: *Deadline Midnight*
A night in the newsroom of a paper preoccupied with scoops.
Not very dramatic, oddly titled and rather pretentious newspaper melodrama confined largely to one set.
w William Bowers d Jack Webb ph Edward Colman m Ray Heindorf
☆ Jack Webb, William Conrad, David Nelson, Whitney Blake, James Bell, Nancy Valentine

Thirty Day Princess *

US   1934   74m   bw
Paramount (B. P. Schulberg)
An actress is hired to impersonate a princess who gets mumps while visiting New York in hope of a loan.
Modest comedy which needed a wittier script but is stylishly played.
w Preston Sturges, Frank Partos *novel* Clarence Budington Kelland d Marion Gering ph Leon Shamroy
☆ Sylvia Sidney, Cary Grant, Edward Arnold, Henry Stephenson, Vince Barnett, Edgar Norton, Lucien Littlefield
'A compact little picture which will entertain generally.' – *Variety*

Thirty Is a Dangerous Age, Cynthia

GB   1967   84m   Technicolor
Columbia/Walter Shenson

🖭

A timid night-club pianist has trouble with women but sells his first musical.
Mild star vehicle for a very mild star, basically a few thin sketches, frantically overdirected.

👪👪 film suitable for family viewing   🖭 VHS video-cassette for the British PAL system   🖭 VHS video-cassette for the British PAL system in wide screen-format   ⟳ Video cassette in a computer-colourised version   🖭 American NTSC video-cassette   ⟳ Laser disc w Dudley Moore, Joe McGrath, John Wells d Joe McGrath ph Billy Williams m Dudley Moore titles Richard Williams

☆ Dudley Moore, Eddie Foy Jnr, Suzy Kendall, John Bird, Duncan Macrae, Patricia Routledge, John Wells

The 39 Steps ****

GB 1935 81m bw
Gaumont British (Ivor Montagu)
📼 🇺🇸 ⚙ ◉ ◉

A spy is murdered; the man who has befriended her is suspected, but eludes the police until a chase across Scotland produces the real villains.
Marvellous comedy thriller with most of the gimmicks found not only in Hitchcock's later work but in anyone else's who has tried the same vein. It has little to do with the original novel, and barely sets foot outside the studio, but it makes every second count, and is unparalleled in its use of timing, atmosphere and comedy relief.
w Charles Bennett, Ian Hay, Alma Reville novel John Buchan d Alfred Hitchcock ph Bernard Knowles m Hubert Bath, Jack Beaver md Louis Levy

☆ Robert Donat, Madeleine Carroll, Godfrey Tearle, Lucie Mannheim, Peggy Ashcroft, John Laurie, Wylie Watson, Helen Haye, Frank Cellier

'A narrative of the unexpected – a humorous, exciting, dramatic, entertaining, pictorial, vivid and novel tale told with a fine sense of character and a keen grasp of the cinematic idea.' – *Sydney W. Carroll*

'A miracle of speed and light.' – *Otis Ferguson*

'Such is the zest of the Hitchcock plot that the original point of the title was totally forgotten, and half a line had to be added at the end by way of explanation.' – *George Perry, 1965*

Thirty Seconds over Tokyo **

US 1944 138m bw
MGM (Sam Zimbalist)
📼 🇺🇸 ⚙

How the first American attack on Japan was planned.
Sturdy World War II action flagwaver, with Tracy guesting as Colonel Dolittle.
w Dalton Trumbo book Ted W. Lawson, Robert Considine d Mervyn Le Roy ph Harold Rosson, Robert Surtees m Herbert Stothart

☆ Spencer Tracy, Van Johnson, Robert Walker, Phyllis Thaxter, Tim Murdock, Don Defore, Robert Mitchum

'All of the production involving planes and technical action is so fine that the film has the tough and literal quality of an air force documentary.' – *Bosley Crowther, New York Times*
'A big studio, big scale film, free of artistic pretensions, it is transformed by its not very imaginative but very dogged sincerity into something forceful, simple and thoroughly sympathetic.' – *James Agee*
�ई
✎ Harold Rosson, Robert Surtees

36 Chowringhee Lane

India 1981 122m colour
Shashi Kapoor
A repressed, elderly Anglo-Indian teacher suffers a life of disappointments and defeats.
Downbeat film, made watchable by Jennifer Kendal's performance.
wd Aparna Sen ph Ashok Mehta md Vanraj Bhatia ad Bansi Chandragupta ed Bhanudas Divkar

☆ Jennifer Kendal, Dhritiman Chatterjee, Debashree Roy, Geoffrey Kendal, Soni Razdan

32 Caliber Killer (dubbed)

Italy 1967 95m Eastmancolor
Explorer '58
original title: *Killer Calibre 32*
A bounty hunter charges $1,000 a head to rid the West of some badmen.
Deservedly obscure spaghetti Western, directed in an exaggerated comic-book style and concentrating on the familiar ingredients of gunfights and bar-room brawls.
w Enzo Gicca d Al Bradley (Alfonso Brescia) ph Bob Roberts m Robby Poitevin

☆ Peter Lee Lawrence, Agnes Spaak, Sherill Morgan, Lucy Slade, Cole Kitosch, Andrew Bosich, Mirko Ellis, Gregory West

32 Short Films about Glenn Gould **

Canada 1993 94m colour
Electric/Rhombus Media (Niv Fichman)
📼 💿 ⚙ ◉

Fragmentary bio-pic and semi-documentary on the life of the reclusive and eccentric Canadian concert pianist Glenn Gould (1932–82), who gave up live performances at the age of 32, with each section accompanied by excerpts from his recordings.
A portrait of the artist as an intellectual and as an individual determined to express himself at whatever cost to himself and others, by turns fascinating and irritating – some of the sequences stop just as they begin to become interesting. Apart from scenes using actors, it also draws on interviews with those who knew him and his own experimental radio documentaries.
w François Girard, Don McKellar d François Girard ph Alain Dostie m Bach, Beethoven and others, played by Glenn Gould ad John Rubino ed Gaétan Huot

☆ Colm Feore

'Manages to hold the watcher in its grip from start to finish.' – *Derek Malcolm, Guardian*
'A uniquely entertaining venture. One need not know Gould's artistry or be attuned to the music to respond to the material.' – *Leonard Klady, Variety*

Thirty Years of Fun **

👪 US 1962 85m bw
Robert Youngson Productions
A compilation of silent comedy, including Chaplin's *The Floorwalker, Easy Street, The Pawnshop* and *The Rink*; Keaton's *The Balloonatic* and *Daydreams*; Langdon's *Smile Please*; and Laurel and Hardy's first meeting in *Lucky Dog*.
Not the most hilarious of the compilations, but historically important, with the usual high quality prints which Youngson alone seemed able to provide.
wd Robert Youngson film quality control Paul Guffanti

The Thirty-Nine Steps

GB 1959 93m Eastmancolor
Rank (Betty E. Box)
📼

Just to show that stars and story aren't everything, this scene-for-scene remake muffs every opportunity for suspense or general effectiveness, and is practically a manual on how not to make a thriller.
w Frank Harvey d Ralph Thomas ph Ernest Steward m Clifton Parker

☆ Kenneth More, Taina Elg, Barry Jones, Faith Brook, Brenda de Banzie, Duncan Lamont, James Hayter, Michael Goodliffe, Reginald Beckwith

The Thirty-Nine Steps *

GB 1978 102m Eastmancolor
Rank/Norfolk International (James Kenelm Clarke)
📼 ⚙

Eager-to-please remake which goes back to the original period and more or less the original story, but rather spoils itself by a cliffhanger climax on the face of Big Ben, absurdly borrowed from Will Hay's *My Learned Friend*.
w Michael Robson d Don Sharp ph John Coquillon m Ed Welch pd Harry Pottle

☆ Robert Powell, Karen Dotrice, John Mills, Eric Porter, David Warner, George Baker, Ronald Pickup, Timothy West, Donald Pickering, Andrew Keir, Robert Flemyng, Miles Anderson

Thirty-Six Hours *

US 1964 115m bw Panavision
MGM/Perlberg-Seaton/Cherokee (William Perlberg)
In 1944 an American major is kidnapped by the Nazis and after drugging is made to think that the war is over.
Well-detailed spy suspenser.
wd George Seaton stories Roald Dahl, Carl K. Hittleman ph Philip Lathrop m Dimitri Tiomkin

☆ James Garner, Rod Taylor, Eva Marie Saint, Werner Peters, John Banner
† The film was remade for cable TV in 1989 under the title *Breaking Point*, directed by Peter Markle and starring Corbin Bernsen and Joanna Pacula.

'What we're fighting for is bigger than you or me!'

This Above All *

US 1942 110m bw
TCF (Darryl F. Zanuck)
A surgeon's daughter on active service during World War II falls in love with a conscientious objector who is also an army deserter: he proves his bravery during an air raid.
Superior studio-set war romance.
w R. C. Sherriff novel Eric Knight d Anatole Litvak ph Arthur Miller m Alfred Newman ad Richard Day, Joseph Wright ed Walter Thompson

☆ Tyrone Power, Joan Fontaine, Thomas Mitchell, Henry Stephenson, Nigel Bruce, Gladys Cooper, Philip Merivale, Alexander Knox, Melville Cooper

'Beautiful, stimulating and occasionally powerful.' – *New York Herald Tribune*
'One of the truly great pictures to come out of this war.' – *Motion Picture Herald*
🏆 Richard Day, Joseph Wright
✎ Arthur Miller; Walter Thompson

This Angry Age

Italy 1957 104m Technirama
Dino de Laurentiis
aka: *The Sea Wall*
original title: *La Diga sul Pacifico*
A French widow in Indo-China struggles to keep her rice fields going despite her family's waning interest.
Curious international production which suffers from the audience's lack of interest in the central situation. Moments of interest and even beauty, though.
w Irwin Shaw, René Clément, Ivo Perelli and Diego Fabbri novel Barrage Contre le Pacifique by Marguerite Duras d René Clément

☆ Silvana Mangano, Jo Van Fleet, Anthony Perkins, Alida Valli, Richard Conte, Nehemiah Persoff

This Boy's Life

US 1993 115m Technicolor
Warner (Art Linson)
📼 🇺🇸 ⚙ ◉

In the 1950s, a teenaged boy finds life hard when his mother settles down with a violent new husband.
An escapist drama, in which a series of dramatic confrontations fail to carry the power they should.
w Robert Getchell book Tobias Wolff d Michael Caton-Jones ph David Watkin m Carter Burwell pd Stephen J. Lineweaver ed Jim Clark, Peter N. Lonsdale

☆ Robert DeNiro, Ellen Barkin, Leonardo DiCaprio, Jonah Blechman, Eliza Dushku, Chris Cooper, Carla Gugino, Zack Ansley

'Despite its admirable strengths and the fact of it being a true story, there is somehow a failure to completely connect with the fierce boy, giving his unhappy and alienating youth an unfortunate air of reality.' – *Angie Errigo, Empire*

This Could Be the Night

US 1957 104m bw Cinemascope
MGM (Joe Pasternak)
📼 ⚙

A schoolteacher becomes secretary to a gangster in his Broadway night-club.
Unlikely romantic melodrama with music, like a more solemn Guys and Dolls.
w Isobel Lennart story Cornelia Baird Gross d Robert Wise ph Russell Harlan m George Stoll

☆ Jean Simmons, Paul Douglas, Tony Franciosa, Julie Wilson, Joan Blondell, J. Carrol Naish, ZaSu Pitts

'The master of inspiring spectacle makes his first great spectacle of modern times!'

This Day and Age *

US 1933 98m bw
Paramount/Cecil B. de Mille
During a youth week, boys put a gangster on trial and by his own methods force him to confess to murder.
A curious aberration for de Mille, this fairly powerful movie was condemned in some quarters as an incitement to fascism.
w Bartlett Cormack d Cecil B. de Mille ph Peverell Marley m Howard Jackson, L. W. Gilbert, Abel Baer

☆ Charles Bickford, Richard Cromwell, Judith Allen, Harry Green, Ben Alexander

'A highly improbable and fantastic story but, as done by de Mille, carries more than average audience appeal.' – *Variety*
'Loaded with that power which excites emotional hysteria … should stimulate audiences to the same pitch of enthusiasm as it did the preview crowd.' – *Motion Picture Herald*
'A strange tale from the Hollywood hills … the technical work is excessively melodramatic.' – *Mordaunt Hall, New York Times*

This Earth Is Mine

US 1959 124m Technicolor Cinemascope
U-I/Vintage (Casey Robinson, Claude Heilman)

A French-American vineyard owner in California brings out his granddaughter from England in the hope that she will consolidate his dynasty.
Solidly efficient film of a solidly efficient novel.
w Casey Robinson novel The Cup and the Sword by Alice Tisdale Hobart d Henry King ph Winton Hoch, Russell Metty m Hugo Friedhofer

☆ Jean Simmons, Claude Rains, Rock Hudson, Dorothy McGuire, Kent Smith, Anna Lee, Ken Scott

This England

GB 1941 84m bw
British National
Landowner and labourer express contrary views through five periods of English history.
Unintentionally hilarious charade with all concerned left with egg on their faces. With propaganda like this, it's a wonder we still won the war.
w Emlyn Williams, A. R. Rawlinson, Bridget Boland d David MacDonald

☆ John Clements, Emlyn Williams, Constance Cummings, Frank Pettingell, Roland Culver, Esmond Knight, Morland Graham, Leslie French
† In Scotland the film was known as *Our Heritage*.

This Gun for Hire ***

US 1942 81m bw
Paramount (Richard M. Blumenthal)
📼 ⚙

A professional killer becomes involved in a fifth columnist plot.
Efficient Americanization of one of its author's more sombre entertainments. The melodrama has an authentic edge and strangeness to it, and it established the star images of both Ladd and Lake, as well as being oddly downbeat for a Hollywood product of this jingoistic time.
w Albert Maltz, W. R. Burnett novel A Gun for Sale by Graham Greene d Frank Tuttle ph John Seitz m David Buttolph

☆ Alan Ladd, Veronica Lake, Robert Preston, Laird Cregar, Tully Marshall, Mikhail Rasumny, Marc Lawrence
† It was remade, less effectively, as a TV movie in 1991, directed by Lou Antonio and starring Robert Wagner.

This Happy Breed **

GB 1944 114m Technicolor
GFD/Two Cities/Cineguild (Noël Coward, Anthony Havelock-Allan)
📼

Life between the wars for a London suburban family.
Coward's domestic epic is unconvincingly written and largely miscast, but sheer professionalism gets it through, and the decor is historically interesting.
w David Lean, Ronald Neame, Anthony Havelock-Allan play Noël Coward d David Lean ph Ronald Neame

☆ Robert Newton, Celia Johnson, Stanley Holloway, John Mills, Kay Walsh, Amy Veness, Alison Leggatt

'Nearly two hours of the pleasure of recognition, which does not come very far up the scale of aesthetic values.' – *Richard Mallett, Punch*

This Happy Feeling

US 1958 92m Eastmancolor Cinemascope
U-I (Ross Hunter)
📼

An ageing actor is invigorated by a mild affair with his secretary.
Flat romantic comedy: the bubbles obstinately refuse to rise.

---

wd Blake Edwards *play* For Love or Money by F. Hugh Herbert *ph* Arthur E. Arling *m* Frank Skinner

☆ Curt Jurgens, Debbie Reynolds, John Saxon, Alexis Smith, Mary Astor, Estelle Winwood

This is Dynamite!: see The Turning Point

This is Elvis *
US   1981   101m   Technicolor
Warner (David L. Wolper)
📼   ▆   ◷   ◉

The life of Elvis Presley, from his first recordings to his death.
This is part-documentary, with some interesting footage, both of Elvis's early performances and of his detractors, whose opposition to his music is unashamedly racist, and part a fictional recreation of his life. Colonel Tom Parker, Elvis's manager, acted as technical adviser, so that the only startling revelation here is Elvis's terrible taste in clothes.
wd Andrew Solt, Malcolm Leo *ph* Gil Hubbs *m* Walter Scharf *ed* Bud Friedgen
☆ David Scott, Paul Boensch III, Johnny Harra, Lawrence Koller, Rhonda Lyn, Debbie Edge, Larry Raspberry, Furry Lewis, Knox Phillips

This Is My Affair: see I Can Get It for You Wholesale (1951)

'What They Whisper To Each Other They Mean Forever!'
This Is My Affair **
US   1937   102m   bw
TCF (Kenneth MacGowan)
GB title: His Affair
When President McKinley is assassinated, one of his top undercover agents is suspected of being a criminal, and threatened with execution.
Jolly good romantic melodrama with excellent period trappings; Hollywood of the thirties at its routine best.
w Allen Rivkin, Lamar Trotti *d* William A. Seiter *ph* Robert Planck *md* Arthur Lange
☆ Robert Taylor, Barbara Stanwyck, Victor McLaglen, Brian Donlevy, Sidney Blackmer, John Carradine, Sig Rumann, Alan Dinehart, Douglas Fowley
'Something of a G-man story in a costume setting.' – Variety
'The best American melodrama of the year ... admirable acting, quick and cunning direction ... a sense of doom, of almost classic suspense.' – Graham Greene

'It's 10 p.m. Do you know where your mother is?'
This Is My Life **
US   1992   94m   DeLuxe
TCF (Lynda Obst)
📼   ▆   ◷   ◉

A mother with two young daughters tries to make it as a stand-up comedian.
Sharply observed movie with a tough comic edge about the problems and conflicts between daughters and a working mother.
w Nora Ephron, Delia Ephron *novel* This Is Your Life by Meg Wolitzer *d* Nora Ephron *ph* Bobby Byrne *m* Carly Simon *pd* David Chapman *ed* Robert Reitano
☆ Julie Kavner, Samantha Mathis, Gaby Hoffman, Carrie Fisher, Dan Aykroyd, Bob Nelson, Marita Geraghty
'Intimate, honestly rendered film looks likely to score some emotional points with the working parents it speaks to, but a funny but frank teen sex scene may somewhat erode its potential as family fare.' – Variety
'Woefully unfunny. If comedy is all about timing then Ephron's directorial watch needs winding.' – Stephen Amidon, Financial Times

This Is My Love
US   1954   91m   Technicolor
RKO
A sensitive young writer gives up everything to help her sister and crippled husband run a restaurant.
Weird, miscast melodrama which ends with Cinderella murdering the ugly sister.
w Hagar Wilde, Hugh Brooke *d* Stuart Heisler *ph* Ray June *m* Franz Waxman
☆ Linda Darnell, Faith Domergue, Dan Duryea, Rick Jason

This Is My Street
GB   1963   94m   bw
Anglo-Amalgamated/Adder (Jack Hanbury)
A Battersea wife has a fling with her mother's lodger.
Unremarkable low-life drama.
w Bill MacIlwraith *novel* Nan Maynard *d* Sidney Hayers *ph* Alan Hume *m* Eric Rogers
☆ June Ritchie, Ian Hendry, Avice Landon, Meredith Edwards, Madge Ryan, John Hurt, Mike Pratt, Tom Adams

This Is Spinal Tap ****
US   1984   82m   CFI color
Mainline/Embassy (Karen Murphy)
📼   ▆   ◷   ◉

Adventures of a British heavy metal rock group on tour in America.
Witty, wickedly accurate satire that skewers the pretensions of rock musicians and their hangers-on, done in documentary style. It hits its target with total precision.
w Christopher Guest, Michael McKean, Harry Shearer, Rob Reiner *d* Rob Reiner *ph* Peter Smokler *m* Christopher Guest, Michael McKean, Harry Shearer, Rob Reiner *pd* Dryan Jones *ed* Robert Leighton
☆ Christopher Guest, Michael McKean, Harry Shearer, Rob Reiner, R. J. Parnell, David Kaff, Tony Hendra, Bruno Kirby
† It is also available on an interactive CD-ROM, which includes extra audio commentary on the film and out-takes.

This Is the Army **
US   1943   121m   Technicolor
Warner (Jack L. Warner, Hal B. Wallis)
▆   ◷

Army recruits put on a musical revue.
Mammoth musical flagwaver.
w Casey Robinson, Claude Binyon *d* Michael Curtiz *ph* Bert Glennon, Sol Polito *m* Ray Heindorf *ad* John Hughes, Lt. John Koenig *songs* Irving Berlin
☆ George Murphy, Joan Leslie, Irving Berlin, George Tobias, Alan Hale, Charles Butterworth, Rosemary de Camp, Dolores Costello, Una Merkel, Stanley Ridges, Ruth Donnelly, Kate Smith, Frances Langford, Gertrude Niesen, Ronald Reagan and also Joe Louis
♫ 'God Bless America'; 'This Is the Army, Mr Jones'; 'I'm Getting Tired So I Can Sleep'; 'I Left My Heart at the Stage Door Canteen'; 'Oh, How I Hate to Get Up in the Morning'; 'This Time'.
🏆 Ray Heindorf
⊗ art direction

This Is the Life
US   1944   87m   bw
Universal
A young girl singer gets a crush on an older man.
Lively youth musical from better-mannered days.
w Wanda Tuchock *play* Angela Is 22 by Fay Wray, Sinclair Lewis *d* Felix Feist
☆ Donald O'Connor, Susanna Foster, Peggy Ryan, Patric Knowles, Louise Allbritton, Dorothy Peterson, Jonathan Hale

This Is the Night *
US   1932   73m   bw
Paramount
A married lady with an eye for other men has an unfortunate habit of getting her dress caught in doors.
Forgotten high comedy in the Lubitsch style, but without his command.
w George Marion Jnr *play* Naughty Cinderella by Avery Hopwood *d* Frank Tuttle
☆ Lili Damita, Charles Ruggles, Roland Young, Thelma Todd, Cary Grant

This Is the Sea
US/Ireland/GB   1996   104m   Technicolor
Panavision
Polygram/Pembridge/Overseas (Michael Garland)
In Northern Ireland, a Protestant woman falls for a Catholic man with IRA connections.
A slight, romantic story set against the background of terrorist activity; it is not particularly rewarding, even if its heart is in the right place.
wd Mary McGuckian *ph* Des Whelan *m* Mike Scott, the Waterboys, Brian Kennedy *pd* Claire Kenny *ed* Kant Pan

☆ Richard Harris, Gabriel Byrne, John Lynch, Dearbhla Molloy, Ian McElhinney, Samantha Morton, Ross McDade
'This Romeo and Juliet story is a winner ... deftly avoiding situations that have turned into clichés from overuse.' – Variety

'The supreme entertainment of our time! Two and a half years in the making!'
This Island Earth **
US   1955   86m   Technicolor
U-I (William Alland)
▆   ◷

Scientists at a mysterious research station are really visitors from a planet in outer space, to which they kidnap brilliant minds who they hope can help them.
Absorbing science fiction mystery with splendid special effects and only one mutant monster to liven the last reels.
w Franklin Coen, Edward G. O'Callaghan *novel* Raymond F. Jones *d* Joseph Newman *m* Henry Mancini, Herman Stein, Hans Salter *ad* Alexander Golitzen, Richard H. Riedel *ph/sp* Clifford Stine, David S. Horsley
☆ Jeff Morrow, Faith Domergue, Rex Reason, Lance Fuller, Russell Johnson, Robert Nicholas, Karl Lindt

'We women who have known love – have learned how to hate!'
This Land Is Mine *
US   1943   103m   bw
RKO (Jean Renoir, Dudley Nichols)
▆   ◷

A European village fights for freedom under occupying Nazis, and a schoolmaster becomes a hero.
Rather superfluous flagwaver with good performances wasted in a totally predictable and rather uninspiring script which gives the director little scope.
w Dudley Nichols *d* Jean Renoir *ph* Frank Redman *m* Lothar Perl
☆ Charles Laughton, Maureen O'Hara, George Sanders, Walter Slezak, Una O'Connor, Kent Smith, Philip Merivale, Thurston Hall, George Coulouris
'Directed with the same Zolaesque intensity, the same excited obsession with locomotives, the same exquisite pictorial sense, that informed La Bête Humaine.' – Guardian
'Dull, prolix and unamusing.' – James Agate
'You cannot afford to dislocate or internationalize your occupied country; or to try to sell it to Americans by making your citizens as well fed, well dressed and comfortably idiomatic as Americans; or to treat the show to the corrupted virtuosities of studio lighting and heavy ballet composition.' – James Agee

This Love of Ours
US   1945   90m   bw
U-I (Edward Dodds)
A jealous doctor leaves his wife but years later saves her from an unhappy second marriage.
Stupid romantic melodrama with characters in whose idiotic behaviour one can take no interest. Remade as Never Say Goodbye (qv).
w Bruce Manning, John Klorer, Leonard Lee *play* Come Prima Meglio di Prima by Luigi Pirandello *d* William Dieterle *ph* Lucien Ballard *m* Hans Salter
☆ Merle Oberon, Charles Korvin, Claude Rains, Carl Esmond, Jess Barker, Harry Davenport, Ralph Morgan, Fritz Leiber
'About as captivating as a funeral dirge.' – Thomas M. Pryor, New York Times
'A juicy example of masochistic team work ... my favourite bad film in two years.' – Richard Winnington
⊗ Hans Salter

This Man Can't Die (dubbed)
Italy   1970   87m   colour
Mercurio/Gerald Fine (Gino Rossi)
An undercover agent and his family become the target of a gang of ruthless gun-runners.
Tired spaghetti Western with a mock-Morricone score, indifferently acted and directed, and lacking any of the spectacular set-pieces that made the genre worth watching.
w Luigi Emmanuele, Gino Mangini, Gianfranco Baldanello *d* Gianfranco Baldanello *ph* Claudio

Cirillo *m* Amedeo Tommasi *ad* Giorgio Giovannini *ed* Alberto Gallitti
☆ Guy Madison, Lucienne Bridou, Rik Battaglia, Peter Martell, Rosalba Neri, Steve Merrich, Anna Liotti, Giola Desideri, Alberto Dell'Acqua

This Man in Paris
GB   1939   86m   bw
Pinebrook
A London reporter in Paris exposes a counterfeiting gang.
Slightly disappointing sequel to the spruce This Man Is News; *no more were made.*
w Allan McKinnon, Roger MacDougall *d* David MacDonald
☆ Barry K. Barnes, Valerie Hobson, Alastair Sim, Edward Lexy, Garry Marsh
'Five years have passed since The Thin Man, and this particular uxorious relationship of loving insults, hygienic sex, and raillery from twin beds is period enough for Punch.' – Graham Greene

This Man Is Dangerous
GB   1941   82m   bw
Rialto
aka: The Patient Vanishes
A police inspector's son solves the case of a fake doctor and a mysterious nursing home.
Nostalgically innocent crime caper; still quite entertaining.
w John Argyle, Edward Dryhurst *novel* They Called Him Death by David Hume *d* Lawrence Huntington
☆ James Mason, Mary Clare, Margaret Vyner, Gordon McLeod, Frederick Valk

This Man Is Mine
US   1934   76m   bw
RKO
A woman wins back her wandering playboy husband.
Tedious marital drama which might have fared better as farce.
w Jane Murfin *play* Love Flies in the Window by Anne Morrison Chapin *d* John Cromwell *ph* David Abel *md* Max Steiner
☆ Irene Dunne, Ralph Bellamy, Constance Cummings, Kay Johnson, Sidney Blackmer, Charles Starrett

This Man Is Mine
GB   1946   103m   bw
Columbia
A family invites a Canadian soldier for Christmas.
Moderate heartwarmer which still exudes a patriotic sentimental glow.
w Doreen Montgomery, Nicholas Phipps, Reginald Beckwith, Mabel Constanduros, Val Valentine, David Evans *play* A Soldier for Christmas by Reginald Beckwith *d* Marcel Varnel
☆ Tom Walls, Glynis Johns, Jeanne de Casalis, Hugh McDermott, Nova Pilbeam, Barry Morse

This Man Is News **
GB   1938   77m   bw
Paramount/Pinebrook (Anthony Havelock-Allan)
A reporter tracks down jewel thieves.
Thoroughly brisk and lively comedy-thriller on Thin Man lines. (See This Man in Paris.)
w Allan MacKinnon, Roger Macdougall, Basil Dearden *d* David MacDonald *ph* Henry Harris *md* Percival Mackey
☆ Barry K. Barnes, Valerie Hobson, Alastair Sim, John Warwick, Garry Marsh

This Man Must Die: see Que la Bête Meure

This Man Reuter: see A Dispatch from Reuter's

This Man's Navy
US   1945   100m   bw
MGM
Two old navy men compare their sons' exploits, especially in the matter of how many submarines destroyed.
Easy-going star flagwaver.
w Borden Chase *d* William Wellman
☆ Wallace Beery, James Gleason, Tom Drake, Noah Beery, Selena Royle

This Modern Age
US   1931   68m   bw
MGM
The socialite child of divorced parents goes to Paris to stay with her sophisticated mother.

Mildly daring melodrama typical of its star and year.
w Sylvia Thalberg, Frank Butler story Mildred Cram d Nick Grinde ph Charles Rosher
☆ Joan Crawford, Pauline Frederick, Monroe Owsley, Neil Hamilton, Hobart Bosworth, Emma Dunn

This Other Eden
GB 1960 85m bw
Regal/Emmet Dalton (Alec C. Snowden)
As a memorial to an IRA hero of the 20s is unveiled, passions in a small Irish town are stirred by the arrival of an Englishman who wants to settle there.
A comedy of misunderstandings that retains a slight charm; it was made on location in Ireland with a cast that included members of Dublin's Abbey Players.
w Patrick Kirwan, Blanaid Irvine play Louis D'Alton d Muriel Box ph Gerald Gibbs m W. Lambert Williamson ad Tommy Inglis ed Henry Richardson
☆ Audrey Dalton, Leslie Phillips, Niall MacGinnis, Hilton Edwards, Paul Farrell, Norman Rodway, Milo O'Shea, Ria Mooney, Harry Brogan, Geoffrey Golden

'Alva was growing up the only way she knew how!'
This Property Is Condemned *
US 1966 110m Technicolor
Paramount/Seven Arts/Ray Stark (John Houseman)
◉ ◎~
Sexual adventures of a tubercular but beautiful girl in her mother's boarding house in a Mississippi town.
The Tennessee Williams mixture as before, quite well done but almost entirely resistible.
w Francis Ford Coppola, Fred Coe, Edith Sommer play Tennessee Williams d Sydney Pollack ph James Wong Howe m Kenyon Hopkins
☆ Natalie Wood, Robert Redford, Mary Badham, Kate Reid, Charles Bronson, Jon Provost, John Harding, Alan Baxter, Robert Blake

This Rebel Age: see *The Beat Generation*

This Side of Heaven
US 1934 78m bw
MGM
A slightly whacky family gets together when father is accused of embezzlement.
Unmemorable but enjoyable domestic comedy drama.
w Zelda Sears, Eve Greene novel Marjorie Paradis d William K. Howard
☆ Lionel Barrymore, Fay Bainter, Mae Clarke, Tom Brown, Una Merkel, Mary Carlisle, Onslow Stevens
'The type of clean picture Will Hays has been telling Hollywood about.' – *Variety*

This Sporting Life ***
GB 1963 134m bw
Rank/Independent Artists (Karel Reisz)
◉ ▣ ⓥ
A tough miner becomes a successful rugby player, but his inner crudeness and violence keep contentment at bay.
Skilful movie-making around an unattractive hero in dismal settings; for all the excellent detail, we do not care sufficiently for the film to become any kind of classic.
w David Storey novel David Storey d Lindsay Anderson ph Denys Coop m Roberto Gerhard
☆ Richard Harris, Rachel Roberts, Alan Badel, William Hartnell, Colin Blakely, Vanda Godsell, Arthur Lowe
⚮ Richard Harris; Rachel Roberts
⚯ Rachel Roberts

This Strange Passion: see *El*

This Thing Called Love *
US 1941 98m bw
Columbia (William Perlberg)
GB title: *Married But Single*
A lady executive insists on proving that marriage is best if the partners start out just good friends.
Amusing comedy which at the time seemed a little saucy, and got itself banned by the Legion of Decency.
w George Seaton, Ken Englund, P. J. Wolfson d Alexander Hall ph Joseph Walker m Werner Heymann md Morris Stoloff
☆ Rosalind Russell, Melvyn Douglas, Binnie Barnes, Allyn Joslyn, Gloria Dickson, Lee J. Cobb, Gloria Holden, Don Beddoe

'One of those laborious forties comedies in which the independent-minded woman has no common sense.' – *New Yorker, 1979*

This Time for Keeps
US 1947 105m Technicolor
MGM (Joe Pasternak)
The son of a famous singer falls in love with a swimming star.
Dim star musical with no outstanding sequences.
w Gladys Lehman d Richard Thorpe ph Karl Freund songs various
☆ Esther Williams, Jimmy Durante, Lauritz Melchior, Johnnie Johnston, Xavier Cugat and his Orchestra
'The money spent on this production might easily have kept Mozart and Schubert alive and busy to the age of sixty, with enough left over to finance five of the best movies ever made. It might even have been invested in a good movie musical.' – *James Agee*

This Was a Woman
GB 1948 104m bw
Excelsior
A paranoid wife, prevented from running the lives of her offspring, tries to poison her husband.
Intolerable, interminable melodrama; a stage event makes a very stagey film.
w Val Valentine play Joan Morgan d Tim Whelan ph Günther Krampf m Mischa Spoliansky
☆ Sonia Dresdel, Barbara White, Walter Fitzgerald, Cyril Raymond, Marjorie Rhodes, Emrys Jones

This Was Paris
GB 1941 88m bw
Warner
Spies suspect each other in Paris just before the Nazi occupation.
Unpersuasive studio-bound potboiler.
w Brock Williams, Edward Dryhurst d John Harlow ph Basil Emmott
☆ Ben Lyon, Ann Dvorak, Griffith Jones, Robert Morley, Harold Huth, Mary Maguire

This Way Please
US 1937 72m bw
Paramount (Mel Shauer)
Romance backstage at a cine-variety theatre.
Uninspired musical now interesting for its sociological detail.
w Maxwell Shane, Bill Thomas, Grant Garrett, Seena Owen, Howard J. Green d Robert Florey
☆ Charles Buddy Rogers, Betty Grable, Ned Sparks, Jim and Marion Jordan, Porter Hall, Lee Bowman, Wally Vernon

This Week of Grace
GB 1933 92m bw
Real Art
An unemployed factory girl goes into service.
Very typical but underproduced star vehicle.
w H. Fowler Mear, Jack Marks d Maurice Elvey
☆ Gracie Fields, Frank Pettingell, Henry Kendall, John Stuart, Douglas Wakefield, Minnie Rayner

'Every inch a lady – till you look at the record!'
This Woman Is Dangerous
US 1952 97m bw
Warner (Robert Sisk)
A woman gangster goes blind and falls in love with her doctor.
Glossy hokum without much dramatic movement; strictly for star fans.
w Geoffrey Homes, George Worthing Yates d Felix Feist ph Ted McCord m David Buttolph
☆ Joan Crawford, David Brian, Dennis Morgan, Mari Aldon, Phil Carey

This Woman Is Mine
US 1941 92m bw
Universal
Fur traders fall out over a beautiful stowaway.
Fairly well-produced but unexciting period drama.
w Seton I. Miller novel I, James Lewis by Gilbert Wolff Gabriel d Frank Lloyd m Richard Hageman
☆ Franchot Tone, John Carroll, Walter Brennan, Carol Bruce, Nigel Bruce, Leo G. Carroll, Sig Rumann
⚮ Richard Hageman

This World, Then the Fireworks *
US 1997 100m DeLuxe
First Independent/Largo (Chris Hanley, Brad Wyman, Larry Gross)
◉ ▣
A man leaves his wife to move in with his unstable mother and sister, a prostitute, and begins an affair with a policewoman, intending to swindle her.
Lurid pulp melodrama of incest, murder and madness, no more than a film noir gone fetid.
w Larry Gross story Jim Thompson d Michael Oblowitz ph Tom Priestley Jnr m Pete Rugolo pd Maia Javan ed Emma E. Hickox
☆ Billy Zane, Gina Gershon, Sheryl Lee, Rue McClanahan, Seymour Cassel, Will Patton, Richard Edson, William Hootkins
'Elegantly stylish, highly erotic, intentionally over-the-top.' – *Variety*

'Everyone's looking for a prince among the pond life.'
This Year's Love *
GB 1999 109m DeLuxe
Entertainment/Kismet/Scottish Arts Council (Michael Camarda)
A London-based Scottish couple split up on their wedding day and find consolation elsewhere.
A trendy comedy of serial affairs, where sex is treated as a fashion accessory.
wd David Kane ph Robert Alazraki m Simon Boswell pd Sarah Greenwood ed Sean Barton
☆ Kathy Burke, Jennifer Ehle, Ian Hart, Douglas Henshall, Catherine McCormack, Dougray Scott, Emily Woof
'If more time had been devoted to the supposed laughs and less to the logistics of bed-hopping the film might've lived up to its gag a minute sales pitch.' – *Lorien Haynes, Film Review*

This'll Make You Whistle *
GB 1936 78m bw
Herbert Wilcox Productions
A playboy pretends to be a crook so as to shock his unwanted fiancée's guardian.
Rather flat comedy from a stage musical; all depends on the star.
w Guy Bolton, Fred Thompson d Herbert Wilcox
☆ Jack Buchanan, Elsie Randolph, Jean Gillie, William Kendall, David Hutcheson, Antony Holles

The Thomas Crown Affair **
US 1968 102m DeLuxe Panavision
UA/Mirisch/Simkoe/Solar (Norman Jewison)
◉ ▣ ◎~
A bored property tycoon masterminds a bank robbery and is chased by a glamorous insurance investigator.
Not so much a movie as an animated colour supplement, this glossy entertainment makes style its prime virtue, plays cute tricks with multiple images and has a famous sexy chess game, but is not above being boring for the rest of the way.
w Alan R. Trustman d Norman Jewison ph Haskell Wexler m Michel Legrand ad Robert Boyle
☆ Steve McQueen, Faye Dunaway, Paul Burke, Jack Weston, Yaphet Kotto
'Jewison and Wexler seem to have gone slightly berserk, piling up tricks and mannerisms until the film itself sinks out of sight, forlorn and forgotten.' – *Tom Milne*
'A glimmering, empty film reminiscent of an haute couture model – stunning on the surface, concave and undernourished beneath.' – *Stefan Kanter*
⚜ song 'The Windmills of Your Mind' (mMichel Legrand, lyAlan and Marilyn Bergman)
⚯ Michel Legrand

The Thomas Crown Affair **
US 1999 110m DeLuxe
MGM/Irish DreamTime (Pierce Brosnan, Beau St. Clair)
◉ ▣ ◎ ◎~
After a billionaire steals a Monet from New York's Metropolitan Museum of Art, he is hounded by a female insurance agent determined to snare him.
Glossy, easily enjoyable thriller that aims for sophistication; it plays a little like a James Bond movie without the big-budget stunts.
w Leslie Dixon, Kurt Wimmer story Alan R. Trustman d John McTiernan ph Tom Priestley m Bill Conti pd Bruno Rubeo ed John Wright

☆ Pierce Brosnan, Rene Russo, Denis Leary, Ben Gazzara, Frankie Faison, Fritz Weaver, Charles Keating, Mark Margolis, Faye Dunaway
'It's updated the older film, but not outclassed it.' – *Alexander Walker*

Thoroughbreds Don't Cry
US 1937 80m bw
MGM
▣ ◎~
Jockeys fight for the chance to ride a valuable English horse.
Ho-hum racetrack yarn significant as the first teaming of two young stars.
w Lawrence Hazard, J. Walter Ruben, Eleanore Griffin d Alfred E. Green
☆ Mickey Rooney, Judy Garland, Ronald Sinclair, Sophie Tucker, C. Aubrey Smith

Thoroughly Modern Millie *
US 1967 138m Technicolor
Universal (Ross Hunter)
◉ ▣ ◎ ◯
In the twenties, a young girl comes to New York, becomes thoroughly modern, falls for her boss, and has various adventures unmasking a white slave racket centring on a Chinese laundry.
Initially most agreeable but subsequently very patchy spoof of twenties fads and films, including a Harold Lloyd thrill sequence which just doesn't work and a comedy performance from Beatrice Lillie which does. Tunes and performances are alike variable.
w Richard Morris d George Roy Hill ph Russell Metty m Elmer Bernstein md André Previn, Joseph Gershenson ch Joe Layton ad Alexander Golitzen, George Webb songs various
☆ Julie Andrews, Mary Tyler Moore, John Gavin, James Fox, Carol Channing, Beatrice Lillie, Jack Soo, Pat Morita, Anthony Dexter
'What a nice 65-minute movie is buried therein!' – *Judith Crist*
⚜ Elmer Bernstein
⚮ André Previn, Joseph Gershenson; title song (mJames Van Heusen, lySammy Cahn); Carol Channing

Those Calloways
↟↟ US 1964 131m Technicolor
Walt Disney (Winston Hibler)
▣
Adventures of a marsh trapper and his family who live near a Maine village and try to protect wild geese from hunters.
Predictable family saga with pleasant backgrounds.
w Louis Pelletier novel Swift Water by Paul Annixter d Norman Tokar ph Edward Colman m Max Steiner
☆ Brian Keith, Vera Miles, Brandon de Wilde, Walter Brennan, Ed Wynn, Linda Evans, Philip Abbott, John Larkin, John Qualen

Those Daring Young Men in Their Jaunty Jalopies
↟↟ US/Italy/France 1969 125m Technicolor Panavision
Paramount/Dino de Laurentiis/Marianne (Ken Annakin, Basil Keys)
◉ ▣
GB title: *Monte Carlo or Bust*
Accidents befall various competitors in the Monte Carlo Rally.
Rough-edged imitation of The Great Race and Those Magnificent Men in Their Flying Machines, much feebler than either but with the waste of a big budget well in evidence.
w Jack Davies, Ken Annakin d Ken Annakin ph Gabor Pogany m Ron Goodwin
☆ Peter Cook, Dudley Moore, Tony Curtis, Bourvil, Walter Chiari, Terry-Thomas, Gert Frobe, Susan Hampshire, Jack Hawkins, Eric Sykes

Those Endearing Young Charms
US 1945 81m bw
RKO (Bert Granet)
An air corps mechanic loves a shopgirl.
Nothing to remember about this light star time-passer.
w Jerome Chodorov play Edward Chodorov d Lewis Allen ph Ted Tetzlaff m Roy Webb
☆ Robert Young, Laraine Day, Bill Williams, Ann Harding, Marc Cramer, Anne Jeffreys
'Well played, well directed, and not quite interesting enough to be worth the time it takes.' – *James Agee*

Those Eyes, That Mouth
France/Italy   1982   100m   colour
Triumph/Columbia/Odissya/Gaumont/RAI/Enca
Ferrario (Enzo Porcelli)
original title: *Gli Occhi, La Bocca*
Returning home for the funeral of his suicidal
brother, a failing actor begins an affair with the
dead man's pregnant fiancée.
*Intense family melodrama that refers back to the
director's first film, Fists in the Pocket, but lacks the
same impact.*
w Marco Bellocchio, Vincenzo Cerami d Marco
Bellocchio ph Giuseppe Lanci m Nicola Piovani
ed Sergio Nuti
☆ Lou Castel, Angela Molina, Emmanuelle Riva,
Antonio Piovanelli, Michel Piccoli

Those Fantastic Flying Fools: see *Jules
Verne's Rocket to the Moon*

Those High Grey Walls
US   1939   80m   bw
Columbia
A doctor is convicted for aiding a criminal.
*Modest variation on a plot used for Prisoner of Shark
Island, Devil's Island, and so on.*
w William A. Ullman, Lewis Meltzer d Charles
Vidor ph John Stumar m Morris Stoloff
☆ Walter Connolly, Onslow Stevens, Iris
Meredith, Paul Fix, Bernard Nedell, Don Beddoe
'Effective prison melodrama … will do all right
where properly booked.' – *Variety*

Those Kids from Town
GB   1941   82m   bw
British National
An earl takes in a group of noisy Cockney kids
evacuated from the city.
*Sentimental wartime crowdpleaser, not especially good
but a fairly rare record of one aspect of the war.*
w Adrian Arlington novel *These Our Strangers* by
Adrian Arlington d Lance Comfort
☆ Shirley Lenner, Jeanne de Casalis, Percy
Marmont, Maire O'Neill, George Cole, Charles
Victor

Those Magnificent Men in Their Flying
Machines, or How I Flew from London
to Paris in 25 hours and 11 Minutes **
🏃 GB   1965   133m   Technicolor   Todd-
AO
TCF (Stan Marguilies, Jack Davies)
In 1910, a newspaper owner sponsors a London to
Paris air race.
*Long-winded, generally agreeable knockabout comedy
with plenty to look at but far too few jokes to sustain it.*
w Jack Davies, Ken Annakin d Ken Annakin
ph Christopher Challis m Ron Goodwin pd Tom
Morahan
☆ Sarah Miles, Stuart Whitman, Robert Morley,
Eric Sykes, Terry-Thomas, James Fox, Alberto
Sordi, Gert Frobe, Jean-Pierre Cassel, Karl Michael
Vogler, Irina Demich, Benny Hill, Flora Robson,
Sam Wanamaker, Red Skelton and also Fred
Emney, Cicely Courtneidge, Gordon Jackson, John
Le Mesurier, Tony Hancock, William Rushton
'There is many a likely gag, but none that
survives the second or third reprise. It could
have been a good bit funnier by being shorter:
the winning time is 25 hours 11 minutes, and by
observing some kind of neo-Aristotelian unity
the film seems to last exactly as long.' – *John
Simon*
🖙 script

Those Marvellous Benchley Shorts: see
Benchley

Those Were the Days *
GB   1934   80m   bw
BIP (Walter C. Mycroft)
In the 1890s, a magistrate seeks out his teenage
stepson in a music hall.
*Lively comedy which is valuable as giving the screen's
best re-creation of an old-time music hall.*
w Fred Thompson, Frank Miller, Frank Launder,
Jack Jordan play *The Magistrate* by Arthur Wing
Pinero d Thomas Bentley ph Otto Kanturek
md Idris Lewis
☆ Will Hay, John Mills, Iris Hoey, Angela
Baddeley, Claud Allister, George Graves, Jane
Carr, H. F. Maltby

† Music hall acts include Gaston and Andrée, Lily
Morris, G. H. Elliott, Sam Curtis, Frank Boston
and Betty

Those Were the Days
US   1940   74m   bw
Paramount (J. Theodore Reed)
GB title: *Good Old Schooldays*
During their 40th anniversary celebrations, a
married couple look back to their courtship days at
college.
Pleasant, light, nostalgic escapades.
w Don Hartman stories George Fitch d J.
Theodore Reed ph Victor Milner
☆ William Holden, Bonita Granville, Ezra Stone,
Judith Barrett, Vaughan Glazer, Lucien Littlefield,
Richard Denning

Those Wonderful Movie Cranks ***
Czechoslovakia   1978   88m   colour
Barrandov (Jan Suster)
A travelling conjuror at the turn of the century
introduces short cinema films into his act, and
solves his woman trouble meanwhile.
*Charming melancholy comedy which adds a little to art
as well as to history.*
w Oldrich Vlcek, Jiri Menzel d Jiri Menzel
ph Jaromir Sofr m Jiri Sust
☆ Rudolf Hrusinsky, Vlasta Fabianova, Blazena
Holisova

A Thousand Acres
US   1997   105m   colour
Buena Vista/Touchstone/Beacon/Propaganda/Via
Rosa/Prairie (Marc Abraham, Lynn Arost, Steve Golin,
Kate Guinzburg, Sigurjon Sighvatsson)
An ageing farmer divides his farm between his
three daughters.
*A variation on King Lear, set in America's Midwest,
this is no more than a melodramatic soap opera that
muddles and muddies not only Shakespeare's play, but
also Smiley's novel.*
w Laura Jones novel Jane Smiley d Jocelyn
Moorhouse ph Tak Fujimoto m Richard Hartley
pd Dan Davis ed Maryann Brandon
☆ Michelle Pfeiffer, Jessica Lange, Jason Robards,
Jennifer Jason Leigh, Colin Firth, Keith Carradine,
Kevin Anderson, Pat Hingle
'What was a careful, moving novel is now a
helping of Hollywood soup. Disasters strike with
cartoonish regularity and mock-horror.' – *Gaby
Wood, Guardian*

A Thousand and One Nights *
🏃 US   1945   92m   Technicolor
Columbia (Samuel Bischoff)
Aladdin seeks his princess.
*Amusing take-off on the Arabian Nights, with good
jokes and music.*
w Wilfrid H. Pettitt, Richard English, Jack Henley
d Alfred E. Green ad Stephen Goosson, Rudolph
Sternad, Ray Rennahan
☆ Cornel Wilde, Phil Silvers, Evelyn Keyes,
Adele Jergens, Dusty Anderson, Dennis Hoey
🖙 art direction

A Thousand Clowns *
US   1965   115m   bw
UA/Harell (Fred Coe)
A New Yorker who has abdicated from work leads
a cheerful, useless life with his young nephew, but
the school board have their doubts.
*Imitative nonconformist comedy with frequent
reminiscences of older, better plays such as You Can't
Take It with You. Good lines occasionally make
themselves felt, but the overall effect is patchy, the lead
is miscast, and the location montages only emphasize
the basic one-room set.*
w Herb Gardner play Herb Gardner d Fred Coe
ph Arthur J. Ornitz m Don Walker
☆ Jason Robards, Martin Balsam, Barry Gordon,
Barbara Harris, William Daniels, Gene Saks
'A broad and joyous comment on the rebellions
and concessions of our daily life, a mature
comedy that mixes its compassion with hilarity.'
– *Judith Crist*
🏆 Martin Balsam
🖙 best picture; Herb Gardner; Don Walker

A Thousand Eyes (dubbed)
West Germany   1984   92m   colour
Filmverlag der Autoren/Radiant/ZDF (Michael Bittins)
original title: *Tausend Augen*
A student of marine biology, who works by night in
a Hamburg strip-show to earn money to enable her
to join her boyfriend in Australia, becomes an
object of obsession for several men.
*Slow-moving and unsatisfactory drama that takes a
long time to make a scarcely perceptible point.*
wd Hans-Christoph Blumenberg ph Martin
Schäfer m Hubert Bartholomae pd Christian
Bussmann ed Helga Borsche
☆ Barbara Rudnik, Armin Mueller-Stahl, Karin
Baal, Peter Kraus, Hannelore Hoger, Mehmet
Yandirer, Vera Tschechowa, Gudrun Landgrebe
† There are cameo appearances by directors Jean-
Marie Straub, Wim Wenders (as a thief in a video
store), George Miller and Phillip Noyce.

The Thousand Eyes of Dr Mabuse *
France/Italy/Germany   1960   103m   bw
CCC/Filmkunst/Incom Criterion/Ajay
Murders in a Berlin hotel are attributed to a
reincarnation of the evil Dr Mabuse.
Lively if belated sequel to the director's silent films.
w Fritz Lang, Jeinz Oskar Wuttig d Fritz Lang
ph Kurt Löb m Bert Grund, Gerhard Becker
☆ Dawn Addams, Peter Van Eyck, Gert Frobe,
Wolfgang Preiss, Werner Peters

Thousand Pieces of Gold *
US   1991   105m   colour
American Playhouse/Maverick/Film Four (Nancy Kelly,
Kenji Yamamoto)
During hard times, a young Chinese woman is sold
by her father and sent to America to work in a
brothel.
*Pioneer days told from the unusual perspective of a
woman and an outsider, an understated drama with a
feminist subtext.*
w Anne Makepeace novel Ruthanne Lum
McCunn d Nancy Kelly ph Bobby Bukowski
m Gary Malkin pd Dan Bishop ed Kenji
Yamamoto
☆ Rosalind Chao, Dennis Dun, Michael Paul
Chan, Chris Cooper

Thousands Cheer *
US   1943   126m   Technicolor
MGM (Joe Pasternak)
An army base stages an all-star variety show.
Ho-hum studio extravaganza with some good numbers.
w Paul Jarrico, Richard Collins d George Sidney
ph George Folsey md Herbert Stothart ad Cedric
Gibbons, Daniel Cathcart songs various
☆ Kathryn Grayson, Gene Kelly, John Boles,
Mary Astor, Jose Iturbi, Kay Kyser and his
Orchestra, Lionel Barrymore, Margaret O'Brien,
June Allyson, Mickey Rooney, Judy Garland, Red
Skelton, Eleanor Powell, Bob Crosby and his
Orchestra, Lena Horne and also Frank Morgan
'A thoroughly routine musical distinguished only
by Gene Kelly with nothing to use his talents
on, a terrible piece of trash by Shostakovich, and
the unpleasant sight of Jose Iturbi proving he is a
real guy by playing the sort of boogie woogie
anyone ought to be able to learn through a
correspondence course.' – *James Agee*
🖙 George Folsey; Herbert Stothart; art direction

Three
GB   1969   105m   DeLuxe
UA/Obelisk (Bruce Becker)
Two American students on holiday in Europe pick
up an English girl to show them the sights.
An aimless road movie.
wd James Salter story *Then We Were Three* by
Irwin Shaw ph Etienne Becker m Laurence
Rosenthal ad Guy Littaye ed Edward Nielson
☆ Charlotte Rampling, Robie Porter, Sam
Waterston, Pascale Roberts, Edina Ronay, Gillian
Hills
'Ambiguous action, coolly inscrutable
characters, dialogue that is little more than half-
heard clichés.' – *Richard Combs, MFB*
† The film was cut to 95m on its British release.

3-4x Jugatsu: see *Boiling Point*

The Three Ages *
US   1923   80m   bw   silent
Joseph Schenck/Metro
Three stories parodying Griffith's *Intolerance.*
*The star's first feature film, not his strongest, is saved
by the final chases.*
w Clyde Bruckman, Jean Havez, Joseph Mitchell
d Buster Keaton, Eddie Cline
☆ Buster Keaton, Wallace Beery, Margaret Leahy,
Joe Roberts

Three Amigos!
🏃 US   1986   105m   Technicolor
Orion (Lorne Michaels, George Folsey Jnr)
Three wimpish cowboy stars find themselves hired
to defend a desert town from a bandit.
*Weak take-off of The Magnificent Seven, with
performances that grate.*
w Steve Martin, Lorne Michaels, Randy Newman
d John Landis ph Ronald W. Browne m Elmer
Bernstein pd Richard Sawyer ed Malcolm
Campbell
☆ Chevy Chase, Steve Martin, Martin Short,
Patrice Martinez, Alfonso Arau

Three Bites of the Apple
US   1966   98m   Metrocolor   Panavision
MGM (Alvin Ganzer)
An English travel courier wins a lot of money in a
Rome casino, and nearly loses it all.
Very dull comedy perked up by attractive locations.
w George Wells d Alvin Ganzer ph Gabor
Pogany m Eddy Manson
☆ David McCallum, Sylva Koscina, Tammy
Grimes, Harvey Korman, Aldo Fabrizi

Three Blind Mice *
US   1938   75m   bw
TCF (Raymond Griffith)
Three Kansas girls in the big city seek rich
husbands.
*Mild comedy remade as Three Little Girls in Blue
and How to Marry a Millionaire, and not all that
different from any of the Gold Diggers comedy
musicals.*
w Brown Holmes, Lynn Starling d William A.
Seiter ph Ernest Palmer m Charles Maxwell
☆ Loretta Young, Joel McCrea, David Niven,
Stuart Erwin, Marjorie Weaver, Pauline Moore,
Binnie Barnes, Jane Darwell, Leonid Kinskey
'More names than can be handled on the
marquee … good summer entertainment.' –
Variety

Three Brave Men *
US   1956   88m   bw   Cinemascope
TCF (Herbert B. Swope Jnr)
A civilian employee in the US Navy is suspended
as a security risk and it takes a lawsuit to set things
straight.
*Semi-factual anti-McCarthy drama proving that
America is a great place to live – when you're winning.
Good courtroom scenes.*
wd Philip Dunne articles Anthony Lewis
ph Charles G. Clarke m Hans Salter
☆ Ray Milland, Ernest Borgnine, Nina Foch, Dean
Jagger, Frank Lovejoy, Edward Andrews, Frank
Faylen, James Westerfield, Joseph Wiseman

The Three Caballeros ***
🏃 US   1945   70m   Technicolor
Walt Disney (Norman Ferguson)
A programme of shorts about South America,
linked by Donald Duck as a tourist.
*Rapid-fire mélange of fragments supporting the good
neighbour policy, following the shorter Saludos
Amigos of 1943. The kaleidoscopic sequences and the
combination of live action with cartoon remain of
absorbing interest.*
w various d various m Edward Plumb, Paul J
Smith, Charles Wolcott
† Stories include Pablo the Penguin, Little
Gauchito, a Mexican sequence and some
adventures with Joe Carioca.
🖙 Edward Plumb, Paul J. Smith, Charles Wolcott

Three Came Home **
US   1950   106m   bw
TCF (Nunnally Johnson)

In 1941 writer Agnes Newton Keith tries to escape from Borneo but is interned and ill-used by the Japanese.
Well-made, harrowing war adventure.
w Nunnally Johnson *book* Agnes Newton Keith d Jean Negulesco *ph* Milton Krasner *m* Hugo Friedhofer *md* Lionel Newman
☆ Claudette Colbert, Patric Knowles, Sessue Hayakawa, Florence Desmond, Sylvia Andrew, Phyllis Morris

'It will shock you, disturb you, tear your heart out. But it will fill you with great respect for a heroic soul.' – *New York Times*

Three Cases of Murder *
GB   1954   99m   bw
British Lion/Wessex/London Films (Ian Dalrymple, Hugh Perceval)

'In the Picture': a painting comes to life. 'You Killed Elizabeth': a man suspects himself of his faithless fiancée's murder. 'Lord Mountdrago': the foreign secretary dreams of killing an MP he hates.
Unlinked compendium, in which the first and third stories are quite interesting and well done, the second very commonplace.
w Donald Wilson, Sidney Caroll, Ian Dalrymple (original stories Roderick Wilkinson, Brett Halliday, W. Somerset Maugham) d Wendy Toye, David Eady, George More O'Ferrall *ph* Georges Périnal *m* Doreen Carwithen
☆ Alan Badel, Hugh Pryse, Leueen MacGrath, Elizabeth Sellars, John Gregson, Emrys Jones, Orson Welles, André Morell

Three Cheers for the Irish
US   1940   100m   bw
Warner (Sam Bischoff)
An Irishman's daughter causes family trouble when she falls for a Scot.
Pleasant, unpretentious but overlong romantic comedy.
w Richard Macaulay, Jerry Wald d Lloyd Bacon *ph* Charles Rosher *m* Adolph Deutsch
☆ Thomas Mitchell, Priscilla Lane, Dennis Morgan, Alan Hale, Virginia Grey, Irene Hervey, William Lundigan

Three Cockeyed Sailors: see Sailors Three

Three Coins in the Fountain **
US   1954   102m   DeLuxe   Cinemascope
TCF (Sol C. Siegel)

Three American girls find romance in Rome.
An enormous box-office hit, the pattern of which was frequently repeated against various backgrounds; it was actually remade in Madrid as The Pleasure Seekers. In itself a thin entertainment, but the title song carried it.
w John Patrick *novel* John H. Secondari d Jean Negulesco *ph* Milton Krasner *m* Victor Young
☆ Clifton Webb, Dorothy McGuire, Louis Jourdan, Jean Peters, Rossano Brazzi, Maggie McNamara, Howard St John, Kathryn Givney, Cathleen Nesbitt
♬ Milton Krasner; title song (*m Jule Styne, ly Sammy Cahn*)
Å best picture

Three Colours: Blue ***
France   1993   98m   Eastmancolor
Artificial Eye/MK2/CED/France 3/CAB/TOR/Canal (Marin Karmitz)

original title: Trois Couleurs: Bleu
A secretive woman, whose husband, a composer, and child are killed in a car crash, destroys his final work, sells all their possessions and sets out to remake her life.
The first part of a trilogy, based on the colours of the French tricolour and dealing with the theme of liberty, as experienced from the viewpoint of its enigmatic central character, for whom liberty often means a refusal to engage with the world, in order to avoid pain.
w Krzysztof Pisiewicz, Krzysztof Kieslowski d Krzysztof Kieslowski *ph* Slawomir Idziak *m* Zbigniew Preisner *ad* Claude Lenoir *ed* Jacques Witta
☆ Juliette Binoche, Benoît Régent, Florence Pernel, Charlotte Véry, Hélène Vincent, Philippe Volter, Claude Duneton, Hugues Quester, Emmanuelle Riva

'What lifts it out of the doldrums is Kieslowski's fascinating use of reflections, focusing techniques and camera angles to give the somewhat pedestrian material a profound and otherworldly East European feel.' – *Kim Newman, Empire*
† The music for the film was written first and the action was filmed to match its rhythms.

Three Colours: Red ***
France/Switzerland/Poland   1994   99m
Eastmancolor
Artificial Eye/MK2/France 3/CAB/Tor (Marin Karmitz)

original title: Trois Couleurs: Rouge
A model confides her fears about her life to a lonely and inquisitive retired judge, who secretly arranges a meeting between her and a young lawyer.
A delicate and intricate study of coincidence and destiny, of the fragile means that link one person to the next; it is a stylish and intriguing end to an impressive trilogy.
w Krzysztof Piesiewicz, Krzysztof Kieslowski d Krzysztof Kieslowski *ph* Piotr Sobocinski *m* Zbigniew Preisner *pd* Claude Lenoir *ed* Jacques Witta
☆ Irene Jacob, Jean-Louis Trintignant, Jean-Pierre Lorit, Frédérique Feder, Juliette Binoche, Julie Delpy

'This is the kind of film that makes you feel intensely alive and sends you out into the streets afterwards eager to talk deeply and urgently to the person you are with.' – *Roger Ebert, Chicago Sun-Times*
'If it's true – as the helmer has announced – that this opus will be his last foray into film directing, Kieslowski retires at a formal and philosophical peak.' – *Variety*
† It is the last part of a trilogy based on the French tricolour and dealing with fraternity.
Å Krzysztof Kieslowski (director); Krzysztof Piesiewicz (screenplay); cinematography

Three Colours: White ***
France/Poland   1993   92m   Eastmancolor
Artificial Eye/MK2/France 3/Cab/TOR/Canal (Marin Karmitz)

original title: Trois Couleurs: Blanc
A Polish hairdresser suffers a series of humiliations in Paris – he becomes impotent, his French wife divorces him and he is reduced to penury – and returns to Warsaw with the aim of becoming rich and winning back his wife.
Elegant and acid comedy of a Chaplinesque little man at large in an entrepreneurial Poland – 'home at last,' says our hero, regaining consciousness on a Warsaw rubbish dump after a nightmare trip from France.
w Krzysztof Piesiewicz, Krzysztof Kieslowski d Krzysztof Kieslowski *ph* Edward Klosiński *m* Zbigniew Preisner *ad* Halina Dobrowolska, Claude Lenoir *ed* Urszula Lesiak
☆ Zbigniew Zamachowski, Julie Delpy, Janusz Gajos, Jerzy Stuhr, Juliette Binoche, Florence Pernel

'Funny, bleak and, like all Kieslowski films, austerely handsome – a festival of minimalist virtuosity.' – *Time*
'A fairly straightforward black comedy that skirts pretentiousness and goes easy on the symbolism while retaining Kieslowski's eerie gift for spinning mystical narrative gold from the simplest of ingredients.' – *Lisa Nesselson, Variety*
† This second part of a trilogy, based on the colours of the French flag, deals with equality.

'Out of the inferno of war came three men and a woman – to live their lives, to strive for happiness, to seek love!'

Three Comrades **
US   1938   98m   bw
MGM (Joseph L. Mankiewicz)

In twenties Germany, three friends find life hard but derive some joy from their love for a high-spirited girl who is dying of tuberculosis.
Despairing romance becomes a sentimental tearjerker with all the stops out; immaculately produced and very appealing to the masses, but prevented by censorship from being the intended indictment of Nazi Germany. The final scene in which the two surviving comrades are joined in the churchyard by their ghostly friends still packs a wallop.
w F. Scott Fitzgerald, Edward E. Paramore *novel* Erich Maria Remarque d Frank Borzage *ph* Joseph Ruttenberg *m* Franz Waxman
☆ Margaret Sullavan, Robert Taylor, Robert Young, Franchot Tone, Guy Kibbee, Lionel Atwill, Henry Hull, Charley Grapewin

'Just what Frank Borzage is trying to prove is very difficult to fathom … there must have been some reason for making this picture, but it certainly isn't in the name of entertainment.' – *Variety*
'A remarkably high combination of talents has made it all very impressive and moving – good writing, a good man at the camera, good actors, and presiding over them a good director … such unforgettable bits as the pursuit of the boy who shot Gottfried, a glimpse from under the muffling blanket of the girl's stricken face, the startling downswoop of the camera's eye upon the girl getting up from bed to remove the burden of her illness from those who love her. These are high moments in a film full of beauty.' – *National Board of Review*
'A love story, beautifully told and consummately acted, but so drenched in hopelessness and heavy with the aroma of death, of wasted youth in a world of foggy shapes and nameless menaces, that its beauty and strength are often clouded and betrayed.' – *Time*
Å Margaret Sullavan

'They might be the family next door – but if they were, you'd move!'

Three Cornered Moon *
US   1933   72m   bw
Paramount
A newly-poor Depression family has trouble finding work.
Slightly screwball romantic comedy, a predecessor of You Can't Take It with You; the humour now seems very faded, but it was a signpost of its day.
w S. K. Lauren, Ray Harris *play* Gertrude Tonkonogy d Elliott Nugent *ph* Leon Shamroy
☆ Claudette Colbert, Mary Boland, Richard Arlen, Wallace Ford, Lyda Roberti, Tom Brown, Hardie Albright

Three Daring Daughters
US   1948   115m   Technicolor
MGM (Joe Pasternak)
GB title: The Birds and the Bees
Three girls are dismayed to hear that their mother is remarrying.
Cheerful comedy with music, but nothing to write home about.
w Albert Mannheimer, Frederick Kohner, Sonya Levien, John Meehan d Fred M. Wilcox *ph* Ray June *md* Georgie Stoll
☆ Jeanette MacDonald, Jose Iturbi, Jane Powell, Ann E. Todd, Mary Elinor Donahue, Larry Adler, Edward Arnold, Harry Davenport, Moyna MacGill

'His code name is Condor. In the next twenty-four hours everyone he trusts will try to kill him.'

Three Days of the Condor **
US   1975   118m   Technicolor   Panavision
Paramount/Dino de Laurentiis/Wildwood (Stanley Schneider)

An innocent researcher for a branch of the CIA finds himself marked for death by assassins employed by another branch.
Entertaining New York-based thriller which shamelessly follows most of the twists of The 39 Steps. It is just possible to follow its complexities, and the dialogue is smart.
w Lorenzo Semple Jnr, David Rayfiel *novel* Six Days of the Condor by James Grady d Sydney Pollack *ph* Owen Roizman *m* Dave Grusin
☆ Robert Redford, Faye Dunaway, Cliff Robertson, Max von Sydow, John Houseman, Walter McGinn

Three Faces East *
US   1930   71m   bw
Warner (Darryl F. Zanuck)
The butler to the British war minister is a German spy, and the German nurse sent to help him is really a British agent …
Slow, melodramatic remake of 1926 silent, later turned into a Karloff vehicle, British Intelligence (qv).
w Oliver H. P. Garrett, Arthur Caesar *play* Anthony Paul Kelly d Roy del Ruth *ph* Chick McGill
☆ Constance Bennett, Erich von Stroheim, Anthony Bushell, William Holden

'Bennett and von Stroheim guarantee a better than average week.' – *Variety*

The Three Faces of Eve **
US   1957   95m   bw   Cinemascope
TCF (Nunnally Johnson)

A psychiatrist discovers that a female patient has three distinct personalities: a drab housewife, a good time girl and a mature sophisticated woman.
Alistair Cooke introduces this tall tale as if he believed it; as presented, it is entertaining but not very convincing. Its box-office success was sufficient to start a schizophrenia cycle.
w Nunnally Johnson *book* Corbett H. Thigpen MD, Hervey M. Cleckley MD d Nunnally Johnson *ph* Stanley Cortez *m* Robert Emmett Dolan
☆ Joanne Woodward, Lee J. Cobb, David Wayne, Nancy Kulp, Edwin Jerome
Å Joanne Woodward

Three Faces West
US   1940   79m   bw
Republic (Sol C. Siegel)

A dust bowl community is helped by an Austrian doctor fleeing from the Nazis, but his daughter is followed by a Nazi suitor.
Unusual modern Western, blandly told.
w F. Hugh Herbert, Joseph Moncure March, Samuel Ornitz d Bernard Vorhaus *ph* John Alton *m* Victor Young
☆ John Wayne, Charles Coburn, Sigrid Gurie, Roland Varno, Spencer Charters, Sonny Bupp

Three for Bedroom C
US   1952   74m   Natural Color
Brenco (Edward L. Alperson Jnr)

Confusion reigns on a train when a film star takes a compartment booked for a Harvard scientist.
Inept farce which never rises above mediocrity and coasts along well below it.
wd Milton H. Bren *ph* Ernest Laszlo *m* Heinz Roemheld
☆ Gloria Swanson, Fred Clark, James Warren, Hans Conried, Steve Brodie, Margaret Dumont

Three for Jamie Dawn
US   1956   81m   bw
AA (Hayes Goetz)
A crooked lawyer bribes three members of a murder jury.
Minor courtroom melodrama, limply developed.
w John Klempner d Thomas Carr *ph* Duke Green *m* Walter Scharf
☆ Laraine Day, Ricardo Montalban, Richard Carlson, June Havoc

Three for the Road
US   1987   88m   DeLuxe
Vista (Herb Jaffe, Mort Engelberg)

A presidential candidate entrusts the task of escorting his delinquent daughter to a Southern reform school to a young, ambitious aide and his friend, a would-be writer.
Dire road movie, about the sort of people that one would wish strenuously to avoid.
w Richard Martini, Tim Metcalfe, Miguel Tejada-Flores d B. W. L. Norton *ph* Stephen L. Posey *m* Barry Goldberg *pd* Linda Allen *ed* Christopher Greenbury
☆ Charlie Sheen, Kerri Green, Alan Ruck, Sally Kellerman, Blair Tefkin, Raymond J. Barry

'One for the songs and dances! Two for the laughs and romances!'

Three for the Show *
US   1955   93m   Technicolor   Cinemascope
Columbia (Jonie Taps)

A married Broadway star finds that her first husband is still alive.
Adequate musical remake of Too Many Husbands (qv); not bad, not good.
w Edward Hope, Leonard Stern *play* Too Many Husbands by W. Somerset Maugham d H. C. Potter *ph* Arthur E. Arling *md* George Duning *ch* Jack Cole *songs* various
☆ Betty Grable, Jack Lemmon, Marge Champion, Gower Champion, Myron McCormick, Paul Harvey

'It has the inimitable zing of vacuity, and it has something more important: a fundamental lilt

◎ Digital Video Disc Region 2   ◎ Digital Video Disc Region 1   ♫ Soundtrack released on compact disc   ☆ Cast in approximate order of importance   † Points of interest   ♬ Notable songs   Å Academy Award   Å Academy Award nomination   ♛ BAFTA that travels from scene to scene and makes the picture musical even when the soundtrack is silent.' – *Time*

Three Fugitives *
US   1989   96m   Metrocolor
Warner/Touchstone/Silver Screen Partners IV (Lauren Shuler-Donner)

An ex-convict, trying to reform, is forced to go on the run with an inept bank robber and his small daughter.
A chase farce that piles up the absurdities with diminishing effect.
wd Francis Veber ph Haskell Wexler m David McHugh pd Rick Carter ed Bruce Green
☆ Nick Nolte, Martin Short, Sarah Rowland Doroff, James Earl Jones, Alan Ruck, Kenneth McMillan, David Arnott, Bruce McGill

Three Girls about Town *
US   1942   71m   bw
Columbia
Three sisters in New York find a corpse in their hotel bedroom.
A funny 'B' picture: fast paced and lively from start to finish.
w Richard Carroll d Leigh Jason ph Franz Planer
☆ Joan Blondell, Binnie Barnes, Janet Blair, John Howard, Robert Benchley, Eric Blore, Una O'Connor

Three Godfathers *
US   1948   106m   Technicolor
MGM/Argosy (John Ford)

Three outlaws escaping across the desert take charge of an orphan baby.
'Orrible sentimental parable partly redeemed by splendid scenery.
w Laurence Stallings, Frank S. Nugent story Peter B. Kyne d John Ford ph Winton Hoch m Richard Hageman
☆ John Wayne, Pedro Armendariz, Harry Carey Jnr, Ward Bond
† The story also appeared in 1909 as *Bronco Billy and the Baby*; in 1916 as *Three Godfathers*, with Harry Carey; in 1920 as *Marked Men*, with Harry Carey; in 1929 as *Hell's Heroes*, with Charles Bickford; in 1936 as *Three Godfathers*, with Chester Morris; and in 1975 as a TV movie, *The Godchild*, with Jack Palance.
†† The film is dedicated 'to the memory of Harry Carey, bright star of the early western sky'.

Three Guys Named Mike
US   1951   90m   bw
MGM (Armand Deutsch)

An accident-prone air hostess has three suitors.
Inconsequential romantic comedy which shows the effort of stretching its thin material to feature length.
w Sidney Sheldon story Ruth Brooks Flippen d Charles Walters ph Paul Vogel m Bronislau Kaper
☆ Jane Wyman, Barry Sullivan, Van Johnson, Howard Keel, Phyllis Kirk, Jeff Donnell

Three Hats for Lisa *
GB   1965   99m   Eastmancolor
Seven Hills/Jack Hanbury
A docker and a taxi driver help a foreign film star to steal three typically English hats.
Minor musical, silly but good to look at.
w Leslie Bricusse, Talbot Rothwell d Sidney Hayers
☆ Joe Brown, Sid James, Sophie Hardy, Una Stubbs, Dave Nelson, Peter Bowles

Three Hearts for Julia
US   1943   90m   bw
MGM
A reporter courts his wife all over again when she threatens to divorce him.
One of those thin romantic comedies which sent its male lead back to the theatre.
w Lionel Houser d Richard Thorpe
☆ Melvyn Douglas, Ann Sothern, Lee Bowman, Felix Bressart, Reginald Owen, Richard Ainley

365 Nights in Hollywood
US   1934   77m   bw
Sol M. Wurtzel/Fox
A down-and-out becomes a director of a fake school of acting.

Slight and casually developed comedy-romance, with comedy interludes by Mitchell and Durant.
w William Conselman, Henry Johnson d George Marshall
☆ James Dunn, Alice Faye, John Bradford, Grant Mitchell
'A picture with no punch and little appeal.' – *Variety*

The 300 Spartans *
US   1962   114m   DeLuxe
Cinemascope
TCF (Rudolph Maté, George St George)
Sparta leads the ancient Greek states against Persia's attack at Thermopylae.
Quite a lively epic with some dignity.
w George St George d Rudolph Maté ph Geoffrey Unsworth m Manos Hadjidakis
☆ Richard Egan, Ralph Richardson, David Farrar, Diane Baker, Barry Coe, Donald Houston, Kieron Moore, John Crawford, Robert Brown

Three Husbands
US   1950   76m   bw
UA/Gloria (I. G. Goldsmith)

Three husbands receive letters from a dead friend claiming that he had affairs with each of their wives.
Silly copy of A Letter to Three Wives, with neither style nor sophistication.
w Vera Caspary, Edward Eliscu d Irving Reis ph Franz Planer m Herschel Burke Gilbert
☆ Emlyn Williams, Eve Arden, Howard da Silva, Ruth Warrick, Shepperd Strudwick, Vanessa Brown, Billie Burke, Jonathan Hale

Three in the Attic
US   1968   90m   Pathécolor
AIP-Hermes (Richard Wilson)

A college Casanova is locked in an attic by three girls who seduce him by rota until he cries for mercy.
One of the first outspoken comedies of the sexual revolution, but not a particularly funny one.
w Stephen Yafa novel Paxton Quigley's Had the Course by Stephen Yafa d Richard Wilson m J. Burgi Contner m Chad Stuart
☆ Chris Jones, Yvette Mimieux, Judy Pace, Maggie Turett, Nan Martin

Three in the Cellar: see Up in the Cellar

'Hello, Mrs Howard, I'm a friend of Mr Howard!'
Three into Two Won't Go *
GB   1969   100m   Technicolor
Universal (Julian Blaustein)
An executive has an affair with a girl hitch-hiker who later moves into his house to his wife's astonishment.
Pulsatable sex drama with good performances, rather flabbily written and directed.
w Edna O'Brien novel Andrea Newman d Peter Hall m Walter Lassally m Francis Lai
☆ Rod Steiger, Claire Bloom, Judy Geeson, Peggy Ashcroft, Paul Rogers

Three Is a Family *
US   1944   81m   bw
Sol Lesser/United Artists
A middle-aged couple find their small apartment invaded by their homeless children and grandchildren.
Quite amusing comedy on a familiar theme.
w Harry Chandlee, Marjorie L. Pfaelzer play Phoebe and Henry Ephron d Edward Ludwig
☆ Charles Ruggles, Fay Bainter, Marjorie Reynolds, Helen Broderick, Arthur Lake, Hattie McDaniel, John Philliber, Jeff Donnell, Walter Catlett, Clarence Kolb, Warren Hymer

Three Kids and a Queen
US   1935   85m   bw
Universal
Three boys decide to kidnap a rich old lady, but are dismayed to find that she enjoys the experience.
Sentimental comedy which seemed to hit the right note.
w Barry Trivers, Samuel Ornitz, Harry Poppe, Chester Beecroft d Edward Ludwig
☆ May Robson, Frankie Darro, Billy Burrud, Billy Benedict, Charlotte Henry, Herman Bing, Henry Armetta, John Miljan, Hedda Hopper
'A cinch for box office satisfaction.' – *Variety*

'They're Deserters, Rebels And Thieves. But In The Nicest Possible Way.'
'It's Good To Be King.'
Three Kings ***
US   1999   115m   Technicolor   Panavision
Warner/Village Roadshow/Village-A.M Film/Coast Ridge/Atlas (Charles Roven, Paul Junger Witt, Edward L. McDonnell)

As the Gulf War ends in 1991, a group US soldiers attempt to steal Saddam Hussein's hoard of gold, buried behind Iraqi lines.
Ironic, blackly humorous drama that manages to take seriously the messy mechanics of war while staying within most of the conventions of a caper movie, and adding some unsettling photographic effects to the genre.
wd David O. Russell story John Ridley ph Newton Thomas Sigel m Carter Burwell pd Catherine Hardwicke ed Robert K. Lambert
☆ George Clooney, Mark Wahlberg, Ice Cube, Spike Jonze, Jamie Kennedy, Mykelti Williamson, Cliff Curtis, Said Taghmaoui, Judy Greer, Liz Stauber
'That most unusual of sights, the grown up, intelligent Hollywood war film.' – *Times*
'There are many clever touches, but there's something tamely conventional at the film's core.' – Janet Maslin, *New York Times*

Three Little Girls in Blue
US   1946   90m   Technicolor
TCF (Mack Gordon)
Musical remake of *Three Blind Mice* (qv); adequate and quite forgettable.
w Valentine Davies d Bruce Humberstone ph Ernest Palmer songs Mack Gordon, Joseph Myrow
☆ June Haver, George Montgomery, Vivian Blaine, Celeste Holm, Vera-Ellen, Frank Latimore, Charles Smith, Charles Halton

Three Little Words *
US   1950   102m   Technicolor
MGM (Jack Cummings)

The careers of songwriters Bert Kalmar and Harry Ruby.
Disappointingly ordinary musical in which two witty people are made to seem dull, and the plot allows Fred Astaire only one dance.
w George Wells d Richard Thorpe ph Harry Jackson md André Previn ch Hermes Pan songs Bert Kalmar, Harry Ruby and various collaborators
☆ Fred Astaire, Red Skelton, Vera-Ellen, Arlene Dahl, Keenan Wynn, Gale Robbins, Gloria de Haven, Phil Regan, *Debbie Reynolds*
† Vera-Ellen's singing was dubbed by Anita Ellis.
♫ André Previn

The Three Lives of Thomasina
GB   1963   97m   Technicolor
Walt Disney

In a Scottish village in 1912, a vet finds that his methods are no match for a local girl who treats animals by giving them love.
Syrupy film for children: the animals are the main interest and one of them narrates…
w Robert Westerby novel Thomasina by Paul Gallico d Don Chaffey ph Paul Beeson m Paul Smith
☆ Susan Hampshire, Patrick McGoohan, Karen Dotrice, Vincent Winter, Laurence Naismith, Finlay Currie, Wilfrid Brambell

Three Loves Has Nancy
US   1938   69m   bw
MGM (Norman Krasna)
A jilted bride takes her time about her next selection.
Adequate star comedy.
w Bella and Sam Spewack, George Oppenheimer, David Hertz d Richard Thorpe ph William Daniels
☆ Janet Gaynor, Robert Montgomery, Franchot Tone, Guy Kibbee, Claire Dodd, Reginald Owen, Charley Grapewin, Emma Dunn, Cora Witherspoon
'This may not be the funniest picture of the season, but it's certainly one of the wackiest.' – *Variety*

The Three Maxims
GB   1937   87m   bw
GFD/Pathé Consortium (Herbert Wilcox)
Two trapezists love the girl member of the team, and the situation leads to attempted murder.
Effective Paris-set treatment of a well worn theme (see Trapeze).
w Herman Mankiewicz d Herbert Wilcox ph Frederick A. Young, Jack Cox
☆ Anna Neagle, Tullio Carminati, Leslie Banks, Horace Hodges

'They changed her diapers – she changed their lives!'
Three Men and a Baby
US   1987   102m   DeLuxe
Touchstone/Silver Screen III (Ted Field, Robert W. Cort)

Three swinging bachelors find a baby on their doorstep.
Slight comedy, given some momentum by a heroin-dealing subplot, which proved surprisingly successful with audiences thanks to energetic playing.
w James Orr, Jim Cruickshank d Leonard Nimoy ph Adam Greenberg m Marvin Hamlisch pd Peter Larkin
☆ Tom Selleck, Steve Guttenberg, Ted Danson, Nancy Travis
† Remake of the more thoughtful and elegant *Trois Hommes et un Couffin* of 1985, whose director Coline Serreau was to have directed the US version but backed out.

Three Men and a Cradle *
France   1985   107m   colour
UKFD/Floch Film/Soprofilm/TF1 Films (Jean-François Lepetit)

original title: *Trois Hommes et un Couffin*
Three bachelors fall for a baby left on their doorstep by a former girl-friend.
Amusing comedy of role reversal which was remade by Hollywood as the glossier Three Men and a Baby.
wd Coline Serreau ph Jean-Yves éscoffier, Jean-Jacques Bouhon pd Yvan Maussion ed Catherine Renault
☆ Roland Giraud, Michel Boujenah, André Dussollier, Philippine Leroy Beaulieu

Three Men and a Girl: see Golden Arrow (1949)

Three Men and a Little Lady
US   1990   100m
Touchstone/Jean François LePetit-Interscope Communications (Ted Field, Robert W. Cort)

Three bachelors prevent the mother of the child they 'adopted' marrying an Englishman.
Dire sequel to Three Men and a Baby, notably silly in its depiction of England as a backward rural country inhabited entirely by eccentrics.
w Charlie Peters story Sara Parriott, Josann McGibbon d Emile Ardolino ph Adam Greenberg m James Newton Howard pd Stuart Wurtzel ad David M. Haber ed Michael A. Stevenson
☆ Tom Selleck, Steve Guttenberg, Ted Danson, Nancy Travis, Robin Weisman, Christopher Cazenove, Sheila Hancock, Fiona Shaw
'Thinking people will be hard-pressed to find a single interesting moment in this relentlessly predictable fantasy.' – *Variety*

Three Men in a Boat
GB   1956   94m   Eastmancolor
Cinemascope
Romulus (Jack Clayton)

In the 1890s, misadventures befall three men holidaying on the Thames.
Flabby burlesque of a celebrated comic novel whose style is never even approached.
w Hubert Gregg, Vernon Harris novel Jerome K. Jerome d Ken Annakin ph Eric Cross m John Addison ad John Howell
☆ David Tomlinson, Jimmy Edwards, Laurence Harvey, Shirley Eaton, Robertson Hare, Jill Ireland, Lisa Gastoni, Martita Hunt, A. E. Matthews, Ernest Thesiger, Adrienne Corri
† A previous version in 1933 starred William Austin, Edmond Breon and Billy Milton; directed by Graham Cutts for ATP.

Three Men on a Horse *
US 1936 85m bw
Warner (Sam Bischoff)
▣

A timid Brooklynite finds he can always pick winners, and gangsters get interested.
Smooth New Yorkish comedy which pleased at the time.
w Laird Doyle *play* John Cecil Holm, George Abbott d Mervyn Le Roy ph Sol Polito
☆ Frank McHugh, Sam Levene, Joan Blondell, Guy Kibbee, Carol Hughes, Allen Jenkins, Edgar Kennedy, Eddie Anderson, Harry Davenport

The Three Mesquiteers
A three-man cowboy team who operated in popular B features at the Hopalong Cassidy level. The make-up of the team varied: the actors most often found in it were John Wayne, Max Terhune, Bob Livingston, Ray Corrigan, Bob Steele, Rufe Davis, Tom Tyler, Raymond Hatton, Duncan Renaldo and Jimmy Dodd. The first film was made for RKO, all the rest for Republic: most frequent directors were George Sherman, Mack V. Wright, Joseph Kane, John English and Lester Orlebeck.
1935 Powdersmoke Range, The Three Mesquiteers
1936 Ghost Town, Gold, Roarin' Lead
1937 Riders of the Whistling Skull, Hit the Saddle, Gunsmoke Ranch, Come On Cowboys, Range Defenders, Heart of the Rockies, The Trigger Trio, Wild Horse Rodeo
1938 The Purple Vigilantes, Call the Mesquiteers, Call of the Mesquiteers, Outlaws of Sonora, Riders of the Black Hills, Heroes of the Hills, Pals of the Saddle, Over-land Stage Raiders, Santa Fe Stampede, Red River Range
1939 The Night Riders, Three Texas Steers, Wyoming Outlaw, New Frontier, The Kansas Terrors, Cowboys from Texas
1940 Heroes of the Saddle, Pioneers of the West, Covered Wagon Days, Rocky Mountain Rangers, Oklahoma Renegades, Under Texas Skies, The Trail Blazers, Lone Star Raiders
1941 Prairie Pioneers, Pals of the Pecos, Saddlemates, Gangs of Sonora, Outlaws of the Cherokee Trail, Gauchos of El Dorado, West of Cimarron
1942 Code of the Outlaw, Riders of the Range, Westward Ho, The Phantom Plainsman, Shadows on the Sage, Valley of Hunted Men
1943 Thundering Trails, The Blocked Trail, Santa Fe Scouts, Riders of the Rio Grande

'A Place Of Betrayal. The Fate Of A King. A Time For Heroes.'
Three Musketeers
👫 US 1993 105m Technicolor Panavision
Buena Vista/Walt Disney/One For All/Caravan (Joe Roth, Roger Birnbaum)
▣ ▤ ◎ ⊘ ⌒

D'Artagnan and the three musketeers save the throne of France despite the machinations of Cardinal Richelieu.
A half-hearted romp by a group of actors to whom swashbuckling is a lost art, this is simply Young Guns with swords, no more than a feeble adventure with little sense of period.
w David Loughery *novel* Alexandre Dumas d Stephen Herek ph Dean Semler m Michael Kamen pd Wolf Kroeger ed John F. Link
☆ Charlie Sheen, Kiefer Sutherland, Chris O'Donnell, Oliver Platt, Tim Curry, Rebecca de Mornay, Gabrielle Anwar, Paul McGann, Julie Delpy
'There should be a better reason for re-making *The Three Musketeers* than to provide a vehicle for whiskery Brat-packers whose careers are on the slide.' – *Sheila Johnston, Independent*

The Three Musketeers
US 1935 97m bw
RKO
▤ ⌒.

See below for synopsis.
A thin and poorly handled version.
w Dudley Nichols, Rowland V. Lee d Rowland V. Lee
☆ Walter Abel, Paul Lukas, Moroni Olsen, Onslow Stevens, Margot Grahame, Heather Angel, Ian Keith, Miles Mander, Nigel de Brulier
'Ineffective and disappointing adaptation ... dull entertainment.' – *Variety*

The Three Musketeers **
US 1939 73m bw
TCF (Raymond Griffith)
▤

GB title: *The Singing Musketeer*
A burlesque of the familiar story with pauses for song.
A very satisfactory entertainment with all concerned in top form.
w M. M. Musselman, William A. Drake, Sam Hellman d Allan Dwan ph Peverell Marley *songs* Samuel Pokrass, Walter Bullock
☆ Don Ameche, the Ritz Brothers, Binnie Barnes, Joseph Schildkraut, Lionel Atwill, Miles Mander, Gloria Stuart, Pauline Moore, John Carradine
'Whenever the action lags, the trio take the rostrum for a slapstick specialty ... moderate b.o., a topper for the key duals.' – *Variety*

The Three Musketeers ***
👫 US 1948 125m Technicolor
MGM (Pandro S. Berman)
▣ ▤ ⌒.

High-spirited version of the famous story, with duels and fights presented like musical numbers.
Its vigour and inventiveness is a pleasure to behold.
w Robert Ardrey d George Sidney ph Robert Planck m Herbert Stothart
☆ Gene Kelly, Lana Turner, June Allyson, Frank Morgan, Van Heflin, Angela Lansbury, Vincent Price, Keenan Wynn, John Sutton, Gig Young, Robert Coote, Reginald Owen, Ian Keith, Patricia Medina
'A heavy, rough-housing mess. As Lady de Winter, Lana Turner sounds like a drive-in waitress exchanging quips with hotrodders, and as Richelieu, Vincent Price might be an especially crooked used car dealer. Angela Lansbury wears the crown of France as though she had won it at a county fair.' – *New Yorker, 1980*
♫ Robert Planck

The Three Musketeers (The Queen's Diamonds) **
👫 Panama 1973 107m Technicolor
Film Trust (Alex Salkind)
▣ ▤ ◎ ⌒

Jokey version with realistic blood; despite very lively highlights it wastes most of its high production cost by not giving its plot a chance; but money was saved by issuing the second half separately as *The Four Musketeers* (*The Revenge of Milady*). The latter section was less attractive.
w George MacDonald Fraser d Richard Lester ph David Watkin m Michel Legrand pd Brian Eatwell
☆ Michael York, Oliver Reed, Richard Chamberlain, Frank Finlay, Raquel Welch, Geraldine Chaplin, Spike Milligan, Faye Dunaway, Charlton Heston, Christopher Lee, Jean-Pierre Cassel
'It's one dragged-out forced laugh. No sweep, no romance, no convincing chivalric tradition to mock.' – *Stanley Kauffmann*

3 Ninjas *
👫 US 1992 84m Technicolor
Buena Vista/Touchstone/Global Venture Hollywood (Martha Chang)
▤ ⌒.

The sons of an FBI agent, taught martial arts by their grandfather, defeat an evil arms dealer.
Amiable martial arts caper that should please the pre-teens.
w Edward Emanuel *story* Kenny Kim d Jon Turteltaub ph Richard Michalak m Rick Marvin pd Kirk Petruccelli ed David Rennie
☆ Victor Wong, Michael Treanor, Max Elliott Slade, Chad Power, Rand Kingsley, Alan McRae, Margarita Franco, Toru Tanaka
'The gracefully choreographed spectacle of three little boys fighting hordes of evil adult ninjas is a surefire juve crowd-pleaser.' – *Variety*

3 Ninjas Kick Back
👫 US 1994 99m Foto-Kem
TriStar/Sheen/Ben-Ami/Leeds (James Kang, Arthur Leeds, Martha Chang)
▤ ⌒.

Three boys travel to Japan to help their grandfather save a ceremonial dagger from an evil businessman who hopes to find buried treasure with its help.

Dreary children's movie that is a mix of fart jokes and violent slapstick; it condescends to its audience, particularly in the bad guy's unmotivated redemption at the end.
w Mark Saltzman *screenplay* Simon Sheen d Charles T. Kanganis ph Christopher Faloona m Richard Marvin pd Hiroyuki Takatsu, Gregory Martin ed Jeffrey Reiner, David Rennie
☆ Victor Wong, Max Elliott Slade, Sean Fox, Evan Bonifant, Caroline Junko King, Dustin Nguyen, Alan McRae, Margarita Franco, Jason Schombing, Angelo Tiffe, Sab Shimono

3 Ninjas Knuckle Up
👫 US 1995 85m colour
TriStar/Sheen (Martha Chang)
▣ ▤

Three brothers who excel at martial arts help defeat a corrupt businessman who is dumping toxic waste on tribal land.
Crude slapstick kiddie picture of minimal interest.
w Alex S. Kim d Simon S. Sheen ph Eugene Shlugleit m Gary Stevan Scott pd Don Day ed Pam Choules
☆ Victor Wong, Charles Napier, Michael Treanor, Max Elliott Slade, Chad Power, Crystle Lightning, Patrick Kilpatrick, Donald L. Shanks
'Thoroughly second-rate in all regards, with slapdash production values, cartoonish performances, by-the-numbers scripting and ridiculous martial arts fight scenes.' – *Variety*
† Made in 1992, but not released until later.

Three O'Clock High
US 1987 101m DeLuxe
Universal (David E. Vogel)
▣ ▤ ⌒.

A timid high school journalist is assigned to write a profile of a thuggish new student, who challenges him to a fight.
Dull, heavy-handed comedy of adolescent life that will mean little outside America; even those who can identify with its notions of student life are likely to find it uninteresting.
w Richard Christian Matheson, Thomas Szollosi d Phil Joanou ph Barry Sonnenfeld (credited as lighting consultant) m Tangerine Dream, Sylvester Levay pd William F. Matthews ed Joe Ann Fogle
☆ Casey Siemaszko, Anne Ryan, Richard Tyson, Jonathan Wise, Stacey Glick, Jeffrey Tambor, Philip Baker Hall, John P. Ryan

'Just your average Girl meets Girl. Girl loses Girl. Girl hires Boy to get Girl back story. With a twist.'
Three of Hearts
US 1992 110m DeLuxe
Guild/Three of Hearts/New Line (Joel B. Michaels, Matthew Irmas)
▣

A gigolo is hired by a lesbian to break the heart of her bisexual lover so that she will return to her.
Trite tale of sexual role-playing that pussyfoots around before coming to a predictable conclusion.
w Adam Greenman, Mitch Glazer d Yurek Bogayevicz ph Andrzej Sekula m Richard Gibbs pd Nelson Coates ed Dennis M. Hill, Suzanne Hines
☆ William Baldwin, Kelly Lynch, Sherilyn Fenn, Joe Pantoliano, Gail Strickland, Cec Verrell, Claire Callaway, Marek Johnson
'Shallow, contrived and less than credible. But marvellously exploiting New York's downtown world, it is a commercially slick and appealing film.' – *Variety*

The Three of Us: see Noi Tre

'Move over, Casanova!'
Three on a Couch
US 1966 109m Technicolor
Columbia/Jerry Lewis Productions (Jerry Lewis)
An artist tries to cure the sexual hang-ups of his psychiatrist fiancée's three female patients.
Intolerably lengthy and witless comedy.
w Bob Ross, Samuel A. Taylor, Arne Sultan, Marvin Worth d Jerry Lewis ph W. Wallace Kelley m Louis Brown
☆ Jerry Lewis, Janet Leigh, James Best, Mary Ann Mobley, Gila Golan, Leslie Parrish, Kathleen Freeman, Fritz Feld
'A long drag through stock situations.' – *MFB*
'Unintentionally unfunny.' – *Leonard Maltin*
'Stay on your own couch and don't bother with Jerry's.' – *Steven Scheuer*

Three on a Match *
US 1932 63m bw
Warner (Sam Bischoff)
▤

Three schoolgirl friends meet again in the big city, after which their paths cross melodramatically.
Predictable, watchable multi-story dramatics with an ironic twist: remade in 1938 as Broadway Musketeers.
w Lucien Hubbard d Mervyn Le Roy ph Sol Polito
☆ Joan Blondell, Bette Davis, Ann Dvorak, Warren William, Grant Mitchell, Lyle Talbot, Humphrey Bogart, Glenda Farrell, Clara Blandick
'A nice picture descending to mediocrity in its final two reels.' – *Variety*

Three on a Weekend: see Bank Holiday

3 Ring Circus
US 1954 103m Technicolor Vistavision
Paramount/Hal B. Wallis
Ex-army veterans join a circus.
The mixture as before from Martin and Lewis: variety acts interspersed with sentiment and heavy mugging.
w Don McGuire d Joseph Pevney ph Loyal Griggs m Walter Scharf
☆ Dean Martin, Jerry Lewis, Joanne Dru, Zsa Zsa Gabor, Wallace Ford, Sig Rumann, Gene Sheldon, Nick Cravat, Elsa Lanchester
'I wouldn't point to 3 Ring Circus with any great deal of pride, and neither would anyone else.' – *Joseph Pevney*

Three Russian Girls
US 1943 80m bw
United Artists (Gregor Rabinovitch)
GB title: *She Who Dares*
A remake of the Russian film *Girl from Stalingrad*, about a nurse called for duty at the front.
Sheer propaganda, almost unwatchable now.
w Maurice Clark, Victor Trivas, Aben Kandel, Dan James d Fedor Ozep, Henry Kesler m W. Franke Harling
☆ Anna Sten, Kent Smith, Mimi Forsythe, Alexander Granach, Kathy Frye, Paul Guilfoyle, Feodor Chaliapin
♫ W. Franke Harling

Three Sailors and a Girl
US 1953 95m Technicolor
Warner (Sammy Cahn)
A ship's funds are unofficially invested in a musical show.
Undernourished comedy musical.
w Roland Kibbee, Devery Freeman *play* The Butter and Egg Man by George S. Kaufman d Roy del Ruth ph Carl Guthrie *songs* Sammy Fain, Sammy Cahn
☆ Jane Powell, Gordon MacRae, Gene Nelson, Sam Levene, George Givot, Veda Ann Borg

'A haunting tale of changes, choices and second chances.'
Three Seasons
US/Vietnam 1999 109m FotoKem
Pathé/October/Open City/The Goatsingers (Jason Kliot, Joana Vicente, Tony Bu)
▤

aka: *Ba Mua*
An American former marine searches for the daughter he left behind in Saigon after the end of the Vietnam war.
Slight, sentimental tale of loss and love, emphasising the beauty of the temples and gardens in which the action takes place.
wd Tony Bui ph Lisa Rinzler m Richard Horowitz pd Wing Lee ed Keith Reamer
☆ Don Duong, Nguyen Ngoc Hiep, Tran Manh Cuong, Harvey Keitel, Zoe Bui, Nguyen Huu Duoc, Diem Kieu, Bui Tuong Trac
'Never rises above mediocrity.' – *Edward Porter, Sunday Times*

Three Secrets *
US 1950 98m bw
Warner/US Pictures (Milton Sperling)
▤

Three women wait anxiously to find out whose child survived a plane crash.
Well-made, formula woman's picture.
w Martin Rackin, Gina Kaus d Robert Wise ph Sid Hickox m David Buttolph

---

⊚ Digital Video Disc Region 2 ⊘ Digital Video Disc Region 1 ⌒ Soundtrack released on compact disc ☆ Cast in approximate order of importance † Points of interest ♫ Notable songs ▲ Academy Award ♫ Academy Award nomination ▽ BAFTA

☆ Eleanor Parker, Patricia Neal, Ruth Roman, Frank Lovejoy, Leif Erickson, Ted de Corsia, Edmon Ryan, Larry Keating

Three Sisters **

Italy/France/Germany 1987 112m colour
Erre/Reteitalia/Bioskop/Cinémax (Angelo Rizzoli)
original title: *Paura e Amore*

In a northern university town, family certainties crumble as three sisters experience unsatisfactory love affairs, two of them with the same married man, and their brother makes an unhappy marriage.

Family drama tinged with melancholy and disappointments, a variation on Chekhov's play of frustration and despair.

w Dacia Maraini, Margerethe von Trotta
d Margarethe von Trotta ph Giuseppe Lanci
m Franco Piersanti ad Giantito Burchiellaro
ed Enzo Meniconi

☆ Fanny Ardant, Greta Scacchi, Valeria Golino, Peter Simonischek, Sergio Castellito, Agnès Soral, Paolo Hendel, Jan-Paul Biczyski

The Three Sisters *

GB 1970 165m Eastmancolor
Alan Clore Films

At the turn of the century, three fatherless sisters dream of abandoning Russian provincial life for the big city.

Filmed Chekhov, better than most but still lacking cinematic vigour.

translator Moura Budberg d Laurence Olivier
ph Geoffrey Unsworth m William Walton

☆ Laurence Olivier, Joan Plowright, Jeanne Watts, Louise Purnell, Derek Jacobi, Alan Bates, Ronald Pickup

Three Smart Girls **

US 1936 86m bw
Universal (Joe Pasternak)

Three sisters bring their parents back together.
Pleasant, efficient family film which made a world star of Deanna Durbin.

w Adele Commandini, Austin Parker story Adele Commandini d Henry Koster ph Joseph Valentine md Charles Previn

☆ Deanna Durbin, Barbara Read, Nan Grey, Charles Winninger, Binnie Barnes, Ray Milland, Alice Brady, Mischa Auer, Ernest Cossart, Hobart Cavanaugh

'Surefire entertainment for any and all types of audiences. It also has that rare quality of making an audience feel better for having seen it.' – *Variety*

'Idiotically tuned in to happiness, but it isn't boring.' – *New Yorker, 1978*

'Clever, intelligent and witty, this delightful bit of entertainment has a genuineness which is rare.' – *Photoplay*

† Remade as *Three Daring Daughters*.
⬩ best picture; original story

Three Smart Girls Grow Up *

US 1939 87m bw
Universal (Joe Pasternak)

A girl helps her sisters to find beaus.
More of the above, quite palatable but inevitably warmed over.

w Bruce Manning, Felix Jackson d Henry Koster
ph Joe Valentine

☆ Deanna Durbin, Helen Parrish, Nan Grey, Charles Winninger, Robert Cummings, William Lundigan, Ernest Cossart, Nella Walker

'The white feminine room which the three sisters share, the quilted beds, the little furry jackets over the pajamas – the whole upholstery is so virginal that it evokes little twitters of nostalgia from the stalls. Pillow fights and first love and being sent to bed without any dinner – the awkward age has never been so laundered and lavendered and laid away.' – *Graham Greene*

Three Strange Loves *

Sweden 1949 84m bw
Svensk Filmindustri
original title: *Törst*
aka: *Thirst*

A married couple tear each other apart on a train journey from Switzerland through Germany to Sweden, while the husband's former lover suffers a breakdown and commits suicide.

Gloomy domestic drama, reminiscent of Strindberg in its depiction of a couple locked together in a struggle neither can win without destroying them both.

w Herbert Grevenius novel Birgit Tengroth
d Ingmar Bergman ph Gunnar Fischer m Erik Nordgren ad Nils Svenwall ed Oscar Rosander

☆ Eva Henning, Birger Malmsten, Birgit Tengroth, Mimi Nelson, Hasse Ekman, Bengt Eklund, Gaby Stenberg, Naima Wifstrand

Three Strangers *

US 1946 92m bw
Warner (Wolfgang Reinhardt)

A sweepstake ticket brings fortune and tragedy to three ill-assorted people.

Humdrum pattern play: the stars work hard to bring a little magic to it.

w John Huston, Howard Koch d Jean Negulesco
ph Arthur Edeson m Adolph Deutsch

☆ Sydney Greenstreet, Peter Lorre, Geraldine Fitzgerald, Joan Lorring, Robert Shayne, Marjorie Riordan, Arthur Shields

Three Stripes in the Sun

US 1955 93m bw
Columbia (Fred Kohlmar)
GB title: *The Gentle Sergeant*

After World War II, a Japanese-hating sergeant in the US occupation forces helps a poverty-stricken orphanage.

Predictable sentimentality based on fact, with good background detail.

wd Richard Murphy articles E. J. Kelly
ph Burnett Guffey m George Duning

☆ Aldo Ray, Phil Carey, Dick York, Chuck Connors, Mitsuko Kimura

3.10 to Yuma **

US 1957 92m bw
Columbia (David Heilwell)

A sheriff has to get his prisoner on to a train despite the threatening presence of the prisoner's outlaw friends.

Tense, well-directed but rather talky low-budget Western: excellent performances and atmosphere flesh out an unconvincing physical situation.

w Halsted Welles d Delmer Daves ph Charles Lawton Jnr m George Duning

☆ Glenn Ford, Van Heflin, Felicia Farr, Leora Dana, Henry Jones, Richard Jaeckel, Robert Emhardt

'A vivid, tense and intelligent story about probable people, enhanced by economical writing and supremely efficient direction and playing.' – *Guardian*

'We experimented by not filling the shadows with reflected light.' – *Delmer Daves*

Three Violent People

US 1956 100m Eastmancolor Vistavision
Paramount (Hugh Brown)

Brother ranchers quarrel over the wife of one of them, an ex-saloon hostess.

Characterless 'character' Western, a long way after Duel in the Sun.

w James Edward Grant d Rudolph Maté ph Loyal Griggs m Walter Scharf

☆ Charlton Heston, Anne Baxter, Gilbert Roland, Tom Tryon, Bruce Bennett, Forrest Tucker, Elaine Stritch, Barton MacLane

The Three Weird Sisters

GB 1948 82m bw
British National (Louis H. Jackson)

Three old maids in a Welsh village plot to kill their rich half-brother but are swept away by a flood.

All-stops-out melodrama which doesn't quite work and is generally remembered, if at all, for the last third of its writing team.

w Louise Birt, David Evans, Dylan Thomas
novel Charlotte Armstrong d Dan Birt ph Ernest Palmer

☆ Nancy Price, Mary Clare, Mary Merrall, Nova Pilbeam, Raymond Lovell, Anthony Hulme

Three Wise Fools

US 1946 90m bw
MGM (William Wright)

Three crusty old gents adopt an orphan, who softens them.

Antediluvian whimsy without the expected fun, remade from a silent.

w John McDermott, James O'Hanlon play Austin Strong d Edward Buzzell m Bronislau Kaper

☆ Margaret O'Brien, Lionel Barrymore, Thomas Mitchell, Edward Arnold, Lewis Stone, Jane Darwell, Harry Davenport, Cyd Charisse

Three Wise Girls

US 1932 80m bw
Columbia

Three small-town girls gain wisdom in New York.
Three millgirls' romances for the price of one. Adequate, predictable romantic fodder of its time.

w Robert Riskin, Agnes C. Johnson d William Beaudine ph Ted Tetzlaff

☆ Jean Harlow, Mae Clarke, Walter Byron, Marie Prevost, Andy Devine, Natalie Moorhead, Jameson Thomas

'Should turn in a respectable score ... Miss Harlow fails to be convincing.' – *Variety*

Three Wishes

🏋 US 1995 114m DeLuxe
Entertainment/Rysher (Gary Lucchesi, Clifford Green, Ellen Green)

In the mid-50s, a widow with two young sons runs over a dog and his owner, a tramp, and takes them home with her.

A fairy tale about getting what you wish for, oozing nostalgia and sweetness, hard to take if you are over ten years old.

w Elizabeth Anderson story Clifford Green, Ellen Green d Martha Coolidge ph Johnny E. Jensen m Cynthia Millar pd John Vallone ed Stephen Cohen

☆ Patrick Swayze, Mary Elizabeth Mastrantonio, Joseph Mazello, Seth Mumy, David Marshall Grant, Michael O'Keefe, Diane Venora

'The kind of sentimental fable that might, in the old days, have made more sense than it does now.' – *Derek Malcolm, Guardian*

Three Women *

US 1924 60m bw silent
Warner

A rake charms three women, each for a different purpose.

Subtle satirical comedy; not one of the director's masterpieces, but with enough barbs to keep one watching.

w Ernst Lubitsch, Hans Kraly novel The Lilie by Yolanthe Marees d Ernst Lubitsch ph Charles Van Enger

☆ Lew Cody, Pauline Frederick, May McAvoy, Marie Prevost

Three Women

US 1977 123m DeLuxe Panavision
TCF/Lion's Gate (Robert Altman)

Three women come to California for different reasons; when their problems become insurmountable they rely on each other.

Tiresomely somnambulistic multi-character drama, half a satire, half a wallow, and never an entertainment.

wd Robert Altman ph Charles Rosher m Gerald Busby

☆ Sissy Spacek, Janice Rule, Shelley Duvall, Robert Fortier, Ruth Nelson, John Cromwell, Sierra Pecheur

Three Women in Love: see *Der Philosoph*

The Three Worlds of Gulliver

🏋 US/Spain 1959 100m Technicolor
Columbia/Morningside (Charles Schneer)

Gulliver's adventures in Lilliput and Brobdingnag.
Flat treatment of marvellous material, with all the excitement squeezed out of it and not even much pizazz in the trick photography.

w Arthur Ross, Jack Sher d Jack Sher ph Wilkie Cooper m Bernard Herrmann sp Ray Harryhausen

☆ Kerwin Mathews, Basil Sydney, Mary Ellis, Jo Morrow, June Thorburn, Grégoire Aslan, Charles Lloyd Pack, Martin Benson

The Threepenny Opera: see *Die Dreigroschenoper*

'One girl, two guys, three possibilities.'

Threesome

US 1994 93m Foto-Kem
Columbia TriStar/MPCA (Bud Krevoy, Steve Stabler)

At university, one woman and two men share a room and their sexuality.

A sophomore version of Jules et Jim, rather too earnest and conventional about its ménage à trois.

wd Andrew Fleming ph Alexander Gruszynski
m Thomas Newman pd Ivo Cristante
ed William C. Carruth

☆ Lara Flynn Boyle, Stephen Baldwin, Josh Charles, Alexis Arquette, Martha Gehman, Mark Arnold, Michele Matheson

'Satisfyingly blunt and truthful under all the pranks and sexual mischief.' – *Variety*

Thrill of a Lifetime

US 1937 72m bw
Paramount

Summer campers put on a show which goes to Broadway.

Stereotyped lower-case musical with agreeable acts.

w Seena Owen, Grant Garrett, Paul Gerard Smith
d George Archainbaud

☆ Judy Canova, Ben Blue, the Yacht Club Boys, Eleanore Whitney, Betty Grable, Johnny Downs, Dorothy Lamour, Larry Crabbe

'Lightweight but pleasant.' – *Variety*

Thrill of a Romance

US 1945 105m Technicolor
MGM (Joe Pasternak)

A lady swimmer falls for a returning serviceman.
Empty musical vehicle with nothing memorable about it except the waste of time and money.

w Richard Connell, Gladys Lehman d Richard Thorpe ph Harry Stradling md George Stoll

☆ Esther Williams, Van Johnson, Lauritz Melchior, Frances Gifford, Henry Travers, Spring Byington, Tommy Dorsey

The Thrill of Brazil

US 1946 90m bw
Columbia (Sidney Biddell)

An American impresario in Brazil tries to win back his estranged wife.

Efficient but unpersuasive musical, another result of the good neighbour policy.

w Allen Rivkin, Harry Clork, Devery Freeman
d S. Sylvan Simon

☆ Evelyn Keyes, Keenan Wynn, Ann Miller, Allyn Joslyn, Tito Guizar, Veloz and Yolanda, Felix Bressart

The Thrill of It All *

US 1963 104m Eastmancolor
U-I/Ross Hunter/Arwin (Ross Hunter, Marty Melcher)

The wife of a gynaecologist becomes an advertising model, and work pressures disrupt her marriage.

Glossy matrimonial farce which starts brightly but eventually flags and becomes exhausting. Its better jokes linger in the memory.

w Carl Reiner d Norman Jewison ph Russell Metty m Frank de Vol

☆ Doris Day, James Garner, Arlene Francis, Edward Andrews, Reginald Owen, ZaSu Pitts, Elliott Reid

'Pleasantly reminiscent of some of the screwball comedies of the thirties.' – *MFB*

Throne of Blood ****

Japan 1957 105m bw
Toho (Akira Kurosawa, Sojiro Motoki)

original title: *Kumonosu-Jo*

A samurai, spurred on by his wife and an old witch, murders his lord at Cobweb Castle.

A Japanese version of Macbeth with a savage and horrifying final sequence. The whole film is a treat to look at.

w Hideo Oguni, Shinobu Hashimoto, Ryuzo Kikushima, Akira Kurosawa play William Shakespeare d Akira Kurosawa ph Asaichi Nakai m Masaru Sato ad Yoshiro Muraki, Kohei Ezaki

☆ Toshiro Mifune, Isuzu Yamada, Takashi Shimura, Minoru Chiaki, Akira Kubo, Takamaru Sasaki, Chieko Naniwa

'Its final impression is of a man who storms into a room with an impassioned speech to deliver and then discovers that he has forgotten what he came to say.' – *Kenneth Cavander, MFB*

🏋 film suitable for family viewing   📼 VHS video-cassette for the British PAL system   📼 VHS video-cassette for the British PAL system in wide screen-format   ⟳ Video cassette in a computer-colourised version   ▤ American NTSC video-cassette   ⌀ Laser disc

Through a Glass Darkly *

Sweden   1961   91m   bw
Svensk Filmindustri

⊚ ▤

Four unfulfilled people on a remote island fail to communicate with each other or to understand what God is.

It sounds like a parody Bergman film, and it almost is. The same themes were carried through in Winter Light *and* The Silence.

wd Ingmar Bergman ph Sven Nykvist m Bach
☆ Harriet Andersson, Gunnar Bjornstrand, Max von Sydow, Lars Passgard

🏆 best foreign film
🏅 Ingmar Bergman (as writer)

Through Different Eyes

US   1942   65m   bw
TCF

A veteran DA cites an old murder case to illustrate the dangers of circumstantial evidence.

Neat and peppy crime programme filler.

w Samuel G. Engel d Thomas Z. Loring
☆ Frank Craven, Donald Woods, Vivian Blaine, Mary Howard, Jerome Cowan

Throw Momma from the Train *

US   1987   88m   DeLuxe
Orion (Larry Brezner)

⊚ ▤ 🎧

After seeing Strangers on a Train, a student tries to persuade his professor to 'swap' murders.

Cheerful black comedy-cum-homage to Hitchcock.

w Stu Silver d Danny DeVito ph Barry Sonnenfeld m David Newman pd Ida Random
☆ Danny DeVito, Billy Crystal, Anne Ramsey, Kim Greist, Kate Mulgrew

'Very clever and engaging from beginning to end.' – Variety
🏅 Anne Ramsey

Thumb Tripping *

US   1972   94m   DeLuxe
Avco (Robert Chartoff, Irwin Winkler)

▤

A boy and a girl hitch-hiker in California have a variety of violent adventures.

Tail end of the Easy Rider fashion, with odd moments of interesting detail.

w Don Mitchell novel Don Mitchell d Quentin Masters ph Harry Stradling Jnr m Bob Thompson
☆ Michael Burns, Meg Foster, Marianna Hill, Bruce Dern

'Follow Your Heart And Nothing Is Impossible.'

Thumbelina

👫 US/Eire   1994   87m   Technicolor
Warner/Don Bluth

⊚ ▤ ⊚ 🎧

aka: Don Bluth's Thumbelina

The adventures of a tiny girl before she is reunited with her fairy prince.

A dull film that cannot stand comparison with Disney's recent animated resurgence; the animation is well done in a traditional style, but the narrative is lifeless.

w Don Bluth d Don Bluth, Gary Goldman m Barry Manilow, William Ross pd Rowland Wilson ed Thomas V. Moss
☆ Featuring Voices of Jodi Benson, Gino Conforti, Barbara Cook, Will Ryan, June Foray, Kenneth Mars, Gary Imhoff, Joe Lynch

'Highly conservative in both its story-telling and character-drawing and eventually rather a let-down.' – Derek Malcolm, Guardian

Thumbs Up

US   1943   67m   bw
Republic (Albert J. Cohen)

An American singing star in London is passed over in favour of talent from the war factories.

Curious hands-across-the-sea filler which gives the weirdest impression of Britain at war.

w Frank Gill Jnr d Joseph Santley
☆ Brenda Joyce, Richard Fraser, Elsa Lanchester, Arthur Margetson, J. Pat O'Malley, Gertrude Niesen, Andre Charlot

Thunder

US   1929   90m   bw   silent
MGM

A train driver has trouble with his sons.

Almost forgotten star melodrama, his last silent one, made when his health was already failing.

w Byron Morgan, Ann Price d William Nigh

☆ Lon Chaney, James Murray, George Duryea, Phyllis Haver

Thunder across the Pacific: see The Wild Blue Yonder

Thunder Afloat

US   1939   95m   bw
MGM

Rival boat owners vie for a 1918 navy contract, and the winner finds he has been trapped into enlisting.

Rumbustious Flagg-and-Quirt style comedy, good enough value for the undemanding.

w Ralph Wheelwright, Wells Root, Harvey Haislip d George B. Seitz
☆ Wallace Beery, Chester Morris, Virginia Grey, Douglass Dumbrille, Regis Toomey, Henry Victor, Jonathan Hale

'Timely actioner, cinch for exploitation.' – Variety

Thunder and Lightning

US   1977   93m   DeLuxe
TCF (Roger Corman)

▤

An independent maker of moonshine whiskey finds himself in competition with his girlfriend's father.

Action-filled comedy, mainly consisting of car and boat chases and crashes.

w William Hjortsberg d Corey Allen ph James Pergola m Andy Stein ed Anthony Redman
☆ David Carradine, Kate Jackson, Roger C. Carmel, Sterling Holloway, Ed Barth

Thunder Bay *

US   1953   102m   Technicolor
U-I (Aaron Rosenberg)

An engineer is convinced that oil can be raised from the Louisiana sea-bed.

Well-produced outdoor actioner.

w Gil Doud, John Michael Hayes d Anthony Mann ph William Daniels m Frank Skinner
☆ James Stewart, Joanne Dru, Dan Duryea, Jay C. Flippen, Antonio Moreno, Gilbert Roland, Marcia Henderson

Thunder Below

US   1932   71m   bw
Paramount

A wife loves her husband's best friend.

Dreary melodrama with a star already seen to be box-office poison.

novel Thomas Rourke d Richard Wallace
☆ Tallulah Bankhead, Charles Bickford, Paul Lukas

'Star as weak as story … dull and uneventful.' – Variety

Thunder Birds: see Thunderbirds

Thunder in the City

GB   1937   88m   bw
Atlantic (Akos Tolnay, Alexander Esway)

An American salesman in London helps a penniless duke promote a non-existent metal.

Mild satire on British and American idiosyncrasies, now very faded.

w Robert Sherwood, Aben Kandel, Akos Tolnay d Marion Gering ph Al Gilks m Miklos Rozsa
☆ Edward G. Robinson, Lulu Deste, Ralph Richardson, Nigel Bruce, Constance Collier, Arthur Wontner

'Cinch to be an important feature and satisfactory booking.' – Variety

Thunder in the East: see The Battle (1934)

Thunder in the East

US   1951   98m   bw
Paramount (Everett Riskin)

When India becomes independent in 1947, an American wanting to sell arms clashes with the peace-loving chief of a principality, but the arms are needed when rebels attack.

Artificial and boring action melodrama with platitudinous conversations.

w Jo Swerling novel Rage of the Vulture by Alan Moorehead d Charles Vidor ph Lee Garmes m Hugo Friedhofer
☆ Alan Ladd, Charles Boyer, Deborah Kerr, Corinne Calvet, Cecil Kellaway

Thunder in the Night

US   1935   69m   bw
Fox

A police captain solves the murder of a blackmailer.

Reasonably snappy mystery set in Budapest.

w Frances Hyland, Eugene Solow play A Woman Lies by Ladislas Fodor d George Archainbaud
☆ Edmund Lowe, Karen Morley, Paul Cavanagh, Una O'Connor, Gene Lockhart, John Qualen, Russell Hicks

'Tops average: deserves to do fairly well.' – Variety

Thunder in the Sun

US   1959   81m   Technicolor
Seven Arts/Carollton (Clarence Greene)

In 1847 an Indian scout guides a group of Basques to California with their vines.

Overwritten and melodramatic wagon train story.

wd Russel Rouse ph Stanley Cortez m Cyril Mockridge
☆ Susan Hayward, Jeff Chandler, Jacques Bergerac, Blanche Yurka, Carl Esmond

Thunder in the Valley: see Bob, Son of Battle

Thunder of Battle: see Coriolanus – Hero without a Country

'I'll make a soldier of you, Mr McQuade – if you don't break first!'

A Thunder of Drums *

US   1961   97m   Metrocolor   Cinemascope
MGM (Robert J. Enders)

Trouble with Apaches at a frontier post in 1870.

Solid, unexciting first-feature Western, some way after Ford.

w James Warner Bellah d Joseph Newman ph William Spencer m Harry Sukman
☆ Richard Boone, George Hamilton, Arthur O'Connell, Luana Patten, Richard Chamberlain, Charles Bronson

Thunder on the Hill

US   1951   84m   bw
U-I (Michael Kraike)
GB title: Bonaventure

In Norfolk, a nun solves a murder mystery during a flood.

Modest whodunnit with an unusual background but not much suspense.

w Oscar Saul, Andrew Solt play Bonaventure by Charlotte Hastings d Douglas Sirk ph William Daniels m Hans Salter
☆ Claudette Colbert, Ann Blyth, Robert Douglas, Anne Crawford, Philip Friend, Gladys Cooper, John Abbott, Connie Gilchrist, Gavin Muir

Thunder over Arizona

US   1956   75m   Trucolor   Naturama
Republic (Joe Kane)

Trouble in Tombstone, where a family fight to save their silver mine from a corrupt mayor and his hired guns.

A familiar cast plod along a well-trodden narrative in a pleasant but undistinguished Western.

w Sloan Nibley d Joe Kane ph Bud Thackery m R. Dale Butts ad Walter Keller ed Tony Martinelli
☆ Skip Homeier, Kristine Miller, George Macready, Wallace Ford, Jack Elam, Gregory Walcott, Nacho Galindo, John Doucette

Thunder over Mexico **

US   1933   60m   bw   silent (with music score)
Principal Pictures

The Upton Sinclair version of the troubled Eisenstein travelogue.

Packed with moments of genius, but not really a finished film in any sense.

m Hugo Reisenfeld

'It will not get to first base either as a critic's picture, or in straight box office parlance … beautiful, slow and dull.' – Variety
† See also Time in the Sun.

Thunder over the Plains

US   1953   82m   Warnercolor
Warner

After the Civil War, a Union officer is posted with his family to the southwest territory, and finds tension.

Busy but uninvolving Western programmer with a reliable star.

Thunder in the East ... (continued)

w Russell Hughes d André de Toth ph Bert Grennon m David Buttolph
☆ Randolph Scott, Phyllis Kirk, Lex Barker, Charles McGraw, Elisha Cook Jnr, Fess Parker

Thunder Road *

US   1958   92m   bw
UA/DRM (Robert Mitchum)

▤

Hillbilly bootleggers defy a Chicago gangster.

Downbeat but actionful crime melodrama with an unusual background and plenty of car chases.

w James Arlee Phillips, Walter Wise story Robert Mitchum d Arthur Ripley ph Alan Stensvold m Jack Marshall
☆ Robert Mitchum, Gene Barry, Jacques Aubuchon, Keely Smith, James Mitchum

Thunder Rock ***

GB   1942   112m   bw
Charter Films (John Boulting)

▤

A journalist disgusted with the world of the thirties retires to a lighthouse on Lake Michigan and is haunted by the ghosts of immigrants drowned a century before.

Subtle adaptation of an impressive and topical anti-isolationist play, very well acted and presented.

w Jeffrey Dell, Bernard Miles play Robert Ardrey d Roy Boulting ph Mutz Greenbaum (Max Greene) m Hans May
☆ Michael Redgrave, Lilli Palmer, Barbara Mullen, James Mason, Frederick Valk, Frederick Cooper, Finlay Currie, Sybilla Binder

'Boldly imaginative in theme and treatment.' – Sunday Express
'More interesting technically than anything since Citizen Kane.' – Manchester Guardian
'If I thought it wouldn't keep too many people away, I'd call it a work of art.' – Daily Express
'What a stimulus to thought it is, this good, brave, outspoken, unfettered picture.' – Observer

Thunder Run

US   1986   91m   DeLuxe
Cannon/Panache (Carol Lynn)

⊚ ▤

A truck driver is hired to drive across Nevada with a load of plutonium that has been targeted by a gang of terrorists.

Dull action thriller, too concerned with adding 'teen interest to maintain any suspense or interest; when it eventually comes, the action is unoriginal and mostly risible.

w Charles Davis, Carol Heyer story Clifford Wenger Snr, Carol Lynn d Gary Hudson ph Harvey Genkins m Jay Levy ad Carol Heyer ed Burton Lee Harry, Marcus Manton
☆ Forrest Tucker, John Ireland, John Shepherd, Jill Whitlow, Wally Ward, Marilyn O'Connor, Cheryl M. Lynn, Graham Ludlow, Alan Rachins, Tom Dugan

Thunderball **

👫 GB   1965   132m   Technicolor
Panavision
UA/Eon/Kevin McClory

⊚ ▤ ▤ ⊚ 🎧

James Bond goes underwater.

Commercially the most successful Bond, but certainly not the best despite a plethora of action sequences.

w Richard Maibaum, John Hopkins novel Ian Fleming d Terence Young ph Ted Moore m John Barry
☆ Sean Connery, Adolfo Celi, Claudine Auger, Luciana Paluzzi, Rik Van Nutter, Bernard Lee, Lois Maxwell, Martine Beswick

'The screenplay stands on tiptoe at the outermost edge of the suggestive and gazes yearningly down into the obscene.' – John Simon
🏆 special visual effects (John Stears)

Thunderbird Six

👫 GB   1968   90m   Techniscope
UA/AP/Century 21 (Gerry and Sylvia Anderson)

International Rescue combats the Black Phantom.

Bright, suspenseful puppetoon based on the TV series.

w Gerry and Sylvia Anderson d David Lane ph Harry Oakes m Barry Gray ad Bob Bell

'Holds some charm for adults, or at least for those who enjoy playing with miniature trains.' – MFB

Thunderbirds

US 1942 79m Technicolor
TCF (Lamar Trotti)
Problems of Arizona flight instructors during
World War II.
Very minor flagwaver.
w Lamar Trotti d William A. Wellman ph Ernest
Palmer m David Buttolph
☆ Gene Tierney, Preston Foster, John Sutton, Jack
Holt, May Whitty, George Barbier, Richard
Haydn, Reginald Denny, Ted North

Thunderbirds

US 1952 99m bw
Republic (John H. Auer)
An Oklahoma unit covers itself in glory during
World War II.
*Scrappy, noisy war actioner with much newsreel
footage.*
w Mary McCall Jnr d John H. Auer ph Reggie
Lanning m Victor Young
☆ John Derek, John Barrymore Jnr, Mona
Freeman, Ward Bond, Gene Evans

Thunderbolt **

US 1929 94m bw
Paramount
A gangster is caught, tried, and repents.
Gloomy melodrama with interesting style and credits.
w Jules Furthman, Herman J. Mankiewicz d Josef
von Sternberg ph Henry Gerrard
☆ George Bancroft, Fay Wray, Richard Arlen,
Tully Marshall, Eugénie Besserer
⅋ George Bancroft

Thunderbolt and Lightfoot *

US 1974 115m DeLuxe Panavision
UA/Malpaso (Robert Daley)
A bank robber escapes prison, disguises himself as a
preacher, befriends a young drifter, and discovers
that a new building stands on the spot where the
loot is hidden.
*Violent melodrama reworking an ancient comedy
situation; well made on its level.*
wd Michael Cimino ph Frank Stanley m Dee
Barton
☆ Clint Eastwood, Jeff Bridges, George Kennedy,
Geoffrey Lewis, Catherine Bach
⅋ Jeff Bridges

Thundercloud: see Colt 45

Thunderhead, Son of Flicka *

♔♔ US 1945 78m Technicolor
TCF (Robert Bassler)
More where My Friend Flicka came from.
*Unexceptionable family film with excellent outdoor
photography.*
w Dwight Cummins, Dorothy Yost novel Mary
O'Hara d Louis King ph Charles Clarke m Cyril
Mockridge
☆ Roddy McDowall, Preston Foster, Rita Johnson,
James Bell, Carleton Young

'Two Men From Different Worlds. Two Cops After
The Same Killer. Together They Must Uncover The
Secrets. Together They Must Discover The Truth.'

Thunderheart **

US 1992 119m DuArt
Columbia TriStar/Tribeca/Waterhorse (Robert DeNiro,
Jane Rosenthal, John Fusco)
A young FBI agent, assigned to help with a murder
investigation in a Sioux reservation, discovers
official connivance behind the killing.
*An enjoyable thriller that manages to deal with
questions of identity and self-discovery along the way.*
w John Fusco d Michael Apted ph Roger
Deakins m James Horner pd Dan Bishop ed Ian
Crafford
☆ Val Kilmer, Sam Shepard, Graham Greene,
Fred Ward, Fred Dalton Thompson, Sheila Tousey,
Chief Ted Thin Elk, John Trudell, Julius Drum,
Sarah Brave
'Reasonably engrossing as a mystery-thriller
despite its overburdened plot, Thunderheart
succeeds most in its captivating portrayal of
mystical Native American ways.' – Variety

Thunderstorm

GB 1955 88m bw
Hemisphere/Binnie Barnes
A Spanish fisherman rescues a mysterious girl from
a derelict yacht and falls in love with her although
the villagers regard her as a witch.
*Heady stuff on a low budget, quite smoothly done for
lovers of peasant drama.*
w George St George, Geoffrey Homes (Daniel
Mainwaring) d John Guillermin ph Manuel
Berenguer m Paul Misraki
☆ Linda Christian, Carlos Thompson, Charles
Korvin

Thursday's Child

GB 1942 81m bw
ABPC
A child from an ordinary family has success in
films and it goes to her head.
*Predictable domestic drama with some good moments,
but rather overpraised at the time.*
w Donald Macardle, Rodney Ackland
novel Donald Macardle d Rodney Ackland
☆ Sally Ann Howes, Wilfrid Lawson, Kathleen
O'Regan, Eileen Bennett, Stewart Granger, Felix
Aylmer

'Visit the future where love is the ultimate crime!'

THX 1138 *

US 1970 95m Technicolor/scope
Warner/American Zoetrope (Francis Ford Coppola,
Lawrence Sturhahn)
In a future society, computer programmed and
emotionless, an automated human begins to break
the rules.
*Orwellian science fiction; a thoughtful, rather cold
affair which is always good to look at.*
w George Lucas, Walter Murch d George Lucas
ph Dave Meyers, Albert Kihn m Lalo Schifrin
☆ Robert Duvall, Donald Pleasence, Don Pedro
Colley, Maggie McOmie, Ian Wolfe

Thy Soul Shall Bear Witness *

Sweden 1920 70m bw silent
Svensk Filmindustri
original title: Korkarlen
aka: The Phantom Carriage
A drunkard is knocked senseless, retraces his
misspent life, hears the carriage of death
approaching and returns to his family.
*Old-fashioned moralistic saga which hit the right note at
the time and has scenes which still impress.*
wd Victor Sjostrom novel Selma Lagerlöf ph J.
Julius Jaenzon
☆ Victor Sjostrom, Hilda Borgstrom, Astrid Holm
† Remade in France in 1939 by Julien Duvivier, as
La Charette Fantôme, with Pierre Fresnay and Louis
Jouvet; and again in Sweden in 1958 as Korkarlen,
by Arne Mattson.

Tiara Tahiti *

GB 1962 100m Eastmancolor
Rank/Ivan Foxwell
An up-from-the-ranks colonel and an aristocratic
smoothie captain continue their antipathy in
peacetime Tahiti, where one is nearly murdered
and the other gets his come-uppance.
*Uneasy mixture of light comedy and character drama;
enjoyable in parts, but flabbily assembled and muddily
photographed.*
w Geoffrey Cotterell, Ivan Foxwell
novel Geoffrey Cotterell d William T. Kotcheff
ph Otto Heller m Philip Green
☆ John Mills, James Mason, Herbert Lom, Claude
Dauphin, Rosenda Monteros

The Tichborne Claimant *

GB 1998 98m colour
Redbus/Bigger Picture/Swiftcall/IoMFC (Tom McCabe)
Sent to Australia to find the missing heir to the
Tichborne fortune, a black servant returns to
England with an imposter whom he has coached in
the role.
*Mildly enjoyable romp through a famous true
happening in Victorian England, one that caught the
imagination of the public; the film is unlikely to enjoy
such success, being ramshackle and not deft enough in
its satire on the high society of the time.*
w Joe Fisher d David Yates ph Peter Thwaites
m Nicholas Hooper pd Brian Sykes ed Jamie
Trevill

☆ Robert Pugh, John Kani, Stephen Fry, Robert
Hardy, John Gielgud, Rachael Dowling, Paola
Dionisotti, Charles Gray, James Villiers, Anita
Dobson, Dudley Sutton
'A fascinating, funny and very handsomely done
charmer.' – Angie Errigo, Empire

Tick, Tick, Tick... *

US 1969 100m Metrocolor Panavision
MGM/Nelson-Barrett (Ralph Nelson, James Lee
Barrett)
The first black sheriff in a Southern community
has trouble with murder and rape cases.
*Socially conscious suspenser, well enough made from
predictable elements and leading surprisingly to an
upbeat ending.*
w James Lee Barrett d Ralph Nelson ph Loyal
Griggs m Jerry Stynes
☆ Jim Brown, George Kennedy, Fredric March,
Lynn Carlin, Don Stroud, Clifton James

Ticket of Leave Man

GB 1937 71m bw
George King Productions (E. M. Smedley-Ashton)
The Tiger, 'the most dangerous killer in London',
falls in love with a singer.
*A ponderous mid-Victorian melodrama complete with
barnstorming acting, and interesting mainly as an
example of an earlier form of popular entertainment
faithfully translated to the screen.*
w H. F. Maltby, A. R. Rawlinson play Tom Taylor
d George King ph H. M. Glendining md Jack
Beaver ad Philip Bawcombe, Jack Hallward
ed Robert Walters
☆ Tod Slaughter, John Warwick, Marjorie Taylor,
Frank Cochran, Robert Adair
† The play was first produced in 1863. A typical
line of dialogue from the film preserves the flavour
of the original. A policeman gloats over the grave
of his adversary: 'You are avenged. And so shall
perish all who fall foul of Hawkshaw the detective.'

Ticket to Heaven *

Canada 1981 108m colour
Ronald Cohen Productions
A rootless young man is taken over by a religious
co-operative.
*Thinly veiled attack on the Moonies, quite well handled
but perhaps better as a straight documentary.*
w Ralph L. Thomas, Anne Cameron
book Moonwebs by Josh Freed d Ralph L. Thomas
ph Richard Leiterman m Maribeth Solomon
☆ Nick Mancuso, Saul Rubinek, Meg Foster, Kim
Cattrall

A Ticket to Tomahawk *

US 1950 90m Technicolor
TCF (Robert Bassler)
A stagecoach line defies the new Western railroad.
*Would-be satirical Western which doesn't quite have
the stamina and after some pleasing touches settles for
dullness.*
w Mary Loos d Richard Sale ph Harry Jackson
m Cyril Mockridge
☆ Anne Baxter, Dan Dailey, Rory Calhoun,
Walter Brennan, Charles Kemper, Connie
Gilchrist, Arthur Hunnicutt, Sen Yung

Tickle Me

US 1965 90m DeLuxe Panavision
AA (Ben Schwalb)
An unemployed rodeo star accepts a job at a health
ranch and helps a girl escape from villains after
hidden treasure.
*Wispy star vehicle with an unexpected haunted ghost
town climax.*
w Elwood Ullman, Edward Bernds d Norman
Taurog ph Loyal Griggs m Walter Scharf
☆ Elvis Presley, Julia Adams, Jocelyn Lane, Jack
Mullaney, Merry Anders, Connie Gilchrist

A Ticklish Affair

US 1963 95m Metrocolor Panavision
MGM/Euterpe (Joe Pasternak)
A naval commander in San Diego falls for a widow
with several children.
Thin romantic comedy with too many juvenile antics.
w Ruth Brooks Flippen d George Sidney
ph Milton Krasner m George Stoll, Robert Van
Eyps

☆ Shirley Jones, Gig Young, Red Buttons, Carolyn
Jones, Edgar Buchanan

'A highly strung love story...'

Tie Me Up! Tie Me Down!

Spain 1989 102m colour
Enterprise/El Deseo (Agustin Almodóvar)
original title: ¡Atame!
A man just released from a psychiatric hospital
kidnaps a drug-addicted pornographic film actress
and threatens to keep her tied up until she falls in
love with him.
*Shallow and glib, all surface and no substance, poorly
constructed and flashily photographed, it nevertheless
found some vociferous admirers.*
wd Pedro Almodóvar ph José Luis Alcaine
m Ennio Morricone ed Jose Salcedo
☆ Victoria Abril, Antonio Banderas, Loles Leon,
Francisco Rabal, Julieta Serrano, Maria Barranco,
Rossy de Palma, Lola Cardona
'The film never stops surprising, moving with
fluid momentum toward a tear-jerker ending
that verges on the comic but – at least the night
I saw it – left most viewers in tears.' – David
Leavitt, New York Times

The Tie that Binds

US 1995 98m Technicolor
Polygram/Interscope (David Madden, Patrick Markey,
John Morrissey, Susan Zachary)
A criminal couple who abandon their young
daughter later return to reclaim her and kill those
who have been caring for her.
*An unprepossessing thriller, crudely directed and given
over to gratuitous violence.*
w Michael Auerbach d Wesley Strick ph Bobby
Bukowski m Graeme Revell pd Marcia Hinds-
Johnson ed Michael N. Knue
☆ Daryl Hannah, Keith Carradine, Moira Kelly,
Vincent Spano, Julia Devin, Cynda Williams
'The drama soon turns into arrant melodrama
which would be laughable were it not so violent.
It's very silly and quite vicious, despite Strick's
ability to crank up the tension nicely.' – Derek
Malcolm, Guardian

Tiempo de Morir: see Time to Die

Tierra *

Spain 1995 125m colour Panavision
Metro/Tartan/Sogetel/Lola/Sogepaq/Canal+ (Lola
Pérez)
On a Spanish farm, a mysterious man with a split
personality becomes involved with a married
woman and her husband's mistress.
*An engrossing but confusing puzzle of a film, which
may, or may not, be about the intervention of an angel
in human affairs.*
wd Julio Medem ph Javier Aguirresarobe
m Alberto Iglesias ad Satur Idarreta ed Ivan
Aledo sp Computer Arts and Development
☆ Carmelo Gómez, Emma Suárez, Karra Elejalde,
Silke Klein, Nancho Nova, Txema Blasco, Ane
Sánchez
'Deliberately obscure but brilliantly made with
erotic intent. It is as clearly the work of a highly
cinematic film-maker. But where it comes from
and where it goes is well beyond me.' – Derek
Malcolm, Guardian

Tiffany Jones

GB 1973 90m Eastmancolor
Hemdale/Peter Walker
A model helps a prince overthrow the dictator who
deposed his father.
*Comic romp in the style of a Carry On movie with
some sex appeal.*
w Alfred Shaughnessy comic strip Pat Tourret,
Jenny Butterworth d Peter Walker ph Peter
Jessop m Cyril Ornadel ed Alan Brett
☆ Anouska Hempel, Ray Brooks, Susan Sheers,
Damien Thomas, Eric Pohlmann, Lynda Baron,
Bill Kerr
'In the place of humour, the production has
recourse to some of the more lethal devices of
British farce – funny foreigners and inflated
third-form puns.' – Gareth Jones, MFB

♔♔ film suitable for
family viewing · VHS video-cassette for
the British PAL system · VHS video-cassette for the British
PAL system in wide screen-format · ☆ Video cassette in a computer-
colourised version · American NTSC video-cassette · Laser disc

Tiger Bay **

GB 1959 105m bw
Rank/Wintle-Parkyn (John Hawkesworth)

A Polish seaman in Cardiff kills his faithless
girlfriend and kidnaps a child who proves more
than a match for him.
*Generally very proficient police chase melodrama with
strong characterizations: a considerable box-office
success of its time.*
w John Hawkesworth, Shelley Smith d J. Lee-
Thompson ph Eric Cross m Laurie Johnson
☆ Hayley Mills, John Mills, Horst Buchholz, Megs
Jenkins, Anthony Dawson, Yvonne Mitchell
ᵼ Hayley Mills (newcomer)

Tiger by the Tail

GB 1955 85m bw
Eros/Tempean (Robert S. Baker, Monty Berman)
An American journalist in London uncovers a
sinister conspiracy.
*Run-of-the-mill thriller which, although sticking to the
same basic narrative, emasculates its far better, more
cryptic source, stripping it of character and of the
genre's first anti-hero.*
w John Gilling, Willis Goldbeck novel Never
Come Back by John Mair d John Gilling ph Eric
Cross md Stanley Black ad Wilfred Arnold
ed Jack Slade
☆ Larry Parks, Constance Smith, Lisa Daniely,
Cyril Chamberlain, Donald Stewart, Thora Hird,
Joan Heal, Alexander Gauge, Doris Hare, Ronald
Leigh-Hunt
† The novel was the only thriller written by John
Mair (1913–42), who died in an RAF flying
accident. It was highly praised on its publication in
1941 by, among others, George Orwell and James
Agate.

Tiger Cage 2

Hong Kong 1990 91m colour
D & B (Stephen Shin)

A former cop, known as The Mad Dragon, and a
female lawyer become accidentally involved with
money-laundering, gangsters and murder.
*Broadly comic action movie, with coarse jokes and
much violence and gore, working up to a climax
involving sword, fist and gunfights.*
w Ip Kwong Kim d Yuen Wo Ping ph Lee Ping
Bing m Richard Yuen
☆ Donnie Yen, Rosamund Kwan, David Wu,
Robin Shou, Gary Chau, Carol Cheng

Tiger in the Sky: see The McConnell Story

Tiger in the Smoke *

GB 1956 94m bw
Rank (Leslie Parkyn)
Ex-commando criminals comb London for hidden
loot and threaten a young girl.
*Odd little melodrama with a complex plot and a
different, Graham Greene-like atmosphere.*
w Anthony Pelissier novel Marjorie Allingham
d Roy Baker ph Geoffrey Unsworth m Malcolm
Arnold
☆ Tony Wright, Muriel Pavlow, Donald Sinden,
Bernard Miles, Alec Clunes, Laurence Naismith,
Christopher Rhodes, Kenneth Griffith, Beatrice
Varley

The Tiger Makes Out *

US 1967 94m Technicolor
Columbia/Elan (George Justin)
A middle-aged New York postman takes revenge
on society by kidnapping a young girl – who rather
enjoys the experience.
*Semi-surrealist comedy misguidedly extended from a
two-character play; frantic pace prevents more than a
few effective moments.*
w Murray Shisgal play Murray Shisgal d Arthur
Hiller ph Arthur J. Ornitz m Milton Rogers
☆ Eli Wallach, Anne Jackson, Bob Dishy, David
Burns, Charles Nelson Reilly
'An attractive and bemusing piece of costume
jewelry – but not comparable to the real thing.' –
Judith Crist

Tiger Man: see The Lady and the Monster

Tiger of the Seven Seas

Italy/France 1963 90m colour
Liber Film/Euro International (Ottavio Poggi)

aka: *La Tigre de Sette Mari*
A pirate's daughter takes over his command to
revenge herself on his killer.
*Mundane swashbuckler with a heroine who lacks the
panache of Errol Flynn.*
w Luigi Capuano, Ottavio Poggi, Arpad de Riso
d Luigi Capuano ph Alvaro Mancori m Carlo
Rustichelli
☆ Gianna Maria Canale, Anthony Steel, Grazia
Maria Spina, Andrea Aureli

Tiger on the Beat

Hong Kong 1988 89m colour
Cinema City (Wellington W. Fung, Tsang Kwok Chi)

An idle, womanizing cop gets a new eager partner;
they are assigned to discover who murdered some
Thai drug dealers.
*An odd mixture of violent and bloody action and broad
comedy which is likely to have a limited appeal for most
Western audiences. (At one point a villain threatens to
have a kidnapped female hostage burned alive. When
that threat doesn't appear to work, he adds, 'Or do you
want her to get screwed by foreigners?', which has the
desired effect.)*
w Tsang Kwok Chi d Lau Kar Leung ph Cho On
Shun, Joe Chan Kwong Hung m Teddy Robin
Kwan ad Eric Lee ed Wong Ming Lam
☆ Chow Yun-Fat, Li Chi, Conan Lee, Ti Lung,
Tsui Shui Keung, Gordon Liu, Shirley Ng, Ko Fai,
Tommy Tam, John Keung, James Wong, Sun Tin
Ha
† The subtitling is erratic in its use of English, as
in 'My brother isn't easy to deal with, he's tear and
I have mucus', and 'I suspect her bra also contains
cock'.

Tiger Shark *

US 1932 80m bw
Warner
A tuna fisherman who has lost a hand to a shark
marries the daughter of an old friend, finds she
loves someone else, and is conveniently killed by
another shark.
*Vivid melodrama with a plot partly borrowed from
Moby Dick and itself partly borrowed by innumerable
other Warner films including Kid Galahad, The
Wagons Roll at Night, Slim and Manpower.*
w Wells Root story Tuna by Houston Branch
d Howard Hawks ph Tony Gaudio
☆ Edward G. Robinson, J. Carrol Naish, Zita
Johann
'Strong and exceedingly well played and directed
sea drama.' – Variety

A Tiger Walks *

ᵼᵼ US 1963 91m Technicolor
Walt Disney (Ron Miller)

In a small Western town, a tiger escapes from the
circus.
*A splendid animal and a happy ending help to make this
a pretty good film for children.*
w Lowell S. Hawley novel Ian Niall d Norman
Tokar ph William Snyder m Buddy Baker
☆ Sabu, Brian Keith, Vera Miles, Pamela
Franklin, Kevin Corcoran, Edward Andrews, Una
Merkel, Frank McHugh
'The Disney message runs true to form – grown-
ups should practise what they preach and
children are right about animals.' – MFB

Tiger Warsaw

US 1988 90m colour
Recorded Releasing/Continental Film Group/Cineplex
(Amin Q. Chaudhri)

After fifteen years away, a former drug-addict, who
shot his father, returns home.
Predictable and ponderous melodrama.
w Roy London d Amin Q. Chaudhri ph Robert
Draper m Ernest Troost pd Tom Targownik
ed Brian Smedley-Aston
☆ Patrick Swayze, Barbara Williams, Piper Laurie,
Lee Richardson, Mary McDonnell, Bobby DiCicco

The Tiger Woman

US 1944 bw serial: 12 eps
Republic

Oil drillers are delayed by jungle people led by a
strange white woman who proves to be an heiress
lost as a child in a plane crash.
Ho-hum hokum.
d Spencer Bennet, Wallace Grissell
☆ Allan Lane, Linda Stirling, Duncan Renaldo,
George J. Lewis, LeRoy Mason

A Tiger's Tale

US 1987 97m colour
Entertainment/Atlantic (Peter Douglas)

A middle-aged woman becomes pregnant as a
result of an affair with a high-school student.
Dire comedy with no visible or audible wit.
wd Peter Douglas novel Love and Other Natural
Disasters by Allen Hanney III ph Tony Pierce-
Roberts m Lee Holdridge pd Shay Austin
ed David Campling
☆ Ann-Margret, C. Thomas Howell, Charles
Durning, Kelly Preston, William Zabka, Ann
Wedgeworth, James Noble

The Tigger Movie

ᵼᵼ US 2000 77m Technicolor
Buena Vista/Walt Disney (Cheryl Abood)
Winnie-the-Pooh and his friends of the Hundred
Acre Wood help Tigger in his search for his
relatives.
*One of Disney's less distinguished efforts, a run-of-the-
mill animated cartoon, in which the bouncy Tigger
becomes a very soft and soppy toy; it may pass muster
with the very young.*
wd Jun Falkenstein story Eddie Guzelian
characters created by A.A. Milne m Harry
Gregson-Williams m/ly Richard M. Sherman,
Robert B. Sherman ad Toby Bluth
☆ Featuring voices of: Jim Cummings, Nikita
Hopkins, Ken Sansom, John Fiedler, Peter Cullen,
Andre Stojka, Kath Soucie, Tom Attenborough,
John Hurt
'By far the least ambitious, and certainly the
least interesting, animated feature to come out of
Disney in quite some time.' – Todd McCarthy,
Variety

Tight Little Island: see Whisky Galore

Tight Shoes

US 1941 67m bw
Universal/Mayfair (Jules Levey)
A political grafter buys tight shoes which have a
series of dramatic consequences.
*Moderately witty little comedy which conveyed the
Runyon flavour as well as any.*
w Leonard Spigelgass, Art Arthur story Damon
Runyon d Albert S. Rogell
☆ Broderick Crawford, Binnie Barnes, John
Howard, Anne Gwynne, Leo Carrillo, Samuel S.
Hinds, Shemp Howard

Tight Spot

US 1955 97m bw
Columbia (Lewis J. Rachmil)

A material witness in the trial of a gangster is
released from prison in the custody of an attorney.
*Fairly routine crime melodrama with unexciting star
performances.*
w William Bowers play Dead Pigeon by Leonard
Kantor d Phil Karlson ph Burnett Guffey
m Morris Stoloff
☆ Edward G. Robinson, Ginger Rogers, Brian
Keith, Lorne Greene, Lucy Marlow, Katherine
Anderson

Tightrope

US 1984 114m Technicolor
Warner/Malpaso (Clint Eastwood, Fritz Manes)

A New Orleans detective investigating a series of
sex murders finds that his own impulses are none
too healthy.
*Boring, dimly lit and generally unappealing low life
thriller.*
wd Richard Tuggle ph Billy Bragg m Lennie
Niehaus
☆ Clint Eastwood, Geneviève Bujold, Dan
Hedaya, Alison Eastwood, Jennifer Beck

Tilai **

Burkina Faso/Switzerland/France 1990 81m
colour
Artificial Eye/Les Films de L'Avenir/Waka Films/Rhea
Films (Idrissa Ouedraogo)

Returning home after being away for two years, a
man discovers that his father has married his
fiancée.
*An African tragedy of domestic conflicts and broken
promises, told with an uncomplicated directness.*
wd Idrissa Ouedraogo ph Jean Monsigny, Pierre
Laurent Chenieux m Abdullah Ibrahim ed Luc
Barnier
☆ Rasmane Ouedraogo, Ina Cisse, Roukietou
Barry, Assane Ouedraogo, Sibidou Sidibe,
Moumouni Ouedraogo, Mariam Barry, Seydou
Ouedraogo
'There is no doubt about Idrissa Ouedraogo's
cinematic mastery.' – MFB

Till Death Us Do Part *

GB 1968 100m Eastmancolor
British Lion/Associated London Films (Jon
Pennington)

From the thirties to the sixties with loud-mouthed,
bigoted Londoner Alf Garnett.
*Unremarkable and frequently misguided opening-up of
a phenomenally successful TV series, adapted for the
US as All in the Family. The original cast wades
cheerfully enough through a bitty script; the sequel,
The Alf Garnett Saga, defeated them.*
w Johnny Speight d Norman Cohen ph Harry
Waxman m Wilfrid Burns
☆ Warren Mitchell, Dandy Nichols, Anthony
Booth, Una Stubbs, Liam Redmond, Bill Maynard,
Sam Kydd, Brian Blessed

Till Glädje: see To Joy

Till the Clouds Roll By **

US 1946 137m Technicolor
MGM (Arthur Freed)

The life and times of composer Jerome Kern.
*Better-than-average biopic with better-than-average
tunes and stars.*
w Myles Connolly, Jean Holloway d Richard
Whorf ph Harry Stradling, George J. Folsey
md Lennie Hayton
☆ Robert Walker, Judy Garland, Lucille Bremer,
Van Heflin, Mary Nash, Dinah Shore, Van
Johnson, June Allyson, Tony Martin, Kathryn
Grayson, Lena Horne, Frank Sinatra, Virginia
O'Brien
'A little like sitting down to a soda fountain de
luxe atomic special of maple walnut on vanilla
on burnt almond on strawberry on butter pecan
on coffee on raspberry sherbert on tutti frutti
with hot fudge, butterscotch, marshmallow,
filberts, pistachios, shredded pineapple, and
rainbow sprills on top, go double on the whipped
cream.' – James Agee
† Lucille Bremer's singing was dubbed by Trudy
Erwin.

Till the End of Time *

US 1946 105m bw
RKO (Dore Schary)

Three returning GIs find romance and problems in
their small town.
*Downbeat variation on The Best Years of Our Lives
with a theme tune which puts words to a Chopin
Polonaise.*
w Allen Rivkin d Edward Dmytryk ph Harry J.
Wild m Leigh Harline
☆ Dorothy McGuire, Guy Madison, Robert
Mitchum

Till There Was You

Australia 1990 95m colour
Rank/Five Arrows/Ayer/Southern Star (Jim McElroy)

An American barman investigates the mysterious
death of his brother in the South Pacific state of
Vanuatu.
*An unconvincing thriller that offers nothing but
occasionally spectacular photography.*
w Michael Thomas d John Seale ph Geoffrey
Simpson, Robert Primes m Graeme Revell
pd George Liddle, Susan Emshwiller ed Jill
Bilcock

☆ Mark Harmon, Deborah Unger, Jeroen Krabbé, Shane Briant, Ivan Kesa

Till We Meet Again

US 1936 87m bw
Paramount
Former sweethearts find themselves both spies, but on opposing sides.
Unconvincing but climactically suspenseful romantic drama.
w Edwin Justus Mayer, Franklin Coen, Brian Marlow *play* Alfred Davis d Robert Florey
☆ Herbert Marshall, Gertrude Michael, Lionel Atwill

'She came from a woman's world – into his world of men – and danger!'

Till We Meet Again

US 1944 88m bw
Paramount (David Lewis)
A French nun helps an American aviator escape from the Nazis.
Very moderate, nicely photographed, romantic war actioner.
w Lenore Coffee *play* Alfred Maury d Frank Borzage ph Theodor Sparkuhl m David Buttolph
☆ Ray Milland, Barbara Britton, Walter Slezak, Lucile Watson, Konstantin Shayne, Vladimir Sokoloff, Mona Freeman

Tillie and Gus *

US 1933 61m bw
Paramount (Douglas MacLean)
Two middle-aged cardsharps return home, help their niece and nephew win an inheritance, and come first in a paddleboat race.
Jumbled comedy with good moments and a rousing climax.
w Walter de Leon, Francis Martin d Francis Martin ph Benjamin Reynolds
☆ W. C. Fields, Alison Skipworth, Baby Le Roy, Jacqueline Wells, Clifford Jones, Clarence Wilson, Edgar Kennedy, Barton MacLane
'Very funny in spots, but not enough spots.' – *Variety*

Tillie's Punctured Romance *

US 1914 60m bw silent
Keystone/Mack Sennett
A country maid falls for a con man who steals her money; but she finally gets her revenge.
Museum piece comedy which no longer irritates the funny bone but has clear historical interest.
w Hampton Del Ruth *play* Tillie's Nightmare by Edgar Smith d Mack Sennett ph Frank D. Williams
☆ Marie Dressler, Charles Chaplin, Mabel Normand, Mack Swain

Tilly of Bloomsbury

GB 1940 83m bw
Hammersmith
The daughter of a boarding house keeper falls for a rich young man.
Basically a millgirl's romance, remembered for one final drunk scene for the star comedian.
w Nils Hostius, Jack Marks *play* Ian Hay d Leslie Hiscott
☆ Sydney Howard, Jean Gillie, Henry Oscar, Athene Seyler, Michael Wilding, Kathleen Harrison, Michael Denison, Martita Hunt, Athole Stewart
† Previous versions: 1921, with Tom Reynolds and Edna Best, for Samuelson; 1931, with Sydney Howard and Phyllis Konstam, for Sterling.

Tim

Australia 1979 98m colour
Pisces Productions (Michael Pate)
A romance develops between a wealthy middle-aged spinster and a young, simple-minded builder.
Sentimental melodrama, notable only as the film that launched the career of Mel Gibson.
wd Michael Pate *novel* Colleen McCullough ph Paul Onorato m Eric Jupp ad John Carroll ed David Stiven
☆ Piper Laurie, Mel Gibson, Alwyn Kurts, Pat Evison, Peter Gwynne, Deborah Kennedy

Tim Burton's The Nightmare before Christmas: see The Nightmare before Christmas

Timberjack

US 1954 94m Trucolor
Republic
A young man seeks his father's killer among forest lumberjacks.
Resiliently cast action story of no great interest.
w Allen Rivkin *novel* Dan Cushman d Joe Kane ph Jack Marta m Victor Young
☆ Sterling Hayden, Vera Ralston, Adolphe Menjou, David Brian, Hoagy Carmichael, Chill Wills, Jim Davis, Elisha Cook Jnr

Timbuktu

US 1958 92m bw
Imperial (Edward Small)
A gun runner quells a desert revolt in the French Sudan during World War II.
Leaden-footed melodrama full of stock characters despite its complex plot.
w Anthony Veiller, Paul Dudley d Jacques Tourneur ph Maury Gertsman m Gerald Fried
☆ Yvonne de Carlo, Victor Mature, George Dolenz, John Dehner, Marcia Henderson

Time after Time *

US 1980 112m Metrocolor Panavision
Warner/Orion (Herb Jaffe)
Jack the Ripper escapes via H. G. Wells's time machine from Victorian London to modern San Francisco; Wells gives chase and eventually projects him into limbo.
Amusing fantasy for those with light literary inclinations, marred by too much gore and a wandering middle section.
wd Nicholas Meyer *story* Karl Alexander, Steve Hayes m Paul Lohmann m Miklos Rozsa pd Edward Carfagno
☆ Malcolm McDowell, David Warner, Mary Steenburgen, Charles Cioffi, Kent Williams

Time Bandits *

GB 1981 113m Technicolor
HandMade Films (Terry Gilliam)
A schoolboy is taken through time by a group of demonic dwarfs.
Curious tall tale in which schoolboy fantasy alternates with violence and black comedy. In general, much less funny than it intended to be, but with some hilarious moments.
w Michael Palin, Terry Gilliam d Terry Gilliam ph Peter Biziou m Mike Moran pd Millie Burns
☆ John Cleese, Sean Connery, Ian Holm, Ralph Richardson, David Warner, Shelley Duvall, Katherine Helmond, Michael Palin, Peter Vaughan, David Rappaport

Time Bomb *

GB 1952 72m bw
MGM (Richard Goldstone)
US title: *Terror on a Train*
A saboteur places a bomb on a goods train travelling from the north of England to Portsmouth.
Tolerable suspenser padded out with domestic asides.
w Ken Bennett *novel* Death at Attention by Ken Bennett d Ted Tetzlaff ph Frederick A. Young m John Addison
☆ Glenn Ford, Anne Vernon, Maurice Denham, Harcourt Williams, Harold Warrender, Bill Fraser, John Horsley, Victor Maddern

Time Flies *

GB 1944 88m bw
GFD/Gainsborough (Edward Black)
A professor invents a time machine and takes his friends back to the court of Good Queen Bess.
Very passable star farce.
w J. O. C. Orton, Ted Kavanagh, Howard Irving Young d Walter Forde ph Basil Emmott md Louis Levy
☆ Tommy Handley, Felix Aylmer, Evelyn Dall, George Moon, Moore Marriott, Graham Moffatt, John Salew, Olga Lindo, Stephane Grappelly

Time for Action: see Tip on a Dead Jockey

A Time for Giving: see Generation

A Time for Killing

US 1967 83m Pathécolor Panavision
Columbia/Sage Western (Harry Joe Brown)
GB title: *The Long Ride Home*
Confederate prisoners escape from a Union fort and the commander sets off in pursuit.
Fairly savage Western with Something to Say about the corruption of war.
w Halsted Welles *novel* Southern Blade by Nelson and Shirley Wolford d Phil Karlson ph Kenneth Peach m Mundell Lowe
☆ Glenn Ford, George Hamilton, Inger Stevens, Max Baer, Paul Petersen, Timothy Carey, Todd Armstrong

A Time for Loving

GB 1971 104m colour
London Screen Plays/Mel Ferrer
Short romantic comedies set at different times in the same Paris flat.
Portmanteau ooh-la-la, quite neat but pitifully undernourished; certainly no Plaza Suite.
w Jean Anouilh d Christopher Miles ph Andreas Winding m Michel Legrand pd Theo Meurisse
☆ Joanna Shimkus, Mel Ferrer, Britt Ekland, Philippe Noiret, Lila Kedrova, Robert Dhery, Mark Burns, Susan Hampshire

Time Gentlemen Please

GB 1952 83m bw
Group Three (Herbert Mason)
A lazy tramp is the one blot on a prize-winning English village.
Artificial, thinly scripted and overlit sub-Ealing comedy with familiar characters and situations.
w Peter Blackmore *novel* Nothing to Lose by R. J. Minney d Lewis Gilbert ph Wilkie Cooper m Antony Hopkins
☆ Eddie Byrne, Hermione Baddeley, Jane Barrett, Robert Brown, Raymond Lovell, Marjorie Rhodes, Dora Bryan, Thora Hird, Sidney James, Edie Martin, Ivor Barnard, Sydney Tafler
'Quite a nice little picture.' – *Karel Reisz*

Time in the Sun ***

Mexico 1933 60m bw
Marie Seton
Unfinished fragments of Eisenstein's incomplete *Que Viva Mexico,* snippets from which were later released in various forms.
This is the longest and presumably best version, with splendidly pictorial sequences of peasant and Indian life culminating with Death Day, all skulls and fireworks. Clearly the work of a master, though if completed the film might well have been a bore.
w Marie Seton, Paul Burnford d Sergei Eisenstein ph Edouard Tissé

Time Limit *

US 1957 95m bw
UA/Richard Widmark, William Reynolds
During the Korean war an officer is courtmartialled for suspected collaboration.
Suspenseful talk piece from a somewhat intellectualized play.
w Henry Denker *play* Henry Denker, Ralph Berkey d Karl Malden ph Sam Leavitt m Fred Steiner
☆ Richard Widmark, Richard Basehart, Dolores Michaels, June Lockhart, Carl Benton Reid, Martin Balsam, Rip Torn
'The tightly constructed story leads logically and unfalteringly to a tense climax.' – *Lindsay Anderson*

Time Lock *

GB 1957 73m bw
Romulus (Peter Rogers)
A small boy is trapped in a bank vault just as it is being locked for the weekend.
Acceptable expansion of a Canadian TV suspenser.
w Peter Rogers *play* Arthur Hailey d Gerald Thomas ph Peter Hennessy m Stanley Black
☆ Robert Beatty, Betty McDowall, Vincent Winter, Lee Patterson, Alan Gifford, Robert Ayres

Time Lost and Time Remembered: see I Was Happy Here

The Time Machine *

US 1960 103m Metrocolor
MGM/Galaxy (George Pal)
A Victorian scientist builds a machine which after some trial and error transports him into the year 802701.
Surprisingly careful recreation of a period, and an undeniably charming machine, go for little when the future, including the villainous Morlocks, is so dull.
w David Duncan *novel* H. G. Wells d George Pal ph Paul C. Vogel m Russell Garcia ad George W. Davis, William Ferrari
☆ Rod Taylor, Yvette Mimieux, Alan Young, Sebastian Cabot, Tom Helmore, Whit Bissell, Doris Lloyd
♟ special effects (Gene Warren, Tim Baar)

A Time of Destiny

US 1988 118m colour
Rank/Columbia/Nelson Entertainment/Alive Films (Anna Thomas)
An immigrant's son swears vengeance on the GI who married his sister and inadvertently caused the death of his father.
Dull revenge drama set in the 1940s.
w Gregory Nava, Anna Thomas d Gregory Nava ph James Glennon m Ennio Morricone pd Henry Bumstead ed Betsy Blankett
☆ William Hurt, Timothy Hutton, Melissa Leo, Francisco Rabal, Concha Hidalgo, Stockard Channing, Megan Follows, Frederick Coffin

The Time of His Life

GB 1955 74m bw
Renown/Shaftesbury (Elizabeth Hiscott)
A former convict reluctantly returns home to his aristocratic daughter, who attempts to pass him off as a dim family servant.
Dull comedy, intended as a vehicle for the slapstick antics of its star in his role as Mr Pastry, but giving him few opportunities to shine.
wd Leslie Hiscott *story* Brock Williams ph Kenneth Talbot m Elizabeth Hiscott md Robin Richmond ad Duncan Sutherland ed Erwin Reiner
☆ Richard Hearne, Ellen Pollock, Richard Wattis, Robert Moreton, Frederick Leister, D'Arcy Conyers, John Downing, Anne Smith, Harry Towb

Time of Miracles *

Yugoslavia 1990 100m colour
Singidunum/Television Belgrad/Channel 4/Metropolitan (Goran Paskaljevic)
original title: *Vrema Cuda*
In September 1945, after the village school burns down, the victorious Communists commandeer the church and whitewash over its religious murals; but the paintings reappear and a stranger arrives who apparently can raise the dead.
Intriguing, if somewhat ponderous, account of faith, belief and their interactions with reality.
w Borislav Pekic, Goran Paskaljevic *novel* Borislav Pekic d Goran Paskaljevic ph Radoslav Vladic m Zoran Simjanovic ad Miodrag Nikolic ed Olga Skrigin, Olga Obradov
☆ Predrag Miki Manojlovic, Dragan Maksimovic, Svetozar Cvetkovic, Mirjana Karanovic, Danilo Bata Stojkovic, Mirjana Jokovic, Ljuba Tadic

Time of the Gypsies *

Yugoslavia 1989 142m colour
Enterprise/Forum Film/Sarajevo TV (Mirza Pasic)
original title: *Dom Za Vesanje*
A young gypsy with magic powers is forced to work with a band of itinerant thieves and beggars.
Cut from a six-part television series, the film, despite some lively episodes, suffers from a disjointed narrative, though that did not prevent Kusturica being voted best director at the Cannes Film Festival.
w Emir Kusturica, Gordan Mihic d Emir Kusturica ph Vilko Filac m Goran Bregovic pd Miljen Kljakovic ed Andrija Zafranovic
☆ Davor Dujmovic, Bora Todorovic, Ljubica Adzovic, Husnija Hasmovic, Sinolicka Trpkova, Zabit Memedov

---

The Time of Their Lives *
US 1946 82m bw
Universal (Val Burton)

Revolutionary ghosts haunt a country estate.
*Unusual, quite effective Abbott and Costello vehicle
with the comedians not playing as a team.*
w Val Burton, Walter de Leon, Bradford Ropes,
John Grant d Charles Barton ph Charles Van
Enger m Milton Rosen
☆ Bud Abbott, Lou Costello, Marjorie Reynolds,
Binnie Barnes, Gale Sondergaard, John Shelton

The Time of Your Life *
US 1948 109m bw
Cagney Productions (William Cagney)

A group of lovable eccentrics spend much of their
time philosophizing in a San Francisco bar.
*Not really a film at all, this essence of Saroyan
contains much to enjoy or to annoy. The performances
are pretty good.*
w Nathaniel Curtis play William Saroyan d H. C.
Potter ph James Wong Howe m Carmen Dragon
☆ James Cagney, William Bendix, Wayne Morris,
Jeanne Cagney, Gale Page, Broderick Crawford,
James Barton, Ward Bond, Paul Draper, James
Lydon, Richard Erdman, Natalie Schafer
'They have done so handsomely by Saroyan that
in the long run everything depends on how
much of Saroyan you can take.' - *Time*

Time Out for Romance
US 1937 75m bw
TCF

A millionairess runs from the altar and teams up
with a car factory driver.
*Weakish rehash of It Happened One Night, but the
script isn't up to the intention.*
w Lou Breslow, John Patrick, Eleanore Griffin,
William Rankin d Malcolm St Clair
☆ Claire Trevor, Michael Whalen, Joan Davis,
Chick Chandler, Douglas Fowley, William
Demarest, Andrew Tombes
'Just misses being able to stand on its own legs as
a solo performer.' - *Variety*

Time out of Mind
US 1947 88m bw
Universal-International (Robert Siodmak)
The housekeeper's daughter finances music studies
for the master's ungrateful son.
*Silly romantic melodrama with few visible
compensations.*
w Abem Finkel, Arnold Phillips novel Rachel
Field d Robert Siodmak ph Maury Gertsman
m Miklos Rozsa
☆ Phyllis Calvert, Robert Hutton, Ella Raines,
Eddie Albert, Leo G. Carroll

A Time out of War *
US 1954 20m bw
Terry and Denis Sanders
Two men on opposite sides of a river during the
American Civil War strike up a brief friendship.
Interesting but overpraised student piece.
wd Denis Sanders story Pickets by Robert W.
Chambers ph Terry Sanders m Frank Hamilton
☆ Barry Atwater, Robert Sherry, Alan Cohen

The Time, the Place and the Girl
US 1946 105m Technicolor
Warner (Alex Gottlieb)
Two night-club owners have problems.
*Lightweight musical, indistinguishable from a dozen
others.*
w Francis Swann, Agnes Christine Johnston, Lynn
Starling d David Butler ph William V. Skall
m Arthur Schwartz
☆ Dennis Morgan, Jack Carson, Janis Paige,
Martha Vickers, S. Z. Sakall, Alan Hale, Donald
Woods, Angela Greene, Florence Bates
♪ song 'A Gal in Calico' (mArthur Schwartz,
lyLeo Robin)

Time to Die **
Columbia/Cuba 1985 94m colour
Artificial Eye/Focine/ICIAC (Gabriel García Marquez)
original title: *Tiempo de Morir*
After serving an eighteen-year sentence for
murder, a man returns home to find that the
victim's sons are waiting to exact revenge.

Basically a Latin American Western, it grips the
attention in its exploration of masculine codes of
honour and duty.
w Gabriel García Marquez d Jorge Ali Triana
ph Mario Garcia Joya m Leo Brower, Nafer Duran
pd Patricia Bonilla ed Nelson Rodriquez
☆ Gustavo Angarita, Sebastian Ospina, Jorge
Emilio Salazar, Maria Eugenia Davila, Lina Botero,
Enrique Almirante

A Time to Kill *
US 1996 149m Technicolor Panavision
Warner/Monarchy/Regency (Arnon Milchan, Michael
Nathanson, Hunt Lowry, John Grisham)
🔲 ▤ ◉. ⊚
In a small Mississippi town, where the Ku Klux
Klan still has power, a young lawyer defends a
black father who killed the two white men arrested
for the rape of his young daughter.
*An old-style Hollywood melodrama, effectively staged
though making little effort to explore the issues
involved; it's content to endorse vigilante action
providing that it's not carried out by the Klan.*
w Akiva Goldsman novel John Grisham d Joel
Schumacher ph Peter Menzies Jnr m Elliot
Goldenthal pd Larry Fulton ed William
Steinkamp
☆ Matthew McConaughey, Sandra Bullock,
Samuel L. Jackson, Kevin Spacey, Oliver Platt,
Charles Dutton, Brenda Fricker, Donald
Sutherland, Kiefer Sutherland, Patrick McGoohan,
Ashley Judd
'Just another Hollywood courtroom drama.' -
Sight and Sound
† The film was among the financial successes of
1996, taking around $109m at the US box-office.

A Time to Live and a Time to Die: see *Le
Feu Follet*

The Time to Live and the Time to Die **
Taiwan 1985 137m colour
Central Motion Pictures
original title: *Tongnian Wangshi*
A Chinese man remembers growing up in Taiwan
in the 1950s and 60s as one of a large family
headed by his consumptive, intellectual father and
his doting, rambling grandmother who dreams of
returning to the mainland.
*An episodic, semi-autobiographical film of family life,
reaching few conclusions, other than those brought
about by death, but affording insight into the tensions
of everyday living.*
w Zu Tianwen, Hou Hsiao-hsien d Hou Hsiao-
hsien ph Li Pingbin m Wu Chuchu
☆ You Anshun, Tian Feng, Mei Fang, Tang
Ruyun, Xiao Ai, Xin Shufen, Hu Xiangping

A Time to Love and a Time to Die *
US 1958 132m Eastmancolor
Cinemascope
U-I (Robert Arthur)
▤
During World War II, a German officer on his last
leave solves problems at home but is killed on his
return to the front.
*Interesting but preachy and generally misguided
attempt, by the studio which made All Quiet on the
Western Front and The Road Back, to repeat the
dose in colour and wide screen.*
w Orin Jannings novel Erich Maria Remarque
d Douglas Sirk ph Russell Metty m Miklos Rozsa
☆ John Gavin, Lilo Pulver, Keenan Wynn, Jock
Mahoney, Thayer David, Agnes Windeck, Erich
Maria Remarque

The Time Travelers *
US 1964 84m Pathécolor
AIP/Dobie (William Redlin)
▤
Scientists venture 107 years into the future, and on
escaping find themselves in a time trap.
*Ingenious and lively low-budget science fiction with a
sobering ending.*
wd Ib Melchior ph William Zsigmond m Richard
La Salle
☆ Preston Foster, Phil Carey, Merry Anders, John
Hoyt, Joan Woodbury

Time without Pity *
GB 1957 88m bw
Harlequin (John Arnold, Anthony Simmons)
An alcoholic arrives in London to seek new
evidence which will prevent his son from being
executed for murder.

*Heavy-going, introspective, hysterical, downbeat
melodrama which takes itself with a seriousness which
is almost deadly.*
w Ben Barzman play Someone Waiting by Emlyn
Williams d Joseph Losey ph Freddie Francis
m Tristam Cary
☆ Michael Redgrave, Alec McCowen, Leo
McKern, Renée Houston, Ann Todd, Peter
Cushing, Paul Daneman, Lois Maxwell, George
Devine, Richard Wordsworth, Joan Plowright
'It hammers home its effects with the
concentration of a heavyweight out for the kill.'
- *Philip Oakes*

Timebomb
US 1991 96m colour
MGM/Raffaella (Raffaella de Laurentiis)
🔲 ▤ ◉. ⊚
A watchmaker and former hitman prevents a CIA
plot to assassinate a liberal politician.
*Confused action adventure that updates The
Manchurian Candidate to no great effect.*
wd Avi Nesher ph Anthony B. Richmond
m Patrick Leonard pd Greg Pruss, Curtis A.
Schnell ed Isaac Sehayek
☆ Michael Biehn, Patsy Kensit, Tracy Scoggins,
Robert Culp, Richard Jordan, Raymond St Jacques
'A throwaway B-picture.' - *Empire*

'They Killed His Wife Ten Years Ago. There's Still Time
To Save Her.'
'Murder Is Forever ... Until Now.'
Timecop
US 1994 98m DeLuxe
UIP/Largo/JVC/Signature/Renaissance/Dark Horse
(Moshe Diamant, Sam Raimi, Robert Tapert)
🔲 ▤ ◉. ⊚
In an era of time travel a cop whose job is to
protect the past discovers that his political boss is
manipulating events in order to become President
and sets out to stop him.
*Over-involved science fiction that does not travel well;
it both exploits and ignores the paradoxes involved in
changing the past, and lacks excitement and the cheap
thrills of comic books.*
w Mark Verheiden, Mike Richardson, based on
their comic series d Peter Hyams ph Peter Hyams
m Mark Isham pd Philip Harrison ed Steven
Kemper
☆ Jean-Claude Van Damme, Mia Sara, Ron
Silver, Bruce McGill, Gloria Reuben, Jason
Schombling, Scott Bellis, Scott Lawrence
'Van Damme and the movie are stiffs.' - *Michael
Sragow, New Yorker*

Times Square
US 1980 113m Technicolor
EMI/Robert Stigwood
▤
Two ill-matched teenage girls form a shabby night-
club act and soon have New York by its ears.
*Sometimes sharply made but generally unpleasant
urban fairy story with suicide as the end, like a cross
between Saturday Night Fever and Midnight
Cowboy. Among a number of forgettable songs is one
called 'Pissing in the River'.*
w Jacob Brackman story Allan Moyle, Leanne
Unger d Allan Moyle ph James A. Contner
m Blue Weaver
☆ Tim Curry, Trini Alvarado, Robin Johnson,
Peter Coffield, Herbert Berghof, David Margulies

Times Square Lady
US 1935 69m bw
MGM
The daughter of a Broadway hustler, being
chiselled by her father's attorney, is helped by one
of his employees.
Flat romantic drama designed as a test for young stars.
w Albert Cohen, Robert Shannon d George B.
Seitz
☆ Robert Taylor, Virginia Bruce, Pinky Tomlin,
Helen Twelvetrees, Isabel Jewell, Nat Pendleton,
Henry Kolker, Jack La Rue
'Not sufficient here to be important.' - *Variety*

Times Square Playboy: see *The Home
Towners*

Timetable *
US 1955 79m bw
UA (Mark Stevens)
An insurance investigator is assigned to a train
robbery which he actually committed himself.
Concise suspenser with good script and treatment.

w Aben Kandel d Mark Stevens ph Charles Van
Enger m Walter Scharf
☆ Mark Stevens, Felicia Farr, King Calder, Wesley
Addy

Tin Cup **
US 1996 135m Technicolor
Warner/Monarchy/Regency (Gary Foster, David
Lester)
🔲 ▤ ◉. ⊚ 🎧
A hapless, small-town golf professional attempts to
clean up his act when he falls for the girlfriend of a
successful rival.
*Engaging romantic comedy, ramshackle in construction
but full of interesting behavourial quirks that give an
individuality missing from much recent homogenized
Hollywood product.*
w John Norville, Ron Shelton d Ron Shelton
ph Russell Boyd m William Ross pd James Bissell
ed Paul Seydor, Kimberly Ray
☆ Kevin Costner, Rene Russo, Cheech Marin,
Don Johnson, Linda Hart, Dennis Burkley, Rex
Linn, Lou Myers
'Gets by on that old standby: if your film lacks a
taut dramatic structure, simply provide the
audience with a bunch of characters they want
to hang out with, and by whatever means
necessary. The sign of a good film.' - *Tom Shone,
Sunday Times*

The Tin Drum ****
West Germany/France 1979 142m
Eastmancolor
UA/Franz Seitz/Bioskop/GGB 14
KG/Hallelujah/Artemis/Argos/Jadran/Film Polski
🔲 ▤ 🎧
original title: *Die Blechtrommel*
Not caring for the world he is growing up in, a
small boy determines to remain a child.
*Brilliantly made version of a labyrinthine satire on
German nationalism and the rise of the Nazis; the
emphasis is sometimes on sex and scatological detail,
for it is intended to be disturbing viewing, succeeding in
its aim of depicting a frightening world where reason is
overthrown.*
w Jean-Claude Carrière, Franz Seitz, Volker
Schlöndorff novel Günter Grass d Volker
Schlöndorff ph Igor Luther m Maurice Jarre
pd Nicos Perakis
☆ David Bennent, Mario Adorf, Angela Winkler,
Daniel Olbrychski
🏆 best foreign film

Tin Men **
US 1987 112m DeLuxe
Touchstone/Silver Screen Partners II (Mark Johnson)
▤ ◉.
In 1960s Baltimore, two aluminium salesmen have
a series of feuds.
*A comedy enjoyable not for its plot but for its authentic
period backgrounds and characters.*
wd Barry Levinson ph Peter Sova m David Steele
pd Peter Jamison ed Stu Linder
☆ Richard Dreyfuss, Danny DeVito, Barbara
Hershey, John Mahoney, Jackie Gayle, Stanley
Brock

Tin Pan Alley ***
US 1940 95m bw
TCF (Kenneth MacGowan)
During World War I and after, two dancing girls
love the same composer.
*Archetypal musical, full of Broadway clichés,
razzmatazz and zip. Remade 1950 as I'll Get By, not
to such peppy effect.*
w Robert Ellis, Helen Logan story Pamela Harris
d Walter Lang ph Leon Shamroy md Alfred
Newman ch Seymour Felix songs Mack Gordon,
Harry Warren
☆ Alice Faye, Betty Grable, John Payne, Jack Oakie,
Allen Jenkins, Esther Ralston, The Nicholas
Brothers, John Loder, Elisha Cook Jnr
♪ 'Moonlight Bay'; 'Honeysuckle Rose'; 'The
Sheik of Araby'; 'K-K-K-Katie'
🏆 Alfred Newman

The Tin Star *
US 1957 93m bw Vistavision
Paramount/Perlberg-Seaton
🔲 ▤ 🎧
An ex-sheriff turned bounty hunter helps a new
young sheriff to catch bandits.
*Dignified and well-characterized Western with
customary pleasures.*

---

w Dudley Nichols *story* Barney Slater, Joel Kane *d* Anthony Mann *ph* Loyal Griggs *m* Elmer Bernstein

☆ Henry Fonda, Anthony Perkins, Betsy Palmer, Michel Ray, Neville Brand, John McIntire, Lee Van Cleef

§ Barney Slater, Joel Kane, Dudley Nichols

Tina: What's Love Got to Do with It: see
What's Love Got to Do with It

'Do you have the guts to sit in this chair?'
The Tingler
US 1959 82m bw
Columbia/William Castle
⬚ ▦ ◉~

Fear (it says here) can create on the spinal column a parasite removable only by screaming. A scientist isolates it and it runs amok in a silent cinema.
Ridiculous shocker with generally dull handling but effective moments.

w Robb White *d* William Castle *ph* Wilfrid Cline *m* Von Dexter

☆ Vincent Price, Judith Evelyn, Darryl Hickman, Patricia Cutts

'The sheer effrontery of this piece of hokum is enjoyable in itself.' – *MFB*

Tinpis Run
France/Belgium/Papua New Guinea 1990 94m colour
JBA/Tinpis/La Sept/RTBF/Femis/Varan/Skul Bilong Wokim Piksa (Jacques Bidou)

A tribal chief who runs a taxi service with his daughter and her boyfriend returns to his village to take part in a war against a neighbouring tribe.
Moderately entertaining anecdotal account of an unusual generation clash – between the peace-loving young and their elders.

w John Barre, Severin Blanchet, Martin Maden, Pengau Nengo *d* Pengau Nengo *ph* Martin Maden *m* Severin Blanchet, Mick Giani *ad* Thomas Gawi *ed* Andrée Davanture

☆ Rhoda Selan, Leo Konga, Oscar Wanu, Gerard Gabud

'More a travelog of the island country than a wholly satisfying dramatic film.' – *Variety*

Tip on a Dead Jockey
US 1957 99m bw
MGM (Edwin H. Knopf)
☊

GB title: *Time for Action*

A flyer loses his nerve and turns international smuggler, but reforms.
Gloomy, pedestrian star melodrama, dully cast.

w Charles Lederer *novel* Irwin Shaw *d* Richard Thorpe *ph* George J. Folsey *m* Miklos Rozsa

☆ Robert Taylor, Dorothy Malone, Gia Scala, Martin Gabel, Marcel Dalio, Jack Lord

Tip-off Girls *
US 1938 61m bw
Paramount

Gangsters use girl employees to get tips on merchandise shipments.
Routine but watchable G-man second.

w Maxwell Shane, Robert Yost, Stuart Anthony *d* Louis King

☆ Lloyd Nolan, Mary Carlisle, J. Carrol Naish, Harvey Stephens, Roscoe Karns, Larry Crabbe, Anthony Quinn

'Excellent meller ... bristles with action, tensity and suspense.' – *Variety*

Tirez sur le Pianiste: see *Shoot the Pianist*

Tish
US 1942 84m bw
Orville O. Dull/MGM

A maiden aunt tries to guide her family's life.
Boring domestic taradiddles which waste a good cast.

w Harry Ruskin *stories* Mary Roberts Rinehart *d* S. Sylvan Simon

☆ Marjorie Main, ZaSu Pitts, Aline MacMahon, Susan Peters, Lee Bowman, Guy Kibbee, Virginia Grey, Richard Quine, Al Shean

The Tit and the Moon **
Spain/France 1994 91m colour
Metro Tartan/Lolafils/Cartel/Sogepaq (Andrés Vicente Gómez)
⬚

original title: *La Teta y la Luna*

Jealous of his newborn baby brother, a young boy seeks maternal comfort from a cabaret artiste married to an impotent and flatulent performer.
Oddly engaging, often charming account of a child attempting to understand adult behaviour through his own emotional turmoil.

w Cuca Canals, Bigas Luna *d* Bigas Luna *ph* José Luis Alcaine *m* Nicola Piovani *ad* Aimé Deudé *ed* Carmen Frias

☆ Biel Duran, Mathilda May, Gérard Darmon, Miguel Poveda, Abel Folk, Genis Sanchez

'It is directed with such a sharp appreciation for childhood obsessions and with such crisp cinematic flair that it becomes a totally enchanting fairy-tale, hilarious and touching by turns.' – *Derek Malcolm, Guardian*

Tit for Tat *
US 1935 20m bw
Hal Roach

Adjoining shopkeepers violently settle an old difference.
Archetypal late star comedy: brilliant timing, but the warmth and sympathy have begun to ebb.

w Stan Laurel *d* Charles Rogers *ph* Art Lloyd *ed* Bert Jordan

☆ Stan Laurel, Oliver Hardy, Charlie Hall, Mae Busch

'A good deal of obvious slapstick and just a thread of a story turns this into only moderate comedy.' – *Box Office*

§ best short

Titanic *
US 1953 98m bw
TCF (Charles Brackett)
▦ ◉~

Personal dramas aboard the *Titanic* in 1912 come to a head as the ship hits an iceberg.
An excellent example of studio production is squandered on a dim script which arouses no excitement.

w Charles Brackett, Walter Reisch, Richard Breen *d* Jean Negulesco *ph* Joe MacDonald *m* Sol Kaplan *ad* Lyle Wheeler, Maurice Ransford

☆ Clifton Webb, Barbara Stanwyck, Robert Wagner, Audrey Dalton, Thelma Ritter, Brian Aherne, Richard Basehart, Allyn Joslyn

⚱ script

§ art direction

'Nothing On Earth Could Come Between Them.'
Titanic **
US 1997 194m DeLuxe Panavision
TCF/Lightstorm (James Cameron, Jon Landau)
⬚ ▦ ◉~ ◉~ ◉~

As the *Titanic* sails for its date with an iceberg, an independent young woman, engaged to a bullying millionaire, and travelling first class, falls for a penniless Wisconsin boy in steerage.
Said Cameron, on accepting one of the many Golden Globe awards for the film: 'So does this prove, once and for all, that size does matter?' To which there are two answers: one supplied by dialogue from the film ('Do you know of Dr Freud? His ideas about the male preoccupation with size may be of interest to you') and the other, only if you confuse quantity with quality. The recreation of the splendour and the disaster of the Titanic is brilliant, and the direction and editing often impeccable; but the dialogue is frequently risible, and the love story banal when it does not indulge in the sort of melodramatics that went out with The Perils of Pauline, which has the effect of diminishing the many real-life tragedies that occurred. Cameron is the modern-day equivalent of the Victorian theatrical designer 'Sensation' Smith of Drury Lane: a master of spectacle, but little else.

wd James Cameron *ph* Russell Carpenter *m* James Horner *pd* Peter Lamont *ed* Conrad Buff, James Cameron, Richard A. Harris *sp* Robert Legato, Mark Lasoff, Thomas L. Fisher, Michael Kanfer; Digital Domain

☆ Leonardo DiCaprio, Kate Winslet, Billy Zane, Kathy Bates, Frances Fisher, Gloria Stuart, Bill Paxton, Bernard Hill, Jonathan Hyde, Victor Garber, David Warner, Danny Nucci, Suzy Amis, Bernard Fox

'The regretful verdict here: Dead in the water.' – *Richard Corliss, Time*
'As Cameron sails his lonely craft toward greatness, he should realise he needs to bring a passenger with him. Preferably someone who can write.' – *Kenneth Turan, Los Angeles Times*
'Suggests the movie Cecil B. DeMille might have made in 1928 had he not been contemplating a more modern disaster flick about a giant dirigible. Not only is the dialogue as floridly stilted as the least literate silent-movie intertitles, but the correlation between the characters' personal lives and their impending doom is absolute.' – *J. Hoberman, Premiere*
'The daring underwater remake of *Harold and Maude*, in which an 18-year-old boy falls in love with an 80-year-old woman. The embryonic facial features of Leonardo DiCaprio (as well as the dialogue, direction and performances) render the love story not merely unconvincing, but almost obscene. Here is a little boy whose face screams "I have not lived", teaching Kate Winslet how to be a woman, giving her permission to play a part in her life.' – *Emma Forrest, Guardian*
† The film, with its 550 computer-generated shots, was the most expensive made so far, at more than $200m, and needed to gross at least $350m to break even; Cameron forewent his salary as costs escalated, keeping only the $1.5m he received as screenwriter. It broke all box-office records around the world to become the highest-grossing film so far, taking more than $1 billion, and also equalled the record set by *Ben Hur* for winning the most Oscars. As a result, Cameron was reportedly to be recompensed with 10 per cent of the gross, which would amount to more than $100m.
†† Papers released by the Public Records Office in 1998 showed that third-class passengers were not locked below decks, as shown in the movie.
⚱ best picture; James Cameron (as director); Russell Carpenter; Peter Lamont; James Horner; Deborah Lynn Scott (costume); editing; visual effects; sound; sound effects editing; song 'My Heart Will Go On' (*m* James Horner, *ly* Will Jennings)
§ Kate Winslet; Gloria Stuart; make-up

Titanic Town *
GB 1998 100m colour
Pandora/BBC/British Screen/Company Pictures (George Faber, Charles Patterson)
⬚

In Belfast in the early 70s, a group of women band together to put an end to violence.
A semi-comic but ultimately downbeat account of the Irish troubles.

w Anne Devlin *novel* Mary Costello *d* Roger Michell *ph* John Daly *m* Trevor Jones *pd* Pat Campbell *ed* Kate Evans

☆ Julie Walters, Ciaran Hinds, Nuala O'Neill, James Loughran, Barry Loughran, Elizabeth Donaghy, Ciaran McMenamin, Jaz Pollock, Aingeal Grehan

'Caught in a no-man's land between gritty realism and upbeat, stylised comedy.' – *Sight and Sound*

The Titfield Thunderbolt ***
🏃🏃 GB 1952 84m Technicolor
Ealing (Michael Truman)
⬚

When a branch railway line is threatened with closure, the villagers take it over as a private concern.
Undervalued on its release in the wake of other Ealing comedies, this now seems among the best of them as well as an immaculate colour production showing the England that is no more; the script has pace, the whole thing is brightly polished and the action works up to a fine climactic frenzy.

w T. E. B. Clarke *d* Charles Crichton *ph* Douglas Slocombe *m* Georges Auric

☆ Stanley Holloway, George Relph, John Gregson, Godfrey Tearle, Edie Martin, Naunton Wayne, Gabrielle Brune, Hugh Griffith, Sidney James, Jack MacGowran, Ewan Roberts, Reginald Beckwith

Title Shot
Canada 1979 98m Film House colour
Regenthall (Rob Iveson)
▦

A troubled detective foils a crooked boxing manager, who will go to any lengths to make a killing.

Dull and diffuse drama, indifferently performed.
w John Saxton *story* Richard Gabourie *d* Les Rose *ph* Henri Fiks *m* Paul James Zaza *ad* Karen Bromley *ed* Ronald Sanders

☆ Tony Curtis, Richard Gabourie, Susan Hogan, Allan Royal, Robert Delbert, Natsuko Ohama

T-Men *
US 1947 96m bw
Eagle Lion (Aubrey Schenck)
▦

Treasury Department detectives trail a gang of counterfeiters.
Tough, well-made crime melodrama which still packs a punch in the traditional vein.

w John C. Higgins *d* Anthony Mann *ph* John Alton *m* Paul Sawtell

☆ Dennis O'Keefe, Alfred Ryder, Mary Meade, Wallace Ford, June Lockhart, Charles McGraw, Jane Randolph, Art Smith

To Be or Not to Be ****
US 1942 99m bw
Alexander Korda/Ernst Lubitsch
⬚ ▦

Warsaw actors get involved in an underground plot and an impersonation of invading Nazis, including Hitler.
Marvellous free-wheeling entertainment which starts as drama and descends through romantic comedy and suspense into farce; accused of bad taste at the time, but now seen as an outstanding example of Hollywood moonshine, kept alight through sheer talent and expertise.

w Edwin Justus Mayer *story* Ernst Lubitsch, Melchior Lengyel *d* Ernst Lubitsch *ph* Rudolph Maté *m* Werner Heymann *ad* Vincent Korda

☆ Jack Benny, Carole Lombard, Robert Stack, Stanley Ridges, Felix Bressart, Lionel Atwill, Sig Rumann, Tom Dugan, Charles Halton

TURA IN DISGUISE (JACK BENNY): 'That great, great Polish actor Joseph Tura – you must have heard of him.'
ERHARDT (SIG RUMANN): 'Ah, yes ... what he did to Shakespeare, we are now doing to Poland!'
ERHARDT (AND OTHERS): 'So they call me Concentration Camp Erhardt!'
'The comedy is hilarious, even when it is hysterically thrilling.' – *Commonweal*
'As effective an example of comic propaganda as *The Great Dictator* and far better directed.' – *Charles Higham, 1972*
'Based on an indiscretion, but undoubtedly a work of art.' – *James Agee*
'In any other medium it would be acknowledged as a classic to rank with *The Alchemist* or *A Modest Proposal*.' – *Peter Barnes*
'Lubitsch's comic genius and corrosive wit are displayed at every turn.' – *John Baxter*
'The actual business at hand ... is nothing less than providing a good time at the expense of Nazi myth ... Lubitsch distinguishes the film's zanier moments with his customary mastery of sly humour and innuendo, and when the story calls for outright melodrama he is more than equal to the occasion.' – *Newsweek*
§ Werner Heymann

To Be or Not to Be
US 1983 107m DeLuxe
TCF/Brooksfilms (Mel Brooks)
⬚ ▦ ◉~

Flat-footed remake of the above, with stagey sets, unconvincing acting (including the unnecessary addition of a gay dresser) and a leading comedian who won't stay still in case his lack of style should be noticed.

w Thomas Meehan, Ronny Graham *d* Alan Johnson *ph* Gerald Hirschfeld *m* John Morris *pd* Terence Marsh

☆ Mel Brooks, Anne Bancroft, Tim Matheson, Charles Durning, José Ferrer, George Gaynes, Christopher Lloyd, James Haake

§ Charles Durning

To Catch a Thief *
US 1955 97m Technicolor Vistavision
Paramount/Alfred Hitchcock
⬚ ▦ ◉~

A famous cat burglar who has retired to the Riviera catches a thief who is imitating his old style.
Very slow, floppy and rather boring entertainment enlivened by the scenery and the odd Hitchcock touch.

🏃🏃 film suitable for family viewing   ⬚ VHS video-cassette for the British PAL system   ⬚ VHS video-cassette for the British PAL system in wide screen-format   ↻ Video cassette in a computer-colourised version   ▦ American NTSC video-cassette   ◉~ Laser disc

w John Michael Hayes *novel* David Dodge
d Alfred Hitchcock *ph* Robert Burks *m* Lyn
Murray *ad* Hal Pereira, Joseph McMillan Johnson
☆ Cary Grant, Grace Kelly, *Jessie Royce Landis,*
John Williams, Charles Vanel, Brigitte Auber
'Billed as a comedy-mystery, it stacks up as a
drawn-out pretentious piece that seldom hits the
comedy level.' – *Variety*
🎗 Robert Burks
⚖ art direction

'Don't let the frilly shirt fool you. This man can kill
without stirring a ruffle.'
To Commit a Murder *(dubbed)*
France/West Germany/Italy 1967 91m
Eastmancolor
Cinerama/SNEG/Gaumont/Waterview/Eichberg/Franca
(Alan Poiré)
original title: Peau d'Espion
A writer becomes involved in a plot to kidnap a
nuclear scientist and take him to China.
*Confused and confusing thriller, long on talk and short
on action.*
w Edouard Molinaro, Jacques Robert *novel Peau
d'Espion* by Jacques Robert d Edouard Molinaro
ph Raymond Le Moigne *m* José Berghmans
ad Robert Clavel, Olivier Girard *ed* Robert
Isnardon, Monique Isnardon
☆ Louis Jourdan, Senta Berger, Edmond O'Brien,
Bernard Blier
'A sleepy espionage yarn which almost grinds to
a halt at the halfway mark.' – *David McGillivray,
Films and Filming*

'Ghost goes Camping!'
To Die For *
GB 1994 97m colour
TDF/London Lighthouse/British Screen (Gary
Fitzpatrick)
▣
The ghost of his lover, who died of AIDS, returns
to haunt a promiscuous gay man.
*An uneven film that, at times, is a witty and affecting
account of a man coming to terms with himself and
making peace with his past, though Slattery's comic-
revue turn as an earnest council official detracts from
its truth and emotional impact.*
w Johnny Byrne *story* Paul McEvoy, Peter
Mackenzie Litten d Peter Mackenzie Litten
ph John Ward *m* Roger Bolton *ed* Jeffrey
Arsenault
☆ Thomas Arklie, Ian Williams, Tony Slattery,
Dillie Keane, Jean Boht, John Altman
'A film of many positive qualities that is neither
smug nor sentimental. Overall, it is much more
satisfying than the likes of *Philadelphia*, in which
all issues readily fit into neat categories and
resolutions.' – *Emanuel Levy, Variety*

'She knew what it took to get to the top. A lot of
heart. And a little head.'
To Die For *
US 1995 107m Technicolor
Rank/Columbia (Laura Ziskin)
▣ ▤ ▨ ⌂
A fame-obsessed weather-woman on a local TV
station describes how she got away with murdering
her husband.
*A deft satire on the worship of celebrity for its own sake
and the way television can elevate the ordinary to
heroic status, though it takes aim at an exceptionally
easy target – a small-town girl – without managing to
hit the bull's-eye.*
w Buck Henry *novel* Joyce Maynard d Gus Van
Sant *ph* Eric Alan Edwards *m* Danny Elfman
pd Missy Stewart *ed* Curtiss Clayton
☆ Nicole Kidman, Matt Dillon, Joaquin Phoenix,
Casey Affleck, Illeana Douglas, Dan Hedaya,
Kurtwood Smith, Buck Henry, David Cronenberg,
George Segal (uncredited)
'Witty, energetic and splendidly acted, this
handcrafted curio will find support among the
specialised, adventurous-minded audiences who
have patronised the director's work in the past.'
– *Todd McCarthy, Variety*

'As long as there are lovers – this picture will live!'
'Paramount proudly brings to the screens of America
one of the three great love stories of all time!'
To Each His Own **
US 1946 100m bw
Paramount (Charles Brackett)
During World War II, a middle-aged woman in
London meets the soldier who is her own
illegitimate and long-since-adopted son.

*The woman's picture par excellence, put together with
tremendous Hollywood flair and extremely enjoyable to
watch.*
w Charles Brackett, Jacques Théry d Mitchell Leisen
ph Daniel L. Fapp *m* Victor Young *ad* Hans
Dreier, Roland Anderson
☆ *Olivia de Havilland,* John Lund, Roland Culver,
Mary Anderson, Philip Terry, Bill Goodwin,
Virginia Welles, Virginia Horne
🎗 Olivia de Havilland
⚖ original story (Charles Brackett)

To Find a Man *
US 1971 93m Eastmancolor
Columbia/Rastar (Irving Pincus)
The spoiled daughter of a rich family becomes
pregnant and is helped by a young chemist.
*Quiet, well-made minor drama about maturity, with
good small-town atmosphere.*
w Arnold Schulman *novel* S. J. Wilson d Buzz
Kulik *ph* Andy Laszlo *m* David Shire
☆ Pamela Martin, Darrell O'Connor, *Lloyd
Bridges,* Phyllis Newman, Tom Ewell, Tom Bosley

To Have and Have Not **
US 1945 100m bw
Warner (Howard Hawks)
▣ ▤ ▨
An American charter boat captain in Martinique
gets involved with Nazis.
*Fairly routinely made studio adventure notable for first
pairing of Bogart and Bacall, as an imitation of
Casablanca, and for its consistent though not
outstanding entertainment value. Remade later as The
Breaking Point (qv) and The Gun Runners (qv),
and not dissimilar from Key Largo (qv).*
w Jules Furthman, William Faulkner *novel* Ernest
Hemingway d Howard Hawks *ph* Sid Hickox
m Franz Waxman (uncredited) *md* Leo F.
Forbstein
☆ *Humphrey Bogart, Lauren Bacall,* Walter
Brennan, Hoagy Carmichael, Dolores Moran,
Sheldon Leonard, Dan Seymour, Marcel Dalio
'Remarkable for the ingenuity and industry with
which the original story and the individualities
of Ernest Hemingway have been rendered down
into Hollywood basic.' – *Richard Winnington*
'Sunlight on the lattice, sex in the corridors, a
new pianist at the café, pistol shots, the fat
sureté man coming round after dark.' – *William
Whitebait*

To Hell and Back *
US 1955 106m Technicolor Cinemascope
U-I (Aaron Rosenberg)
The war career of America's most decorated
infantryman.
*Routine war story which happens to be about a fellow
who later became a film star.*
w Gil Doud *book* Audie Murphy d Jesse Hibbs
ph Maury Gertsman *m* Joseph Gershenson
☆ *Audie Murphy,* Marshall Thompson, Charles
Drake, Gregg Palmer, Jack Kelly, Paul Picerni,
Susan Kohner
'The emotion is congealed and there is no real
personal response to the anguish of war.' – *John
Gillett*

To Joy **
Sweden 1950 98m bw
Svensk Filmindustri (Allan Ekelund)
▤
original title: Till Glädje
After learning of his wife's accidental death, a
provincial violinist remembers the pains and
pleasures of their relationship.
*A frequently bleak but essentially upbeat affirmation of
survival in adversity, and of the satisfactions of
maturity.*
wd Ingmar Bergman *ph* Gunnar Fischer
m Mendelssohn, Mozart, Smetana, Beethoven
ad Nils Svenwall *ed* Oscar Rosander
☆ Maj-Britt Nilsson, Stig Olin, Victor Sjöström,
Birger Malmsten, John Ekman, Margit Carlqvist,
Sif Ruud

To Kill a Clown
GB 1971 104m DeLuxe
Palomar (Theodore Sills)
▤
A painter and his wife move to a New England isle
and are menaced by a crippled Vietnam veteran
and his vicious dogs.

*Pretentious, politically oriented rehash of The Most
Dangerous Game (qv), carefully made but too slow
for suspense.*
w George Bloomfield, I. C. Rapoport
novel Master of the Hounds by Algis Budrys
d George Bloomfield *ph* Walter Lassally
m Richard Hill, John Hawkins
☆ Alan Alda, Blythe Danner, Heath Lamberts,
Eric Clavering

To Kill a Mockingbird **
US 1962 129m bw
U-I (Alan Pakula)
▣ ▤ ▨ ⌂
A lawyer in a small Southern town defends a black
man accused of rape.
*Familiar dollops of social conscience, very well
presented with a child interest and excellent
atmosphere, but a mite overlong.*
w Horton Foote *novel* Harper Lee d Robert
Mulligan *ph* Russell Harlan *m* Elmer Bernstein
☆ *Gregory Peck, Mary Badham,* Philip Alford,
John Megna, Frank Overton, Rosemary Murphy,
Ruth White, Brock Peters
† The narrator is Kim Stanley.
🎗 script; Gregory Peck
⚖ best picture; Robert Mulligan; Russell Harlan;
Elmer Bernstein; Mary Badham

To Kill a Priest
France/US 1988 113m colour
J. P. Productions/FR3/Sofica Valor (Jean-Pierre
Alessandri)
▤ ▨
A militant Polish priest runs foul of the local
police chief.
*Vaguely based on the life and death of Father Jerzy
Popieluszko, a proponent of trade unions, it fails to
make explicit the political and ideological events it
attempts to portray.*
w Agnieszka Holland, Jean-Yves Pitoun
d Agnieszka Holland *ph* Adam Holender
pd Emile Ghigo *ed* Herve de Luze
☆ Christophe Lambert, Ed Harris, Joss Ackland,
Tim Roth, Timothy Spall, Peter Postlethwaite,
Cherie Lunghi, Joanne Whalley, David Suchet

To Koritsi me ta Mavra: see *The Girl in Black*

To Live **
Hong Kong 1994 125m colour
Electric/Century/Era/Shanghai Film Studios (Chiu Fusheng)
▣ ▤
original title: Huozhe
Thirty years in the lives of a Chinese couple living
through the Communist revolution and subsequent
upheavals.
*An engrossing domestic saga of survival, celebrating
fortitude and humour but less compelling than the
director's earlier films.*
w Yu Hua, Lu Wei *novel* Lu Wei d Zhang Yimou
ph Lu Yue *m* Zhao Jiping *ad* Cao Jiuping *ed* Du
Yuan
☆ Ge You, Gong Li, Niu Ben, Guo Tao, Jiang Wu,
Ni Dabong
'A well-crafted but in no way earth-shaking
entry in the helmer's oeuvre.' – *Variety*
🎬 best foreign film

To Live and Die in L.A.
US 1985 116m Technicolor
MGM-UA/New Century/SLM/Irving H. Levin
▣ ▤ ▨ ⌂
A secret service agent nails the counterfeiter who
killed his partner.
*High-gloss, foul-mouthed, hysterical crime melo, a kind
of west coast French Connection.*
w William Friedkin, Gerald Petievich
novel Gerald Petievich d William Friedkin
ph Robby Muller *m* Wang Chung *pd* Lilly
Kilvert *ed* Scott Smith
☆ William L. Petersen, Willem Dafoe, John
Pankow, Debra Feuer, Dean Stockwell, John
Turturro, Darlanne Fluegel
'The intense vulgarity of the characters and
virtuoso stylistic overkill will turn off
mainstream audiences.' – *Variety*

To Mary with Love
US 1936 87m bw
TCF
A businessman thinks back affectionately over ten
years of married life.
Harmless romantic comedy-drama.

w Richard Sherman, Howard Ellis Smith d John
Cromwell
☆ Warner Baxter, Myrna Loy, Ian Hunter, Claire
Trevor, Jean Dixon

To Our Loves *
France 1983 102m colour
Les Films Du Livradois/Gaumont/FR3 (Micheline
Pialat)
▤
original title: A Nos Amours
A teenage girl, whose parents are splitting up,
looks for love and settles for promiscuity.
Domestic misery from a specialist in teenage angst.
w Arlette Langmann, Maurice Pialat d Maurice
Pialat *ph* Jacques Loiseleux *ed* Yann Dedet
☆ Sandrine Bonnaire, Evelyne Ker, Dominique
Besnehard, Maurice Pialat, Christophe Odent

To Paris with Love *
GB 1954 78m Technicolor
GFD/Two Cities (Anthony Darnborough)
A middle-aged widower and his son go to Paris on
holiday and devise matrimonial plans for each
other.
*Thin, disappointing taradiddle which is short but seems
long.*
w Robert Buckner d Robert Hamer *ph* Reg Wyer
m Edwin Astley
☆ Alec Guinness, Vernon Gray, Odile Versois,
Jacques François, Elina Labourdette, Austin Trevor
'The general impression is somehow too aimless,
too muted.' – *Gavin Lambert*
'John Davis came on the set one day and said:
Give us some pratfalls, Alec, give us some
laughs. I realized there and then that I was not
going to fit in.' – *Alec Guinness*

To Please a Lady *
US 1950 91m bw
MGM (Clarence Brown)
A ruthless midget-car racer falls for the lady
journalist who is hounding him.
Good action programmer with no frills.
w Barre Lyndon, Marge Decker d Clarence
Brown *ph* Harold Rosson *m* Bronislau Kaper
☆ Clark Gable, Barbara Stanwyck, Adolphe
Menjou, Will Geer, Roland Winters, Emory
Parnell, Frank Jenks

'A story as fresh as the girls in their minis!'
To Sir with Love
GB 1967 105m Technicolor
Columbia (James Clavell)
▣ ▤ ⦿
A West Indian teacher comes to a tough East End
school.
*Sentimental non-realism patterned after The
Blackboard Jungle but much softer; its influence led to
a TV situation comedy, Please Sir.*
wd James Clavell *novel* E. R. Braithwaite *ph* Paul
Beeson *m* Ron Grainer
☆ Sidney Poitier, Christian Roberts, Judy Geeson,
Suzy Kendall, Lulu, Faith Brook, Geoffrey Bayldon,
Patricia Routledge
'The sententious script sounds as if it has been
written by a zealous Sunday school teacher after
a particularly exhilarating boycott of South
African oranges.' – *MFB*

To Sleep with Anger **
US 1990 102m CFI color
Metro/SVS Films (Caldecott Chubb, Thomas S. Byrnes,
Darin Scott)
▤
A black family which has moved from the South to
Los Angeles finds itself in trouble when an old
friend visits with stories of the past.
Engrossing drama of social disintegration.
wd Charles Burnett *ph* Walt Lloyd *m* Stephen
James Taylor *pd* Penny Barrett *ed* Nancy
Richardson
☆ Danny Glover, Paul Butler, Mary Alice, Carl
Lumbly, Vonetta McGee, Richard Brooks, Sheryl
Lee Ralph, Ethel Ayler, Julius Harris
'With a whole string of superb performances,
dialogue that manages the difficult trick of
hitting notes both lyrical and earthy, and a
magical gospel and blues score, it demonstrates
Burnett's instinct for cinema every inch of the
way.' – *Tom Milne, MFB*

To Telefteo Psemma: see *A Matter of Dignity*

'It's more than just a sport. It's survival.'

To the Death
US 1991 86m Agfacolor
Cannon/Distant Horizon/Tangent (Anant Singh)

📼

A retired kick-boxing champion is lured back into the ring by a corrupt gambler who organizes private fights in which the loser is shot.
Numbingly predictable nonsense, acted and directed with the sensitivity of a boot in the face. The dialogue seems to have strayed from a Victorian melodrama.
w Greg Latter *story* Darrell James Roodt, Greg Latter d Darrell James Roodt ph Mark Vicente m Frank Becker pd David Barkham ed Davedd Heitner
☆ John Barrett, Michel Qissi, Robert Whitehead, Michèle Bestbier, Greg Latter
  HUSBAND TO WIFE SURPRISED IN BED WITH ANOTHER MAN: 'Why? Why? Why? Oh God! I give you everything your heart desires and this is how you repay me!'

To the Devil a Daughter
GB/Germany 1976 93m Technicolor
EMI/Hammer-Terra Filmkunst (Roy Skeggs)

📼 📼

An occult novelist is asked to take care of a girl who has been 'promised' to a group of Satanists.
Confusingly told, high camp diabolic thriller.
w Chris Wicking *novel* Dennis Wheatley d Peter Sykes ph David Watkin m Paul Glass ad Don Picton sp John Trumper sp Les Bowie
☆ Richard Widmark, Christopher Lee, Denholm Elliott, Honor Blackman, Michael Goodliffe, Anthony Valentine, Derek Francis, Nastassja Kinski

To the Ends of the Earth **
US 1948 107m bw
Columbia (Sidney Buchman)
A government agent follows a world-wide trail after a narcotics gang.
Thoroughly riveting conventional thriller, nicely made and photographed.
w Jay Richard Kennedy d Robert Stevenson ph Burnett Guffey m George Duning
☆ Dick Powell, Signe Hasso, Ludwig Donath, Vladimir Sokoloff, Edgar Barrier

To the Shores of Tripoli
US 1942 82m Technicolor
TCF (Milton Sperling)

📼

A cocky playboy becomes a tough marine.
Despite the title, this modest flagwaver with romantic trimmings never moves out of the San Diego training grounds.
w Lamar Trotti d Bruce Humberstone ph Edward Cronjager m Alfred Newman
☆ Maureen O'Hara, John Payne, Randolph Scott, Nancy Kelly, William Tracy, Maxie Rosenbloom, Henry Morgan, Russell Hicks, Minor Watson
⅄ cinematography

To the Starry Island
South Korea 1994 102m colour
Park Kwang-Su/Samsung Nices/Channel 4
A poet, returning for a funeral to the small island community where he was born, remembers the tragic wartime events of 40 years earlier.
Simply told story of rural life that takes a long time to get to the point.
w Lee Chang-Dong, Park Kwang-Su *novel* Im Chul-Woo d Park Kwang-Su ph Yoo Young-Gil m Song Hong-Sup ed Kim Hyun
☆ Ahn Sung-Ki, Moon Sung-Keun, Shim Hae-Jin, Ahn So-Young, Lee Yong-Yi, Im Chul-Woo, Kim Yong-Man, Hur June-Ho, Choi Hyung-In, Lee Kyung-Young, Myung Kae-Nam

To the Victor: see Owd Bob (1938)

To the Victor
US 1948 100m bw
Warner (Jerry Wald)
French collaborators stand trial for war crimes.
Glum melodrama with inadequate cast.
w Richard Brooks d Delmer Daves ph Robert Burks m David Buttolph
☆ Dennis Morgan, Viveca Lindfors, Bruce Bennett, Victor Francen, Dorothy Malone, Tom d'Andrea, Eduardo Ciannelli, Joseph Buloff, Luis Van Rooten, William Conrad

To Trap a Spy
US 1966 92m Metrocolor
MGM (Norman Felton)
American secret agents protect an African diplomat from being killed.
An extended version of the pilot for the television series The Man from U.N.C.L.E.; *despite it, they still went ahead with more episodes.*
w Sam Rolfe d Don Medford ph Joseph Biroc m Jerry Goldsmith ad George W. Davis, Merrill Pye ed Henry Berman
☆ Robert Vaughn, David McCallum, Luciana Paluzzi, Patricia Crowley, Fritz Weaver, Will Kuluva, Leo G. Carroll

To What Red Hell
GB 1929 100m bw
Strand/Twickenham
A young epileptic kills a prostitute and is protected by his mother.
Unpalatable melodrama which failed to be as significant as it wished.
w Leslie Hiscott *play* Percy Robinson d Edwin Greenwood ph Basil Emmott
☆ Sybil Thorndike, John Hamilton, Bramwell Fletcher, Janice Adair

'Attitude Is Everything'
'This Time Snipes and Swayze Face Their Toughest Enemy. Stubble.'
To Wong Foo, Thanks for Everything, Julie Newmar
US 1995 108m DeLuxe
UIP/Universal/Amblin (G. Mac Brown)

📼 📼 ℗ 🎧

Three drag queens, driving to Los Angeles from New York, break down in a small town where they solve the locals' problems.
Tiresome comedy that seems to think it enough to dress its macho stars in women's clothing.
w Douglas Carter Beane d Beeban Kidron ph Steve Mason m Rachel Portman pd Wynn Thomas ed Andrew Mondshein
☆ Wesley Snipes, Patrick Swayze, John Leguizamo, Stockard Channing, Blythe Danner, Arliss Howard, Jason London, Chris Penn, RuPaul, Naomi Campbell

The Toast of New Orleans
US 1950 97m Technicolor
MGM (Joe Pasternak)

📼 ℗

A Bayou villager becomes a star of the New Orleans opera.
Very ordinary setting for a new singing star.
w Sy Gomberg, George Wells d Norman Taurog ph William Snyder md George Stoll ch Eugene Loring
☆ Kathryn Grayson, David Niven, Mario Lanza, J. Carrol Naish, James Mitchell, Richard Hageman, Clinton Sundberg, Sig Arno
  'Sheer excruciation.' – *Pauline Kael, New Yorker*
⅄ song 'Be My Love' (mNicholas Brodszky, lySammy Cahn)

'The screen sensation of a decade, played by a galaxy of stars in a hell-bent world of wine and women!'
The Toast of New York **
US 1937 109m bw
RKO (Edward Small)

📼 ℗

A 19th-century medicine showman becomes a notorious Wall Street financier.
Smart biopic of Jim Fisk; good entertainment with accomplished production.
w Dudley Nichols, John Twist, Joel Sayre d Rowland V. Lee ph Peverell Marley m Nathaniel Shilkret
☆ Edward Arnold, Cary Grant, Frances Farmer, Jack Oakie, Donald Meek, Clarence Kolb, Thelma Leeds
  'Making no pretence for serious consideration as a faithful and accurate reflection of life and manners in the period it depicts, it rates as a piece of hokum aimed at the box office. It will do business.' – *Variety*

Toast of the Legion: see Kiss Me Again (1931)

Tobacco Road ***
US 1941 84m bw
TCF (Darryl F. Zanuck)
Poor whites in Georgia are turned off their land.
This bowdlerized version of a sensational book and play has superbly orchestrated farcical scenes separated by

delightfully pictorial quieter moments: it isn't what was intended, but in its own way it's quite marvellous.
w Nunnally Johnson *play* Jack Kirkland *novel* Erskine Caldwell d John Ford ph Arthur Miller m David Buttolph
☆ Charley Grapewin, Elizabeth Patterson, Dana Andrews, Gene Tierney, Marjorie Rambeau, Ward Bond, William Tracy, Zeffie Tilbury, Slim Summerville, Grant Mitchell, Russell Simpson, Spencer Charters

Tobe Hooper's Night Terrors
US 1993 94m colour
Cannon/Global (Harry Alan Towers)

📼 📼

aka: *Tobe Hooper's Nightmare*
In Alexandria, the silly daughter of an archaeologist begins to read the work of the Marquis de Sade, has erotic fantasies and is kidnapped by his depraved descendant.
Drear, minimal-budget horror of little interest to anyone; for no particular purpose, the action cuts between the 1700s, with scenes of de Sade enjoying being tortured in prison, and the 1990s; neither setting entertains, though masochists might enjoy the movie.
w Daniel Matmor, Rom Globus d Tobe Hooper ph Amnon Solomon m Dov Seltzer ad Yossi Peled ed Alain Jakubowicz sp make-up: David B. Miller
☆ Robert Englund, Zoe Trilling, Alona Kimhi, Juliano Merr, Chandra West, William Finley
  'Bilge.' – *Sight and Sound*
† Tobe Hooper took over the film when the original director, Gerry O'Hara, went to work on another movie. It was originally going to be set in the 1920s, but suitable props and locations could not be found for the Egyptian scenes, shot in Israel, so it was updated to the present day.

Tobruk
US 1967 110m Techniscope
Universal/Corman/Gibraltar (Gene Corman)

📼 📼

During the North African war, a British major and some German Jews try to blow up the Nazi fuel bunkers.
Routine war adventure, quite tough and spectacular but undistinguished.
w Leo V. Gordon d Arthur Hiller ph Russell Harlan m Bronislau Kaper ad Alexander Golitzen, Henry Bumstead ed Robert C. Jones
☆ Rock Hudson, George Peppard, Nigel Green, Guy Stockwell, Jack Watson, Liam Redmond, Leo Gordon, Norman Rossington, Percy Herbert
⅄ special effects

Toby Tyler *
†† US 1959 96m Technicolor
Walt Disney (Bill Walsh)

📼

In 1910, a young orphan runs away to join a travelling circus in the midwest, and with the help of a chimp becomes a famous star.
Acceptable, predictable family fare.
w Bill Walsh, Lillie Hayward *novel* James Otis Kaler d Charles Barton ph William Snyder m Buddy Baker
☆ Kevin Corcoran, Henry Calvin, Gene Sheldon, Bob Sweeney, James Drury

Today It's Me, Tomorrow You! *
Italy 1968 95m Technicolor
PAC/Splendid (Franco Cucca)

📼

original title: *Oggi a Me ... Domani a Te!*
An Indian recruits a gang of gunmen in order to take vengeance on the man who raped and murdered his wife and framed him for the crime.
Spaghetti Western in the style of The Magnificent Seven.
w Dario Argento, Tonino Cervi d Tonino Cervi ph Sergio D'Offizi m Angelo Francesco Lavagnini ad Carlo Gervasi ed Sergio Montanari
☆ Montgomery Ford (Brett Halsey), Bud Spencer (Carlo Pedersoli), William Berger, Tatsuya Nakadai, Wayde Preston, Stanley Gordon

Today We Live *
US 1933 113m bw
MGM (Howard Hawks)
During World War I, an aristocratic English girl and her three lovers all find themselves at the front, and two fail to return.
Stilted romantic melodrama with imposing credentials.

w Edith Fitzgerald, Dwight Taylor, William Faulkner *story* Turnabout by William Faulkner d Howard Hawks ph Oliver T. Marsh
☆ Joan Crawford, Gary Cooper, Robert Young, Franchot Tone, Roscoe Karns, Louise Closser Hale, Rollo Lloyd
  'One of those overly long features which would serve the purpose better in 2000 or more less feet ... but the action, the men and the Crawford name should translate into satisfying figures.' – *Variety*
† Much of the flying footage was taken from the *Hell's Angels* stock.

The Todd Killings *
US 1970 93m Technicolor Panavision
National General (Barry Shear)

🖥

In a small American town, a 23-year-old boy starts out on a rampage of rape and murder.
Violent psychological melodrama, based on fact, with inventive direction.
w Dennis Murphy, Joel Oliansky d Barry Shear ph Harold E. Stine m Leonard Rosenman
☆ Robert F. Lyons, Richard Thomas, Belinda Montgomery, Barbara Bel Geddes, Gloria Grahame
  'The most striking of the many recent film versions of the souring of the American dream.' – *Tony Rayns*

Todo Sobre Mi Madre: see All About My Mother

Together Again
US 1944 93m bw
Columbia (Virginia Van Upp)
The widow of a New England mayor commissions a statue in his honour. The title refers to the reteaming of the stars who were so popular in *Love Affair* and *When Tomorrow Comes*, which is a sign of the lack of invention elsewhere.
A comedy without laughs.
w Virginia Van Upp, F. Hugh Herbert d Charles Vidor ph Joseph Walker m Werner Heymann
☆ Charles Boyer, Irene Dunne, Charles Coburn, Mona Freeman, Jerome Courtland, Elizabeth Patterson, Charles Dingle, Walter Baldwin

Tokyo Cowboy
Canada 1994 94m colour/bw
Big Space (Lodi Butler, Richard Davis)
A Japanese man goes to Canada to meet his female pen-friend and live his fantasy of becoming a cowboy.
Leisurely, almost inert, drama of small-town life, family tensions and lesbian love, interspersed with Western parodies.
w Caroline Adderson d Kathy Garneau ph Kenneth Hewlett m Ari Wise ed Debra Rurak
☆ Hiromoto Ida, Christianne Hirt, Janne Mortil, Anna Ferguson, Alec Willows, Michael Ironside, Christine Lippa, Dwight McFee

Tokyo Drifter **
Japan 1966 83m colour Nikkatsu-Scope
Nikkatsu (Nakagawa Tetsuro)

📼 📼

original title: *Tokyo Nagaremono*
aka: *The Man from Tokyo*
A hitman goes on the run around Japan, followed by killers hired by his former boss.
An enjoyably delirious thriller in which virtually anything goes, including a parody of a bar brawl straight out of a John Wayne Western. It has an exotic appeal, together with a flamboyant visual style.
w Kawauchi Yasunori *novel* Kawauchi Yasunori d Suzuki Seijun ph Mine Shigeyoshi m Kaburagi So ad Kimura Takeo ed Inoue Shinya
☆ Watari Tetsuya, Matsubara Chieko, Nitani Hideaki, Kita Ryuji, Yoshida Tsuyoshi, Esumi Hideaki, Kawachi Tamio, Cho Hiroshi
  'A barrage of aestheticised violence, visual gags, incongruous songs and hairdryers and mind-warping colour effects. This is a reckless reduction of the yazuka genre to its most fundamental elements, strung together with only the most minimal regard for logic or even narrative coherence.' – *Tony Rayns*

'The Self Is The Ultimate Horror.'

Tokyo Fist **
Japan 1995 88m colour
Blue Dolphin/Kaijyu (Shinya Tsukamoto)

An insurance salesman renews his friendship with a school-friend, now a boxer, which results in beatings and the loss of his girlfriend.
A curiously cold, hard-hitting work that will not be to everyone's taste; but its account of violence within a rigid society and between the sexes has a ritualistic power.
wd Shinya Tsukamoto ph Shinya Tsukamoto m Chu Ishikawa ad Shinya Tsukamoto ed Shinya Tsukamoto, Konno Naoto
☆ Kahori Fujii, Shinya Tsukamoto, Kohji Tsukamoto, Naomasa Musaka, Naoto Takenaka
'It suggests that technology has taken over our psyches, and it appears both impassioned and silly at the same time.' – *Derek Malcolm, Guardian*

Tokyo Joe
US 1949 88m bw
Columbia/Santana (Robert Lord)

A former night-club owner returns to postwar Japan to reclaim his fortune and his ex-wife.
Dispirited star melodrama.
w Cyril Hume, Bertram Millhauser d Stuart Heisler ph Charles Lawton Jnr m George Antheil
☆ Humphrey Bogart, Florence Marly, Alexander Knox, Sessue Hayakawa, Lora Lee Michel, Jerome Courtland

Tokyo Monogatari: see Tokyo Story

Tokyo Nagaremono: see Tokyo Drifter

Tokyo Pop
US 1988 99m TVC Color
Fries/Spectrafilm/Lorimar/Kuzui (Kaz Kuzui, Joel Tuber)

A backing singer in a New York punk rock group goes to Tokyo in search of fame.
Mildly entertaining tale of cultural cross-over.
w Fran Rubel Kuzui, Lynn Grossman d Fran Rubel Kuzui ph James Hayman m Alan Brewer pd Terumi Hosoishi ed Camilla Toniolo
☆ Carrie Hamilton, Yutaka Tadokoro, Daisuke Oyama, Hiroshi Kabayashi, Hiroshi Sugita, Satoshi Kanai.

Tokyo Story ****
Japan 1953 135m bw
Shochiku

original title: *Tokyo Monogatari*
An elderly couple, who travel to Tokyo to visit their married son and daughter, discover that their children have little time for them.
Bleak, austere and moving family drama of life's disappointments.
w Kogo Noda, Yasujiro Ozu d Yasujiro Ozu ph Yuharu Atsuta m Kojun Saito ad Tatsuo Hamada ed Yoshiyasu Hamamura
☆ Chishu Ryu, Chieko Higashiyama, Setsuko Hara, Haruko Sugimura, Nobuo Nakamura, So Yamamura, Kuniko Miyake, Eijiro Tono

Tol'able David *
US 1921 80m bw silent
First National/Inspiration

A quiet farming community is disrupted by three marauding convicts, who are finally despatched by the peace-loving youngest son.
Fresh, sympathetic David-and-Goliath story which was a huge popular success on its release.
w Edmund Goulding, Henry King novel Joseph Hergesheimer d Henry King ph Henry Cronjager
☆ Richard Barthelmess, Gladys Hulette, Ernest Torrence, Warner Richmond
'It is sentimental in places, but not sloppy. It is bucolic, but its rusticity is not rubbed in … it is restrained, imaginatively suggestive when not briefly literal. For all these reasons it is stimulating.' – *New York Times*
† Columbia remade the story in 1930 with Richard Cromwell, but its time had passed.

Tom and Huck
👪 US 1996 92m Technicolor Panavision
Buena Vista/Walt Disney (Laurence Mark, John Baldecchi)

Two young witnesses to a murder attempt to clear the innocent man accused of the crime.
Blandly amiable version that manages a modicum of scares and suspense without being in any way memorable.
w Stephen Sommers, David Loughery novel *The Adventures of Tom Sawyer* by Mark Twain d Peter Hewitt ph Bobby Bukowski m Stephen Endelman pd Gemma Jackson ed David Freeman
☆ Jonathan Taylor Thomas, Brad Renfro, Eric Schweig, Charles Rocket, Amy Wright, Michael McShane, Marian Seldes, Rachael Leigh Cook
'Unremarkable but inoffensive.' – *Variety*

Tom and Jerry: The Movie
👪 US 1992 84m CFI color
First Independent/Turner/WMG (Phil Roman)

Tom and Jerry, left homeless, become the best of friends.
A lacklustre cartoon, which replaces the inspired mayhem of the classic shorts with sickly sweetness.
w Dennis Marks d Phil Roman m Henry Mancini ed Julie Ann Gustafson
☆ Featuring the voices of Richard Kind, Dana Hill, Anndi McAfee, Henry Gibson, Tony Jay
'Though slickly animated, this first full-length pic featuring the vintage cat and mouse is misconceived from start to finish. Full of gooey sentimentality in a banal melodramatic plot.' – *Variety*

Tom and Viv *
GB/US 1994 125m Technicolor
Entertainment/Samuelson/Harvey Kass/IRS/British Screen

The unhappy marriage of the poet T. S. Eliot and his first wife, Vivienne Haigh-Wood, whose behaviour causes him increasing embarrassment.
Glossy period movie that only occasionally gets to grips with its fascinating subject-matter.
w Michael Hastings, Adrian Hodges play Michael Hastings d Brian Gilbert ph Martin Fuhrer m Debbie Wiseman pd Jamie Leonard ed Tony Lawson
☆ Willem Dafoe, Miranda Richardson, Rosemary Harris, Tim Dutton, Nickolas Grace, Philip Locke
'A handsomely appointed but overly starched love story that attains real clout only in the final reel … a well-meaning but noble failure.' – *Derek Elley*
Ⅷ Miranda Richardson; Rosemary Harris

Tom Brown of Culver
US 1932 79m bw
Universal

Life at a military cadet school.
Idealized propaganda, with the hero a boy subsidized by the local legion because his dead father was a war hero.
w Tom Buckingham d William Wyler
☆ Tom Brown, H. B. Warner, Slim Summerville, Richard Cromwell, Ben Alexander, Sidney Toler, Betty Blythe
'It will probably make acceptable film fare to other than irritated cadets.' – *Variety*

Tom Brown's Schooldays *
👪 US 1940 86m bw
(RKO) The Play's the Thing (Brian Desmond Hurst)

Tom Brown finds life at Rugby brutal, but helps to become a civilizing influence.
Pretty lively Hollywood version of a rather unattractive semi-classic.
w Walter Ferris, Frank Cavell novel Thomas Hughes d Robert Stevenson ph Nicholas Musuraca m Anthony Collins
☆ Jimmy Lydon, Cedric Hardwicke, Billy Halop, Freddie Bartholomew, Gale Storm, Josephine Hutchinson

Tom Brown's Schooldays
👪 GB 1951 96m bw
Talisman (George Minter)

Unexciting remake featuring one surprisingly strong performance.

Tom, Dick and Harry **
US 1941 86m bw
RKO (Robert Sisk)

A girl daydreams about her three boyfriends, but can't make up her mind.
Brightly-handled comedy which became a minor classic but does seem to have faded a little. Remade as The Girl Most Likely (qv).
w Paul Jarrico d Garson Kanin ph Merritt Gerstad m Roy Webb
☆ Ginger Rogers, Burgess Meredith, Alan Marshal, George Murphy, Phil Silvers, Joe Cunningham, Jane Seymour, Lenore Lonergan
'Foot by foot the best made picture of this year.' – *Otis Ferguson*
Ⅷ Paul Jarrico

Tom Horn
US 1979 97m Technicolor Panavision
Warner/Solar/First Artists (Fred Weintraub)

An ex-cavalry scout gets a job as a stock detective, is framed for murder, and allows himself to be hanged.
Curious pessimistic and unsatisfactory semi-Western in which the star was found to have lost his old charisma after being too long away.
w Thomas McGuane, Bud Shrake, from the alleged autobiography of Tom Horn d William Wiard ph John Alonzo m Ernest Gold
☆ Steve McQueen, Linda Evans, Richard Farnsworth, Billy Green Bush, Slim Pickens, Elisha Cook Jnr
'Imagine a film that opens up with dialogue that can't be heard at all, then proceeds to build up to a fist fight that's never seen, that cuts away to sunsets to fill in other scenes that have no dramatic point, that presents a meal where the sound of knives and forks drowns out what's being said, and you have just the beginning of what's wrong with Tom Horn.' – *Variety*

'The whole world loves him!'
Tom Jones ****
GB 1963 129m Eastmancolor
UA/Woodfall (Tony Richardson)

In 18th-century England a foundling is brought up by the squire and marries his daughter after many adventures.
Fantasia on Old England, at some distance from the original novel, with the director trying every possible jokey approach against a meticulously realistic physical background. Despite trade fears, the Hellzapoppin style made it an astonishing box-office success (the sex helped), though it quickly lost its freshness and was much imitated.
w John Osborne novel Henry Fielding d Tony Richardson ph Walter Lassally, Manny Wynn m John Addison pd Ralph Brinton
☆ Albert Finney, Susannah York, Hugh Griffith, Edith Evans, Joan Greenwood, Diane Cilento, George Devine, Joyce Redman, David Warner, Wilfrid Lawson, Freda Jackson, Rachel Kempson
'Uncertainty, nervousness, muddled method … desperation is writ large over it.' – *Stanley Kauffmann*
'Much of the time it looks like a home movie, made with sporadic talent by a group with more enthusiasm than discipline.' – *Tom Milne*
'It is as though the camera had become a method actor: there are times when you wish you could buy, as on certain juke boxes, five minutes' silence … Obviously a film which elicits such lyric ejaculations from the reviewers cannot be all good.' – *John Simon*
'I just felt I was being used. I wasn't involved … I was bored most of the time.' – *Albert Finney*
† The narrator was Michael MacLiammoir.
🏆 best picture; John Osborne; Tony Richardson; John Addison
Ⅷ Albert Finney; Hugh Griffith; Edith Evans; Diane Cilento; Joyce Redman
🎭 best picture; best British film; John Osborne

Tom Sawyer
👪 US 1973 103m DeLuxe Panavision
UA/Readers Digest (Arthur P. Jacobs)

Reverential, rather tediously over-produced version for family audiences of the seventies, with brief songs and real Mississippi locations.
d Don Taylor ph Frank Stanley md John Williams pd Philip Jefferies w/m/ly Richard and Robert Sherman
☆ Johnnie Whitaker, Celeste Holm, Warren Oates, Jeff East, Jodie Foster
† There had been a version with Jackie Coogan in 1930. Selznick's *The Adventures of Tom Sawyer* followed in 1937. In 1939 Billy Cook was Tom Sawyer, Detective, with Donald O'Connor as Huckleberry Finn.
Ⅷ Richard and Robert Sherman; John Williams

Tom Thumb *
👪 GB 1958 98m Eastmancolor
MGM/Galaxy (George Pal)

A tiny forest boy outwits a couple of thieves.
Slight musical built round the legend of a two-inch boy; good trickwork and songs make it a delightful film for children.
w Ladislas Fodor d George Pal ph Georges Périnal m Douglas Gamley, Kenneth V. Jones sp Tom Howard
☆ Russ Tamblyn, Jessie Matthews, Peter Sellers, Terry-Thomas, Alan Young, June Thorburn, Bernard Miles, Ian Wallace
† Donald O'Connor badly wanted the role, but it went to the MGM contractee.
🏆 special effects

Tomahawk
US 1951 82m Technicolor
Universal-International

GB title: *Battle of Powder River*
An Indian scout helps the Sioux to get their territory rights.
Competent small-scale Western.
w Silvia Richards, Maurice Geraghty d George Sherman ph Charles P. Boyle m Hans Salter
☆ Van Heflin, Yvonne de Carlo, Alex Nicol, Preston Foster, Jack Oakie, Tom Tully, Rock Hudson

The Tomahawk and the Cross: see Pillars of the Sky

The Tomb of Ligeia **
GB 1964 81m Eastmancolor Cinemascope
American International (Roger Corman)

A brooding Victorian metamorphoses his dead wife into a cat, then into the beautiful Lady Rowena.
Complex but rather fascinating horror suspenser which rejigs familiar elements into something new; the best of the Corman Poes.
w Robert Towne story Edgar Allan Poe d Roger Corman ph Arthur Grant m Kenneth V. Jones
☆ Vincent Price, Elizabeth Shepherd, John Westbrook, Oliver Johnston, Richard Johnson, Derek Francis

Tomb of the Living Dead: see The Mad Doctor of Blood Island

Tomboy
US 1984 92m DeLuxe
Crown International/Marimark (Marilyn Jacobs Tenser)

A female mechanic falls for a professional driver, but is determined to beat him in a race.
Unsubtle 'teen flick, an unimaginative, low-budget variation on Flashdance, which even its target audience found wanting; there are rather more shower scenes and bare breasts than the narrative requires, and the rest consists of unattractive visuals to a rock accompaniment.
w Ben Zelig d Herb Freed ph Daniel Yarussi ad Randy Ser ed Richard E. Westover
☆ Betsy Russell, Jerry Dinome, Kristi Somers, Richard Erdman, Philip Sterling, Eric Douglas, Paul Gunning, Toby Iland

---

Tombs of the Blind Dead (dubbed)

Spain/Portugal 1972 86m Eastmancolor
Plata/Interfilme

🎞️ 📼 ⊘

original title: *La Noche del Terror Ciego*
aka: *The Blind Dead*

Devil-worshipping Knights Templar, killed at the time of the Crusades, rise from their graves to kill all they encounter.

Gruesome, low-budget horror with a few original touches; it proved popular enough to spawn a few sequels.

wd Amando de Ossorio ph Pablo Ripoli ad Jaime Duarte de Brito ed José Antonio Rojo
☆ Cesar Burner, Lone Fleming, Joseph Thelman, Helen Harp, Rufino Ingles, Veronica Llimera, Maria Sylva
† It was followed by *The Return of the Evil Dead* (qv).

'Justice is coming.'

Tombstone *

US 1993 129m Technicolor Panavision
Entertainment/Cinergi (James Jacks, Sean Daniel, Bob Misiorowski)

🎞️ 📼 ⟳ ⊘ ⌒

After his brother is killed in Tombstone, Wyatt Earp and his friend Doc Holliday take on the lawless Clanton gang.

Vigorous retelling of the incidents that led up to the famous gunfight at the OK Corral, celebrating Earp as the archetypal Western hero.

w Kevin Jarre d George P. Cosmatos ph William A. Fraker m Bruce Broughton pd Catherine Hardwicke ed Frank J. Urioste, Roberto Silvi, Harvey Rosenstock
☆ Kurt Russell, Val Kilmer, Sam Elliott, Bill Paxton, Powers Boothe, Michael Biehn, Charlton Heston, Jason Priestley, Jon Tenney, Stephen Lang, Robert Mitchum

'A tough-talking but soft-hearted tale that is entertaining in a sprawling, old-fashioned manner.' – *Variety*
† Kevin Jarre was replaced as director during shooting.

'Good men (and women) live in Tombstone – but not for long!'

Tombstone (The Town Too Tough to Die)

US 1942 80m bw
Paramount

How Wyatt Earp cleaned up the town.

Lacklustre low-budget version of a famous story.

w Albert Shelby Le Vino, Edward E. Paramore
d William McGann
☆ Richard Dix, Frances Gifford, Kent Taylor, Edgar Buchanan, Don Castle, Victor Jory

Tommy *

GB 1975 108m colour
Hemdale/Robert Stigwood

🎞️ 📼 ⟳ ⊘ ⌒

A deaf, dumb and blind child is eventually cured and becomes a rock celebrity.

Mystical rock opera screened with the director's usual barrage of effects and an ear-splitting score. Of occasional interest.

w Ken Russell opera Pete Townshend and the Who d Ken Russell ph Dick Bush, Ronnie Taylor m Pete Townshend and the Who
☆ Roger Daltrey, Ann-Margret, Oliver Reed, Elton John, Eric Clapton, Keith Moon
♫ Ann-Margret; score

Tommy Boy

US 1995 96m DeLuxe
Paramount (Lorne Michaels)

🎞️ 📼

A fat and hapless perpetual student inherits the family business when his father dies and saves it from his unscrupulous stepmother with the aid of a skinny friend.

A farce that grows increasingly dim as two television comedians (from Saturday Night Live) flounder helplessly with a witless, cliché-ridden script.

w Bonnie Turner, Terry Turner d Peter Segal ph Victor J. Kemper m David Newman pd Stephen J. Lineweaver ed William Kerr
☆ Chris Farley, David Spade, Brian Dennehy, Bo Derek, Dan Aykroyd, Julie Warner, Sean McCann, Rob Lowe (uncredited)

'The only thing worse than contemplating the oafish antics on screen is imagining the audience of cretins for whom the film was made.' – *Alexander Walker*

The Tommy Steele Story

GB 1957 82m bw
Anglo Amalgamated/Insignia (Herbert Smith)
US title: *Rock around the World*

Tommy Steele tells journalists how he rose from being a steward in the merchant navy to singing in a Soho coffee bar and appearing in cabaret at London's fashionable Café de Paris.

Small-scale movie cashing in on Steele's then status as Britain's first rock singer. The producers don't seem to have had much faith in the drawing power of rock: there is a steel band over the titles, a calypso-styled musical commentary to the action, jazz from Humphrey Lyttleton's Band, and skiffle from Chas McDevitt and Nancy Whiskey. It also avoids the teen rebel clichés of the genre – Steele is shown as a boy who does as his parents tell him.

w Norman Hudis d Gerard Bryant ph Peter Hennessy m/ly Lionel Bart, Tommy Steele, Michael Pratt ad Eric Saw ed Ann Chegwidden
☆ Tommy Steele, Lisa Danieli, Hilda Fenemore, Charles Lamb, Patrick Westwood, Peter Lewiston, Cyril Chamberlain, John Boxer, Mark Daly

Tommy the Toreador

👥 GB 1959 86m Technicolor
Fanfare/AB

🎞️

A seaman takes the place of a bullfighter framed for smuggling.

Acceptable star comedy of its time.

w Nicholas Phipps, Sid Colin, Talbot Rothwell
d John Paddy Carstairs ph Gilbert Taylor
m Stanley Black songs Lionel Bart
☆ Tommy Steele, Sid James, Janet Munro, Pepe Nieto, Noel Purcell, Kenneth Williams, Eric Sykes

Tomorrow and Tomorrow

US 1932 73m bw
Paramount

A happily married woman suddenly falls for a foreign scientist.

Sturdy woman's picture of its day.

w Josephine Lovett play Philip Barry d Richard Wallace
☆ Ruth Chatterton, Paul Lukas, Robert Ames, Harold Minjir, Tad Alexander

'A screen play of the first grade … reflects credit on everybody concerned in its making.' – *Variety*

Tomorrow at Ten *

GB 1962 80m bw
Mancunian (Tom Blakeley)

A crook kidnaps a small boy and locks him up with a time bomb while he makes his demands in person. When the kidnapper is killed, the police have to hunt against time.

Tense second feature, well acted and efficiently done.

w Peter Millar, James Kelly d Lance Comfort ph Basil Emmott m Bernie Fenton
☆ Robert Shaw, John Gregson, Alec Clunes, Alan Wheatley, Ernest Clark, Kenneth Cope

Tomorrow Is Another Day

US 1951 90m bw
Warner

An ex-convict is soon on the run for a crime he didn't commit.

Miserable melodrama apparently left over from John Garfield days.

w Guy Endore, Art Cohn d Felix Feist ph Robert Burks m Daniele Amfitheatrof
☆ Steve Cochran, Ruth Roman, Lurene Tuttle, Bobby Hyatt, Ray Teal

Tomorrow Is Forever *

US 1945 105m bw
RKO-International (David Lewis)

A man supposed dead in the war returns with an altered face to find his wife has remarried.

Enoch Arden rides again in a rampant woman's picture which is well enough made to be generally entertaining.

w Lenore Coffee d Irving Pichel ph Joe Valentine m Max Steiner
☆ Orson Welles, Claudette Colbert, George Brent, Lucile Watson, Richard Long, Natalie Wood

Tomorrow Is Too Late: see Domani è Troppo Tardi

Tomorrow Never Comes

Canada/GB 1977 109m colour
Rank/Classic/Montreal Trust/Neffbourne (Michael Klinger, Julian Melzack)

🎞️

A jealous lover shoots a caller at his girl's beach cabana and a police siege begins.

Far from the class of Le Jour Se Lève, this is an exploitative and violent melodrama which need never have been made.

w David Pursall, Jack Seddon, Sydney Banks
d Peter Collinson ph François Protat m Roy Budd
☆ Oliver Reed, Susan George, Raymond Burr, Stephen McHattie, John Ireland, Donald Pleasence, John Osborne, Cec Linder

Tomorrow Never Dies **

US 1997 119m DeLuxe Panavision
MGM/UA/Eon (Michael G. Wilson, Barbara Broccoli)

🎞️ 📼 ⟳ ⊘ ⌒

James Bond has two days to prevent a world war involving Britain and China.

Action-packed movie that sticks close to the usual 007 formula and has a somewhat lacklustre villain in a megalomaniacal media tycoon, but at least it delivers on its promises.

w Bruce Feirstein d Roger Spottiswoode ph Robert Elswit m David Arnold pd Allan Cameron ed Dominique Fortin, Michel Arcand
☆ Pierce Brosnan, Jonathan Pryce, Michelle Yeoh, Teri Hatcher, Joe Don Baker, Ricky Jay, Götz Otto, Judi Dench, Desmond Llewelyn, Vincent Schiavelli, Geoffrey Palmer

'The filmmakers have steered almost exclusively toward action, at the expense of sex, humor or the sort of jet-set and gaming-room glamour often highlighted in the series.' – *Todd McCarthy, Variety*
† The film's production was a troubled one, owing partly to the producers agreeing to have the film ready for a December release. Brosnan rejected the script after it had been rewritten; it was then rewritten again during filming by the writer of the original script; director and scriptwriter were not talking to one another, and Brosnan and Teri Hatcher were not compatible. The film cost around $90m, and took more than $308m at the box-office worldwide.

Tomorrow the World *

US 1944 86m bw
UA/Lester Cowan

A college professor adopts his orphaned German nephew, who turns out to be an ardent 12-year-old Nazi.

Adequate, predictable screen version of a once-topical play.

w Ring Lardner Jnr, Leopold Atlas play James Gow, Armand D'Usseau d Leslie Fenton ph Henry Sharp m Louis Applebaum
☆ Fredric March, Betty Field, *Skip Homeier*, Agnes Moorehead, Joan Carroll

Tomorrow We Live

GB 1942 85m bw
British Aviation (George King)
US title: *At Dawn We Die*

French villagers help a spy escape to Britain.

Minor flagwaver marred by cheap sets.

w Anatole de Grunwald, Katherine Strueby
d George King
☆ John Clements, Greta Gynt, Hugh Sinclair, Judy Kelly, Godfrey Tearle, Yvonne Arnaud, Bransby Williams

Tongnian Wangshi: see The Time to Live and the Time to Die

Tonight and Every Night

US 1945 92m Technicolor
Columbia (Victor Saville)

🎞️

The lives and loves of London showgirls during the blitz.

Ludicrous concoction looking nothing like London and certainly nothing like the Windmill, the theatre to which it allegedly pays tribute. There are some tolerable numbers along the way.

w Lesser Samuels, Abem Finkel play Heart of a City by Lesley Storm d Victor Saville ph Rudolph Maté md Morris Stoloff, Marlin Skiles
☆ Rita Hayworth, Lee Bowman, Janet Blair, Marc Platt, Leslie Brooks, Dusty Anderson, Florence Bates, Ernest Cossart

† Rita Hayworth's singing was dubbed by Martha Mears.
♫ Morris Stoloff, Marlin Skiles; song 'Anywhere' (mJule Styne, lySammy Cahn)

Tonight Is Ours

US 1932 76m bw
Paramount

A Balkan princess falls for a commoner in Paris.

One of the master's less sparkling plays gets the heavy Hollywood treatment.

w Edwin Justus Mayer play Noël Coward
d Stuart Walker ph Karl Struss
☆ Fredric March, Claudette Colbert, Alison Skipworth, Paul Cavanagh, Arthur Byron, Ethel Griffies

'Slow and talky flicker, better for the class houses.' – *Variety*

Tonight or Never

US 1931 80m bw
Samuel Goldwyn

A prima donna falls for a man she thinks is a Venetian gigolo, but he turns out to be an impresario from New York.

Flimsy comedy which turned out to be its star's last vehicle of any consequence for twenty years.

w Ernest Vajda play Lily Hatvany d Mervyn Le Roy ph Gregg Toland md Alfred Newman
☆ Gloria Swanson, Melvyn Douglas, Ferdinand Gottschalk, Robert Greig, Alison Skipworth, Boris Karloff

Tonight We Raid Calais

US 1943 70m bw
TCF

A British agent lands in occupied France to pave the way for a bombing raid.

Adequate low-budget morale booster.

w Waldo Salt d John Brahm ph Lucien Ballard
☆ John Sutton, Annabella, Lee J. Cobb, Beulah Bondi, Blanche Yurka, Howard Da Silva, Marcel Dalio

Tonight We Sing *

US 1953 109m Technicolor
TCF (George Jessel)

Sol Hurok stifles his own talent to become a great musical impresario.

Blameless uppercrust biopic, with plenty of well-staged guest talent.

w Harry Kurnitz, George Oppenheimer d Mitchell Leisen ph Leon Shamroy md Alfred Newman ch David Lichine
☆ David Wayne, Anne Bancroft, Ezio Pinza, Roberta Peters, Tamara Toumanova, Isaac Stern, Jan Peerce

Tonight's the Night: see Happy Ever After (1954)

Tonka

👥 US 1958 97m Technicolor
Walt Disney

A Sioux Indian tames a magnificent white horse, and after many adventures is reunited with him at Little Big Horn.

Unremarkable and overlong adventure story.

w Lewis R. Foster, Lillie Hayward novel Comanche by David Appel d Lewis R. Foster ph Loyal Griggs
☆ Sal Mineo, Phil Carey, Jerome Courtland, Rafael Campos, H. M. Wynant

Tons of Money

GB 1930 97m bw
B and D/Herbert Wilcox

An inventor poses as his own cousin, and in this guise achieves instant success.

A long-running stage farce makes a grimly overlong movie.

w Herbert Wilcox, Ralph Lynn play Will Evans, Arthur Valentine d Tom Walls ph F. A. Young
☆ Ralph Lynn, Yvonne Arnaud, Mary Brough, Robertson Hare, Gordon James, Madge Saunders

Tony Draws a Horse

GB 1950 91m bw
Pinnacle/GFD

How to deal with a naughty boy causes mounting disagreement in the family.

Very theatrical farce which on screen seems merely silly.

👥 film suitable for family viewing   📼 VHS video-cassette for the British PAL system   📼 VHS video-cassette for the British PAL system in wide screen-format   ⟳ Video cassette in a computer-colourised version   🎞️ American NTSC video-cassette   ⌒ Laser disc

w Brock Williams *play* Lesley Storm *d* John Paddy Carstairs *ph* Jack Hildyard *m* Bretton Byrd *ed* Gerald Thomas
☆ Cecil Parker, Anne Crawford, Derek Bond, Barbara Murray, Mervyn Johns, Edward Rigby

Tony Rome *
US 1967 111m DeLuxe Panavision
TCF/Arcola/Millfield (Aaron Rosenberg)
A seedy Miami private eye runs into murder when he guards a millionaire's daughter.
Complex old-fashioned murder mystery decorated with the new amorality and fashionable violence. Tolerable for its backgrounds and professional expertise. Sequel: Lady in Cement (qv).
w Richard L. Breen *novel* Miami Mayhem by Marvin H. Albert *d* Gordon Douglas *ph* Joe Biroc *m* Billy May
☆ Frank Sinatra, Jill St John, Richard Conte, Gena Rowlands, Simon Oakland, Jeffrey Lynn, Lloyd Bochner, Sue Lyon

Too Beautiful For You: see Trop Belle Pour Toi!

Too Busy to Work
US 1932 76m bw
Fox
A tramp goes looking for his long lost wife.
Amiable remake of one of the star's most successful silents.
w Barry Conners, Philip Klein *story* Jubilo by Ben Ames Williams *d* John Blystone
☆ Will Rogers, Marian Nixon, Dick Powell, Frederick Burton, Louise Beavers
'A homey story of programmer weight … better than average business should be figured on.' – Variety

Too Dangerous to Love: see Perfect Strangers (1950)

Too Hot to Handle: see The Marrying Man

Too Hot to Handle *
US 1938 105m bw
MGM (Lawrence Weingarten)
Adventures of a scoop-seeking newsreel cameraman.
Boisterous comedy-melodrama with as many sags as highlights but generally making a cheerful star entertainment.
w Laurence Stallings, John Lee Mahin *d* Jack Conway *ph* Harold Rosson *m* Franz Waxman
☆ Clark Gable, Myrna Loy, Walter Connolly, Walter Pidgeon, Leo Carrillo, Johnny Hines, Virginia Weidler
'Even more than Test Pilot it's hoked beyond the level of credibility. But it has a driving excitement, crackling dialogue, glittering performances and inescapable romantic pull. So it's a socko audience picture and should make a parachuteful of money.' – Variety
'It's like an old-fashioned serial … no one can call it dull.' – Howard Barnes
'Breathlessly paced, witty, and violent, this is one of the more acid comedies to have been produced by the Thirties.' – John Baxter

Too Hot to Handle
GB 1960 100m Eastmancolor
ABP/Wigmore (Selim Cattan)
aka: Playgirl After Dark
Two Soho strip club owners join forces to hunt down a blackmailer.
Rotten, hilarious British gangster film set in a totally unreal underworld and very uncomfortably cast.
w Herbert Kretzmer *d* Terence Young *ph* Otto Heller *m* Eric Spear
☆ Leo Genn, Jayne Mansfield, Karl Boehm, Danik Patisson, Christopher Lee, Patrick Holt

Too Late Blues
US 1961 100m bw
Paramount (John Cassavetes)
A jazz musician falls for a neurotic girl and has fears of going commercial.
Uninteresting professional feature from a director whose reputation was made with the amateur Shadows.
w John Cassavetes, Richard Carr *d* John Cassavetes *ph* Lionel Lindon *m* David Raksin

☆ Stella Stevens, Bobby Darin, John Cassavetes, Everett Chambers, Nick Dennis, Rupert Crosse, Vince Edwards

Too Late for Tears
US 1949 99m bw
UA/Hunt Stromberg
A lady bluebeard disposes of both husbands and boyfriends.
Silly melodrama, poorly cast.
w Roy Huggins *d* Byron Haskin *ph* William Mellor *m* Dale Butts
☆ Lizabeth Scott, Don Defore, Arthur Kennedy, Dan Duryea, Kristine Miller, Barry Kelley

Too Late the Hero *
US 1969 144m Technicolor 70mm
Associates and Aldrich/Palomar
In World War II the Japanese hold one end of a small Pacific island, British and Americans the other.
Semi-cynical, long and bloody war adventure of competence but no great merit.
w Robert Aldrich, Lukas Heller *d* Robert Aldrich *ph* Joseph Biroc *m* Gerald Fried
☆ Michael Caine, Cliff Robertson, Ian Bannen, Henry Fonda, Harry Andrews, Denholm Elliott, Ronald Fraser, Percy Herbert

Too Many Crooks *
GB 1958 87m bw
Rank/Mario Zampi
Incompetent crooks plot a kidnapping.
Agreeable farce with black edges and an excellent chase sequence.
w Michael Pertwee *d* Mario Zampi *ph* Stan Pavey *m* Stanley Black
☆ Terry-Thomas, George Cole, Brenda de Banzie, Bernard Bresslaw, Sidney James, Joe Melia, Vera Day, John Le Mesurier

Too Many Girls
US 1940 85m bw
RKO (Harry Edgington, George Abbott)
The father of a wealthy co-ed hires four football heroes to protect her.
Witless nonsense, flabbily derived from a Broadway show.
w John Twist *play* George Marion Jnr, Richard Rodgers, Lorenz Hart *d* George Abbott *ph* Frank Redman *songs* Rodgers and Hart
☆ Lucille Ball, Desi Arnaz, Richard Carlson, Ann Miller, Eddie Bracken, Frances Langford, Harry Shannon
† The film on which Ball and Arnaz first met.
†† Lucille Ball's singing was dubbed by Trudy Erwin.

Too Many Husbands *
US 1940 84m bw
Columbia (Wesley Ruggles)
GB title: My Two Husbands
Allegedly drowned on a boat cruise, a man turns up again after his wife has remarried.
Modest variation on a familiar theme, professional but unexciting; later remade as Three for the Show (qv).
w Claude Binyon *play* Home and Beauty by W. Somerset Maugham *d* Wesley Ruggles *ph* Joseph Walker *m* Frederick Hollander
☆ Jean Arthur, Melvyn Douglas, Fred MacMurray, Harry Davenport, Dorothy Peterson, Melville Cooper, Edgar Buchanan

Too Many Lovers
France 1958 102m Eastmancolor
Sirius (Jacques Roitfeld)
original title: Charmants Garçons
A dancer is pursued by a jewel thief, a gigolo, a boxer, a wealthy businessman and several husbands.
Light romantic comedy that offers occasional amusement, as well as a couple of dances by its star.
w Charles Spaak, Dominique Fabre, Etienne Perier *d* Henri Decoin *ph* Pierre Montazel *m* Georges Van Parys *ch* Roland Petit *ad* Robert Clavel *ed* Claude Durand
☆ Zizi Jeanmaire, Daniel Gelin, Henri Vidal, François Perier, Gert Frobe

Too Much Harmony
US 1933 76m bw
Paramount
A star singer helps a promising girl to the top.
Routine light musical which filled a need.
w Harry Ruskin, Joseph L. Mankiewicz *d* Eddie Sutherland
☆ Bing Crosby, Jack Oakie, Judith Allen, Skeets Gallagher, Lilyan Tashman, Harry Green, Ned Sparks
'Should be an easy pleaser.' – Variety

'Always a man! Almost any man!'
Too Much Too Soon *
US 1958 121m bw
Warner (Henry Blanke)
Young actress Diana Barrymore goes to Hollywood to look after her alcoholic father John, but mild success goes to her head and she too turns to drink.
Rather dismal and murkily photographed account of an absorbing real-life situation; one performance holds the first half together.
wd Art Napoleon *memoirs* Diana Barrymore *ph* Nicholas Musuraca, Carl Guthrie *m* Ernest Gold *ad* George James Hopkins
☆ Dorothy Malone, Errol Flynn, Efrem Zimbalist Jnr, Neva Patterson, Martin Milner, Ray Danton, Murray Hamilton

Too Young to Kiss
US 1951 89m bw
MGM (Sam Zimbalist)
A girl pianist poses as an infant prodigy, and falls for the impresario who wants to adopt her.
Dull conveyor belt comedy.
w Frances Goodrich, Albert Hackett *d* Robert Z. Leonard *ph* Joseph Ruttenberg *m* Johnny Green *ad* Cedric Gibbons, Paul Groesse
☆ June Allyson, Van Johnson, Gig Young, Paula Corday, Larry Keating, Hans Conried
℧ art direction

'If this happened to your daughter, would you be to blame?'
Too Young to Love
GB 1959 89m bw
Rank/Welbeck (Herbert Smith)
A 15-year-old prostitute is brought before a Brooklyn juvenile court.
Tepid filming of a popular exploitation play of the fifties, mysteriously made in England.
w Sydney and Muriel Box *play* Pick Up Girl by Elsa Shelley *d* Muriel Box *ph* Gerald Gibbs *m* Bruce Montgomery
☆ Thomas Mitchell, Pauline Hahn, Joan Miller, Austin Willis, Jess Conrad, Bessie Love, Alan Gifford

Tootsie ****
US 1982 116m colour
Columbia/Mirage/Punch (Sydney Pollack, Dick Richards)
An out-of-work actor pretends to be a woman in order to get a job in a soap opera.
As with Genevieve and Whisky Galore, an unlikely comedy subject makes an instant classic. It's all in the handling.
w Larry Gelbart, Murray Shisgal *story* Don McGuire *d* Sydney Pollack *ph* Owen Roizman *m* Dave Grusin *pd* Peter Larkin *ed* Frederic and William Steinkamp
☆ Dustin Hoffman, Jessica Lange, Teri Garr, Dabney Coleman, Charles Durning, Sydney Pollack, George Gaynes
♪ Jessica Lange
℧ best picture; Dustin Hoffman; Teri Garr; Sydney Pollack as director; original screenplay; cinematography; editing; song, 'It Might Be You' (mDave Grusin, lyAlan Bergman, Marilyn Bergman); sound
℧ Dustin Hoffman

Top Banana *
US 1953 100m Color Corporation
Roadshow/Harry M. Popkin
A TV comedian invites an attractive salesgirl to join his show.
A wisp of plot is the excuse for a revue, and the interest is in the old-time burlesque acts, some of which survive the generally shoddy treatment.
w Gene Towne *d* Alfred E. Green *ph* William Bradford *m/ly* Johnny Mercer

☆ Phil Silvers, Rose Marie, Danny Scholl, Jack Albertson

Top Gun
US 1986 110m Metrocolor
Paramount/Don Simpson, Jerry Bruckheimer
Adventures of naval fighter pilots.
A feast of hardware and noisy music; not much story.
w Jim Cash, Jack Epps Jnr *d* Tony Scott *ph* Jeffrey Kimball *m* Harold Faltermeyer *pd* John F. DeCuir Jnr *ed* Billy Weber, Chris Lebenzon
☆ Tom Cruise, Kelly McGillis, Val Kilmer, Anthony Edwards, Tom Skerritt
'Audiences prepared to go with it will be taken for a thrilling ride in the wild blue yonder.' – Variety
♪ song 'Take My Breath Away' (Giorgio Moroder, Tom Whitlock)
℧ editors

Top Hat ****
US 1935 100m bw
RKO (Pandro S. Berman)
The path of true love is roughened by mistaken identities.
Marvellous Astaire-Rogers musical, with a more or less realistic London supplanted by a totally artificial Venice, and show-stopping numbers in a style which is no more, separated by amusing plot complications lightly handled by a team of deft farceurs.
w Dwight Taylor, Allan Scott *d* Mark Sandrich *ph* David Abel, Vernon Walker *m/ly* Irving Berlin *ch* Hermes Pan *ad* Van Nest Polglase, Carroll Clark
☆ Fred Astaire, Ginger Rogers, Edward Everett Horton, Helen Broderick, Eric Blore, Erik Rhodes
'The theatres will hold their own world series with this one. It can't miss.' – Variety
'In 25 years Top Hat has lost nothing of its gaiety and charm.' – Dilys Powell, 1960
℧ best picture; song 'Cheek to Cheek'; Hermes Pan; art direction

Top Man
US 1943 74m bw
Universal
When an officer is recalled to active duty his teenage son becomes head of the family.
Lively little putting-on-a-show comedy musical which established a new young star.
w Zachary Gold *d* Charles Lamont
☆ Donald O'Connor, Richard Dix, Peggy Ryan, Lillian Gish, Susanna Foster, Anne Gwynne

Top o' the Morning
US 1949 100m bw
Paramount (Robert L. Welch)
Investigations follow the theft of the Blarney Stone.
More Irish whimsy from the Going My Way stars.
w Edmund Beloin, James Breen *d* David Miller *ph* Lionel Lindon *m* James Van Heusen
☆ Bing Crosby, Barry Fitzgerald, Ann Blyth, Hume Cronyn, Eileen Crowe, John McIntire

The Top of His Head
Canada 1989 110m colour
Rhombus Media/Grimthorpe Film (Niv Fichman)
A satellite-dish salesman falls in love with a performance artist who is being investigated by the police.
Disastrously pretentious romantic thriller that uses experimental effects to little purpose.
wd Peter Mettler *ph* Peter Mettler *m* Fred Frith *ad* Valanne Ridgeway, Angela Murphy *ed* Peter Mettler, Margaret Van Eerdewijk
☆ Stephen Ouimette, Gary Reineke, Christie MacFadyen, David Main, Julie Wildman, Diane Barrington, David Fox

'A Ravishing Revolution In Screen Revelry!'
Top of the Town
US 1937 86m bw
Universal
The daughter of the owner of the Moonbeam Room wants to oust the swing band and stage a symbolic ballet.
A wisp of plot supports some expensive but not especially attractive numbers in a musical variety show that was supposed to be Universal's answer to other studios' biggies.

w Brown Holmes, Charles Grayson, Lou Brock d Ralph Murphy

☆ George Murphy, Doris Nolan, Hugh Herbert, Gregory Ratoff, Ella Logan, Gertrude Niesen, Henry Armetta, Mischa Auer, Samuel S. Hinds, Peggy Ryan

'A bundle of mediocrity ... it neither goes nor gets anywhere.' – Variety

Top of the World

US   1997   95m   colour

On his first day out of prison, an ex-cop is accidentally implicated in the robbery of a Las Vegas casino.

Trivial thriller that substitutes frenetic action for sense; it is no more than a stupefying succession of car crashes, explosions and gunshots.

w Bart Madison d Sidney J. Furie ph Alan Caso m Robert O. Ragland pd Aaron Osborne ed Alain Jakubowicz

☆ Peter Weller, Dennis Hopper, Tia Carrere, David Alan Grier, Cary-Hiroyuki Tagawa, Martin Kove, Kevin Bernhardt, Peter Coyote, Joe Pantoliano

Top Secret *

GB   1952   94m   bw

ABP (Mario Zampi)

US title: Mr Potts Goes to Moscow

A sanitary engineer, mistaken for a spy, is kidnapped to Moscow when his blueprints are taken for atomic secrets.

Farcical satire full of chases and lavatory humour; much of it comes off nicely.

w Jack Davies, Michael Pertwee d Mario Zampi ph Stan Pavey m Stanley Black

☆ George Cole, Oscar Homolka, Nadia Gray, Frederick Valk, Wilfrid Hyde-White, Geoffrey Sumner, Ronald Adam

Top Secret!

US   1984   90m   Metrocolor

Paramount/Kingsmere (Jon Davison, Hunt Lowry)

An American rock star in Germany gets involved with spies of both sides.

Dull spoof from the folks who gave us Airplane! A very few sight gags stand out among the dross.

w Jim Abrahams, David Zucker, Jerry Zucker, Martyn Burke d Jim Abrahams, David Zucker, Jerry Zucker ph Christopher Challis m Maurice Jarre pd Peter Lamont

☆ Val Kilmer, Lucy Gutteridge, Peter Cushing, Jeremy Kemp, Warren Clarke, Michael Gough, Omar Sharif, Christopher Villiers

'Too far over the top to retain any comic sense of the targets it sets out to lampoon. The overwhelming impression is of a Mad magazine strip in a particularly poor week.' – Martyn Auty, MFB

Top Secret Affair ᴬ

US   1956   100m   bw

Warner/United States (Martin Rackin)

GB title: Their Secret Affair

A female news publisher tries to discredit a military diplomat but falls in love with him.

Curious comedy adaptation of a rather heavy novel, moderately skilled in all departments.

w Roland Kibbee, Allan Scott novel Melville Goodwin USA by John P. Marquand d H. C. Potter ph Stanley Cortez m Roy Webb

☆ Kirk Douglas, Susan Hayward, Jim Backus, Paul Stewart, John Cromwell, Roland Winters

Topaz *

US   1969   124m   Technicolor

Universal/Alfred Hitchcock

In 1962 the CIA enlists a French agent to break up a Russian spy ring.

Oddly halting, desultory and unconvincing spy thriller shot mainly in flat TV style, with just a few short sequences in its director's better manner. A measure of its unsatisfactoriness is that three different endings were shot and actually used at various points of release.

w Samuel Taylor novel Leon Uris d Alfred Hitchcock ph Jack Hildyard m Maurice Jarre

☆ Frederick Stafford, John Forsythe, John Vernon, Roscoe Lee Browne, Dany Robin, Karin Dor, Michel Piccoli, Philippe Noiret

'A larger, slower, duller version of the spy thrillers he used to make in the thirties.' – New Yorker, 1975

Topaze *

US   1933   78m   bw

(RKO)

A simple schoolmaster allows himself to be exploited.

Interesting little comedy with the star playing against type: remade as Mr Topaze (qv).

w Ben Hecht play Marcel Pagnol d Harry d'Abbadie d'Arrast ph Lucien Andriot m Max Steiner

☆ John Barrymore, Myrna Loy, Jobyna Howland, Jackie Searl

'Okay, for metropolitan spots, but scarcely for the subsequents ... there haven't been half a dozen foreign dramas that have clicked on the screen.' – Variety

† In 1952 Howard Hughes announced a remake with Vincent Price, but it never happened.

Topio Stin Omichli: see Landscape in a Mist

Topkapi *

US   1964   119m   Technicolor

UA/Filmways (Jules Dassin)

International thieves try to rob the Istanbul museum.

Light-hearted caper story which gets out of control because of the variety of styles and accents, the director's impression that his wife can do no wrong, and the general slowness and lack of wit; but there are bright moments, colourful backgrounds, and a final suspense sequence in the Rififi manner.

w Monja Danischewsky novel The Light of Day by Eric Ambler d Jules Dassin ph Henri Alekan m Manos Hadjidakis

☆ Melina Mercouri, Maximilian Schell, Peter Ustinov, Robert Morley, Akim Tamiroff, Gilles Segal, Jess Hahn

'Merely silly and boring.' – John Simon

♟ Peter Ustinov

Topper **

US   1937   96m   bw

(MGM) Hal Roach (Milton H. Bren)

A stuffy banker is haunted by the ghosts of his sophisticated friends the Kirbys, who are visible only to him.

Influential supernatural farce, still pretty funny and deftly acted though a shade slow to get going.

w Jack Jevne, Eric Hatch, Eddie Moran novel The Jovial Ghosts by Thorne Smith d Norman Z. McLeod ph Norbert Brodine md Arthur Morton

☆ Cary Grant, Constance Bennett, Roland Young, Billie Burke, Alan Mowbray, Eugene Pallette, Arthur Lake, Hedda Hopper

'How substantial the fan support will be is difficult to anticipate ... None of the other films of similar theme aroused more than mild enthusiasm among a small group who patronize the arty theatres and talk about pictures in terms of art expression ... Effort to excuse the story's absurdities on the theory that the intent is farce comedy does not entirely excuse the production from severe rebuke. Fact also that the living dead are always facetious may be shocking to sensibilities. Some of the situations and dialogue offend conventional good taste.' – Variety

♟ Roland Young

Topper Returns **

US   1941   87m   bw

Hal Roach

A girl ghost helps Topper solve her own murder.

Spirited supernatural farce which spoofs murder mysteries, spooky houses, frightened servants, dumb cops, etc, in a pacy, accomplished and generally delightful manner.

w Jonathan Latimer, Gordon Douglas, with additional dialogue by Paul Gerard Smith d Roy del Ruth ph Norbert Brodine m Werner Heymann

☆ Roland Young, Joan Blondell, Eddie Anderson, Carole Landis, Dennis O'Keefe, H. B. Warner, Billie Burke, Donald McBride, Rafaela Ottiano

'Ectoplasm runs riot and blazes a trail of hilarity from 5th Avenue to the French Riviera!'

Topper Takes a Trip *

US   1939   85m   bw

Hal Roach

Ghostly Mrs Kirby helps Topper to save his wife from a Riviera philanderer.

Mildly pleasant follow-up, with a dog replacing Cary Grant who had become too expensive.

w Eddie Moran, Jack Jevne, Corey Ford d Norman Z. McLeod ph Norbert Brodine m Hugo Friedhofer

☆ Constance Bennett, Roland Young, Billie Burke, Alan Mowbray, Verree Teasdale, Franklin Pangborn, Alexander D'Arcy

'Dandy comedy sequel ... can't miss at the b.o ... the original ended up a fine money-maker ... no doubt one a year about Topper would be welcomed by exhibitors.' – Variety

Tops is the Limit: see Anything Goes

'The Egos. The Battles. The Words. The Music. The Women. The Scandal. Gilbert & Sullivan & So Much More'

Topsy-Turvy ***

GB   1999   160m   colour

Pathé/Thin Man/Greenlight Fund/Newmarket (Simon Channing-Williams)

The trials and tribulations behind Gilbert and Sullivan's creation of The Mikado.

Engrossing, witty drama of a clash between three giant egos, of writer, composer and producer, that takes time to explore the characters of those involved, as well as providing an entertaining glimpse of backstage life and rivalries within a social and political context.

wd Mike Leigh ph Dick Pope m Carl Davis, based on the works of Arthur Sullivan md Gary Yershon pd Eve Stewart ed Robin Sales cos Lindy Hemming

☆ Jim Broadbent, Allan Corduner, Lesley Manville, Eleanor David, Ron Cook, Timothy Spall, Martin Savage, Lely, Shirley Henderson, Jessie Bond, Wendy Nottingham

'One of those films that create a mix of erudition, pageantry and delectable acting opportunities.' – Janet Maslin, New York Times

'An overlong, overdressed and over-indulgent re-creation of an over-familiar story.' – Alexander Walker, London Evening Standard

♟ Lindy Hemming; make-up (Christine Blundell, Trefor Proud)

♟ Mike Leigh (as writer); Eve Stewart

♟ make-up/hair (Christine Blundell)

Tora! Tora! Tora! *

US   1970   144m   DeLuxe   Panavision

TCF (Elmo Williams)

A reconstruction from both sides of the events leading up to Pearl Harbor.

Immense, largely studio-bound, calcified war spectacle with much fidelity to the record but no villains and no hero, therefore no drama and no suspense.

w Larry Forrester, Hideo Oguni, Ryuzo Kikushima d Richard Fleischer, Ray Kellogg, Toshio Masuda, Kinji Fukasaku ph Charles F. Wheeler and Japanese crews m Jerry Goldsmith ad Jack Martin Smith, Yoshiro Muraki, Richard Day, Taizoh Kawashima ed James E. Newcomb, Pembroke J. Herring, Innoue Chikaya sp L. B. Abbott, Art Cruickshank

☆ Martin Balsam, Joseph Cotten, James Whitmore, Jason Robards, Edward Andrews, Leon Ames, George Macready, Soh Yamamura, Takahiro Tamura

'One of the least stirring and least photogenic historical epics ever perpetrated on the screen.' – Gary Arnold

♟ special visual effects (A. D. Flowers, L. B. Abbott)

♟ Charles F. Wheeler, Osami Furuya, Sinsaku Himeda, Masamichi Satoh; art direction; sound; editing

'She sings torch songs to daddies and lullabies to babies!'

Torch Singer

US   1933   72m   bw

Paramount (Albert Lewis)

aka: Broadway Singer

An unwed mother supports her child by singing in night-clubs.

Banal melodrama.

w Lenore Coffee, Lynn Starling play Mike by Grace Perkins d Alexander Hall ph Karl Struss

☆ Claudette Colbert, Ricardo Cortez, David Manners, Lyda Roberti, Baby LeRoy, Florence Roberts, Ethel Griffies, Helen Jerome Eddy

'Unwed mother film not so forte.' – Variety

Torch Song

US   1953   90m   Technicolor

MGM (Henry Berman, Sidney Franklin Jnr)

A temperamental musical comedy star falls for a blind pianist.

Ossified star vehicle which looks great but is too often unintentionally funny.

w John Michael Hayes, Jan Lustig story Why Should I Cry? by I. A. R. Wylie d Charles Walters ph Robert Planck m Adolph Deutsch

☆ Joan Crawford, Michael Wilding, Gig Young, Marjorie Rambeau, Henry Morgan, Dorothy Patrick

'Here is Joan Crawford all over the screen, in command, in love and in color.' – Otis L. Guernsey Jnr

♟ Marjorie Rambeau

Torch Song Trilogy *

US   1988   119m   Metrocolor

Palace/New Line (Howard Gottfried)

Three incidents in the life of a drag artiste: in 1971, there is an on-and-off affair with a school teacher; in 1973, a young man comes to live with him; in 1980, his mother discovers his homosexuality as an old lover moves back in.

A truncated version of a successful Broadway show, the film loses the theatricality of the original and transforms the material into a dated melodrama.

w Harvey Fierstein play Harvey Fierstein d Paul Bogart ph Mikael Salomon m Peter Matz pd Richard Hoover ed Nicholas C. Smith

☆ Harvey Fierstein, Anne Bancroft, Matthew Broderick, Brian Kerwin, Karen Young, Eddie Castrodad, Ken Page, Charles Pierce, Axel Vera

Torchy Blane

Glenda Farrell played the hard-boiled girl reporter and Barton MacLane the tough police inspector who puts up with her in seven out of the nine second features made by Warner in the late 30s. The characters were created in short stories by Frederick Nebel, and the films were mostly directed by William Beaudine or Frank McDonald.

1936 Smart Blonde

1937 Fly Away Baby, The Adventurous Blonde

1938 Blondes at Work, Torchy Blane in Panama (with Lola Lane, Paul Kelly), Torchy Gets Her Man

1939 Torchy Blane in Chinatown, Torchy Runs for Mayor, Torchy Plays with Dynamite (with Jane Wyman, Allen Jenkins)

Torment: see Frenzy (1944)

Torment: see L'Enfer (1993)

Torments: see El

Torn Curtain **

US   1966   119m   Technicolor

Universal/Alfred Hitchcock

A defector who is really a double agent is embarrassed when his girlfriend follows him into East Germany.

Patchy Hitchcock with some mechanically effective suspense sequences, a couple of efforts at something new, a few miscalculations, some evidence of carelessness, and a little enjoyable repetition of old situations.

w Brian Moore d Alfred Hitchcock ph John F. Warren m John Addison

☆ Paul Newman, Julie Andrews, Wolfgang Kieling, Ludwig Donath, Lila Kedrova, Hans-Joerg Felmy, Tamara Toumanova

'The pace is plodding, the political background trite, and the actors stranded by their director's customary lack of concern with performance.' – Time Out, 1984

Torpedo Run *

US   1958   98m   Metrocolor   Cinemascope
MGM (Edmund S. Grainger)

A US submarine in World War II destroys a
Japanese aircraft carrier in Tokyo Bay.
*Well-staged potboiler with excellent action sequences
marred slightly by excessive platitudinizing.*
w Richard Sale, William Wister Haines d Joseph
Pevney ph George J. Folsey
☆ Glenn Ford, Ernest Borgnine, Diane Brewster,
Dean Jones

Torpedoed: see *Our Fighting Navy*

The Torrent *

US   1925   75m   bw   silent
MGM (Hunt Stromberg)
Spanish sweethearts are parted by a domineering
mother, and the girl consoles herself by becoming a
Paris prima donna.
*Adequate emotional vehicle of its day which happened
to be Garbo's first American film.*
w Dorothy Farnum novel Vicente Blasco Ibáñez
d Monta Bell ph William Daniels
☆ Ricardo Cortez, Greta Garbo, Gertrude
Olmsted, Edward Connelly, Lucien Littlefield

Torrents of Spring **

Italy/France   1989   101m   Technicolor
Hobo/Erre Produzione/Reteitalia/Les Films
Ariane/Films A2/Curzon (Angelo Rizzoli)

A young Russian aristocrat is unfaithful to the
beautiful Italian pastrycook he plans to marry.
Charming and evocative treatment of a tragic romance.
w Jerzy Skolimowski, Arcangelo Bonaccorso
novel Ivan Turgenev d Jerzy Skolimowski
ph Dante Spinotti, Witold Sobocinski m Stanley
Myers pd Francesco Bronzi ed Cesare D'Amico,
Andrzej Kostenko
☆ Timothy Hutton, Nastassja Kinski, Valeria
Golino, William Forsythe, Urbano Barberini,
Francesca de Sapio, Jacques Herlin
   'Immensely beguiling.' – Tom Milne, MFB

Torrid Zone **

US   1940   88m   bw
Warner (Mark Hellinger)
In Central America, a banana plantation manager
is tricked by his boss into staying on, and helps a
wandering showgirl as well as foiling bandits.
*Enjoyable, fast-paced hokum with a plot borrowed
from both The Front Page and Red Dust.*
w Richard Macaulay, Jerry Wald d William
Keighley ph James Wong Howe m Adolph
Deutsch
☆ James Cagney, Pat O'Brien, Ann Sheridan, Helen
Vinson, Andy Devine, Jerome Cowan, George
Tobias, George Reeves

Törst: see *Three Strange Loves*

Tortilla Flat *

US   1942   106m   bw
MGM (Sam Zimbalist)

The problems of poor Mexican half-breeds in
California.
*Expensive but unappealing variation on The Grapes
of Wrath, with none of the cast quite getting under the
skin of their parts, and no sense of reality, rather that
of a musical without music.*
w John Lee Mahin, Benjamin Glazer novel John
Steinbeck d Victor Fleming ph Sidney Wagner
m Franz Waxman
☆ Spencer Tracy, Hedy Lamarr, John Garfield,
Frank Morgan, Akim Tamiroff, Connie Gilchrist,
John Qualen, Sheldon Leonard, Donald Meek,
Allen Jenkins, Henry O'Neill
⅋ Frank Morgan

The Torture Chamber of Baron Blood:
see *Baron Blood*

The Torture Chamber of Dr Sadism: see
The Blood Demon

Torture Garden *

GB   1967   93m   Technicolor
Columbia/Amicus (Milton Subotsky)

Five fairground visitors are told their future by the
mysterious Dr Diablo.

*Crude but effective horror portmanteau including one
story about the resurrection of Edgar Allan Poe.*
w Robert Bloch d Freddie Francis ph Norman
Warwick m Don Banks, James Bernard
☆ Burgess Meredith, Jack Palance, Peter Cushing,
Beverly Adams, Michael Bryant, John Standing

Total Eclipse

GB/France/Belgium   1995   110m   colour
Fit-Portman-SFP-K2/Capitol/Canal (Ramsay Levi)

Two poets, Verlaine and Rimbaud, engage in a
destructive love affair.
*Unsuccessful attempt to dramatize a famous literary
conjunction; the concentration is on their behaviour
rather than the work that came out of their mutual
needs, and that is not grounded in any felt experience,
seeming arbitrary and without point.*
w Christopher Hampton d Agnieszka Holland
ph Yorgos Arvanitis m Jan A. P. Kaczmarek
pd Dan Weil ed Isabel Lorente
☆ Leonardo DiCaprio, David Thewlis, Romane
Bohringer, Dominique Blanc
   'Misbegotten … a complete botch in all
respects.' – Todd McCarthy, Variety
   'Unwatchable … The movie is filled with so
many hysterical let's-trash-the-hotel-room
scenes that the audience goes numb.' – Bruce
Diones, New Yorker

'They stole his mind. Now he wants it back.'

Total Recall **

US   1990   109m   Technicolor
Guild/Carolco (Buzz Feitshans, Ronald Shusett)

Following an artificially-induced dream, a labourer
remembers his previous existence as a secret agent
on Mars.
*An over-violent, paranoid and engrossing fantasy, with
more than enough twists of plot to dizzy the mind.*
w Ronald Shusett, Dan O'Bannon, Gary Goldman
story We Can Remember It For You Wholesale by
Philip K. Dick d Paul Verhoeven ph Jost Vacano
m Jerry Goldsmith pd William Sandell ed Frank
J. Urioste
☆ Arnold Schwarzenegger, Rachel Ticotin,
Sharon Stone, Ronny Cox, Michael Ironside,
Marshall Bell, Mel Johnson Jnr, Michael
Champion, Roy Brocksmith, Ray Baker, Rosemary
Dunsmore, Priscilla Allen
   'While the temptation is just to shrug off Total
Recall as an excessive but exciting "no brainer",
enough intelligence and artistry lie behind the
numbing spectacle to also make one regret its
heedless contribution to the accelerating
brutality of its time.' – Variety
🏆 best visual effects

Totally F*ed Up ***

US   1993   80m   colour
Dangerous to Know/desperate pictures/blurco
musclehate (Andrea Sperling, Gregg Araki)

Episodes in the life of six gay teenagers living in
Los Angeles, which end in the suicide of one of
them when he feels abandoned by his friends.
*A flawed but interesting exploration of the fact that a
greater-than-expected number of teenage suicides are
gay, done in semi-documentary style. What it most
obviously reveals is that its provocative director has
talent to spare.*
wd/ph/ed Gregg Araki
☆ James Duval, Roko Belic, Susan Behshid, Jenee
Gill, Gilbert Luna, Lance May, Alan Boyce, Craig
Gilmore
   'A bit of a slog around the houses of those who
see themselves only as irreversibly victimized
and loll around a lot complaining about it.' –
Marianne Gray, Film Review

Toto le Héros **

Belgium/France/Germany   1991   91m   colour
Electric/Ibis/Metropolis/RTBF/FRZ/ZDF/Canal Plus
(Philippe Dussart, Luciano Gloor)

aka: *Toto the Hero*
A bitter old man recalls the past as he plots the
murder of his childhood enemy who married the
woman he loved.
*Strange but largely successful mix of childhood fantasy
and black and bitter comedy.*
w Jaco van Dormael, Laurette Vankeerberghen,
Pascal Lonhay, Didier de Neck d Jaco van
Dormael ph Walther van den Ende m Pierre van
Dormael ad Herbert Pouille ed Susana Rossberg

☆ Michel Bouquet, Jo de Backer, Thomas Godet,
Gisela Uhlen, Mireille Perrier, Sandrine Blancke,
Peter Böhlke, Didier Ferney, Hugo Harold
Harrisson

'When It Comes To Fame And Fortune, Heaven
Knows He's Got The Touch…'

Touch *

US/France   1996   97m   CFI color
Pathé/Lumière (Lila Cazès, Fida Attieh)

A salesman and a right-wing Catholic both try to
exploit for their own purposes a young man who
apparently has the power to heal the sick.
*A surprising story of a miracle-worker, given its hard-
boiled source, and one that lurches uncomfortably
between irony and earnestness.*
wd Paul Schrader novel Elmore Leonard ph Ed
Lachman m David Grohl pd David Waso
ed Cara Silverman
☆ Bridget Fonda, Christopher Walken, Skeet
Ulrich, Tom Arnold, Gina Gershon, Lolita
Davidovich, Paul Mazursky, Janeane Garafalo,
Breckin Mayer, John Doe, Conchata Ferrell
   'Won't quite give you a profound experience but
you won't feel cheated by it either.' – Ian
Calcutt, Film Review

The Touch *

Sweden/US   1970   112m   Eastmancolor
ABC/Cinematograph AB (Lars/Owe Carlburg)
The wife of a provincial surgeon falls in love with
an archaeologist.
*Freedom versus security; the Bergman treatment is
given to a familiar love story, but the expected finesse is
lacking.*
wd Ingmar Bergman ph Sven Nykvist m Jan
Johansson
☆ Bibi Andersson, Elliott Gould, Max von Sydow

Touch and Go *

GB   1955   85m   Technicolor
Ealing (Seth Holt)

US title: *The Light Touch*
A family has doubts about its decision to emigrate
to Australia.
*Very mild comedy which fails to engage sympathy
because the characters don't seem real.*
w William Rose d Michael Truman ph Douglas
Slocombe m John Addison
☆ Jack Hawkins, Margaret Johnston, June
Thorburn, John Fraser, Roland Culver, Alison
Leggatt, James Hayter

'They had the perfect love affair. Until they fell in
love!'

A Touch of Class **

GB   1973   106m   Technicolor   Panavision
Avco/Brut/Gordon Films (Melvin Frank)

A married American businessman in London has a
hectic affair with a dress designer.
*Amiable and very physical sex farce with hilarious
highlights and a few longueurs between; the playing
keeps it above water.*
w Melvin Frank, Jack Rose d Melvin Frank
ph Austin Dempster m John Cameron
☆ Glenda Jackson, George Segal, Paul Sorvino,
Hildegarde Neil
   'Machine-tooled junk.' – William S. Pechter
   'Brightly performed and quite engaging until it
fades into vapid variations on a one-joke theme.'
– Sight and Sound
🏆 Glenda Jackson
⅋ best picture; script; John Cameron; song 'All
That Love Went to Waste' (mGeorge Barrie,
lySammy Cahn)

Touch of Evil ***

US   1958   95m   bw
U-I (Albert Zugsmith)

A Mexican narcotics investigator honeymooning
in a border town clashes with the local police chief
over a murder.
*Overpoweringly atmospheric melodrama crammed with
Wellesian touches, but very cold and unsympathetic,
with rather restrained performances (especially his) and
a plot which takes some following. Hardly the most
auspicious return to Hollywood for a wanderer, but
now a cult classic.*
wd Orson Welles novel Badge of Evil by Whit
Masterson ph Russell Metty m Henry Mancini

☆ Charlton Heston, Orson Welles, Janet Leigh,
Marlene Dietrich, Akim Tamiroff, Joseph Calleia,
Ray Collins, Dennis Weaver
   'Pure Orson Welles and impure balderdash,
which may be the same thing.' – Gerald Weales,
Reporter

A Touch of Larceny *

GB   1959   92m   bw
Paramount/Ivan Foxwell

A naval commander mysteriously disappears in the
hope that he will be branded a traitor and can sue
for libel.
Fairly amusing light comedy with lively performances.
w Roger MacDougall, Guy Hamilton, Ivan
Foxwell novel The Megstone Plot by Andrew Garve
d Guy Hamilton ph John Wilcox m Philip
Green
☆ James Mason, Vera Miles, George Sanders,
Robert Flemyng, Ernest Clark, Duncan Lamont,
Peter Barkworth
   'A beguilingly polished comedy, reminiscent in
its style, urbanity and sheen of the sort of thing
Lubitsch was doing in the 30s.' – Daily Mail

A Touch of Love *

GB   1969   107m   Eastmancolor
Amicus/Palomar (Milton Subotsky)

US title: *Thank You All Very Much*
A pregnant London student tries to get an abortion
but later decides against it.
*Curious bid for serious drama by horror producers; all
very conscientious but rather dreary.*
w Margaret Drabble novel The Millstone by
Margaret Drabble d Waris Hussein ph Peter
Suschitsky m Michael Dress
☆ Sandy Dennis, Ian McKellen, Michael Coles,
John Standing, Eleanor Bron

A Touch of the Sun

GB   1956   80m   bw
Eros/Raystro (Raymond Stross)

A hall porter is left a fortune but after living it up
for a while returns to his old hotel which is on the
rocks.
Limp comedy vehicle.
w Alfred Shaughnessy d Gordon Parry
ph Arthur Grant m Eric Spear
☆ Frankie Howerd, Ruby Murray, Dorothy
Bromiley, Gordon Harker, Reginald Beckwith,
Richard Wattis, Dennis Price, Alfie Bass,
Willoughby Goddard

A Touch of Zen ***

Taiwan   1969   180m   colour
International Film (Hsia Wu Liang-fang)

original title: *Hsia Nu*
In 14th-century China, a poor 30-year-old portrait
painter, who lives with his nagging mother in a
derelict, haunted fort, becomes involved with the
fugitive daughter of a high-ranking official
murdered by a powerful enemy.
*Sprawling, colourful epic with a compelling narrative
and a superb visual style.*
wd King Hu story P'u Sung-ling ph Hua Hui-
ying m Wu Ta-chiang ed King Hu
☆ Hsu Feng, Shih Chun, Pai Ying, Tien Peng,
Hsueh Han, Chiao Hung, Chang Ping-yu
† The film won the Grand Prize at the Cannes
Film Festival in 1975.

Touchez pas au Grisbi *

France/Italy   1953   90m   bw
Del Duca/Antares

aka: *Honour among Thieves*
aka: *Hands Off the Loot*
Two crooks succeed in stealing a consignment of
gold, but that's only the start of their worries.
*Smooth underworld hokum, with a slightly comic
attitude implied if not stated.*
w Jacques Becker, Maurice Griffe novel Albert
Simonin d Jacques Becker ph Pierre Montazel
m Jean Wiener
☆ Jean Gabin, Jeanne Moreau, Gaby Basset,
Daniel Cauchy, Marilyn Buferd, Lino Ventura,
René Dary

Tough Enough

US   1983   107m   Technicolor
TCF/American Cinema (William F. Gilmore)

A failing country singer finds success after he
enters knockout boxing competitions in order to
pay his bills.
*Unengrossing drama enlivened by some rough-house
fight sequences, but it is not a contender.*
w John Leone d Richard O. Fleischer ph James
A. Contner m Michael Lloyd, Steve Wax pd Bill
Kenney ed Dann Cahn
☆ Dennis Quaid, Carlene Watkins, Stan Shaw,
Pam Grier, Warren Oates, Wilford Brimley, Bruce
McGill

Tough Guys

US   1986   104m   DeLuxe   Panavision
Touchstone/Silver Screen/Brynal (Joe Wizan)

The last train robbers are released from prison after
30 years, and, finding that an old people's home is
not for them, return to their old ways.
*Slackly written caper comedy with two former stars in
their seventh teaming.*
w James Orr, Jim Cruickshank d Jeff Kanew
ph King Baggot m James Newton Howard
☆ Burt Lancaster, Kirk Douglas, Charles Durning,
Alexis Smith, Eli Wallach

Tough Guys Don't Dance

US   1987   108m   TVC Color
Zoetrope/Cannon (Menahem Golan, Yoram Globus)

A small businessman in Massachusetts gets
involved in a drugs deal.
*Would-be parody of the Chandler style which works
only fitfully and long outstays its welcome.*
wd Norman Mailer novel Norman Mailer
ph Michael Moyer, Danny Dukovny m Paula
Erickson pd Armin Ganz ed Debra McDermot
☆ Ryan O'Neal, Isabella Rossellini, Debra
Sandlund, Wings Hauser, Lawrence Tierney

Toughest Man in Arizona

US   1952   90m   Trucolor
Republic (Sidney Picker)
In 1861 a US marshal falls in love with the wife of
an outlaw.
*Easy-going, pleasant Western aimed at the top half of a
double bill.*
w John K. Butler d R. G. Springsteen ph Reggie
Lanning m Dale Butts
☆ Vaughn Monroe, Joan Leslie, Edgar Buchanan,
Victor Jory, Jean Parker, Henry Morgan

Tous les matins du monde *

France   1992   115m   colour
Electric/FilmParFilm/D.D./Divali/Sedif/FR3/C.N.C./Canal
/Paravision (Jean-Louis Livi)

Marin Marais, a French musician and composer at
the court of Louis XIV, recalls the man who taught
him musical values, the austere Monsieur de Sainte
Colombe, and an unhappy love affair with his
teacher's daughter.
*Glossy period drama, often delightful to look at and
hear, but hollow-centred.*
w Pascal Quignard, Alain Corneau novel Pascal
Quignard d Alain Corneau ph Yves Angelo
m Jordi Savall ad Bernard Vezat ed Marie-
Josephe Yoyotte
☆ Gérard Depardieu, Jean-Pierre Marielle, Anne
Brochet, Guillaume Depardieu, Caroline Sihol,
Carole Richert, Violaine Lacroix, Nadege Teron
'A memorably audacious parable, performed with
understanding and set out before us with no
evident compromise. But you just have to listen
to the music to realise exactly what it's about.' –
Derek Malcolm, Guardian

Toute une Vie: see And Now My Love

'The most exciting screen event of all time!'

Tovarich **

US   1937   98m   bw
Warner (Robert Lord)
A royal Russian husband and wife flee the
revolution to Paris and take jobs as servants in an
eccentric household.
*A lively comedy of its time; though many of the jokes
now seem obvious, the playing preserves its essential
quality.*

w Casey Robinson play Jacques Deval play
adaptation Robert E. Sherwood d Anatole Litvak
ph Charles Lang m Max Steiner
☆ Claudette Colbert, Charles Boyer, Basil Rathbone,
Anita Louise, Melville Cooper, Isabel Jeans,
Maurice Murphy, Morris Carnovsky, Gregory Gaye,
Montagu Love, Fritz Feld
'A yarn of charming and finely shaded
characterizations. Both humour and heart appeal
spring from intimate acquaintance with the
background and motives of each player. Class
production, magnet for first runs.' – *Variety*

Toward the Unknown

US   1956   115m   Warnercolor   Warnerscope
Warner/Toluca (Mervyn Le Roy)
GB title: *Brink of Hell*
An over-age officer takes part in the X2
experiments with rocket-firing aircraft.
Humourless flagwaver, very forgettable.
w Beirne Lay Jnr d Mervyn Le Roy ph Harold
Rosson m Paul Baron
☆ William Holden, Lloyd Nolan, Virginia Leith,
Charles McGraw, Murray Hamilton, L. Q. Jones,
James Garner, Paul Fix, Karen Steele

Towed in a Hole ***

↟↟   US   1932   20m   bw
Hal Roach
Two would-be fishermen wreck the boat they have
just bought.
*Brilliant star farce, filled with wonderfully lunatic
dialogues and freshly conceived slapstick.*
w Stan Laurel d George Marshall ph Art Lloyd
ed Richard Currier
☆ Stan Laurel, Oliver Hardy, Billy Gilbert

Tower of Evil

GB/US   1972   89m   Technicolor
MGM-EMI/Grenadier/Fanfare (Richard Gordon)

US title: *Horror of Snape Island*
A private investigator takes his family to an island
lighthouse to discover the truth about three
mysterious deaths.
An unoriginal little shocker.
wd Jim O'Connolly story George Baxt
ph Desmond Dickinson m Kenneth V. Jones
ad Disley Jones ed Henry Richardson
☆ Bryant Halliday, Jill Haworth, Anna Palk,
William Lucas, Anthony Valentine, Jack Watson,
Derek Fowlds, Dennis Price, George Coulouris
'As much energy is expended on the self-
conscious nudity and violence as on the
suspense, but the dialogue and performances are
anyway equally unconvincing.' – *David
McGillivray, MFB*

Tower of London **

US   1939   92m   bw
Universal (Rowland V. Lee)

With the help of Mord the executioner, Richard
Crookback kills his way to the throne but is
destroyed at Bosworth.
*The Shakespearean view of history played as a horror
comic: despite an overall lack of pace, spirited scenes
and good performances win the day.*
w Robert N. Lee d Rowland V. Lee ph George
Robinson m Charles Previn
☆ Basil Rathbone, Boris Karloff, Barbara O'Neil,
Ian Hunter, Vincent Price, Nan Grey, John Sutton,
Leo G. Carroll, Miles Mander
'Spine-tingling horror picture … so strong that it
may provide disturbing nightmares as aftermath.'
– *Variety*

Tower of London *

US   1962   79m   bw
AIP/Admiral (Gene Corman)

A variation on the same events, with Price
graduating from Clarence to Crookback, and the
addition of ghostly visions.
*All very cheap, but occasionally vivid melodrama,
despite intrusive American accents.*
w Leo V. Gordon, Amos Powell, James B. Gordon
d Roger Corman ph Arch Dalzell m Michael
Anderson
☆ Vincent Price, Michael Pate, Joan Freeman,
Robert Brown, Justice Eatson, Sarah Selby, Richard
McCauly, Bruce Gordon

The Tower of Terror

GB   1941   78m   bw
ABPC

British and German agents clash in a lighthouse
tended by a mad keeper.
Lurid penny-dreadful, quite amusing in its way.
w John Argyle, John Reinhart d Lawrence
Huntington
☆ Wilfrid Lawson, Movita, Michael Rennie,
Morland Graham, George Woodbridge

'One tiny spark becomes a night of towering
suspense!'

The Towering Inferno ***

US   1974   165m   DeLuxe   Panavision
TCF/Warner (Irwin Allen)

The world's tallest building is destroyed by fire on
the night of its inauguration.
*Showmanlike but relentlessly padded disaster
spectacular, worth seeing for its cast of stars, its sheer
old-fashioned expertise, and its special effects.*
w Stirling Silliphant novels *The Tower* by Richard
Martin Stern, *The Glass Inferno* by Thomas M.
Scortia, Frank M. Robinson d John Guillermin,
Irwin Allen ph Fred Koenekamp, Joseph Biroc
m John Williams pd William Creber ed Harold F.
Kress, Carl Kress sp Bill Abbott
☆ Paul Newman, Steve McQueen, William
Holden, Faye Dunaway, Fred Astaire, Susan
Blakely, Richard Chamberlain, Robert Vaughn,
Jennifer Jones, O. J. Simpson, Robert Wagner
'Several generations of blue-eyed charmers act
their roles as if each were under a separate bell
jar.' – *Verina Glaessner*
'Each scene of someone horribly in flames is
presented as a feat for the audience's
delectation.' – *New Yorker*
'The combination of Grade A spectacle and B-
picture characters induces a feeling of sideline
detachment.' – *Michael Billington, Illustrated
London News*
🏋 photography; song 'We May Never Love Like
This Again' (m/ly Al Kasha, Joel Hirschhorn);
editing
🏆 best picture; John Williams; Fred Astaire; art
direction; sound
🏆 John Williams; Fred Astaire

A Town Called Bastard

GB   1971   97m   Technicolor   Franscope
Benmar/Zurbano (Ben Fisz)
aka: *A Town Called Hell*
Mexican revolutionaries massacre a priest and his
congregation and take over the town. Ten years
later a widow arrives seeking vengeance.
*Sadistic Western with an opening massacre followed by
twenty-two killings (count 'em). Pretty dull otherwise.*
w Richard Aubrey d Robert Parrish ph Manuel
Berenguer m Waldo de Los Rios
☆ Robert Shaw, Stella Stevens, Telly Savalas,
Martin Landau, Michael Craig, Fernando Rey,
Dudley Sutton

A Town Called Hell: see A Town Called Bastard

A Town like Alice **

GB   1956   117m   bw
Rank/Vic Films (Joseph Janni)

US title: *The Rape of Malaya*
Life among women prisoners of the Japanese in
Malaya, especially one who is finally reunited with
her Australian lover.
*Genteelly harrowing war film, formlessly adapted from
the first part of a popular novel; a big commercial
success of its day.*
w W. P. Lipscomb, Richard Mason novel Nevil
Shute d Jack Lee ph Geoffrey Unsworth
m Matyas Seiber
☆ Virginia McKenna, Peter Finch, Takagi, Marie
Lohr, Maureen Swanson, Jean Anderson, Renée
Houston, Nora Nicholson
🏆 Peter Finch; Virginia McKenna

'There she lay, wearing her nylons – right around her
neck!'

Town on Trial *

GB   1956   96m   bw
Columbia/Marksman (Maxwell Setton)
A police inspector solves the murder of a girl after
a tennis club dance in a British country town.
*Straightforward murder mystery shot in Weybridge,
with a wide variety of suspects having something to*

hide; settings and characters are quite realistic and also
a little dreary.
w Ken Hughes, Robert Westerby d John
Guillermin ph Basil Emmott m Tristram Cary
☆ John Mills, Charles Coburn, Derek Farr,
Barbara Bates, Alec McCowen, Geoffrey Keen,
Elizabeth Seal, Margaretta Scott, Fay Compton

The Town Went Wild

US   1945   78m   bw
PRC
Feuding next-door neighbours have children in
love.
*Romeo and Juliet in small-town America, and none of
it sharp enough.*
w Bernard R. Roth, Clarence Greene, Russel
Rouse d Ralph Murphy
☆ Freddie Bartholomew, Edward Everett Horton,
James Lydon, Tom Tully, Jill Browning, Minna
Gombell, Maude Eburne, Charles Halton

Town without Pity *

US/Switzerland/Germany   1961   103m   bw
UA/Mirisch/Osweg/Gloria (Gottfried Reinhardt)

A German girl is raped and four American soldiers
are accused; the defence counsel's wiles lead to the
girl's suicide.
*Dour drama with overpowering expressionist technique
but not much real sympathy, interest or surprise.*
w Silvia Reinhardt, George Hurdalek novel *The
Verdict* by Manfred Gregor d Gottfried Reinhardt
ph Kurt Hasse m Dimitri Tiomkin
☆ Kirk Douglas, E. G. Marshall, Christine
Kaufmann, Barbara Rutting, Robert Blake, Richard
Jaeckel
♫ title song (mDimitri Tiomkin, lyNed
Washington)

The Toxic Avenger

US   1985   76m   colour
Blue Dolphin/Troma/Lloyd Kaufman, Michael Herz

A retarded weakling falls into a vat of radioactive
chemicals and is transformed into a monstrously
ugly super-hero.
*A spoof of the horror genre, but so crudely made and
acted as to be even more offensive than the worst of
what it mocks.*
w Joe Ritter story Lloyd Kaufman d Michael
Herz, Samuel Weil ph James London, Michael
Kaufman ed Richard W. Haines
☆ Andree Maranda, Mitchell Cohen, Pat Ryan
Jnr, Jennifer Babtist, Cindy Manion, Robert
Pritchard, Gary Schneider, Mark Torgl

The Toxic Avenger, Part II

US   1989   95m   TVC Color
Troma/Lloyd Kaufman, Michael Herz

A chemical company wanting to dump its
dangerous waste products attempts to kill the Toxic
Avenger.
*A marginal improvement on the first film, but only
because it could hardly be worse.*
w Gay Partington Terry, Lloyd Kaufman
d Michael Herz, Lloyd Kaufman ph James London
m Christopher Demarco ad Alexis Grey
ed Joseph McGirr
☆ Ron Fazio, John Altamura, Phoebe Legere,
Rich Collins, Rikiya Yasuoka, Tsutomu Sekine,
Mayako Katsuragi, Jessica Dublin

The Toxic Avenger Part III: The Last Temptation Of Toxie

US   1989   89m   TVC Color
Troma/Lloyd Kaufman, Michael Herz

The Toxic Avenger is momentarily transformed
into an upwardly mobile monster before reverting
to type.
*Violence, crude humour and deliberately inept acting
and directing create a cinematic pollution of their own.*
w Gay Partington Terry story Lloyd Kaufman
d Lloyd Kaufman, Michael Herz ph James London
m Barrie Guard ad Alex Grey ed Michael
Schweitzer
☆ Ron Fazio, John Altamura, Phoebe Legere,
Rick Collins, Lisa Gaye, Jessica Dublin, Tsutomu
Sekine

The Toy

US 1983 102m colour
Columbia/Rastar (Phil Feldman)

A black janitor is hired as a toy for a millionaire's nine-year-old son.

Feeble attempt to translate a 1976 French film by Francis Veber. The few laughs are laughs of embarrassment.

w Carol Sobieski d Richard Donner ph Laszlo Kovacs m Patrick Williams pd Charles Rosen
☆ Richard Pryor, Jackie Gleason, Ned Beatty, Scott Schwartz, Teresa Ganzel, Wilfrid Hyde-White, Tony King

'Tasteless in implication, flavourless in execution.' – *Sight and Sound*

The Toy Maker

US 1991 Foto-Kem
Still Silent (Brian Yuzna, Richard N. Gladstein)

The son of a sweet old alcoholic toy-maker creates toys with a difference: they kill.

A nasty little gory horror movie.

w Martin Kitrosser, Brian Yuzna d Martin Kitrosser ph James Mathers m Matthew Morse pd W. Brooke Wheeler ed Norman Buckley sp Screaming Mad George, Ken Tarallo
☆ Jane Higginson, Tracy Fraim, Brian Bremer, William Thorne, Neith Hunter, Mickey Rooney

Toy Soldiers

US 1991 112m Continental Color
Columbia TriStar/Island World (Jack E. Freedman, Wayne S. Williams, Patricia Herskovic)

Wealthy teenage American schoolkids turn the tables on a group of mercenaries, hired by a South American drug dealer, who take them hostage.

Silly, violent action movie presumably aimed at a teen audience that likes plenty of blood and gore.

w Daniel Petrie Jnr, David Koepp novel William P. Kennedy d Daniel Petrie Jnr ph Thomas Burstyn m Robert Folk pd Chester Kaczenski ed Michael Kahn
☆ Sean Astin, Wil Wheaton, Keith Coogan, Andrew Divoff, R. Lee Ermey, Mason Adams, Denholm Elliott, Louis Gossett Jnr, George Perez

'Incompetent botch-up of a potentially good if unlikely story.' – *Derek Malcolm, Guardian*

Toy Story ****

↟↟ US 1995 80m Technicolor
Buena Vista/Walt Disney/Pixar (Ralph Guggenheim, Bonnie Arnold)

A toy cowboy, the long-time favourite of a small boy, is jealous of a new arrival, an astronaut figure who refuses to believe that he is a toy and replaces him in the boy's affections.

A brilliant animated feature, the first to be entirely computer-generated, and notable for its energy and considerable wit; it is darker in tone than most recent Disney movies, but none the worse for that. With its hyper-realism, glossy textures, its dazzling use of perspective and movement, it makes conventional animations look old-fashioned.

w Joss Whedon, Andrew Stanton, Joel Cohen, Joe Ranft, John Lasseter, Pete Docter d John Lasseter m Randy Newman ad Ralph Eggleston ed Robert Gordon, Lee Unkrich
☆ Featuring the voices of: Tom Hanks, Tim Allen, Don Rickles, Jim Varney, Wallace Shawn, John Ratzenberger, Annie Potts

♟ John Lasseter (special achievement)
♫ Randy Newman; song 'You've Got a Friend' (m/ly Randy Newman); screenplay

Toy Story 2 ***

US 1999 92m Technicolor
Buena Vista/Walt Disney/Pixar (Helene Plotkin, Karen Robert Jackson)

A wicked toyshop owner steals the cowboy Woody so that he can complete a set of toys, based on a 50s TV show, and sell them to a Japanese museum.

Witty, brilliantly realised comedy of celebrity and obsolescence; it shows an advance in technique over the original, but its narrative, lacking the darker impulses of the first film, is not as resonant.

w Andrew Stanton, Rita Hsiao, Doug Chamberlin, Chris Webb, John Lasseter, Pete Docter, Ash Brannon d John Lasseter, Lee Unkrich, Ash Brannon ph Sharon Calahan

m Randy Newman pd William Cone, Jim Pearson ed Edie Bleiman, David Ian Salter, Lee Unkrich
☆ Featuring voices of: Tom Hanks, Tim Allen, Joan Cusack, Kelsey Grammer, Don Rickles, Jim Varney, Wallace Shawn, John Ratzenberger, Wayne Knight, John Morris, Laurie Metcalf

'It is not a sequel. It is an upgrade. It is a manufacturer's improvement of staggering ingenuity. It is a software refinement. It is a species leap, a higher order of being.' – *Peter Bradshaw, Guardian*

'A movie that is dazzlingly inventive in its graphic detail, tells an exciting, sophisticated story and raises complex ideas with clarity and wit.' – *Philip French, Observer*
♫ song 'When She Loved Me' (m/l Randy Newman)

Toy Tiger

US 1956 88m Technicolor Cinemascope
U-I (Howard Christie)

The imaginative small son of a widow 'adopts' her business friend as his father.

Flat sentimental comedy off the studio's conveyor belt, a remake of Mad about Music.

w Ted Sherdeman d Jerry Hopper ph George Robinson m Joseph Gershenson
☆ Jeff Chandler, Laraine Day, Tim Hovey, Cecil Kellaway, Richard Haydn, David Janssen

The Toy Wife *

US 1938 95m bw
MGM (Merian C. Cooper)
GB title: Frou Frou

In the early 19th century in Louisiana, a flirtatious girl causes jealousy and tragedy.

Another bid in the Jezebel/Gone with the Wind *stakes, this handsome production proved a commercial misfire and hastened the end of its star's career.*

w Zoe Akins d Richard Thorpe ph Oliver T. Marsh m Edward Ward
☆ Luise Rainer, Melvyn Douglas, Robert Young, Barbara O'Neil, H. B. Warner, Alma Kruger, Walter Kingsford

'Old-fashioned melodrama, beautifully produced but creaky.' – *Variety*

'Laughter Is A State of Mind.'

Toys

⋔ US 1992 121m CFI color
TCF (Mark Johnson, Barry Levinson)

An uptight army officer inherits a toy factory and switches production from cuddly toys to increasingly aggressive ones.

Visually splendid but otherwise totally incoherent movie.

w Valerie Curtin, Barry Levinson d Barry Levinson ph Adam Greenberg m Hans Zimmer, Trevor Horn pd Ferdinando Scarfiotti ed Stu Linder
☆ Robin Williams, Michael Gambon, Joan Cusack, Robin Wright, LL Cool J, Donald O'Connor, Jack Warden

'Only a filmmaker with Barry Levinson's clout would have been so indulged to create such a sprawling, seemingly unsupervised mess … It will be hard to top as the season's major clunker.' – *Variety*

'A disaster … It is quite unlike anything Levinson has done before, and it is sincerely to be hoped that he never does anything like it again.' – *Derek Malcolm, Guardian*
♟ Ferdinando Scarfiotti; Albert Wolsky (costume design)

Toys in the Attic *

US 1963 90m bw Panavision
UA/Claude/Mirisch

In a shabby New Orleans home, two ageing spinsters struggle to look after their ne'er-do-well brother.

Play into film doesn't go in this case, but the script and acting are interesting.

w James Poe play Lillian Hellman d George Roy Hill m Joseph Biroc m George Duning ad Cary Odell
☆ Geraldine Page, Wendy Hiller, Dean Martin, Yvette Mimieux, Gene Tierney, Larry Gates

Traces of Red

US 1992 105m colour
Entertainment/Samuel Goldwyn Company (Mark Gordon)

A cop attempts to solve a series of killings of women with whom he has been involved and for which he is chief suspect.

Deadly dull thriller, of no interest whatsoever.

w Jim Piddock d Andy Wolk ph Tim Suhrstedt m Graeme Revel pd Dan Bishop, Dianna Freas ed Trudy Ship
☆ James Belushi, Lorraine Bracco, Tony Goldwyn, William Russ, Faye Grant, Michelle Joyner, Joe Lisi, Victoria Bass, Jim Piddock

'What could have been, and perhaps was intended to be, a fetching latterday film noir, is constantly stymied by a wooden script, a cast that is at a loss to deal with it, and direction that gives nobody any help.' – *Derek Malcolm, Guardian*

'A dramatic failure but an entertaining exercise in camp.' – *Variety*

Track 29

GB 1988 91m colour
Recorded Releasing/Handmade (Rick McCullum)

A sensual woman, whose husband prefers playing with his electric train-set, is attracted to a mysterious stranger who claims to be her long-lost son.

Offbeat but unsatisfactory psychological drama that loses its way in thickets of sexuality.

w Dennis Potter d Nicolas Roeg ph Alex Thomson m Stanley Myers ad David Brockhurst ed Tony Lawson
☆ Theresa Russell, Gary Oldman, Christopher Lloyd, Sarah Bernhard, Colleen Camp, Seymour Cassel

'A story of how men and women act when they think nobody is looking!'

Track of the Cat *

US 1954 102m Warnercolor Cinemascope
Warner/Wayne-Fellows/Batjac (Robert Fellows)

In the northern California backwoods one winter in the 1880s a farming family is menaced by a marauding mountain lion.

With the lion a symbol of evil, this is real Cold Comfort Farm country and despite good intentions all round becomes irresistibly funny before the end, largely because everyone moves and speaks so s-l-o-w-l-y. The bleached colour is interesting but would suit only snowy settings.

w A. I. Bezzerides novel Walter Van Tilburg Clark d William A. Wellman ph William H. Clothier m Roy Webb
☆ Robert Mitchum, Diana Lynn, Beulah Bondi, Teresa Wright, Tab Hunter, Philip Tonge, William Hopper, Carl Switzer

'Cinemascope's first genuine weirdie … the script is redolent of Eugene O'Neill, and to its presentation the director brings a touch of Poe … Despair hangs in the air like a curse … unfortunately ambition overreaches itself, and the film topples over into barnstorming melodrama.' – *MFB*

'Bill Wellman had the idea: he wanted to make a colour picture with very little colour.' – *William Clothier*

Trackdown

US 1976 98m DeLuxe
UA/Essaness (Bernard Schwarz)

A Montana rancher follows his sister to Los Angeles and avenges her ill-treatment there by gangsters.

Routine action thriller with fashionable realism and violence.

w Paul Edwards d Richard T. Heffron ph Gene Polito m Charles Bernstein
☆ Jim Mitchum, Karen Lamm, Anne Archer, Erik Estrada, Cathy Lee Crosby, Vince Cannon

Tracks

US 1976 90m colour
Rainbow Pictures (Howard Zuker)

A Vietnam veteran begins to lose his reason as he makes a train journey to take back home the coffin of his friend, killed in action.

A movie with an improvised feel, consisting of a series of desultory meetings and conversations between travellers which never quite reach any destination.

wd Henry Jaglom ph Paul Glickman ed George Folsey Jnr
☆ Dennis Hopper, Taryn Power, Dean Stockwell, Topo Swope, Alfred Ryder, Zack Norman, Michael Emil

Trade Winds

US 1938 93m bw
Walter Wanger

A girl who thinks she has committed murder flees to the Far East, and a cynical detective is sent to bring her back. Guess what happens.

Smartly written mixture of comedy, drama, mystery and travelogue which comes off only in spots; it needed a firmer hand.

w Dorothy Parker, Alan Campbell, Frank R. Adams d Tay Garnett ph Rudolph Maté m Alfred Newman
☆ Fredric March, Joan Bennett, Ralph Bellamy, Ann Sothern, Sidney Blackmer, Thomas Mitchell, Robert Elliott

'All the elements that provide broad entertainment are present in this picture, and it should reap healthy grosses.' – *Variety*

Trader Horn *

US 1930 120m bw
MGM (Irving Thalberg)

An experienced African trader overcomes tribal hostility.

Primitive talkie for which second units were sent to Africa amid much publicity hoo-ha. After fifty years, nothing of interest remains to be seen.

w Richard Schayer, Dale Van Every, Thomas Neville novel Alfred Aloysius Horn, Ethelreda Lewis d W. S. Van Dyke ph Clyde de Vinna
☆ Harry Carey, Edwina Booth, Duncan Renaldo, Mutia Omoolu, C. Aubrey Smith

'Sure money-getter. Outstanding animal stuff, great sound effects, and thin story, which has good-looking white girl romping around scantily clad.' – *Variety*

'A movie that contains all the best features of a zoo, a cannibal dance, and a big yarn by Rider Haggard.' – *National Board of Review*
♟ best picture

Trader Horn

US 1973 105m Metrocolor
MGM (Lewis J. Rachmil)

Pitiful remake patched together largely from stock footage.

w William Norton, Edward Harper d Reza Badiyi ph Ronald W. Browne m Shelly Manne
☆ Rod Taylor, Anne Heywood, Jean Sorel

'Laughably inept … it cannot face word of mouth for long.' – *Variety*

Trading Places **

US 1983 116m Technicolor
Paramount/Landis-Folsey (Aaron Russo)

Two rich men arrange a wager on the effects of environment over heredity, and arrange for a con man and a stockbroker to change places.

Surprisingly witty comedy, which while not aspiring to great heights, and marred by a few excesses, brought a refreshing breath of air to a declining genre.

w Timothy Harris, Herschel Weingrod d John Landis ph Robert Paynter m Elmer Bernstein pd Gene Rudolf
☆ Dan Aykroyd, Eddie Murphy, Ralph Bellamy, Don Ameche, Denholm Elliott, Jamie Lee Curtis, Kristin Holby

'Proof positive that the genuine American populist comedy can still attract attention.' – *John Pym, MFB*
♟ Elmer Bernstein
⊎ Jamie Lee Curtis, Denholm Elliott

Traffic *

⋔ France/Italy 1970 96m Eastmancolor
Corona/Gibe/Selenia (Robert Dorfman)

The designer of a camping car has various little accidents on the way from the works to a show.

Rambling comedy with understated jokes and an almost invisible star.

w Jacques Tati, Jacques Lagrange d Jacques Tati (with Bert Haanstra) ph Edouard Van Den Enden, Marcel Weiss m Charles Dumont
☆ Jacques Tati

The Tragedy of a Ridiculous Man ***
Italy   1981   116m   Technicolor
Warner/Ladd Company (Giovanni Bertolucci)

original title: *La Tragedia Di Un Uomo Ridicolo*
A dairy farmer is faced with losing his livelihood in order to pay a ransom demanded by terrorists who have kidnapped his son.
Engrossing study of contemporary terrorism and individual responsibility, though its refusal to explain everything alienated many audiences.
wd Bernardo Bertolucci   ph Carlo Di Palma
m Ennio Morricone   pd Gianni Silvestri
ed Gabriella Cristani
☆ Ugo Tognazzi, Anouk Aimee, Laura Morante, Victor Cavallo, Olympia Carlisi, Riccardo Tognazzi, Vittorio Caprioli

The Tragedy of a Switchboard Operator:
see *The Switchboard Operator*

The Tragic Pursuit: see *Caccia Tragica*

The Trail Beyond
US   1934   57m   bw
Monogram/Lone Star (Paul Malvern)

A cowboy goes to Canada to find missing relatives of his father's best friend and helps an old college friend along the way.
A routine Western, with rather more plot and less action than usual.
w Lindsley Parsons   story *The Wolf Hunters* by James Oliver Curwood   d Robert N. Bradbury
ph Archie Stout   ad E. R. Hickson   ed Charles Hunt
☆ John Wayne, Verna Hillie, Noah Beery Snr, Noah Beery Jnr, Robert Frazer, Iris Lancaster, James Marcus

The Trail of '98 *
US   1928   90m   bw   silent
MGM
San Franciscans leave their homes for the Klondike gold rush.
Impressive spectacular while it stays outdoors; not so good when the plot takes over.
w Waldemar Young, Ben Glazer   novel Robert W. Service   d Clarence Brown
☆ Dolores Del Rio, Ralph Forbes, Harry Carey, Karl Dane, Tully Marshall

'The surging drama of love in the Kentucky hills springs to thrilling life as the first outdoor action romance filmed in colour!'

The Trail of the Lonesome Pine *
US   1936   102m   Technicolor
Paramount (Walter Wanger)
A hillbilly girl goes back home when her brother is killed in a family feud.
Antediluvian Ozarkian melodrama, notable as the first outdoor film to be shot in three-colour Technicolor.
w Grover Jones, Horace McCoy, Harvey Thew
novel John Fox Jnr   d Henry Hathaway
ph Howard Greene   m Hugo Friedhofer, Gerard Carbonara
☆ Sylvia Sidney, Fred MacMurray, Henry Fonda, Fred Stone, Nigel Bruce, Beulah Bondi, Robert Barrat, Spanky McFarland, Fuzzy Knight
'A good show saleable for big grosses, a flicker the ballyhoo boys can and will do tricks with.' – *Variety*
'Unnatural as it is, the colour does no serious damage to the picture. This moldy bit of hokum … takes movies back to the days of their childhood.' – *Newsweek*
† The story was first filmed in 1915 by Cecil B. de Mille.
♫ song 'A Melody from the Sky' (mLouis Alter, lySidney Mitchell)

Trail of the Pink Panther
GB   1982   97m   Technicolor   Panavision
MGM-UA/Titan (Blake Edwards, Tony Adams)

Inspector Clouseau is reported missing at sea and a television reporter interviews those who had known him.
Flimsy, necrophiliac excuse for a movie, with a star cast clearly failing to make bricks without straw two years after the nominal star's death.
w Frank and Tom Waldman, Blake Edwards, Geoffrey Edwards   d Blake Edwards   ph Dick Bush

m Henry Mancini   pd Peter Mullins   ed Alan Jones
☆ Peter Sellers, Joanna Lumley, Herbert Lom, David Niven, Richard Mulligan, Capucine, Robert Loggia, Harvey Korman, Burt Kwouk, Graham Stark, Leonard Rossiter, Peter Arne, Ronald Fraser

Trail of the Vigilantes *
US   1940   78m   bw
Universal
In the old west, a reporter sets out to break up a band of outlaws.
A mild Western which at the time had some reputation as a wild comedy; the fact was that it turned out badly and the editors did the best they could.
w Harold Shumate   d Allan Dwan
☆ Franchot Tone, Warren William, Broderick Crawford, Andy Devine, Mischa Auer, Porter Hall, Peggy Moran
'As light amusement it does all right, but it is amusement in confusion.' – *Otis Ferguson*

Trail Street
US   1947   84m   bw
RKO (Nat Holt)

Wheat is planted in Kansas by the early settlers.
Pretty good, unpretentious Western.
w Norman Houston, Gene Lewis   d Ray Enright
☆ Randolph Scott, Robert Ryan, Anne Jeffreys, Billy House, George 'Gabby' Hayes

'It carried their hopes, their nation's honour!'
The Train **
US   1965   140m   bw
UA/Ariane/Dear (Jules Bricken)

In 1944, the French resistance tries to prevent the Nazis from taking art treasures back to Germany on a special train.
Proficient but longwinded suspense actioner with spectacular sequences; a safe bet for train enthusiasts.
w Franklin Coen, Frank Davis, Walter Bernstein
d John Frankenheimer   ph Jean Tournier, Walter Wottiz   m Maurice Jarre
☆ Burt Lancaster, Paul Scofield, Jeanne Moreau, Michel Simon, Wolfgang Preiss, Suzanne Flon
'Extraordinarily good in many of its parts but rather disappointing as a whole … its greatest virtue is an almost overpowering physical realism.' – *Moira Walsh, America*
♟ script

Train of Dreams
Canada   1987   89m   colour
NFBC (Sam Grana)
An arrogant teenage mugger is sent to a correctional centre for two years.
Earnest but inconsequential social tract, with flashbacks to the protagonist's violent past.
w John N. Smith, Sally Bochner, Sam Grana
d John N. Smith   ph David de Volpi   m Malcolm MacKenzie Jnr   ed John N. Smith
☆ Jason St Amour, Marcella Santa Maria, Fred Ward, Christopher Neil, David Linetsky, Milton Hartman

Train of Events
GB   1949   89m   bw
Ealing (Michael Relph)
Portmanteau of stories à la *Friday the 13th* or *Dead of Night*, linked by a train disaster.
A rather mechanical entertainment, proficiently made.
w Basil Dearden, T. E. B. Clarke, Ronald Millar, Angus MacPhail   d Basil Dearden, Charles Crichton, Sidney Cole   ph Lionel Banes, Gordon Dines   m Leslie Bridgewater
☆ Valerie Hobson, John Clements, Jack Warner, Gladys Henson, Peter Finch, Irina Baronova, Susan Shaw, Patric Doonan, Joan Dowling, Laurence Payne, Mary Morris

The Train Robbers
US   1973   92m   Technicolor   Panavision
Warner/Batjac (Michael Wayne)

A widow asks three gunmen to help her clear her husband's name by retrieving gold he had stolen.
Shaggy-dog Western, sadly lacking in comic situation and detail.
wd Burt Kennedy   ph William Clothier
m Dominic Frontière
☆ John Wayne, Ann-Margret, Rod Taylor, Ben Johnson, Bobby Vinton, Christopher George

Trainspotting ***
GB   1996   94m   colour
Polygram/Channel 4/Figment/Noel Gay (Andrew Macdonald)

Four Scottish friends enjoy the highs, and suffer the lows, of heroin addiction, while indulging in petty theft, sex, booze and violence whenever they are capable of it.
A dark and ironic take on young junkies at their antisocial worst, directed with terrific energy and style, a witty subversion of the usual documentary approach to such subjects, and excellently acted by its ensemble cast.
w John Hodge   novel Irvine Welsh   d Danny Boyle
ph Brian Tufano   pd Kave Quinn   m Masahiro Hirakubo
☆ Ewan McGregor, Ewen Bremner, Jonny Lee Miller, Kevin McKidd, Robert Carlyle, Kelly Macdonald, Peter Mullan, Irvine Welsh
'Spends far too much time with its nose pressed up against the glass of American cinema, desperate for a piece of the action, but merely fogging up the screen with longing. Until British cinema kicks this habit, it will continue to churn out films such as this, which bear the same relation to real film-making that drugs do to real pleasure. It's utterly empty: a cold turkey, despite the fancy trimmings' – *Tom Shone, Sunday Times*
'An extraordinary achievement and a breakthrough British film.' – *Derek Malcolm, Guardian*
'For all its brilliance, the film finally feels sour and hollow.' – *Sheila Johnston*
'Scabrous, brutal and hip, *Trainspotting* is a *Clockwork Orange* for the 90s.' – *Variety*
† The film cost $3m and grossed more than $64 worldwide.
♟ John Hodge
♟ John Hodge

The Traitor *
GB   1957   88m   bw
Fantur (E. J. Fancey)
US title: *The Accused*
At the annual reunion of a resistance group, the host announces that one of their number was a traitor.
Heavy-handed theatrical melodrama, helped by a stout plot and some directional flair.
wd Michael McCarthy   ph Bert Mason   m Jackie Brown
☆ Donald Wolfit, Robert Bray, Jane Griffiths, Carl Jaffe, Anton Diffring, Oscar Quitak, Rupert Davies, John Van Eyssen

The Traitors *
GB   1962   69m   bw
Ello (Jim O'Connolly)
A top scientist is killed and MI5 springs into action.
Commendable second feature with narrative virtues absent in most big films.
w Jim O'Connolly   d Robert Tronson   ph Michael Reed   m Johnny Douglas
☆ Patrick Allen, James Maxwell, Ewan Roberts, Zena Walker

Traitor's Gate
GB   1965   80m   bw
Columbia/Summit (Ted Lloyd)
A London businessman organizes a gang to steal the Crown Jewels.
Modest caper melodrama, routine but watchable.
w John Sansom   novel Edgar Wallace   d Freddie Francis   ph Denys Coop
☆ Albert Lieven, Gary Raymond, Margot Trooger, Klaus Kinski, Catherina von Schell, Edward Underdown

The Tramp *
♟♟ US   1915   20m   bw   silent
Mutual
A tramp saves a girl from crooks, is wounded and cared for by her, deliriously happy – until her lover arrives.
Fairly funny star comedy, the first with sentimental touches and the origin of the into-the-sunset fade-out.
wd Charles Chaplin   ph Rollie Totheroh
☆ Charles Chaplin, Edna Purviance, Bud Jamison, Leo White, Lloyd Bacon

Tramp Tramp Tramp *
♟♟ US   1926   65m   bw   silent
Harry Langdon
Harry enters a cross-country walking contest in order to impress his girl.
Well-staged peripatetic comedy, the star's first feature.
w Frank Capra, Tim Whelan, Hal Conklin, Gerald Duffy, Murray Roth, J. Frank Holliday   d Harry Edwards
☆ Harry Langdon, Joan Crawford, Alec B. Francis

'Jack Deth is back … and he's never been here before!'
Trancers *
US   1985   85m   DeLuxe
Empire Pictures (Charles Band)

aka: *Future Cop*
A tough policeman, Jack Deth, is sent from the future into the present day to hunt down a villain who wants to take over the world by creating Trancers, weak-willed and violent individuals under his psychic influence.
Engaging and occasionally witty low-budget science-fiction action movie, featuring a hero with the manner of a world-weary private eye of the 1930s.
w Paul de Meo, Danny Bilson   d Charles Band
ph Mac Ahlberg   m Mark Ryder, Phil Davies
pd Jeff Staggs   ed Ted Nicolaou   sp John Buechler
☆ Tim Thomerson, Helen Hunt, Michael Stefani, Art La Fleur, Telma Hopkins, Richard Herd, Anne Seymour, Miguel Fernandez, Biff Manard

Trancers II *
US   1991   87m   colour
Full Moon (Charles Band)

aka: *Trancers II: The Return of Jack Deth*
Jack Deth protects the father of a future high official against attacks from Trancers.
Abysmal sequel in which little happens and nothing matters, made, by the look of it, on an even more infinitesimal budget.
w Jackson Barr   story Jackson Barr, Charles Band
d Charles Band   ph Adolfo Bartoli   m Mark Ryder, Phil Davies   pd Kathleen Coates   ed Ted Nicolaou, Andy Hornitch   sp Palah Sandling, Kevin McCarthy
☆ Tim Thomerson, Helen Hunt, Megan Ward, Biff Manard, Richard Lynch, Martine Beswick, Jeffrey Combs, Telma Hopkins
'Some unintentional humor doesn't save this unnecessary sequel, a quickie that's all talk and no action.' – *Variety*

Trancers III *
US   1992   83m   Foto-Kem
Paramount/Full Moon (Albert Band)

aka: *Trancers III: Deth Lives*
While working as a detective in Los Angeles in 1992, Jack Deth is transported to 2352, when the Trancers are destroying the world, to be ordered back to 2005 to kill their creator.
A low-budget variation on the familiar theme of one man single-handedly overcoming a highly trained army; it is also low on skill and imagination.
wd C. Courtney Joyner   ph Adolfo Bartoli
m Mark Ryder, Phil Davies, Richard Band
pd Milo   ed Lauren Schaffer, Margaret-Anne Smith   sp Kurtzman, Nicotero, Berger EFX Group
☆ Tim Thomerson, Melanie Smith, Andrew Robinson, Tony Pierce, Ed Beechner, Dawn Ann Billings, Helen Hunt, Megan Ward, Stephen Macht, Telma Hopkins
'This has some funny lines, smart science fiction riffs, hateworthy villains and, most valuable of all, Thomerson's hard-bitten but hilarious leading performance, to make it worth checking out.' – *Empire*
† The film was cut to 72m on its British video release.

Transatlantic *
US   1931   74m   bw
Fox
Various personal stories come to a climax aboard a transatlantic liner.
Early attempt at what has now become a very worn format; quite lively it must have seemed then.
w Guy Bolton, Lynn Starling   d William K. Howard   ad Gordon Wiles

---

☆ Edmund Lowe, Lois Moran, John Halliday, Greta Nissen, Jean Hersholt, Myrna Loy, Earle Foxe, Billy Bevan

'An aquatic Grand Hotel; should prosper.' – *Variety*

⅄ Gordon Wiles

Transatlantic Merry Go Round

US   1934   92m   bw
Reliance

Romantic misunderstandings on an ocean liner.
Patchy comedy with some good scenes.

w Joseph Moncure March, Harry W. Conn, Leon Gordon d Ben Stoloff ph Ted Tetzlaff md Alfred Newman

☆ Jack Benny, Nancy Carroll, Gene Raymond, Sydney Howard

'Good, popular screen entertainment; certain box office fodder.' – *Variety*

Transatlantic Tunnel: see *The Tunnel*

Trans-Europe Express *

France   1966   90m   bw
Como Film (Samy Halfon)

Film-makers on a train invent a violent plot and then find life aping it.
A theme beloved of Hollywood is treated intellectually, and almost succeeds in attracting all classes.

wd Alain Robbe-Grillet ph Willy Kurant
m Verdi

☆ Jean-Louis Trintignant, Marie-France Pisier, Nadine Verdier, Christian Barbier, Charles Millot, Alain Robbe-Grillet

Transgression

US   1931   70m   bw
RKO

During a Paris vacation, a man forgives his wife for her affair with a Spanish gigolo.
Very routine, matinée drama.

w Elizabeth Meehan novel Kate Jordan
d Herbert Brenon

☆ Kay Francis, Ricardo Cortez, Paul Cavanagh, Nance O'Neil

'Doubtful de luxe subject, principally because its story lacks conviction.' – *Variety*

The Transvestite: see *Glen or Glenda*

The Trap *

US   1958   84m   Technicolor
Paramount/Parkwood-Heath (Melvin Frank, Norman Panama)

GB title: *The Baited Trap*

A lawyer helps a vicious killer to escape into Mexico, but the plan backfires.
Reasonably tense action thriller with desert backgrounds.

w Richard Alan Simmons, Norman Panama
d Norman Panama ph Daniel L. Fapp m Irvin Talbot

☆ Richard Widmark, Lee J. Cobb, Earl Holliman, Tina Louise, Carl Benton Reid, Lorne Greene

The Trap

GB/Canada   1966   106m   Eastmancolor
Panavision
Parallel (George H. Brown)

In 19th-century British Columbia a rough trapper takes a wife, who at first is terrified of him but nurses him when he is hurt ...
Primitive open air melodrama with good action sequences; well made but hardly endearing.

w David Osborn d Sidney Hayers ph Robert Krasker m Ron Goodwin

☆ Oliver Reed, Rita Tushingham, Rex Sevenoaks, Barbara Chilcott

'The Wonder Show Of The World!'

Trapeze **

US   1956   105m   DeLuxe   Cinemascope
UA/Hecht-Lancaster (James Hill)

A circus partnership almost breaks up when a voluptuous third member is engaged.
Concentrated, intense melodrama filmed almost entirely within a French winter circus and giving a very effective feel, almost a smell, of the life therein. Despite great skill in the making, however, the length is too

great for a wisp of plot that goes back to The Three Maxims *and doubtless beyond.*

w James R. Webb d Carol Reed ph Robert Krasker m Malcolm Arnold

☆ Burt Lancaster, Tony Curtis, Gina Lollobrigida, Thomas Gomez, Johnny Puleo, Katy Jurado, Sidney James

† This version was supposedly adapted from a Max Catto novel, *The Killing Frost*, but in 1932 Harmonie of Germany issued a film with the title *Trapeze* and a remarkably similar story. It had a scenario by Alfred Machard and was directed by E. A. Dupont. The Anna Neagle film *The Three Maxims* (qv) was also very similar, but that was supposedly an original by Herman Mankiewicz.

Trapped in Paradise

US   1994   112m   DeLuxe
TCF (Jon Davison, George Gallo)

Three brothers rob a small-town bank on Christmas Eve and try to return the money when the locals show them kindness.
A comedy that just about gets by on seasonal goodwill, though it might have worked better at half its length.

wd George Gallo ph Jack N. Green m Robert Folk pd Bob Ziembicki ed Terry Rawlings

☆ Nicolas Cage, Jon Lovitz, Dana Carvey, John Ashton, Mädchen Amick, Donald Moffat, Richard Jenkins, Jack Heller

'This is a comedy which depends entirely on its playing and certainly not on its script, which is fairly witless.' – *Derek Malcolm, Guardian*

Trash *

US   1970   103m   colour
Vaughn/Andy Warhol

aka: *Andy Warhol's Trash*

A drug addict finds that the women he knows are anxious to cure him of his impotence.
Casually filmed and acted, with casual sexual encounters and moments of comedy along the way.

wd Paul Morrissey

☆ Joe Dallesandro, Geri Miller, Holly Woodlawn, Bruce Pecheur, Jane Forth, Michael Sklar

Trauma

US   1993   105m   Technicolor
Overseas Filmgroup/ADC (Dario Argento)

A couple track down a serial killer who is decapitating his victims.
Argento's first American film has little of the visual flair of the best of his Italian shockers; its predictability soon becomes wearing.

w Dario Argento, T. E. D. Klein, Franco Ferrini, Giovanni Romoli d Dario Argento ph Raffaele Mertes m Pino Donaggio pd Billy Jett
ed Conrad Gonzalez sp Tom Savini

☆ Christopher Rydell, Asia Argento, Piper Laurie, Frederic Forrest, James Russo, Brad Dourif, Laura Johnson

'A by-the-numbers stalker thriller for undemanding genre fans only.' – *Variety*

The Traveling Executioner *

US   1970   95m   Metrocolor   Panavision
MGM (Jack Smight)

In 1918 an ex-carnival showman travels the American South with his portable electric chair and charges a hundred dollars per execution, but falls for one of his proposed victims.
Oddball fable without apparent moral; neither fantastic nor funny enough.

w Garrie Bateson d Jack Smight ph Philip Lathrop m Jerry Goldsmith

☆ Stacy Keach, Marianna Hill, Bud Cort, Graham Jarvis

Traveling Saleslady

US   1935   75m   bw
Warner

A toothpaste manufacturer's daughter shows her father the value of advertising.
Warner stock company comedy which hits no heights but provided reliable entertainment.

w Hugh Herbert, Manuel Seff, Benny Rubin, Frank Howard Clark d Ray Enright

☆ Joan Blondell, Hugh Herbert, Glenda Farrell, William Gargan, Al Shean, Grant Mitchell, Ruth Donnelly, Bert Roach

'It will please and should do all right at the wicket.' – *Variety*

Traveller

US   1997   100m   CFI color
First Independent/MDP/October/Banner (Bill Paxton, Brian Swardstrom, Mickey Liddell, David Blocker)

A con man, who is part of an inward-looking group of travellers, teaches a young hopeful the tricks of his trade.
A tiresome buddy-buddy movie set in an enclosed community, where to be a buddy is to rat on everyone in the wider world.

w Jim McGlynn d Jack Green ph Jack Green (uncredited) m Andy Paley pd Michael Helmy ed Michael Ruscio

☆ Bill Paxton, Mark Wahlberg, Julianna Margulies, James Gammon, Luke Askew, Nikki Deloach

'With muddled characterisation, a slight script and an over-the-top ending, it emerges as an ill-conceived attempt to make a thriller out of almost nothing.' – *Jessica Mellor, Empire*

Traveller's Joy

GB   1949   78m   bw
Gainsborough/Rank

A divorced couple, stranded in Sweden by lack of funds, have to take joint action.
Mild topical comedy from a popular play.

w Allan MacKinnon, Bernard Quayle
play Arthur Macrae d Ralph Thomas ph Jack Cox m Arthur Wilkinson

☆ Googie Withers, John McCallum, Yolande Donlan, Maurice Denham, Geoffrey Sumner, Colin Gordon, Dora Bryan

Travelling North *

Australia   1986   96m   Eastmancolor
View Pictures/CEL (Ben Gannon)

A vigorous 70-year-old leaves Melbourne for sub-tropical Queensland, but his health gives out.
Moving Australian mirror image of On Golden Pond, with good acting and direction.

w David Williamson play David Williamson
d Carl Schultz ph Julian Penney md Alan John
pd Owen Paterson ed Henry Dangar

☆ Leo McKern, Julia Blake, Graham Kennedy, Henri Szeps

Travels with My Aunt *

US   1972   109m   Metrocolor   Panavision
MGM (Robert Fryer, James Cresson)

A staid bank accountant is landed in a series of continental adventures by his eccentric life-loving aunt.
Busy but fairly disastrous adaptation of a delightful novel, ruined by ceaseless chatter, lack of characterization, shapeless incident and an absurdly caricatured central performance.

w Jay Presson Allen, Hugh Wheeler
novel Graham Greene d George Cukor
ph Douglas Slocombe m Tony Hatch pd John Box

☆ Maggie Smith, Alec McCowen, Lou Gossett, Robert Stephens, Cindy Williams

'It seems to run down before it gets started.' – *New Yorker, 1977*

⅄ Douglas Slocombe; Maggie Smith

La Traviata **

Italy   1982   109m   colour
Accent Films/RAI (Tarak Ben Ammar)

A much-acclaimed version of an opera which had previously defied transcription to the screen.

w Francesco Maria Piave, Franco Zeffirelli
opera Verdi d Franco Zeffirelli ph Ennio Guarnieri pd Franco Zeffirelli, Gianni Quaranta ed Peter Taylor, Franca Sylvi

☆ Placido Domingo, Teresa Stratas, Cornell MacNeil, Allan Monk, Axell Gall

'Décors so opulent as on occasion to resemble a three-ring circus.' – *Sight and Sound*

⅄ costume design; art direction
℗ production design

Tread Softly Stranger *

GB   1958   91m   bw
Alderdale (George Minter)

In a north country town, two brothers in love with the same girl rob a safe.
Hilarious murky melodrama full of glum faces, with a well-worn trick ending; rather well photographed.

w George Minter, Denis O'Dell play Jack Popplewell d Gordon Parry ph Douglas Slocombe m Tristram Cary

☆ George Baker, Terence Morgan, Diana Dors, Wilfrid Lawson, Patrick Allen, Jane Griffiths, Joseph Tomelty, Norman MacOwan

Treason: see *Guilty of Treason*

Treasure Hunt

GB   1952   79m   bw
Romulus (Anatole de Grunwald)

The eccentric middle-aged members of an Irish family find their father's fortune is missing.
Theatrical comedy with some charm and humour, but very much a photographed play.

w Anatole de Grunwald play M. J. Perry d John Paddy Carstairs ph C. Pennington-Richards m Mischa Spolianksy

☆ Jimmy Edwards, Martita Hunt, Athene Seyler, Naunton Wayne, June Clyde, Susan Stephen, Brian Worth

Treasure Island **

↟ US   1934   105m   bw
MGM (Hunt Stromberg)

An old pirate map leads to a long sea voyage, a mutiny, and buried treasure.
Nicely mounted Hollywood version of a classic adventure story, a little slow in development but meticulously produced.

w John Lee Mahin novel Robert Louis Stevenson
d Victor Fleming ph Ray June, Clyde de Vinna, Harold Rosson m Herbert Stothart

☆ Wallace Beery, Jackie Cooper, Lewis Stone, Lionel Barrymore, Otto Kruger, Douglass Dumbrille, Nigel Bruce, Chic Sale

'While much of it entrances, the whole is somewhat tiring.' – *Variety*
'The first three-quarters is so lively and well established in its mood as to make the whole quite worth going to.' – *Otis Ferguson*

Treasure Island *

↟ GB   1950   96m   Technicolor
RKO/Walt Disney (Perce Pearce)

Cheerful Disney remake, poor on detail but transfixed by a swaggeringly overplayed and unforgettable leading performance.

w Lawrence Edward Watkin d Byron Haskin
ph F. A. Young m Clifton Parker pd Thomas Morahan ed Alan Jaggs

☆ Robert Newton, Bobby Driscoll, Walter Fitzgerald, Basil Sydney, Denis O'Dea, Geoffrey Wilkinson, Ralph Truman

'Serviceable rather than imaginative.' – *Lindsay Anderson*
'The result is an absolutely super party, but not "the world's greatest adventure story". Walt Disney may have, as Synopsis suggests, "much in common with Stevenson". But not this; shiver my timbers, not *Treasure Island*.' – *C. A. Lejeune.*
'The Long John Silver of Robert Newton ... is the finest I ever saw ... as succulent as peach-fed ham, as sweet as a spoonful of sugar held high over the porridge plate, as darkly oily as a car sump, as tricky as an ageing jockey.' – *Paul Holt*

Treasure Island

↟ GB/France/Germany/Spain   1971   95m
colour
Massfilms/FDL/CCC/Eguiluz (Harry Alan Towers)

Spiritless and characterless international remake with poor acting, production and dubbing.

w Wolf Mankowitz, O. W. Jeeves (Welles) d John Hough m Cicilio Paniagua m Natal Massara

☆ Orson Welles, Kim Burfield, Lionel Stander, Walter Slezak, Rik Battaglia

'Sail the high seas. Battle the pirates. Live the adventure.'

Treasure Island

↟ US   1990   132m   colour
Warner/Agamemnon/British Lion (Fraser C. Heston)

Faithful to the original, but a version lacking in panache, and plodding when it should be exciting.

wd Fraser C. Heston novel Robert Louis Stevenson m Paddy Moloney pd Robert Steadman m Paddy Maloney pd Tony Woollard ed Eric Boyd-Perkins, Bill Parnell, Gregory Gontz

☆ Charlton Heston, Christian Bale, Oliver Reed, Christopher Lee, Richard Johnson, Julian Glover, Clive Wood, John Benfield, Isla Blair

Treasure Island

France/USA 1991 115m colour
BFI/Les Films du Passage/Cannon (Paolo Branco)
French title: L'Île au trésor
A boy dreams, or perhaps lives, a series of events that bear some resemblance to Stevenson's tale of pirates and buried treasure.
A delirious modern-day version, in which events are repeated with variations from different viewpoints, and nothing is what it seems. And nothing is what it amounts to.
wd Raúl Ruiz novel Treasure Island by Robert Louis Stevenson ph Acacio de Almeida m Georges Arriagada ad Maria-José Branco ed Rodolfo Wedeles
☆ Melvil Poupaud, Martin Landau, Vic Tayback, Lou Castel, Jeffrey Kime, Anna Karina, Jean-Pierre Léaud
'One of Ruiz's most seductive films because it so evidently falls short of the grandiose completeness to which it aspires. A richly messy narrative bricolage, it is finally revealed as a game that the viewer is invited to play. It may finally be about very little of serious substance – or indeed about something as trivial as the "future of Western Civilisation", to which the dying Captain portentously alludes – but that in itself makes it all the more worth playing.' – *Jonathan Romney, Sight and Sound*

The Treasure of Lost Canyon

†† US 1952 82m Technicolor
U-I (Leonard Goldstein)
A small boy robbed of his inheritance finds it with the help of a country doctor who turns out to be his uncle.
Modest juvenile adventure, rather boringly narrated.
w Brainerd Duffield, Emerson Crocker story Robert Louis Stevenson d Ted Tetzlaff ph Russell Metty m Joseph Gershenson
☆ William Powell, Julia Adams, Charles Drake, Rosemary de Camp, Henry Hull, Tommy Ivo

Treasure of Matecumbe

†† US 1976 116m Technicolor
Walt Disney (Bill Anderson)
Two boys seek buried gold in the Florida keys.
Cheerful adventure tale with a few nods to Treasure Island; all very competent in the Disney fashion.
w Don Tait d Vincent McEveety ph Frank Phillips m Buddy Baker
☆ Robert Foxworth, Joan Hackett, Peter Ustinov, Vic Morrow, Jane Wyatt, Johnny Duran, Billy Attmore

Treasure of Monte Cristo

US 1949 76m bw
Lippert/Screen Guild
In modern San Francisco, a descendant of Monte Cristo is framed for murder.
Mildly amusing but slackly made variant on a familiar theme.
w Aubrey Wisberg, Jack Pollexfen d William Berke ph Benjamin Kline m Albert Glasser
☆ Glenn Langan, Adele Jergens, Steve Brodie, Robert Jordan, Michael Whalen

The Treasure of Pancho Villa

US 1955 96m Technicolor Superscope
RKO/Edmund Grainger
Mexico 1915: an American adventurer becomes involved with the revolutionary Pancho Villa; both seek a gold consignment but it is buried in an avalanche.
Modestly well made, routine action drama.
w Niven Busch story J. Robert Glen, Gladys Atwater d George Sherman ph William Snyder m Leith Stevens
☆ Rory Calhoun, Shelley Winters, Gilbert Roland, Joseph Calleia

Treasure of San Teresa

GB 1959 81m bw
Orbit (John Nasht, Patrick Filmer-Sankey)
An American secret service agent finds Nazi loot in a Czech convent.
Roughly-made, watchable actioner.

w Jack Andrews, Jeffrey Dell d Alvin Rakoff ph Wilkie Cooper m Philip Martell
☆ Eddie Constantine, Dawn Addams, Marius Goring, Christopher Lee, Walter Gotell

Treasure of the Golden Condor

US 1952 93m Technicolor
TCF (Jules Buck)
A young Frenchman flees to the South Seas but returns to discredit his wicked uncle.
Ineffectual remake of Son of Fury (qv) with Guatemalan backgrounds and no punch at all.
wd Delmer Daves ph Edward Cronjager m Sol Kaplan
☆ Cornel Wilde, Finlay Currie, Constance Smith, George Macready, Walter Hampden, Anne Bancroft, Fay Wray, Leo G. Carroll

'Greed, gold and gunplay on a Mexican mountain of malice!'
'The nearer they got to their treasure the further they got from the law!'

The Treasure of the Sierra Madre **

US 1948 126m bw
Warner (Henry Blanke)
Three gold prospectors come to grief through greed.
Well-acted but partly miscast action fable on the oldest theme in the world; rather tedious and studio-bound for a film with such a high reputation.
wd John Huston novel B. Traven ph Ted McCord m Max Steiner md Leo F. Forbstein
☆ Humphrey Bogart, Walter Huston, Tim Holt, Alfonso Bedoya, John Huston, Bruce Bennett, Barton MacLane
'This bitter fable is told with cinematic integrity and considerable skill.' – *Henry Hart*
'The faces of the men, in close-up or in a group, achieve a kind of formal pattern and always dominate the screen.' – *Peter Ericsson*
'One of the very few movies made since 1927 which I am sure will stand up in the memory and esteem of qualified people alongside the best of the silent movies.' – *James Agee*
👤 John Huston (as writer and director); Walter Huston
🏆 best picture

The Treasure Seekers

US 1977 88m colour
Halart (Sam Manners)
Two old friends search for Henry Morgan's pirate treasure on Jamaica.
Dull thriller, in which very little happens and nothing to catch one's interest or attention.
w Rod Taylor story Walter Brough d Henry Levin ph Richard Kelly, Joe Jackman m Byron Lee ed Keith Stafford
☆ Rod Taylor, Stuart Whitman, Elke Sommer, Jeremy Kemp, Keenan Wynn, Bob Phillips, Jennie Sherman

A Tree Grows in Brooklyn ***

US 1945 128m bw
TCF (Louis D. Lighton)
Life for an Irish family with a drunken father in New York's teeming slums at the turn of the century.
A superbly-detailed studio production of the type they don't make any more: a family drama with interest for everybody.
w Tess Slesinger, Frank Davis novel Betty Smith d Elia Kazan ph Leon Shamroy m Alfred Newman
☆ Peggy Ann Garner, James Dunn, Dorothy McGuire, Joan Blondell, Lloyd Nolan, Ted Donaldson, James Gleason, Ruth Nelson, John Alexander, Adeline de Walt Reynolds, Charles Halton
'He tells a maximum amount of story with a minimum of film. Little touches of humour and human understanding crop up throughout.' – *Frank Ward, NBR*
'An artistically satisfying and emotionally quickening tearjerker.' – *Kine Weekly*
'Its drabness is softened by a glow of love and hope.' – *Picture Show*
👤 James Dunn; Peggy Ann Garner (Special Award as outstanding child actress)
🎵 script

Tree of Hands

GB 1988 89m Eastmancolor
Pathé/Granada/British Screen/Film Four International/Greenpoint (Ann Scott)
After her young son dies, an American writer gives a home to an abused boy kidnapped by her mother.
Turgid and downbeat thriller that offers few pleasures.
w Gordon Williams novel Ruth Rendell d Giles Foster ph Kenneth MacMillan m Richard Hartley pd Adrian Smith ed David Martin
☆ Helen Shaver, Lauren Bacall, Malcolm Stoddard, Peter Firth, Paul McGann, Kate Hardie, Tony Haygarth, Phyllida Law
'The film remains essentially comic-strip in its description of the various milieux and its treatment of the theme of who, in this chaotic selfish world, is best suited to care for the innocent.' – *Louise Sweet, MFB*

The Tree of Liberty: see *The Howards of Virginia*

The Tree of Wooden Clogs *

Italy 1978 186m Gevacolor
Curzon Films/RAI/GPC (Giulio Mandelli)
In 19th-century Lombardy the lives of four peasant families are intertwined.
Sensitive, novel-like investigation of times gone by; never very exciting but certainly never dull, despite the limits of 16mm and a non-professional cast.
wd Ermanno Olmi ph Carlo Petriocioli m Bach md Fernando Germani pd Franco Gambarana

'One man's search for … who knows what.'

Trees Lounge *

US 1996 95m DuArt
Electric/Live Film/Mediaworks (Brad Wyman, Chris Hanley)
An unemployed motor mechanic drinks too much and has problems with women.
A slice of bar-room life, as desultory and apparently aimless as the real thing, but also managing to suggest a few home truths along the way.
wd Steve Buscemi ph Lisa Rinzler m Evan Lurie pd Steve Rosenzweig ed Kate Williams
☆ Steve Buscemi, Chloe Sevigny, Michael Buscemi, Anthony LaPaglia, Elizabeth Bracco, Mark Boone Jnr, Danny Baldwin, Seymour Cassel, Carol Kane, Bronson Dudley, Samuel L. Jackson, Mimi Rogers
'A surprisingly tart and astute chronicle.' – *Movieline*

Trelawny of the Wells: see *The Actress*

Tremors **

US 1989 96m DeLuxe
UIP/Universal/No Frills/Brent Maddock, S. S. Wilson
Giant man-eating worms threaten a small Western town.
Enjoyable monster movie in the style of 50s films, which manages to be both funny and suspenseful.
w S. S. Wilson, Brent Maddock, Ron Underwood d Ron Underwood ph Alexander Gruszynski m Ernest Troost pd Ivo Cristante ed O. Nicholas Brown
☆ Kevin Bacon, Fred Ward, Finn Carter, Michael Gross, Reba McEntire, Bobby Jacoby, Charlotte Stewart, Tony Genaro
'Shrewdly, unpretentiously written, energetically directed and played with high comic conviction, Tremors is bound to become a cult classic.' – *Richard Schickel, Time*

Tremors II: Aftershocks *

US 1995 90m Foto-Kem
Universal/MCA TV/Stampede (Nancy Roberts, Christopher deFaria)
An ostrich farmer is hired to destroy 'graboids', giant man-eating worms that ravage Mexico's biggest oilfield.
Enjoyable sequel, maintaining some of the humour and suspense of the original, though not as polished; it does contain interesting new monsters.
w Brent Maddock, S. S. Wilson d S. S. Wilson ph Virgil Harper m Jay Ferguson pd Ivo Cristante ed Bob Ducsay sp Alec Gillis, Tom Woodruff Jnr; Tippett Studio
☆ Fred Ward, Christopher Gartin, Helen Shaver, Michael Gross, Marcello Tubert, Marco Hernandez

'For some it will be shelter. For others a prison…No-one will ever forget.'
'It Is A Place 8FT Wide, 600 Miles Long, Man-Made and God-Forsaken.'

The Trench

GB/France 1999 99m Technicolor
Entertainment/Blue PM/Skyline/Galatée (Steve Clark-Hall')
A platoon of British soldiers prepare to leave their trench and advance on the enemy at the start of the Somme offensive in 1916.
This is Journey's End revisited, as a small group of men reveal their own fears and insecurities in the face of death; there are many better war movies than this low-budget effort.
wd William Boyd ph Tony Pierce-Roberts m Evelyn Glennie, Greg Malcangi pd Jim Clay ed Jim Clark, Laurence Méry-Clark
☆ Paul Nicholls, Daniel Craig, Julian Rhind-Tutt, Danny Dyer, James D'Arcy, Tam Williams, Antony Strachan, Michael Moreland
'The sort of small, compact, unambitious play you'd have expected to find on TV 20 years ago.' – *Alexander Walker, London Evening Standard*

Trenchcoat

US 1983 91m Technicolor
Buena Vista/Walt Disney (Jerry Leider)
A would-be thriller writer becomes accidentally involved with real-life skulduggery in Malta.
Lacklustre comedy-drama that never finds a satisfactory tone; its style is one of anonymous blandness.
w Jeffrey Price, Peter Seaman d Michael Tuchner ph Tonino delli Colli m Charles Fox pd Rodger Maus ed Frank J. Urioste
☆ Margot Kidder, Robert Hays, David Suchet, Gila von Weitershausen, Ronald Lacey, Daniel Faraldo, John Justin

Trent's Last Case

GB 1952 90m bw
Wilcox-Neagle (Herbert Wilcox)
A journalist suspects that the death of a tycoon was murder.
Desultory version of a famous novel, with none of the original style and a few naïveties of its own.
w Pamela Bower novel E. C. Bentley d Herbert Wilcox ph Max Greene m Anthony Collins
☆ Michael Wilding, Margaret Lockwood, Orson Welles, John McCallum, Miles Malleson

Trespass **

US 1993 101m DeLuxe
Universal (Neil Canton)
Two firemen go on a treasure hunt for a gold cross, which turns out to be hidden in a deserted factory, used as a headquarters by a heavily armed black gang.
Tense and violent thriller, like a modernized, interior, technological version of The Treasure of the Sierra Madre.
w Bob Gale, Robert Zemeckis d Walter Hill ph Lloyd Ahern m Ry Cooder pd Jon Hutman ed Freeman Davies
☆ Bill Paxton, Ice T, William Sadler, Ice Cube, Art Evans, De'Voreaux White, Bruce A. Young, Glenn Plummer
'Fizzles like a Molotov cocktail with a soggy fuse.' – *Kim Newman, Empire*

Trial *

US 1955 109m bw
MGM (Charles Schnee)
A young lawyer defends a Mexican boy accused of rape and murder.
Stereotyped but pacy and watchable racial drama with political overtones, Our Hero having to resist bigots, Commies and McCarthyites.
w Don M. Mankiewicz novel Don M. Mankiewicz d Mark Robson ph Robert Surtees m Daniele Amfitheatrof
☆ Glenn Ford, Dorothy McGuire, Arthur Kennedy, John Hodiak, Katy Jurado, Rafael Campos, Juano Hernandez, Robert Middleton, John Hoyt
🏆 Arthur Kennedy

---

†† film suitable for family viewing   📼 VHS video-cassette for the British PAL system   VHS video-cassette for the British PAL system in wide screen-format   Video cassette in a computer-colourised version   American NTSC video-cassette   Laser disc

The Trial *

France/Italy/West Germany 1962 120m bw
Paris Europe/Ficit/Hisa (Alexander Salkind)

📀 🎬 ▤ ⊙

original title: Le Procès
Joseph K is tried and condemned for an unspecified crime.
Kafka's nightmares tend to go on too long, and this film if one of them is no exception, despite its pin-screen prologue by Alexeieff and its inventive setting in the old Gare d'Orsay. Once again Welles the magician badly needs a Hollywood studio behind him.
ph Edmond Richard m Jean Ledrut pd Jean Mandarut wd/ed Orson Welles
☆ Orson Welles, Jeanne Moreau, Anthony Perkins, Madeleine Robinson, Elsa Martinelli, Suzanne Flon, Akim Tamiroff, Romy Schneider
'The elaboration of scale and decor is as boring as in any biblical spectacular and for the same reason: because it is used without mind or feeling, not to bring out meaning but to distract us from asking for it.' – Dwight MacDonald

The Trial

GB 1992 120m colour
BBC/Europanda (Louis Marks)

📀 🎬 ▤ ⊙

In Prague, Joseph K is arrested, tried and condemned without being able to discover his crime.
Plodding and uninteresting version, with a vacuous central performance and listless direction.
w Harold Pinter novel Franz Kafka d David Jones ph Phil Meheux m Carl Davis pd Don Taylor ed John Stothart
☆ Kyle MacLachlan, Anthony Hopkins, Jason Robards, Juliet Stevenson, Polly Walker, Alfred Molina, Michael Kitchen
'Dull, lifeless and strictly TV-bound in its aesthetics.' – Variety
'The result is like a translation of a translation of a translation; it has zero vitality.' – Michael Sragow, New Yorker

Trial and Error: see The Dock Brief (1962)

Trial and Error

US 1997 98m CFI color Panavision
Entertainment/New Line/Larger Than Life (Gary Ross, Jonathan Lynn)

📀 🎬 ▤ ⊙ 🎧

An incapacitated lawyer gets his friend, an unemployed actor, to impersonate him in court.
Disappointingly heavy-handed and predictable comedy, often sentimental and never funny.
w Sarah Bernstein, Gregory Bernstein d Jonathan Lynn ph Gabriel Beristain m Phil Marshall pd Victoria Paul ed Tony Lombardo
☆ Michael Richards, Jeff Daniels, Charlize Theron, Jessica Steen, Austin Pendleton, Rip Torn, Alexandra Wentworth
'Pleasant, amusing and periodically inspired.' – Variety

Trial by Combat

GB 1976 90m Technicolor
Warner/Combat (Fred Weintraub, Paul Heller)

▤

aka: Choice of Weapons
An apparently harmless secret society of 'medieval knights' rededicates itself to the ritual execution of criminals who have escaped the law.
A rare specimen of comic macabre apparently inspired by the TV series The Avengers. Sadly, not much of it really works.
w Julian Bond, Steven Rossen, Mitchell Smith d Kevin Conner ph Alan Hume m Frank Cordell ed Edward Marshall
☆ John Mills, Donald Pleasence, Peter Cushing, Barbara Hershey, David Birney, Margaret Leighton, Brian Glover

Trial by Jury

US 1994 107m colour
Warner/Morgan Creek (James G. Robinson, Chris Meledandri, Mark Gordon)

📀 🎬 ▤ ⊙

A member of the jury trying a gangland boss is threatened with her son being hurt if she finds him guilty.
Ridiculous courtroom drama, in which a ham-fisted script gets the performances it deserves before toppling over into absurdity.

w Jordan Katz, Heywood Gould d Heywood Gould ph Frederick Elmes m Terence Blanchard pd David Chapman ed Joel Goodman
☆ Joanne Whalley-Kilmer, Armand Assante, Gabriel Byrne, William Hurt, Ed Lauter, Margaret Whitton, Kathleen Quinlan, Stuart Whitman
'Enough laughable dialogue to fill a camp film festival.' – Variety

The Trial of Joan of Arc: see Procès de Jeanne d'Arc

The Trial of Mary Dugan

US 1929 120m bw
MGM

Prosecution and defence counsel both change their feelings towards the girl on trial for murder.
A cast-iron audience pleaser, this adapted stage play was the studio's first all-talking picture. It wouldn't stand the test of time.
w Bayard Veiller, Becky Gardner play Bayard Veiller d Bayard Veiller
☆ Norma Shearer, H. B. Warner, Raymond Hackett, Lewis Stone, Lilyan Tashman
† A 1940 remake directed by Norman Z. McLeod starred Laraine Day, Tom Conway, Robert Young, John Litel and Frieda Inescort, but was not a particular success.

The Trial of Vivienne Ware

US 1932 56m bw
Fox

An attempt is made to kill a woman witness during a murder trial.
Fast, complex courtroom murder mystery which even finds time for frequent bouts of comic relief.
w Philip Klein, Barry Connors novel Kenneth M. Ellis d William K. Howard
☆ Joan Bennett, Donald Cook, Skeets Gallagher, ZaSu Pitts, Lillian Bond, Alan Dinehart, Herbert Mundin, Noel Madison
'A skilful bit of claptrap melodrama.' – Variety

Trial on the Road **

Russia 1985 98m bw
Lenfilm

original title: Proverka Na Dorogakh
A former Red Army sergeant fighting for the Germans in Russia deserts to join the partisans.
Banned for 14 years, a stark, unheroic account of war and its effect on the human spirit, set in a bleak winter landscape.
w Eduard Volodarsky story Yuri Gherman d Alexei Gherman ph L. Kolganov, B. Alexsandrovsky, V. Mironov m I. Shvarts ad V. Yurkevich
☆ Rolan Bykov, Anatoly Solonitsin, Vladimir Zamansky, Oleg Borisov, Fedor Odinokov, Gennady Dindoyev
† Produced in 1971.

Trial Run

New Zealand 1984 89m colour
Cinema and Television/Double Feature (Don Reynolds)

An amateur photographer finds her metier photographing penguins, but in her remote retreat finds herself terrorized by a mysterious prowler.
Suspenseful but overlong thriller with a weak ending and too much psychological probing.
wd Melanie Read ph Allen Guilford m Jan Preston, Blair Greenberg pd Judith Crozier ed Finola Dwyer
☆ Annie Whittle, Judith Gibson, Christopher Broun, Philippa Mayne, Stephen Tozer

The Trials of Oscar Wilde **

GB 1960 123m Super Technirama 70
Warwick/Viceroy (Harold Huth)

US title: The Man with the Green Carnation
Oscar Wilde fatally sues the Marquis of Queensberry for libel, and loses; he is then prosecuted for sodomy.
Plush account of a fascinating event; narrative drive is unfortunately lacking, but one is left with interesting performances.
wd Ken Hughes ph Ted Moore m Ron Goodwin ad Ken Adam, Bill Constable
☆ Peter Finch, Yvonne Mitchell, John Fraser, Lionel Jeffries, Nigel Patrick, James Mason, Emrys Jones, Maxine Audley, Paul Rogers, James Booth
🏆 Peter Finch

Tribute *

Canada 1980 122m colour
TCF/Joel B. Michaels, Garth B. Drabinsky

▤ 🎬

A Broadway press agent comes to know his son by his divorced wife just as he comes to know of his own fatal illness.
Satisfactory screen treatment of a play which is really a vehicle for a charismatic star.
w Bernard Slade play Bernard Slade d Bob Clark ph Reginald H. Morris m various
☆ Jack Lemmon, Lee Remick, Robby Benson, Colleen Dewhurst, Kim Cattrall, John Marley
👤 Jack Lemmon

Tribute to a Bad Man

US 1956 95m Eastmancolor Cinemascope
MGM (Sam Zimbalist)

▤

A Wyoming horse breeder is callous in his treatment of rustlers, and wins the woman he wants when he becomes more understanding.
Somewhere behind an unsympathetic story and hesitant development lies a convincing picture of life in the old west.
w Michael Blankfort story Jack Schaefer d Robert Wise ph Robert Surtees m Miklos Rozsa
☆ James Cagney, Irene Papas, Don Dubbins, Stephen McNally, Vic Morrow, Royal Dano, Lee Van Cleef

'A story about two guys trying to make it in the big city.'

Trick

US 1999 89m colour
Millivres/Roadside Attractions/Good Machine (Eric d'Arbeloff, Jim Fall, Ross Katz)

▤ ⊙

A would-be songwriter in New York falls in love with a dancer.
A gay romantic comedy, pleasant in an unassuming way.
w Jason Schafer d Jim Fall ph Terry Stacey m David Friedman pd Jody Asnes ed Brian A. Kates
☆ Christian Campbell, John Paul Pitoc, Tori Spelling, Steve Hayes, Kevin Chamberlin, Brad Beyer, Lorri Bagley
'The most appealing and most erotic gay date movie ever made.' – Emanuel Levy, Variety

Trigger Happy

US 1996 93m DeLuxe
MGM/UA/Skylight/Dreyfus/James (Judith Rutherford James)

📀 ▤

aka: Mad Dog Time
Returning from a stay in a lunatic asylum, a gang boss demands that his old rivals be eliminated; they also want him out of the way.
An attempt at an ultra-cool gangster movie, in which everyone wisecracks as the gunplay plays; the ever-present attitudinizing quickly wears out its welcome.
wd Larry Bishop ph Frank Byers m Earl Rose pd Dina Lipton ed Norman Hollyn
☆ Ellen Barkin, Gabriel Byrne, Richard Dreyfuss, Jeff Goldblum, Diane Lane, Larry Bishop, Gregory Hines, Kyle MacLachlan, Burt Reynolds, Christopher Jones, Henry Silva
'The problem is, the film doesn't seem to be about anything except ironic detachment. With guns pointed at them, characters simply arch their eyebrows or mutter a throwaway joke, as if genuine emotions were strictly squaresville. If the characters don't seem to care about what's going on, imagine what it's like for the audience.' – Timothy M. Gray, Variety
† The director's father, Joey Bishop, Paul Anka, Richard Pryor, Rob Reiner, Michael J. Pollard and Billy Idol appear in cameo roles.

Trinity Is Still My Name (dubbed)

Italy 1971 90m DeLuxe Scope
Avco Embassy/West Film (Italo Zingarelli)

📀 ▤ 🎬

original title: Continuavamo a Chiamarlo Trinity
Two brothers set out for a life of crime but are sidetracked in rescuing some monks from a gun-runner.
Amiable parody of spaghetti Westerns, high-spirited rather than funny.

wd E. B. Clucher (Enzo Barboni) ph Aldo Giordani m Guido de Angelis, Maurizio de Angelis, Enzo Bulgarelli ed Antonio Siciliano
☆ Terence Hill (Mario Girotti), Bud Spencer (Carlo Pedersoli), Harry Carey Jnr, Jessica Dublin, Yanti Somer, Enzo Tarascio
† The film was originally released in Italy at 121m.

Trio *

GB 1950 91m bw
Rank/Gainsborough (Antony Darnborough)

Following *Quartet* (qv), three more stories from Somerset Maugham: 'The Verger', 'Mr Knowall', and 'Sanatorium'.
An enjoyable package, unpretentiously handled but with full weight to the content.
w W. Somerset Maugham, R. C. Sherriff, Noel Langley stories W. Somerset Maugham d Ken Annakin, Harold French ph Reg Wyer, Geoffrey Unsworth m John Greenwood ad Maurice Carter ed Alfred Roome
☆ James Hayter, Kathleen Harrison, Michael Hordern, Felix Aylmer; Nigel Patrick, Anne Crawford, Naunton Wayne, Wilfrid Hyde-White; Michael Rennie, Jean Simmons, John Laurie, Finlay Currie, Roland Culver, Betty Ann Davies, Raymond Huntley, André Morell
'The casting of all three films with stars and near stars is equally happy. Excellent entertainment.' – Joan Lester

'Listen to the sound of love! Feel people! Taste green!'

The Trip *

US 1967 85m Pathécolor
AIP (Roger Corman)

A director of TV commercials tries LSD and has hallucinations.
Much-banned plotless wallow, the ultimate opt-out movie; well done for those who can take it.
w Jack Nicholson d Roger Corman ph Arch Dalzell psychedelic effects Peter Gardiner montage Dennis Jakob
☆ Peter Fonda, Susan Strasberg, Bruce Dern, Salli Sachse, Dennis Hopper

The Trip to Bountiful *

US 1985 106m Allied and WBS colour
Island/Film Dallas/Bountiful Film Partners (Sterling Vanwagenen, Horton Foote)

▤ 🎬

An old woman leaves her tiresome family to return by bus to the town where she was raised.
A relic of the fifties, when writers were mystical about mid-America, this oddity survives as an acting tour de force.
w Horton Foote play Horton Foote d Peter Masterson ph Fred Murphy m J. A. C. Redford
☆ Geraldine Page, John Heard, Carlin Glynn, Richard Bradford, Rebecca de Mornay
'A wistful tale made for people old enough to appreciate that there is no going back – that the present, however wretched, is all we have.' – Quentin Crisp
🏆 Geraldine Page
👤 adapted screenplay

Triple Bogey on a Par 5 Hole

US 1991 85m colour/bw
ICA/Poe/Island World (Amos Poe)

A researcher questions three rich and spoiled children about the violent deaths of their parents on a golf course 13 years earlier.
Introspective navel-gazing movie that combines many of the least attractive aspects of underground cinema.
wd Amos Poe ph Joe Desalvo m Anna Domino, Michel Delory, Mader, Chic Streetman pd Jocelyne Beaudoin ed Dana Congdon
☆ Eric Mitchell, Daisy Hall, Angela Goethals, Jesse McBride, Alba Clemente, Robbie Coltrane, Olga Bagnasco
'Deeply minimalist, deeply minimal.' – Nigel Andrews, Financial Times
'Deliberately repetitious, funny and slightly threatening at the same time.' – Derek Malcolm, Guardian

Triple Cross

GB 1967 140m colour
Warner/Cineurop (Fred Feldkamp)

▤

A small-time crook imprisoned on Jersey at the start of World War II offers to spy for the Nazis but reports to the English.

Ho-hum biopic of double agent Eddie Chapman; effective scenes merely interrupt the general incoherence.
w René Hardy book The Eddie Chapman Story by Frank Owen d Terence Young ph Henri Alekan m Georges Garvarentz
☆ Christopher Plummer, Yul Brynner, Trevor Howard, Romy Schneider, Gert Frobe, Claudine Auger

Triple Cross
Hong Kong   1991   81m   colour
Rapi Films (Gope T. Samtani)
◙
Rival gangs trying to steal a computer in a suitcase are outwitted by a female security chief.
Car and boat chases, gun and fist fights, and martial arts action with an occasional spectacular stunt take most of the running time so that viewers will have little time to attend to the silly, confused narrative and unsubtle acting, or wonder why so many would kill, or die, for a portable computer.
w Christopher Mitchum story Deddy Armand d Ackyl Anwary ph H. Asmawi m Embie C. Noor ad Hendro Tangkilisan ed Amin Kertaraharia
☆ Cynthia Rothrock, Chris Barnes, Peter O'Brian, Jurek Kylne, Roy Marten, Tanaka, Agust Melasz, Fei Lung, Jack Maland

Triple Echo *
GB   1972   94m   colour
Hemdale/Senta (Graham Cottle)
▤
In 1942, a soldier's wife welcomes another soldier to her farm for tea; he deserts and poses as her sister.
Foolish story which would possibly have worked as a TV play but hardly justifies a film despite the talent on hand.
w Robin Chapman novel H. E. Bates d Michael Apted ph John Coquillon m Marc Wilkinson
☆ Glenda Jackson, Brian Deacon, Oliver Reed

Triple Trouble: see Kentucky Kernels

Tripoli
US   1950   95m   Technicolor
Paramount/Pine-Thomas
In 1805 the United States sends marines to rout the Barbary pirates.
Not a superior actioner, but it passed the time.
w Winston Miller d Will Price ph James Wong Howe m David Chudnow
☆ John Payne, Maureen O'Hara, Howard Da Silva, Philip Reed, Grant Withers, Lowell Gilmore

Tristana ****
Spain/Italy/France   1970   105m   Eastmancolor
Academy/Connoisseur/Epoca/Talia/Selenia/Les Films Corona (Juan Estelrich)
◙ ▤
An impoverished, womanizing aristocrat seduces his young ward and pays the price for his action.
Complex black comedy of obsessive behaviour which also mocks religion and other forms of consolation.
w Luis Buñuel, Julio Alejandro novel Benito Pérez Galdós d Luis Buñuel ph José F. Aguayo ad Enrique Alarcón ed Pedro Del Rey
☆ Catherine Deneuve, Fernando Rey, Franco Nero, Lola Gaos, Antonio Casas, Jesús Fernández
'It is Buñuel at his most majestic.' – Tom Milne, MFB

The Triumph of Sherlock Holmes *
GB   1935   84m   bw
Real Art
▤
Sherlock Holmes solves a murder stemming from enmity between Pennsylvania coal miners.
Solidly satisfying adaptation of Conan Doyle's The Valley of Fear, with more of Moriarty added.
w H. Fowler Mear, Cyril Twyford d Leslie Hiscott
☆ Arthur Wontner, Ian Fleming, Lyn Harding, Jane Carr, Leslie Perrins, Michael Shepley

Triumph of the Spirit *
US   1989   120m   Eastmancolor
Guild/Nova International (Arnold Kopelson, Shimon Arama)
◙ ▤ ⊚ ⌒
A Jewish boxer is forced by the Nazis to fight for his life in a series of boxing matches in Auschwitz.
Tough, sincere but not always convincing drama, based on fact.

w Andrzej Krakowski, Laurence Heath story Shimon Arama, Zion Haen d Robert M. Young ph Curtis Clark m Cliff Eidelman pd Jerzy Maslowska ed Arthur Coburn, Norman Buckley
☆ Willem Dafoe, Edward James Olmos, Robert Loggia, Wendy Gazelle, Kelly Wolf, Costas Mandylor, Kario Salem, Edward Zentara, Hartmut Becker

Triumph of the Will ****
Germany   1936   120m   bw
Leni Riefenstahl/Nazi Party
◙ ▤
The official record of the Nazi party congress held at Nuremberg in 1934.
A devastatingly brilliant piece of filmmaking – right from the opening sequence of Hitler descending from the skies, his plane shadowed against the clouds. The rally scenes are a terrifying example of the camera's power of propaganda. After World War II it was banned for many years because of general fears that it might inspire a new Nazi party.
ph Sepp Allgeier and 36 assistants m Herbert Windt d/ed Leni Riefenstahl

Triumphs of a Man Called Horse
Spain   1982   89m   CFI color
Sandy Howard/Redwing/Transpacific/Hesperia
Third in a dispensable series (A Man Called Horse, Return of a Man Called Horse) of dour Westerns.
In this scrappy item the man dies early on, but his son upholds the tradition.
w Ken Blackwell, Carlos Aured, Jack de Witt d John Hough ph John Alcott m Georges Garvarentz
☆ Richard Harris, Michael Beck, Ana de Sade, Vaughn Armstrong, Buck Taylor

'From a million years back – horror explodes into today!'
Trog
GB   1970   91m   Technicolor
Warner/Herman Cohen
A man-ape is discovered in a pothole and trained by a lady scientist.
Ridiculous semi-horror film which degrades its star.
w Aben Kandel d Freddie Francis ph Desmond Dickinson m John Scott
☆ Joan Crawford, Michael Gough, Bernard Kay, David Griffin

Trois Couleurs: Bleu: see Three Colours: Blue

Trois Hommes et un Couffin: see Three Men and a Cradle

Trojan Eddie *
GB/Ireland   1997   105m   Metrocolor
Film Four/Channel 4/IFB/Initial/Irish Screen (Emma Burge)
◙ ▤
Trapped between his sluttish wife and impatient girlfriend, despised by his thuggish boss, who rules the small community with a gang of travellers, a hangdog salesman finally triumphs.
An intriguing variation on the meek inheriting the earth, set on the fringe of Irish society, in a temporary, shifting world, where nothing seems settled; but the tension of the tale is dissipated by its too-leisurely approach.
w Billy Roche d Gillies MacKinnon ph John de Borman m John Keane pd Frank Conway ed Scott Thomas
☆ Richard Harris, Stephen Rea, Brendan Gleeson, Sean McGinley, Angeline Ball, Brid Brennan, Stuart Townsend, Aislin McGuckin
'This blatant bit of blarney is a joy from start to finish.' – Film Review
'Resembling a slow-moving travelogue for the Irish Lake and Fields Promotions Board.' – Neon

The Trojan Horse: see The Trojan War

The Trojan War
Italy/France   1961   105m   Technicolor
Technoscope
Europa Cinematografica/CICC/Les Films Modernes (Gian Paolo Bigazzi)
original title: La Guerra di Troia
aka: The Wooden Horse of Troy; The Trojan Horse
Aeneas performs heroic deeds before fleeing from his doomed city with his new-born son.

Good-looking, if stolid, epic which is one of the better efforts of its muscular star.
w Ugo Liberatore, Giorgio Stegani, Federico Zardi, Giorgio Ferroni d Giorgio Ferroni ph Rino Filippini m Giovanni Fusco pd Pier Vittorio Marchi ed Antonietta Zita
☆ Steve Reeves, John Drew Barrymore, Juliette Mayniel, Hedy Vessel, Lydia Alfonsi

'The strength of mankind has always been its women'
The Trojan Women *
US   1971   111m   Eastmancolor
Josef Shaftel (Michael Cacoyannis, Anis Nohra)
Troy has fallen to the Greeks and its women bemoan their fate.
And oh, how they bemoan! Even with this cast, Greek tragedy does not fill the big screen.
w Michael Cacoyannis play Euripides d Michael Cacoyannis ph Alfio Contini m Mikis Theodorakis
☆ Katharine Hepburn, Vanessa Redgrave, Geneviève Bujold, Irene Papas, Patrick Magee, Brian Blessed, Pauline Letts

'Waiting! Watching! Wanton!'
'None can escape this slithering terror spawned from a nuclear hell lusting for another taste of human blood … Maybe Yours!'
The Trollenberg Terror
GB   1958   84m   bw
Tempean
US title: The Crawling Eye
Extraterrestrials invade Switzerland.
Tolerable low-budget sci-fi from a BBC serial.
w Jimmy Sangster story Peter Key d Quentin Lawrence ph Monty Berman m Stanley Black
☆ Forrest Tucker, Laurence Payne, Janet Munro, Jennifer Jayne, Warren Mitchell

Tromeo & Juliet
US   1996   107m   colour
Starlight/Troma (Michael Herz, Lloyd Kaufman)
◙ ▤
In Manhattan, a youth falls in love with the daughter of his father's greatest enemy, his former partner in an exploitation film company.
Coarse and crude version that horribly mangles what remains of Shakespeare's verse; the acting is bad and the direction perfunctory, but that seems to be the point of Troma's output.
w James Gunn, Lloyd Kaufman play Romeo and Juliet by William Shakespeare d Lloyd Kaufman ph Brendan Flynt m Willie Wisely pd Roshelle Berliner ed Frank Reynolds
☆ Jane Jensen, Will Keenan, Valentine Miele, Maximilian Shaun, Steve Gibbons, Sean Gunn, Debbie Rochon, Lemmy
'Shakespeare as you never want to see it.' – Film Review

Tron *
US   1982   96m   Technicolor   Super Panavision 70mm
Walt Disney/Lisberger-Kushner
▤ ⊚ ⌀
A computer games designer gets his revenge on an enemy by fighting things out in the computer world he has created.
Complicated science fantasy chiefly interesting for its computerized blend of live action and animation, which isn't always successful.
wd Steven Lisberger ph Bruce Logan m Michael Femer pd Dean Edward Mitzner associate producer (animation) Harrison Ellenshaw
☆ Bruce Boxleitner, Jeff Bridges, David Warner, Barnard Hughes
'Loaded with the expected visual delights, but falls way short of the mark in story and viewer involvement.' – Variety
♫ costume design; sound

Troop Beverly Hills
⋔ US   1989   106m   Metrocolor
Columbia TriStar/Weintraub Entertainment/Fries Entertainment (Ava Ostern Fries, Martin Mickelson, Peter MacGregor-Scott)
◙ ▤
A wealthy mother transforms her daughter's disintegrating Girl Scout troop by giving them badges in shopping and other consumer activities.
A broad and far from sparkling comedy which emphasizes that it is best to be born rich.

w Pamela Norris, Margaret Grieco Oberman story Ava Ostern Fries d Jeff Kanew ph Donald E. Thorin m Randy Edelman, Lou Hemsey pd Robert F. Boyle ed Mark Melnick
☆ Shelley Long, Craig T. Nelson, Betty Thomas, Mary Gross, Stephanie Beacham, David Gautreaux, Karen Kopins, Dinah Lacey, Shelley Morrison

Trooper Hook
US   1957   92m   bw
UA/Sol Baer Fielding
A woman prisoner of the Indians has a half-breed son and becomes an outcast when returned to her people.
Peculiar Western with good moments, but generally very slow and downbeat.
w Charles Marquis Warren, David Victor, Herbert Little Jnr story Jack Schaefer d Charles Marquis Warren ph Ellsworth Fredericks m Gerald Fried
☆ Barbara Stanwyck, Joel McCrea, Earl Holliman, Edward Andrews, John Dehner, Susan Kohner, Royal Dano

Troopship: see Farewell Again

Trop Belle pour Toi! *
France   1989   91m   colour
Artificial Eye/Cine Valse/DD Productions/Orly Films/SEDIF/TF1 (Bernard Marescot)
◙ ▤ ⊚
aka: Too Beautiful for You
A successful car salesman with a beautiful wife begins an affair with his homely secretary.
Mildly amusing romantic comedy, for all that it seems no more than a heterosexual variation on Blier's Tenue de Soirée.
wd Bertrand Blier ph Philippe Rousselot m Schubert ad Theobald Meurisse ed Claudine Merlin
☆ Gérard Depardieu, Josiane Balasko, Carole Bouquet, Roland Blanche, François Cluzet, Didier Benureau, Philippe Loffredo

'Estupendo! Magnifico! Esplendido!'
Tropic Holiday
US   1938   78m   bw
Paramount
A Hollywood scriptwriter finds romance in Mexico.
Musical time-filler with a bit of everything and not much of anything.
w Don Hartman, Frank Butler, John C. Moffett and Duke Atterberry d Theodore Reed
☆ Ray Milland, Dorothy Lamour, Bob Burns, Martha Raye, Binnie Barnes, Tito Guizar
'Will need strong selling to top average business.' – Variety
♫ Boris Morros (music direction)

Tropic of Cancer
US   1970   88m   Eastmancolor
Paramount/Tropic (Joseph Strick)
The sexual exploits of an American writer in Paris.
An adaptation that fails to capture the raw energy of the original, despite, or possibly owing to, quoting from it at great length.
w Joseph Strick, Betty Botley novel Henry Miller d Joseph Strick ph Alain Derobe m Stanley Myers
☆ Rip Torn, James Callahan, Ellen Burstyn, David Bauer, Laurence Ligneres, Phil Brown
'The cinema here pays unfortunate tribute to literary achievement – by erecting a blank and ugly monument with the work itself firmly interred beneath.' – Richard Coombs, MFB
'A trivial but entertaining sex comedy.' – Pauline Kael

Tropic Zone
US   1953   94m   Technicolor
Paramount/Pine-Thomas
In a banana port a man wanted by the police saves a plantation from being taken over by crooks.
Tropical thick ear, not entirely unendurable.
wd Lewis R. Foster novel Tom Gill ph Lionel Linden m Lucien Cailliet
☆ Ronald Reagan, Rhonda Fleming, Noah Beery Jnr, Estelita, Grant Withers, John Wengraf

Tropicana: see The Heat's On

Trottie True *

GB   1949   98m   Technicolor

GFD/Two Cities (Hugh Stewart)

US title: *The Gay Lady*

Adventures of a Gaiety girl who married a lord.

Self-conscious period comedy which could have been highly diverting but manages only to be sporadically charming in a whimsically amateurish way.

w C. Denis Freeman *novel* Caryl Brahms, S. J. Simon *d* Brian Desmond Hurst *ph* Harry Waxman *m* Benjamin Frankel *ad* Ralph Brinton

☆ Jean Kent, James Donald, Hugh Sinclair, Bill Owen, Andrew Crawford, Lana Morris

Le Trou: see *The Hole*

Trouble along the Way

US   1953   110m   bw

Warner (Melville Shavelson)

A famous football coach is co-opted to help a bankrupt college but some of his methods are not quite above board.

American college comedy with dollops of religiosity – a double threat.

w Melville Shavelson, Jack Rose *d* Michael Curtiz *ph* Archie Stout *m* Max Steiner

☆ John Wayne, Donna Reed, Charles Coburn, Tom Tully, Sherry Jackson, Marie Windsor

'No opportunities for a laugh or a tear are missed by the entire cast.' – *MFB*

Trouble at Midnight

US   1937   69m   bw

Universal (Barney A. Sarecky)

A dairy farmer loses his stock in a series of midnight raids, but gets the girl.

A trivial gangster movie in a western setting, with Beery ill-at-ease as a romantic hero.

w Maurice Geraghty, Ford Beebe *d* Ford Beebe *ph* Jerome Ash *ed* John Rawlins

☆ Noah Beery Jnr, Catherine Hughes, Larry Blake, Bernadene Hayes, Louis Mason, Earl Dwire, Charles Halton, Frank Melton

Trouble Bound

US   1993   89m   CFI color

ITC (Tom Kuhn, Fred Weintraub)

A gullible small-time crook finds himself in the middle of a gang war after he picks up a girl on the run from her Mafia family.

Routine road movie that takes the fast lane to clichéville.

w Darrell Fetty, Francis Delia *d* Jeffrey Reiner *ph* Janusz Kaminski *m* Vinny Golia *pd* Richard Sherman *ed* Neil Grieve

☆ Michael Madsen, Patricia Arquette, Florence Stanley, Seymour Cassel, Sal Jenco, Paul Ben-Victor

'A likeable road movie with a couple of decent central performances but few original ideas.' – *Empire*

Trouble Brewing *

GB   1939   87m   bw

ATP

A newspaper printer catches counterfeiters.

Lively star comedy.

w Anthony Kimmins, Angus MacPhail, Michael Hogan *d* Anthony Kimmins *ph* Ronald Neame

☆ George Formby, Googie Withers, Gus MacNaughton, Joss Ambler, Martita Hunt, Garry Marsh, Ronald Shiner, C. Denier Warren, Basil Radford

Trouble for Two *

US   1936   75m   bw

MGM (Louis D. Lighton)

GB title: *The Suicide Club*

A European prince in London for an arranged wedding gets involved with an ingenious organization for murder.

Light-hearted, black-edged Victorian literary spoof which starts nicely but can't quite keep up the pace.

w Manuel Seff, Edward Paramore Jnr *stories* New Arabian Nights by Robert Louis Stevenson *d* J. Walter Rubin *ph* Charles G. Clarke *m* Franz Waxman

☆ Robert Montgomery, Rosalind Russell, Reginald Owen, Frank Morgan, *Louis Hayward*, E. E. Clive, Walter Kingsford

Trouble in Mind

US   1985   111m   colour

Island Alive/Terry Glinwood (Carolyn Pfeiffer, David Blocker)

In some seedy future, the lives of an ex-cop, just out of prison, a petty crook, his innocent girlfriend and their baby interwine in a run-down diner.

Moody, blue-tinged, blues-tinged melodrama, too preoccupied with creating atmosphere, attitudinizing and indulging in windy philosophizing to appeal to any but cultists.

wd Alan Rudolph *ph* Toyomichi Kurita *m* Mark Isham *pd* Stephen Legler *ed* Tom Walls

☆ Kris Kristofferson, Keith Carradine, Lori Singer, Geneviève Bujold, Joe Morton, George Kirby, Divine, John Considine

'At once gritty and weirdly exotic, Rudolph's self-reflective *noir* thriller takes genre commonplaces and pushes them to the limits.' – *Sight and Sound*

Trouble in Paradise ****

US   1932   86m   bw

Paramount (Ernst Lubitsch)

Jewel thieves insinuate themselves into the household of a rich Parisienne, and one falls in love with her.

A masterpiece of light comedy, with sparkling dialogue, innuendo, great performances and masterly cinematic narrative. For connoisseurs, it can't be faulted, and is the masterpiece of American sophisticated comedy.

w Samson Raphaelson, Grover Jones *play* The Honest Finder by Laszlo Aladar *d* Ernst Lubitsch *ph* Victor Milner *m* W. Franke Harling

☆ Herbert Marshall, Miriam Hopkins, Kay Francis, Edward Everett Horton, Charles Ruggles, C. Aubrey Smith, Robert Greig, Leonid Kinskey

'Swell title, poor picture. Better for the class houses than the subsequents.' – *Variety*

'One of the gossamer creations of Lubitsch's narrative art ... it would be impossible in this brief notice to describe the innumerable touches of wit and of narrative skill with which it is unfolded.' – *Alexander Bakshy*

'A shimmering, engaging piece of work ... in virtually every scene a lively imagination shines forth.' – *New York Times*

'An almost continuous musical background pointed up and commented on the action. The settings were the last word in modernistic design.' – *Theodor Huff, 1948*

Trouble in Store *

GB   1953   85m   bw

GFD/Two Cities (Maurice Cowan)

A stock assistant causes chaos in a department store.

First, simplest and best of the Wisdom farces.

w John Paddy Carstairs, Maurice Cowan, Ted Willis *d* John Paddy Carstairs *ph* Ernest Steward *m* Mischa Spoliansky

☆ Norman Wisdom, Jerry Desmonde, Margaret Rutherford, Moira Lister, Derek Bond, Lana Morris, Megs Jenkins, Joan Sims

Ⓥ Norman Wisdom (best newcomer)

Trouble in the Glen

GB   1954   91m   Trucolor

Republic/Wilcox-Neagle (Stuart Robertson)

An Argentinian laird in a Scottish glen causes ill-feeling.

Heavy-handed Celtic comedy whose predictability and sentimentality could have been forgiven were it not for the most garish colour ever seen.

w Frank S. Nugent *novel* Maurice Walsh *d* Herbert Wilcox *ph* Max Greene *m* Victor Young

☆ Margaret Lockwood, Orson Welles, Forrest Tucker, Victor McLaglen, John McCallum, Eddie Byrne, Archie Duncan, Moultrie Kelsall

Trouble in the Sky: see *Cone of Silence*

The Trouble Shooter: see *The Man with the Gun*

The Trouble with Angels

US   1966   112m   Pathécolor

Columbia/William Frye

Two mischievous new pupils cause trouble at a convent school.

Fun with the nuns, for addicts only.

w Blanche Hanalis *novel* Life with Mother Superior by Jane Trahey *d* Ida Lupino *ph* Lionel Lindon *m* Jerry Goldsmith

☆ Rosalind Russell, Hayley Mills, June Harding, Marge Redmond, Binnie Barnes, Gypsy Rose Lee, Camilla Sparv, Mary Wickes, Margalo Gillmore

'A relentless series of prankish escapades.' – *MFB*

Trouble With Eve

GB   1959   64m   bw

Mancunian/Butcher/Blakeley's

A widow who runs a teashop in a small village finds that her reputation for propriety is endangerd when her beatnik daughter comes to stay.

Minor comedy of middle-clsass scandal among the teacups that seemed very dated within a year or so of its release.

w Brock Williams *play* Widows are Dangerous by June Garland *d* Francis Searle *ph* James Harvey *ad* John Earl *ed* Eric Boyd Perkins

☆ Robert Urquhart, Hy Hazel, Garry Marsh, Vera Day, Sally Smith, Tony Quinn, Brenda Hogan, Denis Shaw, Grace Denbeigh-Russell, Bruce Seton

The Trouble with Girls

US   1969   105m   Metrocolor   Panavision

MGM (Lester Welch)

In the twenties the manager of a travelling chautauqua (educational medicine show) gets involved in a small-town murder.

Curious vehicle for a very bored singing star, with some interesting background detail.

w Arnold and Lois Peyser *novel* The Chautauqua by Day Keene, Dwight Babcock *d* Peter Tewkesbury *ph* Jacques Marquette *m* Billy Strange

☆ Elvis Presley, Marlyn Mason, Nicole Jaffe, Sheree North, Edward Andrews, John Carradine, Vincent Price, Joyce Van Patten

The Trouble with Harry **

US   1955   99m   Technicolor   Vistavision

Paramount (Alfred Hitchcock)

In the New England woods, various reasons cause various people to find and bury the same body.

Black comedy which never quite, despite bright moments, catches the style of the book; however, it is finely performed and the autumnal backgrounds are splendid.

w John Michael Hayes *novel* Jack Trevor Story *d* Alfred Hitchcock *ph* Robert Burks *m* Bernard Herrmann

☆ Edmund Gwenn, Mildred Natwick, John Forsythe, Shirley MacLaine, Mildred Dunnock

'Has, I fear, neither the desperation which makes the predicament of its characters wryly enjoyable nor the urbanity which would make their actions sympathetic.' – *Dilys Powell*

The Trouble with Women

US   1947   80m   bw

Paramount

A psychology professor thinks women enjoy being treated rough; a lady reporter tests his theories.

Silly romantic comedy.

w Arthur Sheekman *story* Ruth McKenney *d* Sidney Lanfield

☆ Ray Milland, Brian Donlevy, Teresa Wright, Rose Hobart, Charles Smith, Iris Adrian, Lloyd Bridges

† The film was completed in 1945, but held from release for two years because of overstock.

The Troublemaker

US   1964   80m   bw

Ozymandias/Seneca/Janus (Robert Gaffney)

Arriving in New York to open a coffee house, a gullible chicken farmer learns the hard way that corruption is the way to success.

Amiable, though not often amusing, comedy, performed in an easy-going, easily satisfied manner.

w Buck Henry, Theodore J. Flicker *d* Theodore J. Flicker *ph* Gayne Rescher *m* Cy Coleman *ad* David Moon *ed* John McManus

☆ Tom Aldredge, Joan Darling, James Frawley, Theodore J. Flicker, Buck Henry, Charles White, Godfrey Cambridge

Truck Turner

US   1974   91m   Movielab

Focus/AIP/Sequoia (Paul M. Heller, Fred Weintraub)

Hired to find a thuggish criminal, a bounty hunter finds he has offended a big-time gangster.

Crude blaxploitation thriller, packed with violent action.

w Oscar Williams, Michael Allin, Leigh Chapman *story* Jerry Wilkes *d* Jonathan Kaplan *ph* Charles F. Wheeler *m* Isaac Hayes *ed* Michael Kahn

☆ Isaac Hayes, Yaphet Kotto, Alan Weeks, Nichelle Nichols, Sam Laws, Paul Harris, Scatman Crothers, Dick Miller

'Exceedingly tame even by the genre's current standards.' – *Tony Raynes*, *MFB*

† It was cut to 83m for its British release.

True as a Turtle

GB   1956   96m   Eastmancolor

Rank (Peter de Sarigny)

Honeymooners join a variety of friends on a yacht crossing the Channel, and get involved in smuggling.

Artless, undemanding comedy for those who like messing about in boats.

w Jack Davies, John Coates, Nicholas Phipps *d* Wendy Toye *ph* Reg Wyer *m* Robert Farnon

☆ John Gregson, June Thorburn, Cecil Parker, Elvi Hale, Keith Michell, Avice Landone

True Believer *

US   1989   103m   DeLuxe

Columbia (Walter F. Parkes, Lawrence Lasker)

aka: *Fighting Justice*

A tough, once idealistic lawyer is persuaded to take on the case of an Asian-American who may have been wrongfully imprisoned.

Entertaining thriller, though it would have been as effective on television and, indeed, led to a TV series, Eddie Dodd, based on its central character.

w Wesley Strick *d* Joseph Ruben *ph* John W, Lindley *m* Brad Fiedel *pd* Lawrence Miller *ed* George Bowers

☆ James Woods, Robert Downey Jnr, Margaret Colin, Yuji Okumoto, Kurtwood Smith, Tom Bower, Miguel Fernandes, Charles Hallahan

True Blue

GB   1996   118m   colour

Film Four/Channel 4/Arts Council/Booker/Film and General/Rafford (Clive Parsons, Davina Belling)

As the day of the annual Boat Race between Oxford and Cambridge universities approaches, the Oxford coach faces a crisis when American members of the crew refuse to row.

A true story, based on Oxford's unexpected win in the 1987 Boat Race, makes for a doggedly dull film.

w Rupert Walters *book* Daniel Topolski, Patrick Robinson *d* Ferdinand Fairfax *ph* Brian Tufano *m* Stanislas Syrewicz *pd* Alison Riva *ed* Les Healy

☆ Johan Leysen, Dominic West, Dylan Baker, Geraldine Somerville, Josh Lucas, Brian McGovern, Ryan Bollman, Andrew Tees, Robert Bogue

'An air of ripe ridiculousness hangs over the whole thing.' – *Sunday Times*

True Colors

US   1991   111m   Technicolor

Paramount (Herbert Ross, Laurence Mark)

A principled lawyer watches the rise and fall of his former classmate, who is prepared to use any method to succeed in politics.

Unengrossing story of corruption that never grips, despite its slick presentation.

w Kevin Wade *d* Herbert Ross *ph* Dante Spinotti *m* Trevor Jones *pd* Edward Pisoni *ed* Robert Reitano, Stephen A. Rotter

☆ John Cusack, James Spader, Imogen Stubbs, Mandy Patinkin, Richard Widmark, Dina Merrill, Philip Bosco, Paul Guilfoyle, Brad Sullivan

True Confession **

US   1937   85m   bw

Paramount (Albert Lewin)

A fantasy-prone girl confesses to a murder she didn't commit, and her upright lawyer husband defends her.

Archetypal crazy comedy with fine moments despite longueurs and a lack of cinematic inventiveness. *Remade as Cross My Heart (qv).*

w Claude Binyon *play* Mon Crime by Louis Verneuil, George Berr d Wesley Ruggles *ph* Ted Tetzlaff m Frederick Hollander

☆ Carole Lombard, Fred MacMurray, John Barrymore, Una Merkel, Porter Hall, Edgar Kennedy, Lynne Overman, Fritz Feld, *Irving Bacon*

'Not a big bet but a favourable enough one ... it just falls short of being a smash.' – *Variety*
'The best comedy of the year.' – *Graham Greene*

True Confessions *

US 1981 108m colour
United Artists/Chartoff-Winkler (James D. Brubaker)
⬛ ⬛ ⬅

A policeman working on a murder case finds that his brother, a priest, is involved.
Unnecessary fictional elaboration on a real Los Angeles murder case of the forties (the 'Black Dahlia'); chiefly notable for performances.

w John Gregory Dunne, Joan Didion *novel* John Gregory Dunne d Ulu Grosbard *ph* Owen Roizman m Georges Delerue *pd* Stephen S. Grimes

☆ Robert Duvall, Robert DeNiro, Charles Durning, Kenneth McMillan, Ed Flanders, Cyril Cusack, Burgess Meredith

True Crime *

US 1999 127m Technicolor
Warner/Zanuck/Malpaso (Clint Eastwood, Richard D. Zanuck, Lili Fini Zanuck)
⬛ ⬛

An elderly investigative reporter has 24 hours to prove that a man about to be hanged for murder is innocent.
A predictable against-the-clock thriller is enlivened with a few deft touches of character, but not enough to lift it out of the ordinary.

w Larry Gross, Paul Brickman, Stephen Schiff *novel* Andrew Klavan d Clint Eastwood *ph* Jack N. Green m Lennie Niehaus *pd* Henry Bumstead ed Joel Cox

☆ Clint Eastwood, Isaiah Washington, Denis Leary, Lisa Gay Hamilton, James Woods, Bernard Hill, Diane Venora, Michael McKean, Michael Jeter, Mary McCormack, Hattie Winston

'A wickedly effective thriller.' – *Roger Ebert, Chicago Sun-Times*
'An awkward, if intermittently gripping affair.' – *The Times*

'The Victory You Helped To Make ... Now on the screen in all its glory!'
The True Glory ****

GB/US 1945 90m bw
Ministry of Information/Office of War Information
⬛

The last year of the war, retold by edited newsreels: D-Day to the Fall of Berlin.
A magnificent piece of reportage, worth a dozen fiction films in its exhilarating Shakespearean fervour, though the poetic commentary does occasionally go over the top. One of the finest of all compilations.

w Eric Maschwitz, Arthur Macrae, Jenny Nicholson, Gerald Kersh, Guy Trosper d Carol Reed, Garson Kanin m William Alwyn research Peter Cusick

'Dwarfs all the fiction pictures of the year.' – *Richard Mallett, Punch*
'Bold, welcome but inadequate use of blank verse; much more successful use of many bits of individualized vernacular narration, unusually free of falseness. Very jab-paced, energetic cutting; intelligent selection of shots, of which several hundred are magnificent.' – *James Agee*
'An inspiring recital of human endeavour which all the world will want to see.' – *The Cinema*
🏆 best documentary

True Grit *

US 1969 128m Technicolor
Paramount/Hal B. Wallis (Paul Nathan)
⬛ ⬛ ⬅

In the Old West, a young girl wanting to avenge her murdered father seeks the aid of a hard-drinking old marshal.
Disappointingly slow-moving and uninventive semi-spoof Western with a roistering performance from a veteran star, who won a sentimental Oscar for daring to look fat and old.

w Marguerite Roberts *novel* Charles Portis d Henry Hathaway *ph* Lucien Ballard m Elmer Bernstein

☆ John Wayne, Kim Darby, Glen Campbell, Dennis Hopper, Jeremy Slate, Robert Duvall, Strother Martin, Jeff Corey

'Readers may remember it as a book about a girl, but it's a film about John Wayne.' – *Stanley Kauffmann*
'There is a slight consistent heightening or lowering into absurdity, but there is also a strong feeling for the unvarnished preposterousness of everyday existence.' – *John Simon*

† *Rooster Cogburn featured more adventures of the Wayne character, who also showed up on TV in 1978 in the guise of Warren Oates.*
👤 John Wayne
🎵 title song (*m*Elmer Bernstein, *ly*Don Black)

True Heart Susie *

US 1919 62m bw silent
D. W. Griffith/Artcraft

A country girl sells her cow to send her boyfriend to college, but he is ungrateful.
Lavender-flavoured rustic romance, with the director at his most sentimental. But of its kind it is carefully done.

wd D. W. Griffith *story* Marion Fremont *ph* Billy Bitzer

☆ Lillian Gish, Robert Harron, Clarine Seymour

True Identity

USA 1991 93m Technicolor
Warner/Touchstone/Silver Screen Partners IV/Sandollar (Carol Baum, Teri Schwartz)
⬛ ⬛

On the run from the Mafia, a black actor disguises himself as a white man.
A star vehicle that, despite an engaging central performance, failed, due to a weak script.

w Andy Breckman d Charles Lane *ph* Tom Ackerman m Marc Marder *pd* John DeCuir Jnr ed Kent Beyda

☆ Lenny Henry, Frank Langella, Charles Lane, J. T. Walsh, Anne-Marie Johnson, Andreas Katsulas, Michael McKean, Peggy Lipton

'Mild comedy that works best as a showcase for Lenny Henry.' – *New York Times*

'When he said I do, he never said what he did.'
True Lies

US 1994 141m CFI color
TCF/Lightstorm (James Cameron, Stephanie Austin)
⬛ ⬛ ⬅ ∩

An American secret agent combating Arab terrorism pretends to his wife that he is a very boring computer salesman.
Either a romantic comedy with violent sequences or a Bond-like thriller that ignores the rule that women shouldn't get in the way of action; either way, it long overstays its welcome, though the destruction is on an extremely lavish scale.

wd James Cameron *screenplay* Claude Zidi, Simon Michael, Didier Kaminka *ph* Russell Carpenter m Brad Fiedel *pd* Peter Lamont ed Conrad Buff, Mark Goldblatt, Richard A. Harris *sp* Digital Domain

☆ Arnold Schwarzenegger, Jamie Lee Curtis, Tom Arnold, Bill Paxton, Art Malik, Tia Carrere, Eliza Dushku, Grant Heslov, Charlton Heston

'Every now and then there comes a film with the power to bring criticism to its knees, whimpering. Such a film is the opposite of a masterpiece, nothing so humble as a failure but an astounding condensation of everything that can go wrong with a project. True Lies is just such a reverse classic or anti-paragon.' – *Adam Mars-Jones, Independent*
'Will breed content and contempt in equal measure. With half-an-hour cut, I would certainly have been less inclined to drop an eyelid occasionally.' – *Derek Malcolm, Guardian*
'A loud misfire. It rarely brings its potent themes to life.' – *Richard Corliss, Time*

† *The film, which cost around $120m, was based on Claude Zidi's domestic comedy La Totale, made in 1992.*
†† *The version released on video in Britain runs for 135m and has been 'edited for censorship purposes' to remove some moments of violence so that it could receive a 15 video certificate. The cuts were supervised by the director.*
🎬 visual effects

'If All You Want To Do Is Have A Good Time ... Why Get Married?'
True Love **

US 1989 100m DuArt
Oasis/UA (Richard Guay, Shelley Houis)
⬛ ⬅

A young Italian-American couple in the Bronx prepare for their marriage, she with determination, he with reluctance.
Well-observed, low-budget comedy with a ring of truth about it.

w Nancy Savoca, Richard Guay d Nancy Savoca *ph* Lisa Rinzler *pd* Lester W. Cohen ed John Tintori

☆ Annabella Sciorra, Ron Eldard, Aida Turturro, Roger Rignack, Star Jasper, Michael J. Wolfe, Kelly Cinnante, Rick Shapiro

'...Stealing ... Cheating ... Killing ... who says romance is dead?'
True Romance **

US 1993 119m colour Panvision
Warner/Morgan Creek/Davis (Bill Unger, Steve Perry, Samuel Hadida)
⬛ ⬛ ⬛ ⬅ ◉ ∩

A shop assistant and a callgirl go on the run with a suitcase full of cocaine, chased by gangsters.
A clever, very violent, high-energy thriller, providing opportunity for striking cameos by a variety of actors as well as narrative twists that owe much to farce; the conclusion, a three-way stand-off, brings to mind a minor 30s screwball comedy, The Housekeeper's Daughter, but then the film is stuffed with references to other movies.

w Quentin Tarantino d Tony Scott *ph* Jeffrey L. Kimball m Hans Zimmer *pd* Benjamin Fernandez ed Michael Tronick, Christian Wagner

☆ Christian Slater, Patricia Arquette, *Dennis Hopper*, Val Kilmer, *Gary Oldman*, Brad Pitt, *Christopher Walken*

CLIFF (DENNIS HOPPER): 'I don't know whether you know this or not, Sicilians were spawned by niggers.'
COCCOTTI (CHRISTOPHER WALKEN): 'Come again?'
CLIFF: 'It's a fact. Sicilians have nigger blood pumpin' through their hearts. If you don't believe me, look it up. You see, hundreds and hundreds of years ago the Moors conquered Sicily. And Moors are niggers. Way back then, Sicilians were like the wops in northern Italy. Blond hair. Blue eyes. But, once the Moors moved in there, they changed the whole country. They did so much fuckin' with the Sicilian women, they changed the blood-line for ever, from blond hair and blue eyes to black hair and dark skin. I find it absolutely amazing to think that to this day, hundreds of years later, Sicilians still carry that nigger gene. I'm just quotin' history. It's a fact. It's written. Your ancestors were niggers. Your great, great, great, great, great-grandmother was fucked by a nigger, and had a half-nigger kid. That is a fact. Now tell me, am I lying?'
'Creates a new genre: screwball violence.' – *Tom Hutchinson*
'Provides some amazing encounters, bravura acting turns and gruesome carnage. But it doesn't add up to enough, as preposterous plotting and graphic violence ultimately prove an audience turnoff.' – *Variety*
'Looks like a piece of designer chic searching but unable to find any kind of holding centre.' – *Derek Malcolm, Guardian*

True Stories *

US 1986 89m DuArt
Warner/Edward R. Pressman/Gary Kurfirst
⬛ ⬛ ⬅

A narrator introduces people from the town of Virgil, Texas.
A curious entertainment which plays like a whimsical update of Thornton Wilder's Our Town, though without the subtlety.

w Stephen Tobolowsky, Beth Henley, David Byrne d David Byrne *ph* Ed Lachman m David Byrne

☆ David Byrne, John Goodman, Annie McEnroe, Jo Harvey Allen, Spalding Gray, Alix Elias, Swoosie Kurtz

'The story is just a trick to get your attention. It opens the door and lets the real movie in.' – *David Byrne*

The True Story of Jesse James

US 1956 92m Eastmancolor Cinemascope
TCF (Herbert Swope Jnr)
GB title: *The James Brothers*

After the Civil War, Jesse and Frank James become outlaws and train robbers.
Fairly slavish remake of Jesse James, without the style.

w Walter Newman d Nicholas Ray *ph* Joe MacDonald m Leigh Harline

☆ Robert Wagner, Jeffrey Hunter, Hope Lange, Agnes Moorehead, John Carradine, Alan Hale Jnr, Alan Baxter

True to Life *

US 1943 93m Technicolor
Paramount (Paul Jones)

The writer of a radio soap opera moves in with an average family to get the right atmosphere.
Quite a percipient comedy of its day, though it does not forgo the customary romantic entanglements.

w Don Hartman, Harry Tugend d George Marshall *ph* Charles Lang m Victor Young

☆ Mary Martin, Dick Powell, Franchot Tone, Victor Moore, Mabel Paige, William Demarest, Clarence Kolb, Ernest Truex

True to the Navy

US 1930 70m bw
Paramount

A drug store girl has too many sailor sweethearts for comfort.
Very ordinary star vehicle, with little about it worth remembering next day.

w Keene Thompson, Doris Anderson, Herman Mankiewicz d Frank Tuttle

☆ Clara Bow, Fredric March, Harry Green, Rex Bell, Eddie Fetherston

'Hardly better than fair. Slow in tempo, sappy in story, and bearing the stamp of perfunctory production.' – *Variety*

Truly, Madly, Deeply **

GB 1990 106m colour
Samuel Goldwyn Company/Winston/BBC/Lionheart (Robert Cooper)
⬛ ⬛ ⬅

A woman grieving for the death of her husband is visited by his ghost.
Unusual story of coming to terms with loss, combining wit, insight and excellent acting.

wd Anthony Minghella *ph* Remi Adefarasin m Barrington Pheloung *pd* Barbara Gasnold ed John Stothart

☆ Juliet Stevenson, Alan Rickman, Bill Paterson, Michael Maloney, Jenny Howe, Carolyn Choa, Christopher Rozycki, Keith Bartlett, David Ryall

'Intelligent, charming, ironic and exceptionally well played.' – *Derek Malcolm, Guardian*
🏆 best original screenplay

The Truman Show ***

US 1998 102m DeLuxe
Paramount (Scott Rudin, Andrew Niccol, Edward S. Feldman, Adam Schroeder)
⬛ ⬛ ⬅ ∩

A man who lives happily in an island community discovers that he is the star of an all-day TV soap opera, and that his wife, friends and neighbours are all acting their parts.
A clever (if implausible) conceit that can be taken several ways: as a satire on our all-controlling media, as a comment on television's pervasiveness, and the way everyone wants to appear on it, or as an instance of situationists' desire to disrupt the spectacle, to tear away the false tinsel of everyday life, and reveal the real tinsel beneath. Whichever way, it's a pleasure to watch.

w Andrew Niccol d Peter Weir *ph* Peter Biziou m Burkhard Dallwitz *pd* Dennis Gassner ed William Anderson

☆ Jim Carrey, Laura Linney, Noah Emmerich, Natascha McElhone, Holland Taylor, Ed Harris

'An emerging genre of cheerfully subversive movies finds its first near-masterpiece.' – *David Thomson, Esquire*
🎵 Peter Weir; Andrew Niccol; Ed Harris
🎬 Peter Weir; Andrew Niccol; Dennis Gassner

The Trumpet Blows

US 1934 68m bw
Paramount

A matador comes home to Mexico and quarrels with his bandit brother.
Tedious melodrama with bullring scenes.

---

w Bartlett Cormack, Wallace Smith, Porter Emerson Browne, J. Parker Read Jnr *d* Stephen Roberts

☆ George Raft, Adolphe Menjou, Frances Drake, Sidney Toler, Edward Ellis, Nydia Westman

'Story weak, dialogue bad, casting hopeless.' – *Variety*

Trunk Crime

GB 1939 51m bw

Charter (John Boulting)

A student goes mad and tries to bury his enemy alive.

Now dated, but at the time a smart little programme-filler by an enterprising young producer-director team.

w Francis Miller *play* Edward Percy, Reginald Denham *d* Roy Boulting

☆ Manning Whiley, Barbara Everest, Hay Petrie, Thorley Walters

The Trunk Mystery: see *One New York Night*

'A slightly twisted comedy.'

Trust **

GB/USA 1990 106m colour

Palace/Zenith/True Fiction/Film Four (Bruce Weiss)

▣ ▤ ◎

A pregnant teenager meets a moody, grenade-carrying electronics expert and takes him home with her.

Off-beat film that examines motherhood and marriage with a beady eye.

wd Hal Hartley *ph* Michael Spiller *m* Phillip Reed *pd* Dan Ouellette *ed* Nick Gomez

☆ Adrienne Shelly, Martin Donovan, Marritt Nelson, John MacKay, Edie Falco, Gary Sauer, Matt Malloy

'An existentialist comedy of manners. It comes from the nowhere that its maker grew up in.' – *Terrence Rafferty, New Yorker*

'Brian's About To Discover The Woman He Loves Isn't The Woman He Loves.'

The Truth about Cats & Dogs **

US 1996 97m DeLuxe

TCF/Noon Attack (Cari-Esta Albert)

▣ ▤ ◎ ∩

A radio vet, who thinks of herself as unattractive, gets her beautiful friend to impersonate her on a date with a handsome photographer and his dog.

Charming comic variation on the theme of Cyrano de Bergerac which is witty about the value of good looks and the dangers of self-hatred while delivering a nicely paced romance.

w Audrey Wells *d* Michael Lehmann *ph* Robert Brinkmann *m* Howard Shore *pd* Sharon Seymour *ed* Stephen Semel

☆ Uma Thurman, Janeane Garofalo, Ben Chaplin, Jamie Foxx, James McCaffrey, Richard Coca, Stanley DeSantis

'Cleverly hints at the penalties which women have to pay for achieving feminist success without conforming to a feminine ideal.' – *Alexander Walker*

The Truth about Spring *

GB 1964 102m Technicolor

U-I/Quota Rentals (Alan Brown)

The bored nephew of a millionaire cruising in the Caribbean jumps at the chance to join friends on a scruffy yacht, but they all get involved with pirates.

Pleasing family film with good scenery and a friendly cast.

w James Lee Barrett *novel* H. de Vere Stacpoole *d* Richard Thorpe *ph* Ted Scaife *m* Robert Farnon

☆ Hayley Mills, James MacArthur, David Tomlinson, Lionel Jeffries, John Mills, Harry Andrews, Niall MacGinnis

The Truth about Women

GB 1957 107m Eastmancolor

British Lion/Beaconsfield (Sydney Box)

▤

An old roué recounts to his son-in-law his early amorous adventures.

Tedious charade with neither wit nor grace.

w Muriel and Sydney Box *d* Muriel Box *ph* Otto Heller *m* Bruce Montgomery

☆ Laurence Harvey, Julie Harris, Diane Cilento, Mai Zetterling, Eva Gabor, Michael Denison, Derek Farr, Roland Culver, Wilfrid Hyde-White, Christopher Lee, Marius Goring, Thorley Walters, Ernest Thesiger, Griffith Jones

'It's amazing that with all those talented people nothing happens on the screen.' – *Pauline Kael, 70s*

Truth or Dare *

US 1991 119m colour/bw

Rank/Propaganda/Boy Toy (Tim Clawson, Jay Roewe)

▣ ▤

GB title: *In Bed with Madonna*

Documentary of Madonna's international concert tour of 1990.

Fascinating, if manipulative, look at a current phenomenon, made under the control of Madonna and carefully projecting an image of wild sexuality.

d Alek Keshishian *ph* Robert Leacock *md* Jai Winding *ad* Christopher Ciccone *ed* Barry Alexander Brown, Anne B. Erikson, John Murray

'An ace manipulator's self-portrait, unmediated by interviewers or pundits. Raw, raunchy and epically entertaining, this is pure, unadulterated Madonna.' – *Richard Corliss, Time*

Try and Find It: see *Hi Diddle Diddle*

Try and Get Me *

US 1951 92m bw

(UA)

▤

GB title: *The Sound of Fury*

Two men are arrested for kidnapping and murder, and a journalist stirs the small town to lynch fury.

Harrowing, relentless melodrama, possibly the best on this subject.

w Joe Pagano *novel* *The Condemned* by Joe Pagano *d* Cyril Endfield *ph* Guy Roe *m* Hugo Friedhofer

☆ Frank Lovejoy, Lloyd Bridges, Kathleen Ryan, Richard Carlson, Katherine Locke, Adele Jergens, Art Smith

'The characterization and the handling of the drama are remarkable, at times reaching a complexity rare in films of this type.' – *Gavin Lambert*

'A strange, uncomfortable, sometimes brutal and depressing picture.' – *Richard Mallett, Punch*

The Trygon Factor *

GB 1966 88m Technicolor

Rank/Rialto Film/Preben Phillipsen (Ian Warren)

Bogus nuns plan a million pound bank raid.

When you get used to its mixture of styles, this Anglo-German production is pretty good imitation Edgar Wallace, with bags of mystery and melodramatic goings-on involving larger than life characters most of whom come to sticky ends.

w Derry Quinn, Stanley Munro, Kingsley Amis *d* Cyril Frankel *ph* Harry Waxman *m* Peter Thomas

☆ Stewart Granger, Susan Hampshire, Cathleen Nesbitt, Robert Morley, James Culliford, Brigitte Horney, Sophie Hardy, James Robertson Justice

Tsareubiitsa: see *Assassin of the Tsar*

Tsubaki Sanjuro: see *Sanjuro*

Tsvet Granata: see *The Colour of Pomegranates*

Tucker: The Man and His Dream **

US 1988 115m colour

UIP/Lucasfilm (Fred Roos, Fred Fuchs)

▣ ▤ ◎

A designer is put out of business after he creates a revolutionary new car.

Slick, engaging, well-crafted story, based on fact.

w Arnold Schulman, David Seidler *d* Francis Ford Coppola *ph* Vittorio Storaro *m* Joe Jackson *pd* Dean Tavoularis *ad* Armin Ganz *ed* Priscilla Nedd

☆ Jeff Bridges, Joan Allen, Martin Landau, Frederic Forrest, Mako, Elias Koteas, Christian Slater, Lloyd Bridges, Dean Stockwell

♟ Martin Landau; Dean Tavoularis, Armin Ganz; best costume design

🏆 Dean Tavoularis

Tudor Rose *

GB 1936 78m bw

GFD/Gainsborough (Michael Balcon)

US title: *Nine Days a Queen*

The brief life and reign of Lady Jane Grey.

Modestly well made historical textbook.

w Robert Stevenson, Miles Malleson *d* Robert Stevenson *ph* Max Greene *m* Louis Levy

☆ Cedric Hardwicke, Nova Pilbeam, John Mills, Felix Aylmer, Leslie Perrins, Frank Cellier,

Desmond Tester, Gwen Ffrangcon Davies, Sybil Thorndike, Martita Hunt, Miles Malleson, John Laurie

'There is not a character, not an incident in which history has not been altered for the cheapest of reasons.' – *Graham Greene*

Tuff Turf

US 1985 112m CFI color

Blue Dolphin/New World (Donald P. Borchers)

▤

A street rebel and his moll have trouble understanding themselves and their world.

Audiences had trouble getting interested.

w Jette Rinck *story* Greg Collins O'Neill, Murray Michaels *d* Fritz Kiersch *ph* Willy Kurant *m* Jonathan Elias *ad* Craig Stearns *ed* Marc Grossman

☆ James Spader, Kim Richards, Paul Mones, Robert Downey, Matt Clark

Tugboat Annie **

US 1933 88m bw

MGM (Harry Rapf)

An elderly waterfront lady and her boozy friend smooth out the path of young love.

Hilarious and well-loved comedy vehicle for two great stars of the period.

w Zelda Sears, Eve Greene *stories* Norman Reilly Raine *d* Mervyn Le Roy *ph* Gregg Toland

☆ Marie Dressler, Wallace Beery, Robert Young, Maureen O'Sullivan, Willard Robertson, Paul Hurst

'One of those rare naturals in the picture business – a flicker that sells itself immediately the stars' names go into the lights.' – *Variety*

'A bare outline of the story cannot convey the note of mother love that runs through it, the laughs, the pathos.' – *Picturegoer*

Tugboat Annie Sails Again

US 1940 75m bw

Warner (Edmund Grainger)

The river lady defeats all comers in her efforts to whip up trade.

Badly developed sequel which isn't badly acted but gets nowhere.

w Walter DeLeon *d* Lewis Seiler

☆ Marjorie Rambeau, Alan Hale, Jane Wyman, Ronald Reagan, Clarence Kolb, Charles Halton, Victor Kilian

Tulitikkutehtaan Tytto: see *The Match Factory Girl*

'Meet Cherokee Lansing ... half wildcat ... half angel ... all woman!'

Tulsa *

US 1949 88m Technicolor

Eagle-Lion (Walter Wanger)

▤

The daughter of a cattle owner builds an oil empire.

Splendid Hollywood hokum of the second grade, very predictable but well-oiled.

w Frank Nugent, Curtis Kenyon *d* Stuart Heisler *ph* Winton Hoch *m* Frank Skinner

☆ Susan Hayward, Robert Preston, Pedro Armendariz, Lloyd Gough, Chill Wills, Ed Begley

'Like a damp fuse, it produces a loud bang at the end of a long splutter.' – *Time*

Tumbleweed

US 1953 79m Technicolor

Universal (Ross Hunter)

A cowboy is accused of helping Indians raid the wagon-train he was guarding.

Unpretentious, action-packed minor Western; the horse who plays the title-role takes the acting honours.

d Nathan Juran *ph* Russell Metty *m* Henry Mancini

☆ Audie Murphy, Lori Nelson, Chill Wills, K. T. Stevens, Russell Johnson, Madge Meredith, Roy Roberts, Lee Van Cleef

Tumbleweeds *

US 1925 80m bw silent

United Artists/William S. Hart

▤ ◎

A wandering cowboy helps a family of settlers.

The same plot as Shane works wonders in the last film of William S. Hart, which has the apparently authentic flavour of the old west.

w C. Gardner Sullivan *story* Hal G. Evarts *d* King Baggott *ph* Joseph August

☆ William S. Hart, Barbara Bedford, Lucien Littlefield, Monte Collins

† Reissued in 1939 with an added eight-minute introduction by Hart, showing how the west has changed.

'They ran away from everything...but each other'

Tumbleweeds *

US 1999 103m Foto-Kem

Entertainmeny/ALH/Spanky/Solaris/River One (Greg O'Connor)

▣

A 12-year-old girl rebels against her mother's footloose approach to life.

Slight, well-acted domestic drama of role-reversal, with a feckless adult learning lessons in life from a maturer child.

w Gavin O'Connor, Angela Shelton *d* Gavin O'Connor *ph* Dan Stoloff *m* David Mansfield *pd* Bruce Eric Holtshousen *ed* John Gilroy

☆ Janet McTeer, Kimberly J. Brown, Gavin O'Connor, Jay O'Sanders, Lois Smith, Lolloman, Michael J. Pollard, Noah Emmerich, Ashley Buccille, Cody McMains

'As cute and charming as a mum-and-daughter buddy-picture can be.' – *Cosmo Landesman, Sunday Times*

† A similar movie of a mother-daughter conflict, released around the same time, was *Anywhere But Here* (qv).

♟ Janet McTeer

The Tune **

US 1992 72m colour

▣ ▤ ◎ ∩

A songwriter has problems writing a new song against the clock.

Clever, episodic animated feature, where the wit lies in the surreal visual imagination of its creator, reaching its height in a duel where two men commit ever more bizarre acts of violence upon one another; the musical pastiches also contribute.

wd Bill Plympton *m* Maureen McElheron *ed* Merril Stern

☆ Featuring the voices of: Daniel Neiden, Maureen McElheron, Marty Nelson, Emily Bindinger, Chris Hoffman

'They're having a secret love affair. Only fifty thousand listeners know about it.'

Tune In Tomorrow *

US 1990 104m colour

Hobo/Polar/Odyssey/Cinecom (John Fielder, Mark Tarlov)

▣ ▤ ◎ ∩

GB title: *Aunt Julia and The Scriptwriter*

A writer of a daily radio serial manipulates an affair between a young journalist and his older aunt to provide material for his scripts.

A comedy at the expense of soap operas and the original novel.

w William Boyd *novel* *Aunt Julia and The Scriptwriter* by Mario Vargas Llosa *d* Jon Amiel *ph* Robert Stevens *m* Wynton Marsalis *pd* Jim Clay, James L. Schoppe *ed* Peter Boyle

☆ Barbara Hershey, Keanu Reeves, Peter Falk, Bill McCutcheon, Patricia Clarkson, Richard Portnow, Jerome Dempsey

'A sharp-fanged novel has been turned into an ingratiating puppy walking on its hind legs.' – *Philip French, Observer*

Tunes of Glory ***

GB 1960 107m Technicolor

UA/Knightsbridge (Albert Fennell)

▤

The new disciplinarian CO of a highland regiment crosses swords with his lax, hard drinking predecessor.

Wintry barracks melodrama, finely acted and well made with memorable confrontation scenes compensating for a somewhat underdeveloped script.

w James Kennaway *novel* James Kennaway *d* Ronald Neame *ph* Arthur Ibbetson

☆ Alec Guinness, John Mills, Susannah York, Dennis Price, Kay Walsh, Duncan Macrae, Gordon Jackson, John Fraser, Allan Cuthbertson

'The picture is persuasive. But I daresay one does it wrong by looking too hard for social reflections. Lucky enough to find a film which has life in it.' – *Dilys Powell*

♟ James Kennaway

Tung-Tung-te chia-ch'i: see *A Summer at Grandpa's*

The Tunnel *
GB　1935　94m　bw
Gaumont (Michael Balcon)
▦

US title: *Transatlantic Tunnel*
Crooked finances mar the completion of an
undersea tunnel to America.
*A rare example of British science fiction from this
period, though the film was in fact first made in
German and French versions, the latter with Jean
Gabin.*
w　Curt Siodmak, L. DuGarde Peach, Clemence
Dane *novel* Bernard Kellerman　d　Maurice Elvey
ph　Gunther Krampf　m　Louis Levy
☆　Richard Dix, Leslie Banks, Madge Evans, Helen
Vinson, C. Aubrey Smith, George Arliss, Walter
Huston, Basil Sydney, Jimmy Hanley
　'I was quite unable to sit this film through,
　though by leaving I missed the "courtesy
　appearance" of Mr George Arliss as the Prime
　Minister of Great Britain, an actor from whose
　Athenaeum manner I sometimes derive a rather
　humble pleasure.' – *Graham Greene*

Tunnel 28: see *Escape from East Berlin*

The Tunnel of Love
US　1958　98m　bw　Cinemascope
MGM/Joseph Fields
▦

A husband applying to adopt an orphan thinks he
may, while drunk, have seduced the glamorous
orphan agency official.
*Tasteless and not very funny comedy, somewhat
miscast.*
w　Joseph Fields *play* Joseph Fields, Peter de Vries
novel Peter de Vries　d　Gene Kelly　ph　Robert
Bronner
☆　Richard Widmark, Doris Day, Gig Young, Gia
Scala, Elisabeth Fraser, Elizabeth Wilson

Tunnel Vision
Australia　1994　92m　colour
Beyond/Pro (Phillip Avalon)

A maverick detective is having a hard time: his
marriage is in trouble, his boss hates him, his
female partner is behaving oddly, his investigation
of a serial killer is going badly, and he is suspected
of having killed his wife's business associate.
*Risible thriller that gets sillier, and less interesting, by
the minute.*
wd　Clive Fleury　ph　Paul Murphy　m　David
Hirschfelder, Ric Formosa　pd　Phil Warner
ed　John Scott
☆　Patsy Kensit, Robert Reynolds, Rebecca Rigg,
Gary Day, Shane Briant

'Fear is in the air'
Turbulence
US　1997　100m　colour　Panavision
Entertainment/Rysher (Martin Ransohoff, David
Valdes)
▦　▤　◎　◉

A psychopathic killer, who is being flown from
New York to Los Angeles, takes over a 747 just as
the plane is heading into a major storm.
*Ridiculous thriller that adds violence and special-effects
mayhem to the plot of Airport 1975; it may put you
off going to the cinema again.*
w　Jonathan Brett　d　Robert Butler　ph　Lloyd
Ahern II　m　Shirley Walker　pd　Mayling Cheng
ed　John Duffy
☆　Ray Liotta, Lauren Holly, Brendan Gleeson,
Hector Elizondo, Ben Cross, Rachel Ticotin, Jeffrey
DeMunn, John Finn, Catherine Hicks
　'There's the usual pert air hostess being
　frightfully brave. This should be straight-to-
　video stuff.' – *Derek Malcolm, Guardian*

Turk 182 *
US　1985　98m　TVC Color
TCF (Ted Field, Rene DuPont)
▦

A mystery do-gooder embarrasses the city
bureaucracy into doing right by citizens with a
grievance.
Interesting urban drama with a non-violent vigilante.
w　James Gregory Kingston, Denis and John
Hamill　d　Bob Clark　ph　Reginald H. Morris
m　Paul Zaza　pd　Harry Pottle　ed　Stan Cole

☆　Timothy Hutton, Robert Urich, Kim Cattrall,
Robert Culp, Darren McGavin, Steven Keats,
Peter Boyle, Paul Sorvino

Turkey Time
GB　1933　73m　bw
Gaumont
Family indiscretions come out at Christmas time.
*Vehicle for fruity characterizations by the popular
Aldwych team, but not very strong as a farce.*
w　Ben Travers *play* Ben Travers　d　Tom Walls
ph　Charles Van Enger
☆　Tom Walls, Ralph Lynn, Robertson Hare,
Dorothy Hyson, Mary Brough, Norma Varden

The Turkish Bath: see *Hamam*

Turkish Delight *
Netherlands　1973　106m　colour
Columbia-Warner/Rob Houwer (Mia van't Hof)
▦　▤

original title: *Turks Fruit*
A promiscuous young sculptor marries unhappily
but falls in love with his wife again during her
terminal illness.
*Scabrous satire on Dutch middle-class attitudes
combined with shock tactics and as much sex as the
director could get past the censor; undeniably displaying
talent of a not very likeable kind, it was a box-office
success in Holland.*
w　Gerard Soeteman *novel* Jan Wolkers　d　Paul
Verhoeven　ph　Jan de Bont　m　Rogier van
Otterloo　ad　Ralf van der Elst　ed　Jan Bosdriess
☆　Monique van de Ven, Rutger Hauer, Tonny
Huurdeman, Wim van den Brink, Dolf de Vries
　'Repulsive and meaningless' – *Clyde Jeavons,
　MFB*
　'Underscored by a romanticism which slowly
　accumulates as time goes by. The difficulties of
　combining scatology and tenderness are neatly
　handled.' – *Derek Elley, Films and Filming*

Turks Fruit: see *Turkish Delight*

Turksib *
USSR　1929　60m　bw　silent
Vostok Kino
The making of the Turkestan–Siberia railway.
*A highly fluent and pictorial documentary with an
especially famous climax as the men struggle to lay the
last rails and meet a deadline.*
w　Victor Turin and others　d　Victor Turin
ph　Yevgeni Slavinsky, Boris Frantzisson

Turn Back the Clock *
US　1933　80m　bw
MGM
A man dreams of changing places with his rich
friend.
Unusual, quite pleasing comedy-drama.
w　Edgar Selwyn, Ben Hecht　d　Edgar Selwyn
☆　Lee Tracy, Otto Kruger, Mae Clarke, C. Henry
Gordon, George Barbier
　'Neatly turned domestic comedy with a dramatic
　touch that will please all round.' – *Variety*

The Turn of the Screw
GB/France　1992　95m　colour/bw
Electric Pictures/Michael White/Lakedell/Cinemax
(Staffan Ahrenberg, Nicole Seguin)
▦

A woman in group therapy tells what happened to
her and her brother when, as small children, their
new governess was haunted by the evil ghosts of a
predecessor and her lover.
*Updated for no apparent reason to the 60s, this is a
heavy-handed version, treated as a melodramatic
horror story, and so overburdened with the trappings of
the genre – spooky house, spookier music, sudden
shocks, grinning masks, mechanical toys and disturbing
dolls – that it stifles the subtlety of the original. Despite
his star billing, Sands appears only for a few languid
minutes.*
wd　Rusty Lemorande *story* Henry James
ph　Witold Stok　m　Simon Boswell　pd　Max
Gottlieb　ed　John Victor Smith
☆　Patsy Kensit, Stephane Audran, Julian Sands,
Marianne Faithfull, Olivier Debray, Bryony Brand,
Joseph England, Claire Szekeres
　'This is one screw that needed no further
　turning, especially when it's done in such a
　clumsy, pedestrian manner.' – *Variety*

Turn of the Tide *
GB　1935　80m　bw
British National (John Corfield)
▦

A feud between two fishing families ends in
marriage.
*Low-key, location-set action drama with a moral. The
film which brought J. Arthur Rank into the business,
which he saw had religious possibilities.*
w　L. DuGarde Peach, J. O. C. Orton *novel* Three
Fevers by Leo Walmsley　d　Norman Walker
ph　Franz Planer　m　Arthur Benjamin
☆　Geraldine Fitzgerald, John Garrick, Niall
MacGinnis, J. Fisher White, Joan Maude, Sam
Livesey, Wilfrid Lawson, Moore Marriott
　'Cut to an hour, it should make an acceptable
　second feature.' – *Variety*
　'An unpretentious and truthful film.' – *Graham
　Greene*
†　The film has been released on video together
with *The Man at the Gate*.

Turn Off the Moon
US　1937　79m　bw
Paramount/Fanchon
The proprietor of a department store is persuaded
by an astrologer to stage a big show in celebration
of his 25th anniversary.
*Thinly structured musical with some acceptable gags
and turns.*
w　Marguerite Roberts, Harlan Ware, Paul Gerard
Smith, Mildred Harrington　d　Lewis Seiler
☆　Charles Ruggles, Eleanore Whitney, Johnny
Downs, Kenny Baker, Phil Harris and his
Orchestra, Ben Blue, Andrew Tombes, Marjorie
Gateson, Grady Sutton, Franklin Pangborn
　'B from title to climax.' – *Variety*

Turn the Key Softly
GB　1953　81m　bw
GFD/Chiltern (Maurice Cowan)
The problems of three women released from prison.
*Soppy formula multi-drama with contrived and
uninteresting plots and characters.*
w　Jack Lee, Maurice Cowan *novel* John Brophy
d　Jack Lee　ph　Geoffrey Unsworth　m　Mischa
Spoliansky
☆　Yvonne Mitchell, Terence Morgan, Joan
Collins, Kathleen Harrison, Thora Hird, Dorothy
Alison, Glyn Houston, Geoffrey Keen, Clive
Morton

'Pardon my error, the stork meekly smiled, I've
overlooked wifey, gave hubby the child!'
Turnabout *
US　1940　83m　bw
Hal Roach
A benevolent god enables a quarrelsome couple to
change bodies and see how they like it.
*'The man's had a baby instead of the lady', said the
ads. Well, not quite, but it did seem pretty daring at the
time, and it still provides a hilarious moment or two.*
w　Mickell Novak, Berne Giler, John McLain
novel Thorne Smith　d　Hal Roach　ph　Norbert
Brodine　m　Arthur Morton
☆　Adolphe Menjou, John Hubbard, Carole
Landis, Mary Astor, Verree Teasdale, Donald
Meek, William Gargan, Joyce Compton

Turned Out Nice Again
GB　1941　81m　bw
ATP
An employee teaches an underwear firm to move
with the times.
Tolerable star comedy from his late period.
w　Austin Melford, John Dighton, Basil Dearden
play As You Are by Hugh Mills, Wells Root
d　Marcel Varnel
☆　George Formby, Peggy Bryan, Edward
Chapman, Elliot Mason, Mackenzie Ward, O. B.
Clarence

Turner & Hooch
††　US　1989　99m　Metrocolor
Warner/Touchstone/Silver Screen Partners IV
(Raymond Wagner)
▦　▤　◎

In order to solve a murder, a cop teams up with the
only witness, a large dog.
*The cycle of police buddy-buddy movies reaches its
nadir in this strenuously unfunny release.*
w　Dennis Shryack, Michael Blodgett, Daniel
Petrie Jnr, Jim Cash, Jack Epps Jnr　d　Roger
Spottiswoode　ph　Adam Greenberg　m　Charles

Gross　pd　John DeCuir Jnr　ed　Paul Seydor, Mark
Conte, Kenneth Morrisey, Lois Freeman-Fox
☆　Tom Hanks, Mare Winningham, Craig T.
Nelson, Reginald VelJohnson, Scott Paulin, J. C.
Quinn, John McIntire

The Turners of Prospect Road
GB　1947　88m　bw
Grand National
A taxi driver's family greyhound wins a big race.
Uneasily cast domestic comedy drama.
w　Victor Katona, Patrick Kirwan　d　Maurice J.
Wilson
☆　Wilfrid Lawson, Jeanne de Casalis, Maureen
Glynne, Helena Pickard, Leslie Perrins, Peter
Bull

The Turning
US　1992　87m　Technicolor
White Deer/L. A. Puopolo
▦　▤

Returning home after four years away, a 22-year-old
fascist discovers that his parents are divorcing and
decides that they should stay together.
*Overwrought melodrama that attempts to deal with the
rise of right-wing fundamentalism within the context of
a family breaking apart; it fails to convince as a study
either of politics or of a dysfunctional family.*
w　L. A. Puopolo, Chris Cesaro *play* Home Fires
Burning by Chris Cesaro　d　L. A. Puopolo　ph　J.
Michael McClary　m　Herb Pilhofer　pd　Mike
Moran　ed　Lesley Topping
☆　Karen Allen, Raymond J. Barry, Michael
Dolan, Tess Harper, Gillian Anderson
　'Though it packs an undeniable emotional
　punch, pic comes across as overwritten and
　contrived as a cinema experience.' – *David
　Stratton, Variety*
†　Under the title *Home Fires Burning*, it was shown
at the 1992 Cannes Film Festival in a version
running for 103m.

The Turning Point *
US　1952　85m　bw
Paramount (Irving Asher)
original title: *This is Dynamite!*
A young lawyer is appointed by the state governor
to smash a crime syndicate.
Familiar exposé drama of its time, quite crisply done.
w　Warren Duff　d　William Dieterle　ph　Lionel
Lindon　md　Irwin Talbot
☆　William Holden, Alexis Smith, Edmond
O'Brien, Tom Tully, Ray Teal

'A story of envy, hatred, friendship, triumph and
love!'
The Turning Point *
US　1977　119m　DeLuxe
TCF/Hera (Nora Kaye)
▤

The American Ballet Theatre visits Oklahoma
City, and its ageing star revisits an ex-colleague,
now a housewife.
*Posh person's soap opera, rather boringly made and
interesting only for its performances, which are
certainly vivid.*
w　Arthur Laurents　d　Herbert Ross　ph　Robert
Surtees　m　John Lanchbery　pd　Albert Brenner
ed　William Reynolds
☆　Anne Bancroft, Shirley MacLaine, Mikhail
Baryshnikov, Leslie Browne, Tom Skerritt, Martha
Scott, Marshall Thompson
　'A backstage musical dressed up with smart
　cultural trimmings.' – *Alan Brien*
　'We get a glimpse of something great in the
　movie – Mikhail Baryshnikov dancing – and
　these two harpies out of the soaps block the
　view.' – *New Yorker, 1978*
♀　best picture; Herbert Ross; Robert Surtees;
Anne Bancroft; Shirley MacLaine; Mikhail
Baryshnikov; Leslie Browne; Arthur Laurents; art
direction; editing

Turtle Beach
Australia　1992　88m　colour
Warner/Roadshow/Coote & Carroll
▦　◎

A reporter leaves her husband and children to go
to Malaysia to cover the story of the problems of
Vietnamese boat people and witnesses a massacre.
*An apparent attempt to expose racism and corruption
in Malaysia and Australia, but too muddled to make
much sense.*
w　Ann Turner *novel* Blanche d'Alpuget
d　Stephen Wallace　ph　Russell Boyd　m　Chris

Neal *pd* Brian Thomson *ed* Lee Smith, Louise Innes

☆ Greta Scacchi, Joan Chen, Jack Thompson, Art Malik, Norman Kaye, Victoria Longley, Martin Jacobs, William McInnes, George Whaley

'Rarely has such an interesting story resulted in such drab fare.' – *Variety*

Turtle Diary *
GB 1985 97m Technicolor
CBS/United British Artists/Britannic (Richard Johnson)
🎬 ⊙

Two self-admitted eccentrics take it upon themselves to release turtles from captivity in the London Zoo.
Mainly ineffective character comedy, memorable only for fragments of dialogue and acting.
w Harold Pinter *novel* Russell Hoban *d* John Irvin *ph* Peter Hannan *m* Geoffrey Burgon *pd* Leo Austin *ed* Peter Tanner
☆ Glenda Jackson, Ben Kingsley, Richard Johnson, Michael Gambon, Rosemary Leach, Eleanor Bron, Harriet Walter, Nigel Hawthorne, Michael Aldridge

The Tuttles of Tahiti
US 1942 91m bw
RKO (Sol Lesser)
🎬 ⊙

The Tuttles have one ambition: to do no work.
A negative prospect even for a light comedy, and this one rapidly sinks under a welter of flat dialogue.
w S. Lewis Meltzer, Robert Carson, James Hilton *novel* No More Gas by Charles Nordhoff, James Norman Hall *d* Charles Vidor *ph* Nicholas Musuraca *m* Roy Webb
☆ Charles Laughton, Jon Hall, Victor Francen, Peggy Drake, Florence Bates

Tv Killar Och en Tjej: see *Happy We*

Twelfth Night *
US 1996 133m Technicolor
Entertainment/Fine Line/Twelfth Night/Renaissance (Stephen Evans, David Parfitt)
🎬 ⊙ ⊙

In Illyria, shipwrecked twins become involved in the romantic misunderstandings of a duke and the woman he thinks he loves.
An updated version of Shakespeare's comedy of sexual confusions, set in some unspecified, presumably Edwardian period, in which the farcical elements fare badly and the play's melancholy undercurrent is stressed; it never comes fully to life.
wd Trevor Nunn *play* William Shakespeare *ph* Clive Tickner *m* Shaun Davey *pd* Sophie Becher *ed* Peter Boyle
☆ Helena Bonham Carter, Richard E. Grant, Nigel Hawthorne, Ben Kingsley, Mel Smith, Imelda Staunton, Toby Stephens, Imogen Stubbs, Steven MacKintosh, Nicholas Farrell, Sid Livingstone

'Works best not as a commentary on gender confusion but simply as an old-fashioned actors' showcase. There isn't a weak performance in the ensemble.' – *Stephen Farber, Movieline*
† The American trailer for the film emphasized its cross-dressing aspects, featuring Imogen Stubbs in male attire, accompanied by the song 'Macho Man'. The voice-over began: 'In the tradition of *Some Like It Hot*, *Tootsie* and *The Adventures of Priscilla, Queen of the Desert* comes the classic romantic comedy that proves sometimes clothes really do make the man…'

Twelve Angry Men ****
US 1957 95m bw
(UA) Orion-Nova (Henry Fonda, Reginald Rose)
🎬 ⊙

A murder case jury about to vote guilty is convinced otherwise by one doubting member.
Though unconvincing in detail, this is a brilliantly tight character melodrama which is never less than absorbing to experience. Acting and direction are superlatively right, and the film was important in helping to establish television talents in Hollywood.
w Reginald Rose *play* Reginald Rose *d* Sidney Lumet *ph* Boris Kaufman *m* Kenyon Hopkins
☆ Henry Fonda, Lee J. Cobb, E. G. Marshall, Jack Warden, Ed Begley, Martin Balsam, John Fiedler, Jack Klugman, George Voskovec, Robert Webber, Edward Binns, Joseph Sweeney

'Holds the attention unquestioning. It is one of the most exciting films for months.' – *Dilys Powell*

'Generates more suspense than most thrillers.' – *New Yorker*
⚭ best picture; Reginald Rose; Sidney Lumet
🏆 Henry Fonda

The Twelve Chairs: see *Twelve Plus One*

The Twelve Chairs
US 1970 93m Movielab
UMC/Crossbow (Michael Hertzberg)
🎬 ⊙ ⊙

A Russian bureaucrat chases twelve dining chairs, in one of which is hidden the family jewels.
Tedious Mel Brooks romp with not too many laughs, from a yarn better handled in Keep Your Seats Please and It's in the Bag, from both of which he might have learned something about comedy timing.
w Mel Brooks *novel* Ilya Ilf, Evgeny Petrov *d* Mel Brooks *ph* Dorde Nikolic *m* John Morris
☆ Ron Moody, Frank Langella, Dom DeLuise, Bridget Brice, Diana Coupland, Mel Brooks

'In the end it runs out of both steam and jokes.' – *Michael Billington, Illustrated London News*

Twelve Good Men
GB 1936 64m bw
Warner

A convict escapes to murder the jury who convicted him.
Solidly carpentered suspenser.
w Sidney Gilliat, Frank Launder *novel* Murders in Praed Street by John Rhode *d* Ralph Ince *ph* Basil Emmott
☆ Henry Kendall, Nancy O'Neil, Percy Parsons, Morland Graham, Bernard Miles

'The Future Is History.'
Twelve Monkeys
US 1995 129m colour
Polygram/Universal/Atlas/Classico (Charles Roven)
🎬 ⊙ ⊙ ⊙

In 2035, when the few remaining people live underground to escape the effects of a deadly virus, a convict is sent back to 1996 to discover more about the disease – or perhaps a psychotic is having a bad dream.
A bleak and confused conundrum, which often seems designed for no other purpose than to allow Willis to suffer stoically; despite its visual exuberance, the effect is deadening.
w David Peoples, Janet Peoples *inspired by* La Jetée by Chris Marker *d* Terry Gilliam *ph* Roger Pratt *m* Paul Buckmaster *pd* Jeffrey Beecroft *ed* Mick Audsley
☆ Bruce Willis, Brad Pitt, Madeleine Stowe, Christopher Plummer, Joseph Melito, Jon Seda, Michael Chance, Vernon Campbell

'It's confused, overwrought, illogical and derivative. Far too much is going on inside Gilliam's head, little of it original.' – *Alexander Walker*
'A spectacular mess … long on sensibility, short on sense.' – *Variety*
† The film took more than $60m at the US box-office and more than $120m worldwide.
⚭ Brad Pitt; costume design (Julie Weiss)

'A story of twelve men as their women never knew them!'
Twelve O'Clock High **
US 1949 132m bw
TCF (Darryl F. Zanuck)
🎬 ⊙ ⊙

During World War II, the commander of a US bomber unit in Britain begins to crack under the strain.
Absorbing character drama, justifiably a big box-office success of its day, later revived as a TV series. All production values are excellent.
w Sy Bartlett, Beirne Lay Jnr *d* Henry King *ph* Leon Shamroy *m* Alfred Newman
☆ Gregory Peck, Hugh Marlowe, Gary Merrill, Millard Mitchell, Dean Jagger, Robert Arthur, Paul Stewart, John Kellogg

'The best war film since the fighting stopped.' – *Daily Mirror*
'Integrity all the way down the line.' – *New York Times*
🏆 Dean Jagger
⚭ best picture; Gregory Peck

Twelve Plus One
Italy/France 1969 108m Technicolor
CEF/COFCI (Claude Giroux, Edward J. Pope)
original title: Una su 13
aka: The Twelve Chairs
After he sells some chairs inherited from his aunt, a barber discovers that one of them contains a fortune and sets out to retrieve it.
Broad farce that wastes the talents of its cast, though it contains a bizarrely enjoyable moment by Welles as a barnstorming actor giving a ham performance of Dr Jekyll and Mr Hyde.
w Marc Behm, Dennis Norden, Nicolas Gessner *novel* Twelve Chairs by Ilf and Petrov *d* Nicolas Gessner *ph* Giuseppe Ruzzolini *m* Stelvio Cipriani *ed* Giancarlo Cappelli
☆ Sharon Tate, Vittorio Gassman, Orson Welles, Vittorio de Sica, Terry-Thomas, Mylene Demongeot, Grégoire Aslan, Tim Brooke-Taylor, Lionel Jeffries

Twentieth Century **
US 1934 91m bw
Columbia (Howard Hawks)
🎬 🎬

A temperamental Broadway producer trains an untutored actress, but when a star she proves a match for him.
Though slightly lacking in pace, this is a marvellously sharp and memorable theatrical burlesque, and the second half, set on the train of the title, reaches highly agreeable peaks of insanity.
w Ben Hecht, Charles MacArthur *play* Napoleon of Broadway by Charles Bruce Millholland *d* Howard Hawks *ph* Joseph August
☆ John Barrymore, Carole Lombard, Roscoe Karns, Walter Connolly, Ralph Forbes, Etienne Girardot, Charles Lane, Edgar Kennedy

'Probably too smart for general consumption … a long shot for grosses outside the large cities that boast a cosmopolitan clientele.' – *Variety*
'Notable as the first comedy in which sexually attractive, sophisticated stars indulged in their own slapstick instead of delegating it to their inferiors.' – *Andrew Sarris, 1963*
'In the role of Jaffe John Barrymore fits as wholly and smoothly as a banana in a skin.' – *Otis Ferguson*

'When you pass the buck, the last thing you expect is change.'
Twenty Bucks *
US 1993 91m DeLuxe
Triton/Big Tomorrow (Karen Murphy)
🎬 🎬

The lives of various people are touched by a 20-dollar bill as it passes from one to another.
An old-fashioned notion for a movie which adds up to little more than a succession of slight and not very rewarding anecdotes, though Lloyd provides some interest as a robber who believes in order and discipline.
w Leslie and Endre Bohem *d* Keva Rosenfeld *ph* Emmanuel Lubezki *m* David Robbins *pd* Joseph T. Garrity *ed* Michael Ruscio
☆ Linda Hunt, Christopher Lloyd, Brendan Fraser, Elisabeth Shue, Steve Buscemi, Spalding Gray, Matt Frewer, Gladys Knight

'Delightful if patchy comedy.' – *Film Review*
† Endre Bohem, a Hungarian-born producer and writer, wrote the unproduced script in 1935; it was revised and updated by his son Leslie.

24 Hours
US 1931 65m bw
Paramount
A day in the life of an ultra-rich couple whose marriage has gone sour.
Fairly slick matrimonial drama with an attempt at filmic treatment.
w Louis Weitzenkorn *novel* Louis Bromfield *d* Marion Gering
☆ Clive Brook, Kay Francis, Miriam Hopkins, Regis Toomey, George Barbier, Adrienne Ames

'An absorbing bit of fiction that should engage the attention of the fan regulars and register abundantly at the box office.' – *Variety*

20 Million Miles to Earth
US 1957 82m bw
Columbia/Morningside (Charles Schneer)
🎬 🎬 ⊙

An American rocket ship returning from Venus breaks open and a scaly monster escapes into the Mediterranean and is cornered in the Roman coliseum.

Cheeseparing monster fiction which doesn't wake up till the last five minutes, and looks pretty silly even then.
w Bob Williams, Chris Knopf *d* Nathan Juran *ph* Irving Lippmann *m* Mischa Bakaleinikoff *sp* Ray Harryhausen
☆ William Hopper, Joan Taylor, Frank Puglia, John Zaremba

Twenty Million Sweethearts
US 1934 89m bw
Warner
Singing radio sweethearts are kept apart because of their images.
Thin musical with moderate numbers, remade as My Dream Is Yours.
w Warren Duff, Harry Sauber *d* Ray Enright *ph* Sid Hickox *songs* Harry Warren, Al Dubin
☆ Dick Powell, Ginger Rogers, Pat O'Brien, the Mills Brothers, Ted Fio Rito and his band, the Radio Rogues, Allen Jenkins, Grant Mitchell

'An entry the theatre boys won't have to worry about.' – *Variety*

Twenty Mule Team *
US 1940 84m bw
MGM (J. Walter Ruben)
Rivalry among the borax miners in Death Valley.
Adequate semi-Western with an unusual theme and setting.
w Robert C. DuSoe, Owen Atkinson *d* Richard Thorpe *ph* Clyde de Vinna *m* David Snell
☆ Wallace Beery, Leo Carrillo, Marjorie Rambeau, Anne Baxter, Douglas Fowley, Berton Churchill, Noah Beery Jnr, Arthur Hohl, Clem Bevans, Charles Halton, Minor Watson

29 Acacia Avenue
GB 1945 83m bw
Boca/Columbia (Sydney Box)
Young people are having a good time when their parents return unexpectedly from holiday.
Popular domestic comedy of its day.
w Muriel and Sydney Box *play* Mabel and Denis Constanduros *d* Henry Cass *ph* Ernest Palmer, Nigel Huke *m* Clifton Parker
☆ Gordon Harker, Betty Balfour, Carla Lehmann, Jimmy Hanley, Jill Evans, Hubert Gregg, Dinah Sheridan, Henry Kendall, Guy Middleton

The Twenty Questions Murder Mystery
GB 1949 95m bw
Pax-Pendennis
A killer taunts the police with clues sent to a radio quiz show.
Somewhat heavy comedy mystery with interest arising from the broadcasting background.
w Patrick Kirwan, Victor Katona *d* Paul Stein *ph* Ernest Palmer *m* Hans May
☆ Robert Beatty, Rona Anderson, Clifford Evans, Edward Lexy, Olga Lindo, Richard Dimbleby, Jack Train, Stewart MacPherson, Daphne Padel, Norman Hackforth, Jeanne de Casalis

Twenty Thousand Leagues under the Sea **
👥 US 1954 122m Technicolor
Cinemascope
Walt Disney
🎬 🎬 ⊙

Victorian scientists at sea are wrecked and captured by the mysterious captain of a futuristic submarine.
Pretty full-blooded adaptation of a famous yarn, with strong performances and convincing art and trick work.
w Earl Felton *novel* Jules Verne *d* Richard Fleischer *ph* Franz Planer, Franz Lehy, Ralph Hammeras, Till Gabbani *m* Paul Smith *ad* John Meehan *ed* Elmo Williams
☆ Kirk Douglas, James Mason, Paul Lukas, Peter Lorre, Robert J. Wilke, Carleton Young, Ted de Corsia
🏆 art direction; special effects
⚭ editing

Twenty Thousand Men a Year
US 1939 83m bw
Cosmopolitan/TCF (Sol M. Wurtzel)
Experiences of recruits to college student aviation training.
Very threadbare flagwaver.
w Lou Breslow, Owen Francis, Frank Wead *d* Alfred E. Green
☆ Randolph Scott, Preston Foster, Margaret Lindsay, Robert Shaw, Mary Healy, Kane Richmond, Maxie Rosenbloom, Sen Yung

---

'Needs exploitation as upper-bracket attraction.'
– *Variety*

Twenty Thousand Years in Sing Sing **
US   1933   77m   bw
Warner (Robert Lord)
A tough criminal escapes from prison but his girl kills a man during the attempt, and he takes the blame.
Dated but fast-moving and still-powerful crime melodrama, remade to less effect as Castle on the Hudson *(qv).*
w Wilson Mizner, Brown Holmes *book* Lewis E. Lawes *d* Michael Curtiz *ph* Barney McGill *m* Bernhard Kaun
☆ Spencer Tracy, Bette Davis, Arthur Byron, Lyle Talbot, Louis Calhern, Warren Hymer, Sheila Terry, Edward McNamara
'Good entertainment and good box office with that inside prison routine touch … Finally, it begins to appear Sing Sing wouldn't be a bad place at all to spend a vacation during the depression.' – *Variety*

23:58
France   1993   85m   colour
BFI/MW/Canal
A cop and film buff hunts two former motorbike racers who steal six million francs, the takings of the 24-hour Le Mans motorcycle race, basing their plan on the one in Stanley Kubrick's film *The Killing.*
An odd little act of homage to Kubrick's thriller, although this one has a happier ending; but its effect is to send you back to watch the original again and note how much more interesting it is.
w Pierre William-Glen, Edith Vergne, Frédéric Leroy *d* Pierre William-Glen *m* Jean-Claude Vicquery *m* Laurent Cugny *pd* Jacques Voizet *ed* Anita Perez
☆ Jean-François Stevenin, Jean-Pierre Malo, Gérald Garnier, Yan Epstein, Amelie Glenn, Kader Boukanef
'A superior thriller in all departments, unravelling into an accomplished feature spiked with wry humour.' – *Empire*

The Twenty-Fifth Hour
France/Italy/Yugoslavia   1967   133m
Eastmancolor   Franscope
Concordia/CCC/Avala/Carlo Ponti
When the Nazis deport Rumanian Jews, a simple-minded farmer is sent with them because the officer desires his wife.
Peripatetic adventure with the storm-tossed hero flitting from one symbolic situation to another. All a bit much.
w Henri Verneuil, Wolf Mankowitz, François Boyer *novel* C. Virgil Gheorghiu *d* Henri Verneuil *ph* Andreas Winding *m* Georges Delerue
☆ Anthony Quinn, Virna Lisi, Grégoire Aslan, Michael Redgrave, Serge Reggiani, Marcel Dalio, Marius Goring, Alexander Knox, Liam Redmond, Meier Tzelniker, John Le Mesurier, Françoise Rosay

Twenty-Four Hours of a Woman's Life
GB   1952   90m   Technicolor
ABPC (Ivan Foxwell)
US title: *Affair in Monte Carlo*
A young widow tries to reform an inveterate gambler, but he kills himself.
Stilted, over-literary romantic melodrama with philosophical dialogue, flashback framing and Riviera settings.
w Warren Chetham Strode *novel* Stefan Zweig *d* Victor Saville *ph* Christopher Challis *m* Robert Gill, Philip Green
☆ Merle Oberon, Leo Genn, Richard Todd, Stephen Murray, Peter Illing, Isabel Dean

TwentyFourSeven **
GB   1997   96m   bw
Pathé/BBC/Scala (Imogen West)
▣ ⌒
aka: *24 07*
A one-time amateur boxer remembers the man who started a boxing club for the local youths, and how the enterprise came unstuck.
A throwback in style to the British working-class films of the 60s, and none the worse for that, though the tone is bleaker, and less defiantly rebellious.
w Shane Meadows, Paul Fraser *d* Shane Meadows *ph* Ashley Rowe *m* Neill MacColl, Boo Hewerdine *pd* John-Paul Kelly *ed* Bill Diver

☆ Bob Hoskins, Mat Hand, Sun Hand, Sarah Thom, Sammy Pasha, Gina Aris, James Corden, Frank Harper, Anthony Clarke
'Best described as Ken Loach with a smile.' – *Film Review*
† The title refers to twenty-four hours a day, seven days a week, or, as one character says, 'the people in this town have been living the same day their whole lives'.

'Old enough to know better, young enough not to care.'
Twenty-One
GB   1991   101m   colour
Entertainment/Anglo International (Morgan Mason, John Hardy)
▣ ▤ ⌒
A 21-year-old English girl living in New York recalls her past lovers.
Tedious semi-comedy, full of unconvincing monologues delivered direct to the camera.
w Zoe Heller, Don Boyd *d* Don Boyd *ph* Keith Goddard *m* Michael Berkeley *ed* David Spiers
☆ Patsy Kensit, Jack Shepherd, Patrick Ryecart, Maynard Eziashi, Rufus Sewell, Sophie Thompson, Susan Wooldridge
'A movie that is vulgarly flawed, often made like it was improvised fast on the spot but still managing to contain not only a holding central performance but a certain honesty you can't ignore.' – *Derek Malcolm, Guardian*

Twenty-One Days *
GB   1937   75m   bw
London Films (Alexander Korda)
aka: *The First and the Last*
A barrister's brother accidentally kills a man and lets an old eccentric take the blame.
Watchable but very stilted melodrama with interesting early performances by Olivier and Leigh and a few good moments.
w Graham Greene *play* The First and the Last *by* John Galsworthy *d* Basil Dean *ph* Jan Stallich *m* John Greenwood
☆ Laurence Olivier, Vivien Leigh, Leslie Banks, Hay Petrie, Francis L. Sullivan, Esmé Percy, Robert Newton, Victor Rietti
'I wish I could tell the extraordinary story that lies behind this shelved and resurrected picture, a story involving a theme song, and a bottle of whisky, and camels in Wales. Meanwhile let one guilty man, at any rate, stand in the dock, swearing never to do it again…' – *Graham Greene*
† The film was not shown until 1940.

'Somewhere in the fog there is a voice, a perfume, a glove, a knife – and a victim!'
Twenty-Three Paces to Baker Street *
US   1956   103m   Eastmancolor
Cinemascope
TCF (Henry Ephron)
▤
A blind playwright in a pub overhears a murder plot and follows the trail to the bitter end despite attacks on his life.
Sufficiently engrossing murder mystery with a weird idea of London's geography: the hero's Portman Square apartment has a balcony overlooking the Thames two miles away. Perhaps this is part of the script's light touch.
w Nigel Balchin *novel* Philip MacDonald *d* Henry Hathaway *ph* Milton Krasner *m* Leigh Harline
☆ Van Johnson, Vera Miles, Cecil Parker, Patricia Laffan, Maurice Denham, *Estelle Winwood*, Liam Redmond

Twice Blessed
US   1945   76m   bw
MGM (Arthur L. Field)
Twin daughters of a divorced couple deliberately confuse their parents into a reconciliation.
Paper-thin comedy without much wit.
w Ethel Hill *d* Harry Beaumont
☆ Preston Foster, Gail Patrick, Lee and Lyn Wilde, Richard Gaines, Jean Porter, Ethel Smith at the organ

Twice in a Lifetime
US   1985   117m   colour
Yorkin Company/Bud Yorkin
▣ ▤ ⌒
A man turns fifty and decides to make a clean break with his family.
Comedy drama of the mid-life crisis: nothing new.
w Colin Welland *play* Kisses at 50 *by* Colin Welland *d* Bud Yorkin *ph* Nick McLean *m* Pat Metheny, Paul McCartney *pd* William Creber *ed* Robert Jones
☆ Gene Hackman, Ellen Burstyn, Ann-Margret, Amy Madigan, Ally Sheedy
⌕ Amy Madigan (supporting actress)

Twice round the Daffodils
GB   1962   89m   bw
Anglo Amalgamated/GHW (Peter Rogers)
Comic and serious episodes in the lives of male patients at a TB sanatorium.
Acceptable broadening, almost in Carry On *style, of a modestly successful play.*
w Norman Hudis *play* Ring for Catty *by* Patrick Cargill, Jack Beale *d* Gerald Thomas *ph* Alan Hume *m* Bruce Montgomery
☆ Juliet Mills, Donald Sinden, Donald Houston, Kenneth Williams, Ronald Lewis, Joan Sims, Andrew Ray, Lance Percival, Jill Ireland, Sheila Hancock, Nanette Newman

Twice Two
👪 US   1933   20m   bw
Hal Roach
▣ ♻
Stan and Ollie have each married the other's twin sister …
Strained and laboured trick comedy in which neither the double exposures nor the gags quite come off.
w Stan Laurel *d* James Parrott *ph* Art Lloyd *ed* Bert Jordan
☆ Stan Laurel, Oliver Hardy, Baldwin Cooke, Charlie Hall

'Some people can buy their way out of anything. Except the past.'
Twilight *
US   1998   94m   DeLuxe
Paramount/Cinehaus (Arlene Donovan, Scott Rudin)
▣ ▤ ⌒
Living off the charity of a married film-star couple, an elderly, alcoholic ex-cop finds himself investigating the death of the wife's first husband twenty years before.
A downbeat thriller, tinged with melancholy and an awareness of time running out for its participants; the narrative is a familiar one, but the performances give it a little grace.
w Robert Benton, Richard Russo *d* Robert Benton *ph* Piotr Sobocinski *m* Elmer Bernstein *pd* David Gropman *ed* Carol Littleton
☆ Paul Newman, Susan Sarandon, Gene Hackman, Reese Witherspoon, Stockard Channing, James Garner, Giancarlo Esposito, Liev Schreiber, Margo Martindale, John Spencer, M, Emmet Walsh
'Younger audiences are unlikely to connect with the old-fashioned format and aging thesps, but enough traditionally minded fans should turn out for this beautifully crafted effort.' – *Todd McCarthy, Variety*

The Twilight Avengers (dubbed)
Italy   1970   89m   Eastmancolor
PAC/Caravel
original title: *I Vendicatori dell'Ave Maria*
In California, a travelling circus thwarts the ambitions of a ruthless landowner who murders the sheriff and takes over the town.
Dull spaghetti Western, with the emphasis on slapstick humour.
wd Al Albert (Adalberto Albertini) *ph* Antonio Modica *m* Piero Umiliani *ad* Franco Fontana
☆ Tony Kendall, Alberto Dell'Acqua, Peter Thorrys, Ida Meda, Albert Farley, Spartaco Conversi

Twilight for the Gods
US   1958   120m   Eastmancolor
U-I (Gordon Kay)
The captain of an old sailing ship takes her for a last voyage from Mexico to Tahiti.
Dull and miscast adventure story lacking the spark of the original novel; watchable only for the travelogue elements.

w Ernest K. Gann *novel* Ernest K. Gann *d* Joseph Pevney *ph* Irving Glassberg *m* David Raksin *md* Joseph Gershenson
☆ Rock Hudson, Cyd Charisse, Arthur Kennedy, Leif Erickson, Charles McGraw, Ernest Truex, Richard Haydn, Wallace Ford, Celia Lovsky, Vladimir Sokoloff
'Rock Hudson has difficulty in suggesting a dedicated seaman who has served under sail for thirty years.' – *MFB*

The Twilight Hour
GB   1944   85m   bw
British National
A nobleman's gardener turns out to be the amnesiac father of the girl about to marry into the family.
Plodding and very predictable drama with popular cast.
w Jack Whittingham *novel* Arthur Valentine *d* Paul Stein *ph* James Wilson *m* Hans May
☆ Mervyn Johns, Basil Radford, Marie Lohr, A. E. Matthews, Lesley Brook, Grey Blake

Twilight of Honor
US   1963   115m   bw   Panavision
MGM/Perlsea
GB title: *The Charge Is Murder*
A young small-town lawyer defends a neurotic no-good on a murder charge.
Modest courtroom melodrama in which the detail is better than the main plot.
w Henry Denker *novel* Al Dewlen *d* Boris Sagal *ph* Philip Lathrop *m* John Green
☆ Richard Chamberlain, Claude Rains, Joey Heatherton, Nick Adams, Joan Blackman, James Gregory, Pat Buttram, Jeanette Nolan
⌕ Nick Adams

Twilight of The Dead: see *City of The Living Dead*

Twilight on the Prairie
US   1944   62m   bw
Universal (Warren Wilson)
A cowboy band from New York are forced to find work on a Texas ranch when they become stranded on the way to Hollywood.
Enjoyable low-budget comedy; jazz aficionados will enjoy the bizarre spectacle of trombonist Teagarden, dressed in Stetson and woolly chaps, singing and playing 'The Blues'.
w Clyde Bruckman *story* Warren Wilson *d* Jean Yarbrough *m* Jerome Ash *m* Hans J. Salter *ad* John B. Goodman, Abraham Grossman *ed* Fred Feitshans Jnr
☆ Johnny Downs, Vivian Austin, Leon Errol, Connie Haines, Eddie Quillan, Jack Teagarden, Milburn Stone, Jimmie Dodd, Olin Howlin, Foy Willing and the Riders of the Purple Sage

'You're travelling through another dimension into a wondrous land whose only boundaries are those of the imagination'
Twilight Zone: The Movie *
US   1983   101m   Technicolor
Warner (Steven Spielberg, John Landis)
▤ ⌒
Four supernatural stories in the tradition of Rod Serling's long-running TV series of the fifties.
A disappointing collection on the whole, though with these talents what's on the screen is never quite boring.
w John Landis, George Clayton Johnson, Richard Matheson, Josh Rogan, Rod Serling *d* John Landis, Steven Spielberg, Joe Dante, George Miller *ph* Stevan Larner, Allen Daviau, John Hora *m* Jerry Goldsmith
☆ Dan Aykroyd, Vic Morrow, Scatman Crothers, Bill Quinn, Kathleen Quinlan, Kevin McCarthy, John Lithgow
'If there is an overriding irony to this catalogue of misfortunes, it is that the desire of four up-and-coming directors to honour TV as an imaginative source should have rebounded so disastrously on their cinematic reputations.' – *Richard Combs, MFB*

Twilight's Last Gleaming
US/West Germany   1977   146m   Technicolor
Lorimar/Bavaria Studios (Helmut Jedele)
▤ ⌒
An ex-general commandeers an atomic missile plant and blackmails the president into telling some political truths.

👪 film suitable for family viewing   ▣ VHS video-cassette for the British PAL system   ▤ VHS video-cassette for the British PAL system in wide screen-format   ♻ Video cassette in a computer-colourised version   ▥ American NTSC video-cassette   ⌒ Laser disc

Suspense thriller, fairly incompetent on its level and with ideas above its station. A distinctly overlong and unlikeable entertainment.

w Ronald M. Cohen, Edward Huebsch novel Viper Three by Walter Wager d Robert Aldrich ph Robert Hauser m Jerry Goldsmith ☆ Burt Lancaster, Richard Widmark, Charles Durning, Melvyn Douglas, Paul Winfield, Burt Young, Joseph Cotten, Roscoe Lee Browne, Gerald S. O'Loughlin, Charles Aidman

'It suggests an overextended episode of a TV series, and the attempts at wit are pathetically gross.' – New Yorker

Twin Beds *
US 1942 84m bw
Edward Small

A married couple are embarrassed by the antics of a drunken neighbour.

Slight pretext for a pretty funny old-fashioned farce.

w Curtis Kenyon, Kenneth Earl, E. Edwin Moran play Margaret Mayo, Edward Salisbury Field d Tim Whelan ph Hal Mohr m Dimitri Tiomkin ☆ George Brent, Joan Bennett, Mischa Auer, Una Merkel, Glenda Farrell, Ernest Truex, Margaret Hamilton, Charles Coleman

Twin Dragons (dubbed)
Hong Kong 1992 89m DeLuxe 'Scope
Dimension/Distant Horizon/Media Asia/HK FDG (Teddy Robin)

original title: Shuanglong Hui

Twin brothers are separated at birth, one to become a martial arts expert, the other a concert pianist.

A broad comedy with moments of violent action, this is a likable time-waster, but in no way memorable.

w Barry Wong, Hark, Cheung Tung Jo, Wong Yik d Tsui Hark, Ringo Lam ph Wong Wing Hang, Wong Ngor Tai m Michael Wandmacher, Phe Loung ad Lun Chon Hung, Lam Chun Fai ed Mak Che Sin English adaptation Rod Lean, Val Kuklowsky ☆ Jackie Chan, Maggie Cheung, Nina Li Chi, Anthony Chan, Philip Chan, Sylvia Chang, James Wong, Lai Ying Chow, Kirk Wong, Ringo Lam, John Woo, Tsui Hark

'Sad to say, there's less fighting than mugging: broad Hong Kong comedy is an acquired taste.' – Guardian

† The film was originally made in 1992 and then re-edited in 1998 and dubbed into English to take advantage of Chan's growing US popularity.

Twin Peaks *
US 1989 113m colour Panavision
Lynch-Frost Productions/Propaganda Films (David J. Latt)

An FBI agent is sent to a small town to investigate the murder of a young girl.

The pilot for what became a controversial and cult TV series was released on video in Europe as a surrealist parody of soap opera, full of deliberately over-the-top performances.

w Mark Frost, David Lynch d David Lynch ph Ron Garcia m Angelo Badalamenti pd Patricia Norris ed Duwayne R. Dunham ☆ Kyle MacLachlan, Michael Ontkean, Madchen Amick, Dana Ashbrook, Richard Beymer, Lara Flynn Boyle, Sherilyn Fenn, Warren Frost, Joan Chen, Piper Laurie

'In a town like Twin Peaks, no one is innocent.'
'These are the last seven days of Laura Palmer.'
Twin Peaks: Fire Walk with Me
US 1992 134m CFI color Panavision
Guild/Twin Peaks (Gregg Fienberg)

Events leading up to the murder of the teenage Laura Palmer.

Mystifyingly obscure and dull prequel to the TV series Twin Peaks which tries one's patience with its visions and precognitions.

w David Lynch, Robert Engels d David Lynch ph Ron Garcia m Angelo Badalamenti pd Patricia Norris ed Mark Sweeney ☆ Sheryl Lee, Ray Wise, Mädchen Amick, Dana Ashbrook, Phoebe Augustine, David Bowie, Eric DaRe, Miguel Ferrer, Chris Isaak, Kyle MacLachlan, James Marshall, Jürgen Prochnow, Harry Dean Stanton, Kiefer Sutherland, David Lynch

'Pic will inevitably attract die-hard fans but is too weird and not very meaningful for general audiences.' – Variety

'It looks, in fact, like a very bad movie made by a very good director, tired of fooling around for a television audience.' – Derek Malcolm, Guardian

'Rugby. Tom Jones. Male Voice Choirs. Shirley Bassey. Llanfairpwllgwyngyllgogerychwyrndrobwyllllantisilio gogogoch. Snowdonia. Prince of Wales. Anthony Hopkins. Daffodils. Sheep. Sheep Lovers. Coal. Slate Quarries. The Blaenau Ffestiniog Dinkey-Doo Miniature Railway. Now If That's Your Idea Of Thousands Of Years Of Welsh Culture, You Can't Blame Us For Trying To Liven The Place Up A Little Bit Can You?'
Twin Town **
GB 1997 99m Technicolor
Polygram/Figment/Agenda/Aimimage (Peter McAleese)

Two delinquent brothers take revenge on the local businessman and crooked cop responsible for the deaths of their parents and sister.

The name of Dylan Thomas is invoked, and his cosy Welsh culture rejected, at the beginning of this exuberantly nihilistic demolition of its traditions, where joyriders, karaoke and corruption rule, the police deal drugs and only the old sing. Its bleak, black-comic tone may shock, but is fuelled by a genuine anger.

w Kevin Allen, Paul Durden d Kevin Allen ph John Mathieson m Mark Thomas pd Pat Campbell ed Oral Norrie Ottey ☆ Llyr Evans, Rhys Ifans, Dorien Thomas, Dougray Scott, Brian Hibbard, William Thomas, Jenny Evans, Biddug Williams, Ronnie Williams, Huw Ceredig, Rachel Scorgie, Di Botcher, Keith Allen

'Where the film scores is with its group portrait of a sour but not meaningless Welsh reality – a world that at least has the merit of being trapped in the present rather than the past.' – Adam Mars-Jones, Independent

'The most depressing thing about Twin Town is that it seems to mark the almost instant decay of a new and exciting cinematic language in British films.' – Ben Thompson, Sight and Sound

The Twinkle in God's Eye
US 1955 73m bw
Republic (Mickey Rooney)

A parson rebuilds a church in a Western town where his father was killed by Indians.

Amiable if unlikely Western drama with the star more convincing than one might expect.

w P. J. Wolfson d George Blair ph Bud Thackery m Van Alexander ☆ Mickey Rooney, Hugh O'Brian, Colleen Gray, Michael Connors, Don Barry

Twinkle Twinkle Lucky Stars (dubbed)
Hong Kong 1985 90m colour
Golden Harvest/Paragon (Eric Tsang)

Cops protect an actress from assassination.

Comic martial arts, more under the influence of the Three Stooges than of Bruce Lee. There are, however, some splendidly choreographed fight sequences to compensate for the laborious slapstick.

w Barry Wong story Barry Wong, Szeto Cheuk Hon, Lo Kin d Samo Hung ph Arthur Wong, Johnny Koo m Anders Nelson ad Eddie Ma ed Peter Cheung ☆ Jackie Chan, Samo Hung, Yuen Biao, Richard Ng, Eric Tsang, Fung Shui Fan, Miu Kiu Wai, John Shum, Sibelle Hu, Rosamund Kwan, Richard Norton

Twinky
GB 1969 98m Technicolor
Rank/World Film Services (Clive Sharp)
US title: Lola

A 16-year-old London schoolgirl marries a dissolute 40-year-old American author.

Dreary sex comedy drama, the fag end of London's swinging sixties.

w Norman Thaddeus Vane d Richard Donner ph Walter Lassally m John Scott ☆ Charles Bronson, Susan George, Trevor Howard, Michael Craig, Honor Blackman, Robert Morley, Jack Hawkins

Twins *
↟↟ US 1988 107m DeLuxe
UIP/Universal (Ivan Reitman)

A 36-year-old man, bred in a genetic experiment as the perfect man, discovers that he has a less-than-perfect twin brother.

Amusing, if sometimes ponderous, comedy with the joke depending on the physical disparity of its two protagonists.

w William Davies, William Osborne, Timothy Harris, Herschel Weingrod d Ivan Reitman ph Andrzej Bartkowiak m Georges Delerue, Randy Edelman pd James D. Bissel ed Sheldon Kahn, Donn Cambern ☆ Arnold Schwarzenegger, Danny DeVito, Kelly Preston, Chloe Webb, Bonnie Bartlett, Marshall Bell, Trey Wilson, David Caruso, Hugh O'Brian

'They use the satanic power of their bodies to turn men and women into their blood slaves!'
Twins of Evil
GB 1971 87m Eastmancolor
Rank/Hammer (Harry Fine, Michael Style)

Identical Austrian twins become devotees of a vampire cult.

Vampire-chasing Puritans add a little flavour to a routine Hammer horror.

w Tudor Gates d John Hough ph Dick Bush m Harry Robinson ad Roy Stannard ed Spencer Reeve ☆ Madeleine Collinson, Mary Collinson, Peter Cushing, Kathleen Byron, Dennis Price, Isobel Black

Twist around the Clock
↟↟ US 1961 83m bw
Columbia/Sam Katzman

An astute manager discovers a small-town dance called the twist and promotes it nationally.

Rock around the Clock revisited, with an even lower budget and fewer shreds of talent.

w James B. Gordon d Oscar Rudolph ph Gordon Avil md Fred Karger ☆ Chubby Checker, the Marcels, Dion, John Cronin, Mary Mitchell

Twist of Fate: see Beautiful Stranger

A Twist of Sand
GB 1968 91m DeLuxe
UA/Christina (Fred Engel)

An ill-matched set of criminals seek hidden diamonds on Africa's skeleton coast.

Pattern melodrama of thieves falling out, quite nicely put together but with performances too high pitched.

w Marvin H. Albert novel Geoffrey Jenkins d Don Chaffey ph John Wilcox m Tristram Cary ☆ Richard Johnson, Honor Blackman, Roy Dotrice, Peter Vaughan, Jeremy Kemp

'Enough to make even Hitchcock jump!'
Twisted Nerve
GB 1968 118m Eastmancolor
British Lion/Charter (John Boulting)

A rich, disturbed young man disguises himself as a retarded teenager in order to kill his hated stepfather.

Absurd, unpleasant, longwinded and naïvely scripted shocker, rightly attacked because it asserted that brothers of mongoloids are apt to become murderers. A long way behind the worst Hitchcock.

w Leo Marks, Roy Boulting d Roy Boulting ph Harry Waxman m Bernard Herrmann ☆ Hayley Mills, Hywel Bennett, Phyllis Calvert, Billie Whitelaw, Frank Finlay, Barry Foster, Salmaan Peer

'Curious and in some respects disagreeable … never thrilling enough to reach the Hitchcock level and without sufficient medical credibility to be taken seriously as a case history.' – Michael Billington, Illustrated London News
🎬 Billie Whitelaw

Twister *
US 1996 113m Technicolor Panavision
Warner/Universal/Amblin (Kathleen Kennedy, Ian Bryce, Michael Crichton)

Rival meteorologists chase tornadoes and rediscover romance.

Sensation for its own sake, with all the anarchic destruction an audience could hope for, done with a terrifying hyper-realism; those wanting an equally engaging narrative will be disappointed.

w Michael Crichton, Anne-Marie Martin d Jan de Bont ph Jack N. Green m Mark Mancina pd Joseph Nemec III ed Michael Kahn sp Industrial Light and Magic ☆ Helen Hunt, Bill Paxton, Jami Gertz, Cary Elwes, Lois Smith, Philip Seymour Hoffman, Alan Ruck

'Another theme park ride of a movie without an ounce of emotional credibility to it.' – Todd McCarthy, Variety

'It's the world's first thriller about thin air. No stars, precious little plot to speak of and zero content to hold it back. It's a blast.' – Tom Shone, Sunday Times

† It was among the box-office successes of 1996, grossing more than $493m around the world.
†† Giving evidence in a case involving alleged plagiarism of the idea for Twister, Steven Spielberg told a court that the script accounted for only 5 per cent of the film's success. The action and special effects accounted for 60 per cent, Helen Hunt for 20 per cent, and sound effects for 10 per cent.
⅄ visual effects; sound

Twitch of the Death Nerve: see A Bay of Blood

Two a Penny
GB 1967 98m Eastmancolor
World Wide (Frank R. Jacobson)

An idle art student becomes involved in the drug racket but finally sees the light.

Naïve religious propaganda sponsored by the Billy Graham movement and featuring the evangelist in a cameo. A curiosity.

w Stella Linden d James F. Collier ph Michael Reed m Mike Leander ☆ Cliff Richard, Dora Bryan, Ann Holloway, Avril Angers, Geoffrey Bayldon, Peter Barkworth

Two against the World
US 1936 64m bw
Warner (Bryan Foy)
GB title: The Case of Mrs Pembroke

A gutter newspaper unnecessarily digs up a sordid murder case and causes the suicide of two people involved.

Remake of Five Star Final with the interest boringly shifted to the do-gooders who don't want to publish the story.

w Michel Jacoby play Louis Weitzenkorn d William McGann ph Sid Hickox m Heinz Roemheld ☆ Humphrey Bogart, Beverly Roberts, Helen MacKellar, Henry O'Neill, Linda Perry, Virginia Brissac

Two Alone
US 1934 72m bw
RKO

The orphanage drudge on a remote farm gets herself pregnant.

Heavy-going Cold Comfort Farm melodrama, with virtually no light relief in sight.

w Josephine Lovett, Joseph Moncure March play Wild Birds by Dan Totheroh d Elliott Nugent ph Lucien Andriot md Max Steiner ☆ Jean Parker, Tom Brown, Arthur Byron, ZaSu Pitts, Beulah Bondi, Nydia Westman

Two and Two Make Six
GB 1961 89m bw
Bryanston/Prometheus (Monja Danischewsky)

Two motor cycling couples almost accidentally swap partners.

Reasonably fresh little romantic comedy.

w Monja Danischewsky d Freddie Francis ph Desmond Dickinson, Ronnie Taylor m Norrie Paramor ☆ George Chakiris, Janette Scott, Alfred Lynch, Jackie Lane, Malcolm Keen, Ambrosine Philpotts, Bernard Braden

Two Bright Boys
US 1939 69m bw
Universal (Burt Kelly)

A British boy and his father help an American boy save his oil ranch from a foreclosing villain.

Traditional action stuff, quite pleasantly done for undemanding audiences.

---

w Val Burton, Edmund L. Hartmann d Joseph Santley

☆ Jackie Cooper, Freddie Bartholomew, Melville Cooper, Dorothy Peterson, Alan Dinehart, Willard Robertson

'Adequate support for the duals.' – *Variety*

2 Days in the Valley

US 1996 105m DeLuxe Panavision
Entertainment/Rysher/Redemption (Jeff Wald, Herb Nanas)

📺 ▦ ᗕ ⊚

The lives of two hitmen, a couple of cops, a suicidal director, a wealthy art dealer, an angry woman and an Olympic skier collide, leaving death and destruction behind.

An excessively violent comedy about people behaving badly in Los Angeles; it suffers from overkill.

wd John Herzfeld ph Oliver Wood m Anthony Marinelli pd Catherine Hardwicke ed Jim Miller, Wayne Wahrman

☆ Danny Aiello, Greg Cruttwell, Jeff Daniels, Teri Hatcher, Glenne Headly, Peter Horton, Marsha Mason, Paul Mazursky, James Spader, Eric Stoltz, Keith Carradine, Louise Fletcher, Austin Pendleton, Lawrence Tierney

'Marked by a wearying amount of hostile and antisocial behavior by its criminal and civilian characters alike … Pic does offer some entertainment value for mainstream audiences.' – *Todd McCarthy, Variety*

Two Deaths *

GB 1995 96m colour
BBC/British Screen (Luc Roeg, Carolyn Montagu)

As revolution rages on the streets of Bucharest, three old friends gather at the house of a successful surgeon for a reunion dinner, which ends in confessions of sexual obsessions, pathological behaviour and requited passion.

A well-acted, complex narrative of corruption, of the facing up to unpleasant truths at a moment of national crisis, but the conjunction of political and personal revelations is too contrived to be entirely engaging.

w Allan Scott novel The Two Deaths of Señora Puccini by Stephen Dobyns d Nicolas Roeg ph Witold Stok m Hans Zimmer pd Don Taylor ed Tony Lawson

☆ Michael Gambon, Sonia Braga, Patrick Malahide, Nickolas Grace, Ion Caramitru

'Will connect with filmgoers who relish a stern mix of psychology and politics.' – *Variety*

Two English Girls: see Anne And Muriel

The Two Faces of Dr Jekyll

GB 1960 88m Technicolor Megascope
Hammer (Michael Carreras, Anthony Nelson-Keys)
US title: *House of Fright*

A variation on the much-filmed story: the schizo's evil half is the more handsome.

Surprisingly flat and tedious remake.

w Wolf Mankowitz novel Robert Louis Stevenson d Terence Fisher ph Jack Asher m David Heneker, Monty Norman ad Bernard Robinson ed Jim Needs, Eric Boyd-Perkins

☆ Paul Massie, Dawn Addams, Christopher Lee, David Kossoff, Francis de Wolff

Two Fisted

US 1935 60m bw
Paramount (Harold Hurley)

A prizefighter and his manager join a socialite's household as bodyguards.

Flat comedy which doesn't get very far in any direction; a remake of the silent Is Zat So?

w Sam Hellman, Francis Martin, Eddie Moran play James Gleason, James Taber d James Cruze

☆ Lee Tracy, Roscoe Karns, Grace Bradley, Kent Taylor, Gail Patrick

'Some periods of hilarity.' – *Variety*

Two Flags West *

US 1950 92m bw
TCF (Casey Robinson)

Sixty Confederate prisoners of war are granted an amnesty and go west to fight the Indians.

Laboured but good-looking Civil War Western.

w Casey Robinson d Robert Wise ph Leon Shamroy m Hugo Friedhofer

☆ Joseph Cotten, Jeff Chandler, Linda Darnell, Cornel Wilde, Dale Robertson, Jay C. Flippen, Noah Beery Jnr, Harry von Zell

'Its period reconstruction is remarkable.' – *Gavin Lambert*

Two for the Road *

GB 1966 113m DeLuxe Panavision
TCF/Stanley Donen

📺 ᗕ 🎧

An architect and his wife motoring through France recall the first twelve years of their relationship.

Fractured, fashionable light romantic comedy dressed up to seem of more significance than the gossamer thing it really is; and some of the gossamer has a Woolworth look.

w Frederic Raphael d Stanley Donen ph Christopher Challis m Henry Mancini

☆ Albert Finney, Audrey Hepburn, Eleanor Bron, William Daniels, Claude Dauphin

'The facile, comic bits set off audience expectations which are then betrayed, and the clever, bitter stuff just seems sour.' – *Pauline Kael, New Yorker*

§ Frederic Raphael

Two for the Seesaw

US 1962 120m bw Panavision
UA/Seesaw/Mirisch/Argyle/Talbot (Robert Wise)

📺 ᗕ

A New York dance instructress has a tempestuous affair with an Omaha attorney on the verge of divorce.

Serious comedy or light drama, meticulously detailed but immensely long for its content and too revealing of its stage origins.

w Isobel Lennart play William Gibson d Robert Wise ph Ted McCord m André Previn ad Boris Leven

☆ Robert Mitchum, Shirley MacLaine

§ Ted McCord; song 'Second Chance' (mAndré Previn, lyDory Langdon)

Two for Tonight

US 1935 60m bw
Paramount (Douglas MacLean)

Three half-brothers write a play for a temperamental star.

Much ado about nothing, but not an unpleasant way of passing an hour.

w George Marion Jnr, Jane Storm play Max and J. O. Lief d Frank Tuttle ph Karl Struss

☆ Bing Crosby, Joan Bennett, Mary Boland, Lynne Overman, Thelma Todd, Ernest Cossart

'No wow … the songs, the fetching title, the competent cast and mostly Crosby will have to offset the other deficiencies.' – *Variety*

'A very amusing and well-written entertainment.' – *Graham Greene*

'Thanks to his two girlfriends, Blake's about to learn a new sexual position. Honesty.'

Two Girls and a Guy

US 1997 84m Technicolor
Fox Searchlight/Muse Prods (Edward R. Pressman, Chris Hanley)

📺 ▦ 🎧

Two women discover that they are dating the same actor, and confront him about his duplicity.

An unstructured account of a compulsive womanizer trying to charm his way out of a tight corner that feels as if it is semi-improvised. It is interesting for as long as it lasts, without saying anything new about relationships.

wd James Toback ph Barry Markowitz pd Kevin Thompson ed Alan Oxman

☆ Robert Downey Jnr, Heather Graham, Natasha Gregson Wagner, Angel David, Frederique Van Der Wal

'A work that is as bracingly entertaining at times as it is unfulfilled at others.' – *Todd McCarthy, Variety*

† The film was shot in 11 days.

Two Girls and a Sailor **

US 1944 124m bw
MGM (Joe Pasternak)

📺 ᗕ

The title says it all.

Loosely-linked wartime musical jamboree with first-class talent; a lively entertainment of its type.

w Richard Connell, Gladys Lehman d Richard Thorpe ph Robert Surtees m George Stoll songs various

☆ June Allyson, Gloria de Haven, Van Johnson, Xavier Cugat and his Orchestra, *Jimmy Durante*, Tom Drake, Lena Horne, Carlos Ramirez, Harry James and his Orchestra, Jose Iturbi, *Gracie Allen*, Virginia O'Brien, Albert Coates

§ script

Two Girls on Broadway

US 1940 73m bw
MGM
GB title: *Choose Your Partner*

A song and dance man breaks up a sister act.

Acceptable lower-case vaudeville musical which rewrites the already wispy plot of Broadway Melody.

w Joseph Fields, Jerome Chodorov d S. Sylvan Simon

☆ George Murphy, Joan Blondell, Lana Turner, Kent Taylor, Wallace Ford, Lloyd Corrigan

Two Guys from Milwaukee

US 1946 90m bw
Warner
GB title: *Royal Flush*

A young Balkan prince goes incognito in Brooklyn and befriends a cab driver.

Rumbustious comedy with an amiable cast and gag guest appearances.

w I. A. L. Diamond, Charles Hoffman d David Butler

☆ Dennis Morgan, Jack Carson, Joan Leslie, Janis Paige, S. Z. Sakall, Franklin Pangborn

Two Guys from Texas

US 1948 86m Technicolor
Warner
GB title: *Two Texas Knights*

Two vaudevillians find themselves on the run from crooks.

Little more than a peg on which to hang some clowning and a few musical numbers.

w I. A. L. Diamond, Allen Boretz d David Butler ph Arthur Edeson, William V. Skal m Jule Styne

☆ Dennis Morgan, Jack Carson, Dorothy Malone, Penny Edwards, Fred Clark, Gerald Mohr, Forrest Tucker

'It's 11:59 on New Year's Eve. Do you know where your date is?'

200 Cigarettes

US 1999 101m DeLuxe
Paramount/Lakeshore/MTV/Dogstar (Betsy Beers, David Gale, Van Toffler)

📺 ▦ 🎧

In New York in 1981, various people, all bent on pleasure and sexual gratification, celebrate New Year's Eve.

An uninvolving ensemble piece; some irony or genuine humour might have added a little spice to this stew of the self-absorbed hipsters.

w Shana Larsen d Risa Bramon Garcia ph Frank Prinzi m Bob and Mark Mothersbaugh pd Ina Mayhew ed Lisa Zeno Churgin

☆ Ben Affleck, Casey Affleck, Dave Chappelle, Guillermo Diaz, Angela Featherstone, Janeane Garofalo, Gaby Hoffmann, Kate Hudson, Catherine Kellner, Courtney Love, Brian McCardie, Christina Ricci, Martha Plimpton, Paul Rudd, Jay Mohr and also Elvis Costello

'A dismally unfunny farce.' – *Todd McCarthy*

'Wry ensemble comedy throws up moments of genuine inspiration... the overall effect is charming in an understated way.' – *Sight and Sound*

200 Motels *

US 1971 98m Technicolor
United Artists/Murakami Wolf/Bizarre (Jerry Good, Herb Cohen)

📺 ▦ 🎧

Concert footage of Zappa and The Mothers of Invention is intercut with jokes, sketches and animation, derived from the life of a band on the road – 'touring can make you crazy', as Zappa comments.

A minor cult movie, an often inventive and witty surrealist montage and a notable influence on later rock videos.

wd Frank Zappa, Tony Palmer m Frank Zappa ch Gillian Lynne pd Cal Schenkel ed Rich Harrison

☆ The Mothers of Invention (Mark Volman, Howard Kaylan, Ian Underwood, Aynsley Dunbar, George Duke), Theodore Bikel, Keith Moon, Ringo Starr

† The film was shot on videotape in England at Pinewood Studios. Zappa had intended it as a live concert, but turned to video after it was cancelled on the grounds that the libretto was obscene.

Two If by Sea

US 1996 96m DeLuxe
Warner/Morgan Creek (James G. Robinson)

📺 ▦ ᗕ

GB title: *Stolen Hearts*

An incompetent small-time thief steals a valuable painting and goes off on holiday with his girlfriend, closely followed by the FBI.

Dire mix of romantic comedy and chase movie, poorly plotted and lacking in laughs.

w Denis Leary, Mike Armstrong d Bill Bennett ph Andrew Lesnie m Nick Glennie-Smith, Paddy Moloney pd David Chapman ed Bruce Green

☆ Denis Leary, Sandra Bullock, Stephen Dillane, Yaphet Kotto, Wayne Robson, Jonathan Tucker, Mike Starr

'The dialogue has the crispness of aging lettuce, and the situations rely on coincidence, disbelief and a singular disregard for character.' – *Leonard Klady, Variety*

Two in the Dark

US 1936 72m bw
RKO

An amnesiac tries to find out whether he was involved in the murder of a theatrical producer.

Mildly intriguing mystery.

w Seton I. Miller novel Gelett Burgess d Ben Stoloff

☆ Walter Abel, Margot Grahame, Wallace Ford, Gail Patrick, Alan Hale, Leslie Fenton, Eric Blore

'A programmer that'll suit both audiences and b.o. outside of larger first runs.' – *Variety*

The Two Jakes *

US 1990 138m Technicolor
Blue Dolphin/Paramount (Robert Evans, Harold Schneider)

📺 ▦ ᗕ

A private eye, hired by a real-estate developer to investigate his wife's adultery, tape-records a murder that is part of a complex conspiracy.

Convoluted thriller of small-scale corruption that overstays its welcome.

w Robert Towne d Jack Nicholson ph Vilmos Zsigmond m Van Dyke Parks pd Jeremy Railton, Richard Sawyer ed Anne Goursaud

☆ Jack Nicholson, Harvey Keitel, Meg Tilly, Madeleine Stowe, Eli Wallach, Rubén Blades, Frederic Forrest, David Keith, Richard Farnsworth

'A jumbled, obtuse yet not entirely unsatisfying follow-up.' – *Variety*

† A sequel to Chinatown (qv), it was originally to have been made in 1985 with Robert Towne directing and producer Robert Evans in the role played by Harvey Keitel.

Two Lane Blacktop

US 1971 103m Technicolor scope
Universal/Michael S. Laughlin

In the American southwest, the aimless owners of two souped-up cars have an interminable race.

Occasionally arresting, generally boring eccentricity by a big studio looking for another Easy Rider.

w Rudolph Wurlitzer, Will Corry d Monte Hellman ph Jack Deerson m Billy James

☆ James Taylor, Warren Oates, Laurie Bird, Dennis Wilson

Two Left Feet

GB 1963 93m bw
British Lion/Roy Baker (Leslie Gilliat)

A callow 19-year-old has girl trouble.

Ponderous sex comedy with no apparent purpose but some well observed scenes.

w Roy Baker, John Hopkins novel In My Solitude by David Stuart Leslie d Roy Baker ph Wilkie Cooper m Philip Green

☆ Michael Crawford, Nyree Dawn Porter, Julia Foster, David Hemmings, Dilys Watling, David Lodge, Bernard Lee

The Two Lives of Mattia Pascal **

Italy/West Germany 1985 118m colour
RAI/Excelsior Cinematografica/Cinecitta/Antenne 2/Telemunchen/RTVE/RTS1/Channel 4 (Silvia D'Amico Bendico, Carlo Cucci)

original title: *Le Due Vite di Mattia Pascal*

Cheated out of his inheritance and humiliated by his wife, a man adopts a new identity.

Witty, dark comedy of a personality crisis.

w Suso Cecchi D'Amico, Ennio de Concini, Amanzo Todini, Mario Monicelli novel Il Fu Mattia Pascal by Luigi Pirandello d Mario

Monicelli *ph* Camillo Bazzoni *m* Nicola Piovani *ad* Lorenzo Baraldi *ed* Ruggero Mastroianni
☆ Marcello Mastroianni, Flavio Bucci, Laura Morante, Laura Del Sol, Nestor Garay, Alessandro Haber, Carlo Bagno, Rosalia Maggio, Senta Berger, Bernard Blier

Two Loves
US 1961 100m Metrocolor Cinemascope
MGM/Julian Blaustein
GB title: *Spinster*
An American teacher in New Zealand teaches Maoris and whites and falls for two men.
Pretentious romantic drama with unspeakable dialogue and eccentric characters.
w Ben Maddow *novel* Sylvia Ashton Warner *d* Charles Walters *ph* Joseph Ruttenberg *m* Bronislau Kaper
☆ Shirley MacLaine, Jack Hawkins, Laurence Harvey, Nobu McCarthy

Two Men and a Girl: see *Honeymoon*

Two Minds for Murder: see *Someone Behind the Door*

'91,000 people ... 33 exit gates ... one sniper!'
Two Minute Warning
US 1976 115m Technicolor Panavision
Universal/Filmways (Edward S. Feldman)
🔲 ⊙ 🎧
A sniper terrifies the crowd at a championship football game.
Smartly directed but weakly plotted and scripted disaster movie: the mystery gunman remains a mystery at the end.
w Edward Hume *novel* George LaFountaine *d* Larry Peerce *ph* Gerald Hirschfeld *m* Charles Fox
☆ Charlton Heston, John Cassavetes, Martin Balsam, Beau Bridges, David Janssen, Marilyn Hassett, Jack Klugman, Gena Rowlands, Walter Pidgeon, Brock Peters, Mitch Ryan
'Even by the standards of exploitation movies, this film is an unusually dehumanizing experience. Not only does it exist solely for its gore, but it reduces the victims to the dimensions of plastic ducks at a shooting gallery.' – *Frank Rich, New York Post*

Two Moon Junction
US 1988 105m CFI color
Recorded Releasing/DDM/Samuel Goldwyn Company (Donald P. Borchers)
🔲 🔲 ⊙ 🎧
Despite her approaching marriage, a rich Southern woman begins an affair with a handsome carnival worker.
Ludicrously overwrought romantic melodrama.
wd Zalman King *story* Zalman King, MacGregor Douglas *ph* Mark Plummer *m* Jonathan Elias *pd* Michelle Minch *ed* Marc Grossman
☆ Sherilyn Fenn, Richard Tyson, Louise Fletcher, Burl Ives, Kristy McNichol, Martin Hewitt, Juanita Moore, Don Galloway, Millie Perkins

The Two Mrs Carrolls
US 1947 99m bw
Warner (Mark Hellinger)
🔲
A psychopathic artist paints his wives as the Angel of Death, then murders them with poisoned milk.
Stilted film of an old warhorse of a play, unhappily cast but working up some last-minute tension.
w Thomas Job *play* Martin Vale *d* Peter Godfrey *ph* Peverell Marley *m* Franz Waxman
☆ Barbara Stanwyck, Humphrey Bogart, Alexis Smith, Nigel Bruce, Isobel Elsom, Pat O'Moore, Peter Godfrey
'Most of the show is a clutter of entrance and exit, about as dramatically arresting as a game in and out of the window. Miss Stanwyck, who does well enough with a tough worldly kind of part, is baffled by the sleight of hand required for this one. Humphrey Bogart also appears uncomfortable.' – *Time*
† Made in 1945.

Two Much
Spain/US 1996 118m Technicolor Panavision
Polygram/Sogetel/Lola/Occidental Media/Fernando Trueba
🔲 🔲 🎧
A conniving art dealer, who is engaged to a wealthy woman, invents a twin brother so that he can marry her sister.
A would-be screwball romantic comedy; it might have worked had it been cast with actors capable of comedy acting, or exhibited some wit in the writing.
w Fernando Trueba, David Trueba *novel* Donald E. Westlake *d* Fernando Trueba *ph* José Luis Alcaine *m* Michel Camilo *pd* Juan Botella *ed* Nena Bernard
☆ Antonio Banderas, Melanie Griffith, Daryl Hannah, Danny Aiello, Joan Cusack, Eli Wallach, Gabino Diego, Austin Pendleton
'The comedy is almost entirely misjudged, mistimed and often visually infantile, and while Miami looks appealing, it serves merely as window dressing for a plot that is, frankly, abysmal.' – *Deborah Brown, Empire*

Two Mules for Sister Sara
US 1969 116m Technicolor Panavision
Universal/Malpaso (Martin Rackin)
🔲 🔲
A wandering cowboy kills three men trying to rape a nun, but she is not what she seems.
Vaguely unsatisfactory Western with patches of nasty brutality leading to an action-packed climax.
w Albert Maltz, Budd Boetticher *d* Don Siegel *ph* Gabriel Figueroa, Gabriel Torres *m* Ennio Morricone
☆ Clint Eastwood, Shirley MacLaine, Manolo Fabregas, Alberto Morin

Two O'Clock Courage
US 1945 66m bw
Ben Stoloff/RKO
An amnesia victim is suspected of killing a Broadway producer.
Tepid murder mystery.
w Robert E. Kent *story* Gelett Burgess *d* Anthony Mann *ph* Jack MacKenzie *m* Roy Webb
☆ Tom Conway, Ann Rutherford, Richard Lane, Roland Drew, Emory Parnell, Jane Greer

Two of a Kind
US 1951 75m bw
Columbia (William Dozier)
A man is picked up by a glamorous girl who involves him in an elaborate scheme to defraud an elderly couple.
Modest suspenser.
w Lawrence Kimble, James Grunn *d* Henry Levin *ph* Burnett Guffey *m* George Duning
☆ Edmond O'Brien, Lizabeth Scott, Terry Moore, Alexander Knox, Griff Barnett, Virginia Brissac

Two of a Kind
US 1983 87m DeLuxe
TCF (Roger M. Rothstein, Joe Wizan)
🔲 ⊙
Four angels propose that Earth be spared from a second flood if two arbitrarily chosen human beings can be seen to perform a great sacrifice for each other.
Curious reversion to angelic comedies of the thirties and forties. Lacking the right measures of wit and whimsy, it is totally unsuccessful.
wd John Herzfeld *ph* Fred Koenekamp, Warren Rothenberger *md* Patrick Williams *pd* Albert Brenner
☆ John Travolta, Olivia Newton-John, Charles Durning, Oliver Reed, Beatrice Straight, Scatman Crothers
'It feels as if it must be a remake of something...' – *Sheila Johnston, MFB*

The Two of Us: see *A Nous Deux*

Two on a Guillotine *
US 1965 107m bw Panavision
Warner (William Conrad)
An illusionist arranges to be chained into his coffin at his funeral but promises to return from the dead.
Longwinded and unconvincing shocker with some effectively scary sequences.
w Henry Slesar, John Kneubuhl *d* William Conrad *ph* Sam Leavitt *m* Max Steiner

☆ Connie Stevens, Dean Jones, Cesar Romero, Parley Baer, Virginia Gregg, Connie Gilchrist, John Hoyt

Two or Three Things I Know about Her **
France 1967 95m Eastmancolor Techniscope
Contemporary/Anouchka/Argos/Les Films du Carrosse/Parc Film (Philippe Senné)
🔲 🔲
original title: *Deux ou trois choses que je sais d'elle*
A mother of two spends her day window-shopping and working as a prostitute to maintain her middle-class way of life.
An episodic and critical look at city life – the title refers to Paris, not the central character – and the constraints it puts upon individuals. Godard at his most polemic, by turns infuriating and fascinating.
wd Jean-Luc Godard *ph* Raoul Coutard *m* Beethoven *ed* Françoise Collin, Chantal Delattre
☆ Jean-Luc Godard, Marina Vlady, Anny Duperey, Roger Montsoret, Jean Narboni, Christophe Bourseiller, Marie Bourseiller
'A bit of pontifical journalism, a column and a half, interviews and all, about housing estates, the cost of living and the decay of family life.' – *Dilys Powell*

Two Pennyworth of Hope: see *Due Soldi de Speranza*

'They had just 36 hours to share the love of a lifetime!'
Two People
US 1973 100m Technicolor
Universal (Robert Wise)
An army deserter returns home and falls for a fashion photographer.
Solemn, inconsequential topical drama which made no impact whatever.
w Richard de Roy *d* Robert Wise *ph* Gerald Hirschfeld *m* David Shire
☆ Peter Fonda, Lindsay Wagner, Estelle Parsons, Alan Fudge
'Sluggish pacing, lifeless looping and terminally ludicrous dialogue eventually turn the film into a travesty of its own form.' – *Variety*

Two Rode Together
US 1961 109m Technicolor
Columbia/John Ford/Shpetner
🔲 🔲 ⊙
An army commander and a tough marshal negotiate with Comanches for the return of prisoners.
Substandard Ford, moderately good-looking but uninteresting of plot and dreary of development.
w Frank Nugent *novel* Will Cook *d* John Ford *ph* Charles Lawton Jnr *m* George Duning
☆ James Stewart, Richard Widmark, Shirley Jones, Linda Cristal, Andy Devine, John McIntire

Two Seconds *
US 1932 68m bw
Warner
In the last two seconds of his life a criminal reviews the events leading up to his execution.
Competent, pacy crime melodrama.
w Harvey Thew *play* Elliott Lester *d* Mervyn Le Roy *ph* Sol Polito *m* W. Franke Harling
☆ Edward G. Robinson, Preston Foster, Vivienne Osborne, J. Carrol Naish, Guy Kibbee, Adrienne Dare
'General slowness and stodgy overdramatics won't draw the flaps, nor will a tragic finale help.' – *Variety*
'A film that compels attention.' – *Mordaunt Hall, New York Times*

Two Sinners
US 1935 71m bw
Republic
A man jailed for shooting his wife's lover makes a fresh start.
Curious but tedious romantic drama.
w Jefferson Parker *story* *Two Black Sheep* by Warwick Deeping *d* Arthur Lubin
☆ Otto Kruger, Martha Sleeper, Minna Gombell, Cora Sue Collins

Two Sisters from Boston *
US 1946 112m bw
MGM (Joe Pasternak)
Two girls visiting New York find work in a Bowery saloon.
Nicely-detailed turn-of-the-century musical with pleasant talent.
w Myles Connolly *d* Henry Koster *ph* Robert Surtees *md* Charles Previn *songs* Sammy Fain, Ralph Freed
☆ June Allyson, Kathryn Grayson, Lauritz Melchior, Jimmy Durante, Peter Lawford, Ben Blue
'If MGM think they have disguised the tiredest old musical bore of them all by putting it in period costume they're wrong.' – *Richard Winnington*

Two Smart People
US 1946 93m bw
MGM (Ralph Wheelright)
A con man on parole in New Orleans is chased by a lady crook in search of his hidden loot.
Dog-eared comedy drama.
w Ethel Hill, Leslie Charteris *d* Jules Dassin *ph* Karl Freund *m* George Bassman
☆ Lucille Ball, John Hodiak, Lloyd Nolan, Hugo Haas, Lenore Ulric, Elisha Cook Jnr, Lloyd Corrigan, Vladimir Sokoloff

Two Tars ****
⫟⫟ US 1928 20m bw silent
Hal Roach
🔲
Two sailors in an old banger cause a traffic jam and a consequent escalation of violence.
Marvellous elaboration of a tit-for-tat situation, with the stars already at their technical best.
w Leo McCarey, H. M. Walker *d* James Parrott *ph* George Stevens *ed* Richard Currier
☆ Stan Laurel, Oliver Hardy, Edgar Kennedy, Charley Rogers, Thelma Hill, Ruby Blaine, Charlie Hall

Two Texas Knights: see *Two Guys from Texas*

2001: A Space Odyssey ****
GB 1968 141m Metrocolor Panavision
MGM/Stanley Kubrick (Victor Lyndon)
🔲 🔲 ⊙
From ape to modern space scientist, mankind has striven to reach the unattainable.
A lengthy montage of brilliant model work and obscure symbolism, this curiosity slowly gathered commercial momentum and came to be cherished by longhairs who used it as a trip without LSD.
w Stanley Kubrick, Arthur C. Clarke *story The Sentinel* by Arthur C. Clarke *d* Stanley Kubrick *ph* Geoffrey Unsworth, John Alcott *m* various classics *pd* Tony Masters, Harry Lange, Ernie Archer *ad* John Hoesli
☆ Gary Lockwood, Keir Dullea, William Sylvester, Leonard Rossiter, Robert Beatty, Daniel Richter, Douglas Rain, Margaret Tyzack
'Somewhere between hypnotic and immensely boring.' – *Renata Adler*
'Morally pretentious, intellectually obscure and inordinately long ... intensely exciting visually, with that peculiar artistic power which comes from obsession ... a film out of control, an infuriating combination of exactitude on small points and incoherence on large ones.' – *Arthur Schlesinger Jnr*
'The satire throughout is tepid and half-hearted, and tends to look like unintended stupidity.' – *John Simon*
† Alex North's rejected score for the film has also been released on compact disc.
🎖 special effects
🏆 script; Stanley Kubrick; art direction
🎬 cinematography; production design

2010
US 1984 114m Metrocolor Panavision
MGM-UA (Peter Hyams)
🔲 🔲 ⊙
With Earth on the brink of war, scientists return to Jupiter to decide on the fate of *Discovery* and the meaning of the black monolith.
Tame, almost flatfooted sequel to 2001: A Space Odyssey, with none of the supposed significance and not much else to offer.
wd Peter Hyams *novel* Arthur C. Clarke *m* David Shire *pd* Albert Brenner *ed* James Mitchell

---

☆ Roy Scheider, John Lithgow, Helen Mirren, Bob Balaban, Keir Dullea, Dana Elcar, Madolyn Smith
⌂ art direction

Two Thousand Women
GB   1944   97m   bw
GFD/Gainsborough (Edward Black)
▣

Two pilots try to rescue British women from a French concentration camp.
Routine mix of laughter and tears; hardly an outstanding film of its time, but mildly entertaining.
wd Frank Launder ph Jack Cox md Louis Levy
☆ Phyllis Calvert, Flora Robson, Patricia Roc, Renée Houston, Anne Crawford, Jean Kent, James McKechnie, Reginald Purdell, Robert Arden, Thora Hird, Dulcie Gray, Carl Jaffe, Muriel Aked

Two Tickets to Broadway
US   1951   106m   Technicolor
RKO (Jerry Wald)
▣

Small-town college girl finds romance and success in the big city.
Very mild musical with TV studio backdrop.
w Sid Silvers, Hal Kanter d James V. Kern ph Edward Cronjager, Harry J. Wild m Walter Scharf
☆ Janet Leigh, Eddie Bracken, Gloria de Haven, Tony Martin, Barbara Lawrence, Joe Smith, Charlie Dale

Two Tickets to London
US   1943   78m   bw
Universal

A sailor accused of aiding an enemy submarine escapes and finds the true villain.
Routine wartime thick ear.
w Tom Reed d Edwin L. Marin
☆ Alan Curtis, Michele Morgan, C. Aubrey Smith, Barry Fitzgerald, Dooley Wilson, Mary Gordon

Two Way Stretch **
GB   1960   87m   bw
British Lion/Shepperton (M. Smedley Aston)
▣

Three convicts break jail to rob a maharajah.
Amusing comedy with good performances and situations, unofficially borrowed in part from Convict 99.
w John Warren, Len Heath d Robert Day ph Geoffrey Faithfull m Ken Jones

☆ Peter Sellers, *Lionel Jeffries*, Wilfrid Hyde-White, Bernard Cribbins, David Lodge, Maurice Denham, Beryl Reid, Liz Fraser, Irene Handl, George Woodbridge

Two Weeks in Another Town *
US   1962   107m   Metrocolor   Cinemascope
MGM (John Houseman)
▣   ◉

An ex-alcoholic film director gets his comeback chance in Rome but is plagued by old memories.
Self-indulgent melodrama with entertaining patches for cinéastes, especially those who saw The Bad and the Beautiful.
w Charles Schnee novel Irwin Shaw d Vincente Minnelli ph Milton Krasner m David Raksin
☆ Kirk Douglas, Edward G. Robinson, Cyd Charisse, Daliah Lavi, George Hamilton, Claire Trevor, Rosanna Schiaffino, James Gregory, George Macready
'The result may be a fantasy world, but it is a fantasy which this director understands and makes his own and into which he can breathe an intense, feverish life.' – Dilys Powell

Two Weeks with Love *
US   1950   92m   Technicolor
MGM (Jack Cummings)
▣

Adventures on a family summer holiday at the turn of the century.
Pleasant family musical.
w John Larkin, Dorothy Kingsley d Roy Rowland ph Al Gilks m Georgie Stoll
☆ Jane Powell, Ricardo Montalban, Louis Calhern, Ann Harding, Phyllis Kirk, Debbie Reynolds, Carleton Carpenter, Clinton Sundberg

Two Who Dared: see A Woman Alone

Two Women *
Italy/France   1960   110m   bw
Champion/Marceau/Cocinor/SGC (Carlo Ponti)
▣   ◉
original title: *La Ciociara*
During the Allied bombing of Rome a woman and her daughter travel arduously south and have a hard time at the hands of invading soldiers.
Rather hysterical character drama allowing for a splendid top-note performance from its star.
w Cesare Zavattini, Vittorio de Sica novel Alberto Moravia d Vittorio de Sica ph Gabor Pogany m Armando Trovaioli
☆ Sophia Loren, Eleonora Brown, Jean-Paul Belmondo, Raf Vallone

⌖ Sophia Loren
⌖ Sophia Loren

Two Yanks in Trinidad
US   1942   82m   bw
Samuel Bischoff/Columbia
Minor racketeers join the army and capture a German agent.
One of the many variations on the Flagg and Quirt formula, and not a bad one.
w Sy Bartlett, Richard Carroll, Harry Segall d Gregory Ratoff
☆ Pat O'Brien, Brian Donlevy, Janet Blair, Roger Clark, Donald MacBride, John Emery

Two Years before the Mast *
US   1946   98m   bw
Paramount (Seton I. Miller)
In the mid-19th century, a writer becomes a sailor to expose bad conditions.
Well-made but unconvincing-looking picturization of a famous book.
w Seton I. Miller, George Bruce book Richard Henry Dana d John Farrow ph Ernest Laszlo m Victor Young
☆ Alan Ladd, Brian Donlevy, William Bendix, Barry Fitzgerald, Howard da Silva, Albert Dekker, Luis Van Rooten, Darryl Hickman

Two-Faced Woman *
US   1941   90m   bw
MGM (Gottfried Reinhardt)
▣

A ski instructress, who fears she may be losing her publisher husband to another woman, poses as her own more vivacious twin sister.
The failure of this scatterbrained comedy is alleged to be the reason for Garbo's premature retirement. Looked at half a century later, it is no great shakes but harmless and eager to please; what sabotages it is a shoddy production and flagging pace.
w S. N. Behrman, Salka Viertel, George Oppenheimer play Ludwig Fulda d George Cukor ph Joseph Ruttenberg m Bronislau Kaper
☆ Greta Garbo, Melvyn Douglas, Constance Bennett, Roland Young, Robert Sterling, Ruth Gordon, George Cleveland
'It is almost as shocking as seeing your mother drunk.' – Time

The Two-Headed Spy *
GB   1958   93m   bw
Columbia (Hal E. Chester)
A bogus Nazi worms his way into the Gestapo hierarchy.

Adequate, not too exciting biopic of Colonel Alex Schottland; standard production values.
w James O'Donnell d André de Toth ph Ted Scaife m Gerard Schurmann
☆ Jack Hawkins, Gia Scala, Alexander Knox, Erik Schumann, Felix Aylmer, Laurence Naismith, Donald Pleasence, Kenneth Griffith

Two's Company
GB   1936   74m   bw
B and D/Paul Soskin
An earl's son loves the daughter of an American millionaire.
Not particularly successful hands-across-the-sea comedy.
w Tom Geraghty, Roland Pertwee, J. B. Morton, John Paddy Carstairs, Tim Whelan novel Romeo and Julia by Sidney Horler d Tim Whelan
☆ Gordon Harker, Ned Sparks, Mary Brian, Patric Knowles, Robb Wilton, Morton Selten

Tycoon
US   1947   129m   Technicolor
RKO
An engineer is hired to drive a tunnel through the Andes, and starts a feud with his boss when he falls in love with his daughter.
Boring, studio-set action saga with too many stops for romance.
w Borden Chase, John Twist d Richard Wallace ph Harry J. Wild m Leigh Harline
☆ John Wayne, Cedric Hardwicke, Laraine Day, James Gleason, Judith Anderson, Anthony Quinn, Grant Withers

Typhoon
US   1940   70m   Technicolor
Paramount (Anthony Veiller)
On a Dutch Guianan island, two sailors find a girl who has been a castaway since childhood.
One of Lamour's several sarongers, quite entertaining in its way and commendably brisk.
w Allen Rivkin d Louis King ph William Mellor m Frederick Hollander
☆ Dorothy Lamour, Robert Preston, Lynne Overman, J. Carrol Naish, Frank Reicher
'One of the most emphatically silly pictures I ever saw in my life.' – Richard Mallet, Punch
'The gem of pure, pellucid silliness.' – James

Tystnaden: see The Silence

U

U Boat 29: see *The Spy in Black*

U.F.O.
GB 1993 79m colour
Feature Film/Polygram/George Foster (Simon Wright)
▣

Feminists from outer space kidnap comedian Roy 'Chubby' Brown so that they can try him for telling offensive jokes.
Witless, cheap and nasty movie, starring the self-styled 'rudest, crudest, filthiest comedian in the world'; it is certainly crudely made and performed.
w Richard Hall, Simon Wright, Roy 'Chubby' Brown d Tony Dow ph Paul Wheeler m Clever Music pd David McHenry ed Geoff Hogg
☆ Roy 'Chubby' Brown, Sara Stockbridge, Amanda Symonds, Roger Lloyd Pack, Shirley Anne Field, Sue Lloyd, Kenny Baker
'Wildly uneven, often offensive, but with a cheerful inanity which goes some way to compensate for its grosser shortcomings.' – *Sight and Sound*

'Sex. Murder. Betrayal. Everything That Makes Life Worth Living.'
'A stranger in a strange town ... A wife with murder on her mind ... A husband who wants her dead ... They think their troubles are over ... But they've only just begun.'
U Turn *
US 1997 125m Technicolor
TriStar/Phoenix/Illusion/Clyde is Hungry (Dan Halsted, Clayton Townsend)
▣ ▤ ◉ ◉ ♫

A gambler is having a bad day: his car breaks down in a dreary small town, inhabited by nymphomaniacs and thugs, the money to pay off his debts is lost, and one of the locals wants to hire him as a hitman.
Overblown, overwrought film noir, as seen through a drug-induced haze, in which character and incident are heightened to the point of hysteria.
w John Ridley, novel Stray Dogs by John Ridley d Oliver Stone ph Robert Richardson m Ennio Morricone pd Victor Kempster ed Hank Corwin, Thomas J. Nordberg
☆ Sean Penn, Nick Nolte, Jennifer Lopez, Powers Boothe, Claire Danes, Joaquin Phoenix, Billy Bob Thornton, Jon Voight, Julie Haggerty, Bo Hopkins, Liv Tyler
'Exceedingly raw, imaginative, daring and energized ... loaded with twisted motives, brazen amorality, double dealing, incestuous relationships, subversive intent and hilarious asides.' – *Todd McCarthy*
'Oddly watchable, in the way the ever-circling buzzards find interest in the goings-on beneath them.' – *Alexander Walker, London Evening Standard*

U2 Rattle and Hum *
US 1988 99m colour/bw
Paramount/Midnight (Michael Hamlyn)
▣ ▤

Documentary on the Irish rock group recording a new album and performing at home and in the States, described by its participants as 'a musical journey'. Blues guitarist and singer B. B. King joins them for one number.
Fans will enjoy this celebration of one of the most successful groups of the period, which alternates between coarse-toned black and white and colour photography for no apparent reason; those looking for some deeper insight into the business and art of rock will need to go elsewhere.
d Phil Joanou ph Jordan Cronenweth (colour), Robert Brinkman (bw) ed Phil Joanou

Uccellacci e Uccellini: see *Hawks and Sparrows*

Ucho: see *The Ear*

Ugetsu Monogatari *
Japan 1953 94m bw
Daiei (Masaichi Nagata)

During a 16th-century civil war two potters find a way of profiteering, but their ambitions bring disaster on their families.
Unique mixture of action, comedy and the supernatural, with strong, believable characters participating and a delightfully delicate touch in script and direction. On its first release it began to figure in many best ten lists, but quickly seemed to fade from public approbation.
w Matsutaro Kawaguchi, from 17th-century collection by Akinara Ueda, Tales of a Pale and Mysterious Moon after the Rain d Kenji Mizoguchi ph Kazuo Miyagawa m Fumio Hayasaka
☆ Masayuki Mori, Machiko Kyo, Sakae Ozawa, Mitsuko Mito
'Heavy going in spots, but with marvellous passages that are worth a bit of patience.' – *New Yorker*

'You Can Run. But You Can't Hide.'
The Ugly *
New Zealand 1996 94m colour
Metrodome/NZFC/Essential (Jonathan Dowling)
▣ ▤ ◉

A psychiatrist examines an apparently insane serial killer, who claims that he is forced to murder by the ghosts of his victims.
Unsettling horror movie with a surreal tinge.
wd Scott Reynolds ph Simon Raby m Victoria Kelly pd Grant Major ed Wayne Cook
☆ Paolo Rotondo, Rebecca Hobbs, Roy Ward, Vanessa Burns, Sam Wallace, Paul Glover, Chris Graham, Jennifer Ward-Lealand
'There is a lot to admire and to be disturbed by here.' – *Kim Newman*

The Ugly American
US 1962 120m Eastmancolor
U-I/George Englund
▣

A publisher is made ambassador to a southeast Asian state.
Self-dating anti-communist drama which was muddled and boring when new.
w Stewart Stern novel William J. Lederer, Eugene Burdick d George Englund ph Clifford Stine m Frank Skinner
☆ Marlon Brando, Eiji Okada, Sandra Church, Pat Hingle, Arthur Hill, Jocelyn Brando, Kukrit Pramoj

The Ugly Dachshund *
♠♠ US 1965 93m Technicolor
Walt Disney (Winston Hibler)
▤

A dachshund bitch fosters among its puppies an orphan Great Dane.
Cheerful, fast-moving animal farce.
w Albert Aley novel G. B. Stern d Norman Tokar ph Edward Colman m George Bruns
☆ Dean Jones, Suzanne Pleshette, Charles Ruggles, Kelly Thordsen, Parley Baer, Mako, Charles Lane

'The story of a family on the edge, and a man who brought them back.'
Ulee's Gold *
US 1997 111m DuArt
Orion/Jonathan Demme/Nunez/Gowan/Clinica Estetico
▣ ▤ ◉ ♫

A bee-keeper, a middle-aged widower with family problems, is threatened by two hoodlums, associates of his jailed son and his drug-addicted wife.
A slow-moving drama that builds inexorably to its compelling, emotionally satisfying peak.

wd Victor Nunez ph Virgil Marcus Mirano m Charles Engstrom pd Robert 'Pat' Garner ed Victor Nunez
☆ Peter Fonda, Patricia Richardson, Jessica Biel, J. Kenneth Campbell, Christine Dunford, Steven Flynn, Dewey Weber
'Nunez achieves a rare, and rarely earned, emotional depth that rewards the moderate demands he makes on contemporary viewers' short attention spans.' – *Todd McCarthy, Variety*
♟ Peter Fonda

Ulisse contro Ercole: see *Ulysses versus the Sons of Hercules*

'In his world, brute force isn't enough.'
Ulterior Motives
US 1991 92m DeLuxe
Den Music/Elk/Ian Page (J. Max Kirishíma, Thomas Ian Griffith)
▣ ▤

A *New York Times* journalist hires a high-kicking private eye to help her expose a Japanese research scientist in America who is selling classified information.
Unpleasant paranoid thriller with unsympathetic characters and a little martial arts action thrown in for bad measure.
wd James Becket story James Becket, Thomas Ian Griffith ph Stephen M. Katz m Parmer Fuller pd Michael Helmy ed Virginia Katz
☆ Thomas Ian Griffith, Mary Page Keller, Joe Yamanaka, Ellen Crawford, Tyra Ferrell, M. C. Gainey, Ken Howard
'Spoilt only by the weak ending which negates our hero's most despicable act of violence.' – *Sight and Sound*
'The fight sequences are fair only.' – *Empire*

La Ultima Cena: see *The Last Supper*

La Ultima Siembra: see *The Last Harvest*

Ultimas Imagenes del Naufragio: see *Last Images of the Shipwreck*

Ultimate Revenge: see *Sioux City*

The Ultimate Solution of Grace Quigley: see *Grace Quigley*

The Ultimate Warrior
US 1975 94m Technicolor
Warner (Fred Weintraub, Paul Heller)
▤

In AD 2012 New York is ruled by a gangster, the atmosphere is poisoned, and the only hope is a new community on an island off North Carolina.
Curious pretentious fantasy without the courage of its convictions or much entertainment value.
wd Robert Clouse ph Gerald Hirschfeld m Gil Melle
☆ Yul Brynner, Max von Sydow, Joanna Miles, William Smith, Richard Kelton, Stephen McHattie
'Less a prophetic vision than a kind of thick-ear West Side Story.' – *Richard Combs*

Ultra *
Italy 1991 90m Telecolor
Sacis/Numero Uno/RAI (Claudio Bonivento)
▣
aka: *Hooligans*
A football-obsessed thief comes out of prison in Rome to reassume leadership of a gang of football fans and travels to Turin for a pitched battle with rivals.
A well-observed drama of the rougher passions that football excites, and of a group of fans defined by their exclusion – from the club management and the official supporters, from jobs, family and home.

w Simona Izzo, Graziano Diana, Giuseppe Manfridi, Ricky Tognazzi d Ricky Tognazzi ph Alessio Gelsini m Antonella Venditti ed Carla Simoncelli
☆ Claudio Amendola, Ricky Memphis, Gianmarco Tognazzi, Giuppy Izzo, Alessandro Tiberi, Fabrizio Vidale

'Actually filmed along the route he travelled 3000 years ago!'
Ulysses *
♠♠ Italy 1954 103m Technicolor
Lux Film/Ponti-de Laurentiis (Fernando Cinquini)
▣ ▤ ♫

Ulysses and his crew sail under the curse of Cassandra, and encounter Circe, the sirens and the cyclops.
Peripatetic adventure yarn not too far after Homer; narrative style uncertain but highlights good.
w Franco Brusati, Mario Camerini, Ennio de Concini, Hugh Gray, Ben Hecht, Ivo Perelli, Irwin Shaw poem The Odyssey by Homer d Mario Camerini ph Harold Rosson m Alessandro Cicognini
☆ Kirk Douglas, Silvana Mangano, Anthony Quinn, Rossana Podesta

Ulysses *
GB 1967 132m bw Panavision
Walter Reade (Joseph Strick)
▣ ▤

Twenty-four hours in Dublin with a young poet and a Jewish newspaper man.
A pleasant enough literary exercise, a decent précis of an unmanageably prolix classic novel, this specialized offering would have passed unnoticed were it not for its language, which got it banned in many places but now seems mild indeed.
w Joseph Strick, Fred Haines novel James Joyce d Joseph Strick ph Wolfgang Suschitzky m Stanley Myers
☆ Maurice Roeves, Milo O'Shea, Barbara Jefford, T. P. McKenna, Anna Manahan, Maureen Potter
'No amount of pious invoking of Joyce's name can disguise the fact that a cheaply produced film is being sold at exorbitant prices so that someone can make his boodle off "culture".' – *John Simon*
'An act of homage in the form of readings from the book plus illustrated slides.' – *Pauline Kael*
'A facile and ludicrous reduction.' – *Stanley Kauffmann*
♟ script

Ulysses' Gaze *
Greece/France/Italy 1995 177m colour
Theo Angelopoulos/GFC/Paradis/La Generale d'Images/La Sept/Basic/RAI
▣ ▤ ◉ ♫
original title: *To Vlemma Tou Odyssea*
A Greek-American director returns to his homeland after a gap of 35 years to make a documentary about pioneer film-makers and to search for their lost film.
A brooding, melancholy meditation on the past, rewarding if you can surrender to its slow pace and introspection.
w Theo Angelopoulos, Tonino Guerra, Petros Markaris d Theo Angelopoulos ph Yorgos Arvanitis m Eleni Karaindrou pd Yorgos Patsas, Mile Nicolic ed Giannis Tsitsopoulos
☆ Harvey Keitel, Maia Morgenstern, Erland Josephson, Thanassis Vengos, Yorgos Michalokopoulos, Dora Volonaki
'A tremendously challenging and demanding work that will leave audiences who latch onto its style and mood satisfied but utterly drained.' – *David Stratton, Variety*

Ulysses versus the Sons of Hercules

Italy/France   1961   82m   Eastmancolor
Fidès/CCM (G. Pasquale, A. Fantechi)

🔲

original title: *Ulisse contro Ercole*

The sons of Hercules are told to capture Ulysses so that he can be punished by the Cyclops.
Minor sword-and-sandal epic with a great deal of muscle-flexing.
w Mario Caiano, André Tabet d Mario Caiano
ph Alvaro Mancori m Angelo Francesco Lavagnino pd Piero Filippone ed Renato Cinquini sp Galliano Ricci
☆ Georges Marchal, Michael Lane, Alessandro Panaro, Gianni Santuccio, Yvette Lebon, Eleonora Bianchi, Gabrielle Tinti

'Only one man understood the savagery of the early American west!'

Ulzana's Raid

US   1972   103m   Technicolor
Universal/Carter de Haven/Robert Aldrich

🔲 🔲 🔲 🔲

An ageing Indian fighter and a tenderfoot officer lead a platoon sent out to counter a murderous Apache attack.
Bloodthirsty, reactionary Western with unpleasant shock moments.
w Alan Sharp d Robert Aldrich ph Joseph Biroc
m Frank de Vol
☆ Burt Lancaster, Bruce Davison, Jorge Luke, Richard Jaeckel, Lloyd Bochner

Umberto D **

Italy   1952   89m   bw
Dear Films

🔲 🔲

A retired civil servant can barely afford his rent but won't part with his dog.
Downbeat, immensely moving study of old age in a society which fails to provide for it.
w Cesare Zavattini, Vittorio de Sica d *Vittorio de Sica* ph G. R. Aldo m Alessandro Cicognini
☆ *Carlo Battista*, Maria Pia Casilio, Lina Gennari
'There isn't a minute of banality in this simple, direct film.' – *New Yorker*
🎭 Cesare Zavattini (original story)

The Umbrellas of Cherbourg: see *Les Parapluies de Cherbourg*

Una su 13: see *Twelve Plus One*

Unaccustomed as We Are

🏃 US   1929   20m   bw   silent
Hal Roach
🔲

Ollie takes a friend home to dinner, but his wife walks out, leaving him to get into all kinds of trouble.
The team's first sound comedy, rather hesitant in its use of the new medium. The story was later reworked as the last half hour of Blockheads.
w Leo McCarey, H. M. Walker d Lewis R. Foster
ph George Stevens, Len Powers ed Richard Currier
☆ Stan Laurel, Oliver Hardy, Edgar Kennedy, Mae Busch, Thelma Todd

The Unbearable Lightness of Being **

US   1987   172m   Technicolor/DeLuxe
Saul Zaentz

🔲 🔲 🔲 🔲 🔲

A womanizing brain surgeon and his two lovers painfully achieve maturity after the putting down of the Prague Spring by Soviet troops.
Brave and largely successful attempt to transfer a complex, ironic Czech novel to the screen.
w Jean-Claude Carrière, Philip Kaufman
novel Milan Kundera d *Philip Kaufman* ph Sven Nykvist m Leos Janáček pd Pierre Guffroy
☆ Daniel Day-Lewis, Juliette Binoche, Lena Olin, Erland Josephson, Daniel Olbrychski
'It's a prankish sex comedy that treats modern political events with a delicate – yet almost sly – sense of tragedy. It's touching in sophisticated ways that you don't expect from an American director.' – *Pauline Kael, New Yorker*
🎬 Sven Nykvist; best adapted screenplay
🎬 adapted screenplay

Unbelievable Truth *

US   1989   90m   colour
Electric/Contemporary/Action (Bruce Weiss, Hal Hartley)

🔲 🔲 🔲

A convicted murderer returns to his home town and attracts the intellectual daughter of his employer, a garage owner.
Clever low-budget first feature of an unlikely romance.
wd Hal Hartley ph Michael Spiller m Jim Coleman pd Carla Gerona ed Hal Hartley
☆ Adrienne Shelly, Robert Burke, Christopher Cooke, Julia McNeal, Mark Bailey, Gary Sauer, Katherine Mayfield

The Uncanny

Canada/GB   1977   85m   colour
Rank/Cinevideo/Tor (Claude Héroux, Milton Subotsky)

🔲

An author tells his publisher three stories about evil cats.
Below-par horror compendium with crude effects failing to bolster a sagging script.
w Michel Parry d Denis Héroux ph Harry Waxman, James Bawden m Wilfred Josephs
☆ Peter Cushing, Ray Milland, Susan Penhaligon, Joan Greenwood, Simon Williams, Roland Culver, Alexandra Stewart, Donald Pleasence, Samantha Eggar, John Vernon

Uncensored

GB   1942   108m   bw
GFD/Gainsborough (Edward Black)
In Brussels during the Nazi occupation, the leader of a toe-the-line paper secretly leads the patriots.
Unconvincing underground melodrama with stilted presentation and performances.
w Wolfgang Wilhelm, Terence Rattigan, Rodney Ackland novel Oscar Millard d Anthony Asquith ph Arthur Crabtree m Hans May
☆ Eric Portman, Phyllis Calvert, Griffith Jones, Raymond Lovell, Peter Glenville, Irene Handl, Carl Jaffe, Felix Aylmer

Uncertain Glory

US   1944   102m   bw
Warner (Robert Buckner)

🔲

During World War II, a French playboy sacrifices himself for his country.
Tame star vehicle needing more action and less philosophy.
w Laszlo Vadnay, Max Brand d Raoul Walsh
ph Sid Hickox m Adolph Deutsch
☆ Errol Flynn, Paul Lukas, Jean Sullivan, Lucile Watson, Faye Emerson, James Flavin, Douglass Dumbrille, Dennis Hoey

Uncertain Lady

US   1934   63m   bw
Universal
An executive wife recovers her husband from the clutches of another woman.
Transparent comedy with the principals ill cast.
w Daniel Evena, Martin Brown play Harry Segal
d Karl Freund
☆ Edward Everett Horton, Genevieve Tobin, Renee Gadd, Paul Cavanagh, Mary Nash

Unchained

US   1955   75m   bw
Warner/Hall Bartlett
A new governor experiments with a prison without bars.
Decent documentary drama which reaches no great heights.
wd Hall Bartlett book *Prisoners Are People* by Kenyon J. Scudder ph Virgil Miller m Alex North
☆ Chester Morris, Elroy Hirsch, Barbara Hale, Todd Duncan, Johnny Johnston, Peggy Knudsen, Jerry Paris, John Qualen
🎵 title song (mAlex North, lyHy Zarek)

The Uncle

GB   1964   87m   bw
Play-Pix
A 7-year-old boy finds he is uncle to a boy the same age.
Comedy-drama about the first stirrings of maturity; its failure to find a release got it championed by some critics, but it's essentially a thin piece of work.
w Margaret Abrams, Desmond Davis
novel Margaret Abrams d Desmond Davis

☆ Rupert Davies, Brenda Bruce, Maurice Denham, Christopher Ariss

Uncle Benjamin

France   1969   90m   Eastmancolor
Gaumont International (Robert Sussfeld, Roger Debelmas)
original title: *Mon Oncle Benjamin*
A rakish country doctor tries to seduce the virginal daughter of the local innkeeper.
A Gallic attempt at the bawdy zest of Tom Jones, often coarse in tone and closer to the Carry On films in style.
w André Couteaux, Jean-François Hauduro, Edouard Molinaro d Edouard Molinaro ph Alain Levent m Jacques Brel, François Rauber
ed Robert and Monique Isnardon
☆ Jacques Brel, Claude Jade, Rosy Varte, Bernard Alane, Paul Frankeur, Alfred Adam, Bernard Blier

Uncle Buck *

🏃 US   1989   100m   DeLuxe
UIP/Universal (John Hughes, Tom Jacobson)

🔲 🔲 🔲

A good-natured but slobbish layabout straightens out his sister's warring children and learns to love domesticity.
Rambling, moderately enjoyable comedy, although it is not far removed from a television sit-com.
wd John Hughes ph Ralf D. Bode m Ira Newborn pd John W. Corso ed Lou Lombardo, Tom Lombardo, Peck Prior
☆ John Candy, Jean Louisa Kelly, Gaby Hoffman, Macaulay Culkin, Amy Madigan, Elaine Bromka, Garrett M. Brown

Uncle Harry: see *The Strange Affair of Uncle Harry*

Uncle Silas *

GB   1947   103m   bw
GFD/Two Cities (Josef Somlo, Laurence Irving)

🔲

US title: *The Inheritance*
A young Victorian heiress finds herself menaced by her uncle and his housekeeper.
Slow-starting but superbly made period suspenser; unfortunately the characters are all sticks.
w Ben Travers novel Sheridan Le Fanu d Charles Frank ph Robert Krasker m Alan Rawsthorne
☆ Jean Simmons, Derrick de Marney, Katina Paxinou, Derek Bond, Esmond Knight, Sophie Stewart, Manning Whiley, Reginald Tate, Marjorie Rhodes

Uncommon Valor

US   1983   105m   Movielab
Paramount/Ted Kotcheff (John Milius, Buzz Feitshans)

🔲 🔲 🔲

A retired colonel goes looking for his son, declared missing in action in Vietnam, and is helped by a similarly placed industrialist who backs a rescue raid.
Slam-bang action piece with the customary patriotic and personal sentiment.
w Joe Gayton d Ted Kotcheff ph Stephen H. Burum m James Horner pd James L. Schoppe
☆ Gene Hackman, Robert Stack, Fred Ward, Reb Brown, Randall Cobb, Patrick Swayze

'Plunging over the falls – lashed at the stake – trapped by savages in the mightiest love-spectacle de Mille ever filmed!'
'I bought this woman for my own … and I'll kill the man who touches her!'

Unconquered

US   1947   146m   Technicolor
Paramount/Cecil B. de Mille

🔲

An 18th-century English convict girl is deported to the American colonies and suffers various adventures before marrying a Virginia militiaman.
Cardboard epic, expensive and noisy but totally unpersuasive despite cannon, arrows, fire and dynamite.
w Charles Bennett, Fredric M. Frank, Jesse Lasky Jnr novel Neil H. Swanson d Cecil B. de Mille
ph Ray Rennahan m Victor Young
☆ *Paulette Goddard*, Gary Cooper, Boris Karloff, Howard da Silva, Cecil Kellaway, Ward Bond, Katherine de Mille, Henry Wilcoxon, C. Aubrey Smith, Victor Varconi, Virginia Grey, Porter Hall, Mike Mazurki

'De Mille bangs the drum as loudly as ever but his sideshow has gone cold on us.' – *Richard Winnington*
'A five-million dollar celebration of Gary Cooper's virility, Paulette Goddard's femininity, and the American frontier spirit.' – *Time*

Unconventional Linda: see *Holiday (1938)*

The Undead

US   1956   75m   bw
Balboa Productions (Roger Corman)

🔲

A psychic researcher hypnotizes a prostitute, sending her back to a past life in a medieval world of witchcraft and magic.
A tale told by the devil, but signifying no more than the usual ineptly acted fantasy.
w Charles Griffith, Mark Hanna d Roger Corman
ph William Sickner m Ronald Stein ed Frank Sullivan
☆ Pamela Duncan, Richard Garland, Allison Hayes, Val Dufour, Mel Welles, Dorothy Neumann, Billy Barty

The Undefeated

US   1969   119m   DeLuxe   Panavision
TCF (Robert L. Jacks)

🔲 🔲

After the Civil War, two colonels from opposite sides meet on the Rio Grande.
Sprawling, lethargic star Western with moments of glory.
w James Lee Barrett d Andrew V. McLaglen
ph William H. Clothier m Hugo Montenegro
☆ John Wayne, Rock Hudson, Lee Meriwether, Tony Aguilar, Roman Gabriel

Under a Texas Moon

US   1930   70m   Technicolor
Warner
A rancher of the Don Juan type makes hay with the ladies but also rounds up cattle rustlers.
Lightweight early talkie outdoor spectacle with music, not at all memorable.
w Gordon Rigby, Stewart Edward White
d Michael Curtiz ph Bill Rees song Ray Perkins
☆ *Frank Fay*, Myrna Loy, Raquel Torres, Armida, Noah Beery, George E. Stone, Fred Kohler
'Unusually pleasing western … de luxe programmer of its kind.' – *Variety*

Under California Stars

US   1948   70m   Trucolor
Republic (Edward J. White)
After celebrating his 10th anniversary as a film star, Roy Rogers rides out to deal with the crooks who have kidnapped Trigger, 'the smartest horse in the West', an activity that does not prevent him singing songs at the drop of a stetson.
Amiably daft Western in Rogers' usual mode of music, comedy and occasional mayhem.
w Sloan Nibley, Paul Gangelin d William Witney
ph Jack Marta m Morton Scott ad Frank Hotaling ed Tony Martinelli
☆ Roy Rogers, Jane Frazee, Andy Devine, Bob Nolan and the Sons of the Pioneers.

Under Capricorn

GB   1949   117m   Technicolor
Transatlantic (Sidney Bernstein, Alfred Hitchcock)

🔲 🔲

In Australia in 1830 an English immigrant stays with his cousin Henrietta, who has become a dipsomaniac because of her husband's cruelty.
Cardboard 'woman's picture' with elements of Rebecca, shot with vestiges of Hitch's ten-minute take. A pretty fair disaster.
w James Bridie novel Helen Simpson d Alfred Hitchcock ph Jack Cardiff, Paul Beeson, Ian Craig m Richard Addinsell
☆ Ingrid Bergman, Joseph Cotten, Michael Wilding, Margaret Leighton, Jack Watling, Cecil Parker, Denis O'Dea
'A lengthy, unhurried, and generally quiet picture, directed by Hitchcock with the dreamy contemplation of one embarked on a long sea voyage … I can't feel that the choice of subject is a very happy one, for either Hitchcock or his actors.' – *C. A. Lejeune*

Under Cover of Night

US   1937   70m   bw
MGM (Lucien Hubbard)
A city detective and his wife nab a murderer.

One of many to which this plot might be applied in the wake of The Thin Man, *and not a good example.*
w Bertram Millhauser d George B. Seitz
☆ Edmund Lowe, Florence Rice, Henry Daniell, Nat Pendleton, Sara Haden, Dean Jagger, Frank Reicher

Under Fire *
US 1983 127m Technicolor
Orion/Lion's Gate/Greenberg Brothers (Jonathan Taplin)
◉◉ ▦ ⊗ ⌒
War correspondents in Nicaragua become involved in the dirty politics on both sides.
A thinking man's action piece, but no help to anybody in finding the true facts.
w Ron Shelton, Clayton Frohman d Roger Spottiswoode ph John Alcott m Jerry Goldsmith
☆ Gene Hackman, Nick Nolte, Joanna Cassidy, Jean-Louis Trintignant, Ed Harris, Richard Masur, Rene Enriquez
'A complex, genuinely thrilling drama of commitment, the mercenary mentality and the tortuous ironies of history.' – *Sight and Sound*
♫ Jerry Goldsmith

Under Milk Wood *
GB 1971 88m Technicolor
Timon (Hugo French, Jules Buck)
◉◉ ▦
Life in the Welsh village of Llareggub, as seen by the poet's eye.
Attractive but vaguely unsatisfactory screen rendering of an essentially theatrical event (originally a radio play); everything is much too literal, a real place instead of a fantasy.
wd Andrew Sinclair play Dylan Thomas ph Bob Huke m Brian Gascoigne
☆ Richard Burton, Elizabeth Taylor, Peter O'Toole, Glynis Johns, Vivien Merchant, Sian Phillips, Victor Spinetti, Rachel Thomas, Angharad Rees, Ann Beach

Under My Skin
US 1949 86m bw
TCF (Casey Robinson)
A crooked jockey is idolized by his son and finally reforms rather than disillusion the boy.
Hokey sentimental melodrama with racetrack backgrounds.
w Casey Robinson short story My Old Man by Ernest Hemingway d Jean Negulesco ph Joseph LaShelle m Daniele Amfitheatrof
☆ John Garfield, Micheline Presle, Luther Adler, Orley Lindgren, Ann Codee

Under Satan's Sun *
France 1987 98m colour
Cannon/Erato films/A2/Action Films (Daniel Toscan du Plantier)
▦
original title: *Sous le Soleil du Satan*
A rural priest begins to believe that Satan is controlling mankind.
Austere examination of the nature of religious belief that won the Palme d'Or for best film at the 1987 Cannes Film Festival.
w Sylvie Danton novel Georges Bernanos d Maurice Pialat ph Willy Kurant m Henri Dutilleux ad Katia Vischkof ed Yann Dedet
☆ Gérard Depardieu, Sandrine Bonnaire, Maurice Pialat, Alain Artur, Yann Dedet, Brigitte Legendre

'1992 ... Stop ... Battleship Besieged By Terrorists ... Stop ... Nuclear Warheads Stolen ... Stop ... Crew Helpless ... Stop ... Lone Man Fighting To Save Ship...'
Under Siege
US 1992 102m Technicolor
Warner (Arnon Milchan, Steven Seagal, Steven Reuther)
◉◉ ▦ ⊗ ⊙ ⌒
A ship's cook, aided by a stripper, saves the day after a battleship is hijacked by a force of highly trained killers intent on stealing its nuclear weapons.
Often risible, always predictable action movie in which one man conquers all, and consisting of a succession of slickly done martial arts combats and gun battles. For diehard fans of the star, or fans of Die Hard.
w J. F. Lawton d Andrew Davis ph Frank Tidy m Gary Chang pd Bill Kenney m Robert A. Ferretti

☆ Steven Seagal, Tommy Lee Jones, Gary Busey, Erika Eleniak, Patrick O'Neal, Damian Chapa, Troy Evans, David McKnight, Lee Hinton
'An immensely slick, if also old-fashioned and formulaic, entertainment. Steven Seagal fans and action buffs should eat this up.' – *Variety*
'This delivers lean, suspenseful, he-man heroics with all the whizz-bang aplomb you could wish for.' – *Matt Mueller, Empire*
♫ Sound; sound effects editing

Under Siege 2: Dark Territory
US 1995 99m Technicolor
Warner/Regency (Steven Seagal, Steve Perry, Arnon Milchan)
◉◉ ▦ ⊗ ⊙ ⌒
A former CIA agent finds himself on a train hijacked by a mad military genius who plans to blow up the world if his ransom demands are not met.
Idiotic action film with a dull and doltish hero, enlivened by a few spectacular stunts; rather as vaudeville theatres used to end with a bad act in order to get audiences to leave quickly, Seagal sings a song he wrote himself over the final credits.
w Richard Hatem, Matt Reeves d Geoff Murphy ph Robbie Greenberg, Alexander Witt, Rick Bota m Basil Poledouris pd Albert Brenner ed Michael Tronick
☆ Steven Seagal, Eric Bogosian, Everett McGill, Katherine Heigl, Morris Chestnut, Brenda Bakke, Nick Mancuso
'Muscle-bending, mind-numbing action at high-decibel levels for the lowest and least discriminating common denominator.' – *Leonard Klady, Variety*
'Nothing one says can possibly affect the money-spinning capacity of so routine a corporate product, which does without style, characterisation or even basic coherence in order to give the undemanding audience worldwide what it presumably paid for: a spiralling body count and explosions.' – *Peter Matthews, Sight and Sound*

Under Suspicion *
GB 1991 100m colour
Rank/Carnival/Columbia/LWT (Brian Eastman)
◉◉ ▦ ⊗
In the 1950s, a private detective specializing in divorce is accused of murdering his client and his wife when they are found dead in a hotel room.
Moody attempt at a film noir that looks clumsy when set against the classics of the genre.
wd Simon Moore ph Vernon Layton, Ivan Strasberg m Christopher Gunning pd Tim Hutchinson ed Tariq Anwar
☆ Liam Neeson, Kenneth Cranham, Laura San Giacomo, Maggie O'Neill, Alan Talbot, Malcolm Storry, Martin Grace, Kevin Moore
'Displays most of the virtues of a well-constructed seaside roller-coaster. Twists, switchbacks, lots of flashing lights and gaudy paintwork: no great emotional significance but a thoroughly exhilarating ride.' – *Philip Kemp, Sight and Sound*
'A taut and entertaining mystery melodrama.' – *Vincent Canby, New York Times*

Under Ten Flags
US 1960 92m bw
Paramount/Dino de Laurentiis
In World War II, a German surface raider in disguise menaces British shipping.
Muddled naval epic with too many allegiances.
w Vittorio Petrilli, Duilio Coletti, Ulrich Mohr, William Douglas Home d Duilio Coletti, Silvio Narizzano ph Aldo Tonti m Nino Rota
☆ Van Heflin, Charles Laughton, John Ericson, Mylène Demongeot, Cecil Parker, Folco Lulli, Alex Nicol, Liam Redmond

Under the Clock: see The Clock

Under the Gun
US 1950 83m bw
Universal-International
A racketeer is jailed and tries to escape.
Lower-case prison adventure without much conviction.
w George Zuckerman d Ted Tetzlaff ph Henry Freulich m Joseph Gershenson
☆ Richard Conte, Audrey Totter, John McIntire, Sam Jaffe, Shepperd Strudwick

Under the Pampas Moon
US 1935 78m bw
Fox
A gaucho leader recovers his stolen horse.
Amiable modern adventure set in Argentina.
w Ernest Pascal, Bradley King d James Tinling
☆ Warner Baxter, Ketti Gallian, Rita Hayworth, Jack La Rue, J. Carrol Naish

Under the Rainbow
US 1981 95m colour
Orion/Warner
▦
Nazis and midgets mingle backstage while *The Wizard of Oz* is being filmed.
Zany fantasy which someone must have thought was a good idea. Wrong.
w Pat McCormick, Harry Hurwitz, Martin Smith, Pat Bradley, Fred Bauer d Steve Rash
☆ Chevy Chase, Carrie Fisher, Billy Barty, Eve Arden, Joseph Maher
† The film allegedly cost 20 million dollars and took eight.

Under the Red Robe *
GB 1937 82m bw
New World (Robert T. Kane)
▦
A hell-raising nobleman is persuaded by Cardinal Richelieu to unmask the ringleader of an anti-monarchist conspiracy.
Smart, unusual swashbuckler on the lines of The Prisoner of Zenda, modestly but quite effectively made.
w Lajos Biro, Philip Lindsay, J. L. Hodson novel Stanley J. Weyman d Victor Sjostrom ph Georges Périnal
☆ Conrad Veidt, Raymond Massey, Annabella, Romney Brent, Sophie Stewart, Wyndham Goldie, Lawrence Grant
'Gripping meller of swashbuckling era ... surprisingly fine entertainment.' – *Variety*

Under the Roofs of Paris: see Sous les Toits de Paris

Under the Skin **
GB 1997 83m colour
BFI/Channel 4/Strange Dog/Rouge/MFP (Kate Ogborn)
◉◉
After their mother dies from a brain tumour, two sisters deal with their grief in different ways, one taking refuge in casual sex.
A gritty film about sibling rivalry and reconciliation, powered by excellent acting and observant direction.
wd Carine Adler ph Barry Ackroyd m Ilona Sekacz pd John-Paul Kelly ed Ewa J. Lind
☆ Samantha Morton, Claire Rushbrook, Rita Tushingham, Mark Womack, Matthew Delamere, Christine Tremarco, Stuart Townsend
'Its levels of integrity and accomplishment place it among the most impressive and affecting British films of the year.' – *Richard Williams, Guardian*
† It won the Michael Powell Award for the best British feature at the 1997 Edinburgh Film Festival.

Under the Volcano *
US 1984 111m Technicolor
TCF/Ithaca/Michael and Kathy Fitzgerald (Moritz Borman, Wieland Schulz-Keil)
▦ ⊗
Mexico 1938: the ex-British consul, drinking himself to death, is surprised by a visit from his ex-wife.
A subtle novel has on film become a drunken monologue, fascinating as a tour de force but scarcely tolerable after the first half-hour.
w Guy Gallo novel Malcolm Lowry d John Huston ph Gabriel Figueroa m Alex North pd Gunther Gerzso
☆ Albert Finney, Jacqueline Bisset, Anthony Andrews, Katy Jurado, James Villiers
'Ultimately one is left not, as in the novel, with a man destroyed by the apocalypse of his own imagination, but with little more than another world-weary cuckold following in the wake of Greene's whisky priest and all those other drunkards who have mooned in Mexico.' – *Tom Milne, MFB*
♫ Albert Finney; music

'Here Comes Jack And Those Yum-Yum Girls – With "Yes-Yes" On Their Lips And Yum-Yum In Their Eyes!'
Under the Yum Yum Tree
US 1963 110m Eastmancolor
Columbia/Sonnis/Swift (Frederick Brisson)
Two college students have a trial marriage in an apartment block with a lecherous landlord.
Coy, non-erotic and extremely tedious comedy which runs out of jokes after reel one.
w Lawrence Roman, David Swift d David Swift ph Joseph Biroc m Frank de Vol
☆ Jack Lemmon, Carol Lynley, Dean Jones, Imogene Coca, Edie Adams, Paul Lynde, Robert Lansing
'A disgusting comedy in which we're supposed to be titillated to hear young people speak of sleeping together and then to be reassured when they carry on and on and on about not quite doing so.' – *Brendan Gill, New Yorker*

'Love as burning as Sahara's sands!'
Under Two Flags *
US 1936 111m bw
TCF (Raymond Griffith)
A dashing French Foreign Legionnaire is helped by a café girl.
Despite a highly predictable plot (of Destry Rides Again) this was a solidly-produced epic with a nice deployment of star talent.
w W. P. Lipscomb, Walter Ferris novel 'Ouida' d Frank Lloyd ph Ernest Palmer m Louis Silvers
☆ Ronald Colman, Claudette Colbert, Rosalind Russell, Victor McLaglen, J. Edward Bromberg, Nigel Bruce, Herbert Mundin, Gregory Ratoff, C. Henry Gordon, John Carradine, Onslow Stevens
'How Ouida would have loved the abandon of this picture, the thirty-two thousand rounds of ammunition shot off into the Arizona desert, the cast of more than ten thousand, the five thousand pounds which insured the stars against camel bites ... and, in the words of the programme, a fort two hundred feet square, an Arabian oasis with eight full-sized buildings, a forest of transplanted date palms, two Arabian cities, a horse market and a smaller fort.' – *Graham Greene*

Under Western Skies
US 1945 83m bw
Universal (Warren Wilson)
A small-town schoolmaster falls in love with the singer from a travelling vaudeville show that is down on its luck.
Comic Western with a few indifferent songs and dances; neither cast nor director displays any interest in the creaking narrative.
w Stanley Roberts, Clyde Bruckman d Jean Yarbrough ph Charles Van Enger m/ly Milton Rosen/Everett Carter md H. J. Salter ad John B. Goodman ed Arthur Hilton
☆ Martha O'Driscoll, Noah Beery Jnr, Leo Carrillo, Leon Errol, Ian Keith, Jennifer Holt, Frank Lackteen

Under Your Hat *
GB 1940 79m bw
Grand National (Jack Hulbert)
Film stars chase spies and recover a stolen carburettor.
Light-hearted adaptation of a stage musical, showing the stars in their best film form.
w Rodney Ackland, Anthony Kimmins play Jack Hulbert, Archie Menzies, Geoffrey Kerr, Arthur Macrae d Maurice Elvey ph Mutz Greenbaum (Max Greene)
☆ Jack Hulbert, Cicely Courtneidge, Austin Trevor, Leonora Corbett, Cecil Parker, H. F. Maltby, Glynis Johns, Charles Oliver

Undercover: see Maisie (Undercover Maisie) (1939)

Undercover
GB 1943 80m bw
Ealing (Michael Balcon)
Yugoslavian partisans fight the Nazis.
A rather obviously English cast doesn't help to make this flagwaver convincing.
w John Dighton, Monja Danischewsky story George Slocombe d Sergei Nolbandov ph W. Cooper m Frederic Austin ad Duncan Sutherland ed Sidney Cole, Eily Boland
☆ Tom Walls, Michael Wilding, Mary Morris, John Clements, Godfrey Tearle, Robert Harris, Rachel Thomas, Stephen Murray, Charles Victor

---

Undercover Blues

US　1993　90m　DuArt
MGM (Mike Lobell)

📺 📺 ⏺

A married couple who are also FBI agents have trouble with a vengeful mugger while trying to capture an arms dealer.
A comedy that desperately strains for laughs without delivering any; it is almost a throwback to the spy spoofs of the 60s.
w Ian Abrams d Herbert Ross ph Donald E. Thorin m David Newman pd Ken Adam ed Patricia Nedd-Friendly, Gregg London
☆ Kathleen Turner, Dennis Quaid, Fiona Shaw, Stanley Tucci, Larry Miller, Obba Babatunde, Tom Arnold, Park Overall
'Plays like a big-screen, big-budget pilot for a TV series.' – *Variety*
'Virtually incomprehensible and unfunny to boot. A waste of two good talents.' – *Derek Malcolm*

Undercover Girl

US　1950　80m　bw
Universal-International
A New York policewoman goes undercover to avenge her father's murder.
Rather tedious crime programmer.
w Harry Essex d Joseph Pevney
☆ Alexis Smith, Scott Brady, Richard Egan, Gladys George, Edmon Ryan, Gerald Mohr

Undercover Girl

GB　1958　67m　bw
Butcher's/Bill & Michael Luckwell (Kay Luckwell)
A journalist investigates the murder of his brother-in-law, a crime reporter.
Dull, by-the-numbers thriller, remarkable only for the poverty of imagination shown by all those involved.
w Bernard Lewis, Bill Luckwell d Francis Searle ph Geoffrey Faithfull md Bill Trytel ad Dennis Pavitt ed Douglas Myers
☆ Paul Carpenter, Kay Callard, Bruce Seton, Monica Grey, Jackie Collins, Maya Koumani

Undercover Man

US　1932　74m　bw
Paramount
A man avenges his father's death by going undercover for the FBI and nabbing a bond-stealing gang.
Routine gangster thriller with situations well worn even in 1932.
w Garrett Fort, Francis Faragoh d James Flood
☆ George Raft, Nancy Carroll, Roscoe Karns, Gregory Ratoff, Lew Cody

Undercover Man *

US　1949　89m　bw
Columbia (Robert Rossen)
US treasury agents indict a gang leader for tax evasion.
Good semi-documentary crime melodrama based on the Al Capone case.
w Sydney Boehm, Malvin Wald d Joseph H. Lewis ph Burnett Guffey m George Duning
☆ Glenn Ford, Nina Foch, Barry Kelley, James Whitmore, David Wolf, Esther Minciotti

Undercovers Hero: see *Soft Beds, Hard Battles*

Undercurrent *

US　1946　116m　bw
MGM (Pandro S. Berman)
📺
A professor's daughter marries an industrialist and is frightened and finally endangered by the mystery surrounding his brother.
Overlong suspenser with solid performances and production values; a variation on Gaslight.
w Edward Chodorov story Thelma Strabel d Vincente Minnelli ph Karl Freund m Herbert Stothart
☆ Katharine Hepburn, Robert Taylor, Robert Mitchum, Edmund Gwenn, Marjorie Main, Jayne Meadows, Clinton Sundberg, Dan Tobin
'The indigestible plot, full of false leads and unkept promises, is like a woman's magazine serial consumed at one gulp.' – *Time*

Underground

US　1941　95m　bw
Warner (William Jacobs)
Underground leaders in Germany during World War II send out radio messages under the noses of the Nazis.
Forgotten actioner, quite solidly made.
w Charles Grayson d Vincent Sherman ph Sid Hickox m Adolph Deutsch
☆ Jeffrey Lynn, Philip Dorn, Karen Verne, Mona Maris, Frank Reicher, Martin Kosleck, Ilka Gruning

Underground

US　1970　100m　DeLuxe
UA/Levy-Gardner-Laven
An American paratrooper joins a French resistance group to kidnap a Nazi general.
Routine war actioner.
w Ron Bishop, Andy Lewis d Arthur H. Nadel ph Ken Talbot m Stanley Myers
☆ Robert Goulet, Danièle Gaubert, Lawrence Dobkin, Carl Duering

Underground *

France/Germany/Hungary　1995　170m　colour
Artificial Eye/Mayfair/CiBy 2000/Pandora/Novo (Pierre Spengler)
📺 📺
original title: *Il était une fois un pays*
Two petty crooks in Belgrade survive changing times, from the Second World War to the break-up of Yugoslavia in the 90s.
A long and involved drama on Yugoslavian identity, which it takes to be a myth created for his own purposes by Tito; ranging in time from the 40s to the 90s, it depends on a sort of magic realism, with ghosts from the past still inhabiting the present.
w Dusan Kovacevic, Emir Kusturica play Dusan Kovacevic d Emir Kusturica ph Vilko Filac m Goran Bregovic pd Miljan Kljakovic ed Branka Ceperac
☆ Miki Manojlovic, Lazar Ristovski, Mirjana Jokovic, Slavko Stimac, Ernst Stotzner
'A steamroller circus that leaves the viewer dazed and exhausted, but mightily impressed.' – *Deborah Young, Variety*
† Originally shown at 192m, it won the Palme d'Or at the Cannes Film Festival in 1995.

The Underneath *

US　1995　100m　colour
UIP/Gramercy (John Hardy)
📺 📺
A security guard who rekindles his affair with a former girlfriend plans a way to get rid of her husband, a vicious bank robber.
A movie that takes the heat out of its story of a manipulative woman and a double-crossing man, substituting instead a cool character study of irresponsible individuals.
w Sam Lowry, Daniel Fuchs d Steven Soderbergh ph Elliot Davis m Cliff Martinez pd Howard Cummings ed Stan Salfas
☆ Peter Gallagher, Alison Elliott, William Fichtner, Adam Trese, Joe Don Baker, Paul Dooley, Elisabeth Shue, Anjanette Comer
'It plays more like an art film than as a suspense melodrama, but effort will linger resonantly in the minds of those who tune into its rather rarefied wavelength.' – *Todd McCarthy, Variety*
† A remake of Criss Cross (qv), directed by Robert Siodmak in 1948 and starring Burt Lancaster, Yvonne de Carlo and Dan Duryea.

Underneath the Arches

GB　1937　71m　bw
Julius Hagen/Twickenham
Ship stowaways help to prevent a peace gas from getting into the wrong hands.
Moderate star comedy with music.
w H. Fowler Mear story Alison Booth d Redd Davis m Sydney Blythe
☆ Flanagan and Allen, Stella Moya, Enid Stamp Taylor, Lyn Harding, Edmund Willard, Edward Ashley

The Underpup

US　1939　81m　bw
Joe Pasternak/Universal
A slum girl wins a country holiday among rich folk who ignore her.
Light comedy-drama with music which seemed about to launch a rival to Deanna Durbin.
w Grover Jones d Richard Wallace

☆ Gloria Jean, Robert Cummings, Nan Grey, C. Aubrey Smith, Beulah Bondi, Virginia Weidler, Raymond Walburn, Margaret Lindsay

Undersea Kingdom

US　1936　bw
Republic
At the bottom of the ocean lies Atlantis, where the White Robes are in constant battle with the Black Robes.
Slightly hilarious chapter play.
d B. Reeves Eason, Joseph Kane
☆ Ray 'Crash' Corrigan, Lois Wilde, Monte Blue, William Farnum, Smiley Burnette, Lon Chaney Jnr, Raymond Hatton
† Serial in 12 episodes.

Undertow

US　1949　70m　bw
Universal-International
An ex-racketeer proves his innocence when a big-time gambler is murdered.
Stock suspense crime story, not at all memorable.
w Arthur T. Horman, Lee Loeb d William Castle ph Irving Glassberg
☆ Scott Brady, John Russell, Dorothy Hart, Peggy Dow, Bruce Bennett

Underwater!

US　1955　99m　Technicolor　SuperScope
RKO/Howard Hughes
📺 ⏺
Treasure hunters dive in the Caribbean for sunken pirate treasure.
Flabby adventure yarn, badly designed for the purpose of showing off its star in a variety of dress and undress.
w Walter Newman, Hugh King, Robert B. Bailey d John Sturges ph Harry J. Wild, Lamar Boren m Roy Webb
☆ Jane Russell, Gilbert Roland, Richard Egan, Lori Nelson, Robert Keith, Joseph Calleia
'This presentation of Miss Russell is like one of those fountain pens guaranteed to write under water – novel, but impractical.' – *Bosley Crowther, New York Times*

Underwater Warrior

US　1958　91m　bw　Cinemascope
MGM (Ivan Tors)
A naval reserve commander trains frogmen.
Dry semi-documentary drama, unlikely to win any recruits.
w Gene Levitt d Andrew Marton
☆ Dan Dailey, Ross Martin, James Gregory, Claire Kelly

'Revolvers bark! Figures steal slowly among the shadows of the night! Then all is still ... That's just a bit of the underworld!'
'It takes you to the haunts of the human birds of prey, to the refuge of the hunted!'

Underworld *

US　1927　82m　bw　silent
Paramount (Hector Turnbull)
GB title: *Paying the Penalty*
A gangster is rescued from prison by his moll and his lieutenant, and when he realizes they are in love he allows them to escape when the law closes in.
An innovative film in its time, this melodrama was the first to look at crime from the gangsters' point of view. Its main appeal now lies in its lush direction.
w Ben Hecht, Robert N. Lee, Josef von Sternberg d Josef von Sternberg ph Bert Glennon ad Hans Dreier
☆ George Bancroft, Evelyn Brent, Clive Brook, Larry Semon
† The film was a great international success and had an influence on the pessimistic French school of the thirties.
👤 Ben Hecht

Underworld

GB　1985　100m　colour
Limehouse/Green Man
📺
A mad doctor keeps his mutants underground.
H. G. Wells up to date, but none the better for it.
w Clive Barker, James Caplin d George Pavlou
☆ Denholm Elliott, Steven Berkoff, Larry Lamb, Miranda Richardson, Art Malik, Ingrid Pitt

Underworld Informers: see *The Informers*

The Underworld Story **

US　1950　90m　bw
UA (Hal E. Chester)
📺
An unscrupulous reporter buys a half-share in a small-town newspaper and brings his slick city methods with him when he covers a murder.
Very effective, moodily atmospheric and unpretentious thriller.
w Henry Blankfort, Cyril Endfield story Craig Rice d Cyril Endfield ph Stanley Cortez m David Rose ad Gordon Wiles ed Richard Heermance
☆ Dan Duryea, Herbert Marshall, Gale Storm, Howard Da Silva, Michael O'Shea, Mary Anderson, Gar Moore, Melville Cooper, Frieda Inescort, Art Baker

'A sensational film that puts the finger on today's biggest business – crime.'

Underworld USA *

US　1961　99m　bw
Columbia/Globe (Samuel Fuller)
📺
A young gangster takes elaborate revenge for the killing of his father.
Violent syndicate melodrama with a semi-documentary veneer and some brutal scenes. Well done but heavy going.
wd Samuel Fuller ph Hal Mohr m Harry Sukman ad Robert Peterson ed Jerome Thoms
☆ Cliff Robertson, Beatrice Kay, Larry Gates, Dolores Dorn, Robert Emhardt, Paul Dubov, Richard Rust

'Savage! Sinister! Supernatural! The black fury of a werewolf – sacrificing life and love to the maddening evil that drove him to the most monstrous murders man ever committed!'

The Undying Monster *

US　1943　63m　bw
TCF
📺
GB title: *The Hammond Mystery*
A curse hangs over the English ancestral home of the Hammonds.
Silly but well-photographed and directed minor horror on wolf man lines.
w Lillie Hayward, Michel Jacoby novel Jessie D. Kerruish d John Brahm ph Lucien Ballard m Emil Newman, David Raksin
☆ James Ellison, John Howard, Heather Angel, Bramwell Fletcher, Heather Thatcher, Eily Malyon, Halliwell Hobbes, Aubrey Mather

Unearthly Stranger *

GB　1963　75m　bw
Independent Artists (Julian Wintle, Leslie Parkyn, Albert Fennell)
Scientists working on a time-space formula find that the bride of one of them is an alien in search of their secret.
Surprisingly effective minor science fiction, in some ways all the better for its modest, TV-style production values.
w Rex Carlton d John Krish ph Reg Wyer m Edward Williams
☆ John Neville, Gabriella Licudi, Philip Stone, Jean Marsh, Patrick Newell, Warren Mitchell

Uneasy Terms

GB　1948　91m　bw
British National
Detective Slim Callaghan proves that a blackmail victim is not a murderer.
The film which proved that the British simply can't make crime movies on the American model.
w Peter Cheyney novel Peter Cheyney d Vernon Sewell ph Ernest Palmer m Hans May
☆ Michael Rennie, Moira Lister, Faith Brook, Joy Shelton, Nigel Patrick, Paul Carpenter, Barry Jones

Unexpected Father

US　1939　78m　bw
Universal
GB title: *Sandy Takes a Bow*
A dancer looks after his late partner's baby.
Genial comedy introducing a baby star who was popular until she got out of diapers.
w Leonard Spigelgass, Charles Grayson d Charles Lamont
☆ Baby Sandy, Mischa Auer, Dennis O'Keefe, Shirley Ross, Mayo Methot

Unexpected Uncle
US   1941   67m   bw
RKO
An elderly steel tycoon gives everything up to
become a tramp and play Cupid.
*Money-is-not-everything fable, entirely dependent on
amiable performances.*
w Delmer Daves, Noel Langley *novel* Eric Hatch
d Peter Godfrey
☆ Charles Coburn, Anne Shirley, James Craig,
Ernest Truex, Russell Gleason, Jed Prouty

'If she were yours, would you forgive?'

The Unfaithful *
US   1947   109m   bw
Warner (Jerry Wald)
A wife gets involved in a murder while her
husband is out of town.
Glossy romantic melodrama, an unofficial remake of
The Letter.
w David Goodis, James Gunn d Vincent
Sherman ph Ernest Haller m Max Steiner
☆ Ann Sheridan, Zachary Scott, Lew Ayres, Eve
Arden, Steve Geray, Jerome Cowan, John Hoyt

The Unfaithful Wife: see *La Femme Infidèle*

Unfaithfully Yours **
US   1948   105m   bw
TCF (Preston Sturges)
▣ �
An orchestral conductor believes his wife is
unfaithful, and while conducting a concert thinks
of three different ways of dealing with the
situation.
*A not entirely happy mixture of romance, farce,
melodrama and wit, but in general a pretty entertaining
concoction and the last major film of its talented writer-
director.*
wd Preston Sturges ph Victor Milner m Alfred
Newman
☆ Rex Harrison, Linda Darnell, Barbara Lawrence,
Rudy Vallee, Kurt Kreuger, Lionel Stander, *Edgar
Kennedy*, Al Bridge, Julius Tannen, Torben Meyer,
Robert Greig
  'Harrison discovers more ways of tripping over a
  telephone cable than one can count, and his
  efforts to falsify evidence through a recalcitrant
  tape recorder are as funny as anything thought
  up by Clair in *A Nous La Liberté* or by Chaplin
  in *Modern Times*.' – Basil Wright, 1972
† The Rex Harrison character is named Sir Alfred
de Carter and is meant to be Sir Thomas Beecham.
(In America the equivalent of Beecham's Pills is
Carter's Little Liver Pills.)
♫ The pieces of music played are as follows:
For murder: the *Semiramide Overture* by Rossini
For surrender: the *Venusberg* music from
Tannhäuser, by Wagner
For Russian roulette: *Francesca da Rimini* by
Tchaikovsky

Unfaithfully Yours
US   1983   96m   DeLuxe
TCF (Marvin Worth, Joe Wizan)
▣ ⌐
Modernized and simplified version of the above,
with only one plot instead of three.
*This proves to be an advantage, and the film does
deliver some laughs.*
w Valerie Curtin, Barry Levinson, Robert Klane
d Howard Zieff ph Gregory La Cava
pd Albert Brenner
☆ Dudley Moore, Nastassja Kinski, Armand
Assante, Albert Brooks, Cassie Yates, Richard
Libertini, Richard B. Shull

Unfinished Business
US   1941   95m   bw
Universal (Gregory La Cava)
A wife has thoughts that she should have married
her husband's brother.
*Smooth but disappointing romantic comedy; the detail
is good enough, but it sadly lacks drive.*
w Eugene Thackery pd Gregory La Cava
ph Joseph Valentine m Franz Waxman
☆ Irene Dunne, Robert Montgomery, Eugene
Pallette, Preston Foster, Walter Catlett, June
Clyde, Phyllis Barry, Esther Dale, Samuel S. Hinds
  'Once sentiment gets the upper hand, reach for
  the exit.' – Otis Ferguson

The Unfinished Dance
US   1947   101m   Technicolor
MGM (Joe Pasternak)
The young star of a ballet school becomes jealous
of a talented newcomer, and causes her injury in an
accident.
The delicacies of the French original, La Mort du
Cygne, *give way to standard Hollywood hokum and
produce an accomplished but totally uninteresting film.*
w Myles Connolly story Paul Morand d Henry
Koster ph Robert Surtees md Herbert Stothart
☆ Margaret O'Brien, Cyd Charisse, Karin Booth,
Danny Thomas, Esther Dale
  'The same old story, with pathos, humour and
  ballet substituted for pathos, humour and chorus
  girls.' – MFB

Unforgettable
US   1996   117m   DeLuxe
MGM/Spelling (Dino de Laurentiis, Martha de
Laurentiis)
▣ ▤
A doctor, who is suspected of killing his wife,
makes use of a dangerous experimental technique
to experience other people's memories in order to
discover the real killer.
*Daft thriller from a director and cast worthy of better
things, but here seeming, understandably, uninterested
in events.*
w Bill Geddie d John Dahl ph Jeffrey Jur
m Christopher Young pd Rob Pearson ed Eric L.
Beason, Scott Chestnut
☆ Ray Liotta, Linda Fiorentino, Peter Coyote,
Christopher McDonald, Kim Cattrall, Duncan
Fraser, Garwin Sanford, David Paymer
  'A curious hybrid, a suspense film with a
  scientific theme, but one that is equally
  unsatisfactory in both disciplines.' – Anwar
  Brett, Film Review

Unforgiven ****
US   1992   131m   Technicolor   Panavision
Warner (Clint Eastwood)
▣ ▤ ⌐ ⌐ ⌐
A former hired killer turned unsuccessful farmer,
together with a young would-be gunfighter and an
old friend, set out to collect a thousand-dollar
reward for killing the cowboys who slashed the face
of a prostitute.
*Harsh Western of revenge and needless slaughter that
re-invents and revives the genre to spectacular effect.*
w David Webb Peoples d Clint Eastwood ph Jack
N. Green m Lennie Niehaus pd Henry Bumstead
ed Joel Cox
☆ Clint Eastwood, Gene Hackman, Morgan
Freeman, Richard Harris, Jaimz Woolvett, Saul
Rubinek, Frances Fisher, Anna Thomson, David
Mucci, Rob Campbell, Anthony James
  'The movie's grizzled male ensemble, its gradual
  build, and its juxtaposition of brutality and
  sardonic humor testify to its disdain for box-
  office conventions.' – Michael Sragow, New
  Yorker
  'Eastwood climbs back into the saddle to make a
  classic western.' – Ian Johnstone, Sunday Times
  'A tense, hard-edged, superbly dramatic yarn
  that is also an exceedingly intelligent meditation
  on the West, its myths and its heroes.' – Variety
▮ best picture; Clint Eastwood (as director); Gene
Hackman; Joel Cox
⌥ Clint Eastwood (as actor); Henry Bumstead;
Jack N. Green; David Webb Peoples; best sound
⌦ Gene Hackman

The Unforgiven *
US   1960   125m   Technicolor   Panavision
UA/James Productions/Hecht-Hill-Lancaster (James
Hill)
▣ ▤ ⌐ ⌐
A rancher's daughter is suspected of being an
Indian orphan, and violence results.
*Good-looking, expensive but muddled racist Western,
hard to enjoy.*
w Ben Maddow *novel* Alan le May d John
Huston ph Franz Planer m Dimitri Tiomkin
☆ Burt Lancaster, Audrey Hepburn, Audie
Murphy, Lillian Gish, Charles Bickford, Doug
McClure, John Saxon, Joseph Wiseman, Albert
Salmi
  'How much strain can a director's reputation
  take? Of late, John Huston seems to have been
  trying to find out. I think he has carried the
  experiment too far with *The Unforgiven* ... a
  work of profound phoniness, part adult western,

part that *Oklahoma!* kind of folksy Americana.' –
Dwight MacDonald
  'Ludicrous ... a hodgepodge of crudely stitched
  sententiousness and lame story-conference
  inspirations.' – Stanley Kauffmann

The Unguarded Hour *
US   1936   87m   bw
MGM
A blackmailed woman has evidence to free a man
accused of murder, but dare not reveal it.
Twisty suspense thriller with a rather splendid cast.
w Howard Emmett Rogers, Leon Gordon
play Ladislas Fodor, Bernard Merivale d Sam
Wood
☆ Franchot Tone, Loretta Young, Roland Young,
Henry Daniell, Jessie Ralph, Lewis Stone, Dudley
Digges, E. E. Clive, Robert Greig, Aileen Pringle

The Unguarded Moment
US   1956   85m   Technicolor
U-I (Gordon Kay)
A schoolmistress who receives anonymous love
notes from a psychotic pupil is discredited by his
well-meaning but unbalanced father.
*Well-meaning but boring melodrama with the star
attractively out of her usual element.*
w Herb Meadow, Larry Marcus story Rosalind
Russell d Harry Keller ph William Daniels
m Herman Stein
☆ *Esther Williams*, George Nader, John Saxon,
Edward Andrews, Jack Albertson

The Unholy
US   1987   102m   CFI color
Vestron/Limelight Studios/Team Effort (Matthew
Hayden)
▣ ▤ ⌐
A new priest is sent to a demon-haunted church.
*Routine horror, in which evil seems to be equated with
sexual desire.*
w Philip Yordan, Fernando Fonseca d Camilo
Vilo ph Henry Vargas m Roger Bellon, Fernando
Fonseca pd Fernando Fonseca, Jim Darfus, Cathy
Carlisle ed Mark Melnick
☆ Ben Cross, Ned Beatty, William Russ, Jill
Carroll, Hal Holbrook, Trevor Howard, Peter
Frechette, Claudia Robinson
  'A particularly routine effort in an already
  overcrowded horror sub-genre.' – Julian Petley,
  MFB

The Unholy Four: see *The Stranger Came Home*

The Unholy Garden
US   1931   75m   bw
Samuel Goldwyn
A gentleman thief hides out in a North African
den of misfits.
*Would-be romantic nonsense, much less interesting
than its credits.*
w Ben Hecht, Charles MacArthur d George
Fitzmaurice ph Gregg Toland, George Barnes
m Alfred Newman
☆ Ronald Colman, Fay Wray, Estelle Taylor, Tully
Marshall, Warren Hymer, Mischa Auer, Henry
Armetta, Lawrence Grant
  'Splendid presentation of an ordinary story.' –
  Variety

The Unholy Night
US   1929   94m   bw
MGM
A strangler is caught in the London fog.
*Clumsy and talkative early talkie, chiefly interesting for
its cast.*
w Ben Hecht d Lionel Barrymore
☆ Lionel Barrymore, Roland Young, Boris Karloff,
John Loder, Natalie Moorhead, Ernest Torrence,
Polly Moran, John Miljan

Unholy Partners *
US   1941   95m   bw
MGM (Samuel Marx)
The editor of a sensational newspaper has to accept
finance from a gangster, but friction results when
the newspaper exposes some of the gangster's
activities.
*Agreeable twenties melodrama with two solid stars
battling it out.*
w Earl Baldwin, Lesser Samuels, Bartlett Cormack
d Mervyn Le Roy ph George Barnes m David
Snell

☆ Edward G. Robinson, Edward Arnold, Laraine
Day, Marsha Hunt, William T. Orr, Don Beddoe,
Charles Dingle, Walter Kingsford, Marcel Dalio

The Unholy Three *
US   1925   76m   bw   silent
MGM
▤
A ventriloquist, a dwarf and a strong man carry out
a series of crimes which end in murder.
*Curious melodrama which set its star and director off
on a series of seven more and even weirder
eccentricities.*
w Waldemar Young story Clarence Robbins
d Tod Browning ph David Kesson
☆ Lon Chaney, Harry Earles, Victor McLaglen,
Mae Busch, Matt Moore

The Unholy Three *
US   1930   74m   bw
MGM
▤ ⌐
Remake of the above.
*The star's only talkie – he died before it was released –
is less effective than the silent version.*
w J. C. and Elliott Nugent *novel* Clarence
Robbins d Jack Conway ph Percy Hilburn
☆ *Lon Chaney*, Lila Lee, Harry Earles, Ivan Linow,
Elliott Nugent, John Miljan

'Half-Angel ... Half-Devil. She Made Him Half-A-
Man!'
'All A Guy Had To Do Was Whistle! Frank!
Outspoken!'

The Unholy Wife
US   1957   94m   Technicolor   RKOscope
RKO/Treasure
A bored wife shoots a friend in mistake for her
husband but is sentenced for the accidental death
of her mother-in-law.
Totally uninteresting melodrama in the Double
Indemnity *style, professionally made but turgid.*
w Jonathan Latimer d William A. Seiter ph Lucien
Ballard m Daniele Amfitheatrof
☆ Diana Dors, Rod Steiger, Tom Tryon, Beulah
Bondi, Marie Windsor, Arthur Franz, Luis Van
Rooten

Unhook the Stars
US   1996   103m   Foto-Kem
Miramax/Hachette Première/Gérard Depardieu (René
Cleitman)
▣ ▤
A widow befriends a bedraggled young mother and
her six-year-old son.
*Glossy emotional wallow for the most part,
convincingly acted but never seeming in touch with any
observable reality.*
w Nick Cassavetes, Helen Caldwell d Nick
Cassavetes ph Phedon Papamichael m Steven
Hufsteter pd Phedon Papamichael Snr ed Petra
von Oelffen
☆ Gena Rowlands, Marisa Tomei, Gérard
Depardieu, Jake Lloyd, Moira Kelly, David Sherrill,
David Thornton, Bridgette Wilson, Bobby Cooper,
Clint Howard
  'If the film is a love-letter from a director to his
  mother, it's close to being a rejection-slip sent to
  his dad. Anything less like the American
  independent tradition would be hard to
  imagine.' – Adam Mars-Jones

Unidentified Flying Oddball: see *The
Spaceman and King Arthur*

'A love haunted by nameless evil which fought to live
in their hearts!'

The Uninvited **
US   1944   98m   bw
Paramount (Charles Brackett)
▤ ⌐
A girl returns to her family house and is haunted
by her mother's spirit, which seems to be evil.
*One of the cinema's few genuine ghost stories, and a
good one, though encased in a rather stiff production; it
works up to a fine pitch of frenzy.*
w Dodie Smith *novel Uneasy Freehold* by Dorothy
Macardle d Lewis Allen ph Charles Lang
m Victor Young
☆ Ray Milland, Ruth Hussey, *Gail Russell*, Donald
Crisp, Cornelia Otis Skinner, Dorothy Stickney,
Barbara Everest, Alan Napier

'It will hold audiences glued to their seats.' – *Variety*

'It sets out to give you the shivers – and will do so, if you're readily disposed.' – *New York Times*

'I experienced thirty-five first class jolts, not to mention a well calculated texture of minor frissons.' – *Nation*

'Still manages to ice the blood with its implied horrors … you can almost smell the ghostly mimosa.' – *Peter John Dyer, 1966*

'A superior and satisfying shocker.' – *Newsweek*

† British critics of the time congratulated the director on not showing the ghosts: in fact the visible manifestations had been cut by the British censor.

& Charles Lang

Union Depot

US   1932   68m   bw
Warner

GB title: *Gentleman for a Day*

The fortunes of several people clash in a railway station.

Pale but moderately interesting imitation of Grand Hotel.

w Kenyon Nicholson, Walter de Leon *play* Gene Fowler, Douglas Durkin, Joe Laurie *d* Alfred E. Green

☆ Douglas Fairbanks Jnr, Joan Blondell, Alan Hale, Frank McHugh, George Rosener, Guy Kibbee, David Landau

Union Pacific **

US   1939   133m   bw
Paramount/Cecil B. de Mille

Indians and others cause problems for the railroad builders.

Standard big-scale Western climaxing in a spectacular wreck; not exactly exciting, but very watchable.

w Walter de Leon, C. Gardner Sullivan, Jesse Lasky Jnr *d* Cecil B. de Mille *ph* Victor Milner, Dewey Wrigley *m* John Leipold, Sigmund Krumgold *ad* Hans Dreier, Roland Anderson

☆ Barbara Stanwyck, Joel McCrea, Akim Tamiroff, Robert Preston, Lynne Overman, Brian Donlevy, Robert Barrat, Anthony Quinn, Stanley Ridges, Henry Kolker, Evelyn Keyes, Regis Toomey

'A socko spectacular, surefire for big grosses right down the line.' – *Variety*

'This latest de Mille epic contains all the excelsior qualities we expect of his work – that sense of a Salvationist drum beating round the next corner – but it is never as funny as *The Crusades* and he has lost his touch with crowds.' – *Graham Greene*

'Excitement is the dominant emotion, with swift succession of contrasting materials and episodes, grim and gay, often furious, sometimes funny. The narrative and action take hold at the start and never let go.' – *Motion Picture Herald*

'The largest conglomeration of thrills and cold-blooded murder since Pauline was in peril.' – *Brooklyn Daily Eagle*

'A movie in the old tradition, melodramatic and breathtaking and altogether wonderful.' – *Photoplay*

† De Mille's last picture in black and white.

L'Union Sacrée: see *Brothers in Arms (1989)*

Union Station **

US   1950   80m   bw
Paramount (Jules Schermer)

Kidnappers nominate a crowded railroad station as their ransom collection point.

Compelling little thriller modelled after Naked City, *with real locations and plenty of excitement.*

w Sydney Boehm *novel* Thomas Walsh *d* Rudolph Maté *ph* Daniel L. Fapp *m* David Buttolph, Heinz Roemheld *md* Irvin Talbot

☆ William Holden, Barry Fitzgerald, Nancy Olson, Lyle Bettger, Jan Sterling, Allene Roberts

Universal Soldier

GB   1971   96m   colour
Appaloosa/Ionian (Frank J. Schwarz, Donald L. Factor)

A mercenary returns to London but can't escape his past.

Solemnly meaningful melodrama on a tight budget.

wd Cy Endfield *ph* Tony Imi *m* Philip Goodhand-Tait

☆ George Lazenby, Edward Judd, Benito Carruthers, Germaine Greer, Rudolph Walker

---

'The future has a bad attitude.'

Universal Soldier

US   1992   103m   Technicolor   Panavision
Guild/Carolco (Allen Shapiro, Craig Baumgarten, Joel B. Michaels)

Two soldiers who killed each other in Vietnam are resurrected as androids to form part of an élite group of soldiers for special missions; but one of them goes out of control.

Science-fiction hokum intended to boost the appeal of its two action stars, done with enough energy and containing more than enough mayhem to appeal to fans of action movies.

w Richard Rothstein, Christopher Leitch, Dean Devlin *d* Roland Emmerich *ph* Karl Walter Lindenlaub *m* Christopher Franke *md* Brynmor Jones *pd* Holger Gross *ed* Michael J. Duthie

☆ Jean-Claude Van Damme, Dolph Lundgren, Ally Walker, Ed O'Ross, Jerry Orbach, Leon Rippy, Tico Wells

'To get through the garish mayhem, you need a high vicarious-pain threshold.' – *Michael Sragow, New Yorker*

'A classy rollercoaster ride through the clichés of modern fantasy cinema.' – *Mark Kermode, Sight and Sound*

'Prepare to become obsolete.'

Universal Soldier: The Return

US   1999   83m   DeLuxe
Columbia TriStar/IndieProd/Long Road (Craig Baumgarten, Allen Shapiro, Jean-Claude Van Damme)

Only one man, a bionic commando can save the world when rogue cyborgs, controlled by a super-intelligent computer, go on the rampage.

Extremely dull action movie, with no sense of urgency about it, despite its loud explosions, thumping soundtrack, and endlessly repetitive fights.

w William Malone, John Fasano *ph* Michael A. Benson *m* Don Davis *pd* David Chapman *ed* Peck Prior

☆ Jean-Claude Van Damme, Michael Jai White, Heidi Schanz, Xander Berkeley, Justin Lazard, Kiana Tom, Daniel Von Bargen, James Black, Karis Paige Bryant, Bill Goldberg

'Rot from start to finish.' – *Edward Porter, Sunday Times*

The Unknown

US   1927   65m   bw   silent
MGM

A fake armless wonder has his arms amputated to please a girl who can't stand the touch of a man's hand. (She then changes her mind.)

Weird melodrama which even this contortionist star can't save.

w Waldemar Young *d* Tod Browning

☆ Lon Chaney, Joan Crawford, Norman Kerry

The Unknown

US   1946   70m   bw
Columbia

An amnesiac heiress returns to her family mansion.

Twisty creeper in the I Love a Mystery *series; not bad for a second feature.*

w Malcolm Stuart Boylan, Julian Harmon *d* Henry Levin

☆ Karen Morley, Jeff Donnell, Jim Bannon

Unknown Chaplin ***

GB   1986   157m   colour/bw
Thames Television

A three-part documentary on Chaplin's early years including excerpts from films, out-takes and on-camera rehearsals never seen in public before, much of it taken from Chaplin's own archives, which he had ordered to be destroyed.

First shown as three television programmes, this is by far the finest examination available of Chaplin's genius, which is shown to be due to constant hard work as well as to improvisation.

wd Kevin Brownlow, David Gill *ph* Ted Adcock *m* Carl Davis *ed* Trevor Waite

☆ James Mason

The Unknown Guest

US   1943   61m   bw
Monogram (Maurice King)

A supposedly no-good young man is suspected of murdering his aunt and uncle.

Rather tedious and silly mystery with little happening.

---

w Philip Yordan *d* Kurt Neumann

☆ Victor Jory, Pamela Blake, Harry Hayden, Veda Ann Borg, Nora Cecil

The Unknown Man

US   1951   86m   bw
MGM (Robert Thomsen)

A civil court lawyer of high principles successfully undertakes a criminal case, finds his client was really guilty, and sets matters straight.

Contrived but entertaining morality with standard production and performances.

w Ronald Millar, George Froeschel *d* Richard Thorpe *ph* William Mellor *m* Conrad Salinger

☆ Walter Pidgeon, Ann Harding, Lewis Stone, Barry Sullivan, Keefe Brasselle, Eduard Franz, Richard Anderson, Dawn Addams

Unknown World

US   1951   74m   bw
Lippert/J. R. Rabin, I. A. Block

Scientists burrow down 1,640 miles below the Earth's surface to find a geological shelter in which to preserve civilization from the H-bomb.

Dull, cheap science fiction with a hectoring tone; it raises the question of whether a civilization capable of producing such tedium is worth saving.

w Millard Kaufman *d* Terrell O. Morse *ph* Allen G. Siegler, Henry Freulich *m* Ernest Gold *pd* I. A. Block, J. R. Rabin *ed* Terrell O. Morse

☆ Bruce Kellogg, Marilyn Nash, Otto Waldis, Jim Bannon, Tom Handley, Dick Cogan, George Baxter

Unlawful Entry *

US   1992   111m   DeLuxe
TCF/Largo/JVC (Charles Gordon)

A Los Angeles policeman who befriends a young couple turns out to be a psychopath.

Moderate thriller of a now very familiar kind that deals with a flatmate, tenant, nanny, and, in this instance, a cop from hell.

w Lewis Colick *story* George D. Putnam, John Katchmer, Lewis Colick *d* Jonathan Kaplan *ph* Jamie Anderson *m* James Horner *pd* Lawrence G. Paull *ed* Curtiss Clayton

☆ Kurt Russell, Ray Liotta, Madeleine Stowe, Roger E. Mosley, Ken Lerner, Deborah Offner, Carmen Argenziano, Andy Romano, Johnny Ray McGhee

'The film's main achievement is to fit its trenchant social critique into conventional thriller form … The film catches the fear and paranoia of the couple "home alone".' – *Geoffrey Macnab, Sight and Sound*

Unman, Wittering and Zigo

GB   1971   102m   colour
Paramount/Mediarts (Gareth Wigan)

A nervous schoolmaster discovers that his predecessor was murdered by the boys.

Macabre school story which overreaches itself and peters out.

w Simon Raven *TV play* Giles Cooper *d* John Mackenzie *ph* Geoffrey Unsworth *m* Michael J. Lewis

☆ David Hemmings, Douglas Wilmer, Hamilton Dyce, Carolyn Seymour

Unmarried

US   1939   66m   bw
Paramount

GB title: *Night Club Hostess*

An ex-boxer, shy of marriage, raises an orphan boy.

Modest domestic drama notable as one of the rare non-Western appearances of its star.

w Lillie Hayward, Brian Marlow, Grover Jones *d* Kurt Neumann

☆ Buck Jones, Donald O'Connor, Helen Twelvetrees

An Unmarried Woman *

US   1978   124m   Movielab
TCF (Paul Mazursky, Tony Ray)

A sophisticated New York woman is deserted by her husband, fights with her daughter, and takes up with two men.

Frank, well-observed depiction of one woman in New York's new society; as modern as all get out but not very attractive.

wd Paul Mazursky *ph* Arthur J. Ornitz *m* Bill Conti *pd* Pato Guzman

---

☆ Jill Clayburgh, Alan Bates, Michael Murphy, Cliff Gorman, Pat Quinn, Kelly Bishop

'The motions of the story are not what cripple it – it's the low level of insight and the pervasive sense of exploitation … It's what once would have been called woman's-magazine fiction.' – *Stanley Kauffmann*

& best picture; script; Jill Clayburgh

The Unnamable

Canada   1988   87m   Foto-Kem
Yankee Classic/KP (Dean Ramser, Jean-Paul Ouellette)

Students explore a deserted house and discover a monster that has been imprisoned there for 200 years.

Unexceptional, low-budget, gory rendition of Lovecraft's short stories, padded out with a great deal of irrelevance.

wd Jean-Paul Ouellette *story* The Statement of Randolph Carter *and* The Unnamable *by H. P. Lovecraft* *ph* Tom Fraser *m* David Bergeaud *pd* Gene Abel *ed* Wendy J. Plump *sp* R. Christopher Biggs

☆ Charles King, Mark Kinsey Stephenson, Alexandra Durrell, Laura Albert, Katrin Alexandre, Eben Ham, Blane Wheatley, Mark Parra

The Unnamable Returns

Canada   1992   92m   Foto-Kem
Yankee Classic/AM East/Prism/New Age (Jean-Paul Ouellette)

aka: *H. P. Lovecraft's The Unnamable Returns*

Students dabbling in black magic unleash a murderous demon on the Miskatonic university campus in Arkham.

Supernatural variation on the usual low-budget slasher movie, featuring a cut-price monster.

wd Jean-Paul Ouellette *story* The Statement of Randolph Carter *and* The Unnamable *by H. P. Lovecraft* *m* David Bergeaud *pd* Tim Keating *ed* William C. Williams *sp* R. Christopher Biggs

☆ John Rhys-Davies, Mark Kinsey Stephenson, Charles Klausmeyer, Maria Ford, Julie Strain, Peter Breck, David Warner

Unpublished Story

GB   1942   91m   bw
Columbia/Two Cities (Anthony Havelock-Allan)

A reporter exposes the Nazis behind a pacifist organization.

Ho-hum formula flagwaver with generally stilted production.

w Anatole de Grunwald, Patrick Kirwan *d* Harold French *ph* Bernard Knowles *m* Nicholas Brodzky

☆ Valerie Hobson, Richard Greene, Basil Radford, Roland Culver, Brefni O'Rorke, Miles Malleson, George Carney, André Morell

Unsane: see *Tenebrae*

The Unseen

US   1945   82m   bw
Paramount

A London governess comes to suspect that dark deeds have taken place in the empty house next door.

Period suspenser with good atmosphere but an insubstantial plot.

w Hagar Wilde, Raymond Chandler *d* Lewis Allen *ph* John Seitz *m* Ernst Toch

☆ Joel McCrea, Gail Russell, Herbert Marshall, Richard Lyon, Nona Griffith

† The film seems to have been a hurried attempt to repeat and combine the previous year's successes, *Gaslight* and *The Uninvited*.

Unseen Heroes: see *The Battle of the V1*

Unsichtbare Gegner: see *Invisible Adversaries*

The Unsinkable Molly Brown *

US   1964   128m   Metrocolor   Panavision
MGM/Marten (Lawrence Weingarten)

Western orphan Molly Brown grows up determined to become a member of Denver society.

Semi-Western comedy-musical about a real lady who wound up surviving the Titanic. Bouncy and likeable but not at all memorable.

---

film suitable for family viewing
VHS video-cassette for the British PAL system
VHS video-cassette for the British PAL system in wide screen-format
Video cassette in a computer-colourised version
American NTSC video-cassette
Laser disc

w Helen Deutsch *musical play* Richard Morris *d* Charles Walters *ph* Daniel L. Fapp *md* Robert Armbruster *ad* George W. Davis, Preston Ames
☆ *Debbie Reynolds*, Harve Presnell, Ed Begley, Jack Kruschen, Hermione Baddeley, Martita Hunt
♪ Daniel L. Fapp; Robert Armbruster; Debbie Reynolds

'Sometimes you find your heroes in the most unlikely places.'

Unstrung Heroes *
US   1995   94m   Technicolor
Buena Vista/Hollywood (Susan Arnold, Donna Roth, Bill Badalato)
🎬 🔳 💿 ♫

A 12-year-old, unhappy at home, goes to live with his two eccentric uncles.
Oddball drama of a dysfunctional family; it takes the once-fashionable view that it is the mad who are truly sane and builds on that shaky foundation an affecting domestic drama of people's various strategies for survival.
w Richard LaGravenese *book* Franz Lidz *d* Diane Keaton *ph* Phedon Papamichael *m* Thomas Newman *pd* Garreth Stover *ed* Lisa Churgin
☆ Andie MacDowell, John Turturro, Michael Richards, Maury Chaykin, Nathan Watt, Kendra Krull
'A funny and fond piece of film-making, with a remarkably well-sustained tone – somewhere between an Anne Tyler novel and a Marx Brothers film, if you can imagine that. Keaton has.' – *Tom Shone, Sunday Times*
♪ Thomas Newman

An Unsuitable Job for a Woman
GB   1982   90m   Gevacolor
Gold Crest/NFFC/Boyd's Co (Michael Relph, Peter McKay)
🔳

A young woman, hired to discover why the son of a wealthy businessman killed himself, becomes obsessed by the dead youth.
Tepid and murky thriller that irons out the ambiguities of a convoluted plot.
w Elizabeth McKay, Brian Scobie, Christopher Petit *novel* P. D. James *d* Christopher Petit *ph* Martin Schäfer *m* Chaz Jankel, Philip Bagenal, Pete Van-Hooke *pd* Anton Furst *ed* Mick Audsley
☆ Billie Whitelaw, Paul Freeman, Pippa Guard, Dominic Guard, Elizabeth Spriggs, David Horovitch, Dawn Archibald

The Unsuspected *
US   1947   103m   bw
Warner (Charles Hoffman)
A writer-producer of radio crime shows commits a murder and is forced to follow the clues on air.
Sleek, new look mystery thriller with a disappointing plot which gives its interesting cast little to do, and allows itself to peter out in chases.
w Ranald MacDougall *novel* Charlotte Armstrong *d* Michael Curtiz *ph* Woody Bredell *m* Franz Waxman *ad* Anton Grot
☆ Claude Rains, Joan Caulfield, Audrey Totter, Constance Bennett, Michael North, Hurd Hatfield, Fred Clark

Untamed
US   1940   83m   Technicolor
Paramount (Paul Jones)
A doctor in the frozen north is beset by an epidemic as well as natural hazards.
Old-fashioned melodrama which found an eager audience.
w Frederick Hazlitt Brennan, Frank Butler *novel* Mantrap *by* Sinclair Lewis *d* George Archainbaud *ph* Leo Tover, W. Howard Greene *m* Victor Young
☆ Ray Milland, Patricia Morison, Akim Tamiroff, William Frawley, Jane Darwell, Esther Dale, J. M. Kerrigan, Eily Malyon
† A remake of Clara Bow's 1926 film *Mantrap*.

Untamed
US   1955   109m   Technicolor   Cinemascope
TCF (Bert E. Friedlob, William A. Bacher)
A Dutchman and an Irish girl meet again on a Boer trek to South Africa, and survive Zulu attacks.
A long and involved epic-style plot provides standard excitements and predictable romantic complications.

w Talbot Jennings, Michael Blankfort, Frank Fenton *novel* Helga Moray *d* Henry King *ph* Leo Tover *m* Franz Waxman
☆ Tyrone Power, Susan Hayward, Richard Egan, John Justin, Agnes Moorehead, Rita Moreno, Hope Emerson, Brad Dexter, Henry O'Neill
'A not unenjoyable essay in hokum.' – *MFB*

The Untamed: see Return to Snowy River

Untamed Frontier
US   1952   78m   Technicolor
U-I (Leonard Goldstein)
The son of an unpopular Texan landowner commits murder.
Stolid minor Western.
w Gerald Drayson Adams, Gwen and John Bagni *d* Hugo Fregonese *ph* Charles P. Boyle *m* Hans Salter
☆ Joseph Cotten, Shelley Winters, Scott Brady, Suzan Ball, Minor Watson

'He doesn't make sense. She doesn't make sense. Together they make sense.'

Untamed Heart
US   1993   102m   DeLuxe
MGM (Tony Bill, Helen Buck Bartlett)
🎬 🔳 💿 ♫

A young man with a heart condition begins a tentative love affair with a waitress.
Sickly romantic sob-story, a teenage fantasy of idealized passion which is remote from real life.
w Tom Sierchio *d* Tony Bill *ph* Jost Vacano *m* Cliff Eidelman *pd* Steven Jordan *ed* Mia Goldman
☆ Christian Slater, Marisa Tomei, Rosie Perez, Kyle Secor, Willie Carson
'The movie largely works on its own terms, particularly for those looking for a traditional "good cry".' – *Variety*
'Has the kind of sympathetic handling that isn't totally destroyed by the American propensity for weepie but upbeat endings, and slurpy music to enable even people as silly as ourselves to pinpoint its more dramatic moments.' – *Derek Malcolm, Guardian*

Until September
US   1985   95m   Metrocolor
UA (Michael Gruskoff)
🎬 🔳 ♫

An American woman unexpectedly stuck in Paris begins an affair with a married French banker.
Dull, lightweight romantic comedy of two chauvinistic people divided by their cultures; it is extremely bland and rarely interesting.
w Janice Lee Graham *d* Richard Marquand *ph* Philippe Welt *m* John Barry *pd* Hilton McConnico *ed* Sean Barton
☆ Karen Allen, Thierry L'hermitte, Christopher Cazenove, Marie-Catherine Conti, Hutton Cobb, Michael Mellinger, Nitza Saul

Until the End of the World *
Germany/France/Australia   1991   158m   colour
Warner/Road Movies/Argos/Village Roadshow (Anatole Dauman, Jonathan Taplin)
🎬 🔳 ♫

original title: Bis ans Ende der Welt
As a rogue nuclear satellite threatens to explode, a woman tracks a man with multiple identities across Europe to Japan, China and Australia, where she meets his blind mother and his father, who has invented a camera enabling the blind to see.
Rambling, often confusing, sometimes boring road movie with moments of brilliance.
w Peter Carey, Wim Wenders *d* Wim Wenders *ph* Robby Müller *m* Graeme Revell *pd* Thierry Flamand, Sally Campbell *ed* Peter Przygodda
☆ William Hurt, Solveig Dommartin, Sam Neill, Max von Sydow, Rüdiger Vogler, Ernie Dingo, Jeanne Moreau, Chick Ortega, David Gulpilil, Ryu Chishu
'A dream still partly realised and partly still in the head of the director.' – *Variety*
'Comes across as heavy-handed, chaotic and immensely cluttered, finally leaving one with an overwhelming sense of bewilderment.' – *Julia Knight, Sight and Sound*
† Wenders has announced his intention of releasing a five-hour version of the film on video.

Until They Sail
US   1957   95m   bw   Cinemascope
MGM (Charles Schnee)
🔳

Four New Zealand sisters have wartime romances.
Solid 'woman's picture', well enough presented.
w Robert Anderson *novel* James A. Michener *d* Robert Wise *ph* Joseph Ruttenberg *m* David Raksin
☆ Jean Simmons, Joan Fontaine, Paul Newman, Piper Laurie, Charles Drake, Wally Cassell, Sandra Dee

The Untouchables **
US   1987   119m   Technicolor
Paramount/Art Linson
🎬 🔳 💿 ♫

Law enforcers in 20s Chicago go after Al Capone and other mobsters.
The long-running TV show is given a new polish in this showy, violent gangster picture, which seemed to please all classes.
w David Mamet *d* Brian de Palma *ph* Stephen H. Burum *m* Ennio Morricone *pd* Patrizia von Brandenstein *ad* Hal Gausman *ed* Jerry Greenberg, Bill Pankow
☆ *Kevin Costner*, Sean Connery, Robert DeNiro, Charles Martin Smith, Andy Garcia, Richard Bradford
'Time honoured mayhem in the windy city.' – *Time Out*
'The picture is more like an attempt to visualize the public's collective dream of Chicago gangsters; our movie-fed imagination of the past is enlarged and given new vividness.' – *Pauline Kael, New Yorker*
♣ Sean Connery
♪ Ennio Morricone; art direction; costume design (Marilyn Vance-Straker)
✪ Ennio Morricone

The Unvanquished: see Aparajito

'Unhooked. Undressed. Unhinged.'
'A behind-the-seams look at the world of high fashion.'

Unzipped **
US   1995   73m   Technicolor/bw
Buena Vista/Hachette Filipacchi (Michael Alden)
🎬 🔳

A documentary about fashion designer Isaac Mizrahi who, after his 1994 fashion show is poorly received, returns in triumph with a new collection, inspired by Robert Flaherty's *Nanook of the North*.
An enjoyable insider's account of the often bizarre world of high fashion and its exotic denizens.
d Douglas Keeve *ph* Ellen Kuras *ed* Paula Heredia
'Keeve unzips the false chic to show the real chic beneath. Divine!' – *Alexander Walker*

Up at the Villa
US   2000   114m   Technicolor
UIP/Universal/ntermedia/Mirage/Stanley Buchthal (Geoff Stier)
In Florence in the 1930s, a widow, courted by an English diplomat and an American playboy, finds herself in a compromising situation.
Photogenic, glossy romantic drama that seems extremely dated; it requires an effort of will to summon up any interest in the affairs of this expatriate society just before the beginning of the Second World War.
w Belinda Haas *novella* W. Somerset Maugham *d* Philip Haas *ph* Maurizio Calvesi *m* Pino Donaggio *pd* Paul Brown *ed* Belinda Haas
☆ Kristin Scott Thomas, Sean Penn, Anne Bancroft, James Fox, Jeremy Davies, Derek Jacobi, Massimo Ghini
'A decent period drama that occasionally rises above the reliable.' – *Derek Elley, Variety*

'Every Day We Have Is One More Than We Deserve.'

Up Close and Personal
US   1996   124m   Technicolor
Entertainment/Touchstone/Cinergi (Jon Avnet, David Nicksay, Jordan Kerner)
🎬 🔳

Under the romantic guidance of an experienced executive, a waitress becomes a star TV newscaster.
Very much a 'so what?' movie, a sentimental weepie about what are presumably intended as glamorous and powerful lovers; outside its home territory, it looks and sounds ridiculous.
w Joan Didion, John Gregory Dunne *book* Golden Girl by Alanna Nash *d* Jon Avnet *ph* Karl Walter

Lindenlaub *m* Thomas Newman *pd* Jeremy Conway *ed* Debra Neil-Fisher
☆ Robert Redford, Michelle Pfeiffer, Stockard Channing, Joe Mantegna, Kate Nelligan, Glenn Plummer, James Rebhorn
'A Sunday afternoon time-filling movie.' – *Empire*
♪ song 'Because You Loved Me' (*m/ly* Diane Warren)

Up for the Cup
GB   1931   76m   bw
B & D (Herbert Wilcox)
A Yorkshireman gets into trouble when he comes to London for the Cup Final.
Slap-happy star farce which pleased the public.
w Con West, R. P. Weston, Bert Lee *d* Jack Raymond
☆ Sydney Howard, Joan Wyndham, Stanley Kirk, Moore Marriott
† The same star appeared in *Up for the Derby* in the following year; and in 1950 the original, with much the same script, was refashioned for Albert Modley; it was also directed by Jack Raymond.

'A lone American sergeant on the most impossible mission of the war!'

Up from the Beach *
US   1965   98m   bw   Cinemascope
TCF/Panoramic (Christian Ferry)
Just after D-Day, GIs have trouble in a Normandy village.
A kind of subdued sequel to The Longest Day, well made for war action addicts, but barely memorable.
w Stanley Mann, Claude Brule *novel* Epitaph for an Enemy *by* George Barr *d* Robert Parrish *ph* Walter Wottitz *m* Edgar Cosma
☆ Cliff Robertson, Red Buttons, Françoise Rosay, Marius Goring, Irina Demick, Broderick Crawford, James Robertson Justice, Slim Pickens

Up Goes Maisie
US   1946   89m   bw
MGM (George Haight)
Maisie becomes a secretary and outwits a crooked industrialist trying to steal her boss's invention of an easy-to-fly helicopter.
Lively little programmer.
w Thelma Robinson *d* Harry Beaumont *ph* Robert Planck *m* David Snell *ad* Cedric Gibbons, James Duce *ed* Irvine Warburton
☆ Ann Sothern, George Murphy, Hillary Brooke, Horace McNally, Ray Collins, Jeff York, Murray Alper, Lewis Howard, Jack Davis, Gloria Grafton, John Eldredge

Up in Arms **
👫 US   1944   106m   Technicolor
Samuel Goldwyn
A hypochondriac joins the army.
Loose, generally pleasant introductory vehicle for Danny Kaye.
w Don Hartman, Robert Pirosh, Allen Boretz *d* Elliott Nugent *ph* Ray Rennahan *md* Ray Heindorf, Louis Forbes
☆ Danny Kaye, Dinah Shore, Constance Dowling, Dana Andrews, Louis Calhern, Lyle Talbot
'Not since Greta Garbo made her bow has there been anything so terrific as the inimitable Danny, one of the most exhilarating and spontaneous personalities in film history.' – *New York Daily Mirror*
♪ song 'Now I Know' (*m* Harold Arlen, *ly* Ted Koehler); Ray Heindorf, Louis Forbes

Up in Central Park
US   1948   88m   bw
U-I (Karl Tunberg)
In turn-of-the-century New York, an Irish girl becomes involved in a crooked political set up.
Stiff and unyielding star musical.
w Karl Tunberg *d* William A. Seiter *ph* Milton Krasner *md* John Green *songs* Sigmund Romberg, Dorothy Fields
☆ Deanna Durbin, Vincent Price, Dick Haymes, Albert Sharpe, Tom Powers
'A misery.' – *New Yorker*

Up in Mabel's Room
US   1944   77m   bw
Edward Small
A flustered professor has to retrieve incriminating evidence from an old flame's room.

Antediluvian bedroom farce which keeps several ardent practitioners working happily.
w Tom Reed *play* Wilson Collison, Otto Harbach d Allan Dwan m Edward Paul
☆ Dennis O'Keefe, Mischa Auer, Marjorie Reynolds, Gail Patrick
'As horrible, and wonderful, as watching a Gopher Prairie dramatic club play a mail order farce (6m, 6f).' – *James Agee*
§ Edward Paul

Up in Smoke

US 1978 86m colour
Paramount (Lou Adler, Lou Lombardo)
▣ ◎~

Two dopeheads from a rock band go in search of pot so that they can play.
Direly unamusing; the slapstick is badly timed and the humour infantile. Stoned or sober, Cheech and Chong are the least funny comedy team since The Three Stooges.
w Tommy Chong, Cheech Marin d Lou Adler ph Gene Polito ad Leon Ericksen ed Scott Conrad, Lou Lombardo
☆ Cheech Marin, Tommy Chong, Strother Martin, Edie Adams, Stacy Keach, Tom Skerritt
'The humor is like dogface underclass humor – but without the resentment of the officers. And Cheech and Chong are so gracefully dumb-assed that if you're in a relaxed mood you can't help laughing at them.' – *Pauline Kael, New Yorker*

Up in the Cellar

US 1970 94m Movielab
AIP (William J. Immerman)
▣

A dejected freshman tries various schemes to revenge himself on the college president.
Youth satire aimed at a number of targets which quickly became obsolete; mildly interesting sociologically.
wd Theodore J. Flicker *novel The Late Boy Wonder* by Angus Hall ph Earl Roth m Don Randi
☆ Wes Stern, Joan Collins, Larry Hagman, Judy Pace

Up in the World

GB 1956 91m bw
Rank (Hugh Stewart)

A window cleaner becomes friendly with a boy millionaire.
Slow and unattractive comedy star vehicle.
w Jack Davies, Henry Blyth, Peter Blackmore d John Paddy Carstairs ph Jack Cox m Philip Green
☆ Norman Wisdom, Martin Caridia, Jerry Desmonde, Maureen Swanson, Ambrosine Philpotts, Colin Gordon

Up 'n' Under

GB 1998 100m Rank Colour
Entertainment/Touchdown/Lluniau Lliw (Mark Thomas)
▣

A former rugby league player takes a bet that he can train any team in eight weeks to beat the local champions.
Broad, quite likable comedy, cosy and insular.
wd John Godber *play* John Godber ph Alan M. Trow m Mark Thomas pd Hayden Pearce ed Chris Lawrence
☆ Gary Olsen, Richard Ridings, Samantha Janus, Ralph Brown, Neil Morrissey, Adrian Hood, David MacCreedy, Tony Slattery, Brian Glover, Griff Rhys-Jones
'A game try that still ends up in the second division.' – *Variety*

'Friends are for life.'
Up on the Roof *

GB 1997 101m Rank Colour 'Scope
Rank/Castle Rock/Turner/Carnival/Production Line (Jane Prowse, Pippa Cross, Brian Eastman)
◑

Five people, who shared a house and formed a student vocal group, get together for reunion six, and fifteen, years after their first meeting.
Slight but pleasant drama verging on the bland, with moments of music, which would look better on the television screen.
w Jane Prowse, Simon Moore d Simon Moore ph Nic Morris m Alan Parker pd Tim Hutchinson ed Peter Hollywood

☆ Billy Carter, Clare Cathcart, Adrian Lester, Amy Robbins, Daniel Ryan, Lavinia Bertram, Robin Herford
'The most unfunny, fatuous, irritating and insipid little British "comedy" I have ever had the misfortune to sit and suffer through.' – *Cosmo Landesman, Sunday Times*

Up Periscope

US 1959 111m Technicolor Warnerscope
Warner/Lakeside (Aubrey Schenck)
▣ ◎~

During World War II a submarine frogman is landed on a Pacific island to steal a Japanese code book.
Stock adventure story given stock presentation.
w Richard Landau *novel* Robb White d Gordon Douglas ph Carl Guthrie m Ray Heindorf
☆ James Garner, Edmond O'Brien, Alan Hale Jnr, Carleton Carpenter

Up Pompeii

GB 1971 90m Technicolor
EMI/Associated London Films (Ned Sherrin)
▣

A wily slave outwits Nero and escapes the eruption of Vesuvius.
Yawnmaking spinoff of a lively TV comedy series: the jokes just lie there, and die there.
w Sid Colin d Bob Kellett ph Ian Wilson m Carl Davis
☆ Frankie Howerd, Patrick Cargill, Michael Hordern, Barbara Murray, Lance Percival, Bill Fraser, Adrienne Posta
† Sequels: *Up the Front, Up the Chastity Belt* (qv).

Up Pops the Devil

US 1931 74m bw
Paramount

A wife supports her husband so that he can write novels.
Odd little comedy-drama which struck most people as rather half-hearted.
w Arthur Kober, Eve Unsell *play* Frances Goodrich, Albert Hackett d A. Edward Sutherland
☆ Carole Lombard, Norman Foster, Skeets Gallagher, Stuart Erwin, Lilyan Tashman
'Here's a plenty satisfying strip of celluloid but it won't do any drawing unless it's by word-of-mouth advertising.' – *Variety*

Up She Goes: see Maisie (Up Goes Maisie)

Up the Chastity Belt *

GB 1971 94m Technicolor
EMI/Associated London Films (Ned Sherrin)
▣

Medieval adventures of the serf Lurkalot and his master Sir Coward de Custard.
Patchy pantomime which doesn't always have the courage of its own slapdash vulgarity.
w Sid Colin, Ray Galton, Alan Simpson d Bob Kellett ph Ian Wilson m Carl Davis
☆ Frankie Howerd, Graham Crowden, Bill Fraser, Roy Hudd, Hugh Paddick, Anna Quayle, Eartha Kitt, Dave King, Fred Emney

Up the Creek *

GB 1958 83m bw HammerScope
Byron (Henry Halsted)
▣

A none-too-bright naval lieutenant is assigned command of a broken-down shore establishment.
Cheeky remake of Oh Mr Porter. Jokes fair, atmosphere cheerful and easy-going.
wd Val Guest ph Arthur Grant
☆ David Tomlinson, Peter Sellers, Wilfrid Hyde-White, Vera Day, Tom Gill, Michael Goodliffe, Reginald Beckwith, Lionel Jeffries
† Sequel: *Further Up the Creek.*

Up the Down Staircase *

US 1967 124m Technicolor
Warner/Pakula-Mulligan
▣

Problems of a schoolteacher in one of New York's tough sections.
Earnest, well-acted, not very likeable melodrama.
w Tad Mosel *novel* Bel Kaufman d Robert Mulligan ph Joseph Coffey m Fred Karlin
☆ Sandy Dennis, Patrick Bedford, Eileen Heckart, Ruth White, Jean Stapleton, Sorrell Booke, Roy Poole

'Sandy Dennis, blinking as if she'd taken pills and been awakened in the middle of the night … She reacts confusedly before the situations even develop, but the audience is ahead of her anyway.' – *Pauline Kael, New Yorker*

Up the Front

♟♟ GB 1972 89m Technicolor
EMI/Associated London Films (Ned Sherrin)
▣

A footman is hypnotized into enlisting in World War I and has an enemy 'plan' tattooed on his buttocks.
Threadbare end-of-the-pier romp.
w Sid Colin, Eddie Braben d Bob Kellett ph Tony Spratling m Peter Greenwell ad Seamus Flannery
☆ Frankie Howerd, Bill Fraser, Zsa Zsa Gabor, Stanley Holloway, Hermione Baddeley, Robert Coote, Lance Percival, Dora Bryan

'Don't get caught is what she wasn't taught!'
Up the Junction

GB 1967 119m Techniscope
Paramount/BHE (Anthony Havelock-Allan, John Brabourne)

A well-off girl crosses London's river to live among the workers of Clapham.
Socially obsolete sensationalism based on a television semi-documentary. An irritating heroine moves hygienically among motorbikes.
w Roger Smith *book* Nell Dunn d Peter Collinson ph Arthur Lavis m Mike Hugg, Manfred Mann
☆ Suzy Kendall, Dennis Waterman, Adrienne Posta, Maureen Lipman, Michael Gothard, Liz Fraser, Hylda Baker, Alfie Bass

Up the River

US 1930 80m bw
Fox

An ex-convict is threatened with exposure, but his two pals escape to help him.
Very minor comedy with interesting credits.
w Maurine Watkins d John Ford ph Joseph August
☆ Spencer Tracy, Warren Hymer, Claire Luce, Humphrey Bogart, William Collier Snr
'No cast names to draw, but if the exploitation can make 'em attend, the film will meet its entertainment obligations.' – *Variety*
† In 1938 TCF released a remake directed by Alfred Werker, with Preston Foster, Tony Martin, Slim Summerville and Arthur Treacher.

Up the Sandbox

US 1972 98m Technicolor
Barwood/First Artists (Robert Chartoff, Irwin Winkler)
▣ ◎~

A professor's wife finds she is pregnant again and fantasizes about her future life.
Muddled comedy-drama with little point and less entertainment value.
w Paul Zindel *novel* Anne Richardson Roiphe d Irvin Kershner ph Gordon Willis, Andy Marton m Billy Goldenberg ad Harry Horner
☆ Barbra Streisand, David Selby, Ariane Heller, Jane Hoffman
'A magical mystery tour through the picture book mind of one Manhattan housewife.' – *Richard Combs*

Up Tight

US 1968 104m Technicolor
Paramount/Marlukin (Jules Dassin)

A black street cleaner betrays his criminal pals for money and is hunted down by them.
Ponderous black remake of The Informer, too schematic to make any dramatic or human impression.
w Jules Dassin, Ruby Dee, Julian Mayfield d Jules Dassin ph Boris Kaufman m Booker T. Jones pd Alexander Trauner
☆ Raymond St Jacques, Ruby Dee, Julian Mayfield, Frank Silvera, Roscoe Lee Browne, Juanita Moore

Uphill All the Way

US 1985 86m colour
Melroy/Guardian (Burr Smidt, David L. Ford)
▣

In the early 1900s, two down-and-out confidence tricksters are mistaken for bank robbers and chased across Texas.
Raucous and depressingly unamusing comedy, dependent on heavy-handed slapstick; its two country-

singing stars fail to transfer their hit-making abilities to the screen.
wd Frank Q. Dobbs ph Roland 'Ozzie' Smith m Dennis M. Pratt pd Hal Matheny ed Chuck Weiss
☆ Roy Clark, Mel Tillis, Burl Ives, Glen Campbell, Trish Van Devere, Elaine Joyce, Jacque Lynn Colton, Frank Gorshin, Sheb Wooley, Richard Paul
† Burt Reynolds appears uncredited.

Upperworld

US 1934 75m bw
Warner

A society-conscious wife drives her husband into the arms of a girl from the Bronx.
Smooth romantic melodrama with a murder angle; dated but enjoyable.
w Ben Markson *story* Ben Hecht d Roy del Ruth
☆ Warren William, Mary Astor, Ginger Rogers, Andy Devine, J. Carrol Naish, Henry O'Neill

The Ups and Downs of a Handyman

GB 1975 90m colour
KFR/Nigel A. Marsh (Kenneth F. Rowles)
aka: *Confessions of an Odd-Job Man*

A newly-wed couple move to the country, where the husband finds work servicing the bored wives and daughters of the locals.
Trivial sex farce, of the kind that brought the British film industry to its nadir in the mid-70s.
w Derrick Slater, John Sealey d John Sealey ph Doug Hill m Vic Elms ed Jim Atkinson, John Carr
☆ Barry Stokes, Gay Soper, Sue Lloyd, Bob Todd, Chic Murray, Robert Dorning, Valerie Leon, Penny Meredith, Helli Louise, John Blythe
'Repressive, sniggeringly unfunny soft-core farce.' – *MFB*

Upstairs and Downstairs

GB 1959 101m Eastmancolor
Rank (Betty E. Box)

Newlyweds have trouble with maids and au pair girls.
Glossy, cheerful, empty-headed domestic comedy.
w Frank Harvey *novel* Ronald Scott Thorn d Ralph Thomas ph Ernest Steward m Philip Green
☆ Michael Craig, Anne Heywood, Mylène Demongeot, James Robertson Justice, Sidney James, Daniel Massey, Claudia Cardinale, Joan Hickson, Joan Sims

'Evil Lives Closer Than You Think.'
The Upstairs Neighbor

US 1994 91m colour
Brandon Foley/Matt Devlen
▣ ▣

A novelist begins to believe that the man who lives above him is tapping his phone and involved in occult practices.
A low-budget venture into paranoia and madness, which transverses familiar territory, leaving no trace as it goes.
wd James Merendino ph Greg Littlewood m Bruce Langhorne ad Charlotte Malmlof ed Esther P. Russell
☆ Sebastian Gutierrez, Rustam Branaman, Christina Fulton, Kane Picoy
'An effective, if derivative, slice of mood-driven entertainment.' – *Variety*

Uptown Saturday Night *

US 1974 104m Technicolor
Warner/Verdon/First Artists (Melville Tucker)
▣ ▣

Three friends pursue crooks who have inadvertently stolen a winning lottery ticket.
Witless but high-spirited star comedy for blacks, with a variety of sordid backgrounds.
w Richard Wesley d Sidney Poitier ph Fred J. Koenekamp m Tom Scott
☆ Sidney Poitier, Bill Cosby, Harry Belafonte, Flip Wilson, Roscoe Lee Browne, Richard Pryor, Rosalind Cash, Paula Kelly
'If it had been filmed with a white cast this collection of atrophied comedy routines would have been indistinguishable from a Monogram farce of the forties.' – *David McGillivray*

The Upturned Glass *
GB 1947 86m bw
GFD/Triton (Sydney Box, James Mason)
A Harley Street surgeon murders the woman responsible for the death of the girl he loved.
Rather pointless psychopathology with an ill-explained title; an interesting example of a top star not knowing what's best for him.
w Jon P. Monaghan, Pamela Kellino d Lawrence Huntington ph Reg Wyer m Bernard Stevens
☆ James Mason, Pamela Kellino, Rosamund John, Ann Stephens, Henry Oscar, Morland Graham, Brefni O'Rorke
'The psychology is genuine; so too is the tension; the camera plays some good quiet tricks.' – *William Whitebait*

Upworld
US 1990 88m DeLuxe
Lightning/Interscope/Trilogy (Robert W. Cort, Scott Kroopf, Pen Densham, Richard Lewis)
An undercover cop uncovers corruption and crime with the aid of a gnome called Gnorm from an underground world.
An unsuccessful oddity, with its combination of a paranoid thriller, full of guns and explosions, and an underdeveloped fantasy about a diminutive creature; it is too violent for small children, and too silly for older ones.
w Pen Densham, John Watson d Stan Winston ph Bojan Bazelli m Richard Gibbs pd Marcia Hinds sp Marcus Manton
☆ Anthony Michael Hall, Jerry Orbach, Claudia Christian, Eli Danker, Mark Harelik, Robert Z'Dar

Uranus **
France 1990 99m colour
Artificial Eye/Renn/DD/Sofica (Patrick Bordier)
In the aftermath of the Second World War, political rivalries between Communists and Fascists, Resistance fighters and collaborators, tear apart the inhabitants of a small French town.
Excellently acted and engaging, though wordy, account of postwar witch hunts.
w Claude Berri, Arlette Langmann novel Marcel Aymé d Claude Berri ph Renato Berta m Jean-Claude Petit ad Bernard Vezat ed Hervé de Luze
☆ Philippe Noiret, Gérard Depardieu, Jean-Pierre Marielle, Michel Blanc, Gérard Desarthe, Michel Galabru, Fabrice Luchini
'The intrinsic interest of the subject matter holds us for a while, which is just as well, because this dull, talkative film is dramatically barren.' – *Philip French, Observer*
'The film makes the case against the totalitarian intolerance of empowered Stalinism – in French practice it often amounted to a settling of personal scores – with persuasive force.' – *Richard Schickel, Time*

Urban Cowboy
US 1980 135m Movielab Panavision
Paramount (Robert Evans, Irving Azoff)
A rural Texan finds it difficult to succeed in the big city.
Unpleasant and uninteresting star melodrama with a plot vaguely reminiscent of the first part of An American Tragedy.
w James Bridges novel Aaron Latham d James Bridges ph Ray Villalobos m various songs pd Stephen Grimes
☆ John Travolta, Debra Winger, Scott Glenn, Madolyn Smith
'A fatuous vehicle for John Travolta, requiring him to stride (stiffly and expressionlessly) through various macho torments ... the two-hour-plus running time, incorporating a wealth of cliché characters, is excruciatingly protracted.' – *Tom Milne, MFB*

'It Happened To Someone Who Knows Someone You Know ... You're Next.'
Urban Legend
US 1998 100m colour Super 35
Columbia TriStar/Phoenix (Neil H. Moritz, Gina Matthews, Michael McDonnell)
A serial killer acts out urban legends, such as a driver ignoring a stuttering informant who was trying to tell him that there was someone with an axe hiding in the back of his car.
A horror movie that begins with a clever concept, though otherwise it offers the usual mix of multiple murders and shocks.
w Silvio Horta d Jamie Blanks ph James Chressanthis m Christopher Young pd Charles Breen ed Jay Cassidy
☆ Jared Leto, Alicia Witt, Rebecca Gayheart, Joshua Jackson, Loretta Devine, Tara Reid, Michael Rosenbaum, Robert Englund
'A silly but not unlikeable formula horror picture.' – *Kim Newman, Empire*

Urga **
France/USSR 1991 120m colour
Hachette Première/Studio Trite (Michel Seydoux)
US title: *Close to Eden*
A Mongolian herdsman rescues a Russian lorry-driver who crashes into a river and takes him home to his family.
Delightful and exuberant fable of a clash between urban and rural ways of life.
w Nikita Mikhalkov, Roustam Ibraguimbekov d Nikita Mikhalkov ph Villenn Kaluta m Eduard Artemiev pd Alexei Levchenko ed Joelle Hache
☆ Bayaertu, Badema, Vladimir Gostukhin, Babuskha
'It hardly advances cinematic art, but story and characters resonate with life.' – *Geoff Brown, The Times*
♫ foreign language film

Urotsukidö: see *Legend of the Overfiend*

Urotsukidöji II: see *Legend of the Demon Womb*

Urotsukidoxji III: see *Legend of the Demon Womb*

Ursus (dubbed)
Italy/Spain 1961 95m Eastmancolor Totalscope
UA/Ciné Italia/Atenea (Italo Zingarelli)
aka: *Mighty Ursus*
Ursus returns from the wars to discover that the woman he loves has been kidnapped.
Mundane muscle-man epic, with a dreary narrative and very little action.
w Giuseppe Mangione, Sergio Sollima, Giuliano Carnimeo d Carlo Campogalliani ph Eloy Mella m Roman Vlad ad Romoloa Girolami ed Jolanda Benvenuti, Julia Pena
☆ Ed Fury, Cristina Gajoni, Moira Orfei, Mary Marlon, Mario Scaccia
'The stiff performances and excruciating dialogue come as no surprise, but even the spectacle is gracelessly mounted.' – *David McGillivray*

Ursus and the Tartar Princess (dubbed)
France/Italy 1961 80m Technicolor Techniscope
Explorer Film '58/CFFP (Nino Battiferri)
In 17th-century Poland, a captured nobleman falls in love with the daughter of the leader of an invading Tartar army.

A romantic epic, with strongman Ursus's role reduced to a walk-on; it is a little different from the usual Italian spectacles in preaching a gospel of peace between scenes of swordplay and bloodshed.
w Remigio del Grosso (English dialogue John Hart) d (English-language version) Richard McNamara ph Anchise Brizzi m A. F. Lavagnino ad Antonio Visone ed Antonietta Zita
☆ Yoko Tani, Ettore Manni, Joe Robinson, Akim Tamiroff, Roland Lesaffre, Maria Grazia Spina

'The cop who won't stop is back. But this time he's chasing a lot more than a fugitive.'
US Marshals *
US 1998 133m Technicolor Panavision
Warner (Arnold and Anne Kopelson)
A US marshal tracks down a man accused of killing two FBI agents.
Not only a sequel to The Fugitive, but one that attempts to copy its narrative with only slight variations: a plane crash substituting for a train derailment and so on; but, this time around, they left out human interest.
w John Pogue d Stuart Baird ph Andrzej Bartkowiak m Jerry Goldsmith pd Maher Ahmad ed Terry Rawlings
☆ Tommy Lee Jones, Wesley Snipes, Robert Downey Jnr, Kate Nelligan, Joe Pantoliano, Irene Jacob, Daniel Robuck
'The plot, like nearly every one you see nowadays, defies sense and resists explication.' – *Alexander Walker, London Evening Standard*

Used Cars *
👫 US 1980 111m Metrocolor
Columbia (Bob Gale)
For the love of his boss's daughter, a fast-talking car salesman saves a used-car lot from being taken over by a mean-spirited rival.
Vigorous broad comedy, amusing enough if you're feeling indulgent.
w Robert Zemeckis, Bob Gale d Robert Zemeckis ph Donald M. Morgan m Patrick Williams pd Peter M. Jamison ed Michael Kahn
☆ Kurt Russell, Gerrit Graham, Frank McRae, Deborah Harmon, Jack Russell
'A classic screwball fantasy – a neglected modern comedy that's like a more restless and visually high-spirited version of the W. C. Fields pictures.' – *Pauline Kael, New Yorker*

Used People *
US 1992 116m DeLuxe
TCF/Largo (Peggy Rajski)
An Italian widower courts a Jewish widow whom he has loved from a distance for more than 20 years.
A romantic comedy for the middle-aged, leisurely in pace, giving its cast room to display their skills.
w Todd Graff play *The Grandma Plays* by Todd Graff d Beeban Kidron ph David Watkin m Rachel Portman pd Stuart Wurtzel ed John Tintori
☆ Shirley MacLaine, Marcello Mastroianni, Bob Dishy, Kathy Bates, Jessica Tandy, Marcia Gay Harden, Lee Wallace, Louis Guss
'An actors' showcase, with heightened performances by the ensemble eschewing the naturalism favored by mainstream fare.' – *Variety*
'Funny, touching and very well-observed ... But it finally exposes itself as clichéd, a little shapeless and too long.' – *Derek Malcolm, Guardian*

USS Teakettle: see *You're in the Navy Now*

'Five Criminals. One Line Up. No Coincidence.'
The Usual Suspects ***
US 1995 105m Technicolor Panavision
Polygram/Spelling/Blue Parrot/Bad Hat Harry/Rosco (Bryan Singer, Michael McDonnell)
Five crooks, who meet in a police line-up and decide to work together on a couple of robberies, come to believe that they are being manipulated by a mysterious master criminal.
Excellent, gripping thriller that plays tricks with its audience, leading it down one blind alley after another, dealing in deliberate confusion and double-cross. Its refusal to come clean until its final revelation may infuriate some, but it is part of its appeal, aided by some nicely edgy performances from the actors.
w Christopher McQuarrie d Bryan Singer ph Newton Thomas Sigel m John Ottman pd Howard Cummings ed John Ottman
☆ Gabriel Byrne, Stephen Baldwin, Chazz Palminteri, Kevin Pollak, Pete Postlethwaite, Kevin Spacey, Suzy Amis, Giancarlo Esposito, Dan Hedaya, Benicio del Toro, Paul Bartel
'What The Usual Suspects is not method acting or directorial flair, but its vivid, audacious, relentless intelligence.' – *Stephen Amidon, Sunday Times*
'An ironic, bang-up thriller about the wages of crime. A terrific cast of exciting actors socks over this absorbing complicated yarn.' – *Todd McCarthy, Variety*
🏆 Kevin Spacey; Christopher McQuarrie
🎬 Christopher McQuarrie

Utomlennye Solntsem: see *Burnt by the Sun*

Utopia: see *Robinson Crusoeland*

Utu ***
New Zealand 1983 118m Fujicolour
Glitteron (Geoff Murphy, Don Blakeney)
In New Zealand in the 1870s, a Maori, whose family is massacred by the army, and a farmer, whose wife is killed by the Maoris, are both obsessed by revenge.
Powerful and absorbing drama of imperialistic and colonial attitudes, set against wild, open spaces.
w Geoff Murphy, Keith Aberdein d Geoff Murphy ph Graeme Cowley m John Charles pd Ron Highfield ed Michael Horton, Ian John
☆ Anzac Wallace, Bruno Lawrence, Wi Kuki Kaa, Kelly Johnson, Tim Elliott, Tanya Bristowe, Ilona Rodgers, Merata Mita, Tom Polan

Utvandrarna: see *The Emigrants*

Utz *
GB/Germany/Italy 1992 colour
BBC/NDR/Academy/Cine Electric/Viva (John Goldschmidt)
An American art dealer tries to discover what has happened to a priceless collection of porcelain figures.
Gently civilized entertainment on acquisitive and obsessive pleasures, although one lacking much popular appeal.
w Hugh Whitemore novel Bruce Chatwin d George Sluizer ph Gerard Vandenberg m Nicola Piovani pd Karel Vacek ed Lin Friedman
☆ Armin Mueller-Stahl, Brenda Fricker, Peter Riegert, Paul Scofield, Gaye Brown, Miriam Karlin, Pauline Melville, Vera Soukupova
'The polyglot cast and crew can't provide a cohesive basis on which to pin a frustratingly fragmented screenplay.' – *Variety*

V

V. I. Warshawski

US 1991 89m Technicolor
Warner/Hollywood Pictures/Silver Screen Partners
IV/Chestnut Hill (Jeffrey Lurie)

A female private eye is hired to investigate the murder of a businessman.

Exceedingly dull thriller intended to introduce to film a tough feminist detective from fiction. Its failure to find an audience is likely to mean that the planned sequels will not appear.

w Edward Taylor, David Aaron Cohen, Nick Thiel *novel* Indemnity Only by Sara Paretsky d Jeff Kanew ph Jan Kiesser m Randy Edelman pd Barbara Ling ed C. Timothy O'Meara, Debra Neil

☆ Kathleen Turner, Jay O. Sanders, Charles Durning, Angela Goethals, Nancy Paul, Frederick Coffin, Charles McCaughan, Stephen Meadows, Wayne Knight

'The feebly-plotted movie comes over as a padded-out 90-minute episode of a routine private eye series, or more accurately the black box from a TV pilot that crashed shortly after take-off. It could be shown in film schools as an example of how not to adapt a novel for the screen.' – *Philip French, Observer*

Les Vacances de Monsieur Hulot: see
Monsieur Hulot's Holiday

'A tale of violence, romance and madness.'

Vacas *

Spain 1992 96m colour
ICA/Sogetel (Ricardo Garcia Arrojos)

Rivalry and love between two families, linked by children, continue over three generations.

An intricate, enjoyable story of family feuds and affairs, agreeably tinged with fantasy.

w Julio Medem, Michael Gaztambide d Julio Medem ph Carles Gusi m Alberto Iglesias ed Maria Elena Sainz de Rozas

☆ Emma Suárez, Carmelo Gómez, Ana Torrent, Karra Elejalde, Klara Badiola, Txema Blasco

'With lush cinematography, energetic performances and a strong sense of the mystery and terror to be found in the Great Outdoors, pic lingers in the memory as impressive and unusual.' – *Variety*

'A poetic, boldly directed first film that serves notice of a promising talent.' – *Sheila Johnston, Independent*

Vacation from Marriage: see *Perfect Strangers (GB)*

La Vache et le Prisonnier: see *The Cow and I*

The Vagabond King

US 1956 88m Technicolor Vistavision
Paramount (Pat Duggan)
The life and loves of French medieval poet and rebel François Villon.

Shiny, antiseptic studio-set remake of an old musical warhorse.

w Ken Englund, Noel Langley *operetta* Rudolf Friml d Michael Curtiz ph Robert Burks m/ly Rudolf Friml, Brian Hooker, Johnny Burke md Victor Young ad Hans Dreier

☆ Oreste, Kathryn Grayson, Rita Moreno, Walter Hampden, Leslie Nielsen, Cedric Hardwicke, William Prince

† A 1930 version with Dennis King is lost. Non-musical versions of the story include *If I Were King*, in 1920 with William Farnum, 1928's *The Beloved Rogue* with John Barrymore, and in 1938 with Ronald Colman.

⚬ Hans Dreier

Vagabond Lady

US 1935 72m bw
MGM
The two sons of a department store owner fall for their father's secretary.

Medium romantic comedy which didn't seem to stick in anyone's memory.

w Frank Butler d Sam Taylor

☆ Robert Young, Reginald Denny, Evelyn Venable, Frank Craven, Berton Churchill

'This just misses being a charm picture, the kind they hold over or bring back for repeat dates.' – *Variety*

Vagabonde ***

France 1985 104m colour
Cine-Tamaris/A2/Ministère de la Culture

French title: *Sans Toit ni Loi*
aka: *Vagabond*
After a young woman is found frozen to death in a ditch, people tell of their experiences of her in the last weeks of her life, and of how she abandoned conventional living to become a tramp.

Disturbingly chill movie of the accidental collisions of people's lives, and the changes they cause, with an enigma at its centre.

wd Agnès Varda ph Patrick Blossier m Joanna Bruzdowicz ed Agnès Varda, Patricia Mazuy

☆ Sandrine Bonnaire, Macha Meril, Stéphane Freiss, Laurence Cortadellas, Marthe Jarnais, Yolande Moreau, Joel Fosse

† It won the Golden Lion award for best film at the Venice Film Festival in 1985.

The Vagrant

US/France 1992 91m DeLuxe
TCF/MGM/Pathé Communications/Brooksfilms/Canal+ (Gillian Richardson)

A paranoid office worker is persecuted by a murderous, evil-smelling tramp.

Mind-numbingly dreadful horror comedy, inane from start to finish.

w Richard Jefferies d Chris Walas ph Jack Wallner, John J. Connor m Christopher Young pd Michael Bolton ed Jay Ignaszewski sp Chris Walas

☆ Bill Paxton, Michael Ironside, Marshall Bell, Mitzi Kapture, Colleen Camp, Patrika Darbo

The Valachi Papers

France/Italy 1972 127m Technicolor
Euro France/de Laurentiis Intermarco (Dino de Laurentiis)

A convicted gangster talks to an FBI agent about his life in the Mafia.

Rough, violent gangster melodrama, none the better for being based on actual events.

w Stephen Geller *book* Peter Maas d Terence Young ph Aldo Tonti m Riz Ortolani

☆ Charles Bronson, Fred Valleca, Gerald S. O'Loughlin, Lino Ventura, Walter Chiari, Amedeo Nazzari, Joseph Wiseman

Valborgsmässoafton: see *Walpurgis Night*

Valdez Is Coming

US 1970 90m DeLuxe
UA/Norlan/Ira Steiner

A Mexican confronts a rancher who has double-crossed him.

Simply conceived Western which doesn't quite manage to be the classic intended.

w Roland Kibbee, David Rayfiel *novel* Elmore Leonard d Edwin Sherin ph Gabor Pogany m Charles Gross

☆ Burt Lancaster, Susan Clark, Jon Cypher, Barton Heyman, Frank Silvera

Vale Abraao: see *Abraham Valley*

Valentino

US 1951 105m Technicolor
Columbia (Edward Small)
An Italian immigrant to the US becomes a world-famous romantic film star but dies young.

Disastrously flat attempt to recapture the feel of Hollywood in the twenties as a background to a flatulent romance.

w George Bruce d Lewis Allen ph Harry Stradling m Heinz Roemheld

☆ Anthony Dexter, Eleanor Parker, Richard Carlson, Patricia Medina, Joseph Calleia, Dona Drake, Lloyd Gough, Otto Kruger

'One can almost see the decorated border round the words … it mixes fact, speculation, needless inaccuracy and bathos.' – *Gavin Lambert*

'The dialogue is unbelievably ham, the "entirely imaginary" story commonplace; the players deserve sympathy.' – *Richard Mallett, Punch*

Valentino *

GB 1977 127m DeLuxe
UA/Aperture/Chartoff-Winkler (Harry Benn)

Reporters quiz celebrities at a star's funeral, and his eccentric life unfolds.

Sensationalist 'exposé' of Valentino's rise to fame, with excellent period detail but no sympathy for its subject.

w Ken Russell, Mardik Martin *book* Brad Steiger, Chaw Mank d Ken Russell ph Peter Suschitzky m Ferde Grofe, Stanley Black ad Philip Harrison

☆ Rudolf Nureyev, Leslie Caron, Michelle Phillips, Carol Kane, Felicity Kendal, Huntz Hall, David de Keyser, Alfred Marks, Anton Diffring, Jennie Linden, John Justin

'By attaching the names of actual people to his sadomasochistic fantasies, the director, Ken Russell, gives the picture a nasty inside-joke appeal.' – *Pauline Kael*

Valentino Returns

US 1989 90m Alpha Cine
Owl/Vidmark (Peter Hoffman, David Wisnievitz)

The adolescent son of a mismatched couple buys a pink Cadillac in order to impress his girlfriend.

Low-key, lacklustre drama stuck in a familiar groove.

w Leonard Gardner *story* Christ Has Returned to Earth and Preaches Here Nightly by Leonard Gardner d Peter Hoffman ph Jerzy Zielinski ad Woody Romine ed Denine Rowan

☆ Barry Tubb, Frederic Forrest, Veronica Cartwright, Jenny Wright, Macon McCalman, Kit McDonough, Seth Isler, Miguel Ferrer, Leonard Gardner

Valerie

US 1957 80m bw
UA/Hal R. Makelim
A Western rancher is accused of wounding his wife and murdering her parents.

Curious little Rashomon-like courtroom melodrama, quite well made and acted.

w Leonard Heideman, Emmett Murphy d Gerd Oswald ph Ernest Laszlo m Albert Glasser

☆ Anita Ekberg, Sterling Hayden, Anthony Steel, John Wengraf

Valerie A Týden Divu: see *Valerie and Her Week of Wonders*

Valerie and Her Week of Wonders **

Czechoslovakia 1970 77m Eastmancolor
Contemporary/Ceskoslovensky/Barrandov

original title: *Valerie A Týden Divu*
A young girl on the verge of puberty dreams of vampires and her own death, burned as a witch by a priest who tried to rape her.

A surrealist vision of the awakening of sexuality, full of startling images drawn from myth and religious ritual, somewhat like a more explicit Freudian version of Alice in Wonderland.

w Jaromil Jires, Ester Krumbachová *story* Vitezlav Nezval d Jaromil Jires ph Jan Curik m Jan Klusák ad Jan Oliva ed Josef Valusiak

☆ Jaroslava Schallerová, Helena Anýzová, Petr Kopriva, Jüiri Prymek, Jan Klusák, Libuse Komancová, Karel Engel, Alena Stojáková

'The real and the unreal are disturbingly fused, while the images are continually eloquent.' – *Gordon Gow, Films and Filming*

The Valiant

GB/Italy 1961 89m bw
(UA) BHP/Euro International (Jon Penington)
During World War II, a battleship in Alexandria harbour is mined, and the captain tries desperately to avert disaster.

Ill-made war fodder, of no interest at any level.

w Keith Waterhouse, Willis Hall d Roy Baker ph Wilkie Cooper, Egil Woxholt m Christopher Whelen

☆ John Mills, Ettore Manni, Robert Shaw, Liam Redmond, Ralph Michael, Colin Douglas, Dinsdale Landen

'I who have laughed at love, have fallen in love at last!'

Valiant Is the Word for Carrie

US 1936 110m bw
RKO (Wesley Ruggles)
A childless woman devotes her life to orphan children.

Tedious soap opera.

w Claude Binyon *novel* Barry Benefield d Wesley Ruggles ph Leo Tover m Frederick Hollander

☆ Gladys George, John Howard, Dudley Digges, Arline Judge, Harry Carey, Isabel Jewell

⚬ Gladys George

The Valley of Decision *

US 1945 119m bw
MGM (Edwin H. Knopf)
In old Pittsburgh, an Irish housemaid marries the master's son.

Trouble at t' mill epic romance, American style; starrily cast but not excitingly made.

w John Meehan, Sonya Levien *novel* Marcia Davenport d Tay Garnett ph Joseph Ruttenberg m Herbert Stothart

☆ Greer Garson, Gregory Peck, Lionel Barrymore, Donald Crisp, Preston Foster, Gladys Cooper, Marsha Hunt, Reginald Owen, Dan Duryea, Jessica Tandy, Barbara Everest, Marshall Thompson

⚬ Herbert Stothart, Greer Garson

Valley of Eagles

GB 1951 86m bw
Independent Sovereign/GFD (Nat Bronsten)

A Swedish scientist chases into Lapland after his wife and her lover who have stolen an important formula.

Unconvincing scenery mars what might have been an unusual adventure drama.

w Paul Tabori, Nat Bronsten, Terence Young d Terence Young ph Harry Waxman m Nino Rota

☆ Jack Warner, John McCallum, Nadia Gray, Anthony Dawson, Mary Laura Wood, Christopher Lee

Valley of Fire

US 1951 60m bw
Columbia/Gene Autry (Armand Schaefer)
Gene Autry becomes mayor and cleans up a mining town.

Formula 'B' Western, with a rambling narrative and some dull comedy.

---

w Gerald Geraghty *story* Earle Snell *d* John English *ph* William Bradford *md* Mischa Bakaleinikoff *ad* Charles Clague *ed* James Sweeney

☆ Gene Autry, Pat Buttram, Gail Davis, Russell Hayden, Christine Larson, Harry Lauter, Terry Frost, Barbara Stanley, Teddy Infuhr, Marjorie Liszt

Valley of Fury: see *Chief Crazy Horse*

The Valley of Gwangi
♙♙ US 1968 95m Technicolor
Warner/Morningside (Charles H. Schneer)
◻◻ ▤ ◎~

Cowboys and scientists discover prehistoric monsters in a 'forbidden' Mexican Valley.
Tedious adventure yarn enhanced by good special effects.
w William E. Best *d* Jim O'Connolly *ph* Erwin Hillier *m* Jerome Moross *sp* Ray Harryhausen
☆ Richard Carlson, Laurence Naismith, James Franciscus, Gila Golan, Freda Jackson

Valley of Song
GB 1953 74m bw
ABPC
US title: *Men Are Children Twice*
Members of a Welsh valley choir nearly come to blows over the interpretation of *Messiah*.
Neat, Ealing-style comedy from a well-known radio play.
w Cliff Gordon, Phil Park *play* Choir Practice by Cliff Gordon *d* Gilbert Gunn *ph* Lionel Banes *m* Robert Gill
☆ Mervyn Johns, Clifford Evans, Maureen Swanson, John Fraser, Rachel Thomas, Rachel Roberts, Kenneth Williams

Valley of the Dolls *
US 1967 123m DeLuxe Panavision
TCF/Red Lion (David Weisbart)
▤ ◎~

An innocent young actress is corrupted by Broadway and Hollywood, and takes to drugs.
Cliché-ridden but good-looking road-to-ruin melodrama from a bitchy bestseller; production values high, but the whole thing goes over the top at the end.
w Helen Deutsch, Dorothy Kingsley *novel* Jacqueline Susann *d* Mark Robson *ph* William H. Daniels *m* André Previn *md* John Williams *ad* Jack Martin Smith, Richard Day
☆ Barbara Parkins, Patty Duke, Susan Hayward, Paul Burke, Sharon Tate, Martin Milner, Tony Scotti, Charles Drake, Alex Davion, Lee Grant, Robert H. Harris
  'What kind of pills do you take to sit through a film like this?' – *The Golden Turkey Awards*
  'A skilfully deceptive imitation of a real drama … on a closer look the characters turn out to be images that have almost nothing to do with people.' – *Christian Science Monitor*
  'One of the most stupefyingly clumsy films ever made by alleged professionals.' – *Joseph Morgenstern, Newsweek*
  † Judy Garland was originally slated to play the Susan Hayward part.
  ♫ John Williams

Valley of the Giants
US 1938 79m Technicolor
Warner
A lumberman fights pirates to preserve his beloved redwoods.
Routine outdoor thick ear-to which colour lent the semblance of freshness.
w Seton I. Miller, Michael Fessier *novel* Peter B. Kyne *d* William Keighley
☆ Wayne Morris, Claire Trevor, Frank McHugh, Alan Hale, Donald Crisp, Charles Bickford
  'A yarn which contains nearly all the proven surefire elements of the successful outdoor picture.' – *Variety*
  † This was the third version of the story; the first, in 1919, starred Wallace Reid; the second, in 1927, starred Milton Sills. The 1952 movie *The Big Trees*, with Kirk Douglas, had a suspiciously similar storyline.

Valley of the Kings
US 1954 86m Eastmancolor
MGM
◎
Archaeologists fight looters in the tomb of a Pharaoh.

Thin as drama, with little action or suspense and dispirited acting, this hokum piece nevertheless benefits from splendid locations.
w Robert Pirosh, Karl Tunberg *d* Robert Pirosh *ph* Robert Surtees *m* Miklos Rozsa
☆ Robert Taylor, Eleanor Parker, Carlos Thompson, Kurt Kasznar, Victor Jory

Valley of the Sun
US 1942 79m bw
RKO (Graham Baker)

A government spy in old Arizona outwits a crooked Indian agent.
Cheapjack Western with nothing to commend it.
w Horace McCoy *story* Clarence Budington Kelland *d* George Marshall *ph* Harry J. Wild *m* Paul Sawtell
☆ James Craig, Lucille Ball, Dean Jagger, Billy Gilbert, Cedric Hardwicke, Peter Whitney, Tom Tyler, Antonio Moreno, George Cleveland

Valley of the Zombies
US 1946 56m bw
Republic
A big city zombie goes on a murder spree.
Entirely unpersuasive hokum which wouldn't chill a baby. No valley is apparent.
w The McGowans *d* Philip Ford
☆ Ian Keith, Robert Livingston, Adrian Booth, Thomas Jackson, Charles Trowbridge

Valmont
France/GB 1989 137m colour
Orion/Claude Berri/Renn (Paul Rassam, Michael Hausman)
▤ ◎~

In the 1780s, two aristocrats conspire in the seduction of a young and virginal bride-to-be.
A playful adaptation and one that suggests a fancy dress party rather than a period film, with the tragic ending of the original being altered into something more upbeat and cynical.
w Jean-Claude Carrière *novel* Les Liaisons Dangereuses by Choderlos de Laclos *d* Milos Forman *ph* Miroslav Ondricek *m* Christopher Palmer *pd* Pierre Guffroy *ed* Alan Heim, Nena Danevic
☆ Colin Firth, Annette Bening, Meg Tilly, Fairuza Balk, Sian Phillips, Jeffrey Jones, Henry Thomas, Fabia Drake, T. P. McKenna, Isla Blair, Ronald Lacey
  † A rival, and better, version of the novel was filmed almost simultaneously as *Dangerous Liaisons* (qv).

Les Valseuses **
France 1974 118m Eastmancolor
CAPAC/UPF/SN (Paul Claudon)
◻◻
aka: *Making It; Getting It Up*
US title: *Going Places*
The adventures of two high-spirited layabouts and petty thieves in their wanderings among easy money and willing women.
Enjoyable, though amoral, comedy of two incompetents on the make, lightened by the engaging interplay between its two leads; as it's a French buddy-buddy movie, the male bonding extends to sex.
w Bertrand Blier, Philippe Dumarçay *novel* Bertrand Blier *d* Bertrand Blier *ph* Bruno Nuytten *m* Stéphane Grappelli *ad* Jean-Jacques Caziot *ed* Kénout Peltier
☆ Gérard Depardieu, Patrick Dewaere, Miou-Miou, Jeanne Moreau, Christian Alers, Brigitte Fossey, Michel Peyrelon, Gérard Boucaron, Jacques Chailleux, éva Damien, Isabelle Huppert
  'An explosively funny erotic farce – both a celebration and a satire of men's daydreams – and some people find its gusto revolting in much the same way that the bursting comic force of the sexual hyperbole in Henry Miller's *Tropic of Cancer* was thought revolting.' – *Pauline Kael*
  'This dispiriting romp.' – *Sight and Sound*
  † The French title is slang for 'testicles'.

Value for Money
GB 1955 93m Technicolor Vistavision
Rank/Group Films (Sergei Nolbandov)
A Yorkshire businessman determines to broaden his outlook, and falls in love with a London showgirl.
Highly undistinguished north country romantic farce which wastes a good production and cast.

---

w R. F. Delderfield, William Fairchild *novel* Geoffrey Unsworth *m* Malcolm Arnold
☆ John Gregson, Diana Dors, Susan Stephen, Derek Farr, Frank Pettingell, Jill Adams, Ernest Thesiger, Charles Victor, Joan Hickson

Vamos a Matar, Compañeros!: see *Compañeros*

Vamp
US 1986 94m Metrocolor
New World/Balcor (Donald P. Borchers)
◻◻ ▤ ◎~

Three college boys in search of a stripper find themselves in a den of vampires.
A cheap and gory horror flick, luridly photographed, and most likely to be enjoyed by colour-blind teenagers.
wd Richard Wenk *story* Donald P. Borchers, Richard Wenk *ph* Elliot Davis *m* Jonathan Elias *pd* Alan Roderick-Jones *ed* Marc Grossman *sp* Greg Cannom
☆ Grace Jones, Chris Makepeace, Sandy Baron, Robert Rusler, Dedee Pfeiffer, Gedde Watanabe, Billy Drago

Vampira
GB 1974 88m colour
Columbia/World Film Services (Jack H. Wiener)
US title: *Old Dracula*
A vampire count lures beauty-contest winners to his castle and uses their blood to revive his dead wife.
Would-be spoof which falls flat on its fangs.
w Jeremy Lloyd *d* Clive Donner *ph* Tony Richmond *m* David Whitaker
☆ David Niven, Teresa Graves, Peter Bayliss, Jennie Linden, Linda Hayden, Nicky Henson, Bernard Bresslaw, Veronica Carlson

The Vampire
US 1957 74m bw
UA/Gardner-Levy
▤

A research scientist takes bat essence and becomes a vampire.
Silly attempt to turn a legend into science fiction: more risible than sinister.
w Pat Fielder *d* Paul Landres *ph* Jack Mackenzie *m* Gerald Fried
☆ John Beal, Coleen Gray, Kenneth Tobey, Lydia Reed

  'Mad? I, who have solved the secret of life, you call me mad?'

The Vampire Bat
US 1932 71m bw
Majestic (Phil Goldstone)
◻◻ ▤

A mad doctor kills townsfolk in search of 'blood substitute'.
Primitive but vigorous low budget chiller.
w Edward T. Lowe *d* Frank Strayer *ph* Ira Morgan
☆ Lionel Atwill, Fay Wray, Melvyn Douglas, Maude Eburne, George E. Stone, Dwight Frye, Lionel Belmore
  'Shiver picture, well enough done but coming too late in the cycle to take any money.' – *Variety*

Vampire Circus
GB 1971 87m colour
Rank/Hammer (Wilbur Stark)
◻◻ ▤

In 1825 a plague-ridden village is visited by a circus of animal vampires.
Silly but quite inventive horror thriller.
w Judson Kinberg *d* Robert Young *ph* Moray Grant *m* David Whittaker *ad* Scott MacGregor *ed* Peter Musgrave
☆ Adrienne Corri, Laurence Payne, Thorley Walters, John Moulder Brown, Elizabeth Seal, Lynne Frederick, Robin Hunter

Vampire Cop
US 1993 81m colour
Overseas (Manette Rosen, Marion Zola)
◻◻ ▤

A female cop, bitten by a vampire serial killer, begins to crave blood while trying to track down the monster.
Nasty little shocker, flatly acted apart from its over-the-top vampire.

---

w John Weidner, Ken Lamplugh *d* Joel Bender *ph* Alan Caso *m* Emilio Kauderer *ed* Mark Helfrich, Joel Bender *sp* S.O.T.A. F/X
☆ Michelle Owens, Paul McMillen, Robert Miano, B. J. Gates, Michael Shawn, Gregory A. Greer
  'Some smart one-liners and a tough heroine are the plus points in an otherwise average vampire yarn.' – *Sight and Sound*

Vampire in Brooklyn
US 1995 101m DeLuxe
Paramount (Eddie Murphy, Mark Lipsky)
The last surviving Caribbean vampire goes to Brooklyn in search of a mate.
A dire attempt to combine Murphy's cocksure humour and the mechanics of a horror movie; the result is an unlovely and unfunny mess.
w Charles Murphy, Michael Lucker, Chris Parker *story* Eddie Murphy, Vernon Lynch Jnr, Charles Murphy *d* Wes Craven *ph* Mark Irwin *m* J. Peter Robinson *ad* Gary Diamond, Cynthia Charette *ed* Patrick Lussier *sp* Kurtzman, Nicotero, Berger EFX; Fantasy II
☆ Eddie Murphy, Angela Bassett, Allen Payne, Kadeem Hardison, John Witherspoon, Zakes Mokae, Joanna Cassidy, Simbi Khali
  'Mixes lame blood-pellet effects with lame gags. Its one lingering image is that of Eddie Murphy trying, and failing, to rise from the dead.' – *Owen Gleiberman, Entertainment Weekly*

The Vampire Lovers
GB 1970 91m Technicolor
MGM-EMI/Hammer/AIP (Harry Fine, Michael Style)
▤

A lady vampire worms her way into several noble households.
Reasonably close retelling of Sheridan Le Fanu's Carmilla, complete with lesbian love scenes. Adequate production but not much spirit.
w Tudor Gates, Harry Fine, Michael Styles *story* Carmilla by Sheridan Le Fanu *d* Roy Ward Baker *ph* Moray Grant *m* Harry Robinson *ad* Scott MacGregor *ed* James Needs
☆ Ingrid Pitt, Peter Cushing, Pippa Steele, Madeleine Smith, George Cole, Dawn Addams, Douglas Wilmer, Kate O'Mara

La Vampire Nue (dubbed)
France 1969 90m colour
Tigon/Films ABC (Jean Lavie)
◻◻
aka: *The Naked Vampire*
A son discovers that his father is a member of a private club given over to investigations of ritual suicide, sex and vampirism.
A perversely unconventional horror movie, more concerned with surrealist ornament, nudity and fetishistic costumes than narrative; the director's interest rarely strays beyond striking images and interior decor, but you may be amused by his pretension.
wd Jean Rollin *ph* Jean-Jacques Renon *m* Yvon Serault *ad* Jio Berk
☆ Christine François, Olivier Martin, Maurice Lemaître, Bernard Musson, Jean Aron, Ursule Pauly, Michel Delahaye
  'The essential thinness of the script is reinforced by Rollin's tendency to strive for a sustained mood of mystery by holding shots for several seconds after the action has been completed. Unfortunately, the cumulative effect of these delays is a deadeningly slow pace which appears more contrived than supernatural.' – *David McGillivray, MFB*
  'One of Rollin's most enjoyable films.' – *Peter Tombs and Cathal Tohill, NFT*
  † The British video release runs for 82m. The film was cut to 79m on its British cinema release in 1973.

Vampire of Venice: see *Vampires in Venice*

Vampire Thrills: see *Le Frisson des Vampires*

Vampire Woman: see *Crypt of the Living Dead*

Vampires: see *John Carpenter's Vampires*

The Vampire's Ghost
US 1945 59m bw
Republic (Rudolph E. Abel)
A vampire takes control of a West African plantation.

Unconvincing horror comic with no horror.
w John K. Butler, Leigh Brackett d Lesley Selander
☆ John Abbott, Charles Gordon, Peggy Stewart, Grant Withers

Vampires in Venice
Italy 1988 90m colour
Scena/Reteitalia (Augusto Caminito)
original title: *Nosferatu a Venezia*
aka: *Vampire of Venice*
In Venice, where Nosferatu was last seen 200 years earlier, a princess summons the vampire during a seance.
Despite an atmospheric opening, a muddled and unenticing addition to the endless round of vampire movies, with Kinski reprising his role without visible enthusiasm.
wd Augusto Caminito story Alberto Alfieri, Leandro Luchetti ph Antonio Nardi m Luigi Ceccarelli, Vangelis pd Joseph Teichner, Luca Antonucci ed Claudio Cutry
☆ Klaus Kinski, Donald Pleasence, Christopher Plummer, Barbara de Rossi, Yorgo Voyagis, Anne Knecht

'Seduction. Romance. Murder. The things one does for love.'
Vampire's Kiss
US 1989 103m colour
Hemdale/Magellan Pictures (Barry Shils, Barbara Zitwer)
A literary agent begins to fantasize that he is a vampire and behaves accordingly.
Over-heated film of urban disquiet, too tame for die-hard horror fans and too incoherent to interest any other audience.
w Joseph Minion d Robert Bierman ph Stefan Czapsky m Colin Towns pd Christopher Nowak ed Angus Newton
☆ Nicolas Cage, Maria Conchita Alonso, Jennifer Beals, Elizabeth Ashley, Kasi Lemmons, Bob Lujan, Jessica Lundy, John Walker

Vampyr **
Germany/France 1932 83m bw
Tobis Klangfilm/Carl Dreyer
US title: *Castle of Doom*
aka: *The Strange Adventure of David Gray*
A young man staying in a remote inn suspects that he is surrounded by vampires and has a dream of his own death.
Vague, misty, virtually plotless but occasionally frightening and always interesting to look at, this semi-professional film long since joined the list of minor classics for two scenes: the hero dreaming of his own death and the villain finally buried by flour in a mill.
w Christen Jul, Carl Dreyer story Carmilla by Sheridan Le Fanu d Carl Dreyer ph Rudolph Maté, Louis Née m Wolfgang Zeller
☆ Julian West, Sybille Schmitz, Maurice Schutz, Jan Hieronimko
'It makes our contemporary, explicit Draculas look like advertisements for false teeth.' – *Sunday Times*, 1976
'It is intensely a film of hints, of eerie non sequiturs, of barely perceivable yet striking images ... evil wafts off the screen like a smell of bad breath.' – *New Statesman*, 1976
'Imagine we are sitting in an ordinary room. Suddenly we are told there is a corpse behind the door. In an instant, the room is completely altered; everything in it has taken another look; the light, the atmosphere have changed, though they are physically the same. This is because we have changed, and the objects are as we perceive them. That is the effect I meant to get in my film.' – *Carl Dreyer*
† 'Julian West' was really Baron Nicholas de Gunsberg, who financed the project.

Vampyres *
GB 1974 84m Eastmancolor
Fox-Rank/Essay (Brian Smedley-Aston)
Two murdered lesbian lovers become vampires after their deaths and lure men to a deserted mansion so that they can suck their blood.
Cheaply made, single-minded horror that manages to generate a relentless tension.
w D. Daubeney d Joseph Larraz (José Larraz) ph Harry Waxman m James Clarke ad Ken Bridgeman ed Geoff R. Brown

☆ Marianne Morris, Anulka, Murray Brown, Brian Deacon, Sally Faulkner, Michael Byrne, Karl Lanchbury, Bessie Love
'A sex-horror film about lesbian vampires for which the budget and schedule were insignificant, even by British exploitation standards.' – *David Pirie, MFB*
'A minor masterpiece of erotic fantasy.' – *Peter Tombs and Cathal Tohill, NFT*

Vampyros Lesbos
West Germany/Spain 1971 87m colour
Tele-Cine/Fenix (Karl Heinz Mannchen)
aka: *Erbin des Dracula*
aka: *Lesbian Vampires*
Countess Carody, a man-hating vampire who performs in a lesbian cabaret act in Istanbul, decides to initiate a German woman who comes to the city.
A dull and inept horror movie made worse by Franco's penchant for meaningless zooms, abrupt transitions and inappropriate soundtrack music; the pace is leaden, the cast act as though they're zombies, and the director resorts to scenes of lesbian lovemaking at frequent intervals.
wd Franco Manera (Jesús Franco) ph Manuel Merino m Mannfred Hubler, Siegfried Schwab ed Clarissa Ambach
☆ Susann Korda (Soledad Miranda), Dennis Price, Paul Muller, Ewa Stroemberg, Heidrun Kussin, Michael Berling, Viktor Feldmann
† A different version of the film was released in Spain in 1974. The video release includes the original West German trailer, which describes it as 'a daring film version of the story of Dracula, whose legacy brings fear and terror'.

'A large portion of life...'
The Van
Eire/GB 1996 100m Technicolor
TCF/Deadly/BBC Films/Beacon (Lynda Myles)
In Dublin, a baker uses his redundancy payment to buy a dilapidated van and goes into the mobile fish-and-chip business with a friend.
A flat, small-scale kitchen-sink drama of tensions between friends and family, as experienced by middle-aged men, in which all end battered by life.
w Roddy Doyle novel Roddy Doyle d Stephen Frears ph Oliver Stapleton m Eric Clapton, Richard Hartley pd Mark Geraghty ed Mick Audsley
☆ Colm Meaney, Donal O'Kelly, Ger Ryan, Caroline Rothwell, Neili Conroy, Ruaidhri Conroy, Brendan O'Carroll
'As television drama, this is fine. As a theatrical release, it is sadly a bit flat.' – *Leslie Felperin, Sight and Sound*

Van Gogh *
France 1991 158m colour
Artificial Eye/Erato/Canal/AZ/Livradois (Daniel Tosran du Plantier)
In the final three months of his life, Vincent Van Gogh goes to live in Auvers, where he begins an affair with the young daughter of the local doctor, a collector of paintings, quarrels with his brother and kills himself.
Fictionalized biopic that adds little to an understanding of the artist, even if it sets him in an everyday context as one man among many.
wd Maurice Pialat ph Gilles Henry m A. Bernot, J. M. Bourget, J. Dutronc, P. Revedy
☆ Jacques Dutronc, Alexandra London, Bernard Le Coq, Gerard Sety, Corinne Bourdon, Elsa Zylberstein, Leslie Azoulai, Jacques Vidal, Chantal Barbarit
'The punitive running time and unlovely hero mean that this will hardly be embraced by all cinemagoers, but *Van Gogh* is certainly the best of the Van Gogh movies to date.' – *Kim Newman, Empire*

Vanessa, Her Love Story
US 1935 76m bw
MGM (David O. Selznick)
When her husband becomes insane, a Victorian lady falls for a gypsy.
Very dated romance which finished Helen Hayes's star career, for thirty years at least.
w Lenore Coffee, Hugh Walpole novel Hugh Walpole d William K. Howard ph Ray June m Herbert Stothart

☆ Helen Hayes, Robert Montgomery, May Robson, Otto Kruger, Lewis Stone, Henry Stephenson, Violet Kemble-Cooper, Jessie Ralph
'It drips with agony and dullness.' – *Variety*

Il Vangelo Secondo Matteo: see *The Gospel According to St Matthew*

The Vanishing *
Netherlands/France 1988 106m colour
Metro/Golden Egg Film/Ingrid Productions/MGS Film (Anne Lordo, George Sluizer)
original title: *Spoorloos*
After spending three years searching for his girlfriend who suddenly disappeared while they were on holiday, a man is approached by her kidnapper.
Black thriller with a shock ending.
w Tim Krabbé novel The Golden Egg by Tim Krabbé d George Sluizer ph Toni Kuhn m Henry Vrienten ad Santiago Isidro Pin, Cor Spijk ed George Sluizer, Lin Friedman
☆ Bernard-Pierre Donnadieu, Gene Bervoets, Johanna Ter Steege, Gwen Eckhaus, Bernadette Le Sache, Tania Latarjet
'A consistently bewildering and surprising thriller, chillingly unsentimental and expertly constructed.' – *Kim Newman, MFB*

The Vanishing
US 1993 110m DeLuxe
TCF/Morra, Brezner, Steinberg and Tenenbaum (Larry Brezner, Paul Schiff)
A teacher searches for his kidnapped girlfriend for three years without success; then he gets a call from the kidnapper.
A disastrous remake of a chilling original, so softened and given such a happy Hollywood ending that the narrative loses all point.
w Todd Graff novel The Golden Egg by Tim Krabbé d George Sluizer ph Peter Suschitzky m Jerry Goldsmith pd Jeannine C. Oppewall ed Bruce Green
☆ Jeff Bridges, Kiefer Sutherland, Nancy Travis, Sandra Bullock, Park Overall, Lisa Eichhorn, Maggie Linderman
'This is one remake that sacrifices much of what made the original work so well.' – *Variety*
'Has been systematically and often laughably divested of its subtler moments.' – *Derek Malcolm, Guardian*

The Vanishing American
US 1925 110m bw silent
Paramount
A history of the American Indian.
Solid Western epic, now of historical interest only.
story Zane Grey d George B. Seitz
☆ Richard Dix, Lois Wilson, Noah Beery, Malcolm McGregor, Charles Stevens

The Vanishing Corporal *
France 1962 106m bw
Films du Cyclope (J. W. Beyer)
original title: *Le Caporal Epinglé*
After several attempts, three Frenchmen succeed in escaping from a detention camp.
Symbolic World War II drama told in mainly comic terms. Not one of its director's great films, but a warm and assured one.
w Jean Renoir, Guy Lefranc d Jean Renoir m Georges Leclerc m Joseph Kosma
☆ Jean-Pierre Cassel, Claude Brasseur, Claude Rich, O. E. Hasse
'A comedy which shades sometimes into farce and once into tragedy ... The mood, except in two or three scenes, is deliberately light.' – *Dilys Powell*

The Vanishing Frontier
US 1932 63m bw
Paramount (Larry Darmour)
To quote the opening titles: 'California 1850. A military government which executes its laws by force. A charming pastoral people whose resentment is at times fanned into a tiny flame of defiance. Misunderstanding and discontent where there should be only harmony and happiness.'
Dull Western with Brown as an unconvincing Mexican outlaw protecting the locals from harsh rule; it combines heavy-handed humour and heavier-handed romance.

w Stuart Anthony d Philip E. Rosen ph James S. Brown
☆ Johnny Mack Brown, Evalyn Knapp, ZaSu Pitts, Raymond Hatton, Ben Alexander, J. Farrell Macdonald, 'Deacon' McDaniels

Vanishing Point *
US 1971 107m DeLuxe
TCF/ Cupid (Norman Spencer)
An ex-racing driver who delivers cars for a living becomes hepped up on benzedrine and leads police a rare chase through the Nevada desert.
Strange, fashionable action suspenser which is better to look at than to understand.
w Guillermo Cain d Richard Sarafian ph John A. Alonzo md Jimmy Brown
☆ Barry Newman, Cleavon Little, Dean Jagger, Victoria Medlin, Paul Koslo, Bob Donner
'Uncomfortably reminiscent of Easy Rider as an odyssey through an unknown America in its discovery of strange alliances and unpredictable hostilities.' – *Tom Milne*

The Vanishing Virginian
US 1941 97m bw
MGM (Edwin H. Knopf)
A conservative Virginian finds that he harbours suffragettes in his household.
Life with Father in another setting; rather yawn-provoking.
w Jan Fortune novel Rebecca Yancey Williams d Frank Borzage ph Charles Lawton Jnr m David Snell
☆ Frank Morgan, Spring Byington, Kathryn Grayson, Elizabeth Patterson, Louise Beavers

Vanity Fair
US 1932 78m bw
Hoffman/Allied
The story of Becky Sharp is told in modern dress.
A poorly made independent venture which rapidly dropped from sight.
w F. Hugh Herbert novel W. M. Thackeray d Chester M. Franklin
☆ Myrna Loy, Conway Tearle, Barbara Kent, Walter Byron, Anthony Bushell
'Poor photography, tepid direction, poor dialogue.' – *Variety*

The Vanquished
US 1953 84m Technicolor
Paramount/Pine-Thomas
After the Civil War, a returning Confederate officer finds corruption in his home town.
Uninspiring semi-Western.
w Winston Miller, Frank Moss, Lewis R. Foster novel Karl Brown d Edward Ludwig ph Lionel Lindon m Lucien Cailliet
☆ John Payne, Jan Sterling, Coleen Gray, Lyle Bettger, Willard Parker, Roy Gordon

Vanya on 42nd Street **
US 1994 119m DuArt
Artificial Eye/Laura Pels/Mayfair (Fred Berner)
Actors and a small audience gather in a derelict New York theatre for a rehearsal of *Uncle Vanya*, directed by André Gregory.
A film, part documentary, part recreation, of a theatrical event, performed by a cast that had worked on the play at various times over four years. It works both as a version of the play and as cinema.
w David Mamet play Uncle Vanya by Anton Chekhov d Louis Malle ph Declan Quinn m Joshua Redman pd Eugene Lee ed Nancy Baker
☆ Wallace Shawn, Julianne Moore, Brooke Smith, Larry Pine, George Gaynes, Phoebe Brand, Madhur Jaffrey, André Gregory, Lynn Cohen, Jeffrey Mayer
'A splendid demonstration of how great art seduces us, has its way with us. The movie is designed to give the audience the experience of total surrender to theatrical illusion.' – *Terrence Rafferty, New Yorker*

Vargtimmen: see *The Hour of the Wolf*

Variety **
Germany 1925 104m bw silent
UFA
aka: *Vaudeville*
An ageing acrobat seduces a young girl and later kills another man who is interested in her.

Crude, vivid backstage story, inventively presented to overcome the dullness and tawdriness of the plot.
w E. A. Dupont, Leo Birinsky novel Frederick Hollander d E. A. Dupont ph Karl Freund
☆ Emil Jannings, Lya de Putti, Maly Delschaft, Warwick Ward

'A continually roving lens seizes the best angle for every detail, expression and scene.' – Leon Moussinac

'The enduring power of the movie is not in its far from original story but in the restless, subjective camera and the fast editing which make it an almost voluptuous experience.' – Pauline Kael, 70s

'It was my aim to show a single childish grown-up, devoted, lovable, and his reaction to betrayal and duplicity.' – E. A. Dupont

Variety Girl
US 1947 83m bw
Paramount (Daniel Dare)
Of all the young hopefuls arriving in Hollywood, one girl becomes a star.
The slightest of excuses for a tour of the Paramount studios, with all the contract stars doing bits. It doesn't add up to much.
w Edmund Hartmann, Frank Tashlin, Monte Brice, Robert Welch d George Marshall ph Lionel Lindon, Stuart Thompson md Joseph J. Lilley, Troy Saunders
☆ Mary Hatcher, Olga San Juan, DeForest Kelley, Glenn Tryon, Bob Hope, Bing Crosby, Gary Cooper, Ray Milland, Alan Ladd, Barbara Stanwyck, Paulette Goddard, Dorothy Lamour, Veronica Lake, Sonny Tufts, Joan Caulfield and also William Holden, Lizabeth Scott, Burt Lancaster, Gail Russell, Diana Lynn, Sterling Hayden, Robert Preston, William Bendix, Barry Fitzgerald, Billy de Wolfe, George Pal Puppetoons, Cecil B. de Mille, Mitchell Leisen, George Marshall, Spike Jones and his City Slickers, etc

Variety Jubilee
GB 1942 92m bw
Butcher's
Two generations in the life of a music hall.
Naïve romance with fascinating appearances by some famous names of variety.
w Kathleen Butler d Maclean Rogers ph Geoffrey Faithfull md Percival Mackey
☆ Lesley Brook, Ellis Irving, Reginald Purdell, George Robey, Charles Coborn, Ella Retford, Wilson Keppel and Betty, The Ganjou Brothers and Juanita, Slim Rhyder, Betty Warren, Marie Lloyd Jnr, Tom Finglass, John Rorke

Variety Lights: see Lights of Variety

Variety Time
US 1948 90m bw
RKO (George Bilson)
The film's subtitle puts it, somewhat optimistically, 'a revue of specialities and highlights from RKO film hits'.
It turns out to be a succession of indifferent moments, including two overlong comedy sketches and some ill-advised mockery of silent films, linked by some feeble stand-up comedy from Jack Paar. Little of it retains any interest, other than archaeological.
w Hal Law, Hal Yates, Leo Solomon, Joseph Quillan d Hal Yates (of Edgar Kennedy and Leon Errol's sketches) md C. Bakaleinikoff ad Charles Pyke ed Les Millbrook, Edward W. Williams
☆ Jack Paar, Edgar Kennedy, Leon Errol, Frankie Carle and his orchestra, Pat Rooney, Miguelito Valdes, Harold & Lola, Jesse & James, Lynn, Royce & Vanya

'Make your own rules.'
Varsity Blues
US 1999 104m DeLuxe
Paramount/MTV (Tova Laiter, Mike Tollin, Brian Robbins)
🎧
A Texas high-school student is treated as a local celebrity when he replaces the football team's injured quarterback.
Tiresome teenage drama of small-town worship of athletes that looks merely quaint to audiences not involved in such rituals.
w W. Peter Iliff d Brian Robbins ph Charles Cohen m Mark Isham pd Jaymes Hinkle ed Ned Bastille

☆ James Van Der Beek, Jon Voight, Paul Walker, Ron Lester, Scott Caan, Richard Lineback, Tiffany C. Love, Amy Smart, Eliel Swinton
'An unappetizing mix of raucously vulgar comedy and teen-angst melodrama.' – Joe Leydon, Variety

Varsity Show
US 1937 120m bw
Warner (Louis F. Edelman)
Collegians stage a revue.
Mild musical.
w Warren Duff, Richard Macaulay, Jerry Wald, Sig Herzig d William Keighley ph Sol Polito, George Barnes m/ly Richard Whiting, Johnny Mercer ch Busby Berkeley
☆ Dick Powell, Priscilla Lane, Rosemary Lane, Fred Waring and his Pennsylvanians, Buck and Bubbles, Johnny 'Scat' Davis, Ted Healy, Walter Catlett
'A rah-rah musical entertainment made to order for early autumn business when college boys start pegging out the pigskin.' – Variety
⚓ Busby Berkeley

Vaudeville: see Variety

'Everything that makes life worth leaving!'
Vault of Horror *
GB 1973 86m Eastmancolor
Metromedia/Amicus (Milton Subotsky)
📀 📼
Five men trapped in the basement of a skyscraper tell of their recurring dreams.
All-star horror omnibus, plainly but well staged.
w Milton Subotsky stories William Gaines d Roy Ward Baker ph Denys Coop m Douglas Gamley
☆ Daniel Massey, Anna Massey, Terry-Thomas, Glynis Johns, Curt Jurgens, Dawn Addams, Michael Craig, Edward Judd, Tom Baker, Denholm Elliott

'Leave your expectations at the door.'
Velvet Goldmine **
US 1998 123m Rank Colour
Film Four/Zenith/Killer/Single Cell/Newmarket Capital/Goldwyn/Miramax/Channel 4 (Christine Vachon)
📀 📼 🎧
In Britain in the 80s, a journalist sets out to discover what happened to a glam-rock star of the 70s, who faked his death and disappeared from view.
A camp account of a camp phenomenon, flamboyantly revelling in the fakery and the androgynous appeal of it all.
wd Todd Haynes ph Maryse Alberti m Carter Burwell pd Christopher Hobbs ed James Lyons
☆ Ewan McGregor, Jonathan Rhys Meyers, Toni Collette, Christian Bale, Eddie Izzard, Emily Woof, Michael Feast
'Tells a story the way operas do: blazing with exquisite yet abstract passions, and with quite a lot to look at on the side.' – Janet Maslin, New York Times
⚓ Sandy Powell (costumes)
♛ Sandy Powell (costumes)

The Velvet Touch *
US 1948 97m bw
RKO/Independent Artists (Frederick Brisson)
📼 📀
A famous actress murders her producer and is struck by conscience but allows a detective to find his own way to the truth.
Solid murder melodrama with an excellent theatrical atmosphere.
w Leo Rosten d John Gage ph Joseph Walker m Leigh Harline
☆ Rosalind Russell, Leo Genn, Sydney Greenstreet, Claire Trevor, Leon Ames, Frank McHugh

'Child of the devil, she lives by a secret code!'
Vendetta
US 1950 84m bw
RKO/Howard Hughes
The daughter of an esteemed Corsican family takes vengeance on her father's enemies.
Outmoded ethnic melodrama with nothing to recommend it.
w W. R. Burnett novel Columba by Prosper Mérimée d Mel Ferrer ph Franz Planer, Al Gilks m Roy Webb md Constantin Bakaleinikoff

☆ Faith Domergue, George Dolenz, Donald Buka, Hillary Brooke, Nigel Bruce, Joseph Calleia, Hugo Haas

Vendetta
Italy 1990 120m Fujicolour
Reteitalia/Titanus (Ciro Ippolito)
📀 📼
An Irish hit-man working for the Mafia falls in love with the daughter of a man he shot by mistake.
Interminable and predictable movie, with too little action to work as a thriller and too shallow and stereotypical to be a character study. It also requires the viewer to be sympathetic to the problems of hoodlums and murderers.
w Ennio de Concini, Stuart Margolin, Alan Di Fiore novel Woman of Honor by Svena Casati Modignani d Stuart Margolin ph Ennio Guarnieri m Bruce Ruddel, Stuart Margolin, Riz Ortolani pd Danilo Donati ed Mario Morra
☆ Eric Roberts, Carol Alt, Burt Young, Nick Mancuso, Thomas Calabro, Marcie Leeds, Serena Grandi, Billy Barty, Stuart Margolin, Eli Wallach
† There is also a version, made for TV, that lasts 200m.

La vendetta di Ursus: see The Vengeance of Ursus

I Vendicatori dell'Ave Maria: see The Twilight Avengers

The Venetian Affair
US 1966 92m Metrocolor Panavision
MGM/Jerry Thorpe
A reporter investigates the death in Venice of an American diplomat.
Uninteresting and complicated spy thriller with pleasant locations.
w E. Jack Neuman novel Helen MacInnes d Jerry Thorpe ph Milton Krasner, Enzo Serafin m Lalo Schifrin
☆ Robert Vaughn, Karl Boehm, Elke Sommer, Ed Asner, Boris Karloff, Felicia Farr, Roger C. Carmel, Luciana Paluzzi, Joe de Santis

Venetian Bird *
GB 1952 95m bw
Rank/British Film Makers (Betty E. Box)
US title: The Assassin
A private detective goes to Venice to reward a wartime partisan, who turns out to have become a notorious criminal.
Standard action fare with a nod to The Third Man but not much excitement or sense of place.
w Victor Canning novel Victor Canning d Ralph Thomas ph Ernest Steward m Nino Rota
☆ Richard Todd, Eva Bartok, John Gregson, George Coulouris, Margot Grahame, Walter Rilla, Sidney James

La Venganza Del Sexo: see The Curious Doctor Humpp

Vengeance
GB/Germany 1962 83m bw
CCC/Raymond Stross
aka: The Brain
After a fatal accident, the brain of a tycoon is kept alive and persuades a doctor to find his murderer.
Twisty remake of Donovan's Brain (qv), not too badly done.
w Robert Stewart, Philip Mackie d Freddie Francis ph Bob Hulke m Ken Jones
☆ Anne Heywood, Peter Van Eyck, Cecil Parker, Bernard Lee, Maxine Audley, Jeremy Spenser, Miles Malleson

Vengeance (dubbed) *
Italy/West Germany 1968 100m
Eastmancolor Cromoscope
MGM-EMI/Super International/Top (Renato Savino)
📀
original title: Joko, Invoca Dio ... e Muori
An outlaw takes revenge on the five men who tortured and killed his friend after a bungled bullion robbery.
A bravura and baroque, if violent, spaghetti Western, in which style triumphs over substance.
w Renato Savino, Antonio Margheriti d Anthony Dawson (Antonio Margheriti) ph Riccardo Pallottini m Carlo Savina ed Otello Colangeli

☆ Richard Harrison, Claudio Camaso, Werner Pochath, Paolo Gozlino
'An immensely enjoyable mix of Gothic horror, thriller and Western motifs, the deaths in particular are unusually imaginative.' – Sight and Sound
† The British release was cut to 81m.

The Vengeance of Fu Manchu
GB 1967 92m Eastmancolor
Anglo Amalgamated/Harry Alan Towers
The Yellow Peril plans a crime syndicate to counter Interpol, and creates a double for Nayland Smith...
Limp addition to a series which started well, but was subsequently robbed of period flavour.
w Harry Alan Towers novel Sax Rohmer d Jeremy Summers ph John von Kotze m Malcolm Lockyer
☆ Christopher Lee, Douglas Wilmer, Tony Ferrer, Tsai Chin, Howard Marion Crawford, Wolfgang Kieling

The Vengeance of She
GB 1968 101m Technicolor
Warner-Pathé/Hammer (Aida Young)
📀 📼
A girl is possessed by the spirit of long-dead Queen Ayesha.
Grotesquely unpersuasive reincarnation melodrama, a long way from its inspiration.
w Peter O'Donnell d Cliff Owen ph Wolfgang Suschitsky m Mario Nascimbene pd Lionel Couch ed Raymond Poulton
☆ John Richardson, Olinka Berova, Edward Judd, Colin Blakely, Derek Godfrey, Noel Willman, André Morell, Jill Melford

The Vengeance of Ursus (dubbed)
Italy 1962 90m Eastmancolor Techniscope
Jonia/Splendor
original title: La vendetta di Ursus
aka: The Mighty Warrior
Ursus overthrows a tyrant who plans to marry the princess he loves.
Standard Italian muscleman stuff, following a familiar narrative and with little to distinguish it from similar movies featuring Hercules and Maciste.
w Marcello Ciorciolini, Nino Scolaro, Roberto Gianviti d Luigi Capuano ph Oberdan Troiani m Carlo Innocenzi ad Alfredo Montiori ed Antonietta Zita d (English language) Richard McNamara English dialogue John Hart
☆ Samson Burke, Wandisa Guida, Livio Lorenzon, Nadine Sanders, Nerio Bernardi, Gianni Rizzo, Franco Fantasia, Roberto Chevalier, Gina Rovere

Vengeance: The Demon: see Pumpkinhead

Vengeance Valley
US 1951 82m Technicolor
MGM (Nicholas Nayfack)
📼
A Western rancher keeps his foster-brother's misdeeds from their father.
Well-made character Western, a little short on action.
w Irving Ravetch novel Luke Short d Richard Thorpe ph George Folsey m Rudolph G. Kopp
☆ Burt Lancaster, Robert Walker, Ray Collins, Joanne Dru, Sally Forrest, John Ireland, Carleton Carpenter, Ted de Corsia

Venom
GB 1981 92m Technicolor
Aribage/Morison (Martin Bregman)
📀 📼
A kidnap plan goes awry when a deadly snake is let loose in a besieged house.
Hoary melodrama which veers between dullness, artificial suspense and unpleasant detail.
w Robert Carrington novel Alan Scholefield d Piers Haggard ph Gilbert Taylor m Michael Kamen
☆ Sterling Hayden, Klaus Kinski, Oliver Reed, Sarah Miles, Cornelia Sharpe, Nicol Williamson, Susan George
'Woefully archaic in its British B-picture reliance on very cheap thrills, and without any self-parodic saving grace.' – Time Out

Venus in Furs (dubbed)
Italy   1970   81m   colour
VIP/Roxy
▣
While on holiday, a writer falls in love with, and marries, a woman staying in the next room, believing that she can satisfy his masochistic and voyeuristic sexual fantasies.
Trite, poorly dubbed would-be erotic thriller, updating the original to the swinging 60s and transforming the unreadable into the unwatchable.
w Fabio Massimo *novel* Leopold Sacher-Masoch d Massimo Dallamano ph Sergio D'Offizi m Gian Franco Reverberi ad Alida Cappellini
☆ Laura Antonelli, Régis Vallée, Ewing Loren, Renate Kasche

Venus Peter **
GB   1989   94m   Fujicolour
Recorded Releasing/BFI/Channel 4/British Screen (Christopher Young)
A young boy grows up in a Scottish fishing village in the 1950s.
Nostalgic and enjoyable account of a community on the point of disintegration.
w Ian Sellar, Christopher Rush *book* A Twelve-month and a Day by Christopher Rush d Ian Sellar ph Gabriel Beristain m Jonathan Dove pd Andy Harris ed David Spiers
☆ Ray McAnally, David Hayman, Sinead Cusack, Gordon R. Strachan, Sam Hayman, Caroline Paterson, Alex McAvoy

Vera Cruz **
US   1953   94m   Technicolor   Superscope
UA/Hecht-Lancaster (James Hill)
▤ ◎～
Adventurers in 1860 Mexico become involved in a plot against Emperor Maximilian.
Terse, lively Western melodrama with unusual locations and comedy and suspense touches. Great outdoor entertainment.
w Roland Kibbee, James R. Webb, Borden Chase d Robert Aldrich ph Ernest Laszlo m Hugo Friedhofer
☆ Gary Cooper, Burt Lancaster, Denise Darcel, Cesar Romero, George Macready, Sarita Montiel, Ernest Borgnine, Morris Ankrum, Charles Bronson

'A Mad Generation Spawned In Lust … Consumed By Hate. Where Everything Decent Is…'
Verboten! *
US   1959   93m   bw
Columbia/Globe (Samuel Fuller)
▣▣ ▤
In Germany at the end of the Second World War, an American soldier marries a German girl and faces trouble from people of both nationalities and a secret Nazi organization.
An effective mix of thriller and romance which gives some sense of the messy aftermath and confusions of war.
wd Samuel Fuller ph Joseph Biroc m Harry Sukman, Wagner, Beethoven ad John Mansbridge ed Philip Cahn
☆ James Best, Susan Cummings, Tom Pittman, Paul Dubov, Harold Daye, Dick Kallman, Stuart Randall

Verbrechen am Seelenleben eines Menschens: see *Kaspar Hauser*

Verdict *
France/Italy   1974   97m   Eastmancolor
Concordia/CCC (Carlo Ponti)
A gangster's widow kidnaps the judge who is trying her son for rape and murder.
Tortuous but watchable melodrama with star performances and the director's usual eagerness to exploit legal morality.
w Andre Cayatte, Henri Coupon *novel* Henri Coupon d Andre Cayatte ph Jean Badal m Louiguy
☆ Sophia Loren, Jean Gabin, Henri Garcin, Julien Bertheau
'Not exciting enough to qualify as a thriller nor penetrating enough to make you support Gallic penal reform.' – *Michael Billington, Illustrated London News*

The Verdict *
US   1946   86m   bw
Warner (William Jacobs)
A retired Scotland Yard inspector continues to work on a case which vexes him.

Victorian murder mystery with very unconvincing Hollywood sets and curious casting, but rather nicely detailed.
w Peter Milne *novel* The Big Bow Mystery by Israel Zangwill d Don Siegel ph Ernest Haller m Frederick Hollander
☆ Sydney Greenstreet, Peter Lorre, Joan Lorring, George Coulouris, Rosalind Ivan, Paul Cavanagh, Arthur Shields

'Frank Galvin has one last chance to do something right'
The Verdict *
US   1982   128m   Technicolor
TCF/Zanuck-Brown (Richard D. Zanuck, David Brown)
▣▣ ▤
An ageing and failed attorney is unexpectedly handed a case of medical malpractice and successfully sues a hospital.
Complex and interesting but rather sombrely handled exposé of legal and medical ethics.
w David Mamet *novel* Barry Reed d Sidney Lumet ph Andrzej Bartkowiak m Johnny Mandel pd Edward Pisoni
☆ Paul Newman, James Mason, Charlotte Rampling, Jack Warden, Milo O'Shea, Lindsay Crouse, Edward Binns, Wesley Addy
'When Sidney Lumet gets serious, his energetic, fast-moving style falls apart. The camera sits like Death on the dark, angled images of this anguished movie.' – *New Yorker*
ƪ best picture; Paul Newman; James Mason; Sidney Lumet; screenplay (adaptation)

Verführung: die Grausame Frau: see *Seduction: The Cruel Woman*

Vérités et Mensonges: see *F for Fake*

Veronika Voss **
West Germany   1982   104m   bw
Maura/Tango/Rialto/Trio/Maran (Thomas Schühly)
▣▣ ▤
In the fifties, a distraught star of the previous decade flees from her own image, but finds that her psychiatrist is her own worst enemy.
Fascinatingly convoluted puzzle play with enough to say for a year of late-night discussions; but the bleached-out black and white photography is an unnecessary strain.
w Peter Märtesheimer, Pea Fröhlich, Rainer Werner Fassbinder d Rainer Werner Fassbinder ph Xaver Schwarzenberger m Peer Raben
☆ Rosel Zech, Hilmar Thate, Annemarie Düringer, Doris Schade, Cornelia Froboess
'A dazzling parable of all cinema, of the penalties of living out one another's fantasies.' – *Sight and Sound*

Das Versprechen: see *The Promise*

Vertigo ****
US   1958   128m   Technicolor   Vistavision
Paramount (Alfred Hitchcock)
▣▣ ▤ ◎～ ◔ ⌒
A detective with a fear of heights is drawn into a complex plot in which a girl he loves apparently falls to her death. Then he meets her double …
Double identity thriller which many sequences in Hitchcock's best style. A film as unsettling as the phobia it deals with, keeping its audience dizzy and off balance throughout.
w Alec Coppel, Samuel Taylor *novel* D'entre les Morts by Pierre Boileau, Thomas Narcejac d Alfred Hitchcock ph Robert Burks m Bernard Herrmann ad Hal Pereira, Henry Bumstead
☆ James Stewart, Kim Novak, Barbara Bel Geddes, Tom Helmore, Henry Jones
ƪ art direction

'They've Been Bad. Very Bad.'
Very Bad Things
US   1998   100m   CFI color
Polygram/Initial Entertainment/Interscope/BallPark (Michael Schiffer, Diane Nabatoff, Cindy Cowan)
▣▣ ▤ ◎～ ⌒
Five friends try to cover up the accidental killing of a prostitute on their stag night in Las Vegas.
Gruesome black comedy, of homicidal mania let loose, that escalates into a very sick joke; it will be enjoyed by those who find dead people funny.
wd Peter Berg ph David Hennings m Stewart Copeland pd Dina Lipton ed Dan Lebental
☆ Christian Slater, Cameron Diaz, Daniel Stern, Jeanne Tripplehorn, Jon Favreau, Jeremy Piven,

Leland Orser, Joey Zimmerman, Tyler Malinger, Carla Scott
'The film has a real sense of a situation slipping out of control, with marvellous displays of hysteria matched by movie trickery that spreads the edginess to the audience.' – *Kim Newman, Empire*

'No woman should see this film without a man!'
The Very Edge
GB   1962   89m   bw   Cinevision
British Lion/Garrick/Raymond Stross
▤
An obsessive young man menaces a mother-to-be.
Rather unpleasant suspenser, adequately presented.
w Elizabeth Jane Howard d Cyril Frankel ph Bob Huke m David Lee
☆ Anne Heywood, Richard Todd, Jack Hedley, Jeremy Brett, Nicole Maurey, Barbara Mullen, Maurice Denham, William Lucas

Very Important Person **
GB   1961   98m   bw
Rank/Independent Artists (Julian Wintle, Leslie Parkyn)
US title: *A Coming-Out Party*
A senior British scientist is caught by the Nazis and has to be rescued.
Very satisfactory British comedy with a few suspense scenes; POW fare with a difference.
w Jack Davies d Ken Annakin ph Ernest Steward m Reg Owen
☆ James Robertson Justice, Stanley Baxter, Leslie Phillips, Eric Sykes, Richard Wattis, Colin Gordon

A Very Private Affair: see *Vie Privée*

A Very Special Favor *
US   1965   105m   Technicolor
Universal/Lankershim (Robert Arthur)
A Frenchman with a spinster daughter asks an American lawyer to 'initiate' her.
Tasteless, smirking comedy with several funny scenes, glossily photographed in the lap of luxury and interesting in its early use of homosexuality as a comedy subject.
w Nate Monaster, Stanley Shapiro d Michael Gordon ph Leo Tover m Vic Mizzy
☆ Rock Hudson, Charles Boyer, Leslie Caron, Nita Talbot, Dick Shawn, Walter Slezak, Larry Storch

The Very Thought of You
US   1944   99m   bw
Warner (Jerry Wald)
Problems of a wartime marriage.
Tepid romantic potboiler.
w Alvah Bessie, Delmer Daves d Delmer Daves ph Bert Glennon m Franz Waxman
☆ Dennis Morgan, Eleanor Parker, Dane Clark, Faye Emerson, Beulah Bondi, Henry Travers, William Prince, Andrea King

A Very Young Lady
US   1941   80m   bw
TCF (Robert T. Kane)
A tomboy develops a crush on her headmaster.
Remake of Girls' Dormitory, used as a vehicle for an ageing child star. Predictable comedy, neatly made.
w Ladislas Fodor, Elaine Ryan *play* Ladislas Fodor d Harold Schuster
☆ Jane Withers, John Sutton, Nancy Kelly, Janet Beecher, Cecil Kellaway

Vesnicko Ma Strediskova: see *My Sweet Little Village*

Vesolye Rebyata: see *Jazz Comedy*

Vessel of Wrath **
GB   1938   93m   bw
Mayflower (Erich Pommer)
US title: *The Beachcomber*
In the Dutch East Indies, the missionary's spinster sister falls for a drunken beachcomber.
First-rate character comedy, remade as The Beachcomber (qv).
w Bartlett Cormack, B. Van Thal *story* W. Somerset Maugham d Erich Pommer ph Jules Kruger m Richard Addinsell
☆ Charles Laughton, Elsa Lanchester, Robert Newton, Tyrone Guthrie, Dolly Mollinger, Eliot Makeham

'The moment this film starts you recognize the master touch.' – *Variety*

Viaggio in Italia: see *Voyage to Italy*

El Viaje: see *The Voyage*

Vibes
US   1988   99m   DeLuxe
Imagine (Deborah Blum, Tony Ganz)
▤
A psychic couple go to Ecuador to find a lost city of gold.
Dim comedy that had no future at the box-office.
w Lowell Ganz, Babaloo Mandel d Ken Kwapis ph John Bailey m James Horner pd Richard Sawyer ed Carol Littleton
☆ Cyndi Lauper, Jeff Goldblum, Julian Sands, Peter Falk, Karen Akers, Michael Lerner, Ramon Bieri, Elizabeth Pena

The Vicar of Bray
GB   1937   68m   bw
Twickenham (Julius Hagen)
A clergyman manages to hold on to his living through the reigns of Charles I, Cromwell and Charles II.
Stilted historical comedy, although Stanley Holloway seizes what chances he has to inject a little life and song into the dull pageant.
w H. Fowler Mear *story* Anson Dyer d Henry Edwards ph William Luff md M. de Wolfe ad James A. Carter ed R. T. Verrall
☆ Stanley Holloway, Felix Aylmer, Hugh Miller, K. Hamilton Price, Margaret Vines, Garry Marsh, Esmond Knight, Martin Walker

Vice Squad
US   1953   88m   bw
UA/Jules Levy, Arthur Gardner
GB title: *The Girl in Room 17*
A police captain tracks down two bank robbers who have killed a cop.
A day in the life of a police captain, quite watchable but scarcely engrossing.
w Lawrence Roman *novel* Harness Bull by Leslie T. White d Arnold Laven ph Joseph C. Biroc m Herschel Burke Gilbert
☆ Edward G. Robinson, Paulette Goddard, K. T. Stevens, Porter Hall, Adam Williams, Edward Binns, Lee Van Cleef

The Vice Squad *
US   1931   78m   bw
Paramount
Stool pigeons account for many arrests of supposed prostitutes.
Rather draggy exposé of police methods, allegedly torn from the headlines.
w Oliver H. P. Garrett d John Cromwell
☆ Kay Francis, Paul Lukas, Judith Wood, William B. Davidson, Rockcliffe Fellowes, Esther Howard
'Should draw adult attention in the large cities.' – *Variety*

Vice Versa *
GB   1947   111m   bw
Rank/Two Cities (Peter Ustinov, George H. Brown)
A magic stone enables an unhappy Victorian boy to change places with his pompous father.
Funny moments can't disguise the fact that this overlong comedy is a bit of a fizzle, its talented creator not being a film-maker. A pity, as British films have so rarely entered the realms of fancy.
wd Peter Ustinov *novel* F. Anstey ph Jack Hildyard m Antony Hopkins
☆ Roger Livesey, Kay Walsh, Anthony Newley, James Robertson Justice, David Hutcheson, Petula Clark, Joan Young
'A repository of English oddities.' – *John Russell Taylor*

Vice Versa
US   1988   98m   colour
Columbia (Dick Clement, Ian La Frenais)
▤ ▤ ◎～
A father and his 11-year-old son find their minds transplanted into the other's body by a magic skull.
One of the last and certainly the least of the mid-1980s cycle of role swapping movies.
w Dick Clement, Ian La Frenais d Brian Gilbert m King Baggot m David Shire pd Jim Schoppe ed David Garfield

---

☆ Judge Reinhold, Fred Savage, Corinne Bohrer, Swoosie Kurtz, David Profal, Jane Kaczmarek, Gloria Gifford

The Vicious Circle

US 1948 77m bw
United Artist (W. Lee Wilder)
GB title: *The Woman in Brown*

Five Jewish farmers in Hungary are framed for murder.
Well-meaning but tedious and very static melodrama.
w Heinz Herald, Guy Endore *play The Burning Bush* by Heinz Herald, Geza Herczeg *d* W. Lee Wilder *ph* George Robinson *m* Paul Dessau
☆ Conrad Nagel, Fritz Kortner, Reinhold Schunzel, Philip Van Zandt, Edwin Maxwell, Lyle Talbot

The Vicious Circle *

GB 1957 84m bw
Romulus (Peter Rogers)
US title: *The Circle*

An actress is found dead in Dr Latimer's flat and the weapon turns up in the boot of his car …
Entertaining whodunnit from a TV serial.
w Francis Durbridge *serial The Brass Candlestick* by Francis Durbridge *d* Gerald Thomas *ph* Otto Heller *m* Stanley Black
☆ John Mills, Derek Farr, Noelle Middleton, Roland Culver, Wilfrid Hyde-White, Mervyn Johns, René Ray, Lionel Jeffries, Lisa Daniely

Vicki *

US 1953 85m bw
TCF (Leonard Goldstein)

A girl model is murdered, and her sister proves that her boyfriend is innocent, despite the efforts of a brutal detective.
Very competent if uninspired remake of I Wake Up Screaming (qv).
w Dwight Taylor *d* Harry Horner *ph* Milton Krasner *m* Leigh Harline
☆ Jeanne Crain, Jean Peters, Richard Boone, Elliott Reid, Casey Adams, Alex D'Arcy, Carl Betz, Aaron Spelling

Le Vicomte Règle Ses Comptes: see *The Investigator*

'Fear is the oxygen of blackmail. If Barrett was paying, others are. Find me one!'

Victim ***

GB 1961 100m bw
Rank/Allied Filmmakers/Parkway (Michael Relph)

A barrister with homosexual inclinations tracks down a blackmailer despite the risk to his own reputation.
A plea for a change in the law is very smartly wrapped up as a murder mystery which allows all aspects to be aired, and the London locations are vivid.
w Janet Green, John McCormick *d* Basil Dearden *ph* Otto Heller *m* Philip Green
☆ Dirk Bogarde, Sylvia Syms, John Barrie, Norman Bird, Peter McEnery, Anthony Nicholls, Dennis Price, Charles Lloyd Pack, Derren Nesbitt, John Cairney, Hilton Edwards, Peter Copley, Donald Churchill, Nigel Stock
'Ingenious, moralistic, and moderately amusing.' – Pauline Kael, 70s

La Victoire en Chantant: see *Black and White in Colour*

Victor/Victoria *

GB 1982 134m Technicolor Panavision
MGM/Peerford/Ladbroke Entertainments/Blake Edwards

In 1934 Paris, a girl singer becomes successful when she poses as a female impersonator, but it causes complications in her love life.
The story was previously filmed more innocuously as a Jessie Matthews vehicle, First a Girl; Edwards makes it a sexually harping, grotesque low comedy, but there are pleasurable moments.
wd Blake Edwards, from the German film of 1933 *Viktor und Viktoria* (wd Reinhold Schunzel) *ph* Dick Bush *m* Henry Mancini *pd* Rodger Maus
☆ Julie Andrews, James Garner, Robert Preston, Lesley Ann Warren, Alex Karras, John Rhys-Davies, Graham Stark
'An audience pleaser in the worst sense.' – New Yorker

'Edwards' idea of European sophistication and Gallic naughtiness is seen throughout to be depressingly crude, parochial and second-hand, based on old American farces and reprises of his own Clouseau routines.' – Sunday Times
♪ original song score (Henry Mancini, Leslie Bricusse)
& Julie Andrews; Robert Preston; Lesley Ann Warren; screenplay (adaptation); costume design; art direction

Victoria the Great ***

GB 1937 112m bw (Technicolor sequence)
British Lion/Imperator/Herbert Wilcox

Episodes in the life of Queen Victoria.
A decent film with all the British virtues, and a milestone in the cinema of its time. Script and performances are excellent; production sometimes falters a little.
w Robert Vansittart, Miles Malleson *play Victoria Regina* by Laurence Housman *d* Herbert Wilcox *ph* F. A. Young, William V. Skall *m* Anthony Collins
☆ Anna Neagle, Anton Walbrook, H. B. Warner, Walter Rilla, Mary Morris, C. V. France, Charles Carson, Felix Aylmer, Derrick de Marney
'The effect of the final colour reel is to make the picture look like something enamelled on pottery and labelled "A Present from Blackpool".' – James Agate

'The six most exciting women in the world – in the most expensive entertainment you have ever seen!'

The Victors *

GB 1963 175m bw Panavision
Columbia/Open Road (Carl Foreman)

World War II adventures of an American infantry platoon.
Patchy compendium with moral too heavily stressed but plenty of impressive scenes and performances along the way. The mixture of realism and irony, though, doesn't really mix.
w Carl Foreman *novel The Human Kind* by Alexander Baron *d* Carl Foreman *ph* Christopher Challis *m* Sol Kaplan
☆ George Peppard, George Hamilton, Albert Finney, Melina Mercouri, Eli Wallach, Vince Edwards, Rosanna Schiaffino, James Mitchum, Jeanne Moreau, Elke Sommer, Senta Berger, Peter Fonda, Michael Callan
'Doggerel epic.' – John Coleman
'War has revealed Mr Foreman as a pompous bore.' – John Simon
'Having made a point through an image it continually feels the need to state it all over again by way of dialogue.' – Penelope Houston

Victory *

US 1940 77m bw
Paramount (Anthony Veiller)

A Dutch East Indies recluse rescues a girl and is menaced by three villains who think he is wealthy.
Curious, ineffective but occasionally compelling attempt to translate the untranslatable to the screen.
w John L. Balderston *novel* Joseph Conrad *d* John Cromwell *ph* Leo Tover *m* Frederick Hollander
☆ Fredric March, Betty Field, Cedric Hardwicke, Sig Rumann, Margaret Wycherly, Jerome Cowan, Fritz Feld, Rafaela Ottiano
'There is achieved a combination of amateur theatricals and earnest emptiness of motive and motion that will throw a blanket of reminiscent affection around this solemn, unusual and exotic buffoonery.' – Otis Ferguson
'A mood of impending doom and horror more than makes up for its slow and deliberate action … a fine and penetrating motion picture melodrama.' – New York World Telegram
'This is an unusual film at almost every level, yet it's unusual and disturbing, too.' – Pauline Kael, 70s
'Not a film of flamboyant hues … but it has quality, weight, and above all, compelling drama.' – Philadelphia Record
† The story was previously filmed in 1919 by Maurice Tourneur (with Jack Holt) and in 1930 by William Wellman (with Richard Arlen).

Victory

US 1981 117m Metrocolor Panavision
Lorimar/Victory Company/Tom Stern (Freddie Fields)

alternative and GB release title: *Escape to Victory*
A German POW camp in 1943 houses many international football stars. A Nazi officer sees propaganda in a game against a German side, but the allies make it an opportunity for escape.
Flabby and unconvincing POW story with agreeably old-fashioned values sacrificed to trendy casting and a silly ending.
w Evan Jones, Yabo Yablonsky *d* John Huston *ph* Gerry Fisher *m* Bill Conti *pd* J. Dennis Washington
☆ Sylvester Stallone, Michael Caine, Pele, Bobby Moore, Max von Sydow, George Mikell, Daniel Massey
'Even readers of the Boy's Own Paper might have blenched … ludicrous beyond belief.' – Tom Milne, MFB

Victory through Air Power **

US 1943 65m Technicolor
Walt Disney

The history of aviation and the theories of Major Alexander de Seversky.
What was thought by many to be propaganda was in fact a demonstration of Disney's own fascination with the theories of a controversial figure. The cartoon segments are put together with the studio's accustomed brilliance.
w various *d* H. C. Potter (live action), various *m* Edward H. Plumb, Paul J. Smith, Oliver G. Wallace
& Edward H. Plumb, Paul J. Smith, Oliver G. Wallace

Videodrome

Canada 1982 89m colour
Filmplan International

A videodrome TV channel induces pornographic hallucinations in the viewer.
Dangerous when it is not risible, this thoroughly tawdry concept is made worse by being slickly done.
wd David Cronenberg *ph* Mark Irwin *m* Howard Shore *sp* Michael Lennick
☆ James Woods, Sonja Smits, Deborah Harry, Peter Dvorsky
'Almost as incoherent as it is speculative.' – Sight and Sound

La Vie à l'Envers: see *Life Upside Down*

La Vie de Château **

France 1965 93m bw
Ancinex/Cobela/Guéville (Nicole Stéphane)

aka: *A Matter of Resistance*
aka: *Gracious Living*
In a Normandy château just before the D-Day landings, a husband discovers that his wife is being courted by a Nazi officer and a hero of the Resistance.
A delightful, broad comedy of conflicting desires, marked by slick timing and resourceful performances.
w Jean-Paul Rappeneau, Claude Sautet, Alain Cavalier, Daniel Boulanger *d* Jean-Paul Rappeneau *ph* Pierre Lhomme *m* Michel Legrand *ad* Jacques Saulnier *ed* Jacques Gillette
☆ Catherine Deneuve, Pierre Brasseur, Philippe Noiret, Henri Garcin, Carlos Thompson, Mary Marquet, Donald O'Brien

La Vie Devant Soi: see *Madame Rosa*

La Vie Est un Long Fleuve Tranquille

France 1988 91m colour
Electric/Contemporary/Téléma/MK2/FR3 (Charles Gassot)

GB title: *Life is a Long Quiet River*
Wealthy and respectable parents discover that their child was switched at its birth twelve years before with the baby of a poor and feckless family.
Glossy comedy at the expense of class, demonstrating that environment is more important than breeding in creating character.
w Florence Quentin, Etienne Chatiliez *d* Etienne Chatiliez *ph* Pascal Lebegue *m* Gérard Kawczynski *pd* Geoffroy Larcher *ed* Chantal Delattre

☆ Benoît Magimel, Valerie Lalande, Tara Romer, Jérôme Floc'h, Sylvie Cubertafon, Emmanuel Cendrier

La Vie Est Un Roman: see *Life Is a Bed of Roses*

La Vie et Rien D'Autre: see *Life and Nothing But*

Vie Privée *

France 1961 103m Eastmancolor
Progefi/Cipra/CCM (Christine Gouze-Rénal)

aka: *A Very Private Affair*
A promiscuous movie star who retreats from fame to her home town of Geneva falls again for the theatre director who was her first love.
An unsatisfactory movie given to melodrama, but interesting for its insights into the universe of an actress much like Bardot herself in her strong-willed refusal to conform.
w Jean-Paul Rappeneau, Louis Malle, Jean Ferry *d* Louis Malle *ph* Henri Decaë *m* Fiorenzo Carpi *ad* Bernard Evein *ed* Kenout Peltier
☆ Brigitte Bardot, Marcello Mastroianni, Eleonore Hirt, Grégoire von Rezzori, Dirk Sanders
† The production was troubled, with Bardot and Mastroianni, who played lovers, not hiding their dislike for one another. A dubbed version was cut to 94m by MGM for its American release, despite Malle's protests.

La Vie Rêvée des Anges: see *The Dreamlife of Angels*

La vieille qui marchait dans la mer: see *The Old Lady Who Walked in the Sea*

De Vierde Man: see *The Fourth Man*

Une Vierge chez les Morts Vivants: see *Virgin among the Living Dead*

The View from Pompey's Head *

US 1955 97m Eastmancolor Cinemascope
TCF (Philip Dunne)

GB title: *Secret Interlude*
A New York lawyer returns on a case to the small town of his youth, and falls in love again with his old sweetheart.
Routine Marquand-type novelette, long on atmosphere and short on plot.
wd Philip Dunne *novel* Hamilton Basso *ph* Joe MacDonald *m* Elmer Bernstein
☆ Richard Egan, Dana Wynter, Cameron Mitchell, Sidney Blackmer, Marjorie Rambeau

A View from the Bridge

France 1961 117m bw
Transcontinental (Paul Graetz)

original title: *Vu du Pont*
A longshoreman on the New York waterfront has passionate feelings for his wife's niece, and these erupt when she announces her engagement.
Solemn, self-examining melodrama, poorly adapted from the stage.
w Norman Rosten *play* Arthur Miller *d* Sidney Lumet *ph* Michel Kelber *m* Maurice Leroux
☆ Raf Vallone, Maureen Stapleton, Carol Lawrence, Jean Sorel, Raymond Péllégrin, Morris Carnovsky, Harvey Lembeck, Vincent Gardenia
† The film was shot in several languages.

A View to a Kill

GB 1985 121m Metrocolor Panavision
MGM-UA/Albert R. Broccoli

James Bond tangles with a ruthless international industrialist.
A tedious Bond adventure in which even the expensive highlights are unmemorable.
w Richard Maibaum, Michael G. Wilson *d* John Glen *ph* Alan Hume *m* John Barry *pd* Peter Lamont *ed* Peter Davies
☆ Roger Moore, Christopher Walken, Grace Jones, Tanya Roberts, Patrick Macnee, David Yip, Fiona Fullerton

Vigil *

New Zealand   1984   90m   Eastmancolor
First Blood/Last Rites/John Maynard

On a remote farm, a teenage girl learns about life after her father is killed.
Austere but vaguely impressive drama; one is pleased however when it ends.
w Vincent Ward, Graeme Tetley d Vincent Ward ph Alun Bollinger m Jack Body pd Kai Hawkins ed Simon Reece
☆ Bill Kerr, Fiona Kay, Gordon Shields, Penelope Stewart, Frank Whitten

Vigil in the Night

US   1940   96m   bw
RKO (George Stevens)
Two nurses are attracted to the same doctor; one dies during an epidemic.
Dull, downbeat romantic melodrama with a miscast lead.
w Fred Guiol, P. J. Wolfson, Rowland Leigh novel A. J. Cronin d George Stevens ph Robert de Grasse m Alfred Newman
☆ Carole Lombard, Anne Shirley, Brian Aherne, Julien Mitchell, Robert Coote, Peter Cushing, Ethel Griffies

Vigilante Force

US   1976   89m   DeLuxe
United Artists/Corman Company (Gene Corman)
A Vietnam veteran goes too far in using his wartime skills to crush lawlessness in a small town.
Standard action movie, full of mindless mayhem.
wd George Armitage ph William Cronjager m Gerald Fried ad Jack Fisk ed Morton Tubor
☆ Kris Kristofferson, Jan-Michael Vincent, Victoria Principal, Bernadette Peters, Brad Dexter, Judson Pratt
'Sharp, bright, and not averse to exploitation band-wagons.' – *Tom Milne, MFB*

The Vigilantes Return

US   1947   67m   bw
Universal (Howard Welsch)
A US marshal is framed for murder by the outlaw gang he infiltrates.
Routine minor Western with more plot than action.
w Roy Chanslor d Ray Taylor ph Virgil Miller md Paul Sawtell ad Jack Otterson, Frank A. Richards ed Paul Landres
☆ Jon Hall, Margaret Lindsay, Andy Devine, Paula Drew, Robert Wilcox, Jonathan Hale, Arthur Hohl

Vigo: Passion for Life *

GB/France/Japan/Spain   1997   106m   colour
Channel Four/Little Magic/Impact/Nitrate/MACT (Amanda Temple, Jeremy Bolt)

Biopic of influential French director Jean Vigo, who died at the age of 29 after completing three films.
The passion, heightened by sickness, that marked the life of the tubercular Vigo is nowhere evident in this trudge through his life, which unfortunately reduces him to a conventional portrait of an artist at odds with the world.
w Peter Ettedgui, Anne Devlin, Julien Temple play Love's a Revolution by Chris Ward biography Jean Vigo by Paulo Emilio Salles d Julien Temple ph John Mathieson m Bingen Mendizabal pd Caroline Greville-Morris ed Marie-Thérèse Boiché
☆ Romane Bohringer, James Frain, Jim Carter, Diana Quick, William Scott-Masson, James Faulkner, Francine Bergé, Vernon Dobtcheff, Adolfo Fernandez
'Absolutely dreadful.' – *Sight and Sound*
'Fans of Vigo's slender output will find the works illuminated in fresh and interesting ways. Not incidentally, then, this is Temple's best film to date.' – *Kim Newman, Empire*

The Viking Queen

GB   1967   91m   Technicolor
Warner/Hammer (John Temple-Smith)

During the first century AD, the queen of the Iceni tries to keep peace with the occupying Romans but has trouble with hot-headed Druids.
Stuff and nonsense from the Dark Ages; light should not have been shed upon it.
w Clarke Reynolds story John Temple-Smith d Don Chaffey ph Stephen Dade m Gary Hughes pd George Provis ed James Needs, Peter Boita
☆ Don Murray, Carita, Donald Houston, Andrew Keir, Patrick Troughton, Adrienne Corri, Niall MacGinnis, Wilfrid Lawson, Nicola Pagett

Viking Women

US   1957   66m   bw
AIP (Roger Corman)

A group of Viking women set sail in search of their men, who went on an expedition three years before.
This claims to be 'The Saga of the Viking Women and Their Voyage to the Waters of the Great Sea Serpent'. Viking women, it turns out, are all leggy, slim blondes who wear skin-tight leather and plenty of eyeliner, and look incapable of even fixing their own make-up.
w Lawrence Louis Goldman story Irving Block d Roger Corman ph Monroe P. Askins m Albert Glasser ch Wilda Taylor ad Bob Kinoshita ed Ronald Sinclair
☆ Abby Dalton, Susan Cabot, Brad Jackson, June Kenney, Richard Devon, Betsy Jones-Moreland, Jonathan Haze, Jay Sayer

'Mightiest Of Men ... Mightiest Of Spectacles ... Mightiest Of Motion Pictures!'

The Vikings ***

US   1958   116m   Technirama
UA/KD Productions (Jerry Bresler)

Two Viking half-brothers quarrel over the throne of Northumbria.
Slightly unpleasant and brutal but extremely well-staged and good-looking epic in which you can almost feel the harsh climate. Fine colour, strong performances, natural settings, vivid action, and all production values as they should be.
w Calder Willingham novel The Viking by Edison Marshall d Richard Fleischer ph Jack Cardiff m Mario Nascimbene sp credit titles United Productions of America
☆ Orson Welles, Kirk Douglas, Tony Curtis, Ernest Borgnine, Janet Leigh, Alexander Knox, Frank Thring, James Donald, Maxine Audley, Eileen Way

Villa Rides!

US   1968   125m   Technicolor   Panavision
Paramount (Ted Richmond)
1912 Mexico: an American pilot who has been gun-running for the rebels is pressed into more active service.
Bang-bang actioner which pauses too often for reflection and local colour.
w Robert Towne, Sam Peckinpah d Buzz Kulik ph Jack Hildyard m Maurice Jarre ad Ted Howarth
☆ Yul Brynner, Robert Mitchum, Charles Bronson, Grazia Bucetta, Herbert Lom, Alexander Knox, Fernando Rey, Jill Ireland
'A textbook on How Not To Make a Movie.' – *Robert Towne*

Village of Daughters

GB   1961   86m   bw
MGM (George H. Brown)
An unemployed commercial traveller in an Italian village finds himself choosing a bride for a successful émigré.
Voluble, gesticulating minor comedy.
w David Pursall, Jack Seddon d George Pollock ph Geoffrey Faithfull m Ron Goodwin
☆ Eric Sykes, Warren Mitchell, Scilla Gabel, Carol White, Grégoire Aslan, John Le Mesurier

Village of the Damned **

GB   1960   78m   bw
MGM (Ronald Kinnoch)

Children born simultaneously in an English village prove to be super-intelligent and deadly beings from another planet.
Modestly made but absorbing and logical science fiction, cleanly presented.
w Stirling Silliphant, Wolf Rilla, Geoffrey Barclay novel The Midwich Cuckoos by John Wyndham d Wolf Rilla ph Geoffrey Faithfull m Ron Goodwin
☆ George Sanders, Barbara Shelley, Michael Gwynn, Martin Stephens, Laurence Naismith
† Sequel: Children of the Damned (qv).

Village of the Damned

US   1995   98m   Foto-Kem   Panavision
Universal/Alphaville (Michael Preger, Sandy King)

In a small Californian town, ten women give simultaneous birth to fair-haired children with strange powers.
A drear remake with a somewhat larger budget, but a decrease in skill and interest; there seems no reason to reproduce an old film, unless it is to exhibit the makers' lack of imagination and originality.
w David Himmelstein novel The Midwich Cuckoos by John Wyndham d John Carpenter ph Gary B. Kibbe m John Carpenter, Dave Davies pd Rodger Maus ed Edward A. Warschilka
☆ Christopher Reeve, Kirstie Alley, Linda Kozlowski, Michael Pare, Meredith Salenger, Mark Hamill, Pippa Pearthree
'A risible remake.' – *Variety*

A Village Tale *

US   1935   79m   bw
RKO (David Hempstead)
Envy leads to a clash between two rural landowners.
Unusual but very interesting attempt by Hollywood to film with integrity an old-fashioned country novel. Very dated, but pleasant to watch.
w Allan Scott novel Phil Stong d John Cromwell ph Nicholas Musuraca m Alberto Columbo
☆ Randolph Scott, Robert Barrat, Kay Johnson, Arthur Hohl, Janet Beecher, Edward Ellis, Donald Meek, Dorothy Burgess, Andy Clyde, Guinn Williams
'Depressing story without marquee strength. Restricted in appeal.' – *Variety*

Villain

GB   1971   98m   Technicolor   Panavision
EMI/Kastner/Ladd/Kanter
The come-uppance of a cowardly, sadistic, homosexual East End gang boss with a mother fixation.
Very unpleasant and unentertaining British low life shocker, plainly inspired by White Heat.
w Dick Clement, Ian La Frenais novel The Burden of Proof by James Barlow d Michael Tuchner ph Christopher Challis m Jonathan Hodge
☆ Richard Burton, Ian MacShane, Nigel Davenport, Joss Ackland, Cathleen Nesbitt, Donald Sinden, T. P. McKenna, Fiona Lewis

The Villain

US   1979   89m   Metrocolor
Columbia/Rastar (Paul Maslansky, Mort Engelberg)

GB title: Cactus Jack
An incompetent outlaw rides from one disaster to another.
No doubt amusing in conception, this attempt to put the cartoon character Wile E. Coyote into human form lamentably misfires, six minutes being an ideal length for that kind of comedy.
w Robert G. Kane d Hal Needham ph Bobby Byrne m Bill Justis
☆ Kirk Douglas, Arnold Schwarzenegger, Ann-Margret, Paul Lynde, Ruth Buzzi, Jack Elam, Strother Martin
'Timing is entirely absent from this limp, laughless fiasco, as is any evidence of imagination ... desperation is the keynote.' – *Paul Taylor, MFB*

The Villain Still Pursued Her *

US   1940   66m   bw
RKO (Harold B. Franklin)

An innocent family suffers at the hands of a villainous landlord.
Clumsy burlesque of old time melodrama, interesting that it was done at all and with this cast.
w Elbert Franklin d Edward Cline ph Lucien Ballard m Frank Tours
☆ Buster Keaton, Alan Mowbray, Anita Louise, Hugh Herbert, Joyce Compton, Margaret Hamilton, Billy Gilbert

Vincent and Theo *

France/GB   1990   140m   colour
Blue Dolphin/Belbo Films/Central Films (Ludi Boeken, David Conroy, Emma Hayter)

original title: Vincent et Theo
Biopic of Van Gogh and his supportive, but equally tortured, brother.
Interesting, unsensational account of the brothers' lives, though not particularly illuminating.
w Julian Mitchell d Robert Altman ph Jean Lepine m Gabriel Yared pd Stephen Altman ed Françoise Coispeau, Geraldine Peroni
☆ Tim Roth, Paul Rhys, Johanna Ter Steege, Wladimir Yordanoff, Jip Wijngaarden, Anne Canovas

Vincent: The Life and Death of Vincent van Gogh **

Australia   1987   99m   colour
Illumination/Look/Daska (Tony Llewellyn-Jones)

The life and suicide of the artist is recalled in his letters to his brother Theo.
Intriguing documentary, beautifully filmed and much helped by the passion and urgency of John Hurt's readings.
d Paul Cox
☆ John Hurt

The Vintage

US   1957   92m   Metrocolor   Cinemascope
MGM (Edwin H. Knopf)
Two fugitives from justice cause trouble when they become grape pickers.
Steamy drama with an unconvincing French setting; a Hollywood aberration.
w Michael Blankfort novel Ursula Keir d Jeffrey Hayden ph Joseph Ruttenberg m David Raksin
☆ Mel Ferrer, John Kerr, Michèle Morgan, Pier Angeli, Theodore Bikel, Leif Erickson

Vintage Wine

GB   1935   90m   bw
Gaumont-British/Real Art (Julius Hagen)
A 62-year-old widower upsets his family by marrying a young girl.
Amiable boulevard comedy transferred to the screen in a stagey fashion but providing a vehicle for the well-honed comic skills of Seymour Hicks.
w H. Fowler Mear, Seymour Hicks, Ashley Dukes play Der Ewige Jüngling by Alexander Engel d Henry Edwards ph Sydney Blyth md W. L. Trytel ad James A. Carter ed Ralph Kemplen
☆ Seymour Hicks, Claire Luce, Eva Moore, Judy Gunn, Miles Malleson, Kynaston Reeves, A. Bromley Davenport, Michael Shepley

Violence

US   1947   72m   bw
Monogram
War veterans fall victim to a group spreading civil discord.
Propaganda thick ear.
w Stanley Rubin, Louis Lantz d Jack Bernhard ph Henry Sharp
☆ Nancy Coleman, Michael O'Shea, Sheldon Leonard, Peter Whitney, Emory Parnell

Violent City

Italy/France   1970   100m   Technicolor
Techniscope
Rank/Fono Roma/Unidis/Universal France (Harry Colombo, George Papi)
original title: Città Violenta
aka: The Family
Released from prison, a hitman goes after the man who betrayed him and stole his girlfriend.
Fast-moving, body-strewn melodrama that rarely strays from the obvious.
wd Sauro Scavolini, Gianfranco Calligarich, Lina Wertmüller, Sergio Sollima story Dino Maiuri, Massimo de Rita d Sergio Sollima ph Aldo Tonti m Ennio Morricone ad Francesco Bronzi ed Nino Baragli
☆ Charles Bronson, Jill Ireland, Michel Constantin, Telly Savalas, Umberto Orsini, George Savalas
† The film was cut to 91m for its British release.

Violent Cop *

Japan 1989 103m colour
ICA/Bandai/Shochiku-Fuji (Hisao Nabeshima, Takio
Yoshida, Shozo Ichoyama)

original title: *Sono Otoko Kyobo ni Tsuki*
aka: *Warning, This Man Is Wild*

A maverick homicide cop, while teaching his new
partner the tricks of the trade, discovers that his
crooked colleagues are involved in drug dealing.
*A violent story of revenge and casual brutality, which
resembles Dirty Harry translated to Tokyo.*
w Hisashi Nozawa d Takeshi Kitano ph Yasushi
Sakakibara m Daisaku, Kume, Eric Satie
ad Masuteru Mochizuki ed Nobutake Kamiya
☆ 'Beat' Takeshi (Takeshi Kitano), Maiko
Kawakami, Makoto Ashigawa, Haku Ryu, Ken
Yoshizawa, Shiro Sano, Ittoku Kishibe, Shigeru
Hiraizumi
　'Slow tempo and arty look suits it for film
　festival dates.' – *Variety*

The Violent Enemy

GB 1968 98m Eastmancolor
Trio/Group W. (Wilfrid Eades)

An IRA explosives expert escapes from a British
jail but quarrels with his leaders.
*Dullish political melodrama needlessly rubbing salt in
old wounds.*
w Edmund Ward novel *A Candle for the Dead* by
Hugh Marlowe d Don Sharp ph Alan Hume
m John Scott
☆ Tom Bell, Ed Begley, Susan Hampshire, Noel
Purcell, Michael Standing

The Violent Hour: see *Dial 1119*

The Violent Men *

US 1955 96m Technicolor Cinemascope
Columbia (Lewis J. Rachmil)

GB title: *Rough Company*

A crippled cattle baron drives small landowners
from his valley, while his wife has an affair with his
younger brother.
*So much snarling goes on that this seems like a gangster
film in fancy dress, but it does hold the attention.*
w Harry Kleiner novel Donald Hamilton
d Rudolph Maté ph Burnett Guffey, W. Howard
Greene m Max Steiner
☆ Edward G. Robinson, Barbara Stanwyck, Glenn
Ford, Brian Keith, Dianne Foster, May Wynn,
Warner Anderson, Basil Ruysdael

The Violent Ones *

US 1967 90m Eastmancolor
Madison/Harold Goldman

In a small Mexican town, three American hobos
are interrogated after the rape and murder of a
local girl.
*Rather well-shot murder mystery with emphasis on
character, leading to a desert chase climax.*
w Doug Wilson, Charles Davis d Fernando Lamas
ph Fleet Southcott m Marlin Skiles
☆ Fernando Lamas, Aldo Ray, David Carradine,
Tommy Sands

Violent Playground

GB 1958 108m bw
Rank (Michael Relph)

A junior liaison officer in the Liverpool slums falls
in love with the sister of a fire-raiser.
*'Realistic' melodrama sabotaged by an entirely
schematic and predictable plot; enervatingly dull until
the siege climax.*
w James Kennaway d Basil Dearden ph Reg
Wyer m Philip Green
☆ Stanley Baker, Anne Heywood, David
McCallum, Peter Cushing, John Slater, Clifford
Evans

'The bank robbers that caught a town with its morals
down!'
Violent Saturday *

US 1955 90m DeLuxe Cinemascope
TCF (Buddy Adler)

Crooks move quietly into a small town with the
intention of robbing the bank.
*Interesting little melodrama which the wide screen robs
of its proper tension. Adequate presentation and
performance.*
w Sydney Boehm d Richard Fleischer ph Charles
G. Clarke m Hugo Friedhofer

☆ Richard Egan, Victor Mature, Stephen
McNally, Sylvia Sidney, Virginia Leith, Tommy
Noonan, Lee Marvin, Margaret Hayes, J. Carrol
Naish, Ernest Borgnine

Violent Streets: see *The Thief*

Violent Tradition: see *John Woo's Once a Thief*

Violette Nozière *

France/Canada 1977 122m Eastmancolor
Filmel/Cinevideo (Roger Morand)

In 1933 Paris, an eighteen-year-old girl leads a
double life, gets syphilis, poisons her parents and is
convicted of murder.
*Oddly erratic but interesting recapitulation of a famous
French murder case, not quite typical of its director.*
w Odile Barski, Herve Bromberger, Frederic
Grendel d Claude Chabrol ph Jean Rabier
m Pierre Jansen pd Jacques Brizzio
☆ Isabelle Huppert, Jean Carmier, Stephane
Audran, Bernadette Lafont

The VIPs **

GB 1963 119m Metrocolor Panavision
MGM (Anatole de Grunwald)

Passengers at London Airport are delayed by fog
and spend the night at a hotel.
*Multi-story compendium cunningly designed to exploit
the real-life Burton-Taylor romance. In itself,
competent rather than stimulating.*
w Terence Rattigan d Anthony Asquith ph Jack
Hildyard m Miklos Rozsa
☆ Richard Burton, Elizabeth Taylor, Maggie
Smith, Rod Taylor, Margaret Rutherford, Louis
Jourdan, Elsa Martinelli, Orson Welles, Linda
Christian, Dennis Price, Richard Wattis, David
Frost, Robert Coote, Joan Benham, Michael
Hordern and also Lance Percival, Martin Miller
　'If Mr Rattigan's Aunt Edna still goes to the
　pictures she should like his latest offering,
　especially if she has a good lunch first.' – *Brenda
　Davies*
🏆 Margaret Rutherford

Virgin among the Living Dead

France 1971 85m Eastmancolor
J.K. Films/Prodif (K. H. Mannchen)

original title: *Une Vierge chez les Morts Vivants*
aka: *Christina; Princesse de l'Erotisme*

A young woman visits an isolated chateau for the
reading of her father's will and is haunted by erotic
dreams of death.
*Bizarre but dull attempt at an atmospheric ghost story
coupled with some exploitative nudity; it is shot in the
director's usual clumsy style, with much use of pointless
zooms to uninteresting images.*
wd Jess (Jesús) Franco ph J. Climent ed P. Belair
m/sp Bruno Nicolai
☆ Cristine von Blanc, Howard Vernon, Britt
Nichols, Rosa Palomar, Anne Libert, Jesus Manera,
Paul Muller
　'A rambling, self-indulgent mess that is low on
　scares and high on skin content. Watch at your
　peril.' – *The Dark Side*

The Virgin and the Gypsy *

GB 1970 95m colour
Kenwood/Dimitri de Grunwald (Kenneth Harper)

A Midlands clergyman's daughter falls in love with
a gypsy fortune teller.
*Slow, sensitive, stylish picturization of a Lawrence
novella, with generally good performances.*
w Alan Plater story D. H. Lawrence d Christopher
Miles ph Robert Huke m Patrick Gowers
pd Terence Knight
☆ Joanna Shimkus, Franco Nero, Honor
Blackman, Mark Burns, Maurice Denham, Fay
Compton, Kay Walsh, Norman Bird
　'A minor but lively pleasure.' – *John Simon*

Virgin Island

GB 1958 94m Eastmancolor
British Lion/Countryman (Leon Clore, Graham Tharp)
US title: *Our Virgin Island*

A young couple set up house on a tiny Caribbean
island.
*Pleasant comedy slowed down by lack of plot and too
much conversation.*

w Philip Rush, Pat Jackson book *Our Virgin Island*
by Robb White d Pat Jackson ph Freddie Francis
m Clifton Parker
☆ Virginia Maskell, John Cassavetes, Sidney
Poitier, Isabel Dean, Colin Gordon

'Twentieth Century Fox spectacularly spreads before
you the violent age and velvet cape of Sir Walter
Raleigh!'
The Virgin Queen *

US 1955 92m DeLuxe Cinemascope
TCF (Charles Brackett)

The relationship of Queen Elizabeth I and Sir
Walter Raleigh.
*Unhistorical charade, quite pleasantly made and worth
noting for its star performance.*
w Harry Brown, Mindret Lord d Henry Koster
ph Charles G. Clarke m Franz Waxman
☆ Bette Davis, Richard Todd, Joan Collins,
Herbert Marshall, Jay Robinson, Dan O'Herlihy,
Robert Douglas, Romney Brent

'Sooner or later they're going to get it!'
The Virgin Soldiers **

GB 1969 96m Technicolor
Columbia/Carl Foreman (Leslie Gilliat, Ned Sherrin)

Serio-comic adventures of recruits in the British
army in 1960 Singapore.
*Autobiographical fragments, mostly from below the
belt, sharply observed and often very funny.*
w John Hopkins novel Leslie Thomas d John Dexter
ph Ken Higgins m Peter Greenwell
☆ Hywel Bennett, Nigel Patrick, Lynn Redgrave,
Nigel Davenport, Rachel Kempson, Michael
Gwynn, Tsai Chin
　'A kind of monstrous mating of *Private's Progress*
　and *The Family Way*, with bits of *The Long and
　the Short and the Tall* thrown in for good
　measure.' – *David Pirie*
† Sequel 1977: *Stand Up Virgin Soldiers*.

The Virgin Spring *

Sweden 1959 87m bw
Svensk Filmindustri (Allan Ekelund)

original title: *Jungfrukällan*

When her murderers are killed, a spring bubbles up
from the spot where a young maiden met her
death.
*Stark and rather lovely filming of a medieval legend,
with heavy symbolism and a strong pictorial sense.*
w Ulla Isaakson d Ingmar Bergman ph Sven
Nykvist m Erik Nordgren
☆ Max von Sydow, Birgitta Valberg, Gunnel
Lindblom, Brigitta Pettersson
　'When I first saw the film I thought it merely
　nauseous. At a second view I find it generally
　tedious, occasionally absurd, and always
　retrograde.' – *Dilys Powell*
🏆 best foreign film

Virgin Witch

GB 1971 89m colour
Univista (Ralph Solomons)

Two sisters run away to London and become
involved with the lesbian head of a modelling
agency who persuades them to take part in satanic
rituals.
*Cheaply and ineptly shot horror movie, with script and
acting to match, in which the cast shed their clothes at
the slightest opportunity.*
w Klaus Vogel d Ray Austin ph Gerald Moss
m Ted Dicks ed Philip Barnikel
☆ Patricia Haines, Neil Hallett, Keith Buckley,
James Chase, Vicki Michelle, Ann Michelle

Virginia

US 1940 107m Technicolor
Paramount (Edward H. Griffith)

A showgirl goes home to claim her inheritance,
but thinks of marrying a rich Yankee.
*Languid post-Civil War romantic melodrama, only
memorable for its colour.*
w Virginia Van Upp d Edward H. Griffith
ph Bert Glennon, William V. Skall
☆ Madeleine Carroll, Fred MacMurray, Sterling
Hayden, Helen Broderick, Paul Hurst, Marie
Wilson, Carolyn Lee, Louise Beavers

Virginia City *

US 1940 121m bw
Warner (Robert Fellows)

A dance hall girl is really a Southern spy helping a
rebel colonel to steal a gold shipment from her
Yankee boyfriend.
*Lumpy Western in Warner's best budget but worst
manner: the stars look unhappy and the plot progresses
in fits and starts.*
w Robert Buckner d Michael Curtiz ph Sol
Polito m Max Steiner
☆ Errol Flynn, Randolph Scott, Miriam Hopkins,
Humphrey Bogart, Frank McHugh, Alan Hale,
Guinn Williams, John Litel, Moroni Olsen, Russell
Hicks, Douglass Dumbrille

The Virginia Judge

US 1935 70m bw
Paramount (Charles R. Rogers)

A Southern judge's ne'er-do-well son gets deeper
into trouble.
*Homely vehicle for a star whose 'judge' was for many
years the centre of a vaudeville monologue.*
w Henry Johnson, Frank Adams, Inez Lopez
d Edward Sedgwick
☆ Walter C. Kelly, Marsha Hunt, Stepin Fetchit,
Johnny Downs, Robert Cummings

The Virginian *

US 1929 95m bw
Paramount (Louis D. Lighton)

A stalwart ranch foreman has to see his best friend
hanged for rustling, and defeats the local bad man.
*Standard Western with famous clichés, e.g. 'Smile
when you say that...'*
w Edward E. Paramore Jnr, Howard Estabrook
novel Owen Wister d Victor Fleming ph J. Roy
Hunt
☆ Gary Cooper, Walter Huston, Richard Arlen,
Mary Brian, Chester Conklin, Eugene Pallette

The Virginian

US 1946 90m Technicolor
Paramount (Paul Jones)

Forgettable remake of the above.
w Frances Goodrich, Albert Hackett d Stuart
Gilmore ph Harry Hallenberger m Daniele
Amfitheatrof
☆ Joel McCrea, Brian Donlevy, Sonny Tufts,
Barbara Britton, William Frawley, Henry O'Neill,
Fay Bainter

Virgins and Vampires: see *Requiem for a
Vampire*

Viridiana ****

Spain/Mexico 1961 91m bw
Uninci/Films 59/Gustavo Alatriste (Munoz Suay)

A novice about to take her vows is corrupted by
her wicked uncle and installs a load of beggars in
his house.
*Often hilarious surrealist melodrama packed with
shades of meaning, most of them sacrilegious. A
fascinating film to watch.*
w Luis Buñuel, Julio Alajandro d Luis Buñuel
ph José F. Agayo
☆ Silvia Pinal, Francisco Rabal, Fernando Rey
　'One of the cinema's few major philosophical
　works.' – *Robert Vas*
　'An extraordinary film, a superb film.' – *Dilys
　Powell*

Virtual Assassin: see *Cyberjack*

'The world's last virgin!'
Virtual Sexuality

GB 1999 92m DeLuxe
Columbia TriStar/The Bridge/Noel Gay (Christopher
Figg)

When a computer experiment goes wrong, a
teenage schoolgirl is transformed into two people,
herself and a teenage youth with her mind, with
whom she falls in love.
*A British attempt a a highschool movie with a gender-
changing gimmick and the usual smutty jokes.*
w Nick Fisher novel Chloe Rayban d Nick
Hurran ph Brian Tufano m Rupert Gregson-
Williams pd Chris Edwards ed John Richards

☆ Laura Fraser, Rupert Penry-Jones, Luke De Lacey, Kieran O'Brien, Marcelle Duprey, Natasha Bell, Steve John Shepherd, Laura Macauley
'Vulgar, tacky and creepy.' – *Peter Bradshaw, Guardian*

Virtue
US 1932 68m bw
Columbia
A woman of the streets is regenerated through marriage.
Routine matinée programmer.
w Robert Riskin *story* Ethel Hill d Eddie Buzzell
☆ Carole Lombard, Pat O'Brien, Mayo Methot, Jack La Rue, Ward Bond
'A lot of plot is squeezed into the running time … the picture will be liked.' – *Variety*

Virtuosity
US 1995 105m DeLuxe
Paramount (Gary Lucchesi)
⊞ ⊞ ⊞ 🎧
In 1999, a computer-created psychopathic killer enters the real world, where he is hunted by a former cop.
Frenetic action movie, all show, no substance and not much sense amid the noise.
w Eric Bernt d Brett Leonard ph Gale Tattersall m Christopher Young pd Nilo Rodis ed B. J. Sears, Rob Kobrin sp L2 Communications
☆ Denzel Washington, Kelly Lynch, Russell Crowe, Stephen Spinella, William Forsythe, Louise Fletcher, William Fichtner
'Offers only the evanescent thrills of a videogame, despite a profusion of flashy effects and high-velocity pacing.' – *Variety*

The Virtuous Bigamist: see Four Steps in the Clouds

The Virtuous Sin
US 1930 81m bw
Paramount
GB title: *Cast Iron*
A girl tries to help her student husband when war takes him away from bacteriology.
Stilted romantic drama.
w Martin Brown, Louise Long *novel* Lajos Zilahy d George Cukor, Louis Gasnier ph David Abel
☆ Walter Huston, Kay Francis, Kenneth MacKenna, Paul Cavanagh
'Average programme flicker … cast names all from legit … nor is there much excuse for the picture running 80 minutes when 70 would have been better.' – *Variety*

'Earth is in for a shock.'
Virus
US 1999 100m DeLuxe
Universal/Mutual/Dark Horse/Valhalla (Gale Anne Hurd)
⊞ ⊞
The crew of a salvage tug boards an apparently abandoned Russian ship, but it has been taken over by an extra-terrestrial force that regards humans as a virus to be eradicated.
Frenetic, simple-minded science-fiction that follows an obvious course with few surprises along the way.
w Chuck Pfarrer, Dennis Feldman *comic books* Chuck Pfarrer d John Bruno ph David Eggby m Joel McNeely pd Mayling Cheng ed Scott Smith sp Chuck Gaspar; robotic fx: Steve Johnson, Eric Allard
☆ Jamie Lee Curtis, William Baldwin, Donald Sutherland, Joanna Pacula, Marshall Bell, Julio Oscar Mechoso, Sherman Augustus, Cliff Curtis, Yuri Chervotkin, Keith Flippen
'Derivative sci-fi shocker that isn't likely to spark much interest beyond its target audience of undemanding genre fans.' – *Joe Leydon, Variety*

The Viscount: see The Investigator

Visions of Light ***
US/Japan 1992 92m bw/colour
City Screen/American Film Institute/NHK (Stuart Samuels)
⊞ ⊞ ⊞ ⊘
Documentary tracing the development of cinematography from *The Birth of a Nation* in 1915 through to the present day.
An engrossing look at the contribution to film of the often unsung cinematographers, with excerpts from

125 feature films and interviews with 27 practitioners, from Nestor Almendros to Vilmos Zsigmond.
w Todd McCarthy d Arnold Glassman, Todd McCarthy, Stuart Samuels ph Nancy Schreiber ed Arnold Glassman
☆ Todd McCarthy

The Visit
West Germany/France/Italy/US 1964 100m bw Cinemascope
TCF/Deutschefox/Cinecittà/Dear Film/Films du Siècle/PECF (Julien Derode, Anthony Quinn)
A millionairess offers a fortune to her home town, providing someone will kill her ex-lover.
A realistic production that offers an essentially theatrical play, and all the effort goes for nothing.
w Ben Barzman *play* Friedrich Durrenmatt d Bernhard Wicki ph Armando Nannuzzi m Richard Arnell, Hans-Martin Majewski
☆ Ingrid Bergman, Anthony Quinn, Paolo Stoppa, Hans-Christian Blech, Valentina Cortesa, Irina Demick, Claude Dauphin, Eduardo Ciannelli
† The film's score was written by Richard Arnell with the exception of one sequence retained from Hans-Martin Majewski's otherwise rejected music.

Visit to a Chief's Son
US 1974 92m DeLuxe Panavision
UA/Robert Halmi
An American anthropologist and his son hope to film the rituals of an African tribe.
Minor adventure film with a happy resolution, based on a photomontage by the producer, a Life photographer.
w Albert Ruben d Lamont Johnson ph Ernest Day m Francis Lai
☆ Robert Mulligan, Johnny Sekka, John Philip Hodgdon

Visit to a Small Planet
US 1960 101m bw
Paramount/Wallis-Hazen
⊞
A young man from outer space takes a look at Earth and falls in love.
A satirical play disastrously adapted for the moronic comedy of an unsuitable star.
w Edmund Beloin, Henry Garson *play* Gore Vidal d Norman Taurog ph Loyal Griggs m Leigh Harline
☆ Jerry Lewis, Joan Blackman, Earl Holliman, Fred Clark, John Williams, Jerome Cowan, Gavin Gordon, Lee Patrick
🎨 ad Hal Pereira, Walter Tyler

'They Weren't Born Yesterday!'
Les Visiteurs *
France 1993 107m colour
Arrow/Gaumont/France 3/Alpilles/Amigo (Alain Terzian)
⊞ ⊞ 🎧
A knight and his servant are transported from the 12th century to the modern day.
Broad farce that will appeal to lovers of Carry On films.
w Christian Claiver, Jean-Marie Poiré d Jean-Marie Poiré ph Jean-Yves Le Mener m Eric Lévi pd Hugues Tissandier ed Catherine Kelber
☆ Christian Clavier, Jean Reno, Valérie Lemercier, Marie-Anne Chazel, Christian Bujeau, Isabelle Nanty, Didier Pain
'The French tradition doesn't always recognise the distinction between high and low comedy, and there is certainly a boisterousness about the proceedings which some viewers will find wearing.' – *Adam Mars-Jones*
'People fall over a lot, or hit each other, or shout very loud.' – *Sight and Sound*
† The film was the biggest box-office success of 1993 in France, taking twice as much at the box-office as the No. 2 film, *Jurassic Park.*

Les Visiteurs du Soir *
France 1942 110m bw
André Paulvé
aka: *The Devil's Envoys*
The devil sends messengers to Earth to corrupt two lovers, but he fails: even though he turns them to stone, their hearts still beat.
Made during the Occupation, this stately medieval fable was intended to be significant: the devil was Hitler, and the heartbeat that of France. Perhaps because it is so conscious of hidden meanings, it moves rather stiffly but is often beautiful to behold.

w Jacques Prévert, Pierre Laroche d Marcel Carné ph Roger Hubert m Joseph Kosma, Maurice Thiriet ad Alexandre Trauner, Georges Wakhevitch
☆ Arletty, Jules Berry, Marie Déa, Alain Cuny, Fernand Ledoux, Marcel Herrand
'There are wonderful images, but the movie is heavy on the allegorical and becomes rather slow and stylized.' – *Pauline Kael, 70s*

Visiting Hours
Canada 1981 105m colour Panavision
Filmplan International (Claude Héroux)
⊞
A homicidal maniac is at large in a hospital.
Tedious shocker wasting a reliable idea.
w Brian Taggert d Jean Claude Lord ph René Verzier m Jonathan Goldsmith
☆ Michael Ironside, Lee Grant, Linda Purl, William Shatner, Lenore Zann, Harvey Atkin

The Visitor
Italy 1979 90m colour
Ovidio Assonitis
Creatures from another world come to Earth to deal with a child who is the offspring of an evil mutant alien.
Fussy direction, minimal acting and a plot that makes little sense combine to create an incoherent movie.
w Lou Comici, Robert Mundy *story* Michael J. Paradise, Ovidio Assonitis d Michael J. Paradise (Giulio Paradisi) ph Ennio Guarnieri m Franco Micalizzi ad Frank Vanorio ed Robert Curi
☆ Mel Ferrer, Glenn Ford, Lance Henriksen, John Huston, Joanne Nail, Sam Peckinpah, Shelley Winters, Paige Conner

Viskingar och Rop: see Cries and Whispers

Visszaesök: see Forbidden Relations

La Vita è Bella: see Life Is Beautiful

I Vitelloni
Italy/France 1953 109m bw
Peg/Cité (Lorenzo Pegoraro)
aka: *Spivs*
In a small Italian resort, aimless young people get into various kinds of trouble.
Interesting in its realistic detail, this sharply observed slice of life is long enough for its basic purposelessness to become apparent.
w Federico Fellini, Ennio Flaiano, Tullio Pinelli d Federico Fellini ph Otello Martelli, Tasatti, Carlini m Nino Rota
☆ Franco Fabrizi, Franco Interlenghi, Eleonora Ruffo, Alberto Sordi
🎨 script

Viva Knievel!
US 1977 106m Technicolor Panavision
Warner/Metropolitan (Stan Hough)
⊞ ⊞
Gangsters plan to kill motorcycle stunt rider Evel Knievel in order to use his trailer as a means of smuggling cocaine from Mexico into the United States.
Dreary hagiography, an uneasy mix of fact and fiction that preaches an anti-drug message, while using drugs and gangsters to provide its spurious excitement. In between his stunts, Evel makes the lame walk, causes women to go weak at the knees, cures junkies, reconciles an estranged father and son, and bores cinema audiences.
w Antonio Santillan, Norman Katkov d Gordon Douglas ph Fred Jackman m Charles Bernstein pd Ward Preston ed Harold Kress
☆ Evel Knievel, Gene Kelly, Lauren Hutton, Marjoe Gortner, Red Buttons, Eric Shea, Leslie Nielsen, Cameron Mitchell, Dabney Coleman

Viva Las Vegas!: see Meet Me in Las Vegas (1956)

Viva Las Vegas
👫👫 US 1964 85m Metrocolor Panavision
MGM (Jack Cummings, George Sidney)
⊞ ⊞
GB title: *Love in Las Vegas*
A sports car racer has fun in the gambling city.
Tolerable star musical.
w Sally Benson d George Sidney ph Joseph Biroc md George Stoll

☆ Elvis Presley, Ann-Margret, Cesare Danova, William Demarest, Nicky Blair, Jack Carter

Viva Maria!
France/Italy 1965 120m Eastmancolor Panavision
Nouvelles Editions/Artistes Associés/Vides (Oscar Dancigers, Louis Malle)
An Irish anarchist girl arrives in Central America and joins a group of strolling players.
All show and no substance, this is a colour supplement of a film, neither fish, flesh nor good red herring.
w Louis Malle, Jean-Claude Carrière d Louis Malle ph Henri Decaë m Georges Delerue ad Bernard Evein
☆ Jeanne Moreau, Brigitte Bardot, George Hamilton, Paulette Dubost, Claudio Brook
🎥 Jeanne Moreau

Viva Max
US 1969 93m Eastmancolor
Commonwealth United/Mark Carliner
⊞
A Mexican general marches his troops into Texas and seizes the Alamo.
Flat comedy with mildly amusing passages but too much noise, bluster and sentiment.
w Elliott Baker *novel* James Lehrer d Jerry Paris ph Jack Richards m Hugo Montenegro
☆ Peter Ustinov, John Astin, Pamela Tiffin, Jonathan Winters, Keenan Wynn, Henry Morgan, Alice Ghostley

'1001 nights of glorious romantic adventure!'
Viva Villa! **
US 1934 110m bw
MGM (David O. Selznick)
⊞ ⊘
The career of a Mexican rebel.
Gutsy action drama with some smoothing over of fact in the name of entertainment. A big, highly competent production of its year.
w Ben Hecht d Jack Conway ph James Wong Howe, Charles G. Clarke m Herbert Stothart
☆ Wallace Beery, Fay Wray, Leo Carrillo, Donald Cook, Stuart Erwin, George E. Stone, Joseph Schildkraut, Henry B. Walthall, Katherine de Mille
'Glorified western … strong b.o. fodder, handicapped a bit perhaps by its abnormal masculine appeal.' – *Variety*
'A strange poem of violence.' – *John Baxter, 1968*
'A glorified horse opera … the spectator's excitement is incited by the purely physical impact of the furious riding and war sequences, by the frequent sadism, and by the lively musical score.' – *Irving Lerner*
† Howard Hawks directed some sequences, uncredited.
🎨 best picture; script

Viva Zapata **
US 1952 113m bw
TCF (Darryl F. Zanuck)
⊞ ⊞ ⊘ 🎧
A Mexican revolutionary is finally betrayed by a friend.
Moody, good-looking star vehicle taking a romanticized but glum view of history.
w John Steinbeck d Elia Kazan ph Joe MacDonald m Alex North md Alfred Newman ad Lyle Wheeler, Leland Fuller
☆ Marlon Brando, Jean Peters, Joseph Wiseman, Anthony Quinn, Arnold Moss, Margo, Frank Silvera
🏆 Anthony Quinn
🎨 John Steinbeck; Alex North; Marlon Brando; art direction
🎥 Marlon Brando

Vivacious Lady *
US 1938 90m bw
RKO (George Stevens)
⊞ ⊞
A night-club singer marries a botany professor and has trouble with his parents.
Pleasant romantic comedy for two popular stars.
w P. J. Wolfson, Ernest Pagano d George Stevens ph Robert de Grasse m Roy Webb
☆ Ginger Rogers, James Stewart, Charles Coburn, Beulah Bondi, James Ellison, Frances Mercer, Franklin Pangborn, Grady Sutton, Jack Carson
'A good-natured, unpretentiously entertaining comedy.' – *New Yorker*
🎨 Robert de Grasse

Vivement Dimanche!: see *Finally, Sunday*

Vivre pour Vivre: see *Live for Life*

Vixen
US 1968 71m Eastmancolor
Cinecenta/Eve/Coldstream (Russ Meyer)
A nymphomaniac seduces every passing stranger of either sex.
Comic exploitation film in which the cast, at least, appear to be enjoying themselves.
w Robert Rudelson *story* Russ Meyer, Anthony James Ryan *d* Russ Meyer *ph* Russ Meyer *ad* Wilfred Kues *ed* Russ Meyer, Richard Brummer
☆ Erica Gavin, Harrison Page, Garth Pillsbury, Michael Donovan O'Donnell, Vincene Wallace
† The film was cut to 47m for its British release.

I Vizi Morbosi di una Governante: see *Crazy Desires of a Murderer*

Vogues of 1938 *
US 1937 108m Technicolor
Walter Wanger
reissue title: *All This and Glamour Too*
Rival fashion houses compete at the Seven Arts Ball.
A fashion show with threads of plot, interesting for clothes and cast, all working hard.
w Bella and Samuel Spewack *d* Irving Cummings *ph* Ray Rennahan *m* Victor Young *md* Boris Morros *ch* Seymour Felix *ad* Alexander Toluboff
☆ Joan Bennett, Warner Baxter, Helen Vinson, Mischa Auer, Alan Mowbray, Jerome Cowan, Alma Kruger, Marjorie Gateson, Penny Singleton, Hedda Hopper
♫ song 'That Old Feeling' (*m*Sammy Fain, *ly*Lew Brown); Alexander Toluboff

The Voice in the Mirror
US 1958 102m bw Cinemascope
Universal-International
A reformed alcoholic thinks back on his past life.
Glum case history of no particular point or persuasiveness.
w Larry Marcus *d* Harry Keller *ph* William H. Daniels *m* Henry Mancini
☆ Richard Egan, Julie London, Walter Matthau, Arthur O'Connell, Troy Donahue, Mae Clarke, Ann Doran

A Voice in the Night: see *Freedom Radio*

A Voice in the Wind
US 1944 85m bw
UA/Arthur Ripley
Two refugees from the Nazis meet again and die on a remote island.
Pretentious romantic claptrap, fascinating only for a few of the impressionist effects it contrives on the lowest of budgets.
w Frederick Torberg *d* Arthur Ripley *m* Michel Michelet
☆ Francis Lederer, Sigrid Gurie, J. Carrol Naish
'Like a mid-thirties French melodrama drenched in the Rembrandt-and-molasses manner of German films of the early to middle twenties. Even within those terms it is much less good than it might be, solemn, unimaginative, thinly detailed; but it is also richly nostalgic if you have any feeling for bad period art.' – *James Agee*
♫ Michel Michelet

The Voice of Bugle Ann *
US 1936 70m bw
MGM (John Considine Jnr)
When a dog is killed its embittered owner seeks revenge.
Old-fashioned country tale, rather heavy-going but emotionally strong.
w Harvey Gates, Samuel Hoffenstein *novel* Mackinlay Kantor *d* Richard Thorpe *ph* Ernest Haller
☆ Lionel Barrymore, Maureen O'Sullivan, Eric Linden, Dudley Digges, Spring Byington, Charley Grapewin
'A very fine movie indeed.' – *Pare Lorentz*

The Voice of Merrill
GB 1952 84m bw
Tempean (Robert Baker, Monty Berman)
US title: *Murder Will Out*
Three men are suspected of murder but one becomes a potential victim.

Complicated murder thriller which intrigues but hardly satisfies.
wd John Gilling *ph* Monty Berman *m* Frank Cordell
☆ Valerie Hobson, James Robertson Justice, Edward Underdown, Henry Kendall, Garry Marsh, Sam Kydd

The Voice of the Turtle **
US 1948 103m bw
Warner (Charles Hoffman)
aka: *One for the Book*
A girl shares her apartment with a soldier on leave.
A three-character play is smoothly filmed, slightly broadened, and burnished till its pale wit glows nicely.
w John Van Druten *play* John Van Druten *d* Irving Rapper *ph* Sol Polito *m* Max Steiner
☆ Eleanor Parker, Ronald Reagan, Eve Arden, Wayne Morris, Kent Smith
'A light and lovely comedy.' – *People*

Voices
GB 1973 91m Technicolor
Hemdale/Warden (Robert Enders)
A young couple in an old country house are haunted by the voice of their dead son.
Twisty little ghost story which would have been more effective at one third of its length.
w George Kirgo, Robert Enders *play* Richard Lortz *d* Kevin Billington *ph* Geoffrey Unsworth *m* Richard Rodney Bennett
☆ Gayle Hunnicutt, David Hemmings

La Voie Lactée: see *The Milky Way*

Volcano: see *Les Rendezvous du Diable* (1958)

'The Coast Is Toast.'
Volcano *
US 1997 102m DeLuxe
TCF/Shuler Donner/Donner (Neal H. Moritz, Andrew Z. Davis)
A tunnel being constructed under Los Angeles causes a volcanic eruption that wipes out much of the city.
Hectic disaster flick, played with a straight face by its cast; it's silly enough to be enjoyable.
w Jerome Armstrong, Billy Ray *d* Mick Jackson *ph* Theo van de Sande *m* Alan Silvestri *pd* Jackson DeGovia *ed* Michael Tronick, Don Brochu
☆ Tommy Lee Jones, Anne Heche, Gaby Hoffman, Don Cheadle, Jacqueline Kim, Keith David, John Corbett
'It's all total hokum, and if you don't quake with terror, you can always laugh.' – *The Times*

Volere Volare *
Italy 1991 92m colour
Metro/Italtoons (Ernesto di Sarro, Mario Cecchi Gori, Vittorio Cecchi Gori)
A sound engineer who dubs animated films finds himself changing into a cartoon character as he becomes involved with a psycho-sexual prostitute.
Witty and inventive comedy that mixes live action and animation to amusing effect.
wd Maurizio Nichetti, Guido Manuli *ph* Mario Battistoni *ad* Maria Pio Angelini *ed* Rita Rossi
☆ Maurizio Nichetti, Angela Finocchiaro, Mariella Valentina, Patrizio Roversi
'An offbeat fable for adults. Pic's expensive technical bravura is more impressive than the comedy.' – *Variety*

Les Voleurs
France 1996 116m colour
Metro Tartan/TF1/Rhône-Alpes/DA/Alain Sarde
aka: *Thieves*
A world-weary cop, the brother of a crook, becomes the lover of a petty thief, who is in love with her female philosophy teacher.
A downbeat, tangled tale of dysfunctional families and awkward relationships.
w André Téchiné, Gilles Taurand *d* André Téchiné *ph* Jeanne Lapoirie *m* Philippe Sarde *ad* Ze Branco *ed* Martine Giordano
☆ Catherine Deneuve, Daniel Auteuil, Laurence Côte, Benoite Magimel, Fabienne Babe, Didier Bezace, Julien Riviere, Ivan Desny

'A dense, dark film, filled with pessimism and solitude, but also with a passion for film-making.' – *Ginette Vincendeau, Sight and Sound*

Voltaire *
US 1933 72m bw
Warner (Ray Griffith)
The life and times of the 18th-century French wit.
One of the better Arliss charades, because the film is as stagey as his performance.
w Paul Green, Maude T. Howell *novel* George Gibbs, E. Laurence Dudley *d* John Adolfi *ph* Tony Gaudio
☆ George Arliss, Doris Kenyon, Margaret Lindsay, Reginald Owen, Alan Mowbray, David Torrence, Douglass Dumbrille, Theodore Newton
'Sumptuously staged and photographed ... sufficiently modern story to get interest.' – *Variety*

Volunteers
US 1985 106m Metrocolor
EMI/HBO/Tri-Star/Silver Screen (Richard Shepherd, Walter F. Parkes)
High jinks in the 1962 Peace Corps.
Tawdry comedy about the exploits of a young Home Guard.
w Ken Levine, David Isaacs *story* Keith Critchlow *d* Nicholas Meyer *ph* Ric Waite *m* James Horner *pd* James Schoppe, Delia Castaneda *ed* Ronald Roose, Steven Polivka
☆ Tom Hanks, John Candy, Rita Wilson, Tim Thomerson

Von Richthofen and Brown
US 1971 97m colour
UA/Roger Corman (Gene Corman)
GB title: *The Red Baron*
During World War I, a Canadian pilot takes on Germany's air ace.
The airplanes are nice, but the film is grounded by plot and dialogue.
w John and Joyce Corrington *d* Roger Corman *ph* Michael Reed *m* Hugo Friedhofer
☆ John Phillip Law, Don Stroud, Barry Primus, Karen Huston, Corin Redgrave, Hurd Hatfield

Von Ryan's Express **
US 1965 117m DeLuxe Cinemascope
TCF (Saul David)
In an Italian POW camp during World War II, an unpopular American captain leads English prisoners in a train escape.
Exhilarating action thriller with slow spots atoned for by nail-biting finale, though the downbeat curtain mars the general effect.
w Wendell Mayes, Joseph Landon *novel* Davis Westheimer, Harold Lipstein *m* Jerry Goldsmith
☆ Frank Sinatra, Trevor Howard, Sergio Fantoni, Edward Mulhare, Brad Dexter, John Leyton, Wolfgang Preiss, James Brolin, Adolfo Celi, Rafaela Cara

Voodoo
US 1995 89m CFI color
First Independent/Image/A-pix (Donald P. Borchers)
A student discovers that a university is the headquarters of a voodoo cult practising black magic.
Plodding, unpleasantly nasty little horror, perfunctorily done.
w Brian DiMuccio, Dino Vindeni *d* Rene Eram *ph* Dan Gillham *m* Keith Bilderbeck *pd* Jodi Ginnever *ed* Paolo Mazzucato
☆ Corey Feldman, Joel J. Edwards, Diana Nadeau, Ron Melendez, Sarah Douglas, Maury Ginsberg, Amy Raasch, Jack Nance

Voodoo Man
US 1944 62m bw
Monogram (Sam Katzman)
A mad scientist kidnaps young girls and reduces them to zombies.
Hopeless chiller wasting three stars.
w Robert Charles *d* William Beaudine
☆ Bela Lugosi, John Carradine, George Zucco, Michael Ames, Wanda McKay

Voodoo Woman
US 1956 77m bw
AIP/Carmel (Alex Gordon)
A domineering woman and her weak boyfriend go in search of treasure in the jungle, where a mad scientist in a silly hat has created an indestructible beastlike woman with the aid of voodoo rituals.
Ridiculous horror, with clichéd dialogue and situations; the monster looks like Mighty Joe Young in drag.
w Russell Bender, V. I. Voss *d* Edward L. Cahn *ph* Frederick E. West *m* Darrell Calker *ad* Don Ament *ed* Ronald Sinclair *sp* Harry Thomas
☆ Marla English, Tom Conway, Touch Connors, Lance Fuller, Mary Ellen Kaye
WIFE: 'You're insane.'
HUSBAND: 'Never say that! Never say that to me again!'

The Voyage **
Argentina/France 1991 150m colour
Metro/Cinesur/Du Sud (Fernando E. Solanas)
An isolated and unhappy student sets out on a long journey to find his father, a comic-book artist last heard of in Buenos Aires.
An acerbic, always engaging trip through South American consciousness, part fantasy but never far from being real, as an innocent gains experience of the world.
wd Fernando E. Solanas *ph* Felix Monti *m* Egberto Gismonti, Astor Piazzolla, Fernando E. Solanas *pd* Fernando E. Solanas *ad* Alberto Borello, Jacqueline Meppiel, Jacques Gaillard
☆ Walter Quiroz, Soledad Alfaro, Ricardo Bartis, Cristina Becerra, Marc Berman, Chiquinho Brandao, Franklin Caicedo
'A smooth mixture of stunningly beautiful camerawork and bitter two-fingers-to-them-all political satire.' – *Marcus Trower, Empire*
† Solanas survived an attempt to assassinate him during his post-production work on the film.

Voyage of the Damned *
GB 1976 155m Eastmancolor
ITC/Associated General (Robert Fryer)
In 1939, a ship leaves Hamburg for Cuba with Jewish refugees; but Cuba won't take them.
High-minded, expensive, but poorly devised rehash of Ship of Fools, with too many stars in cameos and not enough central plot.
w Steve Shagan, David Butler *book* Gordon Thomas, Max Morgan-Witts *d* Stuart Rosenberg *ph* Billy Williams *m* Lalo Schifrin
☆ Faye Dunaway, Max von Sydow, Oskar Werner, Malcolm McDowell, James Mason, Orson Welles, Katharine Ross, Ben Gazzara, Lee Grant, Sam Wanamaker, Julie Harris, Helmut Griem, Luther Adler, Wendy Hiller, Nehemiah Persoff and also Maria Schell, Fernando Rey, Donald Houston, José Ferrer, Denholm Elliott, Janet Suzman
'Not a single moment carries any conviction.' – *New Yorker*
'The movie stays surprisingly distanced and impersonal, like a panning shot that moves too quickly for all the details to register.' – *Charles Champlin, Los Angeles Times*
'With a story that is true (or thereabouts), tragic in its detail and implications, and about which it is impossible to take a neutral attitude, you feel an absolute bounder unless you give it the thumbs up.' – *Barry Took, Punch*
♫ script; Lalo Schifrin; Lee Grant

Voyage to Italy **
Italy/France 1953 100m bw
Titanus/Sveva/Junior/Italiafilm (Mario Del Papa, Marcello D'Amico)
original title: *Viaggio in Italia*
aka: *Journey to Italy; The Lonely Woman; Strangers* (US)
During a trip to Italy to sell a property they have inherited, an English couple realize that their marriage is empty and sterile.
Understated narrative of two repressed Northerners failing to respond to the warmth and fecundity of Italians and their landscape. As a portrait of an unhappy marriage it has its moments, but they do not include the film's unsatisfactory resolution.
Undervalued on its first release, it later featured in lists of the top ten films compiled by Italian and French critics.
w Vitaliano Brancati, Roberto Rossellini *d* Roberto Rossellini *ph* Enzo Serafin *m* Renzo

Rossellini *ad* Piero Filippone *ed* Jolanda
Benvenuti

☆ Ingrid Bergman, George Sanders, Maria
Mauban, Anna Proclemer, Paul Muller, Leslie
Daniels, Natalia Rai, Jackie Frost

'It seems impossible to me to see *Viaggio in Italia*
without experiencing, like a whip, the fact that
this film opens a breach that the entire cinema
must pass through under the pain of death.' –
Jacques Rivette, Cahiers du Cinema

'An influential film … marred by banality and
clumsiness.' – *Pauline Kael*

† The film was cut to 80m in its English-language
version, which is the one released on video. The
filming itself was fraught, with both the leads
unhappy. Sanders was sometimes in tears over
Rossellini's habit of giving him his lines at the last
moment.

Voyage to the Bottom of the Sea *

ᴁ US   1961   105m   DeLuxe
Cinemascope

TCF/Windsor (Irwin Allen)

▣▣ ▣▣ ▤ ⌕

USN Admiral Nelson takes scientists in his
futuristic atomic submarine to explode a belt of
radiation.

*Childish but sometimes entertaining science fiction
which spawned a long-running TV series.*

w Irwin Allen, Charles Bennett *d* Irwin Allen
ph Winton Hoch, John Lamb *m* Paul Sawtell,
Bert Shefter *ad* J. M. Smith, Herman A.
Blumenthal

☆ Walter Pidgeon, Robert Sterling, Joan
Fontaine, Peter Lorre, Barbara Eden, Michael
Ansara, Henry Daniell, Regis Toomey, Frankie
Avalon

Voyager

Germany/France   1991   117m   colour
Palace/Bioskop/Action/Stefi 2/Hellas (Eberhard
Junkersdorf)

▣▣ ▤ ⌕ ⌒

A middle-aged engineer begins an affair with a
teenage girl, only to discover that she is the
daughter of his former mistress.

*Involved drama, depending upon a series of
coincidences, that never fully engages its audience.*

w Rudy Wurlitzer *novel* Homo Faber by Max
Frisch *d* Volker Schlöndorff *ph* Yorgos Arvanitis,
Pierre L'homme *m* Stanley Myers *pd* Nicos
Perakis *ed* Dagmar Hirtz

☆ Sam Shepard, Julie Delpy, Barbara Sukowa,
Dieter Kirchlechner, Traci Lind, Deborah Lee-

Furness, August Zirner, Thomas Heinze

'The film's knowing slickness, especially in an
array of visually stunning locations and
masterfully choreographed crowd scenes, may
leave cinema-goers feeling strangely dissatisfied
with the whole enterprise.' – *Screen International*

Le Voyou **

France/Italy   1970   120m   Eastmancolor
UA/Les Films Ariane/Les Films 13/Artistes
Associés/P.E.A. (Alexandre Mnouchkine)

aka: *Simon the Swiss*

US title: *The Crook*

A crooked lawyer escapes from prison so that he
can see his daughter, implicate the accomplice who
put him behind bars and flee the country with his
swag.

*Entertaining, light-hearted thriller, done with great
style.*

w Claude Lelouch, Pierre Uytterhoeven, Claude
Pinoteau *d* Claude Lelouch *ph* Claude Lelouch
m Francis Lai *ad* Albert Volper *ed* Marie-Claude
Lacambre

☆ Jean-Louis Trintignant, Christine Lelouch,
Charles Gérard, Danièle Delorme, Yves Robert,
Amidou, Sacha Distel

'It is all much too good-tempered to be taken

seriously. It is strictly for fun, and on that level it
works very well.' – *Brenda Davies, MFB*

Vredens Dag: see *Day of Wrath*

Vrema Cuda: see *Time of Miracles*

Vssichni Dobršri Rodáci: see *All My Good Countrymen*

Vu du Pont: see *A View from the Bridge*

The Vulture

GB   1967   92m   bw
Lawrence Huntington Productions

▤

A family curse transforms a scientist into a giant
vulture.

*Incredible nonsense – incredible that anyone should try
to get away with it. Fun for those who like to watch
actors in trouble.*

wd Lawrence Huntington *ph* Stephen Dade
m Eric Spear

☆ Robert Hutton, Akim Tamiroff, Broderick
Crawford, Diane Clare

Vzlomshchik: see *The Burglar*

ᴁ film suitable for
   family viewing

▣▣ VHS video-cassette for
   the British PAL system

▣▣ VHS video-cassette for the British
   PAL system in wide screen-format

⇅ Video cassette in a computer-
   colourised version

▤ American NTSC video-cassette

⌕ Laser disc

W
US 1973 95m DeLuxe
Bing Crosby Productions (Mel Ferrer)

A young wife is threatened by her psychotic first husband.
Tedious rehash of several frightened lady themes, all rather sick.
w Gerald di Pego, James Kelly d Richard Quine
ph Gerry Hirschfeld m Johnny Mandell
☆ Twiggy, Michael Witney, Eugene Roche, Dirk Benedict, John Vernon

'On screen he played the child-hating, dog-hating, acid-tongued old swindler. It was no act!'

W. C. Fields and Me
US 1976 112m Technicolor Panavision
Universal (Jay Weston)
The rise to Hollywood fame of alcoholic comedian W. C. Fields.
Untruthful and rather boring biopic, with minor compensations.
w Bob Merrill book Carlotta Monti d Arthur Hiller ph David M. Walsh m Henry Mancini
pd Robert Boyle
☆ Rod Steiger, Valerie Perrine, John Marley, Jack Cassidy, Paul Stewart, Billy Barty, Bernadette Peters

'Steiger's impersonation largely keeps pace with the overriding vulgarity of the enterprise.' – *Sight and Sound*
'A stupid and pointless slander.' – *Judith Crist*
'Just the sort of memorial Fields might have wished for Baby Leroy.' – *Les Keyser, Hollywood in the Seventies*

The W Plan *
GB 1930 105m bw
BIP/Burlington (Victor Saville)
A British spy helps destroy Germany's secret tunnels.
Slightly fantasticated spy/war action which was a big popular success at the time.
w Victor Saville, Miles Malleson, Frank Launder
novel Graham Seton d Victor Saville ph F. A. Young, Werner Brandes
☆ Brian Aherne, Madeleine Carroll, Gordon Harker, Gibb McLaughlin, George Merritt, Mary Jerrold

'One of the best pictures yet from England, but unconvincing b.o. for the US. Lacks punch.' – *Variety*
'Fast, spectacular action, fine acting and notably realistic war scenes.' – *NFT, 1971*

Waati
Mali/France/Burkina Faso 1995 143m colour
Les Films Cissé/Sisé/Erato/La Sept/Kenn/Carthago (Souleymane Cissé)
In South Africa, a young black girl shoots a white policeman after he has murdered her father and brother and escapes to West Africa and a better life.
Sprawling, overlong account of endemic racism and brutality, one that is both too simple and contrived in its narrative to be effective.
wd Souleymane Cissé ph Vincenzo Marano, Gheorghy Rerberg, Alexei Rodionov, Jean-Jacques Bouhon m Bruno Coulais, Dave Pollecutt, Group Ki-Yi, Kaloury Sory pd Joseph Kpobly, Angela Halle ed Andrée Davanture
☆ Linéo Tsolo, Sidi Yaya Cissé, Eric Miyeni, Nakedi Ribane, Vusi Kunen, Mary Twala, Martin Le Maitre, Michelle Burger, Balla Moussa Keita

Wabash Avenue *
US 1950 92m Technicolor
TCF (William Perlberg)
During the Chicago World's Fair of 1892, a shimmy dancer is pursued by two men.
Bright rehash of Coney Island (qv), with solid tunes and performances.

w Harry Tugend, Charles Lederer d Henry Koster
ph Arthur E. Arling md Lionel Newman
☆ Betty Grable, Victor Mature, Phil Harris, Reginald Gardiner, Margaret Hamilton, James Barton, Barry Kelley
♫ song 'Wilhelmina' (mJosef Myrow, lyMack Gordon)

Das Wachsfigurenkabinett: see Waxworks

'The Ocean Roars And So Will You.'

The Wackiest Ship in the Army
US 1960 99m Technicolor Cinemascope
Columbia/Fred Kohlmar

In the South Pacific during World War II a decrepit sailing ship with an inexperienced crew manages to confuse Japanese patrols and land a scout behind enemy lines.
Slapstick war comedy with fragments of action; effect rather muddled.
wd Richard Murphy story Herbert Carlson
ph Charles Lawton m George Duning
☆ Jack Lemmon, Ricky Nelson, John Lund, Chips Rafferty, Tom Tully, Joby Baker, Warren Berlinger, Richard Anderson

'A zany and occasionally amusing farce. Yachtsmen should find it good fun.' – *Bosley Crowther*

Wacko
US 1981 90m Movielab
OSM (Greydon Clark)

A slobbish cop tracks down a Halloween killer armed with a lawn mower.
Dire parody of slasher and horror movies, lacking anything resembling a joke.
w Dana Olsen, Michael Spound, M. James Kouf Jnr, David Greenwalt d Greydon Clark
ph Nicholas J. von Sternberg m Arthur Kempel
ad Chester Kaczenski ed Earl Watson, Curtis Burch
☆ Joe Don Baker, Stella Stevens, George Kennedy, Julia Duffy, Scott McGinnis, Andrew Clay

Waco
US 1966 85m Technicolor
Paramount (A. C. Lyles)
A gunfighter is hired to straighten out a corrupt town.
Routine Western programmer with familiar faces in cameo parts.
w Steve Fisher novel Emporia by Harry Sanford and Max Lamb d R. G. Springsteen ph Robert Pittack m Jimmie Haskell
☆ Howard Keel, Jane Russell, Wendell Corey, Brian Donlevy, John Smith, Gene Evans, DeForest Kelley, Terry Moore, John Agar, Richard Arlen, Robert Lowery, Willard Parker, Fuzzy Knight

'A comedy about truth, justice and other special effects.'
'A Hollywood producer. A Washington spin-doctor. When they get together, they can make you believe anything.'

Wag the Dog **
US 1997 97m Technicolor
Entertainment/New Line/Tribeca/Baltimore/Punch (Jane Rosenthal, Robert de Niro, Barry Levinson)

In order to divert public attention away from a sexual scandal involving the President, his aides hire a Hollywood producer to create the impression of an international crisis.
Enjoyable comedy that skates over the surface of political life with some elegance, but never cuts quite deep enough.
w Hilary Henkin, David Mamet novel American Hero by Larry Beinhart d Barry Levinson

ph Robert Richardson m Mark Knopfler
pd Wynn Thomas ed Stu Linder
☆ Dustin Hoffman, Robert de Niro, Anne Heche, Woody Harrelson, Denis Leary, Willie Nelson, Andrea Martin, Kirsten Dunst, William H. Macy

'Satirizes media culture in a way that hardly delivers real insight or pungency, but shrewdly flatters the educated viewer's knowingness.' – *Godfrey Cheshire, Variety*
♟ Dustin Hoffman; Hilary Henkin, David Mamet

Wages of Fear: see Sorcerer (1977)

The Wages of Fear ***
France/Italy 1953 140m bw
Filmsonor/CICC/Vera

original title: *Le Salaire de la Peur*
The manager of a Central American oilfield offers big money to drivers who will take nitro-glycerine into the jungle to put out an oil well fire.
After too extended an introduction to the less than admirable characters, this fascinating film resolves itself into a suspense shocker with one craftily managed bad moment after another.
wd Henri-Georges Clouzot novel Georges Arnaud ph Armand Thirard m Georges Auric
☆ Yves Montand, Folco Lulli, Peter Van Eyck, Charles Vanel, Vera Clouzot, William Tubbs

'As skilful as, in its preoccupation with violence and its unrelieved pessimism, it is unlikeable.' – *Penelope Houston, Sight and Sound*
'It has some claim to be the greatest suspense thriller of all time; it is the suspense not of mystery but of Damocles' sword.' – *Basil Wright, 1972*
† See *Sorcerer*, a lamentable remake.
♟ best picture

Wagonmaster **
US 1950 86m bw
RKO/Argosy (John Ford, Merian C. Cooper)

Adventures of a Mormon wagon train journeying towards Utah in 1879.
Low-key Ford Western, essentially a collection of incidents, fondly and enjoyably presented.
w Frank Nugent, Patrick Ford d John Ford
ph Bert Glennon m Richard Hageman
☆ Ben Johnson, Joanne Dru, Harry Carey Jnr, Ward Bond, Charles Kemper, Alan Mowbray, Jane Darwell, Russell Simpson

'The feel of the period, the poetry of space and of endeavour, is splendidly communicated.' – *Lindsay Anderson*
'What emerges at the end is nothing less than a view of life itself, the view of a poet.' – *Patrick Gibbs, 1965*

Wagons East!
US 1994 106m Technicolor
Guild/Outlaw (Gary Goodman, Barry Rosen, Robert Newmyer, Jeffrey Silver)

Disgruntled citizens of a Western town hire an alcoholic wagonmaster to take them back to the east.
Lacklustre comedy, recycling old gags in a listless fashion.
w Matthew Carlson story Jerry Abrahamson
d Peter Markle ph Frank Tidy m Michael Small
pd Vince J. Cresciman ed Scott Conrad
☆ John Candy, Richard Lewis, John C. McGinley, Ellen Greene, Robert Picardo, Ed Lauter, William Sanderson, Rodney A. Grant

'It offers an ideal night out for anyone who's spent the past two decades pining for a remake of *Blazing Saddles*.' – *Kevin Jackson, Independent*
† John Candy died while making the movie.

The Wagons Roll at Night
US 1941 83m bw
Warner (Harlan Thompson)
The sweetheart of a circus owner makes a pass at the new young lion-tamer.
Dull remake of Kid Galahad (qv), whose plot was borrowed from Tiger Shark (qv). Warner were good at this kind of retreading, but gradually poor quality began to show.
w Fred Niblo Jnr, Barry Trivers d Ray Enright
ph Sid Hickox m Heinz Roemheld
☆ Humphrey Bogart, Sylvia Sidney, Eddie Albert, Joan Leslie, Sig Rumann, Cliff Clark, Frank Wilcox

Waikiki Wedding *
US 1937 89m bw
Paramount (Arthur Hornblow Jnr)
A press agent in Hawaii promotes a Pineapple Queen contest.
Light-hearted, empty-headed musical very typical of this studio ... except that this one is quite good.
w Frank Butler, Walter de Leon, Don Hartman, Francis Martin d Frank Tuttle ph Karl Struss
m Leo Shukin md Boris Morros ch Leroy Prinz
☆ Bing Crosby, Shirley Ross, Bob Burns, Martha Raye, George Barbier, Leif Erickson, Grady Sutton, Granville Bates, Anthony Quinn

'Shouldn't have any trouble getting by ... it's saccharine celluloid, sugar-coated.' – *Variety*
♫ song 'Sweet Leilani' (m/ly Harry Owens)
♟ Leroy Prinz

Wait 'Til the Sun Shines, Nellie *
US 1952 108m Technicolor
TCF (George Jessel)
The life of a small-town barber, from marriage through tragedy to retirement.
Amiable, leisurely family drama with pleasant settings; small beer, but oddly compulsive.
w Allan Scott novel Ferdinand Reyher d Henry King ph Leon Shamroy m Alfred Newman
☆ David Wayne, Jean Peters, Hugh Marlowe, Albert Dekker, Alan Hale Jnr, Helene Stanley

Wait until Dark **
US 1967 108m Technicolor
Warner Seven Arts (Mel Ferrer)

A photographer unwittingly smuggles a drug-filled doll into New York, and his blind wife, alone in their flat, is terrorized by murderous crooks in search of it.
Sharp suspenser with shock moments, from a successful play; in this case the claustrophobic atmosphere helps, though a lack of light relief makes itself felt.
w Robert and Jane Howard-Carrington
play Frederick Knott d Terence Young
ph Charles Lang m Henry Mancini ad George Jenkins
☆ Audrey Hepburn, Alan Arkin, Richard Crenna, Efrem Zimbalist Jnr, Jack Weston
♟ Audrey Hepburn

Waiting *
Australia 1990 94m colour
Contemporary/Filmside/ABC/Film Four (Ross Matthews)

A group of friends gather in a remote farmhouse as one of their number, an artist who has agreed to bear a baby for a friend, goes into labour.
Interesting and ironic film about surrogate motherhood and doctors' attitudes to childbirth.
wd Jackie McKimmie ph Steve Mason m Martin Arminger pd Murray Picknett ed Michael Honey
☆ Noni Hazelhurst, Deborra-Lee Furness, Frank Whitten, Helen Jones, Denis Moore, Fiona Press, Ray Barrett

Waiting for the Light *
US   1989   94m   DeLuxe
Entertainment/Epic Productions/Sarlui/Diamant
(Caledecot Chubb, Ron Bozman)

Business at a rundown diner is boosted by fake
religious visions.
*Ramshackle comedy of character that yields a
succession of small pleasures.*
wd Christopher Monger ph Gabriel Beristain
m Michael Storey pd Phil Peters ed Eva Gardos
☆ Colin Baumgartner, Clancy Brown, Vincent
Schiavelli, John Bedford Lloyd, Jeff McCracken,
Jack McGee, Louis Guzzo, William Dore
  'A wholly appealing confection that crumbles at
  the first critical touch.' – *Philip Strick, MFB*

Waiting to Exhale *
US   1995   121m   DeLuxe
TCF (Ezra Swerdlow, Deborah Schindler)

Four successful black women friends complain
about the men in their lives.
*Opulent melodrama of female bonding which settles
into an entertaining soap opera rather than a serious
examination of relationships.*
w Terry McMillan, Ron Bass *novel* Terry
McMillan d Forest Whitaker ph Toyomichi
Kurita m Kenneth 'Babyface' Edmonds pd David
Gropman ed Richard Chew
☆ Whitney Houston, Angela Bassett, Loretta
Devine, Lela Rochon, Gregory Hines, Dennis
Haysbert, Mykelti Williamson
  'Smoothly combines the elan and emotional
  luxuriance of old-fashioned woman's mellers
  with a modern black-pop sensibility.' – *Godfrey
  Cheshire, Variety*

Waiting Women *
Sweden   1952   107m   bw
Svensk Filmindustri
original title: *Kvinnors Väntan*
aka: *Secrets of Women*
While waiting for their husbands to arrive, three
wives share secrets about their marriages.
*Deft drama, with occasional comic touches, about
relationships between strong women and weak men,
and about freedom and responsibility.*
wd Ingmar Bergman ph Gunnar Fischer m Erik
Nordgren ad Nils Svenwall ed Oscar Rosander
☆ Anita Björk, Eva Dahlbeck, Maj-Britt Nilsson,
Birger Malmsten, Gunnar Björnstrand, Jarl Kulle,
Karl-Arne Holmsten

Wake in Fright: see *Outback*

'It thrills the women!'
'To the last gun – to the last plane – to the last man!'

Wake Island *
US   1942   78m   bw
Paramount (Joseph Sistrom)

During World War II, marines fight to hold an
American base on a small Pacific island.
Terse, violent flagwaver, well done within its limits.
w W. R. Burnett, Frank Butler d John Farrow
ph Theodor Sparkuhl, William C. Mellor
m David Buttolph
☆ Brian Donlevy, Macdonald Carey, Robert
Preston, William Bendix, Albert Dekker, Walter
Abel, Mikhail Rasumny, Rod Cameron, Barbara
Britton
  'Hollywood's first intelligent, honest and
  completely successful attempt to dramatize the
  deeds of an American force on a fighting front.'
  – *Newsweek*
  § best picture; script; John Farrow; William
  Bendix

Wake Me When It's Over
US   1960   126m   DeLuxe   Cinemascope
TCF/Mervyn Le Roy

Soldiers holding a Pacific island build a de luxe
hotel from surplus war material.
*Aptly-titled army farce on the lines of The Teahouse
of the August Moon but constructed from inferior
material. Yawningly tedious.*
w Richard Breen *novel* Howard Singer d Mervyn
Le Roy ph Leon Shamroy m Cyril Mockridge
☆ Ernie Kovacs, Dick Shawn, Jack Warden,
Margo Moore, Nobu McCarthy, Don Knotts,
Robert Emhardt

Wake of the Red Witch **
US   1948   106m   bw
Republic (Edmund Grainger)

The owner and captain of a ship settle their
differences to seek treasure on an East Indian
island.
*Rattling good action yarn told in flashback, with
adequate production and performances.*
w Harry Brown, Kenneth Gamet *novel* Garland
Roark d Edward Ludwig ph Reggie Lanning
m Nathan Scott
☆ John Wayne, *Luther Adler*, Gail Russell, Gig
Young, Adele Mara, Eduard Franz, Grant Withers,
Henry Daniell, Paul Fix, Dennis Hoey

Wake Up and Dream
US   1946   92m   Technicolor
TCF (Walter Morosco)
A little girl is determined to find her brother who
is missing in action in World War II.
*Ambitious but unappealing whimsy which descends into
sentimentality; either way it bewildered audiences and
critics.*
w Elick Moll *novel* The Enchanted Voyage by
Robert Nathan d Lloyd Bacon ph Harry Jackson
m Cyril Mockridge md Emil Newman
☆ June Haver, John Payne, Connie Marshall,
Charlotte Greenwood, John Ireland, Clem Bevans,
Lee Patrick

'The Sho-wow of Shows! The Hotcha-Topsa Of Them
All!'

Wake Up and Live *
US   1937   91m   bw
TCF (Kenneth MacGowan)
Success and failure in the radio world as a
commentator and a bandleader fight a verbal duel
in public.
*Fast-moving spoof in which something is always
happening, and usually something funny.*
w Harry Tugend, Jack Yellen *book* Dorothea
Brande d Sidney Lanfield ph Edward Cronjager
m Louis Silvers *songs* Mack Gordon, Harry Revel
☆ Walter Winchell, Ben Bernie and his band, Alice
Faye, Jack Haley, Patsy Kelly, Ned Sparks, Grace
Bradley, Walter Catlett, Joan Davis, Douglas
Fowley, Miles Mander, Etienne Girardot
  'Thoroughly satisfying film entertainment.' –
  Variety

Waking Ned *
GB/France/US   1998   91m   Technicolor
Panavision
TCF/Fox Searchlight/Tomboy (Glynis Murray, Richard
Holmes)

US title: *Waking Ned Devine*
In Ireland, villagers conspire in a local's
impersonation of a multimillion-pound lottery
winner, who died of shock before he could collect
his winnings.
*Rumbustious, folksy comedy that rather overdoes the
Irish whimsy.*
wd Kirk Jones ph Henry Braham m Shaun
Davey pd John Ebden ed Alan Strachan
☆ Ian Bannen, David Kelly, Fionnula Flanagan,
Susan Lynch, James Nesbitt, Maura O'Malley,
Robert Hickey, Paddy Ward, James Ryland, Fintan
McKeown, Matthew Devitt
  'Warm-heartedness just short of sentimentality
  … Keeps a steady laugh count rolling.' – *Empire*
  † The film was not shot in Ireland, but on the Isle
  of Man.

Walk a Crooked Mile
US   1948   91m   bw
Columbia (Edward Small)
British and American agents investigate the
leakage of atomic secrets.
Moderate semi-documentary spy thriller.
w George Bruce d Gordon Douglas ph George
Robinson m Paul Sawtell
☆ Louis Hayward, Dennis O'Keefe, Louise
Allbritton, Carl Esmond, Raymond Burr, Onslow
Stevens

Walk a Crooked Path
GB   1969   88m   Eastmancolor
Hanover (John Brason)
A housemaster at a boys' school is accused of
homosexuality.
*Po-faced melodrama in a minor key; reasonably
effective but not exciting.*

w Barry Perowne d John Brason ph John Taylor
m Leslie Bridgewater
☆ Tenniel Evans, Faith Brook, Christopher Coll,
Patricia Haines, Pat Endersby, Margery Mason,
Peter Copley

Walk, Don't Run *
US   1966   114m   Technicolor   Panavision
Columbia/Granley (Sol C. Siegel)

In Tokyo during the Olympics accommodation is
hard to find, and two men move in with a girl.
*Witless reprise of The More the Merrier, notable only
for the Tokyo backgrounds and for Cary Grant's
farewell appearance.*
w Sol Saks d Charles Walters ph Harry Stradling
m Quincy Jones
☆ Cary Grant, Samantha Eggar, Jim Hutton, *John
Standing*, Miiko Taka
  'Too long as are most comedies today, it seems to
  take its title far too literally; but there are several
  very funny sequences, a jaunty score, and the
  unflawed elegance of Mr Grant.' – *Arthur Knight*

Walk East on Beacon *
US   1952   98m   bw
Columbia (Louis de Rochemont)
GB title: *The Crime of the Century*
The FBI exposes communist spies in the US.
*Fast-moving semi-documentary spy thriller modelled on
the same producer's* The House on 92nd Street.
w Leo Rosten d Alfred Werker ph Joseph Brun
m Louis Applebaum
☆ George Murphy, Finlay Currie, Virginia
Gilmore, Karel Stepanek, Louisa Horton

'A man in search. A woman in need. A story of fate.'

A Walk in the Clouds
US   1995   103m   DeLuxe
TCF (Gil Netter, David Zucker, Jerry Zucker)

A travelling chocolate salesman agrees to pretend
to be the husband of a pregnant woman returning
home to her parents' vineyard.
*An over-sweet confection, so resolutely old-fashioned
that in the 40s it would have been described as 'a
woman's picture'; it is unlikely to find an appreciative
audience of any sex these days.*
w Robert Mark Kamen, Mark Miller, Harvey
Weitzman d Alfonso Arau ph Emmanuel Lubezki
m Maurice Jarre pd David Gropman ed Don
Zimmerman
☆ Keanu Reeves, Aitana Sanchez-Gijon,
Anthony Quinn, Giancarlo Giannini, Angelica
Aragon, Evangelina Elizondo, Freddy Rodriguez
  'The filmmaking, so sold on its own fruitiness, is
  cheap, sickly, sodden. It's cinematic
  liebfraumilch.' – *Tom Shone, Sunday Times*
  † The film is a remake of Italian director
  Alessandro Blasetti's *Four Steps in the Clouds*, made
  in 1942

'There weren't supposed to be any more surprises in
their lives. And then they met each other!'

A Walk in the Spring Rain
US   1969   98m   Technicolor   Panavision
Columbia/Pingee (Stirling Silliphant)

A college lecturer's wife, on holiday in the
mountains, falls in love with a local man.
*Romance for the middle-aged, nicely done if lacking in
surprise.*
w Stirling Silliphant *novel* Rachel Maddox
d Guy Green ph Charles B. Lang m Elmer
Bernstein
☆ Ingrid Bergman, Anthony Quinn, Fritz Weaver,
Katherine Crawford
  'Not one line or scene is believably written or
  acted and the direction is so lazy it appears to
  have been mailed in during the postal strike.' –
  Richard Roud

A Walk in the Sun ***
US   1946   117m   bw
Lewis Milestone Productions

The exploits of a single army patrol during the
Salerno landings of 1943, on one vital morning.
*Vivid war film in a minor key, superbly disciplined and
keenly acted.*
w Robert Rossen *novel* Harry Brown d Lewis
Milestone ph Russell Harlan m Fredric Efrem Rich
☆ Dana Andrews, Richard Conte, Sterling
Holloway, John Ireland, George Tyne, Herbert

Rudley, Richard Benedict, Norman Lloyd, Lloyd
Bridges, Huntz Hall
  'Concerned with the individual rather than the
  battlefield, the film is finely perceptive, exciting,
  and very moving.' – *Penelope Houston*
  'A swiftly overpowering piece of work.' – *Bosley
  Crowther*
  'A notable war film, if not the most notable war
  film to come from America.' – *Richard
  Winnington*
  'After nearly two hours one is sorry when it
  ends.' – *Richard Mallett, Punch*

Walk like a Dragon
US   1960   95m   bw
Paramount/James Clavell

In 1870 San Francisco, a cowboy sets free a
Chinese slave girl but incurs racial intolerance
when he takes her home.
*Curious 'liberated' Western which gets itself in a
muddle and doesn't come off at all.*
w James Clavell, Dan Mainwaring d James
Clavell ph Loyal Griggs m Paul Dunlap
☆ Jack Lord, James Shigeta, Nobu McCarthy, Mel
Tormé, Josephine Hutchinson, Rodolfo Acosta

'It was the summer of Woodstock... when she
became the woman she always wanted to be.'

A Walk on the Moon *
US   1998   107m   Technicolor
Miracle/Punch/Village Roadshow/Groucho (Dustin
Hoffman, Tony Goldwyn, Jay Cohen, Neil
Koenigsberg, Lee Gottsegan, Murray Schisgal)
Taking advantage of her husband's absence and an
atmosphere of sexual liberation, a woman begins
an affair, to the distress of her teenage daughter,
and goes to Woodstock with her lover.
*Small scale domestic drama set against a background of
the moon landings and the shifting sensibilities of the
late 60s, centring on a wife who married too young and
feels that she has somehow missed out on life.*
w Pamela Gray d Tony Goldwyn ph Anthony
Richmond m Mason Daring pd Dan Leigh
ed Dana Congdon
☆ Diane Lane, Liev Schreiber, Anna Paquin,
Viggo Mortensen, Tovah Feldshuh, Bobby Boriello,
Stewart Bick, Jess Platt
  'A quietly satisfying piece of work.' – *Adam
  Mars-Jones, Times*

'A side of life you never expected to see on the
screen!'

Walk on the Wild Side
US   1962   114m   bw
Columbia/Famous Artists (Charles K. Feldman)

In the thirties, a penniless farmer finds the girl he
once loved working in a New Orleans brothel.
*A brilliant title sequence heralds the dreariest and most
verbose of self-conscious melodramas, quite missing the
sensational effect promised by the advertising.*
w John Fante, Edmund Morris *novel* Nelson
Algren d Edward Dmytryk ph Joe MacDonald
m Elmer Bernstein *credits* Saul Bass
☆ Jane Fonda, Capucine, Barbara Stanwyck,
Laurence Harvey, Anne Baxter, Richard Rust
  'Since the film prides itself in calling a spade a
  spade, it is surprising to find all concerned
  reacting to their material as though they were up
  to their waists in a quagmire.' – *MFB*
  ♫ title song (mElmer Bernstein, lyMack David)

Walk Softly Stranger
US   1950   81m   bw
RKO (Robert Sparks)

A crook on the run falls for a crippled girl, who
promises to wait for him.
Dismal love-conquers-all melodrama.
w Frank Fenton d Robert Stevenson ph Harry J.
Wild m Frederick Hollander
☆ Alida Valli, Joseph Cotten, Spring Byington,
Paul Stewart, Jack Paar, Jeff Donnell, John
McIntire

Walk the Proud Land
US   1956   88m   Technicolor   Cinemascope
U-I (Aaron Rosenberg)
An Indian agent persuades the army to use less
violent methods.
*Fair standard Western with a thoughtful and
sympathetic attitude.*
w Gil Doud, Jack Sher d Jesse Hibbs ph Harold
Lipstein m Hans Salter

☆ Audie Murphy, Anne Bancroft, Pat Crowley, Robert Warwick, Charles Drake, Tommy Rall, Jay Silverheels

'In a strange and horrifying playground the innocents act out their game of life and death...'

Walkabout ****

Australia 1970 100m DeLuxe

Max L. Raab/Si Litvinoff

▣ ▤ ▥ ∩

A man kills himself in the desert and his small children trek among the aborigines to safety.

Eerily effective contrast of city with native life, a director's and photographer's experimental success.

w Edward Bond *novel* James Vance Marshall
m John Barry *d/ph* Nicolas Roeg

☆ Jenny Agutter, Lucien John, David Gulpilil

'The film is rich enough, especially at a second look, to make you forget the flaws. You are left with the impression of a fresh, powerful and humane imagination.' – *Dilys Powell*

Walker

US 1987 94m colour

Recorded Releasing/Walker Film/Incine (Lorenzo O'Brien, Angel Flores Marini)

▤ ▥

In the 1850s, an American adventurer invades Nicaragua and sets himself up as the country's dictator.

Based on fact, it fails to develop its fascinating theme in a satisfactory way, relying on anachronistic details such as helicopters to point its message.

w Rudy Wurlitzer *d* Alex Cox *ph* David Bridges
m Joe Strummer *pd* Bruno Rubeo, J. Rae Fox
ed Carlos Puente, Alex Cox

☆ Ed Harris, Richard Masur, Rene Auberjonois, Keith Szarabajka, Sy Richardson, Xander Berkeley, John Diehl, Peter Boyle

'Eating & sleeping, fighting & joking, dating & cheating...'

Walking & Talking *

GB/US 1996 86m DuArt

Electric/Zenith (Ted Hope, James Schamus)

▣ ▤ ▥ ∩

Two young professional women, friends from childhood, find that their love affairs are changing their relationship with one another.

Light-hearted gloss on emotional traumas, one that is likely to find its most responsive audience among young, professional women.

wd Nicole Holofcener *ph* Michael Spiller
m Billy Bragg *pd* Anne Stuhler *ed* Alisa Lepselter

☆ Catherine Keener, Anne Heche, Todd Field, Liev Schreiber, Kevin Corrigan, Randall Batinkoff

'A glibly observant comedy about the anxieties of romance and the evolution of a female friendship.' – *Todd McCarthy, Variety*

The Walking Dead *

US 1936 66m bw

Warner (Louis F. Edelman)

A man is revived after electrocution and takes revenge on his enemies.

Dour but well-mounted horror thriller in a shadowy style very typical of its director.

w Ewart Adamson, Peter Milne, Robert Andrews, Lillie Hayward *d* Michael Curtiz *ph* Hal Mohr

☆ Boris Karloff, Edmund Gwenn, Marguerite Churchill, Ricardo Cortez, Barton MacLane, Warren Hull, Henry O'Neill

'Weak story and haphazardly interpolated assortment of scientific abadaba prevent Karloff from making much of a shocker out of this one.' – *Variety*

Walking Down Broadway: see *Hello Sister*

The Walking Hills *

US 1949 78m bw

Columbia (Harry Joe Brown)

Various interests combine to locate gold bullion hidden in Death Valley ... then thieves fall out.

Elementary but fairly satisfying Western.

w Alan LeMay *d* John Sturges

☆ Randolph Scott, Ella Raines, William Bishop, Edgar Buchanan, Arthur Kennedy, John Ireland, Jerome Courtland, Josh White

Walking My Baby Back Home *

US 1953 95m Technicolor

U-I (Ted Richmond)

Ex-army musicians hit on a combination of symphonic and dixieland jazz.

The lightest of light musicals, this highly polished offering remains mildly pleasing though thinly written throughout.

w Don McGuire, Oscar Brodney *d* Lloyd Bacon
ph Irving Glassberg *md* Joseph Gershenson

☆ Donald O'Connor, Janet Leigh, Buddy Hackett, Lori Nelson, Scatman Crothers, Kathleen Lockhart, George Cleveland, John Hubbard

The Walking Stick *

GB 1970 101m Metrocolor Panavision

MGM/Winkast (Alan Ladd Jnr)

A repressed girl polio victim falls reluctantly in love with a painter who involves her in his criminal schemes.

Slow moving character romance which has its heart in the right place but too often promises suspense which never comes, and is made in a chintzy cigarette commercial style.

w George Bluestone *novel* Winston Graham
d Eric Till *ph* Arthur Ibbetson *m* Stanley Myers

☆ David Hemmings, Samantha Eggar, Phyllis Calvert, Ferdy Mayne, Emlyn Williams, Francesca Annis, Dudley Sutton

Walking Tall *

US 1973 125m DeLuxe

Bing Crosby Productions (Mort Briskin)

▤ ▥ ⊙

A Tennessee farmer-sheriff meets violence with violence and becomes a local hero.

True story of an American vigilante, made with modest competence; its great commercial success may have been due to the support of the righteous, or of those who revel in violence.

w Mort Briskin *d* Phil Karlson *ph* Jack Marta
m Walter Scharf

☆ Joe Don Baker, Elizabeth Hartman, Gene Evans, Noah Beery Jnr

'A terrifying image of Nixon's silent majority at work.' – *Gareth Jones*

'It generates a primitive, atavistic sort of power: it awakens more apprehension and dredges up more complicated and contradictory emotions than one anticipates.' – *Gary Arnold*

† Sequel 1976: *Part Two Walking Tall*. (GB title: *Legend of the Lawman*.) 1977: *Walking Tall: Final Chapter*.

The Wall *

France 1983 117m Fujicolour

Contemporary/Guney Productions/MK2 Productions/TFI Films (Marin Karmitz)

original title: *Le Mur*

aka: *Guney's The Wall*

Boys in a Turkish prison revolt against their persecutors.

Powerfully filmed indictment of brutality, based on a true incident and made a year before the director's death.

wd Yilmaz Guney *ph* Izzet Akay *m* Ozan Garip Sahin, Setrak Bakirel, Ali Dede Altuntas, Robert Kempler *ed* Sabine Mamou

☆ Tuncel Kurtiz, Ayse Emel Mesci, Saban, Sisko, Ziya, Garip, Zapata, Mankafa, Malik Berrichi, Nicolas Hossein, Habes Bounabi

The Wall of Death

GB 1950 95m bw

Butcher/Nettlefold (Ernest G. Roy)

aka: *There is Another Sun*

A fairground boxer is led astray by an embittered Wall of Death rider.

Efficient drama, bolstered by a good cast of character actors.

w Guy Morgan *d* Lewis Gilbert *ph* Wilkie Cooper *m* Wilfred Burns *ad* George Provis
ed Charles Hasse

☆ Susan Shaw, Maxwell Reed, Laurence Harvey, Hermione Baddeley, Leslie Dwyer, Meredith Edwards, Earl Cameron, Eric Pohlmann, Robert Adair, Dennis Vance, Harry Fowler

Wall of Noise

US 1963 112m bw

Warner (Joseph Landon)

A racehorse trainer falls for the boss's wife.

Complex but predictable melodrama of the old school, adequately presented and performed.

w Joseph Landon *novel* Daniel Michael Stein
d Richard Wilson *ph* Lucien Ballard *m* William Lava

☆ Suzanne Pleshette, Ty Hardin, Dorothy Provine, Ralph Meeker, Simon Oakland, Murray Matheson, Robert F. Simon

A Wall of Silence: see *Black Flowers*

Wall Street **

US 1987 124m DeLuxe

Edward R. Pressman/American Entertainment

▣ ▤ ▥ ⊙ ∩

An ambitious young financial broker is forced to choose between the values of his Wall Street hero and his own father, an aircraft mechanic.

Almost documentary in its detailed account of financial skulduggery but slipping ultimately into sentimentality, the film is marked by a brilliant performance from Michael Douglas as the scheming megalomaniac Gordon Gekko.

w Stanley Weiser, Oliver Stone *d* Oliver Stone
ph Robert Richardson *m* Stewart Copeland
pd Stephen Hendrickson *ed* Claire Simpson

☆ Charlie Sheen, *Michael Douglas*, Martin Sheen, Daryl Hannah, Terence Stamp, Sean Young, Sylvia Miles, James Spader, Hal Holbrook, Saul Rubinek

♟ Michael Douglas

Wallflower

US 1948 77m bw

Warner

Two sisters chase the same man; the less aggressive gets him.

So-so comedy on familiar lines.

w Phoebe and Henry Ephron *play* Reginald Denham, Mary Orr *d* Frederick de Cordova
ph Karl Freund *m* Frederick Hollander

☆ Joyce Reynolds, Janis Paige, Robert Hutton, Edward Arnold, Jerome Cowan, Barbara Brown

The Walls Came Tumbling Down *

US 1946 81m bw

Columbia (Albert J. Cohen)

A Broadway columnist tracks down the murderer of a priest.

Very acceptable whodunnit with familiar cast.

w Wilfrid H. Pettitt *novel* Jo Eisinger *d* Lothar Mendes

☆ Lee Bowman, Marguerite Chapman, George Macready, Edgar Buchanan, Lee Patrick, Jonathan Hale, J. Edward Bromberg, Elizabeth Risdon, Miles Mander, Moroni Olsen, Robert Ryan

Walls of Glass *

US 1985 86m colour

Tenth Muse (Scott Goldstein, Mark Slater)

A Shakespeare-loving taxi-driver tries to cope with his life's frustrations and return to his first love, the stage.

An engaging character study with a strong central performance.

w Edmond Collins, Scott Goldstein *d* Scott Goldstein *ph* Ivan Strasburg *m* Scott Goldstein
pd Ruth Ammon *ed* Scott Vickrey

☆ Philip Bosco, Geraldine Page, Olympia Dukakis, Brian Bloom, Steven Weber, Louis Zorich, Linda Thorsen

The Walls of Jericho

US 1948 106m bw

TCF (Lamar Trotti)

An influential small-town newspaperman is undermined by his vindictive wife.

Filmed novel of standard competence but minimum interest, ending in a courtroom scene.

w Lamar Trotti *novel* Paul Wellman *d* John M. Stahl *ph* Arthur Miller *m* Cyril Mockridge

☆ Cornel Wilde, Linda Darnell, Anne Baxter, Kirk Douglas, Ann Dvorak, Marjorie Rambeau, Henry Hull, Colleen Townsend

Walpurgis Night

Sweden 1935 80m bw

Svensk Filmindustri

original title: *Valborgsmässoafton*

A secretary falls in love with her unhappily married boss, whose situation is compromised when his wife has an abortion without his knowledge.

Effective, though sometimes heavy-handed, domestic melodrama of love, birth and death, though its happy ending seems contrived.

w Oscar Rydqvist *d* Gustav Edgren *ph* Martin Bodin *m* Eric Bengtson

☆ Ingrid Bergman, Lars Hanson, Karin Kavli, Victor Sjöström, Erik Berglund

Waltz across Texas

US 1982 99m colour

Aster (Martin Jurow)

▥

Love blossoms when an uptight female geologist agrees to help a laid-back Texan search for oil.

Folksy, sentimental, romantic drama, pleasant without being in any way memorable.

w Bill Svanoe *d* Ernest Day *ph* Robert Elswit
m Steve Dorff *ed* Jay Lash Cassidy

☆ Anne Archer, Terry Jastrow, Noah Beery, Richard Farnsworth, Mary Kay Place, Josh Taylor, Ben Piazza

The Waltz King

US 1963 95m Technicolor

Walt Disney (Peter V. Herald)

▥

The life of young Johann Strauss in 1850s Vienna.

Medium-budget international family musical, tolerably well done.

w Maurice Tombragel *d* Steve Previn
ph Gunther Anders *md* Helmuth Froschauer

☆ Kerwin Mathews, Brian Aherne, Senta Berger, Peter Kraus, Fritz Eckhardt

The Waltz of the Toreadors *

GB 1962 105m Technicolor

Rank Wintle-Parkyn (Peter de Sarigny)

▥

A lecherous retired general finds his past creeping up on him and loses his young mistress to his son.

Lukewarm adaptation of a semi-classic comedy, disastrously translated to English setting and characters.

w Wolf Mankowitz *play* Jean Anouilh *d* John Guillermin *ph* John Wilcox *m* Richard Addinsell
pd Wilfrid Shingleton

☆ Peter Sellers, Margaret Leighton, Dany Robin, John Fraser, Cyril Cusack, Prunella Scales

Waltz Time

GB 1933 82m bw

Gaumont

Things are not what they seem to be at a Viennese masked ball.

Pleasant but slight musical comedy vaguely derived from Die Fledermaus.

w A. P. Herbert *d* William Thiele

☆ Evelyn Laye, Fritz Schultz, Gina Malo, Jay Laurier, Frank Titterton

Waltz Time

GB 1945 100m bw

British National

At a Viennese ball, an Empress poses as her masked friend to win a philandering count.

Rather plodding operetta which also has an unattributed allegiance to Die Fledermaus.

w Montgomery Tully, Jack Whittingham, Henry C. James, Karl Rossier *d* Paul Stein *ph* Ernest Palmer *m* Hans May

☆ Carol Raye, Peter Graves, Patricia Medina, Thorley Walters, Richard Tauber, Harry Welchman, George Robey, Anne Ziegler, Webster Booth

Waltzes from Vienna

GB 1933 80m bw

Gaumont (Tom Arnold)

US title: *Strauss's Great Waltz*

A romance of the Strausses.

There is very little music and very little Hitchcock in this extremely mild romantic comedy.

w Alma Reville, Guy Bolton *play* Guy Bolton
d Alfred Hitchcock *ph* Glen MacWilliams

☆ Jessie Matthews, Esmond Knight, Frank Vosper, Fay Compton, Edmund Gwenn, Robert Hale, Hindle Edgar

'I hate this sort of thing. Melodrama is the only thing I can do.' – *Alfred Hitchcock*

Wanda *

US 1971 105m colour

Foundations for Filmakers/F.F. (Harry Shuster)

Divorced by her husband for neglecting him and the children, a woman drifts into a disastrous relationship with a bad-tempered, incompetent robber.

An impressive, if depressing, account of a loveless life, notable for its unflinching, yet sympathetic, approach.

---

wd Barbara Loden *ph* Nicholas T. Proferes
ed Nicholas T. Proferes
☆ Barbara Loden, Michael Higgins, Dorothy Shupenes, Peter Shupenes, Jerome Thier
'The director never falls back on coy tricks or clichés and the performances are admirable, but the movie is such an extremely drab and limited piece of realism that it makes Zola seem like musical comedy.' – *Pauline Kael*

Wanda Nevada
US   1979   105m   Technicolor   Panavision
UA/Pando (Neil Dobrofsky, Dennis Hackin)
■
A gambler wins a 13-year-old girl in a poker game and they go looking for gold in the Grand Canyon.
A casual road movie, easy-going but never getting anywhere very interesting.
w Dennis Hackin *d* Peter Fonda *ph* Michael Butler *m* Ken Lauber *ad* Lynda Paradise *ed* Scott Conrad
☆ Peter Fonda, Brooke Shields, Fiona Lewis, Luke Askew, Ted Markland, Severn Darden, Paul Fix, Henry Fonda

Wandafuru Raifu: see After Life

The Wanderers
US/Netherlands   1979   117m   Technicolor
GTO/PSO/Poly International (Martin Ransohoff)
■   ■
In 1963, teenage street gangs fight in the Bronx.
A bad boys' American Graffiti, all violence and unpleasantness.
w Rose and Philip Kaufman *novel* Richard Price *d* Philip Kaufman *ph* Michael Chapman *ad* Jay Moore *ed* Ronald Roose, Stuart H. Pappe
☆ Ken Wahl, John Friedrich, Karen Allen, Toni Kalem, Linda Manz

The Wandering Jew *
GB   1933   111m   bw
Gaumont/Twickenham (Julius Hagen)
A Jew is condemned to live forever, but dies in the Spanish Inquisition.
Ambitious fantasy which comes off pretty well for those in the mood, but was a curious choice for a British studio at the time.
w H. Fowler Mear *play* E. Temple Thurston *d* Maurice Elvey *ph* Sydney Blythe
☆ Conrad Veidt, Marie Ney, Basil Gill, Anne Grey, Dennis Hoey, John Stuart, Peggy Ashcroft, Francis L. Sullivan, Felix Aylmer, Abraham Sofaer
'A beautiful production, a historic triumph – and most likely a commercial error.' – *Variety*

The Wannsee Conference *
Germany/Austria   1987   87m   colour
Infafilm/Austrian TV/ORF/Bavarian Broadcasting (Manfred Korytowski)
■   ■
original title: *Die Wannseekonferenz*
A group of Nazi officials gather for a conference to discuss Hitler's 'final solution' to exterminate the Jewish people.
Careful re-creation of an historic event, which lasted for 85 minutes, demonstrating the banality of evil. It was originally made for television, to which medium it is better suited.
w Paul Mommertz *d* Heinz Schirk *ph* Horst Schier *ad* Robert Hofer-Ach, Barbara Siebner *ed* Ursula Mollinger
☆ Robert Artzorn, Friedrich Beckhaus, Gerd Bochmann, Jochen Busse, Hans W. Bussinger, Harald Dietl, Peter Fitz, Reinhard Glemnitz, Dieter Groest, Martin Luttge

Wanted for Murder *
GB   1946   103m   bw
Marcel Hellman
A man, obsessed with the fact that his father was the public hangman, becomes a murderer himself.
Curiously stagey melodrama with intermittent use of London backgrounds; an interesting curiosity.
w Emeric Pressburger, Rodney Ackland, Maurice Cowan *d* Lawrence Huntington *ph* Max Greene *m* Mischa Spoliansky
☆ Eric Portman, Dulcie Gray, Derek Farr, Roland Culver, Stanley Holloway, Barbara Everest, Bonar Colleano, Kathleen Harrison
'A pleasant and unpretentious thriller of the second or third grade.' – *James Agee*

Wanted: Jane Turner
US   1936   64m   bw
Cliff Reid/RKO
The postal service tracks down mail van crooks.
Familiar but lively action support.
w John Twist *d* Edward Kelly
☆ Lee Tracy, Gloria Stuart, Judith Blake, John McGuire, Frank M. Thomas

The Wanton: see Manèges

The Wanton Countess: see Senso

'What's worth fighting for?'
The War
US   1994   125m   DeLuxe
UIP/Universal/Island World (Jon Avnet, Jordan Kerner)
■   ■   ■   ◎
In 1970, an unemployed Vietnam veteran tries to teach his son and daughter a non-violent approach to life as they battle with neighbouring children for control of a tree-house.
An earnest and didactic drama that settles for an easy uplift and provides the message that love will conquer all.
w Kathy McWorter *d* Jon Avnet *ph* Geoffrey Simpson *m* Thomas Newman *pd* Kristi Zea *ed* Debra Neil
☆ Kevin Costner, Elijah Wood, Mare Winningham, Lexi Randall, Christine Baranski, Raynor Scheine, Bruce A. Young, LaToya Chisholm, Charlette Julius, Gary Basaraba, Nick Searcy
'For those in quest of severe moral uplift only.' – *Sheila Johnston, Independent*
'Has neither the edge to attract adult tastes nor the action to please youngsters.' – *Denis Seguin, Screen International*

The War against Mrs Hadley *
US   1942   86m   bw
MGM (Irving Asher)
A Washington matron tries to ignore the war and preserve her social life.
Efficient little propaganda piece with a middle-aged heroine.
w George Oppenheimer *d* Harold S. Bucquet *ph* Karl Freund *m* David Snell
☆ Fay Bainter, Edward Arnold, Richard Ney, Jean Rogers, Sara Allgood, Spring Byington, Van Johnson, Isobel Elsom, Halliwell Hobbes, Miles Mander, Frances Rafferty, Connie Gilchrist
'If this film is, as some have labelled it, the American Mrs Miniver, then some of us must have grave illusions about our own (or the English) way of life.' – *Bosley Crowther*
ஃ George Oppenheimer

War and Peace **
US/Italy   1956   208m   Technicolor
Vistavision
Carlo Ponti/Dino de Laurentiis
■   ■   ■   ◎
A Russian family's adventures at the time of Napoleon's invasion.
Despite miscasting and heavy dubbing, the pictorial parts of this précis of a gargantuan novel are powerful and exciting enough; the human side drags a little.
w Bridget Boland, Robert Westerby, King Vidor, Mario Camerini, Ennio de Concini, Ivo Perelli *novel* Leo Tolstoy *d* King Vidor, (battle scenes) Mario Soldati *ph* Jack Cardiff, (battle scenes) Aldo Tonti *m* Nino Rota *ad* Mario Chiari
☆ Audrey Hepburn, Henry Fonda, Mel Ferrer, Herbert Lom, John Mills, Oscar Homolka, Wilfrid Lawson, Vittorio Gassman, Anita Ekberg, Helmut Dantine, Milly Vitale, Barry Jones
'The film has no more warmth than pictures in an art gallery.' – *Philip T. Hartung*
'When I first agreed to do it the screenplay by Irwin Shaw was fine, but what happened? King Vidor used to go home nights with his wife and rewrite it. All the genius of Tolstoy went out the window.' – *Henry Fonda*
ஃ King Vidor; Jack Cardiff

War and Peace ***
USSR   1967   507m   Sovcolor   'Scope 70mm
Mosfilm
■
An immensely long Russian version with some of the most magnificently spectacular battle scenes ever filmed.

A treat for the eyes throughout, and perhaps less taxing than reading the novel, which it follows punctiliously.
w Sergei Bondarchuk, Vasili Solovyov *d* Sergei Bondarchuk *ph* Anatoli Petritsky *m* Vyacheslav Ovchinnikov
☆ Lyudmila Savelyeva, Sergei Bondarchuk, Vyacheslav Tikhonov
† The film was five years in production and cost between 50 and 70 million dollars.
❖ best foreign film

The War at Home
US   1996   119m   Foto-Kem
Buena Vista/Touchstone/Motion Picture Corp/Avatar (Emilio Estevez, Brad Krevoy, Steve Stabler, James Duff)
■
In Texas in the early 70s, a young soldier returns to his family from Vietnam, traumatized by his experience.
Domestic melodrama that begins over the top and just gets louder.
w James Duff *play* Homefront by James Duff *d* Emilio Estevez *ph* Peter Levy *m* Basil Poledouris *pd* Eve Cauley *ed* Craig Bassett
☆ Kathy Bates, Martin Sheen, Kimberly Williams, Emilio Estevez, Carla Gugino, Geoffrey Blake, Corin Nemec, Ann Hearn
'There's a fuzziness of dramatic tone and lack of accruing tension that makes this "War" more a series of skirmishes than a deeply felt analysis.' – *Variety*

The War between Men and Women
US   1972   105m   Technicolor   Panavision
National General/Jalem/Llenroc/4D (Danny Arnold)
A half-blind cartoonist marries a divorcee and is troubled by her ex-husband.
Semi-serious comedy vaguely based on Thurber, but not so that you'd notice, apart from the blind hero; generally neither funny nor affecting.
w Mel Shavelson, Danny Arnold, based on the writings of James Thurber *d* Melville Shavelson *ph* Charles F. Wheeler *m* Marvin Hamlisch *pd* Stan Jolley
☆ Jack Lemmon, Barbara Harris, Jason Robards Jnr, Herb Edelman, Lisa Gerritsen
'Muddle-minded, sloppy and the sappy antithesis of everything the tough-minded Thurber held dear.' – *Paul D. Zimmerman, Newsweek*

War Correspondent: see The Story of GI Joe

War Games *
🏃 US   1983   113m   Metrocolor
MGM-UA/Sherwood (Leonard Goldberg, Harold Schneider)
■   ■   ■   ◎
A teenager unwittingly taps his home computer into the Pentagon and pretends to be Russia on the point of launching missiles.
Mildly intriguing science fantasy which becomes uncomfortable and finally boring because of the excess of jargon and flashing lights.
w Lawrence Lasker, Walter F. Parkes *d* John Badham *ph* William A. Fraker *m* Arthur B. Rubinstein *pd* Angelo P. Graham
☆ Matthew Broderick, Dabney Coleman, John Wood, Ally Sheedy, Barry Corbin, Kent Williams
'All the film's adventure and suspense is inevitably at odds with its ostensible sentiments … [but] the result has a kind of seamless efficiency.' – *Steve Jenkins, MFB*
ஃ screenplay; cinematography

War Gods of the Deep: see City under the Sea

War Hunt
US   1961   83m   bw
TD Enterprises (Terry Sanders)
Korea 1953: a kill-crazy private is befriended by a war orphan but finally has to be shot.
Vaguely commendable but not very expert indictment of the realities of war.
w Stanford Whitmore *d* Denis Sanders *ph* Ted McCord *m* Bud Shank
☆ John Saxon, Robert Redford, Sydney Pollack, Charles Aidman, Tommy Matsuda

The War Is Over: see La Guerre Est Finie

The War Lord **
US   1965   121m   Technicolor   Panavision
Universal/Court (Walter Seltzer)
■   ◎   ■   ∩
An officer of the Duke of Normandy has trouble with Druids and the law of *droit de seigneur*.
Complex medieval melodrama with an air of fantasy about it; generally likeably strange, but the production should have been more stylized and fanciful.
w John Collier, Millard Kaufman *play* The Lovers by Leslie Stevens *d* Franklin Schaffner *ph* Russell Metty *m* Jerome Moross *ad* Alexander Golitzen, Henry Bumstead
☆ Charlton Heston, Richard Boone, Rosemary Forsyth, Maurice Evans, Guy Stockwell, Niall MacGinnis, Henry Wilcoxon, James Farentino

The War Lover
GB   1962   105m   bw
Columbia/Arthur Hornblow Jnr
■   ■   ◎
In 1943, a Flying Fortress commander based in East Anglia has the wrong ideas about women and war.
Solemn character drama punctuated by aerial battles.
w Howard Koch *novel* John Hersey *d* Philip Leacock *ph* Bob Huke *m* Richard Addinsell
☆ Steve McQueen, Shirley Anne Field, Robert Wagner, Gary Cockrell, Michael Crawford

War Nurse
US   1930   79m   bw
MGM
Problems of a nurse behind the lines in World War I.
Ambitious but unsuccessful attempt to do another Big Parade; a lack of style and story kills it.
w Becky Gardner, Joe Farnham, from an anonymous autobiography *d* Edgar Selwyn
☆ Robert Montgomery, Anita Page, June Walker, Robert Ames, ZaSu Pitts, Marie Prevost, Helen Jerome Eddy, Hedda Hopper
'Won't get anywhere in the major houses; too filled with audible suffering to class as entertainment.' – *Variety*

'Most wars last years. This one had to be over by dinner.'
War of the Buttons *
🏃 GB/France   1994   90m   colour
Warner/Enigma/De La Guéville (David Puttnam)
■
In rural Ireland the down-at-heel boys from one village indulge in gang warfare with the posher children from the next village.
A pleasant, light-hearted comedy of a civil war with only a hint of violence.
w Colin Welland *novel* Louis Pergaud *d* John Roberts *ph* Bruno de Keyzer *m* Rachel Portman *pd* Jim Clay *ed* David Freeman
☆ Liam Cunningham, Gregg Fitzgerald, Colm Meaney, John Coffey, Paul Batt, Eveanna Ryan, Dervla Kirwan, Thomas Kavanagh
'Engaging, funny and good-looking dramatic comedy that should appeal to both children and adults.' – *James Cameron-Wilson, Film Review*
† It is a remake of the French film *La Guerre des Boutons*, directed by Yves Robert in 1962.

War of the Colossal Beast
US   1958   68m   bw/colour
AIP (Bert I. Gordon)
■   ■
A 60-foot-tall man, turned bestial by exposure to nuclear radiation and mutilated in a bazooka attack, escapes from his captors and runs amok in Los Angeles.
Dull science fiction movie that runs out of ideas within the first five minutes, after which it tediously repeats not only itself but the movie to which it is a sequel. Originally, the last few minutes were in colour, though surviving prints appear to be monochrome.
w George Worthing Yates *story* Bert I. Gordon *d* Bert I. Gordon *ph* Jack Marta *m* Albert Glasser *ad* Walter Keller *ed* Ronald Sinclair *sp* Bert I. Gordon
☆ Sally Fraser, Roger Pace, Dean Parkin, Russ Bender, John McNamara, Loretta Nicholson, George Navarro
† It was a sequel to *The Amazing Colossal Man* (qv).

'Once in a lifetime comes a motion picture that makes you feel like falling in love all over again. This is not that movie.'

The War of the Roses *
US 1989 116m DeLuxe
Fox/Gracie Films (James L. Brooks, Arnon Milchan)
▣ ▤ ◎~

A couple who decide to divorce fight to the death over who gets the house.
Rancorous comedy, sometimes amusing but too mean-spirited for many laughs.
w Michael Leeson *novel* Warren Adler d Danny DeVito ph Stephen H. Burum m David Newman pd Ida Random ed Lynzee Klingman
☆ Michael Douglas, Kathleen Turner, Danny DeVito, Marianne Sägebrecht, Sean Astin, Heather Fairfield, G. D. Spradlin, Trenton Teigen, Bethany McKinney

War of the Wildcats
US 1943 102m bw
Republic (Robert North)
▣ ▤

aka: *In Old Oklahoma*
A lady writer causes friction between an oil operator and a cowboy.
Action potboiler which once passed an hour and three-quarters quite painlessly.
w Ethel Hill, Eleanore Griffith, Thomson Burtis d Albert S. Rogell ph Jack Marta m Walter Scharf
☆ John Wayne, Martha Scott, Albert Dekker, George 'Gabby' Hayes, Marjorie Rambeau, Dale Evans, Grant Withers, Sidney Blackmer
♫ Walter Scharf

The War of the Worlds *
US 1953 85m Technicolor
Paramount/George Pal
▣ ▤ ◎~ ◎ ◠

Terrifying aliens invade Earth via the American midwest.
Spectacular battle scenes are the mainstay of this violent fantasy, which goes to pieces once the cardboard characters open their mouths.
w Barre Lyndon *novel* H. G. Wells d Byron Haskin ph George Barnes m Leith Stevens ad Al Pereira, Albert Nozaki ed Everett Douglas
☆ Gene Barry, Ann Robinson, Les Tremayne, Robert Cornthwaite, Sandro Giglio, Cedric Hardwicke
🏆 special effects
♫ editing

War Party
US 1989 97m CFI color
Hemdale (John Daly, Derek Gibson)
▣ ▤ ◎~

The centennial re-enactment of a massacre by the US Cavalry of the local Blackfoot Indians leads to a real battle after a white youth murders one of the Indians.
A mundane excuse for a not very interesting modern-day Western.
w Spencer Eastman d Franc Roddam ph Brian Tufano m Chaz Jankel pd Michael Bingham ed Sean Barton
☆ Billy Wirth, Kevin Dillon, Tim Sampson, Jimmie Ray Weeks, Kevyn Major Howard, M. Emmet Walsh, Jerry Hardin, Bill McKinney
'Its message is that it takes danger and excitement to release the pent-up, dulled emotions of both the Indians on the reservation and the white men in town. The result is a straightforward celebration of action-movie clichés.' – *Julian Stringer, MFB*

War Requiem *
GB 1988 93m bw/colour
Anglo International/BBC (Don Boyd)

Images of war, and of the poet Wilfred Owen in the trenches, accompany the music of Benjamin Britten's *War Requiem.*
A series of tableaux, some savagely comic but most tragic, interplay the experience of the music.
d Derek Jarman ph Richard Greatrex m Benjamin Britten pd Lucy Morahan ed Rick Elgood
☆ Nathaniel Parker, Tilda Swinton, Laurence Olivier, Patricia Hayes, Rohan McCillough, Nigel Terry, Owen Teale, Sean Bean, Alex Jennings

The War Wagon **
US 1967 99m Technicolor Panavision
Universal/Batjac (Marvin Schwartz)
▣ ▤ ◎~ ◠

Two cowboys and an Indian plan to ambush the gold wagon of a crooked mining contractor.
Exhilarating but simply-plotted action Western with strong comedy elements and a cast of old reliables.
w Clair Huffaker *novel* Badman by Clair Huffaker d Burt Kennedy ph William H. Clothier m Dimitri Tiomkin
☆ John Wayne, Kirk Douglas, Howard Keel, Robert Walker, Keenan Wynn, Bruce Cabot, Gene Evans, Bruce Dern
'It all works splendidly.' – *MFB*

The War Zone *
GB/Italy 1998 99m colour Panavision
Film Four/Portobello/Fandango/Mikado (Sarah Radclyffe, Dixie Linder)
▣

A teenage boy discovers that his father is having an incestuous relationship with his sister.
Downbeat domestic drama, filmed in bleak colours, that works best in its portrait of traumatised adolescence; its adults are less convincing.
w Alexander Stuart *novel* Alexander Stuart d Tim Roth ph Seamus McGarvey m Simon Boswell pd Michael Carlin ed Trevor Waite
☆ Ray Winstone, Lara Belmont, Freddie Cunliffe, Tilda Swinton, Annabel Apsion, Kate Ashfield, Colin J. Farrell
'It is dismaying that this film misfires so catastrophically, ending up as what can only be described as a soft-core child abuse drama, reeking of good intentions and middlebrow art-house good taste.' – *Peter Bradshaw, Guardian*

Wara Mandel: see *Dance of the Wind*

The Ware Case *
GB 1938 79m bw
Ealing/Capad (S. C. Balcon)

A nobleman is suspected of murdering his wife's rich brother.
Courtroom melodrama twice filmed as a silent; stagey but reasonably compelling in its way.
w Robert Stevenson, Roland Pertwee, E. V. H. Emmett *play* G. P. Bancroft d Robert Stevenson ph Ronald Neame m Ernest Irving
☆ Clive Brook, Jane Baxter, Barry K. Barnes, C. V. France, Francis L. Sullivan, Frank Cellier, Edward Rigby, Peter Bull, Athene Seyler, Ernest Thesiger
† Previous versions had been made in 1917 (with Matheson Lang) and 1930 (with Stewart Rome).

Warlock *
US 1959 123m DeLuxe Cinemascope
TCF (Edward Dmytryk)
▤

The cowardly citizens of a small Western town hire a gunman as their unofficial marshal.
Overlong, talkative and somewhat pretentious star Western with good sequences.
w Robert Alan Aurthur *novel* Oakley Hall d Edward Dmytryk ph Joe MacDonald m Leigh Harline
☆ Henry Fonda, Richard Widmark, Anthony Quinn, Dorothy Malone, Dolores Michaels, Wallace Ford, Tom Drake, Richard Arlen, Regis Toomey, Don Beddoe, DeForest Kelley

Warlock
US 1988 102m DeLuxe
Medusa/New World (Steve Miner)
▣ ▤ ◎~ ◠

A witchfinder and the warlock he is hunting are translated from the 17th century to modern-day Los Angeles.
Enjoyable chase film, energetically performed.
w David T. Twohy d Steve Miner ph David Eggby m Jerry Goldsmith pd Roy Forge Smith ed David Finfer
☆ Richard E. Grant, Julian Sands, Lori Singer, Kevin O'Brien, Mary Woronov, Richard Kuss, Juli Burkhart, Harry Johnson, David Carpenter

Warlock – The Armageddon
US 1993 98m Image Transform colour
Trimark/Tapestry (Peter Abrams, Robert L. Levy)
▣ ▤ ◠

With only two teenage druids to oppose him, the son of Satan has six days to search for five missing runestones that will bring an end to the world.
Moderately effective sequel, with moments of sardonic wit, though dependent on special effects for its shock value; the real horror lies in the opening moments of Shakespeare.
w Kevin Rock, Sam Bernard d Anthony Hickox ph Gerry Lively m Mark McKenzie pd Steve Hardie ed Christopher Cibelli, James D. R. Hickox sp visual effects: BB&J Visual Effects; make-up: Bob Keen
☆ Julian Sands, Chris Young, Paula Marshall, Steve Kahan, Joanna Pacula, Charles Hallahan, R. G. Armstrong, Zach Galligan
'Intriguing, despite the plot's many weaknesses.' – *Sight and Sound*
† The film was released direct to video in Britain.

Warlords of Atlantis
↟↟ GB 1978 96m Technicolor
EMI/John Dark, Kevin Connor
▣

Victorian sea scientists discover a lost land under the Mediterranean.
Predictable compote of monsters and unwearable costumes, without a trace of wit in the script. For infants only.
w Brian Hayles d Kevin Connor ph Alan Hume m Mike Vickers pd Elliot Scott
☆ Doug McClure, Peter Gilmore, Shane Rimmer, Lea Brodie, Michael Gothard

A Warm December
GB/US 1972 101m Technicolor
First Artists/Verdon (Melville Tucker)

A widowed American doctor in London falls for a mysterious African girl who turns out to be the dying niece of a diplomat.
Weird mishmash of Love Story, Brief Encounter and Dark Victory, getting the worst of all worlds.
w Lawrence Roman d Sidney Poitier ph Paul Beeson m Coleridge-Taylor Parkinson
☆ Sidney Poitier, Esther Anderson, George Baker, Johnny Sekka, Earl Cameron

Warm Nights on a Slow Moving Train *
Australia 1988 91m colour
Western Pacific/Ross Dimsey
▣ ▤

An art teacher at a Catholic school, who moonlights as a prostitute on an overnight express at weekends, becomes involved with a shady customer.
An efficient psychological thriller, an account of love and betrayal that is less interested in suspense than in the study of character.
w Bob Ellis, Denny Lawrence d Bob Ellis ph Yuri Sokol m Peter Sullivan pd Tracy Watt ed Tim Lewis
☆ Wendy Hughes, Colin Friels, Norman Kaye, John Clayton, Lewis Fitz-Gerald, Rod Zuanic, Peter Sullivan

Warn London
GB 1934 74m bw
British Lion
A London policeman who is the double of a well-known burglar replaces him and infiltrates an international gang.
Exuberant minor thriller which made a good novelty booking at the time.
w Charles Bennett, Billie Bristow *novel* Denison Clift d T. Hayes Hunter ph Alex Bryce ad Norman Arnold
☆ Edmund Gwenn, John Loder, Leonora Corbett, D. A. Clarke-Smith

Warn That Man
GB 1943 82m bw
ABPC
German spies pose as an English nobleman and his staff but are routed by an unexpected guest.
On the stage this must have been an effective comedy-thriller, but the film is stymied by stiff handling.
w Vernon Sylvaine, Lawrence Huntington play Vernon Sylvaine d Lawrence Huntington
☆ Gordon Harker, Raymond Lovell, Jean Kent, Finlay Currie, Philip Friend, Frederick Cooper
'Slick drama, mounting success, and spectacular military enterprise.' – *The Cinema*

'What's a little bullet between friends?'
Warning Shot *
US 1966 100m Technicolor
Paramount/Bob Banner (Buzz Kulik)
While looking for a psychopathic killer, a cop shoots dead a man who draws a gun on him. But the dead man's gun cannot be found, and the officer is suspended . . .
Watchable mystery decked out with guest stars; possibly intended as a TV movie.
w Mann Rubin *novel* 711–Officer Needs Help by Whit Masterson d Buzz Kulik ph Joseph Biroc m Jerry Goldsmith
☆ David Janssen, Lillian Gish, Ed Begley, Keenan Wynn, Sam Wanamaker, Eleanor Parker, Stefanie Powers, Walter Pidgeon, George Sanders, George Grizzard, Steve Allen, Carroll O'Connor, Joan Collins

Warning Sign
US 1985 100m DeLuxe
TCF/Barwood-Robbins (Jim Bloom)
▤ ◠

A solitary cop combats scientists who may unwittingly unleash a deadly plague.
Unimpressive as propaganda and tedious as suspense.
w Hal Barwood, Matthew Robbins d Hal Barwood ph Dean Cundey m Craig Safan pd Henry Bumstead ed Robert Lawrence
☆ Sam Waterston, Kathleen Quinlan, Yaphet Kotto, Richard Dysart, Jeffrey de Munn

Warning, This Man Is Wild: see *Violent Cop*

Warning to Wantons
GB 1948 104m bw
Aquila/GFD
A nobleman takes in a flirtatious girl and finds she causes trouble for him and his family.
Interminable comedy-drama made even duller by the Independent Frame production method, which cut costs but restricted movement.
w Donald B. Wilson, James Laver *novel* Mary Mitchell d Donald B. Wilson
☆ Harold Warrender, Anne Vernon, David Tomlinson, Sonia Holm, Marie Burke, Judy Kelly

Warpath
US 1951 93m Technicolor
Paramount (Nat Holt)
An ex-army captain tracks down the outlaws who murdered his girl.
Goodish standard Western.
w Frank Gruber d Byron Haskin ph Ray Rennahan m Paul Sawtell
☆ Edmond O'Brien, Dean Jagger, Forrest Tucker, Harry Carey Jnr, Wallace Ford, Polly Bergen

Warrior Queen
US 1986 79m colour
Lightning (Harry Alan Towers)
▣ ▤ ◎~
Berenice, mistress of the Roman Caesar Titus, visits Pompeii and becomes involved with a charioteer and slaves who have been sold to a local brothel.
A movie with no discernible narrative; its director is content to set up scenes involving female nudity and uninspired decadence before reaching a climax with the eruption of Vesuvius which uses footage taken from a 60s Italian film, The Last Days of Pompeii, which is a measure of its penny-pinching unoriginality.
w Rick Marx *story* Peter Welbeck (Harry Alan Towers) d Chuck Vincent ph Lorenzo Battaglia m Ian Shaw, Kai Joffe pd Lucio Parese ed Anthony Delcampo, Chuck Vincent
☆ Sybil Danning, Donald Pleasence, Richard Hill, Josephine Jacqueline Jones, Tally Chanel, Stasia Micula (Samantha Fox), Suzanna Smith
† The US cinema release ran for 69 minutes, after some orgy scenes were cut.

The Warriors: see *The Dark Avenger* (1955)

'These are the armies of the night...'
The Warriors
US 1979 94m Movielab
Paramount (Lawrence Gordon)
▣ ▤ ◎~ ◠
A New York street gang runs into trouble when making a cross-city journey.
A sick exploitation movie about urban violence, poorly made into the bargain.

w David Shaber, Walter Hill *novel* Sol Yurick
d Walter Hill *ph* Andrew Laszlo *m* Barry de
Vorzon
☆ Michael Beck, James Remar, Thomas Waites,
Dorsey Wright, Brian Tyler, David Harris

The Warrior's Husband
US   1933   75m   bw
Fox (Jesse L. Lasky)
The Greeks break into Amazonia and conquer the
women, provoking a worm to turn.
A weird attempt by Hollywood to film a whimsical
comedy which belonged only on Broadway, where the
Greeks no doubt have a word for it.
w Sonya Levien *play* Julian Thompson *d* Walter
Lang
☆ Elissa Landi, Marjorie Rambeau, Ernest Truex,
David Manners, Helen Ware, Maude Eburne
'Novel farce will need astute exploitation aid.' –
Variety

Warriors of Virtue
🏃🏃 US   1997   101m   colour   Panavision
MGM (Dennis Law, Ronald Law, Christopher Law,
Jeremy Law, Patricia Ruben)
▦▦   ▦   ⊘   ◐
A lonely boy is transported into a fantastic world
and joins villagers in a battle against an evil
dictator.
Kung fu kangaroos, the warriors of the title, turn out to
be not much fun in this childish fantasy which mixes a
little preaching with a great deal of fighting.
w Michael Vickerman, Hugh Kelley *d* Ronny Yu
ph Peter Pau *m* Don Davis *pd* Eugenio Zanetti
ed David Wu
☆ Angus MacFadyen, Mario Yedidia, Marley
Shelton, Chao-Li Chi, Dennis Dun, Jack Tate,
Doug Jones
'A slack-jawed kids' adventure in which genre
conventions chafe against cutting-edge martial
arts.' – *Variety*

Warui Yatsu Yoku Nemuru: see *The Bad*
Sleep Well

Washington Masquerade
US   1932   92m   bw
MGM
GB title: *Mad Masquerade*
A high-minded senator is corrupted by a worthless
girl.
Solid star melodrama.
w John Meehan, Samuel Blythe *play* The Claw *by*
Henri Bernstein *d* Charles Brabin
☆ Lionel Barrymore, Karen Morley, Nils Asther,
C. Henry Gordon, William Collier Snr

Washington Merry-go-round *
US   1932   75m   bw
Columbia
A crusading young congressman attacks the crooks
in the government.
Naïve comedy-drama with a miscast star.
w Jo Swerling from an original by Maxwell
Anderson *d* James Cruze
☆ Lee Tracy, Constance Cummings, Alan
Dinehart, Walter Connolly, Clarence Muse,
Arthur Vinton
'Lots of flagwaving and political timeliness the
chief appeal.' – *Variety*

'He was beautiful, passionate and penniless. For a
lonely young heiress, the promise of his love was
worth any price.'
Washington Square
US   1997   115m   Technicolor
Buena Vista/Hollywood/Caravan/Alchemy (Roger
Birnbaum, Julie Bergman Sender)
▦▦   ▦   ⊘   ◐
An ungainly heiress, the daughter of a domineering
man, falls for a fortune hunter.
Clumsily routine adaptation, with generally
unconvincing performances, and given a feminist slant
that confuses the point of James's work.
w Carol Doyle *novel* Henry James *d* Agnieszka
Holland *m* Jerzy Zielinski *m* Jan A. P. Kaczmarek
pd Allan Starski *ed* David Siegel
☆ Jennifer Jason Leigh, Albert Finney, Ben
Chaplin, Maggie Smith, Judith Ivey, Betsy
Brantley, Jennifer Garner
'Emerges with only a portion of its force and
complexity intact.' – *Todd McCarthy, Variety*
† The novel was first filmed in 1949 as *The Heiress*
(qv).

Washington Story
US   1952   82m   bw
MGM (Dore Schary)
GB title: *Target for Scandal*
A lady reporter goes to Washington to expose
corruption, but falls for an honest congressman.
Standard flagwaver which takes itself a shade too
seriously.
wd Robert Pirosh *ph* John Alton *m* Conrad
Salinger
☆ Van Johnson, Patricia Neal, Louis Calhern,
Sidney Blackmer, Philip Ober, Patricia Collinge,
Elizabeth Patterson, Moroni Olsen

Watch It, Sailor
GB   1961   81m   bw
Columbia/Cormorant/Hammer (Maurice Cowan)
A sailor about to be married receives a paternity
accusation.
Glum farce with wasted talent.
w Falkland Cary, Philip King *play* Falkland Cary,
Philip King *d* Wolf Rilla *ph* Arthur Grant
m Douglas Gamley *ad* Bernard Robinson, Don
Mingaye *ed* James Needs, Alfred Cox
☆ Dennis Price, Marjorie Rhodes, Irene Handl,
Liz Fraser, Vera Day, John Meillon, Cyril Smith

Watch Me When I Kill: see *The Cat's Victims*

Watch on the Rhine **
US   1943   114m   bw
Warner (Hal B. Wallis)
▦▦   ▦
A German refugee and his family are pursued by
Nazi agents in Washington.
Talky play doesn't make much of a film, though the talk
is good talk and the performances outstanding; but it
made a prestige point or two for Hollywood.
w Dashiell Hammett *play* Lillian Hellman
d Herman Shumlin *ph* Merritt Gerstad, Hal
Mohr *m* Max Steiner
☆ *Paul Lukas*, Bette Davis, Lucile Watson, *George*
Coulouris, Donald Woods, Geraldine Fitzgerald,
Beulah Bondi, Henry Daniell
🎭 Paul Lukas
🏆 best picture; script; Lucile Watson

Watch the Birdie
US   1950   71m   bw
MGM (Harry Ruskin)
▦▦
A photographer meets a rich girl and saves her
from a crook.
Unhappy remake of Buster Keaton's The
Cameraman, enlivened by a chase finale, but not
helped by the star playing three members of the same
family.
w Ivan Tors, Devery Freeman, Harry Ruskin
d Jack Donohue *ph* Paul C. Vogel *m* George
Stoll
☆ Red Skelton, Arlene Dahl, Ann Miller, Leon
Ames, Pamela Britton, Richard Rober

Watch Your Stern
GB   1960   88m   bw
Allied Artists/GHW (Peter Rogers)
▦▦
A ship's steward pretends to be the inventor of a
homing torpedo.
Routine farce, well handled by its crew of expert comic
actors, but too much driven by its narrative to do more
than intermittently amuse.
w Alan Hackney, Vivian A. Cox *play* Something
about a Sailor by Earle Couttie *d* Gerald Thomas
ph Ted Scaife *m* Bruce Montgomery *ad* Carmen
Dillon *ed* John Shirley
☆ Kenneth Connor, Eric Barker, Leslie Phillips,
Joan Sims, Hattie Jacques, Spike Milligan, Eric
Sykes, Sidney James, Ed Devereaux, David Lodge,
Noel Purcell

The Watcher in the Woods
🏃🏃 US   1980   100m   Technicolor
Walt Disney (Tom Leetch)
▦▦   ▦
The teenage daughter of an American composer
has strange and apparently supernatural
experiences in the British countryside.
Unsatisfactory attempt by the Disney people to aim at
a wider audience than is expected of them. The mixture
of cuteness, menace and the supernatural simply
doesn't gel, and the film was much re-edited between its
two appearances.
w Brian Clemens, Harry Spaulding, Rosemary
Anne Sisson *novel* Florence Engel Randall

d John Hough (and Vincent McEveety) *ph* Alan
Hume *m* Stanley Myers
☆ Bette Davis, Carroll Baker, David McCallum,
Lynn-Holly Johnson, Kyle Richards, Ian Bannen,
Richard Pasco

Watchers
Canada   1988   91m   colour
Guild/Concorde/Centaur/Carolco (Damian Lee, David
Mitchell)
▦▦   ▦
Two experimental animals, an intelligent dog and
an ape-like killer, escape from a top secret
government research laboratory.
Dogged horror movie, with plentiful gore but little
suspense.
w Bill Freed, Damian Lee *novel* Dean R. Koontz
d Jon Hess *ph* Richard Leiterman *m* Joel
Goldsmith *pd* Richard Wilcox *ed* Bill Freda,
Carolle Alain, Rick Fields
☆ Michael Ironside, Christopher Carey, Graeme
Campbell, Dan O'Dowd, Lala, Corey Haim, Dale
Wilson, Blu Mankuma, Colleen Winton

The Watchmaker of St Paul ***
France   1973   105m   Eastmancolor
Lira (Raymond Danon)
▦▦
original title: *L'Horloger de St Paul*
A watchmaker's tranquil life is shattered when he
learns that his son is wanted for murder.
Solid character drama with careful writing and acting.
w Jean Aurenche, Pierre Bost, Bertrand Tavernier
novel L'Horloger d'Everton *by* Georges Simenon
d Bertrand Tavernier *ph* Pierre William Glenn
m Philippe Sarde
☆ Philippe Noiret, Jean Rochefort, Sylvain
Rougerie, Christine Pascal

Water *
GB   1985   95m   colour
HandMade (Ian La Frenais)
▦▦   ▦
Chaos comes to a Caribbean island when
industrialists check it for mineral springs.
Hysterical comedy which never develops a single line
for long, and quickly wears out its welcome.
w Dick Clement, Ian La Frenais, Bill Bersky
d Dick Clement *ph* Douglas Slocombe *m* Mike
Moran
☆ Michael Caine, Valerie Perrine, Brenda
Vaccaro, Leonard Rossiter, Billy Connolly, Fred
Gwynne, Maureen Lipman

The Water Babies
🏃🏃 GB/Poland   1978   92m   colour
Ariadne/Studio Miniatur Filmowych (Peter Shaw)
▦▦
An 1850 chimney sweep evades his pursuers by
jumping into a pool, where he becomes involved in
an underwater adventure.
The live action bookends are strangely subdued, the
animated middle totally characterless and seeming to
bear little relation to the rest. A considerable
disappointment.
w Michael Robson *novel* Charles Kingsley
d Lionel Jeffries *ph* Ted Scaife *m* Phil Coulter
☆ James Mason, Billie Whitelaw, Bernard
Cribbins, Joan Greenwood, David Tomlinson,
Tommy Pender

Water Birds: see *The Living Desert*

The Water Gypsies
GB   1932   80m   bw
ATP
Adventures of two girls who live on a Thames
barge.
Rather naïve and ordinary version of a successful book
which many years later emerged as a stage musical; the
film production has a stagey look throughout.
w Basil Dean, Miles Malleson, Alma Reville, John
Paddy Carstairs *novel* A. P. Herbert *d* Maurice
Elvey
☆ Ann Todd, Sari Maritza, Richard Bird, Frances
Doble, Ian Hunter, Anthony Ireland
'Should do business in the best type of places.' –
Variety

The Waterboy
US   1998   91m   Technicolor
Buena Vista/Touchstone (Robert Simonds, Jack
Giarraputo)
▦▦   ▦   ⊘   ◐
A simple-minded hick becomes a star football
player when he learns to channel all the
humiliation he has suffered into aggression.
An unattractive comedy about stupidity that was a
surprising box-office hit in the United States.
w Tim Herlihy, Adam Sandler *d* Frank Coraci
ph Steven Bernstein *m* Alan Pasqua *pd* Perry
Andelin Blake *ed* Tom Lewis
☆ Adam Sandler, Kathy Bates, Henry Winkler,
Fairuza Balk, Jerry Reed, Larry Gilliard Jnr, Blake
Clark, Rob Schneider, Robert Kokol, Clint
Howard, Al Whiting
'This escapist comedy is so cheerfully outlandish
that it's hard to resist, and so good-hearted that
it's genuinely endearing.' – *Janet Maslin, New*
York Times
'The formulaic mix of mirth and mayhem is
aimed way down the MTV food chain.' – *Glenn*
Lovell, Variety

The Waterdance **
US   1991   107m   colour
Samuel Goldwyn/No Frills (Gale Anne Hurd)
▦▦   ▦   ▦
Three paraplegics in a rehabilitation centre
attempt to come to terms with their condition and
each other.
Graceful, perceptive, quietly effective movie on the
pain of adjustment and the pleasures of friendship.
w Neal Jimenez *d* Neal Jimenez, Michael
Steinberg *ph* Mark Plummer *m* Michael
Convertino *pd* Robert Ziembicki *ed* Jeff Freeman
☆ Eric Stoltz, Wesley Snipes, William Forsythe,
Helen Hunt, Elizabeth Pena, William Allen
Young, Henry Harris, Tony Genaro, Eva Rodriguez,
Grace Zabriskie
'An honest, unsentimental, deeply moving,
often extremely funny account of an adjustment
to a new way of living, of confronting overnight
the deprivations that time will visit on us should
we live into old age, of facing up to the injustices
and misfortunes of life.' – *Philip French, Observer*
'A smashing success if great performances and a
deftly told, thoroughly absorbing tale mean
anything.' – *Variety*

'The desires and loneliness of seafaring men and
their women!'
Waterfront
GB   1950   80m   bw
GFD/Conqueror/Paul Soskin
▦▦
US title: *Waterfront Women*
A drunken ship's fireman comes back to Liverpool
after many years and causes trouble.
Unintentionally funny melodrama which gives the
actors a lot of trouble.
w John Brophy, Paul Soskin *novel* John Brophy
d Michael Anderson *ph* Harry Waxman
md Muir Mathieson
☆ Robert Newton, Richard Burton, Kathleen
Harrison, Susan Shaw, Avis Scott, Kenneth
Griffith

Waterfront Women: see *Waterfront*

Waterhole Three
US   1967   100m   Techniscope
Paramount
▦▦
Sheriff, crooks and a gambler seek buried loot.
Rather irritatingly immoral Western with a hero who
defines rape as assault with a friendly weapon; in
between it tries hard for the ballad style.
w Joseph Steck, Robert R. Young *d* William
Graham *ph* Robert Burks *m* Dave Grusin
☆ James Coburn, Carroll O'Connor, Margaret
Blye, Claude Akins, Joan Blondell, Timothy Carey

Waterland
GB   1992   95m   colour   Scope
Mayfair/Palace/Pandora/Channel 4 Films/British
Screen (Katy McGuinness, Patrick Cassavetti)
▦▦   ▦   ▦
In the 1970s an English history teacher working in
Pittsburgh tells his class of his own difficult past
growing up in East Anglia.
A domestic saga of marital difficulties, incest and
murder that soon slides into glum melodrama.

---

w Peter Prince *novel* Graham Swift *d* Stephen Gyllenhaal *ph* Robert Elswit *m* Carter Burwell *pd* Hugo Luczyc-Wyhowski *ed* Lesley Walker

☆ Jeremy Irons, Sinead Cusack, Ethan Hawke, Grant Warnock, Lena Headey, David Morrissey, John Heard

'A talented but terminally parched piece of literary cinema. Decorous, academic treatment of bizarre and traumatic material makes for a merely unpleasant film rather than an insightful or genuinely disturbing one.' – *Variety*

'The men, the battle, the glory the world will remember forever!'

Waterloo *
🏈 Italy/USSR 1970 132m Technicolor
Panavision
Columbia/DDL/Mosfilm (Dino de Laurentiis)
📼 ⊜ ∩
Historical events leading up to the 1815 battle.
The battle forms the last hour of this historical charade, and looks both exciting and splendid, though confusion is not avoided. The rest is a mixed blessing.
w H. A. L. Craig, Sergei Bondarchuk *d* Sergei Bondarchuk *ph* Armando Nannuzzi *m* Nino Rota *pd* Mario Garbuglia
☆ Rod Steiger, Christopher Plummer, Orson Welles, Jack Hawkins, Virginia McKenna, Dan O'Herlihy, Rupert Davies, Ian Ogilvy, Michael Wilding
🎬 Mario Garbuglia

Waterloo Bridge *
US 1931 72m bw
Universal (Carl Laemmle Jnr)
An army officer marries a ballerina; when he is reported missing his family ignore her and she sinks into prostitution.
One for the ladies, who lapped it up.
w Tom Reed, Benn W. Levy *play* Robert E. Sherwood *d* James Whale *ph* Arthur Edeson
☆ Mae Clarke, Kent Douglass, Doris Lloyd, Ethel Griffies, Enid Bennett, Frederick Kerr, Bette Davis
'Just fair programme fodder, and it ought to be better. Not helped by an uninspiring sad ending.' – *Variety*

Waterloo Bridge **
US 1940 103m bw
MGM (Sidney Franklin)
⊜ ⊚∩
Lush, all-stops-out remake of the above; for yet another version see *Gaby*.
w S. N. Behrman, Hans Rameau, George Froeschel *d* Mervyn Le Roy *ph* Joseph Ruttenberg *m* Herbert Stothart
☆ Vivien Leigh, Robert Taylor, Lucile Watson, Virginia Field, Maria Ouspenskaya, C. Aubrey Smith, Steffi Duna
'The director uses candlelight and rain more effectively than he does the actors.' – *New Yorker, 1977*
⚖ Joseph Ruttenberg; Herbert Stothart

The Waterloo Bridge Handicap *
GB 1978 21m colour
Paramount/Fetter
Commuters enjoy a daily race across Westminster Bridge.
Amusing trifle, well shot and edited.
wd Ross Cramer *ed* Sean Barton
☆ Leonard Rossiter, Lynda Bellingham, John Quentin, Gordon Laye

Waterloo Road
GB 1944 76m bw
GFD/Gainsborough (Edward Black)
A soldier whose wife is enamoured of a petty crook absents himself to settle matters.
What at the time seemed cheerful realism now seems chronically forced, but amusing moments can still be found.
wd Sidney Gilliat *story* Val Valentine *ph* Arthur Crabtree *md* Louis Levy
☆ John Mills, Stewart Granger, Joy Shelton, Alastair Sim, Beatrice Varley, Alison Leggatt, Jean Kent
'The harsh rattle of trains over a viaduct, the clamour of the street market, the wailing of sirens and the crash of bombs are the accompaniment of this wartime love story.' – *Richard Winnington*
'Unpretentious, credible, continuously entertaining and just the right length.' – *Richard Mallett, Punch*

Watermelon Man
US 1970 100m Technicolor
Columbia/Johanna (John B. Bennett)
📼 ⊚∩
A bigoted insurance salesman wakes up one morning to find he has turned into a black man.
Spasmodically funny racial comedy, compromised by the impossibility of a black man playing white even with heavy make-up.
w Herman Raucher *d* Melvin Van Peebles *ph* W. Wallace Kelley *m* Melvin Van Peebles
☆ Godfrey Cambridge, Estelle Parsons, Howard Caine, Mantan Moreland

Watermelon Woman
US 1997 105m DuArt
Dangerous To Know/Dancing Girl/Cheryl Dunye (Barry Swimar, Alexandra Juhasz)
📼 ⊜ ⊚
A lesbian video-shop worker, who wants to be a film-maker, researches the life of an actress who is credited as the Watermelon Woman in films of the 30s and 40s.
A fake documentary, shot in a rough-and-ready manner, that will interest only some of those who share the sexual preferences of its maker.
wd Cheryl Dunye *ph* Michelle Crenshaw *m* Paul Shapiro *pd* Robert 'Ratface' Holtzman *ed* Annie Taylor
☆ Cheryl Dunye, Guinevere Turner, Valerie Walker, Lisa Marie Bronson, Irene Dunye, Brian Freeman, Camille Paglia
'It is very unlikely that it will be seen by anyone who wouldn't otherwise go and see an art movie by a black lesbian film-maker. I wish I could say that this is a shame.' – *Andrea Turner, Sight and Sound*

Waters of Time *
GB 1951 37m bw
Port of London Authority
A poetic impression of the Port of London, from the mouth of the Thames to Kingston.
Notably stylish documentary, made to coincide with the Festival of Britain.
wd Basil Wright, Bill Launder *ed* Basil Wright, Bill Launder

Watership Down
🏈 GB 1978 92m Technicolor
Nepenthe (Martin Rosen)
📼 ⊜ ⊚∩
A colony of rabbits seek a new home following a vision of the destruction of their warren.
A brilliantly written if somewhat pretentious parable becomes a rather flatly made cartoon in which it is difficult to distinguish one rabbit from another; the whole thing becomes a bit doomladen for family audiences, while adults will presumably prefer to re-read the novel.
wd Martin Rosen *novel* Richard Adams *m* Angela Morley *animation director* Tony Guy
☆ Featuring the voices of John Hurt, Richard Briers, Ralph Richardson, Zero Mostel, Roy Kinnear, Denholm Elliott, John Bennett, Simon Cadell

'Beyond The Horizon Lies A Secret To A New Beginning'

Waterworld *
US 1995 135m DeLuxe
UIP/Universal (Charles Gordon, John Davis, Kevin Costner)
📼 ⊜ ⊚ ⊚ ∩
The adventures in the future, when the ice caps have melted and the world is flooded, of a mutant human, who searches across the oceans for land, with the aid of a woman and her adopted daughter.
Overblown action movie with a leaky narrative, relying on stunts to retain an audience's attention; it looks good, though, and is energized by Dennis Hopper as a psychotic villain.
w Peter Rader, David Twohy *d* Kevin Reynolds *ph* Dean Semler *m* James Newton Howard *pd* Dennis Gassner *ed* Peter Boyle *sp* Michael J. McAlister
☆ Kevin Costner, Dennis Hopper, Jeanne Tripplehorn, Tina Majorino, Michael Jeter, Gerard Murphy, Zakes Mokae
'Splashes enough spectacular mayhem up on the screen to divert thrill-seeking audiences through most of its running time.' – *Todd McCarthy, Variety*
'*Waterworld* doesn't suck, but neither will it blow you away, and it spends most of its two hours

with no propulsion whatsoever, save memories of other movies and large, gusty gales of superstar ego.' – *Tom Shone, Sunday Times*
'More like a couple of hours in a flotation tank than a white-knuckle roller coaster ride.' – *Adam Mars-Jones, Independent*
† The film was the most expensive yet made in Hollywood, at a reported cost of $175m (or $1.3m a minute of screen-time). It had its genesis in a script commissioned from Rader as a low-budget variation on *Mad Max*, which was rejected by its original producers when it was estimated that the resulting movie would cost at least $5m. Reynolds left the film during post-production after a disagreement with Costner. It took around $88m at the US box-office and a further $166m elsewhere in the world.
⚖ sound

Watusi
US 1959 85m Technicolor
MGM (Al Zimbalist)
Harry Quarterman retraces his father's footsteps to King Solomon's Mines.
Skilful re-use of King Solomon's Mines footage; acceptable Boy's Own Paper stuff.
w James Clavell *d* Kurt Neumann *ph* Harold E. Wellman
☆ George Montgomery, Taina Elg, David Farrar, Rex Ingram, Dan Seymour

The Wax Mask (dubbed) *
Italy/France 1995 95m colour
Cine 2000/Mediaset/FFI (Giuseppe Colombo)
📼
In Milan, the proprietor of a wax museum is a homicidal maniac.
Stylish, though excessively gory and gruesome, variation on House of Wax with touches of The Terminator thrown in for good measure.
w Lucio Fulci, Daniele Stroppa, Dario Argento *d* Sergio Stivaletti *ph* Sergio Salvati *m* Maurizio Abeni *ad* Antonello Geleng *ed* Paolo Benassi *sp* Sergio Stivaletti; make-up: Benoit Lestang
☆ Robert Hossein, Romina Mondello, Riccardo Serventi Longhi, Gabriella Giorgelli, Umberto Balli, Valery Valmond, Aldo Massasso

Waxwork
US 1988 96m colour
Vestron/Palla Pictures/Filmrullen (Staffen Ahrenberg)
📼 ⊚∩
Students visit a waxworks' chamber of horrors in an old dark house, where the figures come to life.
Direly unimaginative, hammily acted horror movie.
wd Anthony Hickox *ph* Gerry Lively *m* Roger Bellon *pd* Gianni Quaranta *ed* Christopher Cibelli
☆ Zach Galligan, Deborah Freeman, Michelle Johnson, Dana Ashbrook, Miles O'Keeffe, Charles McCaughan, J. Kenneth Campbell, John Rhys-Davies, Patrick Macnee, David Warner
'Film-making by numbers.' – *MFB*

'An eye popping, teeth chattering, mind blowing movie!!!'

Waxwork II: Lost in Time
US 1991 100m Foto-Kem
Electric Pictures (Nancy Paloian)
📼 ⊜
aka: *Lost in Time*
Having destroyed a wax museum where monsters came to life, a couple travel into a parallel universe of 'God's Nintendo game' where the battle between good and evil is fought as scenarios from horror movies.
From Nosferatu to Godzilla and Alien, taking in Frankenstein, Jekyll and Hyde, Edgar Allen Poe and The Haunting along the way, classic horrors are parodied in a clever low-budget style with cut-rate wit, ham acting and a lot of blood-letting. The result may entertain fans of the genre in an indulgent mood.
wd Anthony Hickox *ph* Gerry Lively *m* Steve Schiff *pd* Steve Hardie *ed* Christopher Cibelli *sp* Bob Keen
☆ Zach Galligan, Monika Schnarre, Martin Kemp, Bruce Campbell, Michael Des Barres, Jim Metzler, Sophie Ward, Bill Kane, Juliet Mills, John Ireland, Patrick Macnee, David Carradine, Alexander Godunov
'A loopy gags-and-gore fest striving a mite too self-consciously for cult status.' – *Variety*
'A profound lack of style that confirms just because Hickox loves good horror movies

doesn't necessarily mean he knows how to make them.' – *Shivers*

Waxworks *
Germany 1924 62m bw silent
Neptun-Film
original title: *Das Wachsfigurenkabinett*
A young poet in a fairground waxwork museum concocts stories about Haroun al Raschid, Ivan the Terrible and Jack the Ripper.
The form later became familiar in such horror films as Torture Garden and Tales from the Crypt, but here the emphasis is not on horror but on grotesquerie, and indeed the idea is somewhat more entertaining than the rather plodding execution.
w Henrik Galeen *d* Paul Leni *ph* Helmar Lerski *ad* Paul Leni, Ernst Stern, Alfred Junge
☆ William Dieterle, Emil Jannings, Conrad Veidt, Werner Krauss

The Way: see *Yol*

The Way Ahead ***
GB 1944 115m bw
GFD/Two Cities (John Sutro, Norman Walker)
⊜
US title: *Immortal Battalion*
Adventures of a platoon of raw recruits during World War II.
Memorable semi-documentary originally intended as a training film; the warm humour of the early scenes, however, never leads quite naturally into the final action and tragedy.
w Eric Ambler, Peter Ustinov *d* Carol Reed *ph* Guy Green *m* William Alwyn
☆ David Niven, Stanley Holloway, Raymond Huntley, William Hartnell, James Donald, John Laurie, Leslie Dwyer, Hugh Burden, Jimmy Hanley, Renée Asherson, Penelope Dudley Ward, Reginald Tate, Leo Genn, Mary Jerrold, Peter Ustinov
'Is to be admired and recommended for its direction, its writing and its playing.' – *Dilys Powell*

Way Back Home
US 1932 81m bw
RKO
Problems of a Maine preacher.
Unintentionally hilarious farrago of dark deeds in a small town, from a radio serial.
w Jane Murfin *d* William A. Seiter
☆ Phillips Lord, Bette Davis, Effie Palmer, Bennett Kilpack, Frank Albertson, Mrs Phillips Lord

Way Down East **
US 1920 110m bw (colour sequence)
silent
D. W. Griffith
⊜ ⊚∩
A country girl is seduced; her baby dies; her shame is revealed; but a kindly farmer rescues her from drowning and marries her.
Old-fashioned tearjerker impeccably mounted and very typical of its director in its sentimental mood. The ice floe sequence is famous for its excitement and realism.
w Anthony Paul Kelly, Joseph R. Grismer, D. W. Griffith *play* Lottie Blair Parker *d* D. W. Griffith *ph* Billy Bitzer, Henrik Sortov
☆ Lillian Gish, Richard Barthelmess, Lowell Sherman, Creighton Hale
'Griffith took a creaking, dated stage melodrama and turned it into a melodramatic epic.' – *Pauline Kael, 70s*

Way Down East
US 1935 85m bw
TCF (Winfield Sheehan)
Tedious and unwise remake.
w Howard Estabrook, William Hurlbut *d* Henry King
☆ Rochelle Hudson, Henry Fonda, Slim Summerville, Edward Trevor, Margaret Hamilton, Andy Devine, Spring Byington, Russell Simpson, Sara Haden

Way for a Sailor
US 1930 83m bw
MGM
Adventures of a tough seafarer and a pet seal.
Thin vehicle for a declining star whose talkie voice was at odds with his image.
w Laurence Stallings, W. L. River *novel* Albert Richard Wetjen *d* Sam Wood *ph* Percy Hilburn

☆ John Gilbert, Wallace Beery, Leila Hyams, Jim Tully, Polly Moran, Doris Lloyd

'It throws John Gilbert for a loss, and it's not his fault. His voice is okay.' – *Variety*

Way of a Gaucho

US 1952 91m Technicolor
TCF (Philip Dunne)

An Argentine gaucho joins the militia and fights Indians.

Mildly interesting Western-in-disguise.

w Philip Dunne *novel* Herbert Childs *d* Jacques Tourneur *ph* Harry Jackson *m* Sol Kaplan

☆ Rory Calhoun, Gene Tierney, Richard Boone, Hugh Marlowe, Everett Sloane, Enrique Chaico

The Way of All Flesh *

US 1928 94m bw silent
Paramount (Adolph Zukor, Jesse L. Lasky)

A respectable man leaves his wife, goes to the dogs, and is too ashamed to come back.

Star character drama, most watchable now when it goes over the top.

d Victor Fleming

☆ Emil Jannings, Belle Bennett, Phyllis Haver
♟ Emil Jannings
♟ best picture

'He left his heart behind when he took it!'

The Way of All Flesh

US 1940 82m bw
Paramount (Eugene Zukor)

Remake of the above, well enough done but clearly outmoded.

w Lenore Coffee *story* Jules Furthman, Lajos Biro *novel* Perley Poore Sheehan *d* Louis King *ph* Theodor Sparkuhl

☆ Akim Tamiroff, Gladys George, Muriel Angelus, Berton Churchill, Fritz Leiber

The Way of the Dragon (dubbed)

Hong Kong 1973 99m Cineart Scope
Cathay/Concord/Golden Harvest (Raymond Chow)

aka: Return of the Dragon

A martial arts expert goes to Rome to help a friend save her restaurant which is threatened by gangsters.

A kung fu movie incongruously shifted from the East to Italy, where it seems silly, although the fight sequences are well done.

wd Bruce Lee *ph* Ho Lan Shan *m* Joseph Koo *ad* Chien Hsin *ed* Chang Yao Ching

☆ Bruce Lee, Nora Miao, Chuck Norris, Wei Ping Ao, Wang Chung Hsin

'At once deeply flawed and the most personal film to have come out of Hong Kong.' – Tony Rayns, *MFB*

† The film was cut to 91m on its British release.

Way Out West ****

US 1937 66m bw
Hal Roach (Stan Laurel)

Laurel and Hardy come to Brushwood Gulch to deliver the deed to a gold mine.

Seven reels of perfect joy, with the comedians at their very best in brilliantly-timed routines, plus two song numbers as a bonus.

w Jack Jevne, Charles Rogers, James Parrott, Felix Adler *d* James Horne *ph* Art Lloyd, Walter Lundin *m* Marvin Hatley

☆ Stan Laurel, Oliver Hardy, James Finlayson, Sharon Lynne, Rosina Lawrence

'Thin returns indicated … for added feature on duallers.' – *Variety*
'Not only one of their most perfect films, it ranks with the best screen comedy anywhere.' – David Robinson, 1962
'The film is leisurely in the best sense; you adjust to a different rhythm and come out feeling relaxed as if you'd had a vacation.' – *New Yorker, 1980*

♟ Marvin Hatley

'Of course he's naughty! But that's the way you love him best!'

The Way to Love

US 1933 80m bw
Paramount (Benjamin Glazer)

A would-be Paris tourist guide works as a pavement hawker and helps a showgirl evade her knife-thrower partner.

Thin star vehicle with a few pleasant moments.

w Gene Fowler, Benjamin Glazer *d* Norman Taurog *ph* Charles Lang *m/ly* Ralph Rainger, Leo Robin

☆ Maurice Chevalier, Edward Everett Horton, Ann Dvorak, Arthur Pierson, Minna Gombell, Blanche Frederici, Douglass Dumbrille, John Miljan

'The poorest of the Chevaliers but poor entertainment which will get by on the strength of the star.' – *Variety*

The Way to the Gold

US 1957 94m bw
TCF (David Weisbart)

An ex-convict seeks hidden loot but is pursued by competitors.

Gloomy, self-pitying melodrama.

w Wendell Mayes *novel* Wilber Steele *d* Robert D. Webb *ph* Leo Tover *m* Lionel Newman

☆ Jeffrey Hunter, Sheree North, Barry Sullivan, Walter Brennan, Ruth Donnelly, Neville Brand

The Way to the Stars ****

GB 1945 109m bw
Two Cities (Anatole de Grunwald)

US title: *Johnny in the Clouds*

World War II as seen by the guests at a small hotel near an airfield.

Generally delightful comedy drama suffused with tragic atmosphere but with very few flying shots, one of the few films which instantly bring back the atmosphere of the war in Britain for anyone who was involved.

w Terence Rattigan, Anatole de Grunwald *poem* John Pudney *d* Anthony Asquith *ph* Derick Williams *m* Nicholas Brodszky

☆ John Mills, Rosamund John, Michael Redgrave, Douglass Montgomery, Basil Radford, Stanley Holloway, Joyce Carey, Renée Asherson, Felix Aylmer, Bonar Colleano, Trevor Howard, Jean Simmons

'Not for a long time have I seen a film so satisfying, so memorable, or so successful in evoking the precise mood and atmosphere of the recent past.' – Richard Mallett, *Punch*
'Humour, humanity, and not a sign of mawkishness … a classic opening sequence, with the camera wandering through an abandoned air base, peering in at each detail in the nissen huts, the sleeping quarters, the canteens, noting all the time a procession of objects each of which will have its own special significance in the action of the film.' – Basil Wright, 1972

Way Way Out

US 1966 105m DeLuxe Cinemascope
TCF/Coldwater/Jerry Lewis (Malcolm Stuart)

In 1994 a weather expert on the moon has woman trouble.

Dismal sex farce with an unusual backdrop; painful to sit through.

w William Bowers, Laslo Vadnay *d* Gordon Douglas *ph* William H. Clothier *m* Lalo Schifrin

☆ Jerry Lewis, Connie Stevens, Robert Morley, Dick Shawn, Anita Ekberg, Dennis Weaver, Howard Morris, Brian Keith

'Everything seemed so important then – even love!'

The Way We Were **

US 1973 118m Eastmancolor Panavision
Columbia/Rastar (Ray Stark)

The romance and marriage of an upper-crust young novelist and a Jewish bluestocking girl, from college to Hollywood in the thirties, forties and fifties.

Instant nostalgia for Americans, some fun and a lot of boredom for everybody is provided by this very patchy star vehicle which makes a particular mess of the McCarthy witch hunt sequence but has undeniable moments of vitality.

w Arthur Laurents *novel* Arthur Laurents *d* Sydney Pollack *ph* Harry Stradling Jnr *m* Marvin Hamlisch

☆ Barbra Streisand, Robert Redford, Patrick O'Neal, Viveca Lindfors, Bradford Dillman, Lois Chiles, Allyn Ann McLerie, Herb Edelman, Murray Hamilton

'Not one moment of the picture is anything but garbage under the gravy of false honesty.' – Stanley Kauffmann
'A real curate's egg of a movie, composed of so many disparate parts as to put you in mind of Leacock's knight, who got on his horse and rode off furiously in all directions.' – Benny Green, *Punch*

♟ Marvin Hamlisch; title song (m Marvin Hamlisch, ly Alan and Marilyn Bergman)
♟ Harry Stradling Jnr; Barbra Streisand

The Way West *

US 1967 122m DeLuxe Panavision
UA/Harold Hecht

Hazards of a wagon train between Missouri and Oregon in 1843.

Semi-spectacular Western which looks good but falls apart dramatically, especially in its insistence on a sub-plot about a most unlikely nymphet.

w Ben Maddow, Mitch Lindemann *novel* A. B. Guthrie Jnr *d* Andrew V. McLaglen *ph* William H. Clothier *m* Bronislau Kaper

☆ Kirk Douglas, Robert Mitchum, Richard Widmark, Lola Albright, Michael Witney, Sally Field, Stubby Kaye, Jack Elam

'A jerk's idea of an epic; big stars, big landscapes, bad jokes, folksy-heroic music to plug up the holes, and messy hang-ups.' – Pauline Kael

'You'll laugh. You'll cry. You'll hurl.'

Wayne's World *

US 1992 95m Technicolor
UIP/Paramount (Lorne Michaels)

A ramshackle cable TV show, put together by two girl- and rock-obsessed teenagers, is given big-time exposure by a sleazy TV executive.

Tedious teen comedy, based on characters developed for the Saturday Night Live TV show, which long outstays its welcome. It was, though, one of 1992's surprise hits, ranking sixth at the US box-office and doing well in Europe.

w Mike Myers, Bonnie Turner, Terry Turner *d* Penelope Spheeris *ph* Theo Van de Sande *m* J. Peter Robinson *pd* Gregg Fonseca *ed* Malcolm Campbell

☆ Mike Myers, Dana Carvey, Rob Lowe, Tia Carrere, Brian Doyle-Murray, Lara Flynn Boyle, Michael DeLuise, Dan Bell

'Aggressively pitched at a young white male audience, feature is unlikely to appeal to mainstream moviegoers … Even for fans of the TV comics, the laugh-to-running-time ratio is extremely low.' – *Variety*

Wayne's World 2 *

US 1993 95m DeLuxe
Paramount (Lorne Michaels)

In a dream, Wayne is told to organize Waynestock, the ultimate rock concert.

The mixture is much the same as the first film, but this time around the jokes are slightly better.

w Mike Myers, Bonnie Turner, Terry Turner *d* Stephen Surjik *ph* Francis Kenny *m* Carter Burwell *pd* Gregg Fonseca *ed* Malcolm Campbell

☆ Mike Myers, Dana Carvey, Christopher Walken, Tia Carrere, Ralph Brown, Kim Basinger, Drew Barrymore, Michael Nickles, Aerosmith

'A puerile, misguided and loathsome effort … NOT!' – *Variety*
'Something of a disappointment, though that is not to say that a lot of people won't enjoy it – especially if drunk or on drugs.' – Ben Thompson, *Sight and Sound*

The Wayward Bus

US 1957 89m bw Cinemascope
TCF (Charles Brackett)

A landslide strands an assortment of bus passengers in a lonely farmhouse …

…but not the old dark house, unfortunately: this lot does nothing but talk, and the plot never really forms.

w Ivan Moffat *novel* John Steinbeck *d* Victor Vicas *ph* Charles G. Clarke *m* Leigh Harline

☆ Dan Dailey, Jayne Mansfield, Joan Collins, Rick Jason, Dolores Michaels, Larry Keating, Betty Lou Keim

We Are Not Alone *

US 1939 112m bw
Warner (Henry Blanke)

A man having an innocent affair is accused of murdering his wife.

Gloomy, well-acted drama with a rather uneasy English setting.

w James Hilton, Milton Krims *novel* James Hilton *d* Edmund Goulding *ph* Tony Gaudio *m* Max Steiner

☆ Paul Muni, Jane Bryan, Flora Robson, Raymond Severn, Una O'Connor, Henry Daniell, Montagu Love, James Stephenson, Cecil Kellaway

'It has dignity and warmth and is genuinely moving … handsomely produced, skilfully directed, and eloquently played.' – *Variety*
'An extraordinary moving story, beautifully told and perfectly acted.' – *MFB*

We Dive at Dawn

GB 1943 98m bw
GFD/Gainsborough (Edward Black)

World War II adventures of a British submarine disabled in the Baltic.

Fairly routine war suspenser.

w J. B. Williams, Val Valentine, Frank Launder *d* Anthony Asquith *ph* Jack Cox *md* Louis Levy

☆ John Mills, Eric Portman, Reginald Purdell, Niall MacGinnis, Joan Hopkins, Josephine Wilson, Jack Watling

We Don't Want to Talk about It **

Argentina/Italy 1993 105m colour
Artificial Eye/Aura/Oscar Kramer

original title: *De Eso No Se Habla*

A widow makes sure her daughter, a dwarf, is unaware that there are others like her; the girl marries a sophisticated stranger, but then the circus comes to town.

An oddly enchanting bitter-sweet fable, a satire of conventional life and political correctness, a celebration of growing up, assuming responsibility for oneself and following one's own destiny.

w Maria Luisa Bemberg, Jorge Goldenberg *story* Julio Llinás *d* Maria Luisa Bemberg *ph* Felix Monti *m* Nicola Piovani *pd* Jorge Sarudiansky *ed* Juan Carlos Macias

☆ Marcello Mastroianni, Luisina Brando, Alejandra Podesta, Betiana Blum, Alberto Segado, Roberto Carnaghi, Jorge Luz

'It is a rare feat of enchanted cinema that what could so easily have been grotesque achieves a fairy-tale quality … one of the year's strangest, most mesmeric movies.' – Tom Hutchinson, *Film Review*

We Faw Down

US 1928 20m bw silent
Hal Roach

Stan and Ollie have an evening out, but their lies to their wives become apparent.

Moderate star comedy, later elaborated in Sons of the Desert.

w H. M. Walker *d* Leo McCarey *ed* Richard Currier

☆ Stan Laurel, Oliver Hardy, Bess Flowers, Vivien Oakland, Kay Deslys

We Have Our Moments

US 1937 63m bw
Edmund Grainger/Universal

Gangsters hide their loot in the trunk of a schoolteacher going to Europe on a vacation.

Rather slackly handled comedy with amusing bits.

w Bruce Manning, Charles Grayson, David Belden, Frederick Stephani *d* Alfred Werker

☆ James Dunn, Sally Eilers, Mischa Auer, David Niven, Warren Hymer, Marjorie Gateson, Thurston Hall

'As the number two feature on doubles it will manage to get by.' – *Variety*

We Humans: see Young America

We Joined the Navy

GB 1962 105m Eastmancolor Cinemascope
Dial/Daniel M. Angel

A carefree naval commander and three cadets get involved in the affairs of a small Mediterranean country.

Desperate naval farce which sinks from script malnutrition in reel two.

w Arthur Dales *novel* John Winton *d* Wendy Toye *ph* Otto Heller *m* Ron Grainer

☆ Kenneth More, Lloyd Nolan, Mischa Auer, Joan O'Brien, Jeremy Lloyd, Dinsdale Landen, Derek Fowlds

We Live Again *

US 1934 85m bw

Samuel Goldwyn

A Russian prince is brought up in the country and falls in love with a servant girl whose life later takes a downward path.

Beautifully made but dramatically uninteresting version of a Russian classic.

w Preston Sturges, Maxwell Anderson, Leonard Praskins *novel* Resurrection by Leo Tolstoy d Rouben Mamoulian *ph* Gregg Toland *m* Alfred Newman

☆ Fredric March, Anna Sten, Jane Baxter, C. Aubrey Smith, Ethel Griffies, Jessie Ralph, Sam Jaffe

'It's a class picture basically. That limits its mass b.o. appeal.' – *Variety*

We of the Never Never *

Australia 1982 134m Eastmancolor Technovision

Adams Packer/Film Corporation of Western Australia/GTC (Greg Tepper)

🎵

Around 1900, a city girl marries the owner of an isolated cattle station.

Longwinded but attractively photographed recollections of another time and another place. Not really very memorable despite a plethora of incident.

w Peter Schreck *book* Mrs Aeneas Gunn d Igor Auzins *ph* Gary Hansen *m* Peter Best

☆ Angela Punch-McGregor, Arthur Dignam, Tony Barry, Martin Vaughan

'Tasteful period re-creation, choked-back emotionalism, a *Men of Two Worlds* attempt at assuaging colonial guilt, and the kind of tidily suffering heroine Deborah Kerr used to play.' – *Kim Newman, MFB*

We Think the World of You *

GB 1988 94m Technicolor

Recorded Releasing/Gold Screen/Film Four International/British Screen (Tommaso Jandelli)

🖭 🎵

A middle-aged homosexual becomes devoted to his lover's dog.

Understated and reticent drama, enjoyable mainly for its acting.

w Hugh Stoddart *novel* J. R. Ackerley d Colin Gregg *m* Mike Garfath *m* Julian Jacobson *pd* Jamie Leonard *ed* Peter Delfgou

☆ Alan Bates, Max Wall, Liz Smith, Frances Barber, Gary Oldman, Ryan Batt, Kerry Wise, Sheila Ballantine

We Were Dancing

US 1942 93m bw

MGM (Robert Z. Leonard, Orville Dull)

A Polish princess elopes from her engagement party with a gigolo.

Leaden romantic comedy produced in high style.

w Claudine West, Hans Rameau, George Froeschel *play* Tonight at 8.30 by Noël Coward d Robert Z. Leonard *ph* Robert Planck *m* Bronislau Kaper

☆ Norma Shearer, Melvyn Douglas, Gail Patrick, Lee Bowman, Marjorie Main, Reginald Owen, Alan Mowbray, Florence Bates, Sig Rumann, Dennis Hoey, Heather Thatcher, Connie Gilchrist

We Were Strangers *

US 1949 105m bw

Columbia/Horizon (Sam Spiegel)

Cuban rebels in the thirties plan to assassinate a politician and have to build a tunnel through a cemetery.

Well-made but very downbeat adventure story, too cheerless to be exciting.

w Peter Viertel, John Huston *novel* Rough Sketch by Robert Sylvester d John Huston *ph* Russell Metty *m* Georges Antheil

☆ John Garfield, Jennifer Jones, Pedro Armendariz, Gilbert Roland, Wally Cassell, Ramon Novarro, David Bond, Jose Perez

'There is so much about this film I cannot swallow – the implausibilities of detail, the convention of broken accents, the literary conversaziones, the naïve doctrines of revolution … [but] it continues to haunt the mind and has therefore had its say.' – *Richard Winnington*

We Who Are About to Die

US 1937 82m bw

RKO

Life on Death Row.

Modest prison melodrama with a lot of opportunity for character actors to display hysteria.

w John Twist, David Lamson d Christy Cabanne

☆ Preston Foster, Ann Dvorak, John Beal, Ray Mayer, Gordon Jones, Russell Hopton, J. Carrol Naish, Willie Fung, Paul Hurst, Frank Jenks, Barnett Parker, John Wray, John Carroll

'An action drama of considerable tension that should please the general run of fans with plenty of special charm for the kids and the menfolk.' – *Variety*

The Weak and the Wicked

GB 1953 88m bw

ABPC/Marble Arch (Victor Skutezky)

Flashbacks show how various women came to find themselves in prison.

Predictable portmanteau drama with stalwart performances.

w J. Lee-Thompson, Anne Burnaby *book* Who Lie in Gaol by Joan Henry d J. Lee-Thompson *ph* Gilbert Taylor *m* Leighton Lucas

☆ Glynis Johns, John Gregson, Diana Dors, Jane Hylton, Sidney James, Olive Sloane, Eliot Makeham, A. E. Matthews, Athene Seyler, Sybil Thorndike, Anthony Nicholls, Joan Haythorne

The Weaker Sex

GB 1948 84m bw

Two Cities (Paul Soskin)

Day-to-day problems of a well-to-do war widow.

Mild suburban comedy which sparkled more on stage, with such curtain lines as: 'Quick, the fishmonger's got fish!'

w Esther McCracken, Paul Soskin *play* No Medals by Esther McCracken d Roy Baker *ph* Erwin Hillier *m* Arthur Wilkinson

☆ Ursula Jeans, Cecil Parker, Joan Hopkins, Derek Bond, Lana Morris, Thora Hird, John Stone

The Weapon

GB 1956 81m bw Superscope 235

Periclean (Frank Bevis)

A boy finds a loaded revolver on a bomb site and mistakenly thinks he has killed someone with it.

Standard suspenser with a cast worthy of something more interesting.

w Fred Freiberger d Val Guest *ph* Reg Wyer *m* James Stevens

☆ Lizabeth Scott, Steve Cochran, George Cole, Herbert Marshall, Nicole Maurey, Jon Whiteley, Laurence Naismith

The Web *

US 1947 87m bw

Universal (Jerry Bresler)

A financier hires a young lawyer as his bodyguard and lures him into committing murder.

Modestly well staged and glossy thriller.

w William Bowers, Bertram Millhauser d Michael Gordon *ph* Irving Glassberg *m* Hans Salter

☆ Edmond O'Brien, Vincent Price, Ella Raines, William Bendix

Web of Evidence: see Beyond This Place

Web of Passion: see à Double Tour

The Webster Boy

GB 1961 83m bw

Emmet Dalton

US title: *Middle of Nowhere*

A teenager suffers at the hands of a sadistic schoolmaster.

Curious, totally unbelievable melodrama.

w Ted Allen d Don Chaffey *ph* Gerald Gibbs *m* Wilfrid Joseph

☆ Richard O'Sullivan, John Cassavetes, David Farrar, Elizabeth Sellars, Niall MacGinnis

A Wedding *

US 1978 125m DeLuxe

TCF/Lion's Gate (Thommy Thompson, Robert Altman)

Two families converge for a fashionable wedding, but the day is beset by calamities.

Wide-ranging satirical comedy which despite excellent moments goes on far too long, is rather too black, and is sabotaged by the director's penchant for having fourteen people talking at the same time. An exhausting experience.

w John Considine, Patricia Resnick, Allan Nicholls, Robert Altman d Robert Altman *ph* Charles Rosher *md* Tom Walls

☆ Carol Burnett, Paul Dooley, Amy Stryker, Mia Farrow, Peggy Ann Garner, Lillian Gish, Nina Van Pallandt, Vittorio Gassman, Howard Duff, Desi Arnaz Jnr, Dina Merrill, Geraldine Chaplin, Viveca Lindfors, Lauren Hutton, John Cromwell

'Altman has become our leading silky utilizer of film styles. This time it's quick-sale ugliness. Just because he is so technically accomplished, so vacuously smooth and smart, he is depressing: he seems a kind of walking death sentence on the prospects of American film, much more menacing than clumsy or arrantly sentimental film-makers.' – *Stanley Kauffmann*

'Everyone Wants To Kiss The Bride … Except The Groom.'

The Wedding Banquet ***

Taiwan/US 1993 108m DuArt

Mainline/Central Motion Picture/Good Machine (Ang Lee, Ted Hope, James Schamus)

🖭 🖭 🎵

original title: *Xiyan*

A homosexual American-Taiwanese businessman has to conceal his sexual preferences and his lover when his staid mother and father arrive in New York to celebrate his arranged marriage to a Chinese woman.

A delightful comedy of culture clashes, racial and generational differences and the problems of living up to your parents' expectations; it makes light of situations without concealing their truth and occasional pain.

w Ang Lee, Neil Peng, James Schamus d Ang Lee *ph* Jong Lin *m* Mader *pd* Steve Rosenzweig *ed* Tim Squyres

☆ Mitchell Lichtenstein, Winston Chao, May Chin, Sihung Lung, Ah-Leh Gua, Dion Birney, Jeanne Kuo Chang

'Canny mix of feelgood elements and ethnic color.' – *Variety*

'A wish-fulfilment fantasy on a par with the equally crowd-pleasing *Strictly Ballroom*.' – *Tony Rayns, Sight and Sound*

🏆 best foreign-language film

Wedding Bells: see Royal Wedding

Wedding Breakfast: see The Catered Affair

The Wedding March **

US 1928 196m bw silent

Paramount/Celebrity

A Habsburg prince loves a poor girl but is forced to marry a crippled princess, who dies; he is then murdered by the poor girl's enraged defender.

A marathon dose of Stroheim's favourite subject, sex, with some violence and a few fetishes thrown in. Full of fascinating touches, but desperately overlong; it was originally released in two parts, but failed to draw.

w Harry Carr, Erich von Stroheim d Erich von Stroheim *ph* Hal Mohr, Ben Reynolds *ad* Erich von Stroheim, Richard Day

☆ Erich von Stroheim, Fay Wray, ZaSu Pitts, Matthew Betz, Maude George, Cesare Gravina, George Fawcett

'A pitilessly authentic portrait of decadent Imperialist Austria.' – *Georges Sadoul*

'The slowness, heaviness, mindlessness of this temple of unnaturalness through which man passes as through a forest of clichés defied description.' – *John Simon, 1967*

† In 1975 there was published a pictorial record, *The Complete Wedding March*, by Herman G. Weinberg

The Wedding Night *

US 1935 83m bw

Samuel Goldwyn

A Connecticut author causes tragedy when he takes an interest in the local Polish immigrant farmers and especially in the daughter of one of them.

Interesting and unusual but slightly tediously told drama.

w Edith Fitzgerald d King Vidor *ph* Gregg Toland *md* Alfred Newman

☆ Gary Cooper, Anna Sten, Sig Rumann, Helen Vinson, Ralph Bellamy, Esther Dale

'Fine artistic film, possibly too artistic.' – *Variety*

'Convincing and curiously powerful.' – *New York Herald Tribune*

The Wedding of Lilli Marlene

GB 1953 87m bw

Monarch

The heroine of World War II becomes a success in show business.

Poorly confected programme filler, an unnecessary sequel if ever there was one.

w John Baines d Arthur Crabtree *ph* Arthur Grant *m* Eric Rogers

☆ Lisa Daniely, Hugh McDermott, Sid James, Gabrielle Brune, Robert Ayres

'He gave her something to remember him by!'

Wedding Present *

US 1936 81m bw

Paramount (B. P. Schulberg)

A pair of crack newspaper reporters take their jobs and themselves lightly.

Whimsical star comedy with some funny scenes.

w Joseph Anthony *story* Paul Gallico d Richard Wallace *ph* Leon Shamroy

☆ Cary Grant, Joan Bennett, George Bancroft, Conrad Nagel, Gene Lockhart, William Demarest, Edward Brophy

'Grant and Bennett try hard, but the combination of story, direction and whatnot is pretty much against them.' – *Variety*

Wedding Rehearsal

GB 1932 84m bw

Ideal/London Films/Alexander Korda

A Guards officer foils his grandmother's plans to get him married by finding suitors for all the young ladies offered.

Frail comedy with unsure technique.

w Helen Gardom *story* Lajos Biro, George Grossmith d Alexander Korda *ph* Leslie Rowson *m* Kurt Schroeder *ad* O. F. Werndorff, Vincent Korda *ed* Harold Young

☆ Roland Young, George Grossmith, John Loder, Lady Tree, Wendy Barrie, Maurice Evans, Joan Gardner, Merle Oberon, Kate Cutler, Edmund Breon

'If I were Korda, I would get up in the night, steal the negative, and quietly drop it in the Thames.' – *Marcel Ermans, World Film News*

The Wedding Singer *

US 1998 96m CFI color

Entertainment/New Line (Robert Simonds, Jack Giarraputo)

A singer and a waitress, both involved in unhappy relationships, fall in love.

Broad comedy that succeeds by energy and its delight in the tackier fashions of the 80s.

w Tim Herlihy d Frank Coraci *ph* Tim Suhrstedt *m* Teddy Castellucci *pd* Perry Andelin Blake *ed* Tom Lewis

☆ Adam Sandler, Drew Barrymore, Christine Taylor, Allen Covert, Matthew Glave, Ellen Albertini Dow, Angela Featherstone, Alexis Arquette, Christina Pickles, Jon Lovitz (uncredited), Steve Buscemi (uncredited)

'A good-natured romp, a pantomime for grown-ups that has more charm and more laughs in its 97 minutes than some other comedies can muster in a whole series of sequels.' – *Anwar Brett, Film Review*

Wedlock

US 1991 98m CFI color

Spectacor (Branko Lustig)

🖭 🖭 🎵

aka: *Deadlock*

Two convicts go on the run linked by electronic collars that will explode if they are more than a hundred yards apart.

Plodding, violent thriller which reaches the conclusion that it's acceptable to steal providing you can get away with it.

w Broderick Miller d Lewis Teague *ph* Dietrich Lohmann *m* Richard Gibbs *pd* Veronica Hadfield *ed* Carl Kress

☆ Rutger Hauer, Mimi Rogers, Joan Chen, James Remar

'Nice idea, unsatisfying results.' – *Sight and Sound*

Wee Geordie: see Geordie

'From Rudyard Kipling's Heroic Pen!'
Wee Willie Winkie **
👫 US 1937 99m bw
TCF (Gene Markey)
🎬

A small girl becomes the mascot of a British regiment in India.
Vaguely based on a Kipling tale, this was the most expensive Temple vehicle and a first-rate family action picture with sentimental asides.
w Ernest Pascal, Julien Josephson *story* Rudyard Kipling d John Ford ph Arthur Miller m Alfred Newman ad William S. Darling, David Hall
☆ Shirley Temple, Victor McLaglen, C. Aubrey Smith, June Lang, Michael Whalen, Cesar Romero, Constance Collier, Gavin Muir
'Will add another clean-up to her cycle, but those knees are losing their contour ... a pretentiously produced melodrama which launches the leading feminine box office star into a distinctly new phase of her career and story material.' – *Variety*
⚱ art direction

Weeds
US 1987 115m Technicolor
DEG/Kingsgate (Bill Badalato)

A prisoner serving a life sentence turns playwright and writes himself out of jail.
Intriguing claustrophobic drama of prison life and release, notable for some excellent performances.
w John Hancock, Dorothy Tristan d John Hancock ph Jan Weincke m Angelo Badalamenti pd Joseph T. Garrity ed Dennis M. O'Connor
☆ Nick Nolte, William Forsythe, Lane Smith, John Toles-Bey, Joe Mantegna, Ernie Hudson, Mark Rolston, Rita Taggart
† The film is loosely based on Rick Cluchey, who wrote a play while serving life in San Quentin prison and was paroled, forming a theatre group with other former convicts.

Week of the Killer: see *Cannibal Man*

Weekend ****
France/Italy 1968 103m Eastmancolor
Comacico/Copernic/Lira/Ascot
📼 🎬

A bourgeois couple leave Paris for the weekend and are caught in an endless traffic jam, where cars crash, tempers fray and savagery takes over.
A brilliant black satire at the expense of consumerism and conventional values.
wd Jean-Luc Godard ph Raoul Coutard m Antoine Duhamel, Mozart ed Agnes Guillemot
☆ Mireille Darc, Jean Yanne, Jean-Pierre Kalfon, Valerie Lagrange, Jean-Pierre Léaud, Yves Beneyton, Paul Gegauff
'Though deeply flawed, this film has more depth than any of Godard's earlier work. It's his vision of Hell and it ranks with the greatest.' – *Pauline Kael, New Yorker*

Weekend at Bernie's
US 1989 99m DuArt
Fox/Gladden (Victor Drai)
📼 🎬 🔊

Two minor executives, fearing that they will be blamed when they discover the murdered body of their boss on a weekend visit to his beach house, pretend that he is still alive.
Black farce that manages occasionally to amuse.
w Robert Klane d Ted Kotcheff ph François Protat m Andy Summers pd Peter Jamison ed Joan E. Chapman
☆ Andrew McCarthy, Jonathan Silverman, Catherine Mary Stewart, Terry Kiser, Don Calfa, Catherine Parks, Eloise Broady, Ted Kotcheff

Weekend at Bernie's II
US 1993 97m DeLuxe
Warner/Artimm/Victor Drai
📼 🎬 🔊

Two former employees of a murdered boss, as well as crooks and an insurance investigator, try to get their hands on the dead man's money, an attempt complicated by the fact that his corpse has been semi-revived in a voodoo ceremony.
Witless comedy which even the most frantic efforts at resuscitation by its cast cannot bring back to life.
wd Robert Klane ph Edward Morey III m Peter Wolf pd Michael Bolton ed Peck Prior

☆ Andrew McCarthy, Jonathan Silverman, Terry Kiser, Troy Beyer, Barry Bostwick, Tom Wright, Steve James

Weekend at the Waldorf *
US 1945 130m bw
MGM (Arthur Hornblow Jnr)
🎬

Four stories about guests at New York's largest hotel.
Disguised version of Grand Hotel, with the same stories twisted; the talent at hand, however, is serviceable rather than inspiring.
w Sam and Bella Spewack d Robert Z. Leonard ph Robert Planck md Johnny Green
☆ Ginger Rogers, Walter Pidgeon, Van Johnson, Lana Turner, Robert Benchley, Edward Arnold, Constance Collier, Leon Ames, Warner Anderson, Phyllis Thaxter, Keenan Wynn, Porter Hall, Samuel S. Hinds, George Zucco, Xavier Cugat

Weekend for Three
US 1941 66m bw
RKO (Tay Garnett)
A wife uses a male guest's attentions to excite her husband's jealousy.
Fairly ordinary comedy with moments of wit in the script.
w Dorothy Parker, Alan Campbell d Irving Reis
☆ Dennis O'Keefe, Jane Wyatt, Philip Reed, Edward Everett Horton, ZaSu Pitts, Franklin Pangborn

Weekend in Havana
US 1941 80m Technicolor
TCF (William Le Baron)
A shopgirl in Havana falls for a shipping executive.
Routine Fox musical showcasing familiar talents: adequate wartime escapist fare.
w Karl Tunberg, Darrell Ware d Walter Lang ph Ernest Palmer md Alfred Newman
☆ Alice Faye, John Payne, Carmen Miranda, Cesar Romero, Cobina Wright Jnr, George Barbier, Sheldon Leonard, Leonid Kinskey

Weekend Marriage
US 1932 64m bw
First National
GB title: *Weekend Lives*
A wife wants to remain independent.
Comedy drama with nothing new to say about a familiar subject.
w Sheridan Gibney *novel* Part-Time Wives by Faith Baldwin d Thornton Freeland
☆ Loretta Young, Norman Foster, George Brent, Aline MacMahon, Vivienne Osborne
'Unimportant rewrite on familiar theme minus necessary key strength.' – *Variety*

Weekend of Shadows
Australia 1977 95m Eastmancolor
Samson (Tom Jeffrey, Matt Carroll)
After a farmer's wife is found murdered, townspeople form a posse and search for the obvious suspect, a Polish worker who has gone missing.
A competent but uninspired drama exposing a small town's pettiness and intolerance.
w Peter Yeldham *novel* The Reckoning by Hugh Atkinson d Tom Jeffrey ph Richard Wallace m Charles Marawood ad Christopher Webster ed Rod Adamson
☆ John Waters, Graeme Blundell, Wyn Roberts, Graham Rouse, Melissa Jaffer, Keith Lee, Bill Hunter, Barbara West, Kit Taylor, Les Foxcroft, Bryan Brown

Weekend with Father
US 1951 83m bw
U-I (Ted Richmond)
A widow and a widower fall in love when taking their respective children to a summer camp.
Mechanical comedy of upsets and embarrassments.
w Joseph Hoffman d Douglas Sirk ph Clifford Stine m Frank Skinner
☆ Van Heflin, Patricia Neal, Gigi Perreau, Virginia Field, Richard Denning

Weird Science
US 1985 94m Technicolor
Universal (Joel Silver)
📼 🎬 🔊

Teenage science students create a woman from a computer.

Sex-obsessed frolics which go nowhere.
wd John Hughes ph Matthew F. Leonetti, Joseph Calloway m Ira Newborn pd John W. Corso ed Mark Warner, Christopher Lebenzon, Scott Wallace
☆ Anthony Michael Hall, Kelly Le Brock, Ilan Mitchell-Smith, Bill Paxton, Robert Downey Jnr

'She strikes with the curse of voodoo!'
Weird Woman
US 1944 64m bw
Universal
A professor brings home from the South Seas a wife who seems to bring murder in her wake.
Stiff and stilted thriller from an interesting original; one of the disappointing Inner Sanctum series.
w Brenda Weisberg *novel* Conjure Wife by Fritz Leiber d Reginald Le Borg
☆ Lon Chaney, Evelyn Ankers, Anne Gwynne, Ralph Morgan, Elizabeth Risdon

Welcome Danger *
US 1929 110m bw
Harold Lloyd
The meek son of a police chief gets involved in a tong war.
Moderate early talkie comedy showing the star in some trouble with pace and dialogue.
w Clyde Bruckman, Lex Neal, Felix Adler, Paul Gerard Smith d Clyde Bruckman ph Walter Lundin, Henry Kohler
☆ Harold Lloyd, Barbara Kent, Noah Young, Charles Middleton

Welcome Home: see *SNAFU*

Welcome Home
US 1989 92m Eastmancolor
Rank (Martin Ransohoff)
📼 🎬

Presumed dead in the Vietnamese war, a pilot who has acquired a Cambodian wife and two children returns after a 17-year absence to his American wife, who has remarried, and their teenage son.
Mundane, slow-moving drama that raises more questions than it answers.
w Maggie Kleinman d Franklin J. Schaffner ph Fred J. Koenekamp pd Dan Yarhi, Dennis Davenport ed Bob Swink
☆ Kris Kristofferson, JoBeth Williams, Brian Keith, Sam Waterston, Trey Wilson

Welcome Home Roxy Carmichael
US 1991 96m Technicolor
Castle Premier/ITC (Penney Finkelman Cox)
📼 🎬 🔊 🎧

An adopted teenage girl, who is unhappy at home, convinces herself that she is the illegitimate daughter of her small town's only celebrity.
Limp and unconvincing drama of fame and teenage angst.
w Karen Leigh Hopkins d Jim Abrahams ph Paul Elliott m Thomas Newman pd Dena Roth ed Bruce Green
☆ Winona Ryder, Jeff Daniels, Laila Robins, Thomas Wilson Brown, Joan McMurtrey, Graham Beckel, Frances Fisher, Robby Kiger
'Just another tale about a girl who discovers she's pretty in pink.' – *Sight and Sound*

Welcome Home Soldier Boys
US 1972 92m DeLuxe
TCF
Four war veterans go home and start a wave of violence.
Clumsily brutal anti-war tract which merely repels.
w Guerdon Trueblood d Richard Crompton
☆ Joe Don Baker, Paul Koslo, Alan Vint, Billy Green Bush

Welcome II The Terrordome
GB 1994 90m Technicolor
Metro Tartan/Non Aligned/Channel 4 (Simon Onwurah)
📼

An African family who walk into the sea to escape slavery in the 1650s are reincarnated in an apocalyptic future ghetto, where black gangs fight to control the drug trade before they unite against a common enemy.
An angry film about black suffering at the hands of whites, but couched in such second-hand terms with so unoriginal a scenario that it loses all meaning.

wd Ngozi Onwurah ph Alwin H. Kuchler m John Murphy, David A. Hughes, Black Radical Mk II pd Lindi Pankiv, Miraphora Mina ed Liz Webber
☆ Suzette Llewellyn, Saffron Burrows, Felix Joseph, Valentine Nonyela, Ben Wynter, Sian Martin, Jason Traynor
'Fails on all fronts. It's too ham-fisted to impress in purely cinematic terms, too pleasureless for the multiplexes, and too confused to stir any real debate.' – *Jonathan Romney, Guardian*
'Characters are one-dimensional mouthpieces, the dialogue seemingly pasted together from hip, US-influenced clichés, and Onwurah's visual language largely conservative and immobile. Performances border on the amateur.' – *Derek Elley, Variety*

Welcome Mr Washington
GB 1944 90m bw
British National/Shaftesbury
A US sergeant in an English village falls for a local lady.
Mild plea for harmony between allies; rather embarrassing to watch even at the time.
w Jack Whittingham *novel* Noel Streatfeild d Leslie Hiscott
☆ Barbara Mullen, Donald Stewart, Peggy Cummins, Graham Moffatt, Martita Hunt

Welcome Stranger
US 1947 107m bw
Paramount (Sol C. Siegel)
A genial young doctor fills in for a crusty old one on vacation in a small town.
Formula sentimental comedy, one of several reuniting the stars of Going My Way.
w Arthur Sheekman *story* Frank Butler d Elliott Nugent ph Lionel Lindon m Robert Emmett Dolan
☆ Bing Crosby, Barry Fitzgerald, Joan Caulfield, Wanda Hendrix, Frank Faylen, Elizabeth Patterson, Robert Shayne, Percy Kilbride

Welcome to Arrow Beach
US 1973 99m colour
Brut (Jack Cushingham)
🎬

aka: *Tender Flesh*
A photographer living in a California beach community has become a cannibal after his experiences in the Korean War.
Abysmal horror movie with insufficient plot.
w Wallace C. Bennett, Jack Gross Jnr d Laurence Harvey ph Gerald Perry Finnerman m Tony Camillo
☆ Laurence Harvey, Joanna Pettet, Stuart Whitman, John Ireland, Meg Foster

Welcome to Blood City
GB/Canada 1977 96m colour Panavision
EMI/Ben Herberman (Marilyn Stonehouse)
📼 🎬

A scientist in a totalitarian state becomes emotionally involved in an experiment to find killers by involving them in a fantasy life in a tough western town where murder is encouraged.
Risible science fiction, with a narrative that makes little sense, additionally hampered by mediocre performances.
w Stephen Schenck, Michael Winder d Peter Sasdy ph Reginald H. Morris m Roy Budd pd Jack McAdam ed Keith Palmer
☆ Jack Palance, Keir Dullea, Samantha Eggar, Hollis McLaren, Chris Wiggins, Barry Morse, Allan Royale, Henry Ramer, Ken James, John Evans
'Swiss-cheese script strains coherence and interest with each development.' – *Variety*

Welcome to Hard Times *
US 1967 103m Metrocolor
MGM/Max E. Youngstein, David Carr
GB title: *Killer on a Horse*
A small Western town arms itself against a mysterious bandit.
Curiously likeable, almost symbolic suspense Western which has a good start and middle but not much idea how to end.
wd Burt Kennedy *novel* E. L. Doctorow ph Harry Stradling Jnr m Harry Sukman
☆ Henry Fonda, Janice Rule, Keenan Wynn, Janis Paige, John Anderson, Warren Oates, Fay Spain, Edgar Buchanan, Aldo Ray, Lon Chaney Jnr, Elisha Cook Jnr

---

👫 film suitable for family viewing   📼 VHS video-cassette for the British PAL system   📼 VHS video-cassette for the British PAL system in wide screen-format   🎬 Video cassette in a computer-colourised version   🖥 American NTSC video-cassette   🎬 Laser disc

Welcome to LA *

US 1976 106m DeLuxe
Lion's Gate/Robert Altman

A young composer in Los Angeles has a varied sex life.
Fragmentary, vaguely mystical, momentarily interesting, frequently confusing slice of life as seen through misty glasses.
wd Alan Rudolph ph Dave Myers m Richard Baskin
☆ Keith Carradine, Sally Kellerman, Geraldine Chaplin, Harvey Keitel, Lauren Hutton, Viveca Lindfors, Sissy Spacek, Denver Pyle
'The supposedly free-form, improvisational dynamics of an Altman movie have here become a strictly choreographed ballet.' – *Richard Combs, MFB*

'For this celebrated, outrageous, adrenaline-loving bunch of reporters, home is the latest war zone. Now, one of them is about to do the unthinkable – get emotionally involved.'
'The true story of an extraordinary act of courage.'

Welcome to Sarajevo **

GB/US 1997 101m colour 'Scope
Film Four/Channel 4/Miramax (Graham Broadbent, Damian Jones)
▣ ▤ ℚ

Reporting the siege of Sarajevo by the Bosnian Serbs in 1992, a television journalist smuggles a young girl out to live in Britain with his family.
A fierce, polemical drama of the horrors of a civil war and a lack of political will among the Western powers that suddenly goes soft and manipulative; it is uneven, but very watchable.
w Frank Cottrell Boyce book *Natasha's Story* by Michael Nicholson d Michael Winterbottom ph Daf Hobson m Adrian Johnston pd Mark Geraghty ed Trevor Waite
☆ Stephen Dillane, Woody Harrelson, Marisa Tomei, Emira Nusevic, Kerry Fox, Goran Visnjic, James Nesbitt, Emily Lloyd, Juliet Aubrey
'A film of extremes, then, by turns brash and simplistic and utterly powerful. See it. Then argue.' – *Ian Nathan, Empire*

Welcome to the Club

GB 1970 88m bw
Welcome (Sam Lomberg)
Hiroshima 1945; an American Quaker sergeant upsets military protocol.
Pale satirical comedy shot in Copenhagen.
w Clement Biddle Wood novel Clement Biddle Wood d Walter Shenson ph Mikael Salomon m Ken Thorne
☆ Brian Foley, Jack Warden, Lee Meredith, Andy Jarrell

Welcome to the Dollhouse *

US 1995 88m DuArt
Artificial Eye/Suburban (Ted Skillman, Todd Solondz)
▣ ▤ ℚ ◠

An unattractive 11-year-old girl is ridiculed and ostracized at school and at home.
A tartly observant account of the damage that people can knowingly do to one another.
wd Todd Solondz ph Randy Drummond m Jill Wisoff pd Susan Block ed Alan Oxman
☆ Heather Matarazzo, Victoria Davis, Christina Brucato, Christina Vidal, Siri Howard, Brendan Sexton Jnr, Dana Kalinia, Matthew Faber
'A canny black comedy with plenty of adult appeal even though any school pupil will relate to each and every scene with a nasty chill of recognition.' – *Marianne Gray, Film Review*

'There's No Place Like Hell...'

Welcome to Woop Woop

Australia/GB 1997 102m colour
MGM/Goldwyn/AFFC/Scala/Unthank (Finola Dwyer)
▣ ▤

An American finds himself trapped in a small outback community, and married to the daughter of its tyrannical, boozy boss.
Bizarre comedy that attempts to satirise macho attitudes, but is rarely more than a irritating, slackly scripted muddle.
w Michael Thomas book *The Dead Heart* by Douglas Kennedy d Stephan Elliott ph Mike Molloy m Guy Gross pd Owen Paterson ed Martin Walsh
☆ Johnathon Schaech, Rod Taylor, Susie Porter, Dee Smart, Richard Moir, Maggie Kirkpatrick,

Paul Mercurio, Rachel Griffiths, Barry Humphries, Tina Louise
'Desperately unfunny...An incoherent mess of thrown-together scenes heaping scorn and ridicule on the Australian equivalent of Dogpatch, USA.' – *Stephen Holden, New York Times*

The Well *

US 1951 85m bw
Cardinal/Harry M. Popkin (Clarence Greene, Leo Popkin)
▤

A black child falls down a well, and the town unites to save her.
Forceful high-pitched melodrama, cut to a do-gooder pattern which became very familiar.
w Russel Rouse, Clarence Greene d Leo Popkin Russel Rouse ph Ernest Laszlo m Dimitri Tiomkin ed Chester Schaeffer
☆ Richard Rober, Henry Morgan, Barry Kelley, Christine Larson
⅋ script; editing

The Well Groomed Bride *

US 1946 75m bw
Paramount (Fred Kohlmar)
A naval officer searches San Francisco for a magnum of champagne with which to launch a ship.
Thin but cheerful star comedy.
w Claude Binyon, Robert Russell d Sidney Lanfield ph John F. Seitz m Roy Webb
☆ Ray Milland, Olivia de Havilland, Sonny Tufts, James Gleason, Constance Dowling, Percy Kilbride, Jean Heather

We'll Meet Again

GB 1942 84m bw
Columbia
A girl singer suffers while her boyfriend loves another.
Unassuming star vehicle for the Forces' Sweetheart.
w James Seymour, Howard Thomas d Phil Brandon
☆ Vera Lynn, Geraldo, Patricia Roc, Ronald Ward, Donald Gray, Frederick Leister

The Well-Digger's Daughter: see La Fille du Puisatier

'Paramount's thundering romance of the winning of the west!'

Wells Fargo *

US 1937 115m bw
Paramount (Frank Lloyd)
How the express delivery service was built up.
Large-scale, entertaining Western with overmuch emphasis on domestic issues.
w Paul Schofield, Gerald Geraghty, John Boland story Stuart N. Lake d Frank Lloyd ph Theodor Sparkuhl m Victor Young
☆ Joel McCrea, Bob Burns, Frances Dee, Lloyd Nolan, Henry O'Neill, Mary Nash, Ralph Morgan, John Mack Brown, Porter Hall, Clarence Kolb
'Big b.o. right across the playdate board.' – *Variety*

Wendy Cracked a Walnut

Australia 1990 87m colour
Rosen, Harper, Mortlock/ABC/Rough Diamond (John Edwards)
▤

US video title: *Almost*
An office worker, bored by her marriage to an accident-prone salesman, takes refuge in romantic fantasies.
Turgid comedy, devoid of wit or imagination; it does not work on any level.
w Suzanne Hawley d Michael Pattinson ph Jeffrey Malouf m Bruce Smeaton pd Leigh Tierney ed Michael Honey
☆ Rosanna Arquette, Bruce Spence, Hugo Weaving, Kerry Walker, Doreen Warburton, Desiree Smith
'A listless, laughless affair which suffers from dire miscasting and awkward direction.' – *Variety*

Went the Day Well? ***

GB 1942 92m bw
Ealing (S. C. Balcon)
▤

US title: *Forty-eight Hours*
Villagers resist when German paratroopers invade an English village and the squire proves to be a quisling.
Could-it-happen melodrama which made excellent wartime propaganda; generally well staged.
w Angus MacPhail, John Dighton, Diana Morgan story Graham Greene d Alberto Cavalcanti ph Wilkie Cooper m William Walton
☆ Leslie Banks, Elizabeth Allan, Frank Lawton, Basil Sydney, Valerie Taylor, Mervyn Johns, Edward Rigby, Marie Lohr, C. V. France, David Farrar
'At last, it seems, we are learning to make films with our own native material.' – *Sunday Times*
'It has the sinister, freezing beauty of an Auden prophecy come true.' – *James Agee*
'A refreshing, an exciting and an excellent film.' – *Documentary News Letter*

We're Going to Be Rich

GB 1938 80m bw
TCF
In the South African goldfields in 1880, a singer leaves her worthless husband for a publican.
First American attempt to take over Our Gracie; it didn't work, but the damage was done.
w Monty Banks, James Edward Grant, Rohama Siegel, Sam Hellman d Monty Banks
☆ Gracie Fields, Victor McLaglen, Brian Donlevy, Coral Browne, Gus McNaughton
'Will do well in England. In the States, will slide into the duals.' – *Variety*

We're in the Army Now: see Pack Up Your Troubles

We're in the Money

US 1935 65m bw
Warner
Adventures of female process servers working for a dizzy lawyer.
Minor comedy using up contract artistes.
w F. Hugh Herbert, Brown Holmes, Erwin Gelsey, George Bilson d Ray Enright
☆ Joan Blondell, Glenda Farrell, Hugh Herbert, Ross Alexander, Hobart Cavanaugh
'Only those exhibitors whose clients get hysterical on short notice will profit from it.' – *Variety*

We're No Angels *

US 1954 106m Technicolor Vistavision
Paramount (Pat Duggan)
▣ ▤ ℚ

Three escaped Devil's Island convicts help a downtrodden storekeeper and his family to outwit a scheming relative.
Whimsical, overstretched period comedy suffering from miscasting but with some pleasantries along the way.
w Ranald MacDougall play *La Cuisine des Anges* by Albert Husson d Michael Curtiz ph Loyal Griggs m Frederick Hollander
☆ Humphrey Bogart, Peter Ustinov, Aldo Ray, Joan Bennett, Basil Rathbone, Leo G. Carroll, John Smith

We're No Angels

US 1989 106m Technicolor Panavision
UIP/Paramount (Art Linson)
▣ ▤ ℚ ◠

Convicts on the run disguise themselves as priests and take refuge in a monastery.
Dismal remake that suggests its stars have little talent for comedy.
w David Mamet play *La Cuisine des Anges* by Albert Husson d Neil Jordan ph Philippe Rousselot m George Fenton pd Wolf Kroeger ed Mick Audsley, Joke Van Wijk
☆ Robert DeNiro, Sean Penn, Demi Moore, Hoyt Axton, Bruno Kirby, Ray McAnally, James Russo, Wallace Shawn, John C. Reilly, Jay Brazeau

'It's a circus! Something doing every minute!'

We're Not Dressing *

US 1934 77m bw
Paramount (Benjamin Glazer)
▤ ℚ

A spoiled heiress shipwrecked on a Pacific island is tamed by an easy-going sailor.

Pleasant, madly dated, light-hearted variation on a much-filmed play, resolving itself into a series of comic turns.
w Horace Jackson, Francis Martin, George Marion Jnr play *The Admirable Crichton* by J. M. Barrie d Norman Taurog ph Charles Lang songs Harry Revel, Mack Gordon
☆ Bing Crosby, Carole Lombard, George Burns, Gracie Allen, Leon Errol, Ethel Merman, Jay Henry, Ray Milland
'Tiptop audience appeal musical.' – *Variety*

We're Not Married *

US 1952 85m bw
TCF (Nunnally Johnson)
Six couples find that they were never legally married.
Amiable, smartly-played compendium of sketches on a familiar theme.
w Nunnally Johnson d Edmund Goulding ph Leo Tover m Cyril Mockridge
☆ Ginger Rogers, Fred Allen, Victor Moore, Paul Douglas, Eve Arden, Marilyn Monroe, David Wayne, Louis Calhern, Zsa Zsa Gabor, Mitzi Gaynor, Eddie Bracken, James Gleason, Jane Darwell

We're on the Jury

US 1937 71m bw
RKO
Disagreements break out in the jury room after a murder trial.
More comedy than drama, a modest remake of Ladies of the Jury (qv).
w Franklin Coen play John Frederick Ballard d Ben Holmes
☆ Helen Broderick, Victor Moore, Philip Huston, Louise Latimer, Robert McWade
'Good secondary b.o. value.' – *Variety*

We're Only Human

US 1936 67m bw
RKO (Edward Kaufman)
A police sergeant loses a convicted prisoner and catches him again.
Routine bang-bang melodrama with unconvincing dialogue.
w Rian James story Thomas Walsh d James Flood ph J. Roy Hunt ad Van Nest Polglase
☆ Preston Foster, Jane Wyatt, James Gleason, Arthur Hohl, Jane Darwell, Christian Rub, Moroni Olsen, Mischa Auer
'Nothing which will raise it above double-feature standards.' – *Variety*

The Werewolf

US 1956 80m bw
Columbia/Clover (Sam Katzman)
In a small mountain town, a victim of radiation exposure periodically becomes a werewolf and is hounded down.
Absurd and tedious thriller which wastes an interesting background.
w Robert E. Kent, James B. Gordon d Fred F. Sears ph Edwin Linden m Mischa Bakaleinikoff
☆ Steven Ritch, Don McGowan, Joyce Holden

Werewolf of London *

US 1935 75m bw
Universal (Stanley Bergerman)
▤ ℚ

Werewolves fight for a rare Tibetan flower with curative properties.
Patchy horror film which lurches from excellent suspense scenes to tedious chunks of superfluous dialogue. In many ways a milestone in the history of its kind.
w Robert Harris d Stuart Walker ph Charles Stumar m Karl Hajos
☆ Henry Hull, Warner Oland, Valerie Hobson, Spring Byington, Lester Matthews, Zeffie Tilbury, Ethel Griffies
'Horror attempt that doesn't horrify sufficiently. Requires a build-up and may disappoint.' – *Variety*

The Werewolf of Washington

US 1973 90m colour
Millco (Nina Schulman)
▣ ▤

The US President attempts to cover up the fact that a White House press secretary has turned werewolf and is running amok.

⊚ Digital Video Disc Region 2   ⊚ Digital Video Disc Region 1   ◠ Soundtrack released on compact disc   ✦ Cast in approximate order of importance   † Points of interest   ♫ Notable songs   ▲ Academy Award   ⅋ Academy Award nomination   ⓦ BAFTA

A political satire in the aftermath of Watergate that lacks bite and fails as a horror spoof.
wd Milton Moses Ginsberg ph Bob Baldwin m Arnold Freed ad Nancy Miller-Corwin sp Bob Obradovich
☆ Dean Stockwell, Biff McGuire, Clifton James, Michael Dunn, Beeson Carroll, Thayer David

Werewolf Woman (dubbed)
Italy 1976 100m colour
Agora/Dialchi (Diego Alchimede)
original title: La Lupa Mannara
US title: Legend of the Wolf Woman
A woman becomes a werewolf to satisfy her sexual and murderous appetites.
Trivial mix of sex and horror, directed without style.
wd Rino Di Silvestro ph Mario Capriotti m Coriolano Gori ed Angelo Curi
☆ Annik Borel, Frederick Stafford, Dagmar Lassander, Tino Carraro, Elio Zamuto, Osvaldo Ruggieri, Andrea Scotti, Howard Ross (Renato Rossini)
† According to the credits, the English language version was written and directed by Tony La Penna.

'Freddy's Back in the Best "Nightmare" Ever!'
'...Missed me?'
Wes Craven's New Nightmare
US 1994 112m Foto-Kem
Rank/New Line (Marianne Maddalena)
Wes Craven explains that he is making a new film in a series that concluded with Freddy's Dead: The Final Nightmare because it is the only way to prevent the evil represented by Freddy becoming manifest in the real world.
A strange mixture of fantasy and what passes for reality in Hollywood, with Heather Langenkamp playing herself as the star of the first Elm Street film but being given a fictional life as a wife and mother threatened by Freddy. The result is likely to appeal to the diminishing audience for the series, but to few others.
wd Wes Craven ph Mark Irwin m J. Peter Robinson pd Cynthia Charette ed Patrick Lussier sp visual effects: Flash Film Works; Digital Filmworks; make-up effects: Kurtzman, Nicotero & Berger
☆ Robert Englund, Miko Hughes, David Newsome, Tracy Middendorf, Heather Langenkamp, John Saxon, Wes Craven
'Craven is still one of the horror cinema's most imaginative creators of purely frightening moments.' – Kim Newman, Sight and Sound
† The film is a self-referential sequel to the Nightmare on Elm Street series (qv).

West Beirut: see West Beyrouth

West Beyrouth **
France/Lebanon/Belgium/Norway 1998 109m colour 'Scope
Metrodome/La Sept/Arte/Douri/Ciné Libre/Exposed/Bjorn Eivind Aarskog (Rachid Bouchareb, Jean Brehat)
aka: West Beirut
In 1975, an adolescent Muslim youth experiences the outbreak of a civil war that divided his city.
Energetic, free-wheeling drama of war as seen through the eyes of teenagers, who find freedom and excitement in the situation.
wd Ziad Doueiri ph Ricardo Jacques Gale m Stewart Copeland ad Hamzé Nasrallah ed Dominique Marcombe
☆ Rami Doueiri, Mohamad Chamas, Rola Al Amin, Carmen Lebbos, Joseph Bou Nassar, Liliane Nemry, Leila Karam, Hassan Frahat
'A technically polished, frequently funny and emotionally affecting work.' – Lisa Nesselson, Variety

West Eleven
GB 1963 93m bw
ABP/Daniel M. Angel (Vivian Cox)
A young London drifter is offered £10,000 to commit murder.
Dingy but not very convincing 'realist' melodrama with a jazzy style which induces weariness.
w Keith Waterhouse, Willis Hall novel The Furnished Room by Laura del Rivo d Michael Winner ph Otto Heller m Stanley Black, Acker Bilk

☆ Alfred Lynch, Eric Portman, Kathleen Harrison, Diana Dors, Kathleen Breck, Freda Jackson, Finlay Currie, Harold Lang

West of Broadway
US 1932 68m bw
MGM
A millionaire gets married while drunk and regrets it the next day.
Unappetizing light drama which did no good to anyone concerned with it.
w Gene Markey, J. K. McGuinness, Ralph Graves, Bess Meredyth d Harry Beaumont
☆ John Gilbert, El Brendel, Lois Moran, Madge Evans, Ralph Bellamy, Frank Conroy, Hedda Hopper
'Rates neighbourhood and grind spotting only.' – Variety

West of Montana: see Mail Order Bride

West of Shanghai
US 1937 64m bw
Warner
Fugitives in the Far East are saved by the self-sacrifice of a Chinese war lord.
Unpersuasive melodrama remade from The Bad Man (1930), heavily depending on a star performance.
w Crane Wilbur d John Farrow
☆ Boris Karloff, Beverly Roberts, Ricardo Cortez, Gordon Oliver, Vladimir Sokoloff
† First released as Warlord.

West of the Divide
US 1933 54m bw
Monogram/Lone Star (Paul Malvern)
A cowboy who is searching for his long-lost brother impersonates a killer in order to expose a crooked rancher.
John Wayne gets the girl, the boy and a ranch in this otherwise routine Western.
wd Robert N. Bradbury ph Archie Stout ed Carl Pierson
☆ John Wayne, Virginia Faire Brown, George Hayes, Lloyd Whitlock, Yakima Canutt, Lafe McKee, Billie O'Brien

West of the Pecos
US 1934 70m bw
RKO
In Texas after the Civil War a girl masquerades as a boy in order to get things done.
Moderate Western.
w Milton Krims, John Twist novel Zane Grey d Phil Rosen
☆ Richard Dix, Martha Sleeper, Samuel S. Hinds, Fred Kohler, Louise Beavers, Willie Best ('Sleen 'n Eat')
'Superior entertainment of the horse opera type.' – Variety
† It was remade in 1945, directed by Edward Killy and starring Robert Mitchum and Barbara Hale.

West of Zanzibar
US 1928 70m bw silent
MGM
A paralysed magician turned ivory trader settles an old score.
Corny star vehicle remade in 1932 as Kongo, with Walter Huston.
w Waldemar Young, Elliott Clawson d Tod Browning
☆ Lon Chaney, Lionel Barrymore, Jacqueline Gadsden, Mary Nolan

West of Zanzibar
GB 1954 94m Technicolor
Ealing (Leslie Norman)
Native tribesmen move towards Mombasa and are drawn into ivory smuggling.
Fairly feeble follow-up to Where No Vultures Fly; quite good to look at but clearly not an original.
w Max Catto, Jack Whittingham d Harry Watt ph Paul Beeson m Alan Rawsthorne
☆ Anthony Steel, Sheila Sim, William Simons, Orlando Martins, Martin Benson, Edric Connor, Howard Marion Crawford

West Point of the Air
US 1935 90m bw
MGM (Monta Bell)
The army sergeant father of an air cadet has great hopes for him.
Routine sentimental flagwaver.
w James K. McGuinness, John Monk Saunders, Frank Wead, Arthur J. Beckhard d Richard Rosson ph Clyde de Vinna, Charles A. Marshall, Elmer Dyer m Charles Maxwell
☆ Wallace Beery, Robert Young, Maureen O'Sullivan, Lewis Stone, James Gleason, Rosalind Russell, Russell Hardie, Henry Wadsworth, Robert Taylor
'Trite story holds it down to just moderate entertainment rating.' – Variety

West Point Story *
US 1950 107m bw
Warner (Louis F. Edelman)
GB title: Fine and Dandy
A Broadway producer stages a show at the military academy.
Thin and rather tedious musical saved by its irrepressible star.
w John Monks Jnr, Charles Hoffman, Irving Wallace d Roy del Ruth ph Sid Hickox md Ray Heindorf songs Sammy Cahn, Jule Styne
☆ James Cagney, Virginia Mayo, Doris Day, Gordon MacRae, Gene Nelson, Alan Hale Jnr, Roland Winters, Jerome Cowan
♪ Ray Heindorf

West Side Story ****
US 1961 155m Technicolor
Panavision 70
(UA) Mirisch/Seven Arts (Robert Wise)
The Romeo and Juliet story in a New York dockland setting.
The essentially theatrical conception of this entertainment is nullified by determinedly realistic settings, but production values are fine and the song numbers electrifying.
w Ernest Lehman play Arthur Laurents, after William Shakespeare d Robert Wise, Jerome Robbins ph Daniel L. Fapp m/ly Leonard Bernstein, Stephen Sondheim ch Jerome Robbins pd Boris Leven ed Thomas Stanford cos Irene Sharaff
☆ Natalie Wood (sung by Marni Nixon), Richard Beymer (sung by Jimmy Bryant), Russ Tamblyn, Rita Moreno (sung by Betty Wand), George Chakiris, Simon Oakland, Bill Bramley, Tucker Smith, Tony Mordente, Tony Winters, Eliot Feld
† Jerome Robbins also received an honorary Oscar for 'his brilliant achievements in the art of choreography on film.'
♦ best picture; Robert Wise, Jerome Robbins; Daniel L. Fapp; Rita Moreno; George Chakiris; Thomas Stanford; Irene Sharaff; musical direction (Saul Chaplin, Johnny Green, Sid Ramin, Irwin Kostal); art direction; sound
♪ Ernest Lehman

Westbound
US 1959 69m Warnercolor
Warner
A stagecoach manager is entrusted with Californian gold, which attracts assorted villains.
Stalwart star Western which served its purpose.
w Berne Giler d Budd Boetticher ph J. Peverell Marley m David Buttolph
☆ Randolph Scott, Virginia Mayo, Karen Steele, Andrew Duggan, Michael Pate

Westbound Limited
US 1937 76m bw
Universal (Henry MacRae, Ben Koenig)
A railway employee becomes a fugitive when he is wrongly convicted of causing a train crash that killed 27 passengers.
Conventional melodrama of redemption through love, though the rail system seems more than somewhat accident-prone.
w Maurice Geraghty story Ford Beebe d Ford Beebe ph Elwood Bredell md Charles Previn ad Ralph DeLacy ed Philip Cahn
☆ Lyle Talbot, Polly Rowles, Frank Reicher, Henry Brandon, Henry Hunter, William Lundigan

Western *
France 1997 134m colour Panavision
Artificial Eye/Salomé-Diaphana (Maurice Bernart, Michel Saint-Jean)
A travelling salesman loses his car, his job and his girlfriend but finds friendship on the road with the Russian hitch-hiker who robbed him.
Amiable road movie of contrasting masculinities, marked by a gently observant humour.
w Manuel Poirier, Jean-François Goyet d Manuel Poirier ph Nara Keo Kosal m Bernardo Sandoval ad Roland Mabille ed Yann Dedet
☆ Sergi Lopez, Sacha Bourdo, Elisabeth Vitali, Marie Matheron

Western Approaches ***
GB 1944 83m Technicolor
Crown Film Unit
US title: The Raider
Torpedoed merchantmen in the Atlantic are used by a U-boat as a decoy.
A fictional story is played to great documentary effect by men of the allied navies. One of the outstanding 'factual' films of the war years.
wd Pat Jackson ph Jack Cardiff m Clifton Parker
'Without a doubt the best sea film in existence.' – Daily Mail

Western Union **
US 1941 94m Technicolor
TCF (Harry Joe Brown)
Politicians and crooks hamper the laying of cross-country cables.
First-rate Western with familiar excitements.
w Robert Carson novel Zane Grey d Fritz Lang ph Edward Cronjager m David Buttolph
☆ Randolph Scott, Robert Young, Dean Jagger, Virginia Gilmore, Slim Summerville, John Carradine, Chill Wills, Barton MacLane

'Two women helped him overthrow the most ruthless power in the west!'
The Westerner **
US 1940 99m bw
Samuel Goldwyn
Judge Roy Bean comes to grief through his love for Lily Langtry.
Moody, melodramatic Western with comedy touches; generally entertaining, the villain more so than the hero.
w Jo Swerling, Niven Busch story Stuart N. Lake d William Wyler ph Gregg Toland m Dimitri Tiomkin ad James Basevi
☆ Gary Cooper, Walter Brennan, Doris Davenport, Fred Stone, Paul Hurst, Chill Wills, Charles Halton, Forrest Tucker, Dana Andrews, Lillian Bond, Tom Tyler
♟ Walter Brennan
♪ Stuart N. Lake; James Basevi

Westward Ho the Wagons
US 1956 85m Technicolor
Cinemascope
Walt Disney (Bill Walsh)
A wagon train defends itself against Indians.
Slow and simple-minded family Western.
w Tom Blackburn d William Beaudine ph Charles Boyle m Paul Smith
☆ Fess Parker, Kathleen Crowley, Jeff York, David Stollery, Sebastian Cabot, George Reeves

Westward Passage
US 1932 73m bw
RKO (David O. Selznick)
A wealthy girl weds a poor novelist but wants the rich full life for their children.
Dogged romantic drama with only the casting of interest.
w Bradley King, Humphrey Pearson novel Margaret Ayer Barnes d Robert Milton ph Lucien Andriot m Max Steiner
☆ Ann Harding, Laurence Olivier, ZaSu Pitts, Irving Pichel, Juliette Compton, Florence Roberts
'Slow, prone to be dull, and hardly warm weather theatre inducement.' – Variety

Westward the Women *
US   1951   118m   bw
MGM (Dore Schary)
In the 1850s an Indian scout leads 150 Chicago
women to meet husbands in California.
*Good-looking episodic Western, apparently intended
mainly to amuse but seldom rising to the occasion.*
w Charles Schnee d William Wellman
ph William Mellor m Jeff Alexander
☆ Robert Taylor, Denise Darcel, John McIntire,
Marilyn Erskine, Hope Emerson, Lenore Lonergan,
Julie Bishop

'Where nothing can possibly go worng...'

Westworld **
US   1973   89m   Metrocolor   Panavision
MGM (Paul N. Lazarus III)
◉◉ ▤ ◎ ⊚
In a millionaire holiday resort which recreates the
past, a Western badman robot goes berserk and
relentlessly attacks two visitors.
*Unusual and amusing but under-produced melodrama
with slipshod story development and continuity, atoned
for by memorable moments and underlying excitement.*
wd Michael Crichton ph Gene Polito m Fred
Karlin ad Herman Blumenthal
☆ Yul Brynner, Richard Benjamin, James Brolin,
Norman Bartold, Alan Oppenheimer
† It was followed by a sequel, *Futureworld* (q.v.).

The Wet Parade *
US   1932   122m   bw
MGM (Hunt Stromberg)
A politician points to the corruption caused by
prohibition.
Sociologically interesting melodrama.
w John Lee Mahin novel Upton Sinclair
d Victor Fleming ph George Barnes m William
Axt
☆ Walter Huston, Myrna Loy, Neil Hamilton,
Lewis Stone, Jimmy Durante, Wallace Ford,
Dorothy Jordan, John Miljan, Robert Young
'Final impression strongly anti-liquor, but outside
of reaction that may bring, picture hasn't much
chance. What it lacks as entertainment isn't
covered by propaganda possibilities.' – *Variety*

Wetherby *
GB   1985   97m   Technicolor
Greenpoint/Film Four/Zenith (Simon Relph)
▤
After a party at the home of a lonely and frustrated
woman, a young man shoots himself.
*Interesting if rather irritating drama which leaves as
many puzzles as it solves.*
wd David Hare ph Stuart Harris m Nick Bicat
pd Hayden Griffin
☆ Vanessa Redgrave, Ian Holm, Judi Dench, Tim
McInnerny, Stuart Wilson

We've Never Been Licked
US   1943   103m   bw
Universal (Walter Wanger)
GB title: *Texas to Tokyo*
A young American raised in Japan finds himself on
the wrong side after Pearl Harbor.
Shoddy flagwaver, low on talent and inspiration.
w Norman Reilly Raine, Nick Grinde d John
Rawlins
☆ Richard Quine, Anne Gwynne, Noah Beery
Jnr, Harry Davenport, Martha O'Driscoll, William
Frawley, Robert Mitchum

Whale Music *
Canada   1994   112m   Alpha Cine
Alliance/Cape Scott (Raymond Massey, Steven
DeNure)
The decaying mansion of an ageing, overweight,
reclusive rock musician, who is tormented by the
past, is invaded by a teenage girl on the run from
the law.
*Gently offbeat drama of an unlikely relationship which
gains interest from its leading performance and its
literate script, though the music is less convincing as the
work of a pop genius.*
w Paul Quarrington, Richard J. Lewis novel Paul
Quarrington d Richard J. Lewis ph Vic Sarin
m George Blondheim, Rheostatics pd Rex Raglan
ed Richard Martin
☆ Maury Chaykin, Cyndy Preston, Jennifer Dale,
Paul Gross, Blu Mankuma, Alan Jordan, Kenneth
Welsh
'Has decided artistic assets, but doesn't connect
on an emotional level.' – *Leonard Klady, Variety*

The Whales of August *
US   1987   90m   TVC Color
Circle/Nelson (Carolyn Pfeiffer, Mike Kaplan)
◉◉ ▤ ◎ ◠
Two elderly sisters live on the Maine coast and
think of the past.
*Edgy, sympathetic talk-piece in which old ladies prove
that they are still stars.*
w David Berry novel David Berry d Lindsay
Anderson ph Mike Fash m Alan Price
pd Joselyn Herbert
☆ Bette Davis, Lillian Gish, Vincent Price, Ann
Sothern, Harry Carey Jnr, Mary Steenburgen,
Tisha Sterling
'Lovely on all counts.' – *Daily Variety*
⅄ Ann Sothern

'He had a price on his head ... she had a price on her
heart!'
Wharf Angel
US   1934   65m   bw
Paramount
To quote *Variety*, prostie goes softie for sailor with
murder rap hanging over his head.
Dim little fogbound melodrama.
w Sam Hoffenstein, Frank Partos, Steve Avery,
Frederick Schlick d William Cameron Menzies,
George Somnes
☆ Victor McLaglen, Dorothy Dell, Preston Foster,
Alison Skipworth
'Poor stuff for de luxe audiences: old-fashioned,
drab, lacking in box office draw.' – *Variety*

What?
Italy/France/West Germany   1972   113m
Eastmancolor   Todd-AO 35
Gala/C.C. Champion/Concordia/Dieter Geissler (Carlo
Ponti)
▤
original title: *Che?*
An American hitch-hiker, who is forever losing
her clothes, seeks refuge in the home of an Italian
millionaire full of curious and lecherous guests.
*Eccentric comedy of innocence and experience that
works only fitfully.*
w Gerard Brach, Roman Polanski d Roman
Polanski ph Marcello Gatti, Giuseppe Ruzzolini
m Schubert, Mozart, Beethoven md Claudio Gizzi
pd Aurelio Crugnola ed Alastair McIntyre
☆ Sydne Rome, Marcello Mastroianni, Hugh
Griffith, Romolo Valli, Guido Alberti, Roman
Polanski
'Despite its erratic moments of brilliance, the
overall impression left by the film is of a rather
puerile graffito scrawled in the margins of its
literary antecedants.' – *Jan Dawson, MFB*
'Far from being a masterpiece and several
notches below being even a good film, but it
does stand in danger of being seriously
underrated – not to say dismissed – by virtue of
its gaudy wrapping.' – *Derek Elley, Films and
Filming*

What a Carve Up
GB   1961   88m   bw
New World/Baker-Berman
◉◉ ▤
A madman fakes his own death in order to murder
his relatives.
*Spooky house farce, allegedly a remake of The Ghoul
but bearing little resemblance to it.*
w Ray Cooney, Tony Hilton novel *The Ghoul* by
Frank King d Pat Jackson ph Monty Berman
m Muir Mathieson
☆ Sid James, Kenneth Connor, Shirley Eaton,
Dennis Price, Donald Pleasence, Michael Gough,
Valerie Taylor

What a Chassis: see *La Belle Américaine*

What a Crazy World
⃛ GB   1963   88m   bw
Capricorn/AB Pathé (Michael Carreras)
A working-class London boy sets out to be a rock-
and-roller.
Unsurprising star musical, quite lively of its kind.
w Alan Klein play Alan Klein d Michael
Carreras
☆ Joe Brown, Susan Maughan, Marty Wilde,
Harry H. Corbett, Avis Bunnage

What a Life
US   1939   75m   bw
Paramount
Henry Aldrich has difficulties in high school.
*First of the domestic comedy series (see under Henry)
which became more farcical and had a different cast;
this episode closely followed the Broadway success.*
w Charles Brackett, Billy Wilder play Clifford
Goldsmith d Theodore Reed
☆ Jackie Cooper, Betty Field, John Howard,
Janice Logan, Lionel Stander, Hedda Hopper,
Dorothy Stickney
'A fine comedy drama, excellent for family
trade.' – *Variety*

What a Man: see *Never Give a Sucker an Even
Break*

What a Way to Go *
US   1964   111m   DeLuxe   Cinemascope
TCF/APJAC/Orchard (Arthur P. Jacobs)
An immensely rich girl tells her psychiatrist how
all her husbands proved not only successful but
accident-prone.
*Wild, mainly agreeable, star-and-gag-laden black
comedy which starts on too high a note and fails to
sustain.*
w Betty Comden, Adolph Green d J. Lee-
Thompson ph Leon Shamroy md Nelson Riddle
ly Betty Comden, Adolph Green songs Jule Styne
☆ Shirley MacLaine, Bob Cummings, Dick Van
Dyke, Robert Mitchum, Gene Kelly, Dean Martin,
Paul Newman, Reginald Gardiner, Margaret
Dumont

What a Woman
US   1943   90m   bw
Columbia
aka: *The Beautiful Cheat*
An author's agent gets into romantic escapades
with her writers.
Ho-hum romantic comedy, quickly forgotten.
w Therese Lewis, Barry Trivers d Irving
Cummings
☆ Rosalind Russell, Brian Aherne, Willard Parker,
Ann Savage, Alan Dinehart

What about Bob? *
US   1991   99m   Technicolor
Warner/Touchstone/Touchwood Pacific Partners I
(Laura Ziskin)
◉◉ ▤ ◎
A disturbed patient moves in on holidaying
psychiatrist and his equally disturbed family.
Intermittently amusing black comedy.
w Tom Schulman story Alvin Sargent, Laura
Ziskin d Frank Oz ph Michael Ballhaus m Miles
Goodman pd Les Dilley ed Anne V. Coates
☆ Bill Murray, Richard Dreyfuss, Julie Hagerty,
Charlie Korsmo, Kathryn Erbe, Tom Aldredge,
Susan Willis
'Frank Oz proves that he's a director with just
the mean sense of humor these bland times
desperately need.' – *Richard Schickel, Time*

'Off to grandmother's house they go, For love in the
attic and death down below!'
What Became of Jack and Jill?
GB   1971   90m   DeLuxe
Palomar/Amicus (Milton Subotsky)
A young man tries to hasten his grandmother's
death but she has the last laugh.
Feeble suspenser with a dim ending.
w Roger Marshall novel *The Ruthless Ones* by
Laurence Moody d Bill Bain ph Gerry Turpin
m Carl Davis
☆ Vanessa Howard, Paul Nicholas, Mona
Washbourne, Peter Copley, Peter Jeffrey

What Changed Charley Farthing
GB   1975   101m   Eastmancolor
Patina-Hidalgo (Tristam Cones)
▤
US title: *The Bananas Boat*
A philandering sailor has adventures in Cuba.
*Weirdly ineffective comedy actioner which never gets
started and should never have been thought of.*
w David Pursall, Jack Seddon novel Mark
Hebdon d Sidney Hayers ph Graham Edgar
m Angela Arteaga
☆ Doug McClure, Lionel Jeffries, Warren
Mitchell, Hayley Mills, Dilys Hamlett, Fernando
Sancho

What Did You Do in the War, Daddy?
US   1966   115m   DeLuxe   Panavision
UA/Mirisch/Geoffrey (Owen Crump, Blake Edwards)
▤
In 1943, an Italian town surrenders readily to the
Americans providing its wine festival and football
match can take place.
*Silly war comedy with insufficient jokes for its
wearisome length. The performances are bright enough.*
w William Peter Blatty d Blake Edwards
ph Philip Lathrop m Henry Mancini
☆ James Coburn, Dick Shawn, Sergio Fantoni,
Giovanna Ralli, Aldo Ray, Harry Morgan, Carroll
O'Connor, Leon Askin

'Where One World Ends, Another Begins.'
'After Life There Is More.'
What Dreams May Come
US   1998   113m   Monaco Film Lab
Panavision
Polygram/Interscope/Metafilmics (Stephen Simon,
Barnet Bain)
◉◉ ▤ ◎
A doctor, whose two children die in a car crash, is
himself later killed in another crash; they all meet
in the afterlife, and when his widow commits
suicide, he sets out to rescue her from hell.
*Hollywood's brand of warm, huggy theology gets ever
stranger: heaven here is a gooey oil painting,
psychobabble is the angelic language, there's no deity in
view, and the occupants can't wait to leave the place
and get back to Earth. The mind boggles.*
w Ron Bass novel Richard Matheson d Vincent
Ward ph Eduardo Serra m Michael Kamen
pd Eugenio Zanetti ed David Brenner, Maysie
Hoy sp visual fx: Joel Hynek, Nicholas Brooks,
Stuart Robertson, Kevin Mack
☆ Robin Williams, Cuba Gooding Jnr, Annabella
Sciorra, Max von Sydow, Jessica Brooks Grant,
Josh Paddock, Rosalind Chao
'All the weeping and hugging the characters do
can't make up for the film's fatal lack of texture
and psychological nuance.' – *Stephen Holden,
New York Times*
♨ visual effects
⅄ Eugenio Zanetti

What Every Woman Knows *
US   1934   90m   bw
MGM
A quiet little wife encourages her husband into
parliament.
*Adequate version of the sentimental play, very
pleasantly acted.*
w Monckton Hoffe, John Meehan, James Kevin
McGuinness play J. M. Barrie d Gregory La Cava
☆ Helen Hayes, Brian Aherne, Madge Evans,
Lucile Watson, Dudley Digges, Henry Stephenson,
Donald Crisp, David Torrence
'Cinch b.o., a swell woman's picture.' – *Variety*

What Happened to Santiago *
Puerto Rico   1989   100m   colour
Dios Los Cria (Pedro Muñiz)
original title: *Lo que le pasó de Santiago*
An accountant retires and falls for a woman with a
mysterious past.
*A gently charming domestic drama, most likely to
appeal to the over-50s.*
wd Jacobo Morales ph Augustin Cubano
m Pedro Rivera Toledo ad Ivonne Torres
ed Alfonso Borrell
☆ Tommy Muñiz, Gladys Rodriguez, Johanna
Rosaly, René Monclova, Pedro Javier Muñiz,
Jacobo Morales
⅄ Best foreign language film

What Have I Done to Deserve This? *
Spain   1984   101m   colour
Metro/Tesauro/Kaktus (Tadeo Villalba)
◉◉ ▤ ◎
original title: *Que He Hecho Yo Para Merecer Esto?*
A slum family falls apart, to the indifference of the
busy mother, who takes drugs to keep her awake as
she works hard as a cleaner.
*Fast-paced inconsequential black comedy, lacking any
internal coherence as it rushes from one tasteless joke to
another.*
wd Pedro Almodóvar ph Angel Luis Fernandez
m Bernardo Bonezzi ed Jose Solcedo
☆ Carmen Maura, Luis Hostalot, Angel de
Andres-Lopez, Gonzalo Suarez, Veronica Forque,
Juan Martinez, Miguel Angel Harranz
'Almodóvar is an underground theatre clown.
He may not know how to make anything stay

with you – he may not even care to. He just likes to put on a show. Some of the vignettes might be comedy classics if their timing weren't so sloppy.' – *Pauline Kael, New Yorker*

What Lola Wants: see *Damn Yankees*

What, No Beer?
US   1933   65m   bw
MGM
🎦
A barber rushes to be first on the market with beer after its legalization, but finds himself premature and at odds with gangsters.
Topical farce ending in a slapstick mêlée.
w Carey Wilson, Jack Cluett, Robert E. Hopkins d Edward Sedgwick
☆ Buster Keaton, Jimmy Durante, Roscoe Ates, Phyllis Barry, John Miljan, Henry Armetta
'A commercial little laugh picture.' – *Variety*

What Price Glory? *
US   1952   111m   Technicolor
TCF (Sol C. Siegel)
🎦 🎦
In 1917 France Captain Flagg and Sergeant Quirt spar for the same girl.
Stagey remake of the celebrated silent film and play; watchable if not exactly inspired.
w Phoebe and Henry Ephron *play* Maxwell Anderson, Laurence Stallings d John Ford ph Joe MacDonald m Alfred Newman
☆ James Cagney, Dan Dailey, Corinne Calvet, William Demarest, Robert Wagner, Marisa Pavan, James Gleason

'A heart-touching drama of the world, the flesh and the movies!'
What Price Hollywood? *
US   1932   87m   bw
RKO (Pandro S. Berman)
🎦
A waitress becomes a film star with the help of a drunken director who later commits suicide.
Fairly trenchant early study of the mores of the film city, later revamped as A Star Is Born.
w Ben Markson, Gene Fowler, Rowland Brown, Jane Murfin *story* Adela Rogers St John d George Cukor ph Charles Rosher m Max Steiner montage Slavko Vorkapich
☆ Constance Bennett, Lowell Sherman, Neil Hamilton, Gregory Ratoff, Brooks Benedict, Louise Beavers, Eddie Anderson
'Many of the scenes are like sketches for the later versions, but this film has its own interest, especially because of its glimpses into the studio life of the time.' – *New Yorker, 1977*
👤 Adela Rogers St John, Jane Murfin

What Shall It Profit: see *Hard Steel*

What the Butler Saw
GB   1950   61m   bw
Exclusive/Hammer (Anthony Hinds)
Returning home with his master, the former governor of a tropical island, a butler is followed by the love-struck daughter of the island's king.
A dull comedy that was dated at the time of its release and has acquired no period charm since.
w A. R. Rawlinson, E. J. Mason *story* Roger and Donald Good d Godfrey Grayson ph Walter Harvey md Frank Spencer ed James Needs
☆ Edward Rigby, Henry Mollison, Michael Ward, Eleanor Hallam, Peter Burton, Anne Valery, Mercy Haystead

What Waits Below: see *Secrets of the Phantom Caverns*

Whatever Happened to Aunt Alice? *
US   1969   101m   Metrocolor
Palomar/Associates and Aldrich (Robert Aldrich)
🎦
A genteel widow murders her housekeepers for their private incomes.
Ladylike shocker with some black humour and good performances.
w Theodore Apstein *novel* The Forbidden Garden by Ursula Curtiss d Lee H. Katzin ph Joseph Biroc m Gerald Fried
☆ Geraldine Page, Ruth Gordon, Rosemary Forsyth, Robert Fuller, Mildred Dunnock

'Sister, sister, oh so fair, why is there blood all over your hair?'
Whatever Happened to Baby Jane? *
US   1962   132m   bw
Warner Seven Arts/Associates and Aldrich (Robert Aldrich)
🎦 🎦 🎦
In middle age, a demented ex-child star lives in an old Hollywood mansion with her invalid sister, and tension leads to murder.
Famous for marking the first time Hollywood's ageing first ladies stooped to horror, and followed by Hush Hush Sweet Charlotte and the other Whatevers, this dreary looking melodrama only occasionally grabs the attention and has enough plot for about half its length. The performances, however, are striking.
w Lukas Heller *novel* Henry Farrell d Robert Aldrich ph Ernest Haller m Frank de Vol
☆ Bette Davis, Joan Crawford, Victor Buono, Anna Lee
'It goes on and on, in a light much dimmer than necessary, and the climax, when it belatedly arrives, is a bungled, languid mingling of pursuers and pursued…' – *New Yorker*
👤 Ernest Haller; Bette Davis; Victor Buono

'In 1977, disco wasn't the only magic in town.'
Whatever Happened To Harold Smith? *
GB   1998   94m   DeLuxe
UIP/Intermedia/October/Arts Council/West Eleven (Ruth Jackson, David Brown)
🎧
In Sheffield in the mid-70s, a working class father develops telekinetic powers, while his son tries to pluck up courage to date a middle-class girl.
Lively, inconsequential domestic comedy of misplaced aspirations, set against a background of punk rock and disco.
w Ben Steiner d Pete Hewitt ph David Tattersall m Rupert Gregson-Williams ch Litza Bixler pd Gemma Jackson ed Martin Walsh cos Marie France
☆ Tom Courtenay, Stephen Fry, Michael Legge, Laura Fraser, Lulu, David Thewlis, Rosemary Leach, Amanda Root, Matthew Rhys, James Corden, Charlie Hunnam, Charlotte Roberts
'Busy direction and bright performances partly compensate for a script that goes in too many directions at the same time.' – *Derek Elley, Variety*

What's a Nice Girl Like You Doing in a Place Like This? *
US   1963   10m   bw   16mm
Contemporary/New York University Department of Television, Motion Picture and Radio Presentation Summer Motion Picture Workshop
🎦
A would-be writer tries various ways to overcome his hang-ups.
An exuberant and amusing short, much influenced by the style of the French New Wave.
wd Martin Scorsese *play* James Newman m Richard H. Cole ed Robert Hunsicker
☆ Zeph Michaelis, Mimi Stark, Sarah Braveman, Fred Sica, Robert Uricola
† It was released on video with three other shorts under the title *Scorsese x 4*.

What's Buzzin', Cousin?
US   1943   75m   bw
Columbia (Jack Fier)
An attorney turns band singer and helps revive a droopy hotel.
Listless musical with a few good numbers.
w Harry Sauber d Charles Barton
☆ Ann Miller, John Hubbard, Eddie Anderson, Leslie Brooks, Jeff Donnell

'A film about the love you find … in the last place you look.'
What's Eating Gilbert Grape?
US   1993   118m   DeLuxe
Paramount (Meir Teper, Bertil Ohlsson, David Matalon)
🎦 🎦 🎦
A small-town grocery clerk is the main support of his family: obese, stay-at-home mother, two disturbed sisters and a brain-damaged brother.
Gentle, unsentimental drama, but so low-key that it does not always engage the interest.
w Peter Hedges *novel* Peter Hedges d Lasse Hallstrom ph Sven Nykvist m Alan Parker pd Bernt Capra ed Andrew Monshein

☆ Johnny Depp, Juliette Lewis, Mary Steenburgen, Leonardo DiCaprio, Darlene Cates, Laura Harrington, Mary Kate Schellhardt, Crispin Glover, Kevin Tighe
'An offbeat middleweight charmer that is lent a measure of substance by its astute performances and observational insight.' – *Variety*
'The film is still implicitly condescending since almost all the characters (including the afflicted ones) function as tests of Gilbert's patience.' – *Michael Sragow, New Yorker*
👤 Leonardo DiCaprio

What's Good for the Goose
GB   1969   104m   Eastmancolor
Tigon (Tony Tenser, Norman Wisdom)
An assistant bank manager falls for a girl hitch-hiker and tries to recover his youth.
Embarrassing attempt to build a sexy vehicle for a star whose sentimental mugging always appealed mainly to children.
w Norman Wisdom d Menahem Golan ph William Brayne m Reg Tilsley
☆ Norman Wisdom, Sally Geeson, Sally Bazely, Derek Francis, Terence Alexander

'Who needs a heart when a heart can be broken?'
What's Love Got to Do with It *
US   1993   118m   Technicolor
Buena Vista/Touchstone (Doug Chapin, Barry Krost)
🎦 🎦 🎧
aka: *Tina: What's Love Got to Do with It*
Biopic of the rock singer Tina Turner, from her violent relationship with, and marriage to, Ike Turner to her successful emergence as a solo artist.
Excellent performances by the two leads, some well-staged musical numbers and marital rows and lusty singing by Tina Turner herself make this a better than average picture of its kind.
w Kate Lanier *book* I, Tina by Tina Turner, Kurt Loder d Brian Gibson ph Jamie Anderson m Stanley Clarke pd Stephen Altman ed Stuart Pappé
☆ Angela Bassett, Laurence Fishburne, Vanessa Bell Calloway, Jenifer Lewis, Phyllis Yvonne Stickney, Khandi Alexander, Rae'ven Kelly
'A passionate personal and professional drama that hits both the high and low notes of an extraordinary life and career. An immensely enjoyable saga.' – *Variety*
👤 Laurence Fishburne; Angela Bassett

What's New Pussycat?
US/France   1965   108m   Technicolor
UA/Famous Artists (Charles K. Feldman)
🎦 🎦 🎧
A fashion editor is distracted by beautiful girls.
Zany sex comedy with many more misses than hits, a product of the wildly swinging sixties when it was thought that a big budget and stars making fools of themselves would automatically ensure a success.
w Woody Allen d Clive Donner ph Jean Badal m Burt Bacharach
☆ Peter O'Toole, Peter Sellers, Woody Allen, Ursula Andress, Romy Schneider, Capucine, Paula Prentiss
'Unfortunately for all concerned, to make something enjoyably dirty a lot of taste is required.' – *John Simon*
👤 title song (m Burt Bacharach, ly Hal David)

What's So Bad about Feeling Good?
US   1965   94m   Technicolor
Universal (George Seaton)
A 'happy virus' is carried into New York by a toucan, and affects the lives of various people.
Flimsy pretext for a comedy, further hampered by a less than sparkling script. The actors have their moments.
w George Seaton, Robert Pirosh d George Seaton ph Ernesto Caparros m Frank de Vol
☆ George Peppard, Mary Tyler Moore, Dom DeLuise, John McMartin, Susan St James, Don Stroud, Charles Lane

What's the Matter with Helen? *
US   1971   101m   DeLuxe
Filmways/Raymax (George Edwards, James C. Pratt)
🎦
In 1934 Hollywood, two women run a dancing school for child stars; one of them is a killer.
More Baby Jane melodramatics, quite lively and with interesting period detail.
w Henry Farrell d Curtis Harrington ph Lucien Ballard m David Raksin pd Eugene Lourié

☆ Debbie Reynolds, Shelley Winters, Michael MacLiammoir, Dennis Weaver, Agnes Moorehead
'A cast of seasoned troupers cannot quite alter the impression that they are all working to revive a stiff.' – *Bruce Williamson*

What's Up, Doc? **
👫 US   1972   94m   Technicolor
Warner/Saticoy (Peter Bogdanovich)
🎦 🎦 🎦
In San Francisco, an absent-minded young musicologist is troubled by the attentions of a dotty girl who gets him involved with crooks and a series of accidents.
Madcap comedy, a pastiche of several thirties originals. Spectacular slapstick and willing players are somewhat let down by exhausted patches and a tame final reel.
w Buck Henry, David Newman, Robert Benton d Peter Bogdanovich ph Laszlo Kovacs m Artie Butler pd Polly Platt
☆ Barbra Streisand, Ryan O'Neal, Kenneth Mars, Austin Pendleton, Madeline Kahn, Mabel Albertson, Sorrell Booke
'A comedy made by a man who has seen a lot of movies, knows all the mechanics, and has absolutely no sense of humour. Seeing it is like shaking hands with a joker holding a joy buzzer: the effect is both presumptuous and unpleasant.' – *Jay Cocks*
'It's all rather like a 19th-century imitation of Elizabethan blank verse drama.' – *Stanley Kauffmann*
'It freely borrows from the best screen comedy down the ages but has no discernible style of its own.' – *Michael Billington, Illustrated London News*

What's Up, Tiger Lily? *
US   1966   80m   Eastmancolor   Tohoscope
Benedict/Toho (Woody Allen)
🎦 🎦 🎦
A Japanese agent searches for the world's greatest egg salad recipe.
Woody Allen and his American cast re-dub a Japanese spy film to create an off-beat comedy that is amusing in fits and starts.
w Kazuo Yamada, Woody Allen and others d Senkichi Taniguchi m Jack Lewis, The Lovin' Spoonful ed Richard Krown
☆ Tatsuya Mihashi, Mie Hama, Akiko Wakabayashi, Tadeo Nakamaru, Susumu Kurobe, Woody Allen, Frank Buxton, Len Maxwell, Louise Lasser, Mickey Rose
'The jokes get rather desperate, but there are enough wildly sophomoric ones to keep this pop stunt fairly amusing until about midway.' – *Pauline Kael, New Yorker*

The Wheeler Dealers
US   1963   106m   Metrocolor   Panavision
MGM/Filmways (Martin Ransohoff)
🎦
GB title: *Separate Beds*
A Texas tycoon with a flair for the stock market sets Wall Street agog by manipulating a mysterious and non-existent new product.
Fun for financiers, but barely worth following for the rest. A slick, loud, hollow show.
w G. J. W. Goodman, Ira Wallach d Arthur Hiller ph Charles Lang Jnr m Frank de Vol
☆ James Garner, Lee Remick, Phil Harris, Chill Wills, Jim Backus, Louis Nye, John Astin

Wheels on Meals
Hong Kong   1984   102m   colour
Paragon Films (Leonard K. C. Ho)
🎦 🎦
Two Chinese fast-food operatives working in Spain bring fortune to a local girl.
Bizarre kung-fu comedy with a little romance on the side. Too slow and with not enough action to interest fans of the genre, even if it does include a parody of The Three Musketeers.
d Samo Hung
☆ Jackie Chan, Benny Urquidez, Keith Vitali, Herb Edelman, Samo Hung

When a Man Loves
US   1927   83m   bw   silent with synchronized music
Warner
A hero escapes from a prison ship and gives his all for love of a worthless woman.

Freely adapted version of Manon Lescaut, successful because of the real-life romance of the stars.

w Bess Meredyth d Alan Crosland

☆ John Barrymore, Dolores Costello, Warner Oland, Stuart Holmes, Holmes Herbert

'Through the good times. Through the bad times.'
'It's for all times.'

When a Man Loves a Woman
US 1994 124m Technicolor
Buena Vista/Touchstone (Jordan Kerner, Jon Avnet)
🎞 ▬ ◑ ⊘ ♫

A husband finds that his wife's alcoholism is a problem and her sobriety even worse.
A domestic drama that evades the realities of the situation it shows in its determination to reach a happy ending.

w Ronald Bass, Al Franken d Luis Mandoki ph Lajos Koltai m Zbigniew Preisner pd Stuart Wurtzel ed Garth Craven

☆ Andy Garcia, Meg Ryan, Philip Seymour Hoffman, Lauren Tom, Tina Majorino, Mae Whitman, Ellen Burstyn

'Nothing resonates in this tale of a romance with drink.' – *Time*
'With a little patience, audiences should find themselves emotionally polarized by this adult, intelligent drama that exhumes the detritus of male–female relationships with painful precision.' – *James Cameron-Wilson, Film Review*
'Little more than emotional pornography.' – *Sight and Sound*

'Every baby sitter's nightmare becomes real!'

When a Stranger Calls
US 1979 97m colour
UA/Melvin Simon (Doug Chapin, Steve Feke)
🎞 ▬ ◑

A policeman determinedly chases a baby-murdering maniac.
Middling screamer extended from a short, The Sitter; a passive midsection separates a suspenseful start and finish.

w Steve Feke, Fred Walton d Fred Walton ph Don Peterman m Dana Kaproff pd Elayne Barbara Ceder ed Sam Vitale

☆ Charles Durning, Tony Beckley, Carol Kane, Colleen Dewhurst, Rachel Roberts

When Boys Leave Home: see Downhill

When Comedy Was King ***
†† US 1959 84m bw
Robert Youngson Productions
▬ ◑

Valuable compilation of silent comedy sequences, with the high print quality and poor commentary to be expected from this source. Extracts include Buster Keaton in *Cops*, Laurel and Hardy in *Big Business*, and a Fatty Arbuckle comedy.
ed Robert Youngson

When Dinosaurs Ruled the Earth
†† GB 1969 100m Technicolor
Warner/Hammer (Aida Young)
▬ ◑

In prehistoric times, a girl is swept out to sea by a cyclone and adopted by a dinosaur.
Sequel to One Million Years BC, all very silly but tolerably well done.

wd Val Guest, from a treatment by J. G. Ballard ph Dick Bush m Mario Nascimbene ad John Blezard ed Peter Curran sp Jim Danforth

☆ Victoria Vetri, Patrick Allen, Robin Hawdon, Patrick Holt, Imogen Hassall

'I'm very proud that my first screen credit was for what is, without doubt, the worst film ever made.' – *J. G. Ballard*
& special visual effects (Jim Danforth, Roger Dicken)

When Eight Bells Toll *
GB 1971 94m Eastmancolor Panavision
Winkast (Elliott Kastner)

A naval secret service agent investigates the pirating of gold bullion ships off the Scottish coast.
Acceptable kill-happy thriller: humourless James Bondery graced by splendid Scottish landscapes.

w Alistair MacLean novel Alistair Maclean d Etienne Perier ph Arthur Ibbetson m Wally Stott

☆ Anthony Hopkins, Robert Morley, Corin Redgrave, Jack Hawkins, Ferdy Mayne, Derek Bond, Nathalie Delon

When Father Was Away on Business **
Yugoslavia 1985 136m colour
Cannon/Forum/Sarajevo Film (Vera Mihic-Jolic)
🎞 ▬

original title: *Otac Na Sluašbenom Putu*

Family life in Yugoslavia in the 1950s, as seen through the eyes of a young boy whose father is sent to the mines after being betrayed by his mistress and brother-in-law.
Well-observed study of politics seen from a child's perspective, which adds charm and humour. It won the Palme d'Or for best film at the Cannes Film Festival in 1985.

w Abdulah Sidran d Emir Kusturica ph Vilko Filač m Zoran Simjanović pd Predrag Lukovac ed Andrija Zafranovic

☆ Moreno de Bartoli, Miki Manojlović, Mirjana Karanović, Mustafa Nadarević, Mira Furlan, Zoran Radmilovic, Jelena Covic, Tomislav Gelić, Davor Dujmović, Amir Kapetanović

When Harry Met Sally ****
US 1989 95m DuArt
Palace/Castle Rock/Nelson Entertainment (Rob Reiner, Andrew Scheinman)
🎞 ▬ ◑ ⊘ ♫

Over a period of 12 years, a couple meet occasionally to debate whether there can be friendship without sex between a man and a woman.
Deft, witty romantic comedy, as good of its kind as we're likely to get these days.

w Nora Ephron d Rob Reiner ph Barry Sonnenfeld m Harry Connick Jnr and others pd Jane Musky ed Robert Leighton

☆ Billy Crystal, *Meg Ryan*, Carrie Fisher, Bruno Kirby, Steven Ford, Lisa Jane Persky, Michelle Nicastro

& Nora Ephron
▽ Nora Ephron

When I Fall in Love
US 1988 127m Technicolor
Warner/New Visions (Taylor Hackford, Laura Ziskin, Ian Sander)
▬ ◑

US title: *Everybody's All-American*

A star football player and his beauty queen wife survive 25 years of married life.
A lengthy soap opera, sentimentally indulging in an emotional switchback as its protagonists go from happiness to grief and back.

w Tom Rickman novel Frank Deford d Taylor Hackford ph Stephen Goldblatt m James Newton Howard pd Joe Alves ed Don Zimmerman

☆ Dennis Quaid, Jessica Lange, Timothy Hutton, John Goodman, Carl Lumbly, Raymond Baker, Savannah Smith Boucher, Patricia Clarkson

When I Grow Up *
†† US 1951 90m bw
Horizon (S. P. Eagle)

A boy about to run away changes his mind after reading his grandfather's diaries.
Pleasant, sentimental family film with an unusual approach.

wd Michael Kanin ph Ernest Laszlo m Jerome Moross

☆ Bobby Driscoll, Robert Preston, Charley Grapewin, Martha Scott, Ralph Dumke

When in Rome
US 1952 78m bw
MGM (Clarence Brown)

A gangster in Rome steals a priest's clothes and is accepted in his place.
Typically American religious comedy, nicely made but straying somewhat over the top when the gangster reforms and becomes a monk.

w Charles Schnee, Dorothy Kingsley, Robert Buckner d Clarence Brown ph William Daniels m Carmen Dragon

☆ Van Johnson, Paul Douglas, Joseph Calleia, Carlo Rizzo, Tudor Owen, Aldo Silvani, Dono Nardi

When Johnny Comes Marching Home
US 1942 73m bw
Universal (Bernard W. Burton)

A war hero on leave escapes formalities and returns to the theatrical boarding house he remembers.
And so to the puttin'-on-a-show finale: not bad of its kind.

w Oscar Brodney, Dorothy Bennett d Charles Lamont

☆ Allan Jones, Jane Frazee, Gloria Jean, Donald O'Connor, Peggy Ryan, Phil Spitalny and his all-girl orchestra

When Knights Were Bold
GB 1929 80m bw silent
Herbert Wilcox

An incompetent heir dreams that he lives in medieval times.
Naïve romp which pleased at the time.

w Tim Whelan, Herbert Wilcox play Charles Marlow d Tim Whelan

☆ Nelson Keys, Miriam Seegar, Eric Bransby Williams

† Remade in 1936 with Jack Buchanan, Fay Wray and Garry Marsh; directed by Jack Raymond; for Max Schach.

When Ladies Meet *
US 1933 73m bw
MGM

A successful lady novelist falls in love with her married publisher.
Smartish comedy of manners which still has a sting.

w John Meehan, Leon Gordon play Rachel Crothers d Harry Beaumont ph Ray June ad Cedric Gibbons

☆ Ann Harding, Robert Montgomery, Myrna Loy, Alice Brady, Frank Morgan, Martin Burton, Luis Alberni

'Nice production. Well-spaced comedy helps, and picture should be an outsander.' – *Variety*
& Cedric Gibbons

When Ladies Meet
US 1941 108m bw
MGM (Robert Z. Leonard, Orville O. Dull)
▬ ◑

Over-produced and very talkative remake of the above.

w S. K. Lauren, Anita Loos d Robert Z. Leonard ph Robert Planck m Bronislau Kaper ad Cedric Gibbons, Randall Duell

☆ Joan Crawford, Robert Taylor, Greer Garson, Spring Byington, Herbert Marshall, Rafael Storm, Olaf Hytten

& Cedric Gibbons, Randall Duell

When London Sleeps
GB 1932 78m bw
APD/Twickenham (Julius Hagen)

An unscrupulous Hampstead gambler kidnaps the adopted daughter of a travelling showman, who is heiress to a fortune.
Stilted melodrama, with direction to match.

w H. Fowler Mear, Bernard Merivale play Charles Darrel d Leslie S. Hiscott ph Basil Emmott md W. L. Trytel ad James Carter ed Jack Harris

☆ Harold French, Francis L. Sullivan, Rene Ray, Alexander Field, Ben Field, A. Bromley Davenport, Herbert Lomas, Barbara Everest

When Love Is Young
US 1937 75m bw
Universal (Robert Presnell)

A Broadway stage star returns to her home town in hopes of marrying her old beau, but he is found wanting.
Very moderate comedy to fill a programme.

w Eve Greene, Joseph Fields story Class Prophecy by Eleanore Griffin d Hal Mohr

☆ Virginia Bruce, Kent Taylor, Walter Brennan, Greta Meyer, Christian Rub, Sterling Holloway, Nydia Westman

'Will provide average filmgoers with averagely good amusement.' – *Variety*

When My Baby Smiles at Me
US 1948 98m Technicolor
TCF (George Jessel)

A vaudevillian goes on the skids but is saved by his wife.
Routine musical handling of a dreary drama previously filmed as Dance of Life (1929) and Swing High Swing Low (qv).

w Lamar Trotti play Burlesque by George Manker Walters, Arthur Hopkins d Walter Lang ph Harry Jackson md Alfred Newman

☆ Betty Grable, Dan Dailey, Jack Oakie, June Havoc, Richard Arlen, James Gleason, Jean Wallace

& Alfred Newman; Dan Dailey

When New York Sleeps: see Now I'll Tell

When Night Is Falling
Canada 1995 96m colour
Alliance/Crucial (Barbara Tranter)
🎞 ▬ ◑

A teacher of mythology unexpectedly falls in love with a seductive female circus performer, which changes her attitude to the values of the Christian college where she works, and to the theologian she planned to marry.
Good-looking, intense, serious drama of sexual confusions that founders on overwrought dialogue and its failure to explore the issues of morality and individual choice it raises; its attempt at magic realism, reinterpreting the myth of Cupid and Psyche, is even less successful.

wd Patricia Rozema ph Douglas Koch m Lesley Barber pd John Dondertman ed Susan Shipton

☆ Pascale Bussières, Rachael Crawford, David Fox, Tracy Wright, Don McKellar, Henry Czerny

'Ultimate proof that ravishing photography, crisp cutting and a finely wrought score can't paper over a feeble script.' – *Derek Elley, Variety*

When Saturday Comes
GB 1996 97m colour
Guild/Capitol/A Pint O' Bitter (James Daly, Christopher Lambert)
🎞 ◑

In Sheffield, a brewery worker's ambitions to be a professional footballer are fulfilled.
Risible drama that lacks all credibility, though those who dream of scoring a hat-trick on their debut may enjoy it.

wd Maria Giese story James Daly ph Gerry Fisher m Anne Dudley pd Hugo Luczyc-Wyhowski ed George Akers

☆ Sean Bean, Emily Lloyd, Pete Postlethwaite, John McEnery, Ann Bell, Melanie Hill, Craig Kelly, David Leland

'You can't believe any of this tosh for an instant: it's like *Rocky* blue-tacked to Northern England and washed down with Tennents Extra.' – *James Cameron-Wilson, Film Review*

When Strangers Marry *
US 1944 67m bw
Monogram (Maurice King)
aka: *Betrayed*

A young bride in New York discovers that she may have married a murderer.
Much-praised second feature: a bit stodgy now, but still entertaining.

w Philip Yordan, Dennis Cooper d William Castle ph Ira Morgan m Dimitri Tiomkin

☆ Dean Jagger, Kim Hunter, Robert Mitchum, Neil Hamilton, Lou Lubin, Milt Kibbee, Dewey Robinson

'The obviousness of the low budget is completely overcome by the solid craftsmanship of the direction, script, music, editing and performances.' – *Don Miller*
'Taking it as a whole I have seldom for years now seen one hour so energetically and sensibly used in a film.' – *James Agee*

When the Bough Breaks
GB 1947 81m bw
GFD/Gainsborough (Betty Box)
🎞

The bewildered wife of a bigamist allows her child to be adopted and then regrets it.
Peg's Paper stuff in the then-accepted Gainsborough tradition.

w Peter Rogers story Moie Charles, Herbert Victor d Lawrence Huntington ph Bryan Langley m Clifton Parker ad George Provis ed Gordon Hales

☆ Patricia Roc, Rosamund John, Bill Owen, Patrick Holt, Brenda Bruce, Leslie Dwyer, Jane Hylton

When the Cat's Away **
France 1996 91m colour
Artificial Eye/Vertigo/France 2 (Aïssa Djabri, Farid Lahoussa, Manuel Munz)
🎞

original title: *Chacun cherche son chat*

The adventures, amorous and otherwise, of a woman searching for her missing cat.
Slight but enjoyable drama of life among fashionable young Parisians.

wd Cédric Klapisch ph Benoît Delhomme ad Françoise Emmanuelli

☆ Garance Clavel, Zinedine Soualem, Renée Lecalm, Olivier Py, Joël Brisse, Arapimou, Rambo
'The type of film that several viewings later will still give something new to the audience.' – Marianne Gray, Film Review

When the Daltons Rode *
US   1940   80m   bw
Universal
Adventures of the Dalton Gang.
Good standard Western with whitewashed bad men for heroes.
w Harold Shumate, Stuart Anthony, Lester Cole d George Marshall ph Hal Mohr m Frank Skinner
☆ Randolph Scott, Kay Francis, Brian Donlevy, Andy Devine, George Bancroft, Stuart Erwin

When the Door Opened: see Escape (1940)

When the Legends Die **
US   1972   105m   DeLuxe
Fox-Rank/Sagaponack (Stuart Miller)
🖥
An ageing rodeo rider befriends a young Indian and teaches him the tricks of the trade.
Downbeat tale of the souring of the American dream, with fine performances from the two leads.
w Robert Dozier novel Hal Borland d Stuart Miller ph Richard H. Kline m Glenn Paxton md Lionel Newman ad Angelo Graham ed Louis San Andres
☆ Richard Widmark, Frederic Forrest, Luana Anders, Vito Scotti, Herbert Nelson, John War Eagle

When the Lights go on Again
US   1944   70m   bw
PRC (Leon Fromkess)
An ex-marine comes home with shell shock.
One of the first films to deal with the problems of war veterans: a modest effort, but sincere.
w Milton Lazarus story Frank Craven d William K. Howard
☆ James Lydon, Barbara Belden, Grant Mitchell, Dorothy Peterson, Regis Toomey

When the Whales Came
🏠   GB   1989   100m   Fujicolour
Fox/Golden Swan/Central Television (Simon Channing Williams)
🖥 🖥 🖥 🎧
In 1914, fishermen on one of the Scilly Isles are persuaded by a recluse and a boy to save a beached whale, an act which brings them luck.
Ecologically sound, dramatically dull story, not helped by its insistently soft focus photography.
w Michael Morpurgo novel Why the Whales Came by Michael Morpurgo d Clive Rees ph Robert Paynter m Christopher Gunning pd Bruce Grimes ed Andrew Boulton
☆ Helen Mirren, Paul Scofield, David Suchet, Barbara Jefford, David Threlfall, Barbara Ewing, John Hallam, Jeremy Kemp, Max Rennie, Helen Pearce

When the Wind Blows *
GB   1987   85m   TVC Color
Film Four/Penguin/TVC/NFFC (John Coates)
🖥 🖥 🎧
An elderly man and wife fail to cope with nuclear destruction.
Cartoon picturization of a popular book; the film was less likely, despite its merits, to find an audience.
w Raymond Briggs book Raymond Briggs d Jimmy Murakami m Roger Waters ed John Cary
☆ Featuring the voices of John Mills, Peggy Ashcroft

When Thief Meets Thief: see Jump for Glory

When Time Ran Out
US   1980   109m   Technicolor   Panavision
Warner/Irwin Allen
🖥
Inhabitants of a South Sea island are threatened by a volcano.
Incredibly inept disaster movie, with all clichés on hand in the characters of some downcast actors.
w Carl Foreman, Stirling Silliphant novel The Day the World Ended by Max Morgan Witts and Gordon Thomas d James Goldstone ph Fred J.

Koenekamp m Lalo Schifrin pd Philip M. Jefferies ed Edward Biery, Freeman A. Davies
☆ Paul Newman, Jacqueline Bisset, William Holden, Edward Albert, Burgess Meredith, Valentina Cortesa, Red Buttons, Alex Karras, Ernest Borgnine, James Franciscus
'Disaster movies don't come any more disastrous than this.' – Tom Milne, MFB
† Said to have cost 22 million dollars and taken less than two.
⚱ costumes (Paul Zastupnevich)

When Tomorrow Comes **
US   1939   82m   bw
Universal (John M. Stahl)
A waitress falls for a concert pianist with a mad wife.
Fascinating star romantic drama, a successful follow-up to Love Affair; full of clichés, but impeccably set and acted. The stuff that Hollywood dreams were made of.
w Dwight Taylor story James M. Cain d John M. Stahl ph John Mescall m Charles Previn
☆ Charles Boyer, Irene Dunne, Barbara O'Neil, Nydia Westman, Onslow Stevens
'A persuasive love story … a director's achievement.' – Variety
† The same story was remade twice in 1956, as Serenade and Interlude, and in 1968 as Interlude (all qv).

When We Are Married *
GB   1942   98m   bw
British National (John Baxter)
In 1890s Yorkshire, three couples celebrating their silver wedding are told they were never legally married.
A very funny play smartly filmed with a superb cast of character actors.
w Austin Melford, Barbara K. Emery play J. B. Priestley d Lance Comfort ph James Wilson
☆ Raymond Huntley, Marian Spencer, Lloyd Pearson, Olga Lindo, Ernest Butcher, Ethel Coleridge, Sydney Howard, Barry Morse, Lesley Brook, Marjorie Rhodes, Charles Victor, Cyril Smith, George Carney

'The True Story Of The Rumble In The Jungle.'

When We Were Kings **
US   1996   88m   Technicolor
Polygram/DAS (David Sonenberg, Leon Gast)
🖥 🖥 ⚙ 🎧
Documentary of the world heavyweight fight between the challenger Muhammad Ali and champion George Foreman, which was staged in Zaire in 1974 and marked the emergence of promoter Don King as a not-always-benign influence on the sport.
Enjoyable celebration of a great athlete, even if it is released so long after the event as to lose some of its significance.
d Leon Gast ph Maryse Alberti, Paul Goldsmith, Kevin Keating, Albert Maysles, Roderick Young. ed Leon Gast, Taylor Hackford, Jeffrey Levy-Hinte, Keith Robinson
☆ Muhammad Ali, George Foreman, Don King, President Mobutu Sese Seko, Spike Lee, Norman Mailer
'A genuinely inspiring film about a real twentieth-century hero.' – Sight and Sound
† The director originally planned a film about the concert, featuring James Brown, B. B. King, Miriam Makeba and others, that accompanied the fight; problems of finance and copyright held up that material for many years, and the footage was then fashioned into a documentary about the fight itself.
⚱ documentary

When Willie Comes Marching Home *
US   1950   82m   bw
TCF (Fred Kohlmar)
During World War II, events suddenly transform a small-town air training instructor into a war hero.
Awkwardly paced comedy which could have been much funnier but does amuse in fits and starts.
w Mary Loos, Richard Sale d John Ford ph Leo Tover m Alfred Newman
☆ Dan Dailey, Colleen Townshend, Corinne Calvet, William Demarest, Evelyn Varden, James Lydon, Mae Marsh, Lloyd Corrigan
⚱ original story (Sy Gomberg)

When Worlds Collide
🏠   US   1951   82m   Technicolor
Paramount (George Pal)
🖥 🎧
Another planet is found to be rushing inevitably towards Earth, but before the collision a few people escape in a space ship.
Stolid science fiction with a spectacular but not marvellous climax following seventy minutes of inept talk.
w Sydney Boehm novel Philip Wylie, Edwin Balmer d Rudolph Maté ph John Seitz, W. Howard Greene m Leith Stevens
☆ Richard Derr, Barbara Rush, Larry Keating, Peter Hanson, John Hoyt
🔧 special effects
⚱ John Seitz, W. Howard Greene

When You're in Love *
US   1937   110m   bw
Columbia (Everett Riskin)
GB title: For You Alone
A European opera singer takes on a husband in order to get into the United States.
Pleasing musical star vehicle with comedy touches.
wd Robert Riskin ph Joseph Walker md Alfred Newman
☆ Grace Moore, Cary Grant, Aline MacMahon, Henry Stephenson, Thomas Mitchell, Catherine Doucet, Luis Alberni, Emma Dunn
'Nice musical with fair quota of giggles … should do nice biz.' – Variety

'Two lovers caught between convention and passion…'

Where Angels Fear to Tread
GB   1991   112m   Eastmancolor
Rank/Sovereign/LWT/Stagescreen/Compact (Derek Granger)
🖥 🖥 🎧
A brother and sister travel to Italy to bring back the baby of their sister-in-law who defied family opposition to marry a young Italian and died in childbirth.
Vapid and disjointed adaptation, glossily made but not helped by mannered performances.
w Tim Sullivan, Derek Granger, Charles Sturridge d Charles Sturridge ph Michael Coulter m Rachel Portman pd Simon Holland ed Peter Coulson
☆ Helena Bonham Carter, Judy Davis, Rupert Graves, Giovanni Guidelli, Barbara Jefford, Helen Mirren, Thomas Wheatley, Sophie Kullman
'A story about fine ironies and "fine" behaviour becomes a genre exercise in fine acting and even finer linen.' – MFB

Where Angels Go, Trouble Follows
US   1968   95m   Eastmancolor
Columbia/William Frye
Nuns from a convent school take pupils to a California youth rally, and learn a thing or two.
Peripatetic comedy, rather frantically assembled; a sequel to The Trouble with Angels.
w Blanche Hanalis d James Neilson ph Sam Leavitt m Lalo Schifrin
☆ Rosalind Russell, Stella Stevens, Binnie Barnes, Mary Wickes, Milton Berle, Arthur Godfrey, Robert Taylor, Van Johnson, Susan St James

Where Are Your Children?
US   1943   78m   bw
Monogram (Jeffrey Bernerd)
A wandering rich boy takes up with a hash slinger, and they wind up suspected of murder …
An 'awful warning' melodrama, risible now.
w Hilary Lynn, George W. Sayre d William Nigh
☆ Jackie Cooper, Gale Storm, Patricia Morison, John Litel, Gertrude Michael, Addison Richards, Betty Blythe

Where Danger Lives
US   1950   84m   bw
RKO (Irving Cummings Jnr)
A doctor falls in love with a murderous patient and is drawn into her schemes.
Standard film noir of its time, competent enough in its depressing way.
w Charles Bennett story Leo Rosten d John Farrow ph Nicholas Musuraca m Roy Webb
☆ Faith Domergue, Robert Mitchum, Claude Rains, Maureen O'Sullivan, Charles Kemper

Where Do We Go from Here? *
🏠   US   1945   77m   Technicolor
TCF (William Perlberg)
A writer stumbles on a genie who takes him through periods of American history, including a voyage with Christopher Columbus.
Well-staged and rather funny charade with at least one memorable song.
w Morrie Ryskind d Gregory Ratoff ph Leon Shamroy m David Raksin songs Kurt Weill, Ira Gershwin
☆ Fred MacMurray, June Haver, Joan Leslie, Gene Sheldon, Anthony Quinn, Carlos Ramirez, Fortunio Bonanova, Alan Mowbray, Herman Bing, Otto Preminger
'Nine parts heavy facetiousness to one part very good fun.' – James Agee

'Don't tell your doctor about this film – it could give him ideas!'

Where Does it Hurt?
🏠   US   1971   88m   colour
Josef Shaftel (Rod Amateau, William Schwarz)
Adventures of a profiteering hospital administrator.
Dislikeable, plodding smut in the form of black comedy.
wd Rod Amateau novel The Operator by Budd Robinson, Rod Amateau ph Brick Marquard m Keith Allison
☆ Peter Sellers, Jo Ann Pflug, Rick Lenz, Eve Bruce

Where Eagles Dare **
GB   1969   155m   Metrocolor   Panavision 70
MGM/Winkast (Elliott Kastner)
🖥 🖥 🖥 🎧
During World War II, seven British paratroopers land in the Bavarian Alps to rescue a high-ranking officer from an impregnable castle.
Archetypal schoolboy adventure, rather unattractively photographed but containing a sufficient variety of excitements.
w Alistair MacLean novel Alistair MacLean d Brian G. Hutton ph Arthur Ibbetson, H. A. R. Thompson m Ron Goodwin
☆ Richard Burton, Clint Eastwood, Mary Ure, Patrick Wymark, Michael Hordern, Donald Houston, Peter Barkworth, Robert Beatty

Where It's At
US   1969   106m   DeLuxe
UA/Frank Ross
The owner of a Las Vegas gambling hotel tries to make his son take an interest in the business.
Flaccid comedy drama which belies its credits.
wd Garson Kanin ph Burnett Guffey m Benny Olsen
☆ David Janssen, Rosemary Forsyth, Robert Drivas, Brenda Vaccaro

Where Love Has Gone *
US   1964   114m   Techniscope
Paramount/Embassy (Joseph E. Levine)
A middle-aged man is appalled to hear that his teenage daughter has killed her mother's lover.
Squalid, glossy pulp fiction lightly based on the Lana Turner case, distinguished only by the game performances of its leading ladies.
w John Michael Hayes novel Harold Robbins d Edward Dmytryk ph Joe MacDonald m Walter Scharf
☆ Susan Hayward, Bette Davis, Mike Connors, Joey Heatherton, Jane Greer, George Macready
'A typical Robbins pastiche of newspaper clippings cheaply shellacked with sentiment and glued with sex.' – Newsweek
⚱ title song (mJames Van Heusen, lySammy Cahn)

Where No Vultures Fly *
🏠   GB   1951   107m   Technicolor
Ealing (Leslie Norman)
US title: Ivory Hunter
Adventures of an East African game warden.
Pleasantly improving family film, nicely shot on location; a sequel, West of Zanzibar, was less impressive.
w W. P. Lipscomb, Ralph Smart, Leslie Norman d Harry Watt ph Geoffrey Unsworth m Alan Rawsthorne
☆ Anthony Steel, Dinah Sheridan, Harold Warrender, Meredith Edwards
'These expeditionary films are really journalistic jobs. You get sent out to a country by the studio,

---

🏠 film suitable for family viewing   🖥 VHS video-cassette for the British PAL system   🖥 VHS video-cassette for the British PAL system in wide screen-format   ⚙ Video cassette in a computer-colourised version   🖥 American NTSC video-cassette   🎧 Laser disc stay as long as you can without getting fired, and a story generally crops up.' – *Harry Watt*

'No one will wonder why it was chosen for this year's royal film show. It is not sordid, as so many new films are; it has a theme that almost everyone will find appealing; and the corner of the Empire where it is set is fresh, beautiful and exciting to look at.' – *Daily Telegraph*

Where Sinners Meet
US 1934 68m bw
RKO
GB title: *The Dover Road*

A millionaire eccentric kidnaps eloping couples to find out whether they are making a mistake.
Stagebound whimsy saddled with an absurd American title.
w H. W. Hanemann *play The Dover Road* by A. A. Milne d J. Walter Ruben
☆ Diana Wynyard, Clive Brook, Billie Burke, Reginald Owen, Alan Mowbray, Gilbert Emery, Phyllis Barry
    'Despite fine performances and good production, very dubious.' – *Variety*

Where Sleeping Dogs Lie
US 1991 91m colour
Columbia TriStar/August (Mario Sotela)
▣ ▤

A writer moves into a house where a family was slaughtered and discovers that his new tenant is the murderer.
A dreary thriller that contains a great deal of posturing but not much sense; it is best left alone.
w Charles Finch, Yolande Turner d Charles Finch ph Miles Cooke m Hans Zimmer, Mark Mancina pd Eve Cauley ed B. J. Sears, Gene M. Gamache
☆ Dylan McDermott, Tom Sizemore, Sharon Stone, Charles Finch, Mary Woronov, Ron Karabatsos

Where the Boys Are
US 1960 99m Metrocolor Cinemascope
MGM/Euterpe (Joe Pasternak)
▤ ▣.

Four college girls spend the Easter vacation near a Florida military post in search of conquests.
Mindless, frothy youth musical, quite smoothly done.
w George Wells *novel* Glendon Swarthout d Henry Levin m Robert Bronner m George Stoll
☆ George Hamilton, Dolores Hart, Paula Prentiss, Jim Hutton, Yvette Mimieux, Connie Francis, Frank Gorshin, Chill Wills, Barbara Nichols

Where the Boys Are
US 1984 94m colour
ITC/TriStar (Allan Carr)
▤ ▣.

The 1960 musical becomes a teenage sex movie.
Neither version has much to do with the original novel.
w Stu Krieger, Jeff Burkhart d Hy Averback ph James A. Contner m Sylvester Levay ed Melvin Shapiro, Bobbie Shapiro
☆ Lisa Hartman, Lorna Luft, Wendy Schaal, Lynn-Holly Johnson, Russell Todd, Howard McGillin
    'A travesty ... insufferably coy.' – *Tom Milne, MFB*

Where the Buffalo Roam
US 1980 98m Technicolor Panavision
Universal (Art Linson)
▤

A drug-crazed journalist takes a trip through Nixon's America.
Frenetic, rarely funny comedy, based on the work of self-styled 'gonzo journalist' Hunter S. Thompson.
w John Kaye d Art Linson ph Tak Fujimoto m Mal Young pd Richard Sawyer ed Christopher Greenburg
☆ Peter Boyle, Bill Murray, Bruno Kirby, Rene Auberjonois, R. G. Armstrong, Rafael Campos, Leonard Frey

Where the Day Takes You
US 1992 103m Foto-Kem
New Line/Cinetel (Paul Hertzberg)
▣ ▤

A youth on parole tries to keep the homeless gang of delinquents he leads out of trouble.
Desultory 'teen drama of an unsympathetic, attitudinizing group.

w Michael Hitchcock, Kurt Voss, Marc Rocco d Marc Rocco ph King Baggot m Mark Morgan pd Kirk Petrucelli ed Russell Livingstone
☆ Dermot Mulroney, Lara Flynn Boyle, Balthazar Getty, Sean Astin, James LeGros, Ricki Lake, Kyle MacLachlan, Stephen Tobolowsky, Will Smith, Christian Slater (uncredited)
    'Inevitably winds up giving the runaway's life the kind of romantic-tragic scope that appeals to troubled teens.' – *Variety*

Where the Green Ants Dream
West Germany 1984 100m colour
Werner Herzog Filmproduktion/ZDF (Lucki Stipetić)
▤

original title: *Wo die grünen Ameisen träumen*
Aborigines object to a mining company developing one of their sacred sites.
Dull drama that engages its subject matter only in a desultory way.
w Werner Herzog, Bob Ellis d Werner Herzog ph Jörg Schmidt-Reitwein m Fauré, Wagner and others pd Ulrich Bergfelder ed Beate Mainka-Jellinghaus
☆ Bruce Spence, Wandjuk Marika, Roy Marika, Ray Barrett, Norman Kaye, Colleen Clifford

Where the Heart Is *
US 1990 94m Technicolor
Buena Vista/Touchstone (John Boorman)
▣ ▤ ▣.

A tycoon orders his children to leave their life of luxury and live in a slum tenement.
Domestic comedy with some heavy-handed humour that is never funny enough to be entertaining.
w John Boorman, Telsche Boorman d John Boorman ph Peter Suschitzky m Peter Martin pd Carol Spier ed Ian Crafford
☆ Dabney Coleman, Uma Thurman, Joanna Cassidy, Crispin Glover, Suzy Amis, Christopher Plummer

Where the Hot Wind Blows
France/Italy 1958 125m bw
MGM/Cité Films/Groupe des Quatre/Titanus (Jacques Bar)
▤

original title: *La Loi*
In an Adriatic port, a voluptuous young girl is pursued by the aged local squire, a racketeer, her brother-in-law and a young agriculturist. Guess who wins her.
Hoary melodrama with the emphasis on virility and illicit passion. Long and tiresome, it failed to justify the pretensions with which it announced itself at the time.
w Jules Dassin, Diego Fabbri *novel* Roger Vailland d Jules Dassin ph Otello Martelli m Roman Vlad
☆ Gina Lollobrigida, Yves Montand, Marcello Mastroianni, Pierre Brasseur, Melina Mercouri, Paolo Stoppa
† An English version was generally available.

Where the Lilies Bloom
US 1974 96m DeLuxe
Radnitz/Mattel Productions (Robert B. Radnitz)
▤

Fearful of being sent to an institution, four children living in the Appalachians keep secret the death of their father and fend for themselves.
Slight but charming domestic drama which keeps sentimentality at bay for the most part.
w Earl Hamner Jnr *book* Vera and Bill Cleaver d William A. Graham ph Urs Furrer m Earl Scruggs ad Tambi Larsen ed O. Nicholas Brown
☆ Julie Gholson, Harry Dean Stanton, Jan Smithers, Matthew Burril, Helen Harmon, Sudie Bond, Rance Howard, Tom Spratley, Alice Beardsley, Helen Bragdon

Where the River Bends: see Bend of the River

Where the River Runs Black
US 1986 92m colour
MGM/IPI (Joe Roth, Harry Ufland)
▤

In Brazil a Catholic priest tries to care for the wild, orphaned son of an Indian woman and a priest working in the rain forest.
Slight, sentimental, ecological fable, given over to lyrical nature photography rather than to story-telling.
w Peter Silverman, Neal Jimenez *book* David Kendall d Christopher Cain ph Juan-Ruiz Anchia m James Horner pd Marcos Flaksman ed Richard Chew

☆ Charles Durning, Peter Horton, Ajay Naidu, Conchata Ferrell, Castulo Guerra, Alessandro Rabelo

'A sweeping tale of one man's mission to preserve himself and his way of life.'

Where the Rivers Flow North *
US 1993 106m colour
Ulysse/Caledonia (Bess O'Brien, Jay Craven)
▣ ▤ ▣

In Vermont in the 20s, a woodsman refuses to give up his land so that a new dam can be built.
Intermittently effective backwoods drama, with a deeply flawed protagonist who veers between violent protection of his environment and wilful destruction of it; Cardinal's performance, as a woman fighting to make space for her own life, keeps you watching until the end.
w Don Bredes, Jay Craven *novel* Howard Frank Mosher d Jay Craven ph Paul Ryan pd David Wasco
☆ Rip Torn, *Tantoo Cardinal*, Treat Williams, Michael J. Fox, Bill Raymond, John Griesemer, Mark Margolis, Dennis Mientka, Amy Wright

Where the Sidewalk Ends
US 1950 95m bw
TCF (Otto Preminger)

A tough policeman accidentally kills a suspect and tries to implicate a gang leader.
Gloomy policier with curious moral values.
w Rex Connor (Ben Hecht) *novel* William L. Stuart d Otto Preminger ph Joseph LaShelle m Cyril Mockridge
☆ Dana Andrews, Gene Tierney, Gary Merrill, Bert Freed, Tom Tully, Karl Malden, Ruth Donnelly, Craig Stevens, Robert Simon
    'A pretty beefy affair, not calculated to the taste of customers who shrink from the sight of the male fist contacting with the male or female jawbone.' – *C. A. Lejeune*

Where the Spies Are
GB 1965 113m Metrocolor Panavision
MGM/Val Guest

A country doctor is bribed to become a spy by the promise of a car he greatly covets.
Patchy spy adventure which never settles into a comfortable style but provides occasional entertainment along its bumpy way.
w Wolf Mankowitz, Val Guest *novel* Passport to Oblivion by James Leasor d Val Guest ph Arthur Grant m Mario Nascimbene
☆ David Niven, Françoise Dorleac, Nigel Davenport, John Le Mesurier, Ronald Radd, Cyril Cusack, Eric Pohlmann

Where There's a Will *
GB 1936 81m bw
Gainsborough (Edward Black, Sidney Gilliat)

A seedy education expert sponges on his rich relations but redeems himself by rounding up gangsters at a Christmas party.
Rather slapdash star comedy with very good scenes along the way.
w Will Hay, Robert Edmunds, Ralph Spence *story* Leslie Arliss, Sidney Gilliat d William Beaudine ph Charles Van Enger md Louis Levy
☆ *Will Hay*, Hartley Power, Gibb McLaughlin, Graham Moffatt, Norma Varden, Gina Malo

Where There's a Will
GB 1955 79m bw
Film Locations/Eros

A London family inherits a dilapidated Devon farm and makes a go of it.
Slight comedy with pleasant players.
w R. F. Delderfield *play* R. F. Delderfield d Vernon Sewell ph Basil Emmott m Robert Sharples
☆ Kathleen Harrison, George Cole, Leslie Dwyer, Dandy Nichols, Ann Hanslip, Michael Shepley

'If you laugh yourself sick at this picture – sue Bob Hope!'
Where There's Life
US 1947 75m bw
Paramount (Paul Jones)

A timid New Yorker turns out to be heir to the throne of a Ruritanian country, and is harassed by spies of both sides.
Mild star comedy with slow patches.
w Allen Boretz, Melville Shavelson d Sidney Lanfield ph Charles Lang Jnr md Irvin Talbot

☆ Bob Hope, Signe Hasso, William Bendix, George Coulouris

Where Were You When the Lights Went Out? *
US 1968 94m Metrocolor Panavision
MGM (Everett Freeman, Martin Melcher)

New York's famous electrical blackout in 1965 has its effect on the life of a musical comedy star.
Cheerful sex farce with intriguing beginnings; the later confinement to one set is just a bit harmful.
w Everett Freeman, Karl Tunberg *play* Claude Magnier d Hy Averback ph Ellsworth Fredericks m Dave Grusin
☆ Doris Day, Terry-Thomas, Patrick O'Neal, Robert Morse, Lola Albright, Jim Backus, Ben Blue

Where's Charley? *
♠♠ GB 1952 97m Technicolor
Warner

An Oxford undergraduate impersonates the rich aunt of his best friend.
Slow and rather stately musical version of the famous farce Charley's Aunt, unsatisfactorily shot on a mixture of poor sets and sunlit Oxford locations; worth cherishing for the ebullient performance of its over-age star.
w John Monks Jnr *play* Brandon Thomas (via stage musical) *book* George Abbott d David Butler ph Erwin Hillier m Frank Loesser ch Michael Kidd
☆ Ray Bolger, Robert Shackleton, Mary Germaine, Allyn McLerie, Margaretta Scott, Horace Cooper

Where's Jack? *
GB 1969 119m Eastmancolor
Paramount/Oakhurst (Stanley Baker)
▣ ▤

In 18th-century London Jack Sheppard becomes a romantic highwayman at the behest of underworld leader Jonathan Wild.
Deliberately unromantic, squalid and 'realistic' period piece which takes no hold on the fancy despite the considerable care which was obviously taken in all departments.
w Rafe and David Newhouse d James Clavell ph John Wilcox m Elmer Bernstein pd Cedric Dawe
☆ Tommy Steele, Stanley Baker, Fiona Lewis, Alan Badel, Dudley Foster, Sue Lloyd, Noel Purcell

Where's Poppa? *
US 1970 82m DeLuxe
Jerry Tokovsky/Marvin Worth
▤ ▣.

A Jewish lawyer's aged mother constantly harms his love life, and he considers various means of getting rid of her.
Much-censored black comedy which might have been funnier in a complete form. Even so, it has its moments.
w Robert Klane *novel* Robert Klane d Carl Reiner ph Jack Priestly m Jack Elliott
☆ George Segal, Ruth Gordon, Trish Van Devere, Ron Leibman

Where's That Fire? *
GB 1939 73m bw
TCF (Edward Black)

An incompetent village fire brigade accidentally saves the crown jewels from thieves.
Routine but not despicable star comedy, long thought lost; flat patches are well separated by hilarious sequences.
w Marriott Edgar, Val Guest, J. O. C. Orton d Marcel Varnel ph Arthur Crabtree
☆ Will Hay, Moore Marriott, Graham Moffatt, Peter Gawthorne, Eric Clavering, Charles Hawtrey
    'A superb sequence when they try to fix a pole in the station, otherwise not so funny.' – *Graham Greene*

Which Way to the Front?
US 1970 96m Technicolor
Warner/Jerry Lewis
▤

In 1943, rejected as unfit for military service, the richest man in the world forms his own commando unit with other misfits and decides to kidnap Field Marshal Kesselring to sabotage the Nazis in Italy.
Wretchedly unfunny comedy, the cinematic equivalent of vanity publishing, providing its star with the opportunity to play two frenetic roles: a billionaire who

---

resorts to mouthing gibberish when thwarted and a German commander who does much the same.
w Gerald Gardner, Dee Caruso, Richard Miller d Jerry Lewis ph W. Wallace Kelley m Louis Y. Brown pd John Beckman ed Russell Wiles
☆ Jerry Lewis, Jan Murray, John Wood, Steve Franken, Dack Rambo, Robert Middleton, Willie Davis, Kaye Ballard, Harold J. Stone, Paul Winchell, Sidney Miller

W.H.I.F.F.S.
US 1975 92m Technicolor Panavision
Brut (C. O. Erickson)
⊞ ■
GB title: C.A.S.H.
An impotent army veteran finds that a criminal career, helped by stolen army gas, helps his sex life.
Over-the-top comedy with vaguely anti-war and anti-pollution leanings.
w Malcolm Marmorstein d Ted Post ph David M. Walsh m John Cameron
☆ Elliott Gould, Eddie Albert, Harry Guardino, Godfrey Cambridge, Jennifer O'Neill
† Rather typical of the film was its ambiguous catch line: 'The biggest bang in history!'
♫ song 'Now That We're in Love' (mGeorge Barrie, lySammy Cahn)

While I Live
GB 1947 85m bw
Edward Dryhurst
reissue title: The Dream of Olwen
A Cornishwoman believes an amnesiac girl to be the reincarnation of her dead sister.
Silly melodrama which achieved phenomenal popularity, despite poor production, because of its haunting theme tune The Dream of Olwen by Charles Williams.
w John Harlow, Doreen Montgomery play This Same Garden by Robert Bell d John Harlow ph F. A. Young m Charles Williams
☆ Tom Walls, Sonia Dresdel, Carol Raye, Clifford Evans, Patricia Burke, John Warwick, Edward Lexy
'What cannot be conveyed is the flatulence of the production, the haplessness of the players as they stray heavy-eyed through the sets like lost sheep with Tom Walls yapping around them like a knowing old collie dog.' – Richard Winnington

'A Girl leaves her door open ... A Stranger tiptoes in ... A big city newspaper blazes with murder headlines! Then the chase as newsmen and women feud with each other ... to be the first to find the killer!'
While the City Sleeps
US 1956 100m bw Superscope
RKO (Bert Friedlob)
⊞ ■ ⊛
Three chief executives of a newspaper empire are pitted against each other in a search for a murder scoop.
Star-backed but leaden-paced news bureau melodrama, a major disappointment considering the talent.
w Casey Robinson novel The Bloody Spur by Charles Einstein d Fritz Lang ph Ernest Laszlo m Herschel Burke Gilbert
☆ Dana Andrews, George Sanders, Ida Lupino, Sally Forrest, Thomas Mitchell, Rhonda Fleming, Vincent Price, Howard Duff, James Craig, Robert Warwick, John Barrymore Jnr

While the Patient Slept
US 1935 65m bw
First National
A nurse hired to look after a stricken millionaire finds herself in the middle of a murder case.
Announced as the first of a series of Clue Club Mysteries, this was derived from a source similar to, or possibly the same as, Miss Pinkerton (qv). It sufficed.
w Robert N. Lee novel Mignon G. Eberhart d Ray Enright
☆ Aline MacMahon, Guy Kibbee, Lyle Talbot, Patricia Ellis, Allen Jenkins, Gene Solow, Brown Holmes, Robert Barrat, Hobart Cavanaugh
'Seems probable that it will please wherever mysteries are liked.' – Variety

While the Sun Shines
GB 1946 81m bw
ABPC/International Screenplays (Anatole de Grunwald)
An American soldier and a young Frenchman seek to woo Lady Elizabeth away from her intended.
Mild wartime comedy, rather stagey and considerably undercast.

w Anatole de Grunwald, Terence Rattigan play Terence Rattigan d Anthony Asquith ph Jack Hildyard m Nicholas Brodszky
☆ Brenda Bruce, Ronald Howard, Bonar Colleano, Ronald Squire, Barbara White, Margaret Rutherford, Miles Malleson, Joyce Grenfell

'A story about love at second sight.'
While You Were Sleeping *
US 1995 103m Technicolor
Buena Vista/Hollywood/Caravan (Joe Roth, Roger Birnbaum)
⊞ ■ ⊛ ◎
After a lawyer is mugged and lies in hospital in a coma, his parents mistakenly believe that the woman who saved his life is his fiancée and welcome her into the family.
A pleasing romantic time-waster, with a leading performance that may charm, but it is not a film that will linger long in the memory.
w Daniel G. Sullivan, Frederic Lebow d Jon Turteltaub ph Phedon Papamichael m Randy Edelman pd Garreth Stover ed Bruce Green
☆ Sandra Bullock, Bill Pullman, Peter Gallagher, Peter Boyle, Jack Warden, Glynis Johns, Ally Walker
'There is really nothing exceptional in the film – no stand-out scenes, no real tension about the ending and the usual wallpaper film music that tells us what to feel. But Bullock, the real find of the movie, and Pullman pull it off neatly.' – Derek Malcolm, Guardian

The Whip Hand
US 1951 82m bw
RKO (Lewis J. Rachmil)
A fisherman finds himself unwelcome in a lonely town run by ex-Nazi, now communist, bacteriologists.
Preposterous, pretentious anti-communist low-budgeter, mildly enjoyable for its sheer gall.
w George Bricker, Frank L. Moss ph Nicholas Musuraca m Paul Sawtell d/pd William Cameron Menzies
☆ Elliott Reid, Carla Balenda, Edgar Barrier, Raymond Burr

Whiplash
US 1948 90m bw
Warner (William Jacobs)
A painter becomes a prizefighter.
Hokey, unpersuasive romantic melodrama.
w Maurice Geraghty, Harriet Frank Jnr d Lewis Seiler ph Peverell Marley m Franz Waxman
☆ Dane Clark, Alexis Smith, Zachary Scott, Eve Arden, Jeffrey Lynn, S. Z. Sakall, Alan Hale, Douglas Kennedy

Whipsaw ^
US 1935 88m bw
MGM (Harry Rapf)
A G-man infiltrates a gang by wooing its girl member.
Fairly snappy romantic drama which further established both its stars.
w Howard Emmett Rogers d Sam Wood ph James Wong Howe m William Axt
☆ Spencer Tracy, Myrna Loy, Harvey Stephens, Clay Clement, William Harrigan
'Should do okay biz ... romance and sex angles mingling with the light touch of sophistication so popular nowadays carries events along at a speedy pace that is unabated until the fadeout.' – Variety

Whirlpool
US 1934 69m bw
Columbia
A convict is released and makes contact with the daughter who never knew him.
Heavily plotted melodrama with an unhappy ending; technically quite proficient.
w Dorothy Howell, Ethel Hill, Howard Emmett Rogers d Roy William Neill
☆ Jack Holt, Jean Arthur, Allen Jenkins, Donald Cook, Lila Lee, John Miljan, Ward Bond
'One of the most surefire father and daughter stories ever screened, with heart interest running high throughout ... well above fair in entertainment appeal.' – Variety

Whirlpool *
US 1950 98m bw
TCF (Otto Preminger)
A girl is accused of a murder committed by her hypnotist, who has willed himself out of a hospital bed.
Silly murder melodrama; glossy production makes it entertaining.
w Lester Barstow, Andrew Solt novel Guy Endore d Otto Preminger ph Arthur Miller m David Raksin
☆ Gene Tierney, José Ferrer, Richard Conte, Charles Bickford, Barbara O'Neil, Eduard Franz, Fortunio Bonanova
'It is sometimes difficult to discover from Miss Tierney's playing whether she is or is not under hypnosis.' – MFB
† Lester Barstow = Ben Hecht.

Whirlpool
GB 1959 95m Eastmancolor
Rank (George Pitcher)
A killer escapes in Cologne; his girlfriend separates from him and gets a lift down the Rhine in a barge; the trip reforms her and she betrays her lover.
Modestly attractive travelogue with the burden of a very boring melodrama.
w Lawrence P. Bachmann novel The Lorelei by Lawrence P. Bachmann d Lewis Allen ph Geoffrey Unsworth m Ron Goodwin
☆ Juliette Greco, O. W. Fischer, William Sylvester, Marius Goring, Muriel Pavlow

Whisky Galore ****
♦♦ GB 1948 82m bw
Ealing (Monja Danischewsky)
⊞ ■
US title: Tight Little Island
During World War II, a ship full of whisky is wrecked on a small Hebridean island, and the local customs and excise man has his hands full.
Marvellously precise, fast-moving, well-played and attractively photographed comedy which firmly established the richest Ealing vein.
w Compton Mackenzie, Angus MacPhail novel Compton Mackenzie d Alexander Mackendrick ph Gerald Gibbs m Ernest Irving
☆ Basil Radford, Joan Greenwood, Jean Cadell, Gordon Jackson, James Robertson Justice, Wylie Watson, John Gregson, Morland Graham, Duncan Macrae, Catherine Lacey, Bruce Seton, Henry Mollinson, Compton Mackenzie, A. E. Matthews
'Brilliantly witty and fantastic, but wholly plausible.' – Sunday Chronicle
† Fourteen whisky bottles, said to be the last surviving from the wreck of the SS Politician, the real-life shipwreck that inspired the film, were sold in 1993 at a Glasgow auction for £12,012, with a bottle of Haig Dimple fetching £1,210.

The Whisperers
GB 1966 106m bw
UA/Seven Pines (Michael S. Laughlin, Ronald Shedlo)
⌒
An old lady hears voices and is put upon by her son, her wandering husband, and various others.
Interesting but cold and finally unsatisfactory character melodrama; even the acting, though in a sense admirable, is too genteel.
w Bryan Forbes novel Robert Nicolson d Bryan Forbes ph Gerry Turpin m John Barry
☆ Edith Evans, Eric Portman, Avis Bunnage, Nanette Newman, Gerald Sim, Ronald Fraser
♫ Edith Evans
◈ Gerry Turpin; Edith Evans

Whispering City
Canada 1947 95m bw
Quebec/Eagle Lion
A girl reporter has dangerous information.
Fairly watchable mystery, all Canadian apart from the three leads.
w Rian James, Leonard Lee d Fedor Ozep
☆ Paul Lukas, Mary Anderson, Helmut Dantine, John Pratt, George Alexander

Whispering Ghosts
US 1942 75m bw
TCF (Sol M. Wurtzel)
A radio detective tackles the unsolved murder of an old sea captain.
No ghosts are evident, and not much plot, in this slow mystery comedy which failed to do for Berle what The Cat and the Canary did for Hope.

w Lou Breslow d Alfred Werker
☆ Milton Berle, Brenda Joyce, John Carradine, John Shelton, Willie Best

'The epic spectacle of America's most flaming era!'
Whispering Smith
US 1948 88m Technicolor
Paramount (Mel Epstein)
A government agent investigating robberies finds his friend is implicated.
Fairly entertaining detective Western.
w Frank Butler, Karl Lamb novel Frank H. Spearman d Leslie Fenton ph Ray Rennahan m Adolph Deutsch
☆ Alan Ladd, Robert Preston, Brenda Marshall, Donald Crisp, William Demarest, Fay Holden, Murvyn Vye, Frank Faylen

Whispering Smith Hits London
GB 1951 82m bw
Exclusive/Hammer (Anthony Hinds)
US title: Whispering Smith vs. Scotland Yard
An American detective in London investigates the case of a suicide which may be murder.
Tolerable programmer of its time: competence without inspiration.
w John Gilling story Frank H. Spearman d Francis Searle ph Walter Harvey m Frank Spencer ed James Needs
☆ Richard Carlson, Greta Gynt, Herbert Lom, Rona Anderson, Alan Wheatley, Dora Bryan, Reginald Beckwith

Whispers in the Dark
US 1992 98m DeLuxe
Paramount (Martin Bregman, Michael S. Bregman)
⊞ ■ ⊛
A New York psychiatrist is disturbed to discover that her new and apparently gentle boyfriend seems also to be the sadistic lover who acts out dangerous fantasies with one of her patients.
Mindlessly entertaining thriller that makes few demands on its audience and concludes that psychiatrists need their heads examined.
wd Christopher Crowe ph Michael Chapman m Thomas Newman pd John Jay Moore ed Bill Pankow
☆ Annabella Sciorra, Jamey Sheridan, Anthony LaPaglia, Jill Clayburgh, John Leguizamo, Deborah Unger, Alan Alda, Anthony Heald
'An entertaining pot-boiler, this bypassed the cinemas, but is certainly better value for your rental money than many another upmarket sex slasher.' – Kim Newman, Empire

The Whistle at Eaton Falls *
US 1951 96m bw
Columbia (Louis de Rochemont)
GB title: Richer than the Earth
The story of a strike at a small-town plastics factory.
Reasonably absorbing semi-documentary with a final 'solution' which rather evades the issues.
w Lemist Esler, Virginia Shaler d Robert Siodmak ph Joseph Brun m Louis Applebaum
☆ Lloyd Bridges, Dorothy Gish, Carleton Carpenter, Murray Hamilton, James Westerfield, Lenore Lonergan

Whistle Down the Wind *
♦♦ GB 1961 99m bw
Rank/Allied Film Makers/Beaver (Richard Attenborough)
⊞
Three north country children think a murderer on the run is Jesus Christ.
Charming allegorical study of childhood innocence, extremely well made, amusing, and avoiding sentimentality.
w Keith Waterhouse, Willis Hall novel Mary Hayley Bell d Bryan Forbes ph Arthur Ibbetson m Malcolm Arnold
☆ Hayley Mills, Bernard Lee, Alan Bates, Norman Bird, Elsie Wagstaff, Alan Barnes

Whistle Stop
US 1946 84m bw
United Artists/Nero/Seymour Nebenzal
■
A city girl returns to her small-town home and finds herself torn between a night-club proprietor and an indolent charmer.
Would-be film noir, miscast and rather glum when it isn't unintentionally funny.

---

w Philip Yordan *novel* Maritta M. Wolff
d Leonide Moguy *ph* Russell Metty *m* Dimitri
Tiomkin
☆ George Raft, Ava Gardner, Tom Conway,
Victor McLaglen

The Whistler

Originally a radio series of suspense stories
introduced by someone whistling the theme tune,
this was turned by Columbia into a fairly
workmanlike series of second features quite
unrelated to each other except for the leading
actor, Richard Dix, who alternated as hero and
villain, and William Castle, who directed or
produced most of them.
1944 The Whistler, The Mark of the Whistler
1945 The Power of the Whistler
1946 The Voice of the Whistler
1947 Mysterious Intruder, The Secret of the
Whistler, The 12th Hour
1948 The Return of the Whistler

Whistling in Brooklyn

US 1943 87m bw
MGM (George Haight)
▦
An actor who plays 'The Fox', a radio detective, is
suspected of murder and chased by cops and
robbers.
Amusing, lightweight comedy thriller.
w Nat Perrin, Wilkie Mahoney d S. Sylvan
Simon *ph* Lester White *m* George Bassman
ad Cedric Gibbons *ed* Ben Lewis
☆ Red Skelton, Ann Rutherford, Jean Rogers,
'Rags' Ragland, Ray Collins, Henry O'Neill,
William Frawley, Sam Levene, The Brooklyn
Dodgers
† It was a sequel to *Whistling in the Dark* (qv).

Whistling in Dixie

US 1942 87m bw
MGM (George Haight)
A radio detective known as 'The Fox' solves a
murder while waiting to get married in Georgia.
*Mildly entertaining comedy thriller, though it overplays
the joke of its cowardly hero.*
w Nat Perrin, Wilkie Mahoney d S. Sylvan
Simon *ph* Clyde DeVinna *m* Lennie Hayton
ad Cedric Gibbons *ed* Frank Sullivan
☆ Red Skelton, Ann Rutherford, George
Bancroft, Guy Kibbee, Diana Lewis, Peter Whitney
† It was a sequel to *Whistling in Brooklyn* (qv).

Whistling in the Dark *

US 1941 77m bw
MGM (George Haight)
▦
A radio detective is kidnapped by a criminal who
wants him to devise a perfect murder which will
then be pinned on him.
*Scatty comedy-thriller which, though it now seems slow
to start, was popular enough to warrant two sequels*
(Whistling in Brooklyn, Whistling in Dixie).
w Robert MacGunigle, Harry Clork, Albert
Mannheimer *play* Laurence Gross, Edward Childs
Carpenter d S. Sylvan Simon *ph* Sidney Wagner
m Bronislau Kaper
☆ Red Skelton, Conrad Veidt, Ann Rutherford,
Virginia Grey, Eve Arden, Rags Ragland, Don
Douglas, Lloyd Corrigan
† The play was previously filmed in 1933 with
Ernest Truex, and this version is now shown on TV
as *Scared*.

White Angel

GB 1993 95m colour
Pilgrim/Living Spirit (Genevieve Joliffe)
aka: Interview with a Serial Killer
A crime writer is blackmailed by her lodger, a
dentist and serial killer, when he discovers that she
murdered her violent husband.
*Dull and derivative thriller, no more than another
indication of the current fascination with mass
murderers.*
w Chris Jones, Genevieve Joliffe d Chris Jones
ph Jon Walker *m* Harry Gregson-Williams
ed John Holland
☆ Peter Firth, Harriet Robinson, Don Henderson,
Anne Catherine Arton
'This amateurish thriller wants to plumb some
Silence of the Lambs depths, but silly plot and
lame thesping will soon send it straight to video
prison.' – *Variety*

The White Angel *

US 1936 91m bw
Warner (Henry Blanke)
The life of Florence Nightingale.
*Starchy biopic; the Victorian atmosphere is never quite
caught.*
w Mordaunt Shairp, Michel Jacoby d William
Dieterle *ph* Tony Gaudio
☆ Kay Francis, Ian Hunter, Donald Woods, Nigel
Bruce, Donald Crisp, Henry O'Neill, Billy Mauch,
Halliwell Hobbes
'Miss Kay Francis, handicapped by her beauty,
does her best to sober down this sentimental
version of Florence Nightingale's character, but
she is defeated by the scenario-writers.' –
Graham Greene

The White Balloon **

Iran 1995 85m colour
Electric/CMI/Farabi/Fredos (Kurosh Mozkouri)
▦
original title: Badkonake Sefid
A seven-year-old girl drops her money on the way
to buy a goldfish and sets out to get it back.
*Pleasant, well-observed, rambling tale of street life in
Teheran.*
w Abbas Kiarostami *idea* Parviz Shahbazi d Jafar
Panahi *ph* Farzad Jowdat *pd* Jafar Panahi *ed* Jafar
Panahi
☆ Aida Mohammadkhani, Mohsen Kalifi,
Fereshteh Sadr Orfani, Anna Bourkowska
'By turns suspenseful and amusing, deceptively
slight tale is a charmer with lots of local color.' –
Variety
† The film won the Camera D'Or at the 1995
Cannes Film Festival.

White Banners *

US 1938 88m bw
Warner (Henry Blanke)
A social worker tries to solve the problems of a
troubled family among whom is her own son, a fact
unknown to him.
Moderate middle-class drama.
w Lenore Coffee, Cameron Rogers, Abem Finkel
novel Lloyd C. Douglas d Edmund Goulding
ph Charles Rosher *m* Max Steiner
☆ Fay Bainter, Claude Rains, Jackie Cooper,
Bonita Granville, Henry O'Neill, James
Stephenson, Kay Johnson
'Emotional drama, okay for the family trade ...
there is something fine and tender about it.' –
Variety
⚖ Fay Bainter

White Blood: see The Planter's Wife

The White Buffalo

US 1977 97m Technicolor
Dino de Laurentiis (Pancho Kohner)
Wild Bill Hickok and Chief Crazy Horse join
forces to kill a marauding white buffalo.
*Ridiculous symbolic Western, not helped by the very
artificial looking beast of the title.*
w Richard Sale *novel* Richard Sale d J. Lee-
Thompson *ph* Paul Lohmann *m* John Barry
☆ Charles Bronson, Jack Warden, Will Sampson,
Kim Novak, Clint Walker, Stuart Whitman, John
Carradine, Slim Pickens, Cara Williams, Douglas
Fowley
'The dried husk of a *Moby Dick* allegory seems to
be rattling around here amidst all the other dead
wood.' – *Jonathan Rosenbaum, MFB*

White Captive: see White Savage

White Cargo *

US 1942 90m bw
MGM (Victor Saville)
White rubber planters are driven mad with desire
for a scheming native girl.
*Antediluvian melodrama previously filmed in 1930.
Good for laughing at, and the star looked great as
Tondelayo.*
w Leon Gordon *play* Leon Gordon *novel* Hell's
Playground by Vera Simonton d Richard Thorpe
m Bronislau Kaper
☆ Hedy Lamarr, Walter Pidgeon, Richard
Carlson, Frank Morgan, Bramwell Fletcher,
Richard Ainley, Reginald Owen
† There was also a British version in 1929 (silent)
with Leslie Faber and Gypsy Rhouma; and a few
months later it emerged with added dialogue.

White Cargo

GB 1973 62m Eastmancolor
Border/Negus-Fancey (Mervyn Collard)
A dim-witted civil servant becomes involved in
rescuing some Soho strippers who are being sold to
an Arab harem.
*Limp comedy that mixes poor slapstick and coy sex to
no effect.*
w Ray Selfe, David McGillivray d Ray Selfe
ph John Barnard *m* David Lindup *ad* Jack
Shampan *ed* Peter Austen-Hunt
☆ David Jason, Hugh Lloyd, Imogen Hassall, Tim
Barrett, Dave Prowse, Raymond Cross, John Barber
'Mercifully, there is every sign that the film has
been heavily cut.' – *Tony Rayns, MFB*

White Christmas *

US 1954 120m Technicolor Vistavision
Paramount (Robert Emmett Dolan)
▦▦ ◉ ◎ ⊙
Two entertainers boost the popularity of a winter
resort run by an old army buddy.
*Humdrum musical lifted only by its stars; a revamp of
Holiday Inn, which was much better.*
w Norman Krasna, Norman Panama, Melvin
Frank d Michael Curtiz *ph* Loyal Griggs
songs Irving Berlin
☆ Bing Crosby, Danny Kaye, Rosemary Clooney,
Vera-Ellen, Dean Jagger, Mary Wickes, Sig
Rumann, Grady Sutton
♫ 'Count Your Blessings Instead of Sheep'

The White Cliffs of Dover *

US 1944 126m bw
MGM (Sidney Franklin)
An American girl who marries into the British
aristocracy loses a husband in World War I and a
son in World War II.
*Tearful flagwaver with some entertaining scenes in the
first half and the general sense of an all-stops-out
production.*
w Claudine West, Jan Lustig, George Froeschel
poem Alice Duer Miller d Clarence Brown
ph George Folsey *m* Herbert Stothart
☆ Irene Dunne, Alan Marshal, Frank Morgan,
May Whitty, Roddy McDowall, C. Aubrey Smith,
Gladys Cooper, Peter Lawford, Van Johnson
'A long, earnest, well-intentioned, over-
emotionalized cliché.' – *Richard Mallett, Punch*
'This sterling silver picture ... is such a tribute to
English gentility as only an American studio
would dare to make.' – *New York Times*
'Sentimental patriotism ... a truly monstrous
cultural artifact.' – *Pauline Kael, 70s*
⚖ George Folsey

The White Cockatoo

US 1935 72m bw
Warner
Male and female heirs to a will suffer death threats.
Bland transcription of a popular mystery book.
w Ben Markson, Lillie Hayward *novel* Mignon G.
Eberhart d Alan Crosland
☆ Ricardo Cortez, Jean Muir, Ruth Donnelly,
Minna Gombell, Walter Kingsford, John Eldredge

White Comanche

Spain/US 1968 92m Eastmancolor
Rank/International Producers/Cinematográficas A.B.
(Sam White)
aka: Comancho Blanco
A renegade Comanche is challenged to a duel to
the death by his law-abiding twin brother.
Uninteresting, unconvincing and unoriginal Western.
w José Briz, Manuel G. Rivera *story* Robert I.
Holt, Frank Gruber d Gilbert Lee Kay (José Briz)
ph Francisco Fraile *m* Jean Ledut
☆ William Shatner, Joseph Cotten, Rossana Yani,
Perla Cristal
'The story rambles through stock routines
accommodating stock characters.' – *MFB*
† The film was cut to 83m on its British release.

White Corridors *

GB 1951 102m bw
GFD/Vic (Joseph Janni, John Croydon)
Life in a small Midlands hospital.
Competent multi-drama which found a big audience.
w Jan Read, Pat Jackson *novel* Yeoman's Hospital
by Helen Ashton d Pat Jackson *ph* C.
Pennington-Richards
☆ James Donald, Googie Withers, Godfrey Tearle,
Petula Clark, Jack Watling, Moira Lister, Barry
Jones, Megs Jenkins, Basil Radford

'This quality of professionalism is comparatively
rare in British films.' – *Gavin Lambert*

White Cradle Inn

GB 1947 83m bw
British Lion/Peak (Ivor McLaren, A. G. Hardman)
US title: *High Fury*
A Swiss hotel owner adopts a refugee boy and is
menaced by her ne'er-do-well husband, who finally
sacrifices himself for the boy.
*Unimpressive little drama which wastes its cast, but
provides beautiful scenery.*
w Harold French, Lesley Storm d Harold French
ph Derick Williams *m* Bernard Green
☆ Madeleine Carroll, Michael Rennie, Ian
Hunter, Anne Marie Blanc, Michael McKeag

The White Dawn

US 1976 110m Movielab
Paramount/American Film Properties (Martin
Ransohoff)
▦ ◎
In 1900, survivors from a whaling ship are cared for
by Eskimos, who turn on them when nature proves
unkind.
*Unpleasant fable with lots of bitter weather and
subtitled Eskimos. Scarcely an entertainment, and its
message is mumbled.*
w James Houston, Tom Rickman d Philip
Kaufman *ph* Michael Chapman *m* Henry
Mancini
☆ Warren Oates, Timothy Bottoms, Lou Gossett,
Eskimo cast
'Chief among the pleasures the film offers us is
the sensation of having gained insight into a
distant, primitive culture.' – *Wall Street Journal*

White Dog *

US 1982 90m Metrocolor
Paramount/Edgar J. Scherick
An actress unknowingly acquires a dog that has
been trained to attack blacks only.
*Oddball thriller that attracted unjustified criticism as a
racist work, which prevented it from obtaining a proper
release.*
w Samuel Fuller, Curtis Hanson *book* Romain
Gary d Samuel Fuller *ph* Bruce Surtees *m* Ennio
Morricone
☆ Kristy McNichol, Paul Winfield, Burl Ives,
Jameson Parker, Lynne Moody, Marshall
Thompson

White Fang

↟↟ US 1990 109m Eastmancolor
Warner/Hybrid/Disney/Silver Screen Partners IV
(Marykay Powell)
▦▦ ◉ ◎
A youth, who goes to the Klondike to take over his
dead father's gold-mining claim, befriends a dog
that is half-wolf.
*Tame, youth-oriented version, far closer to Lassie than
to Jack London's original.*
w Jeanne Rosenberg, Nick Thiel, David Fallon
novel Jack London d Randal Kleiser *ph* Tony
Pierce-Roberts *m* Basil Poledouris *pd* Michael
Bolton *ed* Lisa Day
☆ Klaus Maria Brandauer, Ethan Hawke, Seymour
Cassel, Susan Hogan, James Remar, Bill Moseley,
Clint B. Youngreen

White Fang II: The Myth of the White Wolf

↟↟ US 1994 106m Technicolor
Buena Vista/Walt Disney (Preston Fischer)
▦▦ ◉ ◎ ⊙
White Fang's new master helps save from
starvation an Indian tribe who regard him as the
incarnation of a wolf.
*Unsophisticated entertainment for the under-teens, full
of noble savages, nobler dogs and the great outdoors.*
w David Fallon d Ken Olin *ph* Hiro Narita
m John Debney *pd* Cary White *ed* Elba Sanchez-
Short
☆ Scott Bairstow, Charmaine Craig, Al
Harrington, Victoria Racimo, Alfred Molina,
Geoffrey Lewis, Ethan Hawke (uncredited)
'Corny but entertaining outdoor adventure in
the manner of yesteryear's Saturday matinees.' –
Variety

White Feather *

US 1955 100m Technicolor Cinemascope

TCF/Panoramic (Robert L. Jacks)

A cavalry colonel tries to hold back gold prospectors until the Cheyenne have moved on to their new reservations.

Old-fashioned cowboys and (sympathetic) Indians, very efficiently done.

w Delmer Daves, Leo Townsend d Robert Webb ph Lucien Ballard m Hugo Friedhofer ☆ Robert Wagner, John Lund, Jeffrey Hunter, Debra Paget, Eduard Franz, Noah Beery Jnr, Hugh O'Brian, Virginia Leith, Emile Meyer

'Pick up the pieces, folks, Jimmy's in action again!'

White Heat ***

US 1949 114m bw

Warner (Louis F. Edelman)

A violent, mother-fixated gangster gets his come-uppance when a government agent is infiltrated into his gang.

This searing melodrama reintroduced the old Cagney and then some: spellbinding suspense sequences complemented his vivid and hypnotic portrayal.

w Ivan Goff, Ben Roberts story Virginia Kellogg d Raoul Walsh ph Sid Hickox m Max Steiner ☆ James Cagney, Edmond O'Brien, Margaret Wycherly, Virginia Mayo, Steve Cochran, John Archer

'The most gruesome aggregation of brutalities ever presented under the guise of entertainment.' – *Cue*

'In the hurtling tabloid traditions of the gangster movies of the thirties, but its matter-of-fact violence is a new post-war style.' – *Time*

'A wild and exciting picture of mayhem and madness.' – *Life*

§ Virginia Kellogg

The White Hell of Pitz Palu *

Germany 1929 90m bw

UFA

Mountaineers have a difficult ascent of Pitz Palu.

Classic semi-documentary, noted for its pictorial compositions more than its dramatic qualities.

wd G. W. Pabst, Dr Arnold Fank

'An astonishing and, to me, wildly terrifying film.' – *James Agate*

White Hunter

US 1936 65m bw

TCF/Darryl F. Zanuck

An African hunter is hired by an old enemy.

Extremely predictable melodrama with poor technical work.

w Sam Duncan, Kenneth Earl, Gene Markey d Irving Cummings ☆ Warner Baxter, Wilfrid Lawson, June Lang, Gail Patrick, Alison Skipworth

'An adventure in obsession...'

White Hunter Black Heart **

US 1990 112m Technicolor

Warner/Malpaso/Rastar (Clint Eastwood)

A film director goes to Africa ostensibly to make a film but primarily to shoot an elephant.

Based on a novel about John Huston making The African Queen, by a writer involved in that film, it emerges as an entertaining account of Hollywood egotism.

w Peter Viertel, James Bridges, Burt Kennedy novel Peter Viertel d Clint Eastwood ph Jack N. Green m Lennie Niehaus pd John Graysmark ed Joel Cox

☆ Clint Eastwood, Jeff Fahey, Charlotte Cornwell, Norman Lumsden, George Dzundza, Edward Tudor Pole, Roddy Maude-Roxby

'Its chief strength is that it is one of those increasingly rare Hollywood entertainments that treats its audience as adults.' – *Derek Malcolm, Guardian*

'Trapped unhappily between fact and fiction, the film builds up not to a bang but a whimper, leaving one wondering bemusedly what it is trying to say, and about whom.' – *Tom Milne, MFB*

White Lightning

US 1973 101m DeLuxe

United Artists/Levy-Gardner-Laven

A convict escapes to wreak vengeance on the corrupt sheriff who had killed his brother.

Heavy-going Southern melodrama which comes to life only during its occasional fits of violence. Gator was a kind of sequel.

w William Norton d Joseph Sargent ph Edward Rosson m Charles Bernstein ☆ Burt Reynolds, Jennifer Billingsley, Ned Beatty, Matt Clark, Bo Hopkins, Louise Latham, Diane Ladd

White Line Fever

US/Canada 1975 89m Metrocolor

Columbia-Warner/White Line Fever Syndicate/International Cinemedia (John Kemeny)

A poor but honest trucker riles the powerful by refusing to haul stolen goods.

A predictably violent action thriller with little to recommend it.

w Ken Friedman, Jonathan Kaplan d Jonathan Kaplan ph Fred Koenekamp m David Nichtern ad Sydney Litwak ed O. Nicholas Brown ☆ Jan-Michael Vincent, Kay Lenz, Slim Pickens, L. Q. Jones, Don Porter, Sam Laws, Dick Miller

The White Man: see The Squaw Man

White Man's Burden

US/France 1995 89m Technicolor

TCF/UGC/Band Apart (Lawrence Bender)

In an America where the black race holds the power, a white worker kidnaps his boss after he is unfairly sacked.

Feeble and heavy-handed satire that deals unilluminatingly in stereotypical characters and situations.

wd Desmond Nakano ph Willy Kurant m Howard Shore pd Naomi Shohan ed Nancy Richardson

☆ John Travolta, Harry Belafonte, Kelly Lynch, Margaret Avery, Tom Bower, Andrew Lawrence, Bumper Robinson, Tom Wright, Sheryl Lee Ralph

'A noble but dumb idea decimated by uninspired execution and a disastrously misplaced focus.' – *Film Review*

'It Ain't Easy Being This Good.'

White Men Can't Jump **

US 1992 112m DeLuxe

TCF (Don Miller, David Lester)

Two basketball hustlers – one white, one black – team up to part the unwary from their money.

Crisply performed, enjoyable caper with something to say about relationships between races.

wd Ron Shelton ph Russell Boyd m Bennie Wallace pd Dennis Washington ed Paul Seydor ☆ Wesley Snipes, Woody Harrelson, Rosie Perez, Tyra Ferrell, Cylk Cozart, Kadeem Hardison, Ernest Harden Jnr

'As fast, buoyant and full of feinting rubato as basketball itself.' – *Nigel Andrews, Financial Times*

'With a remarkable lack of soap-box oratory, Shelton's film manages to catch the prevailing tone of American race relations, to show us what urban America really looks like, and to depict the moral quandaries that poverty inevitably forces on its victims.' – *Henry Sheehan, Sight and Sound*

White Mischief

GB 1987 107m Agfacolor

Umbrella (Michael White)

Real-life unsolved murder of Lord Erroll in Kenya's Happy Valley.

Starry cast and slick direction fail to engage interest in the sybaritic lifestyle of white settlers in colonial Africa.

w Michael Radford, Jonathan Gems book James Fox d Michael Radford ph Roger Deakins m George Fenton pd Roger Hall ☆ Charles Dance, Greta Scacchi, Joss Ackland, Sarah Miles, John Hurt, Trevor Howard

White Nights

US 1985 135m Metrocolor

Columbia/New Visions/Delphi V (Taylor Hackford, William S. Gilmore)

After a plane crash, a Russian emigré ballet star finds himself a prisoner in Leningrad.

Basically an escape story with silly details, this tries also to be a dance film about relationships. Despite the star's powerful presence, it fails on most counts.

w James Goldman, Eric Hughes d Taylor Hackford ph David Watkin m Michel Colombier pd Philip Harrison ed Fredric and William Steinkamp

☆ Mikhail Baryshnikov, Gregory Hines, Jerzy Skolimowski, Helen Mirren, Geraldine Page, Isabella Rossellini

'Good looks but no style ... neither fish nor fowl, good nor bad, box office gold nor poison.' – *Variety*

♪ song 'Say You, Say Me' (Lionel Richie)

♪ song 'Separate Lives' (m/lStephen Bishop)

White of the Eye

GB 1986 111m colour

Elliott Kastner (Cassian Elwes, Brad Wyman)

A loving father and husband is also a serial killer.

Conventional material is made slightly more interesting by some slick camerawork and editing; but surface gloss is all that it offers.

w China and Donald Cammell novel Mrs White by Margaret Tracy d Donald Cammell ph Alan Jones m Nick Mason, Rick Fenn pd Philip Thomas ed Terry Rawlings

☆ David Keith, Cathy Moriarty, Art Evans, Alan Rosenberg, Mark Hayashi, William Schilling, David Chow, Alberta Watson

'Love is the last thing on their minds.'

White Palace

US 1990 103m colour

UIP/Universal/Mirage/Double Play (Mark Rosenberg, Amy Robinson, Griffin Dunne)

A successful young advertising executive begins an affair with a fortyish waitress in a hamburger joint.

Soft-centred romance in which love conquers social differences and aspirations.

w Ted Tally, Alvin Sargent novel Glenn Savan d Luis Mondoki ph Lajos Koltai m George Fenton pd Jeannine C. Oppewall ed Carol Fischer

☆ Susan Sarandon, James Spader, Jason Alexander, Kathy Bates, Eileen Brennan, Steven Hill, Rachel Levin

'One of the best films of its kind since The Graduate. Rave word-of-mouth should help warm up the box-office grill.' – *Variety*

The White Parade

US 1934 80m bw

TCF (Jesse L. Lasky)

Incidents at the nurses' training school of a midwestern hospital.

Smooth but very predictable semi-documentary.

w Sonya Levien, Ernest Pascal novel Rian James d Irving Cummings ☆ Loretta Young, John Boles, Dorothy Wilson, Muriel Kirkland, Sara Haden, Astrid Allwyn, Jane Darwell, Frank Conroy

'Sympathetic comedy drama with strong *femme* draw value.' – *Variety*

§ best picture

White Room

Canada 1990 91m colour

Vos Productions (Alexandra Raffé)

A voyeuristic youth, upset by witnessing the murder of a famous singer, begins a relationship with a mysterious woman he meets at the funeral.

A modern fairy story, a fantasy on themes of feminism and obsessive voyeurism, but lacking in any magic.

wd Patricia Rozema ph Paul Sarossy m Mark Korven pd Valanne Ridgeway ed Patricia Rozema ☆ Kate Nelligan, Maurice Godin, Margot Kidder, Sheila McCarthy

'The most dangerous way to solve a murder ... become the victim.'

White Sands

US 1992 101m colour

Warner/Morgan Creek (William Sackheim, Scott Rudin)

Investigating a murder in New Mexico, a deputy sheriff finds himself involved with the FBI, the CIA and arms dealers.

Confusing thriller of cross and double-cross that fails to sustain an interest in its many twists and turns.

w Daniel Pyne d Roger Donaldson ph Peter Menzies Jnr m Patrick O'Hearn pd John Graysmark ed Nicholas Beauman, Sue Blainey ☆ Willem Dafoe, Mary Elizabeth Mastrantonio, Mickey Rourke, M. Emmet Walsh, Mimi Rogers, James Rebhorn, Maura Tierney

'An absorbing, tightly coiled thriller not always easy to follow.' – *Variety*

'Initially intriguing, ultimately disappointing, but fun for much of the way.' – *Philip French, Observer*

White Savage: see South of Tahiti (1941)

White Savage

US 1943 75m Technicolor

Universal (George Waggner)

GB title: White Captive

The queen of a beautiful South Sea island has trouble with shark hunters and crooks after her mineral deposits.

Self-admitted hokum strung loosely and colourfully around its star: big box-office in the middle of the war.

w Richard Brooks d Arthur Lubin ph Lester White, William Snyder m Frank Skinner ☆ Maria Montez, Jon Hall, Sabu, Thomas Gomez, Sidney Toler, Paul Guilfoyle, Turhan Bey, Don Terry

'It may be that these semi-burlesques were more fun to make than to watch.' – *Pauline Kael, 70s*

White Shadows in the South Seas *

US 1928 88m bw

MGM

An alcoholic doctor in Tahiti finds happiness with a native girl until he is killed by white colonials.

Rather boring melodrama illuminated by superb photography.

w John Colton, Jack Cunningham book Frederick J. O'Brien d W. S. Van Dyke (and Robert Flaherty) ph Clyde DeVinna and others (including Flaherty) ☆ Monte Blue, Raquel Torres ⚲ Clyde DeVinna

The White Sheik **

Italy 1952 88m bw

PDC/OFI (Luigi Rovere)

original title: Lo Sceicco Bianco

A provincial couple come to Rome on their honeymoon, where the wife is infatuated with a common actor who portrays a dashing, aristocratic lover in a photo-novel.

A gently comic, ironic drama of illusion and reality, based on an idea of Michelangelo Antonioni's.

w Federico Fellini, Tullio Pinelli, Ennio Flaiano d Federico Fellini ph Arturo Gallea m Nino Rota ad Raffaello Tolfo ed Rolando Bebedetti ☆ Brunella Bovo, Leopoldo Trieste, Alberto Sordi, Giulietta Masina

'This affectionate satire on glamour and delusion is probably the most gentle and naturalist of Fellini's films, but it was not a success, maybe because it is a little flat in places.' – *Pauline Kael*

The White Sister

US 1933 110m bw

MGM (Hunt Stromberg)

When her lover is reported killed in the war, an Italian noblewoman takes the veil ... but he comes back.

Tiresome romantic drama from another age, a big prestige production of its time.

w Donald Ogden Stewart novel F. Marion Crawford, Walter Hackett d Victor Fleming ph William Daniels m Herbert Stothart ☆ Helen Hayes, Clark Gable, Lewis Stone, Louise Closser Hale, May Robson, Edward Arnold

'An eloquent yoking of marquee names ... certain money maker for general release.' – *Variety*

🛉🛉 film suitable for family viewing   ▥ VHS video-cassette for the British PAL system   ▤ VHS video-cassette for the British PAL system in wide screen-format   ✿ Video cassette in a computer-colourised version   ▦ American NTSC video-cassette   ⚲ Laser disc

† The silent version of 1923 starred Lillian Gish and Ronald Colman, and bore the tagline: 'A love that outlived passion!'

'The Strongest Force In Nature Is The Will To Survive.'
White Squall *
US   1996   127m   Technicolor
Buena Vista/Hollywood/Largo/Scott Free (Mimi Polk Gitlin, Rocky Lang)

The competence of a captain is questioned after his boat, crewed by teenagers spending a year sailing in the Caribbean, runs into trouble in a sudden storm.
Based on a true story, this is no more than an average rites-of-passage drama, with excitement and interest limited to the storm scenes, which are a long time coming.
w Todd Robinson d Ridley Scott ph Hugh Johnson m Jeff Rona pd Peter J. Hampton ed Gerry Hambling
☆ Jeff Bridges, Caroline Goodall, John Savage, Scott Wolf, Jeremy Sisto, Ryan Phillippe, David Lascher, Eric Michael Cole, Jason Marsden
'Lavish production isn't totally satisfying, coasting aimlessly at times before suddenly leaping into a more intense dramatic plane.' – *Brian Lowry, Variety*

White Tie and Tails
US   1946   81m   bw
Universal
A butler left in charge of the house gets ideas above his station.
Modest comedy which lacks the required high style.
w Bertram Millhauser novel The Victoria Docks at Eight by Rufus King, Charles Leakon d Charles Barton
☆ Dan Duryea, Ella Raines, William Bendix, Richard Gaines, Clarence Kolb, Frank Jenks

The White Tower
US   1950   98m   Technicolor
RKO (Sid Rogell)

Various people have personal reasons for climbing an Alpine mountain.
Pretentiously symbolic melodrama with some good action sequences and curiously stilted performances.
w Paul Jarrico novel James Ramsay Ullman d Ted Tetzlaff ph Ray Rennahan m Roy Webb
☆ Glenn Ford, Claude Rains, Alida Valli, Oscar Homolka, Cedric Hardwicke, Lloyd Bridges, June Clayworth
'The main interest is a curiosity as to who will fall over which precipice when.' – *Penelope Houston*

The White Unicorn
GB   1947   97m   bw
GFD/John Corfield (Harold Huth)
US title: *Bad Sister*
In a home for delinquent girls, the worst offender exchanges reminiscences with the warden.
Peg's Paper melodrama in complex flashback form.
w Robert Westerby, A. R. Rawlinson, Moie Charles novel Flora Sandstrom d Bernard Knowles ph Reginald Wyer m Bretton Byrd
☆ Margaret Lockwood, Joan Greenwood, Ian Hunter, Dennis Price, Guy Middleton, Catherine Lacey, Mabel Constanduros, Paul Dupuis

White Witch Doctor
US   1953   96m   Technicolor
TCF (Otto Lang)
A nurse in the Congo converts a gold-seeking adventurer.
Stale hokum in which the animals are the most interesting feature.
w Ivan Goff, Ben Roberts novel Louise A. Stinetorf d Henry Hathaway ph Leon Shamroy m Bernard Herrmann
☆ Susan Hayward, Robert Mitchum, Walter Slezak, Timothy Carey

'Alone among outcasts who hadn't seen a white woman in ten years!'
White Woman
US   1933   68m   bw
Paramount
A Cockney overseer in the Malaysian jungle takes back a cabaret singer as his bride.
Risible melodrama with an obvious outcome.

w Samuel Hoffenstein, Gladys Lehman story Norman Reilly Raine, Frank Butler d Stuart Walker ph Harry Fischbeck
☆ Charles Laughton, Carole Lombard, Kent Taylor, Charles Bickford, Percy Kilbride, Charles Middleton, James Bell
'Bromidic South Sea stuff ... seems best for dual bills.' – *Variety*
† Remade as *Island of Lost Men*.

White Zombie **
US   1932   74m   bw
American Securities Corporation (Edward Halperin)

Haitian zombies work a sugar mill for a white schemer.
Genuinely eerie horror film with a slow, stagey, out-of-this world quality coupled with an interesting sense of composition.
w Garnett Weston d Victor Halperin ph Arthur Martinelli md Abe Meyer
☆ Bela Lugosi, Madge Bellamy, John Harron, Joseph Cawthorn
'Fine work of Lugosi is backed by good cast and bizarre staging ... not quite up to Broadway.' – *Variety*
'A Gothic fairy tale filled with dreamlike imagery, traditional symbols, echoes of Romanticism, and (probably unintentional) psychosexual overtones.' – *Carlos Clarens*
'For those absolutely dedicated to gothic silliness.' – *New Yorker, 1977*

Whither Germany?: see *Kühle Wampe*

Who?
GB   1974   93m   Eastmancolor
British Lion/Hemisphere/Maclean

An American scientist is captured by the Russians after a car crash and returned six months later as a somewhat suspect android.
So-what mixture of character drama and James Bondery; aiming clearly at no particular audience, it failed to get a release.
w John Gould novel Algis Budrys d Jack Gold ph Petrus Schloemp m John Cameron
☆ Elliott Gould, Trevor Howard, Joseph Bova, Ed Grover, James Noble, Lyndon Brook

Who Am I?
Hong Kong   1998   108m   colour   Panavision
Columbia TriStar/Golden Harvest (Barbie Tung)
original title: *Wo Shi Shui*
In South Africa. the only surviving commando on a special mission suffers amnesia after a deliberately arranged plane crash, and faces death from his corrupt boss.
What begins as a broad comedy in a remote African village gradually segues into a familiar espionage drama, rather in the manner of a cut-price Bond movie; the climax is action-packed, but it's a long wait.
w Jackie Chan, Susan Chan, Lee Reynolds d Jackie Chan, Benny Chan ph Poon Hang Sang m Nathan Wang ad Oliver Wong ed Peter Cheung, Yau Chi Wai
☆ Jackie Chan, Michelle Ferre, Mirai Yamamoto, Ron Smerczak, Ed Nelson, Tom Pompert, Yannick Mbali, Washington Sixolo
'A tired, disjointed effort that neither momentary thrills nor Chan's winning personality can enliven.' – *Leonard Klady, Variety*
† The Hong Kong version, and the film originally shown in the US, ran for 120m.

'The Closest You'll Ever Get To Knowing The Secrets Of The Legendary S.A.S.'
Who Dares Wins
GB   1982   125m   colour
Rank/Richmond Light Horse/Euan Lloyd (Raymond Menmuir)

US title: *The Final Option*
An SAS captain infiltrates a ruthless antinuclear group which finally holds the American Secretary of State to ransom.
Crude exploitation of the SAS's successful relief of the Iranian Embassy. The entertainment is thick ear at best, and some of the dialogue and performances have to be seen to be believed.
w Reginald Rose d Ian Sharp ph Phil Meheux m Roy Budd, Jerry and Marc Donahue pd Syd Cain

☆ Lewis Collins, Judy Davis, Ingrid Pitt, Richard Widmark, Edward Woodward, Robert Webber, Kenneth Griffith, Norman Rodway
'It should manage to offend anybody – punk, pacifist or policeman – inclined to take seriously the subject of global security.' – *Philip Strick, MFB*
'Cinematically antiquated and with hawkish politics poking unappealingly through the thin cloak of fiction.' – *Sight and Sound*

Who Done It?
US   1942   77m   bw
Universal (Alex Gottlieb)

Soda jerks in a New York radio station catch a murderer.
So-so comedy thriller, fatally lacking atmosphere (and good jokes).
w Stanley Roberts, Edmund Joseph, John Grant d Erle C. Kenton ph Charles Van Enger m Frank Skinner
☆ Bud Abbott, Lou Costello, William Gargan, Louise Allbritton, Patric Knowles, Don Porter, Jerome Cowan, William Bendix, Mary Wickes, Thomas Gomez

Who Done It?
GB   1956   85m   bw
Ealing (Michael Relph, Basil Dearden)

An ice-rink sweeper sets up as a private eye and captures a ring of spies.
Lively but disappointing film debut for a star comic whose screen personality proved too bland.
w T. E. B. Clarke d Basil Dearden ph Otto Heller m Philip Green
☆ Benny Hill, Belinda Lee, David Kossoff, Garry Marsh, Ernest Thesiger, Thorley Walters

Who Framed Roger Rabbit ****
US   1988   103m   Rank
Colour/Metrocolor/DeLuxe
Warner/Touchstone/Amblin (Robert Watts, Frank Marshall)

Cartoon characters become involved in Dashiell Hammett-style whodunnit.
Criticisms of thin plotting are irrelevant: the seamless integration of animation and live-action enchanted audiences.
w Jeffrey Price, Peter S. Seaman book Who Censored Roger Rabbit? by Gary K. Wold d Robert Zemeckis ph Dean Cundey m Alan Silvestri pd Elliot Scott ad Arthur Schmidt animation Richard Williams
☆ Bob Hoskins, Christopher Lloyd, Joanna Cassidy, Stubby Kaye and also the voices of Charles Fleischer, Kathleen Turner, Amy Irving, Lou Hirsch, Mel Blanc
'A deplorable development in the possibilities of animation – and a melancholy waste of the gifts of one of our most gifted actors.' – *Dilys Powell*
🏆 Arthur Schmidt; visual effects
🏆 Dean Cundey; art direction

Who Goes There?
GB   1952   85m   bw
British Lion/London Films (Anthony Kimmins)
US title: *The Passionate Sentry*
In a Grace and Favour house near St James's Palace, a guardsman is involved in a trail of romantic intrigue.
Very British romantic farce, dully and quickly filmed from a West End success.
w John Dighton play John Dighton d Anthony Kimmins ph John Wilcox, Ted Scaife m Muir Mathieson
☆ Peggy Cummins, Valerie Hobson, George Cole, Nigel Patrick, A. E. Matthews, Anthony Bushell

Who Is Harry Kellerman and Why Is He Saying These Terrible Things About Me?
US   1971   108m   DeLuxe
Cinema Center (Ulu Grosbard, Herb Gardner)
A New York composer is persecuted by a mysterious figure who turns out to be himself.
Wild, shapeless, satirical psycho-comedy-melodrama. Not very good.
w Herb Gardner d Ulu Grosbard ph Victor Kemper pd Harry Horner
☆ Dustin Hoffman, Barbara Harris, Jack Warden, David Burns, Gabriel Dell, Dom DeLuise
🏆 Barbara Harris

Who Is Killing the Great Chefs of Europe? *
US   1978   112m   Metrocolor
Warner/Aldrich/Lorimar (Merv Adelson, Lee Rich, William Aldrich)

GB title: *Too Many Chefs*
A fast food entrepreneur in London finds himself at the centre of a series of grisly murders.
Unusual and lighthearted black comedy against the background of international gastronomy.
w Peter Stone novel Nan and Ivan Lyons d Ted Kotcheff ph John Alcott m Henry Mancini
☆ George Segal, Jacqueline Bisset, Robert Morley, Jean-Pierre Cassel, Philippe Noiret, Jean Rochefort, Madge Ryan

Who Killed Doc Robbin?
US   1948   55m   Cinecolor
Hal Roach
Local kids prowl a supposedly haunted mansion.
Hesitant revival of the Our Gang comedy style in a semi-feature format; it had only mild success.
w Maurice Geraghty, Dorothy Reid d Bernard Carr ph John Boyle m Heinz Roemheld
☆ George Zucco, Virginia Grey, Don Castle

Who Killed Mary What's Her Name?
US   1971   90m   DeLuxe
Cannon (George Manasse)

An ex-boxer determines to solve the murder of a prostitute.
Old-fashioned whodunnit with something to say grafted on every five minutes: an unsatisfactory mix.
w John O'Toole d Ernest Pintoff ph Greg Sandor m Gary McFarland
☆ Red Buttons, Alice Playten, Sylvia Miles, Sam Waterston

Who Saw Her Die? (dubbed)
Italy/Germany   1972   84m   Technicolor
Techniscope
Doria/Roas/Geissler (Enzo Doria, Dieter Geissler)

original title: *Chi L'ha Vista Morire?*
In Venice, a sculptor investigates the murder of his young daughter.
Slick thriller of no particular distinction, though its setting gives it a sense of style, and Morricone's score adds emphasis to its moments of suspense.
w Massimo D'Avak, Aldo Lado, Francesco Barilli, Rudiger von Spiess d Aldo Lado ph Franco di Giacomo m Ennio Morricone ad Gisella Longo, Alessandro Parenzo ed Angelo Curi, Jutta Brandstaedter
☆ George Lazenby, Anita Strindberg, Peter Chatel, Adolfo Celi, Dominique Boschero, Rosemarie Lindt, Georg Willing
† Aficionados of non-sequiturs may enjoy one line of dialogue: 'If you can't play ping-pong, don't get mixed up in politics.'

Who Shot Patakango?
US   1990   102m   colour
Patakango United Partnership (Halle Brooks)

aka: *Who Shot Pat?*
In the 50s, a group of tough Brooklyn boys fight and play through their final days at high school.
Pleasant, nostalgic rite-of-passage drama to a rock 'n' roll soundtrack.
w Robert and Halle Brooks d Robert Brooks ph Robert Brooks ed Robert and Halle Brooks
☆ David Knight, Sandra Bullock, Kevin Otto, Aaron Ingram, Brad Randall, Chris Cardona, Michael Puzzo, Christopher Creon, Gregg Marc Miller

Who Was That Lady? *
US   1960   115m   bw
Columbia/Ansark/George Sidney (Norman Krasna)
A professor seen kissing a student persuades a friend to tell his wife that they are both FBI agents on duty. Foreign spies believe them ...
Agreeably wacky comedy with a strained and prolonged middle section leading to a totally zany climax.
w Norman Krasna play Norman Krasna d George Sidney ph Harry Stradling m André Previn
☆ Tony Curtis, Dean Martin, Janet Leigh, James Whitmore, John McIntire, Barbara Nichols, Larry Keating

---

Whoever Says the Truth Shall Die *

Holland 1984 52m bw/colour
Vara

A documentary on the life, and especially death, of director Pier Paolo Pasolini which suggests that he was murdered not by a homosexual pick-up but as the victim of a right-wing conspiracy.
Interesting though somewhat inconsequential examination of what made Pasolini a vital and feared figure in modern Italian culture.
wd Philo Bregstein ph Michel Pensato, Alan Jones, Ali Movahed, Richard Laurent ed Mario Steenbergen
☆ Bernardo Bertolucci, Laura Betti, Maria Antonietta Macciochi, Alberto Moravia

'The hand that rocks the cradle has no flesh on it!'

Whoever Slew Auntie Roo?

GB 1972 91m Movielab
EMI-MGM/AIP/Hemdale (Louis M. Heyward)

US title: *Who Slew Auntie Roo?*
A madwoman menaces two orphan children.
Pointless and slenderly plotted adaptation of Hansel and Gretel, crude in all departments.
w Robert Blees, Jimmy Sangster d Curtis Harrington ph Desmond Dickinson m Ken Jones
☆ Shelley Winters, Ralph Richardson, Mark Lester, Lionel Jeffries, Chloe Franks, Hugh Griffith, Rosalie Crutchley, Pat Heywood
'Not content with being a delicate fantasy of childish nightmare, it tries to add a totally inappropriate seasoning of Grand Guignol.' – *Tom Milne*

'In a nice quiet suburb, a hitman with a heart has just moved in.'
'Life's a comedy. It's all in the execution.'

The Whole Nine Yards

US 2000 101m DeLuxe
Warner/Morgan Creek/Franchise/Rational Packaging/Lansdown (David Willis, Allan Kaufman)
A Montreal dentist realises that his new next-door neighbour is a notorious hitman being hunted by the mob for turning informant.
Crude farce, in which Willis does his familiar tough-guy act, Arquette and Pollak use the oddest accents ever heard, and Perry provides the physical comedy; it somehow misses its target.
w Mitchell Kapner d Jonathan Lynn ph David Franco m Randy Edelman pd David L Snyder ed Tom Lewis
☆ Bruce Willis, Matthew Perry, Rosanna Arquette, Matthew Clarke Duncan, Natasha Henstridge, Amanda Peet, Kevin Pollak
'A crudely funny farce that covers no new ground but sees its talented players running some surefire plays.' – *Todd McCarthy, Variety*
'Passable pap.' – *Empire*

The Whole Town's Talking *

US 1935 86m bw
Columbia (Lester Cowan)
GB title: *Passport to Fame*
A gangster finds it convenient occasionally to pose as his double, a meek little clerk.
Pleasingly neat comedy, well staged and acted.
w Jo Swerling, Robert Riskin novel W. R. Burnett d John Ford ph Joseph August
☆ Edward G. Robinson, Jean Arthur, Arthur Hohl, Wallace Ford, Arthur Byron, Donald Meek, Edward Brophy, Etienne Girardot
'Wow comedy-melodrama … swell entertainment.' – *Variety*
'A lively and satisfactory combination of farce and melodrama.' – *Richard Watts Jnr*

The Whole Truth *

GB 1958 84m bw
Columbia/Romulus (Jack Clayton)
A jealous husband poses as a detective in order to murder his wife and incriminate a film producer.
A filmed play, but quite a solidly carpentered murder thriller with a couple of neat twists.
w Jonathan Latimer play Philip Mackie d John Guillermin ph Wilkie Cooper m Mischa Spoliansky
☆ Stewart Granger, George Sanders, Donna Reed, Gianna Maria Canale

Who'll Stop the Rain? *

US 1978 125m colour
UA/Gabriel Katzka, Herb Jaffe

GB title: *Dog Soldiers*
A Vietnam veteran takes to smuggling heroin into the US, but gets his wife and friend involved with gangsters.
Heavy-going, downbeat character drama with action sequences.
w Judith Roscoe novel *Dog Soldiers* by Robert Stone d Karel Reisz ph Richard H. Kline m Laurence Rosenthal
☆ Nick Nolte, Tuesday Weld, Michael Moriarty, Anthony Zerbe, Richard Masur, David Opatoshu, Ray Sharkey, Gail Strickland
'Just another ambition-downer, a wasted effort to make something meaningful out of wasted lives.' – *Richard Schickel, Time*

Wholly Moses

US 1980 109m Metrocolor Panavision
Columbia/David Begelman

A shepherd hears God talking to Moses, and thinks he himself has been ordained to set his people free.
Inept and tasteless biblical spoof which must set back by about ten years the reputations of all connected with it.
w Guy Thomas d Gary Weis ph Frank Stanley m Patrick Williams
☆ Dudley Moore, James Coco, Paul Sand, Jack Gilford, Dom DeLuise, John Houseman, Madeline Kahn
'Deadly dullness of both writing and execution render pointless any attempt to single out blame for misfire, which leaves many talented performers flailing about in desperate attempts to generate laughs.' – *Variety*

Whoopee *

US 1930 94m Technicolor
Samuel Goldwyn, Florenz Ziegfeld

A timid young man is catapulted into various adventures.
Early sound musical from a popular Broadway show, later remade as Up in Arms (qv).
w William Conselman musical play William Anthony McGuire play *The Nervous Wreck* by Owen Davis d Thornton Freeland ph Lee Garmes, Ray Rennahan, Gregg Toland ch Busby Berkeley ad Richard Day songs Walter Donaldson, Gus Kahn
☆ Eddie Cantor, Eleanor Hunt, Paul Gregory, Jack Rutherford, Ethel Shutta
'Dandiest of screen musicals and okay dough-getter.' – *Variety*
⅄ Richard Day

Whoops Apocalypse

GB 1986 91m Eastmancolor
ITC (Brian Eastman)

First woman president of the US tries to avert nuclear attack.
Frenetic but pathetic attempt at Dr Strangelove for the 80s.
w Andrew Marshall, David Renwick d Tom Bussmann ph Ron Robson m Patrick Gowers pd Tony Noble ed Peter Boyle
☆ Loretta Swit, Peter Cook, Rik Mayall, Ian Richardson, Alexei Sayle, Herbert Lom

Whore

US 1991 85m colour
Palace/Trimark (Dan Ireland, Ronaldo Vasconcellos)

A prostitute, hiding from her vicious pimp, recalls good customers and bad.
Dispiriting account of sexual exploitation, not helped by transferring the original's specifically London setting to the United States.
w Ken Russell, Deborah Dalton play *Bondage* by David Hines d Ken Russell ph Amir Mokri m Michael Gibbs pd Richard Lewis ed Brian Tagg
☆ Theresa Russell, Benjamin Mouton, Antonio Fargas, Sanjay, Elizabeth Moorehead, Michael Crabtree

'You are cordially invited to George and Martha's for an evening of fun and games!'

Who's Afraid of Virginia Woolf? ****

US 1966 129m bw
Warner (Ernest Lehman)

A college professor and his wife have an all-night shouting match and embarrass their guests.
As a film of a play, fair to middling; as a milestone in cinematic permissiveness, very important; as an entertainment, sensational for those in the mood.
w Ernest Lehman play Edward Albee d Mike Nichols ph Haskell Wexler m Alex North
☆ Richard Burton, Elizabeth Taylor, George Segal, Sandy Dennis
'A magnificent triumph of determined audacity.' – *Bosley Crowther*
'One of the most scathingly honest American films ever made.' – *Stanley Kauffmann*
🏆 Haskell Wexler; Elizabeth Taylor; Sandy Dennis
⅄ best picture; Ernest Lehman; Mike Nichols; Alex North; Richard Burton; George Segal
🏆 best picture; Richard Burton; Elizabeth Taylor

Who's Been Sleeping in My Bed?

US 1963 103m Technicolor Panavision
Paramount/Amro (Jack Rose)
A TV matinee idol finds he is a sex symbol also in his private life.
Coy bedroom farce with no real action but a smattering of jokes.
w Jack Rose d Daniel Mann ph Joseph Ruttenberg m George Duning
☆ Dean Martin, Elizabeth Montgomery, Martin Balsam, Jill St John, Richard Conte, Carol Burnett, Louis Nye, Yoko Tani, Elisabeth Fraser

'The most riotous bedtime story ever!'

Who's Got the Action?

US 1962 93m Technicolor Panavision
Paramount/Amro (Jack Rose)
A bored wife and her law partner husband have remarkable success betting on horses.
Badly cast and rather slow comedy with flashes of wit.
w Jack Rose novel *Four Horse Players Are Missing* by Alexander Rose d Daniel Mann ph Joseph Ruttenberg m George Duning
☆ Dean Martin, Lana Turner, Eddie Albert, Walter Matthau, Nita Talbot, Margo, Paul Ford, John McGiver

Who's Harry Crumb?

US 1989 90m Technicolor
Columbia TriStar/NBC (Arnon Milchan)

An incompetent, accident-prone private detective investigates the kidnapping of a millionaire's daughter.
Broad, slapstick comedy that offers occasional pleasures.
w Robert Conte, Peter Martin Wortmann d Paul Flaherty ph Stephen M. Katz m Michel Colombier pd Trevor Williams ed Danford B. Greene, Scott Conrad
☆ John Candy, Jeffrey Jones, Annie Potts, Tim Thomerson, Barry Corbin, Shawnee Smith, Valri Bromfield, Doug Steckler, Renee Coleman

Who's Minding the Mint? *

US 1967 97m Technicolor
Columbia/Norman Maurer

An employee of the US mint and his friends find a means of printing bills at night.
Smartly-made action comedy with good performances.
w R. S. Allen, Harvey Bullock d Howard Morris ph Joseph Biroc m Lalo Schifrin
☆ Jim Hutton, Dorothy Provine, Milton Berle, Joey Bishop, Bob Denver, Walter Brennan, Victor Buono, Jack Gilford

Who's Minding the Store? *

US 1963 90m Technicolor
Paramount/York/Jerry Lewis (Paul Jones)
An accident-prone young man gets a job in a department store.
Better-than-average star comedy, slapstick being allowed precedence over sentimentality.
w Frank Tashlin, Harry Tugend d Frank Tashlin ph W. Wallace Kelley m Joseph J. Lilley
☆ Jerry Lewis, Jill St John, Agnes Moorehead, John McGiver, Ray Walston, Nancy Kulp

Who's That Girl?

US 1987 94m Technicolor
Warner/Peter Guber, Jon Peters, Roger Birnbaum

A mild lawyer finds an ex-jailbird starlet his hardest client to handle.
Muddled 'realistic' comedy which starts at screaming pitch and stays there.
w Andrew Smith, Ken Finkleman d James Foley ph Jan DeBont ed Pembroke J. Herring
☆ Madonna, Griffin Dunne, Haviland Morris, John McMartin, Robert Swan, Drew Pillsbury
'What's lacking is pure and simple good humour.' – *Variety*

Who's That Knocking at My Door *

US 1968 90m bw
Cinegate/Tri-Mod (Joseph Weill, Haig Manoogian, Betzi Manoogian)
aka: *I Call First*
aka: *J. R.*
An Italian-American's relationship with a more sophisticated woman is ruined by his working-class Catholic upbringing.
Scorsese's first and an intriguing film, a groping towards the subject-matter that found assured expression in Mean Streets.
wd Martin Scorsese ph Michael Wadleigh, Richard Coll ad Vic Magnotta ed Thelma Schoonmaker
☆ Harvey Keitel, Zina Bethune, Lennard Kuras, Ann Collette, Michael Scala, Harry Northup, Catherine Scorsese, Phil Carlson
† The film was first shown under the title *I Call First* at the Chicago Film Festival in 1967. It was later released under its present title with the addition of a nude scene.

Who's the Man?

US 1993 87m Technicolor
Metro Tartan/New Line/Tin Pan Apple/De Passe/Thomas (Charles Stettler, Maynell Thomas)
Two Harlem barbers become policemen and save the neighbourhood from a wicked developer.
Rappers tread where only Police Academy has trod before in a crudely slapstick comedy that also attempts, and fails, to make a serious point; the reason for it all seems to be the music, which is also an acquired taste.
w Seth Greenland d Ted Demme ph Adam Kimmel m Michael Wolff, Nic ten-Broek pd Ruth Ammon ed Jeffrey Wolf
☆ Ed Lover, Doctor Dre, Badja Djola, Richard Bright, Ice-T
'An enjoyable, kinetic mess of music, low comedy and social drama.' – *Variety*

Whose Life Is It Anyway?

US 1981 118m Metrocolor
MGM/Martin C. Schute, Ray Cooney (Lawrence P. Bachmann)

Totally paralysed after a car crash, a young sculptor lies in hospital wanting to die.
Ill-advised film of a very static play which was a freak success on account of various very good leading performances. It makes a very uneasy movie.
w Brian Clark, Reginald Rose play Brian Clark d John Badham ph Mario Tosi m Arthur B. Rubinstein
☆ Richard Dreyfuss, John Cassavetes, Christine Lahti, Bob Balaban, Kenneth McMillan

Why Bother to Knock: see *Don't Bother to Knock*

Why Did Bodhi-Dharma Leave for the East? *

South Korea 1989 135m colour
ICA/Bae Yong-Kyun
original title: *Dharmaga Tongjoguro Kan Kkadalgun?*
In a remote monastery an old monk prepares for his death, a younger one feels guilt about abandoning his family and his blind mother, and an orphaned child grieves for a moment over a bird he kills accidentally.
A leisurely Zen Buddhist meditation on death and enlightenment that offers few of the usual pleasures of movies, such as narrative and character development.
wd Bae Yong-Kyun ph Bae Yong-Kyun m Chin Kyn-Yong ed Bae Yong-Kyun
☆ Yi Pan-Yong, Sin Won-Sop, Huang Hae-Jin, Ko Su Myoung
† The film won the Golden Leopard award at the 1990 Locarno Film Festival.

Why Me?
US 1989 87m colour
Entertainment/Epic Productions/Sarlui/Diamant
(Marjorie Israel)

Two jewel thieves, who inadvertently steal a
famous ruby ring, double-cross the authorities who
demand its return.
Weakly acted, limp comedy-thriller that fails to sparkle.
w Donald E. Westlake, Leonard Maas Jnr
novel Donald E. Westlake d Gene Quintano
ph Peter Deming m Phil Marshall pd Woody
Crocker ed Alan Balsam
☆ Christopher Lambert, Kim Greist, Christopher
Lloyd, J. T. Walsh, Gregory Millar, Wendel
Meldrum, Michael J. Pollard, John Plana, Tony
Plana

Why Shoot the Teacher?
Canada 1976 99m colour
WSTT/Fraser Films (Lawrence Hertzog)

In 1935 a school teacher finds a chilly reception
when he settles in a Saskatchewan village.
*Unsatisfactory but occasionally quite entertaining
comedy-drama which hovers around the Cold
Comfort Farm mark.*
w James Defelice novel Max Braithwaite d Silvio
Narizzano ph Marc Champion m Ricky Hyslop
☆ Bud Cort, Samantha Eggar, Chris Wiggins,
Gary Reineke

Why We Fight ****
US War Office 1942 bw
Frank Capra
A series of feature-length compilations released
during 1942-5, primarily for showing to the armed
forces, these were superbly vigorous documentaries
which later fascinated the public at large.
Editing, music and diagrams were all used to punch
home the message. Individual titles were:
Prelude to War (53m):
w Eric Knight, Anthony Veiller d Frank Capra
oscarbest documentary
The Nazis Strike (42m):
w and d as above
Divide and Conquer (58m):
w Anthony Veiller, Robert Heller d Frank Capra,
Anatole Litvak
The Battle of Britain (54m):
wd Anthony Veiller
The Battle of Russia (80m):
w Anthony Veiller, Robert Heller, Anatole Litvak d
Anatole Litvak oscar best documentary
The Battle of China (60m):
w Eric Knight, Anthony Veiller d Frank Capra,
Anatole Litvak
War Comes to America (70m)
w Anthony Veiller d Anatole Litvak
All had editing by William Hornbeck, music by
Dimitri Tiomkin and commentary by Walter Huston.

Why Worry? *
US 1923 60m bw silent
Hal Roach-Harold Lloyd
A hypochondriac is cured when he gets mixed up
in a South American revolution.
Moderate star comedy with highlights well spaced out.
d Sam Taylor, Fred Newmeyer
☆ Harold Lloyd, Jobyna Ralston, Leo White

Wichita
US 1955 81m Technicolor Cinemascope
Walter Mirisch/AA

Wyatt Earp is hired to bring law and order to a
wide-open cow town.
*Standard, i.e. romanticized, version of Earp's exploits:
quite entertaining to watch.*
w Daniel Ullman d Jacques Tourneur ph Harold
Lipstein m Hans J. Salter
☆ Joel McCrea, Vera Miles, Lloyd Bridges,
Wallace Ford, Edgar Buchanan, Peter Graves,
Keith Larsen, Carl Benton Reid

Wicked
US 1931 57m bw
Fox
A woman is innocently sent to prison and when
she comes out sets about finding the child she had
to sign away.
Woman's picture, packed with predictable incident.
w anonymous hands d Allan Dwan

☆ Elissa Landi, Victor McLaglen, Theodore von
Eltz, Alan Dinehart, Una Merkel, Oscar Apfel,
Irene Rich
'Old-fashioned tearjerker now too old to jerk
tears or grosses.' – Variety

'If every woman has her price ... there's a reason!'
Wicked As They Come
GB 1956 94m bw
Columbia/Film Locations (Maxwell Setton)
US title: *Portrait in Smoke*
A beauty contest winner from the slums makes
money and luxury her goal.
Busy melodrama which interests without edifying.
wd Ken Hughes ph Basil Emmott m Malcolm
Arnold co-w Robert Westerby, Sigmund Miller
☆ Arlene Dahl, Herbert Marshall, Phil Carey,
Michael Goodliffe, David Kossoff, Sidney James,
Ralph Truman, Faith Brook

Wicked City (dubbed)
Japan 1993 81m colour
Hideyuki Kikuchi/Tokuma Shoten/Video Art/Japan
Home Video/Manga (Kenji Kurada, Makoto Sedani)

A human bodyguard and a woman from the dark
world of monsters are assigned to guard from
assassins a doctor essential to the signing of a peace
treaty between the two worlds.
*A well-animated saga of exotic sex, violence and
sentimentality.*
w Maretoshi Naga novel Hideyuki Kikuchi
d Yoshiaki Kawajiri ph Kinichi Ishikawa
m Yoshimasa Tokai ad Kazuo Oga ed Nobuyuki
Ogata
☆ Featuring the voices of Stuart Miller, Tammy
Holloway, George Littlewood, Bill Richards,
Ronald Baker, Lisa Robinson, Philip Gough

The Wicked Lady *
GB 1945 104m bw
GFD/Gainsborough (R. J. Minney)

In the days of Charles II, Lady Skelton befriends a
highwayman and takes to crime.
*The most commercially successful of the Gainsborough
costume charades because of its atmosphere of gloomy
sin. Dramatically turgid and surprisingly poorly acted
and directed, but with good period detail. It had to be
reshot for America because of the ladies' décolletage.*
wd Leslie Arliss novel The Life and Death of the
Wicked Lady Skelton by Magdalen King-Hall
ph Jack Cox m Hans May md Louis Levy
☆ Margaret Lockwood, James Mason, Griffith
Jones, Patricia Roc, Michael Rennie, Enid Stamp-
Taylor, Felix Aylmer, Martita Hunt, David Horne
'A mixture of hot passion and cold suet
pudding.' – Manchester Guardian
'Rather dull and juvenile in its determination to
be daring.' – Richard Mallett, Punch

The Wicked Lady
GB 1983 99m colour
Columbia/Cannon (Menahem Golan, Yoram Globus)

A remake with colour, sex and violence.
*Pictorially quite attractive, but that's about all. It
caused controversy when the British censor tried to cut
a scene showing Faye Dunaway lashing another
woman with a horse-whip but retracted after Winner
protested. (The fight owed much to a similar scene in
Idol of Paris [qv], directed by Leslie Arliss in 1948.)*
w Leslie Arliss, Michael Winner d Michael
Winner ph Jack Cardiff m Tony Banks ad John
Blezard ed Arnold Crust
☆ Faye Dunaway, Alan Bates, John Gielgud,
Denholm Elliott, Prunella Scales, Oliver Tobias,
Glynis Barber, Joan Hickson
'The images look as cheap as expensive greetings
cards.' – Sunday Times
'A first-class piece of popular entertainment.' –
Lindsay Anderson

Wicked Stepmother
US 1989 92m DeLuxe
MGM/Larco (Robert Littman)

A wife returns from holiday with her husband to
discover that in their absence her father has
married a strange old woman.
*A bizarre oddity: a psychological horror movie that
turned into a broad, occult comedy when its star left in
the early stages. It has a few amusing moments amid*

the chaos, but would probably have been no better had
the production gone smoothly.
wd Larry Cohen ph Bryan England m Robert
Folk ad Gene Abel ed David Kern
☆ Bette Davis, Colleen Camp, Lionel Stander,
David Rasche, Tom Bosley, Barbara Carrera,
Richard Moll, Seymour Cassel, Evelyn Keyes
† Bette Davis (who, at 80, looked shrivelled and
ill) quit the production after she saw herself in
early, unedited scenes, necessitating some swift
rewriting in order to try to incorporate her work in
a new narrative in which she is transformed into
Barbara Carrera. Problems with her false teeth
made it difficult for her to say her lines, which she
also had difficulty remembering. It was her last,
and least, screen appearance.

The Wicked Wife: see Grand National Night

A Wicked Woman
US 1934 71m bw
MGM (Harry Rapf)
A woman kills her drunken husband to protect her
children, later confesses and is exonerated.
*The tail end of the mother love saga, better made than
most.*
w Florence Ryerson, Zelda Sears novel Anne
Austin d Charles Brabin ph Lester White
m William Axt
☆ Mady Christians, Charles Bickford, Betty
Furness, William Henry, Jackie Searl, Robert
Taylor, Paul Harvey

The Wicker Man **
GB 1973 86m Eastmancolor
British Lion (Peter Snell)

A policeman flies to a remote Scottish isle to
investigate the death of a child, and finds himself
in the hands of diabolists.
*Old-fashioned but remarkably well made scare story,
with effective shock moments.*
w Anthony Shaffer d Robin Hardy ph Harry
Waxman m Paul Giovanni ad Seamus Flannery
☆ Edward Woodward, Britt Ekland, Christopher
Lee, Ingrid Pitt, Diane Cilento
'An encouraging achievement for those who had
begun to despair of the British cinema.' – David
McGillivray
† The film also exists in other versions, the longest
running for 102m.

Wide Open Faces
US 1938 67m bw
Columbia (David L. Loew)
Public enemies congregate in a wayside inn where
missing loot is believed to be buried.
Moderately amusing slapstick farce.
w Earle Snell, Clarence Marks, Joe Bigelow,
Richard Flournoy d Kurt Neumann
☆ Joe E. Brown, Jane Wyman, Alison Skipworth,
Lyda Roberti, Alan Baxter, Lucien Littlefield,
Sidney Toler, Berton Churchill
'On the corny side, strictly for dual bills.' –
Variety

'An erotic tale of beauty and bewitchment.'
Wide Sargasso Sea
Australia 1992 98m colour
Rank/Sargasso/New Line/Laughing Kookaburra (Jan
Sharp)

In Jamaica in the mid-1800s, as her marriage to an
English gentleman disintegrates, a plantation
owner fears that, like her mother, she may go mad.
*A prequel to Jane Eyre, concentrating on the fate of
the mad Mrs Rochester, this is a lush and overblown
saga of sex and revenge, bordering on the risible.*
w Jan Sharp, Carole Angier, John Duigan
novel Jean Rhys d John Duigan ph Geoff Burton
m Stewart Copeland pd Franckie D ed Anne
Goursaud
☆ Karina Lombard, Nathaniel Parker, Claudia
Robinson, Michael York, Rachel Ward, Martine
Beswick, Huw Christie Williams
'A faintly absurd erotic melodrama whose
protagonists must have been cast for their looks
and their eagerness to sweat through copious bed
scenes rather than for acting ability.' – Sheila
Johnston, Independent
† The same theme was explored in an earlier film,
I Walked with a Zombie (qv).

The Widow from Chicago
US 1930 63m bw
First National
A woman mixes with a gang to avenge her
brother's murder.
*Bottom-of-the-barrel gangster drama, presented with
little flair.*
w Earl Baldwin d Edward Cline
☆ Alice White, Edward G. Robinson, Neil
Hamilton, Frank McHugh, E. H. Calvert
'Barely makes programme grade ... will have to
struggle to break even.' – Variety

Widow from Monte Carlo
US 1935 60m bw
Warner
The theft of an indiscreet letter causes much
embarrassment in an English country house.
*Society comedy-drama with curious farcical asides: not
an obvious success.*
w F. Hugh Herbert, Charles Belden play Ian
Hunter, A. E. W. Mason d Arthur G. Collins
☆ Warren William, Dolores del Rio, Louise
Fazenda, Colin Clive, Herbert Mundin, Warren
Hymer
'Behind the eight ball where big-time dates are
concerned.' – Variety

Widow's Peak
GB 1993 101m Eastmancolor
Rank/Jo Manuel
An overbearing widow who dominates life in a
small Irish town gets her come-uppance.
*A revenge comedy that begins in a broad and lively
manner and then loses its way.*
w Hugh Leonard d John Irvin ph Ashley Rowe
m Carl Davis pd Leo Austin ed Peter Tanner
☆ Mia Farrow, Joan Plowright, Natasha
Richardson, Jim Broadbent, Adrian Dunbar, John
Kavanagh, Anne Kent
'A forgettable saga worth seeing if only to
immerse yourself in Ireland without seeing it
rain for an hour.' – Neville Judd, Film Review

Wife, Doctor and Nurse *
US 1937 84m bw
TCF (Raymond Griffith)
A romantic triangle as the title suggests.
*Agreeable fluff with a mildly surprising end (for 1937)
suggesting a ménage à trois.*
w Kathryn Scola, Darrell Ware, Lamar Trotti
d Walter Lang ph Edward Cronjager m Arthur
Lange
☆ Loretta Young, Warner Baxter, Virginia Bruce,
Jane Darwell, Sidney Blackmer, Maurice Cass,
Minna Gombell, Elisha Cook Jnr, Lon Chaney Jnr
'A smart comedy that will please all.' – Variety

Wife, Husband and Friend *
US 1939 80m bw
TCF (Nunnally Johnson)
A man sabotages his wife's efforts to become a
professional singer.
*Modestly agreeable romantic comedy later remade as
Everybody Does It (qv).*
w Nunnally Johnson story James M. Cain
d Gregory Ratoff ph Ernest Palmer m David
Buttolph
☆ Loretta Young, Warner Baxter, Binnie Barnes,
Cesar Romero, George Barbier, J. Edward
Bromberg, Eugene Pallette, Helen Westley
'Diverting farce comedy with appeal pointed to
class audiences.' – Variety

The Wife of General Ling
GB 1937 72m bw
John Stafford/Premier
In China, a merchant's white wife unmasks him as
a criminal.
Stilted melodrama.
w Akos Tolnay, Reginald Long, Peter Cheyney,
Dorothy Hope d Ladislas Vajda
☆ Griffith Jones, Inkijinoff, Adrianne Renn, Alan
Napier, Anthony Eustrel, Hugh McDermott,
Gibson Gowland
'Hardly up to West End level.' – Variety

Wife of Monte Cristo
US 1946 83m bw
PRC (Leon Fromkess)
In 1832 Paris, the Count leads an underground
movement against racketeers.
*And the film plays like a Brooklyn melodrama in fancy
dress; as such, not too bad.*

w Dorcas Cochran d Edgar G. Ulmer
☆ John Loder, Lenore Aubert, Charles Dingle, Fritz Kortner, Martin Kosleck, Eduardo Ciannelli, Fritz Feld, Eva Gabor

The Wife Takes a Flyer

US 1942 86m bw
Columbia (B. P. Schulberg)
GB title: A Yank in Dutch

A Dutchwoman whose husband is in the asylum takes in a fugitive USAF pilot in his place although a Nazi officer is billeted on the household.

Downright peculiar World War II comedy which at the time seemed the height of bad taste – and no laughs.

w Gina Kaus, Jay Dratler d Richard Wallace ph Franz Planer m Werner Heyman
☆ Joan Bennett, Franchot Tone, Allyn Joslyn, Cecil Cunningham, Lloyd Corrigan, Georgia Caine

'Kicks in the pants, belching, and exaggerated face-making are lifted from burlesque to decorate this feeble attempt.' – *New York Post*

Wife versus Secretary *

US 1936 88m bw
MGM (Hunt Stromberg)

A publisher's wife starts to believe rumours about his attention to his secretary.

Practised star comedy drama which provided thoroughly satisfactory entertainment of a kind the cinema seems to have forgotten.

w Norman Krasna, Alice Duer Miller, John Lee Mahin novel Faith Baldwin d Clarence Brown ph Ray June m Herbert Stothart, Edward Ward
☆ Clark Gable, Myrna Loy, Jean Harlow, May Robson, George Barbier, James Stewart, Hobart Cavanaugh

'A real box office picture for the sticks and the stems.' – *Variety*
'See this picture if you enjoy the spectacle of three clever stars shining for all they are worth.' – *Film Weekly*

The Wilby Conspiracy *

GB 1975 105m DeLuxe
UA/Optimus/Baum-Dantine (Stanley Sopel)
▤

A British mining engineer is persuaded to help a black revolutionary in his flight from Cape Town to Johannesburg.

· Reasonably exciting political chase thriller with a sufficiency of twists and action sequences; philosophy is present but secondary.

w Rod Amateau, Harold Nebenzal novel Peter Driscoll d Ralph Nelson ph John Coquillon m Stanley Myers ad Harold Pottle ed Ernest Walter
☆ Sidney Poitier, Michael Caine, Nicol Williamson, Prunella Gee, Saeed Jaffrey, Persis Khambatta

The Wild Affair *

GB 1965 87m bw
Seven Arts (Richard Patterson)

An office Christmas party nearly turns into an orgy.

Curious little comedy drama which plays almost like the Road to Ruin and has an attractive but miscast leading lady. Interesting elements.

wd John Krish novel The Last Hours of Sandra Lee by William Sansom ph Arthur Ibbetson m Martin Slavin
☆ Nancy Kwan, Terry-Thomas, Jimmy Logan, Bud Flanagan, Betty Marsden, Gladys Morgan, Paul Whitsun-Jones, Donald Churchill, Victor Spinetti

'Take a ride on the wild side.'

Wild America

👫 US 1997 106m DuArt Panavision
Warner/Morgan Creek/Steve Tisch (James G. Robinson, Irby Smith, Mark Stouffer)
▥ ▤

In the 60s, three brothers in Arkansas set out with a dream to make a documentary on wildlife in America.

Pleasant, rambling family film of scrapes and escapes with animals.

w David Michael Wieger d William Dear ph David Burr m Joel McNeely pd Steve Jordan ed O. Nicholas Brown, Stuart Pappe
☆ Jonathan Taylor Thomas, Devon Sawa, Scott Bairstow, Frances Fisher, Jamie Sheridan, Tracey Walter, Don Stroud

'An abundance of humor, excitement, heart and soul.' – *Michael Medved, New York Post*
'The stuff of second rate children's fiction.' – *Sight and Sound*
† The film is based on a true story of the Stouffer brothers, who became documentary film-makers.

The Wild and the Innocent

US 1959 85m Eastmancolor Cinemascope
Universal-International

A trapper is torn between a mountain girl and a city tart.

Oddly old-fashioned Western, like The Gold Rush without laughs.

w Sy Gomberg, Jack Sher d Jack Sher ph Harold Lipstein m Hans J. Salter
☆ Audie Murphy, Joanne Dru, Gilbert Roland, Sandra Dee, Jim Backus, Peter Breck

The Wild and the Willing

GB 1962 112m bw
Rank/Box-Thomas (Betty E. Box)
US title: Young and Willing

A troublesome student at a provincial university seduces the wife of his professor.

Watchable sex melodrama with an interesting background on which no one seems to have quite enough grip; 'realism' is simply there to be exploited.

w Nicholas Phipps, Mordecai Richler play The Tinker by Laurence Dobie, Robert Sloman d Ralph Thomas ph Ernest Steward m Norrie Paramor
☆ Virginia Maskell, Paul Rogers, Ian McShane, Samantha Eggar, John Hurt, Catherine Woodville, John Standing, Jeremy Brett

Wild and Wonderful

US 1963 88m Eastmancolor
U-I/Harold Hecht

A French film star poodle makes friends with an American gambler.

Amiable zany comedy in a set-bound Gay Paree.

w Larry Markes, Michael Morris, Waldo Salt d Michael Anderson ph Joseph LaShelle m Morton Stevens
☆ Tony Curtis, Christine Kaufmann, Larry Storch, Marty Ingels, Jacques Aubuchon, Jules Munshin

Wild and Woolly

US 1937 90m bw
TCF (John Stone)

During a small-town frontier celebration an attempt to rob the bank is thwarted.

Pleasant family Western with music.

w Lynn Root, Frank Fenton d Alfred Werker
☆ Jane Withers, Walter Brennan, Pauline Moore, Alfalfa Switzer, Jackie Searl, Berton Churchill, Lon Chaney Jnr

'Whatever its companion feature happens to be, this is the one the audience talks about on the way home.' – *Variety*

The Wild Angels *

US 1966 85m Pathécolor Panavision
AIP (Roger Corman)
▥

A Californian motorcycle gang is run on semi-religious, ritualistic, Nazi lines.

Much-banned melodrama, cheaply made but vigorously handled and of some interest on social and historical levels.

w Charles B. Griffith d Roger Corman ph Richard Moore m Mike Curb ad Leon Ericksen ed Monte Hellman
☆ Peter Fonda, Nancy Sinatra, Bruce Dern, Michael J. Pollard, Gayle Hunnicutt

'Roger Corman's color-film account of the orgiastic raping, looting, brawling, pot-smoking, corpse-desecrating, church-wrecking, parson-torturing, swastika-swaddled activities of a gang of motorcyclists. After we've feasted our eyes on the detailing thereof by, incidentally, a thoroughly inept cast, without even the context of good cycling sequences, we're given a one-line moral by the suddenly regenerate gang leader: "There's no place to go," he mumbles. Yes, indeed, there's still room at the bottom.' – *Judith Crist*

Wild at Heart **

US 1990 127m
Palace/Polygram/Propaganda (Monty Montgomery, Steve Golin, Joni Sighvatsson)
▥ ▥ ▤ ◑ 🎧

A petty criminal is redeemed by the love of a histrionic woman.

Over-ripe acting, violent action, and a melodramatic plot combine to produce the cinematic equivalent of Grand Guignol. It won the Palme d'Or at the Cannes Film Festival in 1990.

wd David Lynch novel Barry Gifford ph Fred Elmes m Angelo Badalamenti ed Duwayne Dunham
☆ Nicolas Cage, Laura Dern, Diane Ladd, Willem Dafoe, Isabella Rossellini, Harry Dean Stanton, Crispin Glover, J. E. Freeman, W. Morgan Sheppard

'Joltingly violent, wickedly funny and rivetingly erotic.' – *Variety*
'The picture is packed with so much deranged energy, so many bravura images, that it's hard not to be seduced by the sick wonder of it all.' – *Richard Corliss, Time*
⚖ Diane Ladd

Wild Beauty

👫 US 1946 61m bw
Universal (Wallace W. Fox)

An Indian boy protects his wild horse from men who want to kill the herd he leads for shoe leather.

Amiable minor Western for horse and dog lovers, though it is given to some complacent, if well-meaning, pontification on the plight of Native Americans; the sermon might have been more convincing if the leading role had not been played by an obviously white youth.

w Adele Buffington d Wallace W. Fox ph Maury Gertsman m Paul Sawtell ad Jack Otterson, Abraham Grossman ed D. Patrick Kelley
☆ Don Porter, Lois Collier, Robert 'Buzzy' Henry, Jacqueline de Wit, Robert Wilcox, George Cleveland, Dick Curtis

Wild Bill *

US 1995 97m DeLuxe/bw
MGM/UA/Zanuck Co. (Richard D. Zanuck, Lili Fini Zanuck)
▥ ▤

A Western gunfighter takes to drugs as he examines his life and legend.

A complex, fragmentary look at the life of Wild Bill Hickok that strips away the heroics to present a confused and unhappy killer; spasmodically interesting, if rather too glum.

wd Walter Hill play Fathers and Sons by Thomas Babe novel Deadwood by Pete Dexter ph Lloyd Ahern pd Joseph Nemec III ed Freeman Davies
☆ Jeff Bridges, Ellen Barkin, John Hurt, Diane Lane, David Arquette, Christina Applegate, Bruce Dern, James Gammon, Marjoe Gortner, James Remar, Keith Carradine

'An art Western that manages to shoot itself in both feet.' – *Variety*
† The film cost $30m and took $2.2m at the US box-office.

Wild Bill Hickok Rides

US 1941 81m bw
Warner

Wild Bill helps a homesteader keep his land.

Oddly cast, rather naïve little Western.

w Charles Grayson, Paul Gerard Smith and Raymond Schrock d Ray Enright
☆ Constance Bennett, Bruce Cabot, Warren William, Ward Bond, Howard de Silva

The Wild Blue Yonder

US 1952 98m bw
Republic (Herbert J. Yates)
GB title: Thunder Across the Pacific

Incidents in the lives of bomber pilots in the Pacific during World War II.

Routine action flagwaver.

w Richard Tregaskis d Allan Dwan ph Reggie Lanning m Victor Young
☆ Wendell Corey, Vera Hruba Ralston, Forrest Tucker, Phil Harris, Walter Brennan, Ruth Donnelly

Wild Boys of the Road *

US 1933 88m bw
Warner (Robert Presnell)
GB title: Dangerous Days

Boys of poor families take to the road in gangs.

Vivid social melodrama of its day, now rather overstated.

w Earl Baldwin d William Wellman ph Arthur Todd
☆ Frankie Darro, Rochelle Hudson, Edwin Philips, Arthur Hohl

'A depressing evening in the theatre, one which the general fan public will gladly avoid.' – *Variety*

Wild Brian Kent

US 1936 57m bw
TCF (Sol Lesser)

An amiable Western con man helps a town to rid itself of a villain.

Mild comedy drama.

w Earle Snell, Don Swift novel The Recreation of Brian Kent by Harold Bell Wright d Howard Bretherton
☆ Ralph Bellamy, Mae Clarke, Helen Lowell, Stanley Andrews, Lew Kelly

'Little to commend it.' – *Variety*

'Nine men who came too late and stayed too long!'
'The land had changed. They hadn't. The earth had changed. They couldn't!'

The Wild Bunch ****

US 1969 145m Technicolor Panavision
Warner Seven Arts/Phil Feldman
▥ ▥ ▤ ◑ ⊙ 🎧

In 1914, Texas bandits are ambushed by an old enemy and die bloodily in defence of one of their number against a ruthless Mexican revolutionary.

Arguably the director's best film, and one which set a fashion for blood-spurting violence in Westerns. Undeniably stylish, thoughtful, and in places very exciting.

w Walon Green, Sam Peckinpah d Sam Peckinpah ph Lucien Ballard m Jerry Fielding ad Edward Carrere
☆ William Holden, Ernest Borgnine, Robert Ryan, Edmond O'Brien, Warren Oates, Jaime Sanchez, Ben Johnson, Strother Martin, L. Q. Jones, Albert Dekker

'A western that enlarged the form aesthetically, thematically, demonically.' – *Stanley Kauffmann, 1972*
'We watch endless violence to assure us that violence is not good.' – *Judith Crist, 1976*
'The bloody deaths are voluptuous, frightening, beautiful. Pouring new wine into the bottle of the western, Peckinpah explodes the bottle; his story is too simple for this imagist epic.' – *Pauline Kael, New Yorker*
'One of the most moving elegies for a vanished age ever created within the genre.' – *Time Out, 1984*
⚖ script; Jerry Fielding

The Wild Child: see L'Enfant Sauvage

The Wild Country

US 1970 100m Technicolor
Walt Disney (Ron Miller)

In the late 1880s a farmer buys a dilapidated Wyoming ranch and falls foul of a local rancher who controls the water supply.

Predictable family Western in the familiar Disney style.

w Calvin Clements Jnr, Paul Savage novel Little Britches by Ralph Moody d Robert Totten ph Frank Phillips m Robert Brunner
☆ Steve Forrest, Vera Miles, Jack Elam, Ronny Howard, Morgan Woodward

'The best ******* mercenaries in the business!'

The Wild Geese

GB 1978 134m Eastmancolor Panavision
Rank/Richmond (Euan Lloyd)
▤ ◑ 🎧

Adventures of four British mercenaries in a central African state.

All-star blood and guts with a few breezy touches in the script.

w Reginald Rose novel Daniel Carney d Andrew V. McLaglen m Jack Hildyard m Roy Budd
☆ Roger Moore, Richard Burton, Richard Harris, Hardy Kruger, Stewart Granger, Jack Watson, Frank Finlay, Kenneth Griffith, Barry Foster, Jeff

Corey, Ronald Fraser, Percy Herbert, Patrick Allen, Jane Hylton

Wild Geese Calling
US 1941 77m bw
TCF (Harry Joe Brown)
A young adventurer in Oregon weds the girlfriend of a conniving gambler.
Minor semi-Western which never really finds a style.
w Horace McCoy *novel* Stewart Edward White
d John Brahm *ph* Lucien Ballard *m* Alfred Newman
☆ Joan Bennett, Henry Fonda, Warren William, Ona Munson, Barton MacLane, Russell Simpson, Iris Adrian

Wild Geese II
GB 1985 125m Technicolor
Thorn EMI/Frontier/Euan Lloyd
📀 🎬
A mercenary is commissioned by an American TV station to kidnap Rudolf Hess from Spandau jail.
Ingenious if unlikely premise for another tough adventure; it largely fails because of silly plotting.
w Reginald Rose *novel* The Square Circle by Daniel Carney d Peter Hunt *ph* Michael Reed *m* Roy Budd *pd* Syd Cain *ed* Keith Palmer
☆ Scott Glenn, Barbara Carrera, Edward Fox, Laurence Olivier, Robert Webber, Kenneth Haigh, Stratford Johns

Wild Harvest
US 1947 92m bw
Paramount (Robert Fellows)
A romantic triangle develops among wheat harvesters on the Western plains.
Standard star hokum.
w John Monks Jnr d Tay Garnett *ph* John F. Seitz *m* Hugo Friedhofer
☆ Alan Ladd, Dorothy Lamour, Robert Preston, Lloyd Nolan, Rick Erdman, Allen Jenkins, Will Wright

The Wild Heart: see Gone to Earth

Wild Hearts Can't Be Broken *
🏃🏃 US 1991 88m colour
Buena Vista/Disney/Silver Screen Partners IV (Matt Williams)
📀 🎬
In the early 30s, a young girl struggles to make her way in the world as a horse-riding high diver in a fairground show.
Soft-centred romantic drama, based on a true story, that effectively captures the flavour of its times.
w Matt Williams, Oley Sassone d Steve Miner *ph* Daryn Okada *m* Mason Daring *pd* Randy Ser *ed* Jon Poll
☆ Gabrielle Anwar, Michael Schoeffling, Kathleen York, Dylan Kussman, Cliff Robertson

Wild Heritage
US 1958 78m Eastmancolor Cinemascope
Universal (John E. Horton)
Two pioneer families settling in the west find the going tough, and the bullets flying.
Dull and verbose Western, in which the characters stagger cheerfully through crises that include death, fever, cattle rustling, gunfights and men doing what men have gotta do.
w Paul King, Joseph Stone *story* Steve Frazee d Charles Haas *ph* Philip Lathrop *md* Joseph Gershenson *ad* Alexander Golitzen, Robert Boyle *ed* Edward Mann
☆ Will Rogers Jnr, Maureen O'Sullivan, Rod McKuen, Casey Tibbs, Judy Meredith, Troy Donahue, Gigi Perreau, Jeanette Nolan

Wild in the Country
US 1961 114m DeLuxe Cinemascope
TCF/Company of Artists (Jerry Wald)
📀 🎬
A rebellious hillbilly is involved with three women.
Weird confection designed to show the star in all his facets.
w Clifford Odets *novel* The Lost Country by J. R. Salamanca d Philip Dunne *ph* William C. Mellor *m* Kenyon Hopkins
☆ Elvis Presley, Hope Lange, Tuesday Weld, Millie Perkins, John Ireland, Gary Lockwood
'One can't help feeling he was better off prior to this misguided bid for class.' – *MFB*

Wild in the Sky
US 1971 83m colour
AIP/Bald Eagle (William T. Naud, Dick Gautier)
Three young offenders skyjack a B52 jet bomber.
Black comedy melodrama, uncontrolled but with some engaging absurdities.
w William T. Naud, Dick Gautier d William T. Naud *ph* Thomas E. Spalding *m* Jerry Styner
☆ Brandon de Wilde, Keenan Wynn, Dick Gautier, Tim O'Connor, James Daly, Robert Lansing

Wild in the Streets *
US 1968 97m Perfectcolor
AIP (Jack Cash)
🎬 🎬
In the imminent future, a pop singer becomes president and launches a campaign for teenage emancipation.
Satirical melodrama with a profusion of wild gags, some of which hit the target.
w Robert Thom d Barry Shear *ph* Richard Moore *m* Les Baxter *ed* Fred Feitshans, Eve Newman
☆ Shelley Winters, Chris Jones, Diane Varsi, Hal Holbrook, Millie Perkins
'Blatant, insensitive, crummy-looking … enjoyable at a pop, comic-strip level.' – *New Yorker, 1977*
'It is no less timely a parable today than Orwell's 1984 was 20 years ago.' – *Daily Telegraph*
& *editing*

Wild Is the Wind
US 1957 114m bw Vistavision
Paramount/Hal B. Wallis
🎧
A widowed Italian sheep rancher in Nevada marries his wife's sister from Italy, but she falls for his adopted son.
Intense Cold Comfort Farm melodrama with a strong similarity to They Knew What They Wanted; the strain shows, and the performances are tiresomely noisy.
w Arnold Schulman d George Cukor *ph* Charles Lang Jnr *m* Dimitri Tiomkin
☆ Anna Magnani, Anthony Quinn, Tony Franciosa, Dolores Hart, Joseph Calleia
& *title song* (mDimitri Tiomkin, lyNed Washington); Anna Magnani; Anthony Quinn

Wild Man Blues *
US 1997 105m DuArt
Film Four/Magnolia/Sweetland (Jean Doumanian, Barbara Kopple)
📀 🎬
Documentary of a European tour by Woody Allen and his jazz band, playing music in the New Orleans style.
Enjoyable account of Allen in a different performing context, concentrating not only on the music, but on Allen's relationship with Soon-Yi Previn, and with his unimpressed parents. What is surprising is his clarinet sound: you might have expected him to emulate the piping, everything's-coming-up-neuroses style of Pee Wee Russell; instead he plays in the heart-on-the-sleeve manner of George Lewis.
d Barbara Kopple *ph* Tom Hurwitz *ed* Lawrence Silk
'A hilarious pendant-piece to Deconstructing Harry.' – *Alexander Walker*

The Wild Man of Borneo
US 1941 78m bw
MGM (Joseph L. Mankiewicz)
An unsuccessful braggart comes to live with his daughter in a Manhattan boarding house.
Mildly likeable though very predictable sentimental comedy from an old Broadway warhorse.
w Waldo Scott, John McClain *play* Herman J. Mankiewicz, Marc Connelly d Robert B. Sinclair *ph* Oliver T. Marsh *m* David Snell
☆ Frank Morgan, Mary Howard, Dan Dailey, Billie Burke, Donald Meek, Bonita Granville, Marjorie Main, Connie Gilchrist, Walter Catlett, Andrew Tombes, Phil Silvers, Joe Yule

The Wild North
US 1951 97m Anscocolor
MGM (Stephen Ames)
A mountie gets his man but needs his help getting back to base.
Standard adventure story with avalanche and wolf attacks.

w Frank Fenton d Andrew Marton *ph* Robert Surtees *m* Bronislau Kaper
☆ Stewart Granger, Wendell Corey, Cyd Charisse

'That streetcar man has a new desire!'
The Wild One **
US 1954 79m bw
Columbia/Stanley Kramer
📀 🎬 🎬 🎧
Hoodlum motorcyclists terrorize a small town.
Brooding, compulsive, well-made little melodrama which was much banned because there was no retribution. As a narrative it does somewhat lack dramatic point.
w John Paxton *story* The Cyclists' Raid by Frank Rooney d Laslo Benedek *ph* Hal Mohr *m* Leith Stevens
☆ Marlon Brando, Lee Marvin, Mary Murphy, Robert Keith, Jay C. Flippen
'A picture that tries to grasp an idea, even though the reach falls short.' – *New York Times*
† 'What are you rebelling against?' 'What've you got?' – *sample dialogue.*
†† Sharpness of photography was achieved by the Garutso lens.

Wild Orchid
US 1989 111m DeLuxe
Entertainment/Vision (Mark Damon, Tony Anthony)
📀 🎬 🎬 🎧
An American businessman in Rio plays sexual games with two female lawyers in a struggle over the ownership of a hotel.
Voyeuristic thriller that is less than watchable.
w Patricia Louisianna Knop, Zalman King d Zalman King *ph* Gale Tattersall *m* Geoff MacCormack, Simon Goldenberg *pd* Carlos Conti *ed* Marc Grossman, Glenn A. Morgan
☆ Mickey Rourke, Jacqueline Bisset, Carre Otis, Assumpta Serna, Bruce Greenwood, Jens Peter, Oleg Vidov

The Wild Party
US 1956 81m bw
UA/Security (Sidney Harmon)
An ex-football player and some Los Angeles layabouts plot a kidnap.
Unpleasant melodrama laced with sex, violence and loud music.
w John McPartland d Harry Horner *ph* Sam Leavitt *m* Buddy Bregman
☆ Anthony Quinn, Carol Ohmart, Jay Robinson, Arthur Franz, Nehemiah Persoff, Kathryn Grant, Paul Stewart

The Wild Party
US 1974 91m Movielab
AIP/Edgar Lansbury, Joseph Beruh (Ismail Merchant)
In 1929, a silent film comedian on the skids throws a party to show his latest movie.
Evocative of its period but virtually confined to a single set which becomes boring, this collection of unlikely events and tedious people has only obvious points to make and its final descent into tragedy is not compelling.
w Walter Marks *poem* Joseph Moncure March d James Ivory *ph* Walter Lassally *m* Larry Rosenthal
☆ James Coco, Raquel Welch, Perry King, Tiffany Bolling, Royal Dano, David Dukes, Dena Dietrich
'Seems to promise a pointillist precision about its characters and milieu which it never quite delivers.' – *Jonathan Rosenbaum*

The Wild Reeds: see Les Roseaux Sauvages

Wild River *
US 1960 115m DeLuxe Cinemascope
TCF (Elia Kazan)
In 1933 a Tennessee Valley Authority inspector incurs the wrath of a local matriarch who will not leave her valley even though it is to be flooded.
Interesting liberal-minded sociological drama marred by an added love story, as the similar Last Days of Dolwyn was marred by melodrama. Well made but somehow unmemorable.
w Paul Osborn *novels* Borden Deal, William Bradford Huie d Elia Kazan *ph* Ellsworth Fredericks *m* Kenyon Hopkins
☆ Montgomery Clift, Jo Van Fleet, Lee Remick, Albert Salmi, Jay C. Flippen, James Westerfield, Bruce Dern

Wild Rovers
US 1971 132m Metrocolor Panavision 70
MGM/Geoffrey (Blake Edwards, Ken Wales)
📀 🎬 🎧
A middle-aged cowboy, depressed with the state of his life, joins with a younger man to become a bank robber.
Fashionable, derivative, quite unsuccessful Western tragi-comedy mixing in shades of every director from Ford to Peckinpah.
wd Blake Edwards *ph* Philip Lathrop *m* Jerry Goldsmith
☆ William Holden, Ryan O'Neal, Karl Malden, Lynn Carlin, Tom Skerritt, Joe Don Baker, Rachel Roberts, Leora Dana, Moses Gunn
'An existentialist western which will not do much for existentialism, the western, or the box office.' – *Charles Champlin, Los Angeles Times*

Wild Search
Hong Kong 1989 90m colour
Silver Medal/Born Top (Ringo Lam)
Investigating arms smuggling, a maverick cop falls for the sister of a murdered crook.
Engaging thriller, low-key by the frenetic standards of Hong Kong, with a little romance and comedy on the side.
w Nam Yin d Ringo Lam *ph* Lau Wai Keung *m* Lowell Lo *ad* Luk Tse Fung
☆ Chow Yun-fat, Cherie Chung, Elaine Kam, Paul Chin, Chan Cheuk-Yan, Lau Kong

Wild Seed: see Fargo

The Wild Side: see Suburbia (1983)

Wild Stallion: see Crin Blanc

Wild Strawberries ****
Sweden 1957 93m bw
Svensk Filmindustri (Allan Ekelund)
📀 🎬 🎬
original title: *Smultronstället*
An elderly professor has a nightmare and thinks back over his long life.
A beautifully paced and acted, but somewhat obscure piece of probing symbolism.
wd Ingmar Bergman *ph* Gunnar Fischer *m* Erik Nordgren
☆ Victor Sjostrom, Ingrid Thulin, Gunnar Bjornstrand, Bibi Andersson, Naima Wifstrand, Jullan Kindahl
'The work of a man obsessed by cruelty, especially spiritual cruelty, trying to find some resolution.' – *Kenneth Cavander, MFB*
& *script*

Wild Target *
France 1993 88m colour
Gala/Pelléas/Locofilms/France 2/M6 Films (Philippe Martin)
📀 🎬
original title: *Cible émouvante*
A hitman and his apprentice are hired to kill a woman who has swindled a gangster, but decide to protect her instead.
Amusing blackish comedy, mainly notable for Rochefort's expert comic playing as a prissy killer who finds his precisely ordered life going awry.
wd Pierre Salvadori *ph* Gilles Henry *m* Philippe Eidel *ad* Yan Arlaud *ed* Hélène Viard
☆ Jean Rochefort, Marie Trintignant, Guillaume Depardieu, Patachou, Wladimir Yordanoff, Serge Riaboukine, Charlie Nelson
'Though limited in its ambitions, this is a convincingly quirky experience.' – *Empire*

Wild Things
US 1998 108m Technicolor Panavision
Columbia/Mandalay (Rodney Liber, Steven A. Jones)
📀 🎬 🎧
A teacher faces ruin when a wealthy young girl accuses him of attempted rape.
Convoluted courtroom thriller that plays games with an audience's expectations, but not well enough to capture its interest.
w Stephen Peters d John McNaughton *ph* Jeffrey L. Kimball *m* George S. Clinton *pd* Edward T. McAvoy *ed* Elena Maganini
☆ Kevin Bacon, Matt Dillon, Neve Campbell, Theresa Russell, Denise Richards, Robert Wagner, Bill Murray, Carrie Snodgress, Daphne Rubin-Vega
'Sly, torrid and original.' – *Variety*

Wild West *

GB 1992 100m Metrocolor
Initial/Channel 4/British Screen (Eric Fellner)

Young Asians, living in London and dreaming of stardom, form a country and western band.
Engagingly energetic comedy of cultural misunderstandings and fantasies.

w Harwant Bains d David Attwood ph Nic Knowland m Dominic Miller pd Caroline Hanania ed Martin Walsh

☆ Naveen Andrews, Sarita Choudhury, Ronny Jhutti, Ravi Kapoor, Ameet Chana, Bhasker, Lalita Ahmed, Shaun Scott

'Mangy and artless, this boisterous low-budgeter generates plenty of good laughs and gets lots of mileage from its comic, knowing observations about a vibrant British sub-culture.' – *Variety*

Wild Wild West

US 1999 106m Technicolor
Warner (Jon Peters, Barry Sonnenfeld)

In the 1860s, two ill-matched government agents are dispatched by the President to deal with a Confederate general, who is creating a powerful new weapon with the aid of a wheelchair-bound mad scientist.
Asinine would-be comedy that wastes a great many talents on an ill-thought-out, unfunny narrative and irrelevant special effects.

w S.S. Wilson, Brent Maddock, Jeffrey Price, Peter S. Seaman story Jim Thomas, John Thomas d Barry Sonnenfeld ph Michael Ballhaus m Elmer Bernstein pd Bo Welch ed Jim Miller sp ILM; Cinesite

☆ Will Smith, Kevin Kline, Kenneth Branagh, Salma Hayek, Ted Levine, M. Emmet Walsh, Bai Ling, Rodney A. Grant, Garcelle Beauvais, Musetta Vander, Sofia Eng, Frederique van der Wal

'A would-be blockbuster that figures out how to go thud more often than anything since *Hudson Hawk*.' – *Owen Gleiberman, Entertainment Weekly*

'An extended, incoherent Tourette's-style yelping of design-ideas, soundtrack-styles, FX flourishes, rewrites and mismatched performances.' – *Peter Bradshaw, Guardian*

† The movie was based on the TV series that ran from 1965-1970, starring Robert Conrad as West, Ross Martin as Gordon, and Michael Dunn as the diminutive villain Dr Miguelito Loveless.

†† It grossed more than $113m at the US box-office and a total of $218m around the world.

Wildcat: see *The Great Scout and Cathouse Thursday*

Wildcats

US 1986 107m Technicolor
Warner (Anthea Sylbert)

A girl is appointed football coach at a ghetto school, and of course works wonders.
Silly comedy with few laughs and not much plot development.

w Ezra Sacks d Michael Ritchie ph Donald E. Thorin m Hawk Wolinski, James Newton Howard pd Boris Leven ed Richard A. Harris

☆ Goldie Hawn, Swoosie Kurtz, Robyn Lively, Brandy Gold, James Keach, Bruce McGill, M. Emmet Walsh

The Wildcats of St Trinian's

GB 1980 91m Technicolor
Wildcat (E. M. Smedley-Aston)

The awful schoolgirls get unionized, and kidnap an Arab's daughter to gain attention.
Crude and belated tailpiece to a series which was never very satisfactory. (See The Belles of ... , Blue Murder at ... , The Pure Hell of ... , The Great St Trinian's Train Robbery.)

wd Frank Launder ph Ernest Steward m James Kenelm Clarke

☆ Sheila Hancock, Michael Hordern, Joe Melia, Thorley Walters, Rodney Bewes, Maureen Lipman, Ambrosine Philpotts

'We are all in the gutter, but some of us are looking at the stars.'

Wilde **

GB 1997 115m Metrocolor 'Scope
Polygram/Samuelson/Dove/NDF/Pony Canyon/Pandora/BBC (Mark Samuelson, Peter Samuelson)

Oscar Wilde's love for Lord Alfred Douglas brings about his disgrace and exile from Britain.
A handsome, well-acted, slightly stately biopic that, despite its declared intent to celebrate Wilde's homosexuality, seems determined to reclaim him as a heterosexual and father.

w Julian Mitchell biography Oscar Wilde by Richard Ellmann d Brian Gilbert ph Martin Fuhrer m Debbie Wiseman pd Maria Djurkovic ed Michael Bradsell

☆ Stephen Fry, Jude Law, Vanessa Redgrave, Jennifer Ehle, Gemma Jones, Michael Sheen, Zoe Wanamaker, Tom Wilkinson

'A well-made film in the brass-bound tradition of British heritage cinema.' – *Richard Williams, Guardian*

'A curious mixture of haste and complacency.' – *Tom Shone, Sunday Times*

'In the end *Wilde* triumphs because it manages to do what Wilde himself achieved. In the famous plays he portrayed an English society dominated by the vice of hypocrisy. A hundred years later people are still being destroyed and pilloried in this country for publicly stating that the emperor is wearing a spandex jock strap. *Wilde* gives us a vivid take on this eternal and hateful row.' – *Will Self, New Statesman*

Wilder Napalm

US 1993 110m Technicolor
TriStar/Baltimore (Mark Johnson, Stuart Cornfeld)

Two feuding brothers, who can start fires with the power of thought, quarrel when one makes love to the wife of the other.
Plotless, witless confection about three very uninteresting people.

w Vince Gilligan d Glenn Gordon Caron ph Jerry Hartleben m Michael Kamen pd John Muto ed Artie Mandelberg

☆ Debra Winger, Dennis Quaid, Arliss Howard, M. Emmet Walsh, Jim Varney, Mimi Lieber, Marvin J. McIntyre

'There's little to recommend in the slow-moving, fuzzy-minded yarn.' – *Variety*

Will Any Gentleman?

GB 1953 84m Technicolor
ABPC

A meek bank clerk is hypnotized and becomes a ladies' man.
Efficient comedy from a stage success.

w Vernon Sylvaine play Vernon Sylvaine d Michael Anderson ph Erwin Hillier m Wally Stott

☆ George Cole, Veronica Hurst, Jon Pertwee, Heather Thatcher, James Hayter, William Hartnell, Diana Decker, Joan Sims, Alan Badel

Will It Snow for Christmas? **

France 1996 91m colour
Artificial Eye/Ognon (Danny Lebigot)

original title: *Y'Aura T'il de la Neige à Noël?*

In rural France, a married farmer's lover and their seven children scratch a bare living from the land.
Bleak, minimalist drama of poverty and maternal love that, with its slow rhythms, is hypnotically unforgettable.

wd Sandrine Veysset ph Hélène Louvart m Henri Ancillotti ad Jacques Dubus ed Nelly Quettier

☆ Dominique Reymond, Daniel Duval, Jessica Martinez, Alexandre Roger, Xavier Colonna, Fanny Rochetin

'If it does happen to snow for Christmas, make a snowman, slide down Ben Nevis on a tea tray, teach your grandma to ski, anything – just don't seek shelter in a cinema showing this miserable tale.' – *Giala Murray, Empire*

'Will heats up slow, but when he gets there, he's hell with the hide off!'

Will Penny *

US 1967 109m Technicolor
Paramount/Fred Engel/Walter Seltzer/Tom Gries

A middle-aged cowpuncher falls foul of a family of maniacal cut-throats.
Realistically spare, laconic, uncomforting Western with a curiously melodramatic set of villains.

wd Tom Gries ph Lucien Ballard m David Raksin

☆ Charlton Heston, Joan Hackett, Donald Pleasence, Lee Majors, Bruce Dern, Anthony Zerbe, Clifton James, Ben Johnson

Will Success Spoil Rock Hunter?

US 1957 95m Eastmancolor Cinemascope
TCF (Frank Tashlin)

GB title: *Oh! For a Man!*

A timid advertising executive is touted for a publicity stunt as the world's greatest lover.
A too-wild satire on TV commercials: less frenzied direction and gag-writing would have prised more humour from the situations.

w Frank Tashlin play George Axelrod d Frank Tashlin ph Joe MacDonald m Cyril Mockridge

☆ Jayne Mansfield, Tony Randall, Betsy Drake, Joan Blondell, John Williams, Henry Jones, Mickey Hargitay

Will Tomorrow Ever Come?: see *That's My Man*

'The one film you should not see alone! Where your nightmare ends, Willard *begins!*'

Willard *

US 1971 95m DeLuxe
Cinerama/Bing Crosby (Mort Briskin)

A shy, withdrawn young man breeds and trains rats to kill his enemies.
Modest, rather unusual suspenser which builds well after a slow start; only horrifying to people who can't stand rats. A sequel, Ben (qv), later appeared.

w Gilbert Ralston novel Ratman's Notebooks by Stephen Gilbert d Daniel Mann ph Robert B. Hauser m Alex North rat trainer Moe de Sesso

☆ Bruce Davison, Elsa Lanchester, Ernest Borgnine, Sondra Locke, Michael Dante, J. Pat O'Malley

William at the Circus

GB 1948 89m bw
A. A. Shipman & David Coplan (John R. Sloan)

aka: *William Comes to Town*

William achieves national notoriety and overcomes parental obstacles in his determination to see a circus.
Tired and miscast comedy, with much documentary footage of fun-fair and circus to bad out its trite narrative.

wd Val Guest novel Richmal Crompton ph Bert Mason m Robert Farnon ad Harry Moore ed Carmen Beliaeff

☆ William Graham, Garry Marsh, Jane Walsh, Hugh Cross, Kathleen Stuart, Muriel Aked, A. E. Matthews, Michael Medwin, Michael Balfour, Jon Pertwee

† It was a sequel to *Just William's Luck* (qv).

William Comes to Town: see *William at the Circus*

'Love makes fools of us all.'

William Shakespeare's A Midsummer Night's Dream **

US/Germany 1999 116m DeLuxe
TCF/Fox Searchlight/Regency (Leslie Urdang, Michael Hoffman)

aka: *A Midsummer Night's Dream*

The course of true love does not run smooth for three couples.
Set for no particular reason in an Italian village at the turn of the 19th century, this is a patchy version, with some awkward clashes in acting styles, and much of the verse-speaking disappointing; but the play gradually works its charm and the finale is well-managed.

play William Shakespeare d Michael Hoffman ph Oliver Stapleton m Simon Boswell pd Luciana Arrighi ed Garth Craven cos Gabriella Pescucci

☆ Michelle Pfeiffer, Rupert Everett, Kevin Kline, Stanley Tucci, Calista Flockhart, Anna Friel,

Christian Bale, Dominic West, David Strathairn, Sophie Marceau, Roger Rees, Bernard Hill, Bill Irwin, Sam Rockwell

'Whimsical, intermittently enjoyable but decidedly unmagical.' – *Variety*

'A parade of incongruities with performances ranging from the sublime to the you-know-what.' – *Janet Maslin, New York Times*

'Hope & vengeance. Tragedy & love.'
'The greatest love story the world has ever known.'

William Shakespeare's Romeo and Juliet **

US 1996 120m DeLuxe Panavision
TCF/Bazmark (Gabriella Martinelli, Baz Luhrmann)

In modern-day Verona Beach, two young lovers suffer from family opposition to their affair.
Exuberantly witty version of Shakespeare, where for once the language and the present-day setting match: the weapons toted by its hoodlum cast may be guns, but they bear trademarks such as 'Sword' and 'Dagger'. The poetry of the play tends to get lost in the ethnic mix and loud rock accompaniment, and it dazzles the eye, with its vivid, kitsch settings, rather than the ear, but the updating has been thought through with an invigorating invention that sweeps objections aside.

w Craig Pearce, Baz Luhrmann play William Shakespeare d Baz Luhrmann ph Donald McAlpine m Nellee Hooper, Craig Armstrong, Marius de Vries pd Catherine Martin ed Jill Bilcock

☆ Leonardo DiCaprio, Claire Danes, Brian Dennehy, John Leguizamo, Pete Postlethwaite, Paul Sorvino, Diane Venora

'This acid-house rendition ... is something to behold.' – *Sight and Sound*

'Will undoubtedly do for Shakespeare what *Strictly Ballroom* did for ballroom dancing and make it fresh, vibrant and hot, hot, hot for a whole generation new to the Bard.' – *Marianne Gray, Film Review*

'Luhrmann has produced a splendid rock video.' – *Mark Steyn, Spectator*

† Leonardo DiCaprio won the best actor award at the Berlin Film Festival in 1997.

♪ Catherine Martin

⑦ Baz Luhrmann; Catherine Martin; Nellee Hooper; screenplay

Willie and Phil

US 1980 116m DeLuxe
TCF (Paul Mazursky, Tony Ray)

Two men and a woman enjoy a variable *ménage à trois* throughout the seventies.
Curious attempt at an American Jules et Jim; not badly done if you have to do it, but why do it?

wd Paul Mazursky ph Sven Nykvist m Claude Bolling

☆ Michael Ontkean, Margot Kidder, Ray Sharkey

'Truffaut's film existed both in the real world and in a world of the imagination. Mazursky's has no imagination and doesn't even touch a passable form of reality.' – *Sunday Times*

Will-O'-The-Wisp: see *Le Feu Follet*

Willow *

US 1988 126m colour
UIP/MGM (Nigel Wooll)

In a time of magic, two heroes set out to bring a baby to safety and fulfil a prophecy that will overthrow an evil empire.
Spectacular jaunt around familiar material, plundered from mythology, fairy-tales and old movies, that relies on special effects to maintain interest.

w Bob Dolman story George Lucas d Ron Howard ph Adrian Biddle m James Horner pd Allan Cameron ed Daniel Hanley, Michael Hill sp John Richardson

☆ Val Kilmer, Joanne Whalley, Warwick Davies, Jean Marsh, Patricia Hayes, Billy Barty, Pat Roach, Gavan O'Herlihy, David Steinberg

'It's doubtful if any action-adventure director has a strong enough style to give this script a tone and a shape, and Ron Howard, who's got the job, is lost.' – *Pauline Kael, New Yorker*

Willy Wonka and the Chocolate Factory *

US   1971   100m   Technicolor
David Wolper

A boy wins a tour of the local chocolate factory and finds himself in the power of a magician.
Semi-satiric Grimms Fairy Tale pastiche which looks good but never seems quite happy with itself.
w Roald Dahl *novel* Roald Dahl *d* Mel Stuart *ph* Arthur Ibbetson *md* Walter Scharf *ad* Harper Goff *songs* Leslie Bricusse, Anthony Newley
☆ Gene Wilder, Jack Albertson, Peter Ostrum, Roy Kinnear, Aubrey Woods
⌥ Walter Scharf

Wilson **

US   1944   154m   Technicolor
TCF (Darryl F. Zanuck)

The rise and fall of an American president.
Admirably careful biopic which raises no particular excitement but entertains and instructs on various levels.
w Lamar Trotti *d* Henry King *ph* Leon Shamroy *m* Alfred Newman *ad* James Basevi, Wiard Ihnen *ed* Barbara McLean
☆ Alexander Knox, Charles Coburn, Cedric Hardwicke, Geraldine Fitzgerald, Thomas Mitchell, Ruth Nelson, William Eythe, Vincent Price, Mary Anderson, Ruth Ford, Sidney Blackmer, Stanley Ridges, Eddie Foy Jnr, Charles Halton, Thurston Hall and also J. M. Kerrigan, Francis X. Bushman
'Not without tedium, but worth seeing as an enormous expensive curiosity.' – *Richard Mallett, Punch*
'Rich with the sense of movement and multitude.' – *Daily Sketch*
'Absorbing, significant and entertaining.' – *Time*
† Alexander Knox had 1194 lines in 294 scenes.
⌥ Lamar Trotti; Leon Shamroy; art direction; editing
⌥ best picture; Henry King; Alfred Newman; Alexander Knox

Wilt

GB   1989   93m   Eastmancolor
Rank/LWT/Picture Partnership (Brian Eastman)

A polytechnic lecturer is suspected of having murdered his wife by an inept police inspector.
A low farce which, briskly directed, affords moderate amusement.
w Andrew Marshall, David Renwick *novel* Tom Sharpe *d* Michael Tuchner *ph* Norman Langley *m* Anne Dudley *pd* Leo Austin *ed* Chris Blunden
☆ Griff Rhys Jones, Mel Smith, Alison Steadman, Diana Quick, Jeremy Clyde, Roger Allam, David Ryall, Roger Lloyd Pack, Dermot Crowley, John Normington

Winchester 73 **

US   1950   92m   bw
U-I (Aaron Rosenberg)

Long-time enemies settle an old grudge.
Entertaining, popular, hard-riding, hard-shooting Western of the old school.
w Robert L. Richards, Borden Chase *story* Stuart N. Lake *d* Anthony Mann *ph* William Daniels *m* Frank Skinner *md* Joseph Gershenson
☆ James Stewart, Shelley Winters, Dan Duryea, Stephen McNally, Millard Mitchell, Charles Drake, John McIntire, Will Geer, Jay C. Flippen, Rock Hudson, Tony Curtis, John Alexander, Steve Brodie

Wind

US   1992   125m   Technicolor
Filmlink International/American Zoetrope (Mata Yamamoto, Tom Luddy)

A young sailor, who loses the America's Cup to the Australians, persuades a designer to create a new yacht to win back the title.
Uninteresting and water-logged drama.
w Rudy Wurlitzer, Mac Gudgeon *story* Jeff Benjamin, Roger Vaughan, Kimball Livingston *d* Carroll Ballard *ph* John Toll *m* Basil Poledouris *pd* Laurence Eastwood *ed* Michael Chandler

☆ Matthew Modine, Jennifer Grey, Stellan Skarsgard, Rebecca Miller, Ned Vaughn, Cliff Robertson, Jack Thompson
'Despite the sometimes striking images of expert crews guiding their beautiful boats through challenging waters, predictable story trajectory and bland human element will keep this physically ambitious picture in a b.o. stall.' – *Variety*

The Wind ***

US   1928   75m   bw
MGM

A sheltered Virginia girl goes to live on the rough and windy Texas prairie, marries a man she doesn't love and kills a would-be rapist.
Heavy melodrama with a strong visual sense.
w Frances Marion *novel* Dorothy Scarborough *d* Victor Sjostrom *ph* John Arnold
☆ Lillian Gish, Lars Hanson, Montagu Love, Dorothy Cummings
'So penetrating is the atmosphere that one can almost feel the wind itself and taste the endless dust.' – *Georges Sadoul*
'Unrelieved by the ghost of a smile … but its relentlessness is gripping … a fine and dignified achievement.' – *Pictureplay*
† New version by Thames Silents 1984.

The Wind

Mali   1982   100m   colour
Les Films Cissé
original title: Finyé
The daughter of a military governor becomes involved in political demonstrations against army rule after falling in love with a poor student.
Episodic account of romance and repression in Africa.
wd Souleymane Cissé *ph* Etienne Carton de Grammont *m* Pierre Gorse
☆ Fousseyni Sossoko, Guondo Guisse, Balla Moussa Keita, Ismaila Sarr, Oumou Diarra, Ismaila Cissé, Massitan Ballo, Dioncounda Kone

Wind across the Everglades *

US   1958   93m   Technicolor
(Warner) Schulberg Productions (Stuart Schulberg)
Florida 1900: a young schoolteacher tracks down those responsible for hunting rare birds for their feathers, and becomes a game warden.
Meandering adventure story with a purpose, relying heavily on violence and eccentric characters.
w Budd Schulberg *d* Nicholas Ray *ph* Joseph Brun *ad* Richard Sylbert *ed* Georges Klotz, Joseph Sigman
☆ Christopher Plummer, Burl Ives, Gypsy Rose Lee, Emmett Kelly, George Voskovec, Tony Galento, MacKinlay Kantor, Peter Falk, Chana Eden
† The film was marked by disagreements between Nicholas Ray and Budd Schulberg. Ray was absent for the final two or so weeks, and scenes were shot by Schulberg and Charles Maguire, the assistant director. After seeing the film at a preview, Ray said that he wanted his name removed from the film because 'I cannot allow it to be associated with the style of acting employed by Burl in the death scene'. The scene remained (though Ives wanted to have it shot again), as did Ray's name.
†† The music score used existing music owned by Warner because of a musicians' strike in California.

The Wind and the Lion

US   1975   119m   Metrocolor   Panavision
Columbia/MGM (Herb Jaffe, Phil Rawlins)

In 1904 Tangier, an American widow and her children are kidnapped by a Riffian chief, and the eyes of the world are focused on the incident.
Basing itself very lightly on an actual event, this adventure story is both confused as a narrative and unexciting as an action piece: the camera stops too often to look at sunsets, the plot stops too often to philosophizing, and there are too many underexplained characters and incidents fitting into the international jigsaw.
wd John Milius *ph* Billy Williams *m* Jerry Goldsmith
☆ Sean Connery, Candice Bergen, Brian Keith, John Huston, Geoffrey Lewis, Steve Kanaly, Vladek Sheybal
'When the actors begin to talk (which they do incessantly) the flat-footed dialogue and the amateurish acting take one back to the low-

budget buffoonery of Maria Montez and Turhan Bey.' – *Pauline Kael, New Yorker*
⌥ Jerry Goldsmith

The Wind Cannot Read

GB   1958   115m   Eastmancolor
Rank (Betty E. Box)

In India and Burma during World War II, a flying officer falls in love with a Japanese language instructor suffering from a brain disease.
Or, love is a many-splendoured dark victory. Old-fashioned romance for addicts, well enough produced.
w Richard Mason *novel* Richard Mason *d* Ralph Thomas *m* Ernest Steward *m* Angelo Lavagnino
☆ Dirk Bogarde, Yoko Tani, Ronald Lewis, John Fraser, Anthony Bushell, Michael Medwin
† David Lean was to have directed the film, starring Japanese actress Kishi Keiko; but producer Alexander Korda, who was unhappy about Lean's approach to the subject, died before production began and the project was sold to Rank. Lean signed to make *The Bridge over the River Kwai* instead.

Wind in the Willows: see *Ichabod and Mr Toad (1949)*

The Wind in the Willows

GB   1996   88m   Technicolor
Guild/Allied Filmmakers (John Goldstone, Jake Eberts)

Weasel property developers threaten the homes of a mole and a toad.
Disappointing adaptation of Kenneth Grahame's classic novel of a threatened idyll, given a broad pantomime treatment.
wd Terry Jones *novel* Kenneth Grahame *ph* David Tattersall *m* John Du Prez *m/ly* John Du Prez, André Jacquemin, Terry Jones, Dave Howman *ed* Julian Doyle
☆ Eric Idle, Steve Coogan, Terry Jones, John Cleese, Anthony Sher, Nicol Williamson, Stephen Fry, Bernard Hill, Nigel Planer, Julia Sawalha, Victoria Wood
'The comedy and the songs have a forced desperate quality, as if the filmmakers aren't quite sure whether they're pitching at an adult or child audience, and think that making a lot of noise is the best way of grabbing the attention of both.' – *Geoffrey Macnab, Sight and Sound*

Windbag the Sailor

GB   1936   85m   bw
Gainsborough (Edward Black)
An incompetent seaman is washed away on an old ketch and lands on a South Sea isle.
Rather uninventive star comedy with inevitable pleasing moments.
w Marriott Edgar, Stafford Dickens, Will Hay *d* William Beaudine *ph* Jack Cox *md* Louis Levy
☆ Will Hay, Moore Marriott, Graham Moffatt, Norma Varden

Windom's Way *

GB   1957   108m   Technicolor
Rank (John Bryan)

A doctor on a Far Eastern island tries to quell a native uprising.
Tolerably well intentioned action melodrama, topical because of Malaya; dramatically rather sober and predictable.
w Jill Craigie *novel* James Ramsay Ullman *d* Ronald Neame *ph* Christopher Challis *m* James Bernard
☆ Peter Finch, Mary Ure, Natasha Parry, Robert Flemyng, Michael Hordern

The Window ***

US   1949   73m   bw
RKO (Frederick Ullman)

A New York slum boy is always telling tall tales, so no one believes him when he actually witnesses a murder … except the murderer.
Classic little second feature, entertaining and suspenseful; unfortunately it had few successful imitators.
w Mel Dinelli *d* Ted Tetzlaff *ph* William Steiner *m* Roy Webb *ed* Frederic Knudtson
☆ Bobby Driscoll, Barbara Hale, Arthur Kennedy, Paul Stewart, Ruth Roman

'Logical, well-shaped, cohesive, admirably acted, beautifully photographed and cut to a nicety.' – *Richard Winnington*
⌥ editing

A Window in London *

GB   1939   77m   bw
G and S/GFD

US title: *Lady in Distress*
A crime passionel is witnessed from a passing train. Modest Anglo-Saxon remake of the French film Metropolitan.
w Ian Dalrymple, Brigid Cooper *d* Herbert Mason
☆ Michael Redgrave, Sally Gray, Paul Lukas, Hartley Power, Patricia Roc

A Window to the Sky: see *The Other Side of the Mountain*

Windprints

GB   1989   99m   colour
Virgin/Apex Motion Pictures/United British Artists (Michael L. Games, Raymond Day)

A British journalist and a South African cameraman go in search of a black poet and murderer in Namibia.
Confusing thriller that deals ineffectually with apartheid and its aftermath.
w David Wicht, Johann Potgieter, Heinrich Dahms *d* David Wicht *ph* Brian Tufano *m* John Keane *pd* Michael Phillips *ed* Robin Sales
☆ John Hurt, Sean Bean, Marius Weyers, Eric Nobbs, Lesley Fong, Kurt Egelhof, Dana Niehaus, Trudie Taljaard, Goliath Davids

Windrider

Australia   1986   83m   colour
Barron/Bush Christmas (Paul D. Barron)

A rich, spoilt young man, whose passion is windsurfing, finds his life coming apart when he falls for a rock singer.
A tedious romantic comedy, in which uninteresting people behave in unlikely ways.
w Everett DeRoche, Bonnie Harris *d* Vincent Monton *ph* Joseph Pickering *m* Kevin Peek *ad* Phil Peters *ed* John Scott
☆ Tom Burlinson, Nicole Kidman, Charles Tingwell, Jill Perryman, Simon Chilvers, Kim Bullard

Wing and a Prayer *

US   1944   97m   bw
TCF (William Becker, William Morosco)

Life aboard an aircraft carrier.
Standard action flagwaver.
w Jerome Cady *d* Henry Hathaway *ph* Glen MacWilliams *m* Hugo Friedhofer
☆ Don Ameche, Cedric Hardwicke, Dana Andrews, Charles Bickford, Richard Jaeckel, Henry Morgan
⌥ Jerome Cady

'At The Edge Of Our Universe, All Hell Is About To Break Loose.'

Wing Commander

US   1999   100m   Technicolor
TCF/No Prisoners/Digital Anvil/Origin/Carousel (Todd Moyer)

In the 21st century, a young pilot joins the battle against the evil alien Kilrathi.
A routine war film set in outer space, but otherwise staying close to all the clichés of the genre; the video game that inspired it is a great deal more enjoyable than anything on offer here.
w Kevin Droney *story* Chris Roberts *d* Chris Roberts *ph* Thierry Arbogast *m* Kevin Kiner, David Arnold *pd* Peter Lamont *ed* Peter Davies *sp* Chris Brown
☆ Freddie Prinze Jnr, Saffron Burrows, Matthew Lillard, Tcheky Karyo, Jurgen Prochnow, David Suchet, David Warner
'Based on a video game and has roughly the same degree of character development. That is all most moviegoers will need to know … painfully boring and funny in the wrong places.' – *Anita Gates, New York Times*

The Winged Serpent: see *Q, The Winged Serpent*

Winged Victory **
US 1944 130m bw
TCF (Darryl F. Zanuck)
During World War II, pilots are inducted, trained and sent on dangerous missions.
Solid, competent, best-foot-forward flagwaver of the highest inspirational intention.
w Moss Hart *play* Moss Hart d George Cukor
ph Glen MacWilliams m David Rose
☆ Lon McCallister, Jeanne Crain, Edmond O'Brien, Jane Ball, Mark Daniels, Don Taylor, Lee J. Cobb, Judy Holliday, Peter Lind Hayes, Alan Baxter, Red Buttons, Barry Nelson, Gary Merrill, Karl Malden, Martin Ritt and also Jo-Carroll Dennison
  'I suppose it is all right, but I don't enjoy having anyone tell me, so cheerfully and energetically, that the Air Force personnel is without exception composed of boy scouts old enough to shave.' – *James Agee*
  'There is no question that Mr Hart captured much of the gallantry and pathos of youth rushing towards dangerous adventures with surface enthusiasm and inner dread.' – *Bosley Crowther, New York Times*

Wings *
US 1927 136m bw silent
Paramount (B. P. Schulberg)
▤
Two young men join the Air Service during World War I, and one eventually shoots down the other by accident.
An epic of early aviation, still stirring in its action sequences.
w Hope Loring, Louis D. Lighton d William Wellman m Harry Perry
☆ Clara Bow, Charles Buddy Rogers, Richard Arlen, Gary Cooper, Jobyna Ralston, El Brendel
  'Air battles are photographed from every conceivable angle, producing many bold cinematic effects … so much in fact happens in the air that it is impossible to take it all in.' – *National Board of Review*
  ♟ best picture; best engineering effects (Roy Pomeroy)

Wings and the Woman: see They Flew Alone

Wings for the Eagle
US 1942 85m bw
Warner (Robert Lord)
Aircraft workers do their bit during World War II.
Home Front propaganda, well enough produced.
w Byron Morgan, Harrison Orkow d Lloyd Bacon
ph Tony Gaudio m Frederick Hollander
☆ Ann Sheridan, Dennis Morgan, Jack Carson, George Tobias, Don Defore

Wings in the Dark *
US 1935 75m bw
Paramount (Arthur Hornblow Jnr)
Embittered after being blinded in an accident, a research flyer finally leaps into action when his stranded girlfriend needs help.
Satisfactory romantic melodrama.
w Jack Kirkland, Frank Partos d James Flood
ph William C. Mellor
☆ Cary Grant, Myrna Loy, Roscoe Karns, Hobart Cavanaugh, Dean Jagger, Bert Hanlon, Samuel S. Hinds
  'Unconvincing and improbable story, but handled so deftly that it may nose through to moderate grosses.' – *Variety*

Wings of Danger
GB 1952 73m bw
Exclusive/Hammer (Anthony Hinds)
A pilot, investigating the disappearance of a friend on an apparently routine flight, uncovers a sinister conspiracy.
A programme filler of no particular distinction, taken at too leisurely a pace to maintain any tension.
w John Gilling *novel* Dead on Course by Elleston Trevor, Packham Webb d Terence Fisher
ph Walter Harvey md Malcolm Arnold
ad Andrew Mazzei ed James Needs
☆ Zachary Scott, Robert Beatty, Kay Kendall, Colin Tapley, Naomi Chance, Arthur Lane, Harold Lang, Diane Cilento

Wings of Desire ****
France/West Germany 1987 127m bw/colour
Road Movies/Argos films
▣ ▤ ⌕ ◠
original title: *Der Himmel über Berlin*
One of a pair of angels, visiting Berlin, decides he wants to be human after falling in love with a circus performer.
Marvellously photographed encounter with humanity and recent German history, full of a quiet joy.
w Wim Wenders, Peter Handke d Wim Wenders
ph Henri Alekan m Jürgen Knieper ad Heidi Ludi ed Peter Przygodda
☆ Bruno Ganz, Solveig Dommartin, Otto Sander, Curt Bois, Peter Falk
  'A friend of mine says that he loved every second of this movie and he couldn't wait to leave. To put it simply, *Wings of Desire* has a visual fascination but no animating force – that's part of why it's being acclaimed as art.' – *Pauline Kael, New Yorker*

The Wings of Eagles *
US 1957 110m Metrocolor
MGM (Charles Schnee)
▣ ▤
A navy flyer breaks his neck in an accident and on recovery becomes a Hollywood writer.
Sentimental biopic of Frank 'Spig' Wead, a routine, easy-going assignment for its director (who is caricatured by Ward Bond as John Dodge).
w Frank Fenton, William Wister Haines d John Ford ph Paul C. Vogel m Jeff Alexander
☆ John Wayne, Maureen O'Hara, Ward Bond, Dan Dailey, Ken Curtis, Edmund Lowe, Kenneth Tobey, Sig Rumann, Henry O'Neill

Wings of Fame
Netherlands 1990 109m Agfacolor
Gala/First Floor Features (Laurens Geels, Dick Maas)
After a writer kills a film star, both find themselves in a luxury hotel for the famous dead where they can stay for as long as they are remembered.
Unsuccessful entry in the current cycle of revenant movies.
w Otakar Votoček, Herman Koch d Otakar Votoček ph Alex Thomson m Paul van Brugge
pd Dick Schillemans ed Hans van Dongen
☆ Peter O'Toole, Colin Firth, Marie Trintignant, Ellen Umlauf, Andréa Ferréol, Maria Becker, Gottfried John

The Wings of Honneamise (dubbed) *
♛ Japan 1994 120m colour
Bandai/Gainax (Hirohiko Sueyoshi, Hiroaki Inoue)
▣
A space cadet volunteers to be the first astronaut, while politicians use the occasion to plot war and revolution.
One of the better examples of Japanese animation: a straightforward science-fiction drama well told and with some spectacular moments.
wd Hiroyuki Yamaga ph Hiroshi Isagawa
md Ryuichi Sakamoto ad Hiromasa Ogura
ed Harutoshi Ogata
☆ Featuring the voices of Robert Matthews, Melody Lee, Lee Stone, Steve Blum
  'Anime's own *The Right Stuff* blasts onto the small screen with superb direction and design, sharply realised characters and a fine sound track.' – *Manga Mania*
  'One of the greatest animated films in the world.' – *John Gosling, Movie Collector*

Wings of the Apache
US 1990 85m
Medusa/Inter-Ocean Films (William Badalato)
▣ ▤ ⌕
US title: *Fire Birds*
US pilots go into action against drug barons.
Top Gun with helicopters, but even less interesting.
w Nick Thiel, Paul F. Edwards *story* Step Tyner, John K. Swensson, Dale Dye d David Green
ph Tony Imi m David Newman pd Joseph T. Garrity ed Jon Poll, Norman Buckley, Dennis O'Connor
☆ Nicolas Cage, Tommy Lee Jones, Sean Young, Bryan Kestner, Dale Dye, Mary Ellen Trainor, J. A. Preston, Peter Onorati, Charles Lanyer, Bert Rhine
  'Enjoyable, old-fashioned aerial adventure pic.' – *Variety*

'A couple with everything but money. An heiress with everything but love. A temptation no one could resist.'

The Wings of the Dove **
GB/US 1997 101m Rank Colour 'Scope
Miramax/Renaissance Dove (David Parfitt, Stephen Evans)
▣ ▤ ⌕ ◠
A poor journalist is persuaded by the woman he loves to seduce a wealthy heiress, who is dying.
An updated version of Henry James that takes the basic narrative but little else from the original novel; despite its faltering period sense, it succeeds on its own account as a modest drama of a triangular love affair.
w Hossein Amini *novel* Henry James d Iain Softley ph Eduardo Serra m Edward Shearmur
pd John Beard ed Tariq Anwar
☆ Helena Bonham Carter, Linus Roache, Alison Elliott, Elizabeth McGovern, Charlotte Rampling, Alex Jennings, Michael Gambon
  'One of those rare movies that evokes not just the essence of a great novel but the experience of it. We are enveloped, at every turn, in the hidden pulse of the characters' motivating passions.' – *Owen Gleiberman, Entertainment Weekly*
  ♟ Helena Bonham Carter; Hossein Amini; Eduardo Serra; Sandy Powell (costumes)
  ♗ Eduardo Serra

Wings of the Hawk
US 1953 81m Technicolor 3-D
U-I (Aaron Rosenberg)
Mexico 1911: a gold miner falls into the hands of revolutionaries.
Routine bang-bang, rather sloppily produced.
w James E. Moser d Budd Boetticher ph Clifford Stine m Frank Skinner
☆ Van Heflin, Julie Adams, George Dolenz, Pedro Gonzales-Gonzales, Rodolfo Acosta, Antonio Moreno, Abbe Lane

Wings of the Morning *
GB 1937 89m Technicolor
New World (Robert T. Kane)
In 1899, a gypsy princess marries an Irish nobleman; in 1937, romance again blooms between their descendants.
Britain's first Technicolor film was great to look at and quite charming, though slight; its major attractions being horse races, songs from John McCormack, and a heroine dressed for plot purposes as a boy.
w Tom Geraghty *story* Donn Byrne d Harold Schuster ph Ray Rennahan, Jack Cardiff
m Arthur Benjamin
☆ Henry Fonda, Annabella, Stewart Rome, John McCormack, Leslie Banks, Irene Vanbrugh, Harry Tate, Edward Underdown, Helen Haye
  'A wholesome, refreshing and altogether likeable little romance.' – *Frank S. Nugent*

Wings of the Navy
US 1938 89m bw
Warner (Lou Edelman)
The loves and careers of navy pilots.
Competent animated recruiting poster.
w Michael Fessier d Lloyd Bacon ph Arthur Edeson, Elmer Dyer
☆ George Brent, Olivia de Havilland, John Payne, Frank McHugh, John Litel, Victor Jory, Henry O'Neill, John Ridgely
  'A convincer to mould public opinion and support in favour of current government plans for wide expansion of American air defence forces.' – *Variety*

Wings over Honolulu
US 1937 78m bw
Universal
A young naval airman is posted to Hawaii and followed by his bride.
Lightweight flagwaver, all smiles at the end.
w Isabel Dawn, Boyce DeGaw, Mildred Cram
d H. C. Potter ph Joseph Valentine
☆ Ray Milland, Wendy Barrie, William Gargan, Kent Taylor, Polly Knowles, Samuel S. Hinds
  ♟ Joseph Valentine

The Winner
US/Australia 1996 89m colour
Feature/Mark Damon/Village Roadshow-Clipsal (Ken Schwenker)
⌕
Gangsters and low life gather to fleece a gambler who cannot stop winning at the casinos.

A muddled thriller that was recut by its producers; its director has disowned it as 'incomprehensible' and attempted, unsuccessfully, to have his name removed from the credits.
w Wendy Riss *play* A Darker Purpose by Wendy Riss d Alex Cox ph Denis Maloney m Pray for Rain, Zander Schloss pd Cecilia Montiel
ed Carlos Puente
☆ Vincent D'Onofrio, Rebecca DeMornay, Delroy Lindo, Frank Whaley, Michael Madsen, Billy Bob Thornton, Richard Edson, Saverio Guerra
  'A film that's meant to be quirkily comic but ultimately is more annoying than thrilling.' – *Emanuel Levy, Variety*
  'It's not my film. It was completely re-edited and the music they put on it was just appalling … I don't want anyone to see it.' – *Alex Cox*

Winner Take All *
US 1932 76m bw
Warner
A prizefighter rises to fame and helps a sick girl and her child.
Slightly-plotted comedy-drama allowing its star full rein.
w Wilson Mizner, Robert Lord, Gerald Beaumont
d Roy del Ruth
☆ James Cagney, Marian Nixon, Guy Kibbee, Clarence Muse, Virginia Bruce, Dickie Moore
  'Enjoyable prizefight talker: sprightly gags and bits bolster conventional story.' – *Variety*

Winning *
US 1969 123m Technicolor Panavision 70
Universal/Newman-Foreman (John Foreman)
▣ ▤ ⌕ ◠
A racing driver's professional problems strain his relationship with his wife.
Cliché track melodrama with pretensions, well but needlessly made.
w Howard Rodman d James Goldstone
ph Richard Moore m Dave Grusin
☆ Paul Newman, Joanne Woodward, Richard Thomas, Robert Wagner, David Sheiner, Clu Gulager

The Winning of Barbara Worth *
US 1926 97m bw silent
Samuel Goldwyn
Desert engineers vie for the daughter of a landowner.
Forgettable action romance, a big hit in its day because of the climactic flood sequence, which still thrills.
w Frances Marion *novel* Harold Bell Wright
d Henry King ph George Barnes m Ted Henkel
☆ Ronald Colman, Vilma Banky, Charles Lane, Gary Cooper, Paul McAllister

Winning of the West
US 1953 60m bw
Columbia/Gene Autry (Armand Schaefer)
▤
A cowboy protects a newspaper proprietor from bandits and renegade Indians and redeems his crooked brother.
Better-than-usual Autry Western, with a reasonable narrative and stock footage borrowed from bigger-budget movies between the usual songs and fist fights.
w Norman S. Hall d George Archainbaud
ph William Bradford md Ross DiMaggio
ad George Brooks ed James Sweeney
☆ Gene Autry, Smiley Burnette, Gail Davis, Richard Crane, Robert Livingston, House Peters Jnr, Gregg Barton, William Forrest

The Winning Team
US 1952 98m bw
Warner (Bryan Foy)
▤ ⌕
A telephone linesman becomes a great baseball player despite trouble with his vision after an accident.
Standard biopic of Grover Cleveland Alexander; all very pleasant but no surprises.
w Ted Sherdeman, Seeleg Lester, Merwin Gerard
d Lewis Seiler ph Sid Hickox m David Buttolph
☆ Doris Day, Ronald Reagan, Frank Lovejoy, Eve Miller, James Millican, Russ Tamblyn

The Winning Ticket
US 1935 69m bw
MGM
An Italian barber wins a sweepstake but can't find his ticket.
Modest, lively comedy which pleased at the time.

---

w Ralph Spence, Richard Shayer, Robert Pirosh, George Seaton d Charles F. Reisner
☆ Leo Carrillo, Louise Fazenda, Ted Healy, Irene Hervey, James Ellison, Luis Alberni, Akim Tamiroff

The Winning Way: see *The All-American*

The Winslow Boy *
👫👫 GB 1948 117m bw
British Lion/London Films (Anatole de Grunwald)
◉ ▦

A naval cadet is expelled for stealing a postal order; his father spends all he has on proving his innocence.
Highly enjoyable middle-class British entertainment based on an actual case; performances and period settings are alike excellent, though the film is a trifle overlong.
w Terence Rattigan, Anatole de Grunwald *play* Terence Rattigan d Anthony Asquith ph Frederick Young m William Alwyn
☆ *Robert Donat,* Cedric Hardwicke, Margaret Leighton, Frank Lawton, Jack Watling, Basil Radford, Kathleen Harrison, Francis L. Sullivan, Marie Lohr, Neil North, Wilfrid Hyde-White, Ernest Thesiger
'Only a clod could see this film without excitement, laughter and some slight moisture about the eyes.' – *Daily Telegraph*

'In 1910 A Court Case Concerning A Cadet Accused Of Stealing A Five Shilling Postal Order Brought Down The British Empire.'
The Winslow Boy *
US 1998 104m Technicolor
Columbia TriStar/Sony Pictures Classics (Sarah Green)

In Edwardian England, a father fights to clear his son's name when he is expelled from naval college for stealing a postal order.
Mannered, buttoned-up version of a successful play that gains emotional power from its repression of feelings.
wd David Mamet play Terence Rattigan ph Benoit Delhomme m Alaric Jans pd Gemma Jackson ed Barbara Tulliver
☆ Nigel Hawthorne, Jeremy Northam, Rebecca Pidgeon, Gemma Jones, Guy Edwards, Colin Stinton, Sarah Flind, Neil North, Sara Stewart, Perry Fenwick, Alan Polanski
'Little more than dusty museum piece.' – *Guardian*

Winsor McCay: Animation Legend *
US bw
Milestone/Lumivision (Albert M. Miller)
◉

A collection, released on video, of animated films from La Cinémathèque Québécoise by the pioneering Winsor McCay: *Little Nemo,* made in 1911, *How a Mosquito Operates,* 1912, *Gertie the Dinosaur,* 1914, *The Sinking of the Lusitania,* 1918, *Bug Vaudeville,* c. 1921, *The Pet,* 1921, *The Flying House,* 1921, and fragments of *The Centaurs,* 1918–21, *Gertie on Tour,* 1918–21, and *Flip's Circus,* 1918–21.
Fascinating collection of McCay's early animation that reveals him as far more sophisticated, and much better at portraying people, than his rivals; it also includes glimpses of him at work and play.
m R. J. Miller

Winstanley *
GB 1978 96m colour
Other Cinema/BFI (Andrew Mollo, Kevin Brownlow)
◉ ▦

In 1649, after the English Civil War, the Diggers, a millenarian group who espoused social equality, meet hostility when they form a farming commune in Surrey.
Intense, low-budget ideological drama of the collision of class and greed, distinguished by its cinematography.
w uncredited novel Comrade Jacob by David Caute d Kevin Brownlow, Andrew Mollo ph Ernest Vincze m Sergei Prokoviev ad Andrew Mollo ed Sarah Ellis
☆ Miles Halliwell, Jerome Willis, Terry Higgins, Phil Oliver, David Bramley, Alison Halliwell, Sid Rawle, Dawson France, Barry Shaw

Winter Carnival
US 1939 89m bw
UA (Walter Wanger)
College romances over a holiday weekend.

Nondescript romantic comedy.
w Lester Cole, Budd Schulberg d Charles Riesner ph Merritt Gerstad m Werner Janssen
☆ Ann Sheridan, Richard Carlson, Helen Parrish, Virginia Gilmore, Robert Walker
'Slick production of an undistinguished yarn about the annual Dartmouth winter sports.' – *Variety*

'No matter where you hide, life will always find you.'
The Winter Guest *
GB/US 1996 110m Technicolor
Film Four/Fine Line/Channel 4/Capitol/Scottish Arts Council/Lottery Fund (Ken Lipper, Edward R. Pressman)
◉ ▦ ▦

A mother attempts to re-establish a happy relationship with her recently widowed daughter.
A melancholy drama of family life, over which hangs the shadow of death; it is enlivened by a mordant humour.
w Sharman MacDonald, Alan Rickman d Alan Rickman ph Seamus McGarvey m Michael Kamen pd Robin Cameron Don ed Scott Thomas
☆ Phyllida Law, Emma Thompson, Sheila Reid, Sandra Voe, Arlene Cockburn, Gary Hollywood, Sean Biggerstaff, Douglas Murphy
'Solemn, lengthy and pretentious.' – *Lucy Maycock, New Statesman*

Winter Kills
US 1979 97m colour Panavision
Avco Embassy/Winter Gold (Fred Caruso)
▦ ▦

The brother of an assassinated president tracks down the killers, but finds that his tycoon father is involved.
Heavy-going and confusing melodrama with much flashy editing. Despite its cast, it was never satisfactorily released.
wd William Richert novel Richard Condon ph Vilmos Zsigmond pd Robert Boyle ed David Bretherton
☆ Jeff Bridges, John Huston, Anthony Perkins, Elizabeth Taylor, Sterling Hayden, Eli Wallach, Dorothy Malone, Tomas Milian, Richard Boone, Toshiro Mifune

Winter Light *
Sweden 1962 80m bw
Svensk Filmindustri (Allan Ekelund)
◉ ▦

original title: *Nattvardsgästerna*
A widowed village pastor loses his vocation.
In a sense almost parody Bergman; in another, one of his clearest statements of despair. The middle section of a pessimistic trilogy which also included Through a Glass Darkly and The Silence.
wd Ingmar Bergman ph Sven Nykvist m none
☆ Max von Sydow, Ingrid Thulin, Gunnar Bjornstrand, Gunnel Lindblom
'The film-maker's mastery alone does not guarantee a great film. Winter Light is scarcely even a good one.' – *John Simon, 1967*

Winter Meeting
US 1948 104m bw
Warner (Henry Blanke)
▦

A repressed spinster falls for a naval hero intent on becoming a priest.
Dreary talk marathon which did its star's career no good at all.
w Catherine Turney novel Ethel Vance d Bretaigne Windust ph Ernest Haller m Max Steiner
☆ Bette Davis, James Davis, Janis Paige, John Hoyt, Florence Bates, Walter Baldwin

Winter of Our Dreams *
Australia 1981 90m Eastmancolor
Vega Films (Richard Mason)
▦

A bookseller investigates the suicide of an old girlfriend, and becomes involved with an unhappy prostitute.
Intriguing character drama with a tendency to haunt the mind, though its effectiveness depends largely on its acting.
wd John Duigan ph Tom Cowan m Sharyn Calcraft
☆ Judy Davis, Bryan Brown, Cathy Downes, Baz Luhrmann

Winter People
US 1988 111m DeLuxe
Rank/Nelson Entertainment/Castle Rock (Robert H. Solo)
◉ ▦ ▦

In the 1930s, a wandering clockmaker becomes involved in a feud between two families in a backwoods community.
Frenzied old-fashioned melodrama guaranteed to chill the interest of its audience.
w Carol Sobieski novel John Ehle d Ted Kotcheff ph François Protat m John Scott pd Ron Foreman ed Thom Noble
☆ Kurt Russell, Kelly McGillis, Lloyd Bridges, Mitchell Ryan, Amelia Burnette, Eileen Ryan, Lanny Flaherty

'You Can't Run Away From Destiny.'
Winter Sleepers *
Germany/France 1997 123m colour
original title: *Winterschlafer*
A hit-and-run accident on a snowbound road links the lives of four self-obsessed young people with that of a farmer, seeking the driver who killed his daughter.
An ambitious, slightly ponderous drama that aspires to be a portrait of a disconsolate generation. It is almost worth seeing for one extraordinary sequence of a skier in free-fall.
w Tom Tykwer, Anne-Françoise Pyszora novel Expense of the Spirit by Anne-Françoise Pyszora d Tom Tykwer ph Frank Griebe m Rheinhold Hell, Johnny Klimek, Tom Tykwer ed Katya Dringenberg
☆ Floriane Daniel, Heino Ferch, Ulrich Mattes, Marie-Lou Sellem, Laura Tonke, Sebastian Schipper, Agathe Taffertshofer, Sofia Dirscheri
'At once scary, erotic and desperately sad.' – *Peter Bradshaw, Guardian*

A Winter's Tale: see *Conte d'hiver*

Winterschlafer: see *Winter Sleepers*

'Like a thunderbolt of naked light it struck Broadway – now it tears at your heart on the screen!'
Winterset *
US 1936 78m bw
RKO

On the New York waterfront, a drifter determines to avenge his father's death.
Very dated poetic melodrama, here given a talky, artificial production which at the time impressed many critics but is now fairly difficult to endure.
w Anthony Veiller play Maxwell Anderson d Alfred Santell ph Peverell Marley m Nathaniel Shilkret ad Perry Ferguson
☆ Burgess Meredith, Eduardo Ciannelli, Margo, Paul Guilfoyle, John Carradine, Edward Ellis, Stanley Ridges, Maurice Moscovich, Myron McCormick, Mischa Auer
'Not big box office … in certain locales they may even wonder what it's all about.' – *Variety*
'Still in a grand manner that just won't do on the screen … but there are fine moments in the performances, and there's something childishly touching in the florid dramatic effects.' – *New Yorker, 1978*
𝄞 Nathaniel Shilkret; Perry Ferguson

Wintertime
US 1943 82m bw
TCF (William Le Baron)
A Norwegian skating star comes to Canada where her uncle's winter resort is on its uppers.
The last of the star's Fox musicals is pure routine.
w Edward Moran, Jack Jevne, Lynn Starling d John Brahm ph Glen MacWilliams m Alfred Newman md Charles Henderson
☆ Sonja Henie, Jack Oakie, Cesar Romero, S. Z. Sakall, Carole Landis, Cornel Wilde, Woody Herman and his Band

Wired
US 1989 109m colour
Entertainment/Lion Screen Entertainment (Edward A. Feldman, Charles R. Meeker)
◉ ▦ 𝄞

The ghost of comedian John Belushi, dead from a drug overdose, relives his life, while a journalist interviews his friends.
Fantasy substitutes for the harder, documented facts in a frenetic film that fails to capture Belushi's comic talents.

w Earl MacRauch book Wired: The Short Life and Fast Times of John Belushi by Bob Woodward d Larry Peerce ph Tony Imi m Michael Ruff pd Brian Eatwell ed Eric Sears
☆ Michael Chiklis, Patti D'Arbanville, J. T. Walsh, Lucinda Jenney, Gary Groomes, Ray Sharkey, Alex Rocco, Jere Burns

'No one is entirely human.'
The Wisdom of Crocodiles
GB 1998 98m colour
Entertainment/Zenith/Goldwyn//Film Foundry Partners (David Lascelles, Carolyn Choa)
◉

A vampire can survive only by drinking the blood of women who love him.
Risible would-be horror, bland and bloodless, and lumbered with a script that makes no sense at all.
w Paul Hoffman d Po Chih Leong ph Oliver Curtis m John Lunn, Orlando Gough pd Andy Harris ed Robin Sales
☆ Jude Law, Elina Lowensohn, Timothy Spall, Kerry Fox, Jack Davenport, Colin Salmon, Rick Lamont, Ashley Artus
'Starts intriguingly but ends up thrashing around as a toothless wonder.' – *Derek Elley, Variety*
'Might have got away with being laughable; the fact that it's funded by an Arts Council grant makes it deplorable too.' – *Anthony Quinn, Independent*

Wise Blood *
US/Germany 1979 108m colour
Artificial Eye/Anthea/Ithaca (Michael Fitzgerald, Kathy Fitzgerald)
▦

In the deep South, a war veteran with no beliefs becomes a travelling preacher.
Odd story, not easy to like but with many impressive moments.
w Benedict Fitzgerald novel Flannery O'Connor d John Huston ph Gerry Fisher m Alex North ad Sarah Fitzgerald ed Roberto Silver
☆ Brad Dourif, Ned Beatty, Harry Dean Stanton, Daniel Shor, Amy Wright, John Huston

Wise Girl
US 1937 70m bw
RKO (Edward Kaufman)
A rich girl goes bohemian in Greenwich village.
Pretty absurd romantic comedy which strains the patience.
w Allan Scott, Charles Norman d Leigh Jason
☆ Miriam Hopkins, Ray Milland, Walter Abel, Henry Stephenson, Alec Craig, Guinn Williams, Margaret Dumont
'Slow-moving narrative, considerable silliness, lack of convincing plot.' – *Variety*

Wise Guys
US 1986 91m Technicolor
MGM-UA (Aaron Russo)
▦

Two small-time hoods unwittingly heist Mafia funds.
Haven't we seen this somewhere before? And done better?
w George Gallo d Brian de Palma ph Fred Schuler m Ira Newborn pd Edward Pisoni ed Jerry Greenberg
☆ Danny DeVito, Joe Piscopo, Harvey Keitel, Ray Sharkey, Patti LuPone

The Wiser Sex
US 1932 72m bw
Paramount
A society girl goes undercover to save her public prosecutor boyfriend from smears.
Unattractive comedy-melodrama which never seems to get going.
w Harry Hervey, Caroline Franke play Her Confessions by Clyde Fitch d Berthold Viertel
☆ Claudette Colbert, Melvyn Douglas, Lilyan Tashman, William Boyd, Ross Alexander, Douglass Dumbrille
'Story a handicap: picture suffers accordingly.' – *Variety*

Wish You Were Here *
GB 1987 92m colour
Zenith/Film Four (Sarah Radclyffe)
◉ ▦
The growing pains of a teenage girl in a seaside town.

◎ Digital Video Disc Region 2   ◎ Digital Video Disc Region 1   ♫ Soundtrack released on compact disc   ☆ Cast in approximate order of importance   † Points of interest   🎵 Notable songs   🏆 Academy Award   𝄞 Academy Award nomination   🎖 BAFTA

Noted chiefly for its central performance, this is a film full of telling detail and compassion, despite its apparently defiant mood.
wd David Leland ph Ian Wilson m Stanley Myers
pd Caroline Amies ed George Akers
☆ Emily Lloyd, Tom Bell, Clare Clifford, Barbara Durkin, Geoffrey Hutchings
'What is as depressing as the film itself is the fact that no one has thought even to comment on its one binding quality – the perception of sex, class and history entirely in terms of grotesque appearances.' – *Judith Williamson, New Statesman*
🎭 original screenplay

Wishmaster
US   1997   90m   colour
First Independent/Live/Mediaworks (Pierre David, Clark Peterson, Noel A. Zanitsch)
📼 ▤ ◎ 🎧
An evil spirit, imprisoned for 800 years, is released in modern-day Los Angeles and grants wishes with an umpleasant twist to them.
A violent and nasty horror that numbingly repeats, with diminishing results, its one small idea.
w Peter Atkins d Robert Kurtzman ph Jacques Haitkin m Harry Manfredini pd Dorian Vernaccio, Deborah Raymond ed Dorian Vernaccio
☆ Tammy Lauren, Andrew Divoff, Robert Englund, Tony Todd, Wendy Benson, Tony Crane, Chris Lemmon, Jenny O'Hara, Kane Hodder
'A washout in its painfully obvious attempt to launch a new horror franchise. Unconscionably sadistic, even by genre standards, and mind-numbingly formulaic.' – *Joe Leydon, Variety*
† The cast includes three actors from other horror series: Robert Englund (Freddy Kruger from the *Nightmare on Elm Street* series), Tony Todd (Candyman in the series of the same name), and Kane Hodder (Jason from the *Friday the 13th* series).

The Wistful Widow of Wagon Gap *
US   1947   78m   bw
U-I (Robert Arthur)
▤
In old Montana, an accident-prone wayfarer accidentally kills a man and has to look after his family.
Tame and disappointing comedy vehicle.
w Robert Lees, Frederic I. Rinaldo, John Grant story D. D. Beauchamp, William Bowers
d Charles T. Barton ph Charles Van Enger
m Walter Shumann
☆ Bud Abbott, Lou Costello, Marjorie Main, Audrey Young, George Cleveland

Witch Doctor: see *Men of Two Worlds*

Witch Hunt *
US   1994   98m   CFI color
HBO/Pacific Western (Michael R. Joyce)
📼
Working in a world where magic is real and a witch conjures up Shakespeare to write additional dialogue for movies, Hollywood private eye H. Phillip Lovecraft investigates the death of a film producer, who is turned into an incredible shrinking man and torn apart by his dogs; at the same time, a Congressman investigates magic itself and burns witches at the stake.
An odd and witty mix of cod-Chandler and satirical fantasy, making an oblique comment on McCarthyism and the Hollywood blacklisting of the 50s and including even more film references than Tarantino manages.
w Joseph Dougherty d Paul Schrader ph Jean Yves Escoffier m Angelo Badalamenti pd Curtis A. Schnell ed Kristina Boden
☆ Dennis Hopper, Penelope Ann Miller, Eric Bogosian, Sheryl Lee Ralph, Julian Sands, Valerie Mahaffey, Lypsinka
'Weird, wonderful and quite unlike anything you've ever seen before. Highly recommended.' – *Film Review*
† The film, made for cable TV, was released direct to video in Britain.

Witchcraft *
GB   1964   79m   bw
TCF/Lippert (Robert Lippert, Jack Parsons)
A family of witches take revenge on their longtime enemies.
Spasmodically arresting horror film spoiled by too complex a plot line and some variable acting.

w Harry Spaulding d Don Sharp ph Arthur Lavis m Carlo Martelli
☆ Jack Hedley, Lon Chaney Jnr, Marie Ney, Jill Dixon, David Weston
'Unpretentious and uncommonly gripping.' – *MFB*

Witchcraft through the Ages **
Sweden   1922   83m   bw   silent
Svensk Filmindustri
📼 ▤
original title: *Häxan*
A 'documentary' investigation of the history of witchcraft, with acted examples.
Fascinating reconstruction of ancient rituals, still maintaining its power to frighten.
wd Benjamin Christensen ph Johan Ankarstjerne
☆ Oscar Stribolt, Clara Pontoppidan, Karen Winther

The Witches
GB   1966   91m   Technicolor
Warner/Hammer (Anthony Nelson-Keys)
US title: *The Devil's Own*
A schoolmistress finds witchcraft in an English village.
Chintzy horror with predictable development and risible climax.
w Nigel Kneale novel *The Devil's Own* by Peter Curtis d Cyril Frankel ph Arthur Grant m Richard Rodney Bennett pd Bernard Robinson ed James Needs, Chris Barnes
☆ Joan Fontaine, Kay Walsh, Alec McCowen, Gwen Ffrangcon Davies, Ingrid Brett, John Collin, Michèle Dotrice, Leonard Rossiter, Martin Stephens, Carmel McSharry

The Witches **
👪   US   1990   91m   Eastmancolor
Warner/Lorimar (Mark Shivas)
📼 ▤ 💿
A small boy, who has been turned into a mouse, schemes with his granny to thwart witches' plans to poison all the children in Britain.
Superior entertainment, intended for children, but as likely to be enjoyed by adults.
w Allan Scott novel Roald Dahl d Nicolas Roeg ph Harvey Harrison m Stanley Myers pd Voytek, Andrew Sanders ed Tony Lawson
☆ Anjelica Huston, Mai Zetterling, Jasen Fisher, Rowan Atkinson, Bill Paterson, Brenda Blethyn, Charlie Potter, Anne Lambton, Jane Horrocks
'A controlled and suitably dark piece of filmmaking.' – *Variety*

The Witches of Eastwick **
US   1987   118m   Technicolor
Warner/Guber-Peters/Kennedy Miller
Three divorcees on the make are seduced by the devil.
Horny fantasy, impeccably played, though it could have been shorter.
w Michael Cristofer novel John Updike d George Miller ph Vilmos Zsigmond m John Williams pd Polly Platt
☆ Jack Nicholson, Cher, Susan Sarandon, Michelle Pfeiffer, Veronica Cartwright, Richard Jenkins
👤 John Williams

The Witches of Salem *
France/East Germany   1957   143m   bw
Borderie/CICC/DEFA/Pathé (Raymond Borderie)
original title: *Les Sorcières de Salem*
In 1692 Massachusetts, jealousies lead to accusations of witchcraft and multiple trials and executions.
An account of a horrifying historical fact which was also intended to reflect on the McCarthy witch hunts of the fifties; but the film, despite splendid acting, is too literal and slow-moving.
w Jean-Paul Sartre play *The Crucible* by Arthur Miller d Raymond Rouleau ph Claude Renoir m Georges Auric
☆ Simone Signoret, Yves Montand, Mylène Demongeot, Jean Debucourt
🎭 Simone Signoret

'Keep the children home! And if you're squeamish, stay home with them!'
Witchfinder General *
GB   1968   87m   Eastmancolor
Tigon/American International (Arnold Miller, Philip Waddilove, Louis M. Heyward)
📼 ▤
US title: *The Conqueror Worm*
In 1645 a villainous lawyer finds it profitable to travel the country instigating witch hunts.
Savage, stylish minor horror melodrama with a growing reputation as the best work of its young director. Not for the squeamish despite its pleasing countryside photography.
w Michael Reeves, Tom Baker novel Ronald Bassett d Michael Reeves ph John Coquillon m Paul Ferris, Jim Morahan
☆ Vincent Price, Rupert Davies, Ian Ogilvy, Patrick Wymark, Hilary Dwyer, Wilfrid Brambell

'He made a murderer of the boy who was to marry his own daughter!'
The Witching Hour
US   1934   65m   bw
Paramount (Bayard Veiller)
A gambler hypnotizes a young man into taking the blame for a murder.
Stalwart melodrama, reasonably well done.
w Anthony Veiller, Salisbury Field play Augustus Thomas d Henry Hathaway
☆ John Halliday, Guy Standing, Judith Allen, Tom Brown, William Frawley
† There was a previous (silent) version in 1921.

With a Song in My Heart *
US   1952   117m   Technicolor
TCF (Lamar Trotti)
Singer Jane Froman is crippled in a plane crash but finally makes a comeback.
Romanticized showbiz biopic with the singer providing voice only. Adequate production and plenty of familiar tunes made this a successful mass appeal sob story.
w Lamar Trotti d Walter Lang ph Leon Shamroy md Alfred Newman
☆ Susan Hayward, David Wayne, Rory Calhoun, Thelma Ritter, Una Merkel, Robert Wagner, Helen Westcott
🎵 'Blue Moon'; 'With a Song in My Heart'; 'Embraceable You'; 'Tea for Two'; 'It's a Good Day'; 'I'll Walk Alone'; 'Indiana'; 'Deep in the Heart of Texas'
🏆 Alfred Newman
🎖 Susan Hayward; Thelma Ritter

With Honors
US   1994   100m   Technicolor
Warner/Spring Creek (Paula Weinstein, Amy Robinson)
📼 ▤ 💿
A homeless man persuades a Harvard student to take him home with him in return for giving back, a page at a time, the student's lost thesis.
Saccharine and preachy drama, far removed from any reality and providing little in the way of escapist pleasures.
w William Mastrosimone d Alek Keshishian ph Sven Nykvist m Patrick Leonard pd Barbara Long ed Michael R. Miller
☆ Joe Pesci, Brendan Fraser, Moira Kelly, Patrick Dempsey, John Hamilton, Gore Vidal
'An incredibly mawkish comedy drama.' – *Sight and Sound*

With Six You Get Egg Roll
US   1968   99m   DeLuxe   Panavision
Cinema Center/Arwin (Martin Melcher)
▤
A widow with three sons marries a widower with one daughter.
Quite a bright and inventive family comedy.
w Gwen Bagni, Paul Dubov d Howard Morris ph Ellsworth Fredericks, Harry Stradling Jnr m Robert Mersey
☆ Doris Day, Brian Keith, Pat Carroll, Barbara Hershey

Within a Cloister: see *Behind Convent Walls*

Within the Law: see *Paid (1930)*

Within the Law
US   1939   66m   bw
MGM
A girl wrongly convicted studies law in prison and later takes her revenge on the real culprit.

Reasonably interesting melodrama, filmed several times previously: in 1912, 1917, 1923 and in 1930 as Paid.
w Charles Lederer, Edith Fitzgerald play Bayard Veiller d Gustav Machaty
☆ Ruth Hussey, Tom Neal, Paul Kelly, William Gargan, Paul Cavanagh, Samuel S. Hinds, Rita Johnson, Sidney Blackmer
'Certain of appeal where cops and robbers click.' – *Variety*

Within These Walls
US   1945   71m   bw
TCF (Ben Silvey)
A stern prison governor makes no exceptions when his son becomes a convict.
Formula penitentiary drama with no surprises.
w Charles Trapnell, James R. Fisher, Eugene Ling, Wanda Tuchock d Bruce Humberstone
☆ Thomas Mitchell, Mary Anderson, Edward Ryan, Mark Stevens, Roy Roberts

Withnail and I *
GB   1987   108m   colour
Recorded Releasing/HandMade Films (Paul M. Heller)
📼 📼 ▤ 💿 🎧
In the 60s in Britain two out-of-work actors settle in a dilapidated country cottage.
Deliberately seedy comedy which settles down as a study of character and contrives to be hard to forget.
wd Bruce Robinson ph Peter Hannan m David Dundas pd Michael Pickwoad ed Alan Strachan
☆ Richard E. Grant, Paul McGann, Richard Griffiths, Ralph Brown, Michael Elphick

Without a Clue
US   1988   107m   CFI color
Rank/ITC (Mark Stirdivant)
Dr Watson hires a failed actor to impersonate Sherlock Holmes, a fictional character he has invented to hide his own abilities as a detective.
The mystery is that anyone should have released this witless spoof.
w Gary Murphy, Larry Strawther d Thom Eberhardt ph Alan Hume m Henry Mancini pd Brian Ackland-Snow, Martyn Hebert ed Peter Tanner
☆ Michael Caine, Ben Kingsley, Jeffrey Jones, Lysette Anthony, Paul Freeman, Nigel Davenport, Pat Keen, Peter Cook, Tim Killick

Without a Trace
US   1983   120m   DeLuxe
TCF (Stanley R. Jaffe)
▤
A mother solves the mystery of her missing child.
Fairly interesting modern melodrama with emphasis on character rather than the somewhat arbitrarily resolved plot.
w Beth Gutcheon novel *Still Missing* by Beth Gutcheon d Stanley R. Jaffe ph John Bailey m Jack Nitzsche pd Paul Sylbert
☆ Kate Nelligan, Judd Hirsch, David Dukes, Stockard Channing, Jacqueline Brookes, Keith McDermott, Kathleen Widdoes
'Dignified understatement is the keynote.' – *Tom Milne, MFB*

'Pre. His spirit set a pace only his heart could follow.'
Without Limits
US   1998   118m   Technicolor
Warner (Paula Wagner, Tom Cruise)
▤
After clashing with his coach at the University of Oregon over the best way to win his races, athlete Steve Prefontaine runs poorly in the 1972 Olympics, then tries, too late, to change his approach.
A biopic of a charismatic American long distance runner who died young and failed to win the glittering prizes; at its heart is a sometimes affecting drama of Prefontaine's relationship with his coach.
w Robert Towne, Kenny Moore d Robert Towne ph Conrad L. Hall m Randy Miller pd William Creber ed Claire Simpson
☆ Billy Crudup, Donald Sutherland, Monica Potter, Jeremy Sisto, Gabriel Olds, Judith Ivey, Dean Norris, Billy Burke, Adam Setliff, Nicholas Oleson, William Mapother, Matthew Lillard
'Saddled with a strident soundtrack, the film feels at times like an over-earnest made-for-television feature.' – *Edward Lawrenson, Sight and Sound*
† Prefontaine was also the subject of another biopic *Prefontaine* (qv), made in 1997.

👪 film suitable for family viewing   📼 VHS video-cassette for the British PAL system   📼 VHS video-cassette for the British PAL system in wide screen-format   💿 Video cassette in a computer-colourised version   ▤ American NTSC video-cassette   💿 Laser disc

Without Love *

US 1945 111m bw
MGM (Lawrence Weingarten)
🎞️ 🔊

The housing shortage in wartime Washington causes a widow to allow a scientist to move in with her, quite platonically.
Altered version of a popular play; rather long-drawn-out and disappointing considering the talent on hand.
w Donald Ogden Stewart play Philip Barry
d Harold S. Bucquet ph Karl Freund m Bronislau Kaper
☆ Spencer Tracy, Katharine Hepburn, Lucille Ball, Keenan Wynn, Carl Esmond, Patricia Morison, Felix Bressart, Gloria Grahame
'One of those glossy conversation pieces that MGM does up so handsomely.' – Rose Pelswick

Without Reservations

US 1946 101m bw
RKO/Jesse L. Lasky
🎞️ 🔊

A famous woman writer heads for Hollywood by train and meets a marine who seems ideal for her male lead.
Would-be zany romantic comedy à la It Happened One Night; doesn't quite come off.
w Andrew Solt d Mervyn Le Roy ph Milton Krasner m Roy Webb
☆ Claudette Colbert, John Wayne, Don Defore, Phil Brown, Frank Puglia

Without Warning

US 1952 70m bw
UA/Allart
A sex maniac murders a succession of blondes.
Semi-documentary, low-budget police thriller with all elements adequate for their purpose.
w Bill Raynor d Arnold Laven ph Joseph Biroc m Herschel Burke Gilbert
☆ Adam Williams, Edward Binns, Meg Randall

Without Witnesses: see A Private Conversation

Without You I'm Nothing

US 1990 89m Technicolor
Electric/MCEG (Jonathan D. Krane)
🎞️ 🔊

Stand-up comedian Sandra Bernhard performs her one-woman show.
A self-indulgent ramble through the performer's past, interspersed with a few deft but uninteresting recreations of popular musical styles.
w Sandra Bernhard, John Boscovich d John Boscovich ph Joseph Yacoe m Patrice Rushen pd Kevin Rupnik ed Pamela Malouf-Cundy
☆ Sandra Bernhard, John Doe, Steve Antin, Lu Leonard, Ken Foree, Cynthia Bailey
'It aims for the spin-off thrills of a transgressive act in which much is suggested but nothing really is said.' – Cynthia Rose, Sight and Sound
'One of the sharpest and original comic talents of the past decade.' – Empire

'A big city cop who knows too much. His only witness – a small boy who's seen too much!'

Witness ****

US 1985 112m Technicolor
Paramount/Edward S. Feldman
🎞️ 🔊 🎧

A young Amish boy witnesses a murder, and a big-city detective hides out in the community to protect him.
As much about the meeting of cultures as about cops and robbers, this is one of those lucky movies which works out well on all counts and shows that there are still craftsmen lurking in Hollywood.
w Earl W. Wallace, William Kelley d Peter Weir ph John Seale m Maurice Jarre pd Stan Jolley ed Thom Noble
☆ Harrison Ford, Kelly McGillis, Josef Sommer, Lukas Haas, Jan Rubes, Alexander Godunov
🏆 editing; original screenplay
🏅 best picture; direction; Harrison Ford; photography; music; art direction
🎖️ music

The Witness Chair

US 1936 64m bw
RKO
A secretary accidentally kills her nasty employer and almost allows an associate to take the blame.
Stiff, old-fashioned melodrama that served its purpose.

w Rian James, Gertrude Purcell story Rita Weiman d George Nicholls Jnr
☆ Ann Harding, Walter Abel, Douglass Dumbrille, Frances Sage, Moroni Olsen, Margaret Hamilton

Witness for the Prosecution ***

US 1957 114m bw
UA/Theme/Edward Small (Arthur Hornblow Jnr)
🎞️

A convalescent QC takes on a murder defence and finds himself in a web of trickery.
Thoroughly likeable though relentlessly over-expanded movie version of a clever stage thriller. Some miscasting and artificiality is condoned by smart dialogue and handling, one celebrated performance, and a handful of surprises.
w Billy Wilder, Harry Kurnitz play Agatha Christie d Billy Wilder ph Russell Harlan m Matty Melneck ed Daniel Mandell
☆ Charles Laughton, Tyrone Power, Marlene Dietrich, John Williams, Henry Daniell, Elsa Lanchester, Norma Varden, Una O'Connor, Ian Wolfe
🏅 best picture; Billy Wilder; Charles Laughton; Elsa Lanchester; Daniel Mandell

Witness to Murder *

US 1954 81m bw
UA (Chester Erskine)
A lonely woman sees a strangling in the flat across the street; the police don't believe her but the murderer does.
Predictable but quite effective screamer with a nick-of-time dénouement.
w Chester Erskine d Roy Rowland ph John Alton m Herschel Burke Gilbert
☆ Barbara Stanwyck, George Sanders, Gary Merrill, Jesse White, Harry Shannon, Claire Carleton

Wittgenstein **

GB 1993 75m colour
BFI/Channel 4/Uplink/Bandung (Tariq Ali)
🎞️

Biopic of the linguistic philosopher Ludwig Wittgenstein, from his birth in Austria to his death in Cambridge in 1951.
Made on a tiny budget and shot as a series of scenes, using a minimum of props, against a black background, this is nevertheless a colourful and intriguing work, interested both in Wittgenstein as a person and in what he had to say; inevitably, its appeal will be limited to those interested in philosophy and in the inventive use of film
w Derek Jarman, Terry Eagleton, Ken Butler d Derek Jarman ph James Welland m Jan Latham-Koenig ad Annie Lapaz ed Budge Tremlett
☆ Karl Johnson, Michael Gough, Tilda Swinton, John Quentin, Kevin Collins, Clancy Chassay, Jill Balcon
'Wonderfully theatrical in its execution, this is Jarman pared down to basics – actors, stage, lighting – allowing the script, the real strength of the film, with its equal measures of wit and weight (and surprisingly little pretension) to take centre stage.' – Philippa Bloom, Empire

'You can't tell them apart without a scorecard!'

Wives and Lovers

US 1963 103m bw
Paramount/Hal B. Wallis
A successful author moves his family into Connecticut, where sex rears its ugly head.
Would-be sophisticated comedy with insufficient bubbles.
w Edward Anhalt play The First Wife by Jay Presson Allen d John Rich ph Lucien Ballard m Lyn Murray
☆ Van Johnson, Janet Leigh, Ray Walston, Shelley Winters, Martha Hyer, Jeremy Slate

Wives under Suspicion

US 1938 68m bw
Universal
🎞️

A district attorney involved in a love-triangle murder discovers a similar situation developing in his own life.
Flat remake of the same director's The Kiss Before the Mirror; of little interest.
w Myles Connolly d James Whale
☆ Warren William, Gail Patrick, Ralph Morgan, William Lundigan, Constance Moore

The Wiz *

🔼 US 1978 134m Technicolor
Universal/Motown (Robert Cohen)
🎞️ 🎞️ 🔊 🎧

A black version of The Wizard of Oz, set in New York.
Glossy version of the Broadway musical hit; it offers some rewards, but on the whole the first is the best.
w Joel Schumacher play Charlie Smalls (m/ly) book William Brown d Sidney Lumet ph Oswald Morris m Quincy Jones md Quincy Jones pd Tony Walton songs Charlie Smalls
☆ Diana Ross, Michael Jackson, Nipsey Russell, Ted Ross, Lena Horne, Richard Pryor, Mabel King, Theresa Merritt
🏅 Oswald Morris; Quincy Jones

The Wizard

🔼 US 1989 97m DeLuxe
UIP/Universal (David Chisholm, Ken Topolsky)
A young boy runs away with his almost-mute even younger brother in order to compete in a video-game championship.
Uninteresting pre-teen road movie, which has no other purpose than to sell video games.
w David Chisholm d Todd Holland ph Robert Yeoman m J. Peter Robinson pd Michael Mayer ed Tom Finan
☆ Fred Savage, Luke Edwards, Christian Slater, Beau Bridges, Jenny Leahr, Wendy Phillips, Dea McAllister, Sam McMurray, Will Seltzer

The Wizard of Loneliness

US 1988 110m DuArt
American Playhouse
During the Second World War, a lonely boy goes to stay with his grandparents and observes the complex lives of those around him, centring on his widowed aunt and her former lover, a disturbed soldier on the run.
A good central performance from Haas cannot hold together a rambling narrative.
w Nancy Larsen novel John Nichols d Jenny Bowen ph Richard Bowen m Michel Colombier
☆ Lukas Haas, Lea Thompson, John Randolph, Anne Pitoniak, Dylan Baker, Lance Guest, Jeremiah Warner, Steve Hendrikson

The Wizard of Oz

🔼 US 1925 70m bw silent
Larry Semon
🎞️ 🔊

On her 18th birthday a girl abandoned as a small baby at a Kansas farm discovers that she is the Queen of Oz and, after deposing its dictator, lives there happily ever after.
The emphasis is on farmyard slapstick comedy, mainly executed with a heavy hand, which makes it hard to appreciate why Semon was once almost as popular as Chaplin and Keaton, but it has its moments – particularly a chase sequence in wooden boxes.
w L. Frank Baum Jnr, Leon Lee, Larry Semon novel L. Frank Baum d Larry Semon ph H. F. Koenenkamp, Frank Good, Leonard Smith ad Robert Stevens ed Sam Zimbalist
☆ Larry Semon, Oliver N. Hardy, Dorothy Dwan, Mary Carr, Virginia Pearson, Bryant Washburn, Josef Swickard, Otto Lederer, Charles Murray
† The film is available on video with a musical accompaniment.

The Wizard of Oz ***

🔼 US 1939 102m Technicolor
MGM (Mervyn Le Roy)
🎞️ 🎞️ 🔊 📀 🎧

Unhappy Dorothy runs away from home, has adventures in a fantasy land, but finally decides that happiness was in her own back yard all the time.
Classic fairy tale given vigorous straightforward treatment, made memorable by performances, art direction and hummable tunes.
w Noel Langley, Florence Ryerson, Edgar Allan Woolf book L. Frank Baum d Victor Fleming ph Harold Rosson md Herbert Stothart ad Cedric Gibbons, William A. Horning songs E. Y. Harburg, Harold Arlen
☆ Judy Garland, Frank Morgan, Ray Bolger, Jack Haley, Bert Lahr, Margaret Hamilton, Billie Burke, Charley Grapewin, Clara Blandick
SCARECROW (RAY BOLGER): 'I could while away the hours

Conversin' with the flowers
Consultin' with the rain.
And perhaps I'd deserve you
And be even worthy erv you
If I only had a brain...'
COWARDLY LION (BERT LAHR): 'Oh, it's sad to be admittin'
I'm as vicious as a kitten
Widout de vim and voive;
I could show off my prowess
Be a lion, not a mowess
If I only had de noive.'
GLINDA, THE GOOD WITCH (BILLIE BURKE): 'Close your eyes and tap your heels together three times. And think to yourself, there's no place like home.'
DOROTHY (JUDY GARLAND): 'If I ever go looking for my heart's desire again, I won't look any further than my own back yard, because if it isn't there, I never really lost it to begin with.'
DOROTHY, LION, SCARECROW, TIN MAN: 'We're off to see the Wizard
The wonderful Wizard of Oz.
We hear he is a whiz of a wiz
If ever a wiz there was.
If ever a wever a wiz there was
The Wizard of Oz is one because
Because of the wonderful things he does...'
'There's an audience for it wherever there's a projection machine and a screen.' – Variety
'I don't see why children shouldn't like it, but for adults there isn't very much except Bert Lahr.' – Richard Mallett, Punch
'As for the light touch of fantasy, it weighs like a pound of fruitcake soaking wet.' – Otis Ferguson
† Ray Bolger was originally cast as the tin man but swapped roles with Buddy Ebsen who was to have been the scarecrow. Ebsen then got sick from the aluminium dust and was replaced by Jack Haley. Edna May Oliver was originally cast as the wicked witch. For Dorothy MGM wanted Shirley Temple, but Twentieth Century Fox wouldn't loan her. Richard Thorpe was the original director. He was fired after 12 days. George Cukor did some costume and make-up tests while a new director was found, removing the blonde wig that Judy Garland had been given for her role.
†† The sepia scenes at beginning and end were directed by King Vidor.
††† Aljean Harmetz's book The Making of the Wizard of Oz (Pavilion, 1989) is an entertaining account of the story behind the film.
🎵 song 'Over the Rainbow'; Herbert Stothart; Judy Garland (special award)
🏅 best picture; art direction

Wizards of the Lost Kingdom

US/Argentina 1985 75m colour
Concorde (Frank Isaac, Alex Sessa)
🎞️ 🎞️

A young magician, accompanied by a swordsman and what appears to be a giant two-legged poodle, saves his kingdom from an evil sorcerer.
Cheapskate sword and sorcery, presumably intended for a young audience, and certainly only watchable by an undemanding one; a pity no one was able to conjure up a less banal script.
w Tom Edwards d Hector Olivera ph Leonard Solis m James Horner, Chris Young pd Mary Bertram ed Silvia Roberts sp Richard Lennox
☆ Bo Svenson, Vidal Peterson, Thom Christopher, Barbara Stock, Maria Socas, Dolores Michaels, Rick Gallo

Wo Ai Chufang: see Kitchen

Wo die Grünen Ameisen Träumen: see Where the Green Ants Dream

Wo Shi Shui: see Who Am I?

'The Animal Is Out.'

Wolf *

US 1994 125m Technicolor
Columbia (Douglas Wick)
🎞️ 🎞️ 🔊 📀 🎧

Bitten by a wolf, a mild-mannered publishing executive who is demoted in a takeover finds that he is developing the characteristics of the animal, with keener senses but also with a tendency to grow hair and go around on all fours at the time of the full moon.
A werewolf movie for people who don't like werewolf movies: sometimes witty and clever, particularly in its scenes of office politics, but finally relying on some

dated narrative devices and succumbing to all the usual clichés of the genre.
w Jim Harrison, Wesley Strick d Mike Nichols ph Giuseppe Rotunno m Ennio Morricone pd Bo Welch ed Sam O'Steen sp make-up: Rick Baker
☆ Jack Nicholson, Michelle Pfeiffer, James Spader, Kate Nelligan, Christopher Plummer, Richard Jenkins, Eileen Atkins, David Hyde Pierce, Prunella Scales

'A genre movie for grownups.' – *Richard Schickel, Time*
'It's simply too ridiculous for a mainstream audience and too familiar for horror fans.' – *Kim Newman, Empire*
'Less than entirely convincing, an intriguing thriller more enjoyable for its humor and sophistication than for its scare quotient.' – *Todd McCarthy, Variety*

The Wolf at the Door **
France/Denmark   1986   90m   colour
Dagmar/Famous French/TF1 (Henning Carlsen)
▥

In Paris in 1893, Paul Gaugin returns penniless from Tahiti to show his paintings, expecting acclaim; but he sells few, his friends and lovers desert him, and he has trouble raising the money to go back.
Engrossing, low-key portrait of an artist at odds with conventional society.
w Christopher Hampton *original scenario* Henning Carlsen, Jean-Claude Carriere d Henning Carlsen ph Mikael Salomon m Roger Bourland ad Andre Guerin, Karl-Otto Hedal ed Janus Billeskov Jansen
☆ Donald Sutherland, Max von Sydow, Jean Yanne, Sofie Gråbol, Valerie Glandut, Fanny Bastien, Ghita Norbye, Merete Voldstedlund

Wolf Larsen
US   1958   83m   bw
AA (Lindsley Parsons)
▥

Serviceable remake of *The Sea Wolf* (qv) without the Nietzschean overtones.
w Jack de Witt, Turnley Walker d Harmon Jones ph Floyd Crosby m Paul Dunlap
☆ Barry Sullivan, Peter Graves, Thayer David, Gita Hall

'His hideous howl a dirge of death!'
'Night monster with the blood lust of a savage beast!'
The Wolf Man *
US   1941   70m   bw
Universal (George Waggner)
▦ ▥ ▧ ◠

The son of an English squire comes home, is bitten by a gypsy werewolf, and becomes one himself.
Dazzlingly cast, moderately well staged, but dramatically very disappointing horror piece which established a new Universal monster who later met Frankenstein, Abbott and Costello, and several other eccentrics.
w Curt Siodmak d George Waggner ph Joseph Valentine m Hans Salter, Frank Skinner md Charles Previn
☆ Lon Chaney Jnr, Claude Rains, Warren William, Ralph Bellamy, Bela Lugosi, Maria Ouspenskaya, Patric Knowles, Evelyn Ankers, Fay Helm
MALEVA (MARIA OUSPENSKAYA): 'Even the man who is pure in heart
And says his prayers by night
May become a wolf when the wolf bane bloom
And the moon is pure and bright...'

'It will tear the scream from your throat!'
Wolfen
US   1981   115m   Technicolor   Panavision
Warner/Orion (Rupert Hitzig)
▦ ▥ ▧

Mutilation murders in New York turn out to be the work of savage beasts descended from Indian hunters who went underground in despair at the future of mankind.
Nuthatch horror movie with a message, though providing little of either commodity. Clearly a waste of money.
w David Eyre, Michael Wadleigh *novel* Whitley Strieber d Michael Wadleigh ph Gerry Fisher, Fred Abeles m James Horner pd Paul Sylbert
☆ Albert Finney, Diane Venora, Edward James Olmos, Gregory Hines, Tom Noonan

'A thriller so slow, complicated and frankly rather dull that one's sympathy is all on the side of the predators.' – *Daily Mail*

The Wolves of Willoughby Chase
🏃🏃   GB   1988   93m   colour
Entertainment/Subatomnic/Zenith (Mark Forstater)
▦   ◠

Two girls discover that their wicked governess is attempting to steal the family estate.
Lively children's film with relishable villains.
w William M. Akers *novel* Joan Aiken d Stuart Orme ph Paul Beeson m Colin Towns pd Christopher Hobbs ed Martin Walsh
☆ Stephanie Beacham, Mel Smith, Geraldine James, Richard O'Brien, Emily Hudson, Aleks Darowska, Jane Horrocks, Eleanor David, Jonathan Coy

Woman Accused *
US   1933   73m   bw
Paramount
A woman kills her ex-lover in a struggle and goes on the run.
Intriguing rigmarole written as a magazine serial by ten well-known authors contributing a chapter each. The result confirms the method.
w Bayard Veiller *serial* Rupert Hughes, Vicki Baum, Zane Grey, Vina Delmar, Irvin S. Cobb, Gertrude Atherton, J. P. McEvoy, Ursula Parrott, Polan Banks, Sophie Kerr d Paul Sloane ph Karl Struss
☆ Nancy Carroll, Cary Grant, John Halliday, Irving Pichel, Louis Calhern, Jack La Rue, John Lodge
'It may convince producers and exhibitors that new writing talent should be encouraged ... business possibilities anything but bright on so-so cast names.' – *Variety*

A Woman Alone: see *Sabotage (1936)*

A Woman Alone
GB   1936   78m   bw
Garrett-Klement
US title: *Two Who Dared*
In 19th-century Russia, a captain falls for a peasant girl.
Uninteresting melodrama with stilted actors.
w Leo Lania, Warren Chetham Strode *novel* Fedor Ozep d Eugene Frenke
☆ Anna Sten, Henry Wilcoxon, Viola Keats, John Garrick, Romilly Lunge

The Woman Between: see *The Woman I Love*

A Woman Called Abé Sada *
Japan   1975   77m   colour
Nikkatsu (Yoshiteru Yuuki)
▦
original title: *Jitsuroku Abe Sada*
A maid and former prostitute recalls how, involved in a sado-masochistic affair with her married employer, she strangled and castrated him in an excess of passion.
Chilling drama of love and death that also encompasses the theme of a woman rebelling against her sexually subservient role. It suffers from the fact that Nagisa Oshima made the superior Ai No Corrida (qv) a year later, based on the same true incident that took place in the mid-30s.
w Akio Ido d Noboru Tanaka ph Masaru Mori ad Gunji Kawasaki
☆ Junko Miyashi, Hideaki Azumi, Nagatoshi Sakamoto, Genshu Hanayagi, Ikunosuke Koizumi

Woman Chases Man
US   1937   71m   bw
Samuel Goldwyn
▦
A lady architect persuades a millionaire to help his land developer father.
Thin, lame comedy which constantly amazes by its lack of success.
w Joseph Anthony, Manny Seff, David Hertz *story* Lynn Root, Frank Fenton d John G. Blystone ph Gregg Toland m Alfred Newman
☆ Miriam Hopkins, Joel McCrea, Charles Winninger, Erik Rhodes, Broderick Crawford, Leona Maricle, Ella Logan, Charles Halton
'Laughs stopped at the Music Hall when the action on the screen became so insanely illogical, and dull, that the amazed disappointment of the house expressed itself in chilly silence.' – *Variety*

'A pleasant warm weather fabrication – lightweight, attractively tailored and not meant to withstand the rigours of wear or the chill blasts of the critics.' – *Frank S. Nugent*
† The unhappy production began as a vehicle for Miss Hopkins. Writers who worked on it include Ben Hecht, Sam and Bella Spewack, and Dorothy Parker. Directors involved were Edward Ludwig, William Wyler and Gregory La Cava.

A Woman Commands
US   1932   85m   bw
RKO Pathé
A cabaret entertainer rejects her lover for a king, but regains him when the king is murdered.
Romantic melodrama of the silent school, quite unrevivable.
w Thilde Forster d Paul Stein
☆ Pola Negri, Basil Rathbone, Roland Young, H. B. Warner, Anthony Bushell, Reginald Owen

A Woman Destroyed: see *Smash-Up, The Story of a Woman*

A Woman Disappeared, Portrait of a Woman: see *Une Femme Disparait*

Woman Doctor
US   1939   65m   bw
Republic (Sol C. Siegel)
Her career prospers, her marriage suffers.
Old hat domestic drama, tolerably put over.
w Joseph Moncure March d Sidney Salkow
☆ Frieda Inescort, Henry Wilcoxon, Claire Dodd, Sybil Jason, Cora Witherspoon

The Woman for Joe
GB   1955   91m   Technicolor   VistaVision
Rank/Group
A circus midget falls in love with a singer who falls in love with the circus's owner.
Sentimental little tragedy of misplaced affection, hardly worth a second glance.
w Neil Paterson d George More O'Ferrall ph Georges Perinal m Malcolm Arnold ad Maurice Carter ed Alfred Roome
☆ Diane Cilento, George Baker, Jimmy Karoubi, David Kossoff, Sydney Tafler, Violet Farebrother, Earl Cameron, Derek Sydney

The Woman from Monte Carlo
US   1931   68m   bw
Warner
The wife of a naval officer is suspected of adultery.
Stiff marital melodrama based on a silent film The Night Watch; it worked no wonders for its German star.
w Harvey Thew d Michael Curtiz
☆ Lil Dagover, Walter Huston, Warren William, Robert Warwick, John Wray
'Looks a light draw at best.' – *Variety*

The Woman from Nowhere: see *La Femme de Nulle Part*

Woman Hater
GB   1948   105m   bw
GFD/Two Cities (William Sistrom)
▦
An English nobleman tries to disprove a film star's statement that she hates men and loves solitude.
Incredibly slight material is interminably stretched out, well beyond an excellent cast's ability to help.
w Robert Westerby, Nicholas Phipps d Terence Young ph André Thomas m Lambert Williamson
☆ Stewart Granger, Edwige Feuillère, Ronald Squire, Mary Jerrold, Jeanne de Casalis

Woman Hunt: see *Au Royaume des Cieux*

'Gloriously lifting two great stars to new greatness!'
The Woman I Love *
US   1937   85m   hw
RKO (Albert Lewis)
GB title: *The Woman Between*
In World War I France, a pilot loves his superior officer's wife.
Well-made romantic action melodrama from a well-praised original.
w Mary Borden *novel* L'Equipage by Joseph Kessel d Anatole Litvak ph Charles Rosher m Arthur Honegger, Maurice Thiriet
☆ Paul Muni, Miriam Hopkins, Louis Hayward, Colin Clive, Minor Watson, Elizabeth Risdon, Paul Guilfoyle, Mady Christians

'Needs all the marquee help it can get ... spotty business indicated.' – *Variety*

Woman in a Dressing Gown *
GB   1957   94m   bw
Godwin/Willis/J. Lee-Thompson
After twenty years of marriage, a wife's slatternly ways alienate her once devoted husband, and he asks for a divorce.
Classic British TV play adequately filmed but now rather dated and irritating.
w Ted Willis *play* Ted Willis d J. Lee-Thompson ph Gilbert Taylor m Louis Levy
☆ Yvonne Mitchell, Anthony Quayle, Sylvia Syms, Andrew Ray, Carole Lesley

The Woman in Green
US   1945   68m   bw
Universal (Roy William Neill)
▦   ◠
Sherlock Holmes is called in after the police are baffled by a serial killer who murders women and cuts off their right forefingers as souvenirs.
Deft little thriller that owes little to Conan Doyle but nevertheless manages to entertain.
w Bertram Millhauser d Roy William Neill ph Virgil Miller md Mark Levant ad John B. Goodman, Martin Obzina ed Edward Curtiss
☆ Basil Rathbone, Nigel Bruce, Hillary Brooke, Henry Daniell, Paul Cavanagh, Matthew Boulton, Eve Amber

A Woman in Her Thirties: see *Side Streets*

Woman in Hiding
US   1949   92m   bw
U-I (Michael Kraike)
After escaping her husband's attempts to murder her, a woman goes into hiding while evidence is being accumulated against her.
Modest suspenser with too many near escapes and not much else.
w Oscar Saul d Michael Gordon ph William Daniels m Frank Skinner
☆ Ida Lupino, Howard Duff, Stephen McNally, John Litel, Taylor Holmes, Irving Bacon, Peggy Dow, Joe Besser, Don Beddoe
'The detail is full of things interesting and amusing at the time and pleasant to remember afterwards.' – *Richard Mallett, Punch*

The Woman in His House: see *The Animal Kingdom*

The Woman in Question *
GB   1949   88m   bw
GFD/Javelin (Teddy Baird)
US title: *Five Angles on Murder*
Police investigating a woman's death build up several different impressions of her.
Multi-flashback melodrama which somehow doesn't quite come off despite effort all round.
w John Cresswell d Anthony Asquith ph Desmond Dickinson m John Wooldridge
☆ Jean Kent, Dirk Bogarde, Susan Shaw, John McCallum, Hermione Baddeley, Charles Victor, Duncan Macrae, Lana Morris, Vida Hope

The Woman in Red
US   1935   68m   bw
Warner
A professional horsewoman marries into society and is ill received.
Stiff class melodrama partly redeemed by its star.
w Mary McCall Jnr, Peter Milne *novel* North Shore by Wallace Irwin d Robert Florey
☆ Barbara Stanwyck, Genevieve Tobin, John Eldredge, Gene Raymond, Philip Reed

The Woman in Red *
US   1984   86m   DeLuxe
Orion (Victor Drai)
▦   ▥
A middle-aged married man has fantasies of infidelity.
Moderately successful transfer to America of a French comedy success.
wd Gene Wilder, *from the film* Un Eléphant ça Trompe Enormement by Jean-Loup Dabadie, Yves Robert ph Fred Schuler m John Morris pd David L. Snyder ed Christopher Greenbury
☆ Gene Wilder, Kelly Le Brock, Charles Grodin, Joseph Bologna, Judith Ivey, Gilda Radner
🔔 song 'I Just Called to Say I Love You' (Stevie Wonder)

🏃🏃 film suitable for family viewing   ▦ VHS video-cassette for the British PAL system   ▥ VHS video-cassette for the British PAL system in wide screen-format   ↻ Video cassette in a computer-colourised version   ▧ American NTSC video-cassette   ◠ Laser disc

The Woman in Room 13
US 1932 58m bw
Fox
The wife of an innocent convict tricks the real culprit into a confession.
Stagey melodrama which just about fills an hour.
w Guy Bolton *play* Sam Shipman, Max Marcin, Percival Wilde *d* Henry King
☆ Elissa Landi, Ralph Bellamy, Neil Hamilton, Myrna Loy, Gilbert Roland
'Just another factory-made release.' – *Variety*

Woman in the Dark
US 1935 68m bw
Select/RKO
A man convicted of manslaughter gets himself on his release into another awkward situation.
Moderate semi-crime melodrama.
w Sada Cowan *story* Dashiell Hammett *d* Phil Rosen
☆ Fay Wray, Melvyn Douglas, Ralph Bellamy, Roscoe Ates
'Marquee weakness only thing that may keep it out of single-feature houses … murder mystery fare of sufficient relish to keep 'em from leaving the table.' – *Variety*

Woman in the Dunes: see Woman of the Dunes

The Woman in the Hall
GB 1947 93m bw
GFD/IP/Wessex (Ian Dalrymple)
A well-intentioned woman takes to begging and becomes a bad influence on her daughter.
Finger-wagging novelette makes an unrewarding film.
w G. B. Stern, Ian Dalrymple, Jack Lee *novel* G. B. Stern *d* Jack Lee *ph* C. Pennington-Richards, H. E. Fowle *m* Temple Abady *pd* Peter Proud
☆ Ursula Jeans, Cecil Parker, Jean Simmons, Jill Raymond, Edward Underdown, Joan Miller, Susan Hampshire

The Woman in the Moon *
Germany 1929 125m bw silent
UFA
📼
original title: Frau im Mond
Two scientists are forced to journey to the moon by criminals anxious to mine its gold deposits.
Heavy-handed fantasy which is not among its director's best work.
w Thea von Harbou *d* Fritz Lang
☆ Willy Fritsch, Gerda Maurus, Gusti Stark-Gatettenbaur
'Half of it could be removed; as it is, it winds ponderously on.' – *Variety*

'It was the look in her eyes that did it. How could he resist? How could he know it meant murder?'
The Woman in the Window ***
US 1944 95m bw
International (Nunnally Johnson)
📼
A grass widow professor befriends a girl who gets him involved with murder.
A refreshingly intelligent little thriller which was criticized at the time for a cop-out ending; this can now be seen as a decorative extra to a story which had already ended satisfactorily. Good middlebrow entertainment.
w Nunnally Johnson *novel* Once Off Guard by J. H. Wallis *d* Fritz Lang *ph* Milton Krasner *m* Arthur Lange, Hugo Friedhofer
☆ Edward G. Robinson, Joan Bennett, Raymond Massey, Dan Duryea, Edmund Breon, Thomas Jackson, Dorothy Peterson, Arthur Loft
'A perfect example of its kind, and a very good kind too.' – *James Shelley Hamilton*
'The accumulation of tiny details enlarged as though under a district attorney's magnifying glass gives reality a fantastic and anguishing appearance.' – *Jacques Bourgeois*
'In its rather artificial, club library style an effective and well made piece, absorbing, diverting and full of often painful suspense.' – *Richard Mallett, Punch*
'Art and Mammon, it seems to me, have been very prettily served.' – *Spectator*
♟ Arthur Lange, Hugo Friedhofer

'Born in shame – living in mystery – what is her sinister secret?'
The Woman in White *
US 1948 109m bw
Warner (Henry Blanke)
The new tutor of a strange household finds himself among eccentrics, villains and ill-used ladies.
A Victorian thriller which is long on atmosphere but not so hot on suspense or plot development. The cast helps a lot.
w Stephen Morehouse Avery *novel* Wilkie Collins *d* Peter Godfrey *ph* Carl Guthrie *m* Max Steiner
☆ Gig Young, Eleanor Parker, Sydney Greenstreet, Alexis Smith, Agnes Moorehead, John Emery, John Abbott, Curt Bois
'The Wilkie Collins novel is given the studious, stolid treatment ordinarily reserved for the ritual assassination of a great classic. This is not intended as a recommendation.' – *James Agee*
'Greenstreet and others move through the murky passages of the story like visitors in some massive Gothic museum, and they move, on the whole, with stately discretion, and do not scribble on the objects or show anything but the greatest veneration for them.' – *C. A. Lejeune*

A Woman Is a Woman **
France 1961 85m Eastmancolor Scope
📼 📀
original title: Une Femme est une Femme
A stripper quarrels with her boyfriend because she wants to have a baby and he doesn't.
Exuberantly playful tribute to the high spirits of MGM's classic musicals, even though there is little actual singing and dancing. It has a lovers' bicycle ride that was imitated much later in Butch Cassidy and The Sundance Kid.
wd Jean-Luc Godard *ph* Raoul Coutard *m* Michel Legrand
☆ Jean-Paul Belmondo, Jean-Claude Brialy, Anna Karina, Marie Dubois, Jeanne Moreau
'As bad a film as anyone is ever likely to see.' – *John Simon*

The Woman Next Door
France 1981 106m Fujicolour
Les Films du Carrosse/TF1
📼 📀 📀
An engineer is embarrassed when an old flame, now married, comes to live next door; their love rekindles but ends in tragedy.
Rather uninteresting melodrama with a failure to communicate its apparent personal importance for the director.
w François Truffaut, Suzanne Schiffman, Jean Aurel *d* François Truffaut *ph* William Lubtchansky *m* Georges Delerue
☆ Gérard Depardieu, Fanny Ardant, Henri Garcin, Michele Baumgarner

Woman Obsessed
US 1959 102m DeLuxe Cinemascope
TCF (Sydney Boehm)
In the Canadian Rockies, a pioneer woman's small son does not take to his new stepfather.
Antediluvian pulp fiction with quicksand and a forest fire for highlights. Shades of D. W. Griffith, and badly done into the bargain.
w Sydney Boehm *novel* John Mantley *d* Henry Hathaway *ph* William C. Mellor *m* Hugo Friedhofer
☆ Susan Hayward, Stephen Boyd, Dennis Holmes, Theodore Bikel, Barbara Nichols, Ken Scott, Arthur Franz

A Woman of Affairs
US 1928 90m bw silent
MGM
📼 📀
A wild rich girl goes from man to man and finally kills herself in a car crash.
Romantic star tosh from a fashionable novel of the time.
w Bess Meredyth *novel* The Green Hat by Michael Arlen *d* Clarence Brown *ph* William Daniels
☆ Greta Garbo, Lewis Stone, John Gilbert, John Mack Brown, Douglas Fairbanks Jnr, Hobart Bosworth
♟ Bess Meredyth

Woman of Antwerp: see Dédée d'Anvers

A Woman of Distinction
US 1950 85m bw
Columbia (Buddy Adler)
📼 📀
The lady dean of a New England school falls for a British astronomer.
Pratfall farce for ageing stars. No go.
w Charles Hoffman *d* Edward Buzzell *ph* Joseph Walker *m* Werner Heymann *md* Morris Stoloff
☆ Rosalind Russell, Ray Milland, Edmund Gwenn, Janis Carter, Mary Jane Saunders, Francis Lederer, Jerome Courtland

Woman of Dolwyn: see The Last Days of Dolwyn

A Woman of Paris **
US 1923 85m bw silent (music track added 1976)
Charles Chaplin
A country girl goes to the city, becomes a demi-mondaine, and inadvertently causes the death of the one man she loves.
Remarkably simply-handled 'road to ruin' melodrama; its subtleties of treatment make it still very watchable for those so inclined.
wd Charles Chaplin *ph* Rollie Totheroh, Jack Wilson
☆ Edna Purviance, Adolphe Menjou, Carl Miller, Lydia Knott
'A thoroughly workmanlike entertainment and a candidate for honours and dollars entirely independent of the drawing power built up by Chaplin in other fields.' – *Variety*
'After five minutes of watching the sparkling new print, the spell begins to work. Chaplin is neatly turning the clichés inside out, like a glove.' – *Alan Brien, Sunday Times, 1980*
'Mr Chaplin as writer and director has not done anything radical or anything esoteric; he has merely used his intelligence to the highest degree, an act which for many years has ceased to be expected of motion picture people.' – *Robert E. Sherwood*
'The plot is desperately simple, but played with a control, a complete absence of histrionic vehemence, rare in the early twenties.' – *Dilys Powell, Punch, 1980*
† Chaplin appeared unbilled as a railway porter. The film was not a commercial success and he withdrew it for fifty years.

Woman of Straw *
GB 1964 114m Eastmancolor
UA/Novus (Michael Relph)
A rich old man's nurse conspires with his nephew in a murder plot.
Rather half-hearted but good-looking star melodrama which ventures into Hitchcock territory.
w Robert Muller, Stanley Mann, Michael Relph *novel* Catherine Arley *d* Basil Dearden *ph* Otto Heller *m* Muir Mathieson *pd* Ken Adam
☆ Gina Lollobrigida, Sean Connery, Ralph Richardson, Johnny Sekka, Laurence Hardy, Alexander Knox

Woman of Summer: see The Stripper

Woman of the Dunes *
Japan 1964 127m bw
Teshigahara (Kiichi Ichikawa)
📼 📀 📀 🎧
original title: Suna no Onna
US title: Woman in the Dunes
An entomologist on a deserted beach finds an attractive young widow living in a shack at the bottom of a huge sand pit, spends the night with her, can't escape, and finally doesn't want to.
Unique sex melodrama, all shifting sand and picturesque angles, with a clear meaning; but far too long.
w Kobo Abe *d* Hiroshi Teshigahara *ph* Hiroshi Segawa *m* Toru Takemitsu *ed* F. Susui
☆ Eiji Okada, Kyoko Kishoda
'Teasingly opaque, broodingly erotic.' – *MFB*
♟ Hiroshi Teshigahara; best foreign film

Woman of the North Country
US 1952 90m Trucolor
Republic (Joseph Kane)
Minnesota 1890: rivalry over an iron ore mine erupts between a young engineer and an ambitious woman.
Standard Western.

w Norman Reilly Raine *d* Joseph Kane *ph* Jack Marta *m* R. Dale Butts
☆ Ruth Hussey, Rod Cameron, John Agar, Gale Storm, Jim Davis, J. Carrol Naish

Woman of the River *
Italy/France 1955 95m Technicolor
Ponti/de Laurentiis/Films du Centaure
original title: La Donna del Fiume
A peasant girl has nothing but trouble after falling for a handsome smuggler.
Lively melodrama whose primary purpose was to demonstrate the physical charms of its new star. It succeeded well enough in the Bitter Rice tradition.
w Basilio Franchina, Giorgio Bassani, Pier Paolo Pasolini, Florestano Vancini, Antonio Antoviti, Mario Soldati *story* Alberto Moravia, Ennio Flaiano *d* Mario Soldati *ph* Otello Martelli *m* Angelo Lavagnini, Armando Trovaioli
☆ Sophia Loren, Gerard Oury, Rik Battaglia, Lise Bourdin

The Woman of the Town *
US 1943 87m bw
United Artists (Harry Sherman)
📼
Bat Masterson becomes marshal of Dodge and falls for a saloon singer.
Busy, old-fashioned urban Western with good entertainment values.
w Aeneas Mackenzie *d* George Archainbaud *m* Miklos Rozsa
☆ Albert Dekker, Claire Trevor, Barry Sullivan, Henry Hull, Marion Martin, Porter Hall, Percy Kilbride
♟ Miklos Rozsa

A Woman of the World: see Outcast Lady

Woman of the Year ***
US 1942 114m bw
MGM (Joseph L. Mankiewicz)
📼 📼 📀 📀
A sports columnist marries a lady politician; they have nothing in common but love.
Simple, effective, mildly sophisticated comedy which allows two splendid stars, in harness for the first time, to do their thing to the general benefit.
w Ring Lardner Jnr, Michael Kanin *d* George Stevens *ph* Joseph Ruttenberg *m* Franz Waxman
☆ Spencer Tracy, Katharine Hepburn, Fay Bainter, Reginald Owen, William Bendix, Dan Tobin, Minor Watson, Roscoe Karns
'Between them they have enough charm to keep any ball rolling.' – *William Whitebait*
♟ script
♟ Katharine Hepburn

The Woman on Pier 13
US 1949 73m bw
RKO (Jack J. Gross)
aka: I Married a Communist
A shipping executive is blackmailed by communists, who know of a youthful crime, into helping them spy.
Laboured witch-hunt melodrama.
w Charles Grayson, Robert Hardy Andrews *d* Robert Stevenson *ph* Nicholas Musuraca *m* Leigh Harline
☆ Laraine Day, Robert Ryan, John Agar, Thomas Gomez, Janis Carter, Richard Rober, William Talman

The Woman on the Beach
US 1947 71m bw
RKO (Jack J. Gross)
A mentally ailing coastguard meets a *femme fatale* and comes between her and her sadistic husband.
Nuthouse melodrama which neither convinces nor compels for a moment.
w Frank Davis, Jean Renoir *novel* None So Blind by Mitchell Wilson *d* Jean Renoir *ph* Leo Tover, Harry Wild *m* Hanns Eisler
☆ Joan Bennett, Robert Ryan, Charles Bickford, Nan Leslie, Walter Sande
'One may have to strain to see it as more than an over-aestheticated, interesting failure.' – *Pauline Kael, 70s*

Woman on the Run
US 1950 77m bw
Universal-International/Fidelity (Howard Welsch)
A man runs away after witnessing a murder; his wife is menaced by the killer.

Slightly unusual thriller which alas fails to thrill.
w Norman Foster, Alan Campbell d Norman
Foster ph Hal Mohr m Emil Newman
☆ Ann Sheridan, Dennis O'Keefe, Robert Keith,
Ross Elliott

A Woman or Two: see *Une Femme ou Deux*

A Woman Rebels *
US   1936   88m   bw
RKO (Pandro S. Berman)
A Victorian miss fights for women's rights and has
an illegitimate baby.
Interesting, half-forgotten star drama.
w Anthony Veiller, Ernest Vajda *novel* Portrait of
a Rebel by Netta Syrett d Mark Sandrich
ph Robert de Grasse m Roy Webb ad Van Nest
Polglase
☆ Katharine Hepburn, Herbert Marshall,
Elizabeth Allan, Donald Crisp, Doris Dudley,
David Manners, Van Heflin, Lucile Watson, Eily
Malyon
> 'Delving into the fascinating ugliness of
> Victorian England, RKO Radio have found
> material that is picturesque, humorous and
> tragic.' – *Frank Nugent, New York Times*

The Woman They Almost Lynched
US   1952   90m   bw
Republic
An innocent girl out west is blamed for a crime
wave and almost executed as a spy.
*Incredible, random-plotted Western with a few
entertaining moments.*
w Steve Fisher *story* Michael Fessier d Allan
Dwan ph Reggie Lanning m Stanley Wilson
☆ Joan Leslie, Audrey Totter, John Lund, Brian
Donlevy, Ben Cooper

'As naughty as a black lace nightgown!'
Woman Times Seven
US/France   1967   99m   DeLuxe
TCF/Embassy (Arthur Cohn)
Seven sketches, in each of which a woman behaves
typically of her sex.
Humourless after-dinner entertainment.
w Cesare Zavattini d Vittorio de Sica
ph Christian Matras m Riz Ortolani
☆ Shirley MacLaine, Peter Sellers, Rossano Brazzi,
Vittorio Gassman, Lex Barker, Elsa Martinelli,
Peter Morley, Adrienne Corri, Patrick Wymark,
Alan Arkin, Michael Caine, Anita Ekberg,
Philippe Noiret

Woman to Woman
GB   1923   83m   bw   silent
Balcon, Freedman and Saville
A shell-shocked officer marries into society and
later adopts his son by a French ballerina.
*Far-fetched melodrama in what later became the
Random Harvest style; a great box-office hit of its
time.*
w Alfred Hitchcock *play* Michael Morton
d Graham Cutts
☆ Betty Compson, Clive Brook, Josephine Earle,
Marie Ault
† Victor Saville directed a sound remake in 1929,
with Betty Compson and George Barraud; and in
1946 Maclean Rogers had another shot with Adele
Dixon and Douglass Montgomery.

A Woman under the Influence *
US   1974   155m   colour
Faces International (Sam Shaw)
▭▭   ▭   ⊚
A Los Angeles housewife and mother suffers a
mental breakdown as she increasingly feels at odds
with society.
*Fine acting from Rowlands and Falk lifts an otherwise
overlong domestic drama.*
wd John Cassavetes ph Mitch Breit, Caleb
Deschanel m Bo Harwood ad Phedon
Papamichael ed Tom Cornwell
☆ Peter Falk, Gena Rowlands, Matthew Cassel,
Matthew Laborteaux, Christina Grisanti,
Katherine Cassavetes
> 'Though some in the audience will once again
> accept what is going on as raw, anguishing truth,
> most people will – rightly, I think – take their
> embarrassment as evidence of Cassavetes' self-
> righteous ineptitude.' – *Pauline Kael, New Yorker*
🏆 John Cassavetes (as director); Gena Rowlands

Woman Wanted
US   1935   65m   bw
MGM
A girl accused of murder is helped by an attorney.
*Initially appealing comedy-thriller which moves fast
enough but has a very muddled plotline.*
w Leonard Fields, Dave Silverstein, Wilson
Collison d George B. Seitz
☆ Maureen O'Sullivan, Joel McCrea, Lewis
Stone, Louis Calhern, Edgar Kennedy, Adrienne
Ames, Robert Greig, Noel Madison

The Woman Who Came Back *
US   1945   68m   bw
Republic (Walter Colmes)
▤
A girl returning to her home village in New
England is made to think she is a witch.
Quite an agreeably spooky second feature.
w Dennis Cooper, Lee Willis d Walter Colmes
☆ Nancy Kelly, John Loder, Otto Kruger, Ruth
Ford, Harry Tyler

The Woman with No Name
GB   1950   83m   bw
IFP/ABP
US title: *Her Panelled Door*
An amnesiac wife finds herself threatened from all
sides.
Hoary melodrama with some unintentional laughs.
w Ladislas Vajda, Guy Morgan *novel* Happy Now
I Go by Theresa Charles d Ladislas Vajda, George
More O'Ferrall ph Otto Heller m Allan Gray
☆ Phyllis Calvert, Edward Underdown, Helen
Cherry, Richard Burton, Anthony Nicholls, James
Hayter, Betty Ann Davies

Woman without a Face: see *Mister
Buddwing*

The Woman's Angle
GB   1952   86m   bw
ABP/Leslie Arliss/Bow Belles (Walter Mycroft)
In a divorce court three flashbacks tell of the life of
a composer.
*Damp little formula drama for matinée audiences,
refashioned from a successful silent film.*
wd Leslie Arliss *novel* Three Cups of Coffee by
Ruth Feiner ph Erwin Hillier m Robert Gill; the
Mansell Concerto by Kenneth Leslie Smith
☆ Edward Underdown, Cathy O'Donnell, Lois
Maxwell, Claude Farrell, Peter Reynolds, Marjorie
Fielding

'Whatever I am, men made me!'
A Woman's Face **
US   1941   105m   bw
MGM (Victor Saville)
▤   ▭
A scarred and embittered woman turns to crime
but jibs at murder.
*Curious, unexpected but very entertaining melodrama
with a courtroom frame, Swedish settings, an excellent
cast and some bravura sequences.*
w Donald Ogden Stewart, Elliot Paul *play* Il était
une Fois by François de Croisset d George Cukor
ph Robert Planck m Bronislau Kaper
☆ Joan Crawford, Melvyn Douglas, Conrad Veidt,
Osa Massen, Reginald Owen, Albert Basserman,
Marjorie Main, Donald Meek, Connie Gilchrist
† Also involved in the script were Elliott Paul and
Christopher Isherwood.

A Woman's Secret
US   1949   85m   bw
RKO (Herman J. Mankiewicz)
▤
An ex-singer grooms a girl as her successor but
lives to regret it.
*Downright peculiar little film noir by the co-author of
Citizen Kane (though not so that you'd notice).*
w Herman J. Mankiewicz *novel* Mortgage on Life
by Vicki Baum d Nicholas Ray ph George
Diskant m Frederick Hollander md Constantin
Bakaleinikoff
☆ Maureen O'Hara, Gloria Grahame, Melvyn
Douglas, Bill Williams, Victor Jory, Mary Philips

A Woman's Tale *
Australia   1991   93m   colour
Beyond/Illumination (Paul Cox, Santhana Naidu)
▤   ▭
An old woman prepares for death.
*A low-key drama about a person who insists on how
much she loves life, while disliking, or snubbing, most*

of the people she meets; the result is not as life-
enhancing as it might have been.
w Paul Cox, Barry Dickins d Paul Cox ph Nino
Martinetti m Paul Grabowsky pd Neil Angwin
ed Russell Hurley
☆ Sheila Florance, Gosia Dobrowolska, Norman
Kaye, Chris Haywood, Ernest Gray, Myrtle Woods
† Like the elderly woman she plays, Sheila
Florance was also suffering from cancer, dying a few
days after receiving a best actress award for her
performance.

A Woman's Vengeance *
US   1948   96m   bw
Universal-International (Zoltan Korda)
A man is convicted for the murder of his invalid
wife, actually committed by a jealous woman in
love with him but later spurned.
*Interesting but very stagey melodrama from one of its
author's more commercial ventures.*
w Aldous Huxley *story and play* The Gioconda
Smile by Aldous Huxley d Zoltan Korda ph Russell
Metty m Miklos Rozsa
☆ Charles Boyer, Jessica Tandy, Ann Blyth,
Cedric Hardwicke, Mildred Natwick
> 'A rather literary movie, but most movies aren't
> even that; much less are they real movies.' –
> *James Agee*

'It's a great big wonderful woman's world because
men are in it!'
Woman's World **
US   1954   94m   Technicolor   Cinemascope
TCF (Charles Brackett)
Three top salesmen and their wives are summoned
to New York by the boss, who seeks to choose a
new general manager.
*Amusing, superficial pattern comedy-drama for an all-
star cast, backed by all-round technical competence.*
w Claude Binyon, Mary Loos, Richard Sale
d Jean Negulesco ph Joe MacDonald m Cyril
Mockridge
☆ Clifton Webb, Lauren Bacall, Van Heflin, June
Allyson, Fred MacMurray, Arlene Dahl, Cornel
Wilde, Elliott Reid, Margalo Gillmore

Wombling Free
🏋   GB   1977   96m   Eastmancolor
Rank/Ian Shand
▭▭   ▤
The furry creatures who live under Wimbledon
Common at last make contact with humans.
*Disastrous attempt to film a popular TV series for
children. The series came in five-minute chunks; this
elephantine transcription leaves several talents high and
dry.*
wd Lionel Jeffries, from characters created by
Elizabeth Beresford ph Alan Hume m Mike Batt
☆ David Tomlinson, Frances de la Tour, Bonnie
Langford, Bernard Spear
> 'A fiasco. If you really must take your kids, it
> would be less of a pain to go shopping at the
> same time.' – *Derek Malcolm, Guardian*

'135 women with men on their minds!'
The Women ***
US   1939   132m   bw   (Technicolor sequence)
MGM (Hunt Stromberg)
▤   ▭
A New York socialite gets a divorce but later
thinks better of it.
*Bitchy comedy drama distinguished by an all-girl cast
('135 women with men on their minds'). An over-
generous slice of real theatre, skilfully adapted, with
rich sets, plenty of laughs, and some memorable scenes
between the fighting ladies.*
w Anita Loos, Jane Murfin *play* Clare Boothe
d George Cukor ph Oliver T. Marsh, Joseph
Ruttenberg m Edward Ward, David Snell
☆ Norma Shearer, Joan Crawford, Rosalind Russell,
Mary Boland, Paulette Goddard, Joan Fontaine,
Lucile Watson, Phyllis Povah, Virginia Weidler,
Ruth Hussey, Margaret Dumont, Marjorie Main,
Hedda Hopper
> 'Smash hit of solid proportions for extended runs
> and heavy profits … a strong woman entry but
> still has plenty of spicy lines and situations for
> the men.' – *Variety*
> 'A mordant, mature description of the social
> decay of one corner of the American middle
> class.' – *Time*
> 'So marvellous that we believe every Hollywood
> studio should make at least one thoroughly nasty
> picture a year.' – *New York Times*

> 'Whether you go or not depends on whether you
> can stand Miss Shearer with tears flowing
> steadily in all directions at once, and such an
> endless damn back fence of cats.' – *Otis Ferguson*

Women Are Like That
US   1938   78m   bw
Warner
A separated couple meet again years later and find
each other changed.
*Witless elaboration of a good idea: far too slow and
talky.*
w Horace Jackson, Albert Z. Carr d Stanley
Logan
☆ Kay Francis, Pat O'Brien, Ralph Forbes,
Melville Cooper, Thurston Hall, Grant Mitchell
> 'Terribly tiresome, slow and talky.' – *Variety*

Women in Bondage
US   1943   72m   bw
Monogram (Herman Millakowsky)
How the Nazis treat their women.
*Cheap but vigorous exploitation piece, not quite so
sensational as it now sounds.*
w Houston Branch, Frank Wisbar d Steve Sekely
☆ Gail Patrick, Nancy Kelly, Gertrude Michael,
Anne Nagel, Tala Birell, Maris Wrixon, William
Henry, H. B. Warner, Alan Baxter

Women in Love ***
GB   1969   130m   DeLuxe
UA/Brandywine (Larry Kramer)
▭▭   ⊚
Two girls have their first sexual encounters in the
Midlands during the twenties.
*Satisfactory rendering of a celebrated novel, with
excellent period detail atoning for rather irritating
characters. The nude wrestling scene was a famous
first.*
w Larry Kramer *novel* D. H. Lawrence d Ken
Russell ph Billy Williams m Georges Delerue
☆ Glenda Jackson, Jennie Linden, Alan Bates,
Oliver Reed, Michael Gough, Alan Webb
> 'They should take all the pretentious dialogue off
> the soundtrack and call it Women in Heat.' –
> *Rex Reed*
> 'Two-thirds success, one-third ambitious failure.'
> – *Michael Billington, Illustrated London News*
🏆 Glenda Jackson
🏆 Larry Kramer; Ken Russell; Billy Williams

Women in the Wind
US   1939   63m   bw
Warner (Mark Hellinger)
Conflict arises between contestants in the
Women's Air Derby.
*Formula multi-character picture, only moderately
watchable.*
w Lee Katz, Albert DeMond *novel* Francis
Walton d John Farrow
☆ Kay Francis, William Gargan, Victor Jory,
Maxie Rosenbloom, Eddie Foy Jnr, Eve Arden
> 'Good programmer for duals and cinch for action
> spots.' – *Variety*

Women in War
US   1942   71m   bw
Republic (Sol C. Siegel)
A socialite playgirl is recruited into war nursing in
order to escape a prison sentence.
*Early World War II exploitation piece; lowish marks in
its own right.*
w F. Hugh Herbert, Doris Anderson d John H.
Auer
☆ Elsie Janis, Wendy Barrie, Patric Knowles, Mae
Clarke, Dorothy Peterson, Billy Gilbert

Women of All Nations
US   1931   72m   bw
Fox
Flagg and Quirt, back in the Marines, have
amorous adventures in Sweden, Nicaragua and
Egypt.
*Routine fun and games with the heroes of What Price
Glory (qv).*
w Barry Connors d Raoul Walsh ph Lucien
Andriot m Reginald H. Bassett
☆ Edmund Lowe, Victor McLaglen, Greta Nissen,
El Brendel, Fifi D'Orsay, Bela Lugosi, Humphrey
Bogart

🏋 film suitable for   ▭▭ VHS video-cassette for   ▭▭ VHS video-cassette for the British   ⊹ Video cassette in a computer-   ▤ American NTSC video-cassette   ⊚ Laser disc
family viewing   the British PAL system   PAL system in wide screen-format   colourised version

Women of Glamour

US   1937   65m   bw
Columbia
A man is loved by a society flower and a gold-digger, and chooses the latter.
Minor woman's picture.
w Lynn Starling, Mary McCall Jnr *story* Milton Herbert Gropper d Gordon Wiles
☆ Melvyn Douglas, Virginia Bruce, Reginald Denny, Leona Maricle, Pert Kelton
'Featherweight triangle headed for the dual round-up.' – *Variety*

Women of Twilight

GB   1953   89m   bw
Romulus/Daniel M. Angel
US title: *Twilight Women*
The pregnant lover of a murderer finds lodgings in a boarding house for unmarried mothers run by a money-grasping harridan.
Effective but downbeat domestic melodrama.
w Anatole de Grunwald *play* Sylvia Rayman d Gordon Parry ph Jack Asher m Allan Gray md Philip Martell ad William Kellner ed Ralph Kemplen
☆ Freda Jackson, Rene Ray, Lois Maxwell, Laurence Harvey, Joan Dowling, Dora Bryan, Vida Hope, Mary Germaine, Ingeborg Wells, Dorothy Gordon

Women on the Verge of a Nervous Breakdown **

Spain   1988   89m   Eastmancolor
Rank/El Deseo/Lauren Film/Orion (Agustin Almodóvar)
⊞ ▤ ⌕
original title: *Mujeres al borde de un ataque de nervios*
Three women approach crack-up as their lives entangle: a demented wife whose husband has abandoned her, her husband's estranged mistress, a temperamental actress, and the actress's friend, who has fallen in love with a terrorist.
Frenetic, fashionable farce that manages to amuse most of the time.
wd Pedro Almodóvar ph Jose Luis Alcaine m Bernardo Bonezzi ed Jose Salcedo
☆ Carmen Maura, Antonio Banderas, Julieta Serrano, Maria Barranco, Rossy de Palma, Guillermo Montesinos, Kiti Manver
'The best to be said for *Women on the Verge* is that Almodóvar makes a good interior decorator.' – *Mark Finch, MFB*
⚑ best foreign film

Women without Men

GB   1956   73m   bw
Exclusive/Hammer (Anthony Hinds)
An actress breaks out of prison in order to keep a rendezvous with the man she loves.
Standard programme-filler of a thriller.
w Richard Landau d Elmo Williams ph Walter Harvey m Leonard Salzedo md John Hollingsworth ad John Elphick ed James Needs
☆ Beverly Michaels, Joan Rice, Thora Hird, Avril Angers, Paul Carpenter, Hermione Baddeley, Gordon Jackson, Ralph Michael, Maurice Kaufmann, David Lodge

'Caged emotions, yearning for love!'

Women without Names

US   1940   62m   bw
Paramount (Eugene Zukor)
An innocent girl is accused of murder, is sent to prison, but saves her boyfriend from the gallows.
Eventful second feature; no one would complain.
w William R. Lipman, Horace McCoy d Robert Florey
☆ Ellen Drew, Robert Paige, Judith Barrett, John Miljan, Fay Helm, Louise Beavers, Marjorie Main, Esther Dale

Women's Prison *

US   1955   80m   bw
Columbia (Bryan Foy)
A prison doctor attempts to protect female inmates against the harsh and unjust regime of the warden.
Enjoyable, fast-moving 'B' movie that races through most of the clichés of the genre, including pregnancy and a full-scale riot.
w Crane Wilbur, Jack DeWitt d Lewis Seiler ph Lester H. White md Mischa Bakaleinikoff ad Cary Odell ed Henry Batista

☆ Ida Lupino, Jan Sterling, Cleo Moore, Audrey Totter, Phyllis Thaxter, Howard Duff, Mae Clarke, Juanita Moore

Won Ton Ton, the Dog Who Saved Hollywood

↟↟ US   1976   92m   colour
Paramount/David V. Picker, Arnold Schulman, Michael Winner
In twenties Hollywood, a lost Alsatian dog becomes a movie star but later suffers some ups and downs before being reunited with his mistress.
Scatty, unlikeable comedy with too frantic a pace, apparently in desperation at the dearth of funny lines and situations. The sixty 'guest stars' barely get a look in; the director seems to think (erroneously) that their appearance makes some kind of point even though they have nothing to do. Altogether, an embarrassment.
w Arnold Schulman, Cy Howard d Michael Winner ph Richard H. Kline m Neal Hefti
☆ Madeline Kahn, Art Carney, Bruce Dern, Ron Leibman; and Dennis Morgan, William Demarest, Virginia Mayo, Rory Calhoun, Henry Wilcoxon, Ricardo Montalban, Jackie Coogan, Johnny Weissmuller, Aldo Ray, Ethel Merman, Joan Blondell, Yvonne de Carlo and also Andy Devine, Broderick Crawford, Richard Arlen, Jack La Rue, Dorothy Lamour, Phil Silvers, Gloria de Haven, Stepin Fetchit, Rudy Vallee, George Jessel, Ann Miller, Janet Blair, the Ritz Brothers, Victor Mature, Fernando Lamas, Cyd Charisse, Huntz Hall, Edgar Bergen, Peter Lawford, Regis Toomey, Alice Faye, Milton Berle, John Carradine, Walter Pidgeon, etc.
'The film tries to conceal its deficiencies in comic ideas and comic skill by doing everything at the pace of a clockwork toy with a too-tight spring.' – *Dave Robinson, Times*

Wonder Bar **

US   1934   84m   bw
Warner (Robert Lord)
⌕
Love and hate backstage at a Paris night-club.
Curious musical drama with an interesting cast and fairly stunning numbers.
w Earl Baldwin *play* Geza Herczeg, Karl Farkas, Robert Katscher d Lloyd Bacon ph Sol Polito ch Busby Berkeley ad Jack Okey *songs* Harry Warren, Al Dubin
☆ Al Jolson, Kay Francis, Dolores del Rio, Ricardo Cortez, Dick Powell, Guy Kibbee, Ruth Donnelly, Hugh Herbert, Louise Fazenda, Fifi D'Orsay
'Romance, flash, dash, colour, songs, star-studded talent, and almost every known requisite to ensure sturdy attention and attendance.' – *Variety*
'A tip-top musical.' – *Variety*

Wonder Man **

↟↟ US   1945   97m   Technicolor
Samuel Goldwyn
A mild-mannered student is persuaded by the ghost of his dead twin to avenge his murder.
Smooth, successful mixture of Topper, a night-club musical, a gangster drama and the star's own brand of fooling; this is possibly his best vehicle after The Court Jester.
w Don Hartman, Melville Shavelson, Philip Rapp *story* Arthur Sheekman d Bruce Humberstone ph Victor Milner, William Snyder md Louis Forbes, Ray Heindorf sp John Fulton
☆ Danny Kaye, Vera-Ellen, Virginia Mayo, Steve Cochran, S. Z. Sakall, Allen Jenkins, Ed Brophy, Donald Woods, Otto Kruger, Richard Lane, Natalie Schafer
⚑ Louis Forbes, Ray Heindorf; *song* 'So in Love' (mDavid Rose, lyLeo Robin)

The Wonderful Country

US   1959   96m   Technicolor
UA/DRM (Chester Erskine)
♫
A wandering gunman is offered a job by the Texas Rangers.
Complexly plotted Western offering a range of familiar exploits.
w Robert Ardrey *novel* Tom Lea d Robert Parrish ph Floyd Crosby, Alex Phillips m Alex North
☆ Robert Mitchum, Julie London, Pedro Armendariz, Gary Merrill, Jack Oakie, Albert

Dekker, Charles McGraw, John Banner, Jay Novello

Wonderful Day: see *I've Gotta Horse*

Wonderful Life: see *After Life (1998)*

Wonderful Life *

↟↟ GB   1964   113m   Techniscope
EMI/Elstree Distributors/Ivy (Kenneth Harper)
Four entertainers on a luxury liner are hired by a film crew in Africa.
Slight but zestful youth musical with highly illogical detail; the highlight is a ten-minute spoof history of the movies.
w Peter Myers, Ronald Cass d Sidney J. Furie ph Ken Higgins pd Stanley Dorfman
☆ Cliff Richard, Walter Slezak, Susan Hampshire, Melvyn Hayes, Richard O'Sullivan, Una Stubbs, Derek Bond, Gerald Harper, the Shadows

Wonderful to Be Young: see *The Young Ones*

The Wonderful World of Dogs

Australia   1990   60m   colour
Radio Pictures/Australian Film Commission/ABC/Channel 4 (Mark Lewis)
⊞
A documentary on dogs and their effect on people's lives in an Australian suburb.
Witty and bizarre account of man's best, or worst, friend, one that even cat-lovers should enjoy.
wd Mark Lewis ph Tony Wilson, Steve Windon m Martin Armiger ed Lindsay Frazer

The Wonderful World of the Brothers Grimm *

↟↟ US   1962   134m   Technicolor Cinerama
MGM/Cinerama/George Pal
▤ ⌕
An account of the lives of the German fairy tale writers is supplemented by three of their stories, *The Dancing Princess, The Cobbler and the Elves* and *The Singing Bone.*
Saccharine, heavy-handed pantomime with insufficient comedy, menace or spectacle.
w David P. Harmon, Charles Beaumont, William Roberts d Henry Levin, George Pal ph Paul C. Vogel m Leigh Harline ad George W. Davis, Edward Carfagno *songs* Bob Merrill
☆ Laurence Harvey, Karl Boehm, Claire Bloom, Barbara Eden, Walter Slezak, Oscar Homolka, Martita Hunt, Russ Tamblyn, Yvette Mimieux, Jim Backus, Beulah Bondi, Terry-Thomas, Buddy Hackett, Otto Kruger
⚑ Paul C. Vogel; Leigh Harline

Wonderland *

GB   1999   108m   colour
Universal/BBC/Kismet/Revolution
In London, three sisters have problems with men: they can't get the ones they want, and want to get rid of the ones they have.
Gritty, downbeat, working-class drama in which London features as a harsh and soulless place where lives goes awry without anyone caring very much.
w Laurence Coriat d Michael Winterbottom ph Sean Bobbitt m Michael Nyman pd Mark Tildesley ed Trevor Waite cos Natalie Ward
☆ Shirley Henderson, Gina McKee, Molly Parker, Ian Hart, John Simm, Stuart Townsend, Kika Markham, Jack Shepherd, Enzo Cilenti, Sarah-Jane Potts, David Fahm
'The performances of an ensemble cast are flawless, but it's all so similar to the bleak lives that the telly shows us several times a week.' – *Alexander Walker, London Evening Standard*

The Wonders of Aladdin

↟↟ Italy   1961   92m   Technicolor Cinemascope
Embassy/Lux
▤
With the help of a genie, Aladdin defeats a usurper and wins the princess's hand.
Flat and disappointing pantomime with virtually no charm.
w Luther Davis d Henry Levin, Mario Bava ph Tonino Delli Colli m Angelo Lavagnino
☆ Donald O'Connor, Vittorio de Sica, Aldo Fabrizi, Michèle Mercier

Wonderwall

GB   1968   92m   Eastmancolor
Cinecenta/Alan Clore-Compton (Andrew Braunsberg)
An absent-minded scientist fantasizes about the girl who lives next door after he discovers a hole in the wall of his flat which enables him to spy on her.
One of the last gasps of the 'swinging London' cycle of films, complete with psychedelic settings, mini-skirts, discreet nudity and George Harrison's Indian-style music; it is also vapid and witless.
w G. Cain *story* Gerard Brach d Joe Massot ph Harry Wayman m George Harrison ad Assheton Garton
☆ Jack MacGowran, Jane Birkin, Richard Wattis, Irene Handl, Iain Quarrier, Beatrix Lehmann, Brian Walsh, Sean Lynch

'It's her world... we're just living in it.'

Woo

US   1998   84m   DeLuxe
Entertainment/New Line/New Deal/Gotham (Beth Hubbard, Michael Hubbard)
⊞ ▤ ♪
In New York, encouraged by her fortune-teller, an excessively extroverted woman goes on a blind date with a timid man.
With its unsympathetic, self-obsessed protagonist, this would-be comedy is never less than irritating and more often insufferable.
w David C. Johnson d Daisy V.S. Mayer ph Jean Lepine m Michel Colombier pd Ina Mayhew ed Nicholas Eliopoulos, Janice Hampton
☆ Jada Pinkett Smith, Tommy Davidson, Duane Martin, Michael Ralph, Darrel M. Heath, Dave Chappelle, Paula Jai Parker, LL Cool J, Aida Turturro
'A graceless and gratingly unfunny comedy that brings out the worst in just about everybody involved.' – *Joe Leydon, Variety*

The Woo Woo Kid *

US   1987   100m   CFI color
Guild/Lorimar/Kings Road Entertainment (Gary Adelson, Karen Mack)
⊞ ▤ ⌕
US title: *In the Mood*
A 15-year-old boy marries an older woman and, after the marriage is annulled, runs away with a soldier's wife.
Based on a true story from the 1940s, the comedy has a bizarre period charm.
wd Phil Alden Robinson *story* Bob Kosberg, David Simon, Phil Alden Robinson pd John Lindley m Ralph Burns pd Dennis Gassner ed Patrick Kennedy
☆ Patrick Dempsey, Talia Balsam, Beverly D'Angelo, Michael Constantine, Betty Jinnette, Kathleen Freeman, Peter Hobbs, Tony Longo, Douglas Rowe

'From boyhood to manhood, you can always count on your best friends.'

The Wood

US   1999   107m   DeLuxe
Paramount/MTV/Bona Fide (Albert Berger, Ron Yerxa, David Gale)
On the day he is to marry, a man gathers his childhood friends around him to give him confidence.
A nostalgic movie about growing up and accepting responsibility, with a likeable cast doing their best with shallow material.
d Rick Famuyiwa ph Steven Bernstein m Robert Hurst pd Roger Fortune, Maxine Shepard ed John Carter
☆ Taye Diggs, Omar Epps, Richard T. Jones, Sean Nelson, Trent Cameron, Duane Finley, Malinda Williams, De'Aundre Bonds, Sanaa Lathan, LisaRaye
'A functional feel-good movie, occasionally sweet but predominantly bland.' – *Edward Porter, Sunday Times*

The Wooden Horse **

GB   1950   101m   bw
British Lion/Wessex/London Films (Ian Dalrymple)
⊞ ▤
During World War II, British prisoners escape from Stalag Luft III by tunnelling under a vaulting horse.
Standard, solid POW drama with predictable but exciting and occasionally moving developments.
w Eric Williams *novel* Eric Williams d Jack Lee ph C. Pennington-Richards m Clifton Parker

☆ Leo Genn, *David Tomlinson*, Anthony Steel, David Greene, Michael Goodliffe, Bryan Forbes, Jacques Brunius

'All the suspense I care to take.' – *Sunday Chronicle*

The Wooden Horse of Troy: see *The Trojan War*

Wooden Soldiers: see *Babes in Toyland* (1934)

The Woodlanders *
GB   1997   96m   Technicolor   Panavision
Pathé/Channel 4/Arts Council/River (Barney Reisz, Phil Agland)
▣   ♫

In a rural village in Victorian England, a social-climbing timber merchant marries his daughter to a new doctor, despite his promise that she would marry a local woodsman.
A stolid, painstaking version of Hardy's tale of misplaced love, but one that only occasionally flares into felt life.
w David Rudkin *novel* Thomas Hardy *d* Phil Agland *ph* Ashley Rowe *m* George Fenton *pd* Andy Harris *ed* David Dickie
☆ Rufus Sewell, Emily Woof, Cal MacAninch, Tony Haygarth, Jodhi May, Polly Walker, Walter Sparrow, Sheila Burrell
'A classy and emotionally involving costumer whose only fault is lack of breadth.' – *Variety*

'This time the whole world is watching...'
Woodstock ****
US   1970   184m   Technicolor
Warner/Wadleigh-Maurice (Bob Maurice)
▣   ▣   ≣   ♫

A documentary on the three-day festival ('of peace, music ... and love') that attracted an audience of around 500,000 young people.
A definitive moment of the 60s, with the mood and music brilliantly captured on film. To do it took a team of 20 cameramen, who shot 120 hours of film, as well as eight camera assistants, 20 sound-men and engineers, six still photographers and 30 production assistants.
d Michael Wadleigh *ph* Michael Wadleigh and others *ed* Thelma Schoonmaker, Martin Scorsese
☆ Joan Baez, Canned Heat, Joe Cocker, Country Joe and The Fish, Crosby, Stills, Nash & Young, Arlo Guthrie, Richie Havens, Jimi Hendrix, Santana, John Sebastian, Sha-Na-Na, Sly & The Family Stone, Ten Years After and also The Who
'A joyous, volcanic new film that will make those who missed the festival feel as if they were there. But *Woodstock* is far more than a sound-and-light souvenir of a long weekend concert. Purely as a piece of cinema, it is one of the finest documentaries ever made in the U.S.' – *Time*
'What is distressing about most of the performers at this mammoth mud-in, apart from their obvious lack of musical talent, is, in most cases, their equally obvious hostility. I mean not just laudable hostility to the war, but also profound neurotic hostility.' – *John Simon*
† A 'director's cut' lasting 220m was released in cinemas and on video in 1994.
🏆 best documentary

Words and Music **
US   1948   121m   Technicolor
MGM (Arthur Freed)
≣   ▣   ♫

The songwriting collaboration of Richard Rodgers and Lorenz Hart.
Musical biopic which packs in a lot of good numbers and manages a script which is neither too offensive nor too prominent.
w Guy Bolton, Jean Holloway, Fred Finklehoffe *d* Norman Taurog *ph* Charles Rosher, Harry Stradling *md* Lennie Hayton *ch* Robert Alton, Gene Kelly
☆ *Tom Drake*, Mickey Rooney, Perry Como, Mel Tormé, Betty Garrett, June Allyson, Lena Horne, Ann Sothern, Allyn McLerie, *Gene Kelly*, Vera-Ellen, Cyd Charisse, Janet Leigh, Marshall Thompson

Work Is a Four-Letter Word
GB   1968   93m   Technicolor
Universal/Cavalcade (Thomas Clyde)
A power station attendant is interested only in growing mushrooms, which have a chaotic effect on his private life.

Weakly futuristic industrial fantasy which the author would probably claim to be about lack of communication. Bored audiences might have a similar view.
w Jeremy Brooks *play* Eh? by Henry Livings *d* Peter Hall *ph* Gilbert Taylor *m* Guy Woolfenden
☆ David Warner, Cilla Black, Elizabeth Spriggs, Zia Mohyeddin, Joe Gladwin

Working Girl **
US   1988   113m   DuArt
Fox (Douglas Wick)
▣   ▣   ≣   ♫

A secretary outsmarts her female boss in business and love.
Glossy comedy that owes much to the performances of its leading actors.
w Kevin Wade *d* Mike Nichols *ph* Michael Ballhaus *m* Carly Simon *pd* Patrizia von Brandenstein *ed* Sam O'Steen, Richard Nord
☆ Harrison Ford, Sigourney Weaver, Melanie Griffith, Alec Baldwin, Joan Cusack, Philip Bosco, Nora Dunn, Oliver Platt, James Lally, Olympia Dukakis
🎵 best song
🏆 best picture; Mike Nicholls; Melanie Griffith; Joan Cusack; Sigourney Weaver

Working Girls **
US   1986   90m   colour
Lizzie Borden/Alternate Current (Lizzie Borden, Andi Gladstone)
▣

After a hard day's work and overtime, a prostitute decides to quit working in a New York brothel.
A near-documentary style enlivens an account of workaday prostitutes, an upwardly mobile madame, and their rather sad male clients.
w Lizzie Borden, Sandra Kay *d* Lizzie Borden *ph* Judy Irola *m* David Van Tieghen *pd* Kurt Ossenfort *ed* Lizzie Borden
☆ Louise Smith, Ellen McElduff, Amanda Goodwin, Marusia Zach, Janne Peters, Helen Nicholas

The Working Man
US   1933   78m   bw
Warner
A wealthy shoe manufacturer hands over his business, goes on holiday, and finds himself helping his bitterest rival.
Palatable star parable.
w Maude T. Howell, Charles Kenyon *novel* Edgar Franklin *d* John Adolfi
☆ George Arliss, Bette Davis, Theodore Newton, J. Farrell MacDonald

The World According to Garp *
US   1982   136m   Technicolor
Warner/Pan Arts (George Roy Hill, Robert L. Crawford)
▣   ▣   ≣   ▣

A young man grows up with a determination to become a writer.
Unlikely and uneasy film version of a somewhat cerebral novel; any drama there might have been in the original got lost in the transition, but at least the intention is to be applauded.
w Steve Tesich *novel* John Irving *d* George Roy Hill *m* Miroslav Ondricek *md* David Shire *pd* Henry Bumstead *ed* Stephen A. Rotter
☆ Robin Williams, Mary Beth Hurt, Glenn Close, John Lithgow, Hume Cronyn, Jessica Tandy, Swoosie Kurtz
'Rather like watching a puppy chasing its own tail: engaging, touching, but pointless.' – *Margaret Hinxman, Daily Mail*
'When the movie was over, all I could find to ask myself was: What the hell was all that about?' – *Roger Ebert*
🏆 John Lithgow; Glenn Close (supporting actress)

The World and His Wife: see *State of the Union*

A World Apart **
GB   1987   110m   colour
Palace/British Screen/Atlantic/Working Title (Sarah Radclyffe)
▣   ▣   ▣   ≣

Anti-apartheid struggles in the 1960s seen through the eyes of a 13-year-old South African girl whose mother is imprisoned for her support of the African National Congress.

Excellently acted and moving mix of political and domestic drama.
w Shawn Slovo *d* Chris Menges *ph* Peter Biziou *m* Hans Zimmer *pd* Brian Morris *ed* Nicolas Gaster
☆ Jodhi May, Jeroen Krabbé, Barbara Hershey, Linda Mvusi, David Suchet, Paul Freeman, Tim Roth, Yvonne Bryceland, Albee Lesotho, Rosalie Crutchley
† Shawn Slovo is the daughter of Ruth First, on whose life the story is based.
🎬 Shawn Slovo

The World Changes *
US   1933   91m   bw
Warner (Robert Lord)
A simple farmer becomes a powerful executive, and success goes to his head.
Adequate moral drama of its time, well staged and acted.
w Edward Chodorov *story* Sheridan Gibney *d* Mervyn Le Roy *ph* Tony Gaudio
☆ *Paul Muni*, Aline MacMahon, Mary Astor, Donald Cook, Patricia Ellis, Jean Muir, Margaret Lindsay, Guy Kibbee, Alan Dinehart
'It won't appeal to the hotsy-totsy type of fan, but the parents will bring the youngsters, which should sort of balance things.' – *Variety*

World Gone Wild *
US   1987   90m   colour
Apollo Pictures (Robert L. Rosen)
≣   ▣

In 2087, a small desert community seeks help against an attack from a messianic killer and his disciples.
Inept combination of The Magnificent Seven and Mad Max, lacking in style and substance.
w Jorge Zamacona *d* Lee H. Katzin *ph* Don Burgess *m* Laurence Juber *pd* Donald L. Harris *ed* Gary A. Griffin
☆ Bruce Dern, Michael Pare, Catherine Mary Stewart, Anthony James, Rick Podell, Julius J. Carry III, Alan Autry, Mindy McEnnan, Adam Ant

World in Flames *
US   1940   62m   bw
Paramount (Albert J. Richard)
A newsreel account of the rise to power of dictators during the thirties.
Effective propaganda at the time, and a neat editing job.

The World in His Arms *
US   1952   104m   Technicolor
Universal (Aaron Rosenberg)
≣

In old San Francisco, a seal-poaching sea captain woos a Russian countess.
Romantic melodrama with plushy period backgrounds and a fair measure of action, climaxing in a boat race.
w Borden Chase, Horace McCoy *novel* Rex Beach *d* Raoul Walsh *ph* Russell Metty *m* Frank Skinner
☆ Gregory Peck, Ann Blyth, Anthony Quinn, John McIntire, Andrea King, Carl Esmond, Eugenie Leontovich

World in My Corner *
US   1955   85m   bw
U-I (Aaron Rosenberg)
A penniless would-be prizefighter becomes the protégé of a millionaire and wins his daughter but not the crucial fight.
Well-done minor melodrama.
w Jack Sher *d* Jesse Hibbs *ph* Maury Gertsman *m* Joseph Gershenson
☆ Audie Murphy, Barbara Rush, Jeff Morrow, John McIntire, Tommy Rall, Howard St John

The World in My Pocket: see *On Friday at Eleven*

The World Is Full of Married Men *
GB   1979   106m   Eastmancolor
New Realm/Married Men Productions (Adrienne Fancey)
▣   ▣

The wife of an advertising executive tries to pay him out in kind for his infidelity.
Tedious jet-setting morality play which shows in great detail all the vices it wags a finger at.

w Jackie Collins *novel* Jackie Collins *d* Robert Young *m* Ray Parslow *m* Frank Musker, Dominic Bugatti
☆ Carroll Baker, Anthony Franciosa, Sherrie Cronn, Paul Nicholas, Gareth Hunt, Georgina Hale, Anthony Steel

The World Is Not Enough **
US   1999   125m   DeLuxe   Panavision
MGM/Eon (Michael G. Wilson, Barbara Broccoli)
▣   ▣   ≣   ▣   ♫

James Bond saves the world from a villain who can feel no pain.
A spectacular opening sequence provides most of the thrills, after which Brosnan's charm smooths over the bumpy narrative and second-rate bad guys on offer here; Denise Richards in a wet T-shirt will no doubt do wonders for the image of nuclear scientists everywhere.
w Neal Purvis, Robert Wade, Bruce Feirstein *d* Michael Apted *ph* Adrian Biddle *m* David Arnold *pd* Peter Lamont *ed* Jim Clark *sp* Mara Bryan; Chris Corbould
☆ Pierce Brosnan, Sophie Marceau, Robert Carlyle, Denise Richards, Robbie Coltrane, Judi Dench, Desmond Llewelyn, John Cleese, Maria Grazia Cucinotta, Samantha Bond, Michael Kitchen, Colin Salmon, Goldie, David Calder, Serena Scott Thomas
'Formula film-making, but at least it's Formula One.' – *Adam Mars-Jones, Times*
'19th assignment of Bond's 37-year screen career sees 007 undone by villainous scripting and misguided casting and acting in a couple of key secondary roles.' – *Todd McCarthy, Variety*

The World Moves On *
US   1934   104m   bw
Fox (Winfield Sheehan)
The saga of a Louisiana family up to World War 1.
Careful, good-looking general entertainment.
w Reginald C. Berkeley *d* John Ford *ph* George Schneiderman *m* Louis de Francesco
☆ Madeleine Carroll, Franchot Tone, Reginald Denny, Stepin Fetchit, Lumsden Hare, Louise Dresser, Sig Rumann
'Pacifistic picture inviting endorsement from all bodies. Big on production and cast with six minutes of superb war stuff.' – *Variety*

The World of Apu ****
India   1959   106m   bw
Satyajit Ray Productions
≣

original title: Apur Sansar
An impoverished writer, working as a clerk, who agrees to an arranged marriage, is devastated by the death of his wife in childbirth and rejects his son.
An emotional and satisfyingly moving conclusion to a great artistic experience.
wd Satyajit Ray *novel* Aparajita by Bibhutibhusan Banerjee *ph* Subrata Mitra *m* Ravi Shankar *ad* Bansi Chandragupta *ed* Dulal Dutta
☆ Soumitra Chatterjee, Sarmila Tagore, Alok Chakravarti, Swapan Mukherjee, Dhiresh Majumdar, Sefalika Devi, Dhires Ghosh
'Rich and contemplative, and a great, convincing affirmation.' – *Pauline Kael, New Yorker*
† The film is the final part of a trilogy that began with *Pather Panchali* and continued with *Aparajito* (qqv).

The World of Henry Orient **
US   1964   106m   DeLuxe   Panavision
UA/Pan Arts (Jerome Hellman)
≣   ▣

Two rich 14-year-old New York girls build fantasies around a concert pianist.
Charming, immaculately mounted, refreshingly unusual but overlong comedy.
w Nora and Nunnally Johnson *novel* Nora Johnson *d* George Roy Hill *ph* Boris Kaufman, Arthur J. Ornitz *m* Elmer Bernstein *pd* James Sullivan
☆ Tippy Walker, Merri Spaeth, Peter Sellers, Angela Lansbury, Paula Prentiss, Phyllis Thaxter, Tom Bosley, Bibi Osterwald

World of Plenty ***
GB   1943   45m   bw
The Ministry of Information
How the distribution of food should be handled after the war.
Classic documentary with many new film-making insights, including the use of statistical diagrams.

---

w Paul Rotha, Eric Knight, Miles Malleson *d* Paul Rotha

'Any theatre audience will be grateful for seeing it. It is the epitome of educational picture-making.' – *Variety*

The World of Suzie Wong

GB 1960 129m Technicolor
Paramount/Ray Stark (Hugh Perceval)
▣ ☽

A Hong Kong prostitute falls in love with the artist for whom she poses.

Dull, set-bound romantic melodrama without much gusto.

w John Patrick *play* Paul Osborn *novel* Richard Mason *d* Richard Quine *ph* Geoffrey Unsworth *m* George Duning

☆ William Holden, Nancy Kwan, Sylvia Syms, Michael Wilding, Laurence Naismith, Jackie Chan

'Maybe one day it will all make the grade as a musical.' – *MFB*

The World Owes Me a Living

GB 1944 91m bw
British National

A man gets his memory back and recalls his air force career.

Pointless flagwaving farrago.

w Vernon Sewell, Erwin Reiner *novel* John Llewellyn Rhys *d* Vernon Sewell

☆ David Farrar, Judy Campbell, Sonia Dresdel, Jack Livesey, John Laurie, Wylie Watson

World Premiere *

US 1940 70m bw
Paramount (Sol C. Siegel)

A zany film producer thinks up some wild publicity schemes for his new film and accidentally traps some Nazi spies.

Occasionally amusing farce mainly notable for its star.

w Earl Felton *d* Ted Tetzlaff *ph* Daniel Fapp

☆ John Barrymore, Ricardo Cortez, Frances Farmer, Sig Rumann, Fritz Feld, Eugene Pallette, Luis Alberni, Virginia Dale, Don Castle

The World Ten Times Over

GB 1963 93m bw
Cyclops (Michael Luke)
US title: *Pussycat Alley*

Two semi-prostitutes try to improve their lot.

Dreary, derivative low-life drama with flashy technique.

wd Wolf Rilla *ph* Larry Pizer *m* Edwin Astley

☆ Sylvia Syms, June Ritchie, Edward Judd, William Hartnell, Francis de Wolff

The World, the Flesh and the Devil *

US 1959 95m bw Cinemascope
MGM/Sol C. Siegel/Harbel

Trapped for five days in a mine cave-in, a man struggles to the surface to find a dead world devastated by atomic war; but still alive are the elements of an eternal triangle …

Enterprising but rather disappointing fantasy which tends to become merely glum and rather self-consciously carries a panic button message.

wd Ranald MacDougall *ph* Harold J. Marzorati *m* Miklos Rozsa *ad* William A. Horning, Paul Groesse

☆ Harry Belafonte, Inger Stevens, Mel Ferrer

World without End

US 1956 80m Technicolor Cinemascope
AA (Richard Heermance)

A space ship breaks the time barrier and returns to Earth in 2508, to find that intelligent humans have been driven underground by mutants.

Reasonably lively sci-fi with horror elements, and a plot borrowed from H. G. Wells.

wd Edward Bernds *ph* Ellsworth Fredericks *m* Leith Stevens

☆ Hugh Marlowe, Nancy Gates, Rod Taylor

A World without Pity

France 1989 88m colour
Artificial Eye/Les Productions Lazennec (Alain Rocca)
▣ ☽

A poker-playing youth, living with his young drug-dealing brother, falls in love with a clever student.

A thin romance, whose appeal will depend on how much sympathy can be summoned up for its shiftless, egocentric central character.

wd Eric Rochant *ph* Pierre Novion *m* Gerard Torikian *ad* Thierry François *ed* Michele Darmon

☆ Hippolyte Girardot, Mireille Perrier, Yvan Attal, Jean-Marie Rollin, Cecile Mazan, Aline Still, Paul Pavel

The World's Greatest Athlete

🏌 US 1973 92m Technicolor
Walt Disney (Bill Walsh)

An American sports coach on an African holiday finds a young Tarzan with amazing powers.

Simple-minded comedy with lame tomfoolery and trickwork.

w Gerald Gardiner, Dee Caruso *d* Robert Scheerer *ph* Frank Phillips *m* Marvin Hamlisch

☆ Tim Conway, Jan-Michael Vincent, John Amos, Roscoe Lee Browne

The World's Greatest Lover

US 1977 89m DeLuxe
TCF (Gene Wilder)
▣

In the twenties, a rival studio starts a search for a man to surpass Valentino.

Imitative slapstick extravaganza in which anything goes but hardly anything pleases.

wd Gene Wilder *ph* Gerald Hirschfeld *m* John Morris

☆ Gene Wilder, Carol Kane, Dom DeLuise, Fritz Feld

'Infantile humour for young, slow kids who want everything pounded at them.' – *Pauline Kael, New Yorker*

† The film carries a credit to Federico Fellini, 'for encouragement at the right time'.

Worm's Eye View

GB 1951 77m bw
ABFD/Byron (Henry Halsted)

Incidents in the lives of a group of RAF billetees.

Plotless comedy from a highly successful stage romp; plainly made and empty-headed but not disagreeable.

w R. F. Delderfield *play* R. F. Delderfield *d* Jack Raymond *ph* James Wilson *m* Tony Lowry, Tony Fones

☆ Ronald Shiner, Garry Marsh, Diana Dors, Eric Davis, John Blythe

The Worst Woman in Paris

US 1933 75m bw
Jesse L. Lasky/Fox

An American girl unfairly gets a bad reputation in Paris and on her way home becomes a heroine in Kansas.

Silly, pointless story on which good production values are wasted.

w Marion Dix, Monta Bell, Martin Brown *d* Monta Bell

☆ Benita Hume, Adolphe Menjou, Harvey Stephens, Helen Chandler, Margaret Seddon

'Does not give promise of scoring in any placement.' – *Variety*

WR – Mysteries of the Organism ***

Yugoslavia 1971 86m colour
Neoplanta
▣

original title: *WR Misterije Organizma*

A free-wheeling exploration of the life and teachings of Wilhelm Reich, which resulted in his imprisonment in the United States and the burning of his books, and on the sexual attitudes in the USA and Yugoslavia in the late 60s and early 70s.

A witty, iconoclastic examination of sex and politics and their interaction, using documentary techniques, newsreel footage and fiction; it brought Makavejev an international reputation.

wd Dusan Makavejev *m* Pega Popovic, Aleksandar Petkovic *ad* Dragoljub Ivkov *ed* Ivanka Vukasovic

☆ Milena Dravic, Ivica Vidovic, Jagoda Kaloper, Tuli Kupferberg, Zoran Radmilovic, Jackie Curtis, Miodrag Andric

'The point of view is so unstable that it seems to be more sophomoric than anything else.' – *Pauline Kael, New Yorker*

† The version released on video in Britain is the TV version 'improved by the author for Channel 4', which mainly meant that the scenes showing an erect penis – the first time an erection had been passed by the British Board of Film Censors for exhibition on the screen of a public cinema – were obscured by digital effects.

The Wrath of God

US 1972 111m Metrocolor Panavision
MGM/Rainbow/Cineman (William S. Gilmore Jnr)

During a twenties Central American revolution, a bootlegger joins forces with a defrocked priest.

Noisy, violent adventure yarn which works up to a gory climax but does not take itself too seriously.

wd Ralph Nelson *w* James Graham *ph* Alex Phillips Jnr *m* Lalo Schifrin

☆ Robert Mitchum, Frank Langella, Rita Hayworth, Victor Buono, John Colicos

The Wreck of the Mary Deare *

US 1959 108m Metrocolor Cinemascope
MGM/Blaustein-Baroda (Julian Blaustein)
▣ ☾

An insurance fraud comes to light when a salvage boat is rescued from high seas.

Curious, star-studded amalgam of seafaring action and courtroom melodrama, originally intended for Hitchcock.

w Eric Ambler *novel* Hammond Innes *d* Michael Anderson *ph* Joseph Ruttenberg, F. A. Young *m* George Duning

☆ Charlton Heston, Gary Cooper, Michael Redgrave, Emlyn Williams, Cecil Parker, Alexander Knox, Virginia McKenna, Richard Harris

The Wrecking Crew

US 1968 104m Technicolor
Columbia/Meadway/Claude (Irving Allen)
▣

Special agent Matt Helm recovers bullion stolen from a Danish train.

Camped-up spy buffoonery with the usual nubile ladies and a production which seeks to be flashy but succeeds only in being tatty.

w William McGivern *novel* Donald Hamilton *d* Phil Karlson *ph* Sam Leavitt *m* Hugo Montenegro

☆ Dean Martin, Elke Sommer, Sharon Tate, Nancy Kwan, Nigel Green, Tina Louise, John Larch, John Brascia

Wrestling Ernest Hemingway *

US 1993 122m Technicolor
Warner (Joe Wizan, Todd Black)
▣ ☽ ☾

Two lonely old men – a repressed and fastidious retired barber and an exuberant alcoholic sailor – find consolation in each other's company.

Two accomplished performances by its stars, playing off each other with skill, give some resonance to this otherwise predictable story of the bonding of an odd couple.

w Steve Conrad *d* Randa Haines *ph* Lajos Koltai *m* Michael Convertino *pd* Waldemar Kalinowski *ed* Paul Hirsch

☆ Robert Duvall, Richard Harris, Shirley MacLaine, Sandra Bullock, Micole Mercurio, Piper Laurie, Marty Belafsky

'A poignant tale of intimate friendship between two elderly, eccentric men.' – *Variety*

'The story of a family's ugly secret and the stark moment that thrust their private lives into public view!'

Written on the Wind **

US 1956 99m Technicolor
U-I (Albert Zugsmith)
▣

A secretary marries her oil tycoon boss and finds herself the steadying force in a very rocky family.

The sheerest Hollywood moonshine: high-flying melodramatic hokum which moves fast enough to be very entertaining.

w George Zuckerman *novel* Robert Wilder *d* Douglas Sirk *ph* Russell Metty *m* Frank Skinner

☆ Lauren Bacall, Robert Stack, Dorothy Malone, Rock Hudson, Robert Keith, Grant Williams

🏆 Dorothy Malone

♬ title song (*m* Victor Young, *ly* Sammy Cahn); Robert Stack

Wrong Again

🏌 US 1929 20m bw silent
Hal Roach

A horse instead of a painting is delivered to a rich man's house.

Pleasing but not very inventive star comedy.

w Lewis R. Foster, Leo McCarey, H. M. Walker *d* Leo McCarey *ph* George Stevens *ed* Richard Currier

☆ Stan Laurel, Oliver Hardy, Del Henderson, Josephine Crowell

The Wrong Arm of the Law *

🏌 GB 1962 94m bw
Romulus/Robert Velaise (Aubrey Baring, E. M. Smedley Aston)
▣ ☽

London gangsters plan retaliation against Australian interlopers, and offer Scotland Yard a temporary truce.

Forgettable but pretty funny crook comedy in the British vein, with pacy script and excellent comedy timing.

w Ray Galton, Alan Simpson, John Antrobus *screenplay* Len Heath, John Warren *d* Cliff Owen *ph* Ernest Steward *m* Richard Rodney Bennett

☆ Peter Sellers, Lionel Jeffries, Bernard Cribbins, Davy Kaye, Nanette Newman, Bill Kerr, John Le Mesurier

Wrong Bet: see *A.W.O.L.*

The Wrong Box *

GB 1966 110m Technicolor
Columbia/Salamander (Bryan Forbes)
▣ ☾

Two elderly Victorian brothers are the last survivors of a tontine (an involved form of lottery) and try to murder each other.

Well-intentioned and star-studded black farce in which the excellent period trappings and stray jokes completely overwhelm the plot.

w Larry Gelbart, Burt Shevelove *novel* Robert Louis Stevenson, Lloyd Osbourne *d* Bryan Forbes *ph* Gerry Turpin *m* John Barry *ad* Ray Simm

☆ Ralph Richardson, John Mills, Michael Caine, Wilfrid Lawson, Nanette Newman, Peter Cook, Dudley Moore, Peter Sellers, Tony Hancock, Thorley Walters, Cicely Courtneidge, Irene Handl, John Le Mesurier, Gerald Sim, Norman Bird and also Tutte Lemkow

'A slapdash affair in which anything goes, irrespective of whether or not it fits.' – *Tom Milne*

'Only Patrick Hale Can Prevent A Desperate President, The Head Of The CIA, A Trigger-Happy General, Terrorists, An Arms Dealer, And Religious Fanatics From Destroying The World. But He Has Other Things On His Mind.'

Wrong Is Right

US 1982 117m Metrocolor
Columbia/Richard Brooks
▣ ☾

GB title: *The Man with the Deadly Lens*

An international TV commentator discovers that the world is being manipulated by the CIA.

Wild satiric melodrama which takes potshots at everything and usually misses.

wd Richard Brooks *novel* The Deadly Angels by Charles McCarry *ph* Fred J. Koenekamp *m* Artie Kane *pd* Edward Carfagno *ed* George Grenville

☆ Sean Connery, George Grizzard, Katharine Ross, Robert Conrad, G. D. Spradlin, John Saxon, Henry Silva, Leslie Nielsen, Robert Webber, Rosalind Cash, Hardy Kruger, Dean Stockwell, Ron Moody

'Intended as a sharply cynical overview of the current political scene, it emerges as a drearily murky thriller.' – *Sight and Sound*

The Wrong Kind of Girl: see *Bus Stop*

The Wrong Man *

US 1957 105m bw
Warner (Herbert Coleman)
▣ ☽ ☾

A New York musician is mistaken by police for an armed bandit, and both witnesses and circumstances prevent the truth from emerging.

True but downbeat story from the headlines, filmed with remarkably little persuasion; not its director's métier despite evidence of his usual thoroughness.

w Maxwell Anderson, Angus MacPhail *d* Alfred Hitchcock *ph* Robert Burks *m* Bernard Herrmann

☆ Henry Fonda, Vera Miles, Anthony Quayle, Harold J. Stone, Esther Minciotti

---

Wrongfully Accused
US   1998   85m   Technicolor
Warner/Morgan Creek/Constantin (James
G.Robinson, Bernd Eichinger, Pat Proft)
🎦   ▇

Framed on a murder charge, a violinist escapes on
his way to prison and goes in search of the real
killer, a one-armed, one-legged, one-eyed killer.
A send up of The Fugitive, *but so clumsily done that it
can raise only the slightest of smiles.*
wd Pat Proft *characters created by* Roy Huggins
ph Glen MacPherson m Bill Conti pd Michael
Bolton ed James R. Symons
☆ Leslie Nielsen, Richard Crenna, Kelly Le
Brock, Melinda McGraw, Michael York, Sandra
Bernhard, Aaron Pearl, Leslie Jones, Ben Ratner
   'The broad comedy misses its target except by
   accident, creating more mess than mirth in its
   pie-flinging approach.' – *Leonard Klady, Variety*

WUSA *
US   1970   117m   Technicolor   Panavision
Paramount/Mirror/Coleytown/Stuart Rosenberg (Paul
Newman, John Foreman)

A penniless wanderer causes chaos when he
becomes the announcer for a right-wing radio
station.
*A farcical melodrama for the intelligentsia, and for the
most part a thoroughgoing bore. The last part offers a
compensation or two.*
w Robert Stone *novel Hall of Mirrors by* Robert
Stone d Stuart Rosenberg ph Richard Moore
m Lalo Schifrin
☆ Paul Newman, Joanne Woodward, Laurence
Harvey, Anthony Perkins, Pat Hingle, Cloris
Leachman, Don Gordon, Robert Quarry, Bruce
Cabot, Moses Gunn, Wayne Rogers
   'The most significant film I've ever made and
   the best.' – *Paul Newman*

'Torn with desire … twisted with hate!'
Wuthering Heights ***
US   1939   104m   bw
Samuel Goldwyn
🎦   ▇   ⚘   ◉   🎧

The daughter of an unhappy middle-class Yorkshire
family falls passionately in love with a gypsy who
has been brought up with her.
*Despite American script and settings, this wildly
romantic film makes a pretty fair stab at capturing the
power of at least the first half of a classic Victorian
novel, and in all respects it's a superb Hollywood
production of its day and a typical one, complete with
ghostly finale and a first-rate cast.*
w Ben Hecht, Charles MacArthur *novel* Emily
Brontë d William Wyler ph Gregg Toland m Alfred
Newman ad James Basevi

☆ *Laurence Olivier, Merle Oberon*, David Niven,
Hugh Williams, Flora Robson, Geraldine
Fitzgerald, Donald Crisp, Leo G. Carroll, Cecil
Kellaway, *Miles Mander*
   CATHY (MERLE OBERON): 'I don't think I belong
   in heaven, Ellen. I dreamt once I was there. I
   dreamt I went to heaven and that heaven didn't
   seem to be my home and I broke my heart with
   weeping to come back to earth and the angels were
   so angry they flung me out in the middle of the
   heath on top of Wuthering Heights and I woke up
   sobbing with joy.'
   HEATHCLIFF (LAURENCE OLIVIER): 'What do they
   know of heaven or hell, Cathy, who know nothing
   of life? Oh, they're praying for you, Cathy. I'll pray
   one prayer with them. I'll repeat till my tongue
   stiffens: Catherine Earnshaw, may you not rest
   while I live on. I killed you. Haunt me, then!
   Haunt your murderer! I know that ghosts have
   wandered on the earth. Be with me always – take
   any form – drive me mad! Only do not leave me in
   this dark alone where I cannot find you. I cannot
   live without my life! I cannot die without my
   soul…'
   'Sombre dramatic tragedy, productionally fine,
   but with limited appeal.' – *Variety*
   'Unquestionably one of the most distinguished
   pictures of the year.' – *Frank S. Nugent, New
   York Times*
   'A pattern of constant forward motion, with
   overtones maintained throughout the rise of
   interest and suspense.' – *Otis Ferguson*
   'A strong and sombre film, poetically written as
   the novel not always was, sinister and wild as it
   was meant to be, far more compact dramatically
   than Miss Brontë had made it.' – *Richard Mallett,
   Punch*
🏆 Gregg Toland
🏆 best picture; script; William Wyler; Alfred
Newman; Laurence Olivier; Geraldine Fitzgerald;
art direction

'The power, the passion, the terror!'
Wuthering Heights *
GB   1970   105m   Movielab
AIP (John Pellatt)
▇   ⚘

Somewhat rewritten and overkeen to find a 1970
mood and interpretation for what can only be a
period piece, this disappointing version marks a Z-
film company's first determined effort to enter the
big-time.
w Patrick Tilley d Robert Fuest ph John Coquillon
m Michel Legrand
☆ Anna Calder-Marshall, Timothy Dalton, Harry
Andrews, Pamela Brown, Judy Cornwell, James

Cossins, Rosalie Crutchley, Julian Glover, Hugh
Griffith, Ian Ogilvy, Aubrey Woods

Wuthering Heights
US   1992   106m   colour
UIP/Paramount (Mary Selway)
🎧

Heathcliff, an orphaned gypsy, seeks revenge
on those who humiliated him despite his
passionate love for the girl with whom he was
brought up.
*Unimaginative version, hampered by Binoche's
unconvincing English and the lack of any spark
between her and Fiennes.*
w Anne Devlin *novel* Emily Brontë d Peter
Kosminsky ph Mike Southon m Ryuichi
Sakamoto pd Brian Morris ed Tony Lawson
☆ Juliette Binoche, Ralph Fiennes, Janet
McTeer, Sophie Ward, Simon Shepherd, Jeremy
Northam, Jason Riddington, Simon Ward, John
Woodvine

Wuya Yu Maque: see Crows and Sparrows

WW and the Dixie Dancekings
US   1975   94m   TVC Color
TCF (Stanley S. Canter)

In a Southern state in the 1950s, a crook uses a
travelling band as an alibi and stays to promote
them.
*Combination of American Graffiti and Easy Rider,
either tiresome or tolerable according to one's mood.
Very flashy, anyway.*
w Thomas Rickman d John G. Avildsen ph Jim
Crabe m Dave Grusin
☆ Burt Reynolds, Art Carney, Conny Van Dyke,
Jerry Reed, Ned Beatty

'The Epic Story Of Love And Adventure In A Lawless
Land.'
Wyatt Earp **
US   1994   189m   Technicolor
Warner/Tig/Kasdan (Jim Wilson, Kevin Costner,
Lawrence Kasdan)
🎦   ▇   ⚘   🎧

The life of Wyatt Earp, from his youth to his later
life as horse thief, buffalo hunter and successful
lawman.
*Over-solemn retelling of a story familiar from many
other Westerns, though never before at this length or
detail. Moments of tedium are inevitable, and after a
revisionist beginning the film finally settles for a
celebration of a mythic hero, with Costner playing
Wyatt Earp as a legend rather than a flesh-and-blood
person; but it often works on an epic scale.*
w Dan Gordon, Lawrence Kasdan d Lawrence
Kasdan ph Owen Roizman m James Newton

Howard pd Ida Random ed Carol Littleton
☆ Kevin Costner, Dennis Quaid, Gene Hackman,
Jeff Fahey, Mark Harmon, Michael Madsen,
Catherine O'Hara, Bill Pullman, Isabella
Rossellini, Tom Sizemore, JoBeth Williams, Mare
Winningham, Joanna Going, David Andrews,
Linden Ashby
   'A stately, handsome, grandiose gentleman's
   Western that evenhandedly but too doggedly
   tries to tell more about the famous Tombstone
   lawman than has ever before been put onscreen.'
   – *Todd McCarthy, Variety*
† The film was originally intended as an eight-
hour TV mini-series.
🏆 Owen Roizman

Wyoming
US   1940   88m   bw
MGM
GB title: *Bad Man of Wyoming*

A Missouri badman is persuaded to try an honest
life.
*Well-liked minor Western responsible for the first
teaming of its inelegant stars.*
w Jack Jevne, Hugo Butler d Richard Thorpe
☆ Wallace Beery, Marjorie Main, Leo Carrillo,
Ann Rutherford, Joseph Calleia, Lee Bowman,
Henry Travers

Wyoming
US   1947   84m   bw
Republic
▇

Early settlers in the west meet trouble from
government squatters.
Minor Western for undemanding audiences.
w Lawrence Hazard, Gerald Geraghty d Joe Kane
ph John Alton m Ernest Gold
☆ Bill Elliott, Vera Ralston, John Carroll, George
'Gabby' Hayes, Albert Dekker

The Wyoming Kid: see Cheyenne

Wyoming Mail
US   1950   87m   Technicolor
Universal (Aubrey Schenck)

A government agent pretends to be a bank robber
in order to infiltrate a gang robbing mail trains.
*Trite, glossy Western, focusing more on romance than
action.*
w Harry Essex, Leonard Lee *story* Robert Hardy
Andrew d Reginald LeBorg ph Russell Metty
md Joseph Gershenson ad Bernard Herzbrun,
Hilyard Brown ed Edward Curtiss
☆ Stephen McNally, Alexis Smith, Howard da
Silva, Ed Begley, Whit Bissell, Richard Egan, James
Arness, Richard Jaeckel, Gene Evans

🏃 film suitable for
family viewing
🎦 VHS video-cassette for
the British PAL system
🎦 VHS video-cassette for the British
PAL system in wide screen-format
💾 Video cassette in a computer-
colourised version
▇ American NTSC video-cassette
⚘ Laser disc

'If thine eye offends thee, pluck it out!'
X – the Man with X-Ray Eyes
US 1963 80m Pathécolor 'Spectarama'
AIP (Roger Corman)

GB title: *The Man with the X-Ray Eyes*
A scientist gives himself X-ray vision and goes mad.
Interesting but rather unpleasant horror story with moments of cleverness but a general air of disappointment.
w Robert Dillon, Ray Russell *d* Roger Corman *ph* Floyd Crosby *m* Les Baxter *pd* Daniel Haller *ed* Anthony Carras
☆ Ray Milland, Diana Van Der Vlis, Harold J. Stone, John Hoyt, Don Rickles, John Dierkes
'When the dialogue suggests that Xavier is being driven insane by strange and satanic visions, what one actually sees is rather a comedown.' – *MFB*
'Concise, confident, and not an ounce overweight.' – *NFT, 1967*

X the Unknown *
GB 1956 78m bw
Exclusive/Hammer (Anthony Hinds)
A mysterious force feeds on radiation from a research station on a Scottish moor, and becomes a seeping mass.
Minor sci-fi horror with a monster-like liquid lino, rushed into release to cash in on The Quatermass Experiment.
w Jimmy Sangster *d* Leslie Norman *ph* Gerald Gibbs *m* James Bernard *ed* James Needs

☆ Dean Jagger, Edward Chapman, Leo McKern, William Lucas, John Harvey, Peter Hammond, Michael Ripper, Anthony Newley

X, Y and Zee: see *Zee and Co*

Xala *
Senegal 1974 123m colour
Filmi Domireew/Société Nationale Cinématographique (Paulin Soumanou Vieyra)
GB title: *The Curse*
A leading businessman is humiliated when he finds that he is unable to consummate his marriage to his third wife.
Exuberant satire on corruption and a clash of cultures: tribal and urban, African and European, revolutionary and colonial, feminine and masculine, rich and poor.
wd Ousmane Sembène *novel* Ousmane Sembène *ph* Georges Caristan, Orlando R. Lopez, Seydina D. Gaye, Farba Seck *m* Samba Diabare Samb *ed* Florence Eymon
☆ Thierno Lege, Miriam Niang, Seune Samb, Fatim Diagne, Younouss Seye, Moustapha Toure, Dieynaba Niang

Xanadu
US 1980 93m Technicolor
Universal/Lawrence Gordon
The muse Terpsichore comes to Earth and becomes involved in the opening of a roller-derby disco.
Misguided attempt at a clean nostalgic musical, apparently conceived in a nightmare after somebody saw Down to Earth on the late show.

w Richard Christian Danus, Marc Reid Rubel *d* Robert Greenwald *ph* Victor J. Kemper *m* Barry de Vorzon *pd* John W. Corso *songs* Jeff Lynne, John Farrar
☆ Olivia Newton-John, Gene Kelly, Michael Beck
'Truly a stupendously bad film whose only salvage is the music.' – *Variety*
'A forties musical submerged by contemporary tat.' – *Guardian*
'Mushy and limp, so insubstantial it evaporates before our eyes.' – *Roger Ebert*
† Gene Kelly uses the same character name, Danny McGuire, as he did in *Cover Girl*.

'Fight The Future.'
The X-Files
US 1998 120m DeLuxe Panavision
TCF/Ten Thirteen (Chris Carter, Daniel Sackheim)
FBI agents, who are blamed for a bomb blast in Dallas, discover that there is an alien conspiracy responsible for the event.
Plodding big-screen version of the TV series that will appeal only to fans of the programme and its two glum leads and/or paranoid theorists.
w Chris Carter *d* Rob Bowman *ph* Ward Russell *m* Mark Snow *pd* Christopher Nowak *ed* Stephen Mark *sp* Mat Beck; make-up fx: Alec Gillis, Tom Woodruff Jnr
☆ David Duchovny, Gillian Anderson, Martin Landau, Armin Mueller-Stahl, Blythe Danner, William B. Davis, John Neville, Mitch Pileggi, Jeffrey DeMunn, Terry O'Quinn, Glenne Headly, Lucas Black

'More a grand marketing exercise for its hugely popular TV series than a real movie.' – *Screen International*
'File under unexceptional.' – *Variety*

Xia Dao Gao Fei: see *Full Contact*

Xianggang Zhizao: see *Made in Hong Kong*

Xich Lo: see *Cyclo*

Xiyan: see *The Wedding Banquet*

Xtro
GB 1982 86m colour
New Realm/Ashley/Amalgamated Film Enterprises (Mark Forstater)
An alien on the rampage rapes a woman who gives birth to a man – the clone of one who was abducted by a flying saucer three years earlier.
Weird but not wonderful low-budget horror that is a succession of odd moments rather than a conventional narrative.
w Iain Cassie, Robert Smith, Jo Ann Kaplan, Michel Parry, Harry Bromley Davenport *d* Harry Bromley Davenport *ph* John Metcalfe *m* Harry Bromley Davenport *ad* Andrew Mollo *ed* Nicolas Gaster
☆ Bernice Stegers, Philip Sayer, Danny Brainin, Simon Nash, Maryam D'Abo, David Cardy, Anna Wing, Peter Mandell

Y

Yaaba **
Burkina Faso/France/Switzerland 1989 90m colour
Oasis/Les Films de l'Avenir/Thelma Film/Arcadia Films (Pierre Alain Meier, Freddy Denaës, Idrissa Ouedraogo)
A young boy befriends an old woman, ostracized by the villagers and regarded as a witch.
Riveting account of African village life and a child's growing to maturity, told with directness and humour.
wd Idrissa Ouedraogo ph Matthias Kalin m Francis Bebey ed Loredana Cristelli
☆ Fatima Sanga, Noufou Ouedraogo, Barry Roukietou, Adama Ouedraogo, Amade Toure, Sibidou Ouedraogo, Adame Sidibe

Yacula: see *Female Vampire*

The Yakuza
US 1975 112m Technicolor Panavision
Warner (Sydney Pollack, Michael Hamilburg)
Japanese gangsters kidnap the daughter of a Los Angeles shipping magnate.
Violent thriller roughly exploiting an ancient Japanese genre.
w Paul Schrader, Robert Towne d Sydney Pollack ph Okazaki Kozo, Duke Callaghan m Dave Grusin
☆ Robert Mitchum, Takakura Ken, Brian Keith, Kishi Keiko, Okada Eiji
'No more than a curious footnote to the western exploitation of oriental action movies.' – Tony Rayns

Yam Daabo: see *The Choice*

Yangtse Incident *
GB 1957 113m bw
British Lion/Wilcox/Neagle (Herbert Wilcox)
US title: *Battle Hell*
aka: *Escape of the Amethyst*
In 1949 a British frigate is shelled and held captive by communist shore batteries in the Yangtse.
Stalwart but not very exciting British war heroics.
w Eric Ambler book Franklin Gollings d Michael Anderson ph Gordon Dines m Leighton Lucas
☆ Richard Todd, William Hartnell, Akim Tamiroff, Donald Houston, Keye Luke, Sophie Stewart, Robert Urquhart, James Kenney, Barry Foster

A Yank at Eton
US 1942 88m bw
MGM (John Considine Jnr)
A rich, wild American boy is sent to Eton to cool down.
Tame, tasteless imitation of A Yank at Oxford with younger participants.
w George Oppenheimer, Lionel Houser, Thomas Phipps d Norman Taurog ph Karl Freund, Charles Lawton m Bronislau Kaper
☆ Mickey Rooney, Freddie Bartholomew, Ian Hunter, Edmund Gwenn, Alan Mowbray, Tina Thayer, Marta Linden, Alan Napier, Terry Kilburn

A Yank at Oxford **
GB 1937 105m bw
MGM (Michael Balcon)
A cocky young American student comes to Oxford and meets all kinds of trouble.
A huge pre-war success which now seems naïve, this was the first big Anglo-American production from a team which went on to make The Citadel and Goodbye Mr Chips before war stymied them.
w Malcolm Stuart Boylan, Walter Ferris, George Oppenheimer, Leon Gordon, Roland Pertwee, Sidney Gilliat, Michael Hogan from an idea by John Monk Saunders d Jack Conway ph Harold Rosson m Edward Ward

☆ Robert Taylor, Vivien Leigh, Maureen O'Sullivan, Lionel Barrymore, Robert Coote, Edmund Gwenn, C. V. France, Griffith Jones, Morton Selten
'A draw picture for Taylor at a critical moment in his meteoric bid for fame.' – Variety
† A total of 31 writers are alleged to have worked without credit.

A Yank in Dutch: see *The Wife Takes a Flyer*

A Yank in Ermine
GB 1955 85m colour
Monarch
An American finds that he is really an English earl.
Thin comedy, thinly developed.
w John Paddy Carstairs novel Solid Said the Earl by John Paddy Carstairs d Gordon Parry ph Arthur Grant m Stanley Black
☆ Peter Thompson, Noelle Middleton, Harold Lloyd Jnr, Diana Decker, Jon Pertwee, Reginald Beckwith, Edward Chapman, Richard Wattis

A Yank in London: see *I Live in Grosvenor Square*

A Yank in the RAF *
US 1941 98m bw
TCF (Lou Edelman)
An American chorine stranded in London falls for the titular gentleman.
Silly but entertaining wartime flagwaver.
w Karl Tunberg, Darrell Ware story Melville Crossman (Zanuck) d Henry King ph Leon Shamroy m Alfred Newman
☆ Tyrone Power, Betty Grable, John Sutton, Reginald Gardiner, Donald Stuart, Morton Lowry, Richard Fraser, Bruce Lester

A Yank on the Burma Road
US 1941 66m bw
MGM (Samuel Marx)
GB title: *China Caravan*
A tough truck driver in the Far East abandons profit for heroism when he hears of Pearl Harbor.
Crass action flagwaver.
w George Kahn, Hugo Butler, David Lang d George B. Seitz ph Lester White
☆ Barry Nelson, Laraine Day, Stuart Crawford, Keye Luke, Sen Yung
'Glib humbug, playing tiddleywinks with high stakes.' – Theodore Strauss

Yankee Doodle Dandy ***
US 1942 126m bw
Warner (Hal B. Wallis, William Cagney)
The life story of dancing vaudevillian George M. Cohan.
Outstanding showbiz biopic, with unassuming but effective production, deft patriotic backdrops and a marvellous, strutting, magnetic star performance.
w Robert Buckner, Edmund Joseph d Michael Curtiz ph James Wong Howe m Heinz Roemheld md Heinz Roemheld, Ray Heindorf ed George Amy songs George M. Cohan
☆ James Cagney, Joan Leslie, Walter Huston, Rosemary de Camp, Richard Whorf, George Tobias, Jeanne Cagney, Irene Manning, S. Z. Sakall, George Barbier, Frances Langford, Walter Catlett, Eddie Foy Jnr
COHAN (JAMES CAGNEY) AT END OF VAUDEVILLE ACT: 'My mother thanks you. My father thanks you. My sister thanks you. And I thank you.'
COHAN: 'Where else in the world could a plain guy like me sit down and talk things over with the head man?'
ROOSEVELT (CAPTAIN JACK YOUNG): 'Well now, you know, Mr Cohan, that's as good a description

of America as I've ever heard.'
'Possibly the most genial screen biography ever made.' – Time
♫ 'Harrigan'; 'The Yankee Doodle Boy'; 'Give My Regards to Broadway'; 'Oh, You Wonderful Girl'; 'Mary's a Grand Old Name'; 'So Long, Mary'; 'You're a Grand Old Flag'; 'Over There'.
♪ music direction; James Cagney
♙ best picture; original story (Robert Buckner); Michael Curtiz; Walter Huston; George Amy

A Yankee in King Arthur's Court: see *A Connecticut Yankee in King Arthur's Court*

Yankee Pasha
US 1954 84m Technicolor
Universal-International (Howard Christie)
An American adventurer in 19th-century Marseilles saves his girlfriend from pirates.
Studio-bound hokum for double-featuring.
w Joseph Hoffman novel Edison Marshall d Joseph Pevney ph Carl Guthrie m Joseph Gershenson
☆ Jeff Chandler, Rhonda Fleming, Mamie Van Doren, Lee J. Cobb, Bart Roberts, Hal March

Yanks **
GB 1979 141m Technicolor
United Artists/CIP/Joe Janni-Lester Persky
Romances of American GIs billeted on a Lancashire town during World War II.
Not an entirely promising subject, this overlong piece maintains its interest by sheer skill of dramaturgy and cinematic narrative.
w Colin Welland, Walter Bernstein d John Schlesinger ph Dick Bush m Richard Rodney Bennett pd Brian Morris
☆ Vanessa Redgrave, Richard Gere, William Devane, Lisa Eichhorn, Rachel Roberts, Chick Vennera
Ⓥ Rachel Roberts

Yanzhi Kou: see *Rouge*

Yao a Yao Yao dao Waipo Qiao: see *Shanghai Triad*

Y'Aura T'il de la Neige à Noël?: see *Will it Snow for Christmas?*

The Year My Voice Broke *
Australia 1987 105m colour
Palace/Kennedy Miller Productions (Terry Hayes, Doug Mitchell, George Miller)
A 15-year-old boy, who is having a troubled relationship with an orphaned girl, discovers the shameful secret behind a haunted house in his small town.
An engaging account of growing up that avoids nostalgia and easy sentiment.
wd John Duigan ph Geoff Burton pd Roger Ford ed Neil Thumpston
☆ Noah Taylor, Loene Carmen, Ben Mendelsohn, Graeme Blundell, Lynette Curran, Malcolm Robertson, Judi Farr

'Risking it was all part of the job!'
The Year of Living Dangerously *
Australia 1982 114m Eastmancolor
MGM/McElroy and McElroy (Jim McElroy)
A young Australian journalist takes his first international assignment in Indonesia.
Freshly observed but ultimately pointless political parable which undoubtedly means more to its maker than it will to audiences.
w David Williamson, Peter Weir, A. J. Koch novel C. J. Koch d Peter Weir ph Russell Boyd m Maurice Jarre ed Bill Anderson

☆ Mel Gibson, Sigourney Weaver, Linda Hunt, Michael Murphy, Bill Kerr, Noel Ferrier
'I was held by it and had a very good time, though I didn't believe any of it. And I was held despite my aversion to its gusts of wind about destiny, truth versus appearance and so on.' – Pauline Kael
♙ Linda Hunt

Year of the Comet
US 1992 89m colour
Columbia/Castle Rock/New Line (Peter Yates, Nigel Wooll)
Various people scramble to obtain a 150-year-old bottle of wine, found in a Scottish castle.
A disappointing romantic comedy, given the talents involved, which fails to sparkle.
w William Goldman d Peter Yates ph Roger Pratt m Hummie Mann pd Anthony Pratt ed Ray Lovejoy
☆ Penelope Ann Miller, Tim Daly, Louis Jourdan, Art Malik, Ian Richardson, Ian McNeice, Timothy Bentinck, Julia McCarthy, Jacques Mathou
'This wine-soaked comedy-adventure never really ferments, in part due to a lack of chemistry between its romantic leads.' – Variety

'It's Chinatown – and it's about to explode!'
The Year of the Dragon
US 1985 136m Technicolor Panavision
MGM-UA/Dino de Laurentiis
A tough cop clears Chinatown of a group of murderous youth gangs.
Extremely violent and convoluted thriller with an unpleasant hero.
w Oliver Stone, Michael Cimino novel Robert Daley d Michael Cimino ph Alex Thomson m David Mansfield pd Wolf Kroeger ed Noelle Boisson
☆ Mickey Rourke, John Lone, Ariane, Leonard Termo, Ray Barry
'Never as important as the director thinks it is … nothing is clearly resolved beyond the last dead body.' – Variety

'In A City Bathed In Blood … Who Can You Trust?'
Year of the Gun
US 1991 111m DeLuxe
First Independent/J & M Entertainment/Initial (Edward R. Pressman)
In the 1970s an American journalist working in Rome becomes a target for the terrorist Red Brigades.
Dull political thriller with a bland and uninteresting hero.
w David Ambrose novel Michael Mewshaw d John Frankenheimer ph Blasco Giurato m Bill Conti pd Aurelio Crugnola ed Lee Percy
☆ Andrew McCarthy, Valeria Golino, Sharon Stone, John Pankow, George Murcell, Mattia Sbragia, Roberto Posse
'How can a thriller so stacked with gunfire, chases, twists and red herrings send one to sleep?' – Geoff Brown, The Times

Year of the Horse **
US 1997 106m colour/bw
October/Shakey Pictures (L. A. Johnson)
A documentary on rock singer-songwriter and guitarist Neil Young and Crazy Horse, covering episodes from their 30-odd years on the road.
Revealing glimpse into the dynamics and development of a rock group, one that also celebrates the group's music, with plenty of footage of concert performances.
d Jim Jarmusch ph L. A. Johnson, Jim Jarmusch m Crazy Horse ed Jay Rabinowitz

---

☆ Neil Young, Frank 'Poncho' Sempedro, Billy Talbot, Ralph Molina

'They tamed a tropic wilderness!'
The Yearling **
†† US 1946 134m Technicolor
MGM (Sidney Franklin)
▦ ◎~

The son of an old-time country farmer is attached to a stray deer.
Excellent family film for four-handkerchief patrons.
w Paul Osborn *novel* Marjorie Kinnan Rawlings d Clarence Brown ph Charles Rosher, Leonard Smith m Herbert Stothart ad Cedric Gibbons, Paul Groesse ed Harold Kress
☆ Gregory Peck, Jane Wyman, Claude Jarman Jnr, Chill Wills, Clem Bevans, Margaret Wycherly, Henry Travers, Forrest Tucker
'An unspoilt and simple story of human dignity, patience, struggle, and love, and its appeal should be universal.' – Fred Majdalany, *Daily Mail*
♟ Claude Jarman Jnr (Special Award as outstanding child actor); Charles Rosher, Leonard Smith (and Arthur Arling); art direction
♟ best picture; Clarence Brown; Gregory Peck; Jane Wyman; editing

The Years Between
GB 1946 100m bw
GFD/Sydney Box

An MP returns after being presumed dead in the war and finds his wife has been elected in his place.
Stilted variation on the Enoch Arden theme; plot and performances alike unpersuasive.
w Muriel and Sydney Box *play* Daphne du Maurier d Compton Bennett ph Reg Wyer
☆ Michael Redgrave, Valerie Hobson, Flora Robson, Felix Aylmer, James McKechnie, Dulcie Gray, Edward Rigby

Years without Days: see *Castle on the Hudson*

Yeelen *
Mali 1987 105m colour
Artificial Eye/Les Films Cissé/Souleymane Cissé
US title: *Brightness*

A son struggles to destroy his father, a black magician.
Engrossing and lively mythic tale that holds the attention even when the significance of certain rituals is hard to grasp.
wd Souleymane Cissé ph Jean-Noel Ferragut, Jean-Michel Humeau m Michel Portal, Salif Keita ad Kossa Mody Keita ed Dounamba Coulibaly, Andree Davanture, Marie-Catherine Mique
☆ Issiaka Kane, Niamanto Sanogo, Aoua Sangare, Balla Moussa Keita, Soumba Traore, Ismaila Sarr, Youssouf Cissé, Koke Sangare

The Yellow Balloon
GB 1952 80m bw
ABP (Victor Skutezky)

A small boy who thinks he has killed his friend is terrorized by a murderer.
Tense but not especially rewarding suspenser, clearly borrowed from The Window.
w Anne Burnaby, J. Lee-Thompson d J. Lee-Thompson ph Gilbert Taylor m Philip Green
☆ Kenneth More, William Sylvester, Kathleen Ryan, Andrew Ray, Bernard Lee, Veronica Hurst

The Yellow Cab Man
US 1950 84m bw
MGM (Richard Goldstone)

A taxi-driving inventor is pursued by crooks after his secret formula.
Moderate star comedy.
w Devery Freeman, Albert Beich d Jack Donohue ph Harry Stradling m Scott Bradley
☆ Red Skelton, Gloria de Haven, Walter Slezak, Edward Arnold, James Gleason, Paul Harvey, Jay C. Flippen

Yellow Canary *
GB 1943 98m bw
RKO/Imperator (Herbert Wilcox)

A socialite suspected of being a Nazi sympathizer is really a British spy.
Mild wartime melodrama chiefly notable for allotting an apparently unsympathetic part to the beloved Miss Neagle.
w De Witt Bodeen, Miles Malleson *story* Pamela Bower d Herbert Wilcox ph Max Greene

☆ Anna Neagle, Richard Greene, Nova Pilbeam, Lucie Mannheim, Cyril Fletcher, Albert Lieven, Margaret Rutherford, Marjorie Fielding

Yellow Canary
US 1963 93m bw Cinemascope
TCF/Cooga Mooga (Maury Dexter)

The baby son of a singing idol is kidnapped.
Rather dreary suspenser with too much dialogue.
w Rod Serling *novel* Evil Come, Evil Go by Whit Masterson d Buzz Kulik ph Floyd Crosby m Kenyon Hopkins
☆ Pat Boone, Barbara Eden, Steve Forrest, Jack Klugman, Jesse White, John Banner, Jeff Corey

Yellow Dog
GB 1973 101m Eastmancolor
Scotia-Barber/Akari (Terence Donovan)

A Japanese agent in London keeps watch on a mysterious scientist.
Incoherent spy thriller with a few hybrid oddities.
w Shinobu Hashimoto d Terence Donovan ph David Watkin m Ron Grainer
☆ Jiro Tamiya, Robert Hardy, Carolyn Seymour, Joseph O'Conor

Yellow Earth **
China 1984 89m colour
Guangxi Film Studio
aka: *Huang Tudi*

In 1939, a communist soldier collecting folk songs tries to persuade a peasant family to abandon their traditional ways.
Lyrically photographed against a vast and barren landscape, it celebrates folk traditions in a modern and colourful way.
w Zhang Ziliang *novel* Echo in the Deep Valley by Ke Lan d Chen Kaige ph Zhang Yimou m Zhao Jiping ad He Qun ed Wan Liu, Pei Xiaonan
☆ Xue Bai, Wang Xueqi, Tan Tuo, Liu Qiang

Yellow Jack *
US 1938 83m bw
MGM (Jack Cummings)

In 1899 Cuba a marine offers himself as a guinea pig to combat yellow fever.
Solid, unsurprising, period medical melodrama with conventional romantic sidelights.
w Edward Chodorov *play* Sidney Howard, Paul de Kruif d George B. Seitz ph Lester White m William Axt
☆ Robert Montgomery, Virginia Bruce, Lewis Stone, Andy Devine, Henry Hull, Charles Coburn, Buddy Ebsen, Henry O'Neill, Janet Beecher
'Okay for single billing, but no wow.' – *Variety*

The Yellow Mountain
US 1954 77m Technicolor
Universal (Ross Hunter)

Two old friends fall out over a gold mine and a girl.
Lethargic drama that, after a promising beginning, substitutes talk for action.
w George Zuckerman, Russell Hughes, Robert Blees *Story* Harold Channing Wire d Jesse Hibbs ph George Robinson md Joseph Gershenson ad Alexander Golitzen, Alfred Sweeney ed Edward Curtis
☆ Lex Barker, Mala Powers, Howard Duff, William Demarest, John McIntire, Leo Gordon, Dayton Lummis, Hal K. Dawson, William Fawcett, James Parnell

Yellow Pages
GB 1988 88m Technicolor
Miramax/Norfolk International (John D. Schofield, Jefferson Colegate-Stone)
▦ ▦ ◎~
US title: *Going Undercover*

An incompetent private eye is hired to look after a wild young woman by her wicked stepmother.
Dreary slapstick comedy, directed with a very heavy hand.
d James Kenelm Clarke ph John Coquillon m Alan Hawkshaw ad Jim Dultz ed Eric Boyd Perkins, Danny Retz
☆ Jean Simmons, Lea Thompson, Chris Lemmon, Viveca Lindfors, Mills Watson, Nancy Cartwright, Joe Michael Terry, Jewell Sheppard

The Yellow Passport: see *The Yellow Ticket*

The Yellow Rolls Royce *
GB 1964 122m Metrocolor Panavision
MGM (Anatole de Grunwald)
▦

Three stories about the owners of an expensive car: an aristocrat, a gangster, and a wandering millionairess.
Lukewarm all-star concoction lacking either good stories or a connecting thread.
w Terence Rattigan d Anthony Asquith ph Jack Hildyard m Riz Ortolani pd Vincent Korda
☆ Rex Harrison, Jeanne Moreau, Edmund Purdom, Moira Lister, Roland Culver, Shirley MacLaine, George C. Scott, Alain Delon, Art Carney, Ingrid Bergman, Omar Sharif, Joyce Grenfell
'Tame, bloodless, smothered in elegance and the worst kind of discreetly daring good taste.' – *Peter John Dyer*

Yellow Sands
GB 1938 68m bw
ABPC (Walter C. Mycroft)

A Cornish family sets to bickering over a will.
Reliable comedy from a popular stage original.
w Michael Barringer, Rodney Ackland *play* Eden and Adelaide Phillpotts d Herbert Brenon ph Walter J. Harvey m Hubert Bath
☆ Marie Tempest, Wilfrid Lawson, Belle Chrystal, Robert Newton, Patrick Barr, Edward Rigby

'It was a moment for being a woman ... for only a woman's revenge could keep her alive – now!'
Yellow Sky **
US 1948 98m bw
TCF (Lamar Trotti)

Outlaws on the run take over a desert ghost town.
Gleaming, stylish Western melodrama which benefits from its unusual and confined setting.
w Lamar Trotti *story* W. R. Burnett d William Wellman ph Joe MacDonald m Alfred Newman
☆ Gregory Peck, Anne Baxter, Richard Widmark, Robert Arthur, John Russell, Henry Morgan, James Barton

Yellow Submarine *
†† GB 1968 87m DeLuxe
King Features/Apple (Al Brodax)
▦ ▦ ◎~ ♫

The happy kingdom of Pepperland is attacked by the Blue Meanies.
Way-out cartoon fantasia influenced by Beatlemania and the swinging sixties; hard to watch for non-addicts.
w Lee Minoff, Al Brodax, Jack Mendelsohn, Erich Segal d George Duning ph John Williams m George Martin m/ly John Lennon, Paul McCartney, George Harrison ad Heinz Edelmann ed Brian J. Bishop
☆ John Lennon, Paul McCartney, George Harrison, Ringo Starr and also voices of: John Clive (John), Geoffrey Hughes (Paul), Peter Batten (George), Paul Angelis (Ringo/Chief Blue Meanie), Dick Emery (Nowhere Man/Lord Mayor/Max), Lance Perceval (Old Fred)
'The film is fun, and an animated feature that holds the interest of adults of all ages (I don't think there are children of any age left) is not to be sneezed at.' – *John Simon*
♫ Yellow Submarine; Eleanor Rigby; All Together Now; When I'm 64; Only a Northern Song; With a Little Help from My Friends; Sgt Pepper's Lonely Hearts Club Band; Lucy in the Sky with Diamonds; Nowhere Man; All You Need Is Love; It's All Too Much; Toy Bulldog

'What they learned isn't on any report card!'
The Yellow Teddybears
GB 1964 88m bw
(Robert Hartford-Davis)
▦

Sixth-form girls run the risk of pregnancy because of the lack of sex education in schools.
One of the first British sex films, cashing in on a tabloid report that schoolgirls showed that they were no longer virgins by wearing brooches that were being given away as a sales gimmick by a jam manufacturer; at the time it caused a minor sensation, but now seems merely risible.
w Derek Ford, Donald Ford d Robert Hartford-Davis ph Peter Newbrook m Malcolm Mitchell ad Bernard Sarron ed Teddy Darvas
☆ Jacqueline Ellis, Annette Whiteley, Iain Gregory, Doug Sheldon, Georgina Patterson, Victor Brooks, John Bonney, Anne Kettle, Jill

Adams, Raymond Huntley, Harriette Johns, John Glyn Jones

The Yellow Ticket *
US 1931 76m bw
Fox
GB title: *The Yellow Passport*

In Russia during the pogroms, a Jewish girl pretends to be a prostitute in order to get a travel permit to see her dying father.
Curious anti-Russian melodrama deriving its plot from La Tosca.
w Jules Furthman, Guy Bolton *play* Michael Morton d Raoul Walsh ph James Wong Howe
☆ Elissa Landi, Laurence Olivier, Lionel Barrymore, Walter Byron, Sarah Padden, Mischa Auer, Boris Karloff

'A picture filled with swashbucklers, privateers, public floggings, saucy tarts, looney lords, beggars, queens, and even a very jolly Roger!'
Yellowbeard
†† US 1983 96m DeLuxe
Orion/Seagoat (Carter de Haven Jnr)
▦ ▦ ◎~

Farcical adventures of a 17th-century pirate captain.
A spoofy saga in deliberately bad taste, this ragbag of old gags and new unpleasantness sank rapidly to the bottom of the box-office barrel.
w Graham Chapman, Peter Cook, Bernard McKenna d Mel Damski ph Gerry Fisher m John Morris pd Joseph R. Jennings
☆ Graham Chapman, Peter Boyle, Cheech and Chong, Peter Cook, Marty Feldman, Michael Hordern, Eric Idle, Madeline Kahn, James Mason, John Cleese, Kenneth Mars, Spike Milligan, Susannah York, Beryl Reid, Ferdy Mayne and also Peter Bull
'The atrocious script and haphazard direction elicit generally embarrassing performances from all concerned.' – *Kim Newman, MFB*

Yellowstone Kelly
US 1959 91m Technicolor
Warner

A fur trapper prevents war between Indians and whites.
Standard Western with routine excitements and a cast of TV faces.
w Burt Kennedy d Gordon Douglas ph Carl Guthrie m Howard Jackson
☆ Clint Walker, Edd Byrnes, John Russell, Ray Danton, Claude Akins

Yentl *
GB 1983 133m Technicolor
MGM-UA/Barwood/Ladbroke (Barbra Streisand, Rusty Lemorande)
▦ ▦ ◎~

Many years ago in Poland, a Jewish girl tries to get on in the world by dressing as a boy.
A personal and some would say megalomaniac extravagance by its producer-director-writer-star, who before embarking should have learned the value of brevity. Nevertheless there is about the enterprise a certain heavy style which may appeal strongly to Jews while precluding the interest and understanding of others.
w Jack Rosenthal, Barbra Streisand *story* Isaac Bashevis Singer d Barbra Streisand ph David Watkin m Michel Legrand pd Roy Walker ed Terry Rawlings
☆ Barbra Streisand, Mandy Patinkin, Amy Irving, Nehemiah Persoff, Steven Hill, David de Keyser, Bernard Spear
♟ music
♟ Amy Irving; songs 'Papa, Can You Hear Me?', 'The Way He Makes Me Feel' (mMichel Legrand, lyAlan Bergman, Marilyn Bergman); art director

'A glorious uproarious love story!'
Yes, Giorgio *
US 1982 110m Metrocolor
MGM-UA/Peter Fetterman
▦

A top international tenor falls for the lady throat specialist who cures his ailment.
Nostalgic musical romance, fine in its way but out of key with the modern film business. A treat for television viewers.
w Norman Steinberg *novel* Anne Piper d Franklin J. Schaffner ph Fred J. Koenekamp m John Williams pd William J. Creber

☆ Luciano Pavarotti, Kathryn Harrold, Eddie Albert, Paola Borboni
† The film allegedly cost 19 million and took only one.
♬ original song 'If We Were In Love' (mJohn Williams, lyAlan and Marilyn Bergman)

Yes, Madam?
GB   1938   77m   bw
ABPC
Heirs to a fortune are obliged to act as servants for three months.
Agreeable minor comedy.
w Clifford Grey, Bert Lee and William Freshman novel K. R. G. Browne d Norman Lee ph Walter J. Harvey m Jack Waller
☆ Bobby Howes, Diana Churchill, Billy Milton, Fred Emney, Bertha Belmore, Wylie Watson, Vera Pearce
† Previously filmed in 1933 with Frank Pettingell and Kay Hammond.

Yes Mr Brown *
GB   1933   90m   bw
British and Dominions/Herbert Wilcox
A businessman's secretary pretends to be his wife after the latter has walked out on him.
One of the star's most fondly remembered musical farces, a thin thing but his own.
w Douglas Furber play Business with America by Paul Frank, Ludwig Hershfield d Herbert Wilcox, Jack Buchanan ph F. A. Young m/ly Paul Abraham, Douglas Furber
☆ Jack Buchanan, Elsie Randolph, Hartley Power, Clifford Heatherley, Vera Pearce

Yes My Darling Daughter
US   1939   86m   bw
Warner (Ben Glazer)
Lovers elope and are pursued by her family.
Mildly amusing domestic comedy.
w Casey Robinson play Mark Reed d William Keighley ph Charles Rosher
☆ Priscilla Lane, Jeffrey Lynn, Roland Young, Fay Bainter, May Robson, Genevieve Tobin, Ian Hunter

Yes Sir, That's My Baby
US   1949   82m   Technicolor
U-I (Leonard Goldstein)
Ex-service undergraduates and their wives have trouble settling down to studies.
Witless and exhausting college comedy.
w Oscar Brodney d George Sherman ph Irving Glassberg m Walter Scharf
☆ Donald O'Connor, Gloria de Haven, Charles Coburn, Barbara Brown, Joshua Shelley

Yeshou Xingling: see *Beastcops*

Yesterday Girl: see *Abschied von Gestern*

Yesterday, Today and Tomorrow
Italy/France   1963   119m   Techniscope
CCC/Concordia/Joseph E. Levine (Carlo Ponti)
📼 ▦
Three stories of naughty ladies.
A relentlessly boring compendium with everybody shouting at once.
w Eduardo de Filippo, Cesare Zavattini, others d Vittorio de Sica ph Giuseppe Rotunno m Armando Trovajoli
☆ Marcello Mastroianni, Sophia Loren
'A sad intimation of the sort of rainy day the Italian cinema is currently having.' – *MFB*
'One begins to see, amid the sunsets and sunrises and Roman rooftops, the sheer venality of the creation, the cynical circus thrust upon us on the assumption that breasts and bodies and fornication are all that these leading lights of the Italian cinema need provide to keep us from baying at the moon.' – *Judith Crist*
🏆 best foreign film
🎭 Marcello Mastroianni

Yesterday's Enemy
GB   1959   95m   bw   Megascope
Columbia/Hammer (T. S. Lyndon-Haynes)
In 1942 Burma, a British unit violently takes over a village and finds an unsolved puzzle.
Would-be ironic war suspenser, economically made but quite effective in putting its message across.

w Peter R. Newman *TV play* Peter R. Newman d Val Guest ph Arthur Grant m none ad Bernard Robinson ed James Needs, Alfred Cox
☆ Stanley Baker, Guy Rolfe, Leo McKern, Philip Ahn, Gordon Jackson, David Oxley, Richard Pasco, Russell Waters, Bryan Forbes, David Lodge, Percy Herbert

Yesterday's Hero
GB   1979   95m   colour
Columbia/CinemaSeven (Elliott Kastner)
A successful footballer goes to the bad but redeems himself.
Totally uninteresting sporting version of the Road to Ruin.
w Jackie Collins d Neil Leifer ph Brian West md Stanley Myers pd Keith Wilson
☆ Ian McShane, Suzanne Somers, Adam Faith, Paul Nicholas, Sam Kydd

Les Yeux sans Visage: see *Eyes without a Face*

Yield to the Night *
GB   1956   99m   bw
ABP (Kenneth Harper)
US title: Blonde Sinner
A condemned murderess relives the events which led to her arrest.
Gloomy prison melodrama vaguely based on the Ruth Ellis case and making an emotional plea against capital punishment.
w John Cresswell, Joan Henry *novel* Joan Henry d J. Lee-Thompson ph Gilbert Taylor m Ray Martin
☆ Diana Dors, Yvonne Mitchell, Michael Craig, Marie Ney, Athene Seyler, Geoffrey Keen

Yinshi Nan Nu: see *Eat Drink Man Woman*

Yo, la peor de todas: see *I, The Worst of All*

Yoidore Tenshi: see *Drunken Angel*

Yojimbo ****
Japan   1961   110m   bw
Toho
📼 ▦ ⊚
A wandering samurai tricks two rival gangs of cutthroats into destroying one other.
Masterful, beautifully composed, witty movie that inspired the 'spaghetti Western' cycle when it was remade by Sergio Leone as A Fistful Of Dollars.
w Ryuzo Kikushima, Akira Kurosawa d Akira Kurosawa ph Kazuo Miyagawa m Masuru Sato
☆ Toshiro Mifune, Eijiro Tono, Kamatari Fujiwara, Takashi Shimura, Seizaburo Kawazu, Isuzu Yamada, Hiroshi Tachikawa
'One of the rare Japanese movies that is both great and funny to American audiences.' – *New Yorker*

Yokel Boy
US   1942   69m   bw
Republic (Robert North)
GB title: Hitting the Headlines
A film buff from the sticks comes to Hollywood and gets involved with production.
Spoofy comedy which doesn't come off despite the talent around.
w Isabel Dawn *story* Russel Rouse (the legit musical by Lew Brown was thrown away, together with the songs) d Joseph Santley ph Ernest Miller md Cy Feuer
☆ Eddie Foy Jnr, Joan Davis, Albert Dekker, Alan Mowbray, Roscoe Karns, Mikhail Rasumny, Marc Lawrence, Tom Dugan

Yol ***
Switzerland   1982   114m   Fujicolour
Cactus/Maran/Antenne 2/Swiss Television/Güney (Edi Hubschmid, K. L. Puldi)
📼 ▦ 🎧
Five convicts are released on a week's leave, and their various circumstances lead them to tragedy.
Rewarding if heavy-going Turkish saga which exhausts the spectator almost as much as its long-suffering characters. It feels and looks like an epic.
w Yilmaz Güney d Serif Gören ph Erdogan Engin m Sebastian Argol ed Yilmaz Güney, Elisabeth Waelchli
☆ Tarik Akan, Halil Ergün, Necmettin Cobanoglu, Serif Sezer

Yolanda and the Thief *
US   1945   108m   Technicolor
MGM (Arthur Freed)
▦ ⊚
A con man poses as the guardian angel of a naïve heiress.
Laboured musical fantasy with arty Mexican settings; not a success in any way, but with a few effective moments.
w Irving Brecher *story* Ludwig Bemelmans, Jacques Théry d Vincente Minnelli ph Charles Rosher m Lennie Hayton *songs* Harry Warren, Arthur Freed
☆ Fred Astaire, Lucille Bremer, Frank Morgan, Leon Ames, Mildred Natwick
'The most extreme of the big musical mistakes.' – *New Yorker, 1979*
'It perhaps needs to be seen by anyone who wants to know what killed the MGM musicals.' – *New Yorker*

'Every time she says I love you, she breaks the law!'
You and Me
US   1938   90m   bw
Paramount (Fritz Lang)
A department store owner employs ex-convicts, one of whom has not quite reformed.
Curious comedy drama which never has a hope of coming off.
w Virginia Van Upp *story* Norman Krasna d Fritz Lang ph Charles Lang Jnr m Kurt Weill
☆ Sylvia Sidney, George Raft, Harry Carey, Barton MacLane, Warren Hymer, Roscoe Karns, George E. Stone, Adrian Morris
'Lang's individual touch is visible everywhere ... but for the ordinary George Raft fan it will not only be unappreciated, it will be actually confusing.' – *National Board of Review*
'Given proper control over story and scenario, Lang couldn't have made so bad a film as You and Me; the whole picture is like an elegant and expensive gesture of despair.' – *Graham Greene*

You Belong to Me
US   1934   67m   bw
Paramount (Louis D. Lighton)
An alcoholic vaudeville comic plays father to an orphan.
Muddled backstage melodrama which would be enjoyed by fans of the star.
w Walter DeLeon, Elizabeth Alexander d Alfred Werker
☆ Lee Tracy, Helen Mack, Helen Morgan, Lynne Overman, David Holt
'Should gain attention in the nabe spots.' – *Variety*

You Belong to Me *
US   1941   94m   bw
Columbia (Wesley Ruggles)
GB title: Good Morning, Doctor
A playboy becomes jealous of the male patients of his doctor wife.
Mild comedy for two stars who are well capable of keeping it afloat.
w Claude Binyon, Dalton Trumbo d Wesley Ruggles ph Joseph Walker m Frederick Hollander
☆ Barbara Stanwyck, Henry Fonda, Edgar Buchanan, Roger Clark, Ruth Donnelly, Melville Cooper, Maude Eburne

You Belong to My Heart: see *Mr Imperium*

You Came Along
US   1945   103m   bw
Paramount (Hal B. Wallis)
A girl from the treasury department falls in love with one of three GIs she takes on a war bond tour, but he dies of leukaemia.
Weird mishmash of farce and sentimentality; quite watchable in its way, but an odd showcase for a new female star.
w Robert Smith, Ayn Rand d John Farrow ph Daniel L. Fapp m Victor Young
☆ Lizabeth Scott, Robert Cummings, Don Defore, Charles Drake, Julie Bishop, Kim Hunter, Rhys Williams, Franklin Pangborn, Minor Watson

You Can't Buy Everything *
US   1934   72m   bw
MGM
A woman obsessed by her mounting bank balance almost ruins the lives of her family.

Unusual and rather well-acted period melodrama with a pleasing cast.
w Dudley Nichols, Lamar Trotti d Charles F. Reisner
☆ May Robson, Jean Parker, Lewis Stone, Mary Forbes, Reginald Mason

You Can't Cheat an Honest Man *
US   1939   79m   bw
Universal (Lester Cowan)
Trials and tribulations of a circus owner.
Flat, desultory and generally disappointing comedy vehicle for an irresistible star combination.
w George Marion Jnr, Richard Mack, Everett Freeman *story* Charles Bogle (W. C. Fields) d George Marshall ph Milton Krasner m Charles Previn
☆ W. C. Fields, Edgar Bergen (with Charlie McCarthy and Mortimer Snerd), Constance Moore, Mary Forbes, Thurston Hall, Charles Coleman, Edward Brophy
'Fairly amusing but lacks sustained overall interest.' – *Variety*

You Can't Do That to Me: see *Maisie (Maisie Goes to Reno)*

You Can't Escape Forever
US   1942   77m   bw
Warner (Mark Hellinger)
A girl reporter demoted to the lovelorn column exposes a racket boss.
Untidy remake of Hi Nellie; tolerable on a double bill, but not for close criticism.
w Fred Niblo Jnr, Hector Chevigny *story* Roy Chanslor d Jo Graham
☆ George Brent, Brenda Marshall, Gene Lockhart, Roscoe Karns, Eduardo Ciannelli, Paul Harvey

You Can't Get Away with Murder
US   1939   78m   bw
Warner (Sam Bischoff)
A juvenile delinquent teams up with a gangster and takes a prison rap for him.
Standard post-Dead End crime melodrama with no surprises.
w Robert Buckner, Don Ryan, Kenneth Gamet play Chalked Out by Lewis Lawes, Jonathan Finn d Lewis Seiler ph Sol Polito m Heinz Roemheld
☆ Humphrey Bogart, Billy Halop, Gale Page, John Litel, Henry Travers, Harvey Stephens, Harold Huber
'Strictly a filler for the duals ... ponderous and slow moving.' – *Variety*

You Can't Have Everything *
US   1937   99m   bw
TCF (Lawrence Schwab)
▦
A failed play is turned into a musical.
Lively backstage comedy with good moments.
w Harry Tugend, Jack Yellen, Karl Tunberg *story* Gregory Ratoff d Norman Taurog ph Lucien Andriot md David Buttolph *songs* Mack Gordon, Harry Revel
☆ Alice Faye, *the Ritz Brothers*, Don Ameche, Charles Winninger, Gypsy Rose Lee, Tony Martin, Arthur Treacher, Louis Prima, Tip Tap and Toe, Wally Vernon
'An expert piecing together of story, melody, blackouts, night club specialties and production numbers.' – *Variety*

You Can't Have Everything
US   1970   90m   Eastmancolor
Koala (Lou Brandt)
aka: Cactus in the Snow
An 18-year-old virgin GI is about to leave for Vietnam when he picks up a girl and spends a happy but platonic twenty-four hours.
An agreeably understated little love story for those absorbed by teenage sex problems.
wd Martin Zweiback ph David M. Walsh m Joe Parnello
☆ Richard Thomas, Mary Layne, Lucille Benson, Oscar Beregi

You Can't Ration Love
US   1944   78m   bw
Michel Kraike/Paramount
It's wartime at college, and dates are rationed.
Silly idea for a forgettable musical.
w Val Burton, Hal Fimberg, Muriel Roy Bolton d Lester Fuller

☆ Betty Jane Rhodes, Johnnie Johnston, Bill Edwards, Marjorie Weaver, Marie Wilson, Mabel Paige

You Can't Run Away from It

US 1956 96m Technicolor Cinemascope
Columbia (Dick Powell)
An heiress runs away from a marriage arranged by her father, and falls for an amiable reporter.
Flat remake of It Happened One Night, with practically no comic sense or talent.
w Claude Binyon, Robert Riskin d Dick Powell ph Charles Lawton Jnr m George Duning md Morris Stoloff
☆ June Allyson, Jack Lemmon, Charles Bickford, Jim Backus, Stubby Kaye, Paul Gilbert, Allyn Joslyn

You Can't Sleep Here: see *I Was a Male War Bride*

You Can't Take It with You **

US 1938 127m bw
Columbia (Frank Capra)
🏛 📷
The daughter of a highly eccentric New York family falls for a rich man's son.
A hilarious, warm and witty play is largely changed into a tirade against big business, but the Capra expertise is here in good measure and the stars all pull their weight.
w Robert Riskin play George S. Kaufman, Moss Hart d Frank Capra ph Joseph Walker m Dimitri Tiomkin ed Gene Havlik
☆ Jean Arthur, Lionel Barrymore, James Stewart, Edward Arnold, Spring Byington, Mischa Auer, Ann Miller, Samuel S. Hinds, Donald Meek, H. B. Warner, Halliwell Hobbes, Mary Forbes, Dub Taylor, Lillian Yarbo, Eddie Anderson and also *Harry Davenport*
GRANDPA VANDERHOF (LIONEL BARRYMORE) OFFERING A PRAYER: 'Well, sir, here we are again. We had a little trouble, but that's not your fault. You spread the milk of human kindness, and if some of it gets curdled, that's our look-out. Anyway, things have turned out fine. Alice is going to marry Tony. The Kirbys are going to live with us for a while. And everybody on the block is happy. We've all got our health – and as far as anything else is concerned, we'll leave it up to you. Thank you.'
'The comedy is wholly American, wholesome, homespun, human, appealing, and touching in turn.' – *Variety*
'Shangri-La in a frame house.' – *Otis Ferguson*
⚲ best picture; Frank Capra
⚖ Robert Riskin; Joseph Walker; Spring Byington; Gene Havlik

You Can't Take Money: see *Internes Can't Take Money*

'It's bedlam in Islam!'

You Can't Win 'em All

GB 1970 99m Technicolor Panavision
Columbia/SRO (Gene Corman)
📀 📀
In 1922, two rival American mercenaries have adventures in the Mediterranean.
Hectic, overplotted comedy actioner.
w Leo V. Gordon d Peter Collinson ph Ken Higgins m Bert Kaempfert
☆ Tony Curtis, Charles Bronson, Michèle Mercier, Grégoire Aslan, Patrick Magee

You Don't Need Pajamas at Rosie's: see *The First Time*

You for Me

US 1952 71m bw
MGM (Henry Berman)
A millionaire patient is courted by a needy hospital and falls for a popular nurse.
Cheerful but thin little programme-filler.
w William Roberts d Don Weis ph Paul Vogel md Alberto Colombo
☆ Peter Lawford, Jane Greer, Gig Young, Paula Corday, Elaine Stewart

You Gotta Stay Happy

US 1948 100m bw
Universal (Karl Tunberg)
A runaway heiress joins cargo pilots on a transcontinental hop with some very queer passengers.
Ho-hum imitation of a Capra comedy; the effort shows.
w Karl Tunberg story Robert Carson d H. C. Potter ph Russell Metty m Daniele Amfitheatrof
☆ Joan Fontaine, James Stewart, Eddie Albert, Roland Young, Willard Parker, Percy Kilbride, Porter Hall, Paul Cavanagh, Halliwell Hobbes

You Light Up My Life

US 1977 90m Technicolor
Columbia/Mondial International (Joseph Brooks)
A comedian's daughter tries for success as a composer and singer.
Commonplace showbiz schmaltz, ineptly presented.
wd Joseph Brooks ph Eric Saarinen m Joseph Brooks m/ly Joseph Brooks pd Tom Rasmussen ed Lynzee Klingman
☆ Didi Conn, Joe Silver, Michael Zaslow, Stephen Nathan, Melanie Mayron, Amy Letterman, Jerry Keller
'The movie is both amateurish and slick – it oozes heart. The scenes go on too long and there isn't enough in them.' – *Pauline Kael*
♫ song 'You Light Up My Life' (m/ly Joseph Brooks)

You Live and Learn

GB 1937 80m bw
Warner
American night-club dancers are stranded in Paris and helped by a nitwit Englishman who turns out to be not what he seems.
Rather flat comedy which gets flatter as it goes along.
w Brock Williams, Tom Phipps story Norma Petterson d Arthur Woods
☆ Glenda Farrell, Claude Hulbert, Glen Alyn, John Carol, James Stephenson, George Galleon

You Made Me Love You

GB 1934 69m bw
British International
A temperamental heiress is tamed by an amorous songwriter.
Flimsy comedy with amusing moments.
w Frank Launder story Stanley Lupino d Monty Banks ph John Cox md Harry Acres songs Stanley Lupino, Noel Gay, Clifford Grey
☆ Thelma Todd, Stanley Lupino, John Loder, James Carew, Gerald Rawlinson

You, Me & Marley **

GB 1992 90m colour
BBC
Three friends on a West Belfast estate persist in joy-riding in stolen cars to the annoyance of residents and the IRA.
Excellent drama, tough and authentic in feeling, which deals on a small scale with the complexities of the Irish situation.
w Graham Reid story Richard Spence d Graham Veevers m Stephen Warbeck pd David Wilson ed Greg Miller
☆ Marc O'Shea, Bronagh Gallagher, Michael Liebmann, Michael Gregory, Emma Moylan, Marie Jones, Frank Grimes
† The film was made for TV, but was shown at the 1992 Edinburgh Film Festival, where it won an award.

You Must Be Joking *

GB 1965 100m bw
Columbia/Ameran (Charles H. Schneer)
Assorted army personnel vie in an extended initiative test.
Slam-bang location comedy with more hits than misses: cheerful entertainment.
w Alan Hackney d Michael Winner ph Geoffrey Unsworth m Laurie Johnson
☆ Terry-Thomas, Lionel Jeffries, Michael Callan, Gabriella Licudi, Denholm Elliott, Lee Montague, Bernard Cribbins, Wilfrid Hyde-White, James Robertson Justice, Richard Wattis, James Villiers

You Never Can Tell *

US 1951 78m bw
U-I (Leonard Goldstein)
GB title: *You Never Know*
An Alsatian dog is murdered and is sent back from heaven in the guise of a private detective to expose his killer.
Self-confidently outrageous comedy fantasy in the wake of Here Comes Mr Jordan; not badly done if you accept the premise.
w Lou Breslow, David Chandler d Lou Breslow ph Maury Gertsman m Hans Salter
☆ Dick Powell, Peggy Dow, Charles Drake, Joyce Holden, Albert Sharpe, Sara Taft

You Never Know: see *You Never Can Tell*

'Living, loving – as though any moment a vengeful world might tear her from his arms!'

You Only Live Once **

US 1937 85m bw
Walter Wanger
🏛
A petty crook framed for murder breaks out of prison and tries to escape to Canada with his wife.
Gloomy melodrama partly based on Bonnie and Clyde and incorporating a plea for justice; very well made and acted.
w Graham Baker story Gene Towne d Fritz Lang ph Leon Shamroy m Alfred Newman
☆ Sylvia Sidney, Henry Fonda, Barton MacLane, Jean Dixon, William Gargan, Jerome Cowan, Chic Sale, Margaret Hamilton, Warren Hymer
'Crack blend of spectacular drama and romance … good direction, strong scripting and an arresting production.' – *Variety*
'Again and again in this film we find what can only be described as camera style, the use of the pictorial image to narrate with the maximum of emotional impact.' – *Dilys Powell*

You Only Live Twice **

👪 GB 1967 117m Technicolor Panavision
UA/Eon (Harry Saltzman, Albert R. Broccoli)
📀 📀 🏛 📷 🎵
James Bond goes to Japan.
The Bond saga at its most expensive and expansive, full of local colour and in-jokes, with an enormously impressive set for the climactic action.
w Roald Dahl novel Ian Fleming d Lewis Gilbert ph Freddie Young, Bob Huke m John Barry pd Ken Adam
☆ Sean Connery, Tetsuro Tamba, Akiko Wakabayashi, Mie Hama, Karin Dor, Bernard Lee, Lois Maxwell, Desmond Llewelyn, Charles Gray, Donald Pleasence

You Pay Your Money

GB 1957 67m bw
Butcher's (W. G. Chalmers)
Investigating the shady girlfriend of his boss, a man and his wife uncover an Arab plot to dominate the world.
Mundane low-budget thriller with a narrative that is a little different, but hampered by routine direction and acting.
w Michael Cronin novel Michael Cronin d MacLean Rogers ph James Harvey md Wilfred Burns ad Bill Bennison ed Ben Hipkins
☆ Hugh McDermott, Jane Hylton, Honor Blackman, Hugh Moxey, Ivan Samson, Ferdy Mayne, Shirley Deane, Gerard Heinz

You Said a Mouthful

US 1932 75m bw
Warner
The inventor of an unsinkable bathing suit is mistaken for a champion swimmer.
Tepid star comedy.
w Robert Lord and Bolton Mallory d Lloyd Bacon
☆ Joe E. Brown, Ginger Rogers, Sheila Terry, Guinn Williams, Oscar Apfel

You Were Meant for Me

US 1948 92m bw
TCF (Fred Kohlmar)
A small-town girl marries a bandleader.
Mildly pleasing, muted, musical romance, with good twenties atmosphere.
w Elick Moll, Valentine Davies d Lloyd Bacon ph Victor Milner m/ly various md Lionel Newman

☆ Jeanne Crain, Dan Dailey, Oscar Levant, Barbara Lawrence, Selena Royle, Percy Kilbride, Herbert Anderson

You Were Never Lovelier *

US 1942 97m bw
Columbia (Louis F. Edelman)
📀 🏛 📷
An Argentinian hotel tycoon tries to interest his daughter in marriage by creating a mysterious admirer.
Pleasing musical, a follow-up for the stars of You'll Never Get Rich.
w Michael Fessier, Ernest Pagano, Delmer Daves d William A. Seiter ph Ted Tetzlaff m Leigh Harline m/ly Jerome Kern, Johnny Mercer
☆ Fred Astaire, Rita Hayworth, Adolphe Menjou, Leslie Brooks, Adele Mara, Isobel Elsom, Gus Schilling, Xavier Cugat and his Orchestra, Larry Parks
† Rita Hayworth's singing was dubbed by Nan Wynn.
⚖ Leigh Harline; song 'Dearly Beloved'

You Will Remember

GB 1940 86m bw
Jack Raymond Productions
The life of the late Victorian songwriter Leslie Stuart.
Pleasant, rather surprising, minor British biopic.
w Lydia Hayward d Jack Raymond ph Henry Harris md Percival Mackay
☆ Robert Morley, Emlyn Williams, Dorothy Hyson, Tom E. Finglass, Nicholas Phipps, Allan Jeayes

You'll Find Out *

US 1940 97m bw
RKO (David Butler)
🏛 📷
Kay Kyser's band is hired to play for a 21st birthday party at a gloomy mansion; they help save the life of the girl concerned.
Cheerful if slow-starting spooky house send-up with a splendid trio of villains.
w James V. Kern, David Butler d David Butler ph Frank Redman m Roy Webb m/ly Jimmy McHugh, Johnny Mercer
☆ Kay Kyser, Boris Karloff, Peter Lorre, Bela Lugosi, Dennis O'Keefe, Ginny Simms, Helen Parrish, Alma Kruger, Ish Kabibble
'Generates a fast pace that carries proceedings along in zestful tempo through a maze of humorous and chiller complications.' – *Variety*
⚖ song 'I'd Know You Anywhere'

You'll Like My Mother

US 1972 92m Technicolor
Universal/Bing Crosby Productions (Mort Briskin)
Pregnant widow visits neurotic mother-in-law in a snowbound mansion.
Predictable frightened lady shocker aiming somewhere between Psycho and Fanatic; of strictly routine interest.
w Jo Heims novel Naomi Hintze d Lamont Johnson ph Jack Marta m Gil Melle
☆ Rosemary Murphy, Patty Duke, Richard Thomas, Sian Barbara Allen

You'll Never Get Rich *

US 1941 88m bw
Columbia (Sam Bischoff)
📀 🏛 📷
A Broadway dance director helps his philandering producer by taking a romantically-inclined showgirl off his hands.
Smart comedy-musical which set its female lead as a top star.
w Michael Fessier, Ernest Pagano d Sidney Lanfield ph Philip Tannura m Morris Stoloff m/ly Cole Porter ed Robert Alton
☆ Fred Astaire, Rita Hayworth, Robert Benchley, John Hubbard, Osa Massen, Frieda Inescort, Guinn Williams, Donald MacBride
⚖ Morris Stoloff; song 'Since I Kissed My Baby Goodbye'

Young America

US 1932 74m bw
Fox
GB title: *We Humans*
Two young boys get into trouble with the law.
Dog-eared domestic flagwaver.

---

w William Conselman *play* John Frederick Ballard *d* Frank Borzage *ph* George Schneiderman *md* George Lipschultz
☆ Spencer Tracy, Doris Kenyon, Tommy Conlon, Ralph Bellamy, Beryl Mercer, Sarah Padden
'Hokey propaganda for juvenile courts. Not for smart houses and doubtful elsewhere unless there is a preponderance of mothers.' – *Variety*

'American Drug Wars Come To Britain ... And It Takes A Special Cop To Infiltrate Their World Of Violence.'
The Young Americans *
GB 1993 103m Rank Colour Panavision
Rank/Polygram/Live Entertainment (Paul Trijbits)
An American cop comes to London to help local police investigate drug-related killings.
Loud, frenetic attempt to make an English imitation of an American gangster movie; it is partially successful, though the more it resembles an American film, the more it becomes a lurid fantasy.
wd Danny Cannon, David Hilton *d* Danny Cannon *ph* Vernon Layton *m* David Arnold *pd* Laurence Dorman *ed* Alex Mackie
☆ Harvey Keitel, Iain Glen, John Wood, Terence Rigby, Keith Allen, Craig Kelly, Thandie Newton, Viggo Mortensen
'A high-octane, in-your-face cop thriller that's got everything going for it except a well-rounded script.' – *Variety*

Young and Eager: see *Claudelle Inglish*

Young and Innocent ***
GB 1937 80m bw
GFD/Gainsborough (Edward Black)
US title: *A Girl Was Young*
A girl goes on the run with her boyfriend when he is suspected of murder.
Pleasant, unassuming chase melodrama with a rather weak cast but plenty of its director's touches.
w Charles Bennett, Alma Reville *novel* A Shilling for Candles by Josephine Tey *d* Alfred Hitchcock *ph* Bernard Knowles *m* Louis Levy
☆ Nova Pilbeam, Derrick de Marney, Mary Clare, Edward Rigby, Basil Radford, George Curzon, Percy Marmont, John Longden
'I like it best of all his pictures. It may not be, academically speaking, the cleverest. The adepts who go to a Hitchcock film to grub out bits of montage may be disappointed.' – C. A. *Lejeune*

The Young and the Damned: see *Los Olvidados*

Young and Willing: see *The Wild and the Willing* (1962)

Young and Willing
US 1942 83m bw
UA (made by Paramount) (Edward H. Griffith)
Impecunious actors in a New York boarding house hit on a great play.
Very mild, innocuous comedy which passed quickly from the public memory.
w Virginia Van Upp *play* Francis Swann *d* Edward H. Griffith *ph* Leo Tover *m* Victor Young
☆ William Holden, Susan Hayward, Eddie Bracken, Robert Benchley, Martha O'Driscoll, Barbara Britton, James Brown, Mabel Paige

Young as You Feel *
US 1931 78m bw
Fox
In order to reform his family a father pretends to be as irresponsible as they are.
Medium star vehicle.
w Edwin Burke *play* Father and the Boys by George Ade *d* Frank Borzage
☆ Will Rogers, Fifi D'Orsay, Lucien Littlefield, Donald Dillaway
'Looks fair b.o. due to star.' – *Variety*

Young at Heart **
US 1954 117m Warnercolor
Warner/Arwin (Henry Blanke)
The daughters of a small-town music teacher have romantic problems.
Softened, musicalized remake of Four Daughters (qv), an old-fashioned treat with roses round the door and a high standard of proficiency in all departments.

w Julius J. Epstein, Lenore Coffee *novel* Fannie Hurst *d* Gordon Douglas *ph* Ted McCord *md* Ray Heindorf
☆ Doris Day, Frank Sinatra, Ethel Barrymore, Gig Young, Dorothy Malone, Robert Keith, Elisabeth Fraser, Alan Hale Jnr

Young Bess *
US 1953 112m Technicolor
MGM (Sidney Franklin)
The early years of Elizabeth 1 and her romance with Tom Seymour.
Historical fiction, wildly unreliable as to fact and dramatically not very rewarding. The character actors have the best of it.
w Arthur Wimperis, Jan Lustig *novel* Margaret Irwin *d* George Sidney *m* Charles Rosher *m* Miklos Rozsa *ad* Cedric Gibbons, Urie McCleary
☆ Jean Simmons, Stewart Granger, Charles Laughton, Kay Walsh, Deborah Kerr, Guy Rolfe, Kathleen Byron, Cecil Kellaway, Robert Arthur, Leo G. Carroll, Elaine Stewart, Dawn Addams, Rex Thompson
§ art direction

Young Billy Young
US 1969 89m DeLuxe
UA/Talbot-Youngstein (Max Youngstein)
A young Western gunman is helped out of scrapes by a mysterious stranger bent on revenge.
Good-looking but rather ineffective Western which throws away good production values.
wd Burt Kennedy *novel* Who Rides with Wyatt by Will Henry *ph* Harry Stradling Jnr *m* Shelly Manne
☆ Robert Mitchum, Angie Dickinson, Robert Walker Jnr, David Carradine, John Anderson, Paul Fix

Young Cassidy *
GB 1964 110m Technicolor
MGM/Sextant (Robert D. Graff, Robert Emmett Ginna)
A romantic view of the early Dublin life of writer Sean O'Casey.
Ambling, unconvincing but generally interesting picture of a past time.
w John Whiting, from the writings of Sean O'Casey *d* Jack Cardiff, John Ford *ph* Ted Scaife *m* Sean O'Riada
☆ Rod Taylor, Maggie Smith, Edith Evans, Flora Robson, Michael Redgrave, Julie Christie, Jack MacGowran, Sian Phillips, T. P. McKenna

Young Dillinger
US 1964 102m bw
Alfred Zimbalist
An embittered young convict becomes Public Enemy Number One.
Fantasized forgettable biopic with violent moments.
w Arthur Hoerl, Don Zimbalist *d* Terry Morse *ph* Stanley Cortez *m* Shorty Rogers
☆ Nick Adams, John Ashley, Robert Conrad, Mary Ann Mobley, Victor Buono, John Hoyt, Reed Hadley

The Young Doctors *
US 1961 102m bw
UA/Drexel/Stuart Millar/Laurence Turman
Old Dr Pearson resents his modern young assistant and almost causes a tragedy.
Routine medical melo of the Kildare/Gillespie kind, given a Grade A production and cast.
w Joseph Hayes *novel* The Final Diagnosis by Arthur Hailey *d* Phil Karlson *ph* Arthur J. Ornitz *m* Elmer Bernstein
☆ Fredric March, Ben Gazzara, Dick Clark, Eddie Albert, Ina Balin, Aline MacMahon, Edward Andrews, Arthur Hill, George Segal, Rosemary Murphy

Young Doctors in Love
US 1982 95m Metrocolor
TCF/ABC (Jerry Bruckheimer)
Goings-on in a modern hospital.
Spoof soap opera in the wake of Airplane but seeming more like a flat edition of Carry On.
w Michael Elias, Rich Eustis *d* Garry Marshall *ph* Don Peterman *m* Maurice Jarre
☆ Michael McKean, Sean Young, Harry Dean Stanton, Patrick Macnee, Hector Elizondo, Dabney Coleman

Young Eagles *
US 1930 71m bw
Paramount
The adventures of American aviators in World War 1.
Spirited early sound actioner.
w William McNutt, Grover Jones *d* William Wellman *ph* Archie Stout
☆ Charles Rogers, Jean Arthur, Paul Lukas, Stuart Erwin, Virginia Bruce, James Finlayson
'Pint-sized version of Wings. Comedy and production almost square silly plot.' – *Variety*

Young Einstein *
Australia 1988 91m colour
Warner/Serious Productions (Yahoo Serious, Warwick Ross, David Roach)
Einstein discovers the theory of relativity, falls in love with Marie Curie, and then invents the surfboard, the electric guitar and rock 'n' roll.
A smash-hit in its native land, it is a ramshackle, slapstick comedy that, relatively speaking, does not travel well.
w Yahoo Serious, David Roach *d* Yahoo Serious *ph* Jeff Darling *m* William Motzing, Martin Armiger, Tommy Tycho *ad* Steve Marr, Laurie Faen, Colin Gibson, Ron Highfield *ed* Yahoo Serious
☆ Yahoo Serious, Odile Le Clezio, John Howard, Peewee Wilson, Su Cruikshank
'A film which manages to be innocuous and appalling at the same time.' – *MFB*

Young Frankenstein ***
US 1974 108m bw
TCF/Gruskoff/Venture/Jouer/Crossbow (Michael Gruskoff)
Young Frederick Frankenstein, a brain surgeon, goes back to Transylvania and pores over his grandfather's notebooks.
The most successful of Mel Brooks's parodies, Mad Magazine style; the gleamingly reminiscent photography is the best of it, the script being far from consistently funny, but there are splendid moments.
w Gene Wilder, Mel Brooks *d* Mel Brooks *ph* Gerald Hirschfeld *m* John Morris *ad* Dale Hennesy
☆ Gene Wilder, Marty Feldman, Madeline Kahn, Peter Boyle, Cloris Leachman, Kenneth Mars, Gene Hackman, Richard Haydn
'Like a sketch from the old Sid Caesar show, for which Brooks wrote, spun out ten times as long. Ten times too long. Brooks is a sprinter, and there aren't enough good sprints here.' – *Stanley Kauffmann*
§ script

Young Giants
US 1983 97m DeLuxe Panavision
Entertainment Enterprises (Tom Moyer, Megan Moyer)
A San Diego priest helps a boys' home by re-organizing a football team so that an old priest can die happy.
Shades of Going My Way, but somewhat ineptly done, with a guest appearance from Pele as deus ex machina.
w Tom Moyer, Terrill Tannen, Mike Lammers *d* Terrill Tannen *ph* Raoul Lomas *m* Rick Patterson *ad* Daniel R. Webster *ed* Denine Rowan, Marion W. Cronin, Daniel Gross
☆ Peter Fox, John Huston, Lisa Wills, F. William Parker, Severn Darden
'At least it has the courage of its throwback convictions.' – *Kim Newman, MFB*

The Young Girls of Rochefort
France 1967 126m Eastmancolor Franscope
Parc Film/Madeleine/Seven Arts (Mag Bodard, Gilbert de Goldschmidt)
original title: *Les Demoiselles de Rochefort*
Two country girls join a travelling dancing troupe, and find love on the day of the fair.
Flat, empty tribute to the Hollywood musical, which never inspires despite the presence of one of its greatest stars.
wd Jacques Demy *ph* Ghislain Cloquet *m* Michel Legrand
☆ Catherine Deneuve, Françoise Dorléac, George Chakiris, Gene Kelly, Danielle Darrieux, Grover Dale, Michel Piccoli
§ Michel Legrand

Young Guns
US 1988 107m DeLuxe
Vestron/Morgan Creek Productions (Joe Roth, Christopher Cain)
Billy Bonney joins a group of young ranch hands and they are quickly transformed into Billy the Kid and a gang of outlaws.
Teenage Western, with a background authenticity that does not extend to the characterization.
w John Fusco *d* Christopher Cain *ph* Dean Semler *m* Anthony Marinelli, Brian Banks *pd* Jane Musky *ed* Jack Hofstra
☆ Emilio Estevez, Kiefer Sutherland, Lou Diamond Phillips, Charlie Sheen, Dermot Mulroney, Casey Siemaszko, Terence Stamp, Jack Palance, Patrick Wayne

Young Guns II
US 1990 103m DeLuxe
Fox/Morgan Creek (Paul Schiff, Irby Smith)
Billy the Kid and his gang, on the run from justice, face death as they begin to squabble among themselves.
Continuing from where the first film ended, it provides a similar modern treatment of its youthful anti-heroes.
w John Fusco *d* Geoff Murphy *ph* Dean Semler *m* Alan Silvestri *m/ly* Jon Bon Jovi *pd* Gene Rudolph *ad* Christa Munro *ed* Bruce Green
☆ Emilio Estevez, Kiefer Sutherland, Lou Diamond Phillips, Christian Slater, William Petersen, Alan Ruck, R. D. Call, James Coburn, Balthazar Getty, Jack Kehoe
§ song 'Blaze of Glory' (*m/l* Jon Bon Jovi)

Young Guns of Texas
US 1962 78m DeLuxe Cinemascope
TCF (Maury Dexter)
An Easterner, accompanied by two cowboys and a runaway heiress, rides into Indian territory in search of stolen gold.
Dull, routine Western featuring the untalented offspring of the famous.
w Henry Cross *d* Maury Dexter *ph* John Nickolaus Jnr *m* Paul Sawtell, Bert Shefter *ed* Jodie Copelan, Richard Einfeld
☆ James Mitchum, Alana Ladd, Jody McCrea, Chill Wills, Gary Conway, Barbara Mansell, Robert Lowery

Young Ideas
US 1943 75m bw
MGM (Robert Sisk)
The proposed marriage of two academics is interrupted by the protests of their children.
Predictable light concoction with practised players.
w Ian McLellan Hunter, Bill Noble *d* Jules Dassin
☆ Mary Astor, Herbert Marshall, Susan Peters, Elliott Reid, Richard Carlson, Allyn Joslyn

The Young in Heart ***
US 1938 91m bw
David O. Selznick
A family of charming confidence tricksters move in on a rich old lady but she brings out the best in them.
Delightful, roguish romantic comedy, perfectly cast and pacily handled.
w Paul Osborn, Charles Bennett *novel* The Gay Banditti by I. A. R. Wylie *d* Richard Wallace *ph* Leon Shamroy *m* Franz Waxman
☆ Douglas Fairbanks Jnr, Janet Gaynor, Roland Young, Billie Burke, Minnie Dupree, Paulette Goddard, Richard Carlson, Henry Stephenson
'Sentimental drama, vastly touching and entertaining ... has everything to ensure box office success.' – *Variety*
'It comes as a gentle breeze in the hurricane of hurly burly comedies that have hurtled across the screen of late.' – *Motion Picture Herald*
§ Leon Shamroy; Franz Waxman

The Young Invaders: see *Darby's Rangers*

The Young Land
US 1957 89m Technicolor
Columbia/C. V. Whitney (Patrick Ford)
A young sheriff arrests a gunman and after the trial has to save him from lynching.
Rather stiff attempt at a youth Western.
w Norman Shannon Hall *d* Ted Tetzlaff *ph* Winton C. Hoch, Henry Sharp *m* Dimitri Tiomkin

---

☆ Dan O'Herlihy, Patrick Wayne, Yvonne Craig, Dennis Hopper
♫ song 'Strange Are the Ways of Love' (mDimitri Tiomkin, lyNed Washington)

The Young Lions **
US   1958   167m   bw   Cinemascope
TCF (Al Lichtman)
🔲 🔲 ∿ ∩

World War II adventures of two Americans and a German skiing instructor.
Three strands are loosely interwoven into a would-be modern epic; the result is well mounted and generally absorbing but uneven and decidedly overlong.
w Edward Anhalt *novel* Irwin Shaw d Edward Dmytryk ph Joe MacDonald m Hugo Friedhofer
☆ Marlon Brando, Montgomery Clift, Dean Martin, Hope Lange, Barbara Rush, May Britt, Maximilian Schell, Lee Van Cleef
'Episodic and overproduced, like a wartime *Grand Hotel*.' – *Pauline Kael, 70s*
♒ Joe MacDonald; Hugo Friedhofer

The Young Lovers *
GB   1954   96m   bw
GFD/Group Films (Anthony Havelock-Allan)
US title: Chance Meeting

A US Embassy man in London falls in love with the daughter of an Iron Curtain minister.
Romeo and Juliet, cold war style, quite nicely put together with a thriller climax.
w Robin Estridge *story* George Tabori
d Anthony Asquith ph Jack Asher
m Tchaikovsky
☆ Odile Versois, David Knight, David Kossoff, Joseph Tomelty, Paul Carpenter, Theodore Bikel, Jill Adams
🎬 David Kossoff (best newcomer); Robin Estridge; George Tabori

Young Man of Music: see *Young Man with a Horn*

'Put down your trumpet, jazz man – I'm in the mood for love'

Young Man with a Horn *
US   1950   112m   bw
Warner (Jerry Wald)
🔲 ∿
GB title: Young Man of Music

The professional and romantic tribulations of a trumpet player.
Overwrought character melodrama based on the life of Bix Beiderbecke; quite absorbing though occasionally risible.
w Carl Foreman, Edmund H. North
novel Dorothy Baker d Michael Curtiz ph Ted McCord m Ray Heindorf (trumpet dubbed by Harry James)
☆ Kirk Douglas, Lauren Bacall, Doris Day, Hoagy Carmichael, Juano Hernandez, Jerome Cowan, Mary Beth Hughes, Nestor Paiva

Young Man with Ideas *
US   1952   84m   bw
MGM (Gottfried Reinhardt, William H. Wright)
A small-town lawyer tries to better himself in Los Angeles.
Modestly likeable comedy which doesn't add up to much.
w Arthur Sheekman d Mitchell Leisen
ph Joseph Ruttenberg m David Rose
☆ Glenn Ford, Ruth Roman, Nina Foch, Denise Darcel, Donna Corcoran, Mary Wickes, Sheldon Leonard

Young Man's Fancy
GB   1939   77m   bw
Ealing
A young Victorian lord avoids an unsuitable match by eloping to Paris.
Rather pallid romantic comedy with likeable period detail.
w Roland Pertwee, Rodney Ackland, E. V. H. Emmett d Robert Stevenson
☆ Griffith Jones, Anna Lee, Seymour Hicks, Billy Bennett, Edward Rigby, Francis L. Sullivan

The Young Master
Hong Kong   1980   101m   colour
Golden Harvest (Leonard Ho)
🔲
original title: Shidi Chuma
The adventures of a student in a school for martial arts, searching for a friend who betrayed their master.
An episodic movie with the emphasis on comedy, one of Chan's earliest movies as actor-director in which he is still developing his screen persona.
w Lau Tin Chee, Tung Lu, Edward Tang d Jackie Chan ph Cheng Hui-Jan, Tsai Hua m Ryudo Uzaki, Akira Inoue, Gustav Holst ed Peter Cheung
☆ Jackie Chan, Yuen Biao, Wei Pai, Lily Li, Whong In Sik, Shek Kin (aka Shieh Kien), Tiang Feng

'The Story Of Abraham Lincoln That Has Never Been Told!'

Young Mr Lincoln ***
US   1939   100m   bw
TCF (Kenneth MacGowan)
🔲 ⊙
Abraham Lincoln as a young country lawyer stops a lynching and proves a young man innocent of murder.
Splendid performances and period atmosphere are rather nipped in the bud by second-feature courtroom twists, but this is a marvellous old-fashioned entertainment with its heart in the right place.
w Lamar Trotti d John Ford ph Bert Glennon m Alfred Newman
☆ Henry Fonda, Alice Brady, Marjorie Weaver, Arleen Whelan, Eddie Collins, Richard Cromwell, Donald Meek, Eddie Quillan, Spencer Charters
'A dignified saga of early Lincolniana, paced rather slowly … lack of romance interest is one of the prime factors which deter the film from interpreting itself into big box office.' – *Variety*
'Its simple good faith and understanding are an expression of the country's best life that says as much as forty epics.' – *Otis Ferguson*
'Period details are lovingly sketched in – a log splitting contest, a tug of war, a tar barrel rolling match…' – *Charles Higham*
'Its source is a womb of popular and national spirit. This could account for its unity, its artistry, its genuine beauty.' – *Sergei Eisenstein*
'A film which indisputably has the right to be called Americana.' – *New York Times*
'In spite of the excitements of a murder, a near-lynching and a crackerjack trial, it remains a character study.' – *New York Sun*
'One of John Ford's most memorable films.' – *Pauline Kael, 70s*
♒ Lamar Trotti

The Young Mr Pitt *
GB   1942   118m   bw
TCF (Edward Black)
Britain's youngest prime minister quells the threat of invasion by Napoleon.
Shapeless and overlong but generally diverting historical pastiche timed as wartime propaganda against Hitler.
w Frank Launder, Sidney Gilliat d Carol Reed ph Frederick A. Young m Charles Williams ad Vetchinsky
☆ Robert Donat, Robert Morley, Phyllis Calvert, John Mills, Raymond Lovell, Max Adrian, Felix Aylmer, Albert Lieven

The Young Ones *
👪 GB   1961   108m   Technicolor   Cinemascope
ABP (Kenneth Harper)
🔲
US title: Wonderful to be Young
The son of a tycoon starts a youth club and puts on a musical to raise funds.
A shopworn idea is the springboard for a brave try in a field where Britain was presumed to have failed; despite the enthusiasm with which it was greeted at the time, it has dated badly.
w Peter Myers, Ronald Cass d Sidney J. Furie ph Douglas Slocombe m Stanley Black
☆ Cliff Richard, Robert Morley, Carole Grey, Richard O'Sullivan, Melvyn Hayes, Gerald Harper, Robertson Hare

Young People
US   1940   78m   bw
TCF (Harry Joe Brown)
Vaudevillians retire to give their daughter a proper upbringing, but find that showbiz is in her blood.
Pleasant but unremarkable comedy-drama with music, marking the end of its star's association with the studio.
w Edwin Blum, Don Ettlinger d Allan Dwan ph Edward Cronjager md Alfred Newman
☆ Shirley Temple, Jack Oakie, Charlotte Greenwood, Arleen Whelan, George Montgomery, Kathleen Howard, Mae Marsh

The Young Philadelphians *
US   1959   136m   bw
Warner (producer not credited)
GB title: The City Jungle
A forceful young lawyer pushes his way to the top of the snobbish Philadelphia heap despite threats to expose his illegitimacy.
Novel on film, gleamingly done and acted with assurance.
w James Gunn *novel* The Philadelphian by Richard Powell d Vincent Sherman ph Harry Stradling m Ernest Gold
☆ Paul Newman, Barbara Rush, Alexis Smith, Brian Keith, Billie Burke, John Williams, Otto Kruger, Diane Brewster, Robert Vaughn, Paul Picerni, Robert Douglas
♒ Harry Stradling; Robert Vaughn

'Nothing's More Deadly Than A Poisoned Mind'

The Young Poisoner's Handbook *
GB/Germany   1995   106m   Metrocolor
Electric/Mass/Kinowelt/Haut et Court (Sam Taylor)
🔲 🔲 ∩
A boy obsessed with the power of poisons tries them out on his stepmother and uncle, and is sent to a hospital for the criminally insane, where he is eventually declared cured and released, whereupon he begins poisoning people once more.
A gruesome little tale, approached in a style of black comedy peopled by caricatures; like its hero's concoctions, the result is not always palatable, despite the considerable skills on show.
w Jeff Rawle, Benjamin Ross d Benjamin Ross ph Herbert Taczanowski m Robert Lane, Frankie Strobel pd Maria Djorkovic ed Anne Sopel
☆ Hugh O'Conor, Anthony Sher, Ruth Sheen, Roger Lloyd Pack, Charlotte Coleman, Paul Stacey, Samantha Edmonds
'Will appeal to younger audiences internationally who like their entertainment rude and impudent.' – *Variety*
† The film was based on the life of Graham Young, known as 'The St Albans Poisoner', who was sent to Broadmoor in 1962 at the age of 14 for giving poison to his father, sister and a friend. He was released as 'no longer a danger' in 1971, when he killed two people with poison and damaged six more. He died in prison in 1990.

The Young Rebel: see *Cervantes*

The Young Savages *
US   1961   103m   bw
UA/Contemporary (Pat Duggan)
An assistant DA prosecutes three hoodlums for murder but begins to feel that one is not guilty.
Tough, realistic melodrama of the New York slums, with roughhouse climaxes and a political conscience.
w Edward Anhalt, J. P. Miller *novel* A Matter of Conviction by Evan Hunter d John Frankenheimer ph Lionel Lindon m David Amram
☆ Burt Lancaster, Shelley Winters, John Davis Chandler, Dina Merrill, Edward Andrews, Telly Savalas

Young Scarface: see *Brighton Rock*

Young Sherlock Holmes
👪 US   1985   109m   Technicolor
Paramount/Amblin (Mark Johnson)
🔲 🔲 ∿
GB title: Young Sherlock Holmes and the Pyramid of Fear
Holmes and Watson meet as teenage students, and trace some mysterious murders to an eastern cult.
More expensive gimmickry with acres of tedium in between the technical highlights. Nothing for Holmes buffs.
w Chris Columbus d Barry Levinson ph Stephen Goldblatt m Bruce Broughton pd Norman Reynolds ed Stu Linder

☆ Nicholas Rowe, Alan Cox, Sophie Ward, Anthony Higgins, Freddie Jones, Nigel Stock
'Another Steven Spielberg version of those lamps made from driftwood and coffee tables from redwood burl. It's not art but they all serve their purpose and sell by millions.' – *Variety*
(This one was a box-office disappointment.)
♒ visual effects

Young Soul Rebels *
GB   1991   105m   colour
BFI/Film Four/Sankofa/La Sept/Kinowelt/Iberoamericana (Nadine Marsh-Edwards)
🔲 ∩
In the mid-1970s, two pirate radio disc jockeys specializing in soul music solve the murder of a friend.
Examining black and gay culture in Britain, the movie tries to pack in too much, losing focus as a result.
w Paul Hallam, Derrick Saldaan McClintock, Isaac Julien d Isaac Julien ph Nina Kellgren m Simon Boswell pd Derek Brown ed John Wilson
☆ Valentine Nonyela, Mo Sesay, Dorian Healy, Frances Barber, Sophie Okonedo, Jason Durr, Gary McDonald, Debra Gillet
'It ultimately suffers from trying to say too many things too fast to too many people, the penalty, one suspects, from working in a British film industry where your first film so easily doubles up as your last.' – *Empire*

The Young Stranger *
US   1957   84m   bw
RKO (Stuart Millar)
🔲 🔲
The 16-year-old son of a film executive gets into trouble with the police.
Reasonably stimulating film of a TV play about the kind of causeless rebel who quickly became a cliché.
w Robert Dozier d John Frankenheimer ph Robert Planck m Leonard Rosenman
☆ James MacArthur, Kim Hunter, James Daly, James Gregory, Whit Bissell

Young Tom Edison *
US   1940   82m   bw
MGM (John Considine Jnr)
🔲 ⊙
First of a two-parter (see *Edison the Man*) tracing Edison's first experiments.
Reasonably factual and absorbing junior biopic.
w Bradbury Foote, Dore Schary, Hugo Butler d Norman Taurog ph Sidney Wagner m Edward Ward
☆ Mickey Rooney, Eugene Pallette, George Bancroft, Fay Bainter, Virginia Weidler, Victor Kilian, Lloyd Corrigan
'A picture for all of the people in all of the places.' – *Motion Picture Herald*

Young Warriors
US   1983   103m   colour
Cannon
🔲
After the sister of one of them dies after being raped, high-school graduates set themselves up as vigilantes.
Dangerous rubbish.
w Lawrence D. Foldes, Russell W. Colgin d Lawrence D. Foldes ph Mac Ahlberg m Rob Walsh
☆ Ernest Borgnine, Richard Roundtree, Lynda Day George, James Van Patten, Anne Lockhart, Tom Reilly, Dick Shawn
'A lurid mishmash.' – *Jo Imeson, MFB*

Young Werther: see *Le Jeune Werther*

The Young Widow
US   1946   100m   bw
UA/Hunt Stromberg
The widow of a World War II flyer returns to the Virginia farm where they had spent happy hours.
Glum sudser with talent all at sea.
w Richard Macaulay, Margaret Buell Wilder *novel* Clarissa Fairchild Cushman d Edwin L. Marin ph Lee Garmes m Carmen Dragon pd Nicolai Remisoff
☆ Jane Russell, Louis Hayward, Faith Domergue, Marie Wilson, Kent Taylor, Penny Singleton, Connie Gilchrist, Cora Witherspoon

---

Young, Willing and Eager: see *Rag Doll*

Young Winston **
♀♀   GB   1972   157m   Eastmancolor
Panavision
Columbia/Open Road/Hugh French (Carl Foreman)
▦ ▤
The adventurous life of Winston Churchill up to his becoming an MP.
Generally engaging if lumpy film which switches too frequently from action to family drama to politics to character study and is not helped by irritating directorial tricks.
w Carl Foreman *book* My Early Life by Winston Churchill *d* Richard Attenborough *ph* Gerry Turpin *m* Alfred Ralston *pd* Don Ashton, Geoffrey Drake
☆ *Simon Ward*, Robert Shaw, Anne Bancroft, Jack Hawkins, Ian Holm, *Anthony Hopkins*, John Mills, Patrick Magee, Edward Woodward
♂ Carl Foreman

Young Wives' Tale
GB   1951   79m   bw
ABPC
A playwright and his slaphappy wife share a house with a super-efficient couple.
Very mild but palatable comedy set 'at the wrong end of St John's Wood'.
w Anne Burnaby *play* Ronald Jeans *d* Henry Cass
☆ Joan Greenwood, Nigel Patrick, Derek Farr, Guy Middleton, Athene Seyler, Helen Cherry, Audrey Hepburn, Irene Handl

Young Woodley
GB   1929   79m   bw
BIP
A schoolboy falls in love with his teacher's wife.
Modest early talkie version of a play thought mildly shocking at the time.
w John Van Druten, Victor Kendall *play* John Van Druten *d* Thomas Bentley *ph* Claude Friese-Greene
☆ Madeleine Carroll, Frank Lawton, Sam Livesey, Gerald Rawlinson, Billy Milton
† A silent version made earlier in the same year, with Marjorie Hume and Robin Irvine, was never released.

Youngblood
US   1986   109m   Metrocolor
United Artists/Guber-Peters (Peter Bart, Patrick Wells)
▦ ▤ ◎
Romances of a young hockey star, for those interested; it turned out that there weren't many.
wd Peter Markle *story* Peter Markle, Patrick Wells *ph* Mark Irwin *m* William Orbit *ad* Alicia Keywan *ed* Stephen E. Rivkin, Jack Hofstra
☆ Rob Lowe, Cynthia Gibb, Patrick Swayze, Ed Lauter, Jim Youngs

Youngblood Hawke
US   1964   137m   bw
Warner (Delmer Daves)
A Kentucky truck driver becomes a successful novelist and is spoiled by New York success.
Absurdly archetypal soap opera from a bestseller, spilling over with every imaginable cliché; some of its excesses are glossily entertaining.
wd Delmer Daves *novel* Herman Wouk *ph* Charles Lawton *m* Max Steiner
☆ James Franciscus, Genevieve Page, Suzanne Pleshette, Eva Gabor, *Mary Astor*, Lee Bowman, Edward Andrews, John Emery, Don Porter

Younger & Younger *
Germany/France/Canada   1994   99m   colour
Pelemele/Kushner-Locke/Younger (Eleanore Adlon)
▦ ▤ ◎
A German immigrant, who runs a failing business in Hollywood, is haunted by the memory of his much more capable wife, who died as a result of his infidelity.
A middling comedy of a hapless man forced out of his fantasy world by guilt.
w Percy Adlon, Felix O. Adlon *wd* Percy Adlon *ph* Bernd Heinl *m* Hans Zimmer *pd* Steven Legler *ed* Suzanne Fenn
☆ Donald Sutherland, Lolita Davidovich, Brendan Fraser, Sally Kellerman, Julie Delpy, Linda Hunt

The Younger Brothers
US   1949   76m   Technicolor
Warner (Saul Elkins)
A whitewashed version of the career of the legendary outlaws, who wind up expecting pardons; otherwise routine sagebrush stuff.
w Edna Anhalt *d* Edwin L. Marin *ph* William Snyder
☆ Wayne Morris, Janis Paige, Bruce Bennett, Geraldine Brooks, Robert Hutton, Alan Hale, Fred Clark

The Youngest Profession
US   1943   82m   bw
MGM (B. F. Ziedman)
Teenage autograph hounds cause trouble at the MGM studio.
Innocuous comedy with guest stars.
w George Oppenheimer, Charles Lederer, Leonard Spigelgass *book* Lillian Day *d* Edward Buzzell *ph* Charles Lawton *m* David Snell
☆ Virginia Weidler, Jean Porter, Edward Arnold, John Carroll, Agnes Moorehead, Greer Garson, William Powell, Lana Turner, Walter Pidgeon, Robert Taylor

Your Beating Heart
France   1991   100m   colour
Artifical Eye/Hachette Première/FR3/UGC/Avril (René Cleitman)
A middle-aged married actress begins an affair with a man she meets on the Paris Métro.
Glum story of an adulterous relationship that no one seems to enjoy, least of all an audience.
wd François Dupeyron *ph* Yves Angelo *ad* Carlos Conti *ed* Françoise Collin
☆ Dominique Faysse, Thierry Fortineau, Jean-Marie Winling, Steve Kalfa, Daniel Laloux, Christophe Pichon
'The miasma of doom lies over this gloomy film, remarkable for the unattractiveness of its main characters.' – *George Perry, Sunday Times*

'A Modern Immorality Tale.'
Your Friends & Neighbors *
US   1998   99m   DeLuxe
Polygram/Propaganda/Fleece (Steve Golin, Jason Patric)
▦ ▤ ◎ ◎
Three couples, whose love lives are unsatisfactory, seek partners elsewhere.
A misogynistic comedy of sexual manners, with smart dialogue compensating for the somewhat theatrical situations.
wd Neil LaBute *ph* Nancy Schreiber *m* Metallica, Apocalyptica *pd* Charles Breen *ed* Joel Plotch
☆ Amy Brenneman, Aaron Eckhart, Catherine Keener, Nastassja Kinski, Jason Patric, Ben Stiller
'Callow, nasty-minded movie.' – *Peter Matthews, Sight and Sound*

Your Money Or Your Wife
GB   1960   91m   bw
Rank/Alliance (Norman Williams)
A couple with financial problems resort to letting rooms to lodgers, who turn out to be penniless.
Creaking farce, done without subtlety and resorting to crude slapstick in an attempt to amuse.
w Ronald Jeans *d* Anthony Simmons *ph* Brendan J. Stafford *m* Philip Green *ad* Tony Inglis *ed* Bernard Gribble
☆ Donald Sinden, Peggy Cummins, Richard Wattis, Peter Reynolds, Georgina Cookson, Gladys Boot, Barbara Steele, Betty Baskcomb, Olive Sloane, Ian Fleming

Your Past Is Showing: see *The Naked Truth*

Your Three Minutes Are Up *
US   1973   92m   DeLuxe
Jerry Gershwin
An irresponsible, smooth-talking, penniless con man takes his respectable friend out on one last spree.
Dispiriting comedy of contrasting attitudes to life which plunges into bathos at the end.
w James Dixon *d* Douglas N. Schwartz *ph* Stephen M. Katz *m* Perry Botkin Jnr *ed* Aaron Stell
☆ Beau Bridges, Ron Leibman, Janet Margolin, Kathleen Freeman, David Ketchum, Stu Nisbet, Read Morgan

Your Witness *
GB   1950   100m   bw
Warner/Coronado (Joan Harrison)
US title: *Eye Witness*
An American lawyer comes to an English village to defend a war buddy on a murder charge.
Interesting but ineffective blend of comedy and courtroom procedure intended to contrast English and American ways.
w Hugo Butler, Ian Hunter, William Douglas Home *d* Robert Montgomery *ph* Gerald Gibbs *m* Malcolm Arnold
☆ Robert Montgomery, Leslie Banks, Patricia Cutts, Felix Aylmer, Andrew Cruickshank, Harcourt Williams, Jenny Laird, Michael Ripper

You're a Big Boy Now *
US   1967   96m   Eastmancolor
Warner Seven Arts (William Fadiman)
▤
A young assistant librarian discovers girls.
Freewheeling semi-surrealist comedy with exhilarating moments and the inevitable letdowns associated with this kind of campy high style.
wd Francis Ford Coppola *novel* David Benedictus *ph* Andy Laszlo *m* Bob Prince
☆ Peter Kastner, Elizabeth Hartman, Geraldine Page, Julie Harris, Rip Torn, Tony Bill, Karen Black, Michael Dunn
'A half-kooky, half-sweetly-innocent comedy … which is wonderfully photogenic from a young director's point of view.' – *Judith Crist*
♂ Geraldine Page

You're a Lucky Fellow, Mr Smith
US   1943   63m   bw
Edward Lilley/Universal
A girl must marry quickly in order to secure her inheritance.
Very light musical support.
w Lawrence Riley, Ben Barzman, Louis Lantz *d* Felix Feist
☆ Allan Jones, Evelyn Ankers, Billie Burke, David Bruce, Patsy O'Connor, Stanley Clements

You're a Sweetheart
US   1937   96m   bw
Universal (B. G. de Sylva)
A Broadway star suffers from her press agent's bright ideas.
Muffed musical with all concerned ill at ease with below par material.
w Monte Brice, Charles Grayson *d* David Butler *ph* George Robinson *md* Charles Previn *ad* Jack Otterson *songs* various
☆ Alice Faye, George Murphy, Ken Murray, William Gargan, Frances Hunt, Frank Jenks, Andy Devine, Charles Winninger, Donald Meek
'Just what the doctor ordered for the holiday first runs … enough entertainers for two shows.' – *Variety*

You're Darn Tootin' ***
♀♀   US   1929   20m   bw   silent
Hal Roach
Two musicians get into trouble at work, in their digs and in the street.
Star comedy which though early in their teaming shows Stan and Ollie at their best in a salt shaker routine and in a surreal pants-ripping contest.
w H. M. Walker *d* Edgar Kennedy *ph* Floyd Jackman *ed* Richard Currier
☆ Stan Laurel, Oliver Hardy, Agnes Steele, Otto Lederer

You're Dead…
US/Germany   1999   97m   colour
Entertainment/Atlantic Streamkine (Marco Weber)
An undercover policewoman explains why she is the only survivor of a nine-day siege that resulted after a London bank robbery went wrong.
Frenetic crime caper notable for hammy acting and fussy direction.
wd Andy Hurst *ph* Wedigo von Schultzendorff *m* Robert Folk *pd* Frank Bollinger *ed* Andrew Starke
☆ John Hurt, Claire Skinner, Rhys Ifans, David Schneider, Barbara Flynn, John Benfield, Roger Ashton-Griffiths, Patrick Field, Badi Uzzaman
'A thoroughly stupid piece of work, slightly redeemed by a maniacal devotion to plot twists.' – *Edward Porter, Sunday Times*

You're in the Army Now: see *O.H.M.S. (1936)*

You're in the Army Now **
♀♀   US   1941   79m   bw
Warner (Ben Stoloff)
Two incompetent vacuum cleaner salesmen accidentally join the army.
An excellent vehicle for two star comedians who have often suffered from poor material, with a silent-comedy-style climax involving a house on wheels.
w Paul Gerard Smith, George Beatty *d* Lewis Seiler *ph* James Van Trees *m* Howard Jackson
☆ Jimmy Durante, Phil Silvers, Donald MacBride, Jane Wyman, Regis Toomey

You're in the Navy Now *
US   1951   93m   bw
TCF (Fred Kohlmar)
aka: *USS Teakettle*
Trouble results when the navy instals steam turbines in an experimental patrol craft.
Amusing service comedy with good script touches and capable performances.
w Richard Murphy *d* Henry Hathaway *ph* Joe MacDonald *m* Cyril Mockridge
☆ Gary Cooper, Millard Mitchell, Jane Greer, Eddie Albert, John McIntire, Ray Collins, Harry von Zell, Jack Webb, Richard Erdman

You're My Everything *
US   1949   94m   Technicolor
TCF (Lamar Trotti)
A Boston socialite marries a hoofer and becomes a movie star.
Pleasant twenties comedy with good period detail and lively performances.
w Lamar Trotti, Will Hays Jnr *d* Walter Lang *ph* Arthur E. Arling *m* Alfred Newman
☆ Anne Baxter, Dan Dailey, Anne Revere, Stanley Ridges, Shari Robinson, Henry O'Neill, Selena Royle, Alan Mowbray, Buster Keaton

You're Never Too Young
US   1955   103m   Technicolor   Vistavision
Paramount/Hal B. Wallis (Paul Jones)
An apprentice barber on the run from a murderer poses as a 12-year-old child to travel half fare.
Unattractive revamping of The Major and the Minor (qv), with the star team trying too obviously to make bricks with inferior straw.
w Sidney Sheldon *d* Norman Taurog *ph* Daniel L. Fapp *m* Arthur Schwartz
☆ Dean Martin, Jerry Lewis, Diana Lynn, Nina Foch, Raymond Burr, Veda Ann Borg

You're Only Young Once: see *The Hardy Family*

You're Only Young Twice
GB   1952   81m   bw
Group Three (Terry Bishop)
The puritanical head of a Scottish university is laid low by circumstance and his own folly.
Misfire eccentric comedy which deserves marks for trying but fails to amuse.
w Reginald Beckwith, Lindsay Galloway, Terry Bishop *play* What Say They by James Bridie *d* Terry Bishop *ph* Jo Jago
☆ Duncan Macrae, Charles Hawtrey, Joseph Tomelty, Patrick Barr, Diane Hart, Robert Urquhart

You're Telling Me *
US   1934   66m   bw
Paramount
A small-town inventor meets a princess and makes the social grade.
Meaninglessly-titled star vehicle which is often defiantly unamusing but does include the famous golf routine.
w Walter de Leon, Paul M. Jones *story* Julian Street *d* Erle C. Kenton *ph* Alfred Gilks *m* Arthur Johnston
☆ W. C. Fields, Larry 'Buster' Crabbe, Joan Marsh, Adrienne Ames, Louise Carter
'The kind of comedy that Chaplin used to do in two reels, but stretched out like Carnera's suspenders to run an even six.' – *Variety*

Yours Mine and Ours *
US   1968   111m   Technicolor
UA/Desilu/Walden (Robert F. Blumofe)
▤
[?tb[?A widower with nine children marries a widow with eight, and they settle in an old San Francisco house.

Generally appealing comedy, based on fact and well suited to its stars.

w Mel Shavelson, Mort Lachman d Mel Shavelson ph Charles Wheeler m Fred Karlin

☆ Lucille Ball, Henry Fonda, Van Johnson

Youth Runs Wild

US 1944 67m bw

RKO (Val Lewton)

Indifferent parents are responsible for the problems of teenagers.

Dreary little sermon from the unit which produced semi-classic horrors.

w John Fante, Herbert Kline d Mark Robson

☆ Bonita Granville, Kent Smith, Jean Brooks, Glenn Vernon, Arthur Shields

Youth Takes a Fling

US 1938 77m bw

Universal (Joe Pasternak)

A reluctant truck driver is chased by a department store salesgirl.

Mildly scatty comedy which failed to ring the bell.

w Myles Connolly d Archie Mayo

☆ Joel McCrea, Andrea Leeds, Frank Jenks, Dorothea Kent, Isabel Jeans, Virginia Grey, Grant Mitchell, Willie Best

'Good standard entertainment with many light and diverting passages.' – *Variety*

You've Got Mail *

US 1998 119m Technicolor

Warner (Nora Ephron, Lauren Shuler Donner)

🔲 🟰 ⊚ ⌒

The owner of a small New York bookshop unknowingly conducts a love affair by e-mail with the heir to a large bookshop chain that is putting her out of business.

Almost a sequel to Sleepless in Seattle, this provides the same stars and much the same pleasures, for those sweet on romance.

w Nora Ephron, Delia Ephron play *Parfumerie* by Miklos Laszlo screenplay *The Shop around the Corner* by Samson Raphaelson d Nora Ephron ph John Lindley m George Fenton pd Dan Davis ed Richard Marks

☆ Tom Hanks, Meg Ryan, Parker Posey, Greg Kinnear, Jean Stapleton, Steve Zahn, David Chappelle, Dabney Coleman, John Randolph, Heather Burns

'This winning romantic comedy and great date movie will be propelled to hefty B.O. by its alluring, high-powered stars.' – *Lael Loewenstein, Variety*

† This is the third version of the story, which, after Ernst Lubitsch's 1940 film *The Shop around the Corner* (qv), was also used as the basis of the musical *In the Good Old Summertime* (qv) in 1949.

You've Got to Live Dangerously: see *Il Faut Vivre Dangereusement*

Yukinojo Henge: see *An Actor's Revenge*

Yvonne's Perfume: see *Le Parfum d'Yvonne*

Z

Z ****

France/Algeria 1968 125m Eastmancolor
Reggane/ONCIC/Jacques Pérrin

A leading opposition MP is murdered at a rally. The police are anxious to establish the event as an accident, but the examining magistrate proves otherwise.
An exciting police suspense drama which also recalls events under the Greek colonels and was therefore highly fashionable for a while both as entertainment and as a political roman à clef.
w Costa-Gavras, Jorge Semprun *novel* Vassili Vassilikos d Costa-Gavras ph Raoul Coutard m Mikis Theodorakis
☆ Jean-Louis Trintignant, Jacques Pérrin, Yves Montand, François Périer, Irene Papas, Charles Denner
🏅 best foreign film
🏅 best picture; director; script
🏅 Mikis Theodorakis

'It will blow your mind!'

Zabriskie Point

US 1969 112m Metrocolor Panavision
MGM/Carlo Ponti

A rebellious Los Angeles student steals a private airplane, meets an aimless girl, and finds a revelation in Death Valley …
Highly self-indulgent and unattractive fantasy about escape from the crudities of our over-civilized world. An expensive failure and an awful warning of what happens if you give an arty director carte blanche.
w Michelangelo Antonioni, Fred Gardner, Sam Shepard, Tonino Guerra, Clare Peploe d Michelangelo Antonioni ph Alfio Contini m pop songs
☆ Mark Frechette, Daria Halprin, Rod Taylor, Paul Fix
'Not even a good tourist's notebook … from the choice of Death Valley as a symbol of American civilization to the inclusion of gag signs on bar-room walls to the shots of garish billboards, this film sticks to the surface, stranded.' – *Stanley Kauffman*
'A huge, jerry built, crumbling ruin of a movie.' – *Pauline Kael, New Yorker*
'A small, sad shambles of a film that has obviously been salvaged from a larger shambles. Bad enough to give anti-Americanism a bad name.' – *Joseph Morgenstern, Newsweek*
'He has tried to make a serious movie and hasn't even achieved a beach party level of insight.' – *Roger Ebert*

'The First Electric Western.'

Zachariah

US 1971 93m Metrocolor
Cinerama/ABC (George Englund)

A youth leaves home to become a gunfighter but learns that pacificism is best.
Bizarre rock Western that is never sure whether it's satirical or serious; an audience is likely to be as confused. It was not only the first of its kind, but also the last.
w Joe Massot, The Firesign Theatre (Philip Austin, Peter Bergman, David Ossman, Philip Proctor) d George Englund ph Jorge Shahl m Jimmie Haskell pd Assheton Gorton ed Gary Griffen
☆ John Rubinstein, Pat Quinn, Don Johnson, Country Joe and the Fish, Elvin Jones, Doug Kershaw, William Challee, Dick Van Patten, The James Gang
'Nothing quite works, yet it's a relaxed and generally inoffensive movie.' – *Pauline Kael*

Zamri, Umri, Voskresni! **

USSR 1989 103m bw
Artificial Eye/Lenfilm/Trinity Bridge/First Film Creative Studio (Valentina Tarasova)
aka: *Don't Move, Die and Rise Again!*
In the 1940s in a grim Soviet town, the 12-year-old son of a prostitute is befriended by a girl of his own age.
Supposedly autobiographical film of a depressingly violent semi-criminal childhood marked by tragedy.
wd Vitaly Kanevsky ph Vladimir Bryliakov m Sergei Banevich pd Yury Pashigorev ed G. Kornilova
☆ Dinara Drukarova, Pavel Nazarov, Elena Popova
'It makes a compulsive, unpredictable, unreliable, contradictory, and often remarkably beautiful autobiographical memoir from a powerful and refreshingly undisciplined voice.' – *Philip Strick, Sight and Sound*
'One of those autobiographical first features which suddenly arrives out of nowhere and surprises us with its freshness, power and rough-hewn skill.' – *Derek Malcolm, Guardian*
† The film won the Camera d'Or for best first feature at the Cannes Film Festival in 1990.

'One woman … two men … one driven by desire. The other driven to the edge.'

Zandalee

US 1990 104m colour
Rank/Electric (William Blaycock, Eyal Rimmon)

A hard-drinking artist makes love to the wife of his increasingly unhappy childhood friend.
Appalling dialogue and a ludicrous narrative are combined with lubricious sexual encounters to create a wholly unlovely experience.
w Mari Kornhauser d Sam Pillsbury ph Walt Lloyd m Pray For Rain pd Michael Corenblith ed Michael Horton
☆ Nicolas Cage, Judge Reinhold, Erika Anderson, Viveca Lindfors, Aaron Neville, Joe Pantoliano, Steve Buscemi
'Ill-written, pretentious trash.' – *Philip French, Observer*

Zandy's Bride

US 1974 116m Technicolor Panavision
Warner (Harry Matofsky)

aka: *For Better, For Worse*
Life for a frontier family.
Dour semi-Western.
w Marc Norman *novel The Stranger* by Lillian Bos Ross d Jan Troell ph Jordan Cronenweth m Michael Franks
☆ Gene Hackman, Liv Ullmann, Eileen Heckart, Harry Dean Stanton, Joe Santos, Frank Cady

Zanzibar

US 1940 69m bw
Universal (Warren Douglas)
European powers both want the sacred skull of an African chieftain, but so does a local tribe.
Adventure nonsense patched together with stock shots, including a volcanic finale.
w Maurice Tombragel, Maurice Wright d Harold Schuster
☆ Lola Lane, James Craig, Eduardo Ciannelli, Tom Fadden, Henry Victor, Samuel S. Hinds

Zapped!

US 1982 98m CFI color
Thunder Associates

A high-school boffin discovers his own telekinetic powers, by which he is able to tear everyone's clothes off at the senior prom.
Mild adolescent smut, half-way between Porky's and the unbearable Disney comedies of the sixties.
w Bruce Rubin, Robert J. Rosenthal d Robert J. Rosenthal ph Daniel Pearl m Charles Fox
☆ Scott Baio, Willie Aames, Robert Mandan, Scatman Crothers

Zarak *

GB 1956 99m Technicolor Cinemascope
Columbia/Warwick (Phil C. Samuel)
An Afghan outlaw finally saves a British officer at the cost of his own life.
Box-office actioner, shot in Morocco with a weird cast and the help of old movie clips.
w Richard Maibaum d Terence Young ph John Wilcox, Ted Moore, Cyril Knowles m William Alwyn ad John Box *second unit* Yakima Canutt
☆ Victor Mature, Michael Wilding, Anita Ekberg, Bonar Colleano, Finlay Currie, Bernard Miles, Eunice Gayson, Peter Illing, Frederick Valk, André Morell

Zardoz

GB 1974 105m DeLuxe Panavision
TCF/John Boorman

Life in 2293, when the Earth has become wasteland and a mass of Brutals are ruled by a few Exterminators who have both memory and intelligence.
Pompous, boring fantasy for the so-called intelligentsia.
wd John Boorman ph Geoffrey Unsworth m David Munrow pd Anthony Pratt
☆ Sean Connery, Charlotte Rampling, John Alderton
'A glittering cultural trash pile … the most gloriously fatuous movie since *The Oscar*.' – *New Yorker*

Zärtlichkeit der Wölfe: see Tenderness of Wolves

Zateriannyi v Sibiri: see Lost in Siberia

Zaza

US 1938 83m bw
Paramount (Albert Lewin)
A 1904 French chanteuse is in love with a married aristocrat.
Rather flat period romantic drama with interesting credits.
w Zoe Atkins *play* Pierre Berton, Charles Simon d George Cukor ph Charles Lang *songs* Frank Loesser, Frederick Hollander
☆ Claudette Colbert, Herbert Marshall, Bert Lahr, Constance Collier, Helen Westley, Genevieve Tobin, Walter Catlett, Rex O'Malley
'Fine production with hefty woman-appeal.' – *Variety*
† The original David Belasco stage production made Mrs Leslie Carter famous. Silent film versions starred Pauline Frederick in 1915 and Gloria Swanson in 1923.

Zazie dans le Métro ***

France 1960 88m Eastmancolor
Nouvelles Editions (Irène Leriche)

A naughty little girl has a day in Paris and causes chaos.
Inventive little comedy which almost turns into a French Hellzapoppin, with everybody chasing or fighting everybody else.
wd Louis Malle *novel* Raymond Queneau ph Henri Raichi m Fiorenzo Capri
☆ Catherine Demongeot, Philippe Noiret, Vittorio Caprioli
'There is something not quite innocent or healthy about this film.' – *Bosley Crowther*

Zebra in the Kitchen

US 1965 93m Metrocolor
MGM/Ivan Tors

A young boy tries to improve the lot of zoo animals.
Pleasing family film.
w Art Arthur d Ivan Tors ph Lamar Boren
☆ Jay North, Martin Milner, Andy Devine, Joyce Meadows, Jim Davis

A Zed and Two Noughts **

GB 1985 115m colour
Artificial Eye/BFI/Allarts Enterprises/Film Four International (Peter Sainsbury, Kees Kasander)

An assemblage of images of loss and decay decorate a slim narrative about twin husbands, whose wives are killed in a car crash with a swan, and their relationship with the survivor, a woman whose leg is amputated.
Intriguing, visually compelling and witty, although it may not appeal to those expecting a traditional narrative.
wd Peter Greenaway ph Sacha Vierny m Michael Nyman pd Ben Van Os, Jan Roelfs ed John Wilson
☆ Andrea Ferreol, Eric Deacon, Brian Deacon, Frances Barber, Joss Ackland

Zee and Co *

GB 1971 109m colour
Columbia/Zee Films (Kastner-Ladd-Kanter)

US title: *X, Y and Zee*
A successful architect battles with his termagant wife and seeks an affair.
Overwritten but entertaining sexual melodrama about an absolute bitch. The flow of bad language was new at the time.
w Edna O'Brien d Brian G. Hutton ph Billy Williams m Stanley Myers ad Peter Mullins
☆ Elizabeth Taylor, Michael Caine, Susannah York, Margaret Leighton, John Standing
'Miss Taylor is rapidly turning into a latterday Marie Dressler.' – *Tom Milne*
'A slice-of-jet-set-life nightmare far beyond the dreams of the piggiest male chauvinist … the distinction of this film is that its characters are repulsive, its style vulgar, its situations beyond belief and its dialogue moronic.' – *Judith Crist*

Zelig ***

US 1983 79m bw/colour
Orion/Rollins-Joffe (Robert Greenhut)

A parody documentary tracing a chameleon-like nonentity who contrives to have been associated with all the major events of the 20th century.
The central idea is more elusive than appealing, and the mid-section of psychiatric consultation is downright dull, but considerable amusement derives from the technical trickery which puts Woody Allen in pictorial association with Hitler, Roosevelt and Eugene O'Neill. In all, an after-dinner treat for the intellectuals.
wd Woody Allen ph Gordon Willis m Dick Hyman pd Mel Bourne ed Susan E. Morse
☆ Woody Allen, Mia Farrow, John Buckwater, Marvin Chatinover, Stanley Swerdlow, Paul Nevens, Howard Erskine
'We can all admire the brilliance and economy with which it is made. But is it funny enough? I take leave to doubt it.' – *Derek Malcolm, Guardian*
'Citizen Kane miraculously transformed into side-splitting comedy.' – *New York Times*
'The movie is a technical masterpiece, but in artistic and comic terms, only pretty good.' – *Roger Ebert*
🏅 cinematography; costume design

🏃 film suitable for family viewing 📼 VHS video-cassette for the British PAL system 📼 VHS video-cassette for the British PAL system in wide screen-format ♻ Video cassette in a computer-colourised version ▬ American NTSC video-cassette 💿 Laser disc

Zelly and Me *
US   1988   87m   Technicolor
Columbia/Cypress Films/Tony Mark/Sue Jett

A poor little rich girl, who lives with a grandmother greedy for love, is comforted by her governess.
Unusual in its depiction of the psychological damage an adult can inflict on a child, it handles sympathetically its themes of the failure of love and the need to develop individual strength.
wd Tina Rathbone ph Mikael Salomon m Pino Donaggio pd David Morong ed Cindy Kaplan Rooney
☆ Isabella Rossellini, Glynis Johns, Kaiulani Lee, David Lynch, Joe Morton, Alexandra Johnes

Zemlya: see *Earth*

Zenobia
US   1939   83m   bw
Hal Roach

GB title: *Elephants Never Forget*
A small-town doctor finds himself looking after a performing elephant.
Very mild small-town comedy made during a break-up in the Laurel and Hardy contract.
w Corey Ford, Arnold Belgard, Walter de Leon d Gordon Douglas ph Karl Struss m Marvin Hatley
☆ Oliver Hardy, Harry Langdon, Jean Parker, Billie Burke, Alice Brady, James Ellison, Stepin Fetchit, Hattie McDaniel

Zentropa: see *Europa, Europa*

Zeppelin *
GB   1971   97m   Technicolor   Panavision
Warner/Getty and Fromkess (Owen Crump)

In 1915, the British need to steal secrets from the zeppelin works at Friedrichshafen.
Undistinguished but entertaining period actioner with adequate spectacle but wooden performances.
w Arthur Rowe, Donald Churchill d Etienne Périer ph Alan Hume m Roy Budd sp Wally Veevers
☆ Michael York, Elke Sommer, Peter Carsten, Marius Goring, Anton Diffring, Anton Keir, Rupert Davies

Zéro de Conduite **
France   1933   45m   bw
Gaumont/Franco Film/Aubert

Boys return from the holiday to a nasty little boarding school, where the headmaster is an unpleasant dwarf and all the staff are hateful. A revolution breaks out ...
A clear forerunner of If ... and one of the most famous of surrealist films, though it pales beside Buñuel and is chiefly valuable for being funny.
wd Jean Vigo ph Boris Kaufman m Maurice Jaubert ed Jean Vigo
☆ Jean Dasté, Louis Lefébvre, Gilbert Pruchon, le nain Delphin
'One of the most poetic films ever made and one of the most influential.' – *New Yorker, 1978*

'The World's Most Private Detective.'
Zero Effect *
US   1998   115m   Technicolor
Warner/Castle Rock/Manifest (Lisa Henson, Janet Yang, Jake Kasdan)

A reclusive private eye investigates a case of blackmail.
Quirky mix of comedy, romance and thriller that offers intermittent amusement.
wd Jake Kasdan ph Bill Pope m The Greyboy Allstars ed Gary Frutkoff ed Tara Timpone
☆ Bill Pullman, Ben Stiller, Kim Dickens, Angela Featherstone, Ryan O'Neal, Hugh Ross, Matt O'Toole
'Top heavy with artifice but punctuated with enough off-beat inspiration to make the experience worthwhile.' – *Sight and Sound*

Zero Hour!
US   1957   83m   bw
Paramount/Bartlett/Champion (John Champion)

Half the passengers and all the crew of a jet plane are stricken with food poisoning and a shell-shocked ex-fighter pilot has to land the plane.
Adequate air melodrama with a premise which later served for Terror in the Sky (TV) and Airport 75.
w Arthur Hailey, John Champion, Hall Bartlett teleplay Flight into Danger by Arthur Hailey d Hall Bartlett ph John F. Warren m Ted Dale
☆ Dana Andrews, Linda Darnell, Sterling Hayden, Elroy Hirsch, Jerry Paris

Zero Patience
Canada   1993   88m   colour
Dangerous To Know/Zero Patience/Telefilm Canada/OFDC/Channel 4 (Louise Garfield, Anna Stratton)

English explorer Sir Richard Burton, working at the Natural History Museum in Toronto, is visited by the ghost of the first man to bring AIDS to North America as he plans an exhibition on the disease.
Bizarre gay musical satirizing homophobia in the style of a rock video.
wd John Greyson ph Miroslaw Baszak m/ly Glenn Schellenberg, John Greyson pd Sandra Kybartas ed Miume Jan
☆ John Robinson, Normand Fauteux, Dianne Heatherington, Richardo Keens-Douglas, Maria Lukofsky, Bernard Behrens, Michael Callen
'While one may agree with almost everything it says, the little matter of the way it says it renders the film almost unwatchable.' – Derek Malcolm, *Guardian*
'Enormously entertaining, and perfectly cast ... This is an angry film, a powerful indictment of a society that seems more concerned with finding a scapegoat rather than a cure for one of the biggest killers today.' – Nigel Robinson, *Film Review*

Zero Population Growth
US   1971   96m   Eastmancolor
Sagittarius (Thomas F. Madigan)
In the 21st century there is a death penalty for having children, but a young couple defy the authorities.
Good sci-fi quickly develops into sticky sentimentality.
w Max Ehrlich, Frank de Felitta d Michael Campus ph Michael Reed m Jonathan Hodge pd Tony Masters
☆ Oliver Reed, Geraldine Chaplin, Diane Cilento, Don Gordon, Bill Nagy, Aubrey Woods

Zero Tolerance
US   1994   92m   Foto-Kem
PM Entertainment (Richard Pepin, Joseph Merhi)

An FBI agent takes revenge on the drug-runners who murder his wife and children and force him to smuggle liquid heroin.
Frenetic, melodramatic, violent, repetitious and senseless action movie, a concussive sequence of car crashes, gunshots and explosions, mixed with a little sentimentality.
w Jacobsen Hart d Joseph Merhi ph Ken Blakey m John Gonzalez pd Steve Ramos ed Chris Worland, Chris Maybach
☆ Robert Patrick, Titus Welliver, Kristen Meadows, Mick Fleetwood, Barbara Patrick, Billy Hufsey, Miles O'Keeffe

Zert: see *The Joke*

Zeta One
GB   1969   84m   Eastmancolor
Tigon (George Maynard)

A spy plays strip poker as he explains how he saved the world from being taken over by women wearing orange mini-dresses and white thigh boots.
Based on a comic-strip, an incompetent James Bond spoof with cruder double entendres and more irrelevant sexual activity; tedium sets in very quickly.
w Michael Cort, Alistair McKenzie d Michael Cort ph Jack Atchelor m Johnny Hawksworth ad Martin Gascoigne ed Jack T. Knight, Dennis Lanning
☆ James Robertson Justice, Charles Hawtrey, Robin Hawdon, Anna Gael, Brigitte Skay, Valerie Leon, Yutte Stensgaard, Lionel Murton, Dawn Addams, Rita Webb

Zeus and Roxanne
🏃🏃   US   1997   98m   DeLuxe
MGM/Rysher (Frank Price, Gene Rosow, Ludi Boeken)

When a woman's friendly dolphin bonds with her neighbour's dog, their children know that romance is in the offing.
Pleasant family film with some scene-stealing animals and not too much sentimentality.
w Tom Benedek d George Miller ph David Connell m Bruce Rowland pd Bernt Capra ed Harry Hitner
☆ Steve Guttenberg, Kathleen Quinlan, Arnold Vosloo, Dawn McMillan, Miko Hughes, Majandra Delfino, Jessica Howard
'Simple-minded but efficient piece of filmmaking clearly aimed at small fry.' – *Variety*
† The role of Zeus was played by three dogs.

Zhivoi Trup: see *The Living Corpse*

Ziegfeld Follies **
US   1946   110m   Technicolor
MGM (Arthur Freed)

In heaven, Florenz Ziegfeld dreams up one last spectacular revue.
A rather airless all-star entertainment in which the comedy suffers from the lack of an audience but some of the production numbers are magnificently stylish.
w various d Vincente Minnelli ph George Folsey, Charles Rosher m various md Lennie Hayton ch Robert Alton ad Cedric Gibbons, Merrill Pye, Jack Martin Smith ed Albert Akst cos Florence Bunin, Irene, Helen Rose
☆ Fred Astaire, Lucille Ball, Bunin's Puppets, William Powell, Jimmy Durante, Edward Arnold, Fanny Brice, Lena Horne, Lucille Bremer, Esther Williams, Judy Garland, Red Skelton, Gene Kelly, James Melton, Hume Cronyn and also Victor Moore, Marion Bell
'Between opening and closing is packed a prodigious amount of material, some of which is frankly not deserving of the lavish treatment accorded it.' – *Film Daily*
'The fastidious are advised to head for the lobby while Kathryn Grayson sings "There's Beauty Everywhere" against magenta foam skies.' – *Pauline Kael, 70s*
† Made in 1944, but not released until later.

Ziegfeld Girl *
US   1941   131m   bw
MGM (Pandro S. Berman)

The professional and romantic problems of Ziegfeld chorus girls.
Adequate big-budget drama with music.
w Marguerite Roberts, Sonya Levien d Robert Z. Leonard ph Ray June m Herbert Stothart ch Busby Berkeley songs various
☆ James Stewart, Judy Garland, Hedy Lamarr, Lana Turner, Tony Martin, Jackie Cooper, Ian Hunter, Charles Winninger, Al Shean, Edward Everett Horton, Philip Dorn, Paul Kelly, Eve Arden, Dan Dailey, Fay Holden and also Felix Bressart
'Heaping portions of show life in the opulent days of Flo Ziegfeld, the man who wanted bigger and better staircases.' – C. A. Lejeune
🎵 'You Stepped Out of a Dream'; 'I'm Always Chasing Rainbows'; 'Mr Gallagher and Mr Shean'; 'You Never Looked So Beautiful'.

Zigzag *
US   1970   104m   Metrocolor   Panavision
MGM/Freeman-Enders
GB title: *False Witness*
A dying man frames himself for an unsolved murder so that the reward money, claimed under another name, will go to his wife.
Complex thriller which sustains itself pretty well most of the way, but lacks humour and character.
w John T. Kelley d Richard A. Colla ph James A. Crabe m Oliver Nelson
☆ George Kennedy, Anne Jackson, Eli Wallach, Steve Ihnat, William Marshall, Joe Maross

Zoltan, Hound of Dracula: see *Dracula's Dog*

Zombi 2: see *Zombie Flesh Eaters*

Zombie: see *Zombie Flesh Eaters*

'When The Earth Spits Out The Dead.'
Zombie Flesh Eaters
Italy   1979   93m   Technicolor
Variety Film (Ugo Tucci, Fabrizio de Angelis)

original title: *Zombi 2*
aka: *Zombie; Island of The Living Dead*
After a yacht with a zombie aboard is found floating off New York, a journalist discovers that it originated on a small Caribbean island where a mad scientist's experiments result in the dead, including Spanish conquistadores, rising from their graves.
Visceral, gore-filled horror movie, owing much to the example of George Romero but made by a director who does not understand that less can be more.
w Elisa Briganti d Lucio Fulci sp Sergio Salvati m Fabio Frizzi, Giorgio Tucci pd Walter Patriarca
☆ Ian McCulloch, Tisa Farrow, Richard Johnson, Al Cliver, Auretta Gay
† The film was cut to 85m for its British video release.

Zombie Island Massacre
US   1984   95m   colour
Troma/Broadnax

Tourists who travel to the Caribbean for a voodoo ritual are killed one by one by an apparent zombie.
Dull horror, seemingly designed as a showcase to display the body of former Playboy model Jenrette; its plot owes much to Agatha Christie's Ten Little Indians.
w William Stoddard, Logan O'Neill d John N. Carter m Harry Manfredini ed John N. Carter sp Dennis Eger
☆ David Broadnax, Rita Jenrette, Tom Cantrell, Diane Clayre Holub, Ian MacMillan, George Peters, Dennis Stephenson, Debbie Ewing

The Zombies of Mora Tau
US   1957   71m   bw
Columbia (Sam Katzman)

GB title: *The Dead that Walk*
A diver plans to salvage a subterranean West African treasure: but it is guarded by zombies.
Modest addition to the walking dead cycle.
w Raymond T. Marcus d Edward Cahn ph Benjamin Kline m Mischa Bakaleinikoff
☆ Gregg Palmer, Allison Hayes, Autumn Russell, Morris Ankrum

Zombies on Broadway
US   1945   70m   bw
RKO (Ben Stoloff)

Press agents seek a real zombie for the opening of a new night-club ... and a mad professor provides one.
Knockabout comedy-thriller, just tolerable for addicts of the genre.
w Lawrence Kimble d Gordon Douglas
☆ Wally Brown, Alan Carney, Bela Lugosi, Anne Jeffreys, Sheldon Leonard

Zongheng Sihai: see *Once a Thief (1991)*

Zoo in Budapest *
US   1933   83m   bw
Fox (Jesse Lasky)

An orphan waif runs away to live with a zookeeper.
Curious little romance remembered for its luminescent photography.
w Dan Totheroh, Louise Long, Rowland V. Lee d Rowland V. Lee ph Lee Garmes
☆ Loretta Young, Gene Raymond, O. P. Heggie, Wally Albright, Paul Fix
'Appeal for all classes ... a subject of great photographic and pictorial beauty.' – *Variety*
'Richly composed impressionistic images, assisted by highly imaginative use of sound and background music, create a poem that Murnau himself would have envied.' – *NFT, 1971*

Un Zoo La Nuit: see *Night Zoo*

Zorba the Greek **
GB   1964   142m   bw
TCF/Rockley/Cacoyannis (Michael Cacoyannis)

A young English writer in Crete is befriended by a huge gregarious Greek who comes to dominate his life.
A mainly enjoyable character study of a larger-than-life character, this film made famous by its music does not

really hang together dramatically and has several melodramatic excrescences.

wd Michael Cacoyannis novel Nikos Kazantzakis ph Walter Lassally m Mikis Theodorakis ad Vasseli Fotopoulos ed Alex Archamboult, Michael Cacoyannis

☆ Anthony Quinn, Alan Bates, Lila Kedrova, Irene Papas, George Foundas, Eleni Anousaki

'For all its immense length, the film never gets down to a clear statement of its theme, or comes within measuring distance of its vast pretensions.' – Brenda Davies

† Lila Kedrova replaced Simone Signoret after a week's filming, as Signoret was unable to portray a weak woman.

🏃 Walter Lassally; Lila Kedrova

🏃 best picture; Michael Cacoyannis (as writer and director); Anthony Quinn

Zorro (dubbed)

👫 Italy/France 1975 100m colour
Mondial/Artistes Associés (Vittorio Galiano)
After his friend is assassinated, Zorro takes his place as governor of a Spanish colony where a

corrupt colonel and his friends are terrorizing and exploiting the locals.

Swashbuckling, tongue-in-cheek adventure done with some style and very little bloodshed.

w Giorgio Arlorio d Duccio Tessari ph Giulio Albonico m Guido and Maurizio de Angelis ad Enzo Bulgarelli ed Mario Morra

☆ Alain Delon, Stanley Baker, Ottavia Piccolo, Enzo Cerusico, Moustache, Adriana Asti, Giacomo Rossi Stuart, Gianpiero Albertini, Marino Mase, Rajka Jurcec

'Zany! Zexy! Zensational!'
Zorro the Gay Blade

US 1981 93m DeLuxe
Melvin Simon (George Hamilton, C. O. Erickson)
🎦

Zorro, the masked avenger, not only pretends to be a fop but is one. Luckily he has a twin brother. *Abysmal attempt to do for Zorro what Love at First Bite did for Dracula.*

w Hal Dresner d Peter Medak ph John A. Alonzo m Max Steiner themes

☆ George Hamilton, Lauren Hutton, Brenda

Vaccaro, Ron Leibman, James Booth
'A wonderful giddy farce.' – Pauline Kael

Zotz!

👫 US 1962 87m bw
Columbia/William Castle
🎦

A professor finds a rare coin with occult powers. *Footling farce patterned after The Absent-Minded Professor. Poor, to say the least.*

w Ray Russell novel Walter Karig d William Castle ph Gordon Avil m Bernard Green

☆ Tom Poston, Fred Clark, Jim Backus, Cecil Kellaway, Margaret Dumont

Zuckerbaby: see *Sugarbaby*

Zulu *

👫 GB 1964 135m Technirama
Paramount/Diamond (Stanley Baker, Cyril Endfield)
🎦 🎦 🔍 🎦 🎧
In 1879 British soldiers stand fast against the Zulus at Rorke's Drift.
Standard period heroics, well presented and acted.

w John Prebble, Cy Endfield d Cy Endfield ph Stephen Dade m John Barry

☆ Stanley Baker, Jack Hawkins, Michael Caine, Ulla Jacobsson, James Booth, Nigel Green, Ivor Emmanuel, Paul Daneman

Zulu Dawn

👫 US/Netherlands 1979 117m
Technicolor Panavision
Samarkand/Zulu Dawn NV (Barrie Saint Clair)
🎦 🎦 🔍 🎧
In January 1879, 24,000 Zulus overwhelm and kill 1,300 British and African troops at Isandhlwana. *Confusing historical action adventure, very similar to Zulu but failing in its cross-cut attempt to show both sides.*

w Cy Endfield, Anthony Storey d Douglas Hickox ph Ousama Rawi m Elmer Bernstein pd John Rosewarne

☆ Burt Lancaster, Denholm Elliott, Peter O'Toole, John Mills, Simon Ward, Nigel Davenport, Michael Jayston, Ronald Lacey, Freddie Jones, Christopher Cazenove, Ronald Pickup, Anna Calder-Marshall

---

Academy Award Winners

1927/28
Picture: *Wings*
Unique and Artistic Picture: *Sunrise* (F. W. Murnau)
Director: Frank Borzage (*Seventh Heaven*)
Comedy Director: Lewis Milestone (*Two Arabian Knights*)
Actor: Emil Jannings (*The Last Command, The Way of All Flesh*)
Actress: Janet Gaynor (*Seventh Heaven, Street Angel, Sunrise*)
Original Screenplay: Ben Hecht (*Underworld*)
Adapted Screenplay: Benjamin Glazer (*Seventh Heaven*)
Title Writing: Joseph Farnham (*Telling the World*)

1928/29
Picture: *Broadway Melody*
Director: Frank Lloyd (*The Divine Lady, Weary River, Drag*)
Actor: Warner Baxter (*Old Arizona*)
Actress: Mary Pickford (*Coquette*)
Writing Achievement: Hans Kraly (*The Patriot*)

1929/30
Picture: *All Quiet on the Western Front*
Director: Lewis Milestone (*All Quiet on the Western Front*)
Actor: George Arliss (*Disraeli*)
Actress: Norma Shearer (*The Divorcee*)
Writing Achievement: Frances Marion (*The Big House*)

1930/31
Picture: *Cimarron*
Director: Norman Taurog (*Skippy*)
Actor: Lionel Barrymore (*A Free Soul*)
Actress: Marie Dressler (*Min and Bill*)
Original Screenplay: John Monk Saunders (*The Dawn Patrol*)
Adapted Screenplay: Howard Eastabrook (*Cimarron*)

1931/32
Picture: *Grand Hotel*
Director: Frank Borzage (*Bad Girl*)
Actor: Wallace Beery (*The Champ*), Fredric March (*Dr Jekyll and Mr Hyde*)
Actress: Helen Hayes (*The Sin of Madelon Claudet*)
Original Screenplay: Francis Marion (*The Champ*)
Adapted Screenplay: Edwin Burke (*Bad Girl*)

1932/33
Picture: *Cavalcade*
Director: Frank Lloyd (*Cavalcade*)
Actor: Charles Laughton (*The Private Life of Henry VIII*)
Actress: Katharine Hepburn (*Morning Glory*)
Original Screenplay: Robert Lord (*One Way Passage*)
Adapted Screenplay: Victor Heerman, Sarah Y. Mason (*Little Women*)

1934
Picture: *It Happened One Night*
Director: Frank Capra (*It Happened One Night*)
Actor: Clark Gable (*It Happened One Night*)
Actress: Claudette Colbert (*It Happened One Night*)
Original Screenplay: Arthur Caesar (*Manhattan Melodrama*)
Adapted Screenplay: Robert Riskin (*It Happened One Night*)

1935
Picture: *Mutiny on the Bounty*
Director: John Ford (*The Informer*)
Actor: Victor McLaglen (*The Informer*)
Actress: Bette Davis (*Dangerous*)
Original Screenplay: Ben Hecht, Charles MacArthur (*The Scoundrel*)
Adapted Screenplay: Dudley Nichols (*The Informer*)

1936
Picture: *The Great Ziegfeld*
Director: Frank Capra (*Mr Deeds Goes to Town*)
Actor: Paul Muni (*The Story of Louis Pasteur*)
Actress: Luise Rainer (*The Great Ziegfeld*)
Supporting Actor: Walter Brennan (*Come and Get It*)
Supporting Actress: Gale Sondergaard (*Anthony Adverse*)
Original Screenplay: Pierre Collings, Sheridan Gibney (*The Story of Louis Pasteur*)

1937
Picture: *The Life of Emile Zola*
Director: Leo McCarey (*The Awful Truth*)
Actor: Spencer Tracy (*Captains Courageous*)
Actress: Luise Rainer (*The Good Earth*)
Supporting Actor: Joseph Schildkraut (*The Life of Emile Zola*)
Supporting Actress: Alice Brady (*In Old Chicago*)
Original Story: William A. Wellman, Robert Carson (*A Star Is Born*)
Original Story: Heinz Herald, Geza Herczeg, Norman Reilly Raine (*The Life of Emile Zola*)

1938
Picture: *You Can't Take It with You*
Director: Frank Capra (*You Can't Take It with You*)
Actor: Spencer Tracy (*Boys' Town*)
Actress: Bette Davis (*Jezebel*)
Supporting Actor: Walter Brennan (*Kentucky*)
Supporting Actress: Fay Bainter (*Jezebel*)
Original Story: Eleanore Griffin, Dore Schary (*Boys' Town*)
Screenplay: George Bernard Shaw, adapted by Ian Dalrymple, Cecil Lewis, W. P. Liscomb (*Pygmalion*)

1939
Picture: *Gone with the Wind*
Director: Victor Fleming (*Gone with the Wind*)
Actor: Robert Donat (*Goodbye Mr Chips*)
Actress: Vivien Leigh (*Gone with the Wind*)
Supporting Actor: Thomas Mitchell (*Stagecoach*)
Supporting Actress: Hattie McDaniel (*Gone with the Wind*)
Original Story: Lewis R. Foster (*Mr Deeds Goes to Washington*)
Screenplay: Sidney Howard (*Gone with the Wind*)

1940
Picture: *Rebecca*
Director: John Ford (*The Grapes of Wrath*)
Actor: James Stewart (*The Philadelphia Story*)
Actress: Ginger Rogers (*Kitty Foyle*)
Supporting Actor: Walter Brennan (*The Westerner*)
Supporting Actress: Jane Darwell (*The Grapes of Wrath*)
Original Story: Benjamin Glazer, John S. Toldy (*Arise My Love*)
Original Screenplay: Preston Sturges (*The Great McGinty*)
Screenplay: Donald Ogden Stewart (*The Philadelphia Story*)

1941
Picture: *How Green Was My Valley*
Director: John Ford (*How Green Was My Valley*)
Actor: Gary Cooper (*Sergeant York*)
Actress: Joan Fontaine (*Suspicion*)
Supporting Actor: Donald Crisp (*How Green Was My Valley*)
Supporting Actress: Mary Astor (*The Great Lie*)
Original Story: Harry Segall (*Here Comes Mr Jordan*)
Original Screenplay: Herman J. Mankiewicz, Orson Welles (*Citizen Kane*)
Screenplay: Sidney Buchman, Seton I. Miller (*Here Comes Mr Jordan*)

1942
Picture: *Mrs Miniver*
Director: William Wyler (*Mrs Miniver*)
Actor: James Cagney (*Yankee Doodle Dandy*)
Actress: Greer Garson (*Mrs Miniver*)
Supporting Actor: Van Heflin (*Johnny Eager*)
Supporting Actress: Teresa Wright (*Mrs Miniver*)
Original Story: Emeric Pressburger (*The Invaders*)
Original Screenplay: Michael Kanin, Ring Lardner Jnr (*Woman of the Year*)
Screenplay: George Froeschel, James Hilton, Claudine West, Arthur Wimperis (*Mrs Miniver*)

1943
Picture: *Casablanca*
Director: Michael Curtiz (*Casablanca*)
Actor: Paul Lukas (*Watch on the Rhine*)
Actress: Jennifer Jones (*Song of Bernadette*)
Supporting Actor: Charles Coburn (*The More the Merrier*)
Supporting Actress: Katina Paxinou (*For Whom the Bell Tolls*)
Original Story: William Saroyan (*The Human Comedy*)
Original Screenplay: Norman Krasna (*Princess O'Rourke*)
Screenplay: Julius J. Epstein, Philip G. Epstein, Howard Koch (*Casablanca*)

1944
Picture: *Going My Way*
Director: Leo McCarey (*Going My Way*)
Actor: Bing Crosby (*Going My Way*)
Actress: Ingrid Bergman (*Gaslight*)
Supporting Actor: Barry Fitzgerald (*Going My Way*)
Supporting Actress: Ethel Barrymore (*None but the Lonely Heart*)
Original Story: Leo McCarey (*Going My Way*)
Original Screenplay: Lamar Trotti (*Wilson*)
Screenplay: Frank Butler, Frank Cavett (*Going My Way*)

1945
Picture: *The Lost Weekend*
Director: Billy Wilder (*The Lost Weekend*)
Actor: Ray Milland (*The Lost Weekend*)
Actress: Joan Crawford (*Mildred Pierce*)
Supporting Actor: James Dunn (*A Tree Grows in Brooklyn*)
Supporting Actress: Anne Revere (*National Velvet*)
Original Story: Charles G. Booth (*The House on 92nd Street*)
Original Screenplay: Richard Schweizer (*Marie-Louise*)
Screenplay: Charles Brackett, Billy Wilder (*The Lost Weekend*)

1946
Picture: *The Best Years of Our Lives*
Director: William Wyler (*The Best Years of Our Lives*)
Actor: Fredric March (*The Best Years of Our Lives*)
Actress: Olivia de Havilland (*To Each His Own*)
Supporting Actor: Harold Russell (*The Best Years of Our Lives*)
Supporting Actress: Anne Baxter (*The Razor's Edge*)
Original Story: Clemence Dane (*Vacation from Marriage*)
Original Screenplay: Muriel Box, Sydney Box (*The Seventh Veil*)
Screenplay: Robert E. Sherwood (*The Best Years of Our Lives*)

1947
Picture: *Gentleman's Agreement*
Director: Elia Kazan (*Gentleman's Agreement*)
Actor: Ronald Colman (*A Double Life*)
Actress: Loretta Young (*The Farmer's Daughter*)
Supporting Actor: Edmund Gwenn (*Miracle on 34th Street*)
Supporting Actress: Celeste Holm (*Gentleman's Agreement*)
Original Story: Valentine Davies (*Miracle on 34th Street*)
Original Screenplay: Sidney Sheldon (*The Bachelor and the Bobby-Soxer*)
Screenplay: George Seaton (*Miracle on 34th Street*)

1948
Picture: *Hamlet*
Director: John Huston (*The Treasure of the Sierra Madre*)
Actor: Laurence Olivier (*Hamlet*)
Actress: Jane Wyman (*Johnny Belinda*)
Supporting Actor: Walter Huston (*The Treasure of the Sierra Madre*)
Supporting Actress: Claire Trevor (*Key Largo*)
Motion Picture Story: Richard Sweizer, David Wechsler (*The Search*)
Screenplay: John Huston (*The Treasure of the Sierra Madre*)

1949
Picture: *All the King's Men*
Director: Joseph L. Mankiewicz (*A Letter to Three Wives*)
Actor: Broderick Crawford (*All the King's Men*)
Actress: Olivia de Havilland (*The Heiress*)
Supporting Actor: Dean Jagger (*Twelve O'Clock High*)
Supporting Actress: Mercedes McCambridge (*All the King's Men*)
Motion Picture Story: Douglas Morrow (*The Stratton Story*)
Screenplay: Joseph L. Mankiewicz (*A Letter to Three Wives*)
Story & Screenplay: Robert Pirosh (*Battleground*)

1950
Picture: *All About Eve*
Director: Joseph L. Mankiewicz (*All About Eve*)
Actor: José Ferrer (*Cyrano de Bergerac*)
Actress; Judy Holliday (*Born Yesterday*)
Supporting Actor: George Sanders (*All About Eve*)
Supporting Actress: Josephine Hull (*Harvey*)
Motion Picture Story: Edna Anhalt, Edward Anhalt (*Panic in the Streets*)
Story & Screenplay: Charles Brackett, Billy Wilder, D. M. Marshman Jnr (*Sunset Boulevard*)

1951
Picture: *An American in Paris*
Director: George Stevens (*A Place in the Sun*)
Actor: Humphrey Bogart (*The African Queen*)
Actress: Vivien Leigh (*A Streetcar Named Desire*)
Supporting Actor: Karl Malden (*A Streetcar Named Desire*)
Supporting Actress: Kim Hunter (*A Streetcar Named Desire*)
Motion Picture Story: Paul Dehn, James Bernard (*Seven Days to Noon*)
Screenplay: Michael Wilson, Harry Brown (*A Place in the Sun*)
Story & Screenplay: Alan Jay Lerner (*An American in Paris*)

1952
Picture: *The Greatest Show on Earth*
Director: John Ford (*The Quiet Man*)
Actor: Gary Cooper (*High Noon*)
Actress: Shirley Booth (*Come Back Little Sheba*)
Supporting Actor: Anthony Quinn (*Viva Zapata!*)
Supporting Actress: Gloria Grahame (*The Bad and the Beautiful*)
Motion Picture Story: Frederic M. Frank, Theodore St John, Frank Cavett (*The Greatest Show on Earth*)
Screenplay: Charles Schnee (*The Bad and the Beautiful*)
Story & Screenplay: T. E. B. Clarke (*The Lavender Hill Mob*)

1953
Picture: *From Here to Eternity*
Director: Fred Zinnemann (*From Here to Eternity*)

Actor: William Holden (*Stalag 17*)
Actress: Audrey Hepburn (*Roman Holiday*)
Supporting Actor: Frank Sinatra (*From Here to Eternity*)
Supporting Actress: Donna Reed (*From Here to Eternity*)
Motion Picture Story: Ian McLellan Hunter, fronting for the blacklisted Dalton Trumbo (*Roman Holiday*)
Screenplay: Daniel Taradash (*From Here to Eternity*)
Story & Screenplay: Charles Brackett, Walter Reisch, Richard Breen (*Titanic*)

1954

Picture: *On the Waterfront*
Director: Elia Kazan (*On the Waterfront*)
Actor: Marlon Brando (*On the Waterfront*)
Actress: Grace Kelly (*The Country Girl*)
Supporting Actor: Edmond O'Brien (*The Barefoot Contessa*)
Supporting Actress: Eva Marie Saint (*On the Waterfront*)
Motion Picture Story: Philip Yordan (*Broken Lance*)
Screenplay: George Seaton (*The Country Girl*)
Story & Screenplay: Budd Schulberg (*On the Waterfront*)

1955

Picture: *Marty*
Director: Delbert Mann (*Marty*)
Actor: Ernest Borgnine (*Marty*)
Actress: Anna Magnani (*The Rose Tattoo*)
Supporting Actor: Jack Lemmon (*Mister Roberts*)
Supporting Actress: Jo Van Fleet (*East of Eden*)
Motion Picture Story: Daniel Fuchs (*Love Me or Leave Me*)
Screenplay: Paddy Chayevsky (*Marty*)
Story & Screenplay: William Ludwig, Sonya Levien (*Interrupted Melody*)

1956

Picture: *Around the World in Eighty Days*
Director: George Stevens (*Giant*)
Actor: Yul Brynner (*The King and I*)
Actress: Ingrid Bergman (*Anastasia*)
Supporting Actor: Anthony Quinn (*Lust for Life*)
Supporting Actress: Dorothy Malone (*Written on the Wind*)
Motion Picture Story: Dalton Trumbo (as Robert Rich) (*The Brave One*)
Original Screenplay: Albert Lamorisse (*The Red Balloon*)
Adapted Screenplay: James Poe, John Farrow, S. J. Perelman (*Around the World in Eighty Days*)

1957

Picture: *The Bridge on the River Kwai*
Director: David Lean (*The Bridge on the River Kwai*)
Actor: Alec Guinness (*The Bridge on the River Kwai*)
Actress: Joanne Woodward (*The Three Faces of Eve*)
Supporting Actor: Red Buttons (*Sayonara*)
Supporting Actress: Miyoshi Umeki (*Sayonara*)
Original Story & Screenplay: George Wells (*Designing Woman*)
Adapted Screenplay: Pierre Boulle, Michael Wilson, Carl Foreman (*The Bridge on the River Kwai*)

1958

Picture: *Gigi*
Director: Vincente Minnelli (*Gigi*)
Actor: David Niven (*Separate Tables*)
Actress: Susan Hayward (*I Want to Live*)
Supporting Actor: Burl Ives (*The Big Country*)
Supporting Actress: Wendy Hiller (*Separate Tables*)
Original Story & Screenplay: Nathan E. Douglas (the blacklisted Ned Young), Harold Jacob Smith (*The Defiant Ones*)
Adapted Screenplay: Alan Jay Lerner (*Gigi*)

1959

Picture: *Ben-Hur*
Director: William Wyler (*Ben-Hur*)
Actor: Charlton Heston (*Ben-Hur*)
Actress: Simone Signoret (*Room at the Top*)
Supporting Actor: Hugh Griffith (*Ben-Hur*)
Supporting Actress: Shelley Winters (*The Diary of Anne Frank*)
Original Story & Screenplay: Russell Rouse, Clarence Greene, Stanley Shapiro, Maurice Richlin (*Pillow Talk*)
Adapted Screenplay: Neil Paterson (*Room at the Top*)

1960

Picture: *The Apartment*
Director: Billy Wilder (*The Apartment*)
Actor: Burt Lancaster (*Elmer Gantry*)
Actress: Elizabeth Taylor (*Butterfield 8*)
Supporting Actor: Peter Ustinov (*Spartacus*)
Supporting Actress: Shirley Jones (*Elmer Gantry*)
Original Story & Screenplay: Billy Wilder, I. A. L. Diamond (*The Apartment*)
Adapted Screenplay: Richard Brooks (*Elmer Gantry*)

1961

Picture: *West Side Story*
Director: Jerome Robbins, Robert Wise (*West Side Story*)
Actor: Maximilian Schell (*Judgment at Nuremberg*)
Actress: Sophia Loren (*Two Women*)
Supporting Actor: George Chakiris (*West Side Story*)
Supporting Actress: Rita Moreno (*West Side Story*)
Original Story & Screenplay: William Inge (*Splendor in the Grass*)
Adapted Screenplay: Abby Mann (*Judgment at Nuremberg*)

1962

Picture: *Lawrence of Arabia*
Director: David Lean (*Lawrence of Arabia*)
Actor: Gregory Peck (*To Kill a Mockingbird*)
Actress: Anne Bancroft (*The Miracle Worker*)
Supporting Actor: Ed Begley (*Sweet Bird of Youth*)
Supporting Actress: Patty Duke (*The Miracle Worker*)
Original Story & Screenplay: Ennio de Concini, Alfredo Gianetti, Pietro Germi (*Divorce Italian Style*)
Adapted Screenplay: Horton Foote (*To Kill a Mockingbird*)

1963

Picture: *Tom Jones*
Director: Tony Richardson (*Tom Jones*)
Actor: Sidney Poitier (*Lilies of the Field*)
Actress: Patricia Neal (*Hud*)
Supporting Actor: Melvyn Douglas (*Hud*)
Supporting Actress: Margaret Rutherford (*The VIPs*)
Original Story & Screenplay: James R. Webb (*How the West Was Won*)
Adapted Screenplay: John Osborne (*Tom Jones*)

1964

Picture: *My Fair Lady*
Director: George Cukor (*My Fair Lady*)
Actor: Rex Harrison (*My Fair Lady*)
Actress: Julie Andrews (*Mary Poppins*)
Supporting Actor: Peter Ustinov (*Topkapi*)
Supporting Actress: Lila Kedrova (*Zorba the Greek*)
Original Story & Screenplay: S. H. Barnett, Peter Stone, Frank Tarloff (*Father Goose*)
Adapted Screenplay: Edward Anhalt (*Becket*)

1965

Picture: *The Sound of Music*
Director: Robert Wise (*The Sound of Music*)
Actor: Lee Marvin (*Cat Ballou*)
Actress: Julie Christie (*Darling*)
Supporting Actor: Martin Balsam (*A Thousand Clowns*)
Supporting Actress: Shelley Winters (*A Patch of Blue*)
Original Story & Screenplay: Frederic Raphael (*Darling*)
Adapted Screenplay: Robert Bolt (*Dr Zhivago*)

1966

Picture: *A Man for All Seasons*
Director: Fred Zinnemann (*A Man for All Seasons*)
Actor: Paul Scofield (*A Man for All Seasons*)
Actress: Elizabeth Taylor (*Who's Afraid of Virginia Woolf?*)
Supporting Actor: Walter Matthau (*The Fortune Cookie*)
Supporting Actress: Sandy Dennis (*Who's Afraid of Virginia Woolf?*)
Original Story & Screenplay: Claude Lelouch, Pierre Uytterhoeven (*A Man and a Woman*)
Adapted Screenplay: Robert Bolt (*A Man for All Seasons*)

1967

Picture: *In the Heat of the Night*
Director: Mike Nichols (*The Graduate*)
Actor: Rod Steiger (*In the Heat of the Night*)
Actress: Katharine Hepburn (*Guess Who's Coming to Dinner*)

Supporting Actor: George Kennedy (*Cool Hand Luke*)
Supporting Actress: Estelle Parsons (*Bonnie and Clyde*)
Original Story & Screenplay: William Rose (*Guess Who's Coming to Dinner*)
Adapted Screenplay: Sterling Silliphant (*In the Heat of the Night*)

1968

Picture: *Oliver!*
Director: Carol Reed (*Oliver!*)
Actor: Cliff Robertson (*Charly*)
Actress: Katharine Hepburn (*The Lion in Winter*), Barbra Streisand (*Funny Girl*)
Supporting Actor: Jack Albertson (*The Subject Was Roses*)
Supporting Actress: Ruth Gordon (*Rosemary's Baby*)
Original Story & Screenplay: Mel Brooks (*The Producers*)
Adapted Screenplay: James Goldman (*The Lion in Winter*)

1969

Picture: *Midnight Cowboy*
Director: John Schlesinger (*Midnight Cowboy*)
Actor: John Wayne (*True Grit*)
Actress: Maggie Smith (*The Prime of Miss Jean Brodie*)
Supporting Actor: Gig Young (*They Shoot Horses, Don't They?*)
Supporting Actress: Goldie Hawn (*Cactus Flower*)
Original Story & Screenplay: William Goldman (*Butch Cassidy and the Sundance Kid*)
Adapted Screenplay: Waldo Salt (*Midnight Cowboy*)

1970

Picture: *Patton*
Director: Franklin J. Schaffner (*Patton*)
Actor: George C. Scott (*Patton*)
Actress: Glenda Jackson (*Women in Love*)
Supporting Actor: John Mills (*Ryan's Daughter*)
Supporting Actress: Helen Hayes (*Airport*)
Original Story & Screenplay: Francis Ford Coppola, Edmund H. North (*Patton*)
Adapted Screenplay: Ring Lardner Jnr (*M*A*S*H*)

1971

Picture: *The French Connection*
Director: William Friedkin (*The French Connection*)
Actor: Gene Hackman (*The French Connection*)
Actress: Jane Fonda (*Klute*)
Supporting Actor: Ben Johnson (*The Last Picture Show*)
Supporting Actress: Cloris Leachman (*The Last Picture Show*)
Original Story & Screenplay: Paddy Chayevsky (*The Hospital*)
Adapted Screenplay: Ernest Tidyman (*The French Connection*)

1972

Picture: *The Godfather*
Director: Bob Fosse (*Cabaret*)
Actor: Marlon Brando (*The Godfather*)
Actress: Liza Minnelli (*Cabaret*)
Supporting Actor: Joel Grey (*Cabaret*)
Supporting Actress: Eileen Heckart (*Butterflies Are Free*)
Original Story & Screenplay: Jeremy Larner (*The Candidate*)
Adapted Screenplay: Mario Puzo, Francis Ford Coppola (*The Godfather*)

1973

Picture: *The Sting*
Director: George Roy Hill (*The Sting*)
Actor: Jack Lemmon (*Save the Tiger*)
Actress: Glenda Jackson (*A Touch of Class*)
Supporting Actor: John Houseman (*The Paper Chase*)
Supporting Actress: Tatum O'Neal (*Paper Moon*)
Original Story & Screenplay: David S. Ward (*The Sting*)
Adapted Screenplay: William Peter Blatty (*The Exorcist*)

1974

Picture: *The Godfather Part II*
Director: Francis Ford Coppola (*The Godfather Part II*)

Actor: Art Carney (*Harry and Tonto*)
Actress: Ellen Burstyn (*Alice Doesn't Live Here Any More*)
Supporting Actor: Robert de Niro (*The Godfather Part II*)
Supporting Actress: Ingrid Bergman (*Murder on the Orient Express*)
Original Story & Screenplay: Robert Towne (*Chinatown*)
Adapted Screenplay: Francis Ford Coppola, Mario Puzo (*The Godfather Part II*)

1975

Picture: *One Flew over the Cuckoo's Nest*
Director: Milos Forman (*One Flew over the Cuckoo's Nest*)
Actor: Jack Nicholson (*One Flew over the Cuckoo's Nest*)
Actress: Louise Fletcher (*One Flew over the Cuckoo's Nest*)
Supporting Actor: George Burns (*The Sunshine Boys*)
Supporting Actress: Lee Grant (*Shampoo*)
Original Screenplay: Frank Pierson (*Dog Day Afternoon*)
Adapted Screenplay: Lawrence Hauben, Bo Goldman (*One Flew over the Cuckoo's Nest*)

1976

Picture: *Rocky*
Director: John G. Avildsen (*Rocky*)
Actor: Peter Finch (*Network*)
Actress: Faye Dunaway (*Network*)
Supporting Actor: Jason Robards (*All the President's Men*)
Supporting Actress: Beatrice Straight (*Network*)
Original Screenplay: Paddy Chayevsky (*Network*)
Adapted Screenplay: William Goldman (*All the President's Men*)

1977

Picture: *Annie Hall*
Director: Woody Allen (*Annie Hall*)
Actor: Richard Dreyfuss (*The Goodbye Girl*)
Actress: Diane Keaton (*Annie Hall*)
Supporting Actor: Jason Robards (*Julia*)
Supporting Actress: Vanessa Redgrave (*Julia*)
Original Screenplay: Woody Allen, Marshall Brickman (*Annie Hall*)
Adapted Screenplay: Alvin Sargent (*Julia*)

1978

Picture: *The Deer Hunter*
Director: Michael Cimino (*The Deer Hunter*)
Actor: Jon Voight (*Coming Home*)
Actress: Jane Fonda (*Coming Home*)
Supporting Actor: Christopher Walken (*The Deer Hunter*)
Supporting Actress: Maggie Smith (*California Suite*)
Original Screenplay: Nancy Dowd, Waldo Salt, Robert C. Jones (*Coming Home*)
Adapted Screenplay: Oliver Stone (*Midnight Express*)

1979

Picture: *Kramer versus Kramer*
Director: Robert Benton (*Kramer versus Kramer*)
Actor: Dustin Hoffman (*Kramer versus Kramer*)
Actress: Sally Field (*Norma Rae*)
Supporting Actor: Melvyn Douglas (*Being There*)
Supporting Actress: Meryl Streep (*Kramer versus Kramer*)
Original Screenplay: Steve Tesich (*Breaking Away*)
Adapted Screenplay: Robert Benton (*Kramer versus Kramer*)

1980

Picture: *Ordinary People*
Director: Robert Redford (*Ordinary People*)
Actor: Robert de Niro (*Raging Bull*)
Actress: Sissy Spacek (*Coal Miner's Daughter*)
Supporting Actor: Timothy Hutton (*Ordinary People*)
Supporting Actress: Mary Steenburgen (*Melvin and Howard*)
Original Screenplay: Bo Goldman (*Melvin and Howard*)
Adapted Screenplay: Alvin Sargent (*Ordinary People*)

1981

Picture: *Chariots of Fire*
Director: Warren Beatty (*Reds*)
Actor: Henry Fonda (*On Golden Pond*)

Actress: Katharine Hepburn (*On Golden Pond*)
Supporting Actor: John Gielgud (*Arthur*)
Supporting Actress: Maureen Stapleton (*Reds*)
Original Screenplay: Colin Welland (*Chariots of Fire*)
Adapted Screenplay: Ernest Thompson (*On Golden Pond*)

1982
Picture: *Gandhi*
Director: Richard Attenborough (*Gandhi*)
Actor: Ben Kingsley (*Gandhi*)
Actress: Meryl Streep (*Sophie's Choice*)
Supporting Actor: Louis Gossett Jnr (*An Officer and a Gentleman*)
Supporting Actress: Jessica Lange (*Tootsie*)
Original Screenplay: John Briley (*Gandhi*)
Adapted Screenplay: Costa-Gavras, Donald Stewart (*Missing*)

1983
Picture: *Terms of Endearment*
Director: James L. Brooks (*Terms of Endearment*)
Actor: Robert Duvall (*Tender Mercies*)
Actress: Shirley Maclaine (*Terms of Endearment*)
Supporting Actor: Jack Nicholson (*Terms of Endearment*)
Supporting Actress: Linda Hunt (*The Year of Living Dangerously*)
Original Screenplay: Horton Foote (*Tender Mercies*)
Adapted Screenplay: James L. Brooks (*Terms of Endearment*)

1984
Picture: *Amadeus*
Director: Milos Forman (*Amadeus*)
Actor: F. Murray Abraham (*Amadeus*)
Actress: Sally Field (*Places in the Heart*)
Supporting Actor: Haing S. Ngor (*The Killing Fields*)
Supporting Actress: Peggy Ashcroft (*A Passage to India*)
Original Screenplay: Robert Benton (*Places in the Heart*)
Adapted Screenplay: Peter Shaffer (*Amadeus*)

1985
Picture: *Out of Africa*
Director: Sydney Pollack (*Out of Africa*)
Actor: William Hurt (*Kiss of the Spider Woman*)
Actress: Geraldine Page (*The Trip to Bountiful*)
Supporting Actor: Don Ameche (*Cocoon*)
Supporting Actress: Anjelica Huston (*Prizzi's Honor*)
Original Screenplay: William Kelley, Pamela Wallace, Earl W. Wallace (*Witness*)
Adapted Screenplay: Kurt Luedtke (*Out of Africa*)

1986
Picture: *Platoon*
Director: Oliver Stone (*Platoon*)

Actor: Paul Newman (*The Color of Money*)
Actress: Marlee Matlin (*Children of a Lesser God*)
Supporting Actor: Michael Caine (*Hannah and Her Sisters*)
Supporting Actress: Dianne Wiest (*Hannah and Her Sisters*)
Original Screenplay: Woody Allen (*Hannah and Her Sisters*)
Adapted Screenplay: Ruth Prawer Jhabvala (*A Room with a View*)

1987
Picture: *The Last Emperor*
Director: Bernardo Bertolucci (*The Last Emperor*)
Actor: Michael Douglas (*Wall Street*)
Actress: Cher (*Moonstruck*)
Supporting Actor: Sean Connery (*The Untouchables*)
Supporting Actress: Olympia Dukakis (*Moonstruck*)
Original Screenplay: John Patrick Shanley (*Moonstruck*)
Adapted Screenplay: Mark Peploe, Bernardo Bertolucci (*The Last Emperor*)

1988
Picture: *Rain Man*
Director: Barry Levinson (*Rain Man*)
Actor: Dustin Hoffman (*Rain Man*)
Actress: Jodie Foster (*The Accused*)
Supporting Actor: Kevin Kline (*A Fish Called Wanda*)
Supporting Actress: Geena Davis (*The Accidental Tourist*)
Original Screenplay: Ronald Bass, Barry Morrow (*Rain Man*)
Adapted Screenplay: Christopher Hampton (*Dangerous Liaisons*)

1989
Picture: *Driving Miss Daisy*
Director: Oliver Stone (*Born on the Fourth of July*)
Actor: Daniel Day-Lewis (*My Left Foot*)
Actress: Jessica Tandy (*Driving Miss Daisy*)
Supporting Actor: Denzel Washington (*Glory*)
Supporting Actress: Brenda Fricker (*My Left Foot*)
Original Screenplay: Tom Schulman (*Dead Poets Society*)
Adapted Screenplay: Alfred Uhry (*Driving Miss Daisy*)

1990
Picture: *Dances with Wolves*
Director: Kevin Costner (*Dances with Wolves*)
Actor: Jeremy Irons (*Reversal of Fortune*)
Actress: Kathy Bates (*Misery*)
Supporting Actor: Joe Pesci (*GoodFellas*)
Supporting Actress: Whoopi Goldberg (*Ghost*)
Original Screenplay: Bruce Joel Rubin (*Ghost*)

Adapted Screenplay: Michael Blake (*Dances with Wolves*)

1991
Picture: *Silence of the Lambs*
Director: Jonathan Demme (*Silence of the Lambs*)
Actor: Anthony Hopkins (*Silence of the Lambs*)
Actress: Jodie Foster (*Silence of the Lambs*)
Supporting Actor: Jack Palance (*City Slickers*)
Supporting Actress: Mercedes Ruehl (*The Fisher King*)
Original Screenplay: Callie Khouri (*Thelma and Louise*)
Adapted Screenplay: Ted Tally (*Silence of the Lambs*)

1992
Picture: *Unforgiven*
Director: Clint Eastwood (*Unforgiven*)
Actor: Al Pacino (*Scent of a Woman*)
Actress: Emma Thompson (*Howards End*)
Supporting Actor: Gene Hackman (*Unforgiven*)
Supporting Actress: Marisa Tomei (*My Cousin Vinny*)
Original Screenplay: Neil Jordan (*The Crying Game*)
Adapted Screenplay: Ruth Prawer Jhabvala (*Howards End*)

1993
Picture: *Schindler's List*
Director: Steven Spielberg (*Schindler's List*)
Actor: Tom Hanks (*Philadelphia*)
Actress: Holly Hunter (*The Piano*)
Supporting Actor: Tommy Lee Jones (*The Fugitive*)
Supporting Actress: Anna Paquin (*The Piano*)
Original Screenplay: Jane Campion (*The Piano*)
Adapted Screenplay: Steven Zaillian (*Schindler's List*)

1994
Picture: *Forrest Gump*
Director: Robert Zemeckis (*Forrest Gump*)
Actor: Tom Hanks (*Forrest Gump*)
Actress: Jessica Lange (*Blue Sky*)
Supporting Actor: Martin Landau (*Ed Wood*)
Supporting Actress: Dianne Wiest (*Bullets over Broadway*)
Original Screenplay: Quentin Tarantino, Roger Avary (*Pulp Fiction*)
Adapted Screenplay: Eric Roth (*Forrest Gump*)

1995
Picture: *Braveheart*
Director: Mel Gibson (*Braveheart*)
Actor: Nicolas Cage (*Leaving Las Vegas*)
Actress: Susan Sarandon (*Dead Man Walking*)
Supporting Actor: Kevin Spacey (*The Usual Suspects*)

Supporting Actress: Mira Sorvino (*Mighty Aphrodite*)
Original Screenplay: Christopher McQuarrie (*The Usual Suspects*)
Adapted Screenplay: Emma Thompson (*Sense and Sensibility*)

1996
Picture: *The English Patient*
Director: Anthony Minghella (*The English Patient*)
Actor: Geoffrey Rush (*Shine*)
Actress: Frances McDormand (*Fargo*)
Supporting Actor: Cuba Gooding Jr (*Jerry Maguire*)
Supporting Actress: Juliette Binoche (*The English Patient*)
Original Screenplay: Ethan Coen, Joel Coen (*Fargo*)
Adapted Screenplay: Billy Bob Thornton (*Slingblade*)

1997
Picture: *Titanic*
Director: James Cameron (*Titanic*)
Actor: Jack Nicholson (*As Good As It Gets*)
Actress: Helen Hunt (*As Good As It Gets*)
Supporting Actor: Robin Williams (*Good Will Hunting*)
Supporting Actress: Kim Basinger (*LA Confidential*)
Original Screenplay: Matt Damonn, Ben Affleck (*Good Will Hunting*)
Adapted Screenplay: Curtis Hanson, Brian Helgeland (*LA Confidential*)

1998
Picture: *Shakespeare in Love*
Director: Steven Spielberg (*Saving Private Ryan*)
Actor: Roberto Begnini (*Life is Beautiful*)
Actress: Gwyneth Paltrow (*Shakespeare in Love*)
Supporting Actor: James Coburn (*Affliction*)
Supporting Actress: Judi Dench (*Shakespeare in Love*)
Original Screenplay: Marc Norman, Tom Stoppard (*Shakespeare in Love*)
Adapted Screenplay: Bill Condon (*Gods and Monsters*)

1999
Picture: *American Beauty*
Director: Sam Mendes (*American Beauty*)
Actor: Kevin Spacey (*American Beauty*)
Actress: Hilary Swank (*Boys Don't Cry*)
Supporting Actor: Michael Caine (*The Cider House Rules*)
Supporting Actress: Angelina Jolie (*Girl, Interrupted*)
Original Screenplay: Alan Ball (*American Beauty*)
Adapted Screenplay: John Irving (*The Cider House Rules*)

Four-Star Films – by Title

A Bout de Souffle
A Nous la Liberté
The Adventures of Robin Hood
After Life
Aguirre, Wrath of God
Aladdin
Alexander Nevsky
Alien
All Quiet on the Western Front
All that Money Can Buy
All the President's Men
American Beauty
An American in Paris
And Then There Were None
Andrei Rublev
Angels with Dirty Faces
Annie Hall
Aparajito
Ashes and Diamonds
Au Revoir Les Enfants
Bad Day at Black Rock
Badlands
Bambi
The Band Wagon
The Battle of Algiers
The Battleship Potemkin
Begone Dull Care
Belle de Jour
The Best Years of Our Lives
Big Business
The Birth of a Nation
The Blue Angel
Bonnie and Clyde
Breaking the Waves
The Bride of Frankenstein
The Bridge on the River Kwai
Brief Encounter
Butch Cassidy and the Sundance Kid
Cabaret
The Cabinet of Dr Caligari
Casablanca
The Chant of Jimmie Blacksmith
Chinatown
Cinema Paradiso
Citizen Kane
Cries and Whispers
Crossfire
The Cure
David Copperfield
A Day at the Races
Day for Night
Days of Heaven
The Dead
Dead of Night
Deliverance
Destry Rides Again
The Discreet Charm of the Bourgeoisie
Doctor Jekyll and Mr Hyde
Dr Strangelove; or, How I Learned to Stop
Worrying and Love the Bomb
La Dolce Vita
Don't Look Now

Double Indemnity
The Driver
Duck Soup
Dumbo
E.T. The Extra-Terrestrial
Easy Rider
Easy Street
Eight and a Half
Les Enfants du Paradis
The Enigma of Kaspar Hauser
Face to Face
Fanny and Alexander
Fantasia
Fargo
Fitzcarraldo
Foreign Correspondent
The Four Feathers
Frankenstein
The French Connection
Gaslight
The Gay Divorcee
The General
Genevieve
The Godfather
The Godfather Part II
The Golden Age of Comedy
Gone with the Wind
GoodFellas
The Graduate
The Grapes of Wrath
Great Expectations
A Hard Day's Night
Harold Lloyd's World of Comedy
Henry V
High Noon
His Girl Friday
Hud
The Hunchback of Notre Dame
The Hustler
I Am a Fugitive from a Chain Gang
If...
In the Heat of the Night
In Which We Serve
Intolerance
Invasion of the Body Snatchers
The Invisible Man
It's a Wonderful Life
The Jazz Singer
The Jolson Story
Jules et Jim
Kes
The Kid Brother
A Kind of Loving
King Kong
King of Comedy
Kings Row
The Knack
Kwaidan
LA Confidential
Lacombe, Lucien
The Lady Vanishes
The Last Metro

The Last Picture Show
The Lavender Hill Mob
Lawrence of Arabia
The Leopard
The Letter
Listen to Britain
Little Caesar
London Can Take It
Lost Horizon
The Lost Weekend
Love Me Tonight
M*A*S*H
The Magnificent Ambersons
The Maltese Falcon
A Man for All Seasons
The Man in the White Suit
The Manchurian Candidate
Manhattan
Marty
A Matter of Life and Death
Mean Streets
Mephisto
Midnight Cowboy
Le Million
Les Misérables
Mr Smith Goes to Washington
Monsieur Hulot's Holiday
The Music Box
The Naked City
Napoleon
Network
A Night at the Opera
North by Northwest
October
Oh Mr Porter
The Old Dark House
Oliver Twist
On the Town
On the Waterfront
Once Upon a Time in America
One Flew over the Cuckoo's Nest
The Passion of Joan of Arc
Passport to Pimlico
Pather Panchali
Paths of Glory
Pelle the Conqueror
Persona
The Philadelphia Story
The Piano
Picnic at Hanging Rock
Pinocchio
The Player
The Prisoner of Zenda
Psycho
Pygmalion
Raging Bull
Ran
Rashomon
Rear Window
Rebecca
The Red Balloon
The Red Shoes

Rembrandt
San Francisco
Saturday Night and Sunday Morning
Scarface
Schindler's List
The Searchers
The Seven Samurai
The Seventh Seal
A Short Film about Killing
Singin' in the Rain
Snow White and the Seven Dwarfs
Some Like It Hot
Sons of the Desert
Southern Comfort
Stagecoach
Star Wars
Sullivan's Travels
Sweet Smell of Success
Target for Tonight
Taxi Driver
The Thief of Baghdad
Things to Come
The Third Man
The 39 Steps
This Is Spinal Tap
Throne of Blood
The Tin Drum
To Be or Not to Be
Tokyo Story
Tom Jones
Tootsie
Top Hat
Touch of Evil
Toy Story
Tristana
Triumph of the Will
Trouble in Paradise
The True Glory
Twelve Angry Men
Two Tars
2001: A Space Odyssey
Unforgiven
Vertigo
Viridiana
Walkabout
Way Out West
The Way to the Stars
Weekend
West Side Story
When Harry Met Sally
Whisky Galore
Who Framed Roger Rabbit
Who's Afraid of Virginia Woolf?
Why We Fight
The Wild Bunch
Wild Strawberries
Wings of Desire
Witness
Woodstock
The World of Apu
Yojimbo
Z

Four-Star Films – Year by Year

1915
The Birth of a Nation

1916
Intolerance

1917
The Cure
Easy Street

1919
The Cabinet of Dr Caligari

1925
The Battleship Potemkin

1926
The General

1927
The Jazz Singer
The Kid Brother
Napoleon
October

1928
The Passion of Joan of Arc
Two Tars

1929
Big Business

1930
All Quiet on the Western Front
The Blue Angel

1931
A Nous la Liberté
Doctor Jekyll and Mr Hyde
Frankenstein
Little Caesar
Le Million

1932
I Am a Fugitive from a Chain Gang
Love Me Tonight
The Music Box
The Old Dark House
Scarface
Trouble in Paradise

1933
Duck Soup
The Invisible Man
King Kong

1934
David Copperfield
The Gay Divorcee
Sons of the Desert

1935
The Bride of Frankenstein
Les Misérables
A Night at the Opera
The 39 Steps
Top Hat

1936
Rembrandt
San Francisco
Things to Come
Triumph of the Will

1937
A Day at the Races
Lost Horizon
Oh Mr Porter
The Prisoner of Zenda
Snow White and the Seven Dwarfs
Way Out West

1938
The Adventures of Robin Hood
Alexander Nevsky
Angels with Dirty Faces
The Lady Vanishes
Pygmalion

1939
Destry Rides Again
The Four Feathers
Gone with the Wind
The Hunchback of Notre Dame
Mr Smith Goes to Washington
Stagecoach

1940
Fantasia
Foreign Correspondent
Gaslight
The Grapes of Wrath
His Girl Friday
The Letter
London Can Take It
The Philadelphia Story
Pinocchio
Rebecca
The Thief of Baghdad

1941
All that Money Can Buy
Citizen Kane
Dumbo
Listen to Britain
The Maltese Falcon
Sullivan's Travels
Target for Tonight

1942
Bambi
Casablanca
In Which We Serve
Kings Row
The Magnificent Ambersons
To Be or Not to Be
Why We Fight

1944
Double Indemnity
Henry V

1945
And Then There Were None
Brief Encounter
Dead of Night
Les Enfants du Paradis
The Lost Weekend
The True Glory
The Way to the Stars

1946
The Best Years of Our Lives
Great Expectations
It's a Wonderful Life
The Jolson Story
A Matter of Life and Death

1947
Crossfire

1948
The Naked City
Oliver Twist
The Red Shoes
Whisky Galore

1949
On the Town
Passport to Pimlico
The Third Man

1951
An American in Paris

The Lavender Hill Mob
The Man in the White Suit
Rashomon

1952
High Noon
Singin' in the Rain

1953
The Band Wagon
Begone Dull Care
Genevieve
Monsieur Hulot's Holiday
Tokyo Story

1954
On the Waterfront
Rear Window
The Seven Samurai

1955
Bad Day at Black Rock
Invasion of the Body Snatchers
Marty
Pather Panchali
The Red Balloon

1956
Aparajito
The Searchers

1957
The Bridge on the River Kwai
The Golden Age of Comedy
Paths of Glory
The Seventh Seal
Sweet Smell of Success
Throne of Blood
Twelve Angry Men
Wild Strawberries

1958
Ashes and Diamonds
Touch of Evil
Vertigo

1959
North by Northwest
Some Like It Hot
The World of Apu

1960
A Bout de Souffle
La Dolce Vita
Psycho
Saturday Night and Sunday Morning

1961
The Hustler
Viridiana
West Side Story
Yojimbo

1962
Harold Lloyd's World of Comedy
Jules et Jim
A Kind of Loving
Lawrence of Arabia
The Manchurian Candidate

1963
Dr Strangelove; or, How I Learned to Stop
Worrying and Love the Bomb
Eight and a Half
Hud
The Leopard
Tom Jones

1964
A Hard Day's Night
Kwaidan

1965
The Battle of Algiers
The Knack

1966
Andrei Rublev
A Man for All Seasons
Persona
Who's Afraid of Virginia Woolf?

1967
Belle de Jour
Bonnie and Clyde
The Graduate
In the Heat of the Night

1968
If…
2001: A Space Odyssey
Weekend
Z

1969
Butch Cassidy and the Sundance Kid
Easy Rider
Kes
Midnight Cowboy
The Wild Bunch

1970
M*A*S*H
Tristana
Walkabout
Woodstock

1971
The French Connection
The Last Picture Show

1972
Aguirre, Wrath of God
Cabaret
Cries and Whispers
Deliverance
The Discreet Charm of the Bourgeoisie
The Godfather

1973
Badlands
Day for Night
Don't Look Now
Mean Streets

1974
Chinatown
The Enigma of Kaspar Hauser
The Godfather Part II
Lacombe, Lucien

1975
One Flew over the Cuckoo's Nest
Picnic at Hanging Rock

1976
All the President's Men
Face to Face
Network
Taxi Driver

1977
Annie Hall
Star Wars

1978
The Chant of Jimmie Blacksmith
Days of Heaven
The Driver

1979
Alien
Manhattan
The Tin Drum

1980
The Last Metro
Raging Bull

1981
Mephisto
Southern Comfort

1982
E.T. The Extra-Terrestrial
Fanny and Alexander
Fitzcarraldo
Tootsie

1983
King of Comedy

1984
Once Upon a Time in America
This Is Spinal Tap

1985
Ran
Witness

1987
The Dead
Pelle the Conqueror
Wings of Desire

1988
Au Revoir Les Enfants
A Short Film about Killing
Who Framed Roger Rabbit

1989
Cinema Paradiso
When Harry Met Sally

1990
GoodFellas

1992
Aladdin
The Player
Unforgiven

1993
The Piano
Schindler's List

1995
Toy Story

1996
Breaking the Waves
Fargo

1997
LA Confidential

1998
After Life

1999
American Beauty

Three-Star Films – by Title

The Accidental Tourist
Ace in the Hole
Across 110th Street
Across the Pacific
The Adventurer
The Adventures of Robinson Crusoe
The Adventures of Tom Sawyer
The African Queen
Airport
Alexander's Ragtime Band
Alias Nick Beal
Alice
Alice Doesn't Live Here Any More
All About Eve
All About My Mother
All That Jazz
All the King's Men
Amadeus
American Graffiti
An American Werewolf in London
Angi Vera
Animal Crackers
Anne and Muriel
Antonia's Line
Arise My Love
The Army in the Shadows
Around the World in Eighty Days
Arsenic and Old Lace
As Good as It Gets
The Asphalt Jungle
The Assault
Assault on Precinct 13
The Asthenic Syndrome
Atlantic City
Autobus
An Autumn Afternoon
The Awful Truth
Babe
The Bachelor and the Bobbysoxer
Bachelor Mother
The Bachelor Party
Back to the Future
Bad Company
Bagdad Café
La Balance
The Bank Dick
Barefaced Flatfoot
Barton Fink
Battle for Russia
Battle of Britain
La Beauté du Diable
Beauty and the Beast
The Bedford Incident
Before the Rain
Being John Malkovich
La Belle Noiseuse
Ben-Hur
Berlin, Symphony of a Great City
Best Boy
The Best Intentions
The Best Man
Bicycle Thieves
The Big Country
The Big Parade
The Big Sleep
Billy Liar
The Birds
Black Narcissus
The Black Pirate
Black Robe
The Black Swan
Blackmail
The Blair Witch Project
Blithe Spirit
Blockheads
The Blue Bird
Blue Collar
The Blue Lamp
The Body Snatcher
Bombshell
Boomerang
Le Boucher

Boudu Sauvé des Eaux
The Bowery
Boys Don't Cry
Braveheart
Breaker Morant
A Brighter Summer Day
Brighton Rock
Bringing Out the Dead
Bringing Up Baby
Buena Vista Social Club
The Burmese Harp
Burnt by the Sun
Buster Keaton: A Hard Act to Follow
Butcher Boy
The Butterfly Murders
Cabiria
Call Me Madam
The Cameraman
The Candidate
Cape Fear
Carry On up the Khyber
Casino
Casque d'Or
The Cat and the Canary
The Cat and the Canary
Central Station
César
The Charge of the Light Brigade
Chariots of Fire
Charley Varrick
Charlie Bubbles
The Childhood of Maxim Gorky
The China Syndrome
La Chinoise
Christ Stopped at Eboli
City Lights
City of Hope
City Slickers
Civilization
Claire's Knee
Coal Miner's Daughter
The Colour of Pomegranates
Comrades
Confessions of a Nazi Spy
The Conformist
The Conversation
Cops
The Count of Monte Cristo
The Court Jester
Cousin, Cousine
Creature Comforts
Crimes and Misdemeanors
The Crowd
Crumb
The Crying Game
Cyrano de Bergerac
Dark Star
A Day in the Death of Joe Egg
The Day of the Jackal
Day of Wrath
Days and Nights in the Forest
Days of Thrills and Laughter
Dead End
Dear Diary
Death by Hanging
Death in Venice
Death of a Salesman
Decline of the American Empire
Delicatessen
Desert Victory
Les Diaboliques
Diary for My Children
A Diary for Timothy
The Diary of a Country Priest
Dinner at Eight
Dirty Harry
Dirty Work
Distant Thunder
Do the Right Thing
Dr Ehrlich's Magic Bullet
Doctor Mabuse the Gambler
Doctor No

Doctor Zhivago
Dodge City
Dodsworth
Dog Day Afternoon
Donnie Brasco
Dracula
Dracula
The Dreamlife of Angels
The Dresser
Early Summer
Earth
East is East
Eight Men Out
Election
The Elephant Man
Elizabeth
Empire of the Sun
The Empire Strikes Back
The Enforcer
England Made Me
Erin Brockovich
Ermo
The Exterminating Angel
The Face
A Face in the Crowd
Fail Safe
The Fallen Idol
Family Life
Fanny
Farewell My Concubine
Farewell My Lovely
Farewell, My Lovely
Father Brown
Felicia's Journey
The Fencing Master
Festen
Le Feu Follet
Field of Dreams
Fire over England
A Fistful of Dollars
Five Graves to Cairo
Fog over Frisco
Folies Bergère
Footlight Parade
For Me and My Gal
49th Parallel
42nd Street
Four Daughters
Four Weddings and a Funeral
Fourteen Hours
Friday the Thirteenth
From Here to Eternity
From Russia with Love
From This Day Forward
The Front Page
The Fugitive
The Full Monty
The Further Perils of Laurel and Hardy
Fury
'G' Men
The Game
Gandhi
The General
Gerald McBoing Boing
Germinal
The Ghost Breakers
Ghost Dog: The Way of the Samurai
The Ghost Goes West
Gigi
Gilda
Gimme Shelter
Ginger and Fred
Gladiator
The Go-Between
Gold Diggers of 1933
The Gold Rush
Goldfinger
The Golem
The Good Earth
The Good, the Bad and the Ugly
Goodbye Mr Chips
La Grande Illusion

The Great Lie
The Great Race
The Great Train Robbery
The Great Waltz
Greed
Green for Danger
The Green Pastures
Gregory's Girl
The Grifters
Groundhog Day
The Group
Gunga Din
Hail the Conquering Hero
Hannah and Her Sisters
The Happiest Days of Your Life
Happiness
The Happy Time
Hardcore
Harold Lloyd's Funny Side of Life
Harvey
Heaven Can Wait
Heavenly Creatures
Heimat
Hell's Angels
Hellzapoppin
Helpmates
Henry V
Here Comes Mr Jordan
Hobson's Choice
Hog Wild
Holiday
Hoop Dreams
Horse Feathers
The Hospital
The Hot Rock
House of Games
The House on 92nd Street
How Green Was My Valley
Howards End
Hue and Cry
Husbands and Wives
I Married a Witch
I'm All Right Jack
I'm No Angel
In Cold Blood
In Old Chicago
In Search of the Castaways
The Informer
The Innocent
Innocents with Dirty Hands
The Insider
Intermezzo
Interrogation
Intruder in the Dust
L'Invitation
The Iron Giant
It Always Rains on Sunday
It Happened One Night
It Happened Tomorrow
An Italian Straw Hat
Ivan's Childhood
Jane Eyre
Jason and the Argonauts
Jazz on a Summer's Day
Jesus of Montreal
Jeux Interdits
Jezebel
Johann Mouse
Jour de Fête
Le Jour Se Lève
Journey into Fear
Journey to the Center of the Earth
Julia
Kagemusha
Key Largo
The Kid
The Killers
The Killers
The Killing Fields
Kind Hearts and Coronets
King of Jazz
Kipps

Kiss Me Deadly
Kitty
Klute
Kolya
Kramer versus Kramer
Kühle Wampe
The Lady Eve
Lady for a Day
Lady Killer
The Ladykillers
Lamerica
Lancelot du Lac
Land and Freedom
Last Exit to Brooklyn
The Last Flight
The Last Laugh
The Last Seduction
The Last Waltz
Last Year at Marienbad
Laughing Gravy
Laura
The League of Gentlemen
Lenny
Letter from an Unknown Woman
The Life and Death of Colonel Blimp
Life Is Beautiful
The Life of Emile Zola
The Life of Oharu
Lights of New York
Limelight
The Lion King
The Little Foxes
Little Women
The Living Desert
The Lodger
The Loneliness of the Long Distance Runner
The Long Day Closes
Love Affair
Love on the Dole
Lovers and Other Strangers
Lovers of the Arctic Circle
M
The Madness of King George
Major Barbara
The Man Who Came to Dinner
The Man Who Could Work Miracles
The Man Who Knew Too Much
The Man Who Shot Liberty Valance
Mandy
Manon des Sources
Marathon Man
Margie
The Mark of Zorro
Mary Poppins
The Matrix
Meet John Doe
Meet Me in St Louis
Melvin and Howard
The Men
Metropolis
Metropolitan
Mickey's Christmas Carol
Midnight
A Midsummer Night's Dream
Milou in May
Mine Own Executioner
The Miracle of Morgan's Creek
Miracle on 34th Street
Les Misérables
Mrs Brown
Mr Blandings Builds His Dream House
Mr Deeds Goes to Town
Mr Skeffington
Modern Times
Monkey Business
Monty Python and the Holy Grail
The Moon and Sixpence
Moonlighting
The More the Merrier
Morgan – A Suitable Case for Treatment
Morocco
The Most Dangerous Game
Mother
Mother and Son
The Music Man
Mutiny on the Bounty
My Ain Folk
My American Uncle
My Brilliant Career

My Childhood
My Darling Clementine
My Fair Lady
My Favorite Blonde
My Favorite Wife
My Favorite Year
My Girl Tisa
My Learned Friend
My Man Godfrey
My Name Is Joe
Mystery of the Wax Museum
Nada
The Narrow Margin
Nashville
The Nasty Girl
The Navigator
Newsfront
The Next of Kin
Niagara
The Niebelungen
Night Mail
Night of the Demon
The Night of the Hunter
The Night of the Iguana
The Night of The Living Dead
A Night to Remember
Night Train to Munich
The Nightmare before Christmas
Ninotchka
Nixon
Northwest Frontier
Northwest Passage (Part One, Rogers' Rangers)
Nosferatu
Nothing Sacred
Notorious
Now Voyager
The Nun's Story
O Lucky Man!
Occupe-Toi d'Amélie
Odd Man Out
Of Mice and Men
Oliver!
Olympische Spiele
On Approval
On Golden Pond
Once Upon a Time in the West
Once Were Warriors
One False Move
One Hour with You
One Hundred and One Dalmatians
One Hundred Men and a Girl
Only Two Can Play
The Opposite of Sex
Ordinary People
Orphée
Our Hospitality
Our Relations
Out of Sight
Padre Padrone
The Pajama Game
The Paleface
The Palm Beach Story
Panic in the Streets
The Parallax View
Une Partie de Campagne
Patterns
Patton
The People vs. Larry Flynt
Performance
Peter Pan
The Phantom of Liberty
Phantom of the Opera
Picnic
The Picture of Dorian Gray
Planet of the Apes
The Ploughman's Lunch
Poil de Carotte
Portrait of Jennie
Prelude to War
Pretty Village Pretty Flame
Pride and Prejudice
A Private Conversation
A Private Function
The Private Life of Henry VIII
The Private Life of Sherlock Holmes
Private's Progress
The Prize
The Public Enemy
Pulp Fiction

The Pumpkin Eater
Quai des Brumes
Quartet
Que la Bête Meure
Queen Christina
The Quiet Man
Quiet Wedding
Raiders of the Lost Ark
The Railway Children
The Rains Came
Random Harvest
Red Dust
Red Sorghum
Reds
La Règle du Jeu
Repentance
Reservoir Dogs
Richard III
Richard III
The Roaring Twenties
Robocop
Rocky
The Rocky Horror Picture Show
Rome Express
La Ronde
Room at the Top
A Room with a View
Rosetta
Run Lola Run
Sabotage
Saboteur
Safety Last
The Samurai
Sansho the Bailiff
Saturday Night Fever
Saving Private Ryan
The Scarlet Empress
The Scarlet Pimpernel
Scenes from a Marriage
Scrooge
The Sea Hawk
Secrets and Lies
A Self-Made Hero
Sense and Sensibility
The Set Up
Seven
Seven Days in May
Shadow of a Doubt
Shadowlands
Shakespeare in Love
Shane
Shanghai Express
She Done Him Wrong
Shine
Ship of Fools
Shoah
The Shootist
Short Cuts
Show Business
Showboat
The Sign of the Cross
Silence of the Lambs
A Simple Plan
Since You Went Away
Sing As We Go
Sitting Pretty
The Sixth Sense
A Slight Case of Murder
Smile
Smiles of a Summer Night
Solaris
Son of Frankenstein
Sons and Lovers
Le Souffle au Coeur
The Sound of Music
The Southerner
Speed
The Spiral Staircase
Stage Door
Stanley and Livingstone
A Star Is Born
Star Spangled Rhythm
State of the Union
The Sting
Stormy Weather
The Story of Louis Pasteur
The Story of Qiu Ju
La Strada
The Straight Story

Strangers on a Train
Strictly Ballroom
Strike
Summertime
Sunday, Bloody Sunday
Sunset Boulevard
The Sweet Hereafter
Taking Off
The Tale of the Fox
The Talk of the Town
Tango
Tarzan
A Taste of Honey
Terminus
Thank Your Lucky Stars
Thelma and Louise
They Shoot Horses, Don't They?
They Won't Forget
The Thief
The Thief of Bagdad
The Thin Man
The Thin Red Line
This Gun for Hire
This Sporting Life
Those Wonderful Movie Cranks
The Three Caballeros
Three Colours: Blue
Three Colours: Red
Three Colours: White
Three Kings
The Three Musketeers
Thunder Rock
Time in the Sun
Tin Pan Alley
The Titfield Thunderbolt
Tobacco Road
Topsy-Turvy
A Touch of Zen
Towed in a Hole
The Towering Inferno
Toy Story 2
The Tragedy of a Ridiculous Man
Trainspotting
A Tree Grows in Brooklyn
The Truman Show
Tunes of Glory
Ulee's Gold
Unknown Chaplin
The Usual Suspects
Utu
Vagabonde
Victim
Victoria the Great
The Vikings
Visions of Light
The Wages of Fear
A Walk in the Sun
War and Peace
The Watchmaker of St Paul
The Way Ahead
The Wedding Banquet
Went the Day Well?
Western Approaches
When Comedy Was King
White Heat
Will It Snow for Christmas?
William Shakespeare's Romeo and Juliet
The Wind
The Window
The Winslow Boy
Wise Blood
Witness for the Prosecution
The Wizard of Oz
The Woman in the Window
Woman of the Year
The Women
Women in Love
World of Plenty
WR – Mysteries of the Organism
Wuthering Heights
Yankee Doodle Dandy
Yol
Young and Innocent
Young Frankenstein
The Young in Heart
Young Mr Lincoln
You're Darn Tootin'
Zazie dans le Métro
Zelig

Three-Star Films – Year by Year

1903
The Great Train Robbery

1916
Civilization

1917
The Adventurer

1920
The Golem

1921
The Kid
Nosferatu

1922
Cops
Doctor Mabuse the Gambler

1923
Our Hospitality
Safety Last

1924
Greed
The Last Laugh
The Navigator
The Niebelungen
Strike
The Thief of Bagdad

1925
Ben-Hur
The Big Parade
The Gold Rush
Phantom of the Opera

1926
The Black Pirate
The Lodger
Metropolis
Mother

1927
Berlin, Symphony of a Great City
The Cat and the Canary
An Italian Straw Hat

1928
The Cameraman
The Crowd
Lights of New York
The Wind

1929
Blackmail
You're Darn Tootin'

1930
Animal Crackers
Earth
Hell's Angels
Hog Wild
King of Jazz
Morocco

1931
City Lights
Dracula
The Front Page
The Last Flight
Laughing Gravy
M
Monkey Business
The Public Enemy
The Tale of the Fox

1932
Boudu Sauvé des Eaux
Fanny
Helpmates

Horse Feathers
Kühle Wampe
The Most Dangerous Game
One Hour with You
Poil de Carotte
Red Dust
Rome Express
Shanghai Express
The Sign of the Cross
Towed in a Hole

1933
Bombshell
The Bowery
Dinner at Eight
Dirty Work
Footlight Parade
42nd Street
Friday the Thirteenth
Gold Diggers of 1933
I'm No Angel
Lady for a Day
Lady Killer
Little Women
Mystery of the Wax Museum
The Private Life of Henry VIII
Queen Christina
She Done Him Wrong
Time in the Sun

1934
The Count of Monte Cristo
Fog over Frisco
It Happened One Night
The Man Who Knew Too Much
The Scarlet Empress
The Scarlet Pimpernel
Sing As We Go
The Thin Man

1935
Folies Bergère
'G' Men
The Ghost Goes West
The Informer
A Midsummer Night's Dream
Mutiny on the Bounty

1936
César
The Charge of the Light Brigade
Dodsworth
Fury
The Green Pastures
The Man Who Could Work Miracles
Mr Deeds Goes to Town
Modern Times
My Man Godfrey
Night Mail
Olympische Spiele
Our Relations
Une Partie de Campagne
Sabotage
Showboat
The Story of Louis Pasteur

1937
The Awful Truth
Dead End
Fire over England
The Good Earth
La Grande Illusion
In Old Chicago
The Life of Emile Zola
Nothing Sacred
One Hundred Men and a Girl
Stage Door
A Star Is Born
They Won't Forget
Victoria the Great
Young and Innocent

1938
The Adventures of Tom Sawyer
Alexander's Ragtime Band
Blockheads
Bringing Up Baby
The Childhood of Maxim Gorky
Four Daughters
The Great Waltz
Holiday
Jezebel
Quai des Brumes
A Slight Case of Murder
The Young in Heart

1939
Bachelor Mother
The Cat and the Canary
Confessions of a Nazi Spy
Dodge City
Goodbye Mr Chips
Gunga Din
Intermezzo
Le Jour Se Lève
Love Affair
Midnight
Ninotchka
Of Mice and Men
The Rains Came
La Règle du Jeu
The Roaring Twenties
Son of Frankenstein
Stanley and Livingstone
The Wizard of Oz
The Women
Wuthering Heights
Young Mr Lincoln

1940
Arise My Love
The Bank Dick
The Blue Bird
Dr Ehrlich's Magic Bullet
The Ghost Breakers
The Mark of Zorro
My Favorite Wife
Night Train to Munich
Northwest Passage (Part One, Rogers' Rangers)
Pride and Prejudice
Quiet Wedding
The Sea Hawk
Tin Pan Alley

1941
49th Parallel
The Great Lie
Here Comes Mr Jordan
How Green Was My Valley
Kipps
The Lady Eve
The Little Foxes
Love on the Dole
Major Barbara
The Man Who Came to Dinner
Meet John Doe
Tobacco Road

1942
Across the Pacific
The Black Swan
For Me and My Gal
Hellzapoppin
I Married a Witch
Journey into Fear
My Favorite Blonde
The Next of Kin
Now Voyager
The Palm Beach Story
Random Harvest
Saboteur
Star Spangled Rhythm
The Talk of the Town
This Gun for Hire

Thunder Rock
Went the Day Well?
Woman of the Year
Yankee Doodle Dandy

1943
Battle for Russia
Battle of Britain
Day of Wrath
Desert Victory
Five Graves to Cairo
Heaven Can Wait
Jane Eyre
The Life and Death of Colonel Blimp
The Miracle of Morgan's Creek
The Moon and Sixpence
The More the Merrier
My Learned Friend
On Approval
Prelude to War
Shadow of a Doubt
Stormy Weather
Thank Your Lucky Stars
World of Plenty

1944
Arsenic and Old Lace
Farewell My Lovely
Hail the Conquering Hero
It Happened Tomorrow
Laura
Meet Me in St Louis
Mr Skeffington
Show Business
Since You Went Away
The Way Ahead
Western Approaches
The Woman in the Window

1945
Blithe Spirit
The Body Snatcher
A Diary for Timothy
The House on 92nd Street
Kitty
The Picture of Dorian Gray
The Southerner
The Spiral Staircase
The Three Caballeros
A Tree Grows in Brooklyn

1946
The Big Sleep
From This Day Forward
Gilda
Green for Danger
Hue and Cry
The Killers
Margie
My Darling Clementine
Notorious
Odd Man Out
A Walk in the Sun

1947
The Bachelor and the Bobbysoxer
Black Narcissus
Boomerang
Brighton Rock
It Always Rains on Sunday
Mine Own Executioner
Miracle on 34th Street

1948
Bicycle Thieves
The Fallen Idol
Jour de Fête
Key Largo
Letter from an Unknown Woman
Mr Blandings Builds His Dream House
My Girl Tisa
The Paleface

Portrait of Jennie
Quartet
Sitting Pretty
State of the Union
The Three Musketeers
The Winslow Boy

1949
Alias Nick Beal
All the King's Men
La Beauté du Diable
The Blue Lamp
Intruder in the Dust
Kind Hearts and Coronets
Occupe-Toi d'Amélie
Orphée
The Set Up
White Heat
The Window

1950
All About Eve
The Asphalt Jungle
The Diary of a Country Priest
The Enforcer
The Happiest Days of Your Life
Harvey
The Men
Panic in the Streets
La Ronde
Sunset Boulevard

1951
Ace in the Hole
The African Queen
Death of a Salesman
Early Summer
Fourteen Hours
Gerald McBoing Boing
Scrooge
Strangers on a Train

1952
Barefaced Flatfoot
Casque d'Or
The Happy Time
Jeux Interdits
Johann Mouse
The Life of Oharu
Limelight
Mandy
The Narrow Margin
Niagara
The Quiet Man
The Titfield Thunderbolt

1953
The Adventures of Robinson Crusoe
Call Me Madam
From Here to Eternity
Hobson's Choice
The Living Desert
Peter Pan
Shane
The Wages of Fear

1954
Les Diaboliques
Father Brown
Sansho the Bailiff
La Strada

1955
The Court Jester
Kiss Me Deadly
The Ladykillers
The Night of the Hunter
Picnic
Richard III
Smiles of a Summer Night
Summertime

1956
Around the World in Eighty Days
The Burmese Harp
Patterns
Private's Progress

1957
The Bachelor Party
Cabiria
A Face in the Crowd
Night of the Demon
The Pajama Game
Witness for the Prosecution

1958
The Big Country
Dracula
The Face
Gigi
A Night to Remember
Room at the Top
The Vikings

1959
I'm All Right Jack
Jazz on a Summer's Day
Journey to the Center of the Earth
Northwest Frontier
The Nun's Story
When Comedy Was King

1960
The League of Gentlemen
Sons and Lovers
Tunes of Glory
Zazie dans le Métro

1961
Days of Thrills and Laughter
In Search of the Castaways
Last Year at Marienbad
One Hundred and One Dalmatians
A Taste of Honey
Terminus
Victim

1962
An Autumn Afternoon
Doctor No
The Exterminating Angel
Ivan's Childhood
The Loneliness of the Long Distance Runner
The Man Who Shot Liberty Valance
The Music Man
Only Two Can Play

1963
Billy Liar
The Birds
Le Feu Follet
From Russia with Love
Harold Lloyd's Funny Side of Life
Jason and the Argonauts
The Prize
This Sporting Life

1964
The Best Man
Fail Safe
A Fistful of Dollars
Goldfinger
The Killers
Mary Poppins
My Fair Lady
The Night of the Iguana
The Pumpkin Eater
Seven Days in May

1965
The Bedford Incident
Doctor Zhivago
The Great Race
Ship of Fools
The Sound of Music

1966
The Good, the Bad and the Ugly
The Group
Morgan – A Suitable Case for Treatment

1967
La Chinoise
The Further Perils of Laurel and Hardy
In Cold Blood
The Samurai
War and Peace

1968
Carry On up the Khyber
Charlie Bubbles
Death by Hanging
The Night of The Living Dead
Oliver!
Planet of the Apes

1969
The Army in the Shadows
Le Boucher
The Colour of Pomegranates

The Conformist
Days and Nights in the Forest
Once Upon a Time in the West
Patton
Que la Bête Meure
They Shoot Horses, Don't They?
A Touch of Zen
Women in Love

1970
Airport
Claire's Knee
Gimme Shelter
The Go-Between
Lovers and Other Strangers
Performance
The Private Life of Sherlock Holmes
The Railway Children

1971
Anne and Muriel
A Day in the Death of Joe Egg
Death in Venice
Dirty Harry
Family Life
The Hospital
Klute
Le Souffle au Coeur
Sunday, Bloody Sunday
Taking Off
WR – Mysteries of the Organism

1972
Across 110th Street
Bad Company
The Candidate
England Made Me
The Hot Rock
My Childhood
Solaris

1973
American Graffiti
Charley Varrick
The Day of the Jackal
Distant Thunder
L'Invitation
My Ain Folk
O Lucky Man!
Scenes from a Marriage
The Sting
The Watchmaker of St Paul

1974
Alice Doesn't Live Here Any More
The Conversation
Dark Star
Lancelot du Lac
Lenny
Nada
The Parallax View
The Phantom of Liberty
The Towering Inferno
Young Frankenstein

1975
Cousin, Cousine
Dog Day Afternoon
Farewell, My Lovely
Innocents with Dirty Hands
Monty Python and the Holy Grail
Nashville
The Rocky Horror Picture Show
Smile

1976
Assault on Precinct 13
The Innocent
Marathon Man
Rocky
The Shootist

1977
Julia
Padre Padrone
Saturday Night Fever

1978
Angi Vera
Blue Collar
The Last Waltz
Newsfront
Those Wonderful Movie Cranks

1979
All That Jazz
Best Boy
The Butterfly Murders
The China Syndrome
Christ Stopped at Eboli
Hardcore
Kramer versus Kramer
My Brilliant Career
Wise Blood

1980
Breaker Morant
Coal Miner's Daughter
The Elephant Man
The Empire Strikes Back
Gregory's Girl
Kagemusha
Melvin and Howard
My American Uncle
Ordinary People

1981
An American Werewolf in London
Atlantic City
Chariots of Fire
On Golden Pond
Raiders of the Lost Ark
Reds
The Tragedy of a Ridiculous Man

1982
La Balance
Diary for My Children
Gandhi
Interrogation
Moonlighting
My Favorite Year
Yol

1983
The Dresser
Mickey's Christmas Carol
The Ploughman's Lunch
A Private Conversation
Utu
Zelig

1984
Amadeus
Heimat
The Killing Fields
A Private Function
Repentance

1985
Back to the Future
A Room with a View
Shoah
Vagabonde

1986
The Assault
Decline of the American Empire
Ginger and Fred
Hannah and Her Sisters
Manon des Sources
Unknown Chaplin

1987
Buster Keaton: A Hard Act to Follow
Comrades
Empire of the Sun
House of Games
Red Sorghum
Robocop

1988
The Accidental Tourist
Alice
Bagdad Café
Eight Men Out

1989
The Asthenic Syndrome
Creature Comforts
Crimes and Misdemeanors
Do the Right Thing
Field of Dreams
Henry V
Jesus of Montreal
Last Exit to Brooklyn
Metropolitan
Milou in May

1990
Cyrano de Bergerac
Delicatessen
The Grifters
The Nasty Girl
Silence of the Lambs

1991
Autobus
Barton Fink
Beauty and the Beast
La Belle Noiseuse
Black Robe
A Brighter Summer Day
Cape Fear
City of Hope
City Slickers
Reservoir Dogs
Thelma and Louise

1992
The Best Intentions
The Crying Game
The Fencing Master
Howards End
Husbands and Wives
The Long Day Closes
One False Move
The Story of Qiu Ju
Strictly Ballroom
Visions of Light

1993
Farewell My Concubine
The Fugitive
Germinal

Groundhog Day
The Nightmare before Christmas
Shadowlands
Short Cuts
Tango
Three Colours: Blue
Three Colours: White
The Wedding Banquet

1994
Before the Rain
Burnt by the Sun
Crumb
Dear Diary
Ermo
Four Weddings and a Funeral
Heavenly Creatures
Hoop Dreams
Lamerica
The Last Seduction
The Lion King
The Madness of King George
Once Were Warriors
Pulp Fiction
Speed
Three Colours: Red

1995
Antonia's Line
Babe
Braveheart
Casino
Land and Freedom
Les Misérables
Nixon
Richard III

Secrets and Lies
A Self-Made Hero
Sense and Sensibility
Seven
The Usual Suspects

1996
Kolya
The People vs. Larry Flynt
Pretty Village Pretty Flame
Shine
Trainspotting
Will It Snow for Christmas?
William Shakespeare's Romeo and Juliet

1997
As Good as It Gets
Butcher Boy
Donnie Brasco
The Full Monty
The Game
Life Is Beautiful
Mrs Brown
Mother and Son
The Sweet Hereafter
The Thief
Ulee's Gold

1998
The Blair Witch Project
Buena Vista Social Club
Central Station
The Dreamlife of Angels
Elizabeth
Festen
The General

Happiness
Lovers of the Arctic Circle
My Name Is Joe
The Opposite of Sex
Out of Sight
Run Lola Run
Saving Private Ryan
Shakespeare in Love
A Simple Plan
The Thin Red Line
The Truman Show

1999
All About My Mother
Being John Malkovich
Boys Don't Cry
Bringing Out the Dead
East is East
Election
Felicia's Journey
Ghost Dog: The Way of the Samurai
The Insider
The Iron Giant
The Matrix
Rosetta
The Sixth Sense
The Straight Story
Tarzan
Three Kings
Topsy-Turvy
Toy Story 2

2000
Erin Brockovich
Gladiator

Omitted Films List

Abandoned
Abdulla the Great
The Abysmal Brute
Accused
Ace Drummond
Ace Eli and Rodger of the Skies
Ace High (dubbed)
The Ace of Scotland Yard
Act of the Heart
Action in Arabia
Adam's Woman
Adventure in Diamonds
Adventure in Iraq
Adventure in Washington
Adventures of a Rookie
Adventures of Captain Africa
Adventures of Frank and Jesse James
Adventures of Frank Merriwell
Adventures of Kitty O'Day
Adventures of Red Ryder
Adventures of Rex and Rinty
Adventures of Sir Galahad
Adventures of Smilin' Jack
Adventures of the Flying Cadets
Affairs of a Gentleman
The Affairs of Martha
After Office Hours
Age of Indiscretion
Aggie Appleby Maker of Men
Air Cadet
Air Hawks
The Airmail Mystery
Al Jennings of Oklahoma
Alias a Gentleman
Alias French Gertie
Alias John Preston
Annapolis Farewell
Arabian Nights
Aren't We All?
The Arnelo Affair
Atom Man vs Superman
Baboona
Bachelor Daddy
Bad Men of Tombstone
Badlands of Dakota
Bail Out at 43,000
Barefoot Battalion
The Battle at Apache Pass
Battle Zone
Battling with Buffalo Bill
The Bay of Saint Michel
Beachhead
Beau Sabreur
Bed of Roses
Behind Green Lights
Behind the Make-up
Belle le Grand
Beverly of Graustark
The Big Cube
The Big Guy
Black Arrow
The Black Coin
The Black Panther
The Black Widow
Blackhawk
Blake of Scotland Yard
Blazing the Overland Trail
Bombs Over Burma
Border River
Born to Win

Boys' Ranch
Brenda Starr, Reporter
Brick Bradford
Bride by Mistake
The Bride Wore Crutches
Bruce Gentry – Daredevil of the Skies
Brushfire!
Bunco Squad
Burn 'Em Up Barnes
By Whose Hand?
The Calendar
Calendar Girl
Call of the Blood
Call of the Flesh
The Call of the Savage
Canadian Mounties vs Atomic Invaders
Canaries Sometimes Sing
Canyon Crossroads
Captain America
Captain Lash
Captain Midnight
The Captain's Kid
Carolina Blues
The Case of Sergeant Grischa
The Case of the Black Parrot
The Cavern
The Challenge
Chetniks – The Fighting Guerrillas
Chick Carter, Detective
Child of Manhattan
The City of Beautiful Nonsense
Clancy of the Mounted
Cody of the Pony Express
Collegiate
The Colossus of New York
Column South
Condemned Women
Congo Bill
Corky
The Couch
Crack Up
The Crime of Dr Hallet
The Crimson Ghost
The Crouching Beast
The Cup 2
Custer's Last Stand
Dance Hall
Danger Island
Dangerously Yours
Dangers of the Canadian Mounted
Daredevils of the Red Circle
Daredevils of the West
Darkest Africa
Dead Men Are Dangerous
Deadline for Murder
Death of a Champion
The Desert Hawk
Desirable
Desperadoes of the West
Detective Lloyd
Devil Horse
Dick Tracy (1937)
Dick Tracy Returns
Dick Tracy vs Crime Inc
Dick Tracy's G-Men
Don Daredevil Rides Again
Don Winslow of the Navy
Double Crime in the Maginot Line
Double Crossbones
Dumb Dicks

East of the River
Embraceable You
The End of the Road
Eternal Love
Fanny Foley Herself
Fast Workers
Federal Agents vs Underworld Inc
Federal Operator 99
Fighting Back
Fighting Caravans
Fighting Devil Dogs
Fighting Man of the Plains
Fighting Marines
Fighting with Kit Carson
Fingerprints
Flame of Araby
Flame of Calcutta
Flaming Frontiers
Flesh and Fury
Flirting with Fate
Flying Disc Men from Mars
Flying G-Men
Forbidden (1932)
Forbidden (1949)
Forbidden Cargo
Fugitive Road
The Galloping Ghost
Gambling House
Gang Busters
General Crack
Ghost of Zorro
The Ghost Walks
Girls at Sea
Give Me Your Heart
Glory
G-Men Never Forget
G-Men vs The Black Dragon
Go Chase Yourself
God Is My Co-Pilot
God's Gift to Women
Gold
Golden Dawn
Golden Gloves
The Golden Salamander
Gordon of Ghost City
Government Agents vs The Phantom Legion
The Great Adventures of Captain Kidd
The Great Adventures of Wild Bill Hickok
The Green Archer
The Green Buddha
The Green Hornet
The Green Hornet Strikes Again
The Guilty Generation
Gunfighters of the Northwest
Happiness Ahead
Happy Go Lucky
Haunted Harbor
Hawk of the Wilderness
Hear Me Good
Hellgate
Heroes of the West
The Hidden Hand
High Tide at Noon
Hold 'em Yale
Holt of the Secret Service
Home to Danger
Hop Harrigan
Hot Pepper

Hungry Hill
I Give My Love
Identity Unknown
The Indians Are Coming
The Invisible Monster
Iron Claw
Jack Armstrong
The Jade Box
The James Brothers of Missouri
Jesse James Rides Again
Jungle Drums of Africa
Jungle Girl
Jungle Jim
Jungle Menace
The Jungle Mystery
Jungle Queen
Jungle Raiders
Junior G-Men
Junior G-Men of the Air
King of the Carnival
King of the Congo
King of the Forest Rangers
King of the Mounties
King of the Rocket Men
King of the Royal Mounted
King of the Texas Rangers
King of the Wild
The Last Frontier
The Law of the Wild
The Lightning Express
The Lightning Warrior
The Lone Defender
The Lone Ranger
The Lone Ranger Rides Again
The Lost City
Lost City of the Jungle
The Lost Jungle
The Lost Planet
The Lost Special
The Man with the Steel Whip
Manhunt of Mystery Island
The Masked Marvel
The Master Key
The Miracle Rider
The Monster and the Ape
The Mysterious Dr Satan
Mysterious Island
The Mysterious Mr M
The Mysterious Pilot
Mystery Mountain
Mystery of the River Boat
Mystery Squadron
The New Adventures of Tarzan
The Next Best Thing
Once in a Blue Moon
The Oregon Trail
Overland Mail
Overland with Kit Carson
The Painted Stallion
Panther Girl of the Congo
Paradise Canyon
Perils of Nyoka
The Perils of Pauline
Perils of the Royal Mounted
Perils of the Wilderness
The Phantom
The Phantom Creeps
Phantom Empire
The Phantom of the Air
The Phantom of the West

The Phantom Rider (1936)
The Phantom Rider (1946)
Pirate Treasure
Pirates of the High Seas
Radar Men from the Moon
Radar Patrol vs Spy King
Radio Patrol
Raiders of Ghost City
Red Barry
The Red Rider
The Return of Chandu
Riders of Death Valley
Riding with Buffalo Bill
Roar of the Iron Horse
The Roaring West
Robinson Crusoe of Clipper Island
The Royal Mounted Rides Again
Rustlers of Red Dog
Salut Cousin!
The Scarlet Horseman
Scouts to the Rescue
The Sea Hound
Secret Agent X9 (1937)
Secret Agent X9 (1945)
The Secret Code
The Secret of Treasure Island
Secret Service in Darkest Africa
The Shadow
Shadow of Chinatown
The Shadow of the Eagle
Sky Raiders
A Slight Case of Larceny
Slightly Dangerous
Snow Falling On Cedars
Soldier
Son of Geronimo
Son of the Guardsman
Son of Zorro
SOS Coast Guard
Spell of the Circus
The Spider Returns
The Spider's Web
Spy Smasher
Tailspin Tommy
Tailspin Tommy in the Great Air Mystery
Taza, Son of Cochise
Terry and the Pirates
Terry of the Times
Tex Granger
The Three Musketeers (1933)
Tim Tyler's Luck
Trader Tom of the China Seas
The Valley of Vanishing Men
The Vanishing Legion
The Vanishing Shadow
The Vigilante
The Vigilantes are Coming
Whispering Shadows
White Eagle
Who's Guilty?
Wild West Days
Winners of the West
The Wolf Dog
Young Eagles
Zombies of the Stratosphere
Zorro Rides Again
Zorro's Black Whip
Zorro's Fighting Legion